THE WOMEN'S STUDY BIBLE

NEW LIVING TRANSLATION SECOND EDITION

THE WOMEN'S STUDY BIBLE

NEW LIVING TRANSLATION SECOND EDITION

EDITORS

Catherine Clark Kroeger *and* Mary J. Evans

OXFORD
UNIVERSITY PRESS

OXFORD
UNIVERSITY PRESS

Oxford University Press, Inc., publishes works that further
Oxford University's objective of excellence
in research, scholarship, and education.

Oxford New York

Auckland Cape Town Dar es Salaam Hong Kong Karachi
Kuala Lumpur Madrid Melbourne Mexico City Nairobi
New Delhi Shanghai Taipei Toronto

With offices in

Argentina Austria Brazil Chile Czech Republic France Greece
Guatemala Hungary Italy Japan Poland Portugal Singapore
South Korea Switzerland Thailand Turkey Ukraine Vietnam

Published by Oxford University Press, Inc.
198 Madison Avenue, New York, NY 10016
Oxford is a registered trademark of Oxford University Press

Typesetting by Blue Heron Bookcraft • Battle Ground, Washington

10 9 8 7 6 5 4 3 2 1

Printed in Korea

CONTENTS

NAMES AND ORDER OF THE BOOKS OF THE OLD AND NEW TESTAMENTS

THE OLD TESTAMENT

THE NEW TESTAMENT

ALPHABETICAL LISTING OF THE BOOKS OF THE BIBLE

SIDEBAR ESSAYS AND MAPS

OLD TESTAMENT

NEW TESTAMENT

LIST OF ABBREVIATIONS

OLD TESTAMENT

Genesis	Gen	Ecclesiastes	Eccl
Exodus	Exod	Song of Songs	Song
Leviticus	Lev	Isaiah	Isa
Numbers	Num	Jeremiah	Jer
Deuteronomy	Deut	Lamentations	Lam
Joshua	Josh	Ezekiel	Ezek
Judges	Judg	Daniel	Dan
Ruth	Ruth	Hosea	Hos
1 Samuel	1 Sam	Joel	Joel
2 Samuel	2 Sam	Amos	Amos
1 Kings	1 Kgs	Obadiah	Obad
2 Kings	2 Kgs	Jonah	Jon
1 Chronicles	1 Chr	Micah	Mic
2 Chronicles	2 Chr	Nahum	Nah
Ezra	Ezra	Habakkuk	Hab
Nehemiah	Neh	Zephaniah	Zeph
Esther	Esth	Haggai	Hag
Job	Job	Zechariah	Zech
Psalms	Ps	Malachi	Mal
Proverbs	Prov		

NEW TESTAMENT

Matthew	Matt	1 Timothy	1 Tim
Mark	Mark	2 Timothy	2 Tim
Luke	Luke	Titus	Titus
John	John	Philemon	Phlm
Acts	Acts	Hebrews	Heb
Romans	Rom	James	Jas
1 Corinthians	1 Cor	1 Peter	1 Pet
2 Corinthians	2 Cor	2 Peter	2 Pet
Galatians	Gal	1 John	1 Jn
Ephesians	Eph	2 John	2 Jn
Philippians	Phil	3 John	3 Jn
Colossians	Col	Jude	Jude
1 Thessalonians	1 Thes	Revelation	Rev
2 Thessalonians	2 Thes		

A NOTE TO READERS

The *Holy Bible,* New Living Translation, was first published in 1996. It quickly became one of the most popular Bible translations in the English-speaking world. While the NLT's influence was rapidly growing, the Bible Translation Committee determined that an additional investment in scholarly review and text refinement could make it even better. So shortly after its initial publication, the committee began an eight-year process with the purpose of increasing the level of the NLT's precision without sacrificing its easy-to-understand quality. This second-generation text was completed in 2004 and is reflected in this edition of the New Living Translation. An additional update with minor changes was subequently introduced in 2007.

The goal of any Bible translation is to convey the meaning and content of the ancient Hebrew, Aramaic, and Greek texts as accurately as possible to contemporary readers. The challenge for our translators was to create a text that would communicate as clearly and powerfully to today's readers as the original texts did to readers and listeners in the ancient biblical world. The resulting translation is easy to read and understand, while also accurately communicating the meaning and content of the original biblical texts. The NLT is a general-purpose text especially good for study, devotional reading, and reading aloud in worship services.

We believe that the New Living Translation—which combines the latest biblical scholarship with a clear, dynamic writing style—will communicate God's word powerfully to all who read it. We publish it with the prayer that God will use it to speak his timeless truth to the church and the world in a fresh, new way.

Tyndale House Publishers
October 2007

INTRODUCTION TO THE NEW LIVING TRANSLATION

Translation Philosophy and Methodology

English Bible translations tend to be governed by one of two general translation theories. The first theory has been called "formal-equivalence," "literal," or "word-for-word" translation. According to this theory, the translator attempts to render each word of the original language into English and seeks to preserve the original syntax and sentence structure as much as possible in translation. The second theory has been called "dynamic-equivalence," "functional-equivalence," or "thought-for-thought" translation. The goal of this translation theory is to produce in English the closest natural equivalent of the message expressed by the original-language text, both in meaning and in style.

Both of these translation theories have their strengths. A formal-equivalence translation preserves aspects of the original text—including ancient idioms, term consistency, and original-language syntax—that are valuable for scholars and professional study. It allows a reader to trace formal elements of the original-language text through the English translation. A dynamic-equivalence translation, on the other hand, focuses on translating the message of the original-language text. It ensures that the meaning of the text is readily apparent to the contemporary reader. This allows the message to come through with immediacy, without requiring the reader to struggle with foreign idioms and awkward syntax. It also facilitates serious study of the text's message and clarity in both devotional and public reading.

The pure application of either of these translation philosophies would create translations at opposite ends of the translation spectrum. But in reality, all translations contain a mixture of these two philosophies. A purely formal-equivalence translation would be unintelligible in English, and a purely dynamic-equivalence translation would risk being unfaithful to the original. That is why translations shaped by dynamic-equivalence theory are usually quite literal when the original text is relatively clear, and the translations shaped by formal-equivalence theory are sometimes quite dynamic when the original text is obscure.

The translators of the New Living Translation set out to render the message of the original texts of Scripture into clear, contemporary English. As they did so, they kept the concerns of both formal-equivalence and dynamic-equivalence in mind. On the one hand, they translated as simply and literally as possible when that approach yielded an accurate, clear, and natural English text. Many words and phrases were rendered literally and consistently into English, preserving essential literary and rhetorical devices, ancient metaphors, and word choices that give structure to the text and provide echoes of meaning from one passage to the next.

On the other hand, the translators rendered the message more dynamically when the literal rendering was hard to understand, was misleading, or yielded archaic or foreign wording. They clarified difficult metaphors and terms to aid in the reader's understanding. The translators first struggled with the meaning of the words and phrases in the ancient context; then they rendered the message into clear, natural English. Their goal was to be both faithful to the ancient texts and eminently readable. The result is a translation that is both exegetically accurate and idiomatically powerful.

Translation Process and Team

To produce an accurate translation of the Bible into contemporary English, the translation team needed the skills necessary to enter into the thought patterns of the ancient authors and then to render their ideas, connotations, and effects into clear, contemporary English. To begin this process, qualified biblical scholars were needed to interpret the meaning of the original text and to check it against our base English translation. In order to guard against personal and theological biases, the scholars needed to represent a diverse group of evangelicals who would employ the best exegetical tools. Then to work alongside the scholars, skilled English stylists were needed to shape the text into clear, contemporary English.

With these concerns in mind, the Bible Translation Committee recruited teams of scholars that represented a broad spectrum of denominations, theological perspectives, and backgrounds within the worldwide evangelical community. (These scholars are listed at the end of this introduction.) Each book of the Bible was assigned to three different scholars with proven expertise in the book or group of books to be reviewed. Each of these scholars made a thorough review of a base translation and submitted suggested revisions to the appropriate Senior Translator. The Senior Translator then reviewed and summarized these suggestions and proposed a first-draft revision of the base text. This draft served as the basis for several additional phases of exegetical and stylistic committee review. Then the Bible Translation Committee jointly reviewed and approved every verse of the final translation.

Throughout the translation and editing process, the Senior Translators and their scholar teams were given a chance to review the editing done by the team of stylists. This ensured that exegetical errors would not be introduced late in the process and that the entire Bible Translation Committee was happy with the final result. By choosing a team of qualified scholars and skilled stylists and by setting up a process that allowed their interaction throughout the process, the New Living Translation has been refined to preserve the essential formal elements of the original biblical texts, while also creating a clear, understandable English text.

The New Living Translation was first published in 1996. Shortly after its initial publication, the Bible Translation Committee began a process of further committee review and translation refinement. The purpose of this continued revision was to increase the level of precision without sacrificing the text's easy-to-understand quality. This second-edition text was completed in 2004, and an additional update with minor changes was subequently introduced in 2007. This printing of the New Living Translation reflects the updated 2007 text.

Written to Be Read Aloud

It is evident in Scripture that the biblical documents were written to be read aloud, often in public worship (see Nehemiah 8; Luke 4:16-20; 1 Timothy 4:13; Revelation 1:3). It is still the case today that more people will hear the Bible read aloud in church than are likely to read it for themselves. Therefore, a new translation must communicate with clarity and power when it is read publicly. Clarity was a primary goal for the NLT translators, not only to facilitate private reading and understanding, but also to ensure that it would be excellent for public reading and make an immediate and powerful impact on any listener.

The Texts behind the New Living Translation

The Old Testament translators used the Masoretic Text of the Hebrew Bible as represented in *Biblia Hebraica Stuttgartensia* (1977), with its extensive system of textual notes; this is an update of Rudolf Kittel's *Biblia Hebraica* (Stuttgart, 1937). The translators also further compared the Dead Sea Scrolls, the Septuagint and other Greek manuscripts, the Samaritan Pentateuch, the Syriac Peshitta, the Latin Vulgate, and any other versions or manuscripts that shed light on the meaning of difficult passages.

The New Testament translators used the two standard editions of the Greek New Testament: the *Greek New Testament*, published by the United Bible Societies (UBS, fourth revised edition, 1993), and *Novum Testamentum Graece*, edited by Nestle and Aland (NA, twenty-seventh edition, 1993). These two editions, which have the same text but differ in punctuation and textual notes, represent, for the most part, the best in modern textual scholarship. However, in cases where strong textual or other scholarly evidence supported the decision, the translators sometimes chose to differ from the UBS and NA Greek texts and followed variant readings found in other ancient witnesses. Significant textual variants of this sort are always noted in the textual notes of the New Living Translation.

Translation Issues

The translators have made a conscious effort to provide a text that can be easily understood by the typical reader of modern English. To this end, we sought to use only vocabulary and language structures in common use today. We avoided using language likely to become quickly dated or that reflects only a narrow subdialect of English, with the goal of making the New Living Translation as broadly useful and timeless as possible.

But our concern for readability goes beyond the concerns of vocabulary and sentence structure. We are also concerned about historical and cultural barriers to understanding the Bible, and we have sought to translate terms shrouded in history and culture in ways that can be immediately understood. To this end:

- We have converted ancient weights and measures (for example, "ephah" [a unit of dry volume] or "cubit" [a unit of length]) to modern English (American) equivalents, since the ancient measures are not generally meaningful to today's readers. Then in the textual footnotes we offer the literal Hebrew, Aramaic, or Greek measures, along with modern metric equivalents.
- Instead of translating ancient currency values literally, we have expressed them in common terms that communicate the message. For example, in the Old Testament, "ten shekels of silver" becomes "ten pieces of silver" to convey the intended message. In the New Testament, we have often translated the "denarius" as "the normal daily wage" to facilitate understanding. Then a footnote offers: "Greek *a denarius*, the payment for a full day's wage." In general, we give a clear English rendering and then state the literal Hebrew, Aramaic, or Greek in a textual footnote.
- Since the names of Hebrew months are unknown to most contemporary readers, and since the Hebrew lunar calendar fluctuates from year to year in relation to the solar calendar used today, we have looked for clear ways to communicate the time of year the Hebrew months (such as Abib) refer to. When an expanded or interpretive rendering is given in the text, a textual note gives the literal rendering. Where it is possible to define a specific ancient date in terms of our modern calendar, we use modern dates in the text. A textual footnote then gives the literal Hebrew date and states the rationale for our rendering. For example, Ezra 6:15 pinpoints the date when the postexilic Temple was completed in Jerusalem: "the third day of the month Adar." This was during

the sixth year of King Darius's reign (that is, 515 B.C.). We have translated that date as March 12, with a footnote giving the Hebrew and identifying the year as 515 B.C.

- Since ancient references to the time of day differ from our modern methods of denoting time, we have used renderings that are instantly understandable to the modern reader. Accordingly, we have rendered specific times of day by using approximate equivalents in terms of our common "o'clock" system. On occasion, translations such as "at dawn the next morning" or "as the sun was setting" have been used when the biblical reference is more general.
- When the meaning of a proper name (or a wordplay inherent in a proper name) is relevant to the message of the text, its meaning is often illuminated with a textual footnote. For example, in Exodus 2:10 the text reads: "The princess named him Moses, for she explained, 'I lifted him out of the water.' " The accompanying footnote reads: "*Moses* sounds like a Hebrew term that means 'to lift out.' "

  Sometimes, when the actual meaning of a name is clear, that meaning is included in parentheses within the text itself. For example, the text at Genesis 16:11 reads: "You are to name him Ishmael *(which means 'God hears')*, for the LORD has heard your cry of distress." Since the original hearers and readers would have instantly understood the meaning of the name "Ishmael," we have provided modern readers with the same information so they can experience the text in a similar way.
- Many words and phrases carry a great deal of cultural meaning that was obvious to the original readers but needs explanation in our own culture. For example, the phrase "they beat their breasts" (Luke 23:48) in ancient times meant that people were very upset, often in mourning. In our translation we chose to translate this phrase dynamically for clarity: "They went home *in deep sorrow*." Then we included a footnote with the literal Greek, which reads: "Greek *went home beating their breasts*." In other similar cases, however, we have sometimes chosen to illuminate the existing literal expression to make it immediately understandable. For example, here we might have expanded the literal Greek phrase to read: "They went home beating their breasts *in sorrow*." If we had done this, we would not have included a textual footnote, since the literal Greek clearly appears in translation.
- Metaphorical language is sometimes difficult for contemporary readers to understand, so at times we have chosen to translate or illuminate the meaning of a metaphor. For example, the ancient poet writes, "Your neck is *like* the tower of David" (Song of Songs 4:4). We have rendered it "Your neck is *as beautiful as* the tower of David" to clarify the intended positive meaning of the simile. Another example comes in Ecclesiastes 12:3, which can be literally rendered: "Remember him . . . when the grinding women cease because they are few, and the women who look through the windows see dimly." We have rendered it: "Remember him before your teeth—your few remaining servants—stop grinding; and before your eyes—the women looking through the windows—see dimly." We clarified such metaphors only when we believed a typical reader might be confused by the literal text.
- When the content of the original language text is poetic in character, we have rendered it in English poetic form. We sought to break lines in ways that clarify and highlight the relationships between phrases of the text. Hebrew poetry often uses parallelism, a literary form where a second phrase (or in some instances a third or fourth) echoes the initial phrase in some way. In Hebrew parallelism, the subsequent parallel phrases

continue, while also furthering and sharpening, the thought expressed in the initial line or phrase. Whenever possible, we sought to represent these parallel phrases in natural poetic English.

- The Greek term *hoi Ioudaioi* is literally translated "the Jews" in many English translations. In the Gospel of John, however, this term doesn't always refer to the Jewish people generally. In some contexts, it refers more particularly to the Jewish religious leaders. We have attempted to capture the meaning in these different contexts by using terms such as "the people" (with a footnote: Greek *the Jewish people*) or "the religious leaders," where appropriate.
- One challenge we faced was how to translate accurately the ancient biblical text that was originally written in a context where male-oriented terms were used to refer to humanity generally. We needed to respect the nature of the ancient context while also trying to make the translation clear to a modern audience that tends to read male-oriented language as applying only to males. Often the original text, though using masculine nouns and pronouns, clearly intends that the message be applied to both men and women. A typical example is found in the New Testament letters, where the believers are called "brothers" (*adelphoi*). Yet it is clear from the content of these letters that they were addressed to all the believers—male and female. Thus, we have usually translated this Greek word as "brothers and sisters" in order to represent the historical situation more accurately.

We have also been sensitive to passages where the text applies generally to human beings or to the human condition. In some instances we have used plural pronouns (they, them) in place of the masculine singular (he, him). For example, a traditional rendering of Proverbs 22:6 is: "Train up a child in the way he should go, and when he is old he will not turn from it." We have rendered it: "Direct your children onto the right path, and when they are older, they will not leave it." At times, we have also replaced third person pronouns with the second person to ensure clarity. A traditional rendering of Proverbs 26:27 is: "He who digs a pit will fall into it, and he who rolls a stone, it will come back on him." We have rendered it: "If you set a trap for others, you will get caught in it yourself. If you roll a boulder down on others, it will roll back and crush you."

We should emphasize, however, that all masculine nouns and pronouns used to represent God (for example, "Father") have been maintained without exception. All decisions of this kind have been driven by the concern to reflect accurately the intended meaning of the original texts of Scripture.

Lexical Consistency in Terminology

For the sake of clarity, we have translated certain original-language terms consistently, especially within synoptic passages and for commonly repeated rhetorical phrases, and within certain word categories such as divine names and non-theological technical terminology (e.g., liturgical, legal, cultural, zoological, and botanical terms). For theological terms, we have allowed a greater semantic range of acceptable English words or phrases for a single Hebrew or Greek word. We have avoided some theological terms that are not readily understood by many modern readers. For example, we avoided using words such as "justification" and "sanctification," which are carryovers from Latin translations. In place of these words, we have provided renderings such as "made right with God" and "made holy."

The Spelling of Proper Names

Many individuals in the Bible, especially the Old Testament, are known by more than one name (e.g., Uzziah/Azariah). For the sake of clarity, we have tried to use a single spelling for any one individual, footnoting the literal spelling whenever we differ from it. This is especially helpful in delineating the kings of Israel and Judah. King Joash/Jehoash of Israel has been consistently called Jehoash, while King Joash/Jehoash of Judah is called Joash. A similar distinction has been used to distinguish between Joram/Jehoram of Israel and Joram/Jehoram of Judah. All such decisions were made with the goal of clarifying the text for the reader. When the ancient biblical writers clearly had a theological purpose in their choice of a variant name (e.g., Esh-baal/Ishbosheth), the different names have been maintained with an explanatory footnote.

For the names Jacob and Israel, which are used interchangeably for both the individual patriarch and the nation, we generally render it "Israel" when it refers to the nation and "Jacob" when it refers to the individual. When our rendering of the name differs from the underlying Hebrew text, we provide a textual footnote, which includes this explanation: "The names 'Jacob' and 'Israel' are often interchanged throughout the Old Testament, referring sometimes to the individual patriarch and sometimes to the nation."

The Rendering of Divine Names

All appearances of *'el, 'elohim,* or *'eloah* have been translated "God," except where the context demands the translation "god(s)." We have generally rendered the tetragrammaton (*YHWH*) consistently as "the LORD," utilizing a form with small capitals that is common among English translations. This will distinguish it from the name *'adonai,* which we render "Lord." When *'adonai* and *YHWH* appear together, we have rendered it "Sovereign LORD." This also distinguishes *'adonai YHWH* from cases where *YHWH* appears with *'elohim,* which is rendered "LORD God." When *YH* (the short form of *YHWH*) and *YHWH* appear together, we have rendered it "LORD GOD." When *YHWH* appears with the term *tseba'oth,* we have rendered it "LORD of Heaven's Armies" to translate the meaning of the name. In a few cases, we have utilized the transliteration, *Yahweh,* when the personal character of the name is being invoked in contrast to another divine name or the name of some other god (for example, see Exodus 3:15; 6:2-3).

In the New Testament, the Greek word *christos* has been translated as "Messiah" when the context assumes a Jewish audience. When a Gentile audience can be assumed, *christos* has been translated as "Christ." The Greek word *kurios* is consistently translated "Lord," except that it is translated "LORD" wherever the New Testament text explicitly quotes from the Old Testament, and the text there has it in small capitals.

Textual Footnotes

The New Living Translation provides several kinds of textual footnotes, all designated in the text with an asterisk:

- When for the sake of clarity the NLT renders a difficult or potentially confusing phrase dynamically, we generally give the literal rendering in a textual footnote. This allows the reader to see the literal source of our dynamic rendering and how our translation relates to other more literal translations. These notes are prefaced with "Hebrew," "Aramaic," or "Greek," identifying the language of the underlying source text. For example, in Acts 2:42 we translated the literal "breaking of bread" (from the Greek) as "the Lord's Supper" to clarify that this verse refers to the ceremonial practice of the church rather than just an ordinary meal. Then we attached a footnote to "the Lord's Supper," which reads: "Greek *the breaking of bread.*"

- Textual footnotes are also used to show alternative renderings, prefaced with the word "Or." These normally occur for passages where an aspect of the meaning is debated. On occasion, we also provide notes on words or phrases that represent a departure from long-standing tradition. These notes are prefaced with "Traditionally rendered." For example, the footnote to the translation "serious skin disease" at Leviticus 13:2 says: "Traditionally rendered *leprosy.* The Hebrew word used throughout this passage is used to describe various skin diseases."
- When our translators follow a textual variant that differs significantly from our standard Hebrew or Greek texts (listed earlier), we document that difference with a footnote. We also footnote cases when the NLT excludes a passage that is included in the Greek text known as the *Textus Receptus* (and familiar to readers through its translation in the King James Version). In such cases, we offer a translation of the excluded text in a footnote, even though it is generally recognized as a later addition to the Greek text and not part of the original Greek New Testament.
- All Old Testament passages that are quoted in the New Testament are identified by a textual footnote at the New Testament location. When the New Testament clearly quotes from the Greek translation of the Old Testament, and when it differs significantly in wording from the Hebrew text, we also place a textual footnote at the Old Testament location. This note includes a rendering of the Greek version, along with a cross-reference to the New Testament passage(s) where it is cited (for example, see notes on Proverbs 3:12; Psalms 8:2; 53:3).
- Some textual footnotes provide cultural and historical information on places, things, and people in the Bible that are probably obscure to modern readers. Such notes should aid the reader in understanding the message of the text. For example, in Acts 12:1, "King Herod" is named in this translation as "King Herod Agrippa" and is identified in a footnote as being "the nephew of Herod Antipas and a grandson of Herod the Great."
- When the meaning of a proper name (or a wordplay inherent in a proper name) is relevant to the meaning of the text, it is either illuminated with a textual footnote or included within parentheses in the text itself. For example, the footnote concerning the name "Eve" at Genesis 3:20 reads: "*Eve* sounds like a Hebrew term that means 'to give life.' " This wordplay in the Hebrew illuminates the meaning of the text, which goes on to say that Eve "would be the mother of all who live."

As we submit this translation for publication, we recognize that any translation of the Scriptures is subject to limitations and imperfections. Anyone who has attempted to communicate the richness of God's Word into another language will realize it is impossible to make a perfect translation. Recognizing these limitations, we sought God's guidance and wisdom throughout this project. Now we pray that he will accept our efforts and use this translation for the benefit of the church and of all people.

We pray that the New Living Translation will overcome some of the barriers of history, culture, and language that have kept people from reading and understanding God's Word. We hope that readers unfamiliar with the Bible will find the words clear and easy to understand and that readers well versed in the Scriptures will gain a fresh perspective. We pray that readers will gain insight and wisdom for living, but most of all that they will meet the God of the Bible and be forever changed by knowing him.

The Bible Translation Committee
October 2007

INTRODUCTION TO *THE WOMEN'S STUDY BIBLE*

The majority of comment on the Bible available to today's readers, whether in commentaries or in Study Bibles, is written from the perspective of white, Western, classically educated, middle-class males. The questions asked and issues raised almost always deal with that perspective. Usually the work is done with integrity, insight, and good scholarship, and the usefulness of the comments is by no means limited to those who share the same background as the writers. The answers found in Scripture to questions asked by men often bear great relevance to women; their insights are likely to be genuine insights into what Scripture is saying. Nevertheless, inevitable limitations arise from their curtailed perspective. Many insights into the text are never revealed simply because the questions that might have revealed them have never been asked.

This *Women's Study Bible* is an attempt to redress this imbalance. The annotations and articles unashamedly approach the text from a particular and identified perspective, seeking to provide a resource for the whole church—both women and men—that will allow readers to notice and identify issues within Scripture that relate to women or reflect their unique perspective. It seeks deliberately to ask women's questions. It is not written simply "for" women as opposed to men; it is rather written "from" women. In other words, the notes in this Bible don't just look at passages about women; they look at all of Scripture from a woman's perspective. Texts that are about women or seen as particularly relevant to women are often assumed therefore not to be relevant to men and are rarely if ever preached on in church services. They are assumed to be more properly dealt with in meetings specifically for women. It is interesting that the same attitude is not assumed to apply to passages that are particularly relevant to men! But the whole of the Bible is there for both men and women, and the perspectives of both need to be considered by all.

Certainly women need the opportunity to have the Scriptures explained in ways that are relevant to their lives. The Old Testament bears witness to the importance of the Scriptures being read and interpreted to all God's people (Deut 31:12; Josh 8:34–35; cf. 2 Kgs 23:2). Just as Ezra made sure the Word was not only read but also interpreted for both men and women (Neh 8:1–8), so today the Scriptures need to be read and interpreted for women. All too often, however, the interpretive voices of women have been lacking.

In bringing this material together, it has been exciting and encouraging to note how much there is in the Bible that has often remained unnoticed but, once noted, can clearly be seen as coming from the text and not being read into it. Scripture attests to many women who received and interpreted God's Word within their own contexts—Miriam, Deborah, Hannah, Huldah, Elizabeth, and Mary among them. This Study Bible seeks to help modern believers follow in their footsteps, perhaps fulfilling the psalmist's words "The Lord gives the command: The women who proclaim the *good* tidings are a great host" (Ps 68:11 NASB, cf. ESV, CSB; the feminine plural "host of women" is obscured in many contemporary versions).

Our contributors were encouraged to reflect not only in their university offices and at their kitchen tables but also from serious exegetical study to rumination on the real world in which women live. How does the Scripture speak to their sisters as they birth and breastfeed, bandage and console, earn their daily living, survive intolerable conditions, hold high office, and contemplate their own failures and shattered hopes? We want the annotations to address readers in the most common experiences of everyday life.

At the same time, we could not ignore recent challenges presented to women of faith.

Much contemporary feminist criticism has viewed the Bible as hostile to women because it has been used for unjust oppression in contemporary societies. Some feminists have understandably viewed the Bible as inimical to the concerns of women and have employed what has been called a "hermeneutic of suspicion." Efforts have frequently been made to subvert the text in order to recover an underlying stratum that is supportive of women. This stratum is held to have been deliberately distorted by the biblical writers in order to yield a patriarchal message detrimental to women.

In contrast to such efforts, this commentary is written by women of faith who believe that *all* Scripture is inspired by God and given for the benefit of all humanity. The contributors have examined the difficult texts from a "hermeneutic of faith," a conviction that the Scriptures are meant for healing rather than hurt, for affirmation of all persons, especially those who are oppressed. Our contributors have examined the hard texts, the seeming contradictions and the paradoxes regarding women, and they have sought to move in new, faith-filled directions without minimizing the negative attitudes of individual biblical authors. (Jonah, for instance, had no sympathy for his audience, though he delivered a life-giving message; other figures in biblical history also learned that God had a far nobler and more gracious design than they had originally contemplated.) The Bible is God's Word, and we must deal with both its divine and human authorship—the God of truth communicating through frail and fallen human beings. Faithful believers may appropriately ask some very difficult questions about text and context, original intention, and enduring significance.

Although much relevant material comes through the annotations on the text, certain areas of interest to women cannot be expounded thoroughly in the comments on individual books. For this reason a range of articles (displayed as sidebars) have been included, enabling a number of concerns (such as parental influence, sibling rivalry, and menstruation) to be looked at from a woman's point of view.

The chosen perspective is that of women, but the work of scholars from all around the world and from different denominational backgrounds have been included in recognition that we need to hear from those of different cultures and different backgrounds. Because we have been seeking to provide a voice for women and to ask new questions, the work of some younger and lesser-known writers has been included alongside that of more recognized experts. There are a small number of male contributors, included not simply as a token but as a model, reflecting the conviction that with effort, it is possible to set aside one's own perspective and to ask questions wearing, as it were, someone else's spectacles.

Because of the unique nature of this project, both a complement to other resources and an opportunity to ask different kinds of questions of the biblical text, each writer has been given a great deal of freedom. There is considerable variety in points of view and style—not all agree, and not all reflect the views of the editors or the publisher. What all contributors do share is a conviction that the Scriptures can speak meaningfully to women's and men's lives today. Difficult questions relating to text, context, content, or significance have not been avoided; paradoxes and seeming contradictions have been honestly faced.

This Study Bible should be an invaluable asset for those who wish to gain an understanding of women's approach to Scripture as good news for themselves and others. It argues for the full inspiration of the Bible and the full equality of women. Here is a resource that allows qualified believing women to interpret Scripture from their own stance. It affirms the significance, power, and essential dignity of women in all aspects of life. We offer this work in the conviction of the Puritan divine John Robinson, who proclaimed, "God has yet more things to break forth from his holy Word."

Catherine Clark Kroeger
Mary J. Evans

THE WOMEN'S STUDY BIBLE CONTRIBUTORS

Christine L. Anslow 1 Chronicles

Jill L. Baker 1 and 2 Kings

Kristen Plinke Bentley Philemon (*see also under* Sharyn Dowd)

Kamila A. Blessing John, 1 Timothy

Anthea D. Butler Zephaniah

Philippa Carter Joshua

Lynn H. Cohick Romans

Shirley A. Decker-Lucke Colossians

Sharyn Dowd *and* **Kristen Plinke Bentley** Galatians

Rosemary M. Dowsett Hosea, Matthew, Acts

Mary J. Evans Deuteronomy, James (*see also under* Catherine Clark Kroeger)

Joyce E. Winifred Every-Clayton Daniel

Ailish F. Eves Judges

LeAnn Snow Flesher Job, Lamentations

Conrad Gempf 2 Timothy

Sharon H. Gritz 1 Thessalonians, Hebrews

Elizabeth A. Harper Jonah, Micah

Hannah Karajian Harrington Ezra, Zechariah

Edwin C. Hostetter Habakkuk

L. Ann Jervis 2 Peter

Janet Nasambu Kassilly 2 Thessalonians

Veronica Koperski Philippians

Catherine Clark Kroeger Luke, 1 Corinthians, Titus (*see also under* Gwynneth Marian Napier Raikes and Aida Besançon Spencer)

Catherine Clark Kroeger *and* **Mary J. Evans** Exodus

Richard Clark Kroeger, Jr. Haggai

Alison Le Cornu Proverbs

Jeff H. McCrory, Jr. Nehemiah

Melba Padilla Maggay Esther

Ksenija Magda 2 John, 3 John

Keren E. Morrell Revelation

Margaret A. Motion 1 John

Lai Ling Elizabeth Ngan Amos

Joy Osgood 1 and 2 Samuel

Elaine A. Phillips Ecclesiastes

Susan M. Pigott Leviticus, Numbers

Hyunhye Junia Pokrifka Obadiah

Sandra Hack Polaski 2 Corinthians

Claire M. Powell Ephesians

Gwynneth Marian Napier Raikes Joel

Gwynneth Marian Napier Raikes *and* **Catherine Clark Kroeger** Psalms

Gillian M. Rowell Ruth

Pamela J. Scalise Malachi

Rebecca Skaggs Jude

Aida Besançon Spencer *and* **Catherine Clark Kroeger** 1 Peter

Marion Ann Taylor Ezekiel

Bonnie Bowman Thurston Mark

Ruth Valerio Genesis

Raewynne J. Whiteley Song of Songs

Vivien Whitfield Isaiah

Editors, Oxford University Press 2 Chronicles, Jeremiah, Nahum

THE OLD TESTAMENT

GENESIS

INTRODUCTION

To read Genesis is a privilege, for it is to read the words of extremely old texts and to be given a window into cultures and times long since ended. This also makes Genesis a hard book to understand as it contains much that is unfamiliar to us today: flaming torches passing through severed chunks of meat, sons of God having intercourse with women, talking snakes, and much more.

And yet, despite its strangeness, Genesis contains many stories that resonate deeply with us, and they do so because they speak to us about our "genesis": literally, our origins or beginnings. Genesis is, indeed, the book of beginnings: the beginning of the Bible, of the Old Testament, and of the books of the Pentateuch; it tells of the beginning of the world and of evil, the beginning of the nation of Israel, and of God's purposes for his creation.

Even though no name for an author is given, the traditional understanding among both Jews and Christians is that Genesis (and the Pentateuch as a whole) was written by Moses. Since the late nineteenth century, however, the majority scholarly view has been that Genesis is the result of one author pulling together different sources written at different times during Israel's history (many scholars follow a theory that labels these sources as J, E, D, and P). What is clear about this initial book of the Bible is that the stories that comprise it would have been circulating orally in Israel, some of them for hundreds of years, until an author brought them together and formed them into one literary whole.

The date at which this happened is probably during the period of Israel's exile in Babylon in the sixth century BC, or possibly shortly afterward. This was a crucial time for Israel, a time when she had lost Jerusalem and the Temple, which were key symbols of her identity. What did it mean to be Israel in a strange land (cf. Ps 137)? The answer was partly to be found in going back to the beginning, for the people to rediscover who they were.

The content of Genesis, in particular its opening chapters, has caused many debates and controversies. These revolve around the related issues of how one reads Genesis and what kind of literature it is. At one end of the spectrum are those who read Genesis as historical narrative: The stories relate events as they actually happened, thousands of years ago. At the other end are those who see Genesis as containing myths with no historical basis; myths designed, for example, to explain the origin of a particular custom or sacred place (e.g., 2:32; 28:10–22) or folklore that preserved traditions associated with a particular Israelite hero (such as Abraham or Jacob).

In reading Genesis it is helpful to be aware that the nations around Israel also had their own stories about the beginnings of the world and of humanity. There are many parallels between these writings and the early chapters of Genesis that depict the creation of the world and a flood. Thus, these early chapters can be viewed more as making their own theological statements in light of these other narratives, rather than as history in a literal sense. As the story develops, however, the genre of Genesis becomes one of theological history, which relates the events of years gone by, but in ways that make a definite theological point.

Genesis is the story of God's relationship with his creation, of the breakdown of that relationship, and of the beginnings of God's plans to put that relationship back to rights. That story divides into two parts. The first—Genesis 1 to 11 (often called the *prehistory*)—is the story of God's creation of the heavens and the earth and the first generations of people. The second—Genesis 12 to 50—focuses on the story of the one family that God chooses to be the means of his blessing throughout the earth, and looks at how God's promises to them are outworked through many twists and turns. Within this second part, Genesis 37 to 50 form a novella about Jacob's family, centered around Joseph.

Genesis contains material that has been notorious in relation to women, from Eve's infamous transgression, to Sarai/h's banishment of the slave girl Hagar, to the rape of Dinah. There is much here that needs careful treatment in considering the role and status of women in ancient Israel and what their experiences might teach us today. As we read through this book, though, we will learn much about the character of the Creator God and his promises to his people.—*Ruth Valerio*

✧

The Account of Creation

1 In the beginning God created the heavens and the earth.* 2The earth was formless and empty, and darkness covered the deep waters. And the Spirit of God was hovering over the surface of the waters.

3Then God said, "Let there be light," and there was light. 4And God saw that the light was good. Then he separated the light from the darkness. 5God called the light "day" and the darkness "night."

And evening passed and morning came, marking the first day.

6Then God said, "Let there be a space between the waters, to separate the waters of the heavens from the waters of the earth." 7And that is what happened. God made this space to separate the waters of the earth from the waters of the heavens. 8God called the space "sky."

And evening passed and morning came, marking the second day.

9Then God said, "Let the waters beneath the sky flow together into one place, so dry ground may appear." And that is what happened.
10God called the dry ground "land" and the waters "seas." And God saw that it was good. 11Then God said, "Let the land sprout with vegetation—every sort of seed-bearing plant, and trees that grow seed-bearing fruit. These seeds will then produce the kinds of plants and trees from which they came." And that is what happened. 12The land produced vegetation—all sorts of seed-bearing plants, and trees with seed-bearing fruit. Their seeds produced plants and trees of the same kind. And God saw that it was good.

1:1 Or *In the beginning when God created the heavens and the earth, . . .* Or *When God began to create the heavens and the earth, . . .*

1:1—11:32 The Creation of the World and Beginning of Humankind

1:1—2:4 The First Creation Story. 1:2: God is pictured hovering in anticipation like a great bird. There is potential contained within the formless world that he has created. Unlike the other ancient creation myths, the formlessness is not negative chaos: It is simply empty, waiting for God to act. **3:** For Israel's neighbors, the world was the result of a mighty battle between warring gods. Here, there is only one God and he creates simply by speaking the word. **6–8:** Ancient cosmology saw the universe as turtle-shaped, with a flat earth covered by a dome-shaped sky. This sky pushed up the *waters of the heavens* (as seen in the blue sky) and separated these waters from

13 And evening passed and morning came,
marking the third day.

14 Then God said, "Let lights appear in the sky
to separate the day from the night. Let them
be signs to mark the seasons, days, and years.
15 Let these lights in the sky shine down on
the earth." And that is what happened. 16 God
made two great lights—the larger one to
govern the day, and the smaller one to govern
the night. He also made the stars. 17 God set
these lights in the sky to light the earth, 18 to
govern the day and night, and to separate the
light from the darkness. And God saw that it
was good.
19 And evening passed and morning came,
marking the fourth day.

20 Then God said, "Let the waters swarm with
fish and other life. Let the skies be filled with
birds of every kind." 21 So God created great
sea creatures and every living thing that
scurries and swarms in the water, and every
sort of bird—each producing offspring of the
same kind. And God saw that it was good.
22 Then God blessed them, saying, "Be fruitful
and multiply. Let the fish fill the seas, and let
the birds multiply on the earth."
23 And evening passed and morning came,
marking the fifth day.

24 Then God said, "Let the earth produce every
sort of animal, each producing offspring of
the same kind—livestock, small animals that
scurry along the ground, and wild animals."
And that is what happened. 25 God made all
sorts of wild animals, livestock, and small
animals, each able to produce offspring of the
same kind. And God saw that it was good.

26 Then God said, "Let us make human
beings* in our image, to be like us. They will
reign over the fish in the sea, the birds in the
sky, the livestock, all the wild animals on the
earth, and the small animals that scurry along
the ground."

27 So God created human beings* in his own
image.
In the image of God he created them;
male and female he created them.

28 Then God blessed them and said, "Be
fruitful and multiply. Fill the earth and
govern it. Reign over the fish in the sea, the
birds in the sky, and all the animals that
scurry along the ground."
29 Then God said, "Look! I have given you
every seed-bearing plant throughout the
earth and all the fruit trees for your food.
30 And I have given every green plant as food
for all the wild animals, the birds in the sky,
and the small animals that scurry along the
ground—everything that has life." And that
is what happened.
31 Then God looked over all he had made,
and he saw that it was very good!
And evening passed and morning came,
marking the sixth day.

2 So the creation of the heavens and the
earth and everything in them was
completed. 2 On the seventh day God
had finished his work of creation, so he
rested* from all his work. 3 And God
blessed the seventh day and declared it

1:26 Or *man;* Hebrew reads *adam.* **1:27** Or *the man;* Hebrew reads *ha-adam.* **2:2** Or *ceased;* also in 2:3.

those of the earth. Thus order is brought to the deep waters of verse 2. **14–19:** God continues to bring his order and structure to all parts of the universe. The writer does not say where the daylight of verses 3–5 came from before the sun was created on the fourth day, but that is not the point. The sun, moon, and stars are not to be worshiped as divine celestial beings because they are created things, along with everything else. **22:** The creatures of the sea and the sky are blessed with the same words that God will use for the first humans. **24–25:** All areas of the universe have been filled except for the land. Humans are created on the same day as other animals. **26–27:** The plural *us* and *our image* is not a reference to the Trinity but to the ancient idea of the heavenly council in which God was depicted as surrounded by other heavenly beings (cf. Job 1:6ff). Here, in the Hebrew word for *human beings* (*adam*), the inclusion of women and men is clearly indicated. The word could also mean "earthling/earth being," as is reflected in the way that our modern "human" is linked to the Latin *humus*, "earth." To be made in God's image is to be his representative to the rest of creation. **28:** *Reign* does not imply subordination or abuse but mirrors God's way of servant kingship. **31:** What God has made is very good and is not to be misused. **2:2–3:** Exodus 20:8–11 uses these verses as the basis for the institution of the Sabbath, which comes from the Hebrew verb *shabat*, "to cease."

holy, because it was the day when he
rested from all his work of creation.

4This is the account of the creation of the heavens and the earth.

The Man and Woman in Eden

When the LORD God made the earth and the heavens, 5neither wild plants nor grains were growing on the earth. For the LORD God had not yet sent rain to water the earth, and there were no people to cultivate the soil. 6Instead, springs* came up from the ground and watered all the land. 7Then the LORD God formed the man from the dust of the ground. He breathed the breath of life into the man's nostrils, and the man became a living person.

8Then the LORD God planted a garden in Eden in the east, and there he placed the man he had made. 9The LORD God made all sorts of trees grow up from the ground—trees that were beautiful and that produced delicious fruit. In the middle of the garden he placed the tree of life and the tree of the knowledge of good and evil.

10A river flowed from the land of Eden, watering the garden and then dividing into four branches. 11The first branch, called the Pishon, flowed around the entire land of Havilah, where gold is found. 12The gold of that land is exceptionally pure; aromatic resin and onyx stone are also found there. 13The second branch, called the Gihon, flowed around the entire land of Cush. 14The third branch, called the Tigris, flowed east of the land of Asshur. The fourth branch is called the Euphrates.

15The LORD God placed the man in the Garden of Eden to tend and watch over it. 16But the LORD God warned him, "You may freely eat the fruit of every tree in the garden—17except the tree of the knowledge of good and evil. If you eat its fruit, you are sure to die."

18Then the LORD God said, "It is not good for the man to be alone. I will make a helper who is just right for him." 19So the LORD God formed from the ground all the wild animals and all the birds of the sky. He brought them to the man* to see what he would call them, and the man chose a name for each one. 20He gave names to all the livestock, all the birds of the sky, and all the wild animals. But still there was no helper just right for him.

21So the LORD God caused the man to fall into a deep sleep. While the man slept, the LORD God took out one of the man's ribs* and closed up the opening. 22Then the LORD God made a woman from the rib, and he brought her to the man.

23"At last!" the man exclaimed.

"This one is bone from my bone,
  and flesh from my flesh!
She will be called 'woman,'
  because she was taken from 'man.' "

2:6 Or *mist.* **2:19** Or *Adam,* and so throughout the chapter.
2:21 Or *took a part of the man's side.*

2:4–25 The Man and Woman in Eden. This different account of the creation of the world and its focus on humanity is thought by many to have originated in the tenth century BC, during the period of the United Monarchy. It is notable that *LORD* is used in the divine name here. **4a:** The phrase *the account of* (from Heb., "these are the generations of") is a stylistic phrase that reappears in 6:9; 10:1; 11:27; 25:19; and 37:2. It signals the start of a new section. **4b–9:** The order of creation is different from that in chapter 1 and starts from a dry, infertile earth, rather than watery depths. This reinforces the view that these chapters are not to be taken literally. The man (*adam*), is formed from the ground (*adamah*), establishing an inextricable link. Yet *adam* conveys more than simply dust because the man is the only creature that contains God's breath. **10–14:** The Tigris and Euphrates suggest a location in Mesopotamia (modern-day Iraq and western Iran). The Pishon in Havilah may be in Arabia and the Gishon in Cush could indicate Ethiopia in Africa. These rivers flow over the known world, with the Garden of Eden (lit., "delight") in the center. **15:** The man is created to take care of the garden; the human is given work to do! **16–17:** Despite our yearning to know, the text here does not say what the *tree of the knowledge of good and evil* is (nor the *tree of life* in v. 9). God has placed limits to the human being's freedom in the garden. **18–20:** God creates animals to satisfy the earthling's loneliness, but this fails. The word *helper* does not imply inferiority and is elsewhere used of God (e.g., Pss 10—14). **20b:** This is the first place in which "human being" (*him*) appears without the definite article "the" in the Hebrew; the proper name Adam could rightly be used here. **21–25:** These verses have often been seen from a patriarchal perspective and used to argue both for men's superiority (since woman was made from the man's rib) or for the blatant sexism of the passage. However, seeing the man as a generic earth-being gives a different angle. The poem in verse 23 is the first place where the sexes are differentiated, as this now uses two different but linguistically connected words in Hebrew for woman and man.

24 This explains why a man leaves his father
and mother and is joined to his wife, and the two
are united into one.
25 Now the man and his wife were both naked,
but they felt no shame.

The Man and Woman Sin

3 The serpent was the shrewdest of all the
wild animals the LORD God had made. One
day he asked the woman, "Did God really
say you must not eat the fruit from any of the
trees in the garden?"
2 "Of course we may eat fruit from the trees
in the garden," the woman replied. 3 "It's only the
fruit from the tree in the middle of the garden that
we are not allowed to eat. God said, 'You must not
eat it or even touch it; if you do, you will die.' "
4 "You won't die!" the serpent replied to the
woman. 5 "God knows that your eyes will be
opened as soon as you eat it, and you will be like
God, knowing both good and evil."
6 The woman was convinced. She saw that the
tree was beautiful and its fruit looked delicious,
and she wanted the wisdom it would give her. So
she took some of the fruit and ate it. Then she
gave some to her husband, who was with her, and
he ate it, too. 7 At that moment their eyes were
opened, and they suddenly felt shame at their
nakedness. So they sewed fig leaves together to
cover themselves.
8 When the cool evening breezes were blowing, the man* and his wife heard the LORD God
walking about in the garden. So they hid from
the LORD God among the trees. 9 Then the LORD
God called to the man, "Where are you?"
10 He replied, "I heard you walking in the garden, so I hid. I was afraid because I was naked."
11 "Who told you that you were naked?" the
LORD God asked. "Have you eaten from the tree
whose fruit I commanded you not to eat?"
12 The man replied, "It was the woman you
gave me who gave me the fruit, and I ate it."
13 Then the LORD God asked the woman,
"What have you done?"
"The serpent deceived me," she replied.
"That's why I ate it."
14 Then the LORD God said to the serpent,

"Because you have done this, you are cursed
more than all animals, domestic and wild.
You will crawl on your belly,
groveling in the dust as long as you live.
15 And I will cause hostility between you and
the woman,
and between your offspring and her
offspring.
He will strike* your head,
and you will strike his heel."

16 Then he said to the woman,

"I will sharpen the pain of your pregnancy,
and in pain you will give birth.
And you will desire to control your husband,
but he will rule over you.*"

17 And to the man he said,

"Since you listened to your wife and ate from
the tree
whose fruit I commanded you not to eat,
the ground is cursed because of you.
All your life you will struggle to scratch a
living from it.
18 It will grow thorns and thistles for you,
though you will eat of its grains.
19 By the sweat of your brow
will you have food to eat
until you return to the ground
from which you were made.

3:8 Or *Adam,* and so throughout the chapter. **3:15** Or *bruise;* also in 3:15b. **3:16** Or *And though you will have desire for your husband, / he will rule over you.*

3:1–19 The Man and Woman Sin. 1–3: Craftiness can also be a positive attribute (e.g., Prov 13:16, translated *wise*). There is no indication in the text that the snake is Satan. Both the snake and the woman distort God's command. **4–7:** Some detail is now given about the tree in the middle of the garden. Some commentators see these verses sociologically as referring to the natural process of maturation that occurs within humans. **6:** *Husband* is the translation of the Hebrew word for "man" (cf. 2:23), thus emphasizing the relational dynamic of the Hebrew word. **8–13:** A brief insight into the original relationship between God and humanity is shown, but already that relationship is changed as the man and woman are now afraid of God. The conversation between God and Adam and Eve is one heard every day between parent and child. **14–15:** Only the snake is cursed. The *offspring* of verse 15 is used collectively and refers to the fear or hatred that humans seem naturally to have of snakes, although later interpreters read into it the first announcement of the gospel. **16:** *Desire* is not for romance but for domination (cf. 4:7): The battle of the sexes starts here. **17–19:** Because of Adam, all human beings are now cursed. The effects of humanity's sin extend to the whole created realm (cf. Rom 8:19–23).

For you were made from dust,
and to dust you will return."

Paradise Lost: God's Judgment

[20]Then the man—Adam—named his wife Eve,
because she would be the mother of all who
live.* [21]And the LORD God made clothing from
animal skins for Adam and his wife.
[22]Then the LORD God said, "Look, the human beings* have become like us, knowing both
good and evil. What if they reach out, take fruit
from the tree of life, and eat it? Then they will
live forever!" [23]So the LORD God banished them
from the Garden of Eden, and he sent Adam out
to cultivate the ground from which he had been
made. [24]After sending them out, the LORD God
stationed mighty cherubim to the east of the
Garden of Eden. And he placed a flaming sword
that flashed back and forth to guard the way to
the tree of life.

Cain and Abel

4 Now Adam* had sexual relations with his
wife, Eve, and she became pregnant. When
she gave birth to Cain, she said, "With the
LORD's help, I have produced* a man!" [2]Later she
gave birth to his brother and named him Abel.
When they grew up, Abel became a shepherd,
while Cain cultivated the ground. [3]When it was
time for the harvest, Cain presented some of his
crops as a gift to the LORD. [4]Abel also brought
a gift—the best of the firstborn lambs from his
flock. The LORD accepted Abel and his gift, [5]but
he did not accept Cain and his gift. This made
Cain very angry, and he looked dejected.
[6]"Why are you so angry?" the LORD asked
Cain. "Why do you look so dejected? [7]You will
be accepted if you do what is right. But if you
refuse to do what is right, then watch out! Sin is
crouching at the door, eager to control you. But
you must subdue it and be its master."
[8]One day Cain suggested to his brother,
"Let's go out into the fields."* And while they
were in the field, Cain attacked his brother, Abel,
and killed him.
[9]Afterward the LORD asked Cain, "Where is
your brother? Where is Abel?"
"I don't know," Cain responded. "Am I my
brother's guardian?"
[10]But the LORD said, "What have you done?
Listen! Your brother's blood cries out to me from
the ground! [11]Now you are cursed and banished
from the ground, which has swallowed your
brother's blood. [12]No longer will the ground
yield good crops for you, no matter how hard
you work! From now on you will be a homeless
wanderer on the earth."
[13]Cain replied to the LORD, "My punishment*
is too great for me to bear! [14]You have banished
me from the land and from your presence; you
have made me a homeless wanderer. Anyone
who finds me will kill me!"
[15]The LORD replied, "No, for I will give a sevenfold punishment to anyone who kills you."
Then the LORD put a mark on Cain to warn anyone who might try to kill him. [16]So Cain left the
LORD's presence and settled in the land of Nod,*
east of Eden.

The Descendants of Cain

[17]Cain had sexual relations with his wife, and she
became pregnant and gave birth to Enoch. Then
Cain founded a city, which he named Enoch, after
his son. [18]Enoch had a son named Irad. Irad be-

3:20 *Eve* sounds like a Hebrew term that means "to give life." **3:22** Or *the man;* Hebrew reads *ha-adam.* **4:1a** Or *the man;* also in 4:25. **4:1b** Or *I have acquired. Cain* sounds like a Hebrew term that can mean "produce" or "acquire." **4:8** As in Samaritan Pentateuch, Greek and Syriac versions, and Latin Vulgate; Masoretic Text lacks *"Let's go out into the fields."* **4:13** Or *My sin.* **4:16** *Nod* means "wandering."

3:20–24 Paradise Lost: God's Judgment. 21: God establishes a pattern of following human sin with punishment and then an act of grace (seen also in relation to Cain and the Flood narrative). Prickly fig leaves are replaced by soft leather. **22–24:** Eating from the tree of life would now lead to irrevocable disaster although the text does not tell us why this would result from being able to live forever.

4:1–16 Cain and Abel. 1–5: Abel offers to the LORD *the best* of his produce, while Cain offers only *some of his crops*. Now it is established that only the best is acceptable to God. **6–8:** Cain has a choice over how he responds to God's rejection of his offering. Cain is challenged not to give in to his feelings but to conquer sin. **9:** As in 3:9 God asks a question of the sinful Cain, knowing the answer full well. **10–11:** The curse of Adam is echoed here as Cain is further alienated from the ground. Blood is considered sacred as it contains the person or animal's essence of life. **13–16:** Cain loses all his rights to protection, but as in 3:21 God extends grace toward Cain.

4:17–24 The Descendants of Cain. 17–22: A familiar pattern is established here as only the males of the family line are named, leaving the women hidden. This is the first of many genealogical tables, explaining the origins of major sections of the early Israelite

came the father of* Mehujael. Mehujael became the father of Methushael. Methushael became the father of Lamech.
19 Lamech married two women. The first was named Adah, and the second was Zillah. 20 Adah gave birth to Jabal, who was the first of those who raise livestock and live in tents. 21 His brother's name was Jubal, the first of all who play the harp and flute. 22 Lamech's other wife, Zillah, gave birth to a son named Tubal-cain. He became an expert in forging tools of bronze and iron. Tubal-cain had a sister named Naamah. 23 One day Lamech said to his wives,

"Adah and Zillah, hear my voice;
listen to me, you wives of Lamech.
I have killed a man who attacked me,
a young man who wounded me.
24 If someone who kills Cain is punished seven times,
then the one who kills me will be punished seventy-seven times!"

The Birth of Seth

25 Adam had sexual relations with his wife again, and she gave birth to another son. She named him Seth,* for she said, "God has granted me another son in place of Abel, whom Cain killed."
26 When Seth grew up, he had a son and named him Enosh. At that time people first began to worship the LORD by name.

The Descendants of Adam

5 This is the written account of the descendants of Adam. When God created human beings,* he made them to be like himself. 2 He created them male and female, and he blessed them and called them "human."

3 When Adam was 130 years old, he became the father of a son who was just like him—in his very image. He named his son Seth. 4 After the birth of Seth, Adam lived another 800 years, and he had other sons and daughters. 5 Adam lived 930 years, and then he died.
6 When Seth was 105 years old, he became the father of* Enosh. 7 After the birth of* Enosh, Seth lived another 807 years, and he had other sons and daughters. 8 Seth lived 912 years, and then he died.
9 When Enosh was 90 years old, he became the father of Kenan. 10 After the birth of Kenan, Enosh lived another 815 years, and he had other sons and daughters. 11 Enosh lived 905 years, and then he died.
12 When Kenan was 70 years old, he became the father of Mahalalel. 13 After the birth of Mahalalel, Kenan lived another 840 years, and he had other sons and daughters. 14 Kenan lived 910 years, and then he died.
15 When Mahalalel was 65 years old, he became the father of Jared. 16 After the birth of Jared, Mahalalel lived another 830 years, and he had other sons and daughters. 17 Mahalalel lived 895 years, and then he died.
18 When Jared was 162 years old, he became the father of Enoch. 19 After the birth of Enoch, Jared lived another 800 years, and he had other sons and daughters. 20 Jared lived 962 years, and then he died.
21 When Enoch was 65 years old, he became the father of Methuselah. 22 After the birth of Methuselah, Enoch lived in close fellowship with God for another 300 years, and he had other sons and daughters. 23 Enoch lived 365 years, 24 walking in close fellowship with God. Then one day he disappeared, because God took him.
25 When Methuselah was 187 years old, he became the father of Lamech. 26 After the birth of Lamech, Methuselah lived another 782 years, and he had other sons and daughters. 27 Methuselah lived 969 years, and then he died.

4:18 Or *the ancestor of,* and so throughout the verse. **4:25** *Seth* probably means "granted"; the name may also mean "appointed." **5:1** Or *man;* Hebrew reads *adam;* similarly in 5:2. **5:6** Or *the ancestor of;* also in 5:9, 12, 15, 18, 21, 25. **5:7** Or *the birth of this ancestor of;* also in 5:10, 13, 16, 19, 22, 26.

community. **23–24:** As the human population is increasing, so too is violence and sin.

4:25–26 The Birth of Seth. The genealogy in Luke 3 traces Jesus' ancestry back to Seth.

5:1–32 The Descendants of Adam. Ten generations connect Adam with Noah, suggesting that this genealogy is a stylistic device functioning as a bridge to the next major story, rather than literal history. Only the eldest son is mentioned by name in each generation, reflecting a patriarchal culture that is still seen in many societies today. **21–24:** Interpreters have taken Enoch's disappearance to mean that he did not die, but was simply taken up to be with the LORD, paralleling Elijah in 2 Kings 2:11–12. As a result, Enoch became an important legendary figure within Jewish tradition. **27:** Methuselah is the oldest man in the Bible, reflecting the huge lifespans of the pre-Flood ancestors. If taken literally, these lifespans are

28 When Lamech was 182 years old, he became
the father of a son. 29 Lamech named his
son Noah, for he said, "May he bring us
relief* from our work and the painful labor
of farming this ground that the LORD has
cursed." 30 After the birth of Noah, Lamech
lived another 595 years, and he had other
sons and daughters. 31 Lamech lived 777 years,
and then he died.

32 By the time Noah was 500 years old, he was
the father of Shem, Ham, and Japheth.

A World Gone Wrong

6 Then the people began to multiply on the
earth, and daughters were born to them.
2 The sons of God saw the beautiful wom-
en* and took any they wanted as their wives.
3 Then the LORD said, "My Spirit will not put
up with* humans for such a long time, for they
are only mortal flesh. In the future, their normal
lifespan will be no more than 120 years."

4 In those days, and for some time after, giant
Nephilites lived on the earth, for whenever the
sons of God had intercourse with women, they
gave birth to children who became the heroes
and famous warriors of ancient times.

5 The LORD observed the extent of human
wickedness on the earth, and he saw that everything they thought or imagined was consistently
and totally evil. 6 So the LORD was sorry he had
ever made them and put them on the earth. It
broke his heart. 7 And the LORD said, "I will wipe
this human race I have created from the face
of the earth. Yes, and I will destroy every living thing—all the people, the large animals, the
small animals that scurry along the ground, and
even the birds of the sky. I am sorry I ever made
them." 8 But Noah found favor with the LORD.

The Story of Noah

9 This is the account of Noah and his family. Noah
was a righteous man, the only blameless person
living on earth at the time, and he walked in close
fellowship with God. 10 Noah was the father of
three sons: Shem, Ham, and Japheth.

11 Now God saw that the earth had become
corrupt and was filled with violence. 12 God observed all this corruption in the world, for everyone on earth was corrupt. 13 So God said to Noah,
"I have decided to destroy all living creatures,
for they have filled the earth with violence. Yes, I
will wipe them all out along with the earth!

14 "Build a large boat* from cypress wood*
and waterproof it with tar, inside and out. Then
construct decks and stalls throughout its interior.
15 Make the boat 450 feet long, 75 feet wide, and
45 feet high.* 16 Leave an 18-inch opening* below the roof all the way around the boat. Put the
door on the side, and build three decks inside the
boat—lower, middle, and upper.

17 "Look! I am about to cover the earth with
a flood that will destroy every living thing that
breathes. Everything on earth will die. 18 But I
will confirm my covenant with you. So enter the
boat—you and your wife and your sons and their
wives. 19 Bring a pair of every kind of animal—a
male and a female—into the boat with you to
keep them alive during the flood. 20 Pairs of every
kind of bird, and every kind of animal, and every kind of small animal that scurries along the

5:29 *Noah* sounds like a Hebrew term that can mean "relief" or "comfort." **6:2** Hebrew *daughters of men;* also in 6:4. **6:3** Greek version reads *will not remain in.* **6:14a** Traditionally rendered *an ark.* **6:14b** Or *gopher wood.* **6:15** Hebrew *300 cubits* [138 meters] *long, 50 cubits* [23 meters] *wide, and 30 cubits* [13.8 meters] *high.* **6:16** Hebrew *an opening of 1 cubit* [46 centimeters].

---

such that Adam was still alive when Lamech (Noah's father) was born.

6:1–8 A World Gone Wrong. 1–4: These verses reflect ancient legends about mighty warriors and about the presence of giants and demigods on the earth. What is at play here is the crossing of the boundary between heaven and earth as the human women are seduced by angelic members of the heavenly court (cf. 1:26–27). The *giant Nephilites* reappear in Numbers 13:33 (and their descendants in Deut 1:28 and Josh 11:21–22). **5–6:** There is a contrast here between the human heart (NIV and NRSV have, "every inclination of the thoughts of his/their heart was only evil all the time/continually") and God's heart. We have a beautiful and bold insight into the "mind" of God. **7–8:** In the midst of the punishment there is the third, and final, act of grace in God's election of Noah (cf. 3:21; 4:15).

6:9–22 The Story of Noah. 9: As in 2:4a, *the account of,* as a generations formula, signals the start of a new narrative section. To *walk* with God means to follow and obey him (cf. Deut 10:12; 2 Kgs 21:22; Col 1:10, lit., "walk worthily of the Lord"). **11–13:** In contrast to Noah, violence has filled the earth, which has been corrupted through humanity. **14–16:** The same Hebrew word for boat, *tebah,* is used of Moses' basket in Exod 2:3–5. The boat is 450 feet long, 73 feet wide, 45 feet high, and displaces 43,000 tons. **17–22:** In the Mesopotamian flood narratives, the gods tire of human noise and send the flood, which the hero—Utnapishtim—escapes, thus deceiving the gods. In the biblical account, God is in control and

ground, will come to you to be kept alive. 21 And be sure to take on board enough food for your family and for all the animals."

22 So Noah did everything exactly as God had commanded him.

The Flood Covers the Earth

7 When everything was ready, the LORD said to Noah, "Go into the boat with all your family, for among all the people of the earth, I can see that you alone are righteous. 2 Take with you seven pairs—male and female—of each animal I have approved for eating and for sacrifice,* and take one pair of each of the others. 3 Also take seven pairs of every kind of bird. There must be a male and a female in each pair to ensure that all life will survive on the earth after the flood. 4 Seven days from now I will make the rains pour down on the earth. And it will rain for forty days and forty nights, until I have wiped from the earth all the living things I have created."

5 So Noah did everything as the LORD commanded him.

6 Noah was 600 years old when the flood covered the earth. 7 He went on board the boat to escape the flood—he and his wife and his sons and their wives. 8 With them were all the various kinds of animals—those approved for eating and for sacrifice and those that were not—along with all the birds and the small animals that scurry along the ground. 9 They entered the boat in pairs, male and female, just as God had commanded Noah. 10 After seven days, the waters of the flood came and covered the earth.

11 When Noah was 600 years old, on the seventeenth day of the second month, all the underground waters erupted from the earth, and the rain fell in mighty torrents from the sky. 12 The rain continued to fall for forty days and forty nights.

13 That very day Noah had gone into the boat with his wife and his sons—Shem, Ham, and Japheth—and their wives. 14 With them in the boat were pairs of every kind of animal—domestic and wild, large and small—along with birds of every kind. 15 Two by two they came into the boat, representing every living thing that breathes. 16 A male and female of each kind entered, just as God had commanded Noah. Then the LORD closed the door behind them.

17 For forty days the floodwaters grew deeper, covering the ground and lifting the boat high above the earth. 18 As the waters rose higher and higher above the ground, the boat floated safely on the surface. 19 Finally, the water covered even the highest mountains on the earth, 20 rising more than twenty-two feet* above the highest peaks. 21 All the living things on earth died—birds, domestic animals, wild animals, small animals that scurry along the ground, and all the people. 22 Everything that breathed and lived on dry land died. 23 God wiped out every living thing on the earth—people, livestock, small animals that scurry along the ground, and the birds of the sky. All were destroyed. The only people who survived were Noah and those with him in the boat. 24 And the floodwaters covered the earth for 150 days.

The Flood Recedes

8 But God remembered Noah and all the wild animals and livestock with him in the boat. He sent a wind to blow across the earth, and the floodwaters began to recede. 2 The underground waters stopped flowing, and the torrential rains from the sky were stopped. 3 So the floodwaters gradually receded from the earth. After 150 days, 4 exactly five months from the time the flood began,* the boat came to rest on

7:2 Hebrew *of each clean animal;* similarly in 7:8.
7:20 Hebrew *15 cubits* [6.9 meters]. **8:4** Hebrew *on the seventeenth day of the seventh month;* see 7:11.

purposefully chooses Noah, his family, and representatives of all living things to survive.

7:1–24 The Flood Covers the Earth. 1–5: The distinction between "clean" and "unclean" (see translator's note) reflects Hebrew understandings of living things belonging to their proper order. For example, sea creatures typically have scales and fins, so fish are clean, but crabs or oysters are unclean. Similarly, animals that have a completely split hoof and that chew the cud are clean, but animals that have only one of those characteristics are not (cf. Lev 11). The differing accounts of how many pairs of animals were taken into the boat reflects the possibility that two flood narratives have been woven together. **6–24:** The description in verse 11 mirrors the opening creation account. As God made the world by putting the waters into their proper place, so here he reverses that process and takes the world back into a water chaos. **18:** The boat contains nothing for steering: The occupants are entirely at God's mercy.

8:1–22 The Flood Recedes. 1–3: God remembers his promises to Noah (6:18) and sends a wind (*ruach*, translated "Spirit" in 1:2) to begin his new creation. Noah is the first man born after Adam's death and acts

the mountains of Ararat. 5 Two and a half months
later,* as the waters continued to go down, other
mountain peaks became visible.
6 After another forty days, Noah opened the
window he had made in the boat 7 and released
a raven. The bird flew back and forth until the
floodwaters on the earth had dried up. 8 He also
released a dove to see if the water had receded
and it could find dry ground. 9 But the dove could
find no place to land because the water still covered the ground. So it returned to the boat, and
Noah held out his hand and drew the dove back
inside. 10 After waiting another seven days, Noah
released the dove again. 11 This time the dove returned to him in the evening with a fresh olive
leaf in its beak. Then Noah knew that the floodwaters were almost gone. 12 He waited another
seven days and then released the dove again.
This time it did not come back.
13 Noah was now 601 years old. On the first
day of the new year, ten and a half months after the flood began,* the floodwaters had almost
dried up from the earth. Noah lifted back the
covering of the boat and saw that the surface
of the ground was drying. 14 Two more months
went by,* and at last the earth was dry!
15 Then God said to Noah, 16 "Leave the boat,
all of you—you and your wife, and your sons
and their wives. 17 Release all the animals—the
birds, the livestock, and the small animals that
scurry along the ground—so they can be fruitful
and multiply throughout the earth."
18 So Noah, his wife, and his sons and their
wives left the boat. 19 And all of the large and
small animals and birds came out of the boat,
pair by pair.
20 Then Noah built an altar to the LORD, and
there he sacrificed as burnt offerings the animals and birds that had been approved for that
purpose.* 21 And the LORD was pleased with the
aroma of the sacrifice and said to himself, "I will
never again curse the ground because of the human race, even though everything they think
or imagine is bent toward evil from childhood.
I will never again destroy all living things. 22 As
long as the earth remains, there will be planting
and harvest, cold and heat, summer and winter,
day and night."

God Confirms His Covenant

9 Then God blessed Noah and his sons and
told them, "Be fruitful and multiply. Fill
the earth. 2 All the animals of the earth, all
the birds of the sky, all the small animals that
scurry along the ground, and all the fish in the
sea will look on you with fear and terror. I have
placed them in your power. 3 I have given them to
you for food, just as I have given you grain and
vegetables. 4 But you must never eat any meat
that still has the lifeblood in it.
5 "And I will require the blood of anyone who
takes another person's life. If a wild animal kills
a person, it must die. And anyone who murders
a fellow human must die. 6 If anyone takes a human life, that person's life will also be taken by
human hands. For God made human beings* in
his own image. 7 Now be fruitful and multiply,
and repopulate the earth."
8 Then God told Noah and his sons, 9 "I hereby
confirm my covenant with you and your descen-

8:5 Hebrew *On the first day of the tenth month;* see 7:11 and note on 8:4. **8:13** Hebrew *On the first day of the first month;* see 7:11. **8:14** Hebrew *The twenty-seventh day of the second month arrived;* see note on 8:13. **8:20** Hebrew *every clean animal and every clean bird.* **9:6** Or *man;* Hebrew reads *ha-adam.*

as a new Adam. **4:** Mount Ararat is probably not the modern Ararat on the Turkish/Iranian border but may be located in the kingdom known as Urartu in Assyrian texts (cf. 2 Kgs 19:37). **15–17:** God's blessings to his first creation (1:22, 28) are repeated as Noah, his family, and all the living creatures emerge, at last, from the boat (and again in 9:1). **20–22:** Noah builds the first altar in the Bible. Altars feature prominently in Genesis, built to mark significant encounters with the LORD (e.g., 12:8, 26:25). In the Gilgamesh flood narrative, the gods have grown hungry because they have lost their human servants in the flood; when Utnapishtim leaves the boat and burns an animal in sacrifice they are described as "crowding like flies" around it. God reconciles himself to the reality that the Flood has not purified humanity's heart (see annotation on 6:5–6) and commits himself to maintaining the earthly order, whatever humans do.

9:1–17 God Confirms His Covenant. 2–3: The new creation of the post-Flood world does not perfectly reflect the situation in the garden of Eden due, no doubt, to God's statement regarding humanity's heart in 8:21. The harmonious relationship between humans and the rest of the created order is not restored: Fear and terror will now characterize the relationship as people are permitted to eat any creatures. **4:** See annotation on 4:10–11. **5–6:** The basic foundation for the whole biblical tradition of compassion and social justice is laid here. As former Tanzanian president Julius Nyere said, "I believe in a God who made humanity in his own image. I refuse to believe

dants, 10 and with all the animals that were on the boat with you—the birds, the livestock, and all the wild animals—every living creature on earth. 11 Yes, I am confirming my covenant with you. Never again will floodwaters kill all living creatures; never again will a flood destroy the earth."

12 Then God said, "I am giving you a sign of my covenant with you and with all living creatures, for all generations to come. 13 I have placed my rainbow in the clouds. It is the sign of my covenant with you and with all the earth. 14 When I send clouds over the earth, the rainbow will appear in the clouds, 15 and I will remember my covenant with you and with all living creatures. Never again will the floodwaters destroy all life. 16 When I see the rainbow in the clouds, I will remember the eternal covenant between God and every living creature on earth." 17 Then God said to Noah, "Yes, this rainbow is the sign of the covenant I am confirming with all the creatures on earth."

Noah's Sons

18 The sons of Noah who came out of the boat with their father were Shem, Ham, and Japheth. (Ham is the father of Canaan.) 19 From these three sons of Noah came all the people who now populate the earth.

20 After the flood, Noah began to cultivate the ground, and he planted a vineyard. 21 One day he drank some wine he had made, and he became drunk and lay naked inside his tent. 22 Ham, the father of Canaan, saw that his father was naked and went outside and told his brothers. 23 Then Shem and Japheth took a robe, held it over their shoulders, and backed into the tent to cover their father. As they did this, they looked the other way so they would not see him naked.

24 When Noah woke up from his stupor, he learned what Ham, his youngest son, had done. 25 Then he cursed Canaan, the son of Ham:

"May Canaan be cursed!
May he be the lowest of servants to his relatives."

26 Then Noah said,

"May the LORD, the God of Shem, be blessed,
and may Canaan be his servant!
27 May God expand the territory of Japheth!
May Japheth share the prosperity of Shem,*
and may Canaan be his servant."

28 Noah lived another 350 years after the great flood. 29 He lived 950 years, and then he died.

10 This is the account of the families of Shem, Ham, and Japheth, the three sons of Noah. Many children were born to them after the great flood.

Descendants of Japheth

2 The descendants of Japheth were Gomer, Magog, Madai, Javan, Tubal, Meshech, and Tiras.
3 The descendants of Gomer were Ashkenaz, Riphath, and Togarmah.
4 The descendants of Javan were Elishah, Tarshish, Kittim, and Rodanim.* 5 Their

9:27 Hebrew *May he live in the tents of Shem.* **10:4** As in some Hebrew manuscripts and Greek version (see also 1 Chr 1:7); most Hebrew manuscripts read *Dodanim.*

in a God who is blind, starving and illiterate." **8:** The biblical pattern is continued of seeing only the men in the story (cf. 4:17–22). **9–10:** The covenant is not made with Noah and his sons alone but with all the earth and its creatures (see also vv. 12, 13, 15, and 17). **13, 16:** Some commentators see the rainbow as being associated with the bow used by God to shoot arrows of lightning, so that to hang up the bow in the sky symbolized peace. Others see it as signifying a bow that is pointing up to God, the implied message being, "may I be pierced as if with an arrow if I do not carry out my promise."

9:18–28 Noah's Sons. 18–19: This episode provides the link between the one surviving family and the whole human community that comes from it. **25–27:** The realities of the author's situation is shown to be rooted in stories about individuals from antiquity. This incident eventually provided justification for the conquest of Canaan in Joshua.

10:1–32 The Descendants of Japheth, Ham, and Shem. Chapter 10 is a *branched* genealogy (cf. annotations on 11:10–26) that traces the spreading out of one family. Its intention is to show how all the known peoples of the world come from the one post-Flood family and to provide a historical background to the establishment of the most important cities of the time. Seventy nations are detailed here, which signifies completeness. The genealogy does contain difficulties (e.g., Sheba and Havilah are described as descendants of Ham's son Cush, v. 7, and of Shem's great-grandson Joktan, vv. 28–29). **2–5:** The Japhethites are the ancestors of the people of Europe and

descendants became the seafaring peoples that spread out to various lands, each identified by its own language, clan, and national identity.

Descendants of Ham

6 The descendants of Ham were Cush, Mizraim, Put, and Canaan.
7 The descendants of Cush were Seba, Havilah, Sabtah, Raamah, and Sabteca. The descendants of Raamah were Sheba and Dedan.
8 Cush was also the ancestor of Nimrod, who was the first heroic warrior on earth.
9 Since he was the greatest hunter in the world,* his name became proverbial. People would say, "This man is like Nimrod, the greatest hunter in the world."
10 He built his kingdom in the land of Babylonia,* with the cities of Babylon, Erech, Akkad, and Calneh.
11 From there he expanded his territory to Assyria,* building the cities of Nineveh, Rehoboth-ir, Calah,
12 and Resen (the great city located between Nineveh and Calah).
13 Mizraim was the ancestor of the Ludites, Anamites, Lehabites, Naphtuhites,
14 Pathrusites, Casluhites, and the Caphtorites, from whom the Philistines came.*
15 Canaan's oldest son was Sidon, the ancestor of the Sidonians. Canaan was also the ancestor of the Hittites,*
16 Jebusites, Amorites, Girgashites,
17 Hivites, Arkites, Sinites,
18 Arvadites, Zemarites, and Hamathites. The Canaanite clans eventually spread out,
19 and the territory of Canaan extended from Sidon in the north to Gerar and Gaza in the south, and east as far as Sodom, Gomorrah, Admah, and Zeboiim, near Lasha.
20 These were the descendants of Ham, identified by clan, language, territory, and national identity.

Descendants of Shem

21 Sons were also born to Shem, the older brother of Japheth.* Shem was the ancestor of all the descendants of Eber.
22 The descendants of Shem were Elam, Asshur, Arphaxad, Lud, and Aram.
23 The descendants of Aram were Uz, Hul, Gether, and Mash.
24 Arphaxad was the father of Shelah,* and Shelah was the father of Eber.
25 Eber had two sons. The first was named Peleg (which means "division"), for during his lifetime the people of the world were divided into different language groups. His brother's name was Joktan.
26 Joktan was the ancestor of Almodad, Sheleph, Hazarmaveth, Jerah,
27 Hadoram, Uzal, Diklah,
28 Obal, Abimael, Sheba,
29 Ophir, Havilah, and Jobab. All these were descendants of Joktan.
30 The territory they occupied extended from Mesha all the way to Sephar in the eastern mountains.
31 These were the descendants of Shem, identified by clan, language, territory, and national identity.

Conclusion

32 These are the clans that descended from Noah's sons, arranged by nation according to their lines of descent. All the nations of the earth descended from these clans after the great flood.

The Tower of Babel

11 At one time all the people of the world spoke the same language and used the same words.
2 As the people migrated to the east, they found a plain in the land of Babylonia* and settled there.
3 They began saying to each other, "Let's make bricks and harden them with fire." (In this region bricks were used instead of stone, and tar was used for mortar.)
4 Then they said, "Come, let's build a great city for ourselves with a tower that reaches into the sky. This will make us famous and keep us from being scattered all over the world."

10:9 Hebrew *a great hunter before the LORD;* also in 10:9b. **10:10** Hebrew *Shinar.* **10:11** Or *From that land Assyria went out.* **10:14** Hebrew *Casluhites, from whom the Philistines came, and Caphtorites.* Compare Jer 47:4; Amos 9:7. **10:15** Hebrew *ancestor of Heth.* **10:21** Or *Shem, whose older brother was Japheth.* **10:24** Greek version reads *Arphaxad was the father of Cainan, Cainan was the father of Shelah.* Compare Luke 3:36. **11:2** Hebrew *Shinar.*

Asia Minor. **6–20:** The Hamites represent Egypt and those areas under Egyptian control, including Canaan. **21–31:** The Shemites represent the Semitic people, which will later include Israel. The Shemite line leads to Abram (11:27).

11:1–9 The Tower of Babel. 3: In the Middle East, in the days before oil wells, it was still possible to obtain tar because there were some areas where pools of crude oil sat on the earth's surface. The ancient Greek historian Herodotus described clumps of tar floating down the rivers of Mesopotamia (modern-day Iraq). **4:** The tower is probably one of the ziggurats: towers built in Babylon as temples in which to worship the

[5]But the LORD came down to look at the city
and the tower the people were building. [6]"Look!"
he said. "The people are united, and they all speak
the same language. After this, nothing they set
out to do will be impossible for them! [7]Come,
let's go down and confuse the people with different languages. Then they won't be able to understand each other."
[8]In that way, the LORD scattered them all
over the world, and they stopped building the
city. [9]That is why the city was called Babel,* because that is where the LORD confused the people
with different languages. In this way he scattered
them all over the world.

The Line of Descent from Shem to Abram

[10]This is the account of Shem's family.

Two years after the great flood, when Shem
was 100 years old, he became the father of*
Arphaxad. [11]After the birth of* Arphaxad,
Shem lived another 500 years and had other
sons and daughters.
[12]When Arphaxad was 35 years old, he became
the father of Shelah. [13]After the birth of
Shelah, Arphaxad lived another 403 years and
had other sons and daughters.*
[14]When Shelah was 30 years old, he became
the father of Eber. [15]After the birth of Eber,
Shelah lived another 403 years and had other
sons and daughters.
[16]When Eber was 34 years old, he became the
father of Peleg. [17]After the birth of Peleg,
Eber lived another 430 years and had other
sons and daughters.
[18]When Peleg was 30 years old, he became the
father of Reu. [19]After the birth of Reu, Peleg
lived another 209 years and had other sons
and daughters.
[20]When Reu was 32 years old, he became the
father of Serug. [21]After the birth of Serug,
Reu lived another 207 years and had other
sons and daughters.
[22]When Serug was 30 years old, he became the
father of Nahor. [23]After the birth of Nahor,
Serug lived another 200 years and had other
sons and daughters.
[24]When Nahor was 29 years old, he became the
father of Terah. [25]After the birth of Terah,
Nahor lived another 119 years and had other
sons and daughters.
[26]After Terah was 70 years old, he became the
father of Abram, Nahor, and Haran.

The Family of Terah

[27]This is the account of Terah's family. Terah was
the father of Abram, Nahor, and Haran; and Haran was the father of Lot. [28]But Haran died in
Ur of the Chaldeans, the land of his birth, while
his father, Terah, was still living. [29]Meanwhile,
Abram and Nahor both married. The name of
Abram's wife was Sarai, and the name of Nahor's wife was Milcah. (Milcah and her sister
Iscah were daughters of Nahor's brother Haran.)
[30]But Sarai was unable to become pregnant and
had no children.
[31]One day Terah took his son Abram, his
daughter-in-law Sarai (his son Abram's wife),
and his grandson Lot (his son Haran's child) and
moved away from Ur of the Chaldeans. He was
headed for the land of Canaan, but they stopped
at Haran and settled there. [32]Terah lived for
205 years* and died while still in Haran.

11:9 Or *Babylon. Babel* sounds like a Hebrew term that means "confusion." **11:10** Or *the ancestor of;* also in 11:12, 14, 16, 18, 20, 22, 24. **11:11** Or *the birth of this ancestor of;* also in 11:13, 15, 17, 19, 21, 23, 25. **11:12-13** Greek version reads *[12]When Arphaxad was 135 years old, he became the father of Cainan. [13]After the birth of Cainan, Arphaxad lived another 430 years and had other sons and daughters, and then he died. When Cainan was 130 years old, he became the father of Shelah. After the birth of Shelah, Cainan lived another 330 years and had other sons and daughters, and then he died.* Compare Luke 3:35-36. **11:32** Some ancient versions read *145 years;* compare 11:26 and 12:4.

gods. **5:** There is wonderful irony here as the people aim for the tower to reach right into the sky/heaven, but still *the LORD came down* in order to see it. **6–7:** As in 3:22–24 God recognizes the potential that lies in human beings, which always moves toward evil, and he has to act in order to place limits around that potential. **8–9:** On the face of it this story serves to explain how and why humanity becomes scattered around the world, speaking different languages. If this ancient narrative was being put onto paper around the time of the Exile, however, it could also have served as a critique against the imperialism of Babylon.

11:10–32 The Line of Descent from Shem to Abram. 10–26: This is a *linear* genealogy (cf. annotation on 10:1–32) that traces the family line from Shem to Abram. After the diversion of the Tower of Babel, this genealogy links the Flood to the next main narrative. As in chapter 5, so here there are ten generations. **27–32:** These few verses are pregnant with the story that is to follow. **27:** *The account of* (see annotation on 2:4a) signals the beginning of a major new story line.

The Call of Abram

12 The LORD had said to Abram, "Leave
your native country, your relatives,
and your father's family, and go to
the land that I will show you. [2]I will make you
into a great nation. I will bless you and make you
famous, and you will be a blessing to others. [3]I
will bless those who bless you and curse those
who treat you with contempt. All the families on
earth will be blessed through you."
[4]So Abram departed as the LORD had instructed, and Lot went with him. Abram was seventy-
five years old when he left Haran. [5]He took his
wife, Sarai, his nephew Lot, and all his wealth—
his livestock and all the people he had taken into
his household at Haran—and headed for the land
of Canaan. When they arrived in Canaan, [6]Abram
traveled through the land as far as Shechem. There
he set up camp beside the oak of Moreh. At that
time, the area was inhabited by Canaanites.
[7]Then the LORD appeared to Abram and said,
"I will give this land to your descendants.*" And
Abram built an altar there and dedicated it to
the LORD, who had appeared to him. [8]After that,
Abram traveled south and set up camp in the hill
country, with Bethel to the west and Ai to the
east. There he built another altar and dedicated it
to the LORD, and he worshiped the LORD. [9]Then
Abram continued traveling south by stages toward the Negev.

Abram and Sarai in Egypt

[10]At that time a severe famine struck the land
of Canaan, forcing Abram to go down to Egypt,
where he lived as a foreigner. [11]As he was approaching the border of Egypt, Abram said to
his wife, Sarai, "Look, you are a very beautiful
woman. [12]When the Egyptians see you, they will
say, 'This is his wife. Let's kill him; then we can
have her!' [13]So please tell them you are my sister. Then they will spare my life and treat me
well because of their interest in you."
[14]And sure enough, when Abram arrived in
Egypt, everyone noticed Sarai's beauty. [15]When
the palace officials saw her, they sang her praises
to Pharaoh, their king, and Sarai was taken into
his palace. [16]Then Pharaoh gave Abram many
gifts because of her—sheep, goats, cattle, male
and female donkeys, male and female servants,
and camels.
[17]But the LORD sent terrible plagues upon
Pharaoh and his household because of Sarai,
Abram's wife. [18]So Pharaoh summoned Abram
and accused him sharply. "What have you done
to me?" he demanded. "Why didn't you tell me
she was your wife? [19]Why did you say, 'She is
my sister,' and allow me to take her as my wife?
Now then, here is your wife. Take her and get out
of here!" [20]Pharaoh ordered some of his men to
escort them, and he sent Abram out of the country, along with his wife and all his possessions.

Abram and Lot Separate

13 So Abram left Egypt and traveled
north into the Negev, along with his
wife and Lot and all that they owned.
[2](Abram was very rich in livestock, silver, and
gold.) [3]From the Negev, they continued traveling by stages toward Bethel, and they pitched
their tents between Bethel and Ai, where they
had camped before. [4]This was the same place
where Abram had built the altar, and there he
worshiped the LORD again.
[5]Lot, who was traveling with Abram, had also

12:7 Hebrew *seed.*

12:1—25:18 The Family Stories of Abraham, Sarah, and Isaac

12:1–9 The Call of Abram. 1: Because Abram's father, Terah, settled in Haran instead of reaching Canaan (11:31), Abram is called to go and complete the journey. **2–3:** The significance of these verses cannot be overestimated. The rest of Genesis is the story of how this promise is worked out. God's promise contrasts starkly with the previous efforts of humanity to make a name for themselves (11:4). **5:** We do not know why Abram takes Lot or what has happened to Lot's mother, who is never mentioned (cf. 11:27–30). **7:** The promise of land now accompanies the promise of a nation.

12:10–20 Abram and Sarai in Egypt. The route to the fulfillment of God's promises is not going to be an easy one, and many obstacles will lie in its path, both through the imperfections of the patriarchs and through circumstances outside their control. **11–16:** Sarai is used as an object to ensure Abram's well-being. Nothing is said of how she feels about being taken into Pharaoh's harem (the assumption would be that he slept with her); the story is entirely seen from Abram's perspective. **17–20:** Through Sarai, God's promises begin to be worked out as Abram changes from being a refugee to one with substantial assets.

13:1–18 Abram and Lot Separate. 1–2: This journey parallels the journey that the Israelites will later take: In both cases they have become rich with Egyptian goods. **3–7:** The area of the Negev is a steppe and desert region between Egypt and Canaan and would

become very wealthy with flocks of sheep and goats, herds of cattle, and many tents. 6 But the land could not support both Abram and Lot with all their flocks and herds living so close together. 7 So disputes broke out between the herdsmen of Abram and Lot. (At that time Canaanites and Perizzites were also living in the land.)

8 Finally Abram said to Lot, "Let's not allow this conflict to come between us or our herdsmen. After all, we are close relatives! 9 The whole countryside is open to you. Take your choice of any section of the land you want, and we will separate. If you want the land to the left, then I'll take the land on the right. If you prefer the land on the right, then I'll go to the left."

10 Lot took a long look at the fertile plains of the Jordan Valley in the direction of Zoar. The whole area was well watered everywhere, like the garden of the LORD or the beautiful land of Egypt. (This was before the LORD destroyed Sodom and Gomorrah.) 11 Lot chose for himself the whole Jordan Valley to the east of them. He went there with his flocks and servants and parted company with his uncle Abram. 12 So Abram settled in the land of Canaan, and Lot moved his tents to a place near Sodom and settled among the cities of the plain. 13 But the people of this area were extremely wicked and constantly sinned against the LORD.

14 After Lot had gone, the LORD said to Abram, "Look as far as you can see in every direction—north and south, east and west. 15 I am giving all this land, as far as you can see, to you and your descendants* as a permanent possession. 16 And I will give you so many descendants that, like the dust of the earth, they cannot be counted! 17 Go and walk through the land in every direction, for I am giving it to you."

18 So Abram moved his camp to Hebron and settled near the oak grove belonging to Mamre. There he built another altar to the LORD.

Abram Rescues Lot

14 About this time war broke out in the region. King Amraphel of Babylonia,* King Arioch of Ellasar, King Kedorlaomer of Elam, and King Tidal of Goiim 2 fought against King Bera of Sodom, King Birsha of Gomorrah, King Shinab of Admah, King Shemeber of Zeboiim, and the king of Bela (also called Zoar).

3 This second group of kings joined forces in Siddim Valley (that is, the valley of the Dead Sea*). 4 For twelve years they had been subject to King Kedorlaomer, but in the thirteenth year they rebelled against him.

5 One year later Kedorlaomer and his allies arrived and defeated the Rephaites at Ashteroth-karnaim, the Zuzites at Ham, the Emites at Shaveh-kiriathaim, 6 and the Horites at Mount Seir, as far as El-paran at the edge of the wilderness. 7 Then they turned back and came to En-mishpat (now called Kadesh) and conquered all the territory of the Amalekites, and also the Amorites living in Hazazon-tamar.

8 Then the rebel kings of Sodom, Gomorrah, Admah, Zeboiim, and Bela (also called Zoar) prepared for battle in the valley of the Dead Sea.* 9 They fought against King Kedorlaomer of Elam, King Tidal of Goiim, King Amraphel of Babylonia, and King Arioch of Ellasar—four kings against five. 10 As it happened, the valley of the Dead Sea was filled with tar pits. And as the army of the kings of Sodom and Gomorrah fled, some fell into the tar pits, while the rest escaped into the mountains. 11 The victorious invaders then plundered Sodom and Gomorrah and headed for home, taking with them all the spoils of war and the food supplies. 12 They also captured Lot—Abram's nephew who lived in Sodom—and carried off everything he owned.

13 But one of Lot's men escaped and reported everything to Abram the Hebrew, who was living near the oak grove belonging to Mamre the Amorite. Mamre and his relatives, Eshcol and Aner, were Abram's allies.

14 When Abram heard that his nephew Lot had been captured, he mobilized the 318 trained men who had been born into his household. Then he pursued Kedorlaomer's army until he caught up

13:15 Hebrew *seed;* also in 13:16. **14:1** Hebrew *Shinar;* also in 14:9. **14:3** Hebrew *Salt Sea.* **14:8** Hebrew *Siddim Valley* (see 14:3); also in 14:10.

not have been good for pasture. **8–9:** As the elder uncle, Abram would have had the right to choose first, but he shows himself a peacemaker here as he graciously gives Lot the choice. **13:** The seeds of Sodom's destruction in chapter 19 are sown here in the hearers' minds. **14–18:** God's instruction in verse 17 mirrors the custom of the writer's day whereby kings and landowners walked around their boundaries.

14:1–16 Abram Rescues Lot. 1–3: None of these kings is known of in extrabiblical sources, nor have the cities been identified, except Babylon, Sodom, and Gomorrah. This story may be historical, but to determine that with any certainty is currently impossible. **10:** See annotation on 11:3. **11–16:** The purpose of this episode may have been to continue the seeds sown in 13:13 and demonstrate how unwise Lot was in his decision to settle near Sodom.

with them at Dan. [15]There he divided his men and attacked during the night. Kedorlaomer's army fled, but Abram chased them as far as Hobah, north of Damascus. [16]Abram recovered all the goods that had been taken, and he brought back his nephew Lot with his possessions and all the women and other captives.

Melchizedek Blesses Abram

[17]After Abram returned from his victory over Kedorlaomer and all his allies, the king of Sodom went out to meet him in the valley of Shaveh (that is, the King's Valley).

[18]And Melchizedek, the king of Salem and a priest of God Most High,* brought Abram some bread and wine. [19]Melchizedek blessed Abram with this blessing:

"Blessed be Abram by God Most High,
  Creator of heaven and earth.
[20] And blessed be God Most High,
  who has defeated your enemies for you."

Then Abram gave Melchizedek a tenth of all the goods he had recovered.

[21]The king of Sodom said to Abram, "Give back my people who were captured. But you may keep for yourself all the goods you have recovered."

[22]Abram replied to the king of Sodom, "I solemnly swear to the LORD, God Most High, Creator of heaven and earth, [23]that I will not take so much as a single thread or sandal thong from what belongs to you. Otherwise you might say, 'I am the one who made Abram rich.' [24]I will accept only what my young warriors have already eaten, and I request that you give a fair share of the goods to my allies—Aner, Eshcol, and Mamre."

The LORD's Covenant Promise to Abram

15 Some time later, the LORD spoke to Abram in a vision and said to him, "Do not be afraid, Abram, for I will protect you, and your reward will be great."

[2]But Abram replied, "O Sovereign LORD, what good are all your blessings when I don't even have a son? Since you've given me no children, Eliezer of Damascus, a servant in my household, will inherit all my wealth. [3]You have given me no descendants of my own, so one of my servants will be my heir."

[4]Then the LORD said to him, "No, your servant will not be your heir, for you will have a son of your own who will be your heir." [5]Then the LORD took Abram outside and said to him, "Look up into the sky and count the stars if you can. That's how many descendants you will have!"

[6]And Abram believed the LORD, and the LORD counted him as righteous because of his faith.

[7]Then the LORD told him, "I am the LORD who brought you out of Ur of the Chaldeans to give you this land as your possession."

[8]But Abram replied, "O Sovereign LORD, how can I be sure that I will actually possess it?"

[9]The LORD told him, "Bring me a three-year-old heifer, a three-year-old female goat, a three-year-old ram, a turtledove, and a young pigeon." [10]So Abram presented all these to him and killed them. Then he cut each animal down the middle and laid the halves side by side; he did not, however, cut the birds in half. [11]Some vultures swooped down to eat the carcasses, but Abram chased them away.

[12]As the sun was going down, Abram fell into a deep sleep, and a terrifying darkness came down over him. [13]Then the LORD said to Abram, "You can be sure that your descendants will be strangers in a foreign land, where they will be oppressed as slaves for 400 years. [14]But I will punish the nation that enslaves them, and in the end they will come away with great wealth. [15](As for you, you will die in peace and be buried at a ripe old age.) [16]After four generations your descendants will return here to this land, for the sins of the Amorites do not yet warrant their destruction."

14:18 Hebrew *El-Elyon;* also in 14:19, 20, 22.

14:17–24 Melchizedek Blesses Abram. 18–20: Salem is probably identified as Jerusalem (although this identification happens only in Ps 76:3 and not in extrabiblical sources). *God Most High* (see translator's note) is thought to have been a title of the Canaanite high god. **22–24:** Abram identifies the Canaanite God Most High with the LORD. As he is blessed (v. 19), so Abram blesses his allies, thus showing the unfolding fulfillment of God's promise in 12:2–3.

15:1–21 The LORD's Covenant Promise to Abram. 1–6: This is the first recorded conversation between Abram and the LORD. It follows a pattern of divine promise, human objection, and divine reassurance (cf. Exod 3—4; Judg 6:11–24; Luke 1:26–38). Verse 6 becomes of central importance to Paul's understanding of faith in Jesus Christ (e.g., Gal 3:6–9). **7:** Now the promise turns from descendants to land. Both of these are necessary if Israel is to be a nation that brings blessing to others. **9–10:** This reflects an ancient covenantal ceremony whereby the two sides of each animal were laid opposite each other, thus creating a path for the covenant makers to walk down. The implication is that if they break the covenant, they too will be cut

17 After the sun went down and darkness fell,
Abram saw a smoking firepot and a flaming torch
pass between the halves of the carcasses. 18 So the
LORD made a covenant with Abram that day and
said, "I have given this land to your descendants,
all the way from the border of Egypt* to the
great Euphrates River— 19 the land now occupied
by the Kenites, Kenizzites, Kadmonites, 20 Hittites, Perizzites, Rephaites, 21 Amorites, Canaanites, Girgashites, and Jebusites."

The Birth of Ishmael

16 Now Sarai, Abram's wife, had not
been able to bear children for him.
But she had an Egyptian servant
named Hagar. 2 So Sarai said to Abram, "The
LORD has prevented me from having children.
Go and sleep with my servant. Perhaps I can
have children through her." And Abram agreed
with Sarai's proposal. 3 So Sarai, Abram's wife,
took Hagar the Egyptian servant and gave her to
Abram as a wife. (This happened ten years after
Abram had settled in the land of Canaan.)

4 So Abram had sexual relations with Hagar,
and she became pregnant. But when Hagar knew
she was pregnant, she began to treat her mistress, Sarai, with contempt. 5 Then Sarai said to
Abram, "This is all your fault! I put my servant
into your arms, but now that she's pregnant she
treats me with contempt. The LORD will show
who's wrong—you or me!"

6 Abram replied, "Look, she is your servant, so
deal with her as you see fit." Then Sarai treated
Hagar so harshly that she finally ran away.

7 The angel of the LORD found Hagar beside a
spring of water in the wilderness, along the road
to Shur. 8 The angel said to her, "Hagar, Sarai's
servant, where have you come from, and where
are you going?"

"I'm running away from my mistress, Sarai,"
she replied.

9 The angel of the LORD said to her, "Return
to your mistress, and submit to her authority."
10 Then he added, "I will give you more descendants than you can count."

11 And the angel also said, "You are now pregnant and will give birth to a son. You are to name
him Ishmael (which means 'God hears'), for the
LORD has heard your cry of distress. 12 This son
of yours will be a wild man, as untamed as a wild
donkey! He will raise his fist against everyone,
and everyone will be against him. Yes, he will
live in open hostility against all his relatives."

13 Thereafter, Hagar used another name to
refer to the LORD, who had spoken to her. She
said, "You are the God who sees me."* She also
said, "Have I truly seen the One who sees me?"
14 So that well was named Beer-lahai-roi (which
means "well of the Living One who sees me"). It
can still be found between Kadesh and Bered.

15 So Hagar gave Abram a son, and Abram
named him Ishmael. 16 Abram was eighty-six
years old when Ishmael was born.

Abram Is Named Abraham

17 When Abram was ninety-nine years
old, the LORD appeared to him and
said, "I am El-Shaddai—'God Al-
mighty.' Serve me faithfully and live a blameless
life. 2 I will make a covenant with you, by which
I will guarantee to give you countless descendants."

3 At this, Abram fell face down on the ground.
Then God said to him, 4 "This is my covenant

15:18 Hebrew *the river of Egypt,* referring either to an eastern branch of the Nile River or to the Brook of Egypt in the Sinai (see Num 34:5). **16:13** Hebrew *El-roi.*

---

in half like the animals. **16:** Amorites is another name for Canaanites. **17:** The smoking firepot and flaming torch symbolize God. Only God walks through the pieces, thus making the covenant a unilateral one on God's side. **18–21:** The land of promise is given its clearest definition yet. It plays a central part to this day in the politics of the Middle East.

16:1–16 The Birth of Ishmael. 1–3: We do not know whether Abram told Sarai of his encounters with God, but here Sarai takes matters into her own hands, and Abram readily complies. Regardless of divine promises, to be barren was a social and religious disgrace. **6:** The Hebrew used for Sarai's treatment of Hagar is the same as Egypt's treatment of the Israelites in Exodus 1:11. **7–10:** Hagar, a foreign slave, is the only woman after Eve to receive a direct appearance from the LORD. God's promise is remarkably similar to that made to Abram in 15:5. **11–12:** The LORD is a god of compassion who responds to those who call out to him. This episode begins the history of the Ishmaelites, which will continue in chapters 17, 21, and 25. **13:** This is the only time in the Old Testament that anyone, let alone a woman, gives God a name (see translator's notes).

17:1–8 Abram Is Named Abraham. 1: This is the first occurrence of the title *El-Shaddai* for God. **1–4:** Unlike the covenant of chapter 15, this covenant is bilateral: Abram is given conditions that have to be

with you: I will make you the father of a multitude of nations! [5]What's more, I am changing your name. It will no longer be Abram. Instead, you will be called Abraham,* for you will be the father of many nations. [6]I will make you extremely fruitful. Your descendants will become many nations, and kings will be among them!

[7]"I will confirm my covenant with you and your descendants* after you, from generation to generation. This is the everlasting covenant: I will always be your God and the God of your descendants after you. [8]And I will give the entire land of Canaan, where you now live as a foreigner, to you and your descendants. It will be their possession forever, and I will be their God."

The Mark of the Covenant

[9]Then God said to Abraham, "Your responsibility is to obey the terms of the covenant. You and all your descendants have this continual responsibility. [10]This is the covenant that you and your descendants must keep: Each male among you must be circumcised. [11]You must cut off the flesh of your foreskin as a sign of the covenant between me and you. [12]From generation to generation, every male child must be circumcised on the eighth day after his birth. This applies not only to members of your family but also to the servants born in your household and the foreign-born servants whom you have purchased. [13]All must be circumcised. Your bodies will bear the mark of my everlasting covenant. [14]Any male who fails to be circumcised will be cut off from the covenant family for breaking the covenant."

Sarai Is Named Sarah

[15]Then God said to Abraham, "Regarding Sarai, your wife—her name will no longer be Sarai. From now on her name will be Sarah.* [16]And I will bless her and give you a son from her! Yes, I will bless her richly, and she will become the mother of many nations. Kings of nations will be among her descendants."

[17]Then Abraham bowed down to the ground, but he laughed to himself in disbelief. "How could I become a father at the age of 100?" he thought. "And how can Sarah have a baby when she is ninety years old?" [18]So Abraham said to God, "May Ishmael live under your special blessing!"

[19]But God replied, "No—Sarah, your wife, will give birth to a son for you. You will name him Isaac,* and I will confirm my covenant with him and his descendants as an everlasting covenant. [20]As for Ishmael, I will bless him also, just as you have asked. I will make him extremely fruitful and multiply his descendants. He will become the father of twelve princes, and I will make him a great nation. [21]But my covenant will be confirmed with Isaac, who will be born to you and Sarah about this time next year." [22]When God had finished speaking, he left Abraham.

[23]On that very day Abraham took his son, Ishmael, and every male in his household, including those born there and those he had bought. Then he circumcised them, cutting off their foreskins, just as God had told him. [24]Abraham was ninety-nine years old when he was circumcised, [25]and Ishmael, his son, was thirteen. [26]Both Abraham and his son, Ishmael, were circumcised on that same day, [27]along with all the other men and boys of the household, whether they were born there or bought as servants. All were circumcised with him.

17:5 *Abram* means "exalted father"; *Abraham* sounds like a Hebrew term that means "father of many." **17:7** Hebrew *seed;* also in 17:7b, 8, 9, 10, 19. **17:15** *Sarai* and *Sarah* both mean "princess"; the change in spelling may reflect the difference in dialect between Ur and Canaan. **17:19** *Isaac* means "he laughs."

met on his side. **5:** The name change signals the significance of the covenant and the authority that God has over Abraham. **7:** *Descendants* is literally "seed." As in 3:15 it is not singular, but collective, referring to the people of Israel as a whole.

17:9–14 The Mark of the Covenant. The bilateral nature of the covenant is made explicit here in the command for Abraham and all his male offspring to be circumcised. Circumcision was a custom practiced by Israel's neighbors and is still performed by Jews and Muslims today. Unlike some of Israel's neighbors, both then and now, female circumcision is thankfully not stipulated, but through the emphasis on male circumcision, full access to God's presence now focuses on the men.

17:15–27 Sarai Is Named Sarah. 15–16: Although Sarah is blessed, God's covenant and promises are given exclusively to Abraham, with Sarah effectively excluded. The name change again signifies the importance of the occasion, but Sarah herself is not told of it, and the name is given no special meaning. **17–18:** The drama of the story continues as Abraham and Sarah's old age is emphasized, and Abraham tries once again to engineer the plot's resolution by asking God to focus on the son he already has. **20–21:** All nations of the world are in God's sights, but it is through Isaac that God's plans for salvation are to find their fulfillment.

A Son Is Promised to Sarah

18 The LORD appeared again to Abraham near the oak grove belonging to Mamre. One day Abraham was sitting at the entrance to his tent during the hottest part of the day. 2 He looked up and noticed three men standing nearby. When he saw them, he ran to meet them and welcomed them, bowing low to the ground.

3 "My lord," he said, "if it pleases you, stop here for a while. 4 Rest in the shade of this tree while water is brought to wash your feet. 5 And since you've honored your servant with this visit, let me prepare some food to refresh you before you continue on your journey."

"All right," they said. "Do as you have said."

6 So Abraham ran back to the tent and said to Sarah, "Hurry! Get three large measures* of your best flour, knead it into dough, and bake some bread." 7 Then Abraham ran out to the herd and chose a tender calf and gave it to his servant, who quickly prepared it. 8 When the food was ready, Abraham took some yogurt and milk and the roasted meat, and he served it to the men. As they ate, Abraham waited on them in the shade of the trees.

9 "Where is Sarah, your wife?" the visitors asked.

"She's inside the tent," Abraham replied.

10 Then one of them said, "I will return to you about this time next year, and your wife, Sarah, will have a son!"

Sarah was listening to this conversation from the tent. 11 Abraham and Sarah were both very old by this time, and Sarah was long past the age of having children. 12 So she laughed silently to herself and said, "How could a worn-out woman like me enjoy such pleasure, especially when my master—my husband—is also so old?"

13 Then the LORD said to Abraham, "Why did Sarah laugh? Why did she say, 'Can an old woman like me have a baby?' 14 Is anything too hard for the LORD? I will return about this time next year, and Sarah will have a son."

15 Sarah was afraid, so she denied it, saying, "I didn't laugh."

But the LORD said, "No, you did laugh."

Abraham Intercedes for Sodom

16 Then the men got up from their meal and looked out toward Sodom. As they left, Abraham went with them to send them on their way.

17 "Should I hide my plan from Abraham?" the LORD asked. 18 "For Abraham will certainly become a great and mighty nation, and all the nations of the earth will be blessed through him. 19 I have singled him out so that he will direct his sons and their families to keep the way of the LORD by doing what is right and just. Then I will do for Abraham all that I have promised."

20 So the LORD told Abraham, "I have heard a great outcry from Sodom and Gomorrah, because their sin is so flagrant. 21 I am going down to see if their actions are as wicked as I have heard. If not, I want to know."

22 The other men turned and headed toward Sodom, but the LORD remained with Abraham. 23 Abraham approached him and said, "Will you sweep away both the righteous and the wicked? 24 Suppose you find fifty righteous people living there in the city—will you still sweep it away and not spare it for their sakes? 25 Surely you wouldn't do such a thing, destroying the righteous along with the wicked. Why, you would be treating the righteous and the wicked exactly the same! Surely you wouldn't do that! Should not the Judge of all the earth do what is right?"

26 And the LORD replied, "If I find fifty righteous people in Sodom, I will spare the entire city for their sake."

27 Then Abraham spoke again. "Since I have begun, let me speak further to my Lord, even though I am but dust and ashes. 28 Suppose there are only forty-five righteous people rather than fifty? Will you destroy the whole city for lack of five?"

18:6 Hebrew 3 *seahs,* about 15 quarts or 18 liters.

18:1–15 A Son Is Promised to Sarah. This episode seems to be another version of the story in chapter 17, but this version is more personal and descriptive. The identity of the divine appearance is ambiguous, but probably the three men are divine beings, one of whom is the LORD. **6–8:** Abraham and Sarah demonstrate the hospitality of a Bedouin sheik and prepare a lavish feast for the strangers. **12:** The word *pleasure* has sexual overtones—not just the pleasure of motherhood—and may be related to the word for "moisture," contrasting with Sarah's present condition.

18:16–33 Abraham Intercedes for Sodom. 17–19: This episode gives Abraham the opportunity to work out God's promises for him to be a blessing to others. **22–32:** Abraham no doubt has Lot in his mind as he bargains with the LORD. God is presented as one who connects with humanity and is able to change course. **33:** The writer has no qualms about depicting God moving comfortably about the human world (cf. 3:8).

And the Lord said, "I will not destroy it if I find forty-five righteous people there."

[29]Then Abraham pressed his request further. "Suppose there are only forty?"

And the Lord replied, "I will not destroy it for the sake of the forty."

[30]"Please don't be angry, my Lord," Abraham pleaded. "Let me speak—suppose only thirty righteous people are found?"

And the Lord replied, "I will not destroy it if I find thirty."

[31]Then Abraham said, "Since I have dared to speak to the Lord, let me continue—suppose there are only twenty?"

And the Lord replied, "Then I will not destroy it for the sake of the twenty."

[32]Finally, Abraham said, "Lord, please don't be angry with me if I speak one more time. Suppose only ten are found there?"

And the Lord replied, "Then I will not destroy it for the sake of the ten."

[33]When the Lord had finished his conversation with Abraham, he went on his way, and Abraham returned to his tent.

Sodom and Gomorrah Destroyed

19 That evening the two angels came to the entrance of the city of Sodom. Lot was sitting there, and when he saw them, he stood up to meet them. Then he welcomed them and bowed with his face to the ground. [2]"My lords," he said, "come to my home to wash your feet, and be my guests for the night. You may then get up early in the morning and be on your way again."

"Oh no," they replied. "We'll just spend the night out here in the city square."

[3]But Lot insisted, so at last they went home with him. Lot prepared a feast for them, complete with fresh bread made without yeast, and they ate. [4]But before they retired for the night, all the men of Sodom, young and old, came from all over the city and surrounded the house. [5]They shouted to Lot, "Where are the men who came to spend the night with you? Bring them out to us so we can have sex with them!"

[6]So Lot stepped outside to talk to them, shutting the door behind him. [7]"Please, my brothers," he begged, "don't do such a wicked thing. [8]Look, I have two virgin daughters. Let me bring them out to you, and you can do with them as you wish. But please, leave these men alone, for they are my guests and are under my protection."

[9]"Stand back!" they shouted. "This fellow came to town as an outsider, and now he's acting like our judge! We'll treat you far worse than those other men!" And they lunged toward Lot to break down the door.

[10]But the two angels* reached out, pulled Lot into the house, and bolted the door. [11]Then they blinded all the men, young and old, who were at the door of the house, so they gave up trying to get inside.

[12]Meanwhile, the angels questioned Lot. "Do you have any other relatives here in the city?" they asked. "Get them out of this place—your sons-in-law, sons, daughters, or anyone else. [13]For we are about to destroy this city completely. The outcry against this place is so great it has reached the Lord, and he has sent us to destroy it."

[14]So Lot rushed out to tell his daughters' fiancés, "Quick, get out of the city! The Lord is about to destroy it." But the young men thought he was only joking.

[15]At dawn the next morning the angels became insistent. "Hurry," they said to Lot. "Take your wife and your two daughters who are here. Get out right now, or you will be swept away in the destruction of the city!"

[16]When Lot still hesitated, the angels seized his hand and the hands of his wife and two daughters and rushed them to safety outside the city, for the Lord was merciful. [17]When they were safely out of the city, one of the angels ordered, "Run for your lives! And don't look back or stop anywhere in the valley! Escape to the mountains, or you will be swept away!"

[18]"Oh no, my lord!" Lot begged. [19]"You have been so gracious to me and saved my life, and you have shown such great kindness. But I cannot go to the mountains. Disaster would catch up to me there, and I would soon die. [20]See, there is a small village nearby. Please let me go there instead; don't you see how small it is? Then my life will be saved."

[21]"All right," the angel said, "I will grant your request. I will not destroy the little village. [22]But hurry! Escape to it, for I can do nothing until you arrive there." (This explains why that village was known as Zoar, which means "little place.")

19:10 Hebrew *men;* also in 19:12, 16.

19:1–29 Sodom and Gomorrah Destroyed. 1–3: The two men with the Lord are now identified as angels. They are eating well that day! The implication is that Lot is aware that there will be trouble if the strangers sleep outside in the city square. **4–8:** The sexual and physical sacrifice of women shamefully occurs elsewhere (cf. Judg 11 and 21). **19:** The reason for Lot's fear of the mountains is not given. **24–26:** Tradition

23 Lot reached the village just as the sun was
rising over the horizon. 24 Then the LORD rained
down fire and burning sulfur from the sky on
Sodom and Gomorrah. 25 He utterly destroyed
them, along with the other cities and villages of
the plain, wiping out all the people and every bit
of vegetation. 26 But Lot's wife looked back as she
was following behind him, and she turned into a
pillar of salt.

27 Abraham got up early that morning and
hurried out to the place where he had stood in
the LORD's presence. 28 He looked out across the
plain toward Sodom and Gomorrah and watched
as columns of smoke rose from the cities like
smoke from a furnace.

29 But God had listened to Abraham's request
and kept Lot safe, removing him from the disaster that engulfed the cities on the plain.

Lot and His Daughters

30 Afterward Lot left Zoar because he was afraid
of the people there, and he went to live in a cave
in the mountains with his two daughters. 31 One
day the older daughter said to her sister, "There
are no men left anywhere in this entire area,
so we can't get married like everyone else. And
our father will soon be too old to have children.
32 Come, let's get him drunk with wine, and then
we will have sex with him. That way we will preserve our family line through our father."

33 So that night they got him drunk with
wine, and the older daughter went in and had intercourse with her father. He was unaware of her
lying down or getting up again.

34 The next morning the older daughter said
to her younger sister, "I had sex with our father last night. Let's get him drunk with wine
again tonight, and you go in and have sex with
him. That way we will preserve our family line
through our father." 35 So that night they got
him drunk with wine again, and the younger
daughter went in and had intercourse with him.
As before, he was unaware of her lying down or
getting up again.

36 As a result, both of Lot's daughters became
pregnant by their own father. 37 When the older daughter gave birth to a son, she named him
Moab.* He became the ancestor of the nation
now known as the Moabites. 38 When the younger daughter gave birth to a son, she named him
Ben-ammi.* He became the ancestor of the nation now known as the Ammonites.

Abraham Deceives Abimelech

20 Abraham moved south to the Negev
and lived for a while between Kadesh
and Shur, and then he moved on to
Gerar. While living there as a foreigner, 2 Abraham introduced his wife, Sarah, by saying, "She
is my sister." So King Abimelech of Gerar sent
for Sarah and had her brought to him at his palace.

3 But that night God came to Abimelech in a
dream and told him, "You are a dead man, for that
woman you have taken is already married!"

4 But Abimelech had not slept with her yet,
so he said, "Lord, will you destroy an innocent
nation? 5 Didn't Abraham tell me, 'She is my sister'? And she herself said, 'Yes, he is my brother.' I acted in complete innocence! My hands are
clean."

6 In the dream God responded, "Yes, I know
you are innocent. That's why I kept you from
sinning against me, and why I did not let you
touch her. 7 Now return the woman to her husband, and he will pray for you, for he is a prophet. Then you will live. But if you don't return her
to him, you can be sure that you and all your
people will die."

8 Abimelech got up early the next morning and quickly called all his servants together.
When he told them what had happened, his men
were terrified. 9 Then Abimelech called for Abraham. "What have you done to us?" he demanded. "What crime have I committed that deserves
treatment like this, making me and my kingdom
guilty of this great sin? No one should ever do

19:37 *Moab* sounds like a Hebrew term that means "from father." **19:38** *Ben-ammi* means "son of my kinsman."

places Sodom and Gomorrah in the southeast area of the Dead Sea, where there are large mineral deposits, but archaeological evidence has not been able to locate them. **29:** Despite Abraham's earlier bargaining, Lot appears far from righteous in this story.

19:30–38 Lot and His Daughters. In an ironic twist to the story, Lot's daughters do to him what he was prepared to allow strangers to do to them. It appears that Sodom had had no righteous inhabitants. This episode explains the origins of Moab and Ammon, two nations that bordered Canaan on the east.

20:1–18 Abraham Deceives Abimelech. This may be a second version of the story in chapter 12 or a separate incident. **2:** Taken chronologically, it is hard to see why Abimelech would desire to have the aging Sarah in his harem. **6:** It is important for the narrative to make it clear that the child born to Sarah in the following chapter is *not* Abimelech's. **14–18:** Despite his

what you have done! [10]Whatever possessed you to do such a thing?"

[11]Abraham replied, "I thought, 'This is a godless place. They will want my wife and will kill me to get her.' [12]And she really is my sister, for we both have the same father, but different mothers. And I married her. [13]When God called me to leave my father's home and to travel from place to place, I told her, 'Do me a favor. Wherever we go, tell the people that I am your brother.' "

[14]Then Abimelech took some of his sheep and goats, cattle, and male and female servants, and he presented them to Abraham. He also returned his wife, Sarah, to him. [15]Then Abimelech said, "Look over my land and choose any place where you would like to live." [16]And he said to Sarah, "Look, I am giving your 'brother' 1,000 pieces of silver* in the presence of all these witnesses. This is to compensate you for any wrong I may have done to you. This will settle any claim against me, and your reputation is cleared."

[17]Then Abraham prayed to God, and God healed Abimelech, his wife, and his female servants, so they could have children. [18]For the LORD had caused all the women to be infertile because of what happened with Abraham's wife, Sarah.

The Birth of Isaac

21 The LORD kept his word and did for Sarah exactly what he had promised. [2]She became pregnant, and she gave birth to a son for Abraham in his old age. This happened at just the time God had said it would. [3]And Abraham named their son Isaac. [4]Eight days after Isaac was born, Abraham circumcised him as God had commanded. [5]Abraham was 100 years old when Isaac was born.

[6]And Sarah declared, "God has brought me laughter.* All who hear about this will laugh with me. [7]Who would have said to Abraham that Sarah would nurse a baby? Yet I have given Abraham a son in his old age!"

Hagar and Ishmael Are Sent Away

[8]When Isaac grew up and was about to be weaned, Abraham prepared a huge feast to celebrate the occasion. [9]But Sarah saw Ishmael—the son of Abraham and her Egyptian servant Hagar—making fun of her son, Isaac.* [10]So she turned to Abraham and demanded, "Get rid of that slave woman and her son. He is not going to share the inheritance with my son, Isaac. I won't have it!"

[11]This upset Abraham very much because Ishmael was his son. [12]But God told Abraham, "Do not be upset over the boy and your servant. Do whatever Sarah tells you, for Isaac is the son through whom your descendants will be counted. [13]But I will also make a nation of the descendants of Hagar's son because he is your son, too."

[14]So Abraham got up early the next morning, prepared food and a container of water, and strapped them on Hagar's shoulders. Then he sent her away with their son, and she wandered aimlessly in the wilderness of Beersheba.

[15]When the water was gone, she put the boy in the shade of a bush. [16]Then she went and sat down by herself about a hundred yards* away. "I don't want to watch the boy die," she said, as she burst into tears.

[17]But God heard the boy crying, and the angel of God called to Hagar from heaven, "Hagar, what's wrong? Do not be afraid! God has heard the boy crying as he lies there. [18]Go to him and comfort him, for I will make a great nation from his descendants."

[19]Then God opened Hagar's eyes, and she saw a well full of water. She quickly filled her water container and gave the boy a drink.

[20]And God was with the boy as he grew up in the wilderness. He became a skillful archer, [21]and he settled in the wilderness of Paran. His mother arranged for him to marry a woman from the land of Egypt.

Abraham's Covenant with Abimelech

[22]About this time, Abimelech came with Phicol, his army commander, to visit Abraham. "God is

20:16 Hebrew *1,000 [shekels] of silver,* about 25 pounds or 11.4 kilograms in weight. **21:6** The name *Isaac* means "he laughs." **21:9** As in Greek version and Latin Vulgate; Hebrew lacks *of her son, Isaac.* **21:16** Hebrew *a bowshot.*

---

faults, Abraham is presented as being politically successful and able to mediate God's blessing to others.

21:1–21 The Birth of Isaac. Hagar and Ishmael Are Sent Away. 8: The weaning celebration may have been when Isaac was three to five years old. If we take the chronological details literally, this would make Ishmael somewhere between eighteen and twenty years old (cf. 17:24–25). **9:** The Hebrew text just says Ishmael was "playing," but we do not know whether with Abraham, Isaac, or by himself. **17:** Again we see God's concern for those outside the elected line of Isaac. God's hearing of Ishmael's voice reflects the meaning of Ishmael's name, "God hears."

21:22–34 Abraham's Covenant with Abimelech. 22–24: Having lived in Abimelech's land as a foreigner (cf. 20:1) it is now time to swear peace to each other,

obviously with you, helping you in everything
you do," Abimelech said. 23 "Swear to me in
God's name that you will never deceive me, my
children, or any of my descendants. I have been
loyal to you, so now swear that you will be loyal
to me and to this country where you are living
as a foreigner."

24 Abraham replied, "Yes, I swear to it!" 25 Then
Abraham complained to Abimelech about a well
that Abimelech's servants had taken by force
from Abraham's servants.

26 "This is the first I've heard of it," Abimelech
answered. "I have no idea who is responsible.
You have never complained about this before."

27 Abraham then gave some of his sheep,
goats, and cattle to Abimelech, and they made a
treaty. 28 But Abraham also took seven additional
female lambs and set them off by themselves.
29 Abimelech asked, "Why have you set these
seven apart from the others?"

30 Abraham replied, "Please accept these sev-
en lambs to show your agreement that I dug
this well." 31 Then he named the place Beersheba
(which means "well of the oath"), because that
was where they had sworn the oath.

32 After making their covenant at Beersheba,
Abimelech left with Phicol, the commander of
his army, and they returned home to the land of
the Philistines. 33 Then Abraham planted a tamarisk tree at Beersheba, and there he worshiped
the LORD, the Eternal God.* 34 And Abraham
lived as a foreigner in Philistine country for a
long time.

Abraham's Faith Tested

22 Some time later, God tested Abraham's faith. "Abraham!" God called.
"Yes," he replied. "Here I am."

2 "Take your son, your only son—yes, Isaac,
whom you love so much—and go to the land of
Moriah. Go and sacrifice him as a burnt offering on one of the mountains, which I will show
you."

3 The next morning Abraham got up early. He
saddled his donkey and took two of his servants
with him, along with his son, Isaac. Then he
chopped wood for a fire for a burnt offering and
set out for the place God had told him about. 4 On
the third day of their journey, Abraham looked
up and saw the place in the distance. 5 "Stay here
with the donkey," Abraham told the servants.
"The boy and I will travel a little farther. We
will worship there, and then we will come right
back."

6 So Abraham placed the wood for the burnt
offering on Isaac's shoulders, while he himself
carried the fire and the knife. As the two of them
walked on together, 7 Isaac turned to Abraham
and said, "Father?"

"Yes, my son?" Abraham replied.

"We have the fire and the wood," the boy said,
"but where is the sheep for the burnt offering?"

8 "God will provide a sheep for the burnt offering, my son," Abraham answered. And they
both walked on together.

9 When they arrived at the place where God
had told him to go, Abraham built an altar and
arranged the wood on it. Then he tied his son,
Isaac, and laid him on the altar on top of the
wood. 10 And Abraham picked up the knife to kill
his son as a sacrifice. 11 At that moment the angel
of the LORD called to him from heaven, "Abraham! Abraham!"

"Yes," Abraham replied. "Here I am!"

12 "Don't lay a hand on the boy!" the angel
said. "Do not hurt him in any way, for now I know
that you truly fear God. You have not withheld
from me even your son, your only son."

13 Then Abraham looked up and saw a ram
caught by its horns in a thicket. So he took the ram
and sacrificed it as a burnt offering in place of his
son. 14 Abraham named the place Yahweh-Yireh
(which means "the LORD will provide"). To this
day, people still use that name as a proverb: "On
the mountain of the LORD it will be provided."

15 Then the angel of the LORD called again to

21:33 Hebrew *El-Olam.*

as Abraham's prosperity is increasing. This is another fulfillment of God's promise to Abraham of being a blessing to other nations. **25–34:** This narrative serves to explain how Beersheba, a prominent city in the Negev, got its name. *Beer* means "well," and *sheba* can mean both "seven" or "oath." *The Eternal God* (*El-Olam*) was probably the name of the deity associated with Beersheba before Abraham's arrival, which Abraham added as an appropriate title for the LORD.

22:1–24 Abraham's Faith Tested. 2: Another obstacle comes to stand in the way of God's promises to Abraham, and this time it comes from the LORD himself. Although Moriah is traditionally associated with the mountain that the Temple of Jerusalem stood on (cf. 2 Chr 3:1; even today the Islamic Dome of the Rock is thought to have been built over the place of Isaac's near-sacrifice), the actual location is not known. **6:** We do not know how old Isaac is, but he is apparently old enough to walk some distance carrying wood. **12–14:** The Hebrew words for *fear*, *saw*, and *provide* all sound similar; thus the author is playing on the

Abraham from heaven. [16]"This is what the LORD
says: Because you have obeyed me and have not
withheld even your son, your only son, I swear
by my own name that [17]I will certainly bless
you. I will multiply your descendants* beyond
number, like the stars in the sky and the sand
on the seashore. Your descendants will conquer
the cities of their enemies. [18]And through your
descendants all the nations of the earth will be
blessed—all because you have obeyed me."

[19]Then they returned to the servants and
traveled back to Beersheba, where Abraham continued to live.

[20]Soon after this, Abraham heard that Milcah,
his brother Nahor's wife, had borne Nahor eight
sons. [21]The oldest was named Uz, the next oldest was Buz, followed by Kemuel (the ancestor
of the Arameans), [22]Kesed, Hazo, Pildash, Jid-
laph, and Bethuel. [23](Bethuel became the father
of Rebekah.) In addition to these eight sons from
Milcah, [24]Nahor had four other children from
his concubine Reumah. Their names were Tebah,
Gaham, Tahash, and Maacah.

The Burial of Sarah

23 When Sarah was 127 years old, [2]she
died at Kiriath-arba (now called Hebron) in the land of Canaan. There
Abraham mourned and wept for her.

[3]Then, leaving her body, he said to the Hittite
elders, [4]"Here I am, a stranger and a foreigner
among you. Please sell me a piece of land so I can
give my wife a proper burial."

[5]The Hittites replied to Abraham, [6]"Listen, my
lord, you are an honored prince among us. Choose
the finest of our tombs and bury her there. No one
here will refuse to help you in this way."

[7]Then Abraham bowed low before the Hittites [8]and said, "Since you are willing to help
me in this way, be so kind as to ask Ephron son
of Zohar [9]to let me buy his cave at Machpelah,
down at the end of his field. I will pay the full
price in the presence of witnesses, so I will have a
permanent burial place for my family."

[10]Ephron was sitting there among the others,
and he answered Abraham as the others listened,
speaking publicly before all the Hittite elders of
the town. [11]"No, my lord," he said to Abraham,
"please listen to me. I will give you the field and
the cave. Here in the presence of my people, I
give it to you. Go and bury your dead."

[12]Abraham again bowed low before the citizens of the land, [13]and he replied to Ephron as
everyone listened. "No, listen to me. I will buy it
from you. Let me pay the full price for the field
so I can bury my dead there."

[14]Ephron answered Abraham, [15]"My lord,
please listen to me. The land is worth 400 pieces*
of silver, but what is that between friends? Go
ahead and bury your dead."

[16]So Abraham agreed to Ephron's price and
paid the amount he had suggested—400 pieces of
silver, weighed according to the market standard.
The Hittite elders witnessed the transaction.

[17]So Abraham bought the plot of land belonging to Ephron at Machpelah, near Mamre. This
included the field itself, the cave that was in it,
and all the surrounding trees. [18]It was transferred
to Abraham as his permanent possession in the
presence of the Hittite elders at the city gate.
[19]Then Abraham buried his wife, Sarah, there in
Canaan, in the cave of Machpelah, near Mamre
(also called Hebron). [20]So the field and the cave
were transferred from the Hittites to Abraham
for use as a permanent burial place.

A Wife for Isaac

24 Abraham was now a very old man,
and the LORD had blessed him in
every way. [2]One day Abraham said
to his oldest servant, the man in charge of his
household, "Take an oath by putting your hand
under my thigh. [3]Swear by the LORD, the God of
heaven and earth, that you will not allow my son
to marry one of these local Canaanite women.
[4]Go instead to my homeland, to my relatives,
and find a wife there for my son Isaac."

22:17 Hebrew *seed;* also in 22:17b, 18. **23:15** Hebrew *400 shekels,* about 10 pounds or 4.6 kilograms in weight; also in 23:16.

---

words. **20–24:** This list of children and its mention of Rachel points forward to the next major episode in chapter 24.

23:1–20 The Burial of Sarah. 1–2: This is the only evidence we are given that Abraham entertained any feelings for Sarah! **3–20:** Here we see a wonderful piece of traditional bargaining, conducted in typically indirect and flamboyant manner. The end result is that, through Abraham's paying a high price, Hebron is established as the burial place of the matriarchs and patriarchs.

24:1–67 A Wife for Isaac. Chapters 24—27 focus on the generation between Abraham and Jacob. Although the traditional Israelite formula describes God as "the God of your fathers, Abraham, Isaac, and Jacob," these next chapters are more about Rebekah than Isaac since she features more prominently than does he. **2, 9:** Putting one's hand under the other's

[5]The servant asked, "But what if I can't find a
young woman who is willing to travel so far from
home? Should I then take Isaac there to live among
your relatives in the land you came from?"
[6]"No!" Abraham responded. "Be careful never to take my son there. [7]For the LORD, the God
of heaven, who took me from my father's house
and my native land, solemnly promised to give
this land to my descendants.* He will send his
angel ahead of you, and he will see to it that you
find a wife there for my son. [8]If she is unwilling
to come back with you, then you are free from
this oath of mine. But under no circumstances
are you to take my son there."
[9]So the servant took an oath by putting his
hand under the thigh of his master, Abraham. He
swore to follow Abraham's instructions. [10]Then
he loaded ten of Abraham's camels with all kinds
of expensive gifts from his master, and he traveled to distant Aram-naharaim. There he went to
the town where Abraham's brother Nahor had
settled. [11]He made the camels kneel beside a well
just outside the town. It was evening, and the
women were coming out to draw water.
[12]"O LORD, God of my master, Abraham," he
prayed. "Please give me success today, and show
unfailing love to my master, Abraham. [13]See, I
am standing here beside this spring, and the
young women of the town are coming out to
draw water. [14]This is my request. I will ask one of
them, 'Please give me a drink from your jug.' If
she says, 'Yes, have a drink, and I will water your
camels, too!'—let her be the one you have selected as Isaac's wife. This is how I will know that
you have shown unfailing love to my master."
[15]Before he had finished praying, he saw a
young woman named Rebekah coming out with
her water jug on her shoulder. She was the daughter of Bethuel, who was the son of Abraham's
brother Nahor and his wife, Milcah. [16]Rebekah
was very beautiful and old enough to be married,
but she was still a virgin. She went down to the
spring, filled her jug, and came up again. [17]Run-
ning over to her, the servant said, "Please give
me a little drink of water from your jug."
[18]"Yes, my lord," she answered, "have a
drink." And she quickly lowered her jug from
her shoulder and gave him a drink. [19]When she
had given him a drink, she said, "I'll draw water
for your camels, too, until they have had enough
to drink." [20]So she quickly emptied her jug into
the watering trough and ran back to the well to
draw water for all his camels.
[21]The servant watched her in silence, wondering whether or not the LORD had given him
success in his mission. [22]Then at last, when the
camels had finished drinking, he took out a gold
ring for her nose and two large gold bracelets*
for her wrists.
[23]"Whose daughter are you?" he asked. "And
please tell me, would your father have any room
to put us up for the night?"
[24]"I am the daughter of Bethuel," she replied.
"My grandparents are Nahor and Milcah. [25]Yes,
we have plenty of straw and feed for the camels,
and we have room for guests."
[26]The man bowed low and worshiped the
LORD. [27]"Praise the LORD, the God of my master,
Abraham," he said. "The LORD has shown unfailing love and faithfulness to my master, for he
has led me straight to my master's relatives."
[28]The young woman ran home to tell her
family everything that had happened. [29]Now Rebekah had a brother named Laban, who ran out
to meet the man at the spring. [30]He had seen the
nose-ring and the bracelets on his sister's wrists,
and had heard Rebekah tell what the man had
said. So he rushed out to the spring, where the
man was still standing beside his camels. [31]Laban
said to him, "Come and stay with us, you who are
blessed by the LORD! Why are you standing here
outside the town when I have a room all ready for
you and a place prepared for the camels?"
[32]So the man went home with Laban, and
Laban unloaded the camels, gave him straw for
their bedding, fed them, and provided water for
the man and the camel drivers to wash their feet.
[33]Then food was served. But Abraham's servant
said, "I don't want to eat until I have told you
why I have come."
"All right," Laban said, "tell us."
[34]"I am Abraham's servant," he explained.
[35]"And the LORD has greatly blessed my master;
he has become a wealthy man. The LORD has giv-
en him flocks of sheep and goats, herds of cattle,
a fortune in silver and gold, and many male and
female servants and camels and donkeys.
[36]"When Sarah, my master's wife, was very

24:7 Hebrew *seed;* also in 24:60. **24:22** Hebrew *a gold nose-ring weighing a half shekel* [0.2 ounces or 6 grams] *and two gold bracelets weighing 10 shekels* [4 ounces or 114 grams].

testes (*under the thigh*) signified the importance of the oath being undertaken. **10:** Aram-naharaim and the city of Nahor is very close to Haran. As such it is part of Abraham's original homeland in Mesopotamia, where Abraham and his family lived before setting out to Canaan (cf. 11:27–31). **24:** It was not usual to be identified by one's grandmother, so possibly Milcah's name was well known. **57–58:** As we

old, she gave birth to my master's son, and my master has given him everything he owns. 37 And my master made me take an oath. He said, 'Do not allow my son to marry one of these local Canaanite women. 38 Go instead to my father's house, to my relatives, and find a wife there for my son.'

39 "But I said to my master, 'What if I can't find a young woman who is willing to go back with me?' 40 He responded, 'The LORD, in whose presence I have lived, will send his angel with you and will make your mission successful. Yes, you must find a wife for my son from among my relatives, from my father's family. 41 Then you will have fulfilled your obligation. But if you go to my relatives and they refuse to let her go with you, you will be free from my oath.'

42 "So today when I came to the spring, I prayed this prayer: 'O LORD, God of my master, Abraham, please give me success on this mission. 43 See, I am standing here beside this spring. This is my request. When a young woman comes to draw water, I will say to her, "Please give me a little drink of water from your jug." 44 If she says, "Yes, have a drink, and I will draw water for your camels, too," let her be the one you have selected to be the wife of my master's son.'

45 "Before I had finished praying in my heart, I saw Rebekah coming out with her water jug on her shoulder. She went down to the spring and drew water. So I said to her, 'Please give me a drink.' 46 She quickly lowered her jug from her shoulder and said, 'Yes, have a drink, and I will water your camels, too!' So I drank, and then she watered the camels.

47 "Then I asked, 'Whose daughter are you?' She replied, 'I am the daughter of Bethuel, and my grandparents are Nahor and Milcah.' So I put the ring on her nose, and the bracelets on her wrists.

48 "Then I bowed low and worshiped the LORD. I praised the LORD, the God of my master, Abraham, because he had led me straight to my master's niece to be his son's wife. 49 So tell me—will you or won't you show unfailing love and faithfulness to my master? Please tell me yes or no, and then I'll know what to do next."

50 Then Laban and Bethuel replied, "The LORD has obviously brought you here, so there is nothing we can say. 51 Here is Rebekah; take her and go. Yes, let her be the wife of your master's son, as the LORD has directed."

52 When Abraham's servant heard their answer, he bowed down to the ground and worshiped the LORD. 53 Then he brought out silver and gold jewelry and clothing and presented them to Rebekah. He also gave expensive presents to her brother and mother. 54 Then they ate their meal, and the servant and the men with him stayed there overnight.

But early the next morning, Abraham's servant said, "Send me back to my master."

55 "But we want Rebekah to stay with us at least ten days," her brother and mother said. "Then she can go."

56 But he said, "Don't delay me. The LORD has made my mission successful; now send me back so I can return to my master."

57 "Well," they said, "we'll call Rebekah and ask her what she thinks." 58 So they called Rebekah. "Are you willing to go with this man?" they asked her.

And she replied, "Yes, I will go."

59 So they said good-bye to Rebekah and sent her away with Abraham's servant and his men. The woman who had been Rebekah's childhood nurse went along with her. 60 They gave her this blessing as she parted:

"Our sister, may you become
  the mother of many millions!
May your descendants be strong
  and conquer the cities of their
    enemies."

61 Then Rebekah and her servant girls mounted the camels and followed the man. So Abraham's servant took Rebekah and went on his way.

62 Meanwhile, Isaac, whose home was in the Negev, had returned from Beer-lahai-roi. 63 One evening as he was walking and meditating in the fields, he looked up and saw the camels coming. 64 When Rebekah looked up and saw Isaac, she quickly dismounted from her camel. 65 "Who is that man walking through the fields to meet us?" she asked the servant.

And he replied, "It is my master." So Rebekah covered her face with her veil. 66 Then the servant told Isaac everything he had done.

67 And Isaac brought Rebekah into his mother Sarah's tent, and she became his wife. He loved her deeply, and she was a special comfort to him after the death of his mother.

---

have seen in the stories of Genesis up to this point, it is unusual for the menfolk of a family to take into consideration the feelings of a woman. **59:** Later we hear that Rebekah's childhood nurse is called Deborah and is someone to whom Rebekah is especially close (cf. 35:8). **65:** The face covering was a sign not so much of modesty as of betrothal.

The Death of Abraham

25 Abraham married another wife,
whose name was Keturah. 2 She gave
birth to Zimran, Jokshan, Medan,
Midian, Ishbak, and Shuah. 3 Jokshan was the father of Sheba and Dedan. Dedan's descendants
were the Asshurites, Letushites, and Leummites.
4 Midian's sons were Ephah, Epher, Hanoch,
Abida, and Eldaah. These were all descendants of
Abraham through Keturah.

5 Abraham gave everything he owned to his
son Isaac. 6 But before he died, he gave gifts to
the sons of his concubines and sent them off to a
land in the east, away from Isaac.

7 Abraham lived for 175 years, 8 and he died at
a ripe old age, having lived a long and satisfying
life. He breathed his last and joined his ancestors
in death. 9 His sons Isaac and Ishmael buried him
in the cave of Machpelah, near Mamre, in the
field of Ephron son of Zohar the Hittite. 10 This
was the field Abraham had purchased from the
Hittites and where he had buried his wife Sarah.
11 After Abraham's death, God blessed his son
Isaac, who settled near Beer-lahai-roi in the
Negev.

Ishmael's Descendants

12 This is the account of the family of Ishmael, the
son of Abraham through Hagar, Sarah's Egyptian servant. 13 Here is a list, by their names and
clans, of Ishmael's descendants: The oldest was
Nebaioth, followed by Kedar, Adbeel, Mibsam,
14 Mishma, Dumah, Massa, 15 Hadad, Tema, Jetur, Naphish, and Kedemah. 16 These twelve sons
of Ishmael became the founders of twelve tribes
named after them, listed according to the places they settled and camped. 17 Ishmael lived for
137 years. Then he breathed his last and joined
his ancestors in death. 18 Ishmael's descendants
occupied the region from Havilah to Shur, which
is east of Egypt in the direction of Asshur. There
they lived in open hostility toward all their relatives.*

The Births of Esau and Jacob

19 This is the account of the family of Isaac, the
son of Abraham. 20 When Isaac was forty years
old, he married Rebekah, the daughter of Bethuel the Aramean from Paddan-aram and the sister
of Laban the Aramean.

21 Isaac pleaded with the LORD on behalf of his
wife, because she was unable to have children.
The LORD answered Isaac's prayer, and Rebekah
became pregnant with twins. 22 But the two children struggled with each other in her womb. So
she went to ask the LORD about it. "Why is this
happening to me?" she asked.

23 And the LORD told her, "The sons in your
womb will become two nations. From the very
beginning, the two nations will be rivals. One
nation will be stronger than the other; and your
older son will serve your younger son."

24 And when the time came to give birth, Rebekah discovered that she did indeed have twins!
25 The first one was very red at birth and covered
with thick hair like a fur coat. So they named
him Esau.* 26 Then the other twin was born with
his hand grasping Esau's heel. So they named
him Jacob.* Isaac was sixty years old when the
twins were born.

Esau Sells His Birthright

27 As the boys grew up, Esau became a skillful
hunter. He was an outdoorsman, but Jacob had
a quiet temperament, preferring to stay at home.
28 Isaac loved Esau because he enjoyed eating
the wild game Esau brought home, but Rebekah
loved Jacob.

29 One day when Jacob was cooking some stew,
Esau arrived home from the wilderness exhausted
and hungry. 30 Esau said to Jacob, "I'm starved!
Give me some of that red stew!" (This is how Esau
got his other name, Edom, which means "red.")

25:18 The meaning of the Hebrew is uncertain. **25:25** *Esau* sounds like a Hebrew term that means "hair." **25:26** *Jacob* sounds like the Hebrew words for "heel" and "deceiver."

25:1–18 The Death of Abraham. Ishmael's Descendants. 1–3: Abraham was 137 years old when Sarah died and 175 when he himself died, so this is an astounding age to be marrying and fathering children: Clearly many more sons could indeed be born to a man that old (cf. 17:17)! These sons become the ancestors of the nomadic peoples of Israel's time. **11:** Beer-lahai-roi is the place where the LORD had appeared to Hagar (16:14). These few verses finish the account of Ishmael and show how God's promises to Hagar and Abraham on his behalf have been fulfilled (cf. 16:12; 17:20).

25:19–36:43 The Family Stories of Jacob

25:19–34 Esau and Jacob. 21: The theme of childlessness is prominent in each of the stories of the patriarchs and matriarchs (cf. 29:31), thus emphasizing that the continuation of the LORD's line of promise is due to his miraculous interventions. **23:** From Esau—the oldest—will come Edom and from Jacob—the youngest—will come Israel. Thus we see it established that Israel will be stronger than the nation of Edom and will be served by them (cf. 2 Sam 8:13–14). **30–34:** Wordplays abound in this narrative, as do in-

31 "All right," Jacob replied, "but trade me
your rights as the firstborn son."
32 "Look, I'm dying of starvation!" said Esau.
"What good is my birthright to me now?"
33 But Jacob said, "First you must swear that
your birthright is mine." So Esau swore an oath,
thereby selling all his rights as the firstborn to
his brother, Jacob.
34 Then Jacob gave Esau some bread and lentil
stew. Esau ate the meal, then got up and left. He
showed contempt for his rights as the firstborn.

Isaac Deceives Abimelech

26 A severe famine now struck the land,
as had happened before in Abraham's
time. So Isaac moved to Gerar, where
Abimelech, king of the Philistines, lived.
2 The LORD appeared to Isaac and said, "Do
not go down to Egypt, but do as I tell you. 3 Live
here as a foreigner in this land, and I will be
with you and bless you. I hereby confirm that
I will give all these lands to you and your descendants,* just as I solemnly promised Abraham, your father. 4 I will cause your descendants
to become as numerous as the stars of the sky,
and I will give them all these lands. And through
your descendants all the nations of the earth
will be blessed. 5 I will do this because Abraham
listened to me and obeyed all my requirements,
commands, decrees, and instructions." 6 So Isaac
stayed in Gerar.
7 When the men who lived there asked Isaac
about his wife, Rebekah, he said, "She is my sister." He was afraid to say, "She is my wife." He
thought, "They will kill me to get her, because
she is so beautiful." 8 But some time later, Abimelech, king of the Philistines, looked out his window and saw Isaac caressing Rebekah.
9 Immediately, Abimelech called for Isaac and
exclaimed, "She is obviously your wife! Why did
you say, 'She is my sister'?"
"Because I was afraid someone would kill me
to get her from me," Isaac replied.
10 "How could you do this to us?" Abimelech exclaimed. "One of my people might easily
have taken your wife and slept with her, and you
would have made us guilty of great sin."
11 Then Abimelech issued a public proclamation: "Anyone who touches this man or his wife
will be put to death!"

Conflict over Water Rights

12 When Isaac planted his crops that year, he
harvested a hundred times more grain than he
planted, for the LORD blessed him. 13 He became a
very rich man, and his wealth continued to grow.
14 He acquired so many flocks of sheep and goats,
herds of cattle, and servants that the Philistines
became jealous of him. 15 So the Philistines filled
up all of Isaac's wells with dirt. These were the
wells that had been dug by the servants of his
father, Abraham.
16 Finally, Abimelech ordered Isaac to leave
the country. "Go somewhere else," he said, "for
you have become too powerful for us."
17 So Isaac moved away to the Gerar Valley,
where he set up their tents and settled down.
18 He reopened the wells his father had dug,
which the Philistines had filled in after Abraham's death. Isaac also restored the names Abraham had given them.
19 Isaac's servants also dug in the Gerar Valley
and discovered a well of fresh water. 20 But then
the shepherds from Gerar came and claimed the
spring. "This is our water," they said, and they
argued over it with Isaac's herdsmen. So Isaac
named the well Esek (which means "argument").
21 Isaac's men then dug another well, but again
there was a dispute over it. So Isaac named it
Sitnah (which means "hostility"). 22 Abandoning
that one, Isaac moved on and dug another well.
This time there was no dispute over it, so Isaac
named the place Rehoboth (which means "open
space"), for he said, "At last the LORD has created
enough space for us to prosper in this land."
23 From there Isaac moved to Beersheba,
24 where the LORD appeared to him on the night
of his arrival. "I am the God of your father, Abra-

26:3 Hebrew *seed;* also in 26:4, 24.

dications that neither of the brothers is a particularly upright and virtuous character.

26:1–11 Isaac Deceives Abimelech. 2–5: The promises made to Abraham are reiterated here, thus establishing the continuity into the next generation (cf. 12:1–3; 13:14–17; etc.). **6–11:** This is the third incident of this nature (cf. 12:10–20; 20:1–18), and since both previous times led to the deceiver gaining in riches, it clearly seems a sensible thing for the men to do in such situations!

26:12–35 Conflict over Water Rights. Isaac's Covenant with Abimelech. 23, 33: Beersheba is already associated with Abraham (cf. 21:31–33) and becomes the place where the LORD first reveals himself as *the God of your father, Abraham*. It is notable that the LORD is always the patriarchal God: he is never the God of Sarah, Rebekah, and Rachel. **26–32:** The (presumed) descendant of the Abimelech of chapter

ham," he said. "Do not be afraid, for I am with you and will bless you. I will multiply your descendants, and they will become a great nation. I will do this because of my promise to Abraham, my servant." 25 Then Isaac built an altar there and worshiped the LORD. He set up his camp at that place, and his servants dug another well.

Isaac's Covenant with Abimelech

26 One day King Abimelech came from Gerar with his adviser, Ahuzzath, and also Phicol, his army commander. 27 "Why have you come here?" Isaac asked. "You obviously hate me, since you kicked me off your land."

28 They replied, "We can plainly see that the LORD is with you. So we want to enter into a sworn treaty with you. Let's make a covenant. 29 Swear that you will not harm us, just as we have never troubled you. We have always treated you well, and we sent you away from us in peace. And now look how the LORD has blessed you!"

30 So Isaac prepared a covenant feast to celebrate the treaty, and they ate and drank together. 31 Early the next morning, they each took a solemn oath not to interfere with each other. Then Isaac sent them home again, and they left him in peace.

32 That very day Isaac's servants came and told him about a new well they had dug. "We've found water!" they exclaimed. 33 So Isaac named the well Shibah (which means "oath"). And to this day the town that grew up there is called Beersheba (which means "well of the oath").

34 At the age of forty, Esau married two Hittite wives: Judith, the daughter of Beeri, and Basemath, the daughter of Elon. 35 But Esau's wives made life miserable for Isaac and Rebekah.

Jacob Steals Esau's Blessing

27 One day when Isaac was old and turning blind, he called for Esau, his older son, and said, "My son."

"Yes, Father?" Esau replied.

2 "I am an old man now," Isaac said, "and I don't know when I may die. 3 Take your bow and a quiver full of arrows, and go out into the open country to hunt some wild game for me. 4 Prepare my favorite dish, and bring it here for me to eat. Then I will pronounce the blessing that belongs to you, my firstborn son, before I die."

5 But Rebekah overheard what Isaac had said to his son Esau. So when Esau left to hunt for the wild game, 6 she said to her son Jacob, "Listen. I overheard your father say to Esau, 7 'Bring me some wild game and prepare me a delicious meal. Then I will bless you in the LORD's presence before I die.' 8 Now, my son, listen to me. Do exactly as I tell you. 9 Go out to the flocks, and bring me two fine young goats. I'll use them to prepare your father's favorite dish. 10 Then take the food to your father so he can eat it and bless you before he dies."

11 "But look," Jacob replied to Rebekah, "my brother, Esau, is a hairy man, and my skin is smooth. 12 What if my father touches me? He'll see that I'm trying to trick him, and then he'll curse me instead of blessing me."

13 But his mother replied, "Then let the curse fall on me, my son! Just do what I tell you. Go out and get the goats for me!"

14 So Jacob went out and got the young goats for his mother. Rebekah took them and prepared a delicious meal, just the way Isaac liked it. 15 Then she took Esau's favorite clothes, which were there in the house, and gave them to her younger son, Jacob. 16 She covered his arms and the smooth part of his neck with the skin of the young goats. 17 Then she gave Jacob the delicious meal, including freshly baked bread.

18 So Jacob took the food to his father. "My father?" he said.

"Yes, my son," Isaac answered. "Who are you—Esau or Jacob?"

19 Jacob replied, "It's Esau, your firstborn son. I've done as you told me. Here is the wild game. Now sit up and eat it so you can give me your blessing."

20 Isaac asked, "How did you find it so quickly, my son?"

"The LORD your God put it in my path!" Jacob replied.

21 Then Isaac said to Jacob, "Come closer so I can touch you and make sure that you really are Esau." 22 So Jacob went closer to his father, and Isaac touched him. "The voice is Jacob's, but the hands are Esau's," Isaac said. 23 But he did not recognize Jacob, because Jacob's hands felt hairy just like Esau's. So Isaac prepared to bless Jacob. 24 "But are you really my son Esau?" he asked.

"Yes, I am," Jacob replied.

---

21 now makes a treaty of peace with the descendant of Abraham. Once more, blessing comes both to the recipient of God's promises and to those who associate with him.

27:1—28:9 Jacob Steals Esau's Blessing. 1: The implication is that it is not only Isaac's physical eyesight that is dim but his spiritual eyesight also. **5–17:** Jacob, "the deceiver," here learns deception from his mother. Rebekah uses her cunning to bring about the

25 Then Isaac said, "Now, my son, bring me the wild game. Let me eat it, and then I will give you my blessing." So Jacob took the food to his father, and Isaac ate it. He also drank the wine that Jacob served him. 26 Then Isaac said to Jacob, "Please come a little closer and kiss me, my son."

27 So Jacob went over and kissed him. And when Isaac caught the smell of his clothes, he was finally convinced, and he blessed his son. He said, "Ah! The smell of my son is like the smell of the outdoors, which the LORD has blessed!

28 "From the dew of heaven
and the richness of the earth,
may God always give you abundant harvests of grain
and bountiful new wine.
29 May many nations become your servants,
and may they bow down to you.
May you be the master over your brothers,
and may your mother's sons bow down to you.
All who curse you will be cursed,
and all who bless you will be blessed."

30 As soon as Isaac had finished blessing Jacob, and almost before Jacob had left his father, Esau returned from his hunt. 31 Esau prepared a delicious meal and brought it to his father. Then he said, "Sit up, my father, and eat my wild game so you can give me your blessing."

32 But Isaac asked him, "Who are you?"

Esau replied, "It's your son, your firstborn son, Esau."

33 Isaac began to tremble uncontrollably and said, "Then who just served me wild game? I have already eaten it, and I blessed him just before you came. And yes, that blessing must stand!"

34 When Esau heard his father's words, he let out a loud and bitter cry. "Oh my father, what about me? Bless me, too!" he begged.

35 But Isaac said, "Your brother was here, and he tricked me. He has taken away your blessing."

36 Esau exclaimed, "No wonder his name is Jacob, for now he has cheated me twice.* First he took my rights as the firstborn, and now he has stolen my blessing. Oh, haven't you saved even one blessing for me?"

37 Isaac said to Esau, "I have made Jacob your master and have declared that all his brothers will be his servants. I have guaranteed him an abundance of grain and wine—what is left for me to give you, my son?"

38 Esau pleaded, "But do you have only one blessing? Oh my father, bless me, too!" Then Esau broke down and wept.

39 Finally, his father, Isaac, said to him,

"You will live away from the richness of the earth,
and away from the dew of the heaven above.
40 You will live by your sword,
and you will serve your brother.
But when you decide to break free,
you will shake his yoke from your neck."

Jacob Flees to Paddan-Aram

41 From that time on, Esau hated Jacob because their father had given Jacob the blessing. And Esau began to scheme: "I will soon be mourning my father's death. Then I will kill my brother, Jacob."

42 But Rebekah heard about Esau's plans. So she sent for Jacob and told him, "Listen, Esau is consoling himself by plotting to kill you. 43 So listen carefully, my son. Get ready and flee to my brother, Laban, in Haran. 44 Stay there with him until your brother cools off. 45 When he calms down and forgets what you have done to him, I will send for you to come back. Why should I lose both of you in one day?"

46 Then Rebekah said to Isaac, "I'm sick and tired of these local Hittite women! I would rather die than see Jacob marry one of them."

28 So Isaac called for Jacob, blessed him, and said, "You must not marry any of these Canaanite women. 2 Instead, go at once to Paddan-aram, to the house of your grandfather Bethuel, and marry one of your uncle

27:36 *Jacob* sounds like the Hebrew words for "heel" and "deceiver."

fulfillment of the LORD's words to her in 25:23. **28–20:** The recurring theme of God's promises is reiterated here: The LORD will bless Jacob so that he might be a blessing to those who act favorably toward him. **32–40:** Patriarchal custom demanded that the firstborn son receive the fullness of the father's blessing, but here, as elsewhere, this is turned on its head. This story establishes the principle of the last being first (cf. 48:17–19; 1 Sam 16:1–12). Despite Isaac's words to Esau, the final line (v. 40) reminds us again that God's compassion and sovereignty cover those who lose out, as well as the winners. **41:** These are the last words we hear Esau speak until he meets Jacob again in chapter 33. **46:** Rebekah again uses deception to make sure that Jacob is sent away, out of Esau's murderous reach. **28:2:** Paddan-aram is thought to be

Laban's daughters. 3 May God Almighty* bless you and give you many children. And may your descendants multiply and become many nations! 4 May God pass on to you and your descendants* the blessings he promised to Abraham. May you own this land where you are now living as a foreigner, for God gave this land to Abraham."

5 So Isaac sent Jacob away, and he went to Paddan-aram to stay with his uncle Laban, his mother's brother, the son of Bethuel the Aramean.

6 Esau knew that his father, Isaac, had blessed Jacob and sent him to Paddan-aram to find a wife, and that he had warned Jacob, "You must not marry a Canaanite woman." 7 He also knew that Jacob had obeyed his parents and gone to Paddan-aram. 8 It was now very clear to Esau that his father did not like the local Canaanite women. 9 So Esau visited his uncle Ishmael's family and married one of Ishmael's daughters, in addition to the wives he already had. His new wife's name was Mahalath. She was the sister of Nebaioth and the daughter of Ishmael, Abraham's son.

Jacob's Dream at Bethel

10 Meanwhile, Jacob left Beersheba and traveled toward Haran. 11 At sundown he arrived at a good place to set up camp and stopped there for the night. Jacob found a stone to rest his head against and lay down to sleep. 12 As he slept, he dreamed of a stairway that reached from the earth up to heaven. And he saw the angels of God going up and down the stairway.

13 At the top of the stairway stood the LORD, and he said, "I am the LORD, the God of your grandfather Abraham, and the God of your father, Isaac. The ground you are lying on belongs to you. I am giving it to you and your descendants. 14 Your descendants will be as numerous as the dust of the earth! They will spread out in all directions—to the west and the east, to the north and the south. And all the families of the earth will be blessed through you and your descendants. 15 What's more, I am with you, and I will protect you wherever you go. One day I will bring you back to this land. I will not leave you until I have finished giving you everything I have promised you."

16 Then Jacob awoke from his sleep and said, "Surely the LORD is in this place, and I wasn't even aware of it!" 17 But he was also afraid and said, "What an awesome place this is! It is none other than the house of God, the very gateway to heaven!"

18 The next morning Jacob got up very early. He took the stone he had rested his head against, and he set it upright as a memorial pillar. Then he poured olive oil over it. 19 He named that place Bethel (which means "house of God"), although it was previously called Luz.

20 Then Jacob made this vow: "If God will indeed be with me and protect me on this journey, and if he will provide me with food and clothing, 21 and if I return safely to my father's home, then the LORD will certainly be my God. 22 And this memorial pillar I have set up will become a place for worshiping God, and I will present to God a tenth of everything he gives me."

Jacob Arrives at Paddan-Aram

29 Then Jacob hurried on, finally arriving in the land of the east. 2 He saw a well in the distance. Three flocks of sheep and goats lay in an open field beside it, waiting to be watered. But a heavy stone covered the mouth of the well.

3 It was the custom there to wait for all the flocks to arrive before removing the stone and watering the animals. Afterward the stone would be placed back over the mouth of the well. 4 Jacob went over to the shepherds and asked, "Where are you from, my friends?"

"We are from Haran," they answered.

5 "Do you know a man there named Laban, the grandson of Nahor?" he asked.

"Yes, we do," they replied.

6 "Is he doing well?" Jacob asked.

28:3 Hebrew *El-Shaddai.* **28:4** Hebrew *seed;* also in 28:13, 14.

identical with the Aram-naharaim of 24:10 and so, as with Isaac, Jacob is to get a wife from Abraham's homeland. We first hear of Laban in 24:29. **3–4:** The thread of God's promises to Abraham and then to Isaac are continued here to Jacob.

28:10–22 Jacob's Dream at Bethel. 12: This is the third out of five dreams in which God appears to the sleeper (cf. 15:12–16; 20:3–7; 31:10–13; 31:24). The *angels of God* are probably divine beings in God's heavenly court (cf. 1:26–27; 6:2–4). **13–14:** NRSV has "The LORD stood beside him," and it would seem to be later Jewish sensibilities regarding familiarity with God that changed the text to *At the top . . . stood the LORD* (cf. 18:22). The threefold promise of descendants, land, and blessing-giver are reiterated here. **20–21:** Jacob is the boldest of the patriarchs in setting conditions for God to fulfill!

29:1–30 Jacob Arrives at Paddan-aram. Jacob Marries Leah and Rachel. 6: The Hebrew is literally, "How is his shalom?" This is more than a pleasant

"Yes, he's well," they answered. "Look, here
comes his daughter Rachel with the flock now."
7 Jacob said, "Look, it's still broad daylight—
too early to round up the animals. Why don't
you water the sheep and goats so they can get
back out to pasture?"
8 "We can't water the animals until all the
flocks have arrived," they replied. "Then the
shepherds move the stone from the mouth of
the well, and we water all the sheep and goats."
9 Jacob was still talking with them when Rachel arrived with her father's flock, for she was
a shepherd. 10 And because Rachel was his cousin—the daughter of Laban, his mother's brother—and because the sheep and goats belonged to
his uncle Laban, Jacob went over to the well and
moved the stone from its mouth and watered his
uncle's flock. 11 Then Jacob kissed Rachel, and he
wept aloud. 12 He explained to Rachel that he was
her cousin on her father's side—the son of her
aunt Rebekah. So Rachel quickly ran and told
her father, Laban.
13 As soon as Laban heard that his nephew Jacob had arrived, he ran out to meet him.
He embraced and kissed him and brought him
home. When Jacob had told him his story, 14 Laban exclaimed, "You really are my own flesh and
blood!"

Jacob Marries Leah and Rachel

After Jacob had stayed with Laban for about a
month, 15 Laban said to him, "You shouldn't work
for me without pay just because we are relatives.
Tell me how much your wages should be."
16 Now Laban had two daughters. The older daughter was named Leah, and the younger
one was Rachel. 17 There was no sparkle in Leah's
eyes,* but Rachel had a beautiful figure and a
lovely face. 18 Since Jacob was in love with Rachel, he told her father, "I'll work for you for sev-
en years if you'll give me Rachel, your younger
daughter, as my wife."
19 "Agreed!" Laban replied. "I'd rather give
her to you than to anyone else. Stay and work
with me." 20 So Jacob worked seven years to pay
for Rachel. But his love for her was so strong
that it seemed to him but a few days.
21 Finally, the time came for him to marry her.
"I have fulfilled my agreement," Jacob said to Laban. "Now give me my wife so I can sleep with
her."
22 So Laban invited everyone in the neighborhood and prepared a wedding feast. 23 But that
night, when it was dark, Laban took Leah to Jacob, and he slept with her. 24 (Laban had given
Leah a servant, Zilpah, to be her maid.)
25 But when Jacob woke up in the morning—it
was Leah! "What have you done to me?" Jacob
raged at Laban. "I worked seven years for Rachel! Why have you tricked me?"
26 "It's not our custom here to marry off a
younger daughter ahead of the firstborn," Laban
replied. 27 "But wait until the bridal week is over,
then we'll give you Rachel, too—provided you
promise to work another seven years for me."
28 So Jacob agreed to work seven more years.
A week after Jacob had married Leah, Laban gave
him Rachel, too. 29 (Laban gave Rachel a servant,
Bilhah, to be her maid.) 30 So Jacob slept with
Rachel, too, and he loved her much more than
Leah. He then stayed and worked for Laban the
additional seven years.

Jacob's Many Children

31 When the LORD saw that Leah was unloved, he
enabled her to have children, but Rachel could
not conceive. 32 So Leah became pregnant and
gave birth to a son. She named him Reuben,* for
she said, "The LORD has noticed my misery, and
now my husband will love me."

29:17 Or *Leah had dull eyes*, or *Leah had soft eyes*. The meaning of the Hebrew is uncertain. **29:32** *Reuben* means "Look, a son!" It also sounds like the Hebrew for "He has seen my misery."

greeting; Jacob is finding out what Laban's situation is. **7–8:** Jacob tries to get the shepherds out of the way so he can meet Rachel on his own, but they will not be moved. **17:** Tradition has contrasted Leah's "weak" eyes with Rachel's beauty, but the NRSV translates her eyes as "lovely," thus highlighting the difficulty of this Hebrew word (*rak*). Perhaps Leah has lovely eyes, but all of Rachel is beautiful? Maybe we should see Jacob as fortunate in ending up with two wives with attractive features? All we know is that Jacob loves Rachel and not Leah. **23:** The deception is feasible if Jacob was drunk or if Leah was veiled. Either way we are not told what either of the sisters thinks of this trickery. Maybe they have not even been told who Jacob thinks he is marrying. The contrast with Rebekah in 24:58 is stark. **26–27:** Laban's cunning and dishonest character comes to the fore here, demonstrating he is surely Rebekah's brother!

29:31—30:24 Jacob's Many Children. In this narrative the sons who will become the twelve tribes of Israel are born (and also a daughter, Dinah, mentioned because she features later, in chap. 34). It is an inglorious tale that paints neither of the sisters nor Jacob in a positive light. It also reveals the shame that was attached to childlessness in that ancient society (cf.

33 She soon became pregnant again and gave
birth to another son. She named him Simeon,*
for she said, "The LORD heard that I was unloved
and has given me another son."
34 Then she became pregnant a third time and
gave birth to another son. She named him Levi,*
for she said, "Surely this time my husband will
feel affection for me, since I have given him three
sons!"
35 Once again Leah became pregnant and gave
birth to another son. She named him Judah,* for
she said, "Now I will praise the LORD!" And then
she stopped having children.

30 When Rachel saw that she wasn't
having any children for Jacob, she became jealous of her sister. She pleaded
with Jacob, "Give me children, or I'll die!"
2 Then Jacob became furious with Rachel.
"Am I God?" he asked. "He's the one who has
kept you from having children!"
3 Then Rachel told him, "Take my maid, Bilhah, and sleep with her. She will bear children for
me,* and through her I can have a family, too."
4 So Rachel gave her servant, Bilhah, to Jacob as
a wife, and he slept with her. 5 Bilhah became
pregnant and presented him with a son. 6 Rachel
named him Dan,* for she said, "God has vindicated me! He has heard my request and given
me a son." 7 Then Bilhah became pregnant again
and gave Jacob a second son. 8 Rachel named him
Naphtali,* for she said, "I have struggled hard
with my sister, and I'm winning!"
9 Meanwhile, Leah realized that she wasn't
getting pregnant anymore, so she took her servant, Zilpah, and gave her to Jacob as a wife.
10 Soon Zilpah presented him with a son. 11 Leah
named him Gad,* for she said, "How fortunate
I am!" 12 Then Zilpah gave Jacob a second son.
13 And Leah named him Asher,* for she said,
"What joy is mine! Now the other women will
celebrate with me."
14 One day during the wheat harvest, Reuben
found some mandrakes growing in a field and
brought them to his mother, Leah. Rachel begged
Leah, "Please give me some of your son's mandrakes."
15 But Leah angrily replied, "Wasn't it enough
that you stole my husband? Now will you steal
my son's mandrakes, too?"
Rachel answered, "I will let Jacob sleep with
you tonight if you give me some of the mandrakes."
16 So that evening, as Jacob was coming home
from the fields, Leah went out to meet him. "You
must come and sleep with me tonight!" she said.
"I have paid for you with some mandrakes that
my son found." So that night he slept with Leah.
17 And God answered Leah's prayers. She became
pregnant again and gave birth to a fifth son for
Jacob. 18 She named him Issachar,* for she said,
"God has rewarded me for giving my servant
to my husband as a wife." 19 Then Leah became
pregnant again and gave birth to a sixth son for
Jacob. 20 She named him Zebulun,* for she said,
"God has given me a good reward. Now my husband will treat me with respect, for I have given
him six sons." 21 Later she gave birth to a daughter and named her Dinah.
22 Then God remembered Rachel's plight and
answered her prayers by enabling her to have
children. 23 She became pregnant and gave birth
to a son. "God has removed my disgrace," she
said. 24 And she named him Joseph,* for she said,
"May the LORD add yet another son to my family."

Jacob's Wealth Increases
25 Soon after Rachel had given birth to Joseph,
Jacob said to Laban, "Please release me so I can
go home to my own country. 26 Let me take my
wives and children, for I have earned them by
serving you, and let me be on my way. You certainly know how hard I have worked for you."
27 "Please listen to me," Laban replied. "I have
become wealthy, for* the LORD has blessed me

29:33 *Simeon* probably means "one who hears." **29:34** *Levi* sounds like a Hebrew term that means "being attached" or "feeling affection for." **29:35** *Judah* is related to the Hebrew term for "praise." **30:3** Hebrew *bear children on my knees.* **30:6** *Dan* means "he judged" or "he vindicated." **30:8** *Naphtali* means "my struggle." **30:11** *Gad* means "good fortune." **30:13** *Asher* means "happy." **30:18** *Issachar* sounds like a Hebrew term that means "reward." **30:20** *Zebulun* probably means "honor." **30:24** *Joseph* means "may he add." **30:27** Or *I have learned by divination that.*

30:23), a shame that caused the sisters to engage in a bitter rivalry with each other. Today we know that being childless is not dishonorable and indeed can lead to a greater ability to serve the Lord most effectively (cf. Paul's words on marriage in 1 Cor 7:32–35). **31:** Again we see the LORD's tenderness toward the losers in the story (seen already in relation to Hagar, Ishmael, and Esau). **30:14:** Mandrakes were thought to help fertility, but they are, in fact, poisonous.

30:25–43 Jacob's Wealth Increases. Not only is there rivalry between Leah and Rachel, but there is contention between Jacob and his father-in-law. It is far from a happy family. **27:** As with his father and grandfather,

because of you. [28]Tell me how much I owe you.
Whatever it is, I'll pay it."
[29]Jacob replied, "You know how hard I've
worked for you, and how your flocks and herds
have grown under my care. [30]You had little
indeed before I came, but your wealth has increased enormously. The LORD has blessed you
through everything I've done. But now, what
about me? When can I start providing for my
own family?"
[31]"What wages do you want?" Laban asked
again.
Jacob replied, "Don't give me anything. Just
do this one thing, and I'll continue to tend and
watch over your flocks. [32]Let me inspect your
flocks today and remove all the sheep and goats
that are speckled or spotted, along with all the
black sheep. Give these to me as my wages. [33]In
the future, when you check on the animals you
have given me as my wages, you'll see that I
have been honest. If you find in my flock any
goats without speckles or spots, or any sheep that
are not black, you will know that I have stolen
them from you."
[34]"All right," Laban replied. "It will be as you
say." [35]But that very day Laban went out and
removed the male goats that were streaked and
spotted, all the female goats that were speckled
and spotted or had white patches, and all the
black sheep. He placed them in the care of his
own sons, [36]who took them a three-days' journey from where Jacob was. Meanwhile, Jacob
stayed and cared for the rest of Laban's flock.
[37]Then Jacob took some fresh branches from
poplar, almond, and plane trees and peeled off
strips of bark, making white streaks on them.
[38]Then he placed these peeled branches in the
watering troughs where the flocks came to drink,
for that was where they mated. [39]And when they
mated in front of the white-streaked branches,
they gave birth to young that were streaked,
speckled, and spotted. [40]Jacob separated those
lambs from Laban's flock. And at mating time
he turned the flock to face Laban's animals that
were streaked or black. This is how he built his
own flock instead of increasing Laban's.
[41]Whenever the stronger females were ready
to mate, Jacob would place the peeled branches
in the watering troughs in front of them. Then
they would mate in front of the branches. [42]But
he didn't do this with the weaker ones, so the
weaker lambs belonged to Laban, and the stronger ones were Jacob's. [43]As a result, Jacob became
very wealthy, with large flocks of sheep and
goats, female and male servants, and many camels and donkeys.

Jacob Flees from Laban

31 But Jacob soon learned that Laban's
sons were grumbling about him. "Jacob has robbed our father of everything!" they said. "He has gained all his wealth
at our father's expense." [2]And Jacob began to notice a change in Laban's attitude toward him.
[3]Then the LORD said to Jacob, "Return to the
land of your father and grandfather and to your
relatives there, and I will be with you."
[4]So Jacob called Rachel and Leah out to the
field where he was watching his flock. [5]He said
to them, "I have noticed that your father's attitude toward me has changed. But the God of my
father has been with me. [6]You know how hard I
have worked for your father, [7]but he has cheated me, changing my wages ten times. But God
has not allowed him to do me any harm. [8]For if
he said, 'The speckled animals will be your wages,' the whole flock began to produce speckled
young. And when he changed his mind and said,
'The striped animals will be your wages,' then
the whole flock produced striped young. [9]In this
way, God has taken your father's animals and
given them to me.
[10]"One time during the mating season, I had
a dream and saw that the male goats mating with
the females were streaked, speckled, and spotted.
[11]Then in my dream, the angel of God said to me,
'Jacob!' And I replied, 'Yes, here I am.'
[12]"The angel said, 'Look up, and you will
see that only the streaked, speckled, and spotted males are mating with the females of your
flock. For I have seen how Laban has treated you.
[13]I am the God who appeared to you at Bethel,*
the place where you anointed the pillar of stone
and made your vow to me. Now get ready and
leave this country and return to the land of your
birth.'"
[14]Rachel and Leah responded, "That's fine
with us! We won't inherit any of our father's
wealth anyway. [15]He has reduced our rights to

31:13 As in Greek version and an Aramaic Targum; Hebrew reads *the God of Bethel.*

Jacob blesses those with whom he comes into contact. **34–43:** Despite Laban's dishonesty and trickery, Jacob uses ancient genetic engineering to make sure that he gains the upper hand.

31:1–21 Jacob Flees from Laban. 14–16: The rivalry between the sisters seems ended here as they unite against their father. The years of injustice that they have suffered under him seems to bubble up. The

those of foreign women. And after he sold us, he wasted the money you paid him for us. [16]All the wealth God has given you from our father legally belongs to us and our children. So go ahead and do whatever God has told you."

[17]So Jacob put his wives and children on camels, [18]and he drove all his livestock in front of him. He packed all the belongings he had acquired in Paddan-aram and set out for the land of Canaan, where his father, Isaac, lived. [19]At the time they left, Laban was some distance away, shearing his sheep. Rachel stole her father's household idols and took them with her. [20]Jacob outwitted Laban the Aramean, for they set out secretly and never told Laban they were leaving. [21]So Jacob took all his possessions with him and crossed the Euphrates River,* heading for the hill country of Gilead.

Laban Pursues Jacob

[22]Three days later, Laban was told that Jacob had fled. [23]So he gathered a group of his relatives and set out in hot pursuit. He caught up with Jacob seven days later in the hill country of Gilead. [24]But the previous night God had appeared to Laban the Aramean in a dream and told him, "I'm warning you—leave Jacob alone!"

[25]Laban caught up with Jacob as he was camped in the hill country of Gilead, and he set up his camp not far from Jacob's. [26]"What do you mean by deceiving me like this?" Laban demanded. "How dare you drag my daughters away like prisoners of war? [27]Why did you slip away secretly? Why did you deceive me? And why didn't you say you wanted to leave? I would have given you a farewell feast, with singing and music, accompanied by tambourines and harps. [28]Why didn't you let me kiss my daughters and grandchildren and tell them good-bye? You have acted very foolishly! [29]I could destroy you, but the God of your father appeared to me last night and warned me, 'Leave Jacob alone!' [30]I can understand your feeling that you must go, and your intense longing for your father's home. But why have you stolen my gods?"

[31]"I rushed away because I was afraid," Jacob answered. "I thought you would take your daughters from me by force. [32]But as for your gods, see if you can find them, and let the person who has taken them die! And if you find anything else that belongs to you, identify it before all these relatives of ours, and I will give it back!" But Jacob did not know that Rachel had stolen the household idols.

[33]Laban went first into Jacob's tent to search there, then into Leah's, and then the tents of the two servant wives—but he found nothing. Finally, he went into Rachel's tent. [34]But Rachel had taken the household idols and hidden them in her camel saddle, and now she was sitting on them. When Laban had thoroughly searched her tent without finding them, [35]she said to her father, "Please, sir, forgive me if I don't get up for you. I'm having my monthly period." So Laban continued his search, but he could not find the household idols.

[36]Then Jacob became very angry, and he challenged Laban. "What's my crime?" he demanded. "What have I done wrong to make you chase after me as though I were a criminal? [37]You have rummaged through everything I own. Now show me what you found that belongs to you! Set it out here in front of us, before our relatives, for all to see. Let them judge between us!

[38]"For twenty years I have been with you, caring for your flocks. In all that time your sheep and goats never miscarried. In all those years I never used a single ram of yours for food. [39]If any were attacked and killed by wild animals, I never showed you the carcass and asked you to reduce the count of your flock. No, I took the loss myself! You made me pay for every stolen animal, whether it was taken in broad daylight or in the dark of night.

[40]"I worked for you through the scorching heat of the day and through cold and sleepless nights. [41]Yes, for twenty years I slaved in your house! I worked for fourteen years earning your two daughters, and then six more years for your flock. And you changed my wages ten times! [42]In fact, if the God of my father had not been on my side—the God of Abraham and the fearsome God of Isaac*—you would have sent me away empty-handed. But God has seen your abuse and my hard work. That is why he appeared to you last night and rebuked you!"

31:21 Hebrew *the river.* **31:42** Or *and the Fear of Isaac.*

statement *after he sold us* would appear, finally, to give their version of what happened on that fateful wedding night. **19:** Laban is not a follower of the LORD so it is no surprise that he has idols in his house, reflecting the religion of that area. These idols were thought to bestow good fortune on the household.

31:22–55 Laban Pursues Jacob. Jacob's Treaty with Laban. 26–27: One suspects that this is entirely the opposite of what the lying Laban would have done,

Menstruation

In 2 Samuel 11:2–5, David observes Bathsheba bathing, and the reader is told that she was purifying herself after her menstrual period. A ritual bath, or *mikvah*, following sexual abstinence during menstruation continues to be an important practice for some Jewish women, although such practices are criticized by others (see Purity Laws Related to Women, Lev 15). Scholars who view the regulations concerning menstrual impurity as oppressive, however, often neglect to mention that purification rites, including the washing of clothes and bathing in water, were also prescribed for seminal emissions and unusual penile discharge.

Not only are the discharges of males and females alike regarded as unclean, but chronic or unusual emissions for both males and females require precisely the same purification rites (cf. Lev 15:13–16, 28–30), and in both cases the uncleanness is transferable to other people and objects to a similar degree. Moreover, while a menstruating woman's period of uncleanness is longer than a man's following ejaculation—seven days as opposed to one—this disparity has a basis in physiological reality. The presence of a bodily discharge, not the bodily process itself, renders a person unclean. In the case of menstruation the discharge lasts for five days, and so the law allows for two extra days to be sure that all bleeding has ceased.

Other factors mitigate the apparent harshness of these regulations. First, in comparison with modern women, Israelite women menstruated much less frequently. They married young and had large families. Since menstruation does not occur during pregnancy and seldom occurs during breastfeeding, many women menstruated relatively rarely. Second, within a patriarchal context, in which women were treated more like property than persons, these laws arguably had positive impacts on women and placed some limits on male control of women's lives (see annotation on Matt 9:20–22). Third, there is evidence that women sometimes used these menstrual purity laws to their own advantage. In Genesis 31, for example, Rachel pretends to have her period in order to conceal Laban's stolen household gods and save her own life.

There is, however, textual evidence that in comparison with semen, menstrual blood is the focus of heightened concern. Males who come in contact with menstrual blood during sexual intercourse are rendered unclean for seven days (Lev 15:24), whereas contact with semen during sex renders both the man and the woman unclean only until evening (Lev 15:18). In addition, several passages (Lev 18:19; 20:18; Ezek 22:10) specifically forbid sexual intercourse with a menstruating woman, suggesting that this act is a particularly serious violation. This more intense ritual concern with menstrual blood likely reflects the Israelites' view of blood in general as symbolizing life, belonging to God and hence warranting special precaution (see Lev 17; 19).

An examination of biblical references to menstruation in their cultural context suggests that these texts do not oppress women in the manner or extent to which some critics have claimed. In addition, Jesus' public affirmation of the woman who sought healing for chronic bleeding (Mark 5:34) may imply that his redemptive purpose includes exposing the unjust application of such laws.

Jacob's Treaty with Laban

43 Then Laban replied to Jacob, "These women are my daughters, these children are my grandchildren, and these flocks are my flocks—in fact, everything you see is mine. But what can I do now about my daughters and their children? 44 So come, let's make a covenant, you and I, and it will be a witness to our commitment."

45 So Jacob took a stone and set it up as a monument. 46 Then he told his family members, "Gather some stones." So they gathered stones and piled them in a heap. Then Jacob and Laban sat down beside the pile of stones to eat a covenant meal. 47 To commemorate the event, Laban called the place Jegar-sahadutha (which means "witness pile" in Aramaic), and Jacob called it Galeed (which means "witness pile" in Hebrew).

48 Then Laban declared, "This pile of stones will stand as a witness to remind us of the covenant we have made today." This explains why it was called Galeed—"Witness Pile." 49 But it was also called Mizpah (which means "watchtower"), for Laban said, "May the LORD keep watch between us to make sure that we keep this covenant when

had Jacob told him that he was leaving. **43–54:** This is less of a goodwill covenant of peace, as was cut between Abraham and Abimelech in chapter 21, and more of a contract not to go near each other again.

we are out of each other's sight. 50 If you mistreat
my daughters or if you marry other wives, God
will see it even if no one else does. He is a witness
to this covenant between us.
51 "See this pile of stones," Laban continued,
"and see this monument I have set between us.
52 They stand between us as witnesses of our
vows. I will never pass this pile of stones to harm
you, and you must never pass these stones or
this monument to harm me. 53 I call on the God
of our ancestors—the God of your grandfather
Abraham and the God of my grandfather Nahor—to serve as a judge between us."
So Jacob took an oath before the fearsome
God of his father, Isaac,* to respect the boundary line. 54 Then Jacob offered a sacrifice to God
there on the mountain and invited everyone to a
covenant feast. After they had eaten, they spent
the night on the mountain.
55 *Laban got up early the next morning, and
he kissed his grandchildren and his daughters and
blessed them. Then he left and returned home.

32 1 *As Jacob started on his way again,
angels of God came to meet him.
2 When Jacob saw them, he exclaimed,
"This is God's camp!" So he named the place
Mahanaim.*

Jacob Sends Gifts to Esau

3 Then Jacob sent messengers ahead to his brother, Esau, who was living in the region of Seir
in the land of Edom. 4 He told them, "Give this
message to my master Esau: 'Humble greetings
from your servant Jacob. Until now I have been
living with Uncle Laban, 5 and now I own cattle,
donkeys, flocks of sheep and goats, and many
servants, both men and women. I have sent these
messengers to inform my lord of my coming,
hoping that you will be friendly to me.' "
6 After delivering the message, the messengers returned to Jacob and reported, "We met
your brother, Esau, and he is already on his way
to meet you—with an army of 400 men!" 7 Jacob
was terrified at the news. He divided his household, along with the flocks and herds and camels, into two groups. 8 He thought, "If Esau meets
one group and attacks it, perhaps the other group
can escape."
9 Then Jacob prayed, "O God of my grandfather Abraham, and God of my father, Isaac—
O LORD, you told me, 'Return to your own land
and to your relatives.' And you promised me, 'I
will treat you kindly.' 10 I am not worthy of all
the unfailing love and faithfulness you have
shown to me, your servant. When I left home
and crossed the Jordan River, I owned nothing
except a walking stick. Now my household fills
two large camps! 11 O LORD, please rescue me
from the hand of my brother, Esau. I am afraid
that he is coming to attack me, along with my
wives and children. 12 But you promised me, 'I
will surely treat you kindly, and I will multiply
your descendants until they become as numerous as the sands along the seashore—too many
to count.' "
13 Jacob stayed where he was for the night.
Then he selected these gifts from his possessions
to present to his brother, Esau: 14 200 female
goats, 20 male goats, 200 ewes, 20 rams, 15 30 female camels with their young, 40 cows, 10 bulls,
20 female donkeys, and 10 male donkeys. 16 He
divided these animals into herds and assigned
each to different servants. Then he told his servants, "Go ahead of me with the animals, but
keep some distance between the herds."
17 He gave these instructions to the men leading the first group: "When my brother, Esau,
meets you, he will ask, 'Whose servants are you?
Where are you going? Who owns these animals?' 18 You must reply, 'They belong to your
servant Jacob, but they are a gift for his master
Esau. Look, he is coming right behind us.' "
19 Jacob gave the same instructions to the second and third herdsmen and to all who followed
behind the herds: "You must say the same thing
to Esau when you meet him. 20 And be sure to say,
'Look, your servant Jacob is right behind us.' "
Jacob thought, "I will try to appease him by
sending gifts ahead of me. When I see him in
person, perhaps he will be friendly to me." 21 So
the gifts were sent on ahead, while Jacob himself
spent that night in the camp.

Jacob Wrestles with God

22 During the night Jacob got up and took his two
wives, his two servant wives, and his eleven sons
and crossed the Jabbok River with them. 23 After

31:53 Or *the Fear of his father, Isaac.* **31:55** Verse 31:55 is numbered 32:1 in Hebrew text. **32:1** Verses 32:1-32 are numbered 32:2-33 in Hebrew text. **32:2** *Mahanaim* means "two camps."

32:1–21 Jacob Sends Gifts to Esau. 1–2: Angels meet Jacob both on his journey out (chap. 28) and now on his journey back home. **10:** *Unfailing love* (Heb., *hesed*) is a word that is often used to describe God's disposition toward us (e.g., Exod 34:6; Deut 7:12; Ps 13:5; Jer 9:24).

32:22–32 Jacob Wrestles with God. 25–27: One can

taking them to the other side, he sent over all his possessions.

24 This left Jacob all alone in the camp, and a man came and wrestled with him until the dawn began to break. 25 When the man saw that he would not win the match, he touched Jacob's hip and wrenched it out of its socket. 26 Then the man said, "Let me go, for the dawn is breaking!"

But Jacob said, "I will not let you go unless you bless me."

27 "What is your name?" the man asked.

He replied, "Jacob."

28 "Your name will no longer be Jacob," the man told him. "From now on you will be called Israel,* because you have fought with God and with men and have won."

29 "Please tell me your name," Jacob said.

"Why do you want to know my name?" the man replied. Then he blessed Jacob there.

30 Jacob named the place Peniel (which means "face of God"), for he said, "I have seen God face to face, yet my life has been spared." 31 The sun was rising as Jacob left Peniel,* and he was limping because of the injury to his hip. 32 (Even today the people of Israel don't eat the tendon near the hip socket because of what happened that night when the man strained the tendon of Jacob's hip.)

Jacob and Esau Make Peace

33 Then Jacob looked up and saw Esau coming with his 400 men. So he divided the children among Leah, Rachel, and his two servant wives. 2 He put the servant wives and their children at the front, Leah and her children next, and Rachel and Joseph last. 3 Then Jacob went on ahead. As he approached his brother, he bowed to the ground seven times before him. 4 Then Esau ran to meet him and embraced him, threw his arms around his neck, and kissed him. And they both wept.

5 Then Esau looked at the women and children and asked, "Who are these people with you?"

"These are the children God has graciously given to me, your servant," Jacob replied. 6 Then the servant wives came forward with their children and bowed before him. 7 Next came Leah with her children, and they bowed before him. Finally, Joseph and Rachel came forward and bowed before him.

8 "And what were all the flocks and herds I met as I came?" Esau asked.

Jacob replied, "They are a gift, my lord, to ensure your friendship."

9 "My brother, I have plenty," Esau answered. "Keep what you have for yourself."

10 But Jacob insisted, "No, if I have found favor with you, please accept this gift from me. And what a relief to see your friendly smile. It is like seeing the face of God! 11 Please take this gift I have brought you, for God has been very gracious to me. I have more than enough." And because Jacob insisted, Esau finally accepted the gift.

12 "Well," Esau said, "let's be going. I will lead the way."

13 But Jacob replied, "You can see, my lord, that some of the children are very young, and the flocks and herds have their young, too. If they are driven too hard, even for one day, all the animals could die. 14 Please, my lord, go ahead of your servant. We will follow slowly, at a pace that is comfortable for the livestock and the children. I will meet you at Seir."

15 "All right," Esau said, "but at least let me assign some of my men to guide and protect you."

Jacob responded, "That's not necessary. It's enough that you've received me warmly, my lord!"

32:28 *Jacob* sounds like the Hebrew words for "heel" and "deceiver." *Israel* means "God fights." **32:31** Hebrew *Penuel*, a variant spelling of Peniel.

---

only begin to imagine the pressure that Jacob, alone, is under this night and now a strange *man* appears and wrestles with him. There are many questions we would ask (Why does God fight with Jacob? How is it that God cannot win?), but the text does not say more than what it says. **28:** Now it is revealed that the man is in fact God. As with Abraham (chaps. 17—18) so with Jacob: An intense and strange encounter with the LORD leads to a name change that will prove to be significant in the history of the nation of Israel. **30–31:** The tradition of the Old Testament was that no human could see the LORD's face (*peniel*, "face of God") and live (e.g., Exod 33:11–23; Judg 6:22–23), but Jacob survives. He is, however, left with a disability. **32:** Despite this verse there is no other evidence that this dietary requirement was observed.

33:1–20 Jacob and Esau Make Peace. 1–2: Jacob orders his family in line with patriarchal expectations. **10, 11:** The *gift* is here the same word as the "blessing" of 27:36. Jacob is offering to repay that which he stole so many years ago. **10:** Jacob's declaration here links his reconciliation with Esau with his encounter with God the previous night. **12–16:** Esau is the epitome of fraternal magnanimity, but Jacob is still wary and wishes to put some distance between them, so

16 So Esau turned around and started back to Seir that same day. 17 Jacob, on the other hand, traveled on to Succoth. There he built himself a house and made shelters for his livestock. That is why the place was named Succoth (which means "shelters").

18 Later, having traveled all the way from Paddan-aram, Jacob arrived safely at the town of Shechem, in the land of Canaan. There he set up camp outside the town. 19 Jacob bought the plot of land where he camped from the family of Hamor, the father of Shechem, for 100 pieces of silver.* 20 And there he built an altar and named it El-Elohe-Israel.*

Revenge against Shechem

34 One day Dinah, the daughter of Jacob and Leah, went to visit some of the young women who lived in the area. 2 But when the local prince, Shechem son of Hamor the Hivite, saw Dinah, he seized her and raped her. 3 But then he fell in love with her, and he tried to win her affection with tender words. 4 He said to his father, Hamor, "Get me this young girl. I want to marry her."

5 Soon Jacob heard that Shechem had defiled his daughter, Dinah. But since his sons were out in the fields herding his livestock, he said nothing until they returned. 6 Hamor, Shechem's father, came to discuss the matter with Jacob. 7 Meanwhile, Jacob's sons had come in from the field as soon as they heard what had happened. They were shocked and furious that their sister had been raped. Shechem had done a disgraceful thing against Jacob's family,* something that should never be done.

8 Hamor tried to speak with Jacob and his sons. "My son Shechem is truly in love with your daughter," he said. "Please let him marry her. 9 In fact, let's arrange other marriages, too. You give us your daughters for our sons, and we will give you our daughters for your sons. 10 And you may live among us; the land is open to you! Settle here and trade with us. And feel free to buy property in the area."

11 Then Shechem himself spoke to Dinah's father and brothers. "Please be kind to me, and let me marry her," he begged. "I will give you whatever you ask. 12 No matter what dowry or gift you demand, I will gladly pay it—just give me the girl as my wife."

13 But since Shechem had defiled their sister, Dinah, Jacob's sons responded deceitfully to Shechem and his father, Hamor. 14 They said to them, "We couldn't possibly allow this, because you're not circumcised. It would be a disgrace for our sister to marry a man like you! 15 But here is a solution. If every man among you will be circumcised like we are, 16 then we will give you our daughters, and we'll take your daughters for ourselves. We will live among you and become one people. 17 But if you don't agree to be circumcised, we will take her and be on our way."

18 Hamor and his son Shechem agreed to their proposal. 19 Shechem wasted no time in acting on this request, for he wanted Jacob's daughter desperately. Shechem was a highly respected member of his family, 20 and he went with his father, Hamor, to present this proposal to the leaders at the town gate.

21 "These men are our friends," they said. "Let's invite them to live here among us and trade freely. Look, the land is large enough to hold them. We can take their daughters as wives and let them marry ours. 22 But they will consider staying here and becoming one people with us only if all of our men are circumcised, just as they are. 23 But if we do this, all their livestock and possessions will eventually be ours. Come, let's agree to their terms and let them settle here among us."

24 So all the men in the town council agreed

33:19 Hebrew *100 kesitahs;* the value or weight of the kesitah is no longer known. **33:20** *El-Elohe-Israel* means "God, the God of Israel." **34:7** Hebrew *a disgraceful thing in Israel.*

---

he does not follow Esau to Seir. **18–20:** Jacob's final resting place in Shechem is the first place that his grandfather Abram camped in when he arrived in Canaan (12:6). *Hamor* means "he-ass" in Hebrew, foreshadowing the negative relationship with the Canaanites that is about to begin.

34:1–31 Revenge against Shechem. This episode is extraordinarily ambiguous in its perspective. What is at stake here for the writer is not so much the personal feelings of Dinah as the relationship that Jacob's growing family and descendants are to have with the Canaanites, the present occupiers of the promised land. We know from later texts that God tells Israel that the Canaanites must be exterminated if Israel is to live fully in the land (e.g., Deut 7:1–6; Josh 10:40–42). Here, however, the possibility of living amicably with the Canaanites seems to be hinted at. Maybe the writer is suggesting that had this scenario been dealt with differently, the need to destroy the Canaanites might never have arisen and Israel could, instead, have acted as a blessing, as in Abraham's dealings with the Hittites (chap. 23) and Abimelech (chap. 21)? Or, perhaps, right from the earliest days,

with Hamor and Shechem, and every male in the town was circumcised. 25 But three days later, when their wounds were still sore, two of Jacob's sons, Simeon and Levi, who were Dinah's full brothers, took their swords and entered the town without opposition. Then they slaughtered every male there, 26 including Hamor and his son Shechem. They killed them with their swords, then took Dinah from Shechem's house and returned to their camp.

27 Meanwhile, the rest of Jacob's sons arrived. Finding the men slaughtered, they plundered the town because their sister had been defiled there. 28 They seized all the flocks and herds and donkeys—everything they could lay their hands on, both inside the town and outside in the fields. 29 They looted all their wealth and plundered their houses. They also took all their little children and wives and led them away as captives.

30 Afterward Jacob said to Simeon and Levi, "You have ruined me! You've made me stink among all the people of this land—among all the Canaanites and Perizzites. We are so few that they will join forces and crush us. I will be ruined, and my entire household will be wiped out!"

31 "But why should we let him treat our sister like a prostitute?" they retorted angrily.

Jacob's Return to Bethel

35 Then God said to Jacob, "Get ready and move to Bethel and settle there. Build an altar there to the God who appeared to you when you fled from your brother, Esau."

2 So Jacob told everyone in his household, "Get rid of all your pagan idols, purify yourselves, and put on clean clothing. 3 We are now going to Bethel, where I will build an altar to the God who answered my prayers when I was in distress. He has been with me wherever I have gone."

4 So they gave Jacob all their pagan idols and earrings, and he buried them under the great tree near Shechem. 5 As they set out, a terror from God spread over the people in all the towns of that area, so no one attacked Jacob's family.

6 Eventually, Jacob and his household arrived at Luz (also called Bethel) in Canaan. 7 Jacob built an altar there and named the place El-bethel (which means "God of Bethel"), because God had appeared to him there when he was fleeing from his brother, Esau.

8 Soon after this, Rebekah's old nurse, Deborah, died. She was buried beneath the oak tree in the valley below Bethel. Ever since, the tree has been called Allon-bacuth (which means "oak of weeping").

9 Now that Jacob had returned from Paddan-aram, God appeared to him again at Bethel. God blessed him, 10 saying, "Your name is Jacob, but you will not be called Jacob any longer. From now on your name will be Israel."* So God renamed him Israel.

11 Then God said, "I am El-Shaddai—'God Almighty.' Be fruitful and multiply. You will become a great nation, even many nations. Kings will be among your descendants! 12 And I will give you the land I once gave to Abraham and Isaac. Yes, I will give it to you and your descendants after you." 13 Then God went up from the place where he had spoken to Jacob.

14 Jacob set up a stone pillar to mark the place where God had spoken to him. Then he poured wine over it as an offering to God and anointed the pillar with olive oil. 15 And Jacob named the place Bethel (which means "house of God"), because God had spoken to him there.

The Deaths of Rachel and Isaac

16 Leaving Bethel, Jacob and his clan moved on toward Ephrath. But Rachel went into labor while they were still some distance away. Her labor pains were intense. 17 After a very hard delivery, the midwife finally exclaimed, "Don't be afraid—you have another son!" 18 Rachel

35:10 *Jacob* sounds like the Hebrew words for "heel" and "deceiver." *Israel* means "God fights."

---

the Canaanites were indeed evil and would lead the Israelites astray so that, in order to keep Jacob's line of election pure, they needed to be destroyed?

35:1–15 Jacob's Return to Bethel. 2–4: Evidently Rachel was not the only one to have accumulated *pagan idols* and trinkets. The great tree was probably the sacred oak of Moreh, where Abram had camped (12:6). This area clearly had a reputation for great trees (Deut 11:30). **5:** As a consequence of Jacob's sons' actions, the relationship with the cities around them has changed. **8:** Deborah has been with Rebekah all her life, so the loss must have been great (cf. 24:59). **9–15:** These verses seem to be a combination of the encounters that Jacob has with God in chapters 28 and 32, perhaps coming from a different source.

35:16–29 The Deaths of Rachel and Isaac. 18: *Son of my right hand* denotes the position of honor in sitting at the right hand of an elder. Thus Benjamin is identified as being his father's favorite, linked as he is with

was about to die, but with her last breath she named the baby Ben-oni (which means "son of my sorrow"). The baby's father, however, called him Benjamin (which means "son of my right hand"). 19 So Rachel died and was buried on the way to Ephrath (that is, Bethlehem). 20 Jacob set up a stone monument over Rachel's grave, and it can be seen there to this day.

21 Then Jacob* traveled on and camped beyond Migdal-eder. 22 While he was living there, Reuben had intercourse with Bilhah, his father's concubine, and Jacob soon heard about it.

These are the names of the twelve sons of Jacob:

23 The sons of Leah were Reuben (Jacob's oldest son), Simeon, Levi, Judah, Issachar, and Zebulun.
24 The sons of Rachel were Joseph and Benjamin.
25 The sons of Bilhah, Rachel's servant, were Dan and Naphtali.
26 The sons of Zilpah, Leah's servant, were Gad and Asher.

These are the names of the sons who were born to Jacob at Paddan-aram.

27 So Jacob returned to his father, Isaac, in Mamre, which is near Kiriath-arba (now called Hebron), where Abraham and Isaac had both lived as foreigners. 28 Isaac lived for 180 years. 29 Then he breathed his last and died at a ripe old age, joining his ancestors in death. And his sons, Esau and Jacob, buried him.

Descendants of Esau

36 This is the account of the descendants of Esau (also known as Edom). 2 Esau married two young women from Canaan: Adah, the daughter of Elon the Hittite; and Oholibamah, the daughter of Anah and granddaughter of Zibeon the Hivite. 3 He also married his cousin Basemath, who was the daughter of Ishmael and the sister of Nebaioth. 4 Adah gave birth to a son named Eliphaz for Esau. Basemath gave birth to a son named Reuel. 5 Oholibamah gave birth to sons named Jeush, Jalam, and Korah. All these sons were born to Esau in the land of Canaan.

6 Esau took his wives, his children, and his entire household, along with his livestock and cattle—all the wealth he had acquired in the land of Canaan—and moved away from his brother, Jacob. 7 There was not enough land to support them both because of all the livestock and possessions they had acquired. 8 So Esau (also known as Edom) settled in the hill country of Seir.

9 This is the account of Esau's descendants, the Edomites, who lived in the hill country of Seir.

10 These are the names of Esau's sons: Eliphaz, the son of Esau's wife Adah; and Reuel, the son of Esau's wife Basemath.
11 The descendants of Eliphaz were Teman, Omar, Zepho, Gatam, and Kenaz. 12 Timna, the concubine of Esau's son Eliphaz, gave birth to a son named Amalek. These are the descendants of Esau's wife Adah.
13 The descendants of Reuel were Nahath, Zerah, Shammah, and Mizzah. These are the descendants of Esau's wife Basemath.
14 Esau also had sons through Oholibamah, the daughter of Anah and granddaughter of Zibeon. Their names were Jeush, Jalam, and Korah.

15 These are the descendants of Esau who became the leaders of various clans:

The descendants of Esau's oldest son, Eliphaz, became the leaders of the clans of Teman, Omar, Zepho, Kenaz, 16 Korah, Gatam, and Amalek. These are the clan leaders in the land of Edom who descended from Eliphaz. All these were descendants of Esau's wife Adah.
17 The descendants of Esau's son Reuel became the leaders of the clans of Nahath, Zerah, Shammah, and Mizzah. These are the clan leaders in the land of Edom who descended

35:21 Hebrew *Israel;* also in 35:22a. The names "Jacob" and "Israel" are often interchanged throughout the Old Testament, referring sometimes to the individual patriarch and sometimes to the nation.

his father's favorite wife. **22:** Although nothing seems to happen as a result of Reuben's misconduct, the consequences become apparent later when Jacob gives his sons his final blessings (49:3–4). **27–29:** The life of Isaac comes to a satisfying conclusion as the writer prepares to turn his attention to the final major narrative.

36:1–43 Esau's Descendants. As with other genealogies in Genesis, this provides a bridge between one narrative (that of the patri/matriarchs) and the next (the Joseph story). It also serves to provide an account of the origin of nations that become important enemies to Israel in later history, in particular the Edomites, who descend directly from Esau. **31–39:** This is a list of kings who reigned over Edom before Israel conquered it during David's rule (cf. 2 Sam 8:13–14).

from Reuel. All these were descendants of Esau's wife Basemath.
[18]The descendants of Esau and his wife Oholibamah became the leaders of the clans of Jeush, Jalam, and Korah. These are the clan leaders who descended from Esau's wife Oholibamah, the daughter of Anah.
[19]These are the clans descended from Esau (also known as Edom), identified by their clan leaders.

Original Peoples of Edom

[20]These are the names of the tribes that descended from Seir the Horite. They lived in the land of Edom: Lotan, Shobal, Zibeon, Anah, [21]Dishon, Ezer, and Dishan. These were the Horite clan leaders, the descendants of Seir, who lived in the land of Edom.

[22]The descendants of Lotan were Hori and Hemam. Lotan's sister was named Timna.
[23]The descendants of Shobal were Alvan, Manahath, Ebal, Shepho, and Onam.
[24]The descendants of Zibeon were Aiah and Anah. (This is the Anah who discovered the hot springs in the wilderness while he was grazing his father's donkeys.)
[25]The descendants of Anah were his son, Dishon, and his daughter, Oholibamah.
[26]The descendants of Dishon* were Hemdan, Eshban, Ithran, and Keran.
[27]The descendants of Ezer were Bilhan, Zaavan, and Akan.
[28]The descendants of Dishan were Uz and Aran.
[29]So these were the leaders of the Horite clans: Lotan, Shobal, Zibeon, Anah, [30]Dishon, Ezer, and Dishan. The Horite clans are named after their clan leaders, who lived in the land of Seir.

Rulers of Edom

[31]These are the kings who ruled in the land of Edom before any king ruled over the Israelites*:

[32]Bela son of Beor, who ruled in Edom from his city of Dinhabah.
[33]When Bela died, Jobab son of Zerah from Bozrah became king in his place.
[34]When Jobab died, Husham from the land of the Temanites became king in his place.
[35]When Husham died, Hadad son of Bedad became king in his place and ruled from the city of Avith. He was the one who defeated the Midianites in the land of Moab.
[36]When Hadad died, Samlah from the city of Masrekah became king in his place.
[37]When Samlah died, Shaul from the city of Rehoboth-on-the-River became king in his place.
[38]When Shaul died, Baal-hanan son of Acbor became king in his place.
[39]When Baal-hanan son of Acbor died, Hadad* became king in his place and ruled from the city of Pau. His wife was Mehetabel, the daughter of Matred and granddaughter of Me-zahab.

[40]These are the names of the leaders of the clans descended from Esau, who lived in the places named for them: Timna, Alvah, Jetheth, [41]Oholibamah, Elah, Pinon, [42]Kenaz, Teman, Mibzar, [43]Magdiel, and Iram. These are the leaders of the clans of Edom, listed according to their settlements in the land they occupied. They all descended from Esau, the ancestor of the Edomites.

Joseph's Dreams

37 So Jacob settled again in the land of Canaan, where his father had lived as a foreigner.

[2]This is the account of Jacob and his family. When Joseph was seventeen years old, he often tended his father's flocks. He worked for his half brothers, the sons of his father's wives Bilhah and Zilpah. But Joseph reported to his father some of the bad things his brothers were doing.

[3]Jacob* loved Joseph more than any of his

36:26 Hebrew *Dishan,* a variant spelling of Dishon; compare 36:21, 28. **36:31** Or *before an Israelite king ruled over them.* **36:39** As in some Hebrew manuscripts, Samaritan Pentateuch, and Syriac version (see also 1 Chr 1:50); most Hebrew manuscripts read *Hadar.* **37:3a** Hebrew *Israel;* also in 37:13. See note on 35:21.

37:1—50:26 The Family Stories of Jacob's Sons

37:1–17 Joseph's Dreams. The story of Joseph is entirely male-focused. Even though we know that he had sisters (*family* can be translated "sons and daughters" in v. 35) we do not hear anything more of them. The only major female angle to the story comes in the negative depiction of Potiphar's wife. The image of woman as harlot is one that is often used by the writers of the Old Testament (Samson's Delilah is another classic figure) and is highlighted by feminist writers as one of the main ways in which women were viewed in ancient times. **1:** The Joseph story starts with Israel/Jacob in the land that God had called Abram to, the land of Canaan. God's plans are working out. **2:** *This is the acccount of* again signals the start of a major storyline (cf. 2:4a and the other references given there). **3:** Joseph is his father's fa-

other children because Joseph had been born to
him in his old age. So one day Jacob had a special
gift made for Joseph—a beautiful robe.* 4 But his
brothers hated Joseph because their father loved
him more than the rest of them. They couldn't
say a kind word to him.

5 One night Joseph had a dream, and when he
told his brothers about it, they hated him more
than ever. 6 "Listen to this dream," he said. 7 "We
were out in the field, tying up bundles of grain.
Suddenly my bundle stood up, and your bundles all gathered around and bowed low before
mine!"

8 His brothers responded, "So you think you
will be our king, do you? Do you actually think
you will reign over us?" And they hated him all
the more because of his dreams and the way he
talked about them.

9 Soon Joseph had another dream, and again
he told his brothers about it. "Listen, I have had
another dream," he said. "The sun, moon, and
eleven stars bowed low before me!"

10 This time he told the dream to his father
as well as to his brothers, but his father scolded
him. "What kind of dream is that?" he asked.
"Will your mother and I and your brothers actually come and bow to the ground before you?"
11 But while his brothers were jealous of Joseph,
his father wondered what the dreams meant.

12 Soon after this, Joseph's brothers went to
pasture their father's flocks at Shechem. 13 When
they had been gone for some time, Jacob said to
Joseph, "Your brothers are pasturing the sheep
at Shechem. Get ready, and I will send you to
them."

"I'm ready to go," Joseph replied.

14 "Go and see how your brothers and the
flocks are getting along," Jacob said. "Then come
back and bring me a report." So Jacob sent him
on his way, and Joseph traveled to Shechem from
their home in the valley of Hebron.

15 When he arrived there, a man from the area
noticed him wandering around the countryside.
"What are you looking for?" he asked.

16 "I'm looking for my brothers," Joseph replied. "Do you know where they are pasturing
their sheep?"

17 "Yes," the man told him. "They have moved
on from here, but I heard them say, 'Let's go on
to Dothan.' " So Joseph followed his brothers to
Dothan and found them there.

Joseph Sold into Slavery

18 When Joseph's brothers saw him coming, they
recognized him in the distance. As he approached,
they made plans to kill him. 19 "Here comes the
dreamer!" they said. 20 "Come on, let's kill him
and throw him into one of these cisterns. We can
tell our father, 'A wild animal has eaten him.'
Then we'll see what becomes of his dreams!"

21 But when Reuben heard of their scheme, he
came to Joseph's rescue. "Let's not kill him," he
said. 22 "Why should we shed any blood? Let's
just throw him into this empty cistern here in
the wilderness. Then he'll die without our laying
a hand on him." Reuben was secretly planning to
rescue Joseph and return him to his father.

23 So when Joseph arrived, his brothers ripped
off the beautiful robe he was wearing. 24 Then
they grabbed him and threw him into the cistern. Now the cistern was empty; there was no
water in it. 25 Then, just as they were sitting
down to eat, they looked up and saw a caravan
of camels in the distance coming toward them. It
was a group of Ishmaelite traders taking a load of
gum, balm, and aromatic resin from Gilead down
to Egypt.

26 Judah said to his brothers, "What will we
gain by killing our brother? We'd have to cover
up the crime.* 27 Instead of hurting him, let's sell
him to those Ishmaelite traders. After all, he is
our brother—our own flesh and blood!" And his
brothers agreed. 28 So when the Ishmaelites, who
were Midianite traders, came by, Joseph's brothers pulled him out of the cistern and sold him to
them for twenty pieces* of silver. And the traders took him to Egypt.

29 Some time later, Reuben returned to get Joseph out of the cistern. When he discovered that

37:3b Traditionally rendered *a coat of many colors.* The exact meaning of the Hebrew is uncertain. **37:26** Hebrew *cover his blood.* **37:28** Hebrew *20 shekels,* about 8 ounces or 228 grams in weight.

---

vorite because he is the firstborn of Jacob's favorite wife, Rachel (30:22–24). **4:** The Hebrew says that the brothers could not speak *shalom* or peaceably to him. **5–11:** Dreams will play an important part in the fortunes of Joseph's life.

37:18–36 Joseph Sold into Slavery. 23: The robe was the symbol of Joseph's favoritism and the source of his brothers' envy. Joseph would not have been able to work wearing such a beautiful coat, implying that Joseph was allowed to relax around Jacob's house while his brothers worked. **25–28:** The traders are called Ishmaelites in verse 25 and Midianites in verse 28, both of whom descend from sons of Abraham who were half-brothers. This translation of verse 28 eases the apparent contradiction by its reference to

Joseph was missing, he tore his clothes in grief.
[30]Then he went back to his brothers and lamented, "The boy is gone! What will I do now?"
[31]Then the brothers killed a young goat and
dipped Joseph's robe in its blood. [32]They sent the
beautiful robe to their father with this message:
"Look at what we found. Doesn't this robe belong to your son?"
[33]Their father recognized it immediately.
"Yes," he said, "it is my son's robe. A wild animal
must have eaten him. Joseph has clearly been
torn to pieces!" [34]Then Jacob tore his clothes and
dressed himself in burlap. He mourned deeply
for his son for a long time. [35]His family all tried
to comfort him, but he refused to be comforted.
"I will go to my grave* mourning for my son,"
he would say, and then he would weep.
[36]Meanwhile, the Midianite traders* arrived
in Egypt, where they sold Joseph to Potiphar, an
officer of Pharaoh, the king of Egypt. Potiphar
was captain of the palace guard.

Judah and Tamar

38 About this time, Judah left home and
moved to Adullam, where he stayed
with a man named Hirah. [2]There he
saw a Canaanite woman, the daughter of Shua,
and he married her. When he slept with her, [3]she
became pregnant and gave birth to a son, and he
named the boy Er. [4]Then she became pregnant
again and gave birth to another son, and she
named him Onan. [5]And when she gave birth to a
third son, she named him Shelah. At the time of
Shelah's birth, they were living at Kezib.
[6]In the course of time, Judah arranged for
his firstborn son, Er, to marry a young woman
named Tamar. [7]But Er was a wicked man in the
LORD's sight, so the LORD took his life. [8]Then
Judah said to Er's brother Onan, "Go and marry Tamar, as our law requires of the brother of a
man who has died. You must produce an heir for
your brother."
[9]But Onan was not willing to have a child
who would not be his own heir. So whenever
he had intercourse with his brother's wife, he
spilled the semen on the ground. This prevented
her from having a child who would belong to
his brother. [10]But the LORD considered it evil for
Onan to deny a child to his dead brother. So the
LORD took Onan's life, too.
[11]Then Judah said to Tamar, his daughter-in-
law, "Go back to your parents' home and remain
a widow until my son Shelah is old enough to
marry you." (But Judah didn't really intend to
do this because he was afraid Shelah would also
die, like his two brothers.) So Tamar went back to
live in her father's home.
[12]Some years later Judah's wife died. After the
time of mourning was over, Judah and his friend
Hirah the Adullamite went up to Timnah to supervise the shearing of his sheep. [13]Someone told
Tamar, "Look, your father-in-law is going up to
Timnah to shear his sheep."
[14]Tamar was aware that Shelah had grown up,
but no arrangements had been made for her to
come and marry him. So she changed out of her
widow's clothing and covered herself with a veil
to disguise herself. Then she sat beside the road
at the entrance to the village of Enaim, which is
on the road to Timnah. [15]Judah noticed her and
thought she was a prostitute, since she had covered her face. [16]So he stopped and propositioned
her. "Let me have sex with you," he said, not realizing that she was his own daughter-in-law.
"How much will you pay to have sex with
me?" Tamar asked.
[17]"I'll send you a young goat from my flock,"
Judah promised.
"But what will you give me to guarantee that
you will send the goat?" she asked.

37:35 Hebrew *go down to Sheol.* **37:36** Hebrew *the Medanites.* The relationship between the Midianites and Medanites is unclear; compare 37:28. See also 25:2.

---

the Ishmaelites, which was probably a name given to any nomadic traders, including Midianites. **34:** Burlap is coarse cloth, often used to make sacks or bags (sackcloth).

38:1–30 Judah and Tamar. The inclusion of this story at this point may be because Judah becomes the most prominent of the remaining brothers as the story unfolds; Judah is also the most significant of Jacob's sons in Israel's later history (becoming the Southern Kingdom after the monarchy divides). This episode features a woman's sexual advances, as will also happen in the next chapter. **8–10:** The levirate law stipulated that a childless widow should be married to her dead husband's brother. The son born to that marriage would carry the dead man's name so that his line might continue (cf. Deut 25:5–9; Ruth 3—4). The woman, of course, had no say in the matter: All was done with the interest of the men in mind. The sin of Onan was not masturbation or the practice of a particular form of birth control, but the specific failure to fulfill the duty of the levirate law. **11:** Somehow Tamar carries the blame, in Judah's mind, for the death of his two sons. **12–14:** *Timnah* means "conceal" and *the entrance to . . . Enaim* means "the opening of the eyes." Thus, Tamar is going to use her concealment to

18 "What kind of guarantee do you want?" he replied.

She answered, "Leave me your identification seal and its cord and the walking stick you are carrying." So Judah gave them to her. Then he had intercourse with her, and she became pregnant. 19 Afterward she went back home, took off her veil, and put on her widow's clothing as usual.

20 Later Judah asked his friend Hirah the Adullamite to take the young goat to the woman and to pick up the things he had given her as his guarantee. But Hirah couldn't find her. 21 So he asked the men who lived there, "Where can I find the shrine prostitute who was sitting beside the road at the entrance to Enaim?"

"We've never had a shrine prostitute here," they replied.

22 So Hirah returned to Judah and told him, "I couldn't find her anywhere, and the men of the village claim they've never had a shrine prostitute there."

23 "Then let her keep the things I gave her," Judah said. "I sent the young goat as we agreed, but you couldn't find her. We'd be the laughingstock of the village if we went back again to look for her."

24 About three months later, Judah was told, "Tamar, your daughter-in-law, has acted like a prostitute. And now, because of this, she's pregnant."

"Bring her out, and let her be burned!" Judah demanded.

25 But as they were taking her out to kill her, she sent this message to her father-in-law: "The man who owns these things made me pregnant. Look closely. Whose seal and cord and walking stick are these?"

26 Judah recognized them immediately and said, "She is more righteous than I am, because I didn't arrange for her to marry my son Shelah." And Judah never slept with Tamar again.

27 When the time came for Tamar to give birth, it was discovered that she was carrying twins. 28 While she was in labor, one of the babies reached out his hand. The midwife grabbed it and tied a scarlet string around the child's wrist, announcing, "This one came out first." 29 But then he pulled back his hand, and out came his brother! "What!" the midwife exclaimed. "How did you break out first?" So he was named Perez.* 30 Then the baby with the scarlet string on his wrist was born, and he was named Zerah.*

Joseph in Potiphar's House

39 When Joseph was taken to Egypt by the Ishmaelite traders, he was purchased by Potiphar, an Egyptian officer. Potiphar was captain of the guard for Pharaoh, the king of Egypt.

2 The LORD was with Joseph, so he succeeded in everything he did as he served in the home of his Egyptian master. 3 Potiphar noticed this and realized that the LORD was with Joseph, giving him success in everything he did. 4 This pleased Potiphar, so he soon made Joseph his personal attendant. He put him in charge of his entire household and everything he owned. 5 From the day Joseph was put in charge of his master's household and property, the LORD began to bless Potiphar's household for Joseph's sake. All his household affairs ran smoothly, and his crops and livestock flourished. 6 So Potiphar gave Joseph complete administrative responsibility over everything he owned. With Joseph there, he didn't worry about a thing—except what kind of food to eat!

Joseph was a very handsome and well-built young man, 7 and Potiphar's wife soon began to look at him lustfully. "Come and sleep with me," she demanded.

8 But Joseph refused. "Look," he told her, "my master trusts me with everything in his entire household. 9 No one here has more authority than I do. He has held back nothing from me ex-

38:29 *Perez* means "breaking out." **38:30** *Zerah* means "scarlet" or "brightness."

open Judah's eyes to the injustice he has committed to her. **18:** The seal was used to mark documents with one's personal stamp and was often worn around the neck on a cord. The cord and the staff were the main means of identification, equivalent to a credit card or driver's license today. **21:** A shrine prostitute was socially more acceptable than an ordinary prostitute (vv. 15, 21). **24–26:** Judah exercises absolute authority over his daughter-in-law, but through her cunning she is able to demonstrate that she has been more righteous than he. Her actions become validated in Israelite history (see Ruth 4:12). **27–30:** Perez becomes the ancestor of King David (Ruth 4:18–22) and eventually of Jesus (Matt 1:2–16).

39:1–23 Joseph in Potiphar's House. Joseph Put in Prison. 1–6a: Joseph continues the phenomenon seen with the patriarchs, as those who come into contact with him become materially blessed. **6b:** The words used here to describe Joseph are identical to those used of his mother in 29:17. **7:** In the biblical narrative Potiphar's wife is not named, but in Jew-

cept you, because you are his wife. How could I do such a wicked thing? It would be a great sin against God."

10 She kept putting pressure on Joseph day after day, but he refused to sleep with her, and he kept out of her way as much as possible. 11 One day, however, no one else was around when he went in to do his work. 12 She came and grabbed him by his cloak, demanding, "Come on, sleep with me!" Joseph tore himself away, but he left his cloak in her hand as he ran from the house.

13 When she saw that she was holding his cloak and he had fled, 14 she called out to her servants. Soon all the men came running. "Look!" she said. "My husband has brought this Hebrew slave here to make fools of us! He came into my room to rape me, but I screamed. 15 When he heard me scream, he ran outside and got away, but he left his cloak behind with me."

16 She kept the cloak with her until her husband came home. 17 Then she told him her story. "That Hebrew slave you've brought into our house tried to come in and fool around with me," she said. 18 "But when I screamed, he ran outside, leaving his cloak with me!"

Joseph Put in Prison

19 Potiphar was furious when he heard his wife's story about how Joseph had treated her. 20 So he took Joseph and threw him into the prison where the king's prisoners were held, and there he remained. 21 But the LORD was with Joseph in the prison and showed him his faithful love. And the LORD made Joseph a favorite with the prison warden. 22 Before long, the warden put Joseph in charge of all the other prisoners and over everything that happened in the prison. 23 The warden had no more worries, because Joseph took care of everything. The LORD was with him and caused everything he did to succeed.

Joseph Interprets Two Dreams

40 Some time later, Pharaoh's chief cup-bearer and chief baker offended their royal master. 2 Pharaoh became angry with these two officials, 3 and he put them in the prison where Joseph was, in the palace of the captain of the guard. 4 They remained in prison for quite some time, and the captain of the guard assigned them to Joseph, who looked after them.

5 While they were in prison, Pharaoh's cup-bearer and baker each had a dream one night, and each dream had its own meaning. 6 When Joseph saw them the next morning, he noticed that they both looked upset. 7 "Why do you look so worried today?" he asked them.

8 And they replied, "We both had dreams last night, but no one can tell us what they mean."

"Interpreting dreams is God's business," Joseph replied. "Go ahead and tell me your dreams."

9 So the chief cup-bearer told Joseph his dream first. "In my dream," he said, "I saw a grapevine in front of me. 10 The vine had three branches that began to bud and blossom, and soon it produced clusters of ripe grapes. 11 I was holding Pharaoh's wine cup in my hand, so I took a cluster of grapes and squeezed the juice into the cup. Then I placed the cup in Pharaoh's hand."

12 "This is what the dream means," Joseph said. "The three branches represent three days. 13 Within three days Pharaoh will lift you up and restore you to your position as his chief cup-bearer. 14 And please remember me and do me a favor when things go well for you. Mention me to Pharaoh, so he might let me out of this place. 15 For I was kidnapped from my homeland, the land of the Hebrews, and now I'm here in prison, but I did nothing to deserve it."

16 When the chief baker saw that Joseph had given the first dream such a positive interpretation, he said to Joseph, "I had a dream, too. In my dream there were three baskets of white pastries stacked on my head. 17 The top basket contained all kinds of pastries for Pharaoh, but the birds came and ate them from the basket on my head."

18 "This is what the dream means," Joseph told him. "The three baskets also represent three days. 19 Three days from now Pharaoh will lift you up and impale your body on a pole. Then birds will come and peck away at your flesh."

20 Pharaoh's birthday came three days later, and he prepared a banquet for all his officials and staff. He summoned* his chief cup-bearer and chief baker to join the other officials. 21 He then restored the chief cup-bearer to his former position, so he could again hand Pharaoh his cup.

40:20 Hebrew *He lifted up the head of.*

ish tradition she is called Zuleika. **14–15:** The other servants are silent; we know nothing of what they think about the situation. **23:** The phrase *The LORD was with him* and its linkage to Joseph's success is repeated at the start and end of this chapter.

40:1–23 Joseph Interprets Two Dreams. This chapter functions as a stepping stone in the upward rise of Joseph's fortunes, Joseph having been sold by his brothers into slavery. It establishes Joseph's credibility and shows that he has matured and changed from being

22 But Pharaoh impaled the chief baker, just as
Joseph had predicted when he interpreted his
dream. 23 Pharaoh's chief cup-bearer, however,
forgot all about Joseph, never giving him another
thought.

Pharaoh's Dreams

41 Two full years later, Pharaoh dreamed
that he was standing on the bank of
the Nile River. 2 In his dream he saw
seven fat, healthy cows come up out of the river
and begin grazing in the marsh grass. 3 Then he
saw seven more cows come up behind them from
the Nile, but these were scrawny and thin. These
cows stood beside the fat cows on the riverbank.
4 Then the scrawny, thin cows ate the seven
healthy, fat cows! At this point in the dream,
Pharaoh woke up.
5 But he fell asleep again and had a second
dream. This time he saw seven heads of grain,
plump and beautiful, growing on a single stalk.
6 Then seven more heads of grain appeared, but
these were shriveled and withered by the east
wind. 7 And these thin heads swallowed up the
seven plump, well-formed heads! Then Pharaoh
woke up again and realized it was a dream.
8 The next morning Pharaoh was very disturbed by the dreams. So he called for all the magicians and wise men of Egypt. When Pharaoh
told them his dreams, not one of them could tell
him what they meant.
9 Finally, the king's chief cup-bearer spoke up.
"Today I have been reminded of my failure," he
told Pharaoh. 10 "Some time ago, you were angry
with the chief baker and me, and you imprisoned
us in the palace of the captain of the guard. 11 One
night the chief baker and I each had a dream, and
each dream had its own meaning. 12 There was a
young Hebrew man with us in the prison who
was a slave of the captain of the guard. We told
him our dreams, and he told us what each of our
dreams meant. 13 And everything happened just
as he had predicted. I was restored to my position
as cup-bearer, and the chief baker was executed
and impaled on a pole."
14 Pharaoh sent for Joseph at once, and he was
quickly brought from the prison. After he shaved
and changed his clothes, he went in and stood before Pharaoh. 15 Then Pharaoh said to Joseph, "I
had a dream last night, and no one here can tell
me what it means. But I have heard that when
you hear about a dream you can interpret it."
16 "It is beyond my power to do this," Joseph
replied. "But God can tell you what it means and
set you at ease."
17 So Pharaoh told Joseph his dream. "In my
dream," he said, "I was standing on the bank of
the Nile River, 18 and I saw seven fat, healthy cows
come up out of the river and begin grazing in the
marsh grass. 19 But then I saw seven sick-looking
cows, scrawny and thin, come up after them. I've
never seen such sorry-looking animals in all the
land of Egypt. 20 These thin, scrawny cows ate
the seven fat cows. 21 But afterward you wouldn't
have known it, for they were still as thin and
scrawny as before! Then I woke up.
22 "Then I fell asleep again, and I had another
dream. This time I saw seven heads of grain, full
and beautiful, growing on a single stalk. 23 Then
seven more heads of grain appeared, but these
were blighted, shriveled, and withered by the
east wind. 24 And the shriveled heads swallowed
the seven healthy heads. I told these dreams to
the magicians, but no one could tell me what
they mean."
25 Joseph responded, "Both of Pharaoh's
dreams mean the same thing. God is telling Pharaoh in advance what he is about to do. 26 The
seven healthy cows and the seven healthy heads
of grain both represent seven years of prosperity.
27 The seven thin, scrawny cows that came up later and the seven thin heads of grain, withered by
the east wind, represent seven years of famine.
28 "This will happen just as I have described it,
for God has revealed to Pharaoh in advance what
he is about to do. 29 The next seven years will be a
period of great prosperity throughout the land of
Egypt. 30 But afterward there will be seven years
of famine so great that all the prosperity will be
forgotten in Egypt. Famine will destroy the land.
31 This famine will be so severe that even the
memory of the good years will be erased. 32 As
for having two similar dreams, it means that
these events have been decreed by God, and he
will soon make them happen.
33 "Therefore, Pharaoh should find an intelligent and wise man and put him in charge of
the entire land of Egypt. 34 Then Pharaoh should

---

a dreamer into a dream interpreter. **23:** Perhaps in God's providence the time is not yet right for Joseph to be released.

41:1–36 Pharaoh's Dreams. 8–16: A contrast is made between the *magicians and wise men of Egypt* and the *young Hebrew* who trusts only in God. **32:** All of the dreams in the Joseph narrative have come in pairs, and now the reason for this is given: to provide assurance that God is behind them and will certainly cause them to happen.

appoint supervisors over the land and let them collect one-fifth of all the crops during the seven good years. 35Have them gather all the food produced in the good years that are just ahead and bring it to Pharaoh's storehouses. Store it away, and guard it so there will be food in the cities. 36That way there will be enough to eat when the seven years of famine come to the land of Egypt. Otherwise this famine will destroy the land."

Joseph Made Ruler of Egypt

37Joseph's suggestions were well received by Pharaoh and his officials. 38So Pharaoh asked his officials, "Can we find anyone else like this man so obviously filled with the spirit of God?" 39Then Pharaoh said to Joseph, "Since God has revealed the meaning of the dreams to you, clearly no one else is as intelligent or wise as you are. 40You will be in charge of my court, and all my people will take orders from you. Only I, sitting on my throne, will have a rank higher than yours."

41Pharaoh said to Joseph, "I hereby put you in charge of the entire land of Egypt." 42Then Pharaoh removed his signet ring from his hand and placed it on Joseph's finger. He dressed him in fine linen clothing and hung a gold chain around his neck. 43Then he had Joseph ride in the chariot reserved for his second-in-command. And wherever Joseph went, the command was shouted, "Kneel down!" So Pharaoh put Joseph in charge of all Egypt. 44And Pharaoh said to him, "I am Pharaoh, but no one will lift a hand or foot in the entire land of Egypt without your approval."

45Then Pharaoh gave Joseph a new Egyptian name, Zaphenath-paneah.* He also gave him a wife, whose name was Asenath. She was the daughter of Potiphera, the priest of On.* So Joseph took charge of the entire land of Egypt. 46He was thirty years old when he began serving in the court of Pharaoh, the king of Egypt. And when Joseph left Pharaoh's presence, he inspected the entire land of Egypt.

47As predicted, for seven years the land produced bumper crops. 48During those years, Joseph gathered all the crops grown in Egypt and stored the grain from the surrounding fields in the cities. 49He piled up huge amounts of grain like sand on the seashore. Finally, he stopped keeping records because there was too much to measure.

50During this time, before the first of the famine years, two sons were born to Joseph and his wife, Asenath, the daughter of Potiphera, the priest of On. 51Joseph named his older son Manasseh,* for he said, "God has made me forget all my troubles and everyone in my father's family." 52Joseph named his second son Ephraim,* for he said, "God has made me fruitful in this land of my grief."

53At last the seven years of bumper crops throughout the land of Egypt came to an end. 54Then the seven years of famine began, just as Joseph had predicted. The famine also struck all the surrounding countries, but throughout Egypt there was plenty of food. 55Eventually, however, the famine spread throughout the land of Egypt as well. And when the people cried out to Pharaoh for food, he told them, "Go to Joseph, and do whatever he tells you." 56So with severe famine everywhere, Joseph opened up the storehouses and distributed grain to the Egyptians, for the famine was severe throughout the land of Egypt. 57And people from all around came to Egypt to buy grain from Joseph because the famine was severe throughout the world.

Joseph's Brothers Go to Egypt

42 When Jacob heard that grain was available in Egypt, he said to his sons, "Why are you standing around looking at one another? 2I have heard there is grain in Egypt. Go down there, and buy enough grain to keep us alive. Otherwise we'll die."

3So Joseph's ten older brothers went down to Egypt to buy grain. 4But Jacob wouldn't let Joseph's younger brother, Benjamin, go with them, for fear some harm might come to him. 5So Jacob's* sons arrived in Egypt along with others to buy food, for the famine was in Canaan as well.

6Since Joseph was governor of all Egypt and

41:45a *Zaphenath-paneah* probably means "God speaks and lives." **41:45b** Greek version reads *of Heliopolis;* also in 41:50. **41:51** *Manasseh* sounds like a Hebrew term that means "causing to forget." **41:52** *Ephraim* sounds like a Hebrew term that means "fruitful." **42:5** Hebrew *Israel's.* See note on 35:21.

41:37–57 Joseph Made Ruler of Egypt. 42: The signet ring contains Pharaoh's signature so Joseph can now sign documents in his name. What Joseph wears carries great significance for each stage of the story, from his coat of many colors, both worn and torn, to his cloak left in Potiphar's wife's hands (39:12), to his change of clothes in order to come before Pharaoh (41:14), to now when he gets dressed in *fine linen*. **50–52:** Baby names are significant throughout the book of Genesis and indeed the Old Testament. Here they symbolize the complete reversal in Joseph's fortunes.

42:1–38 Joseph's Brothers Go to Egypt. 6: Joseph's boyhood dreams are fulfilled (37:5–10). **8:** Joseph is

in charge of selling grain to all the people, it was to him that his brothers came. When they arrived, they bowed before him with their faces to the ground. [7]Joseph recognized his brothers instantly, but he pretended to be a stranger and spoke harshly to them. "Where are you from?" he demanded.

"From the land of Canaan," they replied. "We have come to buy food."

[8]Although Joseph recognized his brothers, they didn't recognize him. [9]And he remembered the dreams he'd had about them many years before. He said to them, "You are spies! You have come to see how vulnerable our land has become."

[10]"No, my lord!" they exclaimed. "Your servants have simply come to buy food. [11]We are all brothers—members of the same family. We are honest men, sir! We are not spies!"

[12]"Yes, you are!" Joseph insisted. "You have come to see how vulnerable our land has become."

[13]"Sir," they said, "there are actually twelve of us. We, your servants, are all brothers, sons of a man living in the land of Canaan. Our youngest brother is back there with our father right now, and one of our brothers is no longer with us."

[14]But Joseph insisted, "As I said, you are spies! [15]This is how I will test your story. I swear by the life of Pharaoh that you will never leave Egypt unless your youngest brother comes here! [16]One of you must go and get your brother. I'll keep the rest of you here in prison. Then we'll find out whether or not your story is true. By the life of Pharaoh, if it turns out that you don't have a younger brother, then I'll know you are spies."

[17]So Joseph put them all in prison for three days. [18]On the third day Joseph said to them, "I am a God-fearing man. If you do as I say, you will live. [19]If you really are honest men, choose one of your brothers to remain in prison. The rest of you may go home with grain for your starving families. [20]But you must bring your youngest brother back to me. This will prove that you are telling the truth, and you will not die." To this they agreed.

[21]Speaking among themselves, they said, "Clearly we are being punished because of what we did to Joseph long ago. We saw his anguish when he pleaded for his life, but we wouldn't listen. That's why we're in this trouble."

[22]"Didn't I tell you not to sin against the boy?" Reuben asked. "But you wouldn't listen. And now we have to answer for his blood!"

[23]Of course, they didn't know that Joseph understood them, for he had been speaking to them through an interpreter. [24]Now he turned away from them and began to weep. When he regained his composure, he spoke to them again. Then he chose Simeon from among them and had him tied up right before their eyes.

[25]Joseph then ordered his servants to fill the men's sacks with grain, but he also gave secret instructions to return each brother's payment at the top of his sack. He also gave them supplies for their journey home. [26]So the brothers loaded their donkeys with the grain and headed for home.

[27]But when they stopped for the night and one of them opened his sack to get grain for his donkey, he found his money in the top of his sack. [28]"Look!" he exclaimed to his brothers. "My money has been returned; it's here in my sack!" Then their hearts sank. Trembling, they said to each other, "What has God done to us?"

[29]When the brothers came to their father, Jacob, in the land of Canaan, they told him everything that had happened to them. [30]"The man who is governor of the land spoke very harshly to us," they told him. "He accused us of being spies scouting the land. [31]But we said, 'We are honest men, not spies. [32]We are twelve brothers, sons of one father. One brother is no longer with us, and the youngest is at home with our father in the land of Canaan.'

[33]"Then the man who is governor of the land told us, 'This is how I will find out if you are honest men. Leave one of your brothers here with me, and take grain for your starving families and go on home. [34]But you must bring your youngest brother back to me. Then I will know you are honest men and not spies. Then I will give you back your brother, and you may trade freely in the land.' "

[35]As they emptied out their sacks, there in each man's sack was the bag of money he had paid for the grain! The brothers and their father were terrified when they saw the bags of money. [36]Jacob exclaimed, "You are robbing me of my children! Joseph is gone! Simeon is gone! And now you want to take Benjamin, too. Everything is going against me!"

[37]Then Reuben said to his father, "You may

---

in full Egyptian costume and, as a grown man, now looks very different from when his brothers last saw him. **24:** As the second eldest after Reuben (who tried to stop the brothers from harming Joseph) we can assume that Simeon took the lead in the plot to kill Joseph. **25:** Joseph begins to carry out a plan that will test the character of his brothers before he makes himself known to them. **37:** Reuben again shows

kill my two sons if I don't bring Benjamin back to you. I'll be responsible for him, and I promise to bring him back."

38 But Jacob replied, "My son will not go down with you. His brother Joseph is dead, and he is all I have left. If anything should happen to him on your journey, you would send this grieving, white-haired man to his grave.*"

The Brothers Return to Egypt

43 But the famine continued to ravage the land of Canaan. 2 When the grain they had brought from Egypt was almost gone, Jacob said to his sons, "Go back and buy us a little more food."

3 But Judah said, "The man was serious when he warned us, 'You won't see my face again unless your brother is with you.' 4 If you send Benjamin with us, we will go down and buy more food. 5 But if you don't let Benjamin go, we won't go either. Remember, the man said, 'You won't see my face again unless your brother is with you.' "

6 "Why were you so cruel to me?" Jacob* moaned. "Why did you tell him you had another brother?"

7 "The man kept asking us questions about our family," they replied. "He asked, 'Is your father still alive? Do you have another brother?' So we answered his questions. How could we know he would say, 'Bring your brother down here'?"

8 Judah said to his father, "Send the boy with me, and we will be on our way. Otherwise we will all die of starvation—and not only we, but you and our little ones. 9 I personally guarantee his safety. You may hold me responsible if I don't bring him back to you. Then let me bear the blame forever. 10 If we hadn't wasted all this time, we could have gone and returned twice by now."

11 So their father, Jacob, finally said to them, "If it can't be avoided, then at least do this. Pack your bags with the best products of this land. Take them down to the man as gifts—balm, honey, gum, aromatic resin, pistachio nuts, and almonds. 12 Also take double the money that was put back in your sacks, as it was probably someone's mistake. 13 Then take your brother, and go back to the man. 14 May God Almighty* give you mercy as you go before the man, so that he will release Simeon and let Benjamin return. But if I must lose my children, so be it."

15 So the men packed Jacob's gifts and double the money and headed off with Benjamin. They finally arrived in Egypt and presented themselves to Joseph. 16 When Joseph saw Benjamin with them, he said to the manager of his household, "These men will eat with me this noon. Take them inside the palace. Then go slaughter an animal, and prepare a big feast." 17 So the man did as Joseph told him and took them into Joseph's palace.

18 The brothers were terrified when they saw that they were being taken into Joseph's house. "It's because of the money someone put in our sacks last time we were here," they said. "He plans to pretend that we stole it. Then he will seize us, make us slaves, and take our donkeys."

A Feast at Joseph's Palace

19 The brothers approached the manager of Joseph's household and spoke to him at the entrance to the palace. 20 "Sir," they said, "we came to Egypt once before to buy food. 21 But as we were returning home, we stopped for the night and opened our sacks. Then we discovered that each man's money—the exact amount paid—was in the top of his sack! Here it is; we have brought it back with us. 22 We also have additional money to buy more food. We have no idea who put our money in our sacks."

23 "Relax. Don't be afraid," the household manager told them. "Your God, the God of your father, must have put this treasure into your sacks. I know I received your payment." Then he released Simeon and brought him out to them.

42:38 Hebrew *to Sheol.* **43:6** Hebrew *Israel;* also in 43:11. See note on 35:21. **43:14** Hebrew *El-Shaddai.*

himself as being the honorable one. **38:** *Sheol,* "the grave," was the place where the dead were thought to go. It does not carry with it the expectation of punishment or reward (as in the Christian hell or heaven) but was simply a pit under the earth where the dead existed.

43:1–18 The Brothers Return to Egypt. 1–5: Jacob has clearly prevaricated after the brothers' return and has chosen to ignore Joseph's instructions. **8–10:** Judah takes the lead among the brothers, as he does later in 44:18–34. **11:** These are the sorts of things that might still be around during a drought. **18:** The brothers have no idea what is happening and fear the worst.

43:19–34 A Feast at Joseph's Palace. 19–23: The brothers try to take the initiative in explaining to the household manager what has happened to the money, before they meet Joseph. He does not explain the mystery but reassures them that they have no need to be afraid. The release of Simeon (see 42:19, 34)

[24]The manager then led the men into Joseph's palace. He gave them water to wash their feet and provided food for their donkeys. [25]They were told they would be eating there, so they prepared their gifts for Joseph's arrival at noon.

[26]When Joseph came home, they gave him the gifts they had brought him, then bowed low to the ground before him. [27]After greeting them, he asked, "How is your father, the old man you spoke about? Is he still alive?"

[28]"Yes," they replied. "Our father, your servant, is alive and well." And they bowed low again.

[29]Then Joseph looked at his brother Benjamin, the son of his own mother. "Is this your youngest brother, the one you told me about?" Joseph asked. "May God be gracious to you, my son." [30]Then Joseph hurried from the room because he was overcome with emotion for his brother. He went into his private room, where he broke down and wept. [31]After washing his face, he came back out, keeping himself under control. Then he ordered, "Bring out the food!"

[32]The waiters served Joseph at his own table, and his brothers were served at a separate table. The Egyptians who ate with Joseph sat at their own table, because Egyptians despise Hebrews and refuse to eat with them. [33]Joseph told each of his brothers where to sit, and to their amazement, he seated them according to age, from oldest to youngest. [34]And Joseph filled their plates with food from his own table, giving Benjamin five times as much as he gave the others. So they feasted and drank freely with him.

Joseph's Silver Cup

44 When his brothers were ready to leave, Joseph gave these instructions to his palace manager: "Fill each of their sacks with as much grain as they can carry, and put each man's money back into his sack. [2]Then put my personal silver cup at the top of the youngest brother's sack, along with the money for his grain." So the manager did as Joseph instructed him.

[3]The brothers were up at dawn and were sent on their journey with their loaded donkeys. [4]But when they had gone only a short distance and were barely out of the city, Joseph said to his palace manager, "Chase after them and stop them. When you catch up with them, ask them, 'Why have you repaid my kindness with such evil? [5]Why have you stolen my master's silver cup,* which he uses to predict the future? What a wicked thing you have done!' "

[6]When the palace manager caught up with the men, he spoke to them as he had been instructed.

[7]"What are you talking about?" the brothers responded. "We are your servants and would never do such a thing! [8]Didn't we return the money we found in our sacks? We brought it back all the way from the land of Canaan. Why would we steal silver or gold from your master's house? [9]If you find his cup with any one of us, let that man die. And all the rest of us, my lord, will be your slaves."

[10]"That's fair," the man replied. "But only the one who stole the cup will be my slave. The rest of you may go free."

[11]They all quickly took their sacks from the backs of their donkeys and opened them. [12]The palace manager searched the brothers' sacks, from the oldest to the youngest. And the cup was found in Benjamin's sack! [13]When the brothers saw this, they tore their clothing in despair. Then they loaded their donkeys again and returned to the city.

[14]Joseph was still in his palace when Judah and his brothers arrived, and they fell to the ground before him. [15]"What have you done?" Joseph demanded. "Don't you know that a man like me can predict the future?"

[16]Judah answered, "Oh, my lord, what can we

44:5 As in Greek version; Hebrew lacks this phrase.

must have been an enormous relief to all concerned. **28:** Joseph's boyhood dreams are fulfilled a second time (cf. 42:6). **29:** Benjamin is the only one who is Joseph's full brother because his mother was also Rachel (35:24); thus Benjamin carries particular emotional significance. **32:** Joseph maintains his hidden identity by eating with the Egyptians who, by custom, will not eat with Hebrews. **34:** The presence of alcohol at the meal helps the brothers forget their worries and a jovial atmosphere pervades the meal.

44:1–34 Joseph's Silver Cup. Judah's Speech. 2: Joseph's silver cup is not his favorite drinking cup, but the cup that he uses to practice divination, a practice that is later forbidden in Israel (Deut 18:10). Great irony, of course, revolves around this because it was Joseph's dream divinations that got him into trouble with his brothers, and now this divining cup is getting his brothers into trouble with him. **14:** For a third time Joseph's boyhood dreams are fulfilled (cf. 43:28 and 42:6). **15:** The irony of the situation is emphasized. Joseph's brothers will soon be brought to the realization that Joseph can, indeed, practice divination. **17:** Joseph is testing his brothers to see if they

say to you? How can we explain this? How can
we prove our innocence? God is punishing us
for our sins. My lord, we have all returned to be
your slaves—all of us, not just our brother who
had your cup in his sack."
17 "No," Joseph said. "I would never do such
a thing! Only the man who stole the cup will be
my slave. The rest of you may go back to your
father in peace."

Judah Speaks for His Brothers

18 Then Judah stepped forward and said, "Please,
my lord, let your servant say just one word
to you. Please, do not be angry with me, even
though you are as powerful as Pharaoh himself.
19 "My lord, previously you asked us, your
servants, 'Do you have a father or a brother?'
20 And we responded, 'Yes, my lord, we have a father who is an old man, and his youngest son is a
child of his old age. His full brother is dead, and
he alone is left of his mother's children, and his
father loves him very much.'
21 "And you said to us, 'Bring him here so I
can see him with my own eyes.' 22 But we said to
you, 'My lord, the boy cannot leave his father,
for his father would die.' 23 But you told us, 'Unless your youngest brother comes with you, you
will never see my face again.'
24 "So we returned to your servant, our father,
and told him what you had said. 25 Later, when he
said, 'Go back again and buy us more food,' 26 we
replied, 'We can't go unless you let our youngest brother go with us. We'll never get to see
the man's face unless our youngest brother is
with us.'
27 "Then my father said to us, 'As you know, my
wife had two sons, 28 and one of them went away
and never returned. Doubtless he was torn to
pieces by some wild animal. I have never seen him
since. 29 Now if you take his brother away from
me, and any harm comes to him, you will send
this grieving, white-haired man to his grave.*'
30 "And now, my lord, I cannot go back to my
father without the boy. Our father's life is bound
up in the boy's life. 31 If he sees that the boy is not
with us, our father will die. We, your servants,
will indeed be responsible for sending that grieving, white-haired man to his grave. 32 My lord, I
guaranteed to my father that I would take care of
the boy. I told him, 'If I don't bring him back to
you, I will bear the blame forever.'
33 "So please, my lord, let me stay here as a
slave instead of the boy, and let the boy return
with his brothers. 34 For how can I return to my
father if the boy is not with me? I couldn't bear
to see the anguish this would cause my father!"

Joseph Reveals His Identity

45 Joseph could stand it no longer. There
were many people in the room, and
he said to his attendants, "Out, all of
you!" So he was alone with his brothers when
he told them who he was. 2 Then he broke down
and wept. He wept so loudly the Egyptians could
hear him, and word of it quickly carried to Pharaoh's palace.
3 "I am Joseph!" he said to his brothers. "Is my
father still alive?" But his brothers were speechless! They were stunned to realize that Joseph was
standing there in front of them. 4 "Please, come
closer," he said to them. So they came closer. And
he said again, "I am Joseph, your brother, whom
you sold into slavery in Egypt. 5 But don't be upset, and don't be angry with yourselves for selling
me to this place. It was God who sent me here
ahead of you to preserve your lives. 6 This famine
that has ravaged the land for two years will last
five more years, and there will be neither plowing
nor harvesting. 7 God has sent me ahead of you to
keep you and your families alive and to preserve
many survivors.* 8 So it was God who sent me
here, not you! And he is the one who made me an
adviser* to Pharaoh—the manager of his entire
palace and the governor of all Egypt.
9 "Now hurry back to my father and tell him,
'This is what your son Joseph says: God has
made me master over all the land of Egypt. So
come down to me immediately! 10 You can live in
the region of Goshen, where you can be near me
with all your children and grandchildren, your
flocks and herds, and everything you own. 11 I
will take care of you there, for there are still five
years of famine ahead of us. Otherwise you, your
household, and all your animals will starve.'"

44:29 Hebrew *to Sheol;* also in 44:31. **45:7** Or *and to save you with an extraordinary rescue.* The meaning of the Hebrew is uncertain. **45:8** Hebrew *a father.*

will abandon Benjamin and return to their father, as they did with himself, or if they have changed. **18–34:** Judah's speech shows Joseph that the brothers have, indeed, learned their lesson as they demonstrate remorse for their earlier actions and a deep compassion for their father.

45:1–28 Joseph Reveals His Identity. Pharaoh Invites Jacob to Egypt. 5–8: This programmatic statement by Joseph sums up the purpose of the whole narrative of chapters 37—50. **10:** Goshen is fertile land in the Nile Delta, northeast of Egypt. **15:** Full reconciliation takes place between Joseph and his brothers.

12 Then Joseph added, "Look! You can see for
yourselves, and so can my brother Benjamin,
that I really am Joseph! 13 Go tell my father of
my honored position here in Egypt. Describe for
him everything you have seen, and then bring
my father here quickly." 14 Weeping with joy, he
embraced Benjamin, and Benjamin did the same.
15 Then Joseph kissed each of his brothers and
wept over them, and after that they began talking freely with him.

Pharaoh Invites Jacob to Egypt

16 The news soon reached Pharaoh's palace: "Joseph's brothers have arrived!" Pharaoh and his
officials were all delighted to hear this.
17 Pharaoh said to Joseph, "Tell your brothers, 'This is what you must do: Load your pack
animals, and hurry back to the land of Canaan.
18 Then get your father and all of your families,
and return here to me. I will give you the very
best land in Egypt, and you will eat from the best
that the land produces.' "
19 Then Pharaoh said to Joseph, "Tell your
brothers, 'Take wagons from the land of Egypt
to carry your little children and your wives, and
bring your father here. 20 Don't worry about your
personal belongings, for the best of all the land of
Egypt is yours.' "
21 So the sons of Jacob* did as they were told.
Joseph provided them with wagons, as Pharaoh
had commanded, and he gave them supplies for
the journey. 22 And he gave each of them new
clothes—but to Benjamin he gave five changes
of clothes and 300 pieces* of silver. 23 He also sent
his father ten male donkeys loaded with the finest products of Egypt, and ten female donkeys
loaded with grain and bread and other supplies
he would need on his journey.
24 So Joseph sent his brothers off, and as they
left, he called after them, "Don't quarrel about
all this along the way!" 25 And they left Egypt
and returned to their father, Jacob, in the land
of Canaan.
26 "Joseph is still alive!" they told him. "And
he is governor of all the land of Egypt!" Jacob
was stunned at the news—he couldn't believe it.
27 But when they repeated to Jacob everything Joseph had told them, and when he saw the wagons
Joseph had sent to carry him, their father's spirits revived.
28 Then Jacob exclaimed, "It must be true! My
son Joseph is alive! I must go and see him before
I die."

Jacob's Journey to Egypt

46 So Jacob* set out for Egypt with all
his possessions. And when he came
to Beersheba, he offered sacrifices to
the God of his father, Isaac. 2 During the night
God spoke to him in a vision. "Jacob! Jacob!" he
called.
"Here I am," Jacob replied.
3 "I am God,* the God of your father," the
voice said. "Do not be afraid to go down to Egypt,
for there I will make your family into a great
nation. 4 I will go with you down to Egypt, and I
will bring you back again. You will die in Egypt,
but Joseph will be with you to close your eyes."
5 So Jacob left Beersheba, and his sons took
him to Egypt. They carried him and their little
ones and their wives in the wagons Pharaoh had
provided for them. 6 They also took all their livestock and all the personal belongings they had
acquired in the land of Canaan. So Jacob and his
entire family went to Egypt—7 sons and grandsons, daughters and granddaughters—all his descendants.
8 These are the names of the descendants of
Israel—the sons of Jacob—who went to Egypt:

Reuben was Jacob's oldest son. 9 The sons of
Reuben were Hanoch, Pallu, Hezron, and
Carmi.
10 The sons of Simeon were Jemuel, Jamin,
Ohad, Jakin, Zohar, and Shaul. (Shaul's
mother was a Canaanite woman.)
11 The sons of Levi were Gershon, Kohath, and
Merari.
12 The sons of Judah were Er, Onan, Shelah,
Perez, and Zerah (though Er and Onan had

45:21 Hebrew *Israel;* also in 45:28. See note on 35:21.
45:22 Hebrew *300 shekels,* about 7.5 pounds or 3.4 kilograms in weight. **46:1** Hebrew *Israel;* also in 46:29, 30. See note on 35:21. **46:3** Hebrew *I am El.*

27: The events of these last years have not affected Joseph alone. The contrast between the old man, worn down by the emotional burdens of his life, with the young, energetic deceiver of chapter 27 could not be greater.

46:1–34 Jacob in Egypt. 1: Beersheba carries great significance in the story of Jacob's father and grandfather, the patriarchs (see 21:14, 31–33; 22:19–20). It is no surprise that Jacob wishes to sacrifice to *the God of his father* before setting out on this journey; he must have known that it was taking him away from the land that God had promised him and his ancestors. **3–4:** God reassures Jacob that he is not to be afraid, despite seeming to move away from the promises that God has made to him (cf. 28:13).

died in the land of Canaan). The sons of Perez
were Hezron and Hamul.
13 The sons of Issachar were Tola, Puah,*
Jashub,* and Shimron.
14 The sons of Zebulun were Sered, Elon, and
Jahleel.
15 These were the sons of Leah and Jacob who were
born in Paddan-aram, in addition to their daughter,
Dinah. The number of Jacob's descendants (male
and female) through Leah was thirty-three.

16 The sons of Gad were Zephon,* Haggi, Shuni,
Ezbon, Eri, Arodi, and Areli.
17 The sons of Asher were Imnah, Ishvah, Ishvi,
and Beriah. Their sister was Serah. Beriah's
sons were Heber and Malkiel.
18 These were the sons of Zilpah, the servant giv-
en to Leah by her father, Laban. The number of
Jacob's descendants through Zilpah was sixteen.

19 The sons of Jacob's wife Rachel were Joseph
and Benjamin.
20 Joseph's sons, born in the land of Egypt, were
Manasseh and Ephraim. Their mother was
Asenath, daughter of Potiphera, the priest of
On.*
21 Benjamin's sons were Bela, Beker, Ashbel,
Gera, Naaman, Ehi, Rosh, Muppim, Huppim,
and Ard.
22 These were the sons of Rachel and Jacob. The
number of Jacob's descendants through Rachel
was fourteen.

23 The son of Dan was Hushim.
24 The sons of Naphtali were Jahzeel, Guni, Jezer,
and Shillem.
25 These were the sons of Bilhah, the servant giv-
en to Rachel by her father, Laban. The number of
Jacob's descendants through Bilhah was seven.

26 The total number of Jacob's direct descendants
who went with him to Egypt, not counting his
sons' wives, was sixty-six.
27 In addition, Joseph
had two sons* who were born in Egypt. So altogether, there were seventy* members of Jacob's
family in the land of Egypt.

Jacob's Family Arrives in Goshen

28 As they neared their destination, Jacob sent
Judah ahead to meet Joseph and get directions
to the region of Goshen. And when they finally arrived there,
29 Joseph prepared his chariot
and traveled to Goshen to meet his father, Jacob.
When Joseph arrived, he embraced his father and
wept, holding him for a long time.
30 Finally, Ja-
cob said to Joseph, "Now I am ready to die, since
I have seen your face again and know you are
still alive."

31 And Joseph said to his brothers and to his
father's entire family, "I will go to Pharaoh and
tell him, 'My brothers and my father's entire
family have come to me from the land of Canaan.
32 These men are shepherds, and they raise livestock. They have brought with them their flocks
and herds and everything they own.' "

33 Then he said, "When Pharaoh calls for you
and asks you about your occupation,
34 you must
tell him, 'We, your servants, have raised livestock all our lives, as our ancestors have always
done.' When you tell him this, he will let you live
here in the region of Goshen, for the Egyptians
despise shepherds."

Jacob Blesses Pharaoh

47 Then Joseph went to see Pharaoh
and told him, "My father and my
brothers have arrived from the land
of Canaan. They have come with all their flocks
and herds and possessions, and they are now in
the region of Goshen."
2 Joseph took five of his brothers with him and
presented them to Pharaoh.
3 And Pharaoh asked
the brothers, "What is your occupation?"

They replied, "We, your servants, are shepherds, just like our ancestors.
4 We have come to
live here in Egypt for a while, for there is no pasture for our flocks in Canaan. The famine is very
severe there. So please, we request permission to
live in the region of Goshen."

5 Then Pharaoh said to Joseph, "Now that
your father and brothers have joined you here,

46:13a As in Syriac version and Samaritan Pentateuch (see also 1 Chr 7:1); Hebrew reads *Puvah.* **46:13b** As in some Greek manuscripts and Samaritan Pentateuch (see also Num 26:24; 1 Chr 7:1); Hebrew reads *Iob.* **46:16** As in Greek version and Samaritan Pentateuch (see also Num 26:15); Hebrew reads *Ziphion.* **46:20** Greek version reads *of Heliopolis.* **46:27a** Greek version reads *nine sons,* probably including Joseph's grandsons through Ephraim and Manasseh (see 1 Chr 7:14-20). **46:27b** Greek version reads *seventy-five;* see note on Exod 1:5.

27: Seventy is a number used in Jewish tradition to signal completeness. **31–34:** Joseph realizes that there is a cultural problem. Jacob has not followed Pharaoh's command to leave behind all his possessions, and Joseph knows that the agriculturally based Egyptians look down on nomadic shepherds. Joseph's instructions demonstrate the astute political diplomacy appropriate for his exalted situation.

47:1–12 Jacob Blesses Pharaoh. 3: The five brothers

[6]choose any place in the entire land of Egypt for
them to live. Give them the best land of Egypt.
Let them live in the region of Goshen. And if any
of them have special skills, put them in charge of
my livestock, too."
[7]Then Joseph brought in his father, Jacob, and
presented him to Pharaoh. And Jacob blessed
Pharaoh.
[8]"How old are you?" Pharaoh asked him.
[9]Jacob replied, "I have traveled this earth for
130 hard years. But my life has been short compared to the lives of my ancestors." [10]Then Jacob
blessed Pharaoh again before leaving his court.
[11]So Joseph assigned the best land of Egypt—
the region of Rameses—to his father and his
brothers, and he settled them there, just as Pharaoh had commanded. [12]And Joseph provided
food for his father and his brothers in amounts
appropriate to the number of their dependents,
including the smallest children.

Joseph's Leadership in the Famine

[13]Meanwhile, the famine became so severe that
all the food was used up, and people were starving throughout the lands of Egypt and Canaan.
[14]By selling grain to the people, Joseph eventually collected all the money in Egypt and Canaan,
and he put the money in Pharaoh's treasury.
[15]When the people of Egypt and Canaan ran out
of money, all the Egyptians came to Joseph. "Our
money is gone!" they cried. "But please give us
food, or we will die before your very eyes!"
[16]Joseph replied, "Since your money is gone,
bring me your livestock. I will give you food in
exchange for your livestock." [17]So they brought
their livestock to Joseph in exchange for food.
In exchange for their horses, flocks of sheep and
goats, herds of cattle, and donkeys, Joseph provided them with food for another year.
[18]But that year ended, and the next year they
came again and said, "We cannot hide the truth
from you, my lord. Our money is gone, and all
our livestock and cattle are yours. We have nothing left to give but our bodies and our land. [19]Why
should we die before your very eyes? Buy us and
our land in exchange for food; we offer our land
and ourselves as slaves for Pharaoh. Just give us
grain so we may live and not die, and so the land
does not become empty and desolate."
[20]So Joseph bought all the land of Egypt for
Pharaoh. All the Egyptians sold him their fields
because the famine was so severe, and soon all the
land belonged to Pharaoh. [21]As for the people, he
made them all slaves,* from one end of Egypt to
the other. [22]The only land he did not buy was the
land belonging to the priests. They received an
allotment of food directly from Pharaoh, so they
didn't need to sell their land.
[23]Then Joseph said to the people, "Look, today
I have bought you and your land for Pharaoh. I
will provide you with seed so you can plant the
fields. [24]Then when you harvest it, one-fifth of
your crop will belong to Pharaoh. You may keep
the remaining four-fifths as seed for your fields
and as food for you, your households, and your
little ones."
[25]"You have saved our lives!" they exclaimed.
"May it please you, my lord, to let us be Pharaoh's servants." [26]Joseph then issued a decree
still in effect in the land of Egypt, that Pharaoh
should receive one-fifth of all the crops grown on
his land. Only the land belonging to the priests
was not given to Pharaoh.
[27]Meanwhile, the people of Israel settled in
the region of Goshen in Egypt. There they acquired property, and they were fruitful, and their
population grew rapidly. [28]Jacob lived for seventeen years after his arrival in Egypt, so he lived
147 years in all.
[29]As the time of his death drew near, Jacob*
called for his son Joseph and said to him, "Please
do me this favor. Put your hand under my thigh
and swear that you will treat me with unfailing
love by honoring this last request: Do not bury

47:21 As in Greek version and Samaritan Pentateuch; Hebrew reads *he moved them all into the towns.* **47:29** Hebrew *Israel;* also in 47:31b. See note on 35:21.

stress their ancestry, possibly to make their shepherding occupation more acceptable to Pharaoh. **7–10:** The mighty Pharaoh is blessed by the nomadic refugee. Thus we see the continued fulfillment of God's words to Abram of being a blessing to those who bless him (12:2–3). **11:** Rameses II (1290–1224 BC) made the city of Tanis his capital and this is in the area of Goshen. The author makes the connection.

47:13–31 Joseph's Leadership in the Famine. 13–26: As the famine grows increasingly severe, Joseph gives out the grain that has been carefully horded in exchange for the people's money, livestock, land, and then the people themselves. Thus, through Joseph, the people are enslaved. **27:** Joseph leaves his family alone and enslaves only the Egyptians and Canaanites. In this verse are the seeds of Israel's subsequent enslavement in Egypt and the Exodus. **29:** This method of oath-taking is seen also in 24:1–9. The family burial place is the cave at Machpelah (see 23:1–20, 49:29).

me in Egypt. 30 When I die, please take my body
out of Egypt and bury me with my ancestors."
So Joseph promised, "I will do as you ask."
31 "Swear that you will do it," Jacob insisted.
So Joseph gave his oath, and Jacob bowed humbly at the head of his bed.*

Jacob Blesses Manasseh and Ephraim

48 One day not long after this, word
came to Joseph, "Your father is failing rapidly." So Joseph went to visit
his father, and he took with him his two sons,
Manasseh and Ephraim.
2 When Joseph arrived, Jacob was told, "Your
son Joseph has come to see you." So Jacob* gathered his strength and sat up in his bed.
3 Jacob said to Joseph, "God Almighty* appeared to me at Luz in the land of Canaan and
blessed me. 4 He said to me, 'I will make you
fruitful, and I will multiply your descendants. I
will make you a multitude of nations. And I will
give this land of Canaan to your descendants*
after you as an everlasting possession.'
5 "Now I am claiming as my own sons these
two boys of yours, Ephraim and Manasseh, who
were born here in the land of Egypt before I arrived. They will be my sons, just as Reuben and
Simeon are. 6 But any children born to you in
the future will be your own, and they will inherit land within the territories of their brothers
Ephraim and Manasseh.
7 "Long ago, as I was returning from Paddan-
aram, Rachel died in the land of Canaan. We
were still on the way, some distance from Ephrath (that is, Bethlehem). So with great sorrow I
buried her there beside the road to Ephrath."
8 Then Jacob looked over at the two boys. "Are
these your sons?" he asked.
9 "Yes," Joseph told him, "these are the sons
God has given me here in Egypt."
And Jacob said, "Bring them closer to me, so
I can bless them."
10 Jacob was half blind because of his age and
could hardly see. So Joseph brought the boys
close to him, and Jacob kissed and embraced them.
11 Then Jacob said to Joseph, "I never thought I
would see your face again, but now God has let
me see your children, too!"
12 Joseph moved the boys, who were at their
grandfather's knees, and he bowed with his face
to the ground. 13 Then he positioned the boys in
front of Jacob. With his right hand he directed
Ephraim toward Jacob's left hand, and with his
left hand he put Manasseh at Jacob's right hand.
14 But Jacob crossed his arms as he reached out to
lay his hands on the boys' heads. He put his right
hand on the head of Ephraim, though he was the
younger boy, and his left hand on the head of
Manasseh, though he was the firstborn. 15 Then
he blessed Joseph and said,

"May the God before whom my grandfather
Abraham
and my father, Isaac, walked—
the God who has been my shepherd
all my life, to this very day,
16 the Angel who has redeemed me from all
harm—
may he bless these boys.
May they preserve my name
and the names of Abraham and Isaac.
And may their descendants multiply greatly
throughout the earth."

17 But Joseph was upset when he saw that his
father placed his right hand on Ephraim's head.
So Joseph lifted it to move it from Ephraim's
head to Manasseh's head. 18 "No, my father," he
said. "This one is the firstborn. Put your right
hand on his head."
19 But his father refused. "I know, my son; I
know," he replied. "Manasseh will also become
a great people, but his younger brother will become even greater. And his descendants will become a multitude of nations."
20 So Jacob blessed the boys that day with
this blessing: "The people of Israel will use your
names when they give a blessing. They will say,
'May God make you as prosperous as Ephraim
and Manasseh.' " In this way, Jacob put Ephraim
ahead of Manasseh.
21 Then Jacob said to Joseph, "Look, I am about

47:31 Greek version reads *and Israel bowed in worship as he leaned on his staff.* Compare Heb 11:21. **48:2** Hebrew *Israel;* also in 48:8, 10, 11, 13, 14, 21. See note on 35:21. **48:3** Hebrew *El-Shaddai.* **48:4** Hebrew *seed;* also in 48:19.

48:1–22 Jacob Blesses Manasseh and Ephraim. 3–4: Jacob is referring to the blessing given by God to him in 28:10–22. **5:** Jacob adopts Joseph's two sons, making them equal to Joseph's brothers. This explains why the twelve tribes of Israel have none named after Joseph but do include Manasseh and Ephraim (see Num 1:32–35; Josh 17:17). **12:** If this section is taken chronologically, Joseph's boys would be about nineteen or twenty. Taking them next to his knee may have been a traditional sign of adoption, as seen in 30:1–3. **13–20:** Joseph should not have been so surprised by this reversal in blessings: it was a feature of his family line (20:12–13; 25:23; 38:27–30). **21:** Joseph's bones are taken back to Canaan in Joshua

to die, but God will be with you and will take you back to Canaan, the land of your ancestors.
22 And beyond what I have given your brothers, I am giving you an extra portion of the land* that I took from the Amorites with my sword and bow."

Jacob's Last Words to His Sons

49 Then Jacob called together all his sons and said, "Gather around me, and I will tell you what will happen to each of you in the days to come.

2 "Come and listen, you sons of Jacob;
listen to Israel, your father.

3 "Reuben, you are my firstborn, my strength,
the child of my vigorous youth.
You are first in rank and first in power.
4 But you are as unruly as a flood,
and you will be first no longer.
For you went to bed with my wife;
you defiled my marriage couch.

5 "Simeon and Levi are two of a kind;
their weapons are instruments of violence.
6 May I never join in their meetings;
may I never be a party to their plans.
For in their anger they murdered men,
and they crippled oxen just for sport.
7 A curse on their anger, for it is fierce;
a curse on their wrath, for it is cruel.
I will scatter them among the descendants of Jacob;
I will disperse them throughout Israel.

8 "Judah, your brothers will praise you.
You will grasp your enemies by the neck.
All your relatives will bow before you.
9 Judah, my son, is a young lion
that has finished eating its prey.
Like a lion he crouches and lies down;
like a lioness—who dares to rouse him?
10 The scepter will not depart from Judah,
nor the ruler's staff from his descendants,*
until the coming of the one to whom it belongs,*
the one whom all nations will honor.
11 He ties his foal to a grapevine,
the colt of his donkey to a choice vine.
He washes his clothes in wine,
his robes in the blood of grapes.
12 His eyes are darker than wine,
and his teeth are whiter than milk.

13 "Zebulun will settle by the seashore
and will be a harbor for ships;
his borders will extend to Sidon.

14 "Issachar is a sturdy donkey,
resting between two saddlepacks.*
15 When he sees how good the countryside is
and how pleasant the land,
he will bend his shoulder to the load
and submit himself to hard labor.

16 "Dan will govern his people,
like any other tribe in Israel.
17 Dan will be a snake beside the road,
a poisonous viper along the path
that bites the horse's hooves
so its rider is thrown off.
18 I trust in you for salvation, O LORD!

19 "Gad will be attacked by marauding bands,
but he will attack them when they retreat.

20 "Asher will dine on rich foods
and produce food fit for kings.

48:22 Or *an extra ridge of land.* The meaning of the Hebrew is uncertain. **49:10a** Hebrew *from between his feet.* **49:10b** Or *until tribute is brought to him and the peoples obey;* traditionally rendered *until Shiloh comes.* **49:14** Or *sheepfolds,* or *hearths.*

24:32 (see also Exod 13:19). **22:** The word for *portion* is *shechem,* thus playing on the name of the town of Shechem that Jacob's sons ransacked in 34:25–29. In later Israelite history, Shechem was situated on the border between the tribal lands of Ephraim and Manasseh (see Josh 17:7; 20:20–21).

49:1–28 Jacob's Last Words. These last words of Jacob are poetry, described by some scholars as "tribal ode." The futures predicted to the sons rest on a combination of their maternal line (whether their mother was Leah, Bilhah, Zilpah, or Rachel; see 35:23–26), the role they had played in Joseph's life, and their tribal fortunes at the time this episode was being written down on paper. **4:** Reuben slept with Jacob's concubine Bilhah in 35:22. **5–7:** These words refer back to the destruction of Shechem in 34:25–29. Clearly this action was merely the surface of a nastily violent disposition. The tribe of Simeon was absorbed by Judah (Josh 19:9), and Levi became the landless priestly tribe (Num 18:6–7, 20). **8–12:** Judah becomes the dominant tribe from the time of the monarchy. David came from the line of Judah (1 Sam 17:12).

21 "Naphtali is a doe set free
that bears beautiful fawns.

22 "Joseph is the foal of a wild donkey,
the foal of a wild donkey at a spring—
one of the wild donkeys on the ridge.*
23 Archers attacked him savagely;
they shot at him and harassed him.
24 But his bow remained taut,
and his arms were strengthened
by the hands of the Mighty One of Jacob,
by the Shepherd, the Rock of Israel.
25 May the God of your father help you;
may the Almighty bless you
with the blessings of the heavens above,
and blessings of the watery depths below,
and blessings of the breasts and womb.
26 May the blessings of your father
surpass the blessings of the ancient
mountains,*
reaching to the heights of the eternal hills.
May these blessings rest on the head of
Joseph,
who is a prince among his brothers.

27 "Benjamin is a ravenous wolf,
devouring his enemies in the morning
and dividing his plunder in the evening."

28 These are the twelve tribes of Israel, and
this is what their father said as he told his sons
good-bye. He blessed each one with an appropriate message.

Jacob's Death and Burial

29 Then Jacob instructed them, "Soon I will die
and join my ancestors. Bury me with my father
and grandfather in the cave in the field of Ephron
the Hittite. 30 This is the cave in the field of Machpelah, near Mamre in Canaan, that Abraham
bought from Ephron the Hittite as a permanent
burial site. 31 There Abraham and his wife Sarah
are buried. There Isaac and his wife, Rebekah, are
buried. And there I buried Leah. 32 It is the plot of
land and the cave that my grandfather Abraham
bought from the Hittites."
33 When Jacob had finished this charge to his
sons, he drew his feet into the bed, breathed his
last, and joined his ancestors in death.

50 Joseph threw himself on his father
and wept over him and kissed him.
2 Then Joseph told the physicians who
served him to embalm his father's body; so Jacob* was embalmed. 3 The embalming process
took the usual forty days. And the Egyptians
mourned his death for seventy days.
4 When the period of mourning was over, Joseph approached Pharaoh's advisers and said,
"Please do me this favor and speak to Pharaoh
on my behalf. 5 Tell him that my father made me
swear an oath. He said to me, 'Listen, I am about
to die. Take my body back to the land of Canaan,
and bury me in the tomb I prepared for myself.'
So please allow me to go and bury my father. After his burial, I will return without delay."
6 Pharaoh agreed to Joseph's request. "Go and
bury your father, as he made you promise," he
said. 7 So Joseph went up to bury his father. He
was accompanied by all of Pharaoh's officials, all
the senior members of Pharaoh's household, and
all the senior officers of Egypt. 8 Joseph also took
his entire household and his brothers and their
households. But they left their little children and
flocks and herds in the land of Goshen. 9 A great
number of chariots and charioteers accompanied
Joseph.
10 When they arrived at the threshing floor
of Atad, near the Jordan River, they held a very
great and solemn memorial service, with a seven-day period of mourning for Joseph's father.
11 The local residents, the Canaanites, watched
them mourning at the threshing floor of Atad.
Then they renamed that place (which is near the
Jordan) Abel-mizraim,* for they said, "This is a
place of deep mourning for these Egyptians."
12 So Jacob's sons did as he had commanded
them. 13 They carried his body to the land of Canaan and buried him in the cave in the field of
Machpelah, near Mamre. This is the cave that
Abraham had bought as a permanent burial site
from Ephron the Hittite.

49:22 Or *Joseph is a fruitful tree, / a fruitful tree beside a spring. / His branches reach over the wall.* The meaning of the Hebrew is uncertain. **49:26** Or *of my ancestors.* **50:2** Hebrew *Israel.* See note on 35:21. **50:11** *Abel-mizraim* means "mourning of the Egyptians."

49:29—50:13 Jacob's Death and Burial. 30: Jacob will be the sixth and last person to be buried in the cave, along with Abraham, Sarah, Isaac, Rebekah, and Leah. **2–3:** The Egyptians were unique among ancient Israel's neighbors in their practice of embalming. The length of time given here corresponds well with Egyptian accounts of mourning and embalming. This practice enabled Joseph and his brothers to take the body back to Canaan, as Jacob had requested.

Joseph Reassures His Brothers
[14]After burying Jacob, Joseph returned to Egypt
with his brothers and all who had accompanied
him to his father's burial. [15]But now that their
father was dead, Joseph's brothers became fearful. "Now Joseph will show his anger and pay us
back for all the wrong we did to him," they said.
[16]So they sent this message to Joseph: "Before your father died, he instructed us [17]to say to
you: 'Please forgive your brothers for the great
wrong they did to you—for their sin in treating
you so cruelly.' So we, the servants of the God of
your father, beg you to forgive our sin." When
Joseph received the message, he broke down and
wept. [18]Then his brothers came and threw themselves down before Joseph. "Look, we are your
slaves!" they said.
[19]But Joseph replied, "Don't be afraid of me.
Am I God, that I can punish you? [20]You intended to harm me, but God intended it all for good.
He brought me to this position so I could save
the lives of many people. [21]No, don't be afraid. I
will continue to take care of you and your children." So he reassured them by speaking kindly
to them.

The Death of Joseph
[22]So Joseph and his brothers and their families
continued to live in Egypt. Joseph lived to the
age of 110. [23]He lived to see three generations of
descendants of his son Ephraim, and he lived to
see the birth of the children of Manasseh's son
Makir, whom he claimed as his own.*
[24]"Soon I will die," Joseph told his brothers,
"but God will surely come to help you and lead
you out of this land of Egypt. He will bring you
back to the land he solemnly promised to give to
Abraham, to Isaac, and to Jacob."
[25]Then Joseph made the sons of Israel swear
an oath, and he said, "When God comes to help
you and lead you back, you must take my bones
with you." [26]So Joseph died at the age of 110.
The Egyptians embalmed him, and his body was
placed in a coffin in Egypt.

50:23 Hebrew *who were born on Joseph's knees.*

50:14–21 Joseph Reassures His Brothers. 15: The custom of that era was to hold off taking revenge on one's kin until the period of mourning was over (cf. 27:41). **18:** Once more the brothers bow before Joseph, in fulfillment of his dreams decades earlier (see annotation on 44:14). **19–20:** Joseph highlights the remarkable theme of his life story: that God has been in control, working through the seeming dead ends of Joseph's life to bring about his purposes.

50:22–26 The Death of Joesph. The story ends with the implicit recognition that the family of Abraham, Isaac, and Jacob—of Sarah, Rebekah, and Rachel—are now not in the land that God has called them to. Now a much longer story awaits as to how they return to that land, bringing Joseph's bones with them (see annotation on 48:21).

EXODUS

INTRODUCTION

Exodus is central for the Judeo-Christian tradition's definition of the being and nature of God and in explaining the spiritual origins of those who trust in him. Here we find the account of the great liberating event that set free a slave people and transformed them into a nation with their own law, their own identity, and their own history. Christianity cannot be understood apart from the basic foundation laid by the book of Exodus.

Its narratives supply the stories that mothers tell as they seek to implant faith in their children. Its ethical and moral precepts still guide us through the wilderness of today's turbulent uncertainties. Its many-faceted instructions for worship call us to reflect upon the need for careful preparation, investment of material resources, concern for detail, and utilization in God's service of the highest degree of gifting and talent.

Throughout the ages, the Exodus material has excited the interest and emulation of others. Often the events have served as metaphors for those embarked upon a spiritual journey. The apostle Paul declared the desert experiences to be spiritual examples that could inform faith and guide conduct (1 Cor 10:1–11). The female colleagues of St. Jerome asked about the number of stopping places on the journey from Egypt to the promised land. While the motivation for the query may have been purely academic, it is also possible that this brilliant coterie of women used the locales as symbols for their own spiritual journey—or that they empathized with the mothers who had to move their families so many times.

A significant feature of the book is the retelling of important material more than once. The escape from Egypt, the giving of the law, the enactment of the covenant, the institution of the Passover, and the implementation of carefully detailed worship are all reviewed with considerable precision. Exodus is a document of instruction, intended as a manual to tell each generation how God gave them directives for living, for social justice, for worship. The very retelling of the material was part of its power and displayed the permanence of the lessons taught.

The authorship is traditionally ascribed to Moses, though he may well have had assistance from various colleagues; some of the original material may have been expanded, such as the extensive description of the Tabernacle and its accoutrements. The actual date of the Hebrews' departure from Egypt is a subject of scholarly debate, with the strongest arguments leaning toward either the mid-fifteenth century BC or approximately 1290 to 1280 BC. In the latter case, the pharaoh who ordered the extermination of male Hebrew infants would have been Rameses II.

There are also differences of opinion about its date of composition. At least parts of it go back to the thirteenth century BC. The song of Miriam seems to be an oral memory from the actual event, as the tablets inscribed with the law preserve a written testimony. There is a reference to the importance of keeping a written record as a memorial at 17:14; thus, there is considerable evidence of a determined effort to create a historical document that could be handed down to later generations.—*Catherine Clark Kroeger* and *Mary J. Evans*

The Israelites in Egypt

1 These are the names of the sons of Israel (that is, Jacob) who moved to Egypt with their father, each with his family: 2 Reuben, Simeon, Levi, Judah, 3 Issachar, Zebulun, Benjamin, 4 Dan, Naphtali, Gad, and Asher. 5 In all, Jacob had seventy* descendants in Egypt, including Joseph, who was already there.

6 In time, Joseph and all of his brothers died, ending that entire generation. 7 But their descendants, the Israelites, had many children and grandchildren. In fact, they multiplied so greatly that they became extremely powerful and filled the land.

8 Eventually, a new king came to power in Egypt who knew nothing about Joseph or what he had done. 9 He said to his people, "Look, the people of Israel now outnumber us and are stronger than we are. 10 We must make a plan to keep them from growing even more. If we don't, and if war breaks out, they will join our enemies and fight against us. Then they will escape from the country.*"

11 So the Egyptians made the Israelites their slaves. They appointed brutal slave drivers over them, hoping to wear them down with crushing labor. They forced them to build the cities of Pithom and Rameses as supply centers for the king. 12 But the more the Egyptians oppressed them, the more the Israelites multiplied and spread, and the more alarmed the Egyptians became. 13 So the Egyptians worked the people of Israel without mercy. 14 They made their lives bitter, forcing them to mix mortar and make bricks and do all the work in the fields. They were ruthless in all their demands.

15 Then Pharaoh, the king of Egypt, gave this order to the Hebrew midwives, Shiphrah and Puah: 16 "When you help the Hebrew women as they give birth, watch as they deliver.* If the baby is a boy, kill him; if it is a girl, let her live." 17 But because the midwives feared God, they refused to obey the king's orders. They allowed the boys to live, too.

1:5 Dead Sea Scrolls and Greek version read *seventy-five;* see notes on Gen 46:27. **1:10** Or *will take the country.*
1:16 Hebrew *look upon the two stones;* perhaps the reference is to a birthstool.

1:1–2:25 The Preparation of a Leader

1:1–22 The Israelites in Egypt. The book of Exodus begins with an explanation of how the Israelites come to be living in Egypt and how they have fallen from their original preferred status. It is interesting that the main characters in these early chapters of Exodus are all women: the midwives, the mother and sister of Moses, Pharaoh's daughter. We see the same thing at the beginning of 1 Samuel. The overall history reflects the patriarchal nature of the nation (whose story begins here) and the monarchy (whose story begins in 1 Sam), but the inclusion of women's stories at these crucial beginning moments shows that the biblical perspective does not exactly parallel the attitudes of the time. **8–18:** Fearing that the Hebrews may constitute a military threat, Pharaoh devises a fourfold step to eliminate them: forced hard labor, slavery, secret murder of the males, and an official order for their death. **11:** A series of great building projects was conducted in the eastern delta area during the reign of Rameses II. These would become feasible with the use of massive slave labor. **15:** Exodus tells the story of the great liberating event in the history of Israel, but it is also a story of how women made this possible. The first effort is that of the two midwives, ordered to practice infanticide on all the male children of the Hebrews. Their refusal is an act of civil disobedience that subverts the genocidal purpose of the pharaoh. The names of the two women are Egyptian, and the text does not make it clear whether they were Egyptian midwives who served the

[18] So the king of Egypt called for the midwives. "Why have you done this?" he demanded. "Why have you allowed the boys to live?"

[19] "The Hebrew women are not like the Egyptian women," the midwives replied. "They are more vigorous and have their babies so quickly that we cannot get there in time."

[20] So God was good to the midwives, and the Israelites continued to multiply, growing more and more powerful. [21] And because the midwives feared God, he gave them families of their own.

[22] Then Pharaoh gave this order to all his people: "Throw every newborn Hebrew boy into the Nile River. But you may let the girls live."

The Birth of Moses

2 About this time, a man and woman from the tribe of Levi got married. [2] The woman became pregnant and gave birth to a son. She saw that he was a special baby and kept him hidden for three months. [3] But when she could no longer hide him, she got a basket made of papyrus reeds and waterproofed it with tar and pitch. She put the baby in the basket and laid it among the reeds along the bank of the Nile River. [4] The baby's sister then stood at a distance, watching to see what would happen to him.

[5] Soon Pharaoh's daughter came down to bathe in the river, and her attendants walked along the riverbank. When the princess saw the basket among the reeds, she sent her maid to get it for her. [6] When the princess opened it, she saw the baby. The little boy was crying, and she felt sorry for him. "This must be one of the Hebrew children," she said.

[7] Then the baby's sister approached the princess. "Should I go and find one of the Hebrew women to nurse the baby for you?" she asked.

[8] "Yes, do!" the princess replied. So the girl went and called the baby's mother.

[9] "Take this baby and nurse him for me," the princess told the baby's mother. "I will pay you for your help." So the woman took her baby home and nursed him.

[10] Later, when the boy was older, his mother brought him back to Pharaoh's daughter, who adopted him as her own son. The princess named him Moses,* for she explained, "I lifted him out of the water."

Moses Escapes to Midian

[11] Many years later, when Moses had grown up, he went out to visit his own people, the Hebrews, and he saw how hard they were forced to work. During his visit, he saw an Egyptian beating one of his fellow Hebrews. [12] After looking in all directions to make sure no one was watching, Moses killed the Egyptian and hid the body in the sand.

[13] The next day, when Moses went out to visit his people again, he saw two Hebrew men fight-

2:10 *Moses* sounds like a Hebrew term that means "to lift out."

Hebrew women or if they themselves were Hebrew. In any case, they feared the LORD and refused to carry out the atrocity. **19:** The reply of the midwives is not necessarily a complete untruth. Female athletes and women engaged in hard labor often deliver more quickly than their sedentary sisters. **20–22:** While the midwives enjoy God's blessing, Pharaoh extends to all of his subjects the command to exterminate all newborn male Hebrews.

2:1–10 The Birth of Moses. 1: The role of preserving life now moves to a mother who refuses to surrender her son to death. (The names of the parents, Jochebed and Amram, are given at 6:16–20. Jochebed, mother of the three foremost figures of the Exodus, is mentioned in the genealogy of the Levites at Num 26:59.) **3–4:** Desperation causes her to formulate a plan that will appear to comply with Pharaoh's decree to cast the children into the river. She crafts a basket of papyrus reeds that grow along the Nile, and makes it watertight. Her clever strategy leads her to deposit the floating cradle at a point where the Egyptian princess bathes. Watching nearby is the baby's quick-witted older sister Miriam. **5–6:** The princess and the ladies-in-waiting are aware of the king's decree and of the identity of the child. Nevertheless, they too are swept into the conspiracy of civil disobedience that will lead to the liberation of God's people. **7–9:** Miriam plays her part admirably, and so the scheme advances. **10:** Hebrews nursed their children for an extended period of time—three years and sometimes as late as five years of age. The mother, a descendant of the tribe of Levi, appears to have turned this nursing period into a time of instruction as to the heritage and religion of Israel. (For religious influence during this period, see Ps 22:9.) These early years are the most powerful in the formulation of personal faith. Moses will then meet another religious system in the Egyptian court. "Moses" is an Egyptian word meaning "to give birth," while a Hebrew word with a similar sound means "to draw out." Both names are appropriate as the adoptive mother assumes parentage.

2:11–25 Moses Escapes to Midian. 11–12: The influence of those early years draws Moses back to visit his people. His keen sense of justice leads him to an ill-advised action. **13–15:** Moses comes to the unhappy realization that he does not have the support

ing. "Why are you beating up your friend?" Moses said to the one who had started the fight.
[14]The man replied, "Who appointed you to be
our prince and judge? Are you going to kill me as
you killed that Egyptian yesterday?"
Then Moses was afraid, thinking, "Everyone
knows what I did." [15]And sure enough, Pharaoh
heard what had happened, and he tried to kill
Moses. But Moses fled from Pharaoh and went
to live in the land of Midian.
When Moses arrived in Midian, he sat down
beside a well. [16]Now the priest of Midian had
seven daughters who came as usual to draw water and fill the water troughs for their father's
flocks. [17]But some other shepherds came and
chased them away. So Moses jumped up and rescued the girls from the shepherds. Then he drew
water for their flocks.
[18]When the girls returned to Reuel, their father, he asked, "Why are you back so soon today?"
[19]"An Egyptian rescued us from the shepherds," they answered. "And then he drew water
for us and watered our flocks."
[20]"Then where is he?" their father asked.
"Why did you leave him there? Invite him to
come and eat with us."
[21]Moses accepted the invitation, and he settled there with him. In time, Reuel gave Moses
his daughter Zipporah to be his wife. [22]Later she
gave birth to a son, and Moses named him Gershom,* for he explained, "I have been a foreigner
in a foreign land."
[23]Years passed, and the king of Egypt died. But
the Israelites continued to groan under their burden of slavery. They cried out for help, and their
cry rose up to God. [24]God heard their groaning,
and he remembered his covenant promise to
Abraham, Isaac, and Jacob. [25]He looked down on
the people of Israel and knew it was time to act.*

Moses and the Burning Bush

3 One day Moses was tending the flock of his
father-in-law, Jethro,* the priest of Midian. He led the flock far into the wilderness
and came to Sinai,* the mountain of God. [2]There
the angel of the LORD appeared to him in a blazing fire from the middle of a bush. Moses stared
in amazement. Though the bush was engulfed
in flames, it didn't burn up. [3]"This is amazing,"
Moses said to himself. "Why isn't that bush
burning up? I must go see it."
[4]When the LORD saw Moses coming to take a
closer look, God called to him from the middle of
the bush, "Moses! Moses!"
"Here I am!" Moses replied.
[5]"Do not come any closer," the LORD warned.
"Take off your sandals, for you are standing on
holy ground. [6]I am the God of your father*—the
God of Abraham, the God of Isaac, and the God
of Jacob." When Moses heard this, he covered his
face because he was afraid to look at God.
[7]Then the LORD told him, "I have certainly seen the oppression of my people in Egypt. I
have heard their cries of distress because of their

2:22 *Gershom* sounds like a Hebrew term that means "a foreigner there." **2:25** Or *and acknowledged his obligation to help them.* **3:1a** Moses' father-in-law went by two names, Jethro and Reuel. **3:1b** Hebrew *Horeb,* another name for Sinai. **3:6** Greek version reads *your fathers.*

of the Hebrew community and that his rash effort at social reform has endangered his life. **16–17:** Again his sense of justice comes into play as he defends the rights of the seven women who do the hard work of drawing the water for the flocks. Sheep need large amounts of water; one-third of their body weight is water. The brigands profit daily from the labor of the young shepherdesses. **16:** It is not clear whether he was *priest* of a Midianite deity or whether, like the Gentiles Melchizedek and Balaam, he knew the God of Israel, but Reuel, also known as Jethro, is a marked influence in Moses' spiritual development. **18–20:** The sisters have violated hospitality by not inviting the stranger to their home, perhaps thinking that this travel-weary man, in disheveled Egyptian attire, had fallen into disfavor in his native land. The father welcomes Moses into the family and later accepts him as a son-in-law. **21:** In Numbers 12:1 we read that Moses' wife was a Cushite, a people associated with the modern area of the Sudan. There is considerable debate as to whether Zipporah was the same wife, but to this day inhabitants of the ancient area known as Midian are dark skinned. **25:** God's relationship to the covenant with Abraham, Isaac, and Jacob will be a recurring theme in the liberation of their descendants (cf. 6:8; 33:1).

3:1–4:31 Moses' Commissioning

3:1–22 Moses and the Burning Bush. 1–2: Exiled from the court of Egypt, Moses now herds animals. In the midst of his monotonous tasks, suddenly the presence of God breaks through, not in human form but in flaming fire. The Deity who has been more puzzle than reality has come to meet him. **6:** God is identified in the individual choices that each of the forefathers made to claim the LORD as their God. It is here at the burning bush that Moses must now make the choice for himself. **7:** Moses must have contemplated the plight of his fellow Hebrews in

harsh slave drivers. Yes, I am aware of their suffering. [8]So I have come down to rescue them from the power of the Egyptians and lead them out of Egypt into their own fertile and spacious land. It is a land flowing with milk and honey—the land where the Canaanites, Hittites, Amorites, Perizzites, Hivites, and Jebusites now live.
[9]Look! The cry of the people of Israel has reached me, and I have seen how harshly the Egyptians abuse them. [10]Now go, for I am sending you to Pharaoh. You must lead my people Israel out of Egypt."

[11]But Moses protested to God, "Who am I to appear before Pharaoh? Who am I to lead the people of Israel out of Egypt?"

[12]God answered, "I will be with you. And this is your sign that I am the one who has sent you: When you have brought the people out of Egypt, you will worship God at this very mountain."

[13]But Moses protested, "If I go to the people of Israel and tell them, 'The God of your ancestors has sent me to you,' they will ask me, 'What is his name?' Then what should I tell them?"

[14]God replied to Moses, "I AM WHO I AM.* Say this to the people of Israel: I AM has sent me to you." [15]God also said to Moses, "Say this to the people of Israel: Yahweh,* the God of your ancestors—the God of Abraham, the God of Isaac, and the God of Jacob—has sent me to you.

This is my eternal name,
  my name to remember for all generations.

[16]"Now go and call together all the elders of Israel. Tell them, 'The LORD, the God of your ancestors—the God of Abraham, Isaac, and Jacob—has appeared to me. He told me, "I have been watching closely, and I see how the Egyptians are treating you. [17]I have promised to rescue you from your oppression in Egypt. I will lead you to a land flowing with milk and honey—the land where the Canaanites, Hittites, Amorites, Perizzites, Hivites, and Jebusites now live." '

[18]"The elders of Israel will accept your message. Then you and the elders must go to the king of Egypt and tell him, 'The LORD, the God of the Hebrews, has met with us. So please let us take a three-day journey into the wilderness to offer sacrifices to the LORD, our God.'

[19]"But I know that the king of Egypt will not let you go unless a mighty hand forces him.*
[20]So I will raise my hand and strike the Egyptians, performing all kinds of miracles among them. Then at last he will let you go. [21]And I will cause the Egyptians to look favorably on you. They will give you gifts when you go so you will not leave empty-handed. [22]Every Israelite woman will ask for articles of silver and gold and fine clothing from her Egyptian neighbors and from the foreign women in their houses. You will dress your sons and daughters with these, stripping the Egyptians of their wealth."

Signs of the LORD's Power

4 But Moses protested again, "What if they won't believe me or listen to me? What if they say, 'The LORD never appeared to you'?"

[2]Then the LORD asked him, "What is that in your hand?"

"A shepherd's staff," Moses replied.

[3]"Throw it down on the ground," the LORD

3:14 Or *I WILL BE WHAT I WILL BE.* **3:15** *Yahweh* is a transliteration of the proper name *YHWH* that is sometimes rendered "Jehovah"; in this translation it is usually rendered "the LORD" (note the use of small capitals). **3:19** As in Greek and Latin versions; Hebrew reads *will not let you go, not by a mighty hand.*

Egypt and nursed a bitter frustration that he had been able to do nothing to help them. Now he is assured that God has seen and heard their afflictions. **10–11:** The promise of divine deliverance requires a human component that is to be supplied by the reluctant Moses. **12–14:** He is given a location where he will again worship God and a revelation of God's name. The name "I will be what I will be" (see translator's footnote) perhaps conveys "My nature will become evident from my actions." God's nature is shown by his remarkable acts. **16:** Moses' first act must be the recruitment of a leadership team to work at the highest levels. **17–19:** Other ethnic minorities in Egypt were granted the privilege of holding special religious observances in Egypt so that this petition is not out of line. But Pharaoh's hostility is too deep to grant such a request. Central to the story is that *the LORD, the God of the Hebrews, has met with us*. Moses and the people are developing an increased awareness of the reality of their ancient ancestral God and of his power to lead them into a new life. **22:** The women are to become the financiers of the Exodus (cf. 11:2; 35:25–29). Their relational skills with their neighbors will provide the necessary resources. God's work requires the gifts of human hands.

4:1–17 Signs of the LORD's Power. 1: Gone is the arrogant young man who assumed that he would be recognized as a leader of the Hebrews. Still smarting from the rejection, he must learn to trust in the power and protection of God. **2:** The question may be asked metaphorically as well as physically. The

told him. So Moses threw down the staff, and it
turned into a snake! Moses jumped back.
4 Then the LORD told him, "Reach out and
grab its tail." So Moses reached out and grabbed
it, and it turned back into a shepherd's staff in
his hand.
5 "Perform this sign," the LORD told him.
"Then they will believe that the LORD, the God
of their ancestors—the God of Abraham, the
God of Isaac, and the God of Jacob—really has
appeared to you."
6 Then the LORD said to Moses, "Now put
your hand inside your cloak." So Moses put his
hand inside his cloak, and when he took it out
again, his hand was white as snow with a severe
skin disease.* 7 "Now put your hand back into
your cloak," the LORD said. So Moses put his
hand back in, and when he took it out again, it
was as healthy as the rest of his body.
8 The LORD said to Moses, "If they do not
believe you and are not convinced by the first
miraculous sign, they will be convinced by the
second sign. 9 And if they don't believe you or listen to you even after these two signs, then take
some water from the Nile River and pour it out
on the dry ground. When you do, the water from
the Nile will turn to blood on the ground."
10 But Moses pleaded with the LORD, "O Lord,
I'm not very good with words. I never have been,
and I'm not now, even though you have spoken to
me. I get tongue-tied, and my words get tangled."
11 Then the LORD asked Moses, "Who makes
a person's mouth? Who decides whether people
speak or do not speak, hear or do not hear, see or
do not see? Is it not I, the LORD? 12 Now go! I will
be with you as you speak, and I will instruct you
in what to say."
13 But Moses again pleaded, "Lord, please!
Send anyone else."
14 Then the LORD became angry with Moses.
"All right," he said. "What about your brother,
Aaron the Levite? I know he speaks well. And
look! He is on his way to meet you now. He will
be delighted to see you. 15 Talk to him, and put
the words in his mouth. I will be with both of
you as you speak, and I will instruct you both
in what to do. 16 Aaron will be your spokesman
to the people. He will be your mouthpiece, and
you will stand in the place of God for him, telling him what to say. 17 And take your shepherd's
staff with you, and use it to perform the miraculous signs I have shown you."

Moses Returns to Egypt

18 So Moses went back home to Jethro, his father-
in-law. "Please let me return to my relatives in
Egypt," Moses said. "I don't even know if they
are still alive."
"Go in peace," Jethro replied.
19 Before Moses left Midian, the LORD said to
him, "Return to Egypt, for all those who wanted
to kill you have died."
20 So Moses took his wife and sons, put them
on a donkey, and headed back to the land of
Egypt. In his hand he carried the staff of God.

4:6 Or *with leprosy.* The Hebrew word used here can describe various skin diseases.

---

promising young prince has been reduced to the status of a sheepherder, and he holds only the lowly implement of his trade. God reveals within Moses' staff the potential for leadership and for all the greatness of his soul. Moses must be willing to loose what he holds and to entrust it to God's use. **5:** The overarching theme of the next seven chapters will be the reality of God's character and being. At each point of decision, doubt, or danger, there will be a renewal of this affirmation (3:6, 15, 16; 4:5; 6:2–8). **6:** The next sign lies far closer to Moses' person. The hand placed within his garment comes forth discolored and covered with infection. Bodily health and illness both lie within God's power. In view of the massive health legislation in the Mosaic code, the lesson is an important one. **8–9:** The Nile was the great life-giver of Egypt, irrigating the land each year and bringing fresh topsoil. The ensuing fertility promoted the prosperity and brilliant civilization of the ancient world's mightiest power. The third sign will demonstrate the power of God over the deities and political power of Egypt. **10:** Perhaps Moses suffered from shyness or a speech defect. It is also possible that his command of the Hebrew language was only what he had learned in his home during infancy. He may well have lacked the facility to discuss political and social issues with a slave people struggling to find both their identity and their liberty. **11:** It is God who rules over human communication and God who sends his messages through human instrumentality. **13–14:** Like many of the rest of us, Moses is a slow learner. Nevertheless, God's exasperation will lead to a gracious provision. Aaron will alleviate the loneliness of Moses' task and serve as an able communicator. While Moses has lived with sheep and his own thoughts in the desert, Aaron has been with the people of Israel.

4:18–31 Moses Returns to Egypt. 18–19: Jethro, Moses' father-in-law and Midianite priest, continues to be an important influence in the life and spiritual development of Moses (Jethro is named Reuel in

[21]And the LORD told Moses, "When you arrive back in Egypt, go to Pharaoh and perform all the miracles I have empowered you to do. But I will harden his heart so he will refuse to let the people go. [22]Then you will tell him, 'This is what the LORD says: Israel is my firstborn son. [23]I commanded you, "Let my son go, so he can worship me." But since you have refused, I will now kill your firstborn son!' "

[24]On the way to Egypt, at a place where Moses and his family had stopped for the night, the LORD confronted him and was about to kill him. [25]But Moses' wife, Zipporah, took a flint knife and circumcised her son. She touched his feet* with the foreskin and said, "Now you are a bridegroom of blood to me." [26](When she said "a bridegroom of blood," she was referring to the circumcision.) After that, the LORD left him alone.

[27]Now the LORD had said to Aaron, "Go out into the wilderness to meet Moses." So Aaron went and met Moses at the mountain of God, and he embraced him. [28]Moses then told Aaron everything the LORD had commanded him to say. And he told him about the miraculous signs the LORD had commanded him to perform.

[29]Then Moses and Aaron returned to Egypt and called all the elders of Israel together. [30]Aaron told them everything the LORD had told Moses, and Moses performed the miraculous signs as they watched. [31]Then the people of Israel were convinced that the LORD had sent Moses and Aaron. When they heard that the LORD was concerned about them and had seen their misery, they bowed down and worshiped.

Moses and Aaron Speak to Pharaoh

5 After this presentation to Israel's leaders, Moses and Aaron went and spoke to Pharaoh. They told him, "This is what the LORD, the God of Israel, says: Let my people go so they may hold a festival in my honor in the wilderness."

[2]"Is that so?" retorted Pharaoh. "And who is the LORD? Why should I listen to him and let Israel go? I don't know the LORD, and I will not let Israel go."

[3]But Aaron and Moses persisted. "The God of the Hebrews has met with us," they declared. "So let us take a three-day journey into the wilderness so we can offer sacrifices to the LORD our God. If we don't, he will kill us with a plague or with the sword."

[4]Pharaoh replied, "Moses and Aaron, why are you distracting the people from their tasks? Get back to work! [5]Look, there are many of your people in the land, and you are stopping them from their work."

Making Bricks without Straw

[6]That same day Pharaoh sent this order to the Egyptian slave drivers and the Israelite foremen: [7]"Do not supply any more straw for making bricks. Make the people get it themselves! [8]But still require them to make the same number of bricks as before. Don't reduce the quota. They are lazy. That's why they are crying out, 'Let us go and offer sacrifices to our God.' [9]Load them

4:25 The Hebrew word for "feet" may refer here to the male sex organ.

2:16–22; Jethro here and at 3:1 and 18:1; see also annotation on Num 10:29.) **21:** The stubbornness of Pharaoh is a personal attitude of his own choosing. He will be given repeated evidences of the reality of the LORD, and each rejection will serve only to increase his resistance. What might have created opportunities for faith will instead produce defiance. **24–25:** Zipporah, daughter of a priest, exercises spiritual perception. Some ancient rabbis found it impossible to accept that she should have performed the circumcision, insisting that she passed the knife to her husband. The text is clear however that she herself performs the ritual act and throws the foreskin at Moses' feet (perhaps a euphemism for his genitals). A number of early commentators held that it was an angel who encountered Moses on his journey (cf. Num 22:21–35). **27–31:** The meeting with Aaron leads to a meeting with the leaders who are challenged to accept the reality and message of Yahweh, the ancestral God who had apparently been forgotten. The response to this renewed knowledge is worship.

5:1—10:29 The Contest between God and Pharaoh

5:1–5 Moses and Aaron Speak to Pharaoh. 2: Pharaoh cares little that he is confronted with a direct message from the Hebrew God. He was himself viewed as a deity, and perhaps even saw himself in that way. Furthermore, a three-day vacation for his slave labor force would seriously disrupt his building program.

5:6–23 Making Bricks without Straw. 6–9: This passage, with its verbal and physical abuse, vividly depicts the vicious and despotic character of Pharaoh. **7:** The straw strengthened the bricks. **19:** Pharaoh's

down with more work. Make them sweat! That will teach them to listen to lies!"

10 So the slave drivers and foremen went out and told the people: "This is what Pharaoh says: I will not provide any more straw for you. 11 Go and get it yourselves. Find it wherever you can. But you must produce just as many bricks as before!" 12 So the people scattered throughout the land of Egypt in search of stubble to use as straw.

13 Meanwhile, the Egyptian slave drivers continued to push hard. "Meet your daily quota of bricks, just as you did when we provided you with straw!" they demanded. 14 Then they whipped the Israelite foremen they had put in charge of the work crews. "Why haven't you met your quotas either yesterday or today?" they demanded.

15 So the Israelite foremen went to Pharaoh and pleaded with him. "Please don't treat your servants like this," they begged. 16 "We are given no straw, but the slave drivers still demand, 'Make bricks!' We are being beaten, but it isn't our fault! Your own people are to blame!"

17 But Pharaoh shouted, "You're just lazy! Lazy! That's why you're saying, 'Let us go and offer sacrifices to the LORD.' 18 Now get back to work! No straw will be given to you, but you must still produce the full quota of bricks."

19 The Israelite foremen could see that they were in serious trouble when they were told, "You must not reduce the number of bricks you make each day." 20 As they left Pharaoh's court, they confronted Moses and Aaron, who were waiting outside for them. 21 The foremen said to them, "May the LORD judge and punish you for making us stink before Pharaoh and his officials. You have put a sword into their hands, an excuse to kill us!"

22 Then Moses went back to the LORD and protested, "Why have you brought all this trouble on your own people, Lord? Why did you send me? 23 Ever since I came to Pharaoh as your spokesman, he has been even more brutal to your people. And you have done nothing to rescue them!"

Promises of Deliverance

6 Then the LORD told Moses, "Now you will see what I will do to Pharaoh. When he feels the force of my strong hand, he will let the people go. In fact, he will force them to leave his land!"

2 And God said to Moses, "I am Yahweh—'the LORD.'* 3 I appeared to Abraham, to Isaac, and to Jacob as El-Shaddai—'God Almighty'*—but I did not reveal my name, Yahweh, to them. 4 And I reaffirmed my covenant with them. Under its terms, I promised to give them the land of Canaan, where they were living as foreigners. 5 You can be sure that I have heard the groans of the people of Israel, who are now slaves to the Egyptians. And I am well aware of my covenant with them.

6 "Therefore, say to the people of Israel: 'I am the LORD. I will free you from your oppression and will rescue you from your slavery in Egypt. I will redeem you with a powerful arm and great acts of judgment. 7 I will claim you as my own people, and I will be your God. Then you will know that I am the LORD your God who has freed you from your oppression in Egypt. 8 I will bring you into the land I swore to give to Abraham, Isaac, and Jacob. I will give it to you as your very own possession. I am the LORD!' "

9 So Moses told the people of Israel what the LORD had said, but they refused to listen anymore. They had become too discouraged by the brutality of their slavery.

10 Then the LORD said to Moses, 11 "Go back

6:2 *Yahweh* is a transliteration of the proper name *YHWH* that is sometimes rendered "Jehovah"; in this translation it is usually rendered "the LORD" (note the use of small capitals). **6:3** *El-Shaddai,* which means "God Almighty," is the name for God used in Gen 17:1; 28:3; 35:11; 43:14; 48:3.

---

resistance to Moses' demand has created an intolerable situation. Those who previously accepted his leadership now condemn Moses as a political activist and rabble rouser.

6:1–30 Promises of Deliverance. 1: The contest between God and Pharaoh now begins, and a definitive resolution is promised. **2:** *I am the LORD* becomes a recurring affirmation (vv. 6, 7, 8, 29; 3:14–15; 7:5, 17; 8:22; 10:2; 12:12; 14:4, 18; 16:12). **3:** God presents himself as he has done at every juncture since Moses first met him at the burning bush. Again God declares his relationship with the patriarchs (cf. 3:6, 15, 16; 4:5; 6:8), but this time he states that to Moses only has the divine name been revealed. The fact that earlier passages do use the name YHWH (LORD) could mean that this is anachronistic and they were written at a later time, or it could mean that it was the meaning of a known name that was revealed to Moses. **7–8:** Here is an early introduction of the concept of a covenant between God and these people. Not only is there a promise of a special relationship but also of a special dwelling place. **9:** Despite the renewed promises of God, discouragement has become a terrible deterrent to faith. **10–11:** Although they no longer have popular support, Moses and

to Pharaoh, the king of Egypt, and tell him to let
the people of Israel leave his country."
12 "But LORD!" Moses objected. "My own
people won't listen to me anymore. How can I
expect Pharaoh to listen? I'm such a clumsy
speaker!*"
13 But the LORD spoke to Moses and Aaron
and gave them orders for the Israelites and for
Pharaoh, the king of Egypt. The LORD commanded Moses and Aaron to lead the people of Israel
out of Egypt.

The Ancestors of Moses and Aaron

14 These are the ancestors of some of the clans of
Israel:

The sons of Reuben, Israel's oldest son, were
Hanoch, Pallu, Hezron, and Carmi. Their
descendants became the clans of Reuben.
15 The sons of Simeon were Jemuel, Jamin,
Ohad, Jakin, Zohar, and Shaul. (Shaul's
mother was a Canaanite woman.) Their
descendants became the clans of Simeon.
16 These are the descendants of Levi, as listed in
their family records: The sons of Levi were
Gershon, Kohath, and Merari. (Levi lived to
be 137 years old.)
17 The descendants of Gershon included
Libni and Shimei, each of whom became the
ancestor of a clan.
18 The descendants of Kohath included
Amram, Izhar, Hebron, and Uzziel. (Kohath
lived to be 133 years old.)
19 The descendants of Merari included
Mahli and Mushi.

These are the clans of the Levites, as listed in
their family records.

20 Amram married his father's sister Jochebed,
and she gave birth to his sons, Aaron and
Moses. (Amram lived to be 137 years old.)
21 The sons of Izhar were Korah, Nepheg, and
Zicri.
22 The sons of Uzziel were Mishael, Elzaphan,
and Sithri.
23 Aaron married Elisheba, the daughter of
Amminadab and sister of Nahshon, and she
gave birth to his sons, Nadab, Abihu, Eleazar,
and Ithamar.
24 The sons of Korah were Assir, Elkanah, and
Abiasaph. Their descendants became the clans
of Korah.
25 Eleazar son of Aaron married one of the
daughters of Putiel, and she gave birth to his
son, Phinehas.
These are the ancestors of the Levite families,
listed according to their clans.

26 The Aaron and Moses named in this list are
the same ones to whom the LORD said, "Lead the
people of Israel out of the land of Egypt like an
army." 27 It was Moses and Aaron who spoke to
Pharaoh, the king of Egypt, about leading the
people of Israel out of Egypt.
28 When the LORD spoke to Moses in the land
of Egypt, 29 he said to him, "I am the LORD! Tell
Pharaoh, the king of Egypt, everything I am telling you." 30 But Moses argued with the LORD,
saying, "I can't do it! I'm such a clumsy speaker!
Why should Pharaoh listen to me?"

Aaron's Staff Becomes a Serpent

7 Then the LORD said to Moses, "Pay close
attention to this. I will make you seem like
God to Pharaoh, and your brother, Aaron,
will be your prophet. 2 Tell Aaron everything I
command you, and Aaron must command Pharaoh to let the people of Israel leave his country.
3 But I will make Pharaoh's heart stubborn so I
can multiply my miraculous signs and wonders
in the land of Egypt. 4 Even then Pharaoh will refuse to listen to you. So I will bring down my
fist on Egypt. Then I will rescue my forces—my
people, the Israelites—from the land of Egypt
with great acts of judgment. 5 When I raise my
powerful hand and bring out the Israelites, the
Egyptians will know that I am the LORD."
6 So Moses and Aaron did just as the LORD
had commanded them. 7 Moses was eighty years

6:12 Hebrew *I have uncircumcised lips;* also in 6:30.

Aaron are required to carry on their dangerous mission. Moses' discomfort is heightened by his inability to express himself convincingly in the language of Egypt's royal court (also at v. 30). **14:** The repeated insistence upon the God who had been known to the ancestors is now paralleled with a genealogy of faith. **20–28:** Here the Levitical parentage of Moses and Aaron is detailed and a review given of their own efforts on behalf of the people.

7:1–13 Aaron's Staff Becomes a Serpent. 1–4: The contest will now involve Aaron as a major player, while God's use of marvels will only heighten the resistance of Pharaoh. **5:** A main objective of this great drama is that both Israelites and Egyptians should come to know that the LORD is God (6:7; 7:17; 8:10, 22; 9:14, 29; 10:2; 11:7; 14:4, 18; 16:6, 12; 29:46). **6–7:** Other octogenarians used by God include Daniel, who served as prime minister for more than fifty years, and

old, and Aaron was eighty-three when they made their demands to Pharaoh.

8 Then the LORD said to Moses and Aaron, 9 "Pharaoh will demand, 'Show me a miracle.' When he does this, say to Aaron, 'Take your staff and throw it down in front of Pharaoh, and it will become a serpent.*' "

10 So Moses and Aaron went to Pharaoh and did what the LORD had commanded them. Aaron threw down his staff before Pharaoh and his officials, and it became a serpent! 11 Then Pharaoh called in his own wise men and sorcerers, and these Egyptian magicians did the same thing with their magic. 12 They threw down their staffs, which also became serpents! But then Aaron's staff swallowed up their staffs. 13 Pharaoh's heart, however, remained hard. He still refused to listen, just as the LORD had predicted.

A Plague of Blood

14 Then the LORD said to Moses, "Pharaoh's heart is stubborn,* and he still refuses to let the people go. 15 So go to Pharaoh in the morning as he goes down to the river. Stand on the bank of the Nile and meet him there. Be sure to take along the staff that turned into a snake. 16 Then announce to him, 'The LORD, the God of the Hebrews, has sent me to tell you, "Let my people go, so they can worship me in the wilderness." Until now, you have refused to listen to him. 17 So this is what the LORD says: "I will show you that I am the LORD." Look! I will strike the water of the Nile with this staff in my hand, and the river will turn to blood. 18 The fish in it will die, and the river will stink. The Egyptians will not be able to drink any water from the Nile.' "

19 Then the LORD said to Moses: "Tell Aaron, 'Take your staff and raise your hand over the waters of Egypt—all its rivers, canals, ponds, and all the reservoirs. Turn all the water to blood. Everywhere in Egypt the water will turn to blood, even the water stored in wooden bowls and stone pots.' "

20 So Moses and Aaron did just as the LORD commanded them. As Pharaoh and all of his officials watched, Aaron raised his staff and struck the water of the Nile. Suddenly, the whole river turned to blood! 21 The fish in the river died, and the water became so foul that the Egyptians couldn't drink it. There was blood everywhere throughout the land of Egypt. 22 But again the magicians of Egypt used their magic, and they, too, turned water into blood. So Pharaoh's heart remained hard. He refused to listen to Moses and Aaron, just as the LORD had predicted. 23 Pharaoh returned to his palace and put the whole thing out of his mind. 24 Then all the Egyptians dug along the riverbank to find drinking water, for they couldn't drink the water from the Nile. 25 Seven days passed from the time the LORD struck the Nile.

A Plague of Frogs

8 1 *Then the LORD said to Moses, "Go back to Pharaoh and announce to him, 'This is what the LORD says: Let my people go, so they can worship me. 2 If you refuse to let them go, I will send a plague of frogs across your entire land. 3 The Nile River will swarm with frogs. They will come up out of the river and into your palace, even into your bedroom and onto your bed! They will enter the houses of your officials and your people. They will even jump into your ovens and your kneading bowls. 4 Frogs will jump on you, your people, and all your officials.' "

5 *Then the LORD said to Moses, "Tell Aaron, 'Raise the staff in your hand over all the rivers, canals, and ponds of Egypt, and bring up frogs over all the land.' " 6 So Aaron raised his hand over the waters of Egypt, and frogs came up and covered the whole land! 7 But the magicians were able to do the same thing with their magic. They, too, caused frogs to come up on the land of Egypt.

7:9 Hebrew *tannin*, which elsewhere refers to a sea monster. Greek version translates it "dragon." **7:14** Hebrew *heavy.*
8:1 Verses 8:1-4 are numbered 7:26-29 in Hebrew text.
8:5 Verses 8:5-32 are numbered 8:1-28 in Hebrew text.

the prophet Anna (Luke 2:36–38). **8:** The sign previously given to Moses is now also bestowed on Aaron. The court magicians are able to duplicate the effect, perhaps with the use of charmed snakes that remain stiff until thrown down, a trick still practiced in India.

7:14–25 A Plague of Blood. 17–19: The pollution of the sacred Nile—Egypt's major waterway—is a severe blow to human health and agriculture. To this day the people drink its waters, use it for washing, and depend on its fertile flow. The reddish color may have been produced by algae from farther south or from dust blowing into Egypt from the volcanic eruption of Thera (Santorini). **22:** Contaminated water is always a danger, and the work of the magicians only worsens the danger.

8:1–32 Plagues of Frogs, Gnats, and Flies. 6: The frogs fled the polluted river and infested the land. Some of the plagues would bring particular hardship to women: lack of water for drinking, cooking, and washing; frogs throughout the house; flies; health

8 Then Pharaoh summoned Moses and Aaron and begged, "Plead with the LORD to take the frogs away from me and my people. I will let your people go, so they can offer sacrifices to the LORD."

9 "You set the time!" Moses replied. "Tell me when you want me to pray for you, your officials, and your people. Then you and your houses will be rid of the frogs. They will remain only in the Nile River."

10 "Do it tomorrow," Pharaoh said.

"All right," Moses replied, "it will be as you have said. Then you will know that there is no one like the LORD our God. 11 The frogs will leave you and your houses, your officials, and your people. They will remain only in the Nile River."

12 So Moses and Aaron left Pharaoh's palace, and Moses cried out to the LORD about the frogs he had inflicted on Pharaoh. 13 And the LORD did just what Moses had predicted. The frogs in the houses, the courtyards, and the fields all died. 14 The Egyptians piled them into great heaps, and a terrible stench filled the land. 15 But when Pharaoh saw that relief had come, he became stubborn.* He refused to listen to Moses and Aaron, just as the LORD had predicted.

A Plague of Gnats

16 So the LORD said to Moses, "Tell Aaron, 'Raise your staff and strike the ground. The dust will turn into swarms of gnats throughout the land of Egypt.' " 17 So Moses and Aaron did just as the LORD had commanded them. When Aaron raised his hand and struck the ground with his staff, gnats infested the entire land, covering the Egyptians and their animals. All the dust in the land of Egypt turned into gnats. 18 Pharaoh's magicians tried to do the same thing with their secret arts, but this time they failed. And the gnats covered everyone, people and animals alike.

19 "This is the finger of God!" the magicians exclaimed to Pharaoh. But Pharaoh's heart remained hard. He wouldn't listen to them, just as the LORD had predicted.

A Plague of Flies

20 Then the LORD told Moses, "Get up early in the morning and stand in Pharaoh's way as he goes down to the river. Say to him, 'This is what the LORD says: Let my people go, so they can worship me. 21 If you refuse, then I will send swarms of flies on you, your officials, your people, and all the houses. The Egyptian homes will be filled with flies, and the ground will be covered with them. 22 But this time I will spare the region of Goshen, where my people live. No flies will be found there. Then you will know that I am the LORD and that I am present even in the heart of your land. 23 I will make a clear distinction between* my people and your people. This miraculous sign will happen tomorrow.' "

24 And the LORD did just as he had said. A thick swarm of flies filled Pharaoh's palace and the houses of his officials. The whole land of Egypt was thrown into chaos by the flies.

25 Pharaoh called for Moses and Aaron. "All right! Go ahead and offer sacrifices to your God," he said. "But do it here in this land."

26 But Moses replied, "That wouldn't be right. The Egyptians detest the sacrifices that we offer to the LORD our God. Look, if we offer our sacrifices here where the Egyptians can see us, they will stone us. 27 We must take a three-day trip into the wilderness to offer sacrifices to the LORD our God, just as he has commanded us."

28 "All right, go ahead," Pharaoh replied. "I will let you go into the wilderness to offer sacrifices to the LORD your God. But don't go too far away. Now hurry and pray for me."

29 Moses answered, "As soon as I leave you, I will pray to the LORD, and tomorrow the swarms of flies will disappear from you and your officials and all your people. But I am warning you, Pharaoh, don't lie to us again and refuse to let the people go to sacrifice to the LORD."

30 So Moses left Pharaoh's palace and pleaded with the LORD to remove all the flies. 31 And the LORD did as Moses asked and caused the swarms of flies to disappear from Pharaoh, his officials, and his people. Not a single fly remained. 32 But Pharaoh again became stubborn and refused to let the people go.

8:15 Hebrew *made his heart heavy;* also in 8:32. **8:23** As in Greek and Latin versions; Hebrew reads *I will set redemption between.*

issues; and above all the loss of their precious firstborn. **9:** The precise timing of the removal of the frogs was intended to lead the Egyptians to believe in the reality of the God whom Moses proclaimed. **23:** The distinction between *my people and your people* constitutes not only a sign of God's power but also a concern to spare the innocent Israelites from the afflictions that fall upon those who refuse to acknowledge God and his will. Goshen was the area of Egypt that had been assigned as the habitation of the Hebrews when Joseph was prime minister (Gen 47:5–6, 27).

A Plague against Livestock

9 "Go back to Pharaoh," the LORD commanded Moses. "Tell him, 'This is what the LORD, the God of the Hebrews, says: Let my people go, so they can worship me. 2 If you continue to hold them and refuse to let them go, 3 the hand of the LORD will strike all your livestock—your horses, donkeys, camels, cattle, sheep, and goats—with a deadly plague. 4 But the LORD will again make a distinction between the livestock of the Israelites and that of the Egyptians. Not a single one of Israel's animals will die! 5 The LORD has already set the time for the plague to begin. He has declared that he will strike the land tomorrow.' "

6 And the LORD did just as he had said. The next morning all the livestock of the Egyptians died, but the Israelites didn't lose a single animal. 7 Pharaoh sent his officials to investigate, and they discovered that the Israelites had not lost a single animal! But even so, Pharaoh's heart remained stubborn,* and he still refused to let the people go.

A Plague of Festering Boils

8 Then the LORD said to Moses and Aaron, "Take handfuls of soot from a brick kiln, and have Moses toss it into the air while Pharaoh watches. 9 The ashes will spread like fine dust over the whole land of Egypt, causing festering boils to break out on people and animals throughout the land."

10 So they took soot from a brick kiln and went and stood before Pharaoh. As Pharaoh watched, Moses threw the soot into the air, and boils broke out on people and animals alike. 11 Even the magicians were unable to stand before Moses, because the boils had broken out on them and all the Egyptians. 12 But the LORD hardened Pharaoh's heart, and just as the LORD had predicted to Moses, Pharaoh refused to listen.

A Plague of Hail

13 Then the LORD said to Moses, "Get up early in the morning and stand before Pharaoh. Tell him, 'This is what the LORD, the God of the Hebrews, says: Let my people go, so they can worship me. 14 If you don't, I will send more plagues on you* and your officials and your people. Then you will know that there is no one like me in all the earth. 15 By now I could have lifted my hand and struck you and your people with a plague to wipe you off the face of the earth. 16 But I have spared you for a purpose—to show you my power* and to spread my fame throughout the earth. 17 But you still lord it over my people and refuse to let them go. 18 So tomorrow at this time I will send a hailstorm more devastating than any in all the history of Egypt. 19 Quick! Order your livestock and servants to come in from the fields to find shelter. Any person or animal left outside will die when the hail falls.' "

20 Some of Pharaoh's officials were afraid because of what the LORD had said. They quickly brought their servants and livestock in from the fields. 21 But those who paid no attention to the word of the LORD left theirs out in the open.

22 Then the LORD said to Moses, "Lift your hand toward the sky so hail may fall on the people, the livestock, and all the plants throughout the land of Egypt."

23 So Moses lifted his staff toward the sky, and the LORD sent thunder and hail, and lightning flashed toward the earth. The LORD sent a tremendous hailstorm against all the land of Egypt. 24 Never in all the history of Egypt had there been a storm like that, with such devastating hail and continuous lightning. 25 It left all of Egypt in ruins. The hail struck down everything in the open field—people, animals, and plants alike. Even the trees were destroyed. 26 The only place without hail was the region of Goshen, where the people of Israel lived.

27 Then Pharaoh quickly summoned Moses and Aaron. "This time I have sinned," he confessed. "The LORD is the righteous one, and my people and I are wrong. 28 Please beg the LORD to end this terrifying thunder and hail. We've had enough. I will let you go; you don't need to stay any longer."

9:7 Hebrew *heavy.* **9:14** Hebrew *on your heart.* **9:16** Greek version reads *to display my power in you;* compare Rom 9:17.

9:1–35 Plagues of Animal Disease, Boils, and Hail. 6: The plague was perhaps anthrax. **10:** Again the women must deal not only with their own discomfort but with the misery of their children. **16:** God's purpose has not been to slay the Egyptians but to give them an understanding of the true and living God. The multiplicity of Egyptian gods may have made it exceedingly hard to grasp the concept of a sole Almighty God. **17:** Pharaoh's despotic reign will soon reap its own reward. His cabinet, the nobles in the court, have joined in the resistance to Moses' message (vv. 14, 34; 10:1; 14:5). **20–21:** The warnings of Moses are gaining credence, especially with the officials who previously had rejected them. **27:** Pharaoh concedes that he is the loser in the contest with the LORD, whose power and reality he now acknowl-

29 "All right," Moses replied. "As soon as I leave the city, I will lift my hands and pray to the LORD. Then the thunder and hail will stop, and you will know that the earth belongs to the LORD. 30 But I know that you and your officials still do not fear the LORD God."

31 (All the flax and barley were ruined by the hail, because the barley had formed heads and the flax was budding. 32 But the wheat and the emmer wheat were spared, because they had not yet sprouted from the ground.)

33 So Moses left Pharaoh's court and went out of the city. When he lifted his hands to the LORD, the thunder and hail stopped, and the downpour ceased. 34 But when Pharaoh saw that the rain, hail, and thunder had stopped, he and his officials sinned again, and Pharaoh again became stubborn.* 35 Because his heart was hard, Pharaoh refused to let the people leave, just as the LORD had predicted through Moses.

A Plague of Locusts

10 Then the LORD said to Moses, "Return to Pharaoh and make your demands again. I have made him and his officials stubborn* so I can display my miraculous signs among them. 2 I've also done it so you can tell your children and grandchildren about how I made a mockery of the Egyptians and about the signs I displayed among them—and so you will know that I am the LORD."

3 So Moses and Aaron went to Pharaoh and said, "This is what the LORD, the God of the Hebrews, says: How long will you refuse to submit to me? Let my people go, so they can worship me. 4 If you refuse, watch out! For tomorrow I will bring a swarm of locusts on your country. 5 They will cover the land so that you won't be able to see the ground. They will devour what little is left of your crops after the hailstorm, including all the trees growing in the fields. 6 They will overrun your palaces and the homes of your officials and all the houses in Egypt. Never in the history of Egypt have your ancestors seen a plague like this one!" And with that, Moses turned and left Pharaoh.

7 Pharaoh's officials now came to Pharaoh and appealed to him. "How long will you let this man hold us hostage? Let the men go to worship the LORD their God! Don't you realize that Egypt lies in ruins?"

8 So Moses and Aaron were brought back to Pharaoh. "All right," he told them, "go and worship the LORD your God. But who exactly will be going with you?"

9 Moses replied, "We will all go—young and old, our sons and daughters, and our flocks and herds. We must all join together in celebrating a festival to the LORD."

10 Pharaoh retorted, "The LORD will certainly need to be with you if I let you take your little ones! I can see through your evil plan. 11 Never! Only the men may go and worship the LORD, since that is what you requested." And Pharaoh threw them out of the palace.

12 Then the LORD said to Moses, "Raise your hand over the land of Egypt to bring on the locusts. Let them cover the land and devour every plant that survived the hailstorm."

13 So Moses raised his staff over Egypt, and the LORD caused an east wind to blow over the land all that day and through the night. When morning arrived, the east wind had brought the locusts. 14 And the locusts swarmed over the whole land of Egypt, settling in dense swarms from one end of the country to the other. It was the worst locust plague in Egyptian history, and there has never been another one like it. 15 For the locusts covered the whole country and darkened the land. They devoured every plant in the fields and all the fruit on the trees that had survived the hailstorm. Not a single leaf was left on the trees and plants throughout the land of Egypt.

16 Pharaoh quickly summoned Moses and Aaron. "I have sinned against the LORD your God and against you," he confessed. 17 "Forgive my sin, just this once, and plead with the LORD your God to take away this death from me."

18 So Moses left Pharaoh's court and pleaded with the LORD. 19 The LORD responded by shifting the wind, and the strong west wind blew the locusts into the Red Sea.* Not a single locust re-

9:34 Hebrew *made his heart heavy.* **10:1** Hebrew *have made his heart and his officials' hearts heavy.* **10:19** Hebrew *sea of reeds.*

edges. (For other concessions, see 10:16, 24; 12:31.) **29:** The knowledge includes understanding that God, rather than a series of Egyptian deities, controls the earth. Egyptian gods were represented as insects, reptiles, fish, and four-footed creatures. Against these is the God whose power controls them.

10:1–29 Plagues of Locusts and Darkness. 13–14: Infestations of locusts are not unknown in the Middle East. It is the remarkable timing of one catastrophic event after another that becomes a sign. **25:** The dispute over the proposed worship opportunity progresses in stages. First, Pharaoh totally forbids the en-

mained in all the land of Egypt. [20]But the LORD hardened Pharaoh's heart again, so he refused to let the people go.

A Plague of Darkness

[21]Then the LORD said to Moses, "Lift your hand toward heaven, and the land of Egypt will be covered with a darkness so thick you can feel it." [22]So Moses lifted his hand to the sky, and a deep darkness covered the entire land of Egypt for three days. [23]During all that time the people could not see each other, and no one moved. But there was light as usual where the people of Israel lived.

[24]Finally, Pharaoh called for Moses. "Go and worship the LORD," he said. "But leave your flocks and herds here. You may even take your little ones with you."

[25]"No," Moses said, "you must provide us with animals for sacrifices and burnt offerings to the LORD our God. [26]All our livestock must go with us, too; not a hoof can be left behind. We must choose our sacrifices for the LORD our God from among these animals. And we won't know how we are to worship the LORD until we get there."

[27]But the LORD hardened Pharaoh's heart once more, and he would not let them go. [28]"Get out of here!" Pharaoh shouted at Moses. "I'm warning you. Never come back to see me again! The day you see my face, you will die!"

[29]"Very well," Moses replied. "I will never see your face again."

Death for Egypt's Firstborn

11 Then the LORD said to Moses, "I will strike Pharaoh and the land of Egypt with one more blow. After that, Pharaoh will let you leave this country. In fact, he will be so eager to get rid of you that he will force you all to leave. [2]Tell all the Israelite men and women to ask their Egyptian neighbors for articles of silver and gold." [3](Now the LORD had caused the Egyptians to look favorably on the people of Israel. And Moses was considered a very great man in the land of Egypt, respected by Pharaoh's officials and the Egyptian people alike.)

[4]Moses had announced to Pharaoh, "This is what the LORD says: At midnight tonight I will pass through the heart of Egypt. [5]All the firstborn sons will die in every family in Egypt, from the oldest son of Pharaoh, who sits on his throne, to the oldest son of his lowliest servant girl who grinds the flour. Even the firstborn of all the livestock will die. [6]Then a loud wail will rise throughout the land of Egypt, a wail like no one has heard before or will ever hear again. [7]But among the Israelites it will be so peaceful that not even a dog will bark. Then you will know that the LORD makes a distinction between the Egyptians and the Israelites. [8]All the officials of Egypt will run to me and fall to the ground before me. 'Please leave!' they will beg. 'Hurry! And take all your followers with you.' Only then will I go!" Then, burning with anger, Moses left Pharaoh.

[9]Now the LORD had told Moses earlier, "Pharaoh will not listen to you, but then I will do even more mighty miracles in the land of Egypt." [10]Moses and Aaron performed these miracles in Pharaoh's presence, but the LORD hardened Pharaoh's heart, and he wouldn't let the Israelites leave the country.

The First Passover

12 While the Israelites were still in the land of Egypt, the LORD gave the following instructions to Moses and Aaron: [2]"From now on, this month will be the first month of the year for you. [3]Announce to the whole community of Israel that on the tenth day of this month each family must choose a lamb or a young goat for a sacrifice, one animal for each household. [4]If a family is too small to eat a whole animal, let them share with another family in the neighborhood. Divide the animal according to the size of each family and how much they can eat. [5]The animal you select must be a one-year-old male, either a sheep or a goat, with no defects.

[6]"Take special care of this chosen animal un-

---

terprise, then agrees that the event may go forward if it is not too far removed (9:28); if the children are not included (10:8–11); if they do not bring their property (9:24). Moses insists that true worship will require the totality of their existence.

11:1—14:31 Deliverance from Egypt

11:1–10 Death for Egypt's Firstborn. 2: Some translate this text as the requirement that the men should ask for what they might be able to get, while the women were specifically to ask for gold and silver (cf. 3:21–22). **3:** Throughout the succession of plagues, there has been a rising recognition of God's power and of the stature of Moses as leader of the Hebrew people (8:19; 9:20–21; 10:7–8).

12:1–30 The First Passover. 1–5: The ritual meal is

til the evening of the fourteenth day of this first month. Then the whole assembly of the community of Israel must slaughter their lamb or young goat at twilight. [7]They are to take some of the blood and smear it on the sides and top of the doorframes of the houses where they eat the animal. [8]That same night they must roast the meat over a fire and eat it along with bitter salad greens and bread made without yeast. [9]Do not eat any of the meat raw or boiled in water. The whole animal—including the head, legs, and internal organs—must be roasted over a fire. [10]Do not leave any of it until the next morning. Burn whatever is not eaten before morning.

[11]"These are your instructions for eating this meal: Be fully dressed,* wear your sandals, and carry your walking stick in your hand. Eat the meal with urgency, for this is the LORD's Passover. [12]On that night I will pass through the land of Egypt and strike down every firstborn son and firstborn male animal in the land of Egypt. I will execute judgment against all the gods of Egypt, for I am the LORD! [13]But the blood on your doorposts will serve as a sign, marking the houses where you are staying. When I see the blood, I will pass over you. This plague of death will not touch you when I strike the land of Egypt.

[14]"This is a day to remember. Each year, from generation to generation, you must celebrate it as a special festival to the LORD. This is a law for all time. [15]For seven days the bread you eat must be made without yeast. On the first day of the festival, remove every trace of yeast from your homes. Anyone who eats bread made with yeast during the seven days of the festival will be cut off from the community of Israel. [16]On the first day of the festival and again on the seventh day, all the people must observe an official day for holy assembly. No work of any kind may be done on these days except in the preparation of food.

[17]"Celebrate this Festival of Unleavened Bread, for it will remind you that I brought your forces out of the land of Egypt on this very day. This festival will be a permanent law for you; celebrate this day from generation to generation. [18]The bread you eat must be made without yeast from the evening of the fourteenth day of the first month until the evening of the twenty-first day of that month. [19]During those seven days, there must be no trace of yeast in your homes. Anyone who eats anything made with yeast during this week will be cut off from the community of Israel. These regulations apply both to the foreigners living among you and to the native-born Israelites. [20]During those days you must not eat anything made with yeast. Wherever you live, eat only bread made without yeast."

[21]Then Moses called all the elders of Israel together and said to them, "Go, pick out a lamb or young goat for each of your families, and slaughter the Passover animal. [22]Drain the blood into a basin. Then take a bundle of hyssop branches and dip it into the blood. Brush the hyssop across the top and sides of the doorframes of your houses. And no one may go out through the door until morning. [23]For the LORD will pass through the land to strike down the Egyptians. But when he sees the blood on the top and sides of the doorframe, the LORD will pass over your home. He will not permit his death angel to enter your house and strike you down.

[24]"Remember, these instructions are a permanent law that you and your descendants must observe forever. [25]When you enter the land the LORD has promised to give you, you will continue to observe this ceremony. [26]Then your children will ask, 'What does this ceremony mean?' [27]And you will reply, 'It is the Passover sacrifice to the LORD, for he passed over the houses of the Israelites in Egypt. And though he struck the Egyptians, he spared our families.'" When Moses had finished speaking, all the people bowed down to the ground and worshiped.

[28]So the people of Israel did just as the LORD had commanded through Moses and Aaron. [29]And that night at midnight, the LORD struck down all the firstborn sons in the land of Egypt, from the firstborn son of Pharaoh, who sat on his throne, to the firstborn son of the prisoner in the dungeon. Even the firstborn of their livestock were killed. [30]Pharaoh and all his officials and all the people of Egypt woke up during the night, and loud wailing was heard throughout the land of Egypt. There was not a single house where someone had not died.

Israel's Exodus from Egypt

[31]Pharaoh sent for Moses and Aaron during the night. "Get out!" he ordered. "Leave my people—and take the rest of the Israelites with you!

12:11 Hebrew *Bind up your loins.*

to be a family event, celebrated in small intimate groups. **29:** The death of a child is the most devastating of any human loss. Now the whole nation will be plunged into mourning. The grief will be heightened by the knowledge that a warning had been issued and simply not heeded.

12:31–51 Israel's Exodus from Egypt. 33: Although

Go and worship the LORD as you have requested.
32 Take your flocks and herds, as you said, and be
gone. Go, but bless me as you leave." 33 All the
Egyptians urged the people of Israel to get out of
the land as quickly as possible, for they thought,
"We will all die!"
34 The Israelites took their bread dough before
yeast was added. They wrapped their kneading
boards in their cloaks and carried them on their
shoulders. 35 And the people of Israel did as Moses had instructed; they asked the Egyptians for
clothing and articles of silver and gold. 36 The
LORD caused the Egyptians to look favorably on
the Israelites, and they gave the Israelites whatever they asked for. So they stripped the Egyptians of their wealth!
37 That night the people of Israel left Rameses and started for Succoth. There were about
600,000 men,* plus all the women and children.
38 A rabble of non-Israelites went with them,
along with great flocks and herds of livestock.
39 For bread they baked flat cakes from the dough
without yeast they had brought from Egypt. It
was made without yeast because the people were
driven out of Egypt in such a hurry that they had
no time to prepare the bread or other food.
40 The people of Israel had lived in Egypt*
for 430 years. 41 In fact, it was on the last day of
the 430th year that all the LORD's forces left the
land. 42 On this night the LORD kept his promise
to bring his people out of the land of Egypt. So
this night belongs to him, and it must be commemorated every year by all the Israelites, from
generation to generation.

Instructions for the Passover

43 Then the LORD said to Moses and Aaron,
"These are the instructions for the festival of
Passover. No outsiders are allowed to eat the
Passover meal. 44 But any slave who has been
purchased may eat it if he has been circumcised.
45 Temporary residents and hired servants may
not eat it. 46 Each Passover lamb must be eaten in
one house. Do not carry any of its meat outside,
and do not break any of its bones. 47 The whole
community of Israel must celebrate this Passover festival.
48 "If there are foreigners living among you
who want to celebrate the LORD's Passover, let
all their males be circumcised. Only then may
they celebrate the Passover with you like any
native-born Israelite. But no uncircumcised male
may ever eat the Passover meal. 49 This instruction applies to everyone, whether a native-born
Israelite or a foreigner living among you."
50 So all the people of Israel followed all the
LORD's commands to Moses and Aaron. 51 On
that very day the LORD brought the people of Israel out of the land of Egypt like an army.

Dedication of the Firstborn

13 Then the LORD said to Moses, 2 "Dedicate to me every firstborn among the
Israelites. The first offspring to be
born, of both humans and animals, belongs to
me."
3 So Moses said to the people, "This is a day
to remember forever—the day you left Egypt,
the place of your slavery. Today the LORD has
brought you out by the power of his mighty
hand. (Remember, eat no food containing yeast.)
4 On this day in early spring, in the month of
Abib,* you have been set free. 5 You must celebrate this event in this month each year after

12:37 Or *fighting men;* Hebrew reads *men on foot.* **12:40** Samaritan Pentateuch reads *in Canaan and Egypt;* Greek version reads *in Egypt and Canaan.* **13:4** Hebrew *On this day in the month of Abib.* This first month of the ancient Hebrew lunar calendar usually occurs within the months of March and April.

---

the Exodus is the major salvation occurrence in the Old Testament, the actual event is told briefly and breathlessly as the people scramble to leave. Divinely planned events can still be subject to human confusion and disarray. **34:** The unleavened bread represented the first of the many changes that women would be required to make as they transitioned from settled living to nomadic existence. It would be largely their responsibility to preserve the tradition on a yearly basis. The entire house must be cleaned before Passover and all yeast removed. The apostle Paul, an observant Jew, would remark on this custom when he wrote to the Corinthians (1 Cor 5:7), and Jesus likened the hypocrisy of the Pharisees to yeast that needed to be removed (Luke 12:1). **37–38:** The group that leaves Egypt is a diverse one, with non-Israelites among them. There may have been a host of reasons why they too wished to flee Egypt and cast their lot with a people who worshiped a God who promised them freedom and a new destiny. **39:** Yeast works in bread dough through a time-consuming process of fermentation. It cannot be hurried, and at this point there was not time to prepare the unleavened bread that the Bedouin still bake today when there are unexpected guests. The unbaked dough was wrapped up in cloaks and fastened to people's backs (v. 34), subsequently to be toasted over the coals of a campfire.

13:1–16 Dedication of the Firstborn. 8: The obser-

the LORD brings you into the land of the Canaanites, Hittites, Amorites, Hivites, and Jebusites. (He swore to your ancestors that he would give you this land—a land flowing with milk and honey.) [6] For seven days the bread you eat must be made without yeast. Then on the seventh day, celebrate a feast to the LORD. [7] Eat bread without yeast during those seven days. In fact, there must be no yeast bread or any yeast at all found within the borders of your land during this time.

[8] "On the seventh day you must explain to your children, 'I am celebrating what the LORD did for me when I left Egypt.' [9] This annual festival will be a visible sign to you, like a mark branded on your hand or your forehead. Let it remind you always to recite this teaching of the LORD: 'With a strong hand, the LORD rescued you from Egypt.'* [10] So observe the decree of this festival at the appointed time each year.

[11] "This is what you must do when the LORD fulfills the promise he swore to you and to your ancestors. When he gives you the land where the Canaanites now live, [12] you must present all firstborn sons and firstborn male animals to the LORD, for they belong to him. [13] A firstborn donkey may be bought back from the LORD by presenting a lamb or young goat in its place. But if you do not buy it back, you must break its neck. However, you must buy back every firstborn son.

[14] "And in the future, your children will ask you, 'What does all this mean?' Then you will tell them, 'With the power of his mighty hand, the LORD brought us out of Egypt, the place of our slavery. [15] Pharaoh stubbornly refused to let us go, so the LORD killed all the firstborn males throughout the land of Egypt, both people and animals. That is why I now sacrifice all the firstborn males to the LORD—except that the firstborn sons are always bought back.' [16] This ceremony will be like a mark branded on your hand or your forehead. It is a reminder that the power of the LORD's mighty hand brought us out of Egypt."

Israel's Wilderness Detour

[17] When Pharaoh finally let the people go, God did not lead them along the main road that runs through Philistine territory, even though that was the shortest route to the Promised Land. God said, "If the people are faced with a battle, they might change their minds and return to Egypt." [18] So God led them in a roundabout way through the wilderness toward the Red Sea.* Thus the Israelites left Egypt like an army ready for battle.*

[19] Moses took the bones of Joseph with him, for Joseph had made the sons of Israel swear to do this. He said, "God will certainly come to help you. When he does, you must take my bones with you from this place."

[20] The Israelites left Succoth and camped at Etham on the edge of the wilderness. [21] The LORD went ahead of them. He guided them during the day with a pillar of cloud, and he provided light at night with a pillar of fire. This allowed them to travel by day or by night. [22] And the LORD did not remove the pillar of cloud or pillar of fire from its place in front of the people.

14 Then the LORD gave these instructions to Moses: [2] "Order the Israelites to turn back and camp by Pi-hahiroth between Migdol and the sea. Camp there along the shore, across from Baal-zephon. [3] Then Pharaoh will think, 'The Israelites are confused. They are trapped in the wilderness!' [4] And once again I will harden Pharaoh's heart, and he will chase after you.* I have planned this in order to display my glory through Pharaoh and his whole army. After this the Egyptians will know that I am the LORD!" So the Israelites camped there as they were told.

13:9 Or *Let it remind you always to keep the instructions of the LORD on the tip of your tongue, because with a strong hand, the LORD rescued you from Egypt.* **13:18a** Hebrew *sea of reeds.* **13:18b** Greek version reads *left Egypt in the fifth generation.* **14:4** Hebrew *after them.*

---

vance of Passover now becomes a model of religious education in which children have the story reenacted for them with the aid of ceremonial food. As the text recited at the Passover Seder says, "In every generation one should look upon himself as if he personally had gone out of Egypt . . . It was not only our ancestors whom the Holy One, Blessed is He, redeemed, but also us along with them" (Haggadah). **9, 16:** The memory of God's deliverance will serve as a sign, as would later the frontlet and the phylactery to be bound upon the forehead and the forearm (Deut 6:8; 11:18).

13:17—14:4 Israel's Wilderness Detour. 13:21–22: The God who had again and again told his name to and promised relationship with the people is now manifested in his continuing presence among them day and night. **14:1–4:** Moses is familiar with Egyptian military thinking and leads the people to a place of greater security.

The Egyptians Pursue Israel
5 When word reached the king of Egypt that
the Israelites had fled, Pharaoh and his officials
changed their minds. "What have we done, letting all those Israelite slaves get away?" they
asked. 6 So Pharaoh harnessed his chariot and
called up his troops. 7 He took with him 600 of
Egypt's best chariots, along with the rest of the
chariots of Egypt, each with its commander. 8 The
LORD hardened the heart of Pharaoh, the king
of Egypt, so he chased after the people of Israel,
who had left with fists raised in defiance. 9 The
Egyptians chased after them with all the forces
in Pharaoh's army—all his horses and chariots,
his charioteers, and his troops. The Egyptians
caught up with the people of Israel as they were
camped beside the shore near Pi-hahiroth, across
from Baal-zephon.
10 As Pharaoh approached, the people of Israel looked up and panicked when they saw the
Egyptians overtaking them. They cried out to
the LORD, 11 and they said to Moses, "Why did
you bring us out here to die in the wilderness?
Weren't there enough graves for us in Egypt?
What have you done to us? Why did you make
us leave Egypt? 12 Didn't we tell you this would
happen while we were still in Egypt? We said,
'Leave us alone! Let us be slaves to the Egyptians. It's better to be a slave in Egypt than a
corpse in the wilderness!' "
13 But Moses told the people, "Don't be afraid.
Just stand still and watch the LORD rescue you
today. The Egyptians you see today will never
be seen again. 14 The LORD himself will fight for
you. Just stay calm."

Escape through the Red Sea
15 Then the LORD said to Moses, "Why are you
crying out to me? Tell the people to get moving!
16 Pick up your staff and raise your hand over the
sea. Divide the water so the Israelites can walk
through the middle of the sea on dry ground.
17 And I will harden the hearts of the Egyptians,
and they will charge in after the Israelites. My
great glory will be displayed through Pharaoh
and his troops, his chariots, and his charioteers.
18 When my glory is displayed through them, all
Egypt will see my glory and know that I am the
LORD!"
19 Then the angel of God, who had been leading the people of Israel, moved to the rear of the
camp. The pillar of cloud also moved from the
front and stood behind them. 20 The cloud settled
between the Egyptian and Israelite camps. As
darkness fell, the cloud turned to fire, lighting
up the night. But the Egyptians and Israelites did
not approach each other all night.
21 Then Moses raised his hand over the sea,
and the LORD opened up a path through the water with a strong east wind. The wind blew all
that night, turning the seabed into dry land. 22 So
the people of Israel walked through the middle
of the sea on dry ground, with walls of water on
each side!
23 Then the Egyptians—all of Pharaoh's horses, chariots, and charioteers—chased them into
the middle of the sea. 24 But just before dawn the
LORD looked down on the Egyptian army from
the pillar of fire and cloud, and he threw their
forces into total confusion. 25 He twisted* their
chariot wheels, making their chariots difficult to
drive. "Let's get out of here—away from these
Israelites!" the Egyptians shouted. "The LORD is
fighting for them against Egypt!"
26 When all the Israelites had reached the
other side, the LORD said to Moses, "Raise your
hand over the sea again. Then the waters will
rush back and cover the Egyptians and their
chariots and charioteers." 27 So as the sun began
to rise, Moses raised his hand over the sea, and
the water rushed back into its usual place. The
Egyptians tried to escape, but the LORD swept
them into the sea. 28 Then the waters returned
and covered all the chariots and charioteers—
the entire army of Pharaoh. Of all the Egyptians
who had chased the Israelites into the sea, not a
single one survived.
29 But the people of Israel had walked through
the middle of the sea on dry ground, as the water stood up like a wall on both sides. 30 That is
how the LORD rescued Israel from the hand of

14:25 As in Greek version, Samaritan Pentateuch, and Syriac version; Hebrew reads *He removed.*

14:5–31 Pursuit and Escape. 12: This is the first of several requests to return to slavery in Egypt. **15:** Prayer must be united with action. This verse is sometimes called proof of the slogan that "God helps those who help themselves." **18:** Throughout the Exodus story, God has declared a twofold purpose: (1) the liberation of an oppressed captive people and (2) a revelation of the LORD as true God both to the Egyptians and to the Israelites. Even the army understands the LORD's reality and power (v. 25). **21:** This natural phenomenon has been witnessed in the Red Sea on a few other occasions, and here the timing is providential. It is also possible that the event took place in the marshy Reed Sea, which was smaller and shallower than the Red Sea.

the Egyptians that day. And the Israelites saw
the bodies of the Egyptians washed up on the
seashore. 31 When the people of Israel saw the
mighty power that the LORD had unleashed
against the Egyptians, they were filled with awe
before him. They put their faith in the LORD and
in his servant Moses.

A Song of Deliverance

15 Then Moses and the people of Israel
sang this song to the LORD:

"I will sing to the LORD,
for he has triumphed gloriously;
he has hurled both horse and rider
into the sea.
2 The LORD is my strength and my song;
he has given me victory.
This is my God, and I will praise him—
my father's God, and I will exalt him!
3 The LORD is a warrior;
Yahweh* is his name!
4 Pharaoh's chariots and army
he has hurled into the sea.
The finest of Pharaoh's officers
are drowned in the Red Sea.*
5 The deep waters gushed over them;
they sank to the bottom like a stone.

6 "Your right hand, O LORD,
is glorious in power.
Your right hand, O LORD,
smashes the enemy.
7 In the greatness of your majesty,
you overthrow those who rise against you.
You unleash your blazing fury;
it consumes them like straw.
8 At the blast of your breath,
the waters piled up!
The surging waters stood straight like a wall;
in the heart of the sea the deep waters
became hard.

9 "The enemy boasted, 'I will chase them
and catch up with them.
I will plunder them
and consume them.
I will flash my sword;
my powerful hand will destroy them.'
10 But you blew with your breath,
and the sea covered them.
They sank like lead
in the mighty waters.

11 "Who is like you among the gods, O LORD—
glorious in holiness,
awesome in splendor,
performing great wonders?
12 You raised your right hand,
and the earth swallowed our enemies.

13 "With your unfailing love you lead
the people you have redeemed.
In your might, you guide them
to your sacred home.
14 The peoples hear and tremble;
anguish grips those who live in Philistia.
15 The leaders of Edom are terrified;
the nobles of Moab tremble.
All who live in Canaan melt away;
16 terror and dread fall upon them.
The power of your arm
makes them lifeless as stone
until your people pass by, O LORD,
until the people you purchased pass by.
17 You will bring them in and plant them on
your own mountain—
the place, O LORD, reserved for your own
dwelling,
the sanctuary, O Lord, that your hands
have established.
18 The LORD will reign forever and ever!"

19 When Pharaoh's horses, chariots, and charioteers rushed into the sea, the LORD brought the
water crashing down on them. But the people of
Israel had walked through the middle of the sea
on dry ground!
20 Then Miriam the prophet, Aaron's sister,
took a tambourine and led all the women as they
played their tambourines and danced. 21 And
Miriam sang this song:

15:3 *Yahweh* is a transliteration of the proper name *YHWH* that is sometimes rendered "Jehovah"; in this translation it is usually rendered "the LORD" (note the use of small capitals). **15:4** Hebrew *sea of reeds;* also in 15:22.

15:1–18:27 First Steps of a Newborn Nation

15:1–21 A Song of Deliverance. 1–18: The first act of the newly delivered slaves is one of praise and thanksgiving. **20–21:** Miriam is the first woman in the Bible to be named as a prophet. (For others, see Judg 4 and 5; 2 Kgs 22:8–23 and 2 Chr 34:14–28; Neh 6:7, 14; Isa 8:3; Joel 2:28–29; Luke 2:36). Miriam received special revelations from God (Num 12:2) and was considered to have been a special gift to the leadership team of the Exodus (Mic 6:4). Her memory and influence were long preserved in Israel (Num 20:1; 26:59; 1 Chr 6:3). Miriam initiates the first act of worship for the newborn nation as she leads

"Sing to the LORD,
for he has triumphed gloriously;
he has hurled both horse and rider
into the sea."

Bitter Water at Marah

[22] Then Moses led the people of Israel away from the Red Sea, and they moved out into the desert of Shur. They traveled in this desert for three days without finding any water. [23] When they came to the oasis of Marah, the water was too bitter to drink. So they called the place Marah (which means "bitter").

[24] Then the people complained and turned against Moses. "What are we going to drink?" they demanded. [25] So Moses cried out to the LORD for help, and the LORD showed him a piece of wood. Moses threw it into the water, and this made the water good to drink.

It was there at Marah that the LORD set before them the following decree as a standard to test their faithfulness to him. [26] He said, "If you will listen carefully to the voice of the LORD your God and do what is right in his sight, obeying his commands and keeping all his decrees, then I will not make you suffer any of the diseases I sent on the Egyptians; for I am the LORD who heals you."

[27] After leaving Marah, the Israelites traveled on to the oasis of Elim, where they found twelve springs and seventy palm trees. They camped there beside the water.

Manna and Quail from Heaven

16 Then the whole community of Israel set out from Elim and journeyed into the wilderness of Sin,* between Elim and Mount Sinai. They arrived there on the fifteenth day of the second month, one month after leaving the land of Egypt.* [2] There, too, the whole community of Israel complained about Moses and Aaron.

[3] "If only the LORD had killed us back in Egypt," they moaned. "There we sat around pots filled with meat and ate all the bread we wanted. But now you have brought us into this wilderness to starve us all to death."

16:1a The geographical name *Sin* is related to *Sinai* and should not be confused with the English word *sin*.
16:1b The Exodus had occurred on the fifteenth day of the first month (see Num 33:3).

the women in song and dance. (For the traditional celebration of victory by women's song and dance, see Judg 5:1–31; 11:34; 1 Sam 18:7.) The tambourine (tambour, timbrel) is a rhythm instrument, often used by women, and the song is thought to be one of the earliest written portions of the Hebrew Bible. The women rejoiced in their new freedom, but nomadic life required major adjustments. In Egypt they had lived in settled communities with houses. Now they must adjust to tent life, on the move. The manufacture and pitching of tents was women's work, as was the packing up of household goods in preparation for each move. Care and supervision of children would have become more of a challenge. There were dietary changes, with people hungering for the leeks, garlic, melons, and cucumbers that they had known in Egypt (Num 11:5). Gone were their kitchen gardens. Water for drinking, cooking, and washing was often severely limited. The exaltation of praise was soon to be drowned in a storm of complaints.

15:22–27 Bitter Water at Marah. 22–25: St. Paul sees this saga supplying us with spiritual examples (1 Cor 10:6–11) and invites application of the episodes to our personal lives. In the Exodus narrative, there are several stories about water. Water was carried in animal skins—and after three days any water left must surely have been unappetizing. At last they reach an oasis, only to discover that this water is so nasty that they cannot drink (the name *Marah* means "bitter"). There are many such brackish pools and wells in the desert. To this day Bedouins throw certain shrubs into the water as catalysts so that the precipitates sink to the bottom and remain there. Above them lies excellent drinking water. Some early commentators allegorized the tree of Moses as the cross of Christ, who can bring sweetness into our lives. **25:** Here God gave his people a promise of guidance and protection if they would obey the commands and laws that he would give. Later the concept of covenant would be articulated more fully, but here at the place of bitter waters the concept was introduced. The oppression and degradation of Egypt was left behind, and a renewed people moved on. The purpose of the testing was not to visit the people with affliction but to give them a deeper level of spiritual preparedness (cf. Deut 8:2–3, 16). **26:** Obedience to the law would bring a far higher degree of immunity to the diseases that afflicted ancient populations. Moses has been called the greatest sanitarian in antiquity, and compliance with Israel's legislation greatly enhanced the level of public health. **27:** To this day the twelve springs are still there within a palm grove at Uyn Musa.

16:1–36 Manna and Quail from Heaven. 1–3: The predicament is a cruel one, especially for mothers who have nothing to give their hungry children. Slavery in Egypt now seems preferable to hunger in the wilderness, and again there will be a test of the

4 Then the LORD said to Moses, "Look, I'm going to rain down food from heaven for you. Each day the people can go out and pick up as much food as they need for that day. I will test them in this to see whether or not they will follow my instructions. 5 On the sixth day they will gather food, and when they prepare it, there will be twice as much as usual."

6 So Moses and Aaron said to all the people of Israel, "By evening you will realize it was the LORD who brought you out of the land of Egypt. 7 In the morning you will see the glory of the LORD, because he has heard your complaints, which are against him, not against us. What have we done that you should complain about us?" 8 Then Moses added, "The LORD will give you meat to eat in the evening and bread to satisfy you in the morning, for he has heard all your complaints against him. What have we done? Yes, your complaints are against the LORD, not against us."

9 Then Moses said to Aaron, "Announce this to the entire community of Israel: 'Present yourselves before the LORD, for he has heard your complaining.' " 10 And as Aaron spoke to the whole community of Israel, they looked out toward the wilderness. There they could see the awesome glory of the LORD in the cloud.

11 Then the LORD said to Moses, 12 "I have heard the Israelites' complaints. Now tell them, 'In the evening you will have meat to eat, and in the morning you will have all the bread you want. Then you will know that I am the LORD your God.' "

13 That evening vast numbers of quail flew in and covered the camp. And the next morning the area around the camp was wet with dew. 14 When the dew evaporated, a flaky substance as fine as frost blanketed the ground. 15 The Israelites were puzzled when they saw it. "What is it?" they asked each other. They had no idea what it was.

And Moses told them, "It is the food the LORD has given you to eat. 16 These are the LORD's instructions: Each household should gather as much as it needs. Pick up two quarts* for each person in your tent."

17 So the people of Israel did as they were told. Some gathered a lot, some only a little. 18 But when they measured it out,* everyone had just enough. Those who gathered a lot had nothing left over, and those who gathered only a little had enough. Each family had just what it needed.

19 Then Moses told them, "Do not keep any of it until morning." 20 But some of them didn't listen and kept some of it until morning. But by then it was full of maggots and had a terrible smell. Moses was very angry with them.

21 After this the people gathered the food morning by morning, each family according to its need. And as the sun became hot, the flakes they had not picked up melted and disappeared. 22 On the sixth day, they gathered twice as much as usual—four quarts* for each person instead of two. Then all the leaders of the community came and asked Moses for an explanation. 23 He told them, "This is what the LORD commanded: Tomorrow will be a day of complete rest, a holy Sabbath day set apart for the LORD. So bake or boil as much as you want today, and set aside what is left for tomorrow."

24 So they put some aside until morning, just as Moses had commanded. And in the morning the leftover food was wholesome and good, without maggots or odor. 25 Moses said, "Eat this food

16:16 Hebrew *1 omer* [2 liters]; also in 16:32, 33. **16:18** Hebrew *measured it with an omer.* **16:22** Hebrew *2 omers* [4 liters].

people's readiness to obey. **4:** This time the test lies in the provision of food rather than in its lack. **5–8:** The divinely appointed leaders are reproached for doing their job. St. Paul specifically condemns the murmuring and complaining of the people (1 Cor 10:10), which are based essentially on a negative attitude toward the goodness of God. **10:** As in Numbers 11:4–5 and 14:1–10 when the community also grumbled and wished to return to Egypt, the presence of God is felt in an unusual way. The people have been led to this place by the pillar of cloud and of fire, and to God alone they must turn to meet their needs. **13:** The Sinai is a resting place in the annual migratory pattern of quail as they pass between Africa and Europe. Hunters still find the exhausted birds an easy prey, as did the ancient Israelites. **14–16:** The food was adequate for the nutritional needs of the people, sufficient for everyone, with equitable distribution, and could not be hoarded. Surely this is an important model to be considered by those concerned with global hunger. **17–19:** The provision is heaven-sent, but it requires earthly effort, mostly of women. Once the manna was collected, it was ground up and either boiled or baked in flat cakes (v. 23; Num 11:7–8). The women must also learn safe methods of food storage in the hot desert climate. **22–23:** The Genesis account tells of God's resting on the seventh day, but now the command for its observance falls upon the people. Rest is a fundamental requirement, essential for the well-being of humanity. It is especially difficult for women with overburdened work schedules to achieve. This passage indicates the importance of

today, for today is a Sabbath day dedicated to the LORD. There will be no food on the ground today.
26 You may gather the food for six days, but the seventh day is the Sabbath. There will be no food on the ground that day."
27 Some of the people went out anyway on the seventh day, but they found no food.
28 The LORD asked Moses, "How long will these people refuse to obey my commands and instructions?
29 They must realize that the Sabbath is the LORD's gift to you. That is why he gives you a two-day supply on the sixth day, so there will be enough for two days. On the Sabbath day you must each stay in your place. Do not go out to pick up food on the seventh day."
30 So the people did not gather any food on the seventh day.

31 The Israelites called the food manna.* It was white like coriander seed, and it tasted like honey wafers.

32 Then Moses said, "This is what the LORD has commanded: Fill a two-quart container with manna to preserve it for your descendants. Then later generations will be able to see the food I gave you in the wilderness when I set you free from Egypt."
33 Moses said to Aaron, "Get a jar and fill it with two quarts of manna. Then put it in a sacred place before the LORD to preserve it for all future generations."
34 Aaron did just as the LORD had commanded Moses. He eventually placed it in the Ark of the Covenant—in front of the stone tablets inscribed with the terms of the covenant.*
35 So the people of Israel ate manna for forty years until they arrived at the land where they would settle. They ate manna until they came to the border of the land of Canaan.

36 The container used to measure the manna was an omer, which was one tenth of an ephah; it held about two quarts.*

Water from the Rock

17 At the LORD's command, the whole community of Israel left the wilderness of Sin* and moved from place to place. Eventually they camped at Rephidim, but there was no water there for the people to drink.
2 So once more the people complained against Moses. "Give us water to drink!" they demanded.

"Quiet!" Moses replied. "Why are you complaining against me? And why are you testing the LORD?"

3 But tormented by thirst, they continued to argue with Moses. "Why did you bring us out of Egypt? Are you trying to kill us, our children, and our livestock with thirst?"

4 Then Moses cried out to the LORD, "What should I do with these people? They are ready to stone me!"

5 The LORD said to Moses, "Walk out in front of the people. Take your staff, the one you used when you struck the water of the Nile, and call some of the elders of Israel to join you.
6 I will stand before you on the rock at Mount Sinai.* Strike the rock, and water will come gushing out. Then the people will be able to drink." So Moses struck the rock as he was told, and water gushed out as the elders looked on.

7 Moses named the place Massah (which means "test") and Meribah (which means "arguing") because the people of Israel argued with Moses and tested the LORD by saying, "Is the LORD here with us or not?"

16:31 *Manna* means "What is it?" See 16:15. **16:34** Hebrew *He placed it in front of the Testimony;* see note on 25:16. **16:36** Hebrew *An omer is one tenth of an ephah.* **17:1** The geographical name *Sin* is related to *Sinai* and should not be confused with the English word *sin.* **17:6** Hebrew *Horeb,* another name for Sinai.

---

planning and preparing for rest as much as for work. **27–30:** Here the concept of Sabbath is introduced as a gift to the people of Israel. Later it will become an essential sign of the covenant between the LORD and the Israelite people. **31–35:** The word *manna* is usually understood to mean "What is it?" Its exact identification remains a mystery. Several forms of desert vegetation do indeed produce edible substances, but none is available year-round. In any event, the provision of this sustenance remains a miracle for a desperate people. St. Paul would memorialize the manna as "spiritual food" by which all are fed (1 Cor 10:3). Memorials, such as saving a container of manna, serve as helpful reminders of the event itself and its importance in the life of the nation.

17:1–7 Water from the Rock. 1–4: Once more an episode involving a lack of water and again a resentment of Moses, terminating in a threat of execution (cf. Num 14:10). There remains the question as to whether God is actually still present with the disgruntled people (see v. 7). **6:** The formation of the Sinai is truly a geologist's wonderland. Limestone rock in that area sometimes contains water that could be exposed by a strong blow. According to Talmudic tradition, the water that issued forth from the rock was called "the well of Miriam" and followed the Israelites in their wanderings. St. Paul allegorizes that source as Christ who is our "spiritual water" (1 Cor 10:4).

Israel Defeats the Amalekites
8 While the people of Israel were still at Rephidim, the warriors of Amalek attacked them.
9 Moses commanded Joshua, "Choose some men
to go out and fight the army of Amalek for us.
Tomorrow, I will stand at the top of the hill, holding the staff of God in my hand."
10 So Joshua did what Moses had commanded
and fought the army of Amalek. Meanwhile,
Moses, Aaron, and Hur climbed to the top of a
nearby hill. 11 As long as Moses held up the staff
in his hand, the Israelites had the advantage. But
whenever he dropped his hand, the Amalekites
gained the advantage. 12 Moses' arms soon became so tired he could no longer hold them up.
So Aaron and Hur found a stone for him to sit
on. Then they stood on each side of Moses, holding up his hands. So his hands held steady until
sunset. 13 As a result, Joshua overwhelmed the
army of Amalek in battle.
14 After the victory, the LORD instructed
Moses, "Write this down on a scroll as a permanent reminder, and read it aloud to Joshua:
I will erase the memory of Amalek from under
heaven." 15 Moses built an altar there and named
it Yahweh-nissi (which means "the LORD is my
banner"). 16 He said, "They have raised their fist
against the LORD's throne, so now* the LORD
will be at war with Amalek generation after generation."

Jethro's Visit to Moses
18 Moses' father-in-law, Jethro, the
priest of Midian, heard about everything God had done for Moses and his
people, the Israelites. He heard especially about
how the LORD had rescued them from Egypt.
2 Earlier, Moses had sent his wife, Zipporah, and
his two sons back to Jethro, who had taken them
in. 3 (Moses' first son was named Gershom,* for
Moses had said when the boy was born, "I have
been a foreigner in a foreign land." 4 His second
son was named Eliezer,* for Moses had said, "The
God of my ancestors was my helper; he rescued
me from the sword of Pharaoh.") 5 Jethro, Moses' father-in-law, now came to visit Moses in the
wilderness. He brought Moses' wife and two sons
with him, and they arrived while Moses and the
people were camped near the mountain of God.
6 Jethro had sent a message to Moses, saying, "I,
Jethro, your father-in-law, am coming to see you
with your wife and your two sons."
7 So Moses went out to meet his father-in-law.
He bowed low and kissed him. They asked about
each other's welfare and then went into Moses'
tent. 8 Moses told his father-in-law everything the
LORD had done to Pharaoh and Egypt on behalf
of Israel. He also told about all the hardships they
had experienced along the way and how the LORD
had rescued his people from all their troubles.
9 Jethro was delighted when he heard about all the
good things the LORD had done for Israel as he
rescued them from the hand of the Egyptians.
10 "Praise the LORD," Jethro said, "for he has
rescued you from the Egyptians and from Pharaoh. Yes, he has rescued Israel from the power-

17:16 Or *Hands have been lifted up to the LORD's throne, and now.* **18:3** *Gershom* sounds like a Hebrew term that means "a foreigner there." **18:4** *Eliezer* means "God is my helper."

17:8–16 Israel Defeats the Amalekites. 8–13: The Amalekites attacked the stragglers at the end of the line of march, those least able to defend themselves. The Amalekites were subsequently viewed as traditional enemies, virulent in their hatred of Israel. Joshua serves as the general under Moses and will later assume the leadership of the conquest of Canaan. Hur appears here and at Exodus 24:14 as an associate of Aaron who is able to assume executive duties. The younger leaders are able to identify both the strength and the weaknesses of the aging Moses and to accommodate themselves to both in their pursuit of victory. **14–16:** Again there is to be a memorial, and for the first time writing is mentioned. The book of Exodus contains days of remembrance (12:14; 13:3–10); rituals (12:26–27; 13:14–16); objects (16:32–34). The remembrance of what God has already done enables believers to move forward with faith for the future. Usually the perpetuation of memories and traditions becomes the province of women, especially the vesting of them with meaning. The hands of the Amalekites have been raised in defiance against God's throne, but the hands of Moses have been raised importuning divine grace.

18:1–12 Jethro's Visit. 1–2: After the events of 4:24–26, Moses' wife Zipporah, along with her two children, returns to her father in Midian. **3–4:** He had welcomed Moses into his family after his flight from Pharaoh's wrath. In time Moses married the eldest daughter and sired two sons. The name of the first attested to Moses' discomfort as an alien far from home, while the name of the second spoke of the security he had experienced through God's mercy. **5–7:** The relationship between Moses and Jethro was apparently warm (see 4:18), and Moses is anxious to share his experiences with his old mentor. **10:** Some traditions have maintained that it was through the priest Jethro that Moses learned of the LORD.

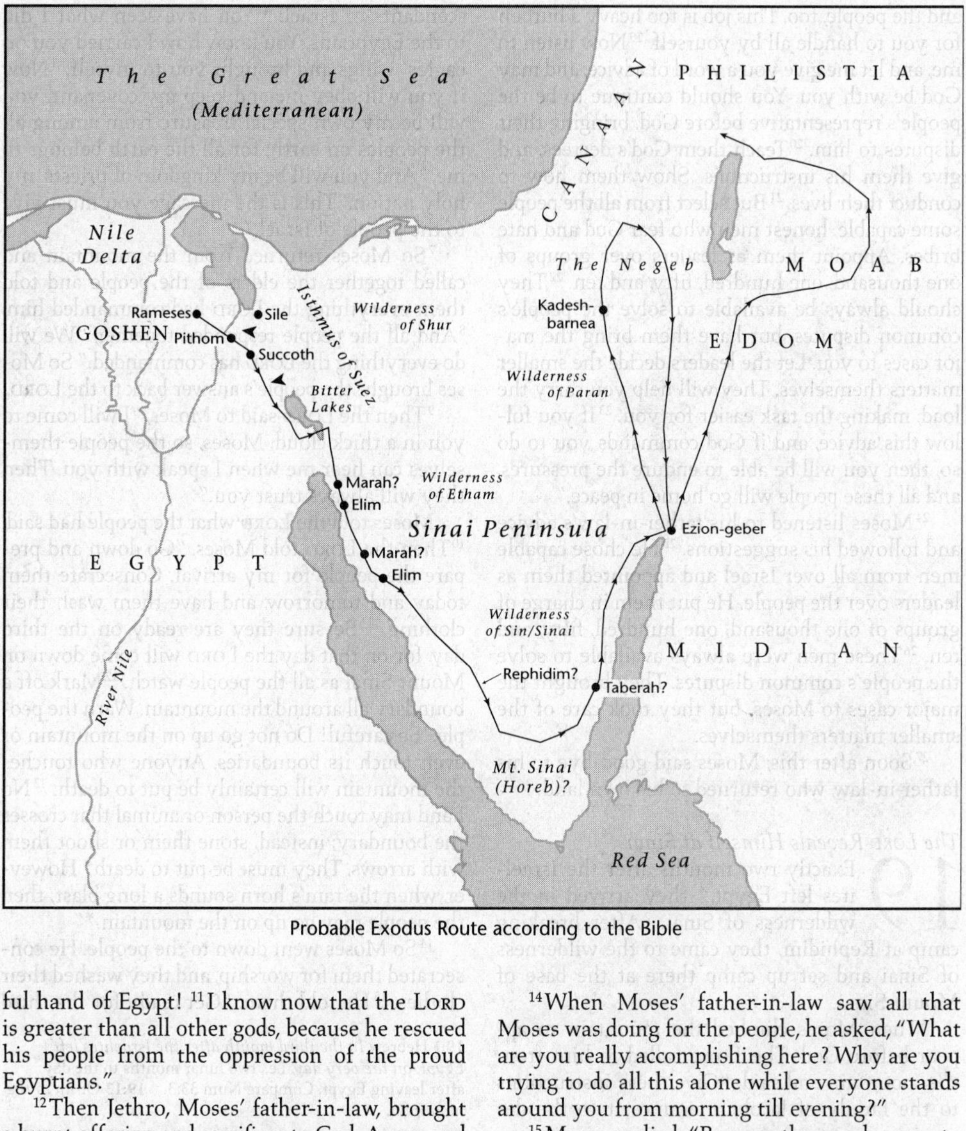

Probable Exodus Route according to the Bible

ful hand of Egypt! [11]I know now that the LORD is greater than all other gods, because he rescued his people from the oppression of the proud Egyptians."

[12]Then Jethro, Moses' father-in-law, brought a burnt offering and sacrifices to God. Aaron and all the elders of Israel came out and joined him in a sacrificial meal in God's presence.

Jethro's Wise Advice

[13]The next day, Moses took his seat to hear the people's disputes against each other. They waited before him from morning till evening.

[14]When Moses' father-in-law saw all that Moses was doing for the people, he asked, "What are you really accomplishing here? Why are you trying to do all this alone while everyone stands around you from morning till evening?"

[15]Moses replied, "Because the people come to me to get a ruling from God. [16]When a dispute arises, they come to me, and I am the one who settles the case between the quarreling parties. I inform the people of God's decrees and give them his instructions."

[17]"This is not good!" Moses' father-in-law exclaimed. [18]"You're going to wear yourself out—

12: The first sacrifice celebrated by the new nation is conducted by Jethro, with Aaron in attendance. The burnt offering was consumed entirely while the meat of other sacrifices was made available to be eaten at the ritual celebration meal.

18:13–27 Jethro's Wise Advice. Here Jethro organizes the judicial system as Moses learns to delegate authority. The people, newly freed from slavery, must begin to bear responsibility for their own governance. **18:** The right to a speedy trial depends upon

and the people, too. This job is too heavy a burden
for you to handle all by yourself. 19 Now listen to
me, and let me give you a word of advice, and may
God be with you. You should continue to be the
people's representative before God, bringing their
disputes to him. 20 Teach them God's decrees, and
give them his instructions. Show them how to
conduct their lives. 21 But select from all the people
some capable, honest men who fear God and hate
bribes. Appoint them as leaders over groups of
one thousand, one hundred, fifty, and ten. 22 They
should always be available to solve the people's
common disputes, but have them bring the major cases to you. Let the leaders decide the smaller
matters themselves. They will help you carry the
load, making the task easier for you. 23 If you follow this advice, and if God commands you to do
so, then you will be able to endure the pressures,
and all these people will go home in peace."

24 Moses listened to his father-in-law's advice
and followed his suggestions. 25 He chose capable
men from all over Israel and appointed them as
leaders over the people. He put them in charge of
groups of one thousand, one hundred, fifty, and
ten. 26 These men were always available to solve
the people's common disputes. They brought the
major cases to Moses, but they took care of the
smaller matters themselves.

27 Soon after this, Moses said good-bye to his
father-in-law, who returned to his own land.

The Lord Reveals Himself at Sinai

19 Exactly two months after the Israelites left Egypt,* they arrived in the
wilderness of Sinai. 2 After breaking
camp at Rephidim, they came to the wilderness
of Sinai and set up camp there at the base of
Mount Sinai.

3 Then Moses climbed the mountain to appear before God. The Lord called to him from
the mountain and said, "Give these instructions
to the family of Jacob; announce it to the descendants of Israel: 4 'You have seen what I did
to the Egyptians. You know how I carried you on
eagles' wings and brought you to myself. 5 Now
if you will obey me and keep my covenant, you
will be my own special treasure from among all
the peoples on earth; for all the earth belongs to
me. 6 And you will be my kingdom of priests, my
holy nation.' This is the message you must give
to the people of Israel."

7 So Moses returned from the mountain and
called together the elders of the people and told
them everything the Lord had commanded him.
8 And all the people responded together, "We will
do everything the Lord has commanded." So Moses brought the people's answer back to the Lord.

9 Then the Lord said to Moses, "I will come to
you in a thick cloud, Moses, so the people themselves can hear me when I speak with you. Then
they will always trust you."

Moses told the Lord what the people had said.
10 Then the Lord told Moses, "Go down and prepare the people for my arrival. Consecrate them
today and tomorrow, and have them wash their
clothing. 11 Be sure they are ready on the third
day, for on that day the Lord will come down on
Mount Sinai as all the people watch. 12 Mark off a
boundary all around the mountain. Warn the people, 'Be careful! Do not go up on the mountain or
even touch its boundaries. Anyone who touches
the mountain will certainly be put to death. 13 No
hand may touch the person or animal that crosses
the boundary; instead, stone them or shoot them
with arrows. They must be put to death.' However, when the ram's horn sounds a long blast, then
the people may go up on the mountain.*"

14 So Moses went down to the people. He consecrated them for worship, and they washed their
clothes. 15 He told them, "Get ready for the third

19:1 Hebrew *In the third month after the Israelites left Egypt, on the very day,* i.e., two lunar months to the day after leaving Egypt. Compare Num 33:3. **19:13** Or *up to the mountain.*

an adequate number of judges to hear cases. **20:** The decision of the judges cannot be arbitrary but must be based upon law that can be administered impartially. Since these instructions presume the existence of written law, the events of chapter 18 may have taken place after those of chapters 19 and 20. The happenings described in Scripture are not always placed in chronological order, so that ancient Jewish scholars declare "there is no earlier or later in the Torah." **21:** We find here articulated the basic premise of a representative government. The decision-making power does not reside in a single individual but in a well-qualified group.

19:1—24:18 The Giving of the Law

19:1–25 The Lord Reveals Himself at Sinai. This part of the book emphasizes the awesome holiness of God and his loving concern for his people. **4–6:** A mother eagle, when she is teaching her young to fly, catches them on her back when they falter. Here the Lord will lead the faltering people to become a *special treasure . . . my kingdom of priests* (cf. 1 Pet 2:9). **10:** Washing the desert-soiled clothing is another indication of the work of women in preparation for the holy event. **15:** Abstinence from food or sex is often required as a preliminary to a sacred ritual.

day, and until then abstain from having sexual intercourse."

[16]On the morning of the third day, thunder roared and lightning flashed, and a dense cloud came down on the mountain. There was a long, loud blast from a ram's horn, and all the people trembled.
[17]Moses led them out from the camp to meet with God, and they stood at the foot of the mountain.
[18]All of Mount Sinai was covered with smoke because the LORD had descended on it in the form of fire. The smoke billowed into the sky like smoke from a brick kiln, and the whole mountain shook violently.
[19]As the blast of the ram's horn grew louder and louder, Moses spoke, and God thundered his reply.
[20]The LORD came down on the top of Mount Sinai and called Moses to the top of the mountain. So Moses climbed the mountain.

[21]Then the LORD told Moses, "Go back down and warn the people not to break through the boundaries to see the LORD, or they will die.
[22]Even the priests who regularly come near to the LORD must purify themselves so that the LORD does not break out and destroy them."

[23]"But LORD," Moses protested, "the people cannot come up to Mount Sinai. You already warned us. You told me, 'Mark off a boundary all around the mountain to set it apart as holy.'"

[24]But the LORD said, "Go down and bring Aaron back up with you. In the meantime, do not let the priests or the people break through to approach the LORD, or he will break out and destroy them."

[25]So Moses went down to the people and told them what the LORD had said.

Ten Commandments for the Covenant Community

20 Then God gave the people all these instructions*:

[2]"I am the LORD your God, who rescued you from the land of Egypt, the place of your slavery.

[3]"You must not have any other god but me.

[4]"You must not make for yourself an idol of any kind or an image of anything in the heavens or on the earth or in the sea.
[5]You must not bow down to them or worship them, for I, the LORD your God, am a jealous God who will not tolerate your affection for any other gods. I lay the sins of the parents upon their children; the entire family is affected—even children in the third and fourth generations of those who reject me.
[6]But I lavish unfailing love for a thousand generations on those* who love me and obey my commands.

[7]"You must not misuse the name of the LORD your God. The LORD will not let you go unpunished if you misuse his name.

[8]"Remember to observe the Sabbath day by keeping it holy.
[9]You have six days each week for your ordinary work,
[10]but the seventh day is a Sabbath day of rest dedicated to the LORD your God. On that day no one in your household may do any work. This includes you, your sons and daughters, your male and female servants, your livestock, and any foreigners living among you.
[11]For in six days the LORD made the heavens, the earth, the sea, and everything in them; but on the seventh day he rested. That is why the LORD blessed the Sabbath day and set it apart as holy.

[12]"Honor your father and mother. Then you will live a long, full life in the land the LORD your God is giving you.

[13]"You must not murder.

[14]"You must not commit adultery.

[15]"You must not steal.

[16]"You must not testify falsely against your neighbor.

[17]"You must not covet your neighbor's house. You must not covet your neighbor's wife,

20:1 Hebrew *all these words.* **20:6** Hebrew *for thousands of those.*

18: The visible presence of God here descends on the mountain and will ultimately transfer to the Tabernacle (40:34).

20:1–21 The Ten Commandments. The law is bestowed as a gift to a free people. They will be governed not by the will of an absolute monarch but by enduring precepts based upon the reality of one true and living God. The first commandments deal with attitudes and actions toward the Deity, while the later ones address social, psychological, and practical issues of people living in community. Those ordinances related to an understanding of God are accompanied by explanatory statements, while those dealing with social relations are more succinct. Throughout these mandates there is a concern for the perpetuation of life and the preservation of human relationships in a meaningful existence. Disregard for these commandments brings tragic consequences not only for the offender but for following generations, but faithful observance brings health, enlightenment, stability, and personal satisfaction.

Adultery

Adultery is forbidden by the Mosaic law (Exod 20:14) and Jesus' teachings (Matt 19), for men and for women. Along with murder, lying, and idolatry—with which it is often linked—it is regarded as a heinous sin punishable by stoning. The grammar of the biblical narrative, however, suggests an underlying gender inequality. A woman's purity is more easily suspect than a man's, evidenced by the uncleanness of menstrual blood (e.g., Lev 22:10) and childbirth, and by the idea that a woman's purity belongs to the honor of the men related to her (see also Purity Laws Related to Women, Lev 15). Note, for example, the extreme vengeance of Dinah's brothers when she is raped at Shechem. Similarly, the sin of adultery is most commonly considered a sin against a husband's honor (e.g., Lev 18:7). This same taint is suggested by laws that prevent a priest from marrying a woman sullied by marriage or prostitution (Lev 21:15).

Although the law always refers to men committing adultery with another's wife, adultery and prostitution are frequently mentioned together and thus are associated with women (e.g., Jer 5:7). In the Prophets the symbol of Israel's unfaithfulness becomes the adulterous woman, and this symbol resonates its charges through Israel's travail and exile (e.g., Jer 3:8). Moreover, Old Testament men appear to be peculiarly insensitive to conviction of their sexual sin, unless confronted directly—witness David and Judah.

The double standard is further suggested by laws that require a virgin woman and her parents to bear the burden of proof of her purity (Deut 22:20–21) and by the ubiquity of male polygamy (see Polygamy, 1 Kgs 11). Moreover, the woman caught in adultery is brought to Jesus without her male partner (John 8:3). Unless one believes that women were the primary adulterers in the ancient world, the close linking of adultery and women must be regarded as a part of a general cultural and religious patriarchy that defines women in terms of sexual status.

The larger trajectory of biblical history, however, suggests a profound reversal. The sons of Tamar and Rahab are a part of the genealogy of Christ (Gen 38; Josh 2; Matt 1:3, 5). Christ promises that "those who seem least important now will be the greatest" (Matt 19:30).

Eschatologically, the New Testament makes explicit what is hinted at by the Prophets: the restoration, in which the new Jerusalem is the bride of Christ (Rev 19:7) and becomes the vindication of Israel and simultaneously of all shamed women. In the new order the bride awaits the bridegroom, but no examination of virginity, no shame is in prospect—only the marriage supper of the Lamb (Rev 19:9). The images of women's adultery and idolatry, which resonated through the Old Testament, are overturned, to be replaced by those of love and honor in the beloved.

male or female servant, ox or donkey, or
anything else that belongs to your neighbor."

[18]When the people heard the thunder and the
loud blast of the ram's horn, and when they saw
the flashes of lightning and the smoke billowing from the mountain, they stood at a distance,
trembling with fear.
[19]And they said to Moses, "You speak to us,
and we will listen. But don't let God speak directly to us, or we will die!"
[20]"Don't be afraid," Moses answered them, "for
God has come in this way to test you, and so that
your fear of him will keep you from sinning!"
[21]As the people stood in the distance, Moses
approached the dark cloud where God was.

Proper Use of Altars

[22]And the LORD said to Moses, "Say this to the
people of Israel: You saw for yourselves that
I spoke to you from heaven. [23]Remember, you
must not make any idols of silver or gold to rival me.
[24]"Build for me an altar made of earth, and
offer your sacrifices to me—your burnt offerings and peace offerings, your sheep and goats,
and your cattle. Build my altar wherever I cause
my name to be remembered, and I will come to
you and bless you. [25]If you use stones to build
my altar, use only natural, uncut stones. Do
not shape the stones with a tool, for that would
make the altar unfit for holy use. [26]And do not
approach my altar by going up steps. If you do,

20:22–26 Proper Use of Altars. Concern is shown for detail and simplicity. Lavish excess is not a necessary sign of worship of God. **26:** Concern for modest propriety in worship will lead to the instruction that the priests wear undergarments (28:42–43).

someone might look up under your clothing and
see your nakedness.

Fair Treatment of Slaves

21 "These are the regulations you must
present to Israel.
2 "If you buy a Hebrew slave, he
may serve for no more than six years. Set him
free in the seventh year, and he will owe you
nothing for his freedom. 3 If he was single when
he became your slave, he shall leave single. But
if he was married before he became a slave, then
his wife must be freed with him.
4 "If his master gave him a wife while he was
a slave and they had sons or daughters, then only
the man will be free in the seventh year, but his
wife and children will still belong to his master.
5 But the slave may declare, 'I love my master, my
wife, and my children. I don't want to go free.' 6 If
he does this, his master must present him before
God.* Then his master must take him to the door
or doorpost and publicly pierce his ear with an
awl. After that, the slave will serve his master
for life.
7 "When a man sells his daughter as a slave,
she will not be freed at the end of six years as the
men are. 8 If she does not satisfy her owner, he
must allow her to be bought back again. But he
is not allowed to sell her to foreigners, since he is
the one who broke the contract with her. 9 But if
the slave's owner arranges for her to marry his
son, he may no longer treat her as a slave but as
a daughter.
10 "If a man who has married a slave wife
takes another wife for himself, he must not neglect the rights of the first wife to food, clothing,
and sexual intimacy. 11 If he fails in any of these
three obligations, she may leave as a free woman
without making any payment.

Cases of Personal Injury

12 "Anyone who assaults and kills another person
must be put to death. 13 But if it was simply an
accident permitted by God, I will appoint a place
of refuge where the slayer can run for safety.
14 However, if someone deliberately kills another
person, then the slayer must be dragged even
from my altar and be put to death.
15 "Anyone who strikes father or mother must
be put to death.
16 "Kidnappers must be put to death, whether
they are caught in possession of their victims or
have already sold them as slaves.
17 "Anyone who dishonors* father or mother
must be put to death.
18 "Now suppose two men quarrel, and one
hits the other with a stone or fist, and the injured
person does not die but is confined to bed. 19 If
he is later able to walk outside again, even with
a crutch, the assailant will not be punished but
must compensate his victim for lost wages and
provide for his full recovery.
20 "If a man beats his male or female slave
with a club and the slave dies as a result, the
owner must be punished. 21 But if the slave re-
covers within a day or two, then the owner shall
not be punished, since the slave is his property.
22 "Now suppose two men are fighting, and in
the process they accidentally strike a pregnant
woman so she gives birth prematurely.* If no
further injury results, the man who struck the
woman must pay the amount of compensation
the woman's husband demands and the judges
approve. 23 But if there is further injury, the punishment must match the injury: a life for a life,
24 an eye for an eye, a tooth for a tooth, a hand
for a hand, a foot for a foot, 25 a burn for a burn, a
wound for a wound, a bruise for a bruise.
26 "If a man hits his male or female slave in
the eye and the eye is blinded, he must let the
slave go free to compensate for the eye. 27 And if

21:6 Or *before the judges.* **21:17** Greek version reads *Anyone who speaks disrespectfully of.* Compare Matt 15:4; Mark 7:10. **21:22** Or *so she has a miscarriage;* Hebrew reads *so her children come out.*

21:1–11 Fair Treatment of Slaves. 2–5: Slavery is not a permanent condition. It is similar to indentured servitude, where one labors for an arranged number of years to gain a specific goal such as freedom from indebtedness or passage to a new country. Hebrew slaves were freed after seven years, and all slaves were freed simultaneously during the Year of Jubilee. Permanent slavery was a status voluntarily chosen. **7–11:** Even for a slave wife, the husband was required to provide food, clothing, and conjugal rights. The neglect of any of these three was considered grounds for divorce. Jewish courts were also to apply the right of divorce on the same stipulation to the nonslave wife.

21:12–36 Cases of Personal Injury. 22–23: Here we find an awareness that violence can endanger the life of the unborn. There is also an understanding that miscarriage brings a sad loss to those expecting to welcome a new member into the family. While money cannot compensate for the loss of a child, the matter was considered worthy of judicial concern. **26–27:** Both male and female slaves who had been victims of violence were to be granted their freedom. This direc-

a man knocks out the tooth of his male or female slave, he must let the slave go free to compensate for the tooth.

[28] "If an ox* gores a man or woman to death, the ox must be stoned, and its flesh may not be eaten. In such a case, however, the owner will not be held liable. [29] But suppose the ox had a reputation for goring, and the owner had been informed but failed to keep it under control. If the ox then kills someone, it must be stoned, and the owner must also be put to death. [30] However, the dead person's relatives may accept payment to compensate for the loss of life. The owner of the ox may redeem his life by paying whatever is demanded.

[31] "The same regulation applies if the ox gores a boy or a girl. [32] But if the ox gores a slave, either male or female, the animal's owner must pay the slave's owner thirty silver coins,* and the ox must be stoned.

[33] "Suppose someone digs or uncovers a pit and fails to cover it, and then an ox or a donkey falls into it. [34] The owner of the pit must pay full compensation to the owner of the animal, but then he gets to keep the dead animal.

[35] "If someone's ox injures a neighbor's ox and the injured ox dies, then the two owners must sell the live ox and divide the price equally between them. They must also divide the dead animal. [36] But if the ox had a reputation for goring, yet its owner failed to keep it under control, he must pay full compensation—a live ox for the dead one—but he may keep the dead ox.

Protection of Property

22 [1]* "If someone steals an ox* or sheep and then kills or sells it, the thief must pay back five oxen for each ox stolen, and four sheep for each sheep stolen.

[2]* "If a thief is caught in the act of breaking into a house and is struck and killed in the process, the person who killed the thief is not guilty of murder. [3] But if it happens in daylight, the one who killed the thief is guilty of murder.

"A thief who is caught must pay in full for everything he stole. If he cannot pay, he must be sold as a slave to pay for his theft. [4] If someone steals an ox or a donkey or a sheep and it is found in the thief's possession, then the thief must pay double the value of the stolen animal.

[5] "If an animal is grazing in a field or vineyard and the owner lets it stray into someone else's field to graze, then the animal's owner must pay compensation from the best of his own grain or grapes.

[6] "If you are burning thornbushes and the fire gets out of control and spreads into another person's field, destroying the sheaves or the uncut grain or the whole crop, the one who started the fire must pay for the lost crop.

[7] "Suppose someone leaves money or goods with a neighbor for safekeeping, and they are stolen from the neighbor's house. If the thief is caught, the compensation is double the value of what was stolen. [8] But if the thief is not caught, the neighbor must appear before God,* who will determine if he stole the property.

[9] "Suppose there is a dispute between two people who both claim to own a particular ox, donkey, sheep, article of clothing, or any lost property. Both parties must come before God, and the person whom God declares* guilty must pay double compensation to the other.

[10] "Now suppose someone leaves a donkey, ox, sheep, or any other animal with a neighbor for safekeeping, but it dies or is injured or gets away, and no one sees what happened. [11] The neighbor must then take an oath in the presence of the LORD. If the LORD confirms that the neighbor did not steal the property, the owner must accept the verdict, and no payment will be required. [12] But if the animal was indeed stolen, the guilty person must pay compensation to the owner. [13] If it was torn to pieces by a wild animal, the remains of the carcass must be shown as evidence, and no compensation will be required.

[14] "If someone borrows an animal from a neighbor and it is injured or dies when the owner is absent, the person who borrowed it must pay full compensation. [15] But if the owner was present, no compensation is required. And no compensation is required if the animal was rented, for this loss is covered by the rental fee.

Social Responsibility

[16] "If a man seduces a virgin who is not engaged to anyone and has sex with her, he must pay the customary bride price and marry her. [17] But if

21:28 Or *bull, or cow;* also in 21:29-36. **21:32** Hebrew *30 shekels of silver,* about 12 ounces or 342 grams in weight. **22:1a** Verse 22:1 is numbered 21:37 in Hebrew text. **22:1b** Or *bull, or cow;* also in 22:4, 9, 10. **22:2** Verses 22:2-31 are numbered 22:1-30 in Hebrew text. **22:8** Or *before the judges.* **22:9** Or *before the judges, and the person whom the judges declare.*

tive is worth pondering for those who wonder whether it is right to leave an abusive home situation. Protection of the law extends to both male and female.

22:1–31 Protection of Property and People. Responsibility for our own actions and other people's well-being was a key element in the law. **16:** Marriage

her father refuses to let him marry her, the man must still pay him an amount equal to the bride price of a virgin.

18 "You must not allow a sorceress to live.

19 "Anyone who has sexual relations with an animal must certainly be put to death.

20 "Anyone who sacrifices to any god other than the LORD must be destroyed.*

21 "You must not mistreat or oppress foreigners in any way. Remember, you yourselves were once foreigners in the land of Egypt.

22 "You must not exploit a widow or an orphan. 23 If you exploit them in any way and they cry out to me, then I will certainly hear their cry. 24 My anger will blaze against you, and I will kill you with the sword. Then your wives will be widows and your children fatherless.

25 "If you lend money to any of my people who are in need, do not charge interest as a money lender would. 26 If you take your neighbor's cloak as security for a loan, you must return it before sunset. 27 This coat may be the only blanket your neighbor has. How can a person sleep without it? If you do not return it and your neighbor cries out to me for help, then I will hear, for I am merciful.

28 "You must not dishonor God or curse any of your rulers.

29 "You must not hold anything back when you give me offerings from your crops and your wine.

"You must give me your firstborn sons.

30 "You must also give me the firstborn of your cattle, sheep, and goats. But leave the newborn animal with its mother for seven days; then give it to me on the eighth day.

31 "You must be my holy people. Therefore, do not eat any animal that has been torn up and killed by wild animals. Throw it to the dogs.

A Call for Justice

23 "You must not pass along false rumors. You must not cooperate with evil people by lying on the witness stand.

2 "You must not follow the crowd in doing wrong. When you are called to testify in a dispute, do not be swayed by the crowd to twist justice. 3 And do not slant your testimony in favor of a person just because that person is poor.

4 "If you come upon your enemy's ox or donkey that has strayed away, take it back to its owner. 5 If you see that the donkey of someone who hates you has collapsed under its load, do not walk by. Instead, stop and help.

6 "In a lawsuit, you must not deny justice to the poor.

7 "Be sure never to charge anyone falsely with evil. Never sentence an innocent or blameless person to death, for I never declare a guilty person to be innocent.

8 "Take no bribes, for a bribe makes you ignore something that you clearly see. A bribe makes even a righteous person twist the truth.

9 "You must not oppress foreigners. You know what it's like to be a foreigner, for you yourselves were once foreigners in the land of Egypt.

10 "Plant and harvest your crops for six years, 11 but let the land be renewed and lie uncultivated during the seventh year. Then let the poor among you harvest whatever grows on its own. Leave the rest for wild animals to eat. The same applies to your vineyards and olive groves.

12 "You have six days each week for your ordinary work, but on the seventh day you must stop working. This gives your ox and your donkey a chance to rest. It also allows your slaves and the foreigners living among you to be refreshed.

13 "Pay close attention to all my instructions. You must not call on the name of any other gods. Do not even speak their names.

Three Annual Festivals

14 "Each year you must celebrate three festivals in my honor. 15 First, celebrate the Festival of

22:20 The Hebrew term used here refers to the complete consecration of things or people to the LORD, either by destroying them or by giving them as an offering.

to a woman's rapist or seducer may seem a most unwelcome option, but in biblical days the arrangement might have been her only chance at suitable provision for herself and her children. **18:** Women who found themselves powerless in other situations sometimes turned to occult practices in the hope of compelling higher powers to do their will. While the shaman commands the gods, the believer humbly beseeches God. **19:** Sexual union is intended to give the deepest form of knowing another person made in the image of God. Copulation with an animal makes a travesty of the divine design.

23:1–13 A Call for Justice. Fairness and integrity was crucial in all aspects of Israelite life. **4–5:** Righteous people must maintain a respect for animal welfare. Cruelty or neglect cannot be tolerated. An overloaded donkey might collapse under the burden or lose its balance. The easiest way to right the animal was for two persons to work together in lifting it, one on each side of the beast. This passage is the basis for the Talmudic obligation not to allow animals to suffer. **13:** The Israelites must leave behind the gods with which they were familiar in Egypt and turn to the true and living God whom their ancestors had served.

Unleavened Bread. For seven days the bread you eat must be made without yeast, just as I commanded you. Celebrate this festival annually at the appointed time in early spring, in the month of Abib,* for that is the anniversary of your departure from Egypt. No one may appear before me without an offering.

16 "Second, celebrate the Festival of Harvest,* when you bring me the first crops of your harvest.

"Finally, celebrate the Festival of the Final Harvest* at the end of the harvest season, when you have harvested all the crops from your fields. 17 At these three times each year, every man in Israel must appear before the Sovereign, the LORD.

18 "You must not offer the blood of my sacrificial offerings together with any baked goods containing yeast. And do not leave the fat from the festival offerings until the next morning.

19 "As you harvest your crops, bring the very best of the first harvest to the house of the LORD your God.

"You must not cook a young goat in its mother's milk.

A Promise of the LORD's Presence

20 "See, I am sending an angel before you to protect you on your journey and lead you safely to the place I have prepared for you. 21 Pay close attention to him, and obey his instructions. Do not rebel against him, for he is my representative, and he will not forgive your rebellion. 22 But if you are careful to obey him, following all my instructions, then I will be an enemy to your enemies, and I will oppose those who oppose you. 23 For my angel will go before you and bring you into the land of the Amorites, Hittites, Perizzites, Canaanites, Hivites, and Jebusites, so you may live there. And I will destroy them completely. 24 You must not worship the gods of these nations or serve them in any way or imitate their evil practices. Instead, you must utterly destroy them and smash their sacred pillars.

25 "You must serve only the LORD your God. If you do, I* will bless you with food and water, and I will protect you from illness. 26 There will be no miscarriages or infertility in your land, and I will give you long, full lives.

27 "I will send my terror ahead of you and create panic among all the people whose lands you invade. I will make all your enemies turn and run. 28 I will send terror* ahead of you to drive out the Hivites, Canaanites, and Hittites. 29 But I will not drive them out in a single year, because the land would become desolate and the wild animals would multiply and threaten you. 30 I will drive them out a little at a time until your population has increased enough to take possession of the land. 31 And I will fix your boundaries from the Red Sea to the Mediterranean Sea,* and from the eastern wilderness to the Euphrates River.* I will hand over to you the people now living in the land, and you will drive them out ahead of you.

32 "Make no treaties with them or their gods. 33 They must not live in your land, or they will cause you to sin against me. If you serve their gods, you will be caught in the trap of idolatry."

Israel Accepts the LORD's Covenant

24 Then the LORD instructed Moses: "Come up here to me, and bring along Aaron, Nadab, Abihu, and seventy of Israel's elders. All of you must worship

23:15 Hebrew *appointed time in the month of Abib.* This first month of the ancient Hebrew lunar calendar usually occurs within the months of March and April. **23:16a** Or *Festival of Weeks.* This was later called the Festival of Pentecost (see Acts 2:1). It is celebrated today as Shavuot (or Shabuoth). **23:16b** Or *Festival of Ingathering.* This was later called the Festival of Shelters or Festival of Tabernacles (see Lev 23:33-36). It is celebrated today as Sukkot (or Succoth). **23:25** As in Greek and Latin versions; Hebrew reads *he.* **23:28** Often rendered *the hornet.* The meaning of the Hebrew is uncertain. **23:31a** Hebrew *from the sea of reeds to the sea of the Philistines.* **23:31b** Hebrew *from the wilderness to the river.*

23:14–19 Three Annual Festivals. 17: Women were welcome although, unlike the men, not required to gather for the three great ceremonies (cf. the attendance of Hannah and Mary the mother of Jesus; see 1 Sam 1:7, 19; Luke 2:41). This gave consideration to those who were pregnant or caring for the young, the sick, or the elderly. **19:** Milk is intended to give life to the young and cannot be used as an implement for death. (See also 34:26.) From this grows the kosher commandment that milk and meat may not be eaten at the same meal.

23:20–33 A Promise of the LORD's Presence. The recurrent motif of God's constant attention to the people is found again here. **28:** Literally "I will send the hornets before you." (See translator's note.) Archaeological excavations sometimes reveal the extinction of a population at a given site and then repopulation some time later. Perhaps the "hornets" were a plague of the type that is known to have wiped out entire communities in the ancient Near East or perhaps the insignia of an invading force.

24:1–18 Israel Accepts the LORD's Covenant. 3–11:

from a distance. 2 Only Moses is allowed to come near to the LORD. The others must not come near, and none of the other people are allowed to climb up the mountain with him."

3 Then Moses went down to the people and repeated all the instructions and regulations the LORD had given him. All the people answered with one voice, "We will do everything the LORD has commanded."

4 Then Moses carefully wrote down all the LORD's instructions. Early the next morning Moses got up and built an altar at the foot of the mountain. He also set up twelve pillars, one for each of the twelve tribes of Israel. 5 Then he sent some of the young Israelite men to present burnt offerings and to sacrifice bulls as peace offerings to the LORD. 6 Moses drained half the blood from these animals into basins. The other half he splattered against the altar.

7 Then he took the Book of the Covenant and read it aloud to the people. Again they all responded, "We will do everything the LORD has commanded. We will obey."

8 Then Moses took the blood from the basins and splattered it over the people, declaring, "Look, this blood confirms the covenant the LORD has made with you in giving you these instructions."

9 Then Moses, Aaron, Nadab, Abihu, and the seventy elders of Israel climbed up the mountain. 10 There they saw the God of Israel. Under his feet there seemed to be a surface of brilliant blue lapis lazuli, as clear as the sky itself. 11 And though these nobles of Israel gazed upon God, he did not destroy them. In fact, they ate a covenant meal, eating and drinking in his presence!

12 Then the LORD said to Moses, "Come up to me on the mountain. Stay there, and I will give you the tablets of stone on which I have inscribed the instructions and commands so you can teach the people." 13 So Moses and his assistant Joshua set out, and Moses climbed up the mountain of God.

14 Moses told the elders, "Stay here and wait for us until we come back. Aaron and Hur are here with you. If anyone has a dispute while I am gone, consult with them."

15 Then Moses climbed up the mountain, and the cloud covered it. 16 And the glory of the LORD settled down on Mount Sinai, and the cloud covered it for six days. On the seventh day the LORD called to Moses from inside the cloud. 17 To the Israelites at the foot of the mountain, the glory of the LORD appeared at the summit like a consuming fire. 18 Then Moses disappeared into the cloud as he climbed higher up the mountain. He remained on the mountain forty days and forty nights.

Offerings for the Tabernacle

25 The LORD said to Moses, 2 "Tell the people of Israel to bring me their sacred offerings. Accept the contributions from all whose hearts are moved to offer them. 3 Here is a list of sacred offerings you may accept from them:

gold, silver, and bronze;
4 blue, purple, and scarlet thread;
fine linen and goat hair for cloth;
5 tanned ram skins and fine goatskin leather;
acacia wood;
6 olive oil for the lamps;
spices for the anointing oil and the fragrant incense;
7 onyx stones, and other gemstones to be set in the ephod and the priest's chestpiece.

8 "Have the people of Israel build me a holy sanctuary so I can live among them. 9 You must build this Tabernacle and its furnishings exactly according to the pattern I will show you.

A typical Near Eastern covenant consisted of an arrangement between a ruler of a great colonial power (suzerain) and the rulers of surrounding conquered nations (vassals). The latter voluntarily agreed to aid the suzerain when called to do so in return for protection and other benefits. The agreement was sealed with a blood sacrifice and a ritual meal (cf. 1 Cor 11:25). God's covenant with Israel is not exactly the same as this, but it did involve free acceptance on Israel's part of both conditions and benefits. **12:** Some of the rocks scattered about the Sinai terrain are extremely soft, and it is possible to mark on them with one's fingernail. Some of the cliffs lend themselves easily to graffiti simply by scratching with a stick.

25:1—31:18 Israel's Preparation for Worship

25:1–40 Plans for Tabernacle, Ark, Table, and Lampstand. 1: Of the forty chapters in the book of Exodus, twelve deal with the establishment of worship. It shows the high priority that worship was given in the life of Israel. **8:** Just as the pillar of cloud and of fire indicated the presence of God in their midst, the traveling sanctuary afforded a holy location for the Israelites to respond in prayer, praise, and sacrifice. Smaller portable objects or shrines that could be used in religious practice were known in the Middle East, but now the people of God were to build a complete sanctuary. The magnitude of a

Plans for the Ark of the Covenant

[10] "Have the people make an Ark of acacia wood—a sacred chest 45 inches long, 27 inches wide, and 27 inches high.* [11] Overlay it inside and outside with pure gold, and run a molding of gold all around it. [12] Cast four gold rings and attach them to its four feet, two rings on each side. [13] Make poles from acacia wood, and overlay them with gold. [14] Insert the poles into the rings at the sides of the Ark to carry it. [15] These carrying poles must stay inside the rings; never remove them. [16] When the Ark is finished, place inside it the stone tablets inscribed with the terms of the covenant,* which I will give to you.

[17] "Then make the Ark's cover—the place of atonement—from pure gold. It must be 45 inches long and 27 inches wide.* [18] Then make two cherubim from hammered gold, and place them on the two ends of the atonement cover. [19] Mold the cherubim on each end of the atonement cover, making it all of one piece of gold. [20] The cherubim will face each other and look down on the atonement cover. With their wings spread above it, they will protect it. [21] Place inside the Ark the stone tablets inscribed with the terms of the covenant, which I will give to you. Then put the atonement cover on top of the Ark. [22] I will meet with you there and talk to you from above the atonement cover between the gold cherubim that hover over the Ark of the Covenant.* From there I will give you my commands for the people of Israel.

Plans for the Table

[23] "Then make a table of acacia wood, 36 inches long, 18 inches wide, and 27 inches high.* [24] Overlay it with pure gold and run a gold molding around the edge. [25] Decorate it with a 3-inch border* all around, and run a gold molding along the border. [26] Make four gold rings for the table and attach them at the four corners next to the four legs. [27] Attach the rings near the border to hold the poles that are used to carry the table. [28] Make these poles from acacia wood, and overlay them with gold. [29] Make special containers of pure gold for the table—bowls, pans, pitchers, and jars—to be used in pouring out liquid offerings. [30] Place the Bread of the Presence on the table to remain before me at all times.

Plans for the Lampstand

[31] "Make a lampstand of pure, hammered gold. Make the entire lampstand and its decorations of one piece—the base, center stem, lamp cups, buds, and petals. [32] Make it with six branches going out from the center stem, three on each side. [33] Each of the six branches will have three lamp cups shaped like almond blossoms, complete with buds and petals. [34] Craft the center stem of the lampstand with four lamp cups shaped like almond blossoms, complete with buds and petals. [35] There will also be an almond bud beneath each pair of branches where the six branches extend from the center stem. [36] The almond buds and branches must all be of one piece with the center stem, and they must be hammered from pure

25:10 Hebrew *2.5 cubits* [115 centimeters] *long, 1.5 cubits* [69 centimeters] *wide, and 1.5 cubits high.* **25:16** Hebrew *Place inside the Ark the Testimony;* similarly in 25:21. The Hebrew word for "testimony" refers to the terms of the LORD's covenant with Israel as written on stone tablets, and also to the covenant itself. **25:17** Hebrew *2.5 cubits* [115 centimeters] *long and 1.5 cubits* [69 centimeters] *wide.* **25:22** Or *Ark of the Testimony.* **25:23** Hebrew *2 cubits* [92 centimeters] *long, 1 cubit* [46 centimeters] *wide, and 1.5 cubits* [69 centimeters] *high.* **25:25** Hebrew *a border of a handbreadth* [8 centimeters].

complete shrine that could be carried about with a nomadic population was a stunningly new concept. The configuration would be that conventionally used in ancient Near Eastern temples: a forecourt where worshipers might gather and then the Holy Place that led into the holiest place of all. The genius of the project lay in its ambitious design and the ease with which the whole might be dismantled and moved to another place. Thus the tent-temple might always be available to a wandering people. **10:** Acacia is an extremely tough wood found abundantly in sturdy shrubs throughout the Sinai. Even twisting off a small twig demands considerable effort. Furniture made of this timber would be very durable, suited to serve generations of God's people. The sacred chest known as the Ark would become the most central of Israel's holy objects. Inside it would be the written record of God's covenant with Israel. The use of poles thrust through rings ensured that the Ark could be carried without being touched by human hands. To this day the holiest part of a Jewish synagogue is the "ark" or niche in which the sacred scrolls of the law are stored. **17:** The golden lid covering the sacred law would represent the platform on which atonement could be made for infractions of those laws. **23:** Like the Ark, the table was to be transported by the means of poles and rings. Fresh loaves of bread were to be placed upon the table each week. **31–40:** Here the decorative motif becomes the almond blossom. The lampstand provided lighting for the interior of the Tabernacle because the roof covering would have kept out the natural light. The seven lamps would have distributed the illumination more evenly.

gold. [37]Then make the seven lamps for the lampstand, and set them so they reflect their light forward. [38]The lamp snuffers and trays must also be
made of pure gold. [39]You will need seventy-five
pounds* of pure gold for the lampstand and its
accessories.
[40]"Be sure that you make everything according to the pattern I have shown you here on the
mountain.

Plans for the Tabernacle

26 "Make the Tabernacle from ten curtains of finely woven linen. Decorate
the curtains with blue, purple, and
scarlet thread and with skillfully embroidered
cherubim. [2]These ten curtains must all be exactly the same size—42 feet long and 6 feet wide.*
[3]Join five of these curtains together to make one
long curtain, then join the other five into a second long curtain. [4]Put loops of blue yarn along
the edge of the last curtain in each set. [5]The fifty
loops along the edge of one curtain are to match
the fifty loops along the edge of the other curtain. [6]Then make fifty gold clasps and fasten the
long curtains together with the clasps. In this
way, the Tabernacle will be made of one continuous piece.
[7]"Make eleven curtains of goat-hair cloth
to serve as a tent covering for the Tabernacle.
[8]These eleven curtains must all be exactly the
same size—45 feet long and 6 feet wide.* [9]Join
five of these curtains together to make one long
curtain, and join the other six into a second long
curtain. Allow 3 feet of material from the second
set of curtains to hang over the front* of the sacred tent. [10]Make fifty loops for one edge of each
large curtain. [11]Then make fifty bronze clasps,
and fasten the loops of the long curtains with the
clasps. In this way, the tent covering will be made
of one continuous piece. [12]The remaining 3 feet*
of this tent covering will be left to hang over the
back of the Tabernacle. [13]Allow 18 inches* of remaining material to hang down over each side,
so the Tabernacle is completely covered. [14]Com-
plete the tent covering with a protective layer
of tanned ram skins and a layer of fine goatskin
leather.
[15]"For the framework of the Tabernacle, construct frames of acacia wood. [16]Each frame must
be 15 feet high and 27 inches wide,* [17]with two
pegs under each frame. Make all the frames identical. [18]Make twenty of these frames to support
the curtains on the south side of the Tabernacle.
[19]Also make forty silver bases—two bases under
each frame, with the pegs fitting securely into
the bases. [20]For the north side of the Tabernacle,
make another twenty frames, [21]with their forty
silver bases, two bases under each frame. [22]Make
six frames for the rear—the west side of the
Tabernacle—[23]along with two additional frames
to reinforce the rear corners of the Tabernacle.
[24]These corner frames will be matched at the
bottom and firmly attached at the top with a single ring, forming a single corner unit. Make both
of these corner units the same way. [25]So there
will be eight frames at the rear of the Tabernacle,
set in sixteen silver bases—two bases under each
frame.
[26]"Make crossbars of acacia wood to link the
frames, five crossbars for the north side of the
Tabernacle [27]and five for the south side. Also
make five crossbars for the rear of the Tabernacle, which will face west. [28]The middle crossbar,
attached halfway up the frames, will run all the
way from one end of the Tabernacle to the other.
[29]Overlay the frames with gold, and make gold
rings to hold the crossbars. Overlay the crossbars
with gold as well.
[30]"Set up this Tabernacle according to the pattern you were shown on the mountain.

25:39 Hebrew *1 talent* [34 kilograms]. **26:2** Hebrew *28 cubits* [12.9 meters] *long and 4 cubits* [1.8 meters] *wide.* **26:8** Hebrew *30 cubits* [13.8 meters] *long and 4 cubits* [1.8 meters] *wide.* **26:9** Hebrew *Double over the sixth sheet at the front.* **26:12** Hebrew *The half sheet that is left over.* **26:13** Hebrew *1 cubit* [46 centimeters]. **26:16** Hebrew *10 cubits* [4.6 meters] *high and 1.5 cubits* [69 centimeters] *wide.*

26:1–37 Plans for the Tabernacle. 1–14: The most extensive need of the tent-sanctuary was for woven curtains. These would enclose not only the Holy Place but also be hung on poles along the outer sides of the larger area surrounding the Tabernacle. It was here that the intricate weaving skills of women would be used. **16–29:** The design to join the various parts was no mean engineering feat. There must be carefully constructed sockets and supports, all handsomely and painstakingly decorated. Artistic expression began to flower in a nomadic people who as slaves had been afforded little time or opportunity for worship. Sometimes this tent-sanctuary is envisioned in terms of primitive crudity, and yet the detailed instructions indicate great care lavished upon this shrine by grateful worshipers. Rather than considering this description a tedious review of a hopelessly antiquated structure, we can see God's blessing on careful planning, ingenious innovation, conscientious execution, and recruitment of top talent. The writer of the book of Hebrews maintains that the pattern of the Tabernacle contained for us a spiritual

31 "For the inside of the Tabernacle, make a
special curtain of finely woven linen. Decorate
it with blue, purple, and scarlet thread and with
skillfully embroidered cherubim. 32 Hang this
curtain on gold hooks attached to four posts of
acacia wood. Overlay the posts with gold, and
set them in four silver bases. 33 Hang the inner
curtain from clasps, and put the Ark of the Covenant* in the room behind it. This curtain will
separate the Holy Place from the Most Holy
Place.
34 "Then put the Ark's cover—the place of
atonement—on top of the Ark of the Covenant
inside the Most Holy Place. 35 Place the table outside the inner curtain on the north side of the
Tabernacle, and place the lampstand across the
room on the south side.
36 "Make another curtain for the entrance to
the sacred tent. Make it of finely woven linen
and embroider it with exquisite designs, using
blue, purple, and scarlet thread. 37 Craft five posts
from acacia wood. Overlay them with gold, and
hang the curtain from them with gold hooks.
Cast five bronze bases for the posts.

Plans for the Altar of Burnt Offering

27 "Using acacia wood, construct a square
altar 7½ feet wide, 7½ feet long, and
4½ feet high.* 2 Make horns for each
of its four corners so that the horns and altar
are all one piece. Overlay the altar with bronze.
3 Make ash buckets, shovels, basins, meat forks,
and firepans, all of bronze. 4 Make a bronze grating for it, and attach four bronze rings at its four
corners. 5 Install the grating halfway down the
side of the altar, under the ledge. 6 For carrying
the altar, make poles from acacia wood, and overlay them with bronze. 7 Insert the poles through
the rings on the two sides of the altar. 8 The altar
must be hollow, made from planks. Build it just
as you were shown on the mountain.

Plans for the Courtyard

9 "Then make the courtyard for the Tabernacle,
enclosed with curtains made of finely woven
linen. On the south side, make the curtains
150 feet long.* 10 They will be held up by twenty posts set securely in twenty bronze bases.
Hang the curtains with silver hooks and rings.
11 Make the curtains the same on the north
side—150 feet of curtains held up by twenty
posts set securely in bronze bases. Hang the
curtains with silver hooks and rings. 12 The curtains on the west end of the courtyard will be
75 feet long,* supported by ten posts set into
ten bases. 13 The east end of the courtyard, the
front, will also be 75 feet long. 14 The courtyard
entrance will be on the east end, flanked by two
curtains. The curtain on the right side will be
22½ feet long,* supported by three posts set
into three bases. 15 The curtain on the left side
will also be 22½ feet long, supported by three
posts set into three bases.
16 "For the entrance to the courtyard, make a
curtain that is 30 feet long.* Make it from finely
woven linen, and decorate it with beautiful embroidery in blue, purple, and scarlet thread. Support it with four posts, each securely set in its
own base. 17 All the posts around the courtyard
must have silver rings and hooks and bronze
bases. 18 So the entire courtyard will be 150 feet
long and 75 feet wide, with curtain walls 7½ feet
high,* made from finely woven linen. The bases
for the posts will be made of bronze.
19 "All the articles used in the rituals of the
Tabernacle, including all the tent pegs used to
support the Tabernacle and the courtyard curtains, must be made of bronze.

Light for the Tabernacle

20 "Command the people of Israel to bring you
pure oil of pressed olives for the light, to keep

26:33 Or *Ark of the Testimony;* also in 26:34. **27:1** Hebrew *5 cubits* [2.3 meters] *wide, 5 cubits long, a square, and 3 cubits* [1.4 meters] *high.* **27:9** Hebrew *100 cubits* [46 meters]; also in 27:11. **27:12** Hebrew *50 cubits* [23 meters]; also in 27:13. **27:14** Hebrew *15 cubits* [6.9 meters]; also in 27:15. **27:16** Hebrew *20 cubits* [9.2 meters]. **27:18** Hebrew *100 cubits* [46 meters] *long and 50 by 50* [23 meters] *wide and 5 cubits* [2.3 meters] *high.*

---

lesson (Heb 9:1–9). **31–36:** Rather than coarse tent cloth, curtains surrounding the Holy Place were of linen, finely woven and gloriously embellished with the use of color. Here the creativity of skilled women shone forth in the designs that they executed in the texture of the fabric. The exterior curtains were spun of goats' hair.

27:1–21 Plans for the Altar and Courtyard. 1: Within the courtyard at the entrance to the Holy Place, stood the altar available to Israelites bringing gifts and sacrifices. The accoutrements are of bronze, rather than gold, and the linen curtains decorated with colored thread. This was the place where all Israelites could come. There is no sign here of the court of the women that Herod incorporated into his temple many centuries later, and no indication of any limitation of access for women as opposed to men who were not priests.

the lamps burning continually. 21 The lampstand will stand in the Tabernacle, in front of the inner curtain that shields the Ark of the Covenant.* Aaron and his sons must keep the lamps burning in the LORD's presence all night. This is a permanent law for the people of Israel, and it must be observed from generation to generation.

Clothing for the Priests

28 "Call for your brother, Aaron, and his sons, Nadab, Abihu, Eleazar, and Ithamar. Set them apart from the rest of the people of Israel so they may minister to me and be my priests. 2 Make sacred garments for Aaron that are glorious and beautiful. 3 Instruct all the skilled craftsmen whom I have filled with the spirit of wisdom. Have them make garments for Aaron that will distinguish him as a priest set apart for my service. 4 These are the garments they are to make: a chestpiece, an ephod, a robe, a patterned tunic, a turban, and a sash. They are to make these sacred garments for your brother, Aaron, and his sons to wear when they serve me as priests. 5 So give them fine linen cloth, gold thread, and blue, purple, and scarlet thread.

Design of the Ephod

6 "The craftsmen must make the ephod of finely woven linen and skillfully embroider it with gold and with blue, purple, and scarlet thread. 7 It will consist of two pieces, front and back, joined at the shoulders with two shoulder-pieces. 8 The decorative sash will be made of the same materials: finely woven linen embroidered with gold and with blue, purple, and scarlet thread.

9 "Take two onyx stones, and engrave on them the names of the tribes of Israel. 10 Six names will be on each stone, arranged in the order of the births of the original sons of Israel. 11 Engrave these names on the two stones in the same way a jeweler engraves a seal. Then mount the stones in settings of gold filigree. 12 Fasten the two stones on the shoulder-pieces of the ephod as a reminder that Aaron represents the people of Israel. Aaron will carry these names on his shoulders as a constant reminder whenever he goes before the LORD. 13 Make the settings of gold filigree, 14 then braid two cords of pure gold and attach them to the filigree settings on the shoulders of the ephod.

Design of the Chestpiece

15 "Then, with great skill and care, make a chestpiece to be worn for seeking a decision from God.* Make it to match the ephod, using finely woven linen embroidered with gold and with blue, purple, and scarlet thread. 16 Make the chestpiece of a single piece of cloth folded to form a pouch nine inches* square. 17 Mount four rows of gemstones* on it. The first row will contain a red carnelian, a pale-green peridot, and an emerald. 18 The second row will contain a turquoise, a blue lapis lazuli, and a white moonstone. 19 The third row will contain an orange jacinth, an agate, and a purple amethyst. 20 The fourth row will contain a blue-green beryl, an onyx, and a green jasper. All these stones will be set in gold filigree. 21 Each stone will represent one of the twelve sons of Israel, and the name of that tribe will be engraved on it like a seal.

22 "To attach the chestpiece to the ephod, make braided cords of pure gold thread. 23 Then make two gold rings and attach them to the top corners of the chestpiece. 24 Tie the two gold cords to the two rings on the chestpiece. 25 Tie the other ends of the cords to the gold settings on the shoulder-pieces of the ephod. 26 Then make two more gold rings and attach them to the inside edges of the chestpiece next to the ephod. 27 And make two more gold rings and attach them to the front of the ephod, below the shoulder-pieces, just above the knot where the decorative sash is fastened to the ephod. 28 Then attach the bottom rings of the chestpiece to the rings on the ephod with blue cords. This will hold the chestpiece securely to the ephod above the decorative sash.

29 "In this way, Aaron will carry the names of the tribes of Israel on the sacred chestpiece* over his heart when he goes into the Holy Place. This will be a continual reminder that he repre-

27:21 Hebrew *in the Tent of Meeting, outside the inner curtain that is in front of the Testimony.* See note on 25:16. **28:15** Hebrew *a chestpiece for decision.* **28:16** Hebrew *1 span* [23 centimeters]. **28:17** The identification of some of these gemstones is uncertain. **28:29** Hebrew *the chestpiece for decision;* also in 28:30. See 28:15.

28:1–43 Priestly Clothing. 1–14: The *ephod* was a sort of vest suspended by shoulder straps. On its breast were attached two stones on which were inscribed the names of the twelve tribes. Thus each time that Aaron entered the sanctuary dressed in his priestly garments, the names would appear before God as a reminder of his people. **15:** The *chestpiece . . . for seeking a decision* was used by the high priest seeking God's will. It was encrusted with precious stones that would have flashed in the sunlight. Attached was a pouch containing the Urim and Thummim. These seem to have been a method of casting lots for answering a yes-or-no question. Perhaps one was drawn out when a difficult decision needed to

sents the people when he comes before the LORD. 30 Insert the Urim and Thummim into the sacred chestpiece so they will be carried over Aaron's heart when he goes into the LORD's presence. In this way, Aaron will always carry over his heart the objects used to determine the LORD's will for his people whenever he goes in before the LORD.

Additional Clothing for the Priests

31 "Make the robe that is worn with the ephod from a single piece of blue cloth, 32 with an opening for Aaron's head in the middle of it. Reinforce the opening with a woven collar* so it will not tear. 33 Make pomegranates out of blue, purple, and scarlet yarn, and attach them to the hem of the robe, with gold bells between them. 34 The gold bells and pomegranates are to alternate all around the hem. 35 Aaron will wear this robe whenever he ministers before the LORD, and the bells will tinkle as he goes in and out of the LORD's presence in the Holy Place. If he wears it, he will not die.

36 "Next make a medallion of pure gold, and engrave it like a seal with these words: HOLY TO THE LORD. 37 Attach the medallion with a blue cord to the front of Aaron's turban, where it must remain. 38 Aaron must wear it on his forehead so he may take on himself any guilt of the people of Israel when they consecrate their sacred offerings. He must always wear it on his forehead so the LORD will accept the people.

39 "Weave Aaron's patterned tunic from fine linen cloth. Fashion the turban from this linen as well. Also make a sash, and decorate it with colorful embroidery.

40 "For Aaron's sons, make tunics, sashes, and special head coverings that are glorious and beautiful. 41 Clothe your brother, Aaron, and his sons with these garments, and then anoint and ordain them. Consecrate them so they can serve as my priests. 42 Also make linen undergarments for them, to be worn next to their bodies, reaching from their hips to their thighs. 43 These must be worn whenever Aaron and his sons enter the Tabernacle* or approach the altar in the Holy Place to perform their priestly duties. Then they will not incur guilt and die. This is a permanent law for Aaron and all his descendants after him.

Dedication of the Priests

29 "This is the ceremony you must follow when you consecrate Aaron and his sons to serve me as priests: Take a young bull and two rams with no defects. 2 Then, using choice wheat flour and no yeast, make loaves of bread, thin cakes mixed with olive oil, and wafers spread with oil. 3 Place them all in a single basket, and present them at the entrance of the Tabernacle, along with the young bull and the two rams.

4 "Present Aaron and his sons at the entrance of the Tabernacle,* and wash them with water. 5 Dress Aaron in his priestly garments—the tunic, the robe worn with the ephod, the ephod itself, and the chestpiece. Then wrap the decorative sash of the ephod around him. 6 Place the turban on his head, and fasten the sacred medallion to the turban. 7 Then anoint him by pouring the anointing oil over his head. 8 Next present his sons, and dress them in their tunics. 9 Wrap the sashes around the waists of Aaron and his sons, and put their special head coverings on them. Then the right to the priesthood will be theirs by law forever. In this way, you will ordain Aaron and his sons.

10 "Bring the young bull to the entrance of the Tabernacle, where Aaron and his sons will lay their hands on its head. 11 Then slaughter the bull in the LORD's presence at the entrance of the Tabernacle. 12 Put some of its blood on the horns of the altar with your finger, and pour out the rest at the base of the altar. 13 Take all the fat around the internal organs, the long lobe of the liver, and the two kidneys and the fat around them, and burn it all on the altar. 14 Then take the rest of the bull, including its hide, meat, and dung, and burn it outside the camp as a sin offering.

15 "Next Aaron and his sons must lay their hands on the head of one of the rams. 16 Then slaughter the ram, and splatter its blood against all sides of the altar. 17 Cut the ram into pieces, and wash off the internal organs and the legs. Set them alongside the head and the other pieces of

28:32 The meaning of the Hebrew is uncertain.
28:43 Hebrew *Tent of Meeting.* **29:4** Hebrew *Tent of Meeting;* also in 29:10, 11, 30, 32, 42, 44.

be made. **33:** Representations of plant life were not forbidden in Hebrew art. Brightly colored woolen tassels shaped like pomegranates were attached to the hem of the priests' garments, interspersed with golden bells (39:24–26). (The pomegranate was used in the decoration of Solomon's Temple, and a small ivory pomegranate from this period has been discovered. It bears the inscription "Belonging to the Temple of the LORD, holy to the priests.") **42:** Apparently other Hebrew males wore no undergarments.

29:1–46 Dedication of the Priests. 3–4: The altar stood in the courtyard before the entrance to the Tabernacle, offering both forgiveness for sin and

the body, [18] then burn the entire animal on the altar. This is a burnt offering to the LORD; it is a pleasing aroma, a special gift presented to the LORD.

[19] "Now take the other ram, and have Aaron and his sons lay their hands on its head. [20] Then slaughter it, and apply some of its blood to the right earlobes of Aaron and his sons. Also put it on the thumbs of their right hands and the big toes of their right feet. Splatter the rest of the blood against all sides of the altar. [21] Then take some of the blood from the altar and some of the anointing oil, and sprinkle it on Aaron and his sons and on their garments. In this way, they and their garments will be set apart as holy.

[22] "Since this is the ram for the ordination of Aaron and his sons, take the fat of the ram, including the fat of the broad tail, the fat around the internal organs, the long lobe of the liver, and the two kidneys and the fat around them, along with the right thigh. [23] Then take one round loaf of bread, one thin cake mixed with olive oil, and one wafer from the basket of bread without yeast that was placed in the LORD's presence. [24] Put all these in the hands of Aaron and his sons to be lifted up as a special offering to the LORD. [25] Afterward take the various breads from their hands, and burn them on the altar along with the burnt offering. It is a pleasing aroma to the LORD, a special gift for him. [26] Then take the breast of Aaron's ordination ram, and lift it up in the LORD's presence as a special offering to him. Then keep it as your own portion.

[27] "Set aside the portions of the ordination ram that belong to Aaron and his sons. This includes the breast and the thigh that were lifted up before the LORD as a special offering. [28] In the future, whenever the people of Israel lift up a peace offering, a portion of it must be set aside for Aaron and his descendants. This is their permanent right, and it is a sacred offering from the Israelites to the LORD.

[29] "Aaron's sacred garments must be preserved for his descendants who succeed him, and they will wear them when they are anointed and ordained. [30] The descendant who succeeds him as high priest will wear these clothes for seven days as he ministers in the Tabernacle and the Holy Place.

[31] "Take the ram used in the ordination ceremony, and boil its meat in a sacred place. [32] Then Aaron and his sons will eat this meat, along with the bread in the basket, at the Tabernacle entrance. [33] They alone may eat the meat and bread used for their purification* in the ordination ceremony. No one else may eat them, for these things are set apart and holy. [34] If any of the ordination meat or bread remains until the morning, it must be burned. It may not be eaten, for it is holy.

[35] "This is how you will ordain Aaron and his sons to their offices, just as I have commanded you. The ordination ceremony will go on for seven days. [36] Each day you must sacrifice a young bull as a sin offering to purify them, making them right with the LORD.* Afterward, cleanse the altar by purifying it*; make it holy by anointing it with oil. [37] Purify the altar, and consecrate it every day for seven days. After that, the altar will be absolutely holy, and whatever touches it will become holy.

[38] "These are the sacrifices you are to offer regularly on the altar. Each day, offer two lambs that are a year old, [39] one in the morning and the other in the evening. [40] With one of them, offer two quarts of choice flour mixed with one quart of pure oil of pressed olives; also, offer one quart of wine* as a liquid offering. [41] Offer the other lamb in the evening, along with the same offerings of flour and wine as in the morning. It will be a pleasing aroma, a special gift presented to the LORD.

[42] "These burnt offerings are to be made each day from generation to generation. Offer them in the LORD's presence at the Tabernacle entrance; there I will meet with you and speak

29:33 Or *their atonement.* **29:36a** Or *to make atonement.* **29:36b** Or *by making atonement for it;* similarly in 29:37. **29:40** Hebrew $^1/_{10}$ *of an ephah* [2.2 liters] *of choice flour . . .* $^1/_4$ *of a hin* [1 liter] *of pure oil . . .* $^1/_4$ *of a hin of wine.*

welcome to the presence of God. **26–28:** The burnt offering was to be burned entirely, but portions of the peace offerings and thanksgiving offerings were shared between the priesthood, the donor of the sacrifice, and their guests. Meat seldom appeared in the ancient diet, unless a sacrifice had taken place. A meal following the sacrifice was an important part of the ritual (cf. 18:12; 24:4–11). **32–34:** The sacred bread (unleavened, consecrated bread) was to be consumed only by the priests, and yet Jesus commended David's action in eating it when he and his followers were desperate for food (Matt 12:3–4; Mark 2:25–28; Luke 6:1–5; cf. 1 Sam 21:6). It may be that the system was not meant to be quite as rigid as it is sometimes assumed to be. **42–45:** Here the altar stood, at the place of meeting between God and his people. It was here that the women ministered (38:8; 1 Sam 2:21). For the importance of this location in other circumstances, see Num 12:5; 25:6.

with you. 43 I will meet the people of Israel there, in the place made holy by my glorious presence. 44 Yes, I will consecrate the Tabernacle and the altar, and I will consecrate Aaron and his sons to serve me as priests. 45 Then I will live among the people of Israel and be their God, 46 and they will know that I am the LORD their God. I am the one who brought them out of the land of Egypt so that I could live among them. I am the LORD their God.

Plans for the Incense Altar

30 "Then make another altar of acacia wood for burning incense. 2 Make it 18 inches square and 36 inches high,* with horns at the corners carved from the same piece of wood as the altar itself. 3 Overlay the top, sides, and horns of the altar with pure gold, and run a gold molding around the entire altar. 4 Make two gold rings, and attach them on opposite sides of the altar below the gold molding to hold the carrying poles. 5 Make the poles of acacia wood and overlay them with gold. 6 Place the incense altar just outside the inner curtain that shields the Ark of the Covenant,* in front of the Ark's cover—the place of atonement—that covers the tablets inscribed with the terms of the covenant.* I will meet with you there.

7 "Every morning when Aaron maintains the lamps, he must burn fragrant incense on the altar. 8 And each evening when he lights the lamps, he must again burn incense in the LORD's presence. This must be done from generation to generation. 9 Do not offer any unholy incense on this altar, or any burnt offerings, grain offerings, or liquid offerings.

10 "Once a year Aaron must purify* the altar by smearing its horns with blood from the offering made to purify the people from their sin. This will be a regular, annual event from generation to generation, for this is the LORD's most holy altar."

Money for the Tabernacle

11 Then the LORD said to Moses, 12 "Whenever you take a census of the people of Israel, each man who is counted must pay a ransom for himself to the LORD. Then no plague will strike the people as you count them. 13 Each person who is counted must give a small piece of silver as a sacred offering to the LORD. (This payment is half a shekel,* based on the sanctuary shekel, which equals twenty gerahs.) 14 All who have reached their twentieth birthday must give this sacred offering to the LORD. 15 When this offering is given to the LORD to purify your lives, making you right with him,* the rich must not give more than the specified amount, and the poor must not give less. 16 Receive this ransom money from the Israelites, and use it for the care of the Tabernacle.* It will bring the Israelites to the LORD's attention, and it will purify your lives."

Plans for the Washbasin

17 Then the LORD said to Moses, 18 "Make a bronze washbasin with a bronze stand. Place it between the Tabernacle and the altar, and fill it with water. 19 Aaron and his sons will wash their hands and feet there. 20 They must wash with water whenever they go into the Tabernacle to appear before the LORD and when they approach the altar to burn up their special gifts to the LORD—or they will die! 21 They must always wash their hands and feet, or they will die. This is a permanent law for Aaron and his descendants, to be observed from generation to generation."

The Anointing Oil

22 Then the LORD said to Moses, 23 "Collect choice spices—12½ pounds of pure myrrh, 6¼ pounds of fragrant cinnamon, 6¼ pounds of fragrant calamus,* 24 and 12½ pounds of cassia*—as measured by the weight of the sanctuary shekel. Also get one gallon of olive oil.* 25 Like a skilled incense maker, blend these ingredients to make a

30:2 Hebrew *1 cubit* [46 centimeters] *long and 1 cubit wide, a square, and 2 cubits* [92 centimeters] *high.* **30:6a** Or *Ark of the Testimony;* also in 30:26. **30:6b** Hebrew *that covers the Testimony;* see note on 25:16. **30:10** Or *make atonement for;* also in 30:10b. **30:13** Or *0.2 ounces, or 6 grams.* **30:15** Or *to make atonement for your lives;* similarly in 30:16. **30:16** Hebrew *Tent of Meeting;* also in 30:18, 20, 26, 36. **30:23** Hebrew *500 shekels* [5.7 kilograms] *of pure myrrh, 250 shekels* [2.9 kilograms] *of fragrant cinnamon, 250 shekels of fragrant calamus.* **30:24a** Hebrew *500 shekels* [5.7 kilograms] *of cassia.* **30:24b** Hebrew *1 hin* [3.8 liters] *of olive oil.*

30:1–38 More Details of the Sanctuary. 1–9: There was a pungent smell of meat roasting, but the odor associated with animal sacrifice was dispelled by the fragrance of the burning incense. **12:** This command is carried out in Numbers 31:25–54. For a plague associated with a census, see 2 Samuel 24:1–25. **15:** All gifts are significant before God, and each donor was of the same value. **17–20:** The sacrificing of animals at the altar was dirty, bloody work, and so the washbasin stood before the entrance to the Holy Place. God's servants must be pure before they came into his presence. **22–37:** Although instructions are given for the preparation of both holy oil and incense, neither is intended for the use of private individuals.

holy anointing oil. 26 Use this sacred oil to anoint
the Tabernacle, the Ark of the Covenant, 27 the
table and all its utensils, the lampstand and all its
accessories, the incense altar, 28 the altar of burnt
offering and all its utensils, and the washbasin
with its stand. 29 Consecrate them to make them
absolutely holy. After this, whatever touches
them will also become holy.

30 "Anoint Aaron and his sons also, consecrating them to serve me as priests. 31 And say to the
people of Israel, 'This holy anointing oil is reserved for me from generation to generation. 32 It
must never be used to anoint anyone else, and
you must never make any blend like it for yourselves. It is holy, and you must treat it as holy.
33 Anyone who makes a blend like it or anoints
someone other than a priest will be cut off from
the community.'"

The Incense

34 Then the LORD said to Moses, "Gather fragrant
spices—resin droplets, mollusk shell, and galba-
num—and mix these fragrant spices with pure
frankincense, weighed out in equal amounts.
35 Using the usual techniques of the incense
maker, blend the spices together and sprinkle
them with salt to produce a pure and holy incense. 36 Grind some of the mixture into a very
fine powder and put it in front of the Ark of the
Covenant,* where I will meet with you in the
Tabernacle. You must treat this incense as most
holy. 37 Never use this formula to make this incense for yourselves. It is reserved for the LORD,
and you must treat it as holy. 38 Anyone who
makes incense like this for personal use will be
cut off from the community."

Craftsmen: Bezalel and Oholiab

31 Then the LORD said to Moses, 2 "Look,
I have specifically chosen Bezalel son
of Uri, grandson of Hur, of the tribe of
Judah. 3 I have filled him with the Spirit of God,
giving him great wisdom, ability, and expertise
in all kinds of crafts. 4 He is a master craftsman,
expert in working with gold, silver, and bronze.
5 He is skilled in engraving and mounting gemstones and in carving wood. He is a master at
every craft!

6 "And I have personally appointed Oholiab
son of Ahisamach, of the tribe of Dan, to be his
assistant. Moreover, I have given special skill to
all the gifted craftsmen so they can make all the
things I have commanded you to make:

7 the Tabernacle;*
the Ark of the Covenant;*
the Ark's cover—the place of atonement;
all the furnishings of the Tabernacle;
8 the table and its utensils;
the pure gold lampstand with all its
accessories;
the incense altar;
9 the altar of burnt offering with all its utensils;
the washbasin with its stand;
10 the beautifully stitched garments—the sacred
garments for Aaron the priest, and the
garments for his sons to wear as they
minister as priests;
11 the anointing oil;
the fragrant incense for the Holy Place.

The craftsmen must make everything as I have
commanded you."

Instructions for the Sabbath

12 The LORD then gave these instructions to Moses: 13 "Tell the people of Israel: 'Be careful to
keep my Sabbath day, for the Sabbath is a sign of
the covenant between me and you from generation to generation. It is given so you may know

30:36 Hebrew *in front of the Testimony;* see note on 25:16.
31:7a Hebrew *the Tent of Meeting.* **31:7b** Hebrew *the Ark of the Testimony.*

31:1–11 Craftsmen: Bezalel and Oholiab. 1–10: The construction and maintenance of the Tabernacle required community effort. There was a need not only for the cleverest artisans but also for all those naturally talented in crafts. The special talents of women were recognized in that the garments of the priests were to be *beautifully stitched*, which was normally a craft where women excelled. Others with no pronounced artistic talents were also necessary. If the Tabernacle was to follow the wandering people, there must be those who had the technical skill to dismantle and reassemble the portable structure as the host moved from place to place. The transportation of the shrine and all its accoutrements was in itself a major project.

31:12–18 Sabbath Instructions. The Sabbath provides not only needful rest but also becomes a mark of the covenantal relationship between God and the holy people (cf. Isa 56:2–6; 58:13–14). Israel, the holy race, was to be set apart by a holy time and a holy place. There are no detailed instructions for keeping the Sabbath, apart from the command to rest. To fail to rest is to fail to trust God. Excessive legalism in Sabbath-keeping later became a problem, but the principle of taking time out because everyone

that I am the LORD, who makes you holy. 14 You
must keep the Sabbath day, for it is a holy day
for you. Anyone who desecrates it must be put
to death; anyone who works on that day will
be cut off from the community. 15 You have six
days each week for your ordinary work, but the
seventh day must be a Sabbath day of complete
rest, a holy day dedicated to the LORD. Anyone
who works on the Sabbath must be put to death.
16 The people of Israel must keep the Sabbath day
by observing it from generation to generation.
This is a covenant obligation for all time. 17 It is a
permanent sign of my covenant with the people
of Israel. For in six days the LORD made heaven
and earth, but on the seventh day he stopped
working and was refreshed.' "

18 When the LORD finished speaking with Moses on Mount Sinai, he gave him the two stone
tablets inscribed with the terms of the covenant,*
written by the finger of God.

The Gold Calf

32 When the people saw how long it
was taking Moses to come back down
the mountain, they gathered around
Aaron. "Come on," they said, "make us some
gods who can lead us. We don't know what happened to this fellow Moses, who brought us here
from the land of Egypt."

2 So Aaron said, "Take the gold rings from the
ears of your wives and sons and daughters, and
bring them to me."

3 All the people took the gold rings from their
ears and brought them to Aaron. 4 Then Aaron
took the gold, melted it down, and molded it into
the shape of a calf. When the people saw it, they
exclaimed, "O Israel, these are the gods who
brought you out of the land of Egypt!"

5 Aaron saw how excited the people were, so
he built an altar in front of the calf. Then he
announced, "Tomorrow will be a festival to the
LORD!"

6 The people got up early the next morning to
sacrifice burnt offerings and peace offerings. After this, they celebrated with feasting and drinking, and they indulged in pagan revelry.

7 The LORD told Moses, "Quick! Go down the
mountain! Your people whom you brought from
the land of Egypt have corrupted themselves.
8 How quickly they have turned away from
the way I commanded them to live! They have
melted down gold and made a calf, and they have
bowed down and sacrificed to it. They are saying,
'These are your gods, O Israel, who brought you
out of the land of Egypt.' "

9 Then the LORD said, "I have seen how stubborn and rebellious these people are. 10 Now leave
me alone so my fierce anger can blaze against
them, and I will destroy them. Then I will make
you, Moses, into a great nation."

11 But Moses tried to pacify the LORD his God.
"O LORD!" he said. "Why are you so angry with
your own people whom you brought from the land
of Egypt with such great power and such a strong
hand? 12 Why let the Egyptians say, 'Their God
rescued them with the evil intention of slaughtering them in the mountains and wiping them
from the face of the earth'? Turn away from your
fierce anger. Change your mind about this terrible
disaster you have threatened against your people!
13 Remember your servants Abraham, Isaac, and
Jacob.* You bound yourself with an oath to them,
saying, 'I will make your descendants as numerous as the stars of heaven. And I will give them all
of this land that I have promised to your descendants, and they will possess it forever.' "

14 So the LORD changed his mind about the
terrible disaster he had threatened to bring on
his people.

15 Then Moses turned and went down the
mountain. He held in his hands the two stone

31:18 Hebrew *the two tablets of the Testimony;* see note on 25:16. **32:13** Hebrew *Israel.* The names "Jacob" and "Israel" are often interchanged throughout the Old Testament, referring sometimes to the individual patriarch and sometimes to the nation.

needs rest and refreshment is also *a covenant obligation* for *a holy day dedicated to the LORD.*

32:1—35:3 Excursus: Failure and Renewal

32:1–29 The Calf of Gold. 5–6: Throughout the period of the Exodus, many Israelites remained committed to the gods of Mesopotamia and Egypt (Josh 24:14, 23) and to the manufacture of idols. Although Israel had been commanded to observe the Passover festival each year, now the people designed a festival of their own. Ritual dancing at such events often became lascivious (see v. 25; cf. 1 Cor 10:7). The defiance of Moses' instruction may imply that sexual misconduct is the cause of the epidemic that afflicts them (v. 35; cf. Num 25:1–9). It may be that Aaron saw the calf as a culturally acceptable way of worshiping the LORD, but it was important for the people to recognize how different the LORD was from their idols. It was not appropriate for them simply to decide for themselves how God should be worshiped. **11–13:** In his effort to deflect the LORD's anger from destroying the people of Israel, Moses turns God's own arguments against him. The Egyptians will think

tablets inscribed with the terms of the covenant.* They were inscribed on both sides, front
and back. 16 These tablets were God's work; the
words on them were written by God himself.
17 When Joshua heard the boisterous noise of
the people shouting below them, he exclaimed to
Moses, "It sounds like war in the camp!"
18 But Moses replied, "No, it's not a shout
of victory nor the wailing of defeat. I hear the
sound of a celebration."
19 When they came near the camp, Moses saw
the calf and the dancing, and he burned with anger. He threw the stone tablets to the ground,
smashing them at the foot of the mountain. 20 He
took the calf they had made and burned it. Then
he ground it into powder, threw it into the water,
and forced the people to drink it.
21 Finally, he turned to Aaron and demanded,
"What did these people do to you to make you
bring such terrible sin upon them?"
22 "Don't get so upset, my lord," Aaron replied. "You yourself know how evil these people
are. 23 They said to me, 'Make us gods who will
lead us. We don't know what happened to this
fellow Moses, who brought us here from the
land of Egypt.' 24 So I told them, 'Whoever has
gold jewelry, take it off.' When they brought it
to me, I simply threw it into the fire—and out
came this calf!"
25 Moses saw that Aaron had let the people get
completely out of control, much to the amusement of their enemies.* 26 So he stood at the entrance to the camp and shouted, "All of you who
are on the LORD's side, come here and join me."
And all the Levites gathered around him.
27 Moses told them, "This is what the LORD,
the God of Israel, says: Each of you, take your
swords and go back and forth from one end of
the camp to the other. Kill everyone—even your
brothers, friends, and neighbors." 28 The Levites
obeyed Moses' command, and about 3,000 people
died that day.
29 Then Moses told the Levites, "Today you
have ordained yourselves* for the service of the
LORD, for you obeyed him even though it meant
killing your own sons and brothers. Today you
have earned a blessing."

Moses Intercedes for Israel

30 The next day Moses said to the people, "You
have committed a terrible sin, but I will go back
up to the LORD on the mountain. Perhaps I will
be able to obtain forgiveness* for your sin."
31 So Moses returned to the LORD and said,
"Oh, what a terrible sin these people have committed. They have made gods of gold for themselves. 32 But now, if you will only forgive their
sin—but if not, erase my name from the record
you have written!"
33 But the LORD replied to Moses, "No, I will
erase the name of everyone who has sinned
against me. 34 Now go, lead the people to the
place I told you about. Look! My angel will lead
the way before you. And when I come to call the
people to account, I will certainly hold them responsible for their sins."
35 Then the LORD sent a great plague upon
the people because they had worshiped the calf
Aaron had made.

33 The LORD said to Moses, "Get going,
you and the people you brought up
from the land of Egypt. Go up to the
land I swore to give to Abraham, Isaac, and Jacob. I told them, 'I will give this land to your descendants.' 2 And I will send an angel before you
to drive out the Canaanites, Amorites, Hittites,
Perizzites, Hivites, and Jebusites. 3 Go up to this
land that flows with milk and honey. But I will

32:15 Hebrew *the two tablets of the Testimony;* see note on 25:16. **32:25** Or *out of control, and they mocked anyone who opposed them.* The meaning of the Hebrew is unclear. **32:29** As in Greek and Latin versions; Hebrew reads *Today ordain yourselves.* **32:30** Or *to make atonement.*

of God as malignant, and he would have to break the ancient covenant with Abraham, Isaac, and Jacob (cf. Num 14:13–19). **15–16:** The giving of the law is variously described in Scripture as the work of God and the work of Moses. The combined sources tell of God's use of Moses to compose and disseminate the divine directives. All of the expertise and experiences of Moses are tools in God's hands: his early childhood training; his familiarity with Egyptian medicine; administration, military, and engineering skills; his knowledge of survival in the Sinai wilderness; and his growing awareness of God's presence and power. **21–25:** Obviously Aaron is telling a falsehood. He refuses to take responsibility for his own wrongdoing. He has done nothing to stop the conduct that brought only humiliation and disgrace upon both the LORD and the people.

32:30—33:11 Moses Intercedes for Israel. 32:31–32: It is sometimes assumed that Moses is asking God to destroy him instead of the people, but that is not his request. He identifies himself with the people—if they are to be blotted out of the record then so should he be. He is very angry with the people he has been called to lead, but they are still his people. Identification with those who are led is an impor-

not travel among you, for you are a stubborn and
rebellious people. If I did, I would surely destroy
you along the way."
4 When the people heard these stern words,
they went into mourning and stopped wearing
their jewelry and fine clothes. 5 For the LORD had
told Moses to tell them, "You are a stubborn and
rebellious people. If I were to travel with you for
even a moment, I would destroy you. Remove
your jewelry and fine clothes while I decide what
to do with you." 6 So from the time they left
Mount Sinai,* the Israelites wore no more jewelry or fine clothes.
7 It was Moses' practice to take the Tent of
Meeting* and set it up some distance from the
camp. Everyone who wanted to make a request
of the LORD would go to the Tent of Meeting
outside the camp.
8 Whenever Moses went out to the Tent of
Meeting, all the people would get up and stand in
the entrances of their own tents. They would all
watch Moses until he disappeared inside. 9 As he
went into the tent, the pillar of cloud would come
down and hover at its entrance while the LORD
spoke with Moses. 10 When the people saw the
cloud standing at the entrance of the tent, they
would stand and bow down in front of their own
tents. 11 Inside the Tent of Meeting, the LORD
would speak to Moses face to face, as one speaks
to a friend. Afterward Moses would return to
the camp, but the young man who assisted him,
Joshua son of Nun, would remain behind in the
Tent of Meeting.

Moses Sees the LORD's Glory

12 One day Moses said to the LORD, "You have
been telling me, 'Take these people up to the
Promised Land.' But you haven't told me whom
you will send with me. You have told me, 'I know
you by name, and I look favorably on you.' 13 If
it is true that you look favorably on me, let me
know your ways so I may understand you more
fully and continue to enjoy your favor. And remember that this nation is your very own people."
14 The LORD replied, "I will personally go with
you, Moses, and I will give you rest—everything
will be fine for you."
15 Then Moses said, "If you don't personally
go with us, don't make us leave this place. 16 How
will anyone know that you look favorably on
me—on me and on your people—if you don't go
with us? For your presence among us sets your
people and me apart from all other people on the
earth."
17 The LORD replied to Moses, "I will indeed
do what you have asked, for I look favorably on
you, and I know you by name."
18 Moses responded, "Then show me your
glorious presence."
19 The LORD replied, "I will make all my goodness pass before you, and I will call out my name,
Yahweh,* before you. For I will show mercy to
anyone I choose, and I will show compassion to
anyone I choose. 20 But you may not look directly at my face, for no one may see me and live."
21 The LORD continued, "Look, stand near me on
this rock. 22 As my glorious presence passes by, I
will hide you in the crevice of the rock and cover
you with my hand until I have passed by. 23 Then
I will remove my hand and let you see me from
behind. But my face will not be seen."

A New Copy of the Covenant

34 Then the LORD told Moses, "Chisel
out two stone tablets like the first
ones. I will write on them the same
words that were on the tablets you smashed. 2 Be
ready in the morning to climb up Mount Sinai
and present yourself to me on the top of the

33:6 Hebrew *Horeb,* another name for Sinai. **33:7** This "Tent of Meeting" is different from the Tabernacle described in chapters 26 and 36. **33:19** *Yahweh* is a transliteration of the proper name *YHWH* that is sometimes rendered "Jehovah"; in this translation it is usually rendered "the LORD" (note the use of small capitals).

---

tant calling for any leader. **33:4–6:** Jewelry acquired by the women at the time of the flight (3:22; 11:2) had provided the molten substance for the gold calf (32:2, 24). Personal adornment was inappropriate during a time of deep contrition.

33:12–23 Moses Sees the LORD's Glory. 16–23: The essential definition of Israel as a nation *set . . . apart* from all others is confirmed by God's accompanying presence (cf. v. 3; 34:9). Moses may long to know the entirety of God's nature, but although only a partial view is possible for any human being, it is significant that God in his awesome glory allows any view at all. The parallel pictures of God's separation and difference from humans and of God's closeness to them remain a motif throughout the Bible.

34:1—35:3 A New Copy of the Covenant. 34:1–4: Not only were the people wrong to have done what they did, but Moses too had been wrong to smash the original tablets. He now has to prepare what God had originally given him. But it is clear and encouraging that God deals with people where they are and provides the opportunity for a new start.

mountain. 3 No one else may come with you. In
fact, no one is to appear anywhere on the mountain. Do not even let the flocks or herds graze
near the mountain."
4 So Moses chiseled out two tablets of stone
like the first ones. Early in the morning he
climbed Mount Sinai as the LORD had commanded him, and he carried the two stone tablets
in his hands.
5 Then the LORD came down in a cloud and
stood there with him; and he called out his own
name, Yahweh.* 6 The LORD passed in front of
Moses, calling out,

"Yahweh!* The LORD!
The God of compassion and mercy!
I am slow to anger
and filled with unfailing love and
faithfulness.
7 I lavish unfailing love to a thousand
generations.*
I forgive iniquity, rebellion, and sin.
But I do not excuse the guilty.
I lay the sins of the parents upon their
children and grandchildren;
the entire family is affected—
even children in the third and fourth
generations."

8 Moses immediately threw himself to the
ground and worshiped. 9 And he said, "O Lord, if
it is true that I have found favor with you, then
please travel with us. Yes, this is a stubborn and
rebellious people, but please forgive our iniquity
and our sins. Claim us as your own special possession."
10 The LORD replied, "Listen, I am making a
covenant with you in the presence of all your
people. I will perform miracles that have never
been performed anywhere in all the earth or in
any nation. And all the people around you will
see the power of the LORD—the awesome power
I will display for you. 11 But listen carefully to
everything I command you today. Then I will
go ahead of you and drive out the Amorites, Canaanites, Hittites, Perizzites, Hivites, and Jebusites.
12 "Be very careful never to make a treaty with
the people who live in the land where you are
going. If you do, you will follow their evil ways
and be trapped. 13 Instead, you must break down
their pagan altars, smash their sacred pillars, and
cut down their Asherah poles. 14 You must worship no other gods, for the LORD, whose very
name is Jealous, is a God who is jealous about his
relationship with you.
15 "You must not make a treaty of any kind
with the people living in the land. They lust after their gods, offering sacrifices to them. They
will invite you to join them in their sacrificial
meals, and you will go with them. 16 Then you
will accept their daughters, who sacrifice to other
gods, as wives for your sons. And they will seduce your sons to commit adultery against me
by worshiping other gods. 17 You must not make
any gods of molten metal for yourselves.
18 "You must celebrate the Festival of Unleavened Bread. For seven days the bread you
eat must be made without yeast, just as I commanded you. Celebrate this festival annually at
the appointed time in early spring, in the month
of Abib,* for that is the anniversary of your departure from Egypt.
19 "The firstborn of every animal belongs to
me, including the firstborn males from your
herds of cattle and your flocks of sheep and goats.
20 A firstborn donkey may be bought back from
the LORD by presenting a lamb or young goat in
its place. But if you do not buy it back, you must
break its neck. However, you must buy back every firstborn son.
"No one may appear before me without an
offering.
21 "You have six days each week for your ordinary work, but on the seventh day you must stop
working, even during the seasons of plowing and
harvest.
22 "You must celebrate the Festival of Harvest* with the first crop of the wheat harvest,
and celebrate the Festival of the Final Harvest*

34:5 *Yahweh* is a transliteration of the proper name *YHWH* that is sometimes rendered "Jehovah"; in this translation it is usually rendered "the LORD" (note the use of small capitals). **34:6** See note on 34:5. **34:7** Hebrew *for thousands.* **34:18** Hebrew *appointed time in the month of Abib.* This first month of the ancient Hebrew lunar calendar usually occurs within the months of March and April. **34:22a** Hebrew *Festival of Weeks;* compare 23:16. This was later called the Festival of Pentecost. It is celebrated today as Shavuot (or Shabuoth). **34:22b** Or *Festival of Ingathering.* This was later called the Festival of Shelters or Festival of Tabernacles (see Lev 23:33-36). It is celebrated today as Sukkot (or Succoth).

5–7: The biblical records ordinarily explain God through a narrative of his deeds. Here is one of the few descriptions of the Deity's essential character: mingling both kindness and justice. **16:** Women are the primary custodians of culture and of household religion. Later history showed that heathen women joining believing families often led to the adoption of pagan worship.

at the end of the harvest season. [23]Three times
each year every man in Israel must appear before
the Sovereign, the LORD, the God of Israel. [24]I
will drive out the other nations ahead of you and
expand your territory, so no one will covet and
conquer your land while you appear before the
LORD your God three times each year.
[25]"You must not offer the blood of my sacrificial offerings together with any baked goods
containing yeast. And none of the meat of the
Passover sacrifice may be kept over until the next
morning.
[26]"As you harvest your crops, bring the very
best of the first harvest to the house of the LORD
your God.

"You must not cook a young goat in its mother's milk."
[27]Then the LORD said to Moses, "Write down
all these instructions, for they represent the
terms of the covenant I am making with you and
with Israel."
[28]Moses remained there on the mountain
with the LORD forty days and forty nights.
In all that time he ate no bread and drank no
water. And the LORD* wrote the terms of the
covenant—the Ten Commandments*—on the
stone tablets.
[29]When Moses came down Mount Sinai carrying the two stone tablets inscribed with the
terms of the covenant,* he wasn't aware that his
face had become radiant because he had spoken
to the LORD. [30]So when Aaron and the people of
Israel saw the radiance of Moses' face, they were
afraid to come near him.
[31]But Moses called out to them and asked
Aaron and all the leaders of the community to
come over, and he talked with them. [32]Then all
the people of Israel approached him, and Moses
gave them all the instructions the LORD had given him on Mount Sinai. [33]When Moses finished
speaking with them, he covered his face with a
veil. [34]But whenever he went into the Tent of
Meeting to speak with the LORD, he would remove the veil until he came out again. Then he
would give the people whatever instructions the
LORD had given him, [35]and the people of Israel
would see the radiant glow of his face. So he
would put the veil over his face until he returned
to speak with the LORD.

Instructions for the Sabbath

35 Then Moses called together the
whole community of Israel and told
them, "These are the instructions the
LORD has commanded you to follow. [2]You have
six days each week for your ordinary work, but
the seventh day must be a Sabbath day of complete rest, a holy day dedicated to the LORD. Anyone who works on that day must be put to death.
[3]You must not even light a fire in any of your
homes on the Sabbath."

Offerings for the Tabernacle

[4]Then Moses said to the whole community of Israel, "This is what the LORD has commanded: [5]Take a
sacred offering for the LORD. Let those with generous hearts present the following gifts to the LORD:

gold, silver, and bronze;
[6]blue, purple, and scarlet thread;
fine linen and goat hair for cloth;
[7]tanned ram skins and fine goatskin leather;
acacia wood;
[8]olive oil for the lamps;
spices for the anointing oil and the fragrant incense;
[9]onyx stones, and other gemstones to be set in the ephod and the priest's chestpiece.

[10]"Come, all of you who are gifted craftsmen.
Construct everything that the LORD has commanded:

[11]the Tabernacle and its sacred tent, its covering, clasps, frames, crossbars, posts, and bases;
[12]the Ark and its carrying poles;
the Ark's cover—the place of atonement;
the inner curtain to shield the Ark;
[13]the table, its carrying poles, and all its utensils;
the Bread of the Presence;
[14]for light, the lampstand, its accessories, the lamp cups, and the olive oil for lighting;
[15]the incense altar and its carrying poles;
the anointing oil and fragrant incense;
the curtain for the entrance of the Tabernacle;

34:28a Hebrew *he.* **34:28b** Hebrew *the ten words.*
34:29 Hebrew *the two tablets of the Testimony;* see note on 25:16.

35:4—40:38 Establishment of Worship

35:4—36:38 More Sabbath and Tabernacle Instructions. 35:4–19: The Tabernacle was not to be an exclusive place for the priests only. Anyone who wanted could offer their gifts whether this meant giving money or other material help or giving their labor. It was important that everyone realized that the Tabernacle belonged to the whole community and that there was a genuine sense of ownership. **16:** The

16 the altar of burnt offering;
the bronze grating of the altar and its carrying
poles and utensils;
the washbasin with its stand;
17 the curtains for the walls of the courtyard;
the posts and their bases;
the curtain for the entrance to the courtyard;
18 the tent pegs of the Tabernacle and courtyard
and their ropes;
19 the beautifully stitched garments for the
priests to wear while ministering in the
Holy Place—the sacred garments for Aaron
the priest, and the garments for his sons to
wear as they minister as priests."

20 So the whole community of Israel left Moses and returned to their tents. 21 All whose hearts
were stirred and whose spirits were moved came
and brought their sacred offerings to the LORD.
They brought all the materials needed for the
Tabernacle,* for the performance of its rituals,
and for the sacred garments. 22 Both men and
women came, all whose hearts were willing. They
brought to the LORD their offerings of gold—
brooches, earrings, rings from their fingers, and
necklaces. They presented gold objects of every kind as a special offering to the LORD. 23 All
those who owned the following items willingly
brought them: blue, purple, and scarlet thread;
fine linen and goat hair for cloth; and tanned ram
skins and fine goatskin leather. 24 And all who had
silver and bronze objects gave them as a sacred
offering to the LORD. And those who had acacia
wood brought it for use in the project.
25 All the women who were skilled in sewing
and spinning prepared blue, purple, and scarlet
thread, and fine linen cloth. 26 All the women who
were willing used their skills to spin the goat hair
into yarn. 27 The leaders brought onyx stones and
the special gemstones to be set in the ephod and
the priest's chestpiece. 28 They also brought spices
and olive oil for the light, the anointing oil, and
the fragrant incense. 29 So the people of Israel—
every man and woman who was eager to help
in the work the LORD had given them through
Moses—brought their gifts and gave them freely
to the LORD.
30 Then Moses told the people of Israel, "The
LORD has specifically chosen Bezalel son of Uri,
grandson of Hur, of the tribe of Judah. 31 The
LORD has filled Bezalel with the Spirit of God,
giving him great wisdom, ability, and expertise
in all kinds of crafts. 32 He is a master craftsman,
expert in working with gold, silver, and bronze.
33 He is skilled in engraving and mounting gemstones and in carving wood. He is a master at every craft. 34 And the LORD has given both him and
Oholiab son of Ahisamach, of the tribe of Dan,
the ability to teach their skills to others. 35 The
LORD has given them special skills as engravers,
designers, embroiderers in blue, purple, and scarlet thread on fine linen cloth, and weavers. They
excel as craftsmen and as designers.

36 "The LORD has gifted Bezalel, Oholiab, and the other skilled craftsmen
with wisdom and ability to perform
any task involved in building the sanctuary. Let
them construct and furnish the Tabernacle, just
as the LORD has commanded."
2 So Moses summoned Bezalel and Oholiab
and all the others who were specially gifted by
the LORD and were eager to get to work. 3 Moses
gave them the materials donated by the people
of Israel as sacred offerings for the completion
of the sanctuary. But the people continued to
bring additional gifts each morning. 4 Finally the
craftsmen who were working on the sanctuary
left their work. 5 They went to Moses and reported, "The people have given more than enough
materials to complete the job the LORD has commanded us to do!"
6 So Moses gave the command, and this message was sent throughout the camp: "Men and
women, don't prepare any more gifts for the
sanctuary. We have enough!" So the people

35:21 Hebrew *Tent of Meeting.*

altar was hollow, and the grating allowed the ashes and remnants of the sacrifice to drop down where they could easily be removed. **20–24:** Egypt was very rich in gold, drawn from its abundance in Cush farther south along the Nile. The jewelry taken from the citizens of Egypt had been used earlier to create the gold calf. Now the precious metal is used in the service of God. Both men and women gave gladly of talent and treasures. The gifts of women are particularly affirmed. **22–23:** *Hearts . . . willing, willingly brought*: Offerings are given freely. **25–29:** Often the decorative arts of women are undervalued, but here we have an appreciation of the various skills in which women excel. The ability to transform the rough goats' hair into smooth cloth bespeaks the way that women are able to produce works of art from humble materials. To create objects of beauty is indeed a worthy endeavor and to dedicate them to God's glory an even greater one. **35:35—36:1:** Part of the LORD's gifting is not only to produce fine quality work but to instruct other gifted persons to perfect their own skills. **8:** Both weaving and embroidery are

stopped bringing their sacred offerings. 7 Their
contributions were more than enough to complete the whole project.

Building the Tabernacle

8 The skilled craftsmen made ten curtains of finely woven linen for the Tabernacle. Then Bezalel*
decorated the curtains with blue, purple, and
scarlet thread and with skillfully embroidered
cherubim. 9 All ten curtains were exactly the
same size—42 feet long and 6 feet wide.* 10 Five
of these curtains were joined together to make
one long curtain, and the other five were joined
to make a second long curtain. 11 He made fifty
loops of blue yarn and put them along the edge
of the last curtain in each set. 12 The fifty loops
along the edge of one curtain matched the fifty
loops along the edge of the other curtain. 13 Then
he made fifty gold clasps and fastened the long
curtains together with the clasps. In this way, the
Tabernacle was made of one continuous piece.

14 He made eleven curtains of goat-hair cloth
to serve as a tent covering for the Tabernacle.
15 These eleven curtains were all exactly the same
size—45 feet long and 6 feet wide.* 16 Bezalel
joined five of these curtains together to make
one long curtain, and the other six were joined to
make a second long curtain. 17 He made fifty loops
for the edge of each large curtain. 18 He also made
fifty bronze clasps to fasten the long curtains together. In this way, the tent covering was made
of one continuous piece. 19 He completed the tent
covering with a layer of tanned ram skins and a
layer of fine goatskin leather.

20 For the framework of the Tabernacle, Bezalel constructed frames of acacia wood. 21 Each
frame was 15 feet high and 27 inches wide,*
22 with two pegs under each frame. All the frames
were identical. 23 He made twenty of these frames
to support the curtains on the south side of the
Tabernacle. 24 He also made forty silver bases—
two bases under each frame, with the pegs fitting securely into the bases. 25 For the north
side of the Tabernacle, he made another twenty
frames, 26 with their forty silver bases, two bases
under each frame. 27 He made six frames for the
rear—the west side of the Tabernacle—28 along
with two additional frames to reinforce the rear
corners of the Tabernacle. 29 These corner frames
were matched at the bottom and firmly attached
at the top with a single ring, forming a single
corner unit. Both of these corner units were
made the same way. 30 So there were eight frames
at the rear of the Tabernacle, set in sixteen silver
bases—two bases under each frame.

31 Then he made crossbars of acacia wood to
link the frames, five crossbars for the north side
of the Tabernacle 32 and five for the south side. He
also made five crossbars for the rear of the Tabernacle, which faced west. 33 He made the middle
crossbar to attach halfway up the frames; it ran
all the way from one end of the Tabernacle to
the other. 34 He overlaid the frames with gold and
made gold rings to hold the crossbars. Then he
overlaid the crossbars with gold as well.

35 For the inside of the Tabernacle, Bezalel
made a special curtain of finely woven linen. He
decorated it with blue, purple, and scarlet thread
and with skillfully embroidered cherubim. 36 For
the curtain, he made four posts of acacia wood
and four gold hooks. He overlaid the posts with
gold and set them in four silver bases.

37 Then he made another curtain for the entrance to the sacred tent. He made it of finely
woven linen and embroidered it with exquisite
designs using blue, purple, and scarlet thread.
38 This curtain was hung on gold hooks attached
to five posts. The posts with their decorated tops
and hooks were overlaid with gold, and the five
bases were cast from bronze.

Building the Ark of the Covenant

37 Next Bezalel made the Ark of acacia
wood—a sacred chest 45 inches long,
27 inches wide, and 27 inches high.*

36:8 Hebrew *he;* also in 36:16, 20, 35. See 37:1. **36:9** Hebrew *28 cubits* [12.9 meters] *long and 4 cubits* [1.8 meters] *wide.* **36:15** Hebrew *30 cubits* [13.8 meters] *long and 4 cubits* [1.8 meters] *wide.* **36:21** Hebrew *10 cubits* [4.6 meters] *high and 1.5 cubits* [69 centimeters] *wide.* **37:1** Hebrew *2.5 cubits* [115 centimeters] *long, 1.5 cubits* [69 centimeters] *wide, and 1.5 cubits high.*

historically the arts of women. Although the representation of any human or animal figures was forbidden, the cherubim were considered to be collective creatures, part human and part animal. In the ancient Near East they were held to be the servants of kings or gods. Thus they are depicted here as servants of the LORD, guarding the throne of God.

37:1—38:20 The Tabernacle Contents. 37:1–24: The Ark, the table, and the lampstand all had great significance as symbols of God's continuing presence with the people, but it was important for everyone to realize that in themselves they were just symbols. Even the Ark was just an ornate box, made like the rest of the Tabernacle by God-gifted artisans. The artistic elements are carefully detailed. A representation of the seven-branched candlestick can be seen in the bas relief on the Arch of Titus in the Roman Forum.

2 He overlaid it inside and outside with pure gold,
and he ran a molding of gold all around it. 3 He
cast four gold rings and attached them to its four
feet, two rings on each side. 4 Then he made poles
from acacia wood and overlaid them with gold.
5 He inserted the poles into the rings at the sides
of the Ark to carry it.
6 Then he made the Ark's cover—the place
of atonement—from pure gold. It was 45 inches
long and 27 inches wide.* 7 He made two cherubim from hammered gold and placed them on the
two ends of the atonement cover. 8 He molded the
cherubim on each end of the atonement cover,
making it all of one piece of gold. 9 The cherubim
faced each other and looked down on the atonement cover. With their wings spread above it,
they protected it.

Building the Table

10 Then Bezalel* made the table of acacia wood,
36 inches long, 18 inches wide, and 27 inches
high.* 11 He overlaid it with pure gold and ran
a gold molding around the edge. 12 He decorated
it with a 3-inch border* all around, and he ran
a gold molding along the border. 13 Then he cast
four gold rings for the table and attached them
at the four corners next to the four legs. 14 The
rings were attached near the border to hold the
poles that were used to carry the table. 15 He
made these poles from acacia wood and overlaid
them with gold. 16 Then he made special containers of pure gold for the table—bowls, pans, jars,
and pitchers—to be used in pouring out liquid
offerings.

Building the Lampstand

17 Then Bezalel made the lampstand of pure, hammered gold. He made the entire lampstand and its
decorations of one piece—the base, center stem,
lamp cups, buds, and petals. 18 The lampstand had
six branches going out from the center stem,
three on each side. 19 Each of the six branches had
three lamp cups shaped like almond blossoms,
complete with buds and petals. 20 The center stem
of the lampstand was crafted with four lamp cups
shaped like almond blossoms, complete with buds
and petals. 21 There was an almond bud beneath
each pair of branches where the six branches
extended from the center stem, all made of one
piece. 22 The almond buds and branches were all
of one piece with the center stem, and they were
hammered from pure gold.
23 He also made seven lamps for the lampstand,
lamp snuffers, and trays, all of pure gold. 24 The
entire lampstand, along with its accessories, was
made from seventy-five pounds* of pure gold.

Building the Incense Altar

25 Then Bezalel made the incense altar of acacia wood. It was 18 inches square and 36 inches
high,* with horns at the corners carved from
the same piece of wood as the altar itself. 26 He
overlaid the top, sides, and horns of the altar with
pure gold, and he ran a gold molding around the
entire altar. 27 He made two gold rings and attached them on opposite sides of the altar below
the gold molding to hold the carrying poles. 28 He
made the poles of acacia wood and overlaid them
with gold.
29 Then he made the sacred anointing oil and
the fragrant incense, using the techniques of a
skilled incense maker.

Building the Altar of Burnt Offering

38 Next Bezalel* used acacia wood to
construct the square altar of burnt
offering. It was 7½ feet wide, 7½ feet
long, and 4½ feet high.* 2 He made horns for
each of its four corners so that the horns and altar were all one piece. He overlaid the altar with
bronze. 3 Then he made all the altar utensils of
bronze—the ash buckets, shovels, basins, meat
forks, and firepans. 4 Next he made a bronze grating and installed it halfway down the side of the
altar, under the ledge. 5 He cast four rings and attached them to the corners of the bronze grating
to hold the carrying poles. 6 He made the poles
from acacia wood and overlaid them with bronze.
7 He inserted the poles through the rings on the
sides of the altar. The altar was hollow and was
made from planks.

Building the Washbasin

8 Bezalel made the bronze washbasin and its
bronze stand from bronze mirrors donated by

37:6 Hebrew *2.5 cubits* [115 centimeters] *long and 1.5 cubits* [69 centimeters] *wide.* **37:10a** Hebrew *he;* also in 37:17, 25. **37:10b** Hebrew *2 cubits* [92 centimeters] *long, 1 cubit* [46 centimeters] *wide, and 1.5 cubits* [69 centimeters] *high.* **37:12** Hebrew *a border of a handbreadth* [8 centimeters]. **37:24** Hebrew *1 talent* [34 kilograms]. **37:25** Hebrew *1 cubit* [46 centimeters] *long and 1 cubit wide, a square, and 2 cubits* [92 centimeters] *high.* **38:1a** Hebrew *he;* also in 38:8, 9. **38:1b** Hebrew *5 cubits* [2.3 meters] *wide, 5 cubits long, a square, and 3 cubits* [1.4 meters] *high.*

38:8: The mirrors that the women had brought from Egypt were of fine brass that could be polished to a very high gloss. The use of this metal brought a shining brilliance to the fixtures of the Tabernacle. The sacrifice of their mirrors must have constituted a real wrench for the women. The women could no longer

the women who served at the entrance of the Tabernacle.*

Building the Courtyard

9 Then Bezalel made the courtyard, which was enclosed with curtains made of finely woven linen. On the south side the curtains were 150 feet long.* 10 They were held up by twenty posts set securely in twenty bronze bases. He hung the curtains with silver hooks and rings. 11 He made a similar set of curtains for the north side—150 feet of curtains held up by twenty posts set securely in bronze bases. He hung the curtains with silver hooks and rings. 12 The curtains on the west end of the courtyard were 75 feet long,* hung with silver hooks and rings and supported by ten posts set into ten bases. 13 The east end, the front, was also 75 feet long.

14 The courtyard entrance was on the east end, flanked by two curtains. The curtain on the right side was 22½ feet long* and was supported by three posts set into three bases. 15 The curtain on the left side was also 22½ feet long and was supported by three posts set into three bases. 16 All the curtains used in the courtyard were made of finely woven linen. 17 Each post had a bronze base, and all the hooks and rings were silver. The tops of the posts of the courtyard were overlaid with silver, and the rings to hold up the curtains were made of silver.

18 He made the curtain for the entrance to the courtyard of finely woven linen, and he decorated it with beautiful embroidery in blue, purple, and scarlet thread. It was 30 feet long, and its height was 7½ feet,* just like the curtains of the courtyard walls. 19 It was supported by four posts, each set securely in its own bronze base. The tops of the posts were overlaid with silver, and the hooks and rings were also made of silver.

20 All the tent pegs used in the Tabernacle and courtyard were made of bronze.

Inventory of Materials

21 This is an inventory of the materials used in building the Tabernacle of the Covenant.* The Levites compiled the figures, as Moses directed, and Ithamar son of Aaron the priest served as recorder. 22 Bezalel son of Uri, grandson of Hur, of the tribe of Judah, made everything just as the LORD had commanded Moses. 23 He was assisted by Oholiab son of Ahisamach, of the tribe of Dan, a craftsman expert at engraving, designing, and embroidering with blue, purple, and scarlet thread on fine linen cloth.

24 The people brought special offerings of gold totaling 2,193 pounds,* as measured by the weight of the sanctuary shekel. This gold was used throughout the Tabernacle.

25 The whole community of Israel gave 7,545 pounds* of silver, as measured by the weight of the sanctuary shekel. 26 This silver came from the tax collected from each man registered in the census. (The tax is one beka, which is half a shekel,* based on the sanctuary shekel.) The tax was collected from 603,550 men who had reached their twentieth birthday. 27 The hundred bases for the frames of the sanctuary walls and for the posts supporting the inner curtain required 7,500 pounds of silver, about 75 pounds for each base.* 28 The remaining 45 pounds* of silver was used to make the hooks and rings and to overlay the tops of the posts.

29 The people also brought as special offerings 5,310 pounds* of bronze, 30 which was used for casting the bases for the posts at the entrance to the Tabernacle, and for the bronze altar with its bronze grating and all the altar utensils. 31 Bronze was also used to make the bases for the posts that supported the curtains around the courtyard, the

38:8 Hebrew *Tent of Meeting;* also in 38:30. **38:9** Hebrew *100 cubits* [46 meters]; also in 38:11. **38:12** Hebrew *50 cubits* [23 meters]; also in 38:13. **38:14** Hebrew *15 cubits* [6.9 meters]; also in 38:15. **38:18** Hebrew *20 cubits* [9.2 meters] *long and 5 cubits* [2.3 meters] *high.* **38:21** Hebrew *the Tabernacle, the Tabernacle of the Testimony.* **38:24** Hebrew *29 talents and 730 shekels* [994 kilograms]. Each shekel weighed about 0.4 ounces. **38:25** Hebrew *100 talents and 1,775 shekels* [3,420 kilograms]. **38:26** Or *0.2 ounces,* or *6 grams.* **38:27** Hebrew *100 talents* [3,400 kilograms] *of silver, 1 talent* [34 kilograms] *for each base.* **38:28** Hebrew *1,775 shekels* [20.2 kilograms]. **38:29** Hebrew *70 talents and 2,400 shekels* [2,407 kilograms].

see their own beauty reflected in their bronze mirrors, yet they could see the radiance of God's Tabernacle. Personal vanity is replaced by collective piety. The women who served at the entrance of the Tabernacle are also mentioned in 1 Samuel 2:22. Thus women are involved not only in the construction of the Tabernacle but also in its active ministry. For the significance of the entry place, see 29:42.

38:21–31 Inventory of Materials. The accoutrements of the holiest place of all were of gold and the hangings the most ornate, shot with threads of gold. The Holy Place was equipped with silver and the outer courtyard with bronze. **23:** Oholiab, a male craftsman, also excels in embroidery. The interest is on ability rather than stereotyped gender roles. Note how carefully the accounts were kept. There is no excuse for slapdash work of any kind in the service of God.

bases for the curtain at the entrance of the courtyard, and all the tent pegs for the Tabernacle and
the courtyard.

Clothing for the Priests

39 The craftsmen made beautiful sacred
garments of blue, purple, and scarlet
cloth—clothing for Aaron to wear
while ministering in the Holy Place, just as the
LORD had commanded Moses.

Making the Ephod

2 Bezalel* made the ephod of finely woven lin-
en and embroidered it with gold and with blue,
purple, and scarlet thread. 3 He made gold thread
by hammering out thin sheets of gold and cutting it into fine strands. With great skill and care,
he worked it into the fine linen with the blue,
purple, and scarlet thread.
4 The ephod consisted of two pieces, front and
back, joined at the shoulders with two shoulder-
pieces. 5 The decorative sash was made of the same
materials: finely woven linen embroidered with
gold and with blue, purple, and scarlet thread,
just as the LORD had commanded Moses. 6 They
mounted the two onyx stones in settings of gold
filigree. The stones were engraved with the names
of the tribes of Israel, just as a seal is engraved.
7 He fastened these stones on the shoulder-pieces
of the ephod as a reminder that the priest represents the people of Israel. All this was done just as
the LORD had commanded Moses.

Making the Chestpiece

8 Bezalel made the chestpiece with great skill
and care. He made it to match the ephod, using
finely woven linen embroidered with gold and
with blue, purple, and scarlet thread. 9 He made
the chestpiece of a single piece of cloth folded
to form a pouch nine inches* square. 10 They
mounted four rows of gemstones* on it. The
first row contained a red carnelian, a pale-green
peridot, and an emerald. 11 The second row contained a turquoise, a blue lapis lazuli, and a white
moonstone. 12 The third row contained an orange
jacinth, an agate, and a purple amethyst. 13 The
fourth row contained a blue-green beryl, an
onyx, and a green jasper. All these stones were
set in gold filigree. 14 Each stone represented one
of the twelve sons of Israel, and the name of that
tribe was engraved on it like a seal.
15 To attach the chestpiece to the ephod, they
made braided cords of pure gold thread. 16 They
also made two settings of gold filigree and two
gold rings and attached them to the top corners
of the chestpiece. 17 They tied the two gold cords
to the rings on the chestpiece. 18 They tied the
other ends of the cords to the gold settings on the
shoulder-pieces of the ephod. 19 Then they made
two more gold rings and attached them to the
inside edges of the chestpiece next to the ephod.
20 Then they made two more gold rings and attached them to the front of the ephod, below
the shoulder-pieces, just above the knot where
the decorative sash was fastened to the ephod.
21 They attached the bottom rings of the chestpiece to the rings on the ephod with blue cords.
In this way, the chestpiece was held securely to
the ephod above the decorative sash. All this was
done just as the LORD had commanded Moses.

Additional Clothing for the Priests

22 Bezalel made the robe that is worn with the
ephod from a single piece of blue woven cloth,
23 with an opening for Aaron's head in the middle
of it. The opening was reinforced with a woven
collar* so it would not tear. 24 They made pomegranates of blue, purple, and scarlet yarn, and
attached them to the hem of the robe. 25 They
also made bells of pure gold and placed them
between the pomegranates along the hem of the
robe, 26 with bells and pomegranates alternating
all around the hem. This robe was to be worn
whenever the priest ministered before the LORD,
just as the LORD had commanded Moses.
27 They made tunics for Aaron and his sons
from fine linen cloth. 28 The turban and the special
head coverings were made of fine linen, and the
undergarments were also made of finely woven
linen. 29 The sashes were made of finely woven lin-
en and embroidered with blue, purple, and scarlet
thread, just as the LORD had commanded Moses.
30 Finally, they made the sacred medallion—
the badge of holiness—of pure gold. They engraved it like a seal with these words: HOLY TO
THE LORD. 31 They attached the medallion with a
blue cord to Aaron's turban, just as the LORD had
commanded Moses.

39:2 Hebrew *He;* also in 39:8, 22. **39:9** Hebrew *1 span* [23 centimeters]. **39:10** The identification of some of these gemstones is uncertain. **39:23** The meaning of the Hebrew is uncertain.

39:1–31 More on the Priest's Clothing. The work that has been described so minutely is now executed in exact detail. The vestments must have been glorious to behold, bespeaking the glory and dignity of the ministry. **3:** Here we have a description of the actual technology that was employed. Gold is the softest of the metals and can be worked the most easily and artistically.

Moses Inspects the Work
32 And so at last the Tabernacle* was finished. The Israelites had done everything just as the LORD had commanded Moses. 33 And they brought the entire Tabernacle to Moses:

the sacred tent with all its furnishings, clasps, frames, crossbars, posts, and bases;
34 the tent coverings of tanned ram skins and fine goatskin leather;
the inner curtain to shield the Ark;
35 the Ark of the Covenant* and its carrying poles;
the Ark's cover—the place of atonement;
36 the table and all its utensils;
the Bread of the Presence;
37 the pure gold lampstand with its symmetrical lamp cups, all its accessories, and the olive oil for lighting;
38 the gold altar;
the anointing oil and fragrant incense;
the curtain for the entrance of the sacred tent;
39 the bronze altar;
the bronze grating and its carrying poles and utensils;
the washbasin with its stand;
40 the curtains for the walls of the courtyard;
the posts and their bases;
the curtain for the entrance to the courtyard;
the ropes and tent pegs;
all the furnishings to be used in worship at the Tabernacle;
41 the beautifully stitched garments for the priests to wear while ministering in the Holy Place—the sacred garments for Aaron the priest, and the garments for his sons to wear as they minister as priests.

42 So the people of Israel followed all of the LORD's instructions to Moses. 43 Then Moses inspected all their work. When he found it had been done just as the LORD had commanded him, he blessed them.

The Tabernacle Completed
40 Then the LORD said to Moses, 2 "Set up the Tabernacle* on the first day of the new year.* 3 Place the Ark of the Covenant* inside, and install the inner curtain to enclose the Ark within the Most Holy Place.
4 Then bring in the table, and arrange the utensils on it. And bring in the lampstand, and set up the lamps.
5 "Place the gold incense altar in front of the Ark of the Covenant. Then hang the curtain at the entrance of the Tabernacle. 6 Place the altar of burnt offering in front of the Tabernacle entrance. 7 Set the washbasin between the Tabernacle* and the altar, and fill it with water. 8 Then set up the courtyard around the outside of the tent, and hang the curtain for the courtyard entrance.
9 "Take the anointing oil and anoint the Tabernacle and all its furnishings to consecrate them and make them holy. 10 Anoint the altar of burnt offering and its utensils to consecrate them. Then the altar will become absolutely holy. 11 Next anoint the washbasin and its stand to consecrate them.
12 "Present Aaron and his sons at the entrance of the Tabernacle, and wash them with water.
13 Dress Aaron with the sacred garments and anoint him, consecrating him to serve me as a priest. 14 Then present his sons and dress them in their tunics. 15 Anoint them as you did their father, so they may also serve me as priests. With their anointing, Aaron's descendants are set apart for the priesthood forever, from generation to generation."
16 Moses proceeded to do everything just as the LORD had commanded him. 17 So the Tabernacle was set up on the first day of the first month of the second year. 18 Moses erected the Tabernacle by setting down its bases, inserting the frames, attaching the crossbars, and setting up the posts. 19 Then he spread the coverings over the Tabernacle framework and put on the protective layers, just as the LORD had commanded him.

39:32 Hebrew *the Tabernacle, the Tent of Meeting;* also in 39:40. **39:35** Or *Ark of the Testimony.* **40:2a** Hebrew *the Tabernacle, the Tent of Meeting;* also in 40:6, 29. **40:2b** Hebrew *the first day of the first month.* This day of the ancient Hebrew lunar calendar occurred in March or April. **40:3** Or *Ark of the Testimony;* also in 40:5, 21. **40:7** Hebrew *Tent of Meeting;* also in 40:12, 22, 24, 26, 30, 32, 34, 35.

39:32–43 Moses Inspects the Work. Moses, who had received the design on the mountain, now sees its realization in the establishment of Israel's worship. Appraisals of any kind can be critical or affirming. This one appears to be the latter. Moses looked over everything not with the expectation of finding things wrong but to rejoice with the people that they had done a wondrous job.

40:1–33 The Tabernacle Completed. All the different parts have been beautifully made, but they are useless until they have been brought together. The Tabernacle, like the covenant itself, is a package deal. We can't pick and choose which elements will be included and which ignored. Similarly all allegiance to God involves the whole of life, not just selected parts.

[20] He took the stone tablets inscribed with the
terms of the covenant and placed them* inside
the Ark. Then he attached the carrying poles to
the Ark, and he set the Ark's cover—the place
of atonement—on top of it. [21] Then he brought
the Ark of the Covenant into the Tabernacle and
hung the inner curtain to shield it from view, just
as the LORD had commanded him.

[22] Next Moses placed the table in the Tabernacle, along the north side of the Holy Place, just
outside the inner curtain. [23] And he arranged the
Bread of the Presence on the table before the
LORD, just as the LORD had commanded him.

[24] He set the lampstand in the Tabernacle
across from the table on the south side of the
Holy Place. [25] Then he lit the lamps in the LORD's
presence, just as the LORD had commanded him.
[26] He also placed the gold incense altar in the Tabernacle, in the Holy Place in front of the inner
curtain. [27] On it he burned the fragrant incense,
just as the LORD had commanded him.

[28] He hung the curtain at the entrance of the
Tabernacle, [29] and he placed the altar of burnt offering near the Tabernacle entrance. On it he offered a burnt offering and a grain offering, just
as the LORD had commanded him.

[30] Next Moses placed the washbasin between
the Tabernacle and the altar. He filled it with water so the priests could wash themselves. [31] Moses
and Aaron and Aaron's sons used water from it
to wash their hands and feet. [32] Whenever they
approached the altar and entered the Tabernacle,
they washed themselves, just as the LORD had
commanded Moses.

[33] Then he hung the curtains forming the
courtyard around the Tabernacle and the altar.
And he set up the curtain at the entrance of the
courtyard. So at last Moses finished the work.

The LORD's Glory Fills the Tabernacle

[34] Then the cloud covered the Tabernacle, and the
glory of the LORD filled the Tabernacle. [35] Moses
could no longer enter the Tabernacle because the
cloud had settled down over it, and the glory of
the LORD filled the Tabernacle.

[36] Now whenever the cloud lifted from the
Tabernacle, the people of Israel would set out on
their journey, following it. [37] But if the cloud did
not rise, they remained where they were until
it lifted. [38] The cloud of the LORD hovered over
the Tabernacle during the day, and at night fire
glowed inside the cloud so the whole family of
Israel could see it. This continued throughout all
their journeys.

40:20 Hebrew *He placed the Testimony;* see note on 25:16.

40:34–38 The LORD's Glory Fills the Tabernacle. The book of Exodus tells how a disenfranchised people were reintroduced to a God whom their forefathers had known long before. They learned his character and his name—Yahweh, a God who existed and acted. This was a God who was always present with his people, in their midst and sharing all their journeys with them.

LEVITICUS

Introduction

What has Leviticus to do with women? On first glance it might seem little, if anything. The regulations are placed in the mouth of a man, Moses, and are directed primarily to men. No women play prominent roles in Leviticus as they do in Genesis, Exodus, and Numbers. The book focuses heavily on the role and responsibilities of the Aaronic priests, none of whom were women. Laws about women focus on childbirth and menstruation, the two most intimate and unique aspects of sexuality that set women apart from men, both of which resulted in the epithet "unclean." And when women vowed themselves to Yahweh, they were valued less than men were.

The fact that Leviticus is perceived to some degree as a man's book is illustrated by the paucity of female commentators on it. Although several essays and journal articles have been written recently by women, men write more about Levitical issues related to women than women do. Women may feel distanced from a book that ostensibly legislates their lower status and demeans their essential bodily functions. How can such a book be understood as canonical Scripture? Does it have a message for women today?

The Hebrew title of Leviticus is *wayyiqra,* which means "and he called" (see Lev 1:1). When the Hebrew Bible was translated into Greek, it was given the title *leuitikos* ("priestly [book]"). The Latin Vulgate rendered this *Liber Leviticus,* from which the current English title is derived.

The date and authorship of Leviticus have been debated for some time and are still the subject of much discussion. The traditional view is that Moses wrote the entire book. The book itself designates Moses as the lawgiver through whom Yahweh communicated the decrees (e.g., 1:1; 4:1; 5:14; 6:1, 8, 19; 8:1; 11:1; 12:1). However, when questions arose regarding Mosaic authorship of the entire Torah, Leviticus was questioned as well.

Critical scholarship of the nineteenth and twentieth centuries generally accepted the view popularized by Julius Wellhausen in *Prolegomena to the History of Ancient Israel* (1878). According to this view, the Torah was composed of four sources (J, E, D, and P) that were gradually redacted together. Leviticus and other portions of the Torah were the product of a priestly writer (P) who wrote long after Moses. Wellhausen asserted that P was written sometime around 450 BC and reflected the priestly interests of the Second Temple period. References to the tent shrine were thinly veiled anachronisms of the Second Temple, and the sacrificial system reproduced the highly structured ritual system of the postexilic era. Because Wellhausen believed that religions developed from simple to complex, he assumed that P's complex religious system represented the latest strand of the Torah. This view of the Torah's composition was widely accepted, and even though Wellhausen's dates for the other three sources (J, E, and D) were subsequently challenged, the postexilic date of P and therefore Leviticus remained virtually uncontested.

The study of comparative religion casts doubt on this scholarly consensus, however. The institutions once thought to be Israelite creations of a late period were discovered in other ancient Near Eastern societies antecedent to and after the Mosaic period. Highly developed ritual systems and priesthoods were common, and extensive law codes elucidated proper sexual relationships, outlined purification procedures for uncleanness, and listed animals acceptable for food and sacrifice. While the existence of ancient Near Eastern parallels did not prove the antiquity of P, since such practices may have continued for some time and influenced P at a later date, the authenticity of Israel's institutions had to be reassessed.

As a result, commentaries on Leviticus increasingly affirm the antiquity of Israel's institutions as depicted in the book, even when a complex composition history is acknowledged. In addition, recent terminological studies comparing P with Deuteronomy and Ezekiel may demonstrate that P's composition date is preexilic, dating to the monarchy and the First Temple.

The books of the Torah are notoriously difficult to date, and this is especially true of Leviticus, which contains no datable referents to the historical world surrounding it, such as wars, invasions, or names of kings. Very little is known about the history of Israel's worship, and reconstructions of it remain speculative. Because interpreters' conclusions are principally determined by their methodological presuppositions, issues of authorship and date will continue to be debated.

The milieu of the ancient Near East provides fertile ground for comparing the institutions and practices prevalent in Leviticus, regardless of when one dates the book. Sacrifice was a common practice in these societies, and sacrifices akin to the ones in Leviticus are evident in other cultures. Priests were expected to maintain a higher degree of sanctity than were laypersons, and strict rules regarding ritual procedures were typical. Animals, particularly pigs and dogs, were regarded as unclean, and sexual discharges and childbirth were ritually regulated. Law codes similar to the ones found in Leviticus demonstrate that other ancient Near Eastern nations had highly developed standards of morality.

Was anything unique to Israel? In terms of practice and procedure Israel's institutions often mirror ancient Near Eastern ones. However, the motivation for Israel's laws is clearly grounded in relationship with Yahweh rather than superstition, demonology, or magic, as in some of the other cultures.

Leviticus plays an integral role in the Torah narrative. Its place between Exodus and Numbers is no accident, for it contains information essential for Israel's survival as the people of God. In Exodus, God provided Moses instructions for building a Tabernacle where God's presence could dwell in the midst of the people. However, while Moses received these instructions, the people attempted to provide themselves with a symbol of God's presence: the gold calf (Exod 32). In light of their stubborn sinfulness, God refused to abide among the people any longer, for "if I did, I would surely destroy you along the way" (Exod 33:3). Moses interceded, focusing on God's merciful and just character (Exod 34:6–7), and God agreed to remain in the midst of the people. One question remained unanswered: The people's sinful character had not changed, so how could God possibly dwell in their midst? Leviticus provides the answer.

Although much of Leviticus deals with laws probably addressed to the whole congregation, certain sections focus on regulations about women: Leviticus 12 (the parturient woman), Leviticus 15 (the menstruant and the woman with an abnormal flow), and Leviticus 18 and Leviticus 20 (laws regulating sexual relations). In addition, Leviticus 21 specifies which women priests could marry, Leviticus 22:10–16 outlines rules regarding who may eat of the priestly sacrifices (specifically when a priest's daughter could partake), and Leviticus 27:2–8 details the valuations of women who offered vows. Interspersed throughout the Holiness Code (Lev 17—26) are individual laws about women. These laws and rituals raise interesting questions about the role of women in the Israelite cult and their status in Israelite society, questions that are fraught with difficulty.

The focus of this commentary is on those sections of Leviticus that deal specifically with women, but the book will also be considered as a whole, especially in light of its significance to women then and now.

How can sinful people live with a holy God in their midst? By becoming pure and holy themselves. And how do they achieve purity and holiness? By observing proper ritual procedures that cleanse and sanctify them, and by living according to God's moral standards. Although modern readers may find the ritual instructions tedious to read, the emphasis on order and detail indicates how seriously procedure, decorum, and preparation in worship were taken. God's holiness is an awesome and formidable thing—it is not something to approach flippantly or without proper regard for one's own sinful state.—*Susan M. Pigott*

1:1—7:38	Grace for People with God in Their Midst: The Sacrificial System
8:1—10:20	Mediators to a Holy God: The Inauguration of the Priesthood
11:1—15:33	Is Cleanliness Next to Godliness? The Laws of Purification
16:1–34	Pollution Control: The Day of Atonement
17:1—26:46	Family Values: The Holiness Code
27:1–34	Sanctuary Economics: The Value of Vows

✧

Procedures for the Burnt Offering

1 The LORD called to Moses from the Tabernacle* and said to him, [2]"Give the following instructions to the people of Israel. When you present an animal as an offering to the LORD, you may take it from your herd of cattle or your flock of sheep and goats.

[3]"If the animal you present as a burnt offering is from the herd, it must be a male with no defects. Bring it to the entrance of the Tabernacle so you* may be accepted by the LORD. [4]Lay your hand on the animal's head, and the LORD will accept its death in your place to purify you, making you right with him.* [5]Then slaughter the young bull in the LORD's presence, and Aaron's sons, the priests, will present the animal's blood by splattering it against all sides of the altar that stands at the entrance to the Tabernacle. [6]Then skin the animal and cut it into pieces. [7]The sons of Aaron the priest will build a wood fire on the altar. [8]They will arrange the pieces of the offering, including the head and fat, on the wood burning on the altar. [9]But the internal organs and the legs must first be washed with water. Then the priest will burn the entire sacrifice on the altar as a burnt offering. It is a special gift, a pleasing aroma to the LORD.

[10]"If the animal you present as a burnt offering is from the flock, it may be either a sheep or a goat, but it must be a male with no defects. [11]Slaughter the animal on the north side of the altar in the LORD's presence, and Aaron's sons, the priests, will splatter its blood against all sides

1:1 Hebrew *Tent of Meeting;* also in 1:3, 5. **1:3** Or *it.* **1:4** Or *to make atonement for you.*

1:1—7:38 The Sacrificial System

The first section of Leviticus is devoted to the most important ritual: sacrifice. Sacrifice served not only to atone for sin but also as a means of fellowship and devotion. As such, it was the language used to communicate between worshiper and deity. It provides procedural instructions for the offerers and the priests, both of whom took part in the ritual. The sacrificial laws do not specifically mention women as participants, though the neutral terms *adam* (1:2; 5:4) and *nefesh* (2:1; 4:2, 27; 5:1, 2, 4, 15, 17, 21; 7:18, 20, 21, 25, 27; 23:29, 30) indicate that both men and women brought sacrifices. **1:1—3:17:** The first three sacrifices—the burnt offering (chap. 1), the grain offering (chap. 2), and the peace offering (chap. 3)—were voluntary sacrifices. They were brought at the offerer's initiative as an expression of gratitude, joy, or dedication to God. This indicates that sacrifices were not solely for expiation. They were a means of fellowship with Yahweh whereby reverence could be expressed publicly through ritual actions. **1:3:** *Tabernacle*: Tent of meeting. Both laywomen and laymen had access to this sacred area. **4:** *Lay your hand on the animal's head*: An act of identification.

of the altar. [12]Then cut the animal in pieces, and the priests will arrange the pieces of the offering, including the head and fat, on the wood burning on the altar. [13]But the internal organs and the legs must first be washed with water. Then the priest will burn the entire sacrifice on the altar as a burnt offering. It is a special gift, a pleasing aroma to the LORD.

[14]"If you present a bird as a burnt offering to the LORD, choose either a turtledove or a young pigeon. [15]The priest will take the bird to the altar, wring off its head, and burn it on the altar. But first he must drain its blood against the side of the altar. [16]The priest must also remove the crop and the feathers* and throw them in the ashes on the east side of the altar. [17]Then, grasping the bird by its wings, the priest will tear the bird open, but without tearing it apart. Then he will burn it as a burnt offering on the wood burning on the altar. It is a special gift, a pleasing aroma to the LORD.

Procedures for the Grain Offering

2 "When you present grain as an offering to the LORD, the offering must consist of choice flour. You are to pour olive oil on it, sprinkle it with frankincense, [2]and bring it to Aaron's sons, the priests. The priest will scoop out a handful of the flour moistened with oil, together with all the frankincense, and burn this representative portion on the altar. It is a special gift, a pleasing aroma to the LORD. [3]The rest of the grain offering will then be given to Aaron and his sons. This offering will be considered a most holy part of the special gifts presented to the LORD.

[4]"If your offering is a grain offering baked in an oven, it must be made of choice flour, but without any yeast. It may be presented in the form of thin cakes mixed with olive oil or wafers spread with olive oil. [5]If your grain offering is cooked on a griddle, it must be made of choice flour mixed with olive oil but without any yeast. [6]Break it in pieces and pour olive oil on it; it is a grain offering. [7]If your grain offering is prepared in a pan, it must be made of choice flour and olive oil.

[8]"No matter how a grain offering for the LORD has been prepared, bring it to the priest, who will present it at the altar. [9]The priest will take a representative portion of the grain offering and burn it on the altar. It is a special gift, a pleasing aroma to the LORD. [10]The rest of the grain offering will then be given to Aaron and his sons as their food. This offering will be considered a most holy part of the special gifts presented to the LORD.

[11]"Do not use yeast in preparing any of the grain offerings you present to the LORD, because no yeast or honey may be burned as a special gift presented to the LORD. [12]You may add yeast and honey to an offering of the first crops of your harvest, but these must never be offered on the altar as a pleasing aroma to the LORD. [13]Season all your grain offerings with salt to remind you of God's eternal covenant. Never forget to add salt to your grain offerings.

[14]"If you present a grain offering to the LORD from the first portion of your harvest, bring fresh grain that is coarsely ground and roasted on a fire. [15]Put olive oil on this grain offering, and sprinkle it with frankincense. [16]The priest will take a representative portion of the grain moistened with oil, together with all the frankincense, and burn it as a special gift presented to the LORD.

Procedures for the Peace Offering

3 "If you present an animal from the herd as a peace offering to the LORD, it may be a male or a female, but it must have no defects. [2]Lay your hand on the animal's head, and slaughter it at the entrance of the Tabernacle.* Then Aaron's sons, the priests, will splatter its blood against all sides of the altar. [3]The priest must present part of this peace offering as a special gift to the LORD. This includes all the fat around the internal organs, [4]the two kidneys and the fat around them near the loins, and the long lobe of the liver. These must be removed with the kidneys, [5]and Aaron's sons will burn them on top of the burnt offering on the wood burning on the altar. It is a special gift, a pleasing aroma to the LORD.

[6]"If you present an animal from the flock as a peace offering to the LORD, it may be a male or a female, but it must have no defects. [7]If you present a sheep as your offering, bring it to the LORD, [8]lay your hand on its head, and slaughter it in front of the Tabernacle. Aaron's sons will then splatter the sheep's blood against all sides of the altar. [9]The priest must present the fat of this peace offering as a special gift to the LORD. This includes the fat of the broad tail cut off near the backbone, all the fat around the internal organs, [10]the two kidneys and the fat around them near the loins, and the long lobe of the liver. These must be removed with the kidneys, [11]and the priest will burn them on the altar. It is a special gift of food presented to the LORD.

1:16 Or *the crop and its contents.* The meaning of the Hebrew is uncertain. **3:2** Hebrew *Tent of Meeting;* also in 3:8, 13.

[12]"If you present a goat as your offering, bring it to the LORD, [13]lay your hand on its head, and slaughter it in front of the Tabernacle. Aaron's sons will then splatter the goat's blood against all sides of the altar. [14]The priest must present part of this offering as a special gift to the LORD. This includes all the fat around the internal organs, [15]the two kidneys and the fat around them near the loins, and the long lobe of the liver. These must be removed with the kidneys, [16]and the priest will burn them on the altar. It is a special gift of food, a pleasing aroma to the LORD. All the fat belongs to the LORD.

[17]"You must never eat any fat or blood. This is a permanent law for you, and it must be observed from generation to generation, wherever you live."

Procedures for the Sin Offering

4 Then the LORD said to Moses, [2]"Give the following instructions to the people of Israel. This is how you are to deal with those who sin unintentionally by doing anything that violates one of the LORD's commands.

[3]"If the high priest* sins, bringing guilt upon the entire community, he must give a sin offering for the sin he has committed. He must present to the LORD a young bull with no defects. [4]He must bring the bull to the LORD at the entrance of the Tabernacle,* lay his hand on the bull's head, and slaughter it before the LORD. [5]The high priest will then take some of the bull's blood into the Tabernacle, [6]dip his finger in the blood, and sprinkle it seven times before the LORD in front of the inner curtain of the sanctuary. [7]The priest will then put some of the blood on the horns of the altar for fragrant incense that stands in the LORD's presence inside the Tabernacle. He will pour out the rest of the bull's blood at the base of the altar for burnt offerings at the entrance of the Tabernacle. [8]Then the priest must remove all the fat of the bull to be offered as a sin offering. This includes all the fat around the internal organs, [9]the two kidneys and the fat around them near the loins, and the long lobe of the liver. He must remove these along with the kidneys, [10]just as he does with cattle offered as a peace offering, and burn them on the altar of burnt offerings. [11]But he must take whatever is left of the bull—its hide, meat, head, legs, internal organs, and dung—[12]and carry it away to a place outside the camp that is ceremonially clean, the place where the ashes are dumped. There, on the ash heap, he will burn it on a wood fire.

[13]"If the entire Israelite community sins by violating one of the LORD's commands, but the people don't realize it, they are still guilty. [14]When they become aware of their sin, the people must bring a young bull as an offering for their sin and present it before the Tabernacle. [15]The elders of the community must then lay their hands on the bull's head and slaughter it before the LORD. [16]The high priest will then take some of the bull's blood into the Tabernacle, [17]dip his finger in the blood, and sprinkle it seven times before the LORD in front of the inner curtain. [18]He will then put some of the blood on the horns of the altar for fragrant incense that stands in the LORD's presence inside the Tabernacle. He will pour out the rest of the blood at the base of the altar for burnt offerings at the entrance of the Tabernacle. [19]Then the priest must remove all the animal's fat and burn it on the altar, [20]just as he does with the bull offered as a sin offering for the high priest. Through this process, the priest will purify the people, making them right with the LORD,* and they will be forgiven. [21]Then the priest must take what is left of the bull and carry it outside the camp and burn it there, just as is done with the sin offering for the high priest. This offering is for the sin of the entire congregation of Israel.

[22]"If one of Israel's leaders sins by violating one of the commands of the LORD his God but doesn't realize it, he is still guilty. [23]When he becomes aware of his sin, he must bring as his offering a male goat with no defects. [24]He must lay his hand on the goat's head and slaughter it at the place where burnt offerings are slaughtered before the LORD. This is an offering for his sin. [25]Then the priest will dip his finger in the blood of the sin offering and put it on the horns of the altar for burnt offerings. He will pour out the rest of the blood at the base of the altar. [26]Then he must burn all the goat's fat on the altar, just as he does with the peace offering. Through this process, the priest will purify the leader from his sin, making him right with the LORD, and he will be forgiven.

4:3 Hebrew *the anointed priest;* also in 4:5, 16. **4:4** Hebrew *Tent of Meeting;* also in 4:5, 7, 14, 16, 18. **4:20** Or *will make atonement for the people;* similarly in 4:26, 31, 35.

4:1—7:38 The sin offering and guilt offering were required sacrifices specifically prescribed for the expiation of sin. In addition, 12:6 and 15:29 clearly state that women were required to offer burnt and purification offerings, and women with skin ailments would have offered the specified sacrifices for their cleansing (reparation, burnt, purification, and grain; 14:10–20).

27 "If any of the common people sin by violating one of the LORD's commands, but they
don't realize it, they are still guilty. 28 When they
become aware of their sin, they must bring as
an offering for their sin a female goat with no
defects. 29 They must lay a hand on the head of
the sin offering and slaughter it at the place
where burnt offerings are slaughtered. 30 Then
the priest will dip his finger in the blood and put
it on the horns of the altar for burnt offerings.
He will pour out the rest of the blood at the base
of the altar. 31 Then he must remove all the goat's
fat, just as he does with the fat of the peace offering. He will burn the fat on the altar, and it will
be a pleasing aroma to the LORD. Through this
process, the priest will purify the people, making them right with the LORD, and they will be
forgiven.

32 "If the people bring a sheep as their sin
offering, it must be a female with no defects.
33 They must lay a hand on the head of the sin offering and slaughter it at the place where burnt
offerings are slaughtered. 34 Then the priest will
dip his finger in the blood of the sin offering and
put it on the horns of the altar for burnt offerings. He will pour out the rest of the blood at
the base of the altar. 35 Then he must remove all
the sheep's fat, just as he does with the fat of a
sheep presented as a peace offering. He will burn
the fat on the altar on top of the special gifts
presented to the LORD. Through this process, the
priest will purify the people from their sin, making them right with the LORD, and they will be
forgiven.

Sins Requiring a Sin Offering

5 "If you are called to testify about something you have seen or that you know
about, it is sinful to refuse to testify, and
you will be punished for your sin.

2 "Or suppose you unknowingly touch something that is ceremonially unclean, such as the
carcass of an unclean animal. When you realize
what you have done, you must admit your defilement and your guilt. This is true whether it
is a wild animal, a domestic animal, or an animal
that scurries along the ground.

3 "Or suppose you unknowingly touch something that makes a person unclean. When you
realize what you have done, you must admit
your guilt.

4 "Or suppose you make a foolish vow of any
kind, whether its purpose is for good or for bad.
When you realize its foolishness, you must admit your guilt.

5 "When you become aware of your guilt in
any of these ways, you must confess your sin.
6 Then you must bring to the LORD as the penalty for your sin a female from the flock, either a
sheep or a goat. This is a sin offering with which
the priest will purify you from your sin, making
you right with the LORD.*

7 "But if you cannot afford to bring a sheep,
you may bring to the LORD two turtledoves or
two young pigeons as the penalty for your sin.
One of the birds will be for a sin offering, and
the other for a burnt offering. 8 You must bring
them to the priest, who will present the first bird
as the sin offering. He will wring its neck but
without severing its head from the body. 9 Then
he will sprinkle some of the blood of the sin offering against the sides of the altar, and the rest
of the blood will be drained out at the base of the
altar. This is an offering for sin. 10 The priest will
then prepare the second bird as a burnt offering, following all the procedures that have been
prescribed. Through this process the priest will
purify you from your sin, making you right with
the LORD, and you will be forgiven.

11 "If you cannot afford to bring two turtledoves or two young pigeons, you may bring
two quarts* of choice flour for your sin offering. Since it is an offering for sin, you must not
moisten it with olive oil or put any frankincense
on it. 12 Take the flour to the priest, who will
scoop out a handful as a representative portion.
He will burn it on the altar on top of the special
gifts presented to the LORD. It is an offering for
sin. 13 Through this process, the priest will purify
those who are guilty of any of these sins, making them right with the LORD, and they will be
forgiven. The rest of the flour will belong to the
priest, just as with the grain offering."

Procedures for the Guilt Offering

14 Then the LORD said to Moses, 15 "If one of you
commits a sin by unintentionally defiling the
LORD's sacred property, you must bring a guilt
offering to the LORD. The offering must be your
own ram with no defects, or you may buy one
of equal value with silver, as measured by the
weight of the sanctuary shekel.* 16 You must
make restitution for the sacred property you
have harmed by paying for the loss, plus an additional 20 percent. When you give the payment to
the priest, he will purify you with the ram sacrificed as a guilt offering, making you right with
the LORD, and you will be forgiven.

5:6 Or *will make atonement for you for your sin;* similarly in 5:10, 13, 16, 18. **5:11** Hebrew $^{1}/_{10}$ *of an ephah* [2.2 liters]. **5:15** Each shekel was about 0.4 ounces or 11 grams in weight.

17 "Suppose you sin by violating one of the LORD's commands. Even if you are unaware of what you have done, you are guilty and will be punished for your sin. 18 For a guilt offering, you must bring to the priest your own ram with no defects, or you may buy one of equal value. Through this process the priest will purify you from your unintentional sin, making you right with the LORD, and you will be forgiven. 19 This is a guilt offering, for you have been guilty of an offense against the LORD."

Sins Requiring a Guilt Offering

6 1 *Then the LORD said to Moses, 2 "Suppose one of you sins against your associate and is unfaithful to the LORD. Suppose you cheat in a deal involving a security deposit, or you steal or commit fraud, 3 or you find lost property and lie about it, or you lie while swearing to tell the truth, or you commit any other such sin. 4 If you have sinned in any of these ways, you are guilty. You must give back whatever you stole, or the money you took by extortion, or the security deposit, or the lost property you found, 5 or anything obtained by swearing falsely. You must make restitution by paying the full price plus an additional 20 percent to the person you have harmed. On the same day you must present a guilt offering. 6 As a guilt offering to the LORD, you must bring to the priest your own ram with no defects, or you may buy one of equal value. 7 Through this process, the priest will purify you before the LORD, making you right with him,* and you will be forgiven for any of these sins you have committed."

Further Instructions for the Burnt Offering

8 *Then the LORD said to Moses, 9 "Give Aaron and his sons the following instructions regarding the burnt offering. The burnt offering must be left on top of the altar until the next morning, and the fire on the altar must be kept burning all night. 10 In the morning, after the priest on duty has put on his official linen clothing and linen undergarments, he must clean out the ashes of the burnt offering and put them beside the altar. 11 Then he must take off these garments, change back into his regular clothes, and carry the ashes outside the camp to a place that is ceremonially clean. 12 Meanwhile, the fire on the altar must be kept burning; it must never go out. Each morning the priest will add fresh wood to the fire and arrange the burnt offering on it. He will then burn the fat of the peace offerings on it. 13 Remember, the fire must be kept burning on the altar at all times. It must never go out.

Further Instructions for the Grain Offering

14 "These are the instructions regarding the grain offering. Aaron's sons must present this offering to the LORD in front of the altar. 15 The priest on duty will take from the grain offering a handful of the choice flour moistened with olive oil, together with all the frankincense. He will burn this representative portion on the altar as a pleasing aroma to the LORD. 16 Aaron and his sons may eat the rest of the flour, but it must be baked without yeast and eaten in a sacred place within the courtyard of the Tabernacle.* 17 Remember, it must never be prepared with yeast. I have given it to the priests as their share of the special gifts presented to me. Like the sin offering and the guilt offering, it is most holy. 18 Any of Aaron's male descendants may eat from the special gifts presented to the LORD. This is their permanent right from generation to generation. Anyone or anything that touches these offerings will become holy."

Procedures for the Ordination Offering

19 Then the LORD said to Moses, 20 "On the day Aaron and his sons are anointed, they must present to the LORD a grain offering of two quarts* of choice flour, half to be offered in the morning and half to be offered in the evening. 21 It must be carefully mixed with olive oil and cooked on a griddle. Then slice* this grain offering and present it as a pleasing aroma to the LORD. 22 In each generation, the high priest* who succeeds Aaron must prepare this same offering. It belongs to the LORD and must be burned up completely. This is a permanent law. 23 All such grain offerings of a priest must be burned up entirely. None of it may be eaten."

Further Instructions for the Sin Offering

24 Then the LORD said to Moses, 25 "Give Aaron and his sons the following instructions regarding the sin offering. The animal given as an offering for sin is a most holy offering, and it must be slaughtered in the LORD's presence at the place where the burnt offerings are slaughtered. 26 The priest who offers the sacrifice as a sin offering must eat his portion in a sacred place within the courtyard of the Tabernacle. 27 Anyone or anything that touches the sacrificial meat will become holy. If any of the sacrificial blood spatters

6:1 Verses 6:1-7 are numbered 5:20-26 in Hebrew text.
6:7 Or *will make atonement for you before the LORD.*
6:8 Verses 6:8-30 are numbered 6:1-23 in Hebrew text.
6:16 Hebrew *Tent of Meeting;* also in 6:26, 30. **6:20** Hebrew *1/10 of an ephah* [2.2 liters]. **6:21** The meaning of this Hebrew term is uncertain. **6:22** Hebrew *the anointed priest.*

on a person's clothing, the soiled garment must be washed in a sacred place. [28]If a clay pot is used to boil the sacrificial meat, it must then be broken. If a bronze pot is used, it must be scoured and thoroughly rinsed with water. [29]Any male from a priest's family may eat from this offering; it is most holy. [30]But the offering for sin may not be eaten if its blood was brought into the Tabernacle as an offering for purification* in the Holy Place. It must be completely burned with fire.

Further Instructions for the Guilt Offering

7 "These are the instructions for the guilt offering. It is most holy. [2]The animal sacrificed as a guilt offering must be slaughtered at the place where the burnt offerings are slaughtered, and its blood must be splattered against all sides of the altar. [3]The priest will then offer all its fat on the altar, including the fat of the broad tail, the fat around the internal organs, [4]the two kidneys and the fat around them near the loins, and the long lobe of the liver. These are to be removed with the kidneys, [5]and the priests will burn them on the altar as a special gift presented to the LORD. This is the guilt offering. [6]Any male from a priest's family may eat the meat. It must be eaten in a sacred place, for it is most holy.

[7]"The same instructions apply to both the guilt offering and the sin offering. Both belong to the priest who uses them to purify someone, making that person right with the LORD.* [8]In the case of the burnt offering, the priest may keep the hide of the sacrificed animal. [9]Any grain offering that has been baked in an oven, prepared in a pan, or cooked on a griddle belongs to the priest who presents it. [10]All other grain offerings, whether made of dry flour or flour moistened with olive oil, are to be shared equally among all the priests, the descendants of Aaron.

Further Instructions for the Peace Offering

[11]"These are the instructions regarding the different kinds of peace offerings that may be presented to the LORD. [12]If you present your peace offering as an expression of thanksgiving, the usual animal sacrifice must be accompanied by various kinds of bread made without yeast—thin cakes mixed with olive oil, wafers spread with oil, and cakes made of choice flour mixed with olive oil. [13]This peace offering of thanksgiving must also be accompanied by loaves of bread made with yeast. [14]One of each kind of bread must be presented as a gift to the LORD. It will then belong to the priest who splatters the blood of the peace offering against the altar. [15]The meat of the peace offering of thanksgiving must be eaten on the same day it is offered. None of it may be saved for the next morning.

[16]"If you bring an offering to fulfill a vow or as a voluntary offering, the meat must be eaten on the same day the sacrifice is offered, but whatever is left over may be eaten on the second day. [17]Any meat left over until the third day must be completely burned up. [18]If any of the meat from the peace offering is eaten on the third day, the person who presented it will not be accepted by the LORD. You will receive no credit for offering it. By then the meat will be contaminated; if you eat it, you will be punished for your sin.

[19]"Meat that touches anything ceremonially unclean may not be eaten; it must be completely burned up. The rest of the meat may be eaten, but only by people who are ceremonially clean. [20]If you are ceremonially unclean and you eat meat from a peace offering that was presented to the LORD, you will be cut off from the community. [21]If you touch anything that is unclean (whether it is human defilement or an unclean animal or any other unclean, detestable thing) and then eat meat from a peace offering presented to the LORD, you will be cut off from the community."

The Forbidden Blood and Fat

[22]Then the LORD said to Moses, [23]"Give the following instructions to the people of Israel. You must never eat fat, whether from cattle, sheep, or goats. [24]The fat of an animal found dead or torn to pieces by wild animals must never be eaten, though it may be used for any other purpose. [25]Anyone who eats fat from an animal presented as a special gift to the LORD will be cut off from the community. [26]No matter where you live, you must never consume the blood of any bird or animal. [27]Anyone who consumes blood will be cut off from the community."

A Portion for the Priests

[28]Then the LORD said to Moses, [29]"Give the following instructions to the people of Israel. When you present a peace offering to the LORD, bring part of it as a gift to the LORD. [30]Present it to the LORD with your own hands as a special gift to the LORD. Bring the fat of the animal, together with the breast, and lift up the breast as a special offering to the LORD. [31]Then the priest will burn the fat on the altar, but the breast will belong to Aaron and his descendants. [32]Give the right thigh of your peace offering to the priest as

6:30 Or *an offering to make atonement.* **7:7** Or *to make atonement.*

a gift. 33 The right thigh must always be given to the priest who offers the blood and the fat of the peace offering. 34 For I have reserved the breast of the special offering and the right thigh of the sacred offering for the priests. It is the permanent right of Aaron and his descendants to share in the peace offerings brought by the people of Israel. 35 This is their rightful share. The special gifts presented to the LORD have been reserved for Aaron and his descendants from the time they were set apart to serve the LORD as priests. 36 On the day they were anointed, the LORD commanded the Israelites to give these portions to the priests as their permanent share from generation to generation."

37 These are the instructions for the burnt offering, the grain offering, the sin offering, and the guilt offering, as well as the ordination offering and the peace offering. 38 The LORD gave these instructions to Moses on Mount Sinai when he commanded the Israelites to present their offerings to the LORD in the wilderness of Sinai.

Ordination of the Priests

8 Then the LORD said to Moses, 2 "Bring Aaron and his sons, along with their sacred garments, the anointing oil, the bull for the sin offering, the two rams, and the basket of bread made without yeast, 3 and call the entire community of Israel together at the entrance of the Tabernacle.*"

4 So Moses followed the LORD's instructions, and the whole community assembled at the Tabernacle entrance. 5 Moses announced to them, "This is what the LORD has commanded us to do!" 6 Then he presented Aaron and his sons and washed them with water. 7 He put the official tunic on Aaron and tied the sash around his waist. He dressed him in the robe, placed the ephod on him, and attached the ephod securely with its decorative sash. 8 Then Moses placed the chestpiece on Aaron and put the Urim and the Thummim inside it. 9 He placed the turban on Aaron's head and attached the gold medallion—the badge of holiness—to the front of the turban, just as the LORD had commanded him.

10 Then Moses took the anointing oil and anointed the Tabernacle and everything in it, making them holy. 11 He sprinkled the oil on the altar seven times, anointing it and all its utensils, as well as the washbasin and its stand, making them holy. 12 Then he poured some of the anointing oil on Aaron's head, anointing him and making him holy for his work. 13 Next Moses presented Aaron's sons. He clothed them in their tunics, tied their sashes around them, and put their special head coverings on them, just as the LORD had commanded him.

14 Then Moses presented the bull for the sin offering. Aaron and his sons laid their hands on the bull's head, 15 and Moses slaughtered it. Moses took some of the blood, and with his finger he put it on the four horns of the altar to purify it. He poured out the rest of the blood at the base of the altar. Through this process, he made the altar holy by purifying it.* 16 Then Moses took all the fat around the internal organs, the long lobe of the liver, and the two kidneys and the fat around them, and he burned it all on the altar. 17 He took the rest of the bull, including its hide, meat, and dung, and burned it on a fire outside the camp, just as the LORD had commanded him.

18 Then Moses presented the ram for the burnt offering. Aaron and his sons laid their hands on the ram's head, 19 and Moses slaughtered it. Then Moses took the ram's blood and splattered it against all sides of the altar. 20 Then he cut the ram into pieces, and he burned the head, some of its pieces, and the fat on the altar. 21 After washing the internal organs and the legs with water, Moses burned the entire ram on the altar as a burnt offering. It was a pleasing aroma, a special gift presented to the LORD, just as the LORD had commanded him.

22 Then Moses presented the other ram, which was the ram of ordination. Aaron and his sons laid their hands on the ram's head, 23 and Moses slaughtered it. Then Moses took some of its blood and applied it to the lobe of Aaron's right ear, the thumb of his right hand, and the big toe of his right foot. 24 Next Moses presented Aaron's sons and applied some of the blood to the lobes of their right ears, the thumbs of their right hands, and the big toes of their right feet. He then splattered the rest of the blood against all sides of the altar.

8:3 Hebrew *Tent of Meeting;* also in 8:4, 31, 33, 35. **8:15** Or *by making atonement for it;* or *that offerings for purification might be made on it.*

8:1–10:20 The Priesthood

The priests were set apart from the rest of Israelite society as members of a holy institution. They alone had access to the most sacred areas of the Tabernacle, and they alone consumed portions of all the sacrifices except the burnt offering. **8:1–36:** The consecration of Aaron and his sons for their priestly duties. **9:1–24:** The inauguration of the sacrifices.

25 Next Moses took the fat, including the fat of the broad tail, the fat around the internal organs, the long lobe of the liver, and the two kidneys and the fat around them, along with the right thigh. 26 On top of these he placed a thin cake of bread made without yeast, a cake of bread mixed with olive oil, and a wafer spread with olive oil. All these were taken from the basket of bread made without yeast that was placed in the LORD's presence. 27 He put all these in the hands of Aaron and his sons, and he lifted them up as a special offering to the LORD. 28 Moses then took all the offerings back from them and burned them on the altar on top of the burnt offering. This was the ordination offering. It was a pleasing aroma, a special gift presented to the LORD. 29 Then Moses took the breast and lifted it up as a special offering to the LORD. This was Moses' portion of the ram of ordination, just as the LORD had commanded him.

30 Next Moses took some of the anointing oil and some of the blood that was on the altar, and he sprinkled them on Aaron and his garments and on his sons and their garments. In this way, he made Aaron and his sons and their garments holy.

31 Then Moses said to Aaron and his sons, "Boil the remaining meat of the offerings at the Tabernacle entrance, and eat it there, along with the bread that is in the basket of offerings for the ordination, just as I commanded when I said, 'Aaron and his sons will eat it.' 32 Any meat or bread that is left over must then be burned up. 33 You must not leave the Tabernacle entrance for seven days, for that is when the ordination ceremony will be completed. 34 Everything we have done today was commanded by the LORD in order to purify you, making you right with him.* 35 Now stay at the entrance of the Tabernacle day and night for seven days, and do everything the LORD requires. If you fail to do this, you will die, for this is what the LORD has commanded." 36 So Aaron and his sons did everything the LORD had commanded through Moses.

The Priests Begin Their Work

9 After the ordination ceremony, on the eighth day, Moses called together Aaron and his sons and the elders of Israel. 2 He said to Aaron, "Take a young bull for a sin offering and a ram for a burnt offering, both without defects, and present them to the LORD. 3 Then tell the Israelites, 'Take a male goat for a sin offering, and take a calf and a lamb, both a year old and without defects, for a burnt offering. 4 Also take a bull* and a ram for a peace offering and flour moistened with olive oil for a grain offering. Present all these offerings to the LORD because the LORD will appear to you today.' "

5 So the people presented all these things at the entrance of the Tabernacle,* just as Moses had commanded. Then the whole community came forward and stood before the LORD. 6 And Moses said, "This is what the LORD has commanded you to do so that the glory of the LORD may appear to you."

7 Then Moses said to Aaron, "Come to the altar and sacrifice your sin offering and your burnt offering to purify yourself and the people. Then present the offerings of the people to purify them, making them right with the LORD,* just as he has commanded."

8 So Aaron went to the altar and slaughtered the calf as a sin offering for himself. 9 His sons brought him the blood, and he dipped his finger in it and put it on the horns of the altar. He poured out the rest of the blood at the base of the altar. 10 Then he burned on the altar the fat, the kidneys, and the long lobe of the liver from the sin offering, just as the LORD had commanded Moses. 11 The meat and the hide, however, he burned outside the camp.

12 Next Aaron slaughtered the animal for the burnt offering. His sons brought him the blood, and he splattered it against all sides of the altar. 13 Then they handed him each piece of the burnt offering, including the head, and he burned them on the altar. 14 Then he washed the internal organs and the legs and burned them on the altar along with the rest of the burnt offering.

15 Next Aaron presented the offerings of the people. He slaughtered the people's goat and presented it as an offering for their sin, just as he had first done with the offering for his own sin. 16 Then he presented the burnt offering and sacrificed it in the prescribed way. 17 He also presented the grain offering, burning a handful of the flour mixture on the altar, in addition to the regular burnt offering for the morning.

18 Then Aaron slaughtered the bull and the ram for the people's peace offering. His sons brought him the blood, and he splattered it against all sides of the altar. 19 Then he took the fat of the bull and the ram—the fat of the broad tail and from around the internal organs—along with the kidneys and the long lobes of the livers. 20 He placed these fat portions on top of the breasts of these animals and burned them on the

8:34 Or *to make atonement for you.* **9:4** Or *cow;* also in 9:18, 19. **9:5** Hebrew *Tent of Meeting;* also in 9:23. **9:7** Or *to make atonement for them.*

altar. 21 Aaron then lifted up the breasts and right thighs as a special offering to the LORD, just as Moses had commanded.

22 After that, Aaron raised his hands toward the people and blessed them. Then, after presenting the sin offering, the burnt offering, and the peace offering, he stepped down from the altar. 23 Then Moses and Aaron went into the Tabernacle, and when they came back out, they blessed the people again, and the glory of the LORD appeared to the whole community. 24 Fire blazed forth from the LORD's presence and consumed the burnt offering and the fat on the altar. When the people saw this, they shouted with joy and fell face down on the ground.

The Sin of Nadab and Abihu

10 Aaron's sons Nadab and Abihu put coals of fire in their incense burners and sprinkled incense over them. In this way, they disobeyed the LORD by burning before him the wrong kind of fire, different than he had commanded. 2 So fire blazed forth from the LORD's presence and burned them up, and they died there before the LORD.

3 Then Moses said to Aaron, "This is what the LORD meant when he said,

'I will display my holiness
through those who come near me.
I will display my glory
before all the people.'"

And Aaron was silent.

4 Then Moses called for Mishael and Elzaphan, Aaron's cousins, the sons of Aaron's uncle Uzziel. He said to them, "Come forward and carry away the bodies of your relatives from in front of the sanctuary to a place outside the camp." 5 So they came forward and picked them up by their garments and carried them out of the camp, just as Moses had commanded.

6 Then Moses said to Aaron and his sons Eleazar and Ithamar, "Do not show grief by leaving your hair uncombed* or by tearing your clothes. If you do, you will die, and the LORD's anger will strike the whole community of Israel. However, the rest of the Israelites, your relatives, may mourn because of the LORD's fiery destruction of Nadab and Abihu. 7 But you must not leave the entrance of the Tabernacle* or you will die, for you have been anointed with the LORD's anointing oil." So they did as Moses commanded.

Instructions for Priestly Conduct

8 Then the LORD said to Aaron, 9 "You and your descendants must never drink wine or any other alcoholic drink before going into the Tabernacle. If you do, you will die. This is a permanent law for you, and it must be observed from generation to generation. 10 You must distinguish between what is sacred and what is common, between what is ceremonially unclean and what is clean. 11 And you must teach the Israelites all the decrees that the LORD has given them through Moses."

12 Then Moses said to Aaron and his remaining sons, Eleazar and Ithamar, "Take what is left of the grain offering after a portion has been presented as a special gift to the LORD, and eat it beside the altar. Make sure it contains no yeast, for it is most holy. 13 You must eat it in a sacred place, for it has been given to you and your descendants as your portion of the special gifts presented to the LORD. These are the commands I have been given. 14 But the breast and thigh that were lifted up as a special offering may be eaten in any place that is ceremonially clean. These parts have been given to you and your descendants as your portion of the peace offerings presented by the people of Israel. 15 You must lift up the thigh and breast as a special offering to the LORD, along with the fat of the special gifts. These parts will belong to you and your descendants as your permanent right, just as the LORD has commanded."

10:6 Or *by uncovering your heads.* **10:7** Hebrew *Tent of Meeting;* also in 10:9.

10:1: *The wrong kind of fire*: Also translated as an unholy fire or a strange fire. **8–20:** Regulations concerning the priests. **10:** The priests were to distinguish between the *sacred* and the *common* or profane; between the *unclean* and the *clean*. Obviously these are opposites. To be unclean did not mean that one was profane or that one had necessarily committed some sort of sin. It meant that one was ritually impure. To be clean did not mean one was holy, since clean persons could still profane holy things (e.g., see Exod 20:25; Lev 18:21; 19:7–8, 12; 20:3; 21:4–6, 9, 12–15, 23; 22:2, 32) and defile the sanctuary by worshiping Molech (Lev 20:3; cf. Ezek 20:26; 23:38). Cleanliness was not the equivalent of godliness; it meant simply that one was ritually appropriate.

The priests were required to live according to different standards (Lev 21), were held responsible for maintaining the sanctity of the offerings made by the Israelites (chap. 22), and paid the ultimate price for abusing their position (10:1–3).

16 Moses then asked them what had happened
to the goat of the sin offering. When he discovered it had been burned up, he became very angry with Eleazar and Ithamar, Aaron's remaining sons. 17 "Why didn't you eat the sin offering
in the sacred area?" he demanded. "It is a holy
offering! The LORD has given it to you to remove the guilt of the community and to purify
the people, making them right with the LORD.*
18 Since the animal's blood was not brought into
the Holy Place, you should have eaten the meat
in the sacred area as I ordered you."

19 Then Aaron answered Moses, "Today my
sons presented both their sin offering and their
burnt offering to the LORD. And yet this tragedy
has happened to me. If I had eaten the people's
sin offering on such a tragic day as this, would
the LORD have been pleased?" 20 And when Moses heard this, he was satisfied.

Ceremonially Clean and Unclean Animals

11 Then the LORD said to Moses and
Aaron, 2 "Give the following instructions to the people of Israel.

"Of all the land animals, these are the ones
you may use for food. 3 You may eat any animal
that has completely split hooves and chews the
cud. 4 You may not, however, eat the following
animals* that have split hooves or that chew the
cud, but not both. The camel chews the cud but
does not have split hooves, so it is ceremonially
unclean for you. 5 The hyrax* chews the cud but
does not have split hooves, so it is unclean. 6 The
hare chews the cud but does not have split hooves,
so it is unclean. 7 The pig has evenly split hooves
but does not chew the cud, so it is unclean. 8 You
may not eat the meat of these animals or even
touch their carcasses. They are ceremonially unclean for you.

9 "Of all the marine animals, these are ones
you may use for food. You may eat anything
from the water if it has both fins and scales,
whether taken from salt water or from streams.
10 But you must never eat animals from the sea or
from rivers that do not have both fins and scales.
They are detestable to you. This applies both to
little creatures that live in shallow water and to
all creatures that live in deep water. 11 They will
always be detestable to you. You must never eat
their meat or even touch their dead bodies. 12 Any
marine animal that does not have both fins and
scales is detestable to you.

13 "These are the birds that are detestable to
you. You must never eat them: the griffon vulture, the bearded vulture, the black vulture, 14 the
kite, falcons of all kinds, 15 ravens of all kinds,
16 the eagle owl, the short-eared owl, the seagull,
hawks of all kinds, 17 the little owl, the cormorant,
the great owl, 18 the barn owl, the desert owl, the
Egyptian vulture, 19 the stork, herons of all kinds,
the hoopoe, and the bat.

20 "You must not eat winged insects that walk
along the ground; they are detestable to you.
21 You may, however, eat winged insects that walk
along the ground and have jointed legs so they
can jump. 22 The insects you are permitted to eat
include all kinds of locusts, bald locusts, crickets,
and grasshoppers. 23 All other winged insects that
walk along the ground are detestable to you.

24 "The following creatures will make you
ceremonially unclean. If any of you touch their
carcasses, you will be defiled until evening. 25 If
you pick up their carcasses, you must wash your
clothes, and you will remain defiled until evening.

26 "Any animal that has split hooves that are
not evenly divided or that does not chew the cud
is unclean for you. If you touch the carcass of
such an animal, you will be defiled. 27 Of the animals that walk on all fours, those that have paws
are unclean. If you touch the carcass of such an
animal, you will be defiled until evening. 28 If you
pick up its carcass, you must wash your clothes,
and you will remain defiled until evening. These
animals are unclean for you.

29 "Of the small animals that scurry along

10:17 Or *to make atonement for the people before the LORD.*
11:4 The identification of some of the animals, birds, and insects in this chapter is uncertain. **11:5** Or *coney,* or *rock badger.*

11:1—15:33 The Laws of Purification

These detailed regulations concern proper food, the uncleanness of childbirth, skin diseases, and bodily discharges. Such matters seem foreign to worship of God since they are physical conditions and, in the case of discharges and skin disease, out of the individual's control.

The laws of purification are organized in four sections: laws of clean and unclean animals (chap. 11); laws concerning the parturient (women who have just given birth; chap. 12); laws of skin ailments (chaps. 13—14), and laws concerning natural and unnatural discharges (chap. 15). Only the purification laws in chapters 12 and 15 specifically concern women. (Women were subject to the food laws and the laws of skin ailments, even when not mentioned. See Purity Laws Related to Women, chap. 15, for general discussion of cleanliness and purity.)

the ground, these are unclean for you: the mole rat, the rat, large lizards of all kinds, 30 the gecko, the monitor lizard, the common lizard, the sand lizard, and the chameleon. 31 All these small animals are unclean for you. If any of you touch the dead body of such an animal, you will be defiled until evening. 32 If such an animal dies and falls on something, that object will be unclean. This is true whether the object is made of wood, cloth, leather, or burlap. Whatever its use, you must dip it in water, and it will remain defiled until evening. After that, it will be ceremonially clean and may be used again.

33 "If such an animal falls into a clay pot, everything in the pot will be defiled, and the pot must be smashed. 34 If the water from such a container spills on any food, the food will be defiled. And any beverage in such a container will be defiled. 35 Any object on which the carcass of such an animal falls will be defiled. If it is an oven or hearth, it must be destroyed, for it is defiled, and you must treat it accordingly.

36 "However, if the carcass of such an animal falls into a spring or a cistern, the water will still be clean. But anyone who touches the carcass will be defiled. 37 If the carcass falls on seed grain to be planted in the field, the seed will still be considered clean. 38 But if the seed is wet when the carcass falls on it, the seed will be defiled.

39 "If an animal you are permitted to eat dies and you touch its carcass, you will be defiled until evening. 40 If you eat any of its meat or carry away its carcass, you must wash your clothes, and you will remain defiled until evening.

41 "All small animals that scurry along the ground are detestable, and you must never eat them. 42 This includes all animals that slither along on their bellies, as well as those with four legs and those with many feet. All such animals that scurry along the ground are detestable, and you must never eat them. 43 Do not defile yourselves by touching them. You must not make yourselves ceremonially unclean because of them. 44 For I am the LORD your God. You must consecrate yourselves and be holy, because I am holy. So do not defile yourselves with any of these small animals that scurry along the ground. 45 For I, the LORD, am the one who brought you up from the land of Egypt, that I might be your God. Therefore, you must be holy because I am holy.

46 "These are the instructions regarding land animals, birds, marine creatures, and animals that scurry along the ground. 47 By these instructions you will know what is unclean and clean, and which animals may be eaten and which may not be eaten."

Purification after Childbirth

12

The LORD said to Moses, 2 "Give the following instructions to the people of Israel. If a woman becomes pregnant and gives birth to a son, she will be ceremonially unclean for seven days, just as she is unclean during her menstrual period. 3 On the eighth day the boy's foreskin must be circumcised. 4 After waiting thirty-three days, she will be purified from the bleeding of childbirth. During this time of purification, she must not touch anything that is set apart as holy. And she must not enter the

12:1–8 Purification after Childbirth. The regulations in this chapter pertain to women's exclusive role in biblical Israel: childbearing. The flow of blood accompanying the birth of a child rendered the woman unclean for a certain period of time, depending on the sex of the child. **2–4:** *Just as she is unclean (niddah) during her menstrual period (dawah)*: Both *niddah* and *dawah* refer to menstruation, although *niddah* is the more common term. Outside of Leviticus this term is often used interchangeably with impurity (Ezek 7:19–20; Lam 1:17; Ezra 9:11) and is sometimes even used in the opposite sense as purification (Zech 13:1; Num 8:7). *Dawah* means "to be ill" and is used three times to refer to the *illness* of parturition or menstruation (Lev 12:2; 15:33; 20:18).

Whether the new mother was considered a menstruant during this time is unclear. In its first stages lochial flow closely resembles a heavy menstrual period. The text does not state that the parturient's uncleanness was communicable to persons or objects as menstrual impurity was (15:19–24), although the use of the term *niddah* may presuppose this. If, however, the mother's uncleanness was communicable, she would have made her child unclean, a fact that seems too significant to be omitted. Unlike some other ancient Near Eastern countries, Israel had no cleansing ceremony for newborns and did not consider them unclean. **4:** This was followed by a thirty-three-day period during which the mother sat (or remained, dwelled) in *the bleeding of childbirth*. Lochia can last up to six weeks, but in its later stages it gradually slows and becomes lighter in color. The priestly writers recognized the uniqueness of this later lochial flow, since they did not relegate the new mother to the status of a *zabah,* a woman with an irregular flow of blood outside of menstruation. Instead, the lochial flow was understood as purificatory blood. The woman was forbidden to touch holy objects or enter the sanctuary *not* because she was unclean but because she was in a unique process of

Uncleanness after the Birth of a Female Child

According to Leviticus 12:5, when a female child was born, the mother was unclean for fourteen days and was unpurified for sixty-six days, double the times for male children (vv. 2, 4). No reason is stated in the text for the doubling, resulting in extensive speculation. A few of these theories are summarized here.

1. A female child was considered less desirable or less valued than a male child (27:2–7). This view is weakened by the fact that the mother was unclean, not the child. If *gender* was the issue, it seems the child would be unclean rather than the mother, as was the case in the Hittite culture. Or if *desirability* or *value* was the issue, it seems there would be regulations for children, male or female, who were born with defects or illness, and this apparently was not the case.

2. A female child was viewed as more vulnerable to disease or demonic attack. Infant mortality was high in the ancient Near East, and childbirth was fraught with danger. Why then would the perceived vulnerability of the child create a state of uncleanness for the mother and not for the child?

3. A female child may produce a vaginal discharge (sometimes bloody) upon birth, and a woman's lochia sometimes lasts longer after the birth of a female child. Although these medical characteristics can occur, they do not account for the extensive time differences between males and females. In addition, it is unclear why a female child's flow would make her mother unclean if the mother's lochia did not render the child unclean.

4. The potential for the female child to menstruate, or possibly her potential motherhood, made the mother unclean. It seems odd that a female's *potential* fertility would have any effect at birth, since she would not reach puberty for many years and at that point would maintain her own uncleanness.

5. Because a male was circumcised on the eighth day (Gen 17:12; Lev 12:3), his mother's uncleanness was abbreviated to seven days. Heavy lochia can last ten days to two weeks, so in the case of the female child who had no circumcision ceremony, the mother's uncleanness extended a full two weeks, in accordance with the heaviest flow. Since the period of uncleanness was doubled, the period of purification was also. The statement of the male's circumcision interrupts the regulations (it is the only verse not focused on the mother), and the circumcision ceremony is the only distinction between male and female births cited in the text, suggesting it as the probable reason for the difference.

sanctuary until her time of purification is over.
[5]If a woman gives birth to a daughter, she will be
ceremonially unclean for two weeks, just as she
is unclean during her menstrual period. After
waiting sixty-six days, she will be purified from
the bleeding of childbirth.
[6]"When the time of purification is completed
for either a son or a daughter, the woman must
bring a one-year-old lamb for a burnt offering
and a young pigeon or turtledove for a purification offering. She must bring her offerings to the
priest at the entrance of the Tabernacle.* [7]The
priest will then present them to the LORD to purify her.* Then she will be ceremonially clean
again after her bleeding at childbirth. These are
the instructions for a woman after the birth of a
son or a daughter.
[8]"If a woman cannot afford to bring a lamb,
she must bring two turtledoves or two young pigeons. One will be for the burnt offering and the
other for the purification offering. The priest will
sacrifice them to purify her, and she will be ceremonially clean."

Serious Skin Diseases

13 The LORD said to Moses and Aaron,
[2]"If anyone has a swelling or a rash
or discolored skin that might develop
into a serious skin disease,* that person must
be brought to Aaron the priest or to one of his
sons.* [3]The priest will examine the affected

12:6 Hebrew *Tent of Meeting.* **12:7** Or *to make atonement for her;* also in 12:8. **13:2a** Traditionally rendered *leprosy.* The Hebrew word used throughout this passage is used to describe various skin diseases. **13:2b** Or *one of his descendants.*

blood purification. **5:** *See* sidebar above. **6–8:** After the proscribed period, the woman brought a year-old lamb for a burnt offering and a pigeon or turtledove for a purification offering to the door of the tent. The priest offered the sacrifices, and the woman's time of purification was complete.

area of the skin. If the hair in the affected area has turned white and the problem appears to be more than skin-deep, it is a serious skin disease, and the priest who examines it must pronounce the person ceremonially unclean.

[4]"But if the affected area of the skin is only a white discoloration and does not appear to be more than skin-deep, and if the hair on the spot has not turned white, the priest will quarantine the person for seven days. [5]On the seventh day the priest will make another examination. If he finds the affected area has not changed and the problem has not spread on the skin, the priest will quarantine the person for seven more days. [6]On the seventh day the priest will make another examination. If he finds the affected area has faded and has not spread, the priest will pronounce the person ceremonially clean. It was only a rash. The person's clothing must be washed, and the person will be ceremonially clean. [7]But if the rash continues to spread after the person has been examined by the priest and has been pronounced clean, the infected person must return to be examined again. [8]If the priest finds that the rash has spread, he must pronounce the person ceremonially unclean, for it is indeed a skin disease.

[9]"Anyone who develops a serious skin disease must go to the priest for an examination. [10]If the priest finds a white swelling on the skin, and some hair on the spot has turned white, and there is an open sore in the affected area, [11]it is a chronic skin disease, and the priest must pronounce the person ceremonially unclean. In such cases the person need not be quarantined, for it is obvious that the skin is defiled by the disease.

[12]"Now suppose the disease has spread all over the person's skin, covering the body from head to foot. [13]When the priest examines the infected person and finds that the disease covers the entire body, he will pronounce the person ceremonially clean. Since the skin has turned completely white, the person is clean. [14]But if any open sores appear, the infected person will be pronounced ceremonially unclean. [15]The priest must make this pronouncement as soon as he sees an open sore, since open sores indicate the presence of a skin disease. [16]However, if the open sores heal and turn white like the rest of the skin, the person must return to the priest [17]for another examination. If the affected areas have indeed turned white, the priest will then pronounce the person ceremonially clean by declaring, 'You are clean!'

[18]"If anyone has a boil on the skin that has started to heal, [19]but a white swelling or a reddish white spot develops in its place, that person must go to the priest to be examined. [20]If the priest examines it and finds it to be more than skin-deep, and if the hair in the affected area has turned white, the priest must pronounce the person ceremonially unclean. The boil has become a serious skin disease. [21]But if the priest finds no white hair on the affected area and the problem appears to be no more than skin-deep and has faded, the priest must quarantine the person for seven days. [22]If during that time the affected area spreads on the skin, the priest must pronounce the person ceremonially unclean, because it is a serious disease. [23]But if the area grows no larger and does not spread, it is merely the scar from the boil, and the priest will pronounce the person ceremonially clean.

[24]"If anyone has suffered a burn on the skin and the burned area changes color, becoming either reddish white or shiny white, [25]the priest must examine it. If he finds that the hair in the affected area has turned white and the problem appears to be more than skin-deep, a skin disease has broken out in the burn. The priest must then pronounce the person ceremonially unclean, for it is clearly a serious skin disease. [26]But if the priest finds no white hair on the affected area and the problem appears to be no more than skin-deep and has faded, the priest must quarantine the infected person for seven days. [27]On the seventh day the priest must examine the person again. If the affected area has spread on the skin, the priest must pronounce that person ceremonially unclean, for it is clearly a serious skin disease. [28]But if the affected area has not changed or spread on the skin and has faded, it is simply a swelling from the burn. The priest will then pronounce the person ceremonially clean, for it is only the scar from the burn.

[29]"If anyone, either a man or woman, has a sore on the head or chin, [30]the priest must examine it. If he finds it is more than skin-deep and has fine yellow hair on it, the priest must pronounce the person ceremonially unclean. It is a scabby sore of the head or chin. [31]If the priest examines the scabby sore and finds that it is only skin-deep but there is no black hair on it, he must quarantine the person for seven days. [32]On the seventh day the priest must examine the sore again. If he finds that the scabby sore has not spread, and there is no yellow hair on it, and it appears to be only skin-deep, [33]the person must shave off all hair except the hair on the affected area. Then the priest must quarantine the person for another seven days. [34]On the seventh day he will examine the sore again. If it

has not spread and appears to be no more than skin-deep, the priest will pronounce the person ceremonially clean. The person's clothing must be washed, and the person will be ceremonially clean. 35 But if the scabby sore begins to spread after the person is pronounced clean, 36 the priest must do another examination. If he finds that the sore has spread, the priest does not need to look for yellow hair. The infected person is ceremonially unclean. 37 But if the color of the scabby sore does not change and black hair has grown on it, it has healed. The priest will then pronounce the person ceremonially clean.

38 "If anyone, either a man or woman, has shiny white patches on the skin, 39 the priest must examine the affected area. If he finds that the shiny patches are only pale white, this is a harmless skin rash, and the person is ceremonially clean.

40 "If a man loses his hair and his head becomes bald, he is still ceremonially clean. 41 And if he loses hair on his forehead, he simply has a bald forehead; he is still clean. 42 However, if a reddish white sore appears on the bald area at the top or back of his head, this is a skin disease. 43 The priest must examine him, and if he finds swelling around the reddish white sore anywhere on the man's head and it looks like a skin disease, 44 the man is indeed infected with a skin disease and is unclean. The priest must pronounce him ceremonially unclean because of the sore on his head.

45 "Those who suffer from a serious skin disease must tear their clothing and leave their hair uncombed.* They must cover their mouth and call out, 'Unclean! Unclean!' 46 As long as the serious disease lasts, they will be ceremonially unclean. They must live in isolation in their place outside the camp.

Treatment of Contaminated Clothing

47 "Now suppose mildew* contaminates some woolen or linen clothing, 48 woolen or linen fabric, the hide of an animal, or anything made of leather. 49 If the contaminated area in the clothing, the animal hide, the fabric, or the leather article has turned greenish or reddish, it is contaminated with mildew and must be shown to the priest. 50 After examining the affected spot, the priest will put the article in quarantine for seven days. 51 On the seventh day the priest must inspect it again. If the contaminated area has spread, the clothing or fabric or leather is clearly contaminated by a serious mildew and is ceremonially unclean. 52 The priest must burn the item—the clothing, the woolen or linen fabric, or piece of leather—for it has been contaminated by a serious mildew. It must be completely destroyed by fire.

53 "But if the priest examines it and finds that the contaminated area has not spread in the clothing, the fabric, or the leather, 54 the priest will order the object to be washed and then quarantined for seven more days. 55 Then the priest must examine the object again. If he finds that the contaminated area has not changed color after being washed, even if it did not spread, the object is defiled. It must be completely burned up, whether the contaminated spot* is on the inside or outside. 56 But if the priest examines it and finds that the contaminated area has faded after being washed, he must cut the spot from the clothing, the fabric, or the leather. 57 If the spot later reappears on the clothing, the fabric, or the leather article, the mildew is clearly spreading, and the contaminated object must be burned up. 58 But if the spot disappears from the clothing, the fabric, or the leather article after it has been washed, it must be washed again; then it will be ceremonially clean.

59 "These are the instructions for dealing with mildew that contaminates woolen or linen clothing or fabric or anything made of leather. This is how the priest will determine whether these items are ceremonially clean or unclean."

Cleansing from Skin Diseases

14 And the LORD said to Moses, 2 "The following instructions are for those seeking ceremonial purification from a skin disease.* Those who have been healed must be brought to the priest, 3 who will examine them at a place outside the camp. If the priest finds that someone has been healed of a serious skin disease, 4 he will perform a purification ceremony, using two live birds that are ceremonially clean, a stick of cedar,* some scarlet yarn, and a hyssop branch. 5 The priest will order that one bird be slaughtered over a clay pot filled with fresh water. 6 He will take the live bird, the cedar stick, the scarlet yarn, and the hyssop branch, and dip them into the blood of the bird that was slaughtered over the fresh water. 7 The priest will then sprinkle the blood of the dead bird seven times on the person being purified of the skin disease. When the priest has purified the person,

13:45 Or *and uncover their heads.* **13:47** Traditionally rendered *leprosy.* The Hebrew term used throughout this passage is the same term used for the various skin diseases described in 13:1-46. **13:55** The meaning of the Hebrew is uncertain. **14:2** Traditionally rendered *leprosy;* see note on 13:2a. **14:4** Or *juniper;* also in 14:6, 49, 51.

he will release the live bird in the open field to
fly away.
8 “The persons being purified must then wash
their clothes, shave off all their hair, and bathe
themselves in water. Then they will be ceremonially clean and may return to the camp. However, they must remain outside their tents for
seven days. 9 On the seventh day they must again
shave all the hair from their heads, including the
hair of the beard and eyebrows. They must also
wash their clothes and bathe themselves in water. Then they will be ceremonially clean.
10 “On the eighth day each person being purified must bring two male lambs and a one-year-
old female lamb, all with no defects, along with
a grain offering of six quarts* of choice flour
moistened with olive oil, and a cup* of olive oil.
11 Then the officiating priest will present that person for purification, along with the offerings, before the LORD at the entrance of the Tabernacle.*
12 The priest will take one of the male lambs and
the olive oil and present them as a guilt offering, lifting them up as a special offering before
the LORD. 13 He will then slaughter the male lamb
in the sacred area where sin offerings and burnt
offerings are slaughtered. As with the sin offering, the guilt offering belongs to the priest. It is
a most holy offering. 14 The priest will then take
some of the blood of the guilt offering and apply
it to the lobe of the right ear, the thumb of the
right hand, and the big toe of the right foot of the
person being purified.
15 “Then the priest will pour some of the olive
oil into the palm of his own left hand. 16 He will
dip his right finger into the oil in his palm and
sprinkle some of it with his finger seven times
before the LORD. 17 The priest will then apply
some of the oil in his palm over the blood from
the guilt offering that is on the lobe of the right
ear, the thumb of the right hand, and the big toe
of the right foot of the person being purified.
18 The priest will apply the oil remaining in his
hand to the head of the person being purified.
Through this process, the priest will purify* the
person before the LORD.
19 “Then the priest must present the sin offering to purify the person who was cured of the
skin disease. After that, the priest will slaughter
the burnt offering 20 and offer it on the altar along
with the grain offering. Through this process, the
priest will purify the person who was healed, and
the person will be ceremonially clean.
21 “But anyone who is too poor and cannot afford these offerings may bring one male lamb for
a guilt offering, to be lifted up as a special offering for purification. The person must also bring
two quarts* of choice flour moistened with olive
oil for the grain offering and a cup of olive oil.
22 The offering must also include two turtledoves
or two young pigeons, whichever the person can
afford. One of the pair must be used for the sin
offering and the other for a burnt offering. 23 On
the eighth day of the purification ceremony, the
person being purified must bring the offerings to
the priest in the LORD's presence at the entrance
of the Tabernacle. 24 The priest will take the lamb
for the guilt offering, along with the olive oil,
and lift them up as a special offering to the LORD.
25 Then the priest will slaughter the lamb for the
guilt offering. He will take some of its blood and
apply it to the lobe of the right ear, the thumb of
the right hand, and the big toe of the right foot
of the person being purified.
26 “The priest will also pour some of the olive
oil into the palm of his own left hand. 27 He will
dip his right finger into the oil in his palm and
sprinkle some of it seven times before the LORD.
28 The priest will then apply some of the oil in his
palm over the blood from the guilt offering that
is on the lobe of the right ear, the thumb of the
right hand, and the big toe of the right foot of
the person being purified. 29 The priest will apply
the oil remaining in his hand to the head of the
person being purified. Through this process, the
priest will purify the person before the LORD.
30 “Then the priest will offer the two turtledoves or the two young pigeons, whichever the
person can afford. 31 One of them is for a sin offering and the other for a burnt offering, to be
presented along with the grain offering. Through
this process, the priest will purify the person before the LORD. 32 These are the instructions for
purification for those who have recovered from
a serious skin disease but who cannot afford to
bring the offerings normally required for the
ceremony of purification.”

Treatment of Contaminated Houses

33 Then the LORD said to Moses and Aaron,
34 “When you arrive in Canaan, the land I am
giving you as your own possession, I may contaminate some of the houses in your land with
mildew.* 35 The owner of such a house must then
go to the priest and say, ‘It appears that my house
has some kind of mildew.’ 36 Before the priest goes
in to inspect the house, he must have the house

14:10a Hebrew $^3/_{10}$ *of an ephah* [6.6 liters]. **14:10b** Hebrew *1 log* [0.3 liters]; also in 14:21. **14:11** Hebrew *Tent of Meeting;* also in 14:23. **14:18** Or *will make atonement for;* similarly in 14:19, 20, 21, 29, 31, 53. **14:21** Hebrew $^1/_{10}$ *of an ephah* [2.2 liters]. **14:34** Traditionally rendered *leprosy;* see note on 13:47.

emptied so nothing inside will be pronounced
ceremonially unclean. [37]Then the priest will go
in and examine the mildew on the walls. If he
finds greenish or reddish streaks and the contamination appears to go deeper than the wall's
surface, [38]the priest will step outside the door
and put the house in quarantine for seven days.
[39]On the seventh day the priest must return for
another inspection. If he finds that the mildew
on the walls of the house has spread, [40]the priest
must order that the stones from those areas be
removed. The contaminated material will then
be taken outside the town to an area designated
as ceremonially unclean. [41]Next the inside walls
of the entire house must be scraped thoroughly
and the scrapings dumped in the unclean place
outside the town. [42]Other stones will be brought
in to replace the ones that were removed, and the
walls will be replastered.
[43]"But if the mildew reappears after all the
stones have been replaced and the house has been
scraped and replastered, [44]the priest must return
and inspect the house again. If he finds that the
mildew has spread, the walls are clearly contaminated with a serious mildew, and the house is
defiled. [45]It must be torn down, and all its stones,
timbers, and plaster must be carried out of town
to the place designated as ceremonially unclean.
[46]Those who enter the house during the period
of quarantine will be ceremonially unclean until
evening, [47]and all who sleep or eat in the house
must wash their clothing.
[48]"But if the priest returns for his inspection
and finds that the mildew has not reappeared
in the house after the fresh plastering, he will
pronounce it clean because the mildew is clearly
gone. [49]To purify the house the priest must take
two birds, a stick of cedar, some scarlet yarn,
and a hyssop branch. [50]He will slaughter one of
the birds over a clay pot filled with fresh water.
[51]He will take the cedar stick, the hyssop branch,
the scarlet yarn, and the live bird, and dip them
into the blood of the slaughtered bird and into
the fresh water. Then he will sprinkle the house
seven times. [52]When the priest has purified the
house in exactly this way, [53]he will release the
live bird in the open fields outside the town.
Through this process, the priest will purify the
house, and it will be ceremonially clean.
[54]"These are the instructions for dealing
with serious skin diseases,* including scabby
sores; [55]and mildew,* whether on clothing or in
a house; [56]and a swelling on the skin, a rash, or
discolored skin. [57]This procedure will determine
whether a person or object is ceremonially clean
or unclean.
"These are the instructions regarding skin
diseases and mildew."

Bodily Discharges

15 The LORD said to Moses and Aaron,
[2]"Give the following instructions to
the people of Israel.
"Any man who has a bodily discharge is ceremonially unclean. [3]This defilement is caused by
his discharge, whether the discharge continues
or stops. In either case the man is unclean. [4]Any
bed on which the man with the discharge lies
and anything on which he sits will be ceremonially unclean. [5]So if you touch the man's bed,
you must wash your clothes and bathe yourself in water, and you will remain unclean until evening. [6]If you sit where the man with the
discharge has sat, you must wash your clothes
and bathe yourself in water, and you will remain unclean until evening. [7]If you touch the
man with the discharge, you must wash your
clothes and bathe yourself in water, and you will
remain unclean until evening. [8]If the man spits
on you, you must wash your clothes and bathe
yourself in water, and you will remain unclean
until evening. [9]Any saddle blanket on which the
man rides will be ceremonially unclean. [10]If you

14:54 Traditionally rendered *leprosy;* see note on 13:2a.
14:55 Traditionally rendered *leprosy;* see note on 13:47.

15:1–33 Bodily Discharges. Five kinds of sexual discharges rendered persons unclean in varying degrees. The discussion of these impurities is arranged so that the two types of male uncleanness (unnatural [vv. 2–15] and natural [vv. 16–17]) and the two types of female uncleanness (natural [vv. 19–24] and unnatural [vv. 25–30]) are parallel, with the rule pertaining to both sexes in the middle (v. 18). **2:** A man who had an unnatural flow *(zab)* from his flesh (penis) was unclean. **3:** The discharge could be either a flow like slimy juice or some sort of stoppage. Gonorrhea is probably the disease being described. **4–12:** The affected man's uncleanness was the most communicable of all the types of sexual uncleanness, implying that it was the most serious. A man could communicate uncleanness to inanimate objects, to humans who touched inanimate objects contaminated by him, and to humans through direct contact with him. This high level of communicability may be due to the fact that an unclean man came into contact with more members of the community than an unclean woman would. However, this would not ex-

touch anything that was under the man, you
will be unclean until evening. You must wash
your clothes and bathe yourself in water, and
you will remain unclean until evening. [11] If the
man touches you without first rinsing his hands,
you must wash your clothes and bathe yourself
in water, and you will remain unclean until evening. [12] Any clay pot the man touches must be
broken, and any wooden utensil he touches must
be rinsed with water.

[13] "When the man with the discharge is healed,
he must count off seven days for the period of
purification. Then he must wash his clothes and
bathe himself in fresh water, and he will be ceremonially clean. [14] On the eighth day he must get
two turtledoves or two young pigeons and come
before the LORD at the entrance of the Tabernacle* and give his offerings to the priest. [15] The
priest will offer one bird for a sin offering and
the other for a burnt offering. Through this process, the priest will purify* the man before the
LORD for his discharge.

[16] "Whenever a man has an emission of semen,
he must bathe his entire body in water, and he
will remain ceremonially unclean until the next
evening.* [17] Any clothing or leather with semen
on it must be washed in water, and it will remain
unclean until evening. [18] After a man and a woman have sexual intercourse, they must each bathe
in water, and they will remain unclean until the
next evening.

[19] "Whenever a woman has her menstrual period, she will be ceremonially unclean for seven
days. Anyone who touches her during that time
will be unclean until evening. [20] Anything on
which the woman lies or sits during the time of
her period will be unclean. [21] If any of you touch
her bed, you must wash your clothes and bathe
yourself in water, and you will remain unclean
until evening. [22] If you touch any object she has
sat on, you must wash your clothes and bathe
yourself in water, and you will remain unclean
until evening. [23] This includes her bed or any
other object she has sat on; you will be unclean
until evening if you touch it. [24] If a man has sexual intercourse with her and her blood touches
him, her menstrual impurity will be transmitted
to him. He will remain unclean for seven days,
and any bed on which he lies will be unclean.

[25] "If a woman has a flow of blood for many

15:14 Hebrew *Tent of Meeting;* also in 15:29. **15:15** Or *will make atonement for;* also in 15:30. **15:16** Hebrew *until evening;* also in 15:18.

---

plain why his communicability within the home was greater. The man could contaminate housewares (v. 12), and in this respect he was comparable to the most reviled of unclean animals, rodents and reptiles (11:32–33). **13–15:** When the unclean man was purified from his flow (i.e., *healed*), he counted seven days for his purification, after which he washed his garments and bathed himself (lit., "his flesh," perhaps here a reference to just his penis or maybe his entire body) in fresh water. This rendered him purified and allowed him to take the prescribed sacrifices to the Tabernacle to complete his atonement. **16–17:** *An emission of semen*: Meaning outside of intercourse. Apparently this uncleanness was communicable only to his garments and bedclothes, which were to be washed in water and were unclean until evening. **18:** Uncleanness from sexual intercourse was apparently not communicable to other persons or to garments and bedclothes. Uncleanness from sexual intercourse was not sin. The Hebrew Bible does not view sex within marriage as sinful but as a God-given command and blessing (Gen 1:28). The reason the participants were unclean is because of semen's role in the production of life. **19:** A menstruating woman was unclean for seven days, apparently regardless of whether her menstrual flow was shorter than that. **19–24:** The menstruant's uncleanness was communicable to others who touched her or who touched anything she had sat or lain upon. The text does not indicate that the woman could render other persons unclean if she touched them. Whether this was because a woman was expected to remain within the home during her menstrual cycle or because she could not contaminate others merely by touching them is unclear. **24:** The most significant communicability was if a man had sex with a woman during her period. A man who had sex with a menstruant became unclean himself and could communicate this uncleanness to inanimate objects. See also 18:19 and 20:18, which are much harsher, stating that a man and woman who engaged in intercourse during the woman's period would be cut off from the community. Leviticus 20:18 may be a strengthening of the law in 15:24, or Leviticus 15:24 may be a less stringent version of 20:18. Possibly the context of the two laws is different. Leviticus 15:24 depicts a situation in which the woman's menstruation began as the partners engaged in sex; thus the couple did not knowingly have intercourse during menstruation. Leviticus 20:18 refers to a man and woman knowingly engaging in sex during menstruation. Leviticus 15 does not state that the menstruant was required to bathe and wash her garments or bedclothes. No sacrifices were required of her; at the end of seven days she was clean. **25–30:** A woman who had a flow of blood that occurred at a time outside of her normal

Purity Laws Related to Women

The Pentateuch contains a system of purity and impurity that undergirds nearly every form of ancient Judaism. Impurities can be organized into three categories: death, skin diseases, and sexual discharges.

Although both men and women are equally susceptible to corpse contamination and skin disease, the sexual discharges of women are more contaminating than are those of men. For both men and women, sexual intercourse brings a one-day impurity, but women have the added impurity of a full week each month due to menstruation (see Menstruation, Gen 31).

A woman who has just given birth is also impure—for forty days if the child is a boy or eighty days if the child is a girl (Lev 12:2–5). The person with the most impure sexual discharge is a woman with an abnormal genital flow (i.e., she is menstruating outside of her normal period). She requires divine healing from her disease before she can undergo purification, an eight-day procedure, including ablutions and sacrifices (15:27–30).

Perhaps the best explanation for the biblical impurity laws is that impurity is a symbol for death. The most impure item in the biblical system is the corpse, and the second to it is the person with a skin disease, a sort of living corpse (cf. Num 12:12; Job 18:13). Sexual discharges are probably impure because they are the fluids that give life but are wasting away from the body. The Israelite system lifts up purity as illustrative of the realm of life, the living God and his people, Israel, as opposed to impurity, representing death, lifeless gods, and pagan nations.

Throughout the Old Testament women's impurities surface in various contexts. Women were forbidden contact with the Israelite military camp on account of purity concerns (Deut 23; 1 Sam 21:4–5). Rachel's declaration that she was menstruating kept her father, Laban, from looking underneath her for his stolen idols (Gen 31:35). The recoil caused by menstruation is often used symbolically in the Bible to describe the repulsion God has toward sin (Isa 30:22).

In the New Testament, Mary offers a sacrifice after the impurity of childbirth (Luke 2:22–24). The woman who had been hemorrhaging for twelve years was undoubtedly a woman with abnormal menstruation (Mark 5:25–34). The woman reaches out fearfully to touch Jesus' garment. However, Jesus reverses the dynamics of impurity. Instead of the woman defiling Jesus' clothes, healing power flows from Jesus to the woman.

days that is unrelated to her menstrual period, or if the blood continues beyond the normal period, she is ceremonially unclean. As during her menstrual period, the woman will be unclean as long as the discharge continues.
26 Any bed she lies on and any object she sits on during that time will be unclean, just as during her normal menstrual period.
27 If any of you touch these things, you will be ceremonially unclean. You must wash your clothes and bathe yourself in water, and you will remain unclean until evening.

28 "When the woman's bleeding stops, she must count off seven days. Then she will be ceremonially clean.
29 On the eighth day she must bring two turtledoves or two young pigeons and present them to the priest at the entrance of the Tabernacle.
30 The priest will offer one for a sin offering and the other for a burnt offering. Through this process, the priest will purify her before the LORD for the ceremonial impurity caused by her bleeding.

31 "This is how you will guard the people of

period or extended many days after her normal period was impure, as she was during her normal period; the uncleanness extended for as long as the unnatural flow. Her uncleanness was communicable to objects (beds, chairs) as it was during her period. When the flow ended, the woman counted seven additional days and after that was purified. Like a man with an unnatural discharge, she brought sacrifices to the Tabernacle to complete her purification and atonement. **31–33:** The final verses of the chapter summarize the laws and indicate the motivation for them. **31:** *Guard . . . from*: The Hebrew verb *nzr* usually means consecration or dedication in the sense of being kept separate, as in the Nazirite vow. This accords well with 10:10, where clean and unclean were to be kept separate or distinct. The Samaritan Pentateuch and Syriac versions replace the verb "to keep separate" with another verb meaning "admonish" or "warn," which is closer to the wording of the NLT. In either case, the only way the people could address their uncleanness was by being cleansed. Failure to be purified would defile the sanctuary, resulting in death (see also Num 19:13, 20).

Israel from ceremonial uncleanness. Otherwise
they would die, for their impurity would defile
my Tabernacle that stands among them. 32 These
are the instructions for dealing with anyone who
has a bodily discharge—a man who is unclean
because of an emission of semen 33 or a woman during her menstrual period. It applies to
any man or woman who has a bodily discharge,
and to a man who has sexual intercourse with a
woman who is ceremonially unclean."

The Day of Atonement

16 The LORD spoke to Moses after the
death of Aaron's two sons, who died
after they entered the LORD's presence and burned the wrong kind of fire before
him. 2 The LORD said to Moses, "Warn your
brother, Aaron, not to enter the Most Holy Place
behind the inner curtain whenever he chooses;
if he does, he will die. For the Ark's cover—the
place of atonement—is there, and I myself am
present in the cloud above the atonement cover.

3 "When Aaron enters the sanctuary area, he
must follow these instructions fully. He must
bring a young bull for a sin offering and a ram
for a burnt offering. 4 He must put on his linen
tunic and the linen undergarments worn next to
his body. He must tie the linen sash around his
waist and put the linen turban on his head. These
are sacred garments, so he must bathe himself in
water before he puts them on. 5 Aaron must take
from the community of Israel two male goats for
a sin offering and a ram for a burnt offering.

6 "Aaron will present his own bull as a sin offering to purify himself and his family, making
them right with the LORD.* 7 Then he must take
the two male goats and present them to the LORD
at the entrance of the Tabernacle.* 8 He is to cast
sacred lots to determine which goat will be reserved as an offering to the LORD and which will
carry the sins of the people to the wilderness of
Azazel. 9 Aaron will then present as a sin offering
the goat chosen by lot for the LORD. 10 The other
goat, the scapegoat chosen by lot to be sent away,
will be kept alive, standing before the LORD.
When it is sent away to Azazel in the wilderness,
the people will be purified and made right with
the LORD.*

11 "Aaron will present his own bull as a sin offering to purify himself and his family, making
them right with the LORD. After he has slaughtered the bull as a sin offering, 12 he will fill an
incense burner with burning coals from the altar
that stands before the LORD. Then he will take
two handfuls of fragrant powdered incense and
will carry the burner and the incense behind the
inner curtain. 13 There in the LORD's presence he
will put the incense on the burning coals so that
a cloud of incense will rise over the Ark's cover—
the place of atonement—that rests on the Ark of
the Covenant.* If he follows these instructions,
he will not die. 14 Then he must take some of the
blood of the bull, dip his finger in it, and sprinkle
it on the east side of the atonement cover. He
must sprinkle blood seven times with his finger
in front of the atonement cover.

15 "Then Aaron must slaughter the first goat as
a sin offering for the people and carry its blood
behind the inner curtain. There he will sprinkle
the goat's blood over the atonement cover and
in front of it, just as he did with the bull's blood.
16 Through this process, he will purify* the Most
Holy Place, and he will do the same for the entire
Tabernacle, because of the defiling sin and rebellion of the Israelites. 17 No one else is allowed inside the Tabernacle when Aaron enters it for the

16:6 Or *to make atonement for himself and his family;* similarly in 16:11, 17b, 24, 34. **16:7** Hebrew *Tent of Meeting;* also in 16:16, 17, 20, 23, 33. **16:10** Or *wilderness, it will make atonement for the people.* **16:13** Hebrew *that is above the Testimony.* The Hebrew word for "testimony" refers to the terms of the LORD's covenant with Israel as written on stone tablets, which were kept in the Ark, and also to the covenant itself. **16:16** Or *make atonement for;* similarly in 16:17a, 18, 20, 27, 33.

16:1–34 The Day of Atonement

Significantly, one purpose of the Day of Atonement was to cleanse the sanctuary from the contamination caused by Israel's uncleanness and sin (vv. 16, 33). This is why the ritual for the day comes immediately after the purification laws. When properly cleansed and atoned for, uncleanness had no effect on the sanctuary. But when unclean persons failed to cleanse themselves or when persons participated in certain sins, the sanctuary was defiled. Apparently these impurities accumulated on the sanctuary throughout the year like an invisible rain of pollution. Thus once a year a cleansing ceremony was performed that eradicated the accumulated filth and atoned for the people. As such, the Day of Atonement became the highest holy day of the sacred year.

The high priest performed the ritual for the Day of Atonement, and that ritual consisted of several rites. One rite cleansed the sanctuary (the Most Holy Place, the Holy Place, and the altar of burnt offerings) from the impurities of the priests. Another cleansed the sanctuary from the impurities of the people. A scapegoat ritual removed the transgressions from the people, and burnt offerings atoned for the priests and the people.

purification ceremony in the Most Holy Place. No one may enter until he comes out again after purifying himself, his family, and all the congregation of Israel, making them right with the LORD.

18 "Then Aaron will come out to purify the altar that stands before the LORD. He will do this by taking some of the blood from the bull and the goat and putting it on each of the horns of the altar. 19 Then he must sprinkle the blood with his finger seven times over the altar. In this way, he will cleanse it from Israel's defilement and make it holy.

20 "When Aaron has finished purifying the Most Holy Place and the Tabernacle and the altar, he must present the live goat. 21 He will lay both of his hands on the goat's head and confess over it all the wickedness, rebellion, and sins of the people of Israel. In this way, he will transfer the people's sins to the head of the goat. Then a man specially chosen for the task will drive the goat into the wilderness. 22 As the goat goes into the wilderness, it will carry all the people's sins upon itself into a desolate land.

23 "When Aaron goes back into the Tabernacle, he must take off the linen garments he was wearing when he entered the Most Holy Place, and he must leave the garments there. 24 Then he must bathe himself with water in a sacred place, put on his regular garments, and go out to sacrifice a burnt offering for himself and a burnt offering for the people. Through this process, he will purify himself and the people, making them right with the LORD. 25 He must then burn all the fat of the sin offering on the altar.

26 "The man chosen to drive the scapegoat into the wilderness of Azazel must wash his clothes and bathe himself in water. Then he may return to the camp.

27 "The bull and the goat presented as sin offerings, whose blood Aaron takes into the Most Holy Place for the purification ceremony, will be carried outside the camp. The animals' hides, internal organs, and dung are all to be burned. 28 The man who burns them must wash his clothes and bathe himself in water before returning to the camp.

29 "On the tenth day of the appointed month in early autumn,* you must deny yourselves.* Neither native-born Israelites nor foreigners living among you may do any kind of work. This is a permanent law for you. 30 On that day offerings of purification will be made for you,* and you will be purified in the LORD's presence from all your sins. 31 It will be a Sabbath day of complete rest for you, and you must deny yourselves. This is a permanent law for you. 32 In future generations, the purification* ceremony will be performed by the priest who has been anointed and ordained to serve as high priest in place of his ancestor Aaron. He will put on the holy linen garments 33 and purify the Most Holy Place, the Tabernacle, the altar, the priests, and the entire congregation. 34 This is a permanent law for you, to purify the people of Israel from their sins, making them right with the LORD once each year."

Moses followed all these instructions exactly as the LORD had commanded him.

Prohibitions against Eating Blood

17 Then the LORD said to Moses, 2 "Give the following instructions to Aaron and his sons and all the people of Israel. This is what the LORD has commanded.

3 "If any native Israelite sacrifices a bull* or a lamb or a goat anywhere inside or outside the camp 4 instead of bringing it to the entrance of the Tabernacle* to present it as an offering to the LORD, that person will be as guilty as a murderer.* Such a person has shed blood and will be cut off from the community. 5 The purpose of this rule is to stop the Israelites from sacrificing animals in the open fields. It will ensure that they bring their sacrifices to the priest at the entrance of the Tabernacle, so he can present them to the LORD as peace offerings. 6 Then the priest will be

16:29a Hebrew *On the tenth day of the seventh month.* This day in the ancient Hebrew lunar calendar occurred in September or October. **16:29b** Or *must fast;* also in 16:31. **16:30** Or *atonement will be made for you, to purify you.* **16:32** Or *atonement.* **17:3** Or *cow.* **17:4a** Hebrew *Tent of Meeting;* also in 17:5, 6, 9. **17:4b** Hebrew *will be guilty of blood.*

17:1–26:46 The Holiness Code

These chapters have long been viewed as a distinct section within Leviticus. Termed the Holiness Code, these chapters probably had a lengthy composition history, originating out of various social settings and reflecting the moral and ethical practices of Israel at various times. How and when the laws were compiled is still the subject of much speculation.

Characterized by the repeated refrain *I am the LORD*, and *Be holy, for I, the LORD your God, am holy*, this portion of Leviticus contains a series of laws for maintaining the community's holiness through proper ritual and relational actions. That the people of Israel were to be separate and distinct from the other nations is a primary emphasis of these laws (esp. chaps. 18—20), yet similar laws are found in ancient Near Eastern law codes indicating common concerns.

able to splatter the blood against the LORD's altar at the entrance of the Tabernacle, and he will burn the fat as a pleasing aroma to the LORD. 7 The people must no longer be unfaithful to the LORD by offering sacrifices to the goat idols.* This is a permanent law for them, to be observed from generation to generation.

8 "Give them this command as well. If any native Israelite or foreigner living among you offers a burnt offering or a sacrifice 9 but does not bring it to the entrance of the Tabernacle to offer it to the LORD, that person will be cut off from the community.

10 "And if any native Israelite or foreigner living among you eats or drinks blood in any form, I will turn against that person and cut him off from the community of your people, 11 for the life of the body is in its blood. I have given you the blood on the altar to purify you, making you right with the LORD.* It is the blood, given in exchange for a life, that makes purification possible. 12 That is why I have said to the people of Israel, 'You must never eat or drink blood—neither you nor the foreigners living among you.'

13 "And if any native Israelite or foreigner living among you goes hunting and kills an animal or bird that is approved for eating, he must drain its blood and cover it with earth. 14 The life of every creature is in its blood. That is why I have said to the people of Israel, 'You must never eat or drink blood, for the life of any creature is in its blood.' So whoever consumes blood will be cut off from the community.

15 "And if any native-born Israelites or foreigners eat the meat of an animal that died naturally or was torn up by wild animals, they must wash their clothes and bathe themselves in water. They will remain ceremonially unclean until evening, but then they will be clean. 16 But if they do not wash their clothes and bathe themselves, they will be punished for their sin."

Forbidden Sexual Practices

18 Then the LORD said to Moses, 2 "Give the following instructions to the people of Israel. I am the LORD your God. 3 So do not act like the people in Egypt, where you used to live, or like the people of Canaan, where I am taking you. You must not imitate their way of life. 4 You must obey all my regulations and be careful to obey my decrees, for I am the LORD your God. 5 If you obey my decrees and my regulations, you will find life through them. I am the LORD.

6 "You must never have sexual relations with a close relative, for I am the LORD.

7 "Do not violate your father by having sexual relations with your mother. She is your mother; you must not have sexual relations with her.

8 "Do not have sexual relations with any of your father's wives, for this would violate your father.

9 "Do not have sexual relations with your sister or half sister, whether she is your father's daughter or your mother's daughter, whether she was born into your household or someone else's.

10 "Do not have sexual relations with your granddaughter, whether she is your son's daughter or your daughter's daughter, for this would violate yourself.

11 "Do not have sexual relations with your stepsister, the daughter of any of your father's wives, for she is your sister.

12 "Do not have sexual relations with your father's sister, for she is your father's close relative.

13 "Do not have sexual relations with your mother's sister, for she is your mother's close relative.

14 "Do not violate your uncle, your father's brother, by having sexual relations with his wife, for she is your aunt.

15 "Do not have sexual relations with your daughter-in-law; she is your son's wife, so you must not have sexual relations with her.

16 "Do not have sexual relations with your brother's wife, for this would violate your brother.

17 "Do not have sexual relations with both a

17:7 Or *goat demons.* **17:11** Or *to make atonement for you.*

18:1–30 Forbidden Sexual Practices. The laws in Leviticus 18 concern two types of forbidden relationships: incest (vv. 6–18), and other forbidden sexual relations (vv. 19–20, 22–23). Every law in this chapter except for one (v. 21) mentions a woman and always in a prohibition regarding sexual intercourse. But the prohibitions are all directed at men (the verbs are second-person masculine singular, except one in v. 23), probably because men were the sexual initiators. The focus of these laws is like that of other Levitical laws: ritual purity. **6–17:** Each verse begins with the equivalent in Hebrew of "the nakedness of *x* do not uncover," which is a euphemism for engaging in intercourse. The fact that sex with a daughter is not prohibited is puzzling. Verse 6 states that a man is not to have intercourse with any flesh relative, so the omitted family members may be subsumed under that prohibition. **19–20, 22–23:** Forbidden sexu-

woman and her daughter. And do not take* her granddaughter, whether her son's daughter or her daughter's daughter, and have sexual relations with her. They are close relatives, and this would be a wicked act.

18 "While your wife is living, do not marry her sister and have sexual relations with her, for they would be rivals.

19 "Do not have sexual relations with a woman during her period of menstrual impurity.

20 "Do not defile yourself by having sexual intercourse with your neighbor's wife.

21 "Do not permit any of your children to be offered as a sacrifice to Molech, for you must not bring shame on the name of your God. I am the LORD.

22 "Do not practice homosexuality, having sex with another man as with a woman. It is a detestable sin.

23 "A man must not defile himself by having sex with an animal. And a woman must not offer herself to a male animal to have intercourse with it. This is a perverse act.

24 "Do not defile yourselves in any of these ways, for the people I am driving out before you have defiled themselves in all these ways. 25 Because the entire land has become defiled, I am punishing the people who live there. I will cause the land to vomit them out. 26 You must obey all my decrees and regulations. You must not commit any of these detestable sins. This applies both to native-born Israelites and to the foreigners living among you.

27 "All these detestable activities are practiced by the people of the land where I am taking you, and this is how the land has become defiled. 28 So do not defile the land and give it a reason to vomit you out, as it will vomit out the people who live there now. 29 Whoever commits any of these detestable sins will be cut off from the community of Israel. 30 So obey my instructions, and do not defile yourselves by committing any of these detestable practices that were committed by the people who lived in the land before you. I am the LORD your God."

Holiness in Personal Conduct

19 The LORD also said to Moses, 2 "Give the following instructions to the entire community of Israel. You must be holy because I, the LORD your God, am holy.

3 "Each of you must show great respect for your mother and father, and you must always observe my Sabbath days of rest. I am the LORD your God.

4 "Do not put your trust in idols or make metal images of gods for yourselves. I am the LORD your God.

18:17 Or *do not marry.*

---

al relationships other than incest, including sex with a menstruant, adultery, homosexuality, and bestiality. **21:** The prohibition against worship of Molech seems out of place in a series of forbidden sexual unions. However, it is connected to the preceding verse by the use of the word "seed." Literally, verse 20 states, "You will not give your lying of seed [intercourse] with your neighbor's wife." Verse 21 states, "You will not give from your seed [descendants] to pass over to Molech." Perhaps just as forbidden sexual unions were inappropriate uses of seed (semen), so was giving over the product of seed (children) to Molech. In addition, worship of Molech and other forms of false worship are often compared with playing the harlot (see 17:7; 20:5–6), a figurative symbol of adultery against Yahweh (cf. Ezek 6:9; 16:1–63, esp. Ezek 16:15; 20:30–31 [Molech worship]; Hos 4:15; 9:1), again tying this prohibition to Leviticus 18:20. **24–30:** These verses relate these restrictions to the practices of the nations whom Israel would drive out. Such sexual unions were abominations, making the entire land ritually unclean (v. 27) as well as the participants (v. 30). Thus the people of Israel were to avoid these practices or face the possibility that they would be *cut off*, or exiled (v. 29) and ultimately *vomited out*, or expelled, by the land itself (v. 28).

19:1–37 Holiness in Personal Conduct. The laws in Leviticus 19 concern proper relationships, both divine-human and human-human. Many of the laws distinctly parallel or expand on the Ten Commandments (cf. vv. 2–4, 11–13, 15–18, 30 and the Decalogues in Exod and Deut). Just as the structure of the Ten Commandments indicates, proper relationship with God expressed through ritual must be mirrored by proper relationship with fellow humans expressed through morality. Laws relating to women include verses 3, 20–22 and 29. **3:** *Great respect* is often translated "fear." The word "fear" is normally used with God as its object and only rarely with humans (Josh 4:14 is the only other example). The formulation here is striking in that mother appears before father, giving her the place of honor (father precedes mother in both versions of the Ten Commandments). In Leviticus this is the first command listed, receiving priority over the Sabbath command and the prohibition against idolatry. A child who cursed rather than honored his parents was subject to the death penalty

5 "When you sacrifice a peace offering to the LORD, offer it properly so you* will be accepted by God. 6 The sacrifice must be eaten on the same day you offer it or on the next day. Whatever is left over until the third day must be completely burned up. 7 If any of the sacrifice is eaten on the third day, it will be contaminated, and I will not accept it. 8 Anyone who eats it on the third day will be punished for defiling what is holy to the LORD and will be cut off from the community.

9 "When you harvest the crops of your land, do not harvest the grain along the edges of your fields, and do not pick up what the harvesters drop. 10 It is the same with your grape crop—do not strip every last bunch of grapes from the vines, and do not pick up the grapes that fall to the ground. Leave them for the poor and the foreigners living among you. I am the LORD your God.

11 "Do not steal.

"Do not deceive or cheat one another.

12 "Do not bring shame on the name of your God by using it to swear falsely. I am the LORD.

13 "Do not defraud or rob your neighbor.

"Do not make your hired workers wait until the next day to receive their pay.

14 "Do not insult the deaf or cause the blind to stumble. You must fear your God; I am the LORD.

15 "Do not twist justice in legal matters by favoring the poor or being partial to the rich and powerful. Always judge people fairly.

16 "Do not spread slanderous gossip among your people.*

"Do not stand idly by when your neighbor's life is threatened. I am the LORD.

17 "Do not nurse hatred in your heart for any of your relatives.* Confront people directly so you will not be held guilty for their sin.

18 "Do not seek revenge or bear a grudge against a fellow Israelite, but love your neighbor as yourself. I am the LORD.

19 "You must obey all my decrees.

"Do not mate two different kinds of animals. Do not plant your field with two different kinds of seed. Do not wear clothing woven from two different kinds of thread.

20 "If a man has sex with a slave girl whose freedom has never been purchased but who is committed to become another man's wife, he must pay full compensation to her master. But since she is not a free woman, neither the man nor the woman will be put to death. 21 The man, however, must bring a ram as a guilt offering and present it to the LORD at the entrance of the Tabernacle.* 22 The priest will then purify him* before the LORD with the ram of the guilt offering, and the man's sin will be forgiven.

23 "When you enter the land and plant fruit trees, leave the fruit unharvested for the first three years and consider it forbidden.* Do not eat it. 24 In the fourth year the entire crop must be consecrated to the LORD as a celebration of praise. 25 Finally, in the fifth year you may eat the fruit. If you follow this pattern, your harvest will increase. I am the LORD your God.

26 "Do not eat meat that has not been drained of its blood.

"Do not practice fortune-telling or witchcraft.

27 "Do not trim off the hair on your temples or trim your beards.

28 "Do not cut your bodies for the dead, and do not mark your skin with tattoos. I am the LORD.

29 "Do not defile your daughter by making her a prostitute, or the land will be filled with prostitution and wickedness.

30 "Keep my Sabbath days of rest, and show reverence toward my sanctuary. I am the LORD.

31 "Do not defile yourselves by turning to mediums or to those who consult the spirits of the dead. I am the LORD your God.

32 "Stand up in the presence of the elderly, and show respect for the aged. Fear your God. I am the LORD.

33 "Do not take advantage of foreigners who live among you in your land. 34 Treat them like native-born Israelites, and love them as you love yourself. Remember that you were once foreign-

19:5 Or *it.* **19:16** Hebrew *Do not act as a merchant toward your own people.* **19:17** Hebrew *for your brother.* **19:21** Hebrew *Tent of Meeting.* **19:22** Or *make atonement for him.* **19:23** Hebrew *consider it uncircumcised.*

(20:9). **20–22:** A man who committed adultery with a slave woman betrothed to another was required to give a reparation offering because he had in essence stolen his companion's property (see 6:2–7). See 20:10, where the punishment for adultery with a free woman is death. **29:** Fathers may have used their daughters as prostitutes in order to remove themselves from debt or to supplement income. However, this verse may refer to prostitution connected with foreign cults, since immediately preceding it is a stipulation against practices related to the cult of the dead (v. 28). Prostituting one's daughter resulted in the prostitution of the land, just as false worship defiled the land (cf. 18:24–30). Thus, making one's daughter a prostitute *defiled* her, and a father was forbidden to use his daughter for monetary or religious gain.

ers living in the land of Egypt. I am the LORD your God.

35 "Do not use dishonest standards when measuring length, weight, or volume. 36 Your scales and weights must be accurate. Your containers for measuring dry materials or liquids must be accurate.* I am the LORD your God who brought you out of the land of Egypt.

37 "You must be careful to keep all of my decrees and regulations by putting them into practice. I am the LORD."

Punishments for Disobedience

20 The LORD said to Moses, 2 "Give the people of Israel these instructions, which apply both to native Israelites and to the foreigners living in Israel.

"If any of them offer their children as a sacrifice to Molech, they must be put to death. The people of the community must stone them to death. 3 I myself will turn against them and cut them off from the community, because they have defiled my sanctuary and brought shame on my holy name by offering their children to Molech. 4 And if the people of the community ignore those who offer their children to Molech and refuse to execute them, 5 I myself will turn against them and their families and will cut them off from the community. This will happen to all who commit spiritual prostitution by worshiping Molech.

6 "I will also turn against those who commit spiritual prostitution by putting their trust in mediums or in those who consult the spirits of the dead. I will cut them off from the community. 7 So set yourselves apart to be holy, for I am the LORD your God. 8 Keep all my decrees by putting them into practice, for I am the LORD who makes you holy.

9 "Anyone who dishonors* father or mother must be put to death. Such a person is guilty of a capital offense.

10 "If a man commits adultery with his neighbor's wife, both the man and the woman who have committed adultery must be put to death.

11 "If a man violates his father by having sex with one of his father's wives, both the man and the woman must be put to death, for they are guilty of a capital offense.

12 "If a man has sex with his daughter-in-law, both must be put to death. They have committed a perverse act and are guilty of a capital offense.

13 "If a man practices homosexuality, having sex with another man as with a woman, both men have committed a detestable act. They must both be put to death, for they are guilty of a capital offense.

14 "If a man marries both a woman and her mother, he has committed a wicked act. The man and both women must be burned to death to wipe out such wickedness from among you.

15 "If a man has sex with an animal, he must be put to death, and the animal must be killed.

16 "If a woman presents herself to a male animal to have intercourse with it, she and the animal must both be put to death. You must kill both, for they are guilty of a capital offense.

17 "If a man marries his sister, the daughter of either his father or his mother, and they have sexual relations, it is a shameful disgrace. They must be publicly cut off from the community. Since the man has violated his sister, he will be punished for his sin.

18 "If a man has sexual relations with a woman during her menstrual period, both of them must be cut off from the community, for together they have exposed the source of her blood flow.

19 "Do not have sexual relations with your aunt, whether your mother's sister or your father's sister. This would dishonor a close relative. Both parties are guilty and will be punished for their sin.

20 "If a man has sex with his uncle's wife, he has violated his uncle. Both the man and woman will be punished for their sin, and they will die childless.

21 "If a man marries his brother's wife, it is an act of impurity. He has violated his brother, and the guilty couple will remain childless.

22 "You must keep all my decrees and regulations by putting them into practice; otherwise the land to which I am bringing you as your new home will vomit you out. 23 Do not live accord-

19:36 Hebrew *Use an honest ephah* [a dry measure] *and an honest hin* [a liquid measure]. **20:9** Greek version reads *Anyone who speaks disrespectfully of.* Compare Matt 15:4; Mark 7:10.

20:1–27 Punishments for Disobedience. Every restriction in Leviticus 20 has a parallel in chapters 18 and/or 19, but the emphasis here is on the penalties for breaking the laws. **2, 9–16:** The death penalty is most often prescribed, although the manner in which it was carried out is usually unspecified. **3, 5, 6, 17, 18:** *Cut them off*: The meaning of this penalty is never spelled out in the biblical material, although usually it occurs in the context of ritual violations. Most likely, being cut off meant exile from the holy community and expulsion from God's presence (cf. Gen 4:14). **20–21:** Childlessness as a penalty indicates that some forbidden sexual unions would produce no fruit.

ing to the customs of the people I am driving out before you. It is because they do these shameful things that I detest them. [24]But I have promised you, 'You will possess their land because I will give it to you as your possession—a land flowing with milk and honey.' I am the LORD your God, who has set you apart from all other people.

[25]"You must therefore make a distinction between ceremonially clean and unclean animals, and between clean and unclean birds. You must not defile yourselves by eating any unclean animal or bird or creature that scurries along the ground. I have identified them as being unclean for you. [26]You must be holy because I, the LORD, am holy. I have set you apart from all other people to be my very own.

[27]"Men and women among you who act as mediums or who consult the spirits of the dead must be put to death by stoning. They are guilty of a capital offense."

Instructions for the Priests

21 The LORD said to Moses, "Give the following instructions to the priests, the descendants of Aaron.

"A priest must not make himself ceremonially unclean by touching the dead body of a relative. [2]The only exceptions are his closest relatives—his mother or father, son or daughter, brother, [3]or his virgin sister who depends on him because she has no husband. [4]But a priest must not defile himself and make himself unclean for someone who is related to him only by marriage.

[5]"The priests must not shave their heads or trim their beards or cut their bodies. [6]They must be set apart as holy to their God and must never bring shame on the name of God. They must be holy, for they are the ones who present the special gifts to the LORD, gifts of food for their God.

[7]"Priests may not marry a woman defiled by prostitution, and they may not marry a woman who is divorced from her husband, for the priests are set apart as holy to their God. [8]You must treat them as holy because they offer up food to your God. You must consider them holy because I, the LORD, am holy, and I make you holy.

[9]"If a priest's daughter defiles herself by becoming a prostitute, she also defiles her father's holiness, and she must be burned to death.

[10]"The high priest has the highest rank of all the priests. The anointing oil has been poured on his head, and he has been ordained to wear the priestly garments. He must never leave his hair uncombed* or tear his clothing. [11]He must not defile himself by going near a dead body. He may not make himself ceremonially unclean even for his father or mother. [12]He must not defile the sanctuary of his God by leaving it to attend to a dead person, for he has been made holy by the anointing oil of his God. I am the LORD.

[13]"The high priest may marry only a virgin. [14]He may not marry a widow, a woman who is divorced, or a woman who has defiled herself by prostitution. She must be a virgin from his own clan, [15]so that he will not dishonor his descendants among his clan, for I am the LORD who makes him holy."

[16]Then the LORD said to Moses, [17]"Give the following instructions to Aaron: In all future generations, none of your descendants who has any defect will qualify to offer food to his God. [18]No one who has a defect qualifies, whether he is blind, lame, disfigured, deformed, [19]or has a broken foot or arm, [20]or is hunchbacked or dwarfed, or has a defective eye, or skin sores or scabs, or damaged testicles. [21]No descendant of Aaron who has a defect may approach the altar to present special gifts to the LORD. Since he has a defect, he may not approach the altar to offer food to his God. [22]However, he may eat from the

21:10 Or *never uncover his head.*

21:1—22:33 Instructions for the Priests. The priests had been set apart by God to be representatives for the people. Therefore, because they themselves were consecrated as holy, the rules they followed were more stringent than those for the people. **21:1–5:** The regular priests could not defile themselves by touching human corpses, except those of their closest family members: parents, children or siblings (cf. Num 19:11–22), and they could not disfigure themselves during mourning. **7:** Marriage restrictions were probably to ensure a pure lineage. **9:** A daughter's prostitution obviously would have compromised the purity of the tribe. In addition, if her prostitution was related to false worship, it would have threatened the sanctity of the priestly office. This presents an intriguing antithesis to Molech worship in which children were burned as sacrifices. In this case, a priest was required to burn his child, not as a sacrifice but as a punishment. **10–15:** The high priest also could not demonstrate any visible signs of mourning, nor could he touch any corpses, not even those of his immediate family. He was required to stay in the sanctuary, lest by leaving he profaned it, and to marry a virgin from among his own people. He could not marry a widow, a divorced woman or a harlot. There was to be no question that the high priest's children were

food offered to God, including the holy offerings and the most holy offerings. 23 Yet because of his physical defect, he may not enter the room behind the inner curtain or approach the altar, for this would defile my holy places. I am the LORD who makes them holy."

24 So Moses gave these instructions to Aaron and his sons and to all the Israelites.

22 The LORD said to Moses, 2 "Tell Aaron and his sons to be very careful with the sacred gifts that the Israelites set apart for me, so they do not bring shame on my holy name. I am the LORD. 3 Give them the following instructions.

"In all future generations, if any of your descendants is ceremonially unclean when he approaches the sacred offerings that the people of Israel consecrate to the LORD, he must be cut off from my presence. I am the LORD.

4 "If any of Aaron's descendants has a skin disease* or any kind of discharge that makes him ceremonially unclean, he may not eat from the sacred offerings until he has been pronounced clean. He also becomes unclean by touching a corpse, or by having an emission of semen, 5 or by touching a small animal that is unclean, or by touching someone who is ceremonially unclean for any reason. 6 The man who is defiled in any of these ways will remain unclean until evening. He may not eat from the sacred offerings until he has bathed himself in water. 7 When the sun goes down, he will be ceremonially clean again and may eat from the sacred offerings, for this is his food. 8 He may not eat an animal that has died a natural death or has been torn apart by wild animals, for this would defile him. I am the LORD.

9 "The priests must follow my instructions carefully. Otherwise they will be punished for their sin and will die for violating my instructions. I am the LORD who makes them holy.

10 "No one outside a priest's family may eat the sacred offerings. Even guests and hired workers in a priest's home are not allowed to eat them. 11 However, if the priest buys a slave for himself, the slave may eat from the sacred offerings. And if his slaves have children, they also may share his food. 12 If a priest's daughter marries someone outside the priestly family, she may no longer eat the sacred offerings. 13 But if she becomes a widow or is divorced and has no children to support her, and she returns to live in her father's home as in her youth, she may eat her father's food again. Otherwise, no one outside a priest's family may eat the sacred offerings.

14 "Any such person who eats the sacred offerings without realizing it must pay the priest for the amount eaten, plus an additional 20 percent. 15 The priests must not let the Israelites defile the sacred offerings brought to the LORD 16 by allowing unauthorized people to eat them. This would bring guilt upon them and require them to pay compensation. I am the LORD who makes them holy."

Worthy and Unworthy Offerings

17 And the LORD said to Moses, 18 "Give Aaron and his sons and all the Israelites these instructions, which apply both to native Israelites and to the foreigners living among you.

"If you present a gift as a burnt offering to the LORD, whether it is to fulfill a vow or is a voluntary offering, 19 you* will be accepted only if your offering is a male animal with no defects. It may be a bull, a ram, or a male goat. 20 Do not present an animal with defects, because the LORD will not accept it on your behalf.

21 "If you present a peace offering to the LORD from the herd or the flock, whether it is to fulfill a vow or is a voluntary offering, you must offer a perfect animal. It may have no defect of any kind. 22 You must not offer an animal that is blind, crippled, or injured, or that has a wart, a skin sore, or scabs. Such animals must never be offered on the altar as special gifts to the LORD. 23 If a bull* or lamb has a leg that is too long or too short, it may be offered as a voluntary offering, but it may not be offered to fulfill a vow. 24 If an animal has damaged testicles or is castrated, you may not offer it to the LORD. You must never do this in your own land, 25 and you must not accept such an animal from foreigners and then offer it as a sacrifice to your God. Such animals will not be accepted on your behalf, for they are mutilated or defective."

26 And the LORD said to Moses, 27 "When a calf

22:4 Traditionally rendered *leprosy;* see note on 13:2a.
22:19 Or *it.* **22:23** Or *cow.*

really his, so he had to marry a virgin. **21:22—22:16:** Priests and their sons were allowed to eat portions of the sacred offerings (6:18, 26, 29; 7:6–10). Daughters, however, were allowed to partake of only the wave (elevation) offerings, not the grain, sin, or guilt offerings (10:14; 22:12–13), and only if she was living as a single woman under her father's roof. These verses indicate that women within the priestly tribe had only limited access to the consecrated food.

or lamb or goat is born, it must be left with its mother for seven days. From the eighth day on, it will be acceptable as a special gift to the LORD. 28 But you must not slaughter a mother animal and her offspring on the same day, whether from the herd or the flock. 29 When you bring a thanksgiving offering to the LORD, sacrifice it properly so you will be accepted. 30 Eat the entire sacrificial animal on the day it is presented. Do not leave any of it until the next morning. I am the LORD.

31 "You must faithfully keep all my commands by putting them into practice, for I am the LORD. 32 Do not bring shame on my holy name, for I will display my holiness among the people of Israel. I am the LORD who makes you holy. 33 It was I who rescued you from the land of Egypt, that I might be your God. I am the LORD."

The Appointed Festivals

23 The LORD said to Moses, 2 "Give the following instructions to the people of Israel. These are the LORD's appointed festivals, which you are to proclaim as official days for holy assembly.

3 "You have six days each week for your ordinary work, but the seventh day is a Sabbath day of complete rest, an official day for holy assembly. It is the LORD's Sabbath day, and it must be observed wherever you live.

4 "In addition to the Sabbath, these are the LORD's appointed festivals, the official days for holy assembly that are to be celebrated at their proper times each year.

Passover and the Festival of Unleavened Bread

5 "The LORD's Passover begins at sundown on the fourteenth day of the first month.* 6 On the next day, the fifteenth day of the month, you must begin celebrating the Festival of Unleavened Bread. This festival to the LORD continues for seven days, and during that time the bread you eat must be made without yeast. 7 On the first day of the festival, all the people must stop their ordinary work and observe an official day for holy assembly. 8 For seven days you must present special gifts to the LORD. On the seventh day the people must again stop all their ordinary work to observe an official day for holy assembly."

Celebration of First Harvest

9 Then the LORD said to Moses, 10 "Give the following instructions to the people of Israel. When you enter the land I am giving you and you harvest its first crops, bring the priest a bundle of grain from the first cutting of your grain harvest. 11 On the day after the Sabbath, the priest will lift it up before the LORD so it may be accepted on your behalf. 12 On that same day you must sacrifice a one-year-old male lamb with no defects as a burnt offering to the LORD. 13 With it you must present a grain offering consisting of four quarts* of choice flour moistened with olive oil. It will be a special gift, a pleasing aroma to the LORD. You must also offer one quart* of wine as a liquid offering. 14 Do not eat any bread or roasted grain or fresh kernels on that day until you bring this offering to your God. This is a permanent law for you, and it must be observed from generation to generation wherever you live.

The Festival of Harvest

15 "From the day after the Sabbath—the day you bring the bundle of grain to be lifted up as a special offering—count off seven full weeks. 16 Keep counting until the day after the seventh Sabbath, fifty days later. Then present an offering of new grain to the LORD. 17 From wherever you live, bring two loaves of bread to be lifted up before the LORD as a special offering. Make these loaves from four quarts of choice flour, and bake them with yeast. They will be an offering to the LORD from the first of your crops. 18 Along with the bread, present seven one-year-old male lambs with no defects, one young bull, and two rams as burnt offerings to the LORD. These burnt offerings, together with the grain offerings and liquid offerings, will be a special gift, a pleasing aroma to the LORD. 19 Then you must offer one male goat as a sin offering and two one-year-old male lambs as a peace offering.

20 "The priest will lift up the two lambs as a special offering to the LORD, together with the loaves representing the first of your crops. These offerings, which are holy to the LORD, belong to the priests. 21 That same day will be proclaimed an official day for holy assembly, a day on which you do no ordinary work. This is a permanent law for you, and it must be observed from generation to generation wherever you live.*

22 "When you harvest the crops of your land, do not harvest the grain along the edges of your fields, and do not pick up what the harvesters drop. Leave it for the poor and the foreigners living among you. I am the LORD your God."

23:5 This day in the ancient Hebrew lunar calendar occurred in late March, April, or early May. **23:13a** Hebrew 2/10 *of an ephah* [4.4 liters]; also in 23:17. **23:13b** Hebrew 1/4 *of a hin* [1 liter]. **23:21** This celebration, called the Festival of Harvest or the Festival of Weeks, was later called the Festival of Pentecost (see Acts 2:1). It is celebrated today as Shavuot (or Shabuoth).

The Festival of Trumpets
23 The LORD said to Moses, 24 "Give the following
instructions to the people of Israel. On the first
day of the appointed month in early autumn,*
you are to observe a day of complete rest. It will
be an official day for holy assembly, a day commemorated with loud blasts of a trumpet. 25 You
must do no ordinary work on that day. Instead,
you are to present special gifts to the LORD."

The Day of Atonement
26 Then the LORD said to Moses, 27 "Be careful to
celebrate the Day of Atonement on the tenth day
of that same month—nine days after the Festival
of Trumpets.* You must observe it as an official
day for holy assembly, a day to deny yourselves*
and present special gifts to the LORD. 28 Do no
work during that entire day because it is the Day
of Atonement, when offerings of purification are
made for you, making you right with* the LORD
your God. 29 All who do not deny themselves that
day will be cut off from God's people. 30 And I
will destroy anyone among you who does any
work on that day. 31 You must not do any work
at all! This is a permanent law for you, and it
must be observed from generation to generation
wherever you live. 32 This will be a Sabbath day
of complete rest for you, and on that day you
must deny yourselves. This day of rest will begin
at sundown on the ninth day of the month and
extend until sundown on the tenth day."

The Festival of Shelters
33 And the LORD said to Moses, 34 "Give the following instructions to the people of Israel. Begin celebrating the Festival of Shelters* on the
fifteenth day of the appointed month—five days
after the Day of Atonement.* This festival to
the LORD will last for seven days. 35 On the first
day of the festival you must proclaim an official
day for holy assembly, when you do no ordinary
work. 36 For seven days you must present special
gifts to the LORD. The eighth day is another holy
day on which you present your special gifts to
the LORD. This will be a solemn occasion, and no
ordinary work may be done that day.
37 ("These are the LORD's appointed festivals.
Celebrate them each year as official days for
holy assembly by presenting special gifts to the
LORD—burnt offerings, grain offerings, sacrifices, and liquid offerings—each on its proper day.
38 These festivals must be observed in addition to
the LORD's regular Sabbath days, and the offerings are in addition to your personal gifts, the
offerings you give to fulfill your vows, and the
voluntary offerings you present to the LORD.)
39 "Remember that this seven-day festival to
the LORD—the Festival of Shelters—begins on
the fifteenth day of the appointed month,* after
you have harvested all the produce of the land.
The first day and the eighth day of the festival
will be days of complete rest. 40 On the first day
gather branches from magnificent trees*—palm
fronds, boughs from leafy trees, and willows that
grow by the streams. Then celebrate with joy before the LORD your God for seven days. 41 You
must observe this festival to the LORD for seven
days every year. This is a permanent law for you,
and it must be observed in the appointed month*
from generation to generation. 42 For seven days
you must live outside in little shelters. All native-born Israelites must live in shelters. 43 This
will remind each new generation of Israelites
that I made their ancestors live in shelters when
I rescued them from the land of Egypt. I am the
LORD your God."
44 So Moses gave the Israelites these instructions regarding the annual festivals of the LORD.

Pure Oil and Holy Bread
24 The LORD said to Moses, 2 "Command
the people of Israel to bring you pure
oil of pressed olives for the light, to
keep the lamps burning continually. 3 This is the
lampstand that stands in the Tabernacle, in front
of the inner curtain that shields the Ark of the
Covenant.* Aaron must keep the lamps burning
in the LORD's presence all night. This is a permanent law for you, and it must be observed from
generation to generation. 4 Aaron and the priests
must tend the lamps on the pure gold lampstand
continually in the LORD's presence.
5 "You must bake twelve loaves of bread from
choice flour, using four quarts* of flour for each
loaf. 6 Place the bread before the LORD on the

23:24 Hebrew *On the first day of the seventh month.* This day in the ancient Hebrew lunar calendar occurred in September or October. This festival is celebrated today as Rosh Hashanah, the Jewish new year. **23:27a** Hebrew *on the tenth day of the seventh month;* see 23:24 and the note there. This day in the ancient Hebrew lunar calendar occurred in September or October. It is celebrated today as Yom Kippur. **23:27b** Or *to fast;* similarly in 23:29, 32. **23:28** Or *when atonement is made for you before.* **23:34a** Or *Festival of Booths,* or *Festival of Tabernacles.* This was earlier called the Festival of the Final Harvest or Festival of Ingathering (see Exod 23:16b). It is celebrated today as Sukkot (or Succoth). **23:34b** Hebrew *on the fifteenth day of the seventh month;* see 23:27a and the note there. **23:39** Hebrew *on the fifteenth day of the seventh month.* **23:40** Or *gather fruit from majestic trees.* **23:41** Hebrew *the seventh month.* **24:3** Hebrew *in the Tent of Meeting, outside the inner curtain of the Testimony;* see note on 16:13. **24:5** Hebrew *2/10 of an ephah* [4.4 liters].

pure gold table, and arrange the loaves in two rows, with six loaves in each row. 7 Put some pure frankincense near each row to serve as a representative offering, a special gift presented to the LORD. 8 Every Sabbath day this bread must be laid out before the LORD. The bread is to be received from the people of Israel as a requirement of the eternal covenant. 9 The loaves of bread will belong to Aaron and his descendants, who must eat them in a sacred place, for they are most holy. It is the permanent right of the priests to claim this portion of the special gifts presented to the LORD."

An Example of Just Punishment

10 One day a man who had an Israelite mother and an Egyptian father came out of his tent and got into a fight with one of the Israelite men. 11 During the fight, this son of an Israelite woman blasphemed the Name of the LORD* with a curse. So the man was brought to Moses for judgment. His mother was Shelomith, the daughter of Dibri of the tribe of Dan. 12 They kept the man in custody until the LORD's will in the matter should become clear to them.

13 Then the LORD said to Moses, 14 "Take the blasphemer outside the camp, and tell all those who heard the curse to lay their hands on his head. Then let the entire community stone him to death. 15 Say to the people of Israel: Those who curse their God will be punished for their sin. 16 Anyone who blasphemes the Name of the LORD must be stoned to death by the whole community of Israel. Any native-born Israelite or foreigner among you who blasphemes the Name of the LORD must be put to death.

17 "Anyone who takes another person's life must be put to death.

18 "Anyone who kills another person's animal must pay for it in full—a live animal for the animal that was killed.

19 "Anyone who injures another person must be dealt with according to the injury inflicted—20 a fracture for a fracture, an eye for an eye, a tooth for a tooth. Whatever anyone does to injure another person must be paid back in kind.

21 "Whoever kills an animal must pay for it in full, but whoever kills another person must be put to death.

22 "This same standard applies both to native-born Israelites and to the foreigners living among you. I am the LORD your God."

23 After Moses gave all these instructions to the Israelites, they took the blasphemer outside the camp and stoned him to death. The Israelites did just as the LORD had commanded Moses.

The Sabbath Year

25 While Moses was on Mount Sinai, the LORD said to him, 2 "Give the following instructions to the people of Israel. When you have entered the land I am giving you, the land itself must observe a Sabbath rest before the LORD every seventh year. 3 For six years you may plant your fields and prune your vineyards and harvest your crops, 4 but during the seventh year the land must have a Sabbath year of complete rest. It is the LORD's Sabbath. Do not plant your fields or prune your vineyards during that year. 5 And don't store away the crops that grow on their own or gather the grapes from your unpruned vines. The land must have a year of complete rest. 6 But you may eat whatever the land produces on its own during its Sabbath. This applies to you, your male and female servants, your hired workers, and the temporary residents who live with you. 7 Your livestock and the wild animals in your land will also be allowed to eat what the land produces.

The Year of Jubilee

8 "In addition, you must count off seven Sabbath years, seven sets of seven years, adding up to forty-nine years in all. 9 Then on the Day of Atonement in the fiftieth year,* blow the ram's horn loud and long throughout the land. 10 Set this year apart as holy, a time to proclaim freedom throughout the land for all who live there. It will be a jubilee year for you, when each of you may return to the land that belonged to your ancestors and return to your own clan. 11 This fiftieth year will be a jubilee for you. During that year you must not plant your fields or store away any of the crops that grow on their own, and don't gather the grapes from your unpruned vines. 12 It will be a jubilee year for you, and you must keep it holy. But you may eat whatever the land produces on its own. 13 In the Year of Jubilee each of you may return to the land that belonged to your ancestors.

14 "When you make an agreement with your neighbor to buy or sell property, you must not take advantage of each other. 15 When you buy land from your neighbor, the price you pay must be based on the number of years since the last jubilee. The seller must set the price by taking into account the number of years remaining until the next Year of Jubilee. 16 The more years until the next jubilee, the higher the price; the fewer

24:11 Hebrew *the Name;* also in 24:16b. **25:9** Hebrew *on the tenth day of the seventh month, on the Day of Atonement;* see 23:27a and the note there.

years, the lower the price. After all, the person selling the land is actually selling you a certain number of harvests. 17 Show your fear of God by not taking advantage of each other. I am the LORD your God.

18 "If you want to live securely in the land, follow my decrees and obey my regulations. 19 Then the land will yield large crops, and you will eat your fill and live securely in it. 20 But you might ask, 'What will we eat during the seventh year, since we are not allowed to plant or harvest crops that year?' 21 Be assured that I will send my blessing for you in the sixth year, so the land will produce a crop large enough for three years. 22 When you plant your fields in the eighth year, you will still be eating from the large crop of the sixth year. In fact, you will still be eating from that large crop when the new crop is harvested in the ninth year.

Redemption of Property

23 "The land must never be sold on a permanent basis, for the land belongs to me. You are only foreigners and tenant farmers working for me.

24 "With every purchase of land you must grant the seller the right to buy it back. 25 If one of your fellow Israelites falls into poverty and is forced to sell some family land, then a close relative should buy it back for him. 26 If there is no close relative to buy the land, but the person who sold it gets enough money to buy it back, 27 he then has the right to redeem it from the one who bought it. The price of the land will be discounted according to the number of years until the next Year of Jubilee. In this way the original owner can then return to the land. 28 But if the original owner cannot afford to buy back the land, it will remain with the new owner until the next Year of Jubilee. In the jubilee year, the land must be returned to the original owners so they can return to their family land.

29 "Anyone who sells a house inside a walled town has the right to buy it back for a full year after its sale. During that year, the seller retains the right to buy it back. 30 But if it is not bought back within a year, the sale of the house within the walled town cannot be reversed. It will become the permanent property of the buyer. It will not be returned to the original owner in the Year of Jubilee. 31 But a house in a village—a settlement without fortified walls—will be treated like property in the countryside. Such a house may be bought back at any time, and it must be returned to the original owner in the Year of Jubilee.

32 "The Levites always have the right to buy back a house they have sold within the towns allotted to them. 33 And any property that is sold by the Levites—all houses within the Levitical towns—must be returned in the Year of Jubilee. After all, the houses in the towns reserved for the Levites are the only property they own in all Israel. 34 The open pastureland around the Levitical towns may never be sold. It is their permanent possession.

Redemption of the Poor and Enslaved

35 "If one of your fellow Israelites falls into poverty and cannot support himself, support him as you would a foreigner or a temporary resident and allow him to live with you. 36 Do not charge interest or make a profit at his expense. Instead, show your fear of God by letting him live with you as your relative. 37 Remember, do not charge interest on money you lend him or make a profit on food you sell him. 38 I am the LORD your God, who brought you out of the land of Egypt to give you the land of Canaan and to be your God.

39 "If one of your fellow Israelites falls into poverty and is forced to sell himself to you, do not treat him as a slave. 40 Treat him instead as a hired worker or as a temporary resident who lives with you, and he will serve you only until the Year of Jubilee. 41 At that time he and his children will no longer be obligated to you, and they will return to their clans and go back to the land originally allotted to their ancestors. 42 The people of Israel are my servants, whom I brought out of the land of Egypt, so they must never be sold as slaves. 43 Show your fear of God by not treating them harshly.

44 "However, you may purchase male and female slaves from among the nations around you. 45 You may also purchase the children of temporary residents who live among you, including those who have been born in your land. You may treat them as your property, 46 passing them on to your children as a permanent inheritance. You may treat them as slaves, but you must never treat your fellow Israelites this way.

47 "Suppose a foreigner or temporary resident becomes rich while living among you. If any of your fellow Israelites fall into poverty and are forced to sell themselves to such a foreigner or to a member of his family, 48 they still retain the right to be bought back, even after they have been purchased. They may be bought back by a brother, 49 an uncle, or a cousin. In fact, anyone from the extended family may buy them back. They may also redeem themselves if they have prospered. 50 They will negotiate the price of their freedom with the person who bought them. The price will be based on the number of years from

the time they were sold until the next Year of Jubilee—whatever it would cost to hire a worker for that period of time. 51 If many years still remain until the jubilee, they will repay the proper proportion of what they received when they sold themselves. 52 If only a few years remain until the Year of Jubilee, they will repay a small amount for their redemption. 53 The foreigner must treat them as workers hired on a yearly basis. You must not allow a foreigner to treat any of your fellow Israelites harshly. 54 If any Israelites have not been bought back by the time the Year of Jubilee arrives, they and their children must be set free at that time. 55 For the people of Israel belong to me. They are my servants, whom I brought out of the land of Egypt. I am the LORD your God.

Blessings for Obedience

26 "Do not make idols or set up carved images, or sacred pillars, or sculptured stones in your land so you may worship them. I am the LORD your God. 2 You must keep my Sabbath days of rest and show reverence for my sanctuary. I am the LORD.

3 "If you follow my decrees and are careful to obey my commands, 4 I will send you the seasonal rains. The land will then yield its crops, and the trees of the field will produce their fruit. 5 Your threshing season will overlap with the grape harvest, and your grape harvest will overlap with the season of planting grain. You will eat your fill and live securely in your own land.

6 "I will give you peace in the land, and you will be able to sleep with no cause for fear. I will rid the land of wild animals and keep your enemies out of your land. 7 In fact, you will chase down your enemies and slaughter them with your swords. 8 Five of you will chase a hundred, and a hundred of you will chase ten thousand! All your enemies will fall beneath your sword.

9 "I will look favorably upon you, making you fertile and multiplying your people. And I will fulfill my covenant with you. 10 You will have such a surplus of crops that you will need to clear out the old grain to make room for the new harvest! 11 I will live among you, and I will not despise you. 12 I will walk among you; I will be your God, and you will be my people. 13 I am the LORD your God, who brought you out of the land of Egypt so you would no longer be their slaves. I broke the yoke of slavery from your neck so you can walk with your heads held high.

Punishments for Disobedience

14 "However, if you do not listen to me or obey all these commands, 15 and if you break my covenant by rejecting my decrees, treating my regulations with contempt, and refusing to obey my commands, 16 I will punish you. I will bring sudden terrors upon you—wasting diseases and burning fevers that will cause your eyes to fail and your life to ebb away. You will plant your crops in vain because your enemies will eat them. 17 I will turn against you, and you will be defeated by your enemies. Those who hate you will rule over you, and you will run even when no one is chasing you!

18 "And if, in spite of all this, you still disobey me, I will punish you seven times over for your sins. 19 I will break your proud spirit by making the skies as unyielding as iron and the earth as hard as bronze. 20 All your work will be for nothing, for your land will yield no crops, and your trees will bear no fruit.

21 "If even then you remain hostile toward me and refuse to obey me, I will inflict disaster on you seven times over for your sins. 22 I will send wild animals that will rob you of your children and destroy your livestock. Your numbers will dwindle, and your roads will be deserted.

23 "And if you fail to learn the lesson and continue your hostility toward me, 24 then I myself will be hostile toward you. I will personally strike you with calamity seven times over for your sins. 25 I will send armies against you to carry out the curse of the covenant you have broken. When you run to your towns for safety, I will send a plague to destroy you there, and you will be handed over to your enemies. 26 I will destroy your food supply, so that ten women will need only one oven to bake bread for their families. They will ration your food by weight, and though you have food to eat, you will not be satisfied.

27 "If in spite of all this you still refuse to listen and still remain hostile toward me, 28 then I will give full vent to my hostility. I myself will punish you seven times over for your sins. 29 Then you will eat the flesh of your own sons and daughters. 30 I will destroy your pagan shrines and knock down your places of worship. I will leave your lifeless corpses piled on top of your lifeless idols,* and I will despise you. 31 I will make your cities desolate and destroy your places of pagan worship. I will take no pleasure in your offerings that should be a pleasing aroma to me. 32 Yes, I myself will devastate your land, and your enemies who come to occupy it will be appalled at what they see. 33 I will scatter you among the na-

26:30 The Hebrew term (literally *round things*) probably alludes to dung.

tions and bring out my sword against you. Your
land will become desolate, and your cities will lie
in ruins. 34 Then at last the land will enjoy its neglected Sabbath years as it lies desolate while you
are in exile in the land of your enemies. Then the
land will finally rest and enjoy the Sabbaths it
missed. 35 As long as the land lies in ruins, it will
enjoy the rest you never allowed it to take every
seventh year while you lived in it.
36 "And for those of you who survive, I will
demoralize you in the land of your enemies. You
will live in such fear that the sound of a leaf driv-
en by the wind will send you fleeing. You will
run as though fleeing from a sword, and you will
fall even when no one pursues you. 37 Though no
one is chasing you, you will stumble over each
other as though fleeing from a sword. You will
have no power to stand up against your enemies.
38 You will die among the foreign nations and be
devoured in the land of your enemies. 39 Those
of you who survive will waste away in your enemies' lands because of their sins and the sins of
their ancestors.
40 "But at last my people will confess their
sins and the sins of their ancestors for betraying
me and being hostile toward me. 41 When I have
turned their hostility back on them and brought
them to the land of their enemies, then at last
their stubborn hearts will be humbled, and they
will pay for their sins. 42 Then I will remember
my covenant with Jacob and my covenant with
Isaac and my covenant with Abraham, and I will
remember the land. 43 For the land must be abandoned to enjoy its years of Sabbath rest as it lies
deserted. At last the people will pay for their sins,
for they have continually rejected my regulations and despised my decrees.
44 "But despite all this, I will not utterly reject or despise them while they are in exile in
the land of their enemies. I will not cancel my
covenant with them by wiping them out, for I
am the LORD their God. 45 For their sakes I will
remember my ancient covenant with their ancestors, whom I brought out of the land of Egypt
in the sight of all the nations, that I might be
their God. I am the LORD."
46 These are the decrees, regulations, and instructions that the LORD gave through Moses on
Mount Sinai as evidence of the relationship between himself and the Israelites.

Redemption of Gifts Offered to the LORD

27 The LORD said to Moses, 2 "Give the
following instructions to the people
of Israel. If anyone makes a special
vow to dedicate someone to the LORD by paying
the value of that person, 3 here is the scale of values to be used. A man between the ages of twenty and sixty is valued at fifty shekels* of silver, as
measured by the sanctuary shekel. 4 A woman of
that age is valued at thirty shekels* of silver. 5 A
boy between the ages of five and twenty is valued at twenty shekels of silver; a girl of that age
is valued at ten shekels* of silver. 6 A boy between
the ages of one month and five years is valued at
five shekels of silver; a girl of that age is valued at
three shekels* of silver. 7 A man older than sixty
is valued at fifteen shekels of silver; a woman of
that age is valued at ten shekels* of silver. 8 If you
desire to make such a vow but cannot afford to

27:3 Or *20 ounces* [570 grams]. **27:4** Or *12 ounces* [342 grams]. **27:5** Or *A boy . . . 8 ounces* [228 grams] *of silver; a girl . . . 4 ounces* [114 grams]. **27:6** Or *A boy . . . 2 ounces* [57 grams] *of silver; a girl . . . 1.2 ounces* [34 grams]. **27:7** Or *A man . . . 6 ounces* [171 grams] *of silver; a woman . . . 4 ounces* [114 grams].

27:1–34 The Value of Vows

The final chapter of Leviticus is usually considered an appendix to the Holiness Code. It addresses vows paid to the sanctuary in the form of persons or animals (vv. 2–13), the dedication of houses or fields to Yahweh (vv. 14–25), and regulations for things dedicated to Yahweh (vv. 26–33).

27:1–8: These verses detail the values placed on human beings who made vows or who were vowed to Yahweh by another person. Because human sacrifice was not practiced in Israel and because the priests were the only ones allowed to serve in the sanctuary, if laypersons wished to dedicate themselves in a special way to God they could do so by paying their equivalent in silver to the sanctuary. Although this is often construed as evidence of the higher social value of males in Israelite society, the higher valuation of males than females is more likely a reflection of each gender's physical strength or the ability of each to contribute to Israel's subsistence. Age and gender together determined the valuations, not gender alone.

In the modern world, where inequality between men and women, especially in wages, has been the source of much contention, Israel's valuation system may seem repugnant. But it was probably a means of standardization based on potential economic contribution, not a commentary on the intrinsic value of human beings. The greatest significance is that both men and women could be vowed or make such a vow as an extraordinary expression of dedication to God.

pay the required amount, take the person to the priest. He will determine the amount for you to pay based on what you can afford.

[9]"If your vow involves giving an animal that is acceptable as an offering to the LORD, any gift to the LORD will be considered holy. [10]You may not exchange or substitute it for another animal—neither a good animal for a bad one nor a bad animal for a good one. But if you do exchange one animal for another, then both the original animal and its substitute will be considered holy. [11]If your vow involves an unclean animal—one that is not acceptable as an offering to the LORD—then you must bring the animal to the priest. [12]He will assess its value, and his assessment will be final, whether high or low. [13]If you want to buy back the animal, you must pay the value set by the priest, plus 20 percent.

[14]"If someone dedicates a house to the LORD, the priest will come to assess its value. The priest's assessment will be final, whether high or low. [15]If the person who dedicated the house wants to buy it back, he must pay the value set by the priest, plus 20 percent. Then the house will again be his.

[16]"If someone dedicates to the LORD a piece of his family property, its value will be assessed according to the amount of seed required to plant it—fifty shekels of silver for a field planted with five bushels of barley seed.* [17]If the field is dedicated to the LORD in the Year of Jubilee, then the entire assessment will apply. [18]But if the field is dedicated after the Year of Jubilee, the priest will assess the land's value in proportion to the number of years left until the next Year of Jubilee. Its assessed value is reduced each year. [19]If the person who dedicated the field wants to buy it back, he must pay the value set by the priest, plus 20 percent. Then the field will again be legally his. [20]But if he does not want to buy it back, and it is sold to someone else, the field can no longer be bought back. [21]When the field is released in the Year of Jubilee, it will be holy, a field specially set apart* for the LORD. It will become the property of the priests.

[22]"If someone dedicates to the LORD a field he has purchased but which is not part of his family property, [23]the priest will assess its value based on the number of years left until the next Year of Jubilee. On that day he must give the assessed value of the land as a sacred donation to the LORD. [24]In the Year of Jubilee the field must be returned to the person from whom he purchased it, the one who inherited it as family property. [25](All the payments must be measured by the weight of the sanctuary shekel,* which equals twenty gerahs.)

[26]"You may not dedicate a firstborn animal to the LORD, for the firstborn of your cattle, sheep, and goats already belong to him. [27]However, you may buy back the firstborn of a ceremonially unclean animal by paying the priest's assessment of its worth, plus 20 percent. If you do not buy it back, the priest will sell it at its assessed value.

[28]"However, anything specially set apart for the LORD—whether a person, an animal, or family property—must never be sold or bought back. Anything devoted in this way has been set apart as holy, and it belongs to the LORD. [29]No person specially set apart for destruction may be bought back. Such a person must be put to death.

[30]"One tenth of the produce of the land, whether grain from the fields or fruit from the trees, belongs to the LORD and must be set apart to him as holy. [31]If you want to buy back the LORD's tenth of the grain or fruit, you must pay its value, plus 20 percent. [32]Count off every tenth animal from your herds and flocks and set them apart for the LORD as holy. [33]You may not pick and choose between good and bad animals, and you may not substitute one for another. But if you do exchange one animal for another, then both the original animal and its substitute will be considered holy and cannot be bought back."

[34]These are the commands that the LORD gave through Moses on Mount Sinai for the Israelites.

27:16 Hebrew *50 shekels* [20 ounces, or 570 grams] *of silver for a homer* [182 liters] *of barley seed.* **27:21** The Hebrew term used here refers to the complete consecration of things or people to the LORD, either by destroying them or by giving them as an offering; also in 27:28, 29. **27:25** Each shekel was about 0.4 ounces [11 grams] in weight.

NUMBERS

INTRODUCTION

The Hebrew title for the book of Numbers means "in the wilderness." As with the other books of the Torah, Numbers derives its title from a word in the first verse in the Hebrew text. The English title, which is based on the Greek Old Testament (Septuagint), reflects the book's many censuses and lists.

According to Jewish and Christian tradition, Numbers was written by Moses, though the book itself claims only that Moses wrote down a travel itinerary (33:2). Occasional references to Moses' writing elsewhere in the Torah (Exod 17:14; 24:4; 34:27; Deut 31:9, 24), and expressions such as "the Law of Moses" (1 Kgs 2:3; Ezra 3:2) or the "Book of Moses" (2 Chr 35:12; Neh 13:1; Mark 12:26) in both testaments led many to conclude that Moses wrote the entire Torah.

The modern scholarly consensus is that the books of the Torah, including Numbers, are the product of multiple authors (sources) and numerous editorial revisions. Originally, this view, known as the Documentary Hypothesis, posited four written sources : J (the Yahwistic source), E (the Elohistic source), D (the Deuteronomic source), and P (the Priestly source). Today, scholars refer to a JE source (a composite of the Yahwistic and Elohistic sources dating sometime around 1200 to 1000 BC), and considerable debate continues regarding the composition date and identification of the various documents. Numbers, with its attention to priestly interests, is primarily ascribed to the priestly writer(s) who probably wrote during the Babylonian exile (586–538 BC) and well into the postexilic era. Chapters 10 through 24 are usually attributed to the earlier JE source, and some scholars believe other older independent sources were incorporated into the book by the priestly writer(s).

The book in its final form is viewed as a postexilic document and reflects the historical context of that time. The priestly writers were living in an era of uncertainty. They dwelled in the "wilderness" of exile created by the previous generation's disobedience and were poised to reenter the promised land. The tribes had been scattered during the Assyrian and Babylonian invasions, leaving unresolved the question of Israel's true identity. The exiles vacillated between the certainty of the past (life in Babylon) and the uncertainty of the future (returning to Israel). With the monarchy dissolved, they faced a crisis in leadership—Who had God's authoritative stamp of approval to lead the postexilic community? With the Temple destroyed, how could acceptable worship be reestablished once they returned to the land? The book of Numbers addresses these concerns through its narrative about a previous generation's wilderness experiences.

The book of Numbers contains two major censuses (1:1—2:34 and 26:1–51) that provide the structural framework for the book. The first census introduces the stories pertaining to the first generation of Israel who depart Sinai after extensive preparations (chaps. 1—10), complain in the wilderness (chaps. 11—12), fail to trust the LORD (chaps. 13—14), and wander in the wilderness for forty years as a result (chaps. 15—25). The second census (chap. 26) enumerates the second generation who inherit the role their forefathers forsook through disobedience. Their stories focus primarily on land inheritance and acquisition

(27:1–11; 31:1–54; 32:1–42; 33:1–56; 34:1—36:13), as well as leadership (27:12–23), offerings (28:1—29:40), and vows (30:1–16).

It makes sense to see the book of Numbers as the story of the postexilic community, interpreting their concerns through narratives about the ancestors. Subsequent generations of readers, both Jewish and Christian, have read Numbers with their own wildernesses in mind—the wilderness of persecution, the wilderness of Holocaust, the wilderness of modernity. In such wildernesses, Numbers provides hope with its focus on God's faithfulness in the face of great disobedience, its enduring promise that future generations will find solace in the promised land, and its challenge to remain faithful and purposeful in worship of God. Numbers reminds readers of every generation that trust in God transforms wildernesses into lands of promise.

Numbers is, unfortunately, a daunting book for many readers. From the first chapter with its detailed census, to the final instructions to Moses, this book frustrates modern audiences with its unrelenting attention to obscure practices and endless lists. Nevertheless, reading Numbers can be a rewarding experience if the reader keeps several things in mind. First, while we may fail to appreciate lengthy lists and excruciating details, the writer(s) of Numbers fashioned such information into powerful theology. For example, the author insists on listing every gift given by the tribal leaders for the Tabernacle's dedication (chap. 7). In doing so, he highlights that all the tribes were equally generous in donating gifts to furnish God's dwelling place. Instead of skipping over the lists in Numbers, the reader should ask herself, "What theological point is the author making with this list?" Second, the book of Numbers serves an important narrative function in the Torah, following Israel's journey from Mount Sinai to the plains of Moab. It explains why this journey took forty years, why the second generation, rather than the first, inherited the land, and why Moses himself was not allowed to enter the land. Third, lest we judge the Israelites too harshly for their ceaseless grumbling and complaining, we should remember our own tendency to prefer the safety of the past to the uncertainty of the future. Like Israel, we struggle to trust God in the midst of trying circumstances.

The book of Numbers is decidedly masculine in its focuses: Only males are counted in the censuses that frame the book; war preparations and the waging of battles are male activities; the extensive priestly legislation in the book applies primarily to men, and land inheritance (a major theme in Numbers) is largely limited to males. Few passages in Numbers focus on women, and those that do are negative: the trial of the suspected adulteress (chap. 5), Miriam's rebellion (chap. 13), and the idolatry instigated by the women of Moab and Midian (chap. 25). One exception to this generally gloomy portrayal is the story of the daughters of Zelophehad, who audaciously demand the right to inherit their father's land and win (chap. 27, cf. chap. 36). In spite of the lack of women's concerns in the book, readers will certainly appreciate the book's major themes, noted above, which are applicable to audiences of both sexes. —*Susan M. Pigott*

Registration of Israel's Troops

1 A year after Israel's departure from Egypt,
the LORD spoke to Moses in the Tabernacle* in the wilderness of Sinai. On the first
day of the second month* of that year he said,
2 "From the whole community of Israel, record
the names of all the warriors by their clans and
families. List all the men 3 twenty years old or
older who are able to go to war. You and Aaron
must register the troops, 4 and you will be assisted by one family leader from each tribe.
5 "These are the tribes and the names of the
leaders who will assist you:

Tribe	*Leader*
Reuben	Elizur son of Shedeur
6 Simeon	Shelumiel son of Zurishaddai
7 Judah	Nahshon son of Amminadab
8 Issachar	Nethanel son of Zuar
9 Zebulun	Eliab son of Helon
10 Ephraim son of Joseph	Elishama son of Ammihud
Manasseh son of Joseph	Gamaliel son of Pedahzur
11 Benjamin	Abidan son of Gideoni
12 Dan	Ahiezer son of Ammishaddai
13 Asher	Pagiel son of Ocran
14 Gad	Eliasaph son of Deuel
15 Naphtali	Ahira son of Enan

16 These are the chosen leaders of the community,
the leaders of their ancestral tribes, the heads of
the clans of Israel."
17 So Moses and Aaron called together these
chosen leaders, 18 and they assembled the whole
community of Israel on that very day.* All the
people were registered according to their ancestry by their clans and families. The men of Israel
who were twenty years old or older were listed
one by one, 19 just as the LORD had commanded
Moses. So Moses recorded their names in the
wilderness of Sinai.
20-21 This is the number of men twenty years
old or older who were able to go to war, as their
names were listed in the records of their clans
and families*:

Tribe	*Number*
Reuben (Jacob's* oldest son)	46,500
22-23 Simeon	59,300
24-25 Gad	45,650
26-27 Judah	74,600
28-29 Issachar	54,400
30-31 Zebulun	57,400
32-33 Ephraim son of Joseph	40,500
34-35 Manasseh son of Joseph	32,200
36-37 Benjamin	35,400
38-39 Dan	62,700
40-41 Asher	41,500
42-43 Naphtali	53,400

44 These were the men registered by Moses and
Aaron and the twelve leaders of Israel, all listed
according to their ancestral descent. 45 They were
registered by families—all the men of Israel who
were twenty years old or older and able to go to
war. 46 The total number was 603,550.
47 But this total did not include the Levites.
48 For the LORD had said to Moses, 49 "Do not include the tribe of Levi in the registration; do not
count them with the rest of the Israelites. 50 Put
the Levites in charge of the Tabernacle of the
Covenant,* along with all its furnishings and
equipment. They must carry the Tabernacle and
all its furnishings as you travel, and they must
take care of it and camp around it. 51 Whenever
it is time for the Tabernacle to move, the Levites
will take it down. And when it is time to stop,
they will set it up again. But any unauthorized
person who goes too near the Tabernacle must be
put to death. 52 Each tribe of Israel will camp in a
designated area with its own family banner. 53 But

1:1a Hebrew *the Tent of Meeting.* **1:1b** This day in the ancient Hebrew lunar calendar occurred in April or May. **1:18** Hebrew *on the first day of the second month;* see 1:1. **1:20-21a** In the Hebrew text, this sentence (*This is the number of men twenty years old or older who were able to go to war, as their names were listed in the records of their clans and families*) is repeated in 1:22, 24, 26, 28, 30, 32, 34, 36, 38, 40, 42. **1:20-21b** Hebrew *Israel's.* The names "Jacob" and "Israel" are often interchanged throughout the Old Testament, referring sometimes to the individual patriarch and sometimes to the nation. **1:50** Or *Tabernacle of the Testimony;* also in 1:53.

1:1—10:36 Preparations for the March

1:1–54 Registration of Israel's Troops. The purpose of the first census is to ascertain the number of able-bodied warriors, ages twenty and up. Theologically, the census establishes Israel's impressive military strength as the camp makes preparations for war. Strikingly, only two men (Joshua and Caleb) from this first census will survive to be counted in the second census (chap. 26), a stark reminder of the consequences of distrusting God in the wilderness. **47–54:** The Levites were exempted from the initial census (and from military service) because of their special service in the Tabernacle. **47–51**: In Numbers, the Levites are portrayed as servants of the Tabernacle who set up and take down the tent and bear its holy contents during travel. They are subordinate to the Aaronide priests (members of the tribe of Levi de-

the Levites will camp around the Tabernacle of
the Covenant to protect the community of Israel
from the LORD's anger. The Levites are responsible to stand guard around the Tabernacle."
54 So the Israelites did everything just as the
LORD had commanded Moses.

Organization for Israel's Camp

2 Then the LORD gave these instructions to
Moses and Aaron: 2 "When the Israelites
set up camp, each tribe will be assigned its
own area. The tribal divisions will camp beneath
their family banners on all four sides of the Tabernacle,* but at some distance from it.
3-4 "The divisions of Judah, Issachar, and Zebulun are to camp toward the sunrise on the east
side of the Tabernacle, beneath their family banners. These are the names of the tribes, their
leaders, and the numbers of their registered
troops:

Tribe	*Leader*	*Number*
Judah	Nahshon son of Amminadab	74,600
5-6 Issachar	Nethanel son of Zuar	54,400
7-8 Zebulun	Eliab son of Helon	57,400

9 So the total of all the troops on Judah's side of
the camp is 186,400. These three tribes are to
lead the way whenever the Israelites travel to a
new campsite.
10-11 "The divisions of Reuben, Simeon, and
Gad are to camp on the south side of the Tabernacle, beneath their family banners. These are
the names of the tribes, their leaders, and the
numbers of their registered troops:

Tribe	*Leader*	*Number*
Reuben	Elizur son of Shedeur	46,500
12-13 Simeon	Shelumiel son of Zurishaddai	59,300
14-15 Gad	Eliasaph son of Deuel*	45,650

16 So the total of all the troops on Reuben's side
of the camp is 151,450. These three tribes will be
second in line whenever the Israelites travel.
17 "Then the Tabernacle, carried by the Levites, will set out from the middle of the camp.
All the tribes are to travel in the same order that
they camp, each in position under the appropriate family banner.
18-19 "The divisions of Ephraim, Manasseh,
and Benjamin are to camp on the west side of the
Tabernacle, beneath their family banners. These
are the names of the tribes, their leaders, and the
numbers of their registered troops:

Tribe	*Leader*	*Number*
Ephraim	Elishama son of Ammihud	40,500
20-21 Manasseh	Gamaliel son of Pedahzur	32,200
22-23 Benjamin	Abidan son of Gideoni	35,400

24 So the total of all the troops on Ephraim's side
of the camp is 108,100. These three tribes will be
third in line whenever the Israelites travel.
25-26 "The divisions of Dan, Asher, and Naphtali are to camp on the north side of the Tabernacle, beneath their family banners. These are
the names of the tribes, their leaders, and the
numbers of their registered troops:

Tribe	*Leader*	*Number*
Dan	Ahiezer son of Ammishaddai	62,700
27-28 Asher	Pagiel son of Ocran	41,500
29-30 Naphtali	Ahira son of Enan	53,400

31 So the total of all the troops on Dan's side of
the camp is 157,600. These three tribes will be
last, marching under their banners whenever the
Israelites travel."

2:2 Hebrew *the Tent of Meeting;* also in 2:17. **2:14-15** As in many Hebrew manuscripts, Samaritan Pentateuch, and Latin Vulgate (see also 1:14); most Hebrew manuscripts read *son of Reuel.*

scended from Aaron). **52–54**: The Levites camped around the Tabernacle, providing a physical (and ritual) barrier to protect the Israelites from venturing too close to God's holiness and experiencing divine wrath. **54:** The chapter concludes with a statement of obedience that appears multiple times (in various forms) in the first ten chapters. Such obedience dramatically contrasts the cynical rebelliousness of first-generation Israelites beginning in chapter 11.

2:1–34 Organization for Israel's Camp. The tribes' positioning around the Tabernacle reflects their status within Israel. Thus, the eastern tribes (Judah, Issachar, and Zebulun) are given the place of greatest prominence closest to the Tabernacle entrance and first in the marching order. The narrator maps the camp clockwise, from east to north, placing the Levites in the middle both geographically and literarily (v. 17 is sandwiched in between vv. 2–16 and vv. 18–31). **32–34:** In these concluding verses, the narrator reiterates the total number of troops and emphasizes, once again, the complete obedience of the people.

[32]In summary, the troops of Israel listed by their families totaled 603,550. [33]But as the LORD had commanded, the Levites were not included in this registration. [34]So the people of Israel did everything as the LORD had commanded Moses. Each clan and family set up camp and marched under their banners exactly as the LORD had instructed them.

Levites Appointed for Service

3 This is the family line of Aaron and Moses as it was recorded when the LORD spoke to Moses on Mount Sinai: [2]The names of Aaron's sons were Nadab (the oldest), Abihu, Eleazar, and Ithamar. [3]These sons of Aaron were anointed and ordained to minister as priests. [4]But Nadab and Abihu died in the LORD's presence in the wilderness of Sinai when they burned before the LORD the wrong kind of fire, different than he had commanded. Since they had no sons, this left only Eleazar and Ithamar to serve as priests with their father, Aaron.

[5]Then the LORD said to Moses, [6]"Call forward the tribe of Levi, and present them to Aaron the priest to serve as his assistants. [7]They will serve Aaron and the whole community, performing their sacred duties in and around the Tabernacle.* [8]They will also maintain all the furnishings of the sacred tent,* serving in the Tabernacle on behalf of all the Israelites. [9]Assign the Levites to Aaron and his sons. They have been given from among all the people of Israel to serve as their assistants. [10]Appoint Aaron and his sons to carry out the duties of the priesthood. But any unauthorized person who goes too near the sanctuary must be put to death."

[11]And the LORD said to Moses, [12]"Look, I have chosen the Levites from among the Israelites to serve as substitutes for all the firstborn sons of the people of Israel. The Levites belong to me, [13]for all the firstborn males are mine. On the day I struck down all the firstborn sons of the Egyptians, I set apart for myself all the firstborn in Israel, both of people and of animals. They are mine; I am the LORD."

Registration of the Levites

[14]The LORD spoke again to Moses in the wilderness of Sinai. He said, [15]"Record the names of the members of the tribe of Levi by their families and clans. List every male who is one month old or older." [16]So Moses listed them, just as the LORD had commanded.

[17]Levi had three sons, whose names were
Gershon, Kohath, and Merari.
[18]The clans descended from Gershon were
named after two of his descendants, Libni and Shimei.
[19]The clans descended from Kohath were named
after four of his descendants, Amram, Izhar, Hebron, and Uzziel.
[20]The clans descended from Merari were named
after two of his descendants, Mahli and Mushi.
These were the Levite clans, listed according to their family groups.

[21]The descendants of Gershon were composed of the clans descended from Libni and Shimei. [22]There were 7,500 males one month old or older among these Gershonite clans. [23]They were assigned the area to the west of the Tabernacle for their camp. [24]The leader of the Gershonite clans was Eliasaph son of Lael. [25]These two clans were responsible to care for the Tabernacle, including the sacred tent with its layers of coverings, the curtain at its entrance, [26]the curtains of the courtyard that surrounded the Tabernacle and altar, the curtain at the courtyard entrance, the ropes, and all the equipment related to their use.

[27]The descendants of Kohath were composed of the clans descended from Amram, Izhar, Hebron, and Uzziel. [28]There were 8,600* males one month old or older among these Kohathite clans. They were responsible for the care of the sanctuary, [29]and they were assigned the area south

3:7 Hebrew *around the Tent of Meeting, doing service at the Tabernacle.* **3:8** Hebrew *the Tent of Meeting;* also in 3:25. **3:28** Some Greek manuscripts read *8,300;* see total in 3:39.

3:1–51 The Levites Appointed for Service. The focus of this chapter is on the Levites, the family tribe of Moses and Aaron. **1–4:** The initial verses set forth Aaron's family, which had preeminence over the other families in the tribe. Nadab and Abihu's demise is originally recorded in Lev 10:1–7. **5–10:** The warning in v. 10 is, perhaps, directed at Levites who attempted to usurp the role of the Aaronides, a problem which is dramatically presented in the story of Korah's rebellion (chap. 16). However, the similar warning in v. 38 is directed at non-Levites. **11–13:** In spite of the Levites' lower status, they play an important role as substitutes for the firstborn men of Israel (cf. Exod 13:1–2), functioning as living sacrifices who served the Tabernacle. **14–39:** Whereas Numbers 1 was a military census and included only adult males, the census of the Levites was strictly for religious purposes and included males one month

of the Tabernacle for their camp. 30 The leader of the Kohathite clans was Elizaphan son of Uzziel. 31 These four clans were responsible for the care of the Ark, the table, the lampstand, the altars, the various articles used in the sanctuary, the inner curtain, and all the equipment related to their use. 32 Eleazar, son of Aaron the priest, was the chief administrator over all the Levites, with special responsibility for the oversight of the sanctuary.

33 The descendants of Merari were composed of the clans descended from Mahli and Mushi. 34 There were 6,200 males one month old or older among these Merarite clans. 35 They were assigned the area north of the Tabernacle for their camp. The leader of the Merarite clans was Zuriel son of Abihail. 36 These two clans were responsible for the care of the frames supporting the Tabernacle, the crossbars, the pillars, the bases, and all the equipment related to their use. 37 They were also responsible for the posts of the courtyard and all their bases, pegs, and ropes.

38 The area in front of the Tabernacle, in the east toward the sunrise,* was reserved for the tents of Moses and of Aaron and his sons, who had the final responsibility for the sanctuary on behalf of the people of Israel. Anyone other than a priest or Levite who went too near the sanctuary was to be put to death.

39 When Moses and Aaron counted the Levite clans at the LORD's command, the total number was 22,000 males one month old or older.

Redeeming the Firstborn Sons

40 Then the LORD said to Moses, "Now count all the firstborn sons in Israel who are one month old or older, and make a list of their names. 41 The Levites must be reserved for me as substitutes for the firstborn sons of Israel; I am the LORD. And the Levites' livestock must be reserved for me as substitutes for the firstborn livestock of the whole nation of Israel."

42 So Moses counted the firstborn sons of the people of Israel, just as the LORD had commanded. 43 The number of firstborn sons who were one month old or older was 22,273.

44 Then the LORD said to Moses, 45 "Take the Levites as substitutes for the firstborn sons of the people of Israel. And take the livestock of the Levites as substitutes for the firstborn livestock of the people of Israel. The Levites belong to me; I am the LORD. 46 There are 273 more firstborn sons of Israel than there are Levites. To redeem these extra firstborn sons, 47 collect five pieces of silver* for each of them (each piece weighing the same as the sanctuary shekel, which equals twenty gerahs). 48 Give the silver to Aaron and his sons as the redemption price for the extra firstborn sons."

49 So Moses collected the silver for redeeming the firstborn sons of Israel who exceeded the number of Levites. 50 He collected 1,365 pieces of silver* on behalf of these firstborn sons of Israel (each piece weighing the same as the sanctuary shekel). 51 And Moses gave the silver for the redemption to Aaron and his sons, just as the LORD had commanded.

Duties of the Kohathite Clan

4 Then the LORD said to Moses and Aaron, 2 "Record the names of the members of the clans and families of the Kohathite division of the tribe of Levi. 3 List all the men between the ages of thirty and fifty who are eligible to serve in the Tabernacle.*

4 "The duties of the Kohathites at the Tabernacle will relate to the most sacred objects. 5 When the camp moves, Aaron and his sons must enter the Tabernacle first to take down the inner curtain and cover the Ark of the Covenant* with it. 6 Then they must cover the inner curtain with fine goatskin leather and spread over that a single piece of blue cloth. Finally, they must put the carrying poles of the Ark in place.

7 "Next they must spread a blue cloth over the table where the Bread of the Presence is displayed, and on the cloth they will place the bowls, pans, jars, pitchers, and the special bread. 8 They must spread a scarlet cloth over all of this,

3:38 Hebrew *toward the sunrise, in front of the Tent of Meeting.* **3:47** Hebrew *5 shekels* [2 ounces or 57 grams]. **3:50** Hebrew *1,365 shekels* [34 pounds or 15.5 kilograms]. **4:3** Hebrew *the Tent of Meeting;* also in 4:4, 15, 23, 25, 28, 30, 31, 33, 35, 37, 39, 41, 43, 47. **4:5** Or *Ark of the Testimony.*

---

old and older (v. 15). **39:** Although the narrator gives a total of 22,000 male Levites, if the numbers listed in v. 22 (7,500), v. 28 (8,600), and v. 34 (6,200) are added, the total comes to 22,300, which is problematic for the verses that follow. The simplest solution is to substitute 8,300 for 8,600 in v. 28. **40–51:** The Levites could serve as substitutes for all but 273 men. To make up for the difference, Moses collected silver for each unredeemed male. Five pieces of silver was the redemption value of a male between one month and five years old (see Lev 27:6).

4:1–49 Another Census. This second census of Levites includes only men who are eligible to serve at the Tabernacle, those between the ages of thirty and fifty (but cf. 8:24). **1–20:** The Kohathites appear first since they

and finally a covering of fine goatskin leather on
top of the scarlet cloth. Then they must insert
the carrying poles into the table.
9 "Next they must cover the lampstand with
a blue cloth, along with its lamps, lamp snuffers, trays, and special jars of olive oil. 10 Then they
must cover the lampstand and its accessories
with fine goatskin leather and place the bundle
on a carrying frame.
11 "Next they must spread a blue cloth over
the gold incense altar and cover this cloth with
fine goatskin leather. Then they must attach the
carrying poles to the altar. 12 They must take all
the remaining furnishings of the sanctuary and
wrap them in a blue cloth, cover them with fine
goatskin leather, and place them on the carrying
frame.
13 "They must remove the ashes from the altar for sacrifices and cover the altar with a purple
cloth. 14 All the altar utensils—the firepans, meat
forks, shovels, basins, and all the containers—
must be placed on the cloth, and a covering of
fine goatskin leather must be spread over them.
Finally, they must put the carrying poles in place.
15 The camp will be ready to move when Aaron
and his sons have finished covering the sanctuary and all the sacred articles. The Kohathites will
come and carry these things to the next destination. But they must not touch the sacred objects,
or they will die. So these are the things from the
Tabernacle that the Kohathites must carry.
16 "Eleazar son of Aaron the priest will be responsible for the oil of the lampstand, the fragrant incense, the daily grain offering, and the
anointing oil. In fact, Eleazar will be responsible
for the entire Tabernacle and everything in it, including the sanctuary and its furnishings."
17 Then the LORD said to Moses and Aaron,
18 "Do not let the Kohathite clans be destroyed
from among the Levites! 19 This is what you
must do so they will live and not die when they
approach the most sacred objects. Aaron and his
sons must always go in with them and assign a
specific duty or load to each person. 20 The Kohathites must never enter the sanctuary to look
at the sacred objects for even a moment, or they
will die."

Duties of the Gershonite Clan

21 And the LORD said to Moses, 22 "Record the
names of the members of the clans and families
of the Gershonite division of the tribe of Levi.
23 List all the men between the ages of thirty and
fifty who are eligible to serve in the Tabernacle.
24 "These Gershonite clans will be responsible
for general service and carrying loads. 25 They
must carry the curtains of the Tabernacle, the
Tabernacle itself with its coverings, the outer covering of fine goatskin leather, and the curtain for
the Tabernacle entrance. 26 They are also to carry
the curtains for the courtyard walls that surround the Tabernacle and altar, the curtain across
the courtyard entrance, the ropes, and all the
equipment related to their use. The Gershonites
are responsible for all these items. 27 Aaron and
his sons will direct the Gershonites regarding
all their duties, whether it involves moving the
equipment or doing other work. They must assign the Gershonites responsibility for the loads
they are to carry. 28 So these are the duties assigned to the Gershonite clans at the Tabernacle.
They will be directly responsible to Ithamar son
of Aaron the priest.

Duties of the Merarite Clan

29 "Now record the names of the members of the
clans and families of the Merarite division of the
tribe of Levi. 30 List all the men between the ages
of thirty and fifty who are eligible to serve in the
Tabernacle.
31 "Their only duty at the Tabernacle will be
to carry loads. They will carry the frames of the
Tabernacle, the crossbars, the posts, and the bases; 32 also the posts for the courtyard walls with
their bases, pegs, and ropes; and all the accessories and everything else related to their use. Assign the various loads to each man by name. 33 So
these are the duties of the Merarite clans at the
Tabernacle. They are directly responsible to Ithamar son of Aaron the priest."

Summary of the Registration

34 So Moses, Aaron, and the other leaders of the
community listed the members of the Kohathite
division by their clans and families. 35 The list in-

are in charge of the most sacred elements of the Tabernacle. **15:** The Aaronide priests must cover all the sacred furniture and insert the carrying poles before the Kohathites can transport it because touching the objects means death. This measure of protection, reiterated in vv. 17–20, emphasizes the author's concern for boundaries. **21–33:** The duties of the Gershonites and Merarites, introduced in 3:25–26 and 3:33–37, are given in slightly more detail here. **34–49:** The narrator concludes the chapter by listing the numbers for each Levitical family followed by the total number of men eligible for service (8,580). Each list highlights the complete obedience of Moses and Aaron in counting the Levites (vv. 37, 41, 44, and 49).

cluded all the men between thirty and fifty years of age who were eligible for service in the Tabernacle, 36 and the total number came to 2,750. 37 So this was the total of all those from the Kohathite clans who were eligible to serve at the Tabernacle. Moses and Aaron listed them, just as the LORD had commanded through Moses.

38 The Gershonite division was also listed by its clans and families. 39 The list included all the men between thirty and fifty years of age who were eligible for service in the Tabernacle, 40 and the total number came to 2,630. 41 So this was the total of all those from the Gershonite clans who were eligible to serve at the Tabernacle. Moses and Aaron listed them, just as the LORD had commanded.

42 The Merarite division was also listed by its clans and families. 43 The list included all the men between thirty and fifty years of age who were eligible for service in the Tabernacle, 44 and the total number came to 3,200. 45 So this was the total of all those from the Merarite clans who were eligible for service. Moses and Aaron listed them, just as the LORD had commanded through Moses.

46 So Moses, Aaron, and the leaders of Israel listed all the Levites by their clans and families. 47 All the men between thirty and fifty years of age who were eligible for service in the Tabernacle and for its transportation 48 numbered 8,580. 49 When their names were recorded, as the LORD had commanded through Moses, each man was assigned his task and told what to carry.

And so the registration was completed, just as the LORD had commanded Moses.

Purity in Israel's Camp

5 The LORD gave these instructions to Moses: 2 "Command the people of Israel to remove from the camp anyone who has a skin disease* or a discharge, or who has become ceremonially unclean by touching a dead person. 3 This command applies to men and women alike. Remove them so they will not defile the camp in which I live among them." 4 So the Israelites did as the LORD had commanded Moses and removed such people from the camp.

5 Then the LORD said to Moses, 6 "Give the following instructions to the people of Israel: If any of the people—men or women—betray the LORD by doing wrong to another person, they are guilty. 7 They must confess their sin and make full restitution for what they have done, adding an additional 20 percent and returning it to the person who was wronged. 8 But if the person who was wronged is dead, and there are no near relatives to whom restitution can be made, the payment belongs to the LORD and must be given to the priest. Those who are guilty must also bring a ram as a sacrifice, and they will be purified and made right with the LORD.* 9 All the sacred offerings that the Israelites bring to a priest will belong to him. 10 Each priest may keep all the sacred donations that he receives."

Protecting Marital Faithfulness

11 And the LORD said to Moses, 12 "Give the following instructions to the people of Israel.

"Suppose a man's wife goes astray, and she is unfaithful to her husband 13 and has sex with another man, but neither her husband nor anyone else knows about it. She has defiled herself, even though there was no witness and she was not caught in the act. 14 If her husband becomes jealous and is suspicious of his wife and needs to know whether or not she has defiled herself, 15 the husband must bring his wife to the priest. He must also bring an offering of two quarts* of barley flour to be presented on her behalf. Do not mix it with olive oil or frankincense, for it is a jealousy offering—an offering to prove whether or not she is guilty.

5:2 Traditionally rendered *leprosy.* The Hebrew word used here describes various skin diseases. **5:8** Or *bring a ram for atonement, which will make atonement for them.* **5:15** Hebrew $^1/_{10}$ *of an ephah* [2.2 liters].

5:1–10 Purity in Israel's Camp. 1–4: Uncleanness was an abnormal condition during which a severely affected person was typically isolated and considered communicable. Uncleanness was by no means considered a sin; rather it was a ritual condition that required ritual purification. **5–10:** The text does not elaborate on the exact nature of the crimes, but the requirement of restitution suggests that property was involved. See also Lev 6:1–7.

5:11–31 Protecting Marital Faithfulness. This passage describes a ritual enacted when a man suspected his wife had committed adultery. Had the woman been caught in the act, she and her partner would have been stoned (cf. Lev 20:10). Although this ritual hardly seems fair from a modern perspective, the woman was at least offered a modicum of justice. Her husband could not simply punish her based on his suspicions but had to allow her guilt or innocence to be determined through public ritual. Nevertheless, the humiliation of being accused would likely have haunted a woman for some time. **15:** The purpose of

16 "The priest will then present her to stand
trial before the LORD. 17 He must take some holy
water in a clay jar and pour into it dust he has
taken from the Tabernacle floor. 18 When the
priest has presented the woman before the LORD,
he must unbind her hair and place in her hands
the offering of proof—the jealousy offering to
determine whether her husband's suspicions are
justified. The priest will stand before her, holding the jar of bitter water that brings a curse to
those who are guilty. 19 The priest will then put
the woman under oath and say to her, 'If no other man has had sex with you, and you have not
gone astray and defiled yourself while under
your husband's authority, may you be immune
from the effects of this bitter water that brings
on the curse. 20 But if you have gone astray by being unfaithful to your husband, and have defiled
yourself by having sex with another man—'
21 "At this point the priest must put the woman under oath by saying, 'May the people know
that the LORD's curse is upon you when he makes
you infertile, causing your womb to shrivel* and
your abdomen to swell. 22 Now may this water that brings the curse enter your body and
cause your abdomen to swell and your womb to
shrivel.*' And the woman will be required to say,
'Yes, let it be so.' 23 And the priest will write these
curses on a piece of leather and wash them off
into the bitter water. 24 He will make the woman
drink the bitter water that brings on the curse.
When the water enters her body, it will cause bitter suffering if she is guilty.
25 "The priest will take the jealousy offering
from the woman's hand, lift it up before the LORD,
and carry it to the altar. 26 He will take a handful
of the flour as a token portion and burn it on the
altar, and he will require the woman to drink the
water. 27 If she has defiled herself by being unfaithful to her husband, the water that brings on
the curse will cause bitter suffering. Her abdomen will swell and her womb will shrink,* and
her name will become a curse among her people.
28 But if she has not defiled herself and is pure,
then she will be unharmed and will still be able
to have children.
29 "This is the ritual law for dealing with suspicion. If a woman goes astray and defiles herself
while under her husband's authority, 30 or if a
man becomes jealous and is suspicious that his
wife has been unfaithful, the husband must present his wife before the LORD, and the priest will
apply this entire ritual law to her. 31 The husband
will be innocent of any guilt in this matter, but
his wife will be held accountable for her sin."

Nazirite Laws

6 Then the LORD said to Moses, 2 "Give the
following instructions to the people of Israel.
"If any of the people, either men or women,
take the special vow of a Nazirite, setting themselves apart to the LORD in a special way, 3 they
must give up wine and other alcoholic drinks.
They must not use vinegar made from wine or
from other alcoholic drinks, they must not drink
fresh grape juice, and they must not eat grapes
or raisins. 4 As long as they are bound by their
Nazirite vow, they are not allowed to eat or drink
anything that comes from a grapevine—not even
the grape seeds or skins.
5 "They must never cut their hair throughout the time of their vow, for they are holy and
set apart to the LORD. Until the time of their
vow has been fulfilled, they must let their hair
grow long. 6 And they must not go near a dead
body during the entire period of their vow to
the LORD. 7 Even if the dead person is their own

5:21 Hebrew *when he causes your thigh to waste away.* **5:22** Hebrew *and your thigh to waste away.* **5:27** Hebrew *and her thigh will waste away.*

the *jealousy offering* is to set the accusation before God who ultimately will decide the woman's guilt or innocence. **17:** Holy water mixed with dirt from the sanctuary became the water of bitterness. Not only would the dirt have made the water unpleasant to drink, but dust was representative of death and mourning (Gen 3:19; Josh 7:6). Note that similar potions in surrounding cultures would have poisoned the woman whereas this liquid was harmless to any who were not destroyed by guilt. **18:** Loosing the hair could represent impurity (Lev 13:45) or mourning (Lev 10:6; 21:10). **19–22:** The exact significance of the curse, expressed in the Hebrew as "may your thigh waste away and your abdomen swell," is unclear. Many interpreters believe the words describe a miscarriage or stillbirth and/or a condition resulting in permanent infertility. The significance is that the woman, if she is guilty, will have no fruit from her illicit union and will never bear children again.

6:1–21 Nazirite Laws. The Nazirite vow was a special vow taken by both men and women to set themselves apart for the LORD for a specified period of time. The strictness of the Nazirite regulations is comparable only to those set for the high priest (see Lev 21:1–5, 11–12), suggesting that the Nazirite vow offered the highest level of sanctification a layperson, male or female, could achieve. It is significant that

father, mother, brother, or sister, they must not defile themselves, for the hair on their head is the symbol of their separation to God. [8]This requirement applies as long as they are set apart to the LORD.

[9]"If someone falls dead beside them, the hair they have dedicated will be defiled. They must wait for seven days and then shave their heads. Then they will be cleansed from their defilement. [10]On the eighth day they must bring two turtledoves or two young pigeons to the priest at the entrance of the Tabernacle.* [11]The priest will offer one of the birds for a sin offering and the other for a burnt offering. In this way, he will purify them* from the guilt they incurred through contact with the dead body. Then they must reaffirm their commitment and let their hair begin to grow again. [12]The days of their vow that were completed before their defilement no longer count. They must rededicate themselves to the LORD as a Nazirite for the full term of their vow, and each must bring a one-year-old male lamb for a guilt offering.

[13]"This is the ritual law for Nazirites. At the conclusion of their time of separation as Nazirites, they must each go to the entrance of the Tabernacle [14]and offer their sacrifices to the LORD: a one-year-old male lamb without defect for a burnt offering, a one-year-old female lamb without defect for a sin offering, a ram without defect for a peace offering, [15]a basket of bread made without yeast—cakes of choice flour mixed with olive oil and wafers spread with olive oil—along with their prescribed grain offerings and liquid offerings. [16]The priest will present these offerings before the LORD: first the sin offering and the burnt offering; [17]then the ram for a peace offering, along with the basket of bread made without yeast. The priest must also present the prescribed grain offering and liquid offering to the LORD.

[18]"Then the Nazirites will shave their heads at the entrance of the Tabernacle. They will take the hair that had been dedicated and place it on the fire beneath the peace-offering sacrifice. [19]After the Nazirite's head has been shaved, the priest will take for each of them the boiled shoulder of the ram, and he will take from the basket a cake and a wafer made without yeast. He will put them all into the Nazirite's hands. [20]Then the priest will lift them up as a special offering before the LORD. These are holy portions for the priest, along with the breast of the special offering and the thigh of the sacred offering that are lifted up before the LORD. After this ceremony the Nazirites may again drink wine.

[21]"This is the ritual law of the Nazirites, who vow to bring these offerings to the LORD. They may also bring additional offerings if they can afford it. And they must be careful to do whatever they vowed when they set themselves apart as Nazirites."

The Priestly Blessing

[22]Then the LORD said to Moses, [23]"Tell Aaron and his sons to bless the people of Israel with this special blessing:

[24] 'May the LORD bless you
and protect you.
[25] May the LORD smile on you
and be gracious to you.
[26] May the LORD show you his favor
and give you his peace.'

[27]Whenever Aaron and his sons bless the people of Israel in my name, I myself will bless them."

Offerings of Dedication

7 On the day Moses set up the Tabernacle, he anointed it and set it apart as holy. He also anointed and set apart all its furnishings and the altar with its utensils. [2]Then the leaders of Israel—the tribal leaders who had registered the troops—came and brought their offerings. [3]Together they brought six large wagons and twelve oxen. There was a wagon for every two leaders and an ox for each leader. They presented these to the LORD in front of the Tabernacle.

6:10 Hebrew *the Tent of Meeting;* also in 6:13, 18. **6:11** Or *make atonement for them.*

such a significant vow is explicitly described as open to women.

6:22–27 The Priestly Blessing. 25: The Hebrew reads "May the LORD shine his face upon you" (NLT, *smile*). The shining of God's face was a sign of favor (cf. Exod 34:29–35) and refers to God looking upon Israel positively and acting for their benefit (Pss 4:6; 31:16; 44:3; 67:1; 80:3, 7, 19; 89:15; 119:135). Similarly, God's graciousness offered physical sustenance, but more importantly conveyed divine forgiveness of sin (cf. Exod 34:6). **26:** Literally, "May the LORD lift up his face to you" (NLT, *show favor*). To "lift up the face," is the opposite of "to hide the face," a sign of disfavor (cf. Deut 31:18; Pss 30:8; 44:25; 104:29). The Hebrew term, *shalom*, refers to well-being and wholeness rather than simply absence of conflict.

4Then the LORD said to Moses, 5"Receive their
gifts, and use these oxen and wagons for transporting the Tabernacle.* Distribute them among
the Levites according to the work they have to
do." 6So Moses took the wagons and oxen and
presented them to the Levites. 7He gave two
wagons and four oxen to the Gershonite division for their work, 8and he gave four wagons
and eight oxen to the Merarite division for their
work. All their work was done under the leadership of Ithamar son of Aaron the priest. 9But he
gave none of the wagons or oxen to the Kohathite division, since they were required to carry the
sacred objects of the Tabernacle on their shoulders.
10The leaders also presented dedication gifts
for the altar at the time it was anointed. They
each placed their gifts before the altar. 11The
LORD said to Moses, "Let one leader bring his
gift each day for the dedication of the altar."

12On the first day Nahshon son of Amminadab,
leader of the tribe of Judah, presented his offering.
13His offering consisted of a silver platter
weighing 3¼ pounds and a silver basin
weighing 1¾ pounds* (as measured by the
weight of the sanctuary shekel). These were
both filled with grain offerings of choice flour
moistened with olive oil. 14He also brought
a gold container weighing four ounces,*
which was filled with incense. 15He brought
a young bull, a ram, and a one-year-old male
lamb for a burnt offering, 16and a male goat
for a sin offering. 17For a peace offering he
brought two bulls, five rams, five male goats,
and five one-year-old male lambs. This was
the offering brought by Nahshon son of
Amminadab.

18On the second day Nethanel son of Zuar, leader
of the tribe of Issachar, presented his offering.
19His offering consisted of a silver platter
weighing 3¼ pounds and a silver basin
weighing 1¾ pounds (as measured by the
weight of the sanctuary shekel). These were
both filled with grain offerings of choice flour
moistened with olive oil. 20He also brought a
gold container weighing four ounces, which
was filled with incense. 21He brought a young
bull, a ram, and a one-year-old male lamb for
a burnt offering, 22and a male goat for a sin
offering. 23For a peace offering he brought
two bulls, five rams, five male goats, and
five one-year-old male lambs. This was the
offering brought by Nethanel son of Zuar.

24On the third day Eliab son of Helon, leader of
the tribe of Zebulun, presented his offering.
25His offering consisted of a silver platter
weighing 3¼ pounds and a silver basin
weighing 1¾ pounds (as measured by the
weight of the sanctuary shekel). These were
both filled with grain offerings of choice flour
moistened with olive oil. 26He also brought a
gold container weighing four ounces, which
was filled with incense. 27He brought a young
bull, a ram, and a one-year-old male lamb for
a burnt offering, 28and a male goat for a sin
offering. 29For a peace offering he brought
two bulls, five rams, five male goats, and
five one-year-old male lambs. This was the
offering brought by Eliab son of Helon.

30On the fourth day Elizur son of Shedeur, leader
of the tribe of Reuben, presented his offering.
31His offering consisted of a silver platter
weighing 3¼ pounds and a silver basin
weighing 1¾ pounds (as measured by the
weight of the sanctuary shekel). These were
both filled with grain offerings of choice flour
moistened with olive oil. 32He also brought a
gold container weighing four ounces, which
was filled with incense. 33He brought a young
bull, a ram, and a one-year-old male lamb for
a burnt offering, 34and a male goat for a sin
offering. 35For a peace offering he brought
two bulls, five rams, five male goats, and
five one-year-old male lambs. This was the
offering brought by Elizur son of Shedeur.

36On the fifth day Shelumiel son of Zurishaddai,
leader of the tribe of Simeon, presented his offering.

7:5 Hebrew *the Tent of Meeting;* also in 7:89. **7:13** Hebrew *silver platter weighing 130 shekels* [1.5 kilograms] *and a silver basin weighing 70 shekels* [800 grams]; also in 7:19, 25, 31, 37, 43, 49, 55, 61, 67, 73, 79, 85. **7:14** Hebrew *10 shekels* [114 grams]; also in 7:20, 26, 32, 38, 44, 50, 56, 62, 68, 74, 80, 86.

7:1–89 Offerings of Dedication. 1–9: The gifts of six large wagons (one for every two tribal leaders) and twelve oxen (one for every leader) provided a practical way for the Gershonites and Merarites to transport the tent curtains and frames. **9:** The Kohathites were not given wagons because they were commanded to carry the most sacred elements of the Tabernacle on their shoulders using poles (see also Num 4:15). **10–88:** The fact that these gifts occur over twelve days highlights the impressive nature of the celebration. In

37 His offering consisted of a silver platter
weighing 3¼ pounds and a silver basin
weighing 1¾ pounds (as measured by the
weight of the sanctuary shekel). These were
both filled with grain offerings of choice flour
moistened with olive oil. 38 He also brought
a gold container weighing four ounces,
which was filled with incense. 39 He brought
a young bull, a ram, and a one-year-old male
lamb for a burnt offering, 40 and a male goat
for a sin offering. 41 For a peace offering he
brought two bulls, five rams, five male goats,
and five one-year-old male lambs. This was
the offering brought by Shelumiel son of
Zurishaddai.

42 On the sixth day Eliasaph son of Deuel, leader
of the tribe of Gad, presented his offering.
43 His offering consisted of a silver platter
weighing 3¼ pounds and a silver basin
weighing 1¾ pounds (as measured by the
weight of the sanctuary shekel). These were
both filled with grain offerings of choice flour
moistened with olive oil. 44 He also brought a
gold container weighing four ounces, which
was filled with incense. 45 He brought a young
bull, a ram, and a one-year-old male lamb for
a burnt offering, 46 and a male goat for a sin
offering. 47 For a peace offering he brought
two bulls, five rams, five male goats, and
five one-year-old male lambs. This was the
offering brought by Eliasaph son of Deuel.

48 On the seventh day Elishama son of Ammihud,
leader of the tribe of Ephraim, presented his offering.
49 His offering consisted of a silver platter
weighing 3¼ pounds and a silver basin
weighing 1¾ pounds (as measured by the
weight of the sanctuary shekel). These were
both filled with grain offerings of choice flour
moistened with olive oil. 50 He also brought
a gold container weighing four ounces,
which was filled with incense. 51 He brought
a young bull, a ram, and a one-year-old male
lamb for a burnt offering, 52 and a male goat
for a sin offering. 53 For a peace offering he
brought two bulls, five rams, five male goats,
and five one-year-old male lambs. This was
the offering brought by Elishama son of
Ammihud.

54 On the eighth day Gamaliel son of Pedahzur,
leader of the tribe of Manasseh, presented his offering.
55 His offering consisted of a silver platter
weighing 3¼ pounds and a silver basin
weighing 1¾ pounds (as measured by the
weight of the sanctuary shekel). These were
both filled with grain offerings of choice flour
moistened with olive oil. 56 He also brought
a gold container weighing four ounces,
which was filled with incense. 57 He brought
a young bull, a ram, and a one-year-old male
lamb for a burnt offering, 58 and a male goat
for a sin offering. 59 For a peace offering he
brought two bulls, five rams, five male goats,
and five one-year-old male lambs. This was
the offering brought by Gamaliel son of
Pedahzur.

60 On the ninth day Abidan son of Gideoni, leader
of the tribe of Benjamin, presented his offering.
61 His offering consisted of a silver platter
weighing 3¼ pounds and a silver basin
weighing 1¾ pounds (as measured by the
weight of the sanctuary shekel). These were
both filled with grain offerings of choice flour
moistened with olive oil. 62 He also brought a
gold container weighing four ounces, which
was filled with incense. 63 He brought a young
bull, a ram, and a one-year-old male lamb for
a burnt offering, 64 and a male goat for a sin
offering. 65 For a peace offering he brought
two bulls, five rams, five male goats, and
five one-year-old male lambs. This was the
offering brought by Abidan son of Gideoni.

66 On the tenth day Ahiezer son of Ammishaddai,
leader of the tribe of Dan, presented his offering.
67 His offering consisted of a silver platter
weighing 3¼ pounds and a silver basin
weighing 1¾ pounds (as measured by the
weight of the sanctuary shekel). These were
both filled with grain offerings of choice flour
moistened with olive oil. 68 He also brought
a gold container weighing four ounces,
which was filled with incense. 69 He brought
a young bull, a ram, and a one-year-old male
lamb for a burnt offering, 70 and a male goat
for a sin offering. 71 For a peace offering he
brought two bulls, five rams, five male goats,
and five one-year-old male lambs. This was
the offering brought by Ahiezer son of
Ammishaddai.

72 On the eleventh day Pagiel son of Ocran, leader of the tribe of Asher, presented his offering.
73 His offering consisted of a silver platter
weighing 3¼ pounds and a silver basin
weighing 1¾ pounds (as measured by the

weight of the sanctuary shekel). These were
both filled with grain offerings of choice flour
moistened with olive oil. 74 He also brought a
gold container weighing four ounces, which
was filled with incense. 75 He brought a young
bull, a ram, and a one-year-old male lamb for
a burnt offering, 76 and a male goat for a sin
offering. 77 For a peace offering he brought
two bulls, five rams, five male goats, and
five one-year-old male lambs. This was the
offering brought by Pagiel son of Ocran.

78 On the twelfth day Ahira son of Enan, leader of
the tribe of Naphtali, presented his offering.
79 His offering consisted of a silver platter
weighing 3¼ pounds and a silver basin
weighing 1¾ pounds (as measured by the
weight of the sanctuary shekel). These were
both filled with grain offerings of choice flour
moistened with olive oil. 80 He also brought a
gold container weighing four ounces, which
was filled with incense. 81 He brought a young
bull, a ram, and a one-year-old male lamb for
a burnt offering, 82 and a male goat for a sin
offering. 83 For a peace offering he brought
two bulls, five rams, five male goats, and
five one-year-old male lambs. This was the
offering brought by Ahira son of Enan.

84 So this was the dedication offering brought
by the leaders of Israel at the time the altar was
anointed: twelve silver platters, twelve silver basins, and twelve gold incense containers. 85 Each
silver platter weighed 3¼ pounds, and each silver basin weighed 1¾ pounds. The total weight
of the silver was 60 pounds* (as measured by
the weight of the sanctuary shekel). 86 Each of
the twelve gold containers that was filled with
incense weighed four ounces (as measured by
the weight of the sanctuary shekel). The total
weight of the gold was three pounds.* 87 Twelve
young bulls, twelve rams, and twelve one-year-
old male lambs were donated for the burnt
offerings, along with their prescribed grain offerings. Twelve male goats were brought for the
sin offerings. 88 Twenty-four bulls, sixty rams,
sixty male goats, and sixty one-year-old male
lambs were donated for the peace offerings. This
was the dedication offering for the altar after it
was anointed.

89 Whenever Moses went into the Tabernacle
to speak with the LORD, he heard the voice speaking to him from between the two cherubim above
the Ark's cover—the place of atonement—that
rests on the Ark of the Covenant.* The LORD
spoke to him from there.

Preparing the Lamps

8 The LORD said to Moses, 2 "Give Aaron
the following instructions: When you set
up the seven lamps in the lampstand, place
them so their light shines forward in front of the
lampstand." 3 So Aaron did this. He set up the
seven lamps so they reflected their light forward,
just as the LORD had commanded Moses. 4 The
entire lampstand, from its base to its decorative blossoms, was made of beaten gold. It was
built according to the exact design the LORD had
shown Moses.

The Levites Dedicated

5 Then the LORD said to Moses, 6 "Now set the Levites apart from the rest of the people of Israel
and make them ceremonially clean. 7 Do this by
sprinkling them with the water of purification,
and have them shave their entire body and wash
their clothing. Then they will be ceremonially
clean. 8 Have them bring a young bull and a grain
offering of choice flour moistened with olive oil,
along with a second young bull for a sin offering.
9 Then assemble the whole community of Israel, and present the Levites at the entrance of the
Tabernacle.* 10 When you present the Levites before the LORD, the people of Israel must lay their

7:85 Hebrew *2,400 shekels* [27.6 kilograms]. **7:86** Hebrew *120 shekels* [1.4 kilograms]. **7:89** Or *Ark of the Testimony.* **8:9** Hebrew *the Tent of Meeting;* also in 8:15, 19, 22, 24, 26.

addition, the details serve to emphasize that each tribe offered exactly the same gifts—no tribe was more generous or less, and all the tribes contributed equally to the Tabernacle's supplies. **89:** Cherubim adorned the lid that covered the Ark. They were winged, nonhuman creatures (probably lions), who sat facing opposite one another with their wings touching in the middle (Exod 25:17–20). God's presence dwelled above the cherubim, and the Ark represented the footstool of God's throne (1 Sam 4:4; 2 Sam 6:2; 2 Kgs 19:15; 1 Chr 13:6; Pss 80:1; 99:1; Isa 37:16).

8:1–4 Preparing the Lamps. The lampstand (or menorah) was made of pure gold and had one central stem with three stems on both sides. On each of the seven stems a lamp was placed (Exod 25:31–40; 37:17–24).

8:5–26 The Levites: A Special Offering. 10: The Israelites laid their hands on the Levites, thereby identifying them as a living sacrifice for the community. Laying on of hands was a common practice in the Old Testament used for setting persons apart for ser-

hands on them. 11 Raising his hands, Aaron must then present the Levites to the LORD as a special offering from the people of Israel, thus dedicating them to the LORD's service.

12 "Next the Levites will lay their hands on the heads of the young bulls. Present one as a sin offering and the other as a burnt offering to the LORD, to purify the Levites and make them right with the LORD.* 13 Then have the Levites stand in front of Aaron and his sons, and raise your hands and present them as a special offering to the LORD. 14 In this way, you will set the Levites apart from the rest of the people of Israel, and the Levites will belong to me. 15 After this, they may go into the Tabernacle to do their work, because you have purified them and presented them as a special offering.

16 "Of all the people of Israel, the Levites are reserved for me. I have claimed them for myself in place of all the firstborn sons of the Israelites; I have taken the Levites as their substitutes. 17 For all the firstborn males among the people of Israel are mine, both of people and of animals. I set them apart for myself on the day I struck down all the firstborn sons of the Egyptians. 18 Yes, I have claimed the Levites in place of all the firstborn sons of Israel. 19 And of all the Israelites, I have assigned the Levites to Aaron and his sons. They will serve in the Tabernacle on behalf of the Israelites and make sacrifices to purify* the people so no plague will strike them when they approach the sanctuary."

20 So Moses, Aaron, and the whole community of Israel dedicated the Levites, carefully following all the LORD's instructions to Moses. 21 The Levites purified themselves from sin and washed their clothes, and Aaron lifted them up and presented them to the LORD as a special offering. He then offered a sacrifice to purify them and make them right with the LORD.* 22 After that the Levites went into the Tabernacle to perform their duties, assisting Aaron and his sons. So they carried out all the commands that the LORD gave Moses concerning the Levites.

23 The LORD also instructed Moses, 24 "This is the rule the Levites must follow: They must begin serving in the Tabernacle at the age of twenty-five, 25 and they must retire at the age of fifty. 26 After retirement they may assist their fellow Levites by serving as guards at the Tabernacle, but they may not officiate in the service. This is how you must assign duties to the Levites."

The Second Passover

9 A year after Israel's departure from Egypt, the LORD spoke to Moses in the wilderness of Sinai. In the first month* of that year he said, 2 "Tell the Israelites to celebrate the Passover at the prescribed time, 3 at twilight on the fourteenth day of the first month.* Be sure to follow all my decrees and regulations concerning this celebration."

4 So Moses told the people to celebrate the Passover 5 in the wilderness of Sinai as twilight fell on the fourteenth day of the month. And they celebrated the festival there, just as the LORD had commanded Moses. 6 But some of the men had been ceremonially defiled by touching a dead body, so they could not celebrate the Passover that day. They came to Moses and Aaron that day 7 and said, "We have become ceremonially unclean by touching a dead body. But why should we be prevented from presenting the LORD's offering at the proper time with the rest of the Israelites?"

8 Moses answered, "Wait here until I have received instructions for you from the LORD."

9 This was the LORD's reply to Moses. 10 "Give the following instructions to the people of Israel: If any of the people now or in future generations are ceremonially unclean at Passover time because of touching a dead body, or if they are on a journey and cannot be present at the ceremony, they may still celebrate the LORD's Pass-

8:12 Or *to make atonement for the Levites.* **8:19** Or *make atonement for.* **8:21** Or *then made atonement for them to purify them.* **9:1** The first month of the ancient Hebrew lunar calendar usually occurs within the months of March and April. **9:3** This day in the ancient Hebrew lunar calendar occurred in late March, April, or early May.

---

vice (Num 27:18, 23), for conferral of blessings (Gen 48:12–14), and for identifying animals for sacrifice (Lev 1:4; 3:2, 8, 13; etc.). **11:** *Special offering* refers to a particular kind of sacrifice known as an elevation offering—an offering that was lifted up before the LORD as a special gift. No other examples exist of human beings being offered in this fashion, another indication of the unique and noble role of the Levites. **23–26:** The beginning age of service (twenty-five years) in verse 24 differs from that specified in Num 4:3 (thirty years). Attempts to resolve this contradiction are all highly speculative, and the best explanation may be that two different traditions existed.

9:1–14 The Second Passover. Passover was celebrated on the fourteenth day of the first month—the equivalent of March/April today. **3:** The Old Testament does not specifically clarify what it means to be "cut off," but the penalty was applied to various infractions, including Sabbath breaking (Exod 12:15–19; 31:12–

over. 11 They must offer the Passover sacrifice one
month later, at twilight on the fourteenth day
of the second month.* They must eat the Passover lamb at that time with bitter salad greens
and bread made without yeast. 12 They must not
leave any of the lamb until the next morning,
and they must not break any of its bones. They
must follow all the normal regulations concerning the Passover.
13 "But those who neglect to celebrate the
Passover at the regular time, even though they
are ceremonially clean and not away on a trip,
will be cut off from the community of Israel. If
they fail to present the LORD's offering at the
proper time, they will suffer the consequences of
their guilt. 14 And if foreigners living among you
want to celebrate the Passover to the LORD, they
must follow these same decrees and regulations.
The same laws apply both to native-born Israelites and to the foreigners living among you."

The Fiery Cloud

15 On the day the Tabernacle was set up, the cloud
covered it.* But from evening until morning the
cloud over the Tabernacle looked like a pillar of
fire. 16 This was the regular pattern—at night
the cloud that covered the Tabernacle had the
appearance of fire. 17 Whenever the cloud lifted
from over the sacred tent, the people of Israel
would break camp and follow it. And wherever
the cloud settled, the people of Israel would set
up camp. 18 In this way, they traveled and camped
at the LORD's command wherever he told them
to go. Then they remained in their camp as long
as the cloud stayed over the Tabernacle. 19 If the
cloud remained over the Tabernacle for a long
time, the Israelites stayed and performed their
duty to the LORD. 20 Sometimes the cloud would
stay over the Tabernacle for only a few days, so
the people would stay for only a few days, as the
LORD commanded. Then at the LORD's command
they would break camp and move on. 21 Sometimes the cloud stayed only overnight and lifted
the next morning. But day or night, when the
cloud lifted, the people broke camp and moved
on. 22 Whether the cloud stayed above the Tabernacle for two days, a month, or a year, the people
of Israel stayed in camp and did not move on. But
as soon as it lifted, they broke camp and moved
on. 23 So they camped or traveled at the LORD's
command, and they did whatever the LORD told
them through Moses.

The Silver Trumpets

10 Now the LORD said to Moses, 2 "Make
two trumpets of hammered silver for
calling the community to assemble
and for signaling the breaking of camp. 3 When
both trumpets are blown, everyone must gather
before you at the entrance of the Tabernacle.*
4 But if only one trumpet is blown, then only the
leaders—the heads of the clans of Israel—must
present themselves to you.
5 "When you sound the signal to move on, the
tribes camped on the east side of the Tabernacle
must break camp and move forward. 6 When you
sound the signal a second time, the tribes camped
on the south will follow. You must sound short
blasts as the signal for moving on. 7 But when you
call the people to an assembly, blow the trumpets
with a different signal. 8 Only the priests, Aaron's
descendants, are allowed to blow the trumpets.
This is a permanent law for you, to be observed
from generation to generation.
9 "When you arrive in your own land and go
to war against your enemies who attack you,
sound the alarm with the trumpets. Then the
LORD your God will remember you and rescue
you from your enemies. 10 Blow the trumpets in
times of gladness, too, sounding them at your

9:11 This day in the ancient Hebrew lunar calendar occurred in late April, May, or early June. **9:15** Hebrew *covered the Tabernacle, the Tent of the Testimony.* **10:3** Hebrew *Tent of Meeting.*

14; Lev 23:29) and sexual impropriety (Lev 18:19; 20:17–18). Being cut off likely refers to permanent exile, though some interpreters suggest it denotes premature death or execution by God's hand (cf. Lev 20:5). **14:** A provision for foreigners to celebrate the Passover highlights the inclusive nature of Israel's celebrations.

9:15–23 The Cloud. See also Exodus 40:36–38. **15–16:** The cloud was a representation of God's earthly presence and appears in various forms throughout the journey from Egypt (Exod 13:21–22; 14:19, 24; 19:9; 33:9–10; 40:34, 38). **17–23:** Two important theological concepts are emphasized through the pillar of cloud: Israel's God was continually present with the community, and their deity was not geographically bound. The belief that gods were confined to the sanctuaries associated with them was common in the ancient Near East. The priestly literature, birthed far from Jerusalem's ruined Temple, steadfastly challenged such a view by emphasizing God's freedom of mobility. The LORD was wherever Israel was, including the wildernesses of Sinai and Babylon.

10:1–10 The Silver Trumpets. 9: Blown during war, the trumpets aroused God's attention, resulting in Is-

annual festivals and at the beginning of each
month. And blow the trumpets over your burnt
offerings and peace offerings. The trumpets will
remind the LORD your God of his covenant with
you. I am the LORD your God."

The Israelites Leave Sinai

11 In the second year after Israel's departure
from Egypt—on the twentieth day of the second
month*—the cloud lifted from the Tabernacle of
the Covenant.* 12 So the Israelites set out from
the wilderness of Sinai and traveled on from
place to place until the cloud stopped in the wilderness of Paran.
13 When the people set out for the first time,
following the instructions the LORD had given
through Moses, 14 Judah's troops led the way.
They marched behind their banner, and their
leader was Nahshon son of Amminadab. 15 They
were joined by the troops of the tribe of Issachar,
led by Nethanel son of Zuar, 16 and the troops of
the tribe of Zebulun, led by Eliab son of Helon.
17 Then the Tabernacle was taken down, and
the Gershonite and Merarite divisions of the Levites were next in the line of march, carrying the
Tabernacle with them. 18 Reuben's troops went
next, marching behind their banner. Their leader
was Elizur son of Shedeur. 19 They were joined
by the troops of the tribe of Simeon, led by Shelumiel son of Zurishaddai, 20 and the troops of the
tribe of Gad, led by Eliasaph son of Deuel.
21 Next came the Kohathite division of the
Levites, carrying the sacred objects from the
Tabernacle. Before they arrived at the next camp,
the Tabernacle would already be set up at its new
location. 22 Ephraim's troops went next, marching
behind their banner. Their leader was Elishama
son of Ammihud. 23 They were joined by the
troops of the tribe of Manasseh, led by Gamaliel
son of Pedahzur, 24 and the troops of the tribe of
Benjamin, led by Abidan son of Gideoni.
25 Dan's troops went last, marching behind
their banner and serving as the rear guard for all
the tribal camps. Their leader was Ahiezer son of
Ammishaddai. 26 They were joined by the troops
of the tribe of Asher, led by Pagiel son of Ocran,
27 and the troops of the tribe of Naphtali, led by
Ahira son of Enan.
28 This was the order in which the Israelites
marched, division by division.
29 One day Moses said to his brother-in-law,
Hobab son of Reuel the Midianite, "We are on
our way to the place the LORD promised us, for
he said, 'I will give it to you.' Come with us and
we will treat you well, for the LORD has promised wonderful blessings for Israel!"
30 But Hobab replied, "No, I will not go. I must
return to my own land and family."
31 "Please don't leave us," Moses pleaded. "You
know the places in the wilderness where we should
camp. Come, be our guide. 32 If you do, we'll share
with you all the blessings the LORD gives us."
33 They marched for three days after leaving
the mountain of the LORD, with the Ark of the
LORD's Covenant moving ahead of them to show
them where to stop and rest. 34 As they moved
on each day, the cloud of the LORD hovered over
them. 35 And whenever the Ark set out, Moses
would shout, "Arise, O LORD, and let your enemies be scattered! Let them flee before you!"
36 And when the Ark was set down, he would say,
"Return, O LORD, to the countless thousands of
Israel!"

The People Complain to Moses

11 Soon the people began to complain
about their hardship, and the LORD
heard everything they said. Then the
LORD's anger blazed against them, and he sent a
fire to rage among them, and he destroyed some

10:11a This day in the ancient Hebrew lunar calendar occurred in late April, May, or early June. **10:11b** Or *Tabernacle of the Testimony.*

---

rael's deliverance. The sound represented God's presence with the people (31:6; cf. Josh 6). **10**: At Sinai God's presence on the mountain was announced with the blast of a ram's horn (Exod 19:16, 19; 20:18); thus every sounding of the silver trumpets served as a reminder of the covenant made with Israel there.

10:11–36 The Israelites Leave Sinai. 12: The Wilderness of Paran was a general designation for the northern Sinai peninsula. **13–28:** The precise order specified in Numbers 2 is followed here, once again highlighting the complete obedience of Israel before the LORD. **29–32:** The exact relationship of Hobab to Moses is uncertain. While the NLT identifies Hobab as Moses' brother-in-law, the Hebrew text can also correctly be translated "father-in-law." In Judg 4:11 (translator's note), Hobab is Moses' father-in-law, but in other traditions, he is called Jethro (Exod 3:1; 4:18; 18:1) and Reuel (Exod 2:18). **32:** Hobab's response following Moses' second plea goes unrecorded, leaving the question of whether Hobab accompanied Israel unanswered. **33–36:** Like the cloud and the silver trumpets, the Ark served as an indicator to go forth or to encamp. **35–36:** The ancient Ark song focuses on God's role as the divine warrior, host of Israel's armies, who, enthroned upon the Ark, led Israel

of the people in the outskirts of the camp. 2 Then
the people screamed to Moses for help, and when
he prayed to the LORD, the fire stopped. 3 After
that, the area was known as Taberah (which
means "the place of burning"), because fire from
the LORD had burned among them there.
4 Then the foreign rabble who were traveling
with the Israelites began to crave the good things
of Egypt. And the people of Israel also began to
complain. "Oh, for some meat!" they exclaimed.
5 "We remember the fish we used to eat for free
in Egypt. And we had all the cucumbers, melons,
leeks, onions, and garlic we wanted. 6 But now
our appetites are gone. All we ever see is this
manna!"
7 The manna looked like small coriander seeds,
and it was pale yellow like gum resin. 8 The people would go out and gather it from the ground.
They made flour by grinding it with hand mills
or pounding it in mortars. Then they boiled it in
a pot and made it into flat cakes. These cakes tasted like pastries baked with olive oil. 9 The manna
came down on the camp with the dew during the
night.
10 Moses heard all the families standing in
the doorways of their tents whining, and the
LORD became extremely angry. Moses was also
very aggravated. 11 And Moses said to the LORD,
"Why are you treating me, your servant, so
harshly? Have mercy on me! What did I do to
deserve the burden of all these people? 12 Did I
give birth to them? Did I bring them into the
world? Why did you tell me to carry them in
my arms like a mother carries a nursing baby?
How can I carry them to the land you swore to
give their ancestors? 13 Where am I supposed to
get meat for all these people? They keep whining to me, saying, 'Give us meat to eat!' 14 I can't
carry all these people by myself! The load is far
too heavy! 15 If this is how you intend to treat
me, just go ahead and kill me. Do me a favor and
spare me this misery!"

Moses Chooses Seventy Leaders

16 Then the LORD said to Moses, "Gather before
me seventy men who are recognized as elders
and leaders of Israel. Bring them to the Tabernacle* to stand there with you. 17 I will come down
and talk to you there. I will take some of the
Spirit that is upon you, and I will put the Spirit
upon them also. They will bear the burden of the
people along with you, so you will not have to
carry it alone.
18 "And say to the people, 'Purify yourselves,
for tomorrow you will have meat to eat. You
were whining, and the LORD heard you when you
cried, "Oh, for some meat! We were better off in
Egypt!" Now the LORD will give you meat, and
you will have to eat it. 19 And it won't be for just a
day or two, or for five or ten or even twenty. 20 You
will eat it for a whole month until you gag and
are sick of it. For you have rejected the LORD, who
is here among you, and you have whined to him,
saying, "Why did we ever leave Egypt?"'"
21 But Moses responded to the LORD, "There
are 600,000 foot soldiers here with me, and
yet you say, 'I will give them meat for a whole
month!' 22 Even if we butchered all our flocks and
herds, would that satisfy them? Even if we caught
all the fish in the sea, would that be enough?"
23 Then the LORD said to Moses, "Has my arm
lost its power? Now you will see whether or not
my word comes true!"
24 So Moses went out and reported the LORD's
words to the people. He gathered the seventy
elders and stationed them around the Tabernacle.* 25 And the LORD came down in the cloud and
spoke to Moses. Then he gave the seventy elders
the same Spirit that was upon Moses. And when
the Spirit rested upon them, they prophesied.
But this never happened again.
26 Two men, Eldad and Medad, had stayed be-

11:16 Hebrew *the Tent of Meeting.* **11:24** Hebrew *the tent;* also in 11:26.

---

into battle and returned them to camp, victorious.

11:1—20:29 Slide into Rebellion and Death

11:1–35 The People Complain to Moses. 1–3: Complaint about hardship at Taberah. **2:** Fire from the LORD can be destructive in nature (Lev 10:2; Num 16:35; 26:10) but can also represent God's presence (Exod 3:2; 19:18). **3:** The place name, Taberah, echoes the Hebrew verb "burn" (NLT, *rage*, v. 1). **4–6:** The *foreign rabble* refers to non-Israelites who fled Egypt with the Hebrews and are at the heart of this rebellion (cf. Exod 12:38; Josh 8:35). **7–9:** The fact that the people complained about manna that had been so generously provided by God (Exod 16:1–36) is an indication of their extreme ungratefulness. **10–14:** The use of birthing imagery is striking and calls attention to God's motherlike role in creating Israel (see similar descriptions of God as mother in Deut 32:18; Job 38:8–11; Ps 22:9–10; Isa 42:14; 49:15; 66:9, 12–13; and Hos 11:1–4). Although feminine imagery for God appears infrequently in the Bible, it is a powerful reminder that we are invited to think of God using a variety of metaphors, not just masculine ones. **17:** In the Old Testament, the Spirit of God is an impersonal, empowering force that is distributed

hind in the camp. They were listed among the elders, but they had not gone out to the Tabernacle.
Yet the Spirit rested upon them as well, so they
prophesied there in the camp. 27 A young man
ran and reported to Moses, "Eldad and Medad
are prophesying in the camp!"
28 Joshua son of Nun, who had been Moses'
assistant since his youth, protested, "Moses, my
master, make them stop!"
29 But Moses replied, "Are you jealous for
my sake? I wish that all the LORD's people were
prophets and that the LORD would put his Spirit
upon them all!" 30 Then Moses returned to the
camp with the elders of Israel.

The LORD Sends Quail

31 Now the LORD sent a wind that brought quail
from the sea and let them fall all around the
camp. For miles in every direction there were
quail flying about three feet above the ground.*
32 So the people went out and caught quail all that
day and throughout the night and all the next
day, too. No one gathered less than fifty bushels*! They spread the quail all around the camp
to dry. 33 But while they were gorging themselves
on the meat—while it was still in their mouths—
the anger of the LORD blazed against the people,
and he struck them with a severe plague. 34 So
that place was called Kibroth-hattaavah (which
means "graves of gluttony") because there they
buried the people who had craved meat from
Egypt. 35 From Kibroth-hattaavah the Israelites traveled to Hazeroth, where they stayed for
some time.

The Complaints of Miriam and Aaron

12 While they were at Hazeroth, Miriam
and Aaron criticized Moses because he
had married a Cushite woman. 2 They
said, "Has the LORD spoken only through Moses?
Hasn't he spoken through us, too?" But the LORD
heard them. 3 (Now Moses was very humble—
more humble than any other person on earth.)
4 So immediately the LORD called to Moses,
Aaron, and Miriam and said, "Go out to the Tabernacle,* all three of you!" So the three of them
went to the Tabernacle. 5 Then the LORD descended in the pillar of cloud and stood at the entrance
of the Tabernacle.* "Aaron and Miriam!" he
called, and they stepped forward. 6 And the LORD
said to them, "Now listen to what I say:

"If there were prophets among you,
I, the LORD, would reveal myself in visions.
I would speak to them in dreams.
7 But not with my servant Moses.
Of all my house, he is the one I trust.
8 I speak to him face to face,
clearly, and not in riddles!
He sees the LORD as he is.
So why were you not afraid
to criticize my servant Moses?"

9 The LORD was very angry with them, and
he departed. 10 As the cloud moved from above
the Tabernacle, there stood Miriam, her skin as
white as snow from leprosy.* When Aaron saw
what had happened to her, 11 he cried out to Moses, "Oh, my master! Please don't punish us for
this sin we have so foolishly committed. 12 Don't
let her be like a stillborn baby, already decayed
at birth."
13 So Moses cried out to the LORD, "O God, I
beg you, please heal her!"
14 But the LORD said to Moses, "If her father
had done nothing more than spit in her face,
wouldn't she be defiled for seven days? So keep
her outside the camp for seven days, and after
that she may be accepted back."
15 So Miriam was kept outside the camp for

11:31 Or *there were quail 3 feet* [2 cubits or 92 centimeters] *deep on the ground.* **11:32** Hebrew *10 homers* [1.8 kiloliters]. **12:4** Hebrew *the Tent of Meeting.* **12:5** Hebrew *the tent;* also in 12:10. **12:10** Or *with a skin disease.* The Hebrew word used here can describe various skin diseases.

---

solely by God and can be removed at will (cf. 1 Sam 16:14). It is placed on certain individuals to provide them the authority and power they need to fulfill their mission. **31–33:** Like manna, the quail fell from the sky and the people had only to gather them. Unlike manna the meat was not a gift but, rather, a plague.

12:1–16 The Complaints of Miriam and Aaron. 1: The fact that Miriam's name appears first may suggest that she was the instigator in this complaining episode. Unfortunately, this wife is not mentioned again, and the nature of the complaint remains unclear. **2:** According to Micah 6:4, Miriam and Aaron were leaders alongside Moses in Israel, but the question here is about who can mediate God's word. **7–8:** God elevated Moses above the rest of the prophets, who only saw through visions and dreams. In essence, God's relationship with Moses was intimate and entirely unique, silencing Miriam and Aaron's claim of equal status. **10:** No explanation is offered for why only Miriam was afflicted and not Aaron, though some think his role as high priest privileged him. *White as snow* refers either to the color of Miriam's skin or to its texture—flaky like snow (see

seven days, and the people waited until she was brought back before they traveled again. 16 Then they left Hazeroth and camped in the wilderness of Paran.

Twelve Scouts Explore Canaan

13 The LORD now said to Moses, 2 "Send out men to explore the land of Canaan, the land I am giving to the Israelites. Send one leader from each of the twelve ancestral tribes." 3 So Moses did as the LORD commanded him. He sent out twelve men, all tribal leaders of Israel, from their camp in the wilderness of Paran. 4 These were the tribes and the names of their leaders:

Tribe	*Leader*
Reuben	Shammua son of Zaccur
5 Simeon	Shaphat son of Hori
6 Judah	Caleb son of Jephunneh
7 Issachar	Igal son of Joseph
8 Ephraim	Hoshea son of Nun
9 Benjamin	Palti son of Raphu
10 Zebulun	Gaddiel son of Sodi
11 Manasseh son of Joseph	Gaddi son of Susi
12 Dan	Ammiel son of Gemalli
13 Asher	Sethur son of Michael
14 Naphtali	Nahbi son of Vophsi
15 Gad	Geuel son of Maki

16 These are the names of the men Moses sent out to explore the land. (Moses called Hoshea son of Nun by the name Joshua.)

17 Moses gave the men these instructions as he sent them out to explore the land: "Go north through the Negev into the hill country. 18 See what the land is like, and find out whether the people living there are strong or weak, few or many. 19 See what kind of land they live in. Is it good or bad? Do their towns have walls, or are they unprotected like open camps? 20 Is the soil fertile or poor? Are there many trees? Do your best to bring back samples of the crops you see." (It happened to be the season for harvesting the first ripe grapes.)

21 So they went up and explored the land from the wilderness of Zin as far as Rehob, near Lebo-hamath. 22 Going north, they passed through the Negev and arrived at Hebron, where Ahiman, Sheshai, and Talmai—all descendants of Anak—lived. (The ancient town of Hebron was founded seven years before the Egyptian city of Zoan.) 23 When they came to the valley of Eshcol, they cut down a branch with a single cluster of grapes so large that it took two of them to carry it on a pole between them! They also brought back samples of the pomegranates and figs. 24 That place was called the valley of Eshcol (which means "cluster"), because of the cluster of grapes the Israelite men cut there.

The Scouting Report

25 After exploring the land for forty days, the men returned 26 to Moses, Aaron, and the whole community of Israel at Kadesh in the wilderness of Paran. They reported to the whole community what they had seen and showed them the fruit they had taken from the land. 27 This was their report to Moses: "We entered the land you sent us to explore, and it is indeed a bountiful country—a land flowing with milk and honey. Here is the kind of fruit it produces. 28 But the people living there are powerful, and their towns are large and fortified. We even saw giants there, the descendants of Anak! 29 The Amalekites live in the Negev, and the Hittites, Jebusites, and Amorites live in the hill country. The Canaanites live along the coast of the Mediterranean Sea* and along the Jordan Valley."

30 But Caleb tried to quiet the people as they stood before Moses. "Let's go at once to take the land," he said. "We can certainly conquer it!"

31 But the other men who had explored the land with him disagreed. "We can't go up against

13:29 Hebrew *the sea.*

also v. 12). **14:** This regulation is not found in the law codes, though a similar law occurs in Lev 15:18. **15:** Even in exile Miriam was still accorded respect by the community, indicating her high position as leader remained intact.

13:1–33 Twelve Scouts Explore Canaan. The choice of twelve men, one from each tribe, to be spies, evokes chapter 1 where twelve men were chosen to assist in the census. The spies' job was to go north through the land; evaluate the military strength of its people, the defensibility of their cities, and the land's fruitfulness; and bring back samples of the crops. **21:** The wilderness of Zin was the southern Negev region. Rehob and Lebo-hamath represent the northernmost extent of Canaan. **22:** Hebron was later given to Caleb as a reward for his role in this episode (Josh 14:6–15), and he defeated the three clans listed here (Josh 15:14). **25:** The number forty, used repeatedly throughout both testaments, symbolizes a complete amount of time. Kadesh was an oasis located in the southern Negev. **29:** This verse identifies enemies to the north, south, east, and west—everywhere Israel might go. **30:** Caleb alone offered a positive re-

them! They are stronger than we are!” 32 So they spread this bad report about the land among the Israelites: “The land we traveled through and explored will devour anyone who goes to live there. All the people we saw were huge. 33 We even saw giants* there, the descendants of Anak. Next to them we felt like grasshoppers, and that's what they thought, too!”

The People Rebel

14 Then the whole community began weeping aloud, and they cried all night. 2 Their voices rose in a great chorus of protest against Moses and Aaron. “If only we had died in Egypt, or even here in the wilderness!” they complained. 3 “Why is the LORD taking us to this country only to have us die in battle? Our wives and our little ones will be carried off as plunder! Wouldn't it be better for us to return to Egypt?” 4 Then they plotted among themselves, “Let's choose a new leader and go back to Egypt!”

5 Then Moses and Aaron fell face down on the ground before the whole community of Israel. 6 Two of the men who had explored the land, Joshua son of Nun and Caleb son of Jephunneh, tore their clothing. 7 They said to all the people of Israel, “The land we traveled through and explored is a wonderful land! 8 And if the LORD is pleased with us, he will bring us safely into that land and give it to us. It is a rich land flowing with milk and honey. 9 Do not rebel against the LORD, and don't be afraid of the people of the land. They are only helpless prey to us! They have no protection, but the LORD is with us! Don't be afraid of them!”

10 But the whole community began to talk about stoning Joshua and Caleb. Then the glorious presence of the LORD appeared to all the Israelites at the Tabernacle.* 11 And the LORD said to Moses, “How long will these people treat me with contempt? Will they never believe me, even after all the miraculous signs I have done among them? 12 I will disown them and destroy them with a plague. Then I will make you into a nation greater and mightier than they are!”

Moses Intercedes for the People

13 But Moses objected. “What will the Egyptians think when they hear about it?” he asked the LORD. “They know full well the power you displayed in rescuing your people from Egypt. 14 Now if you destroy them, the Egyptians will send a report to the inhabitants of this land, who have already heard that you live among your people. They know, LORD, that you have appeared to your people face to face and that your pillar of cloud hovers over them. They know that you go before them in the pillar of cloud by day and the pillar of fire by night. 15 Now if you slaughter all these people with a single blow, the nations that have heard of your fame will say, 16 ‘The LORD was not able to bring them into the land he swore to give them, so he killed them in the wilderness.’

17 “Please, Lord, prove that your power is as great as you have claimed. For you said, 18 ‘The LORD is slow to anger and filled with unfailing love, forgiving every kind of sin and rebellion. But he does not excuse the guilty. He lays the sins of the parents upon their children; the entire family is affected—even children in the third and fourth generations.’ 19 In keeping with your magnificent, unfailing love, please pardon the sins of this people, just as you have forgiven them ever since they left Egypt.”

20 Then the LORD said, “I will pardon them as you have requested. 21 But as surely as I live, and as surely as the earth is filled with the LORD's glory, 22 not one of these people will ever enter that land. They have all seen my glorious presence and the miraculous signs I performed both in Egypt and in the wilderness, but again and again they have tested me by refusing to listen to my voice. 23 They will never even see the land I swore to give their ancestors. None of those who

13:33 Hebrew *nephilim.* **14:10** Hebrew *the Tent of Meeting.*

port; Joshua is not mentioned until the next chapter. **33:** The writer equates the Anakim (v. 22) with the *Nephilim* (NLT, *giants*) of Gen 6:1–4. Although Genesis 6:4 merely identifies the *Nephilim* as heroic men, a tradition developed that they were the unnaturally large offspring of divine beings (sons of God) and human beings (daughters of men). (See annotation on Gen 6:1–4.)

14:1–19 The People Rebel. 1–4: The claim that it would be better to go back to Egypt was, in effect, a repudiation of God's greatest act of deliverance in the Old Testament. **5–9:** By refusing to enter the land, the people denied the power of God's presence among them. **11–12:** This triune threat brought Israel to the brink of complete destruction and offered Moses the opportunity to become a new Abraham and establish a new nation (see also Exod 32:10). **13–19:** Instead, Moses interceded, and based on God's merciful character (see Exod 34:6–7), he asked God to pardon Israel.

have treated me with contempt will ever see it. 24 But my servant Caleb has a different attitude than the others have. He has remained loyal to me, so I will bring him into the land he explored. His descendants will possess their full share of that land. 25 Now turn around, and don't go on toward the land where the Amalekites and Canaanites live. Tomorrow you must set out for the wilderness in the direction of the Red Sea.*"

The LORD Punishes the Israelites

26 Then the LORD said to Moses and Aaron, 27 "How long must I put up with this wicked community and its complaints about me? Yes, I have heard the complaints the Israelites are making against me. 28 Now tell them this: 'As surely as I live, declares the LORD, I will do to you the very things I heard you say. 29 You will all drop dead in this wilderness! Because you complained against me, every one of you who is twenty years old or older and was included in the registration will die. 30 You will not enter and occupy the land I swore to give you. The only exceptions will be Caleb son of Jephunneh and Joshua son of Nun.

31 " 'You said your children would be carried off as plunder. Well, I will bring them safely into the land, and they will enjoy what you have despised. 32 But as for you, you will drop dead in this wilderness. 33 And your children will be like shepherds, wandering in the wilderness for forty years. In this way, they will pay for your faithlessness, until the last of you lies dead in the wilderness.

34 " 'Because your men explored the land for forty days, you must wander in the wilderness for forty years—a year for each day, suffering the consequences of your sins. Then you will discover what it is like to have me for an enemy.' 35 I, the LORD, have spoken! I will certainly do these things to every member of the community who has conspired against me. They will be destroyed here in this wilderness, and here they will die!"

36 The ten men Moses had sent to explore the land—the ones who incited rebellion against the LORD with their bad report— 37 were struck dead with a plague before the LORD. 38 Of the twelve who had explored the land, only Joshua and Caleb remained alive.

39 When Moses reported the LORD's words to all the Israelites, the people were filled with grief. 40 Then they got up early the next morning and went to the top of the range of hills. "Let's go," they said. "We realize that we have sinned, but now we are ready to enter the land the LORD has promised us."

41 But Moses said, "Why are you now disobeying the LORD's orders to return to the wilderness? It won't work. 42 Do not go up into the land now. You will only be crushed by your enemies because the LORD is not with you. 43 When you face the Amalekites and Canaanites in battle, you will be slaughtered. The LORD will abandon you because you have abandoned the LORD."

44 But the people defiantly pushed ahead toward the hill country, even though neither Moses nor the Ark of the LORD's Covenant left the camp. 45 Then the Amalekites and the Canaanites who lived in those hills came down and attacked them and chased them back as far as Hormah.

Laws concerning Offerings

15 Then the LORD told Moses, 2 "Give the following instructions to the people of Israel.

"When you finally settle in the land I am giving you, 3 you will offer special gifts as a pleasing aroma to the LORD. These gifts may take the form of a burnt offering, a sacrifice to fulfill a vow, a

14:25 Hebrew *sea of reeds.*

14:20–45 God Relents, but . . . . 21: For God to swear by the divine self emphasized the unalterable nature of the judgments to follow (see also v. 28). **24:** Caleb alone is commended here, whereas both Joshua and Caleb are commended in verses 30 and 38. **25:** By commanding the people to turn toward the Red Sea, God gave them what they wanted—by all appearances they would be returning to Egypt. **26–27:** While God's mercy was shown in pardoning Israel and exempting them from complete destruction, justice would also be shown to those who so belligerently rebelled. **28–38:** The judgment is spelled out: (1) Everyone twenty years and older would wander in the wilderness until they died (except Joshua and Caleb); (2) the children would enter the land, but they would have to wander for forty years also because of their parents' rebellion; (3) the ten spies would die immediately by the plague originally intended for the entire nation (v. 12). **39–40:** The people's sudden change of heart and confession of sin were not enough to dispel the harsh future promised them. Despite Moses' warning that God had abandoned them, the people rushed to battle. Ironically, the same people who were unwilling to go into the land with God, were doggedly committed to going into the land without God.

15:1–41 Laws and Instructions. 1–16: Special offer-

voluntary offering, or an offering at any of your annual festivals, and they may be taken from your herds of cattle or your flocks of sheep and goats. 4 When you present these offerings, you must also give the LORD a grain offering of two quarts* of choice flour mixed with one quart* of olive oil. 5 For each lamb offered as a burnt offering or a special sacrifice, you must also present one quart of wine as a liquid offering.

6 "If the sacrifice is a ram, give a grain offering of four quarts* of choice flour mixed with a third of a gallon* of olive oil, 7 and give a third of a gallon of wine as a liquid offering. This will be a pleasing aroma to the LORD.

8 "When you present a young bull as a burnt offering or as a sacrifice to fulfill a vow or as a peace offering to the LORD, 9 you must also give a grain offering of six quarts* of choice flour mixed with two quarts* of olive oil, 10 and give two quarts of wine as a liquid offering. This will be a special gift, a pleasing aroma to the LORD.

11 "Each sacrifice of a bull, ram, lamb, or young goat should be prepared in this way. 12 Follow these instructions with each offering you present. 13 All of you native-born Israelites must follow these instructions when you offer a special gift as a pleasing aroma to the LORD. 14 And if any foreigners visit you or live among you and want to present a special gift as a pleasing aroma to the LORD, they must follow these same procedures. 15 Native-born Israelites and foreigners are equal before the LORD and are subject to the same decrees. This is a permanent law for you, to be observed from generation to generation. 16 The same instructions and regulations will apply both to you and to the foreigners living among you."

17 Then the LORD said to Moses, 18 "Give the following instructions to the people of Israel.

"When you arrive in the land where I am taking you, 19 and you eat the crops that grow there, you must set some aside as a sacred offering to the LORD. 20 Present a cake from the first of the flour you grind, and set it aside as a sacred offering, as you do with the first grain from the threshing floor. 21 Throughout the generations to come, you are to present a sacred offering to the LORD each year from the first of your ground flour.

22 "But suppose you unintentionally fail to carry out all these commands that the LORD has given you through Moses. 23 And suppose your descendants in the future fail to do everything the LORD has commanded through Moses. 24 If the mistake was made unintentionally, and the community was unaware of it, the whole community must present a young bull for a burnt offering as a pleasing aroma to the LORD. It must be offered along with its prescribed grain offering and liquid offering and with one male goat for a sin offering. 25 With it the priest will purify the whole community of Israel, making them right with the LORD,* and they will be forgiven. For it was an unintentional sin, and they have corrected it with their offerings to the LORD—the special gift and the sin offering. 26 The whole community of Israel will be forgiven, including the foreigners living among you, for all the people were involved in the sin.

27 "If one individual commits an unintentional sin, the guilty person must bring a one-year-old female goat for a sin offering. 28 The priest will sacrifice it to purify* the guilty person before the LORD, and that person will be forgiven. 29 These same instructions apply both to native-born Israelites and to the foreigners living among you.

30 "But those who brazenly violate the LORD's will, whether native-born Israelites or foreigners, have blasphemed the LORD, and they must be cut off from the community. 31 Since they have treated the LORD's word with contempt and deliberately disobeyed his command, they must be completely cut off and suffer the punishment for their guilt."

Penalty for Breaking the Sabbath

32 One day while the people of Israel were in the wilderness, they discovered a man gathering wood on the Sabbath day. 33 The people who found him doing this took him before Moses,

15:4a Hebrew *1/10 of an ephah* [2.2 liters]. **15:4b** Hebrew *1/4 of a hin* [1 liter]; also in 15:5. **15:6a** Hebrew *2/10 of an ephah* [4.4 liters]. **15:6b** Hebrew *1/3 of a hin* [1.3 liters]; also in 15:7. **15:9a** Hebrew *3/10 of an ephah* [6.6 liters]. **15:9b** Hebrew *1/2 of a hin* [2 liters]; also in 15:10. **15:25** Or *will make atonement for the whole community of Israel.* **15:28** Or *to make atonement for.*

ings were to be accompanied by appropriate grain offerings and wine libations. The recipes for these supplemental offerings required precise amounts just as modern recipes do. **17–21:** Once the Israelites settled in the land and ate its food (lit., "bread"), they were required to bring a firstfruits offering from their baked goods in the form of a cake made of flour. **22–29:** Unintentional violations of God's laws, whether by the community or an individual, could be addressed through sacrifices (see also Lev 4—5). **30–31:** Intentional violations of God's law were viewed as blasphemy and offenders were to be separated from the community. **32–36:** This brief narrative serves as an example of a brazen violation of one

Aaron, and the rest of the community. 34They held him in custody because they did not know what to do with him. 35Then the LORD said to Moses, "The man must be put to death! The whole community must stone him outside the camp." 36So the whole community took the man outside the camp and stoned him to death, just as the LORD had commanded Moses.

Tassels on Clothing

37Then the LORD said to Moses, 38"Give the following instructions to the people of Israel: Throughout the generations to come you must make tassels for the hems of your clothing and attach them with a blue cord. 39When you see the tassels, you will remember and obey all the commands of the LORD instead of following your own desires and defiling yourselves, as you are prone to do. 40The tassels will help you remember that you must obey all my commands and be holy to your God. 41I am the LORD your God who brought you out of the land of Egypt that I might be your God. I am the LORD your God!"

Korah's Rebellion

16 One day Korah son of Izhar, a descendant of Kohath son of Levi, conspired with Dathan and Abiram, the sons of Eliab, and On son of Peleth, from the tribe of Reuben. 2They incited a rebellion against Moses, along with 250 other leaders of the community, all prominent members of the assembly. 3They united against Moses and Aaron and said, "You have gone too far! The whole community of Israel has been set apart by the LORD, and he is with all of us. What right do you have to act as though you are greater than the rest of the LORD's people?"

4When Moses heard what they were saying, he fell face down on the ground. 5Then he said to Korah and his followers, "Tomorrow morning the LORD will show us who belongs to him* and who is holy. The LORD will allow only those whom he selects to enter his own presence. 6Korah, you and all your followers must prepare your incense burners. 7Light fires in them tomorrow, and burn incense before the LORD. Then we will see whom the LORD chooses as his holy one. You Levites are the ones who have gone too far!"

8Then Moses spoke again to Korah: "Now listen, you Levites! 9Does it seem insignificant to you that the God of Israel has chosen you from among all the community of Israel to be near him so you can serve in the LORD's Tabernacle and stand before the people to minister to them? 10Korah, he has already given this special ministry to you and your fellow Levites. Are you now demanding the priesthood as well? 11The LORD is the one you and your followers are really revolting against! For who is Aaron that you are complaining about him?"

12Then Moses summoned Dathan and Abiram, the sons of Eliab, but they replied, "We refuse to come before you! 13Isn't it enough that you brought us out of Egypt, a land flowing with milk and honey, to kill us here in this wilderness, and that you now treat us like your subjects? 14What's more, you haven't brought us into another land flowing with milk and honey. You haven't given us a new homeland with fields and vineyards. Are you trying to fool these men?* We will not come."

15Then Moses became very angry and said to the LORD, "Do not accept their grain offerings! I have not taken so much as a donkey from them, and I have never hurt a single one of them."

16:5 Greek version reads *God has visited and knows those who are his.* Compare 2 Tim 2:19. **16:14** Hebrew *Are you trying to put out the eyes of these men?*

of God's laws (Exod 20:8–11; cf. 35:3). The primary question was not "Did this man sin by gathering wood?" but rather "What punishment is appropriate for him?" **35:** Stoning was the preferred method of execution, perhaps because no single person had to serve as executioner—the community as a whole carried out the punishment. **37–41:** Attaching tassels to garments provided a visible, physical reminder to the wearer to be obedient.

16:1–50 Korah's Rebellion. Two separate rebellions are intertwined in this chapter. The first involves Korah, a Levite, who asserted the right of the Levites to perform the same duties as the Aaronides (see vv. 9–10). The second involves Dathan and Abiram, Reubenites, who challenged Moses' leadership (see vv. 12–14). **1:** Although On is listed as one of the complainers, he appears nowhere else in the story. **2:** The tribal affiliation of the 250 is unclear here, though later they are identified as Levites (v. 8) **3:** All Israel was, indeed, set apart as holy (Exod 19:6), and God's presence was accessible in the Tabernacle. But different degrees of holiness and levels of access to God's presence had been clearly established, especially for the Levites (Num 3—4). **4–7:** Burning incense was a privilege accorded only to the Aaronide priests (Exod 30:7–10). **8–11:** The Levites already had special status among Israel's tribes (Num 3—4; 8:5–26) highlighting the contemptuous nature of Korah's unorthodox demands. **15:** Asking God to reject

16 And Moses said to Korah, "You and all your
followers must come here tomorrow and present
yourselves before the LORD. Aaron will also be
here. 17 You and each of your 250 followers must
prepare an incense burner and put incense on
it, so you can all present them before the LORD.
Aaron will also bring his incense burner."
18 So each of these men prepared an incense
burner, lit the fire, and placed incense on it. Then
they all stood at the entrance of the Tabernacle*
with Moses and Aaron. 19 Meanwhile, Korah had
stirred up the entire community against Moses
and Aaron, and they all gathered at the Tabernacle entrance. Then the glorious presence of the
LORD appeared to the whole community, 20 and
the LORD said to Moses and Aaron, 21 "Get away
from all these people so that I may instantly destroy them!"
22 But Moses and Aaron fell face down on the
ground. "O God," they pleaded, "you are the
God who gives breath to all creatures. Must you
be angry with all the people when only one man
sins?"
23 And the LORD said to Moses, 24 "Then tell all
the people to get away from the tents of Korah,
Dathan, and Abiram."
25 So Moses got up and rushed over to the
tents of Dathan and Abiram, followed by the
elders of Israel. 26 "Quick!" he told the people.
"Get away from the tents of these wicked men,
and don't touch anything that belongs to them.
If you do, you will be destroyed for their sins."
27 So all the people stood back from the tents of
Korah, Dathan, and Abiram. Then Dathan and
Abiram came out and stood at the entrances of
their tents, together with their wives and children and little ones.
28 And Moses said, "This is how you will know
that the LORD has sent me to do all these things
that I have done—for I have not done them on
my own. 29 If these men die a natural death, or
if nothing unusual happens, then the LORD has
not sent me. 30 But if the LORD does something
entirely new and the ground opens its mouth
and swallows them and all their belongings, and
they go down alive into the grave,* then you will
know that these men have shown contempt for
the LORD."
31 He had hardly finished speaking the words
when the ground suddenly split open beneath
them. 32 The earth opened its mouth and swallowed the men, along with their households and
all their followers who were standing with them,
and everything they owned. 33 So they went
down alive into the grave, along with all their
belongings. The earth closed over them, and they
all vanished from among the people of Israel.
34 All the people around them fled when they
heard their screams. "The earth will swallow us,
too!" they cried. 35 Then fire blazed forth from
the LORD and burned up the 250 men who were
offering incense.
36 *And the LORD said to Moses, 37 "Tell Eleazar
son of Aaron the priest to pull all the incense
burners from the fire, for they are holy. Also
tell him to scatter the burning coals. 38 Take the
incense burners of these men who have sinned
at the cost of their lives, and hammer the metal
into a thin sheet to overlay the altar. Since these
burners were used in the LORD's presence, they
have become holy. Let them serve as a warning
to the people of Israel."
39 So Eleazar the priest collected the 250 bronze
incense burners that had been used by the men
who died in the fire, and he hammered them
into a thin sheet to overlay the altar. 40 This
would warn the Israelites that no unauthorized
person—no one who was not a descendant of
Aaron—should ever enter the LORD's presence
to burn incense. If anyone did, the same thing
would happen to him as happened to Korah and
his followers. So the LORD's instructions to Moses were carried out.
41 But the very next morning the whole community of Israel began muttering again against
Moses and Aaron, saying, "You have killed the
LORD's people!" 42 As the community gathered
to protest against Moses and Aaron, they turned
toward the Tabernacle and saw that the cloud had
covered it, and the glorious presence of the LORD
appeared.
43 Moses and Aaron came and stood in front
of the Tabernacle, 44 and the LORD said to Moses,
45 "Get away from all these people so that I can
instantly destroy them!" But Moses and Aaron
fell face down on the ground.

16:18 Hebrew *the Tent of Meeting;* also in 16:19, 42, 43, 50. **16:30** Hebrew *into Sheol;* also in 16:33. **16:36** Verses 16:36–50 are numbered 17:1-15 in Hebrew text.

another person's sacrifices is virtually unheard of in the Old Testament, but when God does reject sacrifices it is in response to extreme disobedience (cf. Amos 5:21–24). **23–35:** Moses and Aaron's right to leadership is established swiftly and dramatically by the unnatural deaths of Korah (and, presumably, Dathan and Abiram). **35:** A fire from God consumed the 250 Levites who were burning incense in a dramatic echo of Nadab and Abihu's fate (Lev 10:1–5). **41:** The community ignored God's very visible repudiation of

46 And Moses said to Aaron, "Quick, take an
incense burner and place burning coals on it
from the altar. Lay incense on it, and carry it
out among the people to purify them and make
them right with the LORD.* The LORD's anger is
blazing against them—the plague has already
begun."
47 Aaron did as Moses told him and ran out
among the people. The plague had already begun to strike down the people, but Aaron burned
the incense and purified* the people. 48 He stood
between the dead and the living, and the plague
stopped. 49 But 14,700 people died in that plague,
in addition to those who had died in the affair
involving Korah. 50 Then because the plague had
stopped, Aaron returned to Moses at the entrance
of the Tabernacle.

The Budding of Aaron's Staff

17 1 *Then the LORD said to Moses, 2 "Tell
the people of Israel to bring you twelve
wooden staffs, one from each leader of
Israel's ancestral tribes, and inscribe each leader's
name on his staff. 3 Inscribe Aaron's name on the
staff of the tribe of Levi, for there must be one
staff for the leader of each ancestral tribe. 4 Place
these staffs in the Tabernacle in front of the Ark
containing the tablets of the Covenant,* where
I meet with you. 5 Buds will sprout on the staff
belonging to the man I choose. Then I will finally
put an end to the people's murmuring and complaining against you."
6 So Moses gave the instructions to the people
of Israel, and each of the twelve tribal leaders,
including Aaron, brought Moses a staff. 7 Moses
placed the staffs in the LORD's presence in the
Tabernacle of the Covenant.* 8 When he went
into the Tabernacle of the Covenant the next
day, he found that Aaron's staff, representing the
tribe of Levi, had sprouted, budded, blossomed,
and produced ripe almonds!
9 When Moses brought all the staffs out from
the LORD's presence, he showed them to the
people. Each man claimed his own staff. 10 And
the LORD said to Moses: "Place Aaron's staff permanently before the Ark of the Covenant* to
serve as a warning to rebels. This should put an
end to their complaints against me and prevent
any further deaths." 11 So Moses did as the LORD
commanded him.
12 Then the people of Israel said to Moses,
"Look, we are doomed! We are dead! We are ruined! 13 Everyone who even comes close to the
Tabernacle of the LORD dies. Are we all doomed
to die?"

Duties of Priests and Levites

18 Then the LORD said to Aaron: "You,
your sons, and your relatives from
the tribe of Levi will be held responsible for any offenses related to the sanctuary. But
you and your sons alone will be held responsible
for violations connected with the priesthood.
2 "Bring your relatives of the tribe of Levi—
your ancestral tribe—to assist you and your
sons as you perform the sacred duties in front
of the Tabernacle of the Covenant.* 3 But as the
Levites go about all their assigned duties at the
Tabernacle, they must be careful not to go near
any of the sacred objects or the altar. If they do,
both you and they will die. 4 The Levites must
join you in fulfilling their responsibilities for the
care and maintenance of the Tabernacle,* but no
unauthorized person may assist you.
5 "You yourselves must perform the sacred
duties inside the sanctuary and at the altar. If you
follow these instructions, the LORD's anger will

16:46 Or *to make atonement for them.* **16:47** Or *and made atonement for.* **17:1** Verses 17:1-13 are numbered 17:16-28 in Hebrew text. **17:4** Hebrew *in the Tent of Meeting before the Testimony.* The Hebrew word for "testimony" refers to the terms of the LORD's covenant with Israel as written on stone tablets, which were kept in the Ark, and also to the covenant itself. **17:7** Or *Tabernacle of the Testimony;* also in 17:8. **17:10** Hebrew *before the Testimony;* see note on 17:4. **18:2** Or *Tabernacle of the Testimony.* **18:4** Hebrew *the Tent of Meeting;* also in 18:6, 21, 22, 23, 31.

the Korahites and Reubenites and launched an attack against Moses and Aaron, suggesting that the original rebellion had been supported by all the tribes. **46:** The job of making atonement for the people in order to avoid a plague was originally given to the Levites (8:19); in their failure Aaron replaces them.

17:1–13 The Budding of Aaron's Staff. 1: The Hebrew word for "staff" is also the word translated as "tribe," a wordplay that emphasizes the leadership theme of the chapter (staffs could represent an official office; cf. Gen 49:10; Num 21:18). **7:** *Tabernacle of the Covenant* refers to the tablets of the Sinaitic covenant that were housed in the Ark (Exod 25:16). **8:** Aaron's staff *sprouted, budded, blossomed, and produced ripe almonds*, completing an entire growth cycle overnight. **12:** The cumulative effect the events in chapters 16—17 have on the people is absolute, unrestrained terror.

18:1–7 Duties of Priests and Levites. 2–7: The repeated notice not to go near the sanctuary or you will die (vv. 3, 7, 22) indicates the major theme of this passage: Only authorized persons can approach

never again blaze against the people of Israel. 6 I myself have chosen your fellow Levites from among the Israelites to be your special assistants. They are a gift to you, dedicated to the LORD for service in the Tabernacle. 7 But you and your sons, the priests, must personally handle all the priestly rituals associated with the altar and with everything behind the inner curtain. I am giving you the priesthood as your special privilege of service. Any unauthorized person who comes too near the sanctuary will be put to death."

Support for the Priests and Levites

8 The LORD gave these further instructions to Aaron: "I myself have put you in charge of all the holy offerings that are brought to me by the people of Israel. I have given all these consecrated offerings to you and your sons as your permanent share. 9 You are allotted the portion of the most holy offerings that is not burned on the fire. This portion of all the most holy offerings—including the grain offerings, sin offerings, and guilt offerings—will be most holy, and it belongs to you and your sons. 10 You must eat it as a most holy offering. All the males may eat of it, and you must treat it as most holy.

11 "All the sacred offerings and special offerings presented to me when the Israelites lift them up before the altar also belong to you. I have given them to you and to your sons and daughters as your permanent share. Any member of your family who is ceremonially clean may eat of these offerings.

12 "I also give you the harvest gifts brought by the people as offerings to the LORD—the best of the olive oil, new wine, and grain. 13 All the first crops of their land that the people present to the LORD belong to you. Any member of your family who is ceremonially clean may eat this food.

14 "Everything in Israel that is specially set apart for the LORD* also belongs to you.

15 "The firstborn of every mother, whether human or animal, that is offered to the LORD will be yours. But you must always redeem your firstborn sons and the firstborn of ceremonially unclean animals. 16 Redeem them when they are one month old. The redemption price is five pieces of silver* (as measured by the weight of the sanctuary shekel, which equals twenty gerahs).

17 "However, you may not redeem the firstborn of cattle, sheep, or goats. They are holy and have been set apart for the LORD. Sprinkle their blood on the altar, and burn their fat as a special gift, a pleasing aroma to the LORD. 18 The meat of these animals will be yours, just like the breast and right thigh that are presented by lifting them up as a special offering before the altar. 19 Yes, I am giving you all these holy offerings that the people of Israel bring to the LORD. They are for you and your sons and daughters, to be eaten as your permanent share. This is an eternal and unbreakable covenant* between the LORD and you, and it also applies to your descendants."

20 And the LORD said to Aaron, "You priests will receive no allotment of land or share of property among the people of Israel. I am your share and your allotment. 21 As for the tribe of Levi, your relatives, I will compensate them for their service in the Tabernacle. Instead of an allotment of land, I will give them the tithes from the entire land of Israel.

22 "From now on, no Israelites except priests or Levites may approach the Tabernacle. If they come too near, they will be judged guilty and will die. 23 Only the Levites may serve at the Tabernacle, and they will be held responsible for any offenses against it. This is a permanent law for you, to be observed from generation to generation. The Levites will receive no allotment of land among the Israelites, 24 because I have given them the Israelites' tithes, which have been presented as sacred offerings to the LORD. This will be the Levites' share. That is why I said they would receive no allotment of land among the Israelites."

25 The LORD also told Moses, 26 "Give these instructions to the Levites: When you receive from the people of Israel the tithes I have assigned as your allotment, give a tenth of the tithes you

18:14 The Hebrew term used here refers to the complete consecration of things or people to the LORD, either by destroying them or by giving them as an offering.
18:16 Hebrew 5 *shekels* [2 ounces or 57 grams] *of silver.*
18:19 Hebrew *a covenant of salt.*

---

the sanctuary, and only authorized Aaronide priests may approach the holiest parts of the sanctuary and offer sacrifices.

18:8–32 Gifts for the Priests and Levites. With the exception of the whole burnt offering, the Aaronide priests received portions of all the sacrifices brought by Israel (cf. Lev 7:28–38). **10–13:** While apparently only males could eat the portions from grain, purification (NLT, *sin*), and reparation (NLT, *guilt*) offerings, all Aaronides, including women (cf. Lev 22:12–13), could partake of the elevation (wave) offerings and firstfruits offerings, as long as they were clean. **24:** Because the Levites did not receive a portion of land, they were given tithes presented by the people of Israel. A tithe represented one-tenth of the Israelites'

receive—a tithe of the tithe—to the LORD as a sacred offering. 27 The LORD will consider this offering to be your harvest offering, as though it were the first grain from your own threshing floor or wine from your own winepress. 28 You must present one-tenth of the tithe received from the Israelites as a sacred offering to the LORD. This is the LORD's sacred portion, and you must present it to Aaron the priest. 29 Be sure to give to the LORD the best portions of the gifts given to you.

30 "Also, give these instructions to the Levites: When you present the best part as your offering, it will be considered as though it came from your own threshing floor or winepress. 31 You Levites and your families may eat this food anywhere you wish, for it is your compensation for serving in the Tabernacle. 32 You will not be considered guilty for accepting the LORD's tithes if you give the best portion to the priests. But be careful not to treat the holy gifts of the people of Israel as though they were common. If you do, you will die."

The Water of Purification

19 The LORD said to Moses and Aaron, 2 "Here is another legal requirement commanded by the LORD: Tell the people of Israel to bring you a red heifer, a perfect animal that has no defects and has never been yoked to a plow. 3 Give it to Eleazar the priest, and it will be taken outside the camp and slaughtered in his presence. 4 Eleazar will take some of its blood on his finger and sprinkle it seven times toward the front of the Tabernacle.* 5 As Eleazar watches, the heifer must be burned—its hide, meat, blood, and dung. 6 Eleazar the priest must then take a stick of cedar,* a hyssop branch, and some scarlet yarn and throw them into the fire where the heifer is burning.

7 "Then the priest must wash his clothes and bathe himself in water. Afterward he may return to the camp, though he will remain ceremonially unclean until evening. 8 The man who burns the animal must also wash his clothes and bathe himself in water, and he, too, will remain unclean until evening. 9 Then someone who is ceremonially clean will gather up the ashes of the heifer and deposit them in a purified place outside the camp. They will be kept there for the community of Israel to use in the water for the purification ceremony. This ceremony is performed for the removal of sin. 10 The man who gathers up the ashes of the heifer must also wash his clothes, and he will remain ceremonially unclean until evening. This is a permanent law for the people of Israel and any foreigners who live among them.

11 "All those who touch a dead human body will be ceremonially unclean for seven days. 12 They must purify themselves on the third and seventh days with the water of purification; then they will be purified. But if they do not do this on the third and seventh days, they will continue to be unclean even after the seventh day. 13 All those who touch a dead body and do not purify themselves in the proper way defile the LORD's Tabernacle, and they will be cut off from the community of Israel. Since the water of purification was not sprinkled on them, their defilement continues.

14 "This is the ritual law that applies when someone dies inside a tent: All those who enter that tent and those who were inside when the death occurred will be ceremonially unclean for seven days. 15 Any open container in the tent that was not covered with a lid is also defiled. 16 And if someone in an open field touches the corpse of someone who was killed with a sword or who died a natural death, or if someone touches a human bone or a grave, that person will be defiled for seven days.

17 "To remove the defilement, put some of the ashes from the burnt purification offering in a jar, and pour fresh water over them. 18 Then someone who is ceremonially clean must take a hyssop branch and dip it into the water. That person must sprinkle the water on the tent, on all the furnishings in the tent, and on the people who were in the tent; also on the person who

19:4 Hebrew *the Tent of Meeting.* **19:6** Or *juniper.*

crops, flocks, etc. **25–32:** The Levites also were expected to offer a tithe to the LORD—a tithe of the tithe given to them by the Israelites.

19:1–22 The Water of Purification. 2: The word *heifer* (a young cow that has not calved) is inferred from the fact that the animal had not been yoked and was probably young. Its red color may be symbolic of blood. **3:** All of the elements for this ritual are prepared outside the camp because death's uncleanness was highly contagious. Death defilement was taken very seriously and required strict observance of the cleansing rituals (vv. 17–22). **6:** Cedar, hyssop, and scarlet yarn are also used in the purification ceremony for those with skin ailments (Lev 14:4, 6) but their exact function in both ceremonies remains uncertain. **11–22:** Cleansing the defilement of death. **17–22:** The seven-day cleansing ritual using the water of

touched a human bone, or touched someone who
was killed or who died naturally, or touched a
grave. [19]On the third and seventh days the person who is ceremonially clean must sprinkle the
water on those who are defiled. Then on the seventh day the people being cleansed must wash
their clothes and bathe themselves, and that evening they will be cleansed of their defilement.
[20]"But those who become defiled and do not
purify themselves will be cut off from the community, for they have defiled the sanctuary of
the LORD. Since the water of purification has
not been sprinkled on them, they remain defiled.
[21]This is a permanent law for the people. Those
who sprinkle the water of purification must afterward wash their clothes, and anyone who
then touches the water used for purification will
remain defiled until evening. [22]Anything and
anyone that a defiled person touches will be ceremonially unclean until evening."

Moses Strikes the Rock

20 In the first month of the year,* the
whole community of Israel arrived in
the wilderness of Zin and camped at
Kadesh. While they were there, Miriam died and
was buried.
[2]There was no water for the people to drink
at that place, so they rebelled against Moses and
Aaron. [3]The people blamed Moses and said, "If
only we had died in the LORD's presence with
our brothers! [4]Why have you brought the congregation of the LORD's people into this wilderness to die, along with all our livestock? [5]Why
did you make us leave Egypt and bring us here
to this terrible place? This land has no grain, no
figs, no grapes, no pomegranates, and no water
to drink!"
[6]Moses and Aaron turned away from the
people and went to the entrance of the Tabernacle,* where they fell face down on the ground.
Then the glorious presence of the LORD appeared
to them, [7]and the LORD said to Moses, [8]"You and
Aaron must take the staff and assemble the entire community. As the people watch, speak to
the rock over there, and it will pour out its water. You will provide enough water from the rock
to satisfy the whole community and their livestock."
[9]So Moses did as he was told. He took the
staff from the place where it was kept before the
LORD. [10]Then he and Aaron summoned the people to come and gather at the rock. "Listen, you
rebels!" he shouted. "Must we bring you water
from this rock?" [11]Then Moses raised his hand
and struck the rock twice with the staff, and water gushed out. So the entire community and
their livestock drank their fill.
[12]But the LORD said to Moses and Aaron,
"Because you did not trust me enough to demonstrate my holiness to the people of Israel,
you will not lead them into the land I am giving them!" [13]This place was known as the waters
of Meribah (which means "arguing") because
there the people of Israel argued with the LORD,
and there he demonstrated his holiness among
them.

Edom Refuses Israel Passage

[14]While Moses was at Kadesh, he sent ambassadors to the king of Edom with this message:

"This is what your relatives, the people of
Israel, say: You know all the hardships we
have been through. [15]Our ancestors went
down to Egypt, and we lived there a long
time, and we and our ancestors were brutally
mistreated by the Egyptians. [16]But when
we cried out to the LORD, he heard us and
sent an angel who brought us out of Egypt.

20:1 The first month of the ancient Hebrew lunar calendar usually occurs within the months of March and April. The number of years since leaving Egypt is not specified. **20:6** Hebrew *the Tent of Meeting.*

purification was the only means by which a person could remove the ritual contamination of death. Failure to observe these laws resulted in being cut off from the community (v. 13).

20:1–13 Moses Strikes the Rock. 1: Miriam's death at Kadesh is reported briefly and without detail. While this contrasts sharply with the more elaborate death report of Aaron which concludes the chapter, her appearance alongside her brothers highlights her role as one of Israel's leaders (cf. Mic 6:4). **9–11:** Two elements of Moses and Aaron's actions differed from God's original instructions: (1) calling the people *rebels* and asking, *"Must we bring you water from this rock?"* and (2) striking the rock instead of speaking to it (cf. Exod 17:1–7). **12:** The LORD rebuked Moses and Aaron for failing to trust God and for failing to demonstrate God's holiness to the people. The consequence, that they would not lead the people into the promised land, parallels the people's punishment for failing to trust God at Kadesh-barnea (Num 14:23, 30). **13:** See also Exodus 17:7. It seems a harsh punishment but Moses' action made it appear that God was angrier than he was. Misrepresenting God is a

Now we are camped at Kadesh, a town on
the border of your land. 17 Please let us travel
through your land. We will be careful not
to go through your fields and vineyards. We
won't even drink water from your wells. We
will stay on the king's road and never leave it
until we have passed through your territory."

18 But the king of Edom said, "Stay out of my
land, or I will meet you with an army!"

19 The Israelites answered, "We will stay on
the main road. If our livestock drink your water,
we will pay for it. Just let us pass through your
country. That's all we ask."

20 But the king of Edom replied, "Stay out!
You may not pass through our land." With that
he mobilized his army and marched out against
them with an imposing force. 21 Because Edom
refused to allow Israel to pass through their
country, Israel was forced to turn around.

The Death of Aaron

22 The whole community of Israel left Kadesh and
arrived at Mount Hor. 23 There, on the border of
the land of Edom, the LORD said to Moses and
Aaron, 24 "The time has come for Aaron to join
his ancestors in death. He will not enter the land
I am giving the people of Israel, because the two
of you rebelled against my instructions concerning the water at Meribah. 25 Now take Aaron and
his son Eleazar up Mount Hor. 26 There you will
remove Aaron's priestly garments and put them
on Eleazar, his son. Aaron will die there and join
his ancestors."

27 So Moses did as the LORD commanded. The
three of them went up Mount Hor together as
the whole community watched. 28 At the summit, Moses removed the priestly garments from
Aaron and put them on Eleazar, Aaron's son.
Then Aaron died there on top of the mountain,
and Moses and Eleazar went back down. 29 When
the people realized that Aaron had died, all Israel
mourned for him thirty days.

Victory over the Canaanites

21 The Canaanite king of Arad, who
lived in the Negev, heard that the
Israelites were approaching on the
road through Atharim. So he attacked the Israelites and took some of them as prisoners.
2 Then the people of Israel made this vow to the
LORD: "If you will hand these people over to us,
we will completely destroy* all their towns."
3 The LORD heard the Israelites' request and
gave them victory over the Canaanites. The
Israelites completely destroyed them and their
towns, and the place has been called Hormah*
ever since.

The Bronze Snake

4 Then the people of Israel set out from Mount
Hor, taking the road to the Red Sea* to go around
the land of Edom. But the people grew impatient
with the long journey, 5 and they began to speak
against God and Moses. "Why have you brought
us out of Egypt to die here in the wilderness?"
they complained. "There is nothing to eat here
and nothing to drink. And we hate this horrible
manna!"

6 So the LORD sent poisonous snakes among
the people, and many were bitten and died. 7 Then
the people came to Moses and cried out, "We
have sinned by speaking against the LORD and
against you. Pray that the LORD will take away
the snakes." So Moses prayed for the people.

8 Then the LORD told him, "Make a replica
of a poisonous snake and attach it to a pole. All
who are bitten will live if they simply look at
it!" 9 So Moses made a snake out of bronze and
attached it to a pole. Then anyone who was bitten by a snake could look at the bronze snake
and be healed!

21:2 The Hebrew term used here refers to the complete consecration of things or people to the LORD, either by destroying them or by giving them as an offering; also in 21:3. **21:3** *Hormah* means "destruction." **21:4** Hebrew *sea of reeds.*

---

very serious offense for a leader.

20:14–29 Edom's Refusal. Death of Aaron. 14: The Edomites were the descendants of Esau, Jacob's brother (Gen 36). **16:** The angel of the LORD, mentioned throughout the Torah (Gen 16:7, 9, 10, 11; 21:17; 22:11, 15; 31:11; Exod 3:2; 14:19; 23:20; 33:2, etc.), is often used interchangeably with God (cf. Gen 18:1 with 18:10) and acted as a visible symbol of God's presence, much like the cloud and the Ark. **22–29:** Aaron's death on Mount Hor parallels Moses' death on Mount Nebo (see Deut 32:48–52; 34:1–8).

21:1–36:13 A New Generation

21:1–35 Travel Experiences. The Bronze Snake. 1–3: This narrative offers an ironic reversal of Israel's first battle at Hormah forty years earlier where they experienced humiliating defeat (Num 14:45). **6:** The word used here for *snake* has connotations of burning, perhaps alluding to the burning sensation caused by the bites. **8–9:** Exactly why and how looking upon the bronze snake caused the afflicted to be healed is not explained. The bronze serpent later became an object of idolatry and was removed from the temple

Israel's Journey to Moab
10 The Israelites traveled next to Oboth and
camped there. 11 Then they went on to Iye-abarim, in the wilderness on the eastern border of
Moab. 12 From there they traveled to the valley of
Zered Brook and set up camp. 13 Then they moved
out and camped on the far side of the Arnon River, in the wilderness adjacent to the territory of
the Amorites. The Arnon is the boundary line
between the Moabites and the Amorites. 14 For
this reason *The Book of the Wars of the Lord*
speaks of "the town of Waheb in the area of Su-
phah, and the ravines of the Arnon River, 15 and
the ravines that extend as far as the settlement of
Ar on the border of Moab."
16 From there the Israelites traveled to Beer,*
which is the well where the Lord said to Moses,
"Assemble the people, and I will give them water." 17 There the Israelites sang this song:

"Spring up, O well!
 Yes, sing its praises!
18 Sing of this well,
 which princes dug,
which great leaders hollowed out
 with their scepters and staffs."

Then the Israelites left the wilderness and
proceeded on through Mattanah, 19 Nahaliel, and
Bamoth. 20 After that they went to the valley in
Moab where Pisgah Peak overlooks the wasteland.*

Victory over Sihon and Og
21 The Israelites sent ambassadors to King Sihon
of the Amorites with this message:

22 "Let us travel through your land. We will
be careful not to go through your fields and
vineyards. We won't even drink water from
your wells. We will stay on the king's road
until we have passed through your territory."

23 But King Sihon refused to let them cross his
territory. Instead, he mobilized his entire army
and attacked Israel in the wilderness, engaging them in battle at Jahaz. 24 But the Israelites
slaughtered them with their swords and occupied
their land from the Arnon River to the Jabbok
River. They went only as far as the Ammonite
border because the boundary of the Ammonites
was fortified.*
25 So Israel captured all the towns of the
Amorites and settled in them, including the city
of Heshbon and its surrounding villages. 26 Heshbon had been the capital of King Sihon of the
Amorites. He had defeated a former Moabite
king and seized all his land as far as the Arnon
River. 27 Therefore, the ancient poets wrote this
about him:

"Come to Heshbon and let it be rebuilt!
 Let the city of Sihon be restored.
28 A fire flamed forth from Heshbon,
 a blaze from the city of Sihon.
It burned the city of Ar in Moab;
 it destroyed the rulers of the Arnon
  heights.
29 What sorrow awaits you, O people of Moab!
 You are finished, O worshipers of
  Chemosh!
Chemosh has left his sons as refugees,
 his daughters as captives of Sihon, the
  Amorite king.
30 We have utterly destroyed them,
 from Heshbon to Dibon.
We have completely wiped them out
 as far away as Nophah and Medeba.*"

31 So the people of Israel occupied the territory
of the Amorites. 32 After Moses sent men to explore the Jazer area, they captured all the towns
in the region and drove out the Amorites who
lived there. 33 Then they turned and marched up
the road to Bashan, but King Og of Bashan and
all his people attacked them at Edrei. 34 The Lord
said to Moses, "Do not be afraid of him, for I have
handed him over to you, along with all his people
and his land. Do the same to him as you did to
King Sihon of the Amorites, who ruled in Heshbon." 35 And Israel killed King Og, his sons, and
all his subjects; not a single survivor remained.
Then Israel occupied their land.

21:16 *Beer* means "well." **21:20** Or *overlooks Jeshimon.* **21:24** Or *because the terrain of the Ammonite frontier was rugged;* Hebrew reads *because the boundary of the Ammonites was strong.* **21:30** Or *until fire spread to Medeba.* The meaning of the Hebrew is uncertain.

(2 Kgs 18:4). The Gospel writer John alludes to this episode in describing Christ's death on the cross (John 3:14–15). **10–20:** The narrator's purpose in giving the itinerary is to move Israel quickly from Mount Hor to the plains of Moab. Three quotations of ancient sources serve to highlight various locations on Israel's journey (vv. 14, 17–18, and 26–30). **21–35:** The victories over Sihon and Og mark Israel's first foray into land they will occupy. That these events are memorialized in other Old Testament literature

Balak Sends for Balaam

22 Then the people of Israel traveled to
the plains of Moab and camped east
of the Jordan River, across from Jer-
icho. [2] Balak son of Zippor, the Moabite king, had
seen everything the Israelites did to the Amorites. [3] And when the people of Moab saw how
many Israelites there were, they were terrified.
[4] The king of Moab said to the elders of Midian,
"This mob will devour everything in sight, like
an ox devours grass in the field!"

So Balak, king of Moab, [5] sent messengers to
call Balaam son of Beor, who was living in his native land of Pethor* near the Euphrates River.*
His message said:

"Look, a vast horde of people has arrived
from Egypt. They cover the face of the earth
and are threatening me. [6] Please come and
curse these people for me because they are
too powerful for me. Then perhaps I will be
able to conquer them and drive them from
the land. I know that blessings fall on any
people you bless, and curses fall on people
you curse."

[7] Balak's messengers, who were elders of Moab
and Midian, set out with money to pay Balaam to
place a curse upon Israel.* They went to Balaam
and delivered Balak's message to him. [8] "Stay
here overnight," Balaam said. "In the morning
I will tell you whatever the LORD directs me to
say." So the officials from Moab stayed there
with Balaam.

[9] That night God came to Balaam and asked
him, "Who are these men visiting you?"

[10] Balaam said to God, "Balak son of Zippor,
king of Moab, has sent me this message: [11] 'Look,
a vast horde of people has arrived from Egypt,
and they cover the face of the earth. Come and
curse these people for me. Then perhaps I will be
able to stand up to them and drive them from
the land.'"

[12] But God told Balaam, "Do not go with them.
You are not to curse these people, for they have
been blessed!"

[13] The next morning Balaam got up and told
Balak's officials, "Go on home! The LORD will
not let me go with you."

[14] So the Moabite officials returned to King
Balak and reported, "Balaam refused to come
with us." [15] Then Balak tried again. This time he
sent a larger number of even more distinguished
officials than those he had sent the first time.
[16] They went to Balaam and delivered this message to him:

"This is what Balak son of Zippor says: Please
don't let anything stop you from coming to
help me. [17] I will pay you very well and do
whatever you tell me. Just come and curse
these people for me!"

[18] But Balaam responded to Balak's messengers, "Even if Balak were to give me his palace
filled with silver and gold, I would be powerless
to do anything against the will of the LORD my
God. [19] But stay here one more night, and I will
see if the LORD has anything else to say to me."

[20] That night God came to Balaam and told him,
"Since these men have come for you, get up and
go with them. But do only what I tell you to do."

Balaam and His Donkey

[21] So the next morning Balaam got up, saddled his
donkey, and started off with the Moabite officials.
[22] But God was angry that Balaam was going, so
he sent the angel of the LORD to stand in the road

22:5a Or *who was at Pethor in the land of the Amavites.* **22:5b** Hebrew *the river.* **22:7** Hebrew *set out with the money of divination in their hand.*

---

indicates their significance (Deut 2:24–37; 3:1–11; Josh 2:10; Pss 135:11; 136:19–22).

22:1—24:25 The Moabites and Balaam. The plains of Moab are the setting for the remainder of Numbers and all of Deuteronomy. **22:2:** Like Pharaoh in Egypt (Exod 1:9–10), Balak, king of Moab, feared Israel's huge numbers (see also v. 5). **6:** The irreversible power and prophetic nature of blessings and curses was taken for granted in the ancient Near East, and sometimes (Gen 27:34–36; 49:1–28) although not always (2 Sam 16:5–14) in the biblical texts. **7:** Some prophets were paid for their work (1 Sam 9:7–8; 1 Kgs 14:3; 2 Kgs 8:8–9), and others would prophesy whatever a person wanted to hear, for the right price (Jer 5:31; 6:13; 8:10; 14:14; 23:16; Ezek 7:6; 13:9; cf. Amos 7:12). Balak offered to pay Balaam generously, believing that the prophet's curse would render Israel powerless before him. **8–14:** Balaam is portrayed here as a prophet who can only repeat the words God gives him; however, later in Numbers he is condemned for leading Israel into idolatry (Num 31:16). It is clear that it is God's wishes rather than any pronounced curse that determine what can happen. **22:** The LORD's anger contradicts the command given in v. 20. This may be explained by the composite na-

to block his way. As Balaam and two servants
were riding along, 23 Balaam's donkey saw the angel of the LORD standing in the road with a drawn
sword in his hand. The donkey bolted off the road
into a field, but Balaam beat it and turned it back
onto the road. 24 Then the angel of the LORD stood
at a place where the road narrowed between two
vineyard walls. 25 When the donkey saw the angel
of the LORD, it tried to squeeze by and crushed
Balaam's foot against the wall. So Balaam beat
the donkey again. 26 Then the angel of the LORD
moved farther down the road and stood in a place
too narrow for the donkey to get by at all. 27 This
time when the donkey saw the angel, it lay down
under Balaam. In a fit of rage Balaam beat the
animal again with his staff.

28 Then the LORD gave the donkey the ability
to speak. "What have I done to you that deserves
your beating me three times?" it asked Balaam.

29 "You have made me look like a fool!" Balaam shouted. "If I had a sword with me, I would
kill you!"

30 "But I am the same donkey you have ridden
all your life," the donkey answered. "Have I ever
done anything like this before?"

"No," Balaam admitted.

31 Then the LORD opened Balaam's eyes, and
he saw the angel of the LORD standing in the
roadway with a drawn sword in his hand. Balaam
bowed his head and fell face down on the ground
before him.

32 "Why did you beat your donkey those three
times?" the angel of the LORD demanded. "Look,
I have come to block your way because you are
stubbornly resisting me. 33 Three times the donkey saw me and shied away; otherwise, I would
certainly have killed you by now and spared the
donkey."

34 Then Balaam confessed to the angel of the
LORD, "I have sinned. I didn't realize you were
standing in the road to block my way. I will return home if you are against my going."

35 But the angel of the LORD told Balaam, "Go
with these men, but say only what I tell you to
say." So Balaam went on with Balak's officials.
36 When King Balak heard that Balaam was on
the way, he went out to meet him at a Moabite
town on the Arnon River at the farthest border
of his land.

37 "Didn't I send you an urgent invitation?
Why didn't you come right away?" Balak asked
Balaam. "Didn't you believe me when I said I
would reward you richly?"

38 Balaam replied, "Look, now I have come,
but I have no power to say whatever I want. I
will speak only the message that God puts in my
mouth." 39 Then Balaam accompanied Balak to
Kiriath-huzoth, 40 where the king sacrificed cattle
and sheep. He sent portions of the meat to Balaam and the officials who were with him. 41 The
next morning Balak took Balaam up to Bamoth-
baal. From there he could see some of the people
of Israel spread out below him.

Balaam Blesses Israel

23 Then Balaam said to King Balak,
"Build me seven altars here, and
prepare seven young bulls and seven
rams for me to sacrifice." 2 Balak followed his
instructions, and the two of them sacrificed a
young bull and a ram on each altar.

3 Then Balaam said to Balak, "Stand here by
your burnt offerings, and I will go to see if the
LORD will respond to me. Then I will tell you
whatever he reveals to me." So Balaam went
alone to the top of a bare hill, 4 and God met him
there. Balaam said to him, "I have prepared seven
altars and have sacrificed a young bull and a ram
on each altar."

5 The LORD gave Balaam a message for King
Balak. Then he said, "Go back to Balak and give
him my message."

6 So Balaam returned and found the king
standing beside his burnt offerings with all the
officials of Moab. 7 This was the message Balaam
delivered:

---

ture of the narrative or by the possibility that Balaam had secretly decided to curse Israel after all (see v. 35). On *angel of the LORD,* see annotation on 20:16. **23–27:** Ironically, the donkey, not Balaam the *seer,* saw the angel, a humorous detail that casts Balaam in a negative light. The prophet's horrifying abuse of the animal raises even more questions about his character. **36–41:** Balak receives Balaam. **38:** Balaam's response to Balak's impatient questions reveals that the oracles will not go as Balak hoped: *I will speak only the message that God puts in my mouth.* This statement is repeated after the first three oracles (23:12, 26; 24:13). **41:** Bamoth-baal was located north of the Arnon River and afforded Balaam a good view of Israel. **23:1–12:** The theological purpose of Balaam's oracles is to portray Israel as a nation blessed by God in spite of its rebelliousness. **1–2:** Sacrifices often preceded theophanies (Exod 24:5; 1 Kgs 3:4–5). Balak likely hoped that the spectacular display would impress God into cursing Israel (see also 23:14, 30). **6–10:** The first oracle recalls God's blessings of Abraham and Jacob (Gen 12:3; 13:16; 28:14). **13:** Balak

"Balak summoned me to come from Aram;
the king of Moab brought me from the eastern hills.
'Come,' he said, 'curse Jacob for me!
Come and announce Israel's doom.'
8 But how can I curse those
whom God has not cursed?
How can I condemn those
whom the LORD has not condemned?
9 I see them from the cliff tops;
I watch them from the hills.
I see a people who live by themselves,
set apart from other nations.
10 Who can count Jacob's descendants, as numerous as dust?
Who can count even a fourth of Israel's people?
Let me die like the righteous;
let my life end like theirs."

11 Then King Balak demanded of Balaam, "What have you done to me? I brought you to curse my enemies. Instead, you have blessed them!"
12 But Balaam replied, "I will speak only the message that the LORD puts in my mouth."

Balaam's Second Message

13 Then King Balak told him, "Come with me to another place. There you will see another part of the nation of Israel, but not all of them. Curse at least that many!" 14 So Balak took Balaam to the plateau of Zophim on Pisgah Peak. He built seven altars there and offered a young bull and a ram on each altar.
15 Then Balaam said to the king, "Stand here by your burnt offerings while I go over there to meet the LORD."
16 And the LORD met Balaam and gave him a message. Then he said, "Go back to Balak and give him my message."
17 So Balaam returned and found the king standing beside his burnt offerings with all the officials of Moab. "What did the LORD say?" Balak asked eagerly.
18 This was the message Balaam delivered:

"Rise up, Balak, and listen!
Hear me, son of Zippor.
19 God is not a man, so he does not lie.
He is not human, so he does not change his mind.
Has he ever spoken and failed to act?
Has he ever promised and not carried it through?
20 Listen, I received a command to bless;
God has blessed, and I cannot reverse it!
21 No misfortune is in his plan for Jacob;
no trouble is in store for Israel.
For the LORD their God is with them;
he has been proclaimed their king.
22 God brought them out of Egypt;
for them he is as strong as a wild ox.
23 No curse can touch Jacob;
no magic has any power against Israel.
For now it will be said of Jacob,
'What wonders God has done for Israel!'
24 These people rise up like a lioness,
like a majestic lion rousing itself.
They refuse to rest
until they have feasted on prey,
drinking the blood of the slaughtered!"

25 Then Balak said to Balaam, "Fine, but if you won't curse them, at least don't bless them!"
26 But Balaam replied to Balak, "Didn't I tell you that I can do only what the LORD tells me?"

Balaam's Third Message

27 Then King Balak said to Balaam, "Come, I will take you to one more place. Perhaps it will please God to let you curse them from there."
28 So Balak took Balaam to the top of Mount Peor, overlooking the wasteland.* 29 Balaam again told Balak, "Build me seven altars, and prepare seven young bulls and seven rams for me to sacrifice." 30 So Balak did as Balaam ordered and offered a young bull and a ram on each altar.

24 By now Balaam realized that the LORD was determined to bless Israel, so he did not resort to divination as before. Instead, he turned and looked out toward the wilderness, 2 where he saw the people of Israel camped, tribe by tribe. Then the Spirit of

23:28 Or *overlooking Jeshimon.*

apparently hoped a change in location would help to change God's mind. Mount Pisgah was the vantage point from which Moses would later view the entire promised land (Deut 3:27; 34:1). **18–24:** The second oracle focuses on Israel's imperviousness to attack because of God's kingly presence with them. **19:** God's mind would not change regarding Israel's blessed status, regardless of what Balak did. **28:** The third oracle is given on Mount Peor, which is likely close to Baal-peor where Israel later commits idolatry (Num 25). **24:1–2:** This time Balaam did not resort to divination, instead *the Spirit of God came upon*

God came upon him, [3] and this is the message he delivered:

"This is the message of Balaam son of Beor,
the message of the man whose eyes see clearly,
[4] the message of one who hears the words of God,
who sees a vision from the Almighty,
who bows down with eyes wide open:
[5] How beautiful are your tents, O Jacob;
how lovely are your homes, O Israel!
[6] They spread before me like palm groves,*
like gardens by the riverside.
They are like tall trees planted by the LORD,
like cedars beside the waters.
[7] Water will flow from their buckets;
their offspring have all they need.
Their king will be greater than Agag;
their kingdom will be exalted.
[8] God brought them out of Egypt;
for them he is as strong as a wild ox.
He devours all the nations that oppose him,
breaking their bones in pieces,
shooting them with arrows.
[9] Like a lion, Israel crouches and lies down;
like a lioness, who dares to arouse her?
Blessed is everyone who blesses you, O Israel,
and cursed is everyone who curses you."

[10] King Balak flew into a rage against Balaam.
He angrily clapped his hands and shouted, "I
called you to curse my enemies! Instead, you
have blessed them three times. [11] Now get out of
here! Go back home! I promised to reward you
richly, but the LORD has kept you from your reward."
[12] Balaam told Balak, "Don't you remember
what I told your messengers? I said, [13] 'Even if
Balak were to give me his palace filled with silver
and gold, I would be powerless to do anything
against the will of the LORD.' I told you that I
could say only what the LORD says! [14] Now I am
returning to my own people. But first let me tell
you what the Israelites will do to your people in
the future."

Balaam's Final Messages

[15] This is the message Balaam delivered:

"This is the message of Balaam son of Beor,
the message of the man whose eyes see clearly,
[16] the message of one who hears the words of God,
who has knowledge from the Most High,
who sees a vision from the Almighty,
who bows down with eyes wide open:
[17] I see him, but not here and now.
I perceive him, but far in the distant future.
A star will rise from Jacob;
a scepter will emerge from Israel.
It will crush the foreheads of Moab's people,
cracking the skulls of the people of Sheth.
[18] Edom will be taken over,
and Seir, its enemy, will be conquered,
while Israel marches on in triumph.
[19] A ruler will rise in Jacob
who will destroy the survivors of Ir."

[20] Then Balaam looked over toward the people of
Amalek and delivered this message:

"Amalek was the greatest of nations,
but its destiny is destruction!"

[21] Then he looked over toward the Kenites and
delivered this message:

"Your home is secure;
your nest is set in the rocks.
[22] But the Kenites will be destroyed
when Assyria* takes you captive."

[23] Balaam concluded his messages by saying:

"Alas, who can survive
unless God has willed it?
[24] Ships will come from the coasts of Cyprus*;

24:6 Or *like a majestic valley.* **24:22** Hebrew *Asshur;* also in 24:24. **24:24** Hebrew *Kittim.*

him (see note on 11:17). **3–9:** The third oracle highlights God's abundant providence for Israel, which has blossomed like a fruitful garden. **4:** *Almighty* is a name for God associated with fertility and multiple descendants (Gen 17:1; 28:3; 35:11; 48:3). It is used here to introduce Israel as a nation blessed with fruitfulness by God (cf. v. 14). **14–24:** Balaam's fourth oracle and messages to nations. **14–19:** The demise of Moab and Edom is the subject of this prophecy. **17:** *A star will rise from Jacob,* likely refers to David, who controlled this region during his reign. **20–22:** The Amalekites dwelled in the southern regions of the Negev and posed a threat to both Saul and David's kingdoms (1 Sam 15; 30). The Kenites were closely related to the Midianites (Judg 1:16; 4:11). **23–24:** Unfortunately, the identities of the groups listed in these verses remain uncertain.

they will oppress Assyria and afflict Eber,
but they, too, will be utterly destroyed."

[25]Then Balaam and Balak returned to their
homes.

Moab Seduces Israel

25 While the Israelites were camped at
Acacia Grove,* some of the men defiled themselves by having* sexual
relations with local Moabite women. [2]These
women invited them to attend sacrifices to their
gods, so the Israelites feasted with them and
worshiped the gods of Moab. [3]In this way, Israel
joined in the worship of Baal of Peor, causing the
LORD's anger to blaze against his people.

[4]The LORD issued the following command
to Moses: "Seize all the ringleaders and execute
them before the LORD in broad daylight, so his
fierce anger will turn away from the people of
Israel."

[5]So Moses ordered Israel's judges, "Each of
you must put to death the men under your authority who have joined in worshiping Baal of
Peor."

[6]Just then one of the Israelite men brought a
Midianite woman into his tent, right before the
eyes of Moses and all the people, as everyone
was weeping at the entrance of the Tabernacle.*
[7]When Phinehas son of Eleazar and grandson
of Aaron the priest saw this, he jumped up and
left the assembly. He took a spear [8]and rushed
after the man into his tent. Phinehas thrust the
spear all the way through the man's body and
into the woman's stomach. So the plague against
the Israelites was stopped, [9]but not before 24,000
people had died.

[10]Then the LORD said to Moses, [11]"Phinehas
son of Eleazar and grandson of Aaron the priest
has turned my anger away from the Israelites
by being as zealous among them as I was. So I
stopped destroying all Israel as I had intended to
do in my zealous anger. [12]Now tell him that I am
making my special covenant of peace with him.
[13]In this covenant, I give him and his descendants a permanent right to the priesthood, for in
his zeal for me, his God, he purified the people of
Israel, making them right with me.*"

[14]The Israelite man killed with the Midianite
woman was named Zimri son of Salu, the leader of a family from the tribe of Simeon. [15]The
woman's name was Cozbi; she was the daughter
of Zur, the leader of a Midianite clan.

[16]Then the LORD said to Moses, [17]"Attack the
Midianites and destroy them, [18]because they
assaulted you with deceit and tricked you into
worshiping Baal of Peor, and because of Cozbi,
the daughter of a Midianite leader, who was
killed at the time of the plague because of what
happened at Peor."

The Second Registration of Israel's Troops

26 After the plague had ended, the LORD
said to Moses and to Eleazar son of
Aaron the priest, [2]"From the whole
community of Israel, record the names of all the
warriors by their families. List all the men twenty years old or older who are able to go to war."
[3]So there on the plains of Moab beside the
Jordan River, across from Jericho, Moses and
Eleazar the priest issued these instructions to
the leaders of Israel: [4]"List all the men of Israel twenty years old and older, just as the LORD
commanded Moses."

This is the record of all the descendants of Israel who came out of Egypt.

25:1a Hebrew *Shittim.* **25:1b** As in Greek version; Hebrew reads *some of the men began having.* **25:6** Hebrew *the Tent of Meeting.* **25:13** Or *he made atonement for the people of Israel.*

25:1–18 Moab Seduces Israel. 2: The Old Testament often blames apostasy on foreigners (especially women) who engage Israel in sex (cf. Exod 34:16; Deut 7:3–4; Josh 23:12–13; 1 Kgs 11:1–8). **3:** Baal, the Canaanite god of fertility, was identified by the shrine where he was worshiped, in this case Peor. **4–5:** Neither God's command to Moses nor Moses' command to the leaders seems to have been carried out. **7:** Phinehas apparently pierced the man and woman through either while they were engaged in intercourse or while they were worshiping false gods. **8:** In the absence of any other leaders carrying out God's commands, Phinehas's actions averted the plague. Perhaps, because Zimri and Cozbi's fathers were leaders (cf. vv. 14–15) their deaths were accepted as symbolic punishment for Israel's leaders. **10–13:** God's covenant with Phinehas is unique in that it establishes his household as priests forever, a promise fulfilled when Phinehas's descendant, Zadok, replaced Abiathar as priest (1 Kgs 2:35). **16–18:** These two incidents, both centering on women, become the basis for Israel's war against Midian (Num 31:1) where the female captives were treated especially harshly (31:15–18).

26:1–65 The Second Registration of Israel's Troops. 1: The narrator introduces the second census by mentioning the plague in chapter 25. That plague would have eliminated any surviving remnants of the first generation preparing the way for the second.

The Tribe of Reuben

5 These were the clans descended from the sons of Reuben, Jacob's* oldest son:

The Hanochite clan, named after their ancestor Hanoch.

The Palluite clan, named after their ancestor Pallu.

6 The Hezronite clan, named after their ancestor Hezron.

The Carmite clan, named after their ancestor Carmi.

7 These were the clans of Reuben. Their registered troops numbered 43,730.

8 Pallu was the ancestor of Eliab, 9 and Eliab
was the father of Nemuel, Dathan, and Abiram.
This Dathan and Abiram are the same community leaders who conspired with Korah against Moses and Aaron, rebelling against the LORD.
10 But the earth opened up its mouth and swallowed them with Korah, and fire devoured 250 of their followers. This served as a warning to the entire nation of Israel.
11 However, the sons of Korah did not die that day.

The Tribe of Simeon

12 These were the clans descended from the sons of Simeon:

The Jemuelite clan, named after their ancestor Jemuel.*

The Jaminite clan, named after their ancestor Jamin.

The Jakinite clan, named after their ancestor Jakin.

13 The Zoharite clan, named after their ancestor Zohar.*

The Shaulite clan, named after their ancestor Shaul.

14 These were the clans of Simeon. Their registered troops numbered 22,200.

The Tribe of Gad

15 These were the clans descended from the sons of Gad:

The Zephonite clan, named after their ancestor Zephon.

The Haggite clan, named after their ancestor Haggi.

The Shunite clan, named after their ancestor Shuni.

16 The Oznite clan, named after their ancestor Ozni.

The Erite clan, named after their ancestor Eri.

17 The Arodite clan, named after their ancestor Arodi.*

The Arelite clan, named after their ancestor Areli.

18 These were the clans of Gad. Their registered troops numbered 40,500.

The Tribe of Judah

19 Judah had two sons, Er and Onan, who had died
in the land of Canaan. 20 These were the clans descended from Judah's surviving sons:

The Shelanite clan, named after their ancestor Shelah.

The Perezite clan, named after their ancestor Perez.

The Zerahite clan, named after their ancestor Zerah.

21 These were the subclans descended from the Perezites:

The Hezronites, named after their ancestor Hezron.

The Hamulites, named after their ancestor Hamul.

22 These were the clans of Judah. Their registered troops numbered 76,500.

The Tribe of Issachar

23 These were the clans descended from the sons of Issachar:

The Tolaite clan, named after their ancestor Tola.

The Puite clan, named after their ancestor Puah.*

24 The Jashubite clan, named after their ancestor Jashub.

The Shimronite clan, named after their ancestor Shimron.

26:5 Hebrew *Israel's*; see note on 1:20-21b. **26:12** As in Syriac version (see also Gen 46:10; Exod 6:15); Hebrew reads *Nemuelite . . . Nemuel.* **26:13** As in parallel texts at Gen 46:10 and Exod 6:15; Hebrew reads *Zerahite . . . Zerah.* **26:17** As in Samaritan Pentateuch and Greek and Syriac versions (see also Gen 46:16); Hebrew reads *Arod.* **26:23** As in Samaritan Pentateuch, Greek and Syriac versions, and Latin Vulgate (see also 1 Chr 7:1); Hebrew reads *The Punite clan, named after its ancestor Puvah.*

5–51: The census total (601,730) indicates that in spite of all the deaths in the wilderness, the new generation was as strong and ready for battle as the first generation had been. **52:** The command to distribute the land comes logically after the census which established each tribe's size and military strength.

25 These were the clans of Issachar. Their registered troops numbered 64,300.

The Tribe of Zebulun

26 These were the clans descended from the sons of Zebulun:

The Seredite clan, named after their ancestor Sered.
The Elonite clan, named after their ancestor Elon.
The Jahleelite clan, named after their ancestor Jahleel.

27 These were the clans of Zebulun. Their registered troops numbered 60,500.

The Tribe of Manasseh

28 Two clans were descended from Joseph through Manasseh and Ephraim.

29 These were the clans descended from Manasseh:

The Makirite clan, named after their ancestor Makir.
The Gileadite clan, named after their ancestor Gilead, Makir's son.

30 These were the subclans descended from the Gileadites:

The Iezerites, named after their ancestor Iezer.
The Helekites, named after their ancestor Helek.
31 The Asrielites, named after their ancestor Asriel.
The Shechemites, named after their ancestor Shechem.
32 The Shemidaites, named after their ancestor Shemida.
The Hepherites, named after their ancestor Hepher.
33 (One of Hepher's descendants, Zelophehad, had no sons, but his daughters' names were Mahlah, Noah, Hoglah, Milcah, and Tirzah.)

34 These were the clans of Manasseh. Their registered troops numbered 52,700.

The Tribe of Ephraim

35 These were the clans descended from the sons of Ephraim:

The Shuthelahite clan, named after their ancestor Shuthelah.
The Bekerite clan, named after their ancestor Beker.
The Tahanite clan, named after their ancestor Tahan.

36 This was the subclan descended from the Shuthelahites:

The Eranites, named after their ancestor Eran.

37 These were the clans of Ephraim. Their registered troops numbered 32,500.

These clans of Manasseh and Ephraim were all descendants of Joseph.

The Tribe of Benjamin

38 These were the clans descended from the sons of Benjamin:

The Belaite clan, named after their ancestor Bela.
The Ashbelite clan, named after their ancestor Ashbel.
The Ahiramite clan, named after their ancestor Ahiram.
39 The Shuphamite clan, named after their ancestor Shupham.*
The Huphamite clan, named after their ancestor Hupham.

40 These were the subclans descended from the Belaites:

The Ardites, named after their ancestor Ard.*
The Naamites, named after their ancestor Naaman.

41 These were the clans of Benjamin. Their registered troops numbered 45,600.

The Tribe of Dan

42 These were the clans descended from the sons of Dan:

The Shuhamite clan, named after their ancestor Shuham.

43 These were the Shuhamite clans of Dan. Their registered troops numbered 64,400.

The Tribe of Asher

44 These were the clans descended from the sons of Asher:

The Imnite clan, named after their ancestor Imnah.
The Ishvite clan, named after their ancestor Ishvi.

26:39 As in some Hebrew manuscripts, Samaritan Pentateuch, Greek and Syriac versions, and Latin Vulgate; most Hebrew manuscripts read *Shephupham.* **26:40** As in Samaritan Pentateuch, some Greek manuscripts, and Latin Vulgate; Hebrew lacks *named after their ancestor Ard.*

The Beriite clan, named after their ancestor Beriah.

45 These were the subclans descended from the Beriites:

The Heberites, named after their ancestor Heber.
The Malkielites, named after their ancestor Malkiel.

46 Asher also had a daughter named Serah.

47 These were the clans of Asher. Their registered troops numbered 53,400.

The Tribe of Naphtali

48 These were the clans descended from the sons of Naphtali:

The Jahzeelite clan, named after their ancestor Jahzeel.
The Gunite clan, named after their ancestor Guni.
49 The Jezerite clan, named after their ancestor Jezer.
The Shillemite clan, named after their ancestor Shillem.

50 These were the clans of Naphtali. Their registered troops numbered 45,400.

Results of the Registration

51 In summary, the registered troops of all Israel numbered 601,730.

52 Then the LORD said to Moses, 53 "Divide the land among the tribes, and distribute the grants of land in proportion to the tribes' populations, as indicated by the number of names on the list. 54 Give the larger tribes more land and the smaller tribes less land, each group receiving a grant in proportion to the size of its population. 55 But you must assign the land by lot, and give land to each ancestral tribe according to the number of names on the list. 56 Each grant of land must be assigned by lot among the larger and smaller tribal groups."

The Tribe of Levi

57 This is the record of the Levites who were counted according to their clans:

The Gershonite clan, named after their ancestor Gershon.
The Kohathite clan, named after their ancestor Kohath.
The Merarite clan, named after their ancestor Merari.

58 The Libnites, the Hebronites, the Mahlites, the Mushites, and the Korahites were all subclans of the Levites.

Now Kohath was the ancestor of Amram, 59 and Amram's wife was named Jochebed. She also was a descendant of Levi, born among the Levites in the land of Egypt. Amram and Jochebed became the parents of Aaron, Moses, and their sister, Miriam. 60 To Aaron were born Nadab, Abihu, Eleazar, and Ithamar. 61 But Nadab and Abihu died when they burned before the LORD the wrong kind of fire, different than he had commanded.

62 The men from the Levite clans who were one month old or older numbered 23,000. But the Levites were not included in the registration of the rest of the people of Israel because they were not given an allotment of land when it was divided among the Israelites.

63 So these are the results of the registration of the people of Israel as conducted by Moses and Eleazar the priest on the plains of Moab beside the Jordan River, across from Jericho. 64 Not one person on this list had been among those listed in the previous registration taken by Moses and Aaron in the wilderness of Sinai. 65 For the LORD had said of them, "They will all die in the wilderness." Not one of them survived except Caleb son of Jephunneh and Joshua son of Nun.

The Daughters of Zelophehad

27 One day a petition was presented by the daughters of Zelophehad—Mahlah, Noah, Hoglah, Milcah, and Tirzah. Their father, Zelophehad, was a descendant of Hepher son of Gilead, son of Makir, son of Manasseh, son of Joseph. 2 These women stood before Moses, Eleazar the priest, the tribal leaders, and the entire community at the entrance of the Tabernacle.* 3 "Our father died in the wilderness," they said. "He was not among Korah's fol-

27:2 Hebrew *the Tent of Meeting.*

57–65: This passage parallels Numbers 3 in counting the Levites. As before, since Levites did not inherit a portion of land their numbers were not included in the registration of the other tribes.

27:1–11 The Daughters of Zelophehad. 2: Standing before the Tabernacle and the community indicates that the daughters were bringing a legal request—a request that was ultimately decided by God. **3:** Distancing their father from Korah's followers was important because, had he been one, his land might have been seized and distributed to other members of the tribe. **4:** The fam-

lowers, who rebelled against the LORD; he died
because of his own sin. But he had no sons. 4 Why
should the name of our father disappear from his
clan just because he had no sons? Give us property along with the rest of our relatives."
5 So Moses brought their case before the LORD.
6 And the LORD replied to Moses, 7 "The claim of
the daughters of Zelophehad is legitimate. You
must give them a grant of land along with their
father's relatives. Assign them the property that
would have been given to their father.
8 "And give the following instructions to the
people of Israel: If a man dies and has no son,
then give his inheritance to his daughters. 9 And
if he has no daughter either, transfer his inheritance to his brothers. 10 If he has no brothers, give
his inheritance to his father's brothers. 11 But if
his father has no brothers, give his inheritance
to the nearest relative in his clan. This is a legal
requirement for the people of Israel, just as the
LORD commanded Moses."

Joshua Chosen to Lead Israel

12 One day the LORD said to Moses, "Climb one
of the mountains east of the river,* and look out
over the land I have given the people of Israel.
13 After you have seen it, you will die like your
brother, Aaron, 14 for you both rebelled against
my instructions in the wilderness of Zin. When
the people of Israel rebelled, you failed to demonstrate my holiness to them at the waters."
(These are the waters of Meribah at Kadesh* in
the wilderness of Zin.)
15 Then Moses said to the LORD, 16 "O LORD,
you are the God who gives breath to all creatures. Please appoint a new man as leader for
the community. 17 Give them someone who will
guide them wherever they go and will lead them
into battle, so the community of the LORD will
not be like sheep without a shepherd."
18 The LORD replied, "Take Joshua son of Nun,
who has the Spirit in him, and lay your hands on
him. 19 Present him to Eleazar the priest before
the whole community, and publicly commission
him to lead the people. 20 Transfer some of your
authority to him so the whole community of Israel will obey him. 21 When direction from the
LORD is needed, Joshua will stand before Eleazar
the priest, who will use the Urim—one of the
sacred lots cast before the LORD—to determine
his will. This is how Joshua and the rest of the
community of Israel will determine everything
they should do."
22 So Moses did as the LORD commanded. He
presented Joshua to Eleazar the priest and the
whole community. 23 Moses laid his hands on him
and commissioned him to lead the people, just as
the LORD had commanded through Moses.

The Daily Offerings

28 The LORD said to Moses, 2 "Give
these instructions to the people of
Israel: The offerings you present as
special gifts are a pleasing aroma to me; they are
my food. See to it that they are brought at the
appointed times and offered according to my instructions.
3 "Say to the people: This is the special gift
you must present to the LORD as your daily
burnt offering. You must offer two one-year-old
male lambs with no defects. 4 Sacrifice one lamb
in the morning and the other in the evening.
5 With each lamb you must offer a grain offering
of two quarts* of choice flour mixed with one
quart* of pure oil of pressed olives. 6 This is the
regular burnt offering instituted at Mount Sinai

27:12 Or *the mountains of Abarim.* **27:14** Hebrew *waters of Meribath-kadesh.* **28:5a** Hebrew *1/10 of an ephah* [2.2 liters]; also in 28:13, 21, 29. **28:5b** Hebrew *1/4 of a hin* [1 liter]; also in 28:7.

ily name was normally passed from father to son. If a man died without sons, his name and land inheritance would be obliterated. The daughters' demand, *Give us property!* was made to preserve their father's name. **5–11:** God not only legitimized the daughters' claim but also turned it into a legal requirement for all subsequent generations. See also Numbers 36.

27:12–23 Moses' Replacement. 12–14: This command is not fulfilled until Deuteronomy 34. **18:** Joshua already had God's Spirit which had been distributed amongst the leaders in response to Moses' cry for help (11:24–25). On the laying of hands, see annotation on Numbers 8:10. **21:** The Urim and Thummim were lot-casting devices prescribed by God in Exodus 28:30. They were typically handled by the high priest who carried them in the breastplate of his priestly garment. The lots were probably two stones marked in some way so that depending on how they landed, a yes or no answer was given.

28:1—29:40 The Appointed Offerings. Chapters 28 and 29 present the required offerings for each event on Israel's liturgical calendar. Readers are sometimes discouraged by the repetition and details in the calendar, but just as we enjoy handing down family traditions for our own holidays, the Israelites passed on theirs. The sacrifices the Israelites were required to offer served as a reminder that their holidays were first and foremost celebrations of what God had done for

as a special gift, a pleasing aroma to the LORD.
7 Along with it you must present the proper liquid offering of one quart of alcoholic drink with
each lamb, poured out in the Holy Place as an offering to the LORD. 8 Offer the second lamb in the
evening with the same grain offering and liquid
offering. It, too, is a special gift, a pleasing aroma
to the LORD.

The Sabbath Offerings

9 "On the Sabbath day, sacrifice two one-year-old
male lambs with no defects. They must be accompanied by a grain offering of four quarts* of
choice flour moistened with olive oil, and a liquid
offering. 10 This is the burnt offering to be presented each Sabbath day, in addition to the regular burnt offering and its accompanying liquid
offering.

The Monthly Offerings

11 "On the first day of each month, present an extra burnt offering to the LORD of two young bulls,
one ram, and seven one-year-old male lambs, all
with no defects. 12 These must be accompanied by
grain offerings of choice flour moistened with olive oil—six quarts* with each bull, four quarts
with the ram, 13 and two quarts with each lamb.
This burnt offering will be a special gift, a pleasing aroma to the LORD. 14 You must also present
a liquid offering with each sacrifice: two quarts*
of wine for each bull, a third of a gallon* for the
ram, and one quart* for each lamb. Present this
monthly burnt offering on the first day of each
month throughout the year.

15 "On the first day of each month, you must
also offer one male goat for a sin offering to the
LORD. This is in addition to the regular burnt offering and its accompanying liquid offering.

Offerings for the Passover

16 "On the fourteenth day of the first month,*
you must celebrate the LORD's Passover. 17 On the
following day—the fifteenth day of the month—
a joyous, seven-day festival will begin, but no
bread made with yeast may be eaten. 18 The first
day of the festival will be an official day for holy
assembly, and no ordinary work may be done on
that day. 19 As a special gift you must present a
burnt offering to the LORD—two young bulls,
one ram, and seven one-year-old male lambs, all
with no defects. 20 These will be accompanied by
grain offerings of choice flour moistened with
olive oil—six quarts with each bull, four quarts
with the ram, 21 and two quarts with each of the
seven lambs. 22 You must also offer a male goat
as a sin offering to purify yourselves and make
yourselves right with the LORD.* 23 Present these
offerings in addition to your regular morning
burnt offering. 24 On each of the seven days of the
festival, this is how you must prepare the food
offering that is presented as a special gift, a pleasing aroma to the LORD. These will be offered in
addition to the regular burnt offerings and liquid
offerings. 25 The seventh day of the festival will
be another official day for holy assembly, and no
ordinary work may be done on that day.

Offerings for the Festival of Harvest

26 "At the Festival of Harvest,* when you present the first of your new grain to the LORD,
you must call an official day for holy assembly,
and you may do no ordinary work on that day.
27 Present a special burnt offering on that day as
a pleasing aroma to the LORD. It will consist of
two young bulls, one ram, and seven one-year-
old male lambs. 28 These will be accompanied by
grain offerings of choice flour moistened with
olive oil—six quarts with each bull, four quarts
with the ram, 29 and two quarts with each of the
seven lambs. 30 Also, offer one male goat to purify yourselves and make yourselves right with

28:9 Hebrew *2/10 of an ephah* [4.4 liters]; also in 28:12, 20, 28. **28:12** Hebrew *3/10 of an ephah* [6.6 liters]; also in 28:20, 28. **28:14a** Hebrew *1/2 of a hin* [2 liters]. **28:14b** Hebrew *1/3 of a hin* [1.3 liters]. **28:14c** Hebrew *1/4 of a hin* [1 liter]. **28:16** This day in the ancient Hebrew lunar calendar occurred in late March, April, or early May. **28:22** Or *to make atonement for yourselves;* also in 28:30. **28:26** Hebrew *Festival of Weeks.* This was later called the Festival of Pentecost (see Acts 2:1). It is celebrated today as Shavuot (or Shabuoth).

them. **28:3–8:** Each day began and ended by honoring God through the daily offerings. **9–10:** Set apart at creation (Gen 2:3), the Sabbath was a day for rest and gathering for worship (Exod 20:8–11; Deut 5:12–15). **11–15:** The new moon festival celebrated the passing of each lunar cycle. Exactly how the festival was celebrated, other than presenting the offerings specified here, is unclear, though 1 Samuel 20:5 alludes to a family feast. **16–25:** The Passover celebration was (and is) a commemoration of God's deliverance of Israel from Egypt. It is remembered as God's premier salvation act in the Old Testament. The main Passover celebration occurred on the fourteenth day of the first month (Num 9:2). One distinctive element of the festival was the prescription that no leavened bread could be eaten, a memorial of the haste with which Israel had departed Egypt (Exod 12:17–20). **26–30:** The harvest festival (firstfruits) (*Shavuot*, Weeks, Pentecost) was a one-day festival fifty days after Passover that celebrated the firstfruits of the wheat harvest.

the LORD. 31 Prepare these special burnt offerings, along with their liquid offerings, in addition to the regular burnt offering and its accompanying grain offering. Be sure that all the animals you sacrifice have no defects.

Offerings for the Festival of Trumpets

29 "Celebrate the Festival of Trumpets each year on the first day of the appointed month in early autumn.* You must call an official day for holy assembly, and you may do no ordinary work. 2 On that day you must present a burnt offering as a pleasing aroma to the LORD. It will consist of one young bull, one ram, and seven one-year-old male lambs, all with no defects. 3 These must be accompanied by grain offerings of choice flour moistened with olive oil—six quarts* with the bull, four quarts* with the ram, 4 and two quarts* with each of the seven lambs. 5 In addition, you must sacrifice a male goat as a sin offering to purify yourselves and make yourselves right with the LORD.* 6 These special sacrifices are in addition to your regular monthly and daily burnt offerings, and they must be given with their prescribed grain offerings and liquid offerings. These offerings are given as a special gift to the LORD, a pleasing aroma to him.

Offerings for the Day of Atonement

7 "Ten days later, on the tenth day of the same month,* you must call another holy assembly. On that day, the Day of Atonement, the people must go without food and must do no ordinary work. 8 You must present a burnt offering as a pleasing aroma to the LORD. It will consist of one young bull, one ram, and seven one-year-old male lambs, all with no defects. 9 These offerings must be accompanied by the prescribed grain offerings of choice flour moistened with olive oil—six quarts of choice flour with the bull, four quarts of choice flour with the ram, 10 and two quarts of choice flour with each of the seven lambs. 11 You must also sacrifice one male goat for a sin offering. This is in addition to the sin offering of atonement and the regular daily burnt offering with its grain offering, and their accompanying liquid offerings.

Offerings for the Festival of Shelters

12 "Five days later, on the fifteenth day of the same month,* you must call another holy assembly of all the people, and you may do no ordinary work on that day. It is the beginning of the Festival of Shelters,* a seven-day festival to the LORD. 13 On the first day of the festival, you must present a burnt offering as a special gift, a pleasing aroma to the LORD. It will consist of thirteen young bulls, two rams, and fourteen one-year-old male lambs, all with no defects. 14 Each of these offerings must be accompanied by a grain offering of choice flour moistened with olive oil—six quarts for each of the thirteen bulls, four quarts for each of the two rams, 15 and two quarts for each of the fourteen lambs. 16 You must also sacrifice a male goat as a sin offering, in addition to the regular burnt offering with its accompanying grain offering and liquid offering.

17 "On the second day of this seven-day festival, sacrifice twelve young bulls, two rams, and fourteen one-year-old male lambs, all with no defects. 18 Each of these offerings of bulls, rams, and lambs must be accompanied by its prescribed grain offering and liquid offering. 19 You must also sacrifice a male goat as a sin offering, in addition to the regular burnt offering with its accompanying grain offering and liquid offering.

29:1 Hebrew *the first day of the seventh month.* This day in the ancient Hebrew lunar calendar occurred in September or October. This festival is celebrated today as Rosh Hashanah, the Jewish new year. **29:3a** Hebrew $^{3}/_{10}$ *of an ephah* [6.6 liters]; also in 29:9, 14. **29:3b** Hebrew $^{2}/_{10}$ *of an ephah* [4.4 liters]; also in 29:9, 14. **29:4** Hebrew $^{1}/_{10}$ *of an ephah* [2.2 liters]; also in 29:10, 15. **29:5** Or *to make atonement for yourselves.* **29:7** Hebrew *On the tenth day of the seventh month;* see 29:1 and the note there. This day in the ancient Hebrew lunar calendar occurred in September or October. It is celebrated today as Yom Kippur. **29:12a** Hebrew *On the fifteenth day of the seventh month;* see 29:1, 7 and the notes there. This day in the ancient Hebrew lunar calendar occurred in late September, October, or early November. **29:12b** Or *Festival of Booths,* or *Festival of Tabernacles.* This was earlier called the Festival of the Final Harvest or Festival of Ingathering (see Exod 23:16b). It is celebrated today as Sukkot (or Succoth).

29:1–6: The first day of the seventh month, heralded by the blowing of trumpets, inaugurated a series of important festivals. Today this feast is associated with Rosh Hashanah. **7–11:** The Day of Atonement (Yom Kippur) was (and is) a solemn day of fasting that took place on the tenth day of the seventh month. According to Leviticus 16, the day was set aside for confession of sins, the ritual cleansing of the Tabernacle, and the atonement of sins. **12–40:** The Festival of Shelters (Sukkoth), also known as the Festival of Ingathering, was the most celebrative of all the feasts. Observed beginning on the fifteenth day of the seventh month, it commemorated the wilderness wanderings and occurred in conjunction with the fall fruit harvest. The numerous sacrifices required during this eight-day feast illustrate its importance.

20 "On the third day of the festival, sacrifice eleven young bulls, two rams, and fourteen one-year-old male lambs, all with no defects. 21 Each of these offerings of bulls, rams, and lambs must be accompanied by its prescribed grain offering and liquid offering. 22 You must also sacrifice a male goat as a sin offering, in addition to the regular burnt offering with its accompanying grain offering and liquid offering.

23 "On the fourth day of the festival, sacrifice ten young bulls, two rams, and fourteen one-year-old male lambs, all with no defects. 24 Each of these offerings of bulls, rams, and lambs must be accompanied by its prescribed grain offering and liquid offering. 25 You must also sacrifice a male goat as a sin offering, in addition to the regular burnt offering with its accompanying grain offering and liquid offering.

26 "On the fifth day of the festival, sacrifice nine young bulls, two rams, and fourteen one-year-old male lambs, all with no defects. 27 Each of these offerings of bulls, rams, and lambs must be accompanied by its prescribed grain offering and liquid offering. 28 You must also sacrifice a male goat as a sin offering, in addition to the regular burnt offering with its accompanying grain offering and liquid offering.

29 "On the sixth day of the festival, sacrifice eight young bulls, two rams, and fourteen one-year-old male lambs, all with no defects. 30 Each of these offerings of bulls, rams, and lambs must be accompanied by its prescribed grain offering and liquid offering. 31 You must also sacrifice a male goat as a sin offering, in addition to the regular burnt offering with its accompanying grain offering and liquid offering.

32 "On the seventh day of the festival, sacrifice seven young bulls, two rams, and fourteen one-year-old male lambs, all with no defects. 33 Each of these offerings of bulls, rams, and lambs must be accompanied by its prescribed grain offering and liquid offering. 34 You must also sacrifice one male goat as a sin offering, in addition to the regular burnt offering with its accompanying grain offering and liquid offering.

35 "On the eighth day of the festival, proclaim another holy day. You must do no ordinary work on that day. 36 You must present a burnt offering as a special gift, a pleasing aroma to the LORD. It will consist of one young bull, one ram, and seven one-year-old male lambs, all with no defects. 37 Each of these offerings must be accompanied by its prescribed grain offering and liquid offering. 38 You must also sacrifice one male goat as a sin offering, in addition to the regular burnt offering with its accompanying grain offering and liquid offering.

39 "You must present these offerings to the LORD at your annual festivals. These are in addition to the sacrifices and offerings you present in connection with vows, or as voluntary offerings, burnt offerings, grain offerings, liquid offerings, or peace offerings."

40 *So Moses gave all of these instructions to the people of Israel as the LORD had commanded him.

Laws concerning Vows

30 1 *Then Moses summoned the leaders of the tribes of Israel and told them, "This is what the LORD has commanded: 2 A man who makes a vow to the LORD or makes a pledge under oath must never break it. He must do exactly what he said he would do.

3 "If a young woman makes a vow to the LORD or a pledge under oath while she is still living at her father's home, 4 and her father hears of the vow or pledge and does not object to it, then all her vows and pledges will stand. 5 But if her father refuses to let her fulfill the vow or pledge on the day he hears of it, then all her vows and pledges will become invalid. The LORD will forgive her because her father would not let her fulfill them.

6 "Now suppose a young woman makes a vow or binds herself with an impulsive pledge and later marries. 7 If her husband learns of her vow or pledge and does not object on the day he hears of it, her vows and pledges will stand. 8 But if her husband refuses to accept her vow or impulsive pledge on the day he hears of it, he nullifies her commitments, and the LORD will forgive her. 9 If,

29:40 Verse 29:40 is numbered 30:1 in Hebrew text.
30:1 Verses 30:1-16 are numbered 30:2-17 in Hebrew text.

30:1–16 Laws concerning Vows. Different sorts of vows are described in the biblical material. Some were simple promises, such as "If God will do X, I will do Y" (Gen 28:20). Other vows involved making a donation of money to the sanctuary (see Lev 27), and this is probably the sort of vow addressed here. **3–16:** In a patriarchal society, women were under the financial authority of their fathers or husbands; thus, any vows they made were subject to a man's approval. In effect, the male (whether father or husband) had to approve or deny his daughter or wife's vow as soon as he heard of it. If he approved, her vow stood. If he did not, her vow was nullified—her husband/father was not required to pay for the vow, and the woman was absolved of any guilt for failing to complete the vow. **9:** Notably, just like men (vv.

however, a woman is a widow or is divorced, she must fulfill all her vows and pledges.

[10] "But suppose a woman is married and living in her husband's home when she makes a vow or binds herself with a pledge. [11] If her husband hears of it and does not object to it, her vow or pledge will stand. [12] But if her husband refuses to accept it on the day he hears of it, her vow or pledge will be nullified, and the LORD will forgive her. [13] So her husband may either confirm or nullify any vows or pledges she makes to deny herself. [14] But if he does not object on the day he hears of it, then he is agreeing to all her vows and pledges. [15] If he waits more than a day and then tries to nullify a vow or pledge, he will be punished for her guilt."

[16] These are the regulations the LORD gave Moses concerning relationships between a man and his wife, and between a father and a young daughter who still lives at home.

Conquest of the Midianites

31 Then the LORD said to Moses, [2] "On behalf of the people of Israel, take revenge on the Midianites for leading them into idolatry. After that, you will die and join your ancestors."

[3] So Moses said to the people, "Choose some men, and arm them to fight the LORD's war of revenge against Midian. [4] From each tribe of Israel, send 1,000 men into battle." [5] So they chose 1,000 men from each tribe of Israel, a total of 12,000 men armed for battle. [6] Then Moses sent them out, 1,000 men from each tribe, and Phinehas son of Eleazar the priest led them into battle. They carried along the holy objects of the sanctuary and the trumpets for sounding the charge. [7] They attacked Midian as the LORD had commanded Moses, and they killed all the men. [8] All five of the Midianite kings—Evi, Rekem, Zur, Hur, and Reba—died in the battle. They also killed Balaam son of Beor with the sword.

[9] Then the Israelite army captured the Midianite women and children and seized their cattle and flocks and all their wealth as plunder. [10] They burned all the towns and villages where the Midianites had lived. [11] After they had gathered the plunder and captives, both people and animals, [12] they brought them all to Moses and Eleazar the priest, and to the whole community of Israel, which was camped on the plains of Moab beside the Jordan River, across from Jericho. [13] Moses, Eleazar the priest, and all the leaders of the community went to meet them outside the camp. [14] But Moses was furious with all the generals and captains* who had returned from the battle.

[15] "Why have you let all the women live?" he demanded. [16] "These are the very ones who followed Balaam's advice and caused the people of Israel to rebel against the LORD at Mount Peor. They are the ones who caused the plague to strike the LORD's people. [17] So kill all the boys and all the women who have had intercourse with a man. [18] Only the young girls who are virgins may live; you may keep them for yourselves. [19] And all of you who have killed anyone or touched a dead body must stay outside the camp for seven days. You must purify yourselves and your captives on the third and seventh days. [20] Purify all your clothing, too, and everything made of leather, goat hair, or wood."

[21] Then Eleazar the priest said to the men who were in the battle, "The LORD has given Moses this legal requirement: [22] Anything made of gold, silver, bronze, iron, tin, or lead—[23] that is, all metals that do not burn—must be passed through fire in order to be made ceremonially pure. These metal objects must then be further purified with the water of purification. But everything that burns must be purified by the water alone. [24] On

31:14 Hebrew *the commanders of thousands, and the commanders of hundreds;* also in 31:48, 52, 54.

1–2), widows and divorced women were responsible to fulfill any vows they made because they were not under a man's financial protection.

31:1–54 Conquest of the Midianites. Division of the Plunder. In fulfillment of God's original command in Numbers 25:17–18, Moses readied the troops for battle. The battle's purpose was to enact vengeance on Midian for leading Israel into idolatry. **7–8:** The dead include all the Midianite men, the five Midianite kings, and Balaam. According to v. 16, Balaam advised the Midianite women to lead Israel into idolatry, a detail not included in the account of chapter 25. **15–18:** Moses' rebuke of the warriors focuses on the female captives who are held solely responsible for Israel's sin at Baal-peor. The command to kill the boys along with the women who were not virgins may seem extremely harsh in the eyes of modern readers, and it is. Unfortunately, captives were allowed to live only if they served a purpose. In this case, the virgin women could be used, presumably as concubines and slaves. Because the older women were not virgins and were blamed as the primary instigators of the idolatry, they were executed. Extermination of all males, including the boys, was required for the annihilation of Midian to be complete.

the seventh day you must wash your clothes and be purified. Then you may return to the camp."

Division of the Plunder

25 And the LORD said to Moses, 26 "You and Eleazar the priest and the family leaders of each tribe are to make a list of all the plunder taken in the battle, including the people and animals. 27 Then divide the plunder into two parts, and give half to the men who fought the battle and half to the rest of the people. 28 From the army's portion, first give the LORD his share of the plunder—one of every 500 of the prisoners and of the cattle, donkeys, sheep, and goats. 29 Give this share of the army's half to Eleazar the priest as an offering to the LORD. 30 From the half that belongs to the people of Israel, take one of every fifty of the prisoners and of the cattle, donkeys, sheep, goats, and other animals. Give this share to the Levites, who are in charge of maintaining the LORD's Tabernacle." 31 So Moses and Eleazar the priest did as the LORD commanded Moses.

32 The plunder remaining from everything the fighting men had taken totaled 675,000 sheep and goats, 33 72,000 cattle, 34 61,000 donkeys, 35 and 32,000 virgin girls.

36 Half of the plunder was given to the fighting men. It totaled 337,500 sheep and goats, 37 of which 675 were the LORD's share; 38 36,000 cattle, of which 72 were the LORD's share; 39 30,500 donkeys, of which 61 were the LORD's share; 40 and 16,000 virgin girls, of whom 32 were the LORD's share. 41 Moses gave all the LORD's share to Eleazar the priest, just as the LORD had directed him.

42 Half of the plunder belonged to the people of Israel, and Moses separated it from the half belonging to the fighting men. 43 It totaled 337,500 sheep and goats, 44 36,000 cattle, 45 30,500 donkeys, 46 and 16,000 virgin girls. 47 From the half-share given to the people, Moses took one of every fifty prisoners and animals and gave them to the Levites, who maintained the LORD's Tabernacle. All this was done as the LORD had commanded Moses.

48 Then all the generals and captains came to Moses 49 and said, "We, your servants, have accounted for all the men who went out to battle under our command; not one of us is missing! 50 So we are presenting the items of gold we captured as an offering to the LORD from our share of the plunder—armbands, bracelets, rings, earrings, and necklaces. This will purify our lives before the LORD and make us right with him.*"

51 So Moses and Eleazar the priest received the gold from all the military commanders—all kinds of jewelry and crafted objects. 52 In all, the gold that the generals and captains presented as a gift to the LORD weighed about 420 pounds.* 53 All the fighting men had taken some of the plunder for themselves. 54 So Moses and Eleazar the priest accepted the gifts from the generals and captains and brought the gold to the Tabernacle* as a reminder to the LORD that the people of Israel belong to him.

The Tribes East of the Jordan

32 The tribes of Reuben and Gad owned vast numbers of livestock. So when they saw that the lands of Jazer and Gilead were ideally suited for their flocks and herds, 2 they came to Moses, Eleazar the priest, and the other leaders of the community. They said, 3 "Notice the towns of Ataroth, Dibon, Jazer, Nimrah, Heshbon, Elealeh, Sibmah,* Nebo, and Beon. 4 The LORD has conquered this whole area for the community of Israel, and it is ideally suited for all our livestock. 5 If we have found favor with you, please let us have this land as our property instead of giving us land across the Jordan River."

6 "Do you intend to stay here while your brothers go across and do all the fighting?" Moses asked the men of Gad and Reuben. 7 "Why do you want to discourage the rest of the people of Israel from going across to the land the LORD has given them? 8 Your ancestors did the same thing when I sent them from Kadesh-barnea

31:50 Or *will make atonement for our lives before the LORD.* **31:52** Hebrew *16,750 shekels* [191 kilograms]. **31:54** Hebrew *the Tent of Meeting.* **32:3** As in Samaritan Pentateuch and Greek version (see also 32:38); Hebrew reads *Sebam.*

48–54: This special offering was given because no men were lost in battle. The second generation remained intact; all of them would enter the promised land as God promised.

32:1–42 The Tribes East of the Jordan. In the Priestly writer's view the land God promised was west of the Jordan (cf. 34:1–12), making Reuben and Gad's request to settle on the east side unorthodox. The problem with their request is masked in the NLT translation, *instead of giving us land across the Jordan River*. The final statement is more forceful in the Hebrew: "Do not make us cross the Jordan." **6–7:** Moses' harsh reply assumes that Reuben and Gad wanted to settle their land immediately and avoid the conquest of the land west of the Jordan. Foregoing entry into the land was tantamount, in Moses' view, to the people's refusal to enter the land

to explore the land. 9 After they went up to the valley of Eshcol and explored the land, they discouraged the people of Israel from entering the land the LORD was giving them. 10 Then the LORD was very angry with them, and he vowed, 11 'Of all those I rescued from Egypt, no one who is twenty years old or older will ever see the land I swore to give to Abraham, Isaac, and Jacob, for they have not obeyed me wholeheartedly. 12 The only exceptions are Caleb son of Jephunneh the Kenizzite and Joshua son of Nun, for they have wholeheartedly followed the LORD.'

13 "The LORD was angry with Israel and made them wander in the wilderness for forty years until the entire generation that sinned in the LORD's sight had died. 14 But here you are, a brood of sinners, doing exactly the same thing! You are making the LORD even angrier with Israel. 15 If you turn away from him like this and he abandons them again in the wilderness, you will be responsible for destroying this entire nation!"

16 But they approached Moses and said, "We simply want to build pens for our livestock and fortified towns for our wives and children. 17 Then we will arm ourselves and lead our fellow Israelites into battle until we have brought them safely to their land. Meanwhile, our families will stay in the fortified towns we build here, so they will be safe from any attacks by the local people. 18 We will not return to our homes until all the people of Israel have received their portions of land. 19 But we do not claim any of the land on the other side of the Jordan. We would rather live here on the east side and accept this as our grant of land."

20 Then Moses said, "If you keep your word and arm yourselves for the LORD's battles, 21 and if your troops cross the Jordan and keep fighting until the LORD has driven out his enemies, 22 then you may return when the LORD has conquered the land. You will have fulfilled your duty to the LORD and to the rest of the people of Israel. And the land on the east side of the Jordan will be your property from the LORD. 23 But if you fail to keep your word, then you will have sinned against the LORD, and you may be sure that your sin will find you out. 24 Go ahead and build towns for your families and pens for your flocks, but do everything you have promised."

25 Then the men of Gad and Reuben replied, "We, your servants, will follow your instructions exactly. 26 Our children, wives, flocks, and cattle will stay here in the towns of Gilead. 27 But all who are able to bear arms will cross over to fight for the LORD, just as you have said."

28 So Moses gave orders to Eleazar the priest, Joshua son of Nun, and the leaders of the clans of Israel. 29 He said, "The men of Gad and Reuben who are armed for battle must cross the Jordan with you to fight for the LORD. If they do, give them the land of Gilead as their property when the land is conquered. 30 But if they refuse to arm themselves and cross over with you, then they must accept land with the rest of you in the land of Canaan."

31 The tribes of Gad and Reuben said again, "We are your servants, and we will do as the LORD has commanded! 32 We will cross the Jordan into Canaan fully armed to fight for the LORD, but our property will be here on this side of the Jordan."

33 So Moses assigned land to the tribes of Gad, Reuben, and half the tribe of Manasseh son of Joseph. He gave them the territory of King Sihon of the Amorites and the land of King Og of Bashan—the whole land with its cities and surrounding lands.

34 The descendants of Gad built the towns of Dibon, Ataroth, Aroer, 35 Atroth-shophan, Jazer, Jogbehah, 36 Beth-nimrah, and Beth-haran. These were all fortified towns with pens for their flocks.

37 The descendants of Reuben built the towns of Heshbon, Elealeh, Kiriathaim, 38 Nebo, Baal-meon, and Sibmah. They changed the names of some of the towns they conquered and rebuilt.

39 Then the descendants of Makir of the tribe of Manasseh went to Gilead and conquered it, and they drove out the Amorites living there. 40 So Moses gave Gilead to the Makirites, descendants of Manasseh, and they settled there. 41 The people of Jair, another clan of the tribe of Manas-

in Numbers 13—14. **16–19:** In response to Moses' accusations, Reuben and Gad reassured Moses that all they wanted was a safe place for their flocks and families. They would fight with the other tribes and return to their homes only after Canaan was conquered. This promise is made two more times in the narrative (vv. 25–27; 31–32) in response to Moses' concerns. **20–31:** Moses settled the dispute by forcing the Reubenites and Gadites to agree that if they failed to assist the other tribes they could not have the land east of the Jordan. If, however, they participated in the conquest, the eastern lands were theirs. **33:** The sudden introduction of Manasseh here is puzzling since that tribe was not included in the negotiations. Because of this, interpreters often suggest that these verses, which may reflect ancient trans-Jordanian settlements, were added to the narrative at a later time.

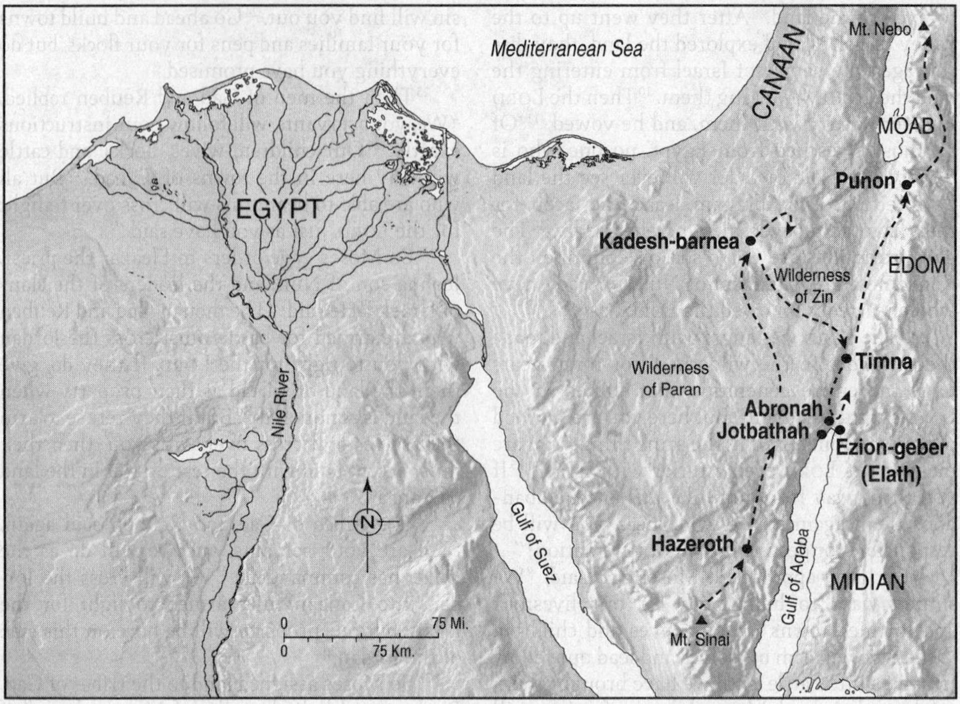

Journey from the Wilderness to Canaan

seh, captured many of the towns in Gilead and changed the name of that region to the Towns of Jair.* 42 Meanwhile, a man named Nobah captured the town of Kenath and its surrounding villages, and he renamed that area Nobah after himself.

Remembering Israel's Journey

33 This is the route the Israelites followed as they marched out of Egypt under the leadership of Moses and Aaron. 2 At the LORD's direction, Moses kept a written record of their progress. These are the stages of their march, identified by the different places where they stopped along the way.

3 They set out from the city of Rameses in early spring—on the fifteenth day of the first month*—on the morning after the first Passover celebration. The people of Israel left defiantly, in full view of all the Egyptians. 4 Meanwhile, the Egyptians were burying all their firstborn sons, whom the LORD had killed the night before. The LORD had defeated the gods of Egypt that night with great acts of judgment!

5 After leaving Rameses, the Israelites set up camp at Succoth.
6 Then they left Succoth and camped at Etham on the edge of the wilderness.
7 They left Etham and turned back toward Pi-hahiroth, opposite Baal-zephon, and camped near Migdol.
8 They left Pi-hahiroth and crossed the Red Sea* into the wilderness beyond. Then they traveled for three days into the Etham wilderness and camped at Marah.
9 They left Marah and camped at Elim, where there were twelve springs of water and seventy palm trees.

32:41 Hebrew *Havvoth-jair.* **33:3** This day in the ancient Hebrew lunar calendar occurred in late March, April, or early May. **33:8** Hebrew *the sea.*

33:1–56 Remembering Israel's Journey. Like a travel brochure, but without the pictures, this itinerary depicts the Israelites' journey, step by step, from Egypt to the plains of Moab. The list identifies forty-two stopping points from Rameses to the plains of Moab, symbolically representing the forty years of wilder-

10 They left Elim and camped beside the Red Sea.*
11 They left the Red Sea and camped in the wilderness of Sin.*
12 They left the wilderness of Sin and camped at Dophkah.
13 They left Dophkah and camped at Alush.
14 They left Alush and camped at Rephidim, where there was no water for the people to drink.
15 They left Rephidim and camped in the wilderness of Sinai.
16 They left the wilderness of Sinai and camped at Kibroth-hattaavah.
17 They left Kibroth-hattaavah and camped at Hazeroth.
18 They left Hazeroth and camped at Rithmah.
19 They left Rithmah and camped at Rimmon-perez.
20 They left Rimmon-perez and camped at Libnah.
21 They left Libnah and camped at Rissah.
22 They left Rissah and camped at Kehelathah.
23 They left Kehelathah and camped at Mount Shepher.
24 They left Mount Shepher and camped at Haradah.
25 They left Haradah and camped at Makheloth.
26 They left Makheloth and camped at Tahath.
27 They left Tahath and camped at Terah.
28 They left Terah and camped at Mithcah.
29 They left Mithcah and camped at Hashmonah.
30 They left Hashmonah and camped at Moseroth.
31 They left Moseroth and camped at Bene-jaakan.
32 They left Bene-jaakan and camped at Hor-haggidgad.
33 They left Hor-haggidgad and camped at Jotbathah.
34 They left Jotbathah and camped at Abronah.
35 They left Abronah and camped at Ezion-geber.
36 They left Ezion-geber and camped at Kadesh in the wilderness of Zin.
37 They left Kadesh and camped at Mount Hor, at the border of Edom. 38 While they were at the foot of Mount Hor, Aaron the priest was directed by the LORD to go up the mountain, and there he died. This happened in midsummer, on the first day of the fifth month* of the fortieth year after Israel's departure from Egypt. 39 Aaron was 123 years old when he died there on Mount Hor.
40 At that time the Canaanite king of Arad, who lived in the Negev in the land of Canaan, heard that the people of Israel were approaching his land.
41 Meanwhile, the Israelites left Mount Hor and camped at Zalmonah.
42 Then they left Zalmonah and camped at Punon.
43 They left Punon and camped at Oboth.
44 They left Oboth and camped at Iye-abarim on the border of Moab.
45 They left Iye-abarim* and camped at Dibon-gad.
46 They left Dibon-gad and camped at Almon-diblathaim.
47 They left Almon-diblathaim and camped in the mountains east of the river,* near Mount Nebo.
48 They left the mountains east of the river and camped on the plains of Moab beside the Jordan River, across from Jericho. 49 Along the Jordan River they camped from Beth-jeshimoth as far as the meadows of Acacia* on the plains of Moab.

50 While they were camped near the Jordan
River on the plains of Moab opposite Jericho,
the LORD said to Moses, 51 "Give the following
instructions to the people of Israel: When you
cross the Jordan River into the land of Canaan,
52 you must drive out all the people living there.
You must destroy all their carved and molten images and demolish all their pagan shrines. 53 Take
possession of the land and settle in it, because I
have given it to you to occupy. 54 You must distribute the land among the clans by sacred lot and in proportion to their size. A larger portion of land will be allotted to each of the larger clans, and a smaller portion will be allotted to each of the smaller clans. The decision of the sacred lot is final. In this way, the portions of land will be divided among your ancestral tribes. 55 But if you
fail to drive out the people who live in the land, those who remain will be like splinters in your eyes and thorns in your sides. They will harass

33:10 Hebrew *sea of reeds;* also in 33:11. **33:11** The geographical name *Sin* is related to *Sinai* and should not be confused with the English word *sin.* **33:38** This day in the ancient Hebrew lunar calendar occurred in July or August. **33:45** As in 33:44; Hebrew reads *Iyim,* another name for Iye-abarim. **33:47** Or *the mountains of Abarim;* also in 33:48. **33:49** Hebrew *as far as Abel-shittim.*

ness wandering. **51–53:** Although it is not made explicit here, other texts indicate that driving out the inhabitants means completely destroying them (cf. Deut 7). **55–56:** Failure would result in the Canaanites becoming *splinters in your eyes and thorns in your sides*—a threat that is fulfilled in Judges 2:1–3.

you in the land where you live. 56 And I will do to
you what I had planned to do to them."

Boundaries of the Land

34 Then the LORD said to Moses, 2 "Give
these instructions to the Israelites:
When you come into the land of
Canaan, which I am giving you as your special
possession, these will be the boundaries. 3 The
southern portion of your country will extend
from the wilderness of Zin, along the edge of
Edom. The southern boundary will begin on the
east at the Dead Sea.* 4 It will then run south past
Scorpion Pass* in the direction of Zin. Its southernmost point will be Kadesh-barnea, from which
it will go to Hazar-addar, and on to Azmon. 5 From
Azmon the boundary will turn toward the Brook
of Egypt and end at the Mediterranean Sea.*
6 "Your western boundary will be the coastline of the Mediterranean Sea.
7 "Your northern boundary will begin at the
Mediterranean Sea and run east to Mount Hor,
8 then to Lebo-hamath, and on through Zedad
9 and Ziphron to Hazar-enan. This will be your
northern boundary.
10 "The eastern boundary will start at Hazar-
enan and run south to Shepham, 11 then down to
Riblah on the east side of Ain. From there the
boundary will run down along the eastern edge
of the Sea of Galilee,* 12 and then along the Jordan River to the Dead Sea. These are the boundaries of your land."
13 Then Moses told the Israelites, "This territory is the homeland you are to divide among
yourselves by sacred lot. The LORD has commanded that the land be divided among the nine
and a half remaining tribes. 14 The families of the
tribes of Reuben, Gad, and half the tribe of Manasseh have already received their grants of land
15 on the east side of the Jordan River, across from
Jericho toward the sunrise."

Leaders to Divide the Land

16 And the LORD said to Moses, 17 "Eleazar the
priest and Joshua son of Nun are the men designated to divide the grants of land among the
people. 18 Enlist one leader from each tribe to help
them with the task. 19 These are the tribes and the
names of the leaders:

Tribe	*Leader*
Judah	Caleb son of Jephunneh
20 Simeon	Shemuel son of Ammihud
21 Benjamin	Elidad son of Kislon
22 Dan	Bukki son of Jogli
23 Manasseh son of Joseph	Hanniel son of Ephod
24 Ephraim son of Joseph	Kemuel son of Shiphtan
25 Zebulun	Elizaphan son of Parnach
26 Issachar	Paltiel son of Azzan
27 Asher	Ahihud son of Shelomi
28 Naphtali	Pedahel son of Ammihud

29 These are the men the LORD has appointed to
divide the grants of land in Canaan among the
Israelites."

Towns for the Levites

35 While Israel was camped beside the
Jordan on the plains of Moab across
from Jericho, the LORD said to Mo-
ses, 2 "Command the people of Israel to give to
the Levites from their property certain towns to
live in, along with the surrounding pasturelands.
3 These towns will be for the Levites to live in,
and the surrounding lands will provide pasture
for their cattle, flocks, and other livestock. 4 The
pastureland assigned to the Levites around these
towns will extend 1,500 feet* from the town
walls in every direction. 5 Measure off 3,000 feet*
outside the town walls in every direction—east,
south, west, north—with the town at the center.
This area will serve as the larger pastureland for
the towns.
6 "Six of the towns you give the Levites will

34:3 Hebrew *Salt Sea;* also in 34:12. **34:4** Or *the ascent of Akrabbim.* **34:5** Hebrew *the sea;* also in 34:6, 7. **34:11** Hebrew *Sea of Kinnereth.* **35:4** Hebrew *1,000 cubits* [460 meters]. **35:5** Hebrew *2,000 cubits* [920 meters].

In essence, if Israel failed to drive out the inhabitants, the Canaanites would tempt Israel into false worship. Consequently, God would enact judgment on Israel for their idolatry and drive them out of the land (exile).

34:1–29 The Boundaries of the Land. A map of Israel's land is depicted in this chapter, identifying the boundaries in each direction of the compass. **13–15:** The land within the boundaries is divided between nine and a half tribes because Reuben, Gad, and half the tribe of Manasseh chose to settle on the east side of the Jordan. **16–29:** The task originally assigned to Moses (26:52–56), then delegated to Eleazar and Joshua (32:28–30), now includes representatives from ten tribes. Reuben and Gad are not represented because all their territory was on the eastern side.

35:1–8 Towns for the Levites. Although the Levites were not given an allotment of land with the other

be cities of refuge, where a person who has accidentally killed someone can flee for safety. In addition, give them forty-two other towns. 7 In all, forty-eight towns with the surrounding pastureland will be given to the Levites. 8 These towns will come from the property of the people of Israel. The larger tribes will give more towns to the Levites, while the smaller tribes will give fewer. Each tribe will give property in proportion to the size of its land."

Cities of Refuge

9 The LORD said to Moses, 10 "Give the following instructions to the people of Israel.

"When you cross the Jordan into the land of Canaan, 11 designate cities of refuge to which people can flee if they have killed someone accidentally. 12 These cities will be places of protection from a dead person's relatives who want to avenge the death. The slayer must not be put to death before being tried by the community. 13 Designate six cities of refuge for yourselves, 14 three on the east side of the Jordan River and three on the west in the land of Canaan. 15 These cities are for the protection of Israelites, foreigners living among you, and traveling merchants. Anyone who accidentally kills someone may flee there for safety.

16 "But if someone strikes and kills another person with a piece of iron, it is murder, and the murderer must be executed. 17 Or if someone with a stone in his hand strikes and kills another person, it is murder, and the murderer must be put to death. 18 Or if someone strikes and kills another person with a wooden object, it is murder, and the murderer must be put to death. 19 The victim's nearest relative is responsible for putting the murderer to death. When they meet, the avenger must put the murderer to death. 20 So if someone hates another person and pushes him or throws a dangerous object at him and he dies, it is murder. 21 Or if someone hates another person and hits him with a fist and he dies, it is murder. In such cases, the avenger must put the murderer to death when they meet.

22 "But suppose someone pushes another person without having shown previous hostility, or throws something that unintentionally hits another person, 23 or accidentally drops a huge stone on someone, though they were not enemies, and the person dies. 24 If this should happen, the community must follow these regulations in making a judgment between the slayer and the avenger, the victim's nearest relative: 25 The community must protect the slayer from the avenger and must escort the slayer back to live in the city of refuge to which he fled. There he must remain until the death of the high priest, who was anointed with the sacred oil.

26 "But if the slayer ever leaves the limits of the city of refuge, 27 and the avenger finds him outside the city and kills him, it will not be considered murder. 28 The slayer should have stayed inside the city of refuge until the death of the high priest. But after the death of the high priest, the slayer may return to his own property. 29 These are legal requirements for you to observe from generation to generation, wherever you may live.

30 "All murderers must be put to death, but only if evidence is presented by more than one witness. No one may be put to death on the testimony of only one witness. 31 Also, you must never accept a ransom payment for the life of someone judged guilty of murder and subject to execution; murderers must always be put to death. 32 And never accept a ransom payment from someone who has fled to a city of refuge, allowing a slayer to return to his property before the death of the high priest. 33 This will ensure that the land where you live will not be polluted, for murder pollutes the land. And no sacrifice except the execution of the murderer can purify the land from murder.* 34 You must not defile the

35:33 Or *can make atonement for murder.*

tribes, the legislation here sets apart forty-eight cities around which the Levites could live and pasture their animals.

35:9–34 Cities of Refuge. A life counted for a life (Gen 9:5–6), so murderers received the death penalty (see Exod 21:12, 14; Lev 24:17; Num 35:30). The death penalty was carried out by a member of the deceased person's family who enacted blood vengeance (see v. 19). In instances where the murder was accidental (i.e., involuntary manslaughter) the accused person was allowed to flee to a city of refuge (cf. Josh 20:7–9). **19:** The *avenger* is elsewhere called the "kinsman redeemer" because, in addition to blood vengeance, he was required to help redeem destitute family members (Lev 25:25, 48; Num 5:8; Ruth 2:20; 3:9, 12; 4:1–10; Jer 32:7–15). **25:** Even if the killing was determined to be unintentional, the murderer was required to live in the city of refuge until the death of the high priest. Symbolically, the high priest's death atoned for the killer. **30:** Accusations of murder required at least two witnesses (cf. Deut 19:15). **31–32:** These verses eliminate the possibility of rich persons buying their way out of proper

Women's Rights in Biblical Times

Women's rights in biblical times were, by modern standards, sharply limited. Patriarchy placed all women, from the Hebrew slave in rural Palestine to the wealthy matron in Rome, under male authority. Yet the experience of an individual woman would have been affected by her situation: whether she was wealthy or poor, Jew or Gentile, Roman citizen or slave, urban or rural, operating in a public or private sphere.

Old Testament Times

In many ways the Old Testament reflects the patriarchal world of its day. Wives and daughters were subject to their husbands and fathers, and they had little right to self-determination: Fathers and husbands could overrule a woman's vows; an injury to a woman was viewed as an injury to her father or husband; and while a man could divorce his wife if she "didn't please him" (Deut 24:1), we read of no such rights for a woman. A raped woman was treated with suspicion and could be killed or forced to marry her rapist. The stories of Lot offering his virginal daughters as sexual appeasements to violent strangers and of Abraham expelling Hagar from her home illustrate the vulnerability of women in this culture (see also the stories of the slave raped to death and of the sacrifice of Jephthah's daughter, both in Judges).

The Old Testament law does, however, provide protections for women. Although a father could sell his daughter (or son) as a slave, he could not turn her into a prostitute. Widows were provided for, and women who were not overruled by their husbands or fathers could make and be held responsible for vows. Although women were dependent upon men to protect their rights, those who were not so provided for could seek recourse: Tamar, for example, took steps to ensure that her right to bear a child was respected. A woman could act with great autonomy, as is the case with the industrious wife (Prov 31:10–31) who earns praise from her husband when she acts decisively and independently.

Arguably, the most important right in the Old Testament was that of membership among the people of God, and this right Israelite women had. Women received blessings, could benefit from the reading of the law, and could participate in worshiping God. They could participate in sacrifices, consult a prophet independently, and take the vow of the Nazirite. Deborah the judge, prophet, and leader, Huldah the prophet, and Miriam the prophet, worshiper, and leader all played respected roles in the life of God's people.

New Testament Times

The women of the New Testament were also under a patriarchal system, but being part of the Roman Empire brought them some freedoms. Some women who had privilege, power, or money obtained divorces; bought, sold, and inherited property; and obtained freedom from slavery. Women such as Lydia, who sold cloth, and Chloe, who appears to be the head of a household, attained a degree of self-determination.

As was the case for Old Testament women, the most significant right for New Testament women was that of full membership in the community of God. In comparison with the surrounding first-century religions, in which women were often excluded and viewed as ritually unclean, women in the early church were given considerable rights of participation. Jesus granted women the right to approach, learn from, be healed by, accompany, and support him; he treated them with respect; and he entrusted them with the first preaching of the gospel. To Paul, women were members of the body of Christ and potential co-laborers for Christ, and thus Paul was far more concerned with what women could do than with what they could not. Women prayed, prophesied, and exhibited many gifts. Prisca and Nympha are examples of women with churches in their homes, in which they possibly were the patron or leader. Prisca taught Apollos, and Junia and Phoebe were called "apostle" and "minister." For New Testament women, their encounter with the church was a liberating experience, granting them the right to approach God, to be a member of God's household, and to exercise their gifts and energies for the work of the church of God.

land where you live, for I live there myself. I am the LORD, who lives among the people of Israel."

Women Who Inherit Property

36 Then the heads of the clans of Gilead—descendants of Makir, son of Manasseh, son of Joseph—came to Moses and the family leaders of Israel with a petition. 2 They said, "Sir, the LORD instructed you to divide the land by sacred lot among the people of Israel. You were told by the LORD to give the grant of land owned by our brother Zelophehad to his daughters. 3 But if they marry men from another tribe, their grants of land will go with them to the tribe into which they marry. In this way, the total area of our tribal land will be reduced. 4 Then when the Year of Jubilee comes, their portion of land will be added to that of the new tribe, causing it to be lost forever to our ancestral tribe."

5 So Moses gave the Israelites this command from the LORD: "The claim of the men of the tribe of Joseph is legitimate. 6 This is what the LORD commands concerning the daughters of Zelophehad: Let them marry anyone they like, as long as it is within their own ancestral tribe. 7 None of the territorial land may pass from tribe to tribe, for all the land given to each tribe must remain within the tribe to which it was first allotted. 8 The daughters throughout the tribes of Israel who are in line to inherit property must marry within their tribe, so that all the Israelites will keep their ancestral property. 9 No grant of land may pass from one tribe to another; each tribe of Israel must keep its allotted portion of land."

10 The daughters of Zelophehad did as the LORD commanded Moses. 11 Mahlah, Tirzah, Hoglah, Milcah, and Noah all married cousins on their father's side. 12 They married into the clans of Manasseh son of Joseph. Thus, their inheritance of land remained within their ancestral tribe.

13 These are the commands and regulations that the LORD gave to the people of Israel through Moses while they were camped on the plains of Moab beside the Jordan River across from Jericho.

---

punishment. Murderers could not pay for their crime with money nor could one purchase an early release from a city of refuge. **33–34:** Murder was considered to pollute the land because human blood was spilled. The only atonement for such an act was the death of another human, either the murderer or, in the case of involuntary manslaughter, the high priest. In the case of murder, no animal sacrifice was sufficient.

36:1–12 Women Who Inherit Property. The story about the daughters of Zelophehad (27:1–11) resurfaces. **4:** During the Year of Jubilee, which occurred every fiftieth year, all land was supposed to be returned to the original owner (Lev 25:24–34). But if the daughters married into other tribes, Zelophehad's land would no longer be considered part of the tribe of Manasseh and would not be returned. **5–6:** The practice of marrying within the tribe, known as endogamy, was not uncommon in Israel, and was actually preferred in order to protect the purity of lineages. **7–9:** These additional regulations stipulate that under no circumstances was land to be transferred from one tribe to another. **10–12:** In accordance with the command, Zelophehad's daughters married paternal cousins, thereby keeping their father's land within the tribe of Manasseh. In effect, daughters who inherited were only temporary custodians of their fathers' land, not true heirs. As soon as they married, their inheritance rights were transferred to their husbands who passed them on to sons.

36:13 A Summary. The final verse of Numbers leaves Israel on the plains of Moab across from Jericho. This is where Moses will deliver his sermons (Deut) and the place from which the second generation will enter the promised land in Joshua.

DEUTERONOMY

INTRODUCTION

Deuteronomy could be described as the most significant book in the Old Testament. It is indissolubly linked to the historical books—Joshua through 2 Kings—because the Deuteronomistic History stems from the links within these books. There are also close connections between the interests and motivation of the Deuteronomist and the prophets. In the New Testament the book of Deuteronomy is quoted directly thirty times, and there are a further eighty clear allusions. Deuteronomy brings together and reflects on the principles of covenant living. It provides a historical background for the nation of Israel, gives a sample selection of laws and rituals, and discusses the consequences, in terms of blessings and curses, if Israel does or does not keep the covenant.

Aims and Objectives

The main purpose of Deuteronomy is not just to provide information about what it means for Israel to live as God's covenant people. Instead, Deuteronomy is a driving force, inspiring loyalty and action. It is in many ways the equivalent of a modern motivational video or seminar. It is the nearest thing that Israel had to a national constitution. It gives the people—of each ongoing generation—a sense of national identity and drives them to take seriously the implications of their identity as the people of God. One of its main links with both New Testament teaching and the teaching of the Prophets is its strong stress that the essence of religion is not a set of beliefs and rules but a personal relationship with the God who has chosen this people as his own. This relationship has to be lived out in the context of everyday life. Deuteronomy provides data as to what this means in practical terms and a stimulus and encouragement to get on and live it. It stands as a refueling station for the people.

There is no doubt that Deuteronomy may be seen as a covenant document. It is structured in the form of a series of speeches given, apparently, by Moses just before the people entered the promised land. It has sometimes been seen as a legal document, but that does not really do this book justice. The laws mentioned are selective, illustrative rather than a comprehensive code. The selection is there to explain rather than to define the covenant and its requirements. We do not have here a text book for lawyers or for leaders, but a challenge for the whole people—children, women, and men alike.

The Speeches

If Israel is to have a clear sense of identity and an effective awareness of the meaning of her covenant partnership with the LORD, then a historical perspective must be vital. Even today, particularly among the older generations and perhaps especially women, interest in family background and genealogical information is growing fast. People like to know where they come from. For women, the awareness of history has always been important: not so much in terms of dates and leaders but in terms of homes and relationships, the stories of the past. The only specific mentions of women in this first speech are when we hear of men, women, and children destroyed by Israel in their progress to the promised land, and in the mention of the wives left behind by the soldiers from the tribes who wished to settle on the eastern side of the Jordan. The history described was their history, women's history, just as much as that of the men.

There are laws and instructions found elsewhere in the Pentateuch that are not contained here. This is not meant to be a comprehensive survey of everything that Israel was or would ever be required to do or not to do. It is a selection, a summary, meant to enable Israelites to get a solid "feel" for the kind of life that God wanted them to lead. It tells them God was concerned about their family life, social life, interaction with their neighbors, religious practices, employment, warfare, food, religious beliefs and understanding, national government, justice system, health and their hygiene. In other words, there was *no* aspect of life that was not relevant to their lives as God's covenant people. There was no separation between the religious and nonreligious aspects of life.

The first two speeches set out the essence of what it means to be Israel, living in covenant relationship with God. The third speech brings home to the Israelites the consequences of allegiance to God and obedience to the law, or of turning from God and disobeying the law. Overall, sixty-five verses speak of curses and only fourteen of blessings. The reason for this apparent imbalance is not discussed. It may be that the editor/author fears (or knows, if he is writing in the seventh century) that Israel will be much more inclined to disobedience than obedience. He therefore spends more time on giving the warnings that might just scare the people into avoiding disaster—perhaps parallel to the health warnings that are becoming more and more prominent on tobacco products throughout the world. This behavior (like smoking) can seriously damage your health!

The fourth speech, or set of speeches, forms a kind of reprise, a review of all that has been covered so far. There is a further look back at Israel's history, an awareness of the importance of the law, a discussion of the consequences of keeping or failing to keep the covenant, a stress on the importance of handing on to their children a realization of their identity as God's people, and finally a sense of urgency about the crucial nature of the decision and the commitment that they as individuals and as a nation are being called upon to make. This really was a life-and-death situation for Israel, and the Deuteronomist was determined that all should be aware of it.

Date and Authorship

Although Deuteronomy itself is formulated as speeches rather than as direct treaty, strong links between Deuteronomy and other ancient Near Eastern treaty documents have been identified. There is some debate as to whether it relates more closely to the Babylonian style of treaty (ca. first millennium BC) or the Hittite style of treaty (ca. second millennium BC). If the Hittite style, then Deuteronomy can be dated as basically Mosaic, and the speeches could be seen as original. On the other hand, if the later Babylonian style is the background, then it supports the view that Deuteronomy was produced in the seventh century BC, around the reign of Josiah, and the speeches are a literary technique used to further the writer's purposes.

The language of Deuteronomy is described as good seventh-century Hebrew, which means that if we are to accept the dating as essentially Mosaic, then we must assume that the language was revised and updated around the time of Josiah—in the same way that modern translations *re-present* the biblical material so that it can be understood by contemporary readers. This would make very good sense: Deuteronomy's prime aim of motivating people to really "own" their identity as a covenant people and to actively live out a covenant lifestyle would be harder to achieve if the language used no longer communicated. In some ways the disagreements over dating can be seen as stemming from the ongoing relevance of the book. It does have a timeless quality, which speaks clearly to each generation.

Themes

The overall theme of Deuteronomy is the call for Israel to be a covenant people and to be aware of herself as that, but it is worthwhile to note a number of subsidiary themes and motifs to look out for as one is reading through the book.

Grace and Law. The Deuteronomist wants to show that God has been and continues to be gracious to Israel, that the LORD is the one who gives them the covenant and provides a stream of blessing for them. But there is also a concern to show the need for the law and for keeping the law—in obedience to their great God but also so that they can imitate and reflect him. As their God is holy, just, and concerned for the poor, so must they be. Grace and law appear to be inextricably linked in the mind of the author: They are not in conflict.

The Deuteronomic Principle. The idea that righteousness will bring blessing and unrighteousness disaster is often seen as at the heart of the Deuteronomist's thinking. It is clear that this principle is present. However, the view that if God blesses the righteous, then those who are blessed—often interpreted as those who are *rich*—must therefore be righteous becomes a travesty of Deuteronomy's teaching.

Humanitarian Interests. The concentration on blessings coming from God does not override the responsibility for others. There is a particular responsibility to care for those who do not seem to be obviously blessed by God, those who if the Deuteronomic principle is applied unthinkingly, could be seen as unrighteous.

Kinship. Related to the humanitarian interests is the sense that the whole community is viewed in family terms; responsibilities of brotherhood and sisterhood carry through to all aspects of life. Business and government must be carried out in the light of this family relationship.

Opposition to Alien Religion. There is within Deuteronomy a consistent stress on the need for the total eradication of all Canaanite worship from within the Israelite community.

The Centralization of Worship. Deuteronomy speaks often of "the place that the LORD your God shall choose." In the light of Israelite history this is interpreted as a single centralized sanctuary—namely the Temple. This is perhaps not quite as clear cut as is sometimes assumed but there does seem to be a strong assumption that corporate worship must take place in officially sanctioned situations. —*Mary J. Evans*

1:1—4:49	Moses' First Speech: Historical Overview and Preliminary Challenge
5:1—26:19	Moses' Second Speech: Overview of the Law
27:1—29:1	Moses' Third Speech: Consequences—Blessings and Curses
29:2—32:52	Moses' Fourth Speech: The Ongoing Challenge
33:1–29	Moses' Fifth Speech: The Blessing on the Tribes
34:1–12	Conclusion: The Baton Is Handed On

✧

Introduction to Moses' First Address

1 These are the words that Moses spoke to all
the people of Israel while they were in the
wilderness east of the Jordan River. They
were camped in the Jordan Valley* near Suph,
between Paran on one side and Tophel, Laban,
Hazeroth, and Di-zahab on the other.
2 Normally it takes only eleven days to travel
from Mount Sinai* to Kadesh-barnea, going
by way of Mount Seir. 3 But forty years after
the Israelites left Egypt, on the first day of the
eleventh month,* Moses addressed the people
of Israel, telling them everything the LORD had
commanded him to say. 4 This took place after he
had defeated King Sihon of the Amorites, who
had ruled in Heshbon, and King Og of Bashan,
who had ruled in Ashtaroth and Edrei.
5 While the Israelites were in the land of
Moab east of the Jordan River, Moses carefully
explained the LORD's instructions as follows.

The Command to Leave Sinai

6 "When we were at Mount Sinai, the LORD our
God said to us, 'You have stayed at this mountain
long enough. 7 It is time to break camp and move
on. Go to the hill country of the Amorites and
to all the neighboring regions—the Jordan Valley, the hill country, the western foothills,* the
Negev, and the coastal plain. Go to the land of
the Canaanites and to Lebanon, and all the way
to the great Euphrates River. 8 Look, I am giving
all this land to you! Go in and occupy it, for it is
the land the LORD swore to give to your ancestors Abraham, Isaac, and Jacob, and to all their
descendants.' "

Moses Appoints Leaders from Each Tribe

9 Moses continued, "At that time I told you,
'You are too great a burden for me to carry all
by myself. 10 The LORD your God has increased
your population, making you as numerous as the
stars! 11 And may the LORD, the God of your ancestors, multiply you a thousand times more and
bless you as he promised! 12 But you are such a
heavy load to carry! How can I deal with all your
problems and bickering? 13 Choose some well-
respected men from each tribe who are known
for their wisdom and understanding, and I will
appoint them as your leaders.'
14 "Then you responded, 'Your plan is a good
one.' 15 So I took the wise and respected men you
had selected from your tribes and appointed them
to serve as judges and officials over you. Some
were responsible for a thousand people, some for
a hundred, some for fifty, and some for ten.
16 "At that time I instructed the judges, 'You
must hear the cases of your fellow Israelites and
the foreigners living among you. Be perfectly
fair in your decisions 17 and impartial in your
judgments. Hear the cases of those who are poor
as well as those who are rich. Don't be afraid
of anyone's anger, for the decision you make is
God's decision. Bring me any cases that are too
difficult for you, and I will handle them.'
18 "At that time I gave you instructions about
everything you were to do.

Scouts Explore the Land

19 "Then, just as the LORD our God commanded
us, we left Mount Sinai and traveled through the
great and terrifying wilderness, as you yourselves remember, and headed toward the hill
country of the Amorites. When we arrived at
Kadesh-barnea, 20 I said to you, 'You have now
reached the hill country of the Amorites that the
LORD our God is giving us. 21 Look! He has placed
the land in front of you. Go and occupy it as the
LORD, the God of your ancestors, has promised
you. Don't be afraid! Don't be discouraged!'
22 "But you all came to me and said, 'First, let's
send out scouts to explore the land for us. They
will advise us on the best route to take and which
towns we should enter.'
23 "This seemed like a good idea to me, so I
chose twelve scouts, one from each of your tribes.

1:1 Hebrew *the Arabah;* also in 1:7. **1:2** Hebrew *Horeb,* another name for Sinai; also in 1:6, 19. **1:3** Hebrew *In the fortieth year, on the first day of the eleventh month.* This day in the ancient Hebrew lunar calendar occurred in January or February. **1:7** Hebrew *the Shephelah.*

1:1—4:49 Moses' First Speech

1:1–8 Introduction. The precise site of the Israelite gathering emphasizes that these are a real people in a real situation. Two key points are that it was forty years since they first set out for the new land, and that it was the LORD himself who was behind the words that Moses spoke.

1:9–18 Moses Appoints Leaders. It is clear that different kinds of leadership are necessary. Verse 13 encourages Israel to choose tribal leaders. This implies a level of democracy that does not seem to be reflected in the practice of Israel elsewhere.

1:19–25 The Scouts. In Numbers 13 the scouts (or spies) are sent out at God's command; here the idea comes first from the people. It is a good idea and means that the people have good information as to what the land was like.

24 They headed for the hill country and came to the valley of Eshcol and explored it. 25 They picked some of its fruit and brought it back to us. And they reported, 'The land the LORD our God has given us is indeed a good land.'

Israel's Rebellion against the LORD

26 "But you rebelled against the command of the LORD your God and refused to go in. 27 You complained in your tents and said, 'The LORD must hate us. That's why he has brought us here from Egypt—to hand us over to the Amorites to be slaughtered. 28 Where can we go? Our brothers have demoralized us with their report. They tell us, "The people of the land are taller and more powerful than we are, and their towns are large, with walls rising high into the sky! We even saw giants there—the descendants of Anak!"'

29 "But I said to you, 'Don't be shocked or afraid of them! 30 The LORD your God is going ahead of you. He will fight for you, just as you saw him do in Egypt. 31 And you saw how the LORD your God cared for you all along the way as you traveled through the wilderness, just as a father cares for his child. Now he has brought you to this place.'

32 "But even after all he did, you refused to trust the LORD your God, 33 who goes before you looking for the best places to camp, guiding you with a pillar of fire by night and a pillar of cloud by day.

34 "When the LORD heard your complaining, he became very angry. So he solemnly swore, 35 'Not one of you from this wicked generation will live to see the good land I swore to give your ancestors, 36 except Caleb son of Jephunneh. He will see this land because he has followed the LORD completely. I will give to him and his descendants some of the very land he explored during his scouting mission.'

37 "And the LORD was also angry with me because of you. He said to me, 'Moses, not even you will enter the Promised Land! 38 Instead, your assistant, Joshua son of Nun, will lead the people into the land. Encourage him, for he will lead Israel as they take possession of it. 39 I will give the land to your little ones—your innocent children. You were afraid they would be captured, but they will be the ones who occupy it. 40 As for you, turn around now and go on back through the wilderness toward the Red Sea.*'

41 "Then you confessed, 'We have sinned against the LORD! We will go into the land and fight for it, as the LORD our God has commanded us.' So your men strapped on their weapons, thinking it would be easy to attack the hill country.

42 "But the LORD told me to tell you, 'Do not attack, for I am not with you. If you go ahead on your own, you will be crushed by your enemies.'

43 "This is what I told you, but you would not listen. Instead, you again rebelled against the LORD's command and arrogantly went into the hill country to fight. 44 But the Amorites who lived there came out against you like a swarm of bees. They chased and battered you all the way from Seir to Hormah. 45 Then you returned and wept before the LORD, but he refused to listen. 46 So you stayed there at Kadesh for a long time.

Remembering Israel's Wanderings

2 "Then we turned around and headed back across the wilderness toward the Red Sea,* just as the LORD had instructed me, and we wandered around in the region of Mount Seir for a long time.

2 "Then at last the LORD said to me, 3 'You have been wandering around in this hill coun-

1:40 Hebrew *sea of reeds.* **2:1** Hebrew *sea of reeds.*

1:26–46 The Land. Information can be a dangerous thing. The people know it is a good land, but they also know the risks, which leads them to reject God's instructions to enter. Verse 37 returns to the question of leadership. Moses states (or perhaps complains) that, *because of you* he was not able to enter the promised land (3:26 picks up the same point). Moses' great longing to enter into the land was not to be fulfilled because of the failures of the people that he led. The account in Numbers 20 is somewhat different. That passage puts the blame securely on Moses' own shoulders. It seems a heavy punishment for a trivial crime, striking the rock instead of speaking to it, but Moses as a leader had a strong responsibility to represent God rightly. Taking it upon himself to misrepresent God as being the source of his own personal anger was a serious offence. It may be here that the elderly Moses is seeking to shift or to share that blame. The Deuteronomist clearly wants to make the point that leadership has implications and consequences. There is perhaps some background here to the directive in James 3:1 that not many should presume to be teachers because they will be judged more strictly.

2:1–25 The Wanderings Begin. This is an abridged record of events, which Exodus and Numbers describe in more detail. The intention here seems to be to provide the people with a sensibility for what had gone on in the past and to bring to mind the whole history, which they would have known from the other sources.

try long enough; turn to the north. [4]Give these orders to the people: "You will pass through the country belonging to your relatives the Edomites, the descendants of Esau, who live in Seir. The Edomites will feel threatened, so be careful. [5]Do not bother them, for I have given them all the hill country around Mount Seir as their property, and I will not give you even one square foot of their land. [6]If you need food to eat or water to drink, pay them for it. [7]For the LORD your God has blessed you in everything you have done. He has watched your every step through this great wilderness. During these forty years, the LORD your God has been with you, and you have lacked nothing." '

[8]"So we bypassed the territory of our relatives, the descendants of Esau, who live in Seir. We avoided the road through the Arabah Valley that comes up from Elath and Ezion-geber.

"Then as we turned north along the desert route through Moab, [9]the LORD warned us, 'Do not bother the Moabites, the descendants of Lot, or start a war with them. I have given them Ar as their property, and I will not give you any of their land.' "

[10](A race of giants called the Emites had once lived in the area of Ar. They were as strong and numerous and tall as the Anakites, another race of giants. [11]Both the Emites and the Anakites are also known as the Rephaites, though the Moabites call them Emites. [12]In earlier times the Horites had lived in Seir, but they were driven out and displaced by the descendants of Esau, just as Israel drove out the people of Canaan when the LORD gave Israel their land.)

[13]Moses continued, "Then the LORD said to us, 'Get moving. Cross the Zered Brook.' So we crossed the brook.

[14]"Thirty-eight years passed from the time we first left Kadesh-barnea until we finally crossed the Zered Brook! By then, all the men old enough to fight in battle had died in the wilderness, as the LORD had vowed would happen. [15]The LORD struck them down until they had all been eliminated from the community.

[16]"When all the men of fighting age had died, [17]the LORD said to me, [18]'Today you will cross the border of Moab at Ar [19]and enter the land of the Ammonites, the descendants of Lot. But do not bother them or start a war with them. I have given the land of Ammon to them as their property, and I will not give you any of their land.' "

[20](That area was once considered the land of the Rephaites, who had lived there, though the Ammonites call them Zamzummites. [21]They were also as strong and numerous and tall as the Anakites. But the LORD destroyed them so the Ammonites could occupy their land. [22]He had done the same for the descendants of Esau who lived in Seir, for he destroyed the Horites so they could settle there in their place. The descendants of Esau live there to this day. [23]A similar thing happened when the Caphtorites from Crete* invaded and destroyed the Avvites, who had lived in villages in the area of Gaza.)

[24]Moses continued, "Then the LORD said, 'Now get moving! Cross the Arnon Gorge. Look, I will hand over to you Sihon the Amorite, king of Heshbon, and I will give you his land. Attack him and begin to occupy the land. [25]Beginning today I will make people throughout the earth terrified because of you. When they hear reports about you, they will tremble with dread and fear.' "

Victory over Sihon of Heshbon

[26]Moses continued, "From the wilderness of Kedemoth I sent ambassadors to King Sihon of Heshbon with this proposal of peace:

> [27]'Let us travel through your land. We will stay on the main road and won't turn off into the fields on either side. [28]Sell us food to eat and water to drink, and we will pay for it. All we want is permission to pass through your land. [29]The descendants of Esau who live in Seir allowed us to go through their country, and so did the Moabites, who live in Ar. Let us pass through until we cross the Jordan into the land the LORD our God is giving us.'

2:23 Hebrew *from Caphtor.*

2:26—3:11 Victory over Heshbon and Bashan. For the modern reader, this section raises uncomfortable issues relating to the conduct of "holy" war. Those who stood in Israel's way were completely destroyed. Whole communities of *men, women, and children* (2:34; 3:6) were slaughtered. For ancient Israelites this would have been a great victory, a reason for pride, and although discussions of innocence and guilt occur elsewhere in the Old Testament, that issue is not raised here. However, 2:9 states, *Do not bother the Moabites . . . I will not give you any of their land,* showing that we must beware of simplistic views of triumphalistic nationalism. The victories of Israel are the main concern here, but the reader must be aware that the God who has instituted a covenant relationship with Israel also has concerns for and dealings with other nations.

30 "But King Sihon of Heshbon refused to allow us to pass through, because the LORD your
God made Sihon stubborn and defiant so he could
help you defeat him, as he has now done.
31 "Then the LORD said to me, 'Look, I have
begun to hand King Sihon and his land over to
you. Begin now to conquer and occupy his land.'
32 "Then King Sihon declared war on us and
mobilized his forces at Jahaz. 33 But the LORD our
God handed him over to us, and we crushed him,
his sons, and all his people. 34 We conquered all
his towns and completely destroyed* everyone—
men, women, and children. Not a single person
was spared. 35 We took all the livestock as plunder
for ourselves, along with anything of value from
the towns we ransacked.
36 "The LORD our God also helped us conquer Aroer on the edge of the Arnon Gorge, and
the town in the gorge, and the whole area as far
as Gilead. No town had walls too strong for us.
37 However, we avoided the land of the Ammonites all along the Jabbok River and the towns in
the hill country—all the places the LORD our
God had commanded us to leave alone.

Victory over Og of Bashan

3 "Next we turned and headed for the land
of Bashan, where King Og and his entire
army attacked us at Edrei. 2 But the LORD
told me, 'Do not be afraid of him, for I have given
you victory over Og and his entire army, and I
will give you all his land. Treat him just as you
treated King Sihon of the Amorites, who ruled
in Heshbon.'
3 "So the LORD our God handed King Og and
all his people over to us, and we killed them all.
Not a single person survived. 4 We conquered all
sixty of his towns—the entire Argob region in
his kingdom of Bashan. Not a single town escaped our conquest. 5 These towns were all fortified with high walls and barred gates. We also
took many unwalled villages at the same time.
6 We completely destroyed* the kingdom of Bashan, just as we had destroyed King Sihon of
Heshbon. We destroyed all the people in every
town we conquered—men, women, and children
alike. 7 But we kept all the livestock for ourselves
and took plunder from all the towns.
8 "So we took the land of the two Amorite
kings east of the Jordan River—all the way from
the Arnon Gorge to Mount Hermon. 9 (Mount
Hermon is called Sirion by the Sidonians, and
the Amorites call it Senir.) 10 We had now conquered all the cities on the plateau and all Gilead
and Bashan, as far as the towns of Salecah and
Edrei, which were part of Og's kingdom in Bashan. 11 (King Og of Bashan was the last survivor
of the giant Rephaites. His bed was made of iron
and was more than thirteen feet long and six feet
wide.* It can still be seen in the Ammonite city
of Rabbah.)

Land Division East of the Jordan

12 "When we took possession of this land, I gave
to the tribes of Reuben and Gad the territory beyond Aroer along the Arnon Gorge, plus half of
the hill country of Gilead with its towns. 13 Then
I gave the rest of Gilead and all of Bashan—Og's
former kingdom—to the half-tribe of Manasseh. (This entire Argob region of Bashan used
to be known as the land of the Rephaites. 14 Jair,
a leader from the tribe of Manasseh, conquered
the whole Argob region in Bashan, all the way
to the border of the Geshurites and Maacathites.
Jair renamed this region after himself, calling it
the Towns of Jair,* as it is still known today.) 15 I
gave Gilead to the clan of Makir. 16 But I also gave
part of Gilead to the tribes of Reuben and Gad.
The area I gave them extended from the middle
of the Arnon Gorge in the south to the Jabbok
River on the Ammonite frontier. 17 They also received the Jordan Valley, all the way from the Sea
of Galilee down to the Dead Sea,* with the Jordan River serving as the western boundary. To
the east were the slopes of Pisgah.
18 "At that time I gave this command to the
tribes that would live east of the Jordan: 'Although the LORD your God has given you this
land as your property, all your fighting men
must cross the Jordan ahead of your Israelite
relatives, armed and ready to assist them. 19 Your
wives, children, and numerous livestock, however, may stay behind in the towns I have given
you. 20 When the LORD has given security to the
rest of the Israelites, as he has to you, and when
they occupy the land the LORD your God is giving them across the Jordan River, then you may
all return here to the land I have given you.'

2:34 The Hebrew term used here refers to the complete consecration of things or people to the LORD, either by destroying them or by giving them as an offering. **3:6** The Hebrew term used here refers to the complete consecration of things or people to the LORD, either by destroying them or by giving them as an offering; also in 3:6b. **3:11** Hebrew *9 cubits* [4.1 meters] *long and 4 cubits* [1.8 meters] *wide.* **3:14** Hebrew *Havvoth-jair.* **3:17** Hebrew *from Kinnereth to the Sea of the Arabah, the Salt Sea.*

3:12–20 The Eastern Area. This section concludes with a brief description of the land assigned to the two and a half tribes who decided to remain on the east side of the Jordan.

Moses Forbidden to Enter the Land
21 “At that time I gave Joshua this charge: ‘You
have seen for yourself everything the LORD your
God has done to these two kings. He will do the
same to all the kingdoms on the west side of the
Jordan. 22 Do not be afraid of the nations there,
for the LORD your God will fight for you.’
23 “At that time I pleaded with the LORD and
said, 24 ‘O Sovereign LORD, you have only begun to show your greatness and the strength
of your hand to me, your servant. Is there any
god in heaven or on earth who can perform such
great and mighty deeds as you do? 25 Please let
me cross the Jordan to see the wonderful land on
the other side, the beautiful hill country and the
Lebanon mountains.’
26 “But the LORD was angry with me because
of you, and he would not listen to me. ‘That’s
enough!’ he declared. ‘Speak of it no more. 27 But
go up to Pisgah Peak, and look over the land in
every direction. Take a good look, but you may
not cross the Jordan River. 28 Instead, commission
Joshua and encourage and strengthen him, for
he will lead the people across the Jordan. He will
give them all the land you now see before you
as their possession.’ 29 So we stayed in the valley
near Beth-peor.

Moses Urges Israel to Obey
4 “And now, Israel, listen carefully to these
decrees and regulations that I am about to
teach you. Obey them so that you may
live, so you may enter and occupy the land that
the LORD, the God of your ancestors, is giving
you. 2 Do not add to or subtract from these commands I am giving you. Just obey the commands
of the LORD your God that I am giving you.
3 “You saw for yourself what the LORD did to
you at Baal-peor. There the LORD your God destroyed everyone who had worshiped Baal, the
god of Peor. 4 But all of you who were faithful to
the LORD your God are still alive today—every
one of you.
5 “Look, I now teach you these decrees and
regulations just as the LORD my God commanded me, so that you may obey them in the land
you are about to enter and occupy. 6 Obey them
completely, and you will display your wisdom
and intelligence among the surrounding nations.
When they hear all these decrees, they will exclaim, ‘How wise and prudent are the people of
this great nation!’ 7 For what great nation has a
god as near to them as the LORD our God is near
to us whenever we call on him? 8 And what great
nation has decrees and regulations as righteous
and fair as this body of instructions that I am
giving you today?
9 “But watch out! Be careful never to forget
what you yourself have seen. Do not let these
memories escape from your mind as long as you
live! And be sure to pass them on to your children and grandchildren. 10 Never forget the day
when you stood before the LORD your God at
Mount Sinai,* where he told me, ‘Summon the
people before me, and I will personally instruct
them. Then they will learn to fear me as long as
they live, and they will teach their children to
fear me also.’
11 “You came near and stood at the foot of
the mountain, while flames from the mountain
shot into the sky. The mountain was shrouded in
black clouds and deep darkness. 12 And the LORD
spoke to you from the heart of the fire. You heard
the sound of his words but didn’t see his form;

4:10 Hebrew *Horeb,* another name for Sinai; also in 4:15.

3:21–29 Moses Forbidden to Enter. The double mention of this prohibition (cf. 1:37) shows how deeply Moses felt about it. One can almost hear the pathos in his voice as he speaks of pleading to be allowed to see the task through. But whatever the basis of the prohibition, the reality remains. Life moves on, new tasks call for new leaders, and it was important that Joshua be seen as fully supported and not just resentfully accepted by Moses. Israel’s leaders needed to accept the concept of graciously handing the reins over to their successors, as some, such as Samuel, later did, and others, such as Saul, did not.

4:1–14 The Need for Obedience. Chapter 4 forms a link between the historical prologue and the overview of the law. It focuses the readers’ minds on experience; their own experience, as individuals and as a nation, and the function of that experience in leading them into relationship with God along with the motivational force of that experience in challenging them into future obedience and service. Verses 1–14 define the relationship between possession of the land and obedience to the laws and decrees that were about to be set out. Both the land and the laws were given to them by the LORD. The God who had cared for their ancestors and themselves in the past would continue to care for them and their descendants in the future. The land was the God-given place where the community could develop and flourish, and the laws defined the pattern of God-ordained living that would enable the community to develop and flourish. The challenge for the community at this crucial stage, is to make it happen. The constant references to children emphasize that this book is not just for the generation

there was only a voice. 13 He proclaimed his covenant—the Ten Commandments*—which he commanded you to keep, and which he wrote on two stone tablets. 14 It was at that time that the LORD commanded me to teach you his decrees and regulations so you would obey them in the land you are about to enter and occupy.

A Warning against Idolatry

15 "But be very careful! You did not see the LORD's form on the day he spoke to you from the heart of the fire at Mount Sinai. 16 So do not corrupt yourselves by making an idol in any form—whether of a man or a woman, 17 an animal on the ground, a bird in the sky, 18 a small animal that scurries along the ground, or a fish in the deepest sea. 19 And when you look up into the sky and see the sun, moon, and stars—all the forces of heaven—don't be seduced into worshiping them. The LORD your God gave them to all the peoples of the earth. 20 Remember that the LORD rescued you from the iron-smelting furnace of Egypt in order to make you his very own people and his special possession, which is what you are today.

21 "But the LORD was angry with me because of you. He vowed that I would not cross the Jordan River into the good land the LORD your God is giving you as your special possession. 22 You will cross the Jordan to occupy the land, but I will not. Instead, I will die here on the east side of the river. 23 So be careful not to break the covenant the LORD your God has made with you. Do not make idols of any shape or form, for the LORD your God has forbidden this. 24 The LORD your God is a devouring fire; he is a jealous God.

25 "In the future, when you have children and grandchildren and have lived in the land a long time, do not corrupt yourselves by making idols of any kind. This is evil in the sight of the LORD your God and will arouse his anger.

26 "Today I call on heaven and earth as witnesses against you. If you break my covenant, you will quickly disappear from the land you are crossing the Jordan to occupy. You will live there only a short time; then you will be utterly destroyed. 27 For the LORD will scatter you among the nations, where only a few of you will survive. 28 There, in a foreign land, you will worship idols made from wood and stone—gods that neither see nor hear nor eat nor smell. 29 But from there you will search again for the LORD your God. And if you search for him with all your heart and soul, you will find him.

30 "In the distant future, when you are suffering all these things, you will finally return to the LORD your God and listen to what he tells you. 31 For the LORD your God is a merciful God; he will not abandon you or destroy you or forget the solemn covenant he made with your ancestors.

There Is Only One God

32 "Now search all of history, from the time God created people on the earth until now, and search from one end of the heavens to the other. Has anything as great as this ever been seen or heard before? 33 Has any nation ever heard the voice of God* speaking from fire—as you did—and survived? 34 Has any other god dared to take a nation for himself out of another nation by means of trials, miraculous signs, wonders, war, a strong hand, a powerful arm, and terrifying acts? Yet that is what the LORD your God did for you in Egypt, right before your eyes.

35 "He showed you these things so you would know that the LORD is God and there is no other. 36 He let you hear his voice from heaven so he could instruct you. He let you see his great fire here on earth so he could speak to you from it. 37 Because he loved your ancestors, he chose to bless their descendants, and he personally brought you out of Egypt with a great display of power. 38 He drove out nations far greater than you, so he could bring you in and give you their land as your special possession, as it is today.

39 "So remember this and keep it firmly in mind: The LORD is God both in heaven and on earth, and there is no other. 40 If you obey all the decrees and commands I am giving you today, all will be well with you and your children. I am giving you these instructions so you will enjoy a

4:13 Hebrew *the ten words.* **4:33** Or *voice of a god.*

---

entering the land at this point but for all those who will live in the land in the future.

4:15–31 Warning against Idolatry. It is clear that the law is not to be kept just for its own sake but because it is God's law. The Israelites' entire national identity is bound up in relationship with God and if they miss out on *that* fact, then everything else is irrelevant. Therefore, the primary prohibition is of idolatry.

4:32–40 The One God. The primary reality is God himself. Israel's task is to *remember this and keep it firmly in mind* (v. 39). If their society is to prosper, they must recognize the uniqueness of their God and the necessity of keeping his commands.

long life in the land the LORD your God is giving you for all time."

Eastern Cities of Refuge

[41] Then Moses set apart three cities of refuge east of the Jordan River. [42] Anyone who killed another person unintentionally, without previous hostility, could flee there to live in safety. [43] These were the cities: Bezer on the wilderness plateau for the tribe of Reuben; Ramoth in Gilead for the tribe of Gad; Golan in Bashan for the tribe of Manasseh.

Introduction to Moses' Second Address

[44] This is the body of instruction that Moses presented to the Israelites. [45] These are the laws, decrees, and regulations that Moses gave to the people of Israel when they left Egypt, [46] and as they camped in the valley near Beth-peor east of the Jordan River. (This land was formerly occupied by the Amorites under King Sihon, who ruled from Heshbon. But Moses and the Israelites destroyed him and his people when they came up from Egypt. [47] Israel took possession of his land and that of King Og of Bashan—the two Amorite kings east of the Jordan. [48] So Israel conquered the entire area from Aroer at the edge of the Arnon Gorge all the way to Mount Sirion,* also called Mount Hermon. [49] And they conquered the eastern bank of the Jordan River as far south as the Dead Sea,* below the slopes of Pisgah.)

Ten Commandments for the Covenant Community

5 Moses called all the people of Israel together and said, "Listen carefully, Israel. Hear the decrees and regulations I am giving you today, so you may learn them and obey them!

[2] "The LORD our God made a covenant with us at Mount Sinai.* [3] The LORD did not make this covenant with our ancestors, but with all of us who are alive today. [4] At the mountain the LORD spoke to you face to face from the heart of the fire. [5] I stood as an intermediary between you and the LORD, for you were afraid of the fire and did not want to approach the mountain. He spoke to me, and I passed his words on to you. This is what he said:

[6] "I am the LORD your God, who rescued you
from the land of Egypt, the place of your
slavery.
[7] "You must not have any other god but me.
[8] "You must not make for yourself an idol of
any kind, or an image of anything in the
heavens or on the earth or in the sea. [9] You
must not bow down to them or worship
them, for I, the LORD your God, am a jealous
God who will not tolerate your affection for
any other gods. I lay the sins of the parents
upon their children; the entire family is
affected—even children in the third and
fourth generations of those who reject me.
[10] But I lavish unfailing love for a thousand
generations on those* who love me and obey
my commands.
[11] "You must not misuse the name of the LORD
your God. The LORD will not let you go
unpunished if you misuse his name.
[12] "Observe the Sabbath day by keeping it holy,
as the LORD your God has commanded you.
[13] You have six days each week for your
ordinary work, [14] but the seventh day is a
Sabbath day of rest dedicated to the LORD
your God. On that day no one in your
household may do any work. This includes
you, your sons and daughters, your male

4:48 As in Syriac version (see also 3:9); Hebrew reads *Mount Sion.* **4:49** Hebrew *took the Arabah on the east side of the Jordan as far as the sea of the Arabah.* **5:2** Hebrew *Horeb,* another name for Sinai. **5:10** Hebrew *for thousands of those.*

4:41–49 Getting Ready. A brief note on the provision of cities of refuge for those in the tribes settling east of the Jordan leads in to the introduction to the law codes.

5:1–26:19 Moses' Second Speech

5:1–33 The Ten Commandments. These form a preliminary summary of all the laws. The commandments, given years before at Sinai are, like the covenant itself, equally applicable to the women and men about to enter the promised land and indeed to women and men throughout the history of God's people. The covenant involves relating not only to God but also to one another. The commandments deal with some of the implications of both. The list is not, and is not intended to be, comprehensive. It is extensive enough for an Israelite to work out what might have been said about their attitudes or behavior in other situations. The New Testament condensation of the Ten Commandments to the twin commands of loving God wholeheartedly and one's neighbor as oneself (Matt 22:39–39; Mark 12:33; Luke 10:27) is fully in line with the presentation in Deuteronomy. Similarly, the Ten Commandments themselves continue to form a good basis for Christian living.

and female servants, your oxen and donkeys
and other livestock, and any foreigners
living among you. All your male and female
servants must rest as you do. 15 Remember
that you were once slaves in Egypt, but the
LORD your God brought you out with his
strong hand and powerful arm. That is why
the LORD your God has commanded you to
rest on the Sabbath day.
16 "Honor your father and mother, as the LORD
your God commanded you. Then you will
live a long, full life in the land the LORD your
God is giving you.
17 "You must not murder.
18 "You must not commit adultery.
19 "You must not steal.
20 "You must not testify falsely against your
neighbor.
21 "You must not covet your neighbor's wife.
You must not covet your neighbor's house or
land, male or female servant, ox or donkey, or
anything else that belongs to your neighbor.

22 "The LORD spoke these words to all of you
assembled there at the foot of the mountain. He
spoke with a loud voice from the heart of the
fire, surrounded by clouds and deep darkness.
This was all he said at that time, and he wrote
his words on two stone tablets and gave them to
me.
23 "But when you heard the voice from the
heart of the darkness, while the mountain was
blazing with fire, all your tribal leaders and elders came to me. 24 They said, 'Look, the LORD
our God has shown us his glory and greatness,
and we have heard his voice from the heart of
the fire. Today we have seen that God can speak
to us humans, and yet we live! 25 But now, why
should we risk death again? If the LORD our God
speaks to us again, we will certainly die and be
consumed by this awesome fire. 26 Can any living
thing hear the voice of the living God from the
heart of the fire as we did and yet survive? 27 Go
yourself and listen to what the LORD our God
says. Then come and tell us everything he tells
you, and we will listen and obey.'
28 "The LORD heard the request you made to
me. And he said, 'I have heard what the people
said to you, and they are right. 29 Oh, that they
would always have hearts like this, that they
might fear me and obey all my commands! If
they did, they and their descendants would prosper forever. 30 Go and tell them, "Return to your
tents." 31 But you stand here with me so I can
give you all my commands, decrees, and regulations. You must teach them to the people so they
can obey them in the land I am giving them as
their possession.' "
32 So Moses told the people, "You must be
careful to obey all the commands of the LORD
your God, following his instructions in every detail. 33 Stay on the path that the LORD your God
has commanded you to follow. Then you will
live long and prosperous lives in the land you are
about to enter and occupy.

A Call for Wholehearted Commitment

6 "These are the commands, decrees, and
regulations that the LORD your God commanded me to teach you. You must obey
them in the land you are about to enter and occupy, 2 and you and your children and grandchildren must fear the LORD your God as long as you
live. If you obey all his decrees and commands,
you will enjoy a long life. 3 Listen closely, Israel,
and be careful to obey. Then all will go well with
you, and you will have many children in the land
flowing with milk and honey, just as the LORD,
the God of your ancestors, promised you.
4 "Listen, O Israel! The LORD is our God, the
LORD alone.* 5 And you must love the LORD

6:4 Or *The LORD our God is one LORD;* or *The LORD our God, the LORD is one;* or *The LORD is our God, the LORD is one.*

It is interesting to note that daughters and female servants are allowed to rest on the Sabbath along with their brothers and male colleagues. This indicates that their need to rest is taken seriously and that their participation in the religious requirements of the covenant is taken for granted. The requirement for the equal honoring of father and mother is paralleled in Deuteronomy 21:13, 19; 22:15; 27:16; 33:9; in fact, in almost every case where parenting comes into question, mother and father are mentioned together.

6:1–25 Wholehearted Commitment. It is possible to see this chapter as the hub around which the rest of Deuteronomy is centered, the heart of the message of covenant relationship. The writer is convinced the covenant was not just about ideas or status but about the whole of life. Lifestyle and belief are intimately linked. What matters most is the love linking God and people together. It would be impossible for Israel to obey the law without loving God because the love of God was at the heart of the law itself. Verses 4–5 beginning *Listen, O Israel* is known as the *Shema* and became, and still is, a key part of the ritual of later Judaism: The instruction to bind it on foreheads and tie it to door frames is interpreted literally. What the

your God with all your heart, all your soul, and all your strength. 6 And you must commit yourselves wholeheartedly to these commands that I am giving you today. 7 Repeat them again and again to your children. Talk about them when you are at home and when you are on the road, when you are going to bed and when you are getting up. 8 Tie them to your hands and wear them on your forehead as reminders. 9 Write them on the doorposts of your house and on your gates.

10 "The LORD your God will soon bring you into the land he swore to give you when he made a vow to your ancestors Abraham, Isaac, and Jacob. It is a land with large, prosperous cities that you did not build. 11 The houses will be richly stocked with goods you did not produce. You will draw water from cisterns you did not dig, and you will eat from vineyards and olive trees you did not plant. When you have eaten your fill in this land, 12 be careful not to forget the LORD, who rescued you from slavery in the land of Egypt. 13 You must fear the LORD your God and serve him. When you take an oath, you must use only his name.

14 "You must not worship any of the gods of neighboring nations, 15 for the LORD your God, who lives among you, is a jealous God. His anger will flare up against you, and he will wipe you from the face of the earth. 16 You must not test the LORD your God as you did when you complained at Massah. 17 You must diligently obey the commands of the LORD your God—all the laws and decrees he has given you. 18 Do what is right and good in the LORD's sight, so all will go well with you. Then you will enter and occupy the good land that the LORD swore to give your ancestors. 19 You will drive out all the enemies living in the land, just as the LORD said you would.

20 "In the future your children will ask you, 'What is the meaning of these laws, decrees, and regulations that the LORD our God has commanded us to obey?'

21 "Then you must tell them, 'We were Pharaoh's slaves in Egypt, but the LORD brought us out of Egypt with his strong hand. 22 The LORD did miraculous signs and wonders before our eyes, dealing terrifying blows against Egypt and Pharaoh and all his people. 23 He brought us out of Egypt so he could give us this land he had sworn to give our ancestors. 24 And the LORD our God commanded us to obey all these decrees and to fear him so he can continue to bless us and preserve our lives, as he has done to this day. 25 For we will be counted as righteous when we obey all the commands the LORD our God has given us.'

The Privilege of Holiness

7 "When the LORD your God brings you into the land you are about to enter and occupy, he will clear away many nations ahead of you: the Hittites, Girgashites, Amorites, Canaanites, Perizzites, Hivites, and Jebusites. These seven nations are greater and more numerous than you. 2 When the LORD your God hands these nations over to you and you con-

---

passage means is that relationship with God is such a major part of their lives that it is perfectly normal to discuss it with their children around the breakfast table or while traveling or at bedtime. The relationship is not something only for special occasions. Parents must make sure that their children understand everything. Without wholehearted allegiance to God there is no relationship; without relationship there is no covenant; without covenant there is no blessing or land or community. For them to survive for more than one generation, the children must fully grasp these ideas.

7:1–26 The Privilege of Holiness. Chapter 7, emphasizing separation from and total destruction of surrounding nations might be read as racist, encouraging the worst form of what is called ethnic cleansing. We must not judge the events in the light of twenty-first-century values, none of which would have been understood at that time. The greatest danger to the survival of the covenant community was the absorption of the beliefs, attitudes, and practices of other inhabitants of the area. This was to be avoided at all costs. God would enable them to overcome their pagan enemies, and these enemies, with God's help, were to be totally wiped out. In particular, all the altars and sacred objects attached to pagan religions were to be destroyed to prevent them from polluting the land. The implication is that nothing and no one from these peoples can be allowed to survive. However, elsewhere in Deuteronomy are sections explaining how the Israelites are to relate to the foreigners living within their communities. Even here, the command not to intermarry implies that there must have been some whom they might have been tempted to marry. The drastic measures described were not applied in such an extreme way as one might have thought. What was absolutely vital was that the Israelites realized just how important it was to be separate and to maintain their own identity and wholehearted allegiance to the LORD. Without this, there would be no Israel.

quer them, you must completely destroy* them. Make no treaties with them and show them no mercy. 3 You must not intermarry with them. Do not let your daughters and sons marry their sons and daughters, 4 for they will lead your children away from me to worship other gods. Then the anger of the LORD will burn against you, and he will quickly destroy you. 5 This is what you must do. You must break down their pagan altars and shatter their sacred pillars. Cut down their Asherah poles and burn their idols. 6 For you are a holy people, who belong to the LORD your God. Of all the people on earth, the LORD your God has chosen you to be his own special treasure.

7 "The LORD did not set his heart on you and choose you because you were more numerous than other nations, for you were the smallest of all nations! 8 Rather, it was simply that the LORD loves you, and he was keeping the oath he had sworn to your ancestors. That is why the LORD rescued you with such a strong hand from your slavery and from the oppressive hand of Pharaoh, king of Egypt. 9 Understand, therefore, that the LORD your God is indeed God. He is the faithful God who keeps his covenant for a thousand generations and lavishes his unfailing love on those who love him and obey his commands. 10 But he does not hesitate to punish and destroy those who reject him. 11 Therefore, you must obey all these commands, decrees, and regulations I am giving you today.

12 "If you listen to these regulations and faithfully obey them, the LORD your God will keep his covenant of unfailing love with you, as he promised with an oath to your ancestors. 13 He will love you and bless you, and he will give you many children. He will give fertility to your land and your animals. When you arrive in the land he swore to give your ancestors, you will have large harvests of grain, new wine, and olive oil, and great herds of cattle, sheep, and goats. 14 You will be blessed above all the nations of the earth. None of your men or women will be childless, and all your livestock will bear young. 15 And the LORD will protect you from all sickness. He will not let you suffer from the terrible diseases you knew in Egypt, but he will inflict them on all your enemies!

16 "You must destroy all the nations the LORD your God hands over to you. Show them no mercy, and do not worship their gods, or they will trap you. 17 Perhaps you will think to yourselves, 'How can we ever conquer these nations that are so much more powerful than we are?' 18 But don't be afraid of them! Just remember what the LORD your God did to Pharaoh and to all the land of Egypt. 19 Remember the great terrors the LORD your God sent against them. You saw it all with your own eyes! And remember the miraculous signs and wonders, and the strong hand and powerful arm with which he brought you out of Egypt. The LORD your God will use this same power against all the people you fear. 20 And then the LORD your God will send terror* to drive out the few survivors still hiding from you!

21 "No, do not be afraid of those nations, for the LORD your God is among you, and he is a great and awesome God. 22 The LORD your God will drive those nations out ahead of you little by little. You will not clear them away all at once, otherwise the wild animals would multiply too quickly for you. 23 But the LORD your God will hand them over to you. He will throw them into complete confusion until they are destroyed. 24 He will put their kings in your power, and you will erase their names from the face of the earth. No one will be able to stand against you, and you will destroy them all.

25 "You must burn their idols in fire, and you must not covet the silver or gold that covers them. You must not take it or it will become a trap to you, for it is detestable to the LORD your God. 26 Do not bring any detestable objects into your home, for then you will be destroyed, just like them. You must utterly detest such things, for they are set apart for destruction.

A Call to Remember and Obey

8 "Be careful to obey all the commands I am giving you today. Then you will live and multiply, and you will enter and occupy the land the LORD swore to give your ancestors. 2 Remember how the LORD your God led you through the wilderness for these forty years,

7:2 The Hebrew term used here refers to the complete consecration of things or people to the LORD, either by destroying them or by giving them as an offering; also in 7:26. **7:20** Often rendered *the hornet.* The meaning of the Hebrew is uncertain.

8:1–20 Learning from History. This short chapter is an extended discussion on God's continuing care for Israel and the importance of remembering what he has done for them. There is a particular concern that the prosperity that God gives them will lead them astray. Their pride may make them think that their wealth is the result of their own cleverness when it is really God-given. Israel's later history shows that this warning was necessary and not always heeded. Amos 4:1 is a well-known example of a rebuke to wealthy women who had set aside their responsibilities to God and to the covenant community.

humbling you and testing you to prove your character, and to find out whether or not you would obey his commands. [3]Yes, he humbled you by letting you go hungry and then feeding you with manna, a food previously unknown to you and your ancestors. He did it to teach you that people do not live by bread alone; rather, we live by every word that comes from the mouth of the LORD. [4]For all these forty years your clothes didn't wear out, and your feet didn't blister or swell. [5]Think about it: Just as a parent disciplines a child, the LORD your God disciplines you for your own good.

[6]"So obey the commands of the LORD your God by walking in his ways and fearing him. [7]For the LORD your God is bringing you into a good land of flowing streams and pools of water, with fountains and springs that gush out in the valleys and hills. [8]It is a land of wheat and barley; of grapevines, fig trees, and pomegranates; of olive oil and honey. [9]It is a land where food is plentiful and nothing is lacking. It is a land where iron is as common as stone, and copper is abundant in the hills. [10]When you have eaten your fill, be sure to praise the LORD your God for the good land he has given you.

[11]"But that is the time to be careful! Beware that in your plenty you do not forget the LORD your God and disobey his commands, regulations, and decrees that I am giving you today. [12]For when you have become full and prosperous and have built fine homes to live in, [13]and when your flocks and herds have become very large and your silver and gold have multiplied along with everything else, be careful! [14]Do not become proud at that time and forget the LORD your God, who rescued you from slavery in the land of Egypt. [15]Do not forget that he led you through the great and terrifying wilderness with its poisonous snakes and scorpions, where it was so hot and dry. He gave you water from the rock! [16]He fed you with manna in the wilderness, a food unknown to your ancestors. He did this to humble you and test you for your own good. [17]He did all this so you would never say to yourself, 'I have achieved this wealth with my own strength and energy.' [18]Remember the LORD your God. He is the one who gives you power to be successful, in order to fulfill the covenant he confirmed to your ancestors with an oath.

[19]"But I assure you of this: If you ever forget the LORD your God and follow other gods, worshiping and bowing down to them, you will certainly be destroyed. [20]Just as the LORD has destroyed other nations in your path, you also will be destroyed if you refuse to obey the LORD your God.

Victory by God's Grace

9 "Listen, O Israel! Today you are about to cross the Jordan River to take over the land belonging to nations much greater and more powerful than you. They live in cities with walls that reach to the sky! [2]The people are strong and tall—descendants of the famous Anakite giants. You've heard the saying, 'Who can stand up to the Anakites?' [3]But recognize today that the LORD your God is the one who will cross over ahead of you like a devouring fire to destroy them. He will subdue them so that you will quickly conquer them and drive them out, just as the LORD has promised.

[4]"After the LORD your God has done this for you, don't say in your hearts, 'The LORD has given us this land because we are such good people!' No, it is because of the wickedness of the other nations that he is pushing them out of your way. [5]It is not because you are so good or have such integrity that you are about to occupy their land. The LORD your God will drive these nations out ahead of you only because of their wickedness, and to fulfill the oath he swore to your ancestors Abraham, Isaac, and Jacob. [6]You must recognize that the LORD your God is not giving you this good land because you are good, for you are not—you are a stubborn people.

Remembering the Gold Calf

[7]"Remember and never forget how angry you made the LORD your God out in the wilderness. From the day you left Egypt until now, you have been constantly rebelling against him. [8]Even at Mount Sinai* you made the LORD so angry he was ready to destroy you. [9]This happened when

9:8 Hebrew *Horeb,* another name for Sinai.

9:1–6: God's Victory. Victory, like prosperity, comes from God and stems from justice. The punishment of the Canaanites shows that their behavior was important to God and warns against any self-satisfaction on Israel's part.

9:7–29 More Lessons from History. The focus moves naturally from memory and forgetfulness to a discussion of Israel's stubbornness. They must embrace endurance, the positive holding onto the things, beliefs, and actions that are good; they must avoid stubbornness, the determined holding onto things, beliefs and actions that God has forbidden and that would lead them away from him.

I was on the mountain receiving the tablets of
stone inscribed with the words of the covenant
that the LORD had made with you. I was there for
forty days and forty nights, and all that time I ate
no food and drank no water. 10 The LORD gave me
the two tablets on which God had written with
his own finger all the words he had spoken to
you from the heart of the fire when you were
assembled at the mountain.

11 "At the end of the forty days and nights,
the LORD handed me the two stone tablets inscribed with the words of the covenant. 12 Then
the LORD said to me, 'Get up! Go down immediately, for the people you brought out of Egypt
have corrupted themselves. How quickly they
have turned away from the way I commanded
them to live! They have melted gold and made
an idol for themselves!'

13 "The LORD also said to me, 'I have seen how
stubborn and rebellious these people are. 14 Leave
me alone so I may destroy them and erase their
name from under heaven. Then I will make
a mighty nation of your descendants, a nation
larger and more powerful than they are.'

15 "So while the mountain was blazing with
fire I turned and came down, holding in my hands
the two stone tablets inscribed with the terms of
the covenant. 16 There below me I could see that
you had sinned against the LORD your God. You
had melted gold and made a calf idol for yourselves. How quickly you had turned away from
the path the LORD had commanded you to follow!
17 So I took the stone tablets and threw them to the
ground, smashing them before your eyes.

18 "Then, as before, I threw myself down before the LORD for forty days and nights. I ate no
bread and drank no water because of the great
sin you had committed by doing what the LORD
hated, provoking him to anger. 19 I feared that the
furious anger of the LORD, which turned him
against you, would drive him to destroy you. But
again he listened to me. 20 The LORD was so angry
with Aaron that he wanted to destroy him, too.
But I prayed for Aaron, and the LORD spared him.
21 I took your sin—the calf you had made—and I
melted it down in the fire and ground it into fine
dust. Then I threw the dust into the stream that
flows down the mountain.

22 "You also made the LORD angry at Taberah,* Massah,* and Kibroth-hattaavah.* 23 And
at Kadesh-barnea the LORD sent you out with
this command: 'Go up and take over the land I
have given you.' But you rebelled against the
command of the LORD your God and refused to
put your trust in him or obey him. 24 Yes, you
have been rebelling against the LORD as long as I
have known you.

25 "That is why I threw myself down before
the LORD for forty days and nights—for the
LORD said he would destroy you. 26 I prayed to
the LORD and said, 'O Sovereign LORD, do not
destroy them. They are your own people. They
are your special possession, whom you redeemed
from Egypt by your mighty power and your
strong hand. 27 Please overlook the stubbornness
and the awful sin of these people, and remember
instead your servants Abraham, Isaac, and Jacob.
28 If you destroy these people, the Egyptians will
say, "The Israelites died because the LORD wasn't
able to bring them to the land he had promised
to give them." Or they might say, "He destroyed
them because he hated them; he deliberately took them into the wilderness to slaughter
them." 29 But they are your people and your special possession, whom you brought out of Egypt
by your great strength and powerful arm.'

A New Copy of the Covenant

10 "At that time the LORD said to me,
'Chisel out two stone tablets like the
first ones. Also make a wooden Ark—
a sacred chest to store them in. Come up to me
on the mountain, 2 and I will write on the tablets the same words that were on the ones you
smashed. Then place the tablets in the Ark.'

3 "So I made an Ark of acacia wood and cut
two stone tablets like the first two. Then I went
up the mountain with the tablets in my hand.
4 Once again the LORD wrote the Ten Commandments* on the tablets and gave them to me. They
were the same words the LORD had spoken to you
from the heart of the fire on the day you were
assembled at the foot of the mountain. 5 Then I
turned and came down the mountain and placed
the tablets in the Ark of the Covenant, which I
had made, just as the LORD commanded me. And
the tablets are still there in the Ark."

6 (The people of Israel set out from the wells
of the people of Jaakan* and traveled to Moserah,

9:22a *Taberah* means "place of burning." See Num 11:1-3.
9:22b *Massah* means "place of testing." See Exod 17:1-7.
9:22c *Kibroth-hattaavah* means "graves of gluttony." See Num 11:31-34. **10:4** Hebrew *the ten words.* **10:6** Or *set out from Beeroth of Bene-jaakan.*

10:1–11 New Stone Tablets. There is an interesting reflection here on the interrelationship between God's gracious provision and human responsibility. God supplies the structure, but Moses and the Levites have to make it happen.

where Aaron died and was buried. His son Eleazar ministered as high priest in his place. [7]Then they journeyed to Gudgodah, and from there to Jotbathah, a land with many brooks and streams. [8]At that time the LORD set apart the tribe of Levi to carry the Ark of the LORD's Covenant, and to stand before the LORD as his ministers, and to pronounce blessings in his name. These are their duties to this day. [9]That is why the Levites have no share of property or possession of land among the other Israelite tribes. The LORD himself is their special possession, as the LORD your God told them.)

[10]"As for me, I stayed on the mountain in the LORD's presence for forty days and nights, as I had done the first time. And once again the LORD listened to my pleas and agreed not to destroy you. [11]Then the LORD said to me, 'Get up and resume the journey, and lead the people to the land I swore to give to their ancestors, so they may take possession of it.'

A Call to Love and Obedience

[12]"And now, Israel, what does the LORD your God require of you? He requires only that you fear the LORD your God, and live in a way that pleases him, and love him and serve him with all your heart and soul. [13]And you must always obey the LORD's commands and decrees that I am giving you today for your own good.

[14]"Look, the highest heavens and the earth and everything in it all belong to the LORD your God. [15]Yet the LORD chose your ancestors as the objects of his love. And he chose you, their descendants, above all other nations, as is evident today. [16]Therefore, change your hearts* and stop being stubborn.

[17]"For the LORD your God is the God of gods and Lord of lords. He is the great God, the mighty and awesome God, who shows no partiality and cannot be bribed. [18]He ensures that orphans and widows receive justice. He shows love to the foreigners living among you and gives them food and clothing. [19]So you, too, must show love to foreigners, for you yourselves were once foreigners in the land of Egypt. [20]You must fear the LORD your God and worship him and cling to him. Your oaths must be in his name alone. [21]He alone is your God, the only one who is worthy of your praise, the one who has done these mighty miracles that you have seen with your own eyes. [22]When your ancestors went down into Egypt, there were only seventy of them. But now the LORD your God has made you as numerous as the stars in the sky!

11 "You must love the LORD your God and obey all his requirements, decrees, regulations, and commands. [2]Keep in mind that I am not talking now to your children, who have never experienced the discipline of the LORD your God or seen his greatness and his strong hand and powerful arm. [3]They didn't see the miraculous signs and wonders he performed in Egypt against Pharaoh and all his land. [4]They didn't see what the LORD did to the armies of Egypt and to their horses and chariots—how he drowned them in the Red Sea* as they were chasing you. He destroyed them, and they have not recovered to this very day!

[5]"Your children didn't see how the LORD cared for you in the wilderness until you arrived here. [6]They didn't see what he did to Dathan and Abiram (the sons of Eliab, a descendant of Reuben) when the earth opened its mouth in the Israelite camp and swallowed them, along with their households and tents and every living thing that belonged to them. [7]But you have seen the LORD perform all these mighty deeds with your own eyes!

The Blessings of Obedience

[8]"Therefore, be careful to obey every command I am giving you today, so you may have strength to go in and take over the land you are about to enter. [9]If you obey, you will enjoy a long life in the land the LORD swore to give to your ancestors and to you, their descendants—a land flowing with milk and honey! [10]For the land you are about to enter and take over is not like the land of Egypt from which you came, where you planted your seed and made irrigation ditches with your foot as in a vegetable garden. [11]Rather, the land

10:16 Hebrew *circumcise the foreskin of your hearts.*
11:4 Hebrew *sea of reeds.*

10:12—11:7 A Call to Service. In 10:16 the people are encouraged to change (see translator's note). This teaching would probably have been quite encouraging to Israelite women. They were only marginally involved in the rite of circumcision, but if what really counted was "circumcision of the heart" then they could be equally involved and their commitment fully recognized.

11:8–32 Obedience Brings Blessings. The point of the law was to enable the people to live in the best way for them. Following God's way was very much to their own benefit. This was how the society would be able to survive and prosper.

you will soon take over is a land of hills and valleys with plenty of rain—12 a land that the LORD your God cares for. He watches over it through each season of the year!

13 "If you carefully obey all the commands I am giving you today, and if you love the LORD your God and serve him with all your heart and soul, 14 then he will send the rains in their proper seasons—the early and late rains—so you can bring in your harvests of grain, new wine, and olive oil. 15 He will give you lush pastureland for your livestock, and you yourselves will have all you want to eat.

16 "But be careful. Don't let your heart be deceived so that you turn away from the LORD and serve and worship other gods. 17 If you do, the LORD's anger will burn against you. He will shut up the sky and hold back the rain, and the ground will fail to produce its harvests. Then you will quickly die in that good land the LORD is giving you.

18 "So commit yourselves wholeheartedly to these words of mine. Tie them to your hands and wear them on your forehead as reminders. 19 Teach them to your children. Talk about them when you are at home and when you are on the road, when you are going to bed and when you are getting up. 20 Write them on the doorposts of your house and on your gates, 21 so that as long as the sky remains above the earth, you and your children may flourish in the land the LORD swore to give your ancestors.

22 "Be careful to obey all these commands I am giving you. Show love to the LORD your God by walking in his ways and holding tightly to him. 23 Then the LORD will drive out all the nations ahead of you, though they are much greater and stronger than you, and you will take over their land. 24 Wherever you set foot, that land will be yours. Your frontiers will stretch from the wilderness in the south to Lebanon in the north, and from the Euphrates River in the east to the Mediterranean Sea in the west.* 25 No one will be able to stand against you, for the LORD your God will cause the people to fear and dread you, as he promised, wherever you go in the whole land.

26 "Look, today I am giving you the choice between a blessing and a curse! 27 You will be blessed if you obey the commands of the LORD your God that I am giving you today. 28 But you will be cursed if you reject the commands of the LORD your God and turn away from him and worship gods you have not known before.

29 "When the LORD your God brings you into the land and helps you take possession of it, you must pronounce the blessing at Mount Gerizim and the curse at Mount Ebal. 30 (These two mountains are west of the Jordan River in the land of the Canaanites who live in the Jordan Valley,* near the town of Gilgal, not far from the oaks of Moreh.) 31 For you are about to cross the Jordan River to take over the land the LORD your God is giving you. When you take that land and are living in it, 32 you must be careful to obey all the decrees and regulations I am giving you today.

The LORD's Chosen Place for Worship

12 "These are the decrees and regulations you must be careful to obey when you live in the land that the LORD, the God of your ancestors, is giving you. You must obey them as long as you live.

2 "When you drive out the nations that live there, you must destroy all the places where they worship their gods—high on the mountains, up on the hills, and under every green tree. 3 Break down their altars and smash their sacred pillars. Burn their Asherah poles and cut down their carved idols. Completely erase the names of their gods!

4 "Do not worship the LORD your God in the way these pagan peoples worship their gods. 5 Rather, you must seek the LORD your God at the place of worship he himself will choose from among all the tribes—the place where his name will be honored. 6 There you will bring your burnt offerings, your sacrifices, your tithes, your sacred offerings, your offerings to fulfill a vow, your voluntary offerings, and your offerings of the firstborn animals of your herds and flocks. 7 There you and your families will feast in the presence of the LORD your God, and you will rejoice in all you have accomplished because the LORD your God has blessed you.

8 "Your pattern of worship will change. Today all of you are doing as you please, 9 because you have not yet arrived at the place of rest, the land the LORD your God is giving you as your special possession. 10 But you will soon cross the

11:24 Hebrew *to the western sea.* **11:30** Hebrew *the Arabah.*

12:1–32 Center of Worship. The Old Testament does not recognize the concept of *private religion.* Coming together to worship is always seen as a vital part of Israel's faith. Verse 12 (like 14:26) illustrates that sacrifices and sacrificial feasts were meant to involve the entire household including *your sons and daughters and all your servants.*

Jordan River and live in the land the LORD your God is giving you. When he gives you rest from all your enemies and you're living safely in the land, [11]you must bring everything I command you—your burnt offerings, your sacrifices, your tithes, your sacred offerings, and your offerings to fulfill a vow—to the designated place of worship, the place the LORD your God chooses for his name to be honored.

[12]"You must celebrate there in the presence of the LORD your God with your sons and daughters and all your servants. And remember to include the Levites who live in your towns, for they will receive no allotment of land among you. [13]Be careful not to sacrifice your burnt offerings just anywhere you like. [14]You may do so only at the place the LORD will choose within one of your tribal territories. There you must offer your burnt offerings and do everything I command you.

[15]"But you may butcher your animals and eat their meat in any town whenever you want. You may freely eat the animals with which the LORD your God blesses you. All of you, whether ceremonially clean or unclean, may eat that meat, just as you now eat gazelle and deer. [16]But you must not consume the blood. You must pour it out on the ground like water.

[17]"But you may not eat your offerings in your hometown—neither the tithe of your grain and new wine and olive oil, nor the firstborn of your flocks and herds, nor any offering to fulfill a vow, nor your voluntary offerings, nor your sacred offerings. [18]You must eat these in the presence of the LORD your God at the place he will choose. Eat them there with your children, your servants, and the Levites who live in your towns, celebrating in the presence of the LORD your God in all you do. [19]And be very careful never to neglect the Levites as long as you live in your land.

[20]"When the LORD your God expands your territory as he has promised, and you have the urge to eat meat, you may freely eat meat whenever you want. [21]It might happen that the designated place of worship—the place the LORD your God chooses for his name to be honored—is a long way from your home. If so, you may butcher any of the cattle, sheep, or goats the LORD has given you, and you may freely eat the meat in your hometown, as I have commanded you. [22]Anyone, whether ceremonially clean or unclean, may eat that meat, just as you do now with gazelle and deer. [23]But never consume the blood, for the blood is the life, and you must not consume the lifeblood with the meat. [24]Instead, pour out the blood on the ground like water. [25]Do not consume the blood, so that all may go well with you and your children after you, because you will be doing what pleases the LORD.

[26]"Take your sacred gifts and your offerings given to fulfill a vow to the place the LORD chooses. [27]You must offer the meat and blood of your burnt offerings on the altar of the LORD your God. The blood of your other sacrifices must be poured out on the altar of the LORD your God, but you may eat the meat. [28]Be careful to obey all my commands, so that all will go well with you and your children after you, because you will be doing what is good and pleasing to the LORD your God.

[29]"When the LORD your God goes ahead of you and destroys the nations and you drive them out and live in their land, [30]do not fall into the trap of following their customs and worshiping their gods. Do not inquire about their gods, saying, 'How do these nations worship their gods? I want to follow their example.' [31]You must not worship the LORD your God the way the other nations worship their gods, for they perform for their gods every detestable act that the LORD hates. They even burn their sons and daughters as sacrifices to their gods.

[32]*"So be careful to obey all the commands I give you. You must not add anything to them or subtract anything from them.

A Warning against Idolatry

13 [1]*"Suppose there are prophets among you or those who dream dreams about the future, and they promise you signs or miracles, [2]and the predicted signs or miracles occur. If they then say, 'Come, let us worship other gods'—gods you have not known before—[3]do not listen to them. The LORD your God is testing you to see if you truly love him with all your heart and soul. [4]Serve only the LORD your God and fear him alone. Obey his commands, listen to his voice, and cling to him. [5]The false prophets

12:32 Verse 12:32 is numbered 13:1 in Hebrew text.
13:1 Verses 13:1-18 are numbered 13:2-19 in Hebrew text.

13:1–18 Warning against Syncretism and Idolatry. The danger of Israel being absorbed into the surrounding tribes was constantly in the mind of the Deuteronomist. Not only intermarrying but also close friendships or even business relationships might entice the Israelites into involvement with the religious beliefs and practices of these tribes. For women, relationships tend to be especially significant, and they

or visionaries who try to lead you astray must
be put to death, for they encourage rebellion
against the LORD your God, who redeemed you
from slavery and brought you out of the land of
Egypt. Since they try to lead you astray from the
way the LORD your God commanded you to live,
you must put them to death. In this way you will
purge the evil from among you.
6"Suppose someone secretly entices you—
even your brother, your son or daughter, your
beloved wife, or your closest friend—and says,
'Let us go worship other gods'—gods that neither you nor your ancestors have known. 7They
might suggest that you worship the gods of peoples who live nearby or who come from the ends
of the earth. 8But do not give in or listen. Have no
pity, and do not spare or protect them. 9You must
put them to death! Strike the first blow yourself,
and then all the people must join in. 10Stone the
guilty ones to death because they have tried to
draw you away from the LORD your God, who
rescued you from the land of Egypt, the place of
slavery. 11Then all Israel will hear about it and be
afraid, and no one will act so wickedly again.
12"When you begin living in the towns the
LORD your God is giving you, you may hear
13that scoundrels among you are leading their
fellow citizens astray by saying, 'Let us go worship other gods'—gods you have not known before. 14In such cases, you must examine the facts
carefully. If you find that the report is true and
such a detestable act has been committed among
you, 15you must attack that town and completely
destroy* all its inhabitants, as well as all the livestock. 16Then you must pile all the plunder in the
middle of the open square and burn it. Burn the
entire town as a burnt offering to the LORD your
God. That town must remain a ruin forever; it
may never be rebuilt. 17Keep none of the plunder that has been set apart for destruction. Then
the LORD will turn from his fierce anger and be
merciful to you. He will have compassion on you
and make you a large nation, just as he swore to
your ancestors.
18"The LORD your God will be merciful only
if you listen to his voice and keep all his commands that I am giving you today, doing what
pleases him.

Ceremonially Clean and Unclean Animals

14 "Since you are the people of the LORD
your God, never cut yourselves or
shave the hair above your foreheads
in mourning for the dead. 2You have been set
apart as holy to the LORD your God, and he has
chosen you from all the nations of the earth to be
his own special treasure.
3"You must not eat any detestable animals
that are ceremonially unclean. 4These are the
animals* you may eat: the ox, the sheep, the
goat, 5the deer, the gazelle, the roe deer, the wild
goat, the addax, the antelope, and the mountain
sheep.
6"You may eat any animal that has completely split hooves and chews the cud, 7but if the
animal doesn't have both, it may not be eaten.
So you may not eat the camel, the hare, or the
hyrax.* They chew the cud but do not have split
hooves, so they are ceremonially unclean for you.
8And you may not eat the pig. It has split hooves
but does not chew the cud, so it is ceremonially
unclean for you. You may not eat the meat of
these animals or even touch their carcasses.
9"Of all the marine animals, you may eat
whatever has both fins and scales. 10You may
not, however, eat marine animals that do not
have both fins and scales. They are ceremonially
unclean for you.
11"You may eat any bird that is ceremonially
clean. 12These are the birds you may not eat: the
griffon vulture, the bearded vulture, the black
vulture, 13the kite, the falcon, buzzards of all
kinds, 14ravens of all kinds, 15the eagle owl, the
short-eared owl, the seagull, hawks of all kinds,
16the little owl, the great owl, the barn owl, 17the
desert owl, the Egyptian vulture, the cormorant,

13:15 The Hebrew term used here refers to the complete consecration of things or people to the LORD, either by destroying them or by giving them as an offering; similarly in 13:17. **14:4** The identification of some of the animals and birds listed in this chapter is uncertain. **14:7** Or *coney,* or *rock badger.*

are also often key players in the transmission of religious beliefs. The warning in vv. 6–11 that anyone who responds to pressures from family or friends and is enticed to worship other gods should be put to death is particularly harsh. But the covenant relationship with God was the basis of the whole community; if that was threatened, the community was at risk.

14:1–21 Ceremonial Regulations. There are good reasons for not eating most of the animals that are classified as unclean, but that is not the point emphasized here. Symbolic ways of keeping separate from those who do not worship the God of Israel are seen as very important. Food plays an important part in life, and in Israel as in most societies, women are the main cooks. The women therefore would have played a major part in making sure that the people remained holy.

18 the stork, herons of all kinds, the hoopoe, and
the bat.
19 "All winged insects that walk along the
ground are ceremonially unclean for you and
may not be eaten. 20 But you may eat any winged
bird or insect that is ceremonially clean.
21 "You must not eat anything that has died a
natural death. You may give it to a foreigner living in your town, or you may sell it to a stranger.
But do not eat it yourselves, for you are set apart
as holy to the LORD your God.
"You must not cook a young goat in its mother's milk.

The Giving of Tithes

22 "You must set aside a tithe of your crops—
one-tenth of all the crops you harvest each
year. 23 Bring this tithe to the designated place of
worship—the place the LORD your God chooses
for his name to be honored—and eat it there in
his presence. This applies to your tithes of grain,
new wine, olive oil, and the firstborn males of
your flocks and herds. Doing this will teach you
always to fear the LORD your God.
24 "Now when the LORD your God blesses
you with a good harvest, the place of worship he
chooses for his name to be honored might be too
far for you to bring the tithe. 25 If so, you may
sell the tithe portion of your crops and herds, put
the money in a pouch, and go to the place the
LORD your God has chosen. 26 When you arrive,
you may use the money to buy any kind of food
you want—cattle, sheep, goats, wine, or other alcoholic drink. Then feast there in the presence
of the LORD your God and celebrate with your
household. 27 And do not neglect the Levites in
your town, for they will receive no allotment of
land among you.
28 "At the end of every third year, bring the
entire tithe of that year's harvest and store it in
the nearest town. 29 Give it to the Levites, who
will receive no allotment of land among you, as
well as to the foreigners living among you, the
orphans, and the widows in your towns, so they
can eat and be satisfied. Then the LORD your God
will bless you in all your work.

Release for Debtors

15 "At the end of every seventh year you
must cancel the debts of everyone
who owes you money. 2 This is how it
must be done. Everyone must cancel the loans
they have made to their fellow Israelites. They
must not demand payment from their neighbors
or relatives, for the LORD's time of release has
arrived. 3 This release from debt, however, applies only to your fellow Israelites—not to the
foreigners living among you.
4 "There should be no poor among you, for
the LORD your God will greatly bless you in
the land he is giving you as a special possession.
5 You will receive this blessing if you are careful
to obey all the commands of the LORD your God
that I am giving you today. 6 The LORD your God
will bless you as he has promised. You will lend
money to many nations but will never need to
borrow. You will rule many nations, but they will
not rule over you.
7 "But if there are any poor Israelites in your
towns when you arrive in the land the LORD
your God is giving you, do not be hard-hearted
or tightfisted toward them. 8 Instead, be generous and lend them whatever they need. 9 Do
not be mean-spirited and refuse someone a loan
because the year for canceling debts is close at
hand. If you refuse to make the loan and the
needy person cries out to the LORD, you will be
considered guilty of sin. 10 Give generously to the
poor, not grudgingly, for the LORD your God will
bless you in everything you do. 11 There will always be some in the land who are poor. That is
why I am commanding you to share freely with
the poor and with other Israelites in need.

Release for Hebrew Slaves

12 "If a fellow Hebrew sells himself or herself to
be your servant* and serves you for six years, in
the seventh year you must set that servant free.
13 "When you release a male servant, do not
send him away empty-handed. 14 Give him a generous farewell gift from your flock, your thresh-

15:12 Or *If a Hebrew man or woman is sold to you.*

14:22–29 Tithes. Any system of government has to be paid for. The details here are sketchy, but it is clear that giving to God and giving to the society are part of the same system and that everyone contributes in a way proportional to his or her means.

15:1–11 Receiving and Giving. The paradox of Deuteronomy comes out clearly here. Riches are a blessing from God, but the rich are also responsible for caring for the poor and therefore bringing blessing to them. Giving riches away seems to bring more blessing than the riches themselves!

15:12–18 Slave Release. This is one of several regulations governing rules of employment. Here the rule is that all ethnic Israelites who have become slaves are to be freed on very generous terms after six years of service. This applies to both female and male slaves.

ing floor, and your winepress. Share with him
some of the bounty with which the LORD your
God has blessed you. 15 Remember that you were
once slaves in the land of Egypt and the LORD
your God redeemed you! That is why I am giving you this command.
16 "But suppose your servant says, 'I will not
leave you,' because he loves you and your family, and he has done well with you. 17 In that case,
take an awl and push it through his earlobe into
the door. After that, he will be your servant for
life. And do the same for your female servants.
18 "You must not consider it a hardship when
you release your servants. Remember that for six
years they have given you services worth double
the wages of hired workers, and the LORD your
God will bless you in all you do.

Sacrificing Firstborn Male Animals

19 "You must set aside for the LORD your God all
the firstborn males from your flocks and herds. Do
not use the firstborn of your herds to work your
fields, and do not shear the firstborn of your flocks.
20 Instead, you and your family must eat these animals in the presence of the LORD your God each
year at the place he chooses. 21 But if this firstborn
animal has any defect, such as lameness or blindness, or if anything else is wrong with it, you must
not sacrifice it to the LORD your God. 22 Instead,
use it for food for your family in your hometown.
Anyone, whether ceremonially clean or unclean,
may eat it, just as anyone may eat a gazelle or deer.
23 But you must not consume the blood. You must
pour it out on the ground like water.

Passover and the Festival of Unleavened Bread

16 "In honor of the LORD your God, celebrate the Passover each year in the
early spring, in the month of Abib,*
for that was the month in which the LORD your
God brought you out of Egypt by night. 2 Your
Passover sacrifice may be from either the flock or
the herd, and it must be sacrificed to the LORD
your God at the designated place of worship—the
place he chooses for his name to be honored. 3 Eat
it with bread made without yeast. For seven days
the bread you eat must be made without yeast,
as when you escaped from Egypt in such a hurry.
Eat this bread—the bread of suffering—so that as
long as you live you will remember the day you
departed from Egypt. 4 Let no yeast be found in
any house throughout your land for those seven
days. And when you sacrifice the Passover lamb
on the evening of the first day, do not let any of
the meat remain until the next morning.
5 "You may not sacrifice the Passover in just
any of the towns that the LORD your God is
giving you. 6 You must offer it only at the designated place of worship—the place the LORD
your God chooses for his name to be honored.
Sacrifice it there in the evening as the sun goes
down on the anniversary of your exodus from
Egypt. 7 Roast the lamb and eat it in the place the
LORD your God chooses. Then you may go back
to your tents the next morning. 8 For the next
six days you may not eat any bread made with
yeast. On the seventh day proclaim another holy
day in honor of the LORD your God, and no work
may be done on that day.

The Festival of Harvest

9 "Count off seven weeks from when you first begin to cut the grain at the time of harvest. 10 Then
celebrate the Festival of Harvest* to honor the
LORD your God. Bring him a voluntary offering

16:1 Hebrew *Observe the month of Abib, and keep the Passover unto the LORD your God.* Abib, the first month of the ancient Hebrew lunar calendar, usually occurs within the months of March and April. **16:10** Hebrew *Festival of Weeks;* also in 16:16. This was later called the Festival of Pentecost (see Acts 2:1). It is celebrated today as Shavuot (or Shabuoth).

Exodus 21:7 states "When a man sells his daughter as a slave, will she not be freed . . . as the men are." However, in Exodus the intention is to provide protection for a woman who has been taken as a slave-wife, preventing her from being cast off after six years, rather than restricting the freedom of all bonded women.

15:19–23: Firstborn males, human or animal, were to be specially dedicated to God. For animals this meant being eaten at a special festival at the Temple, rather than being used in ordinary ways. The reason for this dedication is linked to the plague in Egypt, which killed all the firstborn males except those from Israel (Exod 12—13).

16:1–17 The Festivals. Each of these major festivals (Passover, Harvest, and Shelters) are once again described. Verse 16, *On each of these occasions, all men must appear before the LORD your God* is sometimes used to argue that women were irrelevant to or excluded from Israel's cultic life. The preceding verses make it clear, however, that the whole family was involved in keeping the feasts. The whole family and all the servants, even foreigners, widows, and orphans (vv. 11, 14) celebrate together. Thus the command for attendance by *all men* cannot be interpreted as a restriction on the women. The reason why women are excluded from the command is not made explicit. Possibly it recognizes that for

in proportion to the blessings you have received
from him. 11 This is a time to celebrate before the
LORD your God at the designated place of worship he will choose for his name to be honored.
Celebrate with your sons and daughters, your
male and female servants, the Levites from your
towns, and the foreigners, orphans, and widows
who live among you. 12 Remember that you were
once slaves in Egypt, so be careful to obey all
these decrees.

The Festival of Shelters

13 "You must observe the Festival of Shelters*
for seven days at the end of the harvest season,
after the grain has been threshed and the grapes
have been pressed. 14 This festival will be a happy
time of celebrating with your sons and daughters,
your male and female servants, and the Levites,
foreigners, orphans, and widows from your towns.
15 For seven days you must celebrate this festival to
honor the LORD your God at the place he chooses,
for it is he who blesses you with bountiful harvests and gives you success in all your work. This
festival will be a time of great joy for all.

16 "Each year every man in Israel must celebrate these three festivals: the Festival of Unleavened Bread, the Festival of Harvest, and the
Festival of Shelters. On each of these occasions,
all men must appear before the LORD your God
at the place he chooses, but they must not appear before the LORD without a gift for him. 17 All
must give as they are able, according to the blessings given to them by the LORD your God.

Justice for the People

18 "Appoint judges and officials for yourselves
from each of your tribes in all the towns the
LORD your God is giving you. They must judge
the people fairly. 19 You must never twist justice
or show partiality. Never accept a bribe, for bribes
blind the eyes of the wise and corrupt the decisions of the godly. 20 Let true justice prevail, so
you may live and occupy the land that the LORD
your God is giving you.

21 "You must never set up a wooden Asherah
pole beside the altar you build for the LORD your
God. 22 And never set up sacred pillars for worship, for the LORD your God hates them.

17 "Never sacrifice sick or defective cattle, sheep, or goats to the LORD your
God, for he detests such gifts.

2 "When you begin living in the towns the
LORD your God is giving you, a man or woman among you might do evil in the sight of the
LORD your God and violate the covenant. 3 For
instance, they might serve other gods or worship
the sun, the moon, or any of the stars—the forces of heaven—which I have strictly forbidden.
4 When you hear about it, investigate the matter thoroughly. If it is true that this detestable
thing has been done in Israel, 5 then the man or
woman who has committed such an evil act must
be taken to the gates of the town and stoned to
death. 6 But never put a person to death on the
testimony of only one witness. There must always be two or three witnesses. 7 The witnesses
must throw the first stones, and then all the people may join in. In this way, you will purge the
evil from among you.

8 "Suppose a case arises in a local court that
is too hard for you to decide—for instance,
whether someone is guilty of murder or only
of manslaughter, or a difficult lawsuit, or a case
involving different kinds of assault. Take such
legal cases to the place the LORD your God will
choose, 9 and present them to the Levitical priests
or the judge on duty at that time. They will hear
the case and declare the verdict. 10 You must carry
out the verdict they announce and the sentence
they prescribe at the place the LORD chooses. You
must do exactly what they say. 11 After they have
interpreted the law and declared their verdict,
the sentence they impose must be fully executed;

16:13 Or *Festival of Booths,* or *Festival of Tabernacles;* also in 16:16. This was earlier called the Festival of the Final Harvest or Festival of Ingathering (see Exod 23:16b). It is celebrated today as Sukkot (or Succoth).

pregnant women and those feeding young children travel would be very difficult, and it excuses them from compulsory attendance. In that context, where contraception was not available and weaning did not take place until the child was three years old or older, the proportion of women in those categories would be very high.

16:18—17:13 Local Government. Throughout Deuteronomy all Israelites are responsible for their own actions. Local courts are set up to make sure that everyone is held accountable and judged fairly. Israelite women did not always have full control over their own destinies, but there is no lessening of this personal responsibility for them on those grounds. Women, as much as men, are members of the community and must take responsibility for their own conduct. Chapter 17 reinforces what has already been said in chapter 13: As long as there are at least two or three witnesses to confirm the truth of any accusation, anyone—male or female—who is found guilty of idolatry is to be executed.

do not modify it in any way. 12 Anyone arrogant enough to reject the verdict of the judge or of the priest who represents the LORD your God must die. In this way you will purge the evil from Israel. 13 Then everyone else will hear about it and be afraid to act so arrogantly.

Guidelines for a King

14 "You are about to enter the land the LORD your God is giving you. When you take it over and settle there, you may think, 'We should select a king to rule over us like the other nations around us.' 15 If this happens, be sure to select as king the man the LORD your God chooses. You must appoint a fellow Israelite; he may not be a foreigner.

16 "The king must not build up a large stable of horses for himself or send his people to Egypt to buy horses, for the LORD has told you, 'You must never return to Egypt.' 17 The king must not take many wives for himself, because they will turn his heart away from the LORD. And he must not accumulate large amounts of wealth in silver and gold for himself.

18 "When he sits on the throne as king, he must copy for himself this body of instruction on a scroll in the presence of the Levitical priests. 19 He must always keep that copy with him and read it daily as long as he lives. That way he will learn to fear the LORD his God by obeying all the terms of these instructions and decrees. 20 This regular reading will prevent him from becoming proud and acting as if he is above his fellow citizens. It will also prevent him from turning away from these commands in the smallest way. And it will ensure that he and his descendants will reign for many generations in Israel.

Gifts for the Priests and Levites

18 "Remember that the Levitical priests—that is, the whole of the tribe of Levi—will receive no allotment of land among the other tribes in Israel. Instead, the priests and Levites will eat from the special gifts given to the LORD, for that is their share. 2 They will have no land of their own among the Israelites. The LORD himself is their special possession, just as he promised them.

3 "These are the parts the priests may claim as their share from the cattle, sheep, and goats that the people bring as offerings: the shoulder, the cheeks, and the stomach. 4 You must also give to the priests the first share of the grain, the new wine, the olive oil, and the wool at shearing time. 5 For the LORD your God chose the tribe of Levi out of all your tribes to minister in the LORD's name forever.

6 "Suppose a Levite chooses to move from his town in Israel, wherever he is living, to the place the LORD chooses for worship. 7 He may minister there in the name of the LORD his God, just like all his fellow Levites who are serving the LORD there. 8 He may eat his share of the sacrifices and offerings, even if he also receives support from his family.

A Call to Holy Living

9 "When you enter the land the LORD your God is giving you, be very careful not to imitate the detestable customs of the nations living there. 10 For example, never sacrifice your son or daughter as a burnt offering.* And do not let your people practice fortune-telling, or use sorcery, or interpret omens, or engage in witchcraft, 11 or cast spells, or function as mediums or psychics, or call forth the spirits of the dead. 12 Anyone who does these things is detestable to the LORD. It is because the other nations have done these detestable things that the LORD your God will drive them out ahead of you. 13 But you must be blameless before the LORD your God. 14 The nations you are about to displace consult sorcerers and fortune-tellers, but the LORD your God forbids you to do such things."

True and False Prophets

15 Moses continued, "The LORD your God will raise up for you a prophet like me from among your fellow Israelites. You must listen to him.

18:10 Or *never make your son or daughter pass through the fire.*

17:14–20 National Government. It was late in Israel's history before a king was appointed, but the guidelines for such an appointment are set out clearly here. The key element is not how the king rules but how he lives, and in particular his example in studying and keeping the law. It is interesting that all the things that the king is not to do are set out in the same way as the account in 1 Kings that describes Solomon doing exactly these things.

18:1–22 Religious and National Life. The varied interests of the Deuteronomist are reflected here. The need for proper payment for those in national service, the need to avoid pagan and occult practices, and the importance of critiquing the words and actions of those who claim to speak for God are part of the responsibilities of every Israelite.

16 For this is what you yourselves requested of the LORD your God when you were assembled at Mount Sinai.* You said, 'Don't let us hear the voice of the LORD our God anymore or see this blazing fire, for we will die.'

17 "Then the LORD said to me, 'What they have said is right. 18 I will raise up a prophet like you from among their fellow Israelites. I will put my words in his mouth, and he will tell the people everything I command him. 19 I will personally deal with anyone who will not listen to the messages the prophet proclaims on my behalf. 20 But any prophet who falsely claims to speak in my name or who speaks in the name of another god must die.'

21 "But you may wonder, 'How will we know whether or not a prophecy is from the LORD?' 22 If the prophet speaks in the LORD's name but his prediction does not happen or come true, you will know that the LORD did not give that message. That prophet has spoken without my authority and need not be feared.

Cities of Refuge

19 "When the LORD your God destroys the nations whose land he is giving you, you will take over their land and settle in their towns and homes. 2 Then you must set apart three cities of refuge in the land the LORD your God is giving you. 3 Survey the territory,* and divide the land the LORD your God is giving you into three districts, with one of these cities in each district. Then anyone who has killed someone can flee to one of the cities of refuge for safety.

4 "If someone kills another person unintentionally, without previous hostility, the slayer may flee to any of these cities to live in safety. 5 For example, suppose someone goes into the forest with a neighbor to cut wood. And suppose one of them swings an ax to chop down a tree, and the ax head flies off the handle, killing the other person. In such cases, the slayer may flee to one of the cities of refuge to live in safety.

6 "If the distance to the nearest city of refuge is too far, an enraged avenger might be able to chase down and kill the person who caused the death. Then the slayer would die unfairly, since he had never shown hostility toward the person who died. 7 That is why I am commanding you to set aside three cities of refuge.

8 "And if the LORD your God enlarges your territory, as he swore to your ancestors, and gives you all the land he promised them, 9 you must designate three additional cities of refuge. (He will give you this land if you are careful to obey all the commands I have given you—if you always love the LORD your God and walk in his ways.) 10 That way you will prevent the death of innocent people in the land the LORD your God is giving you as your special possession. You will not be held responsible for the death of innocent people.

11 "But suppose someone is hostile toward a neighbor and deliberately ambushes and murders him and then flees to one of the cities of refuge. 12 In that case, the elders of the murderer's hometown must send agents to the city of refuge to bring him back and hand him over to the dead person's avenger to be put to death. 13 Do not feel sorry for that murderer! Purge from Israel the guilt of murdering innocent people; then all will go well with you.

Concern for Justice

14 "When you arrive in the land the LORD your God is giving you as your special possession, you must never steal anyone's land by moving the boundary markers your ancestors set up to mark their property.

15 "You must not convict anyone of a crime on the testimony of only one witness. The facts of the case must be established by the testimony of two or three witnesses.

16 "If a malicious witness comes forward and accuses someone of a crime, 17 then both the accuser and accused must appear before the LORD by coming to the priests and judges in office at that time. 18 The judges must investigate the case thoroughly. If the accuser has brought false charges against his fellow Israelite, 19 you must impose on the accuser the sentence he intended for the other person. In this way, you will purge

18:16 Hebrew *Horeb,* another name for Sinai. **19:3** Or *Keep the roads in good repair.*

19:1–21 The Justice System. The provision of cities of refuge recognizes that the desire for family revenge was a reality in that society, that accidents happen, and that there is a difference between manslaughter and murder. Further instructions about witnesses are given in vv. 15–20. There is no sign within Deuteronomy of the later ideas that saw the testimony of women as less valuable than that of men. There is no indication, here or elsewhere, that the witnesses whose testimony was required before anyone could be convicted had to be male. The implication is that the responsibility to be truthful and to make sure that injustice is avoided is given to every Israelite, whether they be male or female.

such evil from among you. [20]Then the rest of
the people will hear about it and be afraid to do
such an evil thing. [21]You must show no pity for
the guilty! Your rule should be life for life, eye
for eye, tooth for tooth, hand for hand, foot for
foot.

Regulations concerning War

20 "When you go out to fight your enemies and you face horses and chariots and an army greater than your
own, do not be afraid. The LORD your God, who
brought you out of the land of Egypt, is with
you! [2]When you prepare for battle, the priest
must come forward to speak to the troops. [3]He
will say to them, 'Listen to me, all you men of
Israel! Do not be afraid as you go out to fight
your enemies today! Do not lose heart or panic
or tremble before them. [4]For the LORD your God
is going with you! He will fight for you against
your enemies, and he will give you victory!'
[5]"Then the officers of the army must address
the troops and say, 'Has anyone here just built
a new house but not yet dedicated it? If so, you
may go home! You might be killed in the battle, and someone else would dedicate your house.
[6]Has anyone here just planted a vineyard but
not yet eaten any of its fruit? If so, you may go
home! You might die in battle, and someone else
would eat the first fruit. [7]Has anyone here just
become engaged to a woman but not yet married
her? Well, you may go home and get married!
You might die in the battle, and someone else
would marry her.'
[8]"Then the officers will also say, 'Is anyone
here afraid or worried? If you are, you may go
home before you frighten anyone else.' [9]When
the officers have finished speaking to their troops,
they will appoint the unit commanders.
[10]"As you approach a town to attack it, you
must first offer its people terms for peace. [11]If
they accept your terms and open the gates to
you, then all the people inside will serve you in
forced labor. [12]But if they refuse to make peace
and prepare to fight, you must attack the town.
[13]When the LORD your God hands the town over
to you, use your swords to kill every man in the
town. [14]But you may keep for yourselves all the
women, children, livestock, and other plunder.
You may enjoy the plunder from your enemies
that the LORD your God has given you.
[15]"But these instructions apply only to distant towns, not to the towns of the nations in
the land you will enter. [16]In those towns that the
LORD your God is giving you as a special possession, destroy every living thing. [17]You must
completely destroy* the Hittites, Amorites, Canaanites, Perizzites, Hivites, and Jebusites, just as
the LORD your God has commanded you. [18]This
will prevent the people of the land from teaching you to imitate their detestable customs in the
worship of their gods, which would cause you to
sin deeply against the LORD your God.
[19]"When you are attacking a town and the
war drags on, you must not cut down the trees
with your axes. You may eat the fruit, but do not
cut down the trees. Are the trees your enemies,
that you should attack them? [20]You may only cut
down trees that you know are not valuable for
food. Use them to make the equipment you need
to attack the enemy town until it falls.

Cleansing for Unsolved Murder

21 "When you are in the land the LORD
your God is giving you, someone
may be found murdered in a field,
and you don't know who committed the murder. [2]In such a case, your elders and judges must
measure the distance from the site of the crime
to the nearby towns. [3]When the nearest town
has been determined, that town's elders must
select from the herd a young cow that has never
been trained or yoked to a plow. [4]They must lead
it down to a valley that has not been plowed or
planted and that has a stream running through
it. There in the valley they must break the young
cow's neck. [5]Then the Levitical priests must step
forward, for the LORD your God has chosen them
to minister before him and to pronounce blessings in the LORD's name. They are to decide all
legal and criminal cases.
[6]"The elders of the town must wash their

20:17 The Hebrew term used here refers to the complete consecration of things or people to the LORD, either by destroying them or by giving them as an offering.

20:1–20 Rules for Warfare. War then, as now, was a fact of life, but these regulations are remarkably liberal. There were no call-ups for those who have just married—if a woman was widowed young she would be less likely to have had children to care for her later on; those men who were afraid or worried were sent home, not executed for cowardice; negotiation was always to be the first move, and "scorched-earth" policies were to be avoided.

21:1–21 Case Studies. In this chapter we do not have direct commands but a series of hypothetical case studies all beginning with the word "Suppose." The instructions for the treatment of female captives in vv.

hands over the young cow whose neck was broken. [7]Then they must say, 'Our hands did not shed this person's blood, nor did we see it happen. [8]O LORD, forgive your people Israel whom you have redeemed. Do not charge your people with the guilt of murdering an innocent person.' Then they will be absolved of the guilt of this person's blood. [9]By following these instructions, you will do what is right in the LORD's sight and will cleanse the guilt of murder from your community.

Marriage to a Captive Woman

[10]"Suppose you go out to war against your enemies and the LORD your God hands them over to you, and you take some of them as captives. [11]And suppose you see among the captives a beautiful woman, and you are attracted to her and want to marry her. [12]If this happens, you may take her to your home, where she must shave her head, cut her nails, [13]and change the clothes she was wearing when she was captured. She will stay in your home, but let her mourn for her father and mother for a full month. Then you may marry her, and you will be her husband and she will be your wife. [14]But if you marry her and she does not please you, you must let her go free. You may not sell her or treat her as a slave, for you have humiliated her.

Rights of the Firstborn

[15]"Suppose a man has two wives, but he loves one and not the other, and both have given him sons. And suppose the firstborn son is the son of the wife he does not love. [16]When the man divides his inheritance, he may not give the larger inheritance to his younger son, the son of the wife he loves, as if he were the firstborn son. [17]He must recognize the rights of his oldest son, the son of the wife he does not love, by giving him a double portion. He is the first son of his father's virility, and the rights of the firstborn belong to him.

Dealing with a Rebellious Son

[18]"Suppose a man has a stubborn and rebellious son who will not obey his father or mother, even though they discipline him. [19]In such a case, the father and mother must take the son to the elders as they hold court at the town gate. [20]The parents must say to the elders, 'This son of ours is stubborn and rebellious and refuses to obey. He is a glutton and a drunkard.' [21]Then all the men of his town must stone him to death. In this way, you will purge this evil from among you, and all Israel will hear about it and be afraid.

Various Regulations

[22]"If someone has committed a crime worthy of death and is executed and hung on a tree,* [23]the body must not remain hanging from the tree overnight. You must bury the body that same day, for anyone who is hung* is cursed in the sight of God. In this way, you will prevent the defilement of the land the LORD your God is giving you as your special possession.

22

"If you see your neighbor's ox or sheep or goat wandering away, don't ignore your responsibility.* Take it back to its owner. [2]If its owner does not live nearby or you don't know who the owner is, take it to your place and keep it until the owner comes looking for it. Then you must return it. [3]Do the same if you find your neighbor's donkey, clothing, or anything else your neighbor loses. Don't ignore your responsibility.

[4]"If you see that your neighbor's donkey or ox has collapsed on the road, do not look the other way. Go and help your neighbor get it back on its feet!

[5]"A woman must not put on men's clothing, and a man must not wear women's clothing. Anyone who does this is detestable in the sight of the LORD your God.

[6]"If you happen to find a bird's nest in a tree or on the ground, and there are young ones or eggs in it with the mother sitting in the nest, do

21:22 Or *impaled on a pole;* similarly in 21:23. **21:23** Greek version reads *for everyone who is hung on a tree.* Compare Gal 3:13. **22:1** Hebrew *don't hide yourself;* similarly in 22:3.

10–14 take it for granted that a conquering army has the right to dispose of the conquered population in any way they wish. It is hard for those from a different cultural context to see this as anything other than appalling, but this would have been assumed in the ancient Near East. It is remarkable that, although the woman may have had no choice—the soldier who is attracted to her has every right to make her his wife, her identity as a human being is, at least to some extent, recognized. She must be allowed time to mourn for her parents and her past life. If the man marries her and they don't get along, then she must not be enslaved but allowed to go free.

21:22—22:12: Everything relevant to the community is seen as significant. Rules for burying murderers are set alongside rules for dress, for agriculture, and for egg collecting! One verse (22:5) touches on the importance of sexual integrity.

not take the mother with the young. 7 You may take the young, but let the mother go, so that you may prosper and enjoy a long life.

8 "When you build a new house, you must build a railing around the edge of its flat roof. That way you will not be considered guilty of murder if someone falls from the roof.

9 "You must not plant any other crop between the rows of your vineyard. If you do, you are forbidden to use either the grapes from the vineyard or the other crop.

10 "You must not plow with an ox and a donkey harnessed together.

11 "You must not wear clothing made of wool and linen woven together.

12 "You must put four tassels on the hem of the cloak with which you cover yourself—on the front, back, and sides.

Regulations for Sexual Purity

13 "Suppose a man marries a woman, but after sleeping with her, he turns against her 14 and publicly accuses her of shameful conduct, saying, 'When I married this woman, I discovered she was not a virgin.' 15 Then the woman's father and mother must bring the proof of her virginity to the elders as they hold court at the town gate. 16 Her father must say to them, 'I gave my daughter to this man to be his wife, and now he has turned against her. 17 He has accused her of shameful conduct, saying, "I discovered that your daughter was not a virgin." But here is the proof of my daughter's virginity.' Then they must spread her bed sheet before the elders. 18 The elders must then take the man and punish him. 19 They must also fine him 100 pieces of silver,* which he must pay to the woman's father because he publicly accused a virgin of Israel of shameful conduct. The woman will then remain the man's wife, and he may never divorce her.

20 "But suppose the man's accusations are true, and he can show that she was not a virgin. 21 The woman must be taken to the door of her father's home, and there the men of the town must stone her to death, for she has committed a disgraceful crime in Israel by being promiscuous while living in her parents' home. In this way, you will purge this evil from among you.

22 "If a man is discovered committing adultery, both he and the woman must die. In this way, you will purge Israel of such evil.

23 "Suppose a man meets a young woman, a virgin who is engaged to be married, and he has sexual intercourse with her. If this happens within a town, 24 you must take both of them to the gates of that town and stone them to death. The woman is guilty because she did not scream for help. The man must die because he violated another man's wife. In this way, you will purge this evil from among you.

25 "But if the man meets the engaged woman out in the country, and he rapes her, then only the man must die. 26 Do nothing to the young woman; she has committed no crime worthy of death. She is as innocent as a murder victim. 27 Since the man raped her out in the country, it must be assumed that she screamed, but there was no one to rescue her.

28 "Suppose a man has intercourse with a

22:19 Hebrew *100 shekels of silver,* about 2.5 pounds or 1.1 kilograms in weight.

22:13–30: Again women are viewed as the property of their father or husband. Any married woman having sex outside marriage was automatically condemned. Any harm to a marriage affected the whole community and must be strongly resisted. Therefore both parties to this *crime* must be executed. The death sentence was, in theory at least, mandatory. The concept of an innocent, raped woman is considered only in the case where the woman was engaged rather than married and the rape had taken place in an isolated area. Only then is she innocent, as innocent as a *murder victim* because she may have called for help *but there was no one to rescue her*. The best option for a raped virgin was for her rapist to marry her. He had no choice in this matter, and apparently neither did she. She could be forced into a permanent relationship with the man who assaulted her. Presumably the thinking here is that a raped girl is unmarriageable. Any marriage is better than none; therefore the man must be forced to take responsibility and ensure that she will be married—to him. Any compensation paid for the rape goes not to the girl herself, but to her father. The implication of this seems clear; injury to a woman was viewed primarily as injury to her father or her husband. Surely this is proof that women were regarded as property. This perspective, as you see, does not reflect the whole story. Statements like these are found almost entirely within what is known as casuistic or case law dealing with situations that existed and therefore needed regulating. This certainly does not mean the Deuteronomist was commanding or even encouraging such situations in the first place. In fact, many of these laws include implicit recognition that the situations they describe are oppressive. Within these oppressive situations, the laws are geared to provide at least a level of protection for the women involved.

young woman who is a virgin but is not engaged to be married. If they are discovered, [29]he must pay her father fifty pieces of silver.* Then he must marry the young woman because he violated her, and he may never divorce her as long as he lives.

[30]*"A man must not marry his father's former wife, for this would violate his father.

Regulations concerning Worship

23 [1]*"If a man's testicles are crushed or his penis is cut off, he may not be admitted to the assembly of the LORD.

[2]"If a person is illegitimate by birth, neither he nor his descendants for ten generations may be admitted to the assembly of the LORD.

[3]"No Ammonite or Moabite or any of their descendants for ten generations may be admitted to the assembly of the LORD. [4]These nations did not welcome you with food and water when you came out of Egypt. Instead, they hired Balaam son of Beor from Pethor in distant Aram-naharaim to curse you. [5]But the LORD your God refused to listen to Balaam. He turned the intended curse into a blessing because the LORD your God loves you. [6]As long as you live, you must never promote the welfare and prosperity of the Ammonites or Moabites.

[7]"Do not detest the Edomites or the Egyptians, because the Edomites are your relatives and you lived as foreigners among the Egyptians. [8]The third generation of Edomites and Egyptians may enter the assembly of the LORD.

Miscellaneous Regulations

[9]"When you go to war against your enemies, be sure to stay away from anything that is impure.

[10]"Any man who becomes ceremonially defiled because of a nocturnal emission must leave the camp and stay away all day. [11]Toward evening he must bathe himself, and at sunset he may return to the camp.

[12]"You must have a designated area outside the camp where you can go to relieve yourself. [13]Each of you must have a spade as part of your equipment. Whenever you relieve yourself, dig a hole with the spade and cover the excrement. [14]The camp must be holy, for the LORD your God moves around in your camp to protect you and to defeat your enemies. He must not see any shameful thing among you, or he will turn away from you.

[15]"If slaves should escape from their masters and take refuge with you, you must not hand them over to their masters. [16]Let them live among you in any town they choose, and do not oppress them.

[17]"No Israelite, whether man or woman, may become a temple prostitute. [18]When you are bringing an offering to fulfill a vow, you must not bring to the house of the LORD your God any offering from the earnings of a prostitute, whether a man* or a woman, for both are detestable to the LORD your God.

[19]"Do not charge interest on the loans you make to a fellow Israelite, whether you loan money, or food, or anything else. [20]You may charge interest to foreigners, but you may not charge interest to Israelites, so that the LORD your God may bless you in everything you do in the land you are about to enter and occupy.

[21]"When you make a vow to the LORD your God, be prompt in fulfilling whatever you promised him. For the LORD your God demands that you promptly fulfill all your vows, or you will be guilty of sin. [22]However, it is not a sin to refrain from making a vow. [23]But once you have voluntarily made a vow, be careful to fulfill your promise to the LORD your God.

[24]"When you enter your neighbor's vineyard, you may eat your fill of grapes, but you must not carry any away in a basket. [25]And when you enter your neighbor's field of grain, you may pluck the heads of grain with your hand, but you must not harvest it with a sickle.

24 "Suppose a man marries a woman but she does not please him. Having discovered something wrong with her, he writes her a letter of divorce, hands it to her, and sends her away from his house. [2]When she leaves his house, she is free to marry anoth-

22:29 Hebrew *50 shekels of silver,* about 1.25 pounds or 570 grams in weight. **22:30** Verse 22:30 is numbered 23:1 in Hebrew text. **23:1** Verses 23:1-25 are numbered 23:2-26 in Hebrew text. **23:18** Hebrew *a dog.*

23:1–8 Worship Regulations. The purity of those coming to worship was important; physical disability, illegitimate or foreign birth could exclude people. The inclusion of people like Ruth, the Moabite, shows that these regulations were not always interpreted literally. Otherwise even David would not have been allowed in worship services.

23:9—25:19 Miscellaneous Regulations. The variety of different issues bundled together shows the range of God's interest in the life of the community and how much the interests of women were considered. For example, 24:1 states that if a man divorces his wife, he must do it properly and not leave her in a state of unmarriageable limbo. (In Matt 19:8, Jesus explains

er man. 3But if the second husband also turns against her and divorces her, or if he dies, 4the first husband may not marry her again, for she has been defiled. That would be detestable to the LORD. You must not bring guilt upon the land the LORD your God is giving you as a special possession.

5"A newly married man must not be drafted into the army or be given any other official responsibilities. He must be free to spend one year at home, bringing happiness to the wife he has married.

6"It is wrong to take a set of millstones, or even just the upper millstone, as security for a loan, for the owner uses it to make a living.

7"If anyone kidnaps a fellow Israelite and treats him as a slave or sells him, the kidnapper must die. In this way, you will purge the evil from among you.

8"In all cases involving serious skin diseases,* be careful to follow the instructions of the Levitical priests; obey all the commands I have given them. 9Remember what the LORD your God did to Miriam as you were coming from Egypt.

10"If you lend anything to your neighbor, do not enter his house to pick up the item he is giving as security. 11You must wait outside while he goes in and brings it out to you. 12If your neighbor is poor and gives you his cloak as security for a loan, do not keep the cloak overnight. 13Return the cloak to its owner by sunset so he can stay warm through the night and bless you, and the LORD your God will count you as righteous.

14"Never take advantage of poor and destitute laborers, whether they are fellow Israelites or foreigners living in your towns. 15You must pay them their wages each day before sunset because they are poor and are counting on it. If you don't, they might cry out to the LORD against you, and it would be counted against you as sin.

16"Parents must not be put to death for the sins of their children, nor children for the sins of their parents. Those deserving to die must be put to death for their own crimes.

17"True justice must be given to foreigners living among you and to orphans, and you must never accept a widow's garment as security for her debt. 18Always remember that you were slaves in Egypt and that the LORD your God redeemed you from your slavery. That is why I have given you this command.

19"When you are harvesting your crops and forget to bring in a bundle of grain from your field, don't go back to get it. Leave it for the foreigners, orphans, and widows. Then the LORD your God will bless you in all you do. 20When you beat the olives from your olive trees, don't go over the boughs twice. Leave the remaining olives for the foreigners, orphans, and widows. 21When you gather the grapes in your vineyard, don't glean the vines after they are picked. Leave the remaining grapes for the foreigners, orphans, and widows. 22Remember that you were slaves in the land of Egypt. That is why I am giving you this command.

25 "Suppose two people take a dispute to court, and the judges declare that one is right and the other is wrong. 2If the person in the wrong is sentenced to be flogged, the judge must command him to lie down and be beaten in his presence with the number of lashes appropriate to the crime. 3But never give more than forty lashes; more than forty lashes would publicly humiliate your neighbor.

4"You must not muzzle an ox to keep it from eating as it treads out the grain.

5"If two brothers are living together on the same property and one of them dies without a son, his widow may not be married to anyone from outside the family. Instead, her husband's brother should marry her and have intercourse with her to fulfill the duties of a brother-in-law. 6The first son she bears to him will be considered the son of the dead brother, so that his name will not be forgotten in Israel.

7"But if the man refuses to marry his broth-

24:8 Traditionally rendered *leprosy.* The Hebrew word used here can describe various skin diseases.

that these arrangements for divorce did not imply approval of the process itself. They were a concession rather than an ideal.) Although 24:16 is very explicit that *parents must not be put to death for the sins of their children, nor children for the sins of their parents,* 5:9 speaks of punishing the children for the sins of their parents where "the entire family is affected" but this is apparently meant in very general terms, implying that the behavior of one generation has long-lasting consequences. The significance of each person within the nation is strongly stressed in this interesting chapter. The repeated statement *remember that you were slaves in the land of Egypt* shows that God requires justice for all, rich and poor, men and women, slave or free. Chapter 25 further spells out regulations about property, marriage, merchandise, and the like. It is not clear whether or how often the instruction for a man to marry his brother's widow was carried out (25:7). Even the illustration we have in Ruth 4 is ambiguous. The possibility of the man

er's widow, she must go to the town gate and say to the elders assembled there, 'My husband's brother refuses to preserve his brother's name in Israel—he refuses to fulfill the duties of a brother-in-law by marrying me.' 8 The elders of the town will then summon him and talk with him. If he still refuses and says, 'I don't want to marry her,' 9 the widow must walk over to him in the presence of the elders, pull his sandal from his foot, and spit in his face. Then she must declare, 'This is what happens to a man who refuses to provide his brother with children.' 10 Ever afterward in Israel his family will be referred to as 'the family of the man whose sandal was pulled off'!

11 "If two Israelite men get into a fight and the wife of one tries to rescue her husband by grabbing the testicles of the other man, 12 you must cut off her hand. Show her no pity.

13 "You must use accurate scales when you weigh out merchandise, 14 and you must use full and honest measures. 15 Yes, always use honest weights and measures, so that you may enjoy a long life in the land the LORD your God is giving you. 16 All who cheat with dishonest weights and measures are detestable to the LORD your God.

17 "Never forget what the Amalekites did to you as you came from Egypt. 18 They attacked you when you were exhausted and weary, and they struck down those who were straggling behind. They had no fear of God. 19 Therefore, when the LORD your God has given you rest from all your enemies in the land he is giving you as a special possession, you must destroy the Amalekites and erase their memory from under heaven. Never forget this!

Harvest Offerings and Tithes

26 "When you enter the land the LORD your God is giving you as a special possession and you have conquered it and settled there, 2 put some of the first produce from each crop you harvest into a basket and bring it to the designated place of worship—the place the LORD your God chooses for his name to be honored. 3 Go to the priest in charge at that time and say to him, 'With this gift I acknowledge to the LORD your God that I have entered the land he swore to our ancestors he would give us.' 4 The priest will then take the basket from your hand and set it before the altar of the LORD your God.

5 "You must then say in the presence of the LORD your God, 'My ancestor Jacob was a wandering Aramean who went to live as a foreigner in Egypt. His family arrived few in number, but in Egypt they became a large and mighty nation. 6 When the Egyptians oppressed and humiliated us by making us their slaves, 7 we cried out to the LORD, the God of our ancestors. He heard our cries and saw our hardship, toil, and oppression. 8 So the LORD brought us out of Egypt with a strong hand and powerful arm, with overwhelming terror, and with miraculous signs and wonders. 9 He brought us to this place and gave us this land flowing with milk and honey! 10 And now, O LORD, I have brought you the first portion of the harvest you have given me from the ground.' Then place the produce before the LORD your God, and bow to the ground in worship before him. 11 Afterward you may go and celebrate because of all the good things the LORD your God has given to you and your household. Remember to include the Levites and the foreigners living among you in the celebration.

12 "Every third year you must offer a special tithe of your crops. In this year of the special tithe you must give your tithes to the Levites, foreigners, orphans, and widows, so that they will have enough to eat in your towns. 13 Then you must declare in the presence of the LORD your God, 'I have taken the sacred gift from my house and have given it to the Levites, foreigners, orphans, and widows, just as you commanded me. I have not violated or forgotten any of your commands. 14 I have not eaten any of it while in mourning; I have not handled it while I was ceremonially unclean; and I have not offered any of it to the dead. I have obeyed the LORD my God and have done everything you commanded me. 15 Now look down from your holy dwelling place in heaven and bless your people Israel and the land you swore to our ancestors to give us—a land flowing with milk and honey.'

refusing is clearly recognized. Whether the woman was given a choice is less clear. The rationale given is that the memory of the dead man be preserved, a further indication of the importance of every individual. However, there is no regulation concerning the inheritance of a childless man who died before marriage. Therefore protection for women who otherwise could be left with very bleak prospects may also have been part of the original motivation.

26:1–15: Harvest Gifts. Thanksgiving to God, community celebration, and giving to the needy are all involved in these commands. The law is never simply regulation given for its own sake. It is all about living in the best way possible as the community of God's people.

A Call to Obey the LORD's Commands

16 "Today the LORD your God has commanded you to obey all these decrees and regulations. So be careful to obey them wholeheartedly. 17 You have declared today that the LORD is your God. And you have promised to walk in his ways, and to obey his decrees, commands, and regulations, and to do everything he tells you. 18 The LORD has declared today that you are his people, his own special treasure, just as he promised, and that you must obey all his commands. 19 And if you do, he will set you high above all the other nations he has made. Then you will receive praise, honor, and renown. You will be a nation that is holy to the LORD your God, just as he promised."

The Altar on Mount Ebal

27 Then Moses and the leaders of Israel gave this charge to the people: "Obey all these commands that I am giving you today. 2 When you cross the Jordan River and enter the land the LORD your God is giving you, set up some large stones and coat them with plaster. 3 Write this whole body of instruction on them when you cross the river to enter the land the LORD your God is giving you—a land flowing with milk and honey, just as the LORD, the God of your ancestors, promised you. 4 When you cross the Jordan, set up these stones at Mount Ebal and coat them with plaster, as I am commanding you today. 5 "Then build an altar there to the LORD your God, using natural, uncut stones. You must not shape the stones with an iron tool. 6 Build the altar of uncut stones, and use it to offer burnt offerings to the LORD your God. 7 Also sacrifice peace offerings on it, and celebrate by feasting there before the LORD your God. 8 You must clearly write all these instructions on the stones coated with plaster."

9 Then Moses and the Levitical priests addressed all Israel as follows: "O Israel, be quiet and listen! Today you have become the people of the LORD your God. 10 So you must obey the LORD your God by keeping all these commands and decrees that I am giving you today."

Curses from Mount Ebal

11 That same day Moses also gave this charge to the people: 12 "When you cross the Jordan River, the tribes of Simeon, Levi, Judah, Issachar, Joseph, and Benjamin must stand on Mount Gerizim to proclaim a blessing over the people. 13 And the tribes of Reuben, Gad, Asher, Zebulun, Dan, and Naphtali must stand on Mount Ebal to proclaim a curse.

14 "Then the Levites will shout to all the people of Israel:

15 'Cursed is anyone who carves or casts an idol
and secretly sets it up. These idols, the work
of craftsmen, are detestable to the LORD.'
And all the people will reply, 'Amen.'

26:16–19: This extended selection of regulations ends a final exhortation to obey the LORD's commandments wholeheartedly. The spirit of every Israelite needs to be dedicated to keeping the spirit of the law. Their obedience should stem from commitment to covenant relationship with God and be based on their conviction that the LORD their God has declared his commitment to Israel. They can then in reality be the holy people of a holy God.

27:1—29:1 Moses' Third Speech: Blessings and Curses

27:1–13: There is a great deal of symbolism in this chapter. Visual and even multimedia methods are set out to help the people own their identity as God's covenant nation and to be the people God has called them to be. The words of the law, perhaps meaning only the Ten Commandments representing the whole *body of instruction*, written on large stones, are set up in a public place, on Mount Ebal. The symbolism is clear—the law was for all, to be seen by all, understood by all, obeyed by all. The nearby altar was to be built of ordinary stones picked up from the fields. God cannot be controlled or organized by human activity. The law is presented in the context of worship: burnt offerings recognizing God's sovereignty and peace offerings celebrating relationship with God—in effect, sharing a meal with him. The law, in spite of the curses about to be outlined, is largely about relationship and celebration. Everyone must acknowledge his or her personal ownership of the law and its provisions. The ceremony where the people divided into two, six tribes on Mount Gerizim for blessing and six on Mount Ebal for cursing, enabled this acknowledgment to take place. The two mountains symbolize a choice between two ways: the way of blessing, in relationship with God, and the way of cursing, separated from God. The altar being built on Mount Ebal, from where the curses were to be proclaimed, makes it clear that there was no superstitious significance to the mountains. Both Mount Gerizim and Mount Ebal were part of the land that God had given to them. Joshua 8:30–35 describes the carrying out of the instructions given here.

16 'Cursed is anyone who dishonors father or mother.'
And all the people will reply, 'Amen.'

17 'Cursed is anyone who steals property from a neighbor by moving a boundary marker.'
And all the people will reply, 'Amen.'

18 'Cursed is anyone who leads a blind person astray on the road.'
And all the people will reply, 'Amen.'

19 'Cursed is anyone who denies justice to foreigners, orphans, or widows.'
And all the people will reply, 'Amen.'

20 'Cursed is anyone who has sexual intercourse with one of his father's wives, for he has violated his father.'
And all the people will reply, 'Amen.'

21 'Cursed is anyone who has sexual intercourse with an animal.'
And all the people will reply, 'Amen.'

22 'Cursed is anyone who has sexual intercourse with his sister, whether she is the daughter of his father or his mother.'
And all the people will reply, 'Amen.'

23 'Cursed is anyone who has sexual intercourse with his mother-in-law.'
And all the people will reply, 'Amen.'

24 'Cursed is anyone who attacks a neighbor in secret.'
And all the people will reply, 'Amen.'

25 'Cursed is anyone who accepts payment to kill an innocent person.'
And all the people will reply, 'Amen.'

26 'Cursed is anyone who does not affirm and obey the terms of these instructions.'
And all the people will reply, 'Amen.'

Blessings for Obedience

28 "If you fully obey the LORD your
God and carefully keep all his commands that I am giving you today,
the LORD your God will set you high above all
the nations of the world. 2 You will experience all
these blessings if you obey the LORD your God:

3 Your towns and your fields
will be blessed.
4 Your children and your crops
will be blessed.
The offspring of your herds and flocks
will be blessed.
5 Your fruit baskets and breadboards
will be blessed.
6 Wherever you go and whatever you do,
you will be blessed.

7 "The LORD will conquer your enemies when
they attack you. They will attack you from one
direction, but they will scatter from you in sev-
en!
8 "The LORD will guarantee a blessing on everything you do and will fill your storehouses
with grain. The LORD your God will bless you in
the land he is giving you.
9 "If you obey the commands of the LORD
your God and walk in his ways, the LORD will
establish you as his holy people as he swore he
would do. 10 Then all the nations of the world will
see that you are a people claimed by the LORD,
and they will stand in awe of you.
11 "The LORD will give you prosperity in the
land he swore to your ancestors to give you,
blessing you with many children, numerous livestock, and abundant crops. 12 The LORD will send

---

27:14–26: The dramatic recital of the curses must have been awesome. The whole nation is involved in accepting that those who take part in these activities, who commit these crimes, deserve to be cursed. No legal system can be effective if the people *as a whole* do not accept the validity of its laws. This ceremony is a national ratification of the law. Every person, both women and men, must formally agree that dishonoring parents, depriving widows of justice, incest, and violence against neighbors is unacceptable in their society and weakens the whole community.

28:1–14 Blessings. The pattern of curses and blessings found in Deuteronomy, relating as they do to the breaking and keeping of the covenant between God and Israel, are part of a known system where legal codes are validated by a series of curses. Here, in spite of the amount of space given to the curses, it seems clear that they are there primarily to serve as a backdrop to the blessings. To be in relationship with God, and to demonstrate that by a holy lifestyle, means to be blessed. This blessing is not a reward for keeping the law; rather it is an automatic consequence of being in relationship with God, resting on his promises. This blessing is expressed in material terms. The obedient people can expect tangible benefits, such as fertility, prosperity, peace, and victory because they remain in relationship with God, but

rain at the proper time from his rich treasury
in the heavens and will bless all the work you
do. You will lend to many nations, but you will
never need to borrow from them. 13 If you listen
to these commands of the LORD your God that I
am giving you today, and if you carefully obey
them, the LORD will make you the head and not
the tail, and you will always be on top and never
at the bottom. 14 You must not turn away from
any of the commands I am giving you today, nor
follow after other gods and worship them.

Curses for Disobedience

15 "But if you refuse to listen to the LORD your
God and do not obey all the commands and decrees I am giving you today, all these curses will
come and overwhelm you:

16 Your towns and your fields
will be cursed.
17 Your fruit baskets and breadboards
will be cursed.
18 Your children and your crops
will be cursed.
The offspring of your herds and flocks
will be cursed.
19 Wherever you go and whatever you do,
you will be cursed.

20 "The LORD himself will send on you curses,
confusion, and frustration in everything you do,
until at last you are completely destroyed for doing evil and abandoning me. 21 The LORD will afflict you with diseases until none of you are left
in the land you are about to enter and occupy.
22 The LORD will strike you with wasting diseases,
fever, and inflammation, with scorching heat and
drought, and with blight and mildew. These disasters will pursue you until you die. 23 The skies
above will be as unyielding as bronze, and the
earth beneath will be as hard as iron. 24 The LORD
will change the rain that falls on your land into
powder, and dust will pour down from the sky
until you are destroyed.

25 "The LORD will cause you to be defeated by
your enemies. You will attack your enemies from
one direction, but you will scatter from them in
seven! You will be an object of horror to all the
kingdoms of the earth. 26 Your corpses will be food
for all the scavenging birds and wild animals, and
no one will be there to chase them away.

27 "The LORD will afflict you with the boils
of Egypt and with tumors, scurvy, and the itch,
from which you cannot be cured. 28 The LORD
will strike you with madness, blindness, and panic. 29 You will grope around in broad daylight like
a blind person groping in the darkness, but you
will not find your way. You will be oppressed and
robbed continually, and no one will come to save
you.

30 "You will be engaged to a woman, but another man will sleep with her. You will build a
house, but someone else will live in it. You will
plant a vineyard, but you will never enjoy its
fruit. 31 Your ox will be butchered before your
eyes, but you will not eat a single bite of the meat.
Your donkey will be taken from you, never to be
returned. Your sheep and goats will be given to
your enemies, and no one will be there to help
you. 32 You will watch as your sons and daughters
are taken away as slaves. Your heart will break
for them, but you won't be able to help them.
33 A foreign nation you have never heard about
will eat the crops you worked so hard to grow.
You will suffer under constant oppression and
harsh treatment. 34 You will go mad because of all
the tragedy you see around you. 35 The LORD will
cover your knees and legs with incurable boils. In
fact, you will be covered from head to foot.

36 "The LORD will exile you and your king to

---

the real blessing is the relationship itself. To belong to God's covenant people, that is, to belong to God himself, is to be blessed.

28:15—29:1 Curses. In a similar way, to step outside of that relationship with God is to be cursed. Like the blessings, the curses are also seen in materialistic terms. If the people turn away from God's path, then they will suffer famine, ill health, defeat, and general ignominy. It does not appear that these curses were meant to be applied in a mechanistic way, implying that if they break this particular law they would suffer that particular consequence. Rather the curses serve to persuade Israel that rejecting God or his plans for them will have devastating consequences and that being out of relationship with the LORD is a terrible state, to be avoided at all costs. In the light of this, the curse is presented more as an illustration of what it means to be outside the covenant, outside of relationship with God rather than as a direct punishment for those who do not keep the law. Deuteronomy 27:26 states: *Cursed is anyone who does not affirm and obey the terms of these instructions.* This may be seen as a summary of the more detailed curse statements, supporting the view of a unified curse faced by all who break the law and thus take themselves out of relationship with God. We need to focus our interpretation of the blessings and curses within these covenant documents not on the individual elements of the blessing or curse narratives but rather on the

a nation unknown to you and your ancestors. There in exile you will worship gods of wood and stone! 37 You will become an object of horror, ridicule, and mockery among all the nations to which the LORD sends you.

38 "You will plant much but harvest little, for locusts will eat your crops. 39 You will plant vineyards and care for them, but you will not drink the wine or eat the grapes, for worms will destroy the vines. 40 You will grow olive trees throughout your land, but you will never use the olive oil, for the fruit will drop before it ripens. 41 You will have sons and daughters, but you will lose them, for they will be led away into captivity. 42 Swarms of insects will destroy your trees and crops.

43 "The foreigners living among you will become stronger and stronger, while you become weaker and weaker. 44 They will lend money to you, but you will not lend to them. They will be the head, and you will be the tail!

45 "If you refuse to listen to the LORD your God and to obey the commands and decrees he has given you, all these curses will pursue and overtake you until you are destroyed. 46 These horrors will serve as a sign and warning among you and your descendants forever. 47 If you do not serve the LORD your God with joy and enthusiasm for the abundant benefits you have received, 48 you will serve your enemies whom the LORD will send against you. You will be left hungry, thirsty, naked, and lacking in everything. The LORD will put an iron yoke on your neck, oppressing you harshly until he has destroyed you.

49 "The LORD will bring a distant nation against you from the end of the earth, and it will swoop down on you like a vulture. It is a nation whose language you do not understand, 50 a fierce and heartless nation that shows no respect for the old and no pity for the young. 51 Its armies will devour your livestock and crops, and you will be destroyed. They will leave you no grain, new wine, olive oil, calves, or lambs, and you will starve to death. 52 They will attack your cities until all the fortified walls in your land—the walls you trusted to protect you—are knocked down. They will attack all the towns in the land the LORD your God has given you.

53 "The siege and terrible distress of the enemy's attack will be so severe that you will eat the flesh of your own sons and daughters, whom the LORD your God has given you. 54 The most tenderhearted man among you will have no compassion for his own brother, his beloved wife, and his surviving children. 55 He will refuse to share with them the flesh he is devouring—the flesh of one of his own children—because he has nothing else to eat during the siege and terrible distress that your enemy will inflict on all your towns. 56 The most tender and delicate woman among you—so delicate she would not so much as touch the ground with her foot—will be selfish toward the husband she loves and toward her own son or daughter. 57 She will hide from them the afterbirth and the new baby she has borne, so that she herself can secretly eat them. She will have nothing else to eat during the siege and terrible distress that your enemy will inflict on all your towns.

58 "If you refuse to obey all the words of instruction that are written in this book, and if you do not fear the glorious and awesome name of the LORD your God, 59 then the LORD will overwhelm you and your children with indescribable plagues. These plagues will be intense and without relief, making you miserable and unbearably sick. 60 He will afflict you with all the diseases of Egypt that you feared so much, and you will have no relief. 61 The LORD will afflict you with every sickness and plague there is, even those not mentioned in this Book of Instruction, until you are destroyed. 62 Though you become as

---

single, very significant blessing of being able to relate to God and the single curse of being outside of God's domain, no longer relating to him. To see the curses and blessings in this way and to recognize that God's sovereignty allows him to show mercy when and where he decides, explains why, throughout the Old Testament, individual blessings and curses did not automatically come into play. Not every good, law-keeping person lived a long and happy life; not every disobedient law-breaker suffered devastation and disaster. This was a real problem for Israel on occasion, something that psalmists and prophets alike found very difficult, but it is interesting that they rarely, if ever, discuss the problem in the context of covenantal curses failing to come into play. The Old Testament is full of instances of God's blessing showered on individuals, on families, on the nation—but nowhere do we read of God specifically cursing any human person or any object. God is first of all the one who brings blessings. The people were convinced that because God had chosen Israel as his covenant people, they were guaranteed his blessings—whatever they did. It may be because of this mistaken conviction that Deuteronomy spends so much more time on describing the curses, showing them that God's blessing cannot and must not be taken for granted.

numerous as the stars in the sky, few of you will be left because you would not listen to the LORD your God.

[63] "Just as the LORD has found great pleasure in causing you to prosper and multiply, the LORD will find pleasure in destroying you. You will be torn from the land you are about to enter and occupy. [64] For the LORD will scatter you among all the nations from one end of the earth to the other. There you will worship foreign gods that neither you nor your ancestors have known, gods made of wood and stone! [65] There among those nations you will find no peace or place to rest. And the LORD will cause your heart to tremble, your eyesight to fail, and your soul to despair. [66] Your life will constantly hang in the balance. You will live night and day in fear, unsure if you will survive. [67] In the morning you will say, 'If only it were night!' And in the evening you will say, 'If only it were morning!' For you will be terrified by the awful horrors you see around you. [68] Then the LORD will send you back to Egypt in ships, to a destination I promised you would never see again. There you will offer to sell yourselves to your enemies as slaves, but no one will buy you."

29

[1] *These are the terms of the covenant the LORD commanded Moses to make with the Israelites while they were in the land of Moab, in addition to the covenant he had made with them at Mount Sinai.*

Moses Reviews the Covenant

[2] *Moses summoned all the Israelites and said to them, "You have seen with your own eyes everything the LORD did in the land of Egypt to Pharaoh and to all his servants and to his whole country—[3] all the great tests of strength, the miraculous signs, and the amazing wonders. [4] But to this day the LORD has not given you minds that understand, nor eyes that see, nor ears that hear! [5] For forty years I led you through the wilderness, yet your clothes and sandals did not wear out. [6] You ate no bread and drank no wine or other alcoholic drink, but he gave you food so you would know that he is the LORD your God.

[7] "When we came here, King Sihon of Heshbon and King Og of Bashan came out to fight against us, but we defeated them. [8] We took their land and gave it to the tribes of Reuben and Gad and to the half-tribe of Manasseh as their grant of land.

[9] "Therefore, obey the terms of this covenant so that you will prosper in everything you do. [10] All of you—tribal leaders, elders, officers, all the men of Israel—are standing today in the presence of the LORD your God. [11] Your little ones and your wives are with you, as well as the foreigners living among you who chop your wood and carry your water. [12] You are standing here today to enter into the covenant of the LORD your God. The LORD is making this covenant, including the curses. [13] By entering into the covenant today, he will establish you as his people and confirm that he is your God, just as he promised you and as he swore to your ancestors Abraham, Isaac, and Jacob.

[14] "But you are not the only ones with whom I am making this covenant with its curses. [15] I am making this covenant both with you who stand here today in the presence of the LORD our God, and also with the future generations who are not standing here today.

[16] "You remember how we lived in the land of Egypt and how we traveled through the lands of enemy nations as we left. [17] You have seen their detestable practices and their idols* made of wood, stone, silver, and gold. [18] I am making this

29:1a Verse 29:1 is numbered 28:69 in Hebrew text. **29:1b** Hebrew *Horeb,* another name for Sinai. **29:2** Verses 29:2-29 are numbered 29:1-28 in Hebrew text. **29:17** The Hebrew term (literally *round things*) probably alludes to dung.

29:2—32:52 Moses' Fourth Speech: The Ongoing Challenge

29:2–29 Reviewing the Covenant. This section follows the ancient Near Eastern treaty pattern closely. The first eight verses provide a historical prologue, a brief summary of the history detailed in chapters 1—3. Following the covenantal statement in 29:9, verses 10–15 set out the partners in this covenant. On the one hand is Israel, making sure that it is clearly understood that this included the whole people. All, leaders and led, men and women, adults and children, Israelites and incorporated foreigners, were full participants within the covenant. On the other hand we have the LORD who made promises to their ancestors that he wanted to commit himself to them in this solemn way. For all those who entered into this covenant he was the LORD our God. The basic requirements of the covenant are described in verses 16–19, stressing that this relationship with the LORD was exclusive and that as covenant partners with him they were to behave very differently from the surrounding nations. Women may not have had full recognition or rights within the society as a whole, but they are specifically mentioned here. They, as much as the men, were considered fully responsible as far

covenant with you so that no one among you—
no man, woman, clan, or tribe—will turn away
from the LORD our God to worship these gods
of other nations, and so that no root among you
bears bitter and poisonous fruit.
19"Those who hear the warnings of this curse
should not congratulate themselves, thinking, 'I
am safe, even though I am following the desires
of my own stubborn heart.' This would lead to
utter ruin! 20The LORD will never pardon such
people. Instead his anger and jealousy will burn
against them. All the curses written in this book
will come down on them, and the LORD will erase
their names from under heaven. 21The LORD will
separate them from all the tribes of Israel, to
pour out on them all the curses of the covenant
recorded in this Book of Instruction.
22"Then the generations to come, both your
own descendants and the foreigners who come
from distant lands, will see the devastation of
the land and the diseases the LORD inflicts on
it. 23They will exclaim, 'The whole land is devastated by sulfur and salt. It is a wasteland with
nothing planted and nothing growing, not even
a blade of grass. It is like the cities of Sodom and
Gomorrah, Admah and Zeboiim, which the LORD
destroyed in his intense anger.'
24"And all the surrounding nations will ask,
'Why has the LORD done this to this land? Why
was he so angry?'
25"And the answer will be, 'This happened
because the people of the land abandoned the
covenant that the LORD, the God of their ancestors, made with them when he brought them out
of the land of Egypt. 26Instead, they turned away
to serve and worship gods they had not known
before, gods that were not from the LORD. 27That
is why the LORD's anger has burned against this
land, bringing down on it every curse recorded
in this book. 28In great anger and fury the LORD
uprooted his people from their land and banished them to another land, where they still live
today!'
29"The LORD our God has secrets known to
no one. We are not accountable for them, but we
and our children are accountable forever for all
that he has revealed to us, so that we may obey
all the terms of these instructions.

A Call to Return to the LORD

30 "In the future, when you experience
all these blessings and curses I have
listed for you, and when you are living among the nations to which the LORD your
God has exiled you, take to heart all these instructions. 2If at that time you and your children
return to the LORD your God, and if you obey
with all your heart and all your soul all the commands I have given you today, 3then the LORD
your God will restore your fortunes. He will
have mercy on you and gather you back from all
the nations where he has scattered you. 4Even
though you are banished to the ends of the earth,
the LORD your God will gather you from there
and bring you back again. 5The LORD your God
will return you to the land that belonged to your
ancestors, and you will possess that land again.
Then he will make you even more prosperous
and numerous than your ancestors!
6"The LORD your God will change your
heart* and the hearts of all your descendants, so
that you will love him with all your heart and
soul and so you may live! 7The LORD your God
will inflict all these curses on your enemies and
on those who hate and persecute you. 8Then you
will again obey the LORD and keep all his commands that I am giving you today.
9"The LORD your God will then make you
successful in everything you do. He will give you
many children and numerous livestock, and he
will cause your fields to produce abundant harvests, for the LORD will again delight in being
good to you as he was to your ancestors. 10The
LORD your God will delight in you if you obey

30:6 Hebrew *circumcise your heart.*

---

as the covenant requirements were concerned. Verses 20–28 re-emphasize the disastrous consequences of turning away from God and rejecting his covenant. It was clear that sins could be forgiven, for there were procedures within the system enabling the repentant sinner to be cleansed and restored. Nevertheless, the deliberate and cynical rejection of God and his covenantal requirements would prove fatal. *The LORD will never pardon such people* and *will erase their names from under heaven* (v. 20).

30:1–10 Second Chance. Destruction was not how it was supposed to be, nor how it needed to be. The benefits for those who do keep the covenant will be freely available even for those who fail, if only they recommit themselves fully to God's service. Deuteronomy is realistic. The strong stress on the vital importance of them making the right decision at this point springs from the recognition that they might be tempted to make the wrong decision. They also might fail; indeed there is almost an acceptance that they will fail. But failure—seen as different from the kind of cynical turning away from God—is not necessarily the end of the story. Restoration is possible.

his voice and keep the commands and decrees
written in this Book of Instruction, and if you
turn to the LORD your God with all your heart
and soul.

The Choice of Life or Death

[11]"This command I am giving you today is not
too difficult for you to understand, and it is not
beyond your reach. [12]It is not kept in heaven, so
distant that you must ask, 'Who will go up to
heaven and bring it down so we can hear it and
obey?' [13]It is not kept beyond the sea, so far away
that you must ask, 'Who will cross the sea to
bring it to us so we can hear it and obey?' [14]No,
the message is very close at hand; it is on your
lips and in your heart so that you can obey it.

[15]"Now listen! Today I am giving you a choice
between life and death, between prosperity and
disaster. [16]For I command you this day to love
the LORD your God and to keep his commands,
decrees, and regulations by walking in his ways.
If you do this, you will live and multiply, and the
LORD your God will bless you and the land you
are about to enter and occupy.

[17]"But if your heart turns away and you refuse to listen, and if you are drawn away to serve
and worship other gods, [18]then I warn you now
that you will certainly be destroyed. You will not
live a long, good life in the land you are crossing
the Jordan to occupy.

[19]"Today I have given you the choice between
life and death, between blessings and curses. Now
I call on heaven and earth to witness the choice
you make. Oh, that you would choose life, so that
you and your descendants might live! [20]You can
make this choice by loving the LORD your God,
obeying him, and committing yourself firmly to
him. This* is the key to your life. And if you love
and obey the LORD, you will live long in the land
the LORD swore to give your ancestors Abraham,
Isaac, and Jacob."

Joshua Becomes Israel's Leader

31 When Moses had finished giving
these instructions* to all the people of
Israel, [2]he said, "I am now 120 years
old, and I am no longer able to lead you. The
LORD has told me, 'You will not cross the Jordan River.' [3]But the LORD your God himself will
cross over ahead of you. He will destroy the nations living there, and you will take possession of
their land. Joshua will lead you across the river,
just as the LORD promised.

[4]"The LORD will destroy the nations living in
the land, just as he destroyed Sihon and Og, the
kings of the Amorites. [5]The LORD will hand over
to you the people who live there, and you must
deal with them as I have commanded you. [6]So be
strong and courageous! Do not be afraid and do
not panic before them. For the LORD your God
will personally go ahead of you. He will neither
fail you nor abandon you."

[7]Then Moses called for Joshua, and as all Israel watched, he said to him, "Be strong and courageous! For you will lead these people into the
land that the LORD swore to their ancestors he
would give them. You are the one who will divide
it among them as their grants of land. [8]Do not be
afraid or discouraged, for the LORD will personally go ahead of you. He will be with you; he will
neither fail you nor abandon you."

30:20 Or *He.* **31:1** As in Dead Sea Scrolls and Greek version; Masoretic Text reads *Moses went and spoke.*

30:11–20 The Choice before Them. These verses stress that the commitment Israel was being called upon to make was not impossible. It was, with God's help, well within their grasp. The choice before them was clear: life, or death. The Deuteronomist does not present the options in an objective or dispassionate way. He knew the consequences of each choice, and he cared deeply that they chose the right path. Relating to God is both the requirement of the covenant and its blessing and reward. It is worth repeating that women and children are explicitly included as part of the covenant ceremony in chapters 29—30. The call to *make this choice by loving the LORD* is addressed to the women as much as to the men. The regular reading of the law, which they were commanded to undertake, was to be attended by all the women as well as all the men. It mattered that the women too *hear and learn . . . to fear the LORD your God and carefully obey all the terms of these instructions* (31:12–13).

31:1–8 Joshua. Moses' part in the drama of Israel's life is almost over, but it is important now that there is proper closure for him and a preparation for the new start for the people and for their new leader. These verses describe Moses' public retirement ceremony and his handing over leadership to Joshua. Joshua's leadership is affirmed by Moses, who also makes it clear to Joshua and to the people that this is God's appointment. It is also made clear that Joshua's task is to divide the land among the people. He is to *go with them,* not to lord it over them, and the key to a successful ministry for him is exactly the same as the key to successful life for the people—a trusting relationship with, obedience to and dependence on

Public Reading of the Book of Instruction
9 So Moses wrote this entire body of instruction
in a book and gave it to the priests, who carried
the Ark of the LORD's Covenant, and to the elders of Israel. 10 Then Moses gave them this command: "At the end of every seventh year, the
Year of Release, during the Festival of Shelters,
11 you must read this Book of Instruction to all
the people of Israel when they assemble before
the LORD your God at the place he chooses. 12 Call
them all together—men, women, children, and
the foreigners living in your towns—so they
may hear this Book of Instruction and learn to
fear the LORD your God and carefully obey all
the terms of these instructions. 13 Do this so that
your children who have not known these instructions will hear them and will learn to fear
the LORD your God. Do this as long as you live in
the land you are crossing the Jordan to occupy."

Israel's Disobedience Predicted
14 Then the LORD said to Moses, "The time has
come for you to die. Call Joshua and present
yourselves at the Tabernacle,* so that I may
commission him there." So Moses and Joshua
went and presented themselves at the Tabernacle. 15 And the LORD appeared to them in a pillar
of cloud that stood at the entrance to the sacred
tent.

16 The LORD said to Moses, "You are about to
die and join your ancestors. After you are gone,
these people will begin to worship foreign gods,
the gods of the land where they are going. They
will abandon me and break my covenant that
I have made with them. 17 Then my anger will
blaze forth against them. I will abandon them,
hiding my face from them, and they will be
devoured. Terrible trouble will come down on
them, and on that day they will say, 'These disasters have come down on us because God is no
longer among us!' 18 At that time I will hide my
face from them on account of all the evil they
commit by worshiping other gods.

19 "So write down the words of this song, and
teach it to the people of Israel. Help them learn it,
so it may serve as a witness for me against them.
20 For I will bring them into the land I swore to
give their ancestors—a land flowing with milk
and honey. There they will become prosperous,
eat all the food they want, and become fat. But
they will begin to worship other gods; they will
despise me and break my covenant. 21 And when
great disasters come down on them, this song will
stand as evidence against them, for it will never
be forgotten by their descendants. I know the intentions of these people, even now before they
have entered the land I swore to give them."

22 So that very day Moses wrote down the
words of the song and taught it to the Israelites.

23 Then the LORD commissioned Joshua son
of Nun with these words: "Be strong and courageous, for you must bring the people of Israel
into the land I swore to give them. I will be with
you."

24 When Moses had finished writing this entire body of instruction in a book, 25 he gave this
command to the Levites who carried the Ark of
the LORD's Covenant: 26 "Take this Book of Instruction and place it beside the Ark of the Covenant of the LORD your God, so it may remain
there as a witness against the people of Israel.
27 For I know how rebellious and stubborn you
are. Even now, while I am still alive and am here
with you, you have rebelled against the LORD.
How much more rebellious will you be after my
death!

28 "Now summon all the elders and officials of
your tribes, so that I can speak to them directly and call heaven and earth to witness against
them. 29 I know that after my death you will be-

31:14 Hebrew *Tent of Meeting;* also in 31:14b.

God himself. Moses presents Joshua with a personal mission statement.

31:9–13 Law-reading Ceremony. Instructions are given for the entire law to be read every seven years to all the people—men, women, children, and foreigners. It was perhaps the Deuteronomist's deepest concern that each generation own the covenant and the law for themselves and that each generation realize that the covenant was about life and relationship, not just a list of rules. The law bears constant repetition and so does the encouragement to constant reading for all people.

31:14–29 Problems to Come. In the context of Joshua's official ordination and recognition, the Deuteronomist's sense of reality comes across again. Joshua needs to know the nature of his task and the difficulties that will arise. The people need to know—again—that the covenant needs to be worked at, that although failure is not inevitable, they are likely to fail and therefore to hit disaster *if* they don't recognize the nature of the task ahead of them. There is no unthinking triumphalism here. But for Joshua and for the people there is the clear guarantee that if they walk with God, then God will walk with them.

Images of God as Female

The consistent witness of the church is that biblical references to divine gender must be understood relationally and analogically, for the God of the Bible is neither male nor female (sex), neither feminine nor masculine (gender). If understood univocally, gendered terms would contradict the affirmation that God is Spirit (John 4:24), lacking physicality (Deut 4:15–16), and the Holy One who is qualitatively other (Isa 6:2–3; Hos 11:9; Rev 4:8).

The female or feminine analogies that follow both reflect and transcend their social location. At times their meanings parallel those found in patriarchal constructions, such as nurture (Num 11:12) and immanence (Ps 131:2). At other times patriarchal constructions are transcended, as when the feminine denotes divine power (Isa 42:14; 46:3–4; Hos 13:8) and transcendence (Gen 1:26–28).

Imagery Drawn from Women's Biological Activity

1. A mother suckling her children and responsible for their care (Num 11:12).
2. A mother who gave birth to the Israelites (Deut 32:18). The translation conceals the female analogy: *the Rock who had fathered you*; the Hebrew verb translated "fathered" refers exclusively to birthing by females.
3. A woman in labor whose forceful breaths are an image of divine power (Isa 42:14). God threatens to come in power, a force likened to the air expelled from the lungs of a woman in transition.
4. A mother who births and protects Israel (Isa 46:3–4; see Birth Pain Imagery, John 16). In contrast to idol worshipers, who carry their gods on cattle (Isa 46:1), God carries Israel in the womb. God's promise to redeem Israel is secured by maternal compassion and protective power.
5. A mother who does not forget the child she nurses (Isa 49:14–15).
6. A mother who comforts her children (Isa 66:12–13).
7. A mother who calls, teaches, holds, heals, and feeds her young (Hos 11:1–4). While first person syntax permits either parent to be speaking, the series of activities are those that a mother would likely do. Hosea may be presenting the LORD as Israel's mother over against the Canaanite mother/goddess figure.

come utterly corrupt and will turn from the way I have commanded you to follow. In the days to come, disaster will come down on you, for you will do what is evil in the LORD's sight, making him very angry with your actions."

The Song of Moses

30 So Moses recited this entire song publicly to the assembly of Israel:

32 1 "Listen, O heavens, and I will speak!
Hear, O earth, the words that I say!
2 Let my teaching fall on you like rain;
let my speech settle like dew.
Let my words fall like rain on tender grass,
like gentle showers on young plants.
3 I will proclaim the name of the LORD;
how glorious is our God!
4 He is the Rock; his deeds are perfect.
Everything he does is just and fair.
He is a faithful God who does no wrong;
how just and upright he is!

5 "But they have acted corruptly toward him;
when they act so perversely,
are they really his children?*
They are a deceitful and twisted generation.
6 Is this the way you repay the LORD,
you foolish and senseless people?
Isn't he your Father who created you?
Has he not made you and established you?
7 Remember the days of long ago;
think about the generations past.
Ask your father, and he will inform you.
Inquire of your elders, and they will tell you.

32:5 The meaning of the Hebrew is uncertain.

31:30—32:47 Moses' Song. It is always easier to remember songs than it is to remember speeches. The LORD gave Moses a song to help the people remember and take to heart all that has been told to them so far. The song is a tremendous proclamation of God, of his power and of his goodness, but it is also a warning about the frailty of human beings and the dangers of turning away from God. The last two verses of this

Imagery from Women's Cultural Activity

1. A woman who exercises dominion; bearing the image of the transcendent God, she rules the earth as God's representative (Gen 1:26–28).

2. A seamstress making clothes for Israel to wear (Neh 9:21; cf. Gen 3:21).

3. A midwife attending a birth (Pss 22:9–10, 71:6; Isa 66:9); midwife was a role only for women in ancient Israel.

4. A woman working leaven into bread (Matt 13:33; Luke 13:20–21), equivalent to the masculine image of God in the preceding parable of the mustard seed.

5. A woman seeking a lost coin (Luke 15:8–10), equivalent to the masculine image of God in the preceding parable of the shepherd seeking a lost sheep.

Additional Images

Divine protection is analogous to the action of a bird sheltering her young (Ruth 2:12; Pss 17:8; 36:7; 57:1; 91:1, 4) or hovering overhead (Isa 31:5). Jesus' desire to protect Jerusalem is expressed through imagery of a hen (Matt 23:37; Luke 13:34).

The fierce image of God as a mother bear or lioness is associated with maternal attachment to one's offspring (Hos 13:8). God's rage against those who withhold gratitude is that of a bear "whose cubs have been taken away."

The Holy Spirit is associated with the birthing process (John 3:4–5; cf. John 1:13; 1 Jn 4:7; 5:1, 4, 18; Rom 8:20–23). Some ancient church traditions referred to the Holy Spirit in feminine terms, the Syriac church retaining a feminine pronoun until about AD 400.

Wisdom (Gk., *sophia*), identified with God and personified as a woman (Prov 1:20–33; 8:1–9:6; 31:10–31), develops into wisdom Christology. Jesus Christ does the work that sophia does (Matt 11:16–30; Luke 7:35; Col 1:15–17) and is designated "the sophia (wisdom) of God" (1 Cor 1:24; cf. 1 Cor 1:30; 2:6–8; Eph 3:9–11).

Feminine analogies clarify who God is by enriching the church's vocabulary, as well as clarifying who God is not, by countering idolatry that results from literalizing masculine analogies. These analogies help equalize gender relationships and validate the public ministry of women by challenging patriarchal gender constructions; created in God's image, women and men alike can represent divine transcendence, immanence, power, and nurture. And these analogies enhance spirituality; by seeing their work as work that God also does, women and girls gain a greater sense of their inestimable value.

8 When the Most High assigned lands to the
nations,
when he divided up the human race,
he established the boundaries of the peoples
according to the number in his heavenly
court.*
9 "For the people of Israel belong to the LORD;
Jacob is his special possession.
10 He found them in a desert land,
in an empty, howling wasteland.
He surrounded them and watched over them;
he guarded them as he would guard his
own eyes.*
11 Like an eagle that rouses her chicks
and hovers over her young,
so he spread his wings to take them up
and carried them safely on his pinions.
12 The LORD alone guided them;
they followed no foreign gods.
13 He let them ride over the highlands
and feast on the crops of the fields.
He nourished them with honey from the rock
and olive oil from the stony ground.
14 He fed them yogurt from the herd
and milk from the flock,
together with the fat of lambs.

32:8 As in Dead Sea Scrolls, which read *the number of the sons of God,* and Greek version, which reads *the number of the angels of God;* Masoretic Text reads *the number of the sons of Israel.* **32:10** Hebrew *as the pupil of his eye.*

section, 32:46–47, come as a final reminder of the importance of making sure that the people of Israel and their children—maybe in spite of its somber sections the song was one that a mother could sing to her children as she worked and they played—should take everything to heart. *These . . . are not empty words—they are your life!* (v. 47).

He gave them choice rams from Bashan, and goats,
together with the choicest wheat.
You drank the finest wine,
made from the juice of grapes.

15 "But Israel* soon became fat and unruly;
the people grew heavy, plump, and stuffed!
Then they abandoned the God who had made them;
they made light of the Rock of their salvation.
16 They stirred up his jealousy by worshiping foreign gods;
they provoked his fury with detestable deeds.
17 They offered sacrifices to demons, which are not God,
to gods they had not known before,
to new gods only recently arrived,
to gods their ancestors had never feared.
18 You neglected the Rock who had fathered you;
you forgot the God who had given you birth.

19 "The LORD saw this and drew back,
provoked to anger by his own sons and daughters.
20 He said, 'I will abandon them;
then see what becomes of them.
For they are a twisted generation,
children without integrity.
21 They have roused my jealousy by worshiping things that are not God;
they have provoked my anger with their useless idols.
Now I will rouse their jealousy through people who are not even a people;
I will provoke their anger through the foolish Gentiles.
22 For my anger blazes forth like fire
and burns to the depths of the grave.*
It devours the earth and all its crops
and ignites the foundations of the mountains.
23 I will heap disasters upon them
and shoot them down with my arrows.
24 I will weaken them with famine,
burning fever, and deadly disease.
I will send the fangs of wild beasts
and poisonous snakes that glide in the dust.
25 Outside, the sword will bring death,
and inside, terror will strike
both young men and young women,
both infants and the aged.
26 I would have annihilated them,
wiping out even the memory of them.
27 But I feared the taunt of Israel's enemy,
who might misunderstand and say,
"Our own power has triumphed!
The LORD had nothing to do with this!"'

28 "But Israel is a senseless nation;
the people are foolish, without understanding.
29 Oh, that they were wise and could understand this!
Oh, that they might know their fate!
30 How could one person chase a thousand of them,
and two people put ten thousand to flight,
unless their Rock had sold them,
unless the LORD had given them up?
31 But the rock of our enemies is not like our Rock,
as even they recognize.*
32 Their vine grows from the vine of Sodom,
from the vineyards of Gomorrah.
Their grapes are poison,
and their clusters are bitter.
33 Their wine is the venom of serpents,
the deadly poison of cobras.

34 "The LORD says, 'Am I not storing up these things,
sealing them away in my treasury?
35 I will take revenge; I will pay them back.
In due time their feet will slip.
Their day of disaster will arrive,
and their destiny will overtake them.'

36 "Indeed, the LORD will give justice to his people,
and he will change his mind about* his servants,
when he sees their strength is gone
and no one is left, slave or free.
37 Then he will ask, 'Where are their gods,
the rocks they fled to for refuge?
38 Where now are those gods,
who ate the fat of their sacrifices
and drank the wine of their offerings?
Let those gods arise and help you!
Let them provide you with shelter!
39 Look now; I myself am he!
There is no other god but me!

32:15 Hebrew *Jeshurun,* a term of endearment for Israel. **32:22** Hebrew *of Sheol.* **32:31** The meaning of the Hebrew is uncertain. Greek version reads *our enemies are fools.* **32:36** Or *will take revenge for.*

I am the one who kills and gives life;
I am the one who wounds and heals;
no one can be rescued from my powerful hand!
40 Now I raise my hand to heaven
and declare, "As surely as I live,
41 when I sharpen my flashing sword
and begin to carry out justice,
I will take revenge on my enemies
and repay those who reject me.
42 I will make my arrows drunk with blood,
and my sword will devour flesh—
the blood of the slaughtered and the captives,
and the heads of the enemy leaders." '

43 "Rejoice with him, you heavens,
and let all of God's angels worship him.*
Rejoice with his people, you nations,
and let all the angels be strengthened in him.*
For he will avenge the blood of his servants;
he will take revenge against his enemies.
He will repay those who hate him*
and cleanse the land for his people."

44 So Moses came with Joshua* son of Nun and
recited all the words of this song to the people.
45 When Moses had finished reciting all these
words to the people of Israel, 46 he added: "Take
to heart all the words of warning I have given
you today. Pass them on as a command to your
children so they will obey every word of these
instructions. 47 These instructions are not empty
words—they are your life! By obeying them you
will enjoy a long life in the land you will occupy
when you cross the Jordan River."

Moses' Death Foretold

48 That same day the LORD said to Moses, 49 "Go
to Moab, to the mountains east of the river,* and
climb Mount Nebo, which is across from Jericho.
Look out across the land of Canaan, the land I
am giving to the people of Israel as their own
special possession. 50 Then you will die there on
the mountain. You will join your ancestors, just
as Aaron, your brother, died on Mount Hor and
joined his ancestors. 51 For both of you betrayed
me with the Israelites at the waters of Meribah
at Kadesh* in the wilderness of Zin. You failed to
demonstrate my holiness to the people of Israel
there. 52 So you will see the land from a distance,
but you may not enter the land I am giving to
the people of Israel."

Moses Blesses the People

33 This is the blessing that Moses, the man of God, gave to the people of Israel before his death:

2 "The LORD came from Mount Sinai
and dawned upon us* from Mount Seir;
he shone forth from Mount Paran
and came from Meribah-kadesh
with flaming fire at his right hand.*
3 Indeed, he loves his people;*
all his holy ones are in his hands.
They follow in his steps
and accept his teaching.
4 Moses gave us the LORD's instruction,
the special possession of the people of Israel.*

32:43a As in Dead Sea Scrolls and Greek version; Masoretic Text lacks the first two lines. Compare Heb 1:6. **32:43b** As in Greek version; Hebrew text lacks this line. **32:43c** As in Dead Sea Scrolls and Greek version; Masoretic Text lacks this line. **32:44** Hebrew *Hoshea,* a variant name for Joshua. **32:49** Hebrew *the mountains of Abarim.* **32:51** Hebrew *waters of Meribath-kadesh.* **33:2a** As in Greek and Syriac versions; Hebrew reads *upon them.* **33:2b** Or *came from myriads of holy ones, from the south, from his mountain slopes.* The meaning of the Hebrew is uncertain. **33:3** As in Greek version; Hebrew reads *Indeed, lover of the peoples.* **33:4** Hebrew *of Jacob.* The names "Jacob" and "Israel" are often interchanged throughout the Old Testament, referring sometimes to the individual patriarch and sometimes to the nation.

32:48–52 Moses' Death Foretold. God issues the instruction to Moses to climb up to the mountain for his only chance to look out over the land that he would not enter. Mount Nebo would also be his final resting place.

33:1–29 Moses' Fifth Speech: The Blessing on the Tribes

It is not clear exactly when these blessings on the tribes were given. They are parallel to the blessings that a father might bestow on his children in the last days of his life, not necessarily spoken on his deathbed but counting as his last words (cf. Jacob's blessing on his sons in Gen 49). The blessings are set between two additional statements reflecting on God's glory and care for Israel. The implication is that although Joshua was, without any reservation on Moses' part, proclaimed as leader of the people, it was into God's hands that Moses entrusted the tribes—his surrogate children. The blessings to the tribes of Israel consist of a mixture of prophecy, encouragement, and character assessment. There is no blessing recorded for Simeon. It is not clear whether there was a further verse, now lost, or whether Simeon had already been absorbed into the tribe of Judah.

5 The LORD became king in Israel*—
when the leaders of the people assembled,
when the tribes of Israel gathered as one."

6 Moses said this about the tribe of Reuben:*

"Let the tribe of Reuben live and not die out,
though they are few in number."

7 Moses said this about the tribe of Judah:

"O LORD, hear the cry of Judah
and bring them together as a people.
Give them strength to defend their cause;
help them against their enemies!"

8 Moses said this about the tribe of Levi:

"O LORD, you have given your Thummim
and Urim—the sacred lots—
to your faithful servants the Levites.*
You put them to the test at Massah
and struggled with them at the waters of
Meribah.
9 The Levites obeyed your word
and guarded your covenant.
They were more loyal to you
than to their own parents.
They ignored their relatives
and did not acknowledge their own
children.
10 They teach your regulations to Jacob;
they give your instructions to Israel.
They present incense before you
and offer whole burnt offerings on the
altar.
11 Bless the ministry of the Levites, O LORD,
and accept all the work of their hands.
Hit their enemies where it hurts the most;
strike down their foes so they never rise
again."

12 Moses said this about the tribe of Benjamin:

"The people of Benjamin are loved by the
LORD
and live in safety beside him.
He surrounds them continuously
and preserves them from every harm."

13 Moses said this about the tribes of Joseph:

"May their land be blessed by the LORD
with the precious gift of dew from the
heavens
and water from beneath the earth;
14 with the rich fruit that grows in the sun,
and the rich harvest produced each month;
15 with the finest crops of the ancient
mountains,
and the abundance from the everlasting
hills;
16 with the best gifts of the earth and its
bounty,
and the favor of the one who appeared in
the burning bush.
May these blessings rest on Joseph's head,
crowning the brow of the prince among his
brothers.
17 Joseph has the majesty of a young bull;
he has the horns of a wild ox.
He will gore distant nations,
driving them to the ends of the earth.
This is my blessing for the multitudes of
Ephraim
and the thousands of Manasseh."

18 Moses said this about the tribes of Zebulun and
Issachar*:

"May the people of Zebulun prosper in their
travels.
May the people of Issachar prosper at
home in their tents.
19 They summon the people to the mountain
to offer proper sacrifices there.
They benefit from the riches of the sea
and the hidden treasures in the sand."

20 Moses said this about the tribe of Gad:

"Blessed is the one who enlarges Gad's
territory!
Gad is poised there like a lion
to tear off an arm or a head.
21 The people of Gad took the best land for
themselves;
a leader's share was assigned to them.
When the leaders of the people were
assembled,
they carried out the LORD's justice
and obeyed his regulations for Israel."

22 Moses said this about the tribe of Dan:

"Dan is a lion's cub,
leaping out from Bashan."

33:5 Hebrew *in Jeshurun,* a term of endearment for Israel.
33:6 Hebrew lacks *Moses said this about the tribe of Reuben.* **33:8** As in Greek version; Hebrew lacks *the Levites.*
33:18 Hebrew lacks *and Issachar.*

23 Moses said this about the tribe of Naphtali:

"O Naphtali, you are rich in favor
and full of the LORD's blessings;
may you possess the west and the south."

24 Moses said this about the tribe of Asher:

"May Asher be blessed above other sons;
may he be esteemed by his brothers;
may he bathe his feet in olive oil.
25 May the bolts of your gates be of iron and bronze;
may you be secure all your days."

26 "There is no one like the God of Israel.*
He rides across the heavens to help you,
across the skies in majestic splendor.
27 The eternal God is your refuge,
and his everlasting arms are under you.
He drives out the enemy before you;
he cries out, 'Destroy them!'
28 So Israel will live in safety,
prosperous Jacob in security,
in a land of grain and new wine,
while the heavens drop down dew.
29 How blessed you are, O Israel!
Who else is like you, a people saved by the LORD?
He is your protecting shield
and your triumphant sword!
Your enemies will cringe before you,
and you will stomp on their backs!"

The Death of Moses

34 Then Moses went up to Mount Nebo
from the plains of Moab and climbed
Pisgah Peak, which is across from
Jericho. And the LORD showed him the whole
land, from Gilead as far as Dan; 2 all the land of
Naphtali; the land of Ephraim and Manasseh; all
the land of Judah, extending to the Mediterranean Sea*; 3 the Negev; the Jordan Valley with
Jericho—the city of palms—as far as Zoar. 4 Then
the LORD said to Moses, "This is the land I promised on oath to Abraham, Isaac, and Jacob when
I said, 'I will give it to your descendants.' I have
now allowed you to see it with your own eyes,
but you will not enter the land."
5 So Moses, the servant of the LORD, died
there in the land of Moab, just as the LORD had
said. 6 The LORD buried him* in a valley near
Beth-peor in Moab, but to this day no one knows
the exact place. 7 Moses was 120 years old when
he died, yet his eyesight was clear, and he was as
strong as ever. 8 The people of Israel mourned for
Moses on the plains of Moab for thirty days, until the customary period of mourning was over.
9 Now Joshua son of Nun was full of the spirit
of wisdom, for Moses had laid his hands on him.
So the people of Israel obeyed him, doing just as
the LORD had commanded Moses.
10 There has never been another prophet in
Israel like Moses, whom the LORD knew face to
face. 11 The LORD sent him to perform all the miraculous signs and wonders in the land of Egypt
against Pharaoh, and all his servants, and his entire land. 12 With mighty power, Moses performed
terrifying acts in the sight of all Israel.

33:26 Hebrew *of Jeshurun,* a term of endearment for Israel. **34:2** Hebrew *the western sea.* **34:6** Hebrew *He buried him;* Samaritan Pentateuch and some Greek manuscripts read *They buried him.*

34:1–12 Conclusion: The Baton is Handed On

There has been a lengthy preparation but Moses' death is recorded briefly and simply. He died, was buried, the Israelites grieved, life moved on. Moses was not forgotten; Joshua did not fully replace him. But nevertheless Joshua was now the ruler, and the new adventure was about to begin. God's covenant people were going to enter at last the land that God had set apart for them and all the Deuteronomist's hopes and fears, persuading, encouraging, convincing, and challenging would be put to the test.

JOSHUA

INTRODUCTION

The book of Joshua explains the shift from the nomadic existence of Israel following the Exodus to its settlement in the land God has provided, from bondage in Egypt to sovereignty in the promised land, and most importantly from despair to hope. These transitions are never achieved perfectly. Life can be a messy business even with God on one's side, and at the end of the book Israel has yet to possess the land completely. The book begins and ends, however, with the relationship between God and his people firmly in place.

Despite the emphasis on God's sovereignty over history and care for Israel, his covenant partner, the book of Joshua can be disturbing for any reader. For women it can be especially disaffecting. From the superficial fact that few women appear in the narrative to the more important questions concerning whether the phrase "the people of Israel" includes women, the book poses special challenges for readers interested in the way the Bible speaks about and to women.

Female readers should seek out the women in the text. The most notable woman is Rahab, a prostitute in Jericho, whose memory lived on not only in Israel but also in the writings of early Jews and Christians. Others include the women and girls who constitute part of Israel but whose voices are not heard: the daughters of Achan, who are punished along with their brothers for their father's sin; Acsah (15:13–19); and the daughters of Zelophehad (17:3–6). We must not forget those women and men, girls and boys, who lived in Jericho and the other cities conquered by Joshua and who were to be destroyed under the covenantal policy of *herem* (Deut 20:16–18). Their inherent foreignness, exemplified primarily by their worship of other gods, poses a threat of corruption to the Israelites that must be wiped out. This policy not only emphasizes the loyalty God demands from his people but also acknowledges implicitly the tenuous nature of Israel's devotion to God.

The book of Joshua concentrates on the military conquest of the land. If war is a man's game, then Joshua would appear to be a man's book. But the military conquest of Canaan is contextualized within the larger framework of covenant loyalty. Covenant provides the context for many of the most important biblical themes to emerge and solidify in this book, for in Joshua God's most extravagant promises to his people begin to come to pass. Joshua, like all the biblical books, is primarily about God and his relationship to his people and to his creation. God is portrayed as being interested in and engaged with his people and their welfare. Sometimes, in the popular imagination, the God of the New Testament is loving, forgiving, and merciful, while the God of the Old Testament is possessive, ruthless, and harsh. Such a view oversimplifies God's self-revelation. Nevertheless, as readers of the book of Joshua we are challenged to come to terms with a God who destroys entire cities at the sound of a trumpet and who requires the death of the family of a man who disobeys God. In Joshua conquered cities are placed under the ban (*herem*), so that their inhabitants are slaughtered as an offering to God. God, who so mercifully rescued his people from tyranny in Egypt, now installs them in a land by dispossessing the original inhabitants. While we, like many other exegetes, might struggle with the militaristic, inhumane tone of the book because Israel's victories over the inhabitants of Canaan seem barbarous and cruel, we also detect a view of God who is prepared to show mercy even when it violates the terms of his agreement with Israel. We encounter a God who relates to the marginalized and dispossessed in ways that subvert any attempts to advance a simplistic view of God as harsh, judgmental, and punishing. The prostitute who declares the truth about God is saved with her whole household. In the words of Rahab, "the LORD has given you this land. We are all afraid of you. Everyone in the land is living in terror" (2:9).

The book of Joshua, like all good stories and like human experience, is filled with conflict and opposition. There is little suspense, however. We, like Joshua's original audience, know that God's people will triumph and that the land will be taken. For twenty-first-century readers, though, the book of Joshua poses some special challenges concerning theodicy, but it also assures its readers that no matter how dismal the odds, those who seek God and his will may hope for rescue.

Joshua is set in the period following the Exodus, but it probably achieved its current form later. Scholars detect numerous sources in Joshua. The most basic evidence for its composite nature is the variety of genres we find in the book: from dry lists of Canaanite kings to lively narrative. The book serves as the fulfillment of God's promise to Abraham that he will bring the patriarch's descendants into the land (Gen 12:1–9). Joshua contains reminders both explicit and implicit of what God has achieved in the history of his people already as Israel prepares to consolidate its possession of the land. In many ways, moreover, Joshua's career recalls that of his predecessor, Moses: They both lead their people triumphantly across the water, they both affirm the importance of circumcision, and they both affirm the sanctity and significance of God's law.

Much of the narrative is concerned with how Israel is to prevent Canaanite religious practices from infiltrating its own cultic worship. Scholars are only now coming to reconstruct anywhere near a complete picture of the ancient Canaanite worship, thanks to the discovery of the Ugaritic tablets at Ras Shamra in 1929. Scholarship on these ancient texts from northern Canaan shows how Israelite political and religious formulations were both similar to and different from those of the Canaanites. Pantheons of gods were acknowledged and worshiped by Israel's neighbors, and it is easy to see why much of the biblical record is intent on warning God's people to maintain their covenant loyalty to him.

The inhabitants of Canaan worshiped a variety of gods and goddesses, the most notable of which, given the number of references to them in the biblical record, are Baal and Asherah. Other Canaanite deities posed a threat to the monotheism of Israel, but it is Baal, the Canaanite storm god, with whom the biblical text is most often concerned. The God of Israel is of course depicted as more powerful. Unlike Baal and other ancient Near Eastern deities, he is not confined to a particular geographical area. He has been with and led his people from the dawn of time, in Ur, in Egypt, and now in the land promised to Abraham. That there are so many references to Baal and to other Canaanite gods suggests that not all of Israel maintained unwavering loyalty to the God of Abraham.

More intriguing for many scholars has been the possibility that at least some of the ancient Israelites worshiped a goddess as a consort to God. This view has garnered some credibility among scholars because of repeated references to cultic objects called *asheroth* at various Israelite sites and that Asherah was the name of a Canaanite goddess. Although most scholars do not believe that the worship of a goddess, a consort of God, ever constituted part of the official cultic activity of the ancient Israelites, it is clear that Canaanite religious practices resonated with many of the people since they are warned so often against engaging in them. Most of these warnings come near the end of the book, but the entire narrative demonstrates that in the God of Abraham and Sarah, the God of Israel who brought them out of Egypt, his people find their salvation. It is not only futile but also pernicious to seek it among the local deities of Canaan.

If some or even many Israelites worshiped a goddess, there are no grounds for supposing that such idolatry emerged as a rebellion against the monotheistic worship of a male deity. Although the language used to talk about God in the biblical tradition is grammatically masculine, we need not suppose that the ancient Israelites were so unsophisticated that they could not imagine God as transcending sexuality. The book of Joshua, with its overall depiction of God as warrior, however, offers few resources for thinking about God in less than robustly and traditionally masculine ways. Nevertheless, the book of Joshua also challenges us to think of God as fiercely protective of his people, and as loyal and steadfast, despite their shortcomings. The covenant links God and Israel. The insistence on covenant loyalty, emphasized throughout the book of Deuteronomy, is illustrated with concrete examples of its significance in Joshua. The relationship of the events in Joshua to the presuppositions and theological position of Deuteronomy is important because of the widespread agreement among scholars that Joshua constitutes part of the Deuteronomistic History. Joshua, along with Judges and the books of Kings and Samuel, constitutes a historical narrative that reflects the theological position and interests of Deuteronomy.

The structure of the narrative is illuminating. Although Joshua seems to be primarily about war, it is only in chapters 6—11 that warfare is described. These battles, however, are horrific. They are undertaken by the men of Israel, who serve as the warriors for the nation. The men of Israel had a much greater degree of military obligation than do men in our own time. This aspect of a patriarchal structure is reflected in Joshua in other ways as well. Men wielded authority over the members of their households, whether they were wives, servants, or children. At the same time, however, we should not equate authority with ownership. Although some parts of the Bible suggest that men owned their wives and children, this does not take into account all of the evidence. On occasion—more often than not—the Bible records that the traditional hierarchical social structures were subverted by God. Just as God is not bound by national boundaries, so God is not enslaved by social and political protocols. Repeatedly the oldest son does not inherit and the senior wife is not the most favored.

Similarly, in the case of the land of Canaan, possession may well be nine-tenths of the law, but God's will constitutes the remaining tenth and always prevails. The land belongs neither to the Canaanites nor the Israelites but to God: Human beings have no claim on the land since technically they do not possess it. Having said that, God promises to give the Israelites the land for their own. As Christopher Wright has pointed out, there is some tension between the notion of Israel's possession of the promised land and the idea that God claims sovereignty over all creation. To complicate matters further, when Israel does come to possess the land it is not clear who is envisioned as constituting Israel. The phrases "the people" and "the people of Israel" would seem to be inclusive, yet often it is clear that only men are meant. In Joshua this tension is especially pronounced because of the militaristic theme of the book. Israel is a nation of warriors, of followers of God, the warrior par excellence. Ironically, however, God the warrior is, in Joshua, most clearly understood by a woman, Rahab.

Most scholars agree that the book of Joshua reached its current form long after the events it relates. Critical scholarship classifies it as part of the Deuteronomistic History, those books of the Old Testament (Deut—2 Kgs) in which the theological themes of Deuteronomy are paramount. These themes include the necessity for Israel to maintain covenant loyalty, the centralization of cultic activity, and the shunning of non-Israelites (Deut 10:11; 11:24–25; 31:6–8, 23; see also 5:32–33; 17:18–19; 30:10).

Even the most skeptical scholars agree that Joshua includes ancient sources that have been used to put together a continuous narrative. Many scholars suggest that the book was put together in its present form during the exile in Babylon following the destruction of Jerusalem in 586 BC. We can well imagine how the exilic community would have been both comforted and dismayed on hearing the message of the book of Joshua: comforted because of the repeated assurances throughout the book that God is in solidarity with his people no matter how daunting the opponent, and dismayed by the realization that Israel had forsaken the covenant their ancestors had reaffirmed at Shechem (Josh 24).

The original audience appears to have much greater knowledge of those events than we do today. The author makes several allusions to things we can no longer know and refers to at least one source, the Book of Jashar, no longer extant (10:13). Joshua helps explain why Israel's possession of the land had been so tenuous and why many indigenous inhabitants remained and continued to live, work, and worship alongside their Israelite conquerors. This makes for an enormous degree of narrative tension in the book that is relaxed only because of the repeated assurances, both implied and explicit, that the God of Abraham and Sarah ultimately directs events.

Although Joshua reflects the theological concerns of Deuteronomy, it also looks forward to the practical social and political issues that will confront Israel in the future. Joshua ends on a note of optimism with the renewal of the covenant at Shechem, but the problems that the people of Israel face and indeed create in these early days foreshadow the danger that lies ahead. The covenant is a fragile possession subject to the frailty of the human partners. It depends on the cooperation of all living in the land to keep its requirements. It is also a robust and everlasting mark of God's grace. Although the people of Israel may forsake the covenant and their responsibilities, God is incapable of reneging on his commitment. His loyalty to his people, despite their apostasy, is a mark of grace. It also demands a response: Those who reject that grace suffer the consequences, both in Joshua and throughout the biblical tradition.

Prior to their entry into the promised land the people of Israel had not demonstrated their willingness to maintain covenant relationship with God very consistently. Had they done so, those dimensions of Joshua that appear to be problematic, especially the divinely sanctioned policy of *herem*, might have been eased, since the problem is not so much the Canaanites' cultic practices but the susceptibility of Israel to adopt such false worship. The book of Joshua insists that our acknowledgment of and responsibility to God must come first. —*Philippa Carter*

1:1–18	God Commissions Joshua
2:1–24	Rahab and the Spies
3:1—5:15	Coming Home with God
6:1—8:35	Taking the Land
9:1—12:24	Consolidating Possession of God's Gift
13:1—21:45	Division of the Land
22:1—24:33	Affirmation and Commitment

The Lord's Charge to Joshua

1 After the death of Moses the LORD's servant, the LORD spoke to Joshua son of Nun, Moses' assistant. He said, 2"Moses my servant is dead. Therefore, the time has come for you to lead these people, the Israelites, across the Jordan River into the land I am giving them. 3I promise you what I promised Moses: 'Wherever you set foot, you will be on land I have given you—4from the Negev wilderness in the south to the Lebanon mountains in the north, from the Euphrates River in the east to the Mediterranean Sea* in the west, including all the land of the Hittites.' 5No one will be able to stand against you as long as you live. For I will be with you as I was with Moses. I will not fail you or abandon you.

6"Be strong and courageous, for you are the one who will lead these people to possess all the land I swore to their ancestors I would give them. 7Be strong and very courageous. Be careful to obey all the instructions Moses gave you. Do not deviate from them, turning either to the right or to the left. Then you will be successful in everything you do. 8Study this Book of Instruction continually. Meditate on it day and night so you will be sure to obey everything written in it. Only then will you prosper and succeed in all you do. 9This is my command—be strong and courageous! Do not be afraid or discouraged. For the LORD your God is with you wherever you go."

Joshua's Charge to the Israelites

10Joshua then commanded the officers of Israel, 11"Go through the camp and tell the people to get their provisions ready. In three days you will cross the Jordan River and take possession of the land the LORD your God is giving you."

12Then Joshua called together the tribes of Reuben, Gad, and the half-tribe of Manasseh. He told them, 13"Remember what Moses, the servant of the LORD, commanded you: 'The LORD your God is giving you a place of rest. He has given you this land.' 14Your wives, children, and livestock may remain here in the land Moses assigned to you on the east side of the Jordan River. But your strong warriors, fully armed, must lead the other tribes across the Jordan to help them conquer their territory. Stay with them 15until the LORD gives them rest, as he has given you rest, and until they, too, possess the land the LORD your God is giving them. Only then may you return and settle here on the east side of the Jordan River in the land that Moses, the servant of the LORD, assigned to you."

16They answered Joshua, "We will do whatever you command us, and we will go wherever you send us. 17We will obey you just as we obeyed Moses. And may the LORD your God be with you as he was with Moses. 18Anyone who

1:4 Hebrew *the Great Sea.*

1:1–18 God Commissions Joshua

Some scholars have argued that rather than a fairly rapid conquest, as it is portrayed in the first part of Joshua, we should think in terms of a slow settlement over many years or an uprising of economically exploited people, including, presumably, women. Whatever the case, the book of Joshua emphasizes military conquest. Despite the fact that it begins with fairly explicit militaristic overtones, however, scholars have emphasized the religious nature of the commissioning of Joshua and the preparation of Israel. **1:** Joshua's name means "the LORD is salvation." It is changed, like the names of many biblical heroes, to reflect Joshua's special relationship to God (Num 13:16). Joshua begins his career as an attendant of Moses (Exod 32:17; 24:13; Num 11:28) and as one who guarded the Tabernacle (Exod 33:11). There are several references to his commission to succeed Moses before it occurs in Joshua 1 (Deut 1:38; 3:21, 28; 31:3, 14–15, 23; Num 27:18–23; 34:17). **2–5:** These verses are emphatic that the outcome of Israel's military endeavors is to be credited to God. The bloody slaughter of Canaanites, which is recounted at various points in the book, is God's command to his people. The struggle requires strength, courage, and fidelity to God's law; upon this success depends. In these opening verses Joshua is Moses' right-hand man. **4:** This verse attests to God's extravagance. **5:** The LORD speaks directly to Joshua, assuring him and the reader that he is the legitimate heir to Moses' leadership and will enjoy the same divine protection as did his predecessor. **6–9:** There are conditions, however: Joshua is urged to be strong and courageous (three times), and God insists that the law be kept. This last condition helps explain the failure of Israel to possess the land completely. **10–18:** This exchange shows the strategy of a military campaign with God rather than Joshua as the commander-in-chief. Alliances are solidified: The tribes of Reuben, Gad, and the half-tribe of Manasseh, for example, agree to help with the campaign west of the Jordan even though their own possession will be to the east of the river. The book of Joshua opens and closes with reminders of the importance of God's law and the necessity of the people's fidelity. **17–18:** There is a degree of irony to the promise made here since Israel did not obey Moses in all things. The tribes are loyal both to God

rebels against your orders and does not obey
your words and everything you command will
be put to death. So be strong and courageous!"

Rahab Protects the Spies

2 Then Joshua secretly sent out two spies
from the Israelite camp at Acacia Grove.*
He instructed them, "Scout out the land
on the other side of the Jordan River, especially
around Jericho." So the two men set out and
came to the house of a prostitute named Rahab
and stayed there that night.
2 But someone told the king of Jericho, "Some
Israelites have come here tonight to spy out the
land." 3 So the king of Jericho sent orders to Rahab: "Bring out the men who have come into
your house, for they have come here to spy out
the whole land."
4 Rahab had hidden the two men, but she replied, "Yes, the men were here earlier, but I didn't
know where they were from. 5 They left the town
at dusk, as the gates were about to close. I don't
know where they went. If you hurry, you can
probably catch up with them." 6 (Actually, she
had taken them up to the roof and hidden them
beneath bundles of flax she had laid out.) 7 So the
king's men went looking for the spies along the
road leading to the shallow crossings of the Jordan River. And as soon as the king's men had left,
the gate of Jericho was shut.
8 Before the spies went to sleep that night,
Rahab went up on the roof to talk with them.
9 "I know the LORD has given you this land," she
told them. "We are all afraid of you. Everyone in
the land is living in terror. 10 For we have heard
how the LORD made a dry path for you through
the Red Sea* when you left Egypt. And we know
what you did to Sihon and Og, the two Amorite
kings east of the Jordan River, whose people you
completely destroyed.* 11 No wonder our hearts
have melted in fear! No one has the courage to
fight after hearing such things. For the LORD
your God is the supreme God of the heavens
above and the earth below.
12 "Now swear to me by the LORD that you
will be kind to me and my family since I have
helped you. Give me some guarantee that 13 when
Jericho is conquered, you will let me live, along
with my father and mother, my brothers and sisters, and all their families."
14 "We offer our own lives as a guarantee for
your safety," the men agreed. "If you don't betray us, we will keep our promise and be kind to
you when the LORD gives us the land."
15 Then, since Rahab's house was built into the
town wall, she let them down by a rope through
the window. 16 "Escape to the hill country," she
told them. "Hide there for three days from the
men searching for you. Then, when they have
returned, you can go on your way."

2:1 Hebrew *Shittim.* **2:10a** Hebrew *sea of reeds.* **2:10b** The Hebrew term used here refers to the complete consecration of things or people to the LORD, either by destroying them or by giving them as an offering.

and to Joshua, for they echo the divine exhortation to Joshua to be strong and courageous.

2:1–24 Rahab and the Spies

The story of Rahab represents a sympathetic portrayal of a marginalized Gentile, but more than that it demonstrates that yet again God's purposes are not dictated by social, political, or religious mores and norms. Rahab is the quintessential outsider: Apparently marginalized even among her own people to the extent that she feels no compunction about betraying them, she too can be drawn into the warp and weft of God's design for his people. The narrative directs the reader to the triumph of God's will on behalf of his people. Rahab's confession, rather than her action, is the focal point. In some ways Rahab is yet another example of the biblical theme of the vindication of the one least likely to succeed. Like Israel, the figure of Rahab too is redeemed. She survives and becomes an exemplary figure for Christians in the New Testament, where she appears in lists of one kind or another, including the genealogy of Jesus (Matt 1:5) and as one of several examples of righteousness (Heb 11; Jas 2). **1:** *Prostitute: zonah*. This word is the general term for harlot. Etymologically Rahab's name is connected with the sense of breadth or expansion, and this may have negative connotations. Prostitutes apparently enjoyed a degree of autonomy not accorded to women whose sexuality met the sociolegal model or ideal. **4–6:** Rahab's deception occurs in the interest of preserving God's people, which implicitly at least includes her having recognized God's supremacy. **8–12:** Although Rahab speaks in a Deuteronomic voice by declaring the sovereignty of Israel's God, the agreement the spies make with her violates the guidelines laid out in Deuteronomy 20:10–20 concerning holy war. As a Gentile, her acknowledgment of God's power highlights the frequent inadequacy of Israel's commitment. **15:** Rahab lives on the limits, at the boundary of the city, illustrating that Rahab's status is compromised within the social order by her profession. **17–23:** The amount of reconnaissance the spies engage in is exactly none, and their

17 Before they left, the men told her, "We will be bound by the oath we have taken only if you follow these instructions. 18 When we come into the land, you must leave this scarlet rope hanging from the window through which you let us down. And all your family members—your father, mother, brothers, and all your relatives—must be here inside the house. 19 If they go out into the street and are killed, it will not be our fault. But if anyone lays a hand on people inside this house, we will accept the responsibility for their death. 20 If you betray us, however, we are not bound by this oath in any way."

21 "I accept your terms," she replied. And she sent them on their way, leaving the scarlet rope hanging from the window.

22 The spies went up into the hill country and stayed there three days. The men who were chasing them searched everywhere along the road, but they finally returned without success.

23 Then the two spies came down from the hill country, crossed the Jordan River, and reported to Joshua all that had happened to them. 24 "The LORD has given us the whole land," they said, "for all the people in the land are terrified of us."

The Israelites Cross the Jordan

3 Early the next morning Joshua and all the Israelites left Acacia Grove* and arrived at the banks of the Jordan River, where they camped before crossing. 2 Three days later the Israelite officers went through the camp, 3 giving these instructions to the people: "When you see the Levitical priests carrying the Ark of the Covenant of the LORD your God, move out from your positions and follow them. 4 Since you have never traveled this way before, they will guide you. Stay about a half mile* behind them, keeping a clear distance between you and the Ark. Make sure you don't come any closer."

5 Then Joshua told the people, "Purify yourselves, for tomorrow the LORD will do great wonders among you."

6 In the morning Joshua said to the priests, "Lift up the Ark of the Covenant and lead the people across the river." And so they started out and went ahead of the people.

7 The LORD told Joshua, "Today I will begin to make you a great leader in the eyes of all the Israelites. They will know that I am with you, just as I was with Moses. 8 Give this command to the priests who carry the Ark of the Covenant: 'When you reach the banks of the Jordan River, take a few steps into the river and stop there.'"

9 So Joshua told the Israelites, "Come and listen to what the LORD your God says. 10 Today you will know that the living God is among you. He will surely drive out the Canaanites, Hittites, Hivites, Perizzites, Girgashites, Amorites, and Jebusites ahead of you. 11 Look, the Ark of the Covenant, which belongs to the Lord of the whole earth, will lead you across the Jordan River! 12 Now choose twelve men from the tribes of Israel, one from each tribe. 13 The priests will carry the Ark of the LORD, the Lord of all the earth. As soon as their feet touch the water, the flow of water will be cut off upstream, and the river will stand up like a wall."

14 So the people left their camp to cross the Jordan, and the priests who were carrying the Ark of the Covenant went ahead of them. 15 It was the harvest season, and the Jordan was overflowing its banks. But as soon as the feet of the priests who were carrying the Ark touched the water at the river's edge, 16 the water above that point began backing up a great distance away at a town called Adam, which is near Zarethan. And the water below that point flowed on to the Dead Sea* until the riverbed was dry. Then all the people crossed over near the town of Jericho.

17 Meanwhile, the priests who were carrying the Ark of the LORD's Covenant stood on dry

3:1 Hebrew *Shittim.* **3:4** Hebrew *about 2,000 cubits* [920 meters]. **3:16** Hebrew *the sea of the Arabah, the Salt Sea.*

---

report to Joshua on their return is based entirely on the word of Rahab, who also devises their strategy for evading the king's men before their return to the Israelite camp. Rahab has said all that needs to be said (vv. 9–11), but it is surprising that the spies take her at her word.

3:1—5:15 Coming Home with God

In these chapters the ambiguity in the term "people" or "people of Israel" is especially pronounced. The people who are circumcised are obviously men (5:4), and these chapters focus most clearly on the male priests and warriors who are crossing over, unlike the account in Exodus 14, where we imagine a somewhat ragtag mass of refugees. **3:1—5:1:** The text reminds its readers of the crossing of the Red Sea. Here men constitute both the people of Israel and the army. It is unclear how many women are part of this crossing; see Joshua 1:12–14. **3:8, 14:** Male priests were responsible for transporting the Ark of the Covenant into the promised land.

Parental Influence

"Then God blessed them and said, 'Be fruitful and multiply. Fill the earth and govern it.'" (Gen 1:28). With this mandate God called the first couple to marital partnership in parenting as well as in ruling over the rest of creation. Current research confirms the healthy results when fathers are actively involved in parenting their daughters and sons rather than leaving parenting to mothers. But the climb back to this original partnership has been slow and painful. The pain began when sin disrupted God's created order and resulted in the man's concentration on subduing the earth while the woman focused on child rearing, thus dividing what God had joined together. Biblical history records destructive examples of this division, such as Saul's castigation of Jonathan as a "son of a whore" (1 Sam 20:30) and David's noninvolvement in the training of his rebellious son Adonijah (1 Kgs 1:6), possibly due to his polygamous family (children from polygamous families still report overwhelming noninvolvement of fathers). But Scripture also presents God's continuing call back to healthy partnership in parenting.

God models effective parenting with Israel and then with all who become his children through Christ. He affirms mothers by identifying himself with their special, universal role of breast-feeding (Isa 49:15) and comforting their children (Isa 66:13), thus demonstrating the divine model for maternal care. By presenting himself as a father while modeling nurturing characteristics normally labeled as maternal, however, God redefines the role of father in ways that challenge the cultural models undergirding paternal noninvolvement.

God's modeling blends varying parenting styles. Traditional cultures that value hierarchy and respect use frequent physical contact and holding of infants to comfort and quiet them. Cultures valuing individual achievement, however, rely more heavily on eye contact and talking to infants to comfort them but also to stimulate their learning of speech. Scripture portrays God using both styles in parenting his children. Believers receive comfort from his hands and are carried in his arms (Ps 37:24; Isa 63:9) while he guides them with his eyes and his words (Ps 33:18; Isa 30:21) and listens to them (1 Pet 3:12).

Scripture emphasizes the importance of communication between God and his children as he teaches them his ways. Children's respectful behavior includes talking, listening, and asking questions rather than using silence to denote respect as in the traditional model. God's instructions in Deuteronomy 5—6 call for open communication in family relationships, with the parents being called to love and obey God, and then to teach their children. Children's questions about God are to be answered rather than resisted (Deut 6:20–21). These instructions were given to people in the extremely difficult circumstances of moving as refugees from slavery to an unknown future. Rapid social change challenges parents now as it did then. The biblical model of family communication requires more time together than is acceptable in many traditional families. God's type of family communication helps to bridge the generation gap and also reduces the hypocrisy that so easily neutralizes parental training of children.

Paul commends Timothy's faith, noting the godly influence of his mother and grandmother, who had taught him the Scriptures from his infancy (2 Tim 1:5; 3:15). Although Timothy's father is not mentioned, these women's parental influence on the young Timothy was effective and should encourage all women who lack a father's involvement in parenting.

ground in the middle of the riverbed as the people passed by. They waited there until the whole nation of Israel had crossed the Jordan on dry ground.

Memorials to the Jordan Crossing

4 When all the people had crossed the Jordan, the LORD said to Joshua, 2"Now
choose twelve men, one from each tribe.
3Tell them, 'Take twelve stones from the very
place where the priests are standing in the middle of the Jordan. Carry them out and pile them
up at the place where you will camp tonight.'"
4So Joshua called together the twelve men he
had chosen—one from each of the tribes of Israel.
5He told them, "Go into the middle of the
Jordan, in front of the Ark of the LORD your God. Each of you must pick up one stone and carry it out on your shoulder—twelve stones in all, one for each of the twelve tribes of Israel.
6We will
use these stones to build a memorial. In the future your children will ask you, 'What do these

stones mean?' 7Then you can tell them, 'They remind us that the Jordan River stopped flowing when the Ark of the LORD's Covenant went across.' These stones will stand as a memorial among the people of Israel forever."

8So the men did as Joshua had commanded them. They took twelve stones from the middle of the Jordan River, one for each tribe, just as the LORD had told Joshua. They carried them to the place where they camped for the night and constructed the memorial there.

9Joshua also set up another pile of twelve stones in the middle of the Jordan, at the place where the priests who carried the Ark of the Covenant were standing. And they are there to this day.

10The priests who were carrying the Ark stood in the middle of the river until all of the LORD's commands that Moses had given to Joshua were carried out. Meanwhile, the people hurried across the riverbed. 11And when everyone was safely on the other side, the priests crossed over with the Ark of the LORD as the people watched.

12The armed warriors from the tribes of Reuben, Gad, and the half-tribe of Manasseh led the Israelites across the Jordan, just as Moses had directed. 13These armed men—about 40,000 strong—were ready for battle, and the LORD was with them as they crossed over to the plains of Jericho.

14That day the LORD made Joshua a great leader in the eyes of all the Israelites, and for the rest of his life they revered him as much as they had revered Moses.

15The LORD had said to Joshua, 16"Command the priests carrying the Ark of the Covenant* to come up out of the riverbed." 17So Joshua gave the command. 18As soon as the priests carrying the Ark of the LORD's Covenant came up out of the riverbed and their feet were on high ground, the water of the Jordan returned and overflowed its banks as before.

19The people crossed the Jordan on the tenth day of the first month.* Then they camped at Gilgal, just east of Jericho. 20It was there at Gilgal that Joshua piled up the twelve stones taken from the Jordan River.

21Then Joshua said to the Israelites, "In the future your children will ask, 'What do these stones mean?' 22Then you can tell them, 'This is where the Israelites crossed the Jordan on dry ground.' 23For the LORD your God dried up the river right before your eyes, and he kept it dry until you were all across, just as he did at the Red Sea* when he dried it up until we had all crossed over. 24He did this so all the nations of the earth might know that the LORD's hand is powerful, and so you might fear the LORD your God forever."

5 When all the Amorite kings west of the Jordan and all the Canaanite kings who lived along the Mediterranean coast* heard how the LORD had dried up the Jordan River so the people of Israel could cross, they lost heart and were paralyzed with fear because of them.

Israel Reestablishes Covenant Ceremonies

2At that time the LORD told Joshua, "Make flint knives and circumcise this second generation of Israelites.*" 3So Joshua made flint knives and circumcised the entire male population of Israel at Gibeath-haaraloth.*

4Joshua had to circumcise them because all the men who were old enough to fight in battle when they left Egypt had died in the wilderness. 5Those who left Egypt had all been circumcised, but none of those born after the Exodus, during the years in the wilderness, had been circumcised. 6The Israelites had traveled in the wilderness for forty years until all the men who were old enough to fight in battle when they left Egypt had died. For they had disobeyed the LORD, and the LORD vowed he would not let them enter the land he had sworn to give us—a land flowing with milk and honey. 7So Joshua circumcised their sons—those who had grown up to take their fathers' places—for they had not been circumcised on the way to the Promised Land. 8After all the males had been circumcised, they rested in the camp until they were healed.

9Then the LORD said to Joshua, "Today I have rolled away the shame of your slavery in Egypt." So that place has been called Gilgal* to this day.

10While the Israelites were camped at Gilgal on the plains of Jericho, they celebrated Passover

4:16 Hebrew *Ark of the Testimony.* **4:19** This day in the ancient Hebrew lunar calendar occurred in late March, April, or early May. **4:23** Hebrew *sea of reeds.* **5:1** Hebrew *along the sea.* **5:2** Or *circumcise the Israelites a second time.* **5:3** *Gibeath-haaraloth* means "hill of foreskins." **5:9** *Gilgal* sounds like the Hebrew word *galal,* meaning "to roll."

5:2–9: All the men of Israel reaffirm the covenant by undertaking circumcision. It is not so much that women are excluded as ignored. The rite of circumcision as a sign of the covenant (Gen 17:11) is one that is inscribed on the flesh of men. **10–11:** It is assumed that when Israel celebrated the Passover for the first time in the land the women also participated. **12:** Clearly, *Israelites* here includes women.

on the evening of the fourteenth day of the first month.* 11 The very next day they began to eat unleavened bread and roasted grain harvested from the land. 12 No manna appeared on the day they first ate from the crops of the land, and it was never seen again. So from that time on the Israelites ate from the crops of Canaan.

The LORD's Commander Confronts Joshua

13 When Joshua was near the town of Jericho, he looked up and saw a man standing in front of him with sword in hand. Joshua went up to him and demanded, "Are you friend or foe?"

14 "Neither one," he replied. "I am the commander of the LORD's army."

At this, Joshua fell with his face to the ground in reverence. "I am at your command," Joshua said. "What do you want your servant to do?"

15 The commander of the LORD's army replied, "Take off your sandals, for the place where you are standing is holy." And Joshua did as he was told.

The Fall of Jericho

6 Now the gates of Jericho were tightly shut because the people were afraid of the Israelites. No one was allowed to go out or in. 2 But the LORD said to Joshua, "I have given you Jericho, its king, and all its strong warriors. 3 You and your fighting men should march around the town once a day for six days. 4 Seven priests will walk ahead of the Ark, each carrying a ram's horn. On the seventh day you are to march around the town seven times, with the priests blowing the horns. 5 When you hear the priests give one long blast on the rams' horns, have all the people shout as loud as they can. Then the walls of the town will collapse, and the people can charge straight into the town."

6 So Joshua called together the priests and said, "Take up the Ark of the LORD's Covenant, and assign seven priests to walk in front of it, each carrying a ram's horn." 7 Then he gave orders to the people: "March around the town, and the armed men will lead the way in front of the Ark of the LORD."

8 After Joshua spoke to the people, the seven priests with the rams' horns started marching in the presence of the LORD, blowing the horns as they marched. And the Ark of the LORD's Covenant followed behind them. 9 Some of the armed men marched in front of the priests with the horns and some behind the Ark, with the priests continually blowing the horns. 10 "Do not shout; do not even talk," Joshua commanded. "Not a single word from any of you until I tell you to shout. Then shout!" 11 So the Ark of the LORD was carried around the town once that day, and then everyone returned to spend the night in the camp.

12 Joshua got up early the next morning, and the priests again carried the Ark of the LORD. 13 The seven priests with the rams' horns marched in front of the Ark of the LORD, blowing their horns. Again the armed men marched both in front of the priests with the horns and behind the Ark of the LORD. All this time the priests were blowing their horns. 14 On the second day they again marched around the town once and returned to the camp. They followed this pattern for six days.

15 On the seventh day the Israelites got up at dawn and marched around the town as they had done before. But this time they went around the town seven times. 16 The seventh time around, as the priests sounded the long blast on their horns, Joshua commanded the people, "Shout! For the

5:10 This day in the ancient Hebrew lunar calendar occurred in late March, April, or early May.

13–15: This account of a theophany, an appearance of the divine, has obvious parallels with Moses' encounter with the burning bush (Exod 3). **13:** Joshua does not recognize the man for who he is. **14:** His response is startling; one would anticipate an unequivocal declaration that God is on Israel's side. Joshua's response answers the implicit question: Will Israel be on God's side?

6:1—8:35 Taking the Land

The cities of Jehrico and Ai are devoted to destruction *(herem)* in order to avoid the possibility that their worship of idols and foreign gods might contaminate the Israelites and seduce them into forsaking God. The practice of *herem* is referred to several times in the Hebrew Scriptures (Lev 27:28–29; Num 21:1–3; Deut 20:10–20). It is a sacred act required by God, and consequences follow if it is not practiced.

The Israelites were not the only nation to practice *herem* during times of war. It was practiced by other ethnic and national groups during this period, but we should not shirk from the awful implications. Women did not go to war during this period, but they and their children were slaughtered as brutally as the warrior class due to their guilt by association—whichever side they belonged to. The divine command is the controlling factor determining what Israel may or may not do.

LORD has given you the town! 17 Jericho and everything in it must be completely destroyed* as an offering to the LORD. Only Rahab the prostitute and the others in her house will be spared, for she protected our spies.

18 "Do not take any of the things set apart for destruction, or you yourselves will be completely destroyed, and you will bring trouble on the camp of Israel. 19 Everything made from silver, gold, bronze, or iron is sacred to the LORD and must be brought into his treasury."

20 When the people heard the sound of the rams' horns, they shouted as loud as they could. Suddenly, the walls of Jericho collapsed, and the Israelites charged straight into the town and captured it. 21 They completely destroyed everything in it with their swords—men and women, young and old, cattle, sheep, goats, and donkeys.

22 Meanwhile, Joshua said to the two spies, "Keep your promise. Go to the prostitute's house and bring her out, along with all her family."

23 The men who had been spies went in and brought out Rahab, her father, mother, brothers, and all the other relatives who were with her. They moved her whole family to a safe place near the camp of Israel.

24 Then the Israelites burned the town and everything in it. Only the things made from silver, gold, bronze, or iron were kept for the treasury of the LORD's house. 25 So Joshua spared Rahab the prostitute and her relatives who were with her in the house, because she had hidden the spies Joshua sent to Jericho. And she lives among the Israelites to this day.

26 At that time Joshua invoked this curse:

"May the curse of the LORD fall on anyone
 who tries to rebuild the town of Jericho.
At the cost of his firstborn son,
 he will lay its foundation.
At the cost of his youngest son,
 he will set up its gates."

27 So the LORD was with Joshua, and his reputation spread throughout the land.

Ai Defeats the Israelites

7 But Israel violated the instructions about the things set apart for the LORD.* A man named Achan had stolen some of these dedicated things, so the LORD was very angry with the Israelites. Achan was the son of Carmi, a descendant of Zimri* son of Zerah, of the tribe of Judah.

2 Joshua sent some of his men from Jericho to spy out the town of Ai, east of Bethel, near Beth-aven. 3 When they returned, they told Joshua, "There's no need for all of us to go up there; it won't take more than two or three thousand men to attack Ai. Since there are so few of them, don't make all our people struggle to go up there."

4 So approximately 3,000 warriors were sent, but they were soundly defeated. The men of Ai 5 chased the Israelites from the town gate as far as the quarries,* and they killed about thirty-six who were retreating down the slope. The Israelites were paralyzed with fear at this turn of events, and their courage melted away.

6 Joshua and the elders of Israel tore their clothing in dismay, threw dust on their heads, and bowed face down to the ground before the Ark of the LORD until evening. 7 Then Joshua cried out, "Oh, Sovereign LORD, why did you bring us across the Jordan River if you are going to let the Amorites kill us? If only we had been content to stay on the other side! 8 Lord, what can I say now that Israel has fled from its

6:17 The Hebrew term used here refers to the complete consecration of things or people to the LORD, either by destroying them or by giving them as an offering; similarly in 6:18, 21. **7:1a** The Hebrew term used here refers to the complete consecration of things or people to the LORD, either by destroying them or by giving them as an offering; similarly in 7:11, 12, 13, 15. **7:1b** As in parallel text at 1 Chr 2:6; Hebrew reads *Zabdi*. Also in 7:17, 18. **7:5** Or *as far as Shebarim*.

6:17: While we can celebrate the redemption of Rahab's household out of all the people of Jericho because she alone recognized the truth of God, we should also remember that the other citizens of Jericho are never given the opportunity to declare their allegiance to the God of Israel. **22–25:** Although Rahab and her relatives are saved, they are kept outside the camp. This is probably due to the restrictions imposed on Israel as they engage in warfare. God is present with his warriors in the camp, and the camp is therefore to be kept holy (Deut 23:14). The apparently hard-and-fast policy of *herem* was pliable enough to respond favorably to the entreaties of Rahab. Her household is saved even as her city is reduced to ashes. **7:1:** The notion of collective guilt or—in Rahab's case—innocence is a persistent feature of the biblical understanding of responsibility and accountability. Following the decisive victory at Jericho, Israel's fortunes suddenly shift, and they are almost routed in their next campaign against Ai because Achan has kept back some of Jericho's booty in disobedience to God. **2–5:** The rest of Israel cannot understand why their attempts to take the city of Ai fail so miserably. **7–9:** Joshua uncharacteristically berates God for bringing them into the land, since this failure to take Ai threatens the existence of Israel. He suggests that Israel had a choice concerning where

enemies? [9] For when the Canaanites and all the other people living in the land hear about it, they will surround us and wipe our name off the face of the earth. And then what will happen to the honor of your great name?"

[10] But the LORD said to Joshua, "Get up! Why are you lying on your face like this? [11] Israel has sinned and broken my covenant! They have stolen some of the things that I commanded must be set apart for me. And they have not only stolen them but have lied about it and hidden the things among their own belongings. [12] That is why the Israelites are running from their enemies in defeat. For now Israel itself has been set apart for destruction. I will not remain with you any longer unless you destroy the things among you that were set apart for destruction.

[13] "Get up! Command the people to purify themselves in preparation for tomorrow. For this is what the LORD, the God of Israel, says: Hidden among you, O Israel, are things set apart for the LORD. You will never defeat your enemies until you remove these things from among you.

[14] "In the morning you must present yourselves by tribes, and the LORD will point out the tribe to which the guilty man belongs. That tribe must come forward with its clans, and the LORD will point out the guilty clan. That clan will then come forward, and the LORD will point out the guilty family. Finally, each member of the guilty family must come forward one by one. [15] The one who has stolen what was set apart for destruction will himself be burned with fire, along with everything he has, for he has broken the covenant of the LORD and has done a horrible thing in Israel."

Achan's Sin

[16] Early the next morning Joshua brought the tribes of Israel before the LORD, and the tribe of Judah was singled out. [17] Then the clans of Judah came forward, and the clan of Zerah was singled out. Then the families of Zerah came forward, and the family of Zimri was singled out. [18] Every member of Zimri's family was brought forward person by person, and Achan was singled out.

[19] Then Joshua said to Achan, "My son, give glory to the LORD, the God of Israel, by telling the truth. Make your confession and tell me what you have done. Don't hide it from me."

[20] Achan replied, "It is true! I have sinned against the LORD, the God of Israel. [21] Among the plunder I saw a beautiful robe from Babylon,* 200 silver coins,* and a bar of gold weighing more than a pound.* I wanted them so much that I took them. They are hidden in the ground beneath my tent, with the silver buried deeper than the rest."

[22] So Joshua sent some men to make a search. They ran to the tent and found the stolen goods hidden there, just as Achan had said, with the silver buried beneath the rest. [23] They took the things from the tent and brought them to Joshua and all the Israelites. Then they laid them on the ground in the presence of the LORD.

[24] Then Joshua and all the Israelites took Achan, the silver, the robe, the bar of gold, his sons, daughters, cattle, donkeys, sheep, goats, tent, and everything he had, and they brought them to the valley of Achor. [25] Then Joshua said to Achan, "Why have you brought trouble on us? The LORD will now bring trouble on you." And all the Israelites stoned Achan and his family and burned their bodies. [26] They piled a great heap of stones over Achan, which remains to this

7:21a Hebrew *Shinar.* **7:21b** Hebrew *200 shekels of silver,* about 5 pounds or 2.3 kilograms in weight. **7:21c** Hebrew *50 shekels,* about 20 ounces or 570 grams in weight.

they would wind up despite the divine plan for Israel established in God's conversation with Abraham (Gen 15). **10–15:** God is understandably impatient with Joshua. Israel's sin accounts for the failed offensive against Ai. **12:** God threatens to subject Israel to *herem* unless the sin is discovered and punished. **24:** Although Achan alone is responsible, all or most of his household is destroyed in order to appease God and ensure victory over Ai. Achan's wife is not explicitly mentioned as being subjected to the punishment that the rest of the household undergoes. It is inconceivable that Achan's wife would have escaped the fate of her husband and children unless we assume that Achan was a widower.

The suffering of many (Israel's initial defeat at Ai) or several (the death of Achan's family) for the sin of one (Achan) is an issue that the biblical writers allude to on several occasions (for example, see 2 Sam 11). The Bible as a whole is ambiguous on this topic. There are several assurances that subsequent generations suffer for the sins of their ancestors (Exod 20:5; 34:7; Ps 109:13–15; Isa 65:6–7), but other passages reassure the reader that one is responsible only for one's own wrongdoing (Ezek 18; Jer 31:29–30). The Bible also speaks of those being preserved thanks to the righteousness of their forebears or relatives (such as in Rahab's case). Overall, the biblical literature insists that actions always have consequences. Those passages that speak of those consequences continuing in subsequent generations would be enormously powerful to those whose cultural background emphasizes kinship relationships across generations much

day. That is why the place has been called the Valley of Trouble* ever since. So the LORD was no longer angry.

The Israelites Defeat Ai

8 Then the LORD said to Joshua, "Do not be afraid or discouraged. Take all your fighting men and attack Ai, for I have given you the king of Ai, his people, his town, and his land. 2 You will destroy them as you destroyed Jericho and its king. But this time you may keep the plunder and the livestock for yourselves. Set an ambush behind the town."

3 So Joshua and all the fighting men set out to attack Ai. Joshua chose 30,000 of his best warriors and sent them out at night 4 with these orders: "Hide in ambush close behind the town and be ready for action. 5 When our main army attacks, the men of Ai will come out to fight as they did before, and we will run away from them. 6 We will let them chase us until we have drawn them away from the town. For they will say, 'The Israelites are running away from us as they did before.' Then, while we are running from them, 7 you will jump up from your ambush and take possession of the town, for the LORD your God will give it to you. 8 Set the town on fire, as the LORD has commanded. You have your orders."

9 So they left and went to the place of ambush between Bethel and the west side of Ai. But Joshua remained among the people in the camp that night. 10 Early the next morning Joshua roused his men and started toward Ai, accompanied by the elders of Israel. 11 All the fighting men who were with Joshua marched in front of the town and camped on the north side of Ai, with a valley between them and the town. 12 That night Joshua sent 5,000 men to lie in ambush between Bethel and Ai, on the west side of the town. 13 So they stationed the main army north of the town and the ambush west of the town. Joshua himself spent that night in the valley.

14 When the king of Ai saw the Israelites across the valley, he and all his army hurried out early in the morning and attacked the Israelites at a place overlooking the Jordan Valley.* But he didn't realize there was an ambush behind the town. 15 Joshua and the Israelite army fled toward the wilderness as though they were badly beaten. 16 Then all the men in the town were called out to chase after them. In this way, they were lured away from the town. 17 There was not a man left in Ai or Bethel* who did not chase after the Israelites, and the town was left wide open.

18 Then the LORD said to Joshua, "Point the spear in your hand toward Ai, for I will hand the town over to you." Joshua did as he was commanded. 19 As soon as Joshua gave this signal, all the men in ambush jumped up from their position and poured into the town. They quickly captured it and set it on fire.

20 When the men of Ai looked behind them, smoke from the town was filling the sky, and they had nowhere to go. For the Israelites who had fled in the direction of the wilderness now turned on their pursuers. 21 When Joshua and all the other Israelites saw that the ambush had succeeded and that smoke was rising from the town, they turned and attacked the men of Ai. 22 Meanwhile, the Israelites who were inside the town came out and attacked the enemy from the rear. So the men of Ai were caught in the middle, with Israelite fighters on both sides. Israel attacked them, and not a single person survived or escaped. 23 Only the king of Ai was taken alive and brought to Joshua.

24 When the Israelite army finished chasing and killing all the men of Ai in the open fields, they went back and finished off everyone inside. 25 So the entire population of Ai, including men and women, was wiped out that day—12,000 in all. 26 For Joshua kept holding out his spear until everyone who had lived in Ai was completely destroyed.* 27 Only the livestock and the treasures of the town were not destroyed, for the Israelites kept these as plunder for themselves, as the LORD had commanded Joshua. 28 So Joshua burned the town of Ai,* and it became a permanent mound of ruins, desolate to this very day.

29 Joshua impaled the king of Ai on a sharpened pole and left him there until evening. At sunset the Israelites took down the body, as Joshua commanded, and threw it in front of the town gate. They piled a great heap of stones over him that can still be seen today.

The LORD's Covenant Renewed

30 Then Joshua built an altar to the LORD, the God of Israel, on Mount Ebal. 31 He followed the com-

7:26 Hebrew *valley of Achor.* **8:14** Hebrew *the Arabah.* **8:17** Some manuscripts lack *or Bethel.* **8:26** The Hebrew term used here refers to the complete consecration of things or people to the LORD, either by destroying them or by giving them as an offering. **8:28** *Ai* means "ruin."

---

more than our own does. **8:1:** Now that Achan's sin has been discovered and punished, Israel returns to Ai. **2:** God permits the taking of booty. This surprising concession is all the more jarring following the destruction of Achan's household. **24–28:** Despite God's allowance of plundering, the policy of *herem*

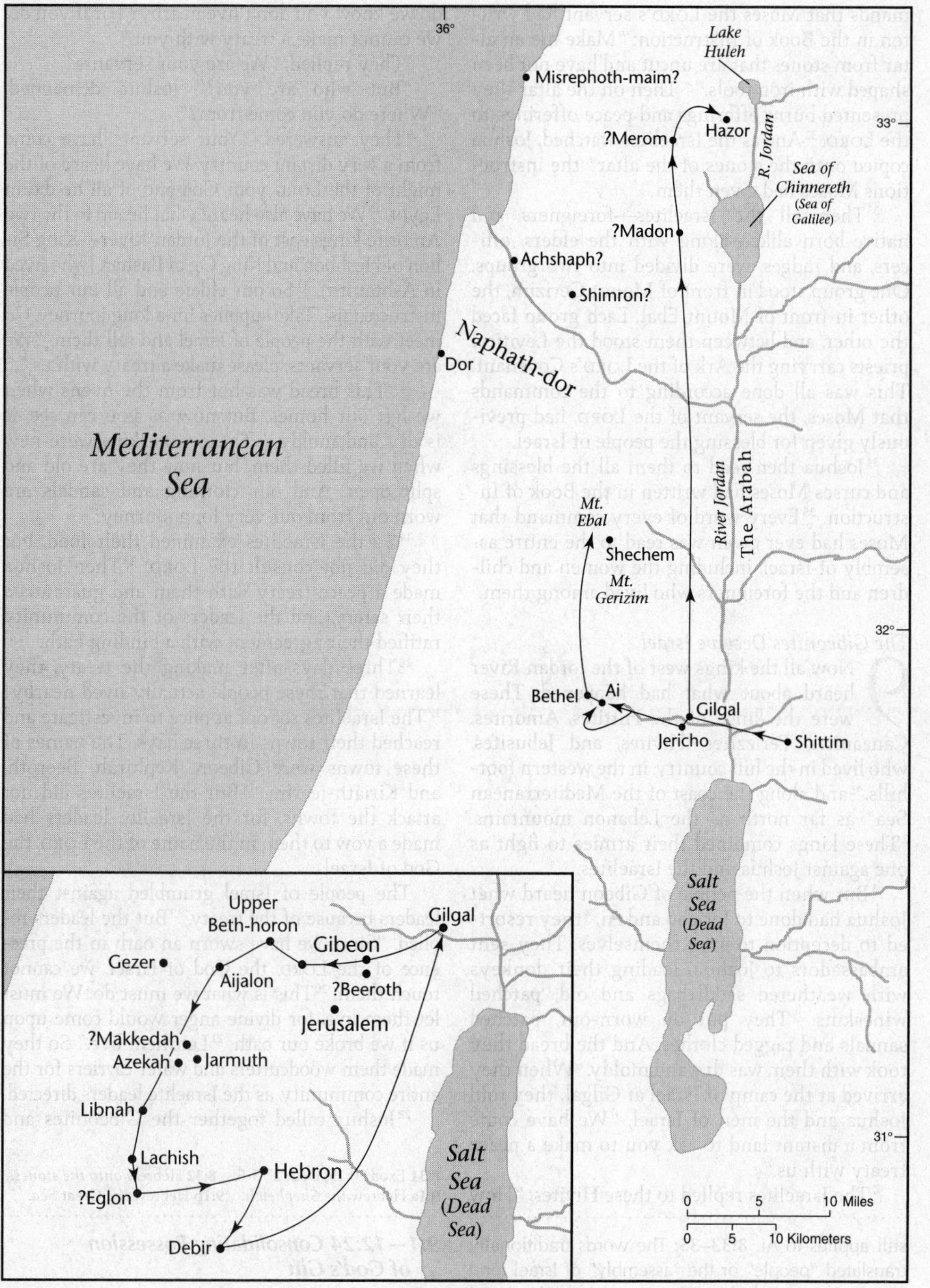

The Conquest of Canaan according to the Book of Joshua

mands that Moses the LORD's servant had written in the Book of Instruction: "Make me an altar from stones that are uncut and have not been shaped with iron tools."* Then on the altar they presented burnt offerings and peace offerings to the LORD. 32 And as the Israelites watched, Joshua copied onto the stones of the altar* the instructions Moses had given them.

33 Then all the Israelites—foreigners and native-born alike—along with the elders, officers, and judges, were divided into two groups. One group stood in front of Mount Gerizim, the other in front of Mount Ebal. Each group faced the other, and between them stood the Levitical priests carrying the Ark of the LORD's Covenant. This was all done according to the commands that Moses, the servant of the LORD, had previously given for blessing the people of Israel.

34 Joshua then read to them all the blessings and curses Moses had written in the Book of Instruction. 35 Every word of every command that Moses had ever given was read to the entire assembly of Israel, including the women and children and the foreigners who lived among them.

The Gibeonites Deceive Israel

9 Now all the kings west of the Jordan River heard about what had happened. These were the kings of the Hittites, Amorites, Canaanites, Perizzites, Hivites, and Jebusites, who lived in the hill country, in the western foothills,* and along the coast of the Mediterranean Sea* as far north as the Lebanon mountains. 2 These kings combined their armies to fight as one against Joshua and the Israelites.

3 But when the people of Gibeon heard what Joshua had done to Jericho and Ai, 4 they resorted to deception to save themselves. They sent ambassadors to Joshua, loading their donkeys with weathered saddlebags and old, patched wineskins. 5 They put on worn-out, patched sandals and ragged clothes. And the bread they took with them was dry and moldy. 6 When they arrived at the camp of Israel at Gilgal, they told Joshua and the men of Israel, "We have come from a distant land to ask you to make a peace treaty with us."

7 The Israelites replied to these Hivites, "How do we know you don't live nearby? For if you do, we cannot make a treaty with you."

8 They replied, "We are your servants."

"But who are you?" Joshua demanded. "Where do you come from?"

9 They answered, "Your servants have come from a very distant country. We have heard of the might of the LORD your God and of all he did in Egypt. 10 We have also heard what he did to the two Amorite kings east of the Jordan River—King Sihon of Heshbon and King Og of Bashan (who lived in Ashtaroth). 11 So our elders and all our people instructed us, 'Take supplies for a long journey. Go meet with the people of Israel and tell them, "We are your servants; please make a treaty with us." '

12 "This bread was hot from the ovens when we left our homes. But now, as you can see, it is dry and moldy. 13 These wineskins were new when we filled them, but now they are old and split open. And our clothing and sandals are worn out from our very long journey."

14 So the Israelites examined their food, but they did not consult the LORD. 15 Then Joshua made a peace treaty with them and guaranteed their safety, and the leaders of the community ratified their agreement with a binding oath.

16 Three days after making the treaty, they learned that these people actually lived nearby! 17 The Israelites set out at once to investigate and reached their towns in three days. The names of these towns were Gibeon, Kephirah, Beeroth, and Kiriath-jearim. 18 But the Israelites did not attack the towns, for the Israelite leaders had made a vow to them in the name of the LORD, the God of Israel.

The people of Israel grumbled against their leaders because of the treaty. 19 But the leaders replied, "Since we have sworn an oath in the presence of the LORD, the God of Israel, we cannot touch them. 20 This is what we must do. We must let them live, for divine anger would come upon us if we broke our oath. 21 Let them live." So they made them woodcutters and water carriers for the entire community, as the Israelite leaders directed.

22 Joshua called together the Gibeonites and

8:31 Exod 20:25; Deut 27:5-6. **8:32** Hebrew *onto the stones.* **9:1a** Hebrew *the Shephelah.* **9:1b** Hebrew *the Great Sea.*

still applies to Ai. **8:33–35:** The words traditionally translated "people" or the "assembly" of Israel tend to refer to men in Joshua. That women, children, and foreigners are specifically mentioned here illustrates their membership in Israel and, more important, their responsibility and accountability under the terms of the covenant.

9:1—12:24 Consolidating Possession of God's Gift

Instead of joining the alliance of local kings against Israel, the Gibeonites convince the Israelites that they do not come from a city nearby but from a land far away, which, according to Deuteronomy, should not

said, "Why did you lie to us? Why did you say
that you live in a distant land when you live right
here among us? 23 May you be cursed! From now
on you will always be servants who cut wood and
carry water for the house of my God."
24 They replied, "We did it because we—your
servants—were clearly told that the LORD your
God commanded his servant Moses to give you
this entire land and to destroy all the people living in it. So we feared greatly for our lives because of you. That is why we have done this.
25 Now we are at your mercy—do to us whatever
you think is right."
26 So Joshua did not allow the people of Israel to kill them. 27 But that day he made the
Gibeonites the woodcutters and water carriers
for the community of Israel and for the altar of
the LORD—wherever the LORD would choose to
build it. And that is what they do to this day.

Israel Defeats the Southern Armies

10 Adoni-zedek, king of Jerusalem, heard
that Joshua had captured and completely destroyed* Ai and killed its king, just
as he had destroyed the town of Jericho and killed
its king. He also learned that the Gibeonites had
made peace with Israel and were now their allies.
2 He and his people became very afraid when they
heard all this because Gibeon was a large town—
as large as the royal cities and larger than Ai. And
the Gibeonite men were strong warriors.
3 So King Adoni-zedek of Jerusalem sent messengers to several other kings: Hoham of Hebron, Piram of Jarmuth, Japhia of Lachish, and
Debir of Eglon. 4 "Come and help me destroy
Gibeon," he urged them, "for they have made
peace with Joshua and the people of Israel." 5 So
these five Amorite kings combined their armies
for a united attack. They moved all their troops
into place and attacked Gibeon.
6 The men of Gibeon quickly sent messengers
to Joshua at his camp in Gilgal. "Don't abandon your servants now!" they pleaded. "Come
at once! Save us! Help us! For all the Amorite
kings who live in the hill country have joined
forces to attack us."
7 So Joshua and his entire army, including his
best warriors, left Gilgal and set out for Gibeon.
8 "Do not be afraid of them," the LORD said to
Joshua, "for I have given you victory over them.
Not a single one of them will be able to stand up
to you."
9 Joshua traveled all night from Gilgal and
took the Amorite armies by surprise. 10 The
LORD threw them into a panic, and the Israelites
slaughtered great numbers of them at Gibeon.
Then the Israelites chased the enemy along the
road to Beth-horon, killing them all along the
way to Azekah and Makkedah. 11 As the Amorites
retreated down the road from Beth-horon, the
LORD destroyed them with a terrible hailstorm
from heaven that continued until they reached
Azekah. The hail killed more of the enemy than
the Israelites killed with the sword.
12 On the day the LORD gave the Israelites
victory over the Amorites, Joshua prayed to the
LORD in front of all the people of Israel. He said,

"Let the sun stand still over Gibeon,
and the moon over the valley of Aijalon."

13 So the sun stood still and the moon stayed in place
until the nation of Israel had defeated its enemies.
Is this event not recorded in *The Book of
Jashar** ? The sun stayed in the middle of the sky,
and it did not set as on a normal day.* 14 There
has never been a day like this one before or since,
when the LORD answered such a prayer. Surely
the LORD fought for Israel that day!

10:1 The Hebrew term used here refers to the complete consecration of things or people to the LORD, either by destroying them or by giving them as an offering; also in 10:28, 35, 37, 39, 40. **10:13a** Or *The Book of the Upright.* **10:13b** Or *did not set for about a whole day.*

---

be subject to the ban, to *herem.* **9:3–15:** The Gibeonites' deception is tempered by their own Deuteronomic confession, which recalls the words of Rahab (2:9–11). **16–21:** Even when the trickery is discovered, the Israelites cannot go back on the treaty. The agreement with Gibeon stands over and above the objections of the Israelites. **21–23:** Because the Gibeonite spokespersons styled themselves as Israel's servants (9:8, 11), Joshua determines that they shall be actual servants: hewers of wood and drawers of water on behalf of Israel. **10:1–5:** The treaty with the Gibeonites is put to the test when Gibeon is attacked by the king of Jerusalem. Jerusalem is one of the last city-states in Canaan to be taken over by the Israelites (much later, during the time of King David). The attack is essentially a preemptive strike to avert a threat from the Israelites. **10–11:** The battle is described as being more between the Canaanites and God than Israel. Although the Canaanite alliance is one made up of fearsome male warriors, the God of Israel is the greatest warrior, whose decisive victory is measured in the greater number of soldiers he kills. The battle is a study in the superiority of divine as opposed to human power. **12–14:** *So the sun stood still and the moon*: The assertion that on this one occasion God heeded a human voice is noteworthy; it suggests that God as a rule acts inde-

15 Then Joshua and the Israelite army returned to their camp at Gilgal.

Joshua Kills the Five Southern Kings

16 During the battle the five kings escaped and hid in a cave at Makkedah. 17 When Joshua heard that they had been found, 18 he issued this command: "Cover the opening of the cave with large rocks, and place guards at the entrance to keep the kings inside. 19 The rest of you continue chasing the enemy and cut them down from the rear. Don't give them a chance to get back to their towns, for the LORD your God has given you victory over them."

20 So Joshua and the Israelite army continued the slaughter and completely crushed the enemy. They totally wiped out the five armies except for a tiny remnant that managed to reach their fortified towns. 21 Then the Israelites returned safely to Joshua in the camp at Makkedah. After that, no one dared to speak even a word against Israel.

22 Then Joshua said, "Remove the rocks covering the opening of the cave, and bring the five kings to me." 23 So they brought the five kings out of the cave—the kings of Jerusalem, Hebron, Jarmuth, Lachish, and Eglon. 24 When they brought them out, Joshua told the commanders of his army, "Come and put your feet on the kings' necks." And they did as they were told.

25 "Don't ever be afraid or discouraged," Joshua told his men. "Be strong and courageous, for the LORD is going to do this to all of your enemies." 26 Then Joshua killed each of the five kings and impaled them on five sharpened poles, where they hung until evening.

27 As the sun was going down, Joshua gave instructions for the bodies of the kings to be taken down from the poles and thrown into the cave where they had been hiding. Then they covered the opening of the cave with a pile of large rocks, which remains to this very day.

Israel Destroys the Southern Towns

28 That same day Joshua captured and destroyed the town of Makkedah. He killed everyone in it, including the king, leaving no survivors. He destroyed them all, and he killed the king of Makkedah as he had killed the king of Jericho. 29 Then Joshua and the Israelites went to Libnah and attacked it. 30 There, too, the LORD gave them the town and its king. He killed everyone in it, leaving no survivors. Then Joshua killed the king of Libnah as he had killed the king of Jericho.

31 From Libnah, Joshua and the Israelites went to Lachish and attacked it. 32 Here again, the LORD gave them Lachish. Joshua took it on the second day and killed everyone in it, just as he had done at Libnah. 33 During the attack on Lachish, King Horam of Gezer arrived with his army to help defend the town. But Joshua's men killed him and his army, leaving no survivors.

34 Then Joshua and the Israelite army went on to Eglon and attacked it. 35 They captured it that day and killed everyone in it. He completely destroyed everyone, just as he had done at Lachish. 36 From Eglon, Joshua and the Israelite army went up to Hebron and attacked it. 37 They captured the town and killed everyone in it, including its king, leaving no survivors. They did the same thing to all of its surrounding villages. And just as he had done at Eglon, he completely destroyed the entire population.

38 Then Joshua and the Israelites turned back and attacked Debir. 39 He captured the town, its king, and all of its surrounding villages. He completely destroyed everyone in it, leaving no survivors. He did to Debir and its king just what he had done to Hebron and to Libnah and its king.

40 So Joshua conquered the whole region—the kings and people of the hill country, the Negev, the western foothills,* and the mountain slopes. He completely destroyed everyone in the land, leaving no survivors, just as the LORD, the God of Israel, had commanded. 41 Joshua slaughtered them from Kadesh-barnea to Gaza and from the region around the town of Goshen up to Gibeon. 42 Joshua conquered all these kings and their land in a single campaign, for the LORD, the God of Israel, was fighting for his people.

43 Then Joshua and the Israelite army returned to their camp at Gilgal.

Israel Defeats the Northern Armies

11 When King Jabin of Hazor heard what had happened, he sent messages to the following kings: King Jobab of Madon; the king of Shimron; the king of Acshaph; 2 all the kings of the northern hill country;

10:40 Hebrew *the Shephelah.*

pendently of human desires and aims, even as he acts on behalf of Israel. **16–27:** The kings who represent the cities in the alliance apparently do not lead the troops into battle. This seems to be a different pattern from that which pervades among the Israelites. Joshua does not shirk the battle. **28–43:** The remainder of the chapter details Joshua's conquest of these and other cities in the south. **11:1–17:** This military campaign is in the north against a formidable alliance equipped with horse-drawn chariots. Again Israel prevails, and

the kings in the Jordan Valley south of Galilee*; the kings in the Galilean foothills*; the kings of Naphoth-dor on the west; [3] the kings of Canaan, both east and west; the kings of the Amorites, the Hittites, the Perizzites, the Jebusites in the hill country, and the Hivites in the towns on the slopes of Mount Hermon in the land of Mizpah.

[4] All these kings came out to fight. Their combined armies formed a vast horde. And with all their horses and chariots, they covered the landscape like the sand on the seashore. [5] The kings joined forces and established their camp around the water near Merom to fight against Israel.

[6] Then the LORD said to Joshua, "Do not be afraid of them. By this time tomorrow I will hand all of them over to Israel as dead men. Then you must cripple their horses and burn their chariots."

[7] So Joshua and all his fighting men traveled to the water near Merom and attacked suddenly. [8] And the LORD gave them victory over their enemies. The Israelites chased them as far as Greater Sidon and Misrephoth-maim, and eastward into the valley of Mizpah, until not one enemy warrior was left alive. [9] Then Joshua crippled the horses and burned all the chariots, as the LORD had instructed.

[10] Joshua then turned back and captured Hazor and killed its king. (Hazor had at one time been the capital of all these kingdoms.) [11] The Israelites completely destroyed* every living thing in the city, leaving no survivors. Not a single person was spared. And then Joshua burned the city.

[12] Joshua slaughtered all the other kings and their people, completely destroying them, just as Moses, the servant of the LORD, had commanded. [13] But the Israelites did not burn any of the towns built on mounds except Hazor, which Joshua burned. [14] And the Israelites took all the plunder and livestock of the ravaged towns for themselves. But they killed all the people, leaving no survivors. [15] As the LORD had commanded his servant Moses, so Moses commanded Joshua. And Joshua did as he was told, carefully obeying all the commands that the LORD had given to Moses.

[16] So Joshua conquered the entire region—the hill country, the entire Negev, the whole area around the town of Goshen, the western foothills, the Jordan Valley,* the mountains of Israel, and the Galilean foothills. [17] The Israelite territory now extended all the way from Mount Halak, which leads up to Seir in the south, as far north as Baal-gad at the foot of Mount Hermon in the valley of Lebanon. Joshua killed all the kings of those territories, [18] waging war for a long time to accomplish this. [19] No one in this region made peace with the Israelites except the Hivites of Gibeon. All the others were defeated. [20] For the LORD hardened their hearts and caused them to fight the Israelites. So they were completely destroyed without mercy, as the LORD had commanded Moses.

[21] During this period Joshua destroyed all the descendants of Anak, who lived in the hill country of Hebron, Debir, Anab, and the entire hill country of Judah and Israel. He killed them all and completely destroyed their towns. [22] None of the descendants of Anak were left in all the land of Israel, though some still remained in Gaza, Gath, and Ashdod.

[23] So Joshua took control of the entire land, just as the LORD had instructed Moses. He gave it to the people of Israel as their special possession, dividing the land among the tribes. So the land finally had rest from war.

Kings Defeated East of the Jordan

12 These are the kings east of the Jordan River who had been killed by the Israelites and whose land was taken. Their territory extended from the Arnon Gorge to Mount Hermon and included all the land east of the Jordan Valley.*

11:2a Hebrew *in the Arabah south of Kinnereth.* **11:2b** Hebrew *the Shephelah;* also in 11:16. **11:11** The Hebrew term used here refers to the complete consecration of things or people to the LORD, either by destroying them or by giving them as an offering; also in 11:12, 20, 21. **11:16** Hebrew *the Shephelah, the Arabah.* **12:1** Hebrew *the Arabah;* also in 12:3, 8.

---

again the duty of *herem* is carried out, although the towns are not burned with the exception of Hazor. In addition, Israel takes booty, although all the people are struck down. Again we are to assume that *all the people* includes women and children. At the conclusion of the chapter we are told how successful Joshua's campaign was, thanks to God. **18–20:** Throughout Joshua those people who concede the power of Israel's God, like Rahab and the Gibeonites, receive mercy. Those whose hearts are hardened, however, who fail to acknowledge God's sovereignty, must, for the sake of Israel's weakness, be destroyed. But God is also merciful, sometimes forsaking even the conditions of his own covenant, toward those who acknowledge his sovereignty and power. **23:** This verse reminds the reader of the continuity between the promise to Moses and Joshua's vocation.

12:1–24: A recounting of Israel's victories on the eastern and western sides of the Jordan River.

[2]King Sihon of the Amorites, who lived in Heshbon, was defeated. His kingdom included Aroer, on the edge of the Arnon Gorge, and extended from the middle of the Arnon Gorge to the Jabbok River, which serves as a border for the Ammonites. This territory included the southern half of the territory of Gilead. [3]Sihon also controlled the Jordan Valley and regions to the east—from as far north as the Sea of Galilee to as far south as the Dead Sea,* including the road to Beth-jeshimoth and southward to the slopes of Pisgah.

[4]King Og of Bashan, the last of the Rephaites, lived at Ashtaroth and Edrei. [5]He ruled a territory stretching from Mount Hermon to Salecah in the north and to all of Bashan in the east, and westward to the borders of the kingdoms of Geshur and Maacah. This territory included the northern half of Gilead, as far as the boundary of King Sihon of Heshbon.

[6]Moses, the servant of the LORD, and the Israelites had destroyed the people of King Sihon and King Og. And Moses gave their land as a possession to the tribes of Reuben, Gad, and the half-tribe of Manasseh.

Kings Defeated West of the Jordan

[7]The following is a list of the kings that Joshua and the Israelite armies defeated on the west side of the Jordan, from Baal-gad in the valley of Lebanon to Mount Halak, which leads up to Seir. (Joshua gave this land to the tribes of Israel as their possession, [8]including the hill country, the western foothills,* the Jordan Valley, the mountain slopes, the Judean wilderness, and the Negev. The people who lived in this region were the Hittites, the Amorites, the Canaanites, the Perizzites, the Hivites, and the Jebusites.) These are the kings Israel defeated:

[9]The king of Jericho
The king of Ai, near Bethel
[10]The king of Jerusalem
The king of Hebron
[11]The king of Jarmuth
The king of Lachish
[12]The king of Eglon
The king of Gezer
[13]The king of Debir
The king of Geder
[14]The king of Hormah
The king of Arad
[15]The king of Libnah
The king of Adullam
[16]The king of Makkedah
The king of Bethel
[17]The king of Tappuah
The king of Hepher
[18]The king of Aphek
The king of Lasharon
[19]The king of Madon
The king of Hazor
[20]The king of Shimron-meron
The king of Acshaph
[21]The king of Taanach
The king of Megiddo
[22]The king of Kedesh
The king of Jokneam in Carmel
[23]The king of Dor in the town of Naphoth-dor*
The king of Goyim in Gilgal*
[24]The king of Tirzah.

In all, thirty-one kings were defeated.

The Land Yet to Be Conquered

13 When Joshua was an old man, the
LORD said to him, "You are growing
old, and much land remains to be conquered. [2]This is the territory that remains: all
the regions of the Philistines and the Geshurites,
[3]and the larger territory of the Canaanites, ex-
tending from the stream of Shihor on the border of Egypt, northward to the boundary of Ekron. It includes the territory of the five Philistine rulers of Gaza, Ashdod, Ashkelon, Gath, and Ekron. The

12:3 Hebrew *from the Sea of Kinnereth to the Sea of the Arabah, which is the Salt Sea.* **12:8** Hebrew *the Shephelah.* **12:23a** Hebrew *Naphath-dor,* a variant spelling of Naphoth-dor. **12:23b** Greek version reads *Goyim in Galilee.*

13:1—21:45 Division of the Land

The chapters concerning the allotment of the land to the tribes and clans of Israel are essentially lists of geographical boundaries with some narrative sections interspersed. The land is divided according to tribe, so that the impression is given of a rigorous, organized apportioning, although several loose ends remain. The failure of the campaign to achieve total success is acknowledged throughout this section of the book (13:13; 15:63; 16:10; 17:12–13). What this section of the book is most interested in is the distribution of the land to the twelve tribes. As God was the primary actor in the first part of the book, here the agency of human beings becomes more prominent; yet it is clear that God approves of the divisions that are made. **13:1–7:** Land that is still to be conquered is noted, giving the impression that God will ultimately triumph and Israel will receive this land too. **4–7:** In fact, the conquest of the towns still to be taken in Phoenicia never took place.

land of the Avvites [4]in the south also remains to be conquered. In the north, the following area has not yet been conquered: all the land of the Canaanites, including Mearah (which belongs to the Sidonians), stretching northward to Aphek on the border of the Amorites; [5]the land of the Gebalites and all of the Lebanon mountain area to the east, from Baal-gad below Mount Hermon to Lebo-hamath; [6]and all the hill country from Lebanon to Misrephoth-maim, including all the land of the Sidonians.

"I myself will drive these people out of the land ahead of the Israelites. So be sure to give this land to Israel as a special possession, just as I have commanded you. [7]Include all this territory as Israel's possession when you divide this land among the nine tribes and the half-tribe of Manasseh."

The Land Divided East of the Jordan

[8]Half the tribe of Manasseh and the tribes of Reuben and Gad had already received their grants of land on the east side of the Jordan, for Moses, the servant of the LORD, had previously assigned this land to them.

[9]Their territory extended from Aroer on
the edge of the Arnon Gorge (including the
town in the middle of the gorge) to the plain
beyond Medeba, as far as Dibon. [10]It also
included all the towns of King Sihon of the
Amorites, who had reigned in Heshbon, and
extended as far as the borders of Ammon. [11]It
included Gilead, the territory of the kingdoms
of Geshur and Maacah, all of Mount Hermon,
all of Bashan as far as Salecah, [12]and all the
territory of King Og of Bashan, who had
reigned in Ashtaroth and Edrei. King Og
was the last of the Rephaites, for Moses had
attacked them and driven them out. [13]But
the Israelites failed to drive out the people of
Geshur and Maacah, so they continue to live
among the Israelites to this day.

An Allotment for the Tribe of Levi

[14]Moses did not assign any allotment of land to the tribe of Levi. Instead, as the LORD had promised them, their allotment came from the offerings burned on the altar to the LORD, the God of Israel.

The Land Given to the Tribe of Reuben

[15]Moses had assigned the following area to the clans of the tribe of Reuben.

[16]Their territory extended from Aroer on
the edge of the Arnon Gorge (including the
town in the middle of the gorge) to the plain
beyond Medeba. [17]It included Heshbon and
the other towns on the plain—Dibon, Bamoth-
baal, Beth-baal-meon, [18]Jahaz, Kedemoth,
Mephaath, [19]Kiriathaim, Sibmah, Zereth-
shahar on the hill above the valley, [20]Beth-
peor, the slopes of Pisgah, and Beth-jeshimoth.
[21]The land of Reuben also included all the
towns of the plain and the entire kingdom
of Sihon. Sihon was the Amorite king who
had reigned in Heshbon and was killed by
Moses along with the leaders of Midian—Evi,
Rekem, Zur, Hur, and Reba—princes living
in the region who were allied with Sihon.
[22]The Israelites had also killed Balaam son of
Beor, who used magic to tell the future. [23]The
Jordan River marked the western boundary
for the tribe of Reuben. The towns and their
surrounding villages in this area were given as
a homeland to the clans of the tribe of Reuben.

The Land Given to the Tribe of Gad

[24]Moses had assigned the following area to the clans of the tribe of Gad.

[25]Their territory included Jazer, all the towns
of Gilead, and half of the land of Ammon, as
far as the town of Aroer just west of* Rabbah.
[26]It extended from Heshbon to Ramath-
mizpeh and Betonim, and from Mahanaim
to the territory of Lo-debar.* [27]In the valley
were Beth-haram, Beth-nimrah, Succoth,
Zaphon, and the rest of the kingdom of King
Sihon of Heshbon. The western boundary
ran along the Jordan River, extended as far
north as the tip of the Sea of Galilee,* and
then turned eastward. [28]The towns and their
surrounding villages in this area were given
as a homeland to the clans of the tribe of Gad.

The Land Given to the Half-Tribe of Manasseh

[29]Moses had assigned the following area to the clans of the half-tribe of Manasseh.

[30]Their territory extended from Mahanaim,
including all of Bashan, all the former
kingdom of King Og, and the sixty towns
of Jair in Bashan. [31]It also included half
of Gilead and King Og's royal cities of
Ashtaroth and Edrei. All this was given to the
clans of the descendants of Makir, who was
Manasseh's son.

13:25 Hebrew *in front of.* **13:26** Hebrew *Li-debir,* apparently a variant spelling of Lo-debar (compare 2 Sam 9:4; 17:27; Amos 6:13). **13:27** Hebrew *Sea of Kinnereth.*

32 These are the allotments Moses had made while he was on the plains of Moab, across the Jordan River, east of Jericho. 33 But Moses gave no allotment of land to the tribe of Levi, for the LORD, the God of Israel, had promised that he himself would be their allotment.

The Land Divided West of the Jordan

14 The remaining tribes of Israel received land in Canaan as allotted by Eleazar the priest, Joshua son of Nun, and the tribal leaders. 2 These nine and a half tribes received their grants of land by means of sacred lots, in accordance with the LORD's command through Moses. 3 Moses had already given a grant of land to the two and a half tribes on the east side of the Jordan River, but he had given the Levites no such allotment. 4 The descendants of Joseph had become two separate tribes—Manasseh and Ephraim. And the Levites were given no land at all, only towns to live in with surrounding pasturelands for their livestock and all their possessions. 5 So the land was distributed in strict accordance with the LORD's commands to Moses.

Caleb Requests His Land

6 A delegation from the tribe of Judah, led by Caleb son of Jephunneh the Kenizzite, came to Joshua at Gilgal. Caleb said to Joshua, "Remember what the LORD said to Moses, the man of God, about you and me when we were at Kadesh-barnea. 7 I was forty years old when Moses, the servant of the LORD, sent me from Kadesh-barnea to explore the land of Canaan. I returned and gave an honest report, 8 but my brothers who went with me frightened the people from entering the Promised Land. For my part, I wholeheartedly followed the LORD my God. 9 So that day Moses solemnly promised me, 'The land of Canaan on which you were just walking will be your grant of land and that of your descendants forever, because you wholeheartedly followed the LORD my God.'

10 "Now, as you can see, the LORD has kept me alive and well as he promised for all these forty-five years since Moses made this promise—even while Israel wandered in the wilderness. Today I am eighty-five years old. 11 I am as strong now as I was when Moses sent me on that journey, and I can still travel and fight as well as I could then. 12 So give me the hill country that the LORD promised me. You will remember that as scouts we found the descendants of Anak living there in great, walled towns. But if the LORD is with me, I will drive them out of the land, just as the LORD said."

13 So Joshua blessed Caleb son of Jephunneh and gave Hebron to him as his portion of land. 14 Hebron still belongs to the descendants of Caleb son of Jephunneh the Kenizzite because he wholeheartedly followed the LORD, the God of Israel. 15 (Previously Hebron had been called Kiriath-arba. It had been named after Arba, a great hero of the descendants of Anak.)

And the land had rest from war.

The Land Given to the Tribe of Judah

15 The allotment for the clans of the tribe of Judah reached southward to the border of Edom, as far south as the wilderness of Zin.

2 The southern boundary began at the south bay of the Dead Sea,* 3 ran south of Scorpion Pass* into the wilderness of Zin, and then went south of Kadesh-barnea to Hezron. Then it went up to Addar, where it turned toward Karka. 4 From there it passed to Azmon until it finally reached the Brook of Egypt, which it followed to the Mediterranean Sea.* This was their* southern boundary.

5 The eastern boundary extended along the Dead Sea to the mouth of the Jordan River.

The northern boundary began at the bay where the Jordan River empties into the Dead Sea, 6 went up from there to Beth-hoglah, then proceeded north of Beth-arabah to the Stone of Bohan. (Bohan was Reuben's son.) 7 From that point it went through the valley of Achor to Debir, turning north toward Gilgal, which is across from the slopes of Adummim on the south side of the valley. From there the boundary extended to the springs at En-shemesh and on to En-rogel. 8 The boundary then passed through the valley of Ben-Hinnom, along the southern slopes of the Jebusites, where the city of Jerusalem is located. Then it went west to

15:2 Hebrew *the Salt Sea;* also in 15:5. **15:3** Hebrew *Akrabbim.* **15:4a** Hebrew *the sea;* also in 15:11. **15:4b** Hebrew *your.*

14:1–5: An explanatory note as to why nine and a half tribes reside west of the Jordan River despite the Levites not being allotted any territory. This is because Joseph's descendants were classed as two tribes: Manasseh, already allotted territory east of the Jordan, and Ephraim, who numbered among the

the top of the mountain above the valley of Hinnom, and on up to the northern end of the valley of Rephaim. [9]From there the boundary extended from the top of the mountain to the spring at the waters of Nephtoah,* and from there to the towns on Mount Ephron. Then it turned toward Baalah (that is, Kiriath-jearim). [10]The boundary circled west of Baalah to Mount Seir, passed along to the town of Kesalon on the northern slope of Mount Jearim, and went down to Beth-shemesh and on to Timnah. [11]The boundary then proceeded to the slope of the hill north of Ekron, where it turned toward Shikkeron and Mount Baalah. It passed Jabneel and ended at the Mediterranean Sea. [12]The western boundary was the shoreline of the Mediterranean Sea.*

These are the boundaries for the clans of the tribe of Judah.

The Land Given to Caleb

[13]The LORD commanded Joshua to assign some of Judah's territory to Caleb son of Jephunneh. So Caleb was given the town of Kiriath-arba (that is, Hebron), which had been named after Anak's ancestor. [14]Caleb drove out the three groups of Anakites—the descendants of Sheshai, Ahiman, and Talmai, the sons of Anak.

[15]From there he went to fight against the people living in the town of Debir (formerly called Kiriath-sepher). [16]Caleb said, "I will give my daughter Acsah in marriage to the one who attacks and captures Kiriath-sepher." [17]Othniel, the son of Caleb's brother Kenaz, was the one who conquered it, so Acsah became Othniel's wife.

[18]When Acsah married Othniel, she urged him* to ask her father for a field. As she got down off her donkey, Caleb asked her, "What's the matter?"

[19]She said, "Give me another gift. You have already given me land in the Negev; now please give me springs of water, too." So Caleb gave her the upper and lower springs.

The Towns Allotted to Judah

[20]This was the homeland allocated to the clans of the tribe of Judah.

[21]The towns of Judah situated along the borders of Edom in the extreme south were Kabzeel, Eder, Jagur, [22]Kinah, Dimonah, Adadah, [23]Kedesh, Hazor, Ithnan, [24]Ziph, Telem, Bealoth, [25]Hazor-hadattah, Kerioth-hezron (that is, Hazor), [26]Amam, Shema, Moladah, [27]Hazar-gaddah, Heshmon, Beth-pelet, [28]Hazar-shual, Beersheba, Biziothiah, [29]Baalah, Iim, Ezem, [30]Eltolad, Kesil, Hormah, [31]Ziklag, Madmannah, Sansannah, [32]Lebaoth, Shilhim, Ain, and Rimmon—twenty-nine towns with their surrounding villages.

[33]The following towns situated in the western foothills* were also given to Judah: Eshtaol, Zorah, Ashnah, [34]Zanoah, En-gannim, Tappuah, Enam, [35]Jarmuth, Adullam, Socoh, Azekah, [36]Shaaraim, Adithaim, Gederah, and Gederothaim—fourteen towns with their surrounding villages.

[37]Also included were Zenan, Hadashah, Migdal-gad, [38]Dilean, Mizpeh, Joktheel, [39]Lachish, Bozkath, Eglon, [40]Cabbon, Lahmam, Kitlish, [41]Gederoth, Beth-dagon, Naamah, and Makkedah—sixteen towns with their surrounding villages.

[42]Besides these, there were Libnah, Ether, Ashan, [43]Iphtah, Ashnah, Nezib, [44]Keilah, Aczib, and Mareshah—nine towns with their surrounding villages.

[45]The territory of the tribe of Judah also included Ekron and its surrounding settlements and villages. [46]From Ekron the boundary extended west and included the towns near Ashdod with their surrounding villages. [47]It also included Ashdod with its surrounding settlements and villages and Gaza with its settlements and villages, as far as the Brook of Egypt and along the coast of the Mediterranean Sea.

[48]Judah also received the following towns in the hill country: Shamir, Jattir, Socoh, [49]Dannah, Kiriath-sannah (that is, Debir), [50]Anab, Eshtemoh, Anim, [51]Goshen, Holon, and Giloh—eleven towns with their surrounding villages.

[52]Also included were the towns of Arab, Dumah, Eshan, [53]Janim, Beth-tappuah, Aphekah, [54]Humtah, Kiriath-arba (that is, Hebron), and Zior—nine towns with their surrounding villages.

[55]Besides these, there were Maon, Carmel, Ziph, Juttah, [56]Jezreel, Jokdeam, Zanoah,

15:9 Or *the spring at Me-nephtoah.* **15:12** Hebrew *the Great Sea;* also in 15:47. **15:18** Some Greek manuscripts read *he urged her.* **15:33** Hebrew *the Shephelah.*

western tribes. **15:15–19:** Othniel receives Acsah as his wife for successfully conquering Debir. Recalling Rahab, we again read of a woman petitioning a man or men as Acsah asks Caleb for springs.

57 Kain, Gibeah, and Timnah—ten towns with
their surrounding villages.
58 In addition, there were Halhul, Beth-zur,
Gedor, 59 Maarath, Beth-anoth, and Eltekon—
six towns with their surrounding villages.
60 There were also Kiriath-baal (that is,
Kiriath-jearim) and Rabbah—two towns with
their surrounding villages.
61 In the wilderness there were the towns
of Beth-arabah, Middin, Secacah, 62 Nibshan,
the City of Salt, and En-gedi—six towns with
their surrounding villages.

63 But the tribe of Judah could not drive out
the Jebusites, who lived in the city of Jerusalem,
so the Jebusites live there among the people of
Judah to this day.

The Land Given to Ephraim and West Manasseh

16 The allotment for the descendants
of Joseph extended from the Jordan
River near Jericho, east of the springs
of Jericho, through the wilderness and into
the hill country of Bethel. 2 From Bethel
(that is, Luz)* it ran over to Ataroth in the
territory of the Arkites. 3 Then it descended
westward to the territory of the Japhletites as
far as Lower Beth-horon, then to Gezer and
over to the Mediterranean Sea.*

4 This was the homeland allocated to the families
of Joseph's sons, Manasseh and Ephraim.

The Land Given to Ephraim

5 The following territory was given to the clans
of the tribe of Ephraim.

The boundary of their homeland began at
Ataroth-addar in the east. From there it
ran to Upper Beth-horon, 6 then on to the
Mediterranean Sea. From Micmethath on the
north, the boundary curved eastward past
Taanath-shiloh to the east of Janoah. 7 From
Janoah it turned southward to Ataroth and
Naarah, touched Jericho, and ended at the
Jordan River. 8 From Tappuah the boundary
extended westward, following the Kanah
Ravine to the Mediterranean Sea. This is the
homeland allocated to the clans of the tribe of
Ephraim.
9 In addition, some towns with their
surrounding villages in the territory allocated
to the half-tribe of Manasseh were set aside
for the tribe of Ephraim. 10 They did not drive
the Canaanites out of Gezer, however, so
the people of Gezer live as slaves among the
people of Ephraim to this day.

The Land Given to West Manasseh

17 The next allotment of land was given
to the half-tribe of Manasseh, the descendants of Joseph's older son. Ma-
kir, the firstborn son of Manasseh, was the father
of Gilead. Because his descendants were experienced soldiers, the regions of Gilead and Bashan
on the east side of the Jordan had already been
given to them. 2 So the allotment on the west
side of the Jordan was for the remaining families within the clans of the tribe of Manasseh:
Abiezer, Helek, Asriel, Shechem, Hepher, and
Shemida. These clans represent the male descendants of Manasseh son of Joseph.
3 However, Zelophehad, a descendant of Hepher son of Gilead, son of Makir, son of Manasseh, had no sons. He had only daughters,
whose names were Mahlah, Noah, Hoglah,
Milcah, and Tirzah. 4 These women came to Eleazar the priest, Joshua son of Nun, and the Israelite leaders and said, "The LORD commanded
Moses to give us a grant of land along with the
men of our tribe."
So Joshua gave them a grant of land along
with their uncles, as the LORD had commanded.
5 As a result, Manasseh's total allocation came
to ten parcels of land, in addition to the land
of Gilead and Bashan across the Jordan River,
6 because the female descendants of Manasseh
received a grant of land along with the male descendants. (The land of Gilead was given to the
rest of the male descendants of Manasseh.)

16:2 As in Greek version (also see 18:13); Hebrew reads *From Bethel to Luz.* **16:3** Hebrew *the sea;* also in 16:6, 8.

17:3–6: The five daughters of Zelophehad—Mahlah, Noah, Hoglah, Milcah, and Tirzah—are forced to petition the priest Eleazar and Joshua to grant them what is rightfully theirs according to the covenant. In Numbers the women take their petition directly to Moses (Num 27:1–11). In that passage they base their claim for land on the need to keep their father's name alive in the absence of any male heirs. In Joshua, however, they simply recall Moses' verdict. Their claim to the land is endorsed by Moses and, of course, God. Women are often forgotten, as in the case of the daughters of Zelophehad, but occasionally heeded: The spies in Jericho apparently judged the voice of Rahab authoritative enough to render any further surveillance of the city unnecessary.

7 The boundary of the tribe of Manasseh extended from the border of Asher to Micmethath, near Shechem. Then the boundary went south from Micmethath to the settlement near the spring of Tappuah. 8 The land surrounding Tappuah belonged to Manasseh, but the town of Tappuah itself, on the border of Manasseh's territory, belonged to the tribe of Ephraim. 9 From the spring of Tappuah, the boundary of Manasseh followed the Kanah Ravine to the Mediterranean Sea.* Several towns south of the ravine were inside Manasseh's territory, but they actually belonged to the tribe of Ephraim. 10 In general, however, the land south of the ravine belonged to Ephraim, and the land north of the ravine belonged to Manasseh. Manasseh's boundary ran along the northern side of the ravine and ended at the Mediterranean Sea. North of Manasseh was the territory of Asher, and to the east was the territory of Issachar.

11 The following towns within the territory of Issachar and Asher, however, were given to Manasseh: Beth-shan,* Ibleam, Dor (that is, Naphoth-dor),* Endor, Taanach, and Megiddo, each with their surrounding settlements.

12 But the descendants of Manasseh were unable to occupy these towns. They could not drive out the Canaanites who continued to live there. 13 Later, however, when the Israelites became strong enough, they forced the Canaanites to work as slaves. But they did not drive them out of the land.

14 The descendants of Joseph came to Joshua and asked, "Why have you given us only one portion of land as our homeland when the LORD has blessed us with so many people?"

15 Joshua replied, "If there are so many of you, and if the hill country of Ephraim is not large enough for you, clear out land for yourselves in the forest where the Perizzites and Rephaites live."

16 The descendants of Joseph responded, "It's true that the hill country is not large enough for us. But all the Canaanites in the lowlands have iron chariots, both those in Beth-shan and its surrounding settlements and those in the valley of Jezreel. They are too strong for us."

17 Then Joshua said to the tribes of Ephraim and Manasseh, the descendants of Joseph, "Since you are so large and strong, you will be given more than one portion. 18 The forests of the hill country will be yours as well. Clear as much of the land as you wish, and take possession of its farthest corners. And you will drive out the Canaanites from the valleys, too, even though they are strong and have iron chariots."

The Allotments of the Remaining Land

18 Now that the land was under Israelite control, the entire community of Israel gathered at Shiloh and set up the Tabernacle.* 2 But there remained seven tribes who had not yet been allotted their grants of land.

3 Then Joshua asked them, "How long are you going to wait before taking possession of the remaining land the LORD, the God of your ancestors, has given to you? 4 Select three men from each tribe, and I will send them out to explore the land and map it out. They will then return to me with a written report of their proposed divisions of their new homeland. 5 Let them divide the land into seven sections, excluding Judah's territory in the south and Joseph's territory in the north. 6 And when you record the seven divisions of the land and bring them to me, I will cast sacred lots in the presence of the LORD our God to assign land to each tribe.

7 "The Levites, however, will not receive any allotment of land. Their role as priests of the LORD is their allotment. And the tribes of Gad, Reuben, and the half-tribe of Manasseh won't receive any more land, for they have already received their grant of land, which Moses, the servant of the LORD, gave them on the east side of the Jordan River."

8 As the men started on their way to map out the land, Joshua commanded them, "Go and explore the land and write a description of it. Then return to me, and I will assign the land to the tribes by casting sacred lots here in the presence of the LORD at Shiloh." 9 The men did as they were told and mapped the entire territory into seven sections, listing the towns in each section. They made a written record and then returned to Joshua in the camp at Shiloh. 10 And there at Shiloh, Joshua cast sacred lots in the presence of the LORD to determine which tribe should have each section.

The Land Given to Benjamin

11 The first allotment of land went to the clans of the tribe of Benjamin. It lay between the territory assigned to the tribes of Judah and Joseph.

17:9 Hebrew *the sea;* also in 17:10. **17:11a** Hebrew *Beth-shean,* a variant spelling of Beth-shan; also in 17:16. **17:11b** The meaning of the Hebrew here is uncertain. **18:1** Hebrew *Tent of Meeting.*

12 The northern boundary of Benjamin's land
began at the Jordan River, went north of the
slope of Jericho, then west through the hill
country and the wilderness of Beth-aven.
13 From there the boundary went south to
Luz (that is, Bethel) and proceeded down to
Ataroth-addar on the hill that lies south of
Lower Beth-horon.
14 The boundary then made a turn and
swung south along the western edge of the
hill facing Beth-horon, ending at the village
of Kiriath-baal (that is, Kiriath-jearim), a
town belonging to the tribe of Judah. This
was the western boundary.
15 The southern boundary began at the
outskirts of Kiriath-jearim. From that
western point it ran* to the spring at the
waters of Nephtoah,* 16 and down to the base
of the mountain beside the valley of Ben-
Hinnom, at the northern end of the valley of
Rephaim. From there it went down the valley
of Hinnom, crossing south of the slope where
the Jebusites lived, and continued down to
En-rogel. 17 From En-rogel the boundary
proceeded in a northerly direction and came
to En-shemesh and on to Geliloth (which
is across from the slopes of Adummim).
Then it went down to the Stone of Bohan.
(Bohan was Reuben's son.) 18 From there
it passed along the north side of the slope
overlooking the Jordan Valley.* The border
then went down into the valley, 19 ran past
the north slope of Beth-hoglah, and ended at
the north bay of the Dead Sea,* which is the
southern end of the Jordan River. This was
the southern boundary.
20 The eastern boundary was the Jordan
River.

These were the boundaries of the homeland allocated to the clans of the tribe of Benjamin.

The Towns Given to Benjamin

21 These were the towns given to the clans of the
tribe of Benjamin.

Jericho, Beth-hoglah, Emek-keziz, 22 Beth-
arabah, Zemaraim, Bethel, 23 Avvim, Parah,
Ophrah, 24 Kephar-ammoni, Ophni, and
Geba—twelve towns with their surrounding
villages. 25 Also Gibeon, Ramah, Beeroth,
26 Mizpah, Kephirah, Mozah, 27 Rekem,
Irpeel, Taralah, 28 Zela, Haeleph, Jebus (that
is, Jerusalem), Gibeah, and Kiriath*—
fourteen towns with their surrounding
villages.

This was the homeland allocated to the clans of the tribe of Benjamin.

The Land Given to Simeon

19 The second allotment of land went to
the clans of the tribe of Simeon. Their
homeland was surrounded by Judah's
territory.

2 Simeon's homeland included Beersheba,
Sheba, Moladah, 3 Hazar-shual, Balah, Ezem,
4 Eltolad, Bethul, Hormah, 5 Ziklag, Beth-
marcaboth, Hazar-susah, 6 Beth-lebaoth,
and Sharuhen—thirteen towns with their
surrounding villages. 7 It also included Ain,
Rimmon, Ether, and Ashan—four towns with
their villages, 8 including all the surrounding
villages as far south as Baalath-beer (also
known as Ramah of the Negev).

This was the homeland allocated to the clans of
the tribe of Simeon. 9 Their allocation of land
came from part of what had been given to Judah
because Judah's territory was too large for them.
So the tribe of Simeon received an allocation
within the territory of Judah.

The Land Given to Zebulun

10 The third allotment of land went to the clans of
the tribe of Zebulun.

The boundary of Zebulun's homeland started
at Sarid. 11 From there it went west, going
past Maralah, touching Dabbesheth, and
proceeding to the brook east of Jokneam. 12 In
the other direction, the boundary went east
from Sarid to the border of Kisloth-tabor,
and from there to Daberath and up to Japhia.
13 Then it continued east to Gath-hepher,
Eth-kazin, and Rimmon and turned toward
Neah. 14 The northern boundary of Zebulun
passed Hannathon and ended at the valley
of Iphtah-el. 15 The towns in these areas
included Kattath, Nahalal, Shimron, Idalah,
and Bethlehem—twelve towns with their
surrounding villages.

16 The homeland allocated to the clans of the tribe
of Zebulun included these towns and their surrounding villages.

18:15a Or *From there it went to Mozah.* The meaning of the Hebrew is uncertain. **18:15b** Or *the spring at Me-nephtoah.* **18:18** Hebrew *overlooking the Arabah,* or *overlooking Beth-arabah.* **18:19** Hebrew *Salt Sea.* **18:28** Some Greek manuscripts read *Kiriath-jearim.*

The Land Given to Issachar
17 The fourth allotment of land went to the clans
of the tribe of Issachar.

18 Its boundaries included the following towns:
Jezreel, Kesulloth, Shunem, 19 Hapharaim,
Shion, Anaharath, 20 Rabbith, Kishion, Ebez,
21 Remeth, En-gannim, En-haddah, and Beth-
pazzez. 22 The boundary also touched Tabor,
Shahazumah, and Beth-shemesh, ending at
the Jordan River—sixteen towns with their
surrounding villages.

23 The homeland allocated to the clans of the tribe
of Issachar included these towns and their surrounding villages.

The Land Given to Asher
24 The fifth allotment of land went to the clans of
the tribe of Asher.

25 Its boundaries included these
towns: Helkath, Hali, Beten, Acshaph,
26 Allammelech, Amad, and Mishal. The
boundary on the west touched Carmel and
Shihor-libnath, 27 then it turned east toward
Beth-dagon, and ran as far as Zebulun in the
valley of Iphtah-el, going north to Beth-emek
and Neiel. It then continued north to Cabul,
28 Abdon,* Rehob, Hammon, Kanah, and as
far as Greater Sidon. 29 Then the boundary
turned toward Ramah and the fortress of
Tyre, where it turned toward Hosah and came
to the Mediterranean Sea.* The territory also
included Mehebel, Aczib, 30 Ummah, Aphek,
and Rehob—twenty-two towns with their
surrounding villages.

31 The homeland allocated to the clans of the tribe
of Asher included these towns and their surrounding villages.

The Land Given to Naphtali
32 The sixth allotment of land went to the clans of
the tribe of Naphtali.

33 Its boundary ran from Heleph, from the
oak at Zaanannim, and extended across to
Adami-nekeb, Jabneel, and as far as Lakkum,
ending at the Jordan River. 34 The western
boundary ran past Aznoth-tabor, then to
Hukkok, and touched the border of Zebulun
in the south, the border of Asher on the west,
and the Jordan River* on the east. 35 The
fortified towns included in this territory were
Ziddim, Zer, Hammath, Rakkath, Kinnereth,
36 Adamah, Ramah, Hazor, 37 Kedesh, Edrei,
En-hazor, 38 Yiron, Migdal-el, Horem, Beth-
anath, and Beth-shemesh—nineteen towns
with their surrounding villages.

39 The homeland allocated to the clans of the tribe
of Naphtali included these towns and their surrounding villages.

The Land Given to Dan
40 The seventh allotment of land went to the clans
of the tribe of Dan.

41 The land allocated as their homeland
included the following towns: Zorah, Eshtaol,
Ir-shemesh, 42 Shaalabbin, Aijalon, Ithlah,
43 Elon, Timnah, Ekron, 44 Eltekeh, Gibbethon,
Baalath, 45 Jehud, Bene-berak, Gath-rimmon,
46 Me-jarkon, Rakkon, and the territory across
from Joppa.
47 But the tribe of Dan had trouble taking
possession of their land,* so they attacked the
town of Laish.* They captured it, slaughtered
its people, and settled there. They renamed
the town Dan after their ancestor.

48 The homeland allocated to the clans of the tribe
of Dan included these towns and their surrounding villages.

The Land Given to Joshua
49 After all the land was divided among the tribes,
the Israelites gave a piece of land to Joshua as his
allocation. 50 For the LORD had said he could have
any town he wanted. He chose Timnath-serah in
the hill country of Ephraim. He rebuilt the town
and lived there.
51 These are the territories that Eleazar the
priest, Joshua son of Nun, and the tribal leaders
allocated as grants of land to the tribes of Israel
by casting sacred lots in the presence of the LORD
at the entrance of the Tabernacle* at Shiloh. So
the division of the land was completed.

The Cities of Refuge
20 The LORD said to Joshua, 2 "Now tell
the Israelites to designate the cities of
refuge, as I instructed Moses. 3 Anyone who kills another person accidentally and
unintentionally can run to one of these cities;

19:28 As in some Hebrew manuscripts (see also 21:30); most Hebrew manuscripts read *Ebron.* **19:29** Hebrew *the sea.* **19:34** Hebrew *and Judah at the Jordan River.* **19:47a** Or *had trouble holding on to their land.* **19:47b** Hebrew *Leshem,* a variant spelling of Laish. **19:51** Hebrew *Tent of Meeting.*

they will be places of refuge from relatives seeking revenge for the person who was killed.

4 "Upon reaching one of these cities, the one who caused the death will appear before the elders at the city gate and present his case. They must allow him to enter the city and give him a place to live among them. 5 If the relatives of the victim come to avenge the killing, the leaders must not release the slayer to them, for he killed the other person unintentionally and without previous hostility. 6 But the slayer must stay in that city and be tried by the local assembly, which will render a judgment. And he must continue to live in that city until the death of the high priest who was in office at the time of the accident. After that, he is free to return to his own home in the town from which he fled."

7 The following cities were designated as cities of refuge: Kedesh of Galilee, in the hill country of Naphtali; Shechem, in the hill country of Ephraim; and Kiriath-arba (that is, Hebron), in the hill country of Judah. 8 On the east side of the Jordan River, across from Jericho, the following cities were designated: Bezer, in the wilderness plain of the tribe of Reuben; Ramoth in Gilead, in the territory of the tribe of Gad; and Golan in Bashan, in the land of the tribe of Manasseh. 9 These cities were set apart for all the Israelites as well as the foreigners living among them. Anyone who accidentally killed another person could take refuge in one of these cities. In this way, they could escape being killed in revenge prior to standing trial before the local assembly.

The Towns Given to the Levites

21 Then the leaders of the tribe of Levi came to consult with Eleazar the priest, Joshua son of Nun, and the leaders of the other tribes of Israel. 2 They came to them at Shiloh in the land of Canaan and said, "The LORD commanded Moses to give us towns to live in and pasturelands for our livestock." 3 So by the command of the LORD the people of Israel gave the Levites the following towns and pasturelands out of their own grants of land.

4 The descendants of Aaron, who were members of the Kohathite clan within the tribe of Levi, were allotted thirteen towns that were originally assigned to the tribes of Judah, Simeon, and Benjamin. 5 The other families of the Kohathite clan were allotted ten towns from the tribes of Ephraim, Dan, and the half-tribe of Manasseh.

6 The clan of Gershon was allotted thirteen towns from the tribes of Issachar, Asher, Naphtali, and the half-tribe of Manasseh in Bashan.

7 The clan of Merari was allotted twelve towns from the tribes of Reuben, Gad, and Zebulun.

8 So the Israelites obeyed the LORD's command to Moses and assigned these towns and pasturelands to the Levites by casting sacred lots.

9 The Israelites gave the following towns from the tribes of Judah and Simeon 10 to the descendants of Aaron, who were members of the Kohathite clan within the tribe of Levi, since the sacred lot fell to them first: 11 Kiriath-arba (that is, Hebron), in the hill country of Judah, along with its surrounding pasturelands. (Arba was an ancestor of Anak.) 12 But the open fields beyond the town and the surrounding villages were given to Caleb son of Jephunneh as his possession.

13 The following towns with their pasturelands were given to the descendants of Aaron the priest: Hebron (a city of refuge for those who accidentally killed someone), Libnah, 14 Jattir, Eshtemoa, 15 Holon, Debir, 16 Ain, Juttah, and Beth-shemesh—nine towns from these two tribes.

17 From the tribe of Benjamin the priests were given the following towns with their pasturelands: Gibeon, Geba, 18 Anathoth, and Almon—four towns. 19 So in all, thirteen towns with their pasturelands were given to the priests, the descendants of Aaron.

20 The rest of the Kohathite clan from the tribe of Levi was allotted the following towns and pasturelands from the tribe of Ephraim: 21 Shechem in the hill country of Ephraim (a city of refuge for those who accidentally killed someone), Gezer, 22 Kibzaim, and Beth-horon—four towns.

23 The following towns and pasturelands were allotted to the priests from the tribe of Dan: Eltekeh, Gibbethon, 24 Aijalon, and Gath-rimmon—four towns.

25 The half-tribe of Manasseh allotted the following towns with their pasturelands to the priests: Taanach and Gath-rimmon—two towns. 26 So in all, ten towns with their pasturelands were given to the rest of the Kohathite clan.

27 The descendants of Gershon, another clan within the tribe of Levi, received the following towns with their pasturelands from the half-tribe of Manasseh: Golan in Bashan (a city of refuge for those who accidentally killed someone) and Be-eshterah—two towns.

28 From the tribe of Issachar they received the following towns with their pasturelands: Kishion, Daberath, 29 Jarmuth, and En-gannim—four towns.

30 From the tribe of Asher they received the following towns with their pasturelands: Mishal, Abdon, 31 Helkath, and Rehob—four towns.

32 From the tribe of Naphtali they received

the following towns with their pasturelands: Kedesh in Galilee (a city of refuge for those who accidentally killed someone), Hammoth-dor, and Kartan—three towns. 33 So in all, thirteen towns with their pasturelands were allotted to the clan of Gershon.

34 The rest of the Levites—the Merari clan—were given the following towns with their pasturelands from the tribe of Zebulun: Jokneam, Kartah, 35 Dimnah, and Nahalal—four towns.

36 From the tribe of Reuben they received the following towns with their pasturelands: Bezer, Jahaz,* 37 Kedemoth, and Mephaath—four towns.

38 From the tribe of Gad they received the following towns with their pasturelands: Ramoth in Gilead (a city of refuge for those who accidentally killed someone), Mahanaim, 39 Heshbon, and Jazer—four towns. 40 So in all, twelve towns were allotted to the clan of Merari.

41 The total number of towns and pasturelands within Israelite territory given to the Levites came to forty-eight. 42 Every one of these towns had pasturelands surrounding it.

43 So the LORD gave to Israel all the land he had sworn to give their ancestors, and they took possession of it and settled there. 44 And the LORD gave them rest on every side, just as he had solemnly promised their ancestors. None of their enemies could stand against them, for the LORD helped them conquer all their enemies. 45 Not a single one of all the good promises the LORD had given to the family of Israel was left unfulfilled; everything he had spoken came true.

The Eastern Tribes Return Home

22 Then Joshua called together the tribes of Reuben, Gad, and the half-tribe of Manasseh. 2 He told them, "You have done as Moses, the servant of the LORD, commanded you, and you have obeyed every order I have given you. 3 During all this time you have not deserted the other tribes. You have been careful to obey the commands of the LORD your God right up to the present day. 4 And now the LORD your God has given the other tribes rest, as he promised them. So go back home to the land that Moses, the servant of the LORD, gave you as your possession on the east side of the Jordan River. 5 But be very careful to obey all the commands and the instructions that Moses gave to you. Love the LORD your God, walk in all his ways, obey his commands, hold firmly to him, and serve him with all your heart and all your soul." 6 So Joshua blessed them and sent them away, and they went home.

7 Moses had given the land of Bashan, east of the Jordan River, to the half-tribe of Manasseh. (The other half of the tribe was given land west of the Jordan.) As Joshua sent them away and blessed them, 8 he said to them, "Go back to your homes with the great wealth you have taken from your enemies—the vast herds of livestock, the silver, gold, bronze, and iron, and the large supply of clothing. Share the plunder with your relatives."

9 So the men of Reuben, Gad, and the half-tribe of Manasseh left the rest of Israel at Shiloh in the land of Canaan. They started the journey back to their own land of Gilead, the territory that belonged to them according to the LORD's command through Moses.

The Eastern Tribes Build an Altar

10 But while they were still in Canaan, and when they came to a place called Geliloth* near the Jordan River, the men of Reuben, Gad, and the half-tribe of Manasseh stopped to build a large and imposing altar.

21:36 Hebrew *Jahzah,* a variant spelling of Jahaz. **22:10** Or *to the circle of stones;* similarly in 22:11.

22:1–24:33 Affirmation and Commitment

Up to this point the reader has had to struggle to remember the tribes east of the Jordan, especially Reuben and Gad. Reuben, although the eldest of Jacob's sons by Leah, does not fare well among the tribes. He is recorded in Genesis as having slept with Bilhah, his father's concubine and the mother of his brothers Dan and Naphtali (Gen 35:22). There is throughout the biblical tradition a bias against the eastern tribes of Reuben, Gad, and Manasseh. Reuben and Gad are descended from Leah, the least favored of Jacob's wives, and Manasseh is the tribe from which arises the clan of Zelophehad, who managed to sire five daughters but no sons and thus elicits a crisis of inheritance (Num 27:1–11). The allotment of the tribes reflects a degree of tension between inheritance norms and divine will. Concerning the tribe of Reuben the incest is not explicit, although is forbidden in the Mosaic law (Lev 18:8). Reuben's act of sex with Bilhah then has far-reaching consequences (cf. 1 Chr 5:1–2). **22:10–34:** The tribes of Reuben, Gad, and Manasseh trigger a crisis when they build an altar west of the Jordan; this act is considered treachery by those tribes settled in Canaan. Fearing that this altar will provoke God to punish the entire nation for disloyalty, the rest of the tribes decide to eradicate these members who appear to have forsaken God's com-

[11]The rest of Israel heard that the people of Reuben, Gad, and the half-tribe of Manasseh had built an altar at Geliloth at the edge of the land of Canaan, on the west side of the Jordan River. [12]So the whole community of Israel gathered at Shiloh and prepared to go to war against them. [13]First, however, they sent a delegation led by Phinehas son of Eleazar, the priest, to talk with the tribes of Reuben, Gad, and the half-tribe of Manasseh. [14]In this delegation were ten leaders of Israel, one from each of the ten tribes, and each the head of his family within the clans of Israel.

[15]When they arrived in the land of Gilead, they said to the tribes of Reuben, Gad, and the half-tribe of Manasseh, [16]"The whole community of the LORD demands to know why you are betraying the God of Israel. How could you turn away from the LORD and build an altar for yourselves in rebellion against him? [17]Was our sin at Peor not enough? To this day we are not fully cleansed of it, even after the plague that struck the entire community of the LORD. [18]And yet today you are turning away from following the LORD. If you rebel against the LORD today, he will be angry with all of us tomorrow.

[19]"If you need the altar because the land you possess is defiled, then join us in the LORD's land, where the Tabernacle of the LORD is situated, and share our land with us. But do not rebel against the LORD or against us by building an altar other than the one true altar of the LORD our God. [20]Didn't divine anger fall on the entire community of Israel when Achan, a member of the clan of Zerah, sinned by stealing the things set apart for the LORD*? He was not the only one who died because of his sin."

[21]Then the people of Reuben, Gad, and the half-tribe of Manasseh answered the heads of the clans of Israel: [22]"The LORD, the Mighty One, is God! The LORD, the Mighty One, is God! He knows the truth, and may Israel know it, too! We have not built the altar in treacherous rebellion against the LORD. If we have done so, do not spare our lives this day. [23]If we have built an altar for ourselves to turn away from the LORD or to offer burnt offerings or grain offerings or peace offerings, may the LORD himself punish us.

[24]"The truth is, we have built this altar because we fear that in the future your descendants will say to ours, 'What right do you have to worship the LORD, the God of Israel? [25]The LORD has placed the Jordan River as a barrier between our people and you people of Reuben and Gad. You have no claim to the LORD.' So your descendants may prevent our descendants from worshiping the LORD.

[26]"So we decided to build the altar, not for burnt offerings or sacrifices, [27]but as a memorial. It will remind our descendants and your descendants that we, too, have the right to worship the LORD at his sanctuary with our burnt offerings, sacrifices, and peace offerings. Then your descendants will not be able to say to ours, 'You have no claim to the LORD.'

[28]"If they say this, our descendants can reply, 'Look at this copy of the LORD's altar that our ancestors made. It is not for burnt offerings or sacrifices; it is a reminder of the relationship both of us have with the LORD.' [29]Far be it from us to rebel against the LORD or turn away from him by building our own altar for burnt offerings, grain offerings, or sacrifices. Only the altar of the LORD our God that stands in front of the Tabernacle may be used for that purpose."

[30]When Phinehas the priest and the leaders of the community—the heads of the clans of Israel—heard this from the tribes of Reuben, Gad, and the half-tribe of Manasseh, they were satisfied. [31]Phinehas son of Eleazar, the priest, replied to them, "Today we know the LORD is among us because you have not committed this treachery against the LORD as we thought. Instead, you have rescued Israel from being destroyed by the hand of the LORD."

[32]Then Phinehas son of Eleazar, the priest, and the other leaders left the tribes of Reuben and Gad in Gilead and returned to the land of Canaan to tell the Israelites what had happened. [33]And all the Israelites were satisfied and praised God and spoke no more of war against Reuben and Gad.

22:20 The Hebrew term used here refers to the complete consecration of things or people to the LORD, either by destroying them or by giving them as an offering.

---

mand. The altar is not meant as a second tabernacle, but as a concrete witness to their loyalty to God.

Although the dispute is settled, there is a clear division in Israel between those tribes living west of the Jordan and those who have helped conquer the land but have returned east. This chapter reflects the episode in which Moses balks at promising the land east of the Jordon to Reuben and Gad since he believes their request to settle there signals cowardice (Num 32). The subtext is one of marginalization. The contribution of the tribes of Reuben and Gad to Israel's victory is undercut by the location of their settlement.

34The people of Reuben and Gad named the
altar "Witness,"* for they said, "It is a witness
between us and them that the LORD is our God,
too."

Joshua's Final Words to Israel

23 The years passed, and the LORD had
given the people of Israel rest from all
their enemies. Joshua, who was now
very old, 2called together all the elders, leaders,
judges, and officers of Israel. He said to them, "I
am now a very old man. 3You have seen everything the LORD your God has done for you during my lifetime. The LORD your God has fought
for you against your enemies. 4I have allotted to
you as your homeland all the land of the nations
yet unconquered, as well as the land of those we
have already conquered—from the Jordan River
to the Mediterranean Sea* in the west. 5This
land will be yours, for the LORD your God will
himself drive out all the people living there now.
You will take possession of their land, just as the
LORD your God promised you.

6"So be very careful to follow everything
Moses wrote in the Book of Instruction. Do not
deviate from it, turning either to the right or to
the left. 7Make sure you do not associate with the
other people still remaining in the land. Do not
even mention the names of their gods, much less
swear by them or serve them or worship them.
8Rather, cling tightly to the LORD your God as
you have done until now.

9"For the LORD has driven out great and powerful nations for you, and no one has yet been
able to defeat you. 10Each one of you will put
to flight a thousand of the enemy, for the LORD
your God fights for you, just as he has promised.
11So be very careful to love the LORD your God.

12"But if you turn away from him and cling
to the customs of the survivors of these nations
remaining among you, and if you intermarry with them, 13then know for certain that the
LORD your God will no longer drive them out of
your land. Instead, they will be a snare and a trap
to you, a whip for your backs and thorny brambles in your eyes, and you will vanish from this
good land the LORD your God has given you.

14"Soon I will die, going the way of everything on earth. Deep in your hearts you know
that every promise of the LORD your God has
come true. Not a single one has failed! 15But as
surely as the LORD your God has given you the
good things he promised, he will also bring disaster on you if you disobey him. He will completely destroy you from this good land he has
given you. 16If you break the covenant of the
LORD your God by worshiping and serving other
gods, his anger will burn against you, and you
will quickly vanish from the good land he has
given you."

The LORD's Covenant Renewed

24 Then Joshua summoned all the tribes
of Israel to Shechem, including their
elders, leaders, judges, and officers. So
they came and presented themselves to God.

2Joshua said to the people, "This is what the
LORD, the God of Israel, says: Long ago your ancestors, including Terah, the father of Abraham
and Nahor, lived beyond the Euphrates River,*
and they worshiped other gods. 3But I took your
ancestor Abraham from the land beyond the
Euphrates and led him into the land of Canaan.
I gave him many descendants through his son
Isaac. 4To Isaac I gave Jacob and Esau. To Esau I
gave the mountains of Seir, while Jacob and his
children went down into Egypt.

5"Then I sent Moses and Aaron, and I
brought terrible plagues on Egypt; and afterward I brought you out as a free people. 6But
when your ancestors arrived at the Red Sea,*
the Egyptians chased after you with chariots and
charioteers. 7When your ancestors cried out to
the LORD, I put darkness between you and the
Egyptians. I brought the sea crashing down on
the Egyptians, drowning them. With your very
own eyes you saw what I did. Then you lived in
the wilderness for many years.

8"Finally, I brought you into the land of the
Amorites on the east side of the Jordan. They

22:34 Some manuscripts lack this word. **23:4** Hebrew *the Great Sea.* **24:2** Hebrew *the river;* also in 24:3, 14, 15. **24:6** Hebrew *sea of reeds.*

23:1–16 Joshua's Farewell Speech. Joshua assures the people that God will continue to work against Israel's enemies provided they remain separate from them. **1–2:** *Elders, leaders, judges, and officers of Israel*: It's likely that this audience was all men. **12–13:** That Joshua has to warn them against intermarriage with Canaanites suggests that Israel has not been entirely successful in fulfilling the requirements of Deuteronomy 7:1–3 or in following the policy of *herem*. **14:** Despite Israel's failings, God has kept his promises.

24:1–28: The people of Israel reaffirm the covenant. Although we cannot be certain that women are present at this ceremony, it is likely that they were; all the people of Israel are responsible to keep the covenant requirements (8:35). **1–13:** Joshua reminds the peo-

fought against you, but I destroyed them before you. I gave you victory over them, and you took possession of their land. 9 Then Balak son of Zippor, king of Moab, started a war against Israel. He summoned Balaam son of Beor to curse you, 10 but I would not listen to him. Instead, I made Balaam bless you, and so I rescued you from Balak.

11 "When you crossed the Jordan River and came to Jericho, the men of Jericho fought against you, as did the Amorites, the Perizzites, the Canaanites, the Hittites, the Girgashites, the Hivites, and the Jebusites. But I gave you victory over them. 12 And I sent terror* ahead of you to drive out the two kings of the Amorites. It was not your swords or bows that brought you victory. 13 I gave you land you had not worked on, and I gave you towns you did not build—the towns where you are now living. I gave you vineyards and olive groves for food, though you did not plant them.

14 "So fear the LORD and serve him wholeheartedly. Put away forever the idols your ancestors worshiped when they lived beyond the Euphrates River and in Egypt. Serve the LORD alone. 15 But if you refuse to serve the LORD, then choose today whom you will serve. Would you prefer the gods your ancestors served beyond the Euphrates? Or will it be the gods of the Amorites in whose land you now live? But as for me and my family, we will serve the LORD."

16 The people replied, "We would never abandon the LORD and serve other gods. 17 For the LORD our God is the one who rescued us and our ancestors from slavery in the land of Egypt. He performed mighty miracles before our very eyes. As we traveled through the wilderness among our enemies, he preserved us. 18 It was the LORD who drove out the Amorites and the other nations living here in the land. So we, too, will serve the LORD, for he alone is our God."

19 Then Joshua warned the people, "You are not able to serve the LORD, for he is a holy and jealous God. He will not forgive your rebellion and your sins. 20 If you abandon the LORD and serve other gods, he will turn against you and destroy you, even though he has been so good to you."

21 But the people answered Joshua, "No, we will serve the LORD!"

22 "You are a witness to your own decision," Joshua said. "You have chosen to serve the LORD."

"Yes," they replied, "we are witnesses to what we have said."

23 "All right then," Joshua said, "destroy the idols among you, and turn your hearts to the LORD, the God of Israel."

24 The people said to Joshua, "We will serve the LORD our God. We will obey him alone."

25 So Joshua made a covenant with the people that day at Shechem, committing them to follow the decrees and regulations of the LORD. 26 Joshua recorded these things in the Book of God's Instructions. As a reminder of their agreement, he took a huge stone and rolled it beneath the terebinth tree beside the Tabernacle of the LORD.

27 Joshua said to all the people, "This stone has heard everything the LORD said to us. It will be a witness to testify against you if you go back on your word to God."

28 Then Joshua sent all the people away to their own homelands.

Leaders Buried in the Promised Land

29 After this, Joshua son of Nun, the servant of the LORD, died at the age of 110. 30 They buried him in the land he had been allocated, at Timnath-serah in the hill country of Ephraim, north of Mount Gaash.

31 The people of Israel served the LORD

24:12 Often rendered *the hornet*. The meaning of the Hebrew is uncertain.

---

ple of Israel of everything God has done for them. **14:** The covenant requirements are essentially reduced to one: absolute loyalty to God, who has chosen Israel and guaranteed its survival. **15–28:** The Israelites' promises to faithfully serve God and observe the law are tragically ironic given their subsequent failures in the succeeding books.

Conclusion

Reading Joshua shows that often things are not as simple as they appear. The voices of the disenfranchised or the marginalized make claims and counterclaims that God's leaders and agents need to hear. Caleb heeded his daughter; Joshua and Eleazar heeded the daughters of Zelophehad. But these women had to speak and make themselves heard. How many others have spoken but were not heard? Civil war is narrowly averted only because the elders hear out the eastern tribes when the tribes west of the Jordan zealously denounce the altar constructed as a witness. How often have the claims and practices of others been condemned by those not patient enough to take the time to listen and learn? Rahab at

throughout the lifetime of Joshua and of the elders who outlived him—those who had personally experienced all that the LORD had done for Israel.

32 The bones of Joseph, which the Israelites
had brought along with them when they left
Egypt, were buried at Shechem, in the parcel of
ground Jacob had bought from the sons of Hamor for 100 pieces of silver.* This land was located in the territory allotted to the descendants
of Joseph.
33 Eleazar son of Aaron also died. He was buried in the hill country of Ephraim, in the town of Gibeah, which had been given to his son Phinehas.

24:32 Hebrew *100 kesitahs;* the value or weight of the kesitah is no longer known.

first seemed to be an enemy, but she spoke the truth about God. How often have people been ignored because they are not from the "right" class, profession, race, or gender? Rahab not only rescues the spies but also teaches that not rules or social structures or traditions or even kings or generals or judges are sovereign but God alone.

As Rahab says, "The LORD your God is the supreme God of the heavens above and the earth below" (2:11). This is probably the most important message we should draw from Joshua. God acts mercifully and graciously on behalf of those who acknowledge his sovereignty and enter into covenant relationship with him. Like the rest of the Bible, the book of Joshua lets us know that backing out of the obligations that are part of this privileged relationship has far-reaching consequences. Only then can we be as confident as Rahab that no matter how appalling the situation, God will act on our behalf. God, unlike his human partners, never fails to hear the voice of his people, no matter how marginalized, and he never, ever reneges on his promises.

JUDGES

INTRODUCTION

Read as a connected narrative, Judges could be advertised as a modern blockbuster novel. Read as a disparate collection of heroic sagas from ancient Israel, it is often presented as exciting fodder for youngsters. But Judges is about adults in history, a story not of sanitized heroes in a saga but of assassins, of violent and sadistic women and men. Although they are real, they are at the same time caricatures, for in its pathos and humor as well as its horror, this kind of storytelling is the generic ancestor of modern action or adventure films. The most pressing question is what led the Hebrew people to preserve among their holy books these accounts of their ancestors' immorality, oppression, and violence.

Judges is an overview of the two hundred years between Joshua and Samuel, about 1230 to 1050 BC. The book of Judges has its own literary unity but is also a further episode in the Deuteronomistic History from Exodus to Exile (Deut—2 Kgs) that was shaped by people sharing the same presuppositions about the LORD's purposes for and demands on his people. Most scholars suggest that the original sources were collected and edited into the canonical book of Judges after the Assyrian captivity of the north in 722 BC, around the time of the Exile in Babylon in the sixth century BC. Nuances in the stories may indicate the political and theological uses to which the stories were put during the long years of oral transmission before the book took its present shape: approval of the monarchy (Judg 21:25) and negative views of Ephraim (12:1–6) and Dan (17–18).

This was the age in which Israel made the transition from being a pastoral, nomadic desert people to being a more agricultural, settled organization. The Canaanite peoples were more advanced civilizations, living in city-states, while across the Jordan on Canaan's eastern flank were the peoples of the desert lands of Ammon and Moab. The early hint of the Iron Age is evident in references to the iron chariots and weapons of the Philistine coastal enclave.

These seminomadic people could initially hope only to colonize the less fertile uplands outside of the fortified cities. There was an obvious need for close cooperation and joint action among the twelve related tribes of the children of Israel, even more so as an unprejudiced eye could see that they would be powerless against the superior equipment of their enemies.

In compiling these diverse accounts of the chaotic years between Israel's conquest of Canaan and the establishment of the monarchy, the editors of the book of Judges discovered a recurring pattern that is explained in Judges 2:6–23. This pattern is the key to the main theological message of the book (see The Cycle of Rebellion, next page).

The repetitive cycle of blessing, defeat and slavery, restoration, and renewed conquest is presented as the result of rebellion against the LORD's covenant and person. Life's pattern for God's people was not meant to be a repetitive cycle of failure but a straight path of obedience and order by living in covenant with him according to his revealed law. The text looks forward to the end of anarchy and the coming of true kings who would be faithful to God (21:25).

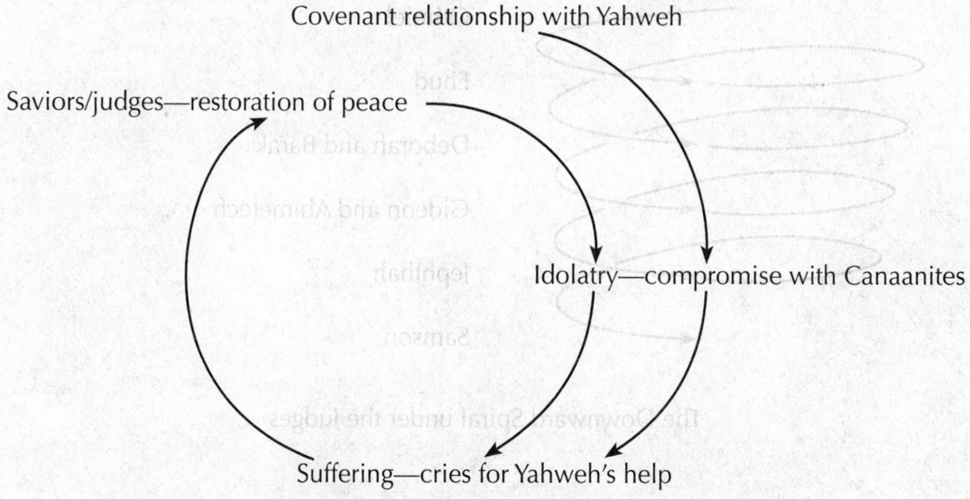

The Cycle of Rebellion, Suffering, and Deliverance

The double story of Gideon and Abimelech is the second key to the book. Here the vicious cycle of repeated failure turns into a downward spiral of accelerating decadence, corruption and defeat in which the judges themselves participate (see The Downward Spiral, next page).

The final chapters (17—21) are an ironic reversal of what was meant by the first entry into Canaan. Victory and displacement are turned against the Israelites; there are no judges and no accepted standards any longer.

Judges is a place for the destruction of an illusory hope in human heroes. The Israelites who had chosen today to follow the LORD in covenant (Josh 24:15, 21) failed to live happily ever after. Here are vivid descriptions of what happens when people fail to keep their part of the promises. Appalling things are done by those purporting to be saviors of God's people, whom we may have been wrongly taught to interpret as types of the Lord Jesus Christ. Yet God is not absent; he uses unexpected, meritless, even dissolute people to display grace in an age of decay. If you want a perfect hero, hear Jephthah: "The LORD . . . is judge" (Judg 11:27).

The excitement of battle stories does not mask the profound moral problem of God's allowing his people to be conquered precisely because they do not implement his genocidal program for the other peoples in Canaan. Yet Judges assumes that readers share the Deuteronomistic view (Deut 9:5) of Canaanite societies: that they were deeply corrupt and that after long patience the LORD intends to judge them through his people. The use of ironic humor to mock powerfully armed opponents beaten by the small, underestimated, and marginalized Israelites signals that this is akin to the cowboy-and-Indian genre of modern storytelling. Narrator and reader stand at a safe distance from the horrors of the historical events. It is not now politically correct to view early United States history in such a way, yet in those lawless days when death and destruction were commonplace, people were much less squeamish than we are. The moral issues are sidelined as far as the worth of Canaanites is concerned (see, however, Judg 18:7, 28), but not for Israelites.

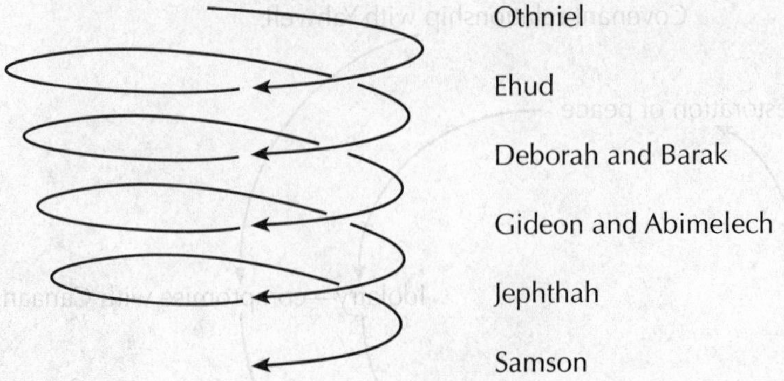

The Downward Spiral under the Judges

The values and culture of a patriarchal tribal society are abhorrent to many modern, Western people. Some modern commentators therefore interpret Judges as exploitative, seeing women as objects of male privilege and programs, used, abused, blamed, and sacrificed. In Judges more than in any other book it is vital to hold to the principle that Scripture is God's Word in all that it affirms. In this light, a study of some female characters shows Yahweh's empowerment as in the case of Deborah (chaps. 4—5), and heroism at the noticeable expense of men (Jael and the woman whose millstone killed Abimelech, 4:11–24; 9:53). Women are comic, stereotypical manipulators in Samson's story (chaps. 14; 16) and stereotypical victims in the last chapters (chaps. 17; 19; 21). In the former, however, we are meant to laugh at Samson, but in the latter we are to shudder at the depths to which the Israelites sink. Even Jephthah's daughter (11:29–40) does not have to be interpreted as the helpless victim of parental egotism and abuse; she is an honored heroine here, as is her father in the view of the writer of Hebrews (Heb 11:32).

Far from being a learned legal figure meting out justice on the basis of God's law, the judge in this book has more affinities with the warlords of China: bandits who ruled and despoiled in times of decayed central government. Each biblical judge, major or minor, differs in function and in action. The judges may be seen as freedom fighters, as terrorists to the opposition, or as charismatic leaders with unusual powers. They are in some sense saviors, and although attention to the geographical references indicates that each operated in a restricted area surrounding his or her tribal position in Canaan, the editors of the book of Judges see them as saving Israel as a whole. By the end of the period, fragmentation and intertribal warfare had replaced the initial attacks on the non-Israelites in the days of Joshua.

After a clear-headed view of the conquest of Canaan, the editors discern in the sagas they have received a recurring pattern of failure. Gideon's ambivalent refusal of kingship and naming of his son Abimelech ("my father, a king") turn the spinning cycle into a downward spiral. These later judges mirror the decay of the LORD's people. In the final reversal the spin is out of control. The Israelites turn the energy and unity needed to face the Canaanites against themselves.—*Ailish F. Eves*

✧

Judah and Simeon Conquer the Land

1 After the death of Joshua, the Israelites asked the LORD, "Which tribe should go first to attack the Canaanites?"

2 The LORD answered, "Judah, for I have given them victory over the land."

3 The men of Judah said to their relatives from the tribe of Simeon, "Join with us to fight against the Canaanites living in the territory allotted to us. Then we will help you conquer your territory." So the men of Simeon went with Judah.

4 When the men of Judah attacked, the LORD gave them victory over the Canaanites and Perizzites, and they killed 10,000 enemy warriors at the town of Bezek. 5 While at Bezek they encountered King Adoni-bezek and fought against him, and the Canaanites and Perizzites were defeated. 6 Adoni-bezek escaped, but the Israelites soon captured him and cut off his thumbs and big toes.

7 Adoni-bezek said, "I once had seventy kings with their thumbs and big toes cut off, eating scraps from under my table. Now God has paid me back for what I did to them." They took him to Jerusalem, and he died there.

8 The men of Judah attacked Jerusalem and captured it, killing all its people and setting the city on fire. 9 Then they went down to fight the Canaanites living in the hill country, the Negev, and the western foothills.* 10 Judah marched against the Canaanites in Hebron (formerly called Kiriath-arba), defeating the forces of Sheshai, Ahiman, and Talmai.

11 From there they went to fight against the people living in the town of Debir (formerly called Kiriath-sepher). 12 Caleb said, "I will give my daughter Acsah in marriage to the one who attacks and captures Kiriath-sepher." 13 Othniel, the son of Caleb's younger brother, Kenaz, was the one who conquered it, so Acsah became Othniel's wife.

14 When Acsah married Othniel, she urged him* to ask her father for a field. As she got down off her donkey, Caleb asked her, "What's the matter?"

15 She said, "Let me have another gift. You have already given me land in the Negev; now please give me springs of water, too." So Caleb gave her the upper and lower springs.

16 When the tribe of Judah left Jericho—the city of palms—the Kenites, who were descendants of Moses' father-in-law, traveled with them into the wilderness of Judah. They settled among the people there, near the town of Arad in the Negev.

17 Then Judah joined with Simeon to fight against the Canaanites living in Zephath, and they completely destroyed* the town. So the town was named Hormah.* 18 In addition, Judah captured the towns of Gaza, Ashkelon, and Ekron, along with their surrounding territories.

Israel Fails to Conquer the Land

19 The LORD was with the people of Judah, and they took possession of the hill country. But they

1:9 Hebrew *the Shephelah*. **1:14** Greek version and Latin Vulgate read *he urged her*. **1:17a** The Hebrew term used here refers to the complete consecration of things or people to the LORD, either by destroying them or by giving them as an offering. **1:17b** *Hormah* means "destruction."

1:1–2:5 Forward with the LORD: An Alternative View of the Conquest

The book of Joshua leaves the impression of total victory and total commitment to the LORD and his covenant. The realities of the situation were to be otherwise. **1:1–26:** The first wave into the south of Canaan, killing tyrants and razing cities, was in consciousness of God's inspiration. There is brotherly unity with Simeon and the exemplars of Caleb's family, including Othniel, later perhaps to function as a model judge (3:7–11). **14–15:** Caleb's daughter epitomizes the adventurous and committed spirit that was her father's legacy. She prefigures the positive leadership and examples of faith given by Deborah and Samson's mother. **17–20:** The Israelites succeeded broadly in the south, but there are hints of trouble. The prior inhabitants' superior weaponry (iron char-

failed to drive out the people living in the plains, who had iron chariots. [20]The town of Hebron was given to Caleb as Moses had promised. And Caleb drove out the people living there, who were descendants of the three sons of Anak.

[21]The tribe of Benjamin, however, failed to drive out the Jebusites, who were living in Jerusalem. So to this day the Jebusites live in Jerusalem among the people of Benjamin.

[22]The descendants of Joseph attacked the town of Bethel, and the LORD was with them. [23]They sent men to scout out Bethel (formerly known as Luz). [24]They confronted a man coming out of the town and said to him, "Show us a way into the town, and we will have mercy on you." [25]So he showed them a way in, and they killed everyone in the town except that man and his family. [26]Later the man moved to the land of the Hittites, where he built a town. He named it Luz, which is its name to this day.

[27]The tribe of Manasseh failed to drive out the people living in Beth-shan,* Taanach, Dor, Ibleam, Megiddo, and all their surrounding settlements, because the Canaanites were determined to stay in that region. [28]When the Israelites grew stronger, they forced the Canaanites to work as slaves, but they never did drive them completely out of the land.

[29]The tribe of Ephraim failed to drive out the Canaanites living in Gezer, so the Canaanites continued to live there among them.

[30]The tribe of Zebulun failed to drive out the residents of Kitron and Nahalol, so the Canaanites continued to live among them. But the Canaanites were forced to work as slaves for the people of Zebulun.

[31]The tribe of Asher failed to drive out the residents of Acco, Sidon, Ahlab, Aczib, Helbah, Aphik, and Rehob. [32]Instead, the people of Asher moved in among the Canaanites, who controlled the land, for they failed to drive them out.

[33]Likewise, the tribe of Naphtali failed to drive out the residents of Beth-shemesh and Beth-anath. Instead, they moved in among the Canaanites, who controlled the land. Nevertheless, the people of Beth-shemesh and Beth-anath were forced to work as slaves for the people of Naphtali.

[34]As for the tribe of Dan, the Amorites forced them back into the hill country and would not let them come down into the plains. [35]The Amorites were determined to stay in Mount Heres, Aijalon, and Shaalbim, but when the descendants of Joseph became stronger, they forced the Amorites to work as slaves. [36]The boundary of the Amorites ran from Scorpion Pass* to Sela and continued upward from there.

The LORD's Messenger Comes to Bokim

2 The angel of the LORD went up from Gilgal to Bokim and said to the Israelites, "I brought you out of Egypt into this land that I swore to give your ancestors, and I said I would never break my covenant with you. [2]For your part, you were not to make any covenants with the people living in this land; instead, you were to destroy their altars. But you disobeyed my command. Why did you do this? [3]So now I declare that I will no longer drive out the people living in your land. They will be thorns in your sides,* and their gods will be a constant temptation to you."

[4]When the angel of the LORD finished speaking to all the Israelites, the people wept loudly. [5]So they called the place Bokim (which means "weeping"), and they offered sacrifices there to the LORD.

The Death of Joshua

[6]After Joshua sent the people away, each of the tribes left to take possession of the land allot-

1:27 Hebrew *Beth-shean,* a variant spelling of Beth-shan. **1:36** Hebrew *Akrabbim.* **2:3** Hebrew *They will be in your sides;* compare Num 33:55.

---

iots) is given as a reason for the Israelites' failure to completely conquer the area. **27–33:** The northern wave of the conquest is characterized by a refrain of failure. The phrase *failed to* suggests compromise with the local inhabitants that is ominous to readers conscious of the LORD's command for the Israelites to be separate as the people of God (Deut 29). **2:1–5:** The first appearance of an angel (cf. Judg. 6:11; 13:3) gives God's perspective. The people failed because they did not listen to God's voice, accepting his commands and obeying him. He is therefore no longer prepared to help them. They mourn but do not appear to repent.

2:6—3:6 The Cycle of Judges

At some point in the transmission and compilation of these tales, a pattern seemed to emerge that ensured their preservation and gave them a permanent theological value. When Israel falters, God provides a leader to bring the people back to the proper path—even if that leader is less than perfect. **2:6–10:** Although Joshua's generation served the LORD, there is an implied criticism. This generation believed only because they had witnessed the LORD's actions, and the Deuteronomic ideal of parents teaching their children the things that the LORD had done for Israel was not fulfilled (Deut

ted to them. 7 And the Israelites served the LORD
throughout the lifetime of Joshua and the leaders who outlived him—those who had seen all
the great things the LORD had done for Israel.
8 Joshua son of Nun, the servant of the LORD,
died at the age of 110. 9 They buried him in the
land he had been allocated, at Timnath-serah*
in the hill country of Ephraim, north of Mount
Gaash.

Israel Disobeys the LORD

10 After that generation died, another generation
grew up who did not acknowledge the LORD or
remember the mighty things he had done for
Israel.
11 The Israelites did evil in the LORD's sight
and served the images of Baal. 12 They abandoned
the LORD, the God of their ancestors, who had
brought them out of Egypt. They went after other gods, worshiping the gods of the people around
them. And they angered the LORD. 13 They abandoned the LORD to serve Baal and the images
of Ashtoreth. 14 This made the LORD burn with
anger against Israel, so he handed them over to
raiders who stole their possessions. He turned
them over to their enemies all around, and they
were no longer able to resist them. 15 Every time
Israel went out to battle, the LORD fought against
them, causing them to be defeated, just as he had
warned. And the people were in great distress.

The LORD Rescues His People

16 Then the LORD raised up judges to rescue the
Israelites from their attackers. 17 Yet Israel did not
listen to the judges but prostituted themselves by
worshiping other gods. How quickly they turned
away from the path of their ancestors, who had
walked in obedience to the LORD's commands.
18 Whenever the LORD raised up a judge
over Israel, he was with that judge and rescued
the people from their enemies throughout the
judge's lifetime. For the LORD took pity on his
people, who were burdened by oppression and
suffering. 19 But when the judge died, the people
returned to their corrupt ways, behaving worse
than those who had lived before them. They
went after other gods, serving and worshiping
them. And they refused to give up their evil
practices and stubborn ways.
20 So the LORD burned with anger against Israel. He said, "Because these people have violated
my covenant, which I made with their ancestors,
and have ignored my commands, 21 I will no longer drive out the nations that Joshua left unconquered when he died. 22 I did this to test Israel—
to see whether or not they would follow the
ways of the LORD as their ancestors did." 23 That
is why the LORD left those nations in place. He
did not quickly drive them out or allow Joshua to
conquer them all.

The Nations Left in Canaan

3 These are the nations that the LORD left
in the land to test those Israelites who had
not experienced the wars of Canaan. 2 He
did this to teach warfare to generations of Israelites who had no experience in battle. 3 These are
the nations: the Philistines (those living under
the five Philistine rulers), all the Canaanites, the
Sidonians, and the Hivites living in the mountains of Lebanon from Mount Baal-hermon to
Lebo-hamath. 4 These people were left to test the
Israelites—to see whether they would obey the
commands the LORD had given to their ancestors
through Moses.
5 So the people of Israel lived among the Canaanites, Hittites, Amorites, Perizzites, Hivites,
and Jebusites, 6 and they intermarried with them.
Israelite sons married their daughters, and Israelite daughters were given in marriage to their
sons. And the Israelites served their gods.

2:9 As in parallel text at Josh 24:30; Hebrew reads *Timnath-heres,* a variant spelling of Timnath-serah.

6:4–9). **11–15:** The ways and gods of the Canaanites are found to be much more attractive than commitment to the LORD. Political as well as spiritual slavery to the pagans follows, sometimes for many years. **16–19:** The theme of the next several chapters: The people's distress and sometimes their prayers (3:15) move the LORD to send a judge to be a savior, guide, or warrior for them. All is renewed; Israel is back at peace and in tenuous relationship with God. The cycle never stops. It is not an arabesque on the horizontal plane but a spiral spinning downward to disintegration.

3:1–6: Testing and Training. Various reasons are given for the tribes' failure to take the land: inferior territory and weaponry (1:19), disobedience (2:13–14), ignorance of the LORD and his power (2:10–11) and a rooted preference for Canaanite culture and religion (2:17–19; 3:6). There are indications, perhaps conflicting ones, that suggest that God is still fulfilling a purpose: to punish (2:3), to test obedience (2:22–23), or to train Israel in warfare (3:2). These may be explanations storytellers offered as they told the sagas to later generations, searching for theological answers and applications to diverse situations and audiences. Facts and experience in human history may not be explicable in only one way.

Othniel Becomes Israel's Judge
7 The Israelites did evil in the LORD's sight. They
forgot about the LORD their God, and they served
the images of Baal and the Asherah poles. 8 Then
the LORD burned with anger against Israel, and
he turned them over to King Cushan-rishathaim
of Aram-naharaim.* And the Israelites served
Cushan-rishathaim for eight years.
9 But when the people of Israel cried out to the
LORD for help, the LORD raised up a rescuer to save
them. His name was Othniel, the son of Caleb's
younger brother, Kenaz. 10 The Spirit of the LORD
came upon him, and he became Israel's judge. He
went to war against King Cushan-rishathaim of
Aram, and the LORD gave Othniel victory over
him. 11 So there was peace in the land for forty
years. Then Othniel son of Kenaz died.

Ehud Becomes Israel's Judge
12 Once again the Israelites did evil in the LORD's
sight, and the LORD gave King Eglon of Moab
control over Israel because of their evil. 13 Eglon
enlisted the Ammonites and Amalekites as allies,
and then he went out and defeated Israel, taking possession of Jericho, the city of palms. 14 And
the Israelites served Eglon of Moab for eighteen
years.
15 But when the people of Israel cried out to
the LORD for help, the LORD again raised up a
rescuer to save them. His name was Ehud son of
Gera, a left-handed man of the tribe of Benjamin.
The Israelites sent Ehud to deliver their tribute
money to King Eglon of Moab. 16 So Ehud made a
double-edged dagger that was about a foot* long,
and he strapped it to his right thigh, keeping it
hidden under his clothing. 17 He brought the tribute money to Eglon, who was very fat.
18 After delivering the payment, Ehud started
home with those who had helped carry the tribute. 19 But when Ehud reached the stone idols
near Gilgal, he turned back. He came to Eglon
and said, "I have a secret message for you."
So the king commanded his servants, "Be
quiet!" and he sent them all out of the room.
20 Ehud walked over to Eglon, who was sitting
alone in a cool upstairs room. And Ehud said, "I
have a message from God for you!" As King Eglon rose from his seat, 21 Ehud reached with his
left hand, pulled out the dagger strapped to his
right thigh, and plunged it into the king's belly.
22 The dagger went so deep that the handle disappeared beneath the king's fat. So Ehud did not
pull out the dagger, and the king's bowels emptied.* 23 Then Ehud closed and locked the doors of
the room and escaped down the latrine.*
24 After Ehud was gone, the king's servants returned and found the doors to the upstairs room
locked. They thought he might be using the latrine in the room, 25 so they waited. But when
the king didn't come out after a long delay, they
became concerned and got a key. And when they
opened the doors, they found their master dead
on the floor.
26 While the servants were waiting, Ehud
escaped, passing the stone idols on his way to
Seirah. 27 When he arrived in the hill country of
Ephraim, Ehud sounded a call to arms. Then he
led a band of Israelites down from the hills.

3:8 *Aram-naharaim* means "Aram of the two rivers," thought to have been located between the Euphrates and Balih Rivers in northwestern Mesopotamia. **3:16** Hebrew *gomed,* the length of which is uncertain. **3:22** Or *and it came out behind.* **3:23** Or *and went out through the porch;* the meaning of the Hebrew is uncertain.

3:7–5:31 Unexpected Heroes

3:7–11 Othniel, a Paradigm. The first specific example of the cycle of events set up in 2:16–19. **9:** Othniel, the first judge, was introduced in 1:15. **10–11:** Othniel wins freedom from Edom, which lasts for the ideal symbolic period of forty years. Othniel's character is unknown to us, but he is a paradigm judge because his experience follows the cycle shown in the previous verses.

3:12–30 Ehud, an Assassin. Ehud is a deceiver and an assassin, yet the text indicates that he is a hero. Distanced from the gruesome realities, told and retold in Israel through the passing years, Ehud's tale becomes a basis for laughter at the enemy's expense. The most unlikely and inadequate of people, it tells us, can defeat the bloated oppressor. **15:** Irony begins the tale. Left-handed Ehud is a man of Benjamin, which means "son of my right hand." People of the Near East always use the right hand; the left is the less honorable hand used for toilet purposes. A child with a tendency to left-handedness would be disciplined out of it. The Hebrew reads "a disability in the right hand." **16:** His disability (or his left-handedness) inspires Ehud and enables him to secrete a blade under his garment on the right side, where anyone who frisks him will not suspect a weapon. **20:** Irony turns to bitter humor at the enemy's expense when Ehud announces to the king, *"I have a message from God for you!"* **26–30:** It is not necessary to presuppose that God approved of Ehud's strategy, but he makes use of it, turning it to a good purpose. This does not remove the moral problem but alerts us to the danger of wanting life's decisions to be wrapped in plastic, free of blood and guts, and devoid of reality.

28 "Follow me," he said, "for the LORD has giv-
en you victory over Moab your enemy." So they
followed him. And the Israelites took control of
the shallow crossings of the Jordan River across
from Moab, preventing anyone from crossing.
29 They attacked the Moabites and killed about
10,000 of their strongest and most able-bodied
warriors. Not one of them escaped. 30 So Moab
was conquered by Israel that day, and there was
peace in the land for eighty years.

Shamgar Becomes Israel's Judge
31 After Ehud, Shamgar son of Anath rescued Israel. He once killed 600 Philistines with an ox goad.

Deborah Becomes Israel's Judge
4 After Ehud's death, the Israelites again
did evil in the LORD's sight. 2 So the LORD
turned them over to King Jabin of Hazor,
a Canaanite king. The commander of his army
was Sisera, who lived in Harosheth-haggoyim.
3 Sisera, who had 900 iron chariots, ruthlessly oppressed the Israelites for twenty years. Then the
people of Israel cried out to the LORD for help.
4 Deborah, the wife of Lappidoth, was a
prophet who was judging Israel at that time.
5 She would sit under the Palm of Deborah, between Ramah and Bethel in the hill country
of Ephraim, and the Israelites would go to her
for judgment. 6 One day she sent for Barak son
of Abinoam, who lived in Kedesh in the land
of Naphtali. She said to him, "This is what the
LORD, the God of Israel, commands you: Call
out 10,000 warriors from the tribes of Naphtali
and Zebulun at Mount Tabor. 7 And I will call out
Sisera, commander of Jabin's army, along with
his chariots and warriors, to the Kishon River.
There I will give you victory over him."
8 Barak told her, "I will go, but only if you go
with me."
9 "Very well," she replied, "I will go with you.
But you will receive no honor in this venture,
for the LORD's victory over Sisera will be at the
hands of a woman." So Deborah went with Barak to Kedesh. 10 At Kedesh, Barak called together
the tribes of Zebulun and Naphtali, and 10,000
warriors went up with him. Deborah also went
with him.
11 Now Heber the Kenite, a descendant of Moses' brother-in-law* Hobab, had moved away
from the other members of his tribe and pitched
his tent by the oak of Zaanannim near Kedesh.
12 When Sisera was told that Barak son of
Abinoam had gone up to Mount Tabor, 13 he
called for all 900 of his iron chariots and all of
his warriors, and they marched from Harosheth-
haggoyim to the Kishon River.
14 Then Deborah said to Barak, "Get ready!
This is the day the LORD will give you victory
over Sisera, for the LORD is marching ahead of
you." So Barak led his 10,000 warriors down the
slopes of Mount Tabor into battle. 15 When Barak
attacked, the LORD threw Sisera and all his chariots and warriors into a panic. Sisera leaped down
from his chariot and escaped on foot. 16 Then Barak chased the chariots and the enemy army all

4:11 Or *father-in-law.*

3:31 Shamgar. This account bears a resemblance to the Samson story in chapter 15. This verse may be a remnant of an incomplete editing process throughout the centuries.

4:1—5:31 Deborah. Israel is a terrorized and oppressed people living in the hills (see 5:6–8). This saga is full of incongruous contrasts. On one side is the overwhelming twenty-year-long military superiority of the Canaanites and their iron-furbished chariotry (4:1–2) based at Hazor, north of the Sea of Galilee. On the other side is Israel, whose "strengths" are a woman prophet, a spineless army commander, and whole tribes that prefer not to get involved (see 5:15–18). Only God can bring victory in that situation, and his main agents are women.

4:1–24 Defeat of Sisera. 4–5: The text takes Deborah's status and responsibilities in Israel for granted. Her standing in society is a secure and accepted one as a prophet through whom God speaks. She is unique in this book in combining roles of prophet and judge. **6–8:** An initiator and a consultant prophet, Deborah passes on God's orders to Barak, who, whatever their relative ages, responds much like a son. Barak, not Deborah, is the unexpected instrument, who triggers the emergency situation by his childlike overdependence on Deborah and implied lack of trust in God. **9:** The incongruity of God's working arises when Deborah has to step out of conventional societal roles, including that of prophetic instruction, to accompany the commander to the battlefield. Then the victor's glory, normally that of the soldier, always male, will go to a woman, whom we expect to be Deborah. **11:** The nomadic Kenites were Midianite in origin; their political alliances are ambivalent at best. It was in their best interest to maintain their role as the blacksmiths (Kenite means "smith") for the Jabinite cavalry. **12–16:** In the main battle the LORD intervenes in some as yet unexplained way as Barak and Deborah take his troops down from Mount Tabor to the Kishon Valley. The Song of Deborah implies an unexpected

the way to Harosheth-haggoyim, killing all of
Sisera's warriors. Not a single one was left alive.
17 Meanwhile, Sisera ran to the tent of Jael,
the wife of Heber the Kenite, because Heber's
family was on friendly terms with King Jabin of
Hazor. 18 Jael went out to meet Sisera and said to
him, "Come into my tent, sir. Come in. Don't be
afraid." So he went into her tent, and she covered
him with a blanket.
19 "Please give me some water," he said. "I'm
thirsty." So she gave him some milk from a
leather bag and covered him again.
20 "Stand at the door of the tent," he told her.
"If anybody comes and asks you if there is anyone here, say no."
21 But when Sisera fell asleep from exhaustion, Jael quietly crept up to him with a hammer
and tent peg in her hand. Then she drove the tent
peg through his temple and into the ground, and
so he died.
22 When Barak came looking for Sisera, Jael
went out to meet him. She said, "Come, and I will
show you the man you are looking for." So he
followed her into the tent and found Sisera lying
there dead, with the tent peg through his temple.
23 So on that day Israel saw God defeat Jabin,
the Canaanite king. 24 And from that time on Israel became stronger and stronger against King
Jabin until they finally destroyed him.

The Song of Deborah

5 On that day Deborah and Barak son of Abinoam sang this song:

2 "Israel's leaders took charge,
and the people gladly followed.
Praise the LORD!

3 "Listen, you kings!
Pay attention, you mighty rulers!
For I will sing to the LORD.
I will make music to the LORD, the God of Israel.

4 "LORD, when you set out from Seir
and marched across the fields of Edom,
the earth trembled,
and the cloudy skies poured down rain.
5 The mountains quaked in the presence of the LORD,
the God of Mount Sinai—
in the presence of the LORD,
the God of Israel.

6 "In the days of Shamgar son of Anath,
and in the days of Jael,
people avoided the main roads,
and travelers stayed on winding pathways.
7 There were few people left in the villages of Israel*—
until Deborah arose as a mother for Israel.
8 When Israel chose new gods,
war erupted at the city gates.
Yet not a shield or spear could be seen
among forty thousand warriors in Israel!
9 My heart is with the commanders of Israel,
with those who volunteered for war.
Praise the LORD!

10 "Consider this, you who ride on fine donkeys,
you who sit on fancy saddle blankets,
and you who walk along the road.
11 Listen to the village musicians*
gathered at the watering holes.
They recount the righteous victories of the LORD
and the victories of his villagers in Israel.

5:7 The meaning of the Hebrew is uncertain. **5:11** The meaning of the Hebrew is uncertain.

---

storm on the plain of Jezreel (5:4–5, 20–21). **18–19:** Jael acts as Sisera—and indeed any other Near Eastern person—would expect from a female, a nomad, and the wife of Heber the nonaligned Kenite. She is kind, hospitable, consoling, and motherly, while even in Sisera's extremity he acts as the dominant male to a woman alone and defenseless. **21:** Tent-pitching was women's work, and Jael knew well how to use the stone tent peg and hammer. A defenseless, statusless, weaponless female becomes the victor over the erstwhile commander of *900 iron chariots*. This sadistic murder of a defenseless man is heightened in effect by the incongruity of a woman acting with such savagery. **22:** The implication of the text is that the failure of the male leader to accomplish his normal task has forced women to step across contemporary Israelite role boundaries and fulfill the divine purpose.

5:1–31 The Song of Deborah. This is in the genre of a triumph song, which emphasizes the triumph of the LORD. **4–5:** There appears to have been a sudden, overwhelming cloudburst that flooded the Kishon Valley and bogged the chariots in mud. The song celebrates the bloodthirsty enjoyment of the oppressors getting their just deserts: shattered bone, smashed brain matter, and spilled blood. **6, 7, 24–27, 28–30:** Three women gain mention: Deborah, Jael, and Sisera's waiting mother (a foil to triumphant Deborah and Jael). Deborah's leadership is celebrated alongside those who willingly responded to the battle call. **15–18:** There is

Women as Psalmists

The Bible is clear that women sang at public events, either in celebration or lament. Often the songs that women sing in the Bible are related to Israel's victory in struggles against an enemy. One such example is the Song of Miriam (Exod 15:20–21). Deborah, a female prophet, praises God in song (Judg 5), calling on kings and princes to listen (Judg 5:3). David's defeat of the Philistines finds women singing and celebrating (1 Sam 18:6–9). Notably, since it is uncharacteristic of the songs that women sing in the Bible, the praise is not of God but of the human warriors.

The most compelling accounts of women as psalmists perhaps are those songs from the lips of women addressing God's response to their individual situations and dilemmas. Hannah, barren for so long and subject to the taunts of her co-wife, Peninnah, praises God when she finally conceives Samuel (1 Sam 2:1–10). In the New Testament, Mary sings a psalm of praise when Elizabeth blesses her pregnancy (Luke 1:41–55). In both cases the women are not only recipients of God's grace but also proclaimers of it. Both Hannah and Mary look beyond the limits of their particular situations to remind all of us that God looks with grace and mercy on the marginalized. Conversely, they warn us of his judgment on the proud and the arrogant. In this, like those of Miriam and Deborah, their songs are prophetic in nature. See the Relevance of Psalms for the Everyday Lives of Women, Psalm 2.

Whether it is the defeat of an enemy or the birth of a baby, all these women, in their capacity as psalmists, prompt us to remember that nothing falls outside the purview of God.

Then the people of the LORD
marched down to the city gates.
12 "Wake up, Deborah, wake up!
Wake up, wake up, and sing a song!
Arise, Barak!
Lead your captives away, son of Abinoam!
13 "Down from Tabor marched the few against
the nobles.
The people of the LORD marched down
against mighty warriors.
14 They came down from Ephraim—
a land that once belonged to the Amalekites;
they followed you, Benjamin, with your
troops.
From Makir the commanders marched down;
from Zebulun came those who carry a
commander's staff.
15 The princes of Issachar were with Deborah
and Barak.
They followed Barak, rushing into the
valley.
But in the tribe of Reuben
there was great indecision.
16 Why did you sit at home among the
sheepfolds—
to hear the shepherds whistle for their
flocks?
Yes, in the tribe of Reuben
there was great indecision.
17 Gilead remained east of the Jordan.
And why did Dan stay home?
Asher sat unmoved at the seashore,
remaining in his harbors.
18 But Zebulun risked his life,
as did Naphtali, on the heights of the
battlefield.

19 "The kings of Canaan came and fought,
at Taanach near Megiddo's springs,
but they carried off no silver treasures.
20 The stars fought from heaven.
The stars in their orbits fought against
Sisera.
21 The Kishon River swept them away—
that ancient torrent, the Kishon.
March on with courage, my soul!
22 Then the horses' hooves hammered the
ground,
the galloping, galloping of Sisera's mighty
steeds.
23 'Let the people of Meroz be cursed,' said the
angel of the LORD.
'Let them be utterly cursed,
because they did not come to help the LORD—
to help the LORD against the mighty
warriors.'

sorrowful mention of the reluctance, neutrality, non-involvement or appeasement policy of the northern tribes, including Naphtali, of whom Barak was not the only fearful and reluctant warrior. He is here only by implication in the song. Tribes in the north were obviously in more danger and were perhaps less free and more endangered by a call emanating from Ephraim, but Israelite disunity is to be noted.

24 "Most blessed among women is Jael,
the wife of Heber the Kenite.
May she be blessed above all women who
live in tents.
25 Sisera asked for water,
and she gave him milk.
In a bowl fit for nobles,
she brought him yogurt.
26 Then with her left hand she reached for a tent
peg,
and with her right hand for the workman's
hammer.
She struck Sisera with the hammer, crushing
his head.
With a shattering blow, she pierced his
temples.
27 He sank, he fell,
he lay still at her feet.
And where he sank,
there he died.

28 "From the window Sisera's mother looked out.
Through the window she watched for his
return, saying,
'Why is his chariot so long in coming?
Why don't we hear the sound of chariot
wheels?'

29 "Her wise women answer,
and she repeats these words to herself:
30 'They must be dividing the captured
plunder—
with a woman or two for every man.
There will be colorful robes for Sisera,
and colorful, embroidered robes for me.
Yes, the plunder will include
colorful robes embroidered on both sides.'

31 "LORD, may all your enemies die like Sisera!
But may those who love you rise like the
sun in all its power!"

Then there was peace in the land for forty years.

Gideon Becomes Israel's Judge

6 The Israelites did evil in the LORD's sight.
So the LORD handed them over to the
Midianites for seven years. 2 The Midianites were so cruel that the Israelites made
hiding places for themselves in the mountains,
caves, and strongholds. 3 Whenever the Israelites planted their crops, marauders from Midian,
Amalek, and the people of the east would attack
Israel, 4 camping in the land and destroying crops
as far away as Gaza. They left the Israelites with
nothing to eat, taking all the sheep, goats, cattle,
and donkeys. 5 These enemy hordes, coming with
their livestock and tents, were as thick as locusts;
they arrived on droves of camels too numerous
to count. And they stayed until the land was
stripped bare. 6 So Israel was reduced to starvation by the Midianites. Then the Israelites cried
out to the LORD for help.
7 When they cried out to the LORD because of
Midian, 8 the LORD sent a prophet to the Israelites. He said, "This is what the LORD, the God
of Israel, says: I brought you up out of slavery
in Egypt. 9 I rescued you from the Egyptians and
from all who oppressed you. I drove out your
enemies and gave you their land. 10 I told you, 'I
am the LORD your God. You must not worship
the gods of the Amorites, in whose land you now
live.' But you have not listened to me."
11 Then the angel of the LORD came and sat
beneath the great tree at Ophrah, which belonged to Joash of the clan of Abiezer. Gideon
son of Joash was threshing wheat at the bottom
of a winepress to hide the grain from the Midianites. 12 The angel of the LORD appeared to him
and said, "Mighty hero, the LORD is with you!"
13 "Sir," Gideon replied, "if the LORD is with
us, why has all this happened to us? And where
are all the miracles our ancestors told us about?
Didn't they say, 'The LORD brought us up out of
Egypt'? But now the LORD has abandoned us and
handed us over to the Midianites."
14 Then the LORD turned to him and said, "Go

6:1—9:57 Monarchy: Yes or No?

6:1—8:32 Gideon, the Doubtful Leader. Gideon is a decidedly ambivalent figure, a doubtful and doubtfull role model. He is perhaps braver than Barak, but the incidents of his life—the call, the fleeces, and the battle—need to be interpreted in the light of the outcome. He descends from the confession *the LORD is peace* (6:24) to idol worship (8:27–33). Gideon is a man struggling and overcoming his doubts, but we see a person who never gets as far as wholehearted commitment to the LORD. **6:1–5:** The devastation and famine created by the locustlike, periodic depredations of the nomadic Bedouin Midianites and other peoples from beyond the Jordan is worse than any so far. **7:** An unnamed prophet, not a judge, is God's first response to their desperation. **8–10:** This passage is a summary of the covenant between the LORD and the Israelites (Josh 24). Before more can be done, they and the reader need to be reminded of their disobedience. **11–16:** Gideon's call. There is a strong vein of irony here. A man hiding from the Midianites is addressed as *mighty hero* and is told to *"Go with the strength you have"* to deliver Israel when he has

with the strength you have, and rescue Israel
from the Midianites. I am sending you!"
15 "But Lord," Gideon replied, "how can I rescue Israel? My clan is the weakest in the whole
tribe of Manasseh, and I am the least in my entire family!"
16 The LORD said to him, "I will be with you.
And you will destroy the Midianites as if you
were fighting against one man."
17 Gideon replied, "If you are truly going to
help me, show me a sign to prove that it is really
the LORD speaking to me. 18 Don't go away until I
come back and bring my offering to you."
He answered, "I will stay here until you return."
19 Gideon hurried home. He cooked a young
goat, and with a basket* of flour he baked some
bread without yeast. Then, carrying the meat in
a basket and the broth in a pot, he brought them
out and presented them to the angel, who was
under the great tree.
20 The angel of God said to him, "Place the
meat and the unleavened bread on this rock, and
pour the broth over it." And Gideon did as he
was told. 21 Then the angel of the LORD touched
the meat and bread with the tip of the staff in
his hand, and fire flamed up from the rock and
consumed all he had brought. And the angel of
the LORD disappeared.
22 When Gideon realized that it was the angel
of the LORD, he cried out, "Oh, Sovereign LORD,
I'm doomed! I have seen the angel of the LORD
face to face!"
23 "It is all right," the LORD replied. "Do not
be afraid. You will not die." 24 And Gideon built
an altar to the LORD there and named it Yahweh-
Shalom (which means "the LORD is peace"). The
altar remains in Ophrah in the land of the clan of
Abiezer to this day.
25 That night the LORD said to Gideon, "Take
the second bull from your father's herd, the one
that is seven years old. Pull down your father's
altar to Baal, and cut down the Asherah pole
standing beside it. 26 Then build an altar to the
LORD your God here on this hilltop sanctuary,
laying the stones carefully. Sacrifice the bull as
a burnt offering on the altar, using as fuel the
wood of the Asherah pole you cut down."
27 So Gideon took ten of his servants and did
as the LORD had commanded. But he did it at
night because he was afraid of the other members of his father's household and the people of
the town.
28 Early the next morning, as the people of the
town began to stir, someone discovered that the
altar of Baal had been broken down and that
the Asherah pole beside it had been cut down. In
their place a new altar had been built, and on it
were the remains of the bull that had been sacrificed. 29 The people said to each other, "Who did
this?" And after asking around and making a careful search, they learned that it was Gideon, the
son of Joash.
30 "Bring out your son," the men of the town
demanded of Joash. "He must die for destroying
the altar of Baal and for cutting down the Asherah pole."
31 But Joash shouted to the mob that confronted him, "Why are you defending Baal? Will you
argue his case? Whoever pleads his case will be
put to death by morning! If Baal truly is a god,
let him defend himself and destroy the one who
broke down his altar!" 32 From then on Gideon
was called Jerub-baal, which means "Let Baal
defend himself," because he broke down Baal's
altar.

Gideon Asks for a Sign

33 Soon afterward the armies of Midian, Amalek,
and the people of the east formed an alliance
against Israel and crossed the Jordan, camping
in the valley of Jezreel. 34 Then the Spirit of the
LORD took possession of Gideon. He blew a ram's
horn as a call to arms, and the men of the clan
of Abiezer came to him. 35 He also sent messengers throughout Manasseh, Asher, Zebulun, and
Naphtali, summoning their warriors, and all of
them responded.
36 Then Gideon said to God, "If you are truly
going to use me to rescue Israel as you promised,

6:19 Hebrew *an ephah* [20 quarts or 22 liters].

---

a mind full of doubts. But God has chosen this man and intends to empower him. **17–23:** The LORD is incredibly patient and willing to give sign after sign to stiffen the resolve and confirm the faith of this judge. **25–31:** Gideon's family is not the most faithful. His father sponsors the altar to Baal that Gideon is ordered to destroy. Joash's reaction to the villagers' outrage indicates a level of noncommitment to either Baal or the LORD that may have been typical of the time. **32:** Gideon's alternative name, Jerub-baal, derives from this incident. He is in opposition to Baal, but still he bears Baal's name. The name symbolizes his semidetached, compromised state of mind. **36–40:** Doubts set in again. This is very human, but a rooted propensity to doubt is not driven out by the Spirit or easily overcome by signs and wonders. The LORD is both gracious and patient in giving the signs, and yet he is not at the beck and call of Gideon.

37 prove it to me in this way. I will put a wool fleece on the threshing floor tonight. If the fleece is wet with dew in the morning but the ground is dry, then I will know that you are going to help me rescue Israel as you promised." 38 And that is just what happened. When Gideon got up early the next morning, he squeezed the fleece and wrung out a whole bowlful of water.

39 Then Gideon said to God, "Please don't be angry with me, but let me make one more request. Let me use the fleece for one more test. This time let the fleece remain dry while the ground around it is wet with dew." 40 So that night God did as Gideon asked. The fleece was dry in the morning, but the ground was covered with dew.

Gideon Defeats the Midianites

7 So Jerub-baal (that is, Gideon) and his army got up early and went as far as the spring of Harod. The armies of Midian were camped north of them in the valley near the hill of Moreh. 2 The LORD said to Gideon, "You have too many warriors with you. If I let all of you fight the Midianites, the Israelites will boast to me that they saved themselves by their own strength. 3 Therefore, tell the people, 'Whoever is timid or afraid may leave this mountain* and go home.' " So 22,000 of them went home, leaving only 10,000 who were willing to fight.

4 But the LORD told Gideon, "There are still too many! Bring them down to the spring, and I will test them to determine who will go with you and who will not." 5 When Gideon took his warriors down to the water, the LORD told him, "Divide the men into two groups. In one group put all those who cup water in their hands and lap it up with their tongues like dogs. In the other group put all those who kneel down and drink with their mouths in the stream." 6 Only 300 of the men drank from their hands. All the others got down on their knees and drank with their mouths in the stream.

7 The LORD told Gideon, "With these 300 men I will rescue you and give you victory over the Midianites. Send all the others home." 8 So Gideon collected the provisions and rams' horns of the other warriors and sent them home. But he kept the 300 men with him.

The Midianite camp was in the valley just below Gideon. 9 That night the LORD said, "Get up! Go down into the Midianite camp, for I have given you victory over them! 10 But if you are afraid to attack, go down to the camp with your servant Purah. 11 Listen to what the Midianites are saying, and you will be greatly encouraged. Then you will be eager to attack."

So Gideon took Purah and went down to the edge of the enemy camp. 12 The armies of Midian, Amalek, and the people of the east had settled in the valley like a swarm of locusts. Their camels were like grains of sand on the seashore—too many to count! 13 Gideon crept up just as a man was telling his companion about a dream. The man said, "I had this dream, and in my dream a loaf of barley bread came tumbling down into the Midianite camp. It hit a tent, turned it over, and knocked it flat!"

14 His companion answered, "Your dream can mean only one thing—God has given Gideon son of Joash, the Israelite, victory over Midian and all its allies!"

15 When Gideon heard the dream and its interpretation, he bowed in worship before the LORD.* Then he returned to the Israelite camp and shouted, "Get up! For the LORD has given you victory over the Midianite hordes!" 16 He divided the 300 men into three groups and gave each man a ram's horn and a clay jar with a torch in it.

17 Then he said to them, "Keep your eyes on me. When I come to the edge of the camp, do just as I do. 18 As soon as I and those with me blow the rams' horns, blow your horns, too, all around the entire camp, and shout, 'For the LORD and for Gideon!' "

19 It was just after midnight,* after the changing of the guard, when Gideon and the 100 men with him reached the edge of the Midianite camp. Suddenly, they blew the rams' horns and broke their clay jars. 20 Then all three groups blew their horns and broke their jars. They held the blazing torches in their left hands and the horns in their right hands, and they all shouted, "A sword for the LORD and for Gideon!"

21 Each man stood at his position around the camp and watched as all the Midianites rushed

7:3 Hebrew *may leave Mount Gilead.* The identity of Mount Gilead is uncertain in this context. It is perhaps used here as another name for Mount Gilboa. **7:15** As in Greek version; Hebrew reads *he bowed.* **7:19** Hebrew *at the beginning of the second watch.*

7:1–8: Yet again the LORD uses the unexpected and inadequate. No human is meant to be able to claim glory in this victory. **9–15:** Anticipating Gideon's need for proof, the LORD sends him at night to hear the Midianite's report of his dream and overcome his fears with the conviction of victory. **19–22:** The nomadic hosts are set to flight, and yet the battle cry is ambivalent: *for the LORD and for Gideon.* **7:23—8:17:**

around in a panic, shouting as they ran to escape. 22 When the 300 Israelites blew their rams' horns, the LORD caused the warriors in the camp to fight against each other with their swords. Those who were not killed fled to places as far away as Beth-shittah near Zererah and to the border of Abel-meholah near Tabbath.

23 Then Gideon sent for the warriors of Naphtali, Asher, and Manasseh, who joined in chasing the army of Midian. 24 Gideon also sent messengers throughout the hill country of Ephraim, saying, "Come down to attack the Midianites. Cut them off at the shallow crossings of the Jordan River at Beth-barah."

So all the men of Ephraim did as they were told. 25 They captured Oreb and Zeeb, the two Midianite commanders, killing Oreb at the rock of Oreb, and Zeeb at the winepress of Zeeb. And they continued to chase the Midianites. Afterward the Israelites brought the heads of Oreb and Zeeb to Gideon, who was by the Jordan River.

Gideon Kills Zebah and Zalmunna

8 Then the people of Ephraim asked Gideon, "Why have you treated us this way? Why didn't you send for us when you first went out to fight the Midianites?" And they argued heatedly with Gideon.

2 But Gideon replied, "What have I accomplished compared to you? Aren't even the leftover grapes of Ephraim's harvest better than the entire crop of my little clan of Abiezer? 3 God gave you victory over Oreb and Zeeb, the commanders of the Midianite army. What have I accomplished compared to that?" When the men of Ephraim heard Gideon's answer, their anger subsided.

4 Gideon then crossed the Jordan River with his 300 men, and though exhausted, they continued to chase the enemy. 5 When they reached Succoth, Gideon asked the leaders of the town, "Please give my warriors some food. They are very tired. I am chasing Zebah and Zalmunna, the kings of Midian."

6 But the officials of Succoth replied, "Catch Zebah and Zalmunna first, and then we will feed your army."

7 So Gideon said, "After the LORD gives me victory over Zebah and Zalmunna, I will return and tear your flesh with the thorns and briers from the wilderness."

8 From there Gideon went up to Peniel* and again asked for food, but he got the same answer. 9 So he said to the people of Peniel, "After I return in victory, I will tear down this tower."

10 By this time Zebah and Zalmunna were in Karkor with 15,000 warriors—all that remained of the allied armies of the east, for 120,000 had already been killed. 11 Gideon circled around by the caravan route east of Nobah and Jogbehah, taking the Midianite army by surprise. 12 Zebah and Zalmunna, the two Midianite kings, fled, but Gideon chased them down and captured all their warriors.

13 After this, Gideon returned from the battle by way of Heres Pass. 14 There he captured a young man from Succoth and demanded that he write down the names of all the seventy-seven officials and elders in the town. 15 Gideon then returned to Succoth and said to the leaders, "Here are Zebah and Zalmunna. When we were here before, you taunted me, saying, 'Catch Zebah and Zalmunna first, and then we will feed your exhausted army.' " 16 Then Gideon took the elders of the town and taught them a lesson, punishing them with thorns and briers from the wilderness. 17 He also tore down the tower of Peniel and killed all the men in the town.

18 Then Gideon asked Zebah and Zalmunna, "The men you killed at Tabor—what were they like?"

"Like you," they replied. "They all had the look of a king's son."

19 "They were my brothers, the sons of my own mother!" Gideon exclaimed. "As surely as the LORD lives, I wouldn't kill you if you hadn't killed them."

20 Turning to Jether, his oldest son, he said, "Kill them!" But Jether did not draw his sword, for he was only a boy and was afraid.

21 Then Zebah and Zalmunna said to Gideon, "Be a man! Kill us yourself!" So Gideon killed them both and took the royal ornaments from the necks of their camels.

Gideon's Sacred Ephod

22 Then the Israelites said to Gideon, "Be our

8:8 Hebrew *Penuel,* a variant spelling of Peniel; also in 8:9, 17.

In the aftermath of this famous and incongruous victory the saga shows Gideon the diplomat, a soother of the susceptibilities of the Ephraimites, who came late to the battle and wanted recognition and a share in the fruits of victory. Yet he is sadistic in his retribution toward those Israelites of Succoth and Peniel east of the Jordan who refused him aid in the pursuit of the Midianite leaders. Such a ruler fulfills the classic pattern of ancient Near Eastern despots. The Israelites recognize and approve these kingly qualities (which Samuel was later to describe, 1 Sam 8:10–22). **8:22–23:** Gideon's decision is for theocracy: the

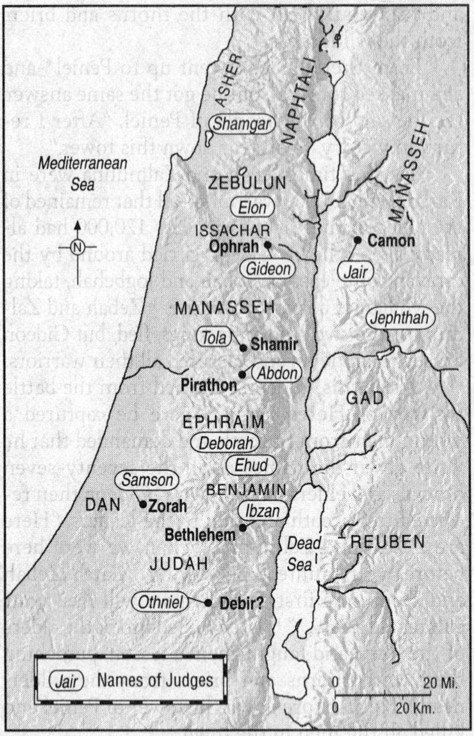

The Twelve Judges

ruler! You and your son and your grandson will
be our rulers, for you have rescued us from Midian."
23 But Gideon replied, "I will not rule over
you, nor will my son. The LORD will rule over
you! 24 However, I do have one request—that
each of you give me an earring from the plunder
you collected from your fallen enemies." (The
enemies, being Ishmaelites, all wore gold earrings.)
25 "Gladly!" they replied. They spread out a
cloak, and each one threw in a gold earring he
had gathered from the plunder. 26 The weight of
the gold earrings was forty-three pounds,* not
including the royal ornaments and pendants, the
purple clothing worn by the kings of Midian, or
the chains around the necks of their camels.
27 Gideon made a sacred ephod from the gold
and put it in Ophrah, his hometown. But soon
all the Israelites prostituted themselves by worshiping it, and it became a trap for Gideon and
his family.
28 That is the story of how the people of Israel defeated Midian, which never recovered.
Throughout the rest of Gideon's lifetime—about
forty years—there was peace in the land.
29 Then Gideon* son of Joash returned home.
30 He had seventy sons born to him, for he had many
wives. 31 He also had a concubine in Shechem, who
gave birth to a son, whom he named Abimelech.
32 Gideon died when he was very old, and he was
buried in the grave of his father, Joash, at Ophrah
in the land of the clan of Abiezer.
33 As soon as Gideon died, the Israelites prostituted themselves by worshiping the images of
Baal, making Baal-berith their god. 34 They forgot the LORD their God, who had rescued them
from all their enemies surrounding them. 35 Nor
did they show any loyalty to the family of Jerub-
baal (that is, Gideon), despite all the good he had
done for Israel.

Abimelech Rules over Shechem

9 One day Gideon's* son Abimelech went to
Shechem to visit his uncles—his mother's
brothers. He said to them and to the rest
of his mother's family, 2 "Ask the leading citizens
of Shechem whether they want to be ruled by
all seventy of Gideon's sons or by one man. And
remember that I am your own flesh and blood!"
3 So Abimelech's uncles gave his message to all
the citizens of Shechem on his behalf. And after
listening to this proposal, the people of Shechem

8:26 Hebrew *1,700 shekels* [19.4 kilograms]. **8:29** Hebrew *Jerub-baal;* see 6:32. **9:1** Hebrew *Jerub-baal's* (see 6:32); also in 9:2, 24.

LORD as king. **24–32:** Monarchy has been offered and ostensibly rejected by Gideon, but his royal lifestyle and his naming of his son Abimelech ("my father, a king") show where his priorities lay. The judge chosen and most closely fostered by God is the one who leads Israel into apostasy and the archetypal pseudomonarchy of Abimelech. **27:** The ephod is perhaps the idol of Baal-berith ("the Lord of the Covenant") worshiped by Israel after his death. **31:** *Shechem* had long been a Canaanite enclave with harmonious interrelationships with the Israelites. As son of his father's Shechemite mistress, Abimelech is the least likely successor to his father's neodynasty.

8:33—9:57 Abimelech, the Pseudo-King. Abimelech breaks the expected next turn of the cycle. Not sent by God, he is a self-appointed half-Israelite who slaughters his way to three years of kingly power. Instead of an external enemy, he is Israel's enemy within. Abimelech is an antihero, a negative embodiment of what monarchy can mean. **9:1–2:** Abimelech is not the LORD's choice of deliverer—none is needed,

decided in favor of Abimelech because he was
their relative. 4 They gave him seventy silver coins
from the temple of Baal-berith, which he used to
hire some reckless troublemakers who agreed to
follow him. 5 He went to his father's home at Ophrah, and there, on one stone, they killed all seventy of his half brothers, the sons of Gideon.* But
the youngest brother, Jotham, escaped and hid.
6 Then all the leading citizens of Shechem and
Beth-millo called a meeting under the oak beside the pillar* at Shechem and made Abimelech
their king.

Jotham's Parable

7 When Jotham heard about this, he climbed to
the top of Mount Gerizim and shouted,

"Listen to me, citizens of Shechem!
Listen to me if you want God to listen to
you!
8 Once upon a time the trees decided to choose
a king.
First they said to the olive tree,
'Be our king!'
9 But the olive tree refused, saying,
'Should I quit producing the olive oil
that blesses both God and people,
just to wave back and forth over the trees?'

10 "Then they said to the fig tree,
'You be our king!'
11 But the fig tree also refused, saying,
'Should I quit producing my sweet fruit
just to wave back and forth over the trees?'

12 "Then they said to the grapevine,
'You be our king!'
13 But the grapevine also refused, saying,
'Should I quit producing the wine
that cheers both God and people,
just to wave back and forth over the trees?'

14 "Then all the trees finally turned to the
thornbush and said,
'Come, you be our king!'
15 And the thornbush replied to the trees,
'If you truly want to make me your king,
come and take shelter in my shade.
If not, let fire come out from me
and devour the cedars of Lebanon.' "

16 Jotham continued, "Now make sure you
have acted honorably and in good faith by making Abimelech your king, and that you have
done right by Gideon and all of his descendants.
Have you treated him with the honor he deserves for all he accomplished? 17 For he fought
for you and risked his life when he rescued you
from the Midianites. 18 But today you have revolted against my father and his descendants,
killing his seventy sons on one stone. And you
have chosen his slave woman's son, Abimelech,
to be your king just because he is your relative.
19 "If you have acted honorably and in good
faith toward Gideon and his descendants today,
then may you find joy in Abimelech, and may
he find joy in you. 20 But if you have not acted
in good faith, then may fire come out from
Abimelech and devour the leading citizens of
Shechem and Beth-millo; and may fire come out
from the citizens of Shechem and Beth-millo and
devour Abimelech!"
21 Then Jotham escaped and lived in Beer because he was afraid of his brother Abimelech.

Shechem Rebels against Abimelech

22 After Abimelech had ruled over Israel for three
years, 23 God sent a spirit that stirred up trouble
between Abimelech and the leading citizens of
Shechem, and they revolted. 24 God was punishing Abimelech for murdering Gideon's seventy
sons, and the citizens of Shechem for supporting
him in this treachery of murdering his brothers. 25 The citizens of Shechem set an ambush
for Abimelech on the hilltops and robbed everyone who passed that way. But someone warned
Abimelech about their plot.

9:5 Hebrew *Jerub-baal* (see 6:32); also in 9:16, 19, 28, 57.
9:6 The meaning of the Hebrew is uncertain.

---

for the land is at peace. **6:** Abimelech's enthronement takes place under the oak at Shechem. Ironically this is the place where Joshua had affirmed loyalty to the covenant with the LORD (Josh 24:1, 25–26). **7–21:** The unexpected mouthpiece of God is Jotham, the surviving youngest son whose fable or parable of the trees picks up on Abimelech's path to leadership. **7:** *Mount Gerizim* was the mount of blessing (Deut 27:12). **15:** The *thornbush* (briar or boxthorn) may make a brushfire blaze and threaten the majestic cedars of Lebanon, but how could such thorny, low bushes offer shade? **21–24:** Jotham disappears, leaving the LORD to repay Abimelech and bring him down. **23–25:** *God . . . stirred up trouble.* The author or editor of Judges believes that nothing that occurs is outside the LORD's overarching ultimate control, his sovereignty. The conflict between Abimelech and his brothers is the result of, literally, "an evil spirit" sent by God. In contrast, his father, Gideon, was moved by "the Spirit of the LORD" (6:34).

26 One day Gaal son of Ebed moved to Shechem with his brothers and gained the confidence of the leading citizens of Shechem. 27 During the annual harvest festival at Shechem, held in the temple of the local god, the wine flowed freely, and everyone began cursing Abimelech. 28 "Who is Abimelech?" Gaal shouted. "He's not a true son of Shechem,* so why should we be his servants? He's merely the son of Gideon, and this Zebul is merely his deputy. Serve the true sons of Hamor, the founder of Shechem. Why should we serve Abimelech? 29 If I were in charge here, I would get rid of Abimelech. I would say* to him, 'Get some soldiers, and come out and fight!' "

30 But when Zebul, the leader of the city, heard what Gaal was saying, he was furious. 31 He sent messengers to Abimelech in Arumah,* telling him, "Gaal son of Ebed and his brothers have come to live in Shechem, and now they are inciting the city to rebel against you. 32 Come by night with an army and hide out in the fields. 33 In the morning, as soon as it is daylight, attack the city. When Gaal and those who are with him come out against you, you can do with them as you wish."

34 So Abimelech and all his men went by night and split into four groups, stationing themselves around Shechem. 35 Gaal was standing at the city gates when Abimelech and his army came out of hiding. 36 When Gaal saw them, he said to Zebul, "Look, there are people coming down from the hilltops!"

Zebul replied, "It's just the shadows on the hills that look like men."

37 But again Gaal said, "No, people are coming down from the hills.* And another group is coming down the road past the Diviners' Oak.*"

38 Then Zebul turned on him and asked, "Now where is that big mouth of yours? Wasn't it you that said, 'Who is Abimelech, and why should we be his servants?' The men you mocked are right outside the city! Go out and fight them!"

39 So Gaal led the leading citizens of Shechem into battle against Abimelech. 40 But Abimelech chased him, and many of Shechem's men were wounded and fell along the road as they retreated to the city gate. 41 Abimelech returned to Arumah, and Zebul drove Gaal and his brothers out of Shechem.

42 The next day the people of Shechem went out into the fields to battle. When Abimelech heard about it, 43 he divided his men into three groups and set an ambush in the fields. When Abimelech saw the people coming out of the city, he and his men jumped up from their hiding places and attacked them. 44 Abimelech and his group stormed the city gate to keep the men of Shechem from getting back in, while Abimelech's other two groups cut them down in the fields. 45 The battle went on all day before Abimelech finally captured the city. He killed the people, leveled the city, and scattered salt all over the ground.

46 When the leading citizens who lived in the tower of Shechem heard what had happened, they ran and hid in the temple of Baal-berith.* 47 Someone reported to Abimelech that the citizens had gathered in the temple, 48 so he led his forces to Mount Zalmon. He took an ax and chopped some branches from a tree, then put them on his shoulder. "Quick, do as I have done!" he told his men. 49 So each of them cut down some branches, following Abimelech's example. They piled the branches against the walls of the temple and set them on fire. So all the people who had lived in the tower of Shechem died—about 1,000 men and women.

50 Then Abimelech attacked the town of Thebez and captured it. 51 But there was a strong tower inside the town, and all the men and women—the entire population—fled to it. They barricaded themselves in and climbed up to the roof of the tower. 52 Abimelech followed them to attack the tower. But as he prepared to set fire to the entrance, 53 a woman on the roof dropped a millstone that landed on Abimelech's head and crushed his skull.

54 He quickly said to his young armor bearer, "Draw your sword and kill me! Don't let it be said that a woman killed Abimelech!" So the young man ran him through with his sword, and he died. 55 When Abimelech's men saw that he was dead, they disbanded and returned to their homes.

9:28 Hebrew *Who is Shechem?* **9:29** As in Greek version; Hebrew reads *And he said.* **9:31** Or *in secret;* Hebrew reads *in Tormah;* compare 9:41. **9:37a** Or *the center of the land.* **9:37b** Hebrew *Elon-meonenim.* **9:46** Hebrew *El-berith,* another name for Baal-berith; compare 9:4.

26–29: An unexpected opponent, Gaal speaks treason against Abimelech, whose father was king in all but title. But Gaal is not the deliverer. **46–52:** Fire is lit against the tower of Shechem and Thebez. The *thornbush* indeed starts a fire (9:15). **53:** Abimelech is not killed by Jotham or the boastful, drunken Gaal. He is killed by a woman without a name—but with a millstone. Like Jael, she uses a weapon with which she is familiar. **54:** Like the general Sisera, Abimelech is mockingly remembered as felled not by a sword but by a common object, not by a warrior but by a mere female.

[56]In this way, God punished Abimelech for
the evil he had done against his father by murdering his seventy brothers. [57]God also punished
the men of Shechem for all their evil. So the
curse of Jotham son of Gideon was fulfilled.

Tola Becomes Israel's Judge

10 After Abimelech died, Tola son of
Puah, son of Dodo, was the next person to rescue Israel. He was from the
tribe of Issachar but lived in the town of Shamir
in the hill country of Ephraim. [2]He judged Israel
for twenty-three years. When he died, he was
buried in Shamir.

Jair Becomes Israel's Judge

[3]After Tola died, Jair from Gilead judged Israel
for twenty-two years. [4]His thirty sons rode
around on thirty donkeys, and they owned thirty
towns in the land of Gilead, which are still called
the Towns of Jair.* [5]When Jair died, he was buried in Kamon.

The Ammonites Oppress Israel

[6]Again the Israelites did evil in the LORD's sight.
They served the images of Baal and Ashtoreth,
and the gods of Aram, Sidon, Moab, Ammon,
and Philistia. They abandoned the LORD and no
longer served him at all. [7]So the LORD burned
with anger against Israel, and he turned them
over to the Philistines and the Ammonites, [8]who
began to oppress them that year. For eighteen
years they oppressed all the Israelites east of the
Jordan River in the land of the Amorites (that is,
in Gilead). [9]The Ammonites also crossed to the
west side of the Jordan and attacked Judah, Benjamin, and Ephraim.

The Israelites were in great distress. [10]Finally,
they cried out to the LORD for help, saying, "We
have sinned against you because we have abandoned you as our God and have served the images of Baal."

[11]The LORD replied, "Did I not rescue you
from the Egyptians, the Amorites, the Ammonites, the Philistines, [12]the Sidonians, the Amalekites, and the Maonites? When they oppressed
you, you cried out to me for help, and I rescued
you. [13]Yet you have abandoned me and served
other gods. So I will not rescue you anymore.
[14]Go and cry out to the gods you have chosen!
Let them rescue you in your hour of distress!"

[15]But the Israelites pleaded with the LORD
and said, "We have sinned. Punish us as you
see fit, only rescue us today from our enemies."
[16]Then the Israelites put aside their foreign gods
and served the LORD. And he was grieved by
their misery.

[17]At that time the armies of Ammon had
gathered for war and were camped in Gilead,
and the people of Israel assembled and camped
at Mizpah. [18]The leaders of Gilead said to each
other, "Whoever attacks the Ammonites first will
become ruler over all the people of Gilead."

Jephthah Becomes Israel's Judge

11 Now Jephthah of Gilead was a great
warrior. He was the son of Gilead, but
his mother was a prostitute. [2]Gilead's
wife also had several sons, and when these half
brothers grew up, they chased Jephthah off the
land. "You will not get any of our father's inheritance," they said, "for you are the son of a
prostitute." [3]So Jephthah fled from his brothers
and lived in the land of Tob. Soon he had a band
of worthless rebels following him.

[4]At about this time, the Ammonites began
their war against Israel. [5]When the Ammonites
attacked, the elders of Gilead sent for Jephthah in
the land of Tob. The elders said, [6]"Come and be
our commander! Help us fight the Ammonites!"

[7]But Jephthah said to them, "Aren't you the
ones who hated me and drove me from my father's house? Why do you come to me now when
you're in trouble?"

10:4 Hebrew *Havvoth-jair.*

10:1—16:31 The Spiral of Decay

10:1–5 Tola and Jair. Two judges are mentioned with minimum detail but will act as contrasts to Abimelech. They have ministries over two decades and are buried in honor.

10:6—12:7 Jephthah: God Is Judge. As a commander, Jephthah invokes the LORD's granting of victory, attempts diplomacy before violence, and seems to be an effective leader. Yet he is ruined by a rash vow. **10:6–16:** The Ammonites and Philistines are the next enemies to attack. Their attack is not limited to a single tribe or location, but spans both sides of the Jordan. This time God's response is bleak. His patience seems to be at an end. But even in his anger, the LORD suffers with his people. **10:17—11:11:** Faced with the enemy, the Gileadites turn to an outcast, illegitimate son of their clan, an outlaw and bandit chief, and choose him as their leader. As illegitimate son of his father's prostitute, Jephthah is paralleled with Abimelech. God spoke of his sense of abandonment (10:13–14); now Jephthah experiences the same. Yet he is the savior that the LORD intends

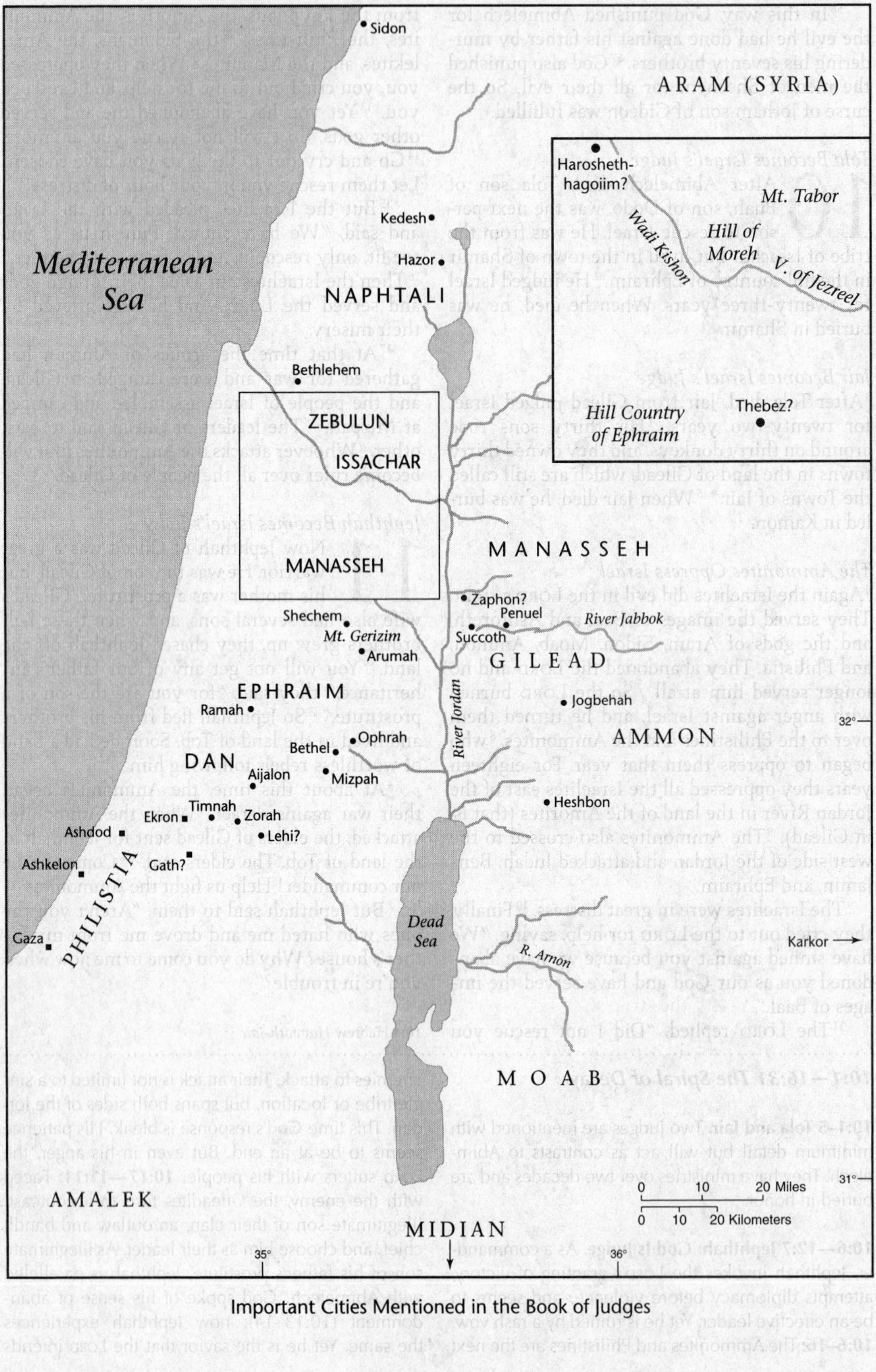
Sidon
ARAM (SYRIA)
Harosheth-
hagoiim?
Mt. Tabor
Wadi Kishon
Hill of
Moreh
V. of Jezreel
Kedesh
Hazor
Mediterranean
Sea
NAPHTALI
Bethlehem
ZEBULUN
ISSACHAR
Hill Country
of Ephraim
Thebez?
MANASSEH
MANASSEH
Zaphon?
Penuel
Shechem
Mt. Gerizim
Succoth
River Jabbok
Arumah
GILEAD
EPHRAIM
Ramah
Jogbehah
River Jordan
Bethel
Ophrah
AMMON
DAN
Aijalon
Mizpah
Timnah
Ekron
Zorah
Heshbon
Ashdod
Lehi?
Gath?
Ashkelon
PHILISTIA
Gaza
Dead
Sea
R. Arnon
Karkor
MOAB
AMALEK
MIDIAN
32°
31°
35°
36°
0 10 20 Miles
0 10 20 Kilometers

Important Cities Mentioned in the Book of Judges

8 "Because we need you," the elders replied. "If you lead us in battle against the Ammonites, we will make you ruler over all the people of Gilead."

9 Jephthah said to the elders, "Let me get this straight. If I come with you and if the LORD gives me victory over the Ammonites, will you really make me ruler over all the people?"

10 "The LORD is our witness," the elders replied. "We promise to do whatever you say."

11 So Jephthah went with the elders of Gilead, and the people made him their ruler and commander of the army. At Mizpah, in the presence of the LORD, Jephthah repeated what he had said to the elders.

12 Then Jephthah sent messengers to the king of Ammon, asking, "Why have you come out to fight against my land?"

13 The king of Ammon answered Jephthah's messengers, "When the Israelites came out of Egypt, they stole my land from the Arnon River to the Jabbok River and all the way to the Jordan. Now then, give back the land peaceably."

14 Jephthah sent this message back to the Ammonite king:

15 "This is what Jephthah says: Israel did not steal any land from Moab or Ammon. 16 When the people of Israel arrived at Kadesh on their journey from Egypt after crossing the Red Sea,* 17 they sent messengers to the king of Edom asking for permission to pass through his land. But their request was denied. Then they asked the king of Moab for similar permission, but he wouldn't let them pass through either. So the people of Israel stayed in Kadesh.

18 "Finally, they went around Edom and Moab through the wilderness. They traveled along Moab's eastern border and camped on the other side of the Arnon River. But they never once crossed the Arnon River into Moab, for the Arnon was the border of Moab.

19 "Then Israel sent messengers to King Sihon of the Amorites, who ruled from Heshbon, asking for permission to cross through his land to get to their destination. 20 But King Sihon didn't trust Israel to pass through his land. Instead, he mobilized his army at Jahaz and attacked them. 21 But the LORD, the God of Israel, gave his people victory over King Sihon. So Israel took control of all the land of the Amorites, who lived in that region, 22 from the Arnon River to the Jabbok River, and from the eastern wilderness to the Jordan.

23 "So you see, it was the LORD, the God of Israel, who took away the land from the Amorites and gave it to Israel. Why, then, should we give it back to you? 24 You keep whatever your god Chemosh gives you, and we will keep whatever the LORD our God gives us. 25 Are you any better than Balak son of Zippor, king of Moab? Did he try to make a case against Israel for disputed land? Did he go to war against them?

26 "Israel has been living here for 300 years, inhabiting Heshbon and its surrounding settlements, all the way to Aroer and its settlements, and in all the towns along the Arnon River. Why have you made no effort to recover it before now? 27 Therefore, I have not sinned against you. Rather, you have wronged me by attacking me. Let the LORD, who is judge, decide today which of us is right—Israel or Ammon."

28 But the king of Ammon paid no attention to Jephthah's message.

Jephthah's Vow

29 At that time the Spirit of the LORD came upon Jephthah, and he went throughout the land of Gilead and Manasseh, including Mizpah in Gilead, and from there he led an army against the Ammonites. 30 And Jephthah made a vow to

11:16 Hebrew *sea of reeds.*

to use: a person wounded by rejection, made hard by suffering. **11:9:** The rejected one is now the preferred candidate of Gilead, whose elders are anxious for Jephthah's leadership. Although he points out the irony, Jephthah is prepared to be their head *ruler* (not their king) and be brought home. **12–28:** The sympathetic portrait of Jephthah continues with mention of diplomatic negotiations. An outlaw bandit engages in diplomatic initiatives on the basis of historical background and careful, God-centered reasoning. **29:** Even without a call narrative or a message from God, it appears that this man is the one he approves, for God's spirit comes upon him. **30–31:** Yet as with Gideon, this endowment does not prevent Jephthah from making mistakes. Jephthah's vow to God, made out of insecurity and doubt and in order to guarantee victory, shows that he thinks and feels from the traumas of an undervalued child. His view of God is that of the Canaanite magic-centered religions, in which unmerited love is unknown and the spiritual bribery of vows may perhaps bring success. Jephthah may have anticipated the need to sacrifice an expend-

the Lord. He said, "If you give me victory over
the Ammonites, 31 I will give to the Lord whatever comes out of my house to meet me when
I return in triumph. I will sacrifice it as a burnt
offering."
32 So Jephthah led his army against the Ammonites, and the Lord gave him victory. 33 He
crushed the Ammonites, devastating about
twenty towns from Aroer to an area near Minnith and as far away as Abel-keramim. In this
way Israel defeated the Ammonites.
34 When Jephthah returned home to Mizpah,
his daughter came out to meet him, playing on a
tambourine and dancing for joy. She was his one
and only child; he had no other sons or daughters. 35 When he saw her, he tore his clothes in
anguish. "Oh, my daughter!" he cried out. "You
have completely destroyed me! You've brought
disaster on me! For I have made a vow to the
Lord, and I cannot take it back."
36 And she said, "Father, if you have made a
vow to the Lord, you must do to me what you
have vowed, for the Lord has given you a great
victory over your enemies, the Ammonites. 37 But
first let me do this one thing: Let me go up and
roam in the hills and weep with my friends for
two months, because I will die a virgin."
38 "You may go," Jephthah said. And he sent
her away for two months. She and her friends
went into the hills and wept because she would
never have children. 39 When she returned home,
her father kept the vow he had made, and she
died a virgin.
So it has become a custom in Israel 40 for young
Israelite women to go away for four days each
year to lament the fate of Jephthah's daughter.

Ephraim Fights with Jephthah

12 Then the people of Ephraim mobilized an army and crossed over the
Jordan River to Zaphon. They sent
this message to Jephthah: "Why didn't you call
for us to help you fight against the Ammonites?
We are going to burn down your house with
you in it!"
2 Jephthah replied, "I summoned you at
the beginning of the dispute, but you refused
to come! You failed to help us in our struggle
against Ammon. 3 So when I realized you weren't
coming, I risked my life and went to battle without you, and the Lord gave me victory over the
Ammonites. So why have you now come to fight
me?"
4 The people of Ephraim responded, "You men
of Gilead are nothing more than fugitives from
Ephraim and Manasseh." So Jephthah gathered
all the men of Gilead and attacked the men of
Ephraim and defeated them.
5 Jephthah captured the shallow crossings of
the Jordan River, and whenever a fugitive from
Ephraim tried to go back across, the men of
Gilead would challenge him. "Are you a member
of the tribe of Ephraim?" they would ask. If the
man said, "No, I'm not," 6 they would tell him
to say "Shibboleth." If he was from Ephraim,
he would say "Sibboleth," because people from
Ephraim cannot pronounce the word correctly.
Then they would take him and kill him at the
shallow crossings of the Jordan. In all, 42,000
Ephraimites were killed at that time.
7 Jephthah judged Israel for six years. When
he died, he was buried in one of the towns of
Gilead.

---

able animal or a household slave (v. 31 may read *whatever* or "whoever"). **34–36:** For God's chosen people, there is no compulsion to make vows, but vows made freely to God must be performed (Deut 23:21–23). Jephthah is committed to his vow, to his determination not to default against the Lord. **35–38:** He treats his daughter as a person in her own right, loved by him. She agrees with the overriding nature of this vow. The narrative arouses pity in the hearer for such a misdirected but honorable father and admiration for such a loving and obedient daughter. To die without the possibility of motherhood was a tragedy in Israelite culture. **39:** Israelite tradition at no point approved human sacrifice, a fact that accounts for the embarrassed, elliptical style by which the writer indicates the fate of the daughter of Jephthah. The father's action is repellent but is a tragically misplaced example of extraordinary determination to honor God by keeping his promise. **39–40:** To remain a virgin is to be lamented, for the resultant childlessness means that this woman, named only by her relation to her father, will be without memorial and so forgotten in the future. Yet ironically she is remembered by the whole people. **12:1–7:** As is their habit, the tribe of Ephraim turns up after the battle is won to complain about their non-selection for this successful attack on Ammon. They threaten Jephthah, but he has had enough. In his state of grief and heroic sacrifice, how can he pander to such a self-serving clan? He is not prepared now for diplomacy and negotiation (cf. Gideon, 8:1–3), so a pitiless internecine slaughter begins. Israelites have now sunk so low that interrelated clans turn against each other, clans recognizably different only by accent and pronunciation (v. 6) but supposedly all one chosen people of God.

Ibzan Becomes Israel's Judge

8 After Jephthah died, Ibzan from Bethlehem judged Israel. 9 He had thirty sons and thirty daughters. He sent his daughters to marry men outside his clan, and he brought in thirty young women from outside his clan to marry his sons. Ibzan judged Israel for seven years. 10 When he died, he was buried at Bethlehem.

Elon Becomes Israel's Judge

11 After Ibzan died, Elon from the tribe of Zebulun judged Israel for ten years. 12 When he died, he was buried at Aijalon in Zebulun.

Abdon Becomes Israel's Judge

13 After Elon died, Abdon son of Hillel, from Pirathon, judged Israel. 14 He had forty sons and thirty grandsons, who rode on seventy donkeys. He judged Israel for eight years. 15 When he died, he was buried at Pirathon in Ephraim, in the hill country of the Amalekites.

The Birth of Samson

13 Again the Israelites did evil in the LORD's sight, so the LORD handed them over to the Philistines, who oppressed them for forty years.

2 In those days a man named Manoah from the tribe of Dan lived in the town of Zorah. His wife was unable to become pregnant, and they had no children. 3 The angel of the LORD appeared to Manoah's wife and said, "Even though you have been unable to have children, you will soon become pregnant and give birth to a son. 4 So be careful; you must not drink wine or any other alcoholic drink nor eat any forbidden food.* 5 You will become pregnant and give birth to a son, and his hair must never be cut. For he will be dedicated to God as a Nazirite from birth. He will begin to rescue Israel from the Philistines."

6 The woman ran and told her husband, "A man of God appeared to me! He looked like one of God's angels, terrifying to see. I didn't ask where he was from, and he didn't tell me his name. 7 But he told me, 'You will become pregnant and give birth to a son. You must not drink wine or any other alcoholic drink nor eat any forbidden food. For your son will be dedicated to God as a Nazirite from the moment of his birth until the day of his death.' "

8 Then Manoah prayed to the LORD, saying, "Lord, please let the man of God come back to us

13:4 Hebrew *any unclean thing;* also in 13:7, 14.

12:8–15 Ibzan, Elon, and Abdon. Like Jephthah, these three judges have short periods of leadership: seven, ten, and eight years. But they contrast with Jephthah in their productivity in terms of their many children. Yet none of these people are named; their parents' contribution to Israelite history is all but forgotten.

13:1—16:31 Samson: Grace and Disgrace. Samson is both superhumanly strong and a buffoon—a type familiar in ancient literature and modern films. The reader can enjoy the discomfiture of the Philistine enemies yet appreciate the irony of Samson's repeated capitulation to the wiles of women and his pitiful blindness at the end. He, who was destined and equipped from conception to fight the enemy, finds all his closest relationships with Philistine (enemy) women. Samson is a parable of Israelite history: chosen and destined for rule, greatly privileged and empowered by the LORD yet consistently wasting his strength and cohabiting with the enemy. He has power without holiness. Most of the women in this saga are used by men, except Samson's mother, Manoah's wife. She is entrusted with the LORD's message, separated to God, mother of the deliverer. Samson uses women: *Get her for me!* (14:2). But these women are used by their people to defeat Samson and destroy his strength. The reader is expected to enjoy the stereotypical humor in the handling of intergender relationships and to not take it too seriously.

13:1–25 An Annunciation Story: Samson's Birth. The Philistines controlled the highlands of Israel from their five towns of Gaza, Ashkelon, Ashdod, Ekron, and Gath on the coastal plain. They were an Iron Age people dominating a Bronze Age Israelite community. **2:** Like their nation, Manoah and his wife are in a barren state. **3–7:** The story of the angel's visit is determinedly focused on Manoah's wife. She receives the message, and she is perceptive and discreet in seeing who it is and not asking the person's name. **4–5:** The restrictions imposed on the mother-to-be and on the child to be born are unique to this annunciation story. (For a woman who had had difficulty conceiving, the ban on alcohol was good prenatal counseling.) Samson was to be a Nazirite, a person who takes a vow to be dedicated to God. But the vow of a Nazirite was usually a voluntary matter entered into by adults and not a matter of inheritance imposed on the unborn child from the womb. It symbolizes a state of separation or consecration to God that is acted out. (See Num 6:1–21 for all the laws Nazirites must follow.) In many traditional spiritist religions, growing long hair or cutting hair have a quasi-religious or magical significance, and this seems to have been the way Samson came to interpret his state and his powers. **8–18:** Her husband bustles about, determined to in-

again and give us more instructions about this son who is to be born."

9 God answered Manoah's prayer, and the angel of God appeared once again to his wife as she was sitting in the field. But her husband, Manoah, was not with her. 10 So she quickly ran and told her husband, "The man who appeared to me the other day is here again!"

11 Manoah ran back with his wife and asked, "Are you the man who spoke to my wife the other day?"

"Yes," he replied, "I am."

12 So Manoah asked him, "When your words come true, what kind of rules should govern the boy's life and work?"

13 The angel of the LORD replied, "Be sure your wife follows the instructions I gave her. 14 She must not eat grapes or raisins, drink wine or any other alcoholic drink, or eat any forbidden food."

15 Then Manoah said to the angel of the LORD, "Please stay here until we can prepare a young goat for you to eat."

16 "I will stay," the angel of the LORD replied, "but I will not eat anything. However, you may prepare a burnt offering as a sacrifice to the LORD." (Manoah didn't realize it was the angel of the LORD.)

17 Then Manoah asked the angel of the LORD, "What is your name? For when all this comes true, we want to honor you."

18 "Why do you ask my name?" the angel of the LORD replied. "It is too wonderful for you to understand."

19 Then Manoah took a young goat and a grain offering and offered it on a rock as a sacrifice to the LORD. And as Manoah and his wife watched, the LORD did an amazing thing. 20 As the flames from the altar shot up toward the sky, the angel of the LORD ascended in the fire. When Manoah and his wife saw this, they fell with their faces to the ground.

21 The angel did not appear again to Manoah and his wife. Manoah finally realized it was the angel of the LORD, 22 and he said to his wife, "We will certainly die, for we have seen God!"

23 But his wife said, "If the LORD were going to kill us, he wouldn't have accepted our burnt offering and grain offering. He wouldn't have appeared to us and told us this wonderful thing and done these miracles."

24 When her son was born, she named him Samson. And the LORD blessed him as he grew up. 25 And the Spirit of the LORD began to stir him while he lived in Mahaneh-dan, which is located between the towns of Zorah and Eshtaol.

Samson's Riddle

14 One day when Samson was in Timnah, one of the Philistine women caught his eye. 2 When he returned home, he told his father and mother, "A young Philistine woman in Timnah caught my eye. I want to marry her. Get her for me."

3 His father and mother objected. "Isn't there even one woman in our tribe or among all the Israelites you could marry?" they asked. "Why must you go to the pagan Philistines to find a wife?"

But Samson told his father, "Get her for me! She looks good to me." 4 His father and mother didn't realize the LORD was at work in this, creating an opportunity to work against the Philistines, who ruled over Israel at that time.

5 As Samson and his parents were going down to Timnah, a young lion suddenly attacked Samson near the vineyards of Timnah. 6 At that moment the Spirit of the LORD came powerfully upon him, and he ripped the lion's jaws apart with his bare hands. He did it as easily as if it

---

terview the man, to check for himself and take the dominant role in this encounter. The angel comes at his own initiative, insists on turning the focus back onto Manoah's wife, and confirms the rightness of her sensitivity: *Why do you ask my name?* **19–23:** After the angel leaves in the sacrificial fire, Manoah is all fear while his wife is the logical and reasonable one who has to calm him. Samson's mother had the balance right!

14:1–20 Timnah and Tantrums. Samson is driven by his hormones, breaking traditions and the commitments of a Nazirite. **1–3:** Without respect to parents or reference to his destiny, Samson breaks covenant by insisting on marrying a woman in Timnah. **3:** The Philistines are not the covenant people but are uncircumcised. **4–6:** Samson is also empowered by God, a wild spirit that comes and goes in his life but is *the Spirit of the LORD*. This seems far from the Holy Spirit and the ethics of the new covenant, but it is a wildfire force. It may be that after the passage of time the tellers of his saga looked back and saw that Samson's uncontrolled outbursts of tantrum and destruction fulfilled God's purposes. So they explain that this unruly physical strength was *the Spirit of the LORD*, as was his desire to marry a girl from Timnah. **5–9:** Samson starts breaking Nazirite rules: Killing a young lion violates the prohibition against contact with corpses, and because the honey came from the lion's carcass, it is unclean. He also involves his par-

were a young goat. But he didn't tell his father or mother about it. 7 When Samson arrived in Timnah, he talked with the woman and was very pleased with her.

8 Later, when he returned to Timnah for the wedding, he turned off the path to look at the carcass of the lion. And he found that a swarm of bees had made some honey in the carcass. 9 He scooped some of the honey into his hands and ate it along the way. He also gave some to his father and mother, and they ate it. But he didn't tell them he had taken the honey from the carcass of the lion.

10 As his father was making final arrangements for the marriage, Samson threw a party at Timnah, as was the custom for elite young men. 11 When the bride's parents* saw him, they selected thirty young men from the town to be his companions.

12 Samson said to them, "Let me tell you a riddle. If you solve my riddle during these seven days of the celebration, I will give you thirty fine linen robes and thirty sets of festive clothing. 13 But if you can't solve it, then you must give me thirty fine linen robes and thirty sets of festive clothing."

"All right," they agreed, "let's hear your riddle."

14 So he said:

"Out of the one who eats came something to eat;
out of the strong came something sweet."

Three days later they were still trying to figure it out. 15 On the fourth* day they said to Samson's wife, "Entice your husband to explain the riddle for us, or we will burn down your father's house with you in it. Did you invite us to this party just to make us poor?"

16 So Samson's wife came to him in tears and said, "You don't love me; you hate me! You have given my people a riddle, but you haven't told me the answer."

"I haven't even given the answer to my father or mother," he replied. "Why should I tell you?" 17 So she cried whenever she was with him and kept it up for the rest of the celebration. At last, on the seventh day he told her the answer because she was tormenting him with her nagging. Then she explained the riddle to the young men.

18 So before sunset of the seventh day, the men of the town came to Samson with their answer:

"What is sweeter than honey?
What is stronger than a lion?"

Samson replied, "If you hadn't plowed with my heifer, you wouldn't have solved my riddle!"

19 Then the Spirit of the LORD came powerfully upon him. He went down to the town of Ashkelon, killed thirty men, took their belongings, and gave their clothing to the men who had solved his riddle. But Samson was furious about what had happened, and he went back home to live with his father and mother. 20 So his wife was given in marriage to the man who had been Samson's best man at the wedding.

Samson's Vengeance on the Philistines

15 Later on, during the wheat harvest, Samson took a young goat as a present to his wife. He said, "I'm going into my wife's room to sleep with her," but her father wouldn't let him in.

14:11 Hebrew *they.* **14:15** As in Greek version; Hebrew reads *seventh.*

ents in unknowingly eating unclean food. **10:** Wine, prohibited to Nazirites, was usual at wedding celebrations. Although the text does not state that Samson himself drank, given his lack of regard for laws about corpses and unclean food, it's probably safe to assume that he did partake. **12–14:** Proposing and solving riddles was a favorite intellectual exercise in the ancient world. **16:** The unnamed wife uses stereotypical tears and nagging, pleading against Samson. Compare this behavior to Delilah's in chapter 16. He claims that his primary loyalty is to his parents rather than to his spouse, which is, ironically unknown to him, his wife's position also. The Torah has a strong covenant concept in marriage of leaving mother and father and uniting with one's wife, involving a change of priorities and a mutual openness (Gen 2:24–25). This is hard enough when the parties are from a shared background, but Samson is marrying out of the covenant. **18–19:** When his wife's deception becomes clear Samson is scathing. His new wife is but a *heifer* to be used by him or by others. He runs amok in Ashkelon in his frustrated rage and loss of face. But at least he is now attacking Philistines rather than sleeping and feasting with them.

15:1–8 Loss of Face, Loss by Fire. 1: Some forms of marriage in the ancient Near East involved the wife continuing to live with her parents after marriage, being visited by her husband. Samson returns to claim his rights. **2–3:** His childish naiveté that all

2 "I truly thought you must hate her," her father explained, "so I gave her in marriage to your
best man. But look, her younger sister is even
more beautiful than she is. Marry her instead."
3 Samson said, "This time I cannot be blamed
for everything I am going to do to you Philistines." 4 Then he went out and caught 300 foxes.
He tied their tails together in pairs, and he fastened a torch to each pair of tails. 5 Then he lit the
torches and let the foxes run through the grain
fields of the Philistines. He burned all their grain
to the ground, including the sheaves and the uncut grain. He also destroyed their vineyards and
olive groves.
6 "Who did this?" the Philistines demanded.
"Samson," was the reply, "because his father-
in-law from Timnah gave Samson's wife to be
married to his best man." So the Philistines went
and got the woman and her father and burned
them to death.
7 "Because you did this," Samson vowed, "I
won't rest until I take my revenge on you!" 8 So
he attacked the Philistines with great fury and
killed many of them. Then he went to live in a
cave in the rock of Etam.
9 The Philistines retaliated by setting up camp
in Judah and spreading out near the town of Lehi.
10 The men of Judah asked the Philistines, "Why
are you attacking us?"
The Philistines replied, "We've come to capture Samson. We've come to pay him back for
what he did to us."
11 So 3,000 men of Judah went down to get
Samson at the cave in the rock of Etam. They
said to Samson, "Don't you realize the Philistines rule over us? What are you doing to us?"
But Samson replied, "I only did to them what
they did to me."
12 But the men of Judah told him, "We have
come to tie you up and hand you over to the Philistines."
"All right," Samson said. "But promise that
you won't kill me yourselves."
13 "We will only tie you up and hand you over
to the Philistines," they replied. "We won't kill
you." So they tied him up with two new ropes
and brought him up from the rock.
14 As Samson arrived at Lehi, the Philistines
came shouting in triumph. But the Spirit of the
LORD came powerfully upon Samson, and he
snapped the ropes on his arms as if they were
burnt strands of flax, and they fell from his
wrists. 15 Then he found the jawbone of a recently
killed donkey. He picked it up and killed 1,000
Philistines with it. 16 Then Samson said,

"With the jawbone of a donkey,
I've piled them in heaps!
With the jawbone of a donkey,
I've killed a thousand men!"

17 When he finished his boasting, he threw away
the jawbone; and the place was named Jawbone
Hill.*
18 Samson was now very thirsty, and he cried
out to the LORD, "You have accomplished this

15:17 Hebrew *Ramath-lehi.*

---

will be back to normal when he arrives with a ritual present is frustrated. He has lost face yet again by his wife being given to another man. Samson is not prepared to take the younger sister, who would be assumed to be the better deal, having more years of fertility before her. Instead he must get his own back. **4–5:** Contemporary Western susceptibilities about cruelty to animals may blind us to the reality that in most societies animals are regarded as pests for destruction or meat for consumption and as being at human disposal. The writers intend us to imagine the harvest destroyed and the prospect of empty stomachs for Timnah's people in the coming months. **6–7:** The Philistines react with the vicious, illogical burning of Samson's ex-wife and her family. They are alike, the Philistines and Samson. **8:** Modern readers might think: "Surely Samson is a sadistic, paranoid manic-depressive. How did his parents let him get to this state? Was this child, whose name may be derived from the Hebrew for 'sun,' the overindulged light of their lives?" In adulthood Samson always has to get what he wants when and how he wants it.

15:9–20 Philistines in Judah. The wild inroads on their people and property provoke the Philistines to move into the hills and raid the territory of Judah. In the conquest of Canaan Judah was the tribe first into battle, most faithful in its separation from and eradication of non-Israelite influences (1:1–8). Yet now they want to keep the status quo and are prepared to surrender Samson. Later generations would see Judah here representing Israel in various points of its later history: a subdued, spiritless, and weaponless people prepared to make the best of the foreign rule. **11–13:** Samson seems to them to be willing to make the heroic sacrifice of his life, but his intent is kept secret from the people of Judah. He knows he can deal with the new ropes that bind him. **14–16:** Samson, in contrast to Judah, cannot be bound and is empowered by God's spirit. Anything that comes to hand can be a weapon. **18–19:** Just as the miraculous

great victory by the strength of your servant. Must I now die of thirst and fall into the hands of these pagans?" [19] So God caused water to gush out of a hollow in the ground at Lehi, and Samson was revived as he drank. Then he named that place "The Spring of the One Who Cried Out,"* and it is still in Lehi to this day.

[20] Samson judged Israel for twenty years during the period when the Philistines dominated the land.

Samson Carries Away Gaza's Gates

16 One day Samson went to the Philistine town of Gaza and spent the night with a prostitute. [2] Word soon spread* that Samson was there, so the men of Gaza gathered together and waited all night at the town gates. They kept quiet during the night, saying to themselves, "When the light of morning comes, we will kill him."

[3] But Samson stayed in bed only until midnight. Then he got up, took hold of the doors of the town gate, including the two posts, and lifted them up, bar and all. He put them on his shoulders and carried them all the way to the top of the hill across from Hebron.

Samson and Delilah

[4] Some time later Samson fell in love with a woman named Delilah, who lived in the valley of Sorek. [5] The rulers of the Philistines went to her and said, "Entice Samson to tell you what makes him so strong and how he can be overpowered and tied up securely. Then each of us will give you 1,100 pieces* of silver."

[6] So Delilah said to Samson, "Please tell me what makes you so strong and what it would take to tie you up securely."

[7] Samson replied, "If I were tied up with seven new bowstrings that have not yet been dried, I would become as weak as anyone else."

[8] So the Philistine rulers brought Delilah seven new bowstrings, and she tied Samson up with them. [9] She had hidden some men in one of the inner rooms of her house, and she cried out, "Samson! The Philistines have come to capture you!" But Samson snapped the bowstrings as a piece of string snaps when it is burned by a fire. So the secret of his strength was not discovered.

[10] Afterward Delilah said to him, "You've been making fun of me and telling me lies! Now please tell me how you can be tied up securely."

[11] Samson replied, "If I were tied up with brand-new ropes that had never been used, I would become as weak as anyone else."

[12] So Delilah took new ropes and tied him up with them. The men were hiding in the inner room as before, and again Delilah cried out, "Samson! The Philistines have come to capture you!" But again Samson snapped the ropes from his arms as if they were thread.

[13] Then Delilah said, "You've been making fun of me and telling me lies! Now tell me how you can be tied up securely."

Samson replied, "If you were to weave the seven braids of my hair into the fabric on your loom and tighten it with the loom shuttle, I would become as weak as anyone else."

So while he slept, Delilah wove the seven braids of his hair into the fabric. [14] Then she

15:19 Hebrew *En-hakkore.* **16:2** As in Greek and Syriac versions and Latin Vulgate; Hebrew lacks *Word soon spread.* **16:5** Hebrew *1,100 shekels,* about 28 pounds or 12.5 kilograms in weight.

story of Samson's birth reminds the reader of the announcement of Isaac's birth to Abraham and Sarah, so this incident has echoes of Moses in the wilderness. Is there hope that Samson is to bring his people out of captivity in a like manner? The request he makes, though duly giving God the credit for his victory, concentrates on his personal safety, his physical needs, and the gratification of the moment. Yet God graciously answers Samson's request. **20:** Samson seems set to rule in peace.

16:1–31 The Same Old Cycle. Like Israel's people as a whole, Samson's life so far is one of commitment, misuse, slavery, and deliverance. At the beginning of this second cycle our hope that he will become the new Moses is swiftly dashed. He ends up an abject, blinded slave. Yet God's purpose for his life is fulfilled in his dying. **1–3:** When it comes to sex, Samson always goes to Philistines. He risks his life in a foolhardy, vainglorious way, confident in his strength, and evades the Philistines yet again. This is a prelude to downfall. **4–20:** The next, inevitable woman is different, for Samson falls in love with her. Yet she, like the wife in Timnah, is loyal to her people and will use her wiles on this congenitally susceptible and gullible man. There are again secrets between Delilah and the Philistine plotters lying in wait (as they had done in Gaza, v. 2) and the secret Samson is determined to keep lest he lose his powers (v. 9). **5:** Delilah is a more despicable character, for she is motivated by money. **6–17:** Bound by bowstrings or ropes or even with his hair woven into the loom, Samson can break free. But he is enslaved to this woman, captured by her assertions of love, her desire to know

tightened it with the loom shuttle.* Again she
cried out, "Samson! The Philistines have come to
capture you!" But Samson woke up, pulled back
the loom shuttle, and yanked his hair away from
the loom and the fabric.
15 Then Delilah pouted, "How can you tell me,
'I love you,' when you don't share your secrets
with me? You've made fun of me three times
now, and you still haven't told me what makes
you so strong!" 16 She tormented him with her
nagging day after day until he was sick to death
of it.
17 Finally, Samson shared his secret with her.
"My hair has never been cut," he confessed, "for
I was dedicated to God as a Nazirite from birth. If
my head were shaved, my strength would leave
me, and I would become as weak as anyone else."
18 Delilah realized he had finally told her the
truth, so she sent for the Philistine rulers. "Come
back one more time," she said, "for he has finally
told me his secret." So the Philistine rulers returned with the money in their hands. 19 Delilah
lulled Samson to sleep with his head in her lap,
and then she called in a man to shave off the
seven locks of his hair. In this way she began to
bring him down,* and his strength left him.
20 Then she cried out, "Samson! The Philistines have come to capture you!"
When he woke up, he thought, "I will do as
before and shake myself free." But he didn't realize the LORD had left him.
21 So the Philistines captured him and gouged
out his eyes. They took him to Gaza, where he
was bound with bronze chains and forced to
grind grain in the prison.
22 But before long, his hair began to grow
back.

Samson's Final Victory

23 The Philistine rulers held a great festival, offering sacrifices and praising their god, Dagon.
They said, "Our god has given us victory over
our enemy Samson!"
24 When the people saw him, they praised
their god, saying, "Our god has delivered our
enemy to us! The one who killed so many of us
is now in our power!"
25 Half drunk by now, the people demanded,
"Bring out Samson so he can amuse us!" So he
was brought from the prison to amuse them, and
they had him stand between the pillars supporting the roof.
26 Samson said to the young servant who
was leading him by the hand, "Place my hands
against the pillars that hold up the temple. I want
to rest against them." 27 Now the temple was
completely filled with people. All the Philistine
rulers were there, and there were about 3,000
men and women on the roof who were watching
as Samson amused them.
28 Then Samson prayed to the LORD, "Sovereign LORD, remember me again. O God, please
strengthen me just one more time. With one
blow let me pay back the Philistines for the loss
of my two eyes." 29 Then Samson put his hands
on the two center pillars that held up the temple. Pushing against them with both hands, 30 he
prayed, "Let me die with the Philistines." And
the temple crashed down on the Philistine rulers
and all the people. So he killed more people when
he died than he had during his entire lifetime.
31 Later his brothers and other relatives went
down to get his body. They took him back home
and buried him between Zorah and Eshtaol,
where his father, Manoah, was buried. Samson
had judged Israel for twenty years.

16:13-14 As in Greek version and Latin Vulgate; Hebrew lacks *I would become as weak as anyone else. / So while he slept, Delilah wove the seven braids of his hair into the fabric.* [14]*Then she tightened it with the loom shuttle.* **16:19** Or *she began to torment him.* Greek version reads *He began to grow weak.*

his secret. By telling her his secret, he becomes helpless, his head in her lap, his hair shorn and unknowingly *weak as anyone else*. **19–20:** His tragedy is to wake and try to shake off his bonds not knowing that *the LORD had left him*. His hair is symbolic—the important thing is that God has now declined to use him further. **21–22:** Despite Samson's blindness and slavery, his growing hair gives the reader a gleam of hope. He is the one who is destined to begin to release Israel from the Philistine yoke, yet he is yoked like an ox or a donkey turning the grinding millstones in the depths of Gaza. **23–31:** In the temple of their god more than three thousand worshipers wait for the entertainment of the Israelite Hercules reduced to a circus event, his God humiliated before theirs. **28:** For the second time Samson calls on the LORD, but his heart is set on revenge for the loss of his eyes, not on his destined task. He is at best an unholy martyr, dying for his own cause rather than God's. Life for a sightless person in ancient times was desperate and purposeless. **29–30:** The saga assumes that the LORD answers with the restored strength that Samson requires, for the LORD's own purposes. **31:** Samson died with the Philistines, but he is returned to the tomb of his father. Samson's story, as with most in Judges, shows God's patience with humans who make perverted use of the gifts he has given and who fail to cooperate with his divine purposes. Even in its de-

Micah's Idols

17 There was a man named Micah, who
lived in the hill country of Ephraim.
[2] One day he said to his mother, "I
heard you place a curse on the person who stole
1,100 pieces* of silver from you. Well, I have the
money. I was the one who took it."
"The LORD bless you for admitting it," his
mother replied. [3] He returned the money to her,
and she said, "I now dedicate these silver coins
to the LORD. In honor of my son, I will have an
image carved and an idol cast."
[4] So when he returned the money to his mother, she took 200 silver coins and gave them to a
silversmith, who made them into an image and
an idol. And these were placed in Micah's house.
[5] Micah set up a shrine for the idol, and he made a
sacred ephod and some household idols. Then he
installed one of his sons as his personal priest.
[6] In those days Israel had no king; all the
people did whatever seemed right in their own
eyes.
[7] One day a young Levite, who had been living
in Bethlehem in Judah, arrived in that area. [8] He
had left Bethlehem in search of another place to
live, and as he traveled, he came to the hill country of Ephraim. He happened to stop at Micah's
house as he was traveling through. [9] "Where are
you from?" Micah asked him.
He replied, "I am a Levite from Bethlehem in
Judah, and I am looking for a place to live."
[10] "Stay here with me," Micah said, "and
you can be a father and priest to me. I will give
you ten pieces* of silver a year, plus a change
of clothes and your food." [11] The Levite agreed
to this, and the young man became like one of
Micah's sons.
[12] So Micah installed the Levite as his personal priest, and he lived in Micah's house. [13] "I
know the LORD will bless me now," Micah said,
"because I have a Levite serving as my priest."

Idolatry in the Tribe of Dan

18 Now in those days Israel had no king.
And the tribe of Dan was trying to
find a place where they could settle,
for they had not yet moved into the land assigned
to them when the land was divided among the
tribes of Israel. [2] So the men of Dan chose from
their clans five capable warriors from the towns
of Zorah and Eshtaol to scout out a land for them
to settle in.
When these warriors arrived in the hill country of Ephraim, they came to Micah's house and

17:2 Hebrew *1,100 shekels,* about 28 pounds or 12.5 kilograms in weight. **17:10** Hebrew *10 shekels,* about 4 ounces or 114 grams in weight.

---

graded motivations and misuse of strength, the story gives hope for Israel's future.

17:1–21:25 The Grand Reversal

On a superficial reading this last section of Judges, held together by the refrain *Israel had no king* (17:6; 18:1; 19:1; 21:25) and sharing two Levites among their characters, seems to be two appendices of undated earlier material cobbled together by someone reluctant to omit any research notes, regardless of their irrelevance. As a musical coda echoes, repeats, and brings to resolution the themes of a piece, however, so these chapters echo past events within and beyond the text: Lot and Sodom, Gideon's ephod, Jephthah's vow, the ambivalent attempts toward monarchy. Then comes the resolution: *In those days Israel had no king; all the people did whatever seemed right in their own eyes* (21:25). Implicit is the approval of the future peaceful days of Davidic monarchy, but the book as a whole shows ambivalence, either because it combines sources from different opinions in the community or because it recognizes that kingship comes in various guises.

17:1–13 Micah's Idols. Micah is a negative person throughout: Stealing from one's own mother is the ultimate in low behavior, and the making of idols is explicitly forbidden by the law. **1:** The Ephraimites are the scapegoat tribe targeted throughout Judges. **2–4:** Family life has reached the ultimate in corruption when his mother responds to the return of the silver with a blessing rather than a rebuke and uses some of it to make an idol for their private shrine. **5–6:** There are echoes of Gideon here (8:27). **7–13:** A Levite, symbol of the separation of the Israelites to the exclusive worship and service of God, leaves his post in Bethlehem of Judah, the idealized or model tribe, to search for a profitable place to be a private priest, instead of going to the place the LORD chooses (see Deut 12:5–7; 18:6–7). Stolen silver has been made into an idol, and a disobedient Levite has become a family chaplain.

18:1–31 Idolatry in the Tribe of Dan. This incident resonates with and repeats (with significant variations) the story of Israel's initial investigation and conquest of the land. It dates back to the days long before Samson, when the tribe of Dan is not yet settled in its region. **2–6:** Spies are sent out as before (Num 13; Josh 2), but they are seeking land according to their own principles and methods. The area of

spent the night there. 3While at Micah's house, they recognized the young Levite's accent, so they went over and asked him, "Who brought you here, and what are you doing in this place? Why are you here?" 4He told them about his agreement with Micah and that he had been hired as Micah's personal priest.

5Then they said, "Ask God whether or not our journey will be successful."

6"Go in peace," the priest replied. "For the LORD is watching over your journey."

7So the five men went on to the town of Laish, where they noticed the people living carefree lives, like the Sidonians; they were peaceful and secure.* The people were also wealthy because their land was very fertile. And they lived a great distance from Sidon and had no allies nearby.

8When the men returned to Zorah and Eshtaol, their relatives asked them, "What did you find?"

9The men replied, "Come on, let's attack them! We have seen the land, and it is very good. What are you waiting for? Don't hesitate to go and take possession of it. 10When you get there, you will find the people living carefree lives. God has given us a spacious and fertile land, lacking in nothing!"

11So 600 men from the tribe of Dan, armed with weapons of war, set out from Zorah and Eshtaol. 12They camped at a place west of Kiriath-jearim in Judah, which is called Mahaneh-dan* to this day. 13Then they went on from there into the hill country of Ephraim and came to the house of Micah.

14The five men who had scouted out the land around Laish explained to the others, "These buildings contain a sacred ephod, as well as some household idols, a carved image, and a cast idol. What do you think you should do?" 15Then the five men turned off the road and went over to Micah's house, where the young Levite lived, and greeted him kindly. 16As the 600 armed warriors from the tribe of Dan stood at the entrance of the gate, 17the five scouts entered the shrine and removed the carved image, the sacred ephod, the household idols, and the cast idol. Meanwhile, the priest was standing at the gate with the 600 armed warriors.

18When the priest saw the men carrying all the sacred objects out of Micah's shrine, he said, "What are you doing?"

19"Be quiet and come with us," they said. "Be a father and priest to all of us. Isn't it better to be a priest for an entire tribe and clan of Israel than for the household of just one man?"

20The young priest was quite happy to go with them, so he took along the sacred ephod, the household idols, and the carved image. 21They turned and started on their way again, placing their children, livestock, and possessions in front of them.

22When the people from the tribe of Dan were quite a distance from Micah's house, the people who lived near Micah came chasing after them. 23They were shouting as they caught up with them. The men of Dan turned around and said to Micah, "What's the matter? Why have you called these men together and chased after us like this?"

24"What do you mean, 'What's the matter?' " Micah replied. "You've taken away all the gods I have made, and my priest, and I have nothing left!"

25The men of Dan said, "Watch what you say! There are some short-tempered men around here who might get angry and kill you and your family." 26So the men of Dan continued on their way. When Micah saw that there were too many of them for him to attack, he turned around and went home.

27Then, with Micah's idols and his priest, the men of Dan came to the town of Laish, whose people were peaceful and secure. They attacked

18:7 The meaning of the Hebrew is uncertain.
18:12 *Mahaneh-dan* means "the camp of Dan."

Laish is occupied by an innocuous, wealthy people, far from neighbors and undefended, not by giants in fortified cities as described by the very first scouts (Num 13). These five spies, like Caleb and Joshua, are full of positive faith that God has ordained the land for them. Laish, however, is not the town set aside for them. See Joshua 19:40–48. **11–26:** As the armed tribe of Dan set off, the erstwhile spies determine to steal the approving Levite priest, the shrine and its furnishings to set up their own center of worship in the far north, away from Judah and Jerusalem. The idol made from stolen silver is itself stolen, and the priest is willing to be seduced into a wider ministry. **22–26:** Micah's desolation is pathetic but self-induced, typical of the people of God in disobedience. **27, 30:** The Danites set up their shrine with their co-opted Levite, stolen silver, and illicit idols (also stolen), emphasizing the illegitimate background of the sanctuary at Dan. Then comes the revelation: This Levite's name was Jonathan, son of Gershom, the grandson of the great Moses. (See translator's note: The manuscripts' reading "Manasseh" rather than "Moses" might have originated in an attempt to avoid offense against the revered giver of the law.) Even that great family had

with swords and burned the town to the ground.
[28]There was no one to rescue the people, for they
lived a great distance from Sidon and had no
allies nearby. This happened in the valley near
Beth-rehob.

Then the people of the tribe of Dan rebuilt
the town and lived there. [29]They renamed the
town Dan after their ancestor, Israel's son, but it
had originally been called Laish.

[30]Then they set up the carved image, and
they appointed Jonathan son of Gershom, son of
Moses,* as their priest. This family continued as
priests for the tribe of Dan until the Exile. [31]So
Micah's carved image was worshiped by the tribe
of Dan as long as the Tabernacle of God remained
at Shiloh.

The Levite and His Concubine

19 Now in those days Israel had no king.
There was a man from the tribe of
Levi living in a remote area of the hill
country of Ephraim. One day he brought home a
woman from Bethlehem in Judah to be his concubine. [2]But she became angry with him* and
returned to her father's home in Bethlehem.

After about four months, [3]her husband set
out for Bethlehem to speak personally to her and
persuade her to come back. He took with him a
servant and a pair of donkeys. When he arrived
at* her father's house, her father saw him and
welcomed him. [4]Her father urged him to stay
awhile, so he stayed three days, eating, drinking,
and sleeping there.

[5]On the fourth day the man was up early,
ready to leave, but the woman's father said to his
son-in-law, "Have something to eat before you
go." [6]So the two men sat down together and had
something to eat and drink. Then the woman's
father said, "Please stay another night and enjoy
yourself." [7]The man got up to leave, but his father-in-law kept urging him to stay, so he finally
gave in and stayed the night.

[8]On the morning of the fifth day he was up
early again, ready to leave, and again the woman's father said, "Have something to eat; then
you can leave later this afternoon." So they had
another day of feasting. [9]Later, as the man and his
concubine and servant were preparing to leave,
his father-in-law said, "Look, it's almost evening.
Stay the night and enjoy yourself. Tomorrow
you can get up early and be on your way."

[10]But this time the man was determined to
leave. So he took his two saddled donkeys and his
concubine and headed in the direction of Jebus
(that is, Jerusalem). [11]It was late in the day when
they neared Jebus, and the man's servant said to
him, "Let's stop at this Jebusite town and spend
the night there."

[12]"No," his master said, "we can't stay in this
foreign town where there are no Israelites. Instead, we will go on to Gibeah. [13]Come on, let's
try to get as far as Gibeah or Ramah, and we'll
spend the night in one of those towns." [14]So they
went on. The sun was setting as they came to
Gibeah, a town in the land of Benjamin, [15]so they
stopped there to spend the night. They rested in
the town square, but no one took them in for the
night.

[16]That evening an old man came home from
his work in the fields. He was from the hill country of Ephraim, but he was living in Gibeah,
where the people were from the tribe of Benjamin. [17]When he saw the travelers sitting in the
town square, he asked them where they were
from and where they were going.

[18]"We have been in Bethlehem in Judah,"
the man replied. "We are on our way to a remote area in the hill country of Ephraim, which
is my home. I traveled to Bethlehem, and now
I'm returning home.* But no one has taken us

18:30 As in an ancient Hebrew tradition, some Greek manuscripts, and Latin Vulgate; Masoretic Text reads *son of Manasseh.* **19:2** Or *she was unfaithful to him.* **19:3** As in Greek version; Hebrew reads *When she brought him to.* **19:18** As in Greek version (see also 19:29); Hebrew reads *now I'm going to the Tabernacle of the LORD.*

been corrupted. When the kingdom of Israel separated into the Northern and Southern kingdoms (ca. 922 BC), Jeroboam I set up a shrine in Dan (1 Kgs 12:29), until the Assyrian captivity (722 BC).

19:1—21:25 The Levite and His Concubine. This Levite, like his woman, remains anonymous. Like Micah, the Levite is no hero but a man corrupt in the midst of a corrupted people. **19:1–3:** His relationship with his common-law wife, although stormy, is recognized and approved in her family. **4–9:** The repetitious account of the father-in-law's delaying tactics serves as a reason for the lateness of their journey and their need to stay overnight along the way. It also serves to point out a deliberate contrast between Bethlehem, David's hometown in Judah, and inhospitable Gibeah, in the territory of Benjamin. **10–15:** We are led to assume that they would have been better off staying in non-Israelite Jerusalem than in Gibeah. **15:** That *no one took them in* would be considered outrageous; hospitality was an important civic virtue. **16–24:** The text echoes with the memory of the angels' visit to Sodom (Gen 19). In contrast, this is not a foreign stranger but a fellow

in for the night, 19 even though we have everything we need. We have straw and feed for our donkeys and plenty of bread and wine for ourselves."

20 "You are welcome to stay with me," the old man said. "I will give you anything you might need. But whatever you do, don't spend the night in the square." 21 So he took them home with him and fed the donkeys. After they washed their feet, they ate and drank together.

22 While they were enjoying themselves, a crowd of troublemakers from the town surrounded the house. They began beating at the door and shouting to the old man, "Bring out the man who is staying with you so we can have sex with him."

23 The old man stepped outside to talk to them. "No, my brothers, don't do such an evil thing. For this man is a guest in my house, and such a thing would be shameful. 24 Here, take my virgin daughter and this man's concubine. I will bring them out to you, and you can abuse them and do whatever you like. But don't do such a shameful thing to this man."

25 But they wouldn't listen to him. So the Levite took hold of his concubine and pushed her out the door. The men of the town abused her all night, taking turns raping her until morning. Finally, at dawn they let her go. 26 At daybreak the woman returned to the house where her husband was staying. She collapsed at the door of the house and lay there until it was light.

27 When her husband opened the door to leave, there lay his concubine with her hands on the threshold. 28 He said, "Get up! Let's go!" But there was no answer.* So he put her body on his donkey and took her home.

29 When he got home, he took a knife and cut his concubine's body into twelve pieces. Then he sent one piece to each tribe throughout all the territory of Israel.

30 Everyone who saw it said, "Such a horrible crime has not been committed in all the time since Israel left Egypt. Think about it! What are we going to do? Who's going to speak up?"

Israel's War with Benjamin

20 Then all the Israelites were united as one man, from Dan in the north to Beersheba in the south, including those from across the Jordan in the land of Gilead. The entire community assembled in the presence of the LORD at Mizpah. 2 The leaders of all the people and all the tribes of Israel—400,000 warriors armed with swords—took their positions in the assembly of the people of God. 3 (Word soon reached the land of Benjamin that the other tribes had gone up to Mizpah.) The Israelites then asked how this terrible crime had happened.

4 The Levite, the husband of the woman who had been murdered, said, "My concubine and I came to spend the night in Gibeah, a town that belongs to the people of Benjamin. 5 That night some of the leading citizens of Gibeah surrounded the house, planning to kill me, and they raped my concubine until she was dead. 6 So I cut her body into twelve pieces and sent the pieces throughout the territory assigned to Israel, for these men have committed a terrible and shameful crime. 7 Now then, all of you—the entire community of Israel—must decide here and now what should be done about this!"

8 And all the people rose to their feet in unison and declared, "None of us will return home! No, not even one of us! 9 Instead, this is what we will do to Gibeah; we will draw lots to decide who will attack it. 10 One tenth of the men* from each tribe will be chosen to supply the warriors with food, and the rest of us will take revenge on Gibeah* of Benjamin for this shameful thing they have done in Israel." 11 So all the Israelites were completely united, and they gathered together to attack the town.

12 The Israelites sent messengers to the tribe of Benjamin, saying, "What a terrible thing has been done among you! 13 Give up those evil men,

19:28 Greek version adds *for she was dead.* **20:10a** Hebrew *10 men from every hundred, 100 men from every thousand, and 1,000 men from every 10,000.* **20:10b** Hebrew *Geba,* in this case a variant spelling of Gibeah; also in 20:33.

Israelite and a Levite at that, yet the townsmen are intent on rape. **24–25:** Their host's offer to surrender his virgin daughter and the man's concubine to the mob comes as an affront beyond bearing, as it does in Genesis 19:8. These men thought of homosexual rape as being much the worse of two evils, involving a sexual connection abominated in Israelite culture and religion. The women are expendable. Their rape is wrong but not seen as so perverse. **25:** The Levite is the crass, egotistic, pitiless male who uses females for his purpose and salvation. **27–28:** The woman is dead. **29:** The dismembering of her body, the gruesome call to arms, may be interpreted as the response of a guilty, traumatized, and grief-filled person driven to the edge of insanity. **19:30—20:3:** Here at last is revulsion against corruption, a call to unity to reject such un-Israelite behavior, unworthy of a people brought out of Egypt. Yet it is also a call to civil war. **20:4–7:** The Levite's tale is a cleaned-up, self-serving version of what happened. **12–15:** Clan loyalty takes

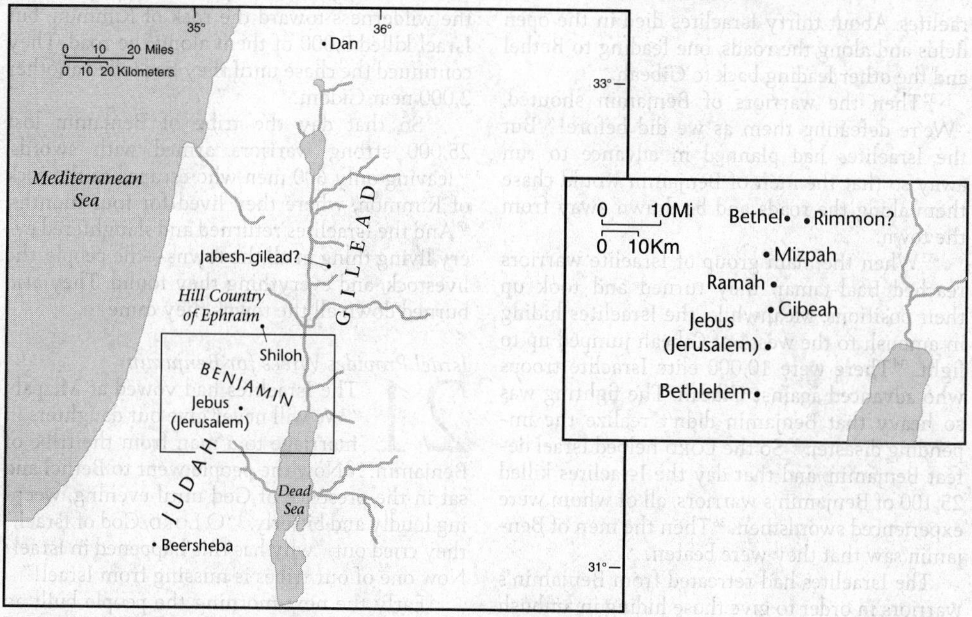

Sites Mentioned in Connection with the Benjaminite War

those troublemakers from Gibeah, so we can execute them and purge Israel of this evil."
But the people of Benjamin would not listen. 14 Instead, they came from their towns and
gathered at Gibeah to fight the Israelites. 15 In all,
26,000 of their warriors armed with swords arrived in Gibeah to join the 700 elite troops who
lived there. 16 Among Benjamin's elite troops,
700 were left-handed, and each of them could
sling a rock and hit a target within a hairsbreadth
without missing. 17 Israel had 400,000 experienced soldiers armed with swords, not counting
Benjamin's warriors.
18 Before the battle the Israelites went to
Bethel and asked God, "Which tribe should go
first to attack the people of Benjamin?"
The LORD answered, "Judah is to go first."
19 So the Israelites left early the next morning
and camped near Gibeah. 20 Then they advanced
toward Gibeah to attack the men of Benjamin.
21 But Benjamin's warriors, who were defending
the town, came out and killed 22,000 Israelites
on the battlefield that day.
22 But the Israelites encouraged each other
and took their positions again at the same place
they had fought the previous day. 23 For they had
gone up to Bethel and wept in the presence of the
LORD until evening. They had asked the LORD,
"Should we fight against our relatives from Benjamin again?"
And the LORD had said, "Go out and fight
against them."
24 So the next day they went out again to fight
against the men of Benjamin, 25 but the men of
Benjamin killed another 18,000 Israelites, all of
whom were experienced with the sword.
26 Then all the Israelites went up to Bethel and
wept in the presence of the LORD and fasted until
evening. They also brought burnt offerings and
peace offerings to the LORD. 27 The Israelites went
up seeking direction from the LORD. (In those
days the Ark of the Covenant of God was in
Bethel, 28 and Phinehas son of Eleazar and grandson of Aaron was the priest.) The Israelites asked
the LORD, "Should we fight against our relatives
from Benjamin again, or should we stop?"
The LORD said, "Go! Tomorrow I will hand
them over to you."
29 So the Israelites set an ambush all around
Gibeah. 30 They went out on the third day and
took their positions at the same place as before.
31 When the men of Benjamin came out to attack,
they were drawn away from the town. And as
they had done before, they began to kill the Is-

precedence over ethical principles. "Our own, right or wrong" seems to be Benjamin's philosophy, not loyalty to Israel as a nation. **18:** The Israelites replay the first scene in Judges, asking the LORD who shall

raelites. About thirty Israelites died in the open
fields and along the roads, one leading to Bethel
and the other leading back to Gibeah.
32 Then the warriors of Benjamin shouted,
"We're defeating them as we did before!" But
the Israelites had planned in advance to run
away so that the men of Benjamin would chase
them along the roads and be drawn away from
the town.
33 When the main group of Israelite warriors
reached Baal-tamar, they turned and took up
their positions. Meanwhile, the Israelites hiding
in ambush to the west* of Gibeah jumped up to
fight. 34 There were 10,000 elite Israelite troops
who advanced against Gibeah. The fighting was
so heavy that Benjamin didn't realize the impending disaster. 35 So the LORD helped Israel defeat Benjamin, and that day the Israelites killed
25,100 of Benjamin's warriors, all of whom were
experienced swordsmen. 36 Then the men of Benjamin saw that they were beaten.
The Israelites had retreated from Benjamin's
warriors in order to give those hiding in ambush
more room to maneuver against Gibeah. 37 Then
those who were hiding rushed in from all sides
and killed everyone in the town. 38 They had arranged to send up a large cloud of smoke from
the town as a signal. 39 When the Israelites saw
the smoke, they turned and attacked Benjamin's
warriors.
By that time Benjamin's warriors had killed
about thirty Israelites, and they shouted, "We're
defeating them as we did in the first battle!"
40 But when the warriors of Benjamin looked
behind them and saw the smoke rising into the
sky from every part of the town, 41 the men of
Israel turned and attacked. At this point the men
of Benjamin became terrified, because they realized disaster was close at hand. 42 So they turned
around and fled before the Israelites toward the
wilderness. But they couldn't escape the battle, and the people who came out of the nearby
towns were also killed.* 43 The Israelites surrounded the men of Benjamin and chased them
relentlessly, finally overtaking them east of Gibeah.* 44 That day 18,000 of Benjamin's strongest
warriors died in battle. 45 The survivors fled into
the wilderness toward the rock of Rimmon, but
Israel killed 5,000 of them along the road. They
continued the chase until they had killed another
2,000 near Gidom.
46 So that day the tribe of Benjamin lost
25,000 strong warriors armed with swords,
47 leaving only 600 men who escaped to the rock
of Rimmon, where they lived for four months.
48 And the Israelites returned and slaughtered every living thing in all the towns—the people, the
livestock, and everything they found. They also
burned down all the towns they came to.

Israel Provides Wives for Benjamin

21 The Israelites had vowed at Mizpah,
"We will never give our daughters in
marriage to a man from the tribe of
Benjamin." 2 Now the people went to Bethel and
sat in the presence of God until evening, weeping loudly and bitterly. 3 "O LORD, God of Israel,"
they cried out, "why has this happened in Israel?
Now one of our tribes is missing from Israel!"
4 Early the next morning the people built an
altar and presented their burnt offerings and
peace offerings on it. 5 Then they said, "Who
among the tribes of Israel did not join us at Mizpah when we held our assembly in the presence
of the LORD?" At that time they had taken a solemn oath in the LORD's presence, vowing that
anyone who refused to come would be put to
death.
6 The Israelites felt sorry for their brother
Benjamin and said, "Today one of the tribes of
Israel has been cut off. 7 How can we find wives
for the few who remain, since we have sworn by
the LORD not to give them our daughters in marriage?"
8 So they asked, "Who among the tribes of
Israel did not join us at Mizpah when we assembled in the presence of the LORD?" And they
discovered that no one from Jabesh-gilead had
attended the assembly. 9 For after they counted

20:33 As in Greek and Syriac versions and Latin Vulgate; Hebrew reads *hiding in the open space.* **20:42** Or *battle, for the people from the nearby towns also came out and killed them.* **20:43** The meaning of the Hebrew is uncertain.

go up first (1:1), and again Judah is indicated. **35–48:** The comprehensive defeat eventually inflicted on Benjamin is attributed to the LORD at work, just as he had been against the Canaanites.

21:1–25 Israel Provides Wives for Benjamin. 1, 5: At Mizpah, associated with Jephthah's commitment to God, the Israelites also made two self-generated vows. Both would have been considered unbreakable. **6–12:** Afraid of the curse on those who do not fulfill vows, they find a loophole in their first vow by activating their second. They provide wives for these Benjaminites while taking the promised retributive killing of the people of Jabesh-gilead, who had not participated in the war. **6:** Israel is yet reluctant that any of the tribes should disappear.

all the people, no one from Jabesh-gilead was present.

10 So the assembly sent 12,000 of their best warriors to Jabesh-gilead with orders to kill everyone there, including women and children. 11 "This is what you are to do," they said. "Completely destroy* all the males and every woman who is not a virgin." 12 Among the residents of Jabesh-gilead they found 400 young virgins who had never slept with a man, and they brought them to the camp at Shiloh in the land of Canaan.

13 The Israelite assembly sent a peace delegation to the remaining people of Benjamin who were living at the rock of Rimmon. 14 Then the men of Benjamin returned to their homes, and the 400 women of Jabesh-gilead who had been spared were given to them as wives. But there were not enough women for all of them.

15 The people felt sorry for Benjamin because the LORD had made this gap among the tribes of Israel. 16 So the elders of the assembly asked, "How can we find wives for the few who remain, since the women of the tribe of Benjamin are dead? 17 There must be heirs for the survivors so that an entire tribe of Israel is not wiped out. 18 But we cannot give them our own daughters in marriage because we have sworn with a solemn oath that anyone who does this will fall under God's curse."

19 Then they thought of the annual festival of the LORD held in Shiloh, south of Lebonah and north of Bethel, along the east side of the road that goes from Bethel to Shechem. 20 They told the men of Benjamin who still needed wives, "Go and hide in the vineyards. 21 When you see the young women of Shiloh come out for their dances, rush out from the vineyards, and each of you can take one of them home to the land of Benjamin to be your wife! 22 And when their fathers and brothers come to us in protest, we will tell them, 'Please be sympathetic. Let them have your daughters, for we didn't find wives for all of them when we destroyed Jabesh-gilead. And you are not guilty of breaking the vow since you did not actually give your daughters to them in marriage.' "

23 So the men of Benjamin did as they were told. Each man caught one of the women as she danced in the celebration and carried her off to be his wife. They returned to their own land, and they rebuilt their towns and lived in them.

24 Then the people of Israel departed by tribes and families, and they returned to their own homes.

25 In those days Israel had no king; all the people did whatever seemed right in their own eyes.

21:11 The Hebrew term used here refers to the complete consecration of things or people to the LORD, either by destroying them or by giving them as an offering.

10–14: The fate of those women is tragic: They are given over to the people their male relatives had refused to fight, men who defended rapists and who were deemed by the other tribes as unworthy of their daughters. **19–23:** Others are abducted during a religious festival to the LORD in Shiloh while their male protectors look away. Yet those abducted women were to be the mothers of the generations to follow. **25:** The people of God who refuse to obey God, make their own strategies and attempt their own deliverances end in degradation. It will be better with a king, hints the text, foreshadowing the Davidic dynasty appointed by God. All the rest is gloom and disintegration.

RUTH

INTRODUCTION

This beautifully constructed narrative tells of Ruth, a Moabite, who, through willing commitment to her impoverished mother-in-law Naomi, Naomi's people, and God (1:16–17), becomes great-grandmother to King David (4:17). God chose an isolated, foreign woman to bring redemption to his chosen people Israel. Ruth is hailed as being worth more than seven (the biblical number for perfection) sons. The book of Ruth is unequivocally a story about God's redemptive love.

Ruth is unusual in that it is a micro-tale concerning women and their struggles in a patriarchal society. For this reason, some scholars argue female authorship, and although this cannot be proven, there is some consensus that it began as an oral story. The canonical book of Ruth may have originated with the women who were aware of Naomi's destitution on her return to Bethlehem and who publicly rejoiced in the restoration of her family line. A written account of an oral tradition would embrace the classical style and language contained within the book and the various dialectical anachronisms while accounting for some editorial explanations and the genealogy (4:18–22). Names in Ruth reveal something of the characters who own them, in keeping with the Hebrew understanding that to know a person's name is to know his or her character. This could suggest that the narrative is a parable, but it conflicts with the historicity of the account (1:1; 4:7, 11–12, 18–22) and its geographical setting. One may conclude that through the passage of time, characters have been given appropriate names in order to emphasize their personalities, the story is indeed historical.

The various arguments regarding date of composition are based on linguistic content, chronological evidence, and the perceived purpose of the book. Evidence is inconclusive regarding precise dating. Assuming the genealogy is integral to the original version, the book was compiled after David became king of Israel, but precise dates remain unknown.

Ruth 1:1 sets the story "in the days when the judges ruled," roughly between 1220 and 1050 BC. Great social weight was accorded to clan loyalty during this time, as was continuance of the family line, always through the male. Israelites were divided into tribes, clans, and families. A clan was united by blood relationship and common ancestry. Land belonged to a family rather than to an individual, and if a man died leaving no sons, the inheritance went to his daughters; if no daughters, to his brothers; and so on (Num 27:8–11). If a married man died, his brother was obliged to act as *levir* (Lat., "brother-in-law") and marry the widow in order to secure his brother's family line (Deut 25:7–9). The firstborn son of this union would be regarded as the son of the dead man. While this law ultimately preserved patriarchal inheritance laws and protected family lineage, it also provided for the widow. Gleaning laws, too, protected the poor and the alien (Lev 19:9–10; 23:22). God was not reinforcing a patriarchal cultural framework through these stipulations; rather, through the provision of them, human integrity and dignity were to be given to those who were vulnerable because of the prevailing culture.

In the telling of Ruth's tale we gain some insight into the vulnerability of women striving for survival in a male domain, where the reality of famine and the vagaries of war were harsh aspects of life, and procreation an essential element of it. —*Gillian M. Rowell*

1:1–22 Death, Destitution, and Covenant
2:1–23 Providence
3:1–18 Covenant
4:1–22 Redemption

✧

Elimelech Moves His Family to Moab

1 In the days when the judges ruled in Israel, a severe famine came upon the land. So a man from Bethlehem in Judah left his home and went to live in the country of Moab, taking his wife and two sons with him. 2 The man's name was Elimelech, and his wife was Naomi. Their two sons were Mahlon and Kilion. They were Ephrathites from Bethlehem in the land of Judah. And when they reached Moab, they settled there.

3 Then Elimelech died, and Naomi was left with her two sons. 4 The two sons married Moabite women. One married a woman named Orpah, and the other a woman named Ruth. But about ten years later, 5 both Mahlon and Kilion died. This left Naomi alone, without her two sons or her husband.

Naomi and Ruth Return

6 Then Naomi heard in Moab that the LORD had blessed his people in Judah by giving them good crops again. So Naomi and her daughters-in-law got ready to leave Moab to return to her homeland. 7 With her two daughters-in-law she set out from the place where she had been living, and they took the road that would lead them back to Judah.

8 But on the way, Naomi said to her two daughters-in-law, "Go back to your mothers' homes. And may the LORD reward you for your kindness to your husbands and to me. 9 May the LORD bless you with the security of another marriage." Then she kissed them good-bye, and they all broke down and wept.

10 "No," they said. "We want to go with you to your people."

11 But Naomi replied, "Why should you go on with me? Can I still give birth to other sons who could grow up to be your husbands? 12 No, my daughters, return to your parents' homes, for I am too old to marry again. And even if it were possible, and I were to get married tonight and bear sons, then what? 13 Would you wait for them to grow up and refuse to marry someone else? No, of course not, my daughters! Things are far more bitter for me than for you, because the LORD himself has raised his fist against me."

14 And again they wept together, and Orpah kissed her mother-in-law good-bye. But Ruth clung tightly to Naomi. 15 "Look," Naomi said to her, "your sister-in-law has gone back to her people and to her gods. You should do the same."

16 But Ruth replied, "Don't ask me to leave you and turn back. Wherever you go, I will go;

1:1–22 Death, Destitution, and Covenant

The first chapter sets the stage for the story of redemption that makes up the majority of the book. **1:** *Bethlehem* means "house of bread," but ironically there is no bread because the land is in famine. *Moab*: Another irony, for the Moabites failed to give food to the Israelites during the Exodus, and they were cursed as a result (Deut 23:2–4). **2:** Circumstantial evidence suggests that an Ephrathite had considerable social standing within the community; the context suggests Ephrathah was a location in Bethlehem. **4:** The marriages to foreign women were possibly for reasons of self-preservation—in order to gain access to land (given as a dowry) that they could farm. There also may have been a shortage of men due to war or famine, and the Moabite women had little choice but to marry foreigners. **5:** Naomi's social standing is precarious, and the extinction of Elimelech's family line is conclusive. Ancient Israel placed a harsh social stigma on women with no children. **6:** The now all-female cast, headed by Naomi, is still in search of food. **8:** Naomi might wish to evade publicly facing up to her sons' marriage to foreigners on arrival in Bethlehem (cf. 4:12; Gen 38:11). Naomi's blessing (repeated in 2:2), reveals a perspective that is almost alien in contemporary society: that of honoring and perpetuating the family of the dead. **12–13:** Naomi's worth is anchored in her status as wife and mother; she interprets her circumstances as being the result of God's judgment against her and not against her husband or sons (cf. Deut 23:2–4). Naomi is past child-bearing, unable to provide sons for Elimelech or husbands for her widowed daughters-in-law. Marriage will not, therefore, secure her future, nor that of her daughters-in-law. **15:** Naomi's appeal to Ruth to follow Orpah's example suggests Naomi's disillusionment with God. She has no desire to convert

Changing Life Circumstances

Women often have to change the circumstances of their lives. Some of these changes come because of personal tragedies, because children bring about much change in their lives, or because their nurturing natures wish to meet the needs of those dependent on their love and care. Role models in the Bible can give courage and wisdom to handle the necessary changes.

A primary example of a biblical character who changed her life's circumstances is Mary Magdalene. Mary was from a small town south of the Plain of Gennesaret, Magdala. She was perhaps afflicted with a mental disorder because Jesus "had cast out seven demons" from her (Luke 8:2). There is little doubt that she must have been a reviled and ostracized woman in her hometown prior to her healing. When she came to Jesus for healing, she changed her life's circumstances. She became a powerful and poised figure who gave of her means as well as of herself to his ministry. Mary didn't let her past deter her from developing into one of the new church's first woman leaders. As a result of her witness about Jesus' resurrection, she experienced a transformation in her life, from material to spiritual.

Other women of the Bible hold a valued place in the honor roll of courageous women who effectively changed their life's circumstances. Rahab, the prostitute of Jericho, was wise enough to understand that the spies were sent by God—the God she didn't know but believed existed—and by assisting them she assured her survival in a turbulent and dangerous time (Josh 2). The widow of Nain had the courage to step out of her subservient and maligned role and implore Jesus to heal her son, her only means of keeping her from destitution (Luke 7). The Syrophoenician woman approached Jesus on behalf of her daughter. Jesus not only used her as an example of faith in action but also admired her courage to act out of character and therefore gain Jesus' blessing, resulting in the healing of her child (Mark 7). Naomi and Ruth worked together to make a better life. The loss of their husbands caused them to bond not just in their relationship as mother-in-law and daughter-in-law but as loyal, supportive friends. They overcame their sorrow and created new lives. Ruth became an ancestor of Jesus, and Naomi found fulfillment in a new family. Esther was an orphan who became the favored of the king in her land of captivity. She took a great risk in making her plea on behalf of her people, therefore changing not only her circumstances but also those of her people. Hers is a dramatic story of a woman who saw opportunities and had the will to change until she became revered in her time and throughout biblical and secular history.

This short honor roll is only a sampling of women who overcame some of life's greatest difficulties. Women of our time who find their lives restricted, hampered, even destroyed, can find no better role models than our spiritual, biblical ancestors.

wherever you live, I will live. Your people will
be my people, and your God will be my God.
17 Wherever you die, I will die, and there I will be
buried. May the LORD punish me severely if I allow anything but death to separate us!" 18 When
Naomi saw that Ruth was determined to go with
her, she said nothing more.
19 So the two of them continued on their journey. When they came to Bethlehem, the entire
town was excited by their arrival. "Is it really
Naomi?" the women asked.
20 "Don't call me Naomi," she responded.
"Instead, call me Mara,* for the Almighty has
made life very bitter for me. 21 I went away full,
but the LORD has brought me home empty. Why
call me Naomi when the LORD has caused me to

1:20 *Naomi* means "pleasant"; *Mara* means "bitter."

Ruth. **16–17:** As a widow Ruth would be an added burden to her family or she would be a servant for her brothers' wives until a husband was found for her. Marriage, however, is not on Ruth's agenda. In committing herself to Naomi, Ruth unknowingly secures for herself the role of redeemer, for her covenantal confession reveals a loyalty and commitment that will be borne out in the rest of the text and will result in God's blessing. Justice is her prime motivating factor. Trapped within their cultural framework, both women face a bleak future. But Ruth proves through her actions that she perceives the God of the Israelites to favor the oppressed, and she is resolute in her determination to follow this through. **19:** The women of the town almost don't recognize the now-desolate Naomi as the one who left Bethlehem more than a decade previously (1:4). **20–21:** Naomi's circumstances have directly affected her outlook on

suffer* and the Almighty has sent such tragedy
upon me?"
22 So Naomi returned from Moab, accompanied by her daughter-in-law Ruth, the young
Moabite woman. They arrived in Bethlehem in
late spring, at the beginning of the barley harvest.

Ruth Works in Boaz's Field

2 Now there was a wealthy and influential
man in Bethlehem named Boaz, who was a
relative of Naomi's husband, Elimelech.
2 One day Ruth the Moabite said to Naomi,
"Let me go out into the harvest fields to pick up
the stalks of grain left behind by anyone who is
kind enough to let me do it."
Naomi replied, "All right, my daughter, go
ahead." 3 So Ruth went out to gather grain behind
the harvesters. And as it happened, she found
herself working in a field that belonged to Boaz,
the relative of her father-in-law, Elimelech.
4 While she was there, Boaz arrived from
Bethlehem and greeted the harvesters. "The
LORD be with you!" he said.
"The LORD bless you!" the harvesters replied.
5 Then Boaz asked his foreman, "Who is that
young woman over there? Who does she belong
to?"
6 And the foreman replied, "She is the young
woman from Moab who came back with Naomi.
7 She asked me this morning if she could gather
grain behind the harvesters. She has been hard
at work ever since, except for a few minutes' rest
in the shelter."
8 Boaz went over and said to Ruth, "Listen,

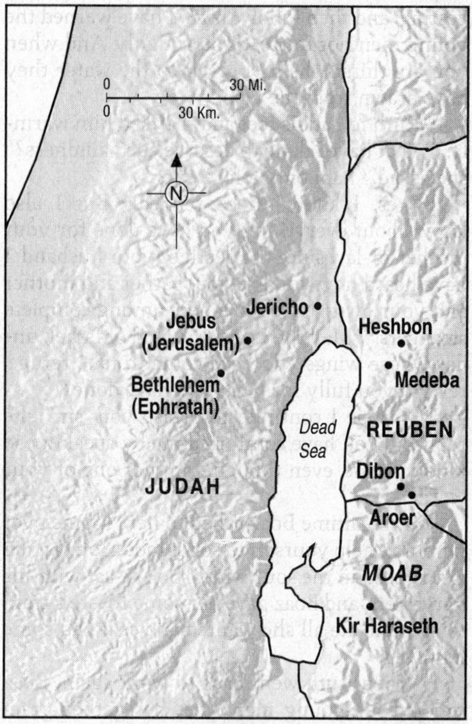

Places in Ruth

my daughter. Stay right here with us when you
gather grain; don't go to any other fields. Stay
right behind the young women working in my
field. 9 See which part of the field they are har-

1:21 Or *has testified against me.*

life. She is consumed with self-pity and hopelessness. Naomi perceives herself as alone, isolated in her affliction and despair, suggesting that her daughter-in-law, Ruth, counts for nothing. Naomi has only one perspective: As a woman she was the facilitator of Elimelech's family line in which was established her security and future. **22:** The famine has ended. The harvest is a fortuitous time to have arrived.

2:1–23 Providence

With the introduction of Boaz to the story, the outlook for Naomi and Ruth becomes brighter; redemption becomes a possibility if Ruth is bold enough to claim it. **1:** The Hebrew words used to describe Boaz mean "man of standing and worth." Not only is he *a wealthy and influential man*, but more importantly, a good one. Matthew 1:5 identifies Boaz's mother as Rahab, the prostitute. Rahab, like Ruth, was an unlikely foreign female who, in her commitment to God's people, was used by God to secure his purposes for Israel (Josh 2; 6:25). **2:** Ruth takes the initiative to provide for her small household. Naomi's social standing, being an Ephrathite, may prevent her from joining Ruth, but it is more likely that she is too weak from age or circumstance to assist with gleaning. **3:** The repetition that Boaz was from Elimelech's family emphasizes his connection to Naomi and paves the way for what is to follow. Ruth is unaware of this connection. **5:** Boaz's question indicates a desire to know who, among his male neighbors, is responsible for the unknown woman working in his field. **6–7:** Whether gleaning was common practice at that time is unclear, but it would indicate to Boaz the extent of Ruth's and Naomi's poverty. **8–9:** Field boundaries were unmarked, often determined only with reference to surrounding ownership. *I have warned the young men not to treat you roughly* could refer to

vesting, and then follow them. I have warned the young men not to treat you roughly. And when you are thirsty, help yourself to the water they have drawn from the well."
10 Ruth fell at his feet and thanked him warmly. "What have I done to deserve such kindness?" she asked. "I am only a foreigner."
11 "Yes, I know," Boaz replied. "But I also know about everything you have done for your mother-in-law since the death of your husband. I have heard how you left your father and mother and your own land to live here among complete strangers.
12 May the LORD, the God of Israel, under whose wings you have come to take refuge, reward you fully for what you have done."
13 "I hope I continue to please you, sir," she replied. "You have comforted me by speaking so kindly to me, even though I am not one of your workers."
14 At mealtime Boaz called to her, "Come over here, and help yourself to some food. You can dip your bread in the sour wine." So she sat with his harvesters, and Boaz gave her some roasted grain to eat. She ate all she wanted and still had some left over.
15 When Ruth went back to work again, Boaz ordered his young men, "Let her gather grain right among the sheaves without stopping her.
16 And pull out some heads of barley from the bundles and drop them on purpose for her. Let her pick them up, and don't give her a hard time!"
17 So Ruth gathered barley there all day, and when she beat out the grain that evening, it filled an entire basket.*
18 She carried it back into town and showed it to her mother-in-law. Ruth also gave her the roasted grain that was left over from her meal.
19 "Where did you gather all this grain today?" Naomi asked. "Where did you work? May the LORD bless the one who helped you!"
So Ruth told her mother-in-law about the man in whose field she had worked. She said, "The man I worked with today is named Boaz."
20 "May the LORD bless him!" Naomi told her daughter-in-law. "He is showing his kindness to us as well as to your dead husband.* That man is one of our closest relatives, one of our family redeemers."
21 Then Ruth* said, "What's more, Boaz even told me to come back and stay with his harvesters until the entire harvest is completed."
22 "Good!" Naomi exclaimed. "Do as he said, my daughter. Stay with his young women right through the whole harvest. You might be harassed in other fields, but you'll be safe with him."
23 So Ruth worked alongside the women in Boaz's fields and gathered grain with them until the end of the barley harvest. Then she continued working with them through the wheat harvest in early summer. And all the while she lived with her mother-in-law.

Ruth at the Threshing Floor

3 One day Naomi said to Ruth, "My daughter, it's time that I found a permanent home for you, so that you will be provided for.
2 Boaz is a close relative of ours, and he's

2:17 Hebrew *it was about an ephah* [20 quarts or 22 liters]. **2:20** Hebrew *to the living and to the dead.* **2:21** Hebrew *Ruth the Moabite.*

Ruth's vulnerable situation in having no man to protect her, leaving her liable to sexual abuse, or it could indicate that gleaners were not welcome during harvest, for they were in effect reducing the quantity of crop gathered. **10:** Ruth is making sure that Boaz takes notice of her. **11:** Ruth is already known and admired in the community. **12:** This pious blessing will be fulfilled through Boaz's actions (3:13; 4:1–10) when Ruth goads Boaz into action on behalf of herself and Naomi. **13:** Working within her culture Ruth gently lays claim to human dignity by emphasizing, to someone powerful, her precarious status. **14–16:** Ruth's tactic, conscious or not, has its effect, and Boaz welcomes Ruth into his household by inviting her to eat and drink with them, and ordering his workers to look after her welfare. **17:** *An entire basket*: Hebrew *ephah* (see translator's note), a little more than half a bushel. **19–20:** Ruth's disclosure of Boaz's name to Naomi emphasizes the key role that Boaz will play in their lives. The narrator labors the point of Boaz's identity when his name is finally revealed to Naomi. Compare Naomi's blessing of Boaz to her blessing in 1:8. **20:** *Our closest relatives*: Ruth's success in gathering food has been rewarded by Naomi's inclusion of Ruth in her clan. **21:** The Hebrew designates Ruth as "the Moabite," a crucial element of the narrative: In focusing on Ruth's foreign origins, the text simultaneously emphasizes God's inclusive love. **23:** The women are temporarily secure in work and food through the providence of God.

3:1–18 Covenant

Ruth and Boaz together on the threshing floor could have compromised both of them. Instead, this exchange becomes the turning point in the story. **1–4:** Naomi devises a scheme to motivate Boaz to fulfill his obligations as a next of kin. It is not clear why Naomi

been very kind by letting you gather grain with
his young women. Tonight he will be winnowing
barley at the threshing floor. 3Now do as I tell
you—take a bath and put on perfume and dress
in your nicest clothes. Then go to the threshing floor, but don't let Boaz see you until he has
finished eating and drinking. 4Be sure to notice
where he lies down; then go and uncover his feet
and lie down there. He will tell you what to do."
5"I will do everything you say," Ruth replied.
6So she went down to the threshing floor that
night and followed the instructions of her mother-in-law.

7After Boaz had finished eating and drinking
and was in good spirits, he lay down at the far end
of the pile of grain and went to sleep. Then Ruth
came quietly, uncovered his feet, and lay down.
8Around midnight Boaz suddenly woke up and
turned over. He was surprised to find a woman lying at his feet! 9"Who are you?" he asked.

"I am your servant Ruth," she replied.
"Spread the corner of your covering over me, for
you are my family redeemer."

10"The Lord bless you, my daughter!" Boaz
exclaimed. "You are showing even more family
loyalty now than you did before, for you have not
gone after a younger man, whether rich or poor.
11Now don't worry about a thing, my daughter.
I will do what is necessary, for everyone in town
knows you are a virtuous woman. 12But while
it's true that I am one of your family redeemers,
there is another man who is more closely related
to you than I am. 13Stay here tonight, and in the
morning I will talk to him. If he is willing to redeem you, very well. Let him marry you. But if
he is not willing, then as surely as the Lord lives,
I will redeem you myself! Now lie down here
until morning."

14So Ruth lay at Boaz's feet until the morning, but she got up before it was light enough for
people to recognize each other. For Boaz had said,
"No one must know that a woman was here at the
threshing floor." 15Then Boaz said to her, "Bring
your cloak and spread it out." He measured six
scoops* of barley into the cloak and placed it on
her back. Then he* returned to the town.

3:15a Hebrew *six measures,* an unknown quantity.
3:15b Most Hebrew manuscripts read *he;* many Hebrew manuscripts, Syriac version, and Latin Vulgate read *she.*

instructs Ruth to approach Boaz in this way. Hebrew *regel,* "feet," is sometimes a euphemism for the sexual organs. It is possible that Naomi is encouraging Ruth to make a sexual advance. Unlike 4:13, the text is not explicit. **5–7:** Ruth acts and is unafraid to claim God's provision for herself and Naomi through Boaz. **8:** *Surprised*: The Hebrew word (sometimes translated "startle" or "tremble") reveals that Boaz, the strong man, was not merely surprised but frightened to find a woman lying near to him, suggesting no expectation on his part to be visited in such a manner. **9:** Ruth challenges Boaz, who is a member of Elimelech's clan, to act as *family redeemer* (see also 2:20) using similar imagery to that which Boaz used of the Lord when he blessed her in 2:12. Ruth, who has sought refuge under the Lord's wings, now seeks refuge under Boaz's cloak. Ezekiel 16:8 uses a similar phrase when the Lord rescues Jerusalem from destitution by spreading his garment over her nakedness. The family redeemer was specifically concerned with buying back ancestral land (Lev 25:25). While no specific mention has been made of Naomi's land, the ancient reader would understand that the redemption of land was a responsibility of the next of kin. But that was not the only responsibility (cf. Gen 38:8–9; Deut 25:5–10; Matt 22:23–25). Because levirate marriage is not possible for Naomi, should Ruth find a male family member willing and able to comply, she could claim a *levir* to continue the family line. **10–11:** Boaz interprets Ruth's actions and appeal as asking him to act as redeemer and brother-in-law, the latter being an invitation to marriage. Not only has Ruth left her family and country; she is now prepared to further the line of her Israelite father-in-law in order to redeem the destitution of her mother-in-law. Self-sacrifice is sometimes perceived as a natural element of a woman's character and role. But Boaz is right to commend Ruth, for her conduct is a model for both genders. Ruth has made an ethical choice, and now she is living by it. As female she initiates; as male Boaz responds. **12–13:** *Another man*: Boaz is content for a closer relative to take on the role of family redeemer, thus indicating that the motivation for his actions is based more on duty than on romantic love. **14:** If it is discovered that Ruth has visited the threshing floor, Boaz may be compromised when challenging the other man to redeem the land and also to marry Ruth (v. 5). If a man was suspected of having intercourse with a Gentile woman, he could not undertake levirate marriage with her. **15:** The gift of barley is a sign for Naomi that Boaz is committed to both of the women and a sign to the reader that the women are still in poverty and in need of food. The theme of covenant pervades the narrative. Ruth has pledged her allegiance to Naomi, and in fulfillment of that pledge goes to the threshing floor to invite Boaz to take up his role. Boaz in response pledges that he will do for her all that she asks, and Naomi is confident this promise, his covenant, is to be relied upon. The barley is a sign of Boaz's covenant to the women.

16 When Ruth went back to her mother-in-law,
Naomi asked, "What happened, my daughter?"
Ruth told Naomi everything Boaz had done
for her, 17 and she added, "He gave me these six
scoops of barley and said, 'Don't go back to your
mother-in-law empty-handed.' "
18 Then Naomi said to her, "Just be patient, my
daughter, until we hear what happens. The man
won't rest until he has settled things today."

Boaz Marries Ruth

4 Boaz went to the town gate and took a seat
there. Just then the family redeemer he
had mentioned came by, so Boaz called out
to him, "Come over here and sit down, friend. I
want to talk to you." So they sat down together. 2 Then Boaz called ten leaders from the town
and asked them to sit as witnesses. 3 And Boaz
said to the family redeemer, "You know Naomi,
who came back from Moab. She is selling the
land that belonged to our relative Elimelech. 4 I
thought I should speak to you about it so that
you can redeem it if you wish. If you want the
land, then buy it here in the presence of these
witnesses. But if you don't want it, let me know
right away, because I am next in line to redeem
it after you."
The man replied, "All right, I'll redeem it."
5 Then Boaz told him, "Of course, your purchase of the land from Naomi also requires that
you marry Ruth, the Moabite widow. That way
she can have children who will carry on her husband's name and keep the land in the family."
6 "Then I can't redeem it," the family redeemer replied, "because this might endanger my own
estate. You redeem the land; I cannot do it."
7 Now in those days it was the custom in Israel for anyone transferring a right of purchase to
remove his sandal and hand it to the other party.
This publicly validated the transaction. 8 So the
other family redeemer drew off his sandal as he
said to Boaz, "You buy the land."
9 Then Boaz said to the elders and to the crowd
standing around, "You are witnesses that today
I have bought from Naomi all the property of
Elimelech, Kilion, and Mahlon. 10 And with the
land I have acquired Ruth, the Moabite widow of
Mahlon, to be my wife. This way she can have a
son to carry on the family name of her dead husband and to inherit the family property here in
his hometown. You are all witnesses today."
11 Then the elders and all the people standing
in the gate replied, "We are witnesses! May the
LORD make this woman who is coming into your

4:1–22 Redemption

The covenants and redemption are fulfilled. Legally there were no provisions enabling a widow to inherit the property of her deceased husband (Num 27:8–11), but in practice it seems that Naomi is using Elimelech's land to galvanize the male members of her clan into action. Leviticus 25:25 indicates that selling the family land is clear confirmation of poverty and testifies to the practice of family members redeeming the land (buying it back) to keep it in the family. If the next near relative(s) will not redeem the land, Naomi will benefit from selling it, but the demise of Elimelech's line will be absolute. **1–2:** In calling the meeting of the town council at the town gate, where matters of legal and public concern were conducted, Boaz serves the purposes of Naomi and Ruth. The men will determine the fate of the women. (See Deut 25:7–9 for a somewhat different scenario.) **4–6:** The anonymous next of kin is initially willing to redeem the land until Boaz also imposes on him the responsibility of acting as *levir*. Boaz has presented the next of kin with a predicament. If the man accepts his duty as next of kin and acts to redeem the land, he will also acquire Ruth, who hopes to carry on Elimelech's line by having children. Levirate marriage is not an option concerning Naomi and poses no threat to the relative's estate, for she is past childbearing. But if he marries Ruth, he would forfeit the redeemed land on the birth of her firstborn son, for the son would be regarded as the firstborn of Mahlon, and all inheritance rights would go to that son. If Ruth were to have no more sons, the *levir* would have restored Elimelech's family line at the expense of his own. **7:** The editorial comment on the practice of sandal exchange indicates a passing of generations after the story is told. **9–10:** Boaz's public announcement is ironic, for Elimelech's and Mahlon's names are omitted from the genealogies. The line of descent is through Boaz in 4:21 and Matthew 1:5, fulfilling the blessing endowed on him by the elders (4:12). It may be that Elimelech's line was also attributable to Salmon; if so, God's redemptive purposes in the restoration of his family have been superbly accomplished. In keeping with the patriarchal framework of which he is a part, Boaz's proclamation is not couched in terms of compassion for the women but rather in terms of maintaining Elimelech's and subsequently Mahlon's name. Naomi embraced this framework wholeheartedly; her identity has been shattered through the loss of male lineage. From her perspective the task of women is to bear children for men. In contrast to this, while Ruth facilitates this agenda, her motivation is based on her commitment to Naomi and ensuring Naomi's survival. In the union of Boaz and Ruth, God has incorporated wealthy male Israelite

home like Rachel and Leah, from whom all the nation of Israel descended! May you prosper in Ephrathah and be famous in Bethlehem. [12]And may the LORD give you descendants by this young woman who will be like those of our ancestor Perez, the son of Tamar and Judah."

The Descendants of Boaz

[13]So Boaz took Ruth into his home, and she became his wife. When he slept with her, the LORD enabled her to become pregnant, and she gave birth to a son. [14]Then the women of the town said to Naomi, "Praise the LORD, who has now provided a redeemer for your family! May this child be famous in Israel. [15]May he restore your youth and care for you in your old age. For he is the son of your daughter-in-law who loves you and has been better to you than seven sons!"

[16]Naomi took the baby and cuddled him to her breast. And she cared for him as if he were her own. [17]The neighbor women said, "Now at last Naomi has a son again!" And they named him Obed. He became the father of Jesse and the grandfather of David.

[18]This is the genealogical record of their ancestor Perez:

Perez was the father of Hezron.
[19]Hezron was the father of Ram.
Ram was the father of Amminadab.
[20]Amminadab was the father of Nahshon.
Nahshon was the father of Salmon.*
[21]Salmon was the father of Boaz.
Boaz was the father of Obed.
[22]Obed was the father of Jesse.
Jesse was the father of David.

4:20 As in some Greek manuscripts (see also 4:21); Hebrew reads *Salma.*

and impoverished female Moabite in his redemptive purposes. **11–12:** *Rachel and Leah,* with their maidservants Bilhah and Zilpah, were the mothers of the twelve sons of Jacob (Gen 29), the ancestors of the twelve tribes of Israel. Ephrathah is where Rachel died in childbirth (Gen 35:16–20); it is also identified as "only a small village among all the people of Judah. Yet a ruler of Israel will come from you, one whose origins are from the distant past" (Mic 5:2; cf. Matt 2:4–6). The reference to *Perez, the son of Tamar and Judah* (see Gen 38) incorporates Boaz's family heritage and also alludes to levirate marriage (Tamar's in this case). The genealogy identifies Perez as Boaz's ancestor, and no mention is made of Elimelech or Mahlon or maintaining the name of the dead with his property. **13:** Obed's conception is orchestrated by God. Ruth provided a grandchild for Naomi that her sons could not. Ruth has redeemed Naomi, Boaz has redeemed Ruth, and together they not only provided a forerunner for the messianic line but also became an essential part of it (Matt 1:5). **14–15:** In extolling Ruth the women gently rebuke Naomi for perceiving the worthiness of her life only in terms of family lineage; in praising the LORD they acknowledge God's providence in redemption. **17:** The women, rather than Boaz, name the child, possibly because as the firstborn of a levirate marriage the boy is reckoned by the women to be Mahlon's. **18–22:** The genealogy straightens things out and attributes paternity to Boaz, rather than Mahlon.

1 SAMUEL

INTRODUCTION

"It was the best of times; it was the worst of times," writes Charles Dickens in his *Tale of Two Cities*—a world in transition where some things never change. In the Hebrew Bible the books of 1 and 2 Samuel directly follow from the verdict of the final editor of the book of Judges. The breakdown in moral and social order is described in Judges 19—21: "In those days Israel had no king; all the people did whatever seemed right in their own eyes" (Judg 21:25). Thus the stage is set for the social and political transition from a society organized as a loose confederation of tribes, organized largely by lineage, to monarchical rule.

The books of 1 and 2 Samuel were originally a single book recounting the beginning of the monarchy and the reigns of its first two kings, Saul and David. The book was named after Samuel because he plays a prominent role in its beginning section. The name is not entirely appropriate, however, since Samuel dies well before 1 Samuel ends (1 Sam 25:1). This book was also part of a larger unit known as the Deuteronomistic History, which incorporates the present books of Deuteronomy, Joshua, Judges, 1–2 Samuel, and 1–2 Kings. The Deuteronomistic History is the central history of Israel in the Hebrew Bible. It covers the events from the giving of the law and the entry into the promised land to the overthrow of the monarchy and the exile of the people to Babylon. As a whole, the history stresses such matters as obedience to the law, God's choice of Jerusalem as a central place of worship for Israel, and David as its king. This history was composed by one or more unknown authors. It was probably written during the Exile (after 586 BC) as a way of collecting Israel's traditions and editing them into a single, running historical account.

The book of 1 Samuel falls into three main sections around its principal characters, Samuel, Saul, and David. Samuel and Saul both prepare the way for David. Samuel is a transitional figure—the last of the judges and the prophet who anoints Saul and then announces Saul's rejection by the LORD and anoints David in his place. Saul is a tragic figure—plucked from obscurity and thrust into a position of power for which he is unfit. Everything he does is a mistake. His rapid decline is balanced by David's meteoric rise. David can do no wrong. Like Saul, he is presented as humble and without personal ambition for kingship. But unlike Saul, "the LORD was with David"—a major theme in the book. David, for his part, consistently trusts in the LORD to guide his movements and actions. Indeed, David is the central character not only in 1–2 Samuel but in the entire Deuteronomistic History.

Despite the changes in governance detailed in 1 Samuel, for the majority of people during this period, life proceeded much as before with its focus primarily on kinship ties and human relationships. Even for those directly caught up in the events surrounding the establishing of the monarchy, family concerns loom large, and much of the action in both 1 and 2 Samuel focuses on the developing and shifting relationships between the various characters. But what makes this story of supreme and lasting value is the divine dimension, for it is the genius of the Judeo-Christian tradition that God is never remote from human affairs but is active in them, working out his mysterious purposes in, through, and sometimes despite the lives of frail and often failing human beings. The books of Samuel may recount Israel's transition to kingship, but the overarching message is that ultimately the LORD rules over all.—*Joy Osgood*

1:1—2:11	A Mother's Prayer
2:12–36	A Father's Failure
3:1–21	A Young Man's Calling
4:1—7:2	The Glory and Power of Yahweh
7:3—8:22	Samuel as Judge
9:1—10:27a	The Anointing and Commissioning of Saul
10:27b—11:15	The Claims of Kinship
12:1–25	Samuel's Farewell
13:1—14:52	Saul under Pressure
15:1–35	Saul's Failure
16:1–23	David as Court Musician
17:1–58	David as Champion of Israel
18:1—20:42	David and the Family of Saul
21:1—22:23	David, Saul, and the Massacre at Nob
23:1—27:4	David on the Run from Saul
27:5—28:2	David in Philistine Territory
28:3–25	Saul's Descent into Despair
29:1–11	David and the King of Gath
30:1–31	David and the Amalekites
31:1–13	The Death of Saul

✧

Elkanah and His Family

1 There was a man named Elkanah who lived
in Ramah in the region of Zuph* in the hill
country of Ephraim. He was the son of Jeroham, son of Elihu, son of Tohu, son of Zuph, of
Ephraim. 2 Elkanah had two wives, Hannah and
Peninnah. Peninnah had children, but Hannah
did not.
3 Each year Elkanah would travel to Shiloh to
worship and sacrifice to the LORD of Heaven's Armies at the Tabernacle. The priests of the LORD at
that time were the two sons of Eli—Hophni and
Phinehas. 4 On the days Elkanah presented his
sacrifice, he would give portions of the meat to
Peninnah and each of her children. 5 And though
he loved Hannah, he would give her only one
choice portion* because the LORD had given her
no children. 6 So Peninnah would taunt Hannah
and make fun of her because the LORD had kept
her from having children. 7 Year after year it was
the same—Peninnah would taunt Hannah as they
went to the Tabernacle.* Each time, Hannah would
be reduced to tears and would not even eat.
8 "Why are you crying, Hannah?" Elkanah
would ask. "Why aren't you eating? Why be

1:1 As in Greek version; Hebrew reads *in Ramathaim-zophim;* compare 1:19. **1:5** Or *And because he loved Hannah, he would give her a choice portion.* The meaning of the Hebrew is uncertain. **1:7** Hebrew *the house of the LORD;* also in 1:24.

1:1—2:11 A Mother's Prayer

The story of Hannah's faith and devotion to God marks a turning point in Israel's history. In ancient society barrenness was regarded as a curse from God, a personal disaster that condemned a woman to an uncertain future. Children, particularly sons, were an effective insurance policy for a mother in the event of her husband's death. **1:1:** Kinship ties were very important in early Israelite society. Membership in a kinship group brought associated rights and duties, privileges and responsibilities. Within the patrilineal framework characteristic of Israelite society, women also ideally found their security and destiny. **2:** Hannah was almost certainly the first wife. In the event of a first wife's being childless, taking a second wife was the norm if the husband's economic status permitted. **6–7:** Peninnah was fruitful, and she exploited

Barrenness and Fertility

The contrasting biblical motifs of barrenness and fertility have their theological roots in the Hebraic concept of God as lifegiver, a concept prominent throughout the Scriptures, from the creation of all living things in Genesis (Gen 1:1—2:25) to the river of the water of life in Revelation (Rev 22:1). Fundamental to the biblical worldview is the confession that God is Creator of all that exists and lifegiver to all that has life.

At its most graphic level the concept of God as lifegiver appears in the depiction of God as a woman giving birth. For the Deuteronomist, God is "the God who had given you birth" (Deut 32:18), while for Isaiah God is the birthing woman: "'Would I ever bring this nation to the point of birth and then not deliver it?' asks the LORD" (Isa 66:9). More frequently, however, God is depicted as the divine agent who bestows fertility upon humans by opening a woman's womb (Gen 29:31; 30:22), in this way enabling childbirth (see Birth Pain Imagery, John 16; Childbearing and Rearing, Col 3).

The biblical records highlight the significance of God's role in enabling childbirth by means of birth predictions delivered by personages divine and human: God (Gen 17:1–21; 18:1–15), the angel of the LORD (Gen 16:1–14; Judg 13:2–25; Matt 1:18-25; Luke 1:5–25, 26–38), a priest (1 Sam 1:17) and a prophet (1 Kgs 13:1–2; 2 Kgs 4:11–17; 2 Sam 7:1–17; 1 Chr 22:6–10; Is 7:14; 9:6–7). For their part the women respond to God's initiatives on their behalf by acknowledging God's essential role in the birth of their children (Gen 4:1, 25; 21:6; 29:32, 33, 35; 30:6, 18, 20, 23–24; 1 Sam 1:20, 27; Luke 1:25).

Alongside the Hebraic concept of God as life-giver stands the correlated concept of barrenness as curse. Barrenness, like fertility, is viewed in terms of divine action. If God opens the womb (Gen 29:31; 30:22), God also closes the womb (Gen 20:18; 1 Sam 1:5) and prevents women from bearing children (Gen 16:2; 30:2). If fertility represents the blessing of God, barrenness represents not merely the absence of that blessing but at its most extreme a curse that God calls down on the disobedient (Deut 28:15, 18). By contrast, for those who obey God's commands, God will remove this curse (Exod 23:26; Deut 7:14).

Barrenness and fertility find their greatest prominence as they are juxtaposed in the accounts of women whose barrenness and desolation have been transformed by God into the joy of conception and childbirth. The biblical writers proclaim God's power to reverse the fortunes of the childless woman (Gen 18:13–14; Isa 54:1–3; Luke 1:36–37; Rom 4:19–21), and they compare God's concern for the barren woman with God's corresponding concerns for the poor and the weak in society (1 Sam 2:2–8; Ps 113:5–9; see God's Call to Social Justice, Amos 5). These writers depict God as one who sees and hears the distress of barren women (Gen 29:31—30:6), grants their petitions (1 Sam 1:17, 27), and heals their barrenness (Gen 20:17). The biblical texts are replete with the stories of women for whom God has turned barrenness into fertility, including Sarah (Gen 11:30; 16:1), the wife of Manoah (Judg 13:2–3), Hannah (1 Sam 1:1–2, 4–6), and Elizabeth (Luke 1:5–7, 18, 36).

Just as with the motif of barrenness, the imagery of fertility functions metaphorically with respect to the life of the nation. If the language of barrenness paints an image of dispersion and exile for the people of God (Isa 49:21; Hos 9:11–14, 16–17), the unexpected fertility of the once barren woman stands as a symbol of God's ultimate reversal of their political fortunes (Isa 54:1).

downhearted just because you have no children? You have me—isn't that better than having ten sons?"

Hannah's Prayer for a Son

[9]Once after a sacrificial meal at Shiloh, Hannah got up and went to pray. Eli the priest was sitting at his customary place beside the entrance of the Tabernacle.* [10]Hannah was in deep anguish, crying bitterly as she prayed to the LORD. [11]And she made this vow: "O LORD of Heaven's Armies, if you will look upon my sorrow and answer my prayer and give me a son, then I will give him back to you. He will be yours for his entire life-

1:9 Hebrew *the Temple of the LORD.*

every opportunity to celebrate her good fortune at the expense of her rival. **8:** It was all very well for Elkanah to suggest that he was better than ten sons, but in the event of his demise, Hannah's future would be bitter. **9–11:** In contrast to later restrictions on women's participation, Hannah takes the initiative and

time, and as a sign that he has been dedicated to
the LORD, his hair will never be cut.*"
12 As she was praying to the LORD, Eli
watched her. 13 Seeing her lips moving but hearing no sound, he thought she had been drinking.
14 "Must you come here drunk?" he demanded.
"Throw away your wine!"
15 "Oh no, sir!" she replied. "I haven't been
drinking wine or anything stronger. But I am
very discouraged, and I was pouring out my
heart to the LORD. 16 Don't think I am a wicked
woman! For I have been praying out of great anguish and sorrow."
17 "In that case," Eli said, "go in peace! May
the God of Israel grant the request you have
asked of him."
18 "Oh, thank you, sir!" she exclaimed. Then
she went back and began to eat again, and she
was no longer sad.

Samuel's Birth and Dedication

19 The entire family got up early the next morning and went to worship the LORD once more.
Then they returned home to Ramah. When Elkanah slept with Hannah, the LORD remembered
her plea, 20 and in due time she gave birth to a
son. She named him Samuel,* for she said, "I
asked the LORD for him."
21 The next year Elkanah and his family went
on their annual trip to offer a sacrifice to the
LORD. 22 But Hannah did not go. She told her
husband, "Wait until the boy is weaned. Then
I will take him to the Tabernacle and leave him
there with the LORD permanently.*"
23 "Whatever you think is best," Elkanah
agreed. "Stay here for now, and may the LORD
help you keep your promise." So she stayed
home and nursed the boy until he was weaned.
24 When the child was weaned, Hannah took
him to the Tabernacle in Shiloh. They brought
along a three-year-old bull* for the sacrifice and a
basket* of flour and some wine. 25 After sacrificing
the bull, they brought the boy to Eli. 26 "Sir, do you
remember me?" Hannah asked. "I am the woman
who stood here several years ago praying to the
LORD. 27 I asked the LORD to give me this boy, and
he has granted my request. 28 Now I am giving him
to the LORD, and he will belong to the LORD his
whole life." And they* worshiped the LORD there.

Hannah's Prayer of Praise

2 Then Hannah prayed:
"My heart rejoices in the LORD!
The LORD has made me strong.*
Now I have an answer for my enemies;
I rejoice because you rescued me.
2 No one is holy like the LORD!
There is no one besides you;
there is no Rock like our God.

1:11 Some manuscripts add *He will drink neither wine nor intoxicants.* **1:20** *Samuel* sounds like the Hebrew term for "asked of God" or "heard by God." **1:22** Some manuscripts add *I will offer him as a Nazirite for all time.* **1:24a** As in Dead Sea Scrolls, Greek and Syriac versions; Masoretic Text reads *three bulls.* **1:24b** Hebrew *and an ephah* [20 quarts or 22 liters]. **1:28** Hebrew *he.* **2:1** Hebrew *has exalted my horn.*

plays an active role. **11:** In a move of breathtaking faith she offers back to God that which she presently lacks, vowing to dedicate her as yet unborn son as a lifelong Nazirite (see Judg 13). **12–14:** In contrast to Hannah's simple faith, Eli's lack of spiritual perception as priest comes as a shock, and his question is a sad reflection on the state of religious practice of the time. **21–28:** For up to three years the child was hers, drawing his life from her breasts, on loan from God until he was weaned. For the rest of his life, Samuel would belong to God. Only a mother can know Hannah's feelings as she nursed her son, or the spiritual resolve required to give him up. The sacrifice Hannah brought that day in fulfillment of her vow (v. 24) was far greater than any offering in accordance with the law. **27:** The Hebrew word for "to ask" can also mean "to lend." God had granted Hannah her request, and a child had been born. Now she in turn loaned that child to him. The same word is similar to the Hebrew form of Saul's name, setting up an implied contrast between Samuel, the child asked for by Hannah in faith, who throughout his life was dedicated to God's service, and Saul, the king asked for by the people in rebellion against God, a king whose dedication and service were to prove a much more complex affair. **2:1–11:** Hannah's prayer is a song of praise to the LORD in which she extends the sovereignty she has experienced in her life to the whole field of human relationships. The language is poetic, the theological principle profound (cf. Hannah's prayer to Mary's song in Luke 1:46–55). Doubt is sometimes expressed regarding the possibility of this song having been composed by a woman, but there is no inherent reason why Hannah could not have expressed her joy in this way, even if she may have adapted for her purposes existing phraseology (cf. Exod 15:1–18). As the story of 1 and 2 Samuel amply demonstrates, the danger for men, especially those in powerful positions, was the temptation to rely on their own resources. Women, lacking such positions of power in society, more easily recognized that their greatest resource was God.

3 "Stop acting so proud and haughty!
Don't speak with such arrogance!
For the LORD is a God who knows what you
have done;
he will judge your actions.
4 The bow of the mighty is now broken,
and those who stumbled are now strong.
5 Those who were well fed are now starving,
and those who were starving are now full.
The childless woman now has seven children,
and the woman with many children wastes
away.
6 The LORD gives both death and life;
he brings some down to the grave* but
raises others up.
7 The LORD makes some poor and others rich;
he brings some down and lifts others up.
8 He lifts the poor from the dust
and the needy from the garbage dump.
He sets them among princes,
placing them in seats of honor.
For all the earth is the LORD's,
and he has set the world in order.

9 "He will protect his faithful ones,
but the wicked will disappear in darkness.
No one will succeed by strength alone.
10 Those who fight against the LORD will be
shattered.
He thunders against them from heaven;
the LORD judges throughout the earth.
He gives power to his king;
he increases the strength* of his anointed
one."

11 Then Elkanah returned home to Ramah
without Samuel. And the boy served the LORD
by assisting Eli the priest.

Eli's Wicked Sons

12 Now the sons of Eli were scoundrels who had no
respect for the LORD 13 or for their duties as priests.
Whenever anyone offered a sacrifice, Eli's sons
would send over a servant with a three-pronged
fork. While the meat of the sacrificed animal was
still boiling, 14 the servant would stick the fork
into the pot and demand that whatever it brought
up be given to Eli's sons. All the Israelites who
came to worship at Shiloh were treated this way.
15 Sometimes the servant would come even before
the animal's fat had been burned on the altar. He
would demand raw meat before it had been boiled
so that it could be used for roasting.

16 The man offering the sacrifice might reply,
"Take as much as you want, but the fat must be
burned first." Then the servant would demand,
"No, give it to me now, or I'll take it by force."
17 So the sin of these young men was very serious
in the LORD's sight, for they treated the LORD's
offerings with contempt.

18 But Samuel, though he was only a boy,
served the LORD. He wore a linen garment like
that of a priest.* 19 Each year his mother made a
small coat for him and brought it to him when she
came with her husband for the sacrifice. 20 Before
they returned home, Eli would bless Elkanah and
his wife and say, "May the LORD give you other
children to take the place of this one she gave to
the LORD.*" 21 And the LORD gave Hannah three
sons and two daughters. Meanwhile, Samuel
grew up in the presence of the LORD.

22 Now Eli was very old, but he was aware of
what his sons were doing to the people of Israel.
He knew, for instance, that his sons were seducing the young women who assisted at the entrance of the Tabernacle.* 23 Eli said to them, "I
have been hearing reports from all the people
about the wicked things you are doing. Why do
you keep sinning? 24 You must stop, my sons!
The reports I hear among the LORD's people are
not good. 25 If someone sins against another person, God* can mediate for the guilty party. But
if someone sins against the LORD, who can in-

2:6 Hebrew *to Sheol.* **2:10** Hebrew *he exalts the horn.* **2:18** Hebrew *He wore a linen ephod.* **2:20** As in Dead Sea Scrolls and Greek version; Masoretic Text reads *this one he requested of the LORD.* **2:22** Hebrew *Tent of Meeting.* Some manuscripts lack this entire sentence. **2:25** Or *the judges.*

2:12–36 A Father's Failure

The remainder of the chapter demonstrates the principle that it is the LORD *who brings some down . . . but raises others up* (v. 6). A contrast is set up between Samuel and Eli's sons, Hophni and Phinehas. **13–17, 22–25:** Hophni and Phinehas abuse their privileges as priests, exploit their position of power over the most vulnerable, and dishonor their father. **22:** At this period of Israel's history it was considered appropriate for women to serve at the entrance of the Tabernacle (cf. Exod 38:8). Perhaps reprobate priests like Hophni and Phinehas contributed to women's subsequent exclusion from service, for it is often easier to remove a source of temptation and consider it blameworthy than to recognize the frailty of our human nature. **19–21, 27–34:** Note the contrast between Hannah, the mother who was willing to relinquish her son to God's service, and Eli, the father who was willing to see the service of God brought into disrepute by his overindulgence of his sons; note also the contrast in God's dealing with them.

tercede?" But Eli's sons wouldn't listen to their father, for the LORD was already planning to put them to death.

26 Meanwhile, the boy Samuel grew taller and grew in favor with the LORD and with the people.

A Warning for Eli's Family

27 One day a man of God came to Eli and gave him this message from the LORD: "I revealed myself* to your ancestors when the people of Israel were slaves in Egypt. 28 I chose your ancestor Aaron* from among all the tribes of Israel to be my priest, to offer sacrifices on my altar, to burn incense, and to wear the priestly vest* as he served me. And I assigned the sacrificial offerings to you priests. 29 So why do you scorn my sacrifices and offerings? Why do you give your sons more honor than you give me—for you and they have become fat from the best offerings of my people Israel!

30 "Therefore, the LORD, the God of Israel, says: I promised that your branch of the tribe of Levi* would always be my priests. But I will honor those who honor me, and I will despise those who think lightly of me. 31 The time is coming when I will put an end to your family, so it will no longer serve as my priests. All the members of your family will die before their time. None will reach old age. 32 You will watch with envy as I pour out prosperity on the people of Israel. But no members of your family will ever live out their days. 33 Those who survive will live in sadness and grief, and their children will die a violent death.* 34 And to prove that what I have said will come true, I will cause your two sons, Hophni and Phinehas, to die on the same day!

35 "Then I will raise up a faithful priest who will serve me and do what I desire. I will establish his family, and they will be priests to my anointed kings forever. 36 Then all of your surviving family will bow before him, begging for money and food. 'Please,' they will say, 'give us jobs among the priests so we will have enough to eat.' "

The LORD Speaks to Samuel

3 Meanwhile, the boy Samuel served the LORD by assisting Eli. Now in those days messages from the LORD were very rare, and visions were quite uncommon.

2 One night Eli, who was almost blind by now, had gone to bed. 3 The lamp of God had not yet gone out, and Samuel was sleeping in the Tabernacle* near the Ark of God. 4 Suddenly the LORD called out, "Samuel!"

"Yes?" Samuel replied. "What is it?" 5 He got up and ran to Eli. "Here I am. Did you call me?"

"I didn't call you," Eli replied. "Go back to bed." So he did.

6 Then the LORD called out again, "Samuel!"

Again Samuel got up and went to Eli. "Here I am. Did you call me?"

"I didn't call you, my son," Eli said. "Go back to bed."

7 Samuel did not yet know the LORD because he had never had a message from the LORD before. 8 So the LORD called a third time, and once more Samuel got up and went to Eli. "Here I am. Did you call me?"

Then Eli realized it was the LORD who was calling the boy. 9 So he said to Samuel, "Go and lie down again, and if someone calls again, say, 'Speak, LORD, your servant is listening.' " So Samuel went back to bed.

10 And the LORD came and called as before, "Samuel! Samuel!"

And Samuel replied, "Speak, your servant is listening."

11 Then the LORD said to Samuel, "I am about to do a shocking thing in Israel. 12 I am going to carry out all my threats against Eli and his family, from beginning to end. 13 I have warned him that judgment is coming upon his family forever, because his sons are blaspheming God* and he hasn't disciplined them. 14 So I have vowed that the sins of Eli and his sons will never be forgiven by sacrifices or offerings."

Samuel Speaks for the LORD

15 Samuel stayed in bed until morning, then got up and opened the doors of the Tabernacle* as usual. He was afraid to tell Eli what the LORD had said to him. 16 But Eli called out to him, "Samuel, my son."

2:27 As in Greek and Syriac versions; Hebrew reads *Did I reveal myself.* **2:28a** Hebrew *your father.* **2:28b** Hebrew *an ephod.* **2:30** Hebrew *that your house and your father's house.* **2:33** As in Dead Sea Scrolls, which read *die by the sword;* Masoretic Text reads *die like mortals.* **3:3** Hebrew *the Temple of the LORD.* **3:13** As in Greek version; Hebrew reads *his sons have made themselves contemptible.* **3:15** Hebrew *the house of the LORD.*

3:1–21 A Young Man's Calling

In the course of Samuel's response to God's call in the night, there is a shift in the relationship between Samuel and Eli. At the start Samuel is ministering to the LORD under Eli; by the end he is ministering to Eli and to Israel under the LORD. **4–10:** Samuel is dependent for his spiritual training on Eli. **15–17:** Samuel's first task as a prophet is to tell Eli of God's judgment. **17–20:** Eli (and the rest of Israel) recog-

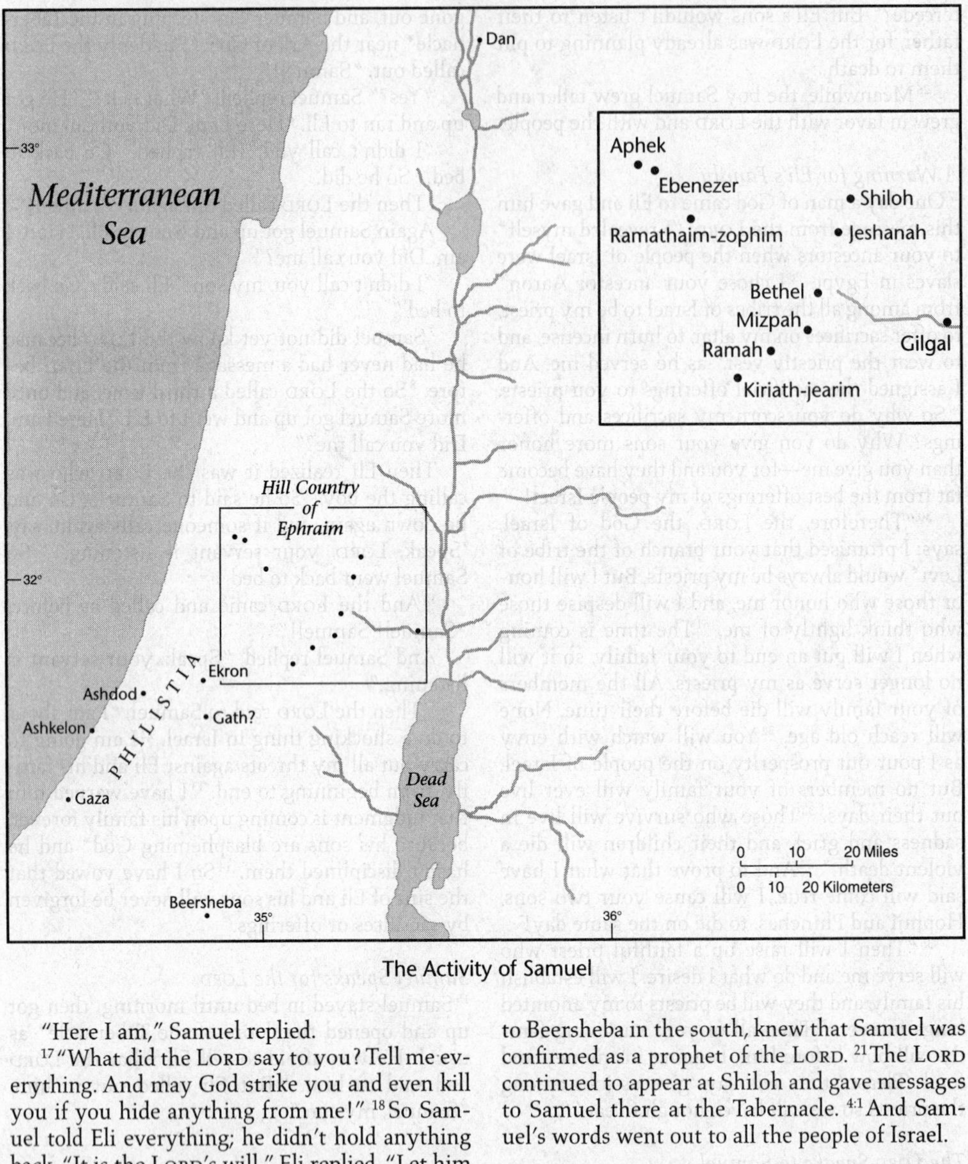

The Activity of Samuel

"Here I am," Samuel replied.
[17]"What did the LORD say to you? Tell me everything. And may God strike you and even kill you if you hide anything from me!" [18]So Samuel told Eli everything; he didn't hold anything back. "It is the LORD's will," Eli replied. "Let him do what he thinks best."
[19]As Samuel grew up, the LORD was with him, and everything Samuel said proved to be reliable. [20]And all Israel, from Dan in the north to Beersheba in the south, knew that Samuel was confirmed as a prophet of the LORD. [21]The LORD continued to appear at Shiloh and gave messages to Samuel there at the Tabernacle. [4:1]And Samuel's words went out to all the people of Israel.

The Philistines Capture the Ark

4 At that time Israel was at war with the Philistines. The Israelite army was camped near Ebenezer, and the Philistines were at

---

nizes his dependence on Samuel for a revelation of God's will.

4:1—7:2 The Glory and Power of Yahweh

4:1–22 The Philistines Capture the Ark. This chapter serves as a bridge, recording the death of Eli's sons and of Eli, thus rounding off the opening unit of 1 Samuel. At the same time it introduces the theme of the awesome power of God, enthroned between the cherubim of the Ark—a power that refused to be manipulated by a sinful people but that remained sufficient to strike terror into Israel's enemies. **1:** The Philistines, Israel's traditional enemy of the time,

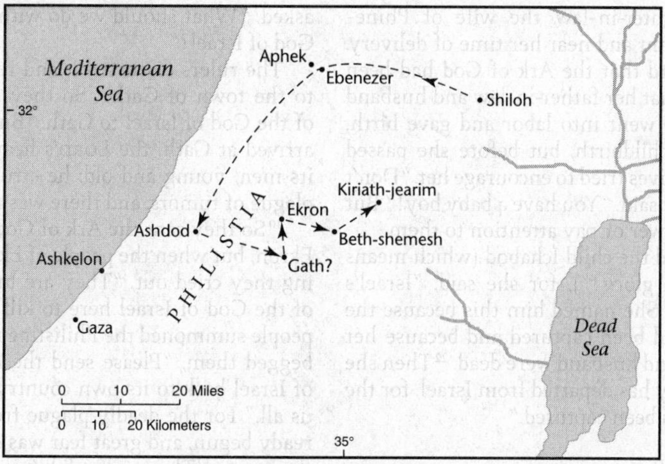

Wanderings of the Ark

Aphek. 2 The Philistines attacked and defeated the army of Israel, killing 4,000 men. 3 After the battle was over, the troops retreated to their camp, and the elders of Israel asked, "Why did the LORD allow us to be defeated by the Philistines?" Then they said, "Let's bring the Ark of the Covenant of the LORD from Shiloh. If we carry it into battle with us, it* will save us from our enemies."

4 So they sent men to Shiloh to bring the Ark of the Covenant of the LORD of Heaven's Armies, who is enthroned between the cherubim. Hophni and Phinehas, the sons of Eli, were also there with the Ark of the Covenant of God. 5 When all the Israelites saw the Ark of the Covenant of the LORD coming into the camp, their shout of joy was so loud it made the ground shake!

6 "What's going on?" the Philistines asked. "What's all the shouting about in the Hebrew camp?" When they were told it was because the Ark of the LORD had arrived, 7 they panicked. "The gods have* come into their camp!" they cried. "This is a disaster! We have never had to face anything like this before! 8 Help! Who can save us from these mighty gods of Israel? They are the same gods who destroyed the Egyptians with plagues when Israel was in the wilderness. 9 Fight as never before, Philistines! If you don't, we will become the Hebrews' slaves just as they have been ours! Stand up like men and fight!"

10 So the Philistines fought desperately, and Israel was defeated again. The slaughter was great; 30,000 Israelite soldiers died that day. The survivors turned and fled to their tents. 11 The Ark of God was captured, and Hophni and Phinehas, the two sons of Eli, were killed.

The Death of Eli

12 A man from the tribe of Benjamin ran from the battlefield and arrived at Shiloh later that same day. He had torn his clothes and put dust on his head to show his grief. 13 Eli was waiting beside the road to hear the news of the battle, for his heart trembled for the safety of the Ark of God. When the messenger arrived and told what had happened, an outcry resounded throughout the town.

14 "What is all the noise about?" Eli asked.

The messenger rushed over to Eli, 15 who was ninety-eight years old and blind. 16 He said to Eli, "I have just come from the battlefield—I was there this very day."

"What happened, my son?" Eli demanded.

17 "Israel has been defeated by the Philistines," the messenger replied. "The people have been slaughtered, and your two sons, Hophni and Phinehas, were also killed. And the Ark of God has been captured."

18 When the messenger mentioned what had happened to the Ark of God, Eli fell backward from his seat beside the gate. He broke his neck and died, for he was old and overweight. He had been Israel's judge for forty years.

4:3 Or *he.* **4:7** Or *A god has.*

came from the northwestern Mediterranean area. **6–9:** The Philistines seem to be sufficiently aware of aspects of Israel's history to quake at the prospect of facing Israel's *gods.* They believed that, like themselves, the Israelites were polytheistic. **10–11:** The Philistines' fear inspires them in battle, and victory

[19]Eli's daughter-in-law, the wife of Phinehas, was pregnant and near her time of delivery. When she heard that the Ark of God had been captured and that her father-in-law and husband were dead, she went into labor and gave birth. [20]She died in childbirth, but before she passed away the midwives tried to encourage her. "Don't be afraid," they said. "You have a baby boy!" But she did not answer or pay attention to them.

[21]She named the child Ichabod (which means "Where is the glory?"), for she said, "Israel's glory is gone." She named him this because the Ark of God had been captured and because her father-in-law and husband were dead. [22]Then she said, "The glory has departed from Israel, for the Ark of God has been captured."

The Ark in Philistia

5 After the Philistines captured the Ark of God, they took it from the battleground at Ebenezer to the town of Ashdod. [2]They carried the Ark of God into the temple of Dagon and placed it beside an idol of Dagon. [3]But when the citizens of Ashdod went to see it the next morning, Dagon had fallen with his face to the ground in front of the Ark of the LORD! So they took Dagon and put him in his place again. [4]But the next morning the same thing happened—Dagon had fallen face down before the Ark of the LORD again. This time his head and hands had broken off and were lying in the doorway. Only the trunk of his body was left intact. [5]That is why to this day neither the priests of Dagon nor anyone who enters the temple of Dagon in Ashdod will step on its threshold.

[6]Then the LORD's heavy hand struck the people of Ashdod and the nearby villages with a plague of tumors.* [7]When the people realized what was happening, they cried out, "We can't keep the Ark of the God of Israel here any longer! He is against us! We will all be destroyed along with Dagon, our god." [8]So they called together the rulers of the Philistine towns and asked, "What should we do with the Ark of the God of Israel?"

The rulers discussed it and replied, "Move it to the town of Gath." So they moved the Ark of the God of Israel to Gath. [9]But when the Ark arrived at Gath, the LORD's heavy hand fell on its men, young and old; he struck them with a plague of tumors, and there was a great panic.

[10]So they sent the Ark of God to the town of Ekron, but when the people of Ekron saw it coming they cried out, "They are bringing the Ark of the God of Israel here to kill us, too!" [11]The people summoned the Philistine rulers again and begged them, "Please send the Ark of the God of Israel back to its own country, or it* will kill us all." For the deadly plague from God had already begun, and great fear was sweeping across the town. [12]Those who didn't die were afflicted with tumors; and the cry from the town rose to heaven.

The Philistines Return the Ark

6 The Ark of the LORD remained in Philistine territory seven months in all. [2]Then the Philistines called in their priests and diviners and asked them, "What should we do about the Ark of the LORD? Tell us how to return it to its own country."

[3]"Send the Ark of the God of Israel back with a gift," they were told. "Send a guilt offering so the plague will stop. Then, if you are healed, you will know it was his hand that caused the plague."

[4]"What sort of guilt offering should we send?" they asked.

And they were told, "Since the plague has struck both you and your five rulers, make five gold tumors and five gold rats, just like those that have ravaged your land. [5]Make these things to

5:6 Greek version and Latin Vulgate read *tumors; and rats appeared in their land, and death and destruction were throughout the city.* **5:11** Or *he.*

was theirs. So also, by virtue of that victory, was the Ark. **21:** *Ichabod*: It was not widowhood that caused Phinehas's wife grief so much as the spiritual insight that *Israel's glory is gone*. Her son's name echoes her lament. God would not assist a corrupt people. She must have been aware of Phinehas's corruption and by extension, that of the land.

5:1–12 The LORD's Triumph. The Philistines concluded that their defeat of the Israelites signified the triumph of their gods over the LORD. Their error, however, became obvious as the statue of Dagon was reduced to a crippled wreck, and the people succumbed to an outbreak of disease. Contemporary wisdom made the connection between the current plight of the inhabitants, the presence of the Ark, and the power of the Israelites' god. **8–12:** The Ark became an object of dread, the very approach of which was sufficient to cause panic and death.

6:1—7:2 The Return of the Ark. The Philistines acknowledge the need for restitution for the wrong they

show honor to the God of Israel. Perhaps then he
will stop afflicting you, your gods, and your land.
6 Don't be stubborn and rebellious as Pharaoh and
the Egyptians were. By the time God was finished
with them, they were eager to let Israel go.
7 "Now build a new cart, and find two cows
that have just given birth to calves. Make sure
the cows have never been yoked to a cart. Hitch
the cows to the cart, but shut their calves away
from them in a pen. 8 Put the Ark of the LORD
on the cart, and beside it place a chest containing
the gold rats and gold tumors you are sending as
a guilt offering. Then let the cows go wherever
they want. 9 If they cross the border of our land
and go to Beth-shemesh, we will know it was the
LORD who brought this great disaster upon us. If
they don't, we will know it was not his hand that
caused the plague. It came simply by chance."
10 So these instructions were carried out. Two
cows were hitched to the cart, and their newborn
calves were shut up in a pen. 11 Then the Ark of
the LORD and the chest containing the gold rats
and gold tumors were placed on the cart. 12 And
sure enough, without veering off in other directions, the cows went straight along the road toward Beth-shemesh, lowing as they went. The
Philistine rulers followed them as far as the border of Beth-shemesh.
13 The people of Beth-shemesh were harvesting wheat in the valley, and when they saw the
Ark, they were overjoyed! 14 The cart came into
the field of a man named Joshua and stopped
beside a large rock. So the people broke up the
wood of the cart for a fire and killed the cows
and sacrificed them to the LORD as a burnt offering. 15 Several men of the tribe of Levi lifted
the Ark of the LORD and the chest containing
the gold rats and gold tumors from the cart and
placed them on the large rock. Many sacrifices
and burnt offerings were offered to the LORD
that day by the people of Beth-shemesh. 16 The
five Philistine rulers watched all this and then
returned to Ekron that same day.
17 The five gold tumors sent by the Philistines
as a guilt offering to the LORD were gifts from
the rulers of Ashdod, Gaza, Ashkelon, Gath, and
Ekron. 18 The five gold rats represented the five
Philistine towns and their surrounding villages,
which were controlled by the five rulers. The
large rock at Beth-shemesh, where they set the
Ark of the LORD, still stands in the field of Joshua
as a witness to what happened there.

The Ark Moved to Kiriath-Jearim

19 But the LORD killed seventy men* from Beth-shemesh because they looked into the Ark of the
LORD. And the people mourned greatly because
of what the LORD had done. 20 "Who is able to
stand in the presence of the LORD, this holy
God?" they cried out. "Where can we send the
Ark from here?"
21 So they sent messengers to the people at
Kiriath-jearim and told them, "The Philistines
have returned the Ark of the LORD. Come here
and get it!"

7 So the men of Kiriath-jearim came to get
the Ark of the LORD. They took it to the
hillside home of Abinadab and ordained
Eleazar, his son, to be in charge of it. 2 The Ark
remained in Kiriath-jearim for a long time—
twenty years in all. During that time all Israel
mourned because it seemed the LORD had abandoned them.

Samuel Leads Israel to Victory

3 Then Samuel said to all the people of Israel, "If
you are really serious about wanting to return to
the LORD, get rid of your foreign gods and your
images of Ashtoreth. Determine to obey only the
LORD; then he will rescue you from the Philistines." 4 So the Israelites got rid of their images
of Baal and Ashtoreth and worshiped only the
LORD.

6:19 As in a few Hebrew manuscripts; most Hebrew manuscripts read *70 men, 50,000 men*. Perhaps the text should be understood to read *the LORD killed 70 men and 50 oxen*.

had committed. **6:7–9:** They mix the spiritual and the pragmatic in the test they devised to discover whether the disasters that had struck them were indeed divinely inspired. For cows to desert their young would be positive proof that a supernatural force was at work and, they hoped, indicate the divine acceptance of their guilt offering. **12:** The cows take the most direct route back to Israel. **19–21:** In the wrong place, handled in the wrong way or approached with a wrong attitude, holiness was potentially dangerous.

7:3—8:22 Samuel as Judge

The return of the Ark does not necessarily mean the return of God's favor. Now Samuel steps into the limelight with instruction for Israel. The Ark had been returned to Israel, but it remained marginalized in the house of Abinadab at Kiriath-jearim. David will restore it to its rightful place at the heart of the nation's life and worship. Yet the people show a renewed desire to return to the LORD. **7:3–6:** Seizing the moment, Samuel issued a prophetic call to repentance,

5 Then Samuel told them, "Gather all of Israel to Mizpah, and I will pray to the LORD for you." 6 So they gathered at Mizpah and, in a great ceremony, drew water from a well and poured it out before the LORD. They also went without food all day and confessed that they had sinned against the LORD. (It was at Mizpah that Samuel became Israel's judge.)

7 When the Philistine rulers heard that Israel had gathered at Mizpah, they mobilized their army and advanced. The Israelites were badly frightened when they learned that the Philistines were approaching. 8 "Don't stop pleading with the LORD our God to save us from the Philistines!" they begged Samuel. 9 So Samuel took a young lamb and offered it to the LORD as a whole burnt offering. He pleaded with the LORD to help Israel, and the LORD answered him.

10 Just as Samuel was sacrificing the burnt offering, the Philistines arrived to attack Israel. But the LORD spoke with a mighty voice of thunder from heaven that day, and the Philistines were thrown into such confusion that the Israelites defeated them. 11 The men of Israel chased them from Mizpah to a place below Beth-car, slaughtering them all along the way.

12 Samuel then took a large stone and placed it between the towns of Mizpah and Jeshanah.* He named it Ebenezer (which means "the stone of help"), for he said, "Up to this point the LORD has helped us!"

13 So the Philistines were subdued and didn't invade Israel again for some time. And throughout Samuel's lifetime, the LORD's powerful hand was raised against the Philistines. 14 The Israelite villages near Ekron and Gath that the Philistines had captured were restored to Israel, along with the rest of the territory that the Philistines had taken. And there was peace between Israel and the Amorites in those days.

15 Samuel continued as Israel's judge for the rest of his life. 16 Each year he traveled around, setting up his court first at Bethel, then at Gilgal, and then at Mizpah. He judged the people of Israel at each of these places. 17 Then he would return to his home at Ramah, and he would hear cases there, too. And Samuel built an altar to the LORD at Ramah.

Israel Requests a King

8

As Samuel grew old, he appointed his sons to be judges over Israel. 2 Joel and Abijah, his oldest sons, held court in Beersheba. 3 But they were not like their father, for they were greedy for money. They accepted bribes and perverted justice.

4 Finally, all the elders of Israel met at Ramah to discuss the matter with Samuel. 5 "Look," they told him, "you are now old, and your sons are not like you. Give us a king to judge us like all the other nations have."

6 Samuel was displeased with their request and went to the LORD for guidance. 7 "Do everything they say to you," the LORD replied, "for it is me they are rejecting, not you. They don't want me to be their king any longer. 8 Ever since I brought them from Egypt they have continually abandoned me and followed other gods. And now they are giving you the same treatment. 9 Do as they ask, but solemnly warn them about the way a king will reign over them."

Samuel Warns against a Kingdom

10 So Samuel passed on the LORD's warning to the people who were asking him for a king. 11 "This is how a king will reign over you," Samuel said. "The king will draft your sons and assign them to his chariots and his charioteers, making them run before his chariots. 12 Some will be generals and captains in his army,* some will be forced to plow in his fields and harvest his crops, and some will make his weapons and chariot equipment. 13 The king will take your daughters from you and force them to cook and bake and make perfumes for him. 14 He will take away the best of your fields and vineyards and olive groves and

7:12 As in Greek and Syriac versions; Hebrew reads *Shen.*
8:12 Hebrew *commanders of thousands and commanders of fifties.*

a single-minded devotion to the LORD, and a steady dependence on his sovereign power to *rescue* [Israel] *from the Philistines*. **7–11:** The restored reliance on the LORD pays off. Divine intervention leads to a dramatic victory. **12:** The setting up of a memorial stone as testimony to the LORD's help is apparently futile, in light of the events of the next chapter. If the people remembered God's help through judges such as Samuel, why did they demand a king? **13–17:** Israel enjoys a tenuous peace throughout the remainder of Samuel's days as judge. **8:6:** Samuel took the people's request as a personal slight, reflecting adversely on his office. **7:** It was God himself being rejected as king. **8:** The sense of betrayal Samuel felt was but a faint echo of God's pain at his people's lack of covenant loyalty. **10–18:** Human power almost inevitably leads to corruption and exploitation, and the monarchy in Israel would be no exception. There is an ominous reiteration of the clause *he will take* and its variants; no family would remain untouched, no

give them to his own officials. 15 He will take a
tenth of your grain and your grape harvest and
distribute it among his officers and attendants.
16 He will take your male and female slaves and
demand the finest of your cattle* and donkeys
for his own use. 17 He will demand a tenth of
your flocks, and you will be his slaves. 18 When
that day comes, you will beg for relief from this
king you are demanding, but then the LORD will
not help you."

19 But the people refused to listen to Samuel's
warning. "Even so, we still want a king," they
said. 20 "We want to be like the nations around us.
Our king will judge us and lead us into battle."

21 So Samuel repeated to the LORD what the
people had said, 22 and the LORD replied, "Do as
they say, and give them a king." Then Samuel
agreed and sent the people home.

Saul Meets Samuel

9 There was a wealthy, influential man
named Kish from the tribe of Benjamin.
He was the son of Abiel, son of Zeror, son
of Becorath, son of Aphiah, of the tribe of Benjamin. 2 His son Saul was the most handsome man
in Israel—head and shoulders taller than anyone
else in the land.

3 One day Kish's donkeys strayed away, and
he told Saul, "Take a servant with you, and go
look for the donkeys." 4 So Saul took one of the
servants and traveled through the hill country
of Ephraim, the land of Shalishah, the Shaalim
area, and the entire land of Benjamin, but they
couldn't find the donkeys anywhere.

5 Finally, they entered the region of Zuph, and
Saul said to his servant, "Let's go home. By now
my father will be more worried about us than
about the donkeys!"

6 But the servant said, "I've just thought of
something! There is a man of God who lives here
in this town. He is held in high honor by all the
people because everything he says comes true.
Let's go find him. Perhaps he can tell us which
way to go."

7 "But we don't have anything to offer him,"
Saul replied. "Even our food is gone, and we
don't have a thing to give him."

8 "Well," the servant said, "I have one small
silver piece.* We can at least offer it to the man
of God and see what happens!" 9 (In those days if
people wanted a message from God, they would
say, "Let's go and ask the seer," for prophets used
to be called seers.)

10 "All right," Saul agreed, "let's try it!" So
they started into the town where the man of God
lived.

11 As they were climbing the hill to the town,
they met some young women coming out to
draw water. So Saul and his servant asked, "Is
the seer here today?"

12 "Yes," they replied. "Stay right on this road.
He is at the town gates. He has just arrived to
take part in a public sacrifice up at the place of
worship. 13 Hurry and catch him before he goes
up there to eat. The guests won't begin eating
until he arrives to bless the food."

14 So they entered the town, and as they passed
through the gates, Samuel was coming out toward them to go up to the place of worship.

15 Now the LORD had told Samuel the previous day, 16 "About this time tomorrow I will send
you a man from the land of Benjamin. Anoint
him to be the leader of my people, Israel. He
will rescue them from the Philistines, for I have
looked down on my people in mercy and have
heard their cry."

17 When Samuel saw Saul, the LORD said,
"That's the man I told you about! He will rule
my people."

18 Just then Saul approached Samuel at the
gateway and asked, "Can you please tell me
where the seer's house is?"

19 "I am the seer!" Samuel replied. "Go up
to the place of worship ahead of me. We will eat
there together, and in the morning I'll tell you
what you want to know and send you on your

8:16 As in Greek version; Hebrew reads *young men*.
9:8 Hebrew 1/4 *shekel of silver*, about 0.1 ounces or 3 grams in weight.

---

aspect of life unaffected. **19–20:** The lure of being like the other nations, instead of remaining significantly different, proved too strong.

9:1–10:27a The Anointing and Commissioning of Saul

This section contains two different accounts of how Saul becomes king. **9:1–4:** Saul is introduced in the context of family life—a handsome young man, sent with one of the family servants to search for some of his father's donkeys. **6:** *Perhaps he can tell us which way to go*: The double significance of this statement was no doubt unintended by the servant. **11–12:** Drawing water was typically the work of women, and most often done in the cool of the morning or evening. **16:** Note the emphasis on Israel as *my people*, the use of the word *leader* instead of "king," the clear echoes of Exodus 3:9–10 (God's words from the burning bush), and the specific refer-

way. 20 And don't worry about those donkeys that were lost three days ago, for they have been found. And I am here to tell you that you and your family are the focus of all Israel's hopes."

21 Saul replied, "But I'm only from the tribe of Benjamin, the smallest tribe in Israel, and my family is the least important of all the families of that tribe! Why are you talking like this to me?"

22 Then Samuel brought Saul and his servant into the hall and placed them at the head of the table, honoring them above the thirty special guests. 23 Samuel then instructed the cook to bring Saul the finest cut of meat, the piece that had been set aside for the guest of honor. 24 So the cook brought in the meat and placed it before Saul. "Go ahead and eat it," Samuel said. "I was saving it for you even before I invited these others!" So Saul ate with Samuel that day.

25 When they came down from the place of worship and returned to town, Samuel took Saul up to the roof of the house and prepared a bed for him there.* 26 At daybreak the next morning, Samuel called to Saul, "Get up! It's time you were on your way." So Saul got ready, and he and Samuel left the house together. 27 When they reached the edge of town, Samuel told Saul to send his servant on ahead. After the servant was gone, Samuel said, "Stay here, for I have received a special message for you from God."

Samuel Anoints Saul as King

10 Then Samuel took a flask of olive oil and poured it over Saul's head. He kissed Saul and said, "I am doing this because the LORD has appointed you to be the ruler over Israel, his special possession.* 2 When you leave me today, you will see two men beside Rachel's tomb at Zelzah, on the border of Benjamin. They will tell you that the donkeys have been found and that your father has stopped worrying about them and is now worried about you. He is asking, 'Have you seen my son?'

3 "When you get to the oak of Tabor, you will see three men coming toward you who are on their way to worship God at Bethel. One will be bringing three young goats, another will have three loaves of bread, and the third will be carrying a wineskin full of wine. 4 They will greet you and offer you two of the loaves, which you are to accept.

5 "When you arrive at Gibeah of God,* where the garrison of the Philistines is located, you will meet a band of prophets coming down from the place of worship. They will be playing a harp, a tambourine, a flute, and a lyre, and they will be prophesying. 6 At that time the Spirit of the LORD will come powerfully upon you, and you will prophesy with them. You will be changed into a different person. 7 After these signs take place, do what must be done, for God is with you. 8 Then go down to Gilgal ahead of me. I will join you there to sacrifice burnt offerings and peace offerings. You must wait for seven days until I arrive and give you further instructions."

Samuel's Signs Are Fulfilled

9 As Saul turned and started to leave, God gave him a new heart, and all Samuel's signs were fulfilled that day. 10 When Saul and his servant arrived at Gibeah, they saw a group of prophets coming toward them. Then the Spirit of God came powerfully upon Saul, and he, too, began to prophesy. 11 When those who knew Saul heard about it, they exclaimed, "What? Is even Saul a prophet? How did the son of Kish become a prophet?"

12 And one of those standing there said, "Can anyone become a prophet, no matter who his father is?"* So that is the origin of the saying "Is even Saul a prophet?"

13 When Saul had finished prophesying, he went up to the place of worship. 14 "Where have you been?" Saul's uncle asked him and his servant.

"We were looking for the donkeys," Saul replied, "but we couldn't find them. So we went to Samuel to ask him where they were."

15 "Oh? And what did he say?" his uncle asked.

16 "He told us that the donkeys had already

9:25 As in Greek version; Hebrew reads *and talked with him there.* **10:1** Greek version reads *over Israel. And you will rule over the LORD's people and save them from their enemies around them. This will be the sign to you that the LORD has appointed you to be leader over his special possession.* **10:5** Hebrew *Gibeath-elohim.* **10:12** Hebrew *said, "Who is their father?"*

ence to deliverance from the hand of the Philistines. **20–21:** Saul's modest reply to Samuel's welcome of him as the *focus of all Israel's hopes* awakens echoes of other leaders' responses to their commission to deliver Israel from the hand of its oppressors. Moses, Gideon, and Jeremiah are three examples. **10:2–6:** These three signs correspond to his earlier expressed concerns about the goats, his lack of food, and his lowliness. **5:** Saul would receive the Spirit at Gibeah of God ("the hill of God"), where, provocatively, a Philistine garrison was located. **7:** *Do what must be done*: This instruction is a military commission.

been found," Saul replied. But Saul didn't tell his
uncle what Samuel said about the kingdom.

Saul Is Acclaimed King

17 Later Samuel called all the people of Israel to
meet before the LORD at Mizpah. 18 And he said,
"This is what the LORD, the God of Israel, has declared: I brought you from Egypt and rescued you
from the Egyptians and from all of the nations
that were oppressing you. 19 But though I have
rescued you from your misery and distress, you
have rejected your God today and have said, 'No,
we want a king instead!' Now, therefore, present
yourselves before the LORD by tribes and clans."
20 So Samuel brought all the tribes of Israel before the LORD, and the tribe of Benjamin was chosen by lot. 21 Then he brought each family of the
tribe of Benjamin before the LORD, and the family of the Matrites was chosen. And finally Saul
son of Kish was chosen from among them. But
when they looked for him, he had disappeared!
22 So they asked the LORD, "Where is he?"
And the LORD replied, "He is hiding among
the baggage." 23 So they found him and brought
him out, and he stood head and shoulders above
anyone else.
24 Then Samuel said to all the people, "This is
the man the LORD has chosen as your king. No
one in all Israel is like him!"
And all the people shouted, "Long live the
king!"
25 Then Samuel told the people what the rights
and duties of a king were. He wrote them down
on a scroll and placed it before the LORD. Then
Samuel sent the people home again.
26 When Saul returned to his home at Gibeah,
a group of men whose hearts God had touched
went with him. 27 But there were some scoundrels who complained, "How can this man save
us?" And they scorned him and refused to bring
him gifts. But Saul ignored them.

[Nahash, king of the Ammonites, had been grievously oppressing the people of Gad and Reuben who lived east of the Jordan River. He gouged out the right eye of each of the Israelites living there, and he didn't allow anyone to come and rescue them. In fact, of all the Israelites east of the Jordan, there wasn't a single one whose right eye Nahash had not gouged out. But there were 7,000 men who had escaped from the Ammonites, and they had settled in Jabesh-gilead.]*

Saul Defeats the Ammonites

11 About a month later,* King Nahash
of Ammon led his army against the
Israelite town of Jabesh-gilead. But
all the citizens of Jabesh asked for peace. "Make
a treaty with us, and we will be your servants,"
they pleaded.
2 "All right," Nahash said, "but only on one
condition. I will gouge out the right eye of every
one of you as a disgrace to all Israel!"
3 "Give us seven days to send messengers
throughout Israel!" replied the elders of Jabesh.
"If no one comes to save us, we will agree to your
terms."
4 When the messengers came to Gibeah of
Saul and told the people about their plight, everyone broke into tears. 5 Saul had been plowing
a field with his oxen, and when he returned to
town, he asked, "What's the matter? Why is everyone crying?" So they told him about the message from Jabesh.
6 Then the Spirit of God came powerfully
upon Saul, and he became very angry. 7 He took
two oxen and cut them into pieces and sent the
messengers to carry them throughout Israel
with this message: "This is what will happen to

10:27 This paragraph, which is not included in the Masoretic Text, is found in Dead Sea Scroll 4QSam[a]. **11:1** As in Greek version; Hebrew lacks *About a month later.*

17–26: If Saul had fulfilled his commission, the people's recognition of him as God's chosen deliverer would have been in little doubt. As it was, a public ceremony was necessary to discover the king. **20–22:** Elsewhere (Josh 7:14; 1 Sam 14:41) lots are used to find a person guilty of breaking a law or vow. No wonder Saul hid!

10:27b—11:15 The Claims of Kinship

The towns of Jabesh-gilead and Gibeah had close kinship ties. See Judges 19—21 for the full story of how daughters from Jabesh-gilead came to marry into the tribe of Benjamin in Gibeah. Although descent was reckoned through the male line, kinship ties through the female line were still significant. Examples include Jacob's fleeing to his mother's brother to escape Esau's wrath (Gen 27:42–44) or David's sending his parents to Moab when he was pursued by Saul (1 Sam 22:3–4). So when the inhabitants of Jabesh-gilead found themselves under threat from Nahash, their request for help from the people of Gibeah was as much a claim on kinship as an appeal to the power of the king. **11:5–6:** Hearing a secondhand report of the threatened assault, Saul reacted in the manner of the judges of former days. **7:** His actions evoke memories of the incident recorded in Judges 19, reenacting the demand of the Levite for

the oxen of anyone who refuses to follow Saul
and Samuel into battle!" And the LORD made
the people afraid of Saul's anger, and all of them
came out together as one. [8]When Saul mobilized
them at Bezek, he found that there were 300,000
men from Israel and 30,000* men from Judah.
[9]So Saul sent the messengers back to Jabesh-
gilead to say, "We will rescue you by noontime
tomorrow!" There was great joy throughout the
town when that message arrived!
[10]The men of Jabesh then told their enemies,
"Tomorrow we will come out to you, and you can
do to us whatever you wish." [11]But before dawn
the next morning, Saul arrived, having divided
his army into three detachments. He launched
a surprise attack against the Ammonites and
slaughtered them the whole morning. The remnant of their army was so badly scattered that no
two of them were left together.
[12]Then the people exclaimed to Samuel, "Now
where are those men who said, 'Why should Saul
rule over us?' Bring them here, and we will kill
them!"
[13]But Saul replied, "No one will be executed
today, for today the LORD has rescued Israel!"
[14]Then Samuel said to the people, "Come, let
us all go to Gilgal to renew the kingdom." [15]So
they all went to Gilgal, and in a solemn ceremony
before the LORD they made Saul king. Then they
offered peace offerings to the LORD, and Saul and
all the Israelites were filled with joy.

Samuel's Farewell Address

12 Then Samuel addressed all Israel: "I
have done as you asked and given you
a king. [2]Your king is now your leader. I stand here before you—an old, gray-haired
man—and my sons serve you. I have served as
your leader from the time I was a boy to this
very day. [3]Now testify against me in the presence of the LORD and before his anointed one.
Whose ox or donkey have I stolen? Have I ever
cheated any of you? Have I ever oppressed you?
Have I ever taken a bribe and perverted justice?
Tell me and I will make right whatever I have
done wrong."
[4]"No," they replied, "you have never cheated
or oppressed us, and you have never taken even
a single bribe."
[5]"The LORD and his anointed one are my witnesses today," Samuel declared, "that my hands
are clean."
"Yes, he is a witness," they replied.
[6]"It was the LORD who appointed Moses and
Aaron," Samuel continued. "He brought your
ancestors out of the land of Egypt. [7]Now stand
here quietly before the LORD as I remind you of
all the great things the LORD has done for you
and your ancestors.
[8]"When the Israelites were* in Egypt and
cried out to the LORD, he sent Moses and Aaron
to rescue them from Egypt and to bring them
into this land. [9]But the people soon forgot about
the LORD their God, so he handed them over to
Sisera, the commander of Hazor's army, and also
to the Philistines and to the king of Moab, who
fought against them.
[10]"Then they cried to the LORD again and
confessed, 'We have sinned by turning away
from the LORD and worshiping the images of
Baal and Ashtoreth. But we will worship you
and you alone if you will rescue us from our enemies.' [11]Then the LORD sent Gideon,* Bedan,*
Jephthah, and Samuel* to save you, and you
lived in safety.
[12]"But when you were afraid of Nahash,
the king of Ammon, you came to me and said
that you wanted a king to reign over you, even
though the LORD your God was already your
king. [13]All right, here is the king you have chosen. You asked for him, and the LORD has granted your request.
[14]"Now if you fear and worship the LORD and
listen to his voice, and if you do not rebel against
the LORD's commands, then both you and your
king will show that you recognize the LORD as

11:8 Dead Sea Scrolls and Greek version read *70,000.*
12:8 Hebrew *When Jacob was.* The names "Jacob" and "Israel" are often interchanged throughout the Old Testament, referring sometimes to the individual patriarch and sometimes to the nation. **12:11a** Hebrew *Jerub-baal,* another name for Gideon; see Judg 6:32. **12:11b** Greek and Syriac versions read *Barak.* **12:11c** Greek and Syriac versions read *Samson.*

justice. **8–15:** Saul's suitability for the role of king was confirmed in action.

12:1–25 Samuel's Farewell

In the aftermath of the celebrations, Samuel makes his farewell speech to the people, declaring his faithfulness as a leader from his youth until old age. **6–12:** Like Moses on the edge of the promised land (Deut 29:2—30:20), Samuel reminded the people of God's faithfulness to his covenant and of Israel's history of disobedience and faithlessness, a disloyalty that had found contemporary expression in the request for a human king. **14–15:** Even with a king, they have to choose between faithful and obedient service to God or the path of rebellion. **16–19:** The visible effect of

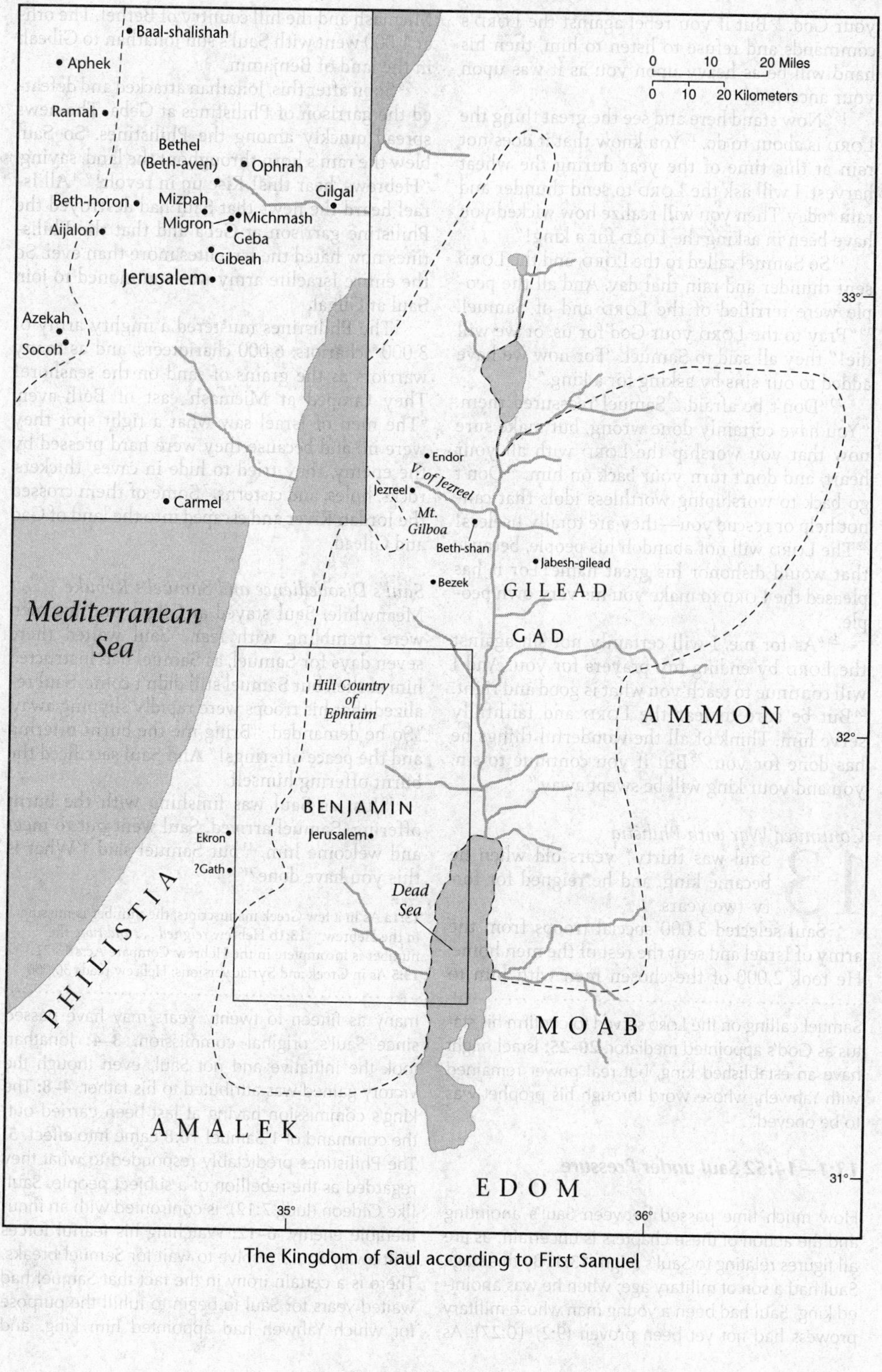

The Kingdom of Saul according to First Samuel

your God. 15 But if you rebel against the LORD's
commands and refuse to listen to him, then his
hand will be as heavy upon you as it was upon
your ancestors.
16 "Now stand here and see the great thing the
LORD is about to do. 17 You know that it does not
rain at this time of the year during the wheat
harvest. I will ask the LORD to send thunder and
rain today. Then you will realize how wicked you
have been in asking the LORD for a king!"
18 So Samuel called to the LORD, and the LORD
sent thunder and rain that day. And all the people were terrified of the LORD and of Samuel.
19 "Pray to the LORD your God for us, or we will
die!" they all said to Samuel. "For now we have
added to our sins by asking for a king."
20 "Don't be afraid," Samuel reassured them.
"You have certainly done wrong, but make sure
now that you worship the LORD with all your
heart, and don't turn your back on him. 21 Don't
go back to worshiping worthless idols that cannot help or rescue you—they are totally useless!
22 The LORD will not abandon his people, because
that would dishonor his great name. For it has
pleased the LORD to make you his very own people.
23 "As for me, I will certainly not sin against
the LORD by ending my prayers for you. And I
will continue to teach you what is good and right.
24 But be sure to fear the LORD and faithfully
serve him. Think of all the wonderful things he
has done for you. 25 But if you continue to sin,
you and your king will be swept away."

Continued War with Philistia

13 Saul was thirty* years old when he
became king, and he reigned for forty-two years.*
2 Saul selected 3,000 special troops from the
army of Israel and sent the rest of the men home.
He took 2,000 of the chosen men with him to
Micmash and the hill country of Bethel. The other 1,000 went with Saul's son Jonathan to Gibeah
in the land of Benjamin.
3 Soon after this, Jonathan attacked and defeated the garrison of Philistines at Geba. The news
spread quickly among the Philistines. So Saul
blew the ram's horn throughout the land, saying,
"Hebrews, hear this! Rise up in revolt!" 4 All Israel heard the news that Saul had destroyed the
Philistine garrison at Geba and that the Philistines now hated the Israelites more than ever. So
the entire Israelite army was summoned to join
Saul at Gilgal.
5 The Philistines mustered a mighty army of
3,000* chariots, 6,000 charioteers, and as many
warriors as the grains of sand on the seashore!
They camped at Micmash east of Beth-aven.
6 The men of Israel saw what a tight spot they
were in; and because they were hard pressed by
the enemy, they tried to hide in caves, thickets,
rocks, holes, and cisterns. 7 Some of them crossed
the Jordan River and escaped into the land of Gad
and Gilead.

Saul's Disobedience and Samuel's Rebuke

Meanwhile, Saul stayed at Gilgal, and his men
were trembling with fear. 8 Saul waited there
seven days for Samuel, as Samuel had instructed
him earlier, but Samuel still didn't come. Saul realized that his troops were rapidly slipping away.
9 So he demanded, "Bring me the burnt offering
and the peace offerings!" And Saul sacrificed the
burnt offering himself.
10 Just as Saul was finishing with the burnt
offering, Samuel arrived. Saul went out to meet
and welcome him, 11 but Samuel said, "What is
this you have done?"

13:1a As in a few Greek manuscripts; the number is missing in the Hebrew. **13:1b** Hebrew *reigned . . . and two;* the number is incomplete in the Hebrew. Compare Acts 13:21. **13:5** As in Greek and Syriac versions; Hebrew reads *30,000.*

Samuel calling on the LORD served to confirm his status as God's appointed mediator. **20–25:** Israel might have an established king, but real power remained with Yahweh, whose word through his prophet was to be obeyed.

13:1–14:52 Saul under Pressure

How much time passed between Saul's anointing and the action of these chapters is uncertain, as are all figures relating to Saul's reign. **13:1:** By this stage Saul had a son of military age; when he was anointed king, Saul had been a young man whose military prowess had not yet been proven (9:2; 10:27). As many as fifteen to twenty years may have passed since Saul's original commission. **3–4:** Jonathan took the initiative and not Saul, even though the victory gained was attributed to his father. **4–8:** The king's commission having at last been carried out, the command of 1 Samuel 10:8 came into effect. **5:** The Philistines predictably responded to what they regarded as the rebellion of a subject people. Saul, like Gideon (Judg 7:12), is confronted with an innumerable enemy. **6–12:** Watching his fearful forces drift away, Saul's resolve to wait for Samuel breaks. There is a certain irony in the fact that Samuel had waited years for Saul to begin to fulfill the purpose for which Yahweh had appointed him king, and

Saul replied, "I saw my men scattering from
me, and you didn't arrive when you said you
would, and the Philistines are at Micmash ready
for battle. [12]So I said, 'The Philistines are ready
to march against us at Gilgal, and I haven't even
asked for the LORD's help!' So I felt compelled
to offer the burnt offering myself before you
came."
[13]"How foolish!" Samuel exclaimed. "You
have not kept the command the LORD your God
gave you. Had you kept it, the LORD would have
established your kingdom over Israel forever.
[14]But now your kingdom must end, for the LORD
has sought out a man after his own heart. The
LORD has already appointed him to be the leader of his people, because you have not kept the
LORD's command."

Israel's Military Disadvantage

[15]Samuel then left Gilgal and went on his way,
but the rest of the troops went with Saul to meet
the army. They went up from Gilgal to Gibeah
in the land of Benjamin.* When Saul counted the men who were still with him, he found
only 600 were left! [16]Saul and Jonathan and the
troops with them were staying at Geba in the
land of Benjamin. The Philistines set up their
camp at Micmash. [17]Three raiding parties soon
left the camp of the Philistines. One went north
toward Ophrah in the land of Shual, [18]another
went west to Beth-horon, and the third moved
toward the border above the valley of Zeboim
near the wilderness.
[19]There were no blacksmiths in the land of
Israel in those days. The Philistines wouldn't
allow them for fear they would make swords
and spears for the Hebrews. [20]So whenever the
Israelites needed to sharpen their plowshares,
picks, axes, or sickles,* they had to take them
to a Philistine blacksmith. [21](The charges were
as follows: a quarter of an ounce of silver* for
sharpening a plowshare or a pick, and an eighth
of an ounce* for sharpening an ax, a sickle, or an
ox goad.) [22]So on the day of the battle none of
the people of Israel had a sword or spear, except
for Saul and Jonathan.
[23]The pass at Micmash had meanwhile
been secured by a contingent of the Philistine
army.

Jonathan's Daring Plan

14 One day Jonathan said to his armor
bearer, "Come on, let's go over to
where the Philistines have their outpost." But Jonathan did not tell his father what
he was doing.
[2]Meanwhile, Saul and his 600 men were
camped on the outskirts of Gibeah, around the
pomegranate tree* at Migron. [3]Among Saul's
men was Ahijah the priest, who was wearing the
ephod, the priestly vest. Ahijah was the son of
Ichabod's brother Ahitub, son of Phinehas, son
of Eli, the priest of the LORD who had served at
Shiloh.
No one realized that Jonathan had left the
Israelite camp. [4]To reach the Philistine outpost,
Jonathan had to go down between two rocky
cliffs that were called Bozez and Seneh. [5]The cliff
on the north was in front of Micmash, and the
one on the south was in front of Geba. [6]"Let's go
across to the outpost of those pagans," Jonathan
said to his armor bearer. "Perhaps the LORD will
help us, for nothing can hinder the LORD. He can
win a battle whether he has many warriors or
only a few!"
[7]"Do what you think is best," the armor bearer replied. "I'm with you completely, whatever
you decide."
[8]"All right then," Jonathan told him. "We will
cross over and let them see us. [9]If they say to us,
'Stay where you are or we'll kill you,' then we
will stop and not go up to them. [10]But if they
say, 'Come on up and fight,' then we will go up.
That will be the LORD's sign that he will help us
defeat them."
[11]When the Philistines saw them coming,
they shouted, "Look! The Hebrews are crawling out of their holes!" [12]Then the men from the
outpost shouted to Jonathan, "Come on up here,
and we'll teach you a lesson!"
"Come on, climb right behind me," Jonathan
said to his armor bearer, "for the LORD will help
us defeat them!"

13:15 As in Greek version; Hebrew reads *Samuel then left Gilgal and went to Gibeah in the land of Benjamin.* **13:20** As in Greek version; Hebrew reads *or plowshares.* **13:21a** Hebrew *1 pim* [8 grams]. **13:21b** Hebrew $^1/_3$ *of a shekel* [4 grams]. **14:2** Or *around the rock of Rimmon;* compare Judg 20:45, 47; 21:13.

---

yet Saul could not wait a week for God's prophet. **13–14:** It was for his disobedience, fear, and ultimate lack of trust in God's sovereign control of the situation that Saul was judged unworthy of the role of leader.

14:1–52 Jonathan's Successes and Saul's Failures. The contrast between Saul and Jonathan continues in the ensuing events of the war against the Philistines. **1–15:** Jonathan takes decisive action with confidence in God and instills such a divine dread in the

13 So they climbed up using both hands and
feet, and the Philistines fell before Jonathan, and
his armor bearer killed those who came behind
them. 14 They killed some twenty men in all, and
their bodies were scattered over about half an
acre.*

15 Suddenly, panic broke out in the Philistine
army, both in the camp and in the field, including
even the outposts and raiding parties. And just
then an earthquake struck, and everyone was
terrified.

Israel Defeats the Philistines

16 Saul's lookouts in Gibeah of Benjamin saw a
strange sight—the vast army of Philistines began to melt away in every direction. 17 "Call the
roll and find out who's missing," Saul ordered.
And when they checked, they found that Jonathan and his armor bearer were gone.

18 Then Saul shouted to Ahijah, "Bring the
ephod here!" For at that time Ahijah was wearing the ephod in front of the Israelites.* 19 But
while Saul was talking to the priest, the confusion in the Philistine camp grew louder and
louder. So Saul said to the priest, "Never mind;
let's get going!"*

20 Then Saul and all his men rushed out to the
battle and found the Philistines killing each other.
There was terrible confusion everywhere. 21 Even
the Hebrews who had previously gone over to the
Philistine army revolted and joined in with Saul,
Jonathan, and the rest of the Israelites. 22 Likewise,
the men of Israel who were hiding in the hill
country of Ephraim joined the chase when they
saw the Philistines running away. 23 So the LORD
saved Israel that day, and the battle continued to
rage even beyond Beth-aven.

Saul's Foolish Oath

24 Now the men of Israel were pressed to exhaustion that day, because Saul had placed them under an oath, saying, "Let a curse fall on anyone
who eats before evening—before I have full revenge on my enemies." So no one ate anything
all day, 25 even though they had all found honeycomb on the ground in the forest. 26 They didn't
dare touch the honey because they all feared the
oath they had taken.

27 But Jonathan had not heard his father's
command, and he dipped the end of his stick into
a piece of honeycomb and ate the honey. After
he had eaten it, he felt refreshed.* 28 But one of
the men saw him and said, "Your father made
the army take a strict oath that anyone who eats
food today will be cursed. That is why everyone
is weary and faint."

29 "My father has made trouble for us all!"
Jonathan exclaimed. "A command like that only
hurts us. See how refreshed I am now that I have
eaten this little bit of honey. 30 If the men had
been allowed to eat freely from the food they
found among our enemies, think how many
more Philistines we could have killed!"

31 They chased and killed the Philistines all
day from Micmash to Aijalon, growing more and
more faint. 32 That evening they rushed for the
battle plunder and butchered the sheep, goats,
cattle, and calves, but they ate them without
draining the blood. 33 Someone reported to Saul,
"Look, the men are sinning against the LORD by
eating meat that still has blood in it."

"That is very wrong," Saul said. "Find a large
stone and roll it over here. 34 Then go out among
the troops and tell them, 'Bring the cattle, sheep,
and goats here to me. Kill them here, and drain
the blood before you eat them. Do not sin against
the LORD by eating meat with the blood still in
it.'"

So that night all the troops brought their
animals and slaughtered them there. 35 Then Saul
built an altar to the LORD; it was the first of the
altars he built to the LORD.

36 Then Saul said, "Let's chase the Philistines
all night and plunder them until sunrise. Let's
destroy every last one of them."

His men replied, "We'll do whatever you
think is best."

But the priest said, "Let's ask God first."

37 So Saul asked God, "Should we go after the
Philistines? Will you help us defeat them?" But
God made no reply that day.

38 Then Saul said to the leaders, "Something's
wrong! I want all my army commanders to come
here. We must find out what sin was committed

14:14 Hebrew *half a yoke;* a "yoke" was the amount of land plowed by a pair of yoked oxen in one day. **14:18** As in some Greek manuscripts; Hebrew reads *"Bring the Ark of God." For at that time the Ark of God was with the Israelites.* **14:19** Hebrew *Withdraw your hand.* **14:27** Or *his eyes brightened;* similarly in 14:29.

Philistine army that they flee in terror. **18–23:** Saul turns to God for counsel and advice but did not wait for an answer. **24–30:** Saul's misguided vow deprives his army of greater success against the Philistines. **31–35:** The enforced fast also led to violation of Israel's food laws. Hungry soldiers slaughtered animals *without draining the blood.* **36–37:** Saul's turning to inquire of God is only on the suggestion of Ahijah the priest. **37–38:** Divine silence signified sin in the camp. **39:** Another rash vow almost ends in disaster.

today. 39 I vow by the name of the LORD who rescued Israel that the sinner will surely die, even if
it is my own son Jonathan!" But no one would
tell him what the trouble was.
40 Then Saul said, "Jonathan and I will stand
over here, and all of you stand over there."
And the people responded to Saul, "Whatever
you think is best."
41 Then Saul prayed, "O LORD, God of Israel,
please show us who is guilty and who is innocent.*" Then they cast sacred lots, and Jonathan
and Saul were chosen as the guilty ones, and the
people were declared innocent.
42 Then Saul said, "Now cast lots again and
choose between me and Jonathan." And Jonathan was shown to be the guilty one.
43 "Tell me what you have done," Saul demanded of Jonathan.
"I tasted a little honey," Jonathan admitted.
"It was only a little bit on the end of my stick.
Does that deserve death?"
44 "Yes, Jonathan," Saul said, "you must die!
May God strike me and even kill me if you do
not die for this."
45 But the people broke in and said to Saul,
"Jonathan has won this great victory for Israel.
Should he die? Far from it! As surely as the LORD
lives, not one hair on his head will be touched,
for God helped him do a great deed today." So
the people rescued Jonathan, and he was not put
to death.
46 Then Saul called back the army from chasing the Philistines, and the Philistines returned
home.

Saul's Military Successes

47 Now when Saul had secured his grasp on Israel's throne, he fought against his enemies in
every direction—against Moab, Ammon, Edom,
the kings of Zobah, and the Philistines. And
wherever he turned, he was victorious.* 48 He
performed great deeds and conquered the Amalekites, saving Israel from all those who had
plundered them.
49 Saul's sons included Jonathan, Ishbosheth,*
and Malkishua. He also had two daughters:
Merab, who was older, and Michal. 50 Saul's wife
was Ahinoam, the daughter of Ahimaaz. The
commander of Saul's army was Abner, the son
of Saul's uncle Ner. 51 Saul's father, Kish, and Abner's father, Ner, were both sons of Abiel.
52 The Israelites fought constantly with the
Philistines throughout Saul's lifetime. So whenever Saul observed a young man who was brave
and strong, he drafted him into his army.

Saul Destroys the Amalekites

15 One day Samuel said to Saul, "It was
the LORD who told me to anoint you
as king of his people, Israel. Now
listen to this message from the LORD! 2 This is
what the LORD of Heaven's Armies has declared:
I have decided to settle accounts with the nation
of Amalek for opposing Israel when they came
from Egypt. 3 Now go and completely destroy*
the entire Amalekite nation—men, women, children, babies, cattle, sheep, goats, camels, and donkeys."
4 So Saul mobilized his army at Telaim. There
were 200,000 soldiers from Israel and 10,000
men from Judah. 5 Then Saul and his army went
to a town of the Amalekites and lay in wait in
the valley. 6 Saul sent this warning to the Kenites:
"Move away from where the Amalekites live, or
you will die with them. For you showed kindness to all the people of Israel when they came
up from Egypt." So the Kenites packed up and
left.
7 Then Saul slaughtered the Amalekites from
Havilah all the way to Shur, east of Egypt. 8 He
captured Agag, the Amalekite king, but completely destroyed everyone else. 9 Saul and his

14:41 Greek version adds *If the fault is with me or my son Jonathan, respond with Urim; but if the men of Israel are at fault, respond with Thummim.* **14:47** As in Greek version; Hebrew reads *he acted wickedly.* **14:49** Hebrew *Ishvi,* a variant name for Ishbosheth; also known as Esh-baal. **15:3** The Hebrew term used here refers to the complete consecration of things or people to the LORD, either by destroying them or by giving them as an offering; also in 15:8, 9, 15, 18, 20, 21.

40–45: The lots indicated Jonathan as the guilty party, but Saul was swayed not by love of his son but by the strong feelings of his troops that the one to whom so much of the victory was owed could not merit death.

15:1–35 Saul's Failure

Despite being king, Saul is still subject to God's word communicated through his prophet. **2–3:** As God's agent of judgment upon the Amalekites because of their ruthless assault upon the Israelites during their journey to the promised land (1 Sam 15:2–3; cf. Exod 17:6–14), Saul was sent to engage in a holy war. **3:** *Completely destroy*: The "ban" or "devotion to destruction" was used by Israel and others in the ancient Middle East. The enemy and all their property were annihilated as a kind of sacrifice to the deity. **8–9:** Saul allows material considerations to determine what was preserved and what was destroyed. **10–21:** Fore-

men spared Agag's life and kept the best of the
sheep and goats, the cattle, the fat calves, and
the lambs—everything, in fact, that appealed to
them. They destroyed only what was worthless
or of poor quality.

The LORD Rejects Saul

[10]Then the LORD said to Samuel, [11]"I am sorry that
I ever made Saul king, for he has not been loyal
to me and has refused to obey my command."
Samuel was so deeply moved when he heard this
that he cried out to the LORD all night.
[12]Early the next morning Samuel went to find
Saul. Someone told him, "Saul went to the town
of Carmel to set up a monument to himself; then
he went on to Gilgal."
[13]When Samuel finally found him, Saul greeted him cheerfully. "May the LORD bless you," he
said. "I have carried out the LORD's command!"
[14]"Then what is all the bleating of sheep and
goats and the lowing of cattle I hear?" Samuel
demanded.
[15]"It's true that the army spared the best of
the sheep, goats, and cattle," Saul admitted. "But
they are going to sacrifice them to the LORD your
God. We have destroyed everything else."
[16]Then Samuel said to Saul, "Stop! Listen to
what the LORD told me last night!"
"What did he tell you?" Saul asked.
[17]And Samuel told him, "Although you may
think little of yourself, are you not the leader
of the tribes of Israel? The LORD has anointed
you king of Israel. [18]And the LORD sent you on
a mission and told you, 'Go and completely destroy the sinners, the Amalekites, until they are
all dead.' [19]Why haven't you obeyed the LORD?
Why did you rush for the plunder and do what
was evil in the LORD's sight?"
[20]"But I did obey the LORD," Saul insisted.
"I carried out the mission he gave me. I brought
back King Agag, but I destroyed everyone else.
[21]Then my troops brought in the best of the
sheep, goats, cattle, and plunder to sacrifice to the
LORD your God in Gilgal."
[22]But Samuel replied,

"What is more pleasing to the LORD:
your burnt offerings and sacrifices
or your obedience to his voice?
Listen! Obedience is better than sacrifice,
and submission is better than offering the
fat of rams.
[23]Rebellion is as sinful as witchcraft,
and stubbornness as bad as worshiping
idols.
So because you have rejected the command of
the LORD,
he has rejected you as king."

Saul Pleads for Forgiveness

[24]Then Saul admitted to Samuel, "Yes, I have
sinned. I have disobeyed your instructions and
the LORD's command, for I was afraid of the
people and did what they demanded. [25]But now,
please forgive my sin and come back with me so
that I may worship the LORD."
[26]But Samuel replied, "I will not go back with
you! Since you have rejected the LORD's command, he has rejected you as king of Israel."
[27]As Samuel turned to go, Saul tried to hold
him back and tore the hem of his robe. [28]And
Samuel said to him, "The LORD has torn the
kingdom of Israel from you today and has given
it to someone else—one who is better than you.
[29]And he who is the Glory of Israel will not lie,
nor will he change his mind, for he is not human
that he should change his mind!"
[30]Then Saul pleaded again, "I know I have
sinned. But please, at least honor me before the
elders of my people and before Israel by coming
back with me so that I may worship the LORD
your God." [31]So Samuel finally agreed and went
back with him, and Saul worshiped the LORD.

Samuel Executes King Agag

[32]Then Samuel said, "Bring King Agag to me."
Agag arrived full of hope, for he thought, "Surely the worst is over, and I have been spared!"*
[33]But Samuel said, "As your sword has killed the
sons of many mothers, now your mother will be
childless." And Samuel cut Agag to pieces before
the LORD at Gilgal.

15:32 Dead Sea Scrolls and Greek version read *Agag arrived hesitantly, for he thought, "Surely this is the bitterness of death."*

warned by God of Saul's disobedience, Samuel proves to be unimpressed by Saul's claims to have fulfilled his commission and brushed aside all his excuses and attempts to shift the blame to his men. **22–23:** To God partial obedience is no obedience. By his refusal to listen to and obey God's word, Saul has disqualified himself as God's appointed ruler. **27–29:** The tearing of the prophet's robe becomes a symbolic act, with Saul's attempt to grasp power that was not his to command matched by God's removal of the kingdom and its power from him in favor of one better qualified. **30–33:** All that was left to Saul was a saving of his face before his troops and an execution of the divine will by Samuel, who killed the Amalekite king.

[34]Then Samuel went home to Ramah, and
Saul returned to his house at Gibeah of Saul.
[35]Samuel never went to meet with Saul again,
but he mourned constantly for him. And the
LORD was sorry he had ever made Saul king of
Israel.

Samuel Anoints David as King

16 Now the LORD said to Samuel, "You
have mourned long enough for Saul. I
have rejected him as king of Israel, so
fill your flask with olive oil and go to Bethlehem.
Find a man named Jesse who lives there, for I
have selected one of his sons to be my king."
[2]But Samuel asked, "How can I do that? If
Saul hears about it, he will kill me."
"Take a heifer with you," the LORD replied,
"and say that you have come to make a sacrifice
to the LORD. [3]Invite Jesse to the sacrifice, and I
will show you which of his sons to anoint for
me."
[4]So Samuel did as the LORD instructed. When
he arrived at Bethlehem, the elders of the town
came trembling to meet him. "What's wrong?"
they asked. "Do you come in peace?"
[5]"Yes," Samuel replied. "I have come to sacrifice to the LORD. Purify yourselves and come with
me to the sacrifice." Then Samuel performed the
purification rite for Jesse and his sons and invited
them to the sacrifice, too.
[6]When they arrived, Samuel took one look
at Eliab and thought, "Surely this is the LORD's
anointed!"
[7]But the LORD said to Samuel, "Don't judge
by his appearance or height, for I have rejected
him. The LORD doesn't see things the way you
see them. People judge by outward appearance,
but the LORD looks at the heart."
[8]Then Jesse told his son Abinadab to step forward and walk in front of Samuel. But Samuel
said, "This is not the one the LORD has chosen."
[9]Next Jesse summoned Shimea,* but Samuel
said, "Neither is this the one the LORD has chosen." [10]In the same way all seven of Jesse's sons
were presented to Samuel. But Samuel said to
Jesse, "The LORD has not chosen any of these."
[11]Then Samuel asked, "Are these all the sons you
have?"
"There is still the youngest," Jesse replied.
"But he's out in the fields watching the sheep
and goats."
"Send for him at once," Samuel said. "We
will not sit down to eat until he arrives."
[12]So Jesse sent for him. He was dark and
handsome, with beautiful eyes.
And the LORD said, "This is the one; anoint
him."
[13]So as David stood there among his brothers,
Samuel took the flask of olive oil he had brought
and anointed David with the oil. And the Spirit
of the LORD came powerfully upon David from
that day on. Then Samuel returned to Ramah.

David Serves in Saul's Court

[14]Now the Spirit of the LORD had left Saul, and
the LORD sent a tormenting spirit* that filled
him with depression and fear.
[15]Some of Saul's servants said to him, "A tormenting spirit from God is troubling you. [16]Let
us find a good musician to play the harp whenever the tormenting spirit troubles you. He will
play soothing music, and you will soon be well
again."
[17]"All right," Saul said. "Find me someone
who plays well, and bring him here."
[18]One of the servants said to Saul, "One of
Jesse's sons from Bethlehem is a talented harp
player. Not only that—he is a brave warrior, a

16:9 Hebrew *Shammah,* a variant spelling of Shimea; compare 1 Chr 2:13; 20:7. **16:14** Or *an evil spirit;* also in 16:15, 16, 23.

16:1–23 David as Court Musician

Since God has rejected Saul as king, a new leader must be found. **2–4:** Samuel's response gives an early hint of the darker side of Saul's character: He will stop at nothing to protect his throne. God's instructions seem to validate Samuel's concern. **5–13:** Note similarities with and contrasts to chapter 9. On both occasions the setting is a community feast. In 1 Samuel 9 the honored guest was the young man Saul; here it is the family of Jesse, among whose sons will be the LORD's anointed. In 1 Samuel 9 attention was drawn to Saul's physique (9:1; cf. 10:23–24), but here it means nothing. In 1 Samuel 9:21 Saul drew attention to the insignificance of his family and tribal connections. Here David is seen as so insignificant, even by his family, that he is not included among those eligible to meet the prophet. **13:** Unlike Saul, David was given no signs and no initial commission to fulfill. **14–23:** Ironically, David's first task as the LORD's anointed was to serve the existing king. **14:** Saul's rebellion against the word of the LORD leads to the removal of the divine protection from him, leaving him susceptible to spiritual forces. The *tormenting spirit* might have been a way of describing mental illness. **15–17:** It was the popular belief of the time that music had calming properties and warded off spirits. **13, 14, 18:** The contrast between Saul and David is

man of war, and has good judgment. He is also
a fine-looking young man, and the LORD is with
him."
19 So Saul sent messengers to Jesse to say,
"Send me your son David, the shepherd." 20 Jesse
responded by sending David to Saul, along with
a young goat, a donkey loaded with bread, and a
wineskin full of wine.
21 So David went to Saul and began serving
him. Saul loved David very much, and David became his armor bearer.
22 Then Saul sent word to Jesse asking, "Please
let David remain in my service, for I am very
pleased with him."
23 And whenever the tormenting spirit from
God troubled Saul, David would play the harp.
Then Saul would feel better, and the tormenting
spirit would go away.

Goliath Challenges the Israelites

17 The Philistines now mustered their
army for battle and camped between
Socoh in Judah and Azekah at Ephes-
dammim. 2 Saul countered by gathering his Israelite troops near the valley of Elah. 3 So the
Philistines and Israelites faced each other on opposite hills, with the valley between them.
4 Then Goliath, a Philistine champion from
Gath, came out of the Philistine ranks to face
the forces of Israel. He was over nine feet* tall!
5 He wore a bronze helmet, and his bronze coat of
mail weighed 125 pounds.* 6 He also wore bronze
leg armor, and he carried a bronze javelin on his
shoulder. 7 The shaft of his spear was as heavy
and thick as a weaver's beam, tipped with an iron
spearhead that weighed 15 pounds.* His armor
bearer walked ahead of him carrying a shield.
8 Goliath stood and shouted a taunt across to
the Israelites. "Why are you all coming out to
fight?" he called. "I am the Philistine champion,
but you are only the servants of Saul. Choose
one man to come down here and fight me! 9 If he
kills me, then we will be your slaves. But if I kill
him, you will be our slaves! 10 I defy the armies
of Israel today! Send me a man who will fight
me!" 11 When Saul and the Israelites heard this,
they were terrified and deeply shaken.

Jesse Sends David to Saul's Camp

12 Now David was the son of a man named Jesse,
an Ephrathite from Bethlehem in the land of Judah. Jesse was an old man at that time, and he
had eight sons. 13 Jesse's three oldest sons—Eliab,
Abinadab, and Shimea*—had already joined
Saul's army to fight the Philistines. 14 David was
the youngest son. David's three oldest brothers
stayed with Saul's army, 15 but David went back
and forth so he could help his father with the
sheep in Bethlehem.
16 For forty days, every morning and evening,
the Philistine champion strutted in front of the
Israelite army.
17 One day Jesse said to David, "Take this
basket* of roasted grain and these ten loaves of
bread, and carry them quickly to your brothers.
18 And give these ten cuts of cheese to their captain. See how your brothers are getting along,
and bring back a report on how they are doing.*"
19 David's brothers were with Saul and the Israelite army at the valley of Elah, fighting against
the Philistines.
20 So David left the sheep with another shepherd and set out early the next morning with
the gifts, as Jesse had directed him. He arrived at
the camp just as the Israelite army was leaving
for the battlefield with shouts and battle cries.
21 Soon the Israelite and Philistine forces stood
facing each other, army against army. 22 David

17:4 Hebrew *6 cubits and 1 span* [which totals about 9.75 feet or 3 meters]; Dead Sea Scrolls and Greek version read *4 cubits and 1 span* [which totals about 6.75 feet or 2 meters]. **17:5** Hebrew *5,000 shekels* [57 kilograms]. **17:7** Hebrew *600 shekels* [6.8 kilograms]. **17:13** Hebrew *Shammah,* a variant spelling of Shimea; compare 1 Chr 2:13; 20:7. **17:17** Hebrew *ephah* [20 quarts or 22 liters]. **17:18** Hebrew *and take their pledge.*

---

summed up by the absence and presence of the Spirit of the LORD, which *had left Saul* and which even a servant recognized as being *with* [David].

17:1–58 David as Champion of Israel

The story of David and Goliath is probably the best known of all the incidents in 1 Samuel, although no summary of that victory can do justice to the subtleties of the narrative as the chapter unfolds. This story may constitute an alternative tradition of how David entered Saul's court, since the court musician (chap. 16) is apparently unknown to the king in this incident (see vv. 55–58). **4–10:** Goliath's effect on the Israelite army was one of dread. Even the king, who stood a head taller than any of the others, had no stomach for the fight. **15:** David is still fulfilling his familial responsibilities by traveling back and forth from Saul's camp to his father's home. **20–32:** The arrival of David brought a new dimension to the scene, even while it awakens echoes of another young man sent on an errand by his father (cf. 9:3–5). Saul's journey led to his secret anointing and (avoided) commission to

left his things with the keeper of supplies and
hurried out to the ranks to greet his brothers.
23 As he was talking with them, Goliath, the Philistine champion from Gath, came out from the
Philistine ranks. Then David heard him shout his
usual taunt to the army of Israel.

24 As soon as the Israelite army saw him, they
began to run away in fright. 25 "Have you seen
the giant?" the men asked. "He comes out each
day to defy Israel. The king has offered a huge
reward to anyone who kills him. He will give
that man one of his daughters for a wife, and the
man's entire family will be exempted from paying taxes!"

26 David asked the soldiers standing nearby,
"What will a man get for killing this Philistine
and ending his defiance of Israel? Who is this pagan Philistine anyway, that he is allowed to defy
the armies of the living God?"

27 And these men gave David the same reply.
They said, "Yes, that is the reward for killing
him."

28 But when David's oldest brother, Eliab,
heard David talking to the men, he was angry.
"What are you doing around here anyway?" he
demanded. "What about those few sheep you're
supposed to be taking care of? I know about
your pride and deceit. You just want to see the
battle!"

29 "What have I done now?" David replied. "I
was only asking a question!" 30 He walked over
to some others and asked them the same thing
and received the same answer. 31 Then David's
question was reported to King Saul, and the king
sent for him.

David Kills Goliath

32 "Don't worry about this Philistine," David told
Saul. "I'll go fight him!"

33 "Don't be ridiculous!" Saul replied. "There's
no way you can fight this Philistine and possibly
win! You're only a boy, and he's been a man of
war since his youth."

34 But David persisted. "I have been taking
care of my father's sheep and goats," he said.
"When a lion or a bear comes to steal a lamb
from the flock, 35 I go after it with a club and
rescue the lamb from its mouth. If the animal
turns on me, I catch it by the jaw and club it
to death. 36 I have done this to both lions and
bears, and I'll do it to this pagan Philistine, too,
for he has defied the armies of the living God!
37 The LORD who rescued me from the claws of
the lion and the bear will rescue me from this
Philistine!"

Saul finally consented. "All right, go ahead,"
he said. "And may the LORD be with you!"

38 Then Saul gave David his own armor—a
bronze helmet and a coat of mail. 39 David put it
on, strapped the sword over it, and took a step or
two to see what it was like, for he had never worn
such things before.

"I can't go in these," he protested to Saul.
"I'm not used to them." So David took them off
again. 40 He picked up five smooth stones from
a stream and put them into his shepherd's bag.
Then, armed only with his shepherd's staff and
sling, he started across the valley to fight the
Philistine.

41 Goliath walked out toward David with his
shield bearer ahead of him, 42 sneering in contempt at this ruddy-faced boy. 43 "Am I a dog,"
he roared at David, "that you come at me with a
stick?" And he cursed David by the names of his
gods. 44 "Come over here, and I'll give your flesh
to the birds and wild animals!" Goliath yelled.

45 David replied to the Philistine, "You come
to me with sword, spear, and javelin, but I come
to you in the name of the LORD of Heaven's
Armies—the God of the armies of Israel, whom
you have defied. 46 Today the LORD will conquer
you, and I will kill you and cut off your head.
And then I will give the dead bodies of your men
to the birds and wild animals, and the whole
world will know that there is a God in Israel!
47 And everyone assembled here will know that
the LORD rescues his people, but not with sword
and spear. This is the LORD's battle, and he will
give you to us!"

48 As Goliath moved closer to attack, David
quickly ran out to meet him. 49 Reaching into his
shepherd's bag and taking out a stone, he hurled
it with his sling and hit the Philistine in the forehead. The stone sank in, and Goliath stumbled
and fell face down on the ground.

50 So David triumphed over the Philistine
with only a sling and a stone, for he had no
sword. 51 Then David ran over and pulled Goliath's sword from its sheath. David used it to kill
him and cut off his head.

---

deal with the Philistine menace; David regards that same Philistine menace as an affront to the living God. **25–26:** Although Saul offers rich rewards to any man who overcame the giant, David's interest in defeating him arises from his wish to stand up for the LORD. **33–37:** Convinced by David's testimony of God's ability to deliver, Saul expressed his desire that the LORD may be with David in the ensuing conflict, unaware that that was precisely the difference between David and himself (cf. 16:13–14).

A Bride Price

"He will give that man one of his daughters for a wife" (17:25). There is much confusion regarding the status of a married woman in ancient Israel, and it is too often assumed that she was her husband's property by virtue of his payment of the *mohar*, a term that is often translated "bride price," confirming the notion that women were bought and sold (see Marriage, Song 2). But marriage was a form of gift exchange, still common in some traditional societies. The gift of the woman, it was hoped, would enable her husband's name and lineage to be preserved. Such generosity on the part of the bride's father required reciprocation in order to maintain the balance and due order in the relationship of the two families involved in the marriage alliance. The nature and size of the *mohar* were determined by the status and relative need of the girl's family. Thus Saul, who needed Goliath killed, could regard that exploit as sufficient *mohar* for his daughter, while the privileges and benefits of becoming the king's son-in-law were considered sufficient to justify the risk involved in killing the giant. See also 18:25.

Israel Routs the Philistines

When the Philistines saw that their champion
was dead, they turned and ran. 52 Then the men
of Israel and Judah gave a great shout of triumph and rushed after the Philistines, chasing
them as far as Gath* and the gates of Ekron. The
bodies of the dead and wounded Philistines were
strewn all along the road from Shaaraim, as far
as Gath and Ekron. 53 Then the Israelite army
returned and plundered the deserted Philistine
camp. 54 (David took the Philistine's head to Jerusalem, but he stored the man's armor in his
own tent.)
55 As Saul watched David go out to fight the
Philistine, he asked Abner, the commander of his
army, "Abner, whose son is this young man?"
"I really don't know," Abner declared.
56 "Well, find out who he is!" the king told
him.
57 As soon as David returned from killing Goliath, Abner brought him to Saul with the Philistine's head still in his hand. 58 "Tell me about
your father, young man," Saul said.
And David replied, "His name is Jesse, and we
live in Bethlehem."

Saul Becomes Jealous of David

18 After David had finished talking with
Saul, he met Jonathan, the king's son.
There was an immediate bond between
them, for Jonathan loved David. 2 From that day
on Saul kept David with him and wouldn't let
him return home. 3 And Jonathan made a solemn pact with David, because he loved him as he
loved himself. 4 Jonathan sealed the pact by taking off his robe and giving it to David, together
with his tunic, sword, bow, and belt.
5 Whatever Saul asked David to do, David did
it successfully. So Saul made him a commander
over the men of war, an appointment that was
welcomed by the people and Saul's officers alike.
6 When the victorious Israelite army was returning home after David had killed the Philistine, women from all the towns of Israel came
out to meet King Saul. They sang and danced for
joy with tambourines and cymbals.* 7 This was
their song:

17:52 As in some Greek manuscripts; Hebrew reads *a valley*. **18:6** The type of instrument represented by the word *cymbals* is uncertain.

55–56: Saul's question to Abner is understandable in the context of his promise to give his daughter in marriage to whoever killed Goliath, for the relative wealth and status of the family involved in such an alliance was an important issue.

18:1—20:42 David and the Family of Saul

The relations between David and the various members of Saul's family are marked primarily by the contrast between Saul's jealousy and his children's high regard for David. **18:1–4:** The covenant formed between Jonathan and David effectively made them brothers, with all the privileges and responsibilities such kinship brought in terms of help in time of need, protection from harm, and preservation of name and honor. The covenant was sealed by the superior party, in this case Jonathan, sharing with David all that marked him off as the king's son and potential heir to the kingdom. **5–19:** Saul saw David's potential for the kingdom but, responding out of his own rejection by the LORD, expressed his jealousy and fear of David by attempting to take his life either directly or by the hand of the Philistines. **17–18:** David displays his

"Saul has killed his thousands,
and David his ten thousands!"

8 This made Saul very angry. "What's this?" he said. "They credit David with ten thousands and me with only thousands. Next they'll be making him their king!" 9 So from that time on Saul kept a jealous eye on David.

10 The very next day a tormenting spirit* from God overwhelmed Saul, and he began to rave in his house like a madman. David was playing the harp, as he did each day. But Saul had a spear in his hand, 11 and he suddenly hurled it at David, intending to pin him to the wall. But David escaped him twice.

12 Saul was then afraid of David, for the LORD was with David and had turned away from Saul. 13 Finally, Saul sent him away and appointed him commander over 1,000 men, and David faithfully led his troops into battle.

14 David continued to succeed in everything he did, for the LORD was with him. 15 When Saul recognized this, he became even more afraid of him. 16 But all Israel and Judah loved David because he was so successful at leading his troops into battle.

David Marries Saul's Daughter

17 One day Saul said to David, "I am ready to give you my older daughter, Merab, as your wife. But first you must prove yourself to be a real warrior by fighting the LORD's battles." For Saul thought, "I'll send him out against the Philistines and let them kill him rather than doing it myself."

18 "Who am I, and what is my family in Israel that I should be the king's son-in-law?" David exclaimed. "My father's family is nothing!" 19 So* when the time came for Saul to give his daughter Merab in marriage to David, he gave her instead to Adriel, a man from Meholah.

20 In the meantime, Saul's daughter Michal had fallen in love with David, and Saul was delighted when he heard about it. 21 "Here's another chance to see him killed by the Philistines!" Saul said to himself. But to David he said, "Today you have a second chance to become my son-in-law!"

22 Then Saul told his men to say to David, "The king really likes you, and so do we. Why don't you accept the king's offer and become his son-in-law?"

23 When Saul's men said these things to David, he replied, "How can a poor man from a humble family afford the bride price for the daughter of a king?"

24 When Saul's men reported this back to the king, 25 he told them, "Tell David that all I want for the bride price is 100 Philistine foreskins! Vengeance on my enemies is all I really want." But what Saul had in mind was that David would be killed in the fight.

26 David was delighted to accept the offer. Before the time limit expired, 27 he and his men went out and killed 200 Philistines. Then David fulfilled the king's requirement by presenting all their foreskins to him. So Saul gave his daughter Michal to David to be his wife.

28 When Saul realized that the LORD was with David and how much his daughter Michal loved him, 29 Saul became even more afraid of him, and he remained David's enemy for the rest of his life.

30 Every time the commanders of the Philistines attacked, David was more successful against them than all the rest of Saul's officers. So David's name became very famous.

Saul Tries to Kill David

19 Saul now urged his servants and his son Jonathan to assassinate David. But Jonathan, because of his strong affection for David, 2 told him what his father was planning. "Tomorrow morning," he warned him, "you must find a hiding place out in the fields. 3 I'll ask my father to go out there with me, and I'll talk to him about you. Then I'll tell you everything I can find out."

4 The next morning Jonathan spoke with his father about David, saying many good things about him. "The king must not sin against his servant David," Jonathan said. "He's never done anything to harm you. He has always helped you in any way he could. 5 Have you forgotten about the time he risked his life to kill the Philistine

18:10 Or *an evil spirit.* **18:19** Or *But.*

humility and lack of ambition to be king, and again reveals that he did not kill Goliath for the reward Saul promised. **25:** The bride price requested for Michal was little more than an invitation to sign his own death warrant. **26–27:** In meeting the king's demand and doubling it, David not only cast doubt on the king's estimation of his daughter's worth but in accordance with the law of reciprocity placed the king in his debt to the tune of one hundred Philistines. (The humor of such a turning of the tables on a king who sought his death would not have been lost on the original audience.) **29:** Killing David became Saul's great obsession, gradually taking over his life. **19:1—20:42:** Saul's jealousy of David adversely affects his

giant and how the LORD brought a great victory
to all Israel as a result? You were certainly happy
about it then. Why should you murder an innocent man like David? There is no reason for it
at all!"

6 So Saul listened to Jonathan and vowed,
"As surely as the LORD lives, David will not be
killed."

7 Afterward Jonathan called David and told
him what had happened. Then he brought David
to Saul, and David served in the court as before.

8 War broke out again after that, and David
led his troops against the Philistines. He attacked
them with such fury that they all ran away.

9 But one day when Saul was sitting at home,
with spear in hand, the tormenting spirit* from
the LORD suddenly came upon him again. As
David played his harp, 10 Saul hurled his spear
at David. But David dodged out of the way, and
leaving the spear stuck in the wall, he fled and
escaped into the night.

Michal Saves David's Life

11 Then Saul sent troops to watch David's house.
They were told to kill David when he came out
the next morning. But Michal, David's wife,
warned him, "If you don't escape tonight, you
will be dead by morning." 12 So she helped him
climb out through a window, and he fled and escaped. 13 Then she took an idol* and put it in his
bed, covered it with blankets, and put a cushion
of goat's hair at its head.

14 When the troops came to arrest David, she
told them he was sick and couldn't get out of
bed.

15 But Saul sent the troops back to get David.
He ordered, "Bring him to me in his bed so I can
kill him!" 16 But when they came to carry David
out, they discovered that it was only an idol in
the bed with a cushion of goat's hair at its head.

17 "Why have you betrayed me like this and
let my enemy escape?" Saul demanded of Michal.

"I had to," Michal replied. "He threatened to
kill me if I didn't help him."

18 So David escaped and went to Ramah to see
Samuel, and he told him all that Saul had done
to him. Then Samuel took David with him to live
at Naioth. 19 When the report reached Saul that
David was at Naioth in Ramah, 20 he sent troops
to capture him. But when they arrived and saw
Samuel leading a group of prophets who were
prophesying, the Spirit of God came upon Saul's
men, and they also began to prophesy. 21 When
Saul heard what had happened, he sent other
troops, but they, too, prophesied! The same thing
happened a third time. 22 Finally, Saul himself
went to Ramah and arrived at the great well in
Secu. "Where are Samuel and David?" he demanded.

"They are at Naioth in Ramah," someone
told him.

23 But on the way to Naioth in Ramah the
Spirit of God came even upon Saul, and he, too,
began to prophesy all the way to Naioth! 24 He
tore off his clothes and lay naked on the ground
all day and all night, prophesying in the presence
of Samuel. The people who were watching exclaimed, "What? Is even Saul a prophet?"

Jonathan Helps David

20 David now fled from Naioth in Ramah and found Jonathan. "What
have I done?" he exclaimed. "What is
my crime? How have I offended your father that
he is so determined to kill me?"

2 "That's not true!" Jonathan protested.
"You're not going to die. He always tells me everything he's going to do, even the little things.
I know my father wouldn't hide something like
this from me. It just isn't so!"

3 Then David took an oath before Jonathan
and said, "Your father knows perfectly well
about our friendship, so he has said to himself,
'I won't tell Jonathan—why should I hurt him?'
But I swear to you that I am only a step away
from death! I swear it by the LORD and by your
own soul!"

4 "Tell me what I can do to help you," Jonathan exclaimed.

5 David replied, "Tomorrow we celebrate the
new moon festival. I've always eaten with the
king on this occasion, but tomorrow I'll hide in
the field and stay there until the evening of the
third day. 6 If your father asks where I am, tell
him I asked permission to go home to Bethle-

19:9 Or *evil spirit.* **19:13** Hebrew *teraphim;* also in 19:16.

relationships with his son and daughter. **19:11–18:** Michal shows daring initiative and insight into her father's intentions, and makes plausible and persuasive arguments to give David time to escape. Her devotion to her husband is clear, though his to her would prove fleeting. **19–24:** Saul's pursuit was ultimately defeated by spiritual forces that overwhelmed not only the soldiers sent to capture David, but also Saul himself, even in his state of rebellion. **20:5–7:** In ancient Israel, family ties and responsibilities were paramount, and David's desire to be present at an annual sacrifice for his clan at Bethlehem would, in

hem for an annual family sacrifice. 7 If he says, 'Fine!' you will know all is well. But if he is angry and loses his temper, you will know he is determined to kill me. 8 Show me this loyalty as my sworn friend—for we made a solemn pact before the LORD—or kill me yourself if I have sinned against your father. But please don't betray me to him!"

9 "Never!" Jonathan exclaimed. "You know that if I had the slightest notion my father was planning to kill you, I would tell you at once."

10 Then David asked, "How will I know whether or not your father is angry?"

11 "Come out to the field with me," Jonathan replied. And they went out there together. 12 Then Jonathan told David, "I promise by the LORD, the God of Israel, that by this time tomorrow, or the next day at the latest, I will talk to my father and let you know at once how he feels about you. If he speaks favorably about you, I will let you know. 13 But if he is angry and wants you killed, may the LORD strike me and even kill me if I don't warn you so you can escape and live. May the LORD be with you as he used to be with my father. 14 And may you treat me with the faithful love of the LORD as long as I live. But if I die, 15 treat my family with this faithful love, even when the LORD destroys all your enemies from the face of the earth."

16 So Jonathan made a solemn pact with David,* saying, "May the LORD destroy all your enemies!" 17 And Jonathan made David reaffirm his vow of friendship again, for Jonathan loved David as he loved himself.

18 Then Jonathan said, "Tomorrow we celebrate the new moon festival. You will be missed when your place at the table is empty. 19 The day after tomorrow, toward evening, go to the place where you hid before, and wait there by the stone pile.* 20 I will come out and shoot three arrows to the side of the stone pile as though I were shooting at a target. 21 Then I will send a boy to bring the arrows back. If you hear me tell him, 'They're on this side,' then you will know, as surely as the LORD lives, that all is well, and there is no trouble. 22 But if I tell him, 'Go farther—the arrows are still ahead of you,' then it will mean that you must leave immediately, for the LORD is sending you away. 23 And may the LORD make us keep our promises to each other, for he has witnessed them."

24 So David hid himself in the field, and when the new moon festival began, the king sat down to eat. 25 He sat at his usual place against the wall, with Jonathan sitting opposite him* and Abner beside him. But David's place was empty. 26 Saul didn't say anything about it that day, for he said to himself, "Something must have made David ceremonially unclean." 27 But when David's place was empty again the next day, Saul asked Jonathan, "Why hasn't the son of Jesse been here for the meal either yesterday or today?"

28 Jonathan replied, "David earnestly asked me if he could go to Bethlehem. 29 He said, 'Please let me go, for we are having a family sacrifice. My brother demanded that I be there. So please let me get away to see my brothers.' That's why he isn't here at the king's table."

30 Saul boiled with rage at Jonathan. "You stupid son of a whore!"* he swore at him. "Do you think I don't know that you want him to be king in your place, shaming yourself and your mother? 31 As long as that son of Jesse is alive, you'll never be king. Now go and get him so I can kill him!"

32 "But why should he be put to death?" Jonathan asked his father. "What has he done?" 33 Then Saul hurled his spear at Jonathan, intending to kill him. So at last Jonathan realized that his father was really determined to kill David.

34 Jonathan left the table in fierce anger and refused to eat on that second day of the festival, for he was crushed by his father's shameful behavior toward David.

35 The next morning, as agreed, Jonathan went out into the field and took a young boy with him to gather his arrows. 36 "Start running," he told the boy, "so you can find the arrows as I shoot them." So the boy ran, and Jonathan shot an ar-

20:16 Hebrew *with the house of David.* **20:19** Hebrew *the stone Ezel.* The meaning of the Hebrew is uncertain. **20:25** As in Greek version; Hebrew reads *with Jonathan standing.* **20:30** Hebrew *You son of a perverse and rebellious woman.*

---

normal circumstances, have been sufficient excuse for his absence from the king's table. **8–17:** David's fears of betrayal were allayed by Jonathan's renewal of the covenant between them, although on this occasion there is a shift in the balance of the two parties. Jonathan acknowledges his dependence on the covenant love of David and the future dependence of his descendants (cf. 2 Sam 9:7; 21:7). **13:** *May the LORD be with you*: Jonathan's prayer recognizes that the future belongs to David, not Saul. **27:** *The son of Jesse*: Saul's phrase introduces a chilling note of distance to the relationship between the king and David. **30:** *Whore*: The Hebrew here more precisely translates as "perverse and rebellious woman." The description is ironic in that it more aptly fits the father.

row beyond him. 37When the boy had almost reached the arrow, Jonathan shouted, "The arrow is still ahead of you. 38Hurry, hurry, don't wait." So the boy quickly gathered up the arrows and ran back to his master. 39He, of course, suspected nothing; only Jonathan and David understood the signal. 40Then Jonathan gave his bow and arrows to the boy and told him to take them back to town.

41As soon as the boy was gone, David came out from where he had been hiding near the stone pile.* Then David bowed three times to Jonathan with his face to the ground. Both of them were in tears as they embraced each other and said good-bye, especially David.

42At last Jonathan said to David, "Go in peace, for we have sworn loyalty to each other in the LORD's name. The LORD is the witness of a bond between us and our children forever." Then David left, and Jonathan returned to the town.*

David Runs from Saul

21 1*David went to the town of Nob to see Ahimelech the priest. Ahimelech trembled when he saw him. "Why are you alone?" he asked. "Why is no one with you?"

2"The king has sent me on a private matter," David said. "He told me not to tell anyone why I am here. I have told my men where to meet me later. 3Now, what is there to eat? Give me five loaves of bread or anything else you have."

4"We don't have any regular bread," the priest replied. "But there is the holy bread, which you can have if your young men have not slept with any women recently."

5"Don't worry," David replied. "I never allow my men to be with women when they are on a campaign. And since they stay clean even on ordinary trips, how much more on this one!"

6Since there was no other food available, the priest gave him the holy bread—the Bread of the Presence that was placed before the LORD in the Tabernacle. It had just been replaced that day with fresh bread.

7Now Doeg the Edomite, Saul's chief herdsman, was there that day, having been detained before the LORD.*

8David asked Ahimelech, "Do you have a spear or sword? The king's business was so urgent that I didn't even have time to grab a weapon!"

9"I only have the sword of Goliath the Philistine, whom you killed in the valley of Elah," the priest replied. "It is wrapped in a cloth behind the ephod. Take that if you want it, for there is nothing else here."

"There is nothing like it!" David replied. "Give it to me!"

10So David escaped from Saul and went to King Achish of Gath. 11But the officers of Achish were unhappy about his being there. "Isn't this David, the king of the land?" they asked. "Isn't he the one the people honor with dances, singing,

'Saul has killed his thousands,
and David his ten thousands'?"

12David heard these comments and was very afraid of what King Achish of Gath might do to him. 13So he pretended to be insane, scratching on doors and drooling down his beard.

14Finally, King Achish said to his men, "Must you bring me a madman? 15We already have enough of them around here! Why should I let someone like this be my guest?"

David at the Cave of Adullam

22 So David left Gath and escaped to the cave of Adullam. Soon his brothers and all his other relatives joined him there. 2Then others began coming—men who were in trouble or in debt or who were just discontented—until David was the captain of about 400 men.

3Later David went to Mizpeh in Moab, where

20:41 As in Greek version; Hebrew reads *near the south edge.* **20:42** This sentence is numbered 21:1 in Hebrew text. **21:1** Verses 21:1-15 are numbered 21:2-16 in Hebrew text. **21:7** The meaning of the Hebrew is uncertain.

21:1—22:23 David, Saul, and the Massacre at Nob

Assistance for David leads to slaughter. **21:1:** On the run for his life, David once again headed for spiritual sanctuary. **2:** Ahimelech's reaction is surprising, for why should a priest be afraid of David, alone and unarmed? Perhaps he was afraid for David, because he was aware of Saul's previous attempts on David's life. **10–11:** Armed and provisioned, David flees to Gath but finds that his reputation as military champion had gone before him. **11:** *Isn't this . . . the king of the land?* The question is heavily ironic in the circumstances, as once again David was displaced and forced to live by his wits. **22:1–2:** David gathers about him a band of four hundred men forced to make a livelihood outside the bounds of normal society or unhappy with Saul. **3–4:** David sought protection for his parents by calling on kinship ties extending back three generations to Ruth, his great-grandmother

he asked the king, "Please allow my father and mother to live here with you until I know what God is going to do for me." [4]So David's parents stayed in Moab with the king during the entire time David was living in his stronghold.

[5]One day the prophet Gad told David, "Leave the stronghold and return to the land of Judah." So David went to the forest of Hereth.

[6]The news of his arrival in Judah soon reached Saul. At the time, the king was sitting beneath the tamarisk tree on the hill at Gibeah, holding his spear and surrounded by his officers.

[7]"Listen here, you men of Benjamin!" Saul shouted to his officers when he heard the news. "Has that son of Jesse promised every one of you fields and vineyards? Has he promised to make you all generals and captains in his army?* [8]Is that why you have conspired against me? For not one of you told me when my own son made a solemn pact with the son of Jesse. You're not even sorry for me. Think of it! My own son—encouraging him to kill me, as he is trying to do this very day!"

[9]Then Doeg the Edomite, who was standing there with Saul's men, spoke up. "When I was at Nob," he said, "I saw the son of Jesse talking to the priest, Ahimelech son of Ahitub. [10]Ahimelech consulted the LORD for him. Then he gave him food and the sword of Goliath the Philistine."

The Slaughter of the Priests

[11]King Saul immediately sent for Ahimelech and all his family, who served as priests at Nob. [12]When they arrived, Saul shouted at him, "Listen to me, you son of Ahitub!"

"What is it, my king?" Ahimelech asked.

[13]"Why have you and the son of Jesse conspired against me?" Saul demanded. "Why did you give him food and a sword? Why have you consulted God for him? Why have you encouraged him to kill me, as he is trying to do this very day?"

[14]"But sir," Ahimelech replied, "is anyone among all your servants as faithful as David, your son-in-law? Why, he is the captain of your bodyguard and a highly honored member of your household! [15]This was certainly not the first time I had consulted God for him! May the king not accuse me and my family in this matter, for I knew nothing at all of any plot against you."

[16]"You will surely die, Ahimelech, along with your entire family!" the king shouted. [17]And he ordered his bodyguards, "Kill these priests of the LORD, for they are allies and conspirators with David! They knew he was running away from me, but they didn't tell me!" But Saul's men refused to kill the LORD's priests.

[18]Then the king said to Doeg, "You do it." So Doeg the Edomite turned on them and killed them that day, eighty-five priests in all, still wearing their priestly garments. [19]Then he went to Nob, the town of the priests, and killed the priests' families—men and women, children and babies—and all the cattle, donkeys, sheep, and goats.

[20]Only Abiathar, one of the sons of Ahimelech, escaped and fled to David. [21]When he told David that Saul had killed the priests of the LORD, [22]David exclaimed, "I knew it! When I saw Doeg the Edomite there that day, I knew he was sure to tell Saul. Now I have caused the death of all your father's family. [23]Stay here with me, and don't be afraid. I will protect you with my own life, for the same person wants to kill us both."

David Protects the Town of Keilah

23 One day news came to David that the Philistines were at Keilah stealing grain from the threshing floors. [2]David asked the LORD, "Should I go and attack them?"

"Yes, go and save Keilah," the LORD told him.

22:7 Hebrew *commanders of thousands and commanders of hundreds?*

(Ruth 4:17). **6–8:** Saul's obsession with David has become all-consuming, leading him to accuse even his closest officials of conspiring against him and his son of inciting David to rebellion. In his imagination, it is David who is plotting murder. **11–15:** Ahimelech's speech marks yet another turning point in the life of Saul: the voice of God, through his priest, coming to Saul for the last time. It was an appeal to reason, but it fell on deaf ears. **16–17:** The king, who on a previous occasion had disobeyed God's command to destroy the Amalekites (15:3), now counteracted God's word by commanding the destruction of the settlement of the priests. **17–19:** Saul's Israelite officials refused to be party to such sacrilege, so it was left to Doeg the Edomite to fulfill the king's command. **18–22:** The slaughter of the priests fulfills the oracle against Eli's family in 2:27–26.

23:1—27:4 David on the Run from Saul

Characteristic of the period covered by these chapters is the contrast in the attitudes and actions of Saul and David, and the manner in which each is guided. David makes use of the divine oracle in order to determine

3 But David's men said, "We're afraid even
here in Judah. We certainly don't want to go to
Keilah to fight the whole Philistine army!"
4 So David asked the LORD again, and again
the LORD replied, "Go down to Keilah, for I will
help you conquer the Philistines."
5 So David and his men went to Keilah. They
slaughtered the Philistines and took all their
livestock and rescued the people of Keilah. 6 Now
when Abiathar son of Ahimelech fled to David at
Keilah, he brought the ephod with him.
7 Saul soon learned that David was at Keilah.
"Good!" he exclaimed. "We've got him now! God
has handed him over to me, for he has trapped
himself in a walled town!" 8 So Saul mobilized
his entire army to march to Keilah and besiege
David and his men.
9 But David learned of Saul's plan and told
Abiathar the priest to bring the ephod and ask the
LORD what he should do. 10 Then David prayed,
"O LORD, God of Israel, I have heard that Saul
is planning to come and destroy Keilah because
I am here. 11 Will the leaders of Keilah betray me
to him?* And will Saul actually come as I have
heard? O LORD, God of Israel, please tell me."
And the LORD said, "He will come."
12 Again David asked, "Will the leaders of
Keilah betray me and my men to Saul?"
And the LORD replied, "Yes, they will betray
you."

David Hides in the Wilderness

13 So David and his men—about 600 of them
now—left Keilah and began roaming the countryside. Word soon reached Saul that David had
escaped, so he didn't go to Keilah after all. 14 David now stayed in the strongholds of the wilderness and in the hill country of Ziph. Saul hunted
him day after day, but God didn't let Saul find
him.
15 One day near Horesh, David received the
news that Saul was on the way to Ziph to search
for him and kill him. 16 Jonathan went to find
David and encouraged him to stay strong in his
faith in God. 17 "Don't be afraid," Jonathan reassured him. "My father will never find you! You
are going to be the king of Israel, and I will be
next to you, as my father, Saul, is well aware."
18 So the two of them renewed their solemn pact
before the LORD. Then Jonathan returned home,
while David stayed at Horesh.
19 But now the men of Ziph went to Saul in
Gibeah and betrayed David to him. "We know
where David is hiding," they said. "He is in
the strongholds of Horesh on the hill of Hakilah, which is in the southern part of Jeshimon.
20 Come down whenever you're ready, O king,
and we will catch him and hand him over to
you!"
21 "The LORD bless you," Saul said. "At last
someone is concerned about me! 22 Go and check
again to be sure of where he is staying and who
has seen him there, for I know that he is very
crafty. 23 Discover his hiding places, and come
back when you are sure. Then I'll go with you.
And if he is in the area at all, I'll track him down,
even if I have to search every hiding place in Judah!" 24 So the men of Ziph returned home ahead
of Saul.
Meanwhile, David and his men had moved
into the wilderness of Maon in the Arabah Valley south of Jeshimon. 25 When David heard
that Saul and his men were searching for him,
he went even farther into the wilderness to the
great rock, and he remained there in the wilderness of Maon. But Saul kept after him in the wilderness.
26 Saul and David were now on opposite sides
of a mountain. Just as Saul and his men began
to close in on David and his men, 27 an urgent
message reached Saul that the Philistines were
raiding Israel again. 28 So Saul quit chasing David
and returned to fight the Philistines. Ever since
that time, the place where David was camped has
been called the Rock of Escape.* 29 *David then
went to live in the strongholds of En-gedi.

David Spares Saul's Life

24 1 *After Saul returned from fighting
the Philistines, he was told that David had gone into the wilderness of
En-gedi. 2 So Saul chose 3,000 elite troops from
all Israel and went to search for David and his
men near the rocks of the wild goats.
3 At the place where the road passes some
sheepfolds, Saul went into a cave to relieve himself. But as it happened, David and his men were
hiding farther back in that very cave!

23:11 Some manuscripts lack the first sentence of 23:11. **23:28** Hebrew *Sela-hammahlekoth.* **23:29** Verse 23:29 is numbered 24:1 in Hebrew text. **24:1** Verses 24:1-22 are numbered 24:2-23 in Hebrew text.

God's way for him. Saul was dependent on information received from human sources as to David's whereabouts. David's determination to wait for God's judgment was rewarded by divine protection and provision for his needs. Saul became the victim of his erratic emotions, driven by his desire to defeat David, even as the Philistine menace pressed in upon his kingdom, demanding his attention and ultimately his life.

4 “Now's your opportunity!” David's men
whispered to him. “Today the LORD is telling
you, ‘I will certainly put your enemy into your
power, to do with as you wish.’ ” So David crept
forward and cut off a piece of the hem of Saul's
robe.
5 But then David's conscience began bothering
him because he had cut Saul's robe. 6 “The LORD
knows I shouldn't have done that to my lord the
king,” he said to his men. “The LORD forbid that
I should do this to my lord the king and attack
the LORD's anointed one, for the LORD himself
has chosen him.” 7 So David restrained his men
and did not let them kill Saul.
After Saul had left the cave and gone on his
way, 8 David came out and shouted after him,
“My lord the king!” And when Saul looked
around, David bowed low before him.
9 Then he shouted to Saul, “Why do you listen to the people who say I am trying to harm
you? 10 This very day you can see with your own
eyes it isn't true. For the LORD placed you at my
mercy back there in the cave. Some of my men
told me to kill you, but I spared you. For I said,
‘I will never harm the king—he is the LORD's
anointed one.’ 11 Look, my father, at what I have
in my hand. It is a piece of the hem of your robe!
I cut it off, but I didn't kill you. This proves that
I am not trying to harm you and that I have not
sinned against you, even though you have been
hunting for me to kill me.
12 “May the LORD judge between us. Perhaps
the LORD will punish you for what you are trying to do to me, but I will never harm you. 13 As
that old proverb says, ‘From evil people come
evil deeds.’ So you can be sure I will never harm
you. 14 Who is the king of Israel trying to catch
anyway? Should he spend his time chasing one
who is as worthless as a dead dog or a single flea?
15 May the LORD therefore judge which of us is
right and punish the guilty one. He is my advocate, and he will rescue me from your power!”
16 When David had finished speaking, Saul
called back, “Is that really you, my son David?”
Then he began to cry. 17 And he said to David,
“You are a better man than I am, for you have
repaid me good for evil. 18 Yes, you have been
amazingly kind to me today, for when the LORD
put me in a place where you could have killed
me, you didn't do it. 19 Who else would let his enemy get away when he had him in his power?
May the LORD reward you well for the kindness
you have shown me today. 20 And now I realize
that you are surely going to be king, and that the
kingdom of Israel will flourish under your rule.
21 Now swear to me by the LORD that when that
happens you will not kill my family and destroy
my line of descendants!”
22 So David promised this to Saul with an
oath. Then Saul went home, but David and his
men went back to their stronghold.

The Death of Samuel

25 Now Samuel died, and all Israel gathered for his funeral. They buried him
at his house in Ramah.

Nabal Angers David

Then David moved down to the wilderness of
Maon.* 2 There was a wealthy man from Maon
who owned property near the town of Carmel.
He had 3,000 sheep and 1,000 goats, and it was
sheep-shearing time. 3 This man's name was
Nabal, and his wife, Abigail, was a sensible and
beautiful woman. But Nabal, a descendant of Caleb, was crude and mean in all his dealings.
4 When David heard that Nabal was shearing his sheep, 5 he sent ten of his young men to
Carmel with this message for Nabal: 6 “Peace and
prosperity to you, your family, and everything
you own! 7 I am told that it is sheep-shearing
time. While your shepherds stayed among us
near Carmel, we never harmed them, and nothing was ever stolen from them. 8 Ask your own
men, and they will tell you this is true. So would
you be kind to us, since we have come at a time
of celebration? Please share any provisions you
might have on hand with us and with your friend
David.” 9 David's young men gave this message
to Nabal in David's name, and they waited for
a reply.
10 “Who is this fellow David?” Nabal sneered
to the young men. “Who does this son of Jesse
think he is? There are lots of servants these days
who run away from their masters. 11 Should I
take my bread and my water and my meat that

25:1 As in Greek version (see also 25:2); Hebrew reads *Paran.*

25:1–44 Abigail's Intercession. The story of Nabal serves as an oblique commentary on the foolishness of a king who was also guilty of treating David in an unworthy manner. It also highlights the role of women. Abigail demonstrates that although women seldom held center stage for long in Israel's history, their intervention at strategic moments was often pivotal. **4–16:** David's assistance of Nabal's shepherds constituted an act of unsolicited generosity for which some reciprocal action of goodwill on Nabal's part was only to be expected. David's request was unremarkable. **10–11:** Nabal's reply is designed to shame and

I've slaughtered for my shearers and give it to
a band of outlaws who come from who knows
where?"
12 So David's young men returned and told
him what Nabal had said. 13 "Get your swords!"
was David's reply as he strapped on his own.
Then 400 men started off with David, and 200 remained behind to guard their equipment.
14 Meanwhile, one of Nabal's servants went
to Abigail and told her, "David sent messengers
from the wilderness to greet our master, but he
screamed insults at them. 15 These men have been
very good to us, and we never suffered any harm
from them. Nothing was stolen from us the
whole time they were with us. 16 In fact, day and
night they were like a wall of protection to us
and the sheep. 17 You need to know this and figure out what to do, for there is going to be trouble for our master and his whole family. He's so
ill-tempered that no one can even talk to him!"
18 Abigail wasted no time. She quickly gathered 200 loaves of bread, two wineskins full
of wine, five sheep that had been slaughtered,
nearly a bushel* of roasted grain, 100 clusters
of raisins, and 200 fig cakes. She packed them
on donkeys 19 and said to her servants, "Go on
ahead. I will follow you shortly." But she didn't
tell her husband Nabal what she was doing.
20 As she was riding her donkey into a mountain ravine, she saw David and his men coming
toward her. 21 David had just been saying, "A lot
of good it did to help this fellow. We protected his
flocks in the wilderness, and nothing he owned
was lost or stolen. But he has repaid me evil for
good. 22 May God strike me and kill me* if even
one man of his household is still alive tomorrow
morning!"

Abigail Intercedes for Nabal

23 When Abigail saw David, she quickly got off
her donkey and bowed low before him. 24 She fell
at his feet and said, "I accept all blame in this
matter, my lord. Please listen to what I have to
say. 25 I know Nabal is a wicked and ill-tempered
man; please don't pay any attention to him. He
is a fool, just as his name suggests.* But I never
even saw the young men you sent.
26 "Now, my lord, as surely as the LORD lives
and you yourself live, since the LORD has kept
you from murdering and taking vengeance into
your own hands, let all your enemies and those
who try to harm you be as cursed as Nabal is.
27 And here is a present that I, your servant, have
brought to you and your young men. 28 Please
forgive me if I have offended you in any way.
The LORD will surely reward you with a lasting
dynasty, for you are fighting the LORD's battles.
And you have not done wrong throughout your
entire life.
29 "Even when you are chased by those who
seek to kill you, your life is safe in the care of the
LORD your God, secure in his treasure pouch! But
the lives of your enemies will disappear like stones
shot from a sling! 30 When the LORD has done all
he promised and has made you leader of Israel,
31 don't let this be a blemish on your record. Then
your conscience won't have to bear the staggering
burden of needless bloodshed and vengeance. And
when the LORD has done these great things for
you, please remember me, your servant!"
32 David replied to Abigail, "Praise the LORD,
the God of Israel, who has sent you to meet me
today! 33 Thank God for your good sense! Bless
you for keeping me from murder and from carrying out vengeance with my own hands. 34 For
I swear by the LORD, the God of Israel, who has
kept me from hurting you, that if you had not
hurried out to meet me, not one of Nabal's men
would still be alive tomorrow morning." 35 Then
David accepted her present and told her, "Return
home in peace. I have heard what you said. We
will not kill your husband."

25:18 Hebrew *5 seahs* [30 liters]. **25:22** As in Greek version; Hebrew reads *May God strike and kill the enemies of David.* **25:25** The name *Nabal* means "fool."

dishonor David among his men. **12–13:** To David, there seemed only one response: Let Nabal discover what his shepherds had been protected from—a marauding band of cutthroats bent on destruction and pillage. **18–31:** If Nabal was Saul's alter ego, then Abigail is Jonathan's, acting decisively to redeem the situation by doing what Nabal should have done. Like Jonathan, she chose not to tell her nearest kin of her actions (cf. 25:19 with 14:1). **18:** Abigail's command of household supplies reflects the general authority of women in the domestic sphere. **22:** The reference to killing all the men leaves unanswered the question of what would happen to the women. **24–31:** This is one of the longest speeches given by a woman in the Old Testament. She prophetically expresses the LORD's ultimate design for David as leader over Israel with a lasting dynasty and urges him to avoid the guilt that would come from a needless shedding of blood. **32–35:** Abigail's tact and diplomacy, eloquence, and persuasive speech dramatically turned the course of action and had the effect of restoring David to an attitude of dependence on God rather than relying on his own schemes of revenge. **37–39:** Nabal's death from a stroke confirmed to David the

[36]When Abigail arrived home, she found that Nabal was throwing a big party and was celebrating like a king. He was very drunk, so she didn't tell him anything about her meeting with David until dawn the next day. [37]In the morning when Nabal was sober, his wife told him what had happened. As a result he had a stroke,* and he lay paralyzed on his bed like a stone. [38]About ten days later, the LORD struck him, and he died.

David Marries Abigail

[39]When David heard that Nabal was dead, he said, "Praise the LORD, who has avenged the insult I received from Nabal and has kept me from doing it myself. Nabal has received the punishment for his sin." Then David sent messengers to Abigail to ask her to become his wife.

[40]When the messengers arrived at Carmel, they told Abigail, "David has sent us to take you back to marry him."

[41]She bowed low to the ground and responded, "I, your servant, would be happy to marry David. I would even be willing to become a slave, washing the feet of his servants!" [42]Quickly getting ready, she took along five of her servant girls as attendants, mounted her donkey, and went with David's messengers. And so she became his wife. [43]David also married Ahinoam from Jezreel, making both of them his wives. [44]Saul, meanwhile, had given his daughter Michal, David's wife, to a man from Gallim named Palti son of Laish.

David Spares Saul Again

26 Now some men from Ziph came to Saul at Gibeah to tell him, "David is hiding on the hill of Hakilah, which overlooks Jeshimon."

[2]So Saul took 3,000 of Israel's elite troops and went to hunt him down in the wilderness of Ziph. [3]Saul camped along the road beside the hill of Hakilah, near Jeshimon, where David was hiding. When David learned that Saul had come after him into the wilderness, [4]he sent out spies to verify the report of Saul's arrival.

[5]David slipped over to Saul's camp one night to look around. Saul and Abner son of Ner, the commander of his army, were sleeping inside a ring formed by the slumbering warriors. [6]"Who will volunteer to go in there with me?" David asked Ahimelech the Hittite and Abishai son of Zeruiah, Joab's brother.

"I'll go with you," Abishai replied. [7]So David and Abishai went right into Saul's camp and found him asleep, with his spear stuck in the ground beside his head. Abner and the soldiers were lying asleep around him.

[8]"God has surely handed your enemy over to you this time!" Abishai whispered to David. "Let me pin him to the ground with one thrust of the spear; I won't need to strike twice!"

[9]"No!" David said. "Don't kill him. For who can remain innocent after attacking the LORD's anointed one? [10]Surely the LORD will strike Saul down someday, or he will die of old age or in battle. [11]The LORD forbid that I should kill the one he has anointed! But take his spear and that jug of water beside his head, and then let's get out of here!"

[12]So David took the spear and jug of water that were near Saul's head. Then he and Abishai got away without anyone seeing them or even waking up, because the LORD had put Saul's men into a deep sleep.

[13]David climbed the hill opposite the camp until he was at a safe distance. [14]Then he shouted down to the soldiers and to Abner son of Ner, "Wake up, Abner!"

"Who is it?" Abner demanded.

[15]"Well, Abner, you're a great man, aren't you?" David taunted. "Where in all Israel is there anyone as mighty? So why haven't you guarded your master the king when someone came to kill him? [16]This isn't good at all! I swear by the LORD that you and your men deserve to die, because you failed to protect your master, the LORD's anointed! Look around! Where are the king's spear and the jug of water that were beside his head?"

[17]Saul recognized David's voice and called out, "Is that you, my son David?"

And David replied, "Yes, my lord the king. [18]Why are you chasing me? What have I done? What is my crime? [19]But now let my lord the king listen to his servant. If the LORD has stirred you up against me, then let him accept my offer-

25:37 Hebrew *his heart failed him.*

---

truth of Abigail's prophecy that his future could safely be left in God's hands. **40–44:** Abigail's freedom to determine her destiny contrasts sharply with that of Michal, who in David's absence had been given by her father to another man in a political move designed to dishonor David and sever any possible future claim to Saul's throne on the grounds of marriage to the king's daughter.

26:1–25 David and Saul's Last Meeting. David again shows honor in his dealings with Saul, sparing his life and pleading his innocence. **21:** The king admits his

ing. But if this is simply a human scheme, then may those involved be cursed by the LORD. For they have driven me from my home, so I can no longer live among the LORD's people, and they have said, 'Go, worship pagan gods.' 20 Must I die on foreign soil, far from the presence of the LORD? Why has the king of Israel come out to search for a single flea? Why does he hunt me down like a partridge on the mountains?"

21 Then Saul confessed, "I have sinned. Come back home, my son, and I will no longer try to harm you, for you valued my life today. I have been a fool and very, very wrong."

22 "Here is your spear, O king," David replied. "Let one of your young men come over and get it. 23 The LORD gives his own reward for doing good and for being loyal, and I refused to kill you even when the LORD placed you in my power, for you are the LORD's anointed one. 24 Now may the LORD value my life, even as I have valued yours today. May he rescue me from all my troubles."

25 And Saul said to David, "Blessings on you, my son David. You will do many heroic deeds, and you will surely succeed." Then David went away, and Saul returned home.

David among the Philistines

27 But David kept thinking to himself, "Someday Saul is going to get me. The best thing I can do is escape to the Philistines. Then Saul will stop hunting for me in Israelite territory, and I will finally be safe."

2 So David took his 600 men and went over and joined Achish son of Maoch, the king of Gath. 3 David and his men and their families settled there with Achish at Gath. David brought his two wives along with him—Ahinoam from Jezreel and Abigail, Nabal's widow from Carmel. 4 Word soon reached Saul that David had fled to Gath, so he stopped hunting for him.

5 One day David said to Achish, "If it is all right with you, we would rather live in one of the country towns instead of here in the royal city."

6 So Achish gave him the town of Ziklag (which still belongs to the kings of Judah to this day), 7 and they lived there among the Philistines for a year and four months.

8 David and his men spent their time raiding the Geshurites, the Girzites, and the Amalekites—people who had lived near Shur, toward the land of Egypt, since ancient times. 9 David did not leave one person alive in the villages he attacked. He took the sheep, goats, cattle, donkeys, camels, and clothing before returning home to see King Achish.

10 "Where did you make your raid today?" Achish would ask.

And David would reply, "Against the south of Judah, the Jerahmeelites, and the Kenites."

11 No one was left alive to come to Gath and tell where he had really been. This happened again and again while he was living among the Philistines. 12 Achish believed David and thought to himself, "By now the people of Israel must hate him bitterly. Now he will have to stay here and serve me forever!"

Saul Consults a Medium

28 About that time the Philistines mustered their armies for another war with Israel. King Achish told David, "You and your men will be expected to join me in battle."

2 "Very well!" David agreed. "Now you will see for yourself what we can do."

Then Achish told David, "I will make you my personal bodyguard for life."

3 Meanwhile, Samuel had died, and all Israel had mourned for him. He was buried in Ramah, his hometown. And Saul had banned from the land of Israel all mediums and those who consult the spirits of the dead.

4 The Philistines set up their camp at Shunem, and Saul gathered all the army of Israel

---

own folly and wrongdoing. Saul and David would never meet again.

27:5—28:2 David in Philistine Territory

David avoids all possibility of death at Saul's hands by taking refuge as an armed mercenary in the service of Achish, king of Gath. **27:8–12:** Fooling Achish about his military actions, David destroyed Israel's enemies in the Negev region, in the southern part of Palestine. **28:1–2:** Only when the Philistines planned a major invasion of Israel did David's position become untenable: As the bodyguard of Achish, who trusted him implicitly, his place at his master's side seemed guaranteed to involve him in fighting against God's people.

28:3–25 Saul's Descent into Despair

Confronted with an invading Philistine army, the mere sight of which was sufficient to inspire terror, Saul was at a loss to know what to do. **4–7:** Faced with divine silence, Saul desperately descends to necromancy, seeking one final encounter with Sam-

and camped at Gilboa. [5]When Saul saw the vast
Philistine army, he became frantic with fear. [6]He
asked the LORD what he should do, but the LORD
refused to answer him, either by dreams or by
sacred lots* or by the prophets. [7]Saul then said
to his advisers, "Find a woman who is a medium,
so I can go and ask her what to do."

His advisers replied, "There is a medium at
Endor."

[8]So Saul disguised himself by wearing ordinary clothing instead of his royal robes. Then he
went to the woman's home at night, accompanied by two of his men.

"I have to talk to a man who has died," he
said. "Will you call up his spirit for me?"

[9]"Are you trying to get me killed?" the woman demanded. "You know that Saul has outlawed
all the mediums and all who consult the spirits of
the dead. Why are you setting a trap for me?"

[10]But Saul took an oath in the name of the
LORD and promised, "As surely as the LORD lives,
nothing bad will happen to you for doing this."

[11]Finally, the woman said, "Well, whose spirit
do you want me to call up?"

"Call up Samuel," Saul replied.

[12]When the woman saw Samuel, she screamed,
"You've deceived me! You are Saul!"

[13]"Don't be afraid!" the king told her. "What
do you see?"

"I see a god* coming up out of the earth," she
said.

[14]"What does he look like?" Saul asked.

"He is an old man wrapped in a robe," she
replied. Saul realized it was Samuel, and he fell
to the ground before him.

[15]"Why have you disturbed me by calling me
back?" Samuel asked Saul.

"Because I am in deep trouble," Saul replied. "The Philistines are at war with me, and
God has left me and won't reply by prophets
or dreams. So I have called for you to tell me
what to do."

[16]But Samuel replied, "Why ask me, since the
LORD has left you and has become your enemy?
[17]The LORD has done just as he said he would.
He has torn the kingdom from you and given it
to your rival, David. [18]The LORD has done this
to you today because you refused to carry out
his fierce anger against the Amalekites. [19]What's
more, the LORD will hand you and the army of
Israel over to the Philistines tomorrow, and you
and your sons will be here with me. The LORD
will bring down the entire army of Israel in defeat."

[20]Saul fell full length on the ground, paralyzed with fright because of Samuel's words.
He was also faint with hunger, for he had eaten
nothing all day and all night.

[21]When the woman saw how distraught he
was, she said, "Sir, I obeyed your command at
the risk of my life. [22]Now do what I say, and let
me give you a little something to eat so you can
regain your strength for the trip back."

[23]But Saul refused to eat anything. Then his
advisers joined the woman in urging him to eat,
so he finally yielded and got up from the ground
and sat on the couch.

[24]The woman had been fattening a calf, so she
hurried out and killed it. She took some flour,
kneaded it into dough and baked unleavened
bread. [25]She brought the meal to Saul and his
advisers, and they ate it. Then they went out into
the night.

The Philistines Reject David

29
The entire Philistine army now mobilized at Aphek, and the Israelites
camped at the spring in Jezreel. [2]As
the Philistine rulers were leading out their troops
in groups of hundreds and thousands, David and
his men marched at the rear with King Achish.
[3]But the Philistine commanders demanded,
"What are these Hebrews doing here?"

And Achish told them, "This is David, the
servant of King Saul of Israel. He's been with me
for years, and I've never found a single fault in
him from the day he arrived until today."

[4]But the Philistine commanders were angry.
"Send him back to the town you've given him!"
they demanded. "He can't go into the battle with
us. What if he turns against us in battle and becomes our adversary? Is there any better way for
him to reconcile himself with his master than by
handing our heads over to him? [5]Isn't this the
same David about whom the women of Israel
sing in their dances,

28:6 Hebrew *by Urim.* **28:13** Or *gods.*

uel. **17–19:** Samuel's answer is no surprise: Saul's failure to do what the prophet had told him had led to his downfall. **20–25:** Overwhelmed with fear of a known future, nothing remained for Saul but the shame of having his basic needs met by a medium—a criminal in Israel.

29:1–11 David and the King of Gath

The narrative focus returns to David to resolve his dilemma as the supposedly loyal subject of a Philistine king. **1–4:** The other Philistine rulers were not so convinced as Achish of David's loyalty. **6:** It is sur-

'Saul has killed his thousands,
and David his ten thousands'?"

[6] So Achish finally summoned David and said to him, "I swear by the LORD that you have been a trustworthy ally. I think you should go with me into battle, for I've never found a single flaw in you from the day you arrived until today. But the other Philistine rulers won't hear of it. [7] Please don't upset them, but go back quietly."

[8] "What have I done to deserve this treatment?" David demanded. "What have you ever found in your servant, that I can't go and fight the enemies of my lord the king?"

[9] But Achish insisted, "As far as I'm concerned, you're as perfect as an angel of God. But the Philistine commanders are afraid to have you with them in the battle. [10] Now get up early in the morning, and leave with your men as soon as it gets light."

[11] So David and his men headed back into the land of the Philistines, while the Philistine army went on to Jezreel.

David Destroys the Amalekites

30 Three days later, when David and his men arrived home at their town of Ziklag, they found that the Amalekites had made a raid into the Negev and Ziklag; they had crushed Ziklag and burned it to the ground. [2] They had carried off the women and children and everyone else but without killing anyone.

[3] When David and his men saw the ruins and realized what had happened to their families, [4] they wept until they could weep no more. [5] David's two wives, Ahinoam from Jezreel and Abigail, the widow of Nabal from Carmel, were among those captured. [6] David was now in great danger because all his men were very bitter about losing their sons and daughters, and they began to talk of stoning him. But David found strength in the LORD his God.

[7] Then he said to Abiathar the priest, "Bring me the ephod!" So Abiathar brought it. [8] Then David asked the LORD, "Should I chase after this band of raiders? Will I catch them?"

And the LORD told him, "Yes, go after them. You will surely recover everything that was taken from you!"

[9] So David and his 600 men set out, and they came to the brook Besor. [10] But 200 of the men were too exhausted to cross the brook, so David continued the pursuit with 400 men.

[11] Along the way they found an Egyptian man in a field and brought him to David. They gave him some bread to eat and water to drink. [12] They also gave him part of a fig cake and two clusters of raisins, for he hadn't had anything to eat or drink for three days and nights. Before long his strength returned.

[13] "To whom do you belong, and where do you come from?" David asked him.

"I am an Egyptian—the slave of an Amalekite," he replied. "My master abandoned me three days ago because I was sick. [14] We were on our way back from raiding the Kerethites in the Negev, the territory of Judah, and the land of Caleb, and we had just burned Ziklag."

[15] "Will you lead me to this band of raiders?" David asked.

The young man replied, "If you take an oath in God's name that you will not kill me or give me back to my master, then I will guide you to them."

[16] So he led David to them, and they found the Amalekites spread out across the fields, eating and drinking and dancing with joy because of the vast amount of plunder they had taken from the Philistines and the land of Judah. [17] David and his men rushed in among them and slaughtered them throughout that night and the entire next day until evening. None of the Amalekites escaped except 400 young men who fled on camels. [18] David got back everything the Amalekites had taken, and he rescued his two wives. [19] Nothing was missing: small or great, son or daughter, nor anything else that had been taken. David brought everything back. [20] He also recovered all the flocks and herds, and his men drove them ahead of the other livestock. "This plunder belongs to David!" they said.

[21] Then David returned to the brook Besor

---

prising that Achish swears by the LORD, the God of Israel. **8:** *My lord the king*: David's protest to Achish is ambiguous. Saul is David's proper lord, but Achish takes it as a reference to himself.

30:1–31 David and the Amalekites

Arriving at Ziklag, David discovered that in his absence the settlement has been attacked by Amalekites. In contrast to Saul, David's victory is assured. **4–6:** Despite his personal grief and the danger from his troops, who doubtless blamed his involvement with the Philistines as the cause of all their woes, David turns to the LORD for guidance. The contrast with Saul's weakness in the face of forthcoming battle could not be more marked. **7–25:** David displays all his virtues: reliance on God, prowess in battle, and fairness to his men. **26–27:** The men of Judah were

and met up with the 200 men who had been
left behind because they were too exhausted
to go with him. They went out to meet David
and his men, and David greeted them joyfully.
22 But some evil troublemakers among David's
men said, "They didn't go with us, so they can't
have any of the plunder we recovered. Give
them their wives and children, and tell them to
be gone."
23 But David said, "No, my brothers! Don't
be selfish with what the LORD has given us. He
has kept us safe and helped us defeat the band of
raiders that attacked us. 24 Who will listen when
you talk like this? We share and share alike—
those who go to battle and those who guard the
equipment." 25 From then on David made this a
decree and regulation for Israel, and it is still followed today.
26 When he arrived at Ziklag, David sent part
of the plunder to the elders of Judah, who were
his friends. "Here is a present for you, taken
from the LORD's enemies," he said.
27 The gifts were sent to the people of the
following towns David had visited: Bethel,
Ramoth-negev, Jattir, 28 Aroer, Siphmoth, Eshtemoa, 29 Racal,* the towns of the Jerahmeelites,
the towns of the Kenites, 30 Hormah, Bor-ashan,
Athach, 31 Hebron, and all the other places David and his men had visited.

The Death of Saul

31 Now the Philistines attacked Israel, and the men of Israel fled before
them. Many were slaughtered on the
slopes of Mount Gilboa. 2 The Philistines closed
in on Saul and his sons, and they killed three of
his sons—Jonathan, Abinadab, and Malkishua.
3 The fighting grew very fierce around Saul, and
the Philistine archers caught up with him and
wounded him severely.
4 Saul groaned to his armor bearer, "Take your
sword and kill me before these pagan Philistines
come to run me through and taunt and torture
me."
But his armor bearer was afraid and would not
do it. So Saul took his own sword and fell on it.
5 When his armor bearer realized that Saul was
dead, he fell on his own sword and died beside the
king. 6 So Saul, his three sons, his armor bearer,
and his troops all died together that same day.
7 When the Israelites on the other side of the
Jezreel Valley and beyond the Jordan saw that
the Israelite army had fled and that Saul and his
sons were dead, they abandoned their towns and
fled. So the Philistines moved in and occupied
their towns.
8 The next day, when the Philistines went out
to strip the dead, they found the bodies of Saul
and his three sons on Mount Gilboa. 9 So they cut
off Saul's head and stripped off his armor. Then
they proclaimed the good news of Saul's death in
their pagan temple and to the people throughout
the land of Philistia. 10 They placed his armor in
the temple of the Ashtoreths, and they fastened
his body to the wall of the city of Beth-shan.
11 But when the people of Jabesh-gilead heard
what the Philistines had done to Saul, 12 all their
mighty warriors traveled through the night to
Beth-shan and took the bodies of Saul and his
sons down from the wall. They brought them
to Jabesh, where they burned the bodies. 13 Then
they took their bones and buried them beneath
the tamarisk tree at Jabesh, and they fasted for
seven days.

30:29 Greek version reads *Carmel.*

to reciprocate David's generous gesture later, when they crowned him king in Hebron (2 Sam 2:4).

31:1–13 The Death of Saul

When Saul was appointed leader of God's people, it was for the purpose of delivering them from the hand of the Philistines. When he met his death, it was at his own hand to avoid capture and abuse by those same enemies. **8–10:** In Israelite thought, for a man to remain unburied was a fate almost worse than death itself. **11–13:** The bodies of Saul and his sons are retrieved by the men of Jabesh-gilead, who reciprocated Saul's earlier action on their behalf when he had intervened to save them from shame and disgrace at the hands of Nahash and by so doing had established himself as the first king of Israel (11:1–15).

2 SAMUEL

INTRODUCTION

The book of 2 Samuel is the continuation of 1 Samuel in the Deuteronomistic History (see the introduction to 1 Samuel). The first half of the book relates how David, after Saul's death, became king of Judah and then of all Israel. It tells how he built a small empire through military conquest and how he established a capital and a dynasty in Jerusalem. The LORD's promise to David of an eternal dynasty (chap. 7) is a key passage. It brings together the themes of Jerusalem as the divinely chosen center for worship and the Davidic line as the chosen family of kings in Judah. The second half of the book describes David's problems, which are all political problems within Israel and arise from within David's extended family. Here women emerge as important catalysts for action and dissent. Key events include David's adultery with Bathsheba, the rape of Tamar and murder of Amnon, and the revolts of Absalom and Sheba.

The date and setting of 2 Samuel are, of course, the same as for 1 Samuel, though there are two possible readings of the book. Some believe the book continues 1 Samuel's defense of David and the monarchy while others see it as strongly anti-Davidic and in opposition to kingship in Israel. The mixture of praise for David with hints of cynical political calculation renders an open-ended interpretation of the book.—*Joy Osgood*

1:1–27	David's Lament
2:1—4:12	Rival Kings in Israel
5:1–25	The Defeat of the Philistines
6:1–23	David, Michal, and the Ark of God
7:1–29	Building a House
8:1–18	David's Military Triumphs
9:1–13	David and Mephibosheth
10:1–19	War with the Ammonites
11:1–27	David and Bathsheba
12:1–31	God's Judgment and Mercy
13:1–39	The Rape of Tamar and Absalom's Revenge
14:1–33	The Return of Absalom
15:1—16:23	Absalom's Rebellion. Ahithophel's Revenge
17:1–29	Hushai's Advice and David's Escape
18:1–33	The Death of Absalom
19:1–43	David's Return
20:1–26	Sheba's Rebellion
21:1—24:25	Appendix

David Learns of Saul's Death

1 After the death of Saul, David returned from his victory over the Amalekites and spent two days in Ziklag. [2] On the third day a man arrived from Saul's army camp. He had torn his clothes and put dirt on his head to show that he was in mourning. He fell to the ground before David in deep respect.

[3] "Where have you come from?" David asked.

"I escaped from the Israelite camp," the man replied.

[4] "What happened?" David demanded. "Tell me how the battle went."

The man replied, "Our entire army fled from the battle. Many of the men are dead, and Saul and his son Jonathan are also dead."

[5] "How do you know Saul and Jonathan are dead?" David demanded of the young man.

[6] The man answered, "I happened to be on Mount Gilboa, and there was Saul leaning on his spear with the enemy chariots and charioteers closing in on him. [7] When he turned and saw me, he cried out for me to come to him. 'How can I help?' I asked him.

[8] "He responded, 'Who are you?'

" 'I am an Amalekite,' I told him.

[9] "Then he begged me, 'Come over here and put me out of my misery, for I am in terrible pain and want to die.'

[10] "So I killed him," the Amalekite told David, "for I knew he couldn't live. Then I took his crown and his armband, and I have brought them here to you, my lord."

[11] David and his men tore their clothes in sorrow when they heard the news. [12] They mourned and wept and fasted all day for Saul and his son Jonathan, and for the LORD's army and the nation of Israel, because they had died by the sword that day.

[13] Then David said to the young man who had brought the news, "Where are you from?"

And he replied, "I am a foreigner, an Amalekite, who lives in your land."

[14] "Why were you not afraid to kill the LORD's anointed one?" David asked.

[15] Then David said to one of his men, "Kill him!" So the man thrust his sword into the Amalekite and killed him. [16] "You have condemned yourself," David said, "for you yourself confessed that you killed the LORD's anointed one."

David's Song for Saul and Jonathan

[17] Then David composed a funeral song for Saul and Jonathan, [18] and he commanded that it be taught to the people of Judah. It is known as the Song of the Bow, and it is recorded in *The Book of Jashar.**

[19] Your pride and joy, O Israel, lies dead on the
hills!
Oh, how the mighty heroes have fallen!
[20] Don't announce the news in Gath,
don't proclaim it in the streets of Ashkelon,
or the daughters of the Philistines will rejoice
and the pagans will laugh in triumph.

[21] O mountains of Gilboa,
let there be no dew or rain upon you,
nor fruitful fields producing offerings of
grain.*
For there the shield of the mighty heroes was
defiled;
the shield of Saul will no longer be
anointed with oil.
[22] The bow of Jonathan was powerful,
and the sword of Saul did its mighty work.
They shed the blood of their enemies
and pierced the bodies of mighty heroes.
[23] How beloved and gracious were Saul and
Jonathan!
They were together in life and in death.
They were swifter than eagles,
stronger than lions.
[24] O women of Israel, weep for Saul,
for he dressed you in luxurious scarlet
clothing,
in garments decorated with gold.

1:18 Or *The Book of the Upright.* **1:21** The meaning of the Hebrew is uncertain.

1:1–27 David's Lament

News of Saul's death and the loss of many men reached David at Ziklag. **1–10:** The opportunist messenger claimed to have been the last person to have seen the king alive. He no doubt hoped to be rewarded. **14–16:** David applied to him the standard by which he had operated, for "who can remain innocent after attacking the LORD's anointed one?" (1 Sam 26:9). **19–27:** David's song of lament describes Saul and Jonathan as Israel's *pride and joy* and *mighty heroes*. **20, 24:** Women were the performers and sometimes the composers of songs of triumph in time of victory (Exod 15:20–21; 1 Sam 18:6–7) or laments in the face of death and defeat. The news of Saul and Jonathan's deaths would have Philistine women singing the former, and the women of Israel the latter. **24–26:** The mention of fine apparel might recall Jon-

25 Oh, how the mighty heroes have fallen in battle!
Jonathan lies dead on the hills.
26 How I weep for you, my brother Jonathan!
Oh, how much I loved you!
And your love for me was deep,
deeper than the love of women!

27 Oh, how the mighty heroes have fallen!
Stripped of their weapons, they lie dead.

David Anointed King of Judah

2 After this, David asked the LORD, "Should I
move back to one of the towns of Judah?"
"Yes," the LORD replied.
Then David asked, "Which town should I go
to?"
"To Hebron," the LORD answered.
2 David's two wives were Ahinoam from Jezreel and Abigail, the widow of Nabal from Carmel. So David and his wives 3 and his men and
their families all moved to Judah, and they settled in the villages near Hebron. 4 Then the men
of Judah came to David and anointed him king
over the people of Judah.
When David heard that the men of Jabesh-
gilead had buried Saul, 5 he sent them this message: "May the LORD bless you for being so loyal
to your master Saul and giving him a decent
burial. 6 May the LORD be loyal to you in return
and reward you with his unfailing love! And I,
too, will reward you for what you have done.
7 Now that Saul is dead, I ask you to be my strong
and loyal subjects like the people of Judah, who
have anointed me as their new king."

Ishbosheth Proclaimed King of Israel

8 But Abner son of Ner, the commander of Saul's
army, had already gone to Mahanaim with Saul's
son Ishbosheth.* 9 There he proclaimed Ishbosheth
king over Gilead, Jezreel, Ephraim, Benjamin, the
land of the Ashurites, and all the rest of Israel.
10 Ishbosheth, Saul's son, was forty years old
when he became king, and he ruled from Mahanaim for two years. Meanwhile, the people of
Judah remained loyal to David. 11 David made
Hebron his capital, and he ruled as king of Judah
for seven and a half years.

War between Israel and Judah

12 One day Abner led Ishbosheth's troops from
Mahanaim to Gibeon. 13 About the same time,
Joab son of Zeruiah led David's troops out and
met them at the pool of Gibeon. The two groups
sat down there, facing each other from opposite
sides of the pool.
14 Then Abner suggested to Joab, "Let's have
a few of our warriors fight hand to hand here in
front of us."
"All right," Joab agreed. 15 So twelve men
were chosen to fight from each side—twelve
men of Benjamin representing Ishbosheth son of
Saul, and twelve representing David. 16 Each one
grabbed his opponent by the hair and thrust his
sword into the other's side so that all of them
died. So this place at Gibeon has been known
ever since as the Field of Swords.*
17 A fierce battle followed that day, and Abner
and the men of Israel were defeated by the forces
of David.

The Death of Asahel

18 Joab, Abishai, and Asahel—the three sons of
Zeruiah—were among David's forces that day.
Asahel could run like a gazelle, 19 and he began
chasing Abner. He pursued him relentlessly, not
stopping for anything. 20 When Abner looked
back and saw him coming, he called out, "Is that
you, Asahel?"
"Yes, it is," he replied.
21 "Go fight someone else!" Abner warned.
"Take on one of the younger men, and strip him
of his weapons." But Asahel kept right on chasing Abner.
22 Again Abner shouted to him, "Get away
from here! I don't want to kill you. How could I
ever face your brother Joab again?"

2:8 *Ishbosheth* is another name for Esh-baal. **2:16** Hebrew *Helkath-hazzurim.*

athan's gift to David of robe and tunic, sword, bow, and belt (1 Sam 18:4). The loss of Jonathan's steadfast love grieved David most of all.

2:1—4:12 Rival Kings in Israel

2:1–32: David continues to rely on the divine oracle about the way ahead (v. 1). **5–6:** David hints broadly that Jabesh-gilead's best interests for the future lay not with their dead master but with himself, the newly anointed king of the house of Judah. **8–10:** Saul's surviving son Ishbosheth rules from Mahanaim, across the Jordan. The real power behind the throne, however, was Abner, the cousin of the late king and commander of the army. **12–17:** Civil war between the opposing forces began when a representational contest escalated into full-scale hostilities in which Abner and his men were defeated and forced to flee. **18:** Asahel and his brothers Joab and Abishai were kin to David (1 Chr 2:16) and employed in his ser-

23 But Asahel refused to turn back, so Abner thrust the butt end of his spear through Asahel's stomach, and the spear came out through his back. He stumbled to the ground and died there. And everyone who came by that spot stopped and stood still when they saw Asahel lying there.
24 When Joab and Abishai found out what had happened, they set out after Abner. The sun was just going down as they arrived at the hill of Ammah near Giah, along the road to the wilderness of Gibeon. 25 Abner's troops from the tribe of Benjamin regrouped there at the top of the hill to take a stand.
26 Abner shouted down to Joab, "Must we always be killing each other? Don't you realize that bitterness is the only result? When will you call off your men from chasing their Israelite brothers?"
27 Then Joab said, "God only knows what would have happened if you hadn't spoken, for we would have chased you all night if necessary." 28 So Joab blew the ram's horn, and his men stopped chasing the troops of Israel.
29 All that night Abner and his men retreated through the Jordan Valley.* They crossed the Jordan River, traveling all through the morning,* and didn't stop until they arrived at Mahanaim.
30 Meanwhile, Joab and his men also returned home. When Joab counted his casualties, he discovered that only 19 men were missing in addition to Asahel. 31 But 360 of Abner's men had been killed, all from the tribe of Benjamin. 32 Joab and his men took Asahel's body to Bethlehem and buried him there in his father's tomb. Then they traveled all night and reached Hebron at daybreak.

3 That was the beginning of a long war between those who were loyal to Saul and those loyal to David. As time passed David became stronger and stronger, while Saul's dynasty became weaker and weaker.

David's Sons Born in Hebron

2 These are the sons who were born to David in Hebron:

The oldest was Amnon, whose mother was Ahinoam from Jezreel.
3 The second was Daniel,* whose mother was Abigail, the widow of Nabal from Carmel.
The third was Absalom, whose mother was Maacah, the daughter of Talmai, king of Geshur.
4 The fourth was Adonijah, whose mother was Haggith.
The fifth was Shephatiah, whose mother was Abital.
5 The sixth was Ithream, whose mother was Eglah, David's wife.

These sons were all born to David in Hebron.

Abner Joins Forces with David

6 As the war between the house of Saul and the house of David went on, Abner became a powerful leader among those loyal to Saul. 7 One day Ishbosheth,* Saul's son, accused Abner of sleeping with one of his father's concubines, a woman named Rizpah, daughter of Aiah.
8 Abner was furious. "Am I some Judean dog to be kicked around like this?" he shouted. "After all I have done for your father, Saul, and his

2:29a Hebrew *the Arabah.* **2:29b** Or *continued on through the Bithron.* The meaning of the Hebrew is uncertain. **3:3** As in parallel text at 1 Chr 3:1 (see also Greek version, which reads *Daluia,* and Dead Sea Scrolls, which read *Dan[iel]*); Hebrew reads *Kileab.* **3:7** *Ishbosheth* is another name for Esh-baal.

vice. **23:** Unwilling to run Asahel through with his spear, Abner turned the butt end toward him with the intention of winding him and effectively bringing his pursuit to an end, but the speed of the young man was such that the force of impact was enough to kill him. On such events the course of history turns, for although the pursuit of Abner and his men ended as the sun went down, the death of Asahel at the hand of Abner was to be long remembered and ultimately avenged in a society in which kinship considerations were still paramount (cf. 2 Sam 3:22–30).

3:1–39 The Defection and Death of Abner. While the civil war dragged on, David's influence, political power, and wealth were increasing. **2–5:** David's status is indicated in the number of wives he was able to support at Hebron. Of the sons born to him there, three were to figure large in his reign: Amnon, Absalom, and Adonijah. Polygamy was a matter of fact in ancient Israel, the number of wives a man had being limited only by his desire and his ability to support them and their offspring. One of the difficulties and dangers of the practice, however, was that although the children shared a common father, they tended to separate into distinct groupings on the basis of maternal bonds. Just as resentment and jealousies might arise among the wives, so it might also arise among their progeny. This would become a serious issue for David later in his life. **6–11:** Unlike wives, concubines were regarded as property and as such were inherited. For Abner to have slept with Rizpah was no slight affair but a direct challenge to Ishbosheth's po-

family and friends by not handing you over to David, is this my reward—that you find fault with me about this woman? 9 May God strike me and even kill me if I don't do everything I can to help David get what the LORD has promised him! 10 I'm going to take Saul's kingdom and give it to David. I will establish the throne of David over Israel as well as Judah, all the way from Dan in the north to Beersheba in the south." 11 Ishbosheth didn't dare say another word because he was afraid of what Abner might do.

12 Then Abner sent messengers to David, saying, "Doesn't the entire land belong to you? Make a solemn pact with me, and I will help turn over all of Israel to you."

13 "All right," David replied, "but I will not negotiate with you unless you bring back my wife Michal, Saul's daughter, when you come."

14 David then sent this message to Ishbosheth, Saul's son: "Give me back my wife Michal, for I bought her with the lives* of 100 Philistines."

15 So Ishbosheth took Michal away from her husband, Palti* son of Laish. 16 Palti followed along behind her as far as Bahurim, weeping as he went. Then Abner told him, "Go back home!" So Palti returned.

17 Meanwhile, Abner had consulted with the elders of Israel. "For some time now," he told them, "you have wanted to make David your king. 18 Now is the time! For the LORD has said, 'I have chosen David to save my people Israel from the hands of the Philistines and from all their other enemies.' " 19 Abner also spoke with the men of Benjamin. Then he went to Hebron to tell David that all the people of Israel and Benjamin had agreed to support him.

20 When Abner and twenty of his men came to Hebron, David entertained them with a great feast. 21 Then Abner said to David, "Let me go and call an assembly of all Israel to support my lord the king. They will make a covenant with you to make you their king, and you will rule over everything your heart desires." So David sent Abner safely on his way.

Joab Murders Abner

22 But just after David had sent Abner away in safety, Joab and some of David's troops returned from a raid, bringing much plunder with them. 23 When Joab arrived, he was told that Abner had just been there visiting the king and had been sent away in safety.

24 Joab rushed to the king and demanded, "What have you done? What do you mean by letting Abner get away? 25 You know perfectly well that he came to spy on you and find out everything you're doing!"

26 Joab then left David and sent messengers to catch up with Abner, asking him to return. They found him at the well of Sirah and brought him back, though David knew nothing about it. 27 When Abner arrived back at Hebron, Joab took him aside at the gateway as if to speak with him privately. But then he stabbed Abner in the stomach and killed him in revenge for killing his brother Asahel.

28 When David heard about it, he declared, "I vow by the LORD that I and my kingdom are forever innocent of this crime against Abner son of Ner. 29 Joab and his family are the guilty ones. May the family of Joab be cursed in every generation with a man who has open sores or leprosy* or who walks on crutches* or dies by the sword or begs for food!"

30 So Joab and his brother Abishai killed Abner because Abner had killed their brother Asahel at the battle of Gibeon.

David Mourns Abner's Death

31 Then David said to Joab and all those who were with him, "Tear your clothes and put on

3:14 Hebrew *the foreskins.* **3:15** As in 1 Sam 25:44; Hebrew reads *Paltiel,* a variant spelling of Palti. **3:29a** Or *or a contagious skin disease.* The Hebrew word used here can describe various skin diseases. **3:29b** Or *who is effeminate;* Hebrew reads *who handles a spindle.*

sition as king. **8–10:** How justified was Ishbosheth's accusation is moot. Abner would not submit to the shame of the accusation. **9:** Abner knew of the divine promise to ultimately give Saul's kingdom to David and considered that the time had come to put that promise into effect. **11–15:** Without Abner behind him, Ishbosheth could do nothing to resist the proposed alliance and meekly complied with David's demand for the return of Michal, David's first wife. **13–16:** Since David had never divorced his wife, his demand for her return was legal, but the contrast between David's inclusion of her in a political deal and the palpable grief of her present husband as his wife is taken away from him is marked. Michal's emotions are never considered. She had loved David dearly at one time. But to become only one of a number of wives in the royal harem would have been a bitter pill to swallow. To have the daughter of Saul as wife would undoubtedly be a point in David's favor when he appealed to the men of Israel to change their allegiance. **20–23:** The repetition of the words *safely* and *in safety* serves to heighten the enormity of Joab's coming crime. **24–30:** Joab puts family vengeance above political considerations and the king's honor.

burlap. Mourn for Abner." And King David himself walked behind the procession to the grave.
32 They buried Abner in Hebron, and the king
and all the people wept at his graveside. 33 Then
the king sang this funeral song for Abner:

"Should Abner have died as fools die?
34 Your hands were not bound;
your feet were not chained.
No, you were murdered—
the victim of a wicked plot."

All the people wept again for Abner. 35 David
had refused to eat anything on the day of the
funeral, and now everyone begged him to eat.
But David had made a vow, saying, "May God
strike me and even kill me if I eat anything before sundown."
36 This pleased the people very much. In fact,
everything the king did pleased them! 37 So everyone in Judah and all Israel understood that
David was not responsible for Abner's murder.
38 Then King David said to his officials, "Don't
you realize that a great commander has fallen today
in Israel? 39 And even though I am the anointed king,
these two sons of Zeruiah—Joab and Abishai—are
too strong for me to control. So may the LORD repay these evil men for their evil deeds."

The Murder of Ishbosheth

4 When Ishbosheth,* Saul's son, heard about
Abner's death at Hebron, he lost all courage, and all Israel became paralyzed with
fear. 2 Now there were two brothers, Baanah and
Recab, who were captains of Ishbosheth's raiding
parties. They were sons of Rimmon, a member of
the tribe of Benjamin who lived in Beeroth. The
town of Beeroth is now part of Benjamin's territory 3 because the original people of Beeroth fled
to Gittaim, where they still live as foreigners.
4 (Saul's son Jonathan had a son named Mephibosheth,* who was crippled as a child. He was
five years old when the report came from Jezreel
that Saul and Jonathan had been killed in battle. When the child's nurse heard the news, she
picked him up and fled. But as she hurried away,
she dropped him, and he became crippled.)
5 One day Recab and Baanah, the sons of Rimmon from Beeroth, went to Ishbosheth's house
around noon as he was taking his midday rest.
6 The doorkeeper, who had been sifting wheat, became drowsy and fell asleep. So Recab and Baanah slipped past her.* 7 They went into the house
and found Ishbosheth sleeping on his bed. They
struck and killed him and cut off his head. Then,
taking his head with them, they fled across the
Jordan Valley* through the night. 8 When they
arrived at Hebron, they presented Ishbosheth's
head to David. "Look!" they exclaimed to the
king. "Here is the head of Ishbosheth, the son
of your enemy Saul who tried to kill you. Today
the LORD has given my lord the king revenge on
Saul and his entire family!"
9 But David said to Recab and Baanah, "The
LORD, who saves me from all my enemies, is my
witness. 10 Someone once told me, 'Saul is dead,'
thinking he was bringing me good news. But I
seized him and killed him at Ziklag. That's the
reward I gave him for his news! 11 How much
more should I reward evil men who have killed
an innocent man in his own house and on his
own bed? Shouldn't I hold you responsible for
his blood and rid the earth of you?"
12 So David ordered his young men to kill
them, and they did. They cut off their hands
and feet and hung their bodies beside the pool in
Hebron. Then they took Ishbosheth's head and
buried it in Abner's tomb in Hebron.

David Becomes King of All Israel

5 Then all the tribes of Israel went to David
at Hebron and told him, "We are your own
flesh and blood. 2 In the past,* when Saul
was our king, you were the one who really led
the forces of Israel. And the LORD told you, 'You
will be the shepherd of my people Israel. You will
be Israel's leader.' "
3 So there at Hebron, King David made a cov-

4:1 *Ishbosheth* is another name for Esh-baal.
4:4 *Mephibosheth* is another name for Merib-baal. **4:6** As in Greek version; Hebrew reads *So they went into the house pretending to fetch wheat, but they stabbed him in the stomach. Then Recab and Baanah escaped.* **4:7** Hebrew *the Arabah.* **5:2** Or *For some time.*

4:1–12 The Death of Ishbosheth. 1: Without Abner, Ishbosheth lost courage and was no longer sufficiently in command of himself to lead. **4:** Jonathan's only surviving son was not a suitable candidate for king, for he was lame and unable to walk without aid, let alone fight. **5–7:** Some decision was called for, so Baanah and Recab, the sons of Rimmon, killed Ishbosheth during his siesta. **8–12:** The brothers' miscalculation of David's character and ignorance of the fate of a previous messenger of death were their undoing. Significantly, David does not refer to Ishbosheth as "the LORD's anointed" but as *an innocent man*.

5:1–25 The Defeat of the Philistines

With the death of Ishbosheth the way was clear for

David's Wives

The Bible records that David had eight named wives and numerous concubines; Jewish tradition accords him more but does not name them. The Bible gives this tradition weight because of Nathan's scathing prophecy in which the LORD says, "I gave you your master's . . . wives" (2 Sam 12:8). Perhaps Saul's wife Ahinoam and his concubine Rizpah became David's wives as well.

David's choice in wives reflects his physical prowess, good fortune, and political astuteness. David won his first wife, Michal, by bringing her father, Saul, two hundred Philistine foreskins (1 Sam 18:27). Michal loved David and saved his life from Saul, but she expressed contempt when he worshiped publicly. She died childless (1 Sam 18:20, 28; 19:9–17; 2 Sam 6:16, 20–23).

David's second wife, Ahinoam of Jezreel, bore him Amnon (1 Sam 25:43). The biblical text lists only two Ahinoams. If David's wife and Saul's wife were the same, perhaps David took her because Saul had given Michal to Palti (1 Sam 25:44).

Abigail, David's third wife, came to him after her husband, Nabal, died. Beautiful and intelligent (the only person in Scripture described by these two adjectives), Abigail brought him wealth and standing in Judah (1 Sam 25:2–3).

Maacah, daughter of Talmai, king of Geshur, bore David Absalom and Tamar. Haggith bore him Adonijah, Abital bore him Shephatiah, and Eglah bore him Ithream (2 Sam 3:2–5). Bathsheba bore him the child of their adulterous union, who died (2 Sam 12:18), and four other sons: Shammua, Shobab, Nathan, and Solomon, his heir (1 Chr 3:5). Jesus' genealogy splits at Nathan and Solomon, showing Bathsheba's preeminence (Matt 1:7; Luke 3:31).

The text depicts David's family as unhappy, perhaps because David did not participate adequately in his children's upbringing (1 Kgs 1:6; see Parental Influence, Josh 4). Amnon seduced his half-sister Tamar; her brother Absalom killed Amnon. Both Absalom and Adonijah rebelled against David, and David grieved mightily at Absalom's death (2 Sam 18:33).

enant before the LORD with all the elders of Israel. And they anointed him king of Israel.
4 David was thirty years old when he began to reign, and he reigned forty years in all. 5 He had reigned over Judah from Hebron for seven years and six months, and from Jerusalem he reigned over all Israel and Judah for thirty-three years.

David Captures Jerusalem

6 David then led his men to Jerusalem to fight against the Jebusites, the original inhabitants of the land who were living there. The Jebusites taunted David, saying, "You'll never get in here! Even the blind and lame could keep you out!" For the Jebusites thought they were safe. 7 But
David captured the fortress of Zion, which is now called the City of David.
8 On the day of the attack, David said to his troops, "I hate those 'lame' and 'blind' Jebusites.*
Whoever attacks them should strike by going into the city through the water tunnel.*" That is the origin of the saying, "The blind and the lame may not enter the house."*
9 So David made the fortress his home, and he called it the City of David. He extended the city, starting at the supporting terraces* and working inward. 10 And David became more and more powerful, because the LORD God of Heaven's Armies was with him.
11 Then King Hiram of Tyre sent messengers to David, along with cedar timber and carpenters and stonemasons, and they built David a palace.
12 And David realized that the LORD had confirmed him as king over Israel and had blessed his kingdom for the sake of his people Israel.
13 After moving from Hebron to Jerusalem, David married more concubines and wives, and they had more sons and daughters. 14 These are the names of David's sons who were born in Je-

5:8a Or *Those 'lame' and 'blind' Jebusites hate me.* **5:8b** Or *with scaling hooks.* The meaning of the Hebrew is uncertain. **5:8c** The meaning of this saying is uncertain. **5:9** Hebrew *the millo.* The meaning of the Hebrew is uncertain.

David to become king over all Israel. **6–10:** David's choice of Jerusalem as capital was politically astute, for its capture from the Jebusites had made it crown property and thus set apart from tribal territory and local allegiances. **9–11:** David begins building a house for himself commensurate with his increasing power. For the palace he formed an economic and political alliance with Hiram, king of Tyre. **13–14:** To build his lineage, he entered into a series of marriages and sexual relationships. None of the women

rusalem: Shammua, Shobab, Nathan, Solomon,
15 Ibhar, Elishua, Nepheg, Japhia, 16 Elishama,
Eliada, and Eliphelet.

David Conquers the Philistines

17 When the Philistines heard that David had
been anointed king of Israel, they mobilized all
their forces to capture him. But David was told
they were coming, so he went into the stronghold. 18 The Philistines arrived and spread out
across the valley of Rephaim. 19 So David asked
the LORD, "Should I go out to fight the Philistines? Will you hand them over to me?"
The LORD replied to David, "Yes, go ahead. I
will certainly hand them over to you."
20 So David went to Baal-perazim and defeated
the Philistines there. "The LORD did it!" David
exclaimed. "He burst through my enemies like
a raging flood!" So he named that place Baal-
perazim (which means "the Lord who bursts
through"). 21 The Philistines had abandoned
their idols there, so David and his men confiscated them.
22 But after a while the Philistines returned and
again spread out across the valley of Rephaim.
23 And again David asked the LORD what to do.
"Do not attack them straight on," the LORD replied. "Instead, circle around behind and attack
them near the poplar* trees. 24 When you hear a
sound like marching feet in the tops of the poplar trees, be on the alert! That will be the signal
that the LORD is moving ahead of you to strike
down the Philistine army." 25 So David did what
the LORD commanded, and he struck down the
Philistines all the way from Gibeon* to Gezer.

Moving the Ark to Jerusalem

6 Then David again gathered all the elite
troops in Israel, 30,000 in all. 2 He led them
to Baalah of Judah* to bring back the Ark
of God, which bears the name of the LORD of
Heaven's Armies,* who is enthroned between
the cherubim. 3 They placed the Ark of God on a
new cart and brought it from Abinadab's house,
which was on a hill. Uzzah and Ahio, Abinadab's
sons, were guiding the cart as it left the house,
4 carrying the Ark of God. Ahio walked in front of
the Ark. 5 David and all the people of Israel were
celebrating before the LORD, singing songs* and
playing all kinds of musical instruments—lyres,
harps, tambourines, castanets, and cymbals.
6 But when they arrived at the threshing floor
of Nacon, the oxen stumbled, and Uzzah reached
out his hand and steadied the Ark of God. 7 Then
the LORD's anger was aroused against Uzzah, and
God struck him dead because of this.* So Uzzah
died right there beside the Ark of God.
8 David was angry because the LORD's anger
had burst out against Uzzah. He named that
place Perez-uzzah (which means "to burst out
against Uzzah"), as it is still called today.
9 David was now afraid of the LORD, and he
asked, "How can I ever bring the Ark of the
LORD back into my care?" 10 So David decided
not to move the Ark of the LORD into the City of
David. Instead, he took it to the house of Obed-
edom of Gath. 11 The Ark of the LORD remained
there in Obed-edom's house for three months,
and the LORD blessed Obed-edom and his entire
household.
12 Then King David was told, "The LORD has
blessed Obed-edom's household and everything
he has because of the Ark of God." So David
went there and brought the Ark of God from
the house of Obed-edom to the City of David
with a great celebration. 13 After the men who
were carrying the Ark of the LORD had gone six
steps, David sacrificed a bull and a fattened calf.
14 And David danced before the LORD with all his
might, wearing a priestly garment.* 15 So David
and all the people of Israel brought up the Ark of

5:23 Or *aspen*, or *balsam;* also in 5:24. The exact identification of this tree is uncertain. **5:25** As in Greek version (see also 1 Chr 14:16); Hebrew reads *Geba*. **6:2a** *Baalah of Judah* is another name for Kiriath-jearim; compare 1 Chr 13:6. **6:2b** Or *the Ark of God where the Name is proclaimed—the name of the LORD of Heaven's Armies.* **6:5** As in Dead Sea Scrolls and Greek version (see also 1 Chr 13:8); Masoretic Text reads *before the LORD with all manner of cypress wood.* **6:7** As in Dead Sea Scrolls; Masoretic Text reads *because of his irreverence.* **6:14** Hebrew *a linen ephod.*

---

are named, although their sons are. **17–25:** In both battles David's dependence on God is stressed. With these victories, the original purpose in granting Israel a king—to "rescue them from the Philistines"—is accomplished (cf. 1 Sam 9:16).

6:1–23 David, Michal, and the Ark of God

Baalah of Judah (v. 2), another name for Kiriath-jearim, was where the Ark was left in 1 Samuel 7:1. The Ark was considered the throne of the LORD. **6–7:** Uzzah's death shows the holiness of the Ark. **14:** *Priestly garment*: The ephod was a linen apron typically worn by priests. It would not provide much coverage. **14–20:** Michal is deeply offended at David's display of enthusiasm. It was one thing for a king to spread his sexual favors around in the privacy of his harem, but to make a public exhibition of himself before every servant girl who chose to ogle at his energetic cavorting was something else. **23:** The next king would not

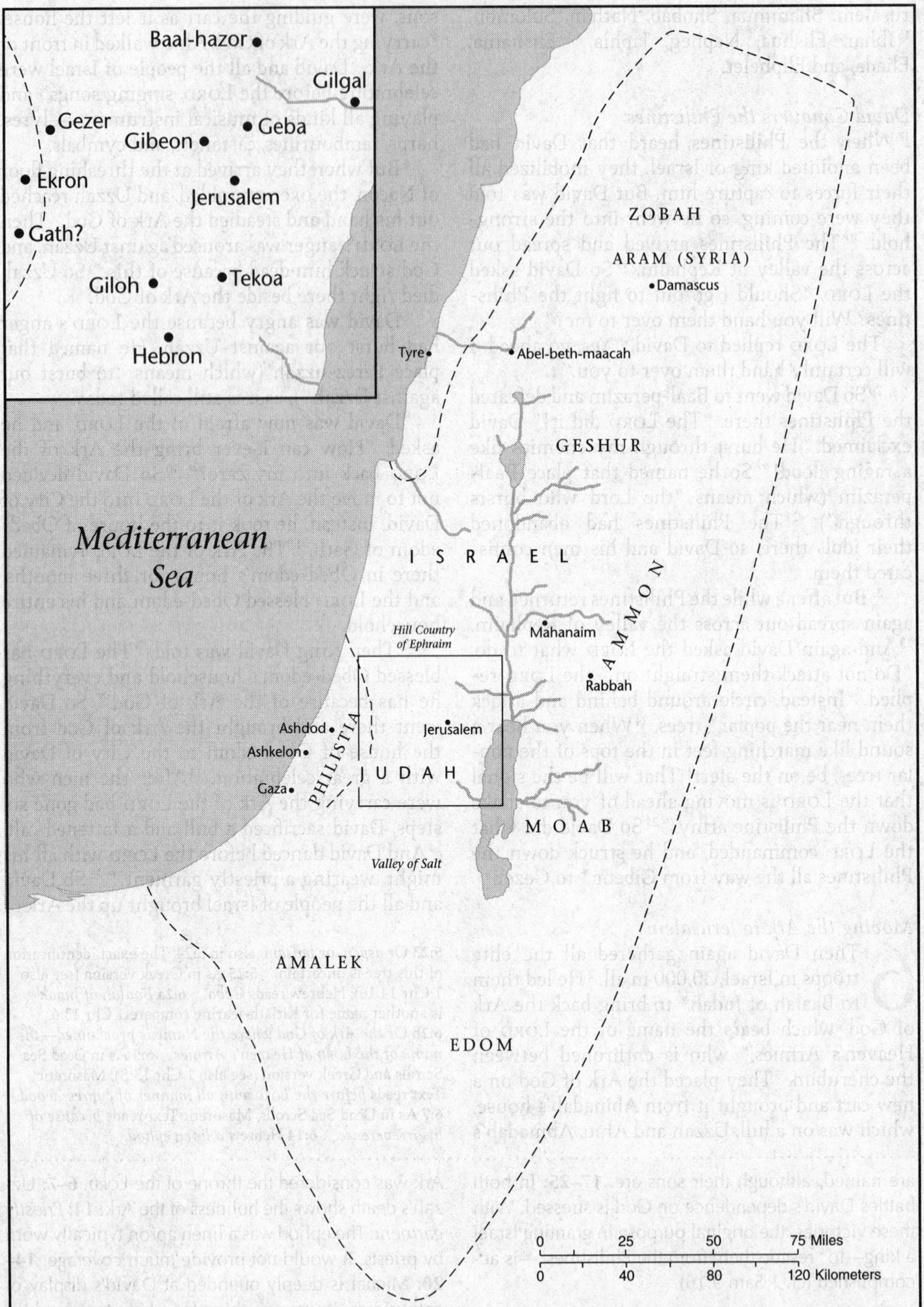

The Kingdom of David according to Second Samuel

the LORD with shouts of joy and the blowing of
rams' horns.

Michal's Contempt for David

16 But as the Ark of the LORD entered the City
of David, Michal, the daughter of Saul, looked
down from her window. When she saw King David leaping and dancing before the LORD, she was
filled with contempt for him.

17 They brought the Ark of the LORD and set it
in its place inside the special tent David had prepared for it. And David sacrificed burnt offerings
and peace offerings to the LORD. 18 When he had
finished his sacrifices, David blessed the people
in the name of the LORD of Heaven's Armies.
19 Then he gave to every Israelite man and woman in the crowd a loaf of bread, a cake of dates,*
and a cake of raisins. Then all the people returned
to their homes.

20 When David returned home to bless his own
family, Michal, the daughter of Saul, came out
to meet him. She said in disgust, "How distinguished the king of Israel looked today, shamelessly exposing himself to the servant girls like
any vulgar person might do!"

21 David retorted to Michal, "I was dancing
before the LORD, who chose me above your father and all his family! He appointed me as the
leader of Israel, the people of the LORD, so I celebrate before the LORD. 22 Yes, and I am willing
to look even more foolish than this, even to be
humiliated in my own eyes! But those servant
girls you mentioned will indeed think I am distinguished!" 23 So Michal, the daughter of Saul,
remained childless throughout her entire life.

The LORD's Covenant Promise to David

7 When King David was settled in his palace
and the LORD had given him rest from all
the surrounding enemies, 2 the king summoned Nathan the prophet. "Look," David said,
"I am living in a beautiful cedar palace,* but the
Ark of God is out there in a tent!"

3 Nathan replied to the king, "Go ahead and
do whatever you have in mind, for the LORD is
with you."

4 But that same night the LORD said to Nathan,

5 "Go and tell my servant David, 'This is what
the LORD has declared: Are you the one to
build a house for me to live in? 6 I have never
lived in a house, from the day I brought the
Israelites out of Egypt until this very day. I
have always moved from one place to another
with a tent and a Tabernacle as my dwelling.
7 Yet no matter where I have gone with the
Israelites, I have never once complained
to Israel's tribal leaders, the shepherds of
my people Israel. I have never asked them,
"Why haven't you built me a beautiful cedar
house?" '

8 "Now go and say to my servant David,
'This is what the LORD of Heaven's Armies
has declared: I took you from tending sheep in
the pasture and selected you to be the leader
of my people Israel. 9 I have been with you
wherever you have gone, and I have destroyed
all your enemies before your eyes. Now I
will make your name as famous as anyone
who has ever lived on the earth! 10 And I will
provide a homeland for my people Israel,
planting them in a secure place where they
will never be disturbed. Evil nations won't
oppress them as they've done in the past,
11 starting from the time I appointed judges to
rule my people Israel. And I will give you rest
from all your enemies.

" 'Furthermore, the LORD declares that
he will make a house for you—a dynasty
of kings! 12 For when you die and are buried
with your ancestors, I will raise up one of
your descendants, your own offspring, and
I will make his kingdom strong. 13 He is the
one who will build a house—a temple—for
my name. And I will secure his royal throne
forever. 14 I will be his father, and he will be
my son. If he sins, I will correct and discipline
him with the rod, like any father would do.

6:19 Or *a portion of meat.* The meaning of the Hebrew is uncertain. **7:2** Hebrew *a house of cedar.*

be a grandson of Saul, either because of God's judgment on Michal or because David had nothing more to do with her after that occasion.

7:1–29 Building a House

God has no need for a fixed house, choosing rather to move from place to place with a tent as his dwelling (v. 6); the statement suggests that the Temple, like kingship, was ultimately a divine concession to human desire (cf. Acts 7:47–50). **8–11:** David had desired to build God a house, but instead God would build *a house* for him, a lasting *dynasty* (Heb., *beth,* "house," can refer to either a building or a human lineage). **11–16:** Successive kings of David's lineage could look to God's promise to be their father and experience in their lifetime the divine love and discipline accorded to them as sons. **17–18:** Nathan's

15 But my favor will not be taken from him
as I took it from Saul, whom I removed from
your sight. 16 Your house and your kingdom
will continue before me* for all time, and
your throne will be secure forever.' "

17 So Nathan went back to David and told him everything the LORD had said in this vision.

David's Prayer of Thanks

18 Then King David went in and sat before the
LORD and prayed,

"Who am I, O Sovereign LORD, and what is
my family, that you have brought me this
far? 19 And now, Sovereign LORD, in addition
to everything else, you speak of giving your
servant a lasting dynasty! Do you deal with
everyone this way, O Sovereign LORD?*

20 "What more can I say to you? You
know what your servant is really like,
Sovereign LORD. 21 Because of your promise
and according to your will, you have done
all these great things and have made them
known to your servant.

22 "How great you are, O Sovereign LORD!
There is no one like you. We have never
even heard of another God like you! 23 What
other nation on earth is like your people
Israel? What other nation, O God, have
you redeemed from slavery to be your own
people? You made a great name for yourself
when you redeemed your people from Egypt.
You performed awesome miracles and drove
out the nations and gods that stood in their
way.* 24 You made Israel your very own people
forever, and you, O LORD, became their God.

25 "And now, O LORD God, I am your
servant; do as you have promised concerning
me and my family. Confirm it as a promise
that will last forever. 26 And may your name
be honored forever so that everyone will say,
'The LORD of Heaven's Armies is God over
Israel!' And may the house of your servant
David continue before you forever.

27 "O LORD of Heaven's Armies, God of
Israel, I have been bold enough to pray this
prayer to you because you have revealed all
this to your servant, saying, 'I will build a
house for you—a dynasty of kings!' 28 For
you are God, O Sovereign LORD. Your words
are truth, and you have promised these good
things to your servant. 29 And now, may it
please you to bless the house of your servant,
so that it may continue forever before you.
For you have spoken, and when you grant a
blessing to your servant, O Sovereign LORD,
it is an eternal blessing!"

David's Military Victories

8 After this, David defeated and subdued the
Philistines by conquering Gath, their largest town.* 2 David also conquered the land
of Moab. He made the people lie down on the
ground in a row, and he measured them off in
groups with a length of rope. He measured off
two groups to be executed for every one group to
be spared. The Moabites who were spared became
David's subjects and paid him tribute money.

3 David also destroyed the forces of Hadadezer
son of Rehob, king of Zobah, when Hadadezer
marched out to strengthen his control along the
Euphrates River. 4 David captured 1,000 chariots,
7,000 charioteers,* and 20,000 foot soldiers. He
crippled all the chariot horses except enough for
100 chariots.

5 When Arameans from Damascus arrived
to help King Hadadezer, David killed 22,000
of them. 6 Then he placed several army garrisons in Damascus, the Aramean capital, and the
Arameans became David's subjects and paid him

7:16 As in Greek version and some Hebrew manuscripts; Masoretic Text reads *before you.* **7:19** Or *This is your instruction for all humanity, O Sovereign LORD.* **7:23** As in Greek version (see also 1 Chr 17:21); Hebrew reads *You made a great name for yourself and performed awesome miracles for your land. You did this in the sight of your people, whom you redeemed from Egypt, from nations and their gods.* **8:1** Hebrew *by conquering Metheg-ammah,* a name that means "the bridle," possibly referring to the size of the town or the tribute money taken from it. Compare 1 Chr 18:1. **8:4** As in Dead Sea Scrolls and Greek version (see also 1 Chr 18:4); Masoretic Text reads *captured 1,700 charioteers.*

faithful communication of God's revelation overwhelmed David. **18:** Once before David had declared *Who am I, . . . and what is my family?* (1 Sam 18:18). Then he had been expressing his reluctance to become the king's son-in-law. **19–29:** Now there is no reluctance in being the LORD's *servant* (the word "servant" is mentioned ten times in David's prayer), only a sense of awe that both he and his people should be singled out for such blessing.

8:1–18 David's Military Triumphs

Because the focus of 2 Samuel is primarily on David and his personal relationships with other human beings and with God, little space is given to the record of his military triumphs, which effectively extended his control from the river Euphrates to the brook of Egypt, as the LORD had promised to Abraham (see Gen 15:18). **15–18:** The beginnings of an adminis-

tribute money. So the LORD made David victorious wherever he went.
[7]David brought the gold shields of Hadadezer's officers to Jerusalem, [8]along with a large
amount of bronze from Hadadezer's towns of
Tebah* and Berothai.
[9]When King Toi of Hamath heard that David
had destroyed the entire army of Hadadezer, [10]he
sent his son Joram to congratulate King David
for his successful campaign. Hadadezer and Toi
had been enemies and were often at war. Joram
presented David with many gifts of silver, gold,
and bronze.
[11]King David dedicated all these gifts to the
LORD, as he did with the silver and gold from the
other nations he had defeated—[12]from Edom,*
Moab, Ammon, Philistia, and Amalek—and from
Hadadezer son of Rehob, king of Zobah.
[13]So David became even more famous when
he returned from destroying 18,000 Edomites*
in the Valley of Salt. [14]He placed army garrisons
throughout Edom, and all the Edomites became
David's subjects. In fact, the LORD made David
victorious wherever he went.
[15]So David reigned over all Israel and did
what was just and right for all his people. [16]Joab
son of Zeruiah was commander of the army. Jehoshaphat son of Ahilud was the royal historian.
[17]Zadok son of Ahitub and Ahimelech son of
Abiathar were the priests. Seraiah was the court
secretary. [18]Benaiah son of Jehoiada was captain of the king's bodyguard.* And David's sons
served as priestly leaders.*

David's Kindness to Mephibosheth

9 One day David asked, "Is anyone in Saul's
family still alive—anyone to whom I can
show kindness for Jonathan's sake?" [2]He
summoned a man named Ziba, who had been
one of Saul's servants. "Are you Ziba?" the king
asked.
"Yes sir, I am," Ziba replied.
[3]The king then asked him, "Is anyone still
alive from Saul's family? If so, I want to show
God's kindness to them."
Ziba replied, "Yes, one of Jonathan's sons is
still alive. He is crippled in both feet."
[4]"Where is he?" the king asked.
"In Lo-debar," Ziba told him, "at the home of
Makir son of Ammiel."
[5]So David sent for him and brought him from
Makir's home. [6]His name was Mephibosheth*;
he was Jonathan's son and Saul's grandson.
When he came to David, he bowed low to the
ground in deep respect. David said, "Greetings,
Mephibosheth."
Mephibosheth replied, "I am your servant."
[7]"Don't be afraid!" David said. "I intend to
show kindness to you because of my promise
to your father, Jonathan. I will give you all the
property that once belonged to your grandfather
Saul, and you will eat here with me at the king's
table!"
[8]Mephibosheth bowed respectfully and exclaimed, "Who is your servant, that you should
show such kindness to a dead dog like me?"
[9]Then the king summoned Saul's servant Ziba
and said, "I have given your master's grandson
everything that belonged to Saul and his family.
[10]You and your sons and servants are to farm the
land for him to produce food for your master's
household.* But Mephibosheth, your master's
grandson, will eat here at my table." (Ziba had
fifteen sons and twenty servants.)
[11]Ziba replied, "Yes, my lord the king; I am
your servant, and I will do all that you have commanded." And from that time on, Mephibosheth
ate regularly at David's table,* like one of the
king's own sons.

8:8 As in some Greek manuscripts (see also 1 Chr 18:8); Hebrew reads *Betah.* **8:12** As in a few Hebrew manuscripts and Greek and Syriac versions (see also 8:14; 1 Chr 18:11); most Hebrew manuscripts read *Aram.* **8:13** As in a few Hebrew manuscripts and Greek and Syriac versions (see also 8:14; 1 Chr 18:12); most Hebrew manuscripts read *Arameans.* **8:18a** Hebrew *of the Kerethites and Pelethites.* **8:18b** Hebrew *David's sons were priests;* compare parallel text at 1 Chr 18:17. **9:6** *Mephibosheth* is another name for Merib-baal. **9:10** As in Greek version; Hebrew reads *your master's grandson.* **9:11** As in Greek version; Hebrew reads *my table.*

trative system, which included David's sons, were set up to assist the king in his just ordering of the country.

9:1–13 David and Mephibosheth

As part of his covenant with Jonathan, David had promised to care for his descendants (1 Sam 20:14–15). **6–7:** *Mephibosheth* had reason to be afraid: As Saul's grandson, he could be considered a rival for the throne. **9–11:** Because of Mephibosheth's incapacity, administration of the property was committed to Ziba, a former servant of Saul and a man of some personal wealth and stature in his own right. **7, 11, 13:** Mephibosheth's new position is noted three times. David's act of kindness had the undoubted political benefit of enabling the king to observe any inclination on Mephibosheth's part to aspire to his grandfather's throne. The reality of Mephibosheth's disability made such a move unlikely.

12 Mephibosheth had a young son named
Mica. From then on, all the members of Ziba's
household were Mephibosheth's servants. 13 And
Mephibosheth, who was crippled in both feet,
lived in Jerusalem and ate regularly at the king's
table.

David Defeats the Ammonites

10 Some time after this, King Nahash*
of the Ammonites died, and his son
Hanun became king. 2 David said,
"I am going to show loyalty to Hanun just as
his father, Nahash, was always loyal to me." So
David sent ambassadors to express sympathy to
Hanun about his father's death.
But when David's ambassadors arrived in
the land of Ammon, 3 the Ammonite commanders said to Hanun, their master, "Do you really
think these men are coming here to honor your
father? No! David has sent them to spy out the
city so they can come in and conquer it!" 4 So
Hanun seized David's ambassadors and shaved
off half of each man's beard, cut off their robes
at the buttocks, and sent them back to David in
shame.
5 When David heard what had happened, he
sent messengers to tell the men, "Stay at Jericho until your beards grow out, and then come
back." For they felt deep shame because of their
appearance.
6 When the people of Ammon realized how
seriously they had angered David, they sent and
hired 20,000 Aramean foot soldiers from the
lands of Beth-rehob and Zobah, 1,000 from the
king of Maacah, and 12,000 from the land of Tob.
7 When David heard about this, he sent Joab and
all his warriors to fight them. 8 The Ammonite
troops came out and drew up their battle lines at
the entrance of the city gate, while the Arameans
from Zobah and Rehob and the men from Tob
and Maacah positioned themselves to fight in the
open fields.
9 When Joab saw that he would have to fight
on both the front and the rear, he chose some
of Israel's elite troops and placed them under his
personal command to fight the Arameans in the
fields. 10 He left the rest of the army under the
command of his brother Abishai, who was to attack the Ammonites. 11 "If the Arameans are too
strong for me, then come over and help me," Joab
told his brother. "And if the Ammonites are too
strong for you, I will come and help you. 12 Be
courageous! Let us fight bravely for our people
and the cities of our God. May the LORD's will
be done."
13 When Joab and his troops attacked, the
Arameans began to run away. 14 And when the
Ammonites saw the Arameans running, they
ran from Abishai and retreated into the city.
After the battle was over, Joab returned to Jerusalem.
15 The Arameans now realized that they
were no match for Israel. So when they regrouped, 16 they were joined by additional
Aramean troops summoned by Hadadezer
from the other side of the Euphrates River.*
These troops arrived at Helam under the command of Shobach, the commander of Hadadezer's forces.
17 When David heard what was happening,
he mobilized all Israel, crossed the Jordan River, and led the army to Helam. The Arameans
positioned themselves in battle formation and
fought against David. 18 But again the Arameans
fled from the Israelites. This time David's forces
killed 700 charioteers and 40,000 foot soldiers,*
including Shobach, the commander of their
army. 19 When all the kings allied with Hadadezer
saw that they had been defeated by Israel, they
surrendered to Israel and became their subjects.
After that, the Arameans were afraid to help the
Ammonites.

10:1 As in parallel text at 1 Chr 19:1; Hebrew reads *the king.* **10:16** Hebrew *the river.* **10:18** As in some Greek manuscripts (see also 1 Chr 19:18); Hebrew reads *charioteers.*

10:1–19 War with the Ammonites

The extensive treatment of Israel's campaign against the Ammonites, rather than mere inclusion in the summary of 2 Samuel 8, is in no small measure due to the fact that it provides the backdrop against which the tragedy of David's affair with Bathsheba is played out. **1–2:** It is not known why the Ammonite king Nahash had shown kindness to David. **3–5:** The misinterpretation of David's motives by the Ammonite nobles led to an unprovoked act of negative reciprocity (cf. 1 Sam 25:21) designed to humiliate the messengers and thus the one who sent them. **6–7:** Fearing reprisal measures for such an assault on David's honor, the Ammonites hired an extensive force of foreign mercenaries and thus precipitated war with Israel. **9–19:** Early battles led by Joab and David so effectively dealt with all the Ammonites' allies that any future help from them could no longer be expected, leaving the Ammonites exposed and vulnerable to attack.

David and Bathsheba

11 In the spring of the year,* when kings
normally go out to war, David sent
Joab and the Israelite army to fight
the Ammonites. They destroyed the Ammonite
army and laid siege to the city of Rabbah. However, David stayed behind in Jerusalem.
2 Late one afternoon, after his midday rest,
David got out of bed and was walking on the roof
of the palace. As he looked out over the city, he
noticed a woman of unusual beauty taking a bath.
3 He sent someone to find out who she was, and
he was told, "She is Bathsheba, the daughter of
Eliam and the wife of Uriah the Hittite." 4 Then
David sent messengers to get her; and when she
came to the palace, he slept with her. She had just
completed the purification rites after having her
menstrual period. Then she returned home. 5 Later,
when Bathsheba discovered that she was pregnant,
she sent David a message, saying, "I'm pregnant."
6 Then David sent word to Joab: "Send me
Uriah the Hittite." So Joab sent him to David.
7 When Uriah arrived, David asked him how Joab
and the army were getting along and how the
war was progressing. 8 Then he told Uriah, "Go
on home and relax.*" David even sent a gift to
Uriah after he had left the palace. 9 But Uriah
didn't go home. He slept that night at the palace
entrance with the king's palace guard.
10 When David heard that Uriah had not gone
home, he summoned him and asked, "What's the
matter? Why didn't you go home last night after
being away for so long?"
11 Uriah replied, "The Ark and the armies of
Israel and Judah are living in tents,* and Joab and
my master's men are camping in the open fields.
How could I go home to wine and dine and sleep
with my wife? I swear that I would never do such
a thing."

11:1 Hebrew *At the turn of the year.* The first day of the year in the ancient Hebrew lunar calendar occurred in March or April. **11:8** Hebrew *and wash your feet,* an expression that may also have a connotation of ritualistic washing. **11:11** Or *at Succoth.*

11:1–27 David and Bathsheba

David's affair with Bathsheba would have repercussions David never could have envisaged. **2:** David's palace would have been built above the other houses clinging to the slopes of the hill on which Jerusalem is located. Bathsheba would have been unaware of her exposure to the view and fantasies of a king with a string of sexual conquests behind him. **3:** It was easy for David to discover whose house it was and who was the woman in residence. According to contemporary convention she was identified as the *daughter of Eliam* and the *wife of Uriah*, one of David's mighty men (cf. 23:39). **4:** The invitation to the palace would have caused Bathsheba no suspicion; she was a married woman, and her grandfather Ahithophel was a member of the court. Her encounter with the king is passed over in a single verse, which effectively communicates how insignificant the whole affair was in the mind and intentions of the king. He sent, she came, he slept with her, she returned home. (See Lev 15:19–28 for the law concerning Bathsheba's ritual bathing.) She was at the most fertile time of her cycle. She could not resist the advances of a man in such a powerful position, a man who was capable of taking whatever or whomever he wanted. She would have had many considerations: What would happen to Uriah if she refused the king? What would happen to her if she acceded to the king's proposal? The law called for both parties of an adulterous affair to be put to death (Lev 20:10), but what would be the use of crying out for help in the king's private chamber? Who would believe her word against that of the king? Perhaps their sin would not be discovered, and the king, having indulged his idle fancy, would forget about her and turn his mind to other conquests of a military variety. **5:** A month or two later, David receives a terse little note: *I'm pregnant*. Only two words in Hebrew, yet they formed the hinge on which the reign of David turned. Readers must imagine Bathsheba's feelings, unlikely to be the excitement of new life stirring within and the prospect of forthcoming celebration but rather a sense of impending shame and doom, for now the whole question of her honor was at stake in the public domain, as was David's—for adultery was adultery, however exalted the position of one of the participants. **6–13:** David saw the situation as a problem to be solved, and the solution, at least in his mind, was simple. Summon Uriah home on some trumped-up military concern, give him a couple of days' leave to spend some time with his wife, and then, when the child was born, pass it off as premature and pray that the community gossips wouldn't notice the child was a full-term baby. **9–11:** The deviousness of the king's plan was undone by the high principles of his loyal soldier who, although a foreigner, had accepted the conditions of holy war to which David had once subscribed, including abstinence (1 Sam 21:4–5). **11:** Uriah's reply to the king is heavy with irony. The rest of the king's troops were camping in the open field, devoid of female company; how could he choose to go home and lie with his wife? The irony was double, for not only had David chosen to stay at home with his own wives, but also he had been sleeping with the wife of Uriah. The very thing Uriah was refusing to do, David had already done. **14–15:** Uriah's strength

[12]"Well, stay here today," David told him, "and tomorrow you may return to the army." So Uriah stayed in Jerusalem that day and the next. [13]Then David invited him to dinner and got him drunk. But even then he couldn't get Uriah to go home to his wife. Again he slept at the palace entrance with the king's palace guard.

David Arranges for Uriah's Death

[14]So the next morning David wrote a letter to Joab and gave it to Uriah to deliver. [15]The letter instructed Joab, "Station Uriah on the front lines where the battle is fiercest. Then pull back so that he will be killed." [16]So Joab assigned Uriah to a spot close to the city wall where he knew the enemy's strongest men were fighting. [17]And when the enemy soldiers came out of the city to fight, Uriah the Hittite was killed along with several other Israelite soldiers.

[18]Then Joab sent a battle report to David. [19]He told his messenger, "Report all the news of the battle to the king. [20]But he might get angry and ask, 'Why did the troops go so close to the city? Didn't they know there would be shooting from the walls? [21]Wasn't Abimelech son of Gideon* killed at Thebez by a woman who threw a millstone down on him from the wall? Why would you get so close to the wall?' Then tell him, 'Uriah the Hittite was killed, too.' "

[22]So the messenger went to Jerusalem and gave a complete report to David. [23]"The enemy came out against us in the open fields," he said. "And as we chased them back to the city gate, [24]the archers on the wall shot arrows at us. Some of the king's men were killed, including Uriah the Hittite."

[25]"Well, tell Joab not to be discouraged," David said. "The sword devours this one today and that one tomorrow! Fight harder next time, and conquer the city!"

[26]When Uriah's wife heard that her husband was dead, she mourned for him. [27]When the period of mourning was over, David sent for her and brought her to the palace, and she became one of his wives. Then she gave birth to a son. But the LORD was displeased with what David had done.

Nathan Rebukes David

12 So the LORD sent Nathan the prophet to tell David this story: "There were two men in a certain town. One was rich, and one was poor. [2]The rich man owned a great many sheep and cattle. [3]The poor man owned nothing but one little lamb he had bought. He raised that little lamb, and it grew up with his children. It ate from the man's own plate and drank from his cup. He cuddled it in his arms like a baby daughter. [4]One day a guest arrived at the home of the rich man. But instead of killing an animal from his own flock or herd, he took the poor man's lamb and killed it and prepared it for his guest."

[5]David was furious. "As surely as the LORD lives," he vowed, "any man who would do such a thing deserves to die! [6]He must repay four lambs to the poor man for the one he stole and for having no pity."

[7]Then Nathan said to David, "You are that man! The LORD, the God of Israel, says: I anointed you king of Israel and saved you from the power of Saul. [8]I gave you your master's house and his wives and the kingdoms of Israel and Judah. And if that had not been enough, I would have given you much, much more. [9]Why, then, have you despised the word of the LORD and done this horrible deed? For you have murdered Uriah the Hittite with the sword of the Ammonites and stolen his wife. [10]From this time on, your family

11:21 Hebrew *son of Jerub-besheth.* Jerub-besheth is a variation on the name Jerub-baal, which is another name for Gideon; see Judg 6:32.

of principle meant he was about to lose his life, as he carried back to Joab the king's instructions for his own death. **22–25:** A military decision that might be regarded as foolhardy is airily dismissed by the king. **27:** *The LORD was displeased with what David had done*, that is, David's lying with Uriah's wife. Other kings in the ancient Near East might assume that they were entitled to take any woman they desired, but kingship in Israel was different. It was the LORD who ruled, and even the king was accountable to God.

12:1–31 God's Judgment and Mercy

While it seems Bathsheba is virtually invisible in chapter 11, several places in chapter 12 show the LORD's concern for her. **1–4:** It is necessary to ask "Who is the lamb in the parable told by Nathan?" in order to realize that Bathsheba was the focus of God's concern. The story Nathan told was perfectly designed to appeal to a king who had once been a shepherd. **5–6:** In passing judgment on the rich man, David unwittingly passed judgment on himself. **7–12:** *You are that man!* The prophet's statement brings home to David the stark truth that all his plans and scheming had been exposed to the view of the LORD all along. **10–12:** The divine judgment perfectly matched the dimensions of David's sin. The *sword* that had so conveniently removed Uriah

will live by the sword because you have despised
me by taking Uriah's wife to be your own.
11 "This is what the LORD says: Because
of what you have done, I will cause your own
household to rebel against you. I will give your
wives to another man before your very eyes, and
he will go to bed with them in public view. 12 You
did it secretly, but I will make this happen to you
openly in the sight of all Israel."

David Confesses His Guilt

13 Then David confessed to Nathan, "I have sinned
against the LORD."

Nathan replied, "Yes, but the LORD has forgiven you, and you won't die for this sin. 14 Nevertheless, because you have shown utter contempt for the LORD* by doing this, your child
will die."
15 After Nathan returned to his home, the
LORD sent a deadly illness to the child of David
and Uriah's wife. 16 David begged God to spare
the child. He went without food and lay all night
on the bare ground. 17 The elders of his household pleaded with him to get up and eat with
them, but he refused.
18 Then on the seventh day the child died.
David's advisers were afraid to tell him. "He
wouldn't listen to reason while the child was ill,"
they said. "What drastic thing will he do when
we tell him the child is dead?"
19 When David saw them whispering, he realized what had happened. "Is the child dead?" he
asked.

"Yes," they replied, "he is dead."
20 Then David got up from the ground, washed
himself, put on lotions,* and changed his clothes.
He went to the Tabernacle and worshiped the
LORD. After that, he returned to the palace and
was served food and ate.
21 His advisers were amazed. "We don't understand you," they told him. "While the child
was still living, you wept and refused to eat. But
now that the child is dead, you have stopped your
mourning and are eating again."
22 David replied, "I fasted and wept while the
child was alive, for I said, 'Perhaps the LORD will
be gracious to me and let the child live.' 23 But
why should I fast when he is dead? Can I bring
him back again? I will go to him one day, but he
cannot return to me."
24 Then David comforted Bathsheba, his wife,
and slept with her. She became pregnant and
gave birth to a son, and David* named him Solomon. The LORD loved the child 25 and sent word
through Nathan the prophet that they should
name him Jedidiah (which means "beloved of the
LORD"), as the LORD had commanded.*

David Captures Rabbah

26 Meanwhile, Joab was fighting against Rabbah,
the capital of Ammon, and he captured the royal
fortifications.* 27 Joab sent messengers to tell David, "I have fought against Rabbah and captured
its water supply.* 28 Now bring the rest of the
army and capture the city. Otherwise, I will capture it and get credit for the victory."
29 So David gathered the rest of the army and
went to Rabbah, and he fought against it and

12:14 As in Dead Sea Scrolls; Masoretic Text reads *the LORD's enemies.* **12:20** Hebrew *anointed himself.* **12:24** Hebrew *he;* an alternate Hebrew reading and some Hebrew manuscripts read *she.* **12:25** As in Greek version; Hebrew reads *because of the LORD.* **12:26** Or *the royal city.* **12:27** Or *captured the city of water.*

in a foreign land would turn back on David's house, bringing death to those he loved. He had dishonored Uriah in taking his wife for himself, so Israel would see him dishonored as his wives were taken by another man. David's action had been shrouded in secrecy, but his public recompense would take place in daylight. **13–14:** His confession of guilt before God secured his forgiveness, but Bathsheba still would have nowhere to hide her shame. **14–18:** As long as their ill-conceived child lived, the palace gossips would have a field day. A little arithmetic would make them realize why David had been in such a hurry to marry Uriah's widow after her husband's unfortunate but possibly convenient death. The death of the child may have been a mercy, a token of the divine compassion for Bathsheba in the longer term. It removed the possibility of any future gossip occasioned by an innocent query as to the child's identity. And without the physical reminder of the king and Bathsheba's adultery, the memory of it would fade all the faster. **15–23:** David prayed that the life of the child might be preserved, but he did not mourn the child's passing. **24:** *His wife*: David's relations with Bathsheba are now acknowledged as legitimate. A child was born, and they named him Solomon, meaning "peace and wholeness," because in him Bathsheba's life was complete once more. The name Jedidiah never recurs.

12:26–31 David Captures Rabbah. Joab captured the citadel and the water supply of Rabbah, the Ammonite capital, so that David's conquest of the rest of the city was fairly simple.

captured it. 30 David removed the crown from the king's head,* and it was placed on his own head. The crown was made of gold and set with gems, and it weighed seventy-five pounds.* David took a vast amount of plunder from the city. 31 He also made slaves of the people of Rabbah and forced them to labor with* saws, iron picks, and iron axes, and to work in the brick kilns.* That is how he dealt with the people of all the Ammonite towns. Then David and all the army returned to Jerusalem.

The Rape of Tamar

13 Now David's son Absalom had a beautiful sister named Tamar. And Amnon, her half brother, fell desperately in love with her. 2 Amnon became so obsessed with Tamar that he became ill. She was a virgin, and Amnon thought he could never have her.

3 But Amnon had a very crafty friend—his cousin Jonadab. He was the son of David's brother Shimea.* 4 One day Jonadab said to Amnon, "What's the trouble? Why should the son of a king look so dejected morning after morning?"

So Amnon told him, "I am in love with Tamar, my brother Absalom's sister."

5 "Well," Jonadab said, "I'll tell you what to do. Go back to bed and pretend you are ill. When your father comes to see you, ask him to let Tamar come and prepare some food for you. Tell him you'll feel better if she prepares it as you watch and feeds you with her own hands."

6 So Amnon lay down and pretended to be sick. And when the king came to see him, Amnon asked him, "Please let my sister Tamar come and cook my favorite dish* as I watch. Then I can eat it from her own hands." 7 So David agreed and sent Tamar to Amnon's house to prepare some food for him.

8 When Tamar arrived at Amnon's house, she went to the place where he was lying down so he could watch her mix some dough. Then she baked his favorite dish for him. 9 But when she set the serving tray before him, he refused to eat. "Everyone get out of here," Amnon told his servants. So they all left.

10 Then he said to Tamar, "Now bring the food into my bedroom and feed it to me here." So Tamar took his favorite dish to him. 11 But as she was feeding him, he grabbed her and demanded, "Come to bed with me, my darling sister."

12 "No, my brother!" she cried. "Don't be foolish! Don't do this to me! Such wicked things aren't done in Israel. 13 Where could I go in my shame? And you would be called one of the greatest fools in Israel. Please, just speak to the king about it, and he will let you marry me."

14 But Amnon wouldn't listen to her, and since he was stronger than she was, he raped her. 15 Then suddenly Amnon's love turned to hate, and he hated her even more than he had loved her. "Get out of here!" he snarled at her.

16 "No, no!" Tamar cried. "Sending me away now is worse than what you've already done to me."

But Amnon wouldn't listen to her. 17 He

12:30a Or *from the head of Milcom* (as in Greek version). Milcom, also called Molech, was the god of the Ammonites. **12:30b** Hebrew *1 talent* [34 kilograms]. **12:31a** Or *He also brought out the people of Rabbah and put them under.* **12:31b** Or *and he made them pass through the brick kilns.* **13:3** Hebrew *Shimeah* (also in 13:32), a variant spelling of Shimea; compare 1 Chr 2:13. **13:6** Or *a couple of cakes;* also in 13:8, 10.

13:1–39 The Rape of Tamar and Absalom's Revenge

The tragedy of Tamar's rape parallels the story of Bathsheba. Like Bathsheba, Tamar was beautiful; like Bathsheba, she became the object of a man's desire, which led to illicit sexual union and subsequent disaster. **1–12:** The sibling relationship between Amnon and Tamar is stressed throughout the story. **3–5:** Jonadab's plan was devised to bring her into his presence that Amnon might look upon her. **6–7:** To the king, this request seemed innocent. **8–10:** The reader can imagine that at some point Tamar's suspicions would be roused that there was more to this encounter than she had been led to expect. **12–13:** Tamar tries to reason with him, to appeal to his better judgment. If he so desired her, let him ask the king. This may have been a ploy to buy time. After all, Abraham had been married to his half sister (Gen 20:12), even though the house rules of Leviticus 18 forbid sexual relations between close relatives, including half sisters and specifically "the daughter of any of your father's wives" (Lev 18:11). When logic fails, she turns to other means of persuasion: What he was suggesting was foolishness. They would be scorned and ridiculed by all. **14–15:** *Love turned to hate*: What Amnon had originally felt could never have been love. His lust satisfied, Amnon's desire turned to revulsion. **16:** Tamar may have the laws that required marriage in similar cases (see Exod 22:16 and Deut 22:28–29) in mind. At least marriage to Amnon would in some measure restore her honor and secure her future. However harsh it might seem, there was no viable alternative, for no other man would ever want to marry a violated woman, and a woman on her own had no future worth contemplating.

shouted for his servant and demanded, "Throw this woman out, and lock the door behind her!"
[18] So the servant put her out and locked the door behind her. She was wearing a long, beautiful robe,* as was the custom in those days for the king's virgin daughters.
[19] But now Tamar tore her robe and put ashes on her head. And then, with her face in her hands, she went away crying.

[20] Her brother Absalom saw her and asked, "Is it true that Amnon has been with you? Well, my sister, keep quiet for now, since he's your brother. Don't you worry about it." So Tamar lived as a desolate woman in her brother Absalom's house.

[21] When King David heard what had happened, he was very angry.*
[22] And though Absalom never spoke to Amnon about this, he hated Amnon deeply because of what he had done to his sister.

Absalom's Revenge on Amnon

[23] Two years later, when Absalom's sheep were being sheared at Baal-hazor near Ephraim, Absalom invited all the king's sons to come to a feast.
[24] He went to the king and said, "My sheep-shearers are now at work. Would the king and his servants please come to celebrate the occasion with me?"

[25] The king replied, "No, my son. If we all came, we would be too much of a burden on you." Absalom pressed him, but the king would not come, though he gave Absalom his blessing.

[26] "Well, then," Absalom said, "if you can't come, how about sending my brother Amnon with us?"

"Why Amnon?" the king asked.
[27] But Absalom kept on pressing the king until he finally agreed to let all his sons attend, including Amnon. So Absalom prepared a feast fit for a king.*

[28] Absalom told his men, "Wait until Amnon gets drunk; then at my signal, kill him! Don't be afraid. I'm the one who has given the command. Take courage and do it!"
[29] So at Absalom's signal they murdered Amnon. Then the other sons of the king jumped on their mules and fled.

[30] As they were on the way back to Jerusalem, this report reached David: "Absalom has killed all the king's sons; not one is left alive!"
[31] The king got up, tore his robe, and threw himself on the ground. His advisers also tore their clothes in horror and sorrow.

[32] But just then Jonadab, the son of David's brother Shimea, arrived and said, "No, don't believe that all the king's sons have been killed! It was only Amnon! Absalom has been plotting this ever since Amnon raped his sister Tamar.
[33] No, my lord the king, your sons aren't all dead! It was only Amnon."
[34] Meanwhile Absalom escaped.

Then the watchman on the Jerusalem wall saw a great crowd coming down the hill on the

13:18 Or *a robe with sleeves,* or *an ornamented robe.* The meaning of the Hebrew is uncertain. **13:21** Dead Sea Scrolls and Greek version add *But he did not punish his son Amnon, because he loved him, for he was his firstborn.* **13:27** As in Greek and Latin versions (compare also Dead Sea Scrolls); the Hebrew text lacks this sentence.

17: *This woman*: Having robbed Tamar of her virginity—and her future—Amnon takes her identity as well. No longer was she his sister but a spurned woman. There is no personal name, no female noun; she is "this female thing," and by this term his true opinion of her is expressed. He may have used the word "sister" to achieve his ends, but in reality she was always only an object in his eyes, and as an object she is now discarded. **18–19:** For Tamar there remains one last appeal for justice, a visible demonstration of her loss of personhood. No longer a virgin, she tears the robe that signified her status and symbolized her own death with the characteristic actions of the bereaved. **20:** The perceptiveness of Absalom's initial question shows an awareness of Amnon's inclinations. Too late to protect Tamar from Amnon's clutches, now he could only offer her shelter. *Desolate*: That is, unmarried. **21:** The responsibility of defending Tamar's honor lay primarily with David, as Tamar's nearest male kin. Although angry, he does not act. His inaction and silence are open to various interpretations, of which the Septuagint addition to the Hebrew text is but one possibility (see translator's note), and even that is ambiguous. Did David maintain silence lest the suitability of Amnon as his successor might be questioned? Or did he see in his firstborn a reflection of his own moral indiscretion that effectively rendered him impotent in his exercise of family discipline? **22:** Absalom's silence was more ominous. His response to Tamar's silent admission of events might suggest an attitude of indifference to her plight and a desire to keep the scandal within the family. As events were to prove, however, Absalom's refusal to say anything was merely restraint as he plotted. **23–29:** The revenge was well-planned, its final execution swift. **30–31:** The report that reached the king was wildly exaggerated: All the king's sons were dead apart from Absalom. This wholesale killing would make sense if Absalom were planning a coup. **32–33:** The clever Jonadab (who helped Amnon earlier) restored a measure of reality. Amnon's fate was sealed from the day he had raped his sis-

road from the west. He ran to tell the king, "I see
a crowd of people coming from the Horonaim
road along the side of the hill."*
35 "Look!" Jonadab told the king. "There they
are now! The king's sons are coming, just as I
said."
36 They soon arrived, weeping and sobbing,
and the king and all his servants wept bitterly
with them. 37 And David mourned many days for
his son Amnon.
Absalom fled to his grandfather, Talmai son of
Ammihud, the king of Geshur. 38 He stayed there
in Geshur for three years. 39 And King David,*
now reconciled to Amnon's death, longed to be
reunited with his son Absalom.*

Joab Arranges for Absalom's Return

14 Joab realized how much the king
longed to see Absalom. 2 So he sent for
a woman from Tekoa who had a repu-
tation for great wisdom. He said to her, "Pretend
you are in mourning; wear mourning clothes
and don't put on lotions.* Act like a woman who
has been mourning for the dead for a long time.
3 Then go to the king and tell him the story I am
about to tell you." Then Joab told her what to
say.
4 When the woman from Tekoa approached
the king, she bowed with her face to the ground
in deep respect and cried out, "O king! Help
me!"
5 "What's the trouble?" the king asked.
"Alas, I am a widow!" she replied. "My husband is dead. 6 My two sons had a fight out in the
field. And since no one was there to stop it, one
of them was killed. 7 Now the rest of the family
is demanding, 'Let us have your son. We will execute him for murdering his brother. He doesn't
deserve to inherit his family's property.' They
want to extinguish the only coal I have left, and
my husband's name and family will disappear
from the face of the earth."
8 "Leave it to me," the king told her. "Go home,
and I'll see to it that no one touches him."
9 "Oh, thank you, my lord the king," the
woman from Tekoa replied. "If you are criticized
for helping me, let the blame fall on me and
on my father's house, and let the king and his
throne be innocent."
10 "If anyone objects," the king said, "bring
him to me. I can assure you he will never complain again!"
11 Then she said, "Please swear to me by
the LORD your God that you won't let anyone
take vengeance against my son. I want no more
bloodshed."
"As surely as the LORD lives," he replied, "not
a hair on your son's head will be disturbed!"
12 "Please allow me to ask one more thing of
my lord the king," she said.
"Go ahead and speak," he responded.
13 She replied, "Why don't you do as much for
the people of God as you have promised to do

13:34 As in Greek version; Hebrew lacks this sentence. **13:39a** Dead Sea Scrolls and Greek version read *And the spirit of the king.* **13:39b** Or *no longer felt a need to go out after Absalom.* **14:2** Hebrew *don't anoint yourself with oil.*

ter and David did not act. **37:** Talmai was Absalom's maternal grandfather. **39:** The end of this verse (see translator's note) might mean that David no longer wished to pursue Absalom—hence his reluctance (14:24) to welcome his son home.

14:1–33 The Return of Absalom

Absalom's return was brought about by Joab, who perceived the king's worry over his son. If he truly *longed to see Absalom* (v. 1), he would not need persuading. **2:** The *woman from Tekoa*, in the hill country of Judah, had earned respect and renown in her village and beyond for her wisdom. **4–11:** Like Nathan, she approached the king with a story that was sufficiently true to life to be a plausible appeal to the king's justice and mercy. **5–7:** The extensive legislation on behalf of widows in Israel is some indication of their precarious position in society, although much depended on whether the widow had children and whether those children were male or female, minors, or old enough to take their place in the adult community. To have adult male sons was to be relatively blessed, for they could look to her interests and protect her rights. But her two sons had fought, and as a result one had died. Contemporary justice demanded revenge, but in this case such justice would leave her vulnerable and lead to the extinction of her husband's lineage. **8–11:** The king's immediate response showed his willingness to temper justice with mercy in the case of the woman's son, but in a masterly exchange, she pressed her point until David swore that not one hair of her son's head would fall to the ground. **13–17:** Once again, in passing judgment on another, the king was passing judgment on himself. To leave his own son banished and estranged was to act in a way contrary to the mercy of God, who does not punish us as we deserve. To a king only too aware of the blood of another man on his own hands it was a powerful message, delivered by a woman whose attitude throughout was one of humble deference to the king's person (the phrase *my lord the king* re-

for me? You have convicted yourself in making this decision, because you have refused to bring home your own banished son. 14 All of us must die eventually. Our lives are like water spilled out on the ground, which cannot be gathered up again. But God does not just sweep life away; instead, he devises ways to bring us back when we have been separated from him.

15 "I have come to plead with my lord the king because people have threatened me. I said to myself, 'Perhaps the king will listen to me 16 and rescue us from those who would cut us off from the inheritance* God has given us. 17 Yes, my lord the king will give us peace of mind again.' I know that you are like an angel of God in discerning good from evil. May the LORD your God be with you."

18 "I must know one thing," the king replied, "and tell me the truth."

"Yes, my lord the king," she responded.

19 "Did Joab put you up to this?"

And the woman replied, "My lord the king, how can I deny it? Nobody can hide anything from you. Yes, Joab sent me and told me what to say. 20 He did it to place the matter before you in a different light. But you are as wise as an angel of God, and you understand everything that happens among us!"

21 So the king sent for Joab and told him, "All right, go and bring back the young man Absalom."

22 Joab bowed with his face to the ground in deep respect and said, "At last I know that I have gained your approval, my lord the king, for you have granted me this request!"

23 Then Joab went to Geshur and brought Absalom back to Jerusalem. 24 But the king gave this order: "Absalom may go to his own house, but he must never come into my presence." So Absalom did not see the king.

Absalom Reconciled to David

25 Now Absalom was praised as the most handsome man in all Israel. He was flawless from head to foot. 26 He cut his hair only once a year, and then only because it was so heavy. When he weighed it out, it came to five pounds!* 27 He had three sons and one daughter. His daughter's name was Tamar, and she was very beautiful.

28 Absalom lived in Jerusalem for two years, but he never got to see the king. 29 Then Absalom sent for Joab to ask him to intercede for him, but Joab refused to come. Absalom sent for him a second time, but again Joab refused to come. 30 So Absalom said to his servants, "Go and set fire to Joab's barley field, the field next to mine." So they set his field on fire, as Absalom had commanded.

31 Then Joab came to Absalom at his house and demanded, "Why did your servants set my field on fire?"

32 And Absalom replied, "Because I wanted you to ask the king why he brought me back from Geshur if he didn't intend to see me. I might as well have stayed there. Let me see the king; if he finds me guilty of anything, then let him kill me."

33 So Joab told the king what Absalom had said. Then at last David summoned Absalom, who came and bowed low before the king, and the king kissed him.

Absalom's Rebellion

15 After this, Absalom bought a chariot and horses, and he hired fifty bodyguards to run ahead of him. 2 He got up early every morning and went out to the gate of the city. When people brought a case to the king for judgment, Absalom would ask where in Israel they were from, and they would tell him their tribe. 3 Then Absalom would say, "You've really got a strong case here! It's too bad the king doesn't have anyone to hear it. 4 I wish I were the judge. Then everyone could bring their cases to me for judgment, and I would give them justice!"

14:16 Or *the property;* or *the people.* **14:26** Hebrew *200 shekels* [2.3 kilograms] *by the royal standard.*

---

curs frequently), wisdom, discernment, and essential goodness. **21–24:** The king's compassion and forgiveness did not quite match that of the woman in the story. Absalom was recalled to Jerusalem but not to the king's presence. **25–33:** It was another two years before Absalom was admitted to the king's presence, and even that audience was obtained only by Absalom taking rash action against Joab to achieve his purpose. Joab always took reciprocal action against any offense. **27:** Absalom's daughter is named for his raped sister.

15:1—16:23 Absalom's Rebellion. Ahithophel's Revenge

Absalom's motivation for rebellion is unclear. Is he still angry with his father for not punishing Amnon? Has his father's coolness toward him convinced him that he had no chance of inheriting his father's throne legally? Or is he simply hungry for power? **15:1:** To improve his image further Absalom obtained the trappings of kingship. **2–4:** He set about winning the hearts of the people by establishing himself as an

[5]When people tried to bow before him, Absalom wouldn't let them. Instead, he took them
by the hand and kissed them. [6]Absalom did this
with everyone who came to the king for judgment, and so he stole the hearts of all the people
of Israel.
[7]After four years,* Absalom said to the king,
"Let me go to Hebron to offer a sacrifice to the
LORD and fulfill a vow I made to him. [8]For while
your servant was at Geshur in Aram, I promised
to sacrifice to the LORD in Hebron* if he would
bring me back to Jerusalem."
[9]"All right," the king told him. "Go and fulfill
your vow."

So Absalom went to Hebron. [10]But while he
was there, he sent secret messengers to all the
tribes of Israel to stir up a rebellion against the
king. "As soon as you hear the ram's horn," his
message read, "you are to say, 'Absalom has been
crowned king in Hebron.' " [11]He took 200 men
from Jerusalem with him as guests, but they
knew nothing of his intentions. [12]While Absalom was offering the sacrifices, he sent for
Ahithophel, one of David's counselors who lived
in Giloh. Soon many others also joined Absalom,
and the conspiracy gained momentum.

David Escapes from Jerusalem

[13]A messenger soon arrived in Jerusalem to tell
David, "All Israel has joined Absalom in a conspiracy against you!"
[14]"Then we must flee at once, or it will be too
late!" David urged his men. "Hurry! If we get
out of the city before Absalom arrives, both we
and the city of Jerusalem will be spared from disaster."
[15]"We are with you," his advisers replied. "Do
what you think is best."
[16]So the king and all his household set out
at once. He left no one behind except ten of his
concubines to look after the palace. [17]The king
and all his people set out on foot, pausing at the
last house [18]to let all the king's men move past
to lead the way. There were 600 men from Gath
who had come with David, along with the king's
bodyguard.*
[19]Then the king turned and said to Ittai, a
leader of the men from Gath, "Why are you
coming with us? Go on back to King Absalom,
for you are a guest in Israel, a foreigner in exile.
[20]You arrived only recently, and should I force
you today to wander with us? I don't even know
where we will go. Go on back and take your kinsmen with you, and may the LORD show you his
unfailing love and faithfulness.*"
[21]But Ittai said to the king, "I vow by the
LORD and by your own life that I will go wherever my lord the king goes, no matter what happens—whether it means life or death."
[22]David replied, "All right, come with us."
So Ittai and all his men and their families went
along.
[23]Everyone cried loudly as the king and his
followers passed by. They crossed the Kidron
Valley and then went out toward the wilderness.
[24]Zadok and all the Levites also came along,
carrying the Ark of the Covenant of God. They set
down the Ark of God, and Abiathar offered sacrifices* until everyone had passed out of the city.
[25]Then the king instructed Zadok to take the
Ark of God back into the city. "If the LORD sees
fit," David said, "he will bring me back to see
the Ark and the Tabernacle* again. [26]But if he
is through with me, then let him do what seems
best to him."
[27]The king also told Zadok the priest, "Look,*
here is my plan. You and Abiathar* should return quietly to the city with your son Ahimaaz
and Abiathar's son Jonathan. [28]I will stop at the
shallows of the Jordan River* and wait there for
a report from you." [29]So Zadok and Abiathar
took the Ark of God back to the city and stayed
there.
[30]David walked up the road to the Mount of

15:7 As in Greek and Syriac versions; Hebrew reads *forty years.* **15:8** As in some Greek manuscripts; Hebrew lacks *in Hebron.* **15:18** Hebrew *the Kerethites and Pelethites.* **15:20** As in Greek version; Hebrew reads *and may unfailing love and faithfulness go with you.* **15:24** Or *Abiathar went up.* **15:25** Hebrew *and his dwelling place.* **15:27a** As in Greek version; Hebrew reads *Are you a seer?* or *Do you see?* **15:27b** Hebrew lacks *and Abiathar;* compare 15:29. **15:28** Hebrew *at the crossing points of the wilderness.*

appeal judge for those who considered local judgment inadequate or unjust or who couldn't get an audience with the king. **7–12:** Having patiently laid his plans, Absalom obtained the king's permission to travel to Hebron, ostensibly to pay a vow made to the LORD during his self-imposed exile in Geshur, but in truth to start his revolt. **13–18:** Unprepared for a full-scale battle and anxious to avoid the sacking of Jerusalem, David fled, accompanied by his officials and personal bodyguard. **24–30:** David left the city as a penitent, walking barefoot with his head covered and weeping as he went, acknowledging once again his dependence on God for the future ordering of events. **27–29:** David's political brain was in gear once more, as he persuaded Abiathar and Zadok to return to the city with the Ark of the Covenant, so that a line of communication might be set up to keep him abreast of events in Jerusalem.

Olives, weeping as he went. His head was covered and his feet were bare as a sign of mourning. And the people who were with him covered their heads and wept as they climbed the hill. [31]When someone told David that his adviser Ahithophel was now backing Absalom, David prayed, "O LORD, let Ahithophel give Absalom foolish advice!"

[32]When David reached the summit of the Mount of Olives where people worshiped God, Hushai the Arkite was waiting there for him. Hushai had torn his clothing and put dirt on his head as a sign of mourning. [33]But David told him, "If you go with me, you will only be a burden. [34]Return to Jerusalem and tell Absalom, 'I will now be your adviser, O king, just as I was your father's adviser in the past.' Then you can frustrate and counter Ahithophel's advice. [35]Zadok and Abiathar, the priests, will be there. Tell them about the plans being made in the king's palace, [36]and they will send their sons Ahimaaz and Jonathan to tell me what is going on."

[37]So David's friend Hushai returned to Jerusalem, getting there just as Absalom arrived.

David and Ziba

16 When David had gone a little beyond the summit of the Mount of Olives, Ziba, the servant of Mephibosheth,* was waiting there for him. He had two donkeys loaded with 200 loaves of bread, 100 clusters of raisins, 100 bunches of summer fruit, and a wineskin full of wine.

[2]"What are these for?" the king asked Ziba.

Ziba replied, "The donkeys are for the king's people to ride on, and the bread and summer fruit are for the young men to eat. The wine is for those who become exhausted in the wilderness."

[3]"And where is Mephibosheth, Saul's grandson?" the king asked him.

"He stayed in Jerusalem," Ziba replied. "He said, 'Today I will get back the kingdom of my grandfather Saul.' "

[4]"In that case," the king told Ziba, "I give you everything Mephibosheth owns."

"I bow before you," Ziba replied. "May I always be pleasing to you, my lord the king."

Shimei Curses David

[5]As King David came to Bahurim, a man came out of the village cursing them. It was Shimei son of Gera, from the same clan as Saul's family. [6]He threw stones at the king and the king's officers and all the mighty warriors who surrounded him. [7]"Get out of here, you murderer, you scoundrel!" he shouted at David. [8]"The LORD is paying you back for all the bloodshed in Saul's clan. You stole his throne, and now the LORD has given it to your son Absalom. At last you will taste some of your own medicine, for you are a murderer!"

[9]"Why should this dead dog curse my lord the king?" Abishai son of Zeruiah demanded. "Let me go over and cut off his head!"

[10]"No!" the king said. "Who asked your opinion, you sons of Zeruiah! If the LORD has told him to curse me, who are you to stop him?"

[11]Then David said to Abishai and to all his servants, "My own son is trying to kill me. Doesn't this relative of Saul* have even more reason to do so? Leave him alone and let him curse, for the LORD has told him to do it. [12]And perhaps the LORD will see that I am being wronged and will bless me because of these curses today." [13]So David and his men continued down the road, and Shimei kept pace with them on a nearby hillside, cursing as he went and throwing stones at David and tossing dust into the air.

[14]The king and all who were with him grew weary along the way, so they rested when they reached the Jordan River.*

Ahithophel Advises Absalom

[15]Meanwhile, Absalom and all the army of Israel arrived at Jerusalem, accompanied by Ahithophel. [16]When David's friend Hushai the Arkite arrived, he went immediately to see Absalom. "Long live the king!" he exclaimed. "Long live the king!"

[17]"Is this the way you treat your friend David?" Absalom asked him. "Why aren't you with him?"

[18]"I'm here because I belong to the man who is chosen by the LORD and by all the men of Israel," Hushai replied. [19]"And anyway, why shouldn't I serve you? Just as I was your father's adviser, now I will be your adviser!"

16:1 *Mephibosheth* is another name for Merib-baal.
16:11 Hebrew *this Benjaminite.* **16:14** As in Greek version (see also 17:16); Hebrew reads *when they reached their destination.*

16:1–4: Ziba's unlikely story about Mephibosheth suggests that he was an opportunist who exploited the present situation to further his interests at the expense of his master. The temporary success of Ziba's plan may reflect David's desperate need of the provisions he had brought or perhaps a deeper underlying suspicion of any of Saul's descendants. **5–13:** The manner in which Shimei curses the king suggests that the events of chapter 21 had already occurred. **15–19:** Hushai's speech is heavy in its ironic affirmation

20 Then Absalom turned to Ahithophel and
asked him, "What should I do next?"
21 Ahithophel told him, "Go and sleep with
your father's concubines, for he has left them
here to look after the palace. Then all Israel will
know that you have insulted your father beyond
hope of reconciliation, and they will throw their
support to you." 22 So they set up a tent on the
palace roof where everyone could see it, and
Absalom went in and had sex with his father's
concubines.
23 Absalom followed Ahithophel's advice, just
as David had done. For every word Ahithophel
spoke seemed as wise as though it had come directly from the mouth of God.

17 Now Ahithophel urged Absalom, "Let
me choose 12,000 men to start out
after David tonight. 2 I will catch up
with him while he is weary and discouraged. He
and his troops will panic, and everyone will run
away. Then I will kill only the king, 3 and I will
bring all the people back to you as a bride returns
to her husband. After all, it is only one man's life
that you seek.* Then you will be at peace with all
the people." 4 This plan seemed good to Absalom
and to all the elders of Israel.

Hushai Counters Ahithophel's Advice

5 But then Absalom said, "Bring in Hushai the
Arkite. Let's see what he thinks about this."
6 When Hushai arrived, Absalom told him what
Ahithophel had said. Then he asked, "What is
your opinion? Should we follow Ahithophel's
advice? If not, what do you suggest?"
7 "Well," Hushai replied to Absalom, "this
time Ahithophel has made a mistake. 8 You know
your father and his men; they are mighty warriors. Right now they are as enraged as a mother
bear who has been robbed of her cubs. And remember that your father is an experienced man
of war. He won't be spending the night among
the troops. 9 He has probably already hidden in
some pit or cave. And when he comes out and
attacks and a few of your men fall, there will
be panic among your troops, and the word will
spread that Absalom's men are being slaughtered. 10 Then even the bravest soldiers, though
they have the heart of a lion, will be paralyzed
with fear. For all Israel knows what a mighty
warrior your father is and how courageous his
men are.
11 "I recommend that you mobilize the entire
army of Israel, bringing them from as far away
as Dan in the north and Beersheba in the south.
That way you will have an army as numerous
as the sand on the seashore. And I advise that
you personally lead the troops. 12 When we find
David, we'll fall on him like dew that falls on the
ground. Then neither he nor any of his men will
be left alive. 13 And if David were to escape into
some town, you will have all Israel there at your
command. Then we can take ropes and drag the
walls of the town into the nearest valley until
every stone is torn down."
14 Then Absalom and all the men of Israel said,
"Hushai's advice is better than Ahithophel's." For
the LORD had determined to defeat the counsel
of Ahithophel, which really was the better plan,
so that he could bring disaster on Absalom!

Hushai Warns David to Escape

15 Hushai told Zadok and Abiathar, the priests,
what Ahithophel had said to Absalom and the
elders of Israel and what he himself had advised
instead. 16 "Quick!" he told them. "Find David
and urge him not to stay at the shallows of the
Jordan River* tonight. He must go across at once
into the wilderness beyond. Otherwise he will
die and his entire army with him."
17 Jonathan and Ahimaaz had been staying at
En-rogel so as not to be seen entering and leav-

17:3 As in Greek version; Hebrew reads *like the return of all is the man whom you seek.* **17:16** Hebrew *at the crossing points of the wilderness.*

of Hushai's loyalty to *the king* as the one *chosen by the LORD* and his people. **21–22:** Ahithophel's advice that Absalom should engage in sexual relations with the concubines of the former king was governed by both political and personal considerations. By taking his father's concubines, Absalom would publicly establish his claim to all of his father's estate, since concubines, being property, were inherited. The fact that David was not dead, however, made Absalom's action a calculated insult. The final element of Nathan's prophecy (12:11–12) was fulfilled in the place where all David's troubles had begun—on the roof of his palace. **23:** Ahithophel may have had a personal desire for revenge against David for the dishonoring of Bathsheba, possibly his granddaughter (cf. 11:3 and 23:34).

17:1–29 Hushai's Advice and David's Escape

Ahithophel's advice is appropriate to the needs of the situation (vv. 1–4, 14). **7–13:** In a speech that conveyed the impression of wisdom by its great length and use of vivid imagery, Hushai deliberately slowed the pace of proceedings, allowing David to

ing the city. Arrangements had been made for a servant girl to bring them the message they were to take to King David. 18 But a boy spotted them at En-rogel, and he told Absalom about it. So they quickly escaped to Bahurim, where a man hid them down inside a well in his courtyard. 19 The man's wife put a cloth over the top of the well and scattered grain on it to dry in the sun; so no one suspected they were there.

20 When Absalom's men arrived, they asked her, "Have you seen Ahimaaz and Jonathan?"

The woman replied, "They were here, but they crossed over the brook." Absalom's men looked for them without success and returned to Jerusalem.

21 Then the two men crawled out of the well and hurried on to King David. "Quick!" they told him, "cross the Jordan tonight!" And they told him how Ahithophel had advised that he be captured and killed. 22 So David and all the people with him went across the Jordan River during the night, and they were all on the other bank before dawn.

23 When Ahithophel realized that his advice had not been followed, he saddled his donkey, went to his hometown, set his affairs in order, and hanged himself. He died there and was buried in the family tomb.

24 David soon arrived at Mahanaim. By now, Absalom had mobilized the entire army of Israel and was leading his troops across the Jordan River. 25 Absalom had appointed Amasa as commander of his army, replacing Joab, who had been commander under David. (Amasa was Joab's cousin. His father was Jether,* an Ishmaelite.* His mother, Abigail daughter of Nahash, was the sister of Joab's mother, Zeruiah.) 26 Absalom and the Israelite army set up camp in the land of Gilead.

27 When David arrived at Mahanaim, he was warmly greeted by Shobi son of Nahash, who came from Rabbah of the Ammonites, and by Makir son of Ammiel from Lo-debar, and by Barzillai of Gilead from Rogelim. 28 They brought sleeping mats, cooking pots, serving bowls, wheat and barley, flour and roasted grain, beans, lentils, 29 honey, butter, sheep, goats, and cheese for David and those who were with him. For they said, "You must all be very hungry and tired and thirsty after your long march through the wilderness."

Absalom's Defeat and Death

18 David now mustered the men who were with him and appointed generals and captains* to lead them. 2 He sent the troops out in three groups, placing one group under Joab, one under Joab's brother Abishai son of Zeruiah, and one under Ittai, the man from Gath. The king told his troops, "I am going out with you."

3 But his men objected strongly. "You must not go," they urged. "If we have to turn and run—and even if half of us die—it will make no difference to Absalom's troops; they will be looking only for you. You are worth 10,000 of us,* and it is better that you stay here in the town and send help if we need it."

4 "If you think that's the best plan, I'll do it," the king answered. So he stood alongside the gate of the town as all the troops marched out in groups of hundreds and of thousands.

5 And the king gave this command to Joab, Abishai, and Ittai: "For my sake, deal gently with young Absalom." And all the troops heard the king give this order to his commanders.

6 So the battle began in the forest of Ephraim, 7 and the Israelite troops were beaten back by David's men. There was a great slaughter that day, and 20,000 men laid down their lives. 8 The battle raged all across the countryside, and more men died because of the forest than were killed by the sword.

17:25a Hebrew *Ithra,* a variant spelling of Jether. **17:25b** As in some Greek manuscripts (see also 1 Chr 2:17); Hebrew reads *an Israelite.* **18:1** Hebrew *appointed commanders of thousands and commanders of hundreds.* **18:3** As in two Hebrew manuscripts and some Greek and Latin manuscripts; most Hebrew manuscripts read *Now there are 10,000 like us.*

recuperate and organize. He also plays on Absalom's ego. **14:** The LORD is still with David. **17–21:** Women have their own part in the intrigue. An important communication link between the priests and their sons was an unnamed servant girl whose movement between Jerusalem and the neighboring village of En-rogel would have aroused no suspicion. Ahimaaz and Jonathan's safety and ultimately that of the king was dependent on the quick thinking of a woman at Bahurim. **23:** Ahithophel knew that in a prolonged campaign the cause of Absalom was doomed. Perhaps he also feared David's retribution.

18:1–33 The Death of Absalom

Not immediately pressed, David takes on his role as army commander. **2–3:** Perhaps David is so involved in his role of army commander that he forgets he is king. His death would be worth more to the forces of Absalom than the loss of even half of his army. **4–5:** Or perhaps the king's heart was not in this battle, giv-

9 During the battle, Absalom happened to
come upon some of David's men. He tried to escape on his mule, but as he rode beneath the thick
branches of a great tree, his hair* got caught in
the tree. His mule kept going and left him dan-
gling in the air. 10 One of David's men saw what
had happened and told Joab, "I saw Absalom dan-
gling from a great tree."

11 "What?" Joab demanded. "You saw him
there and didn't kill him? I would have rewarded
you with ten pieces of silver* and a hero's belt!"

12 "I would not kill the king's son for even
a thousand pieces of silver,*" the man replied
to Joab. "We all heard the king say to you and
Abishai and Ittai, 'For my sake, please spare
young Absalom.' 13 And if I had betrayed the king
by killing his son—and the king would certainly
find out who did it—you yourself would be the
first to abandon me."

14 "Enough of this nonsense," Joab said. Then
he took three daggers and plunged them into
Absalom's heart as he dangled, still alive, in the
great tree. 15 Ten of Joab's young armor bearers
then surrounded Absalom and killed him.

16 Then Joab blew the ram's horn, and his men
returned from chasing the army of Israel. 17 They
threw Absalom's body into a deep pit in the forest and piled a great heap of stones over it. And
all Israel fled to their homes.

18 During his lifetime, Absalom had built a
monument to himself in the King's Valley, for
he said, "I have no son to carry on my name."
He named the monument after himself, and it is
known as Absalom's Monument to this day.

David Mourns Absalom's Death

19 Then Zadok's son Ahimaaz said, "Let me run to
the king with the good news that the LORD has
rescued him from his enemies."

20 "No," Joab told him, "it wouldn't be good
news to the king that his son is dead. You can be
my messenger another time, but not today."

21 Then Joab said to a man from Ethiopia,*
"Go tell the king what you have seen." The man
bowed and ran off.

22 But Ahimaaz continued to plead with Joab,
"Whatever happens, please let me go, too."

"Why should you go, my son?" Joab replied.
"There will be no reward for your news."

23 "Yes, but let me go anyway," he begged.

Joab finally said, "All right, go ahead." So
Ahimaaz took the less demanding route by way
of the plain and ran to Mahanaim ahead of the
Ethiopian.

24 While David was sitting between the inner and outer gates of the town, the watchman
climbed to the roof of the gateway by the wall.
As he looked, he saw a lone man running toward
them. 25 He shouted the news down to David, and
the king replied, "If he is alone, he has news."

As the messenger came closer, 26 the watchman saw another man running toward them. He
shouted down, "Here comes another one!"

The king replied, "He also will have news."

27 "The first man runs like Ahimaaz son of Zadok," the watchman said.

"He is a good man and comes with good
news," the king replied.

28 Then Ahimaaz cried out to the king, "Everything is all right!" He bowed before the king
with his face to the ground and said, "Praise to
the LORD your God, who has handed over the
rebels who dared to stand against my lord the
king."

29 "What about young Absalom?" the king
demanded. "Is he all right?"

Ahimaaz replied, "When Joab told me to
come, there was a lot of commotion. But I didn't
know what was happening."

30 "Wait here," the king told him. So Ahimaaz
stepped aside.

31 Then the man from Ethiopia arrived and
said, "I have good news for my lord the king.
Today the LORD has rescued you from all those
who rebelled against you."

32 "What about young Absalom?" the king
demanded. "Is he all right?"

And the Ethiopian replied, "May all of your
enemies, my lord the king, both now and in the
future, share the fate of that young man!"

18:9 Hebrew *his head.* **18:11** Hebrew *10 shekels of silver,* about 4 ounces or 114 grams in weight. **18:12** Hebrew *1,000 shekels,* about 25 pounds or 11.4 kilograms in weight. **18:21** Hebrew *from Cush;* similarly in 18:23, 31, 32.

en David's strict instructions concerning Absalom. **9–15:** Absalom's hair, which for so long had been his crowning glory, became his downfall. Absalom died as an object of sport, unable to defend himself. **17:** Absalom's body was thrown in a *pit* rather than restored to his father for a proper burial. Burial under a *heap of stones* was a sign of a cursed person. **19–22:** Joab apparently remembers the fate of others who brought the news of unwished-for deaths to David and prefers to send an unnamed foreigner to face David's wrath. **33:** Estranged as they were and ineffectively reconciled, it was only with his son's death that David's true feelings for Absalom found expression in the reiterated use of his name, the repeated phrase *my son, my son,* and the heart-broken statement, *"If only I had died instead of you!"*

33 *The king was overcome with emotion. He
went up to the room over the gateway and burst
into tears. And as he went, he cried, "O my son
Absalom! My son, my son Absalom! If only I
had died instead of you! O Absalom, my son, my
son."

Joab Rebukes the King

19 1 *Word soon reached Joab that the
king was weeping and mourning for
Absalom. 2 As all the people heard of
the king's deep grief for his son, the joy of that
day's victory was turned into deep sadness. 3 They
crept back into the town that day as though they
were ashamed and had deserted in battle. 4 The
king covered his face with his hands and kept on
crying, "O my son Absalom! O Absalom, my
son, my son!"

5 Then Joab went to the king's room and said
to him, "We saved your life today and the lives
of your sons, your daughters, and your wives and
concubines. Yet you act like this, making us feel
ashamed of ourselves. 6 You seem to love those
who hate you and hate those who love you. You
have made it clear today that your commanders
and troops mean nothing to you. It seems that
if Absalom had lived and all of us had died, you
would be pleased. 7 Now go out there and congratulate your troops, for I swear by the LORD
that if you don't go out, not a single one of them
will remain here tonight. Then you will be worse
off than ever before."

8 So the king went out and took his seat at the
town gate, and as the news spread throughout
the town that he was there, everyone went to
him.

Meanwhile, the Israelites who had supported
Absalom fled to their homes. 9 And throughout
all the tribes of Israel there was much discussion
and argument going on. The people were saying,
"The king rescued us from our enemies and saved
us from the Philistines, but Absalom chased him
out of the country. 10 Now Absalom, whom we
anointed to rule over us, is dead. Why not ask
David to come back and be our king again?"

11 Then King David sent Zadok and Abiathar,
the priests, to say to the elders of Judah, "Why
are you the last ones to welcome back the king
into his palace? For I have heard that all Israel
is ready. 12 You are my relatives, my own tribe,
my own flesh and blood! So why are you the
last ones to welcome back the king?" 13 And David told them to tell Amasa, "Since you are my
own flesh and blood, like Joab, may God strike
me and even kill me if I do not appoint you as
commander of my army in his place."

14 Then Amasa* convinced all the men of Judah, and they responded unanimously. They sent
word to the king, "Return to us, and bring back
all who are with you."

David's Return to Jerusalem

15 So the king started back to Jerusalem. And when
he arrived at the Jordan River, the people of Judah
came to Gilgal to meet him and escort him across
the river. 16 Shimei son of Gera, the man from Bahurim in Benjamin, hurried across with the men
of Judah to welcome King David. 17 A thousand
other men from the tribe of Benjamin were with
him, including Ziba, the chief servant of the house
of Saul, and Ziba's fifteen sons and twenty servants. They rushed down to the Jordan to meet
the king. 18 They crossed the shallows of the Jordan to bring the king's household across the river,
helping him in every way they could.

David's Mercy to Shimei

As the king was about to cross the river, Shimei
fell down before him. 19 "My lord the king, please
forgive me," he pleaded. "Forget the terrible
thing your servant did when you left Jerusalem.
May the king put it out of his mind. 20 I know
how much I sinned. That is why I have come
here today, the very first person in all Israel* to
greet my lord the king."

21 Then Abishai son of Zeruiah said, "Shimei
should die, for he cursed the LORD's anointed
king!"

18:33 Verse 18:33 is numbered 19:1 in Hebrew text.
19:1 Verses 19:1-43 are numbered 19:2-44 in Hebrew text.
19:14 Or *David;* Hebrew reads *he.* **19:20** Hebrew *in the house of Joseph.*

19:1–43 David's Return

The day of victory became a day of mourning (v. 2). **5–7:** With an eye for political reality, Joab takes the king to task. Absalom had actively rebelled against his father, seized his throne and taken up arms against the king. David's grief, however, shows love to the disloyal and fails to show love and appreciation for the loyal. **8–10:** The memory of David's exploits against the Philistines was sufficient to earn him renewed support throughout all the tribes of Israel. **11–18:** David's choice to appeal exclusively to his own tribe of Judah to escort him back to his capital would lead to trouble later. **13:** Amasa was David's nephew (17:25) and Absalom's commander. **18–40:** Just as his departure had been marked by a series of encounters with various people, so also was David's return. He is gracious to all, even Shimei, who had cursed him on his way out of

22 "Who asked your opinion, you sons of Zeruiah!" David exclaimed. "Why have you become my adversary* today? This is not a day for execution but for celebration! Today I am once again the king of Israel!" 23 Then, turning to Shimei, David vowed, "Your life will be spared."

David's Kindness to Mephibosheth

24 Now Mephibosheth,* Saul's grandson, came down from Jerusalem to meet the king. He had not cared for his feet, trimmed his beard, or washed his clothes since the day the king left Jerusalem. 25 "Why didn't you come with me, Mephibosheth?" the king asked him.

26 Mephibosheth replied, "My lord the king, my servant Ziba deceived me. I told him, 'Saddle my donkey* so I can go with the king.' For as you know I am crippled. 27 Ziba has slandered me by saying that I refused to come. But I know that my lord the king is like an angel of God, so do what you think is best. 28 All my relatives and I could expect only death from you, my lord, but instead you have honored me by allowing me to eat at your own table! What more can I ask?"

29 "You've said enough," David replied. "I've decided that you and Ziba will divide your land equally between you."

30 "Give him all of it," Mephibosheth said. "I am content just to have you safely back again, my lord the king!"

David's Kindness to Barzillai

31 Barzillai of Gilead had come down from Rogelim to escort the king across the Jordan. 32 He was very old, about eighty, and very wealthy. He was the one who had provided food for the king during his stay in Mahanaim. 33 "Come across with me and live in Jerusalem," the king said to Barzillai. "I will take care of you there."

34 "No," he replied, "I am far too old to go with the king to Jerusalem. 35 I am eighty years old today, and I can no longer enjoy anything. Food and wine are no longer tasty, and I cannot hear the singers as they sing. I would only be a burden to my lord the king. 36 Just to go across the Jordan River with the king is all the honor I need! 37 Then let me return again to die in my own town, where my father and mother are buried. But here is your servant, my son Kimham. Let him go with my lord the king and receive whatever you want to give him."

38 "Good," the king agreed. "Kimham will go with me, and I will help him in any way you would like. And I will do for you anything you want." 39 So all the people crossed the Jordan with the king. After David had blessed Barzillai and kissed him, Barzillai returned to his own home.

40 The king then crossed over to Gilgal, taking Kimham with him. All the troops of Judah and half the troops of Israel escorted the king on his way.

An Argument over the King

41 But all the men of Israel complained to the king, "The men of Judah stole the king and didn't give us the honor of helping take you, your household, and all your men across the Jordan."

42 The men of Judah replied, "The king is one of our own kinsmen. Why should this make you angry? We haven't eaten any of the king's food or received any special favors!"

43 "But there are ten tribes in Israel," the others replied. "So we have ten times as much right to the king as you do. What right do you have to treat us with such contempt? Weren't we the first to speak of bringing him back to be our king again?" The argument continued back and forth, and the men of Judah spoke even more harshly than the men of Israel.

The Revolt of Sheba

20 There happened to be a troublemaker there named Sheba son of Bicri, a man from the tribe of Benjamin. Sheba blew a ram's horn and began to chant:

"Down with the dynasty of David!
We have no interest in the son of Jesse.
Come on, you men of Israel,
back to your homes!"

19:22 Or *my prosecutor.* **19:24** *Mephibosheth* is another name for Merib-baal. **19:26** As in Greek, Syriac, and Latin versions; Hebrew reads *I will saddle a donkey for myself.*

Jerusalem. **29:** That David indicates that Mephibosheth and Ziba should split their assets indicates that he does not know which of them is telling the truth. **41–43:** Judah's escort brings a sour note to his homecoming.

20:1–26 Sheba's Rebellion

More rebellion arises to trouble David. **2:** *All the men of Israel* refers only to the northern tribes. The phrase probably exaggerates the extent of the northern disaffection with David. **3:** Ironically, Absalom's abuse of the concubines condemned them to a fate similar to that which his sister Tamar had experienced because of Amnon—an unnecessary and unnatural widowhood for the rest of their life. David was unwilling to dishonor them further by acting as though his son's vi-

2 So all the men of Israel deserted David and
followed Sheba son of Bicri. But the men of Judah
stayed with their king and escorted him from the
Jordan River to Jerusalem.
3 When David came to his palace in Jerusalem,
he took the ten concubines he had left to look after the palace and placed them in seclusion. Their
needs were provided for, but he no longer slept
with them. So each of them lived like a widow
until she died.
4 Then the king told Amasa, "Mobilize the
army of Judah within three days, and report back
at that time." 5 So Amasa went out to notify Judah, but it took him longer than the time he had
been given.
6 Then David said to Abishai, "Sheba son of
Bicri is going to hurt us more than Absalom did.
Quick, take my troops and chase after him before
he gets into a fortified town where we can't reach
him."
7 So Abishai and Joab,* together with the
king's bodyguard* and all the mighty warriors,
set out from Jerusalem to go after Sheba. 8 As
they arrived at the great stone in Gibeon, Amasa
met them. Joab was wearing his military tunic
with a dagger strapped to his belt. As he stepped
forward to greet Amasa, he slipped the dagger
from its sheath.*
9 "How are you, my cousin?" Joab said and took
him by the beard with his right hand as though
to kiss him. 10 Amasa didn't notice the dagger in
his left hand, and Joab stabbed him in the stomach with it so that his insides gushed out onto
the ground. Joab did not need to strike again, and
Amasa soon died. Joab and his brother Abishai left
him lying there and continued after Sheba.
11 One of Joab's young men shouted to
Amasa's troops, "If you are for Joab and David,
come and follow Joab." 12 But Amasa lay in his
blood in the middle of the road, and Joab's man
saw that everyone was stopping to stare at him.
So he pulled him off the road into a field and
threw a cloak over him. 13 With Amasa's body
out of the way, everyone went on with Joab to
capture Sheba son of Bicri.
14 Meanwhile, Sheba traveled through all the
tribes of Israel and eventually came to the town
of Abel-beth-maacah. All the members of his
own clan, the Bicrites,* assembled for battle and
followed him into the town. 15 When Joab's forces
arrived, they attacked Abel-beth-maacah. They
built a siege ramp against the town's fortifications and began battering down the wall. 16 But
a wise woman in the town called out to Joab,
"Listen to me, Joab. Come over here so I can talk
to you." 17 As he approached, the woman asked,
"Are you Joab?"
"I am," he replied.
So she said, "Listen carefully to your servant."
"I'm listening," he said.
18 Then she continued, "There used to be a
saying, 'If you want to settle an argument, ask
advice at the town of Abel.' 19 I am one who is
peace loving and faithful in Israel. But you are
destroying an important town in Israel.* Why do
you want to devour what belongs to the LORD?"
20 And Joab replied, "Believe me, I don't want
to devour or destroy your town! 21 That's not my
purpose. All I want is a man named Sheba son of
Bicri from the hill country of Ephraim, who has
revolted against King David. If you hand over this
one man to me, I will leave the town in peace."
"All right," the woman replied, "we will throw
his head over the wall to you." 22 Then the woman
went to all the people with her wise advice, and they
cut off Sheba's head and threw it out to Joab. So
he blew the ram's horn and called his troops back
from the attack. They all returned to their homes,
and Joab returned to the king at Jerusalem.
23 Now Joab was the commander of the army
of Israel. Benaiah son of Jehoiada was captain of
the king's bodyguard. 24 Adoniram* was in charge
of the labor force. Jehoshaphat son of Ahilud was

20:7a Hebrew *So Joab's men.* **20:7b** Hebrew *the Kerethites and Pelethites;* also in 20:23. **20:8** Hebrew *As he stepped forward, it fell out.* **20:14** As in Greek and Latin versions; Hebrew reads *All the Berites.* **20:19** Hebrew *a town that is a mother in Israel.* **20:24** As in Greek version (see also 1 Kgs 4:6; 5:14); Hebrew reads *Adoram.*

olation of them was of no account. **7–13:** Joab apparently did not take kindly to his loss of the position of commander to Amasa. **15–22:** Calmly and methodically Joab prepared for a major assault on the city, but he was forestalled by the intervention of a wise woman who offered an alternative way of proceeding, the way of words rather than warfare, of peaceful negotiations rather than unnecessary violence. Although in ancient Israel women lived mainly outside the public arena of power and politics, this often enabled them to approach problems with a fresh perspective and bring divinely inspired wisdom to bear on seemingly intractable situations. Joab listened to the woman, as did the men of her city. Sheba alone died, the town of Abel was preserved, David's kingdom was restored, and his kingship secured. **24:** *Labor force*: This is often translated as "forced labor." Even in the reign of David, the prophetic warning given by Samuel regarding the way a king would treat them was being fulfilled (cf. 1 Sam 8:11–17).

the royal historian. [25]Sheva was the court secretary. Zadok and Abiathar were the priests. [26]And Ira, a descendant of Jair, was David's personal priest.

David Avenges the Gibeonites

21 There was a famine during David's reign that lasted for three years, so David asked the LORD about it. And the LORD said, "The famine has come because Saul and his family are guilty of murdering the Gibeonites."

[2]So the king summoned the Gibeonites. They were not part of Israel but were all that was left of the nation of the Amorites. The people of Israel had sworn not to kill them, but Saul, in his zeal for Israel and Judah, had tried to wipe them out. [3]David asked them, "What can I do for you? How can I make amends so that you will bless the LORD's people again?"

[4]"Well, money can't settle this matter between us and the family of Saul," the Gibeonites replied. "Neither can we demand the life of anyone in Israel."

"What can I do then?" David asked. "Just tell me and I will do it for you."

[5]Then they replied, "It was Saul who planned to destroy us, to keep us from having any place at all in the territory of Israel. [6]So let seven of Saul's sons be handed over to us, and we will execute them before the LORD at Gibeon, on the mountain of the LORD.*"

"All right," the king said, "I will do it." [7]The king spared Jonathan's son Mephibosheth,* who was Saul's grandson, because of the oath David and Jonathan had sworn before the LORD. [8]But he gave them Saul's two sons Armoni and Mephibosheth, whose mother was Rizpah daughter of Aiah. He also gave them the five sons of Saul's daughter Merab,* the wife of Adriel son of Barzillai from Meholah. [9]The men of Gibeon executed them on the mountain before the LORD. So all seven of them died together at the beginning of the barley harvest.

[10]Then Rizpah daughter of Aiah, the mother of two of the men, spread burlap on a rock and stayed there the entire harvest season. She prevented the scavenger birds from tearing at their bodies during the day and stopped wild animals from eating them at night. [11]When David learned what Rizpah, Saul's concubine, had done, [12]he went to the people of Jabesh-gilead and retrieved the bones of Saul and his son Jonathan. (When the Philistines had killed Saul and Jonathan on Mount Gilboa, the people of Jabesh-gilead stole their bodies from the public square of Beth-shan, where the Philistines had hung them.) [13]So David obtained the bones of Saul and Jonathan, as well as the bones of the men the Gibeonites had executed.

[14]Then the king ordered that they bury the bones in the tomb of Kish, Saul's father, at the town of Zela in the land of Benjamin. After that, God ended the famine in the land.

Battles against Philistine Giants

[15]Once again the Philistines were at war with Israel. And when David and his men were in the thick of battle, David became weak and exhausted. [16]Ishbi-benob was a descendant of the giants*; his bronze spearhead weighed more than seven pounds,* and he was armed with a new sword. He had cornered David and was about

21:6 As in Greek version (see also 21:9); Hebrew reads *at Gibeah of Saul, the chosen of the LORD.* **21:7** *Mephibosheth* is another name for Merib-baal. **21:8** As in a few Hebrew and Greek manuscripts and Syriac version (see also 1 Sam 18:19); most Hebrew manuscripts read *Michal.*
21:16a Or *a descendant of the Rapha;* also in 21:18, 20, 22.
21:16b Hebrew *300 shekels* [3.4 kilograms].

21:1–24:25 Appendix

The whole people (of God) were regarded as one, with the offense of any individual affecting the spiritual well-being of all. This principle had determined the defeat of Israel at Ai, after the sin of Achan (Josh 7:1), and it is the same principle that underlies the events of chapter 21, which probably occurred early in the reign of David over all Israel. **21:1:** A famine was regarded as a sign of divine displeasure. Israel had made a covenant with the Gibeonites in the days of Joshua (Josh 9:3–27). **2–6:** Retribution was required from Saul or contemporary representatives of his family who, together with him, were regarded as a single person by law. **8, 10:** Rizpah, bereft of Saul and now also her sons, faced a bleak future, and she wished to honor what remained to her, even if it was only the dead bodies of her children and Saul's grandchildren. Rizpah's devotion throughout a long, hot summer ensured that the dead were at least spared the ignominy of being fed upon by scavengers. **11–14:** As a result of her vigil David honored the remains of Saul, Jonathan, and the seven who had been impaled by returning their bones to their ancestral land. **15–22:** The remaining section of this chapter, a record of a series of local skirmishes with Philistines, honors the prowess of David and his men in battle and provides an insight into the formation of David's reputation as the one who had saved Israel from the hand of the Philistines.

to kill him. 17 But Abishai son of Zeruiah came
to David's rescue and killed the Philistine. Then
David's men declared, "You are not going out to
battle with us again! Why risk snuffing out the
light of Israel?"
18 After this, there was another battle against
the Philistines at Gob. As they fought, Sibbecai
from Hushah killed Saph, another descendant of
the giants.
19 During another battle at Gob, Elhanan son
of Jair* from Bethlehem killed the brother of
Goliath of Gath.* The handle of his spear was as
thick as a weaver's beam!
20 In another battle with the Philistines at
Gath, they encountered a huge man with six
fingers on each hand and six toes on each foot,
twenty-four in all, who was also a descendant
of the giants. 21 But when he defied and taunted
Israel, he was killed by Jonathan, the son of David's brother Shimea.*
22 These four Philistines were descendants of
the giants of Gath, but David and his warriors
killed them.

David's Song of Praise

22 David sang this song to the LORD on
the day the LORD rescued him from
all his enemies and from Saul. 2 He
sang:

"The LORD is my rock, my fortress, and my
savior;
3 my God is my rock, in whom I find
protection.
He is my shield, the power that saves me,
and my place of safety.
He is my refuge, my savior,
the one who saves me from violence.
4 I called on the LORD, who is worthy of
praise,
and he saved me from my enemies.

5 "The waves of death overwhelmed me;
floods of destruction swept over me.
6 The grave* wrapped its ropes around me;
death laid a trap in my path.
7 But in my distress I cried out to the LORD;
yes, I cried to my God for help.
He heard me from his sanctuary;
my cry reached his ears.

8 "Then the earth quaked and trembled.
The foundations of the heavens shook;
they quaked because of his anger.
9 Smoke poured from his nostrils;
fierce flames leaped from his mouth.
Glowing coals blazed forth from him.
10 He opened the heavens and came down;
dark storm clouds were beneath his feet.
11 Mounted on a mighty angelic being,* he flew,
soaring* on the wings of the wind.
12 He shrouded himself in darkness,
veiling his approach with dense rain clouds.
13 A great brightness shone around him,
and burning coals* blazed forth.
14 The LORD thundered from heaven;
the voice of the Most High resounded.
15 He shot arrows and scattered his enemies;
his lightning flashed, and they were
confused.
16 Then at the command of the LORD,
at the blast of his breath,
the bottom of the sea could be seen,
and the foundations of the earth were laid
bare.

17 "He reached down from heaven and rescued
me;
he drew me out of deep waters.
18 He rescued me from my powerful enemies,
from those who hated me and were too
strong for me.
19 They attacked me at a moment when I was in
distress,
but the LORD supported me.
20 He led me to a place of safety;
he rescued me because he delights in me.
21 The LORD rewarded me for doing right;
he restored me because of my innocence.
22 For I have kept the ways of the LORD;
I have not turned from my God to follow
evil.
23 I have followed all his regulations;

21:19a As in parallel text at 1 Chr 20:5; Hebrew reads *son of Jaare-oregim.* **21:19b** As in parallel text at 1 Chr 20:5; Hebrew reads *killed Goliath of Gath.* **21:21** As in parallel text at 1 Chr 20:7; Hebrew reads *Shimei,* a variant spelling of Shimea. **22:6** Hebrew *Sheol.* **22:11a** Hebrew *a cherub.* **22:11b** As in some Hebrew manuscripts (see also Ps 18:10); other Hebrew manuscripts read *appearing.* **22:13** Or *and lightning bolts.*

22:1–51 A Song of Deliverance. This psalm, which is also in the Psalter (Ps 18), expresses David's thanks to God for rescuing him from all his enemies and the dangers to which he had been exposed in the desert. To God alone and his covenant love David ultimately attributes all his success, and to God alone honor and glory are due.

I have never abandoned his decrees.
24 I am blameless before God;
I have kept myself from sin.
25 The LORD rewarded me for doing right.
He has seen my innocence.

26 "To the faithful you show yourself faithful;
to those with integrity you show integrity.
27 To the pure you show yourself pure,
but to the wicked you show yourself hostile.
28 You rescue the humble,
but your eyes watch the proud and
humiliate them.
29 O LORD, you are my lamp.
The LORD lights up my darkness.
30 In your strength I can crush an army;
with my God I can scale any wall.

31 "God's way is perfect.
All the LORD's promises prove true.
He is a shield for all who look to him for
protection.
32 For who is God except the LORD?
Who but our God is a solid rock?
33 God is my strong fortress,
and he makes my way perfect.
34 He makes me as surefooted as a deer,
enabling me to stand on mountain heights.
35 He trains my hands for battle;
he strengthens my arm to draw a bronze
bow.
36 You have given me your shield of victory;
your help* has made me great.
37 You have made a wide path for my feet
to keep them from slipping.

38 "I chased my enemies and destroyed them;
I did not stop until they were conquered.
39 I consumed them;
I struck them down so they did not get up;
they fell beneath my feet.
40 You have armed me with strength for the
battle;
you have subdued my enemies under my
feet.
41 You placed my foot on their necks.
I have destroyed all who hated me.
42 They looked for help, but no one came to
their rescue.
They even cried to the LORD, but he
refused to answer.
43 I ground them as fine as the dust of the earth;
I trampled them* in the gutter like dirt.

44 "You gave me victory over my accusers.
You preserved me as the ruler over nations;
people I don't even know now serve me.
45 Foreign nations cringe before me;
as soon as they hear of me, they submit.
46 They all lose their courage
and come trembling* from their
strongholds.

47 "The LORD lives! Praise to my Rock!
May God, the Rock of my salvation, be
exalted!
48 He is the God who pays back those who harm
me;
he brings down the nations under me
49 and delivers me from my enemies.
You hold me safe beyond the reach of my
enemies;
you save me from violent opponents.
50 For this, O LORD, I will praise you among the
nations;
I will sing praises to your name.
51 You give great victories to your king;
you show unfailing love to your anointed,
to David and all his descendants forever."

David's Last Words

23 These are the last words of David:

"David, the son of Jesse, speaks—
David, the man who was raised up so high,
David, the man anointed by the God of Jacob,
David, the sweet psalmist of Israel.*

2 "The Spirit of the LORD speaks through me;
his words are upon my tongue.
3 The God of Israel spoke.
The Rock of Israel said to me:
'The one who rules righteously,
who rules in the fear of God,
4 is like the light of morning at sunrise,
like a morning without clouds,
like the gleaming of the sun
on new grass after rain.'

5 "Is it not my family God has chosen?
Yes, he has made an everlasting covenant
with me.
His agreement is arranged and guaranteed in
every detail.
He will ensure my safety and success.

22:36 As in Dead Sea Scrolls (see also Ps 18:35); Masoretic Text reads *your answering.* **22:43** As in Dead Sea Scrolls (see also Ps 18:42); Masoretic Text reads *I crushed and trampled them.* **22:46** As in parallel text at Ps 18:45; Hebrew reads *come girding themselves.* **23:1** Or *the favorite subject of the songs of Israel;* or *the favorite of the Strong One of Israel.*

[6] But the godless are like thorns to be thrown
away,
for they tear the hand that touches them.
[7] One must use iron tools to chop them down;
they will be totally consumed by fire."

David's Mightiest Warriors

[8]These are the names of David's mightiest warriors. The first was Jashobeam the Hacmonite,*
who was leader of the Three*—the three mightiest warriors among David's men. He once used
his spear to kill 800 enemy warriors in a single
battle.*
[9]Next in rank among the Three was Eleazar
son of Dodai, a descendant of Ahoah. Once Eleazar and David stood together against the Philistines when the entire Israelite army had fled.
[10]He killed Philistines until his hand was too
tired to lift his sword, and the LORD gave him
a great victory that day. The rest of the army
did not return until it was time to collect the
plunder!
[11]Next in rank was Shammah son of Agee
from Harar. One time the Philistines gathered at
Lehi and attacked the Israelites in a field full of
lentils. The Israelite army fled, [12]but Shammah*
held his ground in the middle of the field and
beat back the Philistines. So the LORD brought
about a great victory.
[13]Once during the harvest, when David was
at the cave of Adullam, the Philistine army was
camped in the valley of Rephaim. The Three
(who were among the Thirty—an elite group
among David's fighting men) went down to meet
him there. [14]David was staying in the stronghold
at the time, and a Philistine detachment had occupied the town of Bethlehem.
[15]David remarked longingly to his men, "Oh,
how I would love some of that good water from
the well by the gate in Bethlehem." [16]So the
Three broke through the Philistine lines, drew
some water from the well by the gate in Bethlehem, and brought it back to David. But he refused to drink it. Instead, he poured it out as an
offering to the LORD. [17]"The LORD forbid that
I should drink this!" he exclaimed. "This water
is as precious as the blood of these men* who
risked their lives to bring it to me." So David did
not drink it. These are examples of the exploits
of the Three.

David's Thirty Mighty Men

[18]Abishai son of Zeruiah, the brother of Joab, was
the leader of the Thirty.* He once used his spear
to kill 300 enemy warriors in a single battle. It
was by such feats that he became as famous as
the Three. [19]Abishai was the most famous of the
Thirty* and was their commander, though he
was not one of the Three.
[20]There was also Benaiah son of Jehoiada,
a valiant warrior* from Kabzeel. He did many
heroic deeds, which included killing two champions* of Moab. Another time, on a snowy day,
he chased a lion down into a pit and killed it.
[21]Once, armed only with a club, he killed a great
Egyptian warrior who was armed with a spear.
Benaiah wrenched the spear from the Egyptian's
hand and killed him with it. [22]Deeds like these
made Benaiah as famous as the Three mightiest
warriors. [23]He was more honored than the other
members of the Thirty, though he was not one
of the Three. And David made him captain of his
bodyguard.
[24]Other members of the Thirty included:

Asahel, Joab's brother;
Elhanan son of Dodo from Bethlehem;
[25]Shammah from Harod;
Elika from Harod;
[26]Helez from Pelon*;
Ira son of Ikkesh from Tekoa;
[27]Abiezer from Anathoth;
Sibbecai* from Hushah;

23:8a As in parallel text at 1 Chr 11:11; Hebrew reads *Josheb-basshebeth the Tahkemonite.* **23:8b** As in Greek and Latin versions (see also 1 Chr 11:11); the meaning of the Hebrew is uncertain. **23:8c** As in some Greek manuscripts (see also 1 Chr 11:11); the meaning of the Hebrew is uncertain, though it might be rendered *the Three. It was Adino the Eznite who killed 800 men at one time.* **23:12** Hebrew *he.* **23:17** Hebrew *Shall I drink the blood of these men?* **23:18** As in a few Hebrew manuscripts and Syriac version; most Hebrew manuscripts read *the Three.* **23:19** As in Syriac version; Hebrew reads *the Three.* **23:20a** Or *son of Jehoiada, son of Ish-hai.* **23:20b** Hebrew *two of Ariel.* **23:26** As in parallel text at 1 Chr 11:27 (see also 1 Chr 27:10); Hebrew reads *from Palti.* **23:27** As in some Greek manuscripts (see also 1 Chr 11:29); Hebrew reads *Mebunnai.*

23:1–39 David as Charismatic Leader. 1–7: David may be king, but God alone has exalted him, and David acknowledges that his exercise of kingship will be of benefit to his people only when it is exercised *in the fear of God.* **8–39:** If David was greatest when he was most dependent on God, the remainder of this chapter illustrates something of that greatness in the list of those whose loyalty he inspired, the *mightiest warriors*, whose devotion to him extended even to their willingness to risk their lives to meet his every wish. **16–17:** David was careful to honor his men's commitment by offering to God as holy the

28 Zalmon from Ahoah;
Maharai from Netophah;
29 Heled* son of Baanah from Netophah;
Ithai* son of Ribai from Gibeah (in the land of
Benjamin);
30 Benaiah from Pirathon;
Hurai* from Nahale-gaash*;
31 Abi-albon from Arabah;
Azmaveth from Bahurim;
32 Eliahba from Shaalbon;
the sons of Jashen;
Jonathan 33 son of Shagee* from Harar;
Ahiam son of Sharar from Harar;
34 Eliphelet son of Ahasbai from Maacah;
Eliam son of Ahithophel from Giloh;
35 Hezro from Carmel;
Paarai from Arba;
36 Igal son of Nathan from Zobah;
Bani from Gad;
37 Zelek from Ammon;
Naharai from Beeroth, Joab's armor bearer;
38 Ira from Jattir;
Gareb from Jattir;
39 Uriah the Hittite.

There were thirty-seven in all.

David Takes a Census

24 Once again the anger of the LORD
burned against Israel, and he caused
David to harm them by taking a cen-
sus. "Go and count the people of Israel and Judah," the LORD told him.
2 So the king said to Joab and the commanders* of the army, "Take a census of all the tribes
of Israel—from Dan in the north to Beersheba
in the south—so I may know how many people
there are."
3 But Joab replied to the king, "May the LORD
your God let you live to see a hundred times as
many people as there are now! But why, my lord
the king, do you want to do this?"
4 But the king insisted that they take the census, so Joab and the commanders of the army
went out to count the people of Israel. 5 First they
crossed the Jordan and camped at Aroer, south of
the town in the valley, in the direction of Gad.
Then they went on to Jazer, 6 then to Gilead in
the land of Tahtim-hodshi* and to Dan-jaan and
around to Sidon. 7 Then they came to the fortress
of Tyre, and all the towns of the Hivites and Canaanites. Finally, they went south to Judah* as
far as Beersheba.
8 Having gone through the entire land for
nine months and twenty days, they returned to
Jerusalem. 9 Joab reported the number of people
to the king. There were 800,000 capable warriors
in Israel who could handle a sword, and 500,000
in Judah.

Judgment for David's Sin

10 But after he had taken the census, David's conscience began to bother him. And he said to the
LORD, "I have sinned greatly by taking this census. Please forgive my guilt, LORD, for doing this
foolish thing."
11 The next morning the word of the LORD
came to the prophet Gad, who was David's seer.
This was the message: 12 "Go and say to David,
'This is what the LORD says: I will give you three
choices. Choose one of these punishments, and I
will inflict it on you.' "
13 So Gad came to David and asked him, "Will
you choose three* years of famine throughout
your land, three months of fleeing from your enemies, or three days of severe plague throughout
your land? Think this over and decide what answer I should give the LORD who sent me."
14 "I'm in a desperate situation!" David replied to Gad. "But let us fall into the hands of the
LORD, for his mercy is great. Do not let me fall
into human hands."
15 So the LORD sent a plague upon Israel that
morning, and it lasted for three days.* A total of

23:29a As in some Hebrew manuscripts (see also 1 Chr 11:30); most Hebrew manuscripts read *Heleb.* **23:29b** As in parallel text at 1 Chr 11:31; Hebrew reads *Ittai.* **23:30a** As in some Greek manuscripts (see also 1 Chr 11:32); Hebrew reads *Hiddai.* **23:30b** Or *from the ravines of Gaash.* **23:33** As in parallel text at 1 Chr 11:34; Hebrew reads *Jonathan, Shammah;* some Greek manuscripts read *Jonathan son of Shammah.* **24:2** As in Greek version (see also 24:4 and 1 Chr 21:2); Hebrew reads *Joab the commander.* **24:6** Greek version reads *to Gilead and to Kadesh in the land of the Hittites.* **24:7** Or *they went to the Negev of Judah.* **24:13** As in Greek version (see also 1 Chr 21:12); Hebrew reads *seven.* **24:15** Hebrew *for the designated time.*

water they had obtained for him at such potential cost to themselves. **39:** *Uriah the Hittite* was Bathsheba's husband. His inclusion is a sober reminder of charisma and power misused.

24:1–25 David's Census. The same story is found in 1 Chronicles 21, where verse 1 says that Satan rather than the LORD caused David to take the census. **1–9:** In the ancient world a census was usually for one of two purposes: to determine a king's military might and human resources or the people's potential to pay taxes to further the king's glory. Neither was appropriate in Israel, for both constituted a fulfillment of the worst of the excesses of kingship predicted by

70,000 people died throughout the nation, from
Dan in the north to Beersheba in the south. 16 But
as the angel was preparing to destroy Jerusalem,
the LORD relented and said to the death angel,
"Stop! That is enough!" At that moment the
angel of the LORD was by the threshing floor of
Araunah the Jebusite.

17 When David saw the angel, he said to the
LORD, "I am the one who has sinned and done
wrong! But these people are as innocent as
sheep—what have they done? Let your anger
fall against me and my family."

David Builds an Altar

18 That day Gad came to David and said to him,
"Go up and build an altar to the LORD on the
threshing floor of Araunah the Jebusite."

19 So David went up to do what the LORD
had commanded him. 20 When Araunah saw the
king and his men coming toward him, he came
and bowed before the king with his face to the
ground. 21 "Why have you come, my lord the
king?" Araunah asked.

David replied, "I have come to buy your
threshing floor and to build an altar to the LORD
there, so that he will stop the plague."

22 "Take it, my lord the king, and use it as you
wish," Araunah said to David. "Here are oxen for
the burnt offering, and you can use the threshing boards and ox yokes for wood to build a fire
on the altar. 23 I will give it all to you, Your Majesty, and may the LORD your God accept your
sacrifice."

24 But the king replied to Araunah, "No, I insist on buying it, for I will not present burnt offerings to the LORD my God that have cost me
nothing." So David paid him fifty pieces of silver* for the threshing floor and the oxen.

25 David built an altar there to the LORD and
sacrificed burnt offerings and peace offerings.
And the LORD answered his prayer for the land,
and the plague on Israel was stopped.

24:24 Hebrew *50 shekels of silver,* about 20 ounces or 570 grams in weight.

Samuel. **10–16:** Ultimately the LORD ruled in Israel, and by his mercy alone his people were preserved. **17:** David remembers his roots as a shepherd and realizes that the people he ruled were as vulnerable to his misuse of power as his sheep had ever been in Bethlehem. **18–25:** These verses indicate that the plague was stopped after David made his offerings.

1 KINGS

INTRODUCTION

The books of 1 and 2 Kings continue the narrative of 1 and 2 Samuel. It is generally accepted that 1 and 2 Kings were originally one volume, since there is no break in the continuous narrative. Kings was divided into two books when it was translated from Hebrew into Greek, perhaps because more space was required for the Greek, since it writes vowels while Hebrew does not. Much of the material from 1 and 2 Kings is paralleled in 1 and 2 Chronicles.

The author of 1 and 2 Kings is not known. Early Jewish tradition attributes authorship to Jeremiah, who was a contemporary of Josiah and the last kings of Judah (639–586 BC). It is thought that he may have written Kings while in exile in Egypt (Jer 43:6–7), since Jeremiah 52 essentially repeats 2 Kings 24:18—25:31, which refers to exile. However, the end of 2 Kings seems to indicate familiarity with events of the Babylonian captivity rather than Egypt. In this case, one may speculate that 1 and 2 Kings were written by an unidentified author in Babylon around 550 BC. It is more likely that several different authors utilized primary sources that no longer exist. The link with Deuteronomy is undisputed, although scholars differ as to whether they see Deuteronomy as the foundation on which the historical writings were based or a conclusion written in the light of the history. The stories of the prophets, including most of the ones about Elijah, do not reflect Deuteronomistic (see the introduction to 1 Samuel) editing and may have been added later.

It is necessary to note that the material that the author(s) of Kings included in this narrative is extremely selective. The author(s) cited several extrabiblical annals, now lost, that chronicled the events of each ruler's reign. From this cited information source, only information that pertained to the relationships among the kings of Judah and Israel, the people, and God was extracted. In other words, the primary concern of the writer(s) of Kings was to show the loyalty or disloyalty of the kings and the people to God. The book of Kings has a direct point to make, and it makes it against the background of the warning of the evil that kings do (1 Sam 8) made at the time of the establishment of the kingship at the people's request.

There are several themes in 1 and 2 Kings. These include proper and improper cultic activities, righteous kingship, loyalty to God, consequences of improper and disloyal behavior toward God, the Jerusalem Temple, prophecy and fulfillment, and united and divided monarchy. Throughout the book the author tries to offer theological explanations for the events of Israel's history, from the division of the kingdom to the success or failure of various kings to follow in David's path. This book is primarily a work of theology, not of history.

The book of Kings also carries good news for women and sheds some light on the significant role of women in the ancient world. Several women play a prominent role in the development of this narrative. Women probably enjoyed a much greater, freer role in ancient Israelite society than many scholars have been willing to admit. The Bible is careful to include powerful, well-respected, well-educated, and intelligent women who helped to shape religious and political history. In the book of Kings, women are shown occupying the same positions as men; this message is conveyed by the writer(s) without shock or disdain, nor is there anticipation of such a reaction from readers. For example, the book of Kings portrays the queen of Sheba and Athaliah as possessing great powers as rulers of their respective lands.

Kings also suggests women and men had equal access to the law. For example, the two prostitutes, one of whose child had died, represent themselves in the high court before Solomon (1 Kgs 3:16–28); there were no male intermediaries. Some scholars have suggested that only women who were widowed, divorced, or prostitutes had their own legal status. However, that view seems to be negated by the actions of the Shunammite woman (2 Kgs 8:1–6), who represented not only herself before the king but her husband and son as well. We may also assume that men and women were subject to equal judgment in decisions, with punishments and rewards commensurate with their deeds and petitions. The two prostitutes and the Shunammite woman had to abide by the king's decision. Jezebel and Athaliah are rulers who commit unforgivable acts in God's estimation: They brought pagan deities into Israel and Judah, and they encouraged the people to worship them. As is seen over and over again, this is the downfall of numerous male rulers who accordingly were also reprimanded by God. Thus God does not distinguish between male and female when it comes to obedience or disobedience—both receive equal treatment. —*Jill L. Baker*

United Kingdom

1:1—2:12	David's Final Days
2:13—11:25	Solomon's Rule

Divided Kingdom

11:26—14:31	Division of the Kingdom
15:1—16:34	Israel and Judah
15:1–8	Abijam of Judah
15:9–24	Asa of Judah
15:25–31	Nadab of Israel
15:32—16:7	Baasha of Israel
16:8–14	Elah of Israel
16:15–20	Zimri of Israel
16:21–28	Omri of Israel
16:29–34	Ahab of Israel
17:1—19:21	Elijah and Elisha
20:1—22:40	Ahab of Israel
22:41–50	Jehoshaphat of Judah
22:51–53	Ahaziah of Israel

David in His Old Age

1 King David was now very old, and no matter how many blankets covered him, he could not keep warm. 2 So his advisers told him, "Let us find a young virgin to wait on you and look after you, my lord. She will lie in your arms and keep you warm."

3 So they searched throughout the land of Israel for a beautiful girl, and they found Abishag from Shunem and brought her to the king. 4 The girl was very beautiful, and she looked after the king and took care of him. But the king had no sexual relations with her.

Adonijah Claims the Throne

5 About that time David's son Adonijah, whose mother was Haggith, began boasting, "I will make myself king." So he provided himself with chariots and charioteers and recruited fifty men to run in front of him. 6 Now his father, King David, had never disciplined him at any time, even by asking, "Why are you doing that?" Adonijah had been born next after Absalom, and he was very handsome.

7 Adonijah took Joab son of Zeruiah and Abiathar the priest into his confidence, and they agreed to help him become king. 8 But Zadok the priest, Benaiah son of Jehoiada, Nathan the prophet, Shimei, Rei, and David's personal bodyguard refused to support Adonijah.

9 Adonijah went to the Stone of Zoheleth* near the spring of En-rogel, where he sacrificed sheep, cattle, and fattened calves. He invited all his brothers—the other sons of King David—and all the royal officials of Judah. 10 But he did not invite Nathan the prophet or Benaiah or the king's bodyguard or his brother Solomon.

11 Then Nathan went to Bathsheba, Solomon's mother, and asked her, "Haven't you heard that Haggith's son, Adonijah, has made himself king, and our lord David doesn't even know about it? 12 If you want to save your own life and the life of your son Solomon, follow my advice. 13 Go at once to King David and say to him, 'My lord the king, didn't you make a vow and say to me, "Your son Solomon will surely be the next king and will sit on my throne"? Why then has Adonijah become king?' 14 And while you are still talking with him, I will come and confirm everything you have said."

15 So Bathsheba went into the king's bedroom. (He was very old now, and Abishag was taking care of him.) 16 Bathsheba bowed down before the king.

"What can I do for you?" he asked her.

17 She replied, "My lord, you made a vow before the LORD your God when you said to me, 'Your son Solomon will surely be the next king and will sit on my throne.' 18 But instead, Adonijah has made himself king, and my lord the king does not even know about it. 19 He has sacrificed many cattle, fattened calves, and sheep, and he has invited all the king's sons to attend the celebration. He also invited Abiathar the priest and Joab, the commander of the army. But he did not invite your servant Solomon. 20 And now, my lord the king, all Israel is waiting for you to announce who will become king after you. 21 If you do not act, my son Solomon and I will be treated as criminals as soon as my lord the king has died."

1:9 Or *to the Serpent's Stone;* Greek version supports reading *Zoheleth* as a proper name.

1:1—11:25 United Kingdom

1:1—2:12 David's Final Days. 1:2: *Virgin*: Hebrew, *betula* ("virgin" or "maid") may refer to someone who has not experienced sexual intercourse (Gen 24:16; Num 31:18) or it may mean "young (unmarried) girl." **3–4:** *Abishag*: Retained to comfort the aged king in his last days. As is seen later in the account, Abishag retains her virginity, since Adonijah attempts to persuade Bathsheba to ask Solomon to give Abishag to Adonijah in marriage (2:13–25). **4–5:** David's abstinence with Abishag may suggest impotence, not only in bed but also as king, leading Adonijah to make a move for the throne. **5–7:** It was a natural assumption that upon David's death Adonijah would become king, since he was the eldest son. He quickly set about gaining supporters. In addition, Adonijah was able to demonstrate military strength, with chariots, horses, and *fifty men to run in front of him*, the trappings of kingship. Their support of Adonijah was crucial if he was to become king. **9:** Adonijah's jubilant group of supporters proceeded to the stone Zoheleth near En-rogel in order to perform a coronation ceremony that would establish him as legitimate king. **11–21:** Nathan and Bathsheba work against Adonijah. It was imperative for David to act quickly and publicly proclaim Solomon his heir. Otherwise, upon David's death there would have been chaos in the kingdom and a divided monarchy would have resulted. These actions seem to represent the culmination of Nathan and Bathsheba's political aspirations. **13, 17:** One may question the accuracy of Bathsheba and Nathan's assertion that Solomon was already heir to the throne. Was this a legitimate promise that David made, or were Bathsheba and Nathan using David's weakened and con-

[22]While she was still speaking with the king,
Nathan the prophet arrived. [23]The king's officials told him, "Nathan the prophet is here to see
you."

Nathan went in and bowed before the king
with his face to the ground. [24]Nathan asked,
"My lord the king, have you decided that Adonijah will be the next king and that he will sit on
your throne? [25]Today he has sacrificed many
cattle, fattened calves, and sheep, and he has invited all the king's sons to attend the celebration.
He also invited the commanders of the army
and Abiathar the priest. They are feasting and
drinking with him and shouting, 'Long live King
Adonijah!' [26]But he did not invite me or Zadok
the priest or Benaiah or your servant Solomon.
[27]Has my lord the king really done this without
letting any of his officials know who should be
the next king?"

David Makes Solomon King

[28]King David responded, "Call Bathsheba!"
So she came back in and stood before the king.
[29]And the king repeated his vow: "As surely as
the LORD lives, who has rescued me from every
danger, [30]your son Solomon will be the next king
and will sit on my throne this very day, just as
I vowed to you before the LORD, the God of Israel."

[31]Then Bathsheba bowed down with her face
to the ground before the king and exclaimed,
"May my lord King David live forever!"

[32]Then King David ordered, "Call Zadok the
priest, Nathan the prophet, and Benaiah son of
Jehoiada." When they came into the king's presence, [33]the king said to them, "Take Solomon
and my officials down to Gihon Spring. Solomon
is to ride on my own mule. [34]There Zadok the
priest and Nathan the prophet are to anoint him
king over Israel. Blow the ram's horn and shout,
'Long live King Solomon!' [35]Then escort him
back here, and he will sit on my throne. He will
succeed me as king, for I have appointed him to
be ruler over Israel and Judah."

[36]"Amen!" Benaiah son of Jehoiada replied.
"May the LORD, the God of my lord the king,
decree that it happen. [37]And may the LORD be
with Solomon as he has been with you, my lord
the king, and may he make Solomon's reign even
greater than yours!"

[38]So Zadok the priest, Nathan the prophet,
Benaiah son of Jehoiada, and the king's bodyguard* took Solomon down to Gihon Spring,
with Solomon riding on King David's own mule.
[39]There Zadok the priest took the flask of olive
oil from the sacred tent and anointed Solomon
with the oil. Then they sounded the ram's horn
and all the people shouted, "Long live King Solomon!" [40]And all the people followed Solomon
into Jerusalem, playing flutes and shouting for
joy. The celebration was so joyous and noisy that
the earth shook with the sound.

[41]Adonijah and his guests heard the celebrating and shouting just as they were finishing
their banquet. When Joab heard the sound of the
ram's horn, he asked, "What's going on? Why is
the city in such an uproar?"

[42]And while he was still speaking, Jonathan
son of Abiathar the priest arrived. "Come in,"
Adonijah said to him, "for you are a good man.
You must have good news."

[43]"Not at all!" Jonathan replied. "Our lord

1:38 Hebrew *the Kerethites and Pelethites;* also in 1:44.

fused state for their political gain? Upon Solomon's accession to the throne, Bathsheba would become queen mother, an important political office. **28–48:** Solomon's accession is sometimes said to mark a departure from charismatic to hereditary kingship in Israel. Charismatic kingship describes the reign of a leader anointed by God regardless of heredity or merit to whom is given special power, such as Solomon's wisdom; the status of such a ruler is further made manifest in his or her gaining support and control of the army. While the king was the political, military, and religious leader of the people, God was ultimately in control—of Israel as a whole and of selecting the ruler. With the appointments of Saul and David, that control is evident. The accession of Solomon, however, marks a transition; Solomon becomes king not only because he was chosen by God but also because of his heredity. From this point on, kings will ascend to the throne based on heredity or military might. **32–40:** Solomon's appointment and anointment were different from Adonijah's self-coronation in that they were conducted with the full support of David and his court. **33:** *Gihon Spring*: An established sacred spring in Jerusalem and the site where the Ark of the Covenant was sheltered. Purification by water has an important significance in the ancient world. **38:** Solomon rode the royal mount. **39:** The act of anointing was an ancient religious rite common among the people of Israel, Canaan, and Egypt. It was considered to confer grace and symbolized that the Spirit of God had taken hold of the recipient (cf. 1 Sam 10:10). Solomon was considered the anointed of the LORD (cf. 1 Sam 24:7, 11; 26:9, 11, 16), having been officially installed as the divinely appointed king of Israel. **39–40:** Solomon's legitimate succession was confirmed through blow-

King David has just declared Solomon king!
44 The king sent him down to Gihon Spring with
Zadok the priest, Nathan the prophet, and Benaiah son of Jehoiada, protected by the king's
bodyguard. They had him ride on the king's own
mule, 45 and Zadok and Nathan have anointed
him at Gihon Spring as the new king. They have
just returned, and the whole city is celebrating
and rejoicing. That's what all the noise is about.
46 What's more, Solomon is now sitting on the
royal throne as king. 47 And all the royal officials
have gone to King David and congratulated him,
saying, 'May your God make Solomon's fame
even greater than your own, and may Solomon's
reign be even greater than yours!' Then the king
bowed his head in worship as he lay in his bed,
48 and he said, 'Praise the LORD, the God of Israel,
who today has chosen a successor to sit on my
throne while I am still alive to see it.'"

49 Then all of Adonijah's guests jumped up in
panic from the banquet table and quickly scattered. 50 Adonijah was afraid of Solomon, so he
rushed to the sacred tent and grabbed on to the
horns of the altar. 51 Word soon reached Solomon
that Adonijah had seized the horns of the altar in
fear, and that he was pleading, "Let King Solomon swear today that he will not kill me!"

52 Solomon replied, "If he proves himself to
be loyal, not a hair on his head will be touched.
But if he makes trouble, he will die." 53 So King
Solomon summoned Adonijah, and they brought
him down from the altar. He came and bowed respectfully before King Solomon, who dismissed
him, saying, "Go on home."

David's Final Instructions to Solomon

2 As the time of King David's death approached, he gave this charge to his son
Solomon:

2 "I am going where everyone on earth must
someday go. Take courage and be a man. 3 Observe the requirements of the LORD your God,
and follow all his ways. Keep the decrees, commands, regulations, and laws written in the Law
of Moses so that you will be successful in all you
do and wherever you go. 4 If you do this, then the
LORD will keep the promise he made to me. He
told me, 'If your descendants live as they should
and follow me faithfully with all their heart and
soul, one of them will always sit on the throne
of Israel.'

5 "And there is something else. You know
what Joab son of Zeruiah did to me when he
murdered my two army commanders, Abner son
of Ner and Amasa son of Jether. He pretended
that it was an act of war, but it was done in a
time of peace,* staining his belt and sandals with
innocent blood.* 6 Do with him what you think
best, but don't let him grow old and go to his
grave in peace.*

7 "Be kind to the sons of Barzillai of Gilead.
Make them permanent guests at your table,
for they took care of me when I fled from your
brother Absalom.

8 "And remember Shimei son of Gera, the man
from Bahurim in Benjamin. He cursed me with
a terrible curse as I was fleeing to Mahanaim.
When he came down to meet me at the Jordan
River, I swore by the LORD that I would not kill
him. 9 But that oath does not make him innocent.
You are a wise man, and you will know how to
arrange a bloody death for him.*"

10 Then David died and was buried with his ancestors in the City of David. 11 David had reigned
over Israel for forty years, seven of them in Hebron and thirty-three in Jerusalem. 12 Solomon
became king and sat on the throne of David his
father, and his kingdom was firmly established.

Solomon Establishes His Rule

13 One day Adonijah, whose mother was Haggith, came to see Bathsheba, Solomon's mother.
"Have you come with peaceful intentions?" she
asked him.

"Yes," he said, "I come in peace. 14 In fact, I
have a favor to ask of you."

2:5a Or *He murdered them during a time of peace as revenge for deaths they had caused in time of war.* **2:5b** As in some Greek and Old Latin manuscripts; Hebrew reads *with the blood of war.* **2:6** Hebrew *don't let his white head go down to Sheol in peace.* **2:9** Hebrew *how to bring his white head down to Sheol in blood.*

---

ing trumpets and shouting *"Long live King Solomon!"* **41–53:** Adonijah was regarded as an enemy of Solomon's court. **2:1–4:** David's instructions include blessings and curses: Follow in the ways of God and you will be blessed; stray from them and you will be cursed. This applied not only to Solomon but also to the nation as a whole. Solomon represented the people and was responsible for the nation's moral character. **5–9:** David's orders justify Solomon's actions in the rest of the chapter. But Solomon's real motivations are political.

2:13—11:25 Solomon's Rule. 2:13–17: Adonijah's request for Abishag represents a significant political move on his part, as he again attempts to acquire power in the kingdom. **13:** Now that Solomon was

"What is it?" she asked.

15 He replied, "As you know, the kingdom was rightfully mine; all Israel wanted me to be the next king. But the tables were turned, and the kingdom went to my brother instead; for that is the way the LORD wanted it. 16 So now I have just one favor to ask of you. Please don't turn me down."

"What is it?" she asked.

17 He replied, "Speak to King Solomon on my behalf, for I know he will do anything you request. Ask him to let me marry Abishag, the girl from Shunem."

18 "All right," Bathsheba replied. "I will speak to the king for you."

19 So Bathsheba went to King Solomon to speak on Adonijah's behalf. The king rose from his throne to meet her, and he bowed down before her. When he sat down on his throne again, the king ordered that a throne be brought for his mother, and she sat at his right hand.

20 "I have one small request to make of you," she said. "I hope you won't turn me down."

"What is it, my mother?" he asked. "You know I won't refuse you."

21 "Then let your brother Adonijah marry Abishag, the girl from Shunem," she replied.

22 "How can you possibly ask me to give Abishag to Adonijah?" King Solomon demanded. "You might as well ask me to give him the kingdom! You know that he is my older brother, and that he has Abiathar the priest and Joab son of Zeruiah on his side."

23 Then King Solomon made a vow before the LORD: "May God strike me and even kill me if Adonijah has not sealed his fate with this request. 24 The LORD has confirmed me and placed me on the throne of my father, David; he has established my dynasty as he promised. So as surely as the LORD lives, Adonijah will die this very day!" 25 So King Solomon ordered Benaiah son of Jehoiada to execute him, and Adonijah was put to death.

26 Then the king said to Abiathar the priest, "Go back to your home in Anathoth. You deserve to die, but I will not kill you now, because you carried the Ark of the Sovereign LORD for David my father and you shared all his hardships." 27 So Solomon deposed Abiathar from his position as priest of the LORD, thereby fulfilling the prophecy the LORD had given at Shiloh concerning the descendants of Eli.

28 Joab had not joined Absalom's earlier rebellion, but he had joined Adonijah's rebellion. So when Joab heard about Adonijah's death, he ran to the sacred tent of the LORD and grabbed on to the horns of the altar. 29 When this was reported to King Solomon, he sent Benaiah son of Jehoiada to execute him.

30 Benaiah went to the sacred tent of the LORD and said to Joab, "The king orders you to come out!"

But Joab answered, "No, I will die here."

So Benaiah returned to the king and told him what Joab had said.

31 "Do as he said," the king replied. "Kill him there beside the altar and bury him. This will remove the guilt of Joab's senseless murders from me and from my father's family. 32 The LORD will repay him* for the murders of two men who were more righteous and better than he. For my father knew nothing about the deaths of Abner son of Ner, commander of the army of Israel, and of Amasa son of Jether, commander of the army of Judah. 33 May their blood be on Joab and his descendants forever, and may the LORD grant peace forever to David, his descendants, his dynasty, and his throne."

34 So Benaiah son of Jehoiada returned to the sacred tent and killed Joab, and he was buried at his home in the wilderness. 35 Then the king appointed Benaiah to command the army in place of Joab, and he installed Zadok the priest to take the place of Abiathar.

36 The king then sent for Shimei and told him, "Build a house here in Jerusalem and live there. But don't step outside the city to go anywhere else. 37 On the day you so much as cross the Kidron Valley, you will surely die; and your blood will be on your own head."

2:32 Hebrew *will return his blood on his own head.*

---

king, Bathsheba enjoyed a great deal of power. **22:** Even though Abishag was not David's wife or concubine, she had been connected to him in a significant way. This association was quite strong, as seen in Solomon's response to Bathsheba. If Adonijah had married Abishag, it would have been equivalent to marrying a newly widowed queen mother or wife of the king. Moreover, if the couple were to have children, the oldest male would pose a threat to Solomon and any heirs or appointed successors of his. **23–25:** Adonijah's request gave Solomon the excuse he needed to put his half brother to death and permanently remove him as a threat to the throne. **26–35:** Solomon eliminates Adonijah's remaining supporters. **36–46:** Solomon may have confined Shimei to Jerusalem to prevent him from causing any trouble in his home tribe of Benjamin (also Saul's tribe).

[38]Shimei replied, "Your sentence is fair; I will do whatever my lord the king commands." So Shimei lived in Jerusalem for a long time.

[39]But three years later two of Shimei's slaves ran away to King Achish son of Maacah of Gath. When Shimei learned where they were, [40]he saddled his donkey and went to Gath to search for them. When he found them, he brought them back to Jerusalem.

[41]Solomon heard that Shimei had left Jerusalem and had gone to Gath and returned. [42]So the king sent for Shimei and demanded, "Didn't I make you swear by the LORD and warn you not to go anywhere else or you would surely die? And you replied, 'The sentence is fair; I will do as you say.' [43]Then why haven't you kept your oath to the LORD and obeyed my command?"

[44]The king also said to Shimei, "You certainly remember all the wicked things you did to my father, David. May the LORD now bring that evil on your own head. [45]But may I, King Solomon, receive the LORD's blessings, and may one of David's descendants always sit on this throne in the presence of the LORD." [46]Then, at the king's command, Benaiah son of Jehoiada took Shimei outside and killed him.

So the kingdom was now firmly in Solomon's grip.

Solomon Asks for Wisdom

3 Solomon made an alliance with Pharaoh, the king of Egypt, and married one of his daughters. He brought her to live in the City of David until he could finish building his palace and the Temple of the LORD and the wall around the city. [2]At that time the people of Israel sacrificed their offerings at local places of worship, for a temple honoring the name of the LORD had not yet been built.

[3]Solomon loved the LORD and followed all the decrees of his father, David, except that Solomon, too, offered sacrifices and burned incense at the local places of worship. [4]The most important of these places of worship was at Gibeon, so the king went there and sacrificed 1,000 burnt offerings. [5]That night the LORD appeared to Solomon in a dream, and God said, "What do you want? Ask, and I will give it to you!"

[6]Solomon replied, "You showed faithful love to your servant my father, David, because he was honest and true and faithful to you. And you have continued your faithful love to him today by giving him a son to sit on his throne.

[7]"Now, O LORD my God, you have made me king instead of my father, David, but I am like a little child who doesn't know his way around. [8]And here I am in the midst of your own chosen people, a nation so great and numerous they cannot be counted! [9]Give me an understanding heart so that I can govern your people well and know the difference between right and wrong. For who by himself is able to govern this great people of yours?"

[10]The Lord was pleased that Solomon had asked for wisdom. [11]So God replied, "Because you have asked for wisdom in governing my people with justice and have not asked for a long life or wealth or the death of your enemies—[12]I will give you what you asked for! I will give you a wise and understanding heart such as no one else has had or ever will have! [13]And I will also give you what you did not ask for—riches and fame! No other king in all the world will be compared to you for the rest of your life! [14]And if you follow me and obey my decrees and my commands as your father, David, did, I will give you a long life."

[15]Then Solomon woke up and realized it had been a dream. He returned to Jerusalem and stood before the Ark of the Lord's Covenant, where he sacrificed burnt offerings and peace offerings. Then he invited all his officials to a great banquet.

3:1—4:34 Solomon's Government. 3:1: It was unusual for a pharaoh to allow a daughter to marry outside Egypt. According to the ordinances put forth in Deuteronomy (Deut 7:1–5), it was also forbidden for Israelites to marry foreigners. Politically, however, Solomon was behaving astutely: Israel would not be attacked by Egypt, since the pharaoh would not want to risk his daughter's safety. Nor would Solomon want to anger his new father-in-law by attacking Egypt. *City of David*: Jerusalem was originally the Jebusite "stronghold of Zion." Early in his reign David captured and occupied this fortification, renaming it the City of David (cf. 2 Sam 5:7, 9; 1 Chr 11:4–7; 8:11). Seven years after conquering this site, David moved his capital there from Hebron. During David's reign this city became the seat of the royal house. **2:** In the ancient world it had long been established that gods lived on mountaintops, because such places were beautiful, grandiose, mysterious, and close to heaven—the perfect place for a god to dwell. Therefore ancient worshipers constructed altars (Heb., lit., "high places") and temples on hilltops and mountain summits to better communicate with their deity. Until the Temple was complete, people worshiped the LORD and offered sacrifices at established sacred high places. Eventually, the Temple would become the only official site for veneration of the LORD. **4:** Solomon offered sacrifices at Gibeon, since it was the most im-

Solomon Judges Wisely

16 Some time later two prostitutes came to the king to have an argument settled. 17 "Please, my lord," one of them began, "this woman and I live in the same house. I gave birth to a baby while she was with me in the house. 18 Three days later this woman also had a baby. We were alone; there were only two of us in the house.

19 "But her baby died during the night when she rolled over on it. 20 Then she got up in the night and took my son from beside me while I was asleep. She laid her dead child in my arms and took mine to sleep beside her. 21 And in the morning when I tried to nurse my son, he was dead! But when I looked more closely in the morning light, I saw that it wasn't my son at all."

22 Then the other woman interrupted, "It certainly was your son, and the living child is mine."

"No," the first woman said, "the living child is mine, and the dead one is yours." And so they argued back and forth before the king.

23 Then the king said, "Let's get the facts straight. Both of you claim the living child is yours, and each says that the dead one belongs to the other. 24 All right, bring me a sword." So a sword was brought to the king.

25 Then he said, "Cut the living child in two, and give half to one woman and half to the other!"

26 Then the woman who was the real mother of the living child, and who loved him very much, cried out, "Oh no, my lord! Give her the child—please do not kill him!"

But the other woman said, "All right, he will be neither yours nor mine; divide him between us!"

27 Then the king said, "Do not kill the child, but give him to the woman who wants him to live, for she is his mother!"

28 When all Israel heard the king's decision, the people were in awe of the king, for they saw the wisdom God had given him for rendering justice.

Solomon's Officials and Governors

4 King Solomon now ruled over all Israel, 2 and these were his high officials:

Azariah son of Zadok was the priest.

3 Elihoreph and Ahijah, the sons of Shisha, were court secretaries.

Jehoshaphat son of Ahilud was the royal historian.

4 Benaiah son of Jehoiada was commander of the army.

Zadok and Abiathar were priests.

5 Azariah son of Nathan was in charge of the district governors.

Zabud son of Nathan, a priest, was a trusted adviser to the king.

6 Ahishar was manager of the palace property.

Adoniram son of Abda was in charge of the labor force.

7 Solomon also had twelve district governors who were over all Israel. They were responsible for providing food for the king's household. Each of them arranged provisions for one month of the year. 8 These are the names of the twelve governors:

Ben-hur, in the hill country of Ephraim.

9 Ben-deker, in Makaz, Shaalbim, Beth-shemesh, and Elon-bethhanan.

10 Ben-hesed, in Arubboth, including Socoh and all the land of Hepher.

11 Ben-abinadab, in all of Naphoth-dor.* (He was married to Taphath, one of Solomon's daughters.)

12 Baana son of Ahilud, in Taanach and Megiddo, all of Beth-shan* near Zarethan below Jezreel, and all the territory from Beth-shan to Abel-meholah and over to Jokmeam.

13 Ben-geber, in Ramoth-gilead, including the Towns of Jair (named for Jair of the tribe of Manasseh*) in Gilead, and in the Argob region of Bashan, including sixty large fortified towns with bronze bars on their gates.

14 Ahinadab son of Iddo, in Mahanaim.

4:11 Hebrew *Naphath-dor,* a variant spelling of Naphoth-dor. **4:12** Hebrew *Beth-shean,* a variant spelling of Beth-shan; also in 4:12b. **4:13** Hebrew *Jair son of Manasseh;* compare 1 Chr 2:22.

portant altar. **16–28:** The story of the two prostitutes was not meant to test the wisdom and judgment of Solomon but rather to establish his abilities. **16:** The two women were able to represent themselves in the highest court of law, before the king. This means they did not need male representation in the legal system, and they enjoyed rights similar to those of men under the law. A high opinion of a mother's care for a child is shown here. **4:1–6:** When a king first comes to power, new officials will be named. Some of these employees were sons of people from David's administration. This suggests continuity in administration and an expectation of loyalty on the part of Solomon and employee alike. **7–21:** Each of the twelve districts was responsible for supplying rations for one month a year to Solomon and his administration. In addition, neighboring nations, such as the Philistines and Egypt, brought tribute (i.e., gifts), as did people who

15 Ahimaaz, in Naphtali. (He was married to Basemath, another of Solomon's daughters.)
16 Baana son of Hushai, in Asher and in Aloth.
17 Jehoshaphat son of Paruah, in Issachar.
18 Shimei son of Ela, in Benjamin.
19 Geber son of Uri, in the land of Gilead,* including the territories of King Sihon of the Amorites and King Og of Bashan.

There was also one governor over the land of Judah.*

Solomon's Prosperity and Wisdom

20 The people of Judah and Israel were as numerous as the sand on the seashore. They were very contented, with plenty to eat and drink. 21 *Solomon ruled over all the kingdoms from the Euphrates River* in the north to the land of the Philistines and the border of Egypt in the south. The conquered peoples of those lands sent tribute money to Solomon and continued to serve him throughout his lifetime.

22 The daily food requirements for Solomon's palace were 150 bushels of choice flour and 300 bushels of meal*; 23 also 10 oxen from the fattening pens, 20 pasture-fed cattle, 100 sheep or goats, as well as deer, gazelles, roe deer, and choice poultry.*

24 Solomon's dominion extended over all the kingdoms west of the Euphrates River, from Tiphsah to Gaza. And there was peace on all his borders. 25 During the lifetime of Solomon, all of Judah and Israel lived in peace and safety. And from Dan in the north to Beersheba in the south, each family had its own home and garden.*

26 Solomon had 4,000* stalls for his chariot horses, and he had 12,000 horses.*

27 The district governors faithfully provided food for King Solomon and his court; each made sure nothing was lacking during the month assigned to him. 28 They also brought the necessary barley and straw for the royal horses in the stables.

29 God gave Solomon very great wisdom and understanding, and knowledge as vast as the sands of the seashore. 30 In fact, his wisdom exceeded that of all the wise men of the East and the wise men of Egypt. 31 He was wiser than anyone else, including Ethan the Ezrahite and the sons of Mahol—Heman, Calcol, and Darda. His fame spread throughout all the surrounding nations. 32 He composed some 3,000 proverbs and wrote 1,005 songs. 33 He could speak with authority about all kinds of plants, from the great cedar of Lebanon to the tiny hyssop that grows from cracks in a wall. He could also speak about animals, birds, small creatures, and fish. 34 And kings from every nation sent their ambassadors to listen to the wisdom of Solomon.

Preparations for Building the Temple

5 1 *King Hiram of Tyre had always been a loyal friend of David. When Hiram learned that David's son Solomon was the new king of Israel, he sent ambassadors to congratulate him.

2 Then Solomon sent this message back to Hiram:

3 "You know that my father, David, was not able to build a Temple to honor the name of the LORD his God because of the many wars waged against him by surrounding nations. He could not build until the LORD gave him victory over all his enemies. 4 But now the LORD my God has given me peace on every side; I have no enemies, and all is well. 5 So I am planning to build a Temple to honor the name of the LORD my God, just as he had instructed my father, David. For the LORD told him, 'Your son, whom I will place on your throne, will build the Temple to honor my name.'

6 "Therefore, please command that cedars from Lebanon be cut for me. Let my men work alongside yours, and I will pay your men whatever wages you ask. As you know, there is no one among us who can cut timber like you Sidonians!"

7 When Hiram received Solomon's message, he was very pleased and said, "Praise the LORD today for giving David a wise son to be king of the great nation of Israel." 8 Then he sent this reply to Solomon:

4:19a Greek version reads *of Gad;* compare 4:13. **4:19b** As in some Greek manuscripts; Hebrew lacks *of Judah.* The meaning of the Hebrew is uncertain. **4:21a** Verses 4:21-34 are numbered 5:1-14 in Hebrew text. **4:21b** Hebrew *the river;* also in 4:24. **4:22** Hebrew *30 cors* [5.5 kiloliters] *of choice flour and 60 cors* [11 kiloliters] *of meal.* **4:23** Or *and fattened geese.* **4:25** Hebrew *each family lived under its own grapevine and under its own fig tree.* **4:26a** As in some Greek manuscripts (see also 2 Chr 9:25); Hebrew reads *40,000.* **4:26b** Or *12,000 charioteers.* **5:1** Verses 5:1-18 are numbered 5:15-32 in Hebrew text.

came to visit the king. **20–34:** The extent, prosperity, and contentedness of Solomon's kingdom may be exaggerated and idealized.

5:1—7:51 Building the Temple. David could never build a temple because he was constantly at war. But Solomon was ruling in peace, and he was ready

"I have received your message, and I will
supply all the cedar and cypress timber you
need. 9 My servants will bring the logs from
the Lebanon mountains to the Mediterranean
Sea* and make them into rafts and float them
along the coast to whatever place you choose.
Then we will break the rafts apart so you
can carry the logs away. You can pay me by
supplying me with food for my household."

10 So Hiram supplied as much cedar and cypress
timber as Solomon desired. 11 In return, Solomon
sent him an annual payment of 100,000 bushels*
of wheat for his household and 110,000 gallons*
of pure olive oil. 12 So the LORD gave wisdom to
Solomon, just as he had promised. And Hiram
and Solomon made a formal alliance of peace.

13 Then King Solomon conscripted a labor
force of 30,000 men from all Israel. 14 He sent
them to Lebanon in shifts, 10,000 every month,
so that each man would be one month in Lebanon and two months at home. Adoniram was in
charge of this labor force. 15 Solomon also had
70,000 common laborers, 80,000 quarry workers
in the hill country, 16 and 3,600* foremen to supervise the work. 17 At the king's command, they
quarried large blocks of high-quality stone and
shaped them to make the foundation of the Temple. 18 Men from the city of Gebal helped Solomon's and Hiram's builders prepare the timber
and stone for the Temple.

Solomon Builds the Temple

6 It was in midspring, in the month of Ziv,*
during the fourth year of Solomon's reign,
that he began to construct the Temple of
the LORD. This was 480 years after the people of
Israel were rescued from their slavery in the land
of Egypt.

2 The Temple that King Solomon built for the
LORD was 90 feet long, 30 feet wide, and 45 feet
high.* 3 The entry room at the front of the Temple
was 30 feet* wide, running across the entire width
of the Temple. It projected outward 15 feet* from
the front of the Temple. 4 Solomon also made narrow recessed windows throughout the Temple.

5 He built a complex of rooms against the
outer walls of the Temple, all the way around the
sides and rear of the building. 6 The complex was
three stories high, the bottom floor being 7½ feet
wide, the second floor 9 feet wide, and the top
floor 10½ feet wide.* The rooms were connected
to the walls of the Temple by beams resting on
ledges built out from the wall. So the beams were
not inserted into the walls themselves.

7 The stones used in the construction of the
Temple were finished at the quarry, so there was
no sound of hammer, ax, or any other iron tool
at the building site.

8 The entrance to the bottom floor* was on
the south side of the Temple. There were winding stairs going up to the second floor, and another flight of stairs between the second and third
floors. 9 After completing the Temple structure,
Solomon put in a ceiling made of cedar beams
and planks. 10 As already stated, he built a complex of rooms on three sides of the building, attached to the Temple walls by cedar timbers. Each
story of the complex was 7½ feet* high.

11 Then the LORD gave this message to Solomon: 12 "Concerning this Temple you are building, if you keep all my decrees and regulations
and obey all my commands, I will fulfill through
you the promise I made to your father, David.
13 I will live among the Israelites and will never
abandon my people Israel."

The Temple's Interior

14 So Solomon finished building the Temple.
15 The entire inside, from floor to ceiling, was

5:9 Hebrew *the sea.* **5:11a** Hebrew *20,000 cors* [3,640 kiloliters]. **5:11b** As in Greek version, which reads *20,000 baths* [420 kiloliters] (see also 2 Chr 2:10); Hebrew reads *20 cors,* about 800 gallons or 3.6 kiloliters in volume. **5:16** As in some Greek manuscripts (see also 2 Chr 2:2, 18); Hebrew reads *3,300.* **6:1** Hebrew *It was in the month of Ziv, which is the second month.* This month of the ancient Hebrew lunar calendar usually occurs within the months of April and May. **6:2** Hebrew *60 cubits* [27.6 meters] *long, 20 cubits* [9.2 meters] *wide, and 30 cubits* [13.8 meters] *high.* **6:3a** Hebrew *20 cubits* [9.2 meters]; also in 6:16, 20. **6:3b** Hebrew *10 cubits* [4.6 meters]. **6:6** Hebrew *the bottom floor being 5 cubits* [2.3 meters] *wide, the second floor 6 cubits* [2.8 meters] *wide, and the top floor 7 cubits* [3.2 meters] *wide.* **6:8** As in Greek version; Hebrew reads *middle floor.* **6:10** Hebrew *5 cubits* [2.3 meters].

to undertake this daunting task. **5:13–18:** Solomon conscripted thousands of men from all over Israel and beyond to work on the Temple. The use of conscripted or forced labor was common practice in the ancient Near East. Slaves of foreign descent were usually war captives from foreign lands and conquered native inhabitants (such as the Canaanites). Solomon's heavy hand took its toll on this labor force, physically and spiritually; ultimately it became a major factor leading to the division of the kingdom (12:4). **6:1—7:51:** Solomon's construction of the Temple, royal palace, and the city plan imitated those of Neo-Hittite and Aramean royal cities. Solomon's intention was to create the Temple under the Davidic dynasty, establish a strong bond between the Temple and royal line, and centralize

paneled with wood. He paneled the walls and
ceilings with cedar, and he used planks of cypress for the floors. [16]He partitioned off an inner
sanctuary—the Most Holy Place—at the far end
of the Temple. It was 30 feet deep and was paneled with cedar from floor to ceiling. [17]The main
room of the Temple, outside the Most Holy Place,
was 60 feet* long. [18]Cedar paneling completely
covered the stone walls throughout the Temple,
and the paneling was decorated with carvings of
gourds and open flowers.

[19]He prepared the inner sanctuary at the far
end of the Temple, where the Ark of the LORD's
Covenant would be placed. [20]This inner sanctuary was 30 feet long, 30 feet wide, and 30 feet
high. He overlaid the inside with solid gold. He
also overlaid the altar made of cedar.* [21]Then
Solomon overlaid the rest of the Temple's interior with solid gold, and he made gold chains
to protect the entrance* to the Most Holy Place.
[22]So he finished overlaying the entire Temple
with gold, including the altar that belonged to
the Most Holy Place.

[23]He made two cherubim of wild olive* wood,
each 15 feet* tall, and placed them in the inner
sanctuary. [24]The wingspan of each of the cherubim was 15 feet, each wing being 7½ feet* long.
[25]The two cherubim were identical in shape and
size; [26]each was 15 feet tall. [27]He placed them
side by side in the inner sanctuary of the Temple.
Their outspread wings reached from wall to wall,
while their inner wings touched at the center of
the room. [28]He overlaid the two cherubim with
gold.

[29]He decorated all the walls of the inner sanctuary and the main room with carvings of cherubim, palm trees, and open flowers. [30]He overlaid
the floor in both rooms with gold.

[31]For the entrance to the inner sanctuary,
he made double doors of wild olive wood with
five-sided doorposts.* [32]These double doors were
decorated with carvings of cherubim, palm trees,
and open flowers. The doors, including the decorations of cherubim and palm trees, were overlaid with gold.

[33]Then he made four-sided doorposts of
wild olive wood for the entrance to the Temple.
[34]There were two folding doors of cypress wood,
and each door was hinged to fold back upon itself. [35]These doors were decorated with carvings
of cherubim, palm trees, and open flowers—all
overlaid evenly with gold.

[36]The walls of the inner courtyard were built
so that there was one layer of cedar beams between every three layers of finished stone.

[37]The foundation of the LORD's Temple was
laid in midspring, in the month of Ziv,* during
the fourth year of Solomon's reign. [38]The entire
building was completed in every detail by midautumn, in the month of Bul,* during the eleventh year of his reign. So it took seven years to
build the Temple.

Solomon Builds His Palace

7 Solomon also built a palace for himself, and
it took him thirteen years to complete the
construction.

[2]One of Solomon's buildings was called the
Palace of the Forest of Lebanon. It was 150 feet
long, 75 feet wide, and 45 feet high.* There were
four rows of cedar pillars, and great cedar beams
rested on the pillars. [3]The hall had a cedar roof.
Above the beams on the pillars were forty-five
side rooms,* arranged in three tiers of fifteen
each. [4]On each end of the long hall were three
rows of windows facing each other. [5]All the door-

6:17 Hebrew *40 cubits* [18.4 meters]. **6:20** Or *overlaid the altar with cedar.* The meaning of the Hebrew is uncertain. **6:21** Or *to draw curtains across.* The meaning of the Hebrew is uncertain. **6:23a** Or *pine;* Hebrew reads *oil tree;* also in 6:31, 33. **6:23b** Hebrew *10 cubits* [4.6 meters]; also in 6:24, 25. **6:24** Hebrew *5 cubits* [2.3 meters]. **6:31** The meaning of the Hebrew is uncertain. **6:37** Hebrew *was laid in the month of Ziv.* This month of the ancient Hebrew lunar calendar usually occurs within the months of April and May. **6:38** Hebrew *by the month of Bul, which is the eighth month.* This month of the ancient Hebrew lunar calendar usually occurs within the months of October and November. **7:2** Hebrew *100 cubits* [46 meters] *long, 50 cubits* [23 meters] *wide, and 30 cubits* [13.5 meters] *high.* **7:3** Or *45 rafters,* or *45 beams,* or *45 pillars.* The architectural details in 7:2-6 can be interpreted in many different ways.

---

the state religion. **6:19–31:** The Most Holy Place was located at the innermost end of the complex. It was a perfect cube; there were no windows and no light wells in the ceiling: Light could not penetrate, and nobody could look in. The Ark of the Covenant was housed in the Most Holy Place. **29, 32, 35:** Solomon included a great deal of artwork in the Temple. It has generally been assumed that the Israelites did not create artwork for fear of violating the second commandment (Exod 20:4), but Solomon's designs illustrate his understanding of this commandment: Artwork in itself is not bad. The problem arises when artistic representation is venerated. **7:1:** Solomon's palace was constructed adjacent to the Temple on the Temple Mount. It took longer to complete the palace than the Temple, about thirteen years. It seems that Solomon's concern for his glory had become greater than his concern for the glory of God. **2–12:** His palace was longer and wider than the Temple and very ornate, bespeak-

ways and doorposts* had rectangular frames and
were arranged in sets of three, facing each other.
6 Solomon also built the Hall of Pillars, which
was 75 feet long and 45 feet wide.* There was
a porch in front, along with a canopy supported
by pillars.
7 Solomon also built the throne room, known
as the Hall of Justice, where he sat to hear legal
matters. It was paneled with cedar from floor to
ceiling.* 8 Solomon's living quarters surrounded
a courtyard behind this hall, and they were constructed the same way. He also built similar living quarters for Pharaoh's daughter, whom he
had married.
9 From foundation to eaves, all these buildings were built from huge blocks of high-quality
stone, cut with saws and trimmed to exact measure on all sides. 10 Some of the huge foundation
stones were 15 feet long, and some were 12 feet*
long. 11 The blocks of high-quality stone used in
the walls were also cut to measure, and cedar
beams were also used. 12 The walls of the great
courtyard were built so that there was one layer
of cedar beams between every three layers of finished stone, just like the walls of the inner courtyard of the LORD's Temple with its entry room.

Furnishings for the Temple

13 King Solomon then asked for a man named
Huram* to come from Tyre. 14 He was half Israelite, since his mother was a widow from the tribe
of Naphtali, and his father had been a craftsman
in bronze from Tyre. Huram was extremely
skillful and talented in any work in bronze, and
he came to do all the metal work for King Solomon.
15 Huram cast two bronze pillars, each 27 feet
tall and 18 feet in circumference.* 16 For the tops
of the pillars he cast bronze capitals, each 7½ feet*
tall. 17 Each capital was decorated with seven sets
of latticework and interwoven chains. 18 He also
encircled the latticework with two rows of pomegranates to decorate the capitals over the pillars.
19 The capitals on the columns inside the entry
room were shaped like water lilies, and they were
six feet* tall. 20 The capitals on the two pillars had
200 pomegranates in two rows around them, beside the rounded surface next to the latticework.
21 Huram set the pillars at the entrance of the
Temple, one toward the south and one toward
the north. He named the one on the south Jakin,
and the one on the north Boaz.* 22 The capitals on
the pillars were shaped like water lilies. And so
the work on the pillars was finished.
23 Then Huram cast a great round basin,
15 feet across from rim to rim, called the Sea.
It was 7½ feet deep and about 45 feet in circumference.* 24 It was encircled just below its rim by
two rows of decorative gourds. There were about
six gourds per foot* all the way around, and they
were cast as part of the basin.
25 The Sea was placed on a base of twelve
bronze oxen,* all facing outward. Three faced
north, three faced west, three faced south, and
three faced east, and the Sea rested on them.
26 The walls of the Sea were about three inches*
thick, and its rim flared out like a cup and resembled a water lily blossom. It could hold about
11,000 gallons* of water.
27 Huram also made ten bronze water carts,
each 6 feet long, 6 feet wide, and 4½ feet tall.*
28 They were constructed with side panels braced
with crossbars. 29 Both the panels and the crossbars were decorated with carved lions, oxen, and
cherubim. Above and below the lions and oxen
were wreath decorations. 30 Each of these carts
had four bronze wheels and bronze axles. There
were supporting posts for the bronze basins at
the corners of the carts; these supports were
decorated on each side with carvings of wreaths.
31 The top of each cart had a rounded frame for
the basin. It projected 1½ feet* above the cart's
top like a round pedestal, and its opening was
2¼ feet* across; it was decorated on the outside
with carvings of wreaths. The panels of the carts
were square, not round. 32 Under the panels were
four wheels that were connected to axles that had

7:5 Greek version reads *windows.* **7:6** Hebrew *50 cubits* [23 meters] *long and 30 cubits* [13.8 meters] *wide.* **7:7** As in Syriac version and Latin Vulgate; Hebrew reads *from floor to floor.* **7:10** Hebrew *10 cubits* [4.6 meters] . . . *8 cubits* [3.7 meters]. **7:13** Hebrew *Hiram* (also in 7:40, 45); compare 2 Chr 2:13. This is not the same person mentioned in 5:1. **7:15** Hebrew *18 cubits* [8.3 meters] *tall and 12 cubits* [5.5 meters] *in circumference.* **7:16** Hebrew *5 cubits* [2.3 meters]. **7:19** Hebrew *4 cubits* [1.8 meters]; also in 7:38. **7:21** *Jakin* probably means "he establishes"; *Boaz* probably means "in him is strength." **7:23** Hebrew *10 cubits* [4.6 meters] *across. . . . 5 cubits* [2.3 meters] *deep and 30 cubits* [13.8 meters] *in circumference.* **7:24** Or *20 gourds per meter;* Hebrew reads *10 per cubit.* **7:25** Hebrew *12 oxen;* compare 2 Kgs 16:17, which specifies *bronze oxen.* **7:26a** Hebrew *a handbreadth* [8 centimeters]. **7:26b** Hebrew *2,000 baths* [42 kiloliters]. **7:27** Hebrew *4 cubits* [1.8 meters] *long, 4 cubits wide, and 3 cubits* [1.4 meters] *high.* **7:31a** Hebrew *a cubit* [46 centimeters]. **7:31b** Hebrew *1½ cubits* [69 centimeters]; also in 7:32.

---

ing a marked extravagance. **13–51:** The furnishings were as elaborate as the Temple itself. Most of the commissioned fittings and utensils were used by the priests while performing ceremonies in the Temple. **7:29:** The cherubim were guardians representing the strength and protection of God.

been cast as one unit with the cart. The wheels were 2¼ feet in diameter 33 and were similar to chariot wheels. The axles, spokes, rims, and hubs were all cast from molten bronze.

34 There were handles at each of the four corners of the carts, and these, too, were cast as one unit with the cart. 35 Around the top of each cart was a rim nine inches wide.* The corner supports and side panels were cast as one unit with the cart. 36 Carvings of cherubim, lions, and palm trees decorated the panels and corner supports wherever there was room, and there were wreaths all around. 37 All ten water carts were the same size and were made alike, for each was cast from the same mold.

38 Huram also made ten smaller bronze basins, one for each cart. Each basin was six feet across and could hold 220 gallons* of water. 39 He set five water carts on the south side of the Temple and five on the north side. The great bronze basin called the Sea was placed near the southeast corner of the Temple. 40 He also made the necessary washbasins, shovels, and bowls.

So at last Huram completed everything King Solomon had assigned him to make for the Temple of the LORD:

41 the two pillars;
the two bowl-shaped capitals on top of the pillars;
the two networks of interwoven chains that decorated the capitals;
42 the 400 pomegranates that hung from the chains on the capitals (two rows of pomegranates for each of the chain networks that decorated the capitals on top of the pillars);
43 the ten water carts holding the ten basins;
44 the Sea and the twelve oxen under it;
45 the ash buckets, the shovels, and the bowls.

Huram made all these things of burnished bronze for the Temple of the LORD, just as King Solomon had directed. 46 The king had them cast in clay molds in the Jordan Valley between Succoth and Zarethan. 47 Solomon did not weigh all these things because there were so many; the weight of the bronze could not be measured.

48 Solomon also made all the furnishings of the Temple of the LORD:

the gold altar;
the gold table for the Bread of the Presence;
49 the lampstands of solid gold, five on the south and five on the north, in front of the Most Holy Place;
the flower decorations, lamps, and tongs—all of gold;
50 the small bowls, lamp snuffers, bowls, dishes, and incense burners—all of solid gold;
the doors for the entrances to the Most Holy Place and the main room of the Temple, with their fronts overlaid with gold.

51 So King Solomon finished all his work on the Temple of the LORD. Then he brought all the gifts his father, David, had dedicated—the silver, the gold, and the various articles—and he stored them in the treasuries of the LORD's Temple.

The Ark Brought to the Temple

8 Solomon then summoned to Jerusalem the elders of Israel and all the heads of the tribes—the leaders of the ancestral families of the Israelites. They were to bring the Ark of the LORD's Covenant to the Temple from its location in the City of David, also known as Zion. 2 So all the men of Israel assembled before King Solomon at the annual Festival of Shelters, which is held in early autumn in the month of Ethanim.*

3 When all the elders of Israel arrived, the priests picked up the Ark. 4 The priests and Levites brought up the Ark of the LORD along with

7:35 Hebrew *half a cubit wide* [23 centimeters]. **7:38** Hebrew *40 baths* [840 liters]. **8:2** Hebrew *at the festival in the month Ethanim, which is the seventh month.* The Festival of Shelters began on the fifteenth day of the seventh month of the ancient Hebrew lunar calendar. This day occurred in late September, October, or early November.

8:1–66 Dedicating the Temple. The Tabernacle, or tent of meeting, had previously sufficed as the house of God. When the Israelites, especially their kings, were becoming more sedentary, only the Temple was a suitable and grand enough residence for the LORD. There was a clear understanding that the Temple in no way contained or restricted God, but it was assumed that the LORD could always be found there. This sort of permanence not only symbolized God's presence among his people but also reflected the fact that the Israelites were no longer nomadic. Their days of wandering were over, for they too had found a permanent dwelling place in the land of Israel. The Temple was thus an important cultural feature that served to unify the nation. **1:** The most important item to be set up in the Temple was the Ark of the Covenant, representing God's permanent presence among his people. **2:** *Festival of Shelters*: Also called the Festival of Tabernacles or Booths (*sukkot*) (Lev 23:33–43; Num 29:12–38). **6–11:** The Ark was

the special tent* and all the sacred items that had
been in it. [5]There, before the Ark, King Solomon
and the entire community of Israel sacrificed so
many sheep, goats, and cattle that no one could
keep count!
[6]Then the priests carried the Ark of the
LORD's Covenant into the inner sanctuary of the
Temple—the Most Holy Place—and placed it
beneath the wings of the cherubim. [7]The cherubim spread their wings over the Ark, forming
a canopy over the Ark and its carrying poles.
[8]These poles were so long that their ends could
be seen from the Temple's main room—the Holy
Place—but not from the outside. They are still
there to this day. [9]Nothing was in the Ark except
the two stone tablets that Moses had placed in it
at Mount Sinai,* where the LORD made a covenant with the people of Israel when they left
the land of Egypt.
[10]When the priests came out of the Holy
Place, a thick cloud filled the Temple of the LORD.
[11]The priests could not continue their service because of the cloud, for the glorious presence of
the LORD filled the Temple.

Solomon Praises the LORD

[12]Then Solomon prayed, "O LORD, you have said
that you would live in a thick cloud of darkness.
[13]Now I have built a glorious Temple for you, a
place where you can live forever!*"
[14]Then the king turned around to the entire
community of Israel standing before him and
gave this blessing: [15]"Praise the LORD, the God of
Israel, who has kept the promise he made to my
father, David. For he told my father, [16]'From the
day I brought my people Israel out of Egypt, I
have never chosen a city among any of the tribes
of Israel as the place where a Temple should be
built to honor my name. But I have chosen David
to be king over my people Israel.' "
[17]Then Solomon said, "My father, David,
wanted to build this Temple to honor the name
of the LORD, the God of Israel. [18]But the LORD
told him, 'You wanted to build the Temple to
honor my name. Your intention is good, [19]but
you are not the one to do it. One of your own
sons will build the Temple to honor me.'
[20]"And now the LORD has fulfilled the promise
he made, for I have become king in my father's
place, and I now sit on the throne of Israel, just
as the LORD promised. I have built this Temple to
honor the name of the LORD, the God of Israel.
[21]And I have prepared a place there for the Ark,
which contains the covenant that the LORD made
with our ancestors when he brought them out
of Egypt."

Solomon's Prayer of Dedication

[22]Then Solomon stood before the altar of the
LORD in front of the entire community of Israel. He lifted his hands toward heaven, [23]and he
prayed,

"O LORD, God of Israel, there is no God like
you in all of heaven above or on the earth
below. You keep your covenant and show
unfailing love to all who walk before you
in wholehearted devotion. [24]You have kept
your promise to your servant David, my
father. You made that promise with your own
mouth, and with your own hands you have
fulfilled it today.
[25]"And now, O LORD, God of Israel, carry
out the additional promise you made to your
servant David, my father. For you said to him,
'If your descendants guard their behavior and
faithfully follow me as you have done, one of
them will always sit on the throne of Israel.'
[26]Now, O God of Israel, fulfill this promise to
your servant David, my father.
[27]"But will God really live on earth? Why,
even the highest heavens cannot contain
you. How much less this Temple I have built!
[28]Nevertheless, listen to my prayer and my
plea, O LORD my God. Hear the cry and the
prayer that your servant is making to you

8:4 Hebrew *the Tent of Meeting;* i.e., the tent mentioned in 2 Sam 6:17 and 1 Chr 16:1. **8:9** Hebrew *at Horeb,* another name for Sinai. **8:13** Some Greek texts add the line *Is this not written in the Book of Jashar?*

placed in the Most Holy Place with the cherubim spreading their protective wings over it. It was not until the priests had left the Holy Place that the glory of the LORD filled the Temple. **12–53:** In the ancient world, cult and state were not separate entities; religion and state were so intimately connected that it is difficult to determine where one ended and the other began. The king was considered to be God's viceroy or regent on earth, managing not only matters of state but the cult as well. Thus Solomon acts as both king and religious leader. This dedication was a joyful ceremony of singing, dancing, ritual, prayer, banquet, and other festivities. **22–26:** Solomon reaffirms the Davidic covenant, which established God's omnipresence, attentiveness to his faithful people, and punishment for disobedience. In this passage God is described as a caring, attentive, patient, and forgiving deity. **27–29:** The LORD's presence is not limited to this place. God's Spirit may be found everywhere in highest heaven and on earth and the depths of the

today. 29 May you watch over this Temple
night and day, this place where you have said,
'My name will be there.' May you always
hear the prayers I make toward this place.
30 May you hear the humble and earnest
requests from me and your people Israel
when we pray toward this place. Yes, hear us
from heaven where you live, and when you
hear, forgive.
31 "If someone wrongs another person and
is required to take an oath of innocence in
front of your altar in this Temple, 32 then
hear from heaven and judge between your
servants—the accuser and the accused.
Punish the guilty as they deserve. Acquit the
innocent because of their innocence.
33 "If your people Israel are defeated by
their enemies because they have sinned
against you, and if they turn to you and
acknowledge your name and pray to you
here in this Temple, 34 then hear from heaven
and forgive the sin of your people Israel
and return them to this land you gave their
ancestors.
35 "If the skies are shut up and there is no
rain because your people have sinned against
you, and if they pray toward this Temple and
acknowledge your name and turn from their
sins because you have punished them, 36 then
hear from heaven and forgive the sins of your
servants, your people Israel. Teach them to
follow the right path, and send rain on your
land that you have given to your people as
their special possession.
37 "If there is a famine in the land or a
plague or crop disease or attacks of locusts or
caterpillars, or if your people's enemies are
in the land besieging their towns—whatever
disaster or disease there is—38 and if your
people Israel pray about their troubles, raising
their hands toward this Temple, 39 then hear
from heaven where you live, and forgive.
Give your people what their actions deserve,
for you alone know each human heart.
40 Then they will fear you as long as they live
in the land you gave to our ancestors.
41 "In the future, foreigners who do not
belong to your people Israel will hear of you.
They will come from distant lands because
of your name, 42 for they will hear of your
great name and your strong hand and your
powerful arm. And when they pray toward
this Temple, 43 then hear from heaven where
you live, and grant what they ask of you.
In this way, all the people of the earth will
come to know and fear you, just as your own
people Israel do. They, too, will know that this
Temple I have built honors your name.
44 "If your people go out where you send
them to fight their enemies, and if they pray
to the LORD by turning toward this city you
have chosen and toward this Temple I have
built to honor your name, 45 then hear their
prayers from heaven and uphold their cause.
46 "If they sin against you—and who has
never sinned?—you might become angry
with them and let their enemies conquer
them and take them captive to their land
far away or near. 47 But in that land of exile,
they might turn to you in repentance and
pray, 'We have sinned, done evil, and acted
wickedly.' 48 If they turn to you with their
whole heart and soul in the land of their
enemies and pray toward the land you gave
to their ancestors—toward this city you have
chosen, and toward this Temple I have built to
honor your name—49 then hear their prayers
and their petition from heaven where you
live, and uphold their cause. 50 Forgive your
people who have sinned against you. Forgive
all the offenses they have committed against
you. Make their captors merciful to them,
51 for they are your people—your special
possession—whom you brought out of the
iron-smelting furnace of Egypt.
52 "May your eyes be open to my requests
and to the requests of your people Israel. May
you hear and answer them whenever they
cry out to you. 53 For when you brought our
ancestors out of Egypt, O Sovereign LORD,
you told your servant Moses that you had set
Israel apart from all the nations of the earth
to be your own special possession."

The Dedication of the Temple

54 When Solomon finished making these prayers
and petitions to the LORD, he stood up in front of
the altar of the LORD, where he had been kneeling with his hands raised toward heaven. 55 He
stood and in a loud voice blessed the entire congregation of Israel:
56 "Praise the LORD who has given rest to his

sea. The Temple holds only the LORD's name. **30–53:** Through God's eyes, ears, and presence, the prayers of the people shall be heard and acted upon. Disobedience will be punished, but forgiveness is available upon confession and repentance. **54–66:** Solomon recalls God's covenant with Moses and the law, and rededicates the people to the LORD, in addition to dedicating the Temple.

people Israel, just as he promised. Not one word has failed of all the wonderful promises he gave through his servant Moses. 57 May the LORD our God be with us as he was with our ancestors; may he never leave us or abandon us. 58 May he give us the desire to do his will in everything and to obey all the commands, decrees, and regulations that he gave our ancestors. 59 And may these words that I have prayed in the presence of the LORD be before him constantly, day and night, so that the LORD our God may give justice to me and to his people Israel, according to each day's needs. 60 Then people all over the earth will know that the LORD alone is God and there is no other. 61 And may you be completely faithful to the LORD our God. May you always obey his decrees and commands, just as you are doing today."

62 Then the king and all Israel with him offered sacrifices to the LORD. 63 Solomon offered to the LORD a peace offering of 22,000 cattle and 120,000 sheep and goats. And so the king and all the people of Israel dedicated the Temple of the LORD.

64 That same day the king consecrated the central area of the courtyard in front of the LORD's Temple. He offered burnt offerings, grain offerings, and the fat of peace offerings there, because the bronze altar in the LORD's presence was too small to hold all the burnt offerings, grain offerings, and the fat of the peace offerings.

65 Then Solomon and all Israel celebrated the Festival of Shelters* in the presence of the LORD our God. A large congregation had gathered from as far away as Lebo-hamath in the north and the Brook of Egypt in the south. The celebration went on for fourteen days in all—seven days for the dedication of the altar and seven days for the Festival of Shelters.* 66 After the festival was over,* Solomon sent the people home. They blessed the king and went to their homes joyful and glad because the LORD had been good to his servant David and to his people Israel.

The LORD's Response to Solomon

9 So Solomon finished building the Temple of the LORD, as well as the royal palace. He completed everything he had planned to do. 2 Then the LORD appeared to Solomon a second time, as he had done before at Gibeon. 3 The LORD said to him,

"I have heard your prayer and your petition.
I have set this Temple apart to be holy—this
place you have built where my name will be
honored forever. I will always watch over it,
for it is dear to my heart.

4 "As for you, if you will follow me with
integrity and godliness, as David your father
did, obeying all my commands, decrees, and
regulations, 5 then I will establish the throne
of your dynasty over Israel forever. For I
made this promise to your father, David: 'One
of your descendants will always sit on the
throne of Israel.'

6 "But if you or your descendants abandon
me and disobey the commands and decrees I
have given you, and if you serve and worship
other gods, 7 then I will uproot Israel from
this land that I have given them. I will reject
this Temple that I have made holy to honor
my name. I will make Israel an object of
mockery and ridicule among the nations.
8 And though this Temple is impressive now,
all who pass by will be appalled and will
shake their heads in amazement. They will
ask, 'Why did the LORD do such terrible
things to this land and to this Temple?'

9 "And the answer will be, 'Because his
people abandoned the LORD their God, who
brought their ancestors out of Egypt, and
they worshiped other gods instead and bowed
down to them. That is why the LORD has
brought all these disasters on them.' "

Solomon's Agreement with Hiram

10 It took Solomon twenty years to build the LORD's Temple and his own royal palace. At the end of that time, 11 he gave twenty towns in the land of Galilee to King Hiram of Tyre. (Hiram had previously provided all the cedar and cypress timber and gold that Solomon had requested.) 12 But when Hiram came from Tyre to see the

8:65a Hebrew *the festival;* see note on 8:2. **8:65b** Hebrew *seven days and seven days, fourteen days;* compare parallel text at 2 Chr 7:8-10. **8:66** Hebrew *On the eighth day,* probably referring to the day following the seven-day Festival of Shelters; compare parallel text at 2 Chr 7:9-10.

9:1–28 God Appears to Solomon. 1–9: The Temple is consecrated by God, and this is where his name will dwell forever. The LORD's name separates him from and elevates him above all other gods. Once again the covenant between God and Israel is renewed. As long as the people are faithful, God will bless and protect them. Verses 6–9 anticipate the disobedience of Solomon and other kings, as well as the Exile. **10–14:** Solomon must give land to Hiram to repay him for supplies for all of his building projects. Apparently, he was not generous in his choice of which cities to hand over. **15–19:** Solomon mounted a great

towns Solomon had given him, he was not at all
pleased with them. [13] "What kind of towns are
these, my brother?" he asked. So Hiram called
that area Cabul (which means "worthless"), as it
is still known today. [14] Nevertheless, Hiram paid*
Solomon 9,000 pounds* of gold.

Solomon's Many Achievements

[15] This is the account of the forced labor that King
Solomon conscripted to build the LORD's Temple,
the royal palace, the supporting terraces,* the
wall of Jerusalem, and the cities of Hazor, Megiddo, and Gezer. [16] (Pharaoh, the king of Egypt, had
attacked and captured Gezer, killing the Canaanite population and burning it down. He gave the
city to his daughter as a wedding gift when she
married Solomon. [17] So Solomon rebuilt the city
of Gezer.) He also built up the towns of Lower
Beth-horon, [18] Baalath, and Tamar* in the wilderness within his land. [19] He built towns as
supply centers and constructed towns where his
chariots and horses* could be stationed. He built
everything he desired in Jerusalem and Lebanon
and throughout his entire realm.

[20] There were still some people living in the
land who were not Israelites, including Amorites,
Hittites, Perizzites, Hivites, and Jebusites. [21] These
were descendants of the nations whom the people
of Israel had not completely destroyed.* So Solomon conscripted them for his labor force, and
they serve in the labor force to this day. [22] But
Solomon did not conscript any of the Israelites
for forced labor. Instead, he assigned them to
serve as fighting men, government officials, officers and captains in his army, commanders of his
chariots, and charioteers. [23] Solomon appointed
550 of them to supervise the people working on
his various projects.

[24] Solomon moved his wife, Pharaoh's daughter, from the City of David to the new palace he
had built for her. Then he constructed the supporting terraces.

[25] Three times each year Solomon presented
burnt offerings and peace offerings on the altar
he had built for the LORD. He also burned incense to the LORD. And so he finished the work of
building the Temple.

[26] King Solomon also built a fleet of ships at
Ezion-geber, a port near Elath* in the land of
Edom, along the shore of the Red Sea.* [27] Hiram
sent experienced crews of sailors to sail the ships
with Solomon's men. [28] They sailed to Ophir and
brought back to Solomon some sixteen tons* of
gold.

Visit of the Queen of Sheba

10 When the queen of Sheba heard
of Solomon's fame, which brought
honor to the name of the LORD,*
she came to test him with hard questions. [2] She
arrived in Jerusalem with a large group of at-

9:14a Or *For Hiram had paid.* **9:14b** Hebrew *120 talents* [4,000 kilograms]. **9:15** Hebrew *the millo;* also in 9:24. The meaning of the Hebrew is uncertain. **9:18** An alternate reading in the Masoretic Text reads *Tadmor.* **9:19** Or *and charioteers.* **9:21** The Hebrew term used here refers to the complete consecration of things or people to the LORD, either by destroying them or by giving them as an offering. **9:26a** As in Greek version (see also 2 Kgs 14:22; 16:6); Hebrew reads *Eloth,* a variant spelling of Elath. **9:26b** Hebrew *sea of reeds.* **9:28** Hebrew *420 talents* [14 metric tons]. **10:1** Or *which was due to the name of the LORD.* The meaning of the Hebrew is uncertain.

building campaign. *Hazor, Megiddo, and Gezer* were placed at militarily strategic points. In contrast, Jerusalem served as Solomon's political and religious center. Since he was ruling during a time of relative peace, his building projects were not interrupted by war. **20–23:** Only non-Israelites were forced to work on these building projects. The Israelites had higher ranking jobs (see 5:13, 11:28, and the events in chap. 12). **26–28:** It is possible this naval port was created to control trade to the south with people such as the Egyptians and the queen of Sheba. Ezion-geber was Solomon's first and only seaport, and Solomon was allowed access to Phoenician ports on the Mediterranean because of his alliance with them (Tyre, where Hiram reigned, was a Phoenician city).

10:1–29 Queen of Sheba. Solomon's reputation as a wise leader, great imparter of wisdom, and follower of the LORD was known far and wide. **1:** Sheba was in Arabia, perhaps modern Yemen. The queen's visit to Solomon may have been a trade mission. Solomon was beginning to expand his sphere of influence, controlling numerous overland trade routes. If the relationship between Sheba and Solomon were to become unfriendly, this could potentially block trade with East Africa, so it was in the queen's best interest to remain on friendly terms with Solomon. She was a powerful leader who was accepted into Solomon's court just as any other head of state would be. Her entourage was large, and there was no question about her ability or legitimacy as a ruler because of her gender. The queen conducted herself with the dignity and stature of a head of state: She did not abuse her power or underestimate it. In order for a woman to achieve her stature and position, she would have had to obtain and retain the respect of the people, the military and religious leaders, and the palace court, all of

tendants and a great caravan of camels loaded
with spices, large quantities of gold, and precious jewels. When she met with Solomon, she
talked with him about everything she had on
her mind. 3 Solomon had answers for all her
questions; nothing was too hard for the king to
explain to her. 4 When the queen of Sheba realized how very wise Solomon was, and when
she saw the palace he had built, 5 she was overwhelmed. She was also amazed at the food on
his tables, the organization of his officials and
their splendid clothing, the cup-bearers, and the
burnt offerings Solomon made at the Temple of
the LORD.
6 She exclaimed to the king, "Everything I
heard in my country about your achievements*
and wisdom is true! 7 I didn't believe what was
said until I arrived here and saw it with my own
eyes. In fact, I had not heard the half of it! Your
wisdom and prosperity are far beyond what I
was told. 8 How happy your people* must be!
What a privilege for your officials to stand here
day after day, listening to your wisdom! 9 Praise
the LORD your God, who delights in you and has
placed you on the throne of Israel. Because of the
LORD's eternal love for Israel, he has made you
king so you can rule with justice and righteousness."
10 Then she gave the king a gift of 9,000
pounds* of gold, great quantities of spices, and
precious jewels. Never again were so many spices
brought in as those the queen of Sheba gave to
King Solomon.
11 (In addition, Hiram's ships brought gold
from Ophir, and they also brought rich cargoes
of red sandalwood* and precious jewels. 12 The
king used the sandalwood to make railings for
the Temple of the LORD and the royal palace, and
to construct lyres and harps for the musicians.
Never before or since has there been such a supply of sandalwood.)
13 King Solomon gave the queen of Sheba
whatever she asked for, besides all the customary
gifts he had so generously given. Then she and
all her attendants returned to their own land.

Solomon's Wealth and Splendor

14 Each year Solomon received about 25 tons* of
gold. 15 This did not include the additional revenue he received from merchants and traders,
all the kings of Arabia, and the governors of the
land.
16 King Solomon made 200 large shields of
hammered gold, each weighing more than fifteen
pounds.* 17 He also made 300 smaller shields
of hammered gold, each weighing nearly four
pounds.* The king placed these shields in the
Palace of the Forest of Lebanon.
18 Then the king made a huge throne, decorated with ivory and overlaid with fine gold. 19 The
throne had six steps and a rounded back. There
were armrests on both sides of the seat, and the
figure of a lion stood on each side of the throne.
20 There were also twelve other lions, one standing on each end of the six steps. No other throne
in all the world could be compared with it!
21 All of King Solomon's drinking cups were
solid gold, as were all the utensils in the Palace
of the Forest of Lebanon. They were not made
of silver, for silver was considered worthless in
Solomon's day!
22 The king had a fleet of trading ships* that
sailed with Hiram's fleet. Once every three years
the ships returned, loaded with gold, silver, ivory,
apes, and peacocks.*
23 So King Solomon became richer and wiser
than any other king on earth. 24 People from every nation came to consult him and to hear the
wisdom God had given him. 25 Year after year everyone who visited brought him gifts of silver and
gold, clothing, weapons, spices, horses, and mules.
26 Solomon built up a huge force of chariots
and horses.* He had 1,400 chariots and 12,000

10:6 Hebrew *your words.* **10:8** Greek and Syriac versions and Latin Vulgate read *your wives.* **10:10** Hebrew *120 talents* [4,000 kilograms]. **10:11** Hebrew *almug wood;* also in 10:12. **10:14** Hebrew *666 talents* [23 metric tons]. **10:16** Hebrew *600 [shekels] of gold* [6.8 kilograms]. **10:17** Hebrew *3 minas* [1.8 kilograms]. **10:22a** Hebrew *fleet of ships of Tarshish.* **10:22b** Or *and baboons.* **10:26** Or *charioteers;* also in 10:26b.

them primarily male-dominated groups. Solomon and the queen of Sheba were immediately friends, and she remained with Solomon, as his guest, for an unknown period of time. According to Ethiopian legend they had a love affair that resulted in the queen's pregnancy, although she was not aware of this consequence upon her departure from Israel. The child, a boy, was born after she had returned to Sheba. **13:** The queen also appears to have been quite shrewd since Solomon's gifts to her exceeded hers to him. **14–15:** Solomon's kingdom controlled most of the trade that passed through Israel, thus accumulating a great deal of wealth from import/export taxes and transit duties. **24–25:** It was unusual for a king to deal directly with people. Kings of other nations usually delegated legal matters to judges or priests, hearing only the most important cases themselves. Solomon dealt directly with his subjects. As a result, gifts and payments made Solomon a very rich man.

Polygamy

Polygamy describes the state of having more than one legal sexual partner, usually wives, rarely husbands. It is part of complex social structures controlling marriage, children, inheritance, and barrenness. Polygamy is not just bound up with meeting male sexual desires.

Although some women use polygamy for their ends, those without choice or status are vulnerable to abuse and misery. Polygamy has usually been restricted to the wealthy and the childless. It has never been widely accepted, especially not in market and industrial economies, with the exception of certain fringe sects.

In ancient Mesopotamia, monogamy was probably the norm, but childlessness could be solved by adopting an heir, using a concubine or the barren wife's slave (i.e., property) in her place or remarrying. The Old Testament reflects this background, but polygamy was not as widespread as commonly thought. Jacob was originally tricked into it. The law accepted the possibility but protected the rights of the most vulnerable (Exod 21:10; Deut 21:10–17) and allowed a wife's divorce when human sin broke the relationship (Deut 24:1–4). The Bible provides evidence of the destructive influence of polygamy and warns that it can lead to the downfall of kings (Deut 17:17; 1 Kgs 11:1–6).

At the same time, the Old Testament laid down the ideal for marriage and the family: one man and one woman equal and identical in their humanity, different in their sexuality, complementing each other and together reflecting the image of God in a lifelong, exclusive, and faithful relationship (Gen 2). The wisdom books never refer to polygamy, and Elkanah is the only ordinary man with two wives mentioned during the monarchy. The prophetic concept of marriage as a picture of God's faithful and exclusive relationship with his people assumes one wife (Hos 2).

Monogamy was also the norm in the New Testament. The early church saw monogamous marriage as a figure of Christ's relationship to the church (Eph 5:21–33). Polygamy apparently existed among new Christians, but leaders could have only one wife (1 Tim 3:2, 12). Polygamy remained legal for Jewish men until the time of the emperor Justinian.

Monogamy comes as the fruit of grace and agape love in marriage, but should not be imposed as a requirement for baptism—an important distinction not always made by past missionaries.

horses. He stationed some of them in the chariot
cities and some near him in Jerusalem. 27 The king
made silver as plentiful in Jerusalem as stone.
And valuable cedar timber was as common as the
sycamore-fig trees that grow in the foothills of
Judah.* 28 Solomon's horses were imported from
Egypt* and from Cilicia*; the king's traders acquired them from Cilicia at the standard price.
29 At that time chariots from Egypt could be purchased for 600 pieces of silver,* and horses for
150 pieces of silver.* They were then exported to
the kings of the Hittites and the kings of Aram.

Solomon's Many Wives

11 Now King Solomon loved many
foreign women. Besides Pharaoh's
daughter, he married women from
Moab, Ammon, Edom, Sidon, and from among
the Hittites. 2 The LORD had clearly instructed
the people of Israel, 'You must not marry them,
because they will turn your hearts to their gods.'
Yet Solomon insisted on loving them anyway.
3 He had 700 wives of royal birth and 300 concubines. And in fact, they did turn his heart away
from the LORD.
4 In Solomon's old age, they turned his heart
to worship other gods instead of being completely faithful to the LORD his God, as his father, Da-

10:27 Hebrew *the Shephelah.* **10:28a** Possibly *Muzur,* a district near Cilicia; also in 10:29. **10:28b** Hebrew *Kue,* probably another name for Cilicia. **10:29a** Hebrew *600 [shekels] of silver,* about 15 pounds or 6.8 kilograms in weight. **10:29b** Hebrew *150 [shekels],* about 3.8 pounds or 1.7 kilograms in weight.

11:1–25 Solomon's Downfall and Death. The writer has divided the account of Solomon's reign into two parts for theological reasons. The first part (chaps. 1—10) told of his successes. Chapter 11 begins the account of his failures and struggles. **1:** It was common for a ruler to have numerous wives. In the ancient world, death during childbirth was common; the survival rate for children and their chances of reaching adulthood were very low. The inability of a couple to bear children was also a common problem. Therefore, numerous wives would ensure a male heir to the throne. Moreover, upon conclusion of a treaty, in order to ensure good relations, a princess or prince would be offered in royal marriage. **2–8:** God's warn-

vid, had been. [5]Solomon worshiped Ashtoreth,
the goddess of the Sidonians, and Molech,* the
detestable god of the Ammonites. [6]In this way,
Solomon did what was evil in the LORD's sight;
he refused to follow the LORD completely, as his
father, David, had done.
[7]On the Mount of Olives, east of Jerusalem,*
he even built a pagan shrine for Chemosh, the
detestable god of Moab, and another for Molech,
the detestable god of the Ammonites. [8]Solomon
built such shrines for all his foreign wives to use
for burning incense and sacrificing to their gods.
[9]The LORD was very angry with Solomon,
for his heart had turned away from the LORD,
the God of Israel, who had appeared to him
twice. [10]He had warned Solomon specifically
about worshiping other gods, but Solomon did
not listen to the LORD's command. [11]So now the
LORD said to him, "Since you have not kept my
covenant and have disobeyed my decrees, I will
surely tear the kingdom away from you and give
it to one of your servants. [12]But for the sake of
your father, David, I will not do this while you
are still alive. I will take the kingdom away from
your son. [13]And even so, I will not take away
the entire kingdom; I will let him be king of one
tribe, for the sake of my servant David and for
the sake of Jerusalem, my chosen city."

Solomon's Adversaries

[14]Then the LORD raised up Hadad the Edomite, a
member of Edom's royal family, to be Solomon's
adversary. [15]Years before, David had defeated
Edom. Joab, his army commander, had stayed to
bury some of the Israelite soldiers who had died
in battle. While there, they killed every male in
Edom. [16]Joab and the army of Israel had stayed
there for six months, killing them.
[17]But Hadad and a few of his father's royal
officials escaped and headed for Egypt. (Hadad
was just a boy at the time.) [18]They set out from
Midian and went to Paran, where others joined
them. Then they traveled to Egypt and went to
Pharaoh, who gave them a home, food, and some
land. [19]Pharaoh grew very fond of Hadad, and he
gave him his wife's sister in marriage—the sister
of Queen Tahpenes. [20]She bore him a son named
Genubath. Tahpenes raised him* in Pharaoh's
palace among Pharaoh's own sons.
[21]When the news reached Hadad in Egypt
that David and his commander Joab were both
dead, he said to Pharaoh, "Let me return to my
own country."
[22]"Why?" Pharaoh asked him. "What do you
lack here that makes you want to go home?"
"Nothing," he replied. "But even so, please let
me return home."
[23]God also raised up Rezon son of Eliada as Solomon's adversary. Rezon had fled from his master,
King Hadadezer of Zobah, [24]and had become the
leader of a gang of rebels. After David conquered
Hadadezer, Rezon and his men fled to Damascus,
where he became king. [25]Rezon was Israel's bitter
adversary for the rest of Solomon's reign, and he
made trouble, just as Hadad did. Rezon hated Israel intensely and continued to reign in Aram.

Jeroboam Rebels against Solomon

[26]Another rebel leader was Jeroboam son of Nebat, one of Solomon's own officials. He came
from the town of Zeredah in Ephraim, and his
mother was Zeruah, a widow.
[27]This is the story behind his rebellion. Solomon was rebuilding the supporting terraces* and
repairing the walls of the city of his father, David. [28]Jeroboam was a very capable young man,
and when Solomon saw how industrious he was,
he put him in charge of the labor force from the
tribes of Ephraim and Manasseh, the descendants of Joseph.
[29]One day as Jeroboam was leaving Jerusalem,
the prophet Ahijah from Shiloh met him along the
way. Ahijah was wearing a new cloak. The two of

11:5 Hebrew *Milcom,* a variant spelling of Molech; also in 11:33. **11:7** Hebrew *On the mountain east of Jerusalem.* **11:20** As in Greek version; Hebrew reads *weaned him.* **11:27** Hebrew *the millo.* The meaning of the Hebrew is uncertain.

---

ing proved true: Solomon began to worship the deities of his wives. **9–13:** Because of this violation, not only Solomon's reign but also the spiritual well-being of Israel would never be as peaceful, strong, and prosperous as it once was. When Solomon decided it was acceptable to worship foreign gods, he made a public statement. A king is inevitably influential, and thus Solomon led the nation down a path to destruction. **14–25:** Both *Hadad the Edomite* and *Rezon* began their careers during David's reign, which indicates that they caused trouble for Solomon early in his reign. The writer has placed their stories here because of the partitioning of the account into "positive" and "negative" sections.

11:26—14:31 Division of the Kingdom

11:26–43: Jeroboam's rebellion was spurred by Ahijah's oracle promising him kingship over the majority of the tribes. **29–32:** One tribe is either missing or presumed in Ahijah's symbolic division of the kingdom, since Jeroboam receives ten pieces of the

them were alone in a field, 30 and Ahijah took hold
of the new cloak he was wearing and tore it into
twelve pieces. 31 Then he said to Jeroboam, "Take
ten of these pieces, for this is what the LORD, the
God of Israel, says: 'I am about to tear the kingdom from the hand of Solomon, and I will give
ten of the tribes to you! 32 But I will leave him
one tribe for the sake of my servant David and for
the sake of Jerusalem, which I have chosen out of
all the tribes of Israel. 33 For Solomon has* abandoned me and worshiped Ashtoreth, the goddess
of the Sidonians; Chemosh, the god of Moab;
and Molech, the god of the Ammonites. He has
not followed my ways and done what is pleasing
in my sight. He has not obeyed my decrees and
regulations as David his father did.
34 " 'But I will not take the entire kingdom
from Solomon at this time. For the sake of my
servant David, the one whom I chose and who
obeyed my commands and decrees, I will keep
Solomon as leader for the rest of his life. 35 But I
will take the kingdom away from his son and give
ten of the tribes to you. 36 His son will have one
tribe so that the descendants of David my servant
will continue to reign, shining like a lamp in Jerusalem, the city I have chosen to be the place for
my name. 37 And I will place you on the throne of
Israel, and you will rule over all that your heart
desires. 38 If you listen to what I tell you and follow my ways and do whatever I consider to be
right, and if you obey my decrees and commands,
as my servant David did, then I will always be
with you. I will establish an enduring dynasty for
you as I did for David, and I will give Israel to
you. 39 Because of Solomon's sin I will punish the
descendants of David—though not forever.' "
40 Solomon tried to kill Jeroboam, but he fled
to King Shishak of Egypt and stayed there until
Solomon died.

Summary of Solomon's Reign

41 The rest of the events in Solomon's reign,
including all his deeds and his wisdom, are recorded in *The Book of the Acts of Solomon.*
42 Solomon ruled in Jerusalem over all Israel for
forty years. 43 When he died, he was buried in the
City of David, named for his father. Then his son
Rehoboam became the next king.

The Northern Tribes Revolt

12 Rehoboam went to Shechem, where
all Israel had gathered to make him
king. 2 When Jeroboam son of Nebat
heard of this, he returned from Egypt,* for he
had fled to Egypt to escape from King Solomon.
3 The leaders of Israel summoned him, and Jeroboam and the whole assembly of Israel went to
speak with Rehoboam. 4 "Your father was a hard
master," they said. "Lighten the harsh labor demands and heavy taxes that your father imposed
on us. Then we will be your loyal subjects."
5 Rehoboam replied, "Give me three days to
think this over. Then come back for my answer."
So the people went away.
6 Then King Rehoboam discussed the matter
with the older men who had counseled his father, Solomon. "What is your advice?" he asked.
"How should I answer these people?"
7 The older counselors replied, "If you are
willing to be a servant to these people today and
give them a favorable answer, they will always be
your loyal subjects."
8 But Rehoboam rejected the advice of the
older men and instead asked the opinion of the
young men who had grown up with him and
were now his advisers. 9 "What is your advice?"
he asked them. "How should I answer these people who want me to lighten the burdens imposed
by my father?"
10 The young men replied, "This is what you
should tell those complainers who want a lighter burden: 'My little finger is thicker than my
father's waist! 11 Yes, my father laid heavy burdens on you, but I'm going to make them even
heavier! My father beat you with whips, but I
will beat you with scorpions!' "
12 Three days later Jeroboam and all the people
returned to hear Rehoboam's decision, just as the

11:33 As in Greek, Syriac, and Latin Vulgate; Hebrew reads *For they have.* **12:2** As in Greek version and Latin Vulgate (see also 2 Chr 10:2); Hebrew reads *he lived in Egypt.*

---

cloak and only one piece is kept for David. Different scholars have proposed that the tribes of Benjamin, Simeon, or Levi are assumed to accompany Judah. **37–38:** Jeroboam receives the same promise of an enduring dynasty that was given to David if he will be obedient to the LORD. **41:** *The Book of the Acts of Solomon* is no longer extant.

12:1–24 Rehoboam as Successor. Upon the death of Solomon, his son Rehoboam attempted to control the Northern Kingdom of Israel and the Southern Kingdom of Judah, but without success. The rupture occurred over the heavy *burdens* that Rehoboam was going to impose, reinforcing his father's forced labor schemes. **10:** *My father's waist* is a euphemism. Rehoboam is saying that he is more of a man than his father, so that the people can expect harsher treatment from him than from Solomon. **19–20:** The northern tribes

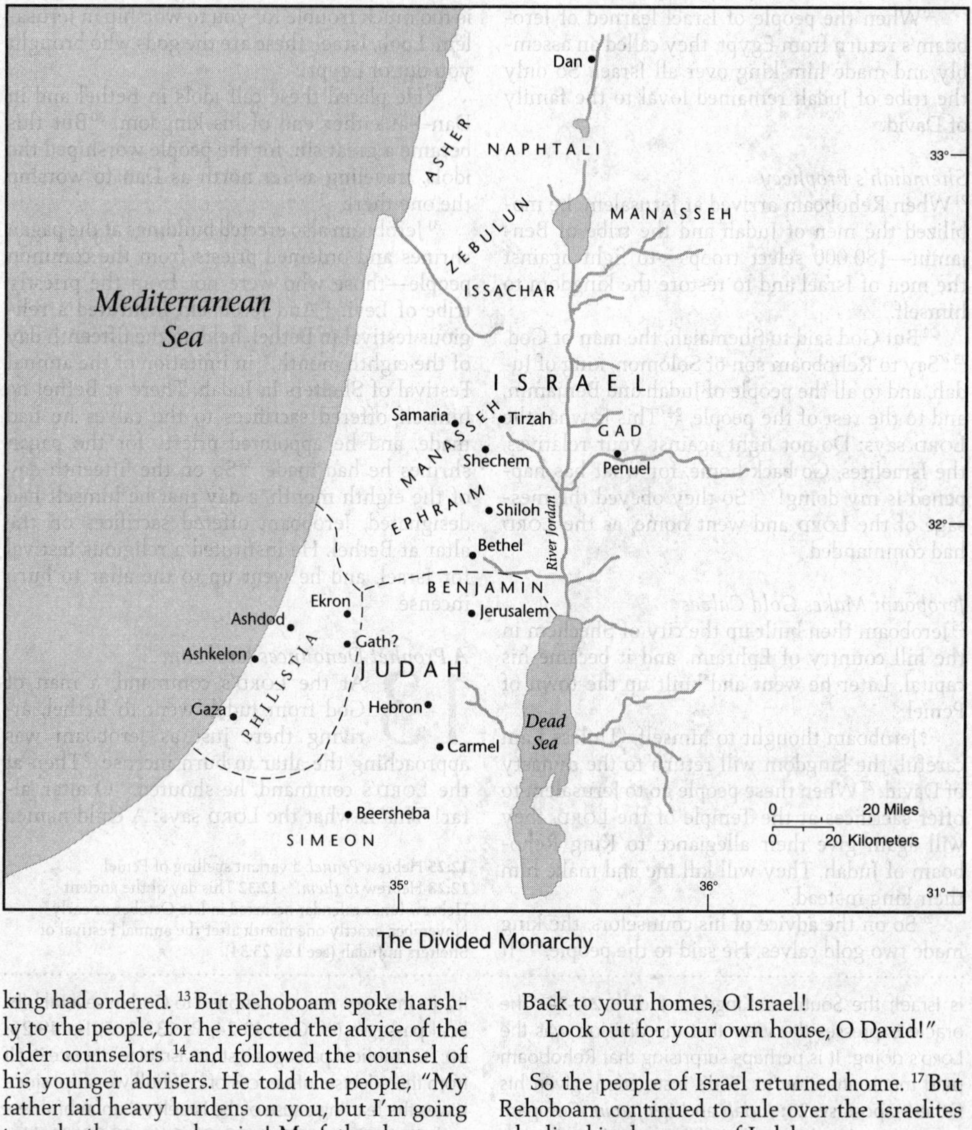

The Divided Monarchy

king had ordered. 13 But Rehoboam spoke harshly to the people, for he rejected the advice of the older counselors 14 and followed the counsel of his younger advisers. He told the people, "My father laid heavy burdens on you, but I'm going to make them even heavier! My father beat you with whips, but I will beat you with scorpions!"

15 So the king paid no attention to the people. This turn of events was the will of the LORD, for it fulfilled the LORD's message to Jeroboam son of Nebat through the prophet Ahijah from Shiloh.

16 When all Israel realized that the king had refused to listen to them, they responded,

"Down with the dynasty of David!
We have no interest in the son of Jesse.
Back to your homes, O Israel!
Look out for your own house, O David!"

So the people of Israel returned home. 17 But Rehoboam continued to rule over the Israelites who lived in the towns of Judah.

18 King Rehoboam sent Adoniram,* who was in charge of the labor force, to restore order, but the people of Israel stoned him to death. When this news reached King Rehoboam, he quickly jumped into his chariot and fled to Jerusalem. 19 And to this day the northern tribes of Israel have refused to be ruled by a descendant of David.

12:18 As in some Greek manuscripts and Syriac version (see also 4:6; 5:14); Hebrew reads *Adoram.*

united behind Jeroboam and broke away from the United Monarchy. This was God's punishment. From this point on, Israel and Judah were two separate nations with two different fates. The Northern Kingdom

20 When the people of Israel learned of Jeroboam's return from Egypt, they called an assembly and made him king over all Israel. So only
the tribe of Judah remained loyal to the family
of David.

Shemaiah's Prophecy

21 When Rehoboam arrived at Jerusalem, he mobilized the men of Judah and the tribe of Benjamin—180,000 select troops—to fight against
the men of Israel and to restore the kingdom to
himself.
22 But God said to Shemaiah, the man of God,
23 "Say to Rehoboam son of Solomon, king of Judah, and to all the people of Judah and Benjamin,
and to the rest of the people, 24 'This is what the
LORD says: Do not fight against your relatives,
the Israelites. Go back home, for what has happened is my doing!' " So they obeyed the message of the LORD and went home, as the LORD
had commanded.

Jeroboam Makes Gold Calves

25 Jeroboam then built up the city of Shechem in
the hill country of Ephraim, and it became his
capital. Later he went and built up the town of
Peniel.*
26 Jeroboam thought to himself, "Unless I am
careful, the kingdom will return to the dynasty
of David. 27 When these people go to Jerusalem to
offer sacrifices at the Temple of the LORD, they
will again give their allegiance to King Rehoboam of Judah. They will kill me and make him
their king instead."
28 So on the advice of his counselors, the king
made two gold calves. He said to the people,* "It
is too much trouble for you to worship in Jerusalem. Look, Israel, these are the gods who brought
you out of Egypt!"
29 He placed these calf idols in Bethel and in
Dan—at either end of his kingdom. 30 But this
became a great sin, for the people worshiped the
idols, traveling as far north as Dan to worship
the one there.
31 Jeroboam also erected buildings at the pagan
shrines and ordained priests from the common
people—those who were not from the priestly
tribe of Levi. 32 And Jeroboam instituted a religious festival in Bethel, held on the fifteenth day
of the eighth month,* in imitation of the annual
Festival of Shelters in Judah. There at Bethel he
himself offered sacrifices to the calves he had
made, and he appointed priests for the pagan
shrines he had made. 33 So on the fifteenth day
of the eighth month, a day that he himself had
designated, Jeroboam offered sacrifices on the
altar at Bethel. He instituted a religious festival
for Israel, and he went up to the altar to burn
incense.

A Prophet Denounces Jeroboam

13 At the LORD's command, a man of
God from Judah went to Bethel, arriving there just as Jeroboam was
approaching the altar to burn incense. 2 Then at
the LORD's command, he shouted, "O altar, altar! This is what the LORD says: A child named

12:25 Hebrew *Penuel,* a variant spelling of Peniel.
12:28 Hebrew *to them.* **12:32** This day of the ancient Hebrew lunar calendar occurred in late October or early November, exactly one month after the annual Festival of Shelters in Judah (see Lev 23:34).

is Israel; the Southern Kingdom Judah. **21–24:** The oracle expresses the view that the division was the LORD's doing. It is perhaps surprising that Rehoboam paid much attention to God's instruction, given his father's apostasy. **23:** *Judah and Benjamin*: Compare to verse 20, in which only Judah is mentioned as the Southern Kingdom. Benjamin was probably divided between the two countries.

12:25–33 Jeroboam Builds New Shrines. Even though the kingdom was divided, everyone's responsibilities to the LORD at the Temple in Jerusalem remained the same. Jeroboam, fearing that the people would transfer their allegiance to Rehoboam, created two new shrines in his kingdom so that his people would not have to go to Jerusalem to satisfy religious obligations. **28:** The gold calves were extremely close in appearance to the bull image found in the Canaanite worship of Baal. Since the bull is a symbol of strength and virility, its imagery was also applied to God in several biblical passages (cf. Gen 49:24; Ps 132:2, 5; Isa 49:26; 60:16). Biblical passages instruct Israel to divorce itself from the adverse influences of calf/bull worship, since it was the leading cause of the Israelites' unfaithfulness to the LORD (Exod 32:2–6, 19–20; 1 Kgs 12:28–31; Hos 13:1–3). **31:** Bethel was in the south and Dan in the north. It is possible that these were shrines to the LORD and the calves were symbols, not intended to be seen as idols, but the writer regards Jerusalem as the only legitimate place to worship the LORD. Compounding Jeroboam's sin was the appointment of non-Levites as priests at the local shrines. He is also accused of changing the religious calendar by establishing a festival to rival the Festival of Shelters—the festival celebrated when the Temple was dedicated.

13:1–34 A Prophet Denounces Jeroboam. The story of the visit of the Judean prophet is enigmatic, but the

Josiah will be born into the dynasty of David. On
you he will sacrifice the priests from the pagan
shrines who come here to burn incense, and human bones will be burned on you." [3]That same
day the man of God gave a sign to prove his message. He said, "The LORD has promised to give
this sign: This altar will split apart, and its ashes
will be poured out on the ground."
[4]When King Jeroboam heard the man of God
speaking against the altar at Bethel, he pointed
at him and shouted, "Seize that man!" But instantly the king's hand became paralyzed in that
position, and he couldn't pull it back. [5]At the
same time a wide crack appeared in the altar, and
the ashes poured out, just as the man of God had
predicted in his message from the LORD.
[6]The king cried out to the man of God,
"Please ask the LORD your God to restore my
hand again!" So the man of God prayed to the
LORD, and the king's hand was restored and he
could move it again.
[7]Then the king said to the man of God, "Come
to the palace with me and have something to eat,
and I will give you a gift."
[8]But the man of God said to the king, "Even
if you gave me half of everything you own, I
would not go with you. I would not eat or drink
anything in this place. [9]For the LORD gave me
this command: 'You must not eat or drink anything while you are there, and do not return to
Judah by the same way you came.' " [10]So he left
Bethel and went home another way.
[11]As it happened, there was an old prophet
living in Bethel, and his sons* came home and
told him what the man of God had done in Bethel that day. They also told their father what the
man had said to the king. [12]The old prophet asked
them, "Which way did he go?" So they showed
their father* which road the man of God had
taken. [13]"Quick, saddle the donkey," the old man
said. So they saddled the donkey for him, and he
mounted it.
[14]Then he rode after the man of God and
found him sitting under a great tree. The old
prophet asked him, "Are you the man of God
who came from Judah?"
"Yes, I am," he replied.
[15]Then he said to the man of God, "Come
home with me and eat some food."
[16]"No, I cannot," he replied. "I am not allowed
to eat or drink anything here in this place. [17]For
the LORD gave me this command: 'You must not
eat or drink anything while you are there, and
do not return to Judah by the same way you
came.' "
[18]But the old prophet answered, "I am a
prophet, too, just as you are. And an angel gave
me this command from the LORD: 'Bring him
home with you so he can have something to eat
and drink.' " But the old man was lying to him.
[19]So they went back together, and the man of
God ate and drank at the prophet's home.
[20]Then while they were sitting at the table, a
command from the LORD came to the old prophet. [21]He cried out to the man of God from Judah,
"This is what the LORD says: You have defied the
word of the LORD and have disobeyed the command the LORD your God gave you. [22]You came
back to this place and ate and drank where he
told you not to eat or drink. Because of this, your
body will not be buried in the grave of your ancestors."
[23]After the man of God had finished eating
and drinking, the old prophet saddled his own
donkey for him, [24]and the man of God started
off again. But as he was traveling along, a lion
came out and killed him. His body lay there on
the road, with the donkey and the lion standing
beside it. [25]People who passed by saw the body
lying in the road and the lion standing beside it,
and they went and reported it in Bethel, where
the old prophet lived.
[26]When the prophet heard the report, he said,
"It is the man of God who disobeyed the LORD's
command. The LORD has fulfilled his word by
causing the lion to attack and kill him."
[27]Then the prophet said to his sons, "Saddle a
donkey for me." So they saddled a donkey, [28]and
he went out and found the body lying in the road.
The donkey and lion were still standing there beside it, for the lion had not eaten the body nor
attacked the donkey. [29]So the prophet laid the
body of the man of God on the donkey and took
it back to the town to mourn over him and bury
him. [30]He laid the body in his own grave, crying
out in grief, "Oh, my brother!"
[31]Afterward the prophet said to his sons,

13:11 As in Greek version; Hebrew reads *son.* **13:12** As in Greek version; Hebrew reads *They had seen.*

point is clear. Jeroboam's failure to keep God's law was the source of his, his family's, and his people's downfall. **9:** Eating and drinking at Bethel would have indicated approval of the shrine there. **11–34:** This part of the story has nothing to do with Jeroboam but concerns obedience to the prophetic word and has affinities with other prophetic legends (see the stories about Elijah and Elisha). **31–32:** The oracle is fulfilled in the purge of Josiah (2 Kgs 23:15–18), who saves the bones of the old prophet.

"When I die, bury me in the grave where the man of God is buried. Lay my bones beside his bones. 32 For the message the LORD told him to proclaim against the altar in Bethel and against the pagan shrines in the towns of Samaria will certainly come true."

33 But even after this, Jeroboam did not turn from his evil ways. He continued to choose priests from the common people. He appointed anyone who wanted to become a priest for the pagan shrines. 34 This became a great sin and resulted in the utter destruction of Jeroboam's dynasty from the face of the earth.

Ahijah's Prophecy against Jeroboam

14 At that time Jeroboam's son Abijah became very sick. 2 So Jeroboam told his wife, "Disguise yourself so that no one will recognize you as my wife. Then go to the prophet Ahijah at Shiloh—the man who told me I would become king. 3 Take him a gift of ten loaves of bread, some cakes, and a jar of honey, and ask him what will happen to the boy."

4 So Jeroboam's wife went to Ahijah's home at Shiloh. He was an old man now and could no longer see. 5 But the LORD had told Ahijah, "Jeroboam's wife will come here, pretending to be someone else. She will ask you about her son, for he is very sick. Give her the answer I give you."

6 So when Ahijah heard her footsteps at the door, he called out, "Come in, wife of Jeroboam! Why are you pretending to be someone else?" Then he told her, "I have bad news for you. 7 Give your husband, Jeroboam, this message from the LORD, the God of Israel: 'I promoted you from the ranks of the common people and made you ruler over my people Israel. 8 I ripped the kingdom away from the family of David and gave it to you. But you have not been like my servant David, who obeyed my commands and followed me with all his heart and always did whatever I wanted. 9 You have done more evil than all who lived before you. You have made other gods for yourself and have made me furious with your gold calves. And since you have turned your back on me, 10 I will bring disaster on your dynasty and will destroy every one of your male descendants, slave and free alike, anywhere in Israel. I will burn up your royal dynasty as one burns up trash until it is all gone. 11 The members of Jeroboam's family who die in the city will be eaten by dogs, and those who die in the field will be eaten by vultures. I, the LORD, have spoken.' "

12 Then Ahijah said to Jeroboam's wife, "Go on home, and when you enter the city, the child will die. 13 All Israel will mourn for him and bury him. He is the only member of your family who will have a proper burial, for this child is the only good thing that the LORD, the God of Israel, sees in the entire family of Jeroboam.

14 "In addition, the LORD will raise up a king over Israel who will destroy the family of Jeroboam. This will happen today, even now! 15 Then the LORD will shake Israel like a reed whipped about in a stream. He will uproot the people of Israel from this good land that he gave their ancestors and will scatter them beyond the Euphrates River,* for they have angered the LORD with the Asherah poles they have set up for worship. 16 He will abandon Israel because Jeroboam sinned and made Israel sin along with him."

17 So Jeroboam's wife returned to Tirzah, and the child died just as she walked through the door of her home. 18 And all Israel buried him and mourned for him, as the LORD had promised through the prophet Ahijah.

19 The rest of the events in Jeroboam's reign, including all his wars and how he ruled, are recorded in *The Book of the History of the Kings of Israel.* 20 Jeroboam reigned in Israel twenty-two years. When Jeroboam died, his son Nadab became the next king.

Rehoboam Rules in Judah

21 Meanwhile, Rehoboam son of Solomon was king in Judah. He was forty-one years old when he became king, and he reigned seventeen years in Jerusalem, the city the LORD had chosen from among all the tribes of Israel as the place to honor his name. Rehoboam's mother was Naamah, an Ammonite woman.

22 During Rehoboam's reign, the people of Judah did what was evil in the LORD's sight, provoking his anger with their sin, for it was even

14:15 Hebrew *the river.*

14:1–20 Jeroboam's Decline. Jeroboam's continued apostasy, even after the prophet's oracle, has ill effects for the king. **1–3:** Jeroboam sends his wife as a representative of the king and the kingdom. She clearly had freedom to travel and freedom to consult the prophet. **12–13:** Jeroboam's son's death is presented positively: As a reward for his faith he was to be buried decently, the only one of Jeroboam's descendants to be properly mourned.

14:21–31 Rehoboam's Decline. Rehoboam, Solomon's son, was not faithful to the LORD and continued to lead Judah astray. He, too, will suffer the consequences. **23–24:** *Pillars* were standing stones used

worse than that of their ancestors. 23 For they also built for themselves pagan shrines and set up sacred pillars and Asherah poles on every high hill and under every green tree. 24 There were even male and female shrine prostitutes throughout the land. The people imitated the detestable practices of the pagan nations the LORD had driven from the land ahead of the Israelites.

25 In the fifth year of King Rehoboam's reign, King Shishak of Egypt came up and attacked Jerusalem. 26 He ransacked the treasuries of the LORD's Temple and the royal palace; he stole everything, including all the gold shields Solomon had made. 27 King Rehoboam later replaced them with bronze shields as substitutes, and he entrusted them to the care of the commanders of the guard who protected the entrance to the royal palace. 28 Whenever the king went to the Temple of the LORD, the guards would also take the shields and then return them to the guardroom.

29 The rest of the events in Rehoboam's reign and everything he did are recorded in *The Book of the History of the Kings of Judah.* 30 There was constant war between Rehoboam and Jeroboam. 31 When Rehoboam died, he was buried among his ancestors in the City of David. His mother was Naamah, an Ammonite woman. Then his son Abijam* became the next king.

Abijam Rules in Judah

15 Abijam* began to rule over Judah in the eighteenth year of Jeroboam's reign in Israel. 2 He reigned in Jerusalem three years. His mother was Maacah, the daughter of Absalom.*

3 He committed the same sins as his father before him, and he was not faithful to the LORD his God, as his ancestor David had been. 4 But for David's sake, the LORD his God allowed his descendants to continue ruling, shining like a lamp, and he gave Abijam a son to rule after him in Jerusalem. 5 For David had done what was pleasing in the LORD's sight and had obeyed the LORD's commands throughout his life, except in the affair concerning Uriah the Hittite.

6 There was war between Abijam and Jeroboam* throughout Abijam's reign. 7 The rest of the events in Abijam's reign and everything he did are recorded in *The Book of the History of the Kings of Judah.* There was constant war between Abijam and Jeroboam. 8 When Abijam died, he was buried in the City of David. Then his son Asa became the next king.

Asa Rules in Judah

9 Asa began to rule over Judah in the twentieth year of Jeroboam's reign in Israel. 10 He reigned in Jerusalem forty-one years. His grandmother* was Maacah, the daughter of Absalom.

11 Asa did what was pleasing in the LORD's sight, as his ancestor David had done. 12 He banished the male and female shrine prostitutes from the land and got rid of all the idols* his ancestors had made. 13 He even deposed his grandmother Maacah from her position as queen mother be-

14:31 Also known as *Abijah.* **15:1** Also known as *Abijah.* **15:2** Hebrew *Abishalom* (also in 15:10), a variant spelling of Absalom; compare 2 Chr 11:20. **15:6** As in a few Hebrew and Greek manuscripts; most Hebrew manuscripts read *between Rehoboam and Jeroboam.* **15:10** Or *The queen mother;* Hebrew reads *His mother* (also in 15:13); compare 15:2. **15:12** The Hebrew term (literally *round things*) probably alludes to dung.

in worship; the biblical writers connect them with service to other gods. *Asherah poles* were fertility symbols used in the worship of the Canaanite goddess Asherah. **25:** *King Shishak* is generally taken to be Sheshonq I (945–924 BC).

15:1—22:53 Israel and Judah

These chapters summarize the character and some of the events of the reigns of the kings of Judah and Israel. The writer(s) of 1 and 2 Kings were mainly concerned with the details of events as they related to the LORD. The reader is invited to learn about all the other events of the kings' reigns in the annals of the kings of Judah or the annals of the kings of Israel, neither of which are extant. The kings of Israel and Judah were seen as good or bad. This determination rested solely on the religious behavior of a king; either he was faithful and worshiped only the LORD, or he was unfaithful and worshiped other gods. Because of confusion over overlapping reigns (co-regencies) and sometimes politicized dating when a king began to seek power rather than when he assumed power, it is extremely difficult to be precise about dating each king's reign. All dates are to some extent approximations. Israel had only one king, Jehu, who is given approval by the authors of Kings, and he reigned for twenty-seven years. Nineteen bad kings ruled for a total of 182 years. Judah had eight good kings and twelve bad kings; the good kings ruled for a total of 224 years, and the bad kings for 121 years.

15:9–24 Asa of Judah. Asa is one of the few kings who is described as good (cf. 2 Chr 13:23—16:14).

cause she had made an obscene Asherah pole. He cut down her obscene pole and burned it in the Kidron Valley. [14]Although the pagan shrines were not removed, Asa's heart remained completely faithful to the LORD throughout his life. [15]He brought into the Temple of the LORD the silver and gold and the various items that he and his father had dedicated.

[16]There was constant war between King Asa of Judah and King Baasha of Israel. [17]King Baasha of Israel invaded Judah and fortified Ramah in order to prevent anyone from entering or leaving King Asa's territory in Judah.

[18]Asa responded by removing all the silver and gold that was left in the treasuries of the Temple of the LORD and the royal palace. He sent it with some of his officials to Ben-hadad son of Tabrimmon, son of Hezion, the king of Aram, who was ruling in Damascus, along with this message:

> [19]"Let there be a treaty* between you and me like the one between your father and my father. See, I am sending you a gift of silver and gold. Break your treaty with King Baasha of Israel so that he will leave me alone."

[20]Ben-hadad agreed to King Asa's request and sent the commanders of his army to attack the towns of Israel. They conquered the towns of Ijon, Dan, Abel-beth-maacah, and all Kinnereth, and all the land of Naphtali. [21]As soon as Baasha of Israel heard what was happening, he abandoned his project of fortifying Ramah and withdrew to Tirzah. [22]Then King Asa sent an order throughout Judah, requiring that everyone, without exception, help to carry away the building stones and timbers that Baasha had been using to fortify Ramah. Asa used these materials to fortify the town of Geba in Benjamin and the town of Mizpah.

[23]The rest of the events in Asa's reign—the extent of his power, everything he did, and the names of the cities he built—are recorded in *The Book of the History of the Kings of Judah.* In his old age his feet became diseased. [24]When Asa died, he was buried with his ancestors in the City of David.

Then Jehoshaphat, Asa's son, became the next king.

Nadab Rules in Israel

[25]Nadab son of Jeroboam began to rule over Israel in the second year of King Asa's reign in Judah. He reigned in Israel two years. [26]But he did what was evil in the LORD's sight and followed the example of his father, continuing the sins that Jeroboam had led Israel to commit.

[27]Then Baasha son of Ahijah, from the tribe of Issachar, plotted against Nadab and assassinated him while he and the Israelite army were laying siege to the Philistine town of Gibbethon. [28]Baasha killed Nadab in the third year of King Asa's reign in Judah, and he became the next king of Israel.

[29]He immediately slaughtered all the descendants of King Jeroboam, so that not one of the royal family was left, just as the LORD had promised concerning Jeroboam by the prophet Ahijah from Shiloh. [30]This was done because Jeroboam had provoked the anger of the LORD, the God of Israel, by the sins he had committed and the sins he had led Israel to commit.

[31]The rest of the events in Nadab's reign and everything he did are recorded in *The Book of the History of the Kings of Israel.*

Baasha Rules in Israel

[32]There was constant war between King Asa of Judah and King Baasha of Israel. [33]Baasha son of Ahijah began to rule over all Israel in the third year of King Asa's reign in Judah. Baasha reigned in Tirzah twenty-four years. [34]But he did what was evil in the LORD's sight and followed the example of Jeroboam, continuing the sins that Jeroboam had led Israel to commit.

16

This message from the LORD was delivered to King Baasha by the prophet Jehu son of Hanani: [2]"I lifted you out of the dust to make you ruler of my people Israel, but you have followed the evil example of Jeroboam. You have provoked my anger by causing my people Israel to sin. [3]So now I will

15:19 As in Greek version; Hebrew reads *There is a treaty.*

He initiated a large-scale and widespread reform. **14–15:** It did not matter that Asa did not remove all of the pagan shrines from the land; he had successfully reestablished the worship of the LORD in Judah. **20:** The places listed are all in northern Israel. Thus, Asa used Ben-hadad to divert Baasha's attention from his southern border with Judah.

15:25—16:7 Nadab. Baasha. Nadab does not last long as king of Israel. Baasha kills Nadab and all of Jeroboam's descendants. This was a customary practice for the founders of new royal houses but here also fulfilled Ahijah's oracle against Jeroboam.

destroy you and your family, just as I destroyed the descendants of Jeroboam son of Nebat. 4 The members of Baasha's family who die in the city will be eaten by dogs, and those who die in the field will be eaten by vultures."

5 The rest of the events in Baasha's reign and the extent of his power are recorded in *The Book of the History of the Kings of Israel.* 6 When Baasha died, he was buried in Tirzah. Then his son Elah became the next king.

7 The message from the LORD against Baasha and his family came through the prophet Jehu son of Hanani. It was delivered because Baasha had done what was evil in the LORD's sight (just as the family of Jeroboam had done), and also because Baasha had destroyed the family of Jeroboam. The LORD's anger was provoked by Baasha's sins.

Elah Rules in Israel

8 Elah son of Baasha began to rule over Israel in the twenty-sixth year of King Asa's reign in Judah. He reigned in the city of Tirzah for two years.

9 Then Zimri, who commanded half of the royal chariots, made plans to kill him. One day in Tirzah, Elah was getting drunk at the home of Arza, the supervisor of the palace. 10 Zimri walked in and struck him down and killed him. This happened in the twenty-seventh year of King Asa's reign in Judah. Then Zimri became the next king.

11 Zimri immediately killed the entire royal family of Baasha, leaving him not even a single male child. He even destroyed distant relatives and friends. 12 So Zimri destroyed the dynasty of Baasha as the LORD had promised through the prophet Jehu. 13 This happened because of all the sins Baasha and his son Elah had committed, and because of the sins they led Israel to commit. They provoked the anger of the LORD, the God of Israel, with their worthless idols.

14 The rest of the events in Elah's reign and everything he did are recorded in *The Book of the History of the Kings of Israel.*

Zimri Rules in Israel

15 Zimri began to rule over Israel in the twenty-seventh year of King Asa's reign in Judah, but his reign in Tirzah lasted only seven days. The army of Israel was then attacking the Philistine town of Gibbethon. 16 When they heard that Zimri had committed treason and had assassinated the king, that very day they chose Omri, commander of the army, as the new king of Israel. 17 So Omri led the entire army of Israel up from Gibbethon to attack Tirzah, Israel's capital. 18 When Zimri saw that the city had been taken, he went into the citadel of the palace and burned it down over himself and died in the flames. 19 For he, too, had done what was evil in the LORD's sight. He followed the example of Jeroboam in all the sins he had committed and led Israel to commit.

20 The rest of the events in Zimri's reign and his conspiracy are recorded in *The Book of the History of the Kings of Israel.*

Omri Rules in Israel

21 But now the people of Israel were split into two factions. Half the people tried to make Tibni son of Ginath their king, while the other half supported Omri. 22 But Omri's supporters defeated the supporters of Tibni. So Tibni was killed, and Omri became the next king.

23 Omri began to rule over Israel in the thirty-first year of King Asa's reign in Judah. He reigned twelve years in all, six of them in Tirzah. 24 Then Omri bought the hill now known as Samaria from its owner, Shemer, for 150 pounds of silver.* He built a city on it and called the city Samaria in honor of Shemer.

25 But Omri did what was evil in the LORD's sight, even more than any of the kings before him. 26 He followed the example of Jeroboam son of Nebat in all the sins he had committed and led Israel to commit. The people provoked the anger of the LORD, the God of Israel, with their worthless idols.

27 The rest of the events in Omri's reign, the extent of his power, and everything he did are recorded in *The Book of the History of the Kings of Israel.* 28 When Omri died, he was buried in Samaria. Then his son Ahab became the next king.

16:24 Hebrew *for 2 talents* [68 kilograms] *of silver.*

16:21–28 Omri of Israel. Omri was the first ruler to bring stability to the northern kingdom, both domestically and on an international level. Because of this solid structure, the Omride dynasty would last longer than any other in Israel, a total of thirty-three years. Historically, Omri was one of the most powerful and important kings of Israel. The author disposes of Omri in just a few verses using the same formulas as for all other kings indicating that his interests are primarily theological rather than historical. **21:** Omri's origin is mysterious, for neither his parents nor his tribe are mentioned; he suddenly appears as "commander of the army" (v. 16). Nevertheless, scholars postulate his origins probably lay in a family who served as foreign mercenaries during David's time.

Ahab Rules in Israel
29 Ahab son of Omri began to rule over Israel in
the thirty-eighth year of King Asa's reign in Judah. He reigned in Samaria twenty-two years.
30 But Ahab son of Omri did what was evil in the
LORD's sight, even more than any of the kings
before him. 31 And as though it were not enough
to follow the example of Jeroboam, he married
Jezebel, the daughter of King Ethbaal of the Sidonians, and he began to bow down in worship
of Baal. 32 First Ahab built a temple and an altar
for Baal in Samaria. 33 Then he set up an Asherah
pole. He did more to provoke the anger of the
LORD, the God of Israel, than any of the other
kings of Israel before him.
34 It was during his reign that Hiel, a man
from Bethel, rebuilt Jericho. When he laid its
foundations, it cost him the life of his oldest son,
Abiram. And when he completed it and set up
its gates, it cost him the life of his youngest son,
Segub.* This all happened according to the message from the LORD concerning Jericho spoken
by Joshua son of Nun.

Elijah Fed by Ravens
17 Now Elijah, who was from Tishbe in
Gilead, told King Ahab, "As surely as
the LORD, the God of Israel, lives—the
God I serve—there will be no dew or rain during
the next few years until I give the word!"
2 Then the LORD said to Elijah, 3 "Go to the
east and hide by Kerith Brook, near where it enters the Jordan River. 4 Drink from the brook and
eat what the ravens bring you, for I have commanded them to bring you food."
5 So Elijah did as the LORD told him and
camped beside Kerith Brook, east of the Jordan.
6 The ravens brought him bread and meat each
morning and evening, and he drank from the
brook. 7 But after a while the brook dried up, for
there was no rainfall anywhere in the land.

The Widow at Zarephath
8 Then the LORD said to Elijah, 9 "Go and live in
the village of Zarephath, near the city of Sidon. I
have instructed a widow there to feed you."
10 So he went to Zarephath. As he arrived at
the gates of the village, he saw a widow gathering sticks, and he asked her, "Would you please
bring me a little water in a cup?" 11 As she was
going to get it, he called to her, "Bring me a bite
of bread, too."
12 But she said, "I swear by the LORD your
God that I don't have a single piece of bread in
the house. And I have only a handful of flour left
in the jar and a little cooking oil in the bottom of
the jug. I was just gathering a few sticks to cook
this last meal, and then my son and I will die."
13 But Elijah said to her, "Don't be afraid! Go
ahead and do just what you've said, but make a
little bread for me first. Then use what's left to
prepare a meal for yourself and your son. 14 For
this is what the LORD, the God of Israel, says:
There will always be flour and olive oil left in
your containers until the time when the LORD
sends rain and the crops grow again!"
15 So she did as Elijah said, and she and Elijah
and her family continued to eat for many days.

16:34 An ancient Hebrew scribal tradition reads *He killed his oldest son when he laid its foundations, and he killed his youngest son when he set up its gates.*

16:29–34 Ahab of Israel. Ahab (874–853 BC) diligently continued the domestic and foreign policies of Omri. He maintained good relations with his neighbors, including marrying Jezebel, the daughter of the king of Sidon, a Phoenician city. **31:** As a Phoenician princess Jezebel would have been high priestess of the chief cult, in this case Baal Melqart, and her father would have been high priest of the cult of Ashtoreth (Astarte). This made an extremely powerful bond between religion and state, as the father and daughter could control the economy, politics, and religion. As readers will see, Jezebel assumed an equally powerful role in Israel's religion and government. She was an essential pillar of Ahab's reign, an important supporter of the Baal and Asherah cults, and she gained the temporary support of the people of Israel. The relationship between Ahab and Jezebel seems to have been one of mutual respect. Jezebel enjoyed a great deal of flexibility, independence, and responsibility in the day-to-day running of the kingdom. She was an active member of the government, functioning as queen and high priestess. She supported 450 prophets of Baal and 400 prophets of Asherah. She had routine access to the king's seal and used it at will. She was seen as the legitimate heir to Ahab's throne. Jezebel knew she had ultimate power and authority as queen. It would have been to Ahab's advantage to give Jezebel such authority, in order to keep the Canaanite population happy. **31–33:** Ahab was supposed to be devoted to the LORD; instead he allowed his foreign wife to lead him, and ultimately Israel, astray.

17:1—19:21 Elijah and Elisha. Elijah's work as prophet began toward the end of Ahab's reign. **17:1:** The drought shows that it is the LORD, not Baal, who controls the elements and the land's fertility. **9:** *Zarephath* was part of Sidon and out of Ahab's jurisdiction.

16 There was always enough flour and olive oil left in the containers, just as the LORD had promised through Elijah.

17 Some time later the woman's son became sick. He grew worse and worse, and finally he died. 18 Then she said to Elijah, "O man of God, what have you done to me? Have you come here to point out my sins and kill my son?"

19 But Elijah replied, "Give me your son." And he took the child's body from her arms, carried him up the stairs to the room where he was staying, and laid the body on his bed. 20 Then Elijah cried out to the LORD, "O LORD my God, why have you brought tragedy to this widow who has opened her home to me, causing her son to die?"

21 And he stretched himself out over the child three times and cried out to the LORD, "O LORD my God, please let this child's life return to him." 22 The LORD heard Elijah's prayer, and the life of the child returned, and he revived! 23 Then Elijah brought him down from the upper room and gave him to his mother. "Look!" he said. "Your son is alive!"

24 Then the woman told Elijah, "Now I know for sure that you are a man of God, and that the LORD truly speaks through you."

The Contest on Mount Carmel

18 Later on, in the third year of the drought, the LORD said to Elijah, "Go and present yourself to King Ahab. Tell him that I will soon send rain!" 2 So Elijah went to appear before Ahab.

Meanwhile, the famine had become very severe in Samaria. 3 So Ahab summoned Obadiah, who was in charge of the palace. (Obadiah was a devoted follower of the LORD. 4 Once when Jezebel had tried to kill all the LORD's prophets, Obadiah had hidden 100 of them in two caves. He put fifty prophets in each cave and supplied them with food and water.) 5 Ahab said to Obadiah, "We must check every spring and valley in the land to see if we can find enough grass to save at least some of my horses and mules." 6 So they divided the land between them. Ahab went one way by himself, and Obadiah went another way by himself.

7 As Obadiah was walking along, he suddenly saw Elijah coming toward him. Obadiah recognized him at once and bowed low to the ground before him. "Is it really you, my lord Elijah?" he asked.

8 "Yes, it is," Elijah replied. "Now go and tell your master, 'Elijah is here.' "

9 "Oh, sir," Obadiah protested, "what harm have I done to you that you are sending me to my death at the hands of Ahab? 10 For I swear by the LORD your God that the king has searched every nation and kingdom on earth from end to end to find you. And each time he was told, 'Elijah isn't here,' King Ahab forced the king of that nation to swear to the truth of his claim. 11 And now you say, 'Go and tell your master, "Elijah is here." ' 12 But as soon as I leave you, the Spirit of the LORD will carry you away to who knows where. When Ahab comes and cannot find you, he will kill me. Yet I have been a true servant of the LORD all my life. 13 Has no one told you, my lord, about the time when Jezebel was trying to kill the LORD's prophets? I hid 100 of them in two caves and supplied them with food and water. 14 And now you say, 'Go and tell your master, "Elijah is here." ' Sir, if I do that, Ahab will certainly kill me."

15 But Elijah said, "I swear by the LORD Almighty, in whose presence I stand, that I will present myself to Ahab this very day."

16 So Obadiah went to tell Ahab that Elijah had come, and Ahab went out to meet Elijah. 17 When Ahab saw him, he exclaimed, "So, is it really you, you troublemaker of Israel?"

18 "I have made no trouble for Israel," Elijah replied. "You and your family are the troublemakers, for you have refused to obey the commands of the LORD and have worshiped the images of Baal instead. 19 Now summon all Israel to join me at Mount Carmel, along with the 450 prophets of Baal and the 400 prophets of Asherah who are supported by Jezebel.*"

18:19 Hebrew *who eat at Jezebel's table.*

15–16: Every time the widow reached for the supplies, she was demonstrating her faith in the LORD as her provider. **17–18:** The widow petitioned Elijah, in order to ascertain the reason for God's great anger toward her, such that he would take away her only son. The implication is that her son's death is divine punishment for some great sin. **21–22:** Elijah's actions suggest that life went from his body into the boy's so that he might be revived. The point of the story, however, is that this was the LORD's doing. **24:** Only after such a dramatic episode could the widow be convinced that the LORD truly is the sovereign God of the universe. **18:5:** Ahab is more concerned about his animals than his people. **9–17:** Elijah was deemed a criminal and enemy of the state because he prophesied against the royal cult of Baal. **19:** Baal and Asherah were the leading male and female deities, respectively, in the fertility region of ancient Caanan. **22:** Elijah's proclamation of him-

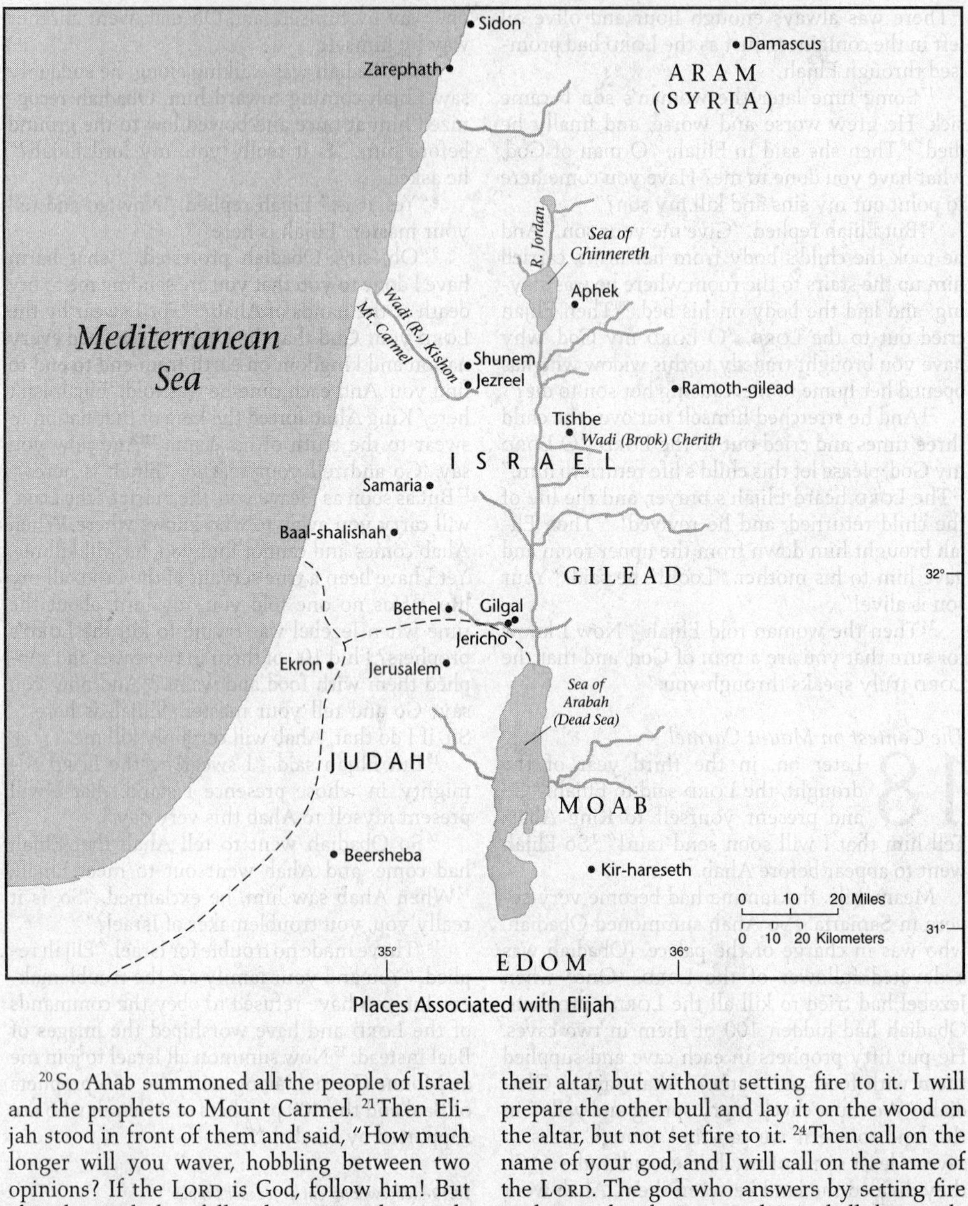

Places Associated with Elijah

[20]So Ahab summoned all the people of Israel and the prophets to Mount Carmel. [21]Then Elijah stood in front of them and said, "How much longer will you waver, hobbling between two opinions? If the LORD is God, follow him! But if Baal is God, then follow him!" But the people were completely silent.

[22]Then Elijah said to them, "I am the only prophet of the LORD who is left, but Baal has 450 prophets. [23]Now bring two bulls. The prophets of Baal may choose whichever one they wish and cut it into pieces and lay it on the wood of their altar, but without setting fire to it. I will prepare the other bull and lay it on the wood on the altar, but not set fire to it. [24]Then call on the name of your god, and I will call on the name of the LORD. The god who answers by setting fire to the wood is the true God!" And all the people agreed.

[25]Then Elijah said to the prophets of Baal, "You go first, for there are many of you. Choose one of the bulls, and prepare it and call on the name of your god. But do not set fire to the wood."

---

self as the last prophet was an exaggeration, since there are at least one hundred that Obadiah saved. In any case, he alone would compete with and be victorious over the assembled prophets of Baal and Asherah. **23–24:** The described test would be decisive in determining which god, Baal or the LORD, controlled

26 So they prepared one of the bulls and placed
it on the altar. Then they called on the name of
Baal from morning until noontime, shouting,
"O Baal, answer us!" But there was no reply of
any kind. Then they danced, hobbling around the
altar they had made.
27 About noontime Elijah began mocking
them. "You'll have to shout louder," he scoffed,
"for surely he is a god! Perhaps he is daydream-
ing, or is relieving himself.* Or maybe he is away
on a trip, or is asleep and needs to be wakened!"
28 So they shouted louder, and following their
normal custom, they cut themselves with knives
and swords until the blood gushed out. 29 They
raved all afternoon until the time of the evening
sacrifice, but still there was no sound, no reply,
no response.
30 Then Elijah called to the people, "Come
over here!" They all crowded around him as he
repaired the altar of the LORD that had been torn
down. 31 He took twelve stones, one to represent
each of the tribes of Israel,* 32 and he used the
stones to rebuild the altar in the name of the
LORD. Then he dug a trench around the altar
large enough to hold about three gallons.* 33 He
piled wood on the altar, cut the bull into pieces,
and laid the pieces on the wood.
Then he said, "Fill four large jars with water, and pour the water over the offering and the
wood."
34 After they had done this, he said, "Do the
same thing again!" And when they were finished, he said, "Now do it a third time!" So they
did as he said, 35 and the water ran around the
altar and even filled the trench.
36 At the usual time for offering the evening
sacrifice, Elijah the prophet walked up to the altar and prayed, "O LORD, God of Abraham, Isaac,
and Jacob,* prove today that you are God in Israel and that I am your servant. Prove that I have
done all this at your command. 37 O LORD, answer
me! Answer me so these people will know that
you, O LORD, are God and that you have brought
them back to yourself."
38 Immediately the fire of the LORD flashed
down from heaven and burned up the young
bull, the wood, the stones, and the dust. It even
licked up all the water in the trench! 39 And when
all the people saw it, they fell face down on the
ground and cried out, "The LORD—he is God!
Yes, the LORD is God!"
40 Then Elijah commanded, "Seize all the prophets of Baal. Don't let a single one escape!" So the
people seized them all, and Elijah took them down
to the Kishon Valley and killed them there.

Elijah Prays for Rain

41 Then Elijah said to Ahab, "Go get something
to eat and drink, for I hear a mighty rainstorm
coming!"
42 So Ahab went to eat and drink. But Elijah
climbed to the top of Mount Carmel and bowed
low to the ground and prayed with his face between his knees.
43 Then he said to his servant, "Go and look
out toward the sea."
The servant went and looked, then returned
to Elijah and said, "I didn't see anything."
Seven times Elijah told him to go and look.
44 Finally the seventh time, his servant told him,
"I saw a little cloud about the size of a man's
hand rising from the sea."
Then Elijah shouted, "Hurry to Ahab and tell
him, 'Climb into your chariot and go back home.
If you don't hurry, the rain will stop you!' "
45 And soon the sky was black with clouds.
A heavy wind brought a terrific rainstorm, and
Ahab left quickly for Jezreel. 46 Then the LORD
gave special strength to Elijah. He tucked his
cloak into his belt* and ran ahead of Ahab's chariot all the way to the entrance of Jezreel.

Elijah Flees to Sinai

19 When Ahab got home, he told Jezebel
everything Elijah had done, including
the way he had killed all the prophets
of Baal. 2 So Jezebel sent this message to Elijah:
"May the gods strike me and even kill me if by
this time tomorrow I have not killed you just as
you killed them."

18:27 Or *is busy somewhere else, or is engaged in business.*
18:31 Hebrew *each of the tribes of the sons of Jacob to whom the LORD had said, "Your name will be Israel."*
18:32 Hebrew *2 seahs* [12 liters] *of seed.* **18:36** Hebrew *and Israel.* The names "Jacob" and "Israel" are often interchanged throughout the Old Testament, referring sometimes to the individual patriarch and sometimes to the nation.
18:46 Hebrew *He bound up his loins.*

the elements. **33–35:** The point of drenching the sacrifice is to make clear that the fire is not accidental and does not originate on the earth. It also makes the test all the more difficult in order to impress the audience with the LORD's power. **40:** The slaughter of the prophets of Baal counters Jezebel's slaughter of the LORD's prophets. **42–45:** Elijah calls for the end of the drought. God's answer is yet one more sign of the LORD's control over the elements and Elijah's prowess as a man of God. **19:1–3:** Upon learning of the fate of her prophets, Jezebel raged against Elijah and threatened his life. Elijah fled to escape her wrath.

[3]Elijah was afraid and fled for his life. He went to Beersheba, a town in Judah, and he left his servant there. [4]Then he went on alone into the wilderness, traveling all day. He sat down under a solitary broom tree and prayed that he might die. "I have had enough, LORD," he said. "Take my life, for I am no better than my ancestors who have already died."

[5]Then he lay down and slept under the broom tree. But as he was sleeping, an angel touched him and told him, "Get up and eat!" [6]He looked around and there beside his head was some bread baked on hot stones and a jar of water! So he ate and drank and lay down again.

[7]Then the angel of the LORD came again and touched him and said, "Get up and eat some more, or the journey ahead will be too much for you."

[8]So he got up and ate and drank, and the food gave him enough strength to travel forty days and forty nights to Mount Sinai,* the mountain of God. [9]There he came to a cave, where he spent the night.

The LORD Speaks to Elijah

But the LORD said to him, "What are you doing here, Elijah?"

[10]Elijah replied, "I have zealously served the LORD God Almighty. But the people of Israel have broken their covenant with you, torn down your altars, and killed every one of your prophets. I am the only one left, and now they are trying to kill me, too."

[11]"Go out and stand before me on the mountain," the LORD told him. And as Elijah stood there, the LORD passed by, and a mighty windstorm hit the mountain. It was such a terrible blast that the rocks were torn loose, but the LORD was not in the wind. After the wind there was an earthquake, but the LORD was not in the earthquake. [12]And after the earthquake there was a fire, but the LORD was not in the fire. And after the fire there was the sound of a gentle whisper. [13]When Elijah heard it, he wrapped his face in his cloak and went out and stood at the entrance of the cave.

And a voice said, "What are you doing here, Elijah?"

[14]He replied again, "I have zealously served the LORD God Almighty. But the people of Israel have broken their covenant with you, torn down your altars, and killed every one of your prophets. I am the only one left, and now they are trying to kill me, too."

[15]Then the LORD told him, "Go back the same way you came, and travel to the wilderness of Damascus. When you arrive there, anoint Hazael to be king of Aram. [16]Then anoint Jehu grandson of Nimshi* to be king of Israel, and anoint Elisha son of Shaphat from the town of Abel-meholah to replace you as my prophet. [17]Anyone who escapes from Hazael will be killed by Jehu, and those who escape Jehu will be killed by Elisha! [18]Yet I will preserve 7,000 others in Israel who have never bowed down to Baal or kissed him!"

The Call of Elisha

[19]So Elijah went and found Elisha son of Shaphat plowing a field. There were twelve teams of oxen in the field, and Elisha was plowing with the twelfth team. Elijah went over to him and threw his cloak across his shoulders and then walked away. [20]Elisha left the oxen standing there, ran

19:8 Hebrew *to Horeb,* another name for Sinai.
19:16 Hebrew *descendant of Nimshi;* compare 2 Kgs 9:2, 14.

4–7, 14–16: In spite of Elijah's feelings of despair and aloneness, God still had work for Elijah. **8:** Mount Sinai is the place where Moses received the law. **11–12:** The storm, earthquake, and fire, none of which represent God, might be associated with the storm god Baal. God appears to be controlling these activities, another show of the LORD's supremacy. **15–18:** God has a succession plan for Elijah. Elisha, not Elijah, will actually anoint Hazael and Jehu in 2 Kings 8—9. **19:** When Elijah found Elisha, he was plowing with twelve teams of oxen, a sign of wealth. Elijah's cloak was a symbol of his prophetic office. By throwing his cloak onto Elisha, Elijah was designating Elisha as his successor. Elijah signaled to Elisha that it was time to go; so, after bidding farewell to his parents, he joined Elijah. Elijah had been delivering unpleasant messages and fighting to stay alive for a long time; in essence, he was burned out and needed a break. God provided a colleague who would become a replacement. A prophet's job was not in general a prestigious position. Rather, it was a dangerous and humble assignment. A prophet was a spokesperson for God, an interpreter of God's will, an intermediary between God and the people. Although prophets did speak of the future, their predictions were usually made with respect to a promise of God's reward or punishment for good or bad behavior. When a prophet was commissioned by the LORD to deliver a message to the people or a king, the communiqué was generally not filled with good news. Prophets frequently conveyed a warning of God's wrath unless the contents of the announcement were obeyed. The prophets' messages were thus paradoxical, including doom and gloom as well as promise and guidance.

after Elijah, and said to him, "First let me go and kiss my father and mother good-bye, and then I will go with you!"

Elijah replied, "Go on back, but think about what I have done to you."

[21] So Elisha returned to his oxen and slaughtered them. He used the wood from the plow to build a fire to roast their flesh. He passed around the meat to the townspeople, and they all ate. Then he went with Elijah as his assistant.

Ben-Hadad Attacks Samaria

20 About that time King Ben-hadad of Aram mobilized his army, supported by the chariots and horses of thirty-two allied kings. They went to besiege Samaria, the capital of Israel, and launched attacks against it. [2] Ben-hadad sent messengers into the city to relay this message to King Ahab of Israel: "This is what Ben-hadad says: [3] 'Your silver and gold are mine, and so are your wives and the best of your children!' "

[4] "All right, my lord the king," Israel's king replied. "All that I have is yours!"

[5] Soon Ben-hadad's messengers returned again and said, "This is what Ben-hadad says: 'I have already demanded that you give me your silver, gold, wives, and children. [6] But about this time tomorrow I will send my officials to search your palace and the homes of your people. They will take away everything you consider valuable!' "

[7] Then Ahab summoned all the elders of the land and said to them, "Look how this man is stirring up trouble! I already agreed with his demand that I give him my wives and children and silver and gold."

[8] "Don't give in to any more demands," all the elders and the people advised.

[9] So Ahab told the messengers from Ben-hadad, "Say this to my lord the king: 'I will give you everything you asked for the first time, but I cannot accept this last demand of yours.' " So the messengers returned to Ben-hadad with that response.

[10] Then Ben-hadad sent this message to Ahab: "May the gods strike me and even kill me if there remains enough dust from Samaria to provide even a handful for each of my soldiers."

[11] The king of Israel sent back this answer: "A warrior putting on his sword for battle should not boast like a warrior who has already won."

[12] Ahab's reply reached Ben-hadad and the other kings as they were drinking in their tents.* "Prepare to attack!" Ben-hadad commanded his officers. So they prepared to attack the city.

Ahab's Victory over Ben-Hadad

[13] Then a certain prophet came to see King Ahab of Israel and told him, "This is what the LORD says: Do you see all these enemy forces? Today I will hand them all over to you. Then you will know that I am the LORD."

[14] Ahab asked, "How will he do it?"

And the prophet replied, "This is what the LORD says: The troops of the provincial commanders will do it."

"Should we attack first?" Ahab asked.

"Yes," the prophet answered.

[15] So Ahab mustered the troops of the 232 provincial commanders. Then he called out the rest of the army of Israel, some 7,000 men. [16] About noontime, as Ben-hadad and the thirty-two allied kings were still in their tents drinking themselves into a stupor, [17] the troops of the provincial commanders marched out of the city as the first contingent.

As they approached, Ben-hadad's scouts reported to him, "Some troops are coming from Samaria."

[18] "Take them alive," Ben-hadad commanded, "whether they have come for peace or for war."

[19] But Ahab's provincial commanders and the entire army had now come out to fight. [20] Each Israelite soldier killed his Aramean opponent, and suddenly the entire Aramean army panicked and fled. The Israelites chased them, but King Ben-hadad and a few of his charioteers escaped on horses. [21] However, the king of Israel destroyed the other horses and chariots and slaughtered the Arameans.

[22] Afterward the prophet said to King Ahab, "Get ready for another attack. Begin making plans now, for the king of Aram will come back next spring.*"

20:12 Or *in Succoth;* also in 20:16. **20:22** Hebrew *at the turn of the year;* similarly in 20:26. The first day of the year in the ancient Hebrew lunar calendar occurred in March or April.

20:1—22:40 Ahab of Israel. 20:1–43: This chapter probably went originally with chapter 22, as in the Greek version of 1 Kings, which has chapters 20 and 21 in reverse order. The stories in chapters 20 and 22 are out of place historically, since they assume a setting in which Israel was dominated by Aram (Syria), which was not the case during Ahab's reign. **1:** *Thirty-two allied kings* were rulers of city-states or chieftains dominated by Damascus. **2:** *Ahab*: This is one of the few places in the story where the king is mentioned by name. Most of the time, he is simply "the king of Israel." **32–33:** The servants of Ben-

Ben-Hadad's Second Attack

23 After their defeat, Ben-hadad's officers said to him, "The Israelite gods are gods of the hills; that is why they won. But we can beat them easily on the plains. 24 Only this time replace the kings with field commanders! 25 Recruit another army like the one you lost. Give us the same number of horses, chariots, and men, and we will fight against them on the plains. There's no doubt that we will beat them." So King Ben-hadad did as they suggested.

26 The following spring he called up the Aramean army and marched out against Israel, this time at Aphek. 27 Israel then mustered its army, set up supply lines, and marched out for battle. But the Israelite army looked like two little flocks of goats in comparison to the vast Aramean forces that filled the countryside!

28 Then the man of God went to the king of Israel and said, "This is what the LORD says: The Arameans have said, 'The LORD is a god of the hills and not of the plains.' So I will defeat this vast army for you. Then you will know that I am the LORD."

29 The two armies camped opposite each other for seven days, and on the seventh day the battle began. The Israelites killed 100,000 Aramean foot soldiers in one day. 30 The rest fled into the town of Aphek, but the wall fell on them and killed another 27,000. Ben-hadad fled into the town and hid in a secret room.

31 Ben-hadad's officers said to him, "Sir, we have heard that the kings of Israel are merciful. So let's humble ourselves by wearing burlap around our waists and putting ropes on our heads, and surrender to the king of Israel. Then perhaps he will let you live."

32 So they put on burlap and ropes, and they went to the king of Israel and begged, "Your servant Ben-hadad says, 'Please let me live!'"

The king of Israel responded, "Is he still alive? He is my brother!"

33 The men took this as a good sign and quickly picked up on his words. "Yes," they said, "your brother Ben-hadad!"

"Go and get him," the king of Israel told them. And when Ben-hadad arrived, Ahab invited him up into his chariot.

34 Ben-hadad told him, "I will give back the towns my father took from your father, and you may establish places of trade in Damascus, as my father did in Samaria."

Then Ahab said, "I will release you under these conditions." So they made a new treaty, and Ben-hadad was set free.

A Prophet Condemns Ahab

35 Meanwhile, the LORD instructed one of the group of prophets to say to another man, "Hit me!" But the man refused to hit the prophet. 36 Then the prophet told him, "Because you have not obeyed the voice of the LORD, a lion will kill you as soon as you leave me." And when he had gone, a lion did attack and kill him.

37 Then the prophet turned to another man and said, "Hit me!" So he struck the prophet and wounded him.

38 The prophet placed a bandage over his eyes to disguise himself and then waited beside the road for the king. 39 As the king passed by, the prophet called out to him, "Sir, I was in the thick of battle, and suddenly a man brought me a prisoner. He said, 'Guard this man; if for any reason he gets away, you will either die or pay a fine of seventy-five pounds* of silver!' 40 But while I was busy doing something else, the prisoner disappeared!"

"Well, it's your own fault," the king replied. "You have brought the judgment on yourself."

41 Then the prophet quickly pulled the bandage from his eyes, and the king of Israel recognized him as one of the prophets. 42 The prophet said to him, "This is what the LORD says: Because you have spared the man I said must be destroyed,* now you must die in his place, and your people will die instead of his people." 43 So the king of Israel went home to Samaria angry and sullen.

Naboth's Vineyard

21 Now there was a man named Naboth, from Jezreel, who owned a vineyard in Jezreel beside the palace of King Ahab of Samaria. 2 One day Ahab said to Naboth, "Since your vineyard is so convenient to my palace, I would like to buy it to use as a vegetable

20:39 Hebrew *1 talent* [34 kilograms]. **20:42** The Hebrew term used here refers to the complete consecration of things or people to the LORD, either by destroying them or by giving them as an offering.

hadad refer to him as the servant of the king of Israel. But the king calls him a brother, thus making him an equal and indicating that the king of Israel wants to be treaty partners with Ben-hadad. **42:** *Destroyed*: The Hebrew term indicates an aspect of holy war in which the enemy was killed as a sacrifice. The king of Israel is condemned for not carrying out the LORD's command, much as Saul is condemned in 1 Samuel 15 for the same offense.

21:1–29 Ahab and Naboth's Vineyard. 3: The land was Naboth's ancestral property; it was the inheritance of

garden. I will give you a better vineyard in exchange, or if you prefer, I will pay you for it."
3 But Naboth replied, "The LORD forbid that I
should give you the inheritance that was passed
down by my ancestors."
4 So Ahab went home angry and sullen because of Naboth's answer. The king went to bed
with his face to the wall and refused to eat!
5 "What's the matter?" his wife Jezebel asked
him. "What's made you so upset that you're not
eating?"
6 "I asked Naboth to sell me his vineyard or
trade it, but he refused!" Ahab told her.
7 "Are you the king of Israel or not?" Jezebel
demanded. "Get up and eat something, and don't
worry about it. I'll get you Naboth's vineyard!"
8 So she wrote letters in Ahab's name, sealed
them with his seal, and sent them to the elders
and other leaders of the town where Naboth
lived. 9 In her letters she commanded: "Call the
citizens together for fasting and prayer, and give
Naboth a place of honor. 10 And then seat two
scoundrels across from him who will accuse him
of cursing God and the king. Then take him out
and stone him to death."
11 So the elders and other town leaders followed the instructions Jezebel had written in the
letters. 12 They called for a fast and put Naboth at
a prominent place before the people. 13 Then the
two scoundrels came and sat down across from
him. And they accused Naboth before all the
people, saying, "He cursed God and the king." So
he was dragged outside the town and stoned to
death. 14 The town leaders then sent word to Jezebel, "Naboth has been stoned to death."
15 When Jezebel heard the news, she said to
Ahab, "You know the vineyard Naboth wouldn't
sell you? Well, you can have it now! He's dead!"
16 So Ahab immediately went down to the vineyard of Naboth to claim it.
17 But the LORD said to Elijah,* 18 "Go down to
meet King Ahab of Israel, who rules in Samaria.
He will be at Naboth's vineyard in Jezreel, claiming it for himself. 19 Give him this message: 'This
is what the LORD says: Wasn't it enough that you
killed Naboth? Must you rob him, too? Because
you have done this, dogs will lick your blood at
the very place where they licked the blood of
Naboth!' "
20 "So, my enemy, you have found me!" Ahab
exclaimed to Elijah.

"Yes," Elijah answered, "I have come because you have sold yourself to what is evil in
the LORD's sight. 21 So now the LORD says, 'I will
bring disaster on you and consume you. I will destroy every one of your male descendants, slave
and free alike, anywhere in Israel! 22 I am going
to destroy your family as I did the family of Jeroboam son of Nebat and the family of Baasha
son of Ahijah, for you have made me very angry
and have led Israel into sin.'
23 "And regarding Jezebel, the LORD says,
'Dogs will eat Jezebel's body at the plot of land
in Jezreel.*'
24 "The members of Ahab's family who die in
the city will be eaten by dogs, and those who die
in the field will be eaten by vultures."
25 (No one else so completely sold himself to
what was evil in the LORD's sight as Ahab did under the influence of his wife Jezebel. 26 His worst
outrage was worshiping idols* just as the Amorites had done—the people whom the LORD had
driven out from the land ahead of the Israelites.)
27 But when Ahab heard this message, he
tore his clothing, dressed in burlap, and fasted.
He even slept in burlap and went about in deep
mourning.

21:17 Hebrew *Elijah the Tishbite;* also in 21:28. **21:23** As in several Hebrew manuscripts, Syriac, and Latin Vulgate (see also 2 Kgs 9:26, 36); most Hebrew manuscripts read *at the city wall.* **21:26** The Hebrew term (literally *round things*) probably alludes to dung.

his forefathers. Thus Naboth's refusal was based on his legal rights, as well as religious principles. The Hebrew word for "inheritance" can refer to property, portion, or inheritance, suggesting God gives or assigns land to Israel, the tribes or individuals (see translator's notes). According to Leviticus 25:23, all land belongs to God, and inhabitants are merely long-term tenants; the LORD determines who holds the land. In addition, the family burial plot would also have been located there. Therefore it was well within Naboth's rights to refuse to sell this land to anyone, even the king. **7:** Behavior such as Naboth's was unacceptable to Jezebel, as a Phoenician; in Phoenicia a subject could not refuse the request of a king in this manner. **8–14:** Jezebel must have received an extensive education as a child, since she was able to write letters, presumably in Phoenician. She apparently knew how to write Hebrew as well, although she may have ordered a scribe to write or translate what she dictated. Nevertheless, she was acutely aware of judicial matters, since she was careful to obtain Naboth's land legally, even if by treachery. **17–24:** Although these were Jezebel's actions, God intended to punish Ahab and Jezebel equally for their actions. Ahab was just as guilty of Naboth's death as was Jezebel. This prophecy was a result not only of his and Jezebel's sins but also for leading Israel astray. **27–29:** Ahab's remorse delays his punishment until after his death, but it will fall on *his sons*.

28 Then another message from the LORD came
to Elijah: 29 "Do you see how Ahab has humbled
himself before me? Because he has done this, I
will not do what I promised during his lifetime.
It will happen to his sons; I will destroy his dynasty."

Jehoshaphat and Ahab

22 For three years there was no war between Aram and Israel. 2 Then during
the third year, King Jehoshaphat of
Judah went to visit King Ahab of Israel. 3 During
the visit, the king of Israel said to his officials,
"Do you realize that the town of Ramoth-gilead
belongs to us? And yet we've done nothing to
recapture it from the king of Aram!"
4 Then he turned to Jehoshaphat and asked,
"Will you join me in battle to recover Ramoth-
gilead?"
Jehoshaphat replied to the king of Israel,
"Why, of course! You and I are as one. My troops
are your troops, and my horses are your horses."
5 Then Jehoshaphat added, "But first let's find out
what the LORD says."
6 So the king of Israel summoned the prophets, about 400 of them, and asked them, "Should
I go to war against Ramoth-gilead, or should I
hold back?"
They all replied, "Yes, go right ahead! The
Lord will give the king victory."
7 But Jehoshaphat asked, "Is there not also a
prophet of the LORD here? We should ask him
the same question."
8 The king of Israel replied to Jehoshaphat,
"There is one more man who could consult the
LORD for us, but I hate him. He never prophesies
anything but trouble for me! His name is Micaiah son of Imlah."
Jehoshaphat replied, "That's not the way a
king should talk! Let's hear what he has to say."
9 So the king of Israel called one of his officials
and said, "Quick! Bring Micaiah son of Imlah."

Micaiah Prophesies against Ahab

10 King Ahab of Israel and King Jehoshaphat of
Judah, dressed in their royal robes, were sitting on thrones at the threshing floor near the
gate of Samaria. All of Ahab's prophets were
prophesying there in front of them. 11 One of
them, Zedekiah son of Kenaanah, made some
iron horns and proclaimed, "This is what the
LORD says: With these horns you will gore the
Arameans to death!"
12 All the other prophets agreed. "Yes," they
said, "go up to Ramoth-gilead and be victorious,
for the LORD will give the king victory!"
13 Meanwhile, the messenger who went to get
Micaiah said to him, "Look, all the prophets are
promising victory for the king. Be sure that you
agree with them and promise success."
14 But Micaiah replied, "As surely as the LORD
lives, I will say only what the LORD tells me to
say."
15 When Micaiah arrived before the king, Ahab
asked him, "Micaiah, should we go to war against
Ramoth-gilead, or should we hold back?"
Micaiah replied sarcastically, "Yes, go up and
be victorious, for the LORD will give the king victory!"
16 But the king replied sharply, "How many
times must I demand that you speak only the
truth to me when you speak for the LORD?"
17 Then Micaiah told him, "In a vision I saw
all Israel scattered on the mountains, like sheep
without a shepherd. And the LORD said, 'Their
master has been killed.* Send them home in
peace.' "
18 "Didn't I tell you?" the king of Israel exclaimed to Jehoshaphat. "He never prophesies
anything but trouble for me."
19 Then Micaiah continued, "Listen to what
the LORD says! I saw the LORD sitting on his
throne with all the armies of heaven around him,
on his right and on his left. 20 And the LORD said,
'Who can entice Ahab to go into battle against
Ramoth-gilead so he can be killed?'
"There were many suggestions, 21 and finally a
spirit approached the LORD and said, 'I can do it!'
22 " 'How will you do this?' the LORD asked.
"And the spirit replied, 'I will go out and inspire all of Ahab's prophets to speak lies.'
" 'You will succeed,' said the LORD. 'Go ahead
and do it.'
23 "So you see, the LORD has put a lying spirit
in the mouths of all your prophets. For the LORD
has pronounced your doom."

22:17 Hebrew *These people have no master.*

22:1–40 Jehoshaphat and Ahab. 2: As in chapter 20, the identification of Ahab as the king of Israel is secondary and probably incorrect. **6:** The prophets are probably court prophets who were sustained by the king. It is not clear whether they were even worshipers of the LORD. **7:** Jehoshaphat is skeptical of the quick answer and so requests a true prophet of the LORD, not associated with the court prophets. **13–23:** Micaiah is an excellent example of someone facing a difficult situation with strength, dignity, and courage. He knew the message he was to deliver would not be to the king's liking, yet he delivered it anyway.

24 Then Zedekiah son of Kenaanah walked
up to Micaiah and slapped him across the face.
"Since when did the Spirit of the LORD leave me
to speak to you?" he demanded.
25 And Micaiah replied, "You will find out
soon enough when you are trying to hide in
some secret room!"
26 "Arrest him!" the king of Israel ordered.
"Take him back to Amon, the governor of the
city, and to my son Joash. 27 Give them this order
from the king: 'Put this man in prison, and feed
him nothing but bread and water until I return
safely from the battle!' "
28 But Micaiah replied, "If you return safely, it
will mean that the LORD has not spoken through
me!" Then he added to those standing around,
"Everyone mark my words!"

The Death of Ahab

29 So King Ahab of Israel and King Jehoshaphat
of Judah led their armies against Ramoth-gilead.
30 The king of Israel said to Jehoshaphat, "As we
go into battle, I will disguise myself so no one
will recognize me, but you wear your royal
robes." So the king of Israel disguised himself,
and they went into battle.
31 Meanwhile, the king of Aram had issued
these orders to his thirty-two chariot commanders: "Attack only the king of Israel. Don't bother with anyone else!" 32 So when the Aramean
chariot commanders saw Jehoshaphat in his royal robes, they went after him. "There is the king
of Israel!" they shouted. But when Jehoshaphat
called out, 33 the chariot commanders realized he
was not the king of Israel, and they stopped chasing him.
34 An Aramean soldier, however, randomly
shot an arrow at the Israelite troops and hit the
king of Israel between the joints of his armor.
"Turn the horses* and get me out of here!" Ahab
groaned to the driver of his chariot. "I'm badly
wounded!"
35 The battle raged all that day, and the king
remained propped up in his chariot facing the
Arameans. The blood from his wound ran down
to the floor of his chariot, and as evening arrived
he died. 36 Just as the sun was setting, the cry ran
through his troops: "We're done for! Run for
your lives!"
37 So the king died, and his body was taken
to Samaria and buried there. 38 Then his chariot
was washed beside the pool of Samaria, and dogs
came and licked his blood at the place where the
prostitutes bathed,* just as the LORD had promised.
39 The rest of the events in Ahab's reign and
everything he did, including the story of the
ivory palace and the towns he built, are recorded
in *The Book of the History of the Kings of Israel.*
40 So Ahab died, and his son Ahaziah became the
next king.

Jehoshaphat Rules in Judah

41 Jehoshaphat son of Asa began to rule over Judah in the fourth year of King Ahab's reign in
Israel. 42 Jehoshaphat was thirty-five years old
when he became king, and he reigned in Jerusalem twenty-five years. His mother was Azubah,
the daughter of Shilhi.
43 Jehoshaphat was a good king, following
the example of his father, Asa. He did what
was pleasing in the LORD's sight. *During his
reign, however, he failed to remove all the pagan
shrines, and the people still offered sacrifices and
burned incense there. 44 Jehoshaphat also made
peace with the king of Israel.
45 The rest of the events in Jehoshaphat's
reign, the extent of his power, and the wars he
waged are recorded in *The Book of the History
of the Kings of Judah.* 46 He banished from the
land the rest of the male and female shrine prostitutes, who still continued their practices from
the days of his father, Asa.
47 (There was no king in Edom at that time,
only a deputy.)
48 Jehoshaphat also built a fleet of trading
ships* to sail to Ophir for gold. But the ships
never set sail, for they met with disaster in their
home port of Ezion-geber. 49 At one time Ahaziah
son of Ahab had proposed to Jehoshaphat, "Let
my men sail with your men in the ships." But
Jehoshaphat refused the request.

22:34 Hebrew *Turn your hand.* **22:38** Or *his blood, and the prostitutes bathed [in it]*; or *his blood, and they washed his armor.* **22:43** Verses 22:43b-53 are numbered 22:44-54 in Hebrew text. **22:48** Hebrew *fleet of ships of Tarshish.*

26–27: Ahab had already made up his mind to go to war. **32–33:** Something about Jehoshaphat's cry, perhaps his accent, alerted the Arameans that he was not the king of Israel. **38:** The dogs *licked* [the king's] *blood* evidently means a fulfillment of Elijah's word in 21:19 (see translator's notes).

22:41–50 Jehoshaphat of Judah. 42: Jehoshaphat was tepidly good, since despite following the LORD, he allowed the people to worship other gods as they pleased.

50 When Jehoshaphat died, he was buried with
his ancestors in the City of David. Then his son
Jehoram became the next king.

Ahaziah Rules in Israel

51 Ahaziah son of Ahab began to rule over Israel
in the seventeenth year of King Jehoshaphat's
reign in Judah. He reigned in Samaria two years.
52 But he did what was evil in the LORD's sight,
following the example of his father and mother
and the example of Jeroboam son of Nebat, who
had led Israel to sin. 53 He served Baal and worshiped him, provoking the anger of the LORD, the
God of Israel, just as his father had done.

22:51–53 Ahaziah of Judah. Most of Ahaziah's story appears in 2 Kings.

2 KINGS

INTRODUCTION

The book of 2 Kings is the continuation of 1 Kings and is the final biblical book of the Deuteronomistic History, which started with the book of Deuteronomy. See the introduction to 1 Kings for information about authorship and dating. In 2 Kings, the kings of Israel are all condemned for perpetuating the sin of Jeroboam in the shrines he built at Dan and Bethel. Several of the kings of Judah, on the other hand, are viewed favorably, although most of them are accused of failing to do away with the shrines other than the Jerusalem Temple, which is considered the only legitimate place for worship. The book recounts the destruction of Jerusalem and the beginning of the Babylonian captivity. In addition, a significant portion of 2 Kings consists of stories about the prophets. Many of these stories may have been inserted by a later writer or editor. The author struggles to explain the cause for the Exile, blaming it on both Manasseh (21:10–15) and Zedekiah and his contemporaries (24:20).

The reader may find the names of the kings unfamiliar and the alternation between Israel and Judah difficult to track. What is more important than knowing the details of this history is understanding the author's overall perspective, which tries to explain Israel's history theologically. Thus, Judah outlasts Israel because of the LORD's reward of a dynasty for David's faithfulness. Israel's destruction is due to its apostasy, as is Judah's captivity. But in Judah's case, there may still be hope for the future. The stories about Elisha and the prophets add another dimension to this narrative. While they emphasize the supremacy of the LORD in contrast to other gods, they also display a legendary quality in describing the deeds of the prophets.—*Jill L. Baker*

1:1–18	Ahaziah of Israel
2:1—8:15	Elisha Stories
8:16–24	Jehoram of Judah
8:25–29	Ahaziah of Judah
9:1—10:36	Jehu's Reform
11:1–20	Athaliah of Judah
11:21—12:21	Jehoash (Joash) of Judah
13:1–13	Jehoahaz and Jehoash of Israel
13:14–25	Elisha's Final Acts
14:1–20	Amaziah of Judah
14:21—15:7	Uzziah (Azariah) of Judah and Jeroboam II of Israel
15:8—17:6	Various Kings of Israel and Judah
15:8–12	Zechariah of Israel
15:13–16	Shallum of Israel
15:17–22	Menahem of Israel
15:23–26	Pekahiah of Israel
15:27–31	Pekah of Israel

15:32–38	Jotham of Judah
16:1–20	Ahaz of Judah
17:1–6	Hoshea of Israel
17:7–41	Fall of the Northern Kingdom to Assyria
18:1—21:26	Various Kings of Judah and Assyria
18:1–16	Hezekiah of Judah
18:17—19:37	Sennacherib Attacks Jerusalem
20:1–21	Hezekiah's Decline
21:1–18	Manasseh of Judah
21:19–26	Amon of Judah
22:1—23:30	Josiah's Reforms
23:31—25:30	The Fall of Judah
23:31–35	Jehoahaz of Judah
23:36—24:7	Jehoiakim of Judah
24:8–17	Jehoiachin of Judah
24:18–20	Zedekiah of Judah
25:1–30	Fall of Jerusalem and Exile

✧

Elijah Confronts King Ahaziah

1 After King Ahab's death, the land of Moab rebelled against Israel.

2 One day Israel's new king, Ahaziah, fell through the latticework of an upper room at his palace in Samaria and was seriously injured. So he sent messengers to the temple of Baal-zebub, the god of Ekron, to ask whether he would recover.

3 But the angel of the LORD told Elijah, who was from Tishbe, "Go and confront the messengers of the king of Samaria and ask them, 'Is there no God in Israel? Why are you going to Baal-zebub, the god of Ekron, to ask whether the king will recover? 4 Now, therefore, this is what the LORD says: You will never leave the bed you are lying on; you will surely die.' " So Elijah went to deliver the message.

5 When the messengers returned to the king, he asked them, "Why have you returned so soon?"

6 They replied, "A man came up to us and told us to go back to the king and give him this message. 'This is what the LORD says: Is there no God in Israel? Why are you sending men to Baal-zebub, the god of Ekron, to ask whether you will recover? Therefore, because you have done this, you will never leave the bed you are lying on; you will surely die.' "

7 "What sort of man was he?" the king demanded. "What did he look like?"

8 They replied, "He was a hairy man,* and he wore a leather belt around his waist."

"Elijah from Tishbe!" the king exclaimed.

9 Then he sent an army captain with fifty soldiers to arrest him. They found him sitting on top of a hill. The captain said to him, "Man of God, the king has commanded you to come down with us."

10 But Elijah replied to the captain, "If I am a man of God, let fire come down from heaven and destroy you and your fifty men!" Then fire fell from heaven and killed them all.

11 So the king sent another captain with fifty men. The captain said to him, "Man of God, the king demands that you come down at once."

12 Elijah replied, "If I am a man of God, let fire come down from heaven and destroy you and

1:8 Or *He was wearing clothing made of hair.*

1:1–18 Ahaziah of Israel

The injured king, Ahaziah, instructed his prophets to seek a prediction of recovery from Baal-zebub, the god of Ekron. Ekron was one of the five cities of the Philistine confederation. **6:** The LORD sends Elijah to intercept Ahaziah's messengers, exhibiting God's superiority over Baal-zebub. **9–12:** The fire that consumed Ahaziah's subsequent messengers is a potent symbol, used throughout the Elijah/Elisha cycles to

your fifty men!" And again the fire of God fell
from heaven and killed them all.
13 Once more the king sent a third captain
with fifty men. But this time the captain went
up the hill and fell to his knees before Elijah. He
pleaded with him, "O man of God, please spare
my life and the lives of these, your fifty servants.
14 See how the fire from heaven came down and
destroyed the first two groups. But now please
spare my life!"
15 Then the angel of the LORD said to Elijah,
"Go down with him, and don't be afraid of him."
So Elijah got up and went with him to the king.
16 And Elijah said to the king, "This is what
the LORD says: Why did you send messengers to
Baal-zebub, the god of Ekron, to ask whether you
will recover? Is there no God in Israel to answer
your question? Therefore, because you have
done this, you will never leave the bed you are
lying on; you will surely die."
17 So Ahaziah died, just as the LORD had promised through Elijah. Since Ahaziah did not have
a son to succeed him, his brother Joram* became
the next king. This took place in the second year
of the reign of Jehoram son of Jehoshaphat, king
of Judah.
18 The rest of the events in Ahaziah's reign are
recorded in *The Book of the History of the Kings
of Israel.*

Elijah Taken into Heaven

2 When the LORD was about to take Elijah
up to heaven in a whirlwind, Elijah and
Elisha were traveling from Gilgal. 2 And
Elijah said to Elisha, "Stay here, for the LORD has
told me to go to Bethel."
But Elisha replied, "As surely as the LORD
lives and you yourself live, I will never leave
you!" So they went down together to Bethel.
3 The group of prophets from Bethel came to
Elisha and asked him, "Did you know that the
LORD is going to take your master away from
you today?"
"Of course I know," Elisha answered. "But be
quiet about it."
4 Then Elijah said to Elisha, "Stay here, for the
LORD has told me to go to Jericho."
But Elisha replied again, "As surely as the
LORD lives and you yourself live, I will never
leave you." So they went on together to Jericho.
5 Then the group of prophets from Jericho
came to Elisha and asked him, "Did you know
that the LORD is going to take your master away
from you today?"
"Of course I know," Elisha answered. "But be
quiet about it."
6 Then Elijah said to Elisha, "Stay here, for the
LORD has told me to go to the Jordan River."
But again Elisha replied, "As surely as the
LORD lives and you yourself live, I will never
leave you." So they went on together.
7 Fifty men from the group of prophets also
went and watched from a distance as Elijah and
Elisha stopped beside the Jordan River. 8 Then
Elijah folded his cloak together and struck the
water with it. The river divided, and the two of
them went across on dry ground!
9 When they came to the other side, Elijah said
to Elisha, "Tell me what I can do for you before I
am taken away."
And Elisha replied, "Please let me inherit a
double share of your spirit and become your successor."
10 "You have asked a difficult thing," Elijah replied. "If you see me when I am taken from you,
then you will get your request. But if not, then
you won't."
11 As they were walking along and talking,
suddenly a chariot of fire appeared, drawn by
horses of fire. It drove between the two men, separating them, and Elijah was carried by a whirlwind into heaven. 12 Elisha saw it and cried out,
"My father! My father! I see the chariots and

1:17 Hebrew *Jehoram,* a variant spelling of *Joram.*

indicate the power of the Spirit of God. **17:** *Joram, Jehoram*: The kings of Israel and Judah have essentially the same name (in some translations, both are *Jehoram*), but are two different men.

2:1—8:15 Elisha Stories

2:1–25 Elijah Goes to Heaven. Elisha Installed. See 1 Kings 19 for the call of Elisha by Elijah. **1–7:** It was no secret to Elijah, Elisha, and all the prophets of the LORD that Elijah would be miraculously taken up into heaven. **9–10:** *Double share of your spirit*: Usually the rightful heir (generally the eldest son) would receive a double portion of the family estate. The other siblings would inherit a single portion. But Elisha had been a loyal underling and perhaps as close to Elijah as an eldest son would be. Elisha was to be Elijah's spiritual heir, having been appointed to succeed Elijah as prophet. **11–15:** The LORD's and Elijah's spirits settled on Elisha, making him a particularly powerful prophet. Elisha was empowered and transformed into a state of being that was similar to Elijah's. Elijah therefore had one portion of divinity (God's Spirit), while Elisha had two, God's and Elijah's spir-

Places Associated with Elisha

charioteers of Israel!" And as they disappeared from sight, Elisha tore his clothes in distress.

13 Elisha picked up Elijah's cloak, which had fallen when he was taken up. Then Elisha returned to the bank of the Jordan River. 14 He struck the water with Elijah's cloak and cried out, "Where is the LORD, the God of Elijah?" Then the river divided, and Elisha went across.

15 When the group of prophets from Jericho saw from a distance what happened, they exclaimed, "Elijah's spirit rests upon Elisha!" And they went to meet him and bowed to the ground before him. 16 "Sir," they said, "just say the word and fifty of our strongest men will search the wilderness for your master. Perhaps the Spirit of the LORD has left him on some mountain or in some valley."

"No," Elisha said, "don't send them." 17 But they kept urging him until they shamed him into agreeing, and he finally said, "All right, send them." So fifty men searched for three days but did not find Elijah. 18 Elisha was still at Jericho when they returned. "Didn't I tell you not to go?" he asked.

its: double the power, twice the intensity. This was demonstrated symbolically when Elisha removed and tore his garment, not only to mourn the passing of his mentor but also to show that he had shed his old being. He had inherited the prophetic spirit of Elijah, symbolized by donning his master's mantle.

Elisha's First Miracles
19 One day the leaders of the town of Jericho visited Elisha. "We have a problem, my lord," they
told him. "This town is located in pleasant surroundings, as you can see. But the water is bad,
and the land is unproductive."
20 Elisha said, "Bring me a new bowl with salt
in it." So they brought it to him. 21 Then he went
out to the spring that supplied the town with water and threw the salt into it. And he said, "This
is what the LORD says: I have purified this water. It will no longer cause death or infertility.*"
22 And the water has remained pure ever since,
just as Elisha said.
23 Elisha left Jericho and went up to Bethel. As
he was walking along the road, a group of boys
from the town began mocking and making fun
of him. "Go away, baldy!" they chanted. "Go
away, baldy!" 24 Elisha turned around and looked
at them, and he cursed them in the name of the
LORD. Then two bears came out of the woods and
mauled forty-two of them. 25 From there Elisha
went to Mount Carmel and finally returned to
Samaria.

War between Israel and Moab
3 Ahab's son Joram* began to rule over Israel in the eighteenth year of King Jehoshaphat's reign in Judah. He reigned in Samaria twelve years. 2 He did what was evil in
the LORD's sight, but not to the same extent as
his father and mother. He at least tore down the
sacred pillar of Baal that his father had set up.
3 Nevertheless, he continued in the sins that Jeroboam son of Nebat had committed and led the
people of Israel to commit.
4 King Mesha of Moab was a sheep breeder.
He used to pay the king of Israel an annual tribute of 100,000 lambs and the wool of 100,000
rams. 5 But after Ahab's death, the king of Moab
rebelled against the king of Israel. 6 So King Joram promptly mustered the army of Israel and
marched from Samaria. 7 On the way, he sent
this message to King Jehoshaphat of Judah: "The
king of Moab has rebelled against me. Will you
join me in battle against him?"
And Jehoshaphat replied, "Why, of course!
You and I are as one. My troops are your troops,
and my horses are your horses." 8 Then Jehoshaphat asked, "What route will we take?"
"We will attack from the wilderness of
Edom," Joram replied.
9 The king of Edom and his troops joined them,
and all three armies traveled along a roundabout
route through the wilderness for seven days. But
there was no water for the men or their animals.
10 "What should we do?" the king of Israel
cried out. "The LORD has brought the three of us
here to let the king of Moab defeat us."
11 But King Jehoshaphat of Judah asked, "Is
there no prophet of the LORD with us? If there is,
we can ask the LORD what to do through him."
One of King Joram's officers replied, "Elisha
son of Shaphat is here. He used to be Elijah's personal assistant.*"
12 Jehoshaphat said, "Yes, the LORD speaks
through him." So the kings of Israel, Judah, and
Edom went to consult with Elisha.
13 "Why are you coming to me?"* Elisha
asked the king of Israel. "Go to the pagan prophets of your father and mother!"
But King Joram of Israel said, "No! For it was
the LORD who called us three kings here—only
to be defeated by the king of Moab!"
14 Elisha replied, "As surely as the LORD Almighty lives, whom I serve, I wouldn't even
bother with you except for my respect for King

2:21 Or *or make the land unproductive;* Hebrew reads *or barrenness.* **3:1** Hebrew *Jehoram,* a variant spelling of Joram; also in 3:6. **3:11** Hebrew *He used to pour water on the hands of Elijah.* **3:13** Hebrew *What is there in common between you and me?*

19–25: These two stories serve to prove that Elisha has inherited Elijah's power. *Bears*: Hebrew, "she-bears," a symbol of the way God protects his children (see also Hos 13:8). This incident is hard for modern readers to comprehend or accept. It seems a gross overreaction on Elisha's part. However, it may be that the mocking of the LORD's prophet is to be seen as a deliberate rejection of the LORD's power and authority, a crime worthy of the death penalty within Israel.

3:1–27 Moab's Revolt. This passage contains a variant account of the ascendancy of Joram to the throne of Israel (1:17–18). Although he tore down the sacred stone of Baal that his father had made, he made his own mistakes. **3:** *The sins that Jeroboam . . . committed* refers to the two shrines at Dan and Bethel (1 Kgs 12:25–33). **4:** Moab was across the Dead Sea from Israel. Mesha, king of Moab, paid a substantial tribute to the king of Israel annually as a subject state of Israel. **8–9:** They traveled by way of the desert of Edom, and after seven days' march they ran out of water. **11:** As in 1 Kings 22:7, the righteous Jehoshaphat of Judah requests a prophet of the LORD who might help them understand the situation. **13:** Elisha wants nothing to do with King Joram of Israel—his father was Ahab and his mother Jezebel. His prophets were worshipers of Baal and Asherah (1 Kgs 18:19). Joram doesn't think much of Elisha and the LORD either.

Jehoshaphat of Judah. 15 Now bring me someone who can play the harp."

While the harp was being played, the power* of the LORD came upon Elisha, 16 and he said, "This is what the LORD says: This dry valley will be filled with pools of water! 17 You will see neither wind nor rain, says the LORD, but this valley will be filled with water. You will have plenty for yourselves and your cattle and other animals. 18 But this is only a simple thing for the LORD, for he will make you victorious over the army of Moab! 19 You will conquer the best of their towns, even the fortified ones. You will cut down all their good trees, stop up all their springs, and ruin all their good land with stones."

20 The next day at about the time when the morning sacrifice was offered, water suddenly appeared! It was flowing from the direction of Edom, and soon there was water everywhere.

21 Meanwhile, when the people of Moab heard about the three armies marching against them, they mobilized every man who was old enough to strap on a sword, and they stationed themselves along their border. 22 But when they got up the next morning, the sun was shining across the water, making it appear red to the Moabites—like blood. 23 "It's blood!" the Moabites exclaimed. "The three armies must have attacked and killed each other! Let's go, men of Moab, and collect the plunder!"

24 But when the Moabites arrived at the Israelite camp, the army of Israel rushed out and attacked them until they turned and ran. The army of Israel chased them into the land of Moab, destroying everything as they went.* 25 They destroyed the towns, covered their good land with stones, stopped up all the springs, and cut down all the good trees. Finally, only Kir-hareseth and its stone walls were left, but men with slings surrounded and attacked it.

26 When the king of Moab saw that he was losing the battle, he led 700 of his swordsmen in a desperate attempt to break through the enemy lines near the king of Edom, but they failed. 27 Then the king of Moab took his oldest son, who would have been the next king, and sacrificed him as a burnt offering on the wall. So there was great anger against Israel,* and the Israelites withdrew and returned to their own land.

Elisha Helps a Poor Widow

4 One day the widow of a member of the group of prophets came to Elisha and cried out, "My husband who served you is dead, and you know how he feared the LORD. But now a creditor has come, threatening to take my two sons as slaves."

2 "What can I do to help you?" Elisha asked. "Tell me, what do you have in the house?"

"Nothing at all, except a flask of olive oil," she replied.

3 And Elisha said, "Borrow as many empty jars as you can from your friends and neighbors. 4 Then go into your house with your sons and shut the door behind you. Pour olive oil from your flask into the jars, setting each one aside when it is filled."

5 So she did as she was told. Her sons kept bringing jars to her, and she filled one after another. 6 Soon every container was full to the brim!

"Bring me another jar," she said to one of her sons.

"There aren't any more!" he told her. And then the olive oil stopped flowing.

7 When she told the man of God what had happened, he said to her, "Now sell the olive oil and pay your debts, and you and your sons can live on what is left over."

Elisha and the Woman from Shunem

8 One day Elisha went to the town of Shunem. A wealthy woman lived there, and she urged him to

3:15 Hebrew *the hand.* **3:24** The meaning of the Hebrew is uncertain. **3:27** Or *So Israel's anger was great.* The meaning of the Hebrew is uncertain.

15: Music was used to induce the prophet's ecstatic experience. **22:** The water, blood-colored in the light of the morning sun, symbolized death to the Moabites and God-given life to the Israelites. **27:** Human sacrifice did sometimes happen in Israel, although it was strongly condemned. There is no mention here of the anguish of the boy's mother or the rest of his family as he is killed in an attempt to influence the course of the battle.

4:1—8:15 More Elisha Stories. 4:1: In the ancient world, when people could not pay their debts, they could sell themselves or their children into slavery for a limited period of time or until the debt was paid. The deceased man's creditors were threatening to take the widow's two sons and indenture them in this way. The widow sought help from God through Elisha. **5–6:** Although there was only a little oil to begin with, it filled all the empty jars. **7:** They were able to sell the jars of oil and not only pay off the debt but live off the profit. Economic and social injustice is not ignored by a just and merciful God who makes special provision for the poor (cf. the story of Elijah and the widow, 1 Kgs 17:8–16). **8–37:** Throughout

come to her home for a meal. After that, whenever he passed that way, he would stop there for
something to eat.
9 She said to her husband, "I am sure this man
who stops in from time to time is a holy man of
God. 10 Let's build a small room for him on the
roof and furnish it with a bed, a table, a chair, and
a lamp. Then he will have a place to stay whenever he comes by."
11 One day Elisha returned to Shunem, and he
went up to this upper room to rest. 12 He said to
his servant Gehazi, "Tell the woman from Shunem I want to speak to her." When she appeared,
13 Elisha said to Gehazi, "Tell her, 'We appreciate the kind concern you have shown us. What
can we do for you? Can we put in a good word
for you to the king or to the commander of the
army?' "
"No," she replied, "my family takes good care
of me."
14 Later Elisha asked Gehazi, "What can we do
for her?"
Gehazi replied, "She doesn't have a son, and
her husband is an old man."
15 "Call her back again," Elisha told him.
When the woman returned, Elisha said to her as
she stood in the doorway, 16 "Next year at this
time you will be holding a son in your arms!"
"No, my lord!" she cried. "O man of God, don't
deceive me and get my hopes up like that."
17 But sure enough, the woman soon became
pregnant. And at that time the following year
she had a son, just as Elisha had said.
18 One day when her child was older, he went
out to help his father, who was working with the
harvesters. 19 Suddenly he cried out, "My head
hurts! My head hurts!"
His father said to one of the servants, "Carry
him home to his mother."
20 So the servant took him home, and his
mother held him on her lap. But around noontime he died. 21 She carried him up and laid him
on the bed of the man of God, then shut the door
and left him there. 22 She sent a message to her
husband: "Send one of the servants and a donkey
so that I can hurry to the man of God and come
right back."
23 "Why go today?" he asked. "It is neither a
new moon festival nor a Sabbath."
But she said, "It will be all right."
24 So she saddled the donkey and said to the
servant, "Hurry! Don't slow down unless I tell
you to."
25 As she approached the man of God at Mount
Carmel, Elisha saw her in the distance. He said
to Gehazi, "Look, the woman from Shunem is
coming. 26 Run out to meet her and ask her, 'Is
everything all right with you, your husband, and
your child?' "
"Yes," the woman told Gehazi, "everything
is fine."
27 But when she came to the man of God at the
mountain, she fell to the ground before him and
caught hold of his feet. Gehazi began to push her
away, but the man of God said, "Leave her alone.
She is deeply troubled, but the LORD has not told
me what it is."
28 Then she said, "Did I ask you for a son, my
lord? And didn't I say, 'Don't deceive me and get
my hopes up'?"
29 Then Elisha said to Gehazi, "Get ready to
travel*; take my staff and go! Don't talk to anyone along the way. Go quickly and lay the staff
on the child's face."
30 But the boy's mother said, "As surely as
the LORD lives and you yourself live, I won't
go home unless you go with me." So Elisha returned with her.
31 Gehazi hurried on ahead and laid the staff
on the child's face, but nothing happened. There
was no sign of life. He returned to meet Elisha
and told him, "The child is still dead."
32 When Elisha arrived, the child was indeed
dead, lying there on the prophet's bed. 33 He

4:29 Hebrew *Bind up your loins.*

---

this passage, the focus is on the woman from Shunem rather than her husband. She is the initiator. This may imply that a greater faith was found in her. **8–10:** The wife makes the original offer of hospitality, and her husband cooperates; she envisages, he supplies. **11–17:** It is to the woman Elisha offers a sign of his gratitude. Note all the singular pronouns in this passage. **21–30:** Her expectation was that only the LORD, through his prophet, could help. **31–35:** Just as Elijah had done (1 Kgs 17:17–24), Elisha was able to bring the boy back to life. Life in the ancient world was hard and sometimes dangerous. It was important that men and woman were not left alone in the world. Domestic life required a great deal of hard work, between household chores and the field. One person could not do it alone; therefore tasks were divided among family members. It is likely there was an age difference between the woman and her husband, so his death would most likely occur before hers. If the woman had been widowed without a son, she would have had to bear all these responsibilities (but see the book of Ruth for the complexities of levirate marriage). If there were a son, the boy would inherit all his father's possessions and be responsible for

went in alone and shut the door behind him and
prayed to the LORD. 34 Then he lay down on the
child's body, placing his mouth on the child's
mouth, his eyes on the child's eyes, and his hands
on the child's hands. And as he stretched out on
him, the child's body began to grow warm again!
35 Elisha got up, walked back and forth across the
room once, and then stretched himself out again
on the child. This time the boy sneezed seven
times and opened his eyes!

36 Then Elisha summoned Gehazi. "Call the
child's mother!" he said. And when she came
in, Elisha said, "Here, take your son!" 37 She fell
at his feet and bowed before him, overwhelmed
with gratitude. Then she took her son in her
arms and carried him downstairs.

Miracles during a Famine

38 Elisha now returned to Gilgal, and there was
a famine in the land. One day as the group of
prophets was seated before him, he said to his
servant, "Put a large pot on the fire, and make
some stew for the rest of the group."

39 One of the young men went out into the
field to gather herbs and came back with a pock-
etful of wild gourds. He shredded them and put
them into the pot without realizing they were
poisonous. 40 Some of the stew was served to the
men. But after they had eaten a bite or two they
cried out, "Man of God, there's poison in this
stew!" So they would not eat it.

41 Elisha said, "Bring me some flour." Then he
threw it into the pot and said, "Now it's all right; go
ahead and eat." And then it did not harm them.

42 One day a man from Baal-shalishah brought
the man of God a sack of fresh grain and twenty
loaves of barley bread made from the first grain
of his harvest. Elisha said, "Give it to the people
so they can eat."

43 "What?" his servant exclaimed. "Feed a
hundred people with only this?"

But Elisha repeated, "Give it to the people
so they can eat, for this is what the LORD says:
Everyone will eat, and there will even be some
left over!" 44 And when they gave it to the people,
there was plenty for all and some left over, just as
the LORD had promised.

The Healing of Naaman

5 The king of Aram had great admiration
for Naaman, the commander of his army,
because through him the LORD had given
Aram great victories. But though Naaman was a
mighty warrior, he suffered from leprosy.*

2 At this time Aramean raiders had invaded
the land of Israel, and among their captives was a
young girl who had been given to Naaman's wife
as a maid. 3 One day the girl said to her mistress,
"I wish my master would go to see the prophet
in Samaria. He would heal him of his leprosy."

4 So Naaman told the king what the young girl
from Israel had said. 5 "Go and visit the prophet,"
the king of Aram told him. "I will send a letter
of introduction for you to take to the king of Israel." So Naaman started out, carrying as gifts
750 pounds of silver, 150 pounds of gold,* and
ten sets of clothing. 6 The letter to the king of Israel said: "With this letter I present my servant
Naaman. I want you to heal him of his leprosy."

7 When the king of Israel read the letter, he
tore his clothes in dismay and said, "This man
sends me a leper to heal! Am I God, that I can
give life and take it away? I can see that he's just
trying to pick a fight with me."

8 But when Elisha, the man of God, heard that
the king of Israel had torn his clothes in dismay,
he sent this message to him: "Why are you so
upset? Send Naaman to me, and he will learn
that there is a true prophet here in Israel."

9 So Naaman went with his horses and chariots and waited at the door of Elisha's house. 10 But

5:1 Or *from a contagious skin disease.* The Hebrew word used here and throughout this passage can describe various skin diseases. **5:5** Hebrew *10 talents* [340 kilograms] *of silver, 6,000 shekels* [68 kilograms] *of gold.*

---

the well-being of his mother. This is why Elisha felt it was so important for this woman to have a son. **38–41:** Whether Elisha's ability to combat the effects of the poisonous stew is a sign of miraculous power or a greater knowledge of the property of foods is not clear. **42–44:** The multiplication and provision of food is a favorite biblical theme (cf. Mark 8:1–21; John 2:1–11). Normally catering is seen as the province of women, and concern for the provision of food affirms the significance of that role.

5:1–27 The Healing of Naaman. Naaman was a powerful commander in the army of the king of Aram, who was greatly respected because, through him, the LORD gave victory to Aram over Israel. The timing of this story is unknown, because neither the king of Aram nor the king of Israel are named. **1:** *Leprosy* is a broad term for several skin diseases. It was considered incurable and highly contagious. **3:** The slave girl displays remarkable initiative. **4–6:** The letter was meant to be a document explaining why a foreign high commander was traveling in Israel, so that the king of Israel would not feel threatened. **10–12:** Naaman expected more than merely being

Elisha sent a messenger out to him with this
message: "Go and wash yourself seven times in
the Jordan River. Then your skin will be restored,
and you will be healed of your leprosy."
11But Naaman became angry and stalked
away. "I thought he would certainly come out to
meet me!" he said. "I expected him to wave his
hand over the leprosy and call on the name of the
LORD his God and heal me! 12Aren't the rivers
of Damascus, the Abana and the Pharpar, better
than any of the rivers of Israel? Why shouldn't I
wash in them and be healed?" So Naaman turned
and went away in a rage.
13But his officers tried to reason with him
and said, "Sir,* if the prophet had told you to
do something very difficult, wouldn't you have
done it? So you should certainly obey him when
he says simply, 'Go and wash and be cured!' "
14So Naaman went down to the Jordan River
and dipped himself seven times, as the man of
God had instructed him. And his skin became as
healthy as the skin of a young child's, and he was
healed!
15Then Naaman and his entire party went
back to find the man of God. They stood before
him, and Naaman said, "Now I know that there
is no God in all the world except in Israel. So
please accept a gift from your servant."
16But Elisha replied, "As surely as the LORD
lives, whom I serve, I will not accept any gifts."
And though Naaman urged him to take the gift,
Elisha refused.
17Then Naaman said, "All right, but please allow me to load two of my mules with earth from
this place, and I will take it back home with me.
From now on I will never again offer burnt offerings or sacrifices to any other god except the
LORD. 18However, may the LORD pardon me in
this one thing: When my master the king goes
into the temple of the god Rimmon to worship
there and leans on my arm, may the LORD pardon me when I bow, too."
19"Go in peace," Elisha said. So Naaman started home again.

The Greed of Gehazi

20But Gehazi, the servant of Elisha, the man of
God, said to himself, "My master should not
have let this Aramean get away without accepting any of his gifts. As surely as the LORD lives,
I will chase after him and get something from
him." 21So Gehazi set off after Naaman.
When Naaman saw Gehazi running after
him, he climbed down from his chariot and went
to meet him. "Is everything all right?" Naaman
asked.
22"Yes," Gehazi said, "but my master has sent
me to tell you that two young prophets from the
hill country of Ephraim have just arrived. He
would like 75 pounds* of silver and two sets of
clothing to give to them."
23"By all means, take twice as much* silver,"
Naaman insisted. He gave him two sets of clothing, tied up the money in two bags, and sent two
of his servants to carry the gifts for Gehazi. 24But
when they arrived at the citadel,* Gehazi took the
gifts from the servants and sent the men back.
Then he went and hid the gifts inside the house.
25When he went in to his master, Elisha asked
him, "Where have you been, Gehazi?"
"I haven't been anywhere," he replied.
26But Elisha asked him, "Don't you realize that
I was there in spirit when Naaman stepped down
from his chariot to meet you? Is this the time
to receive money and clothing, olive groves and
vineyards, sheep and cattle, and male and female
servants? 27Because you have done this, you and
your descendants will suffer from Naaman's leprosy forever." When Gehazi left the room, he was
covered with leprosy; his skin was white as snow.

5:13 Hebrew *My father.* **5:22** Hebrew *1 talent* [34 kilograms]. **5:23** Hebrew *take 2 talents* [68 kilograms]. **5:24** Hebrew *the Ophel.*

sent to the Jordan River for cleansing. But in this way neither Naaman's nor Elisha's actions could be seen as greater than God's. Naaman could conclude without a doubt it was God who cured him, not Elisha. **14:** It was important for Naaman to follow God's instructions, through Elisha, in order to show faith and obedience. In addition, this celebrated military commander was healed in a humble manner, without pomp and circumstance, which was important not only for his physical recovery but his spiritual healing as well. **15–16:** As a true prophet, Elisha was not in the business to become rich, as many false prophets were. Rather, his daily and long-term needs were provided by God, not through riches that were brought to him in return for a prophetic word. **17–18:** Coming from Aram, Naaman assumed that the power of the Israelite God was local—hence the request to take soil back home with him. Jesus uses the story of Naaman to indicate that salvation was not to be restricted to the Jews (Luke 4:27). **19–27:** This episode shows the danger of trying to deceive a prophet. Having lived with Elisha, Gehazi should have known better, but he was consumed by greed. The misrepresentation of the LORD has always been seen as serious offense, particularly for those involved in his service.

The Floating Ax Head

6 One day the group of prophets came to Elisha and told him, "As you can see, this place where we meet with you is too small. 2 Let's go down to the Jordan River, where there are plenty of logs. There we can build a new place for us to meet."

"All right," he told them, "go ahead."

3 "Please come with us," someone suggested.

"I will," he said. 4 So he went with them.

When they arrived at the Jordan, they began cutting down trees. 5 But as one of them was cutting a tree, his ax head fell into the river. "Oh, sir!" he cried. "It was a borrowed ax!"

6 "Where did it fall?" the man of God asked. When he showed him the place, Elisha cut a stick and threw it into the water at that spot. Then the ax head floated to the surface. 7 "Grab it," Elisha said. And the man reached out and grabbed it.

Elisha Traps the Arameans

8 When the king of Aram was at war with Israel, he would confer with his officers and say, "We will mobilize our forces at such and such a place."

9 But immediately Elisha, the man of God, would warn the king of Israel, "Do not go near that place, for the Arameans are planning to mobilize their troops there." 10 So the king of Israel would send word to the place indicated by the man of God. Time and again Elisha warned the king, so that he would be on the alert there.

11 The king of Aram became very upset over this. He called his officers together and demanded, "Which of you is the traitor? Who has been informing the king of Israel of my plans?"

12 "It's not us, my lord the king," one of the officers replied. "Elisha, the prophet in Israel, tells the king of Israel even the words you speak in the privacy of your bedroom!"

13 "Go and find out where he is," the king commanded, "so I can send troops to seize him."

And the report came back: "Elisha is at Dothan." 14 So one night the king of Aram sent a great army with many chariots and horses to surround the city.

15 When the servant of the man of God got up early the next morning and went outside, there were troops, horses, and chariots everywhere. "Oh, sir, what will we do now?" the young man cried to Elisha.

16 "Don't be afraid!" Elisha told him. "For there are more on our side than on theirs!" 17 Then Elisha prayed, "O LORD, open his eyes and let him see!" The LORD opened the young man's eyes, and when he looked up, he saw that the hillside around Elisha was filled with horses and chariots of fire.

18 As the Aramean army advanced toward him, Elisha prayed, "O LORD, please make them blind." So the LORD struck them with blindness as Elisha had asked.

19 Then Elisha went out and told them, "You have come the wrong way! This isn't the right city! Follow me, and I will take you to the man you are looking for." And he led them to the city of Samaria.

20 As soon as they had entered Samaria, Elisha prayed, "O LORD, now open their eyes and let them see." So the LORD opened their eyes, and they discovered that they were in the middle of Samaria.

21 When the king of Israel saw them, he shouted to Elisha, "My father, should I kill them? Should I kill them?"

22 "Of course not!" Elisha replied. "Do we kill prisoners of war? Give them food and drink and send them home again to their master."

23 So the king made a great feast for them and then sent them home to their master. After that, the Aramean raiders stayed away from the land of Israel.

Ben-Hadad Besieges Samaria

24 Some time later, however, King Ben-hadad of Aram mustered his entire army and besieged Samaria. 25 As a result, there was a great famine in the city. The siege lasted so long that a donkey's head sold for eighty pieces of silver, and a cup of dove's dung sold for five pieces* of silver.

26 One day as the king of Israel was walking

6:25 Hebrew *sold for 80 shekels* [2 pounds, or 0.9 kilograms] *of silver, and 1/4 of a cab* [0.3 liters] *of dove's dung sold for 5 shekels* [2 ounces, or 57 grams]. *Dove's dung* may be a variety of wild vegetable.

6:1–23 More Miracles. The stories of Elisha's miracle workings continue. **1–7:** This incident is a further example of Elisha apparently being given miraculous powers to meet the needs of the people. **8–23:** Once again Aram and Israel were at war with one another. Elisha's importance is shown two ways: the strategic advantage he gives Israel by warning the army of the Aramean's action, and the reaction of the king of Aram, leading to all-out invasion just to capture Elisha. **17:** This verse vividly illustrates the title "the LORD of Heaven's Armies" (19:31), since the LORD controls both earthly and heavenly armies.

6:24—7:20 The Siege of Samaria. 6:28–29: The

along the wall of the city, a woman called to him, "Please help me, my lord the king!"

27 He answered, "If the LORD doesn't help you, what can I do? I have neither food from the threshing floor nor wine from the press to give you." 28 But then the king asked, "What is the matter?"

She replied, "This woman said to me: 'Come on, let's eat your son today, then we will eat my son tomorrow.' 29 So we cooked my son and ate him. Then the next day I said to her, 'Kill your son so we can eat him,' but she has hidden her son."

30 When the king heard this, he tore his clothes in despair. And as the king walked along the wall, the people could see that he was wearing burlap under his robe next to his skin. 31 "May God strike me and even kill me if I don't separate Elisha's head from his shoulders this very day," the king vowed.

32 Elisha was sitting in his house with the elders of Israel when the king sent a messenger to summon him. But before the messenger arrived, Elisha said to the elders, "A murderer has sent a man to cut off my head. When he arrives, shut the door and keep him out. We will soon hear his master's steps following him."

33 While Elisha was still saying this, the messenger arrived. And the king* said, "All this misery is from the LORD! Why should I wait for the LORD any longer?"

7 Elisha replied, "Listen to this message from the LORD! This is what the LORD says: By this time tomorrow in the markets of Samaria, five quarts of choice flour will cost only one piece of silver,* and ten quarts of barley grain will cost only one piece of silver.*"

2 The officer assisting the king said to the man of God, "That couldn't happen even if the LORD opened the windows of heaven!"

But Elisha replied, "You will see it happen with your own eyes, but you won't be able to eat any of it!"

Lepers Visit the Enemy Camp

3 Now there were four men with leprosy* sitting at the entrance of the city gates. "Why should we sit here waiting to die?" they asked each other. 4 "We will starve if we stay here, but with the famine in the city, we will starve if we go back there. So we might as well go out and surrender to the Aramean army. If they let us live, so much the better. But if they kill us, we would have died anyway."

5 So at twilight they set out for the camp of the Arameans. But when they came to the edge of the camp, no one was there! 6 For the Lord had caused the Aramean army to hear the clatter of speeding chariots and the galloping of horses and the sounds of a great army approaching. "The king of Israel has hired the Hittites and Egyptians* to attack us!" they cried to one another. 7 So they panicked and ran into the night, abandoning their tents, horses, donkeys, and everything else, as they fled for their lives.

8 When the lepers arrived at the edge of the camp, they went into one tent after another, eating and drinking wine; and they carried off silver and gold and clothing and hid it. 9 Finally, they said to each other, "This is not right. This is a day of good news, and we aren't sharing it with anyone! If we wait until morning, some calamity will certainly fall upon us. Come on, let's go back and tell the people at the palace."

10 So they went back to the city and told the gatekeepers what had happened. "We went out to the Aramean camp," they said, "and no one was there! The horses and donkeys were tethered and the tents were all in order, but there wasn't a single person around!" 11 Then the gatekeepers shouted the news to the people in the palace.

Israel Plunders the Camp

12 The king got out of bed in the middle of the night and told his officers, "I know what has happened. The Arameans know we are starving, so they have left their camp and have hidden in

6:33 Hebrew *he.* **7:1a** Hebrew *1 seah* [6 liters] *of choice flour will cost 1 shekel* [0.4 ounces, or 11 grams]; also in 7:16, 18. **7:1b** Hebrew *2 seahs* [12 liters] *of barley grain will cost 1 shekel* [0.4 ounces, or 11 grams]; also in 7:16, 18. **7:3** Or *with a contagious skin disease.* The Hebrew word used here and throughout this passage can describe various skin diseases. **7:6** Possibly *and the people of Muzur,* a district near Cilicia.

siege, which cuts off the supply of food, lasts so long that people turned to cannibalism. **31:** The king of Israel thought Elisha had caused the problem, somehow influencing God; he did not understand that Elisha was God's messenger. **7:6:** The phrase *the Hittites and Egyptians* is a puzzling one. Most scholars speculate that the Hebrew word *Mitzrayim,* which usually means "Egypt," in this case refers to an area called Mutzri (Muzur; see translator's note) in northern Syria. In addition, these are not the Bronze Age Hittites of central Anatolia; rather, they represent the Iron Age Neo-Hittite kingdoms of Syria. **8–17:** Such deliverance appeared impossible, but God works in unexpected ways. **17–20:** Again, the perils of doubt-

the fields. They are expecting us to leave the city,
and then they will take us alive and capture the
city."
13 One of his officers replied, "We had better
send out scouts to check into this. Let them take
five of the remaining horses. If something happens to them, it will be no worse than if they stay
here and die with the rest of us."
14 So two chariots with horses were prepared,
and the king sent scouts to see what had happened
to the Aramean army. 15 They went all the way to
the Jordan River, following a trail of clothing and
equipment that the Arameans had thrown away
in their mad rush to escape. The scouts returned
and told the king about it. 16 Then the people of
Samaria rushed out and plundered the Aramean
camp. So it was true that five quarts of choice
flour were sold that day for one piece of silver,
and ten quarts of barley grain were sold for one
piece of silver, just as the LORD had promised.
17 The king appointed his officer to control the
traffic at the gate, but he was knocked down and
trampled to death as the people rushed out.
So everything happened exactly as the man
of God had predicted when the king came to his
house. 18 The man of God had said to the king,
"By this time tomorrow in the markets of Samaria, five quarts of choice flour will cost one
piece of silver, and ten quarts of barley grain will
cost one piece of silver."
19 The king's officer had replied, "That couldn't
happen even if the LORD opened the windows of
heaven!" And the man of God had said, "You will
see it happen with your own eyes, but you won't
be able to eat any of it!" 20 And so it was, for the
people trampled him to death at the gate!

The Woman from Shunem Returns Home

8 Elisha had told the woman whose son he
had brought back to life, "Take your family
and move to some other place, for the LORD
has called for a famine on Israel that will last for
seven years." 2 So the woman did as the man of
God instructed. She took her family and settled
in the land of the Philistines for seven years.
3 After the famine ended she returned from
the land of the Philistines, and she went to see
the king about getting back her house and land.
4 As she came in, the king was talking with Gehazi, the servant of the man of God. The king had
just said, "Tell me some stories about the great
things Elisha has done." 5 And Gehazi was telling
the king about the time Elisha had brought a boy
back to life. At that very moment, the mother of
the boy walked in to make her appeal to the king
about her house and land.
"Look, my lord the king!" Gehazi exclaimed.
"Here is the woman now, and this is her son—
the very one Elisha brought back to life!"
6 "Is this true?" the king asked her. And she
told him the story. So he directed one of his officials to see that everything she had lost was
restored to her, including the value of any crops
that had been harvested during her absence.

Hazael Murders Ben-Hadad

7 Elisha went to Damascus, the capital of Aram,
where King Ben-hadad lay sick. When someone
told the king that the man of God had come, 8 the
king said to Hazael, "Take a gift to the man of
God. Then tell him to ask the LORD, 'Will I recover from this illness?' "
9 So Hazael loaded down forty camels with
the finest products of Damascus as a gift for
Elisha. He went to him and said, "Your servant
Ben-hadad, the king of Aram, has sent me to ask,
'Will I recover from this illness?' "
10 And Elisha replied, "Go and tell him, 'You
will surely recover.' But actually the LORD has
shown me that he will surely die!" 11 Elisha
stared at Hazael* with a fixed gaze until Hazael
became uneasy.* Then the man of God started
weeping.

8:11a Hebrew *He stared at him.* **8:11b** The meaning of the Hebrew is uncertain.

---

ing God's word and disrespecting his prophet are displayed.

8:1–6 The Woman of Shunem. This is the sequel to the earlier story (4:8–37). This is another case in which a woman, showing a great deal of initiative, represented herself, her husband, and son before the king (cf. 1 Kgs 3:16–28). **3:** When she had abandoned her house and land, it was taken over by new occupants, which was legal in the ancient world. But since Elisha the prophet had instructed her to do this, the situation was a bit different; the land and house should be returned to the family. **2, 6:** The family returned after seven years, so it may have been that this was a Jubilee year, when all debt was forgiven and loaned property was returned to its rightful owner. However, the image of the seven lean years is another biblical motif.

8:7–17 Ben-Hadad and Hazael. This passage recounts the fate of Ben-hadad, king of Aram, and Hazael, his son. Elisha here apparently carries out the commission given to Elijah in 1 Kings 19:15. **11:** The original Hebrew here is unclear about who *became*

[12] "What's the matter, my lord?" Hazael asked
him.
Elisha replied, "I know the terrible things you
will do to the people of Israel. You will burn their
fortified cities, kill their young men with the
sword, dash their little children to the ground,
and rip open their pregnant women!"
[13] Hazael responded, "How could a nobody
like me* ever accomplish such great things?"
Elisha answered, "The LORD has shown me
that you are going to be the king of Aram."
[14] When Hazael left Elisha and went back, the
king asked him, "What did Elisha tell you?"
And Hazael replied, "He told me that you will
surely recover."
[15] But the next day Hazael took a blanket,
soaked it in water, and held it over the king's face
until he died. Then Hazael became the next king
of Aram.

Jehoram Rules in Judah

[16] Jehoram son of King Jehoshaphat of Judah began to rule over Judah in the fifth year of the
reign of Joram son of Ahab, king of Israel. [17] Jehoram was thirty-two years old when he became
king, and he reigned in Jerusalem eight years.
[18] But Jehoram followed the example of the kings
of Israel and was as wicked as King Ahab, for he
had married one of Ahab's daughters. So Jehoram
did what was evil in the LORD's sight. [19] But the
LORD did not want to destroy Judah, for he had
made a covenant with David and promised that
his descendants would continue to rule, shining
like a lamp forever.
[20] During Jehoram's reign, the Edomites revolted against Judah and crowned their own
king. [21] So Jehoram* went with all his chariots
to attack the town of Zair.* The Edomites surrounded him and his chariot commanders, but
he went out at night and attacked them* under
cover of darkness. But Jehoram's army deserted
him and fled to their homes. [22] So Edom has been
independent from Judah to this day. The town of
Libnah also revolted about that same time.
[23] The rest of the events in Jehoram's reign
and everything he did are recorded in *The Book
of the History of the Kings of Judah*. [24] When Jehoram died, he was buried with his ancestors in
the City of David. Then his son Ahaziah became
the next king.

Ahaziah Rules in Judah

[25] Ahaziah son of Jehoram began to rule over Judah in the twelfth year of the reign of Joram son
of Ahab, king of Israel.
[26] Ahaziah was twenty-two years old when
he became king, and he reigned in Jerusalem one
year. His mother was Athaliah, a granddaughter
of King Omri of Israel. [27] Ahaziah followed the
evil example of King Ahab's family. He did what
was evil in the LORD's sight, just as Ahab's family had done, for he was related by marriage to
the family of Ahab.
[28] Ahaziah joined Joram son of Ahab, the king
of Israel, in his war against King Hazael of Aram
at Ramoth-gilead. When the Arameans wounded
King Joram in the battle, [29] he returned to Jezreel to recover from the wounds he had received
at Ramoth.* Because Joram was wounded, King
Ahaziah of Judah went to Jezreel to visit him.

Jehu Anointed King of Israel

9 Meanwhile, Elisha the prophet had summoned a member of the group of prophets.
"Get ready to travel,"* he told him, "and
take this flask of olive oil with you. Go to Ramoth-gilead, [2] and find Jehu son of Jehoshaphat,
son of Nimshi. Call him into a private room
away from his friends, [3] and pour the oil over his
head. Say to him, 'This is what the LORD says: I
anoint you to be the king over Israel.' Then open
the door and run for your life!"
[4] So the young prophet did as he was told and
went to Ramoth-gilead. [5] When he arrived there,
he found Jehu sitting around with the other
army officers. "I have a message for you, Commander," he said.
"For which one of us?" Jehu asked.
"For you, Commander," he replied.

8:13 Hebrew *a dog*. **8:21a** Hebrew *Joram,* a variant spelling of Jehoram; also in 8:23, 24. **8:21b** Greek version reads *Seir.* **8:21c** Or *he went out and escaped.* The meaning of the Hebrew is uncertain. **8:29** Hebrew *Ramah,* a variant spelling of Ramoth. **9:1** Hebrew *Bind up your loins.*

uneasy. **12:** Elisha foresees that Hazael will be the LORD's instrument to punish Israel.

8:16–29 The Reigns of Jehoram and Ahaziah of Judah

These two reigns are described using the familiar formula found throughout 1 and 2 Kings.

9:1—10:36 Jehu's Reform

Harking back to the time when kingship was a divinely chosen office, rather than a hereditary one, the LORD reached outside the royal family of Israel and chose Jehu as leader, in order to cleanse the nation of the idolatry that had been practiced there for so long. Elisha combined a prophetic role, fulfill-

6 So Jehu left the others and went into the
house. Then the young prophet poured the oil
over Jehu's head and said, "This is what the LORD,
the God of Israel, says: I anoint you king over
the LORD's people, Israel. 7 You are to destroy the
family of Ahab, your master. In this way, I will
avenge the murder of my prophets and all the
LORD's servants who were killed by Jezebel. 8 The
entire family of Ahab must be wiped out. I will
destroy every one of his male descendants, slave
and free alike, anywhere in Israel. 9 I will destroy
the family of Ahab as I destroyed the families
of Jeroboam son of Nebat and of Baasha son of
Ahijah. 10 Dogs will eat Ahab's wife Jezebel at
the plot of land in Jezreel, and no one will bury
her." Then the young prophet opened the door
and ran.

11 Jehu went back to his fellow officers, and
one of them asked him, "What did that madman
want? Is everything all right?"

"You know how a man like that babbles on,"
Jehu replied.

12 "You're hiding something," they said. "Tell
us."

So Jehu told them, "He said to me, 'This is
what the LORD says: I have anointed you to be
king over Israel.' "

13 Then they quickly spread out their cloaks
on the bare steps and blew the ram's horn, shouting, "Jehu is king!"

Jehu Kills Joram and Ahaziah

14 So Jehu son of Jehoshaphat, son of Nimshi, led
a conspiracy against King Joram. (Now Joram
had been with the army at Ramoth-gilead, defending Israel against the forces of King Hazael
of Aram. 15 But King Joram* was wounded in the
fighting and returned to Jezreel to recover from
his wounds.) So Jehu told the men with him, "If
you want me to be king, don't let anyone leave
town and go to Jezreel to report what we have
done."

16 Then Jehu got into a chariot and rode to
Jezreel to find King Joram, who was lying there
wounded. King Ahaziah of Judah was there, too,
for he had gone to visit him. 17 The watchman on
the tower of Jezreel saw Jehu and his company
approaching, so he shouted to Joram, "I see a
company of troops coming!"

"Send out a rider to ask if they are coming in
peace," King Joram ordered.

18 So a horseman went out to meet Jehu and
said, "The king wants to know if you are coming
in peace."

Jehu replied, "What do you know about
peace? Fall in behind me!"

The watchman called out to the king, "The
messenger has met them, but he's not returning."

19 So the king sent out a second horseman.
He rode up to them and said, "The king wants to
know if you come in peace."

Again Jehu answered, "What do you know
about peace? Fall in behind me!"

20 The watchman exclaimed, "The messenger
has met them, but he isn't returning either! It
must be Jehu son of Nimshi, for he's driving like
a madman."

21 "Quick! Get my chariot ready!" King Joram commanded.

Then King Joram of Israel and King Ahaziah of Judah rode out in their chariots to meet
Jehu. They met him at the plot of land that had
belonged to Naboth of Jezreel. 22 King Joram demanded, "Do you come in peace, Jehu?"

Jehu replied, "How can there be peace as long
as the idolatry and witchcraft of your mother,
Jezebel, are all around us?"

23 Then King Joram turned the horses around*
and fled, shouting to King Ahaziah, "Treason,
Ahaziah!" 24 But Jehu drew his bow and shot Joram between the shoulders. The arrow pierced
his heart, and he sank down dead in his chariot.

25 Jehu said to Bidkar, his officer, "Throw him
into the plot of land that belonged to Naboth of
Jezreel. Do you remember when you and I were
riding along behind his father, Ahab? The LORD
pronounced this message against him: 26 'I solemnly swear that I will repay him here on this
plot of land, says the LORD, for the murder of
Naboth and his sons that I saw yesterday.' So
throw him out on Naboth's property, just as the
LORD said."

27 When King Ahaziah of Judah saw what
was happening, he fled along the road to Beth-

9:15 Hebrew *Jehoram,* a variant spelling of Joram; also in 9:17, 21, 22, 23, 24. **9:23** Hebrew *turned his hands.*

ing the command given to Elijah in 1 Kings 19:16, with a political role, inaugurating Jehu's rebellion. **9:13:** By spreading their cloaks before him, the other commanders signal their submission to Jehu as their king.

9:14–29 Jehu Kills Joram and Ahaziah. Jehu's revolt acts as fulfillment of Elijah's oracle in 1 Kings 21 in punishment for the murder of Naboth. If Israel were in any sense to be God's people, then justice must be vital. Crimes like the confiscation of Naboth's vineyard had to be stopped.

haggan. Jehu rode after him, shouting, "Shoot
him, too!" So they shot Ahaziah in his chariot
at the Ascent of Gur, near Ibleam. He was able
to go on as far as Megiddo, but he died there.
28 His servants took him by chariot to Jerusalem,
where they buried him with his ancestors in the
City of David. 29 Ahaziah had become king over
Judah in the eleventh year of the reign of Joram
son of Ahab.

The Death of Jezebel

30 When Jezebel, the queen mother, heard that
Jehu had come to Jezreel, she painted her eyelids
and fixed her hair and sat at a window. 31 When
Jehu entered the gate of the palace, she shouted
at him, "Have you come in peace, you murderer?
You're just like Zimri, who murdered his master!"*

32 Jehu looked up and saw her at the window
and shouted, "Who is on my side?" And two or
three eunuchs looked out at him. 33 "Throw her
down!" Jehu yelled. So they threw her out the
window, and her blood spattered against the wall
and on the horses. And Jehu trampled her body
under his horses' hooves.

34 Then Jehu went into the palace and ate
and drank. Afterward he said, "Someone go and
bury this cursed woman, for she is the daughter
of a king." 35 But when they went out to bury
her, they found only her skull, her feet, and her
hands.

36 When they returned and told Jehu, he
stated, "This fulfills the message from the LORD,
which he spoke through his servant Elijah from
Tishbe: 'At the plot of land in Jezreel, dogs will
eat Jezebel's body. 37 Her remains will be scattered like dung on the plot of land in Jezreel, so
that no one will be able to recognize her.' "

Jehu Kills Ahab's Family

10 Ahab had seventy sons living in the
city of Samaria. So Jehu wrote letters
and sent them to Samaria, to the el-
ders and officials of the city,* and to the guardians of King Ahab's sons. He said, 2 "The king's
sons are with you, and you have at your disposal
chariots, horses, a fortified city, and weapons. As
soon as you receive this letter, 3 select the best
qualified of your master's sons to be your king,
and prepare to fight for Ahab's dynasty."

4 But they were paralyzed with fear and
said, "We've seen that two kings couldn't stand
against this man! What can we do?"

5 So the palace and city administrators, together with the elders and the guardians of the
king's sons, sent this message to Jehu: "We are
your servants and will do anything you tell us.
We will not make anyone king; do whatever you
think is best."

6 Jehu responded with a second letter: "If you
are on my side and are going to obey me, bring
the heads of your master's sons to me at Jezreel
by this time tomorrow." Now the seventy sons
of the king were being cared for by the leaders of

9:31 See 1 Kgs 16:9-10, where Zimri killed his master, King Elah. **10:1** As in some Greek manuscripts and Latin Vulgate (see also 10:6); Hebrew reads *of Jezreel.*

9:30–37 Jehu Kills Jezebel. Jezebel also will meet her prophesied end. Although her husband, Ahab, had long since died, she continued to be a commanding presence in the land. **30:** Jezebel perhaps hopes to seduce Jehu with her painted eyes and fancy hairdo. She may be described this way in order to fit the image of a prostitute. **32–33:** As with many of the kings, Jezebel's actions were intolerable; although she was supported by the people at first, it was clear the tide was turning in favor of Jehu's rule over Israel. Thus, when Jehu ordered three eunuchs to throw her down to the ground, they complied. **34–37:** It had been prophesied that when Jezebel died, the dogs of the city would eat her body, save for the head, which would be unrecognizable (1 Kgs 21:22). Jezebel suffered a death that was commensurate with her great disobedience to the LORD. Although Jezebel had effectively ruled a part of Israel for a short time, she is not recognized as such in the king lists. Her official standing would have been that of queen mother, upon the accession of her son, Ahaziah. Jezebel serves as an excellent example of a woman serving in the highest position possible. She was educated and cunning; she demanded and obtained the respect of the military, religious leaders, and most of the people. She was, for the most part, a great leader. Her failure was her unwillingness to worship only God, maintaining the Baal and Asherah cults. Because of this she was condemned to death, denied a traditional burial, and her memory defiled. Jezebel serves as a positive and negative example to women in leadership positions.

10:1–17 Ahab's Family Killed. Jehu disposes of the surviving male members of Ahab's family, as the LORD had instructed. It was standard practice to rid the land of all surviving members of a rival royal family, so that they did not conspire against the new king. The book of 2 Kings makes no comment and raises no criticism about the extent of the violence used by Jehu, but Hosea 1:4 gives a strong indication that Jehu exceeded his brief.

Samaria, where they had been raised since childhood. 7 When the letter arrived, the leaders killed all seventy of the king's sons. They placed their heads in baskets and presented them to Jehu at Jezreel.

8 A messenger went to Jehu and said, "They have brought the heads of the king's sons."

So Jehu ordered, "Pile them in two heaps at the entrance of the city gate, and leave them there until morning."

9 In the morning he went out and spoke to the crowd that had gathered around them. "You are not to blame," he told them. "I am the one who conspired against my master and killed him. But who killed all these? 10 You can be sure that the message of the LORD that was spoken concerning Ahab's family will not fail. The LORD declared through his servant Elijah that this would happen." 11 Then Jehu killed all who were left of Ahab's relatives living in Jezreel and all his important officials, his personal friends, and his priests. So Ahab was left without a single survivor.

12 Then Jehu set out for Samaria. Along the way, while he was at Beth-eked of the Shepherds, 13 he met some relatives of King Ahaziah of Judah. "Who are you?" he asked them.

And they replied, "We are relatives of King Ahaziah. We are going to visit the sons of King Ahab and the sons of the queen mother."

14 "Take them alive!" Jehu shouted to his men. And they captured all forty-two of them and killed them at the well of Beth-eked. None of them escaped.

15 When Jehu left there, he met Jehonadab son of Recab, who was coming to meet him. After they had greeted each other, Jehu said to him, "Are you as loyal to me as I am to you?"

"Yes, I am," Jehonadab replied.

"If you are," Jehu said, "then give me your hand." So Jehonadab put out his hand, and Jehu helped him into the chariot. 16 Then Jehu said, "Now come with me, and see how devoted I am to the LORD." So Jehonadab rode along with him.

17 When Jehu arrived in Samaria, he killed everyone who was left there from Ahab's family, just as the LORD had promised through Elijah.

Jehu Kills the Priests of Baal

18 Then Jehu called a meeting of all the people of the city and said to them, "Ahab's worship of Baal was nothing compared to the way I will worship him! 19 Therefore, summon all the prophets and worshipers of Baal, and call together all his priests. See to it that every one of them comes, for I am going to offer a great sacrifice to Baal. Anyone who fails to come will be put to death." But Jehu's cunning plan was to destroy all the worshipers of Baal.

20 Then Jehu ordered, "Prepare a solemn assembly to worship Baal!" So they did. 21 He sent messengers throughout all Israel summoning those who worshiped Baal. They all came—not a single one remained behind—and they filled the temple of Baal from one end to the other. 22 And Jehu instructed the keeper of the wardrobe, "Be sure that every worshiper of Baal wears one of these robes." So robes were given to them.

23 Then Jehu went into the temple of Baal with Jehonadab son of Recab. Jehu said to the worshipers of Baal, "Make sure no one who worships the LORD is here—only those who worship Baal." 24 So they were all inside the temple to offer sacrifices and burnt offerings. Now Jehu had stationed eighty of his men outside the building and had warned them, "If you let anyone escape, you will pay for it with your own life."

25 As soon as Jehu had finished sacrificing the burnt offering, he commanded his guards and officers, "Go in and kill all of them. Don't let a single one escape!" So they killed them all with their swords, and the guards and officers dragged their bodies outside.* Then Jehu's men went into the innermost fortress* of the temple of Baal. 26 They dragged out the sacred pillar* used in the worship of Baal and burned it. 27 They smashed the sacred pillar and wrecked the temple of Baal, converting it into a public toilet, as it remains to this day.

28 In this way, Jehu destroyed every trace of Baal worship from Israel. 29 He did not, however, destroy the gold calves at Bethel and Dan, with which Jeroboam son of Nebat had caused Israel to sin.

30 Nonetheless the LORD said to Jehu, "You have done well in following my instructions to destroy the family of Ahab. Therefore, your descendants will be kings of Israel down to the

10:25a Or *they left their bodies lying there;* or *they threw them out into the outermost court.* **10:25b** Hebrew *city.* **10:26** As in Greek and Syriac versions and Latin Vulgate; Hebrew reads *sacred pillars.*

10:18–36 Priests and Prophets of Baal Killed. Jehu uses deception to gather the prophets of Baal from all over the land. **25–28:** Jehu's destruction of the sacred pillar of Baal and the temple effectively destroys Baal worship in Israel. **29:** The author implies that Jehu fell short by not stopping the worship of gold calves at Dan and Bethel. **30–31:** Jehu is rewarded for carrying out God's orders, but he fails to live up to his

fourth generation." [31] But Jehu did not obey the
Law of the LORD, the God of Israel, with all his
heart. He refused to turn from the sins that Jeroboam had led Israel to commit.

The Death of Jehu

[32] At about that time the LORD began to cut down
the size of Israel's territory. King Hazael conquered several sections of the country [33] east of
the Jordan River, including all of Gilead, Gad,
Reuben, and Manasseh. He conquered the area
from the town of Aroer by the Arnon Gorge to
as far north as Gilead and Bashan.

[34] The rest of the events in Jehu's reign—
everything he did and all his achievements—are
recorded in *The Book of the History of the Kings
of Israel.*

[35] When Jehu died, he was buried in Samaria.
Then his son Jehoahaz became the next king.
[36] In all, Jehu reigned over Israel from Samaria
for twenty-eight years.

Queen Athaliah Rules in Judah

11 When Athaliah, the mother of King
Ahaziah of Judah, learned that her
son was dead, she began to destroy
the rest of the royal family. [2] But Ahaziah's sister
Jehosheba, the daughter of King Jehoram,* took
Ahaziah's infant son, Joash, and stole him away
from among the rest of the king's children, who
were about to be killed. She put Joash and his
nurse in a bedroom to hide him from Athaliah,
so the child was not murdered. [3] Joash remained
hidden in the Temple of the LORD for six years
while Athaliah ruled over the land.

Revolt against Athaliah

[4] In the seventh year of Athaliah's reign, Jehoiada
the priest summoned the commanders, the Carite mercenaries, and the palace guards to come to
the Temple of the LORD. He made a solemn pact
with them and made them swear an oath of loyalty there in the LORD's Temple; then he showed
them the king's son.

[5] Jehoiada told them, "This is what you must
do. A third of you who are on duty on the Sabbath are to guard the royal palace itself. [6] Another
third of you are to stand guard at the Sur Gate.
And the final third must stand guard behind the
palace guard. These three groups will all guard
the palace. [7] The other two units who are off duty
on the Sabbath must stand guard for the king at
the LORD's Temple. [8] Form a bodyguard around
the king and keep your weapons in hand. Kill
anyone who tries to break through. Stay with
the king wherever he goes."

[9] So the commanders did everything as Jehoiada the priest ordered. The commanders
took charge of the men reporting for duty that
Sabbath, as well as those who were going off
duty. They brought them all to Jehoiada the
priest, [10] and he supplied them with the spears
and small shields that had once belonged to
King David and were stored in the Temple of
the LORD. [11] The palace guards stationed themselves around the king, with their weapons
ready. They formed a line from the south side
of the Temple around to the north side and all
around the altar.

[12] Then Jehoiada brought out Joash, the king's
son, placed the crown on his head, and presented
him with a copy of God's laws.* They anointed
him and proclaimed him king, and everyone
clapped their hands and shouted, "Long live the
king!"

11:2 Hebrew *Joram,* a variant spelling of Jehoram. **11:12** Or *a copy of the covenant.*

potential. **32–33:** From this time the population and territory of Israel began to decline.

11:1–20 Athaliah of Judah

Athaliah (841–835 BC) was the daughter of Ahab and Jezebel of Israel and widow of Jehoram, king of Judah. Her marriage had evidently been arranged to improve diplomatic ties between the two kingdoms. Athaliah was given in marriage to the Judean crown prince Jehoram as part of a peace settlement. This put an end to hostilities that had existed between Israel and Judah since the death of Solomon, although this new treaty did not remain in effect very long. Nevertheless, Athaliah gained an extremely high rank, that of wife of the king, with the related responsibilities. Once her son, Ahaziah, became king of Judah, Athaliah apparently obtained another powerful position, queen mother and confidant to the new king (cf. 2 Chr 22:3). The writer of 2 Kings did not consider her a legitimate ruler. **1:** Athaliah was educated by Jezebel and thus exposed to the Sidonian princess's influence, both political and religious. She appears to have inherited her mother's cruelty and desire for power. **2–3:** As elsewhere, women are seen as acting in evil and in good, in destructive and creative ways. Jehosheba may well have saved the Davidic line from extinction. **4–12:** Athaliah ruled as an absolute monarch, but the priests of the LORD, some of the military, and Judeans of full citizenship did not support her and conspired to have her removed. **4:** *Carites* were a special detachment of foreigners. **13–**

The Death of Athaliah

[13]When Athaliah heard all the noise made by the palace guards and the people, she hurried to the LORD's Temple to see what was happening. [14]When she arrived, she saw the newly crowned king standing in his place of authority by the pillar, as was the custom at times of coronation. The commanders and trumpeters were surrounding him, and people from all over the land were rejoicing and blowing trumpets. When Athaliah saw all this, she tore her clothes in despair and shouted, "Treason! Treason!"

[15]Then Jehoiada the priest ordered the commanders who were in charge of the troops, "Take her to the soldiers in front of the Temple,* and kill anyone who tries to rescue her." For the priest had said, "She must not be killed in the Temple of the LORD." [16]So they seized her and led her out to the gate where horses enter the palace grounds, and she was killed there.

Jehoiada's Religious Reforms

[17]Then Jehoiada made a covenant between the LORD and the king and the people that they would be the LORD's people. He also made a covenant between the king and the people. [18]And all the people of the land went over to the temple of Baal and tore it down. They demolished the altars and smashed the idols to pieces, and they killed Mattan the priest of Baal in front of the altars.

Jehoiada the priest stationed guards at the Temple of the LORD. [19]Then the commanders, the Carite mercenaries, the palace guards, and all the people of the land escorted the king from the Temple of the LORD. They went through the gate of the guards and into the palace, and the king took his seat on the royal throne. [20]So all the people of the land rejoiced, and the city was peaceful because Athaliah had been killed at the king's palace.

[21]*Joash* was seven years old when he became king.

Joash Repairs the Temple

12 [1]*Joash* began to rule over Judah in the seventh year of King Jehu's reign in Israel. He reigned in Jerusalem forty years. His mother was Zibiah from Beersheba. [2]All his life Joash did what was pleasing in the LORD's sight because Jehoiada the priest instructed him. [3]Yet even so, he did not destroy the pagan shrines, and the people still offered sacrifices and burned incense there.

[4]One day King Joash said to the priests, "Collect all the money brought as a sacred offering to the LORD's Temple, whether it is a regular assessment, a payment of vows, or a voluntary gift. [5]Let the priests take some of that money to pay for whatever repairs are needed at the Temple."

[6]But by the twenty-third year of Joash's reign, the priests still had not repaired the Temple. [7]So King Joash called for Jehoiada and the other priests and asked them, "Why haven't you repaired the Temple? Don't use any more money for your own needs. From now on, it must all be spent on Temple repairs." [8]So the priests agreed not to accept any more money from the people, and they also agreed to let others take responsibility for repairing the Temple.

[9]Then Jehoiada the priest bored a hole in the lid of a large chest and set it on the right-hand side of the altar at the entrance of the Temple of the LORD. The priests guarding the entrance put all of the people's contributions into the chest. [10]Whenever the chest became full, the court secretary and the high priest counted the money that had been brought to the LORD's Temple and put it into bags. [11]Then they gave the money to the construction supervisors, who used it to pay the people working on the LORD's Temple—the carpenters, the

11:15 Or *Bring her out from between the ranks;* or *Take her out of the Temple precincts.* The meaning of the Hebrew is uncertain. **11:21a** Verse 11:21 is numbered 12:1 in Hebrew text. **11:21b** Hebrew *Jehoash,* a variant spelling of Joash. **12:1a** Verses 12:1-21 are numbered 12:2-22 in Hebrew text. **12:1b** Hebrew *Jehoash,* a variant spelling of Joash; also in 12:2, 4, 6, 7, 18.

14: *The LORD's Temple*: The king played an important role in the state religion, especially at the Temple. So Athaliah almost certainly participated in sacrifices, rituals, and ceremonies in her capacity as the representative of God on earth, the basis for her divine right to rule. In fact, Athaliah was comfortable in the temples of the LORD and of Baal. She wielded considerable power religiously and militarily. She was the only female king mentioned in either Judah or Israel. It is disappointing, however, that she could not have been a better religious leader. **14:** Athaliah's cry of *"Treason! Treason!"* was somewhat ironic, since she was a usurper. **17–20:** Indicating a new start for the people as well as a new king, Jehoiada the priest, Joash the king, and the people all promised loyalty to the LORD and to worship only him.

11:21—12:21 Joash of Judah

Like a number of his predecessors, Joash began well, instituting repairs to the Temple. **4–12:** Care for God's house was often seen as a significant sign of recom-

builders, 12 the masons, and the stonecutters. They also used the money to buy the timber and the finished stone needed for repairing the LORD's Temple, and they paid any other expenses related to the Temple's restoration.

13 The money brought to the Temple was not used for making silver bowls, lamp snuffers, basins, trumpets, or other articles of gold or silver for the Temple of the LORD. 14 It was paid to the workmen, who used it for the Temple repairs. 15 No accounting of this money was required from the construction supervisors, because they were honest and trustworthy men. 16 However, the money that was contributed for guilt offerings and sin offerings was not brought into the LORD's Temple. It was given to the priests for their own use.

The End of Joash's Reign

17 About this time King Hazael of Aram went to war against Gath and captured it. Then he turned to attack Jerusalem. 18 King Joash collected all the sacred objects that Jehoshaphat, Jehoram, and Ahaziah, the previous kings of Judah, had dedicated, along with what he himself had dedicated. He sent them all to Hazael, along with all the gold in the treasuries of the LORD's Temple and the royal palace. So Hazael called off his attack on Jerusalem.

19 The rest of the events in Joash's reign and everything he did are recorded in *The Book of the History of the Kings of Judah.*

20 Joash's officers plotted against him and assassinated him at Beth-millo on the road to Silla. 21 The assassins were Jozacar* son of Shimeath and Jehozabad son of Shomer—both trusted advisers. Joash was buried with his ancestors in the City of David. Then his son Amaziah became the next king.

Jehoahaz Rules in Israel

13 Jehoahaz son of Jehu began to rule over Israel in the twenty-third year of King Joash's reign in Judah. He reigned in Samaria seventeen years. 2 But he did what was evil in the LORD's sight. He followed the example of Jeroboam son of Nebat, continuing the sins that Jeroboam had led Israel to commit. 3 So the LORD was very angry with Israel, and he allowed King Hazael of Aram and his son Ben-hadad to defeat them repeatedly.

4 Then Jehoahaz prayed for the LORD's help, and the LORD heard his prayer, for he could see how severely the king of Aram was oppressing Israel. 5 So the LORD provided someone to rescue the Israelites from the tyranny of the Arameans. Then Israel lived in safety again as they had in former days.

6 But they continued to sin, following the evil example of Jeroboam. They also allowed the Asherah pole in Samaria to remain standing. 7 Finally, Jehoahaz's army was reduced to 50 charioteers, 10 chariots, and 10,000 foot soldiers. The king of Aram had killed the others, trampling them like dust under his feet.

8 The rest of the events in Jehoahaz's reign—everything he did and the extent of his power—are recorded in *The Book of the History of the Kings of Israel.* 9 When Jehoahaz died, he was buried in Samaria. Then his son Jehoash* became the next king.

Jehoash Rules in Israel

10 Jehoash son of Jehoahaz began to rule over Israel in the thirty-seventh year of King Joash's reign in Judah. He reigned in Samaria sixteen years. 11 But he did what was evil in the LORD's sight. He refused to turn from the sins that Jeroboam son of Nebat had led Israel to commit.

12 The rest of the events in Jehoash's reign and everything he did, including the extent of his power and his war with King Amaziah of Judah, are recorded in *The Book of the History of the Kings of Israel.* 13 When Jehoash died, he was buried in Samaria with the kings of Israel. Then his son Jeroboam II became the next king.

Elisha's Final Prophecy

14 When Elisha was in his last illness, King Jehoash of Israel visited him and wept over him.

12:21 As in Greek and Syriac versions; Hebrew reads *Jozabad.* **13:9** Hebrew *Joash,* a variant spelling of Jehoash; also in 13:10, 12, 13, 14, 25.

mitment to the LORD. **18:** *Sacred objects* were special items of value that the kings of Judah had dedicated to the Temple. By paying these to Hazael as tribute, Joash capitulated to him and in effect bribed him to prevent him from attacking Jerusalem.

13:1–13 Jehoahaz and Jehoash of Israel

These two kings are passed over quickly with the formulaic words describing the majority of rulers who *did what was evil in the LORD's sight.* **4–7:** Jehoahaz's reformation is short-lived, and the return to sin has typical consequences.

13:14–25 Elisha's Final Acts

This story lies outside of the framework of the regnal formulas. It may be out of place or a later addition.

"My father! My father! I see the chariots and charioteers of Israel!" he cried.

[15] Elisha told him, "Get a bow and some arrows." And the king did as he was told. [16] Elisha told him, "Put your hand on the bow," and Elisha laid his own hands on the king's hands.

[17] Then he commanded, "Open that eastern window," and he opened it. Then he said, "Shoot!" So he shot an arrow. Elisha proclaimed, "This is the LORD's arrow, an arrow of victory over Aram, for you will completely conquer the Arameans at Aphek."

[18] Then he said, "Now pick up the other arrows and strike them against the ground." So the king picked them up and struck the ground three times. [19] But the man of God was angry with him. "You should have struck the ground five or six times!" he exclaimed. "Then you would have beaten Aram until it was entirely destroyed. Now you will be victorious only three times."

[20] Then Elisha died and was buried.

Groups of Moabite raiders used to invade the land each spring. [21] Once when some Israelites were burying a man, they spied a band of these raiders. So they hastily threw the corpse into the tomb of Elisha and fled. But as soon as the body touched Elisha's bones, the dead man revived and jumped to his feet!

[22] King Hazael of Aram had oppressed Israel during the entire reign of King Jehoahaz. [23] But the LORD was gracious and merciful to the people of Israel, and they were not totally destroyed. He pitied them because of his covenant with Abraham, Isaac, and Jacob. And to this day he still has not completely destroyed them or banished them from his presence.

[24] King Hazael of Aram died, and his son Ben-hadad became the next king. [25] Then Jehoash son of Jehoahaz recaptured from Ben-hadad son of Hazael the towns that had been taken from Jehoash's father, Jehoahaz. Jehoash defeated Ben-hadad on three occasions, and he recovered the Israelite towns.

Amaziah Rules in Judah

14 Amaziah son of Joash began to rule over Judah in the second year of the reign of King Jehoash* of Israel. [2] Amaziah was twenty-five years old when he became king, and he reigned in Jerusalem twenty-nine years. His mother was Jehoaddin from Jerusalem. [3] Amaziah did what was pleasing in the LORD's sight, but not like his ancestor David. Instead, he followed the example of his father, Joash. [4] Amaziah did not destroy the pagan shrines, and the people still offered sacrifices and burned incense there.

[5] When Amaziah was well established as king, he executed the officials who had assassinated his father. [6] However, he did not kill the children of the assassins, for he obeyed the command of the LORD as written by Moses in the Book of the Law: "Parents must not be put to death for the sins of their children, nor children for the sins of their parents. Those deserving to die must be put to death for their own crimes."*

[7] Amaziah also killed 10,000 Edomites in the Valley of Salt. He also conquered Sela and changed its name to Joktheel, as it is called to this day.

[8] One day Amaziah sent messengers with this challenge to Israel's king Jehoash, the son of Jehoahaz and grandson of Jehu: "Come and meet me in battle!"*

[9] But King Jehoash of Israel replied to King Amaziah of Judah with this story: "Out in the Lebanon mountains, a thistle sent a message to a mighty cedar tree: 'Give your daughter in marriage to my son.' But just then a wild animal of Lebanon came by and stepped on the thistle, crushing it!

[10] "You have indeed defeated Edom, and you are very proud of it. But be content with your victory and stay at home! Why stir up trouble that will only bring disaster on you and the people of Judah?"

[11] But Amaziah refused to listen, so King Jehoash of Israel mobilized his army against King Amaziah of Judah. The two armies drew up their battle lines at Beth-shemesh in Judah. [12] Judah was routed by the army of Israel, and its army scattered and fled for home. [13] King Jehoash of Israel captured Judah's king, Amaziah son of Joash and grandson of Ahaziah, at Beth-shemesh. Then he marched to Jerusalem, where he demolished 600 feet* of Jerusalem's wall, from the Ephraim Gate to the Corner Gate. [14] He carried off all the gold and silver and all the articles from the Temple of the LORD. He also seized the treasures

14:1 Hebrew *Joash,* a variant spelling of Jehoash; also in 14:13, 23, 27. **14:6** Deut 24:16. **14:8** Hebrew *Come, let us look one another in the face.* **14:13** Hebrew *400 cubits* [180 meters].

15–17: Symbolic acts like this one are frequently carried out by prophets in the Bible. **20–21:** Elisha's miraculous powers continue even after his death. **24–25:** These verses fulfill Elisha's prediction in verse 19.

14:1–20 Amaziah of Judah

The kings in this and following chapters make only brief appearances, despite the varying lengths of their rules.

from the royal palace, along with hostages, and then returned to Samaria.

[15]The rest of the events in Jehoash's reign and everything he did, including the extent of his power and his war with King Amaziah of Judah, are recorded in *The Book of the History of the Kings of Israel.* [16]When Jehoash died, he was buried in Samaria with the kings of Israel. And his son Jeroboam II became the next king.

[17]King Amaziah of Judah lived for fifteen years after the death of King Jehoash of Israel. [18]The rest of the events in Amaziah's reign are recorded in *The Book of the History of the Kings of Judah.*

[19]There was a conspiracy against Amaziah's life in Jerusalem, and he fled to Lachish. But his enemies sent assassins after him, and they killed him there. [20]They brought his body back to Jerusalem on a horse, and he was buried with his ancestors in the City of David.

[21]All the people of Judah had crowned Amaziah's sixteen-year-old son, Uzziah,* as king in place of his father, Amaziah. [22]After his father's death, Uzziah rebuilt the town of Elath and restored it to Judah.

Jeroboam II Rules in Israel

[23]Jeroboam II, the son of Jehoash, began to rule over Israel in the fifteenth year of King Amaziah's reign in Judah. Jeroboam reigned in Samaria forty-one years. [24]He did what was evil in the LORD's sight. He refused to turn from the sins that Jeroboam son of Nebat had led Israel to commit. [25]Jeroboam II recovered the territories of Israel between Lebo-hamath and the Dead Sea,* just as the LORD, the God of Israel, had promised through Jonah son of Amittai, the prophet from Gath-hepher.

[26]For the LORD saw the bitter suffering of everyone in Israel, and that there was no one in Israel, slave or free, to help them. [27]And because the LORD had not said he would blot out the name of Israel completely, he used Jeroboam II, the son of Jehoash, to save them.

[28]The rest of the events in the reign of Jeroboam II and everything he did—including the extent of his power, his wars, and how he recovered for Israel both Damascus and Hamath, which had belonged to Judah*—are recorded in *The Book of the History of the Kings of Israel.* [29]When Jeroboam II died, he was buried in Samaria* with the kings of Israel. Then his son Zechariah became the next king.

Uzziah Rules in Judah

15 Uzziah* son of Amaziah began to rule over Judah in the twenty-seventh year of the reign of King Jeroboam II of Israel. [2]He was sixteen years old when he became king, and he reigned in Jerusalem fifty-two years. His mother was Jecoliah from Jerusalem.

[3]He did what was pleasing in the LORD's sight, just as his father, Amaziah, had done. [4]But he did not destroy the pagan shrines, and the people still offered sacrifices and burned incense there. [5]The LORD struck the king with leprosy,* which lasted until the day he died. He lived in isolation in a separate house. The king's son Jotham was put in charge of the royal palace, and he governed the people of the land.

[6]The rest of the events in Uzziah's reign and everything he did are recorded in *The Book of the History of the Kings of Judah.* [7]When Uzziah died, he was buried with his ancestors in the City of David. And his son Jotham became the next king.

Zechariah Rules in Israel

[8]Zechariah son of Jeroboam II began to rule over Israel in the thirty-eighth year of King Uzziah's

14:21 Hebrew *Azariah,* a variant spelling of Uzziah. **14:25** Hebrew *the sea of the Arabah.* **14:28** Or *to Yaudi.* The meaning of the Hebrew is uncertain. **14:29** As in some Greek manuscripts; Hebrew lacks *he was buried in Samaria.* **15:1** Hebrew *Azariah,* a variant spelling of Uzziah; also in 15:6, 7, 8, 17, 23, 27. **15:5** Or *with a contagious skin disease.* The Hebrew word used here and throughout this passage can describe various skin diseases.

9: The fable does not imply any marriage treaty or relationship between Amaziah and Johoash. Its point is that Amaziah is trying to make himself more important than he is and Jehoash of Israel's parable implies that Amaziah will be *stepped on* and *crush*[ed] if he continues.

14:21—15:7 Uzziah (Azariah) of Judah and Jeroboam II of Israel

The reigns of Jeroboam and Uzziah, coming at a time when world powers like Assyria and Egypt were less interested in this region, brought a great deal of prosperity to both nations. Amos and Hosea in the north and Micah and Isaiah in the south describe the prosperity and the corruption, oppression, and injustice that were brought in with the prosperity. Women were involved as oppressed (Amos 1:13; 2:7) and as oppressors (Amos 4).

15:8—17:6 Various Kings of Israel and Judah

The rapid succession of kings at the end of the Jehu

reign in Judah. He reigned in Samaria six months. [9] Zechariah did what was evil in the LORD's sight, as his ancestors had done. He refused to turn from the sins that Jeroboam son of Nebat had led Israel to commit. [10] Then Shallum son of Jabesh conspired against Zechariah, assassinated him in public,* and became the next king.

[11] The rest of the events in Zechariah's reign are recorded in *The Book of the History of the Kings of Israel.* [12] So the LORD's message to Jehu came true: "Your descendants will be kings of Israel down to the fourth generation."

Shallum Rules in Israel

[13] Shallum son of Jabesh began to rule over Israel in the thirty-ninth year of King Uzziah's reign in Judah. Shallum reigned in Samaria only one month. [14] Then Menahem son of Gadi went to Samaria from Tirzah and assassinated him, and he became the next king.

[15] The rest of the events in Shallum's reign, including his conspiracy, are recorded in *The Book of the History of the Kings of Israel.*

Menahem Rules in Israel

[16] At that time Menahem destroyed the town of Tappuah* and all the surrounding countryside as far as Tirzah, because its citizens refused to surrender the town. He killed the entire population and ripped open the pregnant women.

[17] Menahem son of Gadi began to rule over Israel in the thirty-ninth year of King Uzziah's reign in Judah. He reigned in Samaria ten years. [18] But Menahem did what was evil in the LORD's sight. During his entire reign, he refused to turn from the sins that Jeroboam son of Nebat had led Israel to commit.

[19] Then King Tiglath-pileser* of Assyria invaded the land. But Menahem paid him thirty-seven tons* of silver to gain his support in tightening his grip on royal power. [20] Menahem extorted the money from the rich of Israel, demanding that each of them pay fifty pieces* of silver to the king of Assyria. So the king of Assyria turned from attacking Israel and did not stay in the land.

[21] The rest of the events in Menahem's reign and everything he did are recorded in *The Book of the History of the Kings of Israel.* [22] When Menahem died, his son Pekahiah became the next king.

Pekahiah Rules in Israel

[23] Pekahiah son of Menahem began to rule over Israel in the fiftieth year of King Uzziah's reign in Judah. He reigned in Samaria two years. [24] But Pekahiah did what was evil in the LORD's sight. He refused to turn from the sins that Jeroboam son of Nebat had led Israel to commit.

[25] Then Pekah son of Remaliah, the commander of Pekahiah's army, conspired against him. With fifty men from Gilead, Pekah assassinated the king, along with Argob and Arieh, in the citadel of the palace at Samaria. And Pekah reigned in his place.

[26] The rest of the events in Pekahiah's reign and everything he did are recorded in *The Book of the History of the Kings of Israel.*

Pekah Rules in Israel

[27] Pekah son of Remaliah began to rule over Israel in the fifty-second year of King Uzziah's reign in Judah. He reigned in Samaria twenty years. [28] But Pekah did what was evil in the LORD's sight. He refused to turn from the sins that Jeroboam son of Nebat had led Israel to commit.

[29] During Pekah's reign, King Tiglath-pileser of Assyria attacked Israel again, and he captured the towns of Ijon, Abel-beth-maacah, Janoah, Kedesh, and Hazor. He also conquered the regions of Gilead, Galilee, and all of Naphtali, and he took the people to Assyria as captives. [30] Then Hoshea son of Elah conspired against Pekah and assassinated him. He began to rule over Israel in the twentieth year of Jotham son of Uzziah.

[31] The rest of the events in Pekah's reign and everything he did are recorded in *The Book of the History of the Kings of Israel.*

Jotham Rules in Judah

[32] Jotham son of Uzziah began to rule over Judah in the second year of King Pekah's reign in Israel. [33] He was twenty-five years old when he became

15:10 Or *at Ibleam.* **15:16** As in some Greek manuscripts; other Greek manuscripts read *at Ibleam.* Hebrew reads *Tiphsah.* **15:19a** Hebrew *Pul,* another name for Tiglath-pileser. **15:19b** Hebrew *1,000 talents* [34 metric tons]. **15:20** Hebrew *50 shekels* [20 ounces, or 570 grams].

dynasty in Israel is reminiscent of the last days of Basha's house in 1 Kings 16. **15:12:** The prophecy occurs in 10:30. **16:** The practice of *ripp*[ing] *open the pregnant women* is mentioned elsewhere in the Bible in the context of wars with other countries (2 Kgs 8:12; Hos 13:16; Amos 1:13). If Menahem's army truly *killed the entire population,* this act's purpose could only be as psychological warfare. Tappuah was within Israel, and the reason for Menahem's brutality is unknown, but it has been suggested that this was Shallum's hometown.

king, and he reigned in Jerusalem sixteen years. His mother was Jerusha, the daughter of Zadok.

[34]Jotham did what was pleasing in the LORD's sight. He did everything his father, Uzziah, had done. [35]But he did not destroy the pagan shrines, and the people still offered sacrifices and burned incense there. He rebuilt the upper gate of the Temple of the LORD.

[36]The rest of the events in Jotham's reign and everything he did are recorded in *The Book of the History of the Kings of Judah.* [37]In those days the LORD began to send King Rezin of Aram and King Pekah of Israel to attack Judah. [38]When Jotham died, he was buried with his ancestors in the City of David. And his son Ahaz became the next king.

Ahaz Rules in Judah

16 Ahaz son of Jotham began to rule over Judah in the seventeenth year of King Pekah's reign in Israel. [2]Ahaz was twenty years old when he became king, and he reigned in Jerusalem sixteen years. He did not do what was pleasing in the sight of the LORD his God, as his ancestor David had done. [3]Instead, he followed the example of the kings of Israel, even sacrificing his own son in the fire.* In this way, he followed the detestable practices of the pagan nations the LORD had driven from the land ahead of the Israelites. [4]He offered sacrifices and burned incense at the pagan shrines and on the hills and under every green tree.

[5]Then King Rezin of Aram and King Pekah of Israel came up to attack Jerusalem. They besieged Ahaz but could not conquer him. [6]At that time the king of Edom* recovered the town of Elath for Edom.* He drove out the people of Judah and sent Edomites* to live there, as they do to this day.

[7]King Ahaz sent messengers to King Tiglath-pileser of Assyria with this message: "I am your servant and your vassal.* Come up and rescue me from the attacking armies of Aram and Israel." [8]Then Ahaz took the silver and gold from the Temple of the LORD and the palace treasury and sent it as a payment to the Assyrian king. [9]So the king of Assyria attacked the Aramean capital of Damascus and led its population away as captives, resettling them in Kir. He also killed King Rezin.

[10]King Ahaz then went to Damascus to meet with King Tiglath-pileser of Assyria. While he was there, he took special note of the altar. Then he sent a model of the altar to Uriah the priest, along with its design in full detail. [11]Uriah followed the king's instructions and built an altar just like it, and it was ready before the king returned from Damascus. [12]When the king returned, he inspected the altar and made offerings on it. [13]He presented a burnt offering and a grain offering, he poured out a liquid offering, and he sprinkled the blood of peace offerings on the altar.

[14]Then King Ahaz removed the old bronze altar from its place in front of the LORD's Temple, between the entrance and the new altar, and placed it on the north side of the new altar. [15]He told Uriah the priest, "Use the new altar* for the morning sacrifices of burnt offering, the evening grain offering, the king's burnt offering and grain offering, and the burnt offerings of all the people, as well as their grain offerings and liquid offerings. Sprinkle the blood from all the burnt offerings and sacrifices on the new altar. The bronze altar will be for my personal use only." [16]Uriah the priest did just as King Ahaz commanded him.

[17]Then the king removed the side panels and basins from the portable water carts. He also removed the great bronze basin called the Sea from the backs of the bronze oxen and placed it on the stone pavement. [18]In deference to the king of Assyria, he also removed the canopy that had been constructed inside the palace for use on the Sabbath day,* as well as the king's outer entrance to the Temple of the LORD.

[19]The rest of the events in Ahaz's reign and everything he did are recorded in *The Book of the History of the Kings of Judah.* [20]When Ahaz died, he was buried with his ancestors in the City of David. Then his son Hezekiah became the next king.

Hoshea Rules in Israel

17 Hoshea son of Elah began to rule over Israel in the twelfth year of King Ahaz's reign in Judah. He reigned in

16:3 Or *even making his son pass through the fire.* **16:6a** As in Latin Vulgate; Hebrew reads *Rezin king of Aram.* **16:6b** As in Latin Vulgate; Hebrew reads *Aram.* **16:6c** As in Greek version, Latin Vulgate, and an alternate reading of the Masoretic Text; the other alternate reads *Arameans.* **16:7** Hebrew *your son.* **16:15** Hebrew *the great altar.* **16:18** The meaning of the Hebrew is uncertain.

16:1–20 Ahaz of Judah. The sins of Judah intensify. **17:** Asking Assyria for help was a grave error; Ahaz should have trusted in the LORD. **14–18:** Ahaz dismantles and removes many of the Temple furnishings in deference to the king of Assyria. Ahaz was venerating the king of Assyria the way he should have been revering the LORD. Judah has become a vassal state.

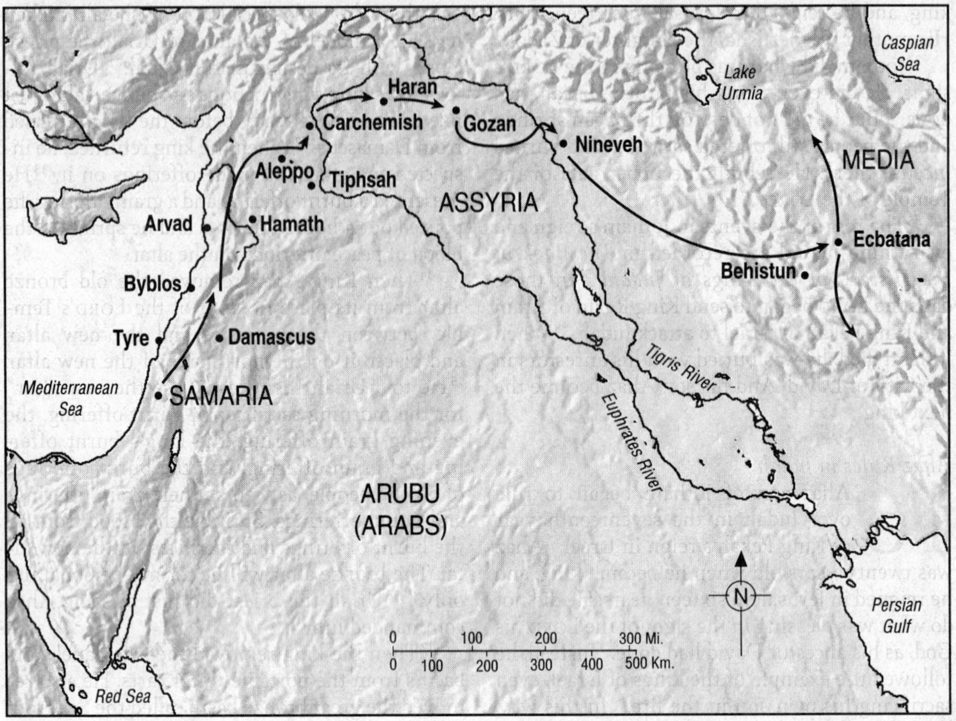

Exile of Northern Kingdom

Samaria nine years. [2]He did what was evil in the LORD's sight, but not to the same extent as the kings of Israel who ruled before him.

[3]King Shalmaneser of Assyria attacked King Hoshea, so Hoshea was forced to pay heavy tribute to Assyria. [4]But Hoshea stopped paying the annual tribute and conspired against the king of Assyria by asking King So of Egypt* to help him shake free of Assyria's power. When the king of Assyria discovered this treachery, he seized Hoshea and put him in prison.

Samaria Falls to Assyria

[5]Then the king of Assyria invaded the entire land, and for three years he besieged the city of Samaria. [6]Finally, in the ninth year of King Hoshea's reign, Samaria fell, and the people of Israel were exiled to Assyria. They were settled in colonies in Halah, along the banks of the Habor River in Gozan, and in the cities of the Medes.

[7]This disaster came upon the people of Israel because they worshiped other gods. They sinned against the LORD their God, who had brought them safely out of Egypt and had rescued them from the power of Pharaoh, the king of Egypt. [8]They had followed the practices of the pagan nations the LORD had driven from the land ahead of them, as well as the practices the kings of Israel had introduced. [9]The people of Israel had also secretly done many things that were not pleasing to the LORD their God. They built pagan shrines for themselves in all their towns, from the smallest outpost to the largest walled city. [10]They set up sacred pillars and Asherah poles

17:4 Or *by asking the king of Egypt at Sais.*

17:1–6 Hoshea of Israel. Since the time of Pekah (15:27–29), the northern half of the kingdom of Israel had been annexed by Tiglath-pileser III. **3–6:** Hoshea, a puppet king, was the last king of Israel. **4:** *King So of Egypt*: He is unknown. **6:** Deportation was a common practice of Assyria.

17:7–41 Fall of the Northern Kingdom to Assyria

The theology of 1 and 2 Kings shows in the list of the multitude of sins that led to Israel's fall. **19–20:** Even after Israel's fall, the kings of Judah gen-

at the top of every hill and under every green tree. 11 They offered sacrifices on all the hilltops, just like the nations the LORD had driven from the land ahead of them. So the people of Israel had done many evil things, arousing the LORD's anger. 12 Yes, they worshiped idols,* despite the LORD's specific and repeated warnings.

13 Again and again the LORD had sent his prophets and seers to warn both Israel and Judah: "Turn from all your evil ways. Obey my commands and decrees—the entire law that I commanded your ancestors to obey, and that I gave you through my servants the prophets."

14 But the Israelites would not listen. They were as stubborn as their ancestors who had refused to believe in the LORD their God. 15 They rejected his decrees and the covenant he had made with their ancestors, and they despised all his warnings. They worshiped worthless idols, so they became worthless themselves. They followed the example of the nations around them, disobeying the LORD's command not to imitate them.

16 They rejected all the commands of the LORD their God and made two calves from metal. They set up an Asherah pole and worshiped Baal and all the forces of heaven. 17 They even sacrificed their own sons and daughters in the fire.* They consulted fortune-tellers and practiced sorcery and sold themselves to evil, arousing the LORD's anger.

18 Because the LORD was very angry with Israel, he swept them away from his presence. Only the tribe of Judah remained in the land. 19 But even the people of Judah refused to obey the commands of the LORD their God, for they followed the evil practices that Israel had introduced. 20 The LORD rejected all the descendants of Israel. He punished them by handing them over to their attackers until he had banished Israel from his presence.

21 For when the LORD* tore Israel away from the kingdom of David, they chose Jeroboam son of Nebat as their king. But Jeroboam drew Israel away from following the LORD and made them commit a great sin. 22 And the people of Israel persisted in all the evil ways of Jeroboam. They did not turn from these sins 23 until the LORD finally swept them away from his presence, just as all his prophets had warned. So Israel was exiled from their land to Assyria, where they remain to this day.

Foreigners Settle in Israel

24 The king of Assyria transported groups of people from Babylon, Cuthah, Avva, Hamath, and Sepharvaim and resettled them in the towns of Samaria, replacing the people of Israel. They took possession of Samaria and lived in its towns. 25 But since these foreign settlers did not worship the LORD when they first arrived, the LORD sent lions among them, which killed some of them.

26 So a message was sent to the king of Assyria: "The people you have sent to live in the towns of Samaria do not know the religious customs of the God of the land. He has sent lions among them to destroy them because they have not worshiped him correctly."

27 The king of Assyria then commanded, "Send one of the exiled priests back to Samaria. Let him live there and teach the new residents the religious customs of the God of the land." 28 So one of the priests who had been exiled from Samaria returned to Bethel and taught the new residents how to worship the LORD.

29 But these various groups of foreigners also continued to worship their own gods. In town after town where they lived, they placed their idols at the pagan shrines that the people of Samaria had built. 30 Those from Babylon worshiped idols of their god Succoth-benoth. Those from Cuthah worshiped their god Nergal. And those from Hamath worshiped Ashima. 31 The Avvites worshiped their gods Nibhaz and Tartak. And the people from Sepharvaim even burned their own children as sacrifices to their gods Adrammelech and Anammelech.

32 These new residents worshiped the LORD,

17:12 The Hebrew term (literally *round things*) probably alludes to dung. **17:17** Or *They even made their sons and daughters pass through the fire.* **17:21** Hebrew *he;* compare 1 Kgs 11:31-32.

erally persisted in their evil practices. *All the descendants of Israel* includes both Israel and Judah. These verses were written in the Exile, after Judah's fall. **21–23:** This explanation differs from the preceding verses. It culminates in the sin of Jeroboam and the shrines at Dan and Bethel (1 Kgs 12:25–33). **24–28:** A widely accepted idea in the ancient Near East was that each country had its own god and each god its own country. It was thought that the lions attacked because the people did not worship the local god. **32–41:** Because the new residents also worshiped their previous gods, their descendants were never seen as part of God's covenant people. Many faithful Jews hated the Samaritans (residents of the province of Samaria) due to their religious practices, which mixed elements from other religions into Jewish observances. Samaritans were also seen as practicing a form of Judaism, particularly at later periods.

but they also appointed from among themselves
all sorts of people as priests to offer sacrifices at
their places of worship. 33 And though they worshiped the LORD, they continued to follow their
own gods according to the religious customs of
the nations from which they came. 34 And this
is still going on today. They continue to follow
their former practices instead of truly worshiping the LORD and obeying the decrees, regulations, instructions, and commands he gave the
descendants of Jacob, whose name he changed to
Israel.

35 For the LORD had made a covenant with the
descendants of Jacob and commanded them: "Do
not worship any other gods or bow before them
or serve them or offer sacrifices to them. 36 But
worship only the LORD, who brought you out of
Egypt with great strength and a powerful arm.
Bow down to him alone, and offer sacrifices only
to him. 37 Be careful at all times to obey the decrees,
regulations, instructions, and commands that he
wrote for you. You must not worship other gods.
38 Do not forget the covenant I made with you, and
do not worship other gods. 39 You must worship
only the LORD your God. He is the one who will
rescue you from all your enemies."

40 But the people would not listen and continued to follow their former practices. 41 So while
these new residents worshiped the LORD, they
also worshiped their idols. And to this day their
descendants do the same.

Hezekiah Rules in Judah

18 Hezekiah son of Ahaz began to rule
over Judah in the third year of King
Hoshea's reign in Israel. 2 He was
twenty-five years old when he became king, and
he reigned in Jerusalem twenty-nine years. His
mother was Abijah,* the daughter of Zechariah.
3 He did what was pleasing in the LORD's sight,
just as his ancestor David had done. 4 He removed
the pagan shrines, smashed the sacred pillars, and
cut down the Asherah poles. He broke up the
bronze serpent that Moses had made, because the
people of Israel had been offering sacrifices to it.
The bronze serpent was called Nehushtan.*

5 Hezekiah trusted in the LORD, the God of
Israel. There was no one like him among all the
kings of Judah, either before or after his time. 6 He
remained faithful to the LORD in everything, and
he carefully obeyed all the commands the LORD
had given Moses. 7 So the LORD was with him,
and Hezekiah was successful in everything he
did. He revolted against the king of Assyria and
refused to pay him tribute. 8 He also conquered
the Philistines as far distant as Gaza and its territory, from their smallest outpost to their largest
walled city.

9 During the fourth year of Hezekiah's reign,
which was the seventh year of King Hoshea's
reign in Israel, King Shalmaneser of Assyria
attacked the city of Samaria and began a siege
against it. 10 Three years later, during the sixth
year of King Hezekiah's reign and the ninth
year of King Hoshea's reign in Israel, Samaria
fell. 11 At that time the king of Assyria exiled the
Israelites to Assyria and placed them in colonies
in Halah, along the banks of the Habor River in
Gozan, and in the cities of the Medes. 12 For they
refused to listen to the LORD their God and obey
him. Instead, they violated his covenant—all the
laws that Moses the LORD's servant had commanded them to obey.

Assyria Invades Judah

13 In the fourteenth year of King Hezekiah's
reign,* King Sennacherib of Assyria came to attack the fortified towns of Judah and conquered
them. 14 King Hezekiah sent this message to the
king of Assyria at Lachish: "I have done wrong.
I will pay whatever tribute money you demand
if you will only withdraw." The king of Assyria
then demanded a settlement of more than eleven
tons of silver and one ton of gold.* 15 To gather
this amount, King Hezekiah used all the silver
stored in the Temple of the LORD and in the palace treasury. 16 Hezekiah even stripped the gold
from the doors of the LORD's Temple and from
the doorposts he had overlaid with gold, and he
gave it all to the Assyrian king.

17 Nevertheless, the king of Assyria sent his
commander in chief, his field commander, and

18:2 As in parallel text at 2 Chr 29:1; Hebrew reads *Abi,* a variant spelling of Abijah. **18:4** *Nehushtan* sounds like the Hebrew terms that mean "snake," "bronze," and "unclean thing." **18:13** The fourteenth year of Hezekiah's reign was 701 B.C. **18:14** Hebrew *300 talents* [10 metric tons] *of silver and 30 talents* [1 metric ton] *of gold.*

18:1—21:26 Various Kings of Judah and Assyria

18:1–16 Hezekiah of Judah. Hezekiah was considered a great king because he genuinely sought to serve the LORD. **5–8:** The writer, emphasizing Hezekiah's righteousness, tells us that God blessed him in *everything he did*—an exaggeration given the extensive defeats also described. **14–16:** These verses directly contradict verse 7.

18:17—19:37 Sennacherib Attacks Jerusalem. Sen-

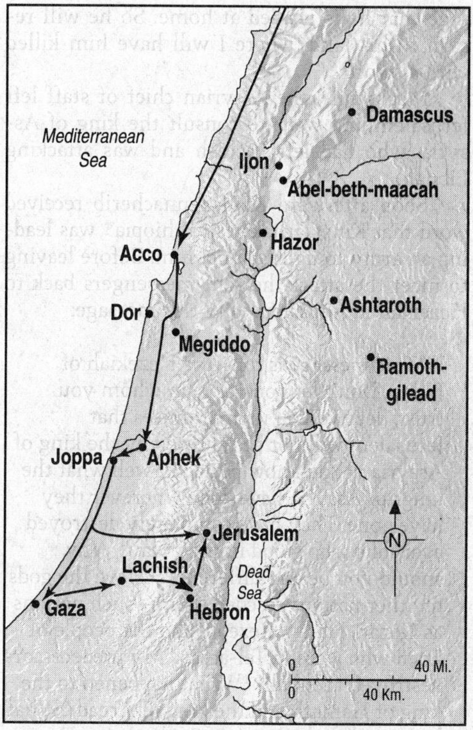

The Campaign of Sennacherib

his chief of staff* from Lachish with a huge army to confront King Hezekiah in Jerusalem. The Assyrians took up a position beside the aqueduct that feeds water into the upper pool, near the road leading to the field where cloth is washed.*
18They summoned King Hezekiah, but the king sent these officials to meet with them: Eliakim son of Hilkiah, the palace administrator; Shebna the court secretary; and Joah son of Asaph, the royal historian.

Sennacherib Threatens Jerusalem

19Then the Assyrian king's chief of staff told them to give this message to Hezekiah:

"This is what the great king of Assyria says:
What are you trusting in that makes you so
confident? 20Do you think that mere words can
substitute for military skill and strength? Who
are you counting on, that you have rebelled
against me? 21On Egypt? If you lean on Egypt,
it will be like a reed that splinters beneath
your weight and pierces your hand. Pharaoh,
the king of Egypt, is completely unreliable!
22"But perhaps you will say to me, 'We
are trusting in the LORD our God!' But isn't
he the one who was insulted by Hezekiah?
Didn't Hezekiah tear down his shrines and
altars and make everyone in Judah and
Jerusalem worship only at the altar here in
Jerusalem?
23"I'll tell you what! Strike a bargain with
my master, the king of Assyria. I will give
you 2,000 horses if you can find that many
men to ride on them! 24With your tiny army,
how can you think of challenging even the
weakest contingent of my master's troops,
even with the help of Egypt's chariots and
charioteers? 25What's more, do you think we
have invaded your land without the LORD's
direction? The LORD himself told us, 'Attack
this land and destroy it!' "

26Then Eliakim son of Hilkiah, Shebna, and
Joah said to the Assyrian chief of staff, "Please
speak to us in Aramaic, for we understand it well.
Don't speak in Hebrew,* for the people on the
wall will hear."
27But Sennacherib's chief of staff replied, "Do
you think my master sent this message only to
you and your master? He wants all the people
to hear it, for when we put this city under siege,
they will suffer along with you. They will be so
hungry and thirsty that they will eat their own
dung and drink their own urine."
28Then the chief of staff stood and shouted in
Hebrew to the people on the wall, "Listen to this
message from the great king of Assyria! 29This
is what the king says: Don't let Hezekiah deceive
you. He will never be able to rescue you from
my power. 30Don't let him fool you into trusting in the LORD by saying, 'The LORD will surely
rescue us. This city will never fall into the hands
of the Assyrian king!'

18:17a Or *the rabshakeh;* also in 18:19, 26, 27, 28, 37.
18:17b Or *bleached.* **18:26** Hebrew *in the dialect of Judah;* also in 18:28.

nacherib is not satisfied with the tribute and invades anyway. **18:19–25:** The essence of Sennacherib's message is that nobody could save Jerusalem from the Assyrians, not even their God, and it would be better to surrender and lead a good life in submission rather than suffering the consequences of futile resistance, thus demoralizing not only Hezekiah but the people of Judah. **22, 25:** The use of religious language to try to manipulate events is nothing new. Discernment was needed then as much as it is today. **26–27:** *Aramaic* was the language of diplomacy. The Assyrians insist on speaking Hebrew, the language

31 "Don't listen to Hezekiah! These are the terms the king of Assyria is offering: Make peace with me—open the gates and come out. Then each of you can continue eating from your own grapevine and fig tree and drinking from your own well. 32 Then I will arrange to take you to another land like this one—a land of grain and new wine, bread and vineyards, olive groves and honey. Choose life instead of death!

"Don't listen to Hezekiah when he tries to mislead you by saying, 'The LORD will rescue us!' 33 Have the gods of any other nations ever saved their people from the king of Assyria? 34 What happened to the gods of Hamath and Arpad? And what about the gods of Sepharvaim, Hena, and Ivvah? Did any god rescue Samaria from my power? 35 What god of any nation has ever been able to save its people from my power? So what makes you think that the LORD can rescue Jerusalem from me?"

36 But the people were silent and did not utter a word because Hezekiah had commanded them, "Do not answer him."

37 Then Eliakim son of Hilkiah, the palace administrator; Shebna the court secretary; and Joah son of Asaph, the royal historian, went back to Hezekiah. They tore their clothes in despair, and they went in to see the king and told him what the Assyrian chief of staff had said.

Hezekiah Seeks the LORD's Help

19 When King Hezekiah heard their report, he tore his clothes and put on burlap and went into the Temple of the LORD. 2 And he sent Eliakim the palace administrator, Shebna the court secretary, and the leading priests, all dressed in burlap, to the prophet Isaiah son of Amoz. 3 They told him, "This is what King Hezekiah says: Today is a day of trouble, insults, and disgrace. It is like when a child is ready to be born, but the mother has no strength to deliver the baby. 4 But perhaps the LORD your God has heard the Assyrian chief of staff,* sent by the king to defy the living God, and will punish him for his words. Oh, pray for those of us who are left!"

5 After King Hezekiah's officials delivered the king's message to Isaiah, 6 the prophet replied, "Say to your master, 'This is what the LORD says: Do not be disturbed by this blasphemous speech against me from the Assyrian king's messengers. 7 Listen! I myself will move against him,* and the king will receive a message that he is needed at home. So he will return to his land, where I will have him killed with a sword.' "

8 Meanwhile, the Assyrian chief of staff left Jerusalem and went to consult the king of Assyria, who had left Lachish and was attacking Libnah.

9 Soon afterward King Sennacherib received word that King Tirhakah of Ethiopia* was leading an army to fight against him. Before leaving to meet the attack, he sent messengers back to Hezekiah in Jerusalem with this message:

> 10 "This message is for King Hezekiah of Judah. Don't let your God, in whom you trust, deceive you with promises that Jerusalem will not be captured by the king of Assyria. 11 You know perfectly well what the kings of Assyria have done wherever they have gone. They have completely destroyed everyone who stood in their way! Why should you be any different? 12 Have the gods of other nations rescued them—such nations as Gozan, Haran, Rezeph, and the people of Eden who were in Tel-assar? My predecessors destroyed them all! 13 What happened to the king of Hamath and the king of Arpad? What happened to the kings of Sepharvaim, Hena, and Ivvah?"

14 After Hezekiah received the letter from the messengers and read it, he went up to the LORD's Temple and spread it out before the LORD. 15 And Hezekiah prayed this prayer before the LORD: "O LORD, God of Israel, you are enthroned between the mighty cherubim! You alone are God of all the kingdoms of the earth. You alone created the heavens and the earth. 16 Bend down, O LORD, and listen! Open your eyes, O LORD, and see! Listen to Sennacherib's words of defiance against the living God.

17 "It is true, LORD, that the kings of Assyria have destroyed all these nations. 18 And they have thrown the gods of these nations into the fire and burned them. But of course the Assyrians could destroy them! They were not gods at all—only idols of wood and stone shaped by human hands. 19 Now, O LORD our God, rescue us from his power; then all the kingdoms of the earth will know that you alone, O LORD, are God."

19:4 Or *the rabshakeh;* also in 19:8. **19:7** Hebrew *I will put a spirit in him.* **19:9** Hebrew *of Cush.*

of the people of Judah, so that they will give up any resistance. **19:1–37:** Hezekiah's trust in the LORD is rewarded. **21:** *The virgin daughter of Zion* is a reference to the city of Jerusalem. *Shak*[ing] *her head*

Africans in Biblical History

While the Israelites hold center stage throughout much of biblical history, Africans play a noteworthy role in the unfolding story of God's salvation. Lack of adequate acknowledgment stems from confusion regarding terminology and location. The term "Africa" does not appear in the Bible, yet its lands and peoples do. Egypt features as Israel's powerful neighbor; Hebrew Cush or Greek Ethiopia (not modern Ethiopia/Abyssinia) or Nubia refers to the upper Nile region, and Libya and Put occupy the northern coast. Disagreement exists concerning the ethnographic classification of these peoples, and racial attitudes color scholarship, particularly when traditions of perverted exegesis attribute the curse of Canaan (Gen 9:25; not Ham) to Black Africans and their descendants.

Despite these problems, African presence in biblical history is unequivocal. The table of nations records Africans among ancient peoples. Moses bears an Egyptian name, as do several Israelite priests (e.g., Aaron's grandson Phinehas, or "the Nubian," Exod 6:25), and Moses "was taught all the wisdom of the Egyptians" (Acts 7:22). Reference is made to Cushites in a proverbial expression concerning their skin color (Jer 13:23).

Examples of African figures in the Old Testament include David's Cushite soldier who brought news of Absalom's death. A Cushite court official, Ebed-melech, confronted King Zedekiah and rescued Jeremiah from the muddy cistern where he'd been cast. Cushite leaders Zerah (2 Chr 14:9–13) and King Tirhakah (Isa 37:9) are noted. Among African women are the Egyptian slave Hagar, the high-ranking Egyptian wives of Joseph and Solomon, and likely the Cushite wife of Moses.

Africans in the New Testament include Simon from Cyrene, who carried Jesus' cross, and Apollos from Alexandria. Egyptian and Libyan Jews were present at Pentecost, and Cyrenian Christians were among those who took the momentous step of preaching to Gentiles in Antioch (Acts 11:20). Best known is the Ethiopian eunuch, an official of Candace, title for the queen of Meroë (Acts 8).

Africa and its peoples play various roles in biblical history. Egypt represents a place of refuge for the patriarchs during famine and for the infant Jesus during persecution from Herod. In contrast, Egypt signifies oppression or "the place of . . . slavery" (Exod 20:2) from which God delivered his people in the Exodus. As major players in the geopolitical world of the ancient Near East, Egypt and Cush are among those nations under God's judgment in the prophetic books (Isa 18—20; Jer 46; Ezek 29—32; Zeph 2:12). Most significantly, however, these African peoples symbolize foreigners who will ultimately worship the God of Israel (Pss 68:31; 87:4; Isa 45:14; Zeph 3:10). Herein lies the theological import of Acts 8:26–40, for the Ethiopian eunuch's conversion to Christ marks the fulfillment of these Old Testament prophecies. Africans are not recent additions to the story of God's salvation; rather, they have been actively present in biblical history from the earliest chapters of Genesis to the earliest expansion of the gospel.

Isaiah Predicts Judah's Deliverance

20 Then Isaiah son of Amoz sent this message to
Hezekiah: "This is what the LORD, the God of Israel, says: I have heard your prayer about King
Sennacherib of Assyria. 21 And the LORD has spoken this word against him:

"The virgin daughter of Zion
despises you and laughs at you.
The daughter of Jerusalem
shakes her head in derision as you flee.

22 "Whom have you been defying and
ridiculing?
Against whom did you raise your voice?
At whom did you look with such haughty
eyes?
It was the Holy One of Israel!
23 By your messengers you have defied the Lord.
You have said, 'With my many chariots
I have conquered the highest mountains—
yes, the remotest peaks of Lebanon.
I have cut down its tallest cedars
and its finest cypress trees.
I have reached its farthest corners
and explored its deepest forests.
24 I have dug wells in many foreign lands
and refreshed myself with their water.
With the sole of my foot
I stopped up all the rivers of Egypt!'

is a sign of contempt: The city of Jerusalem disdains the Assyrian king Sennacherib. **22–28:** Although Sennacherib sees himself as powerful, the LORD is the true source of strength and knowledge. **29–31:** The

25 "But have you not heard?
I decided this long ago.
Long ago I planned it,
and now I am making it happen.
I planned for you to crush fortified cities
into heaps of rubble.
26 That is why their people have so little power
and are so frightened and confused.
They are as weak as grass,
as easily trampled as tender green shoots.
They are like grass sprouting on a housetop,
scorched before it can grow lush and tall.

27 "But I know you well—
where you stay
and when you come and go.
I know the way you have raged against me.
28 And because of your raging against me
and your arrogance, which I have heard for
myself,
I will put my hook in your nose
and my bit in your mouth.
I will make you return
by the same road on which you came."

29 Then Isaiah said to Hezekiah, "Here is the
proof that what I say is true:

"This year you will eat only what grows up
by itself,
and next year you will eat what springs up
from that.
But in the third year you will plant crops and
harvest them;
you will tend vineyards and eat their
fruit.
30 And you who are left in Judah,
who have escaped the ravages of the siege,
will put roots down in your own soil
and will grow up and flourish.
31 For a remnant of my people will spread out
from Jerusalem,
a group of survivors from Mount Zion.
The passionate commitment of the LORD of
Heaven's Armies*
will make this happen!

32 "And this is what the LORD says about the king
of Assyria:

"His armies will not enter Jerusalem.
They will not even shoot an arrow at it.
They will not march outside its gates with
their shields
nor build banks of earth against its walls.
33 The king will return to his own country
by the same road on which he came.
He will not enter this city,
says the LORD.
34 For my own honor and for the sake of my
servant David,
I will defend this city and protect it."

35 That night the angel of the LORD went out
to the Assyrian camp and killed 185,000 Assyrian soldiers. When the surviving Assyrians*
woke up the next morning, they found corpses
everywhere.
36 Then King Sennacherib of Assyr-
ia broke camp and returned to his own land. He
went home to his capital of Nineveh and stayed
there.
37 One day while he was worshiping in the
temple of his god Nisroch, his sons* Adrammelech and Sharezer killed him with their
swords. They then escaped to the land of Ararat,
and another son, Esarhaddon, became the next
king of Assyria.

Hezekiah's Sickness and Recovery

20 About that time Hezekiah became
deathly ill, and the prophet Isaiah son
of Amoz went to visit him. He gave
the king this message: "This is what the LORD
says: Set your affairs in order, for you are going
to die. You will not recover from this illness."
2 When Hezekiah heard this, he turned his
face to the wall and prayed to the LORD,
3 "Re-
member, O LORD, how I have always been faithful to you and have served you single-mindedly,
always doing what pleases you." Then he broke
down and wept bitterly.
4 But before Isaiah had left the middle courtyard,* this message came to him from the LORD:
5 "Go back to Hezekiah, the leader of my people.
Tell him, 'This is what the LORD, the God of your
ancestor David, says: I have heard your prayer

19:31 As in Greek and Syriac versions, Latin Vulgate, and an alternate reading of the Masoretic Text (see also Isa 37:32); the other alternate reads *the LORD.* **19:35** Hebrew *When they.* **19:37** As in Greek version and an alternate reading of the Masoretic Text (see also Isa 37:38); the other alternate reading lacks *his sons.* **20:4** As in Greek version and an alternate reading in the Masoretic Text; the other alternate reads *the middle of the city.*

sign described here is a three-year period before agriculture returns to its normal cycle and the Assyrian threat is finally removed.

20:1–21 Hezekiah's Decline. The stories in this chapter are probably out of place and originally preceded the invasion of Sennacherib, since verse 6 promises

and seen your tears. I will heal you, and three
days from now you will get out of bed and go to
the Temple of the LORD. 6I will add fifteen years
to your life, and I will rescue you and this city
from the king of Assyria. I will defend this city
for my own honor and for the sake of my servant
David.' "
7Then Isaiah said, "Make an ointment from
figs." So Hezekiah's servants spread the ointment
over the boil, and Hezekiah recovered!
8Meanwhile, Hezekiah had said to Isaiah,
"What sign will the LORD give to prove that he
will heal me and that I will go to the Temple of
the LORD three days from now?"
9Isaiah replied, "This is the sign from the
LORD to prove that he will do as he promised.
Would you like the shadow on the sundial to go
forward ten steps or backward ten steps?*"
10"The shadow always moves forward,"
Hezekiah replied, "so that would be easy. Make
it go ten steps backward instead." 11So Isaiah the
prophet asked the LORD to do this, and he caused
the shadow to move ten steps backward on the
sundial* of Ahaz!

Envoys from Babylon

12Soon after this, Merodach-baladan son of Baladan,
king of Babylon, sent Hezekiah his best
wishes and a gift, for he had heard that Hezekiah
had been very sick. 13Hezekiah received the
Babylonian envoys and showed them everything
in his treasure-houses—the silver, the gold, the
spices, and the aromatic oils. He also took them
to see his armory and showed them everything
in his royal treasuries! There was nothing in his
palace or kingdom that Hezekiah did not show
them.
14Then Isaiah the prophet went to King Hezekiah
and asked him, "What did those men want?
Where were they from?"
Hezekiah replied, "They came from the distant
land of Babylon."
15"What did they see in your palace?" Isaiah
asked.
"They saw everything," Hezekiah replied. "I
showed them everything I own—all my royal
treasuries."
16Then Isaiah said to Hezekiah, "Listen to this
message from the LORD: 17The time is coming
when everything in your palace—all the treasures
stored up by your ancestors until now—
will be carried off to Babylon. Nothing will be
left, says the LORD. 18Some of your very own
sons will be taken away into exile. They will
become eunuchs who will serve in the palace of
Babylon's king."
19Then Hezekiah said to Isaiah, "This message
you have given me from the LORD is good."
For the king was thinking, "At least there will be
peace and security during my lifetime."
20The rest of the events in Hezekiah's reign,
including the extent of his power and how he
built a pool and dug a tunnel* to bring water into
the city, are recorded in *The Book of the History
of the Kings of Judah*. 21Hezekiah died, and his
son Manasseh became the next king.

Manasseh Rules in Judah

21 Manasseh was twelve years old when
he became king, and he reigned in Jerusalem
fifty-five years. His mother
was Hephzibah. 2He did what was evil in the
LORD's sight, following the detestable practices
of the pagan nations that the LORD had driven
from the land ahead of the Israelites. 3He rebuilt
the pagan shrines his father, Hezekiah, had destroyed.
He constructed altars for Baal and set up
an Asherah pole, just as King Ahab of Israel had
done. He also bowed before all the powers of the
heavens and worshiped them.
4He built pagan altars in the Temple of the
LORD, the place where the LORD had said, "My
name will remain in Jerusalem forever." 5He
built these altars for all the powers of the heavens
in both courtyards of the LORD's Temple.
6Manasseh also sacrificed his own son in the
fire.* He practiced sorcery and divination, and
he consulted with mediums and psychics. He did
much that was evil in the LORD's sight, arousing
his anger.
7Manasseh even made a carved image of
Asherah and set it up in the Temple, the very
place where the LORD had told David and his
son Solomon: "My name will be honored for-

20:9 Or *The shadow on the sundial has gone forward ten steps; do you want it to go backward ten steps?*
20:11 Hebrew *the steps.* **20:20** Hebrew *watercourse.*
21:6 Or *also made his son pass through the fire.*

rescue from the king of Assyria. **12:** The king of Babylon probably used Hezekiah's illness as an excuse to discuss an alliance against Assyria. **14–18:** Isaiah's anger with Hezekiah almost certainly stems from the possible alliance. Far from supporting Judah, Babylon eventually destroyed it. **20:** Hezekiah's tunnel still exists, and people can walk through it.

21:1–18 Manassah of Judah. Manasseh's fifty-five year reign was the longest reign of any king of Judah or Israel. From this point on, God condemns Judah to destruction.

ever in this Temple and in Jerusalem—the city I have chosen from among all the tribes of Israel. 8 If the Israelites will be careful to obey my commands—all the laws my servant Moses gave them—I will not send them into exile from this land that I gave their ancestors." 9 But the people refused to listen, and Manasseh led them to do even more evil than the pagan nations that the LORD had destroyed when the people of Israel entered the land.

10 Then the LORD said through his servants the prophets: 11 "King Manasseh of Judah has done many detestable things. He is even more wicked than the Amorites, who lived in this land before Israel. He has caused the people of Judah to sin with his idols.* 12 So this is what the LORD, the God of Israel, says: I will bring such disaster on Jerusalem and Judah that the ears of those who hear about it will tingle with horror. 13 I will judge Jerusalem by the same standard I used for Samaria and the same measure* I used for the family of Ahab. I will wipe away the people of Jerusalem as one wipes a dish and turns it upside down. 14 Then I will reject even the remnant of my own people who are left, and I will hand them over as plunder for their enemies. 15 For they have done great evil in my sight and have angered me ever since their ancestors came out of Egypt."

16 Manasseh also murdered many innocent people until Jerusalem was filled from one end to the other with innocent blood. This was in addition to the sin that he caused the people of Judah to commit, leading them to do evil in the LORD's sight.

17 The rest of the events in Manasseh's reign and everything he did, including the sins he committed, are recorded in *The Book of the History of the Kings of Judah.* 18 When Manasseh died, he was buried in the palace garden, the garden of Uzza. Then his son Amon became the next king.

Amon Rules in Judah

19 Amon was twenty-two years old when he became king, and he reigned in Jerusalem two years. His mother was Meshullemeth, the daughter of Haruz from Jotbah. 20 He did what was evil in the LORD's sight, just as his father, Manasseh, had done. 21 He followed the example of his father, worshiping the same idols his father had worshiped. 22 He abandoned the LORD, the God of his ancestors, and he refused to follow the LORD's ways.

23 Then Amon's own officials conspired against him and assassinated him in his palace. 24 But the people of the land killed all those who had conspired against King Amon, and they made his son Josiah the next king.

25 The rest of the events in Amon's reign and what he did are recorded in *The Book of the History of the Kings of Judah.* 26 He was buried in his tomb in the garden of Uzza. Then his son Josiah became the next king.

Josiah Rules in Judah

22 Josiah was eight years old when he became king, and he reigned in Jerusalem thirty-one years. His mother was Jedidah, the daughter of Adaiah from Bozkath. 2 He did what was pleasing in the LORD's sight and followed the example of his ancestor David. He did not turn away from doing what was right.

3 In the eighteenth year of his reign, King Josiah sent Shaphan son of Azaliah and grandson of Meshullam, the court secretary, to the Temple of the LORD. He told him, 4 "Go to Hilkiah the high priest and have him count the money the gatekeepers have collected from the people at the LORD's Temple. 5 Entrust this money to the men assigned to supervise the Temple's restoration. Then they can use it to pay workers to repair the Temple of the LORD. 6 They will need to hire carpenters, builders, and masons. Also have them buy the timber and the finished stone needed to repair the Temple. 7 But don't require the construction supervisors to keep account of the money they receive, for they are honest and trustworthy men."

Hilkiah Discovers God's Law

8 Hilkiah the high priest said to Shaphan the court secretary, "I have found the Book of the Law in the LORD's Temple!" Then Hilkiah gave the scroll to Shaphan, and he read it.

9 Shaphan went to the king and reported, "Your officials have turned over the money collected at the Temple of the LORD to the workers and supervisors at the Temple." 10 Shaphan also told the king, "Hilkiah the priest has given me a scroll." So Shaphan read it to the king.

21:11 The Hebrew term (literally *round things*) probably alludes to dung; also in 21:21. **21:13** Hebrew *the same plumb line I used for Samaria and the same plumb bob.*

21:19–26 Amon of Judah. Amon copied Manasseh's style and was no better a king—his rule ended in assassination and revolt.

22:1—23:30 Josiah's Reforms

Josiah follows Hezekiah's pattern as a good king and

[11]When the king heard what was written in
the Book of the Law, he tore his clothes in despair. [12]Then he gave these orders to Hilkiah the
priest, Ahikam son of Shaphan, Acbor son of Micaiah, Shaphan the court secretary, and Asaiah
the king's personal adviser: [13]"Go to the Temple
and speak to the LORD for me and for the people and for all Judah. Inquire about the words
written in this scroll that has been found. For the
LORD's great anger is burning against us because
our ancestors have not obeyed the words in this
scroll. We have not been doing everything it says
we must do."

[14]So Hilkiah the priest, Ahikam, Acbor,
Shaphan, and Asaiah went to the New Quarter*
of Jerusalem to consult with the prophet Huldah.
She was the wife of Shallum son of Tikvah, son
of Harhas, the keeper of the Temple wardrobe.

[15]She said to them, "The LORD, the God of Israel, has spoken! Go back and tell the man who
sent you, [16]'This is what the LORD says: I am going to bring disaster on this city* and its people.
All the words written in the scroll that the king
of Judah has read will come true. [17]For my people have abandoned me and offered sacrifices to
pagan gods, and I am very angry with them for
everything they have done. My anger will burn
against this place, and it will not be quenched.'

[18]"But go to the king of Judah who sent you
to seek the LORD and tell him: 'This is what the
LORD, the God of Israel, says concerning the
message you have just heard: [19]You were sorry
and humbled yourself before the LORD when
you heard what I said against this city and its
people—that this land would be cursed and become desolate. You tore your clothing in despair
and wept before me in repentance. And I have
indeed heard you, says the LORD. [20]So I will not
send the promised disaster until after you have
died and been buried in peace. You will not see
the disaster I am going to bring on this city.'"

So they took her message back to the king.

Josiah's Religious Reforms

23 Then the king summoned all the elders of Judah and Jerusalem. [2]And
the king went up to the Temple of the
LORD with all the people of Judah and Jerusalem,
along with the priests and the prophets—all the
people from the least to the greatest. There the
king read to them the entire Book of the Covenant that had been found in the LORD's Temple.
[3]The king took his place of authority beside the
pillar and renewed the covenant in the LORD's
presence. He pledged to obey the LORD by keeping all his commands, laws, and decrees with all
his heart and soul. In this way, he confirmed all
the terms of the covenant that were written in
the scroll, and all the people pledged themselves
to the covenant.

[4]Then the king instructed Hilkiah the high
priest and the priests of the second rank and the
Temple gatekeepers to remove from the LORD's
Temple all the articles that were used to worship
Baal, Asherah, and all the powers of the heavens. The king had all these things burned outside
Jerusalem on the terraces of the Kidron Valley,
and he carried the ashes away to Bethel. [5]He did
away with the idolatrous priests, who had been
appointed by the previous kings of Judah, for
they had offered sacrifices at the pagan shrines
throughout Judah and even in the vicinity of Jerusalem. They had also offered sacrifices to Baal,
and to the sun, the moon, the constellations, and
to all the powers of the heavens. [6]The king removed the Asherah pole from the LORD's Temple and took it outside Jerusalem to the Kidron
Valley, where he burned it. Then he ground the
ashes of the pole to dust and threw the dust over
the graves of the people. [7]He also tore down the
living quarters of the male and female shrine

22:14 Or *the Second Quarter,* a newer section of Jerusalem. Hebrew reads *the Mishneh.* **22:16** Hebrew *this place;* also in 22:19, 20.

is renowned for his obedience to the Law. **22:8:** *The Book of the Law* has long been identified as a form of the book of Deuteronomy. **14–20:** Huldah is a prophet of whom we know very little, yet tradition gives her a position of great importance. The two southern gates of the Temple Mount, the Huldah Gates, were named after her. Many think it was odd for Josiah to consult Huldah instead of Jeremiah or Zephaniah. Numerous apologies have been made for this choice, but Jewish tradition has given it importance. Perhaps Huldah possessed greater authority and prominence than originally thought. Huldah delivered the message of God with confidence and obedience. **15–20:** Her message was one of destruction for Jerusalem and a peaceful death for Josiah. The prediction of destruction came to pass; however, Josiah died in the battle of Megiddo (23:20–30; 2 Chr 35:20–24), not peacefully, as foreseen by Huldah. To some, this suggests that the report of her predictions was authentic, that her predictions were made prior to these events rather than being attributed to her anachronistically. **23:1–20:** Huldah's oracle might have originally been conditional, motivating Josiah to carry out extensive reforms and confirm the covenant between the LORD and the people. The possibility is raised that with this full covenant renewal, judgment could be averted.

prostitutes that were inside the Temple of the
LORD, where the women wove coverings for the
Asherah pole.
8 Josiah brought to Jerusalem all the priests
who were living in other towns of Judah. He also
defiled the pagan shrines, where they had offered
sacrifices—all the way from Geba to Beersheba.
He destroyed the shrines at the entrance to the
gate of Joshua, the governor of Jerusalem. This
gate was located to the left of the city gate as
one enters the city. 9 The priests who had served
at the pagan shrines were not allowed* to serve
at the LORD's altar in Jerusalem, but they were
allowed to eat unleavened bread with the other
priests.
10 Then the king defiled the altar of Topheth
in the valley of Ben-Hinnom, so no one could
ever again use it to sacrifice a son or daughter in
the fire* as an offering to Molech. 11 He removed
from the entrance of the LORD's Temple the
horse statues that the former kings of Judah had
dedicated to the sun. They were near the quarters of Nathan-melech the eunuch, an officer of
the court.* The king also burned the chariots
dedicated to the sun.
12 Josiah tore down the altars that the kings of
Judah had built on the palace roof above the upper room of Ahaz. The king destroyed the altars
that Manasseh had built in the two courtyards
of the LORD's Temple. He smashed them to bits*
and scattered the pieces in the Kidron Valley.
13 The king also desecrated the pagan shrines east
of Jerusalem, to the south of the Mount of Corruption, where King Solomon of Israel had built
shrines for Ashtoreth, the detestable goddess of
the Sidonians; and for Chemosh, the detestable
god of the Moabites; and for Molech,* the vile
god of the Ammonites. 14 He smashed the sacred
pillars and cut down the Asherah poles. Then
he desecrated these places by scattering human
bones over them.
15 The king also tore down the altar at Bethel—
the pagan shrine that Jeroboam son of Nebat had
made when he caused Israel to sin. He burned
down the shrine and ground it to dust, and he
burned the Asherah pole. 16 Then Josiah turned
around and noticed several tombs in the side of
the hill. He ordered that the bones be brought
out, and he burned them on the altar at Bethel to
desecrate it. (This happened just as the LORD had
promised through the man of God when Jeroboam stood beside the altar at the festival.)

Then Josiah turned and looked up at the tomb
of the man of God* who had predicted these
things. 17 "What is that monument over there?"
Josiah asked.

And the people of the town told him, "It is the tomb of the man of God who came from Judah and predicted the very things that you have just done to the altar at Bethel!"

18 Josiah replied, "Leave it alone. Don't disturb
his bones." So they did not burn his bones or
those of the old prophet from Samaria.
19 Then Josiah demolished all the buildings at
the pagan shrines in the towns of Samaria, just
as he had done at Bethel. They had been built
by the various kings of Israel and had made the
LORD* very angry. 20 He executed the priests of
the pagan shrines on their own altars, and he
burned human bones on the altars to desecrate
them. Finally, he returned to Jerusalem.

Josiah Celebrates Passover

21 King Josiah then issued this order to all the
people: "You must celebrate the Passover to
the LORD your God, as required in this Book of
the Covenant." 22 There had not been a Passover celebration like that since the time when
the judges ruled in Israel, nor throughout all
the years of the kings of Israel and Judah. 23 This
Passover was celebrated to the LORD in Jerusalem
in the eighteenth year of King Josiah's reign.
24 Josiah also got rid of the mediums and psychics, the household gods, the idols,* and every
other kind of detestable practice, both in Jerusalem and throughout the land of Judah. He did
this in obedience to the laws written in the scroll
that Hilkiah the priest had found in the LORD's
Temple. 25 Never before had there been a king
like Josiah, who turned to the LORD with all his
heart and soul and strength, obeying all the laws
of Moses. And there has never been a king like
him since.
26 Even so, the LORD was very angry with Judah because of all the wicked things Manasseh

23:9 Hebrew *did not come up.* **23:10** Or *to make a son or daughter pass through the fire.* **23:11** The meaning of the Hebrew is uncertain. **23:12** Or *He quickly removed them.* **23:13** Hebrew *Milcom,* a variant spelling of Molech. **23:16** As in Greek version; Hebrew lacks *when Jeroboam stood beside the altar at the festival. Then Josiah turned and looked up at the tomb of the man of God.* **23:19** As in Greek and Syriac versions and Latin Vulgate; Hebrew lacks *the LORD.* **23:24** The Hebrew term (literally *round things*) probably alludes to dung.

15: On Jeroboam's altar, see 1 Kings 12:25–33. **16–18:** The story of this *man of God* is found in 1 Kings 13. **26–27:** These verses are curious because 23:4–14 makes it clear that Josiah corrected Manasseh's apostasies. The writer is apparently struggling to find a theological reason for the Exile and ends up blaming

had done to provoke him. [27] For the LORD said, "I will also banish Judah from my presence just as I have banished Israel. And I will reject my chosen city of Jerusalem and the Temple where my name was to be honored."

[28] The rest of the events in Josiah's reign and all his deeds are recorded in *The Book of the History of the Kings of Judah.*

[29] While Josiah was king, Pharaoh Neco, king of Egypt, went to the Euphrates River to help the king of Assyria. King Josiah and his army marched out to fight him,* but King Neco* killed him when they met at Megiddo. [30] Josiah's officers took his body back in a chariot from Megiddo to Jerusalem and buried him in his own tomb. Then the people of the land anointed Josiah's son Jehoahaz and made him the next king.

Jehoahaz Rules in Judah

[31] Jehoahaz was twenty-three years old when he became king, and he reigned in Jerusalem three months. His mother was Hamutal, the daughter of Jeremiah from Libnah. [32] He did what was evil in the LORD's sight, just as his ancestors had done.

[33] Pharaoh Neco put Jehoahaz in prison at Riblah in the land of Hamath to prevent him from ruling* in Jerusalem. He also demanded that Judah pay 7,500 pounds of silver and 75 pounds of gold* as tribute.

Jehoiakim Rules in Judah

[34] Pharaoh Neco then installed Eliakim, another of Josiah's sons, to reign in place of his father, and he changed Eliakim's name to Jehoiakim. Jehoahaz was taken to Egypt as a prisoner, where he died.

[35] In order to get the silver and gold demanded as tribute by Pharaoh Neco, Jehoiakim collected a tax from the people of Judah, requiring them to pay in proportion to their wealth.

[36] Jehoiakim was twenty-five years old when he became king, and he reigned in Jerusalem eleven years. His mother was Zebidah, the daughter of Pedaiah from Rumah. [37] He did what was evil in the LORD's sight, just as his ancestors had done.

24 During Jehoiakim's reign, King Nebuchadnezzar of Babylon invaded the land of Judah. Jehoiakim surrendered and paid him tribute for three years but then rebelled. [2] Then the LORD sent bands of Babylonian,* Aramean, Moabite, and Ammonite raiders against Judah to destroy it, just as the LORD had promised through his prophets. [3] These disasters happened to Judah because of the LORD's command. He had decided to banish Judah from his presence because of the many sins of Manasseh, [4] who had filled Jerusalem with innocent blood. The LORD would not forgive this.

[5] The rest of the events in Jehoiakim's reign and all his deeds are recorded in *The Book of the History of the Kings of Judah.* [6] When Jehoiakim died, his son Jehoiachin became the next king.

[7] The king of Egypt did not venture out of his country after that, for the king of Babylon captured the entire area formerly claimed by Egypt—from the Brook of Egypt to the Euphrates River.

Jehoiachin Rules in Judah

[8] Jehoiachin was eighteen years old when he became king, and he reigned in Jerusalem three months. His mother was Nehushta, the daughter of Elnathan from Jerusalem. [9] Jehoiachin did what was evil in the LORD's sight, just as his father had done.

[10] During Jehoiachin's reign, the officers of King Nebuchadnezzar of Babylon came up against Jerusalem and besieged it. [11] Nebuchadnezzar himself arrived at the city during the siege. [12] Then King Jehoiachin, along with the queen mother, his advisers, his commanders, and his officials, surrendered to the Babylonians.

In the eighth year of Nebuchadnezzar's reign, he took Jehoiachin prisoner. [13] As the LORD had said beforehand, Nebuchadnezzar carried away all the treasures from the LORD's Temple and the royal palace. He stripped away* all the gold ob-

23:29a Or *Josiah went out to meet him.* **23:29b** Hebrew *he.* **23:33a** The meaning of the Hebrew is uncertain. **23:33b** Hebrew *100 talents* [3,400 kilograms] *of silver and 1 talent* [34 kilograms] *of gold.* **24:2** Or *Chaldean.* **24:13** Or *He cut apart.*

it on Manasseh. **29:** Josiah unwisely sought to prevent Egypt from allying itself with Assyria but succeeded only in bringing Judah under Egyptian control.

23:31—25:30 The Fall of Judah

The last ruling kings of Judah were Jehoahaz and Jehoiakim (both sons of Josiah), Jehoiachin (Jehoiakim's son), and Zedekiah (Jehoiachin's uncle). None of them followed the LORD as they should have; they were harassed and interfered with by the Egyptians and Babylonians, who were vying for control in this territory. **23:32:** The judgment that Jehoahaz *did what was evil in the LORD's sight* is clearly formulaic, since he only reigned for three months. **24:3–4:** As in 23:26, the Babylonian invasion and subsequent

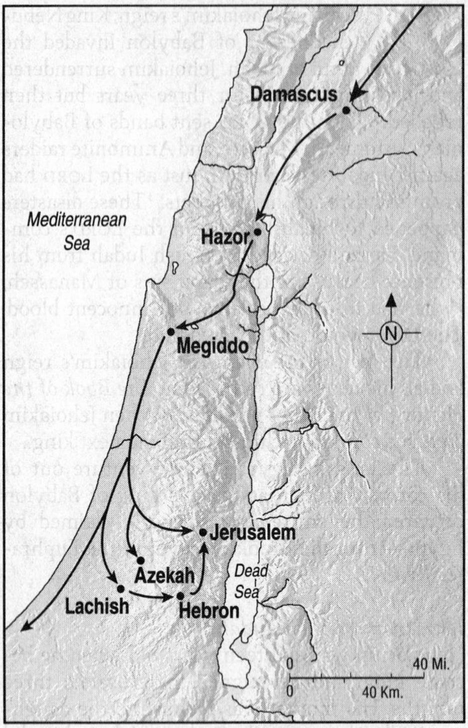

Campaigns of Nebuchadnezzar

jects that King Solomon of Israel had placed in
the Temple. [14]King Nebuchadnezzar took all of
Jerusalem captive, including all the commanders and the best of the soldiers, craftsmen, and
artisans—10,000 in all. Only the poorest people
were left in the land.
[15]Nebuchadnezzar led King Jehoiachin away
as a captive to Babylon, along with the queen
mother, his wives and officials, and all Jerusalem's
elite. [16]He also exiled 7,000 of the best troops and
1,000 craftsmen and artisans, all of whom were
strong and fit for war. [17]Then the king of Babylon installed Mattaniah, Jehoiachin's* uncle, as
the next king, and he changed Mattaniah's name
to Zedekiah.

Zedekiah Rules in Judah

[18]Zedekiah was twenty-one years old when he
became king, and he reigned in Jerusalem eleven
years. His mother was Hamutal, the daughter of
Jeremiah from Libnah. [19]But Zedekiah did what
was evil in the LORD's sight, just as Jehoiakim
had done. [20]These things happened because of
the LORD's anger against the people of Jerusalem
and Judah, until he finally banished them from
his presence and sent them into exile.

The Fall of Jerusalem

Zedekiah rebelled against the king of Babylon.

25 So on January 15,* during the ninth
year of Zedekiah's reign, King Nebuchadnezzar of Babylon led his entire
army against Jerusalem. They surrounded the
city and built siege ramps against its walls. [2]Je-
rusalem was kept under siege until the eleventh
year of King Zedekiah's reign.
[3]By July 18 in the eleventh year of Zedekiah's reign,* the famine in the city had become
very severe, and the last of the food was entirely
gone. [4]Then a section of the city wall was broken
down, and all the soldiers fled. Since the city was
surrounded by the Babylonians,* they waited
for nightfall. Then they slipped through the gate
between the two walls behind the king's garden
and headed toward the Jordan Valley.*
[5]But the Babylonian* troops chased the king
and caught him on the plains of Jericho, for his
men had all deserted him and scattered. [6]They
took him to the king of Babylon at Riblah, where
they pronounced judgment upon Zedekiah.
[7]They made Zedekiah watch as they slaughtered
his sons. Then they gouged out Zedekiah's eyes,
bound him in bronze chains, and led him away
to Babylon.

The Temple Destroyed

[8]On August 14 of that year,* which was the nineteenth year of King Nebuchadnezzar's reign,
Nebuzaradan, the captain of the guard and an official of the Babylonian king, arrived in Jerusalem.
[9]He burned down the Temple of the LORD, the
royal palace, and all the houses of Jerusalem. He

24:17 Hebrew *his.* **25:1** Hebrew *on the tenth day of the tenth month,* of the ancient Hebrew lunar calendar. A number of events in 2 Kings can be cross-checked with dates in surviving Babylonian records and related accurately to our modern calendar. This day was January 15, 588 B.C. **25:3** Hebrew *By the ninth day of the [fourth] month* [in the eleventh year of Zedekiah's reign] (compare Jer 52:6 and the note there). This day was July 18, 586 B.C.; also see note on 25:1. **25:4a** Or *the Chaldeans;* also in 25:13, 25, 26. **25:4b** Hebrew *the Arabah.* **25:5** Or *Chaldean;* also in 25:10, 24. **25:8** Hebrew *On the seventh day of the fifth month,* of the ancient Hebrew lunar calendar. This day was August 14, 586 B.C.; also see note on 25:1.

Exile is blamed on Manasseh. **14–16:** The upper classes are exiled. **24:18—25:21:** This section is very similar to Jeremiah 52, and the first part of it to Jeremiah 39:1–10. **25:2–3:** The city of Jerusalem

destroyed all the important buildings* in the city. [10]Then he supervised the entire Babylonian army as they tore down the walls of Jerusalem on every side. [11]Nebuzaradan, the captain of the guard, then took as exiles the rest of the people who remained in the city, the defectors who had declared their allegiance to the king of Babylon, and the rest of the population. [12]But the captain of the guard allowed some of the poorest people to stay behind in Judah to care for the vineyards and fields.

[13]The Babylonians broke up the bronze pillars in front of the LORD's Temple, the bronze water carts, and the great bronze basin called the Sea, and they carried all the bronze away to Babylon. [14]They also took all the ash buckets, shovels, lamp snuffers, dishes, and all the other bronze articles used for making sacrifices at the Temple. [15]Nebuzaradan, the captain of the guard, also took the incense burners and basins, and all the other articles made of pure gold or silver.

[16]The weight of the bronze from the two pillars, the Sea, and the water carts was too great to be measured. These things had been made for the LORD's Temple in the days of King Solomon. [17]Each of the pillars was 27 feet* tall. The bronze capital on top of each pillar was 7½ feet* high and was decorated with a network of bronze pomegranates all the way around.

[18]Nebuzaradan, the captain of the guard, took with him as prisoners Seraiah the high priest, Zephaniah the priest of the second rank, and the three chief gatekeepers. [19]And from among the people still hiding in the city, he took an officer who had been in charge of the Judean army; five of the king's personal advisers; the army commander's chief secretary, who was in charge of recruitment; and sixty other citizens. [20]Nebuzaradan, the captain of the guard, took them all to the king of Babylon at Riblah. [21]And there at Riblah, in the land of Hamath, the king of Babylon had them all put to death. So the people of Judah were sent into exile from their land.

Gedaliah Governs in Judah

[22]Then King Nebuchadnezzar appointed Gedaliah son of Ahikam and grandson of Shaphan as governor over the people he had left in Judah. [23]When all the army commanders and their men learned that the king of Babylon had appointed Gedaliah as governor, they went to see him at Mizpah. These included Ishmael son of Nethaniah, Johanan son of Kareah, Seraiah son of Tanhumeth the Netophathite, and Jezaniah* son of the Maacathite, and all their men.

[24]Gedaliah vowed to them that the Babylonian officials meant them no harm. "Don't be afraid of them. Live in the land and serve the king of Babylon, and all will go well for you," he promised.

[25]But in midautumn of that year,* Ishmael son of Nethaniah and grandson of Elishama, who was of the royal family, went to Mizpah with ten men and killed Gedaliah. He also killed all the Judeans and Babylonians who were with Gedaliah at Mizpah.

[26]Then all the people of Judah, from the least to the greatest, as well as the army commanders, fled in panic to Egypt, for they were afraid of what the Babylonians would do to them.

Hope for Israel's Royal Line

[27]In the thirty-seventh year of the exile of King Jehoiachin of Judah, Evil-merodach ascended to the Babylonian throne. He was kind to* Jehoiachin and released him from prison on April 2 of that year.* [28]He spoke kindly to Jehoiachin and gave him a higher place than all the other exiled kings in Babylon. [29]He supplied Jehoiachin with new clothes to replace his prison garb and allowed him to dine in the king's presence for the rest of his life. [30]So the Babylonian king gave him a regular food allowance as long as he lived.

25:9 Or *destroyed the houses of all the important people.*
25:17a Hebrew *18 cubits* [8.1 meters]. **25:17b** As in parallel texts at 1 Kgs 7:16, 2 Chr 3:15, and Jer 52:22, all of which read *5 cubits* [2.3 meters]; Hebrew reads *3 cubits,* which is 4.5 feet or 1.4 meters. **25:23** As in parallel text at Jer 40:8; Hebrew reads *Jaazaniah,* a variant spelling of Jezaniah.
25:25 Hebrew *in the seventh month,* of the ancient Hebrew lunar calendar. This month occurred within the months of October and November 586 B.C.; also see note on 25:1.
25:27a Hebrew *He raised the head of.* **25:27b** Hebrew *on the twenty-seventh day of the twelfth month,* of the ancient Hebrew lunar calendar. This day was April 2, 561 B.C.; also see note on 25:1.

---

fell to the Babylonians in 587 or 586 BC. **18–21:** It is likely that these individuals were considered responsible for fostering the rebellion in 24:20b. **24–25:** Gedaliah attempts to convince the remaining Judahites that Babylonian rule would not be so bad, if only they would settle down and respect him. But he was not seen as a legitimate ruler. **26:** This may be when Jeremiah entered into exile in Egypt. **27–30:** The year is around 562, so that there is a gap of about twenty-five years between the events described in these verses and those in the verses. immediately preceding. Some have suggested that these verses subtly express the possibility that God may again restore the Davidic monarchy. **27:** *Evil-merodach*: In Babylon his name was Awel-Marduk, "Man of Marduk."

1 CHRONICLES

INTRODUCTION

The two books of Chronicles (one book in the Hebrew canon) were written after Judah's return from exile in Babylon, around the same time as the books of Ezra and Nehemiah, and perhaps by the same writer. This unknown writer was traditionally thought to have been Ezra. It is possible that they were written about 400 BC, although some scholars place them later.

The exiles returned to Judah, expecting great things. The prophecies of Isaiah, Micah, and others foretold a glorious future for God's people. The reality, however, was quite different. Enemies surrounded them, once again they battled with the temptation to intermarry and integrate with other nations, the rebuilding of the Temple was forbidden for a long period, and their identity as the people of God was in danger of being lost. Ezra, Nehemiah, Haggai, and Zechariah tell of their struggles and the way they overcame their difficulties.

The Chronicler wrote his history to bridge the gap between expectation and reality, to show the continuity of God's plan for his people, and to rekindle their hopes, expectations, and assurance that God was still among them, still working out his purpose for them. He took the pentateuchal genealogies they knew so well and carried them forward to his day. His genealogies are selective; he includes, adds, or omits names according to what he sees as important.

He also demonstrates that the kingdom God established under David survives. Israel, the Northern Kingdom, had, at God's instigation, not accepted the Davidic kingship (1 Kgs 11:31; 2 Chr 10:19), and its kings are barely mentioned in Chronicles. However, representatives of the northern tribes still lived among the people of Judah (2 Chr 11:16) and were a part of the remnant God had preserved. The unity of all Israel under David and Solomon is emphasized.

Since the time of David, Jerusalem was the center of worship of the LORD, so an important emphasis is the Temple in Jerusalem and the regulations laid down for that worship.

Another theme is that God hears and answers prayers when the people of God trust in and obey him. The Chronicler's purpose was to restore and build up God's people in a time of uncertainty and disillusionment, and to do this he focused on continuity and commitment: the continuity of God's plan and purpose for the people, and the people's commitment to faithful worship of and service to their God. —*Christine L. Anslow*

1:1—9:44	Genealogies
10:1–14	Summary of Saul's Reign
11:1—12:40	Establishing David's Reign
13:1—16:43	The Ark Brought to Jerusalem
17:1–27	The LORD Builds a House for David
18:1—20:8	Battles
21:1–30	The Census
22:1–19	Preparations for the Temple
23:1—26:32	Preparations for Temple Worship

✧

From Adam to Noah's Sons

1 The descendants of Adam were Seth,
Enosh, [2] Kenan, Mahalalel, Jared, [3] Enoch,
Methuselah, Lamech, [4] and Noah.
The sons of Noah were* Shem, Ham, and
Japheth.

Descendants of Japheth

[5] The descendants of Japheth were Gomer,
Magog, Madai, Javan, Tubal, Meshech, and
Tiras.
[6] The descendants of Gomer were Ashkenaz,
Riphath,* and Togarmah.
[7] The descendants of Javan were Elishah,
Tarshish, Kittim, and Rodanim.

Descendants of Ham

[8] The descendants of Ham were Cush, Mizraim,*
Put, and Canaan.
[9] The descendants of Cush were Seba,
Havilah, Sabtah, Raamah, and Sabteca.
The descendants of Raamah were Sheba
and Dedan. [10] Cush was also the ancestor of
Nimrod, who was the first heroic warrior on
earth.
[11] Mizraim was the ancestor of the Ludites,
Anamites, Lehabites, Naphtuhites,
[12] Pathrusites, Casluhites, and the Caphtorites,
from whom the Philistines came.*
[13] Canaan's oldest son was Sidon, the ancestor of
the Sidonians. Canaan was also the ancestor
of the Hittites,* [14] Jebusites, Amorites,
Girgashites, [15] Hivites, Arkites, Sinites,
[16] Arvadites, Zemarites, and Hamathites.

Descendants of Shem

[17] The descendants of Shem were Elam, Asshur,
Arphaxad, Lud, and Aram.
The descendants of Aram were* Uz, Hul,
Gether, and Mash.*
[18] Arphaxad was the father of Shelah.
Shelah was the father of Eber.
[19] Eber had two sons. The first was named Peleg
(which means "division"), for during his
lifetime the people of the world were divided
into different language groups. His brother's
name was Joktan.
[20] Joktan was the ancestor of Almodad, Sheleph,
Hazarmaveth, Jerah, [21] Hadoram, Uzal, Diklah,
[22] Obal,* Abimael, Sheba, [23] Ophir, Havilah,
and Jobab. All these were descendants of
Joktan.
[24] So this is the family line descended from
Shem: Arphaxad, Shelah,* [25] Eber, Peleg, Reu,
[26] Serug, Nahor, Terah, [27] and Abram, later
known as Abraham.

Descendants of Abraham

[28] The sons of Abraham were Isaac and Ishmael.
[29] These are their genealogical records:
The sons of Ishmael were Nebaioth (the oldest),
Kedar, Adbeel, Mibsam, [30] Mishma, Dumah,
Massa, Hadad, Tema, [31] Jetur, Naphish, and
Kedemah. These were the sons of Ishmael.

[32] The sons of Keturah, Abraham's concubine,
were Zimran, Jokshan, Medan, Midian,
Ishbak, and Shuah.

1:4 As in Greek version (see also Gen 5:3-32); Hebrew lacks *The sons of Noah were.* **1:6** As in some Hebrew manuscripts and Greek version (see also Gen 10:3); most Hebrew manuscripts read *Diphath.* **1:8** Or *Egypt;* also in 1:11. **1:12** Hebrew *Casluhites, from whom the Philistines came, Caphtorites.* See Jer 47:4; Amos 9:7. **1:13** Hebrew *ancestor of Heth.* **1:17a** As in one Hebrew manuscript and some Greek manuscripts (see also Gen 10:23); most Hebrew manuscripts lack *The descendants of Aram were.* **1:17b** As in parallel text at Gen 10:23; Hebrew reads *and Meshech.* **1:22** As in some Hebrew manuscripts and Syriac version (see also Gen 10:28); most Hebrew manuscripts read *Ebal.* **1:24** Some Greek manuscripts read *Arphaxad, Cainan, Shelah.* See notes on Gen 10:24; 11:12-13.

1:1—9:44 Genealogies

1:1–27 Adam to Abraham. Adam to Noah's sons is a selective list of names that establishes the beginning of Judah's history. Japheth and Ham and their descendants are listed, but these are side shoots. Shem's descendants as far as Abraham are Judah's direct ancestors.

1:28—2:2 Abraham to Jacob. Abraham's sons Ishmael and Isaac are mentioned in 1:28, but the descendants of Keturah are another axillary branch (1:32–33). In 1:32 Keturah is called Abraham's concubine, although in Genesis 25:1 she is called his wife. These verses emphasize the importance of the main line of descent over the side shoots. Isaac, Abraham's son through Sarah, carries on the main line. Sarah was

The sons of Jokshan were Sheba and Dedan.
[33]The sons of Midian were Ephah, Epher, Hanoch, Abida, and Eldaah.
All these were descendants of Abraham through his concubine Keturah.

Descendants of Isaac
[34]Abraham was the father of Isaac. The sons of Isaac were Esau and Israel.*

Descendants of Esau
[35]The sons of Esau were Eliphaz, Reuel, Jeush, Jalam, and Korah.
[36]The descendants of Eliphaz were Teman, Omar, Zepho,* Gatam, Kenaz, and Amalek, who was born to Timna.*
[37]The descendants of Reuel were Nahath, Zerah, Shammah, and Mizzah.

Original Peoples of Edom
[38]The descendants of Seir were Lotan, Shobal, Zibeon, Anah, Dishon, Ezer, and Dishan.
[39]The descendants of Lotan were Hori and Hemam.* Lotan's sister was named Timna.
[40]The descendants of Shobal were Alvan,* Manahath, Ebal, Shepho,* and Onam.
The descendants of Zibeon were Aiah and Anah.
[41]The son of Anah was Dishon.
The descendants of Dishon were Hemdan,* Eshban, Ithran, and Keran.
[42]The descendants of Ezer were Bilhan, Zaavan, and Akan.*
The descendants of Dishan* were Uz and Aran.

Rulers of Edom
[43]These are the kings who ruled in the land of Edom before any king ruled over the Israelites*:

Bela son of Beor, who ruled from his city of Dinhabah.
[44]When Bela died, Jobab son of Zerah from Bozrah became king in his place.
[45]When Jobab died, Husham from the land of the Temanites became king in his place.
[46]When Husham died, Hadad son of Bedad became king in his place and ruled from the city of Avith. He was the one who destroyed the Midianite army in the land of Moab.
[47]When Hadad died, Samlah from the city of Masrekah became king in his place.
[48]When Samlah died, Shaul from the city of Rehoboth-on-the-River became king in his place.
[49]When Shaul died, Baal-hanan son of Acbor became king in his place.
[50]When Baal-hanan died, Hadad became king in his place and ruled from the city of Pau.* His wife was Mehetabel, the daughter of Matred and granddaughter of Me-zahab. [51]Then Hadad died.

The clan leaders of Edom were Timna, Alvah,* Jetheth, [52]Oholibamah, Elah, Pinon, [53]Kenaz, Teman, Mibzar, [54]Magdiel, and Iram. These are the clan leaders of Edom.

Descendants of Israel
2 The sons of Israel* were Reuben, Simeon, Levi, Judah, Issachar, Zebulun, [2]Dan, Joseph, Benjamin, Naphtali, Gad, and Asher.

1:34 *Israel* is the name that God gave to Jacob. **1:36a** As in many Hebrew manuscripts and a few Greek manuscripts (see also Gen 36:11); most Hebrew manuscripts read *Zephi.* **1:36b** As in some Greek manuscripts (see also Gen 36:12); Hebrew reads *Kenaz, Timna, and Amalek.* **1:39** As in parallel text at Gen 36:22; Hebrew reads *and Homam.* **1:40a** As in many Hebrew manuscripts and a few Greek manuscripts (see also Gen 36:23); most Hebrew manuscripts read *Alian.* **1:40b** As in some Hebrew manuscripts (see also Gen 36:23); most Hebrew manuscripts read *Shephi.* **1:41** As in many Hebrew manuscripts and some Greek manuscripts (see also Gen 36:26); most Hebrew manuscripts read *Hamran.* **1:42a** As in many Hebrew and Greek manuscripts (see also Gen 36:27); most Hebrew manuscripts read *Jaakan.* **1:42b** Hebrew *Dishon;* compare 1:38 and parallel text at Gen 36:28. **1:43** Or *before an Israelite king ruled over them.* **1:50** As in many Hebrew manuscripts, some Greek manuscripts, Syriac version, and Latin Vulgate (see also Gen 36:39); most Hebrew manuscripts read *Pai.* **1:51** As in parallel text at Gen 36:40; Hebrew reads *Aliah.* **2:1** *Israel* is the name that God gave to Jacob.

as important as Abraham to the plans of God. **35–54:** Esau and his descendants are a further side shoot explored before Jacob's sons are named in 2:1–2.

2:3–55 Jacob's Descendants (Part 1). The names of several wives and concubines appear in this list, perhaps to identify different branches of a family or because the women were notable in some way. **3–4:** The story of Judah's two wives and their children is briefly told (see Gen 38). Judah had three sons by a Canaanite woman and two by his daughter-in-law, Tamar. Tamar was not given to her brother-in-law Shelah as was her right under law. Because of Judah's betrayal, she tricked Judah into intercourse with her, and from this union came Perez and Zerah. Judah's assessment of her was that she had been more in the right than he (Gen 38:26); she had taken her rights under law that he had withheld from her. God expects his people to fulfill their obligations to others. Even though her actions might not fit in

Descendants of Judah
3 Judah had three sons from Bathshua, a
Canaanite woman. Their names were Er,
Onan, and Shelah. But the LORD saw that the
oldest son, Er, was a wicked man, so he killed
him. 4 Later Judah had twin sons from Tamar,
his widowed daughter-in-law. Their names
were Perez and Zerah. So Judah had five sons
in all.
5 The sons of Perez were Hezron and Hamul.
6 The sons of Zerah were Zimri, Ethan, Heman,
Calcol, and Darda*—five in all.
7 The son of Carmi (a descendant of Zimri) was
Achan,* who brought disaster on Israel by
taking plunder that had been set apart for the
LORD.*
8 The son of Ethan was Azariah.

From Judah's Grandson Hezron to David
9 The sons of Hezron were Jerahmeel, Ram, and
Caleb.*
10 Ram was the father of Amminadab.
Amminadab was the father of Nahshon, a
leader of Judah.
11 Nahshon was the father of Salmon.*
Salmon was the father of Boaz.
12 Boaz was the father of Obed.
Obed was the father of Jesse.
13 Jesse's first son was Eliab, his second was
Abinadab, his third was Shimea, 14 his fourth
was Nethanel, his fifth was Raddai, 15 his sixth
was Ozem, and his seventh was David.
16 Their sisters were named Zeruiah and
Abigail. Zeruiah had three sons named
Abishai, Joab, and Asahel. 17 Abigail married
a man named Jether, an Ishmaelite, and they
had a son named Amasa.

Other Descendants of Hezron
18 Hezron's son Caleb had sons from his wife
Azubah and from Jerioth.* Her sons were
named Jesher, Shobab, and Ardon. 19 After
Azubah died, Caleb married Ephrathah,* and
they had a son named Hur. 20 Hur was the
father of Uri. Uri was the father of Bezalel.
21 When Hezron was sixty years old, he married
Gilead's sister, the daughter of Makir. They
had a son named Segub. 22 Segub was the
father of Jair, who ruled twenty-three
towns in the land of Gilead. 23 (But Geshur
and Aram captured the Towns of Jair* and
also took Kenath and its sixty surrounding
villages.) All these were descendants of Makir,
the father of Gilead.
24 Soon after Hezron died in the town of Caleb-
ephrathah, his wife Abijah gave birth to a son
named Ashhur (the father of* Tekoa).

Descendants of Hezron's Son Jerahmeel
25 The sons of Jerahmeel, the oldest son of
Hezron, were Ram (the firstborn), Bunah,
Oren, Ozem, and Ahijah. 26 Jerahmeel had
a second wife named Atarah. She was the
mother of Onam.
27 The sons of Ram, the oldest son of Jerahmeel,
were Maaz, Jamin, and Eker.
28 The sons of Onam were Shammai and Jada.
The sons of Shammai were Nadab and Abishur.
29 The sons of Abishur and his wife Abihail were
Ahban and Molid.
30 The sons of Nadab were Seled and Appaim.
Seled died without children, 31 but Appaim
had a son named Ishi. The son of Ishi was
Sheshan. Sheshan had a descendant named
Ahlai.
32 The sons of Jada, Shammai's brother, were
Jether and Jonathan. Jether died without
children, 33 but Jonathan had two sons named
Peleth and Zaza.
These were all descendants of Jerahmeel.
34 Sheshan had no sons, though he did have
daughters. He also had an Egyptian servant
named Jarha. 35 Sheshan gave one of his
daughters to be the wife of Jarha, and they
had a son named Attai.
36 Attai was the father of Nathan.

2:6 As in many Hebrew manuscripts, some Greek manuscripts, and Syriac version (see also 1 Kgs 4:31); Hebrew reads *Dara.* **2:7a** Hebrew *Achar;* compare Josh 7:1. *Achar* means "disaster." **2:7b** The Hebrew term used here refers to the complete consecration of things or people to the LORD, either by destroying them or by giving them as an offering. **2:9** Hebrew *Kelubai,* a variant spelling of Caleb; compare 2:18. **2:11** As in Greek version (see also Ruth 4:21); Hebrew reads *Salma.* **2:18** Or *Caleb had a daughter named Jerioth from his wife, Azubah.* The meaning of the Hebrew is uncertain. **2:19** Hebrew *Ephrath,* a variant spelling of Ephrathah; compare 2:50 and 4:4. **2:23** Or *captured Havvoth-jair.* **2:24** Or *the founder of;* also in 2:42, 45, 49.

with our ideas of right and wrong, God vindicated her, and she became an ancestor of Jesus (Matt 1:3). **5–17:** Through Perez the line is carried on down to Jesse and his sons. Zeruiah and Abigail, David's sisters, were, it seems from 2 Samuel 17:25, half sisters, daughters of his mother and a man named Nahash, presumably before her marriage to Jesse. Zeruiah's and Abigail's sons became great leaders in David's army and were rather a handful for him at times (2 Sam 3:39; 19:22–23). Zeruiah, mentioned twenty-six times, must have been a prominent woman. Her husband is never mentioned.

Nathan was the father of Zabad.
37 Zabad was the father of Ephlal.
Ephlal was the father of Obed.
38 Obed was the father of Jehu.
Jehu was the father of Azariah.
39 Azariah was the father of Helez.
Helez was the father of Eleasah.
40 Eleasah was the father of Sismai.
Sismai was the father of Shallum.
41 Shallum was the father of Jekamiah.
Jekamiah was the father of Elishama.

Descendants of Hezron's Son Caleb

42 The descendants of Caleb, the brother of Jerahmeel, included Mesha (the firstborn), who became the father of Ziph. Caleb's descendants also included the sons of Mareshah, the father of Hebron.*
43 The sons of Hebron were Korah, Tappuah,
Rekem, and Shema. 44 Shema was the father
of Raham. Raham was the father of Jorkeam.
Rekem was the father of Shammai. 45 The son
of Shammai was Maon. Maon was the father
of Beth-zur.
46 Caleb's concubine Ephah gave birth to Haran, Moza, and Gazez. Haran was the father of Gazez.
47 The sons of Jahdai were Regem, Jotham, Geshan, Pelet, Ephah, and Shaaph.
48 Another of Caleb's concubines, Maacah, gave
birth to Sheber and Tirhanah. 49 She also gave
birth to Shaaph (the father of Madmannah) and Sheva (the father of Macbenah and Gibea). Caleb also had a daughter named Acsah.
50 These were all descendants of Caleb.

Descendants of Caleb's Son Hur

The sons of Hur, the oldest son of Caleb's wife Ephrathah, were Shobal (the founder
of Kiriath-jearim), 51 Salma (the founder of
Bethlehem), and Hareph (the founder of Beth-gader).
52 The descendants of Shobal (the founder of Kiriath-jearim) were Haroeh, half the
Manahathites, 53 and the families of Kiriath-jearim—the Ithrites, Puthites, Shumathites, and Mishraites, from whom came the people of Zorah and Eshtaol.
54 The descendants of Salma were the people of Bethlehem, the Netophathites, Atroth-beth-joab, the other half of the Manahathites, the
Zorites, 55 and the families of scribes living at Jabez—the Tirathites, Shimeathites, and Sucathites. All these were Kenites who descended from Hammath, the father of the family of Recab.*

Descendants of David

3 These are the sons of David who were born in Hebron:

The oldest was Amnon, whose mother was Ahinoam from Jezreel.
The second was Daniel, whose mother was Abigail from Carmel.
2 The third was Absalom, whose mother was Maacah, the daughter of Talmai, king of Geshur.
The fourth was Adonijah, whose mother was Haggith.
3 The fifth was Shephatiah, whose mother was Abital.
The sixth was Ithream, whose mother was Eglah, David's wife.
4 These six sons were born to David in Hebron, where he reigned seven and a half years.

Then David reigned another thirty-three
years in Jerusalem. 5 The sons born to David in
Jerusalem included Shammua,* Shobab, Nathan,
and Solomon. Their mother was Bathsheba,* the
daughter of Ammiel. 6 David also had nine other
sons: Ibhar, Elishua,* Elpelet,* 7 Nogah, Nepheg,
Japhia, 8 Elishama, Eliada, and Eliphelet.
9 These were the sons of David, not including his sons born to his concubines. Their sister was named Tamar.

Descendants of Solomon

10 The descendants of Solomon were Rehoboam,

2:42 Or *who founded Hebron.* The meaning of the Hebrew is uncertain. **2:55** Or *the founder of Beth-recab.* **3:5a** As in Syriac version (see also 14:4; 2 Sam 5:14); Hebrew reads *Shimea.* **3:5b** Hebrew *Bathshua,* a variant spelling of Bathsheba. **3:6a** As in some Hebrew and Greek manuscripts (see also 14:5-7 and 2 Sam 5:15); most Hebrew manuscripts read *Elishama.* **3:6b** Hebrew *Eliphelet;* compare parallel text at 14:5-7.

42–50: The Caleb spoken of here is the son of Hezron, and the Caleb of Joshua/Judges is the son of Jephunneh, with three sons (see 1 Chr 4:15).

3:1–24 Descendants of David. David's wives and descendants are listed. First we read about his sons and then the line of kings from Solomon to Jehoiachin, who was taken captive into Babylon. Next are seven generations of Jehoiachin's descendants, from the Exile and afterwards, presumably up to the time of the writer—the sons of Elioenai. One sister, Shelomith, is mentioned.

Abijah, Asa, Jehoshaphat, [11] Jehoram,*
Ahaziah, Joash, [12] Amaziah, Uzziah,* Jotham,
[13] Ahaz, Hezekiah, Manasseh, [14] Amon, and
Josiah.
[15] The sons of Josiah were Johanan (the oldest),
Jehoiakim (the second), Zedekiah (the third),
and Jehoahaz* (the fourth).
[16] The successors of Jehoiakim were his son
Jehoiachin and his brother Zedekiah.*

Descendants of Jehoiachin

[17] The sons of Jehoiachin,* who was taken
prisoner by the Babylonians, were Shealtiel,
[18] Malkiram, Pedaiah, Shenazzar, Jekamiah,
Hoshama, and Nedabiah.
[19] The sons of Pedaiah were Zerubbabel and
Shimei.
The sons of Zerubbabel were Meshullam and
Hananiah. (Their sister was Shelomith.)
[20] His five other sons were Hashubah, Ohel,
Berekiah, Hasadiah, and Jushab-hesed.
[21] The sons of Hananiah were Pelatiah and
Jeshaiah. Jeshaiah's son was Rephaiah.
Rephaiah's son was Arnan. Arnan's son was
Obadiah. Obadiah's son was Shecaniah.
[22] The descendants of Shecaniah were Shemaiah
and his sons, Hattush, Igal, Bariah, Neariah,
and Shaphat—six in all.
[23] The sons of Neariah were Elioenai, Hizkiah,
and Azrikam—three in all.
[24] The sons of Elioenai were Hodaviah, Eliashib,
Pelaiah, Akkub, Johanan, Delaiah, and
Anani—seven in all.

Other Descendants of Judah

4 The descendants of Judah were Perez,
Hezron, Carmi, Hur, and Shobal.
[2] Shobal's son Reaiah was the father of
Jahath. Jahath was the father of Ahumai
and Lahad. These were the families of
the Zorathites.
[3] The descendants of* Etam were Jezreel, Ishma,
Idbash, their sister Hazzelelponi, [4] Penuel (the
father of* Gedor), and Ezer (the father of
Hushah). These were the descendants of Hur
(the firstborn of Ephrathah), the ancestor of
Bethlehem.
[5] Ashhur (the father of Tekoa) had two wives,
named Helah and Naarah. [6] Naarah gave
birth to Ahuzzam, Hepher, Temeni, and
Haahashtari. [7] Helah gave birth to Zereth,
Izhar,* Ethnan, [8] and Koz, who became the
ancestor of Anub, Zobebah, and all the
families of Aharhel son of Harum.
[9] There was a man named Jabez who was more
honorable than any of his brothers. His
mother named him Jabez* because his birth
had been so painful. [10] He was the one who
prayed to the God of Israel, "Oh, that you
would bless me and expand my territory!
Please be with me in all that I do, and keep
me from all trouble and pain!" And God
granted him his request.
[11] Kelub (the brother of Shuhah) was the
father of Mehir. Mehir was the father of
Eshton. [12] Eshton was the father of Beth-
rapha, Paseah, and Tehinnah. Tehinnah was
the father of Ir-nahash. These were the
descendants of Recah.
[13] The sons of Kenaz were Othniel and
Seraiah. Othniel's sons were Hathath and
Meonothai.* [14] Meonothai was the father of
Ophrah. Seraiah was the father of Joab, the
founder of the Valley of Craftsmen,* so called
because they were craftsmen.
[15] The sons of Caleb son of Jephunneh were Iru,
Elah, and Naam. The son of Elah was Kenaz.
[16] The sons of Jehallelel were Ziph, Ziphah, Tiria,
and Asarel.
[17] The sons of Ezrah were Jether, Mered, Epher,
and Jalon. One of Mered's wives became*
the mother of Miriam, Shammai, and Ishbah
(the father of Eshtemoa). [18] He married a
woman from Judah, who became the mother
of Jered (the father of Gedor), Heber (the
father of Soco), and Jekuthiel (the father

3:11 Hebrew *Joram,* a variant spelling of Jehoram.
3:12 Hebrew *Azariah,* a variant spelling of Uzziah.
3:15 Hebrew *Shallum,* another name for Jehoahaz.
3:16 Hebrew *The sons of Jehoiakim were his son Jeconiah* [a variant spelling of Jehoiachin] *and his son Zedekiah.*
3:17 Hebrew *Jeconiah,* a variant spelling of Jehoiachin.
4:3 As in Greek version; Hebrew reads *father of.* The meaning of the Hebrew is uncertain. **4:4** Or *the founder of;* also in 4:5, 12, 14, 17, 18, and perhaps other instances where the text reads *the father of.* **4:7** As in an alternate reading in the Masoretic Text (see also Latin Vulgate); the other alternate and the Greek version read *Zohar.* **4:9** *Jabez* sounds like a Hebrew word meaning "distress" or "pain." **4:13** As in some Greek manuscripts and Latin Vulgate; Hebrew lacks *and Meonothai.* **4:14** Or *Joab, the father of Ge-harashim.* **4:17** Or *Jether's wife became;* Hebrew reads *She became.*

4:1—5:26 Descendants of Jacob (Part 2). Chapter 4 goes back to Judah and his descendants. Again, one daughter, Hazzelelponi, is included. **4:9–10:** This story is a picture of the Chronicler's belief that God hears and answers the prayers of his people. The name Jabez, given by his mother, sounds like the word for pain (see translator's note), but instead of changing his name in order to change his circumstances, Jabez called out to God for blessing and his request was granted. Trust in God is better than

of Zanoah). Mered also married Bithia, a daughter of Pharaoh, and she bore him children.
19 Hodiah's wife was the sister of Naham. One of her sons was the father of Keilah the Garmite, and another was the father of Eshtemoa the Maacathite.
20 The sons of Shimon were Amnon, Rinnah, Ben-hanan, and Tilon.
The descendants of Ishi were Zoheth and Ben-zoheth.

Descendants of Judah's Son Shelah

21 Shelah was one of Judah's sons. The descendants of Shelah were Er (the father of Lecah); Laadah (the father of Mareshah); the families of linen workers at Beth-ashbea;
22 Jokim; the men of Cozeba; and Joash and Saraph, who ruled over Moab and Jashubi-lehem. These names all come from ancient records.
23 They were the pottery makers who lived in Netaim and Gederah. They lived there and worked for the king.

Descendants of Simeon

24 The sons of Simeon were Jemuel,* Jamin, Jarib, Zohar,* and Shaul.
25 The descendants of Shaul were Shallum, Mibsam, and Mishma.
26 The descendants of Mishma were Hammuel, Zaccur, and Shimei.
27 Shimei had sixteen sons and six daughters, but none of his brothers had large families. So Simeon's tribe never grew as large as the tribe of Judah.
28 They lived in Beersheba, Moladah, Hazar-shual,
29 Bilhah, Ezem, Tolad,
30 Bethuel, Hormah, Ziklag,
31 Beth-marcaboth, Hazar-susim, Beth-biri, and Shaaraim. These towns were under their control until the time of King David.
32 Their descendants also lived in Etam, Ain, Rimmon, Token, and Ashan—five towns
33 and their surrounding villages as far away as Baalath.* This was their territory, and these names are listed in their genealogical records.
34 Other descendants of Simeon included Meshobab, Jamlech, Joshah son of Amaziah,
35 Joel, Jehu son of Joshibiah, son of Seraiah, son of Asiel,
36 Elioenai, Jaakobah, Jeshohaiah, Asaiah, Adiel, Jesimiel, Benaiah,
37 and Ziza son of Shiphi, son of Allon, son of Jedaiah, son of Shimri, son of Shemaiah.

38 These were the names of some of the leaders of Simeon's wealthy clans. Their families grew,
39 and they traveled to the region of Gerar,* in the east part of the valley, seeking pastureland for their flocks.
40 They found lush pastures there, and the land was quiet and peaceful.

Some of Ham's descendants had been living in that region.
41 But during the reign of King Hezekiah of Judah, these leaders of Simeon invaded the region and completely destroyed* the homes of the descendants of Ham and of the Meunites. No trace of them remains today. They killed everyone who lived there and took the land for themselves, because they wanted its good pastureland for their flocks.
42 Five hundred of these invaders from the tribe of Simeon went to Mount Seir, led by Pelatiah, Neariah, Rephaiah, and Uzziel—all sons of Ishi.
43 They destroyed the few Amalekites who had survived, and they have lived there ever since.

Descendants of Reuben

5 The oldest son of Israel* was Reuben. But since he dishonored his father by sleeping with one of his father's concubines, his birthright was given to the sons of his brother Jo-

4:24a As in Syriac version (see also Gen 46:10; Exod 6:15); Hebrew reads *Nemuel.* **4:24b** As in parallel texts at Gen 46:10 and Exod 6:15; Hebrew reads *Zerah.* **4:33** As in some Greek manuscripts (see also Josh 19:8); Hebrew reads *Baal.* **4:39** As in Greek version; Hebrew reads *Gedor.* **4:41** The Hebrew term used here refers to the complete consecration of things or people to the LORD, either by destroying them or by giving them as an offering. **5:1** *Israel* is the name that God gave to Jacob.

human strategies. **21–23:** Notice how various family clans specialized in linen work and pottery. This would no doubt include men and women using their God-given skills. Uri and Bezalel are mentioned earlier (see 2:20). **4:24—5:26:** The other sons of Jacob are now listed, including the mention of several women (4:17–19, 27). In 4:24–43, Simeon's descendants are given. Their territory was inside Judah's, and during the time of Hezekiah they pushed south and east to find places to settle, destroying the previous inhabitants. **5:1–2:** Reuben was Jacob's firstborn but lost his birthright when he had intercourse with his father's concubine. In doing this he was laying claim to his inheritance as firstborn, but his father was dishonored by this action, seen as rebellion, and Reuben lost his inheritance. Concubines were often used as pawns in power plays (see 2 Sam 16:21–22). Settling across the Jordan River, the Reubenites were in a vulnerable position and were among the first to be taken into exile (5:26). Because of this, the genealogical record is fragmentary, although full records had once been kept (5:17). **11–17:** Gad, living in

seph. For this reason, Reuben is not listed in the genealogical records as the firstborn son. 2 The descendants of Judah became the most powerful tribe and provided a ruler for the nation,* but the birthright belonged to Joseph.

3 The sons of Reuben, the oldest son of Israel,
were Hanoch, Pallu, Hezron, and Carmi.
4 The descendants of Joel were Shemaiah, Gog,
Shimei, 5 Micah, Reaiah, Baal, 6 and Beerah.
Beerah was the leader of the Reubenites
when they were taken into captivity by King
Tiglath-pileser* of Assyria.
7 Beerah's* relatives are listed in their
genealogical records by their clans: Jeiel (the
leader), Zechariah, 8 and Bela son of Azaz, son
of Shema, son of Joel.
The Reubenites lived in the area that stretches
from Aroer to Nebo and Baal-meon. 9 And
since they had so many livestock in the land
of Gilead, they spread east toward the edge
of the desert that stretches to the Euphrates
River.
10 During the reign of Saul, the Reubenites
defeated the Hagrites in battle. Then they
moved into the Hagrite settlements all along
the eastern edge of Gilead.

Descendants of Gad

11 Next to the Reubenites, the descendants of
Gad lived in the land of Bashan as far east
as Salecah. 12 Joel was the leader in the land
of Bashan, and Shapham was second-in-
command, followed by Janai and Shaphat.
13 Their relatives, the leaders of seven other clans,
were Michael, Meshullam, Sheba, Jorai, Jacan,
Zia, and Eber. 14 These were all descendants
of Abihail son of Huri, son of Jaroah, son of
Gilead, son of Michael, son of Jeshishai, son of
Jahdo, son of Buz. 15 Ahi son of Abdiel, son of
Guni, was the leader of their clans.

16 The Gadites lived in the land of Gilead, in
Bashan and its villages, and throughout all the
pasturelands of Sharon. 17 All of these were listed
in the genealogical records during the days of
King Jotham of Judah and King Jeroboam of Israel.

The Tribes East of the Jordan

18 There were 44,760 capable warriors in the armies of Reuben, Gad, and the half-tribe of Manasseh. They were all skilled in combat and armed
with shields, swords, and bows. 19 They waged war
against the Hagrites, the Jeturites, the Naphishites,
and the Nodabites. 20 They cried out to God during
the battle, and he answered their prayer because
they trusted in him. So the Hagrites and all their
allies were defeated. 21 The plunder taken from the
Hagrites included 50,000 camels, 250,000 sheep
and goats, 2,000 donkeys, and 100,000 captives.
22 Many of the Hagrites were killed in the battle
because God was fighting against them. The people of Reuben, Gad, and Manasseh lived in their
land until they were taken into exile.

23 The half-tribe of Manasseh was very large
and spread through the land from Bashan to
Baal-hermon, Senir, and Mount Hermon. 24 These
were the leaders of their clans: Epher,* Ishi, Eliel,
Azriel, Jeremiah, Hodaviah, and Jahdiel. These
men had a great reputation as mighty warriors
and leaders of their clans.

25 But these tribes were unfaithful to the God
of their ancestors. They worshiped the gods of
the nations that God had destroyed. 26 So the God
of Israel caused King Pul of Assyria (also known
as Tiglath-pileser) to invade the land and take
away the people of Reuben, Gad, and the half-tribe of Manasseh as captives. The Assyrians exiled them to Halah, Habor, Hara, and the Gozan
River, where they remain to this day.

The Priestly Line

6 1 *The sons of Levi were Gershon, Kohath,
and Merari.
2 The descendants of Kohath included
Amram, Izhar, Hebron, and Uzziel.

5:2 Or *and from Judah came a prince.* **5:6** Hebrew *Tilgath-pilneser,* a variant spelling of Tiglath-pileser; also in 5:26. **5:7** Hebrew *His.* **5:24** As in Greek version and Latin Vulgate; Hebrew reads *and Epher.* **6:1** Verses 6:1-15 are numbered 5:27-41 in Hebrew text.

Bashan next to Reuben, had joined them and the men of Manasseh in warfare against Arab tribes. **19–26:** Notice again that God heard and answered their prayers because they trusted in him and because they acknowledged that the battle was God's. However, 5:23–26 gives the reason for the capture of the half-tribe of Manasseh by King Tiglath-pileser of Assyria: They were unfaithful to God and worshiped idols. The Chronicler always points out that disobedience and unfaithfulness to God results in disaster.

6:1–81 Priests and Levites. These verses deal with the descendants of Levi. Levites were appointed to serve in the Temple to assist the priests. Some Levites were musicians, some had other duties, but only Aaron's descendants were priests, presenting offerings on the altar and making atonement for the sins of the people. Their towns and pasturelands are listed.

3 The children of Amram were Aaron, Moses,
and Miriam.
The sons of Aaron were Nadab, Abihu, Eleazar,
and Ithamar.
4 Eleazar was the father of Phinehas.
Phinehas was the father of Abishua.
5 Abishua was the father of Bukki.
Bukki was the father of Uzzi.
6 Uzzi was the father of Zerahiah.
Zerahiah was the father of Meraioth.
7 Meraioth was the father of Amariah.
Amariah was the father of Ahitub.
8 Ahitub was the father of Zadok.
Zadok was the father of Ahimaaz.
9 Ahimaaz was the father of Azariah.
Azariah was the father of Johanan.
10 Johanan was the father of Azariah, the high
priest at the Temple* built by Solomon in
Jerusalem.
11 Azariah was the father of Amariah.
Amariah was the father of Ahitub.
12 Ahitub was the father of Zadok.
Zadok was the father of Shallum.
13 Shallum was the father of Hilkiah.
Hilkiah was the father of Azariah.
14 Azariah was the father of Seraiah.
Seraiah was the father of Jehozadak, 15 who
went into exile when the LORD sent
the people of Judah and Jerusalem into
captivity under Nebuchadnezzar.

The Levite Clans

16 *The sons of Levi were Gershon,* Kohath,
and Merari.
17 The descendants of Gershon included Libni
and Shimei.
18 The descendants of Kohath included Amram,
Izhar, Hebron, and Uzziel.
19 The descendants of Merari included Mahli and
Mushi.

The following were the Levite clans, listed according to their ancestral descent:

20 The descendants of Gershon included Libni,
Jahath, Zimmah, 21 Joah, Iddo, Zerah, and
Jeatherai.
22 The descendants of Kohath included
Amminadab, Korah, Assir, 23 Elkanah,
Abiasaph,* Assir, 24 Tahath, Uriel, Uzziah, and
Shaul.
25 The descendants of Elkanah included Amasai,
Ahimoth, 26 Elkanah, Zophai, Nahath, 27 Eliab,
Jeroham, Elkanah, and Samuel.*
28 The sons of Samuel were Joel* (the older) and
Abijah (the second).
29 The descendants of Merari included Mahli,
Libni, Shimei, Uzzah, 30 Shimea, Haggiah, and
Asaiah.

The Temple Musicians

31 David assigned the following men to lead the
music at the house of the LORD after the Ark was
placed there. 32 They ministered with music at
the Tabernacle* until Solomon built the Temple
of the LORD in Jerusalem. They carried out their
work, following all the regulations handed down
to them. 33 These are the men who served, along
with their sons:

Heman the musician was from the clan of
Kohath. His genealogy was traced back
through Joel, Samuel, 34 Elkanah, Jeroham,
Eliel, Toah, 35 Zuph, Elkanah, Mahath, Amasai,
36 Elkanah, Joel, Azariah, Zephaniah, 37 Tahath,
Assir, Abiasaph, Korah, 38 Izhar, Kohath, Levi,
and Israel.*
39 Heman's first assistant was Asaph from the
clan of Gershon.* Asaph's genealogy was
traced back through Berekiah, Shimea,
40 Michael, Baaseiah, Malkijah, 41 Ethni, Zerah,
Adaiah, 42 Ethan, Zimmah, Shimei, 43 Jahath,
Gershon, and Levi.
44 Heman's second assistant was Ethan from
the clan of Merari. Ethan's genealogy was
traced back through Kishi, Abdi, Malluch,
45 Hashabiah, Amaziah, Hilkiah, 46 Amzi,
Bani, Shemer, 47 Mahli, Mushi, Merari, and
Levi.

48 Their fellow Levites were appointed to various
other tasks in the Tabernacle, the house of God.

Aaron's Descendants

49 Only Aaron and his descendants served as
priests. They presented the offerings on the altar of burnt offering and the altar of incense, and
they performed all the other duties related to the
Most Holy Place. They made atonement for Israel by doing everything that Moses, the servant
of God, had commanded them.

6:10 Hebrew *the house.* **6:16a** Verses 6:16-81 are numbered 6:1-66 in Hebrew text. **6:16b** Hebrew *Gershom,* a variant spelling of Gershon (see 6:1); also in 6:17, 20, 43, 62, 71. **6:23** Hebrew *Ebiasaph,* a variant spelling of Abiasaph (also in 6:37); compare parallel text at Exod 6:24. **6:27** As in some Greek manuscripts (see also 6:33-34); Hebrew lacks *and Samuel.* **6:28** As in some Greek manuscripts and the Syriac version (see also 6:33 and 1 Sam 8:2); Hebrew lacks *Joel.* **6:32** Hebrew *the Tabernacle, the Tent of Meeting.* **6:38** *Israel* is the name that God gave to Jacob. **6:39** Hebrew lacks *from the clan of Gershon;* see 6:43.

[50]The descendants of Aaron were Eleazar, Phinehas, Abishua, [51]Bukki, Uzzi, Zerahiah, [52]Meraioth, Amariah, Ahitub, [53]Zadok, and Ahimaaz.

Territory for the Levites

[54]This is a record of the towns and territory assigned by means of sacred lots to the descendants of Aaron, who were from the clan of Kohath. [55]This territory included Hebron and its surrounding pasturelands in Judah, [56]but the fields and outlying areas belonging to the city were given to Caleb son of Jephunneh. [57]So the descendants of Aaron were given the following towns, each with its pasturelands: Hebron (a city of refuge),* Libnah, Jattir, Eshtemoa, [58]Holon,* Debir, [59]Ain,* Juttah,* and Beth-shemesh. [60]And from the territory of Benjamin they were given Gibeon,* Geba, Alemeth, and Anathoth, each with its pasturelands. So thirteen towns were given to the descendants of Aaron. [61]The remaining descendants of Kohath received ten towns from the territory of the half-tribe of Manasseh by means of sacred lots.

[62]The descendants of Gershon received by sacred lots thirteen towns from the territories of Issachar, Asher, Naphtali, and from the Bashan area of Manasseh, east of the Jordan.

[63]The descendants of Merari received by sacred lots twelve towns from the territories of Reuben, Gad, and Zebulun.

[64]So the people of Israel assigned all these towns and pasturelands to the Levites. [65]The towns in the territories of Judah, Simeon, and Benjamin, mentioned above, were assigned to them by means of sacred lots.

[66]The descendants of Kohath were given the following towns from the territory of Ephraim, each with its pasturelands: [67]Shechem (a city of refuge in the hill country of Ephraim),* Gezer, [68]Jokmeam, Beth-horon, [69]Aijalon, and Gath-rimmon. [70]The remaining descendants of Kohath were assigned the towns of Aner and Bileam from the territory of the half-tribe of Manasseh, each with its pasturelands.

[71]The descendants of Gershon received the towns of Golan (in Bashan) and Ashtaroth from the territory of the half-tribe of Manasseh, each with its pasturelands. [72]From the territory of Issachar, they were given Kedesh, Daberath, [73]Ramoth, and Anem, each with its pasturelands. [74]From the territory of Asher, they received Mashal, Abdon, [75]Hukok, and Rehob, each with its pasturelands. [76]From the territory of Naphtali, they were given Kedesh in Galilee, Hammon, and Kiriathaim, each with its pasturelands.

[77]The remaining descendants of Merari received the towns of Jokneam, Kartah,* Rimmon,* and Tabor from the territory of Zebulun, each with its pasturelands. [78]From the territory of Reuben, east of the Jordan River opposite Jericho, they received Bezer (a desert town), Jahaz,* [79]Kedemoth, and Mephaath, each with its pasturelands. [80]And from the territory of Gad, they received Ramoth in Gilead, Mahanaim, [81]Heshbon, and Jazer, each with its pasturelands.

Descendants of Issachar

7 The four sons of Issachar were Tola, Puah, Jashub, and Shimron.

[2]The sons of Tola were Uzzi, Rephaiah, Jeriel, Jahmai, Ibsam, and Shemuel. Each of them was the leader of an ancestral clan. At the time of King David, the total number of mighty warriors listed in the records of these clans was 22,600.

[3]The son of Uzzi was Izrahiah. The sons of Izrahiah were Michael, Obadiah, Joel, and Isshiah. These five became the leaders of clans. [4]All of them had many wives and many sons, so the total number of men available for military service among their descendants was 36,000.

[5]The total number of mighty warriors from all the clans of the tribe of Issachar was 87,000. All of them were listed in their genealogical records.

Descendants of Benjamin

[6]Three of Benjamin's sons were Bela, Beker, and Jediael.

[7]The five sons of Bela were Ezbon, Uzzi, Uzziel,

6:57 As in parallel text at Josh 21:13; Hebrew reads *were given the cities of refuge: Hebron, and the following towns, each with its pasturelands.* **6:58** As in parallel text at Josh 21:15; Masoretic Text reads *Hilez;* other manuscripts read *Hilen.* **6:59a** As in parallel text at Josh 21:16; Hebrew reads *Ashan.* **6:59b** As in Syriac version (see also Josh 21:16); Hebrew lacks *Juttah.* **6:60** As in parallel text at Josh 21:17; Hebrew lacks *Gibeon.* **6:66-67** As in parallel text at Josh 21:21. Hebrew text reads *were given the cities of refuge: Shechem in the hill country of Ephraim, and the following towns, each with its pasturelands.* **6:77a** As in Greek version (see also Josh 21:34); Hebrew lacks *Jokneam, Kartah.* **6:77b** As in Greek version (see also Josh 19:13); Hebrew reads *Rimmono.* **6:78** Hebrew *Jahzah,* a variant spelling of Jahaz.

7:1—8:40 Descendants of Jacob (Part 3). The descendants of Issachar, Benjamin, Naphtali, Manasseh, Ephraim, and Asher are given briefly in chapters 7 and 8 to round off the genealogies; Dan and Zebulun are omitted. Wives and sisters are again noted, particularly Sheerah (7:24), who had a talent for city building. Also mentioned are Zelophehad's daughters (7:15), who spoke up for women as inheritors of

Jerimoth, and Iri. Each of them was the leader of an ancestral clan. The total number of mighty warriors from these clans was 22,034, as listed in their genealogical records.
8 The sons of Beker were Zemirah, Joash, Eliezer, Elioenai, Omri, Jeremoth, Abijah, Anathoth, and Alemeth.
9 Each of them was the leader of an ancestral clan. The total number of mighty warriors and leaders from these clans was 20,200, as listed in their genealogical records.
10 The son of Jediael was Bilhan. The sons of Bilhan were Jeush, Benjamin, Ehud, Kenaanah, Zethan, Tarshish, and Ahishahar.
11 Each of them was the leader of an ancestral clan. From these clans the total number of mighty warriors ready for war was 17,200.
12 The sons of Ir were Shuppim and Huppim. Hushim was the son of Aher.

Descendants of Naphtali

13 The sons of Naphtali were Jahzeel,* Guni, Jezer, and Shillem.* They were all descendants of Jacob's concubine Bilhah.

Descendants of Manasseh

14 The descendants of Manasseh through his Aramean concubine included Asriel. She also bore Makir, the father of Gilead.
15 Makir found wives for* Huppim and Shuppim. Makir had a sister named Maacah. One of his descendants was Zelophehad, who had only daughters.
16 Makir's wife, Maacah, gave birth to a son whom she named Peresh. His brother's name was Sheresh. The sons of Peresh were Ulam and Rakem.
17 The son of Ulam was Bedan. All these were considered Gileadites, descendants of Makir son of Manasseh.
18 Makir's sister Hammoleketh gave birth to Ishhod, Abiezer, and Mahlah.
19 The sons of Shemida were Ahian, Shechem, Likhi, and Aniam.

Descendants of Ephraim

20 The descendants of Ephraim were Shuthelah, Bered, Tahath, Eleadah, Tahath,
21 Zabad, Shuthelah, Ezer, and Elead. These two were killed trying to steal livestock from the local farmers near Gath.
22 Their father, Ephraim, mourned for them a long time, and his relatives came to comfort him.
23 Afterward Ephraim slept with his wife, and she became pregnant and gave birth to a son. Ephraim named him Beriah* because of the tragedy his family had suffered.
24 He had a daughter named Sheerah. She built the towns of Lower and Upper Beth-horon and Uzzen-sheerah.
25 The descendants of Ephraim included Rephah, Resheph, Telah, Tahan,
26 Ladan, Ammihud, Elishama,
27 Nun, and Joshua.

28 The descendants of Ephraim lived in the territory that included Bethel and its surrounding towns to the south, Naaran to the east, Gezer and its villages to the west, and Shechem and its surrounding villages to the north as far as Ayyah and its towns.
29 Along the border of Manasseh were the towns of Beth-shan,* Taanach, Megiddo, Dor, and their surrounding villages. The descendants of Joseph son of Israel* lived in these towns.

Descendants of Asher

30 The sons of Asher were Imnah, Ishvah, Ishvi, and Beriah. They had a sister named Serah.
31 The sons of Beriah were Heber and Malkiel (the father of Birzaith).
32 The sons of Heber were Japhlet, Shomer, and Hotham. They had a sister named Shua.
33 The sons of Japhlet were Pasach, Bimhal, and Ashvath.
34 The sons of Shomer were Ahi,* Rohgah, Hubbah, and Aram.
35 The sons of his brother Helem* were Zophah, Imna, Shelesh, and Amal.
36 The sons of Zophah were Suah, Harnepher, Shual, Beri, Imrah,
37 Bezer, Hod, Shamma, Shilshah, Ithran,* and Beera.
38 The sons of Jether were Jephunneh, Pispah, and Ara.
39 The sons of Ulla were Arah, Hanniel, and Rizia.
40 Each of these descendants of Asher was the head of an ancestral clan. They were all select men—mighty warriors and outstanding leaders. The total number of men available for military service was 26,000, as listed in their genealogical records.

Descendants of Benjamin

8 Benjamin's first son was Bela, the second was Ashbel, the third was Aharah,
2 the fourth was Nohah, and the fifth was Rapha.

7:13a As in parallel text at Gen 46:24; Hebrew reads *Jahziel,* a variant spelling of Jahzeel. **7:13b** As in some Hebrew and Greek manuscripts (see also Gen 46:24; Num 26:49); most Hebrew manuscripts read *Shallum.* **7:15** Or *Makir took a wife from.* The meaning of the Hebrew is uncertain. **7:23** *Beriah* sounds like a Hebrew term meaning "tragedy" or "misfortune." **7:29a** Hebrew *Beth-shean,* a variant spelling of Beth-shan. **7:29b** *Israel* is the name that God gave to Jacob. **7:34** Or *The sons of Shomer, his brother, were.* **7:35** Possibly another name for *Hotham;* compare 7:32. **7:37** Possibly another name for *Jether;* compare 7:38.

3 The sons of Bela were Addar, Gera, Abihud,*
4 Abishua, Naaman, Ahoah, 5 Gera,
Shephuphan, and Huram.
6 The sons of Ehud, leaders of the clans living at
Geba, were exiled to Manahath. 7 Ehud's sons
were Naaman, Ahijah, and Gera. Gera, who
led them into exile, was the father of Uzza
and Ahihud.*
8 After Shaharaim divorced his wives Hushim
and Baara, he had children in the land of
Moab. 9 His wife Hodesh gave birth to Jobab,
Zibia, Mesha, Malcam, 10 Jeuz, Sakia, and
Mirmah. These sons all became the leaders of
clans.
11 Shaharaim's wife Hushim had already given
birth to Abitub and Elpaal. 12 The sons of
Elpaal were Eber, Misham, Shemed (who built
the towns of Ono and Lod and their nearby
villages), 13 Beriah, and Shema. They were the
leaders of the clans living in Aijalon, and they
drove out the inhabitants of Gath.
14 Ahio, Shashak, Jeremoth, 15 Zebadiah, Arad,
Eder, 16 Michael, Ishpah, and Joha were the
sons of Beriah.
17 Zebadiah, Meshullam, Hizki, Heber,
18 Ishmerai, Izliah, and Jobab were the sons of
Elpaal.
19 Jakim, Zicri, Zabdi, 20 Elienai, Zillethai, Eliel,
21 Adaiah, Beraiah, and Shimrath were the
sons of Shimei.
22 Ishpan, Eber, Eliel, 23 Abdon, Zicri, Hanan,
24 Hananiah, Elam, Anthothijah, 25 Iphdeiah,
and Penuel were the sons of Shashak.
26 Shamsherai, Shehariah, Athaliah,
27 Jaareshiah, Elijah, and Zicri were the sons
of Jeroham.
28 These were the leaders of the ancestral clans;
they were listed in their genealogical records,
and they all lived in Jerusalem.

The Family of Saul

29 Jeiel* (the father of* Gibeon) lived in the
town of Gibeon. His wife's name was Maacah,
30 and his oldest son was named Abdon. Jeiel's
other sons were Zur, Kish, Baal, Ner,* Nadab,
31 Gedor, Ahio, Zechariah,* 32 and Mikloth,
who was the father of Shimeam.* All these
families lived near each other in Jerusalem.
33 Ner was the father of Kish.
Kish was the father of Saul.
Saul was the father of Jonathan, Malkishua,
Abinadab, and Esh-baal.
34 Jonathan was the father of Merib-baal.
Merib-baal was the father of Micah.
35 Micah was the father of Pithon, Melech,
Tahrea,* and Ahaz.
36 Ahaz was the father of Jadah.*
Jadah was the father of Alemeth, Azmaveth,
and Zimri.
Zimri was the father of Moza.
37 Moza was the father of Binea.
Binea was the father of Rephaiah.*
Rephaiah was the father of Eleasah.
Eleasah was the father of Azel.
38 Azel had six sons: Azrikam, Bokeru, Ishmael,
Sheariah, Obadiah, and Hanan. These were
the sons of Azel.
39 Azel's brother Eshek had three sons: the first
was Ulam, the second was Jeush, and the
third was Eliphelet. 40 Ulam's sons were all
mighty warriors and expert archers. They had
many sons and grandsons—150 in all.

All these were descendants of Benjamin.

9 So all Israel was listed in the genealogical
records in *The Book of the Kings of Israel.*

The Returning Exiles

The people of Judah were exiled to Babylon because they were unfaithful to the LORD. 2 The

8:3 Possibly *Gera the father of Ehud;* compare 8:6. **8:7** Or *Gera, that is Heglam, was the father of Uzza and Ahihud.* **8:29a** As in some Greek manuscripts (see also 9:35); Hebrew lacks *Jeiel.* **8:29b** Or *the founder of.* **8:30** As in some Greek manuscripts (see also 9:36); Hebrew lacks *Ner.* **8:31** As in parallel text at 9:37; Hebrew reads *Zeker,* a variant spelling of Zechariah. **8:32** As in parallel text at 9:38; Hebrew reads *Shimeah,* a variant spelling of Shimeam. **8:35** As in parallel text at 9:41; Hebrew reads *Tarea,* a variant spelling of Tahrea. **8:36** As in parallel text at 9:42; Hebrew reads *Jehoaddah,* a variant spelling of Jadah. **8:37** As in parallel text at 9:43; Hebrew reads *Raphah,* a variant spelling of Rephaiah.

property because he had only daughters (Num 27:1–11; 36:1–12; Josh 17:3–4). **8:33:** Saul, the eventual king of Israel, makes his first appearance. Throughout the genealogies other women are mentioned, some of whom are foreigners who married into Israel. One of the problems Ezra and Nehemiah faced was intermarriage of Judah's men with women from surrounding nations. They dealt with this strongly, sending the women and children away (Ezra 9—10; Neh 13:23–28). The difference was that these women did not worship God or bring up their children in God's ways. The Chronicler shows that men and women who turn to God are accepted and become God's people, whatever their background.

9:1–34 The Returning Exiles. 1: The Chronicler notes that the genealogies of all Israel were recorded, though not all are included in Chronicles. **2–34:** Af-

first of the exiles to return to their property in their former towns were priests, Levites, Temple servants, and other Israelites. [3] Some of the people from the tribes of Judah, Benjamin, Ephraim, and Manasseh came and settled in Jerusalem.

[4] One family that returned was that of Uthai son of Ammihud, son of Omri, son of Imri, son of Bani, a descendant of Perez son of Judah.
[5] Others returned from the Shilonite clan, including Asaiah (the oldest) and his sons.
[6] From the Zerahite clan, Jeuel returned with his relatives.
In all, 690 families from the tribe of Judah returned.

[7] From the tribe of Benjamin came Sallu son of Meshullam, son of Hodaviah, son of Hassenuah; [8] Ibneiah son of Jeroham; Elah son of Uzzi, son of Micri; and Meshullam son of Shephatiah, son of Reuel, son of Ibnijah.
[9] These men were all leaders of clans, and they were listed in their genealogical records. In all, 956 families from the tribe of Benjamin returned.

The Returning Priests

[10] Among the priests who returned were Jedaiah, Jehoiarib, Jakin, [11] Azariah son of Hilkiah, son of Meshullam, son of Zadok, son of Meraioth, son of Ahitub. Azariah was the chief officer of the house of God.
[12] Other returning priests were Adaiah son of Jeroham, son of Pashhur, son of Malkijah, and Maasai son of Adiel, son of Jahzerah, son of Meshullam, son of Meshillemith, son of Immer.
[13] In all, 1,760 priests returned. They were heads of clans and very able men. They were responsible for ministering at the house of God.

The Returning Levites

[14] The Levites who returned were Shemaiah son of Hasshub, son of Azrikam, son of Hashabiah, a descendant of Merari;
[15] Bakbakkar; Heresh; Galal; Mattaniah son of Mica, son of Zicri, son of Asaph; [16] Obadiah son of Shemaiah, son of Galal, son of Jeduthun; and Berekiah son of Asa, son of Elkanah, who lived in the area of Netophah.
[17] The gatekeepers who returned were Shallum, Akkub, Talmon, Ahiman, and their relatives. Shallum was the chief gatekeeper. [18] Prior to this time, they were responsible for the King's Gate on the east side. These men served as gatekeepers for the camps of the Levites. [19] Shallum was the son of Kore, a descendant of Abiasaph,* from the clan of Korah. He and his relatives, the Korahites, were responsible for guarding the entrance to the sanctuary, just as their ancestors had guarded the Tabernacle in the camp of the LORD.
[20] Phinehas son of Eleazar had been in charge of the gatekeepers in earlier times, and the LORD had been with him. [21] And later Zechariah son of Meshelemiah was responsible for guarding the entrance to the Tabernacle.*

[22] In all, there were 212 gatekeepers in those days, and they were listed according to the genealogies in their villages. David and Samuel the seer had appointed their ancestors because they were reliable men. [23] These gatekeepers and their descendants, by their divisions, were responsible for guarding the entrance to the house of the LORD when that house was a tent. [24] The gatekeepers were stationed on all four sides—east, west, north, and south. [25] Their relatives in the villages came regularly to share their duties for seven-day periods.

[26] The four chief gatekeepers, all Levites, were trusted officials, for they were responsible for the rooms and treasuries at the house of God. [27] They would spend the night around the house of God, since it was their duty to guard it and to open the gates every morning.

[28] Some of the gatekeepers were assigned to care for the various articles used in worship. They checked them in and out to avoid any loss.

9:19 Hebrew *Ebiasaph,* a variant spelling of Abiasaph; compare Exod 6:24. **9:21** Hebrew *Tent of Meeting.*

---

ter a brief mention of the cause of the Exile—Judah's unfaithfulness—the writer comes back to the situation of his time. The exiles had returned to Judah; some had resettled their properties and towns, while others lived in Jerusalem. Among these were representatives from Judah, Benjamin, Ephraim, and Manasseh. **10–32:** Priests, descendants of Aaron, continued the work of the Temple worship with the help of the Levites, including the Levite gatekeepers who traced their lineage back to the earliest gatekeepers of the Tabernacle, and to those appointed by David and Samuel. **28–34:** Various priests and Levites were given special tasks, while musicians, all Levites, were on duty at *all hours,* emphasizing God's continuous presence. Generally speaking, only men are mentioned in the genealogies, but the work of their wives

29 Others were responsible for the furnishings, the items in the sanctuary, and the supplies, such as choice flour, wine, olive oil, frankincense, and spices. 30 But it was the priests who blended the spices. 31 Mattithiah, a Levite and the oldest son of Shallum the Korahite, was entrusted with baking the bread used in the offerings. 32 And some members of the clan of Kohath were in charge of preparing the bread to be set on the table each Sabbath day.

33 The musicians, all prominent Levites, lived at the Temple. They were exempt from other responsibilities since they were on duty at all hours. 34 All these men lived in Jerusalem. They were the heads of Levite families and were listed as prominent leaders in their genealogical records.

King Saul's Family Tree

35 Jeiel (the father of* Gibeon) lived in the town of Gibeon. His wife's name was Maacah,
36 and his oldest son was named Abdon. Jeiel's other sons were Zur, Kish, Baal, Ner, Nadab,
37 Gedor, Ahio, Zechariah, and Mikloth.
38 Mikloth was the father of Shimeam.
All these families lived near each other in Jerusalem.
39 Ner was the father of Kish.
Kish was the father of Saul.
Saul was the father of Jonathan, Malkishua, Abinadab, and Esh-baal.
40 Jonathan was the father of Merib-baal.
Merib-baal was the father of Micah.
41 The sons of Micah were Pithon, Melech, Tahrea, and Ahaz.*
42 Ahaz was the father of Jadah.*
Jadah was the father of Alemeth, Azmaveth, and Zimri.
Zimri was the father of Moza.
43 Moza was the father of Binea.
Binea's son was Rephaiah.
Rephaiah's son was Eleasah.
Eleasah's son was Azel.
44 Azel had six sons, whose names were Azrikam, Bokeru, Ishmael, Sheariah, Obadiah, and Hanan. These were the sons of Azel.

The Death of King Saul

10 Now the Philistines attacked Israel, and the men of Israel fled before them. Many were slaughtered on the slopes of Mount Gilboa. 2 The Philistines closed in on Saul and his sons, and they killed three of his sons—Jonathan, Abinadab, and Malkishua. 3 The fighting grew very fierce around Saul, and the Philistine archers caught up with him and wounded him.

4 Saul groaned to his armor bearer, "Take your sword and kill me before these pagan Philistines come to taunt and torture me."

But his armor bearer was afraid and would not do it. So Saul took his own sword and fell on

9:35 Or *the founder of.* **9:41** As in Syriac version and Latin Vulgate (see also 8:35); Hebrew lacks *and Ahaz.* **9:42** As in some Hebrew manuscripts and Greek version (see also 8:36); Hebrew reads *Jarah.*

is implicit because they care for the children who become the next generation. Their work is vital in every age, whether society recognizes it or not: Proper nurture and care of children is central to the well-being of any nation and is highly valued by God, which is perhaps why women were excused from compulsory attendance at festivals.

9:35–44 Saul's Family Tree. Part of the genealogy of Benjamin (8:29–38) is repeated, listing the immediate ancestors and descendants of Saul. The writer prepares to begin his selective history of Israel, which will encourage readers to worship and trust only God. They already knew the stories, but Chronicles would present them from a different viewpoint. The genealogies have emphasized the tribes of Levi, Judah, and Benjamin. From Levi come the priests and Temple workers; from Benjamin comes King Saul; from Judah comes the enduring kingly line of David. These tribes also form the kingdom of Judah, with the tribe of Simeon and many Levites who moved to Judah after the division of the kingdom (2 Chr 11:14). Kings and priests together are representatives of God to the people and of the people to God. The king is God's representative as ruler and shepherd to care for and protect them, to be an example of godly living. The priest brings the people to God through the sacrifices and teaches them the right way to worship God and to live.

10:1–14 Summary of Saul's Reign

The lessons to be learned are that God will always respond to an obedient, trusting human being. God will always be faithful to his promises; he will always forgive those who repent. But sin will bring judgment on those who will not acknowledge their sins. Saul did not repent, so judgment fell. David did repent, so his sins need not be dwelt on. Rather, the true desire of his heart, to love, serve, and obey God, is emphasized. Other kings and individuals either obeyed or disobeyed God, and each reaped the consequences of the choice—reward or judgment. The Chronicler does not dwell on Saul's life but begins

it. 5 When his armor bearer realized that Saul was dead, he fell on his own sword and died. 6 So Saul and his three sons died there together, bringing his dynasty to an end.

7 When all the Israelites in the Jezreel Valley saw that their army had fled and that Saul and his sons were dead, they abandoned their towns and fled. So the Philistines moved in and occupied their towns.

8 The next day, when the Philistines went out to strip the dead, they found the bodies of Saul and his sons on Mount Gilboa. 9 So they stripped off Saul's armor and cut off his head. Then they proclaimed the good news of Saul's death before their idols and to the people throughout the land of Philistia. 10 They placed his armor in the temple of their gods, and they fastened his head to the temple of Dagon.

11 But when everyone in Jabesh-gilead heard about everything the Philistines had done to Saul, 12 all their mighty warriors brought the bodies of Saul and his sons back to Jabesh. Then they buried their bones beneath the great tree at Jabesh, and they fasted for seven days.

13 So Saul died because he was unfaithful to the LORD. He failed to obey the LORD's command, and he even consulted a medium 14 instead of asking the LORD for guidance. So the LORD killed him and turned the kingdom over to David son of Jesse.

David Becomes King of All Israel

11 Then all Israel gathered before David at Hebron and told him, "We are your own flesh and blood. 2 In the past,* even when Saul was king, you were the one who really led the forces of Israel. And the LORD your God told you, 'You will be the shepherd of my people Israel. You will be the leader of my people Israel.' "

3 So there at Hebron, David made a covenant before the LORD with all the elders of Israel. And they anointed him king of Israel, just as the LORD had promised through Samuel.

David Captures Jerusalem

4 Then David and all Israel went to Jerusalem (or Jebus, as it used to be called), where the Jebusites, the original inhabitants of the land, were living. 5 The people of Jebus taunted David, saying, "You'll never get in here!" But David captured the fortress of Zion, which is now called the City of David.

6 David had said to his troops, "Whoever is first to attack the Jebusites will become the commander of my armies!" And Joab, the son of David's sister Zeruiah, was first to attack, so he became the commander of David's armies.

11:2 Or *For some time.*

---

with the defeat that led to his death. **11–12:** Despite Saul's disobedience, he was nevertheless the king, and the actions of Jabesh-gilead citizens are included to emphasize their loyalty to him as king and their gratitude to him for rescuing them from the Ammonites (1 Sam 11:1–11). **13–14:** Here the results of disobedience and unfaithfulness are spelled out. The Chronicler shows the promises of God flourishing in the ground of obedience, faithfulness, repentance, love, and trust. When Saul failed, God had David ready to take over the kingship.

11:1–12:40 Establishing David's Reign

11:1–3 David's Anointing. When Chronicles was written, David's kingdom was long gone, and the glorious days of his victories were only a memory. But other things flourished in David's reign that could and must still flourish in every age, and the Chronicler wanted his contemporaries to remember these things. The writer skips over the years of hiding from Saul and of David's rule over Judah in Hebron. The account begins as *all Israel* joined to make David king as God had previously promised. The people recognized that David was one of them, that he had led them to victory in the past, and that he was God's choice. They accepted the covenant he made with them, and he was anointed as king. True leadership is not just authority but involves care, commitment, compassion, and humility. David, once the least in his father's family, was raised up by God to a place of power and authority. His task was still to *shepherd* God's people (v. 2) and to care for their spiritual and physical well-being. For this he must humbly rely on God, just as he had done as a shepherd of sheep.

11:4–9 The City of David. The city of Jerusalem is important. It is Zion, the chosen city; there God promised to live among his people and be their God (e.g., Ps 132:13–18). After the Exile God's worship had again been established. To go back to the city's beginnings is to reiterate its importance. It lay in the midst of the United Kingdom of Israel; as a central focus, David's city, it was the historical emblem of a strong center of government and worship. What it once had been it could become again, if the lessons of faithfulness and obedience to God were learned.

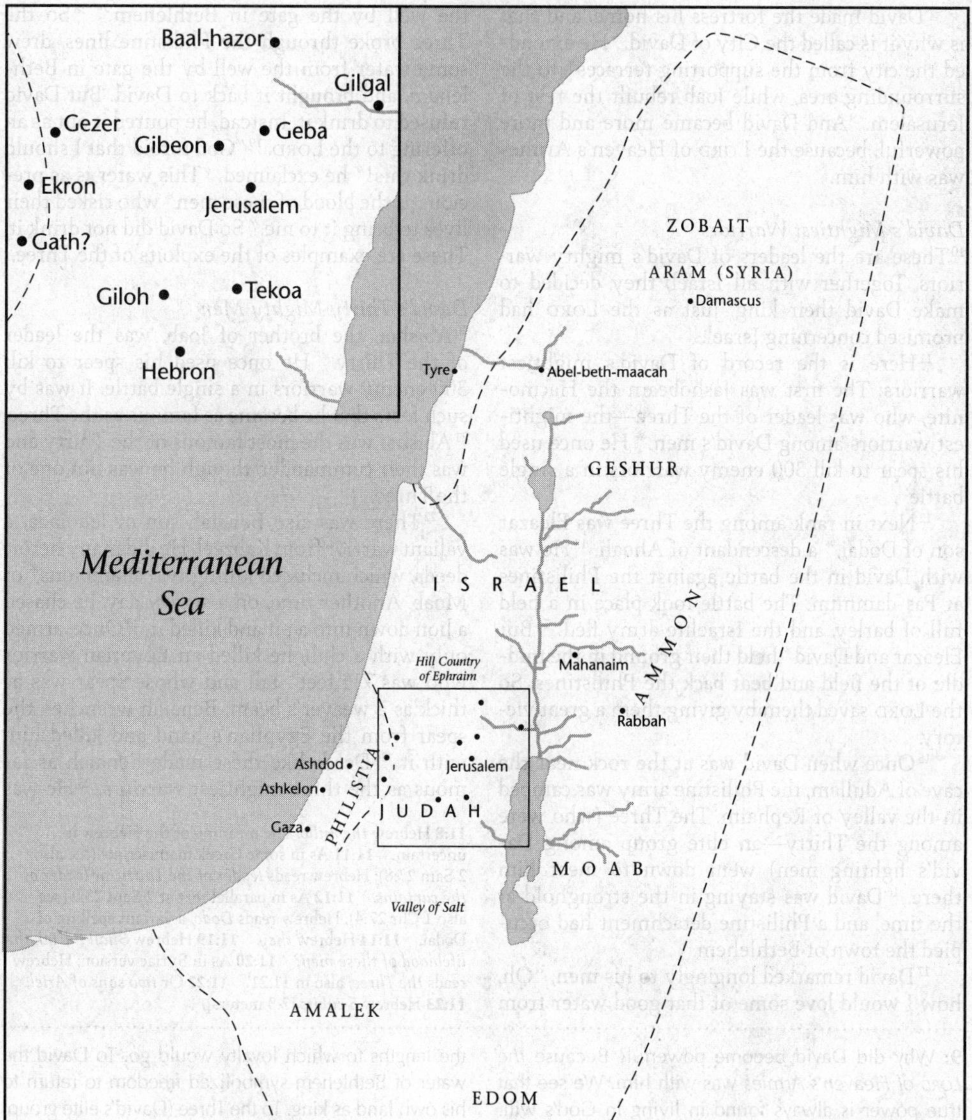

The Kingdom of David according to First Chronicles

7 David made the fortress his home, and that is why it is called the City of David. 8 He extended the city from the supporting terraces* to the surrounding area, while Joab rebuilt the rest of Jerusalem. 9 And David became more and more powerful, because the LORD of Heaven's Armies was with him.

David's Mightiest Warriors

10 These are the leaders of David's mighty warriors. Together with all Israel, they decided to make David their king, just as the LORD had promised concerning Israel.

11 Here is the record of David's mightiest warriors: The first was Jashobeam the Hacmonite, who was leader of the Three—the mightiest warriors among David's men.* He once used his spear to kill 300 enemy warriors in a single battle.

12 Next in rank among the Three was Eleazar son of Dodai,* a descendant of Ahoah. 13 He was with David in the battle against the Philistines at Pas-dammim. The battle took place in a field full of barley, and the Israelite army fled. 14 But Eleazar and David* held their ground in the middle of the field and beat back the Philistines. So the LORD saved them by giving them a great victory.

15 Once when David was at the rock near the cave of Adullam, the Philistine army was camped in the valley of Rephaim. The Three (who were among the Thirty—an elite group among David's fighting men) went down to meet him there. 16 David was staying in the stronghold at the time, and a Philistine detachment had occupied the town of Bethlehem.

17 David remarked longingly to his men, "Oh, how I would love some of that good water from the well by the gate in Bethlehem." 18 So the Three broke through the Philistine lines, drew some water from the well by the gate in Bethlehem, and brought it back to David. But David refused to drink it. Instead, he poured it out as an offering to the LORD. 19 "God forbid that I should drink this!" he exclaimed. "This water is as precious as the blood of these men* who risked their lives to bring it to me." So David did not drink it. These are examples of the exploits of the Three.

David's Thirty Mighty Men

20 Abishai, the brother of Joab, was the leader of the Thirty.* He once used his spear to kill 300 enemy warriors in a single battle. It was by such feats that he became as famous as the Three. 21 Abishai was the most famous of the Thirty and was their commander, though he was not one of the Three.

22 There was also Benaiah son of Jehoiada, a valiant warrior from Kabzeel. He did many heroic deeds, which included killing two champions* of Moab. Another time, on a snowy day, he chased a lion down into a pit and killed it. 23 Once, armed only with a club, he killed an Egyptian warrior who was 7½ feet* tall and whose spear was as thick as a weaver's beam. Benaiah wrenched the spear from the Egyptian's hand and killed him with it. 24 Deeds like these made Benaiah as famous as the three mightiest warriors. 25 He was

11:8 Hebrew *the millo.* The meaning of the Hebrew is uncertain. **11:11** As in some Greek manuscripts (see also 2 Sam 23:8); Hebrew reads *leader of the Thirty,* or *leader of the captains.* **11:12** As in parallel text at 2 Sam 23:9 (see also 1 Chr 27:4); Hebrew reads *Dodo,* a variant spelling of Dodai. **11:14** Hebrew *they.* **11:19** Hebrew *Shall I drink the lifeblood of these men?* **11:20** As in Syriac version; Hebrew reads *the Three;* also in 11:21. **11:22** Or *two sons of Ariel.* **11:23** Hebrew *5 cubits* [2.3 meters].

9: Why did David become powerful? Because *the LORD of Heaven's Armies* was with him. We see that true power is always found in living in God's will. Men and women who rely on and are confident in God are truly powerful, even though they may seem weak and insignificant in the world's eyes.

11:10–47 David's Mighty Men. 10: The chief characteristic of these men is loyalty to David. They gave him support as his kingdom grew. God had promised this extension of territory, but it came about through faithful, brave, devoted men. David had the vision, but these men were God's provision to make it happen. In the New Testament we see how Paul was encouraged by faithful men and women praying for him and working with him in spreading the gospel (see, e.g., Rom 16; Phil 2:19–30; 4:2–3). **15–19:** This story illustrates the lengths to which loyalty would go. To David the water of Bethlehem symbolized freedom to return to his own land as king. To the Three (David's elite group) it was a chance to express loyalty and to show courage and daring. The water they brought back was poured out as an offering to God because such devotion was a worthy offering. The men had risked their lives to obtain it; it appears that David felt unworthy of such devotion, which belonged to God alone. **20–47:** There were degrees of brilliance and greatness of exploits, but each was a *mighty* man. Notice that not all were Israelites (vv. 39, 41, 46). Men and women like these were needed after the Exile, people whose loyalty was to God, who worked for the good of the nation, who were willing to give their lives for God's sake and through whom God could work out his purposes. These were the people the Chronicler was encouraging.

more honored than the other members of the Thirty, though he was not one of the Three. And David made him captain of his bodyguard.
26 David's mighty warriors also included:

Asahel, Joab's brother;
Elhanan son of Dodo from Bethlehem;
27 Shammah from Harod;*
Helez from Pelon;
28 Ira son of Ikkesh from Tekoa;
Abiezer from Anathoth;
29 Sibbecai from Hushah;
Zalmon* from Ahoah;
30 Maharai from Netophah;
Heled son of Baanah from Netophah;
31 Ithai son of Ribai from Gibeah (in the land of Benjamin);
Benaiah from Pirathon;
32 Hurai from near Nahale-gaash*;
Abi-albon* from Arabah;
33 Azmaveth from Bahurim*;
Eliahba from Shaalbon;
34 the sons of Jashen* from Gizon;
Jonathan son of Shagee from Harar;
35 Ahiam son of Sharar* from Harar;
Eliphal son of Ur;
36 Hepher from Mekerah;
Ahijah from Pelon;
37 Hezro from Carmel;
Paarai* son of Ezbai;
38 Joel, the brother of Nathan;
Mibhar son of Hagri;
39 Zelek from Ammon;
Naharai from Beeroth, Joab's armor bearer;
40 Ira from Jattir;
Gareb from Jattir;
41 Uriah the Hittite;
Zabad son of Ahlai;
42 Adina son of Shiza, the Reubenite leader who had thirty men with him;
43 Hanan son of Maacah;
Joshaphat from Mithna;
44 Uzzia from Ashtaroth;
Shama and Jeiel, the sons of Hotham, from Aroer;
45 Jediael son of Shimri;
Joha, his brother, from Tiz;
46 Eliel from Mahavah;
Jeribai and Joshaviah, the sons of Elnaam;
Ithmah from Moab;
47 Eliel and Obed;
Jaasiel from Zobah.*

Warriors Join David's Army

12 The following men joined David at Ziklag while he was hiding from Saul son of Kish. They were among the warriors who fought beside David in battle.
2 All of them were expert archers, and they could shoot arrows or sling stones with their left hand as well as their right. They were all relatives of Saul from the tribe of Benjamin. 3 Their leader was Ahiezer son of Shemaah from Gibeah; his brother Joash was second-in-command. These were the other warriors:

Jeziel and Pelet, sons of Azmaveth;
Beracah;
Jehu from Anathoth;
4 Ishmaiah from Gibeon, a famous warrior and leader among the Thirty;
*Jeremiah, Jahaziel, Johanan, and Jozabad from Gederah;
5 Eluzai, Jerimoth, Bealiah, Shemariah, and Shephatiah from Haruph;
6 Elkanah, Isshiah, Azarel, Joezer, and Jashobeam, who were Korahites;
7 Joelah and Zebadiah, sons of Jeroham from Gedor.

8 Some brave and experienced warriors from the tribe of Gad also defected to David while he was at the stronghold in the wilderness. They were expert with both shield and spear, as fierce as lions and as swift as deer on the mountains.

9 Ezer was their leader.
Obadiah was second.
Eliab was third.
10 Mishmannah was fourth.
Jeremiah was fifth.
11 Attai was sixth.
Eliel was seventh.
12 Johanan was eighth.
Elzabad was ninth.

11:27 As in parallel text at 2 Sam 23:25; Hebrew reads *Shammoth from Haror.* **11:29** As in parallel text at 2 Sam 23:28; Hebrew reads *Ilai.* **11:32a** Or *from the ravines of Gaash.* **11:32b** As in parallel text at 2 Sam 23:31; Hebrew reads *Abiel.* **11:33** As in parallel text at 2 Sam 23:31; Hebrew reads *Baharum.* **11:34** As in parallel text at 2 Sam 23:32; Hebrew reads *sons of Hashem.* **11:35** As in parallel text at 2 Sam 23:33; Hebrew reads *son of Sacar.* **11:37** As in parallel text at 2 Sam 23:35; Hebrew reads *Naarai.* **11:47** Or *the Mezobaite.* **12:4** Verses 12:4b-40 are numbered 12:5-41 in Hebrew text.

12:1–40 Peace and Success. This chapter looks back to David's time in exile. **1–23:** Warriors came to David from Benjamin, Gad, Judah, and Manasseh. Perhaps some knew God's promise that he would be king and wanted to be on the winning side. Perhaps they saw in David a quality lacking in Saul. But their coming

13 Jeremiah was tenth.
Macbannai was eleventh.

14 These warriors from Gad were army commanders. The weakest among them could take
on a hundred regular troops, and the strongest
could take on a thousand! 15 These were the men
who crossed the Jordan River during its seasonal
flooding at the beginning of the year and drove
out all the people living in the lowlands on both
the east and west banks.
16 Others from Benjamin and Judah came to
David at the stronghold. 17 David went out to
meet them and said, "If you have come in peace
to help me, we are friends. But if you have come
to betray me to my enemies when I am innocent, then may the God of our ancestors see it
and punish you."
18 Then the Spirit came upon Amasai, the
leader of the Thirty, and he said,

"We are yours, David!
We are on your side, son of Jesse.
Peace and prosperity be with you,
and success to all who help you,
for your God is the one who helps you."

So David let them join him, and he made them
officers over his troops.
19 Some men from Manasseh defected from
the Israelite army and joined David when he set
out with the Philistines to fight against Saul. But
as it turned out, the Philistine rulers refused to
let David and his men go with them. After much
discussion, they sent them back, for they said, "It
will cost us our heads if David switches loyalties
to Saul and turns against us."
20 Here is a list of the men from Manasseh who
defected to David as he was returning to Ziklag:
Adnah, Jozabad, Jediael, Michael, Jozabad, Elihu,
and Zillethai. Each commanded 1,000 troops from
the tribe of Manasseh. 21 They helped David chase
down bands of raiders, for they were all brave and
able warriors who became commanders in his
army. 22 Day after day more men joined David until he had a great army, like the army of God.

23 These are the numbers of armed warriors
who joined David at Hebron. They were all eager
to see David become king instead of Saul, just as
the LORD had promised.

24 From the tribe of Judah, there were 6,800
warriors armed with shields and spears.
25 From the tribe of Simeon, there were 7,100
brave warriors.
26 From the tribe of Levi, there were 4,600
warriors. 27 This included Jehoiada, leader of
the family of Aaron, who had 3,700 under
his command. 28 This also included Zadok, a
brave young warrior, with 22 members of his
family who were all officers.
29 From the tribe of Benjamin, Saul's relatives,
there were 3,000 warriors. Most of the men
from Benjamin had remained loyal to Saul
until this time.
30 From the tribe of Ephraim, there were 20,800
brave warriors, each highly respected in his
own clan.
31 From the half-tribe of Manasseh west of the
Jordan, 18,000 men were designated by name
to help David become king.
32 From the tribe of Issachar, there were
200 leaders of the tribe with their relatives.
All these men understood the signs of the
times and knew the best course for Israel to
take.
33 From the tribe of Zebulun, there were 50,000
skilled warriors. They were fully armed and
prepared for battle and completely loyal to
David.
34 From the tribe of Naphtali, there were 1,000
officers and 37,000 warriors armed with
shields and spears.
35 From the tribe of Dan, there were 28,600
warriors, all prepared for battle.
36 From the tribe of Asher, there were 40,000
trained warriors, all prepared for battle.
37 From the east side of the Jordan River—
where the tribes of Reuben and Gad and the
half-tribe of Manasseh lived—there were
120,000 troops armed with every kind of
weapon.

---

meant David's success in battle. **16–18:** Saul needed those from his own tribe, Benjamin, but they chose to follow David. David seems to have been wary, but Amasai gave a prophetic message of encouragement. They were with him because God was with him. So while David was in hiding from Saul, a fact that the writer and readers knew well and did not need reiterating, God was building him up by sending strong supporters. Saul's opposition was powerless against God's provision. Likewise, whatever opposition the Chronicler's readers were facing, however strong and invincible it seemed, victory would be theirs if they would trust in God and live in obedience; God's support of them would be powerful and unfailing. **23, 38:** Like these warriors, God's people need to unite in determination to see God's will come to pass, rather than arguing about unimportant things and hindering God's plans. Unity in every thought is not possible,

[38]All these men came in battle array to Hebron with the single purpose of making David the king over all Israel. In fact, everyone in Israel agreed that David should be their king. [39]They feasted and drank with David for three days, for preparations had been made by their relatives for their arrival. [40]And people from as far away as Issachar, Zebulun, and Naphtali brought food on donkeys, camels, mules, and oxen. Vast supplies of flour, fig cakes, clusters of raisins, wine, olive oil, cattle, sheep, and goats were brought to the celebration. There was great joy throughout the land of Israel.

David Attempts to Move the Ark

13 David consulted with all his officials, including the generals and captains of his army.* [2]Then he addressed the entire assembly of Israel as follows: "If you approve and if it is the will of the LORD our God, let us send messages to all the Israelites throughout the land, including the priests and Levites in their towns and pasturelands. Let us invite them to come and join us. [3]It is time to bring back the Ark of our God, for we neglected it during the reign of Saul."

[4]The whole assembly agreed to this, for the people could see it was the right thing to do. [5]So David summoned all Israel, from the Shihor Brook of Egypt in the south all the way to the town of Lebo-hamath in the north, to join in bringing the Ark of God from Kiriath-jearim. [6]Then David and all Israel went to Baalah of Judah (also called Kiriath-jearim) to bring back the Ark of God, which bears the name* of the LORD who is enthroned between the cherubim. [7]They placed the Ark of God on a new cart and brought it from Abinadab's house. Uzzah and Ahio were guiding the cart. [8]David and all Israel were celebrating before God with all their might, singing songs and playing all kinds of musical instruments—lyres, harps, tambourines, cymbals, and trumpets.

[9]But when they arrived at the threshing floor of Nacon,* the oxen stumbled, and Uzzah reached out his hand to steady the Ark. [10]Then the LORD's anger was aroused against Uzzah, and he struck him dead because he had laid his hand on the Ark. So Uzzah died there in the presence of God.

[11]David was angry because the LORD's anger had burst out against Uzzah. He named that place Perez-uzzah (which means "to burst out against Uzzah"), as it is still called today.

[12]David was now afraid of God, and he asked, "How can I ever bring the Ark of God back into my care?" [13]So David did not move the Ark into the City of David. Instead, he took it to the

13:1 Hebrew *the commanders of thousands and of hundreds.* **13:6** Or *the Ark of God, where the Name is proclaimed—the name.* **13:9** As in parallel text at 2 Sam 6:6; Hebrew reads *Kidon.*

---

but unity in purpose and action is. **38–40:** Feasting and joy followed the recognition of David's kingship by representatives of all Israel at Hebron (see 11:1).

13:1–16:43 The Ark Brought to Jerusalem

13:1–14 David Attempts to Move the Ark. The central focus of Israel's identity lay beyond David. It was the worship of the LORD, and loyalty to God would ensure unity. The Ark of the Covenant was where God had promised to meet with his people (Exod 25:22), and yet it had languished in Kiriath-jearim for years after being sent back from the Philistines (1 Sam 7:2). The Philistines had learned that the Ark could not be treated lightly, as God's judgment fell on them (1 Sam 5). The Israelites had learned that it was not a magic talisman with which to manipulate God (1 Sam 4) and that its presence could bring both judgment and blessing (1 Sam 6:19—7:1; cf. Matt 10:34–35). They were to learn these lessons again. **1–4:** David felt that if God were to be the center of the nation, the Ark must be brought to Jerusalem. David's plan met with the approval of military leaders and of all Israelites. **6–8:** The picture is of a celebration in which all Israel could participate with joy and excitement. The Ark is called by the Name (see translator's note; cf. Deut 12:5), and must be brought to Jerusalem in a worthy manner. Hence the new cart with king and people accompanying it, worshiping with music and singing. **9–14:** The celebration abruptly ended as Uzzah was struck dead. His concern apparently was for the safety of the Ark. Perhaps it was his family that had faithfully cared for the Ark for many years, so why did God respond so devastatingly (cf. Exod 19:10–23)? The holiness of God means that his commands cannot be ignored. Numbers 4:5–6, 15, 17–20 clearly states the way the Ark must be carried and touched only by those appointed by God to do so. Uzzah was an innocent victim of the carelessness of the leaders of Israel, king and priests, who had not obeyed God's command. We may not understand God's stipulations, but we must obey; however, Jesus also differentiated between what God says and the way people interpret or add to it (e.g., Matt 12:1–14). **11–12:** David's reactions moved from anger to fear—anger because God had upset his plans and made him look foolish. It may be that pride in his own faithfulness caused him to be angry when God apparently re-

house of Obed-edom of Gath. 14 The Ark of God remained there in Obed-edom's house for three months, and the LORD blessed the household of Obed-edom and everything he owned.

David's Palace and Family

14 Then King Hiram of Tyre sent messengers to David, along with cedar timber, and stonemasons and carpenters to build him a palace. 2 And David realized that the LORD had confirmed him as king over Israel and had greatly blessed his kingdom for the sake of his people Israel.

3 Then David married more wives in Jerusalem, and they had more sons and daughters. 4 These are the names of David's sons who were born in Jerusalem: Shammua, Shobab, Nathan, Solomon, 5 Ibhar, Elishua, Elpelet, 6 Nogah, Nepheg, Japhia, 7 Elishama, Eliada,* and Eliphelet.

David Conquers the Philistines

8 When the Philistines heard that David had been anointed king over all Israel, they mobilized all their forces to capture him. But David was told they were coming, so he marched out to meet them. 9 The Philistines arrived and made a raid in the valley of Rephaim. 10 So David asked God, "Should I go out to fight the Philistines? Will you hand them over to me?"

The LORD replied, "Yes, go ahead. I will hand them over to you."

11 So David and his troops went up to Baal-perazim and defeated the Philistines there. "God did it!" David exclaimed. "He used me to burst through my enemies like a raging flood!" So they named that place Baal-perazim (which means "the Lord who bursts through"). 12 The Philistines had abandoned their gods there, so David gave orders to burn them.

13 But after a while the Philistines returned and raided the valley again. 14 And once again David asked God what to do. "Do not attack them straight on," God replied. "Instead, circle around behind and attack them near the poplar* trees. 15 When you hear a sound like marching feet in the tops of the poplar trees, go out and attack! That will be the signal that God is moving ahead of you to strike down the Philistine army." 16 So David did what God commanded, and they struck down the Philistine army all the way from Gibeon to Gezer.

17 So David's fame spread everywhere, and the LORD caused all the nations to fear David.

14:7 Hebrew *Beeliada,* a variant spelling of Eliada; compare 3:8 and parallel text at 2 Sam 5:16. **14:14** Or *aspen,* or *balsam;* also in 14:15. The exact identification of this tree is uncertain.

jected his efforts. Then came fear as he remembered God's awesome holiness and perhaps became aware of his own arrogance and presumption. **14:** The Ark was left in the house of Obed-edom. If he is the same man mentioned in 15:18, 21, 24, then he was a Levite, although 13:14 calls him a Gittite, a man from Gath. Obed-edom and his household experienced God's blessing upon them in every way as they reverently cared for the Ark. The lesson is that God's requirements must be obeyed and God's holiness honored. If this is not done, the results of disobedience will follow.

14:1–17 David's Blessings. Between the two sections of the Ark story, the writer shows God blessing David in family life, in battles, and among the nations, as if to say that God did not abandon him because he made a mistake. **1:** We see Hiram, king of Tyre, acknowledging David as king of Israel with whom he wanted to establish good relations. **2:** More importantly, we see David acknowledging that God had made him king, not because of who David was but because of God's love for and promises to his people. **3–6:** As was the custom in those days, David had many wives and numerous children. This was a sign of prestige and a way to seal alliances with other nations. The birth of sons was considered a sign of God's blessing. However, we know that the multiplication of wives, despite the warnings of Deut 17:17, brought great tragedy to David. God's plan for man and woman as presented in Genesis 2:24 is that they be one flesh, working together, helping each other. This is not possible with more than one wife, as it creates competition, jealousy, and rivalry among wives and children (see Polygamy, 1 Kgs 11). It is easy to father many children, but it is not easy to be a good father to many children. David clearly failed his many wives and children (see Parental Influence, Josh 4). But the Chronicler describes only the apparent blessings. **8–17:** In contrast to Saul (14:8–12, 13–16), David inquired of God when the Philistines attacked, and received and followed instructions. This time God broke out against David's enemies as he had broken out against Uzzah (13:11). In the previous case it was due to disobedience. The victory over the Philistines followed David's doing things God's way. **16–17:** With God's backing, David's fame and a healthy fear and respect for him spread to the surrounding nations. This summary of what God did for David because he sought God contrasts with the summary of what happened to Saul (10:13).

Preparing to Move the Ark

15 David now built several buildings for
himself in the City of David. He also
prepared a place for the Ark of God and
set up a special tent for it. [2]Then he commanded,
"No one except the Levites may carry the Ark of
God. The LORD has chosen them to carry the Ark
of the LORD and to serve him forever."

[3]Then David summoned all Israel to Jerusalem to bring the Ark of the LORD to the place he
had prepared for it. [4]This is the number of the
descendants of Aaron (the priests) and the Levites who were called together:

[5]From the clan of Kohath, 120, with Uriel as
their leader.
[6]From the clan of Merari, 220, with Asaiah as
their leader.
[7]From the clan of Gershon,* 130, with Joel as
their leader.
[8]From the descendants of Elizaphan, 200, with
Shemaiah as their leader.
[9]From the descendants of Hebron, 80, with Eliel
as their leader.
[10]From the descendants of Uzziel, 112, with
Amminadab as their leader.

[11]Then David summoned the priests, Zadok
and Abiathar, and these Levite leaders: Uriel,
Asaiah, Joel, Shemaiah, Eliel, and Amminadab.
[12]He said to them, "You are the leaders of the
Levite families. You must purify yourselves and
all your fellow Levites, so you can bring the Ark
of the LORD, the God of Israel, to the place I have
prepared for it. [13]Because you Levites did not carry the Ark the first time, the anger of the LORD
our God burst out against us. We failed to ask
God how to move it properly." [14]So the priests
and the Levites purified themselves in order to
bring the Ark of the LORD, the God of Israel, to
Jerusalem. [15]Then the Levites carried the Ark of
God on their shoulders with its carrying poles,
just as the LORD had instructed Moses.

[16]David also ordered the Levite leaders to appoint a choir of Levites who were singers and
musicians to sing joyful songs to the accompaniment of harps, lyres, and cymbals. [17]So the Levites appointed Heman son of Joel along with his
fellow Levites: Asaph son of Berekiah, and Ethan
son of Kushaiah from the clan of Merari. [18]The
following men were chosen as their assistants:
Zechariah, Jaaziel,* Shemiramoth, Jehiel, Unni,
Eliab, Benaiah, Maaseiah, Mattithiah, Eliphelehu, Mikneiah, and the gatekeepers—Obed-edom
and Jeiel.

[19]The musicians Heman, Asaph, and Ethan
were chosen to sound the bronze cymbals.
[20]Zechariah, Aziel, Shemiramoth, Jehiel, Unni,
Eliab, Maaseiah, and Benaiah were chosen to play
the harps.* [21]Mattithiah, Eliphelehu, Mikneiah,
Obed-edom, Jeiel, and Azaziah were chosen to
play the lyres.* [22]Kenaniah, the head Levite, was
chosen as the choir leader because of his skill.

[23]Berekiah and Elkanah were chosen to guard*
the Ark. [24]Shebaniah, Joshaphat, Nethanel,
Amasai, Zechariah, Benaiah, and Eliezer—all of
whom were priests—were chosen to blow the
trumpets as they marched in front of the Ark
of God. Obed-edom and Jehiah were chosen to
guard the Ark.

Moving the Ark to Jerusalem

[25]Then David and the elders of Israel and the generals of the army* went to the house of Obed-
edom to bring the Ark of the LORD's Covenant
up to Jerusalem with a great celebration. [26]And
because God was clearly helping the Levites as

15:7 Hebrew *Gershom,* a variant spelling of Gershon. **15:18** As in several Hebrew manuscripts and Greek version (see also parallel lists in 15:20; 16:5); Masoretic Text reads *Zechariah ben Jaaziel.* **15:20** Hebrew adds *according to Alamoth,* which is probably a musical term. The meaning of the Hebrew is uncertain. **15:21** Hebrew adds *according to the Sheminith,* which is probably a musical term. The meaning of the Hebrew is uncertain. **15:23** Hebrew *chosen as gatekeepers for;* also in 15:24. **15:25** Hebrew *the commanders of thousands.*

15:1—16:6 The Ark Comes to Jerusalem. This time David made careful preparation for the Ark's journey. He prepared a place and a tent for the Ark and followed God's decree that Levites should carry the Ark (see e.g., Num 3:5–10; Deut 10:8), and he again summoned all Israel to accompany the Ark. God is the God of every Israelite; each one belongs to God and owes devotion and service. All must be represented as the Ark is brought to Jerusalem. **15:11–15:** This time the Ark would be carried on poles by Levites, in the way God had stipulated. The Philistines had once sent the Ark back to Israel on a new cart, but they did not have access to God's instructions. God expects his people to know and fulfill his commands. **16–24:** In the celebrations everything was detailed and ordered. Each musician knew what his responsibility was. Much careful study and preparation had been done so that God would be honored. The musicians and singers were skilled and the songs were joyful, because God is worthy of the best and because their hearts were overflowing with joy and thanksgiving. **25–28:** Clothed in fine linen, symbolizing holiness and purity, David and all Israel brought the Ark to Jerusalem with exuberant and wholehearted rejoic-

they carried the Ark of the LORD's Covenant,
they sacrificed seven bulls and seven rams.
27 David was dressed in a robe of fine linen, as
were all the Levites who carried the Ark, and also
the singers, and Kenaniah the choir leader. David
was also wearing a priestly garment.* 28 So all Israel brought up the Ark of the LORD's Covenant
with shouts of joy, the blowing of rams' horns
and trumpets, the crashing of cymbals, and loud
playing on harps and lyres.
29 But as the Ark of the LORD's Covenant entered the City of David, Michal, the daughter of
Saul, looked down from her window. When she
saw King David skipping about and laughing
with joy, she was filled with contempt for him.

16 They brought the Ark of God and
placed it inside the special tent David
had prepared for it. And they presented burnt offerings and peace offerings to
God. 2 When he had finished his sacrifices, David blessed the people in the name of the LORD.
3 Then he gave to every man and woman in all
Israel a loaf of bread, a cake of dates,* and a cake
of raisins.
4 David appointed the following Levites to
lead the people in worship before the Ark of the
LORD—to invoke his blessings, to give thanks,
and to praise the LORD, the God of Israel. 5 Asaph,
the leader of this group, sounded the cymbals.
Second to him was Zechariah, followed by Jeiel,
Shemiramoth, Jehiel, Mattithiah, Eliab, Benaiah,
Obed-edom, and Jeiel. They played the harps and
lyres. 6 The priests, Benaiah and Jahaziel, played
the trumpets regularly before the Ark of God's
Covenant.

David's Song of Praise

7 On that day David gave to Asaph and his fellow
Levites this song of thanksgiving to the LORD:

8 Give thanks to the LORD and proclaim his
greatness.
Let the whole world know what he has
done.
9 Sing to him; yes, sing his praises.
Tell everyone about his wonderful deeds.
10 Exult in his holy name;
rejoice, you who worship the LORD.
11 Search for the LORD and for his strength;
continually seek him.
12 Remember the wonders he has performed,
his miracles, and the rulings he has given,
13 you children of his servant Israel,
you descendants of Jacob, his chosen ones.

15:27 Hebrew *a linen ephod.* **16:3** Or *a portion of meat.* The meaning of the Hebrew is uncertain.

ing. **29:** Michal, Saul's daughter, despised David for his lack of dignity. The Chronicler may be noting the lack of love for the LORD of Saul's house as compared with David's. Michal saw David's actions as demeaning. She did not realize that to exalt God brings not humiliation but a closer fellowship with God. Michal had been a pawn in the hands of both Saul and David. She was given to David as a wife and risked her life for him, and then she was given to another man when David was Saul's enemy (1 Sam 25:44; 2 Sam 3:14). David apparently deserted her but demanded her back when it was convenient. With Michal as his wife, David's claim to the throne had more credibility with Saul's followers. The fact that her husband loved her and presumably she was happy with him didn't concern David (2 Sam 3:15–16). Michal's contempt for David is understandable. Many wives have been suspicious of a devotion to God that is not accompanied by devotion to wife and family, and rightly so, for true love for God is expressed by love for one another. But Michal held on to bitterness and an unforgiving attitude, and her life was blighted (see 2 Sam 6:23). Despite the unfairness of her situation, she could have put her life into God's hands and trusted him, but she did not. **16:1–3:** The Ark was brought and placed in the prepared tent. The king blessed the people, and each Israelite man and woman received a share of the sacrificial meal in Yahweh's name, a symbol of their share in the blessings God promises for his people when they love and seek him. What was the relevance of the Ark to the people of the Chronicler's day, when it was no longer in their possession? The Ark was where God met with his people, and even though it was no longer there, God was still among his people. David's bringing the Ark to Jerusalem symbolizes the need to have God at the center of the nation. **4–6:** Levites ministered before the Ark in prayer, in music, in praise, in thanksgiving—to Yahweh, the God of Israel. This had not been their task previously, but now that the Israelites were settled, their former tasks were to a great extent gone. Notice that God gifted them to take up this new role.

16:7–36 David's Song of Praise. The song in verses 8–22 is the same as Psalm 105:1–15 and calls for thanks and praise for all God's past acts, for God's faithfulness to his covenant promise to Abraham, Isaac, and Jacob, and for God's protection of his people. These promises were made to a people few in number, just as those who returned from the Exile were few in number, and God would be faithful to those promises. **15–18:** The reference here to the

14 He is the LORD our God.
His justice is seen throughout the land.
15 Remember his covenant forever—
the commitment he made to a thousand generations.
16 This is the covenant he made with Abraham
and the oath he swore to Isaac.
17 He confirmed it to Jacob as a decree,
and to the people of Israel as a never-ending covenant:
18 "I will give you the land of Canaan
as your special possession."
19 He said this when you were few in number,
a tiny group of strangers in Canaan.
20 They wandered from nation to nation,
from one kingdom to another.
21 Yet he did not let anyone oppress them.
He warned kings on their behalf:
22 "Do not touch my chosen people,
and do not hurt my prophets."

23 Let the whole earth sing to the LORD!
Each day proclaim the good news that he saves.
24 Publish his glorious deeds among the nations.
Tell everyone about the amazing things he does.
25 Great is the LORD! He is most worthy of praise!
He is to be feared above all gods.
26 The gods of other nations are mere idols,
but the LORD made the heavens!
27 Honor and majesty surround him;
strength and joy fill his dwelling.

28 O nations of the world, recognize the LORD,
recognize that the LORD is glorious and strong.
29 Give to the LORD the glory he deserves!
Bring your offering and come into his presence.
Worship the LORD in all his holy splendor.
30 Let all the earth tremble before him.
The world stands firm and cannot be shaken.

31 Let the heavens be glad, and the earth rejoice!
Tell all the nations, "The LORD reigns!"
32 Let the sea and everything in it shout his praise!
Let the fields and their crops burst out with joy!
33 Let the trees of the forest rustle with praise,
for the LORD is coming to judge the earth.

34 Give thanks to the LORD, for he is good!
His faithful love endures forever.
35 Cry out, "Save us, O God of our salvation!
Gather and rescue us from among the nations,
so we can thank your holy name
and rejoice and praise you."

36 Praise the LORD, the God of Israel,
who lives from everlasting to everlasting!

And all the people shouted "Amen!" and praised the LORD.

Worship at Jerusalem and Gibeon

37 David arranged for Asaph and his fellow Levites to serve regularly before the Ark of the LORD's Covenant, doing whatever needed to be done each day.
38 This group included Obed-edom (son of Jeduthun), Hosah, and sixty-eight other Levites as gatekeepers.
39 Meanwhile, David stationed Zadok the priest and his fellow priests at the Tabernacle of the LORD at the place of worship in Gibeon, where they continued to minister before the LORD.
40 They sacrificed the regular burnt offerings to the LORD each morning and evening on the altar set aside for that purpose, obeying everything written in the Law of the LORD, as he had commanded Israel.
41 David also appointed Heman, Jeduthun, and the others chosen by name to give thanks to the LORD, for "his faithful love endures forever."
42 They used

---

covenant God made with Israel picks up the references to the "Ark of the LORD's Covenant" in 15:25–26, 28–29. The Ark was symbolic of that covenant, and the covenant remained although the Ark had gone. Remembering and telling what God has done in the past is necessary, and so is continual looking to God in the present and into the future (16:11).

16:37–43: The ongoing worship of God before the Ark in Jerusalem and in the Tabernacle at Gibeon was established by David so that everything would be done as God required. There is no other record of the Tabernacle being at Gibeon but that sacrifices continued in the way God had appointed is important to the writer and his readers. Notice, though, that the writer throughout places more emphasis on the Ark and the accompanying worship of the LORD than on the sacrifices, although sacrifices were offered (see 15:26; 16:1–2, 39–40). Many times in Israel's history the people concentrated on ritual performances and sacrifices, not realizing that what really counted was obedient hearts.

their trumpets, cymbals, and other instruments to
accompany their songs of praise to God.* And the
sons of Jeduthun were appointed as gatekeepers.
43 Then all the people returned to their homes,
and David turned and went home to bless his
own family.

The LORD's Covenant Promise to David

17 When David was settled in his palace,
he summoned Nathan the prophet.
"Look," David said, "I am living in a
beautiful cedar palace,* but the Ark of the LORD's
Covenant is out there under a tent!"
2 Nathan replied to David, "Do whatever you
have in mind, for God is with you."
3 But that same night God said to Nathan,

4 "Go and tell my servant David, 'This is what
the LORD has declared: You are not the one to
build a house for me to live in. 5 I have never
lived in a house, from the day I brought the
Israelites out of Egypt until this very day. My
home has always been a tent, moving from
one place to another in a Tabernacle. 6 Yet no
matter where I have gone with the Israelites,
I have never once complained to Israel's
leaders,* the shepherds of my people. I have
never asked them, "Why haven't you built
me a beautiful cedar house?"'
7 "Now go and say to my servant David,
'This is what the LORD of Heaven's Armies
has declared: I took you from tending sheep
in the pasture and selected you to be the
leader of my people Israel. 8 I have been with
you wherever you have gone, and I have
destroyed all your enemies before your eyes.
Now I will make your name as famous as
anyone who has ever lived on the earth!
9 And I will provide a homeland for my people
Israel, planting them in a secure place where
they will never be disturbed. Evil nations
won't oppress them as they've done in the
past, 10 starting from the time I appointed
judges to rule my people Israel. And I will
defeat all your enemies.
" 'Furthermore, I declare that the LORD will
build a house for you—a dynasty of kings!
11 For when you die and join your ancestors,
I will raise up one of your descendants, one
of your sons, and I will make his kingdom
strong. 12 He is the one who will build a
house—a temple—for me. And I will secure
his throne forever. 13 I will be his father, and
he will be my son. I will never take my favor
from him as I took it from the one who ruled
before you. 14 I will confirm him as king over
my house and my kingdom for all time, and
his throne will be secure forever.' "

15 So Nathan went back to David and told him everything the LORD had said in this vision.

David's Prayer of Thanks

16 Then King David went in and sat before the
LORD and prayed,

"Who am I, O LORD God, and what is my
family, that you have brought me this far?

16:42 Or *to accompany the sacred music;* or *to accompany singing to God.* **17:1** Hebrew *a house of cedar.* **17:6** As in Greek version (see also 2 Sam 7:7); Hebrew reads *judges.*

17:1–27 The LORD Builds a House for David

David's plan to build a permanent place for the Ark was a good idea, motivated by a desire to honor God. When David expressed his idea to Nathan the prophet, he too thought it was right, advising David to go ahead because God was with him. **3–6:** However, it was not God's purpose to live in a house (see Isa 55:8–9). God does not require a settled place to live, for he lives everywhere. The Ark had moved through the desert, to Gilgal, to Bethel, to Shiloh, to Philistia, to Beth-shemesh, to Kiriath-jearim. Wherever it went the presence of God had been seen, in judgment or blessing. Its mobility helped to make it clear that God is not limited to any one place. Later experience showed that a temple could hinder worship of God, giving a false sense of security (see, e.g., Jer 7:4). However, verse 4 indicates that a house would be built, but not by David. **11–15:** Rather than David building a house for God, God would build a house for David. God would take David's son, establish his kingdom and throne forever, and he, God, would do the building. (2 Samuel 7:14 states the judgments that would fall if that son disobeyed God, but this is omitted here.) Later, 22:8 and 28:3 tell us the reason preventing David building the Temple was his violent background; Solomon used more peaceful means, such as alliances. The emphasis in Chronicles on David's son is stronger than in 2 Samuel 7, where David's kingdom and throne, rather than his son's, would be established forever. The point is that David's kingdom was dependent upon God, and what God would build far exceeds anything David or his son could build. **16–27:** When David did focus on God, realizing God's greatness and his own insignificance, he expressed this in prayer. He was overwhelmed by the unbelievable grace God had shown him, treating him as

[17]And now, O God, in addition to everything
else, you speak of giving your servant a
lasting dynasty! You speak as though I were
someone very great,* O LORD God!

[18]"What more can I say to you about the
way you have honored me? You know what
your servant is really like. [19]For the sake of
your servant, O LORD, and according to your
will, you have done all these great things and
have made them known.

[20]"O LORD, there is no one like you. We
have never even heard of another God like
you! [21]What other nation on earth is like
your people Israel? What other nation,
O God, have you redeemed from slavery
to be your own people? You made a great
name for yourself when you redeemed your
people from Egypt. You performed awesome
miracles and drove out the nations that stood
in their way. [22]You chose Israel to be your
very own people forever, and you, O LORD,
became their God.

[23]"And now, O LORD, I am your servant;
do as you have promised concerning me and
my family. May it be a promise that will last
forever. [24]And may your name be established
and honored forever so that everyone will
say, 'The LORD of Heaven's Armies, the God
of Israel, is Israel's God!' And may the house
of your servant David continue before you
forever.

[25]"O my God, I have been bold enough
to pray to you because you have revealed
to your servant that you will build a house
for him—a dynasty of kings! [26]For you are
God, O LORD. And you have promised these
good things to your servant. [27]And now, it
has pleased you to bless the house of your
servant, so that it will continue forever before
you. For when you grant a blessing, O LORD,
it is an eternal blessing!"

David's Military Victories

18 After this, David defeated and subdued the Philistines by conquering
Gath and its surrounding towns. [2]Da-
vid also conquered the land of Moab, and the
Moabites who were spared became David's subjects and paid him tribute money.

[3]David also destroyed the forces of Hadadezer, king of Zobah, as far as Hamath,* when
Hadadezer marched out to strengthen his control along the Euphrates River. [4]David captured
1,000 chariots, 7,000 charioteers, and 20,000 foot
soldiers. He crippled all the chariot horses except
enough for 100 chariots.

[5]When Arameans from Damascus arrived
to help King Hadadezer, David killed 22,000 of
them. [6]Then he placed several army garrisons*
in Damascus, the Aramean capital, and the
Arameans became David's subjects and paid him
tribute money. So the LORD made David victorious wherever he went.

[7]David brought the gold shields of Hadadezer's officers to Jerusalem, [8]along with a large
amount of bronze from Hadadezer's towns of
Tebah* and Cun. Later Solomon melted the

17:17 The meaning of the Hebrew is uncertain. **18:3** The meaning of the Hebrew is uncertain. **18:6** As in Greek version and Latin Vulgate (see also 2 Sam 8:6); Hebrew lacks *several army garrisons.* **18:8** Hebrew reads *Tibhath,* a variant spelling of Tebah; compare parallel text at 2 Sam 8:8.

significant instead of someone of little consequence. Why had God made this promise? It was his will to do so. The Chronicler's readers, knowing David's descendants no longer ruled, must have been puzzled by the declaration that David's kingdom would be established forever. The stipulation (in 2 Sam 7) that disobedience would cause God to judge the king had been demonstrated, but why was there no king once the Exile was over? With every promise God makes there must be a response from his people. David responded in belief. Later generations counted on the promise to keep them from destruction (e.g., Amos 6:1–7; Jer 7:1–15) but felt no obligation to obey God's commands. Nor did they believe the words of God spoken through his prophets. The remnant who returned from exile had to learn to listen to God's word through his prophets and to obey him. Although it seemed as if God's promise had failed, they must trust him.

18:1—20:8 Battles

Although David's warring meant he could not build the Temple, his battles were crowned with success by God, who gave him victory. And from the booty won from these battles, much was put aside for the future Temple (18:8). These battles are recorded (in 2 Sam 8—21) alongside details of David's adultery, the murder of Uriah, and the rebellion, rape, and murders among David's family (see Adultery, Exod 20; Violence, Abuse, and Oppression, Eccl 4). In 1 Chronicles the emphasis is on David's expansion of the kingdom and God's blessing on him. It is clear in 2 Samuel 12:13 and in Psalm 51 that David repented and that God continued to use him. This same grace is available to all God's people, and the Chronicler encourages his and future generations to acknowledge sin, to repent, and to press on with confidence in God. The central lesson is that the sov-

bronze and molded it into the great bronze basin
called the Sea, the pillars, and the various bronze
articles used at the Temple.
9 When King Toi* of Hamath heard that David had destroyed the entire army of King Hadadezer of Zobah, 10 he sent his son Joram* to
congratulate King David for his successful campaign. Hadadezer and Toi had been enemies and
were often at war. Joram presented David with
many gifts of gold, silver, and bronze.
11 King David dedicated all these gifts to the
LORD, along with the silver and gold he had tak-
en from the other nations—from Edom, Moab,
Ammon, Philistia, and Amalek.
12 Abishai son of Zeruiah destroyed 18,000
Edomites in the Valley of Salt. 13 He placed army
garrisons in Edom, and all the Edomites became
David's subjects. In fact, the LORD made David
victorious wherever he went.
14 So David reigned over all Israel and did
what was just and right for all his people. 15 Joab
son of Zeruiah was commander of the army.
Jehoshaphat son of Ahilud was the royal historian. 16 Zadok son of Ahitub and Ahimelech* son
of Abiathar were the priests. Seraiah* was the
court secretary. 17 Benaiah son of Jehoiada was
captain of the king's bodyguard.* And David's
sons served as the king's chief assistants.

David Defeats the Ammonites

19 Some time after this, King Nahash of
the Ammonites died, and his son Hanun* became king. 2 David said, "I am
going to show loyalty to Hanun because his father, Nahash, was always loyal to me." So David
sent messengers to express sympathy to Hanun
about his father's death.
But when David's ambassadors arrived in the
land of Ammon, 3 the Ammonite commanders
said to Hanun, "Do you really think these men
are coming here to honor your father? No! David has sent them to spy out the land so they
can come in and conquer it!" 4 So Hanun seized
David's ambassadors and shaved them, cut off
their robes at the buttocks, and sent them back
to David in shame.
5 When David heard what had happened to
the men, he sent messengers to tell them, "Stay
at Jericho until your beards grow out, and then
come back." For they felt deep shame because of
their appearance.
6 When the people of Ammon realized how
seriously they had angered David, Hanun and
the Ammonites sent 75,000 pounds* of silver
to hire chariots and charioteers from Aram-
naharaim, Aram-maacah, and Zobah. 7 They also
hired 32,000 chariots and secured the support of
the king of Maacah and his army. These forces
camped at Medeba, where they were joined by
the Ammonite troops that Hanun had recruited
from his own towns. 8 When David heard about
this, he sent Joab and all his warriors to fight
them. 9 The Ammonite troops came out and drew
up their battle lines at the entrance of the city,
while the other kings positioned themselves to
fight in the open fields.
10 When Joab saw that he would have to fight
on both the front and the rear, he chose some
of Israel's elite troops and placed them under his
personal command to fight the Arameans in the

18:9 As in parallel text at 2 Sam 8:9; Hebrew reads *Tou;* also in 18:10. **18:10** As in parallel text at 2 Sam 8:10; Hebrew reads *Hadoram,* a variant spelling of Joram. **18:16a** As in some Hebrew manuscripts, Syriac version, and Latin Vulgate (see also 2 Sam 8:17); most Hebrew manuscripts read *Abimelech.* **18:16b** As in parallel text at 2 Sam 8:17; Hebrew reads *Shavsha.* **18:17** Hebrew *of the Kerethites and Pelethites.* **19:1** As in parallel text at 2 Sam 10:1; Hebrew lacks *Hanun.* **19:6** Hebrew *1,000 talents* [34,000 kilograms].

---

ereign God will bless those who trust in him. David's God was still sovereign in the Chronicler's day, and his power had been displayed in the exiles' return to their land. **18:14–17:** David as king ruled with justice and righteousness. These characteristics of God are what he expects from his people (see, e.g., Amos 5:24), especially those in leadership. David put into place the necessary structure to organize the kingdom. The royal historian kept official records and probably oversaw the protocol and ceremonial details of the kingdom. Zadok the priest was in charge of the Tabernacle at Gibeon (16:39), and Ahimelech led the worship in Jerusalem. (Zadok came into greater prominence under Solomon; see, e.g., 1 Chr 29:22.) David's bodyguards included non-Israelites, such as the Cherethites and Pelethites. David's sons served as *chief assistants* (2 Sam 8:18 has "priestly leaders"). **19:1–2:** Nahash the Ammonite was Saul's enemy, defeated by him as his reign began (1 Sam 11:1–11). Perhaps the Nahash mentioned here was his son. At some time it seems Nahash and David had made a treaty; the Hebrew word for loyalty is *hesed*, the word used for God's covenant love and faithfulness. **3–5:** To reject David's overtures of friendship, especially in such a humiliating fashion, was to declare war. **6–19:** David did not immediately react, but the Ammonites enlisted Aramean mercenaries, making the intention of war clear. Joab and Abishai routed the first army, and the second, larger one (formed with the addition of more distant Arameans) was defeated by David and *all Israel*. The numbers given in Chronicles vary from, and are generally larg-

fields. 11 He left the rest of the army under the command of his brother Abishai, who was to attack the Ammonites. 12 "If the Arameans are too strong for me, then come over and help me," Joab told his brother. "And if the Ammonites are too strong for you, I will help you. 13 Be courageous! Let us fight bravely for our people and the cities of our God. May the LORD's will be done."

14 When Joab and his troops attacked, the Arameans began to run away. 15 And when the Ammonites saw the Arameans running, they also ran from Abishai and retreated into the city. Then Joab returned to Jerusalem.

16 The Arameans now realized that they were no match for Israel, so they sent messengers and summoned additional Aramean troops from the other side of the Euphrates River.* These troops were under the command of Shobach,* the commander of Hadadezer's forces.

17 When David heard what was happening, he mobilized all Israel, crossed the Jordan River, and positioned his troops in battle formation. Then David engaged the Arameans in battle, and they fought against him. 18 But again the Arameans fled from the Israelites. This time David's forces killed 7,000 charioteers and 40,000 foot soldiers, including Shobach, the commander of their army. 19 When Hadadezer's allies saw that they had been defeated by Israel, they surrendered to David and became his subjects. After that, the Arameans were no longer willing to help the Ammonites.

David Captures Rabbah

20 In the spring of the year,* when kings normally go out to war, Joab led the Israelite army in successful attacks against the land of the Ammonites. In the process he laid siege to the city of Rabbah. However, David stayed behind in Jerusalem.

2 When David arrived at Rabbah, he removed the crown from the king's head,* and it was placed on his own head. The crown was made of gold and set with gems, and he found that it weighed seventy-five pounds.* David took a vast amount of plunder from the city. 3 He also made slaves of the people of Rabbah and forced them to labor with saws, iron picks, and iron axes.* That is how David dealt with the people of all the Ammonite towns. Then David and all the army returned to Jerusalem.

Battles against Philistine Giants

4 After this, war broke out with the Philistines at Gezer. As they fought, Sibbecai from Hushah killed Saph,* a descendant of the giants,* and so the Philistines were subdued.

5 During another battle with the Philistines, Elhanan son of Jair killed Lahmi, the brother of Goliath of Gath. The handle of Lahmi's spear was as thick as a weaver's beam!

6 In another battle with the Philistines at Gath, they encountered a huge man with six fingers on each hand and six toes on each foot, twenty-four in all, who was also a descendant of the giants. 7 But when he defied and taunted Israel, he was killed by Jonathan, the son of David's brother Shimea.

8 These Philistines were descendants of the giants of Gath, but David and his warriors killed them.

David Takes a Census

21 Satan rose up against Israel and caused David to take a census of the people of Israel. 2 So David said to Joab

19:16a Hebrew *the river.* **19:16b** As in parallel text at 2 Sam 10:16; Hebrew reads *Shophach;* also in 19:18. **20:1** Hebrew *At the turn of the year.* The first day of the year in the ancient Hebrew lunar calendar occurred in March or April. **20:2a** Or *from the head of Milcom* (as in Greek version and Latin Vulgate). Milcom, also called Molech, was the god of the Ammonites. **20:2b** Hebrew *1 talent* [34 kilograms]. **20:3** As in parallel text at 2 Sam 12:31; Hebrew reads *and cut them with saws, iron picks, and saws.* **20:4a** As in parallel text at 2 Sam 21:18; Hebrew reads *Sippai.* **20:4b** Hebrew *descendant of the Rephaites;* also in 20:6, 8.

er than, those in 2 Samuel 10 (e.g., 1 Chr 19:18; cf. 2 Sam 10:18). **19:** The groups previously controlled by Arameans then became David's vassals, bringing a further expansion of territory up to the Euphrates River. **20:4–8:** Several battles involve giants. Here Elhanan is said to have killed the brother of Goliath, whereas the Hebrew of 2 Samuel 21:19 says he killed Goliath (cf. 1 Sam 17, where David kills Goliath). It has been suggested that Elhanan was David's family name, but Chronicles could be clarifying the account in 1 Samuel. These three victories over giants show once again the power of Israel's God as the weak overcome the strong.

21:1–30 The Census

This narrative shows how the Temple site was chosen and purchased. David acknowledges his sin and repents; although judgment falls, it is followed by God's mercy and forgiveness and the provision of the Temple site.

1: Satan incited David to take a census. But in 2 Samuel, God incited David to take the census because he was angry with Israel. As in Job 2:10, all things ultimately were seen to come from God's hand, for Satan could not go beyond what God allowed. In Job

and the commanders of the army, "Take a census of all the people of Israel—from Beersheba in the south to Dan in the north—and bring me a report so I may know how many there are."

[3]But Joab replied, "May the LORD increase the number of his people a hundred times over! But why, my lord the king, do you want to do this? Are they not all your servants? Why must you cause Israel to sin?"

[4]But the king insisted that they take the census, so Joab traveled throughout all Israel to count the people. Then he returned to Jerusalem [5]and reported the number of people to David. There were 1,100,000 warriors in all Israel who could handle a sword, and 470,000 in Judah. [6]But Joab did not include the tribes of Levi and Benjamin in the census because he was so distressed at what the king had made him do.

Judgment for David's Sin

[7]God was very displeased with the census, and he punished Israel for it. [8]Then David said to God, "I have sinned greatly by taking this census. Please forgive my guilt for doing this foolish thing."

[9]Then the LORD spoke to Gad, David's seer. This was the message: [10]"Go and say to David, 'This is what the LORD says: I will give you three choices. Choose one of these punishments, and I will inflict it on you.' "

[11]So Gad came to David and said, "These are the choices the LORD has given you. [12]You may choose three years of famine, three months of destruction by the sword of your enemies, or three days of severe plague as the angel of the LORD brings devastation throughout the land of Israel. Decide what answer I should give the LORD who sent me."

[13]"I'm in a desperate situation!" David replied to Gad. "But let me fall into the hands of the LORD, for his mercy is very great. Do not let me fall into human hands."

[14]So the LORD sent a plague upon Israel, and 70,000 people died as a result. [15]And God sent an angel to destroy Jerusalem. But just as the angel was preparing to destroy it, the LORD relented and said to the death angel, "Stop! That is enough!" At that moment the angel of the LORD was standing by the threshing floor of Araunah* the Jebusite.

[16]David looked up and saw the angel of the LORD standing between heaven and earth with his sword drawn, reaching out over Jerusalem. So David and the leaders of Israel put on burlap to show their deep distress and fell face down on the ground. [17]And David said to God, "I am the one who called for the census! I am the one who has sinned and done wrong! But these people are as innocent as sheep—what have they done? O LORD my God, let your anger fall against me and my family, but do not destroy your people."

21:15 As in parallel text at 2 Sam 24:16; Hebrew reads *Ornan,* another name for Araunah; also in 21:18-28.

1—2 and Zechariah 3:1, *the Satan* or the adversary is shown working within God's council or court. However, later Judaism attributes evil to Satan rather than to God. It seems that the Chronicler presents evil as coming from Satan, while still accepting that God is the ultimate authority. **7–8:** Why should taking a census be sinful? Twice in the book of Numbers (Num 1; 26), God told Moses to take a census of the people for a specific purpose. Obviously David was taking this census for his own purposes, not for God's. Perhaps pride made him want to know the numbers of fighting men. Perhaps he was beginning to attribute his victories not to God but to himself because of the size and skill of his army. Satan took advantage of David's wrong motives, and God did not intervene to stop the process. **4–6:** Presumably in all the time it took to conduct the census, David did not seek God. The number of men is smaller in Chronicles than in Samuel, perhaps because the tribes of Levi and Benjamin are not included. **8, 17:** In the end, David recognized that the blame was his. As soon as David recognized his sin, he confessed it, taking responsibility for his actions. Our human tendency is often to blame someone or something else, as Adam and Eve did in the garden. Nevertheless, 2 Samuel 24:1 shows that the sin was not David's alone: Israel too had incurred God's anger. The people were not just innocent victims of David's sin. **9–15:** God forgave David but still meted out punishment. David placed himself and his people in God's hands, even though the three choices that God gave David were dreadful. God sent the destroying angel (as in Exod 12:23), and seventy thousand people died. (If the word *elep* is translated "unit" instead of "thousand," this would give the lesser number of seventy units, but it is not certain how many would be in a unit; see annotation on 1 Chr 23:3–4). **12, 16:** God stopped the destroying angel as he stood over the threshing floor of Araunah (Ornan). David sees the angel of the LORD with his sword drawn. Previously the sword of the destroying angel had been drawn against Israel's enemies (Num 22:22–35; Josh 5:13–15), but now it was extended over Israel. **16–17:** David watched his people suffering, his men dying, his military strength being depleted. He recognized once more that God is the source of all power; God brings victory or defeat. In all the success, prosperity, and victories that God had given him, David had lost his focus; he had ceased to trust

David Builds an Altar
18Then the angel of the LORD told Gad to instruct
David to go up and build an altar to the LORD
on the threshing floor of Araunah the Jebusite.
19So David went up to do what the LORD had
commanded him through Gad. 20Araunah, who
was busy threshing wheat at the time, turned
and saw the angel there. His four sons, who were
with him, ran away and hid. 21When Araunah
saw David approaching, he left his threshing
floor and bowed before David with his face to the
ground.
22David said to Araunah, "Let me buy this
threshing floor from you at its full price. Then I
will build an altar to the LORD there, so that he
will stop the plague."
23"Take it, my lord the king, and use it as you
wish," Araunah said to David. "I will give the
oxen for the burnt offerings, and the threshing
boards for wood to build a fire on the altar, and
the wheat for the grain offering. I will give it all
to you."
24But King David replied to Araunah, "No, I
insist on buying it for the full price. I will not
take what is yours and give it to the LORD. I will
not present burnt offerings that have cost me
nothing!" 25So David gave Araunah 600 pieces of
gold* in payment for the threshing floor.
26David built an altar there to the LORD and
sacrificed burnt offerings and peace offerings.
And when David prayed, the LORD answered him
by sending fire from heaven to burn up the offering on the altar. 27Then the LORD spoke to the
angel, who put the sword back into its sheath.
28When David saw that the LORD had answered his prayer, he offered sacrifices there at
Araunah's threshing floor. 29At that time the
Tabernacle of the LORD and the altar of burnt
offering that Moses had made in the wilderness
were located at the place of worship in Gibeon.
30But David was not able to go there to inquire
of God, because he was terrified by the drawn
sword of the angel of the LORD.

22 Then David said, "This will be the
location for the Temple of the LORD
God and the place of the altar for Israel's burnt offerings!"

Preparations for the Temple
2So David gave orders to call together the foreigners living in Israel, and he assigned them the
task of preparing finished stone for building the
Temple of God. 3David provided large amounts
of iron for the nails that would be needed for the
doors in the gates and for the clamps, and he gave
more bronze than could be weighed. 4He also
provided innumerable cedar logs, for the men of
Tyre and Sidon had brought vast amounts of cedar to David.
5David said, "My son Solomon is still young

21:25 Hebrew *600 shekels of gold,* about 15 pounds or 6.8 kilograms in weight.

God and began to trust only himself. **18–30:** The purchase of the threshing floor has echoes of Abraham's purchase of the field at Machpelah (Gen 23). The full price was paid for land and sacrifice. As he had done for Gideon (Judg 6:26), God sent fire from heaven to consume the sacrifice, signifying his acceptance of the offering, and the plague ended. According to Chronicles, David paid six hundred shekels of gold, whereas Samuel mentions fifty shekels of silver. Perhaps fifty silver shekels was the price for the site of the altar, and the six hundred gold shekels the price of the entire site later used for the Temple. Second Chronicles 3:1 names this as Mount Moriah, perhaps providing a link to the place where many years before Abraham had been stopped from killing Isaac and a substitute sacrifice provided. Once more judgment had been averted by God's mercy at this place.

22:1–19 Preparations for the Temple

The theme of this chapter is the preparation for building the *Temple of the LORD God.* If David could not build it, he could prepare and provide for it. The place where judgment had been stopped and David's prayer answered was where the Temple would be built. Until now the altar had been in Gibeon (21:29). Both it and the Tabernacle would be united in the Temple—sacrifice and worship together again. Jerusalem would be the nation's religious center. **2:** Non-Israelites were used in the preparations. These were likely to have been forced labor gangs (see 2 Sam 20:24). The beginnings of the use of foreigners for forced labor is seen in Joshua 9:21, 27, and 1 Kings 9:21–22. Second Chronicles 2:17–18 and 8:7–8 show Solomon's increased use of non-Israelites in this way. First Kings 5:13 says that Solomon also conscripted Israelites to help build the Temple in shifts of one month in Lebanon and two months at home. This was not a popular move (see 2 Chr 10:4). **5–7, 14:** David was concerned that the house be magnificent, known throughout the world as a reflection of God's magnificence, splendor, and fame. David honored God and expressed that in his provisions for the Temple, which had cost a great deal in money, time, and effort. Some of these materials had been taken as booty from defeated nations (see,

and inexperienced. And since the Temple to be
built for the LORD must be a magnificent structure, famous and glorious throughout the world,
I will begin making preparations for it now." So
David collected vast amounts of building materials before his death.
6Then David sent for his son Solomon and instructed him to build a Temple for the LORD, the
God of Israel. 7"My son, I wanted to build a Temple to honor the name of the LORD my God," David told him. 8"But the LORD said to me, 'You have
killed many men in the battles you have fought.
And since you have shed so much blood in my
sight, you will not be the one to build a Temple
to honor my name. 9But you will have a son who
will be a man of peace. I will give him peace with
his enemies in all the surrounding lands. His name
will be Solomon,* and I will give peace and quiet
to Israel during his reign. 10He is the one who will
build a Temple to honor my name. He will be my
son, and I will be his father. And I will secure the
throne of his kingdom over Israel forever.'
11"Now, my son, may the LORD be with you
and give you success as you follow his directions
in building the Temple of the LORD your God.
12And may the LORD give you wisdom and understanding, that you may obey the Law of the
LORD your God as you rule over Israel. 13For you
will be successful if you carefully obey the decrees and regulations that the LORD gave to Israel through Moses. Be strong and courageous;
do not be afraid or lose heart!
14"I have worked hard to provide materials for
building the Temple of the LORD—nearly 4,000
tons of gold, 40,000 tons of silver,* and so much
iron and bronze that it cannot be weighed. I have
also gathered timber and stone for the walls,
though you may need to add more. 15You have a
large number of skilled stonemasons and carpenters and craftsmen of every kind. 16You have expert goldsmiths and silversmiths and workers of
bronze and iron. Now begin the work, and may
the LORD be with you!"
17Then David ordered all the leaders of Israel
to assist Solomon in this project. 18"The LORD
your God is with you," he declared. "He has giv-
en you peace with the surrounding nations. He
has handed them over to me, and they are now
subject to the LORD and his people. 19Now seek
the LORD your God with all your heart and soul.
Build the sanctuary of the LORD God so that you
can bring the Ark of the LORD's Covenant and
the holy vessels of God into the Temple built to
honor the LORD's name."

Duties of the Levites

23 When David was an old man, he appointed his son Solomon to be king
over Israel. 2David summoned all
the leaders of Israel, together with the priests
and Levites. 3All the Levites who were thirty

22:9 *Solomon* sounds like and is probably derived from the Hebrew word for "peace." **22:14** Hebrew *100,000 talents* [3,400 metric tons] *of gold, 1,000,000 talents* [34,000 metric tons] *of silver.*

e.g., 18:8). **5–13:** David charged Solomon to build the house. Just as Moses had done for Joshua long before, David pointed out Solomon's need for discretion, understanding, obedience, and absolute confidence in God, shown by strength and courage (cf. Deut 12:10–11; Josh 1:6–9). Moses had prepared the people to enter the land; Joshua led them in. David had made preparations for the Temple; Solomon would build it. The parallels show the importance of this Temple. Following David's example, after the Exile Ezra, Nehemiah, Haggai, and Zechariah urged the people not to neglect the rebuilding of the Temple and its service. The prophets exhorted the people to put God first and then begin the building (Hag 1:8), and they promised God's presence and help (Hag 1:13; 2:4; Zech 4:9).

23:1—26:32 Preparations for Temple Worship

Chapters 23—27 seem to break up the narrative, as 28:1 follows on from 23:2 very well (unless they refer to two separate assemblies of leaders). These chapters may have been added at a later date, but they continue the Temple theme of chapter 22 by detailing David's organization of the Levites in its service. They also show the importance of the worship of God in the life of his people. His holy things must be handled by those set apart to do so. Even mundane tasks, such as cleaning, are holy tasks when undertaken for God. Worship of God is to be orderly, not haphazard. Orderliness in worship honors him (1 Cor 14:40), as does giving the best of time, skill, willingness, and obedience. Whether priest, gatekeeper, musician, or worker, each must honor God in ministry, for God had come to dwell in Jerusalem (1 Chr 23:25).

23:1–32 The Levites. 3–4: Some commentators feel that thirty-eight thousand is unnaturally large and prefer to translate the word for *thousand* as "unit," "group," or "clan." This would mean there were thirty-eight units or groups. The original Levites had carried the Tabernacle and its furnishings from place to place in the desert. The twenty-four thousand or

years old or older were counted, and the total
came to 38,000. 4 Then David said, "From all
the Levites, 24,000 will supervise the work at
the Temple of the LORD. Another 6,000 will
serve as officials and judges. 5 Another 4,000
will work as gatekeepers, and 4,000 will praise
the LORD with the musical instruments I have
made." 6 Then David divided the Levites into
divisions named after the clans descended from
the three sons of Levi—Gershon, Kohath, and
Merari.

The Gershonites

7 The Gershonite family units were defined
by their lines of descent from Libni* and
Shimei, the sons of Gershon. 8 Three of the
descendants of Libni were Jehiel (the family
leader), Zetham, and Joel. 9 These were the
leaders of the family of Libni.
Three of the descendants of Shimei were
Shelomoth, Haziel, and Haran. 10 Four other
descendants of Shimei were Jahath, Ziza,*
Jeush, and Beriah. 11 Jahath was the family
leader, and Ziza was next. Jeush and Beriah
were counted as a single family because
neither had many sons.

The Kohathites

12 Four of the descendants of Kohath were
Amram, Izhar, Hebron, and Uzziel.
13 The sons of Amram were Aaron and Moses.
Aaron and his descendants were set apart
to dedicate the most holy things, to offer
sacrifices in the LORD's presence, to serve the
LORD, and to pronounce blessings in his name
forever.
14 As for Moses, the man of God, his sons
were included with the tribe of Levi. 15 The
sons of Moses were Gershom and Eliezer.
16 The descendants of Gershom included
Shebuel, the family leader. 17 Eliezer had
only one son, Rehabiah, the family leader.
Rehabiah had numerous descendants.
18 The descendants of Izhar included Shelomith,
the family leader.
19 The descendants of Hebron included Jeriah
(the family leader), Amariah (the second),
Jahaziel (the third), and Jekameam (the
fourth).
20 The descendants of Uzziel included Micah (the
family leader) and Isshiah (the second).

The Merarites

21 The descendants of Merari included Mahli and
Mushi.
The sons of Mahli were Eleazar and Kish.
22 Eleazar died with no sons, only daughters.
His daughters married their cousins, the sons
of Kish.
23 Three of the descendants of Mushi were
Mahli, Eder, and Jerimoth.

24 These were the descendants of Levi by
clans, the leaders of their family groups, registered carefully by name. Each had to be twenty
years old or older to qualify for service in the
house of the LORD. 25 For David said, "The LORD,
the God of Israel, has given us peace, and he will
always live in Jerusalem. 26 Now the Levites will
no longer need to carry the Tabernacle and its
furnishings from place to place." 27 In accordance
with David's final instructions, all the Levites
twenty years old or older were registered for
service.
28 The work of the Levites was to assist the
priests, the descendants of Aaron, as they served
at the house of the LORD. They also took care of
the courtyards and side rooms, helped perform
the ceremonies of purification, and served in
many other ways in the house of God. 29 They
were in charge of the sacred bread that was set
out on the table, the choice flour for the grain
offerings, the wafers made without yeast, the
cakes cooked in olive oil, and the other mixed
breads. They were also responsible to check all
the weights and measures. 30 And each morning
and evening they stood before the LORD to sing
songs of thanks and praise to him. 31 They assisted
with the burnt offerings that were presented to
the LORD on Sabbath days, at new moon celebrations, and at all the appointed festivals. The
required number of Levites served in the LORD's
presence at all times, following all the procedures
they had been given.
32 And so, under the supervision of the priests,
the Levites watched over the Tabernacle and the
Temple* and faithfully carried out their duties of
service at the house of the LORD.

23:7 Hebrew *Ladan* (also in 23:8, 9), a variant spelling of Libni; compare 6:17. **23:10** As in Greek version and Latin Vulgate (see also 23:11); Hebrew reads *Zina.* **23:32** Hebrew *the Tent of Meeting and the sanctuary.*

---

twenty-four units involved in the Temple service were to help the priests, their duties varied and prescribed by David (vv. 28–32). Praise and worship, service in the outer Temple area, and involvement in preparation of offerings were all part of their responsibilities (cf. Num 3:5–9, 31; 18:1–7).

Duties of the Priests

24 This is how Aaron's descendants, the priests, were divided into groups for service. The sons of Aaron were Nadab, Abihu, Eleazar, and Ithamar. 2 But Nadab and Abihu died before their father, and they had no sons. So only Eleazar and Ithamar were left to carry on as priests.
3 With the help of Zadok, who was a descendant of Eleazar, and of Ahimelech, who was a descendant of Ithamar, David divided Aaron's descendants into groups according to their various duties.
4 Eleazar's descendants were divided into sixteen groups and Ithamar's into eight, for there were more family leaders among the descendants of Eleazar.
5 All tasks were assigned to the various groups by means of sacred lots so that no preference would be shown, for there were many qualified officials serving God in the sanctuary from among the descendants of both Eleazar and Ithamar.
6 Shemaiah son of Nethanel, a Levite, acted as secretary and wrote down the names and assignments in the presence of the king, the officials, Zadok the priest, Ahimelech son of Abiathar, and the family leaders of the priests and Levites. The descendants of Eleazar and Ithamar took turns casting lots.

7 The first lot fell to Jehoiarib.
The second lot fell to Jedaiah.
8 The third lot fell to Harim.
The fourth lot fell to Seorim.
9 The fifth lot fell to Malkijah.
The sixth lot fell to Mijamin.
10 The seventh lot fell to Hakkoz.
The eighth lot fell to Abijah.
11 The ninth lot fell to Jeshua.
The tenth lot fell to Shecaniah.
12 The eleventh lot fell to Eliashib.
The twelfth lot fell to Jakim.
13 The thirteenth lot fell to Huppah.
The fourteenth lot fell to Jeshebeab.
14 The fifteenth lot fell to Bilgah.
The sixteenth lot fell to Immer.
15 The seventeenth lot fell to Hezir.
The eighteenth lot fell to Happizzez.
16 The nineteenth lot fell to Pethahiah.
The twentieth lot fell to Jehezkel.
17 The twenty-first lot fell to Jakin.
The twenty-second lot fell to Gamul.
18 The twenty-third lot fell to Delaiah.
The twenty-fourth lot fell to Maaziah.

19 Each group carried out its appointed duties in the house of the LORD according to the procedures established by their ancestor Aaron in obedience to the commands of the LORD, the God of Israel.

Family Leaders among the Levites

20 These were the other family leaders descended from Levi:

From the descendants of Amram, the leader was Shebuel.*
From the descendants of Shebuel, the leader was Jehdeiah.
21 From the descendants of Rehabiah, the leader was Isshiah.
22 From the descendants of Izhar, the leader was Shelomith.*
From the descendants of Shelomith, the leader was Jahath.
23 From the descendants of Hebron, Jeriah was the leader,* Amariah was second, Jahaziel was third, and Jekameam was fourth.
24 From the descendants of Uzziel, the leader was Micah.
From the descendants of Micah, the leader was Shamir,
25 along with Isshiah, the brother of Micah.
From the descendants of Isshiah, the leader was Zechariah.
26 From the descendants of Merari, the leaders were Mahli and Mushi.
From the descendants of Jaaziah, the leader was Beno.
27 From the descendants of Merari through Jaaziah, the leaders were Beno, Shoham, Zaccur, and Ibri.
28 From the descendants of Mahli, the leader was Eleazar, though he had no sons.

24:20 Hebrew *Shubael* (also in 24:20b), a variant spelling of Shebuel; compare 23:16 and 26:24. **24:22** Hebrew *Shelomoth* (also in 24:22b), a variant spelling of Shelomith; compare 23:18. **24:23** Hebrew *From the descendants of Jeriah;* compare 23:19.

24:1–31 The Priests and Other Levites. The Chronicler breaks into the account of the Levites to deal with Aaron's descendants, the priests, as in 23:13. **1–3:** Nadab and Abihu lost their lives (Lev 10:1–2). Aaron's two other sons, Eleazar and Ithamar, became the ancestors of the priestly line. Two of their descendants, Zadok and Ahimelech, joined with David in dividing the priests into groups for service. **5–6:** Impartiality and fairness in the choice is emphasized. Casting lots indicates that God was being consulted, while the king, the officials, and the heads of priestly families were also involved.

29 From the descendants of Kish, the leader was Jerahmeel.
30 From the descendants of Mushi, the leaders were Mahli, Eder, and Jerimoth.

These were the descendants of Levi in their
various families. 31 Like the descendants of Aar-
on, they were assigned to their duties by means of sacred lots, without regard to age or rank. Lots were drawn in the presence of King David, Zadok, Ahimelech, and the family leaders of the priests and the Levites.

Duties of the Musicians

25 David and the army commanders then appointed men from the families of Asaph, Heman, and Jeduthun to proclaim God's messages to the accompaniment of lyres, harps, and cymbals. Here is a list of their names and their work:

2 From the sons of Asaph, there were Zaccur, Joseph, Nethaniah, and Asarelah. They worked under the direction of their father, Asaph, who proclaimed God's messages by the king's orders.
3 From the sons of Jeduthun, there were Gedaliah, Zeri, Jeshaiah, Shimei,* Hashabiah, and Mattithiah, six in all. They worked under the direction of their father, Jeduthun, who proclaimed God's messages to the accompaniment of the lyre, offering thanks and praise to the LORD.
4 From the sons of Heman, there were Bukkiah, Mattaniah, Uzziel, Shubael,* Jerimoth, Hananiah, Hanani, Eliathah, Giddalti, Romamti-ezer, Joshbekashah, Mallothi, Hothir, and Mahazioth.
5 All these were the sons of Heman, the king's seer, for God had honored him with fourteen sons and three daughters.

6 All these men were under the direction of their fathers as they made music at the house of the LORD. Their responsibilities included the playing of cymbals, harps, and lyres at the house of God. Asaph, Jeduthun, and Heman reported
directly to the king. 7 They and their families were all trained in making music before the LORD, and each of them—288 in all—was an
accomplished musician. 8 The musicians were appointed to their term of service by means of sacred lots, without regard to whether they were young or old, teacher or student.

9 The first lot fell to Joseph of the Asaph clan and twelve of his sons and relatives.*
The second lot fell to Gedaliah and twelve of his sons and relatives.
10 The third lot fell to Zaccur and twelve of his sons and relatives.
11 The fourth lot fell to Zeri* and twelve of his sons and relatives.
12 The fifth lot fell to Nethaniah and twelve of his sons and relatives.
13 The sixth lot fell to Bukkiah and twelve of his sons and relatives.
14 The seventh lot fell to Asarelah* and twelve of his sons and relatives.
15 The eighth lot fell to Jeshaiah and twelve of his sons and relatives.
16 The ninth lot fell to Mattaniah and twelve of his sons and relatives.
17 The tenth lot fell to Shimei and twelve of his sons and relatives.

25:3 As in one Hebrew manuscript and some Greek manuscripts (see also 25:17); most Hebrew manuscripts lack *Shimei.* **25:4** Hebrew *Shebuel,* a variant spelling of Shubael; compare 25:20. **25:9** As in Greek version; Hebrew lacks *and twelve of his sons and relatives.* **25:11** Hebrew *Izri,* a variant spelling of Zeri; compare 25:3. **25:14** Hebrew *Jesarelah,* a variant spelling of Asarelah; compare 25:2.

25:1–31 The Musicians. The musicians are grouped under three family heads: Asaph, Heman, and Jeduthun (or Ethan, see 6:44) who were also descended from Levi (see 6:33–47). Their ministry included prophesying with musical instruments (25:1–3). The trained and skilled musicians' role was vital in the worship of God. **2–3, 6:** They were supervised by the heads of their families and also by the king, because of the huge responsibility involved. **4–5:** The names of Heman's fourteen sons are listed, given by God to exalt him. The names from Hananiah to Mahazioth can be read as poetry, or psalm headings, as follows:

Be gracious to me, Yahweh, be gracious to me;
You are my God.
I exalt, I praise [my] helper,
Sitting in adversity I said,
Clear signs give plentifully.

Heman's three daughters are also mentioned (v. 5) and some think that they too were involved as temple musicians, as verse 6 (*All these*; some translations do not include the word *men*) might imply. In Psalm 68:25–26 girls did take part in the music at the processions into the sanctuary, while Nehemiah 7:67 mentions men and women singers (see Women in Worship, Matt 28). **5:** Heman is named as the king's seer. Asaph and Jeduthun are also called seers (2 Chr 29:30; 35:15).

18 The eleventh lot fell to Uzziel* and twelve of his sons and relatives.
19 The twelfth lot fell to Hashabiah and twelve of his sons and relatives.
20 The thirteenth lot fell to Shubael and twelve of his sons and relatives.
21 The fourteenth lot fell to Mattithiah and twelve of his sons and relatives.
22 The fifteenth lot fell to Jerimoth* and twelve of his sons and relatives.
23 The sixteenth lot fell to Hananiah and twelve of his sons and relatives.
24 The seventeenth lot fell to Joshbekashah* and twelve of his sons and relatives.
25 The eighteenth lot fell to Hanani and twelve of his sons and relatives.
26 The nineteenth lot fell to Mallothi and twelve of his sons and relatives.
27 The twentieth lot fell to Eliathah and twelve of his sons and relatives.
28 The twenty-first lot fell to Hothir and twelve of his sons and relatives.
29 The twenty-second lot fell to Giddalti and twelve of his sons and relatives.
30 The twenty-third lot fell to Mahazioth and twelve of his sons and relatives.
31 The twenty-fourth lot fell to Romamti-ezer and twelve of his sons and relatives.

Duties of the Gatekeepers

26 These are the divisions of the gatekeepers:

From the Korahites, there was Meshelemiah
son of Kore, of the family of Abiasaph.* 2 The
sons of Meshelemiah were Zechariah (the
oldest), Jediael (the second), Zebadiah (the
third), Jathniel (the fourth), 3 Elam (the fifth),
Jehohanan (the sixth), and Eliehoenai (the
seventh).
4 The sons of Obed-edom, also gatekeepers,
were Shemaiah (the oldest), Jehozabad (the
second), Joah (the third), Sacar (the fourth),
Nethanel (the fifth), 5 Ammiel (the sixth),
Issachar (the seventh), and Peullethai (the
eighth). God had richly blessed Obed-edom.
6 Obed-edom's son Shemaiah had sons with
great ability who earned positions of great
authority in the clan. 7 Their names were
Othni, Rephael, Obed, and Elzabad. Their
relatives, Elihu and Semakiah, were also very
capable men.
8 All of these descendants of Obed-edom,
including their sons and grandsons—sixty-
two of them in all—were very capable men,
well qualified for their work.
9 Meshelemiah's eighteen sons and relatives
were also very capable men.
10 Hosah, of the Merari clan, appointed Shimri
as the leader among his sons, though he was
not the oldest. 11 His other sons included
Hilkiah (the second), Tebaliah (the third),
and Zechariah (the fourth). Hosah's sons
and relatives, who served as gatekeepers,
numbered thirteen in all.

12 These divisions of the gatekeepers were
named for their family leaders, and like the other
Levites, they served at the house of the LORD.
13 They were assigned by families for guard duty
at the various gates, without regard to age or
training, for it was all decided by means of sacred lots.
14 The responsibility for the east gate went
to Meshelemiah* and his group. The north gate
was assigned to his son Zechariah, a man of unusual wisdom. 15 The south gate went to Obed-
edom, and his sons were put in charge of the
storehouse. 16 Shuppim and Hosah were assigned
the west gate and the gateway leading up to the
Temple.* Guard duties were divided evenly. 17 Six
Levites were assigned each day to the east gate,
four to the north gate, four to the south gate, and
two pairs at the storehouse. 18 Six were assigned
each day to the west gate, four to the gateway
leading up to the Temple, and two to the courtyard.*
19 These were the divisions of the gatekeepers
from the clans of Korah and Merari.

25:18 Hebrew *Azarel,* a variant spelling of Uzziel; compare 25:4. **25:22** Hebrew *Jeremoth,* a variant spelling of Jerimoth; compare 25:4. **25:24** Hebrew *Joshbekasha,* a variant spelling of Joshbekashah; compare 25:4. **26:1** As in Greek version (see also Exod 6:24); Hebrew reads *Asaph.* **26:14** Hebrew *Shelemiah,* a variant spelling of Meshelemiah; compare 26:2. **26:16** Or *the gate of Shalleketh on the upper road* (also in 26:18). The meaning of the Hebrew is uncertain. **26:18** Or *the colonnade.* The meaning of the Hebrew is uncertain.

26:1–32 The Gatekeepers and Other Officials. 1–19: The gatekeepers (cf. 9:17–27) came from the descendants of Korah and Merari, the sons of Levi. The gatekeepers could assist in other ways, ministering in the Temple, or as 9:28–29 indicates, taking care of articles and furnishings used in the Temple service, and flour, wine, oil, incense, and spices used in the offerings. Gatekeepers guarded the Holy Place, keeping out those who should not enter. Theirs was a place of responsibility and privilege (see Ps 84:10). Many are praised as *very capable* or possessing *great ability* or *authority*. **20–32:** Other officials included

Treasurers and Other Officials

[20] Other Levites, led by Ahijah, were in charge of the treasuries of the house of God and the treasuries of the gifts dedicated to the LORD. [21] From the family of Libni* in the clan of Gershon, Jehiel* was the leader. [22] The sons of Jehiel, Zetham and his brother Joel, were in charge of the treasuries of the house of the LORD.

[23] These are the leaders that descended from Amram, Izhar, Hebron, and Uzziel:

[24] From the clan of Amram, Shebuel was a descendant of Gershom son of Moses. He was the chief officer of the treasuries. [25] His relatives through Eliezer were Rehabiah, Jeshaiah, Joram, Zicri, and Shelomoth.

[26] Shelomoth and his relatives were in charge of the treasuries containing the gifts that King David, the family leaders, and the generals and captains* and other officers of the army had dedicated to the LORD. [27] These men dedicated some of the plunder they had gained in battle to maintain the house of the LORD. [28] Shelomoth* and his relatives also cared for the gifts dedicated to the LORD by Samuel the seer, Saul son of Kish, Abner son of Ner, and Joab son of Zeruiah. All the other dedicated gifts were in their care, too.

[29] From the clan of Izhar came Kenaniah. He and his sons were given administrative responsibilities* over Israel as officials and judges.

[30] From the clan of Hebron came Hashabiah. He and his relatives—1,700 capable men—were put in charge of the Israelite lands west of the Jordan River. They were responsible for all matters related to the things of the LORD and the service of the king in that area.

[31] Also from the clan of Hebron came Jeriah,* who was the leader of the Hebronites according to the genealogical records. (In the fortieth year of David's reign, a search was made in the records, and capable men from the clan of Hebron were found at Jazer in the land of Gilead.) [32] There were 2,700 capable men among the relatives of Jeriah. King David sent them to the east side of the Jordan River and put them in charge of the tribes of Reuben and Gad and the half-tribe of Manasseh. They were responsible for all matters related to God and to the king.

Military Commanders and Divisions

27 This is the list of Israelite generals and captains,* and their officers, who served the king by supervising the army divisions that were on duty each month of the year. Each division served for one month and had 24,000 troops.

[2] Jashobeam son of Zabdiel was commander of the first division of 24,000 troops, which was on duty during the first month. [3] He was a descendant of Perez and was in charge of all the army officers for the first month.

[4] Dodai, a descendant of Ahoah, was commander of the second division of 24,000 troops, which was on duty during the second month. Mikloth was his chief officer.

[5] Benaiah son of Jehoiada the priest was commander of the third division of 24,000 troops, which was on duty during the third month. [6] This was the Benaiah who

26:21a Hebrew *Ladan,* a variant spelling of Libni; compare 6:17. **26:21b** Hebrew *Jehieli* (also in 26:22), a variant spelling of Jehiel; compare 23:8. **26:26** Hebrew *the commanders of thousands and of hundreds.* **26:28** Hebrew *Shelomith,* a variant spelling of Shelomoth. **26:29** Or *were given outside work;* or *were given work away from the Temple area.* **26:31** Hebrew *Jerijah,* a variant spelling of Jeriah; compare 23:19. **27:1** Hebrew *commanders of thousands and of hundreds.*

Levites and others in charge of two treasuries: treasures of the Temple under descendants of Gershon, and treasures of dedicated things, spoils taken in war by David, under Shelomoth. Some of these dedicated things were set aside for repair of the Temple either at this time or after the Temple was built. **24:** Shebuel was descended from Moses' son Gershom. **29:** From the Izharites came officials and judges who moved throughout Israel (see also 2 Chr 19:8–11). **30–32:** The Hebronites were given responsibility in the king's service and in the LORD's work over the tribes west of the Jordan and east of the Jordan. Why more men were required to the east of the Jordan, where there were fewer tribes, is not clarified.

27:1–34 Army and Administration

This chapter expands the description of organization of the Temple to organization of Israel. The leaders of the groups here are included in those whom David summoned to give instructions regarding the Temple in 28:1 and 29:1. Unity in Israel, as in all nations, was difficult to attain. The Chronicler shows that love and worship of Yahweh is what had bound and held Israel together in David's day, and the same would apply after the Exile. **1–15:** Each division served for one month under their commander. Either twenty-four units or twenty-four thousand men were in each division. Presumably the leaders were chosen

commanded David's elite military group known as the Thirty. His son Ammizabad was his chief officer.
7 Asahel, the brother of Joab, was commander of the fourth division of 24,000 troops, which was on duty during the fourth month. Asahel was succeeded by his son Zebadiah.
8 Shammah* the Izrahite was commander of the fifth division of 24,000 troops, which was on duty during the fifth month.
9 Ira son of Ikkesh from Tekoa was commander of the sixth division of 24,000 troops, which was on duty during the sixth month.
10 Helez, a descendant of Ephraim from Pelon, was commander of the seventh division of 24,000 troops, which was on duty during the seventh month.
11 Sibbecai, a descendant of Zerah from Hushah, was commander of the eighth division of 24,000 troops, which was on duty during the eighth month.
12 Abiezer from Anathoth in the territory of Benjamin was commander of the ninth division of 24,000 troops, which was on duty during the ninth month.
13 Maharai, a descendant of Zerah from Netophah, was commander of the tenth division of 24,000 troops, which was on duty during the tenth month.
14 Benaiah from Pirathon in Ephraim was commander of the eleventh division of 24,000 troops, which was on duty during the eleventh month.
15 Heled,* a descendant of Othniel from Netophah, was commander of the twelfth division of 24,000 troops, which was on duty during the twelfth month.

Leaders of the Tribes

16 The following were the tribes of Israel and their leaders:

Tribe	*Leader*
Reuben	Eliezer son of Zicri
Simeon	Shephatiah son of Maacah
17 Levi	Hashabiah son of Kemuel
Aaron (the priests)	Zadok
18 Judah	Elihu (a brother of David)
Issachar	Omri son of Michael
19 Zebulun	Ishmaiah son of Obadiah
Naphtali	Jeremoth son of Azriel
20 Ephraim	Hoshea son of Azaziah
Manasseh (west)	Joel son of Pedaiah
21 Manasseh in Gilead (east)	Iddo son of Zechariah
Benjamin	Jaasiel son of Abner
22 Dan	Azarel son of Jeroham

These were the leaders of the tribes of Israel.
23 When David took his census, he did not count those who were younger than twenty years of age, because the LORD had promised to make the Israelites as numerous as the stars in heaven.
24 Joab son of Zeruiah began the census but never finished it because* the anger of God fell on Israel. The total number was never recorded in King David's official records.

Officials of David's Kingdom

25 Azmaveth son of Adiel was in charge of the palace treasuries.
Jonathan son of Uzziah was in charge of the regional treasuries throughout the towns, villages, and fortresses of Israel.
26 Ezri son of Kelub was in charge of the field workers who farmed the king's lands.
27 Shimei from Ramah was in charge of the king's vineyards.
Zabdi from Shepham was responsible for the grapes and the supplies of wine.
28 Baal-hanan from Geder was in charge of the king's olive groves and sycamore-fig trees in the foothills of Judah.*
Joash was responsible for the supplies of olive oil.
29 Shitrai from Sharon was in charge of the cattle on the Sharon Plain.
Shaphat son of Adlai was responsible for the cattle in the valleys.

27:8 Hebrew *Shamhuth*, a variant spelling of Shammah; compare 11:27 and 2 Sam 23:25. **27:15** Hebrew *Heldai*, a variant spelling of Heled; compare 11:30 and 2 Sam 23:29. **27:24** Or *never finished it, and yet.* **27:28** Hebrew *the Shephelah.*

for their capability. Whether the divisions were an on-call army or used all the time for other purposes is not stated. Many of the same names occur in the list of David's mighty men (11:10–31). **16–24:** In this list the twelve tribes are mentioned, but Gad and Asher are omitted; Ephraim and the two halves of Manasseh make up the twelve. These men are called *leaders* rather than tribal elders, so they may have been appointed by the king, perhaps to take part in the census. **23–24:** These verses give a slightly different slant to the account in 21:2, 5–6. **25–31:** Twelve administrators were placed in charge of David's extensive property in Jerusalem and outlying villages. Some of this property would have been accumulated while he was hiding from Saul in Philistia and attacking Israel's enemies (1 Sam 27:8–9), and some would

30 Obil the Ishmaelite was in charge of the
camels.
Jehdeiah from Meronoth was in charge of the
donkeys.
31 Jaziz the Hagrite was in charge of the king's
flocks of sheep and goats.
All these officials were overseers of King David's
property.

32 Jonathan, David's uncle, was a wise counselor to the king, a man of great insight, and a
scribe. Jehiel the Hacmonite was responsible for
teaching the king's sons. 33 Ahithophel was the
royal adviser. Hushai the Arkite was the king's
friend. 34 Ahithophel was succeeded by Jehoiada
son of Benaiah and by Abiathar. Joab was commander of the king's army.

David's Instructions to Solomon

28 David summoned all the officials of
Israel to Jerusalem—the leaders of
the tribes, the commanders of the
army divisions, the other generals and captains,*
the overseers of the royal property and livestock,
the palace officials, the mighty men, and all the
other brave warriors in the kingdom. 2 David rose
to his feet and said: "My brothers and my people!
It was my desire to build a temple where the Ark
of the LORD's Covenant, God's footstool, could
rest permanently. I made the necessary preparations for building it, 3 but God said to me, 'You
must not build a temple to honor my name, for
you are a warrior and have shed much blood.'
4 "Yet the LORD, the God of Israel, has chosen
me from among all my father's family to be king
over Israel forever. For he has chosen the tribe
of Judah to rule, and from among the families
of Judah he chose my father's family. And from
among my father's sons the LORD was pleased to
make me king over all Israel. 5 And from among
my sons—for the LORD has given me many—
he chose Solomon to succeed me on the throne
of Israel and to rule over the LORD's kingdom.
6 He said to me, 'Your son Solomon will build
my Temple and its courtyards, for I have chosen
him as my son, and I will be his father. 7 And if
he continues to obey my commands and regulations as he does now, I will make his kingdom
last forever.'
8 "So now, with God as our witness, and in the
sight of all Israel—the LORD's assembly—I give
you this charge. Be careful to obey all the commands of the LORD your God, so that you may
continue to possess this good land and leave it to
your children as a permanent inheritance.
9 "And Solomon, my son, learn to know the
God of your ancestors intimately. Worship and
serve him with your whole heart and a willing
mind. For the LORD sees every heart and knows

28:1 Hebrew *the commanders of thousands and commanders of hundreds.*

---

have been booty from wars during his reign. **32–34:** Among these advisers, Jonathan and Jehiel are not mentioned elsewhere. Ahithophel later supported Absalom against David, while Hushai remained loyal (2 Sam 15). Abiathar and Joab had remained loyal during Absalom's rebellion but supported Adonijah over Solomon (1 Kgs 1:7). Jehoiada, son of Benaiah, is not mentioned elsewhere, although Benaiah, son of Jehoiada, is (1 Chr 11:22–24; 18:17; 27:5), and a Jehoiada is mentioned in 12:27.

28:1—29:9 Plans and Gifts for the Temple

We continue the account (broken off after 23:2) of the choosing of Solomon to succeed David. David summoned all those involved in leadership, as detailed in the previous chapters. The Chronicler's account simply records the transition of power from David to Solomon, leaving out the intrigues of 1 Kings 1 as irrelevant to God's plan.

28:1–21 David's Instructions to Solomon. 4–8: God had chosen David from among Jesse's sons to be king, and God had chosen Judah out of all the tribes of Israel. God had chosen in the past, and again he chose for the future. Solomon should be king after David and should build the Temple. God gave him the promise of an established kingdom, just as he had promised David. **9–10:** Solomon was given tremendous privilege, and his responsibility was to be unswerving in obedience. This would involve his choice; it was not forced upon him. God's choices were an assurance to Solomon and to the people that his involvement with them was ongoing. The concept of the king as God's chosen emphasized the king's responsibility to rule as God's representative, with God's justice and love. For the Chronicler's readers, the lessons were clear: God's choice of them as his people remained, but as in the past, their choice must be to remain obedient and faithful. In order to see the promises fulfilled, God's people must trust him and obey him. David charged Solomon to be careful to follow all God's commands. The king's obedience was vital, because the people would follow his example. **9:** The LORD searches, knowing hearts and understanding motives, and Solomon must search for God in the same way, seeking to understand and know God, so that he could walk in his ways. If, rather than search to know

every plan and thought. If you seek him, you will find him. But if you forsake him, he will reject you forever. [10]So take this seriously. The LORD has chosen you to build a Temple as his sanctuary. Be strong, and do the work."

[11]Then David gave Solomon the plans for the Temple and its surroundings, including the entry room, the storerooms, the upstairs rooms, the inner rooms, and the inner sanctuary—which was the place of atonement. [12]David also gave Solomon all the plans he had in mind* for the courtyards of the LORD's Temple, the outside rooms, the treasuries, and the rooms for the gifts dedicated to the LORD. [13]The king also gave Solomon the instructions concerning the work of the various divisions of priests and Levites in the Temple of the LORD. And he gave specifications for the items in the Temple that were to be used for worship.

[14]David gave instructions regarding how much gold and silver should be used to make the items needed for service. [15]He told Solomon the amount of gold needed for the gold lampstands and lamps, and the amount of silver for the silver lampstands and lamps, depending on how each would be used. [16]He designated the amount of gold for the table on which the Bread of the Presence would be placed and the amount of silver for other tables.

[17]David also designated the amount of gold for the solid gold meat hooks used to handle the sacrificial meat and for the basins, pitchers, and dishes, as well as the amount of silver for every dish. [18]He designated the amount of refined gold for the altar of incense. Finally, he gave him a plan for the LORD's "chariot"—the gold cherubim* whose wings were stretched out over the Ark of the LORD's Covenant. [19]"Every part of this plan," David told Solomon, "was given to me in writing from the hand of the LORD.*"

[20]Then David continued, "Be strong and courageous, and do the work. Don't be afraid or discouraged, for the LORD God, my God, is with you. He will not fail you or forsake you. He will see to it that all the work related to the Temple of the LORD is finished correctly. [21]The various divisions of priests and Levites will serve in the Temple of God. Others with skills of every kind will volunteer, and the officials and the entire nation are at your command."

Gifts for Building the Temple

29 Then King David turned to the entire assembly and said, "My son Solomon, whom God has clearly chosen as the next king of Israel, is still young and inexperienced. The work ahead of him is enormous, for the Temple he will build is not for mere mortals—it is for the LORD God himself! [2]Using every resource at my command, I have gathered as much as I could for building the Temple of my God. Now there is enough gold, silver, bronze, iron, and wood, as well as great quantities of onyx, other precious stones, costly jewels, and all kinds of fine stone and marble.

[3]"And now, because of my devotion to the Temple of my God, I am giving all of my own private treasures of gold and silver to help in the construction. This is in addition to the building materials I have already collected for his holy Temple. [4]I am donating more than 112 tons of gold* from Ophir and 262 tons of refined silver*

28:12 Or *the plans of the spirit that was with him.* **28:18** Hebrew *for the gold cherub chariot.* **28:19** Or *was written under the direction of the LORD.* **29:4a** Hebrew *3,000 talents* [102 metric tons] *of gold.* **29:4b** Hebrew *7,000 talents* [238 metric tons] *of silver.*

God, Solomon rejected him, God in turn would reject Solomon. **11–19:** More instructions were given for priests and Levites, along with the details of articles to be used in the Temple service. These were to be of the finest gold and silver. Again David had felt God's hand directing him in all these details. He was concerned that everything be both well organized and God-directed. **18:** The *chariot* on which the Ark was to rest perhaps hints at the Chronicler's recollection of the magnificence of the vision that Ezekiel saw long after David's day (Ezek 1). **20–21:** Prayer, preparation, and planning are prerequisites for service for God. Knowing his will and doing things as he directs are central, and counting on his promise day by day is an ongoing necessity. The people of the Chronicler's day needed to take heart in their difficult situation and know that as they put God first and obeyed him faithfully, they would find him faithful. Times for them had changed; David and Solomon and the glories of their kingdoms were long gone, but God was still the same, his word as true and powerful as ever, and they were still his people.

29:1–9 The Joy of Giving. David's devotion for God led him to give huge quantities of the best of his kingdom's and his own resources (see 22:2–5). The word used for David's personal or special treasures (Heb., *segullah*) is the same as is used of Israel as God's treasure (Exod 19:5). David would not offer to God what had cost him nothing (cf. 21:24) but gave what was personal and valuable, knowing that he owed everything he had to God's generosity. **5:** Having

to be used for overlaying the walls of the buildings 5 and for the other gold and silver work to be done by the craftsmen. Now then, who will follow my example and give offerings to the LORD today?"

6 Then the family leaders, the leaders of the tribes of Israel, the generals and captains of the army,* and the king's administrative officers all gave willingly. 7 For the construction of the Temple of God, they gave about 188 tons of gold,* 10,000 gold coins,* 375 tons of silver,* 675 tons of bronze,* and 3,750 tons of iron.* 8 They also contributed numerous precious stones, which were deposited in the treasury of the house of the LORD under the care of Jehiel, a descendant of Gershon. 9 The people rejoiced over the offerings, for they had given freely and wholeheartedly to the LORD, and King David was filled with joy.

David's Prayer of Praise

10 Then David praised the LORD in the presence of the whole assembly:

"O LORD, the God of our ancestor Israel,*
may you be praised forever and ever! 11 Yours,
O LORD, is the greatness, the power, the glory,
the victory, and the majesty. Everything in
the heavens and on earth is yours, O LORD,
and this is your kingdom. We adore you as
the one who is over all things. 12 Wealth and
honor come from you alone, for you rule
over everything. Power and might are in your
hand, and at your discretion people are made
great and given strength.

13 "O our God, we thank you and praise
your glorious name! 14 But who am I, and
who are my people, that we could give
anything to you? Everything we have has
come from you, and we give you only what
you first gave us! 15 We are here for only a
moment, visitors and strangers in the land
as our ancestors were before us. Our days on
earth are like a passing shadow, gone so soon
without a trace.

16 "O LORD our God, even this material
we have gathered to build a Temple to honor
your holy name comes from you! It all
belongs to you! 17 I know, my God, that you
examine our hearts and rejoice when you find
integrity there. You know I have done all this
with good motives, and I have watched your
people offer their gifts willingly and joyously.

18 "O LORD, the God of our ancestors
Abraham, Isaac, and Israel, make your people
always want to obey you. See to it that their
love for you never changes. 19 Give my son
Solomon the wholehearted desire to obey all
your commands, laws, and decrees, and to do
everything necessary to build this Temple, for
which I have made these preparations."

29:6 Hebrew *the commanders of thousands and commanders of hundreds.* **29:7a** Hebrew *5,000 talents* [170 metric tons] *of gold.* **29:7b** Hebrew *10,000 darics* [a Persian coin] *of gold,* about 185 pounds or 84 kilograms in weight. **29:7c** Hebrew *10,000 talents* [340 metric tons] *of silver.* **29:7d** Hebrew *18,000 talents* [612 metric tons] *of bronze.* **29:7e** Hebrew *100,000 talents* [3,400 metric tons] *of iron.* **29:10** *Israel* is the name that God gave to Jacob.

---

given his best, David challenged the leaders, officers, and officials to consecrate themselves. Priests were consecrated to serve God (see Exod 28:41), which meant a lifetime of devoted obedience to God. Their work and words and actions were to honor God. In the same way, these leaders were challenged to give their whole selves to God, their gifts being an outward expression of their devotion to him. True consecration is always expressed in giving, because consecration comes out of love, and true love always involves sacrifice and giving, as God showed by his example (cf. Mark 12:41–44; Luke 7:47). **6–9:** The leaders gave willingly, just as many years before the Israelites had given willingly and generously for the Tabernacle (Exod 35:20–29).

29:10–30 Solomon's Anointing and David's Death

10–20: Before summarizing Solomon's anointing and David's death, verses 10–20 focus on several aspects of praise. **10–13:** As David thought of God's majesty, power, and splendor, he rejoiced in God's exaltation over all things. God's sovereignty and incomparable greatness are extraordinary and bring forth praise, thanks, and worship from his people, who owe him everything. **14–16:** Recognition of God's greatness brings realization of David's and Israel's insignificance and also the source not only of all they have given but the source of the generous spirit of their giving as well. God's people lived in the land as aliens and strangers and their days there were transient; just as their ancestors had come and gone, so would they all. Like a *passing shadow* they would not have stability in themselves. They were there by God's grace alone, not by right. God does not stint in his giving, which is why the people had been able to give so generously. If God's people will not give, they are implying that their God is not generous. **17–20:** God searches the heart (28:9; see also Pss 26:2; 139:23). David was confident that God would find integrity, willingness, and honesty in his heart.

20 Then David said to the whole assembly,
"Give praise to the LORD your God!" And the
entire assembly praised the LORD, the God of
their ancestors, and they bowed low and knelt
before the LORD and the king.

Solomon Named as King

21 The next day they brought 1,000 bulls, 1,000
rams, and 1,000 male lambs as burnt offerings
to the LORD. They also brought liquid offerings
and many other sacrifices on behalf of all Israel.
22 They feasted and drank in the LORD's presence
with great joy that day.

And again they crowned David's son Solomon as their new king. They anointed him before the LORD as their leader, and they anointed
Zadok as priest. 23 So Solomon took the throne
of the LORD in place of his father, David, and he
succeeded in everything, and all Israel obeyed
him. 24 All the officials, the warriors, and the sons
of King David pledged their loyalty to King Solomon. 25 And the LORD exalted Solomon in the
sight of all Israel, and he gave Solomon greater
royal splendor than any king in Israel before
him.

Summary of David's Reign

26 So David son of Jesse reigned over all Israel.
27 He reigned over Israel for forty years, seven of
them in Hebron and thirty-three in Jerusalem.
28 He died at a ripe old age, having enjoyed long
life, wealth, and honor. Then his son Solomon
ruled in his place.

29 All the events of King David's reign, from
beginning to end, are written in *The Record
of Samuel the Seer, The Record of Nathan the
Prophet,* and *The Record of Gad the Seer.* 30 These
accounts include the mighty deeds of his reign
and everything that happened to him and to Israel and to all the surrounding kingdoms.

He prayed that the same would be true of Solomon, thus ensuring that his kingdom would be established. **21–25:** The second acknowledgment of Solomon as king is recorded. The Chronicler now shows him being accepted by *the whole assembly* (v. 20). **22:** The word *again* does not appear in the Septuagint and may not be in the original, but this re-crowning of Solomon was a separate occasion from that given in 1 Kings 1, which was characterized by factions and divided loyalties (see esp. 1 Kgs 1:9, 19, 25). This acceptance is shown in connection with the officers and mighty men, and Solomon's brothers, the king's sons. These were the ones whose loyalty was divided in 1 Kings 1, but the Chronicler shows these divisions overcome. Zadok the priest replaced Abiathar, who had supported Adonijah's claim to kingship (see 16:39; 1 Kgs 2:35; see also 1 Kgs 1:39, where Zadok anointed Solomon). **26–30:** In a summary of David's life and death, David's reign over *all Israel* is reiterated. The first seven years over Judah only is incorporated into the total rule over Israel (see 2 Sam 5:5; 1 Kgs 2:11). God had kept his promise to David (1 Chr 17:11–14), giving him long life, wealth, and honor, and a son to succeed him as king. **29–30:** The writer gives the sources (see, e.g., 10:13; 11:3; 17:1–15; 21:9–13, 18–19) from which he has chosen the details he wishes to emphasize. David's influence reached not only to Israel but also to many other kingdoms, as did the lives of those kings who followed God after him. It is God's purpose to reach out to other nations, to display his glory to them, through his people, but first his people must become strong in their faith, loyalty, and obedience to God. David's life is an example of how God can use such people.

2 CHRONICLES

INTRODUCTION

The church father Jerome is supposed to have said that "the book of Chronicles . . . is of such importance that without it anyone who claims to have a knowledge of the Scriptures makes himself a fool," and yet this is a neglected book among many Christians.

Second Chronicles tells us about the Temple, the festivals, the Levites, and their various roles. The author of Chronicles emphasized ritual and musical matters. He believed in serving Yahweh through the official and formal worship system, emphasizing the central place of Jerusalem and the Temple. It sounds as if he might have been reading Ezekiel and Malachi. The only hope for the returning refugees was in becoming a worshiping congregation centered in the Temple. And of course no joyful ceremony could be complete without music. In 2 Chronicles there are intricate, detailed descriptions of the festivals.

In the Chronicler's opinion, the Levites' role should have been given more significance than had previously been the case. The book was written from the priestly point of view. Of course, there is emphasis on the prophets too. But there are more references to the Levites in the Chronicler's work than in all the rest of the Old Testament.

The Chronicler also recognizes the principle of retribution. People who sin, especially those who abuse the priests and the prophets, are punished. The wonderful stories of this book illustrate this truth again and again. We may also be surprised and gratified by how many references are significant for women. Two women are particularly important, one negatively, and the other positively: Athaliah and Huldah. —*Editors, Oxford University Press*

1:1—9:31	The Reign of Solomon
10:1—16:14	The Reigns of Rehoboam, Abijah, and Asa
17:1—21:1a	The Reign of Jehoshaphat
21:1b—23:21	The Reigns of Jehoram, Ahaziah, and Athaliah
24:1—25:28	The Reigns of Joash and Amaziah
26:1—28:27	The Reigns of Uzziah, Jotham, and Ahaz
29:1—32:33	The Reign of Hezekiah
33:1–25	The Reigns of Manasseh and Amon
34:1—35:27	The Reign of Josiah
36:1–23	The Reigns of Jehoahaz, Jehoiakim, Jehoiachin, and Zedekiah

Solomon Asks for Wisdom

1 Solomon son of David took firm control
of his kingdom, for the LORD his God was
with him and made him very powerful.
2 Solomon called together all the leaders of
Israel—the generals and captains of the army,*
the judges, and all the political and clan leaders.
3 Then he led the entire assembly to the place of
worship in Gibeon, for God's Tabernacle* was
located there. (This was the Tabernacle that Moses, the LORD's servant, had made in the wilderness.)
4 David had already moved the Ark of God
from Kiriath-jearim to the tent he had prepared
for it in Jerusalem. 5 But the bronze altar made
by Bezalel son of Uri and grandson of Hur was
there* at Gibeon in front of the Tabernacle of
the LORD. So Solomon and the people gathered
in front of it to consult the LORD.* 6 There in
front of the Tabernacle, Solomon went up to the
bronze altar in the LORD's presence and sacrificed
1,000 burnt offerings on it.
7 That night God appeared to Solomon and
said, "What do you want? Ask, and I will give
it to you!"
8 Solomon replied to God, "You showed faithful love to David, my father, and now you have
made me king in his place. 9 O LORD God, please
continue to keep your promise to David my father, for you have made me king over a people as
numerous as the dust of the earth! 10 Give me the
wisdom and knowledge to lead them properly,*
for who could possibly govern this great people
of yours?"
11 God said to Solomon, "Because your greatest desire is to help your people, and you did not
ask for wealth, riches, fame, or even the death of
your enemies or a long life, but rather you asked
for wisdom and knowledge to properly govern
my people—12 I will certainly give you the wisdom and knowledge you requested. But I will
also give you wealth, riches, and fame such as no
other king has had before you or will ever have
in the future!"
13 Then Solomon returned to Jerusalem from
the Tabernacle at the place of worship in Gibeon,
and he reigned over Israel.
14 Solomon built up a huge force of chariots
and horses.* He had 1,400 chariots and 12,000
horses. He stationed some of them in the chariot
cities and some near him in Jerusalem. 15 The
king made silver and gold as plentiful in Jerusalem as stone. And valuable cedar timber was
as common as the sycamore-fig trees that grow
in the foothills of Judah.* 16 Solomon's horses
were imported from Egypt* and from Cilicia*;
the king's traders acquired them from Cilicia at
the standard price. 17 At that time chariots from
Egypt could be purchased for 600 pieces of silver,* and horses for 150 pieces of silver.* They
were then exported to the kings of the Hittites
and the kings of Aram.

Preparations for Building the Temple

2 1 *Solomon decided to build a Temple to
honor the name of the LORD, and also a
royal palace for himself. 2 *He enlisted a
force of 70,000 laborers, 80,000 men to quarry
stone in the hill country, and 3,600 foremen.
3 Solomon also sent this message to King Hiram* at Tyre:

1:2 Hebrew *the commanders of thousands and of hundreds.* **1:3** Hebrew *Tent of Meeting;* also in 1:6, 13. **1:5a** As in Greek version and Latin Vulgate, and some Hebrew manuscripts. Masoretic Text reads *he placed.* **1:5b** Hebrew *to consult him.* **1:10** Hebrew *to go out and come in before this people.* **1:14** Or *charioteers;* also in 1:14b. **1:15** Hebrew *the Shephelah.* **1:16a** Possibly *Muzur,* a district near Cilicia; also in 1:17. **1:16b** Hebrew *Kue,* probably another name for Cilicia. **1:17a** Hebrew *600 [shekels] of silver,* about 15 pounds or 6.8 kilograms in weight. **1:17b** Hebrew *150 [shekels],* about 3.8 pounds or 1.7 kilograms in weight. **2:1** Verse 2:1 is numbered 1:18 in Hebrew text. **2:2** Verses 2:2-18 are numbered 2:1-17 in Hebrew text. **2:3** Hebrew *Huram,* a variant spelling of Hiram; also in 2:11.

1:1—9:31 The Reign of Solomon

First Kings tells all of the good things about Solomon, and then describes how badly he turned out. Second Chronicles, however, concentrates on the good part, leaving many negative aspects of the story to other authors.

1:1–17 Solomon's Good Beginning. According to Chronicles, Solomon was devout without exception. He was selected by the LORD to succeed his father without any of the political manipulations reported in 1 Kings, and—again unlike Kings—he had the full support of his people. The story is so unfailingly positive that one who reads only Chronicles might wonder why the kingdom was divided after his death. **7–12:** Solomon began with humility, and when given his choice of whatever he wanted, he asked for the wisdom and knowledge necessary for leadership. He was granted those gifts, alongside many material blessings. The latter were perhaps given to test whether he would use his wisdom wisely.

2:1—4:22 The Temple Built and Furnished. We know that the Chronicler emphasized ritual and musical matters. This is one reason Solomon was so important

"Send me cedar logs as you did for my
father, David, when he was building his
palace. 4 I am about to build a Temple to
honor the name of the LORD my God. It will
be a place set apart to burn fragrant incense
before him, to display the special sacrificial
bread, and to sacrifice burnt offerings each
morning and evening, on the Sabbaths, at
new moon celebrations, and at the other
appointed festivals of the LORD our God.
He has commanded Israel to do these things
forever.

5 "This must be a magnificent Temple
because our God is greater than all other
gods. 6 But who can really build him a
worthy home? Not even the highest heavens
can contain him! So who am I to consider
building a Temple for him, except as a place to
burn sacrifices to him?

7 "So send me a master craftsman who can
work with gold, silver, bronze, and iron, as
well as with purple, scarlet, and blue cloth. He
must be a skilled engraver who can work with
the craftsmen of Judah and Jerusalem who
were selected by my father, David.

8 "Also send me cedar, cypress, and red
sandalwood* logs from Lebanon, for I know
that your men are without equal at cutting
timber in Lebanon. I will send my men to
help them. 9 An immense amount of timber
will be needed, for the Temple I am going to
build will be very large and magnificent. 10 In
payment for your woodcutters, I will send
100,000 bushels of crushed wheat, 100,000
bushels of barley,* 110,000 gallons of wine,
and 110,000 gallons of olive oil.*"

11 King Hiram sent this letter of reply to Solomon:

"It is because the LORD loves his people
that he has made you their king! 12 Praise
the LORD, the God of Israel, who made
the heavens and the earth! He has given
King David a wise son, gifted with skill and
understanding, who will build a Temple for
the LORD and a royal palace for himself.

13 "I am sending you a master craftsman
named Huram-abi, who is extremely
talented. 14 His mother is from the tribe of
Dan in Israel, and his father is from Tyre.
He is skillful at making things from gold,
silver, bronze, and iron, and he also works
with stone and wood. He can work with
purple, blue, and scarlet cloth and fine linen.
He is also an engraver and can follow any
design given to him. He will work with your
craftsmen and those appointed by my lord
David, your father.

15 "Send along the wheat, barley, olive oil,
and wine that my lord has mentioned. 16 We
will cut whatever timber you need from the
Lebanon mountains and will float the logs
in rafts down the coast of the Mediterranean
Sea* to Joppa. From there you can transport
the logs up to Jerusalem."

17 Solomon took a census of all foreigners in
the land of Israel, like the census his father had
taken, and he counted 153,600. 18 He assigned
70,000 of them as common laborers, 80,000 as
quarry workers in the hill country, and 3,600 as
foremen.

Solomon Builds the Temple

3 So Solomon began to build the Temple of
the LORD in Jerusalem on Mount Moriah,
where the LORD had appeared to David,
his father. The Temple was built on the threshing floor of Araunah* the Jebusite, the site that
David had selected. 2 The construction began in
midspring,* during the fourth year of Solomon's
reign.

3 These are the dimensions Solomon used
for the foundation of the Temple of God (us-

2:8 Or *juniper;* Hebrew reads *algum,* perhaps a variant spelling of *almug;* compare 9:10-11 and parallel text at 1 Kgs 10:11-12. **2:10a** Hebrew *20,000 cors* [3,640 kiloliters] *of crushed wheat, 20,000 cors of barley.* **2:10b** Hebrew *20,000 baths* [420 kiloliters] *of wine, and 20,000 baths of olive oil.* **2:16** Hebrew *the sea.* **3:1** Hebrew reads *Ornan,* a variant spelling of Araunah; compare 2 Sam 24:16. **3:2** Hebrew *on the second day of the second month.* This day of the ancient Hebrew lunar calendar occurred in April or May.

---

and why most of the information about him relates to the Temple. Much of the material in these early chapters repeats and develops that found in 1 Chronicles. Solomon built the Temple, relying on the plans and preparations David had made. He made crucial use of skilled craftsmen and building supplies from their northern allies in Phoenicia, again following David's pattern (2:7–10, 13–16; 4:11–17). The Chronicler provides us with all of the details of the construction. One is touched by the elaborate decorations, which must have been breathtaking. **3:2:** The building began in the second month of the fourth year of Solomon's reign. This may mean there was a delay in beginning the work, or it may mean that Solomon, who was made king before David's death (1 Chr 23:1; 1 Kgs 1:32-40), had been co-regent with David for four years.

ing the old standard of measurement).* It was
90 feet long and 30 feet wide.* [4]The entry room
at the front of the Temple was 30 feet* wide, running across the entire width of the Temple, and
30 feet* high. He overlaid the inside with pure
gold.

[5]He paneled the main room of the Temple
with cypress wood, overlaid it with fine gold,
and decorated it with carvings of palm trees and
chains. [6]He decorated the walls of the Temple
with beautiful jewels and with gold from the
land of Parvaim. [7]He overlaid the beams, thresh-
olds, walls, and doors throughout the Temple
with gold, and he carved figures of cherubim on
the walls.

[8]He made the Most Holy Place 30 feet wide,
corresponding to the width of the Temple,
and 30 feet deep. He overlaid its interior with
23 tons* of fine gold. [9]The gold nails that were
used weighed 20 ounces* each. He also overlaid
the walls of the upper rooms with gold.

[10]He made two figures shaped like cherubim,
overlaid them with gold, and placed them in the
Most Holy Place. [11]The total wingspan of the
two cherubim standing side by side was 30 feet.
One wing of the first figure was 7½ feet* long,
and it touched the Temple wall. The other wing,
also 7½ feet long, touched one of the wings of
the second figure. [12]In the same way, the second
figure had one wing 7½ feet long that touched
the opposite wall. The other wing, also 7½ feet
long, touched the wing of the first figure. [13]So
the wingspan of the two cherubim side by side
was 30 feet. They stood on their feet and faced
out toward the main room of the Temple.

[14]Across the entrance of the Most Holy Place
he hung a curtain made of fine linen, decorated
with blue, purple, and scarlet thread and embroidered with figures of cherubim.

[15]For the front of the Temple, he made two
pillars that were 27 feet* tall, each topped by a
capital extending upward another 7½ feet. [16]He
made a network of interwoven chains and used
them to decorate the tops of the pillars. He also
made 100 decorative pomegranates and attached
them to the chains. [17]Then he set up the two pillars at the entrance of the Temple, one to the
south of the entrance and the other to the north.
He named the one on the south Jakin, and the
one on the north Boaz.*

Furnishings for the Temple

4
Solomon* also made a bronze altar 30 feet
long, 30 feet wide, and 15 feet high.* [2]Then
he cast a great round basin, 15 feet across
from rim to rim, called the Sea. It was 7½ feet
deep and about 45 feet in circumference.* [3]It was
encircled just below its rim by two rows of figures that resembled oxen. There were about six
oxen per foot* all the way around, and they were
cast as part of the basin.

[4]The Sea was placed on a base of twelve bronze
oxen, all facing outward. Three faced north, three
faced west, three faced south, and three faced
east, and the Sea rested on them. [5]The walls of
the Sea were about three inches* thick, and its
rim flared out like a cup and resembled a water
lily blossom. It could hold about 16,500 gallons*
of water.

[6]He also made ten smaller basins for washing
the utensils for the burnt offerings. He set five
on the south side and five on the north. But the
priests washed themselves in the Sea.

[7]He then cast ten gold lampstands according
to the specifications that had been given, and he
put them in the Temple. Five were placed against
the south wall, and five were placed against the
north wall.

[8]He also built ten tables and placed them in
the Temple, five along the south wall and five
along the north wall. Then he molded 100 gold
basins.

[9]He then built a courtyard for the priests, and
also the large outer courtyard. He made doors
for the courtyard entrances and overlaid them
with bronze. [10]The great bronze basin called the
Sea was placed near the southeast corner of the
Temple.

[11]Huram-abi also made the necessary washbasins, shovels, and bowls.

So at last Huram-abi completed everything
King Solomon had assigned him to make for the
Temple of God:

3:3a The "old standard of measurement" was a cubit equal to 18 inches [46 centimeters]. The new standard was a cubit of approximately 21 inches [53 centimeters]. **3:3b** Hebrew *60 cubits* [27.6 meters] *long and 20 cubits* [9.2 meters] *wide.* **3:4a** Hebrew *20 cubits* [9.2 meters]; also in 3:8, 11, 13. **3:4b** As in some Greek and Syriac manuscripts, which read *20 cubits* [9.2 meters]; Hebrew reads *120 [cubits],* which is 180 feet or 55 meters. **3:8** Hebrew *600 talents* [20.4 metric tons]. **3:9** Hebrew *50 shekels* [570 grams]. **3:11** Hebrew *5 cubits* [2.3 meters]; also in 3:11b, 12, 15. **3:15** As in Syriac version (see also 1 Kgs 7:15; 2 Kgs 25:17; Jer 52:21), which reads *18 cubits* [8.3 meters]; Hebrew reads *35 cubits,* which is 52.5 feet or 16.5 meters. **3:17** *Jakin* probably means "he establishes"; *Boaz* probably means "in him is strength." **4:1a** Or *Huram-abi;* Hebrew reads *He.* **4:1b** Hebrew *20 cubits* [9.2 meters] *long, 20 cubits wide, and 10 cubits* [4.6 meters] *high.* **4:2** Hebrew *10 cubits* [4.6 meters] *across . . . 5 cubits* [2.3 meters] *deep and 30 cubits* [13.8 meters] *in circumference.* **4:3** Or *20 oxen per meter;* Hebrew reads *10 per cubit.* **4:5a** Hebrew *a handbreadth* [8 centimeters]. **4:5b** Hebrew *3,000 baths* [63 kiloliters].

12 the two pillars;
the two bowl-shaped capitals on top of the
pillars;
the two networks of interwoven chains that
decorated the capitals;
13 the 400 pomegranates that hung from the chains
on the capitals (two rows of pomegranates for
each of the chain networks that decorated the
capitals on top of the pillars);
14 the water carts holding the basins;
15 the Sea and the twelve oxen under it;
16 the ash buckets, the shovels, the meat hooks,
and all the related articles.

Huram-abi made all these things of burnished
bronze for the Temple of the LORD, just as King
Solomon had directed. 17 The king had them cast
in clay molds in the Jordan Valley between Succoth and Zarethan.* 18 Solomon used such great
quantities of bronze that its weight could not be
determined.

19 Solomon also made all the furnishings for
the Temple of God:

the gold altar;
the tables for the Bread of the Presence;
20 the lampstands and their lamps of solid gold,
to burn in front of the Most Holy Place as
prescribed;
21 the flower decorations, lamps, and tongs—all
of the purest gold;
22 the lamp snuffers, bowls, dishes, and incense
burners—all of solid gold;
the doors for the entrances to the Most Holy
Place and the main room of the Temple,
overlaid with gold.

5 So Solomon finished all his work on the
Temple of the LORD. Then he brought all
the gifts his father, David, had dedicated—
the silver, the gold, and the various articles—and
he stored them in the treasuries of the Temple
of God.

The Ark Brought to the Temple

2 Solomon then summoned to Jerusalem the
elders of Israel and all the heads of tribes—the
leaders of the ancestral families of Israel. They
were to bring the Ark of the LORD's Covenant to
the Temple from its location in the City of David,
also known as Zion. 3 So all the men of Israel assembled before the king at the annual Festival of
Shelters, which is held in early autumn.*

4 When all the elders of Israel arrived, the
Levites picked up the Ark. 5 The priests and Levites brought up the Ark along with the special
tent* and all the sacred items that had been in it.
6 There, before the Ark, King Solomon and the
entire community of Israel sacrificed so many
sheep, goats, and cattle that no one could keep
count!

7 Then the priests carried the Ark of the
LORD's Covenant into the inner sanctuary of the
Temple—the Most Holy Place—and placed it
beneath the wings of the cherubim. 8 The cherubim spread their wings over the Ark, forming
a canopy over the Ark and its carrying poles.
9 These poles were so long that their ends could
be seen from the Temple's main room—the Holy
Place*—but not from the outside. They are still
there to this day. 10 Nothing was in the Ark except the two stone tablets that Moses had placed
in it at Mount Sinai,* where the LORD made a
covenant with the people of Israel when they left
Egypt.

11 Then the priests left the Holy Place. All
the priests who were present had purified themselves, whether or not they were on duty that
day. 12 And the Levites who were musicians—
Asaph, Heman, Jeduthun, and all their sons
and brothers—were dressed in fine linen robes
and stood at the east side of the altar playing
cymbals, lyres, and harps. They were joined by
120 priests who were playing trumpets. 13 The
trumpeters and singers performed together in
unison to praise and give thanks to the LORD.
Accompanied by trumpets, cymbals, and other
instruments, they raised their voices and praised
the LORD with these words:

"He is good!
His faithful love endures forever!"

At that moment a thick cloud filled the Temple of the LORD. 14 The priests could not continue
their service because of the cloud, for the glorious
presence of the LORD filled the Temple of God.

4:17 As in parallel text at 1 Kgs 7:46; Hebrew reads *Zeredah.*
5:3 Hebrew *at the festival that is in the seventh month.* The Festival of Shelters began on the fifteenth day of the seventh month of the ancient Hebrew lunar calendar. This day occurred in late September, October, or early November.
5:5 Hebrew *the Tent of Meeting;* i.e., the tent mentioned in 2 Sam 6:17 and 1 Chr 16:1. **5:9** As in some Hebrew manuscripts and Greek version (see also 1 Kgs 8:8); Masoretic Text reads *from the Ark in front of the Most Holy Place.*
5:10 Hebrew *Horeb,* another name for Sinai.

5:1—7:22 Solomon as Worship Leader. When the Temple was completed, Solomon held an elaborate ceremony of dedication, which included processions, numerous sacrifices, musical praise, and extended

Solomon Praises the Lord

6 Then Solomon prayed, "O Lord, you have said that you would live in a thick cloud of darkness. [2] Now I have built a glorious Temple for you, a place where you can live forever!"

[3] Then the king turned around to the entire community of Israel standing before him and gave this blessing: [4] "Praise the Lord, the God of Israel, who has kept the promise he made to my father, David. For he told my father, [5] 'From the day I brought my people out of the land of Egypt, I have never chosen a city among any of the tribes of Israel as the place where a Temple should be built to honor my name. Nor have I chosen a king to lead my people Israel. [6] But now I have chosen Jerusalem as the place for my name to be honored, and I have chosen David to be king over my people Israel.' "

[7] Then Solomon said, "My father, David, wanted to build this Temple to honor the name of the Lord, the God of Israel. [8] But the Lord told him, 'You wanted to build the Temple to honor my name. Your intention is good, [9] but you are not the one to do it. One of your own sons will build the Temple to honor me.'

[10] "And now the Lord has fulfilled the promise he made, for I have become king in my father's place, and now I sit on the throne of Israel, just as the Lord promised. I have built this Temple to honor the name of the Lord, the God of Israel. [11] There I have placed the Ark, which contains the covenant that the Lord made with the people of Israel."

Solomon's Prayer of Dedication

[12] Then Solomon stood before the altar of the Lord in front of the entire community of Israel, and he lifted his hands in prayer. [13] Now Solomon had made a bronze platform 7½ feet long, 7½ feet wide, and 4½ feet high* and had placed it at the center of the Temple's outer courtyard. He stood on the platform, and then he knelt in front of the entire community of Israel and lifted his hands toward heaven. [14] He prayed,

"O Lord, God of Israel, there is no God like
you in all of heaven and earth. You keep your
covenant and show unfailing love to all who
walk before you in wholehearted devotion.
[15] You have kept your promise to your servant
David, my father. You made that promise
with your own mouth, and with your own
hands you have fulfilled it today.
[16] "And now, O Lord, God of Israel, carry
out the additional promise you made to your
servant David, my father. For you said to him,
'If your descendants guard their behavior and
faithfully follow my Law as you have done,
one of them will always sit on the throne of
Israel.' [17] Now, O Lord, God of Israel, fulfill
this promise to your servant David.
[18] "But will God really live on earth among
people? Why, even the highest heavens cannot
contain you. How much less this Temple I
have built! [19] Nevertheless, listen to my prayer
and my plea, O Lord my God. Hear the cry
and the prayer that your servant is making to
you. [20] May you watch over this Temple day
and night, this place where you have said you
would put your name. May you always hear
the prayers I make toward this place. [21] May
you hear the humble and earnest requests
from me and your people Israel when we pray
toward this place. Yes, hear us from heaven
where you live, and when you hear, forgive.
[22] "If someone wrongs another person
and is required to take an oath of innocence
in front of your altar at this Temple, [23] then
hear from heaven and judge between your
servants—the accuser and the accused. Pay
back the guilty as they deserve. Acquit the
innocent because of their innocence.
[24] "If your people Israel are defeated by
their enemies because they have sinned
against you, and if they turn back and
acknowledge your name and pray to you
here in this Temple, [25] then hear from heaven
and forgive the sin of your people Israel and
return them to this land you gave to them
and to their ancestors.
[26] "If the skies are shut up and there is no
rain because your people have sinned against
you, and if they pray toward this Temple and
acknowledge your name and turn from their
sins because you have punished them, [27] then
hear from heaven and forgive the sins of your
servants, your people Israel. Teach them to
follow the right path, and send rain on your
land that you have given to your people as
their special possession.

6:13 Hebrew *5 cubits* [2.3 meters] *long, 5 cubits wide, and 3 cubits* [1.4 meters] *high.*

public prayer. **6:1–20:** According to Solomon's understanding, the building of the Temple in Jerusalem and the Lord's blessings on it constituted his choice of a place where he would permanently place his name, in fulfillment of the long-given promises such as those in Deuteronomy 12. **7:1–3:** The Lord re-

[28]"If there is a famine in the land or a plague or crop disease or attacks of locusts or caterpillars, or if your people's enemies are in the land besieging their towns—whatever disaster or disease there is—[29]and if your people Israel pray about their troubles or sorrow, raising their hands toward this Temple, [30]then hear from heaven where you live, and forgive. Give your people what their actions deserve, for you alone know each human heart. [31]Then they will fear you and walk in your ways as long as they live in the land you gave to our ancestors.

[32]"In the future, foreigners who do not belong to your people Israel will hear of you. They will come from distant lands when they hear of your great name and your strong hand and your powerful arm. And when they pray toward this Temple, [33]then hear from heaven where you live, and grant what they ask of you. In this way, all the people of the earth will come to know and fear you, just as your own people Israel do. They, too, will know that this Temple I have built honors your name.

[34]"If your people go out where you send them to fight their enemies, and if they pray to you by turning toward this city you have chosen and toward this Temple I have built to honor your name, [35]then hear their prayers from heaven and uphold their cause.

[36]"If they sin against you—and who has never sinned?—you might become angry with them and let their enemies conquer them and take them captive to a foreign land far away or near. [37]But in that land of exile, they might turn to you in repentance and pray, 'We have sinned, done evil, and acted wickedly.' [38]If they turn to you with their whole heart and soul in the land of their captivity and pray toward the land you gave to their ancestors—toward this city you have chosen, and toward this Temple I have built to honor your name—[39]then hear their prayers and their petitions from heaven where you live, and uphold their cause. Forgive your people who have sinned against you.

[40]"O my God, may your eyes be open and your ears attentive to all the prayers made to you in this place.

[41]"And now arise, O LORD God, and enter
your resting place,
along with the Ark, the symbol of your
power.
May your priests, O LORD God, be clothed
with salvation;
may your loyal servants rejoice in your
goodness.
[42]O LORD God, do not reject the king you
have anointed.
Remember your unfailing love for your
servant David."

The Dedication of the Temple

7 When Solomon finished praying, fire flashed down from heaven and burned up the burnt offerings and sacrifices, and the glorious presence of the LORD filled the Temple. [2]The priests could not enter the Temple of the LORD because the glorious presence of the LORD filled it. [3]When all the people of Israel saw the fire coming down and the glorious presence of the LORD filling the Temple, they fell face down on the ground and worshiped and praised the LORD, saying,

"He is good!
His faithful love endures forever!"

[4]Then the king and all the people offered sacrifices to the LORD. [5]King Solomon offered a sacrifice of 22,000 cattle and 120,000 sheep and goats. And so the king and all the people dedicated the Temple of God. [6]The priests took their assigned positions, and so did the Levites who were singing, "His faithful love endures forever!" They accompanied the singing with music from the instruments King David had made for praising the LORD. Across from the Levites, the priests blew the trumpets, while all Israel stood.

[7]Solomon then consecrated the central area of the courtyard in front of the LORD's Temple. He offered burnt offerings and the fat of peace offerings there, because the bronze altar he had built could not hold all the burnt offerings, grain offerings, and sacrificial fat.

[8]For the next seven days Solomon and all Israel celebrated the Festival of Shelters.* A large congregation had gathered from as far away as Lebo-hamath in the north and the Brook of Egypt in the south. [9]On the eighth day they had a closing ceremony, for they had celebrated the dedication of the altar for seven days and the

7:8 Hebrew *the festival* (also in 7:9); see note on 5:3.

sponded to Solomon's elaborate prayer with fire from heaven that consumed the burnt offerings and sacrifices, *and the glorious presence of the LORD filled the Temple*. This was a high point in the history of Israel's

Festival of Shelters for seven days. 10 Then at the
end of the celebration,* Solomon sent the people
home. They were all joyful and glad because the
LORD had been so good to David and to Solomon
and to his people Israel.

The LORD's Response to Solomon

11 So Solomon finished the Temple of the LORD,
as well as the royal palace. He completed everything he had planned to do in the construction of
the Temple and the palace. 12 Then one night the
LORD appeared to Solomon and said,

"I have heard your prayer and have chosen
this Temple as the place for making sacrifices.
13 At times I might shut up the heavens so
that no rain falls, or command grasshoppers
to devour your crops, or send plagues among
you. 14 Then if my people who are called by
my name will humble themselves and pray
and seek my face and turn from their wicked
ways, I will hear from heaven and will forgive
their sins and restore their land. 15 My eyes
will be open and my ears attentive to every
prayer made in this place. 16 For I have chosen
this Temple and set it apart to be holy—a
place where my name will be honored
forever. I will always watch over it, for it is
dear to my heart.

17 "As for you, if you faithfully follow me
as David your father did, obeying all my
commands, decrees, and regulations, 18 then I
will establish the throne of your dynasty. For
I made this covenant with your father, David,
when I said, 'One of your descendants will
always rule over Israel.'

19 "But if you or your descendants abandon
me and disobey the decrees and commands I
have given you, and if you serve and worship
other gods, 20 then I will uproot the people
from this land that I have given them. I will
reject this Temple that I have made holy to
honor my name. I will make it an object of
mockery and ridicule among the nations.
21 And though this Temple is impressive
now, all who pass by will be appalled. They
will ask, 'Why did the LORD do such terrible
things to this land and to this Temple?'

22 "And the answer will be, 'Because his
people abandoned the LORD, the God of their
ancestors, who brought them out of Egypt,
and they worshiped other gods instead and
bowed down to them. That is why he has
brought all these disasters on them.' "

Solomon's Many Achievements

8 It took Solomon twenty years to build the
LORD's Temple and his own royal palace.
At the end of that time, 2 Solomon turned
his attention to rebuilding the towns that King
Hiram* had given him, and he settled Israelites
in them.

3 Solomon also fought against the town of
Hamath-zobah and conquered it. 4 He rebuilt
Tadmor in the wilderness and built towns in the
region of Hamath as supply centers. 5 He fortified the towns of Upper Beth-horon and Lower
Beth-horon, rebuilding their walls and installing
barred gates. 6 He also rebuilt Baalath and other
supply centers and constructed towns where his
chariots and horses* could be stationed. He built
everything he desired in Jerusalem and Lebanon
and throughout his entire realm.

7 There were still some people living in the
land who were not Israelites, including the Hittites, Amorites, Perizzites, Hivites, and Jebusites.
8 These were descendants of the nations whom

7:10 Hebrew *Then on the twenty-third day of the seventh month.* This day of the ancient Hebrew lunar calendar occurred in October or early November. **8:2** Hebrew *Huram,* a variant spelling of Hiram; also in 8:18. **8:6** Or *and charioteers.*

religion, rarely matched in what was to come. **14:** *If my people . . . will humble themselves and pray and seek my face and turn from their wicked ways*: It was a big "if," and the rest of 2 Chronicles shows how far Israel fell short of the ideal.

8:1–18 Solomon's Other Activities. 1–8: Solomon's building projects were an important aspect of his administration. After the Temple he constructed a palace and built (or rebuilt) several cities, fortresses, and storage towns. **11:** Eventually Solomon married, or rather began to marry. He first wife was the daughter of the Egyptian pharaoh. This marriage is important for several reasons. The daughter of the pharaoh was not a believer in the LORD (1 Kgs 11:1–8). A marriage between royal houses was for diplomatic and economic reasons, and these kinds of marriages were how Solomon kept the peace and established trade relations. Apparently spiritual considerations played little or no part in the proceedings. The frequent prohibition against marriage with foreigners was always religious, never racial, but here there is no question of Solomon's wife wishing to become a follower of the LORD. Solomon was evidently highly regarded, because pharaohs had refused previously to give their daughters in marriage to foreign kings. In fact, this is the only Old Testament reference to an Egyptian princess marrying a non-Egyptian.

the people of Israel had not destroyed. So Solomon conscripted them for his labor force, and
they serve in the labor force to this day. [9]But
Solomon did not conscript any of the Israelites
for his labor force. Instead, he assigned them to
serve as fighting men, officers in his army, commanders of his chariots, and charioteers. [10]King
Solomon appointed 250 of them to supervise the
people.

[11]Solomon moved his wife, Pharaoh's daughter, from the City of David to the new palace he
had built for her. He said, "My wife must not live
in King David's palace, for the Ark of the LORD
has been there, and it is holy ground."

[12]Then Solomon presented burnt offerings
to the LORD on the altar he had built for him
in front of the entry room of the Temple. [13]He
offered the sacrifices for the Sabbaths, the new
moon festivals, and the three annual festivals—
the Passover celebration, the Festival of Harvest,* and the Festival of Shelters—as Moses had
commanded.

[14]In assigning the priests to their duties,
Solomon followed the regulations of his father,
David. He also assigned the Levites to lead the
people in praise and to assist the priests in their
daily duties. And he assigned the gatekeepers to
their gates by their divisions, following the commands of David, the man of God. [15]Solomon did
not deviate in any way from David's commands
concerning the priests and Levites and the treasuries.

[16]So Solomon made sure that all the work
related to building the Temple of the LORD was
carried out, from the day its foundation was laid
to the day of its completion.

[17]Later Solomon went to Ezion-geber and
Elath,* ports along the shore of the Red Sea* in
the land of Edom. [18]Hiram sent him ships commanded by his own officers and manned by experienced crews of sailors. These ships sailed to
Ophir with Solomon's men and brought back to
Solomon almost seventeen tons* of gold.

Visit of the Queen of Sheba

9 When the queen of Sheba heard of Solomon's fame, she came to Jerusalem to test
him with hard questions. She arrived with
a large group of attendants and a great caravan
of camels loaded with spices, large quantities of
gold, and precious jewels. When she met with
Solomon, she talked with him about everything
she had on her mind. [2]Solomon had answers for
all her questions; nothing was too hard for him
to explain to her. [3]When the queen of Sheba realized how wise Solomon was, and when she saw
the palace he had built, [4]she was overwhelmed.
She was also amazed at the food on his tables,
the organization of his officials and their splendid clothing, the cup-bearers and their robes, and
the burnt offerings Solomon made at the Temple
of the LORD.

[5]She exclaimed to the king, "Everything I
heard in my country about your achievements*
and wisdom is true! [6]I didn't believe what was
said until I arrived here and saw it with my own
eyes. In fact, I had not heard the half of your
great wisdom! It is far beyond what I was told.
[7]How happy your people must be! What a privilege for your officials to stand here day after day,
listening to your wisdom! [8]Praise the LORD your
God, who delights in you and has placed you on
the throne as king to rule for him. Because God
loves Israel and desires this kingdom to last forever, he has made you king over them so you can
rule with justice and righteousness."

[9]Then she gave the king a gift of 9,000
pounds* of gold, great quantities of spices, and
precious jewels. Never before had there been
spices as fine as those the queen of Sheba gave
to King Solomon.

8:13 Or *Festival of Weeks.* **8:17a** As in Greek version (see also 2 Kgs 14:22; 16:6); Hebrew reads *Eloth,* a variant spelling of Elath. **8:17b** As in parallel text at 1 Kgs 9:26; Hebrew reads *the sea.* **8:18** Hebrew *450 talents* [15.3 metric tons]. **9:5** Hebrew *your words.* **9:9** Hebrew *120 talents* [4,000 kilograms].

12–15: Second Chronicles is greatly concerned with the status of the Levites and their suborders, and with the prescribed feasts and festivals. The Chronicler's Solomon starred at this point, as he had in the Temple construction. **17–18:** He was also active in land and sea trade, which enriched him and his kingdom. These riches are detailed in 9:10–11, 13–28.

9:1–12 Solomon and the Queen of Sheba. The queen of Sheba was the undisputed ruler of an ancient realm. Her story is told to accent Solomon's wisdom and wealth, but the story also indicates her importance and influence. She had *a great caravan of camels loaded with spices, large quantities of gold, and precious jewels.* She was also a woman of considerable intelligence and insight: *She talked with him about everything she had on her mind.* **3–9:** When she became aware of his accomplishments, his lifestyle, and his wealth, she was gracious and voluble in her praise. She provided him with elaborate presents, another indication of her status. It is clear that the approval of this woman adds to Solomon's significance and status, although as she received more than she gave, one wonders whether her diplomatic

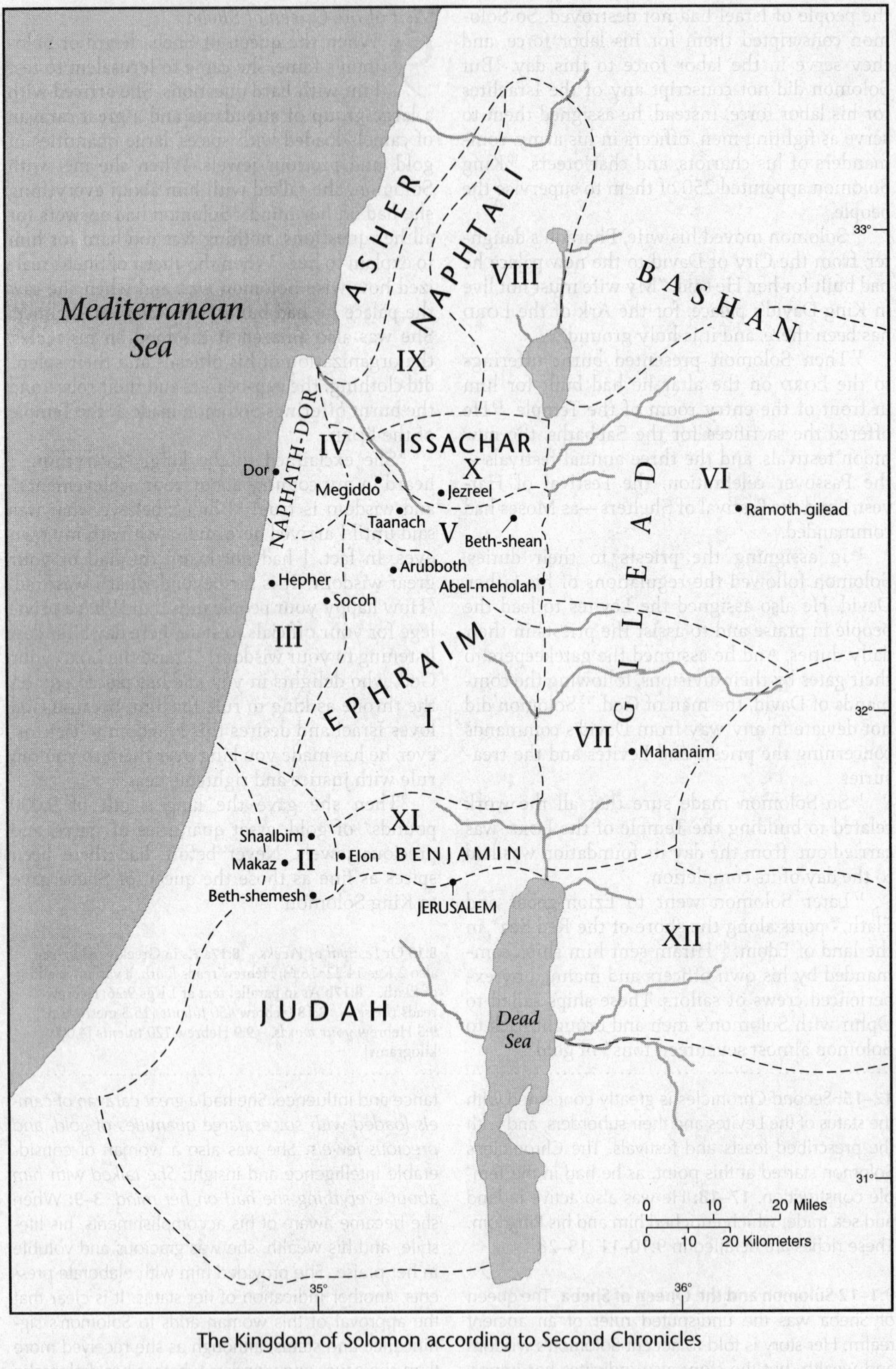

The Kingdom of Solomon according to Second Chronicles

[10](In addition, the crews of Hiram and Solomon brought gold from Ophir, and they also brought red sandalwood* and precious jewels. [11]The king used the sandalwood to make steps* for the Temple of the LORD and the royal palace, and to construct lyres and harps for the musicians. Never before had such beautiful things been seen in Judah.)

[12]King Solomon gave the queen of Sheba whatever she asked for—gifts of greater value than the gifts she had given him. Then she and all her attendants returned to their own land.

Solomon's Wealth and Splendor

[13]Each year Solomon received about 25 tons* of gold. [14]This did not include the additional revenue he received from merchants and traders. All the kings of Arabia and the governors of the provinces also brought gold and silver to Solomon.

[15]King Solomon made 200 large shields of hammered gold, each weighing more than 15 pounds.* [16]He also made 300 smaller shields of hammered gold, each weighing more than 7½ pounds.* The king placed these shields in the Palace of the Forest of Lebanon.

[17]Then the king made a huge throne, decorated with ivory and overlaid with pure gold. [18]The throne had six steps, with a footstool of gold. There were armrests on both sides of the seat, and the figure of a lion stood on each side of the throne. [19]There were also twelve other lions, one standing on each end of the six steps. No other throne in all the world could be compared with it!

[20]All of King Solomon's drinking cups were solid gold, as were all the utensils in the Palace of the Forest of Lebanon. They were not made of silver, for silver was considered worthless in Solomon's day!

[21]The king had a fleet of trading ships* manned by the sailors sent by Hiram.* Once every three years the ships returned, loaded with gold, silver, ivory, apes, and peacocks.*

[22]So King Solomon became richer and wiser than any other king on earth. [23]Kings from every nation came to consult him and to hear the wisdom God had given him. [24]Year after year everyone who visited brought him gifts of silver and gold, clothing, weapons, spices, horses, and mules.

[25]Solomon had 4,000 stalls for his horses and chariots, and he had 12,000 horses.* He stationed some of them in the chariot cities, and some near him in Jerusalem. [26]He ruled over all the kings from the Euphrates River* in the north to the land of the Philistines and the border of Egypt in the south. [27]The king made silver as plentiful in Jerusalem as stone. And valuable cedar timber was as common as the sycamore-fig trees that grow in the foothills of Judah.* [28]Solomon's horses were imported from Egypt* and many other countries.

Summary of Solomon's Reign

[29]The rest of the events of Solomon's reign, from beginning to end, are recorded in *The Record of Nathan the Prophet,* and *The Prophecy of Ahijah from Shiloh,* and also in *The Visions of Iddo the Seer,* concerning Jeroboam son of Nebat. [30]Solomon ruled in Jerusalem over all Israel for forty years. [31]When he died, he was buried in the City of David, named for his father. Then his son Rehoboam became the next king.

The Northern Tribes Revolt

10 Rehoboam went to Shechem, where all Israel had gathered to make him king. [2]When Jeroboam son of Nebat

9:10 Hebrew *algum wood* (also in 9:11); perhaps a variant spelling of *almug.* Compare parallel text at 1 Kgs 10:11-12. **9:11** Or *gateways.* The meaning of the Hebrew is uncertain. **9:13** Hebrew *666 talents* [23 metric tons]. **9:15** Hebrew *600 [shekels] of hammered gold* [6.8 kilograms]. **9:16** Hebrew *300 [shekels] of gold* [3.4 kilograms]. **9:21a** Hebrew *fleet of ships that could sail to Tarshish.* **9:21b** Hebrew *Huram,* a variant spelling of Hiram. **9:21c** Or *and baboons.* **9:25** Or *12,000 charioteers.* **9:26** Hebrew *the river.* **9:27** Hebrew *the Shephelah.* **9:28** Possibly *Muzur,* a district near Cilicia.

---

skills were greater than Solomon realized! **13–28:** The extent of Solomon's wealth is emphasized.

10:1—16:14 The Reigns of Rehoboam, Abijah, and Asa

The Chronicler overlooked Solomon's many shortcomings, even though he had a harder time maintaining that pattern with Solomon's successors. The Chronicler mentioned that the kingdom was divided after Solomon died. The seeds of the catastrophe must have been sown throughout Solomon's years, but the matter came to a head when the young king-to-be, Rehoboam (922–915), sought affirmation of his reign.

10:1-19 The Division of the Kingdom. 2–4: The leader of the northern tribes was Jeroboam the son of Nebat, who eventually became Jeroboam I, the first king of the Northern Kingdom of Israel. Jeroboam expressed his people's desire for relief from the heavy burdens of labor and taxation that Solomon

heard of this, he returned from Egypt, for he had
fled to Egypt to escape from King Solomon. 3 The
leaders of Israel summoned him, and Jeroboam
and all Israel went to speak with Rehoboam.
4 "Your father was a hard master," they said.
"Lighten the harsh labor demands and heavy
taxes that your father imposed on us. Then we
will be your loyal subjects."

5 Rehoboam replied, "Come back in three days
for my answer." So the people went away.

6 Then King Rehoboam discussed the matter
with the older men who had counseled his father, Solomon. "What is your advice?" he asked.
"How should I answer these people?"

7 The older counselors replied, "If you are
good to these people and do your best to please
them and give them a favorable answer, they will
always be your loyal subjects."

8 But Rehoboam rejected the advice of the
older men and instead asked the opinion of the
young men who had grown up with him and
were now his advisers. 9 "What is your advice?"
he asked them. "How should I answer these people who want me to lighten the burdens imposed
by my father?"

10 The young men replied, "This is what you
should tell those complainers who want a lighter burden: 'My little finger is thicker than my
father's waist! 11 Yes, my father laid heavy burdens on you, but I'm going to make them even
heavier! My father beat you with whips, but I
will beat you with scorpions!' "

12 Three days later Jeroboam and all the people returned to hear Rehoboam's decision, just
as the king had ordered. 13 But Rehoboam spoke
harshly to them, for he rejected the advice of the
older counselors 14 and followed the counsel of
his younger advisers. He told the people, "My
father laid* heavy burdens on you, but I'm going
to make them even heavier! My father beat you
with whips, but I will beat you with scorpions!"

15 So the king paid no attention to the people.
This turn of events was the will of God, for it
fulfilled the LORD's message to Jeroboam son of
Nebat through the prophet Ahijah from Shiloh.

16 When all Israel realized* that the king had
refused to listen to them, they responded,

"Down with the dynasty of David!
  We have no interest in the son of Jesse.
Back to your homes, O Israel!
  Look out for your own house, O David!"

So all the people of Israel returned home.
17 But Rehoboam continued to rule over the Israelites who lived in the towns of Judah.

18 King Rehoboam sent Adoniram,* who was
in charge of the labor force, to restore order, but
the people of Israel stoned him to death. When
this news reached King Rehoboam, he quickly
jumped into his chariot and fled to Jerusalem.
19 And to this day the northern tribes of Israel
have refused to be ruled by a descendant of David.

Shemaiah's Prophecy

11 When Rehoboam arrived at Jerusalem, he mobilized the men of Judah and Benjamin—180,000 select
troops—to fight against Israel and to restore the
kingdom to himself.

2 But the LORD said to Shemaiah, the man of
God, 3 "Say to Rehoboam son of Solomon, king of
Judah, and to all the Israelites in Judah and Benjamin: 4 'This is what the LORD says: Do not fight
against your relatives. Go back home, for what
has happened is my doing!' " So they obeyed the
message of the LORD and did not fight against
Jeroboam.

Rehoboam Fortifies Judah

5 Rehoboam remained in Jerusalem and fortified
various towns for the defense of Judah. 6 He built
up Bethlehem, Etam, Tekoa, 7 Beth-zur, Soco,

10:14 As in Greek version and many Hebrew manuscripts (see also 1 Kgs 12:14); Masoretic Text reads *I will lay.* **10:16** As in Syriac version, Latin Vulgate, and many Hebrew manuscripts (see also 1 Kgs 12:16); Masoretic Text lacks *realized.* **10:18** Hebrew *Hadoram,* a variant spelling of Adoniram; compare 1 Kgs 4:6; 5:14; 12:18.

---

had placed on them. **5–16:** Rehoboam, following the wrong instincts and listening to the wrong advisers, decided on a harsh, threatening approach, which was rejected by the northern tribes. In consequence, the one unified nation was instantly turned into two modest kingdoms doomed to generations of struggle against their neighbors and against each other (see 12:15). The division of the kingdom in 922 BC has been called the greatest catastrophe in national history. It certainly had some long-reaching effects. We can only imagine what continued effects this national tragedy had on the wives and mothers of Judah and Israel and their families.

11:1—12:16 Rehoboam's Inept Leadership. This adjective seems ideal to describe Rehoboam of Judah. **1–4:** His pride, naiveté, and attempted tyranny had split the kingdom, so the first thing he did was try to force it back together. The LORD, through his prophet, stopped him. However, Rehoboam had to cope

Adullam, 8 Gath, Mareshah, Ziph, 9 Adoraim, Lachish, Azekah, 10 Zorah, Aijalon, and Hebron. These became the fortified towns of Judah and Benjamin. 11 Rehoboam strengthened their defenses and stationed commanders in them, and he stored supplies of food, olive oil, and wine. 12 He also put shields and spears in these towns as a further safety measure. So only Judah and Benjamin remained under his control.

13 But all the priests and Levites living among the northern tribes of Israel sided with Rehoboam. 14 The Levites even abandoned their pasturelands and property and moved to Judah and Jerusalem, because Jeroboam and his sons would not allow them to serve the LORD as priests. 15 Jeroboam appointed his own priests to serve at the pagan shrines, where they worshiped the goat and calf idols he had made. 16 From all the tribes of Israel, those who sincerely wanted to worship the LORD, the God of Israel, followed the Levites to Jerusalem, where they could offer sacrifices to the LORD, the God of their ancestors. 17 This strengthened the kingdom of Judah, and for three years they supported Rehoboam son of Solomon, for during those years they faithfully followed in the footsteps of David and Solomon.

Rehoboam's Family

18 Rehoboam married his cousin Mahalath, the daughter of David's son Jerimoth and of Abihail, the daughter of Eliab son of Jesse. 19 Mahalath had three sons—Jeush, Shemariah, and Zaham.

20 Later Rehoboam married another cousin, Maacah, the daughter of Absalom. Maacah gave birth to Abijah, Attai, Ziza, and Shelomith. 21 Rehoboam loved Maacah more than any of his other wives and concubines. In all, he had eighteen wives and sixty concubines, and they gave birth to twenty-eight sons and sixty daughters.

22 Rehoboam appointed Maacah's son Abijah as leader among the princes, making it clear that he would be the next king. 23 Rehoboam also wisely gave responsibilities to his other sons and stationed some of them in the fortified towns throughout the land of Judah and Benjamin. He provided them with generous provisions, and he found many wives for them.

Egypt Invades Judah

12 But when Rehoboam was firmly established and strong, he abandoned the Law of the LORD, and all Israel followed him in this sin. 2 Because they were unfaithful to the LORD, King Shishak of Egypt came up and attacked Jerusalem in the fifth year of King Rehoboam's reign. 3 He came with 1,200 chariots, 60,000 horses,* and a countless army of foot soldiers, including Libyans, Sukkites, and Ethiopians.* 4 Shishak conquered Judah's fortified towns and then advanced to attack Jerusalem.

5 The prophet Shemaiah then met with Rehoboam and Judah's leaders, who had all fled to Jerusalem because of Shishak. Shemaiah told them, "This is what the LORD says: You have abandoned me, so I am abandoning you to Shishak."

6 Then the leaders of Israel and the king humbled themselves and said, "The LORD is right in doing this to us!"

7 When the LORD saw their change of heart, he gave this message to Shemaiah: "Since the people have humbled themselves, I will not completely destroy them and will soon give them some relief. I will not use Shishak to pour out my anger on Jerusalem. 8 But they will become his subjects, so they will know the difference between serving me and serving earthly rulers."

9 So King Shishak of Egypt came up and attacked Jerusalem. He ransacked the treasuries of the LORD's Temple and the royal palace; he stole

12:3a Or *charioteers, or horsemen.* **12:3b** Hebrew *and Cushites.*

with the economic loss and political confusion that he had caused. **18–22:** These verses are representative of numerous similar references throughout the book. They refer to Rehoboam's wives, specifically Maacah the mother of the crown prince and, after her husband's death, the queen mother. It is significant that the record is so careful to include these influential women. Often the king's mother seems to be more prominent than his wife. This recognition of the queen mother is an exceptional emphasis in the ancient Near East. (Rehoboam's mother's name is listed in 12:13.) Rehoboam, like many royals and nobles of those times, followed the example of David and Solomon in taking many wives and concubines.

12:1–16: Here, Rehoboam was close to the LORD in the beginning but strayed away later. In contrast, 1 Kings seems to consider him unfaithful from the start. **1:** At this point, *he abandoned the Law of the LORD, and all Israel followed him.* **2–4:** As punishment, the LORD sent the Egyptian pharaoh Shishak against him in 918 BC. This first Egyptian ruler named in the Bible captured Rehoboam's fortifications and threatened Jerusalem. **5–9:** Because Rehoboam heeded the warnings of the prophet Shemaiah, the LORD relented and spared Judah from destruction. This familiar pattern of judgment and grace is found throughout the historical books. Nevertheless, the judgment on Jerusalem was severe: The enemy ruler took away everything, including all the gold shields Solomon had made. 10 King Rehoboam later replaced them with bronze shields as substitutes, and he entrusted them to the care of the commanders of the guard who protected the entrance to the royal palace. 11 Whenever the king went to the Temple of the LORD, the guards would also take the shields and then return them to the guardroom. 12 Because Rehoboam humbled himself, the LORD's anger was turned away, and he did not destroy him completely. There were still some good things in the land of Judah.

Summary of Rehoboam's Reign

13 King Rehoboam firmly established himself in Jerusalem and continued to rule. He was forty-one years old when he became king, and he reigned seventeen years in Jerusalem, the city the LORD had chosen from among all the tribes of Israel as the place to honor his name. Rehoboam's mother was Naamah, a woman from Ammon. 14 But he was an evil king, for he did not seek the LORD with all his heart.

15 The rest of the events of Rehoboam's reign, from beginning to end, are recorded in *The Record of Shemaiah the Prophet* and *The Record of Iddo the Seer,* which are part of the genealogical record. Rehoboam and Jeroboam were continually at war with each other. 16 When Rehoboam died, he was buried in the City of David. Then his son Abijah became the next king.

Abijah's War with Jeroboam

13 Abijah began to rule over Judah in the eighteenth year of Jeroboam's reign in Israel. 2 He reigned in Jerusalem three years. His mother was Maacah,* the daughter of Uriel from Gibeah.

Then war broke out between Abijah and Jeroboam. 3 Judah, led by King Abijah, fielded 400,000 select warriors, while Jeroboam mustered 800,000 select troops from Israel.

4 When the army of Judah arrived in the hill country of Ephraim, Abijah stood on Mount Zemaraim and shouted to Jeroboam and all Israel: "Listen to me! 5 Don't you realize that the LORD, the God of Israel, made a lasting covenant* with David, giving him and his descendants the throne of Israel forever? 6 Yet Jeroboam son of Nebat, a mere servant of David's son Solomon, rebelled against his master. 7 Then a whole gang of scoundrels joined him, defying Solomon's son Rehoboam when he was young and inexperienced and could not stand up to them.

8 "Do you really think you can stand against the kingdom of the LORD that is led by the descendants of David? You may have a vast army, and you have those gold calves that Jeroboam made as your gods. 9 But you have chased away the priests of the LORD (the descendants of Aaron) and the Levites, and you have appointed your own priests, just like the pagan nations. You let anyone become a priest these days! Whoever comes to be dedicated with a young bull and seven rams can become a priest of these so-called gods of yours!

10 "But as for us, the LORD is our God, and we have not abandoned him. Only the descendants of Aaron serve the LORD as priests, and the Levites alone may help them in their work. 11 They present burnt offerings and fragrant incense to the LORD every morning and evening. They place the Bread of the Presence on the holy table, and they light the gold lampstand every evening. We are following the instructions of the LORD our God, but you have abandoned him. 12 So you see, God is with us. He is our leader. His priests blow their trumpets and lead us into battle against you. O people of Israel, do not fight against the LORD, the God of your ancestors, for you will not succeed!"

13 Meanwhile, Jeroboam had secretly sent part of his army around behind the men of Judah to ambush them. 14 When Judah realized that they were being attacked from the front and the rear, they cried out to the LORD for help. Then the priests blew the trumpets, 15 and the men of Judah began to shout. At the sound of their battle cry,

13:2 As in most Greek manuscripts and Syriac version (see also 2 Chr 11:20-21; 1 Kgs 15:2); Hebrew reads *Micaiah,* a variant spelling of Maacah. **13:5** Hebrew *a covenant of salt.*

the treasures of the Temple and the palace. **10–11:** Rehoboam maintained a show of continued dignity by replacing Solomon's famous shields of gold with similar implements of bronze. It is a fitting metaphor for Rehoboam. Through his incompetent leadership, he was able to turn gold into bronze.

13:1–22 Abijah. Rehoboam's son Abijah (915–913) was next in line. His mother's name was Maacah. We do not have enough information to say that Abijah was like his mother, but he was certainly like his father (1 Kgs 15:3)! He too fought against Jeroboam I of Israel (13:2). Unlike Rehoboam, Abijah was at least partially successful, probably because of the LORD's faithfulness to his promises to David and Solomon and his favor for Jerusalem, and because Jeroboam I's sins were always pictured as even worse than those of his counterparts in Judah.

God defeated Jeroboam and all Israel and routed them before Abijah and the army of Judah.

16 The Israelite army fled from Judah, and God handed them over to Judah in defeat. 17 Abijah and his army inflicted heavy losses on them; 500,000 of Israel's select troops were killed that day. 18 So Judah defeated Israel on that occasion because they trusted in the LORD, the God of their ancestors. 19 Abijah and his army pursued Jeroboam's troops and captured some of his towns, including Bethel, Jeshanah, and Ephron, along with their surrounding villages.

20 So Jeroboam of Israel never regained his power during Abijah's lifetime, and finally the LORD struck him down and he died. 21 Meanwhile, Abijah of Judah grew more and more powerful. He married fourteen wives and had twenty-two sons and sixteen daughters.

22 The rest of the events of Abijah's reign, including his words and deeds, are recorded in *The Commentary of Iddo the Prophet.*

Early Years of Asa's Reign

14 1 *When Abijah died, he was buried in the City of David. Then his son Asa became the next king. There was peace in the land for ten years. 2 *Asa did what was pleasing and good in the sight of the LORD his God. 3 He removed the foreign altars and the pagan shrines. He smashed the sacred pillars and cut down the Asherah poles. 4 He commanded the people of Judah to seek the LORD, the God of their ancestors, and to obey his law and his commands. 5 Asa also removed the pagan shrines, as well as the incense altars from every one of Judah's towns. So Asa's kingdom enjoyed a period of peace. 6 During those peaceful years, he was able to build up the fortified towns throughout Judah. No one tried to make war against him at this time, for the LORD was giving him rest from his enemies.

7 Asa told the people of Judah, "Let us build towns and fortify them with walls, towers, gates, and bars. The land is still ours because we sought the LORD our God, and he has given us peace on every side." So they went ahead with these projects and brought them to completion.

8 King Asa had an army of 300,000 warriors from the tribe of Judah, armed with large shields and spears. He also had an army of 280,000 warriors from the tribe of Benjamin, armed with small shields and bows. Both armies were composed of well-trained fighting men.

9 Once an Ethiopian* named Zerah attacked Judah with an army of 1,000,000 men* and 300 chariots. They advanced to the town of Mareshah, 10 so Asa deployed his armies for battle in the valley north of Mareshah.* 11 Then Asa cried out to the LORD his God, "O LORD, no one but you can help the powerless against the mighty! Help us, O LORD our God, for we trust in you alone. It is in your name that we have come against this vast horde. O LORD, you are our God; do not let mere men prevail against you!"

12 So the LORD defeated the Ethiopians* in the presence of Asa and the army of Judah, and the enemy fled. 13 Asa and his army pursued them as far as Gerar, and so many Ethiopians fell that they were unable to rally. They were destroyed by the LORD and his army, and the army of Judah carried off a vast amount of plunder.

14 While they were at Gerar, they attacked all the towns in that area, and terror from the LORD came upon the people there. As a result, a vast amount of plunder was taken from these towns, too. 15 They also attacked the camps of herdsmen and captured many sheep, goats, and camels before finally returning to Jerusalem.

Asa's Religious Reforms

15 Then the Spirit of God came upon Azariah son of Oded, 2 and he went out to meet King Asa as he was returning from the battle. "Listen to me, Asa!" he shouted. "Listen, all you people of Judah and Benjamin! The LORD will stay with you as long as you stay with him! Whenever you seek him, you will find

14:1 Verse 14:1 is numbered 13:23 in Hebrew text.
14:2 Verses 14:2-15 are numbered 14:1-14 in Hebrew text. **14:9a** Hebrew *a Cushite.* **14:9b** Or *an army of thousands and thousands;* Hebrew reads *an army of a thousand thousands.* **14:10** Or *in the Zephathah Valley near Mareshah.* **14:12** Hebrew *Cushites;* also in 14:13.

14:1–15 Asa's Early Years. It is not always true that the good die young. Abijah ruled only three years, while his son, Asa (913–873), reigned for forty. And *Asa did what was pleasing and good* in God's eyes. He was exactly what Judah needed at that time, a reforming king. When an immense Ethiopian army came against Judah, Asa was prepared. He asked the LORD for help, received it, and was victorious. Inspired by prophetic support, he led the people in a far-reaching spiritual renewal, following military victory with spiritual victory.

15:1–19 Asa's Religious Reforms. Asa destroyed the foreign altars and places of pagan worship that had begun to creep into the land during the time of Solomon and the following two reigns. He broke down the symbols of Canaanite fertility religion and encouraged his people by word and example to seek

him. But if you abandon him, he will abandon you. 3 For a long time Israel was without the true God, without a priest to teach them, and without the Law to instruct them. 4 But whenever they were in trouble and turned to the LORD, the God of Israel, and sought him out, they found him.

5 "During those dark times, it was not safe to travel. Problems troubled the people of every land. 6 Nation fought against nation, and city against city, for God was troubling them with every kind of problem. 7 But as for you, be strong and courageous, for your work will be rewarded."

8 When Asa heard this message from Azariah the prophet,* he took courage and removed all the detestable idols from the land of Judah and Benjamin and in the towns he had captured in the hill country of Ephraim. And he repaired the altar of the LORD, which stood in front of the entry room of the LORD's Temple.

9 Then Asa called together all the people of Judah and Benjamin, along with the people of Ephraim, Manasseh, and Simeon who had settled among them. For many from Israel had moved to Judah during Asa's reign when they saw that the LORD his God was with him. 10 The people gathered at Jerusalem in late spring,* during the fifteenth year of Asa's reign.

11 On that day they sacrificed to the LORD 700 cattle and 7,000 sheep and goats from the plunder they had taken in the battle. 12 Then they entered into a covenant to seek the LORD, the God of their ancestors, with all their heart and soul. 13 They agreed that anyone who refused to seek the LORD, the God of Israel, would be put to death—whether young or old, man or woman. 14 They shouted out their oath of loyalty to the LORD with trumpets blaring and rams' horns sounding. 15 All in Judah were happy about this covenant, for they had entered into it with all their heart. They earnestly sought after God, and they found him. And the LORD gave them rest from their enemies on every side.

16 King Asa even deposed his grandmother* Maacah from her position as queen mother because she had made an obscene Asherah pole. He cut down her obscene pole, broke it up, and burned it in the Kidron Valley. 17 Although the pagan shrines were not removed from Israel, Asa's heart remained completely faithful throughout his life. 18 He brought into the Temple of God the silver and gold and the various items that he and his father had dedicated.

19 So there was no more war until the thirty-fifth year of Asa's reign.

Final Years of Asa's Reign

16 In the thirty-sixth year of Asa's reign, King Baasha of Israel invaded Judah and fortified Ramah in order to prevent anyone from entering or leaving King Asa's territory in Judah.

2 Asa responded by removing the silver and gold from the treasuries of the Temple of the LORD and the royal palace. He sent it to King Ben-hadad of Aram, who was ruling in Damascus, along with this message:

> 3 "Let there be a treaty* between you and me like the one between your father and my father. See, I am sending you silver and gold. Break your treaty with King Baasha of Israel so that he will leave me alone."

4 Ben-hadad agreed to King Asa's request and sent the commanders of his army to attack the towns of Israel. They conquered the towns of Ijon, Dan, Abel-beth-maacah,* and all the store cities in Naphtali. 5 As soon as Baasha of Israel heard what was happening, he abandoned his project of fortifying Ramah and stopped all work on it. 6 Then King Asa called out all the men of Judah to carry away the building stones and timbers that Baasha had been using to fortify Ramah. Asa used these materials to fortify the towns of Geba and Mizpah.

7 At that time Hanani the seer came to King

15:8 As in Syriac version and Latin Vulgate (see also 15:1); Hebrew reads *from Oded the prophet.* **15:10** Hebrew *in the third month.* This month of the ancient Hebrew lunar calendar usually occurs within the months of May and June. **15:16** Hebrew *his mother.* **16:3** As in Greek version; Hebrew reads *There is a treaty.* **16:4** As in parallel text at 1 Kgs 15:20; Hebrew reads *Abel-maim,* another name for Abel-beth-maacah.

---

the LORD. Accordingly, the land also rested during his time. **16:** One curious incident involving King Asa's grandmother sheds more light on the influence of women in the royal court of Judah. Maacah, Abijah's mother, clearly had continuing influence. Asa removed her from her position as queen mother because she had made an image for Asherah, the Canaanite goddess. This indicates that women's actions were taken seriously and seen as significant, even when in a negative sense.

16:1–14 Asa's Final Years. Asa spent his final years in continual warfare and in estrangement from the LORD. In order to hire as an ally Ben-hadad of Syria (Aram), he stripped the Temple and palace of their treasures, which had been replaced after Shishak's invasion and

Asa and told him, "Because you have put your
trust in the king of Aram instead of in the LORD
your God, you missed your chance to destroy the
army of the king of Aram. 8Don't you remember
what happened to the Ethiopians* and Libyans
and their vast army, with all of their chariots
and charioteers?* At that time you relied on the
LORD, and he handed them over to you. 9The
eyes of the LORD search the whole earth in order
to strengthen those whose hearts are fully committed to him. What a fool you have been! From
now on you will be at war."
10Asa became so angry with Hanani for saying this that he threw him into prison and put
him in stocks. At that time Asa also began to oppress some of his people.

Summary of Asa's Reign

11The rest of the events of Asa's reign, from beginning to end, are recorded in *The Book of the
Kings of Judah and Israel.* 12In the thirty-ninth
year of his reign, Asa developed a serious foot
disease. Yet even with the severity of his disease,
he did not seek the LORD's help but turned only
to his physicians. 13So he died in the forty-first
year of his reign. 14He was buried in the tomb he
had carved out for himself in the City of David.
He was laid on a bed perfumed with sweet spices
and fragrant ointments, and the people built a
huge funeral fire in his honor.

Jehoshaphat Rules in Judah

17 Then Jehoshaphat, Asa's son, became
the next king. He strengthened Judah
to stand against any attack from Isra-
el. 2He stationed troops in all the fortified towns
of Judah, and he assigned additional garrisons to
the land of Judah and to the towns of Ephraim
that his father, Asa, had captured.
3The LORD was with Jehoshaphat because
he followed the example of his father's early
years* and did not worship the images of Baal.
4He sought his father's God and obeyed his commands instead of following the evil practices of
the kingdom of Israel. 5So the LORD established
Jehoshaphat's control over the kingdom of Judah.
All the people of Judah brought gifts to Jehoshaphat, so he became very wealthy and highly esteemed. 6He was deeply committed to* the ways
of the LORD. He removed the pagan shrines and
Asherah poles from Judah.
7In the third year of his reign Jehoshaphat
sent his officials to teach in all the towns of Judah. These officials included Ben-hail, Obadiah,
Zechariah, Nethanel, and Micaiah. 8He sent
Levites along with them, including Shemaiah,
Nethaniah, Zebadiah, Asahel, Shemiramoth, Jehonathan, Adonijah, Tobijah, and Tob-adonijah.
He also sent out the priests Elishama and Jehoram. 9They took copies of the Book of the Law
of the LORD and traveled around through all the
towns of Judah, teaching the people.
10Then the fear of the LORD fell over all the
surrounding kingdoms so that none of them
wanted to declare war on Jehoshaphat. 11Some
of the Philistines brought him gifts and silver as
tribute, and the Arabs brought 7,700 rams and
7,700 male goats.
12So Jehoshaphat became more and more
powerful and built fortresses and storage cities
throughout Judah. 13He stored numerous supplies in Judah's towns and stationed an army of
seasoned troops at Jerusalem. 14His army was
enrolled according to ancestral clans.

From Judah there were 300,000 troops
organized in units of 1,000, under the
command of Adnah. 15Next in command
was Jehohanan, who commanded 280,000
troops. 16Next was Amasiah son of Zicri,

16:8a Hebrew *Cushites.* **16:8b** Or *and horsemen?*
17:3 Some Hebrew manuscripts read *the example of his father, David.* **17:6** Hebrew *His heart was courageous in.*

would be removed and replaced again. Ben-hadad attacked and defeated Asa's enemy, Baasha, the king of Israel. **7–10:** The problem, according to Hanani the prophet (*seer* is used synonymously with "prophet"), was that Asa relied on foreign allies rather than on the LORD. Asa's response is the first biblical record of royal persecution of a prophet and a sad end to a promising reign.

17:1—21:1a The Reign of Jehoshaphat

If kings like Asa were seen as average and ones like Rehoboam as poor, there were those like Jehoshaphat (873–849) who were viewed more positively. He was somewhat naive, but godly and sincere.

17:1–19 Jehoshaphat's Early Years. 3–6: Jehoshaphat, whose mother was Azubah (20:31), was another reformer. He turned Judah in a better direction. He *sought his father's God and obeyed his commandments. . . . He was deeply committed to the ways of the LORD.* As a result, he removed the high places and sacred poles, or Asherim, from Judah. **7–11:** Jehoshaphat was something of an evangelist; he sent officials and teachers throughout Judah to instruct people in God's law.

who volunteered for the LORD's service, with 200,000 troops under his command.
17 From Benjamin there were 200,000 troops equipped with bows and shields. They were under the command of Eliada, a veteran soldier. 18 Next in command was Jehozabad, who commanded 180,000 armed men.

19 These were the troops stationed in Jerusalem to serve the king, besides those Jehoshaphat stationed in the fortified towns throughout Judah.

Jehoshaphat and Ahab

18 Jehoshaphat enjoyed great riches and high esteem, and he made an alliance with Ahab of Israel by having his son marry Ahab's daughter. 2 A few years later he went to Samaria to visit Ahab, who prepared a great banquet for him and his officials. They butchered great numbers of sheep, goats, and cattle for the feast. Then Ahab enticed Jehoshaphat to join forces with him to recover Ramoth-gilead.

3 "Will you go with me to Ramoth-gilead?" King Ahab of Israel asked King Jehoshaphat of Judah.

Jehoshaphat replied, "Why, of course! You and I are as one, and my troops are your troops. We will certainly join you in battle." 4 Then Jehoshaphat added, "But first let's find out what the LORD says."

5 So the king of Israel summoned the prophets, 400 of them, and asked them, "Should we go to war against Ramoth-gilead, or should I hold back?"

They all replied, "Yes, go right ahead! God will give the king victory."

6 But Jehoshaphat asked, "Is there not also a prophet of the LORD here? We should ask him the same question."

7 The king of Israel replied to Jehoshaphat, "There is one more man who could consult the LORD for us, but I hate him. He never prophesies anything but trouble for me! His name is Micaiah son of Imlah."

Jehoshaphat replied, "That's not the way a king should talk! Let's hear what he has to say."

8 So the king of Israel called one of his officials and said, "Quick! Bring Micaiah son of Imlah."

Micaiah Prophesies against Ahab

9 King Ahab of Israel and King Jehoshaphat of Judah, dressed in their royal robes, were sitting on thrones at the threshing floor near the gate of Samaria. All of Ahab's prophets were prophesying there in front of them. 10 One of them, Zedekiah son of Kenaanah, made some iron horns and proclaimed, "This is what the LORD says: With these horns you will gore the Arameans to death!"

11 All the other prophets agreed. "Yes," they said, "go up to Ramoth-gilead and be victorious, for the LORD will give the king victory!"

12 Meanwhile, the messenger who went to get Micaiah said to him, "Look, all the prophets are promising victory for the king. Be sure that you agree with them and promise success."

13 But Micaiah replied, "As surely as the LORD lives, I will say only what my God says."

14 When Micaiah arrived before the king, Ahab asked him, "Micaiah, should we go to war against Ramoth-gilead, or should I hold back?"

Micaiah replied sarcastically, "Yes, go up and be victorious, for you will have victory over them!"

15 But the king replied sharply, "How many times must I demand that you speak only the truth to me when you speak for the LORD?"

16 Then Micaiah told him, "In a vision I saw all Israel scattered on the mountains, like sheep without a shepherd. And the LORD said, 'Their master has been killed.* Send them home in peace.' "

17 "Didn't I tell you?" the king of Israel exclaimed to Jehoshaphat. "He never prophesies anything but trouble for me."

18 Then Micaiah continued, "Listen to what the LORD says! I saw the LORD sitting on his throne with all the armies of heaven around him, on his right and on his left. 19 And the LORD said, 'Who can entice King Ahab of Israel to go into battle against Ramoth-gilead so he can be killed?'

"There were many suggestions, 20 and finally a spirit approached the LORD and said, 'I can do it!'

" 'How will you do this?' the LORD asked.

21 "And the spirit replied, 'I will go out and inspire all of Ahab's prophets to speak lies.'

18:16 Hebrew *These people have no master.*

18:1–34 Jehoshaphat's Mistakes. Jehoshaphat's naiveté is most evidenced by his cooperation with the corrupt king Ahab of Israel. How else can one explain his close alliance with Ahab, strengthened through the marriage of Ahab and Jezebel's daughter, Athaliah, to Jehoshaphat's son Jehoram? This marriage had later, unfortunate consequences for Judah. **3–27:** This alliance led to Jehoshaphat's fighting alongside Ahab to retake the Transjordanian city of Ramoth-gilead. God warned Jehoshaphat against this inappropriate alliance by using the message and example of the absolutely fearless prophet, Micaiah, who dared to stand alone against Ahab and his sycophantic court prophets. **28–34:** Further evidence of

" 'You will succeed,' said the LORD. 'Go ahead and do it.'

22 "So you see, the LORD has put a lying spirit in the mouths of your prophets. For the LORD has pronounced your doom."

23 Then Zedekiah son of Kenaanah walked up to Micaiah and slapped him across the face. "Since when did the Spirit of the LORD leave me to speak to you?" he demanded.

24 And Micaiah replied, "You will find out soon enough when you are trying to hide in some secret room!"

25 "Arrest him!" the king of Israel ordered. "Take him back to Amon, the governor of the city, and to my son Joash. 26 Give them this order from the king: 'Put this man in prison, and feed him nothing but bread and water until I return safely from the battle!' "

27 But Micaiah replied, "If you return safely, it will mean that the LORD has not spoken through me!" Then he added to those standing around, "Everyone mark my words!"

The Death of Ahab

28 So King Ahab of Israel and King Jehoshaphat of Judah led their armies against Ramoth-gilead. 29 The king of Israel said to Jehoshaphat, "As we go into battle, I will disguise myself so no one will recognize me, but you wear your royal robes." So the king of Israel disguised himself, and they went into battle.

30 Meanwhile, the king of Aram had issued these orders to his chariot commanders: "Attack only the king of Israel! Don't bother with anyone else." 31 So when the Aramean chariot commanders saw Jehoshaphat in his royal robes, they went after him. "There is the king of Israel!" they shouted. But Jehoshaphat called out, and the LORD saved him. God helped him by turning the attackers away from him. 32 As soon as the chariot commanders realized he was not the king of Israel, they stopped chasing him.

33 An Aramean soldier, however, randomly shot an arrow at the Israelite troops and hit the king of Israel between the joints of his armor. "Turn the horses* and get me out of here!" Ahab groaned to the driver of the chariot. "I'm badly wounded!"

34 The battle raged all that day, and the king of Israel propped himself up in his chariot facing the Arameans. In the evening, just as the sun was setting, he died.

Jehoshaphat Appoints Judges

19 When King Jehoshaphat of Judah arrived safely home in Jerusalem, 2 Jehu son of Hanani the seer went out to meet him. "Why should you help the wicked and love those who hate the LORD?" he asked the king. "Because of what you have done, the LORD is very angry with you. 3 Even so, there is some good in you, for you have removed the Asherah poles throughout the land, and you have committed yourself to seeking God."

4 Jehoshaphat lived in Jerusalem, but he went out among the people, traveling from Beersheba to the hill country of Ephraim, encouraging the people to return to the LORD, the God of their ancestors. 5 He appointed judges throughout the nation in all the fortified towns, 6 and he said to them, "Always think carefully before pronouncing judgment. Remember that you do not judge to please people but to please the LORD. He will be with you when you render the verdict in each case. 7 Fear the LORD and judge with integrity, for the LORD our God does not tolerate perverted justice, partiality, or the taking of bribes."

8 In Jerusalem, Jehoshaphat appointed some of the Levites and priests and clan leaders in Israel to serve as judges for cases involving the LORD's regulations and for civil disputes. 9 These were his instructions to them: "You must always act in the fear of the LORD, with faithfulness and an undivided heart. 10 Whenever a case comes to you from fellow citizens in an outlying town, whether a murder case or some other violation of God's laws, commands, decrees, or regulations, you must warn them not to sin against the LORD, so that he will not be angry with you and them. Do this and you will not be guilty.

11 "Amariah the high priest will have final say in all cases involving the LORD. Zebadiah son of Ishmael, a leader from the tribe of Judah, will have final say in all civil cases. The Levites will assist you in making sure that justice is served. Take courage as you fulfill your duties, and may the LORD be with those who do what is right."

18:33 Hebrew *Turn your hand.*

Jehoshaphat's naiveté is apparent in his letting Ahab talk him into dressing in his royal robes and taking Ahab's place in the front of the battle. This almost got him killed.

19:1—20:37 Jehoshaphat's Military and Commercial Campaigns. 19:4–11: Jehoshaphat reformed the judiciary, ensuring justice for his people, and all enjoyed national prosperity and international security.

War with Surrounding Nations

20 After this, the armies of the Moabites,
Ammonites, and some of the Meunites* declared war on Jehoshaphat.
2 Messengers came and told Jehoshaphat, "A vast
army from Edom* is marching against you from
beyond the Dead Sea.* They are already at Hazazon-tamar." (This was another name for En-
gedi.)
3 Jehoshaphat was terrified by this news and
begged the LORD for guidance. He also ordered
everyone in Judah to begin fasting. 4 So people
from all the towns of Judah came to Jerusalem to
seek the LORD's help.
5 Jehoshaphat stood before the community of
Judah and Jerusalem in front of the new courtyard at the Temple of the LORD. 6 He prayed,
"O LORD, God of our ancestors, you alone are
the God who is in heaven. You are ruler of all
the kingdoms of the earth. You are powerful and
mighty; no one can stand against you! 7 O our
God, did you not drive out those who lived in
this land when your people Israel arrived? And
did you not give this land forever to the descendants of your friend Abraham? 8 Your people
settled here and built this Temple to honor your
name. 9 They said, 'Whenever we are faced with
any calamity such as war,* plague, or famine, we
can come to stand in your presence before this
Temple where your name is honored. We can cry
out to you to save us, and you will hear us and
rescue us.'
10 "And now see what the armies of Ammon,
Moab, and Mount Seir are doing. You would not
let our ancestors invade those nations when Israel left Egypt, so they went around them and
did not destroy them. 11 Now see how they reward us! For they have come to throw us out of
your land, which you gave us as an inheritance.
12 O our God, won't you stop them? We are powerless against this mighty army that is about to
attack us. We do not know what to do, but we are
looking to you for help."
13 As all the men of Judah stood before the
LORD with their little ones, wives, and children,
14 the Spirit of the LORD came upon one of the
men standing there. His name was Jahaziel son
of Zechariah, son of Benaiah, son of Jeiel, son
of Mattaniah, a Levite who was a descendant of
Asaph.
15 He said, "Listen, all you people of Judah
and Jerusalem! Listen, King Jehoshaphat! This
is what the LORD says: Do not be afraid! Don't
be discouraged by this mighty army, for the battle is not yours, but God's. 16 Tomorrow, march
out against them. You will find them coming
up through the ascent of Ziz at the end of the
valley that opens into the wilderness of Jeruel.
17 But you will not even need to fight. Take your
positions; then stand still and watch the LORD's
victory. He is with you, O people of Judah and
Jerusalem. Do not be afraid or discouraged. Go
out against them tomorrow, for the LORD is with
you!"
18 Then King Jehoshaphat bowed low with
his face to the ground. And all the people of Judah and Jerusalem did the same, worshiping the
LORD. 19 Then the Levites from the clans of Kohath and Korah stood to praise the LORD, the
God of Israel, with a very loud shout.
20 Early the next morning the army of Judah
went out into the wilderness of Tekoa. On the
way Jehoshaphat stopped and said, "Listen to me,
all you people of Judah and Jerusalem! Believe
in the LORD your God, and you will be able to
stand firm. Believe in his prophets, and you will
succeed."
21 After consulting the people, the king appointed singers to walk ahead of the army, singing to the LORD and praising him for his holy
splendor. This is what they sang:

"Give thanks to the LORD;
his faithful love endures forever!"

22 At the very moment they began to sing
and give praise, the LORD caused the armies of
Ammon, Moab, and Mount Seir to start fighting
among themselves. 23 The armies of Moab and
Ammon turned against their allies from Mount
Seir and killed every one of them. After they had
destroyed the army of Seir, they began attacking
each other. 24 So when the army of Judah arrived
at the lookout point in the wilderness, all they
saw were dead bodies lying on the ground as far
as they could see. Not a single one of the enemy
had escaped.

20:1 As in some Greek manuscripts (see also 26:7); Hebrew repeats *Ammonites.* **20:2a** As in one Hebrew manuscript; most Hebrew manuscripts and ancient versions read *Aram.* **20:2b** Hebrew *the sea.* **20:9** Or *sword of judgment;* or *sword, judgment.*

20:1–30: The Moabites, Ammonites, and Edomites east of the Jordan were longtime bitter enemies, partly because they were related to the Israelites (Gen 19:30–38; 25:30). The king and all of the people of Judah, including the women (2 Chr 20:13), sought the LORD in humility, and he gave them a notable victory over these traditional enemies.

25 King Jehoshaphat and his men went out to
gather the plunder. They found vast amounts
of equipment, clothing,* and other valuables—
more than they could carry. There was so much
plunder that it took them three days just to collect it all! 26 On the fourth day they gathered in
the Valley of Blessing,* which got its name that
day because the people praised and thanked the
LORD there. It is still called the Valley of Blessing today.
27 Then all the men returned to Jerusalem,
with Jehoshaphat leading them, overjoyed that
the LORD had given them victory over their
enemies. 28 They marched into Jerusalem to the
music of harps, lyres, and trumpets, and they
proceeded to the Temple of the LORD.
29 When all the surrounding kingdoms heard
that the LORD himself had fought against the enemies of Israel, the fear of God came over them.
30 So Jehoshaphat's kingdom was at peace, for his
God had given him rest on every side.

Summary of Jehoshaphat's Reign

31 So Jehoshaphat ruled over the land of Judah.
He was thirty-five years old when he became
king, and he reigned in Jerusalem twenty-five
years. His mother was Azubah, the daughter of
Shilhi.
32 Jehoshaphat was a good king, following the
ways of his father, Asa. He did what was pleasing
in the LORD's sight. 33 During his reign, however,
he failed to remove all the pagan shrines, and the
people never fully committed themselves to follow the God of their ancestors.
34 The rest of the events of Jehoshaphat's
reign, from beginning to end, are recorded in *The
Record of Jehu Son of Hanani,* which is included
in *The Book of the Kings of Israel.*
35 Some time later King Jehoshaphat of Judah
made an alliance with King Ahaziah of Israel,
who was very wicked.* 36 Together they built a
fleet of trading ships* at the port of Ezion-geber.
37 Then Eliezer son of Dodavahu from Mareshah prophesied against Jehoshaphat. He said,
"Because you have allied yourself with King
Ahaziah, the LORD will destroy your work." So
the ships met with disaster and never put out
to sea.*

Jehoram Rules in Judah

21 When Jehoshaphat died, he was buried with his ancestors in the City of
David. Then his son Jehoram became
the next king.
2 Jehoram's brothers—the other sons of Jehoshaphat—were Azariah, Jehiel, Zechariah,
Azariahu, Michael, and Shephatiah; all these
were the sons of Jehoshaphat king of Judah.*
3 Their father had given each of them valuable
gifts of silver, gold, and costly items, and also
some of Judah's fortified towns. However, he
designated Jehoram as the next king because he
was the oldest. 4 But when Jehoram had become
solidly established as king, he killed all his brothers and some of the other leaders of Judah.
5 Jehoram was thirty-two years old when he
became king, and he reigned in Jerusalem eight
years. 6 But Jehoram followed the example of the
kings of Israel and was as wicked as King Ahab,
for he had married one of Ahab's daughters. So
Jehoram did what was evil in the LORD's sight.
7 But the LORD did not want to destroy David's
dynasty, for he had made a covenant with David
and promised that his descendants would continue to rule, shining like a lamp forever.
8 During Jehoram's reign, the Edomites revolted against Judah and crowned their own king. 9 So
Jehoram went out with his full army and all his
chariots. The Edomites surrounded him and his
chariot commanders, but he went out at night and
attacked them* under cover of darkness. 10 Even so,
Edom has been independent from Judah to this day.
The town of Libnah also revolted about that same
time. All this happened because Jehoram had abandoned the LORD, the God of his ancestors. 11 He had
built pagan shrines in the hill country of Judah and
had led the people of Jerusalem and Judah to give
themselves to pagan gods and to go astray.

20:25 As in some Hebrew manuscripts and Latin Vulgate; most Hebrew manuscripts read *corpses.* **20:26** Hebrew *valley of Beracah.* **20:35** Or *who made him do what was wicked.* **20:36** Hebrew *fleet of ships that could go to Tarshish.* **20:37** Hebrew *never set sail for Tarshish.* **21:2** Masoretic Text reads *of Israel;* also in 21:4. The author of Chronicles sees Judah as representative of the true Israel. (Some Hebrew manuscripts, Greek and Syriac versions, and Latin Vulgate read *of Judah.*) **21:9** Or *he went out and escaped.* The meaning of the Hebrew is uncertain.

21:1b—23:21 The Reigns of Jehoram, Ahaziah, and Athaliah

21:1–20 Jehoram, Husband of Athaliah. 4: One is not long left in doubt about what sort of king Jehoshaphat's son Jehoram would be. He showed his appreciation for the customary privilege of the firstborn by having his brothers killed. **6:** Significantly, the Chronicler reminds readers that Jehoram had married Athaliah, the daughter of Ahab and Jezebel. **8–17:** A part of the LORD's punishment of Jehoram was the revolt of all Judah's vassal territories. But this did not change Jehoram's life pattern. He not only built regional pagan shrines—but also *led the people of Jerusalem*

12 Then Elijah the prophet wrote Jehoram this letter:

> "This is what the LORD, the God of your ancestor David, says: You have not followed the good example of your father, Jehoshaphat, or your grandfather King Asa of Judah. 13 Instead, you have been as evil as the kings of Israel. You have led the people of Jerusalem and Judah to worship idols, just as King Ahab did in Israel. And you have even killed your own brothers, men who were better than you. 14 So now the LORD is about to strike you, your people, your children, your wives, and all that is yours with a heavy blow. 15 You yourself will suffer with a severe intestinal disease that will get worse each day until your bowels come out."

16 Then the LORD stirred up the Philistines and the Arabs, who lived near the Ethiopians,* to attack Jehoram. 17 They marched against Judah, broke down its defenses, and carried away everything of value in the royal palace, including the king's sons and his wives. Only his youngest son, Ahaziah,* was spared.

18 After all this, the LORD struck Jehoram with the severe intestinal disease. 19 The disease grew worse and worse, and at the end of two years it caused his bowels to come out, and he died in agony. His people did not build a great funeral fire to honor him as they had done for his ancestors. 20 Jehoram was thirty-two years old when he became king, and he reigned in Jerusalem eight years. No one was sorry when he died. They buried him in the City of David, but not in the royal cemetery.

Ahaziah Rules in Judah

22 Then the people of Jerusalem made Ahaziah, Jehoram's youngest son, their next king, since the marauding bands who came with the Arabs* had killed all the older sons. So Ahaziah son of Jehoram reigned as king of Judah.

2 Ahaziah was twenty-two* years old when he became king, and he reigned in Jerusalem one year. His mother was Athaliah, a granddaughter of King Omri. 3 Ahaziah also followed the evil example of King Ahab's family, for his mother encouraged him in doing wrong. 4 He did what was evil in the LORD's sight, just as Ahab's family had done. They even became his advisers after the death of his father, and they led him to ruin.

5 Following their evil advice, Ahaziah joined King Joram,* the son of King Ahab of Israel, in his war against King Hazael of Aram at Ramoth-gilead. When the Arameans wounded Joram in the battle, 6 he returned to Jezreel to recover from the wounds he had received at Ramoth.* Because Joram was wounded, King Ahaziah* of Judah went to Jezreel to visit him.

7 But God had decided that this visit would be Ahaziah's downfall. While he was there, Ahaziah went out with Joram to meet Jehu grandson of Nimshi,* whom the LORD had appointed to destroy the dynasty of Ahab.

8 While Jehu was executing judgment against the family of Ahab, he happened to meet some of Judah's officials and Ahaziah's relatives* who were traveling with Ahaziah. So Jehu killed them all. 9 Then Jehu's men searched for Ahaziah, and they found him hiding in the city of Samaria. They brought him to Jehu, who killed him. Ahaziah was given a decent burial because the people said, "He was the grandson of Jehoshaphat—a man who sought the LORD with all his heart." But none of the surviving members of Ahaziah's family was capable of ruling the kingdom.

21:16 Hebrew *the Cushites.* **21:17** Hebrew *Jehoahaz,* a variant spelling of Ahaziah; compare 22:1. **22:1** Or *marauding bands of Arabs.* **22:2** As in some Greek manuscripts and Syriac version (see also 2 Kgs 8:26); Hebrew reads *forty-two.* **22:5** Hebrew *Jehoram,* a variant spelling of Joram; also in 22:6, 7. **22:6a** Hebrew *Ramah,* a variant spelling of Ramoth. **22:6b** As in some Hebrew manuscripts, Greek and Syriac versions, and Latin Vulgate (see also 2 Kgs 8:29); most Hebrew manuscripts read *Azariah.* **22:7** Hebrew *descendant of Nimshi;* compare 2 Kgs 9:2, 14. **22:8** As in Greek version (see also 2 Kgs 10:13); Hebrew reads *and sons of the brothers of Ahaziah.*

... *to give themselves to pagan gods* (v. 11). **18–20:** His consequent punishment was even more personal and severe. When he died, no one was sorry.

22:1–9 Ahaziah, Son of Jehoram and Athaliah. The good news about Ahaziah (843–842), Jehoram's youngest son, is that he ruled for only one year. The bad news is that his mother was Athaliah. **3:** Significantly, Ahaziah's mother *encouraged him in doing wrong.* Mothers and fathers both bear responsibility for the influence and effect they have on their children (see Parental Influence, Josh 4). **5–9:** During Ahaziah's reign, his uncle Joram was the ruler of Israel. They cooperated in a military expedition against Syria (Aram), and Ahaziah was caught up in Jehu's rebellion against Joram; both kings were killed.

Queen Athaliah Rules in Judah
[10]When Athaliah, the mother of King Ahaziah of
Judah, learned that her son was dead, she began
to destroy the rest of Judah's royal family. [11]But
Ahaziah's sister Jehosheba,* the daughter of
King Jehoram, took Ahaziah's infant son, Joash,
and stole him away from among the rest of the
king's children, who were about to be killed. She
put Joash and his nurse in a bedroom. In this
way, Jehosheba, wife of Jehoiada the priest and
sister of Ahaziah, hid the child so that Athaliah
could not murder him. [12]Joash remained hidden
in the Temple of God for six years while Athaliah
ruled over the land.

Revolt against Athaliah
23 In the seventh year of Athaliah's
reign, Jehoiada the priest decided to
act. He summoned his courage and
made a pact with five army commanders: Azariah son of Jeroham, Ishmael son of Jehohanan,
Azariah son of Obed, Maaseiah son of Adaiah,
and Elishaphat son of Zicri. [2]These men traveled
secretly throughout Judah and summoned the
Levites and clan leaders in all the towns to come
to Jerusalem. [3]They all gathered at the Temple of
God, where they made a solemn pact with Joash,
the young king.
Jehoiada said to them, "Here is the king's
son! The time has come for him to reign! The
LORD has promised that a descendant of David
will be our king. [4]This is what you must do.
When you priests and Levites come on duty
on the Sabbath, a third of you will serve as
gatekeepers. [5]Another third will go over to the
royal palace, and the final third will be at the
Foundation Gate. Everyone else should stay in
the courtyards of the LORD's Temple. [6]Remem-
ber, only the priests and Levites on duty may
enter the Temple of the LORD, for they are set
apart as holy. The rest of the people must obey
the LORD's instructions and stay outside. [7]You
Levites, form a bodyguard around the king and
keep your weapons in hand. Kill anyone who
tries to enter the Temple. Stay with the king
wherever he goes."
[8]So the Levites and all the people of Judah
did everything as Jehoiada the priest ordered.
The commanders took charge of the men reporting for duty that Sabbath, as well as those who
were going off duty. Jehoiada the priest did not let
anyone go home after their shift ended. [9]Then Jehoiada supplied the commanders with the spears
and the large and small shields that had once belonged to King David and were stored in the Temple of God. [10]He stationed all the people around
the king, with their weapons ready. They formed
a line from the south side of the Temple around
to the north side and all around the altar.
[11]Then Jehoiada and his sons brought out
Joash, the king's son, placed the crown on his
head, and presented him with a copy of God's
laws.* They anointed him and proclaimed him
king, and everyone shouted, "Long live the
king!"

The Death of Athaliah
[12]When Athaliah heard the noise of the people
running and the shouts of praise to the king,
she hurried to the LORD's Temple to see what
was happening. [13]When she arrived, she saw the
newly crowned king standing in his place of authority by the pillar at the Temple entrance. The
commanders and trumpeters were surrounding him, and people from all over the land were
rejoicing and blowing trumpets. Singers with
musical instruments were leading the people
in a great celebration. When Athaliah saw all
this, she tore her clothes in despair and shouted,
"Treason! Treason!"
[14]Then Jehoiada the priest ordered the commanders who were in charge of the troops, "Take
her to the soldiers in front of the Temple,* and

22:11 As in parallel text at 2 Kgs 11:2; Hebrew lacks *Ahaziah's sister* and reads *Jehoshabeath* [a variant spelling of Jehosheba]. **23:11** Or *a copy of the covenant.* **23:14** Or *Bring her out from between the ranks;* or *Take her out of the Temple precincts.* The meaning of the Hebrew is uncertain.

22:10—23:21 Athaliah. 22:10–12: Athaliah (842–837), the only woman ever to sit on a Hebrew throne, seized power in Judah. She set out to have all the royal family killed—including her own grandchildren—and would have succeeded but for the heroic efforts of Jehosheba, Ahaziah's sister and the wife of the priest Jehoiada, who hid Ahaziah's son Joash. The young prince lived for six years, hidden in the Temple area while Athaliah reigned. **23:1–11:** Finally Jehoiada felt the time was ripe to act. He enlisted military and spiritual leaders who pledged to support the rightful king of David's line. Plans were carefully laid to present Athaliah with a fait accompli. Thus the existence of Joash, alive and well, was revealed to the citizenry, and he was officially proclaimed king. **12–15:** When Athaliah learned what was going on, it was too late. She charged everyone with treason—rather an ironic charge brought by the woman who had almost all of the royal family destroyed. Athaliah and her followers were executed, though the Chronicler is concerned to point out that she was executed outside of the sacred Temple precincts. **16–21:** Jehoiada then

kill anyone who tries to rescue her." For the
priest had said, "She must not be killed in the
Temple of the LORD." 15 So they seized her and
led her out to the entrance of the Horse Gate on
the palace grounds, and they killed her there.

Jehoiada's Religious Reforms

16 Then Jehoiada made a covenant between himself and the king and the people that they would
be the LORD's people. 17 And all the people went
over to the temple of Baal and tore it down. They
demolished the altars and smashed the idols, and
they killed Mattan the priest of Baal in front of
the altars.
18 Jehoiada now put the priests and Levites
in charge of the Temple of the LORD, following
all the directions given by David. He also commanded them to present burnt offerings to the
LORD, as prescribed by the Law of Moses, and to
sing and rejoice as David had instructed. 19 He
also stationed gatekeepers at the gates of the
LORD's Temple to keep out those who for any
reason were ceremonially unclean.
20 Then the commanders, nobles, rulers, and
all the people of the land escorted the king from
the Temple of the LORD. They went through the
upper gate and into the palace, and they seated
the king on the royal throne. 21 So all the people
of the land rejoiced, and the city was peaceful because Athaliah had been killed.

Joash Repairs the Temple

24 Joash was seven years old when he
became king, and he reigned in Jerusalem forty years. His mother
was Zibiah from Beersheba. 2 Joash did what was
pleasing in the LORD's sight throughout the lifetime of Jehoiada the priest. 3 Jehoiada chose two
wives for Joash, and he had sons and daughters.
4 At one point Joash decided to repair and restore the Temple of the LORD. 5 He summoned
the priests and Levites and gave them these instructions: "Go to all the towns of Judah and collect the required annual offerings, so that we can
repair the Temple of your God. Do not delay!"
But the Levites did not act immediately.
6 So the king called for Jehoiada the high
priest and asked him, "Why haven't you demanded that the Levites go out and collect the
Temple taxes from the towns of Judah and from
Jerusalem? Moses, the servant of the LORD, levied this tax on the community of Israel in order
to maintain the Tabernacle of the Covenant.*"
7 Over the years the followers of wicked Athaliah had broken into the Temple of God, and
they had used all the dedicated things from the
Temple of the LORD to worship the images of
Baal.
8 So now the king ordered a chest to be made
and set outside the gate leading to the Temple
of the LORD. 9 Then a proclamation was sent
throughout Judah and Jerusalem, telling the people to bring to the LORD the tax that Moses, the
servant of God, had required of the Israelites in
the wilderness. 10 This pleased all the leaders and
the people, and they gladly brought their money
and filled the chest with it.
11 Whenever the chest became full, the Levites
would carry it to the king's officials. Then the
court secretary and an officer of the high priest
would come and empty the chest and take it
back to the Temple again. This went on day after
day, and a large amount of money was collected.
12 The king and Jehoiada gave the money to the
construction supervisors, who hired masons and
carpenters to restore the Temple of the LORD.
They also hired metalworkers, who made articles
of iron and bronze for the LORD's Temple.
13 The men in charge of the renovation worked
hard and made steady progress. They restored the
Temple of God according to its original design
and strengthened it. 14 When all the repairs were
finished, they brought the remaining money to
the king and Jehoiada. It was used to make various articles for the Temple of the LORD—articles
for worship services and for burnt offerings, including ladles and other articles made of gold and
silver. And the burnt offerings were sacrificed
continually in the Temple of the LORD during
the lifetime of Jehoiada the priest.
15 Jehoiada lived to a very old age, finally dying at 130. 16 He was buried among the kings in

24:6 Hebrew *Tent of the Testimony.*

led the people in a renewal of the ancient covenant. Note that the Old Testament covenant was not automatic: It had to be renewed by each new generation. Under the leadership of the priest, the people tore down the temple of Baal, with its altars and images, and killed the priests of Baal. True worship was purified and reorganized. Everyone looked forward to a new day under a young, new king.

24:1–25:28 The Reigns of Joash and Amaziah

Joash (837–800), whose mother was Zibiah, was only seven when he became king. Under Jehoiada's influence he made an admirable start.

24:1–27 The Reign of Joash. 4–14: Joash's first signifi-

the City of David, because he had done so much good in Israel for God and his Temple.

Jehoiada's Reforms Reversed

17 But after Jehoiada's death, the leaders of Judah came and bowed before King Joash and persuaded him to listen to their advice. 18 They decided to abandon the Temple of the LORD, the God of their ancestors, and they worshiped Asherah poles and idols instead! Because of this sin, divine anger fell on Judah and Jerusalem. 19 Yet the LORD sent prophets to bring them back to him. The prophets warned them, but still the people would not listen.

20 Then the Spirit of God came upon Zechariah son of Jehoiada the priest. He stood before the people and said, "This is what God says: Why do you disobey the LORD's commands and keep yourselves from prospering? You have abandoned the LORD, and now he has abandoned you!"

21 Then the leaders plotted to kill Zechariah, and King Joash ordered that they stone him to death in the courtyard of the LORD's Temple. 22 That was how King Joash repaid Jehoiada for his loyalty—by killing his son. Zechariah's last words as he died were, "May the LORD see what they are doing and avenge my death!"

The End of Joash's Reign

23 In the spring of the year* the Aramean army marched against Joash. They invaded Judah and Jerusalem and killed all the leaders of the nation. Then they sent all the plunder back to their king in Damascus. 24 Although the Arameans attacked with only a small army, the LORD helped them conquer the much larger army of Judah. The people of Judah had abandoned the LORD, the God of their ancestors, so judgment was carried out against Joash.

25 The Arameans withdrew, leaving Joash severely wounded. But his own officials plotted to kill him for murdering the son* of Jehoiada the priest. They assassinated him as he lay in bed. Then he was buried in the City of David, but not in the royal cemetery. 26 The assassins were Jozacar,* the son of an Ammonite woman named Shimeath, and Jehozabad, the son of a Moabite woman named Shomer.*

27 The account of the sons of Joash, the prophecies about him, and the record of his restoration of the Temple of God are written in *The Commentary on the Book of the Kings.* His son Amaziah became the next king.

Amaziah Rules in Judah

25 Amaziah was twenty-five years old when he became king, and he reigned in Jerusalem twenty-nine years. His mother was Jehoaddin* from Jerusalem. 2 Amaziah did what was pleasing in the LORD's sight, but not wholeheartedly.

3 When Amaziah was well established as king, he executed the officials who had assassinated his father. 4 However, he did not kill the children of the assassins, for he obeyed the command of the LORD as written by Moses in the Book of the Law: "Parents must not be put to death for the sins of their children, nor children for the sins of their parents. Those deserving to die must be put to death for their own crimes."*

5 Then Amaziah organized the army, assigning generals and captains* for all Judah and Benjamin. He took a census and found that he had an army of 300,000 select troops, twenty years old and older, all trained in the use of spear and shield. 6 He also paid about 7,500 pounds* of silver to hire 100,000 experienced fighting men from Israel.

7 But a man of God came to him and said, "Your Majesty, do not hire troops from Israel, for the LORD is not with Israel. He will not help those people of Ephraim! 8 If you let them go

24:23 Hebrew *At the turn of the year.* The first day of the year in the ancient Hebrew lunar calendar occurred in March or April. **24:25** As in Greek version and Latin Vulgate; Hebrew reads *sons.* **24:26a** As in parallel text at 2 Kgs 12:21; Hebrew reads *Zabad.* **24:26b** As in parallel text at 2 Kgs 12:21; Hebrew reads *Shimrith,* a variant spelling of Shomer. **25:1** As in parallel text at 2 Kgs 14:2; Hebrew reads *Jehoaddan,* a variant spelling of Jehoaddin. **25:4** Deut 24:16. **25:5** Hebrew *commanders of thousands and commanders of hundreds.* **25:6** Hebrew *100 talents* [3,400 kilograms].

---

cant act was to properly refurbish the long-abused Temple. The people were generous in their financial support of the project. **16:** Jehoiada had been such an outstanding leader that he had been buried *among the kings in the City of David.* **17–19:** With Jehoiada dead, Joash had a change of heart. He and his people abandoned the LORD and ignored the prophets sent to them. Inevitably they suffered the consequent judgment. **20–26:** Jehoiada's son Zechariah apparently took after his father, but Joash could not cope with his criticism and had him stoned to death. The Chronicler makes his (and the LORD's) disgust at this behavior very clear. Joash was eventually assassinated but unlike Jehoiada, was not buried in "the royal cemetery."

25:1–28 Amaziah, Joash's Mirror Image. Amaziah (800–783), too, began well but, like his father, did not serve Yahweh *wholeheartedly.* **7–12:** In the beginning he listened to God's prophet even when it

with your troops into battle, you will be defeated
by the enemy no matter how well you fight. God
will overthrow you, for he has the power to help
you or to trip you up."
9 Amaziah asked the man of God, "But what
about all that silver I paid to hire the army of
Israel?"

The man of God replied, "The LORD is able to
give you much more than this!" 10 So Amaziah
discharged the hired troops and sent them back
to Ephraim. This made them very angry with Judah, and they returned home in a great rage.
11 Then Amaziah summoned his courage and
led his army to the Valley of Salt, where they
killed 10,000 Edomite troops from Seir. 12 They
captured another 10,000 and took them to the
top of a cliff and threw them off, dashing them to
pieces on the rocks below.
13 Meanwhile, the hired troops that Amaziah
had sent home raided several of the towns of
Judah between Samaria and Beth-horon. They
killed 3,000 people and carried off great quantities of plunder.
14 When King Amaziah returned from slaughtering the Edomites, he brought with him idols
taken from the people of Seir. He set them up
as his own gods, bowed down in front of them,
and offered sacrifices to them! 15 This made the
LORD very angry, and he sent a prophet to ask,
"Why do you turn to gods who could not even
save their own people from you?"
16 But the king interrupted him and said,
"Since when have I made you the king's counselor? Be quiet now before I have you killed!"

So the prophet stopped with this warning: "I
know that God has determined to destroy you
because you have done this and have refused to
accept my counsel."
17 After consulting with his advisers, King
Amaziah of Judah sent this challenge to Israel's
king Jehoash,* the son of Jehoahaz and grandson
of Jehu: "Come and meet me in battle!"*
18 But King Jehoash of Israel replied to King
Amaziah of Judah with this story: "Out in the
Lebanon mountains, a thistle sent a message
to a mighty cedar tree: 'Give your daughter in
marriage to my son.' But just then a wild animal
of Lebanon came by and stepped on the thistle,
crushing it!
19 "You are saying, 'I have defeated Edom,'
and you are very proud of it. But my advice is to
stay at home. Why stir up trouble that will only
bring disaster on you and the people of Judah?"
20 But Amaziah refused to listen, for God was
determined to destroy him for turning to the
gods of Edom. 21 So King Jehoash of Israel mobilized his army against King Amaziah of Judah. The two armies drew up their battle lines
at Beth-shemesh in Judah. 22 Judah was routed
by the army of Israel, and its army scattered and
fled for home. 23 King Jehoash of Israel captured
Judah's king, Amaziah son of Joash and grandson
of Ahaziah, at Beth-shemesh. Then he brought
him to Jerusalem, where he demolished 600 feet*
of Jerusalem's wall, from the Ephraim Gate to
the Corner Gate. 24 He carried off all the gold and
silver and all the articles from the Temple of God
that had been in the care of Obed-edom. He also
seized the treasures of the royal palace, along
with hostages, and then returned to Samaria.
25 King Amaziah of Judah lived on for fifteen
years after the death of King Jehoash of Israel.
26 The rest of the events in Amaziah's reign, from
beginning to end, are recorded in *The Book of the
Kings of Judah and Israel.*
27 After Amaziah turned away from the LORD,
there was a conspiracy against his life in Jerusalem,
and he fled to Lachish. But his enemies sent assassins after him, and they killed him there. 28 They
brought his body back on a horse, and he was buried with his ancestors in the City of David.*

Uzziah Rules in Judah

26 All the people of Judah had crowned
Amaziah's sixteen-year-old son, Uzziah, as king in place of his father.

25:17a Hebrew *Joash,* a variant spelling of Jehoash; also in 25:18, 21, 23, 25. **25:17b** Hebrew *Come, let us look one another in the face.* **25:23** Hebrew *400 cubits* [180 meters]. **25:28** As in some Hebrew manuscripts and other ancient versions (see also 2 Kgs 14:20); most Hebrew manuscripts read *the city of Judah.*

meant serious loss to himself. As prophesied, Amaziah defeated the Edomites. **14–16:** Back in Jerusalem he began to worship the gods of the defeated Edomites. This time, the prophet was ignored. **17–24:** Amaziah was at loggerheads with Jehoash of Israel, and the LORD used this as an avenue of judgment on his idolatry. Judah was soundly defeated; Amaziah and other hostages were captured. Jehoash added to Judah's sorry plight by breaking down a considerable section of the defensive wall of Jerusalem and stripping the Temple and palace of their treasures. **27–28:** Amaziah was assassinated, and the Chronicler's message that actions bring consequences is reiterated.

26:1—28:27 The Reigns of Uzziah, Jotham, and Ahaz

26:1–23 Uzziah, the Best So Far. Uzziah (783–742),

[2] After his father's death, Uzziah rebuilt the town of Elath* and restored it to Judah.

[3] Uzziah was sixteen years old when he became king, and he reigned in Jerusalem fifty-two years. His mother was Jecoliah from Jerusalem. [4] He did what was pleasing in the LORD's sight, just as his father, Amaziah, had done. [5] Uzziah sought God during the days of Zechariah, who taught him to fear God.* And as long as the king sought guidance from the LORD, God gave him success.

[6] Uzziah declared war on the Philistines and broke down the walls of Gath, Jabneh, and Ashdod. Then he built new towns in the Ashdod area and in other parts of Philistia. [7] God helped him in his wars against the Philistines, his battles with the Arabs of Gur,* and his wars with the Meunites. [8] The Meunites* paid annual tribute to him, and his fame spread even to Egypt, for he had become very powerful.

[9] Uzziah built fortified towers in Jerusalem at the Corner Gate, at the Valley Gate, and at the angle in the wall. [10] He also constructed forts in the wilderness and dug many water cisterns, because he kept great herds of livestock in the foothills of Judah* and on the plains. He was also a man who loved the soil. He had many workers who cared for his farms and vineyards, both on the hillsides and in the fertile valleys.

[11] Uzziah had an army of well-trained warriors, ready to march into battle, unit by unit. This army had been mustered and organized by Jeiel, the secretary of the army, and his assistant, Maaseiah. They were under the direction of Hananiah, one of the king's officials. [12] These regiments of mighty warriors were commanded by 2,600 clan leaders. [13] The army consisted of 307,500 men, all elite troops. They were prepared to assist the king against any enemy.

[14] Uzziah provided the entire army with shields, spears, helmets, coats of mail, bows, and sling stones. [15] And he built structures on the walls of Jerusalem, designed by experts to protect those who shot arrows and hurled large stones* from the towers and the corners of the wall. His fame spread far and wide, for the LORD gave him marvelous help, and he became very powerful.

Uzziah's Sin and Punishment

[16] But when he had become powerful, he also became proud, which led to his downfall. He sinned against the LORD his God by entering the sanctuary of the LORD's Temple and personally burning incense on the incense altar. [17] Azariah the high priest went in after him with eighty other priests of the LORD, all brave men. [18] They confronted King Uzziah and said, "It is not for you, Uzziah, to burn incense to the LORD. That is the work of the priests alone, the descendants of Aaron who are set apart for this work. Get out of the sanctuary, for you have sinned. The LORD God will not honor you for this!"

[19] Uzziah, who was holding an incense burner, became furious. But as he was standing there raging at the priests before the incense altar in the LORD's Temple, leprosy* suddenly broke out on his forehead. [20] When Azariah the high priest and all the other priests saw the leprosy, they rushed him out. And the king himself was eager to get out because the LORD had struck him. [21] So King Uzziah had leprosy until the day he died. He lived in isolation in a separate house, for he was excluded from the Temple of the LORD. His son Jotham was put in charge of the royal palace, and he governed the people of the land.

[22] The rest of the events of Uzziah's reign, from beginning to end, are recorded by the prophet Isaiah son of Amoz. [23] When Uzziah died, he was buried with his ancestors; his grave was in a nearby burial field belonging to the kings, for the people said, "He had leprosy." And his son Jotham became the next king.

26:2 As in Greek version (see also 2 Kgs 14:22; 16:6); Hebrew reads *Eloth,* a variant spelling of Elath. **26:5** As in Syriac and Greek versions; Hebrew reads *who instructed him in divine visions.* **26:7** As in Greek version; Hebrew reads *Gur-baal.* **26:8** As in Greek version; Hebrew reads *Ammonites.* Compare 26:7. **26:10** Hebrew *the Shephelah.* **26:15** Or *to shoot arrows and hurl large stones.* **26:19** Or *a contagious skin disease.* The Hebrew word used here and throughout this passage can describe various skin diseases.

---

whose mother was Jecoliah, was only sixteen when he became king, but he reigned well and for an unusually long time. He was effective both in commercial and military ventures. He organized and strengthened the army, and supported agriculture, which contributed to the prosperity of the nation. **16–21:** Uzziah, too, stumbled at the final hurdle. Pride became his downfall. He thought he was above the law and tried to act as priest as well as king. When the priests confronted him, he became furious and a terrible skin disease broke out on his forehead. His anger at the priests was, indirectly, anger at God's chosen means of regulating worship. He spent the rest of his life in quarantine—his *leprosy* (see translator's note) made him unclean according to the Mosaic rules regarding ritual cleanliness—and his son Jotham became regent.

Jotham Rules in Judah

27 Jotham was twenty-five years old
when he became king, and he reigned
in Jerusalem sixteen years. His mother was Jerusha, the daughter of Zadok.
[2]Jotham did what was pleasing in the LORD's
sight. He did everything his father, Uzziah, had
done, except that Jotham did not sin by entering
the Temple of the LORD. But the people continued in their corrupt ways.
[3]Jotham rebuilt the upper gate of the Temple
of the LORD. He also did extensive rebuilding on
the wall at the hill of Ophel. [4]He built towns in
the hill country of Judah and constructed fortresses and towers in the wooded areas. [5]Jotham
went to war against the Ammonites and conquered them. Over the next three years he received from them an annual tribute of 7,500
pounds* of silver, 50,000 bushels of wheat, and
50,000 bushels of barley.*
[6]King Jotham became powerful because he
was careful to live in obedience to the LORD his
God.
[7]The rest of the events of Jotham's reign, including all his wars and other activities, are recorded in *The Book of the Kings of Israel and
Judah.* [8]He was twenty-five years old when he
became king, and he reigned in Jerusalem sixteen
years. [9]When Jotham died, he was buried in the
City of David. And his son Ahaz became the next
king.

Ahaz Rules in Judah

28 Ahaz was twenty years old when he
became king, and he reigned in Jerusalem sixteen years. He did not do
what was pleasing in the sight of the LORD, as his
ancestor David had done. [2]Instead, he followed
the example of the kings of Israel. He cast metal
images for the worship of Baal. [3]He offered sacrifices in the valley of Ben-Hinnom, even sacrificing his own sons in the fire.* In this way, he
followed the detestable practices of the pagan nations the LORD had driven from the land ahead of
the Israelites. [4]He offered sacrifices and burned
incense at the pagan shrines and on the hills and
under every green tree.
[5]Because of all this, the LORD his God allowed
the king of Aram to defeat Ahaz and to exile
large numbers of his people to Damascus. The
armies of the king of Israel also defeated Ahaz
and inflicted many casualties on his army. [6]In a
single day Pekah son of Remaliah, Israel's king,
killed 120,000 of Judah's troops, all of them experienced warriors, because they had abandoned
the LORD, the God of their ancestors. [7]Then Zicri, a warrior from Ephraim, killed Maaseiah, the
king's son; Azrikam, the king's palace commander; and Elkanah, the king's second-in-command.
[8]The armies of Israel captured 200,000 women
and children from Judah and seized tremendous
amounts of plunder, which they took back to Samaria.
[9]But a prophet of the LORD named Oded was
there in Samaria when the army of Israel returned home. He went out to meet them and said,
"The LORD, the God of your ancestors, was angry
with Judah and let you defeat them. But you have
gone too far, killing them without mercy, and all
heaven is disturbed. [10]And now you are planning
to make slaves of these people from Judah and
Jerusalem. What about your own sins against the
LORD your God? [11]Listen to me and return these
prisoners you have taken, for they are your own
relatives. Watch out, because now the LORD's
fierce anger has been turned against you!"
[12]Then some of the leaders of Israel*—Azariah son of Jehohanan, Berekiah son of Meshillemoth, Jehizkiah son of Shallum, and Amasa
son of Hadlai—agreed with this and confronted
the men returning from battle. [13]"You must not
bring the prisoners here!" they declared. "We
cannot afford to add to our sins and guilt. Our
guilt is already great, and the LORD's fierce anger
is already turned against Israel."

27:5a Hebrew *100 talents* [3,400 kilograms]. **27:5b** Hebrew *10,000 cors* [1,820 kiloliters] *of wheat, and 10,000 cors of barley.* **28:3** Or *even making his sons pass through the fire.* **28:12** Hebrew *Ephraim,* referring to the northern kingdom of Israel.

27:1–9 Jotham. Jotham's (742–735) mother was Jerusha. He took after his father's good side, but though he was faithful personally, he failed at leading the people in a closer walk with God.

28:1–15 Ahaz, the Worst So Far. How could good men like Uzziah and Jotham have a grandson and son like Ahaz (735–715)? (Could it have something to do with Ahaz's mother?) The list of his misdeeds makes for discouraging reading: He cast images of Baal, sacrificed his sons as burnt offerings, and worshiped at the pagan high places. The LORD allowed him to be dominated by Aram. When Judah was defeated, the Northern Kingdom took advantage of Judah's weakness to engage in excesses of looting and enslavement. **9–15:** God did not let the plunder get out of hand. Aram and Israel were his instruments of judgment on Ahaz and Judah, but this did not excuse excessive cruelty or inhumanity on their part.

[14]So the warriors released the prisoners and
handed over the plunder in the sight of the leaders and all the people. [15]Then the four men just
mentioned by name came forward and distributed clothes from the plunder to the prisoners
who were naked. They provided clothing and
sandals to wear, gave them enough food and
drink, and dressed their wounds with olive oil.
They put those who were weak on donkeys and
took all the prisoners back to their own people
in Jericho, the city of palms. Then they returned
to Samaria.

Ahaz Closes the Temple

[16]At that time King Ahaz of Judah asked the king
of Assyria for help. [17]The armies of Edom had
again invaded Judah and taken captives. [18]And
the Philistines had raided towns located in the
foothills of Judah* and in the Negev of Judah.
They had already captured and occupied Beth-
shemesh, Aijalon, Gederoth, Soco with its villages, Timnah with its villages, and Gimzo with
its villages. [19]The LORD was humbling Judah
because of King Ahaz of Judah,* for he had encouraged his people to sin and had been utterly
unfaithful to the LORD.
[20]So when King Tiglath-pileser* of Assyria
arrived, he attacked Ahaz instead of helping him.
[21]Ahaz took valuable items from the LORD's
Temple, the royal palace, and from the homes of
his officials and gave them to the king of Assyria
as tribute. But this did not help him.
[22]Even during this time of trouble, King Ahaz
continued to reject the LORD. [23]He offered sacrifices to the gods of Damascus who had defeated
him, for he said, "Since these gods helped the
kings of Aram, they will help me, too, if I sacrifice to them." But instead, they led to his ruin
and the ruin of all Judah.
[24]The king took the various articles from the
Temple of God and broke them into pieces. He
shut the doors of the LORD's Temple so that no
one could worship there, and he set up altars to
pagan gods in every corner of Jerusalem. [25]He
made pagan shrines in all the towns of Judah for
offering sacrifices to other gods. In this way, he
aroused the anger of the LORD, the God of his
ancestors.
[26]The rest of the events of Ahaz's reign and
everything he did, from beginning to end, are
recorded in *The Book of the Kings of Judah and
Israel.* [27]When Ahaz died, he was buried in Jerusalem but not in the royal cemetery of the kings
of Judah. Then his son Hezekiah became the next
king.

Hezekiah Rules in Judah

29 Hezekiah was twenty-five years old
when he became the king of Judah,
and he reigned in Jerusalem twenty-
nine years. His mother was Abijah, the daughter of Zechariah. [2]He did what was pleasing in
the LORD's sight, just as his ancestor David had
done.

Hezekiah Reopens the Temple

[3]In the very first month of the first year of his
reign, Hezekiah reopened the doors of the Temple

28:18 Hebrew *the Shephelah.* **28:19** Masoretic Text reads *of Israel;* also in 28:23, 27. The author of Chronicles sees Judah as representative of the true Israel. (Some Hebrew manuscripts and Greek version read *of Judah.*) **28:20** Hebrew *Tilgath-pilneser,* a variant spelling of Tiglath-pileser.

28:16–26 Ahaz's Most Serious Blunder. Of Ahaz's many mistakes, the one with the longest-lasting consequences was his appeal to Tilgath-pileser of Assyria for help against Aram and Israel. It was like a mouse asking the cat for help to get rid of other mice! Assyria attacked Judah's northern neighbors and within ten years subjugated them. Assyria did not stop there but extended control into Judah. Judah became little more than an Assyrian province. Isaiah 7 tells us more of Ahaz's reign and of the messages from the LORD that Isaiah brought him. **22–25:** Ahaz clearly did not learn his lesson. When trouble came, he became more faithless than ever. He sacrificed to the gods of Damascus—they had defeated him, so they obviously had to be stronger. He closed the Temple and built pagan altars *in every corner of Jerusalem.* **27:** It was a relief to everyone when he was gone. He too was buried outside the royal cemetery.

29:1—32:33 The Reign of Hezekiah

Hezekiah (715–687/6), whose mother was Abijah, was among the best of Judah's kings. His importance can be seen in the Chronicler's giving him about 70 percent more space than did the author(s) of Kings. Hezekiah was a reforming king who undid all Ahaz's perversities. Most important, as far as the Chronicler was concerned, he again centralized worship in Jerusalem.

29:3–36 Hezekiah Reopens the Temple. As soon as Hezekiah became king, he repaired and reopened the Temple; he reconsecrated the priests and Levites; he recognized that previous generations had been unfaithful and had suffered because of it; and, with impressive fanfare and ceremony, he led his people in covenant renewal.

of the LORD and repaired them. [4]He summoned
the priests and Levites to meet him at the courtyard east of the Temple. [5]He said to them, "Listen to me, you Levites! Purify yourselves, and
purify the Temple of the LORD, the God of your
ancestors. Remove all the defiled things from the
sanctuary. [6]Our ancestors were unfaithful and
did what was evil in the sight of the LORD our
God. They abandoned the LORD and his dwelling
place; they turned their backs on him. [7]They also
shut the doors to the Temple's entry room, and
they snuffed out the lamps. They stopped burning incense and presenting burnt offerings at the
sanctuary of the God of Israel.

[8]"That is why the LORD's anger has fallen
upon Judah and Jerusalem. He has made them an
object of dread, horror, and ridicule, as you can
see with your own eyes. [9]Because of this, our fathers have been killed in battle, and our sons and
daughters and wives have been captured. [10]But
now I will make a covenant with the LORD, the
God of Israel, so that his fierce anger will turn
away from us. [11]My sons, do not neglect your
duties any longer! The LORD has chosen you to
stand in his presence, to minister to him, and to
lead the people in worship and present offerings
to him."

[12]Then these Levites got right to work:

From the clan of Kohath: Mahath son of
Amasai and Joel son of Azariah.
From the clan of Merari: Kish son of Abdi and
Azariah son of Jehallelel.
From the clan of Gershon: Joah son of
Zimmah and Eden son of Joah.
[13]From the family of Elizaphan: Shimri and
Jeiel.
From the family of Asaph: Zechariah and
Mattaniah.
[14]From the family of Heman: Jehiel and Shimei.
From the family of Jeduthun: Shemaiah and
Uzziel.

[15]These men called together their fellow Levites, and they all purified themselves. Then they
began to cleanse the Temple of the LORD, just as
the king had commanded. They were careful to
follow all the LORD's instructions in their work.
[16]The priests went into the sanctuary of the
Temple of the LORD to cleanse it, and they took
out to the Temple courtyard all the defiled things
they found. From there the Levites carted it all
out to the Kidron Valley.

[17]They began the work in early spring, on the
first day of the new year,* and in eight days they
had reached the entry room of the LORD's Temple. Then they purified the Temple of the LORD
itself, which took another eight days. So the entire task was completed in sixteen days.

The Temple Rededication

[18]Then the Levites went to King Hezekiah and
gave him this report: "We have cleansed the entire Temple of the LORD, the altar of burnt offering with all its utensils, and the table of the
Bread of the Presence with all its utensils. [19]We
have also recovered all the items discarded by
King Ahaz when he was unfaithful and closed
the Temple. They are now in front of the altar of
the LORD, purified and ready for use."

[20]Early the next morning King Hezekiah
gathered the city officials and went to the Temple
of the LORD. [21]They brought seven bulls, seven
rams, and seven male lambs as a burnt offering,
together with seven male goats as a sin offering
for the kingdom, for the Temple, and for Judah.
The king commanded the priests, who were descendants of Aaron, to sacrifice the animals on
the altar of the LORD.

[22]So they killed the bulls, and the priests took
the blood and sprinkled it on the altar. Next they
killed the rams and sprinkled their blood on the
altar. And finally, they did the same with the male
lambs. [23]The male goats for the sin offering were
then brought before the king and the assembly
of people, who laid their hands on them. [24]The
priests then killed the goats as a sin offering and
sprinkled their blood on the altar to make atonement for the sins of all Israel. The king had specifically commanded that this burnt offering and
sin offering should be made for all Israel.

[25]King Hezekiah then stationed the Levites at
the Temple of the LORD with cymbals, lyres, and
harps. He obeyed all the commands that the LORD
had given to King David through Gad, the king's
seer, and the prophet Nathan. [26]The Levites then
took their positions around the Temple with the
instruments of David, and the priests took their
positions with the trumpets.

[27]Then Hezekiah ordered that the burnt offering be placed on the altar. As the burnt offering
was presented, songs of praise to the LORD were
begun, accompanied by the trumpets and other
instruments of David, the former king of Israel.
[28]The entire assembly worshiped the LORD as the
singers sang and the trumpets blew, until all the
burnt offerings were finished. [29]Then the king
and everyone with him bowed down in worship.

29:17 Hebrew *on the first day of the first month.* This day in the ancient Hebrew lunar calendar occurred in March or early April, 715 B.C.

30 King Hezekiah and the officials ordered the Levites to praise the LORD with the psalms written by David and by Asaph the seer. So they offered joyous praise and bowed down in worship.

31 Then Hezekiah declared, "Now that you have consecrated yourselves to the LORD, bring your sacrifices and thanksgiving offerings to the Temple of the LORD." So the people brought their sacrifices and thanksgiving offerings, and all whose hearts were willing brought burnt offerings, too. 32 The people brought to the LORD 70 bulls, 100 rams, and 200 male lambs for burnt offerings. 33 They also brought 600 cattle and 3,000 sheep and goats as sacred offerings.

34 But there were too few priests to prepare all the burnt offerings. So their relatives the Levites helped them until the work was finished and more priests had been purified, for the Levites had been more conscientious about purifying themselves than the priests had been. 35 There was an abundance of burnt offerings, along with the usual liquid offerings, and a great deal of fat from the many peace offerings.

So the Temple of the LORD was restored to service. 36 And Hezekiah and all the people rejoiced because of what God had done for the people, for everything had been accomplished so quickly.

Preparations for Passover

30 King Hezekiah now sent word to all Israel and Judah, and he wrote letters of invitation to the people of Ephraim and Manasseh. He asked everyone to come to the Temple of the LORD at Jerusalem to celebrate the Passover of the LORD, the God of Israel. 2 The king, his officials, and all the community of Jerusalem decided to celebrate Passover a month later than usual.* 3 They were unable to celebrate it at the prescribed time because not enough priests could be purified by then, and the people had not yet assembled at Jerusalem.

4 This plan for keeping the Passover seemed right to the king and all the people. 5 So they sent a proclamation throughout all Israel, from Beersheba in the south to Dan in the north, inviting everyone to come to Jerusalem to celebrate the Passover of the LORD, the God of Israel. The people had not been celebrating it in great numbers as required in the Law.

6 At the king's command, runners were sent throughout Israel and Judah. They carried letters that said:

"O people of Israel, return to the LORD, the
God of Abraham, Isaac, and Israel,* so that
he will return to the few of us who have
survived the conquest of the Assyrian kings.
7 Do not be like your ancestors and relatives
who abandoned the LORD, the God of their
ancestors, and became an object of derision, as
you yourselves can see. 8 Do not be stubborn,
as they were, but submit yourselves to the
LORD. Come to his Temple, which he has set
apart as holy forever. Worship the LORD your
God so that his fierce anger will turn away
from you.

9 "For if you return to the LORD, your
relatives and your children will be treated
mercifully by their captors, and they will be
able to return to this land. For the LORD your
God is gracious and merciful. If you return
to him, he will not continue to turn his face
from you."

Celebration of Passover

10 The runners went from town to town throughout Ephraim and Manasseh and as far as the territory of Zebulun. But most of the people just laughed at the runners and made fun of them. 11 However, some people from Asher, Manasseh, and Zebulun humbled themselves and went to Jerusalem.

12 At the same time, God's hand was on the people in the land of Judah, giving them all one heart to obey the orders of the king and his officials, who were following the word of the LORD. 13 So a huge crowd assembled at Jerusalem in midspring* to celebrate the Festival of Unleavened Bread. 14 They set to work and removed the pagan altars from Jerusalem. They took away all the incense altars and threw them into the Kidron Valley.

30:2 Hebrew *in the second month.* Passover was normally observed in the first month (of the ancient Hebrew lunar calendar). **30:6** *Israel* is the name that God gave to Jacob. **30:13** Hebrew *in the second month.* The second month of the ancient Hebrew lunar calendar usually occurs within the months of April and May.

30:1—31:21 The Reforms Continue. The kingdom had split under Rehoboam, but Hezekiah and later Josiah did what they could to provide links with the northern tribes. **30:1–27:** Hezekiah encouraged people in Ephraim and Manasseh to return to Jerusalem for the Passover, which had not been properly observed for generations. It was a time of outstanding spiritual opportunity for the people of both areas and for the young king of Judah. **10:** Unfortunately, most of the remaining northerners (Israel had been destroyed by Assyria in 722 BC) were contemptuous of Hezekiah's overtures. **18–20:** Hezekiah's appeal to

15 On the fourteenth day of the second
month, one month later than usual,* the people
slaughtered the Passover lamb. This shamed the
priests and Levites, so they purified themselves
and brought burnt offerings to the Temple of
the LORD. 16 Then they took their places at the
Temple as prescribed in the Law of Moses, the
man of God. The Levites brought the sacrificial
blood to the priests, who then sprinkled it on the
altar.
17 Since many of the people had not purified themselves, the Levites had to slaughter
their Passover lamb for them, to set them apart
for the LORD. 18 Most of those who came from
Ephraim, Manasseh, Issachar, and Zebulun had
not purified themselves. But King Hezekiah
prayed for them, and they were allowed to eat
the Passover meal anyway, even though this
was contrary to the requirements of the Law.
For Hezekiah said, "May the LORD, who is good,
pardon those 19 who decide to follow the LORD,
the God of their ancestors, even though they
are not properly cleansed for the ceremony."
20 And the LORD listened to Hezekiah's prayer
and healed the people.
21 So the people of Israel who were present in
Jerusalem joyously celebrated the Festival of Unleavened Bread for seven days. Each day the Levites and priests sang to the LORD, accompanied
by loud instruments.* 22 Hezekiah encouraged all
the Levites regarding the skill they displayed as
they served the LORD. The celebration continued
for seven days. Peace offerings were sacrificed,
and the people gave thanks to the LORD, the God
of their ancestors.
23 The entire assembly then decided to continue the festival another seven days, so they
celebrated joyfully for another week. 24 King
Hezekiah gave the people 1,000 bulls and 7,000
sheep and goats for offerings, and the officials
donated 1,000 bulls and 10,000 sheep and goats.
Meanwhile, many more priests purified themselves.
25 The entire assembly of Judah rejoiced, including the priests, the Levites, all who came
from the land of Israel, the foreigners who came
to the festival, and all those who lived in Judah.
26 There was great joy in the city, for Jerusalem
had not seen a celebration like this one since the
days of Solomon, King David's son. 27 Then the
priests and Levites stood and blessed the people,
and God heard their prayer from his holy dwelling in heaven.

Hezekiah's Religious Reforms

31 When the festival ended, the Israelites who attended went to all the
towns of Judah, Benjamin, Ephraim,
and Manasseh, and they smashed all the sacred
pillars, cut down the Asherah poles, and removed
the pagan shrines and altars. After this, the Israelites returned to their own towns and homes.
2 Hezekiah then organized the priests and
Levites into divisions to offer the burnt offerings and peace offerings, and to worship and
give thanks and praise to the LORD at the gates
of the Temple. 3 The king also made a personal
contribution of animals for the daily morning
and evening burnt offerings, the weekly Sabbath
festivals, the monthly new moon festivals, and
the annual festivals as prescribed in the Law of
the LORD. 4 In addition, he required the people in
Jerusalem to bring a portion of their goods to the
priests and Levites, so they could devote themselves fully to the Law of the LORD.
5 When the people of Israel heard these requirements, they responded generously by
bringing the first share of their grain, new wine,
olive oil, honey, and all the produce of their
fields. They brought a large quantity—a tithe of
all they produced. 6 The people who had moved
to Judah from Israel, and the people of Judah
themselves, brought in the tithes of their cattle,
sheep, and goats and a tithe of the things that had
been dedicated to the LORD their God, and they
piled them up in great heaps. 7 They began piling
them up in late spring, and the heaps continued
to grow until early autumn.* 8 When Hezekiah
and his officials came and saw these huge piles,
they thanked the LORD and his people Israel!
9 "Where did all this come from?" Hezekiah
asked the priests and Levites.
10 And Azariah the high priest, from the family of Zadok, replied, "Since the people began
bringing their gifts to the LORD's Temple, we
have had enough to eat and plenty to spare. The
LORD has blessed his people, and all this is left
over."
11 Hezekiah ordered that storerooms be pre-

30:15 Hebrew *On the fourteenth day of the second month.* Passover normally began on the fourteenth day of the first month (see Lev 23:5). **30:21** Or *sang to the LORD with all their strength.* **31:7** Hebrew *in the third month . . . until the seventh month.* The third month of the ancient Hebrew lunar calendar usually occurs within the months of May and June; the seventh month usually occurs within September and October.

the LORD to bend the usual purity rules is heard, allowing those from the north to participate in the unified celebrations. **31:1:** Hezekiah's reforms spread beyond Judah and into Israel. **18:** Note that as part

pared in the Temple of the LORD. When this was done, [12]the people faithfully brought all the tithes and gifts to the Temple. Conaniah the Levite was put in charge, assisted by his brother Shimei. [13]The supervisors under them were Jehiel, Azaziah, Nahath, Asahel, Jerimoth, Jozabad, Eliel, Ismakiah, Mahath, and Benaiah. These appointments were made by King Hezekiah and Azariah, the chief official in the Temple of God.

[14]Kore son of Imnah the Levite, who was the gatekeeper at the East Gate, was put in charge of distributing the voluntary offerings given to God, the gifts, and the things that had been dedicated to the LORD. [15]His faithful assistants were Eden, Miniamin, Jeshua, Shemaiah, Amariah, and Shecaniah. They distributed the gifts among the families of priests in their towns by their divisions, dividing the gifts fairly among old and young alike. [16]They distributed the gifts to all males three years old or older, regardless of their place in the genealogical records. The distribution went to all who would come to the LORD's Temple to perform their daily duties according to their divisions. [17]They distributed gifts to the priests who were listed by their families in the genealogical records, and to the Levites twenty years old or older who were listed according to their jobs and their divisions. [18]Food allotments were also given to the families of all those listed in the genealogical records, including their little babies, wives, sons, and daughters. For they had all been faithful in purifying themselves.

[19]As for the priests, the descendants of Aaron, who were living in the open villages around the towns, men were appointed by name to distribute portions to every male among the priests and to all the Levites listed in the genealogical records.

[20]In this way, King Hezekiah handled the distribution throughout all Judah, doing what was pleasing and good in the sight of the LORD his God. [21]In all that he did in the service of the Temple of God and in his efforts to follow God's laws and commands, Hezekiah sought his God wholeheartedly. As a result, he was very successful.

Assyria Invades Judah

32 After Hezekiah had faithfully carried out this work, King Sennacherib of Assyria invaded Judah. He laid siege to the fortified towns, giving orders for his army to break through their walls. [2]When Hezekiah realized that Sennacherib also intended to attack Jerusalem, [3]he consulted with his officials and military advisers, and they decided to stop the flow of the springs outside the city. [4]They organized a huge work crew to stop the flow of the springs, cutting off the brook that ran through the fields. For they said, "Why should the kings of Assyria come here and find plenty of water?"

[5]Then Hezekiah worked hard at repairing all the broken sections of the wall, erecting towers, and constructing a second wall outside the first. He also reinforced the supporting terraces* in the City of David and manufactured large numbers of weapons and shields. [6]He appointed military officers over the people and assembled them before him in the square at the city gate. Then Hezekiah encouraged them by saying: [7]"Be strong and courageous! Don't be afraid or discouraged because of the king of Assyria or his mighty army, for there is a power far greater on our side! [8]He may have a great army, but they are merely men. We have the LORD our God to help us and to fight our battles for us!" Hezekiah's words greatly encouraged the people.

32:5 Hebrew *the millo.* The meaning of the Hebrew is uncertain.

of a census of priestly families, the Chronicler specifically mentions that the daughters of the priests were enrolled on the census lists, another practice that stood out from the common custom of the world of that day.

32:1–23 The Invasion of Sennacherib of Assyria. Hezekiah's greatest military challenge came with the invasion of Judah by the mighty Sennacherib of Assyria in 701 BC. Hezekiah's increasing spirit of independence from his Assyrian overlords was responsible for this invasion. His spiritual reforms were paralleled by political reforms. In those days to be dominated by a power such as Assyria involved at least the implicit recognition of the overlord's gods. By leading his people back to the LORD, Hezekiah distanced himself from the common practice. Sennacherib arrived to bring him back into line. **2–4:** Hezekiah prepared for the onslaught as best he could. Jerusalem has always been short of adequate water. At certain times of the year, the rain-filled reservoirs were virtually empty. Hezekiah's workmen cut a water tunnel a third of a mile long through solid rock underneath Jerusalem. This diverted water from the springs outside the walls, and now, for the first time, Jerusalem had water flowing within its walls. The necessary water would be available to those defending the city instead of to those attacking it. **6–8:** He also particularly urged the people to trust the LORD to help them against

Sennacherib Threatens Jerusalem
[9]While King Sennacherib of Assyria was still besieging the town of Lachish, he sent his officers
to Jerusalem with this message for Hezekiah and
all the people in the city:

[10]"This is what King Sennacherib of Assyria
says: What are you trusting in that makes
you think you can survive my siege of
Jerusalem? [11]Hezekiah has said, 'The LORD
our God will rescue us from the king of
Assyria.' Surely Hezekiah is misleading
you, sentencing you to death by famine and
thirst! [12]Don't you realize that Hezekiah is
the very person who destroyed all the LORD's
shrines and altars? He commanded Judah and
Jerusalem to worship only at the altar at the
Temple and to offer sacrifices on it alone.
[13]"Surely you must realize what I and
the other kings of Assyria before me have
done to all the people of the earth! Were any
of the gods of those nations able to rescue
their people from my power? [14]Which of
their gods was able to rescue its people from
the destructive power of my predecessors?
What makes you think your God can rescue
you from me? [15]Don't let Hezekiah deceive
you! Don't let him fool you like this! I say it
again—no god of any nation or kingdom has
ever yet been able to rescue his people from
me or my ancestors. How much less will your
God rescue you from my power!"

[16]And Sennacherib's officers further mocked
the LORD God and his servant Hezekiah, heaping
insult upon insult. [17]The king also sent letters
scorning the LORD, the God of Israel. He wrote,
"Just as the gods of all the other nations failed to
rescue their people from my power, so the God of
Hezekiah will also fail." [18]The Assyrian officials
who brought the letters shouted this in Hebrew*
to the people gathered on the walls of the city,
trying to terrify them so it would be easier to
capture the city. [19]These officers talked about the
God of Jerusalem as though he were one of the
pagan gods, made by human hands.
[20]Then King Hezekiah and the prophet Isaiah
son of Amoz cried out in prayer to God in heav-
en. [21]And the LORD sent an angel who destroyed
the Assyrian army with all its commanders and
officers. So Sennacherib was forced to return
home in disgrace to his own land. And when he
entered the temple of his god, some of his own
sons killed him there with a sword.
[22]That is how the LORD rescued Hezekiah and
the people of Jerusalem from King Sennacherib of
Assyria and from all the others who threatened
them. So there was peace throughout the land.
[23]From then on King Hezekiah became highly
respected among all the surrounding nations, and
many gifts for the LORD arrived at Jerusalem, with
valuable presents for King Hezekiah, too.

Hezekiah's Sickness and Recovery
[24]About that time Hezekiah became deathly ill.
He prayed to the LORD, who healed him and gave
him a miraculous sign. [25]But Hezekiah did not
respond appropriately to the kindness shown
him, and he became proud. So the LORD's anger
came against him and against Judah and Jerusalem. [26]Then Hezekiah humbled himself and
repented of his pride, as did the people of Jerusalem. So the LORD's anger did not fall on them
during Hezekiah's lifetime.
[27]Hezekiah was very wealthy and highly
honored. He built special treasury buildings for
his silver, gold, precious stones, and spices, and
for his shields and other valuable items. [28]He

32:18 Hebrew *in the dialect of Judah.*

their human foes. **9–19:** However, Sennacherib had already conquered almost all of Judah. According to his records, he captured forty-six towns and had imprisoned Hezekiah in Jerusalem. During the siege of Lachish, the last outpost to fall, Sennacherib sent messengers to Hezekiah to ridicule him and his God, and to demoralize Jerusalem's defenders. The words of the Assyrian messengers indicate that they considerably misunderstood the nature of Hezekiah's spiritual reforms. They boasted that none of the gods of any other nation had been able to protect their people from Assyrian attack. **20–23:** Characteristically, Hezekiah's response was spiritual. He prayed to the LORD and turned to the prophet Isaiah for guidance. The LORD's response was more dramatic than any of them could have dared hope—and far beyond the power of *the pagan gods, made by human hands* (v. 19). Sennacherib was forced to return home in disgrace to Nineveh, where some of his sons killed him.

32:24–33 Hezekiah's Illness and Its Aftermath. At about the same time, Hezekiah became critically ill. He prayed again, this time for physical deliverance, and once again the LORD heard him. **25–26:** Like Uzziah before him, in his time of victory and strength he became proud. Hezekiah, however, learned his lesson—he was like David and acknowledged his shortcomings. He and his people were spared, and he lived to enjoy great riches and prestige.

also constructed many storehouses for his grain, new wine, and olive oil; and he made many stalls for his cattle and pens for his flocks of sheep and goats. [29]He built many towns and acquired vast flocks and herds, for God had given him great wealth. [30]He blocked up the upper spring of Gihon and brought the water down through a tunnel to the west side of the City of David. And so he succeeded in everything he did.

[31]However, when ambassadors arrived from Babylon to ask about the remarkable events that had taken place in the land, God withdrew from Hezekiah in order to test him and to see what was really in his heart.

Summary of Hezekiah's Reign

[32]The rest of the events in Hezekiah's reign and his acts of devotion are recorded in *The Vision of the Prophet Isaiah Son of Amoz,* which is included in *The Book of the Kings of Judah and Israel.* [33]When Hezekiah died, he was buried in the upper area of the royal cemetery, and all Judah and Jerusalem honored him at his death. And his son Manasseh became the next king.

Manasseh Rules in Judah

33 Manasseh was twelve years old when he became king, and he reigned in Jerusalem fifty-five years. [2]He did what was evil in the LORD's sight, following the detestable practices of the pagan nations that the LORD had driven from the land ahead of the Israelites. [3]He rebuilt the pagan shrines his father, Hezekiah, had broken down. He constructed altars for the images of Baal and set up Asherah poles. He also bowed before all the powers of the heavens and worshiped them.

[4]He built pagan altars in the Temple of the LORD, the place where the LORD had said, "My name will remain in Jerusalem forever." [5]He built these altars for all the powers of the heavens in both courtyards of the LORD's Temple. [6]Manasseh also sacrificed his own sons in the fire* in the valley of Ben-Hinnom. He practiced sorcery, divination, and witchcraft, and he consulted with mediums and psychics. He did much that was evil in the LORD's sight, arousing his anger.

[7]Manasseh even took a carved idol he had made and set it up in God's Temple, the very place where God had told David and his son Solomon: "My name will be honored forever in this Temple and in Jerusalem—the city I have chosen from among all the tribes of Israel. [8]If the Israelites will be careful to obey my commands—all the laws, decrees, and regulations given through Moses—I will not send them into exile from this land that I set aside for your ancestors." [9]But Manasseh led the people of Judah and Jerusalem to do even more evil than the pagan nations that the LORD had destroyed when the people of Israel entered the land.

[10]The LORD spoke to Manasseh and his people, but they ignored all his warnings. [11]So the LORD sent the commanders of the Assyrian armies, and they took Manasseh prisoner. They put a ring through his nose, bound him in bronze chains, and led him away to Babylon. [12]But while in deep distress, Manasseh sought the LORD his God and sincerely humbled himself before the God of his ancestors. [13]And when he prayed, the LORD listened to him and was moved by his request. So the LORD brought Manasseh back to Jerusalem and to his kingdom. Then Manasseh finally realized that the LORD alone is God!

[14]After this Manasseh rebuilt the outer wall of the City of David, from west of the Gihon

33:6 Or *also made his sons pass through the fire.*

33:1–25 The Reigns of Manasseh and Amon

Manasseh was the worst Judean king ever, and 2 Kings blames him for the ultimate fall of Judah, despite the fine efforts of his grandson Josiah.

33:1–20 Manasseh. Manasseh (687/6–642) began to reign at the age of twelve, apparently as co-regent with his father. **2–9:** He built altars to pagan gods, like Baal; he built the Asherah poles, sacrificed his own sons, practiced witchcraft; he threatened the Israelites and led the Judahites and the people of Jerusalem into evil doings; he was as evil as the Canaanites. The LORD was considered to be merely one of many gods. Manasseh undid all of Hezekiah's careful reforms, and the people seemed to follow him with enthusiasm. (It seems that Hezekiah's reforms did not outlast him, which is perhaps why they are not mentioned in the book of Isaiah.) **10–13:** The LORD warned Manasseh and his people, but to no effect. Therefore punishment was inevitable. Once again God used Assyria as his instrument of judgment. Second Kings does not tell us that the severe judgment had its desired effect (the purpose of God's judgment is always redemptive, to bring us back): Manasseh had a change of heart. **14–17:** Manasseh's later years were spent in fortifying his capital city, removing the emblems of pagan worship to which he had been so devoted and restoring the true worship of the LORD. Although behavior can be changed, the effects of bad behavior cannot easily be obliterated. The people continued to worship in ways that were questionable.

Spring in the Kidron Valley to the Fish Gate,
and continuing around the hill of Ophel. He
built the wall very high. And he stationed his
military officers in all of the fortified towns of
Judah. 15 Manasseh also removed the foreign
gods and the idol from the LORD's Temple. He
tore down all the altars he had built on the hill
where the Temple stood and all the altars that
were in Jerusalem, and he dumped them outside
the city. 16 Then he restored the altar of the LORD
and sacrificed peace offerings and thanksgiving
offerings on it. He also encouraged the people
of Judah to worship the LORD, the God of Israel.
17 However, the people still sacrificed at the pagan
shrines, though only to the LORD their God.
18 The rest of the events of Manasseh's reign,
his prayer to God, and the words the seers spoke
to him in the name of the LORD, the God of Israel, are recorded in *The Book of the Kings of
Israel.* 19 Manasseh's prayer, the account of the
way God answered him, and an account of all
his sins and unfaithfulness are recorded in *The
Record of the Seers.** It includes a list of the
locations where he built pagan shrines and set
up Asherah poles and idols before he humbled
himself and repented. 20 When Manasseh died,
he was buried in his palace. Then his son Amon
became the next king.

Amon Rules in Judah

21 Amon was twenty-two years old when he became king, and he reigned in Jerusalem two years.
22 He did what was evil in the LORD's sight, just
as his father, Manasseh, had done. He worshiped
and sacrificed to all the idols his father had made.
23 But unlike his father, he did not humble himself before the LORD. Instead, Amon sinned even
more.
24 Then Amon's own officials conspired against
him and assassinated him in his palace. 25 But the
people of the land killed all those who had conspired against King Amon, and they made his
son Josiah the next king.

Josiah Rules in Judah

34 Josiah was eight years old when he
became king, and he reigned in Jerusalem thirty-one years. 2 He did what
was pleasing in the LORD's sight and followed
the example of his ancestor David. He did not
turn away from doing what was right.
3 During the eighth year of his reign, while he
was still young, Josiah began to seek the God of
his ancestor David. Then in the twelfth year he
began to purify Judah and Jerusalem, destroying
all the pagan shrines, the Asherah poles, and the
carved idols and cast images. 4 He ordered that the
altars of Baal be demolished and that the incense
altars which stood above them be broken down.
He also made sure that the Asherah poles, the
carved idols, and the cast images were smashed
and scattered over the graves of those who had
sacrificed to them. 5 He burned the bones of the
pagan priests on their own altars, and so he purified Judah and Jerusalem.
6 He did the same thing in the towns of Manasseh, Ephraim, and Simeon, even as far as
Naphtali, and in the regions* all around them.
7 He destroyed the pagan altars and the Asherah poles, and he crushed the idols into dust.
He cut down all the incense altars throughout
the land of Israel. Finally, he returned to Jerusalem.
8 In the eighteenth year of his reign, after
he had purified the land and the Temple, Josiah appointed Shaphan son of Azaliah, Maaseiah
the governor of Jerusalem, and Joah son of Joahaz, the royal historian, to repair the Temple of
the LORD his God. 9 They gave Hilkiah the high
priest the money that had been collected by the
Levites who served as gatekeepers at the Temple
of God. The gifts were brought by people from
Manasseh, Ephraim, and from all the remnant of

33:19 Or *The Record of Hozai.* **34:6** As in Syriac version. Hebrew reads *in their temples,* or *in their ruins.* The meaning of the Hebrew is uncertain.

33:21–25 Amon's Brief Ungodliness. Amon (642–640) was as bad as Manasseh, but he did not reign as long. He was like his father in his unfaithfulness but unlike him because he never acknowledged his need for God's forgiveness. His servants conspired against him and assassinated him in his palace. He left the throne to his eight-year-old son, Josiah.

34:1—35:27 The Reign of Josiah

Josiah was perhaps the brightest star of the Judean monarchy and is one of true heroes of 2 Chronicles (see also 2 Kgs 23:25). Someone influenced the young man in his spiritual path.

34:1–7: One insight into Josiah's life and character is that he began to seek the LORD early, when he was sixteen, during his eighth year on the throne. He gave practical expression to this impulse four years later when he began reforms to undo the negative influence of his father and grandfather.

34:8–28 Perhaps the most important act of Josiah's kingship came in the eighteenth year of his reign

Expectations of Women

The expectations of women in the Bible are diverse. It might be assumed that, given the ancient and Middle Eastern character of these texts, the place of women would be circumscribed by the expectations of that society. These expectations are evident in much of the law code of ancient Israel described in Leviticus and Numbers. It might also be argued that cultural assumptions account to some degree for the apostle Paul's restrictions on the role of women (1 Cor 14:35; 1 Tim 2:11–14).

Despite this, there is in God's dealings with the people of God a radical inclusivity. The Bible begins with an affirmation that the image of God is borne in the whole of humanity, male and female (Gen 1:27–31), and responsibility for stewardship of the earth is given to men and women. Likewise, God covenants with all Israel, men and women. The women of Israel are freely accountable for their actions in relation to God (Num 6:2; 30:3–9; Deut 17:2–7). Women feature prominently in the ministry of Jesus as supporters and recipients of his ministry. Subsequently the gospel is preached specifically to women (Acts 16:11–15), and women play an active role in the life of the church (1 Cor 11:2–15; Acts 16). It can be argued that women are expected to engage in a full and active life of faith, responding to the call of God in their lives.

Close consideration of the women we meet in the pages of Scripture invites us to ask some new questions. Women are key to the execution of God's plans on many occasions. Many of these women are in some way or other on the margins of society. Sarah's advanced years and infertility set her apart from other women (Gen 18:9–15). Rahab (Josh 2; 6:22–25) was a prostitute in Jericho, and Ruth, a Moabite, ethnically an enemy of Israel (Deut 23:3). Yet all play key roles in bringing about God's purposes for humanity.

The women we meet in the Gospels are equally intriguing. The Syro-Phoenician woman who debates with Jesus (Mark 7:24–30), the woman who risks her reputation to anoint Jesus (Luke 7:36–50), and the Samaritan woman (John 4) stand on the margins of society. Others, such as the women disciples who followed Jesus from Galilee (Luke 23:49–56), have deliberately stepped outside of their social roles to do so. God calls women, no less than men, to give their lives in divine service. Some are freed to do so by their circumstances. For others it is a conscious choice, like that of Abigail (1 Sam 25), to defy the expectations of others. The Scriptures declare God's expectation that women, whether as wives and mothers, prophetic voices (2 Sam 14:1–20), hosts (2 Kgs 4:8–37; Acts 16:14–15, 40), or explicit proclaimers of the gospel (John 4:39; 20:18), will respond boldly to God's call on their lives and give themselves in loving service to God, regardless of the expectations of the world around them.

Israel, as well as from all Judah, Benjamin, and
the people of Jerusalem.
10 He entrusted the money to the men assigned to supervise the restoration of the LORD's
Temple. Then they paid the workers who did the
repairs and renovation of the Temple. 11 They
hired carpenters and builders, who purchased
finished stone for the walls and timber for the
rafters and beams. They restored what earlier
kings of Judah had allowed to fall into ruin.
12 The workers served faithfully under the
leadership of Jahath and Obadiah, Levites of the
Merarite clan, and Zechariah and Meshullam,
Levites of the Kohathite clan. Other Levites, all
of whom were skilled musicians, 13 were put in
charge of the laborers of the various trades. Still
others assisted as secretaries, officials, and gatekeepers.

Hilkiah Discovers God's Law

14 While they were bringing out the money collected at the LORD's Temple, Hilkiah the priest
found the Book of the Law of the LORD that was
written by Moses. 15 Hilkiah said to Shaphan the
court secretary, "I have found the Book of the
Law in the LORD's Temple!" Then Hilkiah gave
the scroll to Shaphan.
16 Shaphan took the scroll to the king and
reported, "Your officials are doing everything
they were assigned to do. 17 The money that was
collected at the Temple of the LORD has been
turned over to the supervisors and workmen."

when he began to refurbish the Temple. **14–21:** During this significant remodeling the workmen uncovered a scroll. To the consternation of Josiah and his senior officials, the book turned out to be a law scroll, containing what may be all or part of our book of Deuteronomy, with commandments which neither

18 Shaphan also told the king, "Hilkiah the priest
has given me a scroll." So Shaphan read it to the
king.
19 When the king heard what was written in
the Law, he tore his clothes in despair. 20 Then
he gave these orders to Hilkiah, Ahikam son of
Shaphan, Acbor son of Micaiah,* Shaphan the
court secretary, and Asaiah the king's personal
adviser: 21 "Go to the Temple and speak to the
LORD for me and for all the remnant of Israel
and Judah. Inquire about the words written in
the scroll that has been found. For the LORD's
great anger has been poured out on us because
our ancestors have not obeyed the word of the
LORD. We have not been doing everything this
scroll says we must do."
22 So Hilkiah and the other men went to the
New Quarter* of Jerusalem to consult with the
prophet Huldah. She was the wife of Shallum
son of Tikvah, son of Harhas,* the keeper of the
Temple wardrobe.
23 She said to them, "The LORD, the God of Israel, has spoken! Go back and tell the man who
sent you, 24 'This is what the LORD says: I am going to bring disaster on this city* and its people.
All the curses written in the scroll that was read
to the king of Judah will come true. 25 For my
people have abandoned me and offered sacrifices
to pagan gods, and I am very angry with them
for everything they have done. My anger will
be poured out on this place, and it will not be
quenched.'
26 "But go to the king of Judah who sent you
to seek the LORD and tell him: 'This is what the
LORD, the God of Israel, says concerning the
message you have just heard: 27 You were sorry
and humbled yourself before God when you
heard his words against this city and its people.
You humbled yourself and tore your clothing in
despair and wept before me in repentance. And I
have indeed heard you, says the LORD. 28 So I will
not send the promised disaster until after you
have died and been buried in peace. You yourself
will not see the disaster I am going to bring on
this city and its people.' "

So they took her message back to the king.

Josiah's Religious Reforms

29 Then the king summoned all the elders of Judah and Jerusalem. 30 And the king went up to
the Temple of the LORD with all the people of
Judah and Jerusalem, along with the priests and
the Levites—all the people from the greatest to
the least. There the king read to them the entire Book of the Covenant that had been found in
the LORD's Temple. 31 The king took his place of
authority beside the pillar and renewed the covenant in the LORD's presence. He pledged to obey
the LORD by keeping all his commands, laws, and
decrees with all his heart and soul. He promised
to obey all the terms of the covenant that were
written in the scroll. 32 And he required everyone
in Jerusalem and the people of Benjamin to make

34:20 As in parallel text at 2 Kgs 22:12; Hebrew reads *Abdon son of Micah.* **34:22a** Or *the Second Quarter,* a newer section of Jerusalem. Hebrew reads *the Mishneh.* **34:22b** As in parallel text at 2 Kgs 22:14; Hebrew reads *son of Tokhath, son of Hasrah.* **34:24** Hebrew *this place;* also in 34:27, 28.

---

king nor people had been observing, in part because they were unaware of them: *Our ancestors have not obeyed the word of the LORD.* **21–28:** It is significant that when Josiah asked for God's guidance, his advisers took the law scroll to a woman. She was a prominent prophet, named Huldah, the most significant female figure in 2 Chronicles. The committee, made up of five of the most highly placed men of the kingdom, clearly saw no problem in taking the scroll to a woman for authentication. Her authority was undisputed. This raises doubts about the common assumption that women of the time were all uneducated and downtrodden (see Expectations of Women, previous page). Huldah was a clear example of a learned and influential woman. She was married to Shallum, the keeper of the Temple wardrobe, and her husband's family had court connections. These were the days of Zephaniah, Habakkuk, and Jeremiah, but the delegation did not go to one of them. We are not told why, but Huldah was seen to be the most important spiritual leader in the Judean capital. **23–24:** Huldah was a true prophet of the LORD. She twice used the traditional prophetic formula: *This is what the LORD says.* Her message of judgment was also in the pattern of the messages of the prophets before the Exile. She was even direct with Josiah: *Tell the man who sent you.* Huldah's message of disaster resulting from their sin was not pleasant, but she did not hesitate to proclaim it boldly. **26–28:** Huldah did have a positive word for Josiah: Because he was penitent and humble, he would not have to live to see the trouble come.

34:29—35:19 Josiah's Response to Huldah's Message. In an appropriate response to Huldah's prophetic proclamation, the king began to lead the people in a dramatic ceremony of covenant renewal. They recommitted themselves to the LORD and to

a similar pledge. The people of Jerusalem did so,
renewing their covenant with God, the God of
their ancestors.
33 So Josiah removed all detestable idols from
the entire land of Israel and required everyone
to worship the LORD their God. And throughout
the rest of his lifetime, they did not turn away
from the LORD, the God of their ancestors.

Josiah Celebrates Passover

35 Then Josiah announced that the Passover of the LORD would be celebrated in Jerusalem, and so the Passover
lamb was slaughtered on the fourteenth day of
the first month.* 2 Josiah also assigned the priests
to their duties and encouraged them in their
work at the Temple of the LORD. 3 He issued this
order to the Levites, who were to teach all Israel
and who had been set apart to serve the LORD:
"Put the holy Ark in the Temple that was built
by Solomon son of David, the king of Israel. You
no longer need to carry it back and forth on your
shoulders. Now spend your time serving the
LORD your God and his people Israel. 4 Report for
duty according to the family divisions of your
ancestors, following the directions of King David
of Israel and the directions of his son Solomon.
5 "Then stand in the sanctuary at the place
appointed for your family division and help the
families assigned to you as they bring their offerings to the Temple. 6 Slaughter the Passover
lambs, purify yourselves, and prepare to help
those who come. Follow all the directions that
the LORD gave through Moses."
7 Then Josiah provided 30,000 lambs and
young goats for the people's Passover offerings,
along with 3,000 cattle, all from the king's own
flocks and herds. 8 The king's officials also made
willing contributions to the people, priests, and
Levites. Hilkiah, Zechariah, and Jehiel, the administrators of God's Temple, gave the priests
2,600 lambs and young goats and 300 cattle as
Passover offerings. 9 The Levite leaders—Conaniah and his brothers Shemaiah and Nethanel,
as well as Hashabiah, Jeiel, and Jozabad—gave
5,000 lambs and young goats and 500 cattle to
the Levites for their Passover offerings.
10 When everything was ready for the Passover
celebration, the priests and the Levites took their
places, organized by their divisions, as the king
had commanded. 11 The Levites then slaughtered
the Passover lambs and presented the blood to
the priests, who sprinkled the blood on the altar
while the Levites prepared the animals. 12 They
divided the burnt offerings among the people
by their family groups, so they could offer them
to the LORD as prescribed in the Book of Moses.
They did the same with the cattle. 13 Then they
roasted the Passover lambs as prescribed; and
they boiled the holy offerings in pots, kettles,
and pans, and brought them out quickly so the
people could eat them.
14 Afterward the Levites prepared Passover offerings for themselves and for the priests—the
descendants of Aaron—because the priests had
been busy from morning till night offering the
burnt offerings and the fat portions. The Levites
took responsibility for all these preparations.
15 The musicians, descendants of Asaph, were
in their assigned places, following the commands that had been given by David, Asaph,
Heman, and Jeduthun, the king's seer. The gatekeepers guarded the gates and did not need to
leave their posts of duty, for their Passover offerings were prepared for them by their fellow
Levites.
16 The entire ceremony for the LORD's Passover was completed that day. All the burnt offerings were sacrificed on the altar of the LORD,
as King Josiah had commanded. 17 All the Israelites present in Jerusalem celebrated Passover
and the Festival of Unleavened Bread for seven
days. 18 Never since the time of the prophet
Samuel had there been such a Passover. None
of the kings of Israel had ever kept a Passover as
Josiah did, involving all the priests and Levites,
all the people of Jerusalem, and people from all
over Judah and Israel. 19 This Passover celebration took place in the eighteenth year of Josiah's reign.

35:1 This day in the ancient Hebrew lunar calendar was April 5, 622 B.C.

---

their covenant obligations. Josiah got rid of the pagan idols and then required everyone to worship the LORD God of Israel. The resulting revival experience was perhaps the most widespread of the Old Testament. Josiah and his people made a strong commitment to follow Yahweh and accept the message of the scroll. **35:1–19:** As a symbol of the renewed covenant relationship, Josiah also led the people in observing the Passover, which had been infrequently or inappropriately observed throughout the generations. This chapter is the final example in the book of the considerable emphasis on the feasts and festivals and on the Levites who were so important in their observance.

Josiah Dies in Battle
20 After Josiah had finished restoring the Temple,
King Neco of Egypt led his army up from Egypt
to do battle at Carchemish on the Euphrates River, and Josiah and his army marched out to fight
him.* 21 But King Neco sent messengers to Josiah
with this message:

"What do you want with me, king of Judah? I
have no quarrel with you today! I am on my
way to fight another nation, and God has told
me to hurry! Do not interfere with God, who
is with me, or he will destroy you."

22 But Josiah refused to listen to Neco, to
whom God had indeed spoken, and he would not
turn back. Instead, he disguised himself and led
his army into battle on the plain of Megiddo.
23 But the enemy archers hit King Josiah with
their arrows and wounded him. He cried out to
his men, "Take me from the battle, for I am badly
wounded!"
24 So they lifted Josiah out of his chariot and
placed him in another chariot. Then they brought
him back to Jerusalem, where he died. He was
buried there in the royal cemetery. And all Judah
and Jerusalem mourned for him. 25 The prophet
Jeremiah composed funeral songs for Josiah, and
to this day choirs still sing these sad songs about
his death. These songs of sorrow have become
a tradition and are recorded in *The Book of Laments.*
26 The rest of the events of Josiah's reign and
his acts of devotion (carried out according to what
was written in the Law of the LORD), 27 from beginning to end—all are recorded in *The Book of
the Kings of Israel and Judah.*

Jehoahaz Rules in Judah
36 Then the people of the land took Josiah's son Jehoahaz and made him the
next king in Jerusalem.
2 Jehoahaz* was twenty-three years old when
he became king, and he reigned in Jerusalem
three months.
3 Then he was deposed by the king of Egypt,
who demanded that Judah pay 7,500 pounds of
silver and 75 pounds of gold* as tribute.

Jehoiakim Rules in Judah
4 The king of Egypt then installed Eliakim, the
brother of Jehoahaz, as the next king of Judah
and Jerusalem, and he changed Eliakim's name
to Jehoiakim. Then Neco took Jehoahaz to Egypt
as a prisoner.
5 Jehoiakim was twenty-five years old when
he became king, and he reigned in Jerusalem
eleven years. He did what was evil in the sight of
the LORD his God.
6 Then King Nebuchadnezzar of Babylon
came to Jerusalem and captured it, and he bound
Jehoiakim in bronze chains and led him away to
Babylon. 7 Nebuchadnezzar also took some of the
treasures from the Temple of the LORD, and he
placed them in his palace* in Babylon.
8 The rest of the events in Jehoiakim's reign,
including all the evil things he did and everything found against him, are recorded in *The
Book of the Kings of Israel and Judah.* Then his
son Jehoiachin became the next king.

35:20 Or *Josiah went out to meet him.* 36:2 Hebrew *Joahaz,* a variant spelling of Jehoahaz; also in 36:4. 36:3 Hebrew *100 talents* [3,400 kilograms] *of silver and 1 talent* [34 kilograms] *of gold.* 36:7 Or *temple.*

35:20–27 Josiah's Untimely End. In the latter years of the seventh century BC, the power struggle in the ancient Near East was approaching its climax. Cruel Assyria, overextended and weakened, was about to reap what it had sown. Babylon had revolted under the father of Nebuchadnezzar and would soon be part of bringing Assyria down. Egypt wanted to maintain the balance of power, so Pharaoh Neco marched eastward through Judah to try to bolster Assyrian resistance. He probably also wanted to carve out a section of Syria-Palestine for himself. Josiah, perhaps foolishly, meddled in the superpowers' fight and was crushed, shot by an enemy archer. He died at the age of thirty-nine and had ruled for thirty-one years. Neco's campaign was too late to help Assyria. Its last outpost fell in 610 BC.

36:1–23 The Reigns of Jehoahaz, Jehoiakim, Jehoiachin, and Zedekiah

The rest of the story of Judah is not a happy one. Forgettable kings came and went quickly, and the final twenty years were rife with political chaos and further spiritual decline.

36:1–4 Jehoahaz (609) was the second son of Josiah, but the people justifiably did not like his older brother, so they made him king instead. **4:** *Neco took Jehoahaz to Egypt as a prisoner.* In a sense, national history begins and ends in Egypt.

36:5–8 Jehoiakim, Strong in His Wickedness. Josiah's oldest son was named Eliakim, but the pharaoh changed his name to Jehoiakim (609–598). This indi-

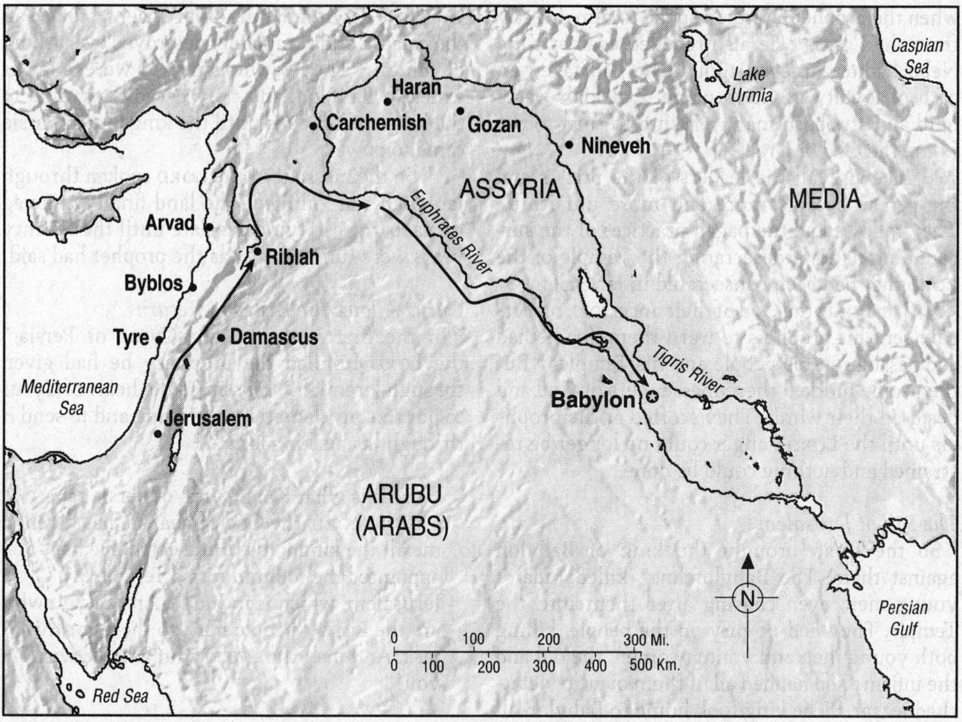

Exile of the Southern Kingdom

Jehoiachin Rules in Judah
9 Jehoiachin was eighteen* years old when he
became king, and he reigned in Jerusalem three
months and ten days. Jehoiachin did what was
evil in the LORD's sight.
10 In the spring of the year* King Nebuchadnezzar took Jehoiachin to Babylon. Many treasures from the Temple of the LORD were also
taken to Babylon at that time. And Nebuchadnezzar installed Jehoiachin's uncle,* Zedekiah, as
the next king in Judah and Jerusalem.

Zedekiah Rules in Judah
11 Zedekiah was twenty-one years old when he
became king, and he reigned in Jerusalem eleven
years. 12 He did what was evil in the sight of the
LORD his God, and he refused to humble himself

36:9 As in one Hebrew manuscript, some Greek manuscripts, and Syriac version (see also 2 Kgs 24:8); most Hebrew manuscripts read *eight*. **36:10a** Hebrew *At the turn of the year.* The first day of this year in the ancient Hebrew lunar calendar was April 13, 597 B.C. **36:10b** As in parallel text at 2 Kgs 24:17; Hebrew reads *brother,* or *relative.*

cates that he was little more than an Egyptian puppet. Remember also that he was not the people's choice. He was selfish, materialistic, and ruthless, and *did what was evil in the sight of the LORD*. Jeremiah had to oppose him every year he ruled. Chronicles states that Jehoiakim was taken into exile in Babylon, but Kings states that he died in Jerusalem during the siege. We can only imagine what was happening in the lives of the women of the land.

36:9–10 Jehoiachin. Jehoiachin (598/7) was a young man when he was suddenly thrust upon the throne. He hardly had time to do much evil before Nebuchadnezzar carted him and his family off to Babylon. In all Jehoiachin ruled for a little more than three months and spent thirty-six years in exile. **10:** Nebuchadnezzar was surprisingly lenient. He looted Jerusalem but did not destroy the city. He took many captives to Babylon, the cream of the leadership of the country, perhaps ten thousand exiles in all. The prophet Ezekiel went to Babylon during this time.

36:11–21 Zedekiah and the End. Zedekiah was the last Judean king, but his fate hung in the balance throughout his ten-year reign. The Chronicler's assessment of Zedekiah is negative and familiar, but perhaps Zedekiah was more weak than wicked, dominated by inferior officials, generally pro-Egypt

when the prophet Jeremiah spoke to him directly from the LORD. 13 He also rebelled against King Nebuchadnezzar, even though he had taken an oath of loyalty in God's name. Zedekiah was a hard and stubborn man, refusing to turn to the LORD, the God of Israel.

14 Likewise, all the leaders of the priests and the people became more and more unfaithful. They followed all the pagan practices of the surrounding nations, desecrating the Temple of the LORD that had been consecrated in Jerusalem.

15 The LORD, the God of their ancestors, repeatedly sent his prophets to warn them, for he had compassion on his people and his Temple. 16 But the people mocked these messengers of God and despised their words. They scoffed at the prophets until the LORD's anger could no longer be restrained and nothing could be done.

The Fall of Jerusalem

17 So the LORD brought the king of Babylon against them. The Babylonians* killed Judah's young men, even chasing after them into the Temple. They had no pity on the people, killing both young men and young women, the old and the infirm. God handed all of them over to Nebuchadnezzar. 18 The king took home to Babylon all the articles, large and small, used in the Temple of God, and the treasures from both the LORD's Temple and from the palace of the king and his officials. 19 Then his army burned the Temple of God, tore down the walls of Jerusalem, burned all the palaces, and completely destroyed everything of value.* 20 The few who survived were taken as exiles to Babylon, and they became servants to the king and his sons until the kingdom of Persia came to power.

21 So the message of the LORD spoken through Jeremiah was fulfilled. The land finally enjoyed its Sabbath rest, lying desolate until the seventy years were fulfilled, just as the prophet had said.

Cyrus Allows the Exiles to Return

22 In the first year of King Cyrus of Persia,* the LORD fulfilled the prophecy he had given through Jeremiah.* He stirred the heart of Cyrus to put this proclamation in writing and to send it throughout his kingdom:

> 23 "This is what King Cyrus of Persia says:
> "The LORD, the God of heaven, has given me all the kingdoms of the earth. He has appointed me to build him a Temple at Jerusalem, which is in Judah. Any of you who are the LORD's people may go there for this task. And may the LORD your God be with you!"

36:17 Or *Chaldeans.* **36:19** Or *destroyed all the valuable articles from the Temple.* **36:22a** The first year of Cyrus's reign over Babylon was 538 B.C. **36:22b** See Jer 25:11-12; 29:10.

---

in sentiment, whom Nebuchadnezzar had thought not important enough to transport to Babylon. He listened to no one but often called on Jeremiah for advice, but neither he nor his people heeded God's message from the faithful, long-suffering prophets. **13, 17–21:** Eventually Zedekiah rebelled against Nebuchadnezzar, who returned, having run out of patience and determined to put an end to the rebellious area. Nebuchadnezzar destroyed the Temple and sacked Jerusalem. Those Judahites who survived became servants to Nebuchadnezzar, and Jeremiah's prophecy was fulfilled. The era of the monarchy was over and Judah *enjoyed its Sabbath rest.*

36:22–23 Even in Despair, Hope. In the short, final paragraph the Chronicler reminds us that fifty years later (538 BC), during the first year of Cyrus the Great, the founder of the mighty Persian Empire that followed Babylon, the LORD began the long and involved process of returning his people home. As Jeremiah had promised, the enlightened Cyrus allowed any captive peoples to return to their homelands and rebuild their lives, including their worship centers. Chronicles concludes with an upbeat reference to the rebuilding of the Temple.

EZRA

INTRODUCTION

Ezra is an account of two returns of the Jewish people from exile in Babylon to Judah. The first takes place in 538 BC, when Cyrus, the Persian emperor, took over the Babylonian Empire and allowed foreign captives to go back to their native lands. The Cyrus Cylinder extols the emperor's generosity in not only allowing conquered people to return to their homelands but also rendering financial assistance to them. Ezra tells how the spirit of God moved upon Cyrus and on fifty thousand Jews of Babylon who took advantage of Cyrus's policy and returned to Judah (1:5). Sheshbazzar and Zerubbabel are the key Jewish leaders of this return. The local population in Palestine did not react favorably to the separatist attitude of the returning Jews or to their claims to property in Judah. The locals fiercely opposed the Jews, who soon became discouraged and stopped their work on the Temple. However, in 520 BC, with the encouragement of God's prophets Haggai and Zechariah, the task was begun anew. The Temple in Jerusalem was completed in 516 BC, seventy years after its destruction by the Babylonians.

The second return took place in 458 BC under Artaxerxes I, another Persian king. Artaxerxes authorized Ezra to go to Judah and establish governance there, including the teaching of the laws of the Jewish God. Close to eighteen hundred Jews accompanied Ezra to Judah. Ezra was noted for his expertise as a scribe and teacher of the law. His interest was not simply academic but also practical: "to study . . . the Law of the LORD and to teach" (7:10).

There are many sources in the book of Ezra. Some of the most obvious are Ezra's memoirs (most of chapters 7—10, both first-person and third-person sections); official memoranda, including the edict of Cyrus in both versions (1:2–4; 6:2–5); letters of Rehum and Shimshai to Artaxerxes and his reply; the letter of Tattenai and Shethar-bozenai to Darius I (5:7–17) and his reply, and Artaxerxes' commission of Ezra (7:12–26); lists of personnel, including those who had returned with Zerubbabel (2:1–70), those returning with Ezra (8:1–14) and those who had married foreign wives (10:18–44); and inventories of important items (vessels and bowls, 1:9–11; 9:26–27). Many of these sources no doubt came from archives in the Jewish community, probably at the Temple, but some may have come from official Persian archives.

One significant issue in the book that involves women is the matter of Israelite men divorcing pagan women who had borne their children. The implication is that a mother will most likely rear her children according to her religion, even if it conflicts with that of the father. To be sure, in ancient times, nurture was even more exclusively the mother's responsibility than it is in many cases today. The power of the one who rocks the baby to sleep is considered more influential than that of the father.

Although God hates divorce in principle (Mal 2:16; Mark 10:9), it was sanctioned in the Old Testament in certain cases, particularly where there had been adultery (Deut 24:1; see also Matt 19:9). Ezra could have argued that the Jews had committed spiritual adultery with God by choosing pagan wives. —*Hannah Karajian Harrington*

✧

Cyrus Allows the Exiles to Return

1 In the first year of King Cyrus of Persia,* the LORD fulfilled the prophecy he had given through Jeremiah.* He stirred the heart of Cyrus to put this proclamation in writing and to send it throughout his kingdom:

2 "This is what King Cyrus of Persia says:

"The LORD, the God of heaven, has given
me all the kingdoms of the earth. He has
appointed me to build him a Temple at
Jerusalem, which is in Judah. 3 Any of you
who are his people may go to Jerusalem in
Judah to rebuild this Temple of the LORD,
the God of Israel, who lives in Jerusalem.
And may your God be with you! 4 Wherever
this Jewish remnant is found, let their
neighbors contribute toward their expenses
by giving them silver and gold, supplies
for the journey, and livestock, as well as a
voluntary offering for the Temple of God in
Jerusalem."

5 Then God stirred the hearts of the priests and Levites and the leaders of the tribes of Judah and Benjamin to go to Jerusalem to rebuild the Temple of the LORD. 6 And all their neighbors assisted by giving them articles of silver and gold, supplies for the journey, and livestock. They gave them many valuable gifts in addition to all the voluntary offerings.

7 King Cyrus himself brought out the articles that King Nebuchadnezzar had taken from the LORD's Temple in Jerusalem and had placed in the temple of his own gods. 8 Cyrus directed Mithredath, the treasurer of Persia, to count these items and present them to Sheshbazzar, the leader of the exiles returning to Judah.* 9 This is a list of the items that were returned:

gold basins	30
silver basins	1,000
silver incense burners*	29
10 gold bowls	30
silver bowls	410
other items	1,000

11 In all, there were 5,400 articles of gold and silver. Sheshbazzar brought all of these along when the exiles went from Babylon to Jerusalem.

Exiles Who Returned with Zerubbabel

2 Here is the list of the Jewish exiles of the provinces who returned from their captivity. King Nebuchadnezzar had deported them to Babylon, but now they returned to Jerusalem and the other towns in Judah where they originally lived. 2 Their leaders were Zerubbabel,

1:1a The first year of Cyrus's reign over Babylon was 538 B.C. **1:1b** See Jer 25:11-12; 29:10. **1:8** Hebrew *Sheshbazzar, the prince of Judah.* **1:9** The meaning of this Hebrew word is uncertain.

1:1–6:22 The First Return of the Jews

1:1–11 Cyrus Allows the Exiles to Return. 1: The prophetic word that the Jews would return from exile after several decades of captivity has been fulfilled (Jer 25:1–12; 29:10). The implication is that God's word can be trusted; his covenant to Israel continued throughout times of chastisement and trouble. Ezra's ministry illustrates the power of God's word. As Ezra teaches the sacred word to the people, they are convicted and make positive changes affecting the course of their lives. **2–4:** When Cyrus took the throne of Babylon he allowed foreign captives to go home. The Cyrus Cylinder tells of the emperor's wish that all captive people in Babylon would return to their homes with their gods and pray to these gods on his behalf. **5–6:** Approximately fifty thousand Jews made the trek from Babylon to Judah. **7–8:** The sacred vessels that Nebuchadnezzar had stolen from the Jerusalem Temple in 586 BC were, with the blessing of Persian authorities, being restored to the site by these Jewish returnees. **11:** The expedition probably took about four months and covered nine hundred miles (see 7:8–9). The caravan would have proceeded from Babylonia north following the Euphrates River and then turned south through the Orontes Valley of Syria to Judah.

2:1–70 Exiles Who Returned with Zerubbabel. 1–2: Zerubbabel, the leader, has the most significant credentials. He is a grandson of Jehoiachin, one of the last kings of Judah. The returnees were the chosen people. This matter was especially important since the returnees would confront local peoples who would either challenge their claim to be the only, true Israel (4:2) or seek to assimilate with them and

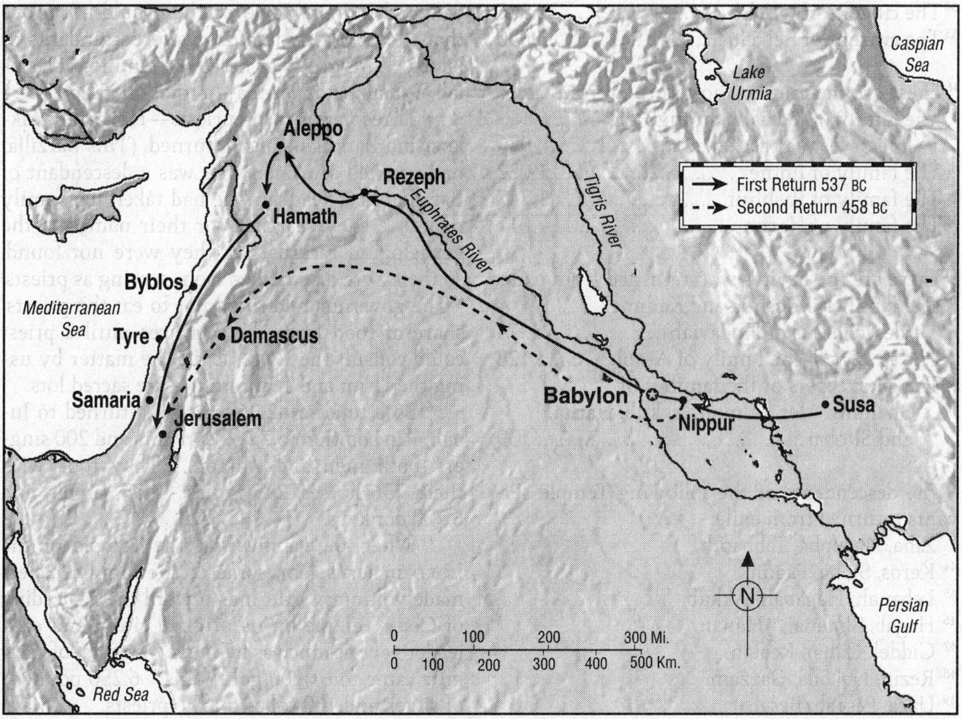

The Return from Exile

Jeshua, Nehemiah, Seraiah, Reelaiah, Mordecai, Bilshan, Mispar, Bigvai, Rehum, and Baanah.

This is the number of the men of Israel who returned from exile:

3 The family of Parosh............2,172
4 The family of Shephatiah............372
5 The family of Arah............775
6 The family of Pahath-moab (descendants of Jeshua and Joab)............2,812
7 The family of Elam............1,254
8 The family of Zattu............945
9 The family of Zaccai............760
10 The family of Bani............642
11 The family of Bebai............623
12 The family of Azgad............1,222
13 The family of Adonikam............666
14 The family of Bigvai............2,056
15 The family of Adin............454
16 The family of Ater (descendants of Hezekiah)............98
17 The family of Bezai............323
18 The family of Jorah............112
19 The family of Hashum............223
20 The family of Gibbar............95
21 The people of Bethlehem............123
22 The people of Netophah............56
23 The people of Anathoth............128
24 The people of Beth-azmaveth*............42
25 The people of Kiriath-jearim,* Kephirah, and Beeroth............743
26 The people of Ramah and Geba............621
27 The people of Micmash............122
28 The people of Bethel and Ai............223
29 The citizens of Nebo............52
30 The citizens of Magbish............156
31 The citizens of West Elam*............1,254
32 The citizens of Harim............320
33 The citizens of Lod, Hadid, and Ono............725

2:24 As in parallel text at Neh 7:28; Hebrew reads *Azmaveth.* **2:25** As in some Hebrew manuscripts and Greek version (see also Neh 7:29); Hebrew reads *Kiriath-arim.* **2:31** Or *of the other Elam.*

thereby contaminate their pure lineage with pagan ways (9:2). **3–42:** Ordinary lay families make up over half of the cited names. The family line was the most common way of personal identification. The maintenance of one's genealogy and its official registry provided credentials for property reclamations in the land.

34 The citizens of Jericho....................................345
35 The citizens of Senaah 3,630

36 These are the priests who returned from exile:
The family of Jedaiah (through the
line of Jeshua)..973
37 The family of Immer 1,052
38 The family of Pashhur 1,247
39 The family of Harim.................................1,017

40 These are the Levites who returned from exile:
The families of Jeshua and Kadmiel
(descendants of Hodaviah).........................74
41 The singers of the family of Asaph 128
42 The gatekeepers of the families of
Shallum, Ater, Talmon, Akkub, Hatita,
and Shobai 139

43 The descendants of the following Temple servants returned from exile:
Ziha, Hasupha, Tabbaoth,
44 Keros, Siaha, Padon,
45 Lebanah, Hagabah, Akkub,
46 Hagab, Shalmai,* Hanan,
47 Giddel, Gahar, Reaiah,
48 Rezin, Nekoda, Gazzam,
49 Uzza, Paseah, Besai,
50 Asnah, Meunim, Nephusim,
51 Bakbuk, Hakupha, Harhur,
52 Bazluth, Mehida, Harsha,
53 Barkos, Sisera, Temah,
54 Neziah, and Hatipha.

55 The descendants of these servants of King Solomon returned from exile:
Sotai, Hassophereth, Peruda,
56 Jaalah, Darkon, Giddel,
57 Shephatiah, Hattil, Pokereth-hazzebaim, and
Ami.

58 In all, the Temple servants and the descendants of Solomon's servants numbered 392.

59 Another group returned at this time from
the towns of Tel-melah, Tel-harsha, Kerub, Addan, and Immer. However, they could not prove
that they or their families were descendants of
Israel. 60 This group included the families of Delaiah, Tobiah, and Nekoda—a total of 652 people.
61 Three families of priests—Hobaiah, Hakkoz, and Barzillai—also returned. (This Barzillai
had married a woman who was a descendant of
Barzillai of Gilead, and he had taken her family
name.) 62 They searched for their names in the
genealogical records, but they were not found,
so they were disqualified from serving as priests.
63 The governor told them not to eat the priests'
share of food from the sacrifices until a priest
could consult the LORD about the matter by using the Urim and Thummim—the sacred lots.
64 So a total of 42,360 people returned to Judah, 65 in addition to 7,337 servants and 200 singers, both men and women. 66 They took with
them 736 horses, 245 mules, 67 435 camels, and
6,720 donkeys.
68 When they arrived at the Temple of the
LORD in Jerusalem, some of the family leaders
made voluntary offerings toward the rebuilding
of God's Temple on its original site, 69 and each
leader gave as much as he could. The total of their
gifts came to 61,000 gold coins,* 6,250 pounds*
of silver, and 100 robes for the priests.
70 So the priests, the Levites, the singers, the
gatekeepers, the Temple servants, and some of
the common people settled in villages near Jerusalem. The rest of the people returned to their own towns throughout Israel.

The Altar Is Rebuilt

3 In early autumn,* when the Israelites had settled in their towns, all the people assembled in Jerusalem with a unified purpose.

2:46 As in an alternate reading of the Masoretic Text (see also Neh 7:48); the other alternate reads *Shamlai.* **2:69a** Hebrew *61,000 darics of gold,* about 1,100 pounds or 500 kilograms in weight. **2:69b** Hebrew *5,000 minas* [3,000 kilograms]. **3:1** Hebrew *in the seventh month.* The year is not specified, so it may have been during Cyrus's first year (538 B.C.) or second year (537 B.C.). The seventh month of the ancient Hebrew lunar calendar occurred within the months of September/October 538 B.C. and October/November 537 B.C.

55: Several women are mentioned in the list of returning exiles, including Hassophereth (or Sophereth; see translator's note, Neh 7:57). While some scholars read these terms as names, the word literally means "the female scribe." Female scribes are rare throughout Jewish history. **61:** The daughter of Barzillai is listed as the individual through whom the bloodline continued. Her husband is identified with his wife's family. Mesopotamian records reveal that when a father had only daughters, the children of these daughters could belong to the mother's family (cf. 1 Chr 2:34–36). **62:** Family registers were maintained by local officials (cf. Neh 7:5) and individual families (1 Chr 5:7–8; 9:22). Without proof people could still remain Israelites, but priests would be disqualified. **64:** The list of cult personnel includes women, singers in the worship service. Thus, at this stage of Israel's history, women participated in cultic functions (see Women in Worship, Matt 28).

3:1–6 The Altar Is Rebuilt. 3–6: Regular daily offer-

[2]Then Jeshua son of Jehozadak* joined his fellow priests and Zerubbabel son of Shealtiel with his family in rebuilding the altar of the God of Israel. They wanted to sacrifice burnt offerings on it, as instructed in the Law of Moses, the man of God. [3]Even though the people were afraid of the local residents, they rebuilt the altar at its old site. Then they began to sacrifice burnt offerings on the altar to the LORD each morning and evening.

[4]They celebrated the Festival of Shelters as prescribed in the Law, sacrificing the number of burnt offerings specified for each day of the festival. [5]They also offered the regular burnt offerings and the offerings required for the new moon celebrations and the annual festivals as prescribed by the LORD. The people also gave voluntary offerings to the LORD. [6]Fifteen days before the Festival of Shelters began,* the priests had begun to sacrifice burnt offerings to the LORD. This was even before they had started to lay the foundation of the LORD's Temple.

The People Begin to Rebuild the Temple

[7]Then the people hired masons and carpenters and bought cedar logs from the people of Tyre and Sidon, paying them with food, wine, and olive oil. The logs were brought down from the Lebanon mountains and floated along the coast of the Mediterranean Sea* to Joppa, for King Cyrus had given permission for this.

[8]The construction of the Temple of God began in midspring,* during the second year after they arrived in Jerusalem. The work force was made up of everyone who had returned from exile, including Zerubbabel son of Shealtiel, Jeshua son of Jehozadak and his fellow priests, and all the Levites. The Levites who were twenty years old or older were put in charge of rebuilding the LORD's Temple. [9]The workers at the Temple of God were supervised by Jeshua with his sons and relatives, and Kadmiel and his sons, all descendants of Hodaviah.* They were helped in this task by the Levites of the family of Henadad.

[10]When the builders completed the foundation of the LORD's Temple, the priests put on their robes and took their places to blow their trumpets. And the Levites, descendants of Asaph, clashed their cymbals to praise the LORD, just as King David had prescribed. [11]With praise and thanks, they sang this song to the LORD:

"He is so good!
His faithful love for Israel endures forever!"

Then all the people gave a great shout, praising the LORD because the foundation of the LORD's Temple had been laid.

[12]But many of the older priests, Levites, and other leaders who had seen the first Temple wept aloud when they saw the new Temple's foundation. The others, however, were shouting for joy. [13]The joyful shouting and weeping mingled together in a loud noise that could be heard far in the distance.

Enemies Oppose the Rebuilding

4 The enemies of Judah and Benjamin heard that the exiles were rebuilding a Temple to the LORD, the God of Israel. [2]So they approached Zerubbabel and the other leaders and said, "Let us build with you, for we worship your God just as you do. We have sacrificed to him ever since King Esarhaddon of Assyria brought us here."

[3]But Zerubbabel, Jeshua, and the other leaders of Israel replied, "You may have no part in this work. We alone will build the Temple for the LORD, the God of Israel, just as King Cyrus of Persia commanded us."

3:2 Hebrew *Jozadak,* a variant spelling of Jehozadak; also in 3:8. **3:6** Hebrew *On the first day of the seventh month.* This day in the ancient Hebrew lunar calendar occurred in September or October. The Festival of Shelters began on the fifteenth day of the seventh month. **3:7** Hebrew *the sea.* **3:8** Hebrew *in the second month.* This month in the ancient Hebrew lunar calendar occurred within the months of April and May 536 B.C. **3:9** Hebrew *sons of Judah* (i.e., *bene Yehudah*). *Bene* might also be read here as the proper name Binnui; *Yehudah* is probably another name for Hodaviah. Compare 2:40; Neh 7:43; 1 Esdras 5:58.

ings were begun as soon as the altar was rebuilt, and the foundation of the Temple was laid. With the restoration of their cult and community in their native land, the Jews experienced a sense of renewal.

3:7–13 The People Rebuild the Temple. 10–11: The priests and Levites provided both vocal and instrumental music. Trumpets were made of beaten silver (Num 10:2) and blown by the priests. Cymbals were played by both priests and Levites. *Anah* ("sang responsively," Ezra 3:11 [NRSV]) is understood to indicate antiphonal singing in which two groups sing responsively. The Jews sang the same song that was sung at the dedication of the first Temple (3:11; 2 Chr 5:13). **12:** The congregation of worshipers was ecstatic, while others wept as they recalled the glorious Solomonic Temple and compared it with the present, humbler edifice.

[4]Then the local residents tried to discourage
and frighten the people of Judah to keep them
from their work. [5]They bribed agents to work
against them and to frustrate their plans. This
went on during the entire reign of King Cyrus
of Persia and lasted until King Darius of Persia
took the throne.*

Later Opposition under Xerxes and Artaxerxes
[6]Years later when Xerxes* began his reign, the
enemies of Judah wrote a letter of accusation
against the people of Judah and Jerusalem.
[7]Even later, during the reign of King Artaxerxes of Persia,* the enemies of Judah, led by
Bishlam, Mithredath, and Tabeel, sent a letter to
Artaxerxes in the Aramaic language, and it was
translated for the king.
[8]*Rehum the governor and Shimshai the
court secretary wrote the letter, telling King Artaxerxes about the situation in Jerusalem. [9]They
greeted the king for all their colleagues—the
judges and local leaders, the people of Tarpel,
the Persians, the Babylonians, and the people of
Erech and Susa (that is, Elam). [10]They also sent
greetings from the rest of the people whom the
great and noble Ashurbanipal* had deported and
relocated in Samaria and throughout the neighboring lands of the province west of the Euphrates River.* [11]This is a copy of their letter:

"To King Artaxerxes, from your loyal
subjects in the province west of the Euphrates
River.
[12]"The king should know that the Jews
who came here to Jerusalem from Babylon
are rebuilding this rebellious and evil city.
They have already laid the foundation and
will soon finish its walls. [13]And the king
should know that if this city is rebuilt and its
walls are completed, it will be much to your
disadvantage, for the Jews will then refuse to
pay their tribute, customs, and tolls to you.
[14]"Since we are your loyal subjects* and
do not want to see the king dishonored
in this way, we have sent the king this
information. [15]We suggest that a search be
made in your ancestors' records, where you
will discover what a rebellious city this has
been in the past. In fact, it was destroyed
because of its long and troublesome history
of revolt against the kings and countries who
controlled it. [16]We declare to the king that if
this city is rebuilt and its walls are completed,
the province west of the Euphrates River will
be lost to you."

[17]Then King Artaxerxes sent this reply:

"To Rehum the governor, Shimshai the
court secretary, and their colleagues living in
Samaria and throughout the province west of
the Euphrates River. Greetings.
[18]"The letter you sent has been translated
and read to me. [19]I ordered a search of the
records and have found that Jerusalem has
indeed been a hotbed of insurrection against
many kings. In fact, rebellion and revolt are
normal there! [20]Powerful kings have ruled
over Jerusalem and the entire province west
of the Euphrates River, receiving tribute,
customs, and tolls. [21]Therefore, issue orders
to have these men stop their work. That city
must not be rebuilt except at my express

4:5 Darius reigned 521–486 B.C. **4:6** Hebrew *Ahasuerus,* another name for Xerxes. He reigned 486–465 B.C. **4:7** Artaxerxes reigned 465–424 B.C. **4:8** The original text of 4:8–6:18 is in Aramaic. **4:10a** Aramaic *Osnappar,* another name for Ashurbanipal. **4:10b** Aramaic *the province beyond the river;* also in 4:11, 16, 17, 20. **4:14** Aramaic *Since we eat the salt of the palace.*

4:1–5 Enemies Oppose the Rebuilding. 4–5: Opposition came from the people who had remained in the land and intermarried with foreigners. They resented the newcomers from Babylon claiming rights to property in Judah and rebuilding their homes and temple. Initially, under Cyrus's reign, the local people had offered to help with the rebuilding effort but had been rebuffed by the returning Jews. The writer of 2 Kings explains that the people of Samaria were syncretistic: *Though they worshiped the LORD, they continued to follow their own gods* (2 Kgs 17:33). Even though they claimed to worship as the returning Jews did, they mixed pagan gods, rituals, and beliefs into the religion of Israel. Ancient wrongs evoke long memories. Ezra 4 gives a review of several occasions of persecution that the Jews faced in the sixth to fifth centuries BC, though the episodes are not in chronological order. Ezra 4:1–5 concerns opposition during the reign of Cyrus (539–530 BC).

4:6–23 Later Opposition under King Artaxerxes. 6: Nearly fifty years later, further harassment occurred during the kingship of Xerxes (486–465 BC). **7–23:** The persistent resistance to the restoration of Jerusalem still endures during the administration of Artaxerxes I (465–424 BC). His decree is issued after the completion of the Temple (516 BC) and is directed against the restoration of the walls and city foundation.

command. 22 Be diligent, and don't neglect this
matter, for we must not permit the situation
to harm the king's interests."

23 When this letter from King Artaxerxes was
read to Rehum, Shimshai, and their colleagues,
they hurried to Jerusalem. Then, with a show of
strength, they forced the Jews to stop building.

The Rebuilding Resumes

24 So the work on the Temple of God in Jerusalem
had stopped, and it remained at a standstill until
the second year of the reign of King Darius of
Persia.*

5 At that time the prophets Haggai and
Zechariah son of Iddo prophesied to the
Jews in Judah and Jerusalem. They prophesied in the name of the God of Israel who was
over them. 2 Zerubbabel son of Shealtiel and Jeshua son of Jehozadak* responded by starting
again to rebuild the Temple of God in Jerusalem.
And the prophets of God were with them and
helped them.

3 But Tattenai, governor of the province west
of the Euphrates River,* and Shethar-bozenai
and their colleagues soon arrived in Jerusalem
and asked, "Who gave you permission to rebuild
this Temple and restore this structure?" 4 They
also asked for the names of all the men working on the Temple. 5 But because their God was
watching over them, the leaders of the Jews were
not prevented from building until a report was
sent to Darius and he returned his decision.

Tattenai's Letter to King Darius

6 This is a copy of the letter that Tattenai the governor, Shethar-bozenai, and the other officials of
the province west of the Euphrates River sent to
King Darius:

7 "To King Darius. Greetings.

8 "The king should know that we went to
the construction site of the Temple of the
great God in the province of Judah. It is being
rebuilt with specially prepared stones, and
timber is being laid in its walls. The work is
going forward with great energy and success.

9 "We asked the leaders, 'Who gave you
permission to rebuild this Temple and restore
this structure?' 10 And we demanded their
names so that we could tell you who the
leaders were.

11 "This was their answer: 'We are the
servants of the God of heaven and earth,
and we are rebuilding the Temple that was
built here many years ago by a great king of
Israel. 12 But because our ancestors angered
the God of heaven, he abandoned them to
King Nebuchadnezzar of Babylon,* who
destroyed this Temple and exiled the people
to Babylonia. 13 However, King Cyrus of
Babylon,* during the first year of his reign,
issued a decree that the Temple of God should
be rebuilt. 14 King Cyrus returned the gold
and silver cups that Nebuchadnezzar had
taken from the Temple of God in Jerusalem
and had placed in the temple of Babylon.
These cups were taken from that temple
and presented to a man named Sheshbazzar,
whom King Cyrus appointed as governor of
Judah. 15 The king instructed him to return
the cups to their place in Jerusalem and
to rebuild the Temple of God there on its

4:24 The second year of Darius's reign was 520 B.C. The narrative started in 4:1-5 is resumed at verse 24. **5:2** Aramaic *Jozadak*, a variant spelling of Jehozadak. **5:3** Aramaic *the province beyond the river;* also in 5:6. **5:12** Aramaic *Nebuchadnezzar the Chaldean.* **5:13** King Cyrus of Persia is here identified as the king of Babylon because Persia had conquered the Babylonian Empire.

4:24—5:5 The Rebuilding Resumes. 4:24: The author ends the chapter by moving backward in history to deal with the current problem: the order of Darius I (522–486 BC) to stop work on the Temple. **5:1:** The prophets Haggai and Zechariah son of Iddo began to prophesy to the Jews in Judah and Jerusalem in about 520 BC. Not only persecution but also economic hardship had taken their toll and stopped the building effort. Haggai admonished the community that they had not put God first but had attended only to their own needs and therefore God had been against their efforts (Hag 1:9). **2:** The community responded promptly with repentance and an eagerness to redouble their efforts on the Temple. Zechariah encouraged the community and its leader Zerubbabel that God's Spirit would enable them to finish the building (Zech 4:6–7). **3:** Tattenai, the governor of the province *Abar Nahara* ("Across the River"), is probably the same individual as Ta-attanni, governor of Ebernari, mentioned in a Babylonian record dated 502 BC. Judah as well as all of Syria-Palestine would have been under his control, and he would have been subject to a higher official, Ushtani, over the combined satrapy of Babylon and Ebernari. Shethar-bozenai was probably Tattenai's assistant.

5:6–17 Tattenai's Letter to King Darius. This letter includes Tattenai's request that Darius search Babylon for the original decree of Cyrus authorizing work on the new Temple.

original site. [16] So this Sheshbazzar came and laid the foundations of the Temple of God in Jerusalem. The people have been working on it ever since, though it is not yet completed.'

[17] "Therefore, if it pleases the king, we request that a search be made in the royal archives of Babylon to discover whether King Cyrus ever issued a decree to rebuild God's Temple in Jerusalem. And then let the king send us his decision in this matter."

Darius Approves the Rebuilding

6 So King Darius issued orders that a search be made in the Babylonian archives, which were stored in the treasury. [2] But it was at the fortress at Ecbatana in the province of Media that a scroll was found. This is what it said:

"Memorandum:

[3] "In the first year of King Cyrus's reign, a decree was sent out concerning the Temple of God at Jerusalem.

"Let the Temple be rebuilt on the site where Jews used to offer their sacrifices, using the original foundations. Its height will be ninety feet, and its width will be ninety feet.* [4] Every three layers of specially prepared stones will be topped by a layer of timber. All expenses will be paid by the royal treasury. [5] Furthermore, the gold and silver cups, which were taken to Babylon by Nebuchadnezzar from the Temple of God in Jerusalem, must be returned to Jerusalem and put back where they belong. Let them be taken back to the Temple of God."

[6] So King Darius sent this message:

"Now therefore, Tattenai, governor of the province west of the Euphrates River,* and Shethar-bozenai, and your colleagues and other officials west of the Euphrates River—stay away from there! [7] Do not disturb the construction of the Temple of God. Let it be rebuilt on its original site, and do not hinder the governor of Judah and the elders of the Jews in their work.

[8] "Moreover, I hereby decree that you are to help these elders of the Jews as they rebuild this Temple of God. You must pay the full construction costs, without delay, from my taxes collected in the province west of the Euphrates River so that the work will not be interrupted.

[9] "Give the priests in Jerusalem whatever is needed in the way of young bulls, rams, and male lambs for the burnt offerings presented to the God of heaven. And without fail, provide them with as much wheat, salt, wine, and olive oil as they need each day. [10] Then they will be able to offer acceptable sacrifices to the God of heaven and pray for the welfare of the king and his sons.

[11] "Those who violate this decree in any way will have a beam pulled from their house. Then they will be tied to it and flogged, and their house will be reduced to a pile of rubble.* [12] May the God who has chosen the city of Jerusalem as the place to honor his name destroy any king or nation that violates this command and destroys this Temple.

"I, Darius, have issued this decree. Let it be obeyed with all diligence."

The Temple's Dedication

[13] Tattenai, governor of the province west of the Euphrates River, and Shethar-bozenai and their colleagues complied at once with the command of King Darius. [14] So the Jewish elders continued their work, and they were greatly encouraged by the preaching of the prophets Haggai and

6:3 Aramaic *Its height will be 60 cubits* [27.6 meters], *and its width will be 60 cubits.* It is commonly held that this verse should be emended to read: "Its height will be 30 cubits [45 feet, or 13.8 meters], its length will be 60 cubits [90 feet, or 27.6 meters], and its width will be 20 cubits [30 feet, or 9.2 meters]"; compare 1 Kgs 6:2. The emendation regarding the width is supported by the Syriac version.
6:6 Aramaic *the province beyond the river;* also in 6:6b, 8, 13.
6:11 Aramaic *a dunghill.*

6:1–12 Darius Approves the Rebuilding. 2: The decree of Cyrus authorizing the building of the Temple at Jerusalem was found in the "fortress of the archives" at Ecbatana, one of the three capitals of the Persian Empire. **6:** Darius had rebuilt other temples throughout the empire, including the temple of Amon in Egypt and the temple of Eanna at Uruk. At the time he was dealing with the Jewish project, he was probably also directing the restoration of the Egyptian temple at Sais. **11–12:** The order of Darius ends with a serious threat. The one who tampers with God's house is punished by the destruction of his own house. The inclusion of a threat of this nature is typical of royal decrees in Assyrian and Aramaic documents. According to the Behistun Inscription, Darius I impaled three thousand leading citizens of Babylonia when he conquered Babylon.

6:13–18 The Temple's Dedication. 16: There were mixed emotions at the dedication of the Temple.

Zechariah son of Iddo. The Temple was finally finished, as had been commanded by the God of Israel and decreed by Cyrus, Darius, and Artaxerxes, the kings of Persia. [15]The Temple was completed on March 12,* during the sixth year of King Darius's reign.

[16]The Temple of God was then dedicated with great joy by the people of Israel, the priests, the Levites, and the rest of the people who had returned from exile. [17]During the dedication ceremony for the Temple of God, 100 young bulls, 200 rams, and 400 male lambs were sacrificed. And 12 male goats were presented as a sin offering for the twelve tribes of Israel. [18]Then the priests and Levites were divided into their various divisions to serve at the Temple of God in Jerusalem, as prescribed in the Book of Moses.

Celebration of Passover

[19]On April 21* the returned exiles celebrated Passover. [20]The priests and Levites had purified themselves and were ceremonially clean. So they slaughtered the Passover lamb for all the returned exiles, for their fellow priests, and for themselves. [21]The Passover meal was eaten by the people of Israel who had returned from exile and by the others in the land who had turned from their immoral customs to worship the LORD, the God of Israel. [22]Then they celebrated the Festival of Unleavened Bread for seven days. There was great joy throughout the land because the LORD had caused the king of Assyria* to be favorable to them, so that he helped them to rebuild the Temple of God, the God of Israel.

Ezra Arrives in Jerusalem

7 Many years later, during the reign of King Artaxerxes of Persia,* there was a man named Ezra. He was the son* of Seraiah, son of Azariah, son of Hilkiah, [2]son of Shallum, son of Zadok, son of Ahitub, [3]son of Amariah, son of Azariah, son* of Meraioth, [4]son of Zerahiah, son of Uzzi, son of Bukki, [5]son of Abishua, son of Phinehas, son of Eleazar, son of Aaron the high priest.* [6]This Ezra was a scribe who was well versed in the Law of Moses, which the LORD, the God of Israel, had given to the people of Israel. He came up to Jerusalem from Babylon, and the king gave him everything he asked for, because the gracious hand of the LORD his God was on him. [7]Some of the people of Israel, as well as some of the priests, Levites, singers, gatekeepers, and Temple servants, traveled up to Jerusalem with him in the seventh year of King Artaxerxes' reign.

[8]Ezra arrived in Jerusalem in August* of that year. [9]He had arranged to leave Babylon on April 8, the first day of the new year,* and he arrived at Jerusalem on August 4,* for the gracious hand of his God was on him. [10]This was because

6:15 Aramaic *on the third day of the month Adar,* of the ancient Hebrew lunar calendar. A number of events in Ezra can be cross-checked with dates in surviving Persian records and related accurately to our modern calendar. This day was March 12, 515 B.C. **6:19** Hebrew *On the fourteenth day of the first month,* of the ancient Hebrew lunar calendar. This day was April 21, 515 B.C.; also see note on 6:15. **6:22** King Darius of Persia is here identified as the king of Assyria because Persia had conquered the Babylonian Empire, which included the earlier Assyrian Empire. **7:1a** Artaxerxes reigned 465–424 B.C. **7:1b** Or *descendant;* see 1 Chr 6:14. **7:3** Or *descendant;* see 1 Chr 6:6-10. **7:5** Or *the first priest.* **7:8** Hebrew *in the fifth month.* This month in the ancient Hebrew lunar calendar occurred within the months of August and September 458 B.C. **7:9a** Hebrew *on the first day of the first month,* of the ancient Hebrew lunar calendar. This day was April 8, 458 B.C.; also see note on 6:15. **7:9b** Hebrew *on the first day of the fifth month,* of the ancient Hebrew lunar calendar. This day was August 4, 458 B.C.; also see note on 6:15.

Some elderly Jews remembered the magnificence of Solomon's Temple and wept at the lesser grandeur of the present Temple. Others, having grown up in Babylon and having seen the more than one thousand temples there dedicated to pagan gods but not a Jewish temple among them, were thrilled that Yahweh too now had a house of worship.

6:19–22 Celebration of Passover. 22: Joy is the dominant emotion in the Temple dedication, and the word is repeated throughout the chapter (vv. 16, 22). The Jews rejoiced as they celebrated the Passover, the feast originally instituted after the Exodus from Egyptian bondage. Indeed a sort of second exodus had taken place among these people. Just as God had miraculously delivered the early Israelites under Moses from the bondage of slavery in Egypt, so also these Jews of the late sixth century BC had been released from captivity in Babylon and allowed to journey to the promised land.

7:1—10:44 The Second Return of the Jews

7:1–10 Ezra Arrives in Jerusalem. 1: The narrative moves ahead several decades. The text changes style from historical narrative to biography and even autobiography as it presents Ezra's memoirs. Ezra was a descendant of Seraiah who was the high priest killed by the Babylonians at the fall of Jerusalem (2 Kgs 25:18–21). **6:** Ezra (lit., "help") was both priest and scribe. *Well versed*: Hebrew, *mahir,* means "quick" not only to study the law but also to do it and teach

Ezra had determined to study and obey the Law of the LORD and to teach those decrees and regulations to the people of Israel.

Artaxerxes' Letter to Ezra

11 King Artaxerxes had given a copy of the following letter to Ezra, the priest and scribe who studied and taught the commands and decrees of the LORD to Israel:

12 *"From Artaxerxes, the king of kings, to Ezra the priest, the teacher of the law of the God of heaven. Greetings.

13 "I decree that any of the people of Israel in my kingdom, including the priests and Levites, may volunteer to return to Jerusalem
with you. 14 I and my council of seven hereby instruct you to conduct an inquiry into the situation in Judah and Jerusalem, based on
your God's law, which is in your hand. 15 We
also commission you to take with you silver and gold, which we are freely presenting as an offering to the God of Israel who lives in Jerusalem.

16 "Furthermore, you are to take any silver and gold that you may obtain from the province of Babylon, as well as the voluntary offerings of the people and the priests that are presented for the Temple of their God
in Jerusalem. 17 These donations are to be
used specifically for the purchase of bulls, rams, male lambs, and the appropriate grain offerings and liquid offerings, all of which will be offered on the altar of the Temple of
your God in Jerusalem. 18 Any silver and gold
that is left over may be used in whatever way you and your colleagues feel is the will of your God.

19 "But as for the cups we are entrusting to you for the service of the Temple of your God, deliver them all to the God of Jerusalem.
20 If you need anything else for your God's Temple or for any similar needs, you may take it from the royal treasury.

21 "I, Artaxerxes the king, hereby send this decree to all the treasurers in the province west of the Euphrates River*: 'You are to give Ezra, the priest and teacher of the law of the God of heaven, whatever he requests
of you. 22 You are to give him up to 7,500
pounds* of silver, 500 bushels* of wheat, 550 gallons of wine, 550 gallons of olive oil,*
and an unlimited supply of salt. 23 Be careful
to provide whatever the God of heaven demands for his Temple, for why should we risk bringing God's anger against the realm
of the king and his sons? 24 I also decree that
no priest, Levite, singer, gatekeeper, Temple servant, or other worker in this Temple of God will be required to pay tribute, customs, or tolls of any kind.'

25 "And you, Ezra, are to use the wisdom your God has given you to appoint magistrates and judges who know your God's laws to govern all the people in the province west of the Euphrates River. Teach the law to
anyone who does not know it. 26 Anyone who
refuses to obey the law of your God and the law of the king will be punished immediately, either by death, banishment, confiscation of goods, or imprisonment."

Ezra Praises the LORD

27 Praise the LORD, the God of our ancestors, who made the king want to beautify the Temple of the
LORD in Jerusalem! 28 And praise him for demonstrating such unfailing love to me by honoring me before the king, his council, and all his mighty nobles! I felt encouraged because the gracious hand of the LORD my God was on me. And I gathered some of the leaders of Israel to return with me to Jerusalem.

7:12 The original text of 7:12-26 is in Aramaic. **7:21** Aramaic *the province beyond the river;* also in 7:25. **7:22a** Aramaic *100 talents* [3,400 kilograms]. **7:22b** Aramaic *100 cors* [18.2 kiloliters]. **7:22c** Aramaic *100 baths* [2.1 kiloliters] *of wine, 100 baths of olive oil.*

it to the Jews. For him, Bible study was not just an intellectual exercise but also relevant to daily life. **10:** As a scribe, Ezra was probably a sort of secretary for Jewish affairs in the Persian government. He had an official position, since he represented the king on his mission, and he had religious as well as political responsibilities.

7:11–26 Artaxerxes' Letter to Ezra. 25–26: Persian kings were known for their interest in codifying law and ensuring stability in the various societies they governed. Thus Ezra is commanded to teach Yahweh's law to the Jews and establish a system of justice in accordance with it. Even capital punishment is put under Ezra's authority.

7:27–28 Ezra Praises the LORD. 27: With a typical Jewish blessing, Ezra gives glory to God for putting it into the heart of the king to support the Temple beautification program.

Exiles Who Returned with Ezra

8 Here is a list of the family leaders and the
genealogies of those who came with me
from Babylon during the reign of King
Artaxerxes:

[2] From the family of Phinehas: Gershom.
From the family of Ithamar: Daniel.
From the family of David: Hattush, [3] a
descendant of Shecaniah.
From the family of Parosh: Zechariah and
150 other men were registered.
[4] From the family of Pahath-moab: Eliehoenai
son of Zerahiah and 200 other men.
[5] From the family of Zattu*: Shecaniah son of
Jahaziel and 300 other men.
[6] From the family of Adin: Ebed son of
Jonathan and 50 other men.
[7] From the family of Elam: Jeshaiah son of
Athaliah and 70 other men.
[8] From the family of Shephatiah: Zebadiah son
of Michael and 80 other men.
[9] From the family of Joab: Obadiah son of
Jehiel and 218 other men.
[10] From the family of Bani*: Shelomith son of
Josiphiah and 160 other men.
[11] From the family of Bebai: Zechariah son of
Bebai and 28 other men.
[12] From the family of Azgad: Johanan son of
Hakkatan and 110 other men.
[13] From the family of Adonikam, who came
later*: Eliphelet, Jeuel, Shemaiah, and
60 other men.
[14] From the family of Bigvai: Uthai, Zaccur,*
and 70 other men.

Ezra's Journey to Jerusalem

[15] I assembled the exiles at the Ahava Canal, and
we camped there for three days while I went over
the lists of the people and the priests who had
arrived. I found that not one Levite had volunteered to come along. [16] So I sent for Eliezer, Ariel, Shemaiah, Elnathan, Jarib, Elnathan, Nathan,
Zechariah, and Meshullam, who were leaders of
the people. I also sent for Joiarib and Elnathan,
who were men of discernment. [17] I sent them to
Iddo, the leader of the Levites at Casiphia, to ask
him and his relatives and the Temple servants to
send us ministers for the Temple of God at Jerusalem.
[18] Since the gracious hand of our God was on
us, they sent us a man named Sherebiah, along
with eighteen of his sons and brothers. He was a
very astute man and a descendant of Mahli, who
was a descendant of Levi son of Israel.* [19] They
also sent Hashabiah, together with Jeshaiah
from the descendants of Merari, and twenty of
his sons and brothers, [20] and 220 Temple servants.
The Temple servants were assistants to the Levites—a group of Temple workers first instituted
by King David and his officials. They were all
listed by name.
[21] And there by the Ahava Canal, I gave orders
for all of us to fast and humble ourselves before
our God. We prayed that he would give us a safe
journey and protect us, our children, and our
goods as we traveled. [22] For I was ashamed to ask
the king for soldiers and horsemen* to accompany us and protect us from enemies along the
way. After all, we had told the king, "Our God's
hand of protection is on all who worship him, but
his fierce anger rages against those who abandon
him." [23] So we fasted and earnestly prayed that
our God would take care of us, and he heard our
prayer.
[24] I appointed twelve leaders of the priests—
Sherebiah, Hashabiah, and ten other priests—[25] to
be in charge of transporting the silver, the gold,
the gold bowls, and the other items that the
king, his council, his officials, and all the people
of Israel had presented for the Temple of God.

8:5 As in some Greek manuscripts (see also 1 Esdras 8:32); Hebrew lacks *Zattu*. **8:10** As in some Greek manuscripts (see also 1 Esdras 8:36); Hebrew lacks *Bani*. **8:13** Or *who were the last of his family.* **8:14** As in Greek and Syriac versions and an alternate reading of the Masoretic Text; the other alternate reads *Zabbud*. **8:18** *Israel* is the name that God gave to Jacob. **8:22** Or *charioteers.*

8:1–14 Exiles Who Returned with Ezra. 1–14: This generation of Babylonian Jews, about eighty years after Zerubbabel's initial caravan, reunite with those among their ancestors who had volunteered to return to the land of Judah under Cyrus's original decree. All but one of the individuals listed here are from families that had been involved with Zerubbabel's return. The inspiration for this journey was not just from Ezra, although he was the inspired leader. The faith of the first returnees was also a catalyst awakening the desire of many individuals to return with Ezra.

8:15–36 Ezra's Journey to Jerusalem. 16–17: From the beginning of Ezra's leadership, one is impressed that he appeals to heads of families rather than commanding people with the authority granted him by the Persian emperor. **18–19:** Two families of Levites contributed thirty-eight ministers to the journey. **21–23:** Perhaps Ezra did not want to arrive in Judah with an ostentatious royal delegation that might immediately put the local population on the defensive and create unnecessary friction (cf. Neh 2:7, 9). **25:** These particular contributions were not just from Babylo-

26 I weighed the treasure as I gave it to them and found the totals to be as follows:

24 tons* of silver,
7,500 pounds* of silver articles,
7,500 pounds of gold,
27 20 gold bowls, equal in value to 1,000 gold coins,*
2 fine articles of polished bronze, as precious as gold.

28 And I said to these priests, "You and these treasures have been set apart as holy to the LORD. This silver and gold is a voluntary offering to the LORD, the God of our ancestors. 29 Guard these treasures well until you present them to the leading priests, the Levites, and the leaders of Israel, who will weigh them at the storerooms of the LORD's Temple in Jerusalem." 30 So the priests and the Levites accepted the task of transporting these treasures of silver and gold to the Temple of our God in Jerusalem.

31 We broke camp at the Ahava Canal on April 19* and started off to Jerusalem. And the gracious hand of our God protected us and saved us from enemies and bandits along the way. 32 So we arrived safely in Jerusalem, where we rested for three days.

33 On the fourth day after our arrival, the silver, gold, and other valuables were weighed at the Temple of our God and entrusted to Meremoth son of Uriah the priest and to Eleazar son of Phinehas, along with Jozabad son of Jeshua and Noadiah son of Binnui—both of whom were Levites. 34 Everything was accounted for by number and weight, and the total weight was officially recorded.

35 Then the exiles who had come out of captivity sacrificed burnt offerings to the God of Israel. They presented twelve bulls for all the people of Israel, as well as ninety-six rams and seventy-seven male lambs. They also offered twelve male goats as a sin offering. All this was given as a burnt offering to the LORD. 36 The king's decrees were delivered to his highest officers and the governors of the province west of the Euphrates River,* who then cooperated by supporting the people and the Temple of God.

Ezra's Prayer concerning Intermarriage

9 When these things had been done, the Jewish leaders came to me and said, "Many of the people of Israel, and even some of the priests and Levites, have not kept themselves separate from the other peoples living in the land. They have taken up the detestable practices of the Canaanites, Hittites, Perizzites, Jebusites, Ammonites, Moabites, Egyptians, and Amorites. 2 For the men of Israel have married women from these people and have taken them as wives for their sons. So the holy race has become polluted by these mixed marriages. Worse yet, the leaders and officials have led the way in this outrage."

3 When I heard this, I tore my cloak and my shirt, pulled hair from my head and beard, and sat down utterly shocked. 4 Then all who trembled at the words of the God of Israel came and sat with me because of this outrage committed by the returned exiles. And I sat there utterly appalled until the time of the evening sacrifice.

8:26a Hebrew *650 talents* [22 metric tons]. **8:26b** Hebrew *100 talents* [3,400 kilograms]; also in 8:26c. **8:27** Hebrew *1,000 darics,* about 19 pounds or 8.6 kilograms in weight. **8:31** Hebrew *on the twelfth day of the first month,* of the ancient Hebrew lunar calendar. This day was April 19, 458 B.C.; also see note on 6:15. **8:36** Hebrew *the province beyond the river.*

---

nian Jews but also from the king and various officials. **29:** As chief cultic personnel, the priests have an obligation to deliver the holy vessels to the Temple personnel at Jerusalem. **35:** Burnt offerings were offered every morning and evening in the Temple cult to ensure the maintenance of Israel's relationship with God as commanded by law. Sin offerings were sacrificed for purification and atonement.

9:1–15 Ezra's Prayer concerning Intermarriage. The last two chapters (9, 10) of Ezra focus on the problem of intermarriage between the Jewish community and the people of the land. Malachi too complains of Jewish men divorcing their Jewish wives and marrying wives "who worship idols" (Mal 2:10–12). Suggestions have been offered as to why the Jews intermarried with pagan women. The latter may reflect wealthy families among the people of Judah and Samaria, an attractive alternative for Jews suffering economic hardship. Maybe there was a lack of available Jewish women, since most of the Jews who had made the arduous journey from Babylon with Ezra were probably men. In any case, Jewish law prohibited marriage with any of the local population of the land of Canaan (Deut 7:1–6). **1–2:** What is surprising about the episode is that Ezra did not bring up the problem. Leaders of the community came to him and told him what many had done. Ezra then meets with the community. This event does not occur until the twentieth day of the ninth month after the group's arrival in Jerusalem (10:9) **3:** Ezra's influence lay in the fact that he was genuinely morally scandalized.

5At the time of the sacrifice, I stood up from
where I had sat in mourning with my clothes
torn. I fell to my knees and lifted my hands to
the LORD my God. 6I prayed,

"O my God, I am utterly ashamed; I blush
to lift up my face to you. For our sins are
piled higher than our heads, and our guilt
has reached to the heavens. 7From the days
of our ancestors until now, we have been
steeped in sin. That is why we and our kings
and our priests have been at the mercy of the
pagan kings of the land. We have been killed,
captured, robbed, and disgraced, just as we are
today.
8"But now we have been given a brief
moment of grace, for the LORD our God has
allowed a few of us to survive as a remnant.
He has given us security in this holy place.
Our God has brightened our eyes and granted
us some relief from our slavery. 9For we
were slaves, but in his unfailing love our God
did not abandon us in our slavery. Instead,
he caused the kings of Persia to treat us
favorably. He revived us so we could rebuild
the Temple of our God and repair its ruins.
He has given us a protective wall in Judah
and Jerusalem.
10"And now, O our God, what can we
say after all of this? For once again we
have abandoned your commands! 11Your
servants the prophets warned us when they
said, 'The land you are entering to possess
is totally defiled by the detestable practices
of the people living there. From one end to
the other, the land is filled with corruption.
12Don't let your daughters marry their sons!
Don't take their daughters as wives for your
sons. Don't ever promote the peace and
prosperity of those nations. If you follow
these instructions, you will be strong and
will enjoy the good things the land produces,
and you will leave this prosperity to your
children forever.'
13"Now we are being punished because of
our wickedness and our great guilt. But we
have actually been punished far less than we
deserve, for you, our God, have allowed some
of us to survive as a remnant. 14But even
so, we are again breaking your commands
and intermarrying with people who do
these detestable things. Won't your anger be
enough to destroy us, so that even this little
remnant no longer survives? 15O LORD, God
of Israel, you are just. We come before you in
our guilt as nothing but an escaped remnant,
though in such a condition none of us can
stand in your presence."

The People Confess Their Sin

10 While Ezra prayed and made this confession, weeping and lying face down
on the ground in front of the Temple
of God, a very large crowd of people from Israel—men, women, and children—gathered and
wept bitterly with him. 2Then Shecaniah son of
Jehiel, a descendant of Elam, said to Ezra, "We
have been unfaithful to our God, for we have
married these pagan women of the land. But in
spite of this there is hope for Israel. 3Let us now
make a covenant with our God to divorce our
pagan wives and to send them away with their
children. We will follow the advice given by you
and by the others who respect the commands of
our God. Let it be done according to the Law of
God. 4Get up, for it is your duty to tell us how to
proceed in setting things straight. We are behind
you, so be strong and take action."
5So Ezra stood up and demanded that the
leaders of the priests and the Levites and all
the people of Israel swear that they would do as
Shecaniah had said. And they all swore a solemn

According to Edwin Yamauchi's translation, Ezra "was reduced to shuddering." **8:** Ezra's prayer reveals his complete identification with his community. Although he is innocent, he intercedes for the offenders in the first-person plural.

10:1–17 The People Confess Their Sin. 1: Initially Ezra did not order these divorces (see Divorce, next page). Rather, he waited for the initiative to come from the people. Although he had the Persian authority to impose any punishment he wished on those who violated the Jewish law, Ezra wanted the community's willing agreement. **2–4:** Shecaniah, a member of the congregation, suggested that the offenders divorce their foreign wives. Jehiel, his father, might be the same Jehiel as mentioned in verses 21, 26, a man of the family of Elam who had married a pagan woman. In fact, six members of Elam were involved in intermarriages.

According to Babylonian custom, divorced women took their children with them and could not remarry until the children were grown. In many ancient cultures the woman had the responsibility to birth and rear her children (see Childbearing and Rearing, Col 3). Fathers were far less significant in these early stages. In addition, men sometimes had multiple wives and many children (see Polygamy, 1 Kgs 11). A mother could be expected to rear her children according

Divorce

Under Mosaic law a man was allowed to divorce his wife by giving her a "bill of divorcement" bearing the words "you are free to marry any man." A husband did not need a bill because male polygamy was tolerated (see Polygamy, 1 Kgs 11). A woman might possibly petition a rabbinic court to put pressure on her husband to divorce her, but only if she could prove he was depriving her of the basic necessities that were held to be the basis of his covenant with her (Exod 21:10–11). Isaiah 54:4–8 reveals God's tender concern for women who suffered rejection and impoverishment in this unequal situation, and Malachi 2:14–16 shows God haranguing those who "broke faith" with their wives.

The principal Old Testament reference to divorce (Deut 24:1–4) prohibits a man from remarrying a woman whom he has already divorced if she has been married again in the meantime. It implies that there is something adulterous about the intervening marriage, and this prohibition protected wives from being used for adulterous purposes in temporary marriages (as in a form of legalized wife-swapping still found in some Middle Eastern countries). The law prohibiting remarriage of the same wife may explain why a compassionate God, having justly divorced Israel for unfaithfulness to the covenant, refuses to divorce unfaithful Judah (Isa 50:1).

In Jesus' day the grounds on which a man could lawfully divorce his wife were the subject of rabbinic debate. In the context of the divorce scandal that cost John the Baptist his life, Jesus entered the Pharisees' debate with sharp moral condemnation of easy divorces (Matt 19:1–9; Mark 10:1–9). The story in Mark has Jesus referring his hearers to God's original intentions in creation, endorsing monogamy for all and gender equality.

Jesus' proverb on the issue (Matt 5:31; 19:9; Mark 10:11–12; Luke 16:18; 1 Cor 7:10–11) is presented in a quasi-legal biblical form used for emphatic moral teaching: Whoever does *x* will receive the penalty *y*. A first-century Jew would have understood it to say, "Whoever breaks the marriage covenant with the spouse is [acting as immorally as if he or she were] committing adultery [and deserves similar punishment]" (cf. Matt 5:28).

As with all issues that deeply affect women, this shows Jesus exhorting his followers to exercise moral integrity with regard to divorce. Paul writes in a similar vein, deploring divorce though recognizing it as a way of escape from a pastorally intolerable situation (e.g., 1 Cor 7:15). In view of the coming apocalypse he counsels against all marriage, including remarriage, particularly against the latter where the divorce has been for an adulterous purpose (i.e., in order to remarry, 1 Cor 7:12–13).

oath. 6 Then Ezra left the front of the Temple of
God and went to the room of Jehohanan son of
Eliashib. He spent the night* there without eating or drinking anything. He was still in mourning because of the unfaithfulness of the returned
exiles.
7 Then a proclamation was made throughout
Judah and Jerusalem that all the exiles should
come to Jerusalem. 8 Those who failed to come
within three days would, if the leaders and elders
so decided, forfeit all their property and be expelled from the assembly of the exiles.
9 Within three days, all the people of Judah
and Benjamin had gathered in Jerusalem. This
took place on December 19,* and all the people
were sitting in the square before the Temple of
God. They were trembling both because of the
seriousness of the matter and because it was
raining. 10 Then Ezra the priest stood and said
to them: "You have committed a terrible sin.
By marrying pagan women, you have increased
Israel's guilt. 11 So now confess your sin to the
LORD, the God of your ancestors, and do what he
demands. Separate yourselves from the people of
the land and from these pagan women."
12 Then the whole assembly raised their voices and answered, "Yes, you are right; we must
do as you say!" 13 Then they added, "This isn't
something that can be done in a day or two, for
many of us are involved in this extremely sinful
affair. And this is the rainy season, so we cannot stay out here much longer. 14 Let our leaders
act on behalf of us all. Let everyone who has a
pagan wife come at a scheduled time, accompanied by the leaders and judges of his city, so that
the fierce anger of our God concerning this affair
may be turned away from us."

10:6 As in parallel text at 1 Esdras 9:2; Hebrew reads *He went.*
10:9 Hebrew *on the twentieth day of the ninth month,* of the ancient Hebrew lunar calendar. This day was December 19, 458 B.C.; also see note on 6:15.

[15]Only Jonathan son of Asahel and Jahzeiah son of Tikvah opposed this course of action, and they were supported by Meshullam and Shabbethai the Levite.
[16]So this was the plan they followed. Ezra selected leaders to represent their families, designating each of the representatives by name. On December 29,* the leaders sat down to investigate the matter. [17]By March 27, the first day of the new year,* they had finished dealing with all the men who had married pagan wives.

Those Guilty of Intermarriage

[18]These are the priests who had married pagan wives:
From the family of Jeshua son of Jehozadak* and his brothers: Maaseiah, Eliezer, Jarib, and Gedaliah. [19]They vowed to divorce their wives, and they each acknowledged their guilt by offering a ram as a guilt offering.
[20]From the family of Immer: Hanani and Zebadiah.
[21]From the family of Harim: Maaseiah, Elijah, Shemaiah, Jehiel, and Uzziah.
[22]From the family of Pashhur: Elioenai, Maaseiah, Ishmael, Nethanel, Jozabad, and Elasah.

[23]These are the Levites who were guilty: Jozabad, Shimei, Kelaiah (also called Kelita), Pethahiah, Judah, and Eliezer.

[24]This is the singer who was guilty: Eliashib.

These are the gatekeepers who were guilty: Shallum, Telem, and Uri.

[25]These are the other people of Israel who were guilty:
From the family of Parosh: Ramiah, Izziah, Malkijah, Mijamin, Eleazar, Hashabiah,* and Benaiah.
[26]From the family of Elam: Mattaniah, Zechariah, Jehiel, Abdi, Jeremoth, and Elijah.
[27]From the family of Zattu: Elioenai, Eliashib, Mattaniah, Jeremoth, Zabad, and Aziza.
[28]From the family of Bebai: Jehohanan, Hananiah, Zabbai, and Athlai.
[29]From the family of Bani: Meshullam, Malluch, Adaiah, Jashub, Sheal, and Jeremoth.
[30]From the family of Pahath-moab: Adna, Kelal, Benaiah, Maaseiah, Mattaniah, Bezalel, Binnui, and Manasseh.
[31]From the family of Harim: Eliezer, Ishijah, Malkijah, Shemaiah, Shimeon, [32]Benjamin, Malluch, and Shemariah.
[33]From the family of Hashum: Mattenai, Mattattah, Zabad, Eliphelet, Jeremai, Manasseh, and Shimei.
[34]From the family of Bani: Maadai, Amram, Uel, [35]Benaiah, Bedeiah, Keluhi, [36]Vaniah, Meremoth, Eliashib, [37]Mattaniah, Mattenai, and Jaasu.
[38]From the family of Binnui*: Shimei,

10:16 Hebrew *On the first day of the tenth month,* of the ancient Hebrew lunar calendar. This day was December 29, 458 B.C.; also see note on 6:15. **10:17** Hebrew *By the first day of the first month,* of the ancient Hebrew lunar calendar. This day was March 27, 457 B.C.; also see note on 6:15. **10:18** Hebrew *Jozadak,* a variant spelling of Jehozadak. **10:25** As in parallel text at 1 Esdras 9:26; Hebrew reads *Malkijah.* **10:37-38** As in Greek version; Hebrew reads *Jaasu, [38]Bani, Binnui.*

to her native religion and customs. Simply put, pagan mothers produce pagan children. **15:** It appears that there were some dissidents. Perhaps they were sheltering relatives or friends or felt that the decree was too harsh. To be sure, God hates divorce (Mal 2:16). Nevertheless, Ezra was faced with a dilemma. If he allowed intermarriage to continue, he would lose the next generation of Jews who, having been brought up by pagan mothers, would not adhere to the law of Moses and would influence their peers and their children to act the same. Thus Ezra chose the lesser of two evils: Divorce, although it would be painful for many families, would preserve the people of Israel into the next generation.

10:18–44 Those Guilty of Intermarriage. 18–24: The list of offenders is shocking. In all, 111 persons, 27 of whom came from priestly families, had intermarried with foreign women. The whole congregation might have numbered 30,000. The offenders even included the descendants of Joshua, the high priest of Zerubbabel's time. **25–43:** In addition to clergy, the list includes mostly upper-class men. None of the Temple servants, whose origin was questionable at best, were offenders. They had clearly forsaken their pagan backgrounds and adopted the pure religion of Israel. They were trusted even with assisting Levites at the Temple courts. The lowest socially acceptable classes appear to be the least involved (cf. 9:2) **44:** The children of these mixed marriages were born in the promised land. Since Ezra had returned to Judah only nine months prior, the children involved were either the fruit of mixed marriages begun in Babylon or the children of Jews already in the land when Ezra came. If the former is the case, one would question how Ezra could have been unaware of the problem. More than likely the problem was not with Babylonian women but with local pagan women. It is more

[39] Shelemiah, Nathan, Adaiah, [40] Macnadebai,
Shashai, Sharai, [41] Azarel, Shelemiah,
Shemariah, [42] Shallum, Amariah, and Joseph.
[43] From the family of Nebo: Jeiel, Mattithiah,
Zabad, Zebina, Jaddai, Joel, and Benaiah.

[44] Each of these men had a pagan wife, and
some even had children by these wives.*

10:44 Or *and they sent them away with their children.* The meaning of the Hebrew is uncertain.

probable that those Jews who had been living in the land of Judah alongside syncretistic families for decades would have been slowly compromised.

In either case, for Ezra's small, struggling community, surgery was necessary to secure the continuation of the people of God. Although proselytization was possible within the law, the situation here seems to be intermarriage with pagans. Thus in Ezra's community the next generation of Jews was threatened by marriage with foreigners. Ezra's radical measures were timely and vital for the continuation of pure religion.

NEHEMIAH

INTRODUCTION

The book of Nehemiah is the second portion of a two-part work, Ezra-Nehemiah, which renders theological evaluation on the early history of the postexilic Israelite community, beginning with the edict of the Persian king Cyrus in 538 BC and extending to the final work of Nehemiah, around 424 BC. The two-part work, as a theological evaluation, presents in narrative not a strict chronological account but a constitution or plan for how the exiles are to live after the fall of Jerusalem—the blessed city—and the monarchy. Of particular interest to this commentary is the question of the emerging community identity in the context of political subjugation by Babylonian, then Persian, and possibly Greek superpowers. "How are we to live and constitute ourselves as the people of God in such an environment?" is the operative question that drives the theological analysis. Such a question is relevant given the postmodern search for identity in the context of competing powers, either in the larger mix of sociopolitical power moves or in the narrower relational matrix of gender issues.

Gradually, through usage in the Christian church, Ezra-Nehemiah evolved into two separate books. The Hebrew Bible knows the two books as one work. In the Hebrew manuscripts, the lack of Masoretic notes at the end of Ezra and the tally for verses at the end of Nehemiah prove this point. Also, thematic and common material unite the two works. Beginning with Origen in the third century, Christian reading practice finally produced a change even in Jewish usage, which resulted in the two separate books of the English Bible. For the purposes of this commentary, however, we will consider only the book of Nehemiah, bringing in passages from Ezra as they touch on theological topics.

Ezra-Nehemiah portrays a history that begins with the edict of Cyrus in 538 BC (Ezra 1:1). According to the text, the edict declares that the Israelite captives may return to Jerusalem and build a temple for their God. Ezra 1—6 narrates the immediate return and subsequent construction of the Temple (515 BC) prior to the arrival of Ezra and Nehemiah. The activity of Ezra and Nehemiah, after the construction of the Temple, coincides with the reign of a later Persian king, Artaxerxes I (465–424 BC). The text tells us that Ezra arrives on the scene in the seventh year of Artaxerxes, or 458 BC, and that Nehemiah subsequently arrives in the twentieth year, or 445 BC. Nehemiah travels back to Persia and later returns to Jerusalem for additional reform prior to 424 BC. The timeline of dates and events is important for the theological analysis of the book of Nehemiah due to the questions raised in such a period of destruction and rebuilding.

People were looking for reasons for the Exile. Why had God judged them? What could they learn from their reliance on temporal power such as the monarchy? During the exilic period, the books of Samuel and Kings took their final shape, both probing for an answer to the question of community identity in relation to temporal power. Furthermore, these people were wondering what they had learned of God's identity and how what they had absorbed affected their self-understanding. Was God resident in the monarchy? Had God really blessed Jerusalem as Isaiah had written? Was the identity of the people of Israel as well determined by the kings and the inviolability of Jerusalem, "the city of the great King"

(Ps 48:2)? Or was it fixed to a deeper understanding of God's presence in their midst, that of the desert sanctuary or with the Judean exiles beside the Kebar River (Ezek 1:1)? These questions and more come to light only if we grasp the significance of the dates and events of Ezra and Nehemiah.

Scholars have debated to no consensus the date and author for Ezra-Nehemiah. The reader may consult the many commentaries and dictionaries for detailed discussion of possibilities. Various people have suggested two different dates for the work, 400 BC or 300 BC. The first option, just after the final events narrated by the text, relates the community identity questions more to early postexilic issues. The latter date places identity questions in the context of subsequent challenges for Israelite self-understanding in light of the rising Samaritan community and its claim for God's presence on Mount Gerazim.

Since the work, as with most biblical texts, does not name its author, we do not know for sure who wrote Ezra-Nehemiah. Scholars have suggested the Chronicler (i.e., the author of 1 and 2 Chronicles), Ezra with help from Nehemiah, or some unnamed redactor/author. Regardless of the author's identity, the two-part work consists of prior existing documents: the memoirs of Ezra (e.g., Ezra 7—10) and Nehemiah (e.g., Neh 1—7), Aramaic letters and documents (e.g., Ezra 6:3–5), lists of exiles and other items (e.g., Ezra 2:1–70; Neh 7:7–73), and third-person accounts (e.g., Ezra 1—6). Thus whoever constructed the final work used previously existing materials in the process. In doing so, this redactor/author shaped the raw materials into a theological paradigm, which helped the Ezra-Nehemiah generation understand its identity in the presence of God and prompts us to examine our struggle for identity in the presence of competing powers.

The analysis of this commentary follows the Christian Bible. The Hebrew Bible verses are at times out of sequence with the English text. Ezra-Nehemiah is a theological report on the exilic community and could be titled "A Narrative Plan for the Postexilic Community."
—*Jeff H. McCrory Jr.*

1:1–11	The Law of Moses and Work
2:1–20	Cooperation with Powers
3:1–32	Shared Tasks and Work
4:1—6:19	Work and Opposition
7:1–73	Reform and Cooperation
8:1–12	The Law of Moses and Celebration
8:13–18	Law and Obedience
9:1–38	Appropriating Tradition
10:1–39	Shared Tasks, the Law of Moses, and Covenant
11:1—12:26	Shared Tasks and Community
12:27—13:31	Reform and Regulation

1 These are the memoirs of Nehemiah son of Hacaliah.

Nehemiah's Concern for Jerusalem

In late autumn, in the month of Kislev, in the twentieth year of King Artaxerxes' reign,* I was at the fortress of Susa. 2 Hanani, one of my brothers, came to visit me with some other men who had just arrived from Judah. I asked them about the Jews who had returned there from captivity and about how things were going in Jerusalem.

3 They said to me, "Things are not going well for those who returned to the province of Judah. They are in great trouble and disgrace. The wall of Jerusalem has been torn down, and the gates have been destroyed by fire."

4 When I heard this, I sat down and wept. In fact, for days I mourned, fasted, and prayed to the God of heaven. 5 Then I said,

"O LORD, God of heaven, the great and
awesome God who keeps his covenant of
unfailing love with those who love him and
obey his commands, 6 listen to my prayer!
Look down and see me praying night and day
for your people Israel. I confess that we have
sinned against you. Yes, even my own family
and I have sinned! 7 We have sinned terribly
by not obeying the commands, decrees, and
regulations that you gave us through your
servant Moses.

8 "Please remember what you told your
servant Moses: 'If you are unfaithful to me,
I will scatter you among the nations. 9 But if
you return to me and obey my commands
and live by them, then even if you are exiled
to the ends of the earth, I will bring you back
to the place I have chosen for my name to be
honored.'

10 "The people you rescued by your great
power and strong hand are your servants.
11 O Lord, please hear my prayer! Listen to
the prayers of those of us who delight in
honoring you. Please grant me success today
by making the king favorable to me.* Put it
into his heart to be kind to me."

In those days I was the king's cup-bearer.

Nehemiah Goes to Jerusalem

2 Early the following spring, in the month of Nisan,* during the twentieth year of King Artaxerxes' reign, I was serving the king his wine. I had never before appeared sad in his presence. 2 So the king asked me, "Why are you looking so sad? You don't look sick to me. You must be deeply troubled."

Then I was terrified, 3 but I replied, "Long

1:1 Hebrew *In the month of Kislev of the twentieth year.* A number of dates in the book of Nehemiah can be cross-checked with dates in surviving Persian records and related accurately to our modern calendar. This month of the ancient Hebrew lunar calendar occurred within the months of November and December 446 B.C. The *twentieth year* probably refers to the reign of King Artaxerxes I; compare 2:1; 5:14. **1:11** Hebrew *today in the sight of this man.*
2:1 Hebrew *In the month of Nisan.* This month of the ancient Hebrew lunar calendar occurred within the months of April and May 445 B.C.

1:1–11 The Law of Moses and Work

1: The narrator is Nehemiah, and he is living in exile in Susa (Persia), supposedly in 445 BC, the twentieth year of Artaxerxes I. **2–11:** The arrival of Hanani, a kinsman of Nehemiah, with word regarding the wall of Jerusalem and the conditions of the people there, raises immediately the issue of community restoration, which has begun in the prior book of Ezra. The condition of the community elicits from Nehemiah a prayer that sets the foundation for community renewal and rebuilding. **7, 8:** Twice in the prayer Nehemiah refers to Moses. Nehemiah grounds community renewal in the *commands, decress, and regulations* of the law. Thus the book of Nehemiah begins as does the work of Ezra with the law of Moses. The reform of the exilic community starts with recognition of God's presence neither in the monarchy nor in the centrality of Jerusalem, but in the Torah or instruction of Moses, which arose before there was a king or a particular place associated with God's presence. By casting back into the foundational experience of early Israel, in the Exodus from Egypt and resultant law giving, the book of Nehemiah sets a theological course different from that of preexilic Israel. The new work to take place begins from this new yet ancient starting point. Feminist theological analysis has critiqued the power structures of society, modern and ancient, exposing the coercive moves of societal structures. It is instructive that Nehemiah does not begin with power structures but with theological description of what it means to be the people of the LORD. It is from the law of Moses, not temporal power, that work will proceed.

2:1–20 Cooperation with Powers

Nehemiah, as cup-bearer of the king, has intimate access to Artaxerxes, such that Artaxerxes notices his moods and feels free to address him with questions. Nehemiah as well does not hesitate to speak frankly with the king. Such intimacy is peculiar in ancient

live the king! How can I not be sad? For the city
where my ancestors are buried is in ruins, and
the gates have been destroyed by fire."
[4]The king asked, "Well, how can I help you?"
With a prayer to the God of heaven, [5]I replied,
"If it please the king, and if you are pleased with
me, your servant, send me to Judah to rebuild the
city where my ancestors are buried."
[6]The king, with the queen sitting beside him,
asked, "How long will you be gone? When will
you return?" After I told him how long I would
be gone, the king agreed to my request.
[7]I also said to the king, "If it please the king,
let me have letters addressed to the governors of
the province west of the Euphrates River,* instructing them to let me travel safely through
their territories on my way to Judah. [8]And please
give me a letter addressed to Asaph, the manager
of the king's forest, instructing him to give me
timber. I will need it to make beams for the gates
of the Temple fortress, for the city walls, and for
a house for myself." And the king granted these
requests, because the gracious hand of God was
on me.
[9]When I came to the governors of the province west of the Euphrates River, I delivered the
king's letters to them. The king, I should add,
had sent along army officers and horsemen* to
protect me. [10]But when Sanballat the Horonite
and Tobiah the Ammonite official heard of my
arrival, they were very displeased that someone
had come to help the people of Israel.

Nehemiah Inspects Jerusalem's Wall

[11]So I arrived in Jerusalem. Three days later, [12]I
slipped out during the night, taking only a few
others with me. I had not told anyone about the
plans God had put in my heart for Jerusalem. We
took no pack animals with us except the donkey
I was riding. [13]After dark I went out through the
Valley Gate, past the Jackal's Well,* and over to
the Dung Gate to inspect the broken walls and
burned gates. [14]Then I went to the Fountain Gate
and to the King's Pool, but my donkey couldn't
get through the rubble. [15]So, though it was still
dark, I went up the Kidron Valley* instead, in-
specting the wall before I turned back and entered again at the Valley Gate.
[16]The city officials did not know I had been out
there or what I was doing, for I had not yet said
anything to anyone about my plans. I had not
yet spoken to the Jewish leaders—the priests, the
nobles, the officials, or anyone else in the administration. [17]But now I said to them, "You know
very well what trouble we are in. Jerusalem lies
in ruins, and its gates have been destroyed by
fire. Let us rebuild the wall of Jerusalem and end
this disgrace!" [18]Then I told them about how the
gracious hand of God had been on me, and about
my conversation with the king.
They replied at once, "Yes, let's rebuild the
wall!" So they began the good work.
[19]But when Sanballat, Tobiah, and Geshem
the Arab heard of our plan, they scoffed contemptuously. "What are you doing? Are you rebelling against the king?" they asked.
[20]I replied, "The God of heaven will help us
succeed. We, his servants, will start rebuilding
this wall. But you have no share, legal right, or
historic claim in Jerusalem."

Rebuilding the Wall of Jerusalem

3 Then Eliashib the high priest and the other
priests started to rebuild at the Sheep Gate.
They dedicated it and set up its doors, building the wall as far as the Tower of the Hundred,

2:7 Hebrew *the province beyond the river;* also in 2:9. **2:9** Or *charioteers.* **2:13** Or *Serpent's Well.* **2:15** Hebrew *the valley.*

royal courts, but it is not peculiar to Ezra-Nehemiah, nor is it out of character in the evaluation of foreign kings as carrying out the will of the LORD (e.g., Ezra 1:1, the edict of Cyrus, and Ezra 7:11–36, the letter of Artaxerxes). **1–8:** By elevating foreign powers to the status of doing the will of the LORD, the text sends the reader in search of God in each person and situation. A person or group can move forward with what is just and right even though not in complete charge of her, his, or their destiny. In spite of elevating foreign powers, the text empowers subjugated individuals to act. Nehemiah can and does do something for the refugees in Jerusalem. He and his people are not without authority and responsibility. They can and do take action, albeit within the power of the Persian state, to make a difference. **9–20:** The return to Jerusalem, the inspection, and opposition emphasize the preceding points, that Nehemiah and the community begin to work within the restricted powers that overshadow them. The work they begin, however, does not proceed without conflict and hardship. Sanballat the Horonite, Tobiah the Ammonite, and Geshem the Arab serve as foils for the protagonist Nehemiah, as do Rehum the royal deputy and Shimshai the scribe, for those who would build the Temple (Ezra 4:9, 23).

3:1–32 Shared Tasks and Work

The shared nature of community restoration is one of

which they dedicated, and the Tower of Hananel.
2 People from the town of Jericho worked next to
them, and beyond them was Zaccur son of Imri.
3 The Fish Gate was built by the sons of Has-
senaah. They laid the beams, set up its doors, and
installed its bolts and bars. 4 Meremoth son of
Uriah and grandson of Hakkoz repaired the next
section of wall. Beside him were Meshullam son
of Berekiah and grandson of Meshezabel, and
then Zadok son of Baana. 5 Next were the people
from Tekoa, though their leaders refused to work
with the construction supervisors.

6 The Old City Gate* was repaired by Joiada
son of Paseah and Meshullam son of Besodeiah.
They laid the beams, set up its doors, and installed its bolts and bars. 7 Next to them were
Melatiah from Gibeon, Jadon from Meronoth,
people from Gibeon, and people from Mizpah,
the headquarters of the governor of the province
west of the Euphrates River.* 8 Next was Uzziel
son of Harhaiah, a goldsmith by trade, who also
worked on the wall. Beyond him was Hananiah,
a manufacturer of perfumes. They left out a section of Jerusalem as they built the Broad Wall.*
9 Rephaiah son of Hur, the leader of half the
district of Jerusalem, was next to them on the
wall. 10 Next Jedaiah son of Harumaph repaired
the wall across from his own house, and next to
him was Hattush son of Hashabneiah. 11 Then
came Malkijah son of Harim and Hasshub son
of Pahath-moab, who repaired another section of
the wall and the Tower of the Ovens. 12 Shallum
son of Hallohesh and his daughters repaired the
next section. He was the leader of the other half
of the district of Jerusalem.

13 The Valley Gate was repaired by the people
from Zanoah, led by Hanun. They set up its doors
and installed its bolts and bars. They also repaired
the 1,500 feet* of wall to the Dung Gate.

14 The Dung Gate was repaired by Malkijah
son of Recab, the leader of the Beth-hakkerem
district. He rebuilt it, set up its doors, and installed its bolts and bars.

15 The Fountain Gate was repaired by Shallum* son of Col-hozeh, the leader of the Mizpah
district. He rebuilt it, roofed it, set up its doors,
and installed its bolts and bars. Then he repaired
the wall of the pool of Siloam* near the king's
garden, and he rebuilt the wall as far as the stairs
that descend from the City of David. 16 Next to
him was Nehemiah son of Azbuk, the leader of
half the district of Beth-zur. He rebuilt the wall
from a place across from the tombs of David's
family as far as the water reservoir and the
House of the Warriors.

17 Next to him, repairs were made by a group
of Levites working under the supervision of Rehum son of Bani. Then came Hashabiah, the leader of half the district of Keilah, who supervised
the building of the wall on behalf of his own district. 18 Next down the line were his countrymen
led by Binnui* son of Henadad, the leader of the
other half of the district of Keilah.

19 Next to them, Ezer son of Jeshua, the leader of Mizpah, repaired another section of wall
across from the ascent to the armory near the
angle in the wall. 20 Next to him was Baruch son
of Zabbai, who zealously repaired an additional
section from the angle to the door of the house
of Eliashib the high priest. 21 Meremoth son of
Uriah and grandson of Hakkoz rebuilt another
section of the wall extending from the door of
Eliashib's house to the end of the house.

22 The next repairs were made by the priests
from the surrounding region. 23 After them, Benjamin and Hasshub repaired the section across
from their house, and Azariah son of Maaseiah
and grandson of Ananiah repaired the section
across from his house. 24 Next was Binnui son of
Henadad, who rebuilt another section of the wall
from Azariah's house to the angle and the corner.
25 Palal son of Uzai carried on the work from a

3:6 Or *The Mishneh Gate,* or *The Jeshanah Gate.* **3:7** Hebrew *the province beyond the river.* **3:8** Or *They fortified Jerusalem up to the Broad Wall.* **3:13** Hebrew *1,000 cubits* [450 meters]. **3:15a** As in Syriac version; Hebrew reads *Shallun.* **3:15b** Hebrew *pool of Shelah,* another name for the pool of Siloam. **3:18** As in a few Hebrew manuscripts, some Greek manuscripts, and Syriac version (see also 3:24; 10:9); most Hebrew manuscripts read *Bavvai.*

the major themes of Ezra-Nehemiah, evident in the many lists. The list in this chapter names each family grouping, where they worked, and what they accomplished on the wall. Lists like this one have a distinct theological purpose: to emphasize the detailed as well as the shared nature of the LORD's work. In an era of foreign subjugation, the community cannot afford to engage in hierarchical leadership paradigms. The text tells through these lists that everyone helps; each has a task, has dignity, and contributes to the work instigated by Nehemiah under the authority of the law of Moses. If one wants to find examples of egalitarian leadership, the book of Nehemiah provides them; it also has much to say to the continuing discussion of how people exercise leadership. **4:** The phrases *beside, next to them,* etc., repeated often through this list, emphasize the importance of community and cooperation. **12:** Note the inclusion of women, *Shallum . . . and his daughters.*

point opposite the angle and the tower that projects up from the king's upper house beside the
court of the guard. Next to him were Pedaiah son
of Parosh, 26 with the Temple servants living on
the hill of Ophel, who repaired the wall as far as a
point across from the Water Gate to the east and
the projecting tower. 27 Then came the people of
Tekoa, who repaired another section across from
the great projecting tower and over to the wall
of Ophel.

28 Above the Horse Gate, the priests repaired
the wall. Each one repaired the section immediately across from his own house. 29 Next Zadok
son of Immer also rebuilt the wall across from
his own house, and beyond him was Shemaiah
son of Shecaniah, the gatekeeper of the East
Gate. 30 Next Hananiah son of Shelemiah and
Hanun, the sixth son of Zalaph, repaired another
section, while Meshullam son of Berekiah rebuilt
the wall across from where he lived. 31 Malkijah,
one of the goldsmiths, repaired the wall as far
as the housing for the Temple servants and merchants, across from the Inspection Gate. Then he
continued as far as the upper room at the corner.
32 The other goldsmiths and merchants repaired
the wall from that corner to the Sheep Gate.

Enemies Oppose the Rebuilding

4 1 *Sanballat was very angry when he
learned that we were rebuilding the wall.
He flew into a rage and mocked the Jews,
2 saying in front of his friends and the Samar-
ian army officers, "What does this bunch of poor,
feeble Jews think they're doing? Do they think
they can build the wall in a single day by just
offering a few sacrifices?* Do they actually think
they can make something of stones from a rub-
bish heap—and charred ones at that?"

3 Tobiah the Ammonite, who was standing beside him, remarked, "That stone wall would collapse if even a fox walked along the top of it!"

4 Then I prayed, "Hear us, our God, for we are
being mocked. May their scoffing fall back on
their own heads, and may they themselves become captives in a foreign land! 5 Do not ignore
their guilt. Do not blot out their sins, for they
have provoked you to anger here in front of* the
builders."

6 At last the wall was completed to half its
height around the entire city, for the people had
worked with enthusiasm.

7 *But when Sanballat and Tobiah and the Arabs, Ammonites, and Ashdodites heard that the
work was going ahead and that the gaps in the
wall of Jerusalem were being repaired, they were
furious. 8 They all made plans to come and fight
against Jerusalem and throw us into confusion.
9 But we prayed to our God and guarded the city
day and night to protect ourselves.

10 Then the people of Judah began to complain, "The workers are getting tired, and there
is so much rubble to be moved. We will never be
able to build the wall by ourselves."

11 Meanwhile, our enemies were saying, "Before they know what's happening, we will swoop
down on them and kill them and end their work."

12 The Jews who lived near the enemy came
and told us again and again, "They will come
from all directions and attack us!"* 13 So I placed
armed guards behind the lowest parts of the
wall in the exposed areas. I stationed the people
to stand guard by families, armed with swords,
spears, and bows.

14 Then as I looked over the situation, I called
together the nobles and the rest of the people and
said to them, "Don't be afraid of the enemy! Remember the Lord, who is great and glorious, and
fight for your brothers, your sons, your daughters, your wives, and your homes!"

15 When our enemies heard that we knew of
their plans and that God had frustrated them, we
all returned to our work on the wall. 16 But from
then on, only half my men worked while the
other half stood guard with spears, shields, bows,
and coats of mail. The leaders stationed themselves behind the people of Judah 17 who were
building the wall. The laborers carried on their

4:1 Verses 4:1-6 are numbered 3:33-38 in Hebrew text. **4:2** The meaning of the Hebrew is uncertain. **4:5** Or *for they have thrown insults in the face of.* **4:7** Verses 4:7-23 are numbered 4:1-17 in Hebrew text. **4:12** The meaning of the Hebrew is uncertain.

4:1—6:19 Work and Opposition

4:1–23 Enemies Oppose the Rebuilding. One of the elements that unites the books of Ezra and Nehemiah is the theme of work and opposition. The flow of the text of Nehemiah moves from outside opposition to inside opposition and then returns to outside opposition. **1:** Opposition begins upon commencement of the building task, as is foreshadowed in 2:19. **12–23:** Nehemiah and others set guards over the wall building, such that some would work and others would guard. The literary mechanism of opposition and response (cf. Ezra 1—6) emphasizes the shared community response as well as the meeting and overcoming of opposition. Those reading such a story would understand first, that in any endeavor there will be opposition, and second, that in order to succeed people must work together.

work with one hand supporting their load and one hand holding a weapon. 18 All the builders had a sword belted to their side. The trumpeter stayed with me to sound the alarm.

19 Then I explained to the nobles and officials and all the people, "The work is very spread out, and we are widely separated from each other along the wall. 20 When you hear the blast of the trumpet, rush to wherever it is sounding. Then our God will fight for us!"

21 We worked early and late, from sunrise to sunset. And half the men were always on guard. 22 I also told everyone living outside the walls to stay in Jerusalem. That way they and their servants could help with guard duty at night and work during the day. 23 During this time, none of us—not I, nor my relatives, nor my servants, nor the guards who were with me—ever took off our clothes. We carried our weapons with us at all times, even when we went for water.*

Nehemiah Defends the Oppressed

5 About this time some of the men and their wives raised a cry of protest against their fellow Jews. 2 They were saying, "We have such large families. We need more food to survive."

3 Others said, "We have mortgaged our fields, vineyards, and homes to get food during the famine."

4 And others said, "We have had to borrow money on our fields and vineyards to pay our taxes. 5 We belong to the same family as those who are wealthy, and our children are just like theirs. Yet we must sell our children into slavery just to get enough money to live. We have already sold some of our daughters, and we are helpless to do anything about it, for our fields and vineyards are already mortgaged to others."

6 When I heard their complaints, I was very angry. 7 After thinking it over, I spoke out against these nobles and officials. I told them, "You are hurting your own relatives by charging interest when they borrow money!" Then I called a public meeting to deal with the problem.

8 At the meeting I said to them, "We are doing all we can to redeem our Jewish relatives who have had to sell themselves to pagan foreigners, but you are selling them back into slavery again. How often must we redeem them?" And they had nothing to say in their defense.

9 Then I pressed further, "What you are doing is not right! Should you not walk in the fear of our God in order to avoid being mocked by enemy nations? 10 I myself, as well as my brothers and my workers, have been lending the people money and grain, but now let us stop this business of charging interest. 11 You must restore their fields, vineyards, olive groves, and homes to them this very day. And repay the interest you charged when you lent them money, grain, new wine, and olive oil."

12 They replied, "We will give back everything and demand nothing more from the people. We will do as you say." Then I called the priests and made the nobles and officials swear to do what they had promised.

13 I shook out the folds of my robe and said, "If you fail to keep your promise, may God shake you like this from your homes and from your property!"

The whole assembly responded, "Amen," and they praised the LORD. And the people did as they had promised.

14 For the entire twelve years that I was governor of Judah—from the twentieth year to the thirty-second year of the reign of King Artaxerxes*—neither I nor my officials drew on our official food allowance. 15 The former governors, in contrast, had laid heavy burdens on the people, demanding a daily ration of food and wine, besides forty pieces* of silver. Even their assistants took advantage of the people. But because I feared God, I did not act that way.

16 I also devoted myself to working on the wall and refused to acquire any land. And I required all my servants to spend time working on the wall. 17 I asked for nothing, even though I regularly fed 150 Jewish officials at my table, besides all the visitors from other lands! 18 The

4:23 Or *Each carried his weapon in his right hand.* Hebrew reads *Each his weapon the water.* The meaning of the Hebrew is uncertain. **5:14** That is, 445–433 B.C. **5:15** Hebrew *40 shekels* [1 pound, or 456 grams].

5:1–19 Nehemiah Defends the Oppressed. There was in the postexilic community infighting between those who had remained in the land and the new immigrants freshly returned from exile. **1:** *And their wives*: As in the case of wall building, women are part of the solution to community building. In this instance, women are at the forefront of justice issues. **2–5:** The problem at hand is economic: Creditors have taken possession of the properties of those who used them for collateral for loans to pay taxes or buy grain, and the situation has reached a point where families are selling the labor of their children in order to pay taxes to the Persian king. **5–19:** Nehemiah responds by calling an assembly to remedy the creditors' malpractice and then in addition serves as a model by limiting his use of tax funds.

Manipulation

Masters and mistresses of the art of manipulation abound in the biblical story. In some instances manipulation is condemned within the narrative—David's attempt to manipulate Uriah after impregnating his wife, or Jezebel's orchestration of Naboth's murder—but some manipulative measures enable the fulfillment of the promises to Abraham. This is true particularly of manipulative actions by women.

Rebekah orchestrates the deception of Isaac by assisting Jacob to steal Esau's blessing; Tamar deceives and seduces Judah in order to continue her husband's line. Shiphrah and Puah save Israelite boys in Egypt; Jochebed and Miriam hatch a plan to save Moses. Rahab the prostitute shields the Israelite spies and engineers their escape; Jael convinces Sisera to come to her for protection and then murders him; Naomi and Ruth arrange a suggestive encounter with Boaz that prompts him to act as Ruth's redeemer. Michal saves the life of David, soon to be king; Esther flatters the king and saves her people.

In almost all of these stories the character and role of the women as women enables their manipulations to succeed and God's purposes to be fulfilled. Jael, because she is a woman, is able to lure a general into a vulnerable position; Shiphrah and Puah are by virtue of their midwifery able to save Israelite baby boys; Esther uses her role as queen and her favor with the king; and Tamar and Ruth use their femininity to ensure the continuation of the lineage of the people, as well as of the Messiah (Matt 1:3, 5; Rahab also is named).

Such manipulations are sometimes the actions of those on the margins of power (Tamar, Ruth, and Rahab). In other cases only subterfuge is effective in the face of brutality (Shiphrah and Puah, Jochebed and Miriam, Rahab, Jael, Michal, and Esther).

Such stories, whether the manipulators are men or women, are less present in the New Testament than in the Old. Ultimately all such manipulation is not in keeping with the New Testament admonition of speaking the truth in love (Eph 4:15).

provisions I paid for each day included one ox, six choice sheep or goats, and a large number of poultry. And every ten days we needed a large supply of all kinds of wine. Yet I refused to claim the governor's food allowance because the people already carried a heavy burden.

[19] Remember, O my God, all that I have done
for these people, and bless me for it.

Continued Opposition to Rebuilding

6 Sanballat, Tobiah, Geshem the Arab, and the rest of our enemies found out that I had finished rebuilding the wall and that no gaps remained—though we had not yet set up
the doors in the gates. [2] So Sanballat and Geshem
sent a message asking me to meet them at one of the villages* in the plain of Ono.

But I realized they were plotting to harm me,
[3] so I replied by sending this message to them: "I am engaged in a great work, so I can't come. Why should I stop working to come and meet with you?"

[4] Four times they sent the same message, and
each time I gave the same reply. [5] The fifth time,
Sanballat's servant came with an open letter in
his hand, [6] and this is what it said:

"There is a rumor among the surrounding nations, and Geshem* tells me it is true, that you and the Jews are planning to rebel and that is why you are building the wall. According to his reports, you plan to be
their king. [7] He also reports that you have
appointed prophets in Jerusalem to proclaim about you, 'Look! There is a king in Judah!'

"You can be very sure that this report will get back to the king, so I suggest that you come and talk it over with me."

6:2 As in Greek version; Hebrew reads *at Kephirim*.
6:6 Hebrew *Gashmu*, a variant spelling of Geshem.

6:1–19 Continued Opposition to Rebuilding. 1–9: Sanballat, Tobiah, and Geshem now plot against Nehemiah through the ruse of a conference, and when this does not work, they threaten him in order to strike fear into the project. In both cases, Nehemiah responds (again the literary mechanism; see annotation on 4:12–23) and the threat is aborted. **5–9:** This section emphasizes the fear that is involved in undertaking a task as a subjugated people. Even though the enemies are in the wrong according to Persian

8 I replied, "There is no truth in any part of
your story. You are making up the whole thing."
9 They were just trying to intimidate us, imagining that they could discourage us and stop the
work. So I continued the work with even greater
determination.*
10 Later I went to visit Shemaiah son of Delaiah and grandson of Mehetabel, who was confined to his home. He said, "Let us meet together
inside the Temple of God and bolt the doors shut.
Your enemies are coming to kill you tonight."
11 But I replied, "Should someone in my position run from danger? Should someone in my
position enter the Temple to save his life? No, I
won't do it!" 12 I realized that God had not spoken to him, but that he had uttered this prophecy against me because Tobiah and Sanballat had
hired him. 13 They were hoping to intimidate me
and make me sin. Then they would be able to accuse and discredit me.

14 Remember, O my God, all the evil things
that Tobiah and Sanballat have done. And
remember Noadiah the prophet and all
the prophets like her who have tried to
intimidate me.

The Builders Complete the Wall

15 So on October 2* the wall was finished—just
fifty-two days after we had begun. 16 When our
enemies and the surrounding nations heard
about it, they were frightened and humiliated.
They realized this work had been done with the
help of our God.
17 During those fifty-two days, many letters
went back and forth between Tobiah and the
nobles of Judah. 18 For many in Judah had sworn
allegiance to him because his father-in-law was
Shecaniah son of Arah, and his son Jehohanan
was married to the daughter of Meshullam son of
Berekiah. 19 They kept telling me about Tobiah's
good deeds, and then they told him everything I
said. And Tobiah kept sending threatening letters
to intimidate me.

7 After the wall was finished and I had set
up the doors in the gates, the gatekeepers,
singers, and Levites were appointed. 2 I gave
the responsibility of governing Jerusalem to my
brother Hanani, along with Hananiah, the commander of the fortress, for he was a faithful man
who feared God more than most. 3 I said to them,
"Do not leave the gates open during the hottest
part of the day.* And even while the gatekeepers
are on duty, have them shut and bar the doors.
Appoint the residents of Jerusalem to act as
guards, everyone on a regular watch. Some will
serve at sentry posts and some in front of their
own homes."

Nehemiah Registers the People

4 At that time the city was large and spacious,
but the population was small, and none of the
houses had been rebuilt. 5 So my God gave me
the idea to call together all the nobles and leaders
of the city, along with the ordinary citizens, for
registration. I had found the genealogical record
of those who had first returned to Judah. This is
what was written there:

6:9 As in Greek version; Hebrew reads *But now to strengthen my hands.* **6:15** Hebrew *on the twenty-fifth day of the month Elul,* of the ancient Hebrew lunar calendar. This day was October 2, 445 B.C.; also see note on 1:1. **7:3** Or *Keep the gates of Jerusalem closed until the sun is hot.*

---

instruction (2:9), they possess power to intimidate. **10–13:** Nehemiah sends a signal to victims of intimidation that they can and should persist with proper behavior despite threats from those who want to disrupt and discourage. **15–16:** Those who do persist will succeed—the wall is completed.

7:1–73 Reform and Cooperation

This unit completes the first half of what is known as the Nehemiah memoir (Neh 1:1—7:73; 11:1—13:31). The unit consists of two parts, the reports of the gate closing and the genealogy of returning exiles. Appropriately, this section of Nehemiah closes the section on building the wall, which is the symbol of community boundary and identity, with a list of those within who returned. The list is identical to the list found in Ezra 2:2–70. **1–3:** The gates are literally and figuratively the outer limit for the community. The city of Jerusalem is yet to be populated, a task that Nehemiah will undertake in chapter 11. Nonetheless it is the location for community identity. The major task of Nehemiah's reform is not just to build a wall but also to establish boundaries for the emerging postexilic community. The wall is the physical symbol of that community. **4:** Guards must stand watch during the night because *the population was small. And none of the houses* had been built. The gate report in verses 1–4, although not specifically aimed at women, does point to the necessity of place in establishing identity. This is true for the homeless on our streets as well as the homeless living in suburbia, who find through either divorce or financial disaster that they no longer have an identity because they no longer can claim a place. With the guarding of Jerusalem, Nehemiah secures a place

[6] Here is the list of the Jewish exiles of the provinces who returned from their captivity. King Nebuchadnezzar had deported them to Babylon, but now they returned to Jerusalem and the other towns in Judah where they originally lived. [7] Their leaders were Zerubbabel, Jeshua, Nehemiah, Seraiah,* Reelaiah,* Nahamani, Mordecai, Bilshan, Mispar,* Bigvai, Rehum,* and Baanah.

This is the number of the men of Israel who returned from exile:

[8] The family of Parosh..........2,172
[9] The family of Shephatiah..........372
[10] The family of Arah..........652
[11] The family of Pahath-moab (descendants of Jeshua and Joab)..........2,818
[12] The family of Elam..........1,254
[13] The family of Zattu..........845
[14] The family of Zaccai..........760
[15] The family of Bani*..........648
[16] The family of Bebai..........628
[17] The family of Azgad..........2,322
[18] The family of Adonikam..........667
[19] The family of Bigvai..........2,067
[20] The family of Adin..........655
[21] The family of Ater (descendants of Hezekiah)..........98
[22] The family of Hashum..........328
[23] The family of Bezai..........324
[24] The family of Jorah*..........112
[25] The family of Gibbar*..........95
[26] The people of Bethlehem and Netophah..........188
[27] The people of Anathoth..........128
[28] The people of Beth-azmaveth..........42
[29] The people of Kiriath-jearim, Kephirah, and Beeroth..........743
[30] The people of Ramah and Geba..........621
[31] The people of Micmash..........122
[32] The people of Bethel and Ai..........123
[33] The people of West Nebo*..........52
[34] The citizens of West Elam*..........1,254
[35] The citizens of Harim..........320
[36] The citizens of Jericho..........345
[37] The citizens of Lod, Hadid, and Ono..........721
[38] The citizens of Senaah..........3,930

[39] These are the priests who returned from exile:

The family of Jedaiah (through the line of Jeshua)..........973
[40] The family of Immer..........1,052
[41] The family of Pashhur..........1,247
[42] The family of Harim..........1,017

[43] These are the Levites who returned from exile:

The families of Jeshua and Kadmiel (descendants of Hodaviah*)..........74
[44] The singers of the family of Asaph..........148
[45] The gatekeepers of the families of Shallum, Ater, Talmon, Akkub, Hatita, and Shobai..........138

[46] The descendants of the following Temple servants returned from exile:

Ziha, Hasupha, Tabbaoth,
[47] Keros, Siaha,* Padon,
[48] Lebanah, Hagabah, Shalmai,
[49] Hanan, Giddel, Gahar,
[50] Reaiah, Rezin, Nekoda,
[51] Gazzam, Uzza, Paseah,
[52] Besai, Meunim, Nephusim,*
[53] Bakbuk, Hakupha, Harhur,
[54] Bazluth,* Mehida, Harsha,
[55] Barkos, Sisera, Temah,
[56] Neziah, and Hatipha.

[57] The descendants of these servants of King Solomon returned from exile:

Sotai, Hassophereth, Peruda,*
[58] Jaalah,* Darkon, Giddel,
[59] Shephatiah, Hattil, Pokereth-hazzebaim, and Ami.*

[60] In all, the Temple servants and the descendants of Solomon's servants numbered 392.

7:7a As in parallel text at Ezra 2:2; Hebrew reads *Azariah.* **7:7b** As in parallel text at Ezra 2:2; Hebrew reads *Raamiah.* **7:7c** As in parallel text at Ezra 2:2; Hebrew reads *Mispereth.* **7:7d** As in parallel text at Ezra 2:2; Hebrew reads *Nehum.* **7:15** As in parallel text at Ezra 2:10; Hebrew reads *Binnui.* **7:24** As in parallel text at Ezra 2:18; Hebrew reads *Hariph.* **7:25** As in parallel text at Ezra 2:20; Hebrew reads *Gibeon.* **7:33** Or *of the other Nebo.* **7:34** Or *of the other Elam.* **7:43** As in parallel text at Ezra 2:40; Hebrew reads *Hodevah.* **7:47** As in parallel text at Ezra 2:44; Hebrew reads *Sia.* **7:52** As in parallel text at Ezra 2:50; Hebrew reads *Nephushesim.* **7:54** As in parallel text at Ezra 2:52; Hebrew reads *Bazlith.* **7:57** As in parallel text at Ezra 2:55; Hebrew reads *Sotai, Sophereth, Perida.* **7:58** As in parallel text at Ezra 2:56; Hebrew reads *Jaala.* **7:59** As in parallel text at Ezra 2:57; Hebrew reads *Amon.*

so that the people can find their identity. **6–73:** The presence of lists in Ezra-Nehemiah sends signals of identity formation as well as egalitarian cooperation. The list appearing here separates those who could prove their ancestry (vv. 6–60) from those who could not (vv. 61–65). Such a division points to the need

[61]Another group returned at this time
from the towns of Tel-melah, Tel-harsha,
Kerub, Addan,* and Immer. However, they
could not prove that they or their families
were descendants of Israel. [62]This group
included the families of Delaiah, Tobiah, and
Nekoda—a total of 642 people.

[63]Three families of priests—Hobaiah,
Hakkoz, and Barzillai—also returned. (This
Barzillai had married a woman who was a
descendant of Barzillai of Gilead, and he had
taken her family name.) [64]They searched
for their names in the genealogical records,
but they were not found, so they were
disqualified from serving as priests. [65]The
governor told them not to eat the priests'
share of food from the sacrifices until a priest
could consult the LORD about the matter by
using the Urim and Thummim—the sacred
lots.

[66]So a total of 42,360 people returned to
Judah, [67]in addition to 7,337 servants and
245 singers, both men and women. [68]They
took with them 736 horses, 245 mules,*
[69]435 camels, and 6,720 donkeys.

[70]Some of the family leaders gave gifts for
the work. The governor gave to the treasury
1,000 gold coins,* 50 gold basins, and
530 robes for the priests. [71]The other leaders
gave to the treasury a total of 20,000 gold
coins* and some 2,750 pounds* of silver for
the work. [72]The rest of the people gave 20,000
gold coins, about 2,500 pounds* of silver, and
67 robes for the priests.

[73]So the priests, the Levites, the gatekeepers,
the singers, the Temple servants, and some of
the common people settled near Jerusalem.
The rest of the people returned to their own
towns throughout Israel.

Ezra Reads the Law

8 In October,* when the Israelites had settled
in their towns, [8:1]all the people assembled
with a unified purpose at the square just
inside the Water Gate. They asked Ezra the scribe
to bring out the Book of the Law of Moses, which
the LORD had given for Israel to obey.

[2]So on October 8* Ezra the priest brought the
Book of the Law before the assembly, which included the men and women and all the children
old enough to understand. [3]He faced the square
just inside the Water Gate from early morning
until noon and read aloud to everyone who could
understand. All the people listened closely to the
Book of the Law.

[4]Ezra the scribe stood on a high wooden platform that had been made for the occasion. To his
right stood Mattithiah, Shema, Anaiah, Uriah,

7:61 As in parallel text at Ezra 2:59; Hebrew reads *Addon.* **7:68** As in some Hebrew manuscripts (see also Ezra 2:66); most Hebrew manuscripts lack this verse. Verses 7:69-73 are numbered 7:68-72 in Hebrew text. **7:70** Hebrew *1,000 darics of gold,* about 19 pounds or 8.6 kilograms in weight. **7:71a** Hebrew *20,000 darics of gold,* about 375 pounds or 170 kilograms in weight; also in 7:72. **7:71b** Hebrew *2,200 minas* [1,300 kilograms]. **7:72** Hebrew *2,000 minas* [1,200 kilograms]. **7:73** Hebrew *in the seventh month.* This month of the ancient Hebrew lunar calendar occurred within the months of October and November 445 B.C. **8:2** Hebrew *on the first day of the seventh month,* of the ancient Hebrew lunar calendar. This day was October 8, 445 B.C.; also see note on 1:1.

to establish community boundaries. **70–72:** The list also tells who contributed to the reform effort, underlining the shared task theme. The building of the wall and the concurrent reform are the result of many hands. These many hands give the community ownership and pride of accomplishment.

8:1–12 The Law of Moses and Celebration

Chapter 8 begins what many think is the center of Ezra-Nehemiah: the reading of the law, and the resultant actions (8:1—12:26). Some interpreters have cited the resumption of the Ezra memoir here, begun in Ezra 7—10. Regardless of literary evaluation, this section does bring together the so far separate reforms of the two postexilic leaders. Ezra the priest/scribe and Nehemiah the governor appear together for the first time, signaling the cooperation of the sacred and secular realms in renewal. Ezra reads the law of Moses establishing the basis upon which the new community will build itself, picking up the uncompromised themes of law and covenant and letting fall the tarnished monarchic tradition. Finally, the law of Moses elicits response from the people, who celebrate the Festival of Shelters (8:13–18) and enter into a new covenant (chap. 9). **1–4:** When Ezra reads from the law he is surrounded by community leaders, who with him address the entire community, which contains women and men. All get a chance to hear the words and respond. The presence of leaders standing alongside and the mixed audience underlines a consistent communal theme running through Ezra-Nehemiah. All read, all hear, all are responsible for their lives under the rule of law. **3–5:** Ezra stands on a platform and reads the law of Moses. This is significant in a society that had for years been a society of kings and privilege. The book of Kings reports that the kings were responsible for the destruction of Jerusalem and the resultant exile. The kings are no longer in charge. The law is now the center of

Hilkiah, and Maaseiah. To his left stood Pedaiah, Mishael, Malkijah, Hashum, Hashbaddanah,
Zechariah, and Meshullam. 5 Ezra stood on the
platform in full view of all the people. When
they saw him open the book, they all rose to
their feet.
6 Then Ezra praised the LORD, the great God,
and all the people chanted, "Amen! Amen!" as
they lifted their hands. Then they bowed down
and worshiped the LORD with their faces to the
ground.
7 The Levites—Jeshua, Bani, Sherebiah, Jamin, Akkub, Shabbethai, Hodiah, Maaseiah, Kelita, Azariah, Jozabad, Hanan, and Pelaiah—then
instructed the people in the Law while everyone
remained in their places. 8 They read from the
Book of the Law of God and clearly explained
the meaning of what was being read, helping the
people understand each passage.
9 Then Nehemiah the governor, Ezra the
priest and scribe, and the Levites who were interpreting for the people said to them, "Don't
mourn or weep on such a day as this! For today
is a sacred day before the LORD your God." For
the people had all been weeping as they listened
to the words of the Law.
10 And Nehemiah* continued, "Go and celebrate with a feast of rich foods and sweet drinks,
and share gifts of food with people who have
nothing prepared. This is a sacred day before our
Lord. Don't be dejected and sad, for the joy of the
LORD is your strength!"
11 And the Levites, too, quieted the people,
telling them, "Hush! Don't weep! For this is a
sacred day." 12 So the people went away to eat
and drink at a festive meal, to share gifts of food,
and to celebrate with great joy because they had
heard God's words and understood them.

The Festival of Shelters

13 On October 9* the family leaders of all the
people, together with the priests and Levites, met
with Ezra the scribe to go over the Law in greater
detail. 14 As they studied the Law, they discovered
that the LORD had commanded through Moses
that the Israelites should live in shelters during
the festival to be held that month.* 15 He had said
that a proclamation should be made throughout
their towns and in Jerusalem, telling the people
to go to the hills to get branches from olive, wild
olive,* myrtle, palm, and other leafy trees. They
were to use these branches to make shelters in
which they would live during the festival, as prescribed in the Law.
16 So the people went out and cut branches and
used them to build shelters on the roofs of their
houses, in their courtyards, in the courtyards of

8:10 Hebrew *he.* **8:13** Hebrew *On the second day,* of the seventh month of the ancient Hebrew lunar calendar. This day was October 9, 445 B.C.; also see notes on 1:1 and 8:2. **8:14** Hebrew *in the seventh month.* This month of the ancient Hebrew lunar calendar usually occurs within the months of September and October. See Lev 23:39-43. **8:15** Or *pine;* Hebrew reads *oil tree.*

---

community identity. **6–9:** People look not to power structures but to a law book, which all hear and obey. Issues of justice and righteousness now rise above temporal rule. For the women in the crowd and for future generations, rule by law opens the possibility for better treatment. In practice it may take time for women to be treated as equal partners with men, but at least this move from a rule of persons to a rule of law, effected in the reforms of Ezra and Nehemiah, pushes in the direction of equal treatment under the law. **7–8:** While Ezra is reading, teachers, the Levites, help the people to understand what is being read and the impact it has on their lives. This sounds like a Reformation church service, where the priests no longer read in Latin but put the Bibles in the pews and preach to the congregation, who all the while read along.

8:13–18 Law and Obedience

The heads of the families come together to study, and upon finding the command of the LORD, they act. They become not only hearers of the word but also doers of the word, evidenced by their observance of the Festival of Shelters (or Booths). **14–18:** The Festival of Shelters is also called Sukkot. It originated as a harvest festival and also commemorated the Israelites' forty years of wandering in the wilderness. Participants build temporary structures and live in them for the week-long festival. In Israel for the first time since Moses' time, the people reinstitute and cooperate with the rule of the LORD and bypass the power structures of the monarchy. And even if the law of Moses contains laws that in the judgment of some may hinder righteous treatment, it nonetheless moves Israel away from the dead end of the abusive monarchy. The fact that Ezra and Nehemiah publish and enact this new system is significant for the postexilic community and for us who seek patterns of rule for our day. The establishment of the rule of law can mitigate abuse of oppressed groups (whether women, tribes, classes, or races) because it raises the criterion for judgment above the coercive force of the rulers. However, the laws may embody the power imbalance that rule of law is meant to redress.

God's Temple, or in the squares just inside the Water Gate and the Ephraim Gate. 17 So everyone who had returned from captivity lived in these shelters during the festival, and they were all filled with great joy! The Israelites had not celebrated like this since the days of Joshua* son of Nun.

18 Ezra read from the Book of the Law of God on each of the seven days of the festival. Then on the eighth day they held a solemn assembly, as was required by law.

The People Confess Their Sins

9 On October 31* the people assembled again, and this time they fasted and dressed in burlap and sprinkled dust on their heads. 2 Those of Israelite descent separated themselves from all foreigners as they confessed their own sins and the sins of their ancestors. 3 They remained standing in place for three hours* while the Book of the Law of the LORD their God was read aloud to them. Then for three more hours they confessed their sins and worshiped the LORD their God. 4 The Levites—Jeshua, Bani, Kadmiel, Shebaniah, Bunni, Sherebiah, Bani, and Kenani—stood on the stairway of the Levites and cried out to the LORD their God with loud voices.

5 Then the leaders of the Levites—Jeshua, Kadmiel, Bani, Hashabneiah, Sherebiah, Hodiah, Shebaniah, and Pethahiah—called out to the people: "Stand up and praise the LORD your God, for he lives from everlasting to everlasting!" Then they prayed:

"May your glorious name be praised! May it
be exalted above all blessing and praise!

6 "You alone are the LORD. You made the
skies and the heavens and all the stars. You
made the earth and the seas and everything
in them. You preserve them all, and the
angels of heaven worship you.

7 "You are the LORD God, who chose Abram
and brought him from Ur of the Chaldeans
and renamed him Abraham. 8 When he had
proved himself faithful, you made a covenant
with him to give him and his descendants the
land of the Canaanites, Hittites, Amorites,
Perizzites, Jebusites, and Girgashites. And you
have done what you promised, for you are
always true to your word.

9 "You saw the misery of our ancestors in
Egypt, and you heard their cries from beside
the Red Sea.* 10 You displayed miraculous
signs and wonders against Pharaoh, his
officials, and all his people, for you knew how
arrogantly they were treating our ancestors.
You have a glorious reputation that has never
been forgotten. 11 You divided the sea for your
people so they could walk through on dry
land! And then you hurled their enemies into
the depths of the sea. They sank like stones
beneath the mighty waters. 12 You led our
ancestors by a pillar of cloud during the day

8:17 Hebrew *Jeshua,* a variant spelling of Joshua.
9:1 Hebrew *On the twenty-fourth day of that same month,* the seventh month of the ancient Hebrew lunar calendar. This day was October 31, 445 B.C.; also see notes on 1:1 and 8:2.
9:3 Hebrew *for a quarter of a day.* **9:9** Hebrew *sea of reeds.*

9:1–38 Appropriating Tradition

A significant question for any renewal movement is how much of the past to keep and how much to reject. The people's confession and the Levites' prayer (sometimes attributed to Ezra) provide an analysis of how the postexilic community envisioned its relationship with the past. The prayer summarizes the history of God's covenant with his chosen people. The prayer is in two parts: the narrative of what the LORD did with Abraham and the post-Egypt community (vv. 7–31), and what Ezra wants the LORD to do with the postexilic community (vv. 32–38). Notice that the trouble, in the assessment of this text, begins not with Abraham but with those who left Egypt.

The significance of the prayer is its analysis of Israel's history under the custom of covenant. Ezra does not reject the history but sees within it what is good, the covenant relationship with the LORD, and wants now to take what is good and reconstitute it for the new community. In doing so Ezra finds Abraham, the covenant, and the LORD's identity worth keeping.

Many people today view tradition as the enemy of establishing a new and better community. Those who hold such a view at times reject the past as the oppressive structure of patriarchy, seeing nothing there to build on for a better future. Conversely, some would lay aside the present for a return to an idyllic past where all was ordered according to goodness and light. Ezra's prayer rejects both these tendencies for a measured sifting of tradition. There is nothing about tradition or currency that makes it of itself good. Ezra's prayer shows that it is the presence of the LORD in justice and righteousness acted out in the covenant relationship with people that is the criterion for whether a movement is good. Thus, in assessing any liberation or reform movement, we must not hail it as valid without the prior sifting according to established criteria: the LORD's presence in our midst.

and a pillar of fire at night so that they could find their way.

13 "You came down at Mount Sinai and spoke to them from heaven. You gave them regulations and instructions that were just, and decrees and commands that were good. 14 You instructed them concerning your holy Sabbath. And you commanded them, through Moses your servant, to obey all your commands, decrees, and instructions.

15 "You gave them bread from heaven when they were hungry and water from the rock when they were thirsty. You commanded them to go and take possession of the land you had sworn to give them.

16 "But our ancestors were proud and stubborn, and they paid no attention to your commands. 17 They refused to obey and did not remember the miracles you had done for them. Instead, they became stubborn and appointed a leader to take them back to their slavery in Egypt! But you are a God of forgiveness, gracious and merciful, slow to become angry, and rich in unfailing love. You did not abandon them, 18 even when they made an idol shaped like a calf and said, 'This is your god who brought you out of Egypt!' They committed terrible blasphemies.

19 "But in your great mercy you did not abandon them to die in the wilderness. The pillar of cloud still led them forward by day, and the pillar of fire showed them the way through the night. 20 You sent your good Spirit to instruct them, and you did not stop giving them manna from heaven or water for their thirst. 21 For forty years you sustained them in the wilderness, and they lacked nothing. Their clothes did not wear out, and their feet did not swell!

22 "Then you helped our ancestors conquer kingdoms and nations, and you placed your people in every corner of the land.* They took over the land of King Sihon of Heshbon and the land of King Og of Bashan. 23 You made their descendants as numerous as the stars in the sky and brought them into the land you had promised to their ancestors.

24 "They went in and took possession of the land. You subdued whole nations before them. Even the Canaanites, who inhabited the land, were powerless! Your people could deal with these nations and their kings as they pleased. 25 Our ancestors captured fortified cities and fertile land. They took over houses full of good things, with cisterns already dug and vineyards and olive groves and fruit trees in abundance. So they ate until they were full and grew fat and enjoyed themselves in all your blessings.

26 "But despite all this, they were disobedient and rebelled against you. They turned their backs on your Law, they killed your prophets who warned them to return to you, and they committed terrible blasphemies. 27 So you handed them over to their enemies, who made them suffer. But in their time of trouble they cried to you, and you heard them from heaven. In your great mercy, you sent them liberators who rescued them from their enemies.

28 "But as soon as they were at peace, your people again committed evil in your sight, and once more you let their enemies conquer them. Yet whenever your people turned and cried to you again for help, you listened once more from heaven. In your wonderful mercy, you rescued them many times!

29 "You warned them to return to your Law, but they became proud and obstinate and disobeyed your commands. They did not follow your regulations, by which people will find life if only they obey. They stubbornly turned their backs on you and refused to listen. 30 In your love, you were patient with them for many years. You sent your Spirit, who warned them through the prophets. But still they wouldn't listen! So once again you allowed the peoples of the land to conquer them. 31 But in your great mercy, you did not destroy them completely or abandon them forever. What a gracious and merciful God you are!

32 "And now, our God, the great and mighty and awesome God, who keeps his covenant of unfailing love, do not let all the hardships we have suffered seem insignificant to you. Great trouble has come upon us and upon our kings and leaders and priests and prophets and ancestors—all of your people—from the days when the kings of Assyria first triumphed over us until now. 33 Every time you punished us you were being just. We have sinned greatly, and you gave us only what we deserved. 34 Our kings, leaders, priests, and ancestors did not obey your Law or listen to the warnings in your commands and laws. 35 Even while they had their own kingdom, they did not serve you, though you showered your goodness on them. You gave

9:22 The meaning of the Hebrew is uncertain.

them a large, fertile land, but they refused to
turn from their wickedness.
36 "So now today we are slaves in the land
of plenty that you gave our ancestors for
their enjoyment! We are slaves here in this
good land. 37 The lush produce of this land
piles up in the hands of the kings whom you
have set over us because of our sins. They
have power over us and our livestock. We
serve them at their pleasure, and we are in
great misery."

The People Agree to Obey

38 *The people responded, "In view of all this,*
we are making a solemn promise and putting
it in writing. On this sealed document are the
names of our leaders and Levites and priests."

10 1 *The document was ratified and
sealed with the following names:

The governor:
Nehemiah son of Hacaliah, and also Zedekiah.
2 The following priests:
Seraiah, Azariah, Jeremiah, 3 Pashhur,
Amariah, Malkijah, 4 Hattush, Shebaniah,
Malluch, 5 Harim, Meremoth, Obadiah,
6 Daniel, Ginnethon, Baruch, 7 Meshullam,
Abijah, Mijamin, 8 Maaziah, Bilgai, and
Shemaiah. These were the priests.
9 The following Levites:
Jeshua son of Azaniah, Binnui from the
family of Henadad, Kadmiel, 10 and their
fellow Levites: Shebaniah, Hodiah, Kelita,
Pelaiah, Hanan, 11 Mica, Rehob, Hashabiah,
12 Zaccur, Sherebiah, Shebaniah, 13 Hodiah,
Bani, and Beninu.
14 The following leaders:
Parosh, Pahath-moab, Elam, Zattu, Bani,
15 Bunni, Azgad, Bebai, 16 Adonijah, Bigvai,
Adin, 17 Ater, Hezekiah, Azzur, 18 Hodiah,
Hashum, Bezai, 19 Hariph, Anathoth, Nebai,
20 Magpiash, Meshullam, Hezir, 21 Meshezabel,
Zadok, Jaddua, 22 Pelatiah, Hanan, Anaiah,
23 Hoshea, Hananiah, Hasshub, 24 Hallohesh,
Pilha, Shobek, 25 Rehum, Hashabnah,
Maaseiah, 26 Ahiah, Hanan, Anan, 27 Malluch,
Harim, and Baanah.

The Vow of the People

28 Then the rest of the people—the priests, Levites,
gatekeepers, singers, Temple servants, and all who
had separated themselves from the pagan people
of the land in order to obey the Law of God, together with their wives, sons, daughters, and all
who were old enough to understand— 29 joined
their leaders and bound themselves with an oath.
They swore a curse on themselves if they failed
to obey the Law of God as issued by his servant
Moses. They solemnly promised to carefully follow all the commands, regulations, and decrees of
the LORD our Lord:

30 "We promise not to let our daughters
marry the pagan people of the land, and not
to let our sons marry their daughters.
31 "We also promise that if the people of
the land should bring any merchandise or
grain to be sold on the Sabbath or on any
other holy day, we will refuse to buy it. Every
seventh year we will let our land rest, and we
will cancel all debts owed to us.
32 "In addition, we promise to obey the
command to pay the annual Temple tax of
one-eighth of an ounce of silver* for the care
of the Temple of our God. 33 This will provide

9:38a Verse 9:38 is numbered 10:1 in Hebrew text. **9:38b** Or *In spite of all this.* **10:1** Verses 10:1-39 are numbered 10:2-40 in Hebrew text. **10:32** Hebrew *tax of 1/3 of a shekel* [4 grams].

38: The reestablished community in Jerusalem recommit themselves to the covenant with God.

10:1–39 Shared Tasks, the Law of Moses, and Covenant

Those who sign the covenant are the leaders of the people. The list underscores the theme that this is not the monarchy but the shared responsibility of the group. In an age of victimization and deflection, it is refreshing to read of a direct claim for responsibility. It is not the problem of our mothers and fathers, it is not the kings—we are the ones who stand before God and acknowledge that the LORD is righteous, not us, and that we are responsible. **28–29:** Not only the leaders but all the people pledge themselves to the covenant and the law of Moses. **30–39:** The communal *we* reinforces the theme of shared responsibility and changed leadership in postexilic Jerusalem. The people recite their promise to follow the law, particularly the laws concerning intermarriage, Sabbath-keeping and Temple tax, tithe, and firstfruits. As was the case originally, the law follows the LORD's actions in establishing the community. At Sinai God gave the people the law as a way of living out the covenant relationship begun in the gracious action at the Exodus. Here God has again acted for the people in bringing them out of exile (note the Exodus themes throughout Ezra-Nehemiah) and consequently gives them the law as a way for establishing good relations.

for the Bread of the Presence; for the regular
grain offerings and burnt offerings; for the
offerings on the Sabbaths, the new moon
celebrations, and the annual festivals; for the
holy offerings; and for the sin offerings to
make atonement for Israel. It will provide
for everything necessary for the work of the
Temple of our God.
34 "We have cast sacred lots to determine
when—at regular times each year—the
families of the priests, Levites, and the
common people should bring wood to God's
Temple to be burned on the altar of the LORD
our God, as is written in the Law.
35 "We promise to bring the first part of
every harvest to the LORD's Temple year after
year—whether it be a crop from the soil or
from our fruit trees. 36 We agree to give God
our oldest sons and the firstborn of all our
herds and flocks, as prescribed in the Law. We
will present them to the priests who minister
in the Temple of our God. 37 We will store the
produce in the storerooms of the Temple of
our God. We will bring the best of our flour
and other grain offerings, the best of our
fruit, and the best of our new wine and olive
oil. And we promise to bring to the Levites a
tenth of everything our land produces, for it
is the Levites who collect the tithes in all our
rural towns.
38 "A priest—a descendant of Aaron—will
be with the Levites as they receive these
tithes. And a tenth of all that is collected
as tithes will be delivered by the Levites to
the Temple of our God and placed in the
storerooms. 39 The people and the Levites
must bring these offerings of grain, new
wine, and olive oil to the storerooms and
place them in the sacred containers near the
ministering priests, the gatekeepers, and the
singers.
"We promise together not to neglect the
Temple of our God."

The People Occupy Jerusalem

11 The leaders of the people were living
in Jerusalem, the holy city. A tenth of
the people from the other towns of
Judah and Benjamin were chosen by sacred lots
to live there, too, while the rest stayed where
they were. 2 And the people commended everyone who volunteered to resettle in Jerusalem.
3 Here is a list of the names of the provincial
officials who came to live in Jerusalem. (Most of
the people, priests, Levites, Temple servants, and
descendants of Solomon's servants continued to
live in their own homes in the various towns of
Judah, 4 but some of the people from Judah and
Benjamin resettled in Jerusalem.)

From the tribe of Judah:
Athaiah son of Uzziah, son of Zechariah,
son of Amariah, son of Shephatiah, son of
Mahalalel, of the family of Perez. 5 Also
Maaseiah son of Baruch, son of Col-hozeh,
son of Hazaiah, son of Adaiah, son of Joiarib,
son of Zechariah, of the family of Shelah.*
6 There were 468 descendants of Perez who
lived in Jerusalem—all outstanding men.
7 From the tribe of Benjamin:
Sallu son of Meshullam, son of Joed, son of
Pedaiah, son of Kolaiah, son of Maaseiah, son
of Ithiel, son of Jeshaiah. 8 After him were
Gabbai and Sallai and a total of 928 relatives.
9 Their chief officer was Joel son of Zicri, who
was assisted by Judah son of Hassenuah,
second-in-command over the city.
10 From the priests:
Jedaiah son of Joiarib; Jakin; 11 and Seraiah
son of Hilkiah, son of Meshullam, son of
Zadok, son of Meraioth, son of Ahitub, the
supervisor of the Temple of God. 12 Also
822 of their associates, who worked at the
Temple. Also Adaiah son of Jeroham, son
of Pelaliah, son of Amzi, son of Zechariah,

11:5 Hebrew *son of the Shilonite.*

God first acts in grace and then in continuing grace gives the law. This is the flow of the book of Exodus as well as Ezra-Nehemiah. The implication of this biblical flow for women's concerns in particular, and for any liberation movement in general, is that the grace and freedom of God contain the restraints of the law. God in grace sets people free, in Egypt and now in the postexilic community, so that they can live within the boundaries of the LORD's reign. God does not set people free to do as they please or to establish their ethos and morality. This is not freedom but license. The Bible, and in particular Ezra-Nehemiah, knows only the freedom to do the right thing, to worship the LORD.

11:1—12:26 Shared Tasks and Community

11:1–36 The People Occupy Jerusalem. Again, the list highlights the shared task theme. **1–2:** Because Jerusalem was still largely empty, moving there was not an attractive prospect; thus, the drawing of lots and honoring those who *volunteered* to live there.

son of Pashhur, son of Malkijah, 13 along
with 242 of his associates, who were heads
of their families. Also Amashsai son of
Azarel, son of Ahzai, son of Meshillemoth,
son of Immer, 14 and 128 of his* outstanding
associates. Their chief officer was Zabdiel son
of Haggedolim.
15 From the Levites:
Shemaiah son of Hasshub, son of Azrikam,
son of Hashabiah, son of Bunni. 16 Also
Shabbethai and Jozabad, who were in charge
of the work outside the Temple of God.
17 Also Mattaniah son of Mica, son of Zabdi, a
descendant of Asaph, who led in thanksgiving
and prayer. Also Bakbukiah, who was
Mattaniah's assistant, and Abda son of
Shammua, son of Galal, son of Jeduthun. 18 In
all, there were 284 Levites in the holy city.
19 From the gatekeepers:
Akkub, Talmon, and 172 of their associates,
who guarded the gates.

20 The other priests, Levites, and the rest of the
Israelites lived wherever their family inheritance
was located in any of the towns of Judah. 21 The
Temple servants, however, whose leaders were
Ziha and Gishpa, all lived on the hill of Ophel.
22 The chief officer of the Levites in Jerusalem
was Uzzi son of Bani, son of Hashabiah, son of
Mattaniah, son of Mica, a descendant of Asaph,
whose family served as singers at God's Temple.
23 Their daily responsibilities were carried out according to the terms of a royal command.
24 Pethahiah son of Meshezabel, a descendant
of Zerah son of Judah, was the royal adviser in all
matters of public administration.
25 As for the surrounding villages with their
open fields, some of the people of Judah lived in
Kiriath-arba with its settlements, Dibon with
its settlements, and Jekabzeel with its villages.
26 They also lived in Jeshua, Moladah, Beth-pelet,
27 Hazar-shual, Beersheba with its settlements,
28 Ziklag, and Meconah with its settlements.
29 They also lived in En-rimmon, Zorah, Jarmuth,
30 Zanoah, and Adullam with their surrounding villages. They also lived in Lachish with its
nearby fields and Azekah with its surrounding
villages. So the people of Judah were living all
the way from Beersheba in the south to the valley of Hinnom.
31 Some of the people of Benjamin lived at
Geba, Micmash, Aija, and Bethel with its settlements. 32 They also lived in Anathoth, Nob, Ananiah, 33 Hazor, Ramah, Gittaim, 34 Hadid, Zeboim,
Neballat, 35 Lod, Ono, and the Valley of Craftsmen.* 36 Some of the Levites who lived in Judah
were sent to live with the tribe of Benjamin.

A History of the Priests and Levites

12 Here is the list of the priests and Levites who returned with Zerubbabel
son of Shealtiel and Jeshua the high
priest:

Seraiah, Jeremiah, Ezra,
2 Amariah, Malluch, Hattush,
3 Shecaniah, Harim,* Meremoth,
4 Iddo, Ginnethon,* Abijah,
5 Miniamin, Moadiah,* Bilgah,
6 Shemaiah, Joiarib, Jedaiah,
7 Sallu, Amok, Hilkiah, and Jedaiah.
These were the leaders of the priests and their
associates in the days of Jeshua.

8 The Levites who returned with them were
Jeshua, Binnui, Kadmiel, Sherebiah, Judah, and
Mattaniah, who with his associates was in charge
of the songs of thanksgiving. 9 Their associates,
Bakbukiah and Unni, stood opposite them during
the service.

10 Jeshua the high priest was the father of
Joiakim.
Joiakim was the father of Eliashib.
Eliashib was the father of Joiada.
11 Joiada was the father of Johanan.*
Johanan was the father of Jaddua.

12 Now when Joiakim was high priest, the family
leaders of the priests were as follows:

Meraiah was leader of the family of Seraiah.
Hananiah was leader of the family of
Jeremiah.
13 Meshullam was leader of the family of Ezra.
Jehohanan was leader of the family of Amariah.

11:14 As in Greek version; Hebrew reads *their.* **11:35** Or *and Ge-harashim.* **12:3** Hebrew *Rehum;* compare 7:42; 12:15; Ezra 2:39. **12:4** As in some Hebrew manuscripts and Latin Vulgate (see also 12:16); most Hebrew manuscripts read *Ginnethoi.* **12:5** Hebrew *Mijamin, Maadiah;* compare 12:17. **12:11** Hebrew *Jonathan;* compare 12:22.

12:1–26: A History of the Priests and Levites. This list of priests and Levites seems out of place in the book of Nehemiah, relating more to the narrative of Ezra in Ezra 1—2. It emphasizes the sacred character of the repopulated city.

14 Jonathan was leader of the family of Malluch.*
Joseph was leader of the family of Shecaniah.*
15 Adna was leader of the family of Harim.
Helkai was leader of the family of
Meremoth.*
16 Zechariah was leader of the family of Iddo.
Meshullam was leader of the family of
Ginnethon.
17 Zicri was leader of the family of Abijah.
There was also a* leader of the family of
Miniamin.
Piltai was leader of the family of Moadiah.
18 Shammua was leader of the family of Bilgah.
Jehonathan was leader of the family of
Shemaiah.
19 Mattenai was leader of the family of Joiarib.
Uzzi was leader of the family of Jedaiah.
20 Kallai was leader of the family of Sallu.*
Eber was leader of the family of Amok.
21 Hashabiah was leader of the family of
Hilkiah.
Nethanel was leader of the family of Jedaiah.

22 A record of the Levite families was kept
during the years when Eliashib, Joiada, Johanan,
and Jaddua served as high priest. Another record
of the priests was kept during the reign of Darius the Persian.* 23 A record of the heads of the
Levite families was kept in *The Book of History*
down to the days of Johanan, the grandson* of
Eliashib.
24 These were the family leaders of the Levites:
Hashabiah, Sherebiah, Jeshua, Binnui,* Kadmiel,
and other associates, who stood opposite them
during the ceremonies of praise and thanksgiving, one section responding to the other, as commanded by David, the man of God. 25 This included Mattaniah, Bakbukiah, and Obadiah.
Meshullam, Talmon, and Akkub were the
gatekeepers in charge of the storerooms at the
gates. 26 These all served in the days of Joiakim
son of Jeshua, son of Jehozadak,* and in the days
of Nehemiah the governor and of Ezra the priest
and scribe.

Dedication of Jerusalem's Wall

27 For the dedication of the new wall of Jerusalem, the Levites throughout the land were asked
to come to Jerusalem to assist in the ceremonies. They were to take part in the joyous occasion with their songs of thanksgiving and with
the music of cymbals, harps, and lyres. 28 The
singers were brought together from the region
around Jerusalem and from the villages of the
Netophathites. 29 They also came from Beth-gilgal and the rural areas near Geba and Azmaveth,
for the singers had built their own settlements
around Jerusalem. 30 The priests and Levites first
purified themselves; then they purified the people, the gates, and the wall.
31 I led the leaders of Judah to the top of the
wall and organized two large choirs to give
thanks. One of the choirs proceeded southward*
along the top of the wall to the Dung Gate. 32 Hoshaiah and half the leaders of Judah followed
them, 33 along with Azariah, Ezra, Meshullam,
34 Judah, Benjamin, Shemaiah, and Jeremiah.
35 Then came some priests who played trumpets,
including Zechariah son of Jonathan, son of Shemaiah, son of Mattaniah, son of Micaiah, son of
Zaccur, a descendant of Asaph. 36 And Zechariah's
colleagues were Shemaiah, Azarel, Milalai, Gil-
alai, Maai, Nethanel, Judah, and Hanani. They
used the musical instruments prescribed by
David, the man of God. Ezra the scribe led this
procession. 37 At the Fountain Gate they went
straight up the steps on the ascent of the city
wall toward the City of David. They passed the
house of David and then proceeded to the Water
Gate on the east.
38 The second choir giving thanks went northward* around the other way to meet them. I followed them, together with the other half of the
people, along the top of the wall past the Tower

12:14a As in Greek version (see also 10:4; 12:2); Hebrew reads *Malluchi.* **12:14b** As in many Hebrew manuscripts, some Greek manuscripts, and Syriac version (see also 12:3); most Hebrew manuscripts read *Shebaniah.* **12:15** As in some Greek manuscripts (see also 12:3); Hebrew reads *Meraioth.* **12:17** Hebrew lacks the name of this family leader. **12:20** Hebrew *Sallai;* compare 12:7. **12:22** *Darius the Persian* is probably Darius II, who reigned 423–404 B.C., or possibly Darius III, who reigned 336–331 B.C. **12:23** Hebrew *descendant;* compare 12:10-11. **12:24** Hebrew *son of* (i.e., *ben*), which should probably be read here as the proper name Binnui; compare Ezra 3:9 and the note there. **12:26** Hebrew *Jozadak,* a variant spelling of Jehozadak. **12:31** Hebrew *to the right.* **12:38** Hebrew *to the left.*

12:27—13:31 Reform and Regulation

12:27–47 Dedication of Jerusalem's Wall. The Nehemiah memoir, which broke off in 7:73, resumes with Nehemiah's report of a celebration at the dedication of the wall. All these activities may have once been part of the report that Nehemiah wrote to the Persian king in order to justify his employment. It is logical that Artaxerxes may have requested such a report and obtained it from Nehemiah when he returned to Susa (13:6). The celebration is once again a symbol of egalitarian cooperation and community identity and endorses the reform efforts of the postexilic community. **31–42:** By including the names of vari-

of the Ovens to the Broad Wall, 39 then past the Ephraim Gate to the Old City Gate,* past the Fish Gate and the Tower of Hananel, and on to the Tower of the Hundred. Then we continued on to the Sheep Gate and stopped at the Guard Gate.

40 The two choirs that were giving thanks then proceeded to the Temple of God, where they took their places. So did I, together with the group of leaders who were with me. 41 We went together with the trumpet-playing priests—Eliakim, Maaseiah, Miniamin, Micaiah, Elioenai, Zechariah, and Hananiah—42 and the singers—Maaseiah, Shemaiah, Eleazar, Uzzi, Jehohanan, Malkijah, Elam, and Ezer. They played and sang loudly under the direction of Jezrahiah the choir director.

43 Many sacrifices were offered on that joyous day, for God had given the people cause for great joy. The women and children also participated in the celebration, and the joy of the people of Jerusalem could be heard far away.

Provisions for Temple Worship

44 On that day men were appointed to be in charge of the storerooms for the offerings, the first part of the harvest, and the tithes. They were responsible to collect from the fields outside the towns the portions required by the Law for the priests and Levites. For all the people of Judah took joy in the priests and Levites and their work. 45 They performed the service of their God and the service of purification, as commanded by David and his son Solomon, and so did the singers and the gatekeepers. 46 The custom of having choir directors to lead the choirs in hymns of praise and thanksgiving to God began long ago in the days of David and Asaph. 47 So now, in the days of Zerubbabel and of Nehemiah, all Israel brought a daily supply of food for the singers, the gatekeepers, and the Levites. The Levites, in turn, gave a portion of what they received to the priests, the descendants of Aaron.

Nehemiah's Various Reforms

13 On that same day, as the Book of Moses was being read to the people, the passage was found that said no Ammonite or Moabite should ever be permitted to enter the assembly of God.* 2 For they had not provided the Israelites with food and water in the wilderness. Instead, they hired Balaam to curse them, though our God turned the curse into a blessing. 3 When this passage of the Law was read, all those of foreign descent were immediately excluded from the assembly.

4 Before this had happened, Eliashib the priest, who had been appointed as supervisor of the storerooms of the Temple of our God and who was also a relative of Tobiah, 5 had converted a large storage room and placed it at Tobiah's disposal. The room had previously been used for storing the grain offerings, the frankincense, various articles for the Temple, and the tithes of grain, new wine, and olive oil (which were prescribed for the Levites, the singers, and the gatekeepers), as well as the offerings for the priests.

6 I was not in Jerusalem at that time, for I had returned to King Artaxerxes of Babylon in the thirty-second year of his reign,* though I later asked his permission to return. 7 When I arrived back in Jerusalem, I learned about Eliashib's evil deed in providing Tobiah with a room in the courtyards of the Temple of God. 8 I became very upset and threw all of Tobiah's belongings out of the room. 9 Then I demanded that the rooms be purified, and I brought back the articles for God's Temple, the grain offerings, and the frankincense.

10 I also discovered that the Levites had not been given their prescribed portions of food, so

12:39 Or *the Mishneh Gate,* or *the Jeshanah Gate.*
13:1 See Deut 23:3-6. **13:6** King Artaxerxes of Persia is here identified as the king of Babylon because Persia had conquered the Babylonian Empire. The thirty-second year of Artaxerxes was 433 B.C.

ous groups, Nehemiah points to the joint effort and now joint celebration. **43:** Shared joy characterizes the report. *God had given the people cause for great joy.* Ezra-Nehemiah's works and reforms were not a false start, but the kind of rule that God intends. The foundation for a biblically valid organization should incorporate the elements of God's law, the Scriptures, and shared work and rule.

13:1–31 Nehemiah's Various Reforms. The latter sections of the Nehemiah memoir cohere in the repeated phrase, *Remember this . . . O my God* (13:14, 22, 29, 30). The reforms of Nehemiah touch the issues of separating from foreigners, removing improper people from the Temple building, enforcing the tithe, policing Sabbath observance, and removing foreign spouses. These reforms may seem petty to modern readers, but to postexilic people they established identity in relationship to the LORD and within the surrounding culture. By separating themselves from foreigners, they declare who they are. In our culture, we might characterize these moves as intolerant or prejudicial. Yet in order for a person or a community to establish identity there must be separation from the surrounding environment.

they and the singers who were to conduct the worship services had all returned to work their fields. 11 I immediately confronted the leaders and demanded, "Why has the Temple of God been neglected?" Then I called all the Levites back again and restored them to their proper duties. 12 And once more all the people of Judah began bringing their tithes of grain, new wine, and olive oil to the Temple storerooms.

13 I assigned supervisors for the storerooms: Shelemiah the priest, Zadok the scribe, and Pedaiah, one of the Levites. And I appointed Hanan son of Zaccur and grandson of Mattaniah as their assistant. These men had an excellent reputation, and it was their job to make honest distributions to their fellow Levites.

14 Remember this good deed, O my God, and
do not forget all that I have faithfully done
for the Temple of my God and its services.

15 In those days I saw men of Judah treading out their winepresses on the Sabbath. They were also bringing in grain, loading it on donkeys, and bringing their wine, grapes, figs, and all sorts of produce to Jerusalem to sell on the Sabbath. So I rebuked them for selling their produce on that day. 16 Some men from Tyre, who lived in Jerusalem, were bringing in fish and all kinds of merchandise. They were selling it on the Sabbath to the people of Judah—and in Jerusalem at that! 17 So I confronted the nobles of Judah. "Why are you profaning the Sabbath in this evil way?" I asked. 18 "Wasn't it just this sort of thing that your ancestors did that caused our God to bring all this trouble upon us and our city? Now you are bringing even more wrath upon Israel by permitting the Sabbath to be desecrated in this way!"

19 Then I commanded that the gates of Jerusalem should be shut as darkness fell every Friday evening,* not to be opened until the Sabbath ended. I sent some of my own servants to guard the gates so that no merchandise could be brought in on the Sabbath day. 20 The merchants and tradesmen with a variety of wares camped outside Jerusalem once or twice. 21 But I spoke sharply to them and said, "What are you doing out here, camping around the wall? If you do this again, I will arrest you!" And that was the last time they came on the Sabbath. 22 Then I commanded the Levites to purify themselves and to guard the gates in order to preserve the holiness of the Sabbath.

Remember this good deed also, O my God!
Have compassion on me according to your
great and unfailing love.

23 About the same time I realized that some of the men of Judah had married women from Ashdod, Ammon, and Moab. 24 Furthermore, half their children spoke the language of Ashdod or of some other people and could not speak the language of Judah at all. 25 So I confronted them and called down curses on them. I beat some of them and pulled out their hair. I made them swear in the name of God that they would not let their children intermarry with the pagan people of the land.

26 "Wasn't this exactly what led King Solomon of Israel into sin?" I demanded. "There was no king from any nation who could compare to him, and God loved him and made him king over all Israel. But even he was led into sin by his foreign wives. 27 How could you even think of committing this sinful deed and acting unfaithfully toward God by marrying foreign women?"

28 One of the sons of Joiada son of Eliashib the high priest had married a daughter of Sanballat the Horonite, so I banished him from my presence.

29 Remember them, O my God, for they have
defiled the priesthood and the solemn vows of
the priests and Levites.

30 So I purged out everything foreign and assigned tasks to the priests and Levites, making certain that each knew his work. 31 I also made sure that the supply of wood for the altar and the first portions of the harvest were brought at the proper times.

Remember this in my favor, O my God.

13:19 Hebrew *on the day before the Sabbath.*

ESTHER

INTRODUCTION

Esther has been compared with such similar pictures of Jewish life in exile as Daniel, where the usual structures that ordered and supported Israel's existence were no longer operative. As in the time of the judges, when Israel's social and political organization was still primitive, crisis brings to the fore men and women like Esther and Mordecai as instruments of deliverance, and they must act even where open profession of their faith and ethnicity can be dangerous.

Set within the reign of Ahasuerus, the Persian king known to the Greeks as Xerxes I, who ruled roughly from 486 to 465 BC, the book in its present form was likely written within a century of the events it describes, probably from Susa or in Palestine. The author is unknown, though Augustine believed it was written by Ezra, while Clement of Alexandria and others thought Mordecai was the author, based on the writer's familiarity with Persian words and customs and access to official documents (9:32). Mordecai's narrative seemed to be one of the sources for whoever organized the final Hebrew material (see 9:20). Scholars posit at least five Esther stories, the most prominent of which are those of the Masoretic and Septuagint texts, the latter a Greek translation with six deuterocanonical chapters added from Semitic and Greek sources. These more devotional sections, written in a later period, seem to have been added to balance the perceived secular nature of the book, making up for a puzzling lack of reference to God or the religion of Israel. This commentary opts for a reading based on the shorter Hebrew or Masoretic version.

Esther as a literary form has been regarded as myth or a historical romance or, on the other extreme, as strictly history. Most likely the book is based on a nucleus of historical material, reworked in such a way that it acquires the quality of fine literature. The work has a symmetry that to others suggests fiction—Gentiles against Jews as personified by "Haman the Agagite" and "Mordecai the Jew"; the contrast between the straightforward intransigence of Vashti and the artful vacillations of Esther; the fall of Haman and the rise of Mordecai as vizier; the prospect of an anti-Semitic pogrom and the eventual slaying of the "enemies of the Jews." Such symmetry, however, seems a function not only of the author's sense of poetic justice but also the sense that the world is providentially ruled. It shows a fine literary hand as well as a confident faith in happy outcomes as arranged by uncanny forces at work in the seemingly ordinary coincidences of everyday life.

The book is primarily a story of deliverance and only secondarily a festal legend, a narrative that recounts the historical grounds for the celebration of the Festival of Purim. The casting of *pur*, or the lot, functions as a central metaphor in the story but is incidental to the main plot, which is the threatened extinction of the Jews and their relief and deliverance through human acts of courage and sagacity combined with what look like accidents of history.

A Jewish woman is queen in a pagan court when Jews were subjects in an alien empire and vulnerable to plots and resentments. This is the central coincidence in the story and explains why our attention is focused on Esther and not on Mordecai even if he seems more like the main hero. Mordecai does appear as a more consistent character, and his greatness is such that it is recorded in Persian annals, his deep and abiding identification with and service to his people extolled in the final chapter (10:2–3). But the work is rightly the book of Esther, for on her the story turns and moves from anxious despair to certain hope. This reversal has been wrought through the inner transformations of this woman who seemed docile and timid but emerged valiant and strong.

There is some substance to the notion that the book is the only one in the Bible that is concerned with showing the politics of gender relations. Here is a society of men who, when thwarted, resort to political power to reinforce a dominant position. The figure of Vashti sets off the patriarchal context of the time without much comment. Her fall represents the discomfort of king and nobles before women of independent will; it prefigures the dangers and risks taken by Esther when she crosses the line to oppose Haman and appeal to an erratic, irascible husband with no apparent principle for governance other than the whim of impulse and the thoughtless carelessness of arbitrary power.

Known simply as the Scroll, one of the five Megilloth (scrolls), Esther is read through in the presence of women as well as men during Purim, observed by Jews in commemoration of their deliverance and the spontaneous rejoicing, feasting and community sharing that followed (Esth 9:18–19). —*Melba Padilla Maggay*

1:1—2:23	The Fall of Vashti and the Rise of Esther
3:1–15	Haman Plots to Destroy the Jews
4:1–17	Esther Chooses to Intervene on Behalf of the Jews
5:1—7:10	A Curious Reversal
8:1—9:19	The Deliverance of the Jews
9:20–32	The Festival of Purim Instituted
10:1–3	Conclusion

✧

The King's Banquet

1 These events happened in the days of King
Xerxes,* who reigned over 127 provinces
stretching from India to Ethiopia.* 2 At
that time Xerxes ruled his empire from his royal
throne at the fortress of Susa. 3 In the third year
of his reign, he gave a banquet for all his nobles
and officials. He invited all the military officers
of Persia and Media as well as the princes and
nobles of the provinces. 4 The celebration lasted
180 days—a tremendous display of the opulent
wealth of his empire and the pomp and splendor
of his majesty.
5 When it was all over, the king gave a banquet for all the people, from the greatest to the
least, who were in the fortress of Susa. It lasted
for seven days and was held in the courtyard of
the palace garden. 6 The courtyard was beautifully decorated with white cotton curtains and blue
hangings, which were fastened with white linen
cords and purple ribbons to silver rings embedded in marble pillars. Gold and silver couches
stood on a mosaic pavement of porphyry, marble,
mother-of-pearl, and other costly stones.
7 Drinks were served in gold goblets of many
designs, and there was an abundance of royal

1:1a Hebrew *Ahasuerus,* another name for Xerxes; also throughout the book of Esther. Xerxes reigned 486–465 B.C.
1:1b Hebrew *to Cush.*

1:1—2:23 The Fall of Vashti and the Rise of Esther

1:1–9 The Social Backdrop. 1: *Xerxes*: The Greek form of the Persian king's name. The Hebrew form is Ahasuerus. **2:** *Susa*: One of three capitals of the Medo-Persian Empire where most of its kings resided in winter. **3–9:** Persian society is depicted as amusing and potentially dangerous, decadently *opulent* but also overregulated. *Edict*: Hebrew, *dat* ("law" or "rule"), any kind of royal decision, from simple instructions to servants to rules for a court audience to imperial edicts announcing the extermination of a people (3:12; 4:11). The law rules over almost ev-

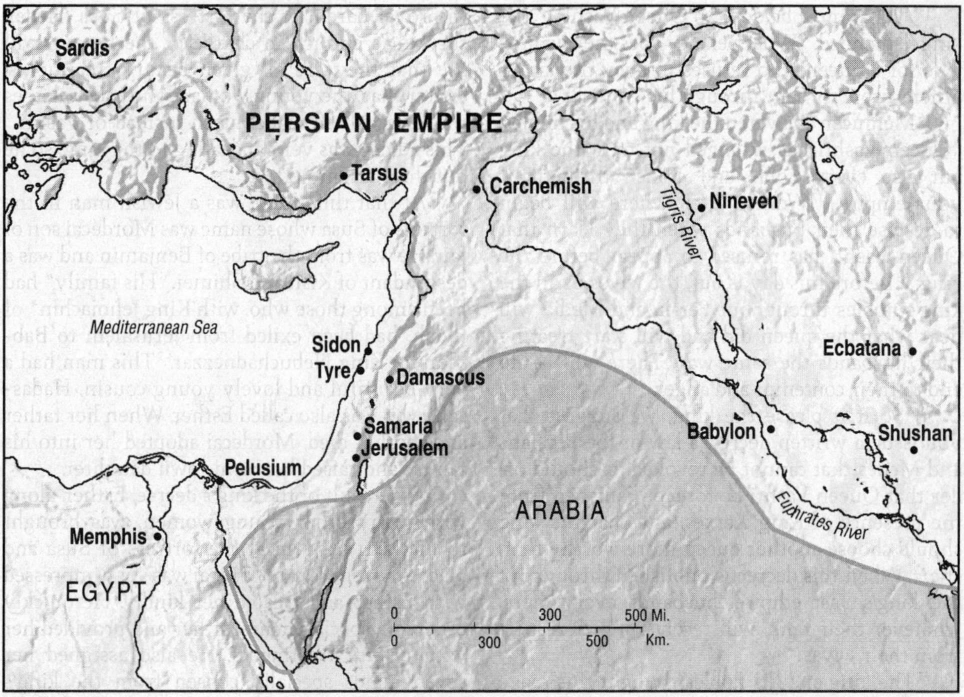

The Persian Empire

wine, reflecting the king's generosity. 8 By edict of the king, no limits were placed on the drinking, for the king had instructed all his palace officials to serve each man as much as he wanted.

9 At the same time, Queen Vashti gave a banquet for the women in the royal palace of King Xerxes.

Queen Vashti Deposed

10 On the seventh day of the feast, when King Xerxes was in high spirits because of the wine, he told the seven eunuchs who attended him—Mehuman, Biztha, Harbona, Bigtha, Abagtha, Zethar, and Carcas—11 to bring Queen Vashti to him with the royal crown on her head. He wanted the nobles and all the other men to gaze on her beauty, for she was a very beautiful woman. 12 But when they conveyed the king's order to Queen Vashti, she refused to come. This made the king furious, and he burned with anger.

13 He immediately consulted with his wise advisers, who knew all the Persian laws and customs, for he always asked their advice. 14 The names of these men were Carshena, Shethar, Admatha, Tarshish, Meres, Marsena, and Memucan—seven nobles of Persia and Media. They met with the king regularly and held the highest positions in the empire.

ery detail of life. **8:** Even drinking was according to the law, a reference perhaps to the relaxation of the strict decorum usually required in royal banquets, where guests drank only whenever the king did or were forced to drink continuously by a king whose wishes cannot be balked at. **9:** Royal parties were segregated according to gender; elsewhere, in Belshazzar's feast, his harem women were present, but the queen came in only on account of the writing on the wall (Dan 5:3, 10).

1:10–22 Vashti's Refusal Turned to Sexual Politics. **12:** The author treats the reasons for Vashti's refusal to attend the king with reticence. It may be out of a sense of rank (the Persian queen by tradition had to come from one of the seven noble families) or dignity—she didn't want to be displayed as one more of Xerxes' prized possessions. Josephus believes Persian law prohibited wives from being viewed by strangers, so Vashti may have refused out of respect for this custom that the king was so flagrantly violating. Tradition has it that Persian wives could be present at banquets but usually left before the drinking. **12–15:** The prescriptive rigidity of Persian law has at its base

15 "What must be done to Queen Vashti?" the
king demanded. "What penalty does the law provide for a queen who refuses to obey the king's
orders, properly sent through his eunuchs?"
16 Memucan answered the king and his nobles,
"Queen Vashti has wronged not only the king
but also every noble and citizen throughout
your empire. 17 Women everywhere will begin
to despise their husbands when they learn that
Queen Vashti has refused to appear before the
king. 18 Before this day is out, the wives of all the
king's nobles throughout Persia and Media will
hear what the queen did and will start treating
their husbands the same way. There will be no
end to their contempt and anger.
19 "So if it please the king, we suggest that
you issue a written decree, a law of the Persians
and Medes that cannot be revoked. It should order that Queen Vashti be forever banished from
the presence of King Xerxes, and that the king
should choose another queen more worthy than
she. 20 When this decree is published throughout
the king's vast empire, husbands everywhere,
whatever their rank, will receive proper respect
from their wives!"
21 The king and his nobles thought this made
good sense, so he followed Memucan's counsel. 22 He sent letters to all parts of the empire,
to each province in its own script and language,
proclaiming that every man should be the ruler
of his own home and should say whatever he
pleases.*

Esther Becomes Queen

2 But after Xerxes' anger had subsided, he
began thinking about Vashti and what she
had done and the decree he had made. 2 So
his personal attendants suggested, "Let us search
the empire to find beautiful young virgins for the
king. 3 Let the king appoint agents in each province to bring these beautiful young women into
the royal harem at the fortress of Susa. Hegai,
the king's eunuch in charge of the harem, will
see that they are all given beauty treatments.
4 After that, the young woman who most pleases
the king will be made queen instead of Vashti."
This advice was very appealing to the king, so he
put the plan into effect.
5 At that time there was a Jewish man in the
fortress of Susa whose name was Mordecai son of
Jair. He was from the tribe of Benjamin and was a
descendant of Kish and Shimei. 6 His family* had
been among those who, with King Jehoiachin* of
Judah, had been exiled from Jerusalem to Babylon by King Nebuchadnezzar. 7 This man had a
very beautiful and lovely young cousin, Hadassah, who was also called Esther. When her father
and mother died, Mordecai adopted her into his
family and raised her as his own daughter.
8 As a result of the king's decree, Esther, along
with many other young women, was brought
to the king's harem at the fortress of Susa and
placed in Hegai's care. 9 Hegai was very impressed
with Esther and treated her kindly. He quickly
ordered a special menu for her and provided her
with beauty treatments. He also assigned her
seven maids specially chosen from the king's
palace, and he moved her and her maids into the
best place in the harem.
10 Esther had not told anyone of her nationality and family background, because Mordecai
had directed her not to do so. 11 Every day Mordecai would take a walk near the courtyard of
the harem to find out about Esther and what was
happening to her.
12 Before each young woman was taken to the
king's bed, she was given the prescribed twelve
months of beauty treatments—six months with

1:22 Or *and should speak in the language of his own people.*
2:6a Hebrew *He.* **2:6b** Hebrew *Jeconiah,* a variant spelling of Jehoiachin.

the fragile ego and volatile temper of a despot. **16–18:** Vashti's refusal made the princes nervous, perceiving a threat to their hegemony. **16–22:** Vashti's fall has been read as a repudiation of strong-willed women. Note, however, that the courtiers are depicted as somewhat ridiculous. *Memucan* unwittingly broadcasts the deed by his counsel. A private act of domestic insurrection gets widely publicized by an official edict, and male-female relations become a matter for yet another state regulation. This prelude to Esther's story licenses a questioning approach to the text; while satire is perhaps too strong a word for it, we are dealing with characters that are not to be taken too seriously.

2:1–23 Esther Is Made Queen. The main characters in this story, Esther and Mordecai, now appear, introduced as representatives of a colonized people, subject to the wishes of a changeable king who is manipulable, susceptible to the self-serving suggestions of those around him. **7–9:** Esther initially appears pliant and passive, a foil to Vashti's intransigence. She obeys Mordecai as a father even after she moves into the palace (vv. 7, 10, 20). **8, 15–16:** The narrative makes no mention of her inner state as she is taken into the palace and later the king's bed; she submits to the beauty contest and the regimen required for it without comment. **12–20:** The contest seems to have neither familial nor political significance; the women

oil of myrrh, followed by six months with special perfumes and ointments. 13 When it was time for her to go to the king's palace, she was given her choice of whatever clothing or jewelry she wanted to take from the harem. 14 That evening she was taken to the king's private rooms, and the next morning she was brought to the second harem,* where the king's wives lived. There she would be under the care of Shaashgaz, the king's eunuch in charge of the concubines. She would never go to the king again unless he had especially enjoyed her and requested her by name.

15 Esther was the daughter of Abihail, who was Mordecai's uncle. (Mordecai had adopted his younger cousin Esther.) When it was Esther's turn to go to the king, she accepted the advice of Hegai, the eunuch in charge of the harem. She asked for nothing except what he suggested, and she was admired by everyone who saw her.

16 Esther was taken to King Xerxes at the royal palace in early winter* of the seventh year of his reign. 17 And the king loved Esther more than any of the other young women. He was so delighted with her that he set the royal crown on her head and declared her queen instead of Vashti. 18 To celebrate the occasion, he gave a great banquet in Esther's honor for all his nobles and officials, declaring a public holiday for the provinces and giving generous gifts to everyone.

19 Even after all the young women had been transferred to the second harem* and Mordecai had become a palace official,* 20 Esther continued to keep her family background and nationality a secret. She was still following Mordecai's directions, just as she did when she lived in his home.

Mordecai's Loyalty to the King

21 One day as Mordecai was on duty at the king's gate, two of the king's eunuchs, Bigthana* and Teresh—who were guards at the door of the king's private quarters—became angry at King Xerxes and plotted to assassinate him. 22 But Mordecai heard about the plot and gave the information to Queen Esther. She then told the king about it and gave Mordecai credit for the report. 23 When an investigation was made and Mordecai's story was found to be true, the two men were impaled on a sharpened pole. This was all recorded in *The Book of the History of King Xerxes' Reign.*

Haman's Plot against the Jews

3 Some time later King Xerxes promoted Haman son of Hammedatha the Agagite over all the other nobles, making him the most powerful official in the empire. 2 All the king's officials would bow down before Haman to show him respect whenever he passed by, for so the king had commanded. But Mordecai refused to bow down or show him respect.

3 Then the palace officials at the king's gate asked Mordecai, "Why are you disobeying the king's command?" 4 They spoke to him day after day, but still he refused to comply with the order. So they spoke to Haman about this to see if he would tolerate Mordecai's conduct, since Mordecai had told them he was a Jew.

5 When Haman saw that Mordecai would not bow down or show him respect, he was filled with rage. 6 He had learned of Mordecai's nationality, so he decided it was not enough to lay hands on Mordecai alone. Instead, he looked for a way to

2:14 Or *to another part of the harem.* **2:16** Hebrew *in the tenth month, the month of Tebeth.* A number of dates in the book of Esther can be cross-checked with dates in surviving Persian records and related accurately to our modern calendar. This month of the ancient Hebrew lunar calendar occurred within the months of December 479 B.C. and January 478 B.C. **2:19a** The meaning of the Hebrew is uncertain. **2:19b** Hebrew *and Mordecai was sitting in the gate of the king.* **2:21** Hebrew *Bigthan;* compare 6:2.

had no need of childbearing potential or the right pedigree that makes for sound alliances, but only beauty and the capacity to please the king sexually (vv. 4, 14). Nevertheless, while she is treated as a sex object, Esther stands out not only for her physical but also personality gifts; naturally winsome, she finds favor in the eyes of all who see her (vv. 9, 15). **21–23:** Although not immediately relevant, this incident will have importance to the story later.

3:1–15 Haman Plots to Destroy the Jews

3:2–4: It is not clear why Mordecai refuses to bow before Haman; like Vashti's, his reasons are unstated, save for a vague reference to his being a Jew. There is no suggestion that obeisance to him has cultic significance as in the book of Daniel. **4:** *If he would tolerate Mordecai's conduct*: Perhaps the court officers bring the matter to Haman to see whether Mordecai's ethnicity exempts him from the king's order. **5–6:** *Rage*: The same word is used for the king's anger (1:12). Besides injured pride, Haman's fury might result from an undercurrent of racial animosity, as shown by his resolve to destroy not only Mordecai but also his people. Whatever the original motive, the conflict now seems more than a personal battle between a recalcitrant subordinate and an overweening court favorite. It has been enlarged into a primal blood feud between "Mordecai the Jew" and "Haman the Agagite," who is four times

destroy all the Jews throughout the entire empire of Xerxes.
7 So in the month of April,* during the
twelfth year of King Xerxes' reign, lots were cast
in Haman's presence (the lots were called *purim*)
to determine the best day and month to take action. And the day selected was March 7, nearly
a year later.*
8 Then Haman approached King Xerxes and
said, "There is a certain race of people scattered
through all the provinces of your empire who
keep themselves separate from everyone else.
Their laws are different from those of any other
people, and they refuse to obey the laws of the
king. So it is not in the king's interest to let them
live. 9 If it please the king, issue a decree that they
be destroyed, and I will give 10,000 large sacks*
of silver to the government administrators to be
deposited in the royal treasury."
10 The king agreed, confirming his decision by
removing his signet ring from his finger and giving it to Haman son of Hammedatha the Agagite, the enemy of the Jews. 11 The king said, "The
money and the people are both yours to do with
as you see fit."
12 So on April 17* the king's secretaries were
summoned, and a decree was written exactly as
Haman dictated. It was sent to the king's highest officers, the governors of the respective provinces, and the nobles of each province in their
own scripts and languages. The decree was written in the name of King Xerxes and sealed with
the king's signet ring. 13 Dispatches were sent by
swift messengers into all the provinces of the
empire, giving the order that all Jews—young
and old, including women and children—must
be killed, slaughtered, and annihilated on a single
day. This was scheduled to happen on March 7 of
the next year.* The property of the Jews would
be given to those who killed them.
14 A copy of this decree was to be issued as law
in every province and proclaimed to all peoples,
so that they would be ready to do their duty on
the appointed day. 15 At the king's command, the
decree went out by swift messengers, and it was
also proclaimed in the fortress of Susa. Then the
king and Haman sat down to drink, but the city
of Susa fell into confusion.

Mordecai Requests Esther's Help

4 When Mordecai learned about all that had
been done, he tore his clothes, put on burlap and ashes, and went out into the city,
crying with a loud and bitter wail. 2 He went as
far as the gate of the palace, for no one was allowed to enter the palace gate while wearing
clothes of mourning. 3 And as news of the king's
decree reached all the provinces, there was great
mourning among the Jews. They fasted, wept,
and wailed, and many people lay in burlap and
ashes.
4 When Queen Esther's maids and eunuchs

3:7a Hebrew *in the first month, the month of Nisan.* This month of the ancient Hebrew lunar calendar occurred within the months of April and May 474 B.C.; also see note on 2:16. **3:7b** As in 3:13, which reads *the thirteenth day of the twelfth month, the month of Adar;* Hebrew reads *in the twelfth month,* of the ancient Hebrew lunar calendar. The date selected was March 7, 473 B.C.; also see note on 2:16. **3:9** Hebrew *10,000 talents,* about 375 tons or 340 metric tons in weight. **3:12** Hebrew *On the thirteenth day of the first month,* of the ancient Hebrew lunar calendar. This day was April 17, 474 B.C.; also see note on 2:16. **3:13** Hebrew *on the thirteenth day of the twelfth month, the month of Adar,* of the ancient Hebrew lunar calendar. The date selected was March 7, 473 B.C.; also see note on 2:16.

described as *enemy of the Jews* (3:10; 8:1; 9:10, 24). **7:** The plight of the Jews is left to chance, the propitious time of their annihilation determined by the casting of *purim,* or *lots*. **8–9:** A mercurial, suggestible monarch too thoughtless and lazy to execute his own decisions controls the existence of a whole people. Described in the abstract as *a certain race of people*, subtly denigrated as *scattered* and therefore powerless and insignificant, the Jews are downgraded to the level of goods: To destroy them is to profit the king with silver, the amount to be gained when the spoils are taken. This fabulous sum is about 68 percent of the total revenue of the Persian Empire, which ran to around 14,560 Euboeic talents, according to Herodotus. **10–11:** The king postures as a munificent benefactor dispensing largesse. **12–13:** The imperial machinery is set into motion, the genocide couched in the passive voice, the fate of the Jews inexorably worked out with the impersonal precision and swiftness of the Persian pony express system. *Their own scripts and languages*: Respect for ethnic diversity ironically is put to the service of destroying a people whose alleged crime is their distinctiveness. **15:** Again the king is portrayed as oblivious to the state of his empire. The vast carelessness and callousness of power is telling.

4:1–17 Esther Chooses to Intervene on Behalf of the Jews

From now on the story is told from Esther's point of view, and it is she who, aided by fortuitous circumstances, moves the plot and brings the crisis to a resolution. **1–9:** News of their threatened extinction brings great lamentation among the Jews. Esther had not heard the decree before Mordecai's mes-

The Power and Potential of Women

The book of Esther has been interpreted as a classic stereotyping of how women shoulder their way to power. Straightforward women like Vashti lose their position, while Esther gets her way through recourse to feminine charm and cunning artifice. She is like Mary and Hannah and other women in the Bible who become national heroines only as they fulfill their assigned roles as wives. She is faulted for lacking an interior life, being uninspired by religious faith, and conforming to a seemingly general biblical policy of allowing women to talk to God only in a procreative context.

Esther needed to deploy all the physical, intellectual, and psychological resources at her disposal. Shrewd strategy and subtlety rather than open confrontation are her only options in a society that requires careful submission to decorum. Like all the Jews, who must adjust to powerlessness in an alien land, Esther had to tread softly through the landmines of power.

From the perspective of a colonized people, her way to power is understandably oblique and roundabout, something that perhaps looks like feminine wiles to those who come from aggressively straightforward cultures and are raised in a political tradition with a highly developed language for rights.

The notion that Esther comes to power largely through a traditional role ignores the fairly marginal influence of a wife in a setting where the king can put her away at will and has a thousand other women to take her place in bed. Like most women who start out with a limited sense of their potential, Esther comes to her own because she grows, moving from fear and timidity to resolute courage. She develops from a woman with a restricted view of the possibilities of her personal attractions and royal position to a woman testing the limits of what she can do.

Contrary to the perception that the Bible exalts women mainly for their procreative functions, we have here a heroine whose importance to the Jewish people does not lie in childbearing. Like Deborah, she rises at a critical moment and rallies her people for a war of resistance. That sometimes women never get the chance to fulfill their potential in the same way is deeply lamented in the haunting story of Jephthah's daughter (Judg 11). In a moving gesture of loyalty to the LORD, before whom her father had made a rash vow, she offers herself for sacrifice. All she asks is that she be left alone to wander on the mountains for two months to bewail her virginity—not merely because she had never had intercourse but that she must die before she sees the full flowering of her womanhood.

It is perhaps an anachronism to criticize the Bible for stories on women whose main significance is in their traditional roles as wives and mothers. God's Word is progressively revealed in history and as such mirrors the status of women as it finds it in a particular time and society. Yet even so, there are subtle shades to each picture, hints toward a future significance defined no longer within the confining terms of gender but by the capacity to respond to God's initiatives. Mary, for instance, is blessed not only because of the fruit of her womb but because she "believed that the Lord would do what he said" (Luke 1:45). Characterized as thoughtful, the mother of Jesus is also author of the Magnificat, the first theological reflection in the New Testament of what the coming of the kingdom means.

There are many and varied ways by which women come to power. Some get there by birth or pedigree and so are naturally self possessed and conscious of what is due them. Some, like Esther, need to rise from a sense of limitation to a sense of what is possible under the sovereign hand of God.

These stories show that all women can grow and find within themselves unsuspected resources and thus win strength out of weakness.

came and told her about Mordecai, she was deeply distressed. She sent clothing to him to replace
the burlap, but he refused it. 5 Then Esther sent
for Hathach, one of the king's eunuchs who had
been appointed as her attendant. She ordered
him to go to Mordecai and find out what was
troubling him and why he was in mourning. 6 So
Hathach went out to Mordecai in the square in
front of the palace gate.
7 Mordecai told him the whole story, includ-

sage through Hathach, underscoring her cloistered existence. **7–17:** The exchange of messages through Hathach indicates knowledge of her Jewishness and friendliness on the part of the court servants.

ing the exact amount of money Haman had
promised to pay into the royal treasury for the
destruction of the Jews. 8 Mordecai gave Hathach
a copy of the decree issued in Susa that called
for the death of all Jews. He asked Hathach to
show it to Esther and explain the situation to her.
He also asked Hathach to direct her to go to the
king to beg for mercy and plead for her people.
9 So Hathach returned to Esther with Mordecai's
message.
10 Then Esther told Hathach to go back and
relay this message to Mordecai: 11 "All the king's
officials and even the people in the provinces
know that anyone who appears before the king in
his inner court without being invited is doomed
to die unless the king holds out his gold scepter. And the king has not called for me to come
to him for thirty days." 12 So Hathach* gave Esther's message to Mordecai.
13 Mordecai sent this reply to Esther: "Don't
think for a moment that because you're in the
palace you will escape when all other Jews are
killed. 14 If you keep quiet at a time like this, deliverance and relief for the Jews will arise from
some other place, but you and your relatives will
die. Who knows if perhaps you were made queen
for just such a time as this?"
15 Then Esther sent this reply to Mordecai:
16 "Go and gather together all the Jews of Susa
and fast for me. Do not eat or drink for three
days, night or day. My maids and I will do the
same. And then, though it is against the law, I
will go in to see the king. If I must die, I must
die." 17 So Mordecai went away and did everything as Esther had ordered him.

Esther's Request to the King

5 On the third day of the fast, Esther put on
her royal robes and entered the inner court
of the palace, just across from the king's
hall. The king was sitting on his royal throne,
facing the entrance. 2 When he saw Queen Esther
standing there in the inner court, he welcomed
her and held out the gold scepter to her. So Esther
approached and touched the end of the scepter.
3 Then the king asked her, "What do you want,
Queen Esther? What is your request? I will give
it to you, even if it is half the kingdom!"
4 And Esther replied, "If it please the king, let
the king and Haman come today to a banquet I
have prepared for the king."
5 The king turned to his attendants and said,
"Tell Haman to come quickly to a banquet, as
Esther has requested." So the king and Haman
went to Esther's banquet.
6 And while they were drinking wine, the king
said to Esther, "Now tell me what you really
want. What is your request? I will give it to you,
even if it is half the kingdom!"
7 Esther replied, "This is my request and deepest wish. 8 If I have found favor with the king,
and if it pleases the king to grant my request and
do what I ask, please come with Haman tomorrow to the banquet I will prepare for you. Then I
will explain what this is all about."

Haman's Plan to Kill Mordecai

9 Haman was a happy man as he left the banquet!
But when he saw Mordecai sitting at the palace

4:12 As in Greek version; Hebrew reads *they*.

10–11: Esther's initial fear and timidity is born out of a sense of the limits set by law and her own doubtful power over the king. **13:** Mordecai's famous reply is a pointed warning and an encouragement. He puts squarely before Esther the fact of her solidarity with her people, a sense of common peril that in her isolation she might have found less compelling than the more immediate danger of death and disfavor from a lover who for a month has been uninterested. At the same time, Mordecai expands Esther's horizon by putting forward a historical opportunity that she could lose if she chooses to keep silence. **14:** There is no mention of God, but there is confidence that Providence so guides history that the possibility of rescue is already in place. And in case Esther fails, some alternative instrument will rise for the Jews' relief and deliverance. **15–16:** Esther becomes her own person, giving orders to her former guardian. She moves from being a docile ward to a decisive, active partner in saving her people, from fear to resolute dauntlessness, and from a diffident faith in her powers to a daring attempt to test the limits of her constraints.

5:1—7:10 A Curious Reversal

5:1–8 Esther's Request to the King. 1: Esther's robes represent the formal grandeur of her office as queen and her attractions as a woman. They increase her chances of winning an audience with the king. **4:** Esther's deliberate inclusion of Haman suggests that she had designed a plan that requires the presence of both principals. A number of speculations have been advanced as to her reasons for doing so, the most straightforward being that she did not wish to give him opportunity for a conspiracy behind her back. **7–8:** It is a puzzle why she delays and passes up another opportunity to state her request. It risks spoiling the king's generous mood, which experience shows

gate, not standing up or trembling nervously before him, Haman became furious. 10 However, he
restrained himself and went on home.
Then Haman gathered together his friends
and Zeresh, his wife, 11 and boasted to them
about his great wealth and his many children.
He bragged about the honors the king had given
him and how he had been promoted over all the
other nobles and officials.
12 Then Haman added, "And that's not all!
Queen Esther invited only me and the king himself to the banquet she prepared for us. And she
has invited me to dine with her and the king
again tomorrow!" 13 Then he added, "But this is
all worth nothing as long as I see Mordecai the
Jew just sitting there at the palace gate."
14 So Haman's wife, Zeresh, and all his friends
suggested, "Set up a sharpened pole that stands
seventy-five feet* tall, and in the morning ask
the king to impale Mordecai on it. When this is
done, you can go on your merry way to the banquet with the king." This pleased Haman, and he
ordered the pole set up.

The King Honors Mordecai

6 That night the king had trouble sleeping,
so he ordered an attendant to bring the
book of the history of his reign so it could
be read to him. 2 In those records he discovered
an account of how Mordecai had exposed the
plot of Bigthana and Teresh, two of the eunuchs
who guarded the door to the king's private
quarters. They had plotted to assassinate King
Xerxes.
3 "What reward or recognition did we ever
give Mordecai for this?" the king asked.
His attendants replied, "Nothing has been
done for him."
4 "Who is that in the outer court?" the king
inquired. As it happened, Haman had just arrived
in the outer court of the palace to ask the king to
impale Mordecai on the pole he had prepared.
5 So the attendants replied to the king, "Haman is out in the court."
"Bring him in," the king ordered. 6 So Haman
came in, and the king said, "What should I do to
honor a man who truly pleases me?"
Haman thought to himself, "Whom would
the king wish to honor more than me?" 7 So he
replied, "If the king wishes to honor someone,
8 he should bring out one of the king's own royal
robes, as well as a horse that the king himself has
ridden—one with a royal emblem on its head.
9 Let the robes and the horse be handed over to
one of the king's most noble officials. And let him
see that the man whom the king wishes to honor
is dressed in the king's robes and led through the
city square on the king's horse. Have the official
shout as they go, 'This is what the king does for
someone he wishes to honor!' "
10 "Excellent!" the king said to Haman.
"Quick! Take the robes and my horse, and do
just as you have said for Mordecai the Jew, who
sits at the gate of the palace. Leave out nothing
you have suggested!"
11 So Haman took the robes and put them on
Mordecai, placed him on the king's own horse,
and led him through the city square, shouting, "This is what the king does for someone
he wishes to honor!" 12 Afterward Mordecai returned to the palace gate, but Haman hurried
home dejected and completely humiliated.
13 When Haman told his wife, Zeresh, and all
his friends what had happened, his wise advisers and his wife said, "Since Mordecai—this man
who has humiliated you—is of Jewish birth, you
will never succeed in your plans against him. It
will be fatal to continue opposing him."
14 While they were still talking, the king's
eunuchs arrived and quickly took Haman to the
banquet Esther had prepared.

5:14 Hebrew *50 cubits* [22.5 meters].

is fairly short-term. It seems that Esther was feeling out the king's disposition; she senses perhaps that the king was merely making a ritual grand gesture and she must cast about for tell-tale signs that her petition would likely turn his expansive impulses into swift and irreversible action. She seizes upon a second invitation as an index of whether he is truly disposed to grant what she wishes. The elaborately deferential preamble of her speech indicates she is aware she might be testing the king's patience.

5:9–14 Haman's Plot. Despite the singular honor of being invited to an intimate dinner with the king and queen, Haman could not bear that Mordecai would neither stand nor tremble.

6:1–14 The King Honors Mordecai. Haman's fall begins with a series of coincidences: the king's insomnia, his recollection of Mordecai's good deed, and Haman's timely arrival. The story is fraught with ironies, turning things upside down. **6–12:** Haman, increasingly caricatured as the prideful buffoon, is forced to perform for Mordecai the honors he intended for himself.

The King Executes Haman

7 So the king and Haman went to Queen Esther's banquet. 2On this second occasion,
while they were drinking wine, the king
again said to Esther, "Tell me what you want,
Queen Esther. What is your request? I will give
it to you, even if it is half the kingdom!"
3Queen Esther replied, "If I have found favor
with the king, and if it pleases the king to grant
my request, I ask that my life and the lives of my
people will be spared. 4For my people and I have
been sold to those who would kill, slaughter,
and annihilate us. If we had merely been sold as
slaves, I could remain quiet, for that would be too
trivial a matter to warrant disturbing the king."
5"Who would do such a thing?" King Xerxes
demanded. "Who would be so presumptuous as
to touch you?"
6Esther replied, "This wicked Haman is our
adversary and our enemy." Haman grew pale
with fright before the king and queen. 7Then the
king jumped to his feet in a rage and went out
into the palace garden.
Haman, however, stayed behind to plead for
his life with Queen Esther, for he knew that the
king intended to kill him. 8In despair he fell on the
couch where Queen Esther was reclining, just as
the king was returning from the palace garden.
The king exclaimed, "Will he even assault the
queen right here in the palace, before my very
eyes?" And as soon as the king spoke, his attendants covered Haman's face, signaling his doom.
9Then Harbona, one of the king's eunuchs, said,
"Haman has set up a sharpened pole that stands
seventy-five feet* tall in his own courtyard. He
intended to use it to impale Mordecai, the man
who saved the king from assassination."
"Then impale Haman on it!" the king ordered.
10So they impaled Haman on the pole he had set
up for Mordecai, and the king's anger subsided.

A Decree to Help the Jews

8 On that same day King Xerxes gave the
property of Haman, the enemy of the
Jews, to Queen Esther. Then Mordecai was
brought before the king, for Esther had told the
king how they were related. 2The king took off
his signet ring—which he had taken back from
Haman—and gave it to Mordecai. And Esther
appointed Mordecai to be in charge of Haman's
property.
3Then Esther went again before the king,
falling down at his feet and begging him with
tears to stop the evil plot devised by Haman the
Agagite against the Jews. 4Again the king held
out the gold scepter to Esther. So she rose and
stood before him.
5Esther said, "If it please the king, and if I
have found favor with him, and if he thinks it is
right, and if I am pleasing to him, let there be a
decree that reverses the orders of Haman son of
Hammedatha the Agagite, who ordered that Jews
throughout all the king's provinces should be destroyed. 6For how can I endure to see my people
and my family slaughtered and destroyed?"
7Then King Xerxes said to Queen Esther and
Mordecai the Jew, "I have given Esther the property of Haman, and he has been impaled on a
pole because he tried to destroy the Jews. 8Now
go ahead and send a message to the Jews in the
king's name, telling them whatever you want,
and seal it with the king's signet ring. But re-

7:9 Hebrew *50 cubits* [22.5 meters].

7:1–10 The King Executes Haman. Haman's downfall continues with still more coincidences. **7–8:** Haman's pleas for mercy from Esther seal his death sentence. **9–10:** The speed with which the eunuch volunteers the information about the gallows demonstrates that for all Haman's pride and demand for deference, he has less respect in the palace than Esther and Mordecai, members of the condemned race. Coincidence and irony operate as a counterforce to the lots, a metaphor for the reckless chance by which the Jews have been fated to perish. By an overwhelming series of coincidences, events are overturned, and we sense an overruling power that orders human life. There is a glaring absence of any reference to God. The Jews get delivered not by miracles but by a chain of events triggered by growth in the inner resources, intellectual and spiritual, of people like Esther who at the outset do not seem to be natural leaders. This book gives us instead an organic sense of God's sovereign strength as it works itself out in history. Even while unnamed, the sense of a Providence disguised as chance compels the recognition that while evil seems strong and life can be fragile, there is at ground level a force for good.

8:1—9:19 The Deliverance of the Jews

8:1–17 A Decree to Help the Jews. The Jews begin their ascendancy. **1–3:** Even though Haman is defeated and Esther and Mordecai are in positions of power, Haman's decree still stands. **4–5:** Esther's speech to the king is prefaced by conditional clauses subtly playing on the king's suggestibility and his evident regard for her. Perhaps this approach rose out of her consciousness that she was asking something unprecedented and needed to fall back on the power

member that whatever has already been written
in the king's name and sealed with his signet ring
can never be revoked."
9 So on June 25* the king's secretaries were
summoned, and a decree was written exactly as
Mordecai dictated. It was sent to the Jews and to
the highest officers, the governors, and the nobles
of all the 127 provinces stretching from India to
Ethiopia.* The decree was written in the scripts
and languages of all the peoples of the empire,
including that of the Jews. 10 The decree was
written in the name of King Xerxes and sealed
with the king's signet ring. Mordecai sent the
dispatches by swift messengers, who rode fast
horses especially bred for the king's service.
11 The king's decree gave the Jews in every city
authority to unite to defend their lives. They were
allowed to kill, slaughter, and annihilate anyone
of any nationality or province who might attack
them or their children and wives, and to take the
property of their enemies. 12 The day chosen for
this event throughout all the provinces of King
Xerxes was March 7 of the next year.*
13 A copy of this decree was to be issued as law
in every province and proclaimed to all peoples,
so that the Jews would be ready to take revenge
on their enemies on the appointed day. 14 So urged
on by the king's command, the messengers rode
out swiftly on fast horses bred for the king's service. The same decree was also proclaimed in the
fortress of Susa.
15 Then Mordecai left the king's presence,
wearing the royal robe of blue and white, the
great crown of gold, and an outer cloak of fine
linen and purple. And the people of Susa celebrated the new decree. 16 The Jews were filled
with joy and gladness and were honored everywhere. 17 In every province and city, wherever the
king's decree arrived, the Jews rejoiced and had
a great celebration and declared a public festival
and holiday. And many of the people of the land
became Jews themselves, for they feared what
the Jews might do to them.

The Victory of the Jews

9 So on March 7* the two decrees of the king
were put into effect. On that day, the enemies of the Jews had hoped to overpower
them, but quite the opposite happened. It was the
Jews who overpowered their enemies. 2 The Jews
gathered in their cities throughout all the king's
provinces to attack anyone who tried to harm
them. But no one could make a stand against
them, for everyone was afraid of them. 3 And all
the nobles of the provinces, the highest officers,
the governors, and the royal officials helped the
Jews for fear of Mordecai. 4 For Mordecai had
been promoted in the king's palace, and his fame
spread throughout all the provinces as he became
more and more powerful.
5 So the Jews went ahead on the appointed day
and struck down their enemies with the sword.
They killed and annihilated their enemies and
did as they pleased with those who hated them.
6 In the fortress of Susa itself, the Jews killed
500 men. 7 They also killed Parshandatha, Dal-
phon, Aspatha, 8 Poratha, Adalia, Aridatha, 9 Par-
mashta, Arisai, Aridai, and Vaizatha—10 the ten
sons of Haman son of Hammedatha, the enemy
of the Jews. But they did not take any plunder.
11 That very day, when the king was informed
of the number of people killed in the fortress of
Susa, 12 he called for Queen Esther. He said, "The
Jews have killed 500 men in the fortress of Susa
alone, as well as Haman's ten sons. If they have
done that here, what has happened in the rest of
the provinces? But now, what more do you want?
It will be granted to you; tell me and I will do it."

8:9a Hebrew *on the twenty-third day of the third month, the month of Sivan,* of the ancient Hebrew lunar calendar. This day was June 25, 474 B.C.; also see note on 2:16. **8:9b** Hebrew *to Cush.* **8:12** Hebrew *the thirteenth day of the twelfth month, the month of Adar,* of the ancient Hebrew lunar calendar. The date selected was March 7, 473 B.C.; also see note on 2:16. **9:1** Hebrew *on the thirteenth day of the twelfth month, the month of Adar,* of the ancient Hebrew lunar calendar. This day was March 7, 473 B.C.; also see note on 2:16.

of her attractions. **8:** The motif of Persian law as both rigidly fixed and randomly fixable takes center stage. **9–14:** Again the machinery of the empire's legal system is put into motion. The writing of the new edict in every people's script and language is especially extended to the Jews. **16–17:** From a subject people fearing for their lives, the Jews find gladness and light and honor among the general population, augured by the resplendent rise of Mordecai. While neither priest nor prophet nor king—leadership roles in the old Jewish society—Mordecai appears in full glory as a new type of leader in an alien empire.

9:1–19 The Victory of the Jews. With Mordecai's ascendancy, fear of the Jews falls upon the peoples, a mixture perhaps of the superstitious awe and obsequious deference accorded those whom the gods seem to regard with peculiar favor. The situation of the Jews reverses from powerlessness to powerful resistance, for the fear of them and of Mordecai has turned the tide of official support and has apparently weakened those who wished to cause them harm. **5–10:** The theme of control, of gaining power and mastery, is reinforced by accounts of the Jews' military victory and the completion of Haman's fall with the slaying of his

13 Esther responded, "If it please the king, give the Jews in Susa permission to do again tomorrow as they have done today, and let the bodies of Haman's ten sons be impaled on a pole."

14 So the king agreed, and the decree was announced in Susa. And they impaled the bodies of Haman's ten sons. 15 Then the Jews at Susa gathered together on March 8* and killed 300 more men, and again they took no plunder.

16 Meanwhile, the other Jews throughout the king's provinces had gathered together to defend their lives. They gained relief from all their enemies, killing 75,000 of those who hated them. But they did not take any plunder. 17 This was done throughout the provinces on March 7, and on March 8 they rested,* celebrating their victory with a day of feasting and gladness. 18 (The Jews at Susa killed their enemies on March 7 and again on March 8, then rested on March 9,* making that their day of feasting and gladness.) 19 So to this day, rural Jews living in remote villages celebrate an annual festival and holiday on the appointed day in late winter,* when they rejoice and send gifts of food to each other.

The Festival of Purim

20 Mordecai recorded these events and sent letters to the Jews near and far, throughout all the provinces of King Xerxes, 21 calling on them to celebrate an annual festival on these two days.* 22 He told them to celebrate these days with feasting and gladness and by giving gifts of food to each other and presents to the poor. This would commemorate a time when the Jews gained relief from their enemies, when their sorrow was turned into gladness and their mourning into joy.

23 So the Jews accepted Mordecai's proposal and adopted this annual custom. 24 Haman son of Hammedatha the Agagite, the enemy of the Jews, had plotted to crush and destroy them on the date determined by casting lots (the lots were called *purim*). 25 But when Esther came before the king, he issued a decree causing Haman's evil plot to backfire, and Haman and his sons were impaled on a sharpened pole. 26 That is why this celebration is called Purim, because it is the ancient word for casting lots.

So because of Mordecai's letter and because of what they had experienced, 27 the Jews throughout the realm agreed to inaugurate this tradition and to pass it on to their descendants and to all who became Jews. They declared they would never fail to celebrate these two prescribed days at the appointed time each year. 28 These days would be remembered and kept from generation to generation and celebrated by every family throughout the provinces and cities of the empire. This Festival of Purim would never cease to be celebrated among the Jews, nor would the memory of what happened ever die out among their descendants.

29 Then Queen Esther, the daughter of Abihail, along with Mordecai the Jew, wrote another letter putting the queen's full authority behind Mordecai's letter to establish the Festival of Purim. 30 Letters wishing peace and security were sent to the Jews throughout the 127 provinces of the empire of Xerxes. 31 These letters established the Festival of Purim—an annual celebration of these days at the appointed time, decreed by both Mordecai the Jew and Queen Esther. (The people decided to observe this festival, just as they had decided for themselves and their descendants to establish

9:15 Hebrew *the fourteenth day of the month of Adar,* of the Hebrew lunar calendar. This day was March 8, 473 B.C.; also see note on 2:16. **9:17** Hebrew *on the thirteenth day of the month of Adar, and on the fourteenth day they rested.* These days were March 7 and 8, 473 B.C.; also see note on 2:16. **9:18** Hebrew *killed their enemies on the thirteenth day and the fourteenth day, and then rested on the fifteenth day,* of the Hebrew month of Adar. **9:19** Hebrew *on the fourteenth day of the month of Adar.* This day of the Hebrew lunar calendar occurs in February or March. **9:21** Hebrew *on the fourteenth and fifteenth days of Adar,* of the Hebrew lunar calendar.

sons. **10–13:** Some have commented that Esther has become bloodthirsty and vindictive, her request for an extension an unnecessary overkill. An alternative reading could be that in the context of intrigue and power play in the capital, she who previously had been shown to be a cool and brilliant strategist saw the need to stamp out remnants of the forces allied with Haman and his sons. **10, 15, 16:** The scrupulous refusal to take the usual spoils of victory suggests that this story is about the claiming of power, not greed, revenge, or bloodletting. **17–19:** The movement from helplessness to mastery, from a sense of threat to relief and of grief to joy, appropriately finds expression in spontaneous celebrations.

9:20–32 The Festival of Purim Instituted

In contrast to the dominant legal system whose legitimacy depends on the wayward whims of a potentate, Mordecai and Esther institutionalize a practice of the Jews: the Festival of Purim. In a social context where a decree can be legal yet lethal, set into motion by fatuous royal fiat, the Jews create an ordinance that originates from popular impulse and finds enduring

the times of fasting and mourning.) 32 So the command of Esther confirmed the practices of Purim, and it was all written down in the records.

The Greatness of Xerxes and Mordecai

10 King Xerxes imposed a tribute throughout his empire, even to the distant coastlands. 2 His great achievements and the full account of the greatness of Mordecai, whom the king had promoted, are recorded in *The Book of the History of the Kings of Media and Persia.* 3 Mordecai the Jew became the prime minister, with authority next to that of King Xerxes himself. He was very great among the Jews, who held him in high esteem, because he continued to work for the good of his people and to speak up for the welfare of all their descendants.

---

force in a community's grateful memory of deliverance.

10:1–3 Conclusion

The Greatness of Xerxes and Mordecai. Mordecai's rise and the story of Esther show that one can lead a significant, rewarding life in a foreign court and use it in the service of one's people, maintaining solidarity and an ethno-religious identity in an alien culture. Human history, it seems, is both free and guided. While we may be subject to thoughtless injustice as exiles in alien lands, there is always the possibility of rescue through the chance provisions of an unseen power and our inner resourcefulness. We are not captive to random fate or to the apparent hopelessness of a history dominated by the vast carelessness of unprincipled power.

JOB

INTRODUCTION

The book of Job is a theodicy, an attempt to defend the justice and goodness of God in spite of the existence of evil in the world. This makes the work significant for women in every time and place, because much violence and evil have been wielded specifically against women. As a result, women have frequently found themselves left alone, in suffering and pain, asking "Why?" and "How long?"

The book of Job seeks to answer the question: Why do the righteous suffer? This question is raised in the light of a traditional emphasis within Old Testament wisdom literature on divine retributive justice, that God will reward the righteous but punish the wicked. The book of Job challenges such an emphasis, exploring experiences that seemingly contradict it and daring to ask difficult, even uncomfortable, questions. In doing so the author or authors challenge the established religious institutions and forge forward to institute a more satisfactory answer to the problem of evil.

The book as it appears in the canon is complex, which strengthens the probability of more than one author and several sources. Two major genres are represented in the book: the introductory and concluding prose narratives (chaps. 1—2; 42), and the poetic texts found in between (chaps. 3—41). The prose passages are simple and reminiscent of folk tales. In contrast, the poetic pieces are difficult and complex, filled with unusual words and thoughts. This has led many commentators to conclude that the two genres represent the work of more than one author and that the poetic pieces have been inserted into what was originally one simple prose narrative. Also, the character Elihu does not appear until chapter 32 and disappears after chapter 37, which leads most scholars to suggest these chapters are a later insertion. Finally, some suggest that God's speeches (chaps. 38—41) were added or modified later.

It seems reasonable to accept the supposition that an astute poet used an existing prose tale as opportunity to stage the debate found in chapters 3—41. Simultaneously, the argument for the later insertion of Elihu's speeches and perhaps the later insertion of chapter 28 is logical. Theories about sources may give us some understanding about differing genres and styles but do not assist our comprehension of the final product. For the purposes of this commentary the book will be read as a unified whole and each piece as a distinct part of an overarching rhetorical conversation.

Also difficult are questions related to date and location. For the latter, there are few clues in the book. The story is situated in Edom, but this does not necessitate Edom as the location for composition. The story provides no clues beyond the initial locating of the characters, and the geographical location plays no significant role for meaning.

The dates proposed for the book range from the tenth to the third century BC. The story is placed in the patriarchal period, but this does not necessitate that date for its authorship or composition. Ezekiel referred to Job as an important person alongside Noah and Daniel (Ezek 14:14–20), and traditionally Job has been understood as one of the oldest books in the canon. But modern scholars are skeptical of this claim to antiquity. The book makes no references to historical events. However, some internal evidences suggest affinities with other canonical books and could lead one to conclude the work in its final form is post-Babylonian exile. Alleged are affinities between Job 3 and Jeremiah 20:7–18 and stylistic similarities between Job and Isaiah 40—55. These connections suggest a time either before the early sixth century BC (if Job is prior) or in the late sixth or early fifth century BC (if Job is later). There is no way of determining which text(s) came first. Job 7:17–18 is related to Psalm 8, but it is impossible to date this psalm. Finally, Job 3:4 seems to reflect on Genesis 1:3, a text often dated around the sixth century BC.

Although Job is an ancient text, the popularity for reading it in contemporary culture is overwhelming due to the age-old struggle to comprehend the juxtaposition of a loving God and the problem of evil. —*LeAnn Snow Flesher*

1:1—2:13	Opening Narrative
3:1–26	Job's Lament
4:1—14:22	First Discourse Cycle
15:1—21:34	Second Discourse Cycle
22:1—31:40	Third Discourse Cycle
32:1—37:24	Discourses of Elihu
38:1—42:6	Discourse Cycle of the LORD
42:7–17	Closing Narrative

✧

Prologue

1 There once was a man named Job who lived in the land of Uz. He was blameless—a man of complete integrity. He feared God and stayed away from evil. 2 He had seven sons and three daughters. 3 He owned 7,000 sheep, 3,000 camels, 500 teams of oxen, and 500 female donkeys. He also had many servants. He was, in fact, the richest person in that entire area.

4 Job's sons would take turns preparing feasts in their homes, and they would also invite their three sisters to celebrate with them. 5 When these celebrations ended—sometimes after several days—Job would purify his children. He would get up early in the morning and offer a burnt offering for each of them. For Job said to himself, "Perhaps my children have sinned and have cursed God in their hearts." This was Job's regular practice.

1:1—2:13 Opening Narrative

The book of Job is bookended with narrative. Here we're introduced to the main character and shown the cause of all his troubles. Although some contemporary scholars assess these opening chapters of Job as historical narrative, many categorize the opening as folk narrative. This is not to suggest that there never has been a Joblike character, and in many ways the point of the book is not lessened whether Job is a single historical figure. If Job is not an actual historical figure, then the ensuing description of his character, family, and wealth are to be understood in this context. This allows the depiction of Job's life as perfect to be understood as exaggerated to make a point. **1:1:** This verse sounds like the beginning of a fairy tale, which consistently begins with a similar phrase, "Once upon a time . . ." *Blameless . . . complete integrity*: This is a key statement for understanding the book. The Hebrew words here will be found many times throughout the book to emphasize and thereby remind the reader that Job is indeed an upright (righteous) and blameless man. If the ensuing discussion is to have any relevance, readers must be aware from the beginning that Job's integrity has been established. If Job is truly without blemish or blame, then he is the perfect foil for the ensuing doctrinal debate. **2–5:** Seven is the number of perfection and completion in the Old Testament, thus the perfect number of sons. In addition, a man does not want to have too many daughters because when they marry, each will require a dowry. Each of the three pairs of numbered items (sons and daughters; sheep and camels; oxen and donkeys) add up to some multiple of ten and thus create an extremely orderly account of Job's wealth. Along with Job's burnt offerings for

Job's First Test

6 One day the members of the heavenly court* came to present themselves before the LORD, and the Accuser, Satan,* came with them. 7 "Where have you come from?" the LORD asked Satan.

Satan answered the LORD, "I have been patrolling the earth, watching everything that's going on."

8 Then the LORD asked Satan, "Have you noticed my servant Job? He is the finest man in all the earth. He is blameless—a man of complete integrity. He fears God and stays away from evil."

9 Satan replied to the LORD, "Yes, but Job has good reason to fear God. 10 You have always put a wall of protection around him and his home and his property. You have made him prosper in everything he does. Look how rich he is! 11 But reach out and take away everything he has, and he will surely curse you to your face!"

12 "All right, you may test him," the LORD said to Satan. "Do whatever you want with everything he possesses, but don't harm him physically." So Satan left the LORD's presence.

13 One day when Job's sons and daughters were feasting at the oldest brother's house, 14 a messenger arrived at Job's home with this news: "Your oxen were plowing, with the donkeys feeding beside them, 15 when the Sabeans raided us. They stole all the animals and killed all the farmhands. I am the only one who escaped to tell you."

16 While he was still speaking, another messenger arrived with this news: "The fire of God has fallen from heaven and burned up your sheep and all the shepherds. I am the only one who escaped to tell you."

17 While he was still speaking, a third messenger arrived with this news: "Three bands of Chaldean raiders have stolen your camels and killed your servants. I am the only one who escaped to tell you."

18 While he was still speaking, another messenger arrived with this news: "Your sons and daughters were feasting in their oldest brother's home. 19 Suddenly, a powerful wind swept in from the wilderness and hit the house on all sides. The house collapsed, and all your children are dead. I am the only one who escaped to tell you."

20 Job stood up and tore his robe in grief. Then he shaved his head and fell to the ground to worship. 21 He said,

"I came naked from my mother's womb,
and I will be naked when I leave.
The LORD gave me what I had,
and the LORD has taken it away.
Praise the name of the LORD!"

22 In all of this, Job did not sin by blaming God.

Job's Second Test

2 One day the members of the heavenly court* came again to present themselves before the LORD, and the Accuser, Satan,* came with them. 2 "Where have you come from?" the LORD asked Satan.

Satan answered the LORD, "I have been patrolling the earth, watching everything that's going on."

3 Then the LORD asked Satan, "Have you noticed my servant Job? He is the finest man in all the earth. He is blameless—a man of complete integrity. He fears God and stays away from evil. And he has maintained his integrity, even though you urged me to harm him without cause."

4 Satan replied to the LORD, "Skin for skin! A man will give up everything he has to save his

1:6a Hebrew *the sons of God.* **1:6b** Hebrew *and the satan;* similarly throughout this chapter. **2:1a** Hebrew *the sons of God.* **2:1b** Hebrew *and the satan;* similarly throughout this chapter.

his children the picture is one of perfection, the ideal worshiper of Yahweh. **6–12:** In Job, Satan is not the supremely evil being humans need deliverance from. Satan is the accuser, the one who travels the earth and brings back a report to God. *Complete integrity*: God describes Job as *tam* and *yashar*, blameless and upright, the same Hebrew words found in verse 1. The repetition is key to the story. Twice within eight verses Job is described this way, first by the narrator, who can be trusted, and now by God. **9–10:** According to Satan, God has been protecting Job from harm as well as assuring the increase of his wealth. This accusation evidences the dogma of divine retributive justice. He questions whether humans—Job in particular—are capable of faith without reward. **13–19:** Satan dismantles Job's fortune and family. Within one day Job loses his herds, his servants, and his children. This is cataclysmic and heightens the narrative: Job has moved from being the wealthiest man in the land to abject poverty. **20–21:** Job's immediate response. **22:** The narrator interprets Job's acts and words of lamentation for us. It would seem Satan was wrong and God was right. Humans are capable of disinterested faith. **2:1–6:** This is a parallel, almost verbatim account of 1:6–8. **3:** God seemingly gloats over Job's response to Satan's test. **4–5:** Satan is not

life. [5] But reach out and take away his health, and
he will surely curse you to your face!"
[6] "All right, do with him as you please," the
LORD said to Satan. "But spare his life." [7] So Satan left the LORD's presence, and he struck Job
with terrible boils from head to foot.
[8] Job scraped his skin with a piece of broken
pottery as he sat among the ashes. [9] His wife said
to him, "Are you still trying to maintain your
integrity? Curse God and die."
[10] But Job replied, "You talk like a foolish
woman. Should we accept only good things from
the hand of God and never anything bad?" So in
all this, Job said nothing wrong.

Job's Three Friends Share His Anguish

[11] When three of Job's friends heard of the tragedy he had suffered, they got together and traveled from their homes to comfort and console
him. Their names were Eliphaz the Temanite,
Bildad the Shuhite, and Zophar the Naamathite. [12] When they saw Job from a distance,
they scarcely recognized him. Wailing loudly,
they tore their robes and threw dust into the air
over their heads to show their grief. [13] Then they
sat on the ground with him for seven days and
nights. No one said a word to Job, for they saw
that his suffering was too great for words.

Job's First Speech

3 At last Job spoke, and he cursed the day of
his birth. [2] He said:

[3] "Let the day of my birth be erased,
and the night I was conceived.
[4] Let that day be turned to darkness.
Let it be lost even to God on high,
and let no light shine on it.
[5] Let the darkness and utter gloom claim that
day for its own.
Let a black cloud overshadow it,
and let the darkness terrify it.
[6] Let that night be blotted off the calendar,
never again to be counted among the days
of the year,
never again to appear among the months.
[7] Let that night be childless.
Let it have no joy.
[8] Let those who are experts at cursing—
whose cursing could rouse Leviathan*—
curse that day.
[9] Let its morning stars remain dark.
Let it hope for light, but in vain;
may it never see the morning light.
[10] Curse that day for failing to shut my
mother's womb,
for letting me be born to see all this
trouble.

[11] "Why wasn't I born dead?
Why didn't I die as I came from the womb?
[12] Why was I laid on my mother's lap?
Why did she nurse me at her breasts?
[13] Had I died at birth, I would now be at peace.
I would be asleep and at rest.
[14] I would rest with the world's kings and prime
ministers,
whose great buildings now lie in ruins.
[15] I would rest with princes, rich in gold,
whose palaces were filled with silver.
[16] Why wasn't I buried like a stillborn child,
like a baby who never lives to see the light?

3:8 The identification of Leviathan is disputed, ranging from an earthly creature to a mythical sea monster in ancient literature.

so easily convinced. If Job himself is threatened, not his property or his children, he will curse God. **8–10:** Satan's final blow has forced Job to leave his community and sit outside its walls as one who is unclean. This is the lowest point one can reach in life; the next level down would be death, something that Job will ask for in the near future. **9–10:** These are the only words spoken by a female in the story, and they do not bode well for women, as Job's wife berates Job for his integrity and exhorts him to curse God and die. She does not have the capacity for disinterested faith. But let us be aware of her literary function in the text. Her words serve as a foil for Job's blameless response. **11–13:** Job's three friends arrive. Their seven days and nights of sitting with Job reflects the extent of his suffering. The reader knows therefore that the friends had tremendous compassion for Job. It is important that we hear their ensuing words within this framework.

3:1–26 Job's Lament

Chapter 3 is a lengthy lament that begins with ten verses of imprecations against the day of Job's birth as though it were an enemy. Job echoes his wife's suggestion that he simply die by essentially wishing himself unborn, even unconceived. Two additional sections—each introduced by the interrogative complaint "Why?"—follow. This complaint is a common form, often found in the lament psalms, that suggests the current distress is incomprehensible to the speaker. **11–19:** Job picks up a second theme,

Midwifery and Birthing Practices

Biblical midwifery incorporated delivery of newborns, counseling of couples, caring for pregnant mothers, assisting during crises such as miscarriage or the death of the mother, and massaging the child in the womb to position the baby for head-first delivery. If the birth is delayed, the child might be given a temporary name and called forth with the formula "[Name], come out!" Many of these functions are combined in Genesis 35:16–20, wherein a midwife assists at Benjamin's difficult birth. Benjamin's temporary name *ben-oni* ("Child of My Labor"), given by Rachel just before her death in childbirth, is a calling-forth name. After the birth, the midwife cleaned and clothed the baby. She also presented the newborn to the parents for adoption—a necessity because relationship was determined by contract rather than kinship.

Most of the biblical references to midwifery describe the work of God or the angel of the LORD. This image is important in the biblical themes of creation (e.g., Job 38:8–11) and salvation. In Isaiah 66:7–11, a prophecy of the new creation, God is presented as midwife to mother Zion. In Psalm 22:9, the speaker acknowledges God as midwife. In Luke 1:26–38, the angel Gabriel acts as midwife to Mary, giving her counseling for the coming pregnancy and birth. In the Synoptic Gospels, Jesus is given two sets of adoption formulas, proclaiming his origins to be divine and human. God implicitly acts as midwife in being the ultimate originator of these adoptions. In the baptism narrative (Matt 3:17 and par.; cf. Matt 17:5 and par.), the formula "This is my dearly loved Son" acknowledges that God is Jesus' legal parent. (God is mother and/or father, since either may adopt.) The human legal adoption occurs when Joseph names Jesus. The angel who instructs Joseph to name Jesus is acting as midwife at God's behest (Matt 1:20–23).

Jesus is presented as midwife when he commands, "Lazarus, come out!" (John 11:43). God as midwife also appears in Paul where the Holy Spirit "helps us in our weakness as all creation has been groaning as in the pains of childbirth" awaiting new birth in Christ (Rom 8:26, 22).

17 For in death the wicked cause no trouble,
and the weary are at rest.
18 Even captives are at ease in death,
with no guards to curse them.
19 Rich and poor are both there,
and the slave is free from his master.

20 "Oh, why give light to those in misery,
and life to those who are bitter?
21 They long for death, and it won't come.
They search for death more eagerly than
for hidden treasure.
22 They're filled with joy when they finally die,
and rejoice when they find the grave.
23 Why is life given to those with no future,
those God has surrounded with
difficulties?
24 I cannot eat for sighing;
my groans pour out like water.
25 What I always feared has happened to me.
What I dreaded has come true.
26 I have no peace, no quietness.
I have no rest; only trouble comes."

Eliphaz's First Response to Job

4 Then Eliphaz the Temanite replied to Job:

2 "Will you be patient and let me say a
word?
For who could keep from speaking out?

summarized by his opening statement, "Why did I not die at birth?" which is closely related to the first. If he had to be born, then he wishes he had died early in life, for to be dead is to be without sorrow. **20–26:** Job completes his lament with a third and final theme: the unfairness of life being forced upon the miserable, those who long only for death. Job's suffering has so overcome him that he longs for relief by means of death. **23:** Compare Job's view of God's role in his life to Satan's in 1:10. Since lament is an acceptable form of expression in the Old Testament, Job still has not sinned with his lips. Although Job has used many words to explicate his pain and suffering, he has not cursed God.

4:1—14:22 First Discourse Cycle

This is the first of three lengthy discourse cycles between Job and his three friends. Throughout these cycles the friends present varying arguments based on their commitments to the doctrine of divine retributive justice. Job responds to every discourse, sometimes addressing the friends' statements and at other times attending to something different. Fre-

3 "In the past you have encouraged many people;
you have strengthened those who were weak.
4 Your words have supported those who were falling;
you encouraged those with shaky knees.
5 But now when trouble strikes, you lose heart.
You are terrified when it touches you.
6 Doesn't your reverence for God give you confidence?
Doesn't your life of integrity give you hope?

7 "Stop and think! Do the innocent die?
When have the upright been destroyed?
8 My experience shows that those who plant trouble
and cultivate evil will harvest the same.
9 A breath from God destroys them.
They vanish in a blast of his anger.
10 The lion roars and the wildcat snarls,
but the teeth of strong lions will be broken.
11 The fierce lion will starve for lack of prey,
and the cubs of the lioness will be scattered.

12 "This truth was given to me in secret,
as though whispered in my ear.
13 It came to me in a disturbing vision at night,
when people are in a deep sleep.
14 Fear gripped me,
and my bones trembled.
15 A spirit* swept past my face,
and my hair stood on end.*
16 The spirit stopped, but I couldn't see its shape.
There was a form before my eyes.
In the silence I heard a voice say,
17 'Can a mortal be innocent before God?
Can anyone be pure before the Creator?'

18 "If God does not trust his own angels
and has charged his messengers with foolishness,
19 how much less will he trust people made of clay!
They are made of dust, crushed as easily as a moth.
20 They are alive in the morning but dead by evening,
gone forever without a trace.
21 Their tent-cords are pulled and the tent collapses,
and they die in ignorance.

Eliphaz's Response Continues

5 1 "Cry for help, but will anyone answer you?
Which of the angels* will help you?
2 Surely resentment destroys the fool,
and jealousy kills the simple.
3 I have seen that fools may be successful for the moment,
but then comes sudden disaster.
4 Their children are abandoned far from help;
they are crushed in court with no one to defend them.
5 The hungry devour their harvest,
even when it is guarded by brambles.*
The thirsty pant after their wealth.
6 But evil does not spring from the soil,
and trouble does not sprout from the earth.
7 People are born for trouble
as readily as sparks fly up from a fire.

8 "If I were you, I would go to God
and present my case to him.
9 He does great things too marvelous to understand.
He performs countless miracles.
10 He gives rain for the earth
and water for the fields.
11 He gives prosperity to the poor
and protects those who suffer.
12 He frustrates the plans of schemers
so the work of their hands will not succeed.
13 He traps the wise in their own cleverness
so their cunning schemes are thwarted.
14 They find it is dark in the daytime,
and they grope at noon as if it were night.
15 He rescues the poor from the cutting words of the strong,
and rescues them from the clutches of the powerful.

4:15a Or *wind;* also in 4:16. **4:15b** Or *its wind sent shivers up my spine.* **5:1** Hebrew *the holy ones.* **5:5** The meaning of the Hebrew for this phrase is uncertain.

quently Job's conversation confronts the dogma of retributive justice.

4:1—5:27 Traditional Doctrine. Eliphaz affirms Job's former virtuous acts, but soon turns to reprimands. **4:5–6:** Eliphaz's initial exhortation is that Job has become impatient and dismayed now that the tables are turned. **17–21:** His argument is built on the simple precept, learned in a vision, that humans cannot be righteous but are imperfect. **5:3–5:** The implication is that Job could be counted among the *fools.* **9–16:** God frustrates the crafty and helps the wise,

16 And so at last the poor have hope,
and the snapping jaws of the wicked are shut.
17 "But consider the joy of those corrected by God!
Do not despise the discipline of the Almighty when you sin.
18 For though he wounds, he also bandages.
He strikes, but his hands also heal.
19 From six disasters he will rescue you;
even in the seventh, he will keep you from evil.
20 He will save you from death in time of famine,
from the power of the sword in time of war.
21 You will be safe from slander
and have no fear when destruction comes.
22 You will laugh at destruction and famine;
wild animals will not terrify you.
23 You will be at peace with the stones of the field,
and its wild animals will be at peace with you.
24 You will know that your home is safe.
When you survey your possessions,
nothing will be missing.
25 You will have many children;
your descendants will be as plentiful as grass!
26 You will go to the grave at a ripe old age,
like a sheaf of grain harvested at the proper time!

27 "We have studied life and found all this to be true.
Listen to my counsel, and apply it to yourself."

Job's Second Speech: A Response to Eliphaz

6 Then Job spoke again:
2 "If my misery could be weighed
and my troubles be put on the scales,
3 they would outweigh all the sands of the sea.
That is why I spoke impulsively.
4 For the Almighty has struck me down with his arrows.
Their poison infects my spirit.
God's terrors are lined up against me.
5 Don't I have a right to complain?
Don't wild donkeys bray when they find no grass,
and oxen bellow when they have no food?
6 Don't people complain about unsalted food?
Does anyone want the tasteless white of an egg?*
7 My appetite disappears when I look at it;
I gag at the thought of eating it!

8 "Oh, that I might have my request,
that God would grant my desire.
9 I wish he would crush me.
I wish he would reach out his hand and kill me.
10 At least I can take comfort in this:
Despite the pain,
I have not denied the words of the Holy One.
11 But I don't have the strength to endure.
I have nothing to live for.
12 Do I have the strength of a stone?
Is my body made of bronze?
13 No, I am utterly helpless,
without any chance of success.

14 "One should be kind to a fainting friend,
but you accuse me without any fear of the Almighty.*
15 My brothers, you have proved as unreliable as a seasonal brook
that overflows its banks in the spring
16 when it is swollen with ice and melting snow.
17 But when the hot weather arrives, the water disappears.
The brook vanishes in the heat.
18 The caravans turn aside to be refreshed,

6:6 Or *the tasteless juice of the mallow plant?* **6:14** Or *friend, / or he might lose his fear of the Almighty.*

but if the wise act in crafty ways then they too shall be frustrated. **17–18:** Those who are disciplined by God are in the end happy because God's discipline is good and leads to healing. **19–26:** Implicit is the assumption that Job has sinned and is being punished accordingly. **27:** Eliphaz's challenge to Job is to turn to God, acknowledge his sin, plead for deliverance, and consequently preserve the idea of divine justice and traditional doctrine.

6:1—7:21 An Opposite Scenario. Job's response must be read in light of the narrator's statement about him in 1:1. Bear in mind that he is blameless and upright. Readers often find such a premise difficult to hold throughout the book and instead accept Eliphaz's argument in chapter 4. The opening narrative, however, intentionally establishes a man of such integrity and righteousness that, given the dogma of divine retributive justice, he should encounter only blessings in his

but there is nothing to drink, so they die.
19 The caravans from Tema search for this water;
the travelers from Sheba hope to find it.
20 They count on it but are disappointed.
When they arrive, their hopes are dashed.
21 You, too, have given no help.
You have seen my calamity, and you are afraid.
22 But why? Have I ever asked you for a gift?
Have I begged for anything of yours for myself?
23 Have I asked you to rescue me from my enemies,
or to save me from ruthless people?
24 Teach me, and I will keep quiet.
Show me what I have done wrong.
25 Honest words can be painful,
but what do your criticisms amount to?
26 Do you think your words are convincing
when you disregard my cry of desperation?
27 You would even send an orphan into slavery*
or sell a friend.
28 Look at me!
Would I lie to your face?
29 Stop assuming my guilt,
for I have done no wrong.
30 Do you think I am lying?
Don't I know the difference between right and wrong?

7 1"Is not all human life a struggle?
Our lives are like that of a hired hand,
2 like a worker who longs for the shade,
like a servant waiting to be paid.
3 I, too, have been assigned months of futility,
long and weary nights of misery.
4 Lying in bed, I think, 'When will it be morning?'
But the night drags on, and I toss till dawn.
5 My body is covered with maggots and scabs.
My skin breaks open, oozing with pus.

Job Cries Out to God

6 "My days fly faster than a weaver's shuttle.
They end without hope.
7 O God, remember that my life is but a breath,
and I will never again feel happiness.
8 You see me now, but not for long.
You will look for me, but I will be gone.
9 Just as a cloud dissipates and vanishes,
those who die* will not come back.
10 They are gone forever from their home—
never to be seen again.

11 "I cannot keep from speaking.
I must express my anguish.
My bitter soul must complain.
12 Am I a sea monster or a dragon
that you must place me under guard?
13 I think, 'My bed will comfort me,
and sleep will ease my misery,'
14 but then you shatter me with dreams
and terrify me with visions.
15 I would rather be strangled—
rather die than suffer like this.
16 I hate my life and don't want to go on living.
Oh, leave me alone for my few remaining days.

17 "What are people, that you should make so much of us,
that you should think of us so often?
18 For you examine us every morning
and test us every moment.
19 Why won't you leave me alone,
at least long enough for me to swallow!
20 If I have sinned, what have I done to you,
O watcher of all humanity?
Why make me your target?
Am I a burden to you?
21 Why not just forgive my sin
and take away my guilt?

6:27 Hebrew *even gamble over an orphan.* **7:9** Hebrew *who go down to Sheol.*

---

life. The subsequent scenario establishes that sometimes bad things happen to good people (and vice versa) and seeks to understand God's justice in the midst of this reality. Job begins with an enigmatic discussion on the weight of his calamity, which exceeds all ordinary misfortunes. He requests death so that he will not curse God or sin. **6:15:** *Brothers*: The Hebrew word is plural: He is rebuking all three friends. He further challenges them to show him his error and establishes his integrity. **7:1–21:** Job complains of the difficulty and brevity of life, a motif frequently found in the lament psalms, and suggests this truth justifies his complaint. In contrast to traditional laments, however, Job blames God for humanity's (and his own) misery. **17–18:** Job parodies Psalm 8: "What are mere mortals that you should think about them, human beings that you should care for them?" The implications of each are opposites: Job is suggesting that God does not care, after all, but only tests and becomes a *watcher of all humanity*. **20–21:** Job is not making a confession of sin; rather he is provoking God to act on his behalf.

For soon I will lie down in the dust and die.
When you look for me, I will be gone."

Bildad's First Response to Job

8 Then Bildad the Shuhite replied to Job:

2 "How long will you go on like this?
You sound like a blustering wind.
3 Does God twist justice?
Does the Almighty twist what is right?
4 Your children must have sinned against him,
so their punishment was well deserved.
5 But if you pray to God
and seek the favor of the Almighty,
6 and if you are pure and live with integrity,
he will surely rise up and restore your happy home.
7 And though you started with little,
you will end with much.

8 "Just ask the previous generation.
Pay attention to the experience of our ancestors.
9 For we were born but yesterday and know nothing.
Our days on earth are as fleeting as a shadow.
10 But those who came before us will teach you.
They will teach you the wisdom of old.

11 "Can papyrus reeds grow tall without a marsh?
Can marsh grass flourish without water?
12 While they are still flowering, not ready to be cut,
they begin to wither more quickly than grass.
13 The same happens to all who forget God.
The hopes of the godless evaporate.
14 Their confidence hangs by a thread.
They are leaning on a spider's web.
15 They cling to their home for security, but it won't last.
They try to hold it tight, but it will not endure.
16 The godless seem like a lush plant growing in the sunshine,
its branches spreading across the garden.
17 Its roots grow down through a pile of stones;
it takes hold on a bed of rocks.
18 But when it is uprooted,
it's as though it never existed!
19 That's the end of its life,
and others spring up from the earth to replace it.

20 "But look, God will not reject a person of integrity,
nor will he lend a hand to the wicked.
21 He will once again fill your mouth with laughter
and your lips with shouts of joy.
22 Those who hate you will be clothed with shame,
and the home of the wicked will be destroyed."

Job's Third Speech: A Response to Bildad

9 Then Job spoke again:

2 "Yes, I know all this is true in principle.
But how can a person be declared innocent in God's sight?
3 If someone wanted to take God to court,*
would it be possible to answer him even once in a thousand times?
4 For God is so wise and so mighty.
Who has ever challenged him successfully?

5 "Without warning, he moves the mountains,
overturning them in his anger.
6 He shakes the earth from its place,
and its foundations tremble.
7 If he commands it, the sun won't rise

9:3 Or *If God wanted to take someone to court.*

8:1–22 Repentance Urged. Bildad, speaking for the first time, also intends to show Job the error of his ways and therefore stimulate him to turn to God in repentance. **2:** Bildad's opener is less courteous than Eliphaz's opening comment. **3–4:** Bildad suggests Job is accusing God of perverting justice and says that if Job is so upright, he must be suffering for his children's sin. **11–19:** Bildad implies that Job has not only sinned somehow but that he has forgotten God altogether. **6–7, 20–22:** As the friends shake their heads in wonderment over who has sinned and where, Bildad proclaims that all Job needs to do is to be upright and blameless, the exact language used to describe Job in the opening chapters.

9:1—10:22 Complaints about Injustice. It seems that Job responds to Eliphaz rather than Bildad in this section (cf. 9:2 with 4:17). **9:3–4:** This is the first of three instances where Job will raise the idea of a hearing before God, but he quickly discards it as impossible to win. Job fears that God will not listen and concludes the idea is futile, because the Creator

and the stars won't shine.
8 He alone has spread out the heavens
and marches on the waves of the sea.
9 He made all the stars—the Bear and Orion,
the Pleiades and the constellations of the southern sky.
10 He does great things too marvelous to understand.
He performs countless miracles.

11 "Yet when he comes near, I cannot see him.
When he moves by, I do not see him go.
12 If he snatches someone in death, who can stop him?
Who dares to ask, 'What are you doing?'
13 And God does not restrain his anger.
Even the monsters of the sea* are crushed beneath his feet.

14 "So who am I, that I should try to answer God
or even reason with him?
15 Even if I were right, I would have no defense.
I could only plead for mercy.
16 And even if I summoned him and he responded,
I'm not sure he would listen to me.
17 For he attacks me with a storm
and repeatedly wounds me without cause.
18 He will not let me catch my breath,
but fills me instead with bitter sorrows.
19 If it's a question of strength, he's the strong one.
If it's a matter of justice, who dares to summon him to court?
20 Though I am innocent, my own mouth would pronounce me guilty.
Though I am blameless, it* would prove me wicked.

21 "I am innocent,
but it makes no difference to me—
I despise my life.
22 Innocent or wicked, it is all the same to God.
That's why I say, 'He destroys both the blameless and the wicked.'
23 When a plague* sweeps through,
he laughs at the death of the innocent.
24 The whole earth is in the hands of the wicked,
and God blinds the eyes of the judges.
If he's not the one who does it, who is?

25 "My life passes more swiftly than a runner.
It flees away without a glimpse of happiness.
26 It disappears like a swift papyrus boat,
like an eagle swooping down on its prey.
27 If I decided to forget my complaints,
to put away my sad face and be cheerful,
28 I would still dread all the pain,
for I know you will not find me innocent, O God.
29 Whatever happens, I will be found guilty.
So what's the use of trying?
30 Even if I were to wash myself with soap
and clean my hands with lye,
31 you would plunge me into a muddy ditch,
and my own filthy clothing would hate me.

32 "God is not a mortal like me,
so I cannot argue with him or take him to trial.
33 If only there were a mediator between us,
someone who could bring us together.
34 The mediator could make God stop beating me,
and I would no longer live in terror of his punishment.
35 Then I could speak to him without fear,
but I cannot do that in my own strength.

Job Frames His Plea to God

10 1 "I am disgusted with my life.
Let me complain freely.
My bitter soul must complain.
2 I will say to God, 'Don't simply condemn me—
tell me the charge you are bringing against me.
3 What do you gain by oppressing me?
Why do you reject me, the work of your own hands,
while smiling on the schemes of the wicked?
4 Are your eyes like those of a human?
Do you see things only as people see them?
5 Is your lifetime only as long as ours?
Is your life so short
6 that you must quickly probe for my guilt

9:13 Hebrew *the helpers of Rahab,* the name of a mythical sea monster that represents chaos in ancient literature. **9:20** Or *he.* **9:23** Or *disaster.*

has the advantage of might and there is no one to act as judge over God. **21–31:** Job accuses God of mocking the calamity of the innocent and prospering the wicked. God would find a way to judge Job guilty, no matter his integrity. **10:1–22:** Job voices the universal question, "Why is this happening to me?" and ques-

and search for my sin?
7 Although you know I am not guilty,
no one can rescue me from your hands.

8 " 'You formed me with your hands; you made me,
yet now you completely destroy me.
9 Remember that you made me from dust—
will you turn me back to dust so soon?
10 You guided my conception
and formed me in the womb.*
11 You clothed me with skin and flesh,
and you knit my bones and sinews together.
12 You gave me life and showed me your unfailing love.
My life was preserved by your care.

13 " 'Yet your real motive—
your true intent—
14 was to watch me, and if I sinned,
you would not forgive my guilt.
15 If I am guilty, too bad for me;
and even if I'm innocent, I can't hold my head high,
because I am filled with shame and misery.
16 And if I hold my head high, you hunt me like a lion
and display your awesome power against me.
17 Again and again you witness against me.
You pour out your growing anger on me
and bring fresh armies against me.

18 " 'Why, then, did you deliver me from my mother's womb?
Why didn't you let me die at birth?
19 It would be as though I had never existed,
going directly from the womb to the grave.
20 I have only a few days left, so leave me alone,
that I may have a moment of comfort
21 before I leave—never to return—
for the land of darkness and utter gloom.
22 It is a land as dark as midnight,
a land of gloom and confusion,
where even the light is dark as midnight.' "

Zophar's First Response to Job

11 Then Zophar the Naamathite replied to Job:

2 "Shouldn't someone answer this torrent of words?
Is a person proved innocent just by a lot of talking?
3 Should I remain silent while you babble on?
When you mock God, shouldn't someone make you ashamed?
4 You claim, 'My beliefs are pure,'
and 'I am clean in the sight of God.'
5 If only God would speak;
if only he would tell you what he thinks!
6 If only he would tell you the secrets of wisdom,
for true wisdom is not a simple matter.
Listen! God is doubtless punishing you
far less than you deserve!

7 "Can you solve the mysteries of God?
Can you discover everything about the Almighty?
8 Such knowledge is higher than the heavens—
and who are you?
It is deeper than the underworld*—
what do you know?
9 It is broader than the earth
and wider than the sea.
10 If God comes and puts a person in prison
or calls the court to order, who can stop him?
11 For he knows those who are false,
and he takes note of all their sins.
12 An empty-headed person won't become wise
any more than a wild donkey can bear a human child.*

10:10 Hebrew *You poured me out like milk / and curdled me like cheese.* **11:8** Hebrew *than Sheol.* **11:12** Or *than a wild male donkey can bear a tame colt.*

---

tions God's intent and justice. **20–21:** Ultimately Job begs God to leave him alone so that he might find some comfort (v. 20).

11:1–20 A Multitude of Words. Zophar begins with biting remarks concerning Job's language, calling it a multitude of words, babble, and mockery. He dismisses Job's statements of innocence while praying that God will speak the secrets of wisdom to Job. **6:** These words are the most crushing: *God is doubtless punishing you far less than you deserve!* **7–11:** Zophar echoes Job's description of God's might and the fruitlessness of pleading innocence to the ultimate judge. Note the differences between this section and 9:15–20. **13–20:** Zophar concludes by exhorting Job to repent of the sin that has led him to this point of suffering so that he may be restored. It is, of course, not sin but righteousness that brought Job to this state.

13 "If only you would prepare your heart
and lift up your hands to him in prayer!
14 Get rid of your sins,
and leave all iniquity behind you.
15 Then your face will brighten with innocence.
You will be strong and free of fear.
16 You will forget your misery;
it will be like water flowing away.
17 Your life will be brighter than the noonday.
Even darkness will be as bright as morning.
18 Having hope will give you courage.
You will be protected and will rest in safety.
19 You will lie down unafraid,
and many will look to you for help.
20 But the wicked will be blinded.
They will have no escape.
Their only hope is death."

Job's Fourth Speech: A Response to Zophar

12 Then Job spoke again:
2 "You people really know
everything, don't you?
And when you die, wisdom will die with
you!
3 Well, I know a few things myself—
and you're no better than I am.
Who doesn't know these things you've
been saying?
4 Yet my friends laugh at me,
for I call on God and expect an answer.
I am a just and blameless man,
yet they laugh at me.
5 People who are at ease mock those in trouble.
They give a push to people who are
stumbling.
6 But robbers are left in peace,
and those who provoke God live in
safety—
though God keeps them in his power.

7 "Just ask the animals, and they will teach
you.
Ask the birds of the sky, and they will tell
you.
8 Speak to the earth, and it will instruct you.
Let the fish in the sea speak to you.
9 For they all know
that my disaster* has come from the hand
of the LORD.
10 For the life of every living thing is in his
hand,
and the breath of every human being.
11 The ear tests the words it hears
just as the mouth distinguishes between
foods.
12 Wisdom belongs to the aged,
and understanding to the old.

13 "But true wisdom and power are found in
God;
counsel and understanding are his.
14 What he destroys cannot be rebuilt.
When he puts someone in prison, there is
no escape.
15 If he holds back the rain, the earth becomes a
desert.
If he releases the waters, they flood the
earth.
16 Yes, strength and wisdom are his;
deceivers and deceived are both in his
power.
17 He leads counselors away, stripped of good
judgment;
wise judges become fools.
18 He removes the royal robe of kings.
They are led away with ropes around their
waist.
19 He leads priests away, stripped of status;
he overthrows those with long years in
power.
20 He silences the trusted adviser
and removes the insight of the elders.
21 He pours disgrace upon princes
and disarms the strong.

22 "He uncovers mysteries hidden in darkness;
he brings light to the deepest gloom.
23 He builds up nations, and he destroys them.
He expands nations, and he abandons them.
24 He strips kings of understanding
and leaves them wandering in a pathless
wasteland.
25 They grope in the darkness without a light.
He makes them stagger like drunkards.

Job Wants to Argue His Case with God

13 1 "Look, I have seen all this with my
own eyes
and heard it with my own ears,
and now I understand.
2 I know as much as you do.

12:9 Hebrew *that this.*

12:1—14:22 Desiring Greater Wisdom. Job begins the final dialogue of this cycle with some biting remarks of his own, mocking his friends' supposed wisdom. Even the birds and beasts know as much as—or more than—they do. For Job also knows the traditional wisdom: God is responsible and is the only source

You are no better than I am.
3 As for me, I would speak directly to the Almighty.
I want to argue my case with God himself.
4 As for you, you smear me with lies.
As physicians, you are worthless quacks.
5 If only you could be silent!
That's the wisest thing you could do.
6 Listen to my charge;
pay attention to my arguments.

7 "Are you defending God with lies?
Do you make your dishonest arguments for his sake?
8 Will you slant your testimony in his favor?
Will you argue God's case for him?
9 What will happen when he finds out what you are doing?
Can you fool him as easily as you fool people?
10 No, you will be in trouble with him
if you secretly slant your testimony in his favor.
11 Doesn't his majesty terrify you?
Doesn't your fear of him overwhelm you?
12 Your platitudes are as valuable as ashes.
Your defense is as fragile as a clay pot.

13 "Be silent now and leave me alone.
Let me speak, and I will face the consequences.
14 Yes, I will take my life in my hands
and say what I really think.
15 God might kill me, but I have no other hope.*
I am going to argue my case with him.
16 But this is what will save me—I am not godless.
If I were, I could not stand before him.

17 "Listen closely to what I am about to say.
Hear me out.
18 I have prepared my case;
I will be proved innocent.
19 Who can argue with me over this?
And if you prove me wrong, I will remain silent and die.

Job Asks How He Has Sinned

20 "O God, grant me these two things,
and then I will be able to face you.
21 Remove your heavy hand from me,
and don't terrify me with your awesome presence.
22 Now summon me, and I will answer!
Or let me speak to you, and you reply.
23 Tell me, what have I done wrong?
Show me my rebellion and my sin.
24 Why do you turn away from me?
Why do you treat me as your enemy?
25 Would you terrify a leaf blown by the wind?
Would you chase dry straw?

26 "You write bitter accusations against me
and bring up all the sins of my youth.
27 You put my feet in stocks.
You examine all my paths.
You trace all my footprints.
28 I waste away like rotting wood,
like a moth-eaten coat.

14

1 "How frail is humanity!
How short is life, how full of trouble!
2 We blossom like a flower and then wither.
Like a passing shadow, we quickly disappear.
3 Must you keep an eye on such a frail creature
and demand an accounting from me?
4 Who can bring purity out of an impure person?
No one!
5 You have decided the length of our lives.
You know how many months we will live,
and we are not given a minute longer.
6 So leave us alone and let us rest!
We are like hired hands, so let us finish our work in peace.

7 "Even a tree has more hope!
If it is cut down, it will sprout again
and grow new branches.
8 Though its roots have grown old in the earth
and its stump decays,

13:15 An alternate reading in the Masoretic Text reads *God might kill me, but I hope in him.*

of true wisdom. **13:3–4, 13–19:** Again Job requests a trial. Job has prepared his case and, despite the risk of coming before God, will speak—confident of his innocence and pending vindication. **4–12:** Job accuses his friends of speaking falsely and foolishly. If they would only keep silent, that would be wisdom. **20–21:** Job's fear of God is evident. **14:1–22:** Again Job laments the shortness and suffering of human lives. Finally Job toys with an idea for escaping the present distress: suggesting that he might be concealed in Sheol, the realm of the dead, until God's wrath dissipates, then be given the chance to speak with God.

9 at the scent of water it will bud
and sprout again like a new seedling.

10 "But when people die, their strength is gone.
They breathe their last, and then where are they?
11 As water evaporates from a lake
and a river disappears in drought,
12 people are laid to rest and do not rise again.
Until the heavens are no more, they will not wake up
nor be roused from their sleep.

13 "I wish you would hide me in the grave*
and forget me there until your anger has passed.
But mark your calendar to think of me again!
14 Can the dead live again?
If so, this would give me hope through all my years of struggle,
and I would eagerly await the release of death.
15 You would call and I would answer,
and you would yearn for me, your handiwork.
16 For then you would guard my steps,
instead of watching for my sins.
17 My sins would be sealed in a pouch,
and you would cover my guilt.

18 "But instead, as mountains fall and crumble
and as rocks fall from a cliff,
19 as water wears away the stones
and floods wash away the soil,
so you destroy people's hope.
20 You always overpower them, and they pass from the scene.
You disfigure them in death and send them away.
21 They never know if their children grow up in honor
or sink to insignificance.
22 They suffer painfully;
their life is full of trouble."

Eliphaz's Second Response to Job

15 Then Eliphaz the Temanite replied:

2 "A wise man wouldn't answer with such empty talk!
You are nothing but a windbag.
3 The wise don't engage in empty chatter.
What good are such words?
4 Have you no fear of God,
no reverence for him?
5 Your sins are telling your mouth what to say.
Your words are based on clever deception.
6 Your own mouth condemns you, not I.
Your own lips testify against you.

7 "Were you the first person ever born?
Were you born before the hills were made?
8 Were you listening at God's secret council?
Do you have a monopoly on wisdom?
9 What do you know that we don't?
What do you understand that we do not?
10 On our side are aged, gray-haired men
much older than your father!

11 "Is God's comfort too little for you?
Is his gentle word not enough?
12 What has taken away your reason?
What has weakened your vision,*
13 that you turn against God
and say all these evil things?
14 Can any mortal be pure?
Can anyone born of a woman be just?
15 Look, God does not even trust the angels.*
Even the heavens are not absolutely pure in his sight.
16 How much less pure is a corrupt and sinful person
with a thirst for wickedness!

17 "If you will listen, I will show you.
I will answer you from my own experience.
18 And it is confirmed by the reports of wise men
who have heard the same thing from their fathers—
19 from those to whom the land was given
long before any foreigners arrived.

20 "The wicked writhe in pain throughout their lives.

14:13 Hebrew *in Sheol.* **15:12** Or *Why do your eyes flash with anger;* Hebrew reads *Why do your eyes blink.* **15:15** Hebrew *the holy ones.*

15:1–21:34 Second Discourse Cycle

The battle lines have been drawn, and Job and his friends become even more confrontational as each one is increasingly more convinced of his stance.

15:1–35 Tradition Threatened. Eliphaz's rhetorical questions are intended to ridicule Job. They build to an accusatory statement that summarizes Eliphaz's primary concern: Job has lost his *fear of God.* **7–17:** Eliphaz's emphasis is upon tradition. **20–35:** The

Years of trouble are stored up for the
ruthless.
21 The sound of terror rings in their ears,
and even on good days they fear the attack
of the destroyer.
22 They dare not go out into the darkness
for fear they will be murdered.
23 They wander around, saying, 'Where can I
find bread?'*
They know their day of destruction is near.
24 That dark day terrifies them.
They live in distress and anguish,
like a king preparing for battle.
25 For they shake their fists at God,
defying the Almighty.
26 Holding their strong shields,
they defiantly charge against him.

27 "These wicked people are heavy and
prosperous;
their waists bulge with fat.
28 But their cities will be ruined.
They will live in abandoned houses
that are ready to tumble down.
29 Their riches will not last,
and their wealth will not endure.
Their possessions will no longer spread
across the horizon.

30 "They will not escape the darkness.
The burning sun will wither their shoots,
and the breath of God will destroy them.
31 Let them no longer fool themselves by
trusting in empty riches,
for emptiness will be their only reward.
32 Like trees, they will be cut down in the prime
of life;
their branches will never again be green.
33 They will be like a vine whose grapes are
harvested too early,
like an olive tree that loses its blossoms
before the fruit can form.
34 For the godless are barren.
Their homes, enriched through bribery,
will burn.
35 They conceive trouble and give birth to evil.
Their womb produces deceit."

Job's Fifth Speech: A Response to Eliphaz

16 Then Job spoke again:
2 "I have heard all this before.
What miserable comforters you are!
3 Won't you ever stop blowing hot air?
What makes you keep on talking?
4 I could say the same things if you were in my
place.
I could spout off criticism and shake my
head at you.
5 But if it were me, I would encourage you.
I would try to take away your grief.
6 Instead, I suffer if I defend myself,
and I suffer no less if I refuse to speak.

7 "O God, you have ground me down
and devastated my family.
8 As if to prove I have sinned, you've reduced
me to skin and bones.
My gaunt flesh testifies against me.
9 God hates me and angrily tears me apart.
He snaps his teeth at me
and pierces me with his eyes.
10 People jeer and laugh at me.
They slap my cheek in contempt.
A mob gathers against me.
11 God has handed me over to sinners.
He has tossed me into the hands of the
wicked.

12 "I was living quietly until he shattered me.
He took me by the neck and broke me in
pieces.
Then he set me up as his target,
13 and now his archers surround me.
His arrows pierce me without mercy.
The ground is wet with my blood.*
14 Again and again he smashes against me,
charging at me like a warrior.
15 I wear burlap to show my grief.
My pride lies in the dust.
16 My eyes are red with weeping;
dark shadows circle my eyes.

15:23 Greek version reads *He is appointed to be food for a vulture.* **16:13** Hebrew *my gall.*

---

retribution visited upon the wicked has been observed by Eliphaz and passed on by the sages. The assumption is that Job will receive the same retribution if he does not turn from his current mode of thought.

16:1—17:16 Miserable Comforters. Job's second response to Eliphaz is one long lament, containing three themes: a lament of his current distress, the lament against the enemies, and the lament against God. **16:7–14:** Job understands God to be the one attacking him. The imagery created is of an enemy warrior's assault or physical torture. **17:** Despite his sufferings, Job proclaims his innocence.

17 Yet I have done no wrong,
and my prayer is pure.
18 "O earth, do not conceal my blood.
Let it cry out on my behalf.
19 Even now my witness is in heaven.
My advocate is there on high.
20 My friends scorn me,
but I pour out my tears to God.
21 I need someone to mediate between God and me,
as a person mediates between friends.
22 For soon I must go down that road
from which I will never return.

Job Continues to Defend His Innocence

17 1"My spirit is crushed,
and my life is nearly snuffed out.
The grave is ready to receive me.
2 I am surrounded by mockers.
I watch how bitterly they taunt me.

3 "You must defend my innocence, O God,
since no one else will stand up for me.
4 You have closed their minds to understanding,
but do not let them triumph.
5 They betray their friends for their own advantage,
so let their children faint with hunger.

6 "God has made a mockery of me among the people;
they spit in my face.
7 My eyes are swollen with weeping,
and I am but a shadow of my former self.
8 The virtuous are horrified when they see me.
The innocent rise up against the ungodly.
9 The righteous keep moving forward,
and those with clean hands become stronger and stronger.

10 "As for all of you, come back with a better argument,
though I still won't find a wise man among you.
11 My days are over.
My hopes have disappeared.
My heart's desires are broken.
12 These men say that night is day;
they claim that the darkness is light.
13 What if I go to the grave*
and make my bed in darkness?
14 What if I call the grave my father,
and the maggot my mother or my sister?
15 Where then is my hope?
Can anyone find it?
16 No, my hope will go down with me to the grave.
We will rest together in the dust!"

Bildad's Second Response to Job

18 Then Bildad the Shuhite replied:
2 "How long before you stop talking?
Speak sense if you want us to answer!
3 Do you think we are mere animals?
Do you think we are stupid?
4 You may tear out your hair in anger,
but will that destroy the earth?
Will it make the rocks tremble?

5 "Surely the light of the wicked will be snuffed out.
The sparks of their fire will not glow.
6 The light in their tent will grow dark.
The lamp hanging above them will be quenched.
7 The confident stride of the wicked will be shortened.
Their own schemes will be their downfall.
8 The wicked walk into a net.
They fall into a pit.
9 A trap grabs them by the heel.
A snare holds them tight.
10 A noose lies hidden on the ground.
A rope is stretched across their path.

11 "Terrors surround the wicked
and trouble them at every step.
12 Hunger depletes their strength,
and calamity waits for them to stumble.
13 Disease eats their skin;
death devours their limbs.

17:13 Hebrew *to Sheol;* also in 17:16.

18: This verse is a powerful allusion to the blood of Abel crying from the ground against Cain (Gen 4:10–11). **19–22:** The imagery is typical for the laments and reflects the manifestation of the doctrine of retributive justice. Anyone who has fallen from blessing, as Job has, was thought to have committed some heinous sin against God. Consequently the community would have ostracized him.

18:1–21 The Extent of Retribution. Bildad's second speech picks up where Eliphaz left off. He accuses Job of giving his lament too much importance and ignoring what is obvious to everyone but Job: Job's suffering stems from wickedness.

14 They are torn from the security of their
homes
and are brought down to the king of
terrors.
15 The homes of the wicked will burn down;
burning sulfur rains on their houses.
16 Their roots will dry up,
and their branches will wither.
17 All memory of their existence will fade from
the earth;
no one will remember their names.
18 They will be thrust from light into darkness,
driven from the world.
19 They will have neither children nor
grandchildren,
nor any survivor in the place where they
lived.
20 People in the west are appalled at their fate;
people in the east are horrified.
21 They will say, 'This was the home of a wicked
person,
the place of one who rejected God.' "

Job's Sixth Speech: A Response to Bildad

19 Then Job spoke again:

2 "How long will you torture me?
How long will you try to crush me with
your words?
3 You have already insulted me ten times.
You should be ashamed of treating me so
badly.
4 Even if I have sinned,
that is my concern, not yours.
5 You think you're better than I am,
using my humiliation as evidence of my
sin.
6 But it is God who has wronged me,
capturing me in his net.*

7 "I cry out, 'Help!' but no one answers me.
I protest, but there is no justice.
8 God has blocked my way so I cannot move.
He has plunged my path into darkness.
9 He has stripped me of my honor
and removed the crown from my head.
10 He has demolished me on every side, and I
am finished.
He has uprooted my hope like a fallen tree.
11 His fury burns against me;
he counts me as an enemy.
12 His troops advance.
They build up roads to attack me.
They camp all around my tent.

13 "My relatives stay far away,
and my friends have turned against me.
14 My family is gone,
and my close friends have forgotten me.
15 My servants and maids consider me a
stranger.
I am like a foreigner to them.
16 When I call my servant, he doesn't come;
I have to plead with him!
17 My breath is repulsive to my wife.
I am rejected by my own family.
18 Even young children despise me.
When I stand to speak, they turn their
backs on me.
19 My close friends detest me.
Those I loved have turned against me.
20 I have been reduced to skin and bones
and have escaped death by the skin of my
teeth.

21 "Have mercy on me, my friends, have mercy,
for the hand of God has struck me.
22 Must you also persecute me, like God does?
Haven't you chewed me up enough?

23 "Oh, that my words could be recorded.
Oh, that they could be inscribed on a
monument,
24 carved with an iron chisel and filled with lead,
engraved forever in the rock.

25 "But as for me, I know that my Redeemer
lives,
and he will stand upon the earth at last.
26 And after my body has decayed,
yet in my body I will see God!*
27 I will see him for myself.

19:6 Or *for I am like a city under siege.* **19:26** Or *without my body I will see God!* The meaning of the Hebrew is uncertain.

19:1–29 Plea for Vindication. The intensity of Job's speech toward his friends is heightened, and he speaks with a new confidence. **4:** *Even if I have sinned*: This is not a confession of sin (cf. 9:21; 10:7; 16:17) but a statement to suggest that the friends' judgment is inappropriate. If Job has sinned that is between him and God. **25:** *Redeemer*: All that is certain is that Job expresses trust in some sort of redeemer (a better translation would be "vindicator"). The Hebrew word refers to a member of one's family who will vindicate one's honor or take care of one's debts (e.g., Lev 25:25; Deut 25:5–10; Ruth 2:20). That person's identity in this text is unclear. But Job is convinced he will be vindicated before

Yes, I will see him with my own eyes.
I am overwhelmed at the thought!

28 "How dare you go on persecuting me,
saying, 'It's his own fault'?
29 You should fear punishment yourselves,
for your attitude deserves punishment.
Then you will know that there is indeed a judgment."

Zophar's Second Response to Job

20 Then Zophar the Naamathite replied:

2 "I must reply
because I am greatly disturbed.
3 I've had to endure your insults,
but now my spirit prompts me to reply.

4 "Don't you realize that from the beginning of time,
ever since people were first placed on the earth,
5 the triumph of the wicked has been short lived
and the joy of the godless has been only temporary?
6 Though the pride of the godless reaches to the heavens
and their heads touch the clouds,
7 yet they will vanish forever,
thrown away like their own dung.
Those who knew them will ask,
'Where are they?'
8 They will fade like a dream and not be found.
They will vanish like a vision in the night.
9 Those who once saw them will see them no more.
Their families will never see them again.
10 Their children will beg from the poor,
for they must give back their stolen riches.
11 Though they are young,
their bones will lie in the dust.

12 "They enjoyed the sweet taste of wickedness,
letting it melt under their tongue.
13 They savored it,
holding it long in their mouths.
14 But suddenly the food in their bellies turns sour,
a poisonous venom in their stomach.
15 They will vomit the wealth they swallowed.
God won't let them keep it down.
16 They will suck the poison of cobras.
The viper will kill them.
17 They will never again enjoy streams of olive oil
or rivers of milk and honey.
18 They will give back everything they worked for.
Their wealth will bring them no joy.
19 For they oppressed the poor and left them destitute.
They foreclosed on their homes.
20 They were always greedy and never satisfied.
Nothing remains of all the things they dreamed about.
21 Nothing is left after they finish gorging themselves.
Therefore, their prosperity will not endure.

22 "In the midst of plenty, they will run into trouble
and be overcome by misery.
23 May God give them a bellyful of trouble.
May God rain down his anger upon them.
24 When they try to escape an iron weapon,
a bronze-tipped arrow will pierce them.
25 The arrow is pulled from their back,
and the arrowhead glistens with blood.*
The terrors of death are upon them.
26 Their treasures will be thrown into deepest darkness.
A wildfire will devour their goods,
consuming all they have left.
27 The heavens will reveal their guilt,
and the earth will testify against them.
28 A flood will sweep away their house.
God's anger will descend on them in torrents.
29 This is the reward that God gives the wicked.
It is the inheritance decreed by God."

20:25 Hebrew *with gall.*

God. **26–27:** This section could be read in such a way as to suggest the idea of resurrection. But the doctrine of resurrection appears quite late in Hebrew thought (cf. Dan 12:1–3) and is not mentioned anywhere else in Job. What is clear is that Job expects to be vindicated in the presence of God, a foreshadowing of the coming theophany (chapters 38—42). Job threatens his friends by suggesting that they will face retribution if they persist in their false accusations against him.

20:1–29 Fate of the Wicked. Zophar gives yet another dogmatic rendition of the fate of the wicked. The only thing new is the concession that the wicked may have prosperity for a time, but it will not endure. This is probably another jab at Job.

Job's Seventh Speech: A Response to Zophar

21 Then Job spoke again:
2 "Listen closely to what I am saying.
That's one consolation you can give me.
3 Bear with me, and let me speak.
After I have spoken, you may resume mocking me.

4 "My complaint is with God, not with people.
I have good reason to be so impatient.
5 Look at me and be stunned.
Put your hand over your mouth in shock.
6 When I think about what I am saying, I shudder.
My body trembles.

7 "Why do the wicked prosper,
growing old and powerful?
8 They live to see their children grow up and settle down,
and they enjoy their grandchildren.
9 Their homes are safe from every fear,
and God does not punish them.
10 Their bulls never fail to breed.
Their cows bear calves and never miscarry.
11 They let their children frisk about like lambs.
Their little ones skip and dance.
12 They sing with tambourine and harp.
They celebrate to the sound of the flute.
13 They spend their days in prosperity,
then go down to the grave* in peace.
14 And yet they say to God, 'Go away.
We want no part of you and your ways.
15 Who is the Almighty, and why should we obey him?
What good will it do us to pray?'
16 (They think their prosperity is of their own doing,
but I will have nothing to do with that kind of thinking.)

17 "Yet the light of the wicked never seems to be extinguished.
Do they ever have trouble?
Does God distribute sorrows to them in anger?
18 Are they driven before the wind like straw?
Are they carried away by the storm like chaff?
Not at all!

19 " 'Well,' you say, 'at least God will punish their children!'
But I say he should punish the ones who sin,
so that they understand his judgment.
20 Let them see their destruction with their own eyes.
Let them drink deeply of the anger of the Almighty.
21 For they will not care what happens to their family
after they are dead.

22 "But who can teach a lesson to God,
since he judges even the most powerful?
23 One person dies in prosperity,
completely comfortable and secure,
24 the picture of good health,
vigorous and fit.
25 Another person dies in bitter poverty,
never having tasted the good life.
26 But both are buried in the same dust,
both eaten by the same maggots.

27 "Look, I know what you're thinking.
I know the schemes you plot against me.
28 You will tell me of rich and wicked people
whose houses have vanished because of their sins.
29 But ask those who have been around,
and they will tell you the truth.
30 Evil people are spared in times of calamity
and are allowed to escape disaster.
31 No one criticizes them openly

21:13 Hebrew *to Sheol.*

21:1–34 Complaints about the Wicked. Job's conclusions depart so radically from traditional teachings that they probably should be classified as complaints. Job concludes that the wicked remain unpunished by God even though they renounce God; the traditional belief that the sins of the fathers are visited on the children is untrue; and the righteous and wicked alike die and are covered by worms. The friends' traditional doctrines on the fate of the wicked are, according to Job, flat-out wrong.

In this discourse cycle Job has made considerable movement theologically. In chapters 16—17 he insisted that God be held accountable. In chapter 19 Job no longer holds to the pretense of respectful, cordial theological debate but ironically shames the behavior of his three friends instead of proclaiming his own shame. Here, Job has recast the image of the fate of the wicked as he insists that they remain unpunished by God though they renounce God. His complaints against God's neglect in this area are a prophetic reminder to all humanity of injustices served and experienced.

or pays them back for what they have
done.
[32] When they are carried to the grave,
an honor guard keeps watch at their tomb.
[33] A great funeral procession goes to the
cemetery.
Many pay their respects as the body is laid
to rest,
and the earth gives sweet repose.

[34] "How can your empty clichés comfort me?
All your explanations are lies!"

Eliphaz's Third Response to Job

22 Then Eliphaz the Temanite replied:
[2] "Can a person do anything to help
God?
Can even a wise person be helpful to him?
[3] Is it any advantage to the Almighty if you are
righteous?
Would it be any gain to him if you were
perfect?
[4] Is it because you're so pious that he accuses
you
and brings judgment against you?
[5] No, it's because of your wickedness!
There's no limit to your sins.

[6] "For example, you must have lent money to
your friend
and demanded clothing as security.
Yes, you stripped him to the bone.
[7] You must have refused water for the thirsty
and food for the hungry.
[8] You probably think the land belongs to the
powerful
and only the privileged have a right to it!
[9] You must have sent widows away
empty-handed
and crushed the hopes of orphans.
[10] That is why you are surrounded by traps
and tremble from sudden fears.
[11] That is why you cannot see in the darkness,
and waves of water cover you.

[12] "God is so great—higher than the heavens,
higher than the farthest stars.
[13] But you reply, 'That's why God can't see what
I am doing!
How can he judge through the thick
darkness?
[14] For thick clouds swirl about him, and he
cannot see us.
He is way up there, walking on the vault of
heaven.'

[15] "Will you continue on the old paths
where evil people have walked?
[16] They were snatched away in the prime of
life,
the foundations of their lives washed away.
[17] For they said to God, 'Leave us alone!
What can the Almighty do to us?'
[18] Yet he was the one who filled their homes
with good things,
so I will have nothing to do with that kind
of thinking.

[19] "The righteous will be happy to see the
wicked destroyed,
and the innocent will laugh in contempt.
[20] They will say, 'See how our enemies have
been destroyed.

22:1—31:40 Third Discourse Cycle

In this discourse cycle Job and his friends have become rigid in their stances. As a result, their speech is extremely candid and confident. The friends, with the exception of Zophar, attribute the characteristics of the wicked to Job. In response Job proclaims his innocence all the more and accuses God of neglecting the poor. In chapters 22—27, textual damage makes it impossible to attribute all the speeches to their proper speaker with certainty. Several passages seem to be out of place or attributed to the wrong person: 24:18–25 is attributed to Job but probably best suits Zophar; 26:1–4, which belongs to Job, seems to be inserted into a speech of Bildad (25:1–6 and 26:5–14); 27:13–24 occurs in a speech of Job but is only appropriate to one of the friends. Job's speech in 26:1–4 prefaces his speech in 27:2–12; 27:13–23 may belong to Zophar. See the annotations in each instance for additional discussion.

22:1–30 A List of Accusations. Eliphaz brings his strongest accusations against Job. His assumption throughout is that Job has sinned. He begins by noting that no humans, not even the wisest, are of use to God. **4:** To this rhetorical question, the reader knows the answer is "Yes." **6–11:** The ensuing inventory of iniquities that Eliphaz attributes to Job reflects the Israelite ethic. One who is righteous and in good standing in the community would respond in a positive manner when confronted with each of the needs listed. **12–20:** All of these accusations are made in an effort to persuade Job to remove his unrighteousness and return to God. Eliphaz concludes with assurances that God will be faithful to forgive and restore if Job will only humble himself.

The last of them have been consumed in
the fire.'

21 "Submit to God, and you will have peace;
then things will go well for you.
22 Listen to his instructions,
and store them in your heart.
23 If you return to the Almighty, you will be
restored—
so clean up your life.
24 If you give up your lust for money
and throw your precious gold into the
river,
25 the Almighty himself will be your treasure.
He will be your precious silver!

26 "Then you will take delight in the Almighty
and look up to God.
27 You will pray to him, and he will hear you,
and you will fulfill your vows to him.
28 You will succeed in whatever you choose
to do,
and light will shine on the road ahead of
you.
29 If people are in trouble and you say, 'Help
them,'
God will save them.
30 Even sinners will be rescued;
they will be rescued because your hands
are pure."

Job's Eighth Speech: A Response to Eliphaz

23 Then Job spoke again:

2 "My complaint today is still a bitter
one,
and I try hard not to groan aloud.
3 If only I knew where to find God,
I would go to his court.
4 I would lay out my case
and present my arguments.
5 Then I would listen to his reply
and understand what he says to me.
6 Would he use his great power to argue with
me?
No, he would give me a fair hearing.
7 Honest people can reason with him,
so I would be forever acquitted by my
judge.
8 I go east, but he is not there.
I go west, but I cannot find him.
9 I do not see him in the north, for he is
hidden.
I look to the south, but he is concealed.

10 "But he knows where I am going.
And when he tests me, I will come out as
pure as gold.
11 For I have stayed on God's paths;
I have followed his ways and not turned
aside.
12 I have not departed from his commands,
but have treasured his words more than
daily food.
13 But once he has made his decision, who can
change his mind?
Whatever he wants to do, he does.
14 So he will do to me whatever he has planned.
He controls my destiny.
15 No wonder I am so terrified in his presence.
When I think of it, terror grips me.
16 God has made me sick at heart;
the Almighty has terrified me.
17 Darkness is all around me;
thick, impenetrable darkness is
everywhere.

Job Asks Why the Wicked Are Not Punished

24 1 "Why doesn't the Almighty bring
the wicked to judgment?
Why must the godly wait for him
in vain?

23:1—24:25 A Turning Point. This is the third time Job has requested a hearing before God (cf. 9:32–34; 13:20–22), and unlike the others, this time Job is convinced that he would be acquitted. But, he concludes, God is nowhere to be found. **23:12–15:** As Job contemplates an encounter with God his focus turns to his continual commitment and devotion to the law, which stands in sharp contrast to God's plans for harm. Job restates his fear of entering God's presence (cf. chap. 13). However, this time Job's confidence in his innocence seemingly overcomes his fear of God. **24:1–17:** Job accuses God of ignoring the prayers of the poor who have been victimized by the wicked. He emphasizes the heinous acts of the wicked against the widow, the orphan, and the needy. While this catalogue of sins stands in parallel to that cited by Eliphaz against Job, this time Job brings the accusation against God. Job suggests the wicked go unpunished for their crimes, while the prayers of the poor for deliverance are ignored. Job is no longer focused solely on his plight and no longer views poverty as a punishment from God for sins committed. Instead he accuses God of ignoring the atrocities that the poor suffer at the hands of the wicked. Although Job has noted several times (e.g., chap. 21) that the wicked go unpunished, this is Job's first acknowledg-

2 Evil people steal land by moving the boundary markers.
They steal livestock and put them in their own pastures.
3 They take the orphan's donkey
and demand the widow's ox as security for a loan.
4 The poor are pushed off the path;
the needy must hide together for safety.
5 Like wild donkeys in the wilderness,
the poor must spend all their time looking for food,
searching even in the desert for food for their children.
6 They harvest a field they do not own,
and they glean in the vineyards of the wicked.
7 All night they lie naked in the cold,
without clothing or covering.
8 They are soaked by mountain showers,
and they huddle against the rocks for want of a home.

9 "The wicked snatch a widow's child from her breast,
taking the baby as security for a loan.
10 The poor must go about naked, without any clothing.
They harvest food for others while they themselves are starving.
11 They press out olive oil without being allowed to taste it,
and they tread in the winepress as they suffer from thirst.
12 The groans of the dying rise from the city,
and the wounded cry for help,
yet God ignores their moaning.

13 "Wicked people rebel against the light.
They refuse to acknowledge its ways
or stay in its paths.
14 The murderer rises in the early dawn
to kill the poor and needy;
at night he is a thief.
15 The adulterer waits for the twilight,
saying, 'No one will see me then.'
He hides his face so no one will know him.
16 Thieves break into houses at night
and sleep in the daytime.
They are not acquainted with the light.
17 The black night is their morning.
They ally themselves with the terrors of the darkness.

18 "But they disappear like foam down a river.
Everything they own is cursed,
and they are afraid to enter their own vineyards.
19 The grave* consumes sinners
just as drought and heat consume snow.
20 Their own mothers will forget them.
Maggots will find them sweet to eat.
No one will remember them.
Wicked people are broken like a tree in the storm.
21 They cheat the woman who has no son to help her.
They refuse to help the needy widow.

22 "God, in his power, drags away the rich.
They may rise high, but they have no assurance of life.
23 They may be allowed to live in security,
but God is always watching them.
24 And though they are great now,
in a moment they will be gone like all others,
cut off like heads of grain.
25 Can anyone claim otherwise?
Who can prove me wrong?"

Bildad's Third Response to Job

25 Then Bildad the Shuhite replied:
2 "God is powerful and dreadful.
He enforces peace in the heavens.
3 Who is able to count his heavenly army?
Doesn't his light shine on all the earth?

24:19 Hebrew *Sheol.*

ment that the poor suffer unjustly. It is therefore a significant turning point in the dialogue. **18–25:** These verses reflect dialogue we are accustomed to hearing from the friends rather than Job. Some scholars suggest the verses are out of place (see annotation on 22:1—31:40). Others suggest the verses should be understood as if Job were quoting the three friends. If we attribute these words against the wicked to Job his discourse appears to be schizophrenic. They could be read, however, as Job's resistance to the severe accusations he has just made. If these are Job's words, then he continues to struggle with the doctrine of divine retributive justice in that he cannot give up the hope that one day the balances will be evened out. Even if this is the case, the traditional dogma has still been significantly altered in that the present-day poor are viewed in a new way, as are the prosperous.

25:1–6 No One Righteous. Bildad's final speech (possibly continued in 26:5–14) is unusually biting.

4 How can a mortal be innocent before God?
Can anyone born of a woman be pure?
5 God is more glorious than the moon;
he shines brighter than the stars.
6 In comparison, people are maggots;
we mortals are mere worms."

Job's Ninth Speech: A Response to Bildad

26 Then Job spoke again:
2 "How you have helped the powerless!
How you have saved the weak!
3 How you have enlightened my stupidity!
What wise advice you have offered!
4 Where have you gotten all these wise sayings?
Whose spirit speaks through you?

5 "The dead tremble—
those who live beneath the waters.
6 The underworld* is naked in God's presence.
The place of destruction* is uncovered.
7 God stretches the northern sky over empty space
and hangs the earth on nothing.
8 He wraps the rain in his thick clouds,
and the clouds don't burst with the weight.
9 He covers the face of the moon,*
shrouding it with his clouds.
10 He created the horizon when he separated the waters;
he set the boundary between day and night.
11 The foundations of heaven tremble;
they shudder at his rebuke.
12 By his power the sea grew calm.
By his skill he crushed the great sea monster.*
13 His Spirit made the heavens beautiful,
and his power pierced the gliding serpent.
14 These are just the beginning of all that he does,
merely a whisper of his power.
Who, then, can comprehend the thunder of his power?"

Job's Final Speech

27 Job continued speaking:
2 "I vow by the living God, who has taken away my rights,
by the Almighty who has embittered my soul—
3 As long as I live,
while I have breath from God,
4 my lips will speak no evil,
and my tongue will speak no lies.
5 I will never concede that you are right;
I will defend my integrity until I die.
6 I will maintain my innocence without wavering.
My conscience is clear for as long as I live.

7 "May my enemy be punished like the wicked,
my adversary like those who do evil.
8 For what hope do the godless have when God cuts them off
and takes away their life?
9 Will God listen to their cry
when trouble comes upon them?
10 Can they take delight in the Almighty?
Can they call to God at any time?
11 I will teach you about God's power.

26:6a Hebrew *Sheol.* **26:6b** Hebrew *Abaddon.* **26:9** Or *covers his throne.* **26:12** Hebrew *Rahab,* the name of a mythical sea monster that represents chaos in ancient literature.

He establishes God's power and might in contrast to a mere mortal. He no longer focuses his attention solely on Job but states that no one can be righteous before God, for human beings are weak and nothing more than worms. A similar theme has been established elsewhere by Eliphaz (cf. 4:17–21; 15:14–26), Zophar (cf. 11:5–12) and Job (cf. 9:2–12; 12:9–25; 14:4), but Bildad portrays a God so powerful and splendid that all else is nothing.

26:1—27:23 The Omnipotence of God. Building off Bildad's power motif, Job's sarcastic response is filled with the same. Job accuses Bildad of speaking the words of a spirit he does not recognize, possibly an evil one. **26:5–14:** These verses proclaim the omnipotence of God in a hymn, and their form matches that of Bildad's preceding speech. Many interpreters have suggested this section should be attached to the end of Bildad's speech. However, they also fit with Job's discourse as a transition from his caustic remarks against Bildad's lack of power and wisdom to his commitment to hold fast to his righteousness (i.e., innocence; 27:6). If Job's, the hymn reveals his agreement with the doctrine of an all-powerful God, but its juxtaposition to 27:1–6 shows his disagreement with Bildad's worm theology. If Job is innocent, then humans have the capacity to be more than worms. **27:2–6:** Job's disagreement with Bildad's doctrine is so intense that he introduces his restatements of innocence with an oath. **7–12:** Job makes statements of ill will against his friends, whom he now calls his enemies, for the first time since the

I will not conceal anything concerning the
Almighty.
12 But you have seen all this,
yet you say all these useless things to me.

13 "This is what the wicked will receive from
God;
this is their inheritance from the Almighty.
14 They may have many children,
but the children will die in war or starve to
death.
15 Those who survive will die of a plague,
and not even their widows will mourn
them.

16 "Evil people may have piles of money
and may store away mounds of clothing.
17 But the righteous will wear that clothing,
and the innocent will divide that money.
18 The wicked build houses as fragile as a
spider's web,*
as flimsy as a shelter made of branches.
19 The wicked go to bed rich
but wake to find that all their wealth is
gone.
20 Terror overwhelms them like a flood,
and they are blown away in the storms of
the night.
21 The east wind carries them away, and they
are gone.
It sweeps them away.
22 It whirls down on them without mercy.
They struggle to flee from its power.
23 But everyone jeers at them
and mocks them.

Job Speaks of Wisdom and Understanding

28 1 "People know where to mine silver
and how to refine gold.
2 They know where to dig iron from
the earth
and how to smelt copper from rock.
3 They know how to shine light in the darkness
and explore the farthest regions of the
earth
as they search in the dark for ore.
4 They sink a mine shaft into the earth
far from where anyone lives.
They descend on ropes, swinging back and
forth.
5 Food is grown on the earth above,
but down below, the earth is melted as by
fire.
6 Here the rocks contain precious lapis lazuli,
and the dust contains gold.
7 These are treasures no bird of prey can see,
no falcon's eye observe.
8 No wild animal has walked upon these
treasures;
no lion has ever set his paw there.
9 People know how to tear apart flinty rocks
and overturn the roots of mountains.
10 They cut tunnels in the rocks
and uncover precious stones.
11 They dam up the trickling streams
and bring to light the hidden treasures.

12 "But do people know where to find wisdom?
Where can they find understanding?
13 No one knows where to find it,
for it is not found among the living.
14 'It is not here,' says the ocean.
'Nor is it here,' says the sea.
15 It cannot be bought with gold.
It cannot be purchased with silver.
16 It's worth more than all the gold of Ophir,
greater than precious onyx or lapis lazuli.
17 Wisdom is more valuable than gold and
crystal.
It cannot be purchased with jewels
mounted in fine gold.
18 Coral and jasper are worthless in trying to
get it.

27:18 As in Greek and Syriac versions (see also 8:14); Hebrew reads *a moth.*

---

dialogues began. **13–23:** Again, many scholars have suggested these verses are the lost speech of Zophar, since the view of the wicked found in this discourse conflicts with Job's earlier comment that the wicked are not punished (cf. 21:7–34; 24:2–17). However, such a view does not take into account the possibility of fluctuating human emotions. Job's statements in chapters 21 and 24 are extreme and might best be understood as reactionary complaints. Total rejection of the doctrine of retributive justice would not allow Job to have any hope for the poor. Consequently it does not seem out of place for Job to swing back to a more moderate position. If our current text is read as an imprecation against Job's enemies, it reveals Job's hope that he will eventually be vindicated and his friends proven to be enemies who will experience the consequences they suppose for Job. Job uses their words against them, which is ironic, and by so doing he condemns them to the fate of the wicked they so confidently proclaim.

28:1–28 Wisdom Inaccessible. The emphasis of this lengthy hymn is the inaccessibility of wisdom. While humans have the capacity to find hidden earthly trea-

The price of wisdom is far above rubies.
19 Precious peridot from Ethiopia* cannot be
exchanged for it.
It's worth more than the purest gold.

20 "But do people know where to find wisdom?
Where can they find understanding?
21 It is hidden from the eyes of all humanity.
Even the sharp-eyed birds in the sky
cannot discover it.
22 Destruction* and Death say,
'We've heard only rumors of where
wisdom can be found.'

23 "God alone understands the way to wisdom;
he knows where it can be found,
24 for he looks throughout the whole earth
and sees everything under the heavens.
25 He decided how hard the winds should blow
and how much rain should fall.
26 He made the laws for the rain
and laid out a path for the lightning.
27 Then he saw wisdom and evaluated it.
He set it in place and examined it
thoroughly.
28 And this is what he says to all humanity:
'The fear of the Lord is true wisdom;
to forsake evil is real understanding.' "

Job Speaks of His Former Blessings

29 Job continued speaking:

2 "I long for the years gone by
when God took care of me,
3 when he lit up the way before me
and I walked safely through the darkness.
4 When I was in my prime,
God's friendship was felt in my home.
5 The Almighty was still with me,
and my children were around me.
6 My cows produced milk in abundance,
and my groves poured out streams of olive
oil.

7 "Those were the days when I went to the city
gate
and took my place among the honored
leaders.
8 The young stepped aside when they saw me,
and even the aged rose in respect at my
coming.
9 The princes stood in silence
and put their hands over their mouths.
10 The highest officials of the city stood quietly,
holding their tongues in respect.

11 "All who heard me praised me.
All who saw me spoke well of me.
12 For I assisted the poor in their need
and the orphans who required help.
13 I helped those without hope, and they
blessed me.
And I caused the widows' hearts to sing for
joy.
14 Everything I did was honest.
Righteousness covered me like a robe,
and I wore justice like a turban.
15 I served as eyes for the blind
and feet for the lame.
16 I was a father to the poor
and assisted strangers who needed help.
17 I broke the jaws of godless oppressors
and plucked their victims from their teeth.

18 "I thought, 'Surely I will die surrounded by
my family
after a long, good life.*
19 For I am like a tree whose roots reach the
water,
whose branches are refreshed with the
dew.
20 New honors are constantly bestowed on me,
and my strength is continually renewed.'

21 "Everyone listened to my advice.
They were silent as they waited for me to
speak.
22 And after I spoke, they had nothing to add,
for my counsel satisfied them.

28:19 Hebrew *from Cush.* **28:22** Hebrew *Abaddon.*
29:18 Hebrew *after I have counted my days like sand.*

sures, they are not able to find the greater treasure, wisdom. God, however, sees everything and has *set wisdom in place.* The hymn ends with a traditional idea: The fear of the LORD is wisdom.

29:1—31:40 Request for a Hearing. These chapters contain Job's final arguments. He will not speak again until commanded to do so by God in the closing chapters. Job 29—31 is one long speech that builds rhetorically, incorporating elements typically found in the lament, to Job's final request for a hearing. Job contrasts his happy past with his present distress and delivers his final plea for a hearing heightened by the language of lament throughout. **29:11–17:** Job claims benevolence to the poor, the widow, and the orphan. These claims counter the accusations made against him by Eliphaz (chap. 22) and stand in sharp contrast to the accusations Job makes against God (chap. 24).

23 They longed for me to speak as people long
for rain.
They drank my words like a refreshing
spring rain.
24 When they were discouraged, I smiled at
them.
My look of approval was precious to them.
25 Like a chief, I told them what to do.
I lived like a king among his troops
and comforted those who mourned.

Job Speaks of His Anguish

30 1 "But now I am mocked by people
younger than I,
by young men whose fathers
are not worthy to run with my
sheepdogs.
2 A lot of good they are to me—
those worn-out wretches!
3 They are gaunt with hunger
and flee to the deserts,
to desolate and gloomy wastelands.
4 They pluck wild greens from among the
bushes
and eat from the roots of broom trees.
5 They are driven from human society,
and people shout at them as if they were
thieves.
6 So now they live in frightening ravines,
in caves and among the rocks.
7 They sound like animals howling among the
bushes,
huddled together beneath the nettles.
8 They are nameless fools,
outcasts from society.

9 "And now they mock me with vulgar songs!
They taunt me!
10 They despise me and won't come near me,
except to spit in my face.
11 For God has cut my bowstring.
He has humbled me,
so they have thrown off all restraint.
12 These outcasts oppose me to my face.
They send me sprawling
and lay traps in my path.
13 They block my road
and do everything they can to destroy me.
They know I have no one to help me.
14 They come at me from all directions.
They jump on me when I am down.
15 I live in terror now.
My honor has blown away in the wind,
and my prosperity has vanished like a
cloud.

16 "And now my life seeps away.
Depression haunts my days.
17 At night my bones are filled with pain,
which gnaws at me relentlessly.
18 With a strong hand, God grabs my shirt.
He grips me by the collar of my coat.
19 He has thrown me into the mud.
I'm nothing more than dust and ashes.

20 "I cry to you, O God, but you don't answer.
I stand before you, but you don't even look.
21 You have become cruel toward me.
You use your power to persecute me.
22 You throw me into the whirlwind
and destroy me in the storm.
23 And I know you are sending me to my
death—
the destination of all who live.

24 "Surely no one would turn against the needy
when they cry for help in their trouble.
25 Did I not weep for those in trouble?
Was I not deeply grieved for the needy?
26 So I looked for good, but evil came instead.
I waited for the light, but darkness fell.
27 My heart is troubled and restless.
Days of suffering torment me.
28 I walk in gloom, without sunlight.
I stand in the public square and cry for help.
29 Instead, I am considered a brother to jackals
and a companion to owls.
30 My skin has turned dark,
and my bones burn with fever.
31 My harp plays sad music,
and my flute accompanies those who weep.

Job's Final Protest of Innocence

31 1 "I made a covenant with my eyes
not to look with lust at a young
woman.
2 For what has God above chosen for us?
What is our inheritance from the Almighty
on high?
3 Isn't it calamity for the wicked
and misfortune for those who do evil?
4 Doesn't he see everything I do
and every step I take?

5 "Have I lied to anyone
or deceived anyone?

31:1–40: Job makes numerous oath statements, each one expressing his conviction of his own innocence. By the close of this discourse cycle Job's confidence in his vindication before God overshadows any fears

[6] Let God weigh me on the scales of justice,
for he knows my integrity.
[7] If I have strayed from his pathway,
or if my heart has lusted for what my eyes have seen,
or if I am guilty of any other sin,
[8] then let someone else eat the crops I have planted.
Let all that I have planted be uprooted.

[9] "If my heart has been seduced by a woman,
or if I have lusted for my neighbor's wife,
[10] then let my wife belong to* another man;
let other men sleep with her.
[11] For lust is a shameful sin,
a crime that should be punished.
[12] It is a fire that burns all the way to hell.*
It would wipe out everything I own.

[13] "If I have been unfair to my male or female servants
when they brought their complaints to me,
[14] how could I face God?
What could I say when he questioned me?
[15] For God created both me and my servants.
He created us both in the womb.

[16] "Have I refused to help the poor,
or crushed the hopes of widows?
[17] Have I been stingy with my food
and refused to share it with orphans?
[18] No, from childhood I have cared for orphans like a father,
and all my life I have cared for widows.
[19] Whenever I saw the homeless without clothes
and the needy with nothing to wear,
[20] did they not praise me
for providing wool clothing to keep them warm?

[21] "If I raised my hand against an orphan,
knowing the judges would take my side,
[22] then let my shoulder be wrenched out of place!
Let my arm be torn from its socket!
[23] That would be better than facing God's judgment.
For if the majesty of God opposes me, what hope is there?

[24] "Have I put my trust in money
or felt secure because of my gold?
[25] Have I gloated about my wealth
and all that I own?

[26] "Have I looked at the sun shining in the skies,
or the moon walking down its silver pathway,
[27] and been secretly enticed in my heart
to throw kisses at them in worship?
[28] If so, I should be punished by the judges,
for it would mean I had denied the God of heaven.

[29] "Have I ever rejoiced when disaster struck my enemies,
or become excited when harm came their way?
[30] No, I have never sinned by cursing anyone
or by asking for revenge.

[31] "My servants have never said,
'He let others go hungry.'
[32] I have never turned away a stranger
but have opened my doors to everyone.

[33] "Have I tried to hide my sins like other people do,
concealing my guilt in my heart?
[34] Have I feared the crowd
or the contempt of the masses,
so that I kept quiet and stayed indoors?

[35] "If only someone would listen to me!
Look, I will sign my name to my defense.
Let the Almighty answer me.
Let my accuser write out the charges against me.
[36] I would face the accusation proudly.
I would wear it like a crown.
[37] For I would tell him exactly what I have done.
I would come before him like a prince.

[38] "If my land accuses me
and all its furrows cry out together,
[39] or if I have stolen its crops
or murdered its owners,
[40] then let thistles grow on that land instead of wheat,
and weeds instead of barley."

Job's words are ended.

31:10 Hebrew *grind for.* **31:12** Hebrew *to Abaddon.*

he may have had (cf. chaps. 13; 23). **35–37:** Again, Job requests a hearing before God that he might hear the charges against him and prove his innocence.

Elihu Responds to Job's Friends

32 Job's three friends refused to reply further to him because he kept insisting on his innocence.

[2]Then Elihu son of Barakel the Buzite, of the
clan of Ram, became angry. He was angry because Job refused to admit that he had sinned
and that God was right in punishing him. [3]He
was also angry with Job's three friends, for they
made God* appear to be wrong by their inability to answer Job's arguments. [4]Elihu had waited
for the others to speak to Job because they were
older than he. [5]But when he saw that they had
no further reply, he spoke out angrily. [6]Elihu son
of Barakel the Buzite said,

"I am young and you are old,
so I held back from telling you what I think.
7 I thought, 'Those who are older should speak,
for wisdom comes with age.'
8 But there is a spirit* within people,
the breath of the Almighty within them,
that makes them intelligent.
9 Sometimes the elders are not wise.
Sometimes the aged do not understand justice.
10 So listen to me,
and let me tell you what I think.

11 "I have waited all this time,
listening very carefully to your arguments,
listening to you grope for words.
12 I have listened,
but not one of you has refuted Job
or answered his arguments.
13 And don't tell me, 'He is too wise for us.
Only God can convince him.'
14 If Job had been arguing with me,
I would not answer with your kind of logic!
15 You sit there baffled,
with nothing more to say.
16 Should I continue to wait, now that you are silent?
Must I also remain silent?
17 No, I will say my piece.
I will speak my mind.
18 For I am full of pent-up words,
and the spirit within me urges me on.
19 I am like a cask of wine without a vent,
like a new wineskin ready to burst!
20 I must speak to find relief,
so let me give my answers.
21 I won't play favorites
or try to flatter anyone.
22 For if I tried flattery,
my Creator would soon destroy me.

Elihu Presents His Case against Job

33 1"Listen to my words, Job;
pay attention to what I have to say.
2 Now that I have begun to speak,
let me continue.
3 I speak with all sincerity;
I speak the truth.
4 For the Spirit of God has made me,
and the breath of the Almighty gives me life.
5 Answer me, if you can;
make your case and take your stand.
6 Look, you and I both belong to God.

32:3 As in ancient Hebrew scribal tradition; the Masoretic Text reads *Job*. **32:8** Or *Spirit;* also in 32:18.

32:1—37:24 Discourses of Elihu

Because of the style and language (there are many Aramaic words) and the seemingly interruptive nature of Elihu's discourses, many scholars suggest that they were written by another author. However, there is no textual evidence to suggest that the book ever existed without these chapters. Thus we will read them as a critical part of the whole and determine their contribution. **32:1–22:** A narrative introduction to Elihu's four discourses. In the first five verses the narrator gives us critical information for understanding this discourse. According to the narrator the three friends cease to speak because Job *kept insisting on his innocence* (i.e., he was self-righteous). The narrator makes much of the fact that Elihu has become angry because Job has sought to justify himself rather than God and because the three friends have found no answer. Also highlighted is the fact that Elihu has waited to speak because the friends are older and supposedly wiser. His dismissal of his elders makes him appear not wiser than they, but less wise. **33:1–33:** Elihu's wisdom is also grounded in the doctrine of divine retributive justice. He makes the simple argument that God is greater than any mortal and therefore challenges Job's right to contend against God. He suggests that God answers humans through dreams and by chastening them with suffering. He even suggests that an angelic mediator may offer a ransom so healing can occur, but this will happen only after a confession of sin. Therefore, Job's

I, too, was formed from clay.
7 So you don't need to be afraid of me.
I won't come down hard on you.

8 "You have spoken in my hearing,
and I have heard your very words.
9 You said, 'I am pure; I am without sin;
I am innocent; I have no guilt.
10 God is picking a quarrel with me,
and he considers me his enemy.
11 He puts my feet in the stocks
and watches my every move.'

12 "But you are wrong, and I will show you why.
For God is greater than any human being.
13 So why are you bringing a charge against him?
Why say he does not respond to people's complaints?
14 For God speaks again and again,
though people do not recognize it.
15 He speaks in dreams, in visions of the night,
when deep sleep falls on people
as they lie in their beds.
16 He whispers in their ears
and terrifies them with warnings.
17 He makes them turn from doing wrong;
he keeps them from pride.
18 He protects them from the grave,
from crossing over the river of death.

19 "Or God disciplines people with pain on their sickbeds,
with ceaseless aching in their bones.
20 They lose their appetite
for even the most delicious food.
21 Their flesh wastes away,
and their bones stick out.
22 They are at death's door;
the angels of death wait for them.

23 "But if an angel from heaven appears—
a special messenger to intercede for a person
and declare that he is upright—
24 he will be gracious and say,
'Rescue him from the grave,
for I have found a ransom for his life.'
25 Then his body will become as healthy as a child's,
firm and youthful again.
26 When he prays to God,
he will be accepted.
And God will receive him with joy
and restore him to good standing.
27 He will declare to his friends,
'I sinned and twisted the truth,
but it was not worth it.*
28 God rescued me from the grave,
and now my life is filled with light.'

29 "Yes, God does these things
again and again for people.
30 He rescues them from the grave
so they may enjoy the light of life.
31 Mark this well, Job. Listen to me,
for I have more to say.
32 But if you have anything to say, go ahead.
Speak, for I am anxious to see you justified.
33 But if not, then listen to me.
Keep silent and I will teach you wisdom!"

Elihu Accuses Job of Arrogance

34 Then Elihu said:
2 "Listen to me, you wise men.
Pay attention, you who have knowledge.
3 Job said, 'The ear tests the words it hears
just as the mouth distinguishes between foods.'
4 So let us discern for ourselves what is right;
let us learn together what is good.
5 For Job also said, 'I am innocent,
but God has taken away my rights.
6 I am innocent, but they call me a liar.
My suffering is incurable, though I have not sinned.'

7 "Tell me, has there ever been a man like Job,
with his thirst for irreverent talk?
8 He chooses evil people as companions.
He spends his time with wicked men.
9 He has even said, 'Why waste time
trying to please God?'

10 "Listen to me, you who have understanding.
Everyone knows that God doesn't sin!
The Almighty can do no wrong.

33:27 Greek version reads *but he* [God] *did not punish me as my sin deserved.*

suffering is the answer from God he has sought. **34:1–37:** The doctrine is so solidified in Elihu's mind that one ought not even question it but assume that one's pain is directly related to one's sin, since God cannot do wickedness and will not pervert justice. He concludes that Job speaks without knowledge and wishes for him to be tried to the limit. Job speaks as a wicked one and adds rebel-

[11] He repays people according to their deeds.
He treats people as they deserve.
[12] Truly, God will not do wrong.
The Almighty will not twist justice.
[13] Did someone else put the world in his care?
Who set the whole world in place?
[14] If God were to take back his spirit
and withdraw his breath,
[15] all life would cease,
and humanity would turn again to dust.

[16] "Now listen to me if you are wise.
Pay attention to what I say.
[17] Could God govern if he hated justice?
Are you going to condemn the almighty judge?
[18] For he says to kings, 'You are wicked,'
and to nobles, 'You are unjust.'
[19] He doesn't care how great a person may be,
and he pays no more attention to the rich than to the poor.
He made them all.
[20] In a moment they die.
In the middle of the night they pass away;
the mighty are removed without human hand.

[21] "For God watches how people live;
he sees everything they do.
[22] No darkness is thick enough
to hide the wicked from his eyes.
[23] We don't set the time
when we will come before God in judgment.
[24] He brings the mighty to ruin without asking anyone,
and he sets up others in their place.
[25] He knows what they do,
and in the night he overturns and destroys them.
[26] He strikes them down because they are wicked,
doing it openly for all to see.
[27] For they turned away from following him.
They have no respect for any of his ways.
[28] They cause the poor to cry out, catching God's attention.
He hears the cries of the needy.
[29] But if he chooses to remain quiet,
who can criticize him?
When he hides his face, no one can find him,
whether an individual or a nation.
[30] He prevents the godless from ruling
so they cannot be a snare to the people.

[31] "Why don't people say to God, 'I have sinned,
but I will sin no more'?
[32] Or 'I don't know what evil I have done—tell me.
If I have done wrong, I will stop at once'?

[33] "Must God tailor his justice to your demands?
But you have rejected him!
The choice is yours, not mine.
Go ahead, share your wisdom with us.
[34] After all, bright people will tell me,
and wise people will hear me say,
[35] 'Job speaks out of ignorance;
his words lack insight.'
[36] Job, you deserve the maximum penalty
for the wicked way you have talked.
[37] For you have added rebellion to your sin;
you show no respect,
and you speak many angry words against God."

Elihu Reminds Job of God's Justice

35 Then Elihu said:

[2] "Do you think it is right for you to claim,
'I am righteous before God'?
[3] For you also ask, 'What's in it for me?
What's the use of living a righteous life?'

[4] "I will answer you
and all your friends, too.
[5] Look up into the sky,
and see the clouds high above you.
[6] If you sin, how does that affect God?
Even if you sin again and again,
what effect will it have on him?
[7] If you are good, is this some great gift to him?
What could you possibly give him?
[8] No, your sins affect only people like yourself,
and your good deeds also affect only humans.

[9] "People cry out when they are oppressed.
They groan beneath the power of the mighty.
[10] Yet they don't ask, 'Where is God my Creator,
the one who gives songs in the night?

lion to his sin. **35:1–16:** Elihu addresses Job's claim that God allows the wicked to go unpunished. Elihu does provide a bit of sound wisdom when he argues, "If you are wicked or righteous, what do you do to God? Your wickedness and righteousness affect other humans" (paraphrasing vv. 7–8). Elihu's

11 Where is the one who makes us smarter than
the animals
and wiser than the birds of the sky?'
12 And when they cry out, God does not answer
because of their pride.
13 But it is wrong to say God doesn't listen,
to say the Almighty isn't concerned.
14 You say you can't see him,
but he will bring justice if you will only
wait.*
15 You say he does not respond to sinners with
anger
and is not greatly concerned about
wickedness.*
16 But you are talking nonsense, Job.
You have spoken like a fool."

36 Elihu continued speaking:
2 "Let me go on, and I will show you
the truth.
For I have not finished defending God!
3 I will present profound arguments
for the righteousness of my Creator.
4 I am telling you nothing but the truth,
for I am a man of great knowledge.

5 "God is mighty, but he does not despise
anyone!
He is mighty in both power and
understanding.
6 He does not let the wicked live
but gives justice to the afflicted.
7 He never takes his eyes off the innocent,
but he sets them on thrones with kings
and exalts them forever.
8 If they are bound in chains
and caught up in a web of trouble,
9 he shows them the reason.
He shows them their sins of pride.
10 He gets their attention
and commands that they turn from evil.

11 "If they listen and obey God,
they will be blessed with prosperity
throughout their lives.
All their years will be pleasant.
12 But if they refuse to listen to him,
they will be killed by the sword*
and die from lack of understanding.
13 For the godless are full of resentment.
Even when he punishes them,
they refuse to cry out to him for help.
14 They die when they are young,
after wasting their lives in immoral living.
15 But by means of their suffering, he rescues
those who suffer.
For he gets their attention through adversity.

16 "God is leading you away from danger, Job,
to a place free from distress.
He is setting your table with the best food.
17 But you are obsessed with whether the
godless will be judged.
Don't worry, judgment and justice will be
upheld.
18 But watch out, or you may be seduced by
wealth.*
Don't let yourself be bribed into sin.
19 Could all your wealth*
or all your mighty efforts
keep you from distress?
20 Do not long for the cover of night,
for that is when people will be destroyed.*
21 Be on guard! Turn back from evil,
for God sent this suffering
to keep you from a life of evil.

Elihu Reminds Job of God's Power

22 "Look, God is all-powerful.
Who is a teacher like him?
23 No one can tell him what to do,
or say to him, 'You have done wrong.'
24 Instead, glorify his mighty works,
singing songs of praise.
25 Everyone has seen these things,
though only from a distance.

35:13-14 These verses can also be translated as follows: [13]*Indeed, God doesn't listen to their empty plea; / the Almighty is not concerned. / *[14]*How much less will he listen when you say you don't see him, / and that your case is before him and you're waiting for justice.* **35:15** As in Greek and Latin versions; the meaning of this Hebrew word is uncertain. **36:12** Or *they will cross the river* [of death]. **36:18** Or *But don't let your anger lead you to mockery.* **36:19** Or *Could all your cries for help.* **36:16-20** The meaning of the Hebrew in this passage is uncertain.

attack on Job is misplaced, but the truth of the statement stands. **36:1–21:** Elihu particularizes his argument by suggesting the afflictions of the wise are intended as motivation for them to turn from their evil ways in order that they might live in prosperity once more. This is the only gracious statement Elihu makes. While a similar argument was made by the three friends early in the discourse cycles, by the end the friends were speaking as if Job had been wicked all along and his punishment simply deferred. Elihu does not discuss the state and plight of the wicked. Instead he emphasizes the revelatory function of suffering (cf. 33:19–33; 36:5–15). **36:22—37:24:** Elihu closes his discourses with a

26 "Look, God is greater than we can understand.
His years cannot be counted.
27 He draws up the water vapor
and then distills it into rain.
28 The rain pours down from the clouds,
and everyone benefits.
29 Who can understand the spreading of the clouds
and the thunder that rolls forth from heaven?
30 See how he spreads the lightning around him
and how it lights up the depths of the sea.
31 By these mighty acts he nourishes* the people,
giving them food in abundance.
32 He fills his hands with lightning bolts
and hurls each at its target.
33 The thunder announces his presence;
the storm announces his indignant anger.*

37

1 "My heart pounds as I think of this.
It trembles within me.
2 Listen carefully to the thunder of God's voice
as it rolls from his mouth.
3 It rolls across the heavens,
and his lightning flashes in every direction.
4 Then comes the roaring of the thunder—
the tremendous voice of his majesty.
He does not restrain it when he speaks.
5 God's voice is glorious in the thunder.
We can't even imagine the greatness of his power.

6 "He directs the snow to fall on the earth
and tells the rain to pour down.
7 Then everyone stops working
so they can watch his power.
8 The wild animals take cover
and stay inside their dens.
9 The stormy wind comes from its chamber,
and the driving winds bring the cold.
10 God's breath sends the ice,
freezing wide expanses of water.
11 He loads the clouds with moisture,
and they flash with his lightning.
12 The clouds churn about at his direction.
They do whatever he commands
throughout the earth.
13 He makes these things happen either to punish people
or to show his unfailing love.

14 "Pay attention to this, Job.
Stop and consider the wonderful miracles of God!
15 Do you know how God controls the storm
and causes the lightning to flash from his clouds?
16 Do you understand how he moves the clouds
with wonderful perfection and skill?
17 When you are sweltering in your clothes
and the south wind dies down and everything is still,
18 he makes the skies reflect the heat like a bronze mirror.
Can you do that?

19 "So teach the rest of us what to say to God.
We are too ignorant to make our own arguments.
20 Should God be notified that I want to speak?
Can people even speak when they are confused?*
21 We cannot look at the sun,
for it shines brightly in the sky
when the wind clears away the clouds.
22 So also, golden splendor comes from the mountain of God.*
He is clothed in dazzling splendor.
23 We cannot imagine the power of the Almighty;
but even though he is just and righteous,
he does not destroy us.
24 No wonder people everywhere fear him.
All who are wise show him reverence."

The LORD Challenges Job

38

1 Then the LORD answered Job from the whirlwind:
2 "Who is this that questions my wisdom
with such ignorant words?
3 Brace yourself like a man,

36:31 Or *he governs.* **36:33** Or *even the cattle know when a storm is coming.* The meaning of the Hebrew is uncertain. **37:20** Or *speak without being swallowed up?* **37:22** Or *from the north;* or *from the abode.*

---

hymn that proclaims the power of God. As he proceeds through the hymn he raises questions for Job: "Do you know the workings of God?" While these questions foreshadow those that will come in the next chapter, when God speaks for the first time, in Elihu's mouth they serve to justify God and condemn Job. But Job will not be condemned when God speaks.

38:1—42:6 Discourse Cycle of the LORD

After thirty-four chapters of human debate over the

because I have some questions for you,
and you must answer them.

4 "Where were you when I laid the foundations of the earth?
Tell me, if you know so much.
5 Who determined its dimensions
and stretched out the surveying line?
6 What supports its foundations,
and who laid its cornerstone
7 as the morning stars sang together
and all the angels* shouted for joy?

8 "Who kept the sea inside its boundaries
as it burst from the womb,
9 and as I clothed it with clouds
and wrapped it in thick darkness?
10 For I locked it behind barred gates,
limiting its shores.
11 I said, 'This far and no farther will you come.
Here your proud waves must stop!'

12 "Have you ever commanded the morning to appear
and caused the dawn to rise in the east?
13 Have you made daylight spread to the ends of the earth,
to bring an end to the night's wickedness?
14 As the light approaches,
the earth takes shape like clay pressed beneath a seal;
it is robed in brilliant colors.*
15 The light disturbs the wicked
and stops the arm that is raised in violence.

16 "Have you explored the springs from which the seas come?
Have you explored their depths?
17 Do you know where the gates of death are located?
Have you seen the gates of utter gloom?
18 Do you realize the extent of the earth?
Tell me about it if you know!

19 "Where does light come from,
and where does darkness go?
20 Can you take each to its home?
Do you know how to get there?
21 But of course you know all this!
For you were born before it was all created,
and you are so very experienced!

22 "Have you visited the storehouses of the snow
or seen the storehouses of hail?
23 (I have reserved them as weapons for the time of trouble,
for the day of battle and war.)
24 Where is the path to the source of light?
Where is the home of the east wind?

25 "Who created a channel for the torrents of rain?
Who laid out the path for the lightning?
26 Who makes the rain fall on barren land,
in a desert where no one lives?
27 Who sends rain to satisfy the parched ground
and make the tender grass spring up?

28 "Does the rain have a father?
Who gives birth to the dew?
29 Who is the mother of the ice?
Who gives birth to the frost from the heavens?
30 For the water turns to ice as hard as rock,
and the surface of the water freezes.

31 "Can you direct the movement of the stars—
binding the cluster of the Pleiades
or loosening the cords of Orion?
32 Can you direct the sequence of the seasons
or guide the Bear with her cubs across the heavens?
33 Do you know the laws of the universe?
Can you use them to regulate the earth?

34 "Can you shout to the clouds
and make it rain?
35 Can you make lightning appear
and cause it to strike as you direct?
36 Who gives intuition to the heart
and instinct to the mind?
37 Who is wise enough to count all the clouds?

38:7 Hebrew *the sons of God.* **38:14** Or *its features stand out like folds in a robe.*

dogma of divine retributive justice, God finally enters the conversation. God speaks out of the whirlwind, which is a frequent setting for theophany (i.e., God appearing to humanity) in the Old Testament. It would seem that God is little concerned with Job's petty questions; God has a much larger agenda. The questions are somewhat playful, at times sarcastic (e.g., 38:21) and seemingly intended to refocus the conversation on the mysteries of the cosmos, of which Job is a small part. **38:4—40:2:** After the first round of questions God demands a response from *God's critic* (40:2). **40:3–5:** Job is speechless for the first time since the

Who can tilt the water jars of heaven
38 when the parched ground is dry
and the soil has hardened into clods?

39 "Can you stalk prey for a lioness
and satisfy the young lions' appetites
40 as they lie in their dens
or crouch in the thicket?
41 Who provides food for the ravens
when their young cry out to God
and wander about in hunger?

The LORD's Challenge Continues

39 1"Do you know when the wild goats
give birth?
Have you watched as deer are
born in the wild?
2 Do you know how many months they carry
their young?
Are you aware of the time of their
delivery?
3 They crouch down to give birth to their
young
and deliver their offspring.
4 Their young grow up in the open fields,
then leave home and never return.

5 "Who gives the wild donkey its freedom?
Who untied its ropes?
6 I have placed it in the wilderness;
its home is the wasteland.
7 It hates the noise of the city
and has no driver to shout at it.
8 The mountains are its pastureland,
where it searches for every blade of grass.

9 "Will the wild ox consent to being tamed?
Will it spend the night in your stall?
10 Can you hitch a wild ox to a plow?
Will it plow a field for you?
11 Given its strength, can you trust it?
Can you leave and trust the ox to do your
work?
12 Can you rely on it to bring home your grain
and deliver it to your threshing floor?

13 "The ostrich flaps her wings grandly,
but they are no match for the feathers of
the stork.
14 She lays her eggs on top of the earth,
letting them be warmed in the dust.
15 She doesn't worry that a foot might crush
them
or a wild animal might destroy them.
16 She is harsh toward her young,
as if they were not her own.
She doesn't care if they die.
17 For God has deprived her of wisdom.
He has given her no understanding.
18 But whenever she jumps up to run,
she passes the swiftest horse with its rider.

19 "Have you given the horse its strength
or clothed its neck with a flowing mane?
20 Did you give it the ability to leap like a
locust?
Its majestic snorting is terrifying!
21 It paws the earth and rejoices in its strength
when it charges out to battle.
22 It laughs at fear and is unafraid.
It does not run from the sword.
23 The arrows rattle against it,
and the spear and javelin flash.
24 It paws the ground fiercely
and rushes forward into battle when the
ram's horn blows.
25 It snorts at the sound of the horn.
It senses the battle in the distance.
It quivers at the captain's commands and
the noise of battle.

26 "Is it your wisdom that makes the hawk soar
and spread its wings toward the south?
27 Is it at your command that the eagle rises
to the heights to make its nest?
28 It lives on the cliffs,
making its home on a distant, rocky crag.
29 From there it hunts its prey,
keeping watch with piercing eyes.
30 Its young gulp down blood.
Where there's a carcass, there you'll
find it."

40 Then the LORD said to Job,
2"Do you still want to argue with
the Almighty?
You are God's critic, but do you have the
answers?"

Job Responds to the LORD

3Then Job replied to the LORD,

4 "I am nothing—how could I ever find the
answers?
I will cover my mouth with my hand.
5 I have said too much already.
I have nothing more to say."

The LORD Challenges Job Again

6Then the LORD answered Job from the whirlwind:

7 "Brace yourself like a man,
because I have some questions for you,
and you must answer them.

8 "Will you discredit my justice
and condemn me just to prove you are right?
9 Are you as strong as God?
Can you thunder with a voice like his?
10 All right, put on your glory and splendor,
your honor and majesty.
11 Give vent to your anger.
Let it overflow against the proud.
12 Humiliate the proud with a glance;
walk on the wicked where they stand.
13 Bury them in the dust.
Imprison them in the world of the dead.
14 Then even I would praise you,
for your own strength would save you.

15 "Take a look at Behemoth,*
which I made, just as I made you.
It eats grass like an ox.
16 See its powerful loins
and the muscles of its belly.
17 Its tail is as strong as a cedar.
The sinews of its thighs are knit tightly together.
18 Its bones are tubes of bronze.
Its limbs are bars of iron.
19 It is a prime example of God's handiwork,
and only its Creator can threaten it.
20 The mountains offer it their best food,
where all the wild animals play.
21 It lies under the lotus plants,*
hidden by the reeds in the marsh.
22 The lotus plants give it shade
among the willows beside the stream.
23 It is not disturbed by the raging river,
not concerned when the swelling Jordan rushes around it.
24 No one can catch it off guard
or put a ring in its nose and lead it away.

The LORD's Challenge Continues

41 1*"Can you catch Leviathan* with a hook
or put a noose around its jaw?
2 Can you tie it with a rope through the nose
or pierce its jaw with a spike?
3 Will it beg you for mercy
or implore you for pity?
4 Will it agree to work for you,
to be your slave for life?
5 Can you make it a pet like a bird,
or give it to your little girls to play with?
6 Will merchants try to buy it
to sell it in their shops?
7 Will its hide be hurt by spears
or its head by a harpoon?
8 If you lay a hand on it,
you will certainly remember the battle that follows.
You won't try that again!
9*No, it is useless to try to capture it.
The hunter who attempts it will be knocked down.
10 And since no one dares to disturb it,
who then can stand up to me?
11 Who has given me anything that I need to pay back?
Everything under heaven is mine.

12 "I want to emphasize Leviathan's limbs
and its enormous strength and graceful form.
13 Who can strip off its hide,
and who can penetrate its double layer of armor?*
14 Who could pry open its jaws?
For its teeth are terrible!
15 Its scales are like rows of shields
tightly sealed together.
16 They are so close together
that no air can get between them.
17 Each scale sticks tight to the next.
They interlock and cannot be penetrated.

18 "When it sneezes, it flashes light!
Its eyes are like the red of dawn.
19 Lightning leaps from its mouth;
flames of fire flash out.

40:15 The identification of Behemoth is disputed, ranging from an earthly creature to a mythical sea monster in ancient literature. **40:21** Or *bramble bushes;* also in 40:22. **41:1a** Verses 41:1-8 are numbered 40:25-32 in Hebrew text. **41:1b** The identification of Leviathan is disputed, ranging from an earthly creature to a mythical sea monster in ancient literature. **41:9** Verses 41:9-34 are numbered 41:1-26 in Hebrew text. **41:13** As in Greek version; Hebrew reads *its bridle?*

inception of the book. **40:6—41:34:** God begins a second set of questions, which focus on God's ability to create and control the chaotic forces of nature as depicted by Behemoth and Leviathan, primeval monsters frequently used in ancient literature as symbols of chaos and evil. The rhetorical effect is to suggest that although humans often experience aspects of creation as overwhelmingly powerful and

20 Smoke streams from its nostrils
like steam from a pot heated over burning
rushes.
21 Its breath would kindle coals,
for flames shoot from its mouth.
22 "The tremendous strength in Leviathan's
neck
strikes terror wherever it goes.
23 Its flesh is hard and firm
and cannot be penetrated.
24 Its heart is hard as rock,
hard as a millstone.
25 When it rises, the mighty are afraid,
gripped by terror.
26 No sword can stop it,
no spear, dart, or javelin.
27 Iron is nothing but straw to that creature,
and bronze is like rotten wood.
28 Arrows cannot make it flee.
Stones shot from a sling are like bits of
grass.
29 Clubs are like a blade of grass,
and it laughs at the swish of javelins.
30 Its belly is covered with scales as sharp as glass.
It plows up the ground as it drags through
the mud.

31 "Leviathan makes the water boil with its
commotion.
It stirs the depths like a pot of ointment.
32 The water glistens in its wake,
making the sea look white.
33 Nothing on earth is its equal,
no other creature so fearless.
34 Of all the creatures, it is the proudest.
It is the king of beasts."

Job Responds to the Lord

42 Then Job replied to the Lord:
2 "I know that you can do anything,
and no one can stop you.
3 You asked, 'Who is this that questions my
wisdom with such ignorance?'
It is I—and I was talking about things I
knew nothing about,
things far too wonderful for me.
4 You said, 'Listen and I will speak!
I have some questions for you,
and you must answer them.'
5 I had only heard about you before,
but now I have seen you with my own
eyes.
6 I take back everything I said,
and I sit in dust and ashes to show my
repentance."

Conclusion: The Lord Blesses Job

7 After the Lord had finished speaking to Job, he
said to Eliphaz the Temanite: "I am angry with
you and your two friends, for you have not spoken accurately about me, as my servant Job has.
8 So take seven bulls and seven rams and go to
my servant Job and offer a burnt offering for
yourselves. My servant Job will pray for you,
and I will accept his prayer on your behalf. I
will not treat you as you deserve, for you have
not spoken accurately about me, as my servant
Job has." 9 So Eliphaz the Temanite, Bildad the
Shuhite, and Zophar the Naamathite did as the
Lord commanded them, and the Lord accepted
Job's prayer.
10 When Job prayed for his friends, the Lord
restored his fortunes. In fact, the Lord gave him

---

chaotic, God is in control. **42:1–6:** Job begins his second and final response to God with two significant summarizing statements: God can do all things, and God's purposes will never be thwarted. These are the only answers Job receives for his question about why the righteous suffer. **6:** His question has not been answered, and yet Job seems satisfied, so much so that he retracts his utterances. It is unclear whether this retraction refers to Job's initial question or some aspect of his dialogue. In any event, it seems the clouds have lifted and he now understands the world as well as his situation in a new way. Job, once so confident in his vindication before the Lord (chap. 23), upon seeing God, despises himself and repents in dust and ashes. Frequently this final statement of repentance creates difficulty for reading the book in its entirety. Job does not deny his pre-catastrophic righteousness. Rather, Job repents of his speech before God throughout the last thirty-four chapters, giving up his legal case against God—but not admitting wrongdoing.

42:7–17 Closing Narrative

These closing verses, the conclusion of God's wager with the Adversary, settle the issue of divine retributive justice, put Eliphaz and Job's friends in their place, and restore Job to prosperity. **7–9:** God himself pronounces a negative verdict on the doctrine of divine retributive justice by telling the four interlocutors that they have spoken wrongly. Rigid adherence to the dogma that the righteous are blessed and the wicked punished is condemned. **8:** That Job is to officiate at the friends' burnt offerings affirms Job as righteous. *I will not treat you as you deserve*: Another proof against divine retributive justice. **10–17:** Many

twice as much as before! [11]Then all his brothers,
sisters, and former friends came and feasted with
him in his home. And they consoled him and
comforted him because of all the trials the LORD
had brought against him. And each of them
brought him a gift of money* and a gold ring.

[12]So the LORD blessed Job in the second half
of his life even more than in the beginning. For
now he had 14,000 sheep, 6,000 camels, 1,000
teams of oxen, and 1,000 female donkeys. [13]He
also gave Job seven more sons and three more
daughters. [14]He named his first daughter Jemi-
mah, the second Keziah, and the third Keren-
happuch. [15]In all the land no women were as
lovely as the daughters of Job. And their father
put them into his will along with their brothers.

[16]Job lived 140 years after that, living to see
four generations of his children and grandchildren. [17]Then he died, an old man who had lived
a long, full life.

42:11 Hebrew *a kesitah;* the value or weight of the kesitah is no longer known.

---

readers struggle with these concluding verses, as they seem to reestablish the doctrine of divine retributive justice. But Job's fortunes are not restored as a result of some righteous act. Job is no more righteous now than he was at the start of the story. The restoration of Job's fortunes and status is an example of God's gracious activity and in no way nullifies the main point of the book: The doctrine of divine retributive justice is an inadequate depiction of God's presence in our world.

Although all people, perhaps women in particular, live immersed in the doctrine of retributive justice, our common hope is God's grace.

PSALMS

INTRODUCTION

The Psalms are personal poems and Israel's hymns. Many have titles indicating authorship and, sometimes, circumstance of writing, though it is possible that "of David," for example, could on occasion mean "for" or "after" David. In the annotations, references to David can refer more generally to the psalmist (see annotation on Ps 27). The titles may classify the psalm as a *maskil* or teaching psalm (e.g., Ps 32:1, translator's note), although the meaning of some descriptions is now lost in the mists of history. We can recognize wisdom psalms (e.g. Pss 37; 73; 78), penitential psalms (e.g., Pss 51; 130), pilgrim psalms (e.g., Pss 120—134), nature psalms (e.g., Pss 29; 104), praise psalms (e.g., Pss 145—150) and so on. The royal psalms (e.g., Pss 2; 45; 110) are worthy of special note. These portray Israel's king as one appointed by the LORD to lead the people in a true fear of the LORD. They can be interpreted as looking beyond the current king to an ideal king yet to come, a king whom the New Testament identifies as Jesus Christ the Messiah.

The most commonly encountered group of women in the psalms are mothers. This reflects the fact that the normative role for women in Israel was a domestic one. They were to marry, bear children, and look after them and the household of which their responsible male was the head. In a family-oriented society, mothers were the link that bonded family members together (Pss 50:20; 69:8). But childbearing and rearing in ancient Israel was a difficult and risky business (reflected in Ps 58:8). To any Israelite, one's mother mattered (Pss 35:14; 116:16). This understanding of motherhood gives added significance to Psalm 87's picture of Zion as a mother city, in whom are the springs of life (Ps 87:5–7).

Another commonly encountered group is that of widows. The Hebrew word for "widow" is closely related to those for "silent" and "desolate." In a society where husbands assumed full economic responsibility for their wives and children, any woman with no male to support her would indeed be desolate. Without a voice to speak for her, even her survival would be at stake. Four of the five references group widows with orphans (Pss 68:5; 94:6; 109:9; 146:9). Together (sometimes with "foreigners" added) they represent the poor, vulnerable, and underprivileged in Israelite society: those without family able to bear the responsibility for supporting them. Such an unenviable position would understandably find its expression in lamentation (Ps 109). The prayer that a man's wife will become a widow (Ps 109:9) seeks not only his death but also lasting shame on his name, as people see his widow and children publicly reduced to a life of poverty, isolation, and destitution.

In a similar way, the barren woman (Ps 113:9) represents those who would normally be considered not blessed or even cursed. As the place where human life begins and is formed, a woman's womb is particularly precious. Here, it was regarded as being under the direct control of the LORD, who opened or closed it at will (Ps 139:13). Since, under the old covenant, children and wealth were promised to those who obeyed the LORD (Deut 7:12–14; Ps 127:3), barrenness was commonly viewed as a sign of his disfavor. Furthermore, children, and sons in particular, were meant to provide for their parents' old age; hence barrenness was a failure of role that could lead to divorce. A woman without children would be vulnerable, at risk of being classed with the poor and needy of Israelite society.

There are hints that the LORD is not content with the status quo. When compared with the Israelite norm, for example, the LORD gives an unusually high priority to caring for widows, orphans, and barren women (Pss 68:5; 113:9). Knowing their particular need for protection from the "evil people" (Ps 94:4–7), the LORD has pity on them and takes on the role of responsible male, becoming their protector, upholder, provider, father, and judge (Pss 68:5–6; 113:9; 146:5–9).

Women reaching out to God in the midst of crisis situations may find great support and consolation in the psalms. Hence we find forthright condemnations of violence (Pss 5:9; 7:1–2; 10:2, 7–10; 17:11; 27:12; 31:4, 10–13; 37:32; 38:11–12; 52:2–3; 54:3; 55:12–14, 20–21; 56:5–6; 59:3; 64:1–6; 69:4, 19–20; 86:14; 140:1–5), passionate appeals to God for deliverance (Pss 59:2; 139:19; 140:1, 4), and deep assurances of God's power to give safety and support (Pss 10:17–18; 12:5; 28:8–9; 34:6; 35:10; 103:6).

As Hebrew poems, the psalms are deeply rhythmic and steeped in many kinds of parallelism. Most are written in couplets or triplets of two or three units per line, with each unit arranged around a tone syllable.

The main themes are adoration, remembrance, confession, thanksgiving, instruction, testimony, petition, and praise. Thus the psalms reveal that worship is essentially a response to God's revelation in creation and salvation, and they still provide a pattern for worship. Organized into five books, each ending with a doxology, the collection emphasizes from beginning to end the truth that to worship the LORD is the greatest possible privilege and brings lasting blessing.

A particular problem is that of the hostile feelings that David so vehemently expresses. The so-called imprecatory psalms are in point of fact remarkable for the honesty of their emotion. More often than we might like to admit, we too have entertained less than charitable thoughts toward others. The psalmists lay these emotions before God and find their way through to a dependence on divine mercy and faithfulness. The appalling sentiments can guide us to attitudes of faith and serenity. —*Gwynneth Marian Napier Raikes* and *Catherine Clark Kroeger*

1:1—41:13	Book 1
42:1—72:20	Book 2
73:1—89:52	Book 3
90:1—106:48	Book 4
107:1—150:6	Book 5

BOOK ONE (Psalms 1–41)

PSALM 1

1 Oh, the joys of those who do not
follow the advice of the wicked,
or stand around with sinners,
or join in with mockers.
2 But they delight in the law of the LORD,
meditating on it day and night.
3 They are like trees planted along the
riverbank,
bearing fruit each season.
Their leaves never wither,
and they prosper in all they do.

4 But not the wicked!
They are like worthless chaff, scattered by
the wind.
5 They will be condemned at the time of
judgment.
Sinners will have no place among the
godly.
6 For the LORD watches over the path of the
godly,
but the path of the wicked leads to
destruction.

PSALM 2

1 Why are the nations so angry?
Why do they waste their time with futile
plans?
2 The kings of the earth prepare for battle;
the rulers plot together
against the LORD
and against his anointed one.
3 "Let us break their chains," they cry,
"and free ourselves from slavery to God."

4 But the one who rules in heaven laughs.
The Lord scoffs at them.
5 Then in anger he rebukes them,
terrifying them with his fierce fury.
6 For the Lord declares, "I have placed my
chosen king on the throne
in Jerusalem,* on my holy mountain."

7 The king proclaims the LORD's decree:
"The LORD said to me, 'You are my son.*
Today I have become your Father.*
8 Only ask, and I will give you the nations as
your inheritance,
the whole earth as your possession.
9 You will break* them with an iron rod
and smash them like clay pots.' "

10 Now then, you kings, act wisely!
Be warned, you rulers of the earth!
11 Serve the LORD with reverent fear,
and rejoice with trembling.
12 Submit to God's royal son,* or he will
become angry,
and you will be destroyed in the midst of
all your activities—
for his anger flares up in an instant.
But what joy for all who take refuge in
him!

PSALM 3

A psalm of David, regarding the time David fled from his son Absalom.

1 O LORD, I have so many enemies;
so many are against me.
2 So many are saying,
"God will never rescue him!" *Interlude**

3 But you, O LORD, are a shield around me;
you are my glory, the one who holds my
head high.
4 I cried out to the LORD,

2:6 Hebrew *on Zion.* **2:7a** Or *Son;* also in 2:12. **2:7b** Or *Today I reveal you as my son.* **2:9** Greek version reads *rule.* Compare Rev 2:27. **2:12** The meaning of the Hebrew is uncertain. **3:2** Hebrew *Selah.* The meaning of this word is uncertain, though it is probably a musical or literary term. It is rendered *Interlude* throughout the Psalms.

1:1—41:13 Book 1

Psalm 1 The only sure and lasting happiness for people is found in friendship with the LORD. This involves deliberately rejecting the *advice* of all wrongdoers and daily delighting instead in *the law of the LORD.* The contrast with *the wicked* reassures the people of God that though sinners may seem prosperous, appearances are deceptive.

Psalm 2 The psalm pictures the LORD emphatically introducing the *king,* to whom he has committed the powers of judgment, originally referring to David (cf. 2 Sam 7:8–11). The New Testament treats this psalm as a prophecy of Christ (e.g., Acts 4:25–26; 13:33).

Psalm 3 This is the first of many psalms written by David when he was in trouble (see title; cf. 2 Sam 15:14). His characteristic response is to turn to the LORD in prayer in spite of discouragement from those around.

The Relevance of Psalms for the Everyday Lives of Women

The Psalms from earliest times have been a source of inspiration and strength. They are used as prayers, sung as hymns, and repeated from memory in times of special need or celebration. These hymns of Israel give expression to the praise in the hearts of believers and reflect at times their deepest despair.

At times of deepest significance the voices of women were essential (see Women as Psalmists, Judg 5). After a victory, women led the expressions of praise and thanksgiving. They too were foremost in expressions of lament (cf. Judg 11:38, 40; 2 Sam 1:24).

The faith and influence of mothers are stressed, and the loss of a mother is mentioned with grief (Ps 35:14).

Psalm 128:3 depicts the joy and blessing of fruitfulness for women. God's presence during childbirth is an important concept for women.

Psalm 22:9–10 pictures God as a midwife. Thus the process of maternal bonding is divinely initiated. God is intimately concerned with both the physical and spiritual dynamics of birth. A similar image occurs at Psalm 71:6, with a representation of God as midwife, bringing to birth and supporting the new child (see Midwifery and Birthing Practices, Job 3). Thus we have here a picture of God as both giver and sustainer of life, present at the time of crisis.

The psalmist prays that sons may be as flourishing young plants (or high towers), and daughters as sculptured pillars in the palace (Ps 144:12). The image bespeaks strength, stability, and beauty. A pillar is critical in bearing the weight of the roof, but its form is an important architectural feature. The key position of the daughters in the palace emphasizes their importance as prime supports in the household of faith.

Expressions of God's love of all persons and the universality of the eschatological response strike a special chord in female readers (Pss 68:31; 72:10; 87:4–6). A particular problem with which women struggle is that of the hostile emotions, which David in particular so vehemently expresses. The so-called imprecatory psalms are in point of fact remarkable for the honesty of their emotion. More often than we might like to admit, we too have entertained less than charitable thoughts toward others. The psalmists lay these emotions before God and find their way through to a dependence on divine mercy and faithfulness. The appalling sentiments can guide us to attitudes of faith and serenity.

This attitude of spiritual expectancy has many ramifications. In Psalm 37:7 the Hebrew command to "be still" is translated in the Septuagint version by the Greek verb usually translated "submit" in its New Testament occurrences as they apply to women. The term has a far broader range of meanings than is often supposed, and these might greatly enrich our understanding of marriage and of interpersonal relationships.

and he answered me from his holy
mountain. *Interlude*

5 I lay down and slept,
yet I woke up in safety,
for the LORD was watching over me.
6 I am not afraid of ten thousand
enemies
who surround me on every side.
7 Arise, O LORD!
Rescue me, my God!
Slap all my enemies in the face!
Shatter the teeth of the wicked!
8 Victory comes from you, O LORD.
May you bless your people. *Interlude*

PSALM 4

For the choir director: A psalm of David, to be accompanied by stringed instruments.

1 Answer me when I call to you,
O God who declares me innocent.
Free me from my troubles.
Have mercy on me and hear my prayer.
2 How long will you people ruin my
reputation?

Psalm 4 is constructed around a tenet of wisdom (v. 4; cf. Job 31:30; Prov 13:3) and its present application. Leading up to it is David's experience: When disturbed by slander against himself, instead of responding in kind, he turned to prayer.

How long will you make groundless
accusations?
How long will you continue your lies?
Interlude
3 You can be sure of this:
The LORD set apart the godly for himself.
The LORD will answer when I call to him.

4 Don't sin by letting anger control you.
Think about it overnight and remain silent.
Interlude
5 Offer sacrifices in the right spirit,
and trust the LORD.

6 Many people say, "Who will show us better
times?"
Let your face smile on us, LORD.
7 You have given me greater joy
than those who have abundant harvests of
grain and new wine.
8 In peace I will lie down and sleep,
for you alone, O LORD, will keep me safe.

PSALM 5

For the choir director: A psalm of David, to be accompanied by the flute.

1 O LORD, hear me as I pray;
pay attention to my groaning.
2 Listen to my cry for help, my King and my
God,
for I pray to no one but you.
3 Listen to my voice in the morning, LORD.
Each morning I bring my requests to you
and wait expectantly.

4 O God, you take no pleasure in wickedness;
you cannot tolerate the sins of the wicked.
5 Therefore, the proud may not stand in your
presence,
for you hate all who do evil.
6 You will destroy those who tell lies.
The LORD detests murderers and
deceivers.

7 Because of your unfailing love, I can enter
your house;
I will worship at your Temple with deepest
awe.
8 Lead me in the right path, O LORD,
or my enemies will conquer me.
Make your way plain for me to follow.

9 My enemies cannot speak a truthful word.
Their deepest desire is to destroy others.
Their talk is foul, like the stench from an
open grave.
Their tongues are filled with flattery.*
10 O God, declare them guilty.
Let them be caught in their own traps.
Drive them away because of their many sins,
for they have rebelled against you.

11 But let all who take refuge in you rejoice;
let them sing joyful praises forever.
Spread your protection over them,
that all who love your name may be filled
with joy.
12 For you bless the godly, O LORD;
you surround them with your shield of
love.

PSALM 6

*For the choir director: A psalm of David, to be accompanied by an eight-stringed instrument.**

1 O LORD, don't rebuke me in your anger
or discipline me in your rage.
2 Have compassion on me, LORD, for I am weak.
Heal me, LORD, for my bones are in agony.
3 I am sick at heart.
How long, O LORD, until you restore me?

4 Return, O LORD, and rescue me.
Save me because of your unfailing love.
5 For the dead do not remember you.
Who can praise you from the grave?*

6 I am worn out from sobbing.
All night I flood my bed with weeping,

5:9 Greek version reads *with lies.* Compare Rom 3:13.
6:TITLE Hebrew *with stringed instruments; according to the sheminith.* **6:5** Hebrew *from Sheol?*

Psalm 5 finds David troubled by the violent duplicity of his enemies. He lays his concerns before the LORD *in the morning*, then watches for an answer. His priorities are to seek first God's guidance for himself, then God's justice for the wicked, and finally God's protective blessing for all his people.

Psalm 6 graphically describes David when suffering from some serious illness. He faces the real prospect of death, filled to the soul with terror at the thought that God must be angry with him (cf. Ps 88). His appeal to the LORD's unfailing love (*hesed,* v. 4) implies that a consideration of his desire to worship and his deep distress will move the LORD to saving action.

drenching it with my tears.
7 My vision is blurred by grief;
my eyes are worn out because of all my enemies.

8 Go away, all you who do evil,
for the LORD has heard my weeping.
9 The LORD has heard my plea;
the LORD will answer my prayer.
10 May all my enemies be disgraced and terrified.
May they suddenly turn back in shame.

PSALM 7

A psalm of David, which he sang to the LORD concerning Cush of the tribe of Benjamin.

1 I come to you for protection, O LORD my God.
Save me from my persecutors—rescue me!
2 If you don't, they will maul me like a lion,
tearing me to pieces with no one to rescue me.
3 O LORD my God, if I have done wrong
or am guilty of injustice,
4 if I have betrayed a friend
or plundered my enemy without cause,
5 then let my enemies capture me.
Let them trample me into the ground
and drag my honor in the dust. *Interlude*

6 Arise, O LORD, in anger!
Stand up against the fury of my enemies!
Wake up, my God, and bring justice!
7 Gather the nations before you.
Rule over them from on high.
8 The LORD judges the nations.
Declare me righteous, O LORD,
for I am innocent, O Most High!
9 End the evil of those who are wicked,
and defend the righteous.
For you look deep within the mind and heart,
O righteous God.

10 God is my shield,
saving those whose hearts are true and right.
11 God is an honest judge.
He is angry with the wicked every day.

12 If a person does not repent,
God* will sharpen his sword;
he will bend and string his bow.
13 He will prepare his deadly weapons
and shoot his flaming arrows.

14 The wicked conceive evil;
they are pregnant with trouble
and give birth to lies.
15 They dig a deep pit to trap others,
then fall into it themselves.
16 The trouble they make for others backfires on them.
The violence they plan falls on their own heads.

17 I will thank the LORD because he is just;
I will sing praise to the name of the LORD Most High.

PSALM 8

*For the choir director: A psalm of David, to be accompanied by a stringed instrument.**

1 O LORD, our Lord, your majestic name fills the earth!
Your glory is higher than the heavens.
2 You have taught children and infants
to tell of your strength,*
silencing your enemies
and all who oppose you.

3 When I look at the night sky and see the work of your fingers—
the moon and the stars you set in place—
4 what are mere mortals that you should think about them,
human beings that you should care for them?*

7:12 Hebrew *he*. **8:TITLE** Hebrew *according to the gittith.* **8:2** Greek version reads *to give you praise.* Compare Matt 21:16. **8:4** Hebrew *what is man that you should think of him, / the son of man that you should care for him?*

Psalm 7 finds David pursued because of an alleged injustice. Cush (see title) is possibly an unknown relative of Abner (see 2 Sam 3). A metaphor of conception, pregnancy, and birthing (v. 14) focuses on the progress of evil rather than good. David's vivid picture of judgment taking place leaves him so sure of the LORD's righteous power that he looks forward in praise.

Psalm 8 is a God-centered celebration of his glory. In delighted wonder, David praises his royal greatness and grace. Yet, paradoxically, this great God commits his defense to humble *children and infants*, which metaphorically includes spiritual children (cf. Matt 18:3). The verbs (v. 5ff.) reflect his grace in creation and redemption.

5 Yet you made them only a little lower than
God*
and crowned them* with glory and honor.
6 You gave them charge of everything you
made,
putting all things under their authority—
7 the flocks and the herds
and all the wild animals,
8 the birds in the sky, the fish in the sea,
and everything that swims the ocean
currents.

9 O LORD, our Lord, your majestic name fills
the earth!

PSALM 9

For the choir director: A psalm of David, to be sung to the tune "Death of the Son."

1 I will praise you, LORD, with all my heart;
I will tell of all the marvelous things you
have done.
2 I will be filled with joy because of you.
I will sing praises to your name, O Most
High.

3 My enemies retreated;
they staggered and died when you
appeared.
4 For you have judged in my favor;
from your throne you have judged with
fairness.
5 You have rebuked the nations and destroyed
the wicked;
you have erased their names forever.
6 The enemy is finished, in endless ruins;
the cities you uprooted are now
forgotten.

7 But the LORD reigns forever,
executing judgment from his throne.
8 He will judge the world with justice
and rule the nations with fairness.
9 The LORD is a shelter for the oppressed,
a refuge in times of trouble.
10 Those who know your name trust in you,
for you, O LORD, do not abandon those
who search for you.
11 Sing praises to the LORD who reigns in
Jerusalem.*
Tell the world about his unforgettable
deeds.
12 For he who avenges murder cares for the
helpless.
He does not ignore the cries of those who
suffer.

13 LORD, have mercy on me.
See how my enemies torment me.
Snatch me back from the jaws of death.
14 Save me so I can praise you publicly at
Jerusalem's gates,
so I can rejoice that you have rescued me.

15 The nations have fallen into the pit they dug
for others.
Their own feet have been caught in the
trap they set.
16 The LORD is known for his justice.
The wicked are trapped by their own deeds.
*Quiet Interlude**

17 The wicked will go down to the grave.*
This is the fate of all the nations who
ignore God.
18 But the needy will not be ignored forever;
the hopes of the poor will not always be
crushed.

19 Arise, O LORD!
Do not let mere mortals defy you!
Judge the nations!
20 Make them tremble in fear, O LORD.
Let the nations know they are merely
human. *Interlude*

PSALM 10

1 O LORD, why do you stand so far away?
Why do you hide when I am in trouble?

8:5a Or *Yet you made them only a little lower than the angels;* Hebrew reads *Yet you made him* [i.e., man] *a little lower than Elohim.* **8:5b** Hebrew *him* [i.e., man]; similarly in 8:6. **9:11** Hebrew *Zion;* also in 9:14. **9:16** Hebrew *Higgaion Selah.* The meaning of this phrase is uncertain. **9:17** Hebrew *to Sheol.*

Psalm 9 gives praise for a recent victory in battle that prompts David to affirm that the LORD *reigns* as the just judge of the whole world. Those who know him trust him to be their stronghold in trouble. In the original Hebrew in verse 14, Jerusalem is described as "daughter" of the land, a term also used by Jeremiah and Zechariah.

Psalm 10 tackles the classic wisdom question: Why do the wicked prosper? They like to think God doesn't exist, doesn't care, doesn't know, or will not judge. The psalmist prays for justice and refutes their arguments. The LORD does know, does care, will hear the prayers of the helpless, and will *bring justice* to them.

2 The wicked arrogantly hunt down the poor.
Let them be caught in the evil they plan for others.
3 For they brag about their evil desires;
they praise the greedy and curse the LORD.

4 The wicked are too proud to seek God.
They seem to think that God is dead.
5 Yet they succeed in everything they do.
They do not see your punishment awaiting them.
They sneer at all their enemies.
6 They think, "Nothing bad will ever happen to us!
We will be free of trouble forever!"

7 Their mouths are full of cursing, lies, and threats.*
Trouble and evil are on the tips of their tongues.
8 They lurk in ambush in the villages,
waiting to murder innocent people.
They are always searching for helpless victims.
9 Like lions crouched in hiding,
they wait to pounce on the helpless.
Like hunters they capture the helpless
and drag them away in nets.
10 Their helpless victims are crushed;
they fall beneath the strength of the wicked.
11 The wicked think, "God isn't watching us!
He has closed his eyes and won't even see what we do!"

12 Arise, O LORD!
Punish the wicked, O God!
Do not ignore the helpless!
13 Why do the wicked get away with despising God?
They think, "God will never call us to account."
14 But you see the trouble and grief they cause.
You take note of it and punish them.
The helpless put their trust in you.
You defend the orphans.

15 Break the arms of these wicked, evil people!
Go after them until the last one is destroyed.
16 The LORD is king forever and ever!
The godless nations will vanish from the land.
17 LORD, you know the hopes of the helpless.
Surely you will hear their cries and comfort them.
18 You will bring justice to the orphans and the oppressed,
so mere people can no longer terrify them.

PSALM 11

For the choir director: A psalm of David.

1 I trust in the LORD for protection.
So why do you say to me,
"Fly like a bird to the mountains for safety!
2 The wicked are stringing their bows
and fitting their arrows on the bowstrings.
They shoot from the shadows
at those whose hearts are right.
3 The foundations of law and order have collapsed.
What can the righteous do?"

4 But the LORD is in his holy Temple;
the LORD still rules from heaven.
He watches everyone closely,
examining every person on earth.
5 The LORD examines both the righteous and the wicked.
He hates those who love violence.
6 He will rain down blazing coals and burning sulfur on the wicked,
punishing them with scorching winds.
7 For the righteous LORD loves justice.
The virtuous will see his face.

PSALM 12

*For the choir director: A psalm of David, to be accompanied by an eight-stringed instrument.**

1 Help, O LORD, for the godly are fast disappearing!
The faithful have vanished from the earth!
2 Neighbors lie to each other,
speaking with flattering lips and deceitful hearts.
3 May the LORD cut off their flattering lips

10:7 Greek version reads *cursing and bitterness.* Compare Rom 3:14. **12:TITLE** Hebrew *according to the sheminith.*

Psalm 11 logically follows Psalm 10. Tempted to abandon trust in God, David replies that because the LORD is enthroned in heaven and their personal *protection*, the righteous do not need to flee from the wicked in fear.

and silence their boastful tongues.
4 They say, "We will lie to our hearts' content.
Our lips are our own—who can stop us?"

5 The LORD replies, "I have seen violence done to the helpless,
and I have heard the groans of the poor.
Now I will rise up to rescue them,
as they have longed for me to do."
6 The LORD's promises are pure,
like silver refined in a furnace,
purified seven times over.
7 Therefore, LORD, we know you will protect the oppressed,
preserving them forever from this lying generation,
8 even though the wicked strut about,
and evil is praised throughout the land.

PSALM 13

For the choir director: A psalm of David.

1 O LORD, how long will you forget me? Forever?
How long will you look the other way?
2 How long must I struggle with anguish in my soul,
with sorrow in my heart every day?
How long will my enemy have the upper hand?

3 Turn and answer me, O LORD my God!
Restore the sparkle to my eyes, or I will die.
4 Don't let my enemies gloat, saying, "We have defeated him!"
Don't let them rejoice at my downfall.

5 But I trust in your unfailing love.
I will rejoice because you have rescued me.
6 I will sing to the LORD
because he is good to me.

PSALM 14

For the choir director: A psalm of David.

1 Only fools say in their hearts,
"There is no God."
They are corrupt, and their actions are evil;
not one of them does good!

2 The LORD looks down from heaven
on the entire human race;
he looks to see if anyone is truly wise,
if anyone seeks God.
3 But no, all have turned away;
all have become corrupt.*
No one does good,
not a single one!

4 Will those who do evil never learn?
They eat up my people like bread
and wouldn't think of praying to the LORD.
5 Terror will grip them,
for God is with those who obey him.
6 The wicked frustrate the plans of the oppressed,
but the LORD will protect his people.

7 Who will come from Mount Zion to rescue Israel?
When the LORD restores his people,
Jacob will shout with joy, and Israel will rejoice.

PSALM 15

A psalm of David.

1 Who may worship in your sanctuary, LORD?
Who may enter your presence on your holy hill?

14:3 Greek version reads *have become useless.* Compare Rom 3:12.

Psalm 12 observes that evil pervades society. David sees people suffering and recognizes the cause as sin. Lies especially are prevalent; they are the manifestation of selfish pride. Note the contrast between the purity of the Word of God and the duplicity of the lies of the wicked.

Psalm 13 finds David, shaken by pain and sorrow, feeling forsaken by God because his enemy has gained the upper hand. For a brief moment he entertains the thought that his enemy may triumph but quickly corrects himself with a reminder of the LORD's *unfailing love* and past goodness (vv. 5–6).

Psalm 14, which is virtually identical to Psalm 53, introduces a character familiar in wisdom literature. The *fool* is one who chooses to ignore God and is morally responsible for the consequences. Israel's present suffering is only his discipline; he will deliver his people and thereby thwart the fools.

Psalm 15 begins with a question. The LORD's home is intended to be the believer's home too, but on what conditions may believers enjoy their privilege? They will demonstrate their fitness in four ways: integrity of character, a disciplined tongue, just dealings with other people, and a right attitude to money.

2 Those who lead blameless lives and do what is right,
speaking the truth from sincere hearts.
3 Those who refuse to gossip
or harm their neighbors
or speak evil of their friends.
4 Those who despise flagrant sinners,
and honor the faithful followers of the Lord,
and keep their promises even when it hurts.
5 Those who lend money without charging interest,
and who cannot be bribed to lie about the innocent.
Such people will stand firm forever.

PSALM 16

A psalm of David.*

1 Keep me safe, O God,
for I have come to you for refuge.

2 I said to the Lord, "You are my Master!
Every good thing I have comes from you."
3 The godly people in the land
are my true heroes!
I take pleasure in them!
4 Troubles multiply for those who chase after other gods.
I will not take part in their sacrifices of blood
or even speak the names of their gods.

5 Lord, you alone are my inheritance, my cup of blessing.
You guard all that is mine.
6 The land you have given me is a pleasant land.
What a wonderful inheritance!

7 I will bless the Lord who guides me;
even at night my heart instructs me.
8 I know the Lord is always with me.
I will not be shaken, for he is right beside me.

9 No wonder my heart is glad, and I rejoice.*
My body rests in safety.
10 For you will not leave my soul among the dead*
or allow your holy one* to rot in the grave.
11 You will show me the way of life,
granting me the joy of your presence
and the pleasures of living with you forever.*

PSALM 17

A prayer of David.

1 O Lord, hear my plea for justice.
Listen to my cry for help.
Pay attention to my prayer,
for it comes from honest lips.
2 Declare me innocent,
for you see those who do right.

3 You have tested my thoughts and examined my heart in the night.
You have scrutinized me and found nothing wrong.
I am determined not to sin in what I say.
4 I have followed your commands,
which keep me from following cruel and evil people.
5 My steps have stayed on your path;
I have not wavered from following you.

6 I am praying to you because I know you will answer, O God.
Bend down and listen as I pray.
7 Show me your unfailing love in wonderful ways.
By your mighty power you rescue
those who seek refuge from their enemies.
8 Guard me as you would guard your own eyes.*
Hide me in the shadow of your wings.
9 Protect me from wicked people who attack me,
from murderous enemies who surround me.

16:title Hebrew *miktam.* This may be a literary or musical term. **16:9** Greek version reads *and my tongue shouts his praises.* Compare Acts 2:26. **16:10a** Hebrew *in Sheol.* **16:10b** Or *your Holy One.* **16:11** Greek version reads *You have shown me the way of life, / and you will fill me with the joy of your presence.* Compare Acts 2:28. **17:8** Hebrew *as the pupil of your eye.*

Psalm 16 is David's personal thanksgiving for preservation from death. The New Testament maintains that David's experience foreshadows a far greater deliverance from death: Christ's resurrection (cf. Acts 2:25–28; 13:35–37).

Psalm 17 finds David being unjustly persecuted, probably by Saul. Knowing his cause is just and his motivation open to God's eyes, he turns to God in urgent, sincere, and confident prayer. He knows that God, like a doting parent (v. 8), will hear, save, guard, and hide him.

10 They are without pity.
Listen to their boasting!
11 They track me down and surround me,
watching for the chance to throw me to the ground.
12 They are like hungry lions, eager to tear me apart—
like young lions hiding in ambush.

13 Arise, O LORD!
Stand against them, and bring them to their knees!
Rescue me from the wicked with your sword!
14 By the power of your hand, O LORD,
destroy those who look to this world for their reward.
But satisfy the hunger of your treasured ones.
May their children have plenty,
leaving an inheritance for their descendants.
15 Because I am righteous, I will see you.
When I awake, I will see you face to face
and be satisfied.

PSALM 18

For the choir director: A psalm of David, the servant of the LORD. He sang this song to the LORD on the day the LORD rescued him from all his enemies and from Saul. He sang:

1 I love you, LORD;
you are my strength.
2 The LORD is my rock, my fortress, and my savior;
my God is my rock, in whom I find protection.
He is my shield, the power that saves me,
and my place of safety.
3 I called on the LORD, who is worthy of praise,
and he saved me from my enemies.

4 The ropes of death entangled me;
floods of destruction swept over me.
5 The grave* wrapped its ropes around me;
death laid a trap in my path.
6 But in my distress I cried out to the LORD;
yes, I prayed to my God for help.
He heard me from his sanctuary;
my cry to him reached his ears.

7 Then the earth quaked and trembled.
The foundations of the mountains shook;
they quaked because of his anger.
8 Smoke poured from his nostrils;
fierce flames leaped from his mouth.
Glowing coals blazed forth from him.
9 He opened the heavens and came down;
dark storm clouds were beneath his feet.
10 Mounted on a mighty angelic being,* he flew,
soaring on the wings of the wind.
11 He shrouded himself in darkness,
veiling his approach with dark rain clouds.
12 Thick clouds shielded the brightness around him
and rained down hail and burning coals.*
13 The LORD thundered from heaven;
the voice of the Most High resounded
amid the hail and burning coals.
14 He shot his arrows and scattered his enemies;
his lightning flashed, and they were greatly confused.
15 Then at your command, O LORD,
at the blast of your breath,
the bottom of the sea could be seen,
and the foundations of the earth were laid bare.

16 He reached down from heaven and rescued me;
he drew me out of deep waters.
17 He rescued me from my powerful enemies,
from those who hated me and were too strong for me.
18 They attacked me at a moment when I was in distress,
but the LORD supported me.
19 He led me to a place of safety;
he rescued me because he delights in me.
20 The LORD rewarded me for doing right;
he restored me because of my innocence.
21 For I have kept the ways of the LORD;
I have not turned from my God to follow evil.
22 I have followed all his regulations;
I have never abandoned his decrees.
23 I am blameless before God;
I have kept myself from sin.

18:5 Hebrew *Sheol.* **18:10** Hebrew *a cherub.* **18:12** Or *and lightning bolts;* also in 18:13.

Psalm 18 is David's thanksgiving to God for rescuing him (see title; cf. 2 Sam 22). With vivid imagery he describes how, motivated by delight in righteousness, the LORD used the forces of nature as instruments of salvation. David attributes his every success to the LORD's strength.

24 The LORD rewarded me for doing right.
He has seen my innocence.
25 To the faithful you show yourself faithful;
to those with integrity you show integrity.
26 To the pure you show yourself pure,
but to the wicked you show yourself hostile.
27 You rescue the humble,
but you humiliate the proud.
28 You light a lamp for me.
The LORD, my God, lights up my darkness.
29 In your strength I can crush an army;
with my God I can scale any wall.

30 God's way is perfect.
All the LORD's promises prove true.
He is a shield for all who look to him for protection.
31 For who is God except the LORD?
Who but our God is a solid rock?
32 God arms me with strength,
and he makes my way perfect.
33 He makes me as surefooted as a deer,
enabling me to stand on mountain heights.
34 He trains my hands for battle;
he strengthens my arm to draw a bronze bow.
35 You have given me your shield of victory.
Your right hand supports me;
your help has made me great.
36 You have made a wide path for my feet
to keep them from slipping.

37 I chased my enemies and caught them;
I did not stop until they were conquered.
38 I struck them down so they could not get up;
they fell beneath my feet.
39 You have armed me with strength for the battle;
you have subdued my enemies under my feet.
40 You placed my foot on their necks.
I have destroyed all who hated me.
41 They called for help, but no one came to their rescue.
They even cried to the LORD, but he refused to answer.
42 I ground them as fine as dust in the wind.
I swept them into the gutter like dirt.
43 You gave me victory over my accusers.
You appointed me ruler over nations;
people I don't even know now serve me.
44 As soon as they hear of me, they submit;
foreign nations cringe before me.
45 They all lose their courage
and come trembling from their strongholds.

46 The LORD lives! Praise to my Rock!
May the God of my salvation be exalted!
47 He is the God who pays back those who harm me;
he subdues the nations under me
48 and rescues me from my enemies.
You hold me safe beyond the reach of my enemies;
you save me from violent opponents.
49 For this, O LORD, I will praise you among the nations;
I will sing praises to your name.
50 You give great victories to your king;
you show unfailing love to your anointed,
to David and all his descendants forever.

PSALM 19

For the choir director: A psalm of David.

1 The heavens proclaim the glory of God.
The skies display his craftsmanship.
2 Day after day they continue to speak;
night after night they make him known.
3 They speak without a sound or word;
their voice is never heard.*
4 Yet their message has gone throughout the earth,
and their words to all the world.

God has made a home in the heavens for the sun.
5 It bursts forth like a radiant bridegroom after his wedding.
It rejoices like a great athlete eager to run the race.
6 The sun rises at one end of the heavens
and follows its course to the other end.
Nothing can hide from its heat.

7 The instructions of the LORD are perfect,
reviving the soul.
The decrees of the LORD are trustworthy,
making wise the simple.

19:3 Or *There is no speech or language where their voice is not heard.*

Psalm 19 The right response to God's revelation, modeled by David, is to seek cleansing and preservation from sin, that one might be acceptable to God, who is Israel's holy covenant LORD. The joyful notion of marriage is noted (v. 5).

8 The commandments of the LORD are right,
bringing joy to the heart.
The commands of the LORD are clear,
giving insight for living.
9 Reverence for the LORD is pure,
lasting forever.
The laws of the LORD are true;
each one is fair.
10 They are more desirable than gold,
even the finest gold.
They are sweeter than honey,
even honey dripping from the comb.
11 They are a warning to your servant,
a great reward for those who obey them.

12 How can I know all the sins lurking in my
heart?
Cleanse me from these hidden faults.
13 Keep your servant from deliberate sins!
Don't let them control me.
Then I will be free of guilt
and innocent of great sin.

14 May the words of my mouth
and the meditation of my heart
be pleasing to you,
O LORD, my rock and my redeemer.

PSALM 20

For the choir director: A psalm of David.

1 In times of trouble, may the LORD answer
your cry.
May the name of the God of Jacob keep
you safe from all harm.
2 May he send you help from his sanctuary
and strengthen you from Jerusalem.*
3 May he remember all your gifts
and look favorably on your burnt offerings.
Interlude

4 May he grant your heart's desires
and make all your plans succeed.
5 May we shout for joy when we hear of your
victory
and raise a victory banner in the name of
our God.
May the LORD answer all your prayers.

6 Now I know that the LORD rescues his
anointed king.
He will answer him from his holy heaven
and rescue him by his great power.
7 Some nations boast of their chariots and
horses,
but we boast in the name of the LORD our
God.
8 Those nations will fall down and collapse,
but we will rise up and stand firm.
9 Give victory to our king, O LORD!
Answer our cry for help.

PSALM 21

For the choir director: A psalm of David.

1 How the king rejoices in your strength,
O LORD!
He shouts with joy because you give him
victory.
2 For you have given him his heart's desire;
you have withheld nothing he requested.
Interlude

3 You welcomed him back with success and
prosperity.
You placed a crown of finest gold on his
head.
4 He asked you to preserve his life,
and you granted his request.
The days of his life stretch on forever.
5 Your victory brings him great honor,
and you have clothed him with splendor
and majesty.
6 You have endowed him with eternal blessings
and given him the joy of your presence.
7 For the king trusts in the LORD.
The unfailing love of the Most High will
keep him from stumbling.

8 You will capture all your enemies.
Your strong right hand will seize all who
hate you.
9 You will throw them in a flaming furnace
when you appear.

20:2 Hebrew *Zion.*

Psalm 20 was probably a prayer before battle. God's people seek his sevenfold blessing in *times of trouble* on the grounds of confidence in his name (i.e., character) and presence with them (signified by Jerusalem). Their confidence in the LORD's holy might assures them that he will hear and help his *anointed king* (cf. Acts 10:38).

Psalm 21 fulfills 20:5. Recognizing that all victory comes from the LORD, God's people gladly give him the glory and praise for victory in battle. Here again David foreshadows the Messiah.

The Lord will consume them in his anger;
fire will devour them.
10 You will wipe their children from the face of the earth;
they will never have descendants.
11 Although they plot against you,
their evil schemes will never succeed.
12 For they will turn and run
when they see your arrows aimed at them.
13 Rise up, O Lord, in all your power.
With music and singing we celebrate your mighty acts.

PSALM 22

For the choir director: A psalm of David, to be sung to the tune "Doe of the Dawn."

1 My God, my God, why have you abandoned me?
Why are you so far away when I groan for help?
2 Every day I call to you, my God, but you do not answer.
Every night you hear my voice, but I find no relief.

3 Yet you are holy,
enthroned on the praises of Israel.
4 Our ancestors trusted in you,
and you rescued them.
5 They cried out to you and were saved.
They trusted in you and were never disgraced.

6 But I am a worm and not a man.
I am scorned and despised by all!
7 Everyone who sees me mocks me.
They sneer and shake their heads, saying,
8 "Is this the one who relies on the Lord?
Then let the Lord save him!
If the Lord loves him so much,
let the Lord rescue him!"

9 Yet you brought me safely from my mother's womb
and led me to trust you at my mother's breast.
10 I was thrust into your arms at my birth.
You have been my God from the moment I was born.

11 Do not stay so far from me,
for trouble is near,
and no one else can help me.
12 My enemies surround me like a herd of bulls;
fierce bulls of Bashan have hemmed me in!
13 Like lions they open their jaws against me,
roaring and tearing into their prey.
14 My life is poured out like water,
and all my bones are out of joint.
My heart is like wax,
melting within me.
15 My strength has dried up like sunbaked clay.
My tongue sticks to the roof of my mouth.
You have laid me in the dust and left me for dead.
16 My enemies surround me like a pack of dogs;
an evil gang closes in on me.
They have pierced my hands and feet.
17 I can count all my bones.
My enemies stare at me and gloat.
18 They divide my garments among themselves
and throw dice* for my clothing.

19 O Lord, do not stay far away!
You are my strength; come quickly to my aid!
20 Save me from the sword;
spare my precious life from these dogs.
21 Snatch me from the lion's jaws
and from the horns of these wild oxen.

22 I will proclaim your name to my brothers and sisters.*
I will praise you among your assembled people.
23 Praise the Lord, all you who fear him!
Honor him, all you descendants of Jacob!

22:18 Hebrew *cast lots.* **22:22** Hebrew *my brothers.*

Psalm 22 finds David in the midst of some tragedy, feeling *abandoned.* Convinced that God has been good to him, David knows he will prove equally good to all nations and generations. The New Testament sees the hope of Psalm 22 fulfilled in Christ's death, resurrection, and exaltation (see Matt 27:39–46; John 19:23–28; Heb 2:9–12).

Verses 9–10 are thought to picture God as a midwife who delivers an infant, places it on her lap in order to clean it off, and then starts it on the process of breastfeeding. Thus the process of maternal bonding is divinely initiated. The Jerusalem Bible translates "You drew me out of the womb, you entrusted me to my mother's breast. You placed me on your lap from my birth, from my mother's womb you have been my God." God is intimately concerned with both the physical and spiritual dynamics of birth. See also 71:2.

Show him reverence, all you descendants
of Israel!
24 For he has not ignored or belittled the
suffering of the needy.
He has not turned his back on them,
but has listened to their cries for help.

25 I will praise you in the great assembly.
I will fulfill my vows in the presence of
those who worship you.
26 The poor will eat and be satisfied.
All who seek the LORD will praise him.
Their hearts will rejoice with everlasting
joy.
27 The whole earth will acknowledge the LORD
and return to him.
All the families of the nations will bow
down before him.
28 For royal power belongs to the LORD.
He rules all the nations.

29 Let the rich of the earth feast and worship.
Bow before him, all who are mortal,
all whose lives will end as dust.
30 Our children will also serve him.
Future generations will hear about the
wonders of the Lord.
31 His righteous acts will be told to those not
yet born.
They will hear about everything he has
done.

PSALM 23

A psalm of David.

1 The LORD is my shepherd;
I have all that I need.
2 He lets me rest in green meadows;
he leads me beside peaceful streams.
3 He renews my strength.
He guides me along right paths,
bringing honor to his name.
4 Even when I walk
through the darkest valley,*
I will not be afraid,
for you are close beside me.
Your rod and your staff
protect and comfort me.
5 You prepare a feast for me
in the presence of my enemies.
You honor me by anointing my head with
oil.
My cup overflows with blessings.
6 Surely your goodness and unfailing love
will pursue me
all the days of my life,
and I will live in the house of the LORD
forever.

PSALM 24

A psalm of David.

1 The earth is the LORD's, and everything in it.
The world and all its people belong to him.
2 For he laid the earth's foundation on the seas
and built it on the ocean depths.

3 Who may climb the mountain of the LORD?
Who may stand in his holy place?
4 Only those whose hands and hearts are pure,
who do not worship idols
and never tell lies.
5 They will receive the LORD's blessing
and have a right relationship with God
their savior.
6 Such people may seek you
and worship in your presence, O God of
Jacob. *Interlude*

7 Open up, ancient gates!
Open up, ancient doors,
and let the King of glory enter.
8 Who is the King of glory?
The LORD, strong and mighty;
the LORD, invincible in battle.
9 Open up, ancient gates!
Open up, ancient doors,
and let the King of glory enter.
10 Who is the King of glory?
The LORD of Heaven's Armies—
he is the King of glory. *Interlude*

23:4 Or *the dark valley of death.*

Psalm 23 The shepherd image implies that God accepts the responsibility to care for those who know him. His priorities are to keep them spiritually healthy and growing (food, water, rest, restoration, and guidance, vv. 1–3). Although they are not protected from the *darkest valley*, the shepherd is always there to protect them through it.

Psalm 24 may perhaps celebrate the return of the Ark, the symbol of God's presence, to Jerusalem (cf. 2 Sam 6:12–15). His holiness necessitates the salvation of those who seek him, so he grants them *a right relationship with* him as a blessing.

PSALM 25*

A psalm of David.

1 O LORD, I give my life to you.
2 I trust in you, my God!
Do not let me be disgraced,
or let my enemies rejoice in my defeat.
3 No one who trusts in you will ever be disgraced,
but disgrace comes to those who try to deceive others.

4 Show me the right path, O LORD;
point out the road for me to follow.
5 Lead me by your truth and teach me,
for you are the God who saves me.
All day long I put my hope in you.
6 Remember, O LORD, your compassion and unfailing love,
which you have shown from long ages past.
7 Do not remember the rebellious sins of my youth.
Remember me in the light of your unfailing love,
for you are merciful, O LORD.

8 The LORD is good and does what is right;
he shows the proper path to those who go astray.
9 He leads the humble in doing right,
teaching them his way.
10 The LORD leads with unfailing love and faithfulness
all who keep his covenant and obey his demands.

11 For the honor of your name, O LORD,
forgive my many, many sins.
12 Who are those who fear the LORD?
He will show them the path they should choose.
13 They will live in prosperity,
and their children will inherit the land.
14 The LORD is a friend to those who fear him.
He teaches them his covenant.
15 My eyes are always on the LORD,
for he rescues me from the traps of my enemies.

16 Turn to me and have mercy,
for I am alone and in deep distress.
17 My problems go from bad to worse.
Oh, save me from them all!
18 Feel my pain and see my trouble.
Forgive all my sins.
19 See how many enemies I have
and how viciously they hate me!
20 Protect me! Rescue my life from them!
Do not let me be disgraced, for in you I take refuge.
21 May integrity and honesty protect me,
for I put my hope in you.

22 O God, ransom Israel
from all its troubles.

PSALM 26

A psalm of David.

1 Declare me innocent, O LORD,
for I have acted with integrity;
I have trusted in the LORD without wavering.
2 Put me on trial, LORD, and cross-examine me.
Test my motives and my heart.
3 For I am always aware of your unfailing love,
and I have lived according to your truth.
4 I do not spend time with liars
or go along with hypocrites.
5 I hate the gatherings of those who do evil,
and I refuse to join in with the wicked.
6 I wash my hands to declare my innocence.
I come to your altar, O LORD,
7 singing a song of thanksgiving
and telling of all your wonders.
8 I love your sanctuary, LORD,
the place where your glorious presence dwells.

25 This psalm is a Hebrew acrostic poem; each verse begins with a successive letter of the Hebrew alphabet.

Psalm 25 In a time of trouble for all Israel, David prays for protection, instruction, pardon, and deliverance. Aware that obedience means loneliness and suffering, he prays for saving grace for himself and all God's people.

Psalm 26 finds David falsely accused but maintaining his innocence. His fidelity is expressed in right inward attitudes (unwavering trust,), and right outward behavior (shunning the wicked, witnessing aloud, and delighting in worship). On this basis he asks the LORD to test him thoroughly and trusts that his prayer for vindication, preservation, and redemption will be answered favorably, with grace to continue faithful.

9 Don't let me suffer the fate of sinners.
Don't condemn me along with murderers.
10 Their hands are dirty with evil schemes,
and they constantly take bribes.
11 But I am not like that; I live with integrity.
So redeem me and show me mercy.
12 Now I stand on solid ground,
and I will publicly praise the LORD.

PSALM 27

A psalm of David.

1 The LORD is my light and my salvation—
so why should I be afraid?
The LORD is my fortress, protecting me from danger,
so why should I tremble?
2 When evil people come to devour me,
when my enemies and foes attack me,
they will stumble and fall.
3 Though a mighty army surrounds me,
my heart will not be afraid.
Even if I am attacked,
I will remain confident.

4 The one thing I ask of the LORD—
the thing I seek most—
is to live in the house of the LORD all the days of my life,
delighting in the LORD's perfections
and meditating in his Temple.
5 For he will conceal me there when troubles come;
he will hide me in his sanctuary.
He will place me out of reach on a high rock.
6 Then I will hold my head high
above my enemies who surround me.
At his sanctuary I will offer sacrifices with shouts of joy,
singing and praising the LORD with music.

7 Hear me as I pray, O LORD.
Be merciful and answer me!
8 My heart has heard you say, "Come and talk with me."
And my heart responds, "LORD, I am coming."
9 Do not turn your back on me.
Do not reject your servant in anger.
You have always been my helper.
Don't leave me now; don't abandon me,
O God of my salvation!
10 Even if my father and mother abandon me,
the LORD will hold me close.

11 Teach me how to live, O LORD.
Lead me along the right path,
for my enemies are waiting for me.
12 Do not let me fall into their hands.
For they accuse me of things I've never done;
with every breath they threaten me with violence.
13 Yet I am confident I will see the LORD's goodness
while I am here in the land of the living.

14 Wait patiently for the LORD.
Be brave and courageous.
Yes, wait patiently for the LORD.

PSALM 28

A psalm of David.

1 I pray to you, O LORD, my rock.
Do not turn a deaf ear to me.
For if you are silent,
I might as well give up and die.
2 Listen to my prayer for mercy
as I cry out to you for help,
as I lift my hands toward your holy sanctuary.

3 Do not drag me away with the wicked—
with those who do evil—
those who speak friendly words to their neighbors
while planning evil in their hearts.
4 Give them the punishment they so richly deserve!

Psalm 27 was written in a time of trouble. The strength of David's faith reveals itself in his courageous confidence and his single-minded longing for the LORD's company, beauty, and wisdom. Even though parental love (v. 10), viewed here as the most steadfast of human relationships, should fail, God will still be faithful. This is one psalm for which "of David" could be interpreted "following David"—the Temple (v. 4) was built by Solomon after David's death.

Psalm 28 begins with David's humble prayer for help, preservation, and justice. Note how inner trust in the LORD leads first to receiving his help, then to inner joy and outward thanksgiving. Clearly David knows God as the builder or breaker of all human lives and the shepherd of his people.

Measure it out in proportion to their
wickedness.
Pay them back for all their evil deeds!
Give them a taste of what they have done
to others.
5 They care nothing for what the LORD has
done
or for what his hands have made.
So he will tear them down,
and they will never be rebuilt!

6 Praise the LORD!
For he has heard my cry for mercy.
7 The LORD is my strength and shield.
I trust him with all my heart.
He helps me, and my heart is filled with joy.
I burst out in songs of thanksgiving.

8 The LORD gives his people strength.
He is a safe fortress for his anointed king.
9 Save your people!
Bless Israel, your special possession.*
Lead them like a shepherd,
and carry them in your arms forever.

PSALM 29

A psalm of David.

1 Honor the LORD, you heavenly beings*;
honor the LORD for his glory and strength.
2 Honor the LORD for the glory of his name.
Worship the LORD in the splendor of his
holiness.

3 The voice of the LORD echoes above the sea.
The God of glory thunders.
The LORD thunders over the mighty sea.
4 The voice of the LORD is powerful;
the voice of the LORD is majestic.
5 The voice of the LORD splits the mighty
cedars;
the LORD shatters the cedars of Lebanon.
6 He makes Lebanon's mountains skip like a
calf;
he makes Mount Hermon* leap like a
young wild ox.
7 The voice of the LORD strikes
with bolts of lightning.
8 The voice of the LORD makes the barren
wilderness quake;
the LORD shakes the wilderness of Kadesh.
9 The voice of the LORD twists mighty oaks*
and strips the forests bare.
In his Temple everyone shouts, "Glory!"

10 The LORD rules over the floodwaters.
The LORD reigns as king forever.
11 The LORD gives his people strength.
The LORD blesses them with peace.

PSALM 30

A psalm of David. A song for the dedication of the Temple.

1 I will exalt you, LORD, for you rescued me.
You refused to let my enemies triumph
over me.
2 O LORD my God, I cried to you for help,
and you restored my health.
3 You brought me up from the grave,* O LORD.
You kept me from falling into the pit of
death.

4 Sing to the LORD, all you godly ones!
Praise his holy name.
5 For his anger lasts only a moment,
but his favor lasts a lifetime!
Weeping may last through the night,
but joy comes with the morning.

6 When I was prosperous, I said,
"Nothing can stop me now!"
7 Your favor, O LORD, made me as secure as a
mountain.
Then you turned away from me, and I was
shattered.

8 I cried out to you, O LORD.
I begged the Lord for mercy, saying,
9 "What will you gain if I die,

28:9 Hebrew *Bless your inheritance.* **29:1** Hebrew *you sons of God.* **29:6** Hebrew *Sirion,* another name for Mount Hermon. **29:9** Or *causes the deer to writhe in labor.* **30:3** Hebrew *from Sheol.*

Psalm 29 focuses on God's transcendent, majestic glory as revealed in a thunderstorm. On earth, *the voice of the LORD* is conveyed in seven strikes of thunder and lightning (vv. 3–9). The devastating destruction they cause signifies especially his sovereign power to judge (e.g., v. 10, the flood). Recognizing only one appropriate response, David calls all heaven to worship.

Psalm 30, though a deeply personal thanksgiving, has an undeniably cultic setting (see title; David never built the Temple but probably dedicated the site; cf. 2 Sam 6—7). The opening and closing personal praise is rooted in experiences of God's favor, especially in answered prayer and in dealing effectively with human pride.

if I sink into the grave?
Can my dust praise you?
Can it tell of your faithfulness?
10 Hear me, LORD, and have mercy on me.
Help me, O LORD."

11 You have turned my mourning into joyful dancing.
You have taken away my clothes of mourning and clothed me with joy,
12 that I might sing praises to you and not be silent.
O LORD my God, I will give you thanks forever!

PSALM 31

For the choir director: A psalm of David.

1 O LORD, I have come to you for protection;
don't let me be disgraced.
Save me, for you do what is right.
2 Turn your ear to listen to me;
rescue me quickly.
Be my rock of protection,
a fortress where I will be safe.
3 You are my rock and my fortress.
For the honor of your name, lead me out of this danger.
4 Pull me from the trap my enemies set for me,
for I find protection in you alone.
5 I entrust my spirit into your hand.
Rescue me, LORD, for you are a faithful God.

6 I hate those who worship worthless idols.
I trust in the LORD.
7 I will be glad and rejoice in your unfailing love,
for you have seen my troubles,
and you care about the anguish of my soul.
8 You have not handed me over to my enemies
but have set me in a safe place.

9 Have mercy on me, LORD, for I am in distress.
Tears blur my eyes.
My body and soul are withering away.
10 I am dying from grief;
my years are shortened by sadness.
Sin has drained my strength;
I am wasting away from within.
11 I am scorned by all my enemies
and despised by my neighbors—
even my friends are afraid to come near me.
When they see me on the street,
they run the other way.
12 I am ignored as if I were dead,
as if I were a broken pot.
13 I have heard the many rumors about me,
and I am surrounded by terror.
My enemies conspire against me,
plotting to take my life.

14 But I am trusting you, O LORD,
saying, "You are my God!"
15 My future is in your hands.
Rescue me from those who hunt me down relentlessly.
16 Let your favor shine on your servant.
In your unfailing love, rescue me.
17 Don't let me be disgraced, O LORD,
for I call out to you for help.
Let the wicked be disgraced;
let them lie silent in the grave.*
18 Silence their lying lips—
those proud and arrogant lips that accuse the godly.

19 How great is the goodness
you have stored up for those who fear you.
You lavish it on those who come to you for protection,
blessing them before the watching world.
20 You hide them in the shelter of your presence,
safe from those who conspire against them.
You shelter them in your presence,
far from accusing tongues.

21 Praise the LORD,
for he has shown me the wonders of his unfailing love.
He kept me safe when my city was under attack.
22 In panic I cried out,
"I am cut off from the LORD!"
But you heard my cry for mercy
and answered my call for help.

23 Love the LORD, all you godly ones!
For the LORD protects those who are loyal to him,

31:17 Hebrew *in Sheol.*

Psalm 31 finds David beset by enemies seeking to trap him. He has succumbed to depression, physical illness, and near paranoia. Note how the protective *hand* of God is contrasted with the violent hands of David's enemies (vv. 5, 8, 15).

but he harshly punishes the arrogant.
24 So be strong and courageous,
all you who put your hope in the LORD!

PSALM 32

A psalm of David.*

1 Oh, what joy for those
whose disobedience is forgiven,
whose sin is put out of sight!
2 Yes, what joy for those
whose record the LORD has cleared of guilt,*
whose lives are lived in complete honesty!
3 When I refused to confess my sin,
my body wasted away,
and I groaned all day long.
4 Day and night your hand of discipline was heavy on me.
My strength evaporated like water in the summer heat. *Interlude*

5 Finally, I confessed all my sins to you
and stopped trying to hide my guilt.
I said to myself, "I will confess my rebellion to the LORD."
And you forgave me! All my guilt is gone. *Interlude*

6 Therefore, let all the godly pray to you while there is still time,
that they may not drown in the floodwaters of judgment.
7 For you are my hiding place;
you protect me from trouble.
You surround me with songs of victory. *Interlude*

8 The LORD says, "I will guide you along the best pathway for your life.
I will advise you and watch over you.
9 Do not be like a senseless horse or mule
that needs a bit and bridle to keep it under control."

10 Many sorrows come to the wicked,
but unfailing love surrounds those who trust the LORD.
11 So rejoice in the LORD and be glad, all you who obey him!
Shout for joy, all you whose hearts are pure!

PSALM 33

1 Let the godly sing for joy to the LORD;
it is fitting for the pure to praise him.
2 Praise the LORD with melodies on the lyre;
make music for him on the ten-stringed harp.
3 Sing a new song of praise to him;
play skillfully on the harp, and sing with joy.
4 For the word of the LORD holds true,
and we can trust everything he does.
5 He loves whatever is just and good;
the unfailing love of the LORD fills the earth.

6 The LORD merely spoke,
and the heavens were created.
He breathed the word,
and all the stars were born.
7 He assigned the sea its boundaries
and locked the oceans in vast reservoirs.
8 Let the whole world fear the LORD,
and let everyone stand in awe of him.
9 For when he spoke, the world began!
It appeared at his command.

10 The LORD frustrates the plans of the nations
and thwarts all their schemes.
11 But the LORD's plans stand firm forever;
his intentions can never be shaken.

12 What joy for the nation whose God is the LORD,
whose people he has chosen as his inheritance.

13 The LORD looks down from heaven
and sees the whole human race.
14 From his throne he observes

32:TITLE Hebrew *maskil.* This may be a literary or musical term. **32:2** Greek version reads *of sin.* Compare Rom 4:7.

Psalm 32 is sometimes held as recording David's experience following his adultery with Bathsheba and murder of Uriah (2 Sam 11). This psalm reveals the devastating effects of sin. It may involve manipulation and exploitative treatment of others, as was the case with David, but it can create an equally deep wound in the soul of the perpetrator (cf. 1 Cor 6:18–19).

Psalm 33 expounds 32:11. The righteous may rejoice for two reasons. Both the *word of the LORD* and the eye of the LORD are indications of his *unfailing love* to all the earth, creating and observing all.

all who live on the earth.
15 He made their hearts,
so he understands everything they do.
16 The best-equipped army cannot save a king,
nor is great strength enough to save a warrior.
17 Don't count on your warhorse to give you victory—
for all its strength, it cannot save you.

18 But the LORD watches over those who fear him,
those who rely on his unfailing love.
19 He rescues them from death
and keeps them alive in times of famine.

20 We put our hope in the LORD.
He is our help and our shield.
21 In him our hearts rejoice,
for we trust in his holy name.
22 Let your unfailing love surround us, LORD,
for our hope is in you alone.

PSALM 34*

A psalm of David, regarding the time he pretended to be insane in front of Abimelech, who sent him away.

1 I will praise the LORD at all times.
I will constantly speak his praises.
2 I will boast only in the LORD;
let all who are helpless take heart.
3 Come, let us tell of the LORD's greatness;
let us exalt his name together.

4 I prayed to the LORD, and he answered me.
He freed me from all my fears.
5 Those who look to him for help will be radiant with joy;
no shadow of shame will darken their faces.
6 In my desperation I prayed, and the LORD listened;
he saved me from all my troubles.
7 For the angel of the LORD is a guard;
he surrounds and defends all who fear him.

8 Taste and see that the LORD is good.
Oh, the joys of those who take refuge in him!
9 Fear the LORD, you his godly people,
for those who fear him will have all they need.
10 Even strong young lions sometimes go hungry,
but those who trust in the LORD will lack no good thing.

11 Come, my children, and listen to me,
and I will teach you to fear the LORD.
12 Does anyone want to live a life
that is long and prosperous?
13 Then keep your tongue from speaking evil
and your lips from telling lies!
14 Turn away from evil and do good.
Search for peace, and work to maintain it.

15 The eyes of the LORD watch over those who do right;
his ears are open to their cries for help.
16 But the LORD turns his face against those who do evil;
he will erase their memory from the earth.
17 The LORD hears his people when they call to him for help.
He rescues them from all their troubles.
18 The LORD is close to the brokenhearted;
he rescues those whose spirits are crushed.

19 The righteous person faces many troubles,
but the LORD comes to the rescue each time.
20 For the LORD protects the bones of the righteous;
not one of them is broken!

21 Calamity will surely overtake the wicked,
and those who hate the righteous will be punished.
22 But the LORD will redeem those who serve him.
No one who takes refuge in him will be condemned.

34 This psalm is a Hebrew acrostic poem; each verse begins with a successive letter of the Hebrew alphabet.

Psalm 34 David had feigned madness in order to avoid the suspicious hostility of the subjects of Abimelech (King Achish of Gath). Presuming him to be insane, the enemies sent him off without incident (cf. 1 Sam 21:10–15). Thrilled by the experience of answered prayer in anxious circumstances, David invites all God's people to discover such happiness by looking to the LORD in reverence. Interestingly, this psalm is an acrostic poem (see translator's note).

PSALM 35

A psalm of David.

1 O LORD, oppose those who oppose me.
Fight those who fight against me.
2 Put on your armor, and take up your shield.
Prepare for battle, and come to my aid.
3 Lift up your spear and javelin
against those who pursue me.
Let me hear you say,
"I will give you victory!"
4 Bring shame and disgrace on those trying to kill me;
turn them back and humiliate those who want to harm me.
5 Blow them away like chaff in the wind—
a wind sent by the angel of the LORD.
6 Make their path dark and slippery,
with the angel of the LORD pursuing them.
7 I did them no wrong, but they laid a trap for me.
I did them no wrong, but they dug a pit to catch me.
8 So let sudden ruin come upon them!
Let them be caught in the trap they set for me!
Let them be destroyed in the pit they dug for me.

9 Then I will rejoice in the LORD.
I will be glad because he rescues me.
10 With every bone in my body I will praise him:
"LORD, who can compare with you?
Who else rescues the helpless from the strong?
Who else protects the helpless and poor from those who rob them?"

11 Malicious witnesses testify against me.
They accuse me of crimes I know nothing about.
12 They repay me evil for good.
I am sick with despair.
13 Yet when they were ill, I grieved for them.
I denied myself by fasting for them,
but my prayers returned unanswered.
14 I was sad, as though they were my friends or family,
as if I were grieving for my own mother.
15 But they are glad now that I am in trouble;
they gleefully join together against me.
I am attacked by people I don't even know;
they slander me constantly.
16 They mock me and call me names;
they snarl at me.

17 How long, O Lord, will you look on and do nothing?
Rescue me from their fierce attacks.
Protect my life from these lions!
18 Then I will thank you in front of the great assembly.
I will praise you before all the people.
19 Don't let my treacherous enemies rejoice over my defeat.
Don't let those who hate me without cause gloat over my sorrow.
20 They don't talk of peace;
they plot against innocent people who mind their own business.
21 They shout, "Aha! Aha!
With our own eyes we saw him do it!"

22 O LORD, you know all about this.
Do not stay silent.
Do not abandon me now, O Lord.
23 Wake up! Rise to my defense!
Take up my case, my God and my Lord.
24 Declare me not guilty, O LORD my God, for you give justice.
Don't let my enemies laugh about me in my troubles.
25 Don't let them say, "Look, we got what we wanted!
Now we will eat him alive!"

26 May those who rejoice at my troubles
be humiliated and disgraced.
May those who triumph over me
be covered with shame and dishonor.
27 But give great joy to those who came to my defense.
Let them continually say, "Great is the LORD,
who delights in blessing his servant with peace!"
28 Then I will proclaim your justice,
and I will praise you all day long.

Psalm 35 is another prayer for salvation and vindication on the grounds of innocence. The unidentified enemies are guilty of conspiracy to murder, false accusation, ingratitude, mockery, and public deceit. Verse 14 recognizes the acute grief occasioned by the loss of one's mother. The deep attachment formed between mother and child was understood as lifelong and powerful.

PSALM 36

For the choir director: A psalm of David, the servant of the LORD.

1 Sin whispers to the wicked, deep within their
hearts.
They have no fear of God at all.
2 In their blind conceit,
they cannot see how wicked they really
are.
3 Everything they say is crooked and deceitful.
They refuse to act wisely or do good.
4 They lie awake at night, hatching sinful plots.
Their actions are never good.
They make no attempt to turn from evil.

5 Your unfailing love, O LORD, is as vast as the
heavens;
your faithfulness reaches beyond the clouds.
6 Your righteousness is like the mighty
mountains,
your justice like the ocean depths.
You care for people and animals alike,
O LORD.
7 How precious is your unfailing love,
O God!
All humanity finds shelter
in the shadow of your wings.
8 You feed them from the abundance of your
own house,
letting them drink from your river of
delights.
9 For you are the fountain of life,
the light by which we see.

10 Pour out your unfailing love on those who
love you;
give justice to those with honest hearts.
11 Don't let the proud trample me
or the wicked push me around.
12 Look! Those who do evil have fallen!
They are thrown down, never to rise again.

PSALM 37*

A psalm of David.

1 Don't worry about the wicked
or envy those who do wrong.
2 For like grass, they soon fade away.
Like spring flowers, they soon wither.

3 Trust in the LORD and do good.
Then you will live safely in the land and
prosper.
4 Take delight in the LORD,
and he will give you your heart's desires.

5 Commit everything you do to the LORD.
Trust him, and he will help you.
6 He will make your innocence radiate like the
dawn,
and the justice of your cause will shine like
the noonday sun.

7 Be still in the presence of the LORD,
and wait patiently for him to act.
Don't worry about evil people who prosper
or fret about their wicked schemes.

8 Stop being angry!
Turn from your rage!
Do not lose your temper—
it only leads to harm.
9 For the wicked will be destroyed,
but those who trust in the LORD will
possess the land.

10 Soon the wicked will disappear.
Though you look for them, they will be
gone.
11 The lowly will possess the land
and will live in peace and prosperity.

12 The wicked plot against the godly;
they snarl at them in defiance.
13 But the Lord just laughs,
for he sees their day of judgment
coming.

14 The wicked draw their swords
and string their bows
to kill the poor and the oppressed,
to slaughter those who do right.

37 This psalm is a Hebrew acrostic poem; each stanza begins with a successive letter of the Hebrew alphabet.

Psalm 36 begins with a meditation on the deceitful sinfulness of the wicked. It then compares that with the LORD's powerful and precious steadfast love, likened to the protection of a mother bird (v. 7). To the faithful, God gives security and the blessings of spiritual food, drink, life, and light.

Psalm 37 In the Septuagint, the Hebrew command to *be still* (v. 7) or "to be receptive" was translated by a Greek verb usually rendered "submit" in its New Testament occurrences applying to women (Eph 5:21; Col 3:18). The term has a far broader range of meanings than is often understood. It can imply loyalty, commitment, alliance, or meaningful relationship.

15 But their swords will stab their own hearts,
and their bows will be broken.

16 It is better to be godly and have little
than to be evil and rich.
17 For the strength of the wicked will be
shattered,
but the LORD takes care of the godly.

18 Day by day the LORD takes care of the
innocent,
and they will receive an inheritance that
lasts forever.
19 They will not be disgraced in hard times;
even in famine they will have more than
enough.

20 But the wicked will die.
The LORD's enemies are like flowers in a
field—
they will disappear like smoke.

21 The wicked borrow and never repay,
but the godly are generous givers.
22 Those the LORD blesses will possess the land,
but those he curses will die.

23 The LORD directs the steps of the godly.
He delights in every detail of their lives.
24 Though they stumble, they will never fall,
for the LORD holds them by the hand.

25 Once I was young, and now I am old.
Yet I have never seen the godly abandoned
or their children begging for bread.
26 The godly always give generous loans to
others,
and their children are a blessing.

27 Turn from evil and do good,
and you will live in the land forever.
28 For the LORD loves justice,
and he will never abandon the godly.

He will keep them safe forever,
but the children of the wicked will die.
29 The godly will possess the land
and will live there forever.

30 The godly offer good counsel;
they teach right from wrong.
31 They have made God's law their own,
so they will never slip from his path.

32 The wicked wait in ambush for the godly,
looking for an excuse to kill them.
33 But the LORD will not let the wicked succeed
or let the godly be condemned when they
are put on trial.

34 Put your hope in the LORD.
Travel steadily along his path.
He will honor you by giving you the land.
You will see the wicked destroyed.

35 I have seen wicked and ruthless people
flourishing like a tree in its native soil.
36 But when I looked again, they were gone!
Though I searched for them, I could not
find them!

37 Look at those who are honest and good,
for a wonderful future awaits those who
love peace.
38 But the rebellious will be destroyed;
they have no future.

39 The LORD rescues the godly;
he is their fortress in times of trouble.
40 The LORD helps them,
rescuing them from the wicked.
He saves them,
and they find shelter in him.

PSALM 38

A psalm of David, asking God to remember him.

1 O LORD, don't rebuke me in your anger
or discipline me in your rage!
2 Your arrows have struck deep,
and your blows are crushing me.
3 Because of your anger, my whole body is
sick;
my health is broken because of my sins.
4 My guilt overwhelms me—
it is a burden too heavy to bear.
5 My wounds fester and stink
because of my foolish sins.
6 I am bent over and racked with pain.
All day long I walk around filled with grief.
7 A raging fever burns within me,
and my health is broken.

Psalm 38 is a penitential psalm in which David's heavy conscience leads him to identify the cause of his present suffering as the LORD's anger. His sin has rendered him vulnerable to illness, depression, isolation, and violent opposition. Yet still he believes God is *my God* and *my savior*; still he sees himself as one who is *pursuing good*. Verses 11–12 parallel the fear and despair of many an abused woman.

8 I am exhausted and completely crushed.
My groans come from an anguished heart.
9 You know what I long for, Lord;
you hear my every sigh.
10 My heart beats wildly, my strength fails,
and I am going blind.
11 My loved ones and friends stay away, fearing
my disease.
Even my own family stands at a distance.
12 Meanwhile, my enemies lay traps to kill me.
Those who wish me harm make plans to
ruin me.
All day long they plan their treachery.

13 But I am deaf to all their threats.
I am silent before them as one who cannot
speak.
14 I choose to hear nothing,
and I make no reply.
15 For I am waiting for you, O LORD.
You must answer for me, O Lord my God.
16 I prayed, "Don't let my enemies gloat over
me
or rejoice at my downfall."

17 I am on the verge of collapse,
facing constant pain.
18 But I confess my sins;
I am deeply sorry for what I have done.
19 I have many aggressive enemies;
they hate me without reason.
20 They repay me evil for good
and oppose me for pursuing good.
21 Do not abandon me, O LORD.
Do not stand at a distance, my God.
22 Come quickly to help me,
O Lord my savior.

PSALM 39

For Jeduthun, the choir director: A psalm of David.

1 I said to myself, "I will watch what I do
and not sin in what I say.
I will hold my tongue
when the ungodly are around me."
2 But as I stood there in silence—
not even speaking of good things—
the turmoil within me grew worse.
3 The more I thought about it,
the hotter I got,
igniting a fire of words:
4 "LORD, remind me how brief my time on
earth will be.
Remind me that my days are numbered—
how fleeting my life is.
5 You have made my life no longer than the
width of my hand.
My entire lifetime is just a moment to you;
at best, each of us is but a breath." *Interlude*

6 We are merely moving shadows,
and all our busy rushing ends in nothing.
We heap up wealth,
not knowing who will spend it.
7 And so, Lord, where do I put my hope?
My only hope is in you.
8 Rescue me from my rebellion.
Do not let fools mock me.
9 I am silent before you; I won't say a word,
for my punishment is from you.
10 But please stop striking me!
I am exhausted by the blows from your
hand.
11 When you discipline us for our sins,
you consume like a moth what is precious
to us.
Each of us is but a breath. *Interlude*

12 Hear my prayer, O LORD!
Listen to my cries for help!
Don't ignore my tears.
For I am your guest—
a traveler passing through,
as my ancestors were before me.
13 Leave me alone so I can smile again
before I am gone and exist no more.

PSALM 40

For the choir director: A psalm of David.

1 I waited patiently for the LORD to help me,
and he turned to me and heard my cry.

Psalm 39 Via a philosophy akin to that of Ecclesiastes (life is fleeting, vv. 4–6, 11–13; cf. Eccl 6:12) David eventually decides to focus on the LORD rather than dwell on life's troubles (vv. 6–7; cf. Ps 77). The psalm's shifting moods—from meditative to confessional to petitioning to hopeful portray despair and hope as simultaneous realities in the life of the faithful.

Psalm 40 Worship is transformed by a new awareness that the LORD requires inner righteousness, and witness becomes more open and unrestrained. The New Testament relates verses 6–8 to the substitutionary work of Christ (see Heb 10:5–9).

2 He lifted me out of the pit of despair,
out of the mud and the mire.
He set my feet on solid ground
and steadied me as I walked along.
3 He has given me a new song to sing,
a hymn of praise to our God.
Many will see what he has done and be amazed.
They will put their trust in the LORD.

4 Oh, the joys of those who trust the LORD,
who have no confidence in the proud
or in those who worship idols.
5 O LORD my God, you have performed many wonders for us.
Your plans for us are too numerous to list.
You have no equal.
If I tried to recite all your wonderful deeds,
I would never come to the end of them.

6 You take no delight in sacrifices or offerings.
Now that you have made me listen, I finally understand*—
you don't require burnt offerings or sin offerings.
7 Then I said, "Look, I have come.
As is written about me in the Scriptures:
8 I take joy in doing your will, my God,
for your instructions are written on my heart."

9 I have told all your people about your justice.
I have not been afraid to speak out,
as you, O LORD, well know.
10 I have not kept the good news of your justice hidden in my heart;
I have talked about your faithfulness and saving power.
I have told everyone in the great assembly
of your unfailing love and faithfulness.

11 LORD, don't hold back your tender mercies from me.
Let your unfailing love and faithfulness always protect me.
12 For troubles surround me—
too many to count!
My sins pile up so high
I can't see my way out.
They outnumber the hairs on my head.
I have lost all courage.

13 Please, LORD, rescue me!
Come quickly, LORD, and help me.
14 May those who try to destroy me
be humiliated and put to shame.
May those who take delight in my trouble
be turned back in disgrace.
15 Let them be horrified by their shame,
for they said, "Aha! We've got him now!"

16 But may all who search for you
be filled with joy and gladness in you.
May those who love your salvation
repeatedly shout, "The LORD is great!"
17 As for me, since I am poor and needy,
let the Lord keep me in his thoughts.
You are my helper and my savior.
O my God, do not delay.

PSALM 41

For the choir director: A psalm of David.

1 Oh, the joys of those who are kind to the poor!
The LORD rescues them when they are in trouble.
2 The LORD protects them
and keeps them alive.
He gives them prosperity in the land
and rescues them from their enemies.
3 The LORD nurses them when they are sick
and restores them to health.

4 "O LORD," I prayed, "have mercy on me.
Heal me, for I have sinned against you."
5 But my enemies say nothing but evil about me.
"How soon will he die and be forgotten?" they ask.
6 They visit me as if they were my friends,
but all the while they gather gossip,
and when they leave, they spread it everywhere.
7 All who hate me whisper about me,
imagining the worst.
8 "He has some fatal disease," they say.
"He will never get out of that bed!"
9 Even my best friend, the one I trusted completely,

40:6 Greek text reads *You have given me a body.* Compare Heb 10:5.

Psalm 41 pictures David suffering from some serious illness. His enemies, including one supposed *friend*, are taking advantage of his weakness to plot and rebel (vv. 5–9; cf. John 13:18). Answered prayer (whether already experienced or still anticipated) leads to reassurance, strengthened faith, and praise, a fitting end to the first book of Psalms.

the one who shared my food, has turned
against me.

10 Lord, have mercy on me.
Make me well again, so I can pay them
back!
11 I know you are pleased with me,
for you have not let my enemies triumph
over me.
12 You have preserved my life because I am
innocent;
you have brought me into your presence
forever.

13 Praise the Lord, the God of Israel,
who lives from everlasting to
everlasting.
Amen and amen!

Book Two (Psalms 42–72)

PSALM 42

For the choir director: A psalm of the descendants of Korah.*

1 As the deer longs for streams of water,
so I long for you, O God.
2 I thirst for God, the living God.
When can I go and stand before him?
3 Day and night I have only tears for food,
while my enemies continually taunt me,
saying,
"Where is this God of yours?"

4 My heart is breaking
as I remember how it used to be:
I walked among the crowds of worshipers,
leading a great procession to the house of
God,
singing for joy and giving thanks
amid the sound of a great celebration!

5 Why am I discouraged?
Why is my heart so sad?
I will put my hope in God!
I will praise him again—
my Savior and 6 my God!

Now I am deeply discouraged,
but I will remember you—
even from distant Mount Hermon, the source
of the Jordan,
from the land of Mount Mizar.
7 I hear the tumult of the raging seas
as your waves and surging tides sweep
over me.
8 But each day the Lord pours his unfailing
love upon me,
and through each night I sing his songs,
praying to God who gives me life.

9 "O God my rock," I cry,
"Why have you forgotten me?
Why must I wander around in grief,
oppressed by my enemies?"
10 Their taunts break my bones.
They scoff, "Where is this God of yours?"

11 Why am I discouraged?
Why is my heart so sad?
I will put my hope in God!
I will praise him again—
my Savior and my God!

PSALM 43

1 Declare me innocent, O God!
Defend me against these ungodly people.
Rescue me from these unjust liars.
2 For you are God, my only safe haven.
Why have you tossed me aside?
Why must I wander around in grief,
oppressed by my enemies?
3 Send out your light and your truth;
let them guide me.
Let them lead me to your holy mountain,
to the place where you live.
4 There I will go to the altar of God,
to God—the source of all my joy.
I will praise you with my harp,
O God, my God!

5 Why am I discouraged?
Why is my heart so sad?
I will put my hope in God!
I will praise him again—
my Savior and my God!

42:TITLE Hebrew *maskil.* This may be a literary or musical term.

42:1–72:20 Book 2

Psalms 42 and 43 are a pair, written by a Temple gatekeeper (cf. 1 Chr 26) while away from Jerusalem (42:6). They portray the same distressing inability to worship at the Temple and the same taunting by onlookers, which leaves the psalmist feeling distant from God. Spiritual hunger leads to joyful memories of past worship, which lead in turn to remembrance of the Lord.

PSALM 44

For the choir director: A psalm of the descendants of Korah.*

1 O God, we have heard it with our own ears—
our ancestors have told us
of all you did in their day,
in days long ago:
2 You drove out the pagan nations by your power
and gave all the land to our ancestors.
You crushed their enemies
and set our ancestors free.
3 They did not conquer the land with their swords;
it was not their own strong arm that gave them victory.
It was your right hand and strong arm
and the blinding light from your face that helped them,
for you loved them.

4 You are my King and my God.
You command victories for Israel.*
5 Only by your power can we push back our enemies;
only in your name can we trample our foes.
6 I do not trust in my bow;
I do not count on my sword to save me.
7 You are the one who gives us victory over our enemies;
you disgrace those who hate us.
8 O God, we give glory to you all day long
and constantly praise your name. *Interlude*

9 But now you have tossed us aside in dishonor.
You no longer lead our armies to battle.
10 You make us retreat from our enemies
and allow those who hate us to plunder our land.
11 You have butchered us like sheep
and scattered us among the nations.
12 You sold your precious people for a pittance,
making nothing on the sale.
13 You let our neighbors mock us.
We are an object of scorn and derision to those around us.
14 You have made us the butt of their jokes;
they shake their heads at us in scorn.
15 We can't escape the constant humiliation;
shame is written across our faces.
16 All we hear are the taunts of our mockers.
All we see are our vengeful enemies.

17 All this has happened though we have not forgotten you.
We have not violated your covenant.
18 Our hearts have not deserted you.
We have not strayed from your path.
19 Yet you have crushed us in the jackal's desert home.
You have covered us with darkness and death.
20 If we had forgotten the name of our God
or spread our hands in prayer to foreign gods,
21 God would surely have known it,
for he knows the secrets of every heart.
22 But for your sake we are killed every day;
we are being slaughtered like sheep.

23 Wake up, O Lord! Why do you sleep?
Get up! Do not reject us forever.
24 Why do you look the other way?
Why do you ignore our suffering and oppression?
25 We collapse in the dust,
lying face down in the dirt.
26 Rise up! Help us!
Ransom us because of your unfailing love.

PSALM 45

For the choir director: A love song to be sung to the tune "Lilies." A psalm of the descendants of Korah.*

1 Beautiful words stir my heart.
I will recite a lovely poem about the king,
for my tongue is like the pen of a skillful poet.

44:TITLE Hebrew *maskil.* This may be a literary or musical term. **44:4** Hebrew *for Jacob.* The names "Jacob" and "Israel" are often interchanged throughout the Old Testament, referring sometimes to the individual patriarch and sometimes to the nation. **45:TITLE** Hebrew *maskil.* This may be a literary or musical term.

Psalm 44 Victory in battle is not the result of military might but the gift of God. Yet what are God's people to make of the reality of present defeat (vv. 9–16)? Three times they ask *Why*? (vv. 23–24) but can only persevere in prayer on the basis of the LORD's unfailing love.

Psalm 45 depicts a wedding against a backdrop of war. The bride is a person of dignity and worth, to be respected near and far. Her function is to forget her past and worship the king. This psalm acknowledges the difficulty that a woman may have in adjusting

[2] You are the most handsome of all.
Gracious words stream from your lips.
God himself has blessed you forever.
[3] Put on your sword, O mighty warrior!
You are so glorious, so majestic!
[4] In your majesty, ride out to victory,
defending truth, humility, and justice.
Go forth to perform awe-inspiring deeds!
[5] Your arrows are sharp, piercing your
enemies' hearts.
The nations fall beneath your feet.
[6] Your throne, O God,* endures forever and
ever.
You rule with a scepter of justice.
[7] You love justice and hate evil.
Therefore God, your God, has anointed
you,
pouring out the oil of joy on you more
than on anyone else.
[8] Myrrh, aloes, and cassia perfume your robes.
In ivory palaces the music of strings
entertains you.
[9] Kings' daughters are among your noble
women.
At your right side stands the queen,
wearing jewelry of finest gold from
Ophir!

[10] Listen to me, O royal daughter; take to heart
what I say.
Forget your people and your family far
away.
[11] For your royal husband delights in your
beauty;
honor him, for he is your lord.
[12] The princess of Tyre* will shower you with
gifts.
The wealthy will beg your favor.
[13] The bride, a princess, looks glorious
in her golden gown.
[14] In her beautiful robes, she is led to the king,
accompanied by her bridesmaids.
[15] What a joyful and enthusiastic procession
as they enter the king's palace!

[16] Your sons will become kings like their father.
You will make them rulers over many
lands.
[17] I will bring honor to your name in every
generation.
Therefore, the nations will praise you
forever and ever.

PSALM 46

*For the choir director: A song of the descendants of Korah, to be sung by soprano voices.**

[1] God is our refuge and strength,
always ready to help in times of trouble.
[2] So we will not fear when earthquakes come
and the mountains crumble into the sea.
[3] Let the oceans roar and foam.
Let the mountains tremble as the waters
surge! *Interlude*

[4] A river brings joy to the city of our God,
the sacred home of the Most High.
[5] God dwells in that city; it cannot be
destroyed.
From the very break of day, God will
protect it.
[6] The nations are in chaos,
and their kingdoms crumble!
God's voice thunders,
and the earth melts!
[7] The LORD of Heaven's Armies is here
among us;
the God of Israel* is our fortress. *Interlude*

[8] Come, see the glorious works of the LORD:
See how he brings destruction upon the
world.
[9] He causes wars to end throughout the earth.
He breaks the bow and snaps the spear;
he burns the shields with fire.

[10] "Be still, and know that I am God!
I will be honored by every nation.
I will be honored throughout the world."

[11] The LORD of Heaven's Armies is here
among us;
the God of Israel is our fortress. *Interlude*

45:6 Or *Your divine throne.* **45:12** Hebrew *The daughter of Tyre.* **46:TITLE** Hebrew *according to alamoth.* **46:7** Hebrew *of Jacob;* also in 46:11. See note on 44:4.

to new surroundings. She must view not only the splendor of marriage but also the inherent worth of the bridegroom. The psalm clearly looks beyond any mortal ruler to Israel's perfect king, identified by the New Testament as Jesus Christ (v. 6; cf. Heb 1:8–9), whose bride is the church (e.g., Rev 19:7–8).

Psalm 46 Perhaps written after a siege has been broken, this psalm's focus on Jerusalem is surrounded by proclamations of God's sovereignty. He is his people's strong *refuge* from trouble (vv. 1–3), a *river that brings joy* (vv. 4–7), and a peacemaker for the world (v. 9).

PSALM 47

For the choir director: A psalm of the descendants of Korah.

1 Come, everyone! Clap your hands!
Shout to God with joyful praise!
2 For the LORD Most High is awesome.
He is the great King of all the earth.
3 He subdues the nations before us,
putting our enemies beneath our feet.
4 He chose the Promised Land as our inheritance,
the proud possession of Jacob's descendants, whom he loves. *Interlude*
5 God has ascended with a mighty shout.
The LORD has ascended with trumpets blaring.
6 Sing praises to God, sing praises;
sing praises to our King, sing praises!
7 For God is the King over all the earth.
Praise him with a psalm.*
8 God reigns above the nations,
sitting on his holy throne.
9 The rulers of the world have gathered together
with the people of the God of Abraham.
For all the kings of the earth belong to God.
He is highly honored everywhere.

PSALM 48

A song. A psalm of the descendants of Korah.

1 How great is the LORD,
how deserving of praise,
in the city of our God,
which sits on his holy mountain!
2 It is high and magnificent;
the whole earth rejoices to see it!
Mount Zion, the holy mountain,*
is the city of the great King!
3 God himself is in Jerusalem's towers,
revealing himself as its defender.

4 The kings of the earth joined forces
and advanced against the city.
5 But when they saw it, they were stunned;
they were terrified and ran away.
6 They were gripped with terror
and writhed in pain like a woman in labor.
7 You destroyed them like the mighty ships of Tarshish
shattered by a powerful east wind.
8 We had heard of the city's glory,
but now we have seen it ourselves—
the city of the LORD of Heaven's Armies.
It is the city of our God;
he will make it safe forever. *Interlude*
9 O God, we meditate on your unfailing love
as we worship in your Temple.
10 As your name deserves, O God,
you will be praised to the ends of the earth.
Your strong right hand is filled with victory.
11 Let the people on Mount Zion rejoice.
Let all the towns of Judah be glad
because of your justice.

12 Go, inspect the city of Jerusalem.*
Walk around and count the many towers.
13 Take note of the fortified walls,
and tour all the citadels,
that you may describe them
to future generations.
14 For that is what God is like.
He is our God forever and ever,
and he will guide us until we die.

PSALM 49

For the choir director: A psalm of the descendants of Korah.

1 Listen to this, all you people!
Pay attention, everyone in the world!
2 High and low,
rich and poor—listen!
3 For my words are wise,
and my thoughts are filled with insight.

47:7 Hebrew *maskil.* This may be a literary or musical term. **48:2** Or *Mount Zion, in the far north;* Hebrew reads *Mount Zion, the heights of Zaphon.* **48:12** Hebrew *Zion.*

Psalm 47 is an enthusiastic song in praise of who the LORD is and what he has done for his people. The loud exuberance of their worship reflects their appreciation of God's great victories and their unashamed desire to witness publicly to him.

Psalm 48 (cf. Rev 21) proclaims that Zion is holy, beautiful, mighty, and enduring, but only because the LORD dwells in her. Verse 6 uses the simile of a woman in labor as describing the extremity of human distress.

Psalm 49, a wisdom psalm, presents a *riddle* (v. 4). Recognizing death as a universal concern, the psalm-

4 I listen carefully to many proverbs
and solve riddles with inspiration from a harp.

5 Why should I fear when trouble comes,
when enemies surround me?
6 They trust in their wealth
and boast of great riches.
7 Yet they cannot redeem themselves from death*
by paying a ransom to God.
8 Redemption does not come so easily,
for no one can ever pay enough
9 to live forever
and never see the grave.

10 Those who are wise must finally die,
just like the foolish and senseless,
leaving all their wealth behind.
11 The grave is their eternal home,
where they will stay forever.
They may name their estates after themselves,
12 but their fame will not last.
They will die, just like animals.
13 This is the fate of fools,
though they are remembered as being wise.* *Interlude*

14 Like sheep, they are led to the grave,*
where death will be their shepherd.
In the morning the godly will rule over them.
Their bodies will rot in the grave,
far from their grand estates.
15 But as for me, God will redeem my life.
He will snatch me from the power of the grave. *Interlude*

16 So don't be dismayed when the wicked grow rich
and their homes become ever more splendid.
17 For when they die, they take nothing with them.
Their wealth will not follow them into the grave.
18 In this life they consider themselves fortunate
and are applauded for their success.
19 But they will die like all before them
and never again see the light of day.
20 People who boast of their wealth don't understand;
they will die, just like animals.

PSALM 50

A psalm of Asaph.

1 The LORD, the Mighty One, is God,
and he has spoken;
he has summoned all humanity
from where the sun rises to where it sets.
2 From Mount Zion, the perfection of beauty,
God shines in glorious radiance.
3 Our God approaches,
and he is not silent.
Fire devours everything in his way,
and a great storm rages around him.
4 He calls on the heavens above and earth below
to witness the judgment of his people.
5 "Bring my faithful people to me—
those who made a covenant with me by giving sacrifices."
6 Then let the heavens proclaim his justice,
for God himself will be the judge. *Interlude*

7 "O my people, listen as I speak.
Here are my charges against you, O Israel:
I am God, your God!
8 I have no complaint about your sacrifices
or the burnt offerings you constantly offer.
9 But I do not need the bulls from your barns
or the goats from your pens.
10 For all the animals of the forest are mine,
and I own the cattle on a thousand hills.
11 I know every bird on the mountains,
and all the animals of the field are mine.
12 If I were hungry, I would not tell you,
for all the world is mine and everything in it.

49:7 Or *no one can redeem the life of another.* **49:13** The meaning of the Hebrew is uncertain. **49:14** Hebrew *Sheol;* also in 49:14b, 15.

ist shows how no one has an answer to its finality. Wisdom recognizes only two ultimate destinies: Either people will go *like sheep* to death or they will be received by God (vv. 14–15). The promise of ransom is fulfilled in Christ (Mark 10:45).

Psalm 50 An awesome picture of God the judge who leads Asaph (cf. 1 Chr 16:4–6) to affirm that judgment begins with God's people, called to be faithful. The wicked slander even their brother (v. 20). The kinship of those who occupied the same womb was considered especially deep. To women living in unsafe environments, verse 15 can be paticularly comforting.

13 Do I eat the meat of bulls?
Do I drink the blood of goats?
14 Make thankfulness your sacrifice to God,
and keep the vows you made to the Most High.
15 Then call on me when you are in trouble,
and I will rescue you,
and you will give me glory."

16 But God says to the wicked:
"Why bother reciting my decrees
and pretending to obey my covenant?
17 For you refuse my discipline
and treat my words like trash.
18 When you see thieves, you approve of them,
and you spend your time with adulterers.
19 Your mouth is filled with wickedness,
and your tongue is full of lies.
20 You sit around and slander your brother—
your own mother's son.
21 While you did all this, I remained silent,
and you thought I didn't care.
But now I will rebuke you,
listing all my charges against you.
22 Repent, all of you who forget me,
or I will tear you apart,
and no one will help you.
23 But giving thanks is a sacrifice that truly honors me.
If you keep to my path,
I will reveal to you the salvation of God."

PSALM 51

For the choir director: A psalm of David, regarding the time Nathan the prophet came to him after David had committed adultery with Bathsheba.

1 Have mercy on me, O God,
because of your unfailing love.
Because of your great compassion,
blot out the stain of my sins.
2 Wash me clean from my guilt.
Purify me from my sin.
3 For I recognize my rebellion;
it haunts me day and night.
4 Against you, and you alone, have I sinned;
I have done what is evil in your sight.
You will be proved right in what you say,
and your judgment against me is just.*
5 For I was born a sinner—
yes, from the moment my mother conceived me.
6 But you desire honesty from the womb,*
teaching me wisdom even there.

7 Purify me from my sins,* and I will be clean;
wash me, and I will be whiter than snow.
8 Oh, give me back my joy again;
you have broken me—
now let me rejoice.
9 Don't keep looking at my sins.
Remove the stain of my guilt.
10 Create in me a clean heart, O God.
Renew a loyal spirit within me.
11 Do not banish me from your presence,
and don't take your Holy Spirit* from me.

12 Restore to me the joy of your salvation,
and make me willing to obey you.
13 Then I will teach your ways to rebels,
and they will return to you.
14 Forgive me for shedding blood, O God who saves;
then I will joyfully sing of your forgiveness.
15 Unseal my lips, O Lord,
that my mouth may praise you.

16 You do not desire a sacrifice, or I would offer one.
You do not want a burnt offering.
17 The sacrifice you desire is a broken spirit.
You will not reject a broken and repentant heart, O God.
18 Look with favor on Zion and help her;
rebuild the walls of Jerusalem.
19 Then you will be pleased with sacrifices offered in the right spirit—
with burnt offerings and whole burnt offerings.
Then bulls will again be sacrificed on your altar.

51:4 Greek version reads *and you will win your case in court.* Compare Rom 3:4. **51:6** Or *from the heart;* Hebrew reads *in the inward parts.* **51:7** Hebrew *Purify me with the hyssop branch.* **51:11** Or *your spirit of holiness.*

Psalm 51, a penitential psalm, clarifies the nature and consequences of all sin by describing David's sin (cf. 2 Sam 11—12). Genuine penitence has led David to recognize the immense damage it has done. His adultery and treachery have enveloped not only two families but also the leadership of the army and hence the entire nation. His idea of having been conceived as a sinner applies less to the event than to his awareness of the depth of sin's hold on him. His confessional prayer for deliverance is thorough, covering every aspect of his need for salvation, from mercy, via cleansing and renewal, to joyful restoration.

PSALM 52

For the choir director: A psalm of David, regarding the time Doeg the Edomite said to Saul, "David has gone to see Ahimelech."*

1 Why do you boast about your crimes, great warrior?
Don't you realize God's justice continues forever?
2 All day long you plot destruction.
Your tongue cuts like a sharp razor;
you're an expert at telling lies.
3 You love evil more than good
and lies more than truth. *Interlude*

4 You love to destroy others with your words,
you liar!
5 But God will strike you down once and for all.
He will pull you from your home
and uproot you from the land of the living. *Interlude*

6 The righteous will see it and be amazed.
They will laugh and say,
7 "Look what happens to mighty warriors
who do not trust in God.
They trust their wealth instead
and grow more and more bold in their wickedness."

8 But I am like an olive tree, thriving in the house of God.
I will always trust in God's unfailing love.
9 I will praise you forever, O God,
for what you have done.
I will trust in your good name
in the presence of your faithful people.

PSALM 53

For the choir director: A meditation; a psalm of David.*

1 Only fools say in their hearts,
"There is no God."
They are corrupt, and their actions are evil;
not one of them does good!
2 God looks down from heaven
on the entire human race;
he looks to see if anyone is truly wise,
if anyone seeks God.
3 But no, all have turned away;
all have become corrupt.*
No one does good,
not a single one!

4 Will those who do evil never learn?
They eat up my people like bread
and wouldn't think of praying to God.
5 Terror will grip them,
terror like they have never known before.
God will scatter the bones of your enemies.
You will put them to shame, for God has rejected them.

6 Who will come from Mount Zion to rescue Israel?
When God restores his people,
Jacob will shout with joy, and Israel will rejoice.

PSALM 54

For the choir director: A psalm of David, regarding the time the Ziphites came and said to Saul, "We know where David is hiding." To be accompanied by stringed instruments.*

1 Come with great power, O God, and rescue me!
Defend me with your might.
2 Listen to my prayer, O God.
Pay attention to my plea.
3 For strangers are attacking me;
violent people are trying to kill me.
They care nothing for God. *Interlude*

52:TITLE Hebrew *maskil.* This may be a literary or musical term. **53:TITLE** Hebrew *According to mahalath; a maskil.* These may be literary or musical terms. **53:3** Greek version reads *have become useless.* Compare Rom 3:12. **54:TITLE** Hebrew *maskil.* This may be a literary or musical term.

Psalm 52 denounces Doeg for a deliberate betrayal and massacre of priests (1 Sam 22). Behind his specific sins, David discerns a love of evil rather than good and a trust in riches rather than God. He prophesies that judgment will be meted out on the principle of Deuteronomy 19:19–21.

Psalm 53 almost repeats Psalm 14, except that *God* replaces "the LORD" (vv. 2, 4, 7), and Psalm 14:6 is replaced by 53:5. These changes shift the psalm's emphasis from salvation of the righteous to God's rejection and judgment of foolish evildoers.

Psalm 54 Twice betrayed by the ruthless Ziphites (1 Sam 23:19–24; 26:1–4), David looks to God's might to save him. Verse 4 marks the turning point in his mood; as prayer brings reassurance so he reaffirms faith in *God . . . my helper.*

4 But God is my helper.
The Lord keeps me alive!
5 May the evil plans of my enemies be turned against them.
Do as you promised and put an end to them.

6 I will sacrifice a voluntary offering to you;
I will praise your name, O LORD,
for it is good.
7 For you have rescued me from my troubles
and helped me to triumph over my enemies.

PSALM 55

For the choir director: A psalm of David, to be accompanied by stringed instruments.*

1 Listen to my prayer, O God.
Do not ignore my cry for help!
2 Please listen and answer me,
for I am overwhelmed by my troubles.
3 My enemies shout at me,
making loud and wicked threats.
They bring trouble on me
and angrily hunt me down.

4 My heart pounds in my chest.
The terror of death assaults me.
5 Fear and trembling overwhelm me,
and I can't stop shaking.
6 Oh, that I had wings like a dove;
then I would fly away and rest!
7 I would fly far away
to the quiet of the wilderness. *Interlude*
8 How quickly I would escape—
far from this wild storm of hatred.

9 Confuse them, Lord, and frustrate their plans,
for I see violence and conflict in the city.
10 Its walls are patrolled day and night against invaders,
but the real danger is wickedness within the city.
11 Everything is falling apart;
threats and cheating are rampant in the streets.

12 It is not an enemy who taunts me—
I could bear that.
It is not my foes who so arrogantly insult me—
I could have hidden from them.
13 Instead, it is you—my equal,
my companion and close friend.
14 What good fellowship we once enjoyed
as we walked together to the house of God.

15 Let death stalk my enemies;
let the grave* swallow them alive,
for evil makes its home within them.

16 But I will call on God,
and the LORD will rescue me.
17 Morning, noon, and night
I cry out in my distress,
and the LORD hears my voice.
18 He ransoms me and keeps me safe
from the battle waged against me,
though many still oppose me.
19 God, who has ruled forever,
will hear me and humble them. *Interlude*
For my enemies refuse to change their ways;
they do not fear God.

20 As for my companion, he betrayed his friends;
he broke his promises.
21 His words are as smooth as butter,
but in his heart is war.
His words are as soothing as lotion,
but underneath are daggers!

22 Give your burdens to the LORD,
and he will take care of you.
He will not permit the godly to slip and fall.

23 But you, O God, will send the wicked
down to the pit of destruction.
Murderers and liars will die young,
but I am trusting you to save me.

55:TITLE Hebrew *maskil.* This may be a literary or musical term. **55:15** Hebrew *let Sheol.*

Psalm 55 has been particularly effective in helping abused women. It describes the feelings of betrayal by an intimate who was trusted (vv. 12–14, 20–21), the mockery of shared spiritual fellowship (v. 14), the terror that the victim knows (vv. 3–5, 9–11), the breach of covenant (v. 20), the deceptive mien (v. 21), and the need for shelter and safety (vv. 6–8). In all of these crises, our hope can be in God, who will hear the prayers of desperation and uphold the oppressed.

PSALM 56

For the choir director: A psalm of David, regarding the time the Philistines seized him in Gath. To be sung to the tune "Dove on Distant Oaks."*

1 O God, have mercy on me,
for people are hounding me.
My foes attack me all day long.
2 I am constantly hounded by those who slander me,
and many are boldly attacking me.
3 But when I am afraid,
I will put my trust in you.
4 I praise God for what he has promised.
I trust in God, so why should I be afraid?
What can mere mortals do to me?

5 They are always twisting what I say;
they spend their days plotting to harm me.
6 They come together to spy on me—
watching my every step, eager to kill me.
7 Don't let them get away with their wickedness;
in your anger, O God, bring them down.

8 You keep track of all my sorrows.*
You have collected all my tears in your bottle.
You have recorded each one in your book.
9 My enemies will retreat when I call to you for help.
This I know: God is on my side!
10 I praise God for what he has promised;
yes, I praise the LORD for what he has promised.
11 I trust in God, so why should I be afraid?
What can mere mortals do to me?

12 I will fulfill my vows to you, O God,
and will offer a sacrifice of thanks for your help.
13 For you have rescued me from death;
you have kept my feet from slipping.
So now I can walk in your presence, O God,
in your life-giving light.

PSALM 57

For the choir director: A psalm of David, regarding the time he fled from Saul and went into the cave. To be sung to the tune "Do Not Destroy!"*

1 Have mercy on me, O God, have mercy!
I look to you for protection.
I will hide beneath the shadow of your wings
until the danger passes by.
2 I cry out to God Most High,*
to God who will fulfill his purpose for me.
3 He will send help from heaven to rescue me,
disgracing those who hound me. *Interlude*
My God will send forth his unfailing love and faithfulness.

4 I am surrounded by fierce lions
who greedily devour human prey—
whose teeth pierce like spears and arrows,
and whose tongues cut like swords.

5 Be exalted, O God, above the highest heavens!
May your glory shine over all the earth.

6 My enemies have set a trap for me.
I am weary from distress.
They have dug a deep pit in my path,
but they themselves have fallen into it. *Interlude*

7 My heart is confident in you, O God;
my heart is confident.
No wonder I can sing your praises!
8 Wake up, my heart!
Wake up, O lyre and harp!
I will wake the dawn with my song.
9 I will thank you, Lord, among all the people.
I will sing your praises among the nations.
10 For your unfailing love is as high as the heavens.
Your faithfulness reaches to the clouds.

56:TITLE Hebrew *miktam.* This may be a literary or musical term. **56:8** Or *my wanderings.* **57:TITLE** Hebrew *miktam.* This may be a literary or musical term. **57:2** Hebrew *Elohim-Elyon.*

Psalm 56 again reflects 1 Samuel 21:10–15 (cf. Ps 34). Outwardly oppressed by enemies who plot his downfall, inwardly David experiences immense conflict between fear and faith, sadness and joy. This prompts a double affirmation of trust in God and his Word. Verses 5–6 can be particularly helpful to those in abusive situations.

Psalm 57 Trapped in a cave with his pursuers (vv. 4, 6; cf. 1 Sam 24), David prays for God's merciful protection on the grounds that God *will fulfill his purpose for me* (v. 2). He pictures God as a mother bird sheltering chicks (v. 1). Salvation is rooted in God's *unfailing love and faithfulness* (vv. 3, 10), in the light of which David can be *confident* and *sing praises*.

11 Be exalted, O God, above the highest heavens.
May your glory shine over all the earth.

PSALM 58

For the choir director: A psalm of David, to be sung to the tune "Do Not Destroy!"*

1 Justice—do you rulers* know the meaning of the word?
Do you judge the people fairly?
2 No! You plot injustice in your hearts.
You spread violence throughout the land.
3 These wicked people are born sinners;
even from birth they have lied and gone their own way.
4 They spit venom like deadly snakes;
they are like cobras that refuse to listen,
5 ignoring the tunes of the snake charmers,
no matter how skillfully they play.

6 Break off their fangs, O God!
Smash the jaws of these lions, O LORD!
7 May they disappear like water into thirsty ground.
Make their weapons useless in their hands.*
8 May they be like snails that dissolve into slime,
like a stillborn child who will never see the sun.
9 God will sweep them away, both young and old,
faster than a pot heats over burning thorns.

10 The godly will rejoice when they see injustice avenged.
They will wash their feet in the blood of the wicked.
11 Then at last everyone will say,
"There truly is a reward for those who live for God;
surely there is a God who judges justly here on earth."

PSALM 59

For the choir director: A psalm of David, regarding the time Saul sent soldiers to watch David's house in order to kill him. To be sung to the tune "Do Not Destroy!"*

1 Rescue me from my enemies, O God.
Protect me from those who have come to destroy me.
2 Rescue me from these criminals;
save me from these murderers.
3 They have set an ambush for me.
Fierce enemies are out there waiting, LORD,
though I have not sinned or offended them.
4 I have done nothing wrong,
yet they prepare to attack me.
Wake up! See what is happening and help me!
5 O LORD God of Heaven's Armies, the God of Israel,
wake up and punish those hostile nations.
Show no mercy to wicked traitors. *Interlude*

6 They come out at night,
snarling like vicious dogs
as they prowl the streets.
7 Listen to the filth that comes from their mouths;
their words cut like swords.
"After all, who can hear us?" they sneer.
8 But LORD, you laugh at them.
You scoff at all the hostile nations.
9 You are my strength; I wait for you to rescue me,
for you, O God, are my fortress.
10 In his unfailing love, my God will stand with me.

58:TITLE Hebrew *miktam*. This may be a literary or musical term. **58:1** Or *you gods*. **58:7** Or *Let them be trodden down and wither like grass*. The meaning of the Hebrew is uncertain. **59:TITLE** Hebrew *miktam*. This may be a literary or musical term.

Psalm 58 begins with David castigating wicked people who have evidently been abusing their positions of power. Their guilt encompasses injustice, wrong thinking, violence, error, lies, and stubborn self-will. The graphically venomous language of the imprecatory prayer that follows is not merely gratuitous; it poetically matches the evildoers' *venom*. The starkness is made yet more vivid by the picture of a mother's dashed hope as she endures the tragedy of a still birth (v. 8). This psalm may be seen as more of a venting of emotions before God rather than an actual supplication for the visitation of such evil upon his enemies.

Psalm 59 David's unnerving experience while living under surveillance and constant threat (cf. 1 Sam 19:1–11) drives him to pray first for his immediate need, then for an outworking of justice that will benefit the LORD and his people. Each prayer is followed by a consideration of the situation, first from a human perspective, then from the perspective of faith.

He will let me look down in triumph on all
my enemies.
11 Don't kill them, for my people soon forget
such lessons;
stagger them with your power, and bring
them to their knees,
O Lord our shield.
12 Because of the sinful things they say,
because of the evil that is on their lips,
let them be captured by their pride,
their curses, and their lies.
13 Destroy them in your anger!
Wipe them out completely!
Then the whole world will know
that God reigns in Israel.* *Interlude*

14 My enemies come out at night,
snarling like vicious dogs
as they prowl the streets.
15 They scavenge for food
but go to sleep unsatisfied.*

16 But as for me, I will sing about your power.
Each morning I will sing with joy about
your unfailing love.
For you have been my refuge,
a place of safety when I am in distress.
17 O my Strength, to you I sing praises,
for you, O God, are my refuge,
the God who shows me unfailing love.

PSALM 60

For the choir director: A psalm of David useful for teaching, regarding the time David fought Aram-naharaim and Aram-zobah, and Joab returned and killed 12,000 Edomites in the Valley of Salt. To be sung to the tune "Lily of the Testimony."*

1 You have rejected us, O God, and broken our
defenses.
You have been angry with us; now restore
us to your favor.
2 You have shaken our land and split it open.
Seal the cracks, for the land trembles.
3 You have been very hard on us,
making us drink wine that sent us reeling.
4 But you have raised a banner for those who
fear you—
a rallying point in the face of attack.
Interlude

5 Now rescue your beloved people.
Answer and save us by your power.
6 God has promised this by his holiness*:
"I will divide up Shechem with joy.
I will measure out the valley of Succoth.
7 Gilead is mine,
and Manasseh, too.
Ephraim, my helmet, will produce my
warriors,
and Judah, my scepter, will produce my
kings.
8 But Moab, my washbasin, will become my
servant,
and I will wipe my feet on Edom
and shout in triumph over Philistia."

9 Who will bring me into the fortified city?
Who will bring me victory over Edom?
10 Have you rejected us, O God?
Will you no longer march with our armies?
11 Oh, please help us against our enemies,
for all human help is useless.
12 With God's help we will do mighty things,
for he will trample down our foes.

PSALM 61

For the choir director: A psalm of David, to be accompanied by stringed instruments.

1 O God, listen to my cry!
Hear my prayer!
2 From the ends of the earth,
I cry to you for help
when my heart is overwhelmed.
Lead me to the towering rock of safety,

59:13 Hebrew *in Jacob.* See note on 44:4. **59:15** Or *and growl if they don't get enough.* **60:TITLE** Hebrew *miktam.* This may be a literary or musical term. **60:6** Or *in his sanctuary.*

Psalm 60 Whether literal or metaphorical, (an earthquake, wine) God's people have been left *reeling* (vv. 2–4). Diagnosing the cause as God's anger, David prays first for restoration and only then for victory. The latter prayer not only confronts God directly but also highlights the *teaching* this psalm aims to convey (see title), namely, the truth that God's people need divine help in battle rather than human help because victory is God's work.

Psalm 61 A heart that is *overwhelmed* suggests the king is running away from trouble (v. 2; cf. 55:6–7) to *the ends of the earth*. Verses 6–7 suggest threats to his life and his throne. Using familiar imagery of a mother bird and of a strong rock (cf. 31:2–3; 57:1) he humbly seeks God's protection and lasting presence.

3 for you are my safe refuge,
a fortress where my enemies cannot reach me.
4 Let me live forever in your sanctuary,
safe beneath the shelter of your wings!
Interlude

5 For you have heard my vows, O God.
You have given me an inheritance reserved for those who fear your name.
6 Add many years to the life of the king!
May his years span the generations!
7 May he reign under God's protection forever.
May your unfailing love and faithfulness watch over him.
8 Then I will sing praises to your name forever
as I fulfill my vows each day.

PSALM 62

For Jeduthun, the choir director: A psalm of David.

1 I wait quietly before God,
for my victory comes from him.
2 He alone is my rock and my salvation,
my fortress where I will never be shaken.

3 So many enemies against one man—
all of them trying to kill me.
To them I'm just a broken-down wall
or a tottering fence.
4 They plan to topple me from my high position.
They delight in telling lies about me.
They praise me to my face
but curse me in their hearts. *Interlude*

5 Let all that I am wait quietly before God,
for my hope is in him.
6 He alone is my rock and my salvation,
my fortress where I will not be shaken.
7 My victory and honor come from God alone.
He is my refuge, a rock where no enemy can reach me.
8 O my people, trust in him at all times.
Pour out your heart to him,
for God is our refuge. *Interlude*

9 Common people are as worthless as a puff of wind,
and the powerful are not what they appear to be.
If you weigh them on the scales,
together they are lighter than a breath of air.

10 Don't make your living by extortion
or put your hope in stealing.
And if your wealth increases,
don't make it the center of your life.

11 God has spoken plainly,
and I have heard it many times:
Power, O God, belongs to you;
12 unfailing love, O Lord, is yours.
Surely you repay all people
according to what they have done.

PSALM 63

A psalm of David, regarding a time when David was in the wilderness of Judah.

1 O God, you are my God;
I earnestly search for you.
My soul thirsts for you;
my whole body longs for you
in this parched and weary land
where there is no water.
2 I have seen you in your sanctuary
and gazed upon your power and glory.
3 Your unfailing love is better than life itself;
how I praise you!
4 I will praise you as long as I live,
lifting up my hands to you in prayer.
5 You satisfy me more than the richest feast.
I will praise you with songs of joy.

6 I lie awake thinking of you,
meditating on you through the night.

Psalm 62 is distinguished by the repeated *alone* (vv. 2, 6, 7). Even though the prolonged lies of his enemies have weakened him, David will neither complain nor *be shaken*. The psalm contrasts their sole purpose (v. 4) and his, which is to *wait* in faith for God his rock, salvation, and fortress. Here, as in Psalm 37:7 the Hebrew term for "wait" was rendered by the ancient Greek translators as "submit" (vv. 1, 5: see annotation on Ps 37). It implies an attitude of trust and joyful expectancy.

Psalm 63 follows the progress of David's soul at a time when he was being pursued into the wilderness by either Saul (1 Sam 23—24) or Absalom (2 Sam 15—18). Regarding insomnia as a welcome opportunity to pray, David discovers that meditating on God's power, glory, and steadfast love satisfies his thirsty soul, prompts a desire to worship God, and renews joy and strength. Like a young nestling, the satisfied soul then clings for protection to God who is pictured as a mother bird.

7 Because you are my helper,
I sing for joy in the shadow of your wings.
8 I cling to you;
your strong right hand holds me securely.

9 But those plotting to destroy me will come to ruin.
They will go down into the depths of the earth.
10 They will die by the sword
and become the food of jackals.
11 But the king will rejoice in God.
All who trust in him will praise him,
while liars will be silenced.

PSALM 64

For the choir director: A psalm of David.

1 O God, listen to my complaint.
Protect my life from my enemies' threats.
2 Hide me from the plots of this evil mob,
from this gang of wrongdoers.
3 They sharpen their tongues like swords
and aim their bitter words like arrows.
4 They shoot from ambush at the innocent,
attacking suddenly and fearlessly.
5 They encourage each other to do evil
and plan how to set their traps in secret.
"Who will ever notice?" they ask.
6 As they plot their crimes, they say,
"We have devised the perfect plan!"
Yes, the human heart and mind are cunning.

7 But God himself will shoot them with his arrows,
suddenly striking them down.
8 Their own tongues will ruin them,
and all who see them will shake their heads in scorn.
9 Then everyone will be afraid;
they will proclaim the mighty acts of God
and realize all the amazing things he does.
10 The godly will rejoice in the LORD
and find shelter in him.
And those who do what is right
will praise him.

PSALM 65

For the choir director: A song. A psalm of David.

1 What mighty praise, O God,
belongs to you in Zion.
We will fulfill our vows to you,
2 for you answer our prayers.
All of us must come to you.
3 Though we are overwhelmed by our sins,
you forgive them all.
4 What joy for those you choose to bring near,
those who live in your holy courts.
What festivities await us
inside your holy Temple.

5 You faithfully answer our prayers with awesome deeds,
O God our savior.
You are the hope of everyone on earth,
even those who sail on distant seas.
6 You formed the mountains by your power
and armed yourself with mighty strength.
7 You quieted the raging oceans
with their pounding waves
and silenced the shouting of the nations.
8 Those who live at the ends of the earth
stand in awe of your wonders.
From where the sun rises to where it sets,
you inspire shouts of joy.

9 You take care of the earth and water it,
making it rich and fertile.
The river of God has plenty of water;
it provides a bountiful harvest of grain,
for you have ordered it so.
10 You drench the plowed ground with rain,
melting the clods and leveling the ridges.
You soften the earth with showers
and bless its abundant crops.
11 You crown the year with a bountiful harvest;
even the hard pathways overflow with abundance.
12 The grasslands of the wilderness become a lush pasture,
and the hillsides blossom with joy.
13 The meadows are clothed with flocks of sheep,
and the valleys are carpeted with grain.
They all shout and sing for joy!

Psalm 64 shows David complaining to God about his enemies' verbal abuse, here depicted as actual weapons of war. But they forget that God has arrows too and will turn their words agsinst them.

Psalm 65, probably originally sung at harvest time, is a thanksgiving for God's goodness. The goodness of God's holy presence is demonstrated especially in answered prayer, forgiven sin, elective privilege, satisfied desire, *awesome deeds* of salvation for his people, and the *hope* (lit., "confidence") of salvation for all.

PSALM 66

For the choir director: A song. A psalm.

1 Shout joyful praises to God, all the earth!
2 Sing about the glory of his name!
Tell the world how glorious he is.
3 Say to God, "How awesome are your deeds!
Your enemies cringe before your mighty power.
4 Everything on earth will worship you;
they will sing your praises,
shouting your name in glorious songs."
Interlude

5 Come and see what our God has done,
what awesome miracles he performs for people!
6 He made a dry path through the Red Sea,*
and his people went across on foot.
There we rejoiced in him.
7 For by his great power he rules forever.
He watches every movement of the nations;
let no rebel rise in defiance. *Interlude*

8 Let the whole world bless our God
and loudly sing his praises.
9 Our lives are in his hands,
and he keeps our feet from stumbling.
10 You have tested us, O God;
you have purified us like silver.
11 You captured us in your net
and laid the burden of slavery on our backs.
12 Then you put a leader over us.*
We went through fire and flood,
but you brought us to a place of great abundance.

13 Now I come to your Temple with burnt offerings
to fulfill the vows I made to you—
14 yes, the sacred vows that I made
when I was in deep trouble.
15 That is why I am sacrificing burnt offerings to you—
the best of my rams as a pleasing aroma,
and a sacrifice of bulls and male goats.
Interlude

16 Come and listen, all you who fear God,
and I will tell you what he did for me.
17 For I cried out to him for help,
praising him as I spoke.
18 If I had not confessed the sin in my heart,
the Lord would not have listened.
19 But God did listen!
He paid attention to my prayer.
20 Praise God, who did not ignore my prayer
or withdraw his unfailing love from me.

PSALM 67

For the choir director: A song. A psalm, to be accompanied by stringed instruments.

1 May God be merciful and bless us.
May his face smile with favor on us.
Interlude

2 May your ways be known throughout the earth,
your saving power among people everywhere.
3 May the nations praise you, O God.
Yes, may all the nations praise you.
4 Let the whole world sing for joy,
because you govern the nations with justice
and guide the people of the whole world.
Interlude

5 May the nations praise you, O God.
Yes, may all the nations praise you.
6 Then the earth will yield its harvests,
and God, our God, will richly bless us.
7 Yes, God will bless us,
and people all over the world will fear him.

PSALM 68

For the choir director: A song. A psalm of David.

1 Rise up, O God, and scatter your enemies.
Let those who hate God run for their lives.
2 Blow them away like smoke.
Melt them like wax in a fire.

66:6 Hebrew *the sea.* **66:12** Or *You made people ride over our heads.*

Psalm 66 Recognizing that God's purpose was to refine his people, the anonymous psalmist issues an invitation to *come and listen* (v. 16) to a personal testimony to answered prayer. Knowing that words and works must match, the psalm closes with a personal example of acceptable worship (v. 20; cf. Ps 50:13–14).

Psalm 67 takes an ancient blessing (v. 1; cf. Num 6:24–25) and relates it to the truth that through the blessing he pours out on his people, God intends all nations to be blessed (Gen 12:2–3; cf. Gal 3:8–9).

Psalm 68 identifies the participation of women in praise, proclamation of the Word, and their involve-

Let the wicked perish in the presence of
God.
3 But let the godly rejoice.
Let them be glad in God's presence.
Let them be filled with joy.
4 Sing praises to God and to his name!
Sing loud praises to him who rides the
clouds.
His name is the LORD—
rejoice in his presence!

5 Father to the fatherless, defender of
widows—
this is God, whose dwelling is holy.
6 God places the lonely in families;
he sets the prisoners free and gives them
joy.
But he makes the rebellious live in a sun-
scorched land.

7 O God, when you led your people out from
Egypt,
when you marched through the dry
wasteland, *Interlude*
8 the earth trembled, and the heavens poured
down rain
before you, the God of Sinai,
before God, the God of Israel.
9 You sent abundant rain, O God,
to refresh the weary land.
10 There your people finally settled,
and with a bountiful harvest, O God,
you provided for your needy people.

11 The Lord gives the word,
and a great army* brings the good news.
12 Enemy kings and their armies flee,
while the women of Israel divide the
plunder.
13 Even those who lived among the sheepfolds
found treasures—
doves with wings of silver
and feathers of gold.
14 The Almighty scattered the enemy kings
like a blowing snowstorm on Mount
Zalmon.

15 The mountains of Bashan are majestic,
with many peaks stretching high into the
sky.
16 Why do you look with envy, O rugged
mountains,
at Mount Zion, where God has chosen to
live,
where the LORD himself will live forever?
17 Surrounded by unnumbered thousands of
chariots,
the Lord came from Mount Sinai into his
sanctuary.
18 When you ascended to the heights,
you led a crowd of captives.
You received gifts from the people,
even from those who rebelled against you.
Now the LORD God will live among us
there.

19 Praise the Lord; praise God our savior!
For each day he carries us in his arms.
Interlude
20 Our God is a God who saves!
The Sovereign LORD rescues us from death.

68:11 Or *a host of women.*

ment in the faith community. The psalm appears to have been composed for a procession in which maidens accompany musicians and singers as they march in celebration (vv. 24–27). The occasion may be the arrival of the Ark of the Covenant in Jerusalem, as singing had accompanied the Ark during its long journey from Sinai to Zion (Num 10:35–36). See the translator's note for verse 11: "A host of women" *brings the good news*. Theirs is the challenge to review the saving acts of God. The gender of those who bring the tidings is feminine and reveals the role of proclamation on the part of women.

The young women play *tambourines* (v. 25), an instrument often used only by women. Not the modern instrument, a tambour was a terra-cotta vessel with the hide of an animal stretched across the open end. Its use was associated with prophesying and dance (Exod 15:20–21; Judg 11:34; 1 Sam 18:6–7; Jer 31:4, 13). At times of victory, women led the expressions of praise and thanksgiving.

The language and sentiments of this psalm are reminiscent of the song of victory sung by Deborah (Judg 5). Indeed, the eighth verse of this psalm is a direct quotation of Judges 5:4ff. (note other similarities at vv. 9, 13, 14, 19, 28), and we may also catch the echoes of Hannah's song (1 Sam 2:1–10). In this case the victory is that of God, who led a slave people out of bondage and through the wilderness into freedom. Now the central shrine will be at Jerusalem, and there a temple will be erected on Mount Zion.

God is mentioned as the protector of widows and orphans who provides a home for the desolate (vv. 5–6) or, as Luther translated it, "gives the lonely woman a house full of children." Women who were sent forth for public proclamation are also active in the domestic sphere, apportioning the spoil (v. 12).

21 But God will smash the heads of his enemies,
crushing the skulls of those who love their guilty ways.
22 The Lord says, "I will bring my enemies down from Bashan;
I will bring them up from the depths of the sea.
23 You, my people, will wash your feet in their blood,
and even your dogs will get their share!"

24 Your procession has come into view, O God—
the procession of my God and King as he goes into the sanctuary.
25 Singers are in front, musicians behind;
between them are young women playing tambourines.
26 Praise God, all you people of Israel;
praise the LORD, the source of Israel's life.
27 Look, the little tribe of Benjamin leads the way.
Then comes a great throng of rulers from Judah
and all the rulers of Zebulun and Naphtali.

28 Summon your might, O God.
Display your power, O God, as you have in the past.
29 The kings of the earth are bringing tribute
to your Temple in Jerusalem.
30 Rebuke these enemy nations—
these wild animals lurking in the reeds,
this herd of bulls among the weaker calves.
Make them bring bars of silver in humble tribute.
Scatter the nations that delight in war.
31 Let Egypt come with gifts of precious metals*;
let Ethiopia* bow in submission to God.
32 Sing to God, you kingdoms of the earth.
Sing praises to the Lord. *Interlude*
33 Sing to the one who rides across the ancient heavens,
his mighty voice thundering from the sky.
34 Tell everyone about God's power.
His majesty shines down on Israel;
his strength is mighty in the heavens.
35 God is awesome in his sanctuary.
The God of Israel gives power and strength to his people.

Praise be to God!

PSALM 69

For the choir director: A psalm of David, to be sung to the tune "Lilies."

1 Save me, O God,
for the floodwaters are up to my neck.
2 Deeper and deeper I sink into the mire;
I can't find a foothold.
I am in deep water,
and the floods overwhelm me.
3 I am exhausted from crying for help;
my throat is parched.
My eyes are swollen with weeping,
waiting for my God to help me.
4 Those who hate me without cause
outnumber the hairs on my head.
Many enemies try to destroy me with lies,
demanding that I give back what I didn't steal.

5 O God, you know how foolish I am;
my sins cannot be hidden from you.
6 Don't let those who trust in you be ashamed because of me,
O Sovereign LORD of Heaven's Armies.
Don't let me cause them to be humiliated,
O God of Israel.
7 For I endure insults for your sake;
humiliation is written all over my face.
8 Even my own brothers pretend they don't know me;
they treat me like a stranger.

9 Passion for your house has consumed me,
and the insults of those who insult you have fallen on me.
10 When I weep and fast,
they scoff at me.
11 When I dress in burlap to show sorrow,
they make fun of me.
12 I am the favorite topic of town gossip,
and all the drunks sing about me.

13 But I keep praying to you, LORD,
hoping this time you will show me favor.
In your unfailing love, O God,
answer my prayer with your sure salvation.

68:31a Or *of rich cloth.* **68:31b** Hebrew *Cush.*

Psalm 69 finds David in *deep* distress, suffering from false accusation, insult, and gossip. He seeks salvation on the basis that though he was not always blameless, his present situation is an undeserved result of spiritual zeal (vv. 1–12; cf. John 2:17). For his oppressors he requests just discipline, on the principle of Deuteronomy 19:19–21.

14 Rescue me from the mud;
don't let me sink any deeper!
Save me from those who hate me,
and pull me from these deep waters.
15 Don't let the floods overwhelm me,
or the deep waters swallow me,
or the pit of death devour me.

16 Answer my prayers, O LORD,
for your unfailing love is wonderful.
Take care of me,
for your mercy is so plentiful.
17 Don't hide from your servant;
answer me quickly, for I am in deep trouble!
18 Come and redeem me;
free me from my enemies.
19 You know of my shame, scorn, and disgrace.
You see all that my enemies are doing.
20 Their insults have broken my heart,
and I am in despair.
If only one person would show some pity;
if only one would turn and comfort me.
21 But instead, they give me poison* for food;
they offer me sour wine for my thirst.

22 Let the bountiful table set before them become a snare
and their prosperity become a trap.*
23 Let their eyes go blind so they cannot see,
and make their bodies shake continually.*
24 Pour out your fury on them;
consume them with your burning anger.
25 Let their homes become desolate
and their tents be deserted.
26 To the one you have punished, they add insult to injury;
they add to the pain of those you have hurt.
27 Pile their sins up high,
and don't let them go free.
28 Erase their names from the Book of Life;
don't let them be counted among the righteous.

29 I am suffering and in pain.
Rescue me, O God, by your saving power.
30 Then I will praise God's name with singing,
and I will honor him with thanksgiving.
31 For this will please the LORD more than sacrificing cattle,
more than presenting a bull with its horns and hooves.
32 The humble will see their God at work and be glad.
Let all who seek God's help be encouraged.
33 For the LORD hears the cries of the needy;
he does not despise his imprisoned people.

34 Praise him, O heaven and earth,
the seas and all that move in them.
35 For God will save Jerusalem*
and rebuild the towns of Judah.
His people will live there
and settle in their own land.
36 The descendants of those who obey him will inherit the land,
and those who love him will live there in safety.

PSALM 70

For the choir director: A psalm of David, asking God to remember him.

1 Please, God, rescue me!
Come quickly, LORD, and help me.
2 May those who try to kill me
be humiliated and put to shame.
May those who take delight in my trouble
be turned back in disgrace.
3 Let them be horrified by their shame,
for they said, "Aha! We've got him now!"
4 But may all who search for you
be filled with joy and gladness in you.
May those who love your salvation
repeatedly shout, "God is great!"
5 But as for me, I am poor and needy;
please hurry to my aid, O God.
You are my helper and my savior;
O LORD, do not delay.

69:21 Or *gall.* **69:22** Greek version reads *Let their bountiful table set before them become a snare, / a trap that makes them think all is well. / Let their blessings cause them to stumble, / and let them get what they deserve.* Compare Rom 11:9. **69:23** Greek version reads *and let their backs be bent forever.* Compare Rom 11:10. **69:35** Hebrew *Zion.*

Psalm 70 is the same prayer for deliverance that ends Psalm 40 (40:13–17). On the basis of his urgent need and his previous experience of God's saving help, David makes five specific requests. For his enemies, he seeks confusion, dishonor, and defeat; for his supporters he seeks joy and the grace to witness to God's greatness.

PSALM 71

1 O LORD, I have come to you for protection;
don't let me be disgraced.
2 Save me and rescue me,
for you do what is right.
Turn your ear to listen to me,
and set me free.
3 Be my rock of safety
where I can always hide.
Give the order to save me,
for you are my rock and my fortress.
4 My God, rescue me from the power of the wicked,
from the clutches of cruel oppressors.
5 O Lord, you alone are my hope.
I've trusted you, O LORD, from childhood.
6 Yes, you have been with me from birth;
from my mother's womb you have cared for me.
No wonder I am always praising you!

7 My life is an example to many,
because you have been my strength and protection.
8 That is why I can never stop praising you;
I declare your glory all day long.
9 And now, in my old age, don't set me aside.
Don't abandon me when my strength is failing.
10 For my enemies are whispering against me.
They are plotting together to kill me.
11 They say, "God has abandoned him.
Let's go and get him,
for no one will help him now."

12 O God, don't stay away.
My God, please hurry to help me.
13 Bring disgrace and destruction on my accusers.
Humiliate and shame those who want to harm me.
14 But I will keep on hoping for your help;
I will praise you more and more.
15 I will tell everyone about your righteousness.
All day long I will proclaim your saving power,
though I am not skilled with words.*
16 I will praise your mighty deeds, O Sovereign LORD.
I will tell everyone that you alone are just.

17 O God, you have taught me from my earliest childhood,
and I constantly tell others about the wonderful things you do.
18 Now that I am old and gray,
do not abandon me, O God.
Let me proclaim your power to this new generation,
your mighty miracles to all who come after me.

19 Your righteousness, O God, reaches to the highest heavens.
You have done such wonderful things.
Who can compare with you, O God?
20 You have allowed me to suffer much hardship,
but you will restore me to life again
and lift me up from the depths of the earth.
21 You will restore me to even greater honor
and comfort me once again.

22 Then I will praise you with music on the harp,
because you are faithful to your promises,
O my God.
I will sing praises to you with a lyre,
O Holy One of Israel.
23 I will shout for joy and sing your praises,
for you have ransomed me.
24 I will tell about your righteous deeds
all day long,
for everyone who tried to hurt me
has been shamed and humiliated.

PSALM 72

A psalm of Solomon.

1 Give your love of justice to the king, O God,
and righteousness to the king's son.
2 Help him judge your people in the right way;
let the poor always be treated fairly.
3 May the mountains yield prosperity for all,
and may the hills be fruitful.
4 Help him to defend the poor,
to rescue the children of the needy,

71:15 Or *though I cannot count it.*

Psalm 71 A prayer for help, its similarities with Psalms 22 and 31 suggest that it may be an anthology of quotations from other psalms. Verse 6 represents God as midwife, bringing to birth and supporting the new child (see 22:9–10 and Midwifery and Birthing Practices, Job 3). The mention of *childhood* in verse 5 pairs with *old age* in verse 9.

Psalm 72 is a king's prayer, at his coronation or soon after he ascended the throne. None of the Judean

and to crush their oppressors.
5 May they fear you* as long as the sun shines,
as long as the moon remains in the sky.
Yes, forever!

6 May the king's rule be refreshing like spring
rain on freshly cut grass,
like the showers that water the earth.
7 May all the godly flourish during his reign.
May there be abundant prosperity until
the moon is no more.
8 May he reign from sea to sea,
and from the Euphrates River* to the ends
of the earth.
9 Desert nomads will bow before him;
his enemies will fall before him in the dust.
10 The western kings of Tarshish and other
distant lands
will bring him tribute.
The eastern kings of Sheba and Seba
will bring him gifts.
11 All kings will bow before him,
and all nations will serve him.

12 He will rescue the poor when they cry to
him;
he will help the oppressed, who have no
one to defend them.
13 He feels pity for the weak and the needy,
and he will rescue them.
14 He will redeem them from oppression and
violence,
for their lives are precious to him.

15 Long live the king!
May the gold of Sheba be given to him.
May the people always pray for him
and bless him all day long.
16 May there be abundant grain throughout the
land,
flourishing even on the hilltops.
May the fruit trees flourish like the trees of
Lebanon,
and may the people thrive like grass in a
field.
17 May the king's name endure forever;
may it continue as long as the sun shines.
May all nations be blessed through him
and bring him praise.

18 Praise the LORD God, the God of Israel,
who alone does such wonderful things.
19 Praise his glorious name forever!
Let the whole earth be filled with his glory.
Amen and amen!

20 (This ends the prayers of David son of Jesse.)

BOOK THREE (Psalms 73–89)

PSALM 73

A psalm of Asaph.

1 Truly God is good to Israel,
to those whose hearts are pure.
2 But as for me, I almost lost my footing.
My feet were slipping, and I was almost
gone.
3 For I envied the proud
when I saw them prosper despite their
wickedness.
4 They seem to live such painless lives;
their bodies are so healthy and strong.
5 They don't have troubles like other people;
they're not plagued with problems like
everyone else.
6 They wear pride like a jeweled necklace
and clothe themselves with cruelty.
7 These fat cats have everything
their hearts could ever wish for!
8 They scoff and speak only evil;
in their pride they seek to crush others.
9 They boast against the very heavens,
and their words strut throughout the
earth.
10 And so the people are dismayed and confused,
drinking in all their words.
11 "What does God know?" they ask.
"Does the Most High even know what's
happening?"
12 Look at these wicked people—
enjoying a life of ease while their riches
multiply.

13 Did I keep my heart pure for nothing?
Did I keep myself innocent for no reason?

72:5 Greek version reads *May they endure.* **72:8** Hebrew *the river.*

kings fulfilled this vision of God's ideal king. The psalm could foreshadow Christ's kingdom of peace, prosperity, and justice reigning *from sea to sea* (v. 8). It ends the second book of Psalms with praise to the God who alone can answer the prayer.

73:1—89:52 Book 3

Psalm 73 Asaph (see 1 Chr 16:4–5) gives poetic testimony to God's goodness. When life became difficult for him, he observed others who mocked God yet

14 I get nothing but trouble all day long;
every morning brings me pain.

15 If I had really spoken this way to others,
I would have been a traitor to your people.
16 So I tried to understand why the wicked
prosper.
But what a difficult task it is!
17 Then I went into your sanctuary, O God,
and I finally understood the destiny of the
wicked.
18 Truly, you put them on a slippery path
and send them sliding over the cliff to
destruction.
19 In an instant they are destroyed,
completely swept away by terrors.
20 When you arise, O Lord,
you will laugh at their silly ideas
as a person laughs at dreams in the
morning.

21 Then I realized that my heart was bitter,
and I was all torn up inside.
22 I was so foolish and ignorant—
I must have seemed like a senseless animal
to you.
23 Yet I still belong to you;
you hold my right hand.
24 You guide me with your counsel,
leading me to a glorious destiny.
25 Whom have I in heaven but you?
I desire you more than anything on earth.
26 My health may fail, and my spirit may grow
weak,
but God remains the strength of my heart;
he is mine forever.

27 Those who desert him will perish,
for you destroy those who abandon you.
28 But as for me, how good it is to be near God!
I have made the Sovereign LORD my shelter,
and I will tell everyone about the
wonderful things you do.

PSALM 74

A psalm of Asaph.*

1 O God, why have you rejected us so long?
Why is your anger so intense against the
sheep of your own pasture?
2 Remember that we are the people you chose
long ago,
the tribe you redeemed as your own special
possession!
And remember Jerusalem,* your home
here on earth.
3 Walk through the awful ruins of the city;
see how the enemy has destroyed your
sanctuary.

4 There your enemies shouted their victorious
battle cries;
there they set up their battle standards.
5 They swung their axes
like woodcutters in a forest.
6 With axes and picks,
they smashed the carved paneling.
7 They burned your sanctuary to the ground.
They defiled the place that bears your
name.
8 Then they thought, "Let's destroy
everything!"
So they burned down all the places where
God was worshiped.

9 We no longer see your miraculous signs.
All the prophets are gone,
and no one can tell us when it will end.
10 How long, O God, will you allow our enemies
to insult you?
Will you let them dishonor your name
forever?
11 Why do you hold back your strong right
hand?
Unleash your powerful fist and destroy
them.

12 You, O God, are my king from ages past,
bringing salvation to the earth.
13 You split the sea by your strength
and smashed the heads of the sea monsters.
14 You crushed the heads of Leviathan*
and let the desert animals eat him.
15 You caused the springs and streams to gush
forth,
and you dried up rivers that never run dry.

74:TITLE Hebrew *maskil.* This may be a literary or musical term. **74:2** Hebrew *Mount Zion.* **74:14** The identification of Leviathan is disputed, ranging from an earthly creature to a mythical sea monster in ancient literature.

lived at ease. The contrast tempted Asaph to self-pity, complaint, and the verge of unbelief until he recovered his spiritual balance: This life, though it is unfair, is not everything.

Psalm 74 conveys the stunned incomprehension of bereavement as Asaph observes a devastated Israel with neither Temple nor prophet (cf. 2 Kgs 25:9–17). However, faith means his questions (vv. 1, 10–11) lead to prayer rather than despair.

16 Both day and night belong to you;
you made the starlight* and the sun.
17 You set the boundaries of the earth,
and you made both summer and winter.

18 See how these enemies insult you, LORD.
A foolish nation has dishonored your name.
19 Don't let these wild beasts destroy your turtledoves.
Don't forget your suffering people forever.

20 Remember your covenant promises,
for the land is full of darkness and violence!
21 Don't let the downtrodden be humiliated again.
Instead, let the poor and needy praise your name.

22 Arise, O God, and defend your cause.
Remember how these fools insult you all day long.
23 Don't overlook what your enemies have said
or their growing uproar.

PSALM 75

For the choir director: A psalm of Asaph. A song to be sung to the tune "Do Not Destroy!"

1 We thank you, O God!
We give thanks because you are near.
People everywhere tell of your wonderful deeds.

2 God says, "At the time I have planned,
I will bring justice against the wicked.
3 When the earth quakes and its people live in turmoil,
I am the one who keeps its foundations firm. *Interlude*

4 "I warned the proud, 'Stop your boasting!'
I told the wicked, 'Don't raise your fists!
5 Don't raise your fists in defiance at the heavens
or speak with such arrogance.' "
6 For no one on earth—from east or west,
or even from the wilderness—
should raise a defiant fist.*
7 It is God alone who judges;
he decides who will rise and who will fall.
8 For the LORD holds a cup in his hand
that is full of foaming wine mixed with spices.
He pours out the wine in judgment,
and all the wicked must drink it,
draining it to the dregs.

9 But as for me, I will always proclaim what God has done;
I will sing praises to the God of Jacob.
10 For God says, "I will break the strength of the wicked,
but I will increase the power of the godly."

PSALM 76

For the choir director: A psalm of Asaph. A song to be accompanied by stringed instruments.

1 God is honored in Judah;
his name is great in Israel.
2 Jerusalem* is where he lives;
Mount Zion is his home.
3 There he has broken the fiery arrows of the enemy,
the shields and swords and weapons of war. *Interlude*

4 You are glorious and more majestic
than the everlasting mountains.*
5 Our boldest enemies have been plundered.
They lie before us in the sleep of death.
No warrior could lift a hand against us.
6 At the blast of your breath, O God of Jacob,
their horses and chariots lay still.

7 No wonder you are greatly feared!
Who can stand before you when your anger explodes?
8 From heaven you sentenced your enemies;

74:16 Or *moon;* Hebrew reads *light.* **75:6** Hebrew *should lift.* **76:2** Hebrew *Salem,* another name for Jerusalem. **76:4** As in Greek version; Hebrew reads *than mountains filled with beasts of prey.*

Psalm 75 answers the questions of 74:10–11. A word from God reminds Asaph that the LORD keeps the earth stable and rules all its peoples, including the wicked (vv. 2–5). The cup in God's hand (v. 8) is a picture of God's will (cf. Jer 25:15).

Psalm 76 praises God for a victory (vv. 5–6), which has vindicated God's mighty presence among his people and revealed his glory (vv. 1–4). On this basis the psalmist foresees a far greater, worldwide victory when God's judgment will surely be revealed in the simultaneous salvation of the *oppressed* (v. 9) and defeat of human opposition.

the earth trembled and stood silent before
you.
9 You stand up to judge those who do evil,
O God,
and to rescue the oppressed of the earth.
Interlude
10 Human defiance only enhances your glory,
for you use it as a weapon.*

11 Make vows to the LORD your God, and keep
them.
Let everyone bring tribute to the Awesome
One.
12 For he breaks the pride of princes,
and the kings of the earth fear him.

PSALM 77

For Jeduthun, the choir director: A psalm of Asaph.

1 I cry out to God; yes, I shout.
Oh, that God would listen to me!
2 When I was in deep trouble,
I searched for the Lord.
All night long I prayed, with hands lifted
toward heaven,
but my soul was not comforted.
3 I think of God, and I moan,
overwhelmed with longing for his help.
Interlude

4 You don't let me sleep.
I am too distressed even to pray!
5 I think of the good old days,
long since ended,
6 when my nights were filled with joyful
songs.
I search my soul and ponder the difference
now.
7 Has the Lord rejected me forever?
Will he never again be kind to me?
8 Is his unfailing love gone forever?
Have his promises permanently failed?
9 Has God forgotten to be gracious?
Has he slammed the door on his
compassion? *Interlude*

10 And I said, "This is my fate;
the Most High has turned his hand
against me."
11 But then I recall all you have done, O LORD;
I remember your wonderful deeds of long
ago.
12 They are constantly in my thoughts.
I cannot stop thinking about your mighty
works.

13 O God, your ways are holy.
Is there any god as mighty as you?
14 You are the God of great wonders!
You demonstrate your awesome power
among the nations.
15 By your strong arm, you redeemed your
people,
the descendants of Jacob and Joseph.
Interlude

16 When the Red Sea* saw you, O God,
its waters looked and trembled!
The sea quaked to its very depths.
17 The clouds poured down rain;
the thunder rumbled in the sky.
Your arrows of lightning flashed.
18 Your thunder roared from the whirlwind;
the lightning lit up the world!
The earth trembled and shook.
19 Your road led through the sea,
your pathway through the mighty
waters—
a pathway no one knew was there!
20 You led your people along that road like a
flock of sheep,
with Moses and Aaron as their shepherds.

PSALM 78

A psalm of Asaph.*

1 O my people, listen to my instructions.
Open your ears to what I am saying,
2 for I will speak to you in a parable.
I will teach you hidden lessons from our
past—
3 stories we have heard and known,
stories our ancestors handed down to us.
4 We will not hide these truths from our
children;
we will tell the next generation
about the glorious deeds of the LORD,

76:10 The meaning of the Hebrew is uncertain.
77:16 Hebrew *the waters.* **78:TITLE** Hebrew *maskil.* This may be a literary or musical term.

Psalm 77 reveals the psalmist struggling because, despite constant prayer, his life is still pervaded by misery. But by choosing to redirect his thoughts from self to the LORD (vv. 11–12), he gains a new perspective.

Psalm 78 tells Israel's history, focusing on the Exodus (cf. Pss 105; 106; 136). The prologue, typical of wisdom literature, explains the purpose: to teach future generations an obedient, trusting faith (vv. 1–8). The

about his power and his mighty wonders.
5 For he issued his laws to Jacob;
he gave his instructions to Israel.
He commanded our ancestors
to teach them to their children,
6 so the next generation might know them—
even the children not yet born—
and they in turn will teach their own children.
7 So each generation should set its hope anew on God,
not forgetting his glorious miracles
and obeying his commands.
8 Then they will not be like their ancestors—
stubborn, rebellious, and unfaithful,
refusing to give their hearts to God.

9 The warriors of Ephraim, though armed with bows,
turned their backs and fled on the day of battle.
10 They did not keep God's covenant
and refused to live by his instructions.
11 They forgot what he had done—
the great wonders he had shown them,
12 the miracles he did for their ancestors
on the plain of Zoan in the land of Egypt.
13 For he divided the sea and led them through,
making the water stand up like walls!
14 In the daytime he led them by a cloud,
and all night by a pillar of fire.
15 He split open the rocks in the wilderness
to give them water, as from a gushing spring.
16 He made streams pour from the rock,
making the waters flow down like a river!

17 Yet they kept on sinning against him,
rebelling against the Most High in the desert.
18 They stubbornly tested God in their hearts,
demanding the foods they craved.
19 They even spoke against God himself, saying,
"God can't give us food in the wilderness.
20 Yes, he can strike a rock so water gushes out,
but he can't give his people bread and meat."
21 When the LORD heard them, he was furious.
The fire of his wrath burned against Jacob.
Yes, his anger rose against Israel,
22 for they did not believe God
or trust him to care for them.
23 But he commanded the skies to open;
he opened the doors of heaven.
24 He rained down manna for them to eat;
he gave them bread from heaven.
25 They ate the food of angels!
God gave them all they could hold.
26 He released the east wind in the heavens
and guided the south wind by his mighty power.
27 He rained down meat as thick as dust—
birds as plentiful as the sand on the seashore!
28 He caused the birds to fall within their camp
and all around their tents.
29 The people ate their fill.
He gave them what they craved.
30 But before they satisfied their craving,
while the meat was yet in their mouths,
31 the anger of God rose against them,
and he killed their strongest men.
He struck down the finest of Israel's young men.

32 But in spite of this, the people kept sinning.
Despite his wonders, they refused to trust him.
33 So he ended their lives in failure,
their years in terror.
34 When God began killing them,
they finally sought him.
They repented and took God seriously.
35 Then they remembered that God was their rock,
that God Most High* was their redeemer.
36 But all they gave him was lip service;
they lied to him with their tongues.
37 Their hearts were not loyal to him.
They did not keep his covenant.
38 Yet he was merciful and forgave their sins
and did not destroy them all.
Many times he held back his anger
and did not unleash his fury!
39 For he remembered that they were merely mortal,
gone like a breath of wind that never returns.

40 Oh, how often they rebelled against him in the wilderness
and grieved his heart in that dry wasteland.

78:35 Hebrew *El-Elyon*.

story is one of persistent care in the face of persistent rebellion. A particular tragedy is that of young women who die before their wedding (v. 63). The role of parents in passing God's law to future generations is stressed (vv. 5–7). An important aspect of motherhood is the perpetuation of her faith in her children.

41 Again and again they tested God's patience
and provoked the Holy One of Israel.
42 They did not remember his power
and how he rescued them from their
enemies.
43 They did not remember his miraculous signs
in Egypt,
his wonders on the plain of Zoan.
44 For he turned their rivers into blood,
so no one could drink from the streams.
45 He sent vast swarms of flies to consume them
and hordes of frogs to ruin them.
46 He gave their crops to caterpillars;
their harvest was consumed by locusts.
47 He destroyed their grapevines with hail
and shattered their sycamore-figs with
sleet.
48 He abandoned their cattle to the hail,
their livestock to bolts of lightning.
49 He loosed on them his fierce anger—
all his fury, rage, and hostility.
He dispatched against them
a band of destroying angels.
50 He turned his anger against them;
he did not spare the Egyptians' lives
but ravaged them with the plague.
51 He killed the oldest son in each Egyptian
family,
the flower of youth throughout the land of
Egypt.*
52 But he led his own people like a flock of
sheep,
guiding them safely through the
wilderness.
53 He kept them safe so they were not afraid;
but the sea covered their enemies.
54 He brought them to the border of his holy
land,
to this land of hills he had won for them.
55 He drove out the nations before them;
he gave them their inheritance by lot.
He settled the tribes of Israel into their
homes.

56 But they kept testing and rebelling against
God Most High.
They did not obey his laws.
57 They turned back and were as faithless as
their parents.
They were as undependable as a crooked
bow.
58 They angered God by building shrines to
other gods;
they made him jealous with their idols.
59 When God heard them, he was very angry,
and he completely rejected Israel.
60 Then he abandoned his dwelling at Shiloh,
the Tabernacle where he had lived among
the people.
61 He allowed the Ark of his might to be
captured;
he surrendered his glory into enemy
hands.
62 He gave his people over to be butchered by
the sword,
because he was so angry with his own
people—his special possession.
63 Their young men were killed by fire;
their young women died before singing
their wedding songs.
64 Their priests were slaughtered,
and their widows could not mourn their
deaths.

65 Then the Lord rose up as though waking
from sleep,
like a warrior aroused from a drunken
stupor.
66 He routed his enemies
and sent them to eternal shame.
67 But he rejected Joseph's descendants;
he did not choose the tribe of Ephraim.
68 He chose instead the tribe of Judah,
and Mount Zion, which he loved.
69 There he built his sanctuary as high as the
heavens,
as solid and enduring as the earth.
70 He chose his servant David,
calling him from the sheep pens.
71 He took David from tending the ewes and
lambs
and made him the shepherd of Jacob's
descendants—
God's own people, Israel.
72 He cared for them with a true heart
and led them with skillful hands.

PSALM 79

A psalm of Asaph.

1 O God, pagan nations have conquered your
land,
your special possession.
They have defiled your holy Temple
and made Jerusalem a heap of ruins.
2 They have left the bodies of your servants
as food for the birds of heaven.
The flesh of your godly ones
has become food for the wild animals.

78:51 Hebrew *in the tents of Ham.*

3 Blood has flowed like water all around
Jerusalem;
no one is left to bury the dead.
4 We are mocked by our neighbors,
an object of scorn and derision to those
around us.

5 O LORD, how long will you be angry with us?
Forever?
How long will your jealousy burn like fire?
6 Pour out your wrath on the nations that
refuse to acknowledge you—
on kingdoms that do not call upon your
name.
7 For they have devoured your people Israel,*
making the land a desolate wilderness.
8 Do not hold us guilty for the sins of our
ancestors!
Let your compassion quickly meet our
needs,
for we are on the brink of despair.

9 Help us, O God of our salvation!
Help us for the glory of your name.
Save us and forgive our sins
for the honor of your name.
10 Why should pagan nations be allowed to scoff,
asking, "Where is their God?"
Show us your vengeance against the nations,
for they have spilled the blood of your
servants.
11 Listen to the moaning of the prisoners.
Demonstrate your great power by saving
those condemned to die.

12 O Lord, pay back our neighbors seven times
for the scorn they have hurled at you.
13 Then we your people, the sheep of your
pasture,
will thank you forever and ever,
praising your greatness from generation to
generation.

PSALM 80

For the choir director: A psalm of Asaph, to be sung to the tune "Lilies of the Covenant."

1 Please listen, O Shepherd of Israel,
you who lead Joseph's descendants like a
flock.
O God, enthroned above the cherubim,
display your radiant glory
2 to Ephraim, Benjamin, and Manasseh.
Show us your mighty power.
Come to rescue us!

3 Turn us again to yourself, O God.
Make your face shine down upon us.
Only then will we be saved.
4 O LORD God of Heaven's Armies,
how long will you be angry with our
prayers?
5 You have fed us with sorrow
and made us drink tears by the bucketful.
6 You have made us the scorn* of neighboring
nations.
Our enemies treat us as a joke.

7 Turn us again to yourself, O God of Heaven's
Armies.
Make your face shine down upon us.
Only then will we be saved.
8 You brought us from Egypt like a grapevine;
you drove away the pagan nations and
transplanted us into your land.
9 You cleared the ground for us,
and we took root and filled the land.
10 Our shade covered the mountains;
our branches covered the mighty cedars.
11 We spread our branches west to the
Mediterranean Sea;
our shoots spread east to the Euphrates
River.*
12 But now, why have you broken down our
walls
so that all who pass by may steal our
fruit?
13 The wild boar from the forest devours it,
and the wild animals feed on it.

14 Come back, we beg you, O God of Heaven's
Armies.
Look down from heaven and see our plight.
Take care of this grapevine
15 that you yourself have planted,
this son you have raised for yourself.

79:7 Hebrew *devoured Jacob.* See note on 44:4. **80:6** As in Syriac version; Hebrew reads *the strife.* **80:11** Hebrew *west to the sea, . . . east to the river.*

Psalm 79 observes Israel's humiliation following the Babylonian invasion (vv. 1–4; cf. Ps 74). The dead lie unburied while the neighbors mock. Yet Asaph's chief concern is for God's name (v. 10). His agonized questions and prayers seek forgiveness and salvation, that they might praise him again (vv. 9, 13). For God's answer, see Psalm 75 and Ezra 1 (cf. Luke 18:7).

Psalm 80 The psalmist is deeply concerned by Israel's suffering, traditionally associated with God's anger.

16 For we are chopped up and burned by our
enemies.
May they perish at the sight of your
frown.
17 Strengthen the man you love,
the son of your choice.
18 Then we will never abandon you again.
Revive us so we can call on your name
once more.

19 Turn us again to yourself, O LORD God of
Heaven's Armies.
Make your face shine down upon us.
Only then will we be saved.

PSALM 81

*For the choir director: A psalm of Asaph, to be accompanied by a stringed instrument.**

1 Sing praises to God, our strength.
Sing to the God of Jacob.
2 Sing! Beat the tambourine.
Play the sweet lyre and the harp.
3 Blow the ram's horn at new moon,
and again at full moon to call a festival!
4 For this is required by the decrees of Israel;
it is a regulation of the God of Jacob.
5 He made it a law for Israel*
when he attacked Egypt to set us free.

I heard an unknown voice say,
6 "Now I will take the load from your
shoulders;
I will free your hands from their heavy
tasks.
7 You cried to me in trouble, and I saved you;
I answered out of the thundercloud
and tested your faith when there was no
water at Meribah. *Interlude*

8 "Listen to me, O my people, while I give you
stern warnings.
O Israel, if you would only listen to me!
9 You must never have a foreign god;
you must not bow down before a false god.
10 For it was I, the LORD your God,
who rescued you from the land of Egypt.
Open your mouth wide, and I will fill it
with good things.

11 "But no, my people wouldn't listen.
Israel did not want me around.
12 So I let them follow their own stubborn
desires,
living according to their own ideas.
13 Oh, that my people would listen to me!
Oh, that Israel would follow me, walking in
my paths!
14 How quickly I would then subdue their
enemies!
How soon my hands would be upon their
foes!
15 Those who hate the LORD would cringe
before him;
they would be doomed forever.
16 But I would feed you with the finest wheat.
I would satisfy you with wild honey from
the rock."

PSALM 82

A psalm of Asaph.

1 God presides over heaven's court;
he pronounces judgment on the heavenly
beings:
2 "How long will you hand down unjust
decisions
by favoring the wicked? *Interlude*

3 "Give justice to the poor and the orphan;
uphold the rights of the oppressed and the
destitute.
4 Rescue the poor and helpless;
deliver them from the grasp of evil people.
5 But these oppressors know nothing;

81:TITLE Hebrew *according to the gittith.* **81:5** Hebrew *for Joseph.*

Using the familiar analogy of a vine, he recalls how it was God, their Shepherd-King (v. 1), who made them great. The specific request to *strengthen . . . the son of your choice* (v. 17) refers originally to the Davidic king but prophetically to the Messiah.

Psalm 81 urges Israel to celebrate a festival, traditionally the Festival of Shelters or Booths (Sukkot), in obedience to God's decree (vv. 3–5; cf. Lev 23:34). To this end Asaph encourages loud praise and attentive listening to God's word (vv. 1–3, 6–16), which reminds the people of God's blessings during the Exodus.

Psalm 82 God the judge demands justice not from humanity, but from *heavenly beings* and *gods.* Verse 5 is probably the explanation preceding God's sentencing of the guilty (vv. 6–7): They do not understand the destabilizing effects of their wickedness. With these unjust rulers out of the way, God can bring true justice to the earth. Jesus understood the guilty to be human leaders rather than spiritual beings (John 10:34–36).

they are so ignorant!
They wander about in darkness,
while the whole world is shaken to the core.
6 I say, 'You are gods;
you are all children of the Most High.
7 But you will die like mere mortals
and fall like every other ruler.' "

8 Rise up, O God, and judge the earth,
for all the nations belong to you.

PSALM 83

A song. A psalm of Asaph.

1 O God, do not be silent!
Do not be deaf.
Do not be quiet, O God.
2 Don't you hear the uproar of your enemies?
Don't you see that your arrogant enemies are rising up?
3 They devise crafty schemes against your people;
they conspire against your precious ones.
4 "Come," they say, "let us wipe out Israel as a nation.
We will destroy the very memory of its existence."
5 Yes, this was their unanimous decision.
They signed a treaty as allies against you—
6 these Edomites and Ishmaelites;
Moabites and Hagrites;
7 Gebalites, Ammonites, and Amalekites;
and people from Philistia and Tyre.
8 Assyria has joined them, too,
and is allied with the descendants of Lot. *Interlude*

9 Do to them as you did to the Midianites
and as you did to Sisera and Jabin at the Kishon River.
10 They were destroyed at Endor,
and their decaying corpses fertilized the soil.
11 Let their mighty nobles die as Oreb and Zeeb did.
Let all their princes die like Zebah and Zalmunna,
12 for they said, "Let us seize for our own use
these pasturelands of God!"
13 O my God, scatter them like tumbleweed,
like chaff before the wind!
14 As a fire burns a forest
and as a flame sets mountains ablaze,
15 chase them with your fierce storm;
terrify them with your tempest.
16 Utterly disgrace them
until they submit to your name, O LORD.
17 Let them be ashamed and terrified forever.
Let them die in disgrace.
18 Then they will learn that you alone are called the LORD,
that you alone are the Most High,
supreme over all the earth.

PSALM 84

*For the choir director: A psalm of the descendants of Korah, to be accompanied by a stringed instrument.**

1 How lovely is your dwelling place,
O LORD of Heaven's Armies.
2 I long, yes, I faint with longing
to enter the courts of the LORD.
With my whole being, body and soul,
I will shout joyfully to the living God.
3 Even the sparrow finds a home,
and the swallow builds her nest and raises her young
at a place near your altar,
O LORD of Heaven's Armies, my King and my God!
4 What joy for those who can live in your house,
always singing your praises. *Interlude*

5 What joy for those whose strength comes from the LORD,
who have set their minds on a pilgrimage to Jerusalem.

84:TITLE Hebrew *according to the gittith.*

Psalm 83 describes an unknown conspiracy to *wipe out Israel* by the nations of verses 6–8. On the basis that Israel's enemies are God's enemies (vv. 2–5), the psalmist prays for their defeat. In particular, he recalls the victory of Deborah and Jael over Sisera and Jabin (cf. Judg 4—5).

Psalm 84 reflects the Korahites' (*gatekeepers*; see 1 Chr 26) seasonal pilgrimage to serve in the Temple, revealing their love and longing for Zion, symbol of God's presence (vv. 1–7; cf. Pss 120—134). Zion meant a safe and happy home, even for small nesting birds (vv. 1–4), a refreshing, growing strength for pilgrims in dry places (vv. 5–8), and unlimited protective blessing for all who *do what is right* (vv. 10–12).

6 When they walk through the Valley of
Weeping,*
it will become a place of refreshing springs.
The autumn rains will clothe it with
blessings.
7 They will continue to grow stronger,
and each of them will appear before God in
Jerusalem.*
8 O LORD God of Heaven's Armies, hear my
prayer.
Listen, O God of Jacob. *Interlude*
9 O God, look with favor upon the king, our
shield!
Show favor to the one you have anointed.
10 A single day in your courts
is better than a thousand anywhere else!
I would rather be a gatekeeper in the house of
my God
than live the good life in the homes of the
wicked.
11 For the LORD God is our sun and our shield.
He gives us grace and glory.
The LORD will withhold no good thing
from those who do what is right.
12 O LORD of Heaven's Armies,
what joy for those who trust in you.

PSALM 85

For the choir director: A psalm of the descendants of Korah.

1 LORD, you poured out blessings on your
land!
You restored the fortunes of Israel.*
2 You forgave the guilt of your people—
yes, you covered all their sins. *Interlude*
3 You held back your fury.
You kept back your blazing anger.
4 Now restore us again, O God of our
salvation.
Put aside your anger against us once
more.
5 Will you be angry with us always?
Will you prolong your wrath to all
generations?
6 Won't you revive us again,
so your people can rejoice in you?
7 Show us your unfailing love, O LORD,
and grant us your salvation.
8 I listen carefully to what God the LORD is
saying,
for he speaks peace to his faithful people.
But let them not return to their foolish
ways.
9 Surely his salvation is near to those who fear
him,
so our land will be filled with his glory.
10 Unfailing love and truth have met together.
Righteousness and peace have kissed!
11 Truth springs up from the earth,
and righteousness smiles down from
heaven.
12 Yes, the LORD pours down his blessings.
Our land will yield its bountiful harvest.
13 Righteousness goes as a herald before him,
preparing the way for his steps.

PSALM 86

A prayer of David.

1 Bend down, O LORD, and hear my prayer;
answer me, for I need your help.
2 Protect me, for I am devoted to you.
Save me, for I serve you and trust you.
You are my God.
3 Be merciful to me, O Lord,
for I am calling on you constantly.
4 Give me happiness, O Lord,
for I give myself to you.
5 O Lord, you are so good, so ready to forgive,
so full of unfailing love for all who ask for
your help.
6 Listen closely to my prayer, O LORD;
hear my urgent cry.
7 I will call to you whenever I'm in trouble,
and you will answer me.
8 No pagan god is like you, O Lord.
None can do what you do!
9 All the nations you made
will come and bow before you, Lord;

84:6 Or *Valley of Poplars;* Hebrew reads *valley of Baca.* **84:7** Hebrew *Zion.* **85:1** Hebrew *of Jacob.* See note on 44:4.

Psalm 85 combines thanksgiving for one undeserved restoration (possibly from exile) with prayer for another. God promises peace, his presence among the people, and good gifts, presumably including revival. The promise depicted exceeds what the people could ever deserve. Some have interpreted verses 9–13 as messianic.

Psalm 86 is composed of fragments of Davidic psalms and other Scriptures. The result is a prayer for help

they will praise your holy name.
10 For you are great and perform wonderful
deeds.
You alone are God.
11 Teach me your ways, O LORD,
that I may live according to your truth!
Grant me purity of heart,
so that I may honor you.
12 With all my heart I will praise you, O Lord
my God.
I will give glory to your name forever,
13 for your love for me is very great.
You have rescued me from the depths of
death.*
14 O God, insolent people rise up against me;
a violent gang is trying to kill me.
You mean nothing to them.
15 But you, O Lord,
are a God of compassion and mercy,
slow to get angry
and filled with unfailing love and
faithfulness.
16 Look down and have mercy on me.
Give your strength to your servant;
save me, the son of your servant.
17 Send me a sign of your favor.
Then those who hate me will be put to
shame,
for you, O LORD, help and comfort me.

PSALM 87

A song. A psalm of the descendants of Korah.

1 On the holy mountain
stands the city founded by the LORD.
2 He loves the city of Jerusalem
more than any other city in Israel.*
3 O city of God,
what glorious things are said of you!
Interlude
4 I will count Egypt* and Babylon among those
who know me—
also Philistia and Tyre, and even distant
Ethiopia.*
They have all become citizens of
Jerusalem!
5 Regarding Jerusalem* it will be said,
"Everyone enjoys the rights of citizenship
there."
And the Most High will personally bless
this city.
6 When the LORD registers the nations, he will
say,
"They have all become citizens of
Jerusalem." *Interlude*
7 The people will play flutes* and sing,
"The source of my life springs from
Jerusalem!"

PSALM 88

For the choir director: A psalm of the descendants of Korah. A song to be sung to the tune "The Suffering of Affliction." A psalm of Heman the Ezrahite.*

1 O LORD, God of my salvation,
I cry out to you by day.
I come to you at night.
2 Now hear my prayer;
listen to my cry.
3 For my life is full of troubles,
and death* draws near.
4 I am as good as dead,
like a strong man with no strength left.
5 They have left me among the dead,
and I lie like a corpse in a grave.
I am forgotten,
cut off from your care.

86:13 Hebrew *of Sheol.* **87:2** Hebrew *He loves the gates of Zion more than all the dwellings of Jacob.* See note on 44:4. **87:4a** Hebrew *Rahab,* the name of a mythical sea monster that represents chaos in ancient literature. The name is used here as a poetic name for Egypt. **87:4b** Hebrew *Cush.* **87:5** Hebrew *Zion.* **87:7** Or *will dance.* **88:TITLE** Hebrew *maskil.* This may be a literary or musical term. **88:3** Hebrew *Sheol.*

based on the psalmist's covenant-servant relationship with the LORD.

Psalm 87 considers God's city (vv. 1–4) and foresees the heavenly city (vv. 5–6; cf. Rev 21). Zion, here translated as *Jerusalem*, is a community of individuals from every nation, including Israel's enemies—Egypt, Philistia, and Babylon. Also noteworthy is the inclusion of Ethiopia (cf. 68:31; Isa 18). In the described change of citizenship, conversion is implicit.

Psalm 88 The psalmist is deeply depressed by some longstanding illness (v. 15) or other urgent situation. Even friends have shunned him (vv. 8, 18). He associates suffering with God's wrath but knows the LORD also as the God of *unfailing love* and *my salvation*. Unlike most similar psalms, this one never turns to explicit trust or praise, ending in *darkness*.

6 You have thrown me into the lowest pit,
into the darkest depths.
7 Your anger weighs me down;
with wave after wave you have engulfed me. *Interlude*
8 You have driven my friends away
by making me repulsive to them.
I am in a trap with no way of escape.
9 My eyes are blinded by my tears.
Each day I beg for your help, O LORD;
I lift my hands to you for mercy.
10 Are your wonderful deeds of any use to the dead?
Do the dead rise up and praise you? *Interlude*
11 Can those in the grave declare your unfailing love?
Can they proclaim your faithfulness in the place of destruction?*
12 Can the darkness speak of your wonderful deeds?
Can anyone in the land of forgetfulness
talk about your righteousness?
13 O LORD, I cry out to you.
I will keep on pleading day by day.
14 O LORD, why do you reject me?
Why do you turn your face from me?

15 I have been sick and close to death since my youth.
I stand helpless and desperate before your terrors.
16 Your fierce anger has overwhelmed me.
Your terrors have paralyzed me.
17 They swirl around me like floodwaters all day long.
They have engulfed me completely.
18 You have taken away my companions and loved ones.
Darkness is my closest friend.

PSALM 89

A psalm of Ethan the Ezrahite.*

1 I will sing of the LORD's unfailing love forever!
Young and old will hear of your faithfulness.
2 Your unfailing love will last forever.
Your faithfulness is as enduring as the heavens.

3 The LORD said, "I have made a covenant with David, my chosen servant.
I have sworn this oath to him:
4 'I will establish your descendants as kings forever;
they will sit on your throne from now until eternity.' " *Interlude*
5 All heaven will praise your great wonders, LORD;
myriads of angels will praise you for your faithfulness.
6 For who in all of heaven can compare with the LORD?
What mightiest angel is anything like the LORD?
7 The highest angelic powers stand in awe of God.
He is far more awesome than all who surround his throne.
8 O LORD God of Heaven's Armies!
Where is there anyone as mighty as you, O LORD?
You are entirely faithful.

9 You rule the oceans.
You subdue their storm-tossed waves.
10 You crushed the great sea monster.*
You scattered your enemies with your mighty arm.
11 The heavens are yours, and the earth is yours;
everything in the world is yours—you created it all.
12 You created north and south.
Mount Tabor and Mount Hermon praise your name.
13 Powerful is your arm!
Strong is your hand!
Your right hand is lifted high in glorious strength.
14 Righteousness and justice are the foundation of your throne.

88:11 Hebrew *in Abaddon?* **89:TITLE** Hebrew *maskil.* This may be a literary or musical term. **89:10** Hebrew *Rahab,* the name of a mythical sea monster that represents chaos in ancient literature.

Psalm 89 The psalmist praises the LORD's *unfailing love,* as seen in the Davidic covenant, and God's mighty rule, as seen in salvation and creation. The LORD promises to remain with Israel's king in intimate father-son relationship and to grant absolute victory and an everlasting dynasty (vv. 20–37). The failures of the Davidic dynasty in Judah led to the downfall described in verses 38–45. Despite the ascendance of Jerusalem's enemies, the psalm ends with words of praise for God.

Unfailing love and truth walk before you
as attendants.
15 Happy are those who hear the joyful call to
worship,
for they will walk in the light of your
presence, LORD.
16 They rejoice all day long in your wonderful
reputation.
They exult in your righteousness.
17 You are their glorious strength.
It pleases you to make us strong.
18 Yes, our protection comes from the LORD,
and he, the Holy One of Israel, has given
us our king.

19 Long ago you spoke in a vision to your
faithful people.
You said, "I have raised up a warrior.
I have selected him from the common
people to be king.
20 I have found my servant David.
I have anointed him with my holy oil.
21 I will steady him with my hand;
with my powerful arm I will make him
strong.
22 His enemies will not defeat him,
nor will the wicked overpower him.
23 I will beat down his adversaries before him
and destroy those who hate him.
24 My faithfulness and unfailing love will be
with him,
and by my authority he will grow in
power.
25 I will extend his rule over the sea,
his dominion over the rivers.
26 And he will call out to me, 'You are my
Father,
my God, and the Rock of my salvation.'
27 I will make him my firstborn son,
the mightiest king on earth.
28 I will love him and be kind to him forever;
my covenant with him will never end.
29 I will preserve an heir for him;
his throne will be as endless as the days of
heaven.
30 But if his descendants forsake my
instructions
and fail to obey my regulations,
31 if they do not obey my decrees
and fail to keep my commands,
32 then I will punish their sin with the rod,
and their disobedience with beating.
33 But I will never stop loving him
nor fail to keep my promise to him.
34 No, I will not break my covenant;
I will not take back a single word I said.
35 I have sworn an oath to David,
and in my holiness I cannot lie:
36 His dynasty will go on forever;
his kingdom will endure as the sun.
37 It will be as eternal as the moon,
my faithful witness in the sky!" *Interlude*

38 But now you have rejected him and cast him
off.
You are angry with your anointed king.
39 You have renounced your covenant with
him;
you have thrown his crown in the dust.
40 You have broken down the walls protecting
him
and ruined every fort defending him.
41 Everyone who comes along has robbed
him,
and he has become a joke to his
neighbors.
42 You have strengthened his enemies
and made them all rejoice.
43 You have made his sword useless
and refused to help him in battle.
44 You have ended his splendor
and overturned his throne.
45 You have made him old before his time
and publicly disgraced him. *Interlude*

46 O LORD, how long will this go on?
Will you hide yourself forever?
How long will your anger burn like fire?
47 Remember how short my life is,
how empty and futile this human
existence!
48 No one can live forever; all will die.
No one can escape the power of the grave.*
Interlude

49 Lord, where is your unfailing love?
You promised it to David with a faithful
pledge.
50 Consider, Lord, how your servants are
disgraced!
I carry in my heart the insults of so many
people.
51 Your enemies have mocked me, O LORD;
they mock your anointed king wherever he
goes.

52 Praise the LORD forever!
Amen and amen!

89:48 Hebrew *of Sheol.*

Book Four (Psalms 90–106)

PSALM 90

A prayer of Moses, the man of God.

1 Lord, through all the generations
you have been our home!
2 Before the mountains were born,
before you gave birth to the earth and the world,
from beginning to end, you are God.

3 You turn people back to dust, saying,
"Return to dust, you mortals!"
4 For you, a thousand years are as a passing day,
as brief as a few night hours.
5 You sweep people away like dreams that disappear.
They are like grass that springs up in the morning.
6 In the morning it blooms and flourishes,
but by evening it is dry and withered.
7 We wither beneath your anger;
we are overwhelmed by your fury.
8 You spread out our sins before you—
our secret sins—and you see them all.
9 We live our lives beneath your wrath,
ending our years with a groan.

10 Seventy years are given to us!
Some even live to eighty.
But even the best years are filled with pain and trouble;
soon they disappear, and we fly away.
11 Who can comprehend the power of your anger?
Your wrath is as awesome as the fear you deserve.
12 Teach us to realize the brevity of life,
so that we may grow in wisdom.

13 O LORD, come back to us!
How long will you delay?
Take pity on your servants!
14 Satisfy us each morning with your unfailing love,
so we may sing for joy to the end of our lives.
15 Give us gladness in proportion to our former misery!
Replace the evil years with good.
16 Let us, your servants, see you work again;
let our children see your glory.
17 And may the Lord our God show us his approval
and make our efforts successful.
Yes, make our efforts successful!

PSALM 91

1 Those who live in the shelter of the Most High
will find rest in the shadow of the Almighty.
2 This I declare about the LORD:
He alone is my refuge, my place of safety;
he is my God, and I trust him.
3 For he will rescue you from every trap
and protect you from deadly disease.
4 He will cover you with his feathers.
He will shelter you with his wings.
His faithful promises are your armor and protection.
5 Do not be afraid of the terrors of the night,
nor the arrow that flies in the day.
6 Do not dread the disease that stalks in darkness,
nor the disaster that strikes at midday.
7 Though a thousand fall at your side,
though ten thousand are dying around you,
these evils will not touch you.
8 Just open your eyes,
and see how the wicked are punished.

9 If you make the LORD your refuge,
if you make the Most High your shelter,

90:1–106:48 Book 4

Psalm 90 This is the only psalm attributed to Moses, yet it also responds to the crisis of exile mentioned in 89:38–51. The psalmist confidently approaches God in prayer on behalf of his people, who find in him a secure and stable *home*. This and the six requests of verses 12–17 evoke both the wilderness wanderings, when Israel was living in tents and grumbling against the LORD, and the Exile.

Psalm 91 vividly testifies that, although believers may face every kind of danger they will survive by abiding and trusting in God, whose four names emphasize his power and covenant love (vv. 1–2). Those who make the LORD their home (v. 9; cf. 90:1) may confidently rely on God's protection. Satan later used Psalm 91:11–12 out of context to tempt Jesus (Matt 4:5–6).

10 no evil will conquer you;
no plague will come near your home.
11 For he will order his angels
to protect you wherever you go.
12 They will hold you up with their hands
so you won't even hurt your foot on a stone.
13 You will trample upon lions and cobras;
you will crush fierce lions and serpents under your feet!

14 The LORD says, "I will rescue those who love me.
I will protect those who trust in my name.
15 When they call on me, I will answer;
I will be with them in trouble.
I will rescue and honor them.
16 I will reward them with a long life
and give them my salvation."

PSALM 92

A psalm. A song to be sung on the Sabbath Day.

1 It is good to give thanks to the LORD,
to sing praises to the Most High.
2 It is good to proclaim your unfailing love in the morning,
your faithfulness in the evening,
3 accompanied by the ten-stringed harp
and the melody of the lyre.

4 You thrill me, LORD, with all you have done for me!
I sing for joy because of what you have done.
5 O LORD, what great works you do!
And how deep are your thoughts.
6 Only a simpleton would not know,
and only a fool would not understand this:
7 Though the wicked sprout like weeds
and evildoers flourish,
they will be destroyed forever.

8 But you, O LORD, will be exalted forever.
9 Your enemies, LORD, will surely perish;
all evildoers will be scattered.
10 But you have made me as strong as a wild ox.
You have anointed me with the finest oil.
11 My eyes have seen the downfall of my enemies;
my ears have heard the defeat of my wicked opponents.
12 But the godly will flourish like palm trees
and grow strong like the cedars of Lebanon.
13 For they are transplanted to the LORD's own house.
They flourish in the courts of our God.
14 Even in old age they will still produce fruit;
they will remain vital and green.
15 They will declare, "The LORD is just!
He is my rock!
There is no evil in him!"

PSALM 93

1 The LORD is king! He is robed in majesty.
Indeed, the LORD is robed in majesty and armed with strength.
The world stands firm
and cannot be shaken.

2 Your throne, O LORD, has stood from time immemorial.
You yourself are from the everlasting past.
3 The floods have risen up, O LORD.
The floods have roared like thunder;
the floods have lifted their pounding waves.
4 But mightier than the violent raging of the seas,
mightier than the breakers on the shore—
the LORD above is mightier than these!
5 Your royal laws cannot be changed.
Your reign, O LORD, is holy forever and ever.

PSALM 94

1 O LORD, the God of vengeance,
O God of vengeance, let your glorious justice shine forth!
2 Arise, O judge of the earth.
Give the proud what they deserve.

Psalm 92 is a Sabbath poem with wisdom features. The Sabbath should be filled with meditation on the LORD's works, especially on the contrast between God's destruction of *the wicked* and exaltation of the *godly*.

Psalm 93 may have been prompted by a recent flood, but it is more likely that God's taming of metaphorical *floods* are be a depiction of God's sovereignty over chaos. This psalm is the first in a collection (93; 95–99) which explicitly proclaims that God *is king*. The psalmist draws three conclusions: The world shall never be moved; the LORD is greater than any force that may threaten Israel; God's word is eternally sure (v. 5; cf. especially Gen 9:11).

Psalm 94 is a prayer for *vengeance* upon *the wicked* who are brazenly abusing God's people, especially

3 How long, O LORD?
How long will the wicked be allowed to gloat?
4 How long will they speak with arrogance?
How long will these evil people boast?
5 They crush your people, LORD,
hurting those you claim as your own.
6 They kill widows and foreigners
and murder orphans.
7 "The LORD isn't looking," they say,
"and besides, the God of Israel* doesn't care."

8 Think again, you fools!
When will you finally catch on?
9 Is he deaf—the one who made your ears?
Is he blind—the one who formed your eyes?
10 He punishes the nations—won't he also punish you?
He knows everything—doesn't he also know what you are doing?
11 The LORD knows people's thoughts;
he knows they are worthless!

12 Joyful are those you discipline, LORD,
those you teach with your instructions.
13 You give them relief from troubled times
until a pit is dug to capture the wicked.
14 The LORD will not reject his people;
he will not abandon his special possession.
15 Judgment will again be founded on justice,
and those with virtuous hearts will pursue it.

16 Who will protect me from the wicked?
Who will stand up for me against evildoers?
17 Unless the LORD had helped me,
I would soon have settled in the silence of the grave.
18 I cried out, "I am slipping!"
but your unfailing love, O LORD, supported me.
19 When doubts filled my mind,
your comfort gave me renewed hope and cheer.
20 Can unjust leaders claim that God is on their side—
leaders whose decrees permit injustice?
21 They gang up against the righteous
and condemn the innocent to death.
22 But the LORD is my fortress;
my God is the mighty rock where I hide.
23 God will turn the sins of evil people back on them.
He will destroy them for their sins.
The LORD our God will destroy them.

PSALM 95

1 Come, let us sing to the LORD!
Let us shout joyfully to the Rock of our salvation.
2 Let us come to him with thanksgiving.
Let us sing psalms of praise to him.
3 For the LORD is a great God,
a great King above all gods.
4 He holds in his hands the depths of the earth
and the mightiest mountains.
5 The sea belongs to him, for he made it.
His hands formed the dry land, too.

6 Come, let us worship and bow down.
Let us kneel before the LORD our maker,
7 for he is our God.
We are the people he watches over,
the flock under his care.

If only you would listen to his voice today!
8 The LORD says, "Don't harden your hearts as Israel did at Meribah,
as they did at Massah in the wilderness.
9 For there your ancestors tested and tried my patience,
even though they saw everything I did.
10 For forty years I was angry with them, and I said,
'They are a people whose hearts turn away from me.
They refuse to do what I tell them.'

94:7 Hebrew *of Jacob.* See note on 44:4.

the vulnerable whom God had promised to protect (vv. 3–6; cf. Deut 10:18). The plight of widows, orphans, and strangers is called to God's attention; the psalmist concludes that God's apparent inactivity means discipline, not desertion. God is the ultimate source of justice—for both the oppressed and the oppressors.

Psalm 95 Worship involves far more than joyful singing; beginning with humble listening, it is ultimately expressed in obedient living. The illustration (vv. 8–11; cf. Exod 17:1–7) warns believers against maintaining the outer rituals of worship with a hardened heart. Hebrews 3:7—4:13 equates God's *rest* (v. 11) with salvation and explains how God's anger against sin means it cannot be regarded with complacency.

11 So in my anger I took an oath:
'They will never enter my place of rest.' "

PSALM 96

1 Sing a new song to the LORD!
Let the whole earth sing to the LORD!
2 Sing to the LORD; praise his name.
Each day proclaim the good news that he saves.
3 Publish his glorious deeds among the nations.
Tell everyone about the amazing things he does.
4 Great is the LORD! He is most worthy of praise!
He is to be feared above all gods.
5 The gods of other nations are mere idols,
but the LORD made the heavens!
6 Honor and majesty surround him;
strength and beauty fill his sanctuary.

7 O nations of the world, recognize the LORD;
recognize that the LORD is glorious and strong.
8 Give to the LORD the glory he deserves!
Bring your offering and come into his courts.
9 Worship the LORD in all his holy splendor.
Let all the earth tremble before him.
10 Tell all the nations, "The LORD reigns!"
The world stands firm and cannot be shaken.
He will judge all peoples fairly.

11 Let the heavens be glad, and the earth rejoice!
Let the sea and everything in it shout his praise!
12 Let the fields and their crops burst out with joy!
Let the trees of the forest rustle with praise
13 before the LORD, for he is coming!
He is coming to judge the earth.
He will judge the world with justice,
and the nations with his truth.

PSALM 97

1 The LORD is king!
Let the earth rejoice!
Let the farthest coastlands be glad.
2 Dark clouds surround him.
Righteousness and justice are the foundation of his throne.
3 Fire spreads ahead of him
and burns up all his foes.
4 His lightning flashes out across the world.
The earth sees and trembles.
5 The mountains melt like wax before the LORD,
before the Lord of all the earth.
6 The heavens proclaim his righteousness;
every nation sees his glory.
7 Those who worship idols are disgraced—
all who brag about their worthless gods—
for every god must bow to him.
8 Jerusalem* has heard and rejoiced,
and all the towns of Judah are glad
because of your justice, O LORD!
9 For you, O LORD, are supreme over all the earth;
you are exalted far above all gods.

10 You who love the LORD, hate evil!
He protects the lives of his godly people
and rescues them from the power of the wicked.
11 Light shines on the godly,
and joy on those whose hearts are right.
12 May all who are godly rejoice in the LORD
and praise his holy name!

PSALM 98

A psalm.

1 Sing a new song to the LORD,
for he has done wonderful deeds.
His right hand has won a mighty victory;

97:8 Hebrew *Zion.*

Psalm 96 (cf. 1 Chr 16:23–33) tells all who know the LORD to praise him and to witness daily to his salvation and his glory. Worship makes sense because God is the whole world's mighty Creator, compared to whom *idols* (v. 5) are powerless.

Psalm 97 looks toward the day when all people will see the LORD's awesome glory (i.e., righteousness made visible, vv. 2–6; cf. Exod 19:16–18; 24:17). *Towns* (v. 8) is literally "daughters," reflecting the family relationship and allegiance of all God's people.

Psalm 98 The psalmist sees an earthly victory as God's vindication in the sight of the nations, as a sign of covenant fidelity to his people and as a foretaste of his final victory (cf. 96:13). The Hebrew word here translated as *victory* is usually translated "salvation," which gives a different atmosphere to the psalm—one recalling the Exodus, perhaps.

his holy arm has shown his saving
power!
2 The LORD has announced his victory
and has revealed his righteousness to every
nation!
3 He has remembered his promise to love and
be faithful to Israel.
The ends of the earth have seen the victory
of our God.

4 Shout to the LORD, all the earth;
break out in praise and sing for joy!
5 Sing your praise to the LORD with the harp,
with the harp and melodious song,
6 with trumpets and the sound of the ram's
horn.
Make a joyful symphony before the LORD,
the King!

7 Let the sea and everything in it shout his
praise!
Let the earth and all living things join in.
8 Let the rivers clap their hands in glee!
Let the hills sing out their songs of joy
9 before the LORD.
For the LORD is coming to judge the earth.
He will judge the world with justice,
and the nations with fairness.

PSALM 99

1 The LORD is king!
Let the nations tremble!
He sits on his throne between the cherubim.
Let the whole earth quake!
2 The LORD sits in majesty in Jerusalem,*
exalted above all the nations.
3 Let them praise your great and awesome
name.
Your name is holy!
4 Mighty King, lover of justice,
you have established fairness.
You have acted with justice
and righteousness throughout Israel.*
5 Exalt the LORD our God!
Bow low before his feet, for he is holy!

6 Moses and Aaron were among his priests;
Samuel also called on his name.
They cried to the LORD for help,
and he answered them.
7 He spoke to Israel from the pillar of cloud,
and they followed the laws and decrees he
gave them.
8 O LORD our God, you answered them.
You were a forgiving God to them,
but you punished them when they went
wrong.
9 Exalt the LORD our God,
and worship at his holy mountain in
Jerusalem,
for the LORD our God is holy!

PSALM 100

A psalm of thanksgiving.

1 Shout with joy to the LORD, all the earth!
2 Worship the LORD with gladness.
Come before him, singing with joy.
3 Acknowledge that the LORD is God!
He made us, and we are his.*
We are his people, the sheep of his pasture.
4 Enter his gates with thanksgiving;
go into his courts with praise.
Give thanks to him and praise his name.
5 For the LORD is good.
His unfailing love continues forever,
and his faithfulness continues to each
generation.

PSALM 101

A psalm of David.

1 I will sing of your love and justice, LORD.
I will praise you with songs.
2 I will be careful to live a blameless life—
when will you come to help me?
I will lead a life of integrity

99:2 Hebrew *Zion.* **99:4** Hebrew *Jacob.* See note on 44:4.
100:3 As in an alternate reading in the Masoretic Text; the other alternate and some ancient versions read *and not we ourselves.*

Psalm 99 This psalm speaks of God's holiness. The *trembl*[ing] and *quak*[ing] is because of the awe of God's presence. Despite the description of obedience in verse 7, *Moses, Aaron,* and *Samuel* interceded when the people disobeyed. God is the Savior in whom perfect justice meets perfect mercy (v. 8).

Psalm 100 The emphasis on joy implies that true worship must be freely offered from a heart full of gratitude and love. Only then will it please God.

Psalm 101 perhaps originally functioned as a king's oath of office or after the Exile as an implicit plea for restoration. The speaker is far more aware of the responsibilities of kingship than the perquisites. First he aimed to be a good servant and witness to the LORD (vv. 1, 8). By striving to be *blameless,* the king vows to embody God's character.

in my own home.
[3] I will refuse to look at
anything vile and vulgar.
I hate all who deal crookedly;
I will have nothing to do with them.
[4] I will reject perverse ideas
and stay away from every evil.
[5] I will not tolerate people who slander their neighbors.
I will not endure conceit and pride.

[6] I will search for faithful people
to be my companions.
Only those who are above reproach
will be allowed to serve me.
[7] I will not allow deceivers to serve in my house,
and liars will not stay in my presence.
[8] My daily task will be to ferret out the wicked
and free the city of the LORD from their grip.

PSALM 102

A prayer of one overwhelmed with trouble, pouring out problems before the LORD.

[1] LORD, hear my prayer!
Listen to my plea!
[2] Don't turn away from me
in my time of distress.
Bend down to listen,
and answer me quickly when I call to you.
[3] For my days disappear like smoke,
and my bones burn like red-hot coals.
[4] My heart is sick, withered like grass,
and I have lost my appetite.
[5] Because of my groaning,
I am reduced to skin and bones.
[6] I am like an owl in the desert,
like a little owl in a far-off wilderness.
[7] I lie awake,
lonely as a solitary bird on the roof.
[8] My enemies taunt me day after day.
They mock and curse me.
[9] I eat ashes for food.
My tears run down into my drink
[10] because of your anger and wrath.
For you have picked me up and thrown me out.
[11] My life passes as swiftly as the evening shadows.
I am withering away like grass.

[12] But you, O LORD, will sit on your throne forever.
Your fame will endure to every generation.
[13] You will arise and have mercy on Jerusalem*—
and now is the time to pity her,
now is the time you promised to help.
[14] For your people love every stone in her walls
and cherish even the dust in her streets.
[15] Then the nations will tremble before the LORD.
The kings of the earth will tremble before his glory.
[16] For the LORD will rebuild Jerusalem.
He will appear in his glory.
[17] He will listen to the prayers of the destitute.
He will not reject their pleas.

[18] Let this be recorded for future generations,
so that a people not yet born will praise the LORD.
[19] Tell them the LORD looked down
from his heavenly sanctuary.
He looked down to earth from heaven
[20] to hear the groans of the prisoners,
to release those condemned to die.
[21] And so the LORD's fame will be celebrated in Zion,
his praises in Jerusalem,
[22] when multitudes gather together
and kingdoms come to worship the LORD.

[23] He broke my strength in midlife,
cutting short my days.
[24] But I cried to him, "O my God, who lives forever,
don't take my life while I am so young!
[25] Long ago you laid the foundation of the earth
and made the heavens with your hands.
[26] They will perish, but you remain forever;
they will wear out like old clothing.
You will change them like a garment
and discard them.
[27] But you are always the same;
you will live forever.
[28] The children of your people
will live in security.
Their children's children
will thrive in your presence."

102:13 Hebrew *Zion;* also in 102:16.

Psalm 102 The psalmist trusts the time for action has come, praying and hearing the answer: The LORD does not change, and therefore his people are secure. The distress might be that of exile, based on the language of restoration in verses 12–22.

PSALM 103

A psalm of David.

1 Let all that I am praise the LORD;
with my whole heart, I will praise his holy name.
2 Let all that I am praise the LORD;
may I never forget the good things he does for me.
3 He forgives all my sins
and heals all my diseases.
4 He redeems me from death
and crowns me with love and tender mercies.
5 He fills my life with good things.
My youth is renewed like the eagle's!

6 The LORD gives righteousness
and justice to all who are treated unfairly.
7 He revealed his character to Moses
and his deeds to the people of Israel.
8 The LORD is compassionate and merciful,
slow to get angry and filled with unfailing love.
9 He will not constantly accuse us,
nor remain angry forever.
10 He does not punish us for all our sins;
he does not deal harshly with us, as we deserve.
11 For his unfailing love toward those who fear him
is as great as the height of the heavens above the earth.
12 He has removed our sins as far from us
as the east is from the west.
13 The LORD is like a father to his children,
tender and compassionate to those who fear him.
14 For he knows how weak we are;
he remembers we are only dust.
15 Our days on earth are like grass;
like wildflowers, we bloom and die.
16 The wind blows, and we are gone—
as though we had never been here.
17 But the love of the LORD remains forever
with those who fear him.
His salvation extends to the children's children
18 of those who are faithful to his covenant,
of those who obey his commandments!

19 The LORD has made the heavens his throne;
from there he rules over everything.

20 Praise the LORD, you angels,
you mighty ones who carry out his plans,
listening for each of his commands.
21 Yes, praise the LORD, you armies of angels
who serve him and do his will!
22 Praise the LORD, everything he has created,
everything in all his kingdom.

Let all that I am praise the LORD.

PSALM 104

1 Let all that I am praise the LORD.

O LORD my God, how great you are!
You are robed with honor and majesty.
2 You are dressed in a robe of light.
You stretch out the starry curtain of the heavens;
3 you lay out the rafters of your home in the rain clouds.
You make the clouds your chariot;
you ride upon the wings of the wind.
4 The winds are your messengers;
flames of fire are your servants.*
5 You placed the world on its foundation
so it would never be moved.
6 You clothed the earth with floods of water,
water that covered even the mountains.
7 At your command, the water fled;
at the sound of your thunder, it hurried away.
8 Mountains rose and valleys sank
to the levels you decreed.
9 Then you set a firm boundary for the seas,
so they would never again cover the earth.

10 You make springs pour water into the ravines,
so streams gush down from the mountains.

104:4 Greek version reads *He sends his angels like the winds, / his servants like flames of fire.* Compare Heb 1:7.

Psalm 103 David remembers how the LORD's nature has remained the same since Moses' day (vv. 6–18; cf. Exod 34:6–7). God is the eternal Ruler of all creation yet understands our transient human nature and cares for his people as a father cares for his children.

Psalm 104 People are part of creation, yet special. God provides abundantly for the physical needs of all living things, but provision for people also meets their inner needs.

11 They provide water for all the animals,
and the wild donkeys quench their thirst.
12 The birds nest beside the streams
and sing among the branches of the trees.
13 You send rain on the mountains from your heavenly home,
and you fill the earth with the fruit of your labor.
14 You cause grass to grow for the livestock
and plants for people to use.
You allow them to produce food from the earth—
15 wine to make them glad,
olive oil to soothe their skin,
and bread to give them strength.
16 The trees of the LORD are well cared for—
the cedars of Lebanon that he planted.
17 There the birds make their nests,
and the storks make their homes in the cypresses.
18 High in the mountains live the wild goats,
and the rocks form a refuge for the hyraxes.*

19 You made the moon to mark the seasons,
and the sun knows when to set.
20 You send the darkness, and it becomes night,
when all the forest animals prowl about.
21 Then the young lions roar for their prey,
stalking the food provided by God.
22 At dawn they slink back
into their dens to rest.
23 Then people go off to their work,
where they labor until evening.

24 O LORD, what a variety of things you have made!
In wisdom you have made them all.
The earth is full of your creatures.
25 Here is the ocean, vast and wide,
teeming with life of every kind,
both large and small.
26 See the ships sailing along,
and Leviathan,* which you made to play in the sea.

27 They all depend on you
to give them food as they need it.
28 When you supply it, they gather it.
You open your hand to feed them,
and they are richly satisfied.
29 But if you turn away from them, they panic.
When you take away their breath,
they die and turn again to dust.
30 When you give them your breath,* life is created,
and you renew the face of the earth.

31 May the glory of the LORD continue forever!
The LORD takes pleasure in all he has made!
32 The earth trembles at his glance;
the mountains smoke at his touch.

33 I will sing to the LORD as long as I live.
I will praise my God to my last breath!
34 May all my thoughts be pleasing to him,
for I rejoice in the LORD.
35 Let all sinners vanish from the face of the earth;
let the wicked disappear forever.

Let all that I am praise the LORD.

Praise the LORD!

PSALM 105

1 Give thanks to the LORD and proclaim his greatness.
Let the whole world know what he has done.
2 Sing to him; yes, sing his praises.
Tell everyone about his wonderful deeds.
3 Exult in his holy name;
rejoice, you who worship the LORD.
4 Search for the LORD and for his strength;
continually seek him.
5 Remember the wonders he has performed,
his miracles, and the rulings he has given,
6 you children of his servant Abraham,
you descendants of Jacob, his chosen ones.
7 He is the LORD our God.
His justice is seen throughout the land.
8 He always stands by his covenant—
the commitment he made to a thousand generations.

104:18 Or *coneys*, or *rock badgers*. **104:26** The identification of Leviathan is disputed, ranging from an earthly creature to a mythical sea monster in ancient literature. **104:30** Or *When you send your Spirit*.

Psalm 105 God's *wonderful deeds* arise out of fidelity to his covenant with Abraham. They are evident in God's historical provision for Israel, especially in his special protective relationship with the patriarchs during famine and throughout the events of the Exodus culminating in possession of the promised land and the law. These works reveal God's purpose: to produce a people as faithful to him as he is to them (v. 45).

9 This is the covenant he made with Abraham
and the oath he swore to Isaac.
10 He confirmed it to Jacob as a decree,
and to the people of Israel as a never-ending covenant:
11 "I will give you the land of Canaan
as your special possession."

12 He said this when they were few in number,
a tiny group of strangers in Canaan.
13 They wandered from nation to nation,
from one kingdom to another.
14 Yet he did not let anyone oppress them.
He warned kings on their behalf:
15 "Do not touch my chosen people,
and do not hurt my prophets."

16 He called for a famine on the land of Canaan,
cutting off its food supply.
17 Then he sent someone to Egypt ahead of them—
Joseph, who was sold as a slave.
18 They bruised his feet with fetters
and placed his neck in an iron collar.
19 Until the time came to fulfill his dreams,*
the LORD tested Joseph's character.
20 Then Pharaoh sent for him and set him free;
the ruler of the nation opened his prison door.
21 Joseph was put in charge of all the king's household;
he became ruler over all the king's possessions.
22 He could instruct the king's aides as he pleased
and teach the king's advisers.

23 Then Israel arrived in Egypt;
Jacob lived as a foreigner in the land of Ham.
24 And the LORD multiplied the people of Israel
until they became too mighty for their enemies.
25 Then he turned the Egyptians against the Israelites,
and they plotted against the LORD's servants.

26 But the LORD sent his servant Moses,
along with Aaron, whom he had chosen.
27 They performed miraculous signs among the Egyptians,
and wonders in the land of Ham.
28 The LORD blanketed Egypt in darkness,
for they had defied his commands to let his people go.
29 He turned their water into blood,
poisoning all the fish.
30 Then frogs overran the land
and even invaded the king's bedrooms.
31 When the LORD spoke, flies descended on the Egyptians,
and gnats swarmed across Egypt.
32 He sent them hail instead of rain,
and lightning flashed over the land.
33 He ruined their grapevines and fig trees
and shattered all the trees.
34 He spoke, and hordes of locusts came—
young locusts beyond number.
35 They ate up everything green in the land,
destroying all the crops in their fields.
36 Then he killed the oldest son in each Egyptian home,
the pride and joy of each family.

37 The LORD brought his people out of Egypt,
loaded with silver and gold;
and not one among the tribes of Israel even stumbled.
38 Egypt was glad when they were gone,
for they feared them greatly.
39 The LORD spread a cloud above them as a covering
and gave them a great fire to light the darkness.
40 They asked for meat, and he sent them quail;
he satisfied their hunger with manna—
bread from heaven.
41 He split open a rock, and water gushed out
to form a river through the dry wasteland.
42 For he remembered his sacred promise
to his servant Abraham.
43 So he brought his people out of Egypt with joy,
his chosen ones with rejoicing.
44 He gave his people the lands of pagan nations,
and they harvested crops that others had planted.
45 All this happened so they would follow his decrees
and obey his instructions.

Praise the LORD!

PSALM 106

1 Praise the LORD!

Give thanks to the LORD, for he is good!
His faithful love endures forever.

105:19 Hebrew *his word.*

2 Who can list the glorious miracles of the
Lord?
Who can ever praise him enough?
3 There is joy for those who deal justly with
others
and always do what is right.

4 Remember me, Lord, when you show favor
to your people;
come near and rescue me.
5 Let me share in the prosperity of your chosen
ones.
Let me rejoice in the joy of your people;
let me praise you with those who are your
heritage.

6 Like our ancestors, we have sinned.
We have done wrong! We have acted
wickedly!
7 Our ancestors in Egypt
were not impressed by the Lord's
miraculous deeds.
They soon forgot his many acts of kindness
to them.
Instead, they rebelled against him at the
Red Sea.*
8 Even so, he saved them—
to defend the honor of his name
and to demonstrate his mighty power.
9 He commanded the Red Sea* to dry up.
He led Israel across the sea as if it were a
desert.
10 So he rescued them from their enemies
and redeemed them from their foes.
11 Then the water returned and covered their
enemies;
not one of them survived.
12 Then his people believed his promises.
Then they sang his praise.

13 Yet how quickly they forgot what he had
done!
They wouldn't wait for his counsel!
14 In the wilderness their desires ran wild,
testing God's patience in that dry
wasteland.
15 So he gave them what they asked for,
but he sent a plague along with it.
16 The people in the camp were jealous of Moses
and envious of Aaron, the Lord's holy
priest.
17 Because of this, the earth opened up;
it swallowed Dathan
and buried Abiram and the other rebels.
18 Fire fell upon their followers;
a flame consumed the wicked.

19 The people made a calf at Mount Sinai*;
they bowed before an image made of gold.
20 They traded their glorious God
for a statue of a grass-eating bull.
21 They forgot God, their savior,
who had done such great things in
Egypt—
22 such wonderful things in the land of Ham,
such awesome deeds at the Red Sea.
23 So he declared he would destroy them.
But Moses, his chosen one, stepped
between the Lord and the people.
He begged him to turn from his anger and
not destroy them.

24 The people refused to enter the pleasant land,
for they wouldn't believe his promise to
care for them.
25 Instead, they grumbled in their tents
and refused to obey the Lord.
26 Therefore, he solemnly swore
that he would kill them in the wilderness,
27 that he would scatter their descendants
among the nations,
exiling them to distant lands.

28 Then our ancestors joined in the worship of
Baal at Peor;
they even ate sacrifices offered to the dead!
29 They angered the Lord with all these things,
so a plague broke out among them.
30 But Phinehas had the courage to intervene,
and the plague was stopped.
31 So he has been regarded as a righteous man
ever since that time.

106:7 Hebrew *at the sea, the sea of reeds.* **106:9** Hebrew *sea of reeds;* also in 106:22. **106:19** Hebrew *at Horeb,* another name for Sinai.

Psalm 106, the first of four psalms that use a common refrain (v. 1; cf. 2 Chr 7:3; Ezra 3:11), encourages God's people to give thanks for his faithfulness despite their persistent sin from the Exodus on. They were forgetful, rebellious, lustful, jealous, idolatrous, faithless, grumbling, and disobedient, which provoked the Lord to anger and punishment. Verses 28–31 recall the seduction of Israelite men by Moabite cult prostitutes. Phinehas intervened when a sexually transmitted disease raged through the camp (Num 25). Acculturation and intermarriage brought pagan worship, including the sacrifice of sons and daughters to Canaanite gods (vv. 34–39). In its infidelity, Israel is likened to a prostitute (cf. Hos 2:2–13).

32 At Meribah, too, they angered the LORD,
causing Moses serious trouble.
33 They made Moses angry,*
and he spoke foolishly.

34 Israel failed to destroy the nations in the land,
as the LORD had commanded them.
35 Instead, they mingled among the pagans
and adopted their evil customs.
36 They worshiped their idols,
which led to their downfall.
37 They even sacrificed their sons
and their daughters to the demons.
38 They shed innocent blood,
the blood of their sons and daughters.
By sacrificing them to the idols of Canaan,
they polluted the land with murder.
39 They defiled themselves by their evil deeds,
and their love of idols was adultery in the LORD's sight.

40 That is why the LORD's anger burned against his people,
and he abhorred his own special possession.
41 He handed them over to pagan nations,
and they were ruled by those who hated them.
42 Their enemies crushed them
and brought them under their cruel power.
43 Again and again he rescued them,
but they chose to rebel against him,
and they were finally destroyed by their sin.
44 Even so, he pitied them in their distress
and listened to their cries.
45 He remembered his covenant with them
and relented because of his unfailing love.
46 He even caused their captors
to treat them with kindness.

47 Save us, O LORD our God!
Gather us back from among the nations,
so we can thank your holy name
and rejoice and praise you.

48 Praise the LORD, the God of Israel,
who lives from everlasting to everlasting!
Let all the people say, "Amen!"

Praise the LORD!

BOOK FIVE (Psalms 107–150)

PSALM 107

1 Give thanks to the LORD, for he is good!
His faithful love endures forever.
2 Has the LORD redeemed you? Then speak out!
Tell others he has redeemed you from your enemies.
3 For he has gathered the exiles from many lands,
from east and west,
from north and south.

4 Some wandered in the wilderness,
lost and homeless.
5 Hungry and thirsty,
they nearly died.
6 "LORD, help!" they cried in their trouble,
and he rescued them from their distress.
7 He led them straight to safety,
to a city where they could live.
8 Let them praise the LORD for his great love
and for the wonderful things he has done for them.
9 For he satisfies the thirsty
and fills the hungry with good things.

10 Some sat in darkness and deepest gloom,
imprisoned in iron chains of misery.
11 They rebelled against the words of God,
scorning the counsel of the Most High.
12 That is why he broke them with hard labor;
they fell, and no one was there to help them.
13 "LORD, help!" they cried in their trouble,
and he saved them from their distress.

106:33 Hebrew *They embittered his spirit.*

107:1—150:6 Book 5

Psalm 107 echoes 106:1, telling how God has *redeemed* four groups of people. The *lost* (vv. 4–9) wandered in the wilderness and became weak. The *rebels* (vv. 10–16) disobeyed God's word and brought imprisonment upon themselves. The *fools* (vv. 17–22) allowed sin in their lives and brought sickness upon themselves. The storm-tossed (vv. 23–32) relied on themselves until the LORD's storm humbled them. In each case, when they cried to God, he saved them, providing (respectively) guidance, liberation, healing, and peace.

14 He led them from the darkness and deepest
gloom;
he snapped their chains.
15 Let them praise the LORD for his great love
and for the wonderful things he has done
for them.
16 For he broke down their prison gates of
bronze;
he cut apart their bars of iron.
17 Some were fools; they rebelled
and suffered for their sins.
18 They couldn't stand the thought of food,
and they were knocking on death's door.
19 "LORD, help!" they cried in their trouble,
and he saved them from their distress.
20 He sent out his word and healed them,
snatching them from the door of death.
21 Let them praise the LORD for his great love
and for the wonderful things he has done
for them.
22 Let them offer sacrifices of thanksgiving
and sing joyfully about his glorious acts.

23 Some went off to sea in ships,
plying the trade routes of the world.
24 They, too, observed the LORD's power in
action,
his impressive works on the deepest seas.
25 He spoke, and the winds rose,
stirring up the waves.
26 Their ships were tossed to the heavens
and plunged again to the depths;
the sailors cringed in terror.
27 They reeled and staggered like drunkards
and were at their wits' end.
28 "LORD, help!" they cried in their trouble,
and he saved them from their distress.
29 He calmed the storm to a whisper
and stilled the waves.
30 What a blessing was that stillness
as he brought them safely into harbor!
31 Let them praise the LORD for his great love
and for the wonderful things he has done
for them.
32 Let them exalt him publicly before the
congregation
and before the leaders of the nation.

33 He changes rivers into deserts,
and springs of water into dry, thirsty
land.
34 He turns the fruitful land into salty
wastelands,
because of the wickedness of those who live
there.
35 But he also turns deserts into pools of water,
the dry land into springs of water.
36 He brings the hungry to settle there
and to build their cities.
37 They sow their fields, plant their vineyards,
and harvest their bumper crops.
38 How he blesses them!
They raise large families there,
and their herds of livestock increase.

39 When they decrease in number and become
impoverished
through oppression, trouble, and sorrow,
40 the LORD pours contempt on their princes,
causing them to wander in trackless
wastelands.
41 But he rescues the poor from trouble
and increases their families like flocks of
sheep.
42 The godly will see these things and be glad,
while the wicked are struck silent.
43 Those who are wise will take all this to heart;
they will see in our history the faithful
love of the LORD.

PSALM 108

A song. A psalm of David.

1 My heart is confident in you, O God;
no wonder I can sing your praises with all
my heart!
2 Wake up, lyre and harp!
I will wake the dawn with my song.
3 I will thank you, LORD, among all the people.
I will sing your praises among the nations.
4 For your unfailing love is higher than the
heavens.
Your faithfulness reaches to the clouds.
5 Be exalted, O God, above the highest heavens.
May your glory shine over all the earth.

6 Now rescue your beloved people.
Answer and save us by your power.
7 God has promised this by his holiness*:
"I will divide up Shechem with joy.
I will measure out the valley of Succoth.

108:7 Or *in his sanctuary.*

Psalm 108 combines the second halves of Psalm 57 and Psalm 60, both of which are attributed to specific incidents in David's life (vv. 1–5 are Ps 57:7–11; vv. 6–13 are Ps 60:5–12). The purpose of combining them in this way is unclear.

8 Gilead is mine,
and Manasseh, too.
Ephraim, my helmet, will produce my warriors,
and Judah, my scepter, will produce my kings.
9 But Moab, my washbasin, will become my servant,
and I will wipe my feet on Edom
and shout in triumph over Philistia."

10 Who will bring me into the fortified city?
Who will bring me victory over Edom?
11 Have you rejected us, O God?
Will you no longer march with our armies?
12 Oh, please help us against our enemies,
for all human help is useless.
13 With God's help we will do mighty things,
for he will trample down our foes.

PSALM 109

For the choir director: A psalm of David.

1 O God, whom I praise,
don't stand silent and aloof
2 while the wicked slander me
and tell lies about me.
3 They surround me with hateful words
and fight against me for no reason.
4 I love them, but they try to destroy me with accusations
even as I am praying for them!
5 They repay evil for good,
and hatred for my love.

6 They say,* "Get an evil person to turn against him.
Send an accuser to bring him to trial.
7 When his case comes up for judgment,
let him be pronounced guilty.
Count his prayers as sins.
8 Let his years be few;
let someone else take his position.
9 May his children become fatherless,
and his wife a widow.
10 May his children wander as beggars
and be driven from their ruined homes.
11 May creditors seize his entire estate,
and strangers take all he has earned.
12 Let no one be kind to him;
let no one pity his fatherless children.
13 May all his offspring die.
May his family name be blotted out in a single generation.
14 May the LORD never forget the sins of his fathers;
may his mother's sins never be erased from the record.
15 May the LORD always remember these sins,
and may his name disappear from human memory.
16 For he refused all kindness to others;
he persecuted the poor and needy,
and he hounded the brokenhearted to death.
17 He loved to curse others;
now you curse him.
He never blessed others;
now don't you bless him.
18 Cursing is as natural to him as his clothing,
or the water he drinks,
or the rich food he eats.
19 Now may his curses return and cling to him like clothing;
may they be tied around him like a belt."

20 May those curses become the LORD's punishment
for my accusers who speak evil of me.
21 But deal well with me, O Sovereign LORD,
for the sake of your own reputation!
Rescue me
because you are so faithful and good.
22 For I am poor and needy,
and my heart is full of pain.
23 I am fading like a shadow at dusk;
I am brushed off like a locust.
24 My knees are weak from fasting,
and I am skin and bones.
25 I am a joke to people everywhere;
when they see me, they shake their heads in scorn.

26 Help me, O LORD my God!
Save me because of your unfailing love.
27 Let them see that this is your doing,
that you yourself have done it, LORD.
28 Then let them curse me if they like,

109:6 Hebrew lacks *They say.*

Psalm 109 sees David facing verbal vitriol from people he loves (vv. 2–5). Though hot with anger, David preferred prayer to personal revenge (see Rom 12:19). Verses 9–15 reflect the dependence of wives and children on the man who headed their household. See the translator's note for verse 6: Verses 9–19 can also be seen as expressing the psalmist's wishes. The psalmist presents his plea for help as a way to glorify God (vv. 21, 26–27).

but you will bless me!
When they attack me, they will be
disgraced!
But I, your servant, will go right on
rejoicing!
29 May my accusers be clothed with disgrace;
may their humiliation cover them like a
cloak.
30 But I will give repeated thanks to the LORD,
praising him to everyone.
31 For he stands beside the needy,
ready to save them from those who
condemn them.

PSALM 110

A psalm of David.

1 The LORD said to my Lord,
"Sit in the place of honor at my right
hand
until I humble your enemies,
making them a footstool under your feet."
2 The LORD will extend your powerful
kingdom from Jerusalem*;
you will rule over your enemies.
3 When you go to war,
your people will serve you willingly.
You are arrayed in holy garments,
and your strength will be renewed each
day like the morning dew.

4 The LORD has taken an oath and will not
break his vow:
"You are a priest forever in the order of
Melchizedek."

5 The Lord stands at your right hand to protect
you.
He will strike down many kings when his
anger erupts.
6 He will punish the nations
and fill their lands with corpses;
he will shatter heads over the whole earth.
7 But he himself will be refreshed from brooks
along the way.
He will be victorious.

PSALM 111*

1 Praise the LORD!

I will thank the LORD with all my heart
as I meet with his godly people.
2 How amazing are the deeds of the LORD!
All who delight in him should ponder
them.
3 Everything he does reveals his glory and
majesty.
His righteousness never fails.
4 He causes us to remember his wonderful
works.
How gracious and merciful is our LORD!
5 He gives food to those who fear him;
he always remembers his covenant.
6 He has shown his great power to his people
by giving them the lands of other nations.
7 All he does is just and good,
and all his commandments are
trustworthy.
8 They are forever true,
to be obeyed faithfully and with integrity.
9 He has paid a full ransom for his people.
He has guaranteed his covenant with them
forever.
What a holy, awe-inspiring name he has!
10 Fear of the LORD is the foundation of true
wisdom.
All who obey his commandments will
grow in wisdom.

Praise him forever!

PSALM 112*

1 Praise the LORD!

How joyful are those who fear the LORD
and delight in obeying his commands.

110:2 Hebrew *Zion.* **111** This psalm is a Hebrew acrostic poem; after the introductory note of praise, each line begins with a successive letter of the Hebrew alphabet. **112** This psalm is a Hebrew acrostic poem; after the introductory note of praise, each line begins with a successive letter of the Hebrew alphabet.

Psalm 110, possibly used for coronations, begins with two promises from the LORD. Verses 1–3 picture the king exalted by God and ruling alongside him. The New Testament applies this text messianically to the ascended Jesus Christ fifteen times (e.g., Mark 16:19; Heb 10:12–13). Verse 4 promises he will also be a *priest forever*. For the significance , see Hebrews 5—7 (cf. Melchizedek, Gen 14:18–20).

Psalms 111—112 These two psalms are acrostics, probably meant to be recited or learned together.

Psalm 111 reflects God's character as seen in his *deeds*, especially those done for the covenant people. They reveal God to be righteous, gracious, merciful, generous, faithful, just, holy, and awesome.

2 Their children will be successful
everywhere;
an entire generation of godly people will
be blessed.
3 They themselves will be wealthy,
and their good deeds will last forever.
4 Light shines in the darkness for the godly.
They are generous, compassionate, and
righteous.
5 Good comes to those who lend money
generously
and conduct their business fairly.
6 Such people will not be overcome by evil.
Those who are righteous will be long
remembered.
7 They do not fear bad news;
they confidently trust the LORD to care for
them.
8 They are confident and fearless
and can face their foes triumphantly.
9 They share freely and give generously to
those in need.
Their good deeds will be remembered
forever.
They will have influence and honor.
10 The wicked will see this and be infuriated.
They will grind their teeth in anger;
they will slink away, their hopes thwarted.

PSALM 113

1 Praise the LORD!

Yes, give praise, O servants of the LORD.
Praise the name of the LORD!
2 Blessed be the name of the LORD
now and forever.
3 Everywhere—from east to west—
praise the name of the LORD.
4 For the LORD is high above the nations;
his glory is higher than the heavens.
5 Who can be compared with the LORD our
God,
who is enthroned on high?
6 He stoops to look down
on heaven and on earth.
7 He lifts the poor from the dust
and the needy from the garbage dump.
8 He sets them among princes,
even the princes of his own people!
9 He gives the childless woman a family,
making her a happy mother.

Praise the LORD!

PSALM 114

1 When the Israelites escaped from Egypt—
when the family of Jacob left that foreign
land—
2 the land of Judah became God's sanctuary,
and Israel became his kingdom.
3 The Red Sea* saw them coming and hurried
out of their way!
The water of the Jordan River turned away.
4 The mountains skipped like rams,
the hills like lambs!
5 What's wrong, Red Sea, that made you hurry
out of their way?
What happened, Jordan River, that you
turned away?
6 Why, mountains, did you skip like rams?
Why, hills, like lambs?

7 Tremble, O earth, at the presence of the Lord,
at the presence of the God of Jacob.
8 He turned the rock into a pool of water;
yes, a spring of water flowed from solid
rock.

114:3 Hebrew *the sea;* also in 114:5.

Psalm 112 Children and riches were generally understood as blessings (v. 1, *joyful* can be translated as "blessed") promised by the LORD to those who kept the covenant. Good comes to those who do good.

Psalm 113 The repetition of *the name of the LORD* and *the LORD* in the first four verses raises the issue of God's identity, which is addressed in verses 5–9. He reveals it in his personal care for poor and needy individuals. The psalmist's example is someone like Hannah, whose words are quoted (vv. 7–8; 1 Sam 2:8). Whether the psalmist quotes Hannah, or Hannah recalled this psalm as appropriate praise for the LORD, is impossible to know. A *childless woman* could be rejected by her husband and consequently be homeless. A woman enthroned among her children could indeed be joyful.

Psalm 114 The LORD brought Israel out of Egypt to the promised land to make a holy dwelling place (*sanctuary*) over which to rule (v. 2). Verses 3–6 vividly picture creation on three occasions during the Exodus (Red Sea, Jordan River, Mount Sinai) responding supernaturally to the commanding presence of its mighty Creator (v. 7). As God brought water from rock (Exod 17:6; Num 20:10–11; cf. 1 Cor 10:4), so he still works miracles for his chosen people.

PSALM 115

1 Not to us, O LORD, not to us,
but to your name goes all the glory
for your unfailing love and faithfulness.
2 Why let the nations say,
"Where is their God?"
3 Our God is in the heavens,
and he does as he wishes.
4 Their idols are merely things of silver and
gold,
shaped by human hands.
5 They have mouths but cannot speak,
and eyes but cannot see.
6 They have ears but cannot hear,
and noses but cannot smell.
7 They have hands but cannot feel,
and feet but cannot walk,
and throats but cannot make a sound.
8 And those who make idols are just like
them,
as are all who trust in them.

9 O Israel, trust the LORD!
He is your helper and your shield.
10 O priests, descendants of Aaron, trust the
LORD!
He is your helper and your shield.
11 All you who fear the LORD, trust the LORD!
He is your helper and your shield.

12 The LORD remembers us and will bless us.
He will bless the people of Israel
and bless the priests, the descendants of
Aaron.
13 He will bless those who fear the LORD,
both great and lowly.

14 May the LORD richly bless
both you and your children.
15 May you be blessed by the LORD,
who made heaven and earth.
16 The heavens belong to the LORD,
but he has given the earth to all humanity.
17 The dead cannot sing praises to the LORD,
for they have gone into the silence of the
grave.
18 But we can praise the LORD
both now and forever!

Praise the LORD!

PSALM 116

1 I love the LORD because he hears my voice
and my prayer for mercy.
2 Because he bends down to listen,
I will pray as long as I have breath!
3 Death wrapped its ropes around me;
the terrors of the grave* overtook me.
I saw only trouble and sorrow.
4 Then I called on the name of the LORD:
"Please, LORD, save me!"
5 How kind the LORD is! How good he is!
So merciful, this God of ours!
6 The LORD protects those of childlike faith;
I was facing death, and he saved me.
7 Let my soul be at rest again,
for the LORD has been good to me.
8 He has saved me from death,
my eyes from tears,
my feet from stumbling.
9 And so I walk in the LORD's presence
as I live here on earth!
10 I believed in you, so I said,
"I am deeply troubled, LORD."
11 In my anxiety I cried out to you,
"These people are all liars!"
12 What can I offer the LORD
for all he has done for me?
13 I will lift up the cup of salvation
and praise the LORD's name for saving me.
14 I will keep my promises to the LORD
in the presence of all his people.

15 The LORD cares deeply
when his loved ones die.
16 O LORD, I am your servant;
yes, I am your servant, born into your
household;
you have freed me from my chains.
17 I will offer you a sacrifice of thanksgiving

116:3 Hebrew *of Sheol.*

Psalm 115 prays for help, not simply because God's people need it but also for God's sake because the watching world denounces him (v. 2). If priests and people trust in the LORD, they can confidently look and pray toward future blessing (vv. 12–15). God has chosen to share dominion of *the earth* with humanity. The people should therefore choose to praise the LORD.

Psalm 116 The psalmist was facing death, prayed for help, and gave thanks for deliverance. In verse 16, *born into your household* could be more precisely translated "child of your serving girl." The psalmist is not only a servant but an especially lowly one, freed by God's saving grace.

and call on the name of the LORD.
18 I will fulfill my vows to the LORD
in the presence of all his people—
19 in the house of the LORD
in the heart of Jerusalem.

Praise the LORD!

PSALM 117

1 Praise the LORD, all you nations.
Praise him, all you people of the earth.
2 For he loves us with unfailing love;
the LORD's faithfulness endures forever.

Praise the LORD!

PSALM 118

1 Give thanks to the LORD, for he is good!
His faithful love endures forever.

2 Let all Israel repeat:
"His faithful love endures forever."
3 Let Aaron's descendants, the priests, repeat:
"His faithful love endures forever."
4 Let all who fear the LORD repeat:
"His faithful love endures forever."

5 In my distress I prayed to the LORD,
and the LORD answered me and set me free.
6 The LORD is for me, so I will have no fear.
What can mere people do to me?
7 Yes, the LORD is for me; he will help me.
I will look in triumph at those who hate me.
8 It is better to take refuge in the LORD
than to trust in people.
9 It is better to take refuge in the LORD
than to trust in princes.

10 Though hostile nations surrounded me,
I destroyed them all with the authority of the LORD.
11 Yes, they surrounded and attacked me,
but I destroyed them all with the authority of the LORD.
12 They swarmed around me like bees;
they blazed against me like a crackling fire.
But I destroyed them all with the authority of the LORD.
13 My enemies did their best to kill me,
but the LORD rescued me.
14 The LORD is my strength and my song;
he has given me victory.
15 Songs of joy and victory are sung in the camp of the godly.
The strong right arm of the LORD has done glorious things!
16 The strong right arm of the LORD is raised in triumph.
The strong right arm of the LORD has done glorious things!
17 I will not die; instead, I will live
to tell what the LORD has done.
18 The LORD has punished me severely,
but he did not let me die.

19 Open for me the gates where the righteous enter,
and I will go in and thank the LORD.
20 These gates lead to the presence of the LORD,
and the godly enter there.
21 I thank you for answering my prayer
and giving me victory!

22 The stone that the builders rejected
has now become the cornerstone.
23 This is the LORD's doing,
and it is wonderful to see.
24 This is the day the LORD has made.
We will rejoice and be glad in it.
25 Please, LORD, please save us.
Please, LORD, please give us success.
26 Bless the one who comes in the name of the LORD.
We bless you from the house of the LORD.
27 The LORD is God, shining upon us.
Take the sacrifice and bind it with cords on the altar.

Psalm 117 is a call to *all . . . nations* to praise the LORD for his *unfailing love* and *faithfulness* or truth to Israel (cf. Ps 100). God never intended that those who knew his covenant love should keep it to themselves; they were meant to witness to all peoples that his love is great and his truth eternal.

Psalm 118 (cf. Pss 106; 107; 136) was probably sung in festival procession. It is a thanksgiving for deliverance, and since the psalm was and is used at Passover, it is appropriate to consider the *distress* to have been the Exodus. The king leads the procession. At the Temple gates, he seeks admission (v. 19). The gatekeeper implies that sinners are unacceptable in the LORD's presence (v. 20; cf. 24:3–4), but the king is welcomed. Verse 22 is often used in the New Testament to refer to Jesus (Matt 21:9, 42; Eph 2:20; 1 Pet 2:4–8).

28 You are my God, and I will praise you!
You are my God, and I will exalt you!

29 Give thanks to the LORD, for he is good!
His faithful love endures forever.

PSALM 119*

Aleph

1 Joyful are people of integrity,
who follow the instructions of the LORD.
2 Joyful are those who obey his laws
and search for him with all their hearts.
3 They do not compromise with evil,
and they walk only in his paths.
4 You have charged us
to keep your commandments carefully.
5 Oh, that my actions would consistently
reflect your decrees!
6 Then I will not be ashamed
when I compare my life with your
commands.
7 As I learn your righteous regulations,
I will thank you by living as I should!
8 I will obey your decrees.
Please don't give up on me!

Beth

9 How can a young person stay pure?
By obeying your word.
10 I have tried hard to find you—
don't let me wander from your commands.
11 I have hidden your word in my heart,
that I might not sin against you.
12 I praise you, O LORD;
teach me your decrees.
13 I have recited aloud
all the regulations you have given us.
14 I have rejoiced in your laws
as much as in riches.
15 I will study your commandments
and reflect on your ways.
16 I will delight in your decrees
and not forget your word.

Gimel

17 Be good to your servant,
that I may live and obey your word.
18 Open my eyes to see
the wonderful truths in your instructions.
19 I am only a foreigner in the land.
Don't hide your commands from me!
20 I am always overwhelmed
with a desire for your regulations.
21 You rebuke the arrogant;
those who wander from your commands
are cursed.
22 Don't let them scorn and insult me,
for I have obeyed your laws.
23 Even princes sit and speak against me,
but I will meditate on your decrees.
24 Your laws please me;
they give me wise advice.

Daleth

25 I lie in the dust;
revive me by your word.
26 I told you my plans, and you answered.
Now teach me your decrees.
27 Help me understand the meaning of your
commandments,
and I will meditate on your wonderful
deeds.
28 I weep with sorrow;
encourage me by your word.
29 Keep me from lying to myself;
give me the privilege of knowing your
instructions.
30 I have chosen to be faithful;
I have determined to live by your
regulations.
31 I cling to your laws.
LORD, don't let me be put to shame!
32 I will pursue your commands,
for you expand my understanding.

He

33 Teach me your decrees, O LORD;
I will keep them to the end.
34 Give me understanding and I will obey your
instructions;
I will put them into practice with all my
heart.
35 Make me walk along the path of your
commands,
for that is where my happiness is found.

119 This psalm is a Hebrew acrostic poem; there are twenty-two stanzas, one for each successive letter of the Hebrew alphabet. Each of the eight verses within each stanza begins with the Hebrew letter named in its heading.

Psalm 119, another acrostic, pictures the believer as a pilgrim (vv. 19, 54) encountering various difficulties, among them temptation (vv. 36–37), mockery (v. 42), despair (vv. 81–82), and persecution (v. 150). The pilgrim's wholehearted response is to look to Scripture and pray to its author in a telling mix of praise and supplication. Almost every verse is a prayer incorporating a different synonym for God's Word.

36 Give me an eagerness for your laws
rather than a love for money!
37 Turn my eyes from worthless things,
and give me life through your word.*
38 Reassure me of your promise,
made to those who fear you.
39 Help me abandon my shameful ways;
for your regulations are good.
40 I long to obey your commandments!
Renew my life with your goodness.

Waw

41 LORD, give me your unfailing love,
the salvation that you promised me.
42 Then I can answer those who taunt me,
for I trust in your word.
43 Do not snatch your word of truth from me,
for your regulations are my only hope.
44 I will keep on obeying your instructions
forever and ever.
45 I will walk in freedom,
for I have devoted myself to your
commandments.
46 I will speak to kings about your laws,
and I will not be ashamed.
47 How I delight in your commands!
How I love them!
48 I honor and love your commands.
I meditate on your decrees.

Zayin

49 Remember your promise to me;
it is my only hope.
50 Your promise revives me;
it comforts me in all my troubles.
51 The proud hold me in utter contempt,
but I do not turn away from your
instructions.
52 I meditate on your age-old regulations;
O LORD, they comfort me.
53 I become furious with the wicked,
because they reject your instructions.
54 Your decrees have been the theme of my
songs
wherever I have lived.
55 I reflect at night on who you are, O LORD;
therefore, I obey your instructions.
56 This is how I spend my life:
obeying your commandments.

Heth

57 LORD, you are mine!
I promise to obey your words!
58 With all my heart I want your blessings.
Be merciful as you promised.
59 I pondered the direction of my life,
and I turned to follow your laws.
60 I will hurry, without delay,
to obey your commands.
61 Evil people try to drag me into sin,
but I am firmly anchored to your
instructions.
62 I rise at midnight to thank you
for your just regulations.
63 I am a friend to anyone who fears you—
anyone who obeys your commandments.
64 O LORD, your unfailing love fills the earth;
teach me your decrees.

Teth

65 You have done many good things for me,
LORD,
just as you promised.
66 I believe in your commands;
now teach me good judgment and
knowledge.
67 I used to wander off until you disciplined me;
but now I closely follow your word.
68 You are good and do only good;
teach me your decrees.
69 Arrogant people smear me with lies,
but in truth I obey your commandments
with all my heart.
70 Their hearts are dull and stupid,
but I delight in your instructions.
71 My suffering was good for me,
for it taught me to pay attention to your
decrees.
72 Your instructions are more valuable to me
than millions in gold and silver.

Yodh

73 You made me; you created me.
Now give me the sense to follow your
commands.
74 May all who fear you find in me a cause for
joy,
for I have put my hope in your word.
75 I know, O LORD, that your regulations are
fair;
you disciplined me because I needed it.
76 Now let your unfailing love comfort me,
just as you promised me, your servant.
77 Surround me with your tender mercies so I
may live,
for your instructions are my delight.
78 Bring disgrace upon the arrogant people who
lied about me;
meanwhile, I will concentrate on your
commandments.

119:37 Some manuscripts read *in your ways.*

79 Let me be united with all who fear you,
with those who know your laws.
80 May I be blameless in keeping your decrees;
then I will never be ashamed.

Kaph

81 I am worn out waiting for your rescue,
but I have put my hope in your word.
82 My eyes are straining to see your promises
come true.
When will you comfort me?
83 I am shriveled like a wineskin in the smoke,
but I have not forgotten to obey your
decrees.
84 How long must I wait?
When will you punish those who persecute
me?
85 These arrogant people who hate your
instructions
have dug deep pits to trap me.
86 All your commands are trustworthy.
Protect me from those who hunt me down
without cause.
87 They almost finished me off,
but I refused to abandon your
commandments.
88 In your unfailing love, spare my life;
then I can continue to obey your laws.

Lamedh

89 Your eternal word, O LORD,
stands firm in heaven.
90 Your faithfulness extends to every
generation,
as enduring as the earth you created.
91 Your regulations remain true to this day,
for everything serves your plans.
92 If your instructions hadn't sustained me with
joy,
I would have died in my misery.
93 I will never forget your commandments,
for by them you give me life.
94 I am yours; rescue me!
For I have worked hard at obeying your
commandments.
95 Though the wicked hide along the way to kill
me,
I will quietly keep my mind on your laws.
96 Even perfection has its limits,
but your commands have no limit.

Mem

97 Oh, how I love your instructions!
I think about them all day long.
98 Your commands make me wiser than my
enemies,
for they are my constant guide.
99 Yes, I have more insight than my teachers,
for I am always thinking of your laws.
100 I am even wiser than my elders,
for I have kept your commandments.
101 I have refused to walk on any evil path,
so that I may remain obedient to your
word.
102 I haven't turned away from your regulations,
for you have taught me well.
103 How sweet your words taste to me;
they are sweeter than honey.
104 Your commandments give me understanding;
no wonder I hate every false way of life.

Nun

105 Your word is a lamp to guide my feet
and a light for my path.
106 I've promised it once, and I'll promise it
again:
I will obey your righteous regulations.
107 I have suffered much, O LORD;
restore my life again as you promised.
108 LORD, accept my offering of praise,
and teach me your regulations.
109 My life constantly hangs in the balance,
but I will not stop obeying your
instructions.
110 The wicked have set their traps for me,
but I will not turn from your
commandments.
111 Your laws are my treasure;
they are my heart's delight.
112 I am determined to keep your decrees
to the very end.

Samekh

113 I hate those with divided loyalties,
but I love your instructions.
114 You are my refuge and my shield;
your word is my source of hope.
115 Get out of my life, you evil-minded people,
for I intend to obey the commands of my
God.
116 LORD, sustain me as you promised, that I may
live!
Do not let my hope be crushed.
117 Sustain me, and I will be rescued;
then I will meditate continually on your
decrees.
118 But you have rejected all who stray from
your decrees.
They are only fooling themselves.
119 You skim off the wicked of the earth like
scum;
no wonder I love to obey your laws!

120 I tremble in fear of you;
I stand in awe of your regulations.

Ayin

121 Don't leave me to the mercy of my enemies,
for I have done what is just and right.
122 Please guarantee a blessing for me.
Don't let the arrogant oppress me!
123 My eyes strain to see your rescue,
to see the truth of your promise fulfilled.
124 I am your servant; deal with me in unfailing love,
and teach me your decrees.
125 Give discernment to me, your servant;
then I will understand your laws.
126 LORD, it is time for you to act,
for these evil people have violated your instructions.
127 Truly, I love your commands
more than gold, even the finest gold.
128 Each of your commandments is right.
That is why I hate every false way.

Pe

129 Your laws are wonderful.
No wonder I obey them!
130 The teaching of your word gives light,
so even the simple can understand.
131 I pant with expectation,
longing for your commands.
132 Come and show me your mercy,
as you do for all who love your name.
133 Guide my steps by your word,
so I will not be overcome by evil.
134 Ransom me from the oppression of evil people;
then I can obey your commandments.
135 Look upon me with love;
teach me your decrees.
136 Rivers of tears gush from my eyes
because people disobey your instructions.

Tsadhe

137 O LORD, you are righteous,
and your regulations are fair.
138 Your laws are perfect
and completely trustworthy.
139 I am overwhelmed with indignation,
for my enemies have disregarded your words.
140 Your promises have been thoroughly tested;
that is why I love them so much.
141 I am insignificant and despised,
but I don't forget your commandments.
142 Your justice is eternal,
and your instructions are perfectly true.
143 As pressure and stress bear down on me,
I find joy in your commands.
144 Your laws are always right;
help me to understand them so I may live.

Qoph

145 I pray with all my heart; answer me, LORD!
I will obey your decrees.
146 I cry out to you; rescue me,
that I may obey your laws.
147 I rise early, before the sun is up;
I cry out for help and put my hope in your words.
148 I stay awake through the night,
thinking about your promise.
149 In your faithful love, O LORD, hear my cry;
let me be revived by following your regulations.
150 Lawless people are coming to attack me;
they live far from your instructions.
151 But you are near, O LORD,
and all your commands are true.
152 I have known from my earliest days
that your laws will last forever.

Resh

153 Look upon my suffering and rescue me,
for I have not forgotten your instructions.
154 Argue my case; take my side!
Protect my life as you promised.
155 The wicked are far from rescue,
for they do not bother with your decrees.
156 LORD, how great is your mercy;
let me be revived by following your regulations.
157 Many persecute and trouble me,
yet I have not swerved from your laws.
158 Seeing these traitors makes me sick at heart,
because they care nothing for your word.
159 See how I love your commandments, LORD.
Give back my life because of your unfailing love.
160 The very essence of your words is truth;
all your just regulations will stand forever.

Shin

161 Powerful people harass me without cause,
but my heart trembles only at your word.
162 I rejoice in your word
like one who discovers a great treasure.
163 I hate and abhor all falsehood,
but I love your instructions.
164 I will praise you seven times a day
because all your regulations are just.
165 Those who love your instructions have great peace
and do not stumble.

166 I long for your rescue, LORD,
so I have obeyed your commands.
167 I have obeyed your laws,
for I love them very much.
168 Yes, I obey your commandments and laws
because you know everything I do.

Taw

169 O LORD, listen to my cry;
give me the discerning mind you promised.
170 Listen to my prayer;
rescue me as you promised.
171 Let praise flow from my lips,
for you have taught me your decrees.
172 Let my tongue sing about your word,
for all your commands are right.
173 Give me a helping hand,
for I have chosen to follow your commandments.
174 O LORD, I have longed for your rescue,
and your instructions are my delight.
175 Let me live so I can praise you,
and may your regulations help me.
176 I have wandered away like a lost sheep;
come and find me,
for I have not forgotten your commands.

PSALM 120

A song for pilgrims ascending to Jerusalem.

1 I took my troubles to the LORD;
I cried out to him, and he answered my prayer.
2 Rescue me, O LORD, from liars
and from all deceitful people.
3 O deceptive tongue, what will God do to you?
How will he increase your punishment?
4 You will be pierced with sharp arrows
and burned with glowing coals.

5 How I suffer in far-off Meshech.
It pains me to live in distant Kedar.
6 I am tired of living
among people who hate peace.
7 I search for peace;
but when I speak of peace, they want war!

PSALM 121

A song for pilgrims ascending to Jerusalem.

1 I look up to the mountains—
does my help come from there?
2 My help comes from the LORD,
who made heaven and earth!

3 He will not let you stumble;
the one who watches over you will not slumber.
4 Indeed, he who watches over Israel
never slumbers or sleeps.

5 The LORD himself watches over you!
The LORD stands beside you as your protective shade.
6 The sun will not harm you by day,
nor the moon at night.

7 The LORD keeps you from all harm
and watches over your life.
8 The LORD keeps watch over you as you come and go,
both now and forever.

PSALM 122

A song for pilgrims ascending to Jerusalem. A psalm of David.

1 I was glad when they said to me,
"Let us go to the house of the LORD."
2 And now here we are,
standing inside your gates,
O Jerusalem.
3 Jerusalem is a well-built city;
its seamless walls cannot be breached.
4 All the tribes of Israel—the LORD's people—
make their pilgrimage here.
They come to give thanks to the name of the LORD,
as the law requires of Israel.
5 Here stand the thrones where judgment is given,
the thrones of the dynasty of David.

Psalms 120—134 Called the Songs of Ascents, these psalms were sung by pilgrims traveling to the Temple in Jerusalem.

Psalm 120 is the cry of the believer in the world facing hostility and a basic incompatibility: *I search for peace; . . they want war* (v. 7).

Psalm 121 Traveling through hills, the home of outlaws, would frighten any Israelite pilgrim. The believer's reaction is to look to the almighty, all-knowing Creator of the hills (who is the perfect helper).

Psalm 122 The believer finds security in Jerusalem (cf. Heb 12:22–23, which equates Jerusalem with the invisible church). The hostility and alienation one experiences in the world is replaced by joy and fellowship in *the house of the LORD.*

6 Pray for peace in Jerusalem.
May all who love this city prosper.
7 O Jerusalem, may there be peace within your walls
and prosperity in your palaces.
8 For the sake of my family and friends, I will say,
"May you have peace."
9 For the sake of the house of the LORD our God,
I will seek what is best for you,
O Jerusalem.

PSALM 123

A song for pilgrims ascending to Jerusalem.

1 I lift my eyes to you,
O God, enthroned in heaven.
2 We keep looking to the LORD our God for his mercy,
just as servants keep their eyes on their master,
as a slave girl watches her mistress for the slightest signal.
3 Have mercy on us, LORD, have mercy,
for we have had our fill of contempt.
4 We have had more than our fill of the scoffing of the proud
and the contempt of the arrogant.

PSALM 124

A song for pilgrims ascending to Jerusalem.
A psalm of David.

1 What if the LORD had not been on our side?
Let all Israel repeat:
2 What if the LORD had not been on our side
when people attacked us?
3 They would have swallowed us alive
in their burning anger.
4 The waters would have engulfed us;
a torrent would have overwhelmed us.
5 Yes, the raging waters of their fury
would have overwhelmed our very lives.

6 Praise the LORD,
who did not let their teeth tear us apart!
7 We escaped like a bird from a hunter's trap.
The trap is broken, and we are free!
8 Our help is from the LORD,
who made heaven and earth.

PSALM 125

A song for pilgrims ascending to Jerusalem.

1 Those who trust in the LORD are as secure as Mount Zion;
they will not be defeated but will endure forever.
2 Just as the mountains surround Jerusalem,
so the LORD surrounds his people, both now and forever.
3 The wicked will not rule the land of the godly,
for then the godly might be tempted to do wrong.
4 O LORD, do good to those who are good,
whose hearts are in tune with you.
5 But banish those who turn to crooked ways, O LORD.
Take them away with those who do evil.

May Israel have peace!

PSALM 126

A song for pilgrims ascending to Jerusalem.

1 When the LORD brought back his exiles to Jerusalem,*
it was like a dream!
2 We were filled with laughter,
and we sang for joy.
And the other nations said,

126:1 Hebrew *Zion.*

Psalm 123 Whether one is male or female (v. 2), access to God in prayer is constant; the believer adopts the attitude of a servant and looks to the LORD. God is pictured both as master and as mistress of a large household who assign tasks to both male and female staff (cf. Prov 31:15; see Images of God as Female, Deut 32).

Psalm 124 The psalmist illustrates his experience of deliverance through images of a beast (vv. 3, 6), a flood (vv. 4–5), and a trap (v. 7). Whether these imply one deliverance or more, God's help is common to all (cf. Ps 121).

Psalm 125 God's people are threatened by wickedness (v. 3), perhaps referring to Assyria. The response is to *trust in the LORD* (v. 1). They will then know lasting stability, like Zion; security, for the LORD surrounds them; and assurance, for God is in control.

Psalm 126 looks back to a restoration beyond Israel's wildest dreams (v. 1). Recognizing it as solely an act of God, the people responded with exuberant praise, a witness to the watching world. They pray for further restoration (vv. 4–5), in confident trust that the LORD will give what they seek (cf. 30:5).

"What amazing things the LORD has done
for them."
3 Yes, the LORD has done amazing things
for us!
What joy!

4 Restore our fortunes, LORD,
as streams renew the desert.
5 Those who plant in tears
will harvest with shouts of joy.
6 They weep as they go to plant their seed,
but they sing as they return with the
harvest.

PSALM 127

A song for pilgrims ascending to Jerusalem.
A psalm of Solomon.

1 Unless the LORD builds a house,
the work of the builders is wasted.
Unless the LORD protects a city,
guarding it with sentries will do no good.
2 It is useless for you to work so hard
from early morning until late at night,
anxiously working for food to eat;
for God gives rest to his loved ones.

3 Children are a gift from the LORD;
they are a reward from him.
4 Children born to a young man
are like arrows in a warrior's hands.
5 How joyful is the man whose quiver is full of
them!
He will not be put to shame when he
confronts his accusers at the city gates.

PSALM 128

A song for pilgrims ascending to Jerusalem.

1 How joyful are those who fear the LORD—
all who follow his ways!
2 You will enjoy the fruit of your labor.
How joyful and prosperous you will be!
3 Your wife will be like a fruitful grapevine,
flourishing within your home.
Your children will be like vigorous young
olive trees
as they sit around your table.
4 That is the LORD's blessing
for those who fear him.

5 May the LORD continually bless you from Zion.
May you see Jerusalem prosper as long as
you live.
6 May you live to enjoy your grandchildren.
May Israel have peace!

PSALM 129

A song for pilgrims ascending to Jerusalem.

1 From my earliest youth my enemies have
persecuted me.
Let all Israel repeat this:
2 From my earliest youth my enemies have
persecuted me,
but they have never defeated me.
3 My back is covered with cuts,
as if a farmer had plowed long furrows.
4 But the LORD is good;
he has cut me free from the ropes of the
ungodly.

5 May all who hate Jerusalem*
be turned back in shameful defeat.
6 May they be as useless as grass on a rooftop,
turning yellow when only half grown,
7 ignored by the harvester,
despised by the binder.
8 And may those who pass by
refuse to give them this blessing:
"The LORD bless you;
we bless you in the LORD's name."

PSALM 130

A song for pilgrims ascending to Jerusalem.

1 From the depths of despair, O LORD,
I call for your help.

129:5 Hebrew *Zion.*

Psalm 127 Any and every activity, including raising children, will be purposeless unless oriented to God. Children are a joyful gift from God, and generations of offspring can fill God's house with enduring purpose and praise.

Psalm 128 promises blessings in the present and in the future. It pictures a secure, healthy family, with loving and joyful relationships. The wife's fruitfulness refers to every part of her life, not only to her children. Her meaningful role in the home is appeciated and affirmed.

Psalm 129 Those who attack God's people provoke his righteous wrath, and God punishes them (the *ropes* of v. 4 probably relate to the plowing image of v. 3). The believer is confidently looking forward to what God wills and has already promised.

Psalm 130 Alongside beliefs about sin are beliefs about

2 Hear my cry, O Lord.
Pay attention to my prayer.

3 Lord, if you kept a record of our sins,
who, O Lord, could ever survive?
4 But you offer forgiveness,
that we might learn to fear you.

5 I am counting on the Lord;
yes, I am counting on him.
I have put my hope in his word.
6 I long for the Lord
more than sentries long for the dawn,
yes, more than sentries long for the dawn.

7 O Israel, hope in the Lord;
for with the Lord there is unfailing love.
His redemption overflows.
8 He himself will redeem Israel
from every kind of sin.

PSALM 131

A song for pilgrims ascending to Jerusalem. A psalm of David.

1 Lord, my heart is not proud;
my eyes are not haughty.
I don't concern myself with matters too great
or too awesome for me to grasp.
2 Instead, I have calmed and quieted myself,
like a weaned child who no longer cries for its mother's milk.
Yes, like a weaned child is my soul within me.

3 O Israel, put your hope in the Lord—
now and always.

PSALM 132

A song for pilgrims ascending to Jerusalem.

1 Lord, remember David
and all that he suffered.
2 He made a solemn promise to the Lord.
He vowed to the Mighty One of Israel,*
3 "I will not go home;
I will not let myself rest.
4 I will not let my eyes sleep
nor close my eyelids in slumber
5 until I find a place to build a house for the Lord,
a sanctuary for the Mighty One of Israel."

6 We heard that the Ark was in Ephrathah;
then we found it in the distant countryside of Jaar.
7 Let us go to the sanctuary of the Lord;
let us worship at the footstool of his throne.
8 Arise, O Lord, and enter your resting place,
along with the Ark, the symbol of your power.
9 May your priests be clothed in godliness;
may your loyal servants sing for joy.
10 For the sake of your servant David,
do not reject the king you have anointed.
11 The Lord swore an oath to David
with a promise he will never take back:
"I will place one of your descendants
on your throne.
12 If your descendants obey the terms of my covenant
and the laws that I teach them,
then your royal line
will continue forever and ever."

13 For the Lord has chosen Jerusalem*;
he has desired it for his home.
14 "This is my resting place forever," he said.
"I will live here, for this is the home I desired.
15 I will bless this city and make it prosperous;
I will satisfy its poor with food.
16 I will clothe its priests with godliness;
its faithful servants will sing for joy.
17 Here I will increase the power of David;
my anointed one will be a light for my people.
18 I will clothe his enemies with shame,
but he will be a glorious king."

132:2 Hebrew *of Jacob;* also in 132:5. See note on 44:4.
132:13 Hebrew *Zion.*

God that lead simultaneously to urgent prayer, trusting and confident waiting; the morning always comes.

Psalm 131 The Hebrew text speaks of a newly weaned child finding comfort at its mother's breast. In the final stages of the difficult weaning process, a frantically crying baby can be calmed by a visit to the familiar source of sustenance. As in Isaiah 49:14–16; 66:13, God is pictured as a nursing mother. The image has prompted the question as to whether the composer of this psalm may have been a woman.

Psalm 132 articulates the reasons that Jerusalem is the pilgrim's destination.The royal city was a home for the Ark (cf. 2 Sam 6), the symbol of the Lord's powerful presence. The Lord promised to make Zion his home, to bless Zion and David as well as his descendants.

PSALM 133

A song for pilgrims ascending to Jerusalem. A psalm of David.

1 How wonderful and pleasant it is
when brothers live together in harmony!
2 For harmony is as precious as the anointing oil
that was poured over Aaron's head,
that ran down his beard
and onto the border of his robe.
3 Harmony is as refreshing as the dew from Mount Hermon
that falls on the mountains of Zion.
And there the LORD has pronounced his blessing,
even life everlasting.

PSALM 134

A song for pilgrims ascending to Jerusalem.

1 Oh, praise the LORD, all you servants of the LORD,
you who serve at night in the house of the LORD.
2 Lift up holy hands in prayer,
and praise the LORD.
3 May the LORD, who made heaven and earth,
bless you from Jerusalem.*

PSALM 135

1 Praise the LORD!

Praise the name of the LORD!
Praise him, you who serve the LORD,
2 you who serve in the house of the LORD,
in the courts of the house of our God.
3 Praise the LORD, for the LORD is good;
celebrate his lovely name with music.
4 For the LORD has chosen Jacob for himself,
Israel for his own special treasure.
5 I know the greatness of the LORD—
that our Lord is greater than any other god.
6 The LORD does whatever pleases him
throughout all heaven and earth,
and on the seas and in their depths.
7 He causes the clouds to rise over the whole earth.
He sends the lightning with the rain
and releases the wind from his storehouses.

8 He destroyed the firstborn in each Egyptian home,
both people and animals.
9 He performed miraculous signs and wonders in Egypt
against Pharaoh and all his people.
10 He struck down great nations
and slaughtered mighty kings—
11 Sihon king of the Amorites,
Og king of Bashan,
and all the kings of Canaan.
12 He gave their land as an inheritance,
a special possession to his people Israel.

13 Your name, O LORD, endures forever;
your fame, O LORD, is known to every generation.
14 For the LORD will give justice to his people
and have compassion on his servants.

15 The idols of the nations are merely things of silver and gold,
shaped by human hands.
16 They have mouths but cannot speak,
and eyes but cannot see.
17 They have ears but cannot hear,
and noses but cannot smell.
18 And those who make idols are just like them,
as are all who trust in them.

19 O Israel, praise the LORD!
O priests—descendants of Aaron—praise the LORD!

134:3 Hebrew *Zion.*

Psalm 133 Harmony in the home is compared to the pouring of the anointing oil used at the consecration of the high priest and the king (Lev 8:12). It spilled over in abundant richness, bringing blessing to all that it touched. Harmony is also compared to the effect of Mount Hermon, from its heights to the north, as it sent down cooling winds accompanied by life-giving moisture. A harmonious home life is not achieved by measures of power and control but by openness to the shared blessing of a life lived in God.

Psalm 134 pictures the pilgrims entering the Temple on Mount Zion, God's home, open day and night, from which he blesses his people as they worship him.

Psalm 135 is a compilation of other Scriptures (e.g., 115:3–8; 136:18–22). The result is a psalm of praise grounded in the LORD's choosing of Israel as *his own special treaure* (v. 4). God never abandons his people.

20 O Levites, praise the LORD!
All you who fear the LORD, praise the LORD!
21 The LORD be praised from Zion,
for he lives here in Jerusalem.

Praise the LORD!

PSALM 136

1 Give thanks to the LORD, for he is good!
His faithful love endures forever.
2 Give thanks to the God of gods.
His faithful love endures forever.
3 Give thanks to the Lord of lords.
His faithful love endures forever.

4 Give thanks to him who alone does mighty miracles.
His faithful love endures forever.
5 Give thanks to him who made the heavens so skillfully.
His faithful love endures forever.
6 Give thanks to him who placed the earth among the waters.
His faithful love endures forever.
7 Give thanks to him who made the heavenly lights—
His faithful love endures forever.
8 the sun to rule the day,
His faithful love endures forever.
9 and the moon and stars to rule the night.
His faithful love endures forever.

10 Give thanks to him who killed the firstborn of Egypt.
His faithful love endures forever.
11 He brought Israel out of Egypt.
His faithful love endures forever.
12 He acted with a strong hand and powerful arm.
His faithful love endures forever.
13 Give thanks to him who parted the Red Sea.*
His faithful love endures forever.
14 He led Israel safely through,
His faithful love endures forever.
15 but he hurled Pharaoh and his army into the Red Sea.
His faithful love endures forever.
16 Give thanks to him who led his people through the wilderness.
His faithful love endures forever.

17 Give thanks to him who struck down mighty kings.
His faithful love endures forever.
18 He killed powerful kings—
His faithful love endures forever.
19 Sihon king of the Amorites,
His faithful love endures forever.
20 and Og king of Bashan.
His faithful love endures forever.
21 God gave the land of these kings as an inheritance—
His faithful love endures forever.
22 a special possession to his servant Israel.
His faithful love endures forever.

23 He remembered us in our weakness.
His faithful love endures forever.
24 He saved us from our enemies.
His faithful love endures forever.
25 He gives food to every living thing.
His faithful love endures forever.
26 Give thanks to the God of heaven.
His faithful love endures forever.

PSALM 137

1 Beside the rivers of Babylon, we sat and wept
as we thought of Jerusalem.*
2 We put away our harps,
hanging them on the branches of poplar trees.
3 For our captors demanded a song from us.
Our tormentors insisted on a joyful hymn:
"Sing us one of those songs of Jerusalem!"
4 But how can we sing the songs of the LORD
while in a pagan land?

136:13 Hebrew *sea of reeds;* also in 136:15. **137:1** Hebrew *Zion;* also in 137:3.

Psalm 136 is the fourth psalm to expound the theme of the first verse (cf. Pss 106; 107; 118). Designed for antiphonal singing, it testifies to God's *faithful love,* as seen in creation and redemption (amplifying 135:8–12).

Psalm 137 is a lament dating from the Exile. The Babylonians treated captives well (Jer 29:4–7) and preferred to see them happy, but the faithful tearfully continued to remember their home and the LORD's. They also remembered that at the time of Jerusalem's capture, their own kinsfolk, the Edomites, sided with the Babylonians and did nothing to help (cf. Obad 10–14; Ezek 25:1–6). The lament ends with a malicious wish that allows us a glimpse into the resentment harbored in the souls of the exiles, expressing an honest exposure of raw human emotion.

5 If I forget you, O Jerusalem,
let my right hand forget how to play the harp.
6 May my tongue stick to the roof of my mouth
if I fail to remember you,
if I don't make Jerusalem my greatest joy.

7 O LORD, remember what the Edomites did
on the day the armies of Babylon captured Jerusalem.
"Destroy it!" they yelled.
"Level it to the ground!"
8 O Babylon, you will be destroyed.
Happy is the one who pays you back
for what you have done to us.
9 Happy is the one who takes your babies
and smashes them against the rocks!

PSALM 138

A psalm of David.

1 I give you thanks, O LORD, with all my heart;
I will sing your praises before the gods.
2 I bow before your holy Temple as I worship.
I praise your name for your unfailing love and faithfulness;
for your promises are backed
by all the honor of your name.
3 As soon as I pray, you answer me;
you encourage me by giving me strength.

4 Every king in all the earth will thank you, LORD,
for all of them will hear your words.
5 Yes, they will sing about the LORD's ways,
for the glory of the LORD is very great.
6 Though the LORD is great, he cares for the humble,
but he keeps his distance from the proud.

7 Though I am surrounded by troubles,
you will protect me from the anger of my enemies.
You reach out your hand,
and the power of your right hand saves me.
8 The LORD will work out his plans for my life—
for your faithful love, O LORD, endures forever.
Don't abandon me, for you made me.

PSALM 139

For the choir director: A psalm of David.

1 O LORD, you have examined my heart
and know everything about me.
2 You know when I sit down or stand up.
You know my thoughts even when I'm far away.
3 You see me when I travel
and when I rest at home.
You know everything I do.
4 You know what I am going to say
even before I say it, LORD.
5 You go before me and follow me.
You place your hand of blessing on my head.
6 Such knowledge is too wonderful for me,
too great for me to understand!

7 I can never escape from your Spirit!
I can never get away from your presence!
8 If I go up to heaven, you are there;
if I go down to the grave,* you are there.
9 If I ride the wings of the morning,
if I dwell by the farthest oceans,
10 even there your hand will guide me,
and your strength will support me.
11 I could ask the darkness to hide me
and the light around me to become night—
12 but even in darkness I cannot hide from you.
To you the night shines as bright as day.
Darkness and light are the same to you.

13 You made all the delicate, inner parts of my body
and knit me together in my mother's womb.

139:8 Hebrew *to Sheol.*

Psalm 138 is a thanksgiving for answered prayer in the midst of trouble. The answer did not change the situation; it strengthened the one who prayed and led to worship, witness, and trust in the LORD. The attribution may mean "of the Davidic school," as there was no Temple (v. 2) in David's lifetime.

Psalm 139 All human lives belong to God, who has the power of life and death. No one can escape God's presence, and nothing is hidden from him. The understanding of a fetus as an individual person known by God (vv. 13–16) and the continuity of identity from embryo can bring meaning to a mother during the weary months of pregnancy. Prenatal influence is profound both mentally and spiritually. The mind and body of a pregnant woman become agents with whom God is at work on a human soul.

14 Thank you for making me so wonderfully complex!
Your workmanship is marvelous—how well I know it.
15 You watched me as I was being formed in utter seclusion,
as I was woven together in the dark of the womb.
16 You saw me before I was born.
Every day of my life was recorded in your book.
Every moment was laid out
before a single day had passed.

17 How precious are your thoughts about me,* O God.
They cannot be numbered!
18 I can't even count them;
they outnumber the grains of sand!
And when I wake up,
you are still with me!

19 O God, if only you would destroy the wicked!
Get out of my life, you murderers!
20 They blaspheme you;
your enemies misuse your name.
21 O LORD, shouldn't I hate those who hate you?
Shouldn't I despise those who oppose you?
22 Yes, I hate them with total hatred,
for your enemies are my enemies.

23 Search me, O God, and know my heart;
test me and know my anxious thoughts.
24 Point out anything in me that offends you,
and lead me along the path of everlasting life.

PSALM 140

For the choir director: A psalm of David.

1 O LORD, rescue me from evil people.
Protect me from those who are violent,
2 those who plot evil in their hearts
and stir up trouble all day long.
3 Their tongues sting like a snake;
the venom of a viper drips from their lips.
Interlude

4 O LORD, keep me out of the hands of the wicked.
Protect me from those who are violent,
for they are plotting against me.
5 The proud have set a trap to catch me;
they have stretched out a net;
they have placed traps all along the way.
Interlude

6 I said to the LORD, "You are my God!"
Listen, O LORD, to my cries for mercy!
7 O Sovereign LORD, the strong one who rescued me,
you protected me on the day of battle.
8 LORD, do not let evil people have their way.
Do not let their evil schemes succeed,
or they will become proud. *Interlude*

9 Let my enemies be destroyed
by the very evil they have planned for me.
10 Let burning coals fall down on their heads.
Let them be thrown into the fire
or into watery pits from which they can't escape.
11 Don't let liars prosper here in our land.
Cause great disasters to fall on the violent.

12 But I know the LORD will help those they persecute;
he will give justice to the poor.
13 Surely righteous people are praising your name;
the godly will live in your presence.

PSALM 141

A psalm of David.

1 O LORD, I am calling to you. Please hurry!
Listen when I cry to you for help!
2 Accept my prayer as incense offered to you,
and my upraised hands as an evening offering.
3 Take control of what I say, O LORD,
and guard my lips.

139:17 Or *How precious to me are your thoughts.*

Psalm 140 The psalmist is suffering from the evil plans, words, and deeds of *those who are violent,* who seek to trap him. Verse 3 contains a trenchant description of verbal abuse. With its condemnation of violence and appeal to God for deliverance, this psalm is helpful for the meditations of battered and abused women.

Psalm 141 Still oppressed by evildoers who want to trap him (cf. Ps 140), the psalmist's response is again prayer. He would accept rebuke from *the godly* but wants nothing to do with *the wicked* except to pray against them. Not only is the prayer for rescue from oppression but for the will and ability to continue in righteousness.

4 Don't let me drift toward evil
or take part in acts of wickedness.
Don't let me share in the delicacies
of those who do wrong.

5 Let the godly strike me!
It will be a kindness!
If they correct me, it is soothing medicine.
Don't let me refuse it.

But I pray constantly
against the wicked and their deeds.
6 When their leaders are thrown down from a cliff,
the wicked will listen to my words and find them true.
7 Like rocks brought up by a plow,
the bones of the wicked will lie scattered without burial.*

8 I look to you for help, O Sovereign LORD.
You are my refuge; don't let them kill me.
9 Keep me from the traps they have set for me,
from the snares of those who do wrong.
10 Let the wicked fall into their own nets,
but let me escape.

PSALM 142

A psalm of David, regarding his experience in the cave. A prayer.*

1 I cry out to the LORD;
I plead for the LORD's mercy.
2 I pour out my complaints before him
and tell him all my troubles.
3 When I am overwhelmed,
you alone know the way I should turn.
Wherever I go,
my enemies have set traps for me.
4 I look for someone to come and help me,
but no one gives me a passing thought!
No one will help me;
no one cares a bit what happens to me.
5 Then I pray to you, O LORD.
I say, "You are my place of refuge.
You are all I really want in life.
6 Hear my cry,
for I am very low.
Rescue me from my persecutors,
for they are too strong for me.
7 Bring me out of prison
so I can thank you.
The godly will crowd around me,
for you are good to me."

PSALM 143

A psalm of David.

1 Hear my prayer, O LORD;
listen to my plea!
Answer me because you are faithful and righteous.
2 Don't put your servant on trial,
for no one is innocent before you.
3 My enemy has chased me.
He has knocked me to the ground
and forces me to live in darkness like those in the grave.
4 I am losing all hope;
I am paralyzed with fear.
5 I remember the days of old.
I ponder all your great works
and think about what you have done.
6 I lift my hands to you in prayer.
I thirst for you as parched land thirsts for rain. *Interlude*

7 Come quickly, LORD, and answer me,
for my depression deepens.
Don't turn away from me,
or I will die.
8 Let me hear of your unfailing love each morning,
for I am trusting you.
Show me where to walk,
for I give myself to you.
9 Rescue me from my enemies, LORD;
I run to you to hide me.
10 Teach me to do your will,
for you are my God.
May your gracious Spirit lead me forward
on a firm footing.
11 For the glory of your name, O LORD, preserve my life.

141:7 Hebrew *scattered at the mouth of Sheol.*
142:TITLE Hebrew *maskil.* This may be a literary or musical term.

Psalm 142 is specifically attributed to the period when David was hiding from Saul (1 Sam 22—26). Feeling imprisoned and alone he takes his *troubles* to God in prayer. This psalm is particularly helpful to women hiding from abusers or anyone who simply feels *overwhelmed* by life.

Psalm 143 This is the final psalm in a series of prayers for help. It presents eleven distinct needs or petitions, including assurance of God's covenant love (v. 8), instruction and guidance (vv. 8, 10), deliverance and preservation (vv. 9, 11), and the destruction of his enemies (v. 12).

Because of your faithfulness, bring me out
of this distress.
12 In your unfailing love, silence all my enemies
and destroy all my foes,
for I am your servant.

PSALM 144

A psalm of David.

1 Praise the LORD, who is my rock.
He trains my hands for war
and gives my fingers skill for battle.
2 He is my loving ally and my fortress,
my tower of safety, my rescuer.
He is my shield, and I take refuge in him.
He makes the nations* submit to me.

3 O LORD, what are human beings that you
should notice them,
mere mortals that you should think about
them?
4 For they are like a breath of air;
their days are like a passing shadow.

5 Open the heavens, LORD, and come down.
Touch the mountains so they billow smoke.
6 Hurl your lightning bolts and scatter your
enemies!
Shoot your arrows and confuse them!
7 Reach down from heaven and rescue me;
rescue me from deep waters,
from the power of my enemies.
8 Their mouths are full of lies;
they swear to tell the truth, but they lie
instead.

9 I will sing a new song to you, O God!
I will sing your praises with a ten-stringed
harp.
10 For you grant victory to kings!
You rescued your servant David from the
fatal sword.
11 Save me!
Rescue me from the power of my enemies.
Their mouths are full of lies;
they swear to tell the truth, but they lie
instead.

12 May our sons flourish in their youth
like well-nurtured plants.
May our daughters be like graceful pillars,
carved to beautify a palace.
13 May our barns be filled
with crops of every kind.
May the flocks in our fields multiply by the
thousands,
even tens of thousands,
14 and may our oxen be loaded down with
produce.
May there be no enemy breaking through
our walls,
no going into captivity,
no cries of alarm in our town squares.
15 Yes, joyful are those who live like this!
Joyful indeed are those whose God is the
LORD.

PSALM 145*

A psalm of praise of David.

1 I will exalt you, my God and King,
and praise your name forever and ever.
2 I will praise you every day;
yes, I will praise you forever.
3 Great is the LORD! He is most worthy of
praise!
No one can measure his greatness.

4 Let each generation tell its children of your
mighty acts;
let them proclaim your power.
5 I will meditate* on your majestic, glorious
splendor
and your wonderful miracles.

144:2 Some manuscripts read *my people.* **145** This psalm is a Hebrew acrostic poem; each verse (including 13b) begins with a successive letter of the Hebrew alphabet. **145:5** Some manuscripts read *They will speak.*

Psalms 144—150 This set of seven psalms close the Psalter with effervescent praise.

Psalm 144 The psalmist prays that sons may be as flourishing young plants (or high towers), and daughters as sculptured pillars in the palace (v. 12). The image bespeaks strength, stability, and beauty. The Jerusalem Bible suggests that perhaps the psalmist has in mind carved female figures used to decorate the exterior of the building, beautiful yet capable of supporting tremendous strength. The most famous example would be the caryatids adorning the Porch of the Maidens in the Erechtheum on Athens' Acropolis (see The Relevance of Psalms for the Everyday Lives of Women, Ps 2).

Psalm 145 God is described as great, good, merciful, faithful, gracious, and kind. The repetition of the word *kingdom* reinforces the focus on God's sovereignty.

6 Your awe-inspiring deeds will be on every tongue;
I will proclaim your greatness.
7 Everyone will share the story of your wonderful goodness;
they will sing with joy about your righteousness.

8 The LORD is merciful and compassionate,
slow to get angry and filled with unfailing love.
9 The LORD is good to everyone.
He showers compassion on all his creation.
10 All of your works will thank you, LORD,
and your faithful followers will praise you.
11 They will speak of the glory of your kingdom;
they will give examples of your power.
12 They will tell about your mighty deeds
and about the majesty and glory of your reign.
13 For your kingdom is an everlasting kingdom.
You rule throughout all generations.

The LORD always keeps his promises;
he is gracious in all he does.*
14 The LORD helps the fallen
and lifts those bent beneath their loads.
15 The eyes of all look to you in hope;
you give them their food as they need it.
16 When you open your hand,
you satisfy the hunger and thirst of every living thing.
17 The LORD is righteous in everything he does;
he is filled with kindness.
18 The LORD is close to all who call on him,
yes, to all who call on him in truth.
19 He grants the desires of those who fear him;
he hears their cries for help and rescues them.
20 The LORD protects all those who love him,
but he destroys the wicked.

21 I will praise the LORD,
and may everyone on earth bless his holy name
forever and ever.

PSALM 146

1 Praise the LORD!

Let all that I am praise the LORD.
2 I will praise the LORD as long as I live.
I will sing praises to my God with my dying breath.

3 Don't put your confidence in powerful people;
there is no help for you there.
4 When they breathe their last, they return to the earth,
and all their plans die with them.
5 But joyful are those who have the God of Israel* as their helper,
whose hope is in the LORD their God.
6 He made heaven and earth,
the sea, and everything in them.
He keeps every promise forever.
7 He gives justice to the oppressed
and food to the hungry.
The LORD frees the prisoners.
8 The LORD opens the eyes of the blind.
The LORD lifts up those who are weighed down.
The LORD loves the godly.
9 The LORD protects the foreigners among us.
He cares for the orphans and widows,
but he frustrates the plans of the wicked.

10 The LORD will reign forever.
He will be your God, O Jerusalem,*
throughout the generations.

Praise the LORD!

PSALM 147

1 Praise the LORD!

How good to sing praises to our God!
How delightful and how fitting!
2 The LORD is rebuilding Jerusalem

145:13 The last two lines of 145:13 are not found in many of the ancient manuscripts. **146:5** Hebrew *of Jacob.* See note on 44:4. **146:10** Hebrew *Zion.*

Psalm 146 focuses praise on the happiness of having the LORD in whom we can trust. Mortality renders people unreliable but experience of God proves him always trustworthy. Verses 7–9 recall God's special care for the needy and how God meets their various needs.

Psalm 147 is corporate praise from all God's people. The imperatives *praise, sing,* and *glorify* (vv. 1, 7, 12) begin three sections that each juxtapose themes of redemption and creation. God's many blessings form the backdrop for the greatest blessing of all, the agent of all other blessings: God's Word (vv. 15–20).

and bringing the exiles back to Israel.
3 He heals the brokenhearted
and bandages their wounds.
4 He counts the stars
and calls them all by name.
5 How great is our Lord! His power is absolute!
His understanding is beyond
comprehension!
6 The LORD supports the humble,
but he brings the wicked down into the dust.

7 Sing out your thanks to the LORD;
sing praises to our God with a harp.
8 He covers the heavens with clouds,
provides rain for the earth,
and makes the grass grow in mountain
pastures.
9 He gives food to the wild animals
and feeds the young ravens when they cry.
10 He takes no pleasure in the strength of a
horse
or in human might.
11 No, the LORD's delight is in those who fear
him,
those who put their hope in his unfailing
love.

12 Glorify the LORD, O Jerusalem!
Praise your God, O Zion!
13 For he has strengthened the bars of your
gates
and blessed your children within your
walls.
14 He sends peace across your nation
and satisfies your hunger with the finest
wheat.
15 He sends his orders to the world—
how swiftly his word flies!
16 He sends the snow like white wool;
he scatters frost upon the ground like
ashes.
17 He hurls the hail like stones.*
Who can stand against his freezing cold?
18 Then, at his command, it all melts.
He sends his winds, and the ice thaws.
19 He has revealed his words to Jacob,
his decrees and regulations to Israel.
20 He has not done this for any other nation;
they do not know his regulations.

Praise the LORD!

PSALM 148

1 Praise the LORD!

Praise the LORD from the heavens!
Praise him from the skies!
2 Praise him, all his angels!
Praise him, all the armies of heaven!
3 Praise him, sun and moon!
Praise him, all you twinkling stars!
4 Praise him, skies above!
Praise him, vapors high above the clouds!
5 Let every created thing give praise to the
LORD,
for he issued his command, and they came
into being.
6 He set them in place forever and ever.
His decree will never be revoked.

7 Praise the LORD from the earth,
you creatures of the ocean depths,
8 fire and hail, snow and clouds,*
wind and weather that obey him,
9 mountains and all hills,
fruit trees and all cedars,
10 wild animals and all livestock,
small scurrying animals and birds,
11 kings of the earth and all people,
rulers and judges of the earth,
12 young men and young women,
old men and children.

13 Let them all praise the name of the LORD.
For his name is very great;
his glory towers over the earth and
heaven!
14 He has made his people strong,
honoring his faithful ones—
the people of Israel who are close to him.

Praise the LORD!

PSALM 149

1 Praise the LORD!

Sing to the LORD a new song.
Sing his praises in the assembly of the
faithful.

147:17 Hebrew *like bread crumbs.* **148:8** Or *mist,* or *smoke.*

Psalm 148 calls for universal praise in the heavens and on earth. The downward order of praise (vv. 1–6, from greater to lesser) poetically balances the upward order (vv. 7–14, lesser to greater), culminating in the specifically equal call to people of both sexes and all ages (v. 12).

Psalm 149 The task of God's people is to cooperate in

2 O Israel, rejoice in your Maker.
O people of Jerusalem,* exult in your King.
3 Praise his name with dancing,
accompanied by tambourine and harp.
4 For the LORD delights in his people;
he crowns the humble with victory.
5 Let the faithful rejoice that he honors them.
Let them sing for joy as they lie on their beds.

6 Let the praises of God be in their mouths,
and a sharp sword in their hands—
7 to execute vengeance on the nations
and punishment on the peoples,
8 to bind their kings with shackles
and their leaders with iron chains,
9 to execute the judgment written against them.
This is the glorious privilege of his faithful ones.

Praise the LORD!

PSALM 150

1 Praise the LORD!

Praise God in his sanctuary;
praise him in his mighty heaven!
2 Praise him for his mighty works;
praise his unequaled greatness!
3 Praise him with a blast of the ram's horn;
praise him with the lyre and harp!
4 Praise him with the tambourine and dancing;
praise him with strings and flutes!
5 Praise him with a clash of cymbals;
praise him with loud clanging cymbals.
6 Let everything that breathes sing praises to the LORD!

Praise the LORD!

149:2 Hebrew *Zion.*

---

accomplishing God's will; hence the picture of them, happily relaxed yet with swords in their hands (vv. 5–6). The tension between resting in victory accomplished and fighting for victory still to come is one with which every believer continually lives. The task of establishing justice belongs to the *faithful*.

Psalm 150 turns the final words of Book 4 (106:48) into a tenfold doxology, an imperative to unceasing and all-encompassing praise, including human praise, by every available musical means. The cosmic God invites the response of every creature. No less a congregation will suffice.

PROVERBS

INTRODUCTION

The book of Proverbs belongs to the corpus of biblical and extrabiblical literature known as wisdom literature. This corpus is characterized principally by its focus on life on earth, giving the collective wise words probably passed down and modified through the decades and centuries about the joys and pitfalls to be encountered and handled.

There is evidence to indicate multiple sources in Proverbs, incorporated by various authors and coupled with an overall editorial working that may have taken place at different stages. The book attributes certain sections to various individuals: Solomon (1:1; 10:1; 25:1), Agur (30:1), and Lemuel (31:1), as well as indicating the involvement of scribes (25:1) and hinting at a wider, more generally public origin in the "words of the wise" (22:17; 24:23). Efforts at dating the various sections allow for Solomonic authorship at least of chapters 10:1—22:16 and probably of chapters 25—29, but the book may have taken its current form much later. Many scholars believe it happened in the postexilic period.

In the opinion of certain scholars, the proverbial form originally grew among ordinary (illiterate?) people and was passed down orally as folk sayings, often in the home. Other scholars have long talked of wisdom schools based in the royal court; in these schools, wisdom sayings were compiled from various sources, including that of surrounding nations and folk sayings, and used to train young male bureaucrats in response to the need for stable state administration. Some now favor a setting of the home rather than the royal court.

The various indications of authorship in the text also largely correspond with significant distinctions in literary style. There is general agreement that the book subdivides into eight readily identifiable sections (1:1—9:18; 10:1—22:16; 22:17—24:22; 24:23–34; 25:1—29:27; 30:1–33; 31:1–9; 31:10–31, albeit with minor modifications among scholars) that correspond generally to movement between sources and authors. Three primary literary styles also permit grouping as instruction literature (1:1—9:18; 22:17—24:22; 31:1–9), sentence literature (10:1—22:16; 24:23–34; 25:1—29:27) and poems and numerical sayings (30:1–33; 31:10–31). —*Alison Le Cornu*

1:1—9:18	Acquiring Wisdom
10:1—29:27	Acting Wisely
30:1–33	The Truth of God's Words
31:1–31	A Final Portrait of Wisdom

The Purpose of Proverbs

1 These are the proverbs of Solomon, David's son, king of Israel.

2 Their purpose is to teach people wisdom and discipline,
to help them understand the insights of the wise.
3 Their purpose is to teach people to live disciplined and successful lives,
to help them do what is right, just, and fair.
4 These proverbs will give insight to the simple,
knowledge and discernment to the young.

5 Let the wise listen to these proverbs and become even wiser.
Let those with understanding receive guidance
6 by exploring the meaning in these proverbs and parables,
the words of the wise and their riddles.

7 Fear of the LORD is the foundation of true knowledge,
but fools despise wisdom and discipline.

A Father's Exhortation: Acquire Wisdom

8 My child,* listen when your father corrects you.
Don't neglect your mother's instruction.
9 What you learn from them will crown you with grace
and be a chain of honor around your neck.

10 My child, if sinners entice you,
turn your back on them!
11 They may say, "Come and join us.
Let's hide and kill someone!
Just for fun, let's ambush the innocent!
12 Let's swallow them alive, like the grave*;
let's swallow them whole, like those who go down to the pit of death.
13 Think of the great things we'll get!
We'll fill our houses with all the stuff we take.
14 Come, throw in your lot with us;
we'll all share the loot."

15 My child, don't go along with them!
Stay far away from their paths.
16 They rush to commit evil deeds.
They hurry to commit murder.
17 If a bird sees a trap being set,
it knows to stay away.
18 But these people set an ambush for themselves;
they are trying to get themselves killed.

1:8 Hebrew *My son;* also in 1:10, 15. **1:12** Hebrew *like Sheol.*

1:1—9:18 Acquiring Wisdom

1:1–7 A Call to Understanding. 1–6: These verses provide the key to all that follows. Highlighting the weaknesses of youth (simplicity; lack of prudence, reflecting youth's characteristic impetuosity) and maturity of age (a tendency to rest on laurels; thinking themselves already wise through lifelong experience), all are encouraged to acquire and to go on acquiring wisdom. The purpose of the book is thus to impart wisdom and instruction in such a way that they can be known and received. Common sense is also called for: Observation and reflection should reveal that certain courses of action have beneficial results while others have negative repercussions. This is where the need for God's revealed wisdom becomes apparent, since there are occasions when either the expected or the logically deserved doesn't come to pass. **7:** The *fear of the LORD* is cited as the beginning of wisdom (9:10), which results in the ability to avoid evil (16:6) and is a fountain of life through which one may avoid death (14:27). Terms such as awe, reverence, respect, and devotion might illuminate the concept further. This contrasts significantly with the arrogance displayed by fools, who despise instruction through pride and self-sufficiency. The human tendency to analyze, structure, dissect, reconstruct, and hence dominate, control, and master must find its correct locus in God, the giver of these skills and the origin of knowledge.

1:8—2:22 Learning the Lesson. 1:8–9: Here the mother's teaching is specifically mentioned. This verse, like many others in Proverbs, takes a stylized form: two lines written in such a way that the second line backs up, sheds light on, or contrasts the first. Thus mothers feature alongside fathers in these couplets to make primarily a literary point, although references to mothers teaching (1:8; 6:20; 29:15; 31:2) may indicate a more prominent instructive role in Hebrew society than the notion of wisdom schools might allow. **10–17:** Functioning as a type of subsection, this passage presents an instance in which wisdom needs to be exercised and walks the son through its outworking. The son is to understand that situations will arise that will potentially pull him down. **18–19:** One reaps the fruit of one's ways but illicit gain rots life to the core, choking to death the freedom of honesty

19 Such is the fate of all who are greedy for
money;
it robs them of life.

Wisdom Shouts in the Streets

20 Wisdom shouts in the streets.
She cries out in the public square.
21 She calls to the crowds along the main street,
to those gathered in front of the city gate:
22 "How long, you simpletons,
will you insist on being simpleminded?
How long will you mockers relish your
mocking?
How long will you fools hate knowledge?
23 Come and listen to my counsel.
I'll share my heart with you
and make you wise.

24 "I called you so often, but you wouldn't
come.
I reached out to you, but you paid no
attention.
25 You ignored my advice
and rejected the correction I offered.
26 So I will laugh when you are in trouble!
I will mock you when disaster overtakes
you—
27 when calamity overtakes you like a storm,
when disaster engulfs you like a cyclone,
and anguish and distress overwhelm you.

28 "When they cry for help, I will not answer.
Though they anxiously search for me, they
will not find me.
29 For they hated knowledge
and chose not to fear the LORD.
30 They rejected my advice
and paid no attention when I corrected
them.
31 Therefore, they must eat the bitter fruit of
living their own way,
choking on their own schemes.
32 For simpletons turn away from me—to
death.
Fools are destroyed by their own
complacency.
33 But all who listen to me will live in peace,
untroubled by fear of harm."

The Benefits of Wisdom

2 1My child,* listen to what I say,
and treasure my commands.
2Tune your ears to wisdom,
and concentrate on understanding.
3 Cry out for insight,
and ask for understanding.
4 Search for them as you would for silver;
seek them like hidden treasures.
5 Then you will understand what it means to
fear the LORD,
and you will gain knowledge of God.
6 For the LORD grants wisdom!
From his mouth come knowledge and
understanding.
7 He grants a treasure of common sense to the
honest.
He is a shield to those who walk with
integrity.

2:1 Hebrew *My son.*

and integrity. **20–27:** Wisdom speaks as one with authority but no desire or perhaps ability to coerce; she employs no wiles, in direct contrast to the alluring but open enticement of the sinners (v. 10), yet she is equally forthright in her desire to influence the young man's course of action. She is also communicating a message about herself. **20–21:** Found in the most public places, she is evident and available to all. At the same time she is often found precisely where she is not expected—these public places would not have been commonly frequented by women. **28:** Herein lies a further thrust of her message: Responsibility for listening and taking action is the hearer's, not hers. The sobering fact is that there comes a time when it is too late to seek her. To seek Wisdom diligently after calamity is to mock her, a hypocritical act; therefore she goes into hiding. **29–31:** This section gathers the observations and pleas under the overall umbrella of the fear of the LORD. Those who reject this, choosing another authority, as did the sinners, must reap the benefit of their actions. **32:** A complacent attitude is particularly dangerous as opposed to fools, who despise wisdom, and the simple, who turn away from following wisdom, refusing to evaluate, consider, listen, understand, and thoughtlessly follow all their inappropriate impulses. **2:1–5:** The father aims to make sure that the son will understand. *Treasure my commands*: Just as Wisdom cried out to passersby, so the son must cry out with equal urgency for insight and understanding. **6:** Wisdom belongs to the LORD, who communicates knowledge and understanding. Neither can be comprehended as a gift suddenly bestowed; instead both demand perpetual listening. **7–10:** While thus emphasizing the ongoing process of the acquisition of wisdom, the son should also gain encouragement from the fact that the LORD stores up sound wisdom for the upright, an indication that the more experience in walking wisely one has, the more upright one is and the more one can have confidence. As a result—note, not as

8 He guards the paths of the just
and protects those who are faithful to him.
9 Then you will understand what is right, just, and fair,
and you will find the right way to go.
10 For wisdom will enter your heart,
and knowledge will fill you with joy.
11 Wise choices will watch over you.
Understanding will keep you safe.

12 Wisdom will save you from evil people,
from those whose words are twisted.
13 These men turn from the right way
to walk down dark paths.
14 They take pleasure in doing wrong,
and they enjoy the twisted ways of evil.
15 Their actions are crooked,
and their ways are wrong.

16 Wisdom will save you from the immoral woman,
from the seductive words of the promiscuous woman.
17 She has abandoned her husband
and ignores the covenant she made before God.
18 Entering her house leads to death;
it is the road to the grave.*
19 The man who visits her is doomed.
He will never reach the paths of life.
20 Follow the steps of good men instead,
and stay on the paths of the righteous.
21 For only the godly will live in the land,
and those with integrity will remain in it.
22 But the wicked will be removed from the land,
and the treacherous will be uprooted.

Trusting in the LORD

3 1My child,* never forget the things I have taught you.
Store my commands in your heart.
2 If you do this, you will live many years,
and your life will be satisfying.
3 Never let loyalty and kindness leave you!
Tie them around your neck as a reminder.
Write them deep within your heart.
4 Then you will find favor with both God and people,
and you will earn a good reputation.

5 Trust in the LORD with all your heart;
do not depend on your own understanding.
6 Seek his will in all you do,
and he will show you which path to take.

7 Don't be impressed with your own wisdom.
Instead, fear the LORD and turn away from evil.

2:18 Hebrew *to the spirits of the dead.* **3:1** Hebrew *My son;* also in 3:11, 21.

a reward—the son will experience the protection of the LORD. **12–17:** The odd switch to the first warning about *the immoral . . . promiscuous woman* seems to be provoked by the reference to perverted speech (referring to 1:11–14?), although with the subtler link of forbidden fruit. At one level the father appears to be warning the son against an adulterous woman—a natural warning should the son be preparing for marriage or adulthood. This latter could well help to explain the frequent references to women, who would be in many ways an unknown in terms of relationships other than the maternal and sororital (sisterly). Marriage would involve leaving the parental home, accepting new responsibilities, and getting to know a new wife with whom the young man would rear a family. Avoiding marriage to a difficult wife would be important. **18–19:** The son must understand that here is a new type, one that will creep up on him imperceptibly, that he won't instantly recognize it for what it is, one that will strike where he is most vulnerable, taking him by surprise, flattering him and appealing to his vanity and manhood. The vocabulary emphasizes how gradual the descent to death is. As opposed to a quick death of violence that comes almost as rightful dues from easily identifiable foolish actions, this path to death can start without the son realizing it. It is doubly dangerous because death—the inevitable consequence—is not immediately evident. **20–22:** The father concludes by encouraging the son to learn the lesson just presented. In so doing, he will join the ranks of the upright, with the corresponding expectation of living a life of security and blessing.

3:1—4:27 Commending Wisdom. 3:1–4: The father goes on to flesh out his teachings as he introduces new aspects of wisdom. These include loyalty and faithfulness, with the urge to make them part of one's being: The heart is the place of understanding, and the neck, a particularly vulnerable part of the body, is a place of beauty. **5–8:** A real danger of living wisely lies in the temptation to trust in these attributes per se and in the corresponding blessings of favor and good repute, which also potentially lead to self-sufficiency and complacency. So wisdom involves recognizing the dangers of wisdom. **11–12:** Disregard may in-

8 Then you will have healing for your body
and strength for your bones.

9 Honor the LORD with your wealth
and with the best part of everything you produce.
10 Then he will fill your barns with grain,
and your vats will overflow with good wine.

11 My child, don't reject the LORD's discipline,
and don't be upset when he corrects you.
12 For the LORD corrects those he loves,
just as a father corrects a child in whom he delights.*

13 Joyful is the person who finds wisdom,
the one who gains understanding.
14 For wisdom is more profitable than silver,
and her wages are better than gold.
15 Wisdom is more precious than rubies;
nothing you desire can compare with her.
16 She offers you long life in her right hand,
and riches and honor in her left.
17 She will guide you down delightful paths;
all her ways are satisfying.
18 Wisdom is a tree of life to those who embrace her;
happy are those who hold her tightly.

19 By wisdom the LORD founded the earth;
by understanding he created the heavens.
20 By his knowledge the deep fountains of the earth burst forth,
and the dew settles beneath the night sky.

21 My child, don't lose sight of common sense and discernment.
Hang on to them,
22 for they will refresh your soul.
They are like jewels on a necklace.
23 They keep you safe on your way,
and your feet will not stumble.
24 You can go to bed without fear;
you will lie down and sleep soundly.
25 You need not be afraid of sudden disaster
or the destruction that comes upon the wicked,
26 for the LORD is your security.
He will keep your foot from being caught in a trap.

27 Do not withhold good from those who deserve it
when it's in your power to help them.
28 If you can help your neighbor now, don't say,
"Come back tomorrow, and then I'll help you."

29 Don't plot harm against your neighbor,
for those who live nearby trust you.
30 Don't pick a fight without reason,
when no one has done you harm.

31 Don't envy violent people
or copy their ways.
32 Such wicked people are detestable to the LORD,
but he offers his friendship to the godly.
33 The LORD curses the house of the wicked,
but he blesses the home of the upright.

34 The LORD mocks the mockers
but is gracious to the humble.*
35 The wise inherit honor,
but fools are put to shame!

A Father's Wise Advice

4 1My children,* listen when your father corrects you.
Pay attention and learn good judgment,
2 for I am giving you good guidance.
Don't turn away from my instructions.
3 For I, too, was once my father's son,
tenderly loved as my mother's only child.

3:12 Greek version reads *And he punishes those he accepts as his children.* Compare Heb 12:6. **3:34** Greek version reads *The LORD opposes the proud / but favors the humble.* Compare Jas 4:6; 1 Pet 5:5. **4:1** Hebrew *My sons.*

voke God's loving discipline, a much more comforting concept than inevitable negative consequences. **13–20:** Wisdom is part of the created order, and humanity's task is to work in conjunction with this, acknowledging God's far superior knowledge and understanding. **21–22:** Once the skill of understanding is acquired, then it must be kept in the forefront of life. **25–26:** When the unexpected arrives and takes you by surprise, your previous experiences and the father's teaching will guide you through (cf. 4:1–5). **27–35:** Here we find explicit instruction on social relationships, including a caution against avoiding the patterns associated with violent persons. **4:1–4:** Now begins the concept of early instruction for small children to be accomplished within the structure of the family. The father himself was instructed at a very young age when he was *tenderly loved* by his mother. Clearly, the maternal influence was also powerful.

4 My father taught me,
"Take my words to heart.
Follow my commands, and you will live.
5 Get wisdom; develop good judgment.
Don't forget my words or turn away from them.
6 Don't turn your back on wisdom, for she will protect you.
Love her, and she will guard you.
7 Getting wisdom is the wisest thing you can do!
And whatever else you do, develop good judgment.
8 If you prize wisdom, she will make you great.
Embrace her, and she will honor you.
9 She will place a lovely wreath on your head;
she will present you with a beautiful crown."

10 My child,* listen to me and do as I say,
and you will have a long, good life.
11 I will teach you wisdom's ways
and lead you in straight paths.
12 When you walk, you won't be held back;
when you run, you won't stumble.
13 Take hold of my instructions; don't let them go.
Guard them, for they are the key to life.

14 Don't do as the wicked do,
and don't follow the path of evildoers.
15 Don't even think about it; don't go that way.
Turn away and keep moving.
16 For evil people can't sleep until they've done their evil deed for the day.
They can't rest until they've caused someone to stumble.
17 They eat the food of wickedness
and drink the wine of violence!

18 The way of the righteous is like the first gleam of dawn,
which shines ever brighter until the full light of day.
19 But the way of the wicked is like total darkness.
They have no idea what they are stumbling over.

20 My child, pay attention to what I say.
Listen carefully to my words.
21 Don't lose sight of them.
Let them penetrate deep into your heart,
22 for they bring life to those who find them,
and healing to their whole body.
23 Guard your heart above all else,
for it determines the course of your life.

24 Avoid all perverse talk;
stay away from corrupt speech.

25 Look straight ahead,
and fix your eyes on what lies before you.
26 Mark out a straight path for your feet;
stay on the safe path.
27 Don't get sidetracked;
keep your feet from following evil.

Avoid Immoral Women

5 1 My son, pay attention to my wisdom;
listen carefully to my wise counsel.
2 Then you will show discernment,
and your lips will express what you've learned.
3 For the lips of an immoral woman are as sweet as honey,
and her mouth is smoother than oil.
4 But in the end she is as bitter as poison,
as dangerous as a double-edged sword.
5 Her feet go down to death;
her steps lead straight to the grave.*
6 For she cares nothing about the path to life.
She staggers down a crooked trail and doesn't realize it.

7 So now, my sons, listen to me.
Never stray from what I am about to say:
8 Stay away from her!
Don't go near the door of her house!

4:10 Hebrew *My son;* also in 4:20. **5:5** Hebrew *to Sheol.*

Earliest impressions are the most lasting. **5–9:** Simply to recognize that wisdom is a vital requisite of life is already to be wise. The entire tone bespeaks kindly parental guidance, done in a one-on-one situation. **10–27:** Peppered throughout these chapters is the notion of blessing resulting from wisdom: life (3:22); long life, often associated with the land (4:10; 2:21); healing (4:22); and security (1:33). We do better to view these benefits as generally but not guaranteeably true in a fallen world. They are principles rather than promises.

5:1–23 Warnings against Foolishness. 3–6: Once again the appearance of the *immoral woman* seems to be provoked by reference to speech (cf. 1:12, 16). We have the impression that the father means to go in another direction but is always drawn back—perhaps himself a prisoner of the influences he warns against?

9 If you do, you will lose your honor
and will lose to merciless people all you have achieved.
10 Strangers will consume your wealth,
and someone else will enjoy the fruit of your labor.
11 In the end you will groan in anguish
when disease consumes your body.
12 You will say, "How I hated discipline!
If only I had not ignored all the warnings!
13 Oh, why didn't I listen to my teachers?
Why didn't I pay attention to my instructors?
14 I have come to the brink of utter ruin,
and now I must face public disgrace."

15 Drink water from your own well—
share your love only with your wife.*
16 Why spill the water of your springs in the streets,
having sex with just anyone?*
17 You should reserve it for yourselves.
Never share it with strangers.

18 Let your wife be a fountain of blessing for you.
Rejoice in the wife of your youth.
19 She is a loving deer, a graceful doe.
Let her breasts satisfy you always.
May you always be captivated by her love.
20 Why be captivated, my son, by an immoral woman,
or fondle the breasts of a promiscuous woman?

21 For the LORD sees clearly what a man does,
examining every path he takes.
22 An evil man is held captive by his own sins;
they are ropes that catch and hold him.
23 He will die for lack of self-control;
he will be lost because of his great foolishness.

Lessons for Daily Life

6 1My child,* if you have put up security for a friend's debt
or agreed to guarantee the debt of a stranger—
2 if you have trapped yourself by your agreement
and are caught by what you said—
3 follow my advice and save yourself,
for you have placed yourself at your friend's mercy.
Now swallow your pride;
go and beg to have your name erased.
4 Don't put it off; do it now!
Don't rest until you do.
5 Save yourself like a gazelle escaping from a hunter,
like a bird fleeing from a net.

6 Take a lesson from the ants, you lazybones.
Learn from their ways and become wise!
7 Though they have no prince
or governor or ruler to make them work,
8 they labor hard all summer,
gathering food for the winter.
9 But you, lazybones, how long will you sleep?
When will you wake up?
10 A little extra sleep, a little more slumber,
a little folding of the hands to rest—
11 then poverty will pounce on you like a bandit;
scarcity will attack you like an armed robber.

12 What are worthless and wicked people like?
They are constant liars,

5:15 Hebrew *Drink water from your own cistern, / flowing water from your own well.* **5:16** Hebrew *Why spill your springs in the streets, / your streams in the city squares?* **6:1** Hebrew *My son.*

7–14: Of particular note are the penalties for listening to her, many of which are negative parallels to the blessings received through being wise. As before, it is appropriate to take the text on two levels: a genuine warning against an adulterous relationship with its draining, life-sucking, debilitating effects, and a lived example of how external, tempting influences, once given room, will imperceptibly invade and take on ever greater dimensions. **15–20:** There are many metaphors of sex in the Bible. One is that of water, desperately needed for survival and refreshment in the parched Middle East. This text uses the images of a well and a fountain to describe the abundant joy of a permanent marriage, intimating that sex only gets better with age. Sexual expression should not spill out into the streets but be saved for one another alone. Song of Songs 4:12–15 speaks in a parallel way of the bride as a spring that no one else can drink from, a "hidden fountain" that becomes a well of flowing water. In Proverbs, the contrasts between the *immoral woman* (5:3–14) and the *wife of your youth* (v. 18) are distinctly marked, with the latter embodying beauty, love, and affection.

6:1–19 Living Wisely. 1–5: Chapter 6 prepares the reader for living in society. We are not to exercise any manipulative or controlling power over others; neither should we give others the same sort of power

[13] signaling their deceit with a wink of the eye,
a nudge of the foot, or the wiggle of fingers.
[14] Their perverted hearts plot evil,
and they constantly stir up trouble.
[15] But they will be destroyed suddenly,
broken in an instant beyond all hope of healing.

[16] There are six things the LORD hates—
no, seven things he detests:
[17] haughty eyes,
a lying tongue,
hands that kill the innocent,
[18] a heart that plots evil,
feet that race to do wrong,
[19] a false witness who pours out lies,
a person who sows discord in a family.

[20] My son, obey your father's commands,
and don't neglect your mother's instruction.
[21] Keep their words always in your heart.
Tie them around your neck.
[22] When you walk, their counsel will lead you.
When you sleep, they will protect you.
When you wake up, they will advise you.
[23] For their command is a lamp
and their instruction a light;
their corrective discipline
is the way to life.
[24] It will keep you from the immoral woman,
from the smooth tongue of a promiscuous woman.
[25] Don't lust for her beauty.
Don't let her coy glances seduce you.
[26] For a prostitute will bring you to poverty,*
but sleeping with another man's wife will cost you your life.
[27] Can a man scoop a flame into his lap
and not have his clothes catch on fire?
[28] Can he walk on hot coals
and not blister his feet?
[29] So it is with the man who sleeps with another man's wife.
He who embraces her will not go unpunished.

[30] Excuses might be found for a thief
who steals because he is starving.
[31] But if he is caught, he must pay back seven times what he stole,
even if he has to sell everything in his house.
[32] But the man who commits adultery is an utter fool,
for he destroys himself.
[33] He will be wounded and disgraced.
His shame will never be erased.
[34] For the woman's jealous husband will be furious,
and he will show no mercy when he takes revenge.
[35] He will accept no compensation,
nor be satisfied with a payoff of any size.

Another Warning about Immoral Women

7 [1]Follow my advice, my son;
always treasure my commands.
[2]Obey my commands and live!
Guard my instructions as you guard your own eyes.*
[3] Tie them on your fingers as a reminder.
Write them deep within your heart.

[4] Love wisdom like a sister;
make insight a beloved member of your family.

6:26 Hebrew *to a loaf of bread.* **7:2** Hebrew *as the pupil of your eye.*

---

over us. **16–19:** This list of the seven things that God hates might well be set in juxtaposition to God's hatred of divorce and spousal abuse (Mal 2:16). **17:** The allusion to *a lying tongue* recalls the same in 4:24 ("perverse talk . . . corrupt speech") and contrasts with looking straight ahead as well as bringing evil to mind. Those who look sideways allow themselves to be deflected from the path of righteousness and will create havoc for themselves and others, spending time on worthless pursuits.

6:20—8:36 Influences and Temptations. 6:20–23: Both father and mother have given instruction in wisdom, portrayed in female form, representing the emotional and moral pulls and desires exerted on one's life. **24–25:** The *immoral woman* flits on stage one last time before making her grand finale just to make sure there is no uncertainty regarding her identity. **26–32:** This text seems to blur the edges between the *immoral woman* as a somewhat surreal representation of evil temptation, a readily available prostitute, and an adulterous woman. It seems reasonable to allow those three distinctions to stand, noting that the emphasis is of concern for the son's well-being and right action. They are presented as analogies of danger to beware of, not because of their gender but through the use of gender in this way the son is better equipped to learn the required lessons. **7:4–5:** Wisdom can preserve the son from the immoral woman, particularly from her words. She is readily identifi-

5 Let them protect you from an affair with an
immoral woman,
from listening to the flattery of a
promiscuous woman.

6 While I was at the window of my house,
looking through the curtain,
7 I saw some naive young men,
and one in particular who lacked common
sense.
8 He was crossing the street near the house of
an immoral woman,
strolling down the path by her house.
9 It was at twilight, in the evening,
as deep darkness fell.
10 The woman approached him,
seductively dressed and sly of heart.
11 She was the brash, rebellious type,
never content to stay at home.
12 She is often in the streets and markets,
soliciting at every corner.
13 She threw her arms around him and kissed
him,
and with a brazen look she said,
14 "I've just made my peace offerings
and fulfilled my vows.
15 You're the one I was looking for!
I came out to find you, and here you are!
16 My bed is spread with beautiful blankets,
with colored sheets of Egyptian linen.
17 I've perfumed my bed
with myrrh, aloes, and cinnamon.
18 Come, let's drink our fill of love until
morning.
Let's enjoy each other's caresses,
19 for my husband is not home.
He's away on a long trip.
20 He has taken a wallet full of money with him
and won't return until later this month.*"

21 So she seduced him with her pretty speech
and enticed him with her flattery.
22 He followed her at once,
like an ox going to the slaughter.
He was like a stag caught in a trap,
23 awaiting the arrow that would pierce its
heart.
He was like a bird flying into a snare,
little knowing it would cost him his life.

24 So listen to me, my sons,
and pay attention to my words.
25 Don't let your hearts stray away toward her.
Don't wander down her wayward path.
26 For she has been the ruin of many;
many men have been her victims.
27 Her house is the road to the grave.*
Her bedroom is the den of death.

Wisdom Calls for a Hearing

8 1Listen as Wisdom calls out!
Hear as understanding raises her voice!
2 On the hilltop along the road,
she takes her stand at the crossroads.
3 By the gates at the entrance to the town,
on the road leading in, she cries aloud,
4 "I call to you, to all of you!
I raise my voice to all people.
5 You simple people, use good judgment.
You foolish people, show some
understanding.
6 Listen to me! For I have important things to
tell you.
Everything I say is right,
7 for I speak the truth
and detest every kind of deception.
8 My advice is wholesome.
There is nothing devious or crooked in it.
9 My words are plain to anyone with
understanding,
clear to those with knowledge.
10 Choose my instruction rather than silver,

7:20 Hebrew *until the moon is full.* **7:27** Hebrew *to Sheol.*

able through her dress (v. 10), already suggesting that any wise son should distance himself if he saw fit. **6–20:** The promiscuous and immoral woman, rather than being an actual human being, may be the personification of evil and temptation, just as Wisdom personifies wisdom. **7:** The vignette depends on the son's simplicity and aims to equip him in the skills of sobriety and watchfulness by alerting him to the existence and the way of working of a form of evil temptation able to destroy him. **24–27:** Femme Fatale leads the son to believe that he can play with fire and not be burned, or more precisely, that the experience is pleasurable and the repercussions insignificant. **8:1–5:** Now Wisdom takes the stage, vying with Femme Fatale for the son's attention. Wisdom's message is still to the *simple people* (in contrast to the foolish) and her appeal begins by her declaring the benefits of accepting her. **6–9:** Little has changed from her previous messages, and again we are struck by the emphasis on words. Wisdom speaks what is noble and right, but she still depends on the listener to understand and to seek knowledge in order for the truth of her words to become apparent. Only by taking her at her word and experiencing it is her message proved true. **10–16:** Wisdom reveals her role in just government (her presence therefore

and knowledge rather than pure gold.
11 For wisdom is far more valuable than rubies.
Nothing you desire can compare with it.

12 "I, Wisdom, live together with good judgment.
I know where to discover knowledge and discernment.
13 All who fear the LORD will hate evil.
Therefore, I hate pride and arrogance,
corruption and perverse speech.
14 Common sense and success belong to me.
Insight and strength are mine.
15 Because of me, kings reign,
and rulers make just decrees.
16 Rulers lead with my help,
and nobles make righteous judgments.*

17 "I love all who love me.
Those who search will surely find me.
18 I have riches and honor,
as well as enduring wealth and justice.
19 My gifts are better than gold, even the purest gold,
my wages better than sterling silver!
20 I walk in righteousness,
in paths of justice.
21 Those who love me inherit wealth.
I will fill their treasuries.

22 "The LORD formed me from the beginning,
before he created anything else.
23 I was appointed in ages past,
at the very first, before the earth began.
24 I was born before the oceans were created,
before the springs bubbled forth their waters.
25 Before the mountains were formed,
before the hills, I was born—
26 before he had made the earth and fields
and the first handfuls of soil.
27 I was there when he established the heavens,
when he drew the horizon on the oceans.
28 I was there when he set the clouds above,
when he established springs deep in the earth.
29 I was there when he set the limits of the seas,
so they would not spread beyond their boundaries.
And when he marked off the earth's foundations,
30 I was the architect at his side.
I was his constant delight,
rejoicing always in his presence.
31 And how happy I was with the world he created;
how I rejoiced with the human family!

32 "And so, my children,* listen to me,
for all who follow my ways are joyful.
33 Listen to my instruction and be wise.
Don't ignore it.
34 Joyful are those who listen to me,
watching for me daily at my gates,
waiting for me outside my home!
35 For whoever finds me finds life
and receives favor from the LORD.
36 But those who miss me injure themselves.
All who hate me love death."

9

1 Wisdom has built her house;
she has carved its seven columns.
2 She has prepared a great banquet,
mixed the wines, and set the table.
3 She has sent her servants to invite everyone to come.
She calls out from the heights overlooking the city.
4 "Come in with me," she urges the simple.
To those who lack good judgment, she says,
5 "Come, eat my food,
and drink the wine I have mixed.

8:16 Some Hebrew manuscripts and Greek version read *and nobles are judges over the earth.* **8:32** Hebrew *my sons.*

---

aiding in issues of authority and responsibility). She is unabashed at proclaiming her inestimable worth (v. 11), which constitutes truth, counsel, sound wisdom, insight, and strength (v. 14)—indispensable properties for ruling, since they ensure peace, justice, and stability. **17–21:** Then, as if overcome by her glory, as a bud finally breaks open to allow the full flower to reflect the sun's glory, she presents her credentials—and what a curriculum vitae! Present at the creation of the world, used by God in that creation, and now rejoicing in that created world, she enjoys an intimate relationship with God, is his own, and is the principle by which he ordered the world. **22–35:** Not only is she the means by which humanity fears the LORD, but she is also the means by which the universe is structured. By implication, those who find her and live by her align themselves to that same order, finding peace and tranquillity.

9:1–18 Application. 1–7: Wisdom offers the simple—*those who lack good judgment*—her feast, a potent invitation, given the need for the simple to so practice the art of understanding that it becomes akin to eating and inwardly digesting, then becoming a

6 Leave your simple ways behind, and begin to live;
learn to use good judgment."
7 Anyone who rebukes a mocker will get an insult in return.
Anyone who corrects the wicked will get hurt.
8 So don't bother correcting mockers;
they will only hate you.
But correct the wise,
and they will love you.
9 Instruct the wise,
and they will be even wiser.
Teach the righteous,
and they will learn even more.
10 Fear of the LORD is the foundation of wisdom.
Knowledge of the Holy One results in good judgment.
11 Wisdom will multiply your days
and add years to your life.
12 If you become wise, you will be the one to benefit.
If you scorn wisdom, you will be the one to suffer.

Folly Calls for a Hearing

13 The woman named Folly is brash.
She is ignorant and doesn't know it.
14 She sits in her doorway
on the heights overlooking the city.
15 She calls out to men going by
who are minding their own business.
16 "Come in with me," she urges the simple.
To those who lack good judgment, she says,
17 "Stolen water is refreshing;
food eaten in secret tastes the best!"
18 But little do they know that the dead are there.
Her guests are in the depths of the grave.*

The Proverbs of Solomon

10 The proverbs of Solomon:
A wise child* brings joy to a father;
a foolish child brings grief to a mother.

2 Tainted wealth has no lasting value,
but right living can save your life.

3 The LORD will not let the godly go hungry,
but he refuses to satisfy the craving of the wicked.

4 Lazy people are soon poor;
hard workers get rich.

5 A wise youth harvests in the summer,
but one who sleeps during harvest is a disgrace.

6 The godly are showered with blessings;
the words of the wicked conceal violent intentions.

7 We have happy memories of the godly,
but the name of a wicked person rots away.

8 The wise are glad to be instructed,
but babbling fools fall flat on their faces.

9 People with integrity walk safely,
but those who follow crooked paths will slip and fall.

10 People who wink at wrong cause trouble,
but a bold reproof promotes peace.*

11 The words of the godly are a life-giving fountain;
the words of the wicked conceal violent intentions.

9:18 Hebrew *in Sheol.* **10:1** Hebrew *son;* also in 10:1b. **10:10** As in Greek version; Hebrew reads *but babbling fools fall flat on their faces.*

source of nourishment and well-being (note the analogy of eating honey in 24:13–14). **7–12:** These might seem to be an odd collection of unrelated sayings, yet they have their place as a practical application of what has gone before as well as preparation for that to come. **13–17:** Femme Fatale's final sortie gives the impression of a damp firecracker, her message vain, empty, and unappealing, her voice petering into insignificance when set against that of Wisdom.

10:1—29:27 Acting Wisely

Of major concern is the type of person one is. **10:1–32:** The fool is roundly condemned, accredited with numerous failings: hasty, unconsidered, or slanderous speech (vv. 8, 14, 18), lack of common sense (v. 21), enjoyment of wrongdoing (v. 23), and embarrassment to her or his mother (v. 1). Unchanneled or inappropriately directed energy is unproductive and

12 Hatred stirs up quarrels,
but love makes up for all offenses.

13 Wise words come from the lips of people with understanding,
but those lacking sense will be beaten with a rod.

14 Wise people treasure knowledge,
but the babbling of a fool invites disaster.

15 The wealth of the rich is their fortress;
the poverty of the poor is their destruction.

16 The earnings of the godly enhance their lives,
but evil people squander their money on sin.

17 People who accept discipline are on the pathway to life,
but those who ignore correction will go astray.

18 Hiding hatred makes you a liar;
slandering others makes you a fool.

19 Too much talk leads to sin.
Be sensible and keep your mouth shut.

20 The words of the godly are like sterling silver;
the heart of a fool is worthless.

21 The words of the godly encourage many,
but fools are destroyed by their lack of common sense.

22 The blessing of the LORD makes a person rich,
and he adds no sorrow with it.

23 Doing wrong is fun for a fool,
but living wisely brings pleasure to the sensible.

24 The fears of the wicked will be fulfilled;
the hopes of the godly will be granted.

25 When the storms of life come, the wicked are whirled away,
but the godly have a lasting foundation.

26 Lazy people irritate their employers,
like vinegar to the teeth or smoke in the eyes.

27 Fear of the LORD lengthens one's life,
but the years of the wicked are cut short.

28 The hopes of the godly result in happiness,
but the expectations of the wicked come to nothing.

29 The way of the LORD is a stronghold to those with integrity,
but it destroys the wicked.

30 The godly will never be disturbed,
but the wicked will be removed from the land.

31 The mouth of the godly person gives wise advice,
but the tongue that deceives will be cut off.

32 The lips of the godly speak helpful words,
but the mouth of the wicked speaks perverse words.

11 1The LORD detests the use of dishonest scales,
but he delights in accurate weights.

2 Pride leads to disgrace,
but with humility comes wisdom.

3 Honesty guides good people;
dishonesty destroys treacherous people.

4 Riches won't help on the day of judgment,
but right living can save you from death.

5 The godly are directed by honesty;
the wicked fall beneath their load of sin.

6 The godliness of good people rescues them;
the ambition of treacherous people traps them.

7 When the wicked die, their hopes die with them,
for they rely on their own feeble strength.

senseless and can be harmful. **11:1–31:** The righteous are a blessing to the society in which they live (v. 11). They have every hope that their desires and hopes will be fulfilled (v. 23; cf. 10:24). They are rewarded by joy and satisfaction (v. 28; 10:6) their righteousness is linked with delivery from death (v. 4; cf. 10:2), of their being saved (v. 6) and of walking in a straight way (v. 5). The physical charms of a beautiful woman may attract wealth (v. 16) that is unreliable at best (vv. 4, 28). She who lacks good

[8] The godly are rescued from trouble,
and it falls on the wicked instead.

[9] With their words, the godless destroy their friends,
but knowledge will rescue the righteous.

[10] The whole city celebrates when the godly succeed;
they shout for joy when the wicked die.

[11] Upright citizens are good for a city and make it prosper,
but the talk of the wicked tears it apart.

[12] It is foolish to belittle one's neighbor;
a sensible person keeps quiet.

[13] A gossip goes around telling secrets,
but those who are trustworthy can keep a confidence.

[14] Without wise leadership, a nation falls;
there is safety in having many advisers.

[15] There's danger in putting up security for a stranger's debt;
it's safer not to guarantee another person's debt.

[16] A gracious woman gains respect,
but ruthless men gain only wealth.

[17] Your kindness will reward you,
but your cruelty will destroy you.

[18] Evil people get rich for the moment,
but the reward of the godly will last.

[19] Godly people find life;
evil people find death.

[20] The LORD detests people with crooked hearts,
but he delights in those with integrity.

[21] Evil people will surely be punished,
but the children of the godly will go free.

[22] A beautiful woman who lacks discretion
is like a gold ring in a pig's snout.

[23] The godly can look forward to a reward,
while the wicked can expect only judgment.

[24] Give freely and become more wealthy;
be stingy and lose everything.

[25] The generous will prosper;
those who refresh others will themselves be refreshed.

[26] People curse those who hoard their grain,
but they bless the one who sells in time of need.

[27] If you search for good, you will find favor;
but if you search for evil, it will find you!

[28] Trust in your money and down you go!
But the godly flourish like leaves in spring.

[29] Those who bring trouble on their families inherit the wind.
The fool will be a servant to the wise.

[30] The seeds of good deeds become a tree of life;
a wise person wins friends.*

[31] If the righteous are rewarded here on earth,
what will happen to wicked sinners?*

12 [1] To learn, you must love discipline;
it is stupid to hate correction.

[2] The LORD approves of those who are good,
but he condemns those who plan wickedness.

[3] Wickedness never brings stability,
but the godly have deep roots.

11:30 Or *and those who win souls are wise.* **11:31** Greek version reads *If the righteous are barely saved, / what will happen to godless sinners?* Compare 1 Pet 4:18.

---

sense is an object of particular scorn (v. 22) while the children of the godly inherit great blessing (v. 21). **12:1–28:** Possession of a godly wife and children is appreciated by the wise (vv. 4, 6). The righteous are considerate even to animals (v. 10). One's well-being is directly related to the common sense exercised in the making of choices (v. 8), and these chapters often have a pragmatic flavor: Do what is right, not just because of its intrinsic rightness but because the results are to one's benefit (11:17). Words are a means of perpetuating or desecrating justice (12:17, 19, 22; cf. 14:5, 25) and of initiating, maintaining, or disabling constructive and peaceful relationships (12:18; cf. 15:1; 21:23). Gossip is identified as the

4 A worthy wife is a crown for her husband,
but a disgraceful woman is like cancer in his bones.

5 The plans of the godly are just;
the advice of the wicked is treacherous.

6 The words of the wicked are like a murderous ambush,
but the words of the godly save lives.

7 The wicked die and disappear,
but the family of the godly stands firm.

8 A sensible person wins admiration,
but a warped mind is despised.

9 Better to be an ordinary person with a servant
than to be self-important but have no food.

10 The godly care for their animals,
but the wicked are always cruel.

11 A hard worker has plenty of food,
but a person who chases fantasies has no sense.

12 Thieves are jealous of each other's loot,
but the godly are well rooted and bear their own fruit.

13 The wicked are trapped by their own words,
but the godly escape such trouble.

14 Wise words bring many benefits,
and hard work brings rewards.

15 Fools think their own way is right,
but the wise listen to others.

16 A fool is quick-tempered,
but a wise person stays calm when insulted.

17 An honest witness tells the truth;
a false witness tells lies.

18 Some people make cutting remarks,
but the words of the wise bring healing.

19 Truthful words stand the test of time,
but lies are soon exposed.

20 Deceit fills hearts that are plotting evil;
joy fills hearts that are planning peace!

21 No harm comes to the godly,
but the wicked have their fill of trouble.

22 The LORD detests lying lips,
but he delights in those who tell the truth.

23 The wise don't make a show of their knowledge,
but fools broadcast their foolishness.

24 Work hard and become a leader;
be lazy and become a slave.

25 Worry weighs a person down;
an encouraging word cheers a person up.

26 The godly give good advice to their friends;*
the wicked lead them astray.

27 Lazy people don't even cook the game they catch,
but the diligent make use of everything they find.

28 The way of the godly leads to life;
that path does not lead to death.

13

1 A wise child accepts a parent's discipline;*
a mocker refuses to listen to correction.

2 Wise words will win you a good meal,
but treacherous people have an appetite for violence.

3 Those who control their tongue will have a long life;
opening your mouth can ruin everything.

4 Lazy people want much but get little,
but those who work hard will prosper.

5 The godly hate lies;
the wicked cause shame and disgrace.

12:26 Or *The godly are cautious in friendship;* or *The godly are freed from evil.* The meaning of the Hebrew is uncertain.
13:1 Hebrew *A wise son accepts his father's discipline.*

cause of much mischief (cf. 26:20–22). The need to be able to ignore damaging words is highlighted here (12:16). **13:1–25:** Parents who withhold guidance and control from their children do them a pro-

6 Godliness guards the path of the blameless,
but the evil are misled by sin.

7 Some who are poor pretend to be rich;
others who are rich pretend to be poor.

8 The rich can pay a ransom for their lives,
but the poor won't even get threatened.

9 The life of the godly is full of light and joy,
but the light of the wicked will be snuffed out.

10 Pride leads to conflict;
those who take advice are wise.

11 Wealth from get-rich-quick schemes quickly disappears;
wealth from hard work grows over time.

12 Hope deferred makes the heart sick,
but a dream fulfilled is a tree of life.

13 People who despise advice are asking for trouble;
those who respect a command will succeed.

14 The instruction of the wise is like a life-giving fountain;
those who accept it avoid the snares of death.

15 A person with good sense is respected;
a treacherous person is headed for destruction.*

16 Wise people think before they act;
fools don't—and even brag about their foolishness.

17 An unreliable messenger stumbles into trouble,
but a reliable messenger brings healing.

18 If you ignore criticism, you will end in poverty and disgrace;
if you accept correction, you will be honored.

19 It is pleasant to see dreams come true,
but fools refuse to turn from evil to attain them.

20 Walk with the wise and become wise;
associate with fools and get in trouble.

21 Trouble chases sinners,
while blessings reward the righteous.

22 Good people leave an inheritance to their grandchildren,
but the sinner's wealth passes to the godly.

23 A poor person's farm may produce much food,
but injustice sweeps it all away.

24 Those who spare the rod of discipline hate their children.
Those who love their children care enough to discipline them.

25 The godly eat to their hearts' content,
but the belly of the wicked goes hungry.

14

1 A wise woman builds her home,
but a foolish woman tears it down with her own hands.

2 Those who follow the right path fear the LORD;
those who take the wrong path despise him.

3 A fool's proud talk becomes a rod that beats him,
but the words of the wise keep them safe.

4 Without oxen a stable stays clean,
but you need a strong ox for a large harvest.

5 An honest witness does not lie;
a false witness breathes lies.

13:15 As in Greek version; Hebrew reads *the way of the treacherous is lasting.*

found disservice. Those who love their children are careful to discipline them, but the guidance is to be positive and affirming (vv. 1, 24). **14:1–14:** In contrast to the beautiful but foolish woman (11:22) is the wise woman who builds her house (cf. 9:1; 24:2). She constructs the home atmosphere with positive attitudes, conscientious guidance, and creative solutions to the challenges (cf. 31:10–31). She builds not only with the bearing and rearing of children but also by the companionship that she affords her husband (12:4) and her influence on those around her (31:20, 25). For affirmations of women

[6] A mocker seeks wisdom and never finds it,
but knowledge comes easily to those with understanding.

[7] Stay away from fools,
for you won't find knowledge on their lips.

[8] The prudent understand where they are going,
but fools deceive themselves.

[9] Fools make fun of guilt,
but the godly acknowledge it and seek reconciliation.

[10] Each heart knows its own bitterness,
and no one else can fully share its joy.

[11] The house of the wicked will be destroyed,
but the tent of the godly will flourish.

[12] There is a path before each person that seems right,
but it ends in death.

[13] Laughter can conceal a heavy heart,
but when the laughter ends, the grief remains.

[14] Backsliders get what they deserve;
good people receive their reward.

[15] Only simpletons believe everything they're told!
The prudent carefully consider their steps.

[16] The wise are cautious* and avoid danger;
fools plunge ahead with reckless confidence.

[17] Short-tempered people do foolish things,
and schemers are hated.

[18] Simpletons are clothed with foolishness,*
but the prudent are crowned with knowledge.

[19] Evil people will bow before good people;
the wicked will bow at the gates of the godly.

[20] The poor are despised even by their neighbors,
while the rich have many "friends."

[21] It is a sin to belittle one's neighbor;
blessed are those who help the poor.

[22] If you plan to do evil, you will be lost;
if you plan to do good, you will receive unfailing love and faithfulness.

[23] Work brings profit,
but mere talk leads to poverty!

[24] Wealth is a crown for the wise;
the effort of fools yields only foolishness.

[25] A truthful witness saves lives,
but a false witness is a traitor.

[26] Those who fear the LORD are secure;
he will be a refuge for their children.

[27] Fear of the LORD is a life-giving fountain;
it offers escape from the snares of death.

[28] A growing population is a king's glory;
a prince without subjects has nothing.

[29] People with understanding control their anger;
a hot temper shows great foolishness.

[30] A peaceful heart leads to a healthy body;
jealousy is like cancer in the bones.

[31] Those who oppress the poor insult their Maker,
but helping the poor honors him.

[32] The wicked are crushed by disaster,
but the godly have a refuge when they die.

[33] Wisdom is enshrined in an understanding heart;
wisdom is not* found among fools.

[34] Godliness makes a nation great,
but sin is a disgrace to any people.

[35] A king rejoices in wise servants
but is angry with those who disgrace him.

15

[1] A gentle answer deflects anger,
but harsh words make tempers flare.

14:16 Hebrew *The wise fear.* **14:18** Or *inherit foolishness.*
14:33 As in Greek and Syriac versions; Hebrew lacks *not.*

as home builders see 5:18–19; 12:4; 18:22; 19:14 (see also Lev 19:3; Deut 5:16; Mal 2:14–15; 1 Tim 5:10). **15:1–33:** Gentleness of speech can impart wisdom while making learning a joy (vv. 1, 4). Coun-

2 The tongue of the wise makes knowledge
appealing,
but the mouth of a fool belches out
foolishness.
3 The LORD is watching everywhere,
keeping his eye on both the evil and the
good.

4 Gentle words are a tree of life;
a deceitful tongue crushes the spirit.
5 Only a fool despises a parent's* discipline;
whoever learns from correction is wise.

6 There is treasure in the house of the godly,
but the earnings of the wicked bring
trouble.

7 The lips of the wise give good advice;
the heart of a fool has none to give.

8 The LORD detests the sacrifice of the wicked,
but he delights in the prayers of the
upright.
9 The LORD detests the way of the wicked,
but he loves those who pursue godliness.

10 Whoever abandons the right path will be
severely disciplined;
whoever hates correction will die.

11 Even Death and Destruction* hold no secrets
from the LORD.
How much more does he know the human
heart!

12 Mockers hate to be corrected,
so they stay away from the wise.

13 A glad heart makes a happy face;
a broken heart crushes the spirit.

14 A wise person is hungry for knowledge,
while the fool feeds on trash.

15 For the despondent, every day brings trouble;
for the happy heart, life is a continual feast.

16 Better to have little, with fear for the LORD,
than to have great treasure and inner
turmoil.
17 A bowl of vegetables with someone you love
is better than steak with someone you hate.

18 A hot-tempered person starts fights;
a cool-tempered person stops them.

19 A lazy person's way is blocked with briers,
but the path of the upright is an open
highway.

20 Sensible children bring joy to their father;
foolish children despise their mother.

21 Foolishness brings joy to those with no
sense;
a sensible person stays on the right path.

22 Plans go wrong for lack of advice;
many advisers bring success.

23 Everyone enjoys a fitting reply;
it is wonderful to say the right thing at the
right time!

24 The path of life leads upward for the wise;
they leave the grave* behind.

25 The LORD tears down the house of the
proud,
but he protects the property of widows.

26 The LORD detests evil plans,
but he delights in pure words.

27 Greed brings grief to the whole family,
but those who hate bribes will live.

28 The heart of the godly thinks carefully before
speaking;
the mouth of the wicked overflows with
evil words.

29 The LORD is far from the wicked,
but he hears the prayers of the righteous.

30 A cheerful look brings joy to the heart;
good news makes for good health.

31 If you listen to constructive criticism,
you will be at home among the wise.

15:5 Hebrew *father's.* **15:11** Hebrew *Sheol and Abaddon.*
15:24 Hebrew *Sheol.*

sel from others is required in the process of gaining wisdom (vv. 5, 22) in part because one's own view is limited (14:12). Verse 5 repeats the purpose stated in 1:4: to train the young. Departure from that instruc-

32 If you reject discipline, you only harm
yourself;
but if you listen to correction, you grow in
understanding.

33 Fear of the LORD teaches wisdom;
humility precedes honor.

16 1We can make our own plans,
but the LORD gives the right
answer.

2 People may be pure in their own eyes,
but the LORD examines their motives.

3 Commit your actions to the LORD,
and your plans will succeed.

4 The LORD has made everything for his own
purposes,
even the wicked for a day of disaster.

5 The LORD detests the proud;
they will surely be punished.

6 Unfailing love and faithfulness make
atonement for sin.
By fearing the LORD, people avoid evil.

7 When people's lives please the LORD,
even their enemies are at peace with them.

8 Better to have little, with godliness,
than to be rich and dishonest.

9 We can make our plans,
but the LORD determines our steps.

10 The king speaks with divine wisdom;
he must never judge unfairly.

11 The LORD demands accurate scales and
balances;
he sets the standards for fairness.

12 A king detests wrongdoing,
for his rule is built on justice.

13 The king is pleased with words from
righteous lips;
he loves those who speak honestly.

14 The anger of the king is a deadly threat;
the wise will try to appease it.

15 When the king smiles, there is life;
his favor refreshes like a spring rain.

16 How much better to get wisdom than gold,
and good judgment than silver!

17 The path of the virtuous leads away from
evil;
whoever follows that path is safe.

18 Pride goes before destruction,
and haughtiness before a fall.

19 Better to live humbly with the poor
than to share plunder with the proud.

20 Those who listen to instruction will prosper;
those who trust the LORD will be joyful.

21 The wise are known for their understanding,
and pleasant words are persuasive.

22 Discretion is a life-giving fountain to those
who possess it,
but discipline is wasted on fools.

23 From a wise mind comes wise speech;
the words of the wise are persuasive.

24 Kind words are like honey—
sweet to the soul and healthy for the
body.

25 There is a path before each person that seems
right,
but it ends in death.

26 It is good for workers to have an appetite;
an empty stomach drives them on.

27 Scoundrels create trouble;
their words are a destructive blaze.

28 A troublemaker plants seeds of strife;
gossip separates the best of friends.

---

tion brings grief to the mother (v. 20). (For advocacy of gentle discipline for children, see Eph 6:4; Col 3:21.) **16:1–33:** The first eleven verses of Proverbs 16 focus on contrasting human ways, plans, thoughts, and intentions with God's, while the following verses (vv. 12–33) speak of earthly kingship almost as if to emphasize the need for those who are the most exalted in earthly terms to judge themselves according to God's person and ordinances. The LORD is also seen to take an active part in the establishment and

29 Violent people mislead their companions,
leading them down a harmful path.

30 With narrowed eyes, people plot evil;
with a smirk, they plan their mischief.

31 Gray hair is a crown of glory;
it is gained by living a godly life.

32 Better to be patient than powerful;
better to have self-control than to conquer
a city.

33 We may throw the dice,*
but the LORD determines how they fall.

17

1 Better a dry crust eaten in peace
than a house filled with feasting—
and conflict.

2 A wise servant will rule over the master's
disgraceful son
and will share the inheritance of the
master's children.

3 Fire tests the purity of silver and gold,
but the LORD tests the heart.

4 Wrongdoers eagerly listen to gossip;
liars pay close attention to slander.

5 Those who mock the poor insult their Maker;
those who rejoice at the misfortune of
others will be punished.

6 Grandchildren are the crowning glory of the
aged;
parents* are the pride of their children.

7 Eloquent words are not fitting for a fool;
even less are lies fitting for a ruler.

8 A bribe is like a lucky charm;
whoever gives one will prosper!

9 Love prospers when a fault is forgiven,
but dwelling on it separates close friends.

10 A single rebuke does more for a person of
understanding
than a hundred lashes on the back of a
fool.

11 Evil people are eager for rebellion,
but they will be severely punished.

12 It is safer to meet a bear robbed of her cubs
than to confront a fool caught in
foolishness.

13 If you repay good with evil,
evil will never leave your house.

14 Starting a quarrel is like opening a
floodgate,
so stop before a dispute breaks out.

15 Acquitting the guilty and condemning the
innocent—
both are detestable to the LORD.

16 It is senseless to pay tuition to educate a fool,
since he has no heart for learning.

17 A friend is always loyal,
and a brother is born to help in time of
need.

18 It's poor judgment to guarantee another
person's debt
or put up security for a friend.

19 Anyone who loves to quarrel loves sin;
anyone who trusts in high walls invites
disaster.

20 The crooked heart will not prosper;
the lying tongue tumbles into trouble.

21 It is painful to be the parent of a fool;
there is no joy for the father of a rebel.

22 A cheerful heart is good medicine,
but a broken spirit saps a person's
strength.

23 The wicked take secret bribes
to pervert the course of justice.

16:33 Hebrew *We may cast lots.* **17:6** Hebrew *fathers.*

---

outworking of justice (v. 11; 22:22–23), with the same expectation being made of the wise. **17:1–28:** The multigenerational value of the family brings satisfaction and appreciation of its various members (v. 6). One of the potent aspects of the book is its hand-me-down nature, from father to son(s), from those times to these. This wisdom needs the mind and cannot be bought (v. 16), and it demands a wholehearted commitment (v. 24). Wisdom is dynamic, ever-changing: a person (Wisdom personi-

24 Sensible people keep their eyes glued on
wisdom,
but a fool's eyes wander to the ends of the
earth.

25 Foolish children* bring grief to their father
and bitterness to the one who gave them
birth.

26 It is wrong to punish the godly for being
good
or to flog leaders for being honest.

27 A truly wise person uses few words;
a person with understanding is even-
tempered.

28 Even fools are thought wise when they keep
silent;
with their mouths shut, they seem
intelligent.

18 1Unfriendly people care only about
themselves;
they lash out at common sense.

2 Fools have no interest in understanding;
they only want to air their own opinions.

3 Doing wrong leads to disgrace,
and scandalous behavior brings
contempt.

4 Wise words are like deep waters;
wisdom flows from the wise like a bubbling
brook.

5 It is not right to acquit the guilty
or deny justice to the innocent.

6 Fools' words get them into constant
quarrels;
they are asking for a beating.

7 The mouths of fools are their ruin;
they trap themselves with their lips.

8 Rumors are dainty morsels
that sink deep into one's heart.

9 A lazy person is as bad as
someone who destroys things.

10 The name of the LORD is a strong fortress;
the godly run to him and are safe.

11 The rich think of their wealth as a strong
defense;
they imagine it to be a high wall of safety.

12 Haughtiness goes before destruction;
humility precedes honor.

13 Spouting off before listening to the facts
is both shameful and foolish.

14 The human spirit can endure a sick body,
but who can bear a crushed spirit?

15 Intelligent people are always ready to learn.
Their ears are open for knowledge.

16 Giving a gift can open doors;
it gives access to important people!

17 The first to speak in court sounds right—
until the cross-examination begins.

18 Flipping a coin* can end arguments;
it settles disputes between powerful
opponents.

19 An offended friend is harder to win back than
a fortified city.
Arguments separate friends like a gate
locked with bars.

20 Wise words satisfy like a good meal;
the right words bring satisfaction.

21 The tongue can bring death or life;
those who love to talk will reap the
consequences.

22 The man who finds a wife finds a treasure,
and he receives favor from the LORD.

23 The poor plead for mercy;
the rich answer with insults.

24 There are "friends" who destroy each other,
but a real friend sticks closer than a
brother.

17:25 Hebrew *A foolish son.* **18:18** Hebrew *Casting lots.*

fied as a female) rather than a text, a skill rather than a dogma. **18:1–24:** In the midst of many unrelated topics, we find an affirmation of a wife as a treasure (v. 22), a crown (12:4), and a prize divinely given (19:14). Far from the "beautiful woman who lacks discretion" of 11:22, the "virtuous and capable wife"

19 [1]Better to be poor and honest
than to be dishonest and a fool.

2 Enthusiasm without knowledge is no good;
haste makes mistakes.

3 People ruin their lives by their own
foolishness
and then are angry at the LORD.

4 Wealth makes many "friends";
poverty drives them all away.

5 A false witness will not go unpunished,
nor will a liar escape.

6 Many seek favors from a ruler;
everyone is the friend of a person who
gives gifts!

7 The relatives of the poor despise them;
how much more will their friends avoid
them!
Though the poor plead with them,
their friends are gone.

8 To acquire wisdom is to love oneself;
people who cherish understanding will
prosper.

9 A false witness will not go unpunished,
and a liar will be destroyed.

10 It isn't right for a fool to live in luxury
or for a slave to rule over princes!

11 Sensible people control their temper;
they earn respect by overlooking
wrongs.

12 The king's anger is like a lion's roar,
but his favor is like dew on the grass.

13 A foolish child* is a calamity to a father;
a quarrelsome wife is as annoying as
constant dripping.

14 Fathers can give their sons an inheritance of
houses and wealth,
but only the LORD can give an
understanding wife.

15 Lazy people sleep soundly,
but idleness leaves them hungry.

16 Keep the commandments and keep your life;
despising them leads to death.

17 If you help the poor, you are lending to the
LORD—
and he will repay you!

18 Discipline your children while there is hope.
Otherwise you will ruin their lives.

19 Hot-tempered people must pay the penalty.
If you rescue them once, you will have to
do it again.

20 Get all the advice and instruction you can,
so you will be wise the rest of your life.

21 You can make many plans,
but the LORD's purpose will prevail.

22 Loyalty makes a person attractive.
It is better to be poor than dishonest.

23 Fear of the LORD leads to life,
bringing security and protection from
harm.

24 Lazy people take food in their hand
but don't even lift it to their mouth.

25 If you punish a mocker, the simpleminded
will learn a lesson;
if you correct the wise, they will be all the
wiser.

26 Children who mistreat their father or chase
away their mother
are an embarrassment and a public
disgrace.

27 If you stop listening to instruction, my child,
you will turn your back on knowledge.

28 A corrupt witness makes a mockery of
justice;
the mouth of the wicked gulps down evil.

19:13 Hebrew *son;* also in 19:27.

is of noble character and commands the respect of all (31:10–31). **19:1–29:** Unlike goods and chattels, an understanding wife is not inherited (cf. v. 14) but is rather a gift from the LORD. Despite the statement about finding a good wife, (18:22), most of the wives mentioned are sources of irritation (19:13; 21:9, 19) and even a means of the LORD's punishment (22:14). The likening of a nagging wife to the annoyance of

29 Punishment is made for mockers,
and the backs of fools are made to be beaten.

20 1Wine produces mockers; alcohol leads to brawls.
Those led astray by drink cannot be wise.

2 The king's fury is like a lion's roar;
to rouse his anger is to risk your life.

3 Avoiding a fight is a mark of honor;
only fools insist on quarreling.

4 Those too lazy to plow in the right season
will have no food at the harvest.

5 Though good advice lies deep within the heart,
a person with understanding will draw it out.

6 Many will say they are loyal friends,
but who can find one who is truly reliable?

7 The godly walk with integrity;
blessed are their children who follow them.

8 When a king sits in judgment, he weighs all the evidence,
distinguishing the bad from the good.

9 Who can say, "I have cleansed my heart;
I am pure and free from sin"?

10 False weights and unequal measures*—
the LORD detests double standards of every kind.

11 Even children are known by the way they act,
whether their conduct is pure, and whether it is right.

12 Ears to hear and eyes to see—
both are gifts from the LORD.

13 If you love sleep, you will end in poverty.
Keep your eyes open, and there will be plenty to eat!

14 The buyer haggles over the price, saying, "It's worthless,"
then brags about getting a bargain!

15 Wise words are more valuable
than much gold and many rubies.

16 Get security from someone who guarantees a stranger's debt.
Get a deposit if he does it for foreigners.*

17 Stolen bread tastes sweet,
but it turns to gravel in the mouth.

18 Plans succeed through good counsel;
don't go to war without wise advice.

19 A gossip goes around telling secrets,
so don't hang around with chatterers.

20 If you insult your father or mother,
your light will be snuffed out in total darkness.

21 An inheritance obtained too early in life
is not a blessing in the end.

22 Don't say, "I will get even for this wrong."
Wait for the LORD to handle the matter.

23 The LORD detests double standards;
he is not pleased by dishonest scales.

24 The LORD directs our steps,
so why try to understand everything along the way?

25 Don't trap yourself by making a rash promise to God
and only later counting the cost.

26 A wise king scatters the wicked like wheat,
then runs his threshing wheel over them.

27 The LORD's light penetrates the human spirit,*
exposing every hidden motive.

20:10 Hebrew *A stone and a stone, an ephah and an ephah.* **20:16** An alternate reading in the Masoretic Text is *for a promiscuous woman.* **20:27** Or *The human spirit is the LORD's light.*

dripping water (19:13) is repeated at 27:15. **20:1–30:** The lives of the righteous have long-term influence morally (v. 7) and practically. The responsibility each has for his or her actions is emphasized as the means by which one's reputation is established (v. 11). The stability of society is something seen as essentially maintained through the family, with a reiteration of the need for parental respect (v. 20; 10:1;

[28] Unfailing love and faithfulness protect the
king;
his throne is made secure through love.

[29] The glory of the young is their strength;
the gray hair of experience is the splendor
of the old.

[30] Physical punishment cleanses away evil;*
such discipline purifies the heart.

21

[1]The king's heart is like a stream of
water directed by the LORD;
he guides it wherever he pleases.

[2] People may be right in their own eyes,
but the LORD examines their heart.

[3] The LORD is more pleased when we do what
is right and just
than when we offer him sacrifices.

[4] Haughty eyes, a proud heart,
and evil actions are all sin.

[5] Good planning and hard work lead to
prosperity,
but hasty shortcuts lead to poverty.

[6] Wealth created by a lying tongue
is a vanishing mist and a deadly trap.*

[7] The violence of the wicked sweeps them away,
because they refuse to do what is just.

[8] The guilty walk a crooked path;
the innocent travel a straight road.

[9] It's better to live alone in the corner of an
attic
than with a quarrelsome wife in a lovely
home.

[10] Evil people desire evil;
their neighbors get no mercy from them.

[11] If you punish a mocker, the simpleminded
become wise;
if you instruct the wise, they will be all the
wiser.

[12] The Righteous One* knows what is going on
in the homes of the wicked;
he will bring disaster on them.

[13] Those who shut their ears to the cries of the
poor
will be ignored in their own time of need.

[14] A secret gift calms anger;
a bribe under the table pacifies fury.

[15] Justice is a joy to the godly,
but it terrifies evildoers.

[16] The person who strays from common sense
will end up in the company of the dead.

[17] Those who love pleasure become poor;
those who love wine and luxury will never
be rich.

[18] The wicked are punished in place of the godly,
and traitors in place of the honest.

[19] It's better to live alone in the desert
than with a quarrelsome, complaining wife.

[20] The wise have wealth and luxury,
but fools spend whatever they get.

[21] Whoever pursues righteousness and unfailing
love
will find life, righteousness, and honor.

[22] The wise conquer the city of the strong
and level the fortress in which they trust.

[23] Watch your tongue and keep your mouth
shut,
and you will stay out of trouble.

[24] Mockers are proud and haughty;
they act with boundless arrogance.

[25] Despite their desires, the lazy will come to ruin,
for their hands refuse to work.

20:30 The meaning of the Hebrew is uncertain. **21:6** As in Greek version; Hebrew reads *mist for those who seek death.* **21:12** Or *The righteous man.*

13:1; 15:20) generally for the well-being of the child but also stated as an nonnegotiable principle (v. 20). **21:1–31:** The sages extol the righteous, whose virtues are multiple. Portrayed as being those whose thoughts are just (v. 1; 12:5) and who rejoice in seeing justice done (v. 15), these people stand firmly rooted and secure, a blessing to the society in which they live. They are generous (vv. 25–26), upright, and able to plan carefully for the future (v. 29). The theme of living with a difficult spouse recurs twice

[26] Some people are always greedy for more,
but the godly love to give!

[27] The sacrifice of an evil person is detestable,
especially when it is offered with wrong motives.

[28] A false witness will be cut off,
but a credible witness will be allowed to speak.

[29] The wicked bluff their way through,
but the virtuous think before they act.

[30] No human wisdom or understanding or plan
can stand against the LORD.

[31] The horse is prepared for the day of battle,
but the victory belongs to the LORD.

22 [1]Choose a good reputation over great riches;
being held in high esteem is better than silver or gold.

[2] The rich and poor have this in common:
The LORD made them both.

[3] A prudent person foresees danger and takes precautions.
The simpleton goes blindly on and suffers the consequences.

[4] True humility and fear of the LORD
lead to riches, honor, and long life.

[5] Corrupt people walk a thorny, treacherous road;
whoever values life will avoid it.

[6] Direct your children onto the right path,
and when they are older, they will not leave it.

[7] Just as the rich rule the poor,
so the borrower is servant to the lender.

[8] Those who plant injustice will harvest disaster,
and their reign of terror will come to an end.*

[9] Blessed are those who are generous,
because they feed the poor.

[10] Throw out the mocker, and fighting goes, too.
Quarrels and insults will disappear.

[11] Whoever loves a pure heart and gracious speech
will have the king as a friend.

[12] The LORD preserves those with knowledge,
but he ruins the plans of the treacherous.

[13] The lazy person claims, "There's a lion out there!
If I go outside, I might be killed!"

[14] The mouth of an immoral woman is a dangerous trap;
those who make the LORD angry will fall into it.

[15] A youngster's heart is filled with foolishness,
but physical discipline will drive it far away.

[16] A person who gets ahead by oppressing the poor
or by showering gifts on the rich will end in poverty.

Sayings of the Wise

[17] Listen to the words of the wise;
apply your heart to my instruction.
[18] For it is good to keep these sayings in your heart
and always ready on your lips.
[19] I am teaching you today—yes, you—
so you will trust in the LORD.
[20] I have written thirty sayings* for you,
filled with advice and knowledge.
[21] In this way, you may know the truth

22:8 The Greek version includes an additional proverb: *God blesses a man who gives cheerfully, / but his worthless deeds will come to an end.* Compare 2 Cor 9:7. **22:20** Or *excellent sayings;* the meaning of the Hebrew is uncertain.

(vv. 9, 19). Perhaps the answer lies in the treatment suggested in verse 21. **22:1–29:** Again the immoral woman appears with her destructive power (v. 14). Women's role in society is portrayed in fairly realistic terms: capable teachers in the home, appreciated wives, but with their weaknesses and foibles just as throughout all generations. These portraits are presented generally with a view to the effect and influence, positive yet mostly negative, that diverse types of women have on men (never the reverse). It is disconcerting only until one realizes that this section depends on the contrast of gender in order to com-

and take an accurate report to those who
sent you.

22 Don't rob the poor just because you can,
or exploit the needy in court.
23 For the LORD is their defender.
He will ruin anyone who ruins them.

24 Don't befriend angry people
or associate with hot-tempered people,
25 or you will learn to be like them
and endanger your soul.

26 Don't agree to guarantee another person's debt
or put up security for someone else.
27 If you can't pay it,
even your bed will be snatched from under
you.

28 Don't cheat your neighbor by moving the
ancient boundary markers
set up by previous generations.

29 Do you see any truly competent workers?
They will serve kings
rather than working for ordinary people.

23 1While dining with a ruler,
pay attention to what is put
before you.
2 If you are a big eater,
put a knife to your throat;
3 don't desire all the delicacies,
for he might be trying to trick you.

4 Don't wear yourself out trying to get rich.
Be wise enough to know when to quit.
5 In the blink of an eye wealth disappears,
for it will sprout wings
and fly away like an eagle.

6 Don't eat with people who are stingy;
don't desire their delicacies.
7 They are always thinking about how much it
costs.*
"Eat and drink," they say, but they don't
mean it.
8 You will throw up what little you've eaten,
and your compliments will be wasted.

9 Don't waste your breath on fools,
for they will despise the wisest advice.

10 Don't cheat your neighbor by moving the
ancient boundary markers;
don't take the land of defenseless orphans.
11 For their Redeemer* is strong;
he himself will bring their charges against
you.

12 Commit yourself to instruction;
listen carefully to words of knowledge.

13 Don't fail to discipline your children.
They won't die if you spank them.
14 Physical discipline
may well save them from death.*

15 My child,* if your heart is wise,
my own heart will rejoice!
16 Everything in me will celebrate
when you speak what is right.

17 Don't envy sinners,
but always continue to fear the LORD.
18 You will be rewarded for this;
your hope will not be disappointed.

19 My child, listen and be wise:
Keep your heart on the right course.
20 Do not carouse with drunkards
or feast with gluttons,

23:7 The meaning of the Hebrew is uncertain. **23:11** Or *redeemer.* **23:14** Hebrew *from Sheol.* **23:15** Hebrew *My son;* also in 23:19.

municate its message. The key is possibly found in the fact that the female is used principally to portray a source of influence and an occasional example. **24–25:** These verses constitute a call to zero tolerance for violent behavior (cf. 3:31; 24:1–2). **23:1–35:** There is recurrent emphasis on the need for parental respect and the pleasure parents experience when their children exhibit wisdom (vv. 22–25). The reference to corporal punishment (vv. 13–14), is best understood metaphorically. The Hebrew word for "rod," *shebet*, is used a metaphor in the biblical texts (Ps 23:4; Isa 10:15; 2 Sam 7:14; Mic 5:1), and appears in connection with the training of children (Prov 13:24; 22:15; 23:13–14; 29:15). It is frequently a metaphor for correction, (Prov 10:13; 13:24; 22:15; Job 9:34; 21:9; 37:13; Isa 10:5, 24; 30:31), and in Isaiah 11:4 refers specifically to verbal correction. Significantly, in Leviticus 27:32 and Psalm 23:4 *shebet* denotes the shepherd's crook, useful to hook around the leg of an animal in order to pull it back from danger. The *shebet* was used as a means of counting sheep (Lev 27:32) and appears in a figurative sense in Ezekiel 20:37 as a tool to guide Israel back to a covenant relationship with God. The rod

[21] for they are on their way to poverty,
and too much sleep clothes them in rags.
[22] Listen to your father, who gave you life,
and don't despise your mother when she is old.
[23] Get the truth and never sell it;
also get wisdom, discipline, and good judgment.
[24] The father of godly children has cause for joy.
What a pleasure to have children who are wise.*
[25] So give your father and mother joy!
May she who gave you birth be happy.
[26] O my son, give me your heart.
May your eyes take delight in following my ways.
[27] A prostitute is a dangerous trap;
a promiscuous woman is as dangerous as falling into a narrow well.
[28] She hides and waits like a robber,
eager to make more men unfaithful.

[29] Who has anguish? Who has sorrow?
Who is always fighting? Who is always complaining?
Who has unnecessary bruises? Who has bloodshot eyes?
[30] It is the one who spends long hours in the taverns,
trying out new drinks.
[31] Don't gaze at the wine, seeing how red it is,
how it sparkles in the cup, how smoothly it goes down.
[32] For in the end it bites like a poisonous snake;
it stings like a viper.
[33] You will see hallucinations,
and you will say crazy things.
[34] You will stagger like a sailor tossed at sea,
clinging to a swaying mast.
[35] And you will say, "They hit me, but I didn't feel it.
I didn't even know it when they beat me up.
When will I wake up
so I can look for another drink?"

24 [1] Don't envy evil people
or desire their company.
[2] For their hearts plot violence,
and their words always stir up trouble.
[3] A house is built by wisdom
and becomes strong through good sense.
[4] Through knowledge its rooms are filled
with all sorts of precious riches and valuables.

[5] The wise are mightier than the strong,*
and those with knowledge grow stronger and stronger.
[6] So don't go to war without wise guidance;
victory depends on having many advisers.

[7] Wisdom is too lofty for fools.
Among leaders at the city gate, they have nothing to say.

[8] A person who plans evil
will get a reputation as a troublemaker.
[9] The schemes of a fool are sinful;
everyone detests a mocker.

[10] If you fail under pressure,
your strength is too small.

[11] Rescue those who are unjustly sentenced to die;
save them as they stagger to their death.
[12] Don't excuse yourself by saying, "Look, we didn't know."
For God understands all hearts, and he sees you.
He who guards your soul knows you knew.
He will repay all people as their actions deserve.

[13] My child,* eat honey, for it is good,
and the honeycomb is sweet to the taste.
[14] In the same way, wisdom is sweet to your soul.
If you find it, you will have a bright future,
and your hopes will not be cut short.

[15] Don't wait in ambush at the home of the godly,
and don't raid the house where the godly live.
[16] The godly may trip seven times, but they will get up again.

23:24 Hebrew *to have a wise son.* **24:5** As in Greek version; Hebrew reads *A wise man is strength.* **24:13** Hebrew *My son;* also in 24:21.

could be used to protect the sheep (Ps 23:4; Mic 7:14) or to keep them headed on the right path. Thus, the use of the rod should not be used to justify child abuse. **24:1–34:** Verses 30–34 function as a vignette exemplifying some of the components of acting wisely: observing what happens all around, be-

But one disaster is enough to overthrow
the wicked.

17 Don't rejoice when your enemies fall;
don't be happy when they stumble.
18 For the LORD will be displeased with you
and will turn his anger away from them.

19 Don't fret because of evildoers;
don't envy the wicked.
20 For evil people have no future;
the light of the wicked will be snuffed out.

21 My child, fear the LORD and the king.
Don't associate with rebels,
22 for disaster will hit them suddenly.
Who knows what punishment will come
from the LORD and the king?

More Sayings of the Wise

23 Here are some further sayings of the wise:

It is wrong to show favoritism when passing
judgment.
24 A judge who says to the wicked, "You are
innocent,"
will be cursed by many people and
denounced by the nations.
25 But it will go well for those who convict the
guilty;
rich blessings will be showered on them.

26 An honest answer
is like a kiss of friendship.

27 Do your planning and prepare your fields
before building your house.

28 Don't testify against your neighbors without
cause;
don't lie about them.
29 And don't say, "Now I can pay them back for
what they've done to me!
I'll get even with them!"

30 I walked by the field of a lazy person,
the vineyard of one with no common sense.
31 I saw that it was overgrown with nettles.
It was covered with weeds,
and its walls were broken down.
32 Then, as I looked and thought about it,
I learned this lesson:
33 A little extra sleep, a little more slumber,
a little folding of the hands to rest—
34 then poverty will pounce on you like a bandit;
scarcity will attack you like an armed
robber.

More Proverbs of Solomon

25 These are more proverbs of Solomon, collected by the advisers of King Hezekiah of Judah.

2 It is God's privilege to conceal things
and the king's privilege to discover them.

3 No one can comprehend the height of heaven,
the depth of the earth,
or all that goes on in the king's mind!

4 Remove the impurities from silver,
and the sterling will be ready for the
silversmith.
5 Remove the wicked from the king's court,
and his reign will be made secure by
justice.

6 Don't demand an audience with the king
or push for a place among the great.
7 It's better to wait for an invitation to the head
table
than to be sent away in public disgrace.

Just because you've seen something,
8 don't be in a hurry to go to court.
For what will you do in the end
if your neighbor deals you a shameful
defeat?

9 When arguing with your neighbor,
don't betray another person's secret.
10 Others may accuse you of gossip,
and you will never regain your good
reputation.

11 Timely advice is lovely,
like golden apples in a silver basket.

12 To one who listens, valid criticism
is like a gold earring or other gold jewelry.

13 Trustworthy messengers refresh like snow in
summer.
They revive the spirit of their employer.

---

ing aware of one's surroundings, focusing on an element that attracts attention for some reason, considering, and understanding. **25:1–28:** Rulers are often singled out as a result of their particular responsibilities. Issues of justice arise when considering the vulnerable, and the need to exercise justice

14 A person who promises a gift but doesn't give it
is like clouds and wind that bring no rain.

15 Patience can persuade a prince,
and soft speech can break bones.

16 Do you like honey?
Don't eat too much, or it will make you sick!

17 Don't visit your neighbors too often,
or you will wear out your welcome.

18 Telling lies about others
is as harmful as hitting them with an ax,
wounding them with a sword,
or shooting them with a sharp arrow.

19 Putting confidence in an unreliable person in times of trouble
is like chewing with a broken tooth or walking on a lame foot.

20 Singing cheerful songs to a person with a heavy heart
is like taking someone's coat in cold weather
or pouring vinegar in a wound.*

21 If your enemies are hungry, give them food to eat.
If they are thirsty, give them water to drink.
22 You will heap burning coals of shame on their heads,
and the LORD will reward you.

23 As surely as a north wind brings rain,
so a gossiping tongue causes anger!

24 It's better to live alone in the corner of an attic
than with a quarrelsome wife in a lovely home.

25 Good news from far away
is like cold water to the thirsty.

26 If the godly give in to the wicked,
it's like polluting a fountain or muddying a spring.

27 It's not good to eat too much honey,
and it's not good to seek honors for yourself.

28 A person without self-control
is like a city with broken-down walls.

26 [1]Honor is no more associated with fools
than snow with summer or rain with harvest.

2 Like a fluttering sparrow or a darting swallow,
an undeserved curse will not land on its intended victim.

3 Guide a horse with a whip, a donkey with a bridle,
and a fool with a rod to his back!

4 Don't answer the foolish arguments of fools,
or you will become as foolish as they are.

5 Be sure to answer the foolish arguments of fools,
or they will become wise in their own estimation.

6 Trusting a fool to convey a message
is like cutting off one's feet or drinking poison!

7 A proverb in the mouth of a fool
is as useless as a paralyzed leg.

8 Honoring a fool
is as foolish as tying a stone to a slingshot.

9 A proverb in the mouth of a fool
is like a thorny branch brandished by a drunk.

10 An employer who hires a fool or a bystander
is like an archer who shoots at random.

11 As a dog returns to its vomit,
so a fool repeats his foolishness.

12 There is more hope for fools
than for people who think they are wise.

25:20 As in Greek version; Hebrew reads *pouring vinegar on soda.*

---

is another theme omnipresent throughout the book. Discretion in speech is applauded, as is the ability to hold one's tongue (vv. 2–7). Difficulties of life with an unpleasant spouse are repeated in verse 24 (see 21:9,19). **26:1–28:** The sluggard is lethargic, even when his personal safety and well-being are con-

13 The lazy person claims, "There's a lion on the road!
Yes, I'm sure there's a lion out there!"

14 As a door swings back and forth on its hinges,
so the lazy person turns over in bed.

15 Lazy people take food in their hand
but don't even lift it to their mouth.

16 Lazy people consider themselves smarter
than seven wise counselors.

17 Interfering in someone else's argument
is as foolish as yanking a dog's ears.

18 Just as damaging
as a madman shooting a deadly weapon
19 is someone who lies to a friend
and then says, "I was only joking."

20 Fire goes out without wood,
and quarrels disappear when gossip stops.

21 A quarrelsome person starts fights
as easily as hot embers light charcoal or fire lights wood.

22 Rumors are dainty morsels
that sink deep into one's heart.

23 Smooth* words may hide a wicked heart,
just as a pretty glaze covers a clay pot.

24 People may cover their hatred with pleasant words,
but they're deceiving you.
25 They pretend to be kind, but don't believe them.
Their hearts are full of many evils.*
26 While their hatred may be concealed by trickery,
their wrongdoing will be exposed in public.

27 If you set a trap for others,
you will get caught in it yourself.
If you roll a boulder down on others,
it will crush you instead.

28 A lying tongue hates its victims,
and flattering words cause ruin.

27

1 Don't brag about tomorrow,
since you don't know what the day will bring.

2 Let someone else praise you, not your own mouth—
a stranger, not your own lips.

3 A stone is heavy and sand is weighty,
but the resentment caused by a fool is even heavier.

4 Anger is cruel, and wrath is like a flood,
but jealousy is even more dangerous.

5 An open rebuke
is better than hidden love!

6 Wounds from a sincere friend
are better than many kisses from an enemy.

7 A person who is full refuses honey,
but even bitter food tastes sweet to the hungry.

8 A person who strays from home
is like a bird that strays from its nest.

9 The heartfelt counsel of a friend
is as sweet as perfume and incense.

10 Never abandon a friend—
either yours or your father's.
When disaster strikes, you won't have to ask your brother for assistance.
It's better to go to a neighbor than to a brother who lives far away.

11 Be wise, my child,* and make my heart glad.
Then I will be able to answer my critics.

12 A prudent person foresees danger and takes precautions.
The simpleton goes blindly on and suffers the consequences.

26:23 As in Greek version; Hebrew reads *Burning.*
26:25 Hebrew *seven evils.* **27:11** Hebrew *my son.*

---

cerned (vv. 13–16), always wanting but never getting (13:4) and therefore endangering his life (21:25). **27:1–27:** Specific topics include treatment of neighbors, who must be respected (14:21), whose good nature must not be abused (27:14; 25:17), and whose friendship is often more worthwhile than that of a close relative (27:10). But their presence can all too easily tempt one to envy, anger, and wrath (v. 4).

13 Get security from someone who guarantees a stranger's debt.
Get a deposit if he does it for foreigners.*

14 A loud and cheerful greeting early in the morning
will be taken as a curse!

15 A quarrelsome wife is as annoying
as constant dripping on a rainy day.
16 Stopping her complaints is like trying to stop the wind
or trying to hold something with greased hands.

17 As iron sharpens iron,
so a friend sharpens a friend.
18 As workers who tend a fig tree are allowed to eat the fruit,
so workers who protect their employer's interests will be rewarded.

19 As a face is reflected in water,
so the heart reflects the real person.

20 Just as Death and Destruction* are never satisfied,
so human desire is never satisfied.

21 Fire tests the purity of silver and gold,
but a person is tested by being praised.*

22 You cannot separate fools from their foolishness,
even though you grind them like grain with mortar and pestle.

23 Know the state of your flocks,
and put your heart into caring for your herds,
24 for riches don't last forever,
and the crown might not be passed to the next generation.
25 After the hay is harvested and the new crop appears
and the mountain grasses are gathered in,
26 your sheep will provide wool for clothing,
and your goats will provide the price of a field.
27 And you will have enough goats' milk for yourself,
your family, and your servant girls.

28

1 The wicked run away when no one is chasing them,
but the godly are as bold as lions.

2 When there is moral rot within a nation, its government topples easily.
But wise and knowledgeable leaders bring stability.

3 A poor person who oppresses the poor
is like a pounding rain that destroys the crops.

4 To reject the law is to praise the wicked;
to obey the law is to fight them.

5 Evil people don't understand justice,
but those who follow the LORD understand completely.

6 Better to be poor and honest
than to be dishonest and rich.

7 Young people who obey the law are wise;
those with wild friends bring shame to their parents.*

8 Income from charging high interest rates
will end up in the pocket of someone who is kind to the poor.

9 God detests the prayers
of a person who ignores the law.

10 Those who lead good people along an evil path
will fall into their own trap,
but the honest will inherit good things.

11 Rich people may think they are wise,
but a poor person with discernment can see right through them.

12 When the godly succeed, everyone is glad.
When the wicked take charge, people go into hiding.

13 People who conceal their sins will not prosper,
but if they confess and turn from them, they will receive mercy.

27:13 As in Greek and Latin versions (see also 20:16); Hebrew reads *for a promiscuous woman.* **27:20** Hebrew *Sheol and Abaddon.* **27:21** Or *by flattery.* **28:7** Hebrew *their father.*

Verse 12, recurring also at 22:3, can be utilized effectively by those encouraging the development of safety plans for victims of abuse. **28:1–28:** Compare verse 24 with Jesus' statement in Mark 7:11–13.

14 Blessed are those who fear to do wrong,*
but the stubborn are headed for serious trouble.

15 A wicked ruler is as dangerous to the poor
as a roaring lion or an attacking bear.

16 A ruler with no understanding will oppress his people,
but one who hates corruption will have a long life.

17 A murderer's tormented conscience will drive him into the grave.
Don't protect him!

18 The blameless will be rescued from harm,
but the crooked will be suddenly destroyed.

19 A hard worker has plenty of food,
but a person who chases fantasies ends up in poverty.

20 The trustworthy person will get a rich reward,
but a person who wants quick riches will get into trouble.

21 Showing partiality is never good,
yet some will do wrong for a mere piece of bread.

22 Greedy people try to get rich quick
but don't realize they're headed for poverty.

23 In the end, people appreciate honest criticism
far more than flattery.

24 Anyone who steals from his father and mother
and says, "What's wrong with that?"
is no better than a murderer.

25 Greed causes fighting;
trusting the LORD leads to prosperity.

26 Those who trust their own insight are foolish,
but anyone who walks in wisdom is safe.

27 Whoever gives to the poor will lack nothing,
but those who close their eyes to poverty will be cursed.

28 When the wicked take charge, people go into hiding.
When the wicked meet disaster, the godly flourish.

29

1 Whoever stubbornly refuses to accept criticism
will suddenly be destroyed beyond recovery.

2 When the godly are in authority, the people rejoice.
But when the wicked are in power, they groan.

3 The man who loves wisdom brings joy to his father,
but if he hangs around with prostitutes, his wealth is wasted.

4 A just king gives stability to his nation,
but one who demands bribes destroys it.

5 To flatter friends
is to lay a trap for their feet.

6 Evil people are trapped by sin,
but the righteous escape, shouting for joy.

7 The godly care about the rights of the poor;
the wicked don't care at all.

8 Mockers can get a whole town agitated,
but the wise will calm anger.

9 If a wise person takes a fool to court,
there will be ranting and ridicule but no satisfaction.

10 The bloodthirsty hate blameless people,
but the upright seek to help them.*

11 Fools vent their anger,
but the wise quietly hold it back.

12 If a ruler pays attention to liars,
all his advisers will be wicked.

28:14 Or *those who fear the LORD;* Hebrew reads *those who fear.* **29:10** Or *The bloodthirsty hate blameless people, / and they seek to kill the upright;* Hebrew reads *The bloodthirsty hate blameless people; / as for the upright, they seek their life.*

29:1–27: The first source of instruction in wisdom must be that of the child's mother (v. 15). While reproach for lack of training falls upon her, well-disciplined children are a source of great satisfaction.

13 The poor and the oppressor have this in
common—
the LORD gives sight to the eyes of both.

14 If a king judges the poor fairly,
his throne will last forever.

15 To discipline a child produces wisdom,
but a mother is disgraced by an
undisciplined child.

16 When the wicked are in authority, sin
flourishes,
but the godly will live to see their
downfall.

17 Discipline your children, and they will give
you peace of mind
and will make your heart glad.

18 When people do not accept divine guidance,
they run wild.
But whoever obeys the law is joyful.

19 Words alone will not discipline a servant;
the words may be understood, but they are
not heeded.

20 There is more hope for a fool
than for someone who speaks without
thinking.

21 A servant pampered from childhood
will become a rebel.

22 An angry person starts fights;
a hot-tempered person commits all kinds of
sin.

23 Pride ends in humiliation,
while humility brings honor.

24 If you assist a thief, you only hurt
yourself.
You are sworn to tell the truth, but you
dare not testify.

25 Fearing people is a dangerous trap,
but trusting the LORD means safety.

26 Many seek the ruler's favor,
but justice comes from the LORD.

27 The righteous despise the unjust;
the wicked despise the godly.

The Sayings of Agur

30 The sayings of Agur son of Jakeh
contain this message.*

I am weary, O God;
I am weary and worn out, O God.*
2 I am too stupid to be human,
and I lack common sense.
3 I have not mastered human wisdom,
nor do I know the Holy One.

4 Who but God goes up to heaven and comes
back down?
Who holds the wind in his fists?
Who wraps up the oceans in his cloak?
Who has created the whole wide world?
What is his name—and his son's name?
Tell me if you know!

5 Every word of God proves true.
He is a shield to all who come to him for
protection.
6 Do not add to his words,
or he may rebuke you and expose you as a
liar.

7 O God, I beg two favors from you;
let me have them before I die.
8 First, help me never to tell a lie.
Second, give me neither poverty nor
riches!
Give me just enough to satisfy my needs.
9 For if I grow rich, I may deny you and say,
"Who is the LORD?"
And if I am too poor, I may steal and thus
insult God's holy name.

10 Never slander a worker to the employer,
or the person will curse you, and you will
pay for it.

11 Some people curse their father
and do not thank their mother.
12 They are pure in their own eyes,
but they are filthy and unwashed.

30:1a Or *son of Jakeh from Massa;* or *son of Jakeh, an oracle.*
30:1b The Hebrew can also be translated *The man declares this to Ithiel, / to Ithiel and to Ucal.*

30:1–33 The Truth of God's Words

The change of authorship not only signals a further change of style but also introduces the only occasion in the book in which self-confessed lack of wisdom is bemoaned (v. 1).

13 They look proudly around,
casting disdainful glances.
14 They have teeth like swords
and fangs like knives.
They devour the poor from the earth
and the needy from among humanity.

15 The leech has two suckers
that cry out, "More, more!"*

There are three things that are never
satisfied—
no, four that never say, "Enough!":
16 the grave,*
the barren womb,
the thirsty desert,
the blazing fire.

17 The eye that mocks a father
and despises a mother's instructions
will be plucked out by ravens of the valley
and eaten by vultures.

18 There are three things that amaze me—
no, four things that I don't understand:
19 how an eagle glides through the sky,
how a snake slithers on a rock,
how a ship navigates the ocean,
how a man loves a woman.

20 An adulterous woman consumes a man,
then wipes her mouth and says, "What's
wrong with that?"

21 There are three things that make the earth
tremble—
no, four it cannot endure:
22 a slave who becomes a king,
an overbearing fool who prospers,
23 a bitter woman who finally gets a
husband,
a servant girl who supplants her mistress.

24 There are four things on earth that are small
but unusually wise:
25 Ants—they aren't strong,
but they store up food all summer.
26 Hyraxes*—they aren't powerful,
but they make their homes among the
rocks.
27 Locusts—they have no king,
but they march in formation.
28 Lizards—they are easy to catch,
but they are found even in kings' palaces.

29 There are three things that walk with stately
stride—
no, four that strut about:
30 the lion, king of animals, who won't turn
aside for anything,
31 the strutting rooster,
the male goat,
a king as he leads his army.

32 If you have been a fool by being proud or
plotting evil,
cover your mouth in shame.

33 As the beating of cream yields butter
and striking the nose causes bleeding,
so stirring up anger causes quarrels.

The Sayings of King Lemuel

31 The sayings of King Lemuel contain this message,* which his mother taught him.

2 O my son, O son of my womb,
O son of my vows,
3 do not waste your strength on women,
on those who ruin kings.

30:15 Hebrew *two daughters who cry out, "Give, give!"* **30:16** Hebrew *Sheol.* **30:26** Or *Coneys,* or *Rock badgers.* **31:1** Or *of Lemuel, king of Massa;* or *of King Lemuel, an oracle.*

15–31: The numerical sayings generally follow a pattern in which the last of the cited examples provides the climax and often its real raison d'être. The leech's two daughters are thought to be the two suckers found at the head and tail of the leech. **18–19:** The relative unattractiveness of these scenarios is contrasted by instances of fulfillment and satisfaction in which each plays its ordained role. In so doing, a mysterious yet beautiful liberty is exercised that defies comprehension and provokes wonder and awe. **20:** The adulterous woman is then presented as one who demonstrates an illegitimate fulfillment, satisfying her hunger yet becoming prisoner of a need to defend herself from her conscience, and thus unable to fly free. **21:** The earth's trembling may reflect fear of the consequences at the hand of ineptitude or revenge but equally affirms the dignity of each person regardless of status—a dignity lost should the bearer find himself or herself out of one's depth or making use of an inappropriate resource.

31:1–30 A Final Portrait of Wisdom

The last chapter of this book is divided into two separate sections (vv. 1–9, 10–31). Of immediate note is the heavy female emphasis throughout. Lemuel's

The Wise Woman, the Foolish Woman, and the Righteous Woman

The book of Proverbs offers a kaleidoscope of womanly images. A "mother's instruction" is offered in counterpoint to a "father's" correction (1:8; cf. 6:20; 31). Wisdom, allegorized in the majestic feminine, prophetically confronts society. Wisdom is to be attended to as the source of understanding the "knowledge of God" (2:5), as well as the way to long life, riches, and honor.

The writer does not see Wisdom as one with God but rather as an attribute of God and, metaphorically, as the agency of divine action in creation. Wisdom is a metaphoric figure akin to allegorized attributes of God in Psalm 85:10, which medieval thinkers rendered as the Four Daughters of God—love, faithfulness, righteousness, and peace.

Proverbs presents three types of woman: the wise woman, the foolish woman, and the righteous woman. Examples of each and discussions about them are to be found throughout the Bible. Allegorized or personified Wisdom also occurs in Job 28, suggesting it to be a very ancient concept. A number of wise women are described in the Old Testament, including Tamar (Gen 38), Abigail (1 Sam 25), and Esther.

Wise women emerge from within the New Testament as well. Priscilla, with her husband, Aquila, teaches and disciples new converts at Ephesus and Rome (Acts 18:18–26; 1 Cor 16:19; Rom 16:3). Eunice and Lois teach Timothy the Scriptures (2 Tim 1:5; cf. 3:15). Phoebe is commended as "a deacon in the church" (Rom 16:1).

But as there are examples of wise and righteous women, so also are there examples of unsound, faithless, and dangerous women—or of the dangers of unsoundness and faithlessness characterized or allegorized in feminine form. The preacher of Ecclesiastes complains of the woman whose "passion is a snare" (Eccl 7:26). Delilah, who betrays Samson to the Philistines (Judg 16), is not only a person but also a paradigm. When Israel turns away from God's wisdom, the nation becomes the faithless wife portrayed in Proverbs, and God becomes the betrayed husband.

Biblical allegorical images of the wise, foolish, and righteous woman are glimpsed again in Revelation. The church or perhaps the nation of Israel becomes the childbearing mother who is under supernatural protection (Rev 12). The world system of commerce is portrayed as Babylon, the "great whore" who defies God and his rule (Rev 17; cf. Isa 13—21). The new Jerusalem is seen as a bride wearing "pure white linen" with the explanation that the linen represents "the good deeds of God's holy people" (Rev 19:8).

4 It is not for kings, O Lemuel, to guzzle wine.
Rulers should not crave alcohol.
5 For if they drink, they may forget the law
and not give justice to the oppressed.
6 Alcohol is for the dying,
and wine for those in bitter distress.
7 Let them drink to forget their poverty
and remember their troubles no more.

8 Speak up for those who cannot speak for themselves;
ensure justice for those being crushed.
9 Yes, speak up for the poor and helpless,
and see that they get justice.

A Wife of Noble Character

10* Who can find a virtuous and capable wife?
She is more precious than rubies.
11 Her husband can trust her,
and she will greatly enrich his life.

31:10 Verses 10-31 comprise a Hebrew acrostic poem; each verse begins with a successive letter of the Hebrew alphabet.

mother (possibly the queen or a queen mother; see v. 4) addresses her son in verses 1–9. **10–31:** The final twenty-one verses are in the form of an acrostic poem in which each verse begins with a successive letter of the Hebrew alphabet. An omnicompetent woman is introduced who has no blemish other than her perceived perfection. She provides food and clothing for the family, she oversees the servants, she buys and sells and conducts business, she rolls up her sleeves and works. She even has time and energy to look to the needs of the poor, offer charity, and teach. She makes independent decisions (v. 16), evaluates her own performance (v. 18), and exercises sound judgment (v. 26). She is active in both the public and the private spheres. The husband, meanwhile, confident in his wife's abilities and in her desire to do him good (vv. 11–12), devotes himself to civic causes (v. 23), taking his place as judge at

12 She brings him good, not harm,
all the days of her life.

13 She finds wool and flax
and busily spins it.
14 She is like a merchant's ship,
bringing her food from afar.
15 She gets up before dawn to prepare breakfast
for her household
and plan the day's work for her servant girls.

16 She goes to inspect a field and buys it;
with her earnings she plants a vineyard.
17 She is energetic and strong,
a hard worker.
18 She makes sure her dealings are profitable;
her lamp burns late into the night.

19 Her hands are busy spinning thread,
her fingers twisting fiber.
20 She extends a helping hand to the poor
and opens her arms to the needy.
21 She has no fear of winter for her household,
for everyone has warm* clothes.

22 She makes her own bedspreads.
She dresses in fine linen and purple gowns.
23 Her husband is well known at the city gates,
where he sits with the other civic leaders.
24 She makes belted linen garments
and sashes to sell to the merchants.
25 She is clothed with strength and dignity,
and she laughs without fear of the future.
26 When she speaks, her words are wise,
and she gives instructions with kindness.
27 She carefully watches everything in her
household
and suffers nothing from laziness.

28 Her children stand and bless her.
Her husband praises her:
29 "There are many virtuous and capable
women in the world,
but you surpass them all!"

30 Charm is deceptive, and beauty does not
last;
but a woman who fears the LORD will be
greatly praised.
31 Reward her for all she has done.
Let her deeds publicly declare her praise.

31:21 As in Greek and Latin versions; Hebrew reads *scarlet.*

the city gate among those who administer justice (cf. Gen 19:1; 23:10; Ruth 4:1–12). The passage reflects a remarkable perception of the value and dignity in women's occupations. The housewifely skills—not the most recent technology—sustain and nurture human life. Women's abilities in the marketplace and in real estate are no less admired. The woman herself takes pride and pleasure in her excellent work (v. 13). Both husband and wife exhibit qualities of wisdom and contribute to the good order of society. Their children grow to mature adulthood, standing on their own two feet and expressing their own opinions. The passage clearly indicates that the husband appreciates his good fortune, in no way sees himself diminished, and is thus able to give all credit to his wife (vv. 28–29). It seems likely therefore that this chapter is not intended to be exemplary or exhortatory. Scholars now recognize the ways in which this female paradigm of virtue mirrors aspects of Wisdom's person and message. Wisdom's parting invitation (9:4–6) was to enter her house and eat and drink with her; this final chapter can be seen as a phenomenological portrayal of her overall message set in the now-established household of wisdom.

ECCLESIASTES

INTRODUCTION

Women who investigate the biblical text eventually encounter the alternately disturbing and reassuring realities expressed in Ecclesiastes. While scholars differ as to whether these views are a comfortable fit with orthodoxy and debate how to label and understand the various attitudes expressed, Ecclesiastes unquestionably speaks to the frustrating and tedious nature of much of life, the anguish over the brevity of life and finality of death, and the pain of incessant injustice.

Recurring expressions and the structure of the book contribute to its profound message to women. Foremost among the expressions is the phrase that frames the message (1:2 and 12:8) and is the hallmark of Ecclesiastes: "Vanity of vanities! All is vanity" (NRSV) or "Everything is meaningless! . . . Completely meaningless!" (NLT). It is significant to note that the Hebrew word *hebel*, which is translated "vanity" or "meaningless," means literally "vapor" or "breath." In other words, it refers to the transitory nature of all of existence and is an appropriate metaphor for life. This is a sobering thought, but it does not necessarily follow that everything is meaningless. Instead, the expression is frequently used in the superlative form, indicating ultimate pain and frustration at the temporary and elusive nature of all aspects of life that are so profoundly important.

Several additional phrases maintain a high profile. The first is "I observed" (1:14); what follows is a sensitive perception of the way things are. Second, most of the book speaks from the perspective of "under the sun" (1:9, 14). The writer observed the complex and often perverse functioning of the universe as a result of the Fall (cf. Rom 8:20–21). Thus the text speaks frankly in terms that sound pessimistic, wounded, even fatalistic. A third phrase is "chasing the wind" (1:17; 2:11, 26), an apt metaphor that is used in conjunction with *hebel* to describe an enterprise that yields no tangible results. Finally, the author repeatedly returned to the refrain "to enjoy food and drink and to find satisfaction in work" (2:24; 5:18), urging the immediate appreciation and enjoyment of what is present and known, wholesome advice in light of the uncertainty of all that is yet to come.

From the standpoint of structure, there is a constant counterpoint in Ecclesiastes between the presentation of a transitory and pain-ridden life, and life that acknowledges the divine presence. The former is more prominent because that is the majority of each person's experience. Nevertheless, there are those fleeting moments when the presence and participation of God in the world is profoundly evident. This literary structure helps to convey the message that is also clearly articulated in words.

Additionally there is a slow evolution of thought throughout the book from overwhelmingly negative attitudes at the outset to a more balanced outlook, even to the point of including two sets of tart, down-to-earth proverbs (7:1–14; 10:1—11:6). After the midpoint of 5:1–7, which addresses intentional approach to God, there is a noticeable increase in the expressed perception that life is not only transitory; aspects of it are fundamentally evil (5:13, 16; 6:1–2; 8:8–13; 9:3; 10:5). The observations take on a moral character, neutral objectivity is distinctly out of the question, and the end of the matter is the basic need to fear the judgment of God (8:12; 11:9; 12:13–14).

The Hebrew title of the text is *Qohelet* and is related to *qahal*, which means "assembly" or "congregation." Perhaps Qohelet was one who addressed a congregation; in other words, a preacher. In light of what is said in the text, this is a rather interesting sermon. It becomes even more intriguing when the issue of authorship is raised. There is a wide range of suggestions as to the actual date of composition, all based on differing analyses of linguistic considerations as well as references within the text. It is evident, however, that the reader is supposed to think of Solomon, the paradigmatic wisdom figure, recording his observations about the multifaceted life he had lived (1:1, 12, 16; 2:1–9; 4:13; 12:9). The ambiguous identity of this personage is heightened by the fact that *qohelet*, used only in this book, is a feminine noun form. There are possible parallels with the public and challenging preaching of the woman Wisdom in Proverbs 1:20–33. Even though the descriptions of this author uniformly depict a man, *qohelet* once is accompanied by the corresponding feminine form of the verb (7:27).

No human enterprise, no matter how earnest and valuable, is sufficient to meet life's ultimate needs. "Under the sun," the following are true: The more knowledge one has, the more grief (1: 3, 18; 8:16–17); even after expending a life's effort, the very things striven for are empty and must be left upon death (2:11, 18–23; 4:7–8; 5:10–12, 14–15); pleasure provides no lasting satisfaction and yet the desire for pleasure is insatiable (1:17; 2:1–3, 10–11; 6:7); the injustices of life are inescapable (4:1–2; 5:8–9); in the face of inevitable death, there is a lack of lasting personal importance (2:15–16; 3:18–20; 9:11–12).

Nevertheless, a new perspective is gained in God's presence. Because Qohelet painted the world with all its intolerable darkness, the faint glimmers of light at the recurring mentions of God are all the more tantalizing and thought provoking. What humankind needs is supplied by God, beginning with time and stability (3:1–14), work and pleasure, relationships and knowledge (2:24–26; 4:9–12; 5:18–20; 9:9). In the midst of this counterpoint comes the ultimate paradox that hope and meaning are found in the prospect of judgment (3:17; 11:9). Nothing is trivial, no injustice will be overlooked forever, and fear of the Judge will be the best security (12:13–14).

Ecclesiastes does not easily fall into an outline form, but it may be addressed in successive units. The division points are arbitrary, as will be evident in the obvious flow from one section to the next. —*Elaine A. Phillips*

1:1–11	Prologue: Statement of Primary Themes
1:12—2:16	Initial Program of Investigation: Research, Exploration, and Reporting
2:17–26	The Emotional Side: Despair Followed by Acknowledgment of the Hand of God
3:1–17	God and Time
3:18—4:16	Investigating Social and Psychological Stresses 1
5:1–7	In the Presence of God Perspectives Change
5:8—6:12	Investigating Social and Psychological Stresses 2
7:1–14	A Collection of Proverbs
7:15—8:6	Observations of a Pragmatist
8:7—9:12	How to Think about the Future: Death, Justice, Enjoyment
9:13—11:6	Making the Case for Wisdom Literature
11:7—12:7	At the Threshold of Darkness: Thinking Now about Old Age
12:8–14	Epilogue

✧

1 These are the words of the Teacher,* King
David's son, who ruled in Jerusalem.

Everything Is Meaningless
2 "Everything is meaningless," says the Teacher,
"completely meaningless!"
3 What do people get for all their hard work
under the sun? 4 Generations come and generations go, but the earth never changes. 5 The sun
rises and the sun sets, then hurries around to
rise again. 6 The wind blows south, and then
turns north. Around and around it goes, blowing in circles. 7 Rivers run into the sea, but the
sea is never full. Then the water returns again
to the rivers and flows out again to the sea. 8 Everything is wearisome beyond description. No
matter how much we see, we are never satisfied. No matter how much we hear, we are not
content.
9 History merely repeats itself. It has all been
done before. Nothing under the sun is truly new.
10 Sometimes people say, "Here is something
new!" But actually it is old; nothing is ever truly
new. 11 We don't remember what happened in the
past, and in future generations, no one will remember what we are doing now.

The Teacher Speaks: The Futility of Wisdom
12 I, the Teacher, was king of Israel, and I lived in
Jerusalem. 13 I devoted myself to search for understanding and to explore by wisdom everything being done under heaven. I soon discovered that God has dealt a tragic existence to the
human race. 14 I observed everything going on
under the sun, and really, it is all meaningless—
like chasing the wind.

15 What is wrong cannot be made right.
What is missing cannot be recovered.

16 I said to myself, "Look, I am wiser than
any of the kings who ruled in Jerusalem before
me. I have greater wisdom and knowledge than
any of them." 17 So I set out to learn everything
from wisdom to madness and folly. But I learned
firsthand that pursuing all this is like chasing the
wind.

18 The greater my wisdom, the greater my grief.
To increase knowledge only increases
sorrow.

The Futility of Pleasure
2 I said to myself, "Come on, let's try pleasure. Let's look for the 'good things' in life."
But I found that this, too, was meaningless.
2 So I said, "Laughter is silly. What good does it
do to seek pleasure?" 3 After much thought, I
decided to cheer myself with wine. And while
still seeking wisdom, I clutched at foolishness.
In this way, I tried to experience the only happiness most people find during their brief life in
this world.
4 I also tried to find meaning by building huge
homes for myself and by planting beautiful vineyards. 5 I made gardens and parks, filling them
with all kinds of fruit trees. 6 I built reservoirs to
collect the water to irrigate my many flourishing
groves. 7 I bought slaves, both men and women,
and others were born into my household. I also

1:1 Hebrew *Qoheleth;* this term is rendered "the Teacher" throughout this book.

1:1–11 Prologue: Statement of Primary Themes

The varied sources of personal anguish are introduced at the outset of the sermon and resonate in each woman's heart. Weariness and endless toil are foremost among them, perhaps as a reflection of the curse pronounced on the ground and human effort (Gen 3:17–19). The intrinsic lack of satisfaction and constant desire for something more are pitted against monotony from every perceivable direction. Finally, the ultimate insult to the rigor of laboring through life is the anonymity that death brings. There is another side to the picture even at this point. While the repetitive nature of existence does lead to ennui and frustration, it also bespeaks stability. That the natural world is predictable has a degree of assurance in the face of uncertainty, especially the uncertainty associated with death.

1:12—2:16 Initial Program of Investigation: Research, Exploration, and Reporting

The descriptions of Qohelet that are suggestive of Solomon appear primarily in this section. Qohelet held a royal position in Jerusalem (v. 12). His wisdom was the defining factor pressing him to investigate all that is done under heaven and guiding him through the potential pitfalls of his chosen course. **1:13–18:** Even in the early stages of investigation, the pain of knowledge is evident. God has laid a *tragic existence* on humankind; some things are irreparably twisted; and with wisdom is bound to come anger or distress and pain. **2:1–11:** His wealth and status enabled him to engage in the varied projects described here. These statements are reminiscent of the wealth that Solomon amassed as a result of commerce and tribute (2 Chr 9). Three times (1:17; 2:3, 12) Qohelet indicated that his research program ranged into areas

owned large herds and flocks, more than any of the kings who had lived in Jerusalem before me. 8 I collected great sums of silver and gold, the treasure of many kings and provinces. I hired wonderful singers, both men and women, and had many beautiful concubines. I had everything a man could desire!

9 So I became greater than all who had lived in Jerusalem before me, and my wisdom never failed me. 10 Anything I wanted, I would take. I denied myself no pleasure. I even found great pleasure in hard work, a reward for all my labors. 11 But as I looked at everything I had worked so hard to accomplish, it was all so meaningless—like chasing the wind. There was nothing really worthwhile anywhere.

The Wise and the Foolish

12 So I decided to compare wisdom with foolishness and madness (for who can do this better than I, the king?*). 13 I thought, "Wisdom is better than foolishness, just as light is better than darkness. 14 For the wise can see where they are going, but fools walk in the dark." Yet I saw that the wise and the foolish share the same fate. 15 Both will die. So I said to myself, "Since I will end up the same as the fool, what's the value of all my wisdom? This is all so meaningless!" 16 For the wise and the foolish both die. The wise will not be remembered any longer than the fool. In the days to come, both will be forgotten.

17 So I came to hate life because everything done here under the sun is so troubling. Everything is meaningless—like chasing the wind.

The Futility of Work

18 I came to hate all my hard work here on earth, for I must leave to others everything I have earned. 19 And who can tell whether my successors will be wise or foolish? Yet they will control everything I have gained by my skill and hard work under the sun. How meaningless! 20 So I gave up in despair, questioning the value of all my hard work in this world.

21 Some people work wisely with knowledge and skill, then must leave the fruit of their efforts to someone who hasn't worked for it. This, too, is meaningless, a great tragedy. 22 So what do people get in this life for all their hard work and anxiety? 23 Their days of labor are filled with pain and grief; even at night their minds cannot rest. It is all meaningless.

24 So I decided there is nothing better than to enjoy food and drink and to find satisfaction in work. Then I realized that these pleasures are from the hand of God. 25 For who can eat or enjoy anything apart from him?* 26 God gives wisdom, knowledge, and joy to those who please him. But if a sinner becomes wealthy, God takes the wealth away and gives it to those who please him. This, too, is meaningless—like chasing the wind.

A Time for Everything

3 1 For everything there is a season,
a time for every activity under heaven.

2:12 The meaning of the Hebrew is uncertain. **2:25** As in Greek and Syriac versions; Hebrew reads *apart from me?*

---

of folly as well as wisdom. **8:** His attitude toward women appears to have been part of that folly (cf. 1 Kgs 11:1–8). **15–16:** His preliminary conclusion was a capsule of what follows in the book. Objectively something about wisdom seemed to be better than folly, but the prospect of personal mortality dampened the moral compulsion to act wisely.

2:17–26 The Emotional Side: Despair Followed by Acknowledgment of the Hand of God

Qohelet's response to the inevitability of death and the apparent futility of hard work intensified. He expressed hatred for life and its inevitable stresses. All were pronounced evil and a vapor because that for which everyone labors passes out of one's control, a crisis of significant proportions. Each of the book's characteristic phrases appears in this context, and the emotional anguish associated with the enterprise is palpable. It is evil and accompanied by anger and pain. Nevertheless, the heart that perceives the giving hand of God in all things will enjoy God's provision, even in the midst of distress.

3:1–17 God and Time

Implicit in the preceding conclusion is a call to rein in the anxious imagination about the unknowns in the future. **1–8:** This poem about time imparts confidence that there is appropriate and planned order to all circumstances. In the ancient world, where the individual was bound into the community, women were integral to each passing phase of life. The poem commences with the extreme points, giving birth and accepting death. Events that are parallel to starting and stopping life come next—planting and uprooting, killing and healing. Work in the fields and the home, relationships and emotional responses are all represented. As even the structure of the poetry indicates, life's experiences are balanced, and both good and evil are to be expected. These good and

2 A time to be born and a time to die.
A time to plant and a time to harvest.
3 A time to kill and a time to heal.
A time to tear down and a time to build up.
4 A time to cry and a time to laugh.
A time to grieve and a time to dance.
5 A time to scatter stones and a time to gather
stones.
A time to embrace and a time to turn away.
6 A time to search and a time to quit searching.
A time to keep and a time to throw away.
7 A time to tear and a time to mend.
A time to be quiet and a time to speak.
8 A time to love and a time to hate.
A time for war and a time for peace.

9 What do people really get for all their hard
work? 10 I have seen the burden God has placed on
us all. 11 Yet God has made everything beautiful
for its own time. He has planted eternity in the
human heart, but even so, people cannot see the
whole scope of God's work from beginning to end.
12 So I concluded there is nothing better than to
be happy and enjoy ourselves as long as we can.
13 And people should eat and drink and enjoy the
fruits of their labor, for these are gifts from God.
14 And I know that whatever God does is final.
Nothing can be added to it or taken from it. God's
purpose is that people should fear him. 15 What is
happening now has happened before, and what
will happen in the future has happened before,
because God makes the same things happen over
and over again.

The Injustices of Life

16 I also noticed that under the sun there is evil
in the courtroom. Yes, even the courts of law are
corrupt! 17 I said to myself, "In due season God
will judge everyone, both good and bad, for all
their deeds."
18 I also thought about the human condition—
how God proves to people that they are like animals. 19 For people and animals share the same
fate—both breathe* and both must die. So people
have no real advantage over the animals. How
meaningless! 20 Both go to the same place—they
came from dust and they return to dust. 21 For
who can prove that the human spirit goes up and
the spirit of animals goes down into the earth?
22 So I saw that there is nothing better for people
than to be happy in their work. That is why we
are here! No one will bring us back from death
to enjoy life after we die.

4 Again, I observed all the oppression that
takes place under the sun. I saw the tears
of the oppressed, with no one to comfort
them. The oppressors have great power, and
their victims are helpless. 2 So I concluded that
the dead are better off than the living. 3 But most
fortunate of all are those who are not yet born.
For they have not seen all the evil that is done
under the sun.
4 Then I observed that most people are motivated to success because they envy their neighbors. But this, too, is meaningless—like chasing
the wind.

5 "Fools fold their idle hands,
leading them to ruin."

3:19 Or *both have the same spirit.*

---

evil counterpoints are not presented with uncompromising rigidity. On the contrary, the aspects that are good switch positions with those that are evil as the poetry develops, which is reflective of the experienced uncertainty as humankind progresses from milestone to milestone in the time-bound sphere. The closure to the list has the significant pairing of love and hate, followed by war and peace. **9–17:** Then comes another paradox. While there is a profound sense of eternity planted deep in the hearts of humankind, it is impossible to know anything beyond the present. Instead, there is a call to trust God and to act in accordance with belief in God's providential ordering of events. The premise that what God does will endure forever introduces a forceful moral component into the way humankind chooses to deal with the vicissitudes of life; people are to fear God because the injustices of all time, past, present and future, will be brought to judgment.

3:18—4:16 Investigating Social and Psychological Stresses 1

Qohelet returned to the painful reality of mortality, coming to grips with its humiliating aspects. In the disintegration of the physical body and the return to dust, humans are no different from animals. That, in conjunction with the call to enjoy work, is again reminiscent of Genesis 3:17–19. After the honor of being given the mandate to care for the earth (Gen 2:15), being reduced to dust was a searing reminder of the corruption of sin and death.

Qohelet remarked on the tainted motives, envy and lack of contentment, that prompt all human achievement and drive a person to endless striving. **4:5:** And yet the fools who do not work but fold their

Violence, Abuse, and Oppression

Women, especially Christian women, can have difficulty determining what counts as violence, abuse, and oppression. It may be easier to recognize the victimization of others than to identify such problems within our circle and family. These difficulties in recognizing abuse come honestly. The Christian belief system and scriptures are often understood to teach unrestricted self-sacrifice, endless forgiveness, humility as a chief virtue, and sin as pride and self-will. While these can represent valid components of a Christian theology, an uncritical appropriation of them often blinds women to the violence in their lives and in the lives of those close to them. It can also stop women from following Christ in opposing such injustice.

Identifying Violence, Abuse, and Oppression
Violence, abuse, and oppression are about coercion. A person or group uses methods of control, normally considered illegitimate, to further their goals. This control can be interpersonal or institutionalized, overt or covert. All forms further the unequal distribution of power. Racism, sexism, and ageism are institutionalized forms of violence, abuse, and oppression. When religion is used to justify coercion, it can be especially hard to detect and oppose. But religion can also bring reconciliation and peace, and that is the undergirding message of the gospel.

Making distinctions among these three forms of control can alert women to the subtle harm that exists here. Bodily harm is an overt form of coercion, but threats, intimidation, or reminders of past harmful acts can count as violence. Abuse can be a more elusive form of coercion, including withdrawal, neglect, or deceit. Abuse can be slow acting and cumulative. Scripture makes clear that abuse can include scorn, mockery, and insult (Job 30:9; Ps 22:5–7; Luke 6:22).

Oppression is often on the social level. It is about setting up a hierarchy in which one person or group is privileged and others dispossessed. Scripture uses a number of different words to describe oppression, but all involve harming and gaining control over others. Passages often pair oppression with affliction, misery, and poverty. Social oppression from within Israel is the kind most often referred to in the Old Testament. People are often blindsided by this injustice, since most expect oppression to come from outside our community, to be obvious, or to happen to others.

Women experience these three forms of harm more often than they realize. Because it is so deeply rooted in history and society, no one can expect intelligence, education, class, wealth, or status to provide protection. Yet there are deep resources of help in faith and Scripture, if readers are able to see them and receive God's grace in new ways.

The Effect: Bondage to Anguish
Scripture identifies what it feels like to receive violence, abuse, and oppression. One feels abandoned, overpowered, reduced, foolish, and even insane. The victim becomes "broken spirited" and experiences affliction, suffering, and loss. One may often feel angry at God, be unable to keep God's precepts and despair of life. There are good reasons for these feelings—the abused have been abandoned, let down or used by others, often by the people closest to us.

6 And yet,

"Better to have one handful with quietness
than two handfuls with hard work
and chasing the wind."

The Advantages of Companionship
7 I observed yet another example of something meaningless under the sun. 8 This is the case of a man who is all alone, without a child or a brother, yet who works hard to gain as much wealth as he can. But then he asks himself, "Who am I working for? Why am I giving up so much pleasure now?" It is all so meaningless and depressing.
9 Two people are better off than one, for they can help each other succeed. 10 If one person falls, the other can reach out and help. But someone who falls alone is in real trouble. 11 Likewise, two

hands are ruined. **9:** Qohelet recognized the nurturing power of mutually interdependent relationships, especially in contexts where human frailty is particularly evident. **12:** Lack of contentment on the individual level is paralleled in the sociopolitical arena; loyalty fades fast with each successive ruler.

The victim feels anguish: the pain of being sinned against to the point of powerlessness. Anguish needs to be marked out as different from personal wrongdoing or sin. Anguish happens when our healthy expectation for interpersonal interdependency is subverted. Someone has used us for his or her ends. The distinguishing experience from the victim's perspective is that she has been rendered helpless.

All people have trouble motivating their wills to turn toward God, but victims have an additional problem. The trauma of being victimized can paralyze or reduce the ability of the will to break free. The more powerful the abuse or the fewer the resources, the more deeply one is put in bondage to one's anguish. Once trapped, the will is weakened or paralyzed, and outside intervention is necessary to break the grip (e.g., Exod 6:6).

Theological Pitfalls and Helps

Christian theology, with its focus on personal sin, does not often help victims. While it is true that "everyone has sinned; we all fall short of God's glorious standard" (Rom 3:23), it is also true that we are all sinned against, some more and some less.

Victims often wonder if God condones what has happened to them, especially since in the Bible God gets angry and even acts violently on occasion. There is a subtle distinction here, for Scripture indicates that God hates violence, abuse, and oppression, especially when done to the most vulnerable, such as aliens, orphans, and widows. When God exhibits anger it is not the uncontrolled passion that humans exert. Instead, God allows perpetrators to have their sins turn back upon them. This serves a higher goal than retributive justice, that is, good being rewarded and evil being punished. God's fury is against sin in order to restrain it (Exod 22:21–27).

Thus God's relationship to chaos and order is not one-sided. God restrains evil and preserves order to keep chaos at bay, but sometimes disruption is necessary. Then God is free to disturb the status quo, especially when that system has perpetuated such evils as oppression and alienation. Not all human order has divine mandate, especially when it has become the purveyor of violence, abuse, and oppression. This wisdom can help victims who feel guilty about disrupting human structures, even a marriage that has become abusive. Alternatively it counsels caution to those who feel they must take revenge. The Bible promises that evils such as violence, abuse, and oppression will ultimately be done away with by God. In the meantime, God disrupts or protects human order.

This does not mean, however, that victims must practice immediate, unlimited forgiveness or that they should not exercise legal means to have their abuse addressed. Both assumptions can come from an unbalanced use of Christian teaching on personal sin, humility, and Jesus' work on the cross. While forgiveness is a worthy goal and can free the victim from spiritual bondage, true reconciliation is not achieved without the repentance of the sinner. Ideally the most complete healing comes when the perpetrator helps in the victim's restoration. As for appropriate legal redress, it can be part of healing and re-empowerment for the victim, while also serving to warn against or restrain evil. Finally, the witness of Jesus does not teach us to welcome or endure victimization but to work against it. We see the deep human propensity to scapegoat and victimize when we see the misunderstanding and mistreatment of this righteous, innocent God-man. Jesus' life, words, and actions condemn and undercut, rather than condone, this human sin.

people lying close together can keep each other
warm. But how can one be warm alone? 12 A person standing alone can be attacked and defeated,
but two can stand back-to-back and conquer.
Three are even better, for a triple-braided cord is
not easily broken.

The Futility of Political Power

13 It is better to be a poor but wise youth than
an old and foolish king who refuses all advice.
14 Such a youth could rise from poverty and succeed. He might even become king, though he
has been in prison. 15 But then everyone rushes
to the side of yet another youth* who replaces
him. 16 Endless crowds stand around him,* but
then another generation grows up and rejects
him, too. So it is all meaningless—like chasing
the wind.

4:15 Hebrew *the second youth.* **4:16** Hebrew *There is no end to all the people, to all those who are before them.*

Approaching God with Care

5 1*As you enter the house of God, keep
your ears open and your mouth shut. It
is evil to make mindless offerings to God.
2*Don't make rash promises, and don't be hasty
in bringing matters before God. After all, God is
in heaven, and you are here on earth. So let your
words be few.
3Too much activity gives you restless dreams;
too many words make you a fool.
4When you make a promise to God, don't delay in following through, for God takes no pleasure in fools. Keep all the promises you make to
him. 5It is better to say nothing than to make a
promise and not keep it. 6Don't let your mouth
make you sin. And don't defend yourself by telling the Temple messenger that the promise you
made was a mistake. That would make God angry, and he might wipe out everything you have
achieved.
7Talk is cheap, like daydreams and other useless activities. Fear God instead.

The Futility of Wealth

8Don't be surprised if you see a poor person being
oppressed by the powerful and if justice is being
miscarried throughout the land. For every official
is under orders from higher up, and matters of
justice get lost in red tape and bureaucracy. 9Even
the king milks the land for his own profit!*
10Those who love money will never have
enough. How meaningless to think that wealth
brings true happiness! 11The more you have, the
more people come to help you spend it. So what
good is wealth—except perhaps to watch it slip
through your fingers!
12People who work hard sleep well, whether
they eat little or much. But the rich seldom get a
good night's sleep.
13There is another serious problem I have
seen under the sun. Hoarding riches harms the
saver. 14Money is put into risky investments
that turn sour, and everything is lost. In the end,
there is nothing left to pass on to one's children.
15We all come to the end of our lives as naked
and empty-handed as on the day we were born.
We can't take our riches with us.
16And this, too, is a very serious problem.
People leave this world no better off than when
they came. All their hard work is for nothing—
like working for the wind. 17Throughout their
lives, they live under a cloud—frustrated, discouraged, and angry.
18Even so, I have noticed one thing, at least,
that is good. It is good for people to eat, drink,
and enjoy their work under the sun during the
short life God has given them, and to accept
their lot in life. 19And it is a good thing to receive
wealth from God and the good health to enjoy it.
To enjoy your work and accept your lot in life—
this is indeed a gift from God. 20God keeps such
people so busy enjoying life that they take no
time to brood over the past.

6 There is another serious tragedy I have
seen under the sun, and it weighs heavily on humanity. 2God gives some people
great wealth and honor and everything they
could ever want, but then he doesn't give them
the chance to enjoy these things. They die, and
someone else, even a stranger, ends up enjoying
their wealth! This is meaningless—a sickening
tragedy.
3A man might have a hundred children and

5:1 Verse 5:1 is numbered 4:17 in Hebrew text. **5:2** Verses 5:2-20 are numbered 5:1-19 in Hebrew text. **5:9** The meaning of the Hebrew in verses 8 and 9 is uncertain.

5:1–7 In the Presence of God Perspectives Change

Even when God is the primary objective of the quest, there are cautions for the one who seeks that encounter. It is a fool who approaches God with no sense of remorse over evil and with an excess of words. Qohelet twice used the figure of dreams, which come and go haphazardly and are beyond conscious control, to illustrate the dangerous potential toward sin that lies in multiple words. The text is particularly emphatic about vows, words uttered with moral intent in the presence of God, and the necessity of carrying through on them. Recognizing that God is actively and personally responsive to words, Qohelet's advice is simple and profound: Listen, and fear God.

5:8—6:12 Investigating Social and Psychological Stresses 2

5:13, 16; 6:1–2: In light of the divine Presence, the previously articulated sources of personal anguish are now recognized as a grievous evil. Qohelet cast a somewhat jaded and resigned glance at oppression, injustice, and lack of contentment. What continued to bring distress, however, was that personal effort seemed to be thwarted no matter what the context, and death nullified all endeavors. The weight of wealth and honor and labor contrasted sharply with *hebel* and chasing after wind. What Qohelet continued to see with frightening clarity was that a death-ridden world is an unmitigated evil; *under the sun* is darkness, but the toil that enables a person to eat and

live to be very old. But if he finds no satisfaction in life and doesn't even get a decent burial, it
would have been better for him to be born dead.
4 His birth would have been meaningless, and he
would have ended in darkness. He wouldn't even
have had a name, 5 and he would never have seen
the sun or known of its existence. Yet he would
have had more peace than in growing up to be
an unhappy man. 6 He might live a thousand
years twice over but still not find contentment.
And since he must die like everyone else—well,
what's the use?
7 All people spend their lives scratching for
food, but they never seem to have enough. 8 So
are wise people really better off than fools? Do
poor people gain anything by being wise and
knowing how to act in front of others?
9 Enjoy what you have rather than desiring
what you don't have. Just dreaming about nice
things is meaningless—like chasing the wind.

The Future—Determined and Unknown

10 Everything has already been decided. It was
known long ago what each person would be. So
there's no use arguing with God about your destiny.
11 The more words you speak, the less they
mean. So what good are they?
12 In the few days of our meaningless lives,
who knows how our days can best be spent? Our
lives are like a shadow. Who can tell what will
happen on this earth after we are gone?

Wisdom for Life

7 1 A good reputation is more valuable than
costly perfume.
And the day you die is better than the
day you are born.
2 Better to spend your time at funerals than at
parties.
After all, everyone dies—
so the living should take this to heart.
3 Sorrow is better than laughter,
for sadness has a refining influence on us.
4 A wise person thinks a lot about death,
while a fool thinks only about having a
good time.

5 Better to be criticized by a wise person
than to be praised by a fool.
6 A fool's laughter is quickly gone,
like thorns crackling in a fire.
This also is meaningless.

7 Extortion turns wise people into fools,
and bribes corrupt the heart.

8 Finishing is better than starting.
Patience is better than pride.

9 Control your temper,
for anger labels you a fool.

10 Don't long for "the good old days."
This is not wise.

11 Wisdom is even better when you have
money.
Both are a benefit as you go through life.
12 Wisdom and money can get you almost
anything,
but only wisdom can save your life.

13 Accept the way God does things,
for who can straighten what he has made
crooked?
14 Enjoy prosperity while you can,
but when hard times strike, realize that
both come from God.
Remember that nothing is certain in this
life.

The Limits of Human Wisdom

15 I have seen everything in this meaningless life,
including the death of good young people and
the long life of wicked people. 16 So don't be too

---

drink is a gift of God. All can and must be enjoyed, fleeting as the experiences might be.

7:1–14 A Collection of Proverbs

Contemplating death and mourning continues as a persistent theme, and it is better than the frivolity in which the author had also engaged. Many of the proverbs are evaluative; recognition of something that is better implies the ability to discern between good and evil. Qohelet explored wisdom and folly and concluded that wisdom and knowledge have a protective function that wealth does not have. Another glance at the matter from "above the sun" follows: God ordains good and evil, and it is an exercise in futility and hubris to think that humans can change these things.

7:15—8:6 Observations of a Pragmatist

Qohelet's statement in 7:15 sets the stage for the forthcoming observations: literally, "I have seen everything in the days of my breath [*hebel*]." Life was exceedingly transient, yet it had been sufficient for

good or too wise! Why destroy yourself? [17]On
the other hand, don't be too wicked either. Don't
be a fool! Why die before your time? [18]Pay attention to these instructions, for anyone who
fears God will avoid both extremes.*
[19]One wise person is stronger than ten leading citizens of a town!
[20]Not a single person on earth is always good
and never sins.
[21]Don't eavesdrop on others—you may hear
your servant curse you. [22]For you know how often you yourself have cursed others.
[23]I have always tried my best to let wisdom
guide my thoughts and actions. I said to myself, "I am determined to be wise." But it didn't
work. [24]Wisdom is always distant and difficult
to find. [25]I searched everywhere, determined to
find wisdom and to understand the reason for
things. I was determined to prove to myself
that wickedness is stupid and that foolishness
is madness.
[26]I discovered that a seductive woman* is
a trap more bitter than death. Her passion is a
snare, and her soft hands are chains. Those who
are pleasing to God will escape her, but sinners
will be caught in her snare.
[27]"This is my conclusion," says the Teacher. "I
discovered this after looking at the matter from
every possible angle. [28]Though I have searched
repeatedly, I have not found what I was looking
for. Only one out of a thousand men is virtuous,
but not one woman! [29]But I did find this: God
created people to be virtuous, but they have each
turned to follow their own downward path."

8 [1]How wonderful to be wise,
to analyze and interpret things.
Wisdom lights up a person's face,
softening its harshness.

Obedience to the King

[2]Obey the king since you vowed to God that
you would. [3]Don't try to avoid doing your duty,
and don't stand with those who plot evil, for the
king can do whatever he wants. [4]His command is
backed by great power. No one can resist or question it. [5]Those who obey him will not be punished. Those who are wise will find a time and a
way to do what is right, [6]for there is a time and
a way for everything, even when a person is in
trouble.
[7]Indeed, how can people avoid what they
don't know is going to happen? [8]None of us can
hold back our spirit from departing. None of us
has the power to prevent the day of our death.
There is no escaping that obligation, that dark
battle. And in the face of death, wickedness will
certainly not rescue the wicked.

The Wicked and the Righteous

[9]I have thought deeply about all that goes on
here under the sun, where people have the power
to hurt each other. [10]I have seen wicked people
buried with honor. Yet they were the very ones
who frequented the Temple and are now praised*

7:18 Or *will follow them both.* **7:26** Hebrew *a woman.* **8:10** As in some Hebrew manuscripts and Greek version; many Hebrew manuscripts read *and are forgotten.*

him to experience all the perversities under the sun, and he was left without idealistic expectations or a false sense of personal righteousness or wisdom. **7:24–26:** Qohelet was driven again to determine as much as possible about the depths of wisdom, all the while recognizing that it was impossibly far off. The irony is that Qohelet more systematically than ever pursued the quest. Again this intention included a foray into the dark side of folly and madness, but now Qohelet linked them with wickedness. The mention of folly, joined in Proverbs with the figure of an adulterous woman and the known experiences of Solomon, may have prompted the next rueful observations about the woman whose heart and hands are snares and chains. This is not the statement of a misogynist. Instead it acknowledges from the perspective of the Solomon figure the horrifying bondage of relationships with evil partners and is reminiscent of the good advice King Lemuel received from his mother (Prov 31:1–3). Avoiding this trap is dependent on one's relationship with God. **27–29:** Qohelet's next utterance, introduced here with the feminine verb form, posed again the incomprehensible riddle of being human. Driven to seek order, Qohelet meticulously went through the data one by one, this time in terms of persons, but still the results were impossible to categorize: literally "One man [*'adam*] among a thousand I found, but a woman among all these I did not find. See, this alone I found, that God made human beings [*ha 'adam*] straightforward [or upright], but they have devised many schemes." In other words, the perversity of the human heart and mind complicates existence exceedingly; the ambiguity of the poetry reinforces that conclusion.

8:7—9:12 How to Think about the Future: Death, Justice, Enjoyment

Qohelet again confronted present and future unknowns and the power of death and wickedness, and more firmly lodged the discussion in the context of God's inscrutable but ever present control (8:12–13,

in the same city where they committed their
crimes! This, too, is meaningless. 11When a crime
is not punished quickly, people feel it is safe to
do wrong. 12But even though a person sins a
hundred times and still lives a long time, I know
that those who fear God will be better off. 13The
wicked will not prosper, for they do not fear God.
Their days will never grow long like the evening
shadows.

14And this is not all that is meaningless in our
world. In this life, good people are often treated
as though they were wicked, and wicked people
are often treated as though they were good. This
is so meaningless!

15So I recommend having fun, because there
is nothing better for people in this world than to
eat, drink, and enjoy life. That way they will experience some happiness along with all the hard
work God gives them under the sun.

16In my search for wisdom and in my observation of people's burdens here on earth, I discovered that there is ceaseless activity, day and
night. 17I realized that no one can discover everything God is doing under the sun. Not even
the wisest people discover everything, no matter
what they claim.

Death Comes to All

9 This, too, I carefully explored: Even though
the actions of godly and wise people are in
God's hands, no one knows whether God
will show them favor. 2The same destiny ultimately awaits everyone, whether righteous
or wicked, good or bad,* ceremonially clean or
unclean, religious or irreligious. Good people receive the same treatment as sinners, and people
who make promises to God are treated like people who don't.

3It seems so tragic that everyone under the
sun suffers the same fate. That is why people
are not more careful to be good. Instead, they
choose their own mad course, for they have no
hope. There is nothing ahead but death anyway.
4There is hope only for the living. As they say,
"It's better to be a live dog than a dead lion!"

5The living at least know they will die, but
the dead know nothing. They have no further reward, nor are they remembered. 6Whatever they
did in their lifetime—loving, hating, envying—
is all long gone. They no longer play a part in
anything here on earth. 7So go ahead. Eat your
food with joy, and drink your wine with a happy heart, for God approves of this! 8Wear fine
clothes, with a splash of cologne!

9Live happily with the woman you love
through all the meaningless days of life that
God has given you under the sun. The wife God
gives you is your reward for all your earthly toil.
10Whatever you do, do well. For when you go to
the grave,* there will be no work or planning or
knowledge or wisdom.

11I have observed something else under the
sun. The fastest runner doesn't always win the
race, and the strongest warrior doesn't always
win the battle. The wise sometimes go hungry,
and the skillful are not necessarily wealthy. And
those who are educated don't always lead successful lives. It is all decided by chance, by being
in the right place at the right time.

12People can never predict when hard times
might come. Like fish in a net or birds in a trap,
people are caught by sudden tragedy.

Thoughts on Wisdom and Folly

13Here is another bit of wisdom that has impressed me as I have watched the way our world
works. 14There was a small town with only a few
people, and a great king came with his army and
besieged it. 15A poor, wise man knew how to save
the town, and so it was rescued. But afterward no
one thought to thank him. 16So even though wis-

9:2 As in Greek and Syriac versions and Latin Vulgate; Hebrew lacks *or bad.* **9:10** Hebrew *to Sheol.*

15, 17; 9:1, 7, 9). **9:2–3:** There is a blending and merging of opposites; the righteous and the wicked all face the same encounter with death. **11–12:** No one knows when the divide will be crossed and how. In that framework, life is then opposed to death and life is deemed better; cruel as it might be, life still has memory, deep emotions, companionship, and the prospect of personal engagement.

9:13—11:6 Making the Case for Wisdom Literature

The second collection of proverbs is introduced by a narrative with a predictable twist; the wisdom of a poor man saved a city, and yet he was neither remembered nor honored for his wisdom (cf. a similar story involving a woman; see 2 Sam 20:14–22). The value of wisdom is recognized, and there follows a series of memorable word pictures and tidbits of advice that encapsulate keen observations about nature and human nature. The fool is prominent, illustrating characteristics to avoid. Reversals and ironies abound, chance is acknowledged, and yet there is also some degree of predictability in cause-and-effect sequences. There comes a point, however, beyond which advice and observation cannot pen-

dom is better than strength, those who are wise will be despised if they are poor. What they say will not be appreciated for long.

17 Better to hear the quiet words of a wise person
than the shouts of a foolish king.
18 Better to have wisdom than weapons of war,
but one sinner can destroy much that is good.

10 1As dead flies cause even a bottle of perfume to stink,
so a little foolishness spoils great wisdom and honor.

2 A wise person chooses the right road;
a fool takes the wrong one.

3 You can identify fools
just by the way they walk down the street!

4 If your boss is angry at you, don't quit!
A quiet spirit can overcome even great mistakes.

The Ironies of Life

5There is another evil I have seen under the sun.
Kings and rulers make a grave mistake 6when
they give great authority to foolish people and
low positions to people of proven worth. 7I have
even seen servants riding horseback like princes—and princes walking like servants!

8 When you dig a well,
you might fall in.
When you demolish an old wall,
you could be bitten by a snake.
9 When you work in a quarry,
stones might fall and crush you.
When you chop wood,
there is danger with each stroke of your ax.

10 Using a dull ax requires great strength,
so sharpen the blade.
That's the value of wisdom;
it helps you succeed.

11 If a snake bites before you charm it,
what's the use of being a snake charmer?

12 Wise words bring approval,
but fools are destroyed by their own words.

13 Fools base their thoughts on foolish assumptions,
so their conclusions will be wicked madness;
14 they chatter on and on.

No one really knows what is going to happen;
no one can predict the future.

15 Fools are so exhausted by a little work
that they can't even find their way home.

16 What sorrow for the land ruled by a servant,*
the land whose leaders feast in the morning.
17 Happy is the land whose king is a noble leader
and whose leaders feast at the proper time
to gain strength for their work, not to get drunk.

18 Laziness leads to a sagging roof;
idleness leads to a leaky house.

19 A party gives laughter,
wine gives happiness,
and money gives everything!

20 Never make light of the king, even in your thoughts.
And don't make fun of the powerful, even in your own bedroom.
For a little bird might deliver your message
and tell them what you said.

The Uncertainties of Life

11 1Send your grain across the seas,
and in time, profits will flow back to you.*
2 But divide your investments among many places,*
for you do not know what risks might lie ahead.

3 When clouds are heavy, the rains come down.
Whether a tree falls north or south, it stays where it falls.

4 Farmers who wait for perfect weather never plant.
If they watch every cloud, they never harvest.

10:16 Or *a child.* **11:1** Or *Give generously, / for your gifts will return to you later.* Hebrew reads *Throw your bread on the waters, / for after many days you will find it again.* **11:2** Hebrew *among seven or even eight.*

5 Just as you cannot understand the path of the
wind or the mystery of a tiny baby growing in
its mother's womb,* so you cannot understand
the activity of God, who does all things.
6 Plant your seed in the morning and keep
busy all afternoon, for you don't know if profit
will come from one activity or another—or maybe both.

Advice for Young and Old
7 Light is sweet; how pleasant to see a new day
dawning.
8 When people live to be very old, let them
rejoice in every day of life. But let them also
remember there will be many dark days. Everything still to come is meaningless.
9 Young people,* it's wonderful to be young!
Enjoy every minute of it. Do everything you
want to do; take it all in. But remember that you
must give an account to God for everything you
do. 10 So refuse to worry, and keep your body
healthy. But remember that youth, with a whole
life before you, is meaningless.

12 Don't let the excitement of youth
cause you to forget your Creator.
Honor him in your youth before
you grow old and say, "Life is not pleasant anymore." 2 Remember him before the light of the
sun, moon, and stars is dim to your old eyes, and
rain clouds continually darken your sky. 3 Remember him before your legs—the guards of
your house—start to tremble; and before your
shoulders—the strong men—stoop. Remember
him before your teeth—your few remaining
servants—stop grinding; and before your eyes—
the women looking through the windows—see
dimly.
4 Remember him before the door to life's opportunities is closed and the sound of work fades.
Now you rise at the first chirping of the birds,
but then all their sounds will grow faint.
5 Remember him before you become fearful
of falling and worry about danger in the streets;
before your hair turns white like an almond tree
in bloom, and you drag along without energy
like a dying grasshopper, and the caperberry no
longer inspires sexual desire. Remember him before you near the grave, your everlasting home,
when the mourners will weep at your funeral.
6 Yes, remember your Creator now while you
are young, before the silver cord of life snaps and
the golden bowl is broken. Don't wait until the
water jar is smashed at the spring and the pul-
ley is broken at the well. 7 For then the dust will
return to the earth, and the spirit will return to
God who gave it.

Concluding Thoughts about the Teacher
8 "Everything is meaningless," says the Teacher,
"completely meaningless."
9 Keep this in mind: The Teacher was consid-

11:5 Some manuscripts read *Just as you cannot understand how breath comes to a tiny baby in its mother's womb.*
11:9 Hebrew *Young man.*

---

etrate. **11:5:** The mystery of God's creation is likened to the miracle of life ("bones," NRSV) developing in the mother's womb. Humankind is given the mandate to be active stewards of creation in spite of the fundamental inability to predict or control the outcomes of those endeavors.

11:7—12:7 At the Threshold of Darkness: Thinking Now about Old Age

From the vantage point of light and vigorous youth, the audience of Qohelet is urged to think ahead to the vast time chasm of darkness and to the test that is old age. While everything is *hebel*, nothing is inconsequential because God will bring each person into judgment, a good reason to fear God and remember the One who created humankind. Only that mind-set will provide sufficient preparation for the grim task of navigating through physical disintegration until death and assisting others on that journey. The poignant metaphors of old age and death are heartrending. These are the days in which no pleasure is found, when vision dims into darkness, limbs once strong give way, teeth fall out and hearing fades, sleep escapes, all desire is gone, and terrors invade because of frailty. The vessel bearing life is shattered and returns to dust (Gen 3:19). At this extremity, Qohelet extended a profound source of hope: The spirit goes into the care of God who gave it. This is the closing answer to all the expressed despair at the prospect of death.

12:8–14 Epilogue

Having acknowledged the spirit's return to God, it is difficult to construe verse 8 as a final frustrated outcry against lack of meaning. Rather, it reiterates the brevity, from beginning to end, of the human endeavor. The epilogue then presents the qualifications of Qohelet and the value of carefully articulated words of wisdom. Finally, lest the message have gotten lost, the best-chosen lifestyle is one that is founded on the fear of God and obedience. In the prospect of judgment lies ultimate hope.

ered wise, and he taught the people everything
he knew. He listened carefully to many proverbs,
studying and classifying them. 10 The Teacher
sought to find just the right words to express
truths clearly.*
11 The words of the wise are like cattle prods—
painful but helpful. Their collected sayings are
like a nail-studded stick with which a shepherd*
drives the sheep.
12 But, my child,* let me give you some further advice: Be careful, for writing books is endless, and much study wears you out.
13 That's the whole story. Here now is my final
conclusion: Fear God and obey his commands, for
this is everyone's duty. 14 God will judge us for
everything we do, including every secret thing,
whether good or bad.

12:10 Or *sought to write what was upright and true.*
12:11 Or *one shepherd.* **12:12** Hebrew *my son.*

SONG OF SONGS

INTRODUCTION

The Song of Songs is one of the most beautifully written books in the Bible, full of evocative imagery and superb use of language. Yet it is one of the most difficult books to interpret. In essence it is love poetry, and as such it is unashamedly erotic, so much so that early Christian commentators quote a Jewish saying that the book should not be studied until the reader has reached the age of thirty. Issues of authorship, date, form, canonicity, and interpretation are controversial and interwoven; key themes include the voice of the woman, the community of women, eroticism and the Bible, the place of God, links with the Garden of Eden, and notions of beauty and richness of imagery.

The title "Song of Songs" is the literal translation of the Hebrew in 1:1 and refers to the superlative nature of this song or poem. The attribution "Solomon's . . . " has been taken to mean either that he was the author (in 1 Kgs 4:32 Solomon is said to have written 1,005 songs) or that it was written about him.

If the author is Solomon, then it must have been written in the mid-tenth century BC. The bulk of modern scholarship tends toward a later date, possibly the fifth century BC, a date supported by the placement of the book at the end of the Writings in the Hebrew Bible.

There are two main strands of interpretive tradition for the Song of Songs. The first is the natural, literal meaning, whereby the Song is a poetic composition that explores the dimensions of human love. Such an interpretation is consistent with a reading of the Song of Songs as wisdom literature, testifying by implication to a God who is concerned with every detail of human life.

The allegorical strand of interpretation, in which the Song is understood as expressing the relationship between God and Israel (in Jewish exegesis) and Christ and the church (in Christian exegesis), provided a rich resource for sermons and commentaries. Such an allegorical reading emphasizes links between the Song and prophetic literature, in which the marriage relationship is used as a model of the relationship between God and Israel (see Hos 1—3; Jer 2—3; Ezek 16; 23; Isa 50; 54; 62); in Christian thought it also reflects the language of Ephesians 5.

In contemporary interpretation there is a move to draw together allegorical and literal readings of the text in order to more fully experience its richness. In this view the Song is understood as more than just a celebration of human love; it is intended by its authors to be read symbolically, describing the intense love between God and God's people, using the language of human love as the least inadequate way of describing that love.

Perhaps the most conspicuous characteristic of the Song of Songs is that well over half the book is spoken by a woman. Women are largely silent in the Bible, whether by deliberate choice or simple omission; female authorship is rarely seriously posited of biblical texts. The lovers, male and female, are equal in the way they give voice to their relationship; the volume of the woman's speech outweighs the man's speech. Nor, in contrast with other writings of the period, is any inferiority implied in the woman's appearance, intelligence, will, or emotions. The man and the woman each have freedom in word and act, although there are hints of the limit of the woman's freedom in the actions of the night watchmen (3:3; 5:7). Desire is reciprocal: Man and woman meet in full mutuality in the Song, each enriching the other's life.

Throughout the Song the woman appeals to the women of Jerusalem. This chorus functions as her peers, those to whom she gives advice as one who has learned from experience. They allow the woman to give voice to her love and represent the role of the hearer—the community—in validating love. Communities of women have traditionally provided support, encouragement, and advice. In the Song of Songs they are similarly called on to be tradition bearers in the wisdom of love—that between a woman and a man, and between humanity and God.

The Song contains a vast number of quotes from and allusions to other Old Testament texts, placing it firmly within the tradition of the covenant relationship of God with Israel. Thus, the allegorical interpretation of the Song finds God in the person of the male lover. The language is dominated by garden imagery. This evokes recollections of the Garden of Eden (Gen 2—3), the place where man and woman live in harmony and walk with God.

Images, similes, and metaphors are drawn from nature, art, and architecture, particularly in the lovers' praise of each other's bodies. These descriptions are not intended to be literal but rather to evoke the beauty they find in one another. A sense of playfulness pervades the Song. —*Raewynne J. Whiteley*

1:1	A Frame of Reference
1:2–6	Inviting Love
1:7—2:7	Finding Complementarity
2:8–17	Yearning Fulfilled
3:1—6:3	Searching for the Lover
6:4—8:4	Exploring Dimensions of Love
8:5–14	Universalizing Love

✧

1 This is Solomon's song of songs, more wonderful than any other.

*Young Woman**

2 Kiss me and kiss me again,
for your love is sweeter than wine.
3 How fragrant your cologne;
your name is like its spreading fragrance.
No wonder all the young women love you!
4 Take me with you; come, let's run!
The king has brought me into his bedroom.

Young Women of Jerusalem

How happy we are for you, O king.
We praise your love even more than wine.

Young Woman

How right they are to adore you.

1:1 The headings identifying the speakers are not in the original text, though the Hebrew usually gives clues by means of the gender of the person speaking.

1:1 A Frame of Reference

The opening verse provides a frame of reference for the book. The title "Song of Songs," a superlative form, denotes this as the highest of all songs. Identifying the Song as Solomon's establishes the book's significance within the Writings and points to wisdom as a possible premise for interpretation.

1:2–6 Inviting Love

The woman, with an invitation to love and a brief self-description, introduces the Song. The love invited encompasses all aspects of lovemaking (cf. Prov 7:18; Ezek 16:8; 23:17; cf. Song 1:4; 4:10; 5:1; 7:13). The woman is the initiator in the Song's presentation of the relationship, as she proclaims the superla-

5 I am dark but beautiful,
O women of Jerusalem—
dark as the tents of Kedar,
dark as the curtains of Solomon's tents.
6 Don't stare at me because I am dark—
the sun has darkened my skin.
My brothers were angry with me;
they forced me to care for their vineyards,
so I couldn't care for myself—my own vineyard.

7 Tell me, my love, where are you leading your flock today?
Where will you rest your sheep at noon?
For why should I wander like a prostitute*
among your friends and their flocks?

Young Man
8 If you don't know, O most beautiful woman,
follow the trail of my flock,
and graze your young goats by the shepherds' tents.
9 You are as exciting, my darling,
as a mare among Pharaoh's stallions.
10 How lovely are your cheeks;
your earrings set them afire!
How lovely is your neck,
enhanced by a string of jewels.
11 We will make for you earrings of gold
and beads of silver.

Young Woman
12 The king is lying on his couch,
enchanted by the fragrance of my perfume.
13 My lover is like a sachet of myrrh
lying between my breasts.
14 He is like a bouquet of sweet henna blossoms
from the vineyards of En-gedi.

Young Man
15 How beautiful you are, my darling,
how beautiful!
Your eyes are like doves.

Young Woman
16 You are so handsome, my love,
pleasing beyond words!
The soft grass is our bed;
17 fragrant cedar branches are the beams of our house,
and pleasant smelling firs are the rafters.

Young Woman
2 1 I am the spring crocus blooming on the Sharon Plain,*
the lily of the valley.

1:7 Hebrew *like a veiled woman.* **2:1** Traditionally rendered *I am the rose of Sharon.* Sharon Plain is a region in the coastal plain of Palestine.

tive nature of her lover and of their love. The self-description of the woman, speaking to the chorus, the women of Jerusalem, challenges stereotypes of beauty within some traditions. No longer is beauty akin to fairness of skin; here, darkness of skin, accentuated by time in the vineyards, is celebrated.

1:7—2:7 Finding Complementarity

What follows is a dialogue between the lovers, each extolling the beauty of the other using imagery drawn from the world around them. It begins with the woman's question to her lover, using language that he then adopts and develops in his response, a pattern that is often repeated in the Song. Where one pauses, the other picks up the conversation, creating a sense of the complementarity of the lovers. The woman's opening question is of particular interest, as she demands that her lover tell her the whereabouts of his flocks. Whether she means this literally or figuratively, as an allusion to his dwelling, this is no submissive or passive stereotype of a woman.

The woman's reference to her lover as shepherd and king (1:7, 12) has precipitated a great deal of speculation about the identity of her lover. The shepherd analogy is consistent with the lover's drawing upon pastoral imagery in his description of the woman (4:1–2; 6:5–6); however, some interpreters have questioned this on the grounds of incompatibility with the description of him as king. This assumes that the language of love in the Song is uncharacteristically literal. Furthermore, the Bible provides a precedent for a shepherd king in the person of David. And if the Song is interpreted allegorically, it coheres with the wider biblical witness of God as shepherd and king.

The mutual extolling of beauty, which assumes the presence of both lovers, shifts to remembrances of the past and a sense of yearning on the part of the woman for her now apparently absent lover. She concludes with a formal caution *not to awaken love until the time is right* (2:7). This formula reappears twice more (3:5; 8:4) and speaks of the pain experienced when love comes at the wrong time, when one is unable, unwilling, or not yet ready to consummate it. This caution anticipates two late scenes (3:1–5; 5:2–7) in which the mistiming of love is dramatically portrayed.

Marriage

The union of a man and woman in an exclusive and procreative covenant of marriage is presented as God's creative intention in the two creation stories. In Genesis 1, God creates humans male and female together. In Genesis 2, God first creates the male and then determines that it is not good that the man should be alone. God remedies the solitariness of the man by creating the woman to be his "helper" (Gen 2:20), a word most commonly used in the Old Testament to refer to someone who rescues another from distress. The woman is one who corresponds to him and complements him, so that together they are complete.

Few marriages in the Old Testament conform to the pattern set out in Genesis 1—2. While there are examples in the Bible of marriages that are faithful, loving, and in harmony with the purposes of God, there are many more examples of marriages that are disrupted by polygamy, infidelity, and divorce. Marriages in the Old Testament are just as untidy and complex as marriages in postbiblical societies, and do not necessarily reflect God's will.

Scattered throughout the various legal codes in the Old Testament are laws that address such matters as whom one may or may not marry, the dissolution of marriage, and remarriage. Some laws regulate situations that appear to be inconsistent with God's creative intent for marriage. For example, monogamy is presented as an ideal, but there is a law that requires fairness from a man who is married to two wives at the same time (Deut 21:15–17). Similarly, lifelong marriage is presented as an ideal, but there are laws regulating divorce.

Deuteronomy 25:5–10 addresses the question of what is to become of a childless widow. If a woman's husband dies without offspring, the brother of the deceased man is to marry her and father a son with her "so that his [the deceased's] name will not be forgotten in Israel." This is called levirate marriage. Levirate marriage persisted into the New Testament period, as evidenced by the Sadducees' question to Jesus about the childless widow who was married in turn to each of seven brothers (Matt 22:23; Mark 12:18–27; Luke 20:27–40).

In the genealogies of the sons born to Tamar (Gen 38) and to Ruth, the biological fathers are named, not the deceased husbands. Perhaps, then, an unmentioned but equally important purpose of levirate marriage was the support of widows, not just the continuation of a man's line.

The Prophets

The prophets use the metaphor of marriage to describe God's relationship to the covenant people, Israel. The prophet Hosea's tragically broken marriage to Gomer becomes in Hosea's prophetic utterances an illustration of Israel's unfaithfulness to God and God's consequent heartbrokenness over her infidelity. As Hosea anticipates his eventual reconciliation with his wife, this also becomes an illustration of God's reconciliation with his spouse, Israel. Hosea looks forward to the time when Israel will call God not "my master" but "my husband" (Hos 2:16). This juxtaposition of "master" with "husband" constitutes a strong affirmation that a wife is not meant to be a slave but a trusted covenant partner and friend.

Young Man

2 Like a lily among thistles
is my darling among young women.

Young Woman

3 Like the finest apple tree in the orchard
is my lover among other young men.
I sit in his delightful shade
and taste his delicious fruit.
4 He escorts me to the banquet hall;
it's obvious how much he loves me.
5 Strengthen me with raisin cakes,
refresh me with apples,
for I am weak with love.
6 His left arm is under my head,
and his right arm embraces me.

7 Promise me, O women of Jerusalem,
by the gazelles and wild deer,
not to awaken love until the time is right.*

8 Ah, I hear my lover coming!
He is leaping over the mountains,
bounding over the hills.
9 My lover is like a swift gazelle
or a young stag.

2:7 Or *not to awaken love until it is ready.*

Jeremiah follows Hosea in using the language of infidelity to describe Judah's unfaithfulness to God (Jer 2:20–25; 3:1–3). Ezekiel 16:8 uses two expressions to speak of God's marriage to Judah: "I wrapped my cloak around you," that is, "I married you" (cf. Ruth 3:9); and "I made a covenant with you." The remainder of Ezekiel 16 is an extended description of Judah's unfaithfulness as shameless adultery and of God's efforts to call her back to fidelity and to reestablish his covenant with her (Ezek 16:60). Isaiah and Malachi also use this metaphor.

The Gospels

Marriage is presented in the Gospels as an ordinary and unremarkable aspect of human life, like eating and drinking (cf. Matt 24:28; Luke 17:27). Within that context, Jesus calls all persons to follow him. The only person whose marital status Jesus addresses is the Samaritan woman (John 4:7–30), and the effect is to make her a disciple and an evangelist.

Jesus emphasizes the importance of marital fidelity (Mark 10:19; Matt 19:3–9; Luke 18:20; see also John 8:11) and explains that the commandment "do not commit adultery" forbids lust as well (Matt 5:28). Jesus refuses to specify circumstances under which divorce is legitimate and instead emphasizes God's intention that marriage be indissoluble; he stresses the serious moral consequences that attend divorce.

The Epistles

A prominent emphasis in the Epistles is on the importance of sexual fidelity in marriage. Marital fidelity is a way in which Christians image the holiness and purity of God (1 Thes 4:3–7). Conversely, sexual impurity is just as incompatible with the kingdom of God as is idolatry. This spiritual dimension of marriage makes it important that a Christian marry another Christian (1 Cor 7:39; 2 Cor 6:14–18).

In light of the demands of God's kingdom, Paul expresses a preference for singleness (1 Cor 7:1, 8, 26, 32–35, 40) but acknowledges that most people will marry (1 Cor 7:2, 9, 28, 36–38). Scripture speaks twice of the relationship of husband and wife in terms of headship and likens this to the relationships among the church, Christ and God (1 Cor 11:3; Eph 5:21–33). Given the perfect peace and mutuality obtained between Christ and his head, God, and the self-emptying love with which Christ poured out himself for the Church, of which he is the head, the headship that a husband is to exercise with respect to his wife is presumably to be characterized by similar peace, mutuality, and self-emptying love.

Marriage is a practical as well as a spiritual reality, and all Christians are to take care that their marriages are in good order and to respect the covenant between husband and wife (Heb 13:4).

Look, there he is behind the wall,
looking through the window,
peering into the room.

10 My lover said to me,
"Rise up, my darling!
Come away with me, my fair one!
11 Look, the winter is past,
and the rains are over and gone.
12 The flowers are springing up,
the season of singing birds* has come,
and the cooing of turtledoves fills the air.
13 The fig trees are forming young fruit,
and the fragrant grapevines are blossoming.
Rise up, my darling!
Come away with me, my fair one!"

Young Man

14 My dove is hiding behind the rocks,
behind an outcrop on the cliff.
Let me see your face;
let me hear your voice.
For your voice is pleasant,
and your face is lovely.

2:12 Or *the season of pruning vines.*

2:8–17 Yearning Fulfilled

Here the yearning is fulfilled—the desired lover appears. This section is dominated by the image of the beloved as a young stag or gazelle and the incredible bounty of creation, reminiscent of the Garden of Eden (Gen 1—2). Spring will inevitably follow winter, yet it is a source of surprise and joy; so too the arrival of the lover is heralded as inevitable, also bringing joyous surprise.

Young Women of Jerusalem

15 Catch all the foxes,
those little foxes,
before they ruin the vineyard of love,
for the grapevines are blossoming!

Young Woman

16 My lover is mine, and I am his.
He browses among the lilies.
17 Before the dawn breezes blow
and the night shadows flee,
return to me, my love, like a gazelle
or a young stag on the rugged mountains.*

Young Woman

3 1 One night as I lay in bed, I yearned for
my lover.
I yearned for him, but he did not come.
2 So I said to myself, "I will get up and roam
the city,
searching in all its streets and squares.
I will search for the one I love."
So I searched everywhere but did not find
him.
3 The watchmen stopped me as they made their
rounds,
and I asked, "Have you seen the one I
love?"
4 Then scarcely had I left them
when I found my love!
I caught and held him tightly,
then I brought him to my mother's house,
into my mother's bed, where I had been
conceived.

5 Promise me, O women of Jerusalem,
by the gazelles and wild deer,
not to awaken love until the time is right.*

Young Women of Jerusalem

6 Who is this sweeping in from the wilderness
like a cloud of smoke?
Who is it, fragrant with myrrh and
frankincense
and every kind of spice?
7 Look, it is Solomon's carriage,
surrounded by sixty heroic men,
the best of Israel's soldiers.
8 They are all skilled swordsmen,
experienced warriors.
Each wears a sword on his thigh,
ready to defend the king against an attack
in the night.
9 King Solomon's carriage is built
of wood imported from Lebanon.
10 Its posts are silver,
its canopy gold;
its cushions are purple.
It was decorated with love
by the young women of Jerusalem.

Young Woman

11 Come out to see King Solomon,
young women of Jerusalem.*
He wears the crown his mother gave him on
his wedding day,
his most joyous day.

Young Man

4 1 You are beautiful, my darling,
beautiful beyond words.
Your eyes are like doves
behind your veil.
Your hair falls in waves,

2:17 Or *on the hills of Bether.* **3:5** Or *not to awaken love until it is ready.* **3:11** Hebrew *of Zion.*

2:16–17: We find a reminder of the mutuality of the lovers, each belonging to the other, a principle taken up in 1 Corinthians 7:4.

3:1—6:3 Searching for the Lover

The third chapter of the Song begins with the woman's search for her missing lover. This and the similar account in 5:2–8 speak of the dangers inherent in love that is ill-timed. They have been particularly rich grounds for allegorical interpretation, with images of the soul's search for God and God's search for the soul (particularly 5:2) and the need to respond to God's love. The depth of human passion becomes an expression for the passionate love of God.

Although the woman searches for her lover, the compromised position of women is seen in the actions of the watchmen, who not only find her (3:3) but also beat her (5:7). Those who are supposed to be the protectors become the aggressors. **3:6–11:** The description of Solomon has little connection with what precedes or follows it; it intrudes into the flow of the Song. It contrasts strongly with the monologues and dialogues of the lovers, and while some commentators have seen this section as evidence that the Song is by or about Solomon, it is perhaps more helpful to understand it, with its references to a royal wedding, as an idealizing of the love of the woman and her lover. **4:1:** We return to the lovers. This is the first extended description of the physical beauty of the woman, using evocative similes from the world around the lovers. There is a rich use of garden imagery, harking back to the Garden of Eden, when all creation was good. Unlike many stereotypes of

like a flock of goats winding down the
slopes of Gilead.
2 Your teeth are as white as sheep,
recently shorn and freshly washed.
Your smile is flawless,
each tooth matched with its twin.*
3 Your lips are like scarlet ribbon;
your mouth is inviting.
Your cheeks are like rosy pomegranates
behind your veil.
4 Your neck is as beautiful as the tower of David,
jeweled with the shields of a thousand
heroes.
5 Your breasts are like two fawns,
twin fawns of a gazelle grazing among the
lilies.
6 Before the dawn breezes blow
and the night shadows flee,
I will hurry to the mountain of myrrh
and to the hill of frankincense.
7 You are altogether beautiful, my darling,
beautiful in every way.

8 Come with me from Lebanon, my bride,
come with me from Lebanon.
Come down* from Mount Amana,
from the peaks of Senir and Hermon,
where the lions have their dens
and leopards live among the hills.

9 You have captured my heart,
my treasure,* my bride.
You hold it hostage with one glance of your
eyes,
with a single jewel of your necklace.
10 Your love delights me,
my treasure, my bride.
Your love is better than wine,
your perfume more fragrant than spices.
11 Your lips are as sweet as nectar, my bride.
Honey and milk are under your tongue.
Your clothes are scented
like the cedars of Lebanon.

12 You are my private garden, my treasure, my
bride,
a secluded spring, a hidden fountain.
13 Your thighs shelter a paradise of
pomegranates
with rare spices—
henna with nard,
14 nard and saffron,
fragrant calamus and cinnamon,
with all the trees of frankincense, myrrh, and
aloes,
and every other lovely spice.
15 You are a garden fountain,
a well of fresh water
streaming down from Lebanon's mountains.

Young Woman

16 Awake, north wind!
Rise up, south wind!
Blow on my garden
and spread its fragrance all around.
Come into your garden, my love;
taste its finest fruits.

Young Man

5 1 I have entered my garden, my treasure,*
my bride!
I gather myrrh with my spices
and eat honeycomb with my honey.
I drink wine with my milk.

Young Women of Jerusalem

Oh, lover and beloved, eat and drink!
Yes, drink deeply of your love!

Young Woman

2 I slept, but my heart was awake,
when I heard my lover knocking and
calling:
"Open to me, my treasure, my darling,
my dove, my perfect one.
My head is drenched with dew,
my hair with the dampness of the night."

3 But I responded,
"I have taken off my robe.

4:2 Hebrew *Not one is missing; each has a twin.* **4:8** Or *Look down.* **4:9** Hebrew *my sister;* also in 4:10, 12.
5:1 Hebrew *my sister;* also in 5:2.

woman as temptress, here her physical beauty is something to be celebrated and enjoyed, the very gift of God. If we follow the allegorical interpretation, this section suggests that humanity is a source of great joy for God; it speaks of the great love and tenderness felt by God for God's people. **5:1—6:3:** A similar pattern can be found here. The search for the lover is again followed by a vivid description of the beloved. This time the search, the mistiming of love, is tragic. The lover comes to the woman; she is too slow, and he leaves. Her search for him ends not in the joy of reunion but in the sorrow of assault. The extended description of the beloved is, unlike 4:1–15, of the lover, the one who is absent.

Should I get dressed again?
I have washed my feet.
Should I get them soiled?"

4 My lover tried to unlatch the door,
and my heart thrilled within me.
5 I jumped up to open the door for my love,
and my hands dripped with perfume.
My fingers dripped with lovely myrrh
as I pulled back the bolt.
6 I opened to my lover,
but he was gone!
My heart sank.
I searched for him
but could not find him anywhere.
I called to him,
but there was no reply.
7 The night watchmen found me
as they made their rounds.
They beat and bruised me
and stripped off my veil,
those watchmen on the walls.

8 Make this promise, O women of Jerusalem—
If you find my lover,
tell him I am weak with love.

Young Women of Jerusalem

9 Why is your lover better than all others,
O woman of rare beauty?
What makes your lover so special
that we must promise this?

Young Woman

10 My lover is dark and dazzling,
better than ten thousand others!
11 His head is finest gold,
his wavy hair is black as a raven.
12 His eyes sparkle like doves
beside springs of water;
they are set like jewels
washed in milk.
13 His cheeks are like gardens of spices
giving off fragrance.
His lips are like lilies,
perfumed with myrrh.
14 His arms are like rounded bars of gold,
set with beryl.
His body is like bright ivory,
glowing with lapis lazuli.
15 His legs are like marble pillars
set in sockets of finest gold.
His posture is stately,
like the noble cedars of Lebanon.
16 His mouth is sweetness itself;
he is desirable in every way.
Such, O women of Jerusalem,
is my lover, my friend.

Young Women of Jerusalem

6
1 Where has your lover gone,
O woman of rare beauty?
Which way did he turn
so we can help you find him?

Young Woman

2 My lover has gone down to his garden,
to his spice beds,
to browse in the gardens
and gather the lilies.
3 I am my lover's, and my lover is mine.
He browses among the lilies.

Young Man

4 You are beautiful, my darling,
like the lovely city of Tirzah.
Yes, as beautiful as Jerusalem,
as majestic as an army with billowing
banners.
5 Turn your eyes away,

6:4—8:4 Exploring Dimensions of Love

The descriptions become more explicit, with a sense of growing passion. The language of the Song is unashamedly erotic. Some commentators have in recognition of this opted for an allegorical reading of the Song of Songs as less offensive. However, the offense of such language lies in a view of human embodiment and sexuality as fundamentally evil, part of creation marred by the Fall. An alternative view, grounded in creation, is that the human body and sexuality are part of the rich blessing of God and therefore to be celebrated. Like so many of God's gifts in creation, sexuality has the potential for great good but can be misused for evil. The pleasure of love exhibited in the Song coincides with the general tenor of wisdom literature, which identifies the place of God in everyday life.

Song of Songs is lavish in its descriptions of beauty, perceived through the eyes of love. The language depicting the beauty of man and woman is concrete and visual. One would not be wise to use these images to try to create a portrait of either the man or the woman; taken literally the images appear ludicrous. A description of a woman as dark and beautiful (1:5) or more sustained descriptions (e.g., 4:1–15) affirm notions of beauty other than traditional white Western stereotypes and challenge assumptions associating light with good and pure, and dark or black with bad and sin.

for they overpower me.
Your hair falls in waves,
like a flock of goats winding down the slopes of Gilead.
6 Your teeth are as white as sheep
that are freshly washed.
Your smile is flawless,
each tooth matched with its twin.*
7 Your cheeks are like rosy pomegranates
behind your veil.

8 Even among sixty queens
and eighty concubines
and countless young women,
9 I would still choose my dove, my perfect one—
the favorite of her mother,
dearly loved by the one who bore her.
The young women see her and praise her;
even queens and royal concubines sing her praises:
10 "Who is this, arising like the dawn,
as fair as the moon,
as bright as the sun,
as majestic as an army with billowing banners?"

Young Woman
11 I went down to the grove of walnut trees
and out to the valley to see the new spring growth,
to see whether the grapevines had budded
or the pomegranates were in bloom.
12 Before I realized it,
my strong desires had taken me to the chariot of a noble man.*

Young Women of Jerusalem
13* Return, return to us, O maid of Shulam.
Come back, come back, that we may see you again.

Young Man
Why do you stare at this young woman of Shulam,
as she moves so gracefully between two lines of dancers?*

7
1* How beautiful are your sandaled feet,
O queenly maiden.
Your rounded thighs are like jewels,
the work of a skilled craftsman.
2 Your navel is perfectly formed
like a goblet filled with mixed wine.
Between your thighs lies a mound of wheat
bordered with lilies.
3 Your breasts are like two fawns,
twin fawns of a gazelle.
4 Your neck is as beautiful as an ivory tower.
Your eyes are like the sparkling pools in Heshbon
by the gate of Bath-rabbim.
Your nose is as fine as the tower of Lebanon
overlooking Damascus.
5 Your head is as majestic as Mount Carmel,
and the sheen of your hair radiates royalty.
The king is held captive by its tresses.
6 Oh, how beautiful you are!
How pleasing, my love, how full of delights!
7 You are slender like a palm tree,
and your breasts are like its clusters of fruit.
8 I said, "I will climb the palm tree
and take hold of its fruit."
May your breasts be like grape clusters,
and the fragrance of your breath like apples.
9 May your kisses be as exciting as the best wine,
flowing gently over lips and teeth.*

Young Woman
10 I am my lover's,
and he claims me as his own.
11 Come, my love, let us go out to the fields
and spend the night among the wildflowers.*
12 Let us get up early and go to the vineyards
to see if the grapevines have budded,
if the blossoms have opened,
and if the pomegranates have bloomed.
There I will give you my love.
13 There the mandrakes give off their fragrance,
and the finest fruits are at our door,
new delights as well as old,
which I have saved for you, my lover.

Young Woman
8
1 Oh, I wish you were my brother,
who nursed at my mother's breasts.
Then I could kiss you no matter who was watching,

6:6 Hebrew *Not one is missing; each has a twin.* **6:12** Or *to the royal chariots of my people,* or *to the chariots of Amminadab.* The meaning of the Hebrew is uncertain. **6:13a** Verse 6:13 is numbered 7:1 in Hebrew text. **6:13b** Or *as you would at the movements of two armies?* or *as you would at the dance of Mahanaim?* The meaning of the Hebrew is uncertain. **7:1** Verses 7:1-13 are numbered 7:2-14 in Hebrew text. **7:9** As in Greek and Syriac versions and Latin Vulgate; Hebrew reads *over lips of sleepers.* **7:11** Or *in the villages.*

and no one would criticize me.
2 I would bring you to my childhood home,
and there you would teach me.*
I would give you spiced wine to drink,
my sweet pomegranate wine.
3 Your left arm would be under my head,
and your right arm would embrace me.

4 Promise me, O women of Jerusalem,
not to awaken love until the time is right.*

Young Women of Jerusalem

5 Who is this sweeping in from the desert,
leaning on her lover?

Young Woman

I aroused you under the apple tree,
where your mother gave you birth,
where in great pain she delivered you.
6 Place me like a seal over your heart,
like a seal on your arm.
For love is as strong as death,
its jealousy* as enduring as the grave.*
Love flashes like fire,
the brightest kind of flame.
7 Many waters cannot quench love,
nor can rivers drown it.
If a man tried to buy love
with all his wealth,
his offer would be utterly scorned.

The Young Woman's Brothers

8 We have a little sister
too young to have breasts.
What will we do for our sister
if someone asks to marry her?
9 If she is a virgin, like a wall,
we will protect her with a silver tower.
But if she is promiscuous, like a swinging
door,
we will block her door with a cedar bar.

Young Woman

10 I was a virgin, like a wall;
now my breasts are like towers.
When my lover looks at me,
he is delighted with what he sees.

11 Solomon has a vineyard at Baal-hamon,
which he leases out to tenant farmers.
Each of them pays a thousand pieces of
silver*
for harvesting its fruit.
12 But my vineyard is mine to give,
and Solomon need not pay a thousand
pieces of silver.
But I will give two hundred pieces
to those who care for its vines.

Young Man

13 O my darling, lingering in the gardens,
your companions are fortunate to hear
your voice.
Let me hear it, too!

Young Woman

14 Come away, my love! Be like a gazelle
or a young stag on the mountains of spices.

8:2 Or *there she will teach me;* or *there she bore me.* **8:4** Or *not to awaken love until it is ready.* **8:6a** Or *its passion.* **8:6b** Hebrew *as Sheol.* **8:11** Hebrew *1,000 shekels of silver.*

8:5–14 Universalizing Love

This section contains a number of apparently disparate fragments that echo other parts of the Song. **6–7:** Love is portrayed as a primeval force of intimacy, stronger than the chaos of a creation marred by sin and death. **8–12:** These five verses form a fitting conclusion to the song. It follows the lofty pronouncement about love with the story of the awakening of that love—from childhood, past the protective custody of the brothers (8:8–9), to the woman's affirmation of her beauty, maturity, independence and love (8:10–12)—returning to the imagery of the vineyard (cf. 1:6). The structure of the beginning of the song is repeated in inversion, first a section of self-description and then in conclusion, the woman's call to her lover. However, this story of love is not completed. There is no ending, only an unresolved invitation to love.

The Song of Songs could be understood as a superb love poem, evocative and rich in imagery. As such, it sets forth a high standard for mutual love and encourages the celebration of love and beauty. However, as we understand the further dimension of God's love, it becomes an intimate invitation into relationship with God, celebrating the goodness of love, the beauty of passion, and the tenderness of God.

ISAIAH

INTRODUCTION

The book of Isaiah contains some of the most expressive and well-known passages in the Bible. In it we hear echoes of Handel's famous oratorio *Messiah*; we read beautiful poetic verses, familiar to all; and we understand that these messages from God to all nations are as important today as they were in Isaiah's time.

In addition, there are several allusions to themes of interest to women in the book of Isaiah. But first, some background.

Name and authorship

The name "Isaiah" means "The LORD is salvation," and since the thrust of the book is the hope of a restored future after judgment, the prophet's name neatly sums up his message. The book divides readily into three main sections (chaps. 1—39 [First Isaiah], 40—55 [Second Isaiah], 56—66 [Third Isaiah]), and there has been much scholarly discussion about whether Isaiah of Jerusalem wrote the entire book or only chapters 1 through 39, and even whether all of that. Most modern scholars suggest that separate authors ("Deutero-Isaiah" and "Trito-Isaiah") were responsible for chapters 40—55 and 56—66 respectively, partly because of scepticism over whether prophets could predict the future and partly because the content seems to point to having been written in different eras. Others, however, see the unanimous testimony of both Jewish and Christian tradition crediting Isaiah with the authorship of the entire book and cite literary, geographical, historical, and theological reasons for continuing this tradition. The arguments, however, are strong on both sides, leaving us uncertain about definitive authorship.

Literary Compilation and Dates of Composition

The book of Isaiah shows some chronological arrangement, but this is not always followed. There are sections of the book offering similar subject matter (e.g., oracles about foreign nations in chaps. 13—23), but that does not mean the book is consistently organized this way. In terms of style, the second main section (chaps. 40—55) is of a very high quality of poetry compared with the other two sections. But this is not consistent either, as there are examples of similar style elsewhere (e.g., 4:2–6 and 35:1–10). Those who advocate a single author include these considerations in their argument, and of course the history of how the book was put together depends very much on whether it was written by one or several people.

Those who believe that there were several authors rely on an assumption that there was some kind of "Isaianic school" of the prophet's followers, who continued his work (and in much the same kind of vein). There is no external evidence for this, but that does not mean such a group did not exist. If that was so, then there must also have been a group of archivists who gathered all the material and put it together, perhaps in the late fifth century BC, well after the return from the Exile. Those who believe that Isaiah of Jerusalem was responsible for the whole book will inevitably date it to the eighth and early seventh centuries BC. Isaiah would naturally want his prophecies written down for posterity (see 8:16), not in strict date order but using his material to convey his main themes of God's holiness and mercy and their implications. This would have been particularly urgent during the dark days under king Manasseh.

Historical Context

Isaiah prophesied in the Southern Kingdom of Judah (capital Jerusalem) during the reigns of Uzziah, Jotham, Ahaz, and Hezekiah, i.e., between 792 and 686 BC. The mid-eighth century saw the rise to imperial power of Assyria (capital Nineveh), which provoked two major crises for Judah. First, under Ahaz, the Assyrian threat had driven the Northern Kingdom of Israel (capital Samaria) into a pact with Syria (capital Damascus); these two tried to compel Judah to join them against their common enemy. Isaiah speaks to this in 7:1–9. At the same time, Edomites and Philistines were invading Judah from the south and west. Ahaz panicked, ignored Isaiah's call to faith, and made a treaty with Assyria requesting help against these invaders (2 Kgs 16:1–9; 2 Chr 28:16–18). The result was an uneasy subjection to the dominant power. This was still the case when Hezekiah became king in 715 BC. True to Isaiah's word, Damascus had fallen to Assyria in 732 and Samaria fell in 722. Judah was being gripped by Assyria from the north, and now it was Egypt's turn in the south to press Judah to join them in a concerted rebellion. Babylon, too, was making overtures to Hezekiah (39:1–2). What should he do? In the name of the LORD Isaiah promised that the king and his city of Jerusalem would be delivered. But like Ahaz, Hezekiah fell under the lure of political expediency and signed a treaty with Egypt, one that would prove useless (30:1–7). Assyria smashed Egypt and switched its attention to Judah (36:1). Belatedly, Hezekiah turned to the LORD, who honored his faith and delivered him and the city (chaps. 36 and 37).

Assyria itself fell in 612 BC to the emerging power of Babylon. Meanwhile, Hezekiah's successor, Manasseh, turned Judah farther away from the LORD, although he knew that the fate of the nation was inextricably linked with their faithfulness (or otherwise) to God. Despite an attempt by the later king Josiah to bring the nation to repentance, the downward spiral continued; after a run of incompetent kings, Jerusalem too fell to the enemy army in 587 BC, its people taken into exile in Babylon. In 539 Babylon fell to Cyrus of Persia, and the following year saw the start of a return to the land of Israel. Chapters 40 on speak to the situation of exile and postexile, looking to the future.

Guide to Reading Isaiah

Isaiah's call (chap. 6) is a good starting point, introducing the concept of the LORD's holiness and human sinfulness, yet with assurance of forgiveness and the commission to trust in the LORD. The passages in 9:2–7 and 11:1–9 are often read at Christmas, because they hint at a coming One who will save his people. The later passage 52:13—53:12 depicts the Suffering Servant, used by the New Testament writers as a graphic picture of what Jesus underwent on the cross. And in Luke 4:14–30 Jesus identifies himself with the anointed one of Isaiah 61:1–3. New Testament writers have also linked the servant in 49:6, who brings light to the world, to Jesus (Luke 2:32) and to Paul and Barnabas (Acts 13:47).

Other passages have brought comfort to Christians of every age. Those who feel inadequate may like to read how God's servant, and indeed God himself, deals gently with people (42:1–4) and loves them intensely, calling them by name (43:1–4). He welcomes them freely (55:1–13), yet challenges them to the kind of worship that overflows in caring for the poor and marginalized (58:6–11).

Readers who wish to study more widely in the book may wish to follow the suggested section divisions in the outline, or follow through the themes indicated in the following section.

Major Themes in Isaiah

God's holiness. The word "holy" is used to describe God thirty-three times in Isaiah, compared with only twenty-six times elsewhere in the Old Testament. Isaiah's call sets the scene (6:3). The prophet is constantly aware that God will brook no rivals and requires his people to reflect his holy character (1:2–4, 11–17; 58:6–12). Human pride and arrogance will perish under God's judgment (2:11; 9:8–9).

A gospel of grace. Throughout Isaiah, God's undeserved mercy and grace are apparent: God is forgiving and will restore his people at great personal cost if they will turn back to him (1:16–18; 30:15; 53:4–6, 11; 54:9–10); he is preparing a glorious future for them (60:15–22). Despite terrible judgment, there would be a remnant of believers (4:3; 6:13; 7:3a [see translator's note]; 10:20; 11:11, 16; 37:31–32).

Messianic hope. Isaiah paints a portrait of a messianic figure who will come as a Savior. He will be given God's own Spirit (11:1–2; 42:1; 61:1–3); he will bring justice and righteousness (9:7; 11:4; 53:11; 61:10–11); and his concern will be as much for the Gentiles as for Israel—his mercy extends to the whole world (2:2–4; 11:9; 19:23–25; 42:1–4; 49:1–6; 66:18–19). Isaiah's view of the Messiah is clearly both human and divine: a king born of David's line (11:1, 10) yet "Mighty God" (9:6); a human suffering servant (52:13—53:12) yet the "arm of the LORD," himself bringing salvation (53:1; cf. 51:5; 59:16).

Issues Relevant to Women

God cares for people who suffer. There are several references to the LORD's care for orphans and widows (1:17, 23; 10:1–2), but only when they are victims of oppression, not perpetrators of it (9:17). We frequently see the LORD's compassion toward those who suffer and are weak (3:15; 11:4; 30:18–19; 40:1–2; 42:3); God is even likened to a mother bird caring for its young (31:5).

Motherhood. Motherhood is a strong motif in Isaiah. Isaiah's wife becomes pregnant, and their children's names are symbolic of their father's message (7:3; 8:1–4). A special child is promised (7:14; cf. Matt 1:23) to be called Immanuel ("God is with us"); and his names, too, are significant (9:6). God carried Israel in the womb, and still carries her (46:3–4); just like a mother with a newborn baby, God can never forget his child (49:14–15). Israel is urged to drink joyfully of the LORD's comfort, as a baby drinks its mother's milk (66:10–13). Indeed, childlessness is looked on as a symbol of desolation (23:4; cf. 54:1). However, there is a darker side of motherhood. Frequently Isaiah compares the suffering of the coming judgment to the pain of childbirth (13:8; 21:3; 26:16–18). Yet God himself suffers such birth pains in restoring Israel (42:14).

Wifely infidelity. Jerusalem is likened to a prostitute and adulterer because she has turned away from her "husband," the LORD (1:21). She flirts with other gods and is consequently raped by them (3:16–26; 57:7–9). But she will be washed from her filth (4:4), reconciled to her husband (54:4–8), and made beautiful again (54:11–12; 61:3). —*Vivien Whitfield*

First Isaiah: 1:1—39:8	Warnings and Promises before the Exile
1:1—6:13	Isaiah's Earliest Messages
7:1—12:6	Historical and Political Insights
13:1—23:18	Prophetic Oracles
24:1—35:10	Blessings, Judgments, and Messages for the Nations
36:1—39:8	A Window into History
Second Isaiah: 40:1—55:13	Experience of God in Exile
40:1—44:20	Comfort after Judgment
44:21—55:13	Promises of Deliverance to All Nations
Third Isaiah: 56:1—66:24	A Glorious Future after the Exile
56:1—59:21	Warnings about False Worship and Sin
60:1—66:24	Transformation for God's people

✧

1 These are the visions that Isaiah son of Amoz saw concerning Judah and Jerusalem. He saw these visions during the years when Uzziah, Jotham, Ahaz, and Hezekiah were kings of Judah.*

A Message for Rebellious Judah

2 Listen, O heavens! Pay attention, earth!
This is what the LORD says:
"The children I raised and cared for
have rebelled against me.
3 Even an ox knows its owner,
and a donkey recognizes its master's care—
but Israel doesn't know its master.
My people don't recognize my care for them."
4 Oh, what a sinful nation they are—
loaded down with a burden of guilt.
They are evil people,
corrupt children who have rejected the LORD.
They have despised the Holy One of Israel
and turned their backs on him.

5 Why do you continue to invite punishment?
Must you rebel forever?
Your head is injured,
and your heart is sick.
6 You are battered from head to foot—
covered with bruises, welts, and infected wounds—

1:1 These kings reigned from 792 to 686 B.C.

1:1—39:8 First Isaiah: Warnings and Promises before the Exile

1:1—6:13 Isaiah's Earliest Messages

Isaiah's earliest messages (visions) warn Judah about sin and idolatry, and the consequent coming judgment by the LORD. Interspersed are glimpses of salvation, promises of blessings and a better future, and oracles concerning neighboring nations. Hymns, laments, praise psalms, even love poetry can be found throughout, showing that Isaiah spoke directly to the people in ways they could easily understand and relate. Isaiah's call to prophesy in chapter 6 leads into several historical and political insights, while continuing the themes of judgment and hope, including the "messianic" passages in chapters 9 and 11, often read at Christmas. Prophetic oracles and messages to Judah's neighbors mix with complex political relationships, again in the context of coming judgment and salvation, and written in forceful, beautiful poetry. A prose section ends First Isaiah with reports of a crucial period in King Hezekiah's reign and Isaiah's interaction with him.

1:1–20 A Message for Rebellious Judah. God's people have rebelled, rejecting his ways, despite his loving care. They cannot see that the battering they are receiving from Assyria is their own fault. Indeed, they could have been annihilated by now, but for God's mercy. They go through the motions of worship, but their sacrifices and rituals are useless without a corresponding change in attitude. God cannot hear their prayers until they adopt his ways of caring and justice. If they do that, all will be well. If not, they will be destroyed by Assyria.

without any soothing ointments or
bandages.
7 Your country lies in ruins,
and your towns are burned.
Foreigners plunder your fields before your
eyes
and destroy everything they see.
8 Beautiful Jerusalem* stands abandoned
like a watchman's shelter in a vineyard,
like a lean-to in a cucumber field after the
harvest,
like a helpless city under siege.
9 If the LORD of Heaven's Armies
had not spared a few of us,*
we would have been wiped out like Sodom,
destroyed like Gomorrah.

10 Listen to the LORD, you leaders of "Sodom."
Listen to the law of our God, people of
"Gomorrah."
11 "What makes you think I want all your
sacrifices?"
says the LORD.
"I am sick of your burnt offerings of rams
and the fat of fattened cattle.
I get no pleasure from the blood
of bulls and lambs and goats.
12 When you come to worship me,
who asked you to parade through my
courts with all your ceremony?
13 Stop bringing me your meaningless gifts;
the incense of your offerings disgusts me!
As for your celebrations of the new moon
and the Sabbath
and your special days for fasting—
they are all sinful and false.
I want no more of your pious meetings.
14 I hate your new moon celebrations and your
annual festivals.
They are a burden to me. I cannot stand
them!
15 When you lift up your hands in prayer, I will
not look.
Though you offer many prayers, I will not
listen,
for your hands are covered with the blood
of innocent victims.
16 Wash yourselves and be clean!
Get your sins out of my sight.
Give up your evil ways.
17 Learn to do good.
Seek justice.
Help the oppressed.
Defend the cause of orphans.
Fight for the rights of widows.

18 "Come now, let's settle this,"
says the LORD.
"Though your sins are like scarlet,
I will make them as white as snow.
Though they are red like crimson,
I will make them as white as wool.
19 If you will only obey me,
you will have plenty to eat.
20 But if you turn away and refuse to listen,
you will be devoured by the sword of your
enemies.
I, the LORD, have spoken!"

Unfaithful Jerusalem

21 See how Jerusalem, once so faithful,
has become a prostitute.
Once the home of justice and righteousness,
she is now filled with murderers.
22 Once like pure silver,
you have become like worthless slag.
Once so pure,
you are now like watered-down wine.
23 Your leaders are rebels,
the companions of thieves.
All of them love bribes
and demand payoffs,
but they refuse to defend the cause of
orphans
or fight for the rights of widows.

24 Therefore, the Lord, the LORD of Heaven's
Armies,
the Mighty One of Israel, says,
"I will take revenge on my enemies
and pay back my foes!
25 I will raise my fist against you.
I will melt you down and skim off your slag.
I will remove all your impurities.
26 Then I will give you good judges again
and wise counselors like you used to have.
Then Jerusalem will again be called the Home
of Justice
and the Faithful City."

1:8 Hebrew *The daughter of Zion.* **1:9** Greek version reads *a few of our children.* Compare Rom 9:29.

1:21–31 Unfaithful Jerusalem. Judah's capital has degenerated from former glory into spiritual prostitution; instead of worshiping the LORD her people worship idols. Her leaders are corrupt. Moral collapse inevitably follows rejection of God. The way back to justice and faithfulness is repentance; the alternative is utter destruction.

27 Zion will be restored by justice;
those who repent will be revived by righteousness.
28 But rebels and sinners will be completely destroyed,
and those who desert the LORD will be consumed.

29 You will be ashamed of your idol worship
in groves of sacred oaks.
You will blush because you worshiped
in gardens dedicated to idols.
30 You will be like a great tree with withered leaves,
like a garden without water.
31 The strongest among you will disappear like straw;
their evil deeds will be the spark that sets it on fire.
They and their evil works will burn up together,
and no one will be able to put out the fire.

The LORD's Future Reign

2 This is a vision that Isaiah son of Amoz saw concerning Judah and Jerusalem:

2 In the last days, the mountain of the LORD's house
will be the highest of all—
the most important place on earth.
It will be raised above the other hills,
and people from all over the world will stream there to worship.
3 People from many nations will come and say,
"Come, let us go up to the mountain of the LORD,
to the house of Jacob's God.
There he will teach us his ways,
and we will walk in his paths."
For the LORD's teaching will go out from Zion;
his word will go out from Jerusalem.
4 The LORD will mediate between nations
and will settle international disputes.
They will hammer their swords into plowshares
and their spears into pruning hooks.
Nation will no longer fight against nation,
nor train for war anymore.

A Warning of Judgment

5 Come, descendants of Jacob,
let us walk in the light of the LORD!
6 For the LORD has rejected his people,
the descendants of Jacob,
because they have filled their land with practices from the East
and with sorcerers, as the Philistines do.
They have made alliances with pagans.
7 Israel is full of silver and gold;
there is no end to its treasures.
Their land is full of warhorses;
there is no end to its chariots.
8 Their land is full of idols;
the people worship things they have made
with their own hands.
9 So now they will be humbled,
and all will be brought low—
do not forgive them.
10 Crawl into caves in the rocks.
Hide in the dust
from the terror of the LORD
and the glory of his majesty.
11 Human pride will be brought down,
and human arrogance will be humbled.
Only the LORD will be exalted
on that day of judgment.

12 For the LORD of Heaven's Armies
has a day of reckoning.
He will punish the proud and mighty
and bring down everything that is exalted.
13 He will cut down the tall cedars of Lebanon
and all the mighty oaks of Bashan.
14 He will level all the high mountains
and all the lofty hills.
15 He will break down every high tower
and every fortified wall.
16 He will destroy all the great trading ships*
and every magnificent vessel.
17 Human pride will be humbled,
and human arrogance will be brought down.

2:16 Hebrew *every ship of Tarshish.*

2:1–4 The LORD's Future Reign. Isaiah sees beyond the present murkiness to when Jerusalem will again be glorious, attracting all nations to the LORD.

2:5–22 A Warning of Judgment. People have made *alliances with pagans,* including occult practices and worshiping idols. They are filled with *pride* and *arrogance*; the latest military technology brings them only temporary victory. Isaiah's prayer that God would not forgive them (v. 9) is a recognition that simply sweeping sin under the carpet is no solution. Human pride must fall, if God is to be exalted. So there will be a time of terror, when human support proves useless.

Only the LORD will be exalted
on that day of judgment.

18 Idols will completely disappear.
19 When the LORD rises to shake the earth,
his enemies will crawl into holes in the ground.
They will hide in caves in the rocks
from the terror of the LORD
and the glory of his majesty.
20 On that day of judgment they will abandon
the gold and silver idols
they made for themselves to worship.
They will leave their gods to the rodents and bats,
21 while they crawl away into caverns
and hide among the jagged rocks in the cliffs.
They will try to escape the terror of the LORD
and the glory of his majesty
as he rises to shake the earth.
22 Don't put your trust in mere humans.
They are as frail as breath.
What good are they?

Judgment against Judah

3 [1]The Lord, the LORD of Heaven's Armies,
will take away from Jerusalem and Judah
everything they depend on:
every bit of bread
and every drop of water,
2 all their heroes and soldiers,
judges and prophets,
fortune-tellers and elders,
3 army officers and high officials,
advisers, skilled craftsmen, and astrologers.

4 I will make boys their leaders,
and toddlers their rulers.
5 People will oppress each other—
man against man,
neighbor against neighbor.
Young people will insult their elders,
and vulgar people will sneer at the honorable.

6 In those days a man will say to his brother,
"Since you have a coat, you be our leader!
Take charge of this heap of ruins!"
7 But he will reply,
"No! I can't help.
I don't have any extra food or clothes.
Don't put me in charge!"

8 For Jerusalem will stumble,
and Judah will fall,
because they speak out against the LORD and
refuse to obey him.
They provoke him to his face.
9 The very look on their faces gives them away.
They display their sin like the people of Sodom
and don't even try to hide it.
They are doomed!
They have brought destruction upon themselves.

10 Tell the godly that all will be well for them.
They will enjoy the rich reward they have earned!
11 But the wicked are doomed,
for they will get exactly what they deserve.

12 Childish leaders oppress my people,
and women rule over them.
O my people, your leaders mislead you;
they send you down the wrong road.
13 The LORD takes his place in court
and presents his case against his people!
14 The LORD comes forward to pronounce judgment
on the elders and rulers of his people:
"You have ruined Israel, my vineyard.
Your houses are filled with things stolen from the poor.
15 How dare you crush my people,
grinding the faces of the poor into the dust?"
demands the Lord, the LORD of Heaven's Armies.

A Warning to Jerusalem

16 The LORD says, "Beautiful Zion* is haughty:
craning her elegant neck,

3:16 Or *The women of Zion* (with corresponding changes to plural forms through verse 24); Hebrew reads *The daughters of Zion;* also in 3:17.

3:1–15 Judgement against Judah. God will remove Judah's resources and props; civil unrest, disrespect, and an unwillingness to take responsibility will characterize society because people blatantly refuse to obey God. Judgment will fall first on the leaders, referred to as *childish leaders*, and women who oppress and mislead their people. God cares about those who are crushed by other people.

3:16—4:1 A Warning to Jerusalem. Jerusalem is

Feminine Adornment

Feminine adornment refers to methods used to highlight a woman's appearance, including cosmetics, perfumes, and fashion. Eye paint enhanced and enlarged the eyes and eyebrows but may also have reduced glare from the sun, deterred disease-carrying flies, and alleviated dryness of the skin. Three Old Testament passages seem to disapprove of eye painting (2 Kgs 9:30; Jer 4:30; Ezek 23:40), but Job 42:14 refers to Job's third daughter as Keren-happuch, the "horn of paint" or "antimony" (horn being a small container used for eye-paint powder), and Job 42:15 refers to the same daughter with high regard. This passage could indicate that only the overuse of cosmetics was viewed with disapproval.

The use of perfume was hygienic and social. Since water was sometimes scarce, the more expeditious method of caring for the body was with oils and perfumes. Oils and ointments were essential for maintaining the skin in such a dry climate. Manufacture of these items required skilled workers and was an accepted vocation (1 Sam 8:13).

Jewelry was sometimes worn for superstitious reasons (e.g., as a good-luck charm). Many biblical passages mention jewelry, specific gemstones, metals, or bones, wood, or plants from which jewelry was fashioned. Some ancient jewelry forms are necklaces, bracelets, armlets, anklets, hairpins and hair ornaments, pins for securing tunics, earrings, nose rings, finger rings, belts, and pendants. Reportedly no gemstone deposits have been found in Palestine, but many are located in Egypt and Mesopotamia. This helps in understanding why much Israelite acquisition of gemstone jewelry came through trade, purchase, or conquest (cf. Isa 1).

In the Greco-Roman world, sumptuary laws (that is, laws regulating personal behavior) were passed from time to time, but they did little to restrain women's love of elegance and fashion. Classical statuary reveals the care with which fine fabric was draped about the female form and with which hair was arranged, often requiring the specialized labor of at least two slaves (cf. 1 Pet 3:4). Pearls were greatly prized, even though they were acquired at the risk of a pearl diver's life; ostentation in jewelry and fine clothing required funds that might better be employed to feed the poor (cf. 1 Tim 2:9). The noble Roman widow Cornelia was once visited by women anxious to show off their jewels. When asked in turn to show her own, Cornelia summoned her two young sons, the Gracchi, and declared, "These are my jewels."

flirting with her eyes,
walking with dainty steps,
tinkling her ankle bracelets.
17 So the Lord will send scabs on her head;
the LORD will make beautiful Zion
bald."

18 On that day of judgment
the Lord will strip away everything that
makes her beautiful:
ornaments, headbands, crescent necklaces,
19 earrings, bracelets, and veils;
20 scarves, ankle bracelets, sashes,
perfumes, and charms;
21 rings, jewels,
22 party clothes, gowns, capes, and purses;
23 mirrors, fine linen garments,
head ornaments, and shawls.

24 Instead of smelling of sweet perfume, she will
stink.
She will wear a rope for a sash,
and her elegant hair will fall out.
She will wear rough burlap instead of rich
robes.
Shame will replace her beauty.*
25 The men of the city will be killed with the
sword,
and her warriors will die in battle.
26 The gates of Zion will weep and mourn.
The city will be like a ravaged
woman,
huddled on the ground.

3:24 As in Dead Sea Scrolls; Masoretic Text reads *robes / because instead of beauty.*

compared to a beautiful woman who is stripped of her finery and raped, ending as a smelly heap in the gutter. This may reflect actual females, bent on luxury and sex, with no thought of God. These will be desperate to find a mate, when the males have died in battle. Ending up unmarried in those days was a terrible fate.

4 In that day so few men will be left that seven women will fight for each man, saying, "Let us all marry you! We will provide our own food and clothing. Only let us take your name so we won't be mocked as old maids."

A Promise of Restoration

2 But in that day, the branch* of the LORD
will be beautiful and glorious;
the fruit of the land will be the pride and glory
of all who survive in Israel.
3 All who remain in Zion
will be a holy people—
those who survive the destruction of Jerusalem
and are recorded among the living.
4 The Lord will wash the filth from beautiful Zion*
and cleanse Jerusalem of its bloodstains
with the hot breath of fiery judgment.
5 Then the LORD will provide shade for Mount Zion
and all who assemble there.
He will provide a canopy of cloud during the day
and smoke and flaming fire at night,
covering the glorious land.
6 It will be a shelter from daytime heat
and a hiding place from storms and rain.

A Song about the LORD's Vineyard

5 [1]Now I will sing for the one I love
a song about his vineyard:
My beloved had a vineyard
on a rich and fertile hill.
2 He plowed the land, cleared its stones,
and planted it with the best vines.
In the middle he built a watchtower
and carved a winepress in the nearby rocks.
Then he waited for a harvest of sweet grapes,
but the grapes that grew were bitter.
3 Now, you people of Jerusalem and Judah,
you judge between me and my vineyard.
4 What more could I have done for my vineyard
that I have not already done?
When I expected sweet grapes,
why did my vineyard give me bitter grapes?

5 Now let me tell you
what I will do to my vineyard:
I will tear down its hedges
and let it be destroyed.
I will break down its walls
and let the animals trample it.
6 I will make it a wild place
where the vines are not pruned and the ground is not hoed,
a place overgrown with briers and thorns.
I will command the clouds
to drop no rain on it.
7 The nation of Israel is the vineyard of the LORD of Heaven's Armies.
The people of Judah are his pleasant garden.
He expected a crop of justice,
but instead he found oppression.
He expected to find righteousness,
but instead he heard cries of violence.

Judah's Guilt and Judgment

8 What sorrow for you who buy up house after house and field after field,

4:2 Or *the Branch.* **4:4** Or *from the women of Zion;* Hebrew reads *from the daughters of Zion.*

4:2–6 A Promise of Restoration. God will cleanse those who survive, wiping away their sins and making them holy and beautiful. He will provide shelter and protection. Note the idea of cloud by day and fire by night, evoking memories of his protection of Israel in the wilderness (Num 9:15ff.).

5:1–7 A Song about the LORD's Vineyard. God's people are his vineyard, for whom he has done everything necessary for the best possible harvest. But their fruit is bitter, inedible. The logical response is to uproot the vines, leaving a wasteland, just as God views Judah's output of oppression and violence instead of righteousness and justice.

5:8–30 Judah's Guilt and Judgment. As the population decreases once God's judgment begins to bite, opportunists will buy up deserted properties. But how sad this is, because one day there will only be ghost towns left. Isaiah points to the irony of having wild parties now without giving a thought to God—it will all end in the tragedy of exile and death. Humanity will be humiliated, but God will finally have the glory his people have not given him. Not only are they piling up wickedness and getting their values and priorities upside down, they are also mocking the very One who could save them, but God will not save them because they have despised him. Indeed, God will call a pagan power to destroy Judah—note the vivid drama in the poetry of verses 26–36.

until everyone is evicted and you live alone
in the land.
9 But I have heard the LORD of Heaven's Armies
swear a solemn oath:
"Many houses will stand deserted;
even beautiful mansions will be empty.
10 Ten acres* of vineyard will not produce even
six gallons* of wine.
Ten baskets of seed will yield only one
basket* of grain."

11 What sorrow for those who get up early in
the morning
looking for a drink of alcohol
and spend long evenings drinking wine
to make themselves flaming drunk.
12 They furnish wine and lovely music at their
grand parties—
lyre and harp, tambourine and flute—
but they never think about the LORD
or notice what he is doing.

13 So my people will go into exile far away
because they do not know me.
Those who are great and honored will starve,
and the common people will die of thirst.
14 The grave* is licking its lips in anticipation,
opening its mouth wide.
The great and the lowly
and all the drunken mob will be swallowed
up.
15 Humanity will be destroyed, and people
brought down;
even the arrogant will lower their eyes in
humiliation.
16 But the LORD of Heaven's Armies will be
exalted by his justice.
The holiness of God will be displayed by
his righteousness.
17 In that day lambs will find good pastures,
and fattened sheep and young goats* will
feed among the ruins.

18 What sorrow for those who drag their sins
behind them
with ropes made of lies,
who drag wickedness behind them like a
cart!
19 They even mock God and say,
"Hurry up and do something!
We want to see what you can do.
Let the Holy One of Israel carry out his plan,
for we want to know what it is."

20 What sorrow for those who say
that evil is good and good is evil,
that dark is light and light is dark,
that bitter is sweet and sweet is bitter.
21 What sorrow for those who are wise in their
own eyes
and think themselves so clever.
22 What sorrow for those who are heroes at
drinking wine
and boast about all the alcohol they can
hold.
23 They take bribes to let the wicked go free,
and they punish the innocent.

24 Therefore, just as fire licks up stubble
and dry grass shrivels in the flame,
so their roots will rot
and their flowers wither.
For they have rejected the law of the LORD of
Heaven's Armies;
they have despised the word of the Holy
One of Israel.
25 That is why the LORD's anger burns against
his people,
and why he has raised his fist to crush
them.
The mountains tremble,
and the corpses of his people litter the
streets like garbage.
But even then the LORD's anger is not
satisfied.
His fist is still poised to strike!

26 He will send a signal to distant nations far
away
and whistle to those at the ends of the
earth.
They will come racing toward Jerusalem.
27 They will not get tired or stumble.
They will not stop for rest or sleep.
Not a belt will be loose,
not a sandal strap broken.
28 Their arrows will be sharp
and their bows ready for battle.
Sparks will fly from their horses' hooves,
and the wheels of their chariots will spin
like a whirlwind.
29 They will roar like lions,
like the strongest of lions.
Growling, they will pounce on their victims
and carry them off,
and no one will be there to rescue them.

5:10a Hebrew *A ten yoke,* that is, the area of land plowed by ten teams of oxen in one day. **5:10b** Hebrew *a bath* [21 liters]. **5:10c** Hebrew *A homer* [5 bushels or 182 liters] *of seed will yield only an ephah* [20 quarts or 22 liters]. **5:14** Hebrew *Sheol.* **5:17** As in Greek version; Hebrew reads *and strangers.*

30 They will roar over their victims on that day
of destruction
like the roaring of the sea.
If someone looks across the land,
only darkness and distress will be seen;
even the light will be darkened by clouds.

Isaiah's Cleansing and Call

6 It was in the year King Uzziah died* that
I saw the Lord. He was sitting on a lofty
throne, and the train of his robe filled the
Temple. 2 Attending him were mighty seraphim,
each having six wings. With two wings they covered their faces, with two they covered their feet,
and with two they flew. 3 They were calling out
to each other,

"Holy, holy, holy is the LORD of Heaven's
Armies!
The whole earth is filled with his glory!"

4 Their voices shook the Temple to its foundations, and the entire building was filled with
smoke.
5 Then I said, "It's all over! I am doomed, for
I am a sinful man. I have filthy lips, and I live
among a people with filthy lips. Yet I have seen
the King, the LORD of Heaven's Armies."
6 Then one of the seraphim flew to me with a
burning coal he had taken from the altar with a
pair of tongs. 7 He touched my lips with it and said,
"See, this coal has touched your lips. Now your
guilt is removed, and your sins are forgiven."
8 Then I heard the Lord asking, "Whom
should I send as a messenger to this people? Who
will go for us?"
I said, "Here I am. Send me."
9 And he said, "Yes, go, and say to this people,

'Listen carefully, but do not understand.
Watch closely, but learn nothing.'
10 Harden the hearts of these people.
Plug their ears and shut their eyes.
That way, they will not see with their eyes,
nor hear with their ears,
nor understand with their hearts
and turn to me for healing."*

11 Then I said, "Lord, how long will this go on?"
And he replied,

"Until their towns are empty,
their houses are deserted,
and the whole country is a wasteland;
12 until the LORD has sent everyone away,
and the entire land of Israel lies deserted.
13 If even a tenth—a remnant—survive,
it will be invaded again and burned.
But as a terebinth or oak tree leaves a stump
when it is cut down,
so Israel's stump will be a holy seed."

A Message for Ahaz

7 When Ahaz, son of Jotham and grandson
of Uzziah, was king of Judah, King Rezin of
Syria* and Pekah son of Remaliah, the king
of Israel, set out to attack Jerusalem. However,
they were unable to carry out their plan.
2 The news had come to the royal court of Judah: "Syria is allied with Israel* against us!" So
the hearts of the king and his people trembled
with fear, like trees shaking in a storm.

6:1 King Uzziah died in 740 B.C. **6:9-10** Greek version reads *And he said, "Go and say to this people, / 'When you hear what I say, you will not understand. / When you see what I do, you will not comprehend.' / For the hearts of these people are hardened, / and their ears cannot hear, and they have closed their eyes— / so their eyes cannot see, / and their ears cannot hear, / and their hearts cannot understand, / and they cannot turn to me and let me heal them."* Compare Matt 13:14-15; Mark 4:12; Luke 8:10; Acts 28:26-27. **7:1** Hebrew *Aram;* also in 7:2, 4, 5, 8. **7:2** Hebrew *Ephraim,* referring to the northern kingdom of Israel; also in 7:5, 8, 9, 17.

6:1–13 Isaiah's Cleansing and Call. Uzziah's story is told in 2 Kings 15:1–7. Politically, the Assyrians were beginning to invade the Northern Kingdom of Israel (2 Kgs 15:17–20) and were therefore a threat to Judah in the south. Spiritually, Judah's people were blatantly worshiping at pagan shrines. The young Isaiah identifies himself with the nation's guilt, as he experiences a vision of God's holiness. His forgiveness and subsequent commission is a model of what God wanted Israel to be: a forgiven, missionary people. Instead, they will resist Isaiah's message to the bitter end. Yet even then, there is hope of a remnant. Note that Isaiah was not told to make his message obscure or complex (cf. 28:9–10, where he is accused of being too simple!). The imperatives here reflect people's inevitable response to his ministry.

7:1—12:6 Historical and Political Insights

The scene is set with Judah's king Ahaz facing a double attack by Israel and Syria in an attempt to ward off the common enemy, Assyria.

7:1–9 A Message for Ahaz. Isaiah and his son, whose name promises hope (see translator's note on 7:3a), try to get Ahaz to stop worrying because neither Syria nor Israel has any real power.

3 Then the LORD said to Isaiah, "Take your son Shear-jashub* and go out to meet King Ahaz. You will find him at the end of the aqueduct that feeds water into the upper pool, near the road leading to the field where cloth is washed.* 4 Tell him to stop worrying. Tell him he doesn't need to fear the fierce anger of those two burned-out embers, King Rezin of Syria and Pekah son of Remaliah. 5 Yes, the kings of Syria and Israel are plotting against him, saying, 6 'We will attack Judah and capture it for ourselves. Then we will install the son of Tabeel as Judah's king.' 7 But this is what the Sovereign LORD says:

"This invasion will never happen;
 it will never take place;
8 for Syria is no stronger than its capital,
 Damascus,
 and Damascus is no stronger than its king,
 Rezin.
As for Israel, within sixty-five years
 it will be crushed and completely
 destroyed.
9 Israel is no stronger than its capital, Samaria,
 and Samaria is no stronger than its king,
 Pekah son of Remaliah.
Unless your faith is firm,
 I cannot make you stand firm."

The Sign of Immanuel

10 Later, the LORD sent this message to King Ahaz: 11 "Ask the LORD your God for a sign of confirmation, Ahaz. Make it as difficult as you want—as high as heaven or as deep as the place of the dead.*"

12 But the king refused. "No," he said, "I will not test the LORD like that."

13 Then Isaiah said, "Listen well, you royal family of David! Isn't it enough to exhaust human patience? Must you exhaust the patience of my God as well? 14 All right then, the Lord himself will give you the sign. Look! The virgin* will conceive a child! She will give birth to a son and will call him Immanuel (which means 'God is with us'). 15 By the time this child is old enough to choose what is right and reject what is wrong, he will be eating yogurt* and honey. 16 For before the child is that old, the lands of the two kings you fear so much will both be deserted.

17 "Then the LORD will bring things on you, your nation, and your family unlike anything since Israel broke away from Judah. He will bring the king of Assyria upon you!"

18 In that day the LORD will whistle for the army of southern Egypt and for the army of Assyria. They will swarm around you like flies and bees. 19 They will come in vast hordes and settle in the fertile areas and also in the desolate valleys, caves, and thorny places. 20 In that day the Lord will hire a "razor" from beyond the Euphrates River*—the king of Assyria—and use it to shave off everything: your land, your crops, and your people.*

21 In that day a farmer will be fortunate to have a cow and two sheep or goats left. 22 Nevertheless, there will be enough milk for everyone because so few people will be left in the land. They will eat their fill of yogurt and honey. 23 In that day the lush vineyards, now worth 1,000 pieces of silver,* will become patches of briers and thorns. 24 The entire land will become a vast expanse of briers and thorns, a hunting ground overrun by wildlife. 25 No one will go to the fertile hillsides where the gardens once grew, for briers and thorns will cover them. Cattle, sheep, and goats will graze there.

The Coming Assyrian Invasion

8 Then the LORD said to me, "Make a large signboard and clearly write this name on it: Maher-shalal-hash-baz.*" 2 I asked Uriah

7:3a *Shear-jashub* means "A remnant will return." **7:3b** Or *bleached.* **7:11** Hebrew *as deep as Sheol.* **7:14** Or *young woman.* **7:15** Or *curds;* also in 7:22. **7:20a** Hebrew *the river.* **7:20b** Hebrew *shave off the head, the hair of the legs, and the beard.* **7:23** Hebrew *1,000 shekels of silver,* about 25 pounds or 11.4 kilograms in weight. **8:1** *Maher-shalal-hash-baz* means "Swift to plunder and quick to carry away."

7:10–25 The Sign of Immanuel. Ahaz demonstrates his unbelieving attitude by refusing God's proffered sign, which will nevertheless come true. An unmarried young woman will have a child called Immanuel, "God with us." There is a tension between the immediate and the future here. The baby is possibly current headline news—perhaps of a well-known contemporary woman—and gives a timeline for when Ahaz's immediate enemies will be no more. But it is more than that. Isaiah later places the child *after* all the darkness to come (9:1–7), and Matthew 1:23 picks this up this thread as a messianic reference to Jesus. Meanwhile, God will whistle up a much more feared enemy to ravage the land. The Egyptian Nile River's annual floods brought swarms of flies, and Assyria's hills were known for their bees, hence the metaphors.

8:1–10 The Coming Assyrian Invasion. Isaiah's second son's name is also significant, warning of the imminent demise of the Northern Kingdom, Israel (see 2 Kgs 17:1–6). Judah's glee at the downfall of their

the priest and Zechariah son of Jeberekiah, both
known as honest men, to witness my doing this.
3 Then I slept with my wife, and she became
pregnant and gave birth to a son. And the LORD
said, "Call him Maher-shalal-hash-baz. 4 For before
this child is old enough to say 'Papa' or 'Mama,'
the king of Assyria will carry away both the abundance of Damascus and the riches of Samaria."
5 Then the LORD spoke to me again and said,
6 "My care for the people of Judah is like the gently flowing waters of Shiloah, but they have rejected it. They are rejoicing over what will happen
to* King Rezin and King Pekah.* 7 Therefore, the
Lord will overwhelm them with a mighty flood
from the Euphrates River*—the king of Assyria
and all his glory. This flood will overflow all its
channels 8 and sweep into Judah until it is chin
deep. It will spread its wings, submerging your
land from one end to the other, O Immanuel.

9 "Huddle together, you nations, and be terrified.
Listen, all you distant lands.
Prepare for battle, but you will be crushed!
Yes, prepare for battle, but you will be
crushed!
10 Call your councils of war, but they will be
worthless.
Develop your strategies, but they will not
succeed.
For God is with us!*"

A Call to Trust the LORD

11 The LORD has given me a strong warning not
to think like everyone else does. He said,

12 "Don't call everything a conspiracy, like
they do,
and don't live in dread of what frightens
them.
13 Make the LORD of Heaven's Armies holy in
your life.
He is the one you should fear.
He is the one who should make you tremble.
14 He will keep you safe.
But to Israel and Judah
he will be a stone that makes people stumble,
a rock that makes them fall.
And for the people of Jerusalem
he will be a trap and a snare.
15 Many will stumble and fall,
never to rise again.
They will be snared and captured."

16 Preserve the teaching of God;
entrust his instructions to those who
follow me.
17 I will wait for the LORD,
who has turned away from the descendants
of Jacob.
I will put my hope in him.

18 I and the children the LORD has given me
serve as signs and warnings to Israel from the
LORD of Heaven's Armies who dwells in his
Temple on Mount Zion.
19 Someone may say to you, "Let's ask the
mediums and those who consult the spirits of
the dead. With their whisperings and mutter-
ings, they will tell us what to do." But shouldn't
people ask God for guidance? Should the living
seek guidance from the dead?
20 Look to God's instructions and teachings!
People who contradict his word are completely in
the dark. 21 They will go from one place to another, weary and hungry. And because they are hungry, they will rage and curse their king and their
God. They will look up to heaven 22 and down at
the earth, but wherever they look, there will be
trouble and anguish and dark despair. They will
be thrown out into the darkness.

Hope in the Messiah

9 1 *Nevertheless, that time of darkness and
despair will not go on forever. The land of
Zebulun and Naphtali will be humbled, but
there will be a time in the future when Galilee of

8:6a Or *They are rejoicing because of.* **8:6b** Hebrew *and the son of Remaliah.* **8:7** Hebrew *the river.* **8:10** Hebrew *Immanuel!* **9:1** Verse 9:1 is numbered 8:23 in Hebrew text.

enemy will be short-lived, and their trust in Assyria is misplaced; Immanuel's land will also suffer at the hands of their "rescuer." And yet, in what may be a quotation from a temple hymn, international hostility will ultimately be ineffectual against a nation that has "God with us," Immanuel.

8:11–22 A Call to Trust the LORD. Isaiah is to make sure that God is supreme in his life. For everyone else in Israel and Judah, God himself will be a *stone* and a *rock* to cause their downfall, another messianic allusion, which the New Testament applies to Jesus (Rom 9:33; 1 Pet 2:8). Isaiah is told to ensure God's teaching is preserved for faithful people, and he responds in trust. Those who look elsewhere for guidance are in darkness.

9:1–7 Hope in the Messiah. There is light at the end of the tunnel. The darkness of God's judgment will end with glory! The northern tribes of Zebulun and

the Gentiles, which lies along the road that runs between the Jordan and the sea, will be filled with glory.

2*The people who walk in darkness
will see a great light.
For those who live in a land of deep darkness,*
a light will shine.
3 You will enlarge the nation of Israel,
and its people will rejoice.
They will rejoice before you
as people rejoice at the harvest
and like warriors dividing the plunder.
4 For you will break the yoke of their slavery
and lift the heavy burden from their shoulders.
You will break the oppressor's rod,
just as you did when you destroyed the army of Midian.
5 The boots of the warrior
and the uniforms bloodstained by war
will all be burned.
They will be fuel for the fire.
6 For a child is born to us,
a son is given to us.
The government will rest on his shoulders.
And he will be called:
Wonderful Counselor,* Mighty God,
Everlasting Father, Prince of Peace.
7 His government and its peace
will never end.
He will rule with fairness and justice from
the throne of his ancestor David
for all eternity.
The passionate commitment of the LORD of Heaven's Armies
will make this happen!

The LORD's Anger against Israel

8 The Lord has spoken out against Jacob;
his judgment has fallen upon Israel.
9 And the people of Israel* and Samaria,
who spoke with such pride and arrogance,
will soon know it.
10 They said, "We will replace the broken bricks
of our ruins with finished stone,
and replant the felled sycamore-fig trees
with cedars."

11 But the LORD will bring Rezin's enemies
against Israel
and stir up all their foes.
12 The Syrians* from the east and the Philistines from the west
will bare their fangs and devour Israel.
But even then the LORD's anger will not be satisfied.
His fist is still poised to strike.
13 For after all this punishment, the people will still not repent.
They will not seek the LORD of Heaven's Armies.
14 Therefore, in a single day the LORD will
destroy both the head and the tail,
the noble palm branch and the lowly reed.
15 The leaders of Israel are the head,
and the lying prophets are the tail.
16 For the leaders of the people have misled them.
They have led them down the path of destruction.
17 That is why the Lord takes no pleasure in the young men
and shows no mercy even to the widows and orphans.
For they are all wicked hypocrites,
and they all speak foolishness.

9:2a Verses 9:2-21 are numbered 9:1-20 in Hebrew text. **9:2b** Greek version reads *a land where death casts its shadow.* Compare Matt 4:16. **9:6** Or *Wonderful, Counselor.* **9:9** Hebrew *of Ephraim,* referring to the northern kingdom of Israel. **9:12** Hebrew *Arameans.*

Naphtali occupied the area around the Sea of Galilee and had been the first to fall to Assyria. Only here is it called *Galilee of the Gentiles*; the Messiah is for all nations. The *great light* that is the Messiah-child will bring joy, breaking the burden of oppression. (For *army of Midian* see Judg 6—7.) The Messiah-child is more than simply David's descendant; he is the divine Ruler, with an eternal reign of peace, fairness, and justice.

9:8—10:4 The LORD's Anger against Israel. Isaiah turns his attention to Israel and Syria, so arrogant, but so soon to be destroyed. Rezin is Syria's king; his enemies are the Assyrians. The region is a melting pot of unrest; much is already ruined. Despite everything, Israel remains unrepentant. So God will destroy all, both noble and lowly, especially the leaders and false prophets (the head and tail) who have led the nation away from him. Even widows and orphans, normally God's special concern, are shunned for their hypocrisy. Evil has a habit of spreading like a forest fire, and in the horror of suffering and starvation everyone will turn on each other; parents will even eat their children. Corruption in the courts receives special condemnation, because as always it is the poor who are deprived of justice, among them widows and orphans who have no one to support them.

But even then the LORD's anger will not be
satisfied.
His fist is still poised to strike.

18 This wickedness is like a brushfire.
It burns not only briers and thorns
but also sets the forests ablaze.
Its burning sends up clouds of smoke.
19 The land will be blackened
by the fury of the LORD of Heaven's Armies.
The people will be fuel for the fire,
and no one will spare even his own brother.
20 They will attack their neighbor on the right
but will still be hungry.
They will devour their neighbor on the left
but will not be satisfied.
In the end they will even eat their own
children.*
21 Manasseh will feed on Ephraim,
Ephraim will feed on Manasseh,
and both will devour Judah.
But even then the LORD's anger will not be
satisfied.
His fist is still poised to strike.

10 [1]What sorrow awaits the unjust
judges
and those who issue unfair laws.
2 They deprive the poor of justice
and deny the rights of the needy among
my people.
They prey on widows
and take advantage of orphans.
3 What will you do when I punish you,
when I send disaster upon you from a
distant land?
To whom will you turn for help?
Where will your treasures be safe?
4 You will stumble along as prisoners
or lie among the dead.
But even then the LORD's anger will not be
satisfied.
His fist is still poised to strike.

Judgment against Assyria

5 "What sorrow awaits Assyria, the rod of my
anger.
I use it as a club to express my anger.
6 I am sending Assyria against a godless nation,
against a people with whom I am angry.
Assyria will plunder them,
trampling them like dirt beneath its feet.
7 But the king of Assyria will not understand
that he is my tool;
his mind does not work that way.
His plan is simply to destroy,
to cut down nation after nation.
8 He will say,
'Each of my princes will soon be a king.
9 We destroyed Calno just as we did
Carchemish.
Hamath fell before us as Arpad did.
And we destroyed Samaria just as we did
Damascus.
10 Yes, we have finished off many a kingdom
whose gods were greater than those in
Jerusalem and Samaria.
11 So we will defeat Jerusalem and her gods,
just as we destroyed Samaria with hers.' "

12 After the Lord has used the king of Assyria
to accomplish his purposes on Mount Zion and
in Jerusalem, he will turn against the king of Assyria and punish him—for he is proud and arrogant. 13 He boasts,

"By my own powerful arm I have done this.
With my own shrewd wisdom I planned it.
I have broken down the defenses of nations
and carried off their treasures.
I have knocked down their kings like a bull.
14 I have robbed their nests of riches
and gathered up kingdoms as a farmer
gathers eggs.
No one can even flap a wing against me
or utter a peep of protest."
15 But can the ax boast greater power than the
person who uses it?
Is the saw greater than the person who saws?
Can a rod strike unless a hand moves it?
Can a wooden cane walk by itself?
16 Therefore, the Lord, the LORD of Heaven's
Armies,
will send a plague among Assyria's proud
troops,
and a flaming fire will consume its glory.
17 The LORD, the Light of Israel, will be a fire;

9:20 Or *eat their own arms.*

10:5–19 Judgment against Assyria. How often God uses unbelievers to teach his people a lesson! Here, Assyria is God's tool for judgment, but their king gets the wrong idea. He thinks he is unassailable and that Jerusalem's God is just like the rest—easily conquered. But the LORD will punish Assyria for its arrogance (note the vivid analogies of fire and plague), with few survivors.

the Holy One will be a flame.
He will devour the thorns and briers with fire,
burning up the enemy in a single night.
18 The LORD will consume Assyria's glory
like a fire consumes a forest in a fruitful land;
it will waste away like sick people in a plague.
19 Of all that glorious forest, only a few trees will survive—
so few that a child could count them!

Hope for the LORD's People

20 In that day the remnant left in Israel,
the survivors in the house of Jacob,
will no longer depend on allies
who seek to destroy them.
But they will faithfully trust the LORD,
the Holy One of Israel.
21 A remnant will return;*
yes, the remnant of Jacob will return to the Mighty God.
22 But though the people of Israel are as numerous
as the sand of the seashore,
only a remnant of them will return.
The LORD has rightly decided to destroy his people.
23 Yes, the Lord, the LORD of Heaven's Armies,
has already decided to destroy the entire land.*

24 So this is what the Lord, the LORD of Heav-
en's Armies, says: "O my people in Zion, do not
be afraid of the Assyrians when they oppress
you with rod and club as the Egyptians did long
ago. 25 In a little while my anger against you will
end, and then my anger will rise up to destroy
them." 26 The LORD of Heaven's Armies will lash
them with his whip, as he did when Gideon triumphed over the Midianites at the rock of Oreb,
or when the LORD's staff was raised to drown the
Egyptian army in the sea.

27 In that day the LORD will end the bondage of his people.
He will break the yoke of slavery
and lift it from their shoulders.*
28 Look, the Assyrians are now at Aiath.
They are passing through Migron
and are storing their equipment at Micmash.
29 They are crossing the pass
and are camping at Geba.
Fear strikes the town of Ramah.
All the people of Gibeah, the hometown of Saul,
are running for their lives.
30 Scream in terror,
you people of Gallim!
Shout out a warning to Laishah.
Oh, poor Anathoth!
31 There go the people of Madmenah, all fleeing.
The citizens of Gebim are trying to hide.
32 The enemy stops at Nob for the rest of that day.
He shakes his fist at beautiful Mount Zion,
the mountain of Jerusalem.
33 But look! The Lord, the LORD of Heaven's Armies,
will chop down the mighty tree of Assyria with great power!
He will cut down the proud.
That lofty tree will be brought down.
34 He will cut down the forest trees with an ax.
Lebanon will fall to the Mighty One.*

A Branch from David's Line

11 1 Out of the stump of David's family*
will grow a shoot—
yes, a new Branch bearing fruit
from the old root.
2 And the Spirit of the LORD will rest on him—
the Spirit of wisdom and understanding,

10:21 Hebrew *Shear-jashub;* see 7:3; 8:18. **10:22-23** Greek version reads *only a remnant of them will be saved. / For he will carry out his sentence quickly and with finality and righteousness; / for God will carry out his sentence upon all the world with finality.* Compare Rom 9:27-28. **10:27** As in Greek version; Hebrew reads *The yoke will be broken, / for you have grown so fat.* **10:34** Or *with an ax / as even the mighty trees of Lebanon fall.* **11:1** Hebrew *the stump of the line of Jesse.* Jesse was King David's father.

10:20–34 Hope for the LORD's People. A remnant from Israel will survive, though, returning to the LORD their God. Meanwhile, Isaiah encourages Jerusalem's inhabitants with a picture of God's vengeance on Assyria, just as he punished his people's enemies in the past (see Judg 6—7, and Exod 14). When that happens, his people will go free. But now, Assyria is marching toward and into Judah, and the residents are fleeing in terror. The army is only a few miles from Jerusalem. It seems hopeless—but God has other plans. Unlike Israel, Judah will be spared for the time being. Lebanon (with its forests) is a metaphor for the mighty and *lofty tree*, Assyria, which will be chopped down.

11:1–16 A Branch from David's Line. Isaiah continues the analogy of felling trees, promising that out of the *stump* that remains from Judah (David's family line)

the Spirit of counsel and might,
the Spirit of knowledge and the fear of the LORD.
3 He will delight in obeying the LORD.
He will not judge by appearance
nor make a decision based on hearsay.
4 He will give justice to the poor
and make fair decisions for the exploited.
The earth will shake at the force of his word,
and one breath from his mouth will destroy the wicked.
5 He will wear righteousness like a belt
and truth like an undergarment.

6 In that day the wolf and the lamb will live together;
the leopard will lie down with the baby goat.
The calf and the yearling will be safe with the lion,
and a little child will lead them all.
7 The cow will graze near the bear.
The cub and the calf will lie down together.
The lion will eat hay like a cow.
8 The baby will play safely near the hole of a cobra.
Yes, a little child will put its hand in a nest of deadly snakes without harm.
9 Nothing will hurt or destroy in all my holy mountain,
for as the waters fill the sea,
so the earth will be filled with people who know the LORD.

10 In that day the heir to David's throne*
will be a banner of salvation to all the world.
The nations will rally to him,
and the land where he lives will be a glorious place.*
11 In that day the Lord will reach out his hand a second time
to bring back the remnant of his people—
those who remain in Assyria and northern Egypt;
in southern Egypt, Ethiopia,* and Elam;
in Babylonia,* Hamath, and all the distant coastlands.
12 He will raise a flag among the nations
and assemble the exiles of Israel.
He will gather the scattered people of Judah
from the ends of the earth.

13 Then at last the jealousy between Israel* and Judah will end.
They will not be rivals anymore.
14 They will join forces to swoop down on Philistia to the west.
Together they will attack and plunder the nations to the east.
They will occupy the lands of Edom and Moab,
and Ammon will obey them.
15 The LORD will make a dry path through the gulf of the Red Sea.*
He will wave his hand over the Euphrates River,*
sending a mighty wind to divide it into seven streams
so it can easily be crossed on foot.
16 He will make a highway for the remnant of his people,
the remnant coming from Assyria,
just as he did for Israel long ago
when they returned from Egypt.

Songs of Praise for Salvation

12 1In that day you will sing:
"I will praise you, O LORD!
You were angry with me, but not any more.
Now you comfort me.
2 See, God has come to save me.
I will trust in him and not be afraid.
The LORD GOD is my strength and my song;
he has given me victory."

11:10a Hebrew *the root of Jesse.* **11:10b** Greek version reads *In that day the heir to David's throne* [literally *the root of Jesse*] *will come, / and he will rule over the Gentiles. / They will place their hopes on him.* Compare Rom 15:12. **11:11a** Hebrew *in Pathros, Cush.* **11:11b** Hebrew *in Shinar.* **11:13** Hebrew *Ephraim,* referring to the northern kingdom of Israel. **11:15a** Hebrew *will destroy the tongue of the sea of Egypt.* **11:15b** Hebrew *the river.*

---

will arise a new *shoot,* the Messiah. He will be clothed in God's Spirit, and delight in justice and fairness, righteousness and truth. Under his rule all creation will be at peace; he will be the Savior of the whole world. All God's scattered people will be brought together and relationships mended. Isaiah uses warrior terms to describe success against all foes; this is possibly also a metaphor for the spread of the Messiah's reign.

12:1–6 Songs of Praise for Salvation. Looking forward to this glorious future, God's people will spontaneously sing his praise. Trust, joy, and a testimony to the nations characterizes those who have experienced his salvation and restoration.

3 With joy you will drink deeply
from the fountain of salvation!
4 In that wonderful day you will sing:
"Thank the LORD! Praise his name!
Tell the nations what he has done.
Let them know how mighty he is!
5 Sing to the LORD, for he has done wonderful things.
Make known his praise around the world.
6 Let all the people of Jerusalem* shout his praise with joy!
For great is the Holy One of Israel who lives among you."

A Message about Babylon

13 Isaiah son of Amoz received this message concerning the destruction of Babylon:

2 "Raise a signal flag on a bare hilltop.
Call up an army against Babylon.
Wave your hand to encourage them
as they march into the palaces of the high and mighty.
3 I, the LORD, have dedicated these soldiers for this task.
Yes, I have called mighty warriors to express my anger,
and they will rejoice when I am exalted."

4 Hear the noise on the mountains!
Listen, as the vast armies march!
It is the noise and shouting of many nations.
The LORD of Heaven's Armies has called this army together.
5 They come from distant countries,
from beyond the farthest horizons.
They are the LORD's weapons to carry out his anger.
With them he will destroy the whole land.

6 Scream in terror, for the day of the LORD has arrived—
the time for the Almighty to destroy.
7 Every arm is paralyzed with fear.
Every heart melts,
8 and people are terrified.
Pangs of anguish grip them,
like those of a woman in labor.
They look helplessly at one another,
their faces aflame with fear.

9 For see, the day of the LORD is coming—
the terrible day of his fury and fierce anger.
The land will be made desolate,
and all the sinners destroyed with it.
10 The heavens will be black above them;
the stars will give no light.
The sun will be dark when it rises,
and the moon will provide no light.

11 "I, the LORD, will punish the world for its evil
and the wicked for their sin.
I will crush the arrogance of the proud
and humble the pride of the mighty.
12 I will make people scarcer than gold—
more rare than the fine gold of Ophir.
13 For I will shake the heavens.
The earth will move from its place
when the LORD of Heaven's Armies displays his wrath
in the day of his fierce anger."

14 Everyone in Babylon will run about like a hunted gazelle,
like sheep without a shepherd.
They will try to find their own people
and flee to their own land.
15 Anyone who is captured will be cut down—
run through with a sword.
16 Their little children will be dashed to death before their eyes.
Their homes will be sacked, and their wives will be raped.

17 "Look, I will stir up the Medes against Babylon.
They cannot be tempted by silver
or bribed with gold.

12:6 Hebrew *Zion.*

13:1—23:18 Prophetic Oracles

We see a vivid picture of the army God has raised, comprising different people groups who in turn had been dispersed when conquered.

13:1–22 A Message about Babylon. It was to Babylon that Judah finally fell, yet this was not the end of the story; proud Babylon herself would fall to the Medes and Persians, under God's judgment. We feel the Babylonians' terror—likened to probably the physical anguish women experience during childbirth. A dark day indeed, symbolized metaphorically by the extinguishing of all light in the sky. The savagery against babies and little children, and the raping of their mothers is devastating. The city will be left for wildlife to inhabit.

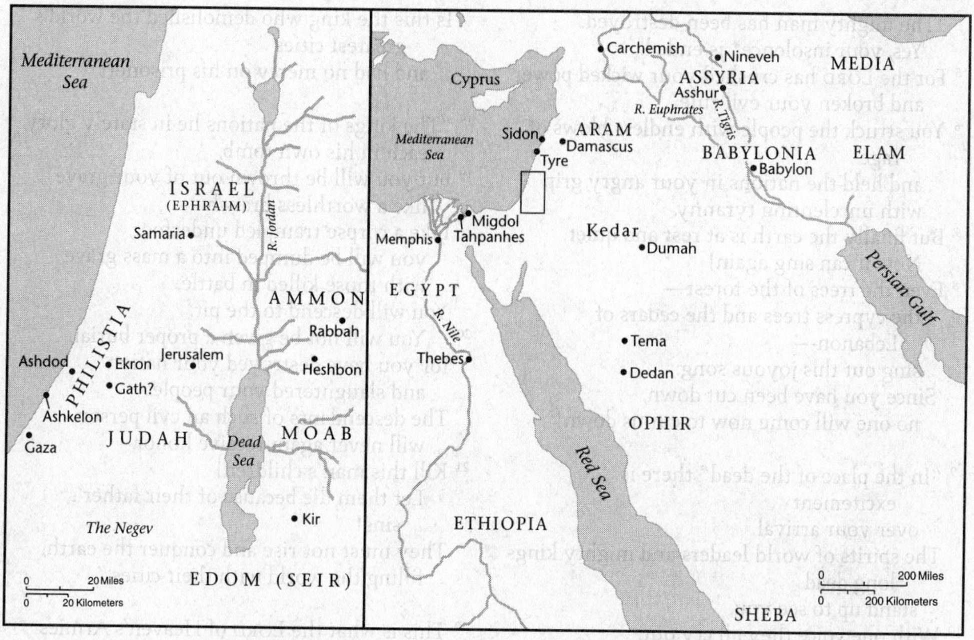

Places Mentioned in the Oracles against the Nations

18 The attacking armies will shoot down the
young men with arrows.
They will have no mercy on helpless babies
and will show no compassion for children."

19 Babylon, the most glorious of kingdoms,
the flower of Chaldean pride,
will be devastated like Sodom and Gomorrah
when God destroyed them.
20 Babylon will never be inhabited again.
It will remain empty for generation after
generation.
Nomads will refuse to camp there,
and shepherds will not bed down their
sheep.
21 Desert animals will move into the ruined city,
and the houses will be haunted by howling
creatures.
Owls will live among the ruins,
and wild goats will go there to dance.
22 Hyenas will howl in its fortresses,
and jackals will make dens in its luxurious
palaces.
Babylon's days are numbered;
its time of destruction will soon arrive.

A Taunt for Babylon's King

14 But the LORD will have mercy on the
descendants of Jacob. He will choose
Israel as his special people once again.
He will bring them back to settle once again in
their own land. And people from many different
nations will come and join them there and unite
with the people of Israel.* 2 The nations of the
world will help the LORD's people to return, and
those who come to live in their land will serve
them. Those who captured Israel will themselves
be captured, and Israel will rule over its enemies.
3 In that wonderful day when the LORD gives
his people rest from sorrow and fear, from slavery and chains, 4 you will taunt the king of Babylon. You will say,

14:1 Hebrew *the house of Jacob.* The names "Jacob" and "Israel" are often interchanged throughout the Old Testament, referring sometimes to the individual patriarch and sometimes to the nation.

14:1–23 A Taunt for Babylon's King. The tables are reversed, and it is Israel's turn to taunt their enemies. (Here, the term *Israel* is not the Northern Kingdom; it looks ahead to the remnant of God's people after the Exile—the surviving descendants of the patriarch Jacob/Israel.) Experiencing God's mercy, welcoming people from many nations, no wonder they sing! Incredibly, Babylon's king has fallen to rock bottom because of his lofty pride—his aspirations to godhead. Neither he nor his descendants must be given the chance to repeat their evil.

"The mighty man has been destroyed.
Yes, your insolence* is ended.
5 For the LORD has crushed your wicked power
and broken your evil rule.
6 You struck the people with endless blows of rage
and held the nations in your angry grip
with unrelenting tyranny.
7 But finally the earth is at rest and quiet.
Now it can sing again!
8 Even the trees of the forest—
the cypress trees and the cedars of Lebanon—
sing out this joyous song:
'Since you have been cut down,
no one will come now to cut us down!'

9 "In the place of the dead* there is excitement
over your arrival.
The spirits of world leaders and mighty kings long dead
stand up to see you.
10 With one voice they all cry out,
'Now you are as weak as we are!
11 Your might and power were buried with you.*
The sound of the harp in your palace has ceased.
Now maggots are your sheet,
and worms your blanket.'

12 "How you are fallen from heaven,
O shining star, son of the morning!
You have been thrown down to the earth,
you who destroyed the nations of the world.
13 For you said to yourself,
'I will ascend to heaven and set my throne
above God's stars.
I will preside on the mountain of the gods
far away in the north.*
14 I will climb to the highest heavens
and be like the Most High.'
15 Instead, you will be brought down to the place of the dead,
down to its lowest depths.
16 Everyone there will stare at you and ask,
'Can this be the one who shook the earth
and made the kingdoms of the world tremble?
17 Is this the one who destroyed the world
and made it into a wasteland?
Is this the king who demolished the world's greatest cities
and had no mercy on his prisoners?'

18 "The kings of the nations lie in stately glory,
each in his own tomb,
19 but you will be thrown out of your grave
like a worthless branch.
Like a corpse trampled underfoot,
you will be dumped into a mass grave
with those killed in battle.
You will descend to the pit.
20 You will not be given a proper burial,
for you have destroyed your nation
and slaughtered your people.
The descendants of such an evil person
will never again receive honor.
21 Kill this man's children!
Let them die because of their father's sins!
They must not rise and conquer the earth,
filling the world with their cities."

22 This is what the LORD of Heaven's Armies says:
"I, myself, have risen against Babylon!
I will destroy its children and its children's children,"
says the LORD.
23 "I will make Babylon a desolate place of owls,
filled with swamps and marshes.
I will sweep the land with the broom of destruction.
I, the LORD of Heaven's Armies, have spoken!"

A Message about Assyria

24 The LORD of Heaven's Armies has sworn this oath:
"It will all happen as I have planned.
It will be as I have decided.
25 I will break the Assyrians when they are in Israel;
I will trample them on my mountains.
My people will no longer be their slaves
nor bow down under their heavy loads.
26 I have a plan for the whole earth,
a hand of judgment upon all the nations.

14:4 As in Dead Sea Scrolls; the meaning of the Masoretic Text is uncertain. **14:9** Hebrew *Sheol;* also in 14:15. **14:11** Hebrew *were brought down to Sheol.* **14:13** Or *on the heights of Zaphon.*

14:24–27 A Message about Assyria. God's retribution extends to Assyria, which had exiled and enslaved the Northern Kingdom, Israel. God will fulfill his plans!

27 The LORD of Heaven's Armies has spoken—
who can change his plans?
When his hand is raised,
who can stop him?"

A Message about Philistia

28 This message came to me the year King Ahaz died:*

29 Do not rejoice, you Philistines,
that the rod that struck you is broken—
that the king who attacked you is dead.
For from that snake a more poisonous snake
will be born,
a fiery serpent to destroy you!
30 I will feed the poor in my pasture;
the needy will lie down in peace.
But as for you, I will wipe you out with famine
and destroy the few who remain.
31 Wail at the gates! Weep in the cities!
Melt with fear, you Philistines!
A powerful army comes like smoke from the
north.
Each soldier rushes forward eager to fight.

32 What should we tell the Philistine messengers? Tell them,

"The LORD has built Jerusalem*;
its walls will give refuge to his oppressed
people."

A Message about Moab

15 This message came to me concerning Moab:

In one night the town of Ar will be leveled,
and the city of Kir will be destroyed.
2 Your people will go to their temple in Dibon
to mourn.
They will go to their sacred shrines to
weep.
They will wail for the fate of Nebo and
Medeba,
shaving their heads in sorrow and cutting
off their beards.
3 They will wear burlap as they wander the
streets.
From every home and public square will
come the sound of wailing.
4 The people of Heshbon and Elealeh will cry
out;
their voices will be heard as far away as
Jahaz!
The bravest warriors of Moab will cry out in
utter terror.
They will be helpless with fear.

5 My heart weeps for Moab.
Its people flee to Zoar and Eglath-shelishiyah.
Weeping, they climb the road to Luhith.
Their cries of distress can be heard all
along the road to Horonaim.
6 Even the waters of Nimrim are dried up!
The grassy banks are scorched.
The tender plants are gone;
nothing green remains.
7 The people grab their possessions
and carry them across the Ravine of
Willows.
8 A cry of distress echoes through the land of
Moab
from one end to the other—
from Eglaim to Beer-elim.
9 The stream near Dibon* runs red with blood,
but I am still not finished with Dibon!
Lions will hunt down the survivors—
both those who try to escape
and those who remain behind.

16 1 Send lambs from Sela as tribute
to the ruler of the land.
Send them through the desert
to the mountain of beautiful Zion.
2 The women of Moab are left like homeless
birds
at the shallow crossings of the Arnon River.

14:28 King Ahaz died in 715 B.C. **14:32** Hebrew *Zion.*
15:9 As in Dead Sea Scrolls, some Greek manuscripts, and Latin Vulgate; Masoretic Text reads *Dimon;* also in 15:9b.

14:28–32 A Message about Philistia. The Philistines had threatened Judah in Ahaz's reign, and Ahaz had applied to Assyria for help against his enemies. Now that Ahaz is dead, Isaiah warns the Philistines that they are doomed. But God's people will find refuge in Jerusalem.

15:1—16:14 A Message about Moab. The relentless scouring of the region by Assyria continues as the small country of Moab is caught up in the turmoil. The main thrust is on the heartrending plight of the stream of refugees. We can picture the women and girls fleeing from all directions, a people-jam at the narrow Arnon River crossings; begging for refuge in Jerusalem, for fear their pursuers will ravish them as they've ravished their land of lush grapevines. Yet in the midst of the terror, there comes a reminder that one day the messiah-king from David's line will rule with mercy, justice, and truth.

3 "Help us," they cry.
"Defend us against our enemies.
Protect us from their relentless attack.
Do not betray us now that we have escaped.
4 Let our refugees stay among you.
Hide them from our enemies until the terror is past."

When oppression and destruction have ended
and enemy raiders have disappeared,
5 then God will establish one of David's descendants as king.
He will rule with mercy and truth.
He will always do what is just
and be eager to do what is right.

6 We have heard about proud Moab—
about its pride and arrogance and rage.
But all that boasting has disappeared.
7 The entire land of Moab weeps.
Yes, everyone in Moab mourns
for the cakes of raisins from Kir-hareseth.
They are all gone now.
8 The farms of Heshbon are abandoned;
the vineyards at Sibmah are deserted.
The rulers of the nations have broken down Moab—
that beautiful grapevine.
Its tendrils spread north as far as the town of Jazer
and trailed eastward into the wilderness.
Its shoots reached so far west
that they crossed over the Dead Sea.*

9 So now I weep for Jazer and the vineyards of Sibmah;
my tears will flow for Heshbon and Elealeh.
There are no more shouts of joy
over your summer fruits and harvest.
10 Gone now is the gladness,
gone the joy of harvest.
There will be no singing in the vineyards,
no more happy shouts,
no treading of grapes in the winepresses.
I have ended all their harvest joys.
11 My heart's cry for Moab is like a lament on a harp.
I am filled with anguish for Kir-hareseth.*
12 The people of Moab will worship at their pagan shrines,
but it will do them no good.
They will cry to the gods in their temples,
but no one will be able to save them.

13 The LORD has already said these things about Moab in the past. 14 But now the LORD says, "Within three years, counting each day,* the glory of Moab will be ended. From its great population, only a few of its people will be left alive."

A Message about Damascus and Israel

17 This message came to me concerning Damascus:

"Look, the city of Damascus will disappear!
It will become a heap of ruins.
2 The towns of Aroer will be deserted.
Flocks will graze in the streets and lie down undisturbed,
with no one to chase them away.
3 The fortified towns of Israel* will also be destroyed,
and the royal power of Damascus will end.
All that remains of Syria*
will share the fate of Israel's departed glory,"
declares the LORD of Heaven's Armies.

4 "In that day Israel's* glory will grow dim;
its robust body will waste away.
5 The whole land will look like a grainfield
after the harvesters have gathered the grain.
It will be desolate,
like the fields in the valley of Rephaim
after the harvest.
6 Only a few of its people will be left,
like stray olives left on a tree after the harvest.
Only two or three remain in the highest branches,

16:8 Hebrew *the sea.* **16:11** Hebrew *Kir-heres,* a variant spelling of Kir-hareseth. **16:14** Hebrew *Within three years, as a servant bound by contract would count them.* **17:3a** Hebrew *of Ephraim,* referring to the northern kingdom of Israel. **17:3b** Hebrew *Aram.* **17:4** Hebrew *Jacob's.* See note on 14:1.

17:1–14 A Message about Damascus and Israel. Syria (capital Damascus) joined forces with Israel in the face of the Assyrian threat, but there will be no escape. As Israel watches the destruction of their land they will finally realize the folly of turning away from God. The poles associated with worship of the goddess Asherah symbolized life and fertility; now they give way to death and desolation. Yet in the end God has the last word; judgment is not the end of the story.

four or five scattered here and there on the
limbs,"
declares the LORD, the God of Israel.

7 Then at last the people will look to their
Creator
and turn their eyes to the Holy One of
Israel.
8 They will no longer look to their idols for
help
or worship what their own hands have
made.
They will never again bow down to their
Asherah poles
or worship at the pagan shrines they have
built.
9 Their largest cities will be like a deserted
forest,
like the land the Hivites and Amorites
abandoned*
when the Israelites came here so long ago.
It will be utterly desolate.
10 Why? Because you have turned from the God
who can save you.
You have forgotten the Rock who can hide
you.
So you may plant the finest grapevines
and import the most expensive seedlings.
11 They may sprout on the day you set them
out;
yes, they may blossom on the very
morning you plant them,
but you will never pick any grapes from
them.
Your only harvest will be a load of grief
and unrelieved pain.

12 Listen! The armies of many nations
roar like the roaring of the sea.
Hear the thunder of the mighty forces
as they rush forward like thundering
waves.
13 But though they thunder like breakers on a
beach,
God will silence them, and they will run
away.
They will flee like chaff scattered by the wind,
like a tumbleweed whirling before a storm.
14 In the evening Israel waits in terror,
but by dawn its enemies are dead.
This is the just reward of those who
plunder us,
a fitting end for those who destroy us.

A Message about Ethiopia

18 1 Listen, Ethiopia*—land of fluttering
sails*
that lies at the headwaters of the
Nile,
2 that sends ambassadors
in swift boats down the river.

Go, swift messengers!
Take a message to a tall, smooth-skinned
people,
who are feared far and wide
for their conquests and destruction,
and whose land is divided by rivers.

3 All you people of the world,
everyone who lives on the earth—
when I raise my battle flag on the mountain,
look!
When I blow the ram's horn, listen!
4 For the LORD has told me this:
"I will watch quietly from my dwelling
place—
as quietly as the heat rises on a summer
day,
or as the morning dew forms during the
harvest."
5 Even before you begin your attack,
while your plans are ripening like grapes,
the LORD will cut off your new growth with
pruning shears.
He will snip off and discard your spreading
branches.
6 Your mighty army will be left dead in the
fields
for the mountain vultures and wild
animals.
The vultures will tear at the corpses all
summer.
The wild animals will gnaw at the bones all
winter.

17:9 As in Greek version; Hebrew reads *like places of the wood and the highest bough.* **18:1a** Hebrew *Cush.* **18:1b** Or *land of many locusts;* Hebrew reads *land of whirring wings.*

18:1–7 A Message about Ethiopia. Situated at the southern border of Egypt, Ethiopia symbolized the most far-flung parts of the known world. Its *tall, smooth-skinned people* had joined the anti-Assyrian diplomats sending envoys to Jerusalem. Isaiah makes them his own envoys, to share a message back home: God quietly observes and then acts. The Assyrians will be left for dead, and the Ethiopians will bring homage to the LORD.

7 At that time the LORD of Heaven's Armies
will receive gifts
from this land divided by rivers,
from this tall, smooth-skinned people,
who are feared far and wide for their
conquests and destruction.
They will bring the gifts to Jerusalem,*
where the LORD of Heaven's Armies dwells.

A Message about Egypt

19 This message came to me concerning
Egypt:

Look! The LORD is advancing against Egypt,
riding on a swift cloud.
The idols of Egypt tremble.
The hearts of the Egyptians melt with fear.

2 "I will make Egyptian fight against
Egyptian—
brother against brother,
neighbor against neighbor,
city against city,
province against province.
3 The Egyptians will lose heart,
and I will confuse their plans.
They will plead with their idols for wisdom
and call on spirits, mediums, and those who
consult the spirits of the dead.
4 I will hand Egypt over
to a hard, cruel master.
A fierce king will rule them,"
says the Lord, the LORD of Heaven's Armies.

5 The waters of the Nile will fail to rise and
flood the fields.
The riverbed will be parched and dry.
6 The canals of the Nile will dry up,
and the streams of Egypt will stink
with rotting reeds and rushes.
7 All the greenery along the riverbank
and all the crops along the river
will dry up and blow away.
8 The fishermen will lament for lack of work.
Those who cast hooks into the Nile will
groan,
and those who use nets will lose heart.
9 There will be no flax for the harvesters,
no thread for the weavers.
10 They will be in despair,
and all the workers will be sick at heart.

11 What fools are the officials of Zoan!
Their best counsel to the king of Egypt is
stupid and wrong.
Will they still boast to Pharaoh of their
wisdom?
Will they dare brag about all their wise
ancestors?
12 Where are your wise counselors, Pharaoh?
Let them tell you what God plans,
what the LORD of Heaven's Armies is going
to do to Egypt.
13 The officials of Zoan are fools,
and the officials of Memphis* are deluded.
The leaders of the people
have led Egypt astray.
14 The LORD has sent a spirit of foolishness on
them,
so all their suggestions are wrong.
They cause Egypt to stagger
like a drunk in his vomit.
15 There is nothing Egypt can do.
All are helpless—
the head and the tail,
the noble palm branch and the lowly reed.

16 In that day the Egyptians will be as weak as
women. They will cower in fear beneath the upraised fist of the LORD of Heaven's Armies. 17 Just
to speak the name of Israel will terrorize them,
for the LORD of Heaven's Armies has laid out his
plans against them.
18 In that day five of Egypt's cities will follow
the LORD of Heaven's Armies. They will even
begin to speak Hebrew, the language of Canaan.
One of these cities will be Heliopolis, the City of
the Sun.*
19 In that day there will be an altar to the LORD
in the heart of Egypt, and there will be a monument to the LORD at its border. 20 It will be a sign
and a witness that the LORD of Heaven's Armies is
worshiped in the land of Egypt. When the people

18:7 Hebrew *to Mount Zion.* **19:13** Hebrew *Noph.*
19:18 Or *will be the City of Destruction.*

19:1–25 A Message about Egypt. Israel's oldest adversary, Egypt, which was behind all the contemporary anti-Assyrian movements, will also suffer God's judgment—through social collapse, conquest, and climate chaos. (The annual flooding of the Nile was crucial; if it failed, people starved.) Egypt's leaders have led people astray. But at their lowest point, when they feel *as weak as women* (a male view!), wonderfully many will turn from their idols and sun-worship to the LORD, and find he is their Savior. The kind of close relationship that God has had with Israel will extend to Egypt too. Furthermore, at some point even Assyria will worship God and know his blessing and care, and political enemies will become allies.

cry to the LORD for help against those who oppress
them, he will send them a savior who will rescue
them. [21]The LORD will make himself known to the
Egyptians. Yes, they will know the LORD and will
give their sacrifices and offerings to him. They will
make a vow to the LORD and will keep it. [22]The
LORD will strike Egypt, and then he will bring
healing. For the Egyptians will turn to the LORD,
and he will listen to their pleas and heal them.

[23]In that day Egypt and Assyria will be connected by a highway. The Egyptians and Assyrians will move freely between their lands, and
they will both worship God. [24]And Israel will be
their ally. The three will be together, and Israel
will be a blessing to them. [25]For the LORD of
Heaven's Armies will say, "Blessed be Egypt, my
people. Blessed be Assyria, the land I have made.
Blessed be Israel, my special possession!"

A Message about Egypt and Ethiopia

20 In the year when King Sargon of Assyria sent his commander in chief to capture the Philistine city of Ashdod,* [2]the LORD told Isaiah son of Amoz, "Take off the burlap you have been wearing, and remove your sandals." Isaiah did as he was told and walked around naked and barefoot.

[3]Then the LORD said, "My servant Isaiah has
been walking around naked and barefoot for the
last three years. This is a sign—a symbol of the
terrible troubles I will bring upon Egypt and Ethiopia.* [4]For the king of Assyria will take away the
Egyptians and Ethiopians* as prisoners. He will
make them walk naked and barefoot, both young
and old, their buttocks bared, to the shame of
Egypt. [5]Then the Philistines will be thrown into
panic, for they counted on the power of Ethiopia
and boasted of their allies in Egypt! [6]They will
say, 'If this can happen to Egypt, what chance do
we have? We were counting on Egypt to protect
us from the king of Assyria.' "

A Message about Babylon

21 This message came to me concerning Babylon—the desert by the sea*:

Disaster is roaring down on you from the
desert,
like a whirlwind sweeping in from the
Negev.
[2] I see a terrifying vision:
I see the betrayer betraying,
the destroyer destroying.
Go ahead, you Elamites and Medes,
attack and lay siege.
I will make an end
to all the groaning Babylon caused.
[3] My stomach aches and burns with pain.
Sharp pangs of anguish are upon me,
like those of a woman in labor.
I grow faint when I hear what God is
planning;
I am too afraid to look.
[4] My mind reels and my heart races.
I longed for evening to come,
but now I am terrified of the dark.

[5] Look! They are preparing a great feast.
They are spreading rugs for people to
sit on.
Everyone is eating and drinking.
But quick! Grab your shields and prepare for
battle.
You are being attacked!

[6] Meanwhile, the Lord said to me,
"Put a watchman on the city wall.
Let him shout out what he sees.
[7] He should look for chariots
drawn by pairs of horses,
and for riders on donkeys and camels.
Let the watchman be fully alert."

[8] Then the watchman* called out,
"Day after day I have stood on the
watchtower, my lord.
Night after night I have remained at my
post.
[9] Now at last—look!
Here comes a man in a chariot
with a pair of horses!"

20:1 Ashdod was captured by Assyria in 711 B.C.
20:3 Hebrew *Cush;* also in 20:5. **20:4** Hebrew *Cushites.*
21:1 Hebrew *concerning the desert by the sea.* **21:8** As in Dead Sea Scrolls and Syriac version; Masoretic Text reads *a lion.*

20:1–6 A Message about Egypt and Ethiopia. Isaiah's graphic visual aid effectively describes the fate of Egypt and Ethiopia at the hands of Assyria, throwing their ally Philistia into panic.

21:1–10 A Message about Babylon. This may be an oracle to Hezekiah and his advisers as they considered joining forces with Babylon's current king, Merodach-baladan, against Assyria (see chap. 39), the latest in proffered diplomatic liaisons. Despite their celebratory ambassadorial feasts, Babylon too would fall to Assyria and prove powerless to help God's *threshed and winnowed* people at this stage. This causes Isaiah great anguish.

Then the watchman said,
"Babylon is fallen, fallen!
All the idols of Babylon
lie broken on the ground!"
10 O my people, threshed and winnowed,
I have told you everything the LORD of Heaven's Armies has said,
everything the God of Israel has told me.

A Message about Edom
11 This message came to me concerning Edom*:

Someone from Edom* keeps calling to me,
"Watchman, how much longer until morning?
When will the night be over?"
12 The watchman replies,
"Morning is coming, but night will soon return.
If you wish to ask again, then come back and ask."

A Message about Arabia
13 This message came to me concerning Arabia:

O caravans from Dedan,
hide in the deserts of Arabia.
14 O people of Tema,
bring water to these thirsty people,
food to these weary refugees.
15 They have fled from the sword,
from the drawn sword,
from the bent bow
and the terrors of battle.

16 The Lord said to me, "Within a year, counting each day,* all the glory of Kedar will come
to an end. 17 Only a few of its courageous archers
will survive. I, the LORD, the God of Israel, have
spoken!"

A Message about Jerusalem
22 This message came to me concerning Jerusalem—the Valley of Vision*:

What is happening?
Why is everyone running to the rooftops?
2 The whole city is in a terrible uproar.
What do I see in this reveling city?
Bodies are lying everywhere,
killed not in battle but by famine and disease.
3 All your leaders have fled.
They surrendered without resistance.
The people tried to slip away,
but they were captured, too.
4 That's why I said, "Leave me alone to weep;
do not try to comfort me.
Let me cry for my people
as I watch them being destroyed."
5 Oh, what a day of crushing defeat!
What a day of confusion and terror
brought by the Lord, the LORD of Heaven's Armies,
upon the Valley of Vision!
The walls of Jerusalem have been broken,
and cries of death echo from the mountainsides.
6 Elamites are the archers,
with their chariots and charioteers.
The men of Kir hold up the shields.
7 Chariots fill your beautiful valleys,
and charioteers storm your gates.
8 Judah's defenses have been stripped away.
You run to the armory* for your weapons.
9 You inspect the breaks in the walls of Jerusalem.*
You store up water in the lower pool.
10 You survey the houses and tear some down
for stone to strengthen the walls.
11 Between the city walls, you build a reservoir
for water from the old pool.
But you never ask for help from the One who did all this.

21:11a Hebrew *Dumah,* which means "silence" or "stillness." It is a wordplay on the word *Edom.* **21:11b** Hebrew *Seir,* another name for Edom. **21:16** Hebrew *Within a year, as a servant bound by contract would count it.* Some ancient manuscripts read *Within three years,* as in 16:14. **22:1** Hebrew *concerning the Valley of Vision.* **22:8** Hebrew *to the House of the Forest;* see 1 Kgs 7:2-5. **22:9** Hebrew *the city of David.*

21:11–12 A Message about Edom. In the developing international darkness, uncertainty is rife. A lone Edomite longs to know how long the night of terror will continue. Isaiah has no easy answer; the time is protracted, and any respite is only temporary.

21:13–16 A Message about Arabia. The whole Arabian region is caught up in the current suffering. One group may offer refuge to another, but ultimately few people will survive.

22:1–14 A Message about Jerusalem. The picture takes in initial reveling, perhaps at Jerusalem's escape referred to in 2 Kings 18:13–18, but quickly turns to the reality of famine, disease, and capture. The city's inhabitants shore up their defenses and ensure a

You never considered the One who planned
this long ago.
12 At that time the Lord, the LORD of Heaven's
Armies,
called you to weep and mourn.
He told you to shave your heads in sorrow
for your sins
and to wear clothes of burlap to show your
remorse.
13 But instead, you dance and play;
you slaughter cattle and kill sheep.
You feast on meat and drink wine.
You say, "Let's feast and drink,
for tomorrow we die!"
14 The LORD of Heaven's Armies has revealed this
to me: "Till the day you die, you will never be
forgiven for this sin." That is the judgment of
the Lord, the LORD of Heaven's Armies.

A Message for Shebna

15 This is what the Lord, the LORD of Heaven's
Armies, said to me: "Confront Shebna, the palace
administrator, and give him this message:

16 "Who do you think you are,
and what are you doing here,
building a beautiful tomb for yourself—
a monument high up in the rock?
17 For the LORD is about to hurl you away,
mighty man.
He is going to grab you,
18 crumple you into a ball,
and toss you away into a distant, barren land.
There you will die,
and your glorious chariots will be broken
and useless.
You are a disgrace to your master!

19 "Yes, I will drive you out of office," says the
LORD. "I will pull you down from your high position. 20 And then I will call my servant Eliakim
son of Hilkiah to replace you. 21 I will dress him
in your royal robes and will give him your title
and your authority. And he will be a father to
the people of Jerusalem and Judah. 22 I will give
him the key to the house of David—the highest
position in the royal court. When he opens doors,
no one will be able to close them; when he closes
doors, no one will be able to open them. 23 He will
bring honor to his family name, for I will drive
him firmly in place like a nail in the wall. 24 They
will give him great responsibility, and he will
bring honor to even the lowliest members of his
family.*"
25 But the LORD of Heaven's Armies also says:
"The time will come when I will pull out the nail
that seemed so firm. It will come out and fall to
the ground. Everything it supports will fall with
it. I, the LORD, have spoken!"

A Message about Tyre

23 This message came to me concerning
Tyre:

Weep, O ships of Tarshish,
for the harbor and houses of Tyre are gone!
The rumors you heard in Cyprus*
are all true.
2 Mourn in silence, you people of the coast
and you merchants of Sidon.
Your traders crossed the sea,
3 sailing over deep waters.
They brought you grain from Egypt*

22:24 Hebrew *They will hang on him all the glory of his father's house: its offspring and offshoots, all its lesser vessels, from the bowls to all the jars.* **23:1** Hebrew *Kittim;* also in 23:12. **23:3** Hebrew *from Shihor,* a branch of the Nile River.

good water supply (see 2 Kgs 20:20). But instead of turning to God in repentance they feel self-sufficient, which is ultimately fatal.

22:15–25 A Message for Shebna. Both Shebna and Eliakim feature in the events of chapters 36 and 37. Shebna may have led the pro-Egypt party that scoffed at Isaiah's preaching; here he is denounced for his ostentatiousness. God would replace him with Eliakim, who would give the support and security that Judah needed—for a time, at least. However, would-be hangers-on will prove too heavy; when society's dependence is on humans rather than God, everything collapses.

23:1–18 A Message about Tyre. The exact location of Tarshish is unknown, but it represents a city a great distance away, whose merchant ships were famous. Tarshish and Tyre were partners in trade. But now, although the rock citadel itself withstood attacks until much later (it finally fell under Alexander the Great in 332 BC), in destroying the harbor Assyria has rendered Tyre unsafe for shipping—a huge mercenary blow. Tyre is pictured as without children. In those times, to be childless was desolation indeed; an apt description of a once bustling and prosperous area. Again, it is pride that is the given reason for the reversal of their fortunes. They will have a second chance; but human nature does not easily change, and they will continue to do all for mercenary motives in the way that prostitutes do. They will find, though, that God has the last word, and their wealth will provide for his priests.

and harvests from along the Nile.
You were the marketplace of the world.

4 But now you are put to shame, city of Sidon,
for Tyre, the fortress of the sea, says,
"Now I am childless;
I have no sons or daughters."
5 When Egypt hears the news about Tyre,
there will be great sorrow.
6 Send word now to Tarshish!
Wail, you people who live in distant lands!
7 Is this silent ruin all that is left of your once
joyous city?
What a long history was yours!
Think of all the colonists you sent to
distant places.

8 Who has brought this disaster on Tyre,
that great creator of kingdoms?
Her traders were all princes,
her merchants were nobles.
9 The LORD of Heaven's Armies has done it
to destroy your pride
and bring low all earth's nobility.
10 Come, people of Tarshish,
sweep over the land like the flooding Nile,
for Tyre is defenseless.*
11 The LORD held out his hand over the sea
and shook the kingdoms of the earth.
He has spoken out against Phoenicia,*
ordering that her fortresses be destroyed.
12 He says, "Never again will you rejoice,
O daughter of Sidon, for you have been
crushed.
Even if you flee to Cyprus,
you will find no rest."

13 Look at the land of Babylonia*—
the people of that land are gone!
The Assyrians have handed Babylon over
to the wild animals of the desert.
They have built siege ramps against its
walls,
torn down its palaces,
and turned it to a heap of rubble.

14 Wail, O ships of Tarshish,
for your harbor is destroyed!

15 For seventy years, the length of a king's
life, Tyre will be forgotten. But then the city will
come back to life as in the song about the prostitute:

16 Take a harp and walk the streets,
you forgotten harlot.
Make sweet melody and sing your songs
so you will be remembered again.

17 Yes, after seventy years the LORD will revive Tyre. But she will be no different than she
was before. She will again be a prostitute to all
kingdoms around the world. 18 But in the end her
profits will be given to the LORD. Her wealth will
not be hoarded but will provide good food and
fine clothing for the LORD's priests.

Destruction of the Earth

24 1 Look! The LORD is about to destroy
the earth
and make it a vast wasteland.
He devastates the surface of the earth
and scatters the people.
2 Priests and laypeople,
servants and masters,
maids and mistresses,
buyers and sellers,
lenders and borrowers,
bankers and debtors—none will be spared.
3 The earth will be completely emptied and
looted.
The LORD has spoken!

4 The earth mourns and dries up,
and the crops waste away and wither.
Even the greatest people on earth waste
away.
5 The earth suffers for the sins of its people,
for they have twisted God's instructions,
violated his laws,
and broken his everlasting covenant.
6 Therefore, a curse consumes the earth.
Its people must pay the price for their sin.
They are destroyed by fire,

23:10 The meaning of the Hebrew in this verse is uncertain.
23:11 Hebrew *Canaan.* **23:13** Or *Chaldea.*

24:1—35:10 Blessings, Judgments, and Messages for the Nations

24:1–23 Destruction of the Earth. With so much carnage and terror it feels as though the entire earth is being systematically destroyed by its Creator. Women, men, and the land itself are suffering a curse because people have rebelled against God. Music and merrymaking is a thing of the past, replaced by chaos, fear, deceit, and treachery. There is always a price to pay for sin, with no escape. And yet, in the midst of this cosmic collapse Isaiah sees a glimpse of how joyful things could be for anyone who submits to the LORD's rule and gives him praise and glory. There is hope!

and only a few are left alive.
7 The grapevines waste away,
and there is no new wine.
All the merrymakers sigh and mourn.
8 The cheerful sound of tambourines is stilled;
the happy cries of celebration are heard no more.
The melodious chords of the harp are silent.
9 Gone are the joys of wine and song;
alcoholic drink turns bitter in the mouth.
10 The city writhes in chaos;
every home is locked to keep out intruders.
11 Mobs gather in the streets, crying out for wine.
Joy has turned to gloom.
Gladness has been banished from the land.
12 The city is left in ruins,
its gates battered down.
13 Throughout the earth the story is the same—
only a remnant is left,
like the stray olives left on the tree
or the few grapes left on the vine after harvest.

14 But all who are left shout and sing for joy.
Those in the west praise the LORD's majesty.
15 In eastern lands, give glory to the LORD.
In the lands beyond the sea, praise the name of the LORD, the God of Israel.
16 We hear songs of praise from the ends of the earth,
songs that give glory to the Righteous One!

But my heart is heavy with grief.
Weep for me, for I wither away.
Deceit still prevails,
and treachery is everywhere.
17 Terror and traps and snares will be your lot,
you people of the earth.
18 Those who flee in terror will fall into a trap,
and those who escape the trap will be caught in a snare.

Destruction falls like rain from the heavens;
the foundations of the earth shake.
19 The earth has broken up.
It has utterly collapsed;
it is violently shaken.
20 The earth staggers like a drunk.
It trembles like a tent in a storm.
It falls and will not rise again,
for the guilt of its rebellion is very heavy.

21 In that day the LORD will punish the gods in the heavens
and the proud rulers of the nations on earth.
22 They will be rounded up and put in prison.
They will be shut up in prison
and will finally be punished.
23 Then the glory of the moon will wane,
and the brightness of the sun will fade,
for the LORD of Heaven's Armies will rule on Mount Zion.
He will rule in great glory in Jerusalem,
in the sight of all the leaders of his people.

Praise for Judgment and Salvation

25 1 O LORD, I will honor and praise your name,
for you are my God.
You do such wonderful things!
You planned them long ago,
and now you have accomplished them.
2 You turn mighty cities into heaps of ruins.
Cities with strong walls are turned to rubble.
Beautiful palaces in distant lands disappear
and will never be rebuilt.
3 Therefore, strong nations will declare your glory;
ruthless nations will fear you.

4 But you are a tower of refuge to the poor, O LORD,
a tower of refuge to the needy in distress.
You are a refuge from the storm
and a shelter from the heat.
For the oppressive acts of ruthless people
are like a storm beating against a wall,
5 or like the relentless heat of the desert.
But you silence the roar of foreign nations.
As the shade of a cloud cools relentless heat,
so the boastful songs of ruthless people are stilled.

25:1–12 Praise for Judgment and Salvation. Perhaps this song is one of those envisaged in 24:16a. God is praised for what he does. Even the strongest cities are no match for him and also for who he is—a safe shelter for the needy who seek refuge in him. God silences the relentless roar of ruthless oppressors and cools the heat of their attacks. He spreads a feast of good things for people of all nations. He wipes away tears and swallows up the ultimate curse—death. No wonder his people sing! And yet Moab—perhaps representative of all who refuse to humble themselves before God—is still caught up in judgment (see chaps. 15—16).

6 In Jerusalem,* the LORD of Heaven's Armies
will spread a wonderful feast
for all the people of the world.
It will be a delicious banquet
with clear, well-aged wine and choice meat.
7 There he will remove the cloud of gloom,
the shadow of death that hangs over the earth.
8 He will swallow up death forever!*
The Sovereign LORD will wipe away all tears.
He will remove forever all insults and mockery
against his land and people.
The LORD has spoken!

9 In that day the people will proclaim,
"This is our God!
We trusted in him, and he saved us!
This is the LORD, in whom we trusted.
Let us rejoice in the salvation he brings!"
10 For the LORD's hand of blessing will rest on Jerusalem.
But Moab will be crushed.
It will be like straw trampled down and left to rot.
11 God will push down Moab's people
as a swimmer pushes down water with his hands.
He will end their pride
and all their evil works.
12 The high walls of Moab will be demolished.
They will be brought down to the ground,
down into the dust.

A Song of Praise to the LORD

26 In that day, everyone in the land of Judah will sing this song:

Our city is strong!
We are surrounded by the walls of God's salvation.
2 Open the gates to all who are righteous;
allow the faithful to enter.
3 You will keep in perfect peace
all who trust in you,
all whose thoughts are fixed on you!
4 Trust in the LORD always,
for the LORD GOD is the eternal Rock.
5 He humbles the proud
and brings down the arrogant city.
He brings it down to the dust.
6 The poor and oppressed trample it underfoot,
and the needy walk all over it.

7 But for those who are righteous,
the way is not steep and rough.
You are a God who does what is right,
and you smooth out the path ahead of them.
8 LORD, we show our trust in you by obeying your laws;
our heart's desire is to glorify your name.
9 All night long I search for you;
in the morning I earnestly seek for God.
For only when you come to judge the earth
will people learn what is right.
10 Your kindness to the wicked
does not make them do good.
Although others do right, the wicked keep doing wrong
and take no notice of the LORD's majesty.
11 O LORD, they pay no attention to your upraised fist.
Show them your eagerness to defend your people.
Then they will be ashamed.
Let your fire consume your enemies.

12 LORD, you will grant us peace;
all we have accomplished is really from you.
13 O LORD our God, others have ruled us,
but you alone are the one we worship.
14 Those we served before are dead and gone.
Their departed spirits will never return!
You attacked them and destroyed them,

25:6 Hebrew *On this mountain;* also in 25:10. **25:8** Greek version reads *Death is swallowed up in victory.* Compare 1 Cor 15:54.

26:1–19 A Song of Praise to the LORD. The joyful singing continues, as Judah recognizes that its strength and security is in God's salvation. Pride and self-reliance are replaced by humble trust in God, an earnest seeking for him, and a heartfelt desire to glorify his name. There is a welcome for all who are in right relationship with him. Such righteousness is seen in obedience to God's ways, which is itself a demonstration of faith, and becomes a testimony of God's life and salvation for the world. But mission is hard work, as the wicked are blind to the LORD's majesty. God's people can do nothing without him. Their experience of agonizing suffering (note the allusion to childbirth again) has brought no fruit of salvation to the world. But such discouragement is banished in a moment in the light of the promise of resurrection for those who belong to the LORD—one of the few indications in the Old Testament of an emerging belief in life after death.

and they are long forgotten.
15 O LORD, you have made our nation great;
yes, you have made us great.
You have extended our borders,
and we give you the glory!

16 LORD, in distress we searched for you.
We prayed beneath the burden of your discipline.
17 Just as a pregnant woman
writhes and cries out in pain as she gives birth,
so were we in your presence, LORD.
18 We, too, writhe in agony,
but nothing comes of our suffering.
We have not given salvation to the earth,
nor brought life into the world.
19 But those who die in the LORD will live;
their bodies will rise again!
Those who sleep in the earth
will rise up and sing for joy!
For your life-giving light will fall like dew
on your people in the place of the dead!

Restoration for Israel
20 Go home, my people,
and lock your doors!
Hide yourselves for a little while
until the LORD's anger has passed.
21 Look! The LORD is coming from heaven
to punish the people of the earth for their sins.
The earth will no longer hide those who have been killed.
They will be brought out for all to see.

27 In that day the LORD will take his terrible, swift sword and punish Leviathan,* the swiftly moving serpent, the coiling, writhing serpent. He will kill the dragon of the sea.

2 "In that day,
sing about the fruitful vineyard.
3 I, the LORD, will watch over it,
watering it carefully.
Day and night I will watch so no one can harm it.
4 My anger will be gone.
If I find briers and thorns growing,
I will attack them;
I will burn them up—
5 unless they turn to me for help.
Let them make peace with me;
yes, let them make peace with me."
6 The time is coming when Jacob's descendants will take root.
Israel will bud and blossom
and fill the whole earth with fruit!

7 Has the LORD struck Israel
as he struck her enemies?
Has he punished her
as he punished them?
8 No, but he exiled Israel to call her to account.
She was exiled from her land
as though blown away in a storm from the east.
9 The LORD did this to purge Israel's* wickedness,
to take away all her sin.
As a result, all the pagan altars will be crushed to dust.
No Asherah pole or pagan shrine will be left standing.
10 The fortified towns will be silent and empty,
the houses abandoned, the streets overgrown with weeds.
Calves will graze there,
chewing on twigs and branches.
11 The people are like the dead branches of a tree,
broken off and used for kindling beneath the cooking pots.
Israel is a foolish and stupid nation,
for its people have turned away from God.
Therefore, the one who made them
will show them no pity or mercy.

27:1 The identification of Leviathan is disputed, ranging from an earthly creature to a mythical sea monster in ancient literature. **27:9** Hebrew *Jacob's.* See note on 14:1.

26:20—27:13 Restoration for Israel. Meanwhile there is a waiting time, for God has yet to avenge innocent blood—a process in which the earth will cooperate in some way. For ancient Near Eastern peoples, the sea was a symbol of chaos, and mythological sea monsters are often used metaphorically in the Old Testament to describe an immense power ranged against God. Israel will become the vineyard she was always meant to be (see 5:1–7, and compare with John 15:1–16). Then at last, purged from all sin by the experience of invasion and exile, she will bear fruit in the world; even her enemies (*thorns*) will be forgiven if they turn to God. Israel's dead vine branches have been broken off and used as fuel for the cooking pots—a rare glimpse of an ancient kitchen. God's true people are handpicked; from far-flung corners they will return to Jerusalem, united in worship.

[12] Yet the time will come when the LORD will
gather them together like handpicked grain. One
by one he will gather them—from the Euphrates
River* in the east to the Brook of Egypt in the
west. [13] In that day the great trumpet will sound.
Many who were dying in exile in Assyria and
Egypt will return to Jerusalem to worship the
LORD on his holy mountain.

A Message about Samaria

28 [1] What sorrow awaits the proud city
of Samaria—
the glorious crown of the drunks
of Israel.*
It sits at the head of a fertile valley,
but its glorious beauty will fade like a
flower.
It is the pride of a people
brought down by wine.
[2] For the Lord will send a mighty army
against it.
Like a mighty hailstorm and a torrential
rain,
they will burst upon it like a surging flood
and smash it to the ground.
[3] The proud city of Samaria—
the glorious crown of the drunks of
Israel*—
will be trampled beneath its enemies' feet.
[4] It sits at the head of a fertile valley,
but its glorious beauty will fade like a
flower.
Whoever sees it will snatch it up,
as an early fig is quickly picked and eaten.

[5] Then at last the LORD of Heaven's Armies
will himself be Israel's glorious crown.
He will be the pride and joy
of the remnant of his people.
[6] He will give a longing for justice
to their judges.
He will give great courage
to their warriors who stand at the gates.

[7] Now, however, Israel is led by drunks
who reel with wine and stagger with
alcohol.
The priests and prophets stagger with alcohol
and lose themselves in wine.
They reel when they see visions
and stagger as they render decisions.
[8] Their tables are covered with vomit;
filth is everywhere.
[9] "Who does the LORD think we are?" they ask.
"Why does he speak to us like this?
Are we little children,
just recently weaned?
[10] He tells us everything over and over—
one line at a time,
one line at a time,
a little here,
and a little there!"

[11] So now God will have to speak to his people
through foreign oppressors who speak a
strange language!
[12] God has told his people,
"Here is a place of rest;
let the weary rest here.
This is a place of quiet rest."
But they would not listen.
[13] So the LORD will spell out his message for
them again,
one line at a time,
one line at a time,
a little here,
and a little there,
so that they will stumble and fall.
They will be injured, trapped, and
captured.

[14] Therefore, listen to this message from the
LORD,
you scoffing rulers in Jerusalem.
[15] You boast, "We have struck a bargain to cheat
death
and have made a deal to dodge the grave.*
The coming destruction can never touch us,
for we have built a strong refuge made of
lies and deception."

[16] Therefore, this is what the Sovereign LORD
says:

27:12 Hebrew *the river.* **28:1** Hebrew *What sorrow awaits the crowning glory of the drunks of Ephraim,* referring to Samaria, capital of the northern kingdom of Israel. **28:3** Hebrew *The crowning glory of the drunks of Ephraim;* see note on 28:1. **28:15** Hebrew *Sheol;* also in 28:18.

28:1–29 A Message about Samaria. How often alcohol has been people's downfall! The Northern Kingdom, Israel (capital Samaria), is facing the consequences of their behavior; they will be devoured by Assyria. Note the reference to playschool teaching (vv. 9–10); because the priests and prophets refuse to be taught through caring means, God has to resort to more violent lessons. Despite their scoffing, their defenses will be knocked down. Yet at the same time God is providing a solid foundation for his people and their future. He knows how best to teach his people, just as a farmer knows how to cultivate different crops.

"Look! I am placing a foundation stone in
Jerusalem,*
a firm and tested stone.
It is a precious cornerstone that is safe to
build on.
Whoever believes need never be shaken.*
17 I will test you with the measuring line of
justice
and the plumb line of righteousness.
Since your refuge is made of lies,
a hailstorm will knock it down.
Since it is made of deception,
a flood will sweep it away.
18 I will cancel the bargain you made to cheat
death,
and I will overturn your deal to dodge the
grave.
When the terrible enemy sweeps through,
you will be trampled into the ground.
19 Again and again that flood will come,
morning after morning,
day and night,
until you are carried away."

This message will bring terror to your
people.
20 The bed you have made is too short to lie on.
The blankets are too narrow to cover you.
21 The LORD will come as he did against the
Philistines at Mount Perazim
and against the Amorites at Gibeon.
He will come to do a strange thing;
he will come to do an unusual deed:
22 For the Lord, the LORD of Heaven's Armies,
has plainly said that he is determined to
crush the whole land.
So scoff no more,
or your punishment will be even greater.

23 Listen to me;
listen, and pay close attention.
24 Does a farmer always plow and never sow?
Is he forever cultivating the soil and never
planting?
25 Does he not finally plant his seeds—
black cumin, cumin, wheat, barley, and
emmer wheat—
each in its proper way,
and each in its proper place?
26 The farmer knows just what to do,
for God has given him understanding.
27 A heavy sledge is never used to thresh black
cumin;
rather, it is beaten with a light stick.
A threshing wheel is never rolled on cumin;
instead, it is beaten lightly with a flail.
28 Grain for bread is easily crushed,
so he doesn't keep on pounding it.
He threshes it under the wheels of a cart,
but he doesn't pulverize it.
29 The LORD of Heaven's Armies is a wonderful
teacher,
and he gives the farmer great wisdom.

A Message about Jerusalem

29

1 "What sorrow awaits Ariel,* the
City of David.
Year after year you celebrate your
feasts.
2 Yet I will bring disaster upon you,
and there will be much weeping and
sorrow.
For Jerusalem will become what her name
Ariel means—
an altar covered with blood.
3 I will be your enemy,
surrounding Jerusalem and attacking its
walls.
I will build siege towers
and destroy it.
4 Then deep from the earth you will speak;
from low in the dust your words will come.
Your voice will whisper from the ground
like a ghost conjured up from the grave.

5 "But suddenly, your ruthless enemies will be
crushed
like the finest of dust.
Your many attackers will be driven away
like chaff before the wind.
Suddenly, in an instant,
6 I, the LORD of Heaven's Armies, will act for
you
with thunder and earthquake and great noise,
with whirlwind and storm and consuming
fire.

28:16a Hebrew *in Zion.* **28:16b** Greek version reads *Look! I am placing a stone in the foundation of Jerusalem* [literally *Zion*], */ a precious cornerstone for its foundation, chosen for great honor. / Anyone who trusts in him will never be disgraced.* Compare Rom 9:33; 1 Pet 2:6. **29:1** *Ariel* sounds like a Hebrew term that means "hearth" or "altar."

29:1–24 A Message about Jerusalem. Judah's capital also has much to learn. God uses both disaster and rescue (typified by the name *Ariel*, meaning "hearth"—the burning and the comfort) to bring his people to true wisdom and genuine devotion. He is molding his people; one day they will recognize him and rejoice, standing in awe of his holiness.

7 All the nations fighting against Jerusalem*
will vanish like a dream!
Those who are attacking her walls
will vanish like a vision in the night.
8 A hungry person dreams of eating
but wakes up still hungry.
A thirsty person dreams of drinking
but is still faint from thirst when morning comes.
So it will be with your enemies,
with those who attack Mount Zion."

9 Are you amazed and incredulous?
Don't you believe it?
Then go ahead and be blind.
You are stupid, but not from wine!
You stagger, but not from liquor!
10 For the LORD has poured out on you a spirit of deep sleep.
He has closed the eyes of your prophets and visionaries.

11 All the future events in this vision are like
a sealed book to them. When you give it to those
who can read, they will say, "We can't read it because it is sealed." 12 When you give it to those
who cannot read, they will say, "We don't know
how to read."

13 And so the Lord says,
"These people say they are mine.
They honor me with their lips,
but their hearts are far from me.
And their worship of me
is nothing but man-made rules learned by rote.*
14 Because of this, I will once again astound these hypocrites
with amazing wonders.
The wisdom of the wise will pass away,
and the intelligence of the intelligent will disappear."
15 What sorrow awaits those who try to hide their plans from the LORD,
who do their evil deeds in the dark!
"The LORD can't see us," they say.
"He doesn't know what's going on!"
16 How foolish can you be?
He is the Potter, and he is certainly greater than you, the clay!
Should the created thing say of the one who made it,
"He didn't make me"?
Does a jar ever say,
"The potter who made me is stupid"?

17 Soon—and it will not be very long—
the forests of Lebanon will become a fertile field,
and the fertile field will yield bountiful crops.
18 In that day the deaf will hear words read from a book,
and the blind will see through the gloom and darkness.
19 The humble will be filled with fresh joy from the LORD.
The poor will rejoice in the Holy One of Israel.
20 The scoffer will be gone,
the arrogant will disappear,
and those who plot evil will be killed.
21 Those who convict the innocent
by their false testimony will disappear.
A similar fate awaits those who use trickery to pervert justice
and who tell lies to destroy the innocent.

22 That is why the LORD, who redeemed Abraham, says to the people of Israel,*

"My people will no longer be ashamed
or turn pale with fear.
23 For when they see their many children
and all the blessings I have given them,
they will recognize the holiness of the Holy One of Israel.
They will stand in awe of the God of Jacob.
24 Then the wayward will gain understanding,
and complainers will accept instruction.

Judah's Worthless Treaty with Egypt

30 1 "What sorrow awaits my rebellious children,"
says the LORD.
"You make plans that are contrary to mine.
You make alliances not directed by my Spirit,
thus piling up your sins.
2 For without consulting me,

29:7 Hebrew *Ariel.* **29:13** Greek version reads *Their worship is a farce, / for they teach man-made ideas as commands from God.* Compare Mark 7:7. **29:22** Hebrew *of Jacob.* See note on 14:1.

30:1–7 Judah's Worthless Treaty with Egypt. Judah's alliance with Egypt is expensive, yet will prove worse than useless.

you have gone down to Egypt for help.
You have put your trust in Pharaoh's
protection.
You have tried to hide in his shade.
3 But by trusting Pharaoh, you will be
humiliated,
and by depending on him, you will be
disgraced.
4 For though his power extends to Zoan
and his officials have arrived in Hanes,
5 all who trust in him will be ashamed.
He will not help you.
Instead, he will disgrace you."

6 This message came to me concerning the animals in the Negev:

The caravan moves slowly
across the terrible desert to Egypt—
donkeys weighed down with riches
and camels loaded with treasure—
all to pay for Egypt's protection.
They travel through the wilderness,
a place of lionesses and lions,
a place where vipers and poisonous snakes
live.
All this, and Egypt will give you nothing in
return.
7 Egypt's promises are worthless!
Therefore, I call her Rahab—
the Harmless Dragon.*

A Warning for Rebellious Judah

8 Now go and write down these words.
Write them in a book.
They will stand until the end of time
as a witness
9 that these people are stubborn rebels
who refuse to pay attention to the LORD's
instructions.
10 They tell the seers,
"Stop seeing visions!"
They tell the prophets,
"Don't tell us what is right.
Tell us nice things.
Tell us lies.
11 Forget all this gloom.
Get off your narrow path.
Stop telling us about your
'Holy One of Israel.' "

12 This is the reply of the Holy One of Israel:

"Because you despise what I tell you
and trust instead in oppression and lies,
13 calamity will come upon you suddenly—
like a bulging wall that bursts and falls.
In an instant it will collapse
and come crashing down.
14 You will be smashed like a piece of pottery—
shattered so completely that
there won't be a piece big enough
to carry coals from a fireplace
or a little water from the well."

15 This is what the Sovereign LORD,
the Holy One of Israel, says:
"Only in returning to me
and resting in me will you be saved.
In quietness and confidence is your strength.
But you would have none of it.
16 You said, 'No, we will get our help from
Egypt.
They will give us swift horses for riding
into battle.'
But the only swiftness you are going to see
is the swiftness of your enemies chasing
you!
17 One of them will chase a thousand of you.
Five of them will make all of you flee.
You will be left like a lonely flagpole on a
hill
or a tattered banner on a distant
mountaintop."

Blessings for the LORD's People

18 So the LORD must wait for you to come to
him
so he can show you his love and
compassion.
For the LORD is a faithful God.
Blessed are those who wait for his help.

30:7 Hebrew *Rahab who sits still.* Rahab is the name of a mythical sea monster that represents chaos in ancient literature. The name is used here as a poetic name for Egypt.

30:8–17 A Warning for Rebellious Judah. Not only are people rebelling against God, they close their ears to prophetic warnings. Their misplaced trust in Egypt will collapse in tatters. Their only hope is to return to the LORD—yet they ignore him.

30:18–33 Blessings for the LORD's People. But those who do come to him will find God to be a loving and compassionate teacher, faithful and responsive, offering blessing and healing. Isaiah uses volcanic and extreme weather terminology to describe God's passionate care for his people, who will sing with joy at the destruction of their enemies.

19 O people of Zion, who live in Jerusalem,
you will weep no more.
He will be gracious if you ask for help.
He will surely respond to the sound of your cries.
20 Though the Lord gave you adversity for food
and suffering for drink,
he will still be with you to teach you.
You will see your teacher with your own eyes.
21 Your own ears will hear him.
Right behind you a voice will say,
"This is the way you should go,"
whether to the right or to the left.
22 Then you will destroy all your silver idols
and your precious gold images.
You will throw them out like filthy rags,
saying to them, "Good riddance!"

23 Then the LORD will bless you with rain at
planting time. There will be wonderful harvests
and plenty of pastureland for your livestock.
24 The oxen and donkeys that till the ground will
eat good grain, its chaff blown away by the wind.
25 In that day, when your enemies are slaughtered and the towers fall, there will be streams
of water flowing down every mountain and hill.
26 The moon will be as bright as the sun, and the
sun will be seven times brighter—like the light
of seven days in one! So it will be when the LORD
begins to heal his people and cure the wounds he
gave them.

27 Look! The LORD is coming from far away,
burning with anger,
surrounded by thick, rising smoke.
His lips are filled with fury;
his words consume like fire.
28 His hot breath pours out like a flood
up to the neck of his enemies.
He will sift out the proud nations for destruction.
He will bridle them and lead them away to ruin.

29 But the people of God will sing a song of joy,
like the songs at the holy festivals.
You will be filled with joy,
as when a flutist leads a group of pilgrims
to Jerusalem, the mountain of the LORD—
to the Rock of Israel.
30 And the LORD will make his majestic voice heard.
He will display the strength of his mighty arm.
It will descend with devouring flames,
with cloudbursts, thunderstorms, and huge hailstones.
31 At the LORD's command, the Assyrians will be shattered.
He will strike them down with his royal scepter.
32 And as the LORD strikes them with his rod of punishment,
his people will celebrate with tambourines and harps.
Lifting his mighty arm, he will fight the Assyrians.
33 Topheth—the place of burning—
has long been ready for the Assyrian king;
the pyre is piled high with wood.
The breath of the LORD, like fire from a volcano,
will set it ablaze.

The Futility of Relying on Egypt

31 1 What sorrow awaits those who look
to Egypt for help,
trusting their horses, chariots, and charioteers
and depending on the strength of human armies
instead of looking to the LORD,
the Holy One of Israel.
2 In his wisdom, the LORD will send great disaster;
he will not change his mind.
He will rise against the wicked
and against their helpers.
3 For these Egyptians are mere humans, not God!
Their horses are puny flesh, not mighty spirits!
When the LORD raises his fist against them,
those who help will stumble,
and those being helped will fall.
They will all fall down and die together.

4 But this is what the LORD has told me:

"When a strong young lion
stands growling over a sheep it has killed,
it is not frightened by the shouts and noise
of a whole crowd of shepherds.
In the same way, the LORD of Heaven's Armies

31:1–9 The Futility of Relying on Egypt. Despite the foolishness of relying on human help rather than divine, God will—amazingly—protect Jerusalem and rout the Assyrians.

will come down and fight on Mount Zion.
[5] The LORD of Heaven's Armies will hover over
Jerusalem
and protect it like a bird protecting its nest.
He will defend and save the city;
he will pass over it and rescue it."

[6] Though you are such wicked rebels, my people, come and return to the LORD. [7] I know the
glorious day will come when each of you will
throw away the gold idols and silver images your
sinful hands have made.

[8] "The Assyrians will be destroyed,
but not by the swords of men.
The sword of God will strike them,
and they will panic and flee.
The strong young Assyrians
will be taken away as captives.
[9] Even the strongest will quake with terror,
and princes will flee when they see your
battle flags,"
says the LORD, whose fire burns in Zion,
whose flame blazes from Jerusalem.

Israel's Ultimate Deliverance

32 [1] Look, a righteous king is coming!
And honest princes will rule under
him.
[2] Each one will be like a shelter from the wind
and a refuge from the storm,
like streams of water in the desert
and the shadow of a great rock in a parched
land.

[3] Then everyone who has eyes will be able to
see the truth,
and everyone who has ears will be able to
hear it.
[4] Even the hotheads will be full of sense and
understanding.
Those who stammer will speak out plainly.
[5] In that day ungodly fools will not be heroes.
Scoundrels will not be respected.
[6] For fools speak foolishness
and make evil plans.
They practice ungodliness
and spread false teachings about the LORD.
They deprive the hungry of food
and give no water to the thirsty.
[7] The smooth tricks of scoundrels are evil.
They plot crooked schemes.
They lie to convict the poor,
even when the cause of the poor is just.
[8] But generous people plan to do what is
generous,
and they stand firm in their generosity.

[9] Listen, you women who lie around in ease.
Listen to me, you who are so smug.
[10] In a short time—just a little more than a
year—
you careless ones will suddenly begin to
care.
For your fruit crops will fail,
and the harvest will never take place.
[11] Tremble, you women of ease;
throw off your complacency.
Strip off your pretty clothes,
and put on burlap to show your grief.
[12] Beat your breasts in sorrow for your
bountiful farms
and your fruitful grapevines.
[13] For your land will be overgrown with thorns
and briers.
Your joyful homes and happy towns will
be gone.
[14] The palace and the city will be deserted,
and busy towns will be empty.
Wild donkeys will frolic and flocks will graze
in the empty forts* and watchtowers
[15] until at last the Spirit is poured out
on us from heaven.
Then the wilderness will become a fertile
field,
and the fertile field will yield bountiful
crops.

[16] Justice will rule in the wilderness
and righteousness in the fertile field.
[17] And this righteousness will bring peace.
Yes, it will bring quietness and confidence
forever.
[18] My people will live in safety, quietly at home.
They will be at rest.
[19] Even if the forest should be destroyed
and the city torn down,
[20] the LORD will greatly bless his people.

32:14 Hebrew *the Ophel.*

32:1–20 Israel's Ultimate Deliverance. Isaiah looks forward to a day when, under a righteous king, generosity will win out over the injustice of scoundrels. Some of the women are, perhaps surprisingly, among the worst offenders, for their complacency and indifference to the needs of others. Isaiah bids them prepare to become prisoners of war, wearing rough clothes and beating their breasts in sorrow. But one day all will change, as the Spirit is poured out on the land and people will feel safe at last.

Wherever they plant seed, bountiful crops
will spring up.
Their cattle and donkeys will graze freely.

A Message about Assyria

33 [1]What sorrow awaits you Assyrians,
who have destroyed others*
but have never been destroyed
yourselves.
You betray others,
but you have never been betrayed.
When you are done destroying,
you will be destroyed.
When you are done betraying,
you will be betrayed.
2 But LORD, be merciful to us,
for we have waited for you.
Be our strong arm each day
and our salvation in times of trouble.
3 The enemy runs at the sound of your voice.
When you stand up, the nations flee!
4 Just as caterpillars and locusts strip the fields
and vines,
so the fallen army of Assyria will be
stripped!

5 Though the LORD is very great and lives in
heaven,
he will make Jerusalem* his home of
justice and righteousness.
6 In that day he will be your sure foundation,
providing a rich store of salvation, wisdom,
and knowledge.
The fear of the LORD will be your treasure.

7 But now your brave warriors weep in public.
Your ambassadors of peace cry in bitter
disappointment.
8 Your roads are deserted;
no one travels them anymore.
The Assyrians have broken their peace treaty
and care nothing for the promises they
made before witnesses.*
They have no respect for anyone.
9 The land of Israel wilts in mourning.
Lebanon withers with shame.
The plain of Sharon is now a wilderness.
Bashan and Carmel have been plundered.

10 But the LORD says: "Now I will stand up.
Now I will show my power and might.
11 You Assyrians produce nothing but dry grass
and stubble.
Your own breath will turn to fire and
consume you.
12 Your people will be burned up completely,
like thornbushes cut down and tossed in a
fire.
13 Listen to what I have done, you nations far
away!
And you that are near, acknowledge my
might!"

14 The sinners in Jerusalem shake with fear.
Terror seizes the godless.
"Who can live with this devouring fire?" they
cry.
"Who can survive this all-consuming fire?"
15 Those who are honest and fair,
who refuse to profit by fraud,
who stay far away from bribes,
who refuse to listen to those who plot
murder,
who shut their eyes to all enticement to do
wrong—
16 these are the ones who will dwell on high.
The rocks of the mountains will be their
fortress.
Food will be supplied to them,
and they will have water in abundance.

17 Your eyes will see the king in all his
splendor,
and you will see a land that stretches into
the distance.
18 You will think back to this time of terror,
asking,
"Where are the Assyrian officers
who counted our towers?
Where are the bookkeepers
who recorded the plunder taken from our
fallen city?"
19 You will no longer see these fierce, violent
people
with their strange, unknown language.

33:1 Hebrew *What sorrow awaits you, O destroyer.* The Hebrew text does not specifically name Assyria as the object of the prophecy in this chapter. **33:5** Hebrew *Zion;* also in 33:14. **33:8** As in Dead Sea Scrolls; Masoretic Text reads *care nothing for the cities.*

33:1–24 A Message about Assyria. The Assyrians will experience the destruction and treachery they have heaped on others. But God in his mercy will transform Jerusalem from a place of danger and weeping to a center for justice, righteousness, and abundance for those who demonstrate their honesty. Instead of Assyrian officers babbling a disorienting foreign language, people will see the coming righteous king, the LORD, and feel secure in him.

20 Instead, you will see Zion as a place of holy
festivals.
You will see Jerusalem, a city quiet and
secure.
It will be like a tent whose ropes are taut
and whose stakes are firmly fixed.
21 The LORD will be our Mighty One.
He will be like a wide river of protection
that no enemy can cross,
that no enemy ship can sail upon.
22 For the LORD is our judge,
our lawgiver, and our king.
He will care for us and save us.
23 The enemies' sails hang loose
on broken masts with useless tackle.
Their treasure will be divided by the people
of God.
Even the lame will take their share!
24 The people of Israel will no longer say,
"We are sick and helpless,"
for the LORD will forgive their sins.

A Message for the Nations

34 1Come here and listen, O nations of
the earth.
Let the world and everything in it
hear my words.
2 For the LORD is enraged against the nations.
His fury is against all their armies.
He will completely destroy* them,
dooming them to slaughter.
3 Their dead will be left unburied,
and the stench of rotting bodies will fill the
land.
The mountains will flow with their
blood.
4 The heavens above will melt away
and disappear like a rolled-up scroll.
The stars will fall from the sky
like withered leaves from a grapevine,
or shriveled figs from a fig tree.

5 And when my sword has finished its work in
the heavens,
it will fall upon Edom,
the nation I have marked for destruction.
6 The sword of the LORD is drenched with
blood
and covered with fat—
with the blood of lambs and goats,
with the fat of rams prepared for sacrifice.
Yes, the LORD will offer a sacrifice in the city
of Bozrah.
He will make a mighty slaughter in Edom.
7 Even men as strong as wild oxen will die—
the young men alongside the veterans.
The land will be soaked with blood
and the soil enriched with fat.

8 For it is the day of the LORD's revenge,
the year when Edom will be paid back for
all it did to Israel.*
9 The streams of Edom will be filled with
burning pitch,
and the ground will be covered with fire.
10 This judgment on Edom will never end;
the smoke of its burning will rise forever.
The land will lie deserted from generation to
generation.
No one will live there anymore.
11 It will be haunted by the desert owl and the
screech owl,
the great owl and the raven.*
For God will measure that land carefully;
he will measure it for chaos and
destruction.
12 It will be called the Land of Nothing,
and all its nobles will soon be gone.*
13 Thorns will overrun its palaces;
nettles and thistles will grow in its forts.
The ruins will become a haunt for jackals
and a home for owls.
14 Desert animals will mingle there with
hyenas,
their howls filling the night.
Wild goats will bleat at one another among
the ruins,
and night creatures* will come there to
rest.
15 There the owl will make her nest and lay her
eggs.
She will hatch her young and cover them
with her wings.
And the buzzards will come,
each one with its mate.

34:2 The Hebrew term used here refers to the complete consecration of things or people to the LORD, either by destroying them or by giving them as an offering; similarly in 34:5. **34:8** Hebrew *to Zion.* **34:11** The identification of some of these birds is uncertain. **34:12** The meaning of the Hebrew is uncertain. **34:14** Hebrew *Lilith,* possibly a reference to a mythical demon of the night.

34:1–17 A Message for the Nations. This apparently ferocious chapter *against the nations* clearly does not contradict God's love for all peoples expressed elsewhere. It majors on Edom, soon to experience judgment for their contempt of God's people in the past (see Num 20:14–21 and subsequent history). Edom epitomizes the ultimate enemy of God, to be overthrown and replaced with a sanctuary for wildlife.

16 Search the book of the LORD,
and see what he will do.
Not one of these birds and animals will be missing,
and none will lack a mate,
for the LORD has promised this.
His Spirit will make it all come true.
17 He has surveyed and divided the land
and deeded it over to those creatures.
They will possess it forever,
from generation to generation.

Hope for Restoration

35 1Even the wilderness and desert will be glad in those days.
The wasteland will rejoice and blossom with spring crocuses.
2 Yes, there will be an abundance of flowers
and singing and joy!
The deserts will become as green as the mountains of Lebanon,
as lovely as Mount Carmel or the plain of Sharon.
There the LORD will display his glory,
the splendor of our God.
3 With this news, strengthen those who have tired hands,
and encourage those who have weak knees.
4 Say to those with fearful hearts,
"Be strong, and do not fear,
for your God is coming to destroy your enemies.
He is coming to save you."

5 And when he comes, he will open the eyes of the blind
and unplug the ears of the deaf.
6 The lame will leap like a deer,
and those who cannot speak will sing for joy!
Springs will gush forth in the wilderness,
and streams will water the wasteland.
7 The parched ground will become a pool,
and springs of water will satisfy the thirsty land.
Marsh grass and reeds and rushes will flourish
where desert jackals once lived.

8 And a great road will go through that once deserted land.
It will be named the Highway of Holiness.
Evil-minded people will never travel on it.
It will be only for those who walk in God's ways;
fools will never walk there.
9 Lions will not lurk along its course,
nor any other ferocious beasts.
There will be no other dangers.
Only the redeemed will walk on it.
10 Those who have been ransomed by the LORD will return.
They will enter Jerusalem* singing,
crowned with everlasting joy.
Sorrow and mourning will disappear,
and they will be filled with joy and gladness.

Assyria Invades Judah

36 In the fourteenth year of King Hezekiah's reign,* King Sennacherib of
Assyria came to attack the fortified
towns of Judah and conquered them. 2Then the
king of Assyria sent his chief of staff* from Lachish with a huge army to confront King Hezekiah in Jerusalem. The Assyrians took up a position beside the aqueduct that feeds water into
the upper pool, near the road leading to the field
where cloth is washed.*
3These are the officials who went out to meet
with them: Eliakim son of Hilkiah, the palace administrator; Shebna the court secretary; and Joah
son of Asaph, the royal historian.

Sennacherib Threatens Jerusalem

4Then the Assyrian king's chief of staff told them
to give this message to Hezekiah:

35:10 Hebrew *Zion.* **36:1** The fourteenth year of Hezekiah's reign was 701 B.C. **36:2a** Or *the rabshakeh;* also in 36:4, 11, 12, 22. **36:2b** Or *bleached.*

35:1–10 Hope for Restoration. Thought of wildlife spurs Isaiah to offer hope that all deserts, whether physical or in the human heart, will blossom and flourish when the LORD comes. A great *Highway of Holiness* will lead repentant exiles back to Jerusalem in overwhelming joy. All obstacles and dangers will be overcome.

36:1—39:8 A Window into History

The end of this large First Isaiah section highlights a particular period in the life of Judah under king Hezekiah, giving some historical background to Isaiah's words.

36:1–3 Assyria Invades Judah. King Sennacherib of Assyria, having conquered the Northern Kingdom, Israel, moves to attack Judah, sending envoys to meet Hezekiah's officials.

36:4–22 Sennacherib Threatens Jerusalem. There is a lot of truth in what Sennacherib's envoy says.

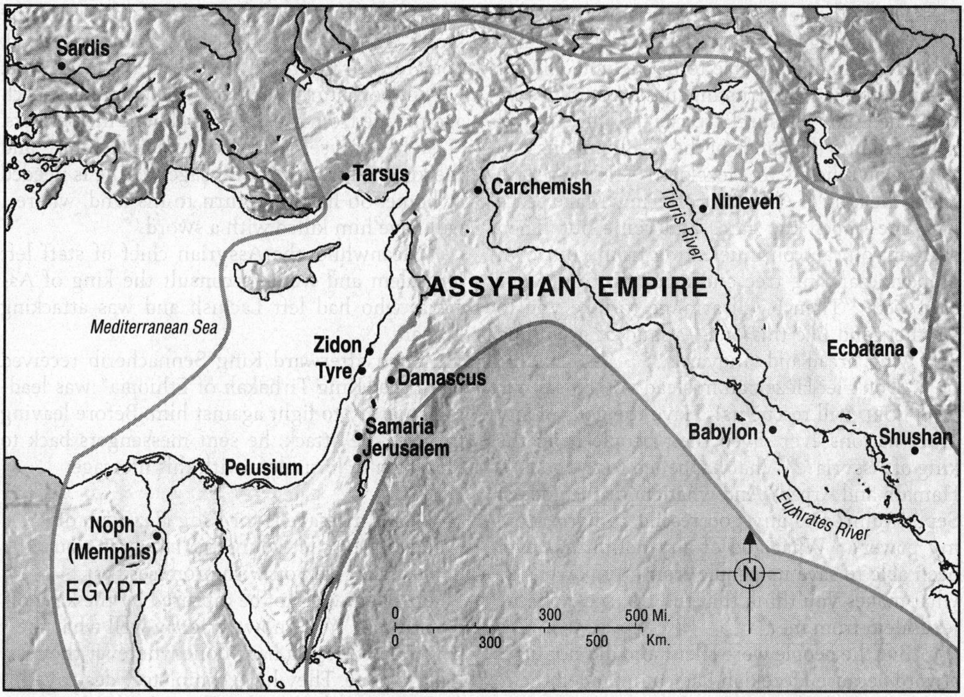

The Assyrian Empire

"This is what the great king of Assyria says:
What are you trusting in that makes you so
confident? 5Do you think that mere words
can substitute for military skill and strength?
Who are you counting on, that you have
rebelled against me? 6On Egypt? If you lean
on Egypt, it will be like a reed that splinters
beneath your weight and pierces your hand.
Pharaoh, the king of Egypt, is completely
unreliable!

7"But perhaps you will say to me, 'We
are trusting in the LORD our God!' But isn't
he the one who was insulted by Hezekiah?
Didn't Hezekiah tear down his shrines and
altars and make everyone in Judah and
Jerusalem worship only at the altar here in
Jerusalem?

8"I'll tell you what! Strike a bargain with
my master, the king of Assyria. I will give
you 2,000 horses if you can find that many
men to ride on them! 9With your tiny army,
how can you think of challenging even the
weakest contingent of my master's troops,
even with the help of Egypt's chariots and
charioteers? 10What's more, do you think we
have invaded your land without the LORD's
direction? The LORD himself told us, 'Attack
this land and destroy it!' "

11Then Eliakim, Shebna, and Joah said to the
Assyrian chief of staff, "Please speak to us in Aramaic, for we understand it well. Don't speak in
Hebrew,* for the people on the wall will hear."
12But Sennacherib's chief of staff replied, "Do
you think my master sent this message only to
you and your master? He wants all the people
to hear it, for when we put this city under siege,
they will suffer along with you. They will be so
hungry and thirsty that they will eat their own
dung and drink their own urine."

13Then the chief of staff stood and shouted in
Hebrew to the people on the wall, "Listen to this

36:11 Hebrew *in the dialect of Judah;* also in 36:13.

Egypt is indeed a reed, and Isaiah has been warning of God's judgment for a long time. But he misunderstands Hezekiah's religious reforms. The Judean officials recognize the debilitating power of threatening words on the public, hence the request to speak in Aramaic, the Assyrian language. The request is refused, and the next shouted message insults the LORD as well as the king.

message from the great king of Assyria! 14 This
is what the king says: Don't let Hezekiah deceive
you. He will never be able to rescue you. 15 Don't
let him fool you into trusting in the LORD by saying, 'The LORD will surely rescue us. This city will
never fall into the hands of the Assyrian king!'
16 "Don't listen to Hezekiah! These are the
terms the king of Assyria is offering: Make peace
with me—open the gates and come out. Then
each of you can continue eating from your own
grapevine and fig tree and drinking from your
own well. 17 Then I will arrange to take you to
another land like this one—a land of grain and
new wine, bread and vineyards.
18 "Don't let Hezekiah mislead you by saying,
'The LORD will rescue us!' Have the gods of any
other nations ever saved their people from the
king of Assyria? 19 What happened to the gods of
Hamath and Arpad? And what about the gods of
Sepharvaim? Did any god rescue Samaria from
my power? 20 What god of any nation has ever
been able to save its people from my power? So
what makes you think that the LORD can rescue
Jerusalem from me?"
21 But the people were silent and did not utter
a word because Hezekiah had commanded them,
"Do not answer him."
22 Then Eliakim son of Hilkiah, the palace administrator; Shebna the court secretary; and Joah
son of Asaph, the royal historian, went back to
Hezekiah. They tore their clothes in despair, and
they went in to see the king and told him what
the Assyrian chief of staff had said.

Hezekiah Seeks the LORD's Help

37 When King Hezekiah heard their report, he tore his clothes and put on
burlap and went into the Temple of
the LORD. 2 And he sent Eliakim the palace administrator, Shebna the court secretary, and
the leading priests, all dressed in burlap, to the
prophet Isaiah son of Amoz. 3 They told him,
"This is what King Hezekiah says: Today is a day
of trouble, insults, and disgrace. It is like when
a child is ready to be born, but the mother has
no strength to deliver the baby. 4 But perhaps the
LORD your God has heard the Assyrian chief of
staff,* sent by the king to defy the living God,
and will punish him for his words. Oh, pray for
those of us who are left!"
5 After King Hezekiah's officials delivered the
king's message to Isaiah, 6 the prophet replied,
"Say to your master, 'This is what the LORD says:
Do not be disturbed by this blasphemous speech
against me from the Assyrian king's messengers.
7 Listen! I myself will move against him,* and
the king will receive a message that he is needed
at home. So he will return to his land, where I
will have him killed with a sword.' "
8 Meanwhile, the Assyrian chief of staff left
Jerusalem and went to consult the king of Assyria, who had left Lachish and was attacking
Libnah.
9 Soon afterward King Sennacherib received
word that King Tirhakah of Ethiopia* was leading an army to fight against him. Before leaving
to meet the attack, he sent messengers back to
Hezekiah in Jerusalem with this message:

10 "This message is for King Hezekiah of
Judah. Don't let your God, in whom you
trust, deceive you with promises that
Jerusalem will not be captured by the king of
Assyria. 11 You know perfectly well what the
kings of Assyria have done wherever they
have gone. They have completely destroyed
everyone who stood in their way! Why
should you be any different? 12 Have the gods
of other nations rescued them—such nations
as Gozan, Haran, Rezeph, and the people of
Eden who were in Tel-assar? My predecessors
destroyed them all! 13 What happened to the
king of Hamath and the king of Arpad? What
happened to the kings of Sepharvaim, Hena,
and Ivvah?"

14 After Hezekiah received the letter from the
messengers and read it, he went up to the LORD's
Temple and spread it out before the LORD. 15 And
Hezekiah prayed this prayer before the LORD:
16 "O LORD of Heaven's Armies, God of Israel,
you are enthroned between the mighty cherubim! You alone are God of all the kingdoms of
the earth. You alone created the heavens and the
earth. 17 Bend down, O LORD, and listen! Open
your eyes, O LORD, and see! Listen to Sennacherib's words of defiance against the living God.

37:4 Or *the rabshakeh;* also in 37:8. **37:7** Hebrew *I will put a spirit in him.* **37:9** Hebrew *of Cush.*

37:1–20 Hezekiah Seeks the LORD's Help. Brought to the point of utter helplessness, a devastated Hezekiah sends his officials to humbly seek God's help through Isaiah. Isaiah reassures them that despite the seemingly impossible situation, God is in control. Sennacherib is diverted, though not before repeating his defiance against the LORD. This time, Hezekiah goes to seek God himself. His prayer focuses on the LORD's sovereignty over all kingdoms and expresses his faith that Israel's God is different from those of other nations.

18 "It is true, LORD, that the kings of Assyria
have destroyed all these nations. 19 And they have
thrown the gods of these nations into the fire and
burned them. But of course the Assyrians could
destroy them! They were not gods at all—only
idols of wood and stone shaped by human hands.
20 Now, O LORD our God, rescue us from his power; then all the kingdoms of the earth will know
that you alone, O LORD, are God.*"

Isaiah Predicts Judah's Deliverance

21 Then Isaiah son of Amoz sent this message to
Hezekiah: "This is what the LORD, the God of Israel, says: Because you prayed about King Sennacherib of Assyria, 22 the LORD has spoken this
word against him:

"The virgin daughter of Zion
despises you and laughs at you.
The daughter of Jerusalem
shakes her head in derision as you flee.

23 "Whom have you been defying and ridiculing?
Against whom did you raise your voice?
At whom did you look with such haughty eyes?
It was the Holy One of Israel!
24 By your messengers you have defied the Lord.
You have said, 'With my many chariots
I have conquered the highest mountains—
yes, the remotest peaks of Lebanon.
I have cut down its tallest cedars
and its finest cypress trees.
I have reached its farthest heights
and explored its deepest forests.
25 I have dug wells in many foreign lands*
and refreshed myself with their water.
With the sole of my foot,
I stopped up all the rivers of Egypt!'

26 "But have you not heard?
I decided this long ago.
Long ago I planned it,
and now I am making it happen.
I planned for you to crush fortified cities
into heaps of rubble.
27 That is why their people have so little power
and are so frightened and confused.
They are as weak as grass,
as easily trampled as tender green shoots.
They are like grass sprouting on a housetop,
scorched* before it can grow lush and tall.

28 "But I know you well—
where you stay
and when you come and go.
I know the way you have raged against me.
29 And because of your raging against me
and your arrogance, which I have heard for myself,
I will put my hook in your nose
and my bit in your mouth.
I will make you return
by the same road on which you came."

30 Then Isaiah said to Hezekiah, "Here is the
proof that what I say is true:

"This year you will eat only what grows up by itself,
and next year you will eat what springs up from that.
But in the third year you will plant crops and harvest them;
you will tend vineyards and eat their fruit.
31 And you who are left in Judah,
who have escaped the ravages of the siege,
will put roots down in your own soil
and grow up and flourish.
32 For a remnant of my people will spread out from Jerusalem,
a group of survivors from Mount Zion.
The passionate commitment of the LORD of Heaven's Armies
will make this happen!

33 "And this is what the LORD says about the king
of Assyria:

" 'His armies will not enter Jerusalem.
They will not even shoot an arrow at it.
They will not march outside its gates with their shields
nor build banks of earth against its walls.
34 The king will return to his own country
by the same road on which he came.

37:20 As in Dead Sea Scrolls (see also 2 Kgs 19:19); Masoretic Text reads *you alone are the LORD.* **37:25** As in Dead Sea Scrolls (see also 2 Kgs 19:24); Masoretic Text lacks *in many foreign lands.* **37:27** As in Dead Sea Scrolls and some Greek manuscripts (see also 2 Kgs 19:26); most Hebrew manuscripts read *like a terraced field.*

37:21–38 Isaiah Predicts Judah's Deliverance. Prayer changes things! Sennacherib versus the LORD—how laughable! God's honor is at stake, and all will be well. Judah's survivors will flourish, and Sennacherib's doom is sealed.

He will not enter this city,'
says the LORD.
35 'For my own honor and for the sake of my
servant David,
I will defend this city and protect it.' "

36 That night the angel of the LORD went out
to the Assyrian camp and killed 185,000 Assyrian
soldiers. When the surviving Assyrians* woke up
the next morning, they found corpses everywhere.
37 Then King Sennacherib of Assyria broke camp
and returned to his own land. He went home to
his capital of Nineveh and stayed there.
38 One day while he was worshiping in the temple of his god Nisroch, his sons Adrammelech and
Sharezer killed him with their swords. They then
escaped to the land of Ararat, and another son,
Esarhaddon, became the next king of Assyria.

Hezekiah's Sickness and Recovery

38 About that time Hezekiah became
deathly ill, and the prophet Isaiah son
of Amoz went to visit him. He gave
the king this message: "This is what the LORD
says: 'Set your affairs in order, for you are going
to die. You will not recover from this illness.' "
2 When Hezekiah heard this, he turned his
face to the wall and prayed to the LORD, 3 "Remember, O LORD, how I have always been faithful to you and have served you single-mindedly,
always doing what pleases you." Then he broke
down and wept bitterly.
4 Then this message came to Isaiah from the
LORD: 5 "Go back to Hezekiah and tell him, 'This
is what the LORD, the God of your ancestor David, says: I have heard your prayer and seen your
tears. I will add fifteen years to your life, 6 and I
will rescue you and this city from the king of
Assyria. Yes, I will defend this city.
7 " 'And this is the sign from the LORD to
prove that he will do as he promised: 8 I will cause
the sun's shadow to move ten steps backward on
the sundial* of Ahaz!' " So the shadow on the
sundial moved backward ten steps.

Hezekiah's Poem of Praise

9 When King Hezekiah was well again, he wrote
this poem:

10 I said, "In the prime of my life,
must I now enter the place of the dead?*
Am I to be robbed of the rest of my years?"
11 I said, "Never again will I see the LORD GOD
while still in the land of the living.
Never again will I see my friends
or be with those who live in this world.
12 My life has been blown away
like a shepherd's tent in a storm.
It has been cut short,
as when a weaver cuts cloth from a loom.
Suddenly, my life was over.
13 I waited patiently all night,
but I was torn apart as though by lions.
Suddenly, my life was over.
14 Delirious, I chattered like a swallow or a crane,
and then I moaned like a mourning dove.
My eyes grew tired of looking to heaven for
help.
I am in trouble, Lord. Help me!"

15 But what could I say?
For he himself sent this sickness.
Now I will walk humbly throughout my years
because of this anguish I have felt.
16 Lord, your discipline is good,
for it leads to life and health.
You restore my health
and allow me to live!
17 Yes, this anguish was good for me,
for you have rescued me from death
and forgiven all my sins.
18 For the dead* cannot praise you;
they cannot raise their voices in praise.
Those who go down to the grave
can no longer hope in your faithfulness.
19 Only the living can praise you as I do today.
Each generation tells of your faithfulness
to the next.
20 Think of it—the LORD is ready to heal me!
I will sing his praises with instruments
every day of my life
in the Temple of the LORD.

21 Isaiah had said to Hezekiah's servants,
"Make an ointment from figs and spread it over
the boil, and Hezekiah will recover."
22 And Hezekiah had asked, "What sign will
prove that I will go to the Temple of the LORD?"

37:36 Hebrew *When they.* **38:8** Hebrew *the steps.*
38:10 Hebrew *enter the gates of Sheol?* **38:18** Hebrew
Sheol.

38:1–8 Hezekiah's Sickness and Recovery. The young king's grief at the initial prognosis of his illness is the impulse for further prayer, through which his life is extended. The exact nature of the sign is unclear.

38:9–22 Hezekiah's Poem of Praise. Hezekiah's recognition of God's discipline being good for him results in humble praise. The poultice of figs for a skin disorder is typical of ancient folk medicine.

Envoys from Babylon

39 Soon after this, Merodach-baladan son of Baladan, king of Babylon, sent Hezekiah his best wishes and a gift. He had heard that Hezekiah had been very sick and that he had recovered. 2 Hezekiah was delighted with the Babylonian envoys and showed them everything in his treasure-houses—the silver, the gold, the spices, and the aromatic oils. He also took them to see his armory and showed them everything in his royal treasuries! There was nothing in his palace or kingdom that Hezekiah did not show them.

3 Then Isaiah the prophet went to King Hezekiah and asked him, "What did those men want? Where were they from?"

Hezekiah replied, "They came from the distant land of Babylon."

4 "What did they see in your palace?" asked Isaiah.

"They saw everything," Hezekiah replied. "I showed them everything I own—all my royal treasuries."

5 Then Isaiah said to Hezekiah, "Listen to this message from the LORD of Heaven's Armies:
6 'The time is coming when everything in your palace—all the treasures stored up by your ancestors until now—will be carried off to Babylon. Nothing will be left,' says the LORD. 7 'Some of your very own sons will be taken away into exile. They will become eunuchs who will serve in the palace of Babylon's king.' "

8 Then Hezekiah said to Isaiah, "This message you have given me from the LORD is good." For the king was thinking, "At least there will be peace and security during my lifetime."

Comfort for God's People

40 1 "Comfort, comfort my people,"
says your God.
2 "Speak tenderly to Jerusalem.
Tell her that her sad days are gone
and her sins are pardoned.
Yes, the LORD has punished her twice over
for all her sins."

3 Listen! It's the voice of someone shouting,
"Clear the way through the wilderness
for the LORD!
Make a straight highway through the
wasteland
for our God!
4 Fill in the valleys,
and level the mountains and hills.
Straighten the curves,
and smooth out the rough places.
5 Then the glory of the LORD will be revealed,
and all people will see it together.
The LORD has spoken!"*

6 A voice said, "Shout!"
I asked, "What should I shout?"

"Shout that people are like the grass.
Their beauty fades as quickly
as the flowers in a field.
7 The grass withers and the flowers fade
beneath the breath of the LORD.
And so it is with people.
8 The grass withers and the flowers fade,
but the word of our God stands forever."

9 O Zion, messenger of good news,
shout from the mountaintops!

40:3-5 Greek version reads *He is a voice shouting in the wilderness, / "Prepare the way for the LORD's coming! / Clear a road for our God! / Fill in the valleys, / and level the mountains and hills. / And then the glory of the LORD will be revealed, / and all people will see the salvation sent from God. / The LORD has spoken!"* Compare Matt 3:3; Mark 1:3; Luke 3:4-6.

39:1–8 Envoys from Babylon. However, Hezekiah's trust is short-lived. When Babylonian envoys come with gifts, he is somewhat too open with them. Their visit is tantamount to a proffered political alliance, and Isaiah is sceptical. He knows that Babylon is set to grow into greatness, and one day Judah will be taken into exile there. This sets the scene for the next chapters, which envisage life after deportation to Babylon.

40:1—55:13 Second Isaiah: Experience of God in Exile

40:1—44:20 Comfort after Judgment

The focus now shifts to the days immediately following judgment. The prophet Isaiah brings great comfort to God's people, looking beyond their suffering. The idea of the *servant* of the LORD is introduced, a multifaceted concept meaning at different times the nation, Isaiah himself, political individuals, and a messianic figure. We read repeatedly *Israel my servant, Jacob my servant, my chosen one*.

40:1–11 Comfort for God's People. God's people are in exile in Babylon, because they rebelled against him and rejected his ways. Now Isaiah hears God's message of comfort and reassurance; their punishment is over, and they are forgiven. God is coming to tenderly lead his people again. This is good news, to be shouted everywhere!

Shout it louder, O Jerusalem.*
Shout, and do not be afraid.
Tell the towns of Judah,
"Your God is coming!"
10 Yes, the Sovereign LORD is coming in power.
He will rule with a powerful arm.
See, he brings his reward with him as he comes.
11 He will feed his flock like a shepherd.
He will carry the lambs in his arms,
holding them close to his heart.
He will gently lead the mother sheep with their young.

The LORD Has No Equal

12 Who else has held the oceans in his hand?
Who has measured off the heavens with his fingers?
Who else knows the weight of the earth
or has weighed the mountains and hills on a scale?
13 Who is able to advise the Spirit of the LORD?*
Who knows enough to give him advice or teach him?
14 Has the LORD ever needed anyone's advice?
Does he need instruction about what is good?
Did someone teach him what is right
or show him the path of justice?

15 No, for all the nations of the world
are but a drop in the bucket.
They are nothing more
than dust on the scales.
He picks up the whole earth
as though it were a grain of sand.
16 All the wood in Lebanon's forests
and all Lebanon's animals would not be enough
to make a burnt offering worthy of our God.
17 The nations of the world are worth nothing to him.
In his eyes they count for less than nothing—
mere emptiness and froth.

18 To whom can you compare God?
What image can you find to resemble him?
19 Can he be compared to an idol formed in a mold,
overlaid with gold, and decorated with silver chains?
20 Or if people are too poor for that,
they might at least choose wood that won't decay
and a skilled craftsman
to carve an image that won't fall down!

21 Haven't you heard? Don't you understand?
Are you deaf to the words of God—
the words he gave before the world began?
Are you so ignorant?
22 God sits above the circle of the earth.
The people below seem like grasshoppers to him!
He spreads out the heavens like a curtain
and makes his tent from them.
23 He judges the great people of the world
and brings them all to nothing.
24 They hardly get started, barely taking root,
when he blows on them and they wither.
The wind carries them off like chaff.

25 "To whom will you compare me?
Who is my equal?" asks the Holy One.

26 Look up into the heavens.
Who created all the stars?
He brings them out like an army, one after another,
calling each by its name.
Because of his great power and incomparable strength,
not a single one is missing.
27 O Jacob, how can you say the LORD does not see your troubles?
O Israel, how can you say God ignores your rights?
28 Have you never heard?
Have you never understood?
The LORD is the everlasting God,
the Creator of all the earth.
He never grows weak or weary.
No one can measure the depths of his understanding.
29 He gives power to the weak
and strength to the powerless.
30 Even youths will become weak and tired,

40:9 Or *O messenger of good news, shout to Zion from the mountaintops! Shout it louder to Jerusalem.* **40:13** Greek version reads *Who can know the LORD's thoughts?* Compare Rom 11:34; 1 Cor 2:16.

40:12–31 The LORD Has No Equal. In view of their earlier apostasy, Isaiah invites the exiles to compare the LORD with images and idols—but the outcome is ridiculously obvious! This is a glorious portrayal of the Creator, who gives strength to those who trust him.

and young men will fall in exhaustion.
31 But those who trust in the LORD will find
new strength.
They will soar high on wings like eagles.
They will run and not grow weary.
They will walk and not faint.

God's Help for Israel

41 1"Listen in silence before me, you
lands beyond the sea.
Bring your strongest arguments.
Come now and speak.
The court is ready for your case.

2 "Who has stirred up this king from the east,
rightly calling him to God's service?
Who gives this man victory over many
nations
and permits him to trample their kings
underfoot?
With his sword, he reduces armies to dust.
With his bow, he scatters them like chaff
before the wind.
3 He chases them away and goes on safely,
though he is walking over unfamiliar
ground.
4 Who has done such mighty deeds,
summoning each new generation from the
beginning of time?
It is I, the LORD, the First and the Last.
I alone am he."

5 The lands beyond the sea watch in fear.
Remote lands tremble and mobilize for war.
6 The idol makers encourage one another,
saying to each other, "Be strong!"
7 The carver encourages the goldsmith,
and the molder helps at the anvil.
"Good," they say. "It's coming along fine."
Carefully they join the parts together,
then fasten the thing in place so it won't
fall over.

8 "But as for you, Israel my servant,
Jacob my chosen one,
descended from Abraham my friend,
9 I have called you back from the ends of the
earth,
saying, 'You are my servant.'
For I have chosen you
and will not throw you away.
10 Don't be afraid, for I am with you.
Don't be discouraged, for I am your God.
I will strengthen you and help you.
I will hold you up with my victorious right
hand.

11 "See, all your angry enemies lie there,
confused and humiliated.
Anyone who opposes you will die
and come to nothing.
12 You will look in vain
for those who tried to conquer you.
Those who attack you
will come to nothing.
13 For I hold you by your right hand—
I, the LORD your God.
And I say to you,
'Don't be afraid. I am here to help you.
14 Though you are a lowly worm, O Jacob,
don't be afraid, people of Israel, for I will
help you.
I am the LORD, your Redeemer.
I am the Holy One of Israel.'
15 You will be a new threshing instrument
with many sharp teeth.
You will tear your enemies apart,
making chaff of mountains.
16 You will toss them into the air,
and the wind will blow them all away;
a whirlwind will scatter them.
Then you will rejoice in the LORD.
You will glory in the Holy One of Israel.

17 "When the poor and needy search for water
and there is none,
and their tongues are parched from thirst,
then I, the LORD, will answer them.
I, the God of Israel, will never abandon
them.
18 I will open up rivers for them on the high
plateaus.
I will give them fountains of water in the
valleys.
I will fill the desert with pools of water.
Rivers fed by springs will flow across the
parched ground.
19 I will plant trees in the barren desert—
cedar, acacia, myrtle, olive, cypress, fir, and
pine.

41:1–29 God's Help for Israel. In a simulated court hearing, God takes legal responsibility for the devastation that has happened, and challenges Israel about her former idols. Now, in contrast to the idol makers, Israel—God's *servant*—is told not to fear, for God will help her against her enemies and will transform her desert experiences, creating new life and great joy. He is stirring up a new leader (Cyrus; see 44:28) who will be good news for ruined Jerusalem.

20 I am doing this so all who see this miracle
will understand what it means—
that it is the LORD who has done this,
the Holy One of Israel who created it.
21 "Present the case for your idols,"
says the LORD.
"Let them show what they can do,"
says the King of Israel.*
22 "Let them try to tell us what happened long ago
so that we may consider the evidence.
Or let them tell us what the future holds,
so we can know what's going to happen.
23 Yes, tell us what will occur in the days ahead.
Then we will know you are gods.
In fact, do anything—good or bad!
Do something that will amaze and frighten us.
24 But no! You are less than nothing and can do nothing at all.
Those who choose you pollute themselves.

25 "But I have stirred up a leader who will come from the north.
I have called him by name from the east.
I will give him victory over kings and princes.
He will trample them as a potter treads on clay.
26 "Who told you from the beginning
that this would happen?
Who predicted this,
making you admit that he was right?
No one said a word!
27 I was the first to tell Zion,
'Look! Help is on the way!'*
I will send Jerusalem a messenger with good news.
28 Not one of your idols told you this.
Not one gave any answer when I asked.
29 See, they are all foolish, worthless things.
All your idols are as empty as the wind.

The LORD's Chosen Servant

42 1"Look at my servant, whom I strengthen.
He is my chosen one, who pleases me.
I have put my Spirit upon him.
He will bring justice to the nations.
2 He will not shout
or raise his voice in public.
3 He will not crush the weakest reed
or put out a flickering candle.
He will bring justice to all who have been wronged.
4 He will not falter or lose heart
until justice prevails throughout the earth.
Even distant lands beyond the sea will wait for his instruction.*"

5 God, the LORD, created the heavens and stretched them out.
He created the earth and everything in it.
He gives breath to everyone,
life to everyone who walks the earth.
And it is he who says,
6 "I, the LORD, have called you to demonstrate my righteousness.
I will take you by the hand and guard you,
and I will give you to my people, Israel,
as a symbol of my covenant with them.
And you will be a light to guide the nations.
7 You will open the eyes of the blind.
You will free the captives from prison,
releasing those who sit in dark dungeons.

8 "I am the LORD; that is my name!
I will not give my glory to anyone else,
nor share my praise with carved idols.
9 Everything I prophesied has come true,
and now I will prophesy again.
I will tell you the future before it happens."

A Song of Praise to the LORD

10 Sing a new song to the LORD!
Sing his praises from the ends of the earth!
Sing, all you who sail the seas,
all you who live in distant coastlands.
11 Join in the chorus, you desert towns;
let the villages of Kedar rejoice!
Let the people of Sela sing for joy;
shout praises from the mountaintops!
12 Let the whole world glorify the LORD;
let it sing his praise.

41:21 Hebrew *the King of Jacob.* See note on 14:1. **41:27** Or *'Look! They are coming home.'* **42:4** Greek version reads *And his name will be the hope of all the world.* Compare Matt 12:21.

42:1–9 The LORD's Chosen Servant. This is the first of four "servant songs." Here we simply see the servant's task: Endowed by God's Spirit, he will bring justice throughout the earth, thus demonstrating God's own character.

42:10–17 A Song of Praise to the LORD. The whole world is invited to respond in joyful praise to the LORD. God will put huge effort into smoothing Israel's path—note the imagery of childbirth again, but this time God himself is in labor!

13 The LORD will march forth like a mighty hero;
he will come out like a warrior, full of fury.
He will shout his battle cry
and crush all his enemies.

14 He will say, "I have long been silent;
yes, I have restrained myself.
But now, like a woman in labor,
I will cry and groan and pant.
15 I will level the mountains and hills
and blight all their greenery.
I will turn the rivers into dry land
and will dry up all the pools.
16 I will lead blind Israel down a new path,
guiding them along an unfamiliar way.
I will brighten the darkness before them
and smooth out the road ahead of them.
Yes, I will indeed do these things;
I will not forsake them.
17 But those who trust in idols,
who say, 'You are our gods,'
will be turned away in shame.

Israel's Failure to Listen and See

18 "Listen, you who are deaf!
Look and see, you blind!
19 Who is as blind as my own people, my servant?
Who is as deaf as my messenger?
Who is as blind as my chosen people,
the servant of the LORD?
20 You see and recognize what is right
but refuse to act on it.
You hear with your ears,
but you don't really listen."

21 Because he is righteous,
the LORD has exalted his glorious law.
22 But his own people have been robbed and plundered,
enslaved, imprisoned, and trapped.
They are fair game for anyone
and have no one to protect them,
no one to take them back home.

23 Who will hear these lessons from the past
and see the ruin that awaits you in the future?
24 Who allowed Israel to be robbed and hurt?
It was the LORD, against whom we sinned,
for the people would not walk in his path,
nor would they obey his law.
25 Therefore, he poured out his fury on them
and destroyed them in battle.
They were enveloped in flames,
but they still refused to understand.
They were consumed by fire,
but they did not learn their lesson.

The Savior of Israel

43 1But now, O Jacob, listen to the LORD who created you.
O Israel, the one who formed you says,
"Do not be afraid, for I have ransomed you.
I have called you by name; you are mine.
2 When you go through deep waters,
I will be with you.
When you go through rivers of difficulty,
you will not drown.
When you walk through the fire of oppression,
you will not be burned up;
the flames will not consume you.
3 For I am the LORD, your God,
the Holy One of Israel, your Savior.
I gave Egypt as a ransom for your freedom;
I gave Ethiopia* and Seba in your place.
4 Others were given in exchange for you.
I traded their lives for yours
because you are precious to me.
You are honored, and I love you.

5 "Do not be afraid, for I am with you.
I will gather you and your children from east and west.
6 I will say to the north and south,
'Bring my sons and daughters back to Israel
from the distant corners of the earth.
7 Bring all who claim me as their God,
for I have made them for my glory.
It was I who created them.' "

8 Bring out the people who have eyes but are blind,
who have ears but are deaf.

43:3 Hebrew *Cush.*

42:18–25 Israel's Failure to Listen and See. Even God's servants can fail to heed him, which is why he allowed their suffering. Some never learn!

43:1–13 The Savior of Israel. The extent of God's love is beyond imagination! In this hypothetical situation, it is as if he would sacrifice the entire world for the sake of the loved one, if necessary—a choice spelled out further in Isaiah 53 and in the New Testament. What God has done in saving his people is unique.

9 Gather the nations together!
Assemble the peoples of the world!
Which of their idols has ever foretold such things?
Which can predict what will happen tomorrow?
Where are the witnesses of such predictions?
Who can verify that they spoke the truth?

10 "But you are my witnesses, O Israel!" says the LORD.
"You are my servant.
You have been chosen to know me, believe in me,
and understand that I alone am God.
There is no other God—
there never has been, and there never will be.
11 I, yes I, am the LORD,
and there is no other Savior.
12 First I predicted your rescue,
then I saved you and proclaimed it to the world.
No foreign god has ever done this.
You are witnesses that I am the only God,"
says the LORD.
13 "From eternity to eternity I am God.
No one can snatch anyone out of my hand.
No one can undo what I have done."

The LORD's Promise of Victory

14 This is what the LORD says—your Redeemer, the Holy One of Israel:

"For your sakes I will send an army against Babylon,
forcing the Babylonians* to flee in those ships they are so proud of.
15 I am the LORD, your Holy One,
Israel's Creator and King.
16 I am the LORD, who opened a way through the waters,
making a dry path through the sea.
17 I called forth the mighty army of Egypt
with all its chariots and horses.
I drew them beneath the waves, and they drowned,
their lives snuffed out like a smoldering candlewick.

18 "But forget all that—
it is nothing compared to what I am going to do.
19 For I am about to do something new.
See, I have already begun! Do you not see it?
I will make a pathway through the wilderness.
I will create rivers in the dry wasteland.
20 The wild animals in the fields will thank me,
the jackals and owls, too,
for giving them water in the desert.
Yes, I will make rivers in the dry wasteland
so my chosen people can be refreshed.
21 I have made Israel for myself,
and they will someday honor me before the whole world.

22 "But, dear family of Jacob, you refuse to ask for my help.
You have grown tired of me, O Israel!
23 You have not brought me sheep or goats for burnt offerings.
You have not honored me with sacrifices,
though I have not burdened and wearied you
with requests for grain offerings and frankincense.
24 You have not brought me fragrant calamus
or pleased me with the fat from sacrifices.
Instead, you have burdened me with your sins
and wearied me with your faults.

25 "I—yes, I alone—will blot out your sins for my own sake
and will never think of them again.
26 Let us review the situation together,
and you can present your case to prove your innocence.
27 From the very beginning, your first ancestor sinned against me;
all your leaders broke my laws.
28 That is why I have disgraced your priests;
I have decreed complete destruction* for Jacob
and shame for Israel.

43:14 Or *Chaldeans.* **43:28** The Hebrew term used here refers to the complete consecration of things or people to the LORD, either by destroying them or by giving them as an offering.

43:14—44:5 The LORD's Promise of Victory. God will do a new thing, comparable to the Exodus from Egypt: Now he will arrange their own exodus from Babylon. But first God talks things through with his people. They tired of him, broke his laws, and were punished, but now they can expect help, reassurance, and blessing as they claim the LORD as their God.

44

1"But now, listen to me, Jacob my servant,
Israel my chosen one.
2 The LORD who made you and helps you says:
Do not be afraid, O Jacob, my servant,
O dear Israel,* my chosen one.
3 For I will pour out water to quench your thirst
and to irrigate your parched fields.
And I will pour out my Spirit on your descendants,
and my blessing on your children.
4 They will thrive like watered grass,
like willows on a riverbank.
5 Some will proudly claim, 'I belong to the LORD.'
Others will say, 'I am a descendant of Jacob.'
Some will write the LORD's name on their hands
and will take the name of Israel as their own."

The Foolishness of Idols

6This is what the LORD says—Israel's King and Redeemer, the LORD of Heaven's Armies:

"I am the First and the Last;
there is no other God.
7 Who is like me?
Let him step forward and prove to you his power.
Let him do as I have done since ancient times
when I established a people and explained its future.
8 Do not tremble; do not be afraid.
Did I not proclaim my purposes for you long ago?
You are my witnesses—is there any other God?
No! There is no other Rock—not one!"

9 How foolish are those who manufacture idols.
These prized objects are really worthless.
The people who worship idols don't know this,
so they are all put to shame.
10 Who but a fool would make his own god—
an idol that cannot help him one bit?
11 All who worship idols will be disgraced
along with all these craftsmen—mere humans—
who claim they can make a god.
They may all stand together,
but they will stand in terror and shame.

12 The blacksmith stands at his forge to make a sharp tool,
pounding and shaping it with all his might.
His work makes him hungry and weak.
It makes him thirsty and faint.
13 Then the wood-carver measures a block of wood
and draws a pattern on it.
He works with chisel and plane
and carves it into a human figure.
He gives it human beauty
and puts it in a little shrine.
14 He cuts down cedars;
he selects the cypress and the oak;
he plants the pine in the forest
to be nourished by the rain.
15 Then he uses part of the wood to make a fire.
With it he warms himself and bakes his bread.
Then—yes, it's true—he takes the rest of it
and makes himself a god to worship!
He makes an idol
and bows down in front of it!
16 He burns part of the tree to roast his meat
and to keep himself warm.
He says, "Ah, that fire feels good."
17 Then he takes what's left
and makes his god: a carved idol!
He falls down in front of it,
worshiping and praying to it.
"Rescue me!" he says.
"You are my god!"

18 Such stupidity and ignorance!
Their eyes are closed, and they cannot see.
Their minds are shut, and they cannot think.
19 The person who made the idol never stops to reflect,
"Why, it's just a block of wood!
I burned half of it for heat
and used it to bake my bread and roast my meat.
How can the rest of it be a god?
Should I bow down to worship a piece of wood?"

44:2 Hebrew *Jeshurun,* a term of endearment for Israel.

44:6–20 The Foolishness of Idols. Isaiah pictures the LORD of Heaven's Armies ridiculing those who think they can manufacture an idol from a block of firewood and expect it to rescue people! It is like feeding on ashes.

20 The poor, deluded fool feeds on ashes.
He trusts something that can't help him at all.
Yet he cannot bring himself to ask,
"Is this idol that I'm holding in my hand a lie?"

Restoration for Jerusalem

21 "Pay attention, O Jacob,
for you are my servant, O Israel.
I, the LORD, made you,
and I will not forget you.
22 I have swept away your sins like a cloud.
I have scattered your offenses like the morning mist.
Oh, return to me,
for I have paid the price to set you free."

23 Sing, O heavens, for the LORD has done this wondrous thing.
Shout for joy, O depths of the earth!
Break into song,
O mountains and forests and every tree!
For the LORD has redeemed Jacob
and is glorified in Israel.

24 This is what the LORD says—
your Redeemer and Creator:
"I am the LORD, who made all things.
I alone stretched out the heavens.
Who was with me
when I made the earth?
25 I expose the false prophets as liars
and make fools of fortune-tellers.
I cause the wise to give bad advice,
thus proving them to be fools.
26 But I carry out the predictions of my prophets!
By them I say to Jerusalem, 'People will live here again,'
and to the towns of Judah, 'You will be rebuilt;
I will restore all your ruins!'
27 When I speak to the rivers and say, 'Dry up!'
they will be dry.
28 When I say of Cyrus, 'He is my shepherd,'
he will certainly do as I say.
He will command, 'Rebuild Jerusalem';
he will say, 'Restore the Temple.' "

Cyrus, the LORD's Chosen One

45 1 This is what the LORD says to Cyrus, his anointed one,
whose right hand he will empower.
Before him, mighty kings will be paralyzed with fear.
Their fortress gates will be opened,
never to shut again.
2 This is what the LORD says:

"I will go before you, Cyrus,
and level the mountains.*
I will smash down gates of bronze
and cut through bars of iron.
3 And I will give you treasures hidden in the darkness—
secret riches.
I will do this so you may know that I am the LORD,
the God of Israel, the one who calls you by name.

4 "And why have I called you for this work?
Why did I call you by name when you did not know me?
It is for the sake of Jacob my servant,
Israel my chosen one.
5 I am the LORD;
there is no other God.
I have equipped you for battle,
though you don't even know me,

45:2 As in Dead Sea Scrolls and Greek version; Masoretic Text reads *the swellings.*

44:21—55:13 Promises of Deliverance to All Nations

Again we read about the *chosen ones*, the *servants* Israel and Jacob, as these chapters contain the promise of deliverance and restoration for Jerusalem. Cyrus is God's servant politically, but there will be another kind of servant who will pay the cost and deliver God's people from their sin and rebellion. Furthermore, membership of the people of God will be opened to all nations.

44:21–28 Restoration for Jerusalem. God has paid the price to free his people, and calls them to return to him. His servant Cyrus of Persia will conquer Babylon and allow the exiles to return home to restore their temple. Judah's ruined cities will be rebuilt.

45:1–13 Cyrus, the LORD's Chosen One. Just as God earlier used Babylon's king to destroy Jerusalem, now Cyrus, another unbeliever, is God's chosen instrument for restoring her. Sometimes God's ways are surprising. But arguing with his plan is as ridiculous as the idea of a newborn baby arguing its very existence with its parents. The God who orders the stars also guides history.

6 so all the world from east to west
will know there is no other God.
I am the LORD, and there is no other.
7 I create the light and make the darkness.
I send good times and bad times.
I, the LORD, am the one who does these things.

8 "Open up, O heavens,
and pour out your righteousness.
Let the earth open wide
so salvation and righteousness can sprout up together.
I, the LORD, created them.

9 "What sorrow awaits those who argue with their Creator.
Does a clay pot argue with its maker?
Does the clay dispute with the one who shapes it, saying,
'Stop, you're doing it wrong!'
Does the pot exclaim,
'How clumsy can you be?'
10 How terrible it would be if a newborn baby said to its father,
'Why was I born?'
or if it said to its mother,
'Why did you make me this way?' "

11 This is what the LORD says—
the Holy One of Israel and your Creator:
"Do you question what I do for my children?
Do you give me orders about the work of my hands?
12 I am the one who made the earth
and created people to live on it.
With my hands I stretched out the heavens.
All the stars are at my command.
13 I will raise up Cyrus to fulfill my righteous purpose,
and I will guide his actions.
He will restore my city and free my captive people—
without seeking a reward!
I, the LORD of Heaven's Armies, have spoken!"

Future Conversion of Gentiles

14 This is what the LORD says:

"You will rule the Egyptians,
the Ethiopians,* and the Sabeans.
They will come to you with all their merchandise,
and it will all be yours.
They will follow you as prisoners in chains.
They will fall to their knees in front of you and say,
'God is with you, and he is the only God.
There is no other.' "

15 Truly, O God of Israel, our Savior,
you work in mysterious ways.
16 All craftsmen who make idols will be humiliated.
They will all be disgraced together.
17 But the LORD will save the people of Israel
with eternal salvation.
Throughout everlasting ages,
they will never again be humiliated and disgraced.

18 For the LORD is God,
and he created the heavens and earth
and put everything in place.
He made the world to be lived in,
not to be a place of empty chaos.
"I am the LORD," he says,
"and there is no other.
19 I publicly proclaim bold promises.
I do not whisper obscurities in some dark corner.
I would not have told the people of Israel* to seek me
if I could not be found.
I, the LORD, speak only what is true
and declare only what is right.

20 "Gather together and come,
you fugitives from surrounding nations.
What fools they are who carry around their wooden idols
and pray to gods that cannot save!
21 Consult together, argue your case.
Get together and decide what to say.
Who made these things known so long ago?
What idol ever told you they would happen?
Was it not I, the LORD?
For there is no other God but me,
a righteous God and Savior.

45:14 Hebrew *Cushites.* **45:19** Hebrew *of Jacob.* See note on 14:1.

45:14–25 Future Conversion of Gentiles. Israel will be a magnet for foreigners who recognize the futility of their idols and the uniqueness of Israel's God. They are invited to join Israel as God's saved people. One day every knee will bow to the LORD, whether willingly, or in shame.

There is none but me.
22 Let all the world look to me for salvation!
For I am God; there is no other.
23 I have sworn by my own name;
I have spoken the truth,
and I will never go back on my word:
Every knee will bend to me,
and every tongue will confess allegiance
to me.*"
24 The people will declare,
"The LORD is the source of all my
righteousness and strength."
And all who were angry with him
will come to him and be ashamed.
25 In the LORD all the generations of Israel will
be justified,
and in him they will boast.

Babylon's False Gods

46 1Bel and Nebo, the gods of Babylon,
bow as they are lowered to the
ground.
They are being hauled away on ox carts.
The poor beasts stagger under the weight.
2 Both the idols and their owners are bowed
down.
The gods cannot protect the people,
and the people cannot protect the gods.
They go off into captivity together.

3 "Listen to me, descendants of Jacob,
all you who remain in Israel.
I have cared for you since you were born.
Yes, I carried you before you were born.
4 I will be your God throughout your
lifetime—
until your hair is white with age.
I made you, and I will care for you.
I will carry you along and save you.

5 "To whom will you compare me?
Who is my equal?
6 Some people pour out their silver and gold
and hire a craftsman to make a god from it.
Then they bow down and worship it!
7 They carry it around on their shoulders,
and when they set it down, it stays there.
It can't even move!
And when someone prays to it, there is no
answer.
It can't rescue anyone from trouble.

8 "Do not forget this! Keep it in mind!
Remember this, you guilty ones.
9 Remember the things I have done in the past.
For I alone am God!
I am God, and there is none like me.
10 Only I can tell you the future
before it even happens.
Everything I plan will come to pass,
for I do whatever I wish.
11 I will call a swift bird of prey from the east—
a leader from a distant land to come and do
my bidding.
I have said what I would do,
and I will do it.

12 "Listen to me, you stubborn people
who are so far from doing right.
13 For I am ready to set things right,
not in the distant future, but right now!
I am ready to save Jerusalem*
and show my glory to Israel.

Prediction of Babylon's Fall

47 1"Come down, virgin daughter of
Babylon, and sit in the dust.
For your days of sitting on a
throne have ended.
O daughter of Babylonia,* never again will
you be
the lovely princess, tender and delicate.
2 Take heavy millstones and grind flour.
Remove your veil, and strip off your robe.
Expose yourself to public view.
3 You will be naked and burdened with shame.

45:23 Hebrew *will confess;* Greek version reads *will confess and give praise to God.* Compare Rom 14:11. **46:13** Hebrew *Zion.* **47:1** Or *Chaldea;* also in 47:5.

46:1–13 Babylon's False Gods. There is a stark contrast here between gods who are being carried into captivity on a cart by Cyrus (the *bird of prey*), and the God who carries his people throughout their lives, as a mother carries her child. Israel has the choice: homemade, impotent gods (Bel, or Marduk, was the head of the pantheon of Babylon's gods; Nebo was his son)—or the God who acts.

47:1–15 Prediction of Babylon's Fall. Isaiah uses the metaphor of a virgin who is stripped naked and made to grind in the mills, to bring home the reality of Babylon's fate. God had used Babylon to punish his people, but in arrogant queenly fashion she had overstepped the boundaries and had mercilessly oppressed the helpless, believing herself secure. Now she herself would be deprived of help. The metaphor changes, and the virgin becomes the widow who loses her children, signifying all those who made her great.

I will take vengeance against you without
pity."

4 Our Redeemer, whose name is the LORD of
Heaven's Armies,
is the Holy One of Israel.

5 "O beautiful Babylon, sit now in darkness
and silence.
Never again will you be known as the
queen of kingdoms.
6 For I was angry with my chosen people
and punished them by letting them fall
into your hands.
But you, Babylon, showed them no mercy.
You oppressed even the elderly.
7 You said, 'I will reign forever as queen of the
world!'
You did not reflect on your actions
or think about their consequences.

8 "Listen to this, you pleasure-loving kingdom,
living at ease and feeling secure.
You say, 'I am the only one, and there is no
other.
I will never be a widow or lose my
children.'
9 Well, both these things will come upon you
in a moment:
widowhood and the loss of your children.
Yes, these calamities will come upon you,
despite all your witchcraft and magic.

10 "You felt secure in your wickedness.
'No one sees me,' you said.
But your 'wisdom' and 'knowledge' have led
you astray,
and you said, 'I am the only one, and there
is no other.'
11 So disaster will overtake you,
and you won't be able to charm it away.
Calamity will fall upon you,
and you won't be able to buy your way
out.
A catastrophe will strike you suddenly,
one for which you are not prepared.

12 "Now use your magical charms!
Use the spells you have worked at all these
years!
Maybe they will do you some good.
Maybe they can make someone afraid of
you.
13 All the advice you receive has made you tired.
Where are all your astrologers,
those stargazers who make predictions each
month?
Let them stand up and save you from what
the future holds.
14 But they are like straw burning in a fire;
they cannot save themselves from the
flame.
You will get no help from them at all;
their hearth is no place to sit for warmth.
15 And all your friends,
those with whom you've done business
since childhood,
will go their own ways,
turning a deaf ear to your cries.

God's Stubborn People

48 1"Listen to me, O family of Jacob,
you who are called by the name
of Israel
and born into the family of Judah.
Listen, you who take oaths in the name of the
LORD
and call on the God of Israel.
You don't keep your promises,
2 even though you call yourself the holy city
and talk about depending on the God of
Israel,
whose name is the LORD of Heaven's
Armies.
3 Long ago I told you what was going to
happen.
Then suddenly I took action,
and all my predictions came true.
4 For I know how stubborn and obstinate you
are.
Your necks are as unbending as iron.
Your heads are as hard as bronze.
5 That is why I told you what would happen;
I told you beforehand what I was going
to do.
Then you could never say, 'My idols did it.
My wooden image and metal god
commanded it to happen!'
6 You have heard my predictions and seen
them fulfilled,
but you refuse to admit it.
Now I will tell you new things,

48:1–11 God's Stubborn People. Lest his people should take their forgiveness for granted, God reminds them of their stubborn human nature. He tells them beforehand what he will do, so that when it happens, they cannot attribute it to their idols. God never gives up on his people, but he will not be shared. Now that they have been cleansed through their suffering, he will tell them new things.

secrets you have not yet heard.
7 They are brand new, not things from the past.
So you cannot say, 'We knew that all the time!'

8 "Yes, I will tell you of things that are entirely new,
things you never heard of before.
For I know so well what traitors you are.
You have been rebels from birth.
9 Yet for my own sake and for the honor of my name,
I will hold back my anger and not wipe you out.
10 I have refined you, but not as silver is refined.
Rather, I have refined you in the furnace of suffering.
11 I will rescue you for my sake—
yes, for my own sake!
I will not let my reputation be tarnished,
and I will not share my glory with idols!

Freedom from Babylon

12 "Listen to me, O family of Jacob,
Israel my chosen one!
I alone am God,
the First and the Last.
13 It was my hand that laid the foundations of the earth,
my right hand that spread out the heavens above.
When I call out the stars,
they all appear in order."

14 Have any of your idols ever told you this?
Come, all of you, and listen:
The LORD has chosen Cyrus as his ally.
He will use him to put an end to the empire of Babylon
and to destroy the Babylonian* armies.

15 "I have said it: I am calling Cyrus!
I will send him on this errand and will help him succeed.
16 Come closer, and listen to this.
From the beginning I have told you plainly what would happen."
And now the Sovereign LORD and his Spirit
have sent me with this message.
17 This is what the LORD says—
your Redeemer, the Holy One of Israel:
"I am the LORD your God,
who teaches you what is good for you
and leads you along the paths you should follow.
18 Oh, that you had listened to my commands!
Then you would have had peace flowing like a gentle river
and righteousness rolling over you like waves in the sea.
19 Your descendants would have been like the sands along the seashore—
too many to count!
There would have been no need for your destruction,
or for cutting off your family name."

20 Yet even now, be free from your captivity!
Leave Babylon and the Babylonians.*
Sing out this message!
Shout it to the ends of the earth!
The LORD has redeemed his servants,
the people of Israel.*
21 They were not thirsty
when he led them through the desert.
He divided the rock,
and water gushed out for them to drink.
22 "But there is no peace for the wicked,"
says the LORD.

The LORD's Servant Commissioned

49 1 Listen to me, all you in distant lands!
Pay attention, you who are far away!
The LORD called me before my birth;
from within the womb he called me by name.
2 He made my words of judgment as sharp as a sword.
He has hidden me in the shadow of his hand.
I am like a sharp arrow in his quiver.

48:14 Or *Chaldean.* **48:20a** Or *the Chaldeans.* **48:20b** Hebrew *his servant, Jacob.* See note on 14:1.

48:12–22 Freedom from Babylon. A reminder that God alone created the universe and controls history. He has chosen Cyrus to destroy Babylon. If only Israel had obeyed God in the first place, they would not have needed to go through all their suffering. But now they are free!

49:1–7 The LORD's Servant Commissioned. In this second servant song, the identity of God's chosen servant is ambiguous—he is Israel, yet serves Israel. He will both *restore* Israel to relationship with God and be a *light to the Gentiles.* He is *despised and rejected*; yet kings will bow to him.

[3] He said to me, "You are my servant, Israel,
and you will bring me glory."

[4] I replied, "But my work seems so useless!
I have spent my strength for nothing and
to no purpose.
Yet I leave it all in the LORD's hand;
I will trust God for my reward."

[5] And now the LORD speaks—
the one who formed me in my mother's
womb to be his servant,
who commissioned me to bring Israel back
to him.
The LORD has honored me,
and my God has given me strength.

[6] He says, "You will do more than restore the
people of Israel to me.
I will make you a light to the Gentiles,
and you will bring my salvation to the
ends of the earth."

[7] The LORD, the Redeemer
and Holy One of Israel,
says to the one who is despised and rejected
by the nations,
to the one who is the servant of rulers:
"Kings will stand at attention when you
pass by.
Princes will also bow low
because of the LORD, the faithful one,
the Holy One of Israel, who has chosen
you."

Promises of Israel's Restoration

[8]This is what the LORD says:

"At just the right time, I will respond to you.*
On the day of salvation I will help you.
I will protect you and give you to the people
as my covenant with them.
Through you I will reestablish the land of
Israel
and assign it to its own people again.

[9] I will say to the prisoners, 'Come out in
freedom,'
and to those in darkness, 'Come into the
light.'
They will be my sheep, grazing in green
pastures
and on hills that were previously bare.

[10] They will neither hunger nor thirst.
The searing sun will not reach them
anymore.
For the LORD in his mercy will lead them;
he will lead them beside cool waters.

[11] And I will make my mountains into level
paths for them.
The highways will be raised above the
valleys.

[12] See, my people will return from far away,
from lands to the north and west,
and from as far south as Egypt.*"

[13] Sing for joy, O heavens!
Rejoice, O earth!
Burst into song, O mountains!
For the LORD has comforted his people
and will have compassion on them in their
suffering.

[14] Yet Jerusalem* says, "The LORD has
deserted us;
the Lord has forgotten us."

[15] "Never! Can a mother forget her nursing
child?
Can she feel no love for the child she has
borne?
But even if that were possible,
I would not forget you!

[16] See, I have written your name on the palms
of my hands.
Always in my mind is a picture of
Jerusalem's walls in ruins.

[17] Soon your descendants will come back,
and all who are trying to destroy you will
go away.

[18] Look around you and see,
for all your children will come back to you.
As surely as I live," says the LORD,
"they will be like jewels or bridal
ornaments for you to display.

[19] "Even the most desolate parts of your
abandoned land

49:8 Greek version reads *I heard you.* Compare 2 Cor 6:2. **49:12** As in Dead Sea Scrolls, which read *from the region of Aswan,* which is in southern Egypt. Masoretic Text reads *from the region of Sinim.* **49:14** Hebrew *Zion.*

49:8—50:3 Promises of Israel's Restoration. The servant will be God's instrument in restoring Israel to her land, after exile. Isaiah's idealistic picture describes God's provision and care for his renewed people—cause for rejoicing! It may seem as if he has deserted them, but that can never be. He is more committed to them than a mother to her child. Against all the odds, so many will return that it will feel crowded, and the whole world will know that the LORD is Israel's Savior. Separation from God has ended in rescue.

will soon be crowded with your people.
Your enemies who enslaved you
will be far away.
20 The generations born in exile will return and say,
'We need more room! It's crowded here!'
21 Then you will think to yourself,
'Who has given me all these descendants?
For most of my children were killed,
and the rest were carried away into exile.
I was left here all alone.
Where did all these people come from?
Who bore these children?
Who raised them for me?' "

22 This is what the Sovereign LORD says:
"See, I will give a signal to the godless nations.
They will carry your little sons back to you in their arms;
they will bring your daughters on their shoulders.
23 Kings and queens will serve you
and care for all your needs.
They will bow to the earth before you
and lick the dust from your feet.
Then you will know that I am the LORD.
Those who trust in me will never be put to shame."

24 Who can snatch the plunder of war from the hands of a warrior?
Who can demand that a tyrant* let his captives go?
25 But the LORD says,
"The captives of warriors will be released,
and the plunder of tyrants will be retrieved.
For I will fight those who fight you,
and I will save your children.
26 I will feed your enemies with their own flesh.
They will be drunk with rivers of their own blood.
All the world will know that I, the LORD,
am your Savior and your Redeemer,
the Mighty One of Israel.*"

50 This is what the LORD says:
"Was your mother sent away
because I divorced her?
Did I sell you as slaves to my creditors?
No, you were sold because of your sins.
And your mother, too, was taken because of your sins.
2 Why was no one there when I came?
Why didn't anyone answer when I called?
Is it because I have no power to rescue?
No, that is not the reason!
For I can speak to the sea and make it dry up!
I can turn rivers into deserts covered with dying fish.
3 I dress the skies in darkness,
covering them with clothes of mourning."

The LORD's Obedient Servant

4 The Sovereign LORD has given me his words of wisdom,
so that I know how to comfort the weary.
Morning by morning he wakens me
and opens my understanding to his will.
5 The Sovereign LORD has spoken to me,
and I have listened.
I have not rebelled or turned away.
6 I offered my back to those who beat me
and my cheeks to those who pulled out my beard.
I did not hide my face
from mockery and spitting.

7 Because the Sovereign LORD helps me,
I will not be disgraced.
Therefore, I have set my face like a stone,
determined to do his will.
And I know that I will not be put to shame.
8 He who gives me justice is near.
Who will dare to bring charges against me now?
Where are my accusers?
Let them appear!
9 See, the Sovereign LORD is on my side!
Who will declare me guilty?
All my enemies will be destroyed
like old clothes that have been eaten by moths!

10 Who among you fears the LORD
and obeys his servant?
If you are walking in darkness,
without a ray of light,

49:24 As in Dead Sea Scrolls, Syriac version, and Latin Vulgate (also see 49:25); Masoretic Text reads *a righteous person.* **49:26** Hebrew *of Jacob.* See note on 14:1.

50:4–11 The LORD's Obedient Servant. Unlike Israel, the servant listens obediently to God each day and is therefore used to comfort others. His determination to do God's will involves personal suffering, but God will vindicate him. Faithful people currently experiencing darkness are encouraged to trust God.

trust in the LORD
and rely on your God.
[11] But watch out, you who live in your own light
and warm yourselves by your own fires.
This is the reward you will receive from me:
You will soon fall down in great torment.

A Call to Trust the LORD

51 [1] "Listen to me, all who hope for
deliverance—
all who seek the LORD!
Consider the rock from which you were cut,
the quarry from which you were mined.
[2] Yes, think about Abraham, your ancestor,
and Sarah, who gave birth to your nation.
Abraham was only one man when I called him.
But when I blessed him, he became a great
nation."

[3] The LORD will comfort Israel* again
and have pity on her ruins.
Her desert will blossom like Eden,
her barren wilderness like the garden of
the LORD.
Joy and gladness will be found there.
Songs of thanksgiving will fill the air.

[4] "Listen to me, my people.
Hear me, Israel,
for my law will be proclaimed,
and my justice will become a light to the
nations.
[5] My mercy and justice are coming soon.
My salvation is on the way.
My strong arm will bring justice to the
nations.
All distant lands will look to me
and wait in hope for my powerful arm.
[6] Look up to the skies above,
and gaze down on the earth below.
For the skies will disappear like smoke,
and the earth will wear out like a piece of
clothing.
The people of the earth will die like flies,
but my salvation lasts forever.
My righteous rule will never end!

[7] "Listen to me, you who know right from
wrong,
you who cherish my law in your hearts.
Do not be afraid of people's scorn,
nor fear their insults.
[8] For the moth will devour them as it devours
clothing.
The worm will eat at them as it eats wool.
But my righteousness will last forever.
My salvation will continue from
generation to generation."

[9] Wake up, wake up, O LORD! Clothe yourself
with strength!
Flex your mighty right arm!
Rouse yourself as in the days of old
when you slew Egypt, the dragon of the
Nile.*
[10] Are you not the same today,
the one who dried up the sea,
making a path of escape through the depths
so that your people could cross over?
[11] Those who have been ransomed by the LORD
will return.
They will enter Jerusalem* singing,
crowned with everlasting joy.
Sorrow and mourning will disappear,
and they will be filled with joy and gladness.

[12] "I, yes I, am the one who comforts you.
So why are you afraid of mere humans,
who wither like the grass and disappear?
[13] Yet you have forgotten the LORD, your
Creator,
the one who stretched out the sky like a
canopy
and laid the foundations of the earth.
Will you remain in constant dread of human
oppressors?
Will you continue to fear the anger of your
enemies?
Where is their fury and anger now?
It is gone!
[14] Soon all you captives will be released!
Imprisonment, starvation, and death will
not be your fate!

51:3 Hebrew *Zion;* also in 51:16. **51:9** Hebrew *You slew Rahab; you pierced the dragon.* Rahab is the name of a mythical sea monster that represents chaos in ancient literature. The name is used here as a poetic name for Egypt. **51:11** Hebrew *Zion.*

51:1–23 A Call to Trust the LORD. To those who seek him, God gives reassurance. Just as he blessed in the past, so he will again. His rule of justice, mercy, and salvation are for all peoples and will last forever, whatever the opposition may be. So Isaiah prays for God to act once again in their history, knowing the end result will be joy. Present fear must go! The *dragon of the Nile* (an ancient euphemism for chaos) is slain; the LORD of Heaven's Armies controls the roaring waves of life. His people are safe in his hand now, after the terror of recent times.

15 For I am the LORD your God,
who stirs up the sea, causing its waves to roar.
My name is the LORD of Heaven's Armies.
16 And I have put my words in your mouth
and hidden you safely in my hand.
I stretched out* the sky like a canopy
and laid the foundations of the earth.
I am the one who says to Israel,
'You are my people!' "

17 Wake up, wake up, O Jerusalem!
You have drunk the cup of the LORD's fury.
You have drunk the cup of terror,
tipping out its last drops.
18 Not one of your children is left alive
to take your hand and guide you.
19 These two calamities have fallen on you:
desolation and destruction, famine and war.
And who is left to sympathize with you?
Who is left to comfort you?*
20 For your children have fainted and lie in the streets,
helpless as antelopes caught in a net.
The LORD has poured out his fury;
God has rebuked them.

21 But now listen to this, you afflicted ones
who sit in a drunken stupor,
though not from drinking wine.
22 This is what the Sovereign LORD,
your God and Defender, says:
"See, I have taken the terrible cup from your hands.
You will drink no more of my fury.
23 Instead, I will hand that cup to your tormentors,
those who said, 'We will trample you into the dust
and walk on your backs.' "

Deliverance for Jerusalem

52 1 Wake up, wake up, O Zion!
Clothe yourself with strength.
Put on your beautiful clothes,
O holy city of Jerusalem,
for unclean and godless people will enter
your gates no longer.
2 Rise from the dust, O Jerusalem.
Sit in a place of honor.
Remove the chains of slavery from your neck,
O captive daughter of Zion.
3 For this is what the LORD says:
"When I sold you into exile,
I received no payment.
Now I can redeem you
without having to pay for you."

4 This is what the Sovereign LORD says: "Long
ago my people chose to live in Egypt. Now they
are oppressed by Assyria. 5 What is this?" asks
the LORD. "Why are my people enslaved again?
Those who rule them shout in exultation. My
name is blasphemed all day long.* 6 But I will reveal my name to my people, and they will come
to know its power. Then at last they will recognize that I am the one who speaks to them."

7 How beautiful on the mountains
are the feet of the messenger who brings good news,
the good news of peace and salvation,
the news that the God of Israel* reigns!
8 The watchmen shout and sing with joy,
for before their very eyes
they see the LORD returning to Jerusalem.*
9 Let the ruins of Jerusalem break into joyful song,
for the LORD has comforted his people.
He has redeemed Jerusalem.
10 The LORD has demonstrated his holy power
before the eyes of all the nations.
All the ends of the earth will see
the victory of our God.

11 Get out! Get out and leave your captivity,
where everything you touch is unclean.
Get out of there and purify yourselves,
you who carry home the sacred objects of the LORD.
12 You will not leave in a hurry,
running for your lives.
For the LORD will go ahead of you;
yes, the God of Israel will protect you from behind.

51:16 As in Syriac version (see also 51:13); Hebrew reads *planted.* **51:19** As in Dead Sea Scrolls and Greek, Latin, and Syriac versions; Masoretic Text reads *How can I comfort you?* **52:5** Greek version reads *The Gentiles continually blaspheme my name because of you.* Compare Rom 2:24. **52:7** Hebrew *of Zion.* **52:8** Hebrew *to Zion.*

52:1–12 Deliverance for Jerusalem. Holiness will mark the city that had been invaded by pagans. Just as God once *sold* Jerusalem in judgment, now he will come to the rescue and *redeem* his people—but without using money. This is good news to be shared and sung about! God reigns, and the world will see it. Those returning are to leave behind all that dishonors God.

The LORD's Suffering Servant

13 See, my servant will prosper;
he will be highly exalted.
14 But many were amazed when they saw him.*
His face was so disfigured he seemed
hardly human,
and from his appearance, one would
scarcely know he was a man.
15 And he will startle* many nations.
Kings will stand speechless in his presence.
For they will see what they had not been told;
they will understand what they had not
heard about.*

53 1 Who has believed our message?
To whom has the LORD revealed
his powerful arm?
2 My servant grew up in the LORD's presence
like a tender green shoot,
like a root in dry ground.
There was nothing beautiful or majestic
about his appearance,
nothing to attract us to him.
3 He was despised and rejected—
a man of sorrows, acquainted with deepest
grief.
We turned our backs on him and looked the
other way.
He was despised, and we did not care.
4 Yet it was our weaknesses he carried;
it was our sorrows* that weighed him
down.
And we thought his troubles were a
punishment from God,
a punishment for his own sins!
5 But he was pierced for our rebellion,
crushed for our sins.
He was beaten so we could be whole.
He was whipped so we could be healed.
6 All of us, like sheep, have strayed away.
We have left God's paths to follow our own.
Yet the LORD laid on him
the sins of us all.

7 He was oppressed and treated harshly,
yet he never said a word.
He was led like a lamb to the slaughter.
And as a sheep is silent before the shearers,
he did not open his mouth.
8 Unjustly condemned,
he was led away.*
No one cared that he died without
descendants,
that his life was cut short in midstream.*
But he was struck down
for the rebellion of my people.
9 He had done no wrong
and had never deceived anyone.
But he was buried like a criminal;
he was put in a rich man's grave.

10 But it was the LORD's good plan to crush him
and cause him grief.
Yet when his life is made an offering for sin,
he will have many descendants.
He will enjoy a long life,
and the LORD's good plan will prosper in
his hands.
11 When he sees all that is accomplished by his
anguish,
he will be satisfied.
And because of his experience,
my righteous servant will make it possible
for many to be counted righteous,
for he will bear all their sins.
12 I will give him the honors of a victorious
soldier,
because he exposed himself to death.
He was counted among the rebels.
He bore the sins of many and interceded
for rebels.

Future Glory for Jerusalem

54 1 "Sing, O childless woman,
you who have never given birth!
Break into loud and joyful song,
O Jerusalem,

52:14 As in Syriac version; Hebrew reads *you.* **52:15a** Or *cleanse.* **52:15b** Greek version reads *Those who have never been told about him will see, / and those who have never heard of him will understand.* Compare Rom 15:21. **53:4** Or *Yet it was our sicknesses he carried; / it was our diseases.* **53:8a** Greek version reads *He was humiliated and received no justice.* Compare Acts 8:33. **53:8b** Or *As for his contemporaries, / who cared that his life was cut short in midstream?* Greek version reads *Who can speak of his descendants? / For his life was taken from the earth.* Compare Acts 8:33.

52:13—53:12 The LORD's Suffering Servant. God's servant will be exalted, but first he will be brutally disfigured; he will suffer greatly and be killed. Now it is clear how God will buy back his people: His innocent servant will pay the price for Israel's sins and rebellion. The New Testament sees in this startling passage a description of the suffering of Jesus on the cross, *a man of sorrows* as he carried the sins of the world, thereby making it possible for many to be put right with God.

54:1–17 Future Glory for Jerusalem. No wonder Jerusalem can sing! It is as if she were childless all her life

you who have never been in labor.
For the desolate woman now has more children
than the woman who lives with her
husband,"
says the LORD.
2 "Enlarge your house; build an addition.
Spread out your home, and spare no
expense!
3 For you will soon be bursting at the seams.
Your descendants will occupy other nations
and resettle the ruined cities.

4 "Fear not; you will no longer live in shame.
Don't be afraid; there is no more disgrace
for you.
You will no longer remember the shame of
your youth
and the sorrows of widowhood.
5 For your Creator will be your husband;
the LORD of Heaven's Armies is his name!
He is your Redeemer, the Holy One of Israel,
the God of all the earth.
6 For the LORD has called you back from your
grief—
as though you were a young wife
abandoned by her husband,"
says your God.
7 "For a brief moment I abandoned you,
but with great compassion I will take you
back.
8 In a burst of anger I turned my face away for
a little while.
But with everlasting love I will have
compassion on you,"
says the LORD, your Redeemer.

9 "Just as I swore in the time of Noah
that I would never again let a flood cover
the earth,
so now I swear
that I will never again be angry and punish
you.
10 For the mountains may move
and the hills disappear,
but even then my faithful love for you will
remain.
My covenant of blessing will never be
broken,"
says the LORD, who has mercy on you.

11 "O storm-battered city,
troubled and desolate!
I will rebuild you with precious jewels
and make your foundations from lapis
lazuli.
12 I will make your towers of sparkling rubies,
your gates of shining gems,
and your walls of precious stones.
13 I will teach all your children,
and they will enjoy great peace.
14 You will be secure under a government that is
just and fair.
Your enemies will stay far away.
You will live in peace,
and terror will not come near.
15 If any nation comes to fight you,
it is not because I sent them.
Whoever attacks you will go down in
defeat.

16 "I have created the blacksmith
who fans the coals beneath the forge
and makes the weapons of destruction.
And I have created the armies that destroy.
17 But in that coming day
no weapon turned against you will succeed.
You will silence every voice
raised up to accuse you.
These benefits are enjoyed by the servants of
the LORD;
their vindication will come from me.
I, the LORD, have spoken!

Invitation to the LORD's Salvation

55 1"Is anyone thirsty?
Come and drink—
even if you have no money!
Come, take your choice of wine or milk—
it's all free!
2 Why spend your money on food that does
not give you strength?
Why pay for food that does you no good?

---

and suddenly has the children she has always longed for. Numerous children and a bigger home is needed for them! People will blossom in their renewed intimate relationship with God. God deserted them, as a husband who walks out on his wife, but he loves them too much to stay away for long. Whatever happens in the future, his love and mercy are everlasting. Jerusalem's husband will make her beautiful. She will feel safe and live in peace, all enemies vanquished.

55:1–13 Invitation to the LORD's Salvation. All these blessings are free. God invites people to come to him, rather than to that which cannot satisfy. In him they will find life and love, just as in the past when David was king over Israel (probably the best era in their history). God will fulfill all he has promised, and if they seek him they will find mercy and forgiveness, and live in joy and peace, even with the natural world. And this will bring honor to his name!

Listen to me, and you will eat what is good.
You will enjoy the finest food.

3 "Come to me with your ears wide open.
Listen, and you will find life.
I will make an everlasting covenant with you.
I will give you all the unfailing love I promised to David.
4 See how I used him to display my power among the peoples.
I made him a leader among the nations.
5 You also will command nations you do not know,
and peoples unknown to you will come running to obey,
because I, the LORD your God,
the Holy One of Israel, have made you glorious."

6 Seek the LORD while you can find him.
Call on him now while he is near.
7 Let the wicked change their ways
and banish the very thought of doing wrong.
Let them turn to the LORD that he may have mercy on them.
Yes, turn to our God, for he will forgive generously.

8 "My thoughts are nothing like your thoughts," says the LORD.
"And my ways are far beyond anything you could imagine.
9 For just as the heavens are higher than the earth,
so my ways are higher than your ways
and my thoughts higher than your thoughts.

10 "The rain and snow come down from the heavens
and stay on the ground to water the earth.
They cause the grain to grow,
producing seed for the farmer
and bread for the hungry.
11 It is the same with my word.
I send it out, and it always produces fruit.
It will accomplish all I want it to,
and it will prosper everywhere I send it.
12 You will live in joy and peace.
The mountains and hills will burst into song,
and the trees of the field will clap their hands!
13 Where once there were thorns, cypress trees will grow.
Where nettles grew, myrtles will sprout up.
These events will bring great honor to the LORD's name;
they will be an everlasting sign of his power and love."

Blessings for All Nations

56 This is what the LORD says:
"Be just and fair to all.
Do what is right and good,
for I am coming soon to rescue you
and to display my righteousness among you.
2 Blessed are all those
who are careful to do this.
Blessed are those who honor my Sabbath days of rest
and keep themselves from doing wrong.

3 "Don't let foreigners who commit themselves to the LORD say,
'The LORD will never let me be part of his people.'
And don't let the eunuchs say,
'I'm a dried-up tree with no children and no future.'
4 For this is what the LORD says:
I will bless those eunuchs
who keep my Sabbath days holy
and who choose to do what pleases me
and commit their lives to me.
5 I will give them—within the walls of my house—

56:1—66:24 Third Isaiah: A Glorious Future after the Exile

56:1—59:21 Warnings about False Worship and Sin

Isaiah continues the global perspective, first with blessings, then with warnings that would again cut people off from God. The final chapters in this book stress God's deliverance, mercy, and pardon once more; and the transformation there will be for all who put themselves under his rule.

56:1–8 Blessings for All Nations. Those who commit their lives to God must reflect his character in their relationships with others, being careful to follow his ways. Foreigners and those with personal defects are equally welcome to belong to the LORD, with equal personal significance (they will have *a memorial and a name*), and equal responsibilities. God's family is for people of all nations and circumstances.

a memorial and a name
far greater than sons and daughters could give.
For the name I give them is an everlasting one.
It will never disappear!

6 "I will also bless the foreigners who commit themselves to the LORD,
who serve him and love his name,
who worship him and do not desecrate the Sabbath day of rest,
and who hold fast to my covenant.
7 I will bring them to my holy mountain of Jerusalem
and will fill them with joy in my house of prayer.
I will accept their burnt offerings and sacrifices,
because my Temple will be called a house of prayer for all nations.
8 For the Sovereign LORD,
who brings back the outcasts of Israel,
says:
I will bring others, too,
besides my people Israel."

Sinful Leaders Condemned

9 Come, wild animals of the field!
Come, wild animals of the forest!
Come and devour my people!
10 For the leaders of my people—
the LORD's watchmen, his shepherds—
are blind and ignorant.
They are like silent watchdogs
that give no warning when danger comes.
They love to lie around, sleeping and dreaming.
11 Like greedy dogs, they are never satisfied.
They are ignorant shepherds,
all following their own path
and intent on personal gain.
12 "Come," they say, "let's get some wine and have a party.
Let's all get drunk.
Then tomorrow we'll do it again
and have an even bigger party!"

57 1 Good people pass away;
the godly often die before their time.
But no one seems to care or wonder why.
No one seems to understand
that God is protecting them from the evil to come.
2 For those who follow godly paths
will rest in peace when they die.

Idolatrous Worship Condemned

3 "But you—come here, you witches' children,
you offspring of adulterers and prostitutes!
4 Whom do you mock,
making faces and sticking out your tongues?
You children of sinners and liars!
5 You worship your idols with great passion
beneath the oaks and under every green tree.
You sacrifice your children down in the valleys,
among the jagged rocks in the cliffs.
6 Your gods are the smooth stones in the valleys.
You worship them with liquid offerings
and grain offerings.
They, not I, are your inheritance.
Do you think all this makes me happy?
7 You have committed adultery on every high mountain.
There you have worshiped idols
and have been unfaithful to me.
8 You have put pagan symbols
on your doorposts and behind your doors.
You have left me
and climbed into bed with these detestable gods.
You have committed yourselves to them.
You love to look at their naked bodies.
9 You have given olive oil to Molech*
with many gifts of perfume.
You have traveled far,
even into the world of the dead,*
to find new gods to love.
10 You grew weary in your search,

57:9a Or *to the king.* **57:9b** Hebrew *into Sheol.*

56:9—57:2 Sinful Leaders Condemned. Leaders have huge responsibility for caring for those under them, rather than selfishly indulging themselves. Meanwhile, there is reassurance concerning God's people who die unexpectedly early.

57:3–13 Idolatrous Worship Condemned. Isaiah vehemently condemns those who exchange their worship of the true God for regional pagan gods. Idolatry is spiritual adultery; people are being unfaithful to the LORD, and have *climbed into bed* with the well-known gods such as Molech (linked to human sacrifice) or with the latest new find. But how can these compare with the LORD?

but you never gave up.
Desire gave you renewed strength,
and you did not grow weary.

11 "Are you afraid of these idols?
Do they terrify you?
Is that why you have lied to me
and forgotten me and my words?
Is it because of my long silence
that you no longer fear me?
12 Now I will expose your so-called good
deeds.
None of them will help you.
13 Let's see if your idols can save you
when you cry to them for help.
Why, a puff of wind can knock them down!
If you just breathe on them, they fall over!
But whoever trusts in me will inherit the
land
and possess my holy mountain."

God Forgives the Repentant

14 God says, "Rebuild the road!
Clear away the rocks and stones
so my people can return from captivity."
15 The high and lofty one who lives in eternity,
the Holy One, says this:
"I live in the high and holy place
with those whose spirits are contrite and
humble.
I restore the crushed spirit of the humble
and revive the courage of those with
repentant hearts.
16 For I will not fight against you forever;
I will not always be angry.
If I were, all people would pass away—
all the souls I have made.
17 I was angry,
so I punished these greedy people.
I withdrew from them,
but they kept going on their own stubborn
way.
18 I have seen what they do,
but I will heal them anyway!
I will lead them.
I will comfort those who mourn,
19 bringing words of praise to their lips.
May they have abundant peace, both near and
far,"
says the LORD, who heals them.
20 "But those who still reject me are like the
restless sea,
which is never still
but continually churns up mud and dirt.
21 There is no peace for the wicked,"
says my God.

True and False Worship

58 1"Shout with the voice of a trumpet
blast.
Shout aloud! Don't be timid.
Tell my people Israel* of their sins!
2 Yet they act so pious!
They come to the Temple every day
and seem delighted to learn all about me.
They act like a righteous nation
that would never abandon the laws of its
God.
They ask me to take action on their behalf,
pretending they want to be near me.
3 'We have fasted before you!' they say.
'Why aren't you impressed?
We have been very hard on ourselves,
and you don't even notice it!'

"I will tell you why!" I respond.
"It's because you are fasting to please
yourselves.
Even while you fast,
you keep oppressing your workers.
4 What good is fasting
when you keep on fighting and
quarreling?
This kind of fasting
will never get you anywhere with me.
5 You humble yourselves
by going through the motions of penance,
bowing your heads
like reeds bending in the wind.
You dress in burlap
and cover yourselves with ashes.
Is this what you call fasting?

58:1 Hebrew *Jacob.* See note on 14:1.

57:14–21 God Forgives the Repentant. Those who return with humble, repentant hearts will be healed and comforted, but those who continue to reject God will never find peace.

58:1–14 True and False Worship. Isaiah condemns the kind of worship that is merely mechanical: seemingly pious outwardly but with no matching inner attitude. God is not impressed by religious rituals and fasting. What he requires is much more costly: freedom for the oppressed, practical help for the poor and hungry, and giving up self-interests one day a week. Only when his people are actively demonstrating what they profess in worship will they know his presence, guidance, and provision, along with true satisfaction.

Do you really think this will please the
LORD?

6 "No, this is the kind of fasting I want:
Free those who are wrongly imprisoned;
lighten the burden of those who work for
you.
Let the oppressed go free,
and remove the chains that bind people.
7 Share your food with the hungry,
and give shelter to the homeless.
Give clothes to those who need them,
and do not hide from relatives who need
your help.

8 "Then your salvation will come like the
dawn,
and your wounds will quickly heal.
Your godliness will lead you forward,
and the glory of the LORD will protect you
from behind.
9 Then when you call, the LORD will answer.
'Yes, I am here,' he will quickly reply.

"Remove the heavy yoke of oppression.
Stop pointing your finger and spreading
vicious rumors!
10 Feed the hungry,
and help those in trouble.
Then your light will shine out from the
darkness,
and the darkness around you will be as
bright as noon.
11 The LORD will guide you continually,
giving you water when you are dry
and restoring your strength.
You will be like a well-watered garden,
like an ever-flowing spring.
12 Some of you will rebuild the deserted ruins
of your cities.
Then you will be known as a rebuilder of
walls
and a restorer of homes.

13 "Keep the Sabbath day holy.
Don't pursue your own interests on that day,
but enjoy the Sabbath
and speak of it with delight as the LORD's
holy day.
Honor the Sabbath in everything you do on
that day,
and don't follow your own desires or talk
idly.
14 Then the LORD will be your delight.
I will give you great honor
and satisfy you with the inheritance I
promised to your ancestor Jacob.
I, the LORD, have spoken!"

Warnings against Sin

59 1Listen! The LORD's arm is not too
weak to save you,
nor is his ear too deaf to hear you
call.
2 It's your sins that have cut you off from God.
Because of your sins, he has turned away
and will not listen anymore.
3 Your hands are the hands of murderers,
and your fingers are filthy with sin.
Your lips are full of lies,
and your mouth spews corruption.

4 No one cares about being fair and honest.
The people's lawsuits are based on lies.
They conceive evil deeds
and then give birth to sin.
5 They hatch deadly snakes
and weave spiders' webs.
Whoever falls into their webs will die,
and there's danger even in getting near
them.
6 Their webs can't be made into clothing,
and nothing they do is productive.
All their activity is filled with sin,
and violence is their trademark.
7 Their feet run to do evil,
and they rush to commit murder.
They think only about sinning.
Misery and destruction always follow
them.
8 They don't know where to find peace
or what it means to be just and good.
They have mapped out crooked roads,
and no one who follows them knows a
moment's peace.

9 So there is no justice among us,
and we know nothing about right living.
We look for light but find only darkness.
We look for bright skies but walk in gloom.
10 We grope like the blind along a wall,
feeling our way like people without eyes.

59:1–21 Warnings against Sin. God and sin are totally incompatible. This is a grim description of a people from whom the LORD has turned away, and it shows how hard it is for anyone to go against the grain and renounce evil within such a society. But God, who is silent toward sinners, personally steps in to save those who have turned from their sin. They will have his Spirit and his words to sustain them.

Even at brightest noontime,
we stumble as though it were dark.
Among the living,
we are like the dead.
11 We growl like hungry bears;
we moan like mournful doves.
We look for justice, but it never comes.
We look for rescue, but it is far away
from us.
12 For our sins are piled up before God
and testify against us.
Yes, we know what sinners we are.
13 We know we have rebelled and have denied
the LORD.
We have turned our backs on our God.
We know how unfair and oppressive we have
been,
carefully planning our deceitful lies.
14 Our courts oppose the righteous,
and justice is nowhere to be found.
Truth stumbles in the streets,
and honesty has been outlawed.
15 Yes, truth is gone,
and anyone who renounces evil is attacked.

The LORD looked and was displeased
to find there was no justice.
16 He was amazed to see that no one intervened
to help the oppressed.
So he himself stepped in to save them with
his strong arm,
and his justice sustained him.
17 He put on righteousness as his body armor
and placed the helmet of salvation on his
head.
He clothed himself with a robe of vengeance
and wrapped himself in a cloak of divine
passion.
18 He will repay his enemies for their evil deeds.
His fury will fall on his foes.
He will pay them back even to the ends of
the earth.
19 In the west, people will respect the name of
the LORD;
in the east, they will glorify him.
For he will come like a raging flood tide
driven by the breath of the LORD.*

20 "The Redeemer will come to Jerusalem
to buy back those in Israel
who have turned from their sins,"*
says the LORD.

21 "And this is my covenant with them," says
the LORD. "My Spirit will not leave them, and
neither will these words I have given you. They
will be on your lips and on the lips of your children and your children's children forever. I, the
LORD, have spoken!

Future Glory for Jerusalem

60 1 "Arise, Jerusalem! Let your light
shine for all to see.
For the glory of the LORD rises to
shine on you.
2 Darkness as black as night covers all the
nations of the earth,
but the glory of the LORD rises and appears
over you.
3 All nations will come to your light;
mighty kings will come to see your
radiance.

4 "Look and see, for everyone is coming home!
Your sons are coming from distant lands;
your little daughters will be carried home.
5 Your eyes will shine,
and your heart will thrill with joy,
for merchants from around the world will
come to you.
They will bring you the wealth of many
lands.

59:19 Or *When the enemy comes like a raging flood tide, / the Spirit of the LORD will drive him back.* **59:20** Hebrew *The Redeemer will come to Zion / to buy back those in Jacob / who have turned from their sins.* Greek version reads *The one who rescues will come on behalf of Zion, / and he will turn Jacob away from ungodliness.* Compare Rom 11:26.

60:1—66:24 Transformation for God's People

Using apocalyptic language (prophecy that goes beyond history, that which understands that God will one day inaugurate a new age of justice and righteousness and inexpressible glory), Isaiah sees that God will then be all in all to his people.

60:1–22 Future Glory for Jerusalem. The city is seen not so much as a civic entity as an ideal portrayal of God's people everywhere. As the LORD's glory shines on her, so she in turn is a radiant beacon for people living in darkness who seek light, *for everyone is coming home* to God. Imagine a mother's joy as she welcomes home her long-lost children! They come bringing their treasures as offerings to honor the LORD. In a series of reversals, the people who were once despised will be made beautiful; oppression will turn to utter satisfaction (breastfeeding conjures up the sense of deeply loving intimacy and care); violence will turn to peace; desolation to praise. As Isaiah reflects on all this, time becomes irrelevant.

6 Vast caravans of camels will converge on you,
the camels of Midian and Ephah.
The people of Sheba will bring gold and
frankincense
and will come worshiping the LORD.
7 The flocks of Kedar will be given to you,
and the rams of Nebaioth will be brought
for my altars.
I will accept their offerings,
and I will make my Temple glorious.

8 "And what do I see flying like clouds to Israel,
like doves to their nests?
9 They are ships from the ends of the earth,
from lands that trust in me,
led by the great ships of Tarshish.
They are bringing the people of Israel home
from far away,
carrying their silver and gold.
They will honor the LORD your God,
the Holy One of Israel,
for he has filled you with splendor.

10 "Foreigners will come to rebuild your towns,
and their kings will serve you.
For though I have destroyed you in my anger,
I will now have mercy on you through my
grace.
11 Your gates will stay open day and night
to receive the wealth of many lands.
The kings of the world will be led as captives
in a victory procession.
12 For the nations that refuse to serve you
will be destroyed.

13 "The glory of Lebanon will be yours—
the forests of cypress, fir, and pine—
to beautify my sanctuary.
My Temple will be glorious!
14 The descendants of your tormentors
will come and bow before you.
Those who despised you
will kiss your feet.
They will call you the City of the LORD,
and Zion of the Holy One of Israel.

15 "Though you were once despised and hated,
with no one traveling through you,
I will make you beautiful forever,
a joy to all generations.
16 Powerful kings and mighty nations
will satisfy your every need,
as though you were a child
nursing at the breast of a queen.
You will know at last that I, the LORD,
am your Savior and your Redeemer,
the Mighty One of Israel.*
17 I will exchange your bronze for gold,
your iron for silver,
your wood for bronze,
and your stones for iron.
I will make peace your leader
and righteousness your ruler.
18 Violence will disappear from your land;
the desolation and destruction of war will
end.
Salvation will surround you like city walls,
and praise will be on the lips of all who
enter there.

19 "No longer will you need the sun to shine by
day,
nor the moon to give its light by night,
for the LORD your God will be your
everlasting light,
and your God will be your glory.
20 Your sun will never set;
your moon will not go down.
For the LORD will be your everlasting light.
Your days of mourning will come to an
end.
21 All your people will be righteous.
They will possess their land forever,
for I will plant them there with my own
hands
in order to bring myself glory.
22 The smallest family will become a thousand
people,
and the tiniest group will become a mighty
nation.
At the right time, I, the LORD, will make it
happen."

Good News for the Oppressed

61 1The Spirit of the Sovereign LORD is
upon me,
for the LORD has anointed me
to bring good news to the poor.

60:16 Hebrew *of Jacob.* See note on 14:1.

61:1–11 Good News for the Oppressed. The anointed servant of 49:1–7 now explains his task in more detail. It is good news indeed! The overall theme is the turning of past grief and despair into joy and praise, because of God's favor toward his people. There will be a new start. Different nationalities will cooperate together; former aliens taking their place among God's people, who will be honored by all. And God himself will be praised by the entire world. Isaiah's joy at this thought of the future almost overwhelms him.

He has sent me to comfort the brokenhearted
and to proclaim that captives will be released
and prisoners will be freed.*
2 He has sent me to tell those who mourn
that the time of the LORD's favor has come,*
and with it, the day of God's anger against their enemies.
3 To all who mourn in Israel,*
he will give a crown of beauty for ashes,
a joyous blessing instead of mourning,
festive praise instead of despair.
In their righteousness, they will be like great oaks
that the LORD has planted for his own glory.

4 They will rebuild the ancient ruins,
repairing cities destroyed long ago.
They will revive them,
though they have been deserted for many generations.
5 Foreigners will be your servants.
They will feed your flocks
and plow your fields
and tend your vineyards.
6 You will be called priests of the LORD,
ministers of our God.
You will feed on the treasures of the nations
and boast in their riches.
7 Instead of shame and dishonor,
you will enjoy a double share of honor.
You will possess a double portion of prosperity in your land,
and everlasting joy will be yours.

8 "For I, the LORD, love justice.
I hate robbery and wrongdoing.
I will faithfully reward my people for their suffering
and make an everlasting covenant with them.
9 Their descendants will be recognized
and honored among the nations.
Everyone will realize that they are a people
the LORD has blessed."

10 I am overwhelmed with joy in the LORD my God!
For he has dressed me with the clothing of salvation
and draped me in a robe of righteousness.
I am like a bridegroom in his wedding suit
or a bride with her jewels.
11 The Sovereign LORD will show his justice to the nations of the world.
Everyone will praise him!
His righteousness will be like a garden in early spring,
with plants springing up everywhere.

Isaiah's Prayer for Jerusalem

62 [1]Because I love Zion,
I will not keep still.
Because my heart yearns for Jerusalem,
I cannot remain silent.
I will not stop praying for her
until her righteousness shines like the dawn,
and her salvation blazes like a burning torch.
2 The nations will see your righteousness.
World leaders will be blinded by your glory.
And you will be given a new name
by the LORD's own mouth.
3 The LORD will hold you in his hand for all to see—
a splendid crown in the hand of God.
4 Never again will you be called "The Forsaken City"*
or "The Desolate Land."*
Your new name will be "The City of God's Delight"*
and "The Bride of God,"*
for the LORD delights in you
and will claim you as his bride.
5 Your children will commit themselves to you, O Jerusalem,
just as a young man commits himself to his bride.
Then God will rejoice over you
as a bridegroom rejoices over his bride.

61:1 Greek version reads *and the blind will see.* Compare Luke 4:18. **61:2** Or *to proclaim the acceptable year of the LORD.* **61:3** Hebrew *in Zion.* **62:4a** Hebrew *Azubah,* which means "forsaken." **62:4b** Hebrew *Shemamah,* which means "desolate." **62:4c** Hebrew *Hephzibah,* which means "my delight is in her." **62:4d** Hebrew *Beulah,* which means "married."

62:1–12 Isaiah's Prayer for Jerusalem. Isaiah's joy leads to intercessory prayer for Jerusalem that her people will indeed radiate God's glory to the world and take their place as his *bride*—the most intimate and joyous relationship imaginable. Names are important for a sense of personal identity, and here God's people are showered with significant new names that demonstrate his commitment to them.

6 O Jerusalem, I have posted watchmen on
your walls;
they will pray day and night, continually.
Take no rest, all you who pray to the LORD.
7 Give the LORD no rest until he completes his
work,
until he makes Jerusalem the pride of the
earth.
8 The LORD has sworn to Jerusalem by his own
strength:
"I will never again hand you over to your
enemies.
Never again will foreign warriors come
and take away your grain and new wine.
9 You raised the grain, and you will eat it,
praising the LORD.
Within the courtyards of the Temple,
you yourselves will drink the wine you
have pressed."

10 Go out through the gates!
Prepare the highway for my people to
return!
Smooth out the road; pull out the boulders;
raise a flag for all the nations to see.
11 The LORD has sent this message to every land:
"Tell the people of Israel,*
'Look, your Savior is coming.
See, he brings his reward with him as he
comes.' "
12 They will be called "The Holy People"
and "The People Redeemed by the LORD."
And Jerusalem will be known as "The
Desirable Place"
and "The City No Longer Forsaken."

Judgment against the LORD's Enemies

63 1Who is this who comes from Edom,
from the city of Bozrah,
with his clothing stained red?
Who is this in royal robes,
marching in his great strength?

"It is I, the LORD, announcing your salvation!
It is I, the LORD, who has the power to
save!"

2 Why are your clothes so red,
as if you have been treading out grapes?
3 "I have been treading the winepress alone;
no one was there to help me.
In my anger I have trampled my enemies
as if they were grapes.
In my fury I have trampled my foes.
Their blood has stained my clothes.
4 For the time has come for me to avenge my
people,
to ransom them from their oppressors.
5 I was amazed to see that no one intervened
to help the oppressed.
So I myself stepped in to save them with my
strong arm,
and my wrath sustained me.
6 I crushed the nations in my anger
and made them stagger and fall to the
ground,
spilling their blood upon the earth."

Praise for Deliverance

7 I will tell of the LORD's unfailing love.
I will praise the LORD for all he has done.
I will rejoice in his great goodness to Israel,
which he has granted according to his
mercy and love.
8 He said, "They are my very own people.
Surely they will not betray me again."
And he became their Savior.
9 In all their suffering he also suffered,
and he personally* rescued them.
In his love and mercy he redeemed them.
He lifted them up and carried them
through all the years.
10 But they rebelled against him
and grieved his Holy Spirit.
So he became their enemy
and fought against them.

11 Then they remembered those days of old
when Moses led his people out of Egypt.
They cried out, "Where is the one who
brought Israel through the sea,
with Moses as their shepherd?
Where is the one who sent his Holy Spirit
to be among his people?
12 Where is the one whose power was displayed

62:11 Hebrew *Tell the daughter of Zion.* **63:9** Hebrew *and the angel of his presence.*

63:1–6 Judgment against the LORD's Enemies. Edom (capital Bozrah) typifies the unrepentant world (cf. 34:6). Edom translates as "red," and Bozrah as "vintage." In this play on words (*stained red, treading . . . grapes, blood . . . stained*) Isaiah sees God coming to avenge his people and save them. Judgment and salvation are necessarily his alone.

63:7–14 Praise for Deliverance. This brief cameo of Israel's history is a testimony to what God has done in their lives.

when Moses lifted up his hand—
the one who divided the sea before them,
making himself famous forever?
13 Where is the one who led them through the bottom of the sea?
They were like fine stallions
racing through the desert, never stumbling.
14 As with cattle going down into a peaceful valley,
the Spirit of the LORD gave them rest.
You led your people, LORD,
and gained a magnificent reputation."

Prayer for Mercy and Pardon

15 LORD, look down from heaven;
look from your holy, glorious home, and see us.
Where is the passion and the might
you used to show on our behalf?
Where are your mercy and compassion now?
16 Surely you are still our Father!
Even if Abraham and Jacob* would disown us,
LORD, you would still be our Father.
You are our Redeemer from ages past.
17 LORD, why have you allowed us to turn from your path?
Why have you given us stubborn hearts so we no longer fear you?
Return and help us, for we are your servants,
the tribes that are your special possession.
18 How briefly your holy people possessed your holy place,
and now our enemies have destroyed it.
19 Sometimes it seems as though we never belonged to you,
as though we had never been known as your people.

64

1*Oh, that you would burst from the heavens and come down!
How the mountains would quake in your presence!
2*As fire causes wood to burn
and water to boil,
your coming would make the nations tremble.
Then your enemies would learn the reason for your fame!
3 When you came down long ago,
you did awesome deeds beyond our highest expectations.
And oh, how the mountains quaked!
4 For since the world began,
no ear has heard
and no eye has seen a God like you,
who works for those who wait for him!
5 You welcome those who gladly do good,
who follow godly ways.
But you have been very angry with us,
for we are not godly.
We are constant sinners;
how can people like us be saved?
6 We are all infected and impure with sin.
When we display our righteous deeds,
they are nothing but filthy rags.
Like autumn leaves, we wither and fall,
and our sins sweep us away like the wind.
7 Yet no one calls on your name
or pleads with you for mercy.
Therefore, you have turned away from us
and turned us over* to our sins.

8 And yet, O LORD, you are our Father.
We are the clay, and you are the potter.
We all are formed by your hand.
9 Don't be so angry with us, LORD.
Please don't remember our sins forever.
Look at us, we pray,
and see that we are all your people.
10 Your holy cities are destroyed.
Zion is a wilderness;
yes, Jerusalem is a desolate ruin.
11 The holy and beautiful Temple
where our ancestors praised you
has been burned down,
and all the things of beauty are destroyed.
12 After all this, LORD, must you still refuse to help us?
Will you continue to be silent and punish us?

63:16 Hebrew *Israel.* See note on 14:1. **64:1** In the Hebrew text this verse is included in 63:19. **64:2** Verses 64:2-12 are numbered 64:1-11 in Hebrew text. **64:7** As in Greek, Syriac, and Aramaic versions; Hebrew reads *melted us.*

63:15—64:12 Prayer for Mercy and Pardon. Remembering all this focuses Isaiah's mind on present reality. In determined faith he demands answers to the difficult questions. *Why* did God allow them to go wrong, with such disastrous consequences? He longs for him to come and put everything right. Isaiah owns the nation's sinfulness, recognizing God's justice in turning from them. But . . . he is their Father! Parents go on loving their children no matter how wayward they are! So can he continue to ignore them?

Judgment and Final Salvation

65 The LORD says,
"I was ready to respond, but no one asked for help.
I was ready to be found, but no one was looking for me.
I said, 'Here I am, here I am!'
to a nation that did not call on my name.*
2 All day long I opened my arms to a rebellious people.*
But they follow their own evil paths
and their own crooked schemes.
3 All day long they insult me to my face
by worshiping idols in their sacred gardens.
They burn incense on pagan altars.
4 At night they go out among the graves,
worshiping the dead.
They eat the flesh of pigs
and make stews with other forbidden foods.
5 Yet they say to each other,
'Don't come too close or you will defile me!
I am holier than you!'
These people are a stench in my nostrils,
an acrid smell that never goes away.

6 "Look, my decree is written out* in front of me:
I will not stand silent;
I will repay them in full!
Yes, I will repay them—
7 both for their own sins
and for those of their ancestors,"
says the LORD.
"For they also burned incense on the mountains
and insulted me on the hills.
I will pay them back in full!

8 "But I will not destroy them all,"
says the LORD.
"For just as good grapes are found among a cluster of bad ones
(and someone will say, 'Don't throw them all away—
some of those grapes are good!'),
so I will not destroy all Israel.
For I still have true servants there.
9 I will preserve a remnant of the people of Israel*
and of Judah to possess my land.
Those I choose will inherit it,
and my servants will live there.
10 The plain of Sharon will again be filled with flocks
for my people who have searched for me,
and the valley of Achor will be a place to pasture herds.

11 "But because the rest of you have forsaken the LORD
and have forgotten his Temple,
and because you have prepared feasts to honor the god of Fate
and have offered mixed wine to the god of Destiny,
12 now I will 'destine' you for the sword.
All of you will bow down before the executioner.
For when I called, you did not answer.
When I spoke, you did not listen.
You deliberately sinned—before my very eyes—
and chose to do what you know I despise."

13 Therefore, this is what the Sovereign LORD says:
"My servants will eat,

65:1 Or *to a nation that did not bear my name.*
65:1-2 Greek version reads *I was found by people who were not looking for me. / I showed myself to those who were not asking for me. / All day long I opened my arms to them, / but they were disobedient and rebellious.* Compare Rom 10:20-21. **65:6** Or *their sins are written out;* Hebrew reads *it stands written.* **65:9** Hebrew *remnant of Jacob.* See note on 14:1.

65:1—66:24 Judgment and Final Salvation. And God answers. He has always been there waiting for them to turn back to him. He could not ignore their evil rebellion any more than a parent can ignore the smell of their soiled child. He had to do something about it. And that meant destroying the evil and releasing a *remnant* of faithful and true servants who have searched for him. There are two categories of people—the good *grapes* and the bad—and their destinies will be entirely different. After judgment comes a new creation for his servants, where there will be only joy and delight. No more grief, no more premature deaths, no more insecurity and fear, no more hurts. The great Creator will bless those who humble themselves before him. In the present, many will scoff at God's servants, but such will receive their comeuppance. It is almost as if God himself gives birth to a new people. The call is to be fully identified with them; drinking in all that God offers, as a baby feeds at the breast; and in turn giving nourishment, comfort, and security to others. God will send his people to all nations to declare his glory and bring home the remnant of believers, to serve him and worship him forever. Yet always there is the grim reminder of the fate of those who stubbornly rebel against the LORD.

but you will starve.
My servants will drink,
but you will be thirsty.
My servants will rejoice,
but you will be sad and ashamed.
14 My servants will sing for joy,
but you will cry in sorrow and despair.
15 Your name will be a curse word among my people,
for the Sovereign LORD will destroy you
and will call his true servants by another name.
16 All who invoke a blessing or take an oath
will do so by the God of truth.
For I will put aside my anger
and forget the evil of earlier days.

17 "Look! I am creating new heavens and a new earth,
and no one will even think about the old ones anymore.
18 Be glad; rejoice forever in my creation!
And look! I will create Jerusalem as a place of happiness.
Her people will be a source of joy.
19 I will rejoice over Jerusalem
and delight in my people.
And the sound of weeping and crying
will be heard in it no more.

20 "No longer will babies die when only a few days old.
No longer will adults die before they have lived a full life.
No longer will people be considered old at one hundred!
Only the cursed will die that young!
21 In those days people will live in the houses they build
and eat the fruit of their own vineyards.
22 Unlike the past, invaders will not take their houses
and confiscate their vineyards.
For my people will live as long as trees,
and my chosen ones will have time to enjoy their hard-won gains.
23 They will not work in vain,
and their children will not be doomed to misfortune.
For they are people blessed by the LORD,
and their children, too, will be blessed.
24 I will answer them before they even call to me.
While they are still talking about their needs,
I will go ahead and answer their prayers!
25 The wolf and the lamb will feed together.
The lion will eat hay like a cow.
But the snakes will eat dust.
In those days no one will be hurt or destroyed on my holy mountain.
I, the LORD, have spoken!"

66 This is what the LORD says:
"Heaven is my throne,
and the earth is my footstool.
Could you build me a temple as good as that?
Could you build me such a resting place?
2 My hands have made both heaven and earth;
they and everything in them are mine.*
I, the LORD, have spoken!

"I will bless those who have humble and contrite hearts,
who tremble at my word.
3 But those who choose their own ways—
delighting in their detestable sins—
will not have their offerings accepted.
When such people sacrifice a bull,
it is no more acceptable than a human sacrifice.
When they sacrifice a lamb,
it's as though they had sacrificed a dog!
When they bring an offering of grain,
they might as well offer the blood of a pig.
When they burn frankincense,
it's as if they had blessed an idol.
4 I will send them great trouble—
all the things they feared.
For when I called, they did not answer.
When I spoke, they did not listen.
They deliberately sinned before my very eyes
and chose to do what they know I despise."

5 Hear this message from the LORD,
all you who tremble at his words:
"Your own people hate you
and throw you out for being loyal to my name.
'Let the LORD be honored!' they scoff.
'Be joyful in him!'
But they will be put to shame.
6 What is all the commotion in the city?
What is that terrible noise from the Temple?
It is the voice of the LORD
taking vengeance against his enemies.

66:2 As in Greek, Latin, and Syriac versions; Hebrew reads *these things are.*

7 "Before the birth pains even begin,
Jerusalem gives birth to a son.
8 Who has ever seen anything as strange as this?
Who ever heard of such a thing?
Has a nation ever been born in a single day?
Has a country ever come forth in a mere moment?
But by the time Jerusalem's* birth pains begin,
her children will be born.
9 Would I ever bring this nation to the point of birth
and then not deliver it?" asks the LORD.
"No! I would never keep this nation from being born,"
says your God.

10 "Rejoice with Jerusalem!
Be glad with her, all you who love her
and all you who mourn for her.
11 Drink deeply of her glory
even as an infant drinks at its mother's comforting breasts."

12 This is what the LORD says:
"I will give Jerusalem a river of peace and prosperity.
The wealth of the nations will flow to her.
Her children will be nursed at her breasts,
carried in her arms, and held on her lap.
13 I will comfort you there in Jerusalem
as a mother comforts her child."

14 When you see these things, your heart will rejoice.
You will flourish like the grass!
Everyone will see the LORD's hand of blessing on his servants—
and his anger against his enemies.
15 See, the LORD is coming with fire,
and his swift chariots roar like a whirlwind.
He will bring punishment with the fury of his anger
and the flaming fire of his hot rebuke.
16 The LORD will punish the world by fire
and by his sword.
He will judge the earth,
and many will be killed by him.

17 "Those who 'consecrate' and 'purify' themselves in a sacred garden with its idol in the
center—feasting on pork and rats and other detestable meats—will come to a terrible end," says
the LORD.
18 "I can see what they are doing, and I know
what they are thinking. So I will gather all nations and peoples together, and they will see my
glory. 19 I will perform a sign among them. And
I will send those who survive to be messengers
to the nations—to Tarshish, to the Libyans* and
Lydians* (who are famous as archers), to Tubal
and Greece,* and to all the lands beyond the
sea that have not heard of my fame or seen my
glory. There they will declare my glory to the
nations. 20 They will bring the remnant of your
people back from every nation. They will bring
them to my holy mountain in Jerusalem as an
offering to the LORD. They will ride on horses,
in chariots and wagons, and on mules and camels," says the LORD. 21 "And I will appoint some
of them to be my priests and Levites. I, the LORD,
have spoken!

22 "As surely as my new heavens and earth will remain,
so will you always be my people,
with a name that will never disappear,"
says the LORD.
23 "All humanity will come to worship me
from week to week
and from month to month.
24 And as they go out, they will see
the dead bodies of those who have rebelled against me.
For the worms that devour them will never die,
and the fire that burns them will never go out.
All who pass by
will view them with utter horror."

66:8 Hebrew *Zion's.* **66:19a** As in some Greek manuscripts, which read *Put* [that is, *Libya*]; Hebrew reads *Pul.* **66:19b** Hebrew *Lud.* **66:19c** Hebrew *Javan.*

JEREMIAH

INTRODUCTION

The book of Jeremiah reveals God's presence in a disintegrating world and God's gift of hope for life beyond catastrophe. God's word through Jeremiah provides a theological basis for comprehending this chaos and believing in the future.

The book is not arranged chronologically or logically. Jeremiah and assisting scribes who composed the book help readers discover words or ideas linking the disparate parts and reflect on how juxtaposed passages interpret one another. In Jeremiah two paradigms for God's dealings with the people remain in tension. God upholds the covenant requirement of judgment and simultaneously reaches out to help.

Jeremiah's ministry began in Josiah's thirteenth year (627/6 BC) and continued past the conquest of Jerusalem (587/6 BC). Jeremiah's prophecies provided God-given analyses of conditions within the whole region. When he began, the Assyrian Empire was in decline. Judah enjoyed increasing security and independence. Under Josiah's leadership, Judah briefly renewed its covenant commitment to God. When he finished, however, the king was imprisoned and the people were deported to Babylon or fled to Egypt.

The latest date referred to is 561 BC (52:31–34), and the narrative continues for a number of years afterward. The earliest possible date for the completed book is therefore several years after 561 BC.

The book addresses questions of exiles about why the Exile happened and what its implications are. One purpose of the book is that Judah will repent so that God "will be able to forgive their sins" (36:3).

In order to understand Jeremiah, readers must know something of the context and timing.

In 721 BC, Israel, the Northern Kingdom, was, as a result of their idolatry (Hos; 2 Kgs 17), destroyed by Assyria. A large part of the population was deported. Jeremiah points to the similarities between Israel and Judah who remained under Assyrian influence.

In 605 BC, in the fourth year of Jehoiakim, the Babylonians (Chaldeans), under Nebuchadnezzar, defeated Egypt and Assyria at Carchemish and took over Assyria's empire.

In 598–597 BC, after Jehoiakim rebelled, the Babylonians besieged Jerusalem. During the siege Jehoiakim died and Jehoiachin succeeded him. When the Babylonians conquered the city they took Jehoiachin and other exiles to Babylon, looted the Temple, and appointed Zedekiah as their vassal king.

In 588–587 BC Zedekiah rebelled, and Babylon besieged Jerusalem. In 587–586 BC the Babylonians conquered and burned Jerusalem and the Temple, exiled Zedekiah and many others, and appointed Gedaliah governor over the remainder of Judah. In 539 BC Cyrus conquered Babylon, and the Persian Empire replaced that of Babylon. —*Editors, Oxford University Press*

1:1–3	Superscription
1:4–19	Jeremiah's Call
2:1—4:2	Israel Breaks Faith with God
4:3—6:30	The Enemy from the North

✧

1 These are the words of Jeremiah son of
Hilkiah, one of the priests from the town
of Anathoth in the land of Benjamin. 2 The
LORD first gave messages to Jeremiah during
the thirteenth year of the reign of Josiah son
of Amon, king of Judah.* 3 The LORD's messages continued throughout the reign of King
Jehoiakim, Josiah's son, until the eleventh year
of the reign of King Zedekiah, another of Josiah's sons. In August* of that eleventh year
the people of Jerusalem were taken away as
captives.

Jeremiah's Call and First Visions

4 The LORD gave me this message:

5 "I knew you before I formed you in your
mother's womb.
Before you were born I set you apart
and appointed you as my prophet to the
nations."

6 "O Sovereign LORD," I said, "I can't speak
for you! I'm too young!"

1:2 The thirteenth year of Josiah's reign was 627 B.C.
1:3 Hebrew *In the fifth month*, of the ancient Hebrew lunar calendar. A number of events in Jeremiah can be cross-checked with dates in surviving Babylonian records and related accurately to our modern calendar. The fifth month in the eleventh year of Zedekiah's reign occurred within the months of August and September 586 B.C. Also see 52:12 and the note there.

1:1–3 Superscription

Jeremiah was born into a priestly family living in Anathoth, two miles north of Jerusalem, in Benjaminite territory. Centuries earlier Solomon had banished the priest Abiathar to Anathoth (1 Kgs 2:26). Jeremiah's family may have been Abiathar's descendants. Jeremiah began to convey God's messages in Josiah's thirteenth year and continued until Jerusalem fell to the Babylonians in Zedekiah's eleventh year. In Jeremiah 40—44, however, Jeremiah's prophesying continues for some time after that date.

1:4–19 Jeremiah's Call

The book's main themes are set out here along with their relation to Jeremiah's role. Judah is guilty of idolatry and deserves judgment, which God will bring through conquerors from the north. Judah's fortified cities will fall, but God's presence to save and protect is also revealed by Jeremiah. Jeremiah will himself have to suffer like a city under attack but will not be defeated. **4–5:** Before Jeremiah's birth God had set him apart, but unlike with Jacob and Samson there is no evidence that Jeremiah's mother knew this. Hannah also dedicated Samuel to God's service before his birth. All three women had been childless before bearing their chosen, dedicated sons. The only link between Jeremiah's mother and these other mothers is a possible meaning of Jeremiah's name, "Yahweh loosened," which could be a testimony by a previously childless woman that God had "loosened" her womb, enabling her to conceive. **6:** Jeremiah is concerned about his youth. For Levites their service began at age twenty (1 Chr 23:24), twenty-five (Num 8:24), or thirty (Num 4:3). Whatever his age, Jeremiah

[7]The LORD replied, "Don't say, 'I'm too
young,' for you must go wherever I send you and
say whatever I tell you. [8]And don't be afraid of
the people, for I will be with you and will protect
you. I, the LORD, have spoken!" [9]Then the LORD
reached out and touched my mouth and said,

"Look, I have put my words in your mouth!
[10] Today I appoint you to stand up
against nations and kingdoms.
Some you must uproot and tear down,
destroy and overthrow.
Others you must build up
and plant."

[11]Then the LORD said to me, "Look, Jeremiah!
What do you see?"
And I replied, "I see a branch from an almond
tree."
[12]And the LORD said, "That's right, and it
means that I am watching,* and I will certainly
carry out all my plans."
[13]Then the LORD spoke to me again and asked,
"What do you see now?"
And I replied, "I see a pot of boiling water,
spilling from the north."
[14]"Yes," the LORD said, "for terror from the
north will boil out on the people of this land.
[15]Listen! I am calling the armies of the kingdoms
of the north to come to Jerusalem. I, the LORD,
have spoken!

"They will set their thrones
at the gates of the city.
They will attack its walls
and all the other towns of Judah.
[16] I will pronounce judgment
on my people for all their evil—
for deserting me and burning incense to other
gods.
Yes, they worship idols made with their
own hands!

[17] "Get up and prepare for action.
Go out and tell them everything I tell you
to say.
Do not be afraid of them,
or I will make you look foolish in front of
them.
[18] For see, today I have made you strong
like a fortified city that cannot be captured,
like an iron pillar or a bronze wall.
You will stand against the whole land—
the kings, officials, priests, and people of
Judah.
[19] They will fight you, but they will fail.
For I am with you, and I will take care of
you.
I, the LORD, have spoken!"

The LORD's Case against His People

2 The LORD gave me another message. He
said, [2]"Go and shout this message to Jerusalem. This is what the LORD says:

"I remember how eager you were to
please me
as a young bride long ago,
how you loved me and followed me
even through the barren wilderness.
[3] In those days Israel was holy to the LORD,
the first of his children.*
All who harmed his people were declared
guilty,
and disaster fell on them.
I, the LORD, have spoken!"

[4]Listen to the word of the LORD, people of
Jacob—all you families of Israel! [5]This is what
the LORD says:

"What did your ancestors find wrong with me
that led them to stray so far from me?
They worshiped worthless idols,
only to become worthless themselves.
[6] They did not ask, 'Where is the LORD
who brought us safely out of Egypt
and led us through the barren wilderness—
a land of deserts and pits,
a land of drought and death,
where no one lives or even travels?'

[7] "And when I brought you into a fruitful land
to enjoy its bounty and goodness,

1:12 The Hebrew word for "watching" *(shoqed)* sounds like the word for "almond tree" *(shaqed)*. **2:3** Hebrew *the firstfruits of his harvest.*

will become a responsible adult when he accepts his commission and begins to speak God's messages.

2:1–4:2 Israel Breaks Faith with God

Underlying this collection of short, mostly poetic sayings is the story of God's relationship with Israel and Judah.

2:1–22 God's Case against His People. 6–7: He brought Israel out of Egypt, preserved them in the wilderness, and gave them the land. Jeremiah pro-

you defiled my land and
corrupted the possession I had promised
you.
8 The priests did not ask,
'Where is the LORD?'
Those who taught my word ignored me,
the rulers turned against me,
and the prophets spoke in the name of Baal,
wasting their time on worthless idols.
9 Therefore, I will bring my case against you,"
says the LORD.
"I will even bring charges against your
children's children
in the years to come.

10 "Go west and look in the land of Cyprus*;
go east and search through the land of
Kedar.
Has anyone ever heard of anything
as strange as this?
11 Has any nation ever traded its gods for new
ones,
even though they are not gods at all?
Yet my people have exchanged their glorious
God*
for worthless idols!
12 The heavens are shocked at such a thing
and shrink back in horror and dismay,"
says the LORD.
13 "For my people have done two evil things:
They have abandoned me—
the fountain of living water.
And they have dug for themselves cracked
cisterns
that can hold no water at all!

The Results of Israel's Sin
14 "Why has Israel become a slave?
Why has he been carried away as plunder?
15 Strong lions have roared against him,
and the land has been destroyed.
The towns are now in ruins,
and no one lives in them anymore.
16 Egyptians, marching from their cities of
Memphis* and Tahpanhes,
have destroyed Israel's glory and power.
17 And you have brought this upon yourselves
by rebelling against the LORD your God,
even though he was leading you on the
way!
18 "What have you gained by your alliances
with Egypt
and your covenants with Assyria?
What good to you are the streams of the
Nile*
or the waters of the Euphrates River?*
19 Your wickedness will bring its own
punishment.
Your turning from me will shame you.
You will see what an evil, bitter thing it is
to abandon the LORD your God and not to
fear him.
I, the Lord, the LORD of Heaven's Armies,
have spoken!

20 "Long ago I broke the yoke that oppressed
you
and tore away the chains of your slavery,
but still you said,
'I will not serve you.'
On every hill and under every green tree,
you have prostituted yourselves by bowing
down to idols.
21 But I was the one who planted you,
choosing a vine of the purest stock—the
very best.
How did you grow into this corrupt wild
vine?
22 No amount of soap or lye can make you
clean.
I still see the stain of your guilt.
I, the Sovereign LORD, have spoken!

Israel, an Unfaithful Wife
23 "You say, 'That's not true!
I haven't worshiped the images of Baal!'
But how can you say that?

2:10 Hebrew *Kittim.* **2:11** Hebrew *their glory.* **2:16** Hebrew *Noph.* **2:18a** Hebrew *of Shihor,* a branch of the Nile River. **2:18b** Hebrew *the river?*

vides an outline of events up to the time he wrote and challenges his fellow Judeans. **14–16:** Judah has not heeded the Northern Kingdom's example. God urges those remaining from both countries to acknowledge their rebellion, and to return. If they do, they will come back to the land, Israel and Judah will be reunited, and the nations will come peacefully to Jerusalem. Jeremiah wants to persuade the people of Judah to acknowledge their guilt and the justice of divine judgment, and to repent. **18–22:** Jeremiah sets out his conviction that their behavior, in particular their alliances (both political and religious) with other nations, had done them nothing but harm. He also says that judgment on Judah is not only coming but is thoroughly deserved.

2:23—3:5 Israel, an Unfaithful Wife. The image of God and his people being in a marriage relationship

Go and look in any valley in the land!
Face the awful sins you have done.
You are like a restless female camel
desperately searching for a mate.
24 You are like a wild donkey,
sniffing the wind at mating time.
Who can restrain her lust?
Those who desire her don't need to search,
for she goes running to them!
25 When will you stop running?
When will you stop panting after other gods?
But you say, 'Save your breath.
I'm in love with these foreign gods,
and I can't stop loving them now!'
26 "Israel is like a thief
who feels shame only when he gets caught.
They, their kings, officials, priests, and prophets—
all are alike in this.
27 To an image carved from a piece of wood they say,
'You are my father.'
To an idol chiseled from a block of stone they say,
'You are my mother.'
They turn their backs on me,
but in times of trouble they cry out to me,
'Come and save us!'
28 But why not call on these gods you have made?
When trouble comes, let them save you if they can!
For you have as many gods
as there are towns in Judah.
29 Why do you accuse me of doing wrong?
You are the ones who have rebelled,"
says the LORD.
30 "I have punished your children,
but they did not respond to my discipline.
You yourselves have killed your prophets
as a lion kills its prey.

31 "O my people, listen to the words of the LORD!
Have I been like a desert to Israel?
Have I been to them a land of darkness?
Why then do my people say, 'At last we are free from God!
We don't need him anymore!'
32 Does a young woman forget her jewelry?
Does a bride hide her wedding dress?
Yet for years on end
my people have forgotten me.

33 "How you plot and scheme to win your lovers.
Even an experienced prostitute could learn from you!
34 Your clothing is stained with the blood of the innocent and the poor,
though you didn't catch them breaking into your houses!
35 And yet you say,
'I have done nothing wrong.
Surely God isn't angry with me!'
But now I will punish you severely
because you claim you have not sinned.
36 First here, then there—
you flit from one ally to another asking for help.
But your new friends in Egypt will let you down,
just as Assyria did before.

---

comes into focus. **2:24–25:** The marriage began happily, but Israel behaved like a harlot. The LORD waited, hoping that she would return. The poetry likens Israel to a female donkey or camel in heat, crudely searching for a mate. The audience was expected to feel revulsion for this foolish behavior. If they acknowledged this picture of themselves they would have to admit their guilt. **26:** Accusation was necessary because Israel refused to acknowledge her sin. Israel did not return to the LORD, so he divorced her, sending her into exile. Judah observed Israel's harlotry and its consequences yet also committed adultery. **27:** Apostasy made less sense for Israel than for anyone else because deities other than the LORD are worthless and powerless. Yet the people worshiped those deities ignorantly, saying *my father* to the tree that represented Asherah, a goddess, and addressing the stone representing the male deity Baal as their *mother*. **31–35:** Accusations against Israel for betraying this relationship and rebelling against God fill most of this section. Negative, offensive rhetoric is used to break down Judah's refusal to admit they had sinned. Note that the accused parties are the nations or governments of Israel or Judah rather than individuals. The imagery is never intended to make statements about individual marriages. God's relationship to Israel originated with deliverance and blessing. God was a fountain of living, life-giving water to them. The divine farmer protected Israel as the best of the harvest; he planted them as a vine from the best stock. **33:** Israel as the LORD's bride at the Exodus and Israel and Judah as unfaithful wives are the most prominent images of their relationship with God. Israel tried to hide and deny its promiscuity, yet even the strongest soap could not remove the guilty stain. God charges Israel with teaching even an *experienced prostitute* how to find lovers.

37 In despair, you will be led into exile
with your hands on your heads,
for the LORD has rejected the nations you trust.
They will not help you at all.

3 1"If a man divorces a woman
and she goes and marries someone else,
he will not take her back again,
for that would surely corrupt the land.
But you have prostituted yourself with many lovers,
so why are you trying to come back to me?"
says the LORD.
2 "Look at the shrines on every hilltop.
Is there any place you have not been defiled
by your adultery with other gods?
You sit like a prostitute beside the road
waiting for a customer.
You sit alone like a nomad in the desert.
You have polluted the land with your prostitution
and your wickedness.
3 That's why even the spring rains have failed.
For you are a brazen prostitute and completely shameless.
4 Yet you say to me,
'Father, you have been my guide since my youth.
5 Surely you won't be angry forever!
Surely you can forget about it!'
So you talk,
but you keep on doing all the evil you can."

Judah Follows Israel's Example

6 During the reign of King Josiah, the LORD said
to me, "Have you seen what fickle Israel has
done? Like a wife who commits adultery, Israel
has worshiped other gods on every hill and under every green tree. 7 I thought, 'After she has
done all this, she will return to me.' But she did
not return, and her faithless sister Judah saw this.
8 She saw that I divorced faithless Israel because
of her adultery. But that treacherous sister Judah
had no fear, and now she, too, has left me and
given herself to prostitution. 9 Israel treated it all
so lightly—she thought nothing of committing
adultery by worshiping idols made of wood and
stone. So now the land has been polluted. 10 But
despite all this, her faithless sister Judah has never sincerely returned to me. She has only pretended to be sorry. I, the LORD, have spoken!"

Hope for Wayward Israel

11 Then the LORD said to me, "Even faithless Israel is less guilty than treacherous Judah! 12 Therefore, go and give this message to Israel.* This is
what the LORD says:

3:12 Hebrew *toward the north.*

3:6—4:2 Judah Follows Israel's Example. These messages stem from Josiah's reign, a hundred years after the Northern Kingdom fell. **3:6–11:** These verses, with the metaphor of a husband and his unfaithful wives, provide the interpretative key (cf. 2:2). The social and legal aspects of marriage made it a very suitable image. A husband might have several wives, but a wife could have only one husband and was required to remain loyal. A wife could not initiate divorce. If she left her husband for another man, she committed adultery. The husband, however, could divorce his wife if he found something objectionable. The intimacy of marriage adds a dimension of compassion and anguish to the metaphor, which could simultaneously convey God's freedom and authority, Israel's dependence, and their love for each other. Using this metaphor, Jeremiah shows the impossibility of Judah's initiating reconciliation with God. The law forbids remarriage of a woman to the husband who divorced her if she had meanwhile married another man. Only God can initiate this reconciliation by inviting Israel to return and repent. **12–14:** The wording of God's invitation goes beyond the marriage metaphor. Rebel is a political term, used often of the people's transgressions against God but never of a wife's behavior against her husband. Guilt has a broad range of meanings not limited to sexual sin. Personified Israel is also guilty of violating the ethical standards of the LORD's community by murdering innocent poor. The people by their whorings have polluted the land given to them as a heritage. Marriage imagery is one, but not the only, way of describing their infidelity (cf. 2:7). The idea of a wife deserting her husband and proudly choosing a life of prostitution would have appalled Jeremiah's hearers. It is another image of the senseless, inexplicable choice Israel made in turning away from the LORD. Contemporary readers living in societies where women enjoy legal and economic independence may find this imagery difficult. A woman leaves her husband because she has been abused. We have rightly learned to reject justifications given by men and women for abusing children or spouses and to conclude that the abuser is at fault (see Violence, Abuse, and Oppression, Eccl 4). What was meant to demonstrate God's justice and lead hearers to recognize their sin now prompts some readers to take sides against God. Since nothing can justify abusing one's spouse or children, they reason, then nothing that

"O Israel, my faithless people,
come home to me again,
for I am merciful.
I will not be angry with you forever.
13 Only acknowledge your guilt.
Admit that you rebelled against the LORD
your God
and committed adultery against him
by worshiping idols under every green
tree.
Confess that you refused to listen to my
voice.
I, the LORD, have spoken!

14 "Return home, you wayward children,"
says the LORD,
"for I am your master.
I will bring you back to the land of Israel*—
one from this town and two from that
family—
from wherever you are scattered.
15 And I will give you shepherds after my own
heart,
who will guide you with knowledge and
understanding.

16 "And when your land is once more filled
with people," says the LORD, "you will no longer wish for 'the good old days' when you possessed the Ark of the LORD's Covenant. You will
not miss those days or even remember them, and
there will be no need to rebuild the Ark. 17 In that
day Jerusalem will be known as 'The Throne of
the LORD.' All nations will come there to honor
the LORD. They will no longer stubbornly follow
their own evil desires. 18 In those days the people
of Judah and Israel will return together from exile in the north. They will return to the land I
gave their ancestors as an inheritance forever.

19 "I thought to myself,
'I would love to treat you as my own
children!'
I wanted nothing more than to give you this
beautiful land—
the finest possession in the world.
I looked forward to your calling me 'Father,'
and I wanted you never to turn from me.
20 But you have been unfaithful to me, you
people of Israel!
You have been like a faithless wife who
leaves her husband.
I, the LORD, have spoken."

21 Voices are heard high on the windswept
mountains,
the weeping and pleading of Israel's
people.
For they have chosen crooked paths
and have forgotten the LORD their God.

22 "My wayward children," says the LORD,
"come back to me, and I will heal your
wayward hearts."

"Yes, we're coming," the people reply,
"for you are the LORD our God.
23 Our worship of idols on the hills
and our religious orgies on the
mountains
are a delusion.
Only in the LORD our God
will Israel ever find salvation.
24 From childhood we have watched
as everything our ancestors worked for—
their flocks and herds, their sons and
daughters—
was squandered on a delusion.
25 Let us now lie down in shame
and cover ourselves with dishonor,
for we and our ancestors have sinned
against the LORD our God.
From our childhood to this day
we have never obeyed him."

3:14 Hebrew *to Zion.*

Israel did can justify God's judgment. This reasoning becomes another way of saying that a God who judges in wrath is incompatible with a God who saves and nurtures in love. But the imagery must be seen in its own context. **19–20:** The ethical implications of this image are also serious. If God as husband must punish Israel and Judah as wives, then aren't human husbands desiring to imitate God obligated to punish their wives in analogous ways? This reasoning is tempting, but it misunderstands completely the point: It is not intended to teach human husbands how to treat their wives. Other images or nonpictorial expressions depicting God's relationship to Israel and Judah are regularly used. God is not merely a husband, he is sovereign LORD and Creator. Israel and Judah are not individual women but nation-states possessing God-granted territory and responsible for conducting national affairs in accordance with God's will. The marriage image is a powerful rhetorical tool but must not divert attention from the full scope of the message. **22–25:** Even the remnant from the north have yet another opportunity to confess their rebellion, acknowledging the truth of the prophetic accusations and the justice of God's judgment.

4 [1]"O Israel," says the LORD,
"if you wanted to return to me, you could.
You could throw away your detestable idols
and stray away no more.
[2] Then when you swear by my name, saying,
'As surely as the LORD lives,'
you could do so
with truth, justice, and righteousness.
Then you would be a blessing to the nations of the world,
and all people would come and praise my name."

Coming Judgment against Judah

[3]This is what the LORD says to the people of Judah and Jerusalem:

"Plow up the hard ground of your hearts!
Do not waste your good seed among thorns.
[4] O people of Judah and Jerusalem,
surrender your pride and power.
Change your hearts before the LORD,*
or my anger will burn like an unquenchable fire
because of all your sins.

[5] "Shout to Judah, and broadcast to Jerusalem!
Tell them to sound the alarm throughout the land:
'Run for your lives!
Flee to the fortified cities!'
[6] Raise a signal flag as a warning for Jerusalem*:
'Flee now! Do not delay!'
For I am bringing terrible destruction upon you
from the north."

[7] A lion stalks from its den,
a destroyer of nations.
It has left its lair and is headed your way.
It's going to devastate your land!
Your towns will lie in ruins,
with no one living in them anymore.
[8] So put on clothes of mourning
and weep with broken hearts,
for the fierce anger of the LORD
is still upon us.

[9] "In that day," says the LORD,
"the king and the officials will tremble in fear.
The priests will be struck with horror,
and the prophets will be appalled."

[10] Then I said, "O Sovereign LORD,
the people have been deceived by what you said,
for you promised peace for Jerusalem.
But the sword is held at their throats!"

[11] The time is coming when the LORD will say
to the people of Jerusalem,
"My dear people, a burning wind is blowing
in from the desert,
and it's not a gentle breeze useful for winnowing grain.
[12] It is a roaring blast sent by me!
Now I will pronounce your destruction!"
[13] Our enemy rushes down on us like storm clouds!
His chariots are like whirlwinds.
His horses are swifter than eagles.

4:4 Hebrew *Circumcise yourselves to the LORD, and take away the foreskins of your heart.* **4:6** Hebrew *Zion.*

4:3—6:30 The Enemy from the North

As elsewhere, this section is not arranged chronologically. The purpose of these oracles is again to convince God's people of the justice of divine judgment and to provoke repentance. Some are warnings; others cite invitations the people had rejected or previous warnings they had ignored and thus present suffering as discipline or refining to which they had refused to respond. This collection addresses those for whom Babylonian conquest was certain. The audience is instructed to accept the prophet's explanation of Babylon's success as divine judgment.

4:3–18 Coming Judgment. 4: Judah sinned just like Israel, and prophetic accusations against Israel also apply to Judah. But Judah and Jerusalem had an opportunity to repent and thus avoid at least some of the judgment. **13–17:** Many of the short poetic sayings in 4:3b—6:30 describe the enemy coming from the north to execute God's judgment. Judah lay in the fertile strip between the Mediterranean Sea and the Arabian desert. Invaders from Mesopotamia passed around the desert and approached from the north (cf. 6:1). **13:** This enemy, typical of ancient Near Eastern conquerors, comes on horses and chariots, equipped with the most effective armaments. The army will attack cruelly, show no mercy, and kill efficiently, like predatory beasts. Their power will be so awesome that the description approaches mythic proportions.

How terrible it will be, for we are
doomed!
14 O Jerusalem, cleanse your heart
that you may be saved.
How long will you harbor
your evil thoughts?
15 Your destruction has been announced
from Dan and the hill country of Ephraim.

16 "Warn the surrounding nations
and announce this to Jerusalem:
The enemy is coming from a distant land,
raising a battle cry against the towns of
Judah.
17 They surround Jerusalem like watchmen
around a field,
for my people have rebelled against me,"
says the LORD.
18 "Your own actions have brought this upon
you.
This punishment is bitter, piercing you to
the heart!"

Jeremiah Weeps for His People
19 My heart, my heart—I writhe in pain!
My heart pounds within me! I cannot be
still.
For I have heard the blast of enemy trumpets
and the roar of their battle cries.
20 Waves of destruction roll over the land,
until it lies in complete desolation.
Suddenly my tents are destroyed;
in a moment my shelters are crushed.
21 How long must I see the battle flags
and hear the trumpets of war?

22 "My people are foolish
and do not know me," says the LORD.
"They are stupid children
who have no understanding.
They are clever enough at doing wrong,
but they have no idea how to do right!"

Jeremiah's Vision of Coming Disaster
23 I looked at the earth, and it was empty and
formless.
I looked at the heavens, and there was no
light.
24 I looked at the mountains and hills,
and they trembled and shook.
25 I looked, and all the people were gone.
All the birds of the sky had flown away.
26 I looked, and the fertile fields had become a
wilderness.
The towns lay in ruins,
crushed by the LORD's fierce anger.

27 This is what the LORD says:
"The whole land will be ruined,
but I will not destroy it completely.
28 The earth will mourn
and the heavens will be draped in black
because of my decree against my people.
I have made up my mind and will not
change it."

29 At the noise of charioteers and archers,
the people flee in terror.
They hide in the bushes
and run for the mountains.
All the towns have been abandoned—
not a person remains!
30 What are you doing,
you who have been plundered?
Why do you dress up in beautiful clothing
and put on gold jewelry?
Why do you brighten your eyes with
mascara?
Your primping will do you no good!
The allies who were your lovers
despise you and seek to kill you.

31 I hear a cry, like that of a woman in labor,
the groans of a woman giving birth to her
first child.

4:19–22 Jeremiah Weeps for His People. 19: Neither the LORD nor the prophet rejoices in the judgment. God's efforts to find a reason to pardon and the recognition of Judah as *my people* are consistent with other images of tender care in 2:1—4:2 (husband, parent) and the references to the good that God had done for them. This cry of anguish expresses the prophet's participation in the people's despair amid judgment. He feels his heart *pounds within* him and can't help but cry out in pain. He wants the enemy army to disappear.

4:23–31 Jeremiah's Vision of Coming Disaster. 30: The metaphor probably again describes a prostitute, although dyed clothing, jewelry, and makeup were normal marks of wealth and position (David praises Saul for having enriched the nation so Israelite women could possess these luxury items; 2 Sam 1:24). Gold jewelry was worn not just by brides (Isa 61:10; Ezek 16:11, 13) but also by any rich man or woman (Isa 3:16, 18–23; Exod 33:4–6). A prostitute dressed to display her wealth to potential clients because success evidenced expertise (cf. Ezek 23:40). A city seeking allies would show off the strength of its armies, the abundance of its provisions, and the popularity of its leaders. Jerusalem's efforts, however,

It is beautiful Jerusalem*
  gasping for breath and crying out,
  "Help! I'm being murdered!"

The Sins of Judah

5 [1]"Run up and down every street in
    Jerusalem," says the LORD.
  "Look high and low; search throughout
    the city!
If you can find even one just and honest
    person,
  I will not destroy the city.
2 But even when they are under oath,
  saying, 'As surely as the LORD lives,'
  they are still telling lies!"
3 LORD, you are searching for honesty.
You struck your people,
  but they paid no attention.
You crushed them,
  but they refused to be corrected.
They are determined, with faces set like
    stone;
  they have refused to repent.

4 Then I said, "But what can we expect from
    the poor?
  They are ignorant.
They don't know the ways of the LORD.
  They don't understand God's laws.
5 So I will go and speak to their leaders.
  Surely they know the ways of the LORD
  and understand God's laws."
But the leaders, too, as one man,
  had thrown off God's yoke
  and broken his chains.
6 So now a lion from the forest will attack
    them;
  a wolf from the desert will pounce on
    them.
A leopard will lurk near their towns,
  tearing apart any who dare to venture out.
For their rebellion is great,
  and their sins are many.

7 "How can I pardon you?
  For even your children have turned
    from me.
They have sworn by gods that are not gods at
    all!
  I fed my people until they were full.
But they thanked me by committing adultery
  and lining up at the brothels.
8 They are well-fed, lusty stallions,
  each neighing for his neighbor's wife.
9 Should I not punish them for this?" says the
    LORD.
  "Should I not avenge myself against such a
    nation?

10 "Go down the rows of the vineyards and
    destroy the grapevines,
  leaving a scattered few alive.
Strip the branches from the vines,
  for these people do not belong to the LORD.
11 The people of Israel and Judah
  are full of treachery against me,"
  says the LORD.
12 "They have lied about the LORD
  and said, 'He won't bother us!
No disasters will come upon us.
  There will be no war or famine.
13 God's prophets are all windbags
  who don't really speak for him.
  Let their predictions of disaster fall on
    themselves!' "

14 Therefore, this is what the LORD God of Heaven's Armies says:

"Because the people are talking like this,
  my messages will flame out of your mouth
  and burn the people like kindling wood.
15 O Israel, I will bring a distant nation against
    you,"
  says the LORD.
"It is a mighty nation,

4:31 Hebrew *the daughter of Zion.*

will fail. **31:** This failure is depicted with another feminine metaphor, that of a woman in labor. The picture, serving as an image of military conquest, is one of pain and vulnerability. The pregnant woman cannot avoid labor, nor control its beginning or its length. The woman in labor cannot escape or fight back. This is a picture of a city without defense or hope of avoiding judgment.

5:1–19 The Sins of Judah. 1: The whole nation was involved; Jeremiah could find no one to use as an example to persuade God to pardon them. **11:** The key word translated "faithless" in 3:4–14 reappears here without the marriage metaphor but reaffirming Jeremiah's conviction that all kinds of *treachery,* from people or leaders, from children or parents, will only bring disaster. **10, 18:** The small encouragement is that the inevitable destruction of Judah will not be total. **19:** The question articulates Judah's reaction to the judgment. The many sins and wrong attitudes listed here provide the answer.

an ancient nation,
a people whose language you do not know,
whose speech you cannot understand.
16 Their weapons are deadly;
their warriors are mighty.
17 They will devour the food of your harvest;
they will devour your sons and daughters.
They will devour your flocks and herds;
they will devour your grapes and figs.
And they will destroy your fortified towns,
which you think are so safe.

18 "Yet even in those days I will not blot you
out completely," says the LORD. 19 "And when
your people ask, 'Why did the LORD our God do
all this to us?' you must reply, 'You rejected him
and gave yourselves to foreign gods in your own
land. Now you will serve foreigners in a land
that is not your own.'

A Warning for God's People

20 "Make this announcement to Israel,*
and say this to Judah:
21 Listen, you foolish and senseless people,
with eyes that do not see
and ears that do not hear.
22 Have you no respect for me?
Why don't you tremble in my presence?
I, the LORD, define the ocean's sandy shoreline
as an everlasting boundary that the waters cannot cross.
The waves may toss and roar,
but they can never pass the boundaries I set.
23 But my people have stubborn and rebellious hearts.
They have turned away and abandoned me.
24 They do not say from the heart,
'Let us live in awe of the LORD our God,
for he gives us rain each spring and fall,
assuring us of a harvest when the time is right.'
25 Your wickedness has deprived you of these wonderful blessings.
Your sin has robbed you of all these good things.
26 "Among my people are wicked men
who lie in wait for victims like a hunter hiding in a blind.
They continually set traps
to catch people.
27 Like a cage filled with birds,
their homes are filled with evil plots.
And now they are great and rich.
28 They are fat and sleek,
and there is no limit to their wicked deeds.
They refuse to provide justice to orphans
and deny the rights of the poor.
29 Should I not punish them for this?" says the LORD.
"Should I not avenge myself against such a nation?
30 A horrible and shocking thing
has happened in this land—
31 the prophets give false prophecies,
and the priests rule with an iron hand.
Worse yet, my people like it that way!
But what will you do when the end comes?

Jerusalem's Last Warning

6 1 "Run for your lives, you people of Benjamin!
Get out of Jerusalem!
Sound the alarm in Tekoa!
Send up a signal at Beth-hakkerem!
A powerful army is coming from the north,
coming with disaster and destruction.
2 O Jerusalem,* you are my beautiful and delicate daughter—
but I will destroy you!
3 Enemies will surround you, like shepherds
camped around the city.
Each chooses a place for his troops to devour.
4 They shout, 'Prepare for battle!
Attack at noon!'
'No, it's too late; the day is fading,
and the evening shadows are falling.'

5:20 Hebrew *to the house of Jacob.* The names "Jacob" and "Israel" are often interchanged throughout the Old Testament, referring sometimes to the individual patriarch and sometimes to the nation. **6:2** Hebrew *Daughter of Zion.*

5:20–31 A Warning for God's People. 29: The rhetorical question from verse 9 is repeated here. Given Judah's behavior, the charges of idolatry and seeking only illicit alliances illustrate many indictments. Jeremiah's surprise that anyone would doubt that judgment was inevitable comes across clearly. All their crimes relate to their refusal to heed God's law. Judah's and Jerusalem's suffering at Babylon's hands is pictured as the result of Babylon's imperial ambitions but also as God's punishment and (cf. 4:18) as entirely their own responsibility. It happened because they refused to heed warnings and turn back to God's way.

6:1–15 Jerusalem's Last Warning. In 4:10 Jeremiah implies that God had, through his prophets, deceived the people into a false confidence, but the constant proclamation of judgment makes it clear the prophetic reassurances were not from God. **14:** A medi-

5 'Well then, let's attack at night
and destroy her palaces!'"
6 This is what the LORD of Heaven's Armies
says:
"Cut down the trees for battering rams.
Build siege ramps against the walls of
Jerusalem.
This is the city to be punished,
for she is wicked through and through.
7 She spouts evil like a fountain.
Her streets echo with the sounds of
violence and destruction.
I always see her sickness and sores.
8 Listen to this warning, Jerusalem,
or I will turn from you in disgust.
Listen, or I will turn you into a heap of ruins,
a land where no one lives."

9 This is what the LORD of Heaven's Armies
says:
"Even the few who remain in Israel
will be picked over again,
as when a harvester checks each vine a second
time
to pick the grapes that were missed."

Israel's Constant Rebellion

10 To whom can I give warning?
Who will listen when I speak?
Their ears are closed,
and they cannot hear.
They scorn the word of the LORD.
They don't want to listen at all.
11 So now I am filled with the LORD's fury.
Yes, I am tired of holding it in!

"I will pour out my fury on children playing
in the streets
and on gatherings of young men,
on husbands and wives
and on those who are old and gray.
12 Their homes will be turned over to their
enemies,
as will their fields and their wives.
For I will raise my powerful fist
against the people of this land,"
says the LORD.

13 "From the least to the greatest,
their lives are ruled by greed.
From prophets to priests,
they are all frauds.
14 They offer superficial treatments
for my people's mortal wound.
They give assurances of peace
when there is no peace.
15 Are they ashamed of their disgusting actions?
Not at all—they don't even know how to
blush!
Therefore, they will lie among the slaughtered.
They will be brought down when I punish
them,"
says the LORD.

Israel Rejects the LORD's Way

16 This is what the LORD says:
"Stop at the crossroads and look around.
Ask for the old, godly way, and walk in it.
Travel its path, and you will find rest for your
souls.
But you reply, 'No, that's not the road we
want!'
17 I posted watchmen over you who said,
'Listen for the sound of the alarm.'
But you replied,
'No! We won't pay attention!'

18 "Therefore, listen to this, all you nations.
Take note of my people's situation.
19 Listen, all the earth!
I will bring disaster on my people.
It is the fruit of their own schemes,
because they refuse to listen to me.
They have rejected my word.
20 There's no use offering me sweet
frankincense from Sheba.
Keep your fragrant calamus imported from
distant lands!
I will not accept your burnt offerings.
Your sacrifices have no pleasing aroma
for me."

21 Therefore, this is what the LORD says:
"I will put obstacles in my people's path.
Fathers and sons will both fall over them.
Neighbors and friends will die together."

---

cal metaphor—*my people's mortal wound*—is used to expose the damage done by prophets who persuaded the people to complacently reject the LORD's warnings of judgment (cf. 5:12–13).

6:16–30 Israel Rejects the LORD's Way. 22: Neither Babylon nor Nebuchadnezzar is mentioned by name in chapters 4—6, but the rest of the book makes the identification obvious. The Babylonians besieged and conquered Jerusalem twice during Jeremiah's ministry, in 597 and 587/6 BC. The devastation envisioned in these chapters matches other Old Testament depictions of the result of Babylonian conquest (e.g., Jer 33:10; Lam 2:15–16).

An Invasion from the North

22 This is what the LORD says:
"Look! A great army coming from the north!
A great nation is rising against you from
far-off lands.
23 They are armed with bows and spears.
They are cruel and show no mercy.
They sound like a roaring sea
as they ride forward on horses.
They are coming in battle formation,
planning to destroy you, beautiful
Jerusalem.*"
24 We have heard reports about the enemy,
and we wring our hands in fright.
Pangs of anguish have gripped us,
like those of a woman in labor.
25 Don't go out to the fields!
Don't travel on the roads!
The enemy's sword is everywhere
and terrorizes us at every turn!
26 Oh, my people, dress yourselves in burlap
and sit among the ashes.
Mourn and weep bitterly, as for the loss of an
only son.
For suddenly the destroying armies will be
upon you!
27 "Jeremiah, I have made you a tester of metals,*
that you may determine the quality of my
people.
28 They are the worst kind of rebel,
full of slander.
They are as hard as bronze and iron,
and they lead others into corruption.
29 The bellows fiercely fan the flames
to burn out the corruption.
But it does not purify them,
for the wickedness remains.
30 I will label them 'Rejected Silver,'
for I, the LORD, am discarding them."

Jeremiah Speaks at the Temple

7 The LORD gave another message to Jeremiah. He said, 2 "Go to the entrance of
the LORD's Temple, and give this message
to the people: 'O Judah, listen to this message
from the LORD! Listen to it, all of you who worship here! 3 This is what the LORD of Heaven's
Armies, the God of Israel, says:
" 'Even now, if you quit your evil ways, I
will let you stay in your own land. 4 But don't be
fooled by those who promise you safety simply
because the LORD's Temple is here. They chant,
"The LORD's Temple is here! The LORD's Temple
is here!" 5 But I will be merciful only if you stop
your evil thoughts and deeds and start treating
each other with justice; 6 only if you stop exploiting foreigners, orphans, and widows; only if you
stop your murdering; and only if you stop harming yourselves by worshiping idols. 7 Then I will
let you stay in this land that I gave to your ancestors to keep forever.
8 " 'Don't be fooled into thinking that you
will never suffer because the Temple is here.
It's a lie! 9 Do you really think you can steal,
murder, commit adultery, lie, and burn incense
to Baal and all those other new gods of yours,
10 and then come here and stand before me in my
Temple and chant, "We are safe!"—only to go
right back to all those evils again? 11 Don't you
yourselves admit that this Temple, which bears
my name, has become a den of thieves? Surely I
see all the evil going on there. I, the LORD, have
spoken!
12 " 'Go now to the place at Shiloh where I
once put the Tabernacle that bore my name. See
what I did there because of all the wickedness of
my people, the Israelites. 13 While you were doing these wicked things, says the LORD, I spoke
to you about it repeatedly, but you would not
listen. I called out to you, but you refused to answer. 14 So just as I destroyed Shiloh, I will now
destroy this Temple that bears my name, this
Temple that you trust in for help, this place that
I gave to you and your ancestors. 15 And I will
send you out of my sight into exile, just as I did
your relatives, the people of Israel.*'

6:23 Hebrew *daughter of Zion.* **6:27** As in Greek version; Hebrew reads *a tester of my people a fortress.* **7:15** Hebrew *of Ephraim,* referring to the northern kingdom of Israel.

7:1—10:25 False Worship

A loose collection of prophetic sayings accuses and condemns Judah and Jerusalem for various forms of false worship.

7:1–15 Jeremiah Speaks at the Temple. 2: Jeremiah must speak out at the Temple, which should have been the site of exclusive, pure worship of the LORD. The people thought that the Temple's existence guaranteed their security because God would always defend it. God reminds them that it was only a symbol of relationship based on God's law. Sacrifices were pointless when the people were violating the Ten Commandments. The Temple would be destroyed, as the earlier sanctuary at Shiloh had been, and the people would be exiled.

Judah's Persistent Idolatry
16 "Pray no more for these people, Jeremiah. Do
not weep or pray for them, and don't beg me to
help them, for I will not listen to you. 17 Don't
you see what they are doing throughout the
towns of Judah and in the streets of Jerusalem?
18 No wonder I am so angry! Watch how the children gather wood and the fathers build sacrificial
fires. See how the women knead dough and make
cakes to offer to the Queen of Heaven. And they
pour out liquid offerings to their other idol gods!
19 Am I the one they are hurting?" asks the LORD.
"Most of all, they hurt themselves, to their own
shame."
20 So this is what the Sovereign LORD says:
"I will pour out my terrible fury on this place.
Its people, animals, trees, and crops will be consumed by the unquenchable fire of my anger."
21 This is what the LORD of Heaven's Armies,
the God of Israel, says: "Take your burnt offerings and your other sacrifices and eat them
yourselves! 22 When I led your ancestors out of
Egypt, it was not burnt offerings and sacrifices
I wanted from them. 23 This is what I told them:
'Obey me, and I will be your God, and you will
be my people. Do everything as I say, and all will
be well!'
24 "But my people would not listen to me.
They kept doing whatever they wanted, following the stubborn desires of their evil hearts. They
went backward instead of forward. 25 From the
day your ancestors left Egypt until now, I have
continued to send my servants, the prophets—
day in and day out. 26 But my people have not
listened to me or even tried to hear. They have
been stubborn and sinful—even worse than their
ancestors.
27 "Tell them all this, but do not expect them
to listen. Shout out your warnings, but do not
expect them to respond. 28 Say to them, 'This is
the nation whose people will not obey the LORD
their God and who refuse to be taught. Truth has
vanished from among them; it is no longer heard
on their lips. 29 Shave your head in mourning,
and weep alone on the mountains. For the LORD
has rejected and forsaken this generation that
has provoked his fury.'

The Valley of Slaughter
30 "The people of Judah have sinned before my
very eyes," says the LORD. "They have set up
their abominable idols right in the Temple that
bears my name, defiling it. 31 They have built
pagan shrines at Topheth, the garbage dump in
the valley of Ben-Hinnom, and there they burn
their sons and daughters in the fire. I have never
commanded such a horrible deed; it never even
crossed my mind to command such a thing! 32 So
beware, for the time is coming," says the LORD,
"when that garbage dump will no longer be
called Topheth or the valley of Ben-Hinnom, but
the Valley of Slaughter. They will bury the bodies in Topheth until there is no more room for
them. 33 The bodies of my people will be food for
the vultures and wild animals, and no one will
be left to scare them away. 34 I will put an end to
the happy singing and laughter in the streets of
Jerusalem. The joyful voices of bridegrooms and
brides will no longer be heard in the towns of
Judah. The land will lie in complete desolation.

8 "In that day," says the LORD, "the enemy
will break open the graves of the kings and
officials of Judah, and the graves of the
priests, prophets, and common people of Jerusalem. 2 They will spread out their bones on the
ground before the sun, moon, and stars—the
gods my people have loved, served, and worshiped. Their bones will not be gathered up again
or buried but will be scattered on the ground like
manure. 3 And the people of this evil nation who
survive will wish to die rather than live where I

7:16–29 Judah's Persistent Idolatry. 18: The Queen of Heaven was one of the other gods worshiped in Judah. This is possibly the Sidonian Ashtoreth or the Babylonian Ishtar, the consort of Tammuz (cf. Ezek 8:14). As her title indicates, she was a high god with a wide range of powers. Her devotees believed she granted fertility as well as success in battle. She was a deity for entire families, not just for women. Worship of the Queen of Heaven persisted in Israel throughout the monarchy; even Solomon constructed a high place for her outside Jerusalem (1 Kgs 11:5, 33). The refugees who forcibly removed Jeremiah and Baruch with them to Egypt determined to resume worshiping her there (see Jer 37—44).

7:30—8:3 The Valley of Slaughter. 7:31: At Topheth (the "fireplace"), the people of Judah sacrificed daughters and sons to Baal by burning them. Such a thing was unthinkable to God. They could not excuse themselves by claiming to emulate Abraham or fulfill the command to dedicate firstborn sons to the LORD. The law regarding the firstborn required an animal substitute. Child sacrifice did sometimes happen in Judah, as by Ahaz (2 Kgs 16:3), but is always seen as abhorrent. Such corruption of the people's spirit and of the land will bring a terrible judgment. This valley, just outside Jerusalem, will be filled with corpses, buried and unburied, that will become food for carrion-eating beasts and birds.

will send them. I, the LORD of Heaven's Armies,
have spoken!

Deception by False Prophets
4"Jeremiah, say to the people, 'This is what the
LORD says:

" 'When people fall down, don't they get up
again?
When they discover they're on the wrong
road, don't they turn back?
5 Then why do these people stay on their self-
destructive path?
Why do the people of Jerusalem refuse to
turn back?
They cling tightly to their lies
and will not turn around.
6 I listen to their conversations
and don't hear a word of truth.
Is anyone sorry for doing wrong?
Does anyone say, "What a terrible thing I
have done"?
No! All are running down the path of sin
as swiftly as a horse galloping into battle!
7 Even the stork that flies across the sky
knows the time of her migration,
as do the turtledove, the swallow, and the
crane.*
They all return at the proper time each
year.
But not my people!
They do not know the LORD's laws.

8 " 'How can you say, "We are wise because we
have the word of the LORD,"
when your teachers have twisted it by
writing lies?
9 These wise teachers will fall
into the trap of their own foolishness,
for they have rejected the word of the LORD.
Are they so wise after all?
10 I will give their wives to others
and their farms to strangers.
From the least to the greatest,
their lives are ruled by greed.
Yes, even my prophets and priests are like
that.
They are all frauds.
11 They offer superficial treatments
for my people's mortal wound.
They give assurances of peace
when there is no peace.
12 Are they ashamed of these disgusting
actions?
Not at all—they don't even know how to
blush!
Therefore, they will lie among the slaughtered.
They will be brought down when I punish
them,
says the LORD.
13 I will surely consume them.
There will be no more harvests of figs and
grapes.
Their fruit trees will all die.
Whatever I gave them will soon be gone.
I, the LORD, have spoken!'

14 "Then the people will say,
'Why should we wait here to die?
Come, let's go to the fortified towns and die
there.
For the LORD our God has decreed our
destruction
and has given us a cup of poison to drink
because we sinned against the LORD.
15 We hoped for peace, but no peace came.
We hoped for a time of healing, but found
only terror.'

16 "The snorting of the enemies' warhorses can
be heard
all the way from the land of Dan in the
north!
The neighing of their stallions makes the
whole land tremble.
They are coming to devour the land and
everything in it—
cities and people alike.
17 I will send these enemy troops among you
like poisonous snakes you cannot charm.
They will bite you, and you will die.
I, the Lord, have spoken!"

Jeremiah Weeps for Sinful Judah
18 My grief is beyond healing;
my heart is broken.

8:7 The identification of some of these birds is uncertain.

8:4–17 Deception by False Prophets. 8: The twisted teaching of the prophets mentioned earlier (4:10; 5:12; 6:14) is again described and condemned. It is made clear that those claiming to speak God's words have a tremendous responsibility to do so accurately, and that those who listen must be discerning and cannot leave the responsibility for reading and discerning God's word entirely to others.

8:18—9:26: The prophet describes his own and God's grief over the people of Jerusalem's suffering and despair. They are called *my people* four times

19 Listen to the weeping of my people;
it can be heard all across the land.
"Has the LORD abandoned Jerusalem?*" the people ask.
"Is her King no longer there?"
"Oh, why have they provoked my anger with their carved idols
and their worthless foreign gods?" says the LORD.

20 "The harvest is finished,
and the summer is gone," the people cry,
"yet we are not saved!"

21 I hurt with the hurt of my people.
I mourn and am overcome with grief.
22 Is there no medicine in Gilead?
Is there no physician there?
Why is there no healing
for the wounds of my people?

9 1*If only my head were a pool of water
and my eyes a fountain of tears,
I would weep day and night
for all my people who have been slaughtered.
2* Oh, that I could go away and forget my people
and live in a travelers' shack in the desert.
For they are all adulterers—
a pack of treacherous liars.

Judgment for Disobedience

3 "My people bend their tongues like bows
to shoot out lies.
They refuse to stand up for the truth.
They only go from bad to worse.
They do not know me,"
says the LORD.

4 "Beware of your neighbor!
Don't even trust your brother!
For brother takes advantage of brother,
and friend slanders friend.
5 They all fool and defraud each other;
no one tells the truth.
With practiced tongues they tell lies;
they wear themselves out with all their sinning.
6 They pile lie upon lie
and utterly refuse to acknowledge me,"
says the LORD.

7 Therefore, this is what the LORD of Heaven's Armies says:
"See, I will melt them down in a crucible
and test them like metal.
What else can I do with my people?*
8 For their tongues shoot lies like poisoned arrows.
They speak friendly words to their neighbors
while scheming in their heart to kill them.
9 Should I not punish them for this?" says the LORD.
"Should I not avenge myself against such a nation?"

10 I will weep for the mountains
and wail for the wilderness pastures.
For they are desolate and empty of life;
the lowing of cattle is heard no more;
the birds and wild animals have all fled.

11 "I will make Jerusalem into a heap of ruins,"
says the LORD.
"It will be a place haunted by jackals.
The towns of Judah will be ghost towns,
with no one living in them."

12 Who is wise enough to understand all this?
Who has been instructed by the LORD and can
explain it to others? Why has the land been so
ruined that no one dares to travel through it?
13 The LORD replies, "This has happened because my people have abandoned my instructions; they have refused to obey what I said.
14 Instead, they have stubbornly followed their
own desires and worshiped the images of Baal,
as their ancestors taught them. 15 So now, this is

8:19 Hebrew *Zion?* **9:1** Verse 9:1 is numbered 8:23 in Hebrew text. **9:2** Verses 9:2-26 are numbered 9:1-25 in Hebrew text. **9:7** Hebrew *with the daughter of my people?* Greek version reads *with the evil daughter of my people?*

in 8:1—9:1. This term of endearment (lit., "daughter, my people") is God's special name for the Israelites. The reasons for the people's suffering are clear—it is the result of judgment for unfaithfulness (i.e., idolatry and falsehood). However, both God and his prophet find only pain not satisfaction from this. The poem demonstrates that wrath did not destroy or replace God's love for Israel. **8:19:** The whole people are called to lament and wail in anticipation of devastating judgment to come. Wailing for the dead was done publicly, in streets and public squares, by relatives and colleagues. Women or men skilled in composing and performing dirges led the public mourning. David (2 Sam 1:17; 3:33) and Jeremiah (2 Chr 35:25) are the only named authors of dirges for the dead in the Old Testament.

what the LORD of Heaven's Armies, the God of Israel, says: Look! I will feed them with bitterness and give them poison to drink. [16] I will scatter them around the world, in places they and their ancestors never heard of, and even there I will chase them with the sword until I have destroyed them completely."

Weeping in Jerusalem

[17] This is what the LORD of Heaven's Armies
says:
"Consider all this, and call for the mourners.
Send for the women who mourn at
funerals.
[18] Quick! Begin your weeping!
Let the tears flow from your eyes.
[19] Hear the people of Jerusalem* crying in
despair,
'We are ruined! We are completely
humiliated!
We must leave our land,
because our homes have been torn down.' "

[20] Listen, you women, to the words of
the LORD;
open your ears to what he has to say.
Teach your daughters to wail;
teach one another how to lament.
[21] For death has crept in through our windows
and has entered our mansions.
It has killed off the flower of our youth:
Children no longer play in the streets,
and young men no longer gather in the
squares.

[22] This is what the LORD says:
"Bodies will be scattered across the fields like
clumps of manure,
like bundles of grain after the harvest.
No one will be left to bury them."

[23] This is what the LORD says:
"Don't let the wise boast in their wisdom,
or the powerful boast in their power,
or the rich boast in their riches.
[24] But those who wish to boast
should boast in this alone:
that they truly know me and understand that
I am the LORD
who demonstrates unfailing love
and who brings justice and righteousness
to the earth,
and that I delight in these things.
I, the LORD, have spoken!

[25] "A time is coming," says the LORD, "when I
will punish all those who are circumcised in body
but not in spirit—[26] the Egyptians, Edomites,
Ammonites, Moabites, the people who live in
the desert in remote places,* and yes, even the
people of Judah. And like all these pagan nations, the people of Israel also have uncircumcised hearts."

Idolatry Brings Destruction

10 Hear the word that the LORD speaks to you, O Israel! [2] This is what the
LORD says:

"Do not act like the other nations,
who try to read their future in the stars.
Do not be afraid of their predictions,
even though other nations are terrified by
them.
[3] Their ways are futile and foolish.
They cut down a tree, and a craftsman
carves an idol.
[4] They decorate it with gold and silver
and then fasten it securely with hammer
and nails
so it won't fall over.
[5] Their gods are like
helpless scarecrows in a cucumber field!
They cannot speak,
and they need to be carried because they
cannot walk.
Do not be afraid of such gods,
for they can neither harm you nor do you
any good."

9:19 Hebrew *Zion.* **9:26** Or *in the desert and clip the corners of their hair.*

9:20: The dirge sung and taught by these women is a word from God. The ministry of women skilled in mourning will enable the people to weep. Music touches the heart and inspires tears, but more is at stake here than emotional release. Jeremiah's audience will mourn under the leadership of these skilled women only when they acknowledge the truth of God's judgment. **25:** This prose comment summarizes the paradoxical divine character, recognized by all who truly know the LORD who delights in love and justice.

10:1–25 Idolatry Brings Destruction. 2–16: A long poem contrasts God, the Creator, with manufactured idols. The poem's humor is sarcastic. One need not fear gods of other nations because one can see them being made. The LORD, the living God who made earth and heaven, claims authority over the nations because

[6] LORD, there is no one like you!
For you are great, and your name is full of power.
[7] Who would not fear you, O King of nations?
That title belongs to you alone!
Among all the wise people of the earth
and in all the kingdoms of the world,
there is no one like you.

[8] People who worship idols are stupid and foolish.
The things they worship are made of wood!
[9] They bring beaten sheets of silver from Tarshish
and gold from Uphaz,
and they give these materials to skillful craftsmen
who make their idols.
Then they dress these gods in royal blue and purple robes
made by expert tailors.
[10] But the LORD is the only true God.
He is the living God and the everlasting King!
The whole earth trembles at his anger.
The nations cannot stand up to his wrath.

[11] Say this to those who worship other gods:
"Your so-called gods, who did not make the
heavens and earth, will vanish from the earth
and from under the heavens."*

[12] But God made the earth by his power,
and he preserves it by his wisdom.
With his own understanding
he stretched out the heavens.
[13] When he speaks in the thunder,
the heavens roar with rain.
He causes the clouds to rise over the earth.
He sends the lightning with the rain
and releases the wind from his storehouses.
[14] The whole human race is foolish and has no knowledge!
The craftsmen are disgraced by the idols they make,
for their carefully shaped works are a fraud.
These idols have no breath or power.
[15] Idols are worthless; they are ridiculous lies!
On the day of reckoning they will all be destroyed.
[16] But the God of Israel* is no idol!
He is the Creator of everything that exists,
including Israel, his own special possession.
The LORD of Heaven's Armies is his name!

The Coming Destruction

[17] Pack your bags and prepare to leave;
the siege is about to begin.
[18] For this is what the LORD says:
"Suddenly, I will fling out
all you who live in this land.
I will pour great troubles upon you,
and at last you will feel my anger."

[19] My wound is severe,
and my grief is great.
My sickness is incurable,
but I must bear it.
[20] My home is gone,
and no one is left to help me rebuild it.
My children have been taken away,
and I will never see them again.
[21] The shepherds of my people have lost their senses.
They no longer seek wisdom from the LORD.
Therefore, they fail completely,
and their flocks are scattered.
[22] Listen! Hear the terrifying roar of great armies
as they roll down from the north.
The towns of Judah will be destroyed
and become a haunt for jackals.

Jeremiah's Prayer

[23] I know, LORD, that our lives are not our own.
We are not able to plan our own course.
[24] So correct me, LORD, but please be gentle.
Do not correct me in anger, for I would die.
[25] Pour out your wrath on the nations that refuse to acknowledge you—
on the peoples that do not call upon your name.
For they have devoured your people Israel*;
they have devoured and consumed them,
making the land a desolate wilderness.

10:11 The original text of this verse is in Aramaic.
10:16 Hebrew *the Portion of Jacob.* See note on 5:20.
10:25 Hebrew *devoured Jacob.* See note on 5:20.

their deities are a delusion, incapable of speech or moral action. **17–25:** The poem continues, describing the coming destruction. **23–25:** Salvation and restoration are offered to God's people when their just measure of correction is complete, but they still suffer because their conquerors extend oppression beyond their warrant from God. Objects of just judgment become recipients of divine mercy, as the prayer asks.

Judah's Broken Covenant

11 The LORD gave another message to Jeremiah. He said, [2]"Remind the people of Judah and Jerusalem about the terms of my covenant with them. [3]Say to them, 'This is what the LORD, the God of Israel, says: Cursed is anyone who does not obey the terms of my covenant! [4]For I said to your ancestors when I brought them out of the iron-smelting furnace of Egypt, "If you obey me and do whatever I command you, then you will be my people, and I will be your God." [5]I said this so I could keep my promise to your ancestors to give you a land flowing with milk and honey—the land you live in today.' "

Then I replied, "Amen, LORD! May it be so."

[6]Then the LORD said, "Broadcast this message in the streets of Jerusalem. Go from town to town throughout the land and say, 'Remember the ancient covenant, and do everything it requires. [7]For I solemnly warned your ancestors when I brought them out of Egypt, "Obey me!" I have repeated this warning over and over to this day, [8]but your ancestors did not listen or even pay attention. Instead, they stubbornly followed their own evil desires. And because they refused to obey, I brought upon them all the curses described in this covenant.' "

[9]Again the LORD spoke to me and said, "I have discovered a conspiracy against me among the people of Judah and Jerusalem. [10]They have returned to the sins of their forefathers. They have refused to listen to me and are worshiping other gods. Israel and Judah have both broken the covenant I made with their ancestors. [11]Therefore, this is what the LORD says: I am going to bring calamity upon them, and they will not escape. Though they beg for mercy, I will not listen to their cries. [12]Then the people of Judah and Jerusalem will pray to their idols and burn incense before them. But the idols will not save them when disaster strikes! [13]Look now, people of Judah; you have as many gods as you have towns. You have as many altars of shame—altars for burning incense to your god Baal—as there are streets in Jerusalem.

[14]"Pray no more for these people, Jeremiah. Do not weep or pray for them, for I will not listen to them when they cry out to me in distress.

[15] "What right do my beloved people have to
come to my Temple,
when they have done so many immoral
things?
Can their vows and sacrifices prevent their
destruction?
They actually rejoice in doing evil!
[16] I, the LORD, once called them a thriving olive
tree,
beautiful to see and full of good fruit.
But now I have sent the fury of their
enemies
to burn them with fire,
leaving them charred and broken.

[17]"I, the LORD of Heaven's Armies, who planted this olive tree, have ordered it destroyed. For the people of Israel and Judah have done evil, arousing my anger by burning incense to Baal."

A Plot against Jeremiah

[18]Then the LORD told me about the plots my enemies were making against me. [19]I was like a lamb being led to the slaughter. I had no idea that they were planning to kill me! "Let's destroy this man and all his words," they said. "Let's cut him down, so his name will be forgotten forever."

[20] O LORD of Heaven's Armies,
you make righteous judgments,
and you examine the deepest thoughts and
secrets.
Let me see your vengeance against them,
for I have committed my cause to you.

11:1—17:27 The Broken Covenant and Prayers for Help

Most of Jeremiah 11—17 deals with a particular consequence of the broken covenant. The point has been reached when God will not enter into negotiations for covenant renewal. The covenant curses must come into effect. Moses had interceded effectively on behalf of Israel on two occasions when God was ready to break all ties with them.

11:1–17 Judah's Broken Covenant. 2–5: The LORD's covenant with Israel will no longer protect them. Their distant ancestors had accepted God's terms at Sinai—obedience and exclusive worship—but while living in the land they had persistently refused to keep those terms. The LORD declared the covenant broken only after the people refused to heed repeated warnings. **14:** Therefore God will not listen to their prayers for help or to intercession by Jeremiah. The covenant theology in verses 1–17 offers a rationale for the despair and hope expressed in the following prayers and prophecies.

11:18—13:14 Jeremiah's Personal Struggles. 11:18: Anyone speaking out against his own culture is in-

[21]This is what the LORD says about the men of Anathoth who wanted me dead. They had said, "We will kill you if you do not stop prophesying in the LORD's name." [22]So this is what the LORD of Heaven's Armies says about them: "I will punish them! Their young men will die in battle, and their boys and girls will starve to death. [23]Not one of these plotters from Anathoth will survive, for I will bring disaster upon them when their time of punishment comes."

Jeremiah Questions the LORD's Justice

12 [1]LORD, you always give me justice
when I bring a case before you.
So let me bring you this complaint:
Why are the wicked so prosperous?
Why are evil people so happy?
[2]You have planted them,
and they have taken root and prospered.
Your name is on their lips,
but you are far from their hearts.
[3]But as for me, LORD, you know my heart.
You see me and test my thoughts.
Drag these people away like sheep to be butchered!
Set them aside to be slaughtered!
[4]How long must this land mourn?
Even the grass in the fields has withered.
The wild animals and birds have disappeared
because of the evil in the land.
For the people have said,
"The LORD doesn't see what's ahead for us!"

The LORD's Reply to Jeremiah

[5]"If racing against mere men makes you tired,
how will you race against horses?
If you stumble and fall on open ground,
what will you do in the thickets near the Jordan?
[6]Even your brothers, members of your own family,
have turned against you.
They plot and raise complaints against you.
Do not trust them,
no matter how pleasantly they speak.
[7]"I have abandoned my people, my special possession.
I have surrendered my dearest ones to their enemies.
[8]My chosen people have roared at me like a lion of the forest,
so I have treated them with contempt.
[9]My chosen people act like speckled vultures,*
but they themselves are surrounded by vultures.
Bring on the wild animals to pick their corpses clean!
[10]"Many rulers have ravaged my vineyard,
trampling down the vines
and turning all its beauty into a barren wilderness.
[11]They have made it an empty wasteland;
I hear its mournful cry.
The whole land is desolate,
and no one even cares.
[12]On all the bare hilltops,
destroying armies can be seen.
The sword of the LORD devours people
from one end of the nation to the other.
No one will escape!
[13]My people have planted wheat
but are harvesting thorns.
They have worn themselves out,
but it has done them no good.
They will harvest a crop of shame
because of the fierce anger of the LORD."

A Message for Israel's Neighbors

[14]Now this is what the LORD says: "I will uproot
from their land all the evil nations reaching out
for the possession I gave my people Israel. And
I will uproot Judah from among them. [15]But afterward I will return and have compassion on all
of them. I will bring them home to their own
lands again, each nation to its own possession.
[16]And if these nations truly learn the ways of my
people, and if they learn to swear by my name,
saying, 'As surely as the LORD lives' (just as they
taught my people to swear by the name of Baal),
then they will be given a place among my people.

12:9 Or *speckled hyenas.*

evitably going to meet with opposition. **12:1–4:** For Jeremiah, the pain of having to speak judgment is made worse by the pain of rejection and threat from the people he desperately wanted to help. A further agony comes with his own questioning. He knows what he must proclaim but it seems as if the wicked are doing very nicely. (Because of Jeremiah's constant complaining, a "jeremiad" has come to mean a lengthy complaint, a cautionary harangue.) **5–13:** God's response is fairly bracing. He acknowledges Jeremiah's struggles but simply repeats the original message. It could be that the inclusion of the message that Israel's neighbors will not escape the judgment is meant to reassure Jeremiah that this is not a person-

17 But any nation who refuses to obey me will be
uprooted and destroyed. I, the LORD, have spoken!"

Jeremiah's Linen Loincloth

13 This is what the LORD said to me: "Go
and buy a linen loincloth and put it
on, but do not wash it." 2 So I bought
the loincloth as the LORD directed me, and I put
it on.
3 Then the LORD gave me another message:
4 "Take the linen loincloth you are wearing, and
go to the Euphrates River.* Hide it there in a
hole in the rocks." 5 So I went and hid it by the
Euphrates as the LORD had instructed me.
6 A long time afterward the LORD said to me,
"Go back to the Euphrates and get the loincloth I
told you to hide there." 7 So I went to the Euphrates and dug it out of the hole where I had hidden
it. But now it was rotting and falling apart. The
loincloth was good for nothing.
8 Then I received this message from the LORD:
9 "This is what the LORD says: This shows how I
will rot away the pride of Judah and Jerusalem.
10 These wicked people refuse to listen to me. They
stubbornly follow their own desires and worship
other gods. Therefore, they will become like this
loincloth—good for nothing! 11 As a loincloth
clings to a man's waist, so I created Judah and
Israel to cling to me, says the LORD. They were to
be my people, my pride, my glory—an honor to
my name. But they would not listen to me.
12 "So tell them, 'This is what the LORD, the
God of Israel, says: May all your jars be filled
with wine.' And they will reply, 'Of course! Jars
are made to be filled with wine!'
13 "Then tell them, 'No, this is what the LORD
means: I will fill everyone in this land with
drunkenness—from the king sitting on David's
throne to the priests and the prophets, right
down to the common people of Jerusalem. 14 I
will smash them against each other, even parents
against children, says the LORD. I will not let my
pity or mercy or compassion keep me from destroying them.' "

A Warning against Pride

15 Listen and pay attention!
Do not be arrogant, for the LORD has
spoken.
16 Give glory to the LORD your God
before it is too late.
Acknowledge him before he brings darkness
upon you,
causing you to stumble and fall on the
darkening mountains.
For then, when you look for light,
you will find only terrible darkness and
gloom.
17 And if you still refuse to listen,
I will weep alone because of your pride.
My eyes will overflow with tears,
because the LORD's flock will be led away
into exile.

18 Say to the king and his mother,
"Come down from your thrones
and sit in the dust,
for your glorious crowns
will soon be snatched from your heads."

13:4 Hebrew *Perath;* also in 13:5, 6, 7.

---

al campaign against Judah. **13:1–14:** The symbolic picture of Jeremiah's rotted linen underwear depicts the closeness of Judah to God and yet the total destruction that corruption brings. God does have great compassion for his people, but this cannot override his passion for justice and holiness.

13:15–27 Warning against Pride. The consequences of pride listed here illustrate a frequent phenomenon in Jeremiah: God and the Babylonians do the same things. Compare, for example, verse 14 (God: *I will not let my pity or mercy or compassion keep me from destroying them*) and 21:7 (Nebuchadnezzar *will slaughter them and show . . . no mercy, pity, or compassion*). God has chosen to bring the kingdom of Judah to an end "by his [Nebuchadnezzar's] hand" (ESV, Jer 27:8; cf. *I* [the LORD] *will punish any nation that refuses to be his* [Nebuchadnezzar's] *slave*). As a result, a large part of the portrayal of God in Jeremiah corresponds to the portrayal of the Babylonians. One might even say that God takes responsibility for the horrors of warfare as practiced by Babylonians. The LORD took a risk by choosing to depend on Nebuchadnezzar and the Babylonians to execute his judgment, for they retained freedom to act according to their values and ambitions. They exceeded their mandate from God and they suffered judgment. The theme of God's anguish and grief over the suffering of the people under just judgment and excessive Babylonian violence distinguishes the LORD's plan from Nebuchadnezzar's imperial goals. **18:** Pride will destroy rulers and ruled alike. The queen mother and the king addressed here may be Jehoiachin and his mother, Nehushta, who were exiled together. Other queen mothers probably used their political skills and the power of their families to keep their sons in power and secure their own influential position. For instance, Athaliah (the grand-

19 The towns of the Negev will close their gates,
and no one will be able to open them.
The people of Judah will be taken away as captives.
All will be carried into exile.
20 Open up your eyes and see
the armies marching down from the north!
Where is your flock—
your beautiful flock—
that he gave you to care for?
21 What will you say when the LORD takes the allies you have cultivated
and appoints them as your rulers?
Pangs of anguish will grip you,
like those of a woman in labor!
22 You may ask yourself,
"Why is all this happening to me?"
It is because of your many sins!
That is why you have been stripped
and raped by invading armies.
23 Can an Ethiopian* change the color of his skin?
Can a leopard take away its spots?
Neither can you start doing good,
for you have always done evil.

24 "I will scatter you like chaff
that is blown away by the desert winds.
25 This is your allotment,
the portion I have assigned to you,"
says the LORD,
"for you have forgotten me,
putting your trust in false gods.
26 I myself will strip you
and expose you to shame.
27 I have seen your adultery and lust,
and your disgusting idol worship out in the fields and on the hills.
What sorrow awaits you, Jerusalem!
How long before you are pure?"

Judah's Terrible Drought

14 This message came to Jeremiah from the LORD, explaining why he was holding back the rain:

2 "Judah wilts;
commerce at the city gates grinds to a halt.
All the people sit on the ground in mourning,
and a great cry rises from Jerusalem.
3 The nobles send servants to get water,
but all the wells are dry.
The servants return with empty pitchers,
confused and desperate,
covering their heads in grief.
4 The ground is parched
and cracked for lack of rain.
The farmers are deeply troubled;
they, too, cover their heads.
5 Even the doe abandons her newborn fawn
because there is no grass in the field.
6 The wild donkeys stand on the bare hills
panting like thirsty jackals.
They strain their eyes looking for grass,
but there is none to be found."

7 The people say, "Our wickedness has caught up with us, LORD,
but help us for the sake of your own reputation.
We have turned away from you
and sinned against you again and again.
8 O Hope of Israel, our Savior in times of trouble,
why are you like a stranger to us?
Why are you like a traveler passing through the land,
stopping only for the night?
9 Are you also confused?
Is our champion helpless to save us?

13:23 Hebrew *a Cushite.*

---

mother of Joash, 2 Kgs 11) certainly did this. Asa, in his religious reforms, removed Maacah as queen mother because she set up an Asherah image. Nehushta's status at court is implied when in the 597 BC list of exiles she comes after the king and before other court officials (2 Kgs 24:8, 15). **20–27:** Jerusalem is personified as a woman who will be humbled by conquest because she worshiped other gods. The humiliation of nakedness is emphasized (see also 2 Sam 10:1–5; Isa 20:1–4). Having the freedom and means to maintain the privacy of one's body is a basic human need. By exposing private parts of the conquered enemy the victors deprived them of dignity and revealed their powerlessness to defend themselves or others in their care. When applied to a nation or city, the threat of exposing nakedness is metaphorical, and it is the conqueror's act, not the husband's. Fortifications constituted a city's clothes: A naked city has had its walls breached or gate broken so she can no longer control who enters to plunder and kill. **22, 26:** Knowledge of human nature and the violence done by conquering armies makes it likely that the rape mentioned is literal.

14:1–22 Judah's Terrible Drought. 11: After declaring the covenant broken, God forbids Jeremiah to pray for the people. A series of prayers by the people alternating with words from God illustrate this deci-

You are right here among us, LORD.
We are known as your people.
Please don't abandon us now!"

10 So this is what the LORD says to his people:
"You love to wander far from me
and do not restrain yourselves.
Therefore, I will no longer accept you as my people.
Now I will remember all your wickedness
and will punish you for your sins."

The LORD Forbids Jeremiah to Intercede

11 Then the LORD said to me, "Do not pray for
these people anymore. 12 When they fast, I will
pay no attention. When they present their burnt
offerings and grain offerings to me, I will not accept them. Instead, I will devour them with war,
famine, and disease."

13 Then I said, "O Sovereign LORD, their
prophets are telling them, 'All is well—no war
or famine will come. The LORD will surely send
you peace.' "

14 Then the LORD said, "These prophets are
telling lies in my name. I did not send them
or tell them to speak. I did not give them any
messages. They prophesy of visions and revelations they have never seen or heard. They speak
foolishness made up in their own lying hearts.
15 Therefore, this is what the LORD says: I will
punish these lying prophets, for they have spoken in my name even though I never sent them.
They say that no war or famine will come, but
they themselves will die by war and famine!
16 As for the people to whom they prophesy—
their bodies will be thrown out into the streets of
Jerusalem, victims of famine and war. There will
be no one left to bury them. Husbands, wives,
sons, and daughters—all will be gone. For I will
pour out their own wickedness on them. 17 Now,
Jeremiah, say this to them:

"Night and day my eyes overflow with tears.
I cannot stop weeping,
for my virgin daughter—my precious people—
has been struck down
and lies mortally wounded.
18 If I go out into the fields,
I see the bodies of people slaughtered by the enemy.
If I walk the city streets,
I see people who have died of starvation.
The prophets and priests continue with their work,
but they don't know what they're doing."

A Prayer for Healing

19 LORD, have you completely rejected Judah?
Do you really hate Jerusalem?*
Why have you wounded us past all hope of healing?
We hoped for peace, but no peace came.
We hoped for a time of healing, but found only terror.
20 LORD, we confess our wickedness
and that of our ancestors, too.
We all have sinned against you.
21 For the sake of your reputation, LORD, do not abandon us.
Do not disgrace your own glorious throne.
Please remember us,
and do not break your covenant with us.

22 Can any of the worthless foreign gods send us rain?
Does it fall from the sky by itself?
No, you are the one, O LORD our God!
Only you can do such things.
So we will wait for you to help us.

Judah's Inevitable Doom

15 Then the LORD said to me, "Even if
Moses and Samuel stood before me
pleading for these people, I wouldn't
help them. Away with them! Get them out of my
sight! 2 And if they say to you, 'But where can we
go?' tell them, 'This is what the LORD says:

" 'Those who are destined for death, to death;
those who are destined for war, to war;
those who are destined for famine, to famine;
those who are destined for captivity, to captivity.'

3 "I will send four kinds of destroyers against
them," says the LORD. "I will send the sword to
kill, the dogs to drag away, the vultures to devour, and the wild animals to finish up what is

14:19 Hebrew *Zion?*

sion (14:7—15:9). **20–21:** Although the people confess their faults and plead with God not to abandon them, it seems it is too little, too late.

15:1–9 Judah's Inevitable Doom. The people's pleading does not make God relent. Exile, loss of the land, and dissolution of institutions of national life are the unchangeable consequences of covenant violation. The sufferings of individual women and of personified Jerusalem are highlighted.

left. [4] Because of the wicked things Manasseh son of Hezekiah, king of Judah, did in Jerusalem, I will make my people an object of horror to all the kingdoms of the earth.

[5] "Who will feel sorry for you, Jerusalem?
Who will weep for you?
Who will even bother to ask how you are?
[6] You have abandoned me
and turned your back on me,"
says the LORD.
"Therefore, I will raise my fist to destroy you.
I am tired of always giving you another chance.
[7] I will winnow you like grain at the gates of your cities
and take away the children you hold dear.
I will destroy my own people,
because they refuse to change their evil ways.
[8] There will be more widows
than the grains of sand on the seashore.
At noontime I will bring a destroyer
against the mothers of young men.
I will cause anguish and terror
to come upon them suddenly.
[9] The mother of seven grows faint and gasps for breath;
her sun has gone down while it is still day.
She sits childless now,
disgraced and humiliated.
And I will hand over those who are left
to be killed by the enemy.
I, the LORD, have spoken!"

Jeremiah's Complaint

[10] Then I said,

"What sorrow is mine, my mother.
Oh, that I had died at birth!
I am hated everywhere I go.
I am neither a lender who threatens to foreclose
nor a borrower who refuses to pay—
yet they all curse me."

[11] The LORD replied,

"I will take care of you, Jeremiah.
Your enemies will ask you to plead on their behalf
in times of trouble and distress.
[12] Can a man break a bar of iron from the north,
or a bar of bronze?
[13] At no cost to them,
I will hand over your wealth and treasures
as plunder to your enemies,
for sin runs rampant in your land.
[14] I will tell your enemies to take you
as captives to a foreign land.
For my anger blazes like a fire
that will burn forever.*"

[15] Then I said,

"LORD, you know what's happening to me.
Please step in and help me. Punish my persecutors!
Please give me time; don't let me die young.
It's for your sake that I am suffering.
[16] When I discovered your words, I devoured them.
They are my joy and my heart's delight,
for I bear your name,
O LORD God of Heaven's Armies.
[17] I never joined the people in their merry feasts.
I sat alone because your hand was on me.
I was filled with indignation at their sins.
[18] Why then does my suffering continue?
Why is my wound so incurable?
Your help seems as uncertain as a seasonal brook,
like a spring that has gone dry."

[19] This is how the LORD responds:

"If you return to me, I will restore you
so you can continue to serve me.
If you speak good words rather than worthless ones,
you will be my spokesman.
You must influence them;
do not let them influence you!
[20] They will fight against you like an attacking army,
but I will make you as secure as a fortified wall of bronze.
They will not conquer you,

15:14 As in some Hebrew manuscripts (see also 17:4); most Hebrew manuscripts read *will burn against you.*

8–9: Instead of picturing soldiers dead on the battlefield, Jeremiah indicates uncountable widows and bereaved mothers. God had promised Abraham descendants as numerous as grains of sand on the shore; here, the number of widows will exceed that count.

15:10—16:4 Jeremiah's Complaint. 15:10: The focus on women continues as Jeremiah requests his mother to witness his own struggles. His task seems too hard to bear. **19:** It is interesting that God's message to him parallels the message to Judah: If he

for I am with you to protect and rescue you.
I, the LORD, have spoken!
21 Yes, I will certainly keep you safe from these
wicked men.
I will rescue you from their cruel hands."

Jeremiah Forbidden to Marry

16 The LORD gave me another message.
He said, 2 "Do not get married or have
children in this place. 3 For this is what
the LORD says about the children born here in
this city and about their mothers and fathers:
4 They will die from terrible diseases. No one will
mourn for them or bury them, and they will lie
scattered on the ground like manure. They will
die from war and famine, and their bodies will be
food for the vultures and wild animals."

Judah's Coming Punishment

5 This is what the LORD says: "Do not go to funerals to mourn and show sympathy for these
people, for I have removed my protection and
peace from them. I have taken away my unfailing love and my mercy. 6 Both the great and
the lowly will die in this land. No one will bury
them or mourn for them. Their friends will not
cut themselves in sorrow or shave their heads
in sadness. 7 No one will offer a meal to comfort
those who mourn for the dead—not even at the
death of a mother or father. No one will send a
cup of wine to console them.
8 "And do not go to their feasts and parties.
Do not eat and drink with them at all. 9 For this
is what the LORD of Heaven's Armies, the God
of Israel, says: In your own lifetime, before your
very eyes, I will put an end to the happy singing and laughter in this land. The joyful voices of
bridegrooms and brides will no longer be heard.
10 "When you tell the people all these things,
they will ask, 'Why has the LORD decreed such
terrible things against us? What have we done to
deserve such treatment? What is our sin against
the LORD our God?'
11 "Then you will give them the LORD's reply:
'It is because your ancestors were unfaithful to
me. They worshiped other gods and served them.
They abandoned me and did not obey my word.
12 And you are even worse than your ancestors!
You stubbornly follow your own evil desires
and refuse to listen to me. 13 So I will throw you
out of this land and send you into a foreign land
where you and your ancestors have never been.
There you can worship idols day and night—and
I will grant you no favors!'

Hope despite the Disaster

14 "But the time is coming," says the LORD, "when
people who are taking an oath will no longer say,
'As surely as the LORD lives, who rescued the
people of Israel from the land of Egypt.' 15 Instead, they will say, 'As surely as the LORD lives,
who brought the people of Israel back to their
own land from the land of the north and from
all the countries to which he had exiled them.'
For I will bring them back to this land that I gave
their ancestors.
16 "But now I am sending for many fishermen who will catch them," says the LORD. "I am
sending for hunters who will hunt them down
in the mountains, hills, and caves. 17 I am watching them closely, and I see every sin. They cannot hope to hide from me. 18 I will double their
punishment for all their sins, because they have
defiled my land with lifeless images of their detestable gods and have filled my territory with
their evil deeds."

Jeremiah's Prayer of Confidence

19 LORD, you are my strength and fortress,
my refuge in the day of trouble!
Nations from around the world
will come to you and say,
"Our ancestors left us a foolish heritage,
for they worshiped worthless idols.
20 Can people make their own gods?
These are not real gods at all!"

21 The LORD says,
"Now I will show them my power;
now I will show them my might.
At last they will know and understand
that I am the LORD.

---

returns, he will be restored. Here, Jeremiah needs to refocus; his task will never be easy, but he will be kept safe. **16:1–4:** The LORD commanded him to remain unmarried and childless *in this place*. This unique way of life would be a demonstration of the judgment to come. Jeremiah was deprived of children and therefore a future for his name, just like the people. Throughout this chapter, there is a constant repetition of the phrase *what the LORD says*.

16:5–21 Hope Does Follow Punishment. The description of the coming disaster is again reinforced, but after all these struggles and problems, a note of hope is introduced. God summarizes his plan for Israel, including restoration after exile: *I will bring them back to this land that I gave their ancestors.*

Judah's Sin and Punishment

17 [1]"The sin of Judah
is inscribed with an iron chisel—
engraved with a diamond point on
their stony hearts
and on the corners of their altars.
[2] Even their children go to worship
at their pagan altars and Asherah poles,
beneath every green tree
and on every high hill.
[3] So I will hand over my holy mountain—
along with all your wealth and treasures
and your pagan shrines—
as plunder to your enemies,
for sin runs rampant in your land.
[4] The wonderful possession I have reserved for
you
will slip from your hands.
I will tell your enemies to take you
as captives to a foreign land.
For my anger blazes like a fire
that will burn forever."

Wisdom from the LORD

[5] This is what the LORD says:
"Cursed are those who put their trust in mere
humans,
who rely on human strength
and turn their hearts away from the LORD.
[6] They are like stunted shrubs in the desert,
with no hope for the future.
They will live in the barren wilderness,
in an uninhabited salty land.

[7] "But blessed are those who trust in the LORD
and have made the LORD their hope and
confidence.
[8] They are like trees planted along a riverbank,
with roots that reach deep into the water.
Such trees are not bothered by the heat
or worried by long months of drought.
Their leaves stay green,
and they never stop producing fruit.

[9] "The human heart is the most deceitful of all
things,
and desperately wicked.
Who really knows how bad it is?
[10] But I, the LORD, search all hearts
and examine secret motives.
I give all people their due rewards,
according to what their actions deserve."

Jeremiah's Trust in the LORD

[11] Like a partridge that hatches eggs she has not
laid,
so are those who get their wealth by unjust
means.
At midlife they will lose their riches;
in the end, they will become poor old fools.
[12] But we worship at your throne—
eternal, high, and glorious!
[13] O LORD, the hope of Israel,
all who turn away from you will be
disgraced.
They will be buried in the dust of the earth,
for they have abandoned the LORD, the
fountain of living water.

[14] O LORD, if you heal me, I will be truly
healed;
if you save me, I will be truly saved.
My praises are for you alone!
[15] People scoff at me and say,
"What is this 'message from the LORD' you
talk about?
Why don't your predictions come true?"

[16] LORD, I have not abandoned my job
as a shepherd for your people.
I have not urged you to send disaster.
You have heard everything I've said.
[17] LORD, don't terrorize me!
You alone are my hope in the day of
disaster.
[18] Bring shame and dismay on all who
persecute me,

Jeremiah's concluding prayer echoes Psalm 46.

17:1–10: Judah has turned everything upside down; evil rather than good is seen as the law. Jeremiah's wonderful ability with images comes out again as he speaks of inscriptions with diamond points on stony hearts, of great treasures slipping away, and of barren wilderness chosen in preference to luxurious riverside growth. It was important that the people understood what they were doing, the consequences of their actions, and the alternative future for those who were not party to such actions.

17:11–18 Jeremiah's Trust in the LORD. 14–18: Here we have the third of Jeremiah's prayers or confessions (11:18—12:6; 15:10–21). In each instance Jeremiah contends with God over the pain and distress he suffers as a prophet. Jeremiah's complaints serve as further evidence against the people. His enemies stand under divine judgment, and persecuting Jeremiah compounds their guilt. Jeremiah follows the conventions of other laments and asks for vindication from his enemies. When judgment falls on Judah and Jerusalem those prayers will be fulfilled. Jeremiah's survival depends solely on

but don't let me experience shame and
dismay.
Bring a day of terror on them.
Yes, bring double destruction upon them!

Observing the Sabbath

19 This is what the LORD said to me: "Go and
stand in the gates of Jerusalem, first in the gate
where the king goes in and out, and then in each
of the other gates. 20 Say to all the people, 'Listen to this message from the LORD, you kings
of Judah and all you people of Judah and everyone living in Jerusalem. 21 This is what the LORD
says: Listen to my warning! Stop carrying on
your trade at Jerusalem's gates on the Sabbath
day. 22 Do not do your work on the Sabbath,
but make it a holy day. I gave this command to
your ancestors, 23 but they did not listen or obey.
They stubbornly refused to pay attention or accept my discipline.
24 " 'But if you obey me, says the LORD, and do
not carry on your trade at the gates or work on the
Sabbath day, and if you keep it holy, 25 then kings
and their officials will go in and out of these gates
forever. There will always be a descendant of David
sitting on the throne here in Jerusalem. Kings and
their officials will always ride in and out among
the people of Judah in chariots and on horses,
and this city will remain forever. 26 And from all
around Jerusalem, from the towns of Judah and
Benjamin, from the western foothills* and the hill
country and the Negev, the people will come with
their burnt offerings and sacrifices. They will bring
their grain offerings, frankincense, and thanksgiving offerings to the LORD's Temple.
27 " 'But if you do not listen to me and refuse
to keep the Sabbath holy, and if on the Sabbath
day you bring loads of merchandise through the
gates of Jerusalem just as on other days, then I
will set fire to these gates. The fire will spread to
the palaces, and no one will be able to put out the
roaring flames.' "

The Potter and the Clay

18 The LORD gave another message to
Jeremiah. He said, 2 "Go down to the
potter's shop, and I will speak to you
there." 3 So I did as he told me and found the
potter working at his wheel. 4 But the jar he was
making did not turn out as he had hoped, so he
crushed it into a lump of clay again and started
over.
5 Then the LORD gave me this message:
6 "O Israel, can I not do to you as this potter has
done to his clay? As the clay is in the potter's
hand, so are you in my hand. 7 If I announce that
a certain nation or kingdom is to be uprooted,
torn down, and destroyed, 8 but then that nation
renounces its evil ways, I will not destroy it as I
had planned. 9 And if I announce that I will plant
and build up a certain nation or kingdom, 10 but
then that nation turns to evil and refuses to obey
me, I will not bless it as I said I would.
11 "Therefore, Jeremiah, go and warn all Judah and Jerusalem. Say to them, 'This is what
the LORD says: I am planning disaster for you instead of good. So turn from your evil ways, each
of you, and do what is right.' "
12 But the people replied, "Don't waste your
breath. We will continue to live as we want to,
stubbornly following our own evil desires."
13 So this is what the LORD says:

"Has anyone ever heard of such a thing,
even among the pagan nations?
My virgin daughter Israel
has done something terrible!
14 Does the snow ever disappear from the
mountaintops of Lebanon?
Do the cold streams flowing from those
distant mountains ever run dry?
15 But my people are not so reliable, for they
have deserted me;

17:26 Hebrew *the Shephelah.*

God, who had promised to be with him and defend him.

17:19–27: Again we hear the repeated phrases of this book: *This is what the LORD said*. An obvious sign that Judah had rejected God was a refusal to keep the Sabbath. Making money was more important than obeying God. There are strong parallels here with the situation in Nehemiah 13:15–22 (cf. Neh 10:31). The Sabbath breaking may have only been a small part of their offense against God, but it was a good test of the people's willingness to change.

18:1—20:18 The Last Chance Refused

These chapters show the people refusing their last chance to repent and be spared. **18:1–17:** Two examples from pottery making illustrate this development. **2–10:** In the first a potter changes his plan for a lump of clay. It could be remade into another shape while it was still moist and malleable. God had planned good things for Israel, but they had disobeyed. **11–17:** Through Jeremiah the LORD had declared the plan to break and destroy them, but they could still choose to turn from their wick-

they burn incense to worthless idols.
They have stumbled off the ancient highways
and walk in muddy paths.
16 Therefore, their land will become desolate,
a monument to their stupidity.
All who pass by will be astonished
and will shake their heads in amazement.
17 I will scatter my people before their enemies
as the east wind scatters dust.
And in all their trouble I will turn my back
on them
and refuse to notice their distress."

A Plot against Jeremiah

18 Then the people said, "Come on, let's plot a way to stop Jeremiah. We have plenty of priests and wise men and prophets. We don't need him to teach the word and give us advice and prophecies. Let's spread rumors about him and ignore what he says."

19 LORD, hear me and help me!
Listen to what my enemies are saying.
20 Should they repay evil for good?
They have dug a pit to kill me,
though I pleaded for them
and tried to protect them from your anger.
21 So let their children starve!
Let them die by the sword!
Let their wives become childless widows.
Let their old men die in a plague,
and let their young men be killed in battle!
22 Let screaming be heard from their homes
as warriors come suddenly upon them.
For they have dug a pit for me
and have hidden traps along my path.
23 LORD, you know all about their murderous
plots against me.
Don't forgive their crimes and blot out
their sins.
Let them die before you.
Deal with them in your anger.

Jeremiah's Shattered Jar

19 This is what the LORD said to me: "Go
and buy a clay jar. Then ask some of
the leaders of the people and of the
priests to follow you. 2 Go out through the Gate
of Broken Pots to the garbage dump in the valley of Ben-Hinnom, and give them this message.
3 Say to them, 'Listen to this message from the
LORD, you kings of Judah and citizens of Jerusalem! This is what the LORD of Heaven's Armies,
the God of Israel, says: I will bring a terrible disaster on this place, and the ears of those who
hear about it will ring!
4 " 'For Israel has forsaken me and turned
this valley into a place of wickedness. The people
burn incense to foreign gods—idols never before
acknowledged by this generation, by their ancestors, or by the kings of Judah. And they have
filled this place with the blood of innocent children. 5 They have built pagan shrines to Baal, and
there they burn their sons as sacrifices to Baal. I
have never commanded such a horrible deed; it
never even crossed my mind to command such a
thing! 6 So beware, for the time is coming, says
the LORD, when this garbage dump will no longer
be called Topheth or the valley of Ben-Hinnom,
but the Valley of Slaughter.
7 " 'For I will upset the careful plans of Judah and Jerusalem. I will allow the people to be
slaughtered by invading armies, and I will leave
their dead bodies as food for the vultures and
wild animals. 8 I will reduce Jerusalem to ruins,
making it a monument to their stupidity. All
who pass by will be astonished and will gasp at
the destruction they see there. 9 I will see to it
that your enemies lay siege to the city until all
the food is gone. Then those trapped inside will
eat their own sons and daughters and friends.
They will be driven to utter despair.'
10 "As these men watch you, Jeremiah, smash
the jar you brought. 11 Then say to them, 'This is
what the LORD of Heaven's Armies says: As this

---

ed ways and let God shape their future for good. They refused, however, and chose to be shaped by their own plans. Their national life and institutions would maintain their way rather than the LORD's. **18–23:** Jeremiah was a constant thorn in the flesh of his listeners, and they made constant attempts to remove him—this time not by violence but by discrediting him. He again turns to God for help and expresses all his anger and frustration against them. It is noteworthy that God does not respond to this particular plea! **19:1–15:** Here, we have another reference to pottery. **1, 10:** Once a pot was fired, the only way to change its shape was to break it, rendering it useless. The city shattered by divine judgment is like an unmendable shattered pot. After the decision there will be no turning back from disaster. **4–8:** Once again idolatry is presented as the reason for judgment. The city gate near the pottery shop led to the valley of Ben-Hinnom, where people burned their children as offerings to Baal. Whatever the motivation for such sacrifices verse 4 uses the language of murder to describe the results. **9:** *Utter despair:* A particularly horrible picture of judgment follows this indictment. Jerusalem will be besieged, and the starving people will resort to cannibalism (cf. Ezek 5:10; 2 Kgs 6:24–30 provides a narrative account of

jar lies shattered, so I will shatter the people of Judah and Jerusalem beyond all hope of repair. They
will bury the bodies here in Topheth, the garbage
dump, until there is no more room for them. 12 This
is what I will do to this place and its people, says
the LORD. I will cause this city to become defiled
like Topheth. 13 Yes, all the houses in Jerusalem,
including the palace of Judah's kings, will become
like Topheth—all the houses where you burned incense on the rooftops to your star gods, and where
liquid offerings were poured out to your idols.' "

14 Then Jeremiah returned from Topheth, the
garbage dump where he had delivered this message, and he stopped in front of the Temple of the
LORD. He said to the people there, 15 "This is what
the LORD of Heaven's Armies, the God of Israel,
says: 'I will bring disaster upon this city and its
surrounding towns as I promised, because you
have stubbornly refused to listen to me.' "

Jeremiah and Pashhur

20 Now Pashhur son of Immer, the priest
in charge of the Temple of the LORD,
heard what Jeremiah was prophesy-
ing. 2 So he arrested Jeremiah the prophet and
had him whipped and put in stocks at the Benjamin Gate of the LORD's Temple.

3 The next day, when Pashhur finally released
him, Jeremiah said, "Pashhur, the LORD has
changed your name. From now on you are to be
called 'The Man Who Lives in Terror.'* 4 For this is
what the LORD says: 'I will send terror upon you
and all your friends, and you will watch as they are
slaughtered by the swords of the enemy. I will hand
the people of Judah over to the king of Babylon.
He will take them captive to Babylon or run them
through with the sword. 5 And I will let your enemies plunder Jerusalem. All the famed treasures
of the city—the precious jewels and gold and silver
of your kings—will be carried off to Babylon. 6 As
for you, Pashhur, you and all your household will
go as captives to Babylon. There you will die and
be buried, you and all your friends to whom you
prophesied that everything would be all right.' "

Jeremiah's Complaint

7 O LORD, you misled me,
and I allowed myself to be misled.
You are stronger than I am,
and you overpowered me.
Now I am mocked every day;
everyone laughs at me.
8 When I speak, the words burst out.
"Violence and destruction!" I shout.
So these messages from the LORD
have made me a household joke.
9 But if I say I'll never mention the LORD
or speak in his name,
his word burns in my heart like a fire.
It's like a fire in my bones!
I am worn out trying to hold it in!
I can't do it!
10 I have heard the many rumors about me.
They call me "The Man Who Lives in
Terror."
They threaten, "If you say anything, we will
report it."
Even my old friends are watching me,
waiting for a fatal slip.
"He will trap himself," they say,
"and then we will get our revenge on him."
11 But the LORD stands beside me like a great
warrior.
Before him my persecutors will stumble.
They cannot defeat me.
They will fail and be thoroughly humiliated.
Their dishonor will never be forgotten.
12 O LORD of Heaven's Armies,
you test those who are righteous,
and you examine the deepest thoughts and
secrets.
Let me see your vengeance against them,
for I have committed my cause to you.
13 Sing to the LORD!
Praise the LORD!
For though I was poor and needy,
he rescued me from my oppressors.

14 Yet I curse the day I was born!
May no one celebrate the day of my birth.
15 I curse the messenger who told my father,
"Good news—you have a son!"

20:3 Hebrew *Magor-missabib,* which means "surrounded by terror"; also in 20:10.

this measure of desperation). **20:1–6:** Rejection of the divine word takes the form of persecuting the LORD's prophet. His enemies plotted against Jeremiah, beat him, put him in stocks, and planned to kill him. This time Jeremiah's prayer for vindication coincides with God's announced judgment. **7–18:** Jeremiah's prayer once again follows lament conventions and blames his suffering on God. **10:** He accuses God of persuading or deceiving him and prevailing over him, just like his treacherous friends. God succeeded where they had only planned. **11–13:** Nevertheless, this prayer also expresses confidence in God's help. Jeremiah believes the truth of the judgment oracles he has delivered. **14:** This sixth and final prayer for

[16] Let him be destroyed like the cities of old
that the LORD overthrew without mercy.
Terrify him all day long with battle shouts,
[17] because he did not kill me at birth.
Oh, that I had died in my mother's womb,
that her body had been my grave!
[18] Why was I ever born?
My entire life has been filled
with trouble, sorrow, and shame.

No Deliverance from Babylon

21 The LORD spoke through Jeremiah when King Zedekiah sent Pashhur son of Malkijah and Zephaniah son of Maaseiah, the priest, to speak with him. They begged Jeremiah, [2]"Please speak to the LORD for us and ask him to help us. King Nebuchadnezzar* of Babylon is attacking Judah. Perhaps the LORD will be gracious and do a mighty miracle as he has done in the past. Perhaps he will force Nebuchadnezzar to withdraw his armies."

[3]Jeremiah replied, "Go back to King Zedekiah and tell him, [4]'This is what the LORD, the God of Israel, says: I will make your weapons useless against the king of Babylon and the Babylonians* who are outside your walls attacking you. In fact, I will bring your enemies right into the heart of this city. [5]I myself will fight against you with a strong hand and a powerful arm, for I am very angry. You have made me furious! [6]I will send a terrible plague upon this city, and both people and animals will die. [7]And after all that, says the LORD, I will hand over King Zedekiah, his staff, and everyone else in the city who survives the disease, war, and famine. I will hand them over to King Nebuchadnezzar of Babylon and to their other enemies. He will slaughter them and show them no mercy, pity, or compassion.'

[8]"Tell all the people, 'This is what the LORD says: Take your choice of life or death! [9]Everyone who stays in Jerusalem will die from war, famine, or disease, but those who go out and surrender to the Babylonians will live. Their reward will be life! [10]For I have decided to bring disaster and not good upon this city, says the LORD. It will be handed over to the king of Babylon, and he will reduce it to ashes.'

Judgment on Judah's Kings

[11]"Say to the royal family of Judah, 'Listen to this message from the LORD! [12]This is what the LORD says to the dynasty of David:

"'Give justice each morning to the people
you judge!
Help those who have been robbed;
rescue them from their oppressors.
Otherwise, my anger will burn like an
unquenchable fire
because of all your sins.
[13] I will personally fight against the people in
Jerusalem,
that mighty fortress—
the people who boast, "No one can touch us
here.
No one can break in here."
[14] And I myself will punish you for your
sinfulness,
says the LORD.
I will light a fire in your forests
that will burn up everything around you.'"

A Message for Judah's Kings

22 This is what the LORD said to me: "Go over and speak directly to the king of Judah. Say to him, [2]'Listen

21:2 Hebrew *Nebuchadrezzar,* a variant spelling of Nebuchadnezzar; also in 21:7. **21:4** Or *Chaldeans;* also in 21:9.

help is uniformly negative. Jeremiah's misery is expressed by cursing the day he was born. The LORD had consecrated Jeremiah before birth, so he could have avoided the burden of God's call only by never being born (cf. 15:10). **15:** His father had joyfully received the announcement of his birth, but Jeremiah curses this messenger. If he had been stillborn, he could have avoided the sorrow and shame that fill his life. Jeremiah's question about his own life suggests a parallel question about why Israel was ever born: They have turned down their final opportunity to repent and forfeited their special role as God's chosen people. What has been the meaning of their national life if it ends like this? Jeremiah's survival provides a hint that there will be a future for God's people too. Although Jeremiah's hearers decided against God's word, they were not able to kill God's prophet.

21:1—24:10 Failed Monarchy and False Prophecy

The monarchy was the heart of pride, security, and hope for Judah but it was not going to endure. The last four kings of Judah failed God's basic requirement to execute justice and righteousness. Kings were responsible for delivering the oppressed and protecting the weak. A message is given for each of these kings.

21:1—22:30 Messages for Judah's Kings. 21:3–7:

to this message from the LORD, you king of Judah, sitting on David's throne. Let your attendants and your people listen, too. 3 This is what
the LORD says: Be fair-minded and just. Do what
is right! Help those who have been robbed; rescue them from their oppressors. Quit your evil
deeds! Do not mistreat foreigners, orphans, and
widows. Stop murdering the innocent! 4 If you
obey me, there will always be a descendant of
David sitting on the throne here in Jerusalem.
The king will ride through the palace gates in
chariots and on horses, with his parade of attendants and subjects. 5 But if you refuse to pay
attention to this warning, I swear by my own
name, says the LORD, that this palace will become a pile of rubble.' "

A Message about the Palace

6 Now this is what the LORD says concerning Judah's royal palace:

"I love you as much as fruitful Gilead
and the green forests of Lebanon.
But I will turn you into a desert,
with no one living within your walls.
7 I will call for wreckers,
who will bring out their tools to dismantle
you.
They will tear out all your fine cedar beams
and throw them on the fire.

8 "People from many nations will pass by the
ruins of this city and say to one another, 'Why
did the LORD destroy such a great city?' 9 And
the answer will be, 'Because they violated their
covenant with the LORD their God by worshiping other gods.' "

A Message about Jehoahaz

10 Do not weep for the dead king or mourn his
loss.
Instead, weep for the captive king being led
away!
For he will never return to see his native
land again.

11 For this is what the LORD says about Jehoahaz,* who succeeded his father, King Josiah,
and was taken away as a captive: "He will never
return. 12 He will die in a distant land and will
never again see his own country."

A Message about Jehoiakim

13 And the LORD says, "What sorrow awaits
Jehoiakim,*
who builds his palace with forced labor.*
He builds injustice into its walls,
for he makes his neighbors work for
nothing.
He does not pay them for their labor.
14 He says, 'I will build a magnificent palace
with huge rooms and many windows.
I will panel it throughout with fragrant cedar
and paint it a lovely red.'
15 But a beautiful cedar palace does not make a
great king!
Your father, Josiah, also had plenty to eat
and drink.
But he was just and right in all his dealings.
That is why God blessed him.
16 He gave justice and help to the poor and
needy,
and everything went well for him.
Isn't that what it means to know me?"
says the LORD.
17 "But you! You have eyes only for greed and
dishonesty!
You murder the innocent,
oppress the poor, and reign ruthlessly."

18 Therefore, this is what the LORD says about Jehoiakim, son of King Josiah:

"The people will not mourn for him, crying
to one another,
'Alas, my brother! Alas, my sister!'
His subjects will not mourn for him, crying,
'Alas, our master is dead! Alas, his splendor
is gone!'
19 He will be buried like a dead donkey—
dragged out of Jerusalem and dumped
outside the gates!
20 Weep for your allies in Lebanon.
Shout for them in Bashan.
Search for them in the regions east of the
river.*
See, they are all destroyed.
Not one is left to help you.
21 I warned you when you were prosperous,

22:11 Hebrew *Shallum,* another name for Jehoahaz. **22:13a** The brother and successor of the exiled Jehoahaz. See 22:18. **22:13b** Hebrew *by unrighteousness.* **22:20** Or *in Abarim.*

Zedekiah will be handed over to Nebuchadnezzar, whose victory is certain. Yet again, we read as a constant reminder: *This is what the LORD says.* **22:10–12:** Shallum (Jehoahaz) will never see Judah again; he will die in *a distant land.* **13–23:** Jehoiakim, who had been one of the oppressors, receives a devastating condemnation. No one will mourn him; his body will be treated like a donkey's, *dumped outside the*

but you replied, 'Don't bother me.'
You have been that way since childhood—
you simply will not obey me!
22 And now the wind will blow away your allies.
All your friends will be taken away as
captives.
Surely then you will see your wickedness
and be ashamed.
23 It may be nice to live in a beautiful palace
paneled with wood from the cedars of
Lebanon,
but soon you will groan with pangs of
anguish—
anguish like that of a woman in labor.

A Message for Jehoiachin

24 "As surely as I live," says the LORD, "I will
abandon you, Jehoiachin* son of Jehoiakim, king
of Judah. Even if you were the signet ring on my
right hand, I would pull you off. 25 I will hand
you over to those who seek to kill you, those you
so desperately fear—to King Nebuchadnezzar*
of Babylon and the mighty Babylonian* army.
26 I will expel you and your mother from this
land, and you will die in a foreign country, not in
your native land. 27 You will never again return
to the land you yearn for.

28 "Why is this man Jehoiachin like a discarded,
broken jar?
Why are he and his children to be exiled to
a foreign land?
29 O earth, earth, earth!
Listen to this message from the LORD!
30 This is what the LORD says:
'Let the record show that this man Jehoiachin
was childless.
He is a failure,
for none of his children will succeed him on
the throne of David
to rule over Judah.'

The Righteous Descendant

23 "What sorrow awaits the leaders of
my people—the shepherds of my
sheep—for they have destroyed and
scattered the very ones they were expected to
care for," says the LORD.

2 Therefore, this is what the LORD, the God of
Israel, says to these shepherds: "Instead of caring
for my flock and leading them to safety, you have
deserted them and driven them to destruction.
Now I will pour out judgment on you for the
evil you have done to them. 3 But I will gather
together the remnant of my flock from the
countries where I have driven them. I will bring
them back to their own sheepfold, and they will
be fruitful and increase in number. 4 Then I will
appoint responsible shepherds who will care for
them, and they will never be afraid again. Not
a single one will be lost or missing. I, the LORD,
have spoken!

5 "For the time is coming,"
says the LORD,
"when I will raise up a righteous descendant*
from King David's line.
He will be a King who rules with wisdom.
He will do what is just and right
throughout the land.
6 And this will be his name:
'The LORD Is Our Righteousness.'*
In that day Judah will be saved,
and Israel will live in safety.

7 "In that day," says the LORD, "when people
are taking an oath, they will no longer say, 'As
surely as the LORD lives, who rescued the people of Israel from the land of Egypt.' 8 Instead,
they will say, 'As surely as the LORD lives, who
brought the people of Israel back to their own
land from the land of the north and from all the
countries to which he had exiled them.' Then
they will live in their own land."

Judgment on False Prophets

9 My heart is broken because of the false
prophets,
and my bones tremble.
I stagger like a drunkard,
like someone overcome by wine,
because of the holy words

22:24 Hebrew *Coniah,* a variant spelling of Jehoiachin; also 22:28. **22:25a** Hebrew *Nebuchadrezzar,* a variant spelling of Nebuchadnezzar. **22:25b** Or *Chaldean.* **23:5** Hebrew *a righteous branch.* **23:6** Hebrew *Yahweh Tsidqenu.*

gates of Jerusalem. **24–30:** Coniah (Jehoiachin) will die childless in exile. These kings failed to care for the nation, so they too will be uncared for.

23:1—24:10: In spite of the failure of current leaders, the LORD's plan will include both return from exile and a new king. **23:6:** This descendant of David will so reflect God's will, that he will be named *the LORD Is Our Righteousness*. **9–39:** False prophets, who claimed to speak God's word although God had never spoken to them, or they had never listened, bore much responsibility for Judah's attitudes (v. 18). Jeremiah saw false prophets undermining Judah by encouraging disobedience to God, although any who encourage wor-

the LORD has spoken against them.
10 For the land is full of adultery,
and it lies under a curse.
The land itself is in mourning—
its wilderness pastures are dried up.
For they all do evil
and abuse what power they have.

11 "Even the priests and prophets
are ungodly, wicked men.
I have seen their despicable acts
right here in my own Temple,"
says the LORD.
12 "Therefore, the paths they take
will become slippery.
They will be chased through the dark,
and there they will fall.
For I will bring disaster upon them
at the time fixed for their punishment.
I, the LORD, have spoken!

13 "I saw that the prophets of Samaria were
terribly evil,
for they prophesied in the name of Baal
and led my people of Israel into sin.
14 But now I see that the prophets of Jerusalem
are even worse!
They commit adultery and love
dishonesty.
They encourage those who are doing evil
so that no one turns away from their sins.
These prophets are as wicked
as the people of Sodom and Gomorrah once
were."

15 Therefore, this is what the LORD of Heaven's Armies says concerning the prophets:

"I will feed them with bitterness
and give them poison to drink.
For it is because of Jerusalem's prophets
that wickedness has filled this land."

16 This is what the LORD of Heaven's Armies says to his people:

"Do not listen to these prophets when they
prophesy to you,
filling you with futile hopes.
They are making up everything they say.
They do not speak for the LORD!
17 They keep saying to those who despise my
word,
'Don't worry! The LORD says you will have
peace!'
And to those who stubbornly follow their
own desires,
they say, 'No harm will come your way!'

18 "Have any of these prophets been in the
LORD's presence
to hear what he is really saying?
Has even one of them cared enough to
listen?
19 Look! The LORD's anger bursts out like a
storm,
a whirlwind that swirls down on the heads
of the wicked.
20 The anger of the LORD will not diminish
until it has finished all he has planned.
In the days to come
you will understand all this very clearly.

21 "I have not sent these prophets,
yet they run around claiming to speak for
me.
I have given them no message,
yet they go on prophesying.
22 If they had stood before me and listened to me,
they would have spoken my words,
and they would have turned my people
from their evil ways and deeds.
23 Am I a God who is only close at hand?" says
the LORD.
"No, I am far away at the same time.
24 Can anyone hide from me in a secret place?
Am I not everywhere in all the heavens
and earth?"
says the LORD.

25 "I have heard these prophets say, 'Listen to
the dream I had from God last night.' And then
they proceed to tell lies in my name.
26 How long
will this go on? If they are prophets, they are
prophets of deceit, inventing everything they
say.
27 By telling these false dreams, they are trying to get my people to forget me, just as their
ancestors did by worshiping the idols of Baal.

28 "Let these false prophets tell their dreams,
but let my true messengers faithfully
proclaim my every word.

ship of other gods deserve death (Deut 13:1–5). True prophets should have the opposite effect, turning the people away from evil and back to God. **25–39:** Preaching judgment helped people to recognize their need to repent. False prophets preached peace and well-being, so people saw no need to change. They insisted that Babylon would not conquer and destroy as Jeremiah prophesied. Even after the first conquest

There is a difference between straw and
grain!
29 Does not my word burn like fire?"
says the LORD.
"Is it not like a mighty hammer
that smashes a rock to pieces?

30 "Therefore," says the LORD, "I am against
these prophets who steal messages from each
other and claim they are from me. 31 I am against
these smooth-tongued prophets who say, 'This
prophecy is from the LORD!' 32 I am against
these false prophets. Their imaginary dreams
are flagrant lies that lead my people into sin. I
did not send or appoint them, and they have no
message at all for my people. I, the LORD, have
spoken!

False Prophecies and False Prophets

33 "Suppose one of the people or one of the prophets or priests asks you, 'What prophecy has the
LORD burdened you with now?' You must reply,
'You are the burden!* The LORD says he will
abandon you!'

34 "If any prophet, priest, or anyone else says,
'I have a prophecy from the LORD,' I will punish
that person along with his entire family. 35 You
should keep asking each other, 'What is the
LORD's answer?' or 'What is the LORD saying?'
36 But stop using this phrase, 'prophecy from the
LORD.' For people are using it to give authority to
their own ideas, turning upside down the words
of our God, the living God, the LORD of Heaven's
Armies.

37 "This is what you should say to the prophets: 'What is the LORD's answer?' or 'What is
the LORD saying?' 38 But suppose they respond,
'This is a prophecy from the LORD!' Then you
should say, 'This is what the LORD says: Because
you have used this phrase, "prophecy from the
LORD," even though I warned you not to use
it, 39 I will forget you completely.* I will expel
you from my presence, along with this city that
I gave to you and your ancestors. 40 And I will
make you an object of ridicule, and your name
will be infamous throughout the ages.' "

Good and Bad Figs

24 After King Nebuchadnezzar* of Babylon exiled Jehoiachin* son of Jehoiakim, king of Judah, to Babylon along
with the officials of Judah and all the craftsmen
and artisans, the LORD gave me this vision. I saw
two baskets of figs placed in front of the LORD's
Temple in Jerusalem. 2 One basket was filled with
fresh, ripe figs, while the other was filled with
bad figs that were too rotten to eat.

3 Then the LORD said to me, "What do you
see, Jeremiah?"

I replied, "Figs, some very good and some
very bad, too rotten to eat."

4 Then the LORD gave me this message: 5 "This
is what the LORD, the God of Israel, says: The good
figs represent the exiles I sent from Judah to the
land of the Babylonians.* 6 I will watch over and
care for them, and I will bring them back here
again. I will build them up and not tear them
down. I will plant them and not uproot them. 7 I
will give them hearts that recognize me as the
LORD. They will be my people, and I will be their
God, for they will return to me wholeheartedly.

8 "But the bad figs," the LORD said, "represent King Zedekiah of Judah, his officials, all the
people left in Jerusalem, and those who live in
Egypt. I will treat them like bad figs, too rotten to eat. 9 I will make them an object of horror
and a symbol of evil to every nation on earth.
They will be disgraced and mocked, taunted and
cursed, wherever I scatter them. 10 And I will send
war, famine, and disease until they have vanished
from the land of Israel, which I gave to them and
their ancestors."

Seventy Years of Captivity

25 This message for all the people of Judah came to Jeremiah from the LORD
during the fourth year of Jehoiakim's

23:33 As in Greek version and Latin Vulgate; Hebrew reads *What burden?* **23:39** Some Hebrew manuscripts and Greek version read *I will surely lift you up.* **24:1a** Hebrew *Nebuchadrezzar,* a variant spelling of Nebuchadnezzar. **24:1b** Hebrew *Jeconiah,* a variant spelling of Jehoiachin. **24:5** Or *Chaldeans.*

of Jerusalem and the exile of Jehoiachin, the false prophets preached peace, suggesting that the worst was now over. They were wrong! **24:1–10:** A parable of good versus rotten figs illustrates the contrast. Figs that were too rotten to eat represented Zedekiah and his colleagues, who would be similarly destroyed. **4:** The exiles of 597 BC, however, were represented by good figs. Those who accept divine judgment receive God's promised future. They will return and be built up in the land. Their hearts will be changed and they will follow only the LORD, once again becoming God's covenant people.

25:1–38 The LORD's People among the Nations

The God of Israel claims a scope of authority as wide as the known world and a direct responsibility for the affairs of other nations. (In the Septuagint the oracles

reign over Judah.* This was the year when King
Nebuchadnezzar* of Babylon began his reign.
2 Jeremiah the prophet said to all the people
in Judah and Jerusalem, 3 "For the past twenty-
three years—from the thirteenth year of the
reign of Josiah son of Amon,* king of Judah, until now—the LORD has been giving me his messages. I have faithfully passed them on to you,
but you have not listened.
4 "Again and again the LORD has sent you his
servants, the prophets, but you have not listened
or even paid attention. 5 Each time the message
was this: 'Turn from the evil road you are traveling and from the evil things you are doing. Only
then will I let you live in this land that the LORD
gave to you and your ancestors forever. 6 Do not
provoke my anger by worshiping idols you made
with your own hands. Then I will not harm you.'
7 "But you would not listen to me," says the
LORD. "You made me furious by worshiping idols
you made with your own hands, bringing on yourselves all the disasters you now suffer. 8 And now
the LORD of Heaven's Armies says: Because you
have not listened to me, 9 I will gather together all
the armies of the north under King Nebuchadnezzar of Babylon, whom I have appointed as my
deputy. I will bring them all against this land and
its people and against the surrounding nations. I
will completely destroy* you and make you an
object of horror and contempt and a ruin forever.
10 I will take away your happy singing and laughter. The joyful voices of bridegrooms and brides
will no longer be heard. Your millstones will fall
silent, and the lights in your homes will go out.
11 This entire land will become a desolate wasteland. Israel and her neighboring lands will serve
the king of Babylon for seventy years.
12 "Then, after the seventy years of captivity
are over, I will punish the king of Babylon and
his people for their sins," says the LORD. "I will
make the country of the Babylonians* a wasteland forever. 13 I will bring upon them all the terrors I have promised in this book—all the penalties announced by Jeremiah against the nations.
14 Many nations and great kings will enslave the
Babylonians, just as they enslaved my people. I
will punish them in proportion to the suffering
they cause my people."

The Cup of the LORD's Anger

15 This is what the LORD, the God of Israel, said
to me: "Take from my hand this cup filled to the
brim with my anger, and make all the nations
to whom I send you drink from it. 16 When they
drink from it, they will stagger, crazed by the
warfare I will send against them."
17 So I took the cup of anger from the LORD
and made all the nations drink from it—every
nation to which the LORD sent me. 18 I went to Jerusalem and the other towns of Judah, and their
kings and officials drank from the cup. From that
day until this, they have been a desolate ruin,
an object of horror, contempt, and cursing. 19 I
gave the cup to Pharaoh, king of Egypt, his attendants, his officials, and all his people, 20 along
with all the foreigners living in that land. I also
gave it to all the kings of the land of Uz and the
kings of the Philistine cities of Ashkelon, Gaza,
Ekron, and what remains of Ashdod. 21 Then I
gave the cup to the nations of Edom, Moab, and
Ammon, 22 and the kings of Tyre and Sidon, and
the kings of the regions across the sea. 23 I gave it
to Dedan, Tema, and Buz, and to the people who
live in distant places.* 24 I gave it to the kings of
Arabia, the kings of the nomadic tribes of the
desert, 25 and to the kings of Zimri, Elam, and
Media. 26 And I gave it to the kings of the northern countries, far and near, one after the other—
all the kingdoms of the world. And finally, the
king of Babylon* himself drank from the cup of
the LORD's anger.
27 Then the LORD said to me, "Now tell them,
'This is what the LORD of Heaven's Armies,
the God of Israel, says: Drink from this cup of
my anger. Get drunk and vomit; fall to rise no
more, for I am sending terrible wars against you.'
28 And if they refuse to accept the cup, tell them,
'The LORD of Heaven's Armies says: You have
no choice but to drink from it. 29 I have begun to
punish Jerusalem, the city that bears my name.
Now should I let you go unpunished? No, you
will not escape disaster. I will call for war against
all the nations of the earth. I, the LORD of Heav-
en's Armies, have spoken!'
30 "Now prophesy all these things, and say to
them,

25:1a The fourth year of Jehoiakim's reign and the accession year of Nebuchadnezzar's reign was 605 B.C. **25:1b** Hebrew *Nebuchadrezzar,* a variant spelling of Nebuchadnezzar; also in 25:9. **25:3** The thirteenth year of Josiah's reign was 627 B.C. **25:9** The Hebrew term used here refers to the complete consecration of things or people to the LORD, either by destroying them or by giving them as an offering. **25:12** Or *Chaldeans.* **25:23** Or *who clip the corners of their hair.* **25:26** Hebrew *of Sheshach,* a code name for Babylon.

against foreign nations [chaps. 46—51] are all found in the middle of chap. 25.) The world of the ancient Near East was falling apart, but the LORD had not lost control. The Babylonians' domination would last seventy years; then they will be repaid by the use of their own methods.

" 'The LORD will roar against his own land
from his holy dwelling in heaven.
He will shout like those who tread grapes;
he will shout against everyone on earth.
[31] His cry of judgment will reach the ends of the
earth,
for the LORD will bring his case against all
the nations.
He will judge all the people of the earth,
slaughtering the wicked with the sword.
I, the LORD, have spoken!' "

[32] This is what the LORD of Heaven's Armies
says:
"Look! Disaster will fall upon nation after
nation!
A great whirlwind of fury is rising
from the most distant corners of the earth!"

[33] In that day those the LORD has slaughtered
will fill the earth from one end to the other. No
one will mourn for them or gather up their bodies to bury them. They will be scattered on the
ground like manure.

[34] Weep and moan, you evil shepherds!
Roll in the dust, you leaders of the flock!
The time of your slaughter has arrived;
you will fall and shatter like a fragile vase.
[35] You will find no place to hide;
there will be no way to escape.
[36] Listen to the frantic cries of the shepherds.
The leaders of the flock are wailing in
despair,
for the LORD is ruining their pastures.
[37] Peaceful meadows will be turned into a
wasteland
by the LORD's fierce anger.
[38] He has left his den like a strong lion seeking
its prey,
and their land will be made desolate
by the sword of the enemy
and the LORD's fierce anger.

Jeremiah's Escape from Death

26 This message came to Jeremiah from
the LORD early in the reign of Jehoiakim son of Josiah,* king of Ju-
dah. [2] "This is what the LORD says: Stand in the
courtyard in front of the Temple of the LORD, and
make an announcement to the people who have
come there to worship from all over Judah. Give
them my entire message; include every word.
[3] Perhaps they will listen and turn from their evil
ways. Then I will change my mind about the disaster I am ready to pour out on them because
of their sins.
[4] "Say to them, 'This is what the LORD says:
If you will not listen to me and obey my word
I have given you, [5] and if you will not listen to
my servants, the prophets—for I sent them again
and again to warn you, but you would not listen
to them—[6] then I will destroy this Temple as I
destroyed Shiloh, the place where the Tabernacle
was located. And I will make Jerusalem an object
of cursing in every nation on earth.' "
[7] The priests, the prophets, and all the people
listened to Jeremiah as he spoke in front of the
LORD's Temple. [8] But when Jeremiah had finished his message, saying everything the LORD
had told him to say, the priests and prophets and
all the people at the Temple mobbed him. "Kill
him!" they shouted. [9] "What right do you have
to prophesy in the LORD's name that this Temple
will be destroyed like Shiloh? What do you mean,
saying that Jerusalem will be destroyed and left
with no inhabitants?" And all the people threatened him as he stood in front of the Temple.
[10] When the officials of Judah heard what was
happening, they rushed over from the palace and
sat down at the New Gate of the Temple to hold
court. [11] The priests and prophets presented their
accusations to the officials and the people. "This
man should die!" they said. "You have heard
with your own ears what a traitor he is, for he
has prophesied against this city."
[12] Then Jeremiah spoke to the officials and the
people in his own defense. "The LORD sent me to
prophesy against this Temple and this city," he
said. "The LORD gave me every word that I have
spoken. [13] But if you stop your sinning and begin
to obey the LORD your God, he will change his
mind about this disaster that he has announced
against you. [14] As for me, I am in your hands—do

26:1 The first year of Jehoiakim's reign was 608 B.C.

26:1–24 Jeremiah among the Prophets

Jeremiah followed many earlier prophets sent to call Israel to repentance. The purpose of their prophesying had always been that people would listen and change, so God would withhold the threatened disaster. **10–16:** Jeremiah's trial evidences his true prophethood. His proclamation of the destruction of the Temple led to a capital charge. Such a word could, in their view, never have come from God (cf. Deut 18:20). Yet the court ruled that he had spoken God's word in God's name. Readers know that his

with me as you think best. 15 But if you kill me,
rest assured that you will be killing an innocent
man! The responsibility for such a deed will lie
on you, on this city, and on every person living
in it. For it is absolutely true that the LORD sent
me to speak every word you have heard."
16 Then the officials and the people said to the
priests and prophets, "This man does not deserve
the death sentence, for he has spoken to us in the
name of the LORD our God."
17 Then some of the wise old men stood and
spoke to all the people assembled there. 18 They
said, "Remember when Micah of Moresheth
prophesied during the reign of King Hezekiah of
Judah. He told the people of Judah,

'This is what the LORD of Heaven's Armies
says:
Mount Zion will be plowed like an open field;
Jerusalem will be reduced to ruins!
A thicket will grow on the heights
where the Temple now stands.'*

19 But did King Hezekiah and the people kill him
for saying this? No, they turned from their sins
and worshiped the LORD. They begged him for
mercy. Then the LORD changed his mind about
the terrible disaster he had pronounced against
them. So we are about to do ourselves great
harm."
20 At this time Uriah son of Shemaiah from
Kiriath-jearim was also prophesying for the
LORD. And he predicted the same terrible disaster against the city and nation as Jeremiah did.
21 When King Jehoiakim and the army officers
and officials heard what he was saying, the king
sent someone to kill him. But Uriah heard about
the plan and escaped in fear to Egypt. 22 Then
King Jehoiakim sent Elnathan son of Acbor to
Egypt along with several other men to capture
Uriah. 23 They took him prisoner and brought
him back to King Jehoiakim. The king then killed
Uriah with a sword and had him buried in an unmarked grave.
24 Nevertheless, Ahikam son of Shaphan stood
up for Jeremiah and persuaded the court not to
turn him over to the mob to be killed.

Jeremiah Wears an Ox Yoke

27 This message came to Jeremiah from
the LORD early in the reign of Zedekiah* son of Josiah, king of Judah.
2 This is what the LORD said to me: "Make
a yoke, and fasten it on your neck with leather
straps. 3 Then send messages to the kings of Edom,
Moab, Ammon, Tyre, and Sidon through their
ambassadors who have come to see King Zedekiah
in Jerusalem. 4 Give them this message for their
masters: 'This is what the LORD of Heaven's
Armies, the God of Israel, says: 5 With my great
strength and powerful arm I made the earth and
all its people and every animal. I can give these
things of mine to anyone I choose. 6 Now I will
give your countries to King Nebuchadnezzar of
Babylon, who is my servant. I have put everything, even the wild animals, under his control.
7 All the nations will serve him, his son, and his
grandson until his time is up. Then many nations
and great kings will conquer and rule over Babylon. 8 So you must submit to Babylon's king and
serve him; put your neck under Babylon's yoke! I
will punish any nation that refuses to be his slave,
says the LORD. I will send war, famine, and disease
upon that nation until Babylon has conquered it.
9 " 'Do not listen to your false prophets, fortune-tellers, interpreters of dreams, mediums,
and sorcerers who say, "The king of Babylon
will not conquer you." 10 They are all liars, and
their lies will lead to your being driven out of
your land. I will drive you out and send you far

26:18 Mic 3:12. **27:1** As in some Hebrew manuscripts and Syriac version (see also 27:3, 12); most Hebrew manuscripts read *Jehoiakim.*

prophecy came true. **17–24:** The elders' response shows that there were still some "listeners" in the court, but Uriah's death indicates their rarity and the reality of the danger faced by Jeremiah himself. The fear expressed in his earlier prayers was a very real threat.

27:1—29:32 The LORD Reigns

Another message from the LORD to Jeremiah concerning submission to the king of Babylon, and contrasting a wooden ox yoke with a yoke of iron. **27:1–11:** Early in Zedekiah's reign emissaries from surrounding nations came to Jerusalem, apparently to plot rebellion against Nebuchadnezzar. Jeremiah met them with a message, backed by the authority of the Creator God, telling them all to submit to Nebuchadnezzar. As an illustration, Jeremiah wore a yoke, a familiar image of political servitude. If they accepted Nebuchadnezzar's yoke peacefully they would avoid exile or ruin. Similarly, Judah had already experienced one deportation, in 597 BC, but Jerusalem might be spared destruction. **7:** The LORD had granted the Babylonians three generations of rule (cf. seventy years in 25:12; 29:10). Their domination had a time limit, but it was long enough so that Jeremiah's hearers

away to die. 11 But the people of any nation that submits to the king of Babylon will be allowed to stay in their own country to farm the land as usual. I, the LORD, have spoken!' "

12 Then I repeated this same message to King Zedekiah of Judah. "If you want to live, submit to the yoke of the king of Babylon and his people. 13 Why do you insist on dying—you and your people? Why should you choose war, famine, and disease, which the LORD will bring against every nation that refuses to submit to Babylon's king? 14 Do not listen to the false prophets who keep telling you, 'The king of Babylon will not conquer you.' They are liars. 15 This is what the LORD says: 'I have not sent these prophets! They are telling you lies in my name, so I will drive you from this land. You will all die—you and all these prophets, too.' "

16 Then I spoke to the priests and the people and said, "This is what the LORD says: 'Do not listen to your prophets who claim that soon the gold articles taken from my Temple will be returned from Babylon. It is all a lie! 17 Do not listen to them. Surrender to the king of Babylon, and you will live. Why should this whole city be destroyed? 18 If they really are prophets and speak the LORD's messages, let them pray to the LORD of Heaven's Armies. Let them pray that the articles remaining in the LORD's Temple and in the king's palace and in the palaces of Jerusalem will not be carried away to Babylon!'

19 "For the LORD of Heaven's Armies has spoken about the pillars in front of the Temple, the great bronze basin called the Sea, the water carts, and all the other ceremonial articles. 20 King Nebuchadnezzar of Babylon left them here when he exiled Jehoiachin* son of Jehoiakim, king of Judah, to Babylon, along with all the other nobles of Judah and Jerusalem. 21 Yes, this is what the LORD of Heaven's Armies, the God of Israel, says about the precious things still in the Temple and in the palace of Judah's king: 22 'They will all be carried away to Babylon and will stay there until I send for them,' says the LORD. 'Then I will bring them back to Jerusalem again.' "

Jeremiah Condemns Hananiah

28 One day in late summer* of that same year—the fourth year of the reign of Zedekiah, king of Judah—Hananiah son of Azzur, a prophet from Gibeon, addressed me publicly in the Temple while all the priests and people listened. He said, 2 "This is what the LORD of Heaven's Armies, the God of Israel, says: 'I will remove the yoke of the king of Babylon from your necks. 3 Within two years I will bring back all the Temple treasures that King Nebuchadnezzar carried off to Babylon. 4 And I will bring back Jehoiachin* son of Jehoiakim, king of Judah, and all the other captives that were taken to Babylon. I will surely break the yoke that the king of Babylon has put on your necks. I, the LORD, have spoken!' "

5 Jeremiah responded to Hananiah as they stood in front of all the priests and people at the Temple. 6 He said, "Amen! May your prophecies come true! I hope the LORD does everything you say. I hope he does bring back from Babylon the treasures of this Temple and all the captives. 7 But listen now to the solemn words I speak to you in the presence of all these people. 8 The ancient prophets who preceded you and me spoke against many nations, always warning of war, disaster, and disease. 9 So a prophet who predicts peace must show he is right. Only when his predictions come true can we know that he is really from the LORD."

10 Then Hananiah the prophet took the yoke off Jeremiah's neck and broke it in pieces. 11 And Hananiah said again to the crowd that had gathered, "This is what the LORD says: 'Just as this yoke has been broken, within two years I will break the yoke of oppression from all the nations now subject to King Nebuchadnezzar of Babylon.' " With that, Jeremiah left the Temple area.

12 Soon after this confrontation with Hananiah, the LORD gave this message to Jeremiah: 13 "Go and tell Hananiah, 'This is what the LORD says: You have broken a wooden yoke, but you have replaced it with a yoke of iron. 14 The LORD of Heaven's Armies, the God of Israel, says: I have put a yoke of iron on the necks of all these nations, forcing them into slavery under King Nebuchadnezzar of Babylon. I have put every-

27:20 Hebrew *Jeconiah,* a variant spelling of Jehoiachin.
28:1 Hebrew *In the fifth month,* of the ancient Hebrew lunar calendar. The fifth month in the fourth year of Zedekiah's reign occurred within the months of August and September 593 B.C. Also see note on 1:3. **28:4** Hebrew *Jeconiah,* a variant spelling of Jehoiachin.

would not see the end and Judah could never be the same. **28:1–17:** Jeremiah seemed to be a lone voice. Others, like Hananiah in Jerusalem and Ahab and Zedekiah in Babylon, predicted that God would defeat Nebuchadnezzar. Within two years both exiles and plunder would be returned. The worst was over. Repentance was unnecessary. Hananiah made his point by breaking Jeremiah's wooden yoke but that changed nothing, as the LORD replaced that yoke with a stronger one (*a yoke of iron*) on all the nations under

thing, even the wild animals, under his control.' "

15 Then Jeremiah the prophet said to Hananiah, "Listen, Hananiah! The LORD has not sent you, but the people believe your lies. 16 Therefore, this is what the LORD says: 'You must die. Your life will end this very year because you have rebelled against the LORD.' "

17 Two months later* the prophet Hananiah died.

A Letter to the Exiles

29 Jeremiah wrote a letter from Jerusalem to the elders, priests, prophets, and all the people who had been exiled to Babylon by King Nebuchadnezzar. 2 This was after King Jehoiachin,* the queen mother, the court officials, the other officials of Judah, and all the craftsmen and artisans had been deported from Jerusalem. 3 He sent the letter with Elasah son of Shaphan and Gemariah son of Hilkiah when they went to Babylon as King Zedekiah's ambassadors to Nebuchadnezzar. This is what Jeremiah's letter said:

4 This is what the LORD of Heaven's Armies, the God of Israel, says to all the captives he has exiled to Babylon from Jerusalem: 5 "Build homes, and plan to stay. Plant gardens, and eat the food they produce. 6 Marry and have children. Then find spouses for them so that you may have many grandchildren. Multiply! Do not dwindle away! 7 And work for the peace and prosperity of the city where I sent you into exile. Pray to the LORD for it, for its welfare will determine your welfare."

8 This is what the LORD of Heaven's Armies, the God of Israel, says: "Do not let your prophets and fortune-tellers who are with you in the land of Babylon trick you. Do not listen to their dreams, 9 because they are telling you lies in my name. I have not sent them," says the LORD.

10 This is what the LORD says: "You will be in Babylon for seventy years. But then I will come and do for you all the good things I have promised, and I will bring you home again. 11 For I know the plans I have for you," says the LORD. "They are plans for good and not for disaster, to give you a future and a hope. 12 In those days when you pray, I will listen. 13 If you look for me wholeheartedly, you will find me. 14 I will be found by you," says the LORD. "I will end your captivity and restore your fortunes. I will gather you out of the nations where I sent you and will bring you home again to your own land."

15 You claim that the LORD has raised up prophets for you in Babylon. 16 But this is what the LORD says about the king who sits on David's throne and all those still living here in Jerusalem—your relatives who were not exiled to Babylon. 17 This is what the LORD of Heaven's Armies says: "I will send war, famine, and disease upon them and make them like bad figs, too rotten to eat. 18 Yes, I will pursue them with war, famine, and disease, and I will scatter them around the world. In every nation where I send them, I will make them an object of damnation, horror, contempt, and mockery. 19 For they refuse to listen to me, though I have spoken to them repeatedly through the prophets I sent. And you who are in exile have not listened either," says the LORD.

20 Therefore, listen to this message from the LORD, all you captives there in Babylon. 21 This is what the LORD of Heaven's Armies, the God of Israel, says about your prophets—Ahab son of Kolaiah and Zedekiah son of Maaseiah—who are telling you lies in my name: "I will turn them over to Nebuchadnezzar* for execution before your eyes. 22 Their terrible fate will become proverbial, so that the Judean exiles will curse someone by saying, 'May the LORD make you like Zedekiah and Ahab, whom the king of Babylon burned alive!' 23 For these men have done terrible things among my people. They have committed adultery with their neighbors' wives and have lied in my name,

28:17 Hebrew *In the seventh month of that same year.* See 28:1 and the note there. **29:2** Hebrew *Jeconiah,* a variant spelling of Jehoiachin. **29:21** Hebrew *Nebuchadrezzar,* a variant spelling of Nebuchadnezzar.

Nebuchadnezzar. Wishful thinking is no replacement for truth, however uncomfortable. **29:1–23:** Jeremiah now wrote a letter to the current Babylonian exiles. They had been kept together for the most part, and God told them to settle down and carry on with normal life, working *for the peace and prosperity of the city where I sent you into exile.* **6–7:** The three generations corresponds to the three generations of Babylonian kings. During this time, the exiles' well-being will coincide with Babylon's. Therefore they should pray for the good of Babylon, as they had once prayed for Jerusalem. Their mandate was to survive and flourish until Babylon's time was over. The adults addressed would not live to see it, but if they heed-

saying things I did not command. I am a
witness to this. I, the LORD, have spoken."

A Message for Shemaiah

24 The LORD sent this message to Shemaiah the
Nehelamite in Babylon: 25 "This is what the LORD
of Heaven's Armies, the God of Israel, says: You
wrote a letter on your own authority to Zephaniah son of Maaseiah, the priest, and you sent
copies to the other priests and people in Jerusalem. You wrote to Zephaniah,

26 "The LORD has appointed you to replace
Jehoiada as the priest in charge of the house
of the LORD. You are responsible to put
into stocks and neck irons any crazy man
who claims to be a prophet. 27 So why have
you done nothing to stop Jeremiah from
Anathoth, who pretends to be a prophet
among you? 28 Jeremiah sent a letter here to
Babylon, predicting that our captivity will be
a long one. He said, 'Build homes, and plan
to stay. Plant gardens, and eat the food they
produce.'"

29 But when Zephaniah the priest received
Shemaiah's letter, he took it to Jeremiah and read
it to him. 30 Then the LORD gave this message to
Jeremiah: 31 "Send an open letter to all the exiles
in Babylon. Tell them, 'This is what the LORD
says concerning Shemaiah the Nehelamite: Since
he has prophesied to you when I did not send
him and has tricked you into believing his lies,
32 I will punish him and his family. None of his
descendants will see the good things I will do for
my people, for he has incited you to rebel against
me. I, the LORD, have spoken!'"

Promises of Deliverance

30 The LORD gave another message to
Jeremiah. He said, 2 "This is what the
LORD, the God of Israel, says: Write
down for the record everything I have said to
you, Jeremiah. 3 For the time is coming when I
will restore the fortunes of my people of Israel
and Judah. I will bring them home to this land
that I gave to their ancestors, and they will possess it again. I, the LORD, have spoken!"

4 This is the message the LORD gave concerning
Israel and Judah. 5 This is what the LORD says:

"I hear cries of fear;
there is terror and no peace.
6 Now let me ask you a question:
Do men give birth to babies?
Then why do they stand there, ashen-faced,
hands pressed against their sides
like a woman in labor?
7 In all history there has never been such a
time of terror.
It will be a time of trouble for my people
Israel.*
Yet in the end they will be saved!
8 For in that day,"
says the LORD of Heaven's Armies,
"I will break the yoke from their necks
and snap their chains.
Foreigners will no longer be their masters.
9 For my people will serve the LORD their
God
and their king descended from David—
the king I will raise up for them.

10 "So do not be afraid, Jacob, my servant;
do not be dismayed, Israel,"
says the LORD.
"For I will bring you home again from distant
lands,
and your children will return from their
exile.
Israel will return to a life of peace and quiet,
and no one will terrorize them.
11 For I am with you and will save you,"
says the LORD.

30:7 Hebrew *Jacob;* also in 30:10b, 18. See note on 5:20.

---

ed, then their grandchildren would have a hopeful future. **24–32:** The LORD sent a message to Shemaiah accusing him of lying to the other priests and people. Shemaiah's refusal to recognize the validity of God's word through Jeremiah meant that neither he (Shemaiah) nor his family would live to see the *good things I will do for my people.* God's people will emerge from Babylon's seventy years transformed and renewed.

30:1—33:26 The Book of Comfort and Hope

The LORD's promises of restoration for Israel and Judah receive their fullest description. These chapters employ many forms and they jump around chronologically, but the words consistently present the new future planned by God alongside present judgment. They have been told why judgment is necessary, and they learn why God's people will be saved. **30:5–11:** Their terror and distress is real, but so will their salvation be. **12–17:** Their sin-caused pain seems incurable, but God will heal. **18–24:** Once the judgment is complete, Jerusalem will be rebuilt, repopulated, and ruled by God's appointed prince. The principle of measured judgment is also present. Punishment

"I will completely destroy the nations where
I have scattered you,
but I will not completely destroy you.
I will discipline you, but with justice;
I cannot let you go unpunished."

12 This is what the LORD says:
"Your injury is incurable—
a terrible wound.
13 There is no one to help you
or to bind up your injury.
No medicine can heal you.
14 All your lovers—your allies—have left you
and do not care about you anymore.
I have wounded you cruelly,
as though I were your enemy.
For your sins are many,
and your guilt is great.
15 Why do you protest your punishment—
this wound that has no cure?
I have had to punish you
because your sins are many
and your guilt is great.

16 "But all who devour you will be devoured,
and all your enemies will be sent into exile.
All who plunder you will be plundered,
and all who attack you will be attacked.
17 I will give you back your health
and heal your wounds," says the LORD.
"For you are called an outcast—
'Jerusalem* for whom no one cares.'"

18 This is what the LORD says:
"When I bring Israel home again from
captivity
and restore their fortunes,
Jerusalem will be rebuilt on its ruins,
and the palace reconstructed as before.
19 There will be joy and songs of thanksgiving,
and I will multiply my people, not diminish
them;
I will honor them, not despise them.
20 Their children will prosper as they did long
ago.
I will establish them as a nation before me,
and I will punish anyone who hurts them.
21 They will have their own ruler again,
and he will come from their own people.
I will invite him to approach me," says the
LORD,
"for who would dare to come unless
invited?
22 You will be my people,
and I will be your God."
23 Look! The LORD's anger bursts out like a
storm,
a driving wind that swirls down on the
heads of the wicked.
24 The fierce anger of the LORD will not diminish
until it has finished all he has planned.
In the days to come
you will understand all this.

Hope for Restoration

31 "In that day," says the LORD, "I will
be the God of all the families of Israel,
and they will be my people. 2This is
what the LORD says:

"Those who survive the coming destruction
will find blessings even in the barren land,
for I will give rest to the people of Israel."

3 Long ago the LORD said to Israel:
"I have loved you, my people, with an
everlasting love.
With unfailing love I have drawn you to
myself.
4 I will rebuild you, my virgin Israel.
You will again be happy
and dance merrily with your tambourines.
5 Again you will plant your vineyards on the
mountains of Samaria
and eat from your own gardens there.
6 The day will come when watchmen will shout
from the hill country of Ephraim,
'Come, let us go up to Jerusalem*
to worship the LORD our God.' "
7 Now this is what the LORD says:
"Sing with joy for Israel.*

30:17 Hebrew *Zion.* **31:6** Hebrew *Zion;* also in 31:12.
31:7 Hebrew *Jacob;* also in 31:11. See note on 5:20.

will continue until God's plan is accomplished, but when Israel's conquerors exceed that just measure of punishment, God will bring deliverance. **31:1–14:** Salvation and restoration will be possible because of God's everlasting love and faithfulness. Throughout we hear the repeated mantra: *This is what the LORD says.* **2–6:** The people who survive will be built up in the land. Crops will grow, festivals will be celebrated in gratitude to God. **4:** The people are addressed as *virgin Israel.* Although they were guilty of unfaithfulness in the past, they will be wholly true to God. **7–14:** Jeremiah reflects on all that has happened and describes how people will return to the land and resettle. The LORD will make the return

Shout for the greatest of nations!
Shout out with praise and joy:
'Save your people, O LORD,
the remnant of Israel!'
8 For I will bring them from the north
and from the distant corners of the earth.
I will not forget the blind and lame,
the expectant mothers and women in labor.
A great company will return!
9 Tears of joy will stream down their faces,
and I will lead them home with great care.
They will walk beside quiet streams
and on smooth paths where they will not stumble.
For I am Israel's father,
and Ephraim is my oldest child.

10 "Listen to this message from the LORD,
you nations of the world;
proclaim it in distant coastlands:
The LORD, who scattered his people,
will gather them and watch over them
as a shepherd does his flock.
11 For the LORD has redeemed Israel
from those too strong for them.
12 They will come home and sing songs of joy
on the heights of Jerusalem.
They will be radiant because of the LORD's good gifts—
the abundant crops of grain, new wine, and olive oil,
and the healthy flocks and herds.
Their life will be like a watered garden,
and all their sorrows will be gone.
13 The young women will dance for joy,
and the men—old and young—will join in the celebration.
I will turn their mourning into joy.
I will comfort them and exchange their sorrow for rejoicing.
14 The priests will enjoy abundance,
and my people will feast on my good gifts.
I, the LORD, have spoken!"

Rachel's Sadness Turns to Joy
15 This is what the LORD says:
"A cry is heard in Ramah—
deep anguish and bitter weeping.
Rachel weeps for her children,
refusing to be comforted—
for her children are gone."

16 But now this is what the LORD says:
"Do not weep any longer,
for I will reward you," says the LORD.
"Your children will come back to you
from the distant land of the enemy.
17 There is hope for your future," says the LORD.
"Your children will come again to their own land.
18 I have heard Israel* saying,
'You disciplined me severely,
like a calf that needs training for the yoke.
Turn me again to you and restore me,
for you alone are the LORD my God.
19 I turned away from God,
but then I was sorry.
I kicked myself for my stupidity!
I was thoroughly ashamed of all I did in my younger days.'

20 "Is not Israel still my son,
my darling child?" says the LORD.
"I often have to punish him,
but I still love him.
That's why I long for him
and surely will have mercy on him.
21 Set up road signs;
put up guideposts.
Mark well the path
by which you came.
Come back again, my virgin Israel;
return to your towns here.
22 How long will you wander,
my wayward daughter?
For the LORD will cause something new to happen—
Israel will embrace her God.*"

31:18 Hebrew *Ephraim,* referring to the northern kingdom of Israel; also in 31:20. **31:22** Hebrew *a woman will surround a man.*

and re-settlement process smooth. Even the weakest travelers will be able to come, including women pregnant or in labor. Once judgment is over, people who once needed the services of women skilled in mourning will be led by women dancing with joy. **15–22:** The final poem begins by recalling Rachel, who died in childbirth. She weeps for the exiled children of Israel, and her weeping is answered like a prayer. These lost children acknowledge sin, repent, and pray for restoration: *Do not weep . . . for I will reward you*. God, as their father, has shown discipline but is merciful. *Virgin Israel*, God's daughter, has repeatedly turned from God, but God will forget her unfaithfulness and welcome her home. **22:** The enigmatic *new* creation (Heb., a woman will surround a man) has many possible interpretations. The dead nation will live again, so Rachel (Israel) will embrace a strong son. The status of women will improve so

23 This is what the LORD of Heaven's Armies,
the God of Israel, says: "When I bring them back
from captivity, the people of Judah and its towns
will again say, 'The LORD bless you, O righteous
home, O holy mountain!' 24 Townspeople and
farmers and shepherds alike will live together in
peace and happiness. 25 For I have given rest to
the weary and joy to the sorrowing."
26 At this, I woke up and looked around. My
sleep had been very sweet.
27 "The day is coming," says the LORD, "when
I will greatly increase the human population and
the number of animals here in Israel and Judah.
28 In the past I deliberately uprooted and tore
down this nation. I overthrew it, destroyed it,
and brought disaster upon it. But in the future I
will just as deliberately plant it and build it up. I,
the LORD, have spoken!
29 "The people will no longer quote this proverb:

'The parents have eaten sour grapes,
but their children's mouths pucker at the
taste.'

30 All people will die for their own sins—those
who eat the sour grapes will be the ones whose
mouths will pucker.
31 "The day is coming," says the LORD, "when
I will make a new covenant with the people of
Israel and Judah. 32 This covenant will not be like
the one I made with their ancestors when I took
them by the hand and brought them out of the
land of Egypt. They broke that covenant, though
I loved them as a husband loves his wife," says
the LORD.
33 "But this is the new covenant I will make
with the people of Israel on that day," says the
LORD. "I will put my instructions deep within
them, and I will write them on their hearts. I will
be their God, and they will be my people. 34 And
they will not need to teach their neighbors, nor
will they need to teach their relatives, saying,
'You should know the LORD.' For everyone, from
the least to the greatest, will know me already,"
says the LORD. "And I will forgive their wickedness, and I will never again remember their
sins."

35 It is the LORD who provides the sun to light
the day
and the moon and stars to light the night,
and who stirs the sea into roaring waves.
His name is the LORD of Heaven's Armies,
and this is what he says:
36 "I am as likely to reject my people Israel
as I am to abolish the laws of nature!"
37 This is what the LORD says:
"Just as the heavens cannot be measured
and the foundations of the earth cannot be
explored,
so I will not consider casting them away
for the evil they have done.
I, the LORD, have spoken!

38 "The day is coming," says the LORD, "when
all Jerusalem will be rebuilt for me, from the
Tower of Hananel to the Corner Gate. 39 A measuring line will be stretched out over the hill
of Gareb and across to Goah. 40 And the entire
area—including the graveyard and ash dump
in the valley, and all the fields out to the Kidron
Valley on the east as far as the Horse Gate—will
be holy to the LORD. The city will never again be
captured or destroyed."

Jeremiah's Land Purchase

32 The following message came to Jeremiah from the LORD in the tenth
year of the reign of Zedekiah,* king
of Judah. This was also the eighteenth year of the
reign of King Nebuchadnezzar.* 2 Jerusalem was
then under siege from the Babylonian army, and
Jeremiah was imprisoned in the courtyard of the

32:1a The tenth year of Zedekiah's reign and the eighteenth year of Nebuchadnezzar's reign was 587 B.C. **32:1b** Hebrew *Nebuchadrezzar,* a variant spelling of Nebuchadnezzar; also in 32:28.

a woman can protect a male warrior as well as he can protect her. God will transform people spiritually so that Israel, as fickle daughter, will firmly embrace faith in the LORD. **34:** God promises a new and different covenant. Sins will be forgiven; not even the memory of them will cloud the new relationship (cf. Num 14:20–23; Matt 26:28). God will transform every person's will and desire to be consistent with his will. No one will have to teach them to choose the LORD's way. **32:1–15:** During the final siege of Jerusalem, Jeremiah fulfilled the obligation of redeemer for his cousin, Hanamel, by buying his field, ensuring that ancestral land was kept within the family. However, Hanamel's field in Anathoth may have already been occupied by Babylonians. In spite of being under arrest, Jeremiah obeyed God's command and used the transaction as a sealed deed. The deed was signed, witnessed, sealed, and safely stored to demonstrate God's promise. This was not foolish; it was a wise investment in God's sure, promised future.

guard in the royal palace. 3 King Zedekiah had put him there, asking why he kept giving this prophecy: "This is what the LORD says: 'I am about to hand this city over to the king of Babylon, and he will take it. 4 King Zedekiah will be captured by the Babylonians* and taken to meet the king of Babylon face to face. 5 He will take Zedekiah to Babylon, and I will deal with him there,' says the LORD. 'If you fight against the Babylonians, you will never succeed.' "

6 At that time the LORD sent me a message. He said, 7 "Your cousin Hanamel son of Shallum will come and say to you, 'Buy my field at Anathoth. By law you have the right to buy it before it is offered to anyone else.' "

8 Then, just as the LORD had said he would, my cousin Hanamel came and visited me in the prison. He said, "Please buy my field at Anathoth in the land of Benjamin. By law you have the right to buy it before it is offered to anyone else, so buy it for yourself." Then I knew that the message I had heard was from the LORD.

9 So I bought the field at Anathoth, paying Hanamel seventeen pieces* of silver for it. 10 I signed and sealed the deed of purchase before witnesses, weighed out the silver, and paid him. 11 Then I took the sealed deed and an unsealed copy of the deed, which contained the terms and conditions of the purchase, 12 and I handed them to Baruch son of Neriah and grandson of Mahseiah. I did all this in the presence of my cousin Hanamel, the witnesses who had signed the deed, and all the men of Judah who were there in the courtyard of the guardhouse.

13 Then I said to Baruch as they all listened, 14 "This is what the LORD of Heaven's Armies, the God of Israel, says: 'Take both this sealed deed and the unsealed copy, and put them into a pottery jar to preserve them for a long time.' 15 For this is what the LORD of Heaven's Armies, the God of Israel, says: 'Someday people will again own property here in this land and will buy and sell houses and vineyards and fields.' "

Jeremiah's Prayer

16 Then after I had given the papers to Baruch, I prayed to the LORD:

17 "O Sovereign LORD! You made the heavens
and earth by your strong hand and powerful
arm. Nothing is too hard for you! 18 You show
unfailing love to thousands, but you also
bring the consequences of one generation's
sin upon the next. You are the great and
powerful God, the LORD of Heaven's Armies.
19 You have all wisdom and do great and
mighty miracles. You see the conduct of
all people, and you give them what they
deserve. 20 You performed miraculous signs
and wonders in the land of Egypt—things
still remembered to this day! And you have
continued to do great miracles in Israel and
all around the world. You have made your
name famous to this day.

21 "You brought Israel out of Egypt
with mighty signs and wonders, with a
strong hand and powerful arm, and with
overwhelming terror. 22 You gave the people
of Israel this land that you had promised their
ancestors long before—a land flowing with
milk and honey. 23 Our ancestors came and
conquered it and lived in it, but they refused
to obey you or follow your word. They have
not done anything you commanded. That is
why you have sent this terrible disaster upon
them.

24 "See how the siege ramps have been
built against the city walls! Through war,
famine, and disease, the city will be handed
over to the Babylonians, who will conquer
it. Everything has happened just as you said.
25 And yet, O Sovereign LORD, you have told
me to buy the field—paying good money
for it before these witnesses—even though
the city will soon be handed over to the
Babylonians."

A Prediction of Jerusalem's Fall

26 Then this message came to Jeremiah from the LORD: 27 "I am the LORD, the God of all the peoples of the world. Is anything too hard for me? 28 Therefore, this is what the LORD says: I will hand this city over to the Babylonians and to Nebuchadnezzar, king of Babylon, and he will capture it. 29 The Babylonians outside the walls will come in and set fire to the city. They will burn down all these houses where the people provoked my anger by burning incense to Baal

32:4 Or *Chaldeans;* also in 32:5, 24, 25, 28, 29, 43.
32:9 Hebrew *17 shekels,* about 7 ounces or 194 grams in weight.

16–25: Once again, Jeremiah's prayer and God's answers set this apparently foolish act in the context of Israel's past and the LORD's plan. God's people were about to lose the land because of persistent disobedience. How could they hope to hold it again? **17:** The answer is in God's character: For God *nothing is too hard* (cf. v. 27 and Gen 18:12–15). The LORD will give the new covenant people a single-minded capacity

on the rooftops and by pouring out liquid offerings to other gods. [30] Israel and Judah have done nothing but wrong since their earliest days. They have infuriated me with all their evil deeds," says the LORD. [31] "From the time this city was built until now, it has done nothing but anger me, so I am determined to get rid of it.

[32] "The sins of Israel and Judah—the sins of the people of Jerusalem, the kings, the officials, the priests, and the prophets—have stirred up my anger. [33] My people have turned their backs on me and have refused to return. Even though I diligently taught them, they would not receive instruction or obey. [34] They have set up their abominable idols right in my own Temple, defiling it. [35] They have built pagan shrines to Baal in the valley of Ben-Hinnom, and there they sacrifice their sons and daughters to Molech. I have never commanded such a horrible deed; it never even crossed my mind to command such a thing. What an incredible evil, causing Judah to sin so greatly!

A Promise of Restoration

[36] "Now I want to say something more about this city. You have been saying, 'It will fall to the king of Babylon through war, famine, and disease.' But this is what the LORD, the God of Israel, says: [37] I will certainly bring my people back again from all the countries where I will scatter them in my fury. I will bring them back to this very city and let them live in peace and safety. [38] They will be my people, and I will be their God. [39] And I will give them one heart and one purpose: to worship me forever, for their own good and for the good of all their descendants. [40] And I will make an everlasting covenant with them: I will never stop doing good for them. I will put a desire in their hearts to worship me, and they will never leave me. [41] I will find joy doing good for them and will faithfully and wholeheartedly replant them in this land.

[42] "This is what the LORD says: Just as I have brought all these calamities on them, so I will do all the good I have promised them. [43] Fields will again be bought and sold in this land about which you now say, 'It has been ravaged by the Babylonians, a desolate land where people and animals have all disappeared.' [44] Yes, fields will once again be bought and sold—deeds signed and sealed and witnessed—in the land of Benjamin and here in Jerusalem, in the towns of Judah and in the hill country, in the foothills of Judah* and in the Negev, too. For someday I will restore prosperity to them. I, the LORD, have spoken!"

Promises of Peace and Prosperity

33 While Jeremiah was still confined in the courtyard of the guard, the LORD gave him this second message: [2] "This is what the LORD says—the LORD who made the earth, who formed and established it, whose name is the LORD: [3] Ask me and I will tell you remarkable secrets you do not know about things to come. [4] For this is what the LORD, the God of Israel, says: You have torn down the houses of this city and even the king's palace to get materials to strengthen the walls against the siege ramps and swords of the enemy. [5] You expect to fight the Babylonians,* but the men of this city are already as good as dead, for I have determined to destroy them in my terrible anger. I have abandoned them because of all their wickedness.

[6] "Nevertheless, the time will come when I will heal Jerusalem's wounds and give it prosperity and true peace. [7] I will restore the fortunes of Judah and Israel and rebuild their towns. [8] I will cleanse them of their sins against me and forgive all their sins of rebellion. [9] Then this city will bring me joy, glory, and honor before all the nations of the earth! The people of the world will see all the good I do for my people, and they will tremble with awe at the peace and prosperity I provide for them.

[10] "This is what the LORD says: You have said, 'This is a desolate land where people and animals have all disappeared.' Yet in the empty streets of Jerusalem and Judah's other towns, there will be heard once more [11] the sounds of joy and laughter. The joyful voices of bridegrooms and brides will be heard again, along with the joyous songs of people bringing thanksgiving offerings to the LORD. They will sing,

'Give thanks to the LORD of Heaven's Armies,
for the LORD is good.
His faithful love endures forever!'

For I will restore the prosperity of this land to what it was in the past, says the LORD.

32:44 Hebrew *the Shephelah.* **33:5** Or *Chaldeans.*

to honor and obey. **32:36—33:26:** Just as the earlier chapters have emphasized the certainty and extent of the destruction of Judah, now the certainty and extent of the promised future restoration is brought into focus. It mattered that the people understood both. The current generation would not see it but could stake their children's future on its happening.

12 "This is what the LORD of Heaven's Armies says: This land—though it is now desolate and has no people and animals—will once more have pastures where shepherds can lead their flocks. 13 Once again shepherds will count their flocks in the towns of the hill country, the foothills of Judah,* the Negev, the land of Benjamin, the vicinity of Jerusalem, and all the towns of Judah. I, the LORD, have spoken!

14 "The day will come, says the LORD, when I will do for Israel and Judah all the good things I have promised them.

15 "In those days and at that time
I will raise up a righteous descendant*
from King David's line.
He will do what is just and right
throughout the land.
16 In that day Judah will be saved,
and Jerusalem will live in safety.
And this will be its name:
'The LORD Is Our Righteousness.'*

17 For this is what the LORD says: David will have a descendant sitting on the throne of Israel forever. 18 And there will always be Levitical priests to offer burnt offerings and grain offerings and sacrifices to me."

19 Then this message came to Jeremiah from the LORD: 20 "This is what the LORD says: If you can break my covenant with the day and the night so that one does not follow the other, 21 only then will my covenant with my servant David be broken. Only then will he no longer have a descendant to reign on his throne. The same is true for my covenant with the Levitical priests who minister before me. 22 And as the stars of the sky cannot be counted and the sand on the seashore cannot be measured, so I will multiply the descendants of my servant David and the Levites who minister before me."

23 The LORD gave another message to Jeremiah. He said, 24 "Have you noticed what people are saying?—'The LORD chose Judah and Israel and then abandoned them!' They are sneering and saying that Israel is not worthy to be counted as a nation. 25 But this is what the LORD says: I would no more reject my people than I would change my laws that govern night and day, earth and sky. 26 I will never abandon the descendants of Jacob or David, my servant, or change the plan that David's descendants will rule the descendants of Abraham, Isaac, and Jacob. Instead, I will restore them to their land and have mercy on them."

A Warning for Zedekiah

34 King Nebuchadnezzar of Babylon came with all the armies from the kingdoms he ruled, and he fought against Jerusalem and the towns of Judah. At that time this message came to Jeremiah from the LORD: 2 "Go to King Zedekiah of Judah, and tell him, 'This is what the LORD, the God of Israel, says: I am about to hand this city over to the king of Babylon, and he will burn it down. 3 You will not escape his grasp but will be captured and taken to meet the king of Babylon face to face. Then you will be exiled to Babylon.

4 "'But listen to this promise from the LORD, O Zedekiah, king of Judah. This is what the LORD says: You will not be killed in war 5 but will die peacefully. People will burn incense in your memory, just as they did for your ancestors, the kings who preceded you. They will mourn for you, crying, "Alas, our master is dead!" This I have decreed, says the LORD.'"

6 So Jeremiah the prophet delivered the message to King Zedekiah of Judah. 7 At this time the Babylonian army was besieging Jerusalem, Lachish, and Azekah—the only fortified cities of Judah not yet captured.

Freedom for Hebrew Slaves

8 This message came to Jeremiah from the LORD after King Zedekiah made a covenant with the people, proclaiming freedom for the slaves. 9 He

33:13 Hebrew *the Shephelah.* **33:15** Hebrew *a righteous branch.* **33:16** Hebrew *Yahweh Tsidqenu.*

34:1—36:32 Examples of Faithlessness and Faith

Contrasting examples of faith and faithlessness are arranged in reverse chronological order. Looking backward, judgment on Judah is justified. Looking ahead, continuing adherence to God's word is called for. **34:1–7:** Zedekiah knew Jeremiah believed Judah would face heavy defeat. So the first half of the latest message was no surprise. Perhaps also hearing that he would survive and die in peace would have been some reassurance as the end approached. (One wonders whether this reassurance outlived his being made blind [2 Kgs 25:7].) **8–22:** During the siege of Jerusalem Zedekiah freed all male and female debt slaves. Like Josiah, he led the people to renew their adherence to the Sinai covenant. Slave holders may have agreed because they thought feeding slaves was beginning to cost more than their worth. The only reason given here, however, was

had ordered all the people to free their Hebrew
slaves—both men and women. No one was to
keep a fellow Judean in bondage. 10 The officials
and all the people had obeyed the king's command, 11 but later they changed their minds.
They took back the men and women they had
freed, forcing them to be slaves again.
12 So the LORD gave them this message
through Jeremiah: 13 "This is what the LORD,
the God of Israel, says: I made a covenant with
your ancestors long ago when I rescued them
from their slavery in Egypt. 14 I told them that
every Hebrew slave must be freed after serving
six years. But your ancestors paid no attention to
me. 15 Recently you repented and did what was
right, following my command. You freed your
slaves and made a solemn covenant with me in
the Temple that bears my name. 16 But now you
have shrugged off your oath and defiled my
name by taking back the men and women you
had freed, forcing them to be slaves once again.
17 "Therefore, this is what the LORD says:
Since you have not obeyed me by setting your
countrymen free, I will set you free to be destroyed by war, disease, and famine. You will be
an object of horror to all the nations of the earth.
18 Because you have broken the terms of our covenant, I will cut you apart just as you cut apart
the calf when you walked between its halves to
solemnize your vows. 19 Yes, I will cut you apart,
whether you are officials of Judah or Jerusalem,
court officials, priests, or common people—for
you have broken your oath. 20 I will give you to
your enemies, and they will kill you. Your bodies
will be food for the vultures and wild animals.
21 "I will hand over King Zedekiah of Judah
and his officials to the army of the king of Babylon. And although Babylon's king has left Jerusalem for a while, 22 I will call the Babylonian
armies back again. They will fight against this
city and will capture it and burn it down. I will
see to it that all the towns of Judah are destroyed,
with no one living there."

The Faithful Recabites

35 This is the message the LORD gave
Jeremiah when Jehoiakim son of Josiah was king of Judah: 2 "Go to the
settlement where the families of the Recabites
live, and invite them to the LORD's Temple. Take
them into one of the inner rooms, and offer them
some wine."
3 So I went to see Jaazaniah son of Jeremiah
and grandson of Habazziniah and all his brothers
and sons—representing all the Recabite families.
4 I took them to the Temple, and we went into the
room assigned to the sons of Hanan son of Igda-
liah, a man of God. This room was located next
to the one used by the Temple officials, directly
above the room of Maaseiah son of Shallum, the
Temple gatekeeper.
5 I set cups and jugs of wine before them and
invited them to have a drink, 6 but they refused.
"No," they said, "we don't drink wine, because
our ancestor Jehonadab* son of Recab gave us
this command: 'You and your descendants must
never drink wine. 7 And do not build houses or
plant crops or vineyards, but always live in tents.
If you follow these commands, you will live long,
good lives in the land.' 8 So we have obeyed him
in all these things. We have never had a drink of
wine to this day, nor have our wives, our sons, or
our daughters. 9 We haven't built houses or owned
vineyards or farms or planted crops. 10 We have
lived in tents and have fully obeyed all the com-

35:6 Hebrew *Jonadab,* a variant spelling of Jehonadab; also in 35:10, 14, 16, 18, 19. See 2 Kgs 10:15.

the requirement that no Judean should hold another as a slave. Although the covenant law allowed someone to sell herself or a child into servitude to pay debts, this service was limited to six years. The people in Jerusalem who held slaves had not been releasing them at the end of their term. Zedekiah's proclamation of release resembles the ancient Near Eastern custom of a king alleviating some burdens of the poor in order to gain personal support. **11:** However, when the Babylonian forces temporarily withdrew from Jerusalem, the people hoped or believed that the Babylonians would not return. However, the slaveholders reneged on their promise, *forcing them to be slaves again*. This not only broke the law but violated the covenant oath that they had sworn. They—as once again *the LORD says*—would suffer under the curses of the covenants they had violated. **35:1–19:** The Recabites were a mysterious, isolated group originating from the ninth century BC (see 2 Kgs 10:15–28). Women, men, and children did not live in houses, engage in agriculture, or drink wine *as* their *ancestor Jehonadab* had commanded. At God's command Jeremiah used them as an example calling Judah to account. When the Recabites refused to drink offered wine, still obeying their ancestor's command, Jeremiah challenged his audience to examine themselves. The Recabites, despite regular pressure, had obeyed their ancestor's stringent commands over many generations. The people of Israel and Judah, however, had not been obedient to God's word for even one generation, even though God had spoken many times through many people.

mands of Jehonadab, our ancestor. 11But when King Nebuchadnezzar* of Babylon attacked this country, we were afraid of the Babylonian and Syrian* armies. So we decided to move to Jerusalem. That is why we are here."

12Then the LORD gave this message to Jeremiah: 13"This is what the LORD of Heaven's Armies, the God of Israel, says: Go and say to the people in Judah and Jerusalem, 'Come and learn a lesson about how to obey me. 14The Recabites do not drink wine to this day because their ancestor Jehonadab told them not to. But I have spoken to you again and again, and you refuse to obey me. 15Time after time I sent you prophets, who told you, "Turn from your wicked ways, and start doing things right. Stop worshiping other gods so that you might live in peace here in the land I have given to you and your ancestors." But you would not listen to me or obey me. 16The descendants of Jehonadab son of Recab have obeyed their ancestor completely, but you have refused to listen to me.'

17"Therefore, this is what the LORD God of Heaven's Armies, the God of Israel, says: 'Because you refuse to listen or answer when I call, I will send upon Judah and Jerusalem all the disasters I have threatened.' "

18Then Jeremiah turned to the Recabites and said, "This is what the LORD of Heaven's Armies, the God of Israel, says: 'You have obeyed your ancestor Jehonadab in every respect, following all his instructions.' 19Therefore, this is what the LORD of Heaven's Armies, the God of Israel, says: 'Jehonadab son of Recab will always have descendants who serve me.' "

Baruch Reads the LORD's Messages

36 During the fourth year that Jehoiakim son of Josiah was king in Judah,* the LORD gave this message to Jeremiah: 2"Get a scroll, and write down all my messages against Israel, Judah, and the other nations. Begin with the first message back in the days of Josiah, and write down every message, right up to the present time. 3Perhaps the people of Judah will repent when they hear again all the terrible things I have planned for them. Then I will be able to forgive their sins and wrongdoings."

4So Jeremiah sent for Baruch son of Neriah, and as Jeremiah dictated all the prophecies that the LORD had given him, Baruch wrote them on a scroll. 5Then Jeremiah said to Baruch, "I am a prisoner here and unable to go to the Temple. 6So you go to the Temple on the next day of fasting, and read the messages from the LORD that I have had you write on this scroll. Read them so the people who are there from all over Judah will hear them. 7Perhaps even yet they will turn from their evil ways and ask the LORD's forgiveness before it is too late. For the LORD has threatened them with his terrible anger."

8Baruch did as Jeremiah told him and read these messages from the LORD to the people at the Temple. 9He did this on a day of sacred fasting held in late autumn,* during the fifth year of the reign of Jehoiakim son of Josiah. People from all over Judah had come to Jerusalem to attend the services at the Temple on that day. 10Baruch read Jeremiah's words on the scroll to all the people. He stood in front of the Temple room of Gemariah, son of Shaphan the secretary. This room was just off the upper courtyard of the Temple, near the New Gate entrance.

11When Micaiah son of Gemariah and grandson of Shaphan heard the messages from the LORD, 12he went down to the secretary's room in the palace where the administrative officials were meeting. Elishama the secretary was there, along with Delaiah son of Shemaiah, Elnathan son of Acbor, Gemariah son of Shaphan, Zedekiah son of Hananiah, and all the other officials. 13When Micaiah told them about the messages Baruch was reading to the people, 14the officials sent Jehudi son of Nethaniah, grandson of Shelemiah and great-grandson of Cushi, to ask Baruch to

35:11a Hebrew *Nebuchadrezzar,* a variant spelling of Nebuchadnezzar. **35:11b** Or *Chaldean and Aramean.*
36:1 The fourth year of Jehoiakim's reign was 605 B.C.
36:9 Hebrew *in the ninth month,* of the ancient Hebrew lunar calendar (also in 36:22). The ninth month in the fifth year of Jehoiakim's reign occurred within the months of November and December 604 B.C. Also see note on 1:3.

36:1–32: These events occurred in the year Nebuchadnezzar defeated the Egyptians at Carchemish and became king of Babylon and overlord of Judah. They are another example of unfaithfulness and disobedience to the LORD. The scroll described the disasters threatened against Judah. King Jehoiakim's response epitomizes contempt and rejection of God's word. Instead of tearing his clothes in contrition as Josiah had done when he read the law scroll (2 Kgs 23), Jehoiakim cut the scroll into strips. Instead of allowing a prophet to authenticate the scroll, he sent men to arrest Jeremiah and Baruch. Instead of instituting changes in reponse to God's word, Jehoiakim burned the scroll so that no one else could hear it. Jeremiah then heard what the LORD said and rewrote the scroll, adding more punishments and similar disasters.

come and read the messages to them, too. So Baruch took the scroll and went to them. 15 "Sit down and read the scroll to us," the officials said, and Baruch did as they requested.

16 When they heard all the messages, they looked at one another in alarm. "We must tell the king what we have heard," they said to Baruch. 17 "But first, tell us how you got these messages. Did they come directly from Jeremiah?"

18 So Baruch explained, "Jeremiah dictated them, and I wrote them down in ink, word for word, on this scroll."

19 "You and Jeremiah should both hide," the officials told Baruch. "Don't tell anyone where you are!" 20 Then the officials left the scroll for safekeeping in the room of Elishama the secretary and went to tell the king what had happened.

King Jehoiakim Burns the Scroll

21 The king sent Jehudi to get the scroll. Jehudi brought it from Elishama's room and read it to the king as all his officials stood by. 22 It was late autumn, and the king was in a winterized part of the palace, sitting in front of a fire to keep warm. 23 Each time Jehudi finished reading three or four columns, the king took a knife and cut off that section of the scroll. He then threw it into the fire, section by section, until the whole scroll was burned up. 24 Neither the king nor his attendants showed any signs of fear or repentance at what they heard. 25 Even when Elnathan, Delaiah, and Gemariah begged the king not to burn the scroll, he wouldn't listen.

26 Then the king commanded his son Jerahmeel, Seraiah son of Azriel, and Shelemiah son of Abdeel to arrest Baruch and Jeremiah. But the LORD had hidden them.

Jeremiah Rewrites the Scroll

27 After the king had burned the scroll on which Baruch had written Jeremiah's words, the LORD gave Jeremiah another message. He said, 28 "Get another scroll, and write everything again just as you did on the scroll King Jehoiakim burned. 29 Then say to the king, 'This is what the LORD says: You burned the scroll because it said the king of Babylon would destroy this land and empty it of people and animals. 30 Now this is what the LORD says about King Jehoiakim of Judah: He will have no heirs to sit on the throne of David. His dead body will be thrown out to lie unburied—exposed to the heat of the day and the frost of the night. 31 I will punish him and his family and his attendants for their sins. I will pour out on them and on all the people of Jerusalem and Judah all the disasters I promised, for they would not listen to my warnings.' "

32 So Jeremiah took another scroll and dictated again to his secretary, Baruch. He wrote everything that had been on the scroll King Jehoiakim had burned in the fire. Only this time he added much more!

Zedekiah Calls for Jeremiah

37 Zedekiah son of Josiah succeeded Jehoiachin* son of Jehoiakim as the king of Judah. He was appointed by King Nebuchadnezzar* of Babylon. 2 But neither King Zedekiah nor his attendants nor the people who were left in the land listened to what the LORD said through Jeremiah.

3 Nevertheless, King Zedekiah sent Jehucal son of Shelemiah, and Zephaniah the priest, son of Maaseiah, to ask Jeremiah, "Please pray to the LORD our God for us." 4 Jeremiah had not yet been imprisoned, so he could come and go among the people as he pleased.

5 At this time the army of Pharaoh Hophra* of Egypt appeared at the southern border of Judah. When the Babylonian* army heard about it, they withdrew from their siege of Jerusalem.

6 Then the LORD gave this message to Jeremiah: 7 "This is what the LORD, the God of Israel, says: The king of Judah sent you to ask me what is going to happen. Tell him, 'Pharaoh's army is about to return to Egypt, though he came here to help you. 8 Then the Babylonians*

37:1a Hebrew *Coniah,* a variant spelling of Jehoiachin. **37:1b** Hebrew *Nebuchadrezzar,* a variant spelling of Nebuchadnezzar. **37:5a** Hebrew *army of Pharaoh;* see 44:30. **37:5b** Or *Chaldean;* also in 37:10, 11. **37:8** Or *Chaldeans;* also in 37:9, 13.

37:1—44:30 Siege, Conquest, and Aftermath

These eight chapters, bracketed by reference to the people's false hope in Egypt as refuge, recount the last months or years of Jeremiah's ministry, highlighting the political aspect of Jeremiah's message, which constantly called for submission to Babylon. **37:1–10:** During the Babylonian siege Pharaoh Hophra's army approached Jerusalem. Zedekiah, perhaps with new hope, sent for Jeremiah. When the Babylonians withdrew to face Egypt, the Jews hoped they were saved. God, through Jeremiah, however, denied all such hopes. Pharaoh would return home, and the Babylonians would defeat and burn Jerusalem. Later some Jews tried to escape Babylonian rule by emigrating to Egypt, even though Jeremiah warned them against doing this and prophesied the conquest of Egypt.

will come back and capture this city and burn it to the ground.'

[9]"This is what the LORD says: Do not fool yourselves into thinking that the Babylonians are gone for good. They aren't! [10]Even if you were to destroy the entire Babylonian army, leaving only a handful of wounded survivors, they would still stagger from their tents and burn this city to the ground!"

Jeremiah Is Imprisoned

[11]When the Babylonian army left Jerusalem because of Pharaoh's approaching army, [12]Jeremiah started to leave the city on his way to the territory of Benjamin, to claim his share of the property among his relatives there.* [13]But as he was walking through the Benjamin Gate, a sentry arrested him and said, "You are defecting to the Babylonians!" The sentry making the arrest was Irijah son of Shelemiah, grandson of Hananiah.

[14]"That's not true!" Jeremiah protested. "I had no intention of doing any such thing." But Irijah wouldn't listen, and he took Jeremiah before the officials. [15]They were furious with Jeremiah and had him flogged and imprisoned in the house of Jonathan the secretary. Jonathan's house had been converted into a prison. [16]Jeremiah was put into a dungeon cell, where he remained for many days.

[17]Later King Zedekiah secretly requested that Jeremiah come to the palace, where the king asked him, "Do you have any messages from the LORD?"

"Yes, I do!" said Jeremiah. "You will be defeated by the king of Babylon."

[18]Then Jeremiah asked the king, "What crime have I committed? What have I done against you, your attendants, or the people that I should be imprisoned like this? [19]Where are your prophets now who told you the king of Babylon would not attack you or this land? [20]Listen, my lord the king, I beg you. Don't send me back to the dungeon in the house of Jonathan the secretary, for I will die there."

[21]So King Zedekiah commanded that Jeremiah not be returned to the dungeon. Instead, he was imprisoned in the courtyard of the guard in the royal palace. The king also commanded that Jeremiah be given a loaf of fresh bread every day as long as there was any left in the city. So Jeremiah was put in the palace prison.

Jeremiah in a Cistern

38 Now Shephatiah son of Mattan, Gedaliah son of Pashhur, Jehucal* son of Shelemiah, and Pashhur son of Malkijah heard what Jeremiah had been telling the people. He had been saying, [2]"This is what the LORD says: 'Everyone who stays in Jerusalem will die from war, famine, or disease, but those who surrender to the Babylonians* will live. Their reward will be life. They will live!' [3]The LORD also says: 'The city of Jerusalem will certainly be handed over to the army of the king of Babylon, who will capture it.'"

[4]So these officials went to the king and said, "Sir, this man must die! That kind of talk will undermine the morale of the few fighting men we have left, as well as that of all the people. This man is a traitor!"

[5]King Zedekiah agreed. "All right," he said. "Do as you like. I can't stop you."

[6]So the officials took Jeremiah from his cell and lowered him by ropes into an empty cistern in the prison yard. It belonged to Malkijah, a member of the royal family. There was no water in the cistern, but there was a thick layer of mud at the bottom, and Jeremiah sank down into it.

[7]But Ebed-melech the Ethiopian,* an important court official, heard that Jeremiah was in the cistern. At that time the king was holding court at the Benjamin Gate, [8]so Ebed-melech rushed from the palace to speak with him. [9]"My lord the king," he said, "these men have done a very evil

37:12 Hebrew *to separate from there in the midst of the people.* **38:1** Hebrew *Jucal,* a variant spelling of Jehucal; see 37:3. **38:2** Or *Chaldeans;* also in 38:18, 19, 23. **38:7** Hebrew *the Cushite.*

11–21: The temporary lifting of the siege led to Jeremiah's imprisonment in Jerusalem on a charge of desertion. He had set off for Anathoth to check his new field and was arrested at the city gate, beaten, and incarcerated. Before Jerusalem fell, individuals could save themselves by deserting to the besieging forces. The king could have saved the city and his own life if he surrendered. The king's ambiguous attitude to Jeremiah is shown by his summons. Although he preserved Jeremiah's life by ameliorating his situation, Zedekiah never submitted to God's word.

38:1–13 Jeremiah in the Cistern. Jeremiah had one courageous ally while he was being held in the court of the guard. Ebed-melech, from Ethiopia, or Nubia, was an official in the palace (see Africans in Biblical History, 2 Kgs 19). He gained permission from the king to remove Jeremiah from the muddy cistern where the anti-Babylonian advisers had left him to die. It is interesting that this foreigner had more compassion and insight than the Judean establishment. His trust in God was acknowledged and rewarded (cf. 39:15–18).

thing in putting Jeremiah the prophet into the
cistern. He will soon die of hunger, for almost all
the bread in the city is gone."
10 So the king told Ebed-melech, "Take thirty
of my men with you, and pull Jeremiah out of
the cistern before he dies."
11 So Ebed-melech took the men with him and
went to a room in the palace beneath the treasury, where he found some old rags and discarded
clothing. He carried these to the cistern and lowered them to Jeremiah on a rope. 12 Ebed-melech
called down to Jeremiah, "Put these rags under
your armpits to protect you from the ropes."
Then when Jeremiah was ready, 13 they pulled
him out. So Jeremiah was returned to the courtyard of the guard—the palace prison—where he
remained.

Zedekiah Questions Jeremiah

14 One day King Zedekiah sent for Jeremiah and
had him brought to the third entrance of the
LORD's Temple. "I want to ask you something,"
the king said. "And don't try to hide the truth."
15 Jeremiah said, "If I tell you the truth, you
will kill me. And if I give you advice, you won't
listen to me anyway."
16 So King Zedekiah secretly promised him,
"As surely as the LORD our Creator lives, I will
not kill you or hand you over to the men who
want you dead."
17 Then Jeremiah said to Zedekiah, "This is
what the LORD God of Heaven's Armies, the God
of Israel, says: 'If you surrender to the Babylonian officers, you and your family will live, and
the city will not be burned down. 18 But if you refuse to surrender, you will not escape! This city
will be handed over to the Babylonians, and they
will burn it to the ground.' "
19 "But I am afraid to surrender," the king
said, "for the Babylonians may hand me over to
the Judeans who have defected to them. And who
knows what they will do to me!"
20 Jeremiah replied, "You won't be handed
over to them if you choose to obey the LORD.
Your life will be spared, and all will go well for
you. 21 But if you refuse to surrender, this is what
the LORD has revealed to me: 22 All the women
left in your palace will be brought out and given
to the officers of the Babylonian army. Then the
women will taunt you, saying,

'What fine friends you have!
They have betrayed and misled you.
When your feet sank in the mud,
they left you to your fate!'

23 All your wives and children will be led out to
the Babylonians, and you will not escape. You
will be seized by the king of Babylon, and this
city will be burned down."
24 Then Zedekiah said to Jeremiah, "Don't tell
anyone you told me this, or you will die! 25 My
officials may hear that I spoke to you, and they
may say, 'Tell us what you and the king were
talking about. If you don't tell us, we will kill
you.' 26 If this happens, just tell them you begged
me not to send you back to Jonathan's dungeon,
for fear you would die there."
27 Sure enough, it wasn't long before the
king's officials came to Jeremiah and asked him
why the king had called for him. But Jeremiah
followed the king's instructions, and they left
without finding out the truth. No one had overheard the conversation between Jeremiah and
the king. 28 And Jeremiah remained a prisoner in
the courtyard of the guard until the day Jerusalem was captured.

The Fall of Jerusalem

39 In January* of the ninth year of King
Zedekiah's reign, King Nebuchadnezzar* came with his army to be-
siege Jerusalem. 2 Two and a half years later, on
July 18* in the eleventh year of Zedekiah's reign,

39:1a Hebrew *in the tenth month,* of the ancient Hebrew lunar calendar. A number of events in Jeremiah can be cross-checked with dates in surviving Babylonian records and related accurately to our modern calendar. This event occurred on January 15, 588 B.C.; see 52:4a and the note there. **39:1b** Hebrew *Nebuchadrezzar,* a variant spelling of Nebuchadnezzar; also in 39:11. **39:2** Hebrew *On the ninth day of the fourth month.* This day was July 18, 586 B.C.; also see note on 39:1a.

38:14–28 Zedekiah questions Jeremiah. Jeremiah's last word for Zedekiah included a vision of the women of the king's household being led out of the conquered city to the Babylonian leaders and taunting the king for listening to unreliable advisers. The courtiers who opposed the LORD's word thought Jeremiah should die for undermining the courage of Jerusalem's residents with his announcements of Babylon's certain victory.

39:1–10 Fall of Jerusalem. In the eleventh year of Zedekiah, after almost two years of siege, the Babylonian forces breached the wall and took the city. Rather than surrender, Zedekiah fled but was captured near Jericho, brought before Nebuchadnezzar, and suffered agonizing punishments. The last thing he saw before being blinded was the slaughter of his family and friends. In chains, Zedekiah was exiled to Babylon along with the Judeans who

the Babylonians broke through the wall, and the
city fell. 3All the officers of the Babylonian army
came in and sat in triumph at the Middle Gate:
Nergal-sharezer of Samgar, and Nebo-sarsekim,*
a chief officer, and Nergal-sharezer, the king's adviser, and all the other officers.
4When King Zedekiah and all the soldiers
saw that the Babylonians had broken into the
city, they fled. They waited for nightfall and then
slipped through the gate between the two walls
behind the king's garden and headed toward the
Jordan Valley.*
5But the Babylonian* troops chased the king
and caught him on the plains of Jericho. They took
him to King Nebuchadnezzar of Babylon, who was
at Riblah in the land of Hamath. There the king of
Babylon pronounced judgment upon Zedekiah.
6He made Zedekiah watch as they slaughtered
his sons and all the nobles of Judah. 7Then they
gouged out Zedekiah's eyes, bound him in bronze
chains, and led him away to Babylon.
8Meanwhile, the Babylonians burned Jerusalem, including the palace, and tore down the
walls of the city. 9Then Nebuzaradan, the captain of the guard, sent to Babylon the rest of the
people who remained in the city as well as those
who had defected to him. 10But Nebuzaradan left
a few of the poorest people in Judah, and he assigned them vineyards and fields to care for.

Jeremiah Remains in Judah

11King Nebuchadnezzar had told Nebuzaradan,
the captain of the guard, to find Jeremiah. 12"See
that he isn't hurt," he said. "Look after him well,
and give him anything he wants." 13So Nebuzaradan, the captain of the guard; Nebushazban,
a chief officer; Nergal-sharezer, the king's adviser; and the other officers of Babylon's king 14sent
messengers to bring Jeremiah out of the prison.
They put him under the care of Gedaliah son of
Ahikam and grandson of Shaphan, who took him
back to his home. So Jeremiah stayed in Judah
among his own people.
15The LORD had given the following message
to Jeremiah while he was still in prison: 16"Say
to Ebed-melech the Ethiopian,* 'This is what
the LORD of Heaven's Armies, the God of Israel, says: I will do to this city everything I have
threatened. I will send disaster, not prosperity.
You will see its destruction, 17but I will rescue
you from those you fear so much. 18Because you
trusted me, I will give you your life as a reward.
I will rescue you and keep you safe. I, the LORD,
have spoken!' "

40 The LORD gave a message to Jeremiah
after Nebuzaradan, the captain of the
guard, had released him at Ramah.
He had found Jeremiah bound in chains among
all the other captives of Jerusalem and Judah who
were being sent to exile in Babylon.
2The captain of the guard called for Jeremiah
and said, "The LORD your God has brought this
disaster on this land, 3just as he said he would.
For these people have sinned against the LORD
and disobeyed him. That is why it happened.
4But I am going to take off your chains and let
you go. If you want to come with me to Babylon, you are welcome. I will see that you are
well cared for. But if you don't want to come, you
may stay here. The whole land is before you—go
wherever you like. 5If you decide to stay, then
return to Gedaliah son of Ahikam and grandson
of Shaphan. He has been appointed governor of
Judah by the king of Babylon. Stay there with
the people he rules. But it's up to you; go wherever you like."
Then Nebuzaradan, the captain of the guard,
gave Jeremiah some food and money and let him
go. 6So Jeremiah returned to Gedaliah son of
Ahikam at Mizpah, and he lived in Judah with
the few who were still left in the land.

Gedaliah Governs in Judah

7The leaders of the Judean guerrilla bands in
the countryside heard that the king of Babylon

39:3 Or *Nergal-sharezer, Samgar-nebo, Sarsekim.* **39:4** Hebrew *the Arabah.* **39:5** Or *Chaldean;* similarly in 39:8. **39:16** Hebrew *the Cushite.*

had surrendered and other siege survivors.

39:11—41:18: Because of Nebuchadnezzar's kindness, the Babylonians treated Jeremiah differently. He was taken with the other captive survivors but was released and allowed to remain in Judah. Jeremiah was entrusted to the care of Gedaliah, whom the Babylonians had appointed governor. Gedaliah came from a family of courtiers who had supported Jeremiah's ministry in various ways. **40:7–16:** Gedaliah's leadership offered hope to the remaining remnant. Poor people owning nothing had been left behind and given farmland and vineyards once owned by exiles. Judeans who had fled during the crisis returned and received a share in the harvest. Somehow, part of Judah's army had survived in the open country. Gedaliah persuaded some of them to accept Babylonian rule and submit to his authority. He assured them that they would suffer no reprisals and granted them support. Not everyone was happy

had appointed Gedaliah son of Ahikam as governor over the poor people who were left behind
in Judah—the men, women, and children who
hadn't been exiled to Babylon. 8 So they went to
see Gedaliah at Mizpah. These included: Ishmael
son of Nethaniah, Johanan and Jonathan sons
of Kareah, Seraiah son of Tanhumeth, the sons
of Ephai the Netophathite, Jezaniah son of the
Maacathite, and all their men.
9 Gedaliah vowed to them that the Babylonians* meant them no harm. "Don't be afraid
to serve them. Live in the land and serve the
king of Babylon, and all will go well for you," he
promised. 10 "As for me, I will stay at Mizpah to
represent you before the Babylonians who come
to meet with us. Settle in the towns you have
taken, and live off the land. Harvest the grapes
and summer fruits and olives, and store them
away."
11 When the Judeans in Moab, Ammon, Edom,
and the other nearby countries heard that the
king of Babylon had left a few people in Judah
and that Gedaliah was the governor, 12 they began to return to Judah from the places to which
they had fled. They stopped at Mizpah to meet
with Gedaliah and then went into the Judean
countryside to gather a great harvest of grapes
and other crops.

A Plot against Gedaliah

13 Soon after this, Johanan son of Kareah and
the other guerrilla leaders came to Gedaliah at
Mizpah. 14 They said to him, "Did you know that
Baalis, king of Ammon, has sent Ishmael son of
Nethaniah to assassinate you?" But Gedaliah refused to believe them.
15 Later Johanan had a private conference with
Gedaliah and volunteered to kill Ishmael secretly. "Why should we let him come and murder
you?" Johanan asked. "What will happen then
to the Judeans who have returned? Why should
the few of us who are still left be scattered and
lost?"
16 But Gedaliah said to Johanan, "I forbid you
to do any such thing, for you are lying about
Ishmael."

The Murder of Gedaliah

41 But in midautumn,* Ishmael son of
Nethaniah and grandson of Elishama, who was a member of the royal
family and had been one of the king's high officials, went to Mizpah with ten men to meet
Gedaliah. While they were eating together, 2 Ishmael and his ten men suddenly jumped up, drew
their swords, and killed Gedaliah, whom the king
of Babylon had appointed governor. 3 Ishmael
also killed all the Judeans and the Babylonian*
soldiers who were with Gedaliah at Mizpah.
4 The next day, before anyone had heard about
Gedaliah's murder, 5 eighty men arrived from
Shechem, Shiloh, and Samaria to worship at the
Temple of the LORD. They had shaved off their
beards, torn their clothes, and cut themselves,
and had brought along grain offerings and frankincense. 6 Ishmael left Mizpah to meet them,
weeping as he went. When he reached them, he
said, "Oh, come and see what has happened to
Gedaliah!"
7 But as soon as they were all inside the town,
Ishmael and his men killed all but ten of them
and threw their bodies into a cistern. 8 The other
ten had talked Ishmael into letting them go by
promising to bring him their stores of wheat,
barley, olive oil, and honey that they had hidden away. 9 The cistern where Ishmael dumped
the bodies of the men he murdered was the large
one dug by King Asa when he fortified Mizpah
to protect himself against King Baasha of Israel.
Ishmael son of Nethaniah filled it with corpses.
10 Then Ishmael made captives of the king's
daughters and the other people who had been
left under Gedaliah's care in Mizpah by Nebuzaradan, the captain of the guard. Taking them
with him, he started back toward the land of Ammon.
11 But when Johanan son of Kareah and the
other guerrilla leaders heard about Ishmael's
crimes, 12 they took all their men and set out to

40:9 Or *Chaldeans;* also in 40:10. **41:1** Hebrew *in the seventh month,* of the ancient Hebrew lunar calendar. This month occurred within the months of October and November 586 B.C.; also see note on 39:1a. **41:3** Or *Chaldean.*

with the conditions in Judah, however. **41:1–18:** One of the commanders did not accept Gedaliah's terms. Ishmael, a member of the royal family, plotted with Baalis, king of the Ammonites, to assassinate Gedaliah and overthrow Babylonian rule. To Jeremiah this plot represented continued resistance to the LORD's will, not admirable patriotism. Another commander, Johanan, warned Gedaliah, but his refusal to heed the warning led to his death. Ishmael's rebellion prevented a first step toward return and reunion for the eighty Northern Kingdom Israelites. These men were clearly mourning the destruction of Judah and seeking simply to worship God. All but the ten who bribed him were killed, showing that Ishmael's motivation was greed, not patriotism. Johanan and his forces caught up with Ishmael and freed his captives. Even in this situation courage, kindness, and some awareness of righteousness did exist.

stop him. They caught up with him at the large pool near Gibeon. 13The people Ishmael had captured shouted for joy when they saw Johanan and the other guerrilla leaders. 14And all the captives from Mizpah escaped and began to help Johanan. 15Meanwhile, Ishmael and eight of his men escaped from Johanan into the land of Ammon.

16Then Johanan son of Kareah and the other guerrilla leaders took all the people they had rescued in Gibeon—the soldiers, women, children, and court officials* whom Ishmael had captured after he killed Gedaliah. 17They took them all to the village of Geruth-kimham near Bethlehem, where they prepared to leave for Egypt. 18They were afraid of what the Babylonians* would do when they heard that Ishmael had killed Gedaliah, the governor appointed by the Babylonian king.

Warning to Stay in Judah

42 Then all the guerrilla leaders, including Johanan son of Kareah and Jezaniah* son of Hoshaiah, and all the people, from the least to the greatest, approached 2Jeremiah the prophet. They said, "Please pray to the LORD your God for us. As you can see, we are only a tiny remnant compared to what we were before. 3Pray that the LORD your God will show us what to do and where to go."

4"All right," Jeremiah replied. "I will pray to the LORD your God, as you have asked, and I will tell you everything he says. I will hide nothing from you."

5Then they said to Jeremiah, "May the LORD your God be a faithful witness against us if we refuse to obey whatever he tells us to do! 6Whether we like it or not, we will obey the LORD our God to whom we are sending you with our plea. For if we obey him, everything will turn out well for us."

7Ten days later the LORD gave his reply to Jeremiah. 8So he called for Johanan son of Kareah and the other guerrilla leaders, and for all the people, from the least to the greatest. 9He said to them, "You sent me to the LORD, the God of Israel, with your request, and this is his reply: 10'Stay here in this land. If you do, I will build you up and not tear you down; I will plant you and not uproot you. For I am sorry about all the punishment I have had to bring upon you. 11Do not fear the king of Babylon anymore,' says the LORD. 'For I am with you and will save you and rescue you from his power. 12I will be merciful to you by making him kind, so he will let you stay here in your land.'

13"But if you refuse to obey the LORD your God, and if you say, 'We will not stay here; 14instead, we will go to Egypt where we will be free from war, the call to arms, and hunger,' 15then hear the LORD's message to the remnant of Judah. This is what the LORD of Heaven's Armies, the God of Israel, says: 'If you are determined to go to Egypt and live there, 16the very war and famine you fear will catch up to you, and you will die there. 17That is the fate awaiting every one of you who insists on going to live in Egypt. Yes, you will die from war, famine, and disease. None of you will escape the disaster I will bring upon you there.'

18"This is what the LORD of Heaven's Armies, the God of Israel, says: 'Just as my anger and fury have been poured out on the people of Jerusalem, so they will be poured out on you when you enter Egypt. You will be an object of damnation, horror, cursing, and mockery. And you will never see your homeland again.'

19"Listen, you remnant of Judah. The LORD has told you: 'Do not go to Egypt!' Don't forget this warning I have given you today. 20For you were not being honest when you sent me to pray to the LORD your God for you. You said, 'Just tell us what the LORD our God says, and we will do it!' 21And today I have told you exactly what he said, but you will not obey the LORD your God any better now than you have in the past. 22So you can be sure that you will die from war, famine, and disease in Egypt, where you insist on going."

Jeremiah Taken to Egypt

43 When Jeremiah had finished giving this message from the LORD their God to all the people, 2Azariah son of Hoshaiah and Johanan son of Kareah and all the other proud men said to Jeremiah, "You lie! The LORD our God hasn't forbidden us to go to Egypt! 3Baruch son of Neriah has convinced you to say this, because he wants us to stay here and be killed by the Babylonians* or be carried off into exile."

4So Johanan and the other guerrilla leaders

41:16 Or *eunuchs.* **41:18** Or *Chaldeans.* **42:1** Greek version reads *Azariah;* compare 43:2. **43:3** Or *Chaldeans.*

42:1—43:13 Warning to Stay in Judah. Johanan and his people inquired of the LORD through Jeremiah. The divine word was unequivocal: Egypt was not the way to go. But the fearful people, in spite of Jeremiah's track record, were unconvinced and refused to obey. Jeremiah was even accused of colluding with Baruch in order to hand them over to the Babylonians. The group emigrated to Egypt, taking Jeremiah and Baruch with them.

and all the people refused to obey the LORD's command to stay in Judah. 5Johanan and the other leaders took with them all the people who had returned from the nearby countries to which they had fled. 6In the crowd were men, women, and children, the king's daughters, and all those whom Nebuzaradan, the captain of the guard, had left with Gedaliah. The prophet Jeremiah and Baruch were also included. 7The people refused to obey the voice of the LORD and went to Egypt, going as far as the city of Tahpanhes.

8Then at Tahpanhes, the LORD gave another message to Jeremiah. He said, 9"While the people of Judah are watching, take some large rocks and bury them under the pavement stones at the entrance of Pharaoh's palace here in Tahpanhes. 10Then say to the people of Judah, 'This is what the LORD of Heaven's Armies, the God of Israel, says: I will certainly bring my servant Nebuchadnezzar,* king of Babylon, here to Egypt. I will set his throne over these stones that I have hidden. He will spread his royal canopy over them. 11And when he comes, he will destroy the land of Egypt. He will bring death to those destined for death, captivity to those destined for captivity, and war to those destined for war. 12He will set fire to the temples of Egypt's gods; he will burn the temples and carry the idols away as plunder. He will pick clean the land of Egypt as a shepherd picks fleas from his cloak. And he himself will leave unharmed. 13He will break down the sacred pillars standing in the temple of the sun* in Egypt, and he will burn down the temples of Egypt's gods.'"

Judgment for Idolatry

44 This is the message Jeremiah received concerning the Judeans living in northern Egypt in the cities of Migdol, Tahpanhes, and Memphis,* and in southern Egypt* as well: 2"This is what the LORD of Heaven's Armies, the God of Israel, says: You saw the calamity I brought on Jerusalem and all the towns of Judah. They now lie deserted and in ruins. 3They provoked my anger with all their wickedness. They burned incense and worshiped other gods—gods that neither they nor you nor any of your ancestors had ever even known.

4"Again and again I sent my servants, the prophets, to plead with them, 'Don't do these horrible things that I hate so much.' 5But my people would not listen or turn back from their wicked ways. They kept on burning incense to these gods. 6And so my fury boiled over and fell like fire on the towns of Judah and into the streets of Jerusalem, and they are still a desolate ruin today.

7"And now the LORD God of Heaven's Armies, the God of Israel, asks you: Why are you destroying yourselves? For not one of you will survive—not a man, woman, or child among you who has come here from Judah, not even the babies in your arms. 8Why provoke my anger by burning incense to the idols you have made here in Egypt? You will only destroy yourselves and make yourselves an object of cursing and mockery for all the nations of the earth. 9Have you forgotten the sins of your ancestors, the sins of the kings and queens of Judah, and the sins you and your wives committed in Judah and Jerusalem? 10To this very hour you have shown no remorse or reverence. No one has chosen to follow my word and the decrees I gave to you and your ancestors before you.

11"Therefore, this is what the LORD of Heaven's Armies, the God of Israel, says: I am determined to destroy every one of you! 12I will take this remnant of Judah—those who were determined to come here and live in Egypt—and I will consume them. They will fall here in Egypt, killed by war and famine. All will die, from the least to the greatest. They will be an object of damnation, horror, cursing, and mockery. 13I will punish them in Egypt just as I punished them in Jerusalem, by war, famine, and disease. 14Of that remnant who fled to Egypt, hoping someday to return to Judah, there will be no survivors. Even though they long to return home, only a handful will do so."

15Then all the women present and all the men who knew that their wives had burned incense to idols—a great crowd of all the Judeans living in northern Egypt and southern Egypt*—answered Jeremiah, 16"We will not listen to your messages

43:10 Hebrew *Nebuchadrezzar,* a variant spelling of Nebuchadnezzar. **43:13** Or *in Heliopolis.* **44:1a** Hebrew *Noph.* **44:1b** Hebrew *in Pathros.* **44:15** Hebrew *in Egypt, in Pathros.*

44:1–30: The last phase of Jeremiah's ministry returns to the core issue of disobedience and false worship. **15–18:** The Jewish refugees in Egypt, although they had experienced disaster and now had God's word readily available, chose once more to worship the Queen of Heaven. They had worked out an alternate theological explanation for past events, one that contradicted God's word through Jeremiah. Earlier, the Queen of Heaven had been worshiped and the people prospered, enjoying peace and plenty of food. Josiah's religious reformation, beginning in 621 BC, had put a stop to her veneration. The people believed that neglect of her offerings had obviously caused the suffering Judah experienced in the years that followed.

from the LORD! 17 We will do whatever we want. We will burn incense and pour out liquid offerings to the Queen of Heaven just as much as we like—just as we, and our ancestors, and our kings and officials have always done in the towns of Judah and in the streets of Jerusalem. For in those days we had plenty to eat, and we were well off and had no troubles! 18 But ever since we quit burning incense to the Queen of Heaven and stopped worshiping her with liquid offerings, we have been in great trouble and have been dying from war and famine."

19 "Besides," the women added, "do you suppose that we were burning incense and pouring out liquid offerings to the Queen of Heaven, and making cakes marked with her image, without our husbands knowing it and helping us? Of course not!"

20 Then Jeremiah said to all of them, men and women alike, who had given him that answer, 21 "Do you think the LORD did not know that you and your ancestors, your kings and officials, and all the people were burning incense to idols in the towns of Judah and in the streets of Jerusalem? 22 It was because the LORD could no longer bear all the disgusting things you were doing that he made your land an object of cursing—a desolate ruin without inhabitants—as it is today. 23 All these terrible things happened to you because you have burned incense to idols and sinned against the LORD. You have refused to obey him and have not followed his instructions, his decrees, and his laws."

24 Then Jeremiah said to them all, including the women, "Listen to this message from the LORD, all you citizens of Judah who live in Egypt. 25 This is what the LORD of Heaven's Armies, the God of Israel, says: 'You and your wives have said, "We will keep our promises to burn incense and pour out liquid offerings to the Queen of Heaven," and you have proved by your actions that you meant it. So go ahead and carry out your promises and vows to her!'

26 "But listen to this message from the LORD, all you Judeans now living in Egypt: 'I have sworn by my great name,' says the LORD, 'that my name will no longer be spoken by any of the Judeans in the land of Egypt. None of you may invoke my name or use this oath: "As surely as the Sovereign LORD lives." 27 For I will watch over you to bring you disaster and not good. Everyone from Judah who is now living in Egypt will suffer war and famine until all of you are dead. 28 Only a small number will escape death and return to Judah from Egypt. Then all those who came to Egypt will find out whose words are true—mine or theirs!

29 " 'And this is the proof I give you,' says the LORD, 'that all I have threatened will happen to you and that I will punish you here.' 30 This is what the LORD says: 'I will turn Pharaoh Hophra, king of Egypt, over to his enemies who want to kill him, just as I turned King Zedekiah of Judah over to King Nebuchadnezzar* of Babylon.' "

A Message for Baruch

45 The prophet Jeremiah gave a message to Baruch son of Neriah in the fourth year of the reign of Jehoiakim son of Josiah,* after Baruch had written down everything Jeremiah had dictated to him. He said, 2 "This is what the LORD, the God of Israel, says to you, Baruch: 3 You have said, 'I am overwhelmed with trouble! Haven't I had enough pain already? And now the LORD has added more! I am worn out from sighing and can find no rest.'

4 "Baruch, this is what the LORD says: 'I will destroy this nation that I built. I will uproot what I planted. 5 Are you seeking great things for yourself? Don't do it! I will bring great disaster upon all these people; but I will give you your

44:30 Hebrew *Nebuchadrezzar,* a variant spelling of Nebuchadnezzar. **45:1** The fourth year of Jehoiakim's reign was 605 B.C.

20–30: The final word of prophecy reported from Jeremiah in Egypt is therefore another announcement of judgment. People who had experienced the consequences of idolatry in Judah will experience it again. The truth of God's judgment against them had been confirmed by the Babylonian conquest. Disbelieving, they had disobeyed again. So proof will be offered once more when God gives Pharaoh into the hands of Nebuchadnezzar. No one knows what happened to Jeremiah, but the book that bears his name continues to bring the living word of God to the nations.

45:1–5 A Promise for Baruch

This portion of the book comes from the year in which Baruch wrote the scroll at Jeremiah's dictation. **3:** Because of his service, the LORD promised Baruch his life as a prize of war during the chaotic, dangerous years. Jehoiakim had closed his mind to the LORD's word, but Baruch had responded in sorrow because he believed it. **5:** Baruch the believer contrasts with the idolatrous Jews in Egypt. It also gives another example of God's trustworthiness. Baruch had survived through all these disasters because God had promised.

Household Gods

Mesopotamian families had various household deities: deceased ancestors, personal deities and protective spirits. The ancestors of Laban and Jacob were Mesopotamian, so the household gods of Genesis 31 and other Old Testament references may parallel Mesopotamian "little gods" that fifteenth- to fourteenth-century BC texts mention as figurines that represented deified ancestors. These deified ancestors functioned in divination in a family's house.

Personal gods assisted by protective spirits, both often feminine, were thought to protect the members and interests of the household. The biblical narrative in which Rachel steals her family household gods seems to distinguish between them and the personal guardian deities of the family. Since Laban makes a treaty with Jacob that depends on Nahor's god as witness while the household gods are missing, he must be referring to another deity.

Texts also distinguish between ancestors and personal deities with respect to their offerings. Whereas families executed prayer and offering ceremonies to personal deities each morning and evening, they made ritual offerings for deceased relatives only once a year. Burning incense or oil invoked the presence of protective deities. Lamps and incense burners are present frequently in excavated household shrines in the ancient Near East.

From the group of publicly known deities, patriarchs chose personal deities that related to their interests or to the neighborhoods in which they lived. Family members shared the same personal deity, and a woman's allegiance changed from her father's deity to her husband's when she married. Babylonian letters indicate that personal deities functioned as intercessors with national or city deities.

Archaeologists have found female clay figurines throughout Israel and Judah, with a large number of them in Jerusalem; they probably exemplify the "carved image" and "idols, dung balls" that the Deuteronomists and prophets so vigorously opposed. The prevalence of such figurines throughout Israel and Judah is evidenced in that almost every domestic dwelling in tenth-century Tirzah (Tell el-Far'ah) and 45 percent of divided monarchy-era houses at Mizpah (Tell Beit Mirsim) had a female or an animal figurine. The jewelry, textile production tools, and cooking equipment that surround the female figurines and other ritual artifacts at these and other sites like Beersheba and Tell Halif suggest that women petitioned images of the goddess for aid and protection, particularly while childrearing. The writing prophets consistently denounced syncretism just as they opposed the oppression of the poor. While the veneration of secondary deities, often imaged in concrete form, diminished after the Exile, it continued in various branches of Judaism and thrives even in some forms of Christianity today.

life as a reward wherever you go. I, the LORD, have spoken!' "

Messages for the Nations

46 The following messages were given to Jeremiah the prophet from the LORD concerning foreign nations.

Messages about Egypt

2This message concerning Egypt was given in the fourth year of the reign of Jehoiakim son of Josiah, the king of Judah, on the occasion of the battle of Carchemish* when Pharaoh Neco, king of Egypt, and his army were defeated beside the Euphrates River by King Nebuchadnezzar* of Babylon.

46:2a This event occurred in 605 B.C., during the fourth year of Jehoiakim's reign (according to the calendar system in which the new year begins in the spring). **46:2b** Hebrew *Nebuchadrezzar,* a variant spelling of Nebuchadnezzar; also in 46:13, 26.

46:1—49:39 Prophecies against the Nations

Babylonian expansion through Syria-Palestine and into Egypt appeared to be the result of their ambition and military prowess, but Jeremiah revealed another cause. The LORD as Creator claims sovereignty over all nations and exercises the authority to appoint their ruler by naming the king of Babylon. Nebuchadnezzar will be God's instrument for bringing judgment upon Judah and its neighbors. The upheaval and suffering that accompanied Babylon's rise were not proof of the victory of Marduk, patron deity of Babylon. On the contrary, the king of Babylon was the LORD's servant. Each nation is addressed (Egypt, Philistia, Moab, Ammon, Edom, Damascus, Kedar, Hazor, Elam, and Babylon) by predictions of war, famine, and other great disasters.

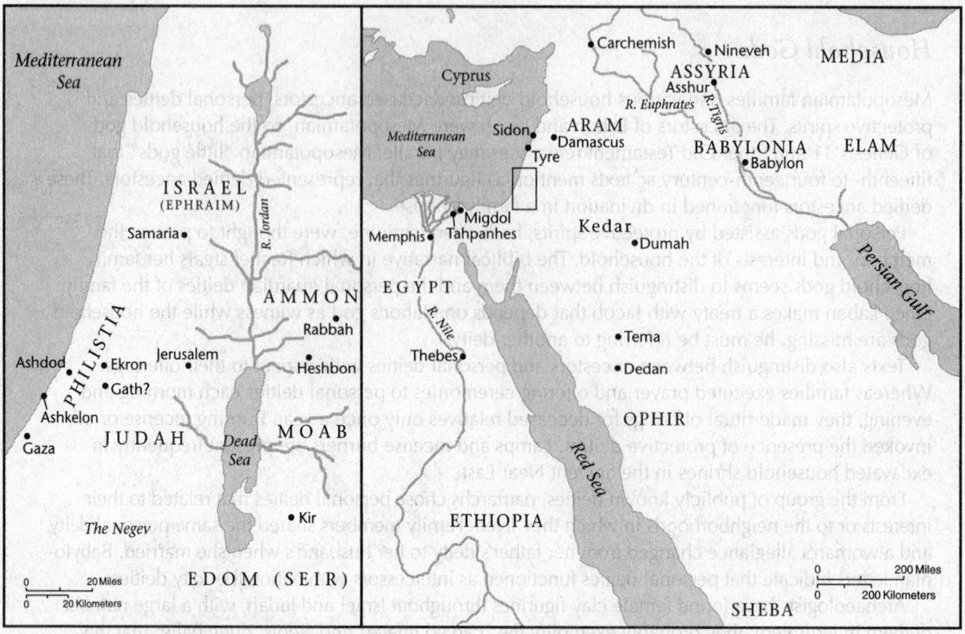

Places Mentioned in the Oracles against the Nations

3 "Prepare your shields,
and advance into battle!
4 Harness the horses,
and mount the stallions.
Take your positions.
Put on your helmets.
Sharpen your spears,
and prepare your armor.
5 But what do I see?
The Egyptian army flees in terror.
The bravest of its fighting men run
without a backward glance.
They are terrorized at every turn,"
says the LORD.
6 "The swiftest runners cannot flee;
the mightiest warriors cannot escape.
By the Euphrates River to the north,
they stumble and fall.

7 "Who is this, rising like the Nile at floodtime,
overflowing all the land?
8 It is the Egyptian army,
overflowing all the land,
boasting that it will cover the earth like a flood,
destroying cities and their people.
9 Charge, you horses and chariots;
attack, you mighty warriors of Egypt!
Come, all you allies from Ethiopia, Libya, and Lydia*
who are skilled with the shield and bow!
10 For this is the day of the Lord, the LORD of Heaven's Armies,
a day of vengeance on his enemies.
The sword will devour until it is satisfied,
yes, until it is drunk with your blood!
The Lord, the LORD of Heaven's Armies, will receive a sacrifice today
in the north country beside the Euphrates River.
11 "Go up to Gilead to get medicine,
O virgin daughter of Egypt!
But your many treatments
will bring you no healing.
12 The nations have heard of your shame.
The earth is filled with your cries of despair.
Your mightiest warriors will run into each other
and fall down together."

46:9 Hebrew *from Cush, Put, and Lud.*

46:2–28 Egypt. 3–12: Prophecies against Egypt are related to Babylon's victories. Jeremiah describes the failure of Egypt's ambitions. Egyptian forces had defeated the Babylonians and made Judah Egypt's vassal, but at Carchemish, Nebuchadnezzar was victorious. This oracle claimed that Babylon's victory was

13 Then the LORD gave the prophet Jeremiah this message about King Nebuchadnezzar's plans to attack Egypt.

14 "Shout it out in Egypt!
Publish it in the cities of Migdol,
Memphis,* and Tahpanhes!
Mobilize for battle,
for the sword will devour everyone around you.
15 Why have your warriors fallen?
They cannot stand, for the LORD has knocked them down.
16 They stumble and fall over each other
and say among themselves,
'Come, let's go back to our people,
to the land of our birth.
Let's get away from the sword of the enemy!'
17 There they will say,
'Pharaoh, the king of Egypt, is a loudmouth
who missed his opportunity!'

18 "As surely as I live," says the King,
whose name is the LORD of Heaven's Armies,
"one is coming against Egypt
who is as tall as Mount Tabor,
or as Mount Carmel by the sea!
19 Pack up! Get ready to leave for exile,
you citizens of Egypt!
The city of Memphis will be destroyed,
without a single inhabitant.
20 Egypt is as sleek as a beautiful young cow,
but a horsefly from the north is on its way!
21 Egypt's mercenaries have become like fattened calves.
They, too, will turn and run,
for it is a day of great disaster for Egypt,
a time of great punishment.
22 Egypt flees, silent as a serpent gliding away.
The invading army marches in;
they come against her with axes like woodsmen.
23 They will cut down her people like trees,"
says the LORD,
"for they are more numerous than locusts.
24 Egypt will be humiliated;
she will be handed over to people from the north."

25 The LORD of Heaven's Armies, the God
of Israel, says: "I will punish Amon, the god of
Thebes,* and all the other gods of Egypt. I will
punish its rulers and Pharaoh, too, and all who
trust in him. 26 I will hand them over to those
who want them killed—to King Nebuchadnezzar of Babylon and his army. But afterward the land will recover from the ravages of war. I, the LORD, have spoken!

27 "But do not be afraid, Jacob, my servant;
do not be dismayed, Israel.
For I will bring you home again from distant lands,
and your children will return from their exile.
Israel* will return to a life of peace and quiet,
and no one will terrorize them.
28 Do not be afraid, Jacob, my servant,
for I am with you," says the LORD.
"I will completely destroy the nations to which I have exiled you,
but I will not completely destroy you.
I will discipline you, but with justice;
I cannot let you go unpunished."

A Message about Philistia

47 This is the LORD's message to the prophet Jeremiah concerning the Philistines of Gaza, before it was

46:14 Hebrew *Noph;* also in 46:19. **46:25** Hebrew *of No.* **46:27** Hebrew *Jacob.* See note on 5:20.

---

because God was behind them. **14–26:** Some in Judah continued to put their hopes in Egypt. God warns against this misplaced trust. Pharaoh, Egypt's gods, and their armies will fall before the LORD and the enemy invader from the north. The Egyptians could not save Judah from the judgment, and they could not save themselves. Since Nebuchadnezzar did not invade Egypt until 568 BC, this oracle had continuing relevance after the fall of Jerusalem. Egypt would not be a safe place for refugees. **27–28:** These final two verses repeat 30:10–11. Again Nebuchadnezzar's victories are balanced with the promise of a limit to Babylonian rule. When Israel's just measure of punishment is complete, the LORD will make an end of Babylon and bring his people back from captivity.

47:1–7 Philistia. The Philistine cities along the Mediterranean coast lay in the path of imperial armies. Babylon defeated Ashkelon in 604 BC, and Egypt conquered Gaza in 601. This oracle about the first occasion could have been reused in preparation for the second. Prophecies about Babylonian victories supported Jeremiah's unwelcome message that Judah and Jerusalem must submit. Ashkelon's conqueror was a sword in the LORD's hand. Resisting Babylon was resisting the LORD and was, therefore, pointless.

captured by the Egyptian army. [2]This is what the
LORD says:

"A flood is coming from the north
to overflow the land.
It will destroy the land and everything in it—
cities and people alike.
People will scream in terror,
and everyone in the land will wail.
3 Hear the clatter of stallions' hooves
and the rumble of wheels as the chariots
rush by.
Terrified fathers run madly,
without a backward glance at their helpless
children.
4 "The time has come for the Philistines to be
destroyed,
along with their allies from Tyre and Sidon.
Yes, the LORD is destroying the remnant of
the Philistines,
those colonists from the island of Crete.*
5 Gaza will be humiliated, its head shaved bald;
Ashkelon will lie silent.
You remnant from the Mediterranean coast,*
how long will you lament and mourn?

6 "Now, O sword of the LORD,
when will you be at rest again?
Go back into your sheath;
rest and be still.

7 "But how can it be still
when the LORD has sent it on a mission?
For the city of Ashkelon
and the people living along the sea
must be destroyed."

A Message about Moab

48 This message was given concerning Moab. This is what the LORD of Heaven's Armies, the God of Israel, says:

"What sorrow awaits the city of Nebo;
it will soon lie in ruins.
The city of Kiriathaim will be humiliated and
captured;
the fortress will be humiliated and broken
down.
2 No one will ever brag about Moab again,
for in Heshbon there is a plot to destroy her.
'Come,' they say, 'we will cut her off from
being a nation.'
The town of Madmen,* too, will be silenced;
the sword will follow you there.
3 Listen to the cries from Horonaim,
cries of devastation and great destruction.
4 All Moab is destroyed.
Her little ones will cry out.*
5 Her refugees weep bitterly,
climbing the slope to Luhith.
They cry out in terror,
descending the slope to Horonaim.
6 Flee for your lives!
Hide* in the wilderness!
7 Because you have trusted in your wealth and
skill,
you will be taken captive.
Your god Chemosh, with his priests and
officials,
will be hauled off to distant lands!

8 "All the towns will be destroyed,
and no one will escape—
either on the plateaus or in the valleys,
for the LORD has spoken.
9 Oh, that Moab had wings
so she could fly away,*
for her towns will be left empty,
with no one living in them.
10 Cursed are those who refuse to do the LORD's
work,
who hold back their swords from shedding
blood!

11 "From his earliest history, Moab has lived in
peace,

47:4 Hebrew *from Caphtor.* **47:5** Hebrew *the plain.* **48:2** *Madmen* sounds like the Hebrew word for "silence"; it should not be confused with the English word *madmen.* **48:4** Greek version reads *Her cries are heard as far away as Zoar.* **48:6** Or *Hide like a wild donkey;* or *Hide like a juniper shrub;* or *Be like* [the town of] *Aroer.* The meaning of the Hebrew is uncertain. **48:9** Or *Put salt on Moab, / for she will be laid waste.*

48:1–47 Moab. Envoys from Moab, Ammon, Edom, Tyre, and Sidon met with Zedekiah in 594 BC to plan a revolt against Nebuchadnezzar. God's response via Jeremiah (cf. chap. 27) provides a context for reading the prophecies concerning Moab, the Ammonites, and Edom. The LORD, the Creator, delivered these lands to Nebuchadnezzar. Any nation refusing to submit to Babylon would suffer. The judgment prophecies in chapters 48—49 assert God's authority over these nations and give vivid descriptions of their terror and loss. **7:** The main reason for judgment in each case was pride and misplaced trust. Moab was arrogant and relied on its citadels, wealth, and its god Chemosh.

never going into exile.
He is like wine that has been allowed to settle.
He has not been poured from flask to flask,
and he is now fragrant and smooth.
12 But the time is coming soon," says the LORD,
"when I will send men to pour him from his jar.
They will pour him out,
then shatter the jar!
13 At last Moab will be ashamed of his idol Chemosh,
as the people of Israel were ashamed of their gold calf at Bethel.*

14 "You used to boast, 'We are heroes,
mighty men of war.'
15 But now Moab and his towns will be destroyed.
His most promising youth are doomed to slaughter,"
says the King, whose name is the LORD of Heaven's Armies.
16 "Destruction is coming fast for Moab;
calamity threatens ominously.
17 You friends of Moab,
weep for him and cry!
See how the strong scepter is broken,
how the beautiful staff is shattered!

18 "Come down from your glory
and sit in the dust, you people of Dibon,
for those who destroy Moab will shatter Dibon, too.
They will tear down all your towers.
19 You people of Aroer,
stand beside the road and watch.
Shout to those who flee from Moab,
'What has happened there?'

20 "And the reply comes back,
'Moab lies in ruins, disgraced;
weep and wail!
Tell it by the banks of the Arnon River:
Moab has been destroyed!'
21 Judgment has been poured out on the towns of the plateau—
on Holon and Jahaz* and Mephaath,
22 on Dibon and Nebo and Beth-diblathaim,
23 on Kiriathaim and Beth-gamul and Beth-meon,
24 on Kerioth and Bozrah—
all the towns of Moab, far and near.

25 "The strength of Moab has ended.
His arm has been broken," says the LORD.
26 "Let him stagger and fall like a drunkard,
for he has rebelled against the LORD.
Moab will wallow in his own vomit,
ridiculed by all.
27 Did you not ridicule the people of Israel?
Were they caught in the company of thieves
that you should despise them as you do?

28 "You people of Moab,
flee from your towns and live in the caves.
Hide like doves that nest
in the clefts of the rocks.
29 We have all heard of the pride of Moab,
for his pride is very great.
We know of his lofty pride,
his arrogance, and his haughty heart.
30 I know about his insolence,"
says the LORD,
"but his boasts are empty—
as empty as his deeds.
31 So now I wail for Moab;
yes, I will mourn for Moab.
My heart is broken for the men of Kir-hareseth.*

32 "You people of Sibmah, rich in vineyards,
I will weep for you even more than I did for Jazer.
Your spreading vines once reached as far as the Dead Sea,*
but the destroyer has stripped you bare!
He has harvested your grapes and summer fruits.
33 Joy and gladness are gone from fruitful Moab.
The presses yield no wine.
No one treads the grapes with shouts of joy.
There is shouting, yes, but not of joy.

34 "Instead, their awful cries of terror can be
heard from Heshbon clear across to Elealeh and
Jahaz; from Zoar all the way to Horonaim and
Eglath-shelishiyah. Even the waters of Nimrim
are dried up now.
35 "I will put an end to Moab," says the LORD,
"for the people offer sacrifices at the pagan shrines
and burn incense to their false gods. 36 My heart
moans like a flute for Moab and Kir-hareseth,
for all their wealth has disappeared. 37 The people shave their heads and beards in mourning.
They slash their hands and put on clothes made

48:13 Hebrew *ashamed when they trusted in Bethel.*
48:21 Hebrew *Jahzah,* a variant spelling of Jahaz.
48:31 Hebrew *Kir-heres,* a variant spelling of Kir-hareseth; also in 48:36. **48:32** Hebrew *the sea of Jazer.*

of burlap. [38]There is crying and sorrow in every Moabite home and on every street. For I have smashed Moab like an old, unwanted jar. [39]How it is shattered! Hear the wailing! See the shame of Moab! It has become an object of ridicule, an example of ruin to all its neighbors."

[40]This is what the LORD says:

"Look! The enemy swoops down like an eagle,
spreading his wings over Moab.
[41] Its cities will fall,
and its strongholds will be seized.
Even the mightiest warriors will be in anguish
like a woman in labor.
[42] Moab will no longer be a nation,
for it has boasted against the LORD.
[43] "Terror and traps and snares will be your lot,
O Moab," says the LORD.
[44] "Those who flee in terror will fall into a trap,
and those who escape the trap will step into a snare.
I will see to it that you do not get away,
for the time of your judgment has come,"
says the LORD.
[45] "The people flee as far as Heshbon
but are unable to go on.
For a fire comes from Heshbon,
King Sihon's ancient home,
to devour the entire land
with all its rebellious people.
[46] "O Moab, they weep for you!
The people of the god Chemosh are destroyed!
Your sons and your daughters
have been taken away as captives.
[47] But I will restore the fortunes of Moab
in days to come.
I, the LORD, have spoken!"

This is the end of Jeremiah's prophecy concerning Moab.

A Message about Ammon

49 This message was given concerning the Ammonites. This is what the LORD says:

"Are there no descendants of Israel
to inherit the land of Gad?
Why are you, who worship Molech,*
living in its towns?
[2] In the days to come," says the LORD,
"I will sound the battle cry against your city of Rabbah.
It will become a desolate heap of ruins,
and the neighboring towns will be burned.
Then Israel will take back the land
you took from her," says the LORD.
[3] "Cry out, O Heshbon,
for the town of Ai is destroyed.
Weep, O people of Rabbah!
Put on your clothes of mourning.
Weep and wail, hiding in the hedges,
for your god Molech, with his priests and officials,
will be hauled off to distant lands.
[4] You are proud of your fertile valleys,
but they will soon be ruined.
You trusted in your wealth,
you rebellious daughter,
and thought no one could ever harm you.
[5] But look! I will bring terror upon you,"
says the Lord, the LORD of Heaven's Armies.
"Your neighbors will chase you from your land,
and no one will help your exiles as they flee.
[6] But I will restore the fortunes of the Ammonites
in days to come.
I, the LORD, have spoken."

Messages about Edom

[7]This message was given concerning Edom. This is what the LORD of Heaven's Armies says:

"Is there no wisdom in Teman?
Is no one left to give wise counsel?
[8] Turn and flee!
Hide in deep caves, you people of Dedan!
For when I bring disaster on Edom,*
I will punish you, too!
[9] Those who harvest grapes

49:1 Hebrew *Malcam,* a variant spelling of Molech; also in 49:3. **49:8** Hebrew *Esau;* also in 49:10.

49:1–39 Ammon, Edom, Damascus, Kedar, Hazor, Elam. 1–22: These messages (as well as the one to Moab, chap. 48), are about nations related to Israel. Edom came from Esau, and Moab and Ammon were sons of Lot. Their territories bordered Israel and Judah on the east, and they were regularly at each others' throats. Moab had ridiculed Israel, and Ammon had taken land and towns from the tribe of Gad. **1–6:** The Ammonites also believed their treasures made them secure; Edom trusted in its brute strength. All this trust will prove misplaced. Shame and mourning will replace pride. Yet God is also concerned for

always leave a few for the poor.
If thieves came at night,
they would not take everything.
10 But I will strip bare the land of Edom,
and there will be no place left to hide.
Its children, its brothers, and its neighbors
will all be destroyed,
and Edom itself will be no more.
11 But I will protect the orphans who remain
among you.
Your widows, too, can depend on me for
help."

12 And this is what the LORD says: "If the innocent must suffer, how much more must you!
You will not go unpunished! You must drink this
cup of judgment! 13 For I have sworn by my own
name," says the LORD, "that Bozrah will become
an object of horror and a heap of ruins; it will
be mocked and cursed. All its towns and villages
will be desolate forever."

14 I have heard a message from the LORD
that an ambassador was sent to the nations
to say,
"Form a coalition against Edom,
and prepare for battle!"
15 The LORD says to Edom,
"I will cut you down to size among the nations.
You will be despised by all.
16 You have been deceived
by the fear you inspire in others
and by your own pride.
You live in a rock fortress
and control the mountain heights.
But even if you make your nest among the
peaks with the eagles,
I will bring you crashing down,"
says the LORD.

17 "Edom will be an object of horror.
All who pass by will be appalled
and will gasp at the destruction they see
there.
18 It will be like the destruction of Sodom and
Gomorrah
and their neighboring towns," says the
LORD.
"No one will live there;
no one will inhabit it.
19 I will come like a lion from the thickets of the
Jordan,
leaping on the sheep in the pasture.
I will chase Edom from its land,
and I will appoint the leader of my choice.
For who is like me, and who can challenge
me?
What ruler can oppose my will?"
20 Listen to the LORD's plans against Edom
and the people of Teman.
Even the little children will be dragged off
like sheep,
and their homes will be destroyed.
21 The earth will shake with the noise of Edom's
fall,
and its cry of despair will be heard all the
way to the Red Sea.*
22 Look! The enemy swoops down like an
eagle,
spreading his wings over Bozrah.
Even the mightiest warriors will be in
anguish
like a woman in labor.

A Message about Damascus

23 This message was given concerning Damascus.
This is what the LORD says:

"The towns of Hamath and Arpad are struck
with fear,
for they have heard the news of their
destruction.
Their hearts are troubled
like a wild sea in a raging storm.
24 Damascus has become feeble,
and all her people turn to flee.
Fear, anguish, and pain have gripped her
as they grip a woman in labor.
25 That famous city, a city of joy,
will be forsaken!
26 Her young men will fall in the streets and
die.
Her soldiers will all be killed,"
says the LORD of Heaven's Armies.
27 "And I will set fire to the walls of Damascus
that will burn up the palaces of Ben-hadad."

49:21 Hebrew *sea of reeds.*

these nations. **4:** Ammon is described by the same title by which God addressed Israel in 31:22. **11:** The LORD offers shelter to Edom's widows and orphans. After the judgment, God promises to restore the Moabites and the Ammonites to their lands. **23–39:** The remaining three messages are about peoples increasingly distant from Israel. God's sovereignty covers the whole world. These prophecies have been included in Jeremiah because they support the LORD's authority to rule all nations.

A Message about Kedar and Hazor

28 This message was given concerning Kedar and the kingdoms of Hazor, which were attacked by King Nebuchadnezzar* of Babylon. This is what the LORD says:

"Advance against Kedar!
Destroy the warriors from the East!
29 Their flocks and tents will be captured,
and their household goods and camels will be taken away.
Everywhere shouts of panic will be heard:
'We are terrorized at every turn!'
30 Run for your lives," says the LORD.
"Hide yourselves in deep caves, you people of Hazor,
for King Nebuchadnezzar of Babylon has plotted against you
and is preparing to destroy you.

31 "Go up and attack that complacent nation,"
says the LORD.
"Its people live alone in the desert
without walls or gates.
32 Their camels and other livestock will all be yours.
I will scatter to the winds these people
who live in remote places.*
I will bring calamity upon them
from every direction," says the LORD.
33 "Hazor will be inhabited by jackals,
and it will be desolate forever.
No one will live there;
no one will inhabit it."

A Message about Elam

34 This message concerning Elam came to the
prophet Jeremiah from the LORD at the beginning
of the reign of King Zedekiah of Judah. 35 This is
what the LORD of Heaven's Armies says:

"I will destroy the archers of Elam—
the best of their forces.
36 I will bring enemies from all directions,
and I will scatter the people of Elam to the four winds.
They will be exiled to countries around the world.
37 I myself will go with Elam's enemies to shatter it.
In my fierce anger, I will bring great disaster
upon the people of Elam," says the LORD.
"Their enemies will chase them with the sword
until I have destroyed them completely.
38 I will set my throne in Elam," says the LORD,
"and I will destroy its king and officials.
39 But I will restore the fortunes of Elam
in days to come.
I, the LORD, have spoken!"

A Message about Babylon

50 The LORD gave Jeremiah the prophet
this message concerning Babylon and
the land of the Babylonians.* 2 This is
what the LORD says:

"Tell the whole world,
and keep nothing back.
Raise a signal flag
to tell everyone that Babylon will fall!
Her images and idols* will be shattered.
Her gods Bel and Marduk will be utterly disgraced.
3 For a nation will attack her from the north
and bring such destruction that no one will live there again.
Everything will be gone;
both people and animals will flee.

Hope for Israel and Judah

4 "In those coming days,"
says the LORD,
"the people of Israel will return home
together with the people of Judah.
They will come weeping
and seeking the LORD their God.

49:28 Hebrew *Nebuchadrezzar,* a variant spelling of Nebuchadnezzar; also in 49:30. **49:32** Or *who clip the corners of their hair.* **50:1** Or *Chaldeans;* also in 50:8, 25, 35, 45. **50:2** The Hebrew term (literally *round things*) probably alludes to dung.

50:1—51:64 Judgment on Babylon

This collection of judgment prophecies against Babylon seems to contradict the commands to serve Babylon (27:7, 12) and to pray for Babylon (29:7). The book explains this difference by the promise of a limited period of power, seventy years, for Babylon. The promised return of the exiles and their descendants will be linked to the end of Babylon's power. God will summon the exiles to flee before Babylon is destroyed. Babylon's destruction will be followed by some restoration for Egypt, Moab, Ammon, and Elam. **50:4–20:** The message of destruction is followed by an additional message from the LORD about hope for

5 They will ask the way to Jerusalem*
and will start back home again.
They will bind themselves to the LORD
with an eternal covenant that will never be forgotten.
6 "My people have been lost sheep.
Their shepherds have led them astray
and turned them loose in the mountains.
They have lost their way
and can't remember how to get back to the sheepfold.
7 All who found them devoured them.
Their enemies said,
'We did nothing wrong in attacking them,
for they sinned against the LORD,
their true place of rest,
and the hope of their ancestors.'
8 "But now, flee from Babylon!
Leave the land of the Babylonians.
Like male goats at the head of the flock,
lead my people home again.
9 For I am raising up an army
of great nations from the north.
They will join forces to attack Babylon,
and she will be captured.
The enemies' arrows will go straight to the mark;
they will not miss!
10 Babylonia* will be looted
until the attackers are glutted with loot.
I, the LORD, have spoken!

Babylon's Sure Fall

11 "You rejoice and are glad,
you who plundered my chosen people.
You frisk about like a calf in a meadow
and neigh like a stallion.
12 But your homeland* will be overwhelmed
with shame and disgrace.
You will become the least of nations—
a wilderness, a dry and desolate land.
13 Because of the LORD's anger,
Babylon will become a deserted wasteland.
All who pass by will be horrified
and will gasp at the destruction they see there.

14 "Yes, prepare to attack Babylon,
all you surrounding nations.
Let your archers shoot at her; spare no arrows.
For she has sinned against the LORD.
15 Shout war cries against her from every side.
Look! She surrenders!
Her walls have fallen.
It is the LORD's vengeance,
so take vengeance on her.
Do to her as she has done to others!
16 Take from Babylon all those who plant crops;
send all the harvesters away.
Because of the sword of the enemy,
everyone will run away and rush back to their own lands.

Hope for God's People

17 "The Israelites are like sheep
that have been scattered by lions.
First the king of Assyria ate them up.
Then King Nebuchadnezzar* of Babylon
cracked their bones."
18 Therefore, this is what the LORD of Heaven's Armies,
the God of Israel, says:
"Now I will punish the king of Babylon and his land,
just as I punished the king of Assyria.
19 And I will bring Israel home again to its own land,
to feed in the fields of Carmel and Bashan,
and to be satisfied once more
in the hill country of Ephraim and Gilead.
20 In those days," says the LORD,
"no sin will be found in Israel or in Judah,
for I will forgive the remnant I preserve.

The LORD's Judgment on Babylon

21 "Go up, my warriors, against the land of Merathaim
and against the people of Pekod.
Pursue, kill, and completely destroy* them,
as I have commanded you," says the LORD.
22 "Let the battle cry be heard in the land,
a shout of great destruction.
23 Babylon, the mightiest hammer in all the earth,
lies broken and shattered.
Babylon is desolate among the nations!

50:5 Hebrew *Zion;* also in 50:28. **50:10** Or *Chaldea.* **50:12** Hebrew *your mother.* **50:17** Hebrew *Nebuchadrezzar,* a variant spelling of Nebuchadnezzar. **50:21** The Hebrew term used here refers to the complete consecration of things or people to the LORD, either by destroying them or by giving them as an offering.

Israel and Judah. **21–28:** Babylon was used by God to destroy Jerusalem, yet the LORD says, *I have set a trap . . . Destroy her completely,* announcing judgment on Babylon for cruel oppression and for sinning against

24 Listen, Babylon, for I have set a trap for you.
You are caught, for you have fought against the LORD.
25 The LORD has opened his armory
and brought out weapons to vent his fury.
The terror that falls upon the Babylonians
will be the work of the Sovereign LORD of Heaven's Armies.
26 Yes, come against her from distant lands.
Break open her granaries.
Crush her walls and houses into heaps of rubble.
Destroy her completely, and leave nothing!
27 Destroy even her young bulls—
it will be terrible for them, too!
Slaughter them all!
For Babylon's day of reckoning has come.
28 Listen to the people who have escaped from Babylon,
as they tell in Jerusalem
how the LORD our God has taken vengeance
against those who destroyed his Temple.

29 "Send out a call for archers to come to Babylon.
Surround the city so none can escape.
Do to her as she has done to others,
for she has defied the LORD, the Holy One of Israel.
30 Her young men will fall in the streets and die.
Her soldiers will all be killed,"
says the LORD.

31 "See, I am your enemy, you arrogant people,"
says the Lord, the LORD of Heaven's Armies.
"Your day of reckoning has arrived—
the day when I will punish you.
32 O land of arrogance, you will stumble and fall,
and no one will raise you up.
For I will light a fire in the cities of Babylon
that will burn up everything around them."

33 This is what the LORD of Heaven's Armies says:
"The people of Israel and Judah have been wronged.
Their captors hold them and refuse to let them go.
34 But the one who redeems them is strong.
His name is the LORD of Heaven's Armies.
He will defend them
and give them rest again in Israel.
But for the people of Babylon
there will be no rest!

35 "The sword of destruction will strike the Babylonians,"
says the LORD.
"It will strike the people of Babylon—
her officials and wise men, too.
36 The sword will strike her wise counselors,
and they will become fools.
The sword will strike her mightiest warriors,
and panic will seize them.
37 The sword will strike her horses and chariots
and her allies from other lands,
and they will all become like women.
The sword will strike her treasures,
and they all will be plundered.
38 The sword will even strike her water supply,
causing it to dry up.
And why? Because the whole land is filled with idols,
and the people are madly in love with them.

39 "Soon Babylon will be inhabited by desert animals and hyenas.
It will be a home for owls.
Never again will people live there;
it will lie desolate forever.
40 I will destroy it as I* destroyed Sodom and Gomorrah
and their neighboring towns," says the LORD.
"No one will live there;
no one will inhabit it.

41 "Look! A great army is coming from the north.
A great nation and many kings

50:40 Hebrew *as God.*

God. **29:** *Do to her as she has done* summarizes the principle exemplified in 30:16. This transformation mirrors changes seen earlier especially in 30:12–17. In a gracious non sequitur, God's word transforms the exiles and survivors from objects of just punishment to the recipients of mercy and vindication. The concept of a "just measure" of punishment helps to explain this change (30:11, cf. 10:24). **41–43:** The oracles against Babylon repeat several themes and specific expressions from the judgment sayings against Judah earlier in the book. This one duplicates the description of the invaders from Jeremiah 6:22–24 but substitutes *Babylon* for "Jerusalem." Babylon's warriors will become weak like women, and

are rising against you from far-off lands.
42 They are armed with bows and spears.
They are cruel and show no mercy.
As they ride forward on horses,
they sound like a roaring sea.
They are coming in battle formation,
planning to destroy you, Babylon.
43 The king of Babylon has heard reports about the enemy,
and he is weak with fright.
Pangs of anguish have gripped him,
like those of a woman in labor.

44 "I will come like a lion from the thickets of the Jordan,
leaping on the sheep in the pasture.
I will chase Babylon from its land,
and I will appoint the leader of my choice.
For who is like me, and who can challenge me?
What ruler can oppose my will?"

45 Listen to the LORD's plans against Babylon
and the land of the Babylonians.
Even the little children will be dragged off like sheep,
and their homes will be destroyed.
46 The earth will shake with the shout,
"Babylon has been taken!"
and its cry of despair will be heard around the world.

51 [1]This is what the LORD says:
"I will stir up a destroyer against Babylon
and the people of Babylonia.*
2 Foreigners will come and winnow her,
blowing her away as chaff.
They will come from every side
to rise against her in her day of trouble.
3 Don't let the archers put on their armor
or draw their bows.
Don't spare even her best soldiers!
Let her army be completely destroyed.*
4 They will fall dead in the land of the Babylonians,*
slashed to death in her streets.
5 For the LORD of Heaven's Armies
has not abandoned Israel and Judah.
He is still their God,
even though their land was filled with sin
against the Holy One of Israel."

6 Flee from Babylon! Save yourselves!
Don't get trapped in her punishment!
It is the LORD's time for vengeance;
he will repay her in full.
7 Babylon has been a gold cup in the LORD's hands,
a cup that made the whole earth drunk.
The nations drank Babylon's wine,
and it drove them all mad.
8 But suddenly Babylon, too, has fallen.
Weep for her.
Give her medicine.
Perhaps she can yet be healed.
9 We would have helped her if we could,
but nothing can save her now.
Let her go; abandon her.
Return now to your own land.
For her punishment reaches to the heavens;
it is so great it cannot be measured.
10 The LORD has vindicated us.
Come, let us announce in Jerusalem*
everything the LORD our God has done.

11 Sharpen the arrows!
Lift up the shields!*
For the LORD has inspired the kings of the Medes
to march against Babylon and destroy her.
This is his vengeance against those
who desecrated his Temple.
12 Raise the battle flag against Babylon!
Reinforce the guard and station the watchmen.
Prepare an ambush,
for the LORD will fulfill all his plans against Babylon.
13 You are a city by a great river,
a great center of commerce,
but your end has come.
The thread of your life is cut.
14 The LORD of Heaven's Armies has taken this vow
and has sworn to it by his own name:
"Your cities will be filled with enemies,
like fields swarming with locusts,
and they will shout in triumph over you."

51:1 Hebrew *of Leb-kamai,* a code name for Babylonia. **51:3** The Hebrew term used here refers to the complete consecration of things or people to the LORD, either by destroying them or by giving them as an offering. **51:4** Or *Chaldeans;* also in 51:54. **51:10** Hebrew *Zion;* also in 51:24. **51:11** Greek version reads *Fill up the quivers.*

its king will suffer anguish like a woman in labor. They will be powerless to defend and save the city. The city of Babylon personified as a woman appears frequently in these chapters, intensifying the picture of the city as a victim. **51:1–14:** More judgments against Babylon, interrupted by a hymn of praise

A Hymn of Praise to the Lord

15 The Lord made the earth by his power,
and he preserves it by his wisdom.
With his own understanding
he stretched out the heavens.
16 When he speaks in the thunder,
the heavens are filled with water.
He causes the clouds to rise over the earth.
He sends the lightning with the rain
and releases the wind from his storehouses.

17 The whole human race is foolish and has no knowledge!
The craftsmen are disgraced by the idols they make,
for their carefully shaped works are a fraud.
These idols have no breath or power.
18 Idols are worthless; they are ridiculous lies!
On the day of reckoning they will all be destroyed.
19 But the God of Israel* is no idol!
He is the Creator of everything that exists,
including his people, his own special possession.
The Lord of Heaven's Armies is his name!

Babylon's Great Punishment

20 "You* are my battle-ax and sword,"
says the Lord.
"With you I will shatter nations
and destroy many kingdoms.
21 With you I will shatter armies—
destroying the horse and rider,
the chariot and charioteer.
22 With you I will shatter men and women,
old people and children,
young men and maidens.
23 With you I will shatter shepherds and flocks,
farmers and oxen,
captains and officers.

24 "I will repay Babylon
and the people of Babylonia*
for all the wrong they have done
to my people in Jerusalem," says the Lord.

25 "Look, O mighty mountain, destroyer of the earth!
I am your enemy," says the Lord.
"I will raise my fist against you,
to knock you down from the heights.
When I am finished,
you will be nothing but a heap of burnt rubble.
26 You will be desolate forever.
Even your stones will never again be used for building.
You will be completely wiped out,"
says the Lord.

27 Raise a signal flag to the nations.
Sound the battle cry!
Mobilize them all against Babylon.
Prepare them to fight against her!
Bring out the armies of Ararat, Minni, and Ashkenaz.
Appoint a commander,
and bring a multitude of horses like swarming locusts!
28 Bring against her the armies of the nations—
led by the kings of the Medes
and all their captains and officers.

29 The earth trembles and writhes in pain,
for everything the Lord has planned
against Babylon stands unchanged.
Babylon will be left desolate without a single inhabitant.
30 Her mightiest warriors no longer fight.
They stay in their barracks, their courage gone.
They have become like women.
The invaders have burned the houses
and broken down the city gates.
31 The news is passed from one runner to the next
as the messengers hurry to tell the king
that his city has been captured.
32 All the escape routes are blocked.
The marshes have been set aflame,
and the army is in a panic.

33 This is what the Lord of Heaven's Armies,
the God of Israel, says:
"Babylon is like wheat on a threshing floor,
about to be trampled.
In just a little while
her harvest will begin."

51:19 Hebrew *the Portion of Jacob.* See note on 5:20. **51:20** Possibly Cyrus, whom God used to conquer Babylon. Compare Isa 44:28; 45:1. **51:24** Or *Chaldea;* also in 51:35.

at 15–19. God did not change sides arbitrarily. The Creator who had granted power to Nebuchadnezzar is also free to take it away (51:15–19, a duplicate of vv. 12–16). **20–44:** The narrator returns to judgments against Babylon and her great punishment. **34–35:** Like Judah, the Babylonians will be judged because

34 "King Nebuchadnezzar* of Babylon has eaten
and crushed us
and drained us of strength.
He has swallowed us like a great monster
and filled his belly with our riches.
He has thrown us out of our own country.
35 Make Babylon suffer as she made us suffer,"
say the people of Zion.
"Make the people of Babylonia pay for
spilling our blood,"
says Jerusalem.

The LORD's Vengeance on Babylon

36 This is what the LORD says to Jerusalem:

"I will be your lawyer to plead your case,
and I will avenge you.
I will dry up her river,
as well as her springs,
37 and Babylon will become a heap of ruins,
haunted by jackals.
She will be an object of horror and contempt,
a place where no one lives.
38 Her people will roar together like strong
lions.
They will growl like lion cubs.
39 And while they lie inflamed with all their
wine,
I will prepare a different kind of feast for
them.
I will make them drink until they fall asleep,
and they will never wake up again,"
says the LORD.
40 "I will bring them down
like lambs to the slaughter,
like rams and goats to be sacrificed.

41 "How Babylon* is fallen—
great Babylon, praised throughout the
earth!
Now she has become an object of horror
among the nations.
42 The sea has risen over Babylon;
she is covered by its crashing waves.
43 Her cities now lie in ruins;
she is a dry wasteland
where no one lives or even passes by.
44 And I will punish Bel, the god of Babylon,
and make him vomit up all he has eaten.
The nations will no longer come and worship
him.
The wall of Babylon has fallen!

A Message for the Exiles

45 "Come out, my people, flee from Babylon.
Save yourselves! Run from the LORD's
fierce anger.
46 But do not panic; don't be afraid
when you hear the first rumor of
approaching forces.
For rumors will keep coming year by year.
Violence will erupt in the land
as the leaders fight against each other.
47 For the time is surely coming
when I will punish this great city and all
her idols.
Her whole land will be disgraced,
and her dead will lie in the streets.
48 Then the heavens and earth will rejoice,
for out of the north will come destroying
armies
against Babylon," says the LORD.
49 "Just as Babylon killed the people of Israel
and others throughout the world,
so must her people be killed.
50 Get out, all you who have escaped the sword!
Do not stand and watch—flee while you
can!
Remember the LORD, though you are in a far-
off land,
and think about your home in Jerusalem."

51 "We are ashamed," the people say.
"We are insulted and disgraced
because the LORD's Temple
has been defiled by foreigners."

52 "Yes," says the LORD, "but the time is coming
when I will destroy Babylon's idols.
The groans of her wounded people

51:34 Hebrew *Nebuchadrezzar,* a variant spelling of Nebuchadnezzar. **51:41** Hebrew *Sheshach,* a code name for Babylon.

they had sinned against, challenged, and arrogantly defied the LORD. In answer to lament prayers like those of Jerusalem, the LORD will redeem Judah and take revenge for city and Temple. Babylon will be killed as she killed. **32, 37:** Jeremiah 52:13 reports that the Babylonian commander burned the Temple and other large buildings. The same threat is spoken against Babylon here. Like Jerusalem, Babylon will be burned and become a deserted *heap of ruins.* **45–64:** The principle of corresponding judgments eventually breaks down. God will pardon the Jewish remnant and will not abandon them. Israel and Judah will join in an everlasting covenant with the LORD while Babylon will remain abandoned forever.

will be heard throughout the land.
53 Though Babylon reaches as high as the
heavens
and makes her fortifications incredibly
strong,
I will still send enemies to plunder her.
I, the LORD, have spoken!

Babylon's Complete Destruction

54 "Listen! Hear the cry of Babylon,
the sound of great destruction from the
land of the Babylonians.
55 For the LORD is destroying Babylon.
He will silence her loud voice.
Waves of enemies pound against her;
the noise of battle rings through the city.
56 Destroying armies come against Babylon.
Her mighty men are captured,
and their weapons break in their hands.
For the LORD is a God who gives just
punishment;
he always repays in full.
57 I will make her officials and wise men drunk,
along with her captains, officers, and warriors.
They will fall asleep
and never wake up again!"
says the King, whose name is
the LORD of Heaven's Armies.

58 This is what the LORD of Heaven's Armies
says:
"The thick walls of Babylon will be leveled to
the ground,
and her massive gates will be burned.
The builders from many lands have worked
in vain,
for their work will be destroyed by fire!"

Jeremiah's Message Sent to Babylon

59 The prophet Jeremiah gave this message to Seraiah son of Neriah and grandson of Mahseiah, a
staff officer, when Seraiah went to Babylon with
King Zedekiah of Judah. This was during the
fourth year of Zedekiah's reign.* 60 Jeremiah had
recorded on a scroll all the terrible disasters that
would soon come upon Babylon—all the words
written here. 61 He said to Seraiah, "When you
get to Babylon, read aloud everything on this
scroll. 62 Then say, 'LORD, you have said that you
will destroy Babylon so that neither people nor
animals will remain here. She will lie empty and
abandoned forever.' 63 When you have finished
reading the scroll, tie it to a stone and throw
it into the Euphrates River. 64 Then say, 'In this
same way Babylon and her people will sink,
never again to rise, because of the disasters I will
bring upon her.'"

This is the end of Jeremiah's messages.

The Fall of Jerusalem

52 Zedekiah was twenty-one years old
when he became king, and he reigned
in Jerusalem eleven years. His mother was Hamutal, the daughter of Jeremiah from
Libnah. 2 But Zedekiah did what was evil in the
LORD's sight, just as Jehoiakim had done. 3 These
things happened because of the LORD's anger
against the people of Jerusalem and Judah, until
he finally banished them from his presence and
sent them into exile.

Zedekiah rebelled against the king of Babylon.
4 So on January 15,* during the ninth year of
Zedekiah's reign, King Nebuchadnezzar* of Babylon led his entire army against Jerusalem. They
surrounded the city and built siege ramps against
its walls. 5 Jerusalem was kept under siege until
the eleventh year of King Zedekiah's reign.

6 By July 18 in the eleventh year of Zedekiah's reign,* the famine in the city had become

51:59 The fourth year of Zedekiah's reign was 593 B.C.
52:4a Hebrew *on the tenth day of the tenth month,* of the ancient Hebrew lunar calendar. A number of events in Jeremiah can be cross-checked with dates in surviving Babylonian records and related accurately to our modern calendar. This day was January 15, 588 B.C. **52:4b** Hebrew *Nebuchadrezzar,* a variant spelling of Nebuchadnezzar; also in 52:12, 28, 29, 30. **52:6** Hebrew *By the ninth day of the fourth month* [in the eleventh year of Zedekiah's reign]. This day was July 18, 586 B.C.; also see note on 52:4a.

59–62: Jeremiah's announcement concerning the final message dates to the fourth year of Zedekiah, only shortly after the message of Jeremiah in chapters 27—28.

52:1–34 The End of Judah and Jerusalem

The book concludes with a chapter borrowed from 2 Kings 24:18—25:30 reporting the fall of Jerusalem and its immediate aftermath; then the text jumps (v. 31) to the thirty-seventh year of Jehoiachin's exile (561 BC). Jews were subject to the king of Babylon, Evil-merodach, but the former, rightful king of Judah still lived. Roughly halfway through the predicted seventy years, Evil-merodach released Jehoiachin from prison, acknowledged his royal status, and gave him the dubious honors accorded to other captured kings. Fragments of documents detailing the allowance of grain, wine, and oil for Jehoiachin's family have been discovered in excavations of ancient Babylon. By the addition of Jeremiah 52, the completed form of the book communicates important assurances to later readers.

very severe, and the last of the food was entirely
gone. 7 Then a section of the city wall was broken
down, and all the soldiers fled. Since the city was
surrounded by the Babylonians,* they waited
for nightfall. Then they slipped through the gate
between the two walls behind the king's garden
and headed toward the Jordan Valley.*

8 But the Babylonian troops chased King
Zedekiah and caught him on the plains of Jericho, for his men had all deserted him and scattered. 9 They took him to the king of Babylon at
Riblah in the land of Hamath. There the king of
Babylon pronounced judgment upon Zedekiah.
10 He made Zedekiah watch as they slaughtered
his sons and all the other officials of Judah.
11 Then they gouged out Zedekiah's eyes, bound
him in bronze chains, and led him away to Babylon. Zedekiah remained there in prison until
the day of his death.

The Temple Destroyed

12 On August 17 of that year,* which was the
nineteenth year of King Nebuchadnezzar's reign,
Nebuzaradan, the captain of the guard and an official of the Babylonian king, arrived in Jerusalem. 13 He burned down the Temple of the LORD,
the royal palace, and all the houses of Jerusalem.
He destroyed all the important buildings* in the
city. 14 Then he supervised the entire Babylonian*
army as they tore down the walls of Jerusalem
on every side. 15 Nebuzaradan, the captain of the
guard, then took as exiles some of the poorest of
the people, the rest of the people who remained
in the city, the defectors who had declared their
allegiance to the king of Babylon, and the rest of
the craftsmen. 16 But Nebuzaradan allowed some
of the poorest people to stay behind in Judah to
care for the vineyards and fields.

17 The Babylonians broke up the bronze pillars in front of the LORD's Temple, the bronze
water carts, and the great bronze basin called
the Sea, and they carried all the bronze away to
Babylon. 18 They also took all the ash buckets,
shovels, lamp snuffers, basins, dishes, and all the
other bronze articles used for making sacrifices
at the Temple. 19 Nebuzaradan, the captain of the
guard, also took the small bowls, incense burners,
basins, pots, lampstands, dishes, bowls used for
liquid offerings, and all the other articles made
of pure gold or silver.

20 The weight of the bronze from the two pillars, the Sea with the twelve bronze oxen beneath
it, and the water carts was too great to be measured. These things had been made for the LORD's
Temple in the days of King Solomon. 21 Each of
the pillars was 27 feet tall and 18 feet in circumference.* They were hollow, with walls 3 inches
thick.* 22 The bronze capital on top of each pillar
was 7½ feet* high and was decorated with a network of bronze pomegranates all the way around.
23 There were 96 pomegranates on the sides, and a
total of 100 on the network around the top.

24 Nebuzaradan, the captain of the guard, took
with him as prisoners Seraiah the high priest,
Zephaniah the priest of the second rank, and
the three chief gatekeepers. 25 And from among
the people still hiding in the city, he took an officer who had been in charge of the Judean army;
seven of the king's personal advisers; the army
commander's chief secretary, who was in charge
of recruitment; and sixty other citizens. 26 Nebuzaradan, the captain of the guard, took them all
to the king of Babylon at Riblah. 27 And there at
Riblah, in the land of Hamath, the king of Babylon had them all put to death. So the people of
Judah were sent into exile from their land.

28 The number of captives taken to Babylon in
the seventh year of Nebuchadnezzar's reign* was
3,023. 29 Then in Nebuchadnezzar's eighteenth
year* he took 832 more. 30 In Nebuchadnezzar's
twenty-third year* he sent Nebuzaradan, the
captain of the guard, who took 745 more—a total
of 4,600 captives in all.

Hope for Israel's Royal Line

31 In the thirty-seventh year of the exile of King
Jehoiachin of Judah, Evil-merodach ascended to
the Babylonian throne. He was kind to* Jehoiachin and released him from prison on March 31
of that year.* 32 He spoke kindly to Jehoiachin
and gave him a higher place than all the other
exiled kings in Babylon. 33 He supplied Jehoiachin with new clothes to replace his prison garb
and allowed him to dine in the king's presence
for the rest of his life. 34 So the Babylonian king
gave him a regular food allowance as long as he
lived. This continued until the day of his death.

52:7a Or *the Chaldeans;* similarly in 52:8, 17. **52:7b** Hebrew *the Arabah.* **52:12** Hebrew *On the tenth day of the fifth month,* of the ancient Hebrew lunar calendar. This day was August 17, 586 B.C.; also see note on 52:4a. **52:13** Or *destroyed the houses of all the important people.* **52:14** Or *Chaldean.* **52:21a** Hebrew *18 cubits* [8.1 meters] *tall and 12 cubits* [5.4 meters] *in circumference.* **52:21b** Hebrew *4 fingers thick* [8 centimeters]. **52:22** Hebrew *5 cubits* [2.3 meters]. **52:28** This exile in the seventh year of Nebuchadnezzar's reign occurred in 597 B.C. **52:29** This exile in the eighteenth year of Nebuchadnezzar's reign occurred in 586 B.C. **52:30** This exile in the twenty-third year of Nebuchadnezzar's reign occurred in 581 B.C. **52:31a** Hebrew *He raised the head of.* **52:31b** Hebrew *on the twenty-fifth day of the twelfth month,* of the ancient Hebrew lunar calendar. This day was March 31, 561 B.C.; also see note on 52:4a.

LAMENTATIONS

INTRODUCTION

Lamentation is a common genre in the ancient Near East. There are numerous examples in the Old Testament, in particular in Psalms. The book of Lamentations is a compilation of corporate laments responding to Jerusalem's destruction by the Neo-Babylonians in 587/6 BC. Many interpreters suggest these laments were recited annually during the fasting days held regularly at the ruined Temple site (cf. Jer 41:5; Zech 7:1–7; 8:19).

There are five laments artfully redacted into one rhetorical piece. Lamentations 1—4 share common vocabulary, stylistic devices, and an acrostic structure. Such consistency suggests an individual or group of lament experts as composer(s). Second Chronicles 35:25 was often used to ascribe authorship to Jeremiah, but the laments here are for Jerusalem's destruction not, as there, for Josiah's death.

Scholars identify links between imagery and language in Lamentations and that of prophetic, wisdom, Deuteronomistic, and kingship traditions. The greatest similarities between the laments and prophetic traditions are in the use of female imagery and personification. In Lamentations, Jerusalem is personified as female, sometimes a woman scorned, sometimes a young girl, but most often as God's daughter (sometimes "virgin daughter"; e.g., 2:13). In the prophetic literature, however, Israel is most often personified as an adulterous wife who must be punished.

Female imagery is used rhetorically in prophetic literature to shame Israel into repentance. In Lamentations the imagery is used to persuade God to deliver Jerusalem from her distress (i.e., exile). While the result is the same—reconciliation between Israel and God—the object of persuasion differs in each genre. *—LeAnn Snow Flesher*

Sorrow in Jerusalem

1 * [1]Jerusalem, once so full of people,
is now deserted.
She who was once great among the nations
now sits alone like a widow.
Once the queen of all the earth,
she is now a slave.

[2] She sobs through the night;
tears stream down her cheeks.
Among all her lovers,
there is no one left to comfort her.
All her friends have betrayed her
and become her enemies.

[3] Judah has been led away into captivity,
oppressed with cruel slavery.
She lives among foreign nations
and has no place of rest.
Her enemies have chased her down,
and she has nowhere to turn.

[4] The roads to Jerusalem* are in mourning,
for crowds no longer come to celebrate the festivals.
The city gates are silent,
her priests groan,
her young women are crying—
how bitter is her fate!

[5] Her oppressors have become her masters,
and her enemies prosper,
for the LORD has punished Jerusalem
for her many sins.
Her children have been captured
and taken away to distant lands.

[6] All the majesty of beautiful Jerusalem*
has been stripped away.
Her princes are like starving deer
searching for pasture.
They are too weak to run
from the pursuing enemy.

[7] In the midst of her sadness and wandering,
Jerusalem remembers her ancient splendor.
But now she has fallen to her enemy,
and there is no one to help her.
Her enemy struck her down
and laughed as she fell.

[8] Jerusalem has sinned greatly,
so she has been tossed away like a filthy rag.
All who once honored her now despise her,
for they have seen her stripped naked and humiliated.
All she can do is groan
and hide her face.

[9] She defiled herself with immorality
and gave no thought to her future.
Now she lies in the gutter
with no one to lift her out.
"LORD, see my misery," she cries.
"The enemy has triumphed."

[10] The enemy has plundered her completely,
taking every precious thing she owns.
She has seen foreigners violate her sacred Temple,
the place the LORD had forbidden them to enter.

1 Each of the first four chapters of this book is an acrostic, laid out in the order of the Hebrew alphabet. The first word of each verse begins with a successive Hebrew letter. Chapters 1, 2, and 4 have one verse for each of the 22 Hebrew letters. Chapter 3 contains 22 stanzas of three verses each. Though chapter 5 has 22 verses, it is not an acrostic. **1:4** Hebrew *Zion;* also in 1:17. **1:6** Hebrew *of the daughter of Zion.*

1:1–22 Jerusalem Personified as Female

Jerusalem is consistently personified, using several images, as female. Jerusalem is a lonely widow who was formerly a queen. None of her lovers (i.e., allies) have comforted her; she is now an exiled slave. **6–8:** Daughter Zion (see translator's note on v. 6) has lost her majesty. The reference to nakedness implies both shame and wantonness. **9–11:** Her downfall directly relates to sin, specifically *immorality*, an allusion to prophetic imagery of a harlot. However, the emphasis is on the helpless, victimized female, with Jerusalem the lonely widow and slave, the inhabitants as young girls and children, and Zion as daughter, mocked and oppressed by enemies. The images of distressed females intertwined with laments over enemy victory alongside confessions of sin suggest Jerusalem's failure in her responsibility (as a parent) to discipline and protect a child. Ignoring the protection element brings shame onto parent as well as children; similarly, widows should be cared for by family or community. In other words, God is being called into account for not protecting his children. Although God's discipline is understandable and acceptable, destruction by the hand of unclean enemies is not. Note that the only petition found in these opening lines (v. 9b) is for God to observe the enemy's triumph and Jerusalem's

11 Her people groan as they search for bread.
They have sold their treasures for food to stay alive.
"O LORD, look," she mourns,
"and see how I am despised.

12 "Does it mean nothing to you, all you who pass by?
Look around and see if there is any suffering like mine,
which the LORD brought on me
when he erupted in fierce anger.

13 "He has sent fire from heaven that burns in my bones.
He has placed a trap in my path and turned me back.
He has left me devastated,
racked with sickness all day long.

14 "He wove my sins into ropes
to hitch me to a yoke of captivity.
The Lord sapped my strength and turned me over to my enemies;
I am helpless in their hands.

15 "The Lord has treated my mighty men
with contempt.
At his command a great army has come
to crush my young warriors.
The Lord has trampled his beloved city*
like grapes are trampled in a winepress.

16 "For all these things I weep;
tears flow down my cheeks.
No one is here to comfort me;
any who might encourage me are far away.
My children have no future,
for the enemy has conquered us."

17 Jerusalem reaches out for help,
but no one comforts her.
Regarding his people Israel,*
the LORD has said,
"Let their neighbors be their enemies!
Let them be thrown away like a filthy rag!"

18 "The LORD is right," Jerusalem says,
"for I rebelled against him.
Listen, people everywhere;
look upon my anguish and despair,
for my sons and daughters
have been taken captive to distant lands.

19 "I begged my allies for help,
but they betrayed me.
My priests and leaders
starved to death in the city,
even as they searched for food
to save their lives.

20 "LORD, see my anguish!
My heart is broken
and my soul despairs,
for I have rebelled against you.
In the streets the sword kills,
and at home there is only death.

21 "Others heard my groans,
but no one turned to comfort me.
When my enemies heard about my troubles,
they were happy to see what you had done.
Oh, bring the day you promised,
when they will suffer as I have suffered.

22 "Look at all their evil deeds, LORD.
Punish them,
as you have punished me
for all my sins.
My groans are many,
and I am sick at heart."

1:15 Hebrew *the virgin daughter of Judah.* **1:17** Hebrew *Jacob.* The names "Jacob" and "Israel" are often interchanged throughout the Old Testament, referring sometimes to the individual patriarch and sometimes to the nation.

affliction. **11b:** The speaker changes as Jerusalem laments for herself. Again God is asked to notice Jerusalem's pitiful state and is accused of attacking Jerusalem. Although Jerusalem has fallen to the Neo-Babylonians, she holds God accountable. **13–16:** The images become increasingly more severe: fire from heaven penetrating deep into bones, transgressions forming a yoke hung around Jerusalem's neck, rejecting mighty men and crushing young warriors, treading on the virgin daughter (see translator's note) as if in a winepress. **17–22:** These accusations sharply contrast with the image of the virgin daughter stretching out her arms searching hopelessly for a comforter. Juxtaposed is the image of mother Jerusalem concerned for her helpless children. Jerusalem is an exiled orphan. Her final appeal is that God should also discipline her enemies. God is held accountable for severe parental discipline of a weak virgin daughter while evil dominating enemies rejoice. Implicit within these contrasting metaphors is a petition for God to redeem and restore.

God's Anger at Sin

2 [1]The Lord in his anger
has cast a dark shadow over beautiful Jerusalem.*
The fairest of Israel's cities lies in the dust,
thrown down from the heights of heaven.
In his day of great anger,
the Lord has shown no mercy even to his Temple.*

2 Without mercy the Lord has destroyed
every home in Israel.*
In his anger he has broken down
the fortress walls of beautiful Jerusalem.*
He has brought them to the ground,
dishonoring the kingdom and its rulers.

3 All the strength of Israel
vanishes beneath his fierce anger.
The Lord has withdrawn his protection
as the enemy attacks.
He consumes the whole land of Israel
like a raging fire.

4 He bends his bow against his people,
as though he were their enemy.
His strength is used against them
to kill their finest youth.
His fury is poured out like fire
on beautiful Jerusalem.*

5 Yes, the Lord has vanquished Israel
like an enemy.
He has destroyed her palaces
and demolished her fortresses.
He has brought unending sorrow and tears
upon beautiful Jerusalem.

6 He has broken down his Temple
as though it were merely a garden shelter.
The LORD has blotted out all memory
of the holy festivals and Sabbath days.
Kings and priests fall together
before his fierce anger.

7 The Lord has rejected his own altar;
he despises his own sanctuary.
He has given Jerusalem's palaces
to her enemies.
They shout in the LORD's Temple
as though it were a day of celebration.

8 The LORD was determined
to destroy the walls of beautiful Jerusalem.
He made careful plans for their destruction,
then did what he had planned.
Therefore, the ramparts and walls
have fallen down before him.

9 Jerusalem's gates have sunk into the ground.
He has smashed their locks and bars.
Her kings and princes have been exiled to distant lands;
her law has ceased to exist.
Her prophets receive
no more visions from the LORD.

10 The leaders of beautiful Jerusalem
sit on the ground in silence.
They are clothed in burlap
and throw dust on their heads.
The young women of Jerusalem
hang their heads in shame.

11 I have cried until the tears no longer come;
my heart is broken.
My spirit is poured out in agony
as I see the desperate plight of my people.
Little children and tiny babies
are fainting and dying in the streets.

12 They cry out to their mothers,
"We need food and drink!"
Their lives ebb away in the streets
like the life of a warrior wounded in battle.
They gasp for life
as they collapse in their mothers' arms.

2:1a Hebrew *the daughter of Zion;* also in 2:8, 10, 18. **2:1b** Hebrew *his footstool.* **2:2a** Hebrew *Jacob;* also in 2:3b. See note on 1:17. **2:2b** Hebrew *the daughter of Judah;* also in 2:5. **2:4** Hebrew *on the tent of the daughter of Zion.*

2:1–22 The Day of the LORD's Anger

Like the prophets, the poet emhasizes the day of God's anger and the ensuing destruction of Jerusalem. He depicts God as destroyer of city, Temple, and traditions. **1–10:** God's severe discipline leaves Jerusalem humiliated, destroyed without mercy. The destruction climaxes with the ironical description(s) of God destroying God's sanctuary. God's fierce anger juxtaposed to the destruction of daughter Zion exhibits God's obligation to discipline, preparing for and legitimating following laments. **11–19:** Jerusalem's inhabitants are portrayed as small children. Attempting to console, the poet emphasizes Jerusalem's innocence by using feminine epithets and by claiming her prophets were deceptive. Simultaneously enemies continually mock her destruction. Ultimately Jerusalem is exhorted to cry to God for deliverance

13 What can I say about you?
Who has ever seen such sorrow?
O daughter of Jerusalem,
to what can I compare your anguish?
O virgin daughter of Zion,
how can I comfort you?
For your wound is as deep as the sea.
Who can heal you?

14 Your prophets have said
so many foolish things, false to the core.
They did not save you from exile
by pointing out your sins.
Instead, they painted false pictures,
filling you with false hope.

15 All who pass by jeer at you.
They scoff and insult beautiful Jerusalem,*
saying,
"Is this the city called 'Most Beautiful in All the World'
and 'Joy of All the Earth'?"

16 All your enemies mock you.
They scoff and snarl and say,
"We have destroyed her at last!
We have long waited for this day,
and it is finally here!"

17 But it is the LORD who did just as he planned.
He has fulfilled the promises of disaster
he made long ago.
He has destroyed Jerusalem without mercy.
He has caused her enemies to gloat over her
and has given them power over her.

18 Cry aloud* before the Lord,
O walls of beautiful Jerusalem!
Let your tears flow like a river
day and night.
Give yourselves no rest;
give your eyes no relief.

19 Rise during the night and cry out.
Pour out your hearts like water to the Lord.
Lift up your hands to him in prayer,
pleading for your children,
for in every street
they are faint with hunger.

20 "O LORD, think about this!
Should you treat your own people this way?
Should mothers eat their own children,
those they once bounced on their knees?
Should priests and prophets be killed
within the Lord's Temple?

21 "See them lying in the streets—
young and old,
boys and girls,
killed by the swords of the enemy.
You have killed them in your anger,
slaughtering them without mercy.

22 "You have invited terrors from all around,
as though you were calling them to a day of feasting.
In the day of the LORD's anger,
no one has escaped or survived.
The enemy has killed all the children
whom I carried and raised."

Hope in the LORD's Faithfulness

3 1 I am the one who has seen the afflictions
that come from the rod of the LORD's anger.
2 He has led me into darkness,
shutting out all light.
3 He has turned his hand against me
again and again, all day long.
4 He has made my skin and flesh grow old.
He has broken my bones.
5 He has besieged and surrounded me
with anguish and distress.
6 He has buried me in a dark place,
like those long dead.

2:15 Hebrew *the daughter of Jerusalem.* **2:18** Hebrew *Their heart cried.*

because her punishment has been fulfilled. **20–22:** Daughter Zion then laments over her children's destruction asking pointedly: "To whom have you done this?" (NRSV), set in contrast to the festivities of enemies. The concluding focus on the unsurvivable day of the LORD mirrors the emphasis of the book's opening verses creating an inclusio. In the end, the lament obligates God to redeem and restore Jerusalem, now replacing the deserved discipline and protecting his daughter from the mockery of enemies.

3:1–66 Traditional Responses to Suffering

Chapter 3 contains allusions to three Old Testament genres: Joblike expressions of despair and trust (vv. 1–24), wisdom teachings on suffering (vv. 25–39), and an individual lament psalm (vv. 40–66). **1–24:** If this is an intentional allusion to Job (cf. v. 1 and Job 9:34; v. 2 and Job 19:8; v. 4 and Job 30:30), then it functions to proclaim Jerusalem's distress incomprehensible while justifying God's acts (i.e., theodicy).

[7] He has walled me in, and I cannot escape.
He has bound me in heavy chains.
[8] And though I cry and shout,
he has shut out my prayers.
[9] He has blocked my way with a high stone wall;
he has made my road crooked.

[10] He has hidden like a bear or a lion,
waiting to attack me.
[11] He has dragged me off the path and torn me in pieces,
leaving me helpless and devastated.
[12] He has drawn his bow
and made me the target for his arrows.

[13] He shot his arrows
deep into my heart.
[14] My own people laugh at me.
All day long they sing their mocking songs.
[15] He has filled me with bitterness
and given me a bitter cup of sorrow to drink.

[16] He has made me chew on gravel.
He has rolled me in the dust.
[17] Peace has been stripped away,
and I have forgotten what prosperity is.
[18] I cry out, "My splendor is gone!
Everything I had hoped for from the LORD is lost!"

[19] The thought of my suffering and homelessness
is bitter beyond words.*
[20] I will never forget this awful time,
as I grieve over my loss.
[21] Yet I still dare to hope
when I remember this:

[22] The faithful love of the LORD never ends!*
His mercies never cease.
[23] Great is his faithfulness;
his mercies begin afresh each morning.
[24] I say to myself, "The LORD is my inheritance;
therefore, I will hope in him!"

[25] The LORD is good to those who depend on him,
to those who search for him.
[26] So it is good to wait quietly
for salvation from the LORD.
[27] And it is good for people to submit at an early age
to the yoke of his discipline:

[28] Let them sit alone in silence
beneath the LORD's demands.
[29] Let them lie face down in the dust,
for there may be hope at last.
[30] Let them turn the other cheek to those who strike them
and accept the insults of their enemies.

[31] For no one is abandoned
by the Lord forever.
[32] Though he brings grief, he also shows compassion
because of the greatness of his unfailing love.
[33] For he does not enjoy hurting people
or causing them sorrow.

[34] If people crush underfoot
all the prisoners of the land,
[35] if they deprive others of their rights
in defiance of the Most High,
[36] if they twist justice in the courts—
doesn't the Lord see all these things?

[37] Who can command things to happen
without the Lord's permission?
[38] Does not the Most High
send both calamity and good?
[39] Then why should we, mere humans, complain
when we are punished for our sins?

[40] Instead, let us test and examine our ways.
Let us turn back to the LORD.
[41] Let us lift our hearts and hands
to God in heaven and say,

3:19 Or *is wormwood and gall.* **3:22** As in Syriac version; Hebrew reads *of the LORD keeps us from destruction.*

Theodicy, then as today, was a common means of coping with suffering. **25–39:** We see here traditional responses to suffering found in Proverbs. **25–30:** The emphasis is on teachings on patience and taking the long view (cf. Eccl 7:8). **31–39:** Patience will be rewarded; God will not reject forever (cf. Ps 30:5) because of his steadfast love (cf. Ps 36:5, 7, 10). The LORD sees all their sins (cf. Pss 10:14; 35:22); both blessing and calamity come from him (cf. Job 2:10; Isa 45:7). **40–66:** The chapter closes with a typical individual psalm of lament emphasizing God's shunning, resulting in enemy victory, and the poet's complaint. The poet cries for God to hear and deliver. In verse 57 God responds to this cry, and the poet reviews the crimes of enemies and petitions for their destruction. Uniquely this lament describes the fate

42 "We have sinned and rebelled,
and you have not forgiven us.

43 "You have engulfed us with your anger,
chased us down,
and slaughtered us without mercy.
44 You have hidden yourself in a cloud
so our prayers cannot reach you.
45 You have discarded us as refuse and garbage
among the nations.

46 "All our enemies
have spoken out against us.
47 We are filled with fear,
for we are trapped, devastated, and
ruined."
48 Tears stream from my eyes
because of the destruction of my people!

49 My tears flow endlessly;
they will not stop
50 until the LORD looks down
from heaven and sees.
51 My heart is breaking
over the fate of all the women of
Jerusalem.

52 My enemies, whom I have never harmed,
hunted me down like a bird.
53 They threw me into a pit
and dropped stones on me.
54 The water rose over my head,
and I cried out, "This is the end!"

55 But I called on your name, LORD,
from deep within the pit.
56 You heard me when I cried, "Listen to my
pleading!
Hear my cry for help!"
57 Yes, you came when I called;
you told me, "Do not fear."

58 Lord, you are my lawyer! Plead my case!
For you have redeemed my life.
59 You have seen the wrong they have done to
me, LORD.
Be my judge, and prove me right.
60 You have seen the vengeful plots
my enemies have laid against me.

61 LORD, you have heard the vile names they
call me.
You know all about the plans they have
made.
62 My enemies whisper and mutter
as they plot against me all day long.
63 Look at them! Whether they sit or stand,
I am the object of their mocking songs.

64 Pay them back, LORD,
for all the evil they have done.
65 Give them hard and stubborn hearts,
and then let your curse fall on them!
66 Chase them down in your anger,
destroying them beneath the LORD's
heavens.

God's Anger Satisfied

4 [1]How the gold has lost its luster!
Even the finest gold has become dull.
The sacred gemstones
lie scattered in the streets!

2 See how the precious children of Jerusalem,*
worth their weight in fine gold,
are now treated like pots of clay
made by a common potter.

3 Even the jackals feed their young,
but not my people Israel.
They ignore their children's cries,
like ostriches in the desert.

4 The parched tongues of their little ones
stick to the roofs of their mouths in
thirst.
The children cry for bread,
but no one has any to give them.

5 The people who once ate the richest foods
now beg in the streets for anything they
can get.
Those who once wore the finest clothes
now search the garbage dumps for food.

6 The guilt* of my people
is greater than that of Sodom,

4:2 Hebrew *precious sons of Zion.* **4:6** Or *punishment.*

of the city's young women (v. 51). Substituting a petition for deliverance with imprecations against enemies does reflect a malicious, backward approach to deliverance.

4:1–22 Jerusalem's Punishment Too Severe Jerusalem, formerly God's precious child, is now an impoverished mother unable to feed her children. Her precious royalty now sits on ash heaps. **6:** This

where utter disaster struck in a moment
and no hand offered help.

7 Our princes once glowed with health—
brighter than snow, whiter than milk.
Their faces were as ruddy as rubies,
their appearance like fine jewels.*

8 But now their faces are blacker than soot.
No one recognizes them in the streets.
Their skin sticks to their bones;
it is as dry and hard as wood.

9 Those killed by the sword are better off
than those who die of hunger.
Starving, they waste away
for lack of food from the fields.

10 Tenderhearted women
have cooked their own children.
They have eaten them
to survive the siege.

11 But now the anger of the LORD is satisfied.
His fierce anger has been poured out.
He started a fire in Jerusalem*
that burned the city to its foundations.

12 Not a king in all the earth—
no one in all the world—
would have believed that an enemy
could march through the gates of
Jerusalem.

13 Yet it happened because of the sins of her
prophets
and the sins of her priests,
who defiled the city
by shedding innocent blood.

14 They wandered blindly
through the streets,
so defiled by blood
that no one dared touch them.

15 "Get away!" the people shouted at them.
"You're defiled! Don't touch us!"
So they fled to distant lands
and wandered among foreign nations,
but none would let them stay.

16 The LORD himself has scattered them,
and he no longer helps them.
People show no respect for the priests
and no longer honor the leaders.

17 We looked in vain for our allies
to come and save us,
but we were looking to nations
that could not help us.

18 We couldn't go into the streets
without danger to our lives.
Our end was near; our days were
numbered.
We were doomed!

19 Our enemies were swifter than eagles in
flight.
If we fled to the mountains, they found
us.
If we hid in the wilderness,
they were waiting for us there.

20 Our king—the LORD's anointed, the very life
of our nation—
was caught in their snares.
We had thought that his shadow
would protect us against any nation on
earth!

21 Are you rejoicing in the land of Uz,
O people of Edom?
But you, too, must drink from the cup of the
LORD's anger.
You, too, will be stripped naked in your
drunkenness.

4:7 Hebrew *like lapis lazuli.* **4:11** Hebrew *in Zion.*

further allusion to Job is combined with accusation proclaiming the current chastisement too severe. Sodom's desolation was quick and complete, but Jerusalem's life slowly drains away. **10:** The final imagery drives home the point—Israel's devastation is so severe mothers eat their own children. **11:** God's anger here reflects the day of the LORD proclaimed by prophets (e.g., Amos 5:18–20). God was assumed to be coming to destroy Israel's enemies. **13–20:** Lamentations, like the prophets, turned it back onto Israel (cf. 2:1–10). **21–22:** Curiously, the lament ends, not with any kind of petition. Instead, personified Jerusalem directs God's attention to Jerusalem's incapable allies (probably Egypt, 4:17–19; cf. Jer 37:5–10) and proclaims that Jerusalem's punishment is completed and Edom's about to come. Edom (descended from Esau), who should have been an ally, probably played some role in Jerusalem's destruction by Neo-Babylonians (see Obad, Ezek 25:12; 35:3, 15; Ps 137:7; Jer 40:11; Isa 34; Mal 1:2–5; Joel 3:19). Jerusalem's shame before the nations, also shames her God.

22 O beautiful Jerusalem,* your punishment
will end;
you will soon return from exile.
But Edom, your punishment is just
beginning;
soon your many sins will be exposed.

Prayer for Restoration

5 1LORD, remember what has happened
to us.
See how we have been disgraced!
2 Our inheritance has been turned over to
strangers,
our homes to foreigners.
3 We are orphaned and fatherless.
Our mothers are widowed.
4 We have to pay for water to drink,
and even firewood is expensive.
5 Those who pursue us are at our heels;
we are exhausted but are given no rest.
6 We submitted to Egypt and Assyria
to get enough food to survive.
7 Our ancestors sinned, but they have died—
and we are suffering the punishment they
deserved!

8 Slaves have now become our masters;
there is no one left to rescue us.
9 We hunt for food at the risk of our lives,
for violence rules the countryside.
10 The famine has blackened our skin
as though baked in an oven.
11 Our enemies rape the women in Jerusalem*
and the young girls in all the towns of
Judah.
12 Our princes are being hanged by their
thumbs,
and our elders are treated with contempt.
13 Young men are led away to work at
millstones,
and boys stagger under heavy loads of
wood.
14 The elders no longer sit in the city gates;
the young men no longer dance and sing.
15 Joy has left our hearts;
our dancing has turned to mourning.
16 The garlands have* fallen from our heads.
Weep for us because we have sinned.
17 Our hearts are sick and weary,
and our eyes grow dim with tears.
18 For Jerusalem* is empty and desolate,
a place haunted by jackals.

19 But LORD, you remain the same forever!
Your throne continues from generation to
generation.
20 Why do you continue to forget us?
Why have you abandoned us for so long?
21 Restore us, O LORD, and bring us back to you
again!
Give us back the joys we once had!
22 Or have you utterly rejected us?
Are you angry with us still?

4:22 Hebrew *O daughter of Zion.* **5:11** Hebrew *in Zion.* **5:16** Or *The crown has.* **5:18** Hebrew *Mount Zion.*

5:1–22 The Cry for Restoration

The closing lament begins by asking God to remember Jerusalem's shame. **1–18:** The imagery is of the vulnerable orphan enslaved under a foreign master and scraping for life. The treatment is difficult and cruel, causing community mourning. The monarchy is no more, and Mount Zion is desolate, because she has sinned. The current generation pays for the sins of their ancestors. **19–22:** The implicit finally becomes overt as Jerusalem petitions for restoration. A masterful redaction of independent sources has built to this moment. Juxtaposed to the eternal nature of God's reign are two interrogative complaints: *Why do you continue to forget us? Why have you abandoned us for so long?* These address the severity and the duration of the discipline. Given the preceding arguments, the only comprehensible reason for God not to restore would be an utter rejection of Jerusalem, which is inconceivable. The book ends with the poet's ultimate argument: Jerusalem must be restored because she belongs to God.

EZEKIEL

INTRODUCTION

The book of Ezekiel, a carefully structured collection of writings to the exiles in Babylon, contains insights into life in Jerusalem and wrestles with deep questions surrounding the Exile. Although some are skeptical, many scholars have now returned to the earlier consensus about the book's essential unity and Ezekiel's role as author.

Although little of Ezekiel's personal life is revealed, his experiences of God and his dramatic sign presentations have made him the subject of psychological studies. Some features of Ezekiel's prophecy could be—and have been by some—attributed to a pathological fear and hatred of female sexuality arising from possible sexual abuse Ezekiel suffered as a child. This approach, although problematic and not affirmed by most commentators and psychologists, nonetheless highlights an important interpretive issue, namely, the predominantly violent and negative images of women. A more fruitful approach involves considering the book's purpose and context, the rhetorical function of prophecy, separation of women as literary figures or metaphors from real women, and appreciation of the differences between life in the ancient and modern world.

Dates within the book place Ezekiel's ministry between his call in 593 BC, the fifth year of exile (1:2), and 571 BC, the twenty-seventh year of exile (29:17). The book is set in Babylon, though Ezekiel's visions transport him back to Jerusalem, and thus provides insights into life in exile. King Jehoiachin, his family, and many other leaders and upper-class Judeans, including Ezekiel, were taken to Babylon in 598 BC as prisoners (2 Kgs 24:11–16). The number of captives is debated, and it is not clear whether women and children were included in the numbers. However, there is little doubt that Nebuchadnezzar took whole families into captivity.

Like the Assyrians, the Neo-Babylonians used exile as a way of controlling conquered peoples. Some indication of the treatment of women in exile is afforded by stone reliefs showing women and children walking or in ox or mule carts, separated from men who were sometimes in chains. Touching scenes of women and children weeping with hands raised in prayer, of mothers nursing babies and bending to give a small child a drink all call attention to the difficulties faced by families journeying into captivity.

Their journey ended with settlement in small communities in Nippur. The settlement conditions are unclear, but an extant letter listing the rations for Jehoiachin suggests that the king's family were well provided for. Also positive is Jeremiah's letter (Jer 29:5–7). The mention of elders points to some form of self-government; Ezekiel clearly exercised considerable independence in terms of his own ministry.

Still, the emotional and practical challenges the exiles faced were immense. Moreover, many women sent into exile were women of status, power, and ability. The discovery of Hebrew seals belonging to women suggests that some, during the eighth to sixth centuries, were accustomed to having legal rights that involved signing contracts and other such documents. Some women may have been literate (seals, consisting of words and not pictures, may indicate this).

Women's primary focus would have continued to be the family. Hence, marriage, birth rituals, preparation and production of food, and clothing, nurture, and education of children would have been central to a woman's life. Moreover, women's responsibilities included the care of the sick, dying, and dead. In the context of exile, women would have learned new skills because of economic constraints, their changed status, and differences in climate, geography, and environment.

Faced with different socioeconomic conditions, women and men may have experienced shifts in gender roles. Ezekiel's message about individual responsibility would accord with this. Little is known about women's roles outside the family, although some women were professional mourners and others prophets. Believing Judean women and men would have had to take a stand against the pressures and temptations of Babylonian society, but they may also have had things to learn from the positive aspects.

While Ezekiel portrays the male leaders of the community deliberating about the theological issues related to the captivity, women undoubtedly discussed these issues among themselves and with their husbands. They were expected to respond to the challenges of Ezekiel's message. To the women would have fallen the vital task of teaching their children lessons, which must have included resisting the pressures of their new home, both religious and social.

We are given few glimpses into the lives of individual women. Ezekiel's wife is the only real woman in the book, and information about her is limited. Women are mentioned as weeping for Tammuz and as prophets, and also as potential defilers of righteous men, victims of war, and perhaps the intended audience of the story of Samaria and Jerusalem. Moreover, women feature prominently in Ezekiel's imagery, particularly in the book's first half.

The most important and problematic female image is Jerusalem as the LORD's wife. Cities in the ancient Near East often had a patron deity, and women were frequently envisaged as the wife of that deity. Hosea, Isaiah, and Jeremiah used this commonplace notion, picturing Jerusalem as God's unfaithful wife. Ezekiel, however, graphically depicts Jerusalem and Samaria as unfaithful women, punished by their lovers at their husband's request.

The language and images Ezekiel uses to depict God's relationship with Jerusalem and Samaria present challenges for women because the prophet depicts women's bodies, bodily functions, and sexuality explicitly and negatively. Most contemporary readers find Ezekiel's negative images of women problematic and offensive.

Critical here is the nature of metaphorical language. Some interpreters focus on what was meant or signified by Ezekiel's metaphoric language in its historical and canonical context. Others suggest that metaphorical language itself is not significant but should be heard or read as a finger pointing beyond itself. An example of letting the metaphor take over would be seeing Ezekiel's image of God as the shamed husband violently retaliating against his wife as modeling or justifying spousal abuse.

Ezekiel's purpose was to offend and shock his readers. His mission was to confront God's people with their sin that had severed the covenant bond, to correct their faulty ideas (about God, God's promises, and the nature of the covenant), to warn of the imminent fall of Jerusalem, and to inform them of God's plans for restoration. However, modern readers experience even more shock and offense because they do not share the ancients' assumptions.

Still, the focus on woman's uncleanness and infidelity is largely restricted to texts that feature the unfaithful female city. Other references to real and imagined women are much more positive (e.g., Ezekiel's wife, the lioness, the women prophets judged for their actions alongside their male counterparts and not for their womanhood, and the feminine images linked to the new Temple).

Even though the book of Ezekiel presents numerous interpretive challenges, it continues to draw women and men into a deeper understanding of God, of sin, of grace, and the demands of a covenanted life with God. It also holds a message of hope of restoration and new life for those who, like the suffering exiles of the sixth century, need to be filled with God's life-giving Spirit and given hope for the future. —*Marion Ann Taylor*

1:1—3:27	Ezekiel's Initial Vision and Call
4:1—5:17	Messages of Judgment
6:1—7:27	Oracles of Judgment and the Knowledge of the LORD
8:1—11:25	The Temple Vision
12:1–20	Exile Reenacted
12:21—14:11	True and False Prophecy
14:12—15:8	A Righteous Few Cannot Save
16:1–63	A Love Story Gone Wrong
17:1—18:32	A Riddle and a Proverb
19:1–14	The Lioness and the Vine
20:1–44	Israel's History Revisited
20:45—21:32	The Sword
22:1–31	Jerusalem, the Guilty City
23:1–49	The Story of Two Sisters
24:1–14	The Cooking Pot
24:15–27	The Death of Ezekiel's Wife
25:1—32:32	Oracles against the Nations
33:1–33	Ezekiel, the Watchman
34:1–31	Shepherds of Israel and a Covenant of Peace
35:1—36:38	Judgment and Restoration
37:1–28	Restoration of the House of Israel
38:1—39:29	Prophecies against Gog
40:1—48:35	The New Temple

✧

A Vision of Living Beings

1 On July 31* of my thirtieth year,* while I
was with the Judean exiles beside the Kebar
River in Babylon, the heavens were opened
and I saw visions of God. 2This happened during the fifth year of King Jehoiachin's captivity.
3(The LORD gave this message to Ezekiel son of
Buzi, a priest, beside the Kebar River in the land
of the Babylonians,* and he felt the hand of the
LORD take hold of him.)
4As I looked, I saw a great storm coming from
the north, driving before it a huge cloud that
flashed with lightning and shone with brilliant
light. There was fire inside the cloud, and in the
middle of the fire glowed something like gleaming amber.* 5From the center of the cloud came

1:1a Hebrew *On the fifth day of the fourth month,* of the ancient Hebrew lunar calendar. A number of dates in Ezekiel can be cross-checked with dates in surviving Babylonian records and related accurately to our modern calendar. This event occurred on July 31, 593 B.C. **1:1b** Or *in the thirtieth year.* **1:3** Or *Chaldeans.* **1:4** Or *like burnished metal;* also in 1:27.

1:1—3:27 Ezekiel's Initial Vision and Call

Ezekiel, the son of Buzi and a priest, was one of those taken from Jerusalem and relocated by the Kebar River in Babylon. Cut off from the Temple, Ezekiel could not exercise his priestly duties. However, in the fifth year of exile, Ezekiel was given a new vocation as prophet. **1:1-28:** Ezekiel's initial vision was of four astoundingly brilliant creatures reminiscent of the cherubim that supported the Ark of the Covenant (1 Sam 4:4; Ezek 10:14–19). The creatures seemed to carry a four-wheeled, chariot-like vehicle that could

four living beings that looked human, [6]except that each had four faces and four wings. [7]Their legs were straight, and their feet had hooves like those of a calf and shone like burnished bronze. [8]Under each of their four wings I could see human hands. So each of the four beings had four faces and four wings. [9]The wings of each living being touched the wings of the beings beside it. Each one moved straight forward in any direction without turning around.

[10]Each had a human face in the front, the face of a lion on the right side, the face of an ox on the left side, and the face of an eagle at the back. [11]Each had two pairs of outstretched wings—one pair stretched out to touch the wings of the living beings on either side of it, and the other pair covered its body. [12]They went in whatever direction the spirit chose, and they moved straight forward in any direction without turning around.

[13]The living beings looked like bright coals of fire or brilliant torches, and lightning seemed to flash back and forth among them. [14]And the living beings darted to and fro like flashes of lightning.

[15]As I looked at these beings, I saw four wheels touching the ground beside them, one wheel belonging to each. [16]The wheels sparkled as if made of beryl. All four wheels looked alike and were made the same; each wheel had a second wheel turning crosswise within it. [17]The beings could move in any of the four directions they faced, without turning as they moved. [18]The rims of the four wheels were tall and frightening, and they were covered with eyes all around.

[19]When the living beings moved, the wheels moved with them. When they flew upward, the wheels went up, too. [20]The spirit of the living beings was in the wheels. So wherever the spirit went, the wheels and the living beings also went. [21]When the beings moved, the wheels moved. When the beings stopped, the wheels stopped. When the beings flew upward, the wheels rose up, for the spirit of the living beings was in the wheels.

[22]Spread out above them was a surface like the sky, glittering like crystal. [23]Beneath this surface the wings of each living being stretched out to touch the others' wings, and each had two wings covering its body. [24]As they flew, their wings sounded to me like waves crashing against the shore or like the voice of the Almighty* or like the shouting of a mighty army. When they stopped, they let down their wings. [25]As they stood with wings lowered, a voice spoke from beyond the crystal surface above them.

[26]Above this surface was something that looked like a throne made of blue lapis lazuli. And on this throne high above was a figure whose appearance resembled a man. [27]From what appeared to be his waist up, he looked like gleaming amber, flickering like a fire. And from his waist down, he looked like a burning flame, shining with splendor. [28]All around him was a glowing halo, like a rainbow shining in the clouds on a rainy day. This is what the glory of the LORD looked like to me. When I saw it, I fell face down on the ground, and I heard someone's voice speaking to me.

Ezekiel's Call and Commission

2

"Stand up, son of man," said the voice. "I want to speak with you." [2]The Spirit came into me as he spoke, and he set me on my feet. I listened carefully to his words. [3]"Son of man," he said, "I am sending you to the nation of Israel, a rebellious nation that has rebelled against me. They and their ancestors have been rebelling against me to this very day. [4]They are a stubborn and hard-hearted people. But I am sending you to say to them, 'This is what the

1:24 Hebrew *Shaddai.*

---

move everywhere (the Ark was called a chariot, 1 Chr 28:18). **24:** *The Almighty*: *El-Shaddai*, in Hebrew. The etymology of *Shaddai* is obscure, but one option is "the God of the two breasts" or "the double breasted One." **25–28:** Enthroned on this vehicle was something reminiscent of the glory of the LORD. Ezekiel's response indicates the vision's theological significance: God was not confined to the Temple in Jerusalem. Instead, God's throne could easily move and God was therefore present among the exiles. Ezekiel 1 has inspired artists and songwriters and the hearts of the faithful who, like the exiles, need a renewed vision of God. When circumstances make normal worship impossible or difficult (e.g., caring for newborns or the sick), an assurance of God's presence, power, holiness, and accessibility brings hope and comfort. It offers a new perspective on circumstances that seem unchangeable or unjust (cf. Rom 8:38–39 and the lives of African American slaves). A renewed vision of God's holiness also prepared the way for the message of judgment that Ezekiel was to bring.

2:1—3:15 Ezekiel's Call. 2:1–2: *Son of man* means "human." Although addressed by God as "mortal" or "human," the Spirit enters Ezekiel and sets him on his feet to hear his assignment. **3–7:** The charge of Israel's rebellion against God is a constant theme to justify Israel's suffering as an act of divine punishment.

Sovereign LORD says!' [5]And whether they listen or refuse to listen—for remember, they are
rebels—at least they will know they have had a
prophet among them.
[6]"Son of man, do not fear them or their
words. Don't be afraid even though their threats
surround you like nettles and briers and stinging scorpions. Do not be dismayed by their dark
scowls, even though they are rebels. [7]You must
give them my messages whether they listen or
not. But they won't listen, for they are completely rebellious! [8]Son of man, listen to what I say
to you. Do not join them in their rebellion. Open
your mouth, and eat what I give you."
[9]Then I looked and saw a hand reaching out
to me. It held a scroll, [10]which he unrolled. And
I saw that both sides were covered with funeral
songs, words of sorrow, and pronouncements of
doom.

3 The voice said to me, "Son of man, eat
what I am giving you—eat this scroll!
Then go and give its message to the people
of Israel." [2]So I opened my mouth, and he fed me
the scroll. [3]"Fill your stomach with this," he said.
And when I ate it, it tasted as sweet as honey in
my mouth.
[4]Then he said, "Son of man, go to the people
of Israel and give them my messages. [5]I am not
sending you to a foreign people whose language
you cannot understand. [6]No, I am not sending
you to people with strange and difficult speech. If
I did, they would listen! [7]But the people of Israel
won't listen to you any more than they listen to
me! For the whole lot of them are hard-hearted
and stubborn. [8]But look, I have made you as
obstinate and hard-hearted as they are. [9]I have
made your forehead as hard as the hardest rock!
So don't be afraid of them or fear their angry
looks, even though they are rebels."
[10]Then he added, "Son of man, let all my
words sink deep into your own heart first. Listen
to them carefully for yourself. [11]Then go to your
people in exile and say to them, 'This is what the
Sovereign LORD says!' Do this whether they listen to you or not."
[12]Then the Spirit lifted me up, and I heard a
loud rumbling sound behind me. (May the glory
of the LORD be praised in his place!)* [13]It was the
sound of the wings of the living beings as they
brushed against each other and the rumbling of
their wheels beneath them.
[14]The Spirit lifted me up and took me away.
I went in bitterness and turmoil, but the LORD's
hold on me was strong. [15]Then I came to the colony of Judean exiles in Tel-abib, beside the Kebar
River. I was overwhelmed and sat among them
for seven days.

A Watchman for Israel

[16]After seven days the LORD gave me a message.
He said, [17]"Son of man, I have appointed you as
a watchman for Israel. Whenever you receive
a message from me, warn people immediately.
[18]If I warn the wicked, saying, 'You are under
the penalty of death,' but you fail to deliver the
warning, they will die in their sins. And I will
hold you responsible for their deaths. [19]If you
warn them and they refuse to repent and keep on
sinning, they will die in their sins. But you will
have saved yourself because you obeyed me.
[20]"If righteous people turn away from their
righteous behavior and ignore the obstacles I
put in their way, they will die. And if you do not
warn them, they will die in their sins. None of
their righteous acts will be remembered, and I
will hold you responsible for their deaths. [21]But
if you warn righteous people not to sin and they
listen to you and do not sin, they will live, and
you will have saved yourself, too."
[22]Then the LORD took hold of me and said,
"Get up and go out into the valley, and I will
speak to you there." [23]So I got up and went, and
there I saw the glory of the LORD, just as I had

3:12 A possible reading for this verse is *Then the Spirit lifted me up, and as the glory of the LORD rose from its place, I heard a loud rumbling sound behind me.*

2:8—3:3: Ezekiel obediently eats a scroll containing words of lamentation, mourning, and woe; ironically, it tastes as sweet as honey. By eating the scroll, Ezekiel internalizes the divine message. **3:5–6:** Exiles from other countries had also been brought to Babylonia, but this message is for Israel alone.

3:16–27 Watchman for Israel. 16–21: Ezekiel's job was to warn the people of God's judgments and to beware the death sentence if they wouldn't repent. The messenger is held responsible for delivering God's warning, though not for the people's response. **22–27:** As God's chosen, Spirit-filled prophet, Ezekiel must carry out God's orders explicitly. God fixes the limits of the prophetic task, and Ezekiel's words will be God's words. What follows in the book of Ezekiel must be read in light of these opening chapters, which establish God's character as holy, transcendent, relational, and omnipresent; the nation's character as rebellious and stubborn; and the prophet's character as obedient messenger and his task as sentinel.

seen in my first vision by the Kebar River. And I
fell face down on the ground.
24 Then the Spirit came into me and set me
on my feet. He spoke to me and said, "Go to
your house and shut yourself in. 25 There, son
of man, you will be tied with ropes so you cannot go out among the people. 26 And I will make
your tongue stick to the roof of your mouth so
that you will be speechless and unable to rebuke
them, for they are rebels. 27 But when I give you
a message, I will loosen your tongue and let you
speak. Then you will say to them, 'This is what
the Sovereign LORD says!' Those who choose to
listen will listen, but those who refuse will refuse, for they are rebels.

A Sign of the Coming Siege

4 "And now, son of man, take a large clay
brick and set it down in front of you. Then
draw a map of the city of Jerusalem on it.
2 Show the city under siege. Build a wall around
it so no one can escape. Set up the enemy camp,
and surround the city with siege ramps and battering rams. 3 Then take an iron griddle and place
it between you and the city. Turn toward the city
and demonstrate how harsh the siege will be
against Jerusalem. This will be a warning to the
people of Israel.
4 "Now lie on your left side and place the sins
of Israel on yourself. You are to bear their sins
for the number of days you lie there on your
side. 5 I am requiring you to bear Israel's sins
for 390 days—one day for each year of their sin.
6 After that, turn over and lie on your right side
for 40 days—one day for each year of Judah's
sin.
7 "Meanwhile, keep staring at the siege of
Jerusalem. Lie there with your arm bared and
prophesy her destruction. 8 I will tie you up with
ropes so you won't be able to turn from side to
side until the days of your siege have been completed.
9 "Now go and get some wheat, barley, beans,
lentils, millet, and emmer wheat, and mix them
together in a storage jar. Use them to make bread
for yourself during the 390 days you will be lying on your side. 10 Ration this out to yourself,
eight ounces* of food for each day, and eat it at
set times. 11 Then measure out a jar* of water for
each day, and drink it at set times. 12 Prepare and
eat this food as you would barley cakes. While
all the people are watching, bake it over a fire
using dried human dung as fuel and then eat the
bread." 13 Then the LORD said, "This is how Israel will eat defiled bread in the Gentile lands to
which I will banish them!"
14 Then I said, "O Sovereign LORD, must I be
defiled by using human dung? For I have never
been defiled before. From the time I was a child
until now I have never eaten any animal that
died of sickness or was killed by other animals.
I have never eaten any meat forbidden by the
law."
15 "All right," the LORD said. "You may bake
your bread with cow dung instead of human
dung." 16 Then he told me, "Son of man, I will
make food very scarce in Jerusalem. It will be
weighed out with great care and eaten fearfully.
The water will be rationed out drop by drop, and
the people will drink it with dismay. 17 Lacking
food and water, people will look at one another
in terror, and they will waste away under their
punishment.

4:10 Hebrew *20 shekels* [228 grams]. **4:11** Hebrew $1/6$ *of a hin* [about 1 pint or 0.6 liters].

4:1–5:17 Messages of Judgment

Through a series of sign acts, Ezekiel conveys God's message. **4:3:** The iron griddle blocks the view of the prophet by those in the *city*. Ezekiel represented God, whose separation from Jerusalem was symbolized in this way. God was allowing his wrath to be enacted on his beloved Jerusalem. The message would have unnerved and bewildered the exiles, who had assumed that the covenant protected them. **4–6:** The other signs also portray siege. Ezekiel's action of lying on his left side for 390 days may symbolize the duration of Israel's sin (390 years from the fall of Jerusalem in 586 BC to the time of Solomon). The action of lying on his right side for 40 days may represent the exiled generation. The significance of the numbers, however, is debated. **9–17:** In the third sign act, Ezekiel takes on a traditional woman's task: He takes six different grains and vegetables and makes bread for himself in front of an audience. The recipe highlights the shortage of ritually clean food, which would accompany the siege and that bread would be made with whatever grain and vegetables could be found. This bread was to be cooked on human dung, rendering it unclean. When Ezekiel protests, the LORD empathizes with his feelings of revulsion and allows him to cook on cow dung. Ezekiel may have had to consult his wife about how to prepare the grains and vegetables. The sight of a male preparing an unusual loaf of bread in an unusual fashion would have caused a stir, particularly among the women exiles. The message conveyed was one that women especially might have taken to heart.

A Sign of the Coming Judgment

5 "Son of man, take a sharp sword and use it as a razor to shave your head and beard. Use a scale to weigh the hair into three equal parts. 2 Place a third of it at the center of your map of Jerusalem. After acting out the siege, burn it there. Scatter another third across your map and chop it with a sword. Scatter the last third to the wind, for I will scatter my people with the sword. 3 Keep just a bit of the hair and tie it up in your robe. 4 Then take some of these hairs out and throw them into the fire, burning them up. A fire will then spread from this remnant and destroy all of Israel.

5 "This is what the Sovereign LORD says: This is an illustration of what will happen to Jerusalem. I placed her at the center of the nations, 6 but she has rebelled against my regulations and decrees and has been even more wicked than the surrounding nations. She has refused to obey the regulations and decrees I gave her to follow.

7 "Therefore, this is what the Sovereign LORD says: You people have behaved worse than your neighbors and have refused to obey my decrees and regulations. You have not even lived up to the standards of the nations around you. 8 Therefore, I myself, the Sovereign LORD, am now your enemy. I will punish you publicly while all the nations watch. 9 Because of your detestable idols, I will punish you like I have never punished anyone before or ever will again. 10 Parents will eat their own children, and children will eat their parents. I will punish you and scatter to the winds the few who survive.

11 "As surely as I live, says the Sovereign LORD, I will cut you off completely. I will show you no pity at all because you have defiled my Temple with your vile images and detestable sins. 12 A third of your people will die in the city from disease and famine. A third of them will be slaughtered by the enemy outside the city walls. And I will scatter a third to the winds, chasing them with my sword. 13 Then at last my anger will be spent, and I will be satisfied. And when my fury against them has subsided, all Israel will know that I, the LORD, have spoken to them in my jealous anger.

14 "So I will turn you into a ruin, a mockery in the eyes of the surrounding nations and to all who pass by. 15 You will become an object of mockery and taunting and horror. You will be a warning to all the nations around you. They will see what happens when the LORD punishes a nation in anger and rebukes it, says the LORD.

16 "I will shower you with the deadly arrows of famine to destroy you. The famine will become more and more severe until every crumb of food is gone. 17 And along with the famine, wild animals will attack you and rob you of your children. Disease and war will stalk your land, and I will bring the sword of the enemy against you. I, the LORD, have spoken!"

Judgment against Israel's Mountains

6 Again a message came to me from the LORD: 2 "Son of man, turn and face the mountains of Israel and prophesy against them. 3 Proclaim this message from the Sovereign LORD against the mountains of Israel. This is what the Sovereign LORD says to the mountains and hills and to the ravines and valleys: I am about to bring war upon you, and I will smash your pagan shrines. 4 All your altars will be demolished, and your places of worship will be destroyed. I will kill your people in front of your idols.* 5 I will lay your corpses in front of your idols and scatter your bones around your altars. 6 Wherever you live there will be desolation, and I will destroy your pagan shrines. Your altars will be demol-

6:4 The Hebrew term (literally *round things*) probably alludes to dung; also in 6:5, 6, 9, 13.

5:1–17 The Shearing of Ezekiel and Jerusalem. In yet another sign act, Ezekiel shaves his head and beard, a sign of shame or mourning. The hair is then weighed and divided symbolizing the fate of Jerusalem's inhabitants. The interpretation rehashes Jerusalem's failures. The city has rebelled against God and defiled God's sanctuary. God's response is one of jealous anger. Men, women, and children will be judged and punished through famine, pestilence, wild animals, bloodshed, and the sword. It is difficult to imagine the desperation leading parents to eat their children and vice versa. The motif of cannibalism, however, is found in a number of ancient treaty curses (Lev 26:29; Deut 28:53–57). The story of the mother who shared the flesh of her son with another mother during the siege of Samaria (2 Kgs 6:24–31) puts a human face on this harsh message.

6:1—7:27 Oracles of Judgment and the Knowledge of the LORD

Ezekiel identifies the cause of punishment in the various altars and shrines—usually built on the tops of hills or mountains and so often called "high places"—where the people worship. For Ezekiel, legitimate worship of God must take place only in the Jerusalem Temple. **6:1:** *The mountains of Israel*: The homeland of Israel in the hills of Samaria and Judah. **5:** *Corpses*

ished, your idols will be smashed, your places of
worship will be torn down, and all the religious
objects you have made will be destroyed. 7 The
place will be littered with corpses, and you will
know that I alone am the LORD.
8 "But I will let a few of my people escape destruction, and they will be scattered among the
nations of the world. 9 Then when they are exiled among the nations, they will remember me.
They will recognize how hurt I am by their unfaithful hearts and lustful eyes that long for their
idols. Then at last they will hate themselves for
all their detestable sins. 10 They will know that I
alone am the LORD and that I was serious when I
said I would bring this calamity on them.
11 "This is what the Sovereign LORD says: Clap
your hands in horror, and stamp your feet. Cry
out because of all the detestable sins the people of
Israel have committed. Now they are going to die
from war and famine and disease. 12 Disease will
strike down those who are far away in exile. War
will destroy those who are nearby. And anyone
who survives will be killed by famine. So at last
I will spend my fury on them. 13 They will know
that I am the LORD when their dead lie scattered
among their idols and altars on every hill and
mountain and under every green tree and every
great shade tree—the places where they offered
sacrifices to their idols. 14 I will crush them and
make their cities desolate from the wilderness in
the south to Riblah* in the north. Then they will
know that I am the LORD."

The Coming of the End

7 Then this message came to me from the
LORD: 2 "Son of man, this is what the Sovereign LORD says to Israel:

"The end is here!
Wherever you look—
east, west, north, or south—
your land is finished.
3 No hope remains,
for I will unleash my anger against you.
I will call you to account
for all your detestable sins.
4 I will turn my eyes away and show no pity.
I will repay you for all your detestable sins.
Then you will know that I am the LORD.

5 "This is what the Sovereign LORD says:
Disaster after disaster
is coming your way!
6 The end has come.
It has finally arrived.
Your final doom is waiting!
7 O people of Israel, the day of your
destruction is dawning.
The time has come; the day of trouble is
near.
Shouts of anguish will be heard on the
mountains,
not shouts of joy.
8 Soon I will pour out my fury on you
and unleash my anger against you.
I will call you to account
for all your detestable sins.
9 I will turn my eyes away and show no pity.
I will repay you for all your detestable
sins.
Then you will know that it is I, the LORD,
who is striking the blow.

10 "The day of judgment is here;
your destruction awaits!
The people's wickedness and pride
have blossomed to full flower.
11 Their violence has grown into a rod
that will beat them for their wickedness.
None of these proud and wicked people will
survive.
All their wealth and prestige will be swept
away.
12 Yes, the time has come;
the day is here!
Buyers should not rejoice over bargains,
nor sellers grieve over losses,
for all of them will fall
under my terrible anger.
13 Even if the merchants survive,
they will never return to their business.
For what God has said applies to everyone—
it will not be changed!
Not one person whose life is twisted by sin
will ever recover.

6:14 As in some Hebrew manuscripts; most Hebrew manuscripts read *Diblah.*

render the land impure. **7:1–13:** Ezekiel develops the theme of judgment further by emphasizing the imminence of *the end* for the land of Israel. To the exiles, whose hopes for release and return centered on God's presence in the land, these oracles would be disturbing. God is portrayed as an angry covenant God whose longstanding patience and compassion are spent. The cry of Ezekiel, the sentinel, is again that God must punish. But God's actions as judge are not seen as impetuous, capricious, or even unexpected. The inhabitants would be judged according to their ways. **14–22:** The description of the time of war con-

The Desolation of Israel

14 "The trumpet calls Israel's army to mobilize,
but no one listens,
for my fury is against them all.
15 There is war outside the city
and disease and famine within.
Those outside the city walls
will be killed by enemy swords.
Those inside the city
will die of famine and disease.
16 The survivors who escape to the mountains
will moan like doves, weeping for their
sins.
17 Their hands will hang limp,
their knees will be weak as water.
18 They will dress themselves in burlap;
horror and shame will cover them.
They will shave their heads
in sorrow and remorse.

19 "They will throw their money in the streets,
tossing it out like worthless trash.
Their silver and gold won't save them
on that day of the LORD's anger.
It will neither satisfy nor feed them,
for their greed can only trip them up.
20 They were proud of their beautiful jewelry
and used it to make detestable idols and
vile images.
Therefore, I will make all their wealth
disgusting to them.
21 I will give it as plunder to foreigners,
to the most wicked of nations,
and they will defile it.
22 I will turn my eyes from them
as these robbers invade and defile my
treasured land.

23 "Prepare chains for my people,
for the land is bloodied by terrible crimes.
Jerusalem is filled with violence.
24 I will bring the most ruthless of nations
to occupy their homes.
I will break down their proud fortresses
and defile their sanctuaries.
25 Terror and trembling will overcome my
people.
They will look for peace but not find it.
26 Calamity will follow calamity;
rumor will follow rumor.
They will look in vain
for a vision from the prophets.
They will receive no teaching from the priests
and no counsel from the leaders.
27 The king and the prince will stand helpless,
weeping in despair,
and the people's hands
will tremble with fear.
I will bring on them
the evil they have done to others,
and they will receive the punishment
they so richly deserve.
Then they will know that I am the LORD."

Idolatry in the Temple

8 Then on September 17,* during the sixth
year of King Jehoiachin's captivity, while
the leaders of Judah were in my home, the
Sovereign LORD took hold of me. 2 I saw a figure
that appeared to be a man. From what appeared
to be his waist down, he looked like a burning
flame. From the waist up he looked like gleaming amber.* 3 He reached out what seemed to be
a hand and took me by the hair. Then the Spirit
lifted me up into the sky and transported me
to Jerusalem in a vision from God. I was taken
to the north gate of the inner courtyard of the
Temple, where there is a large idol that has made
the LORD very jealous. 4 Suddenly, the glory of
the God of Israel was there, just as I had seen it
before in the valley.
5 Then the LORD said to me, "Son of man, look

8:1 Hebrew *on the fifth day of the sixth month,* of the ancient Hebrew lunar calendar. This event occurred on September 17, 592 B.C.; also see note on 1:1. **8:2** Or *like burnished metal.*

tains appropriately male images. **23–24:** *Defile*: Ezekiel's training as a priest sensitized him to issues of purity and impurity; most likely he had this in mind as he attempted to shake his hearers out of their lethargy and bring them to an awareness of the imminence of God's judgment and of their personal accountability for what had happened and would happen.

8:1—11:25 The Temple Vision

Although the reason for the leaders' visit is not given, the leaders seem to have recognized Ezekiel as God's prophet and came to hear God's message. They would then spread God's message to others, including women. The message of these scenes of cultic sin is that God demands exclusive worship. The presence of rivals in God's sanctuary evokes not only God's jealousy but also his pain as those he loves bring other lovers into his presence. **8:3–5:** Though the identity of this *idol* is not certain, it was most likely the Canaanite goddess Asherah. In Ugaritic texts she is the consort of the chief god, El, and the mother of gods, perhaps even Baal. In these syncretistic times, maybe in the minds of some, Asherah was God's female con-

toward the north." So I looked, and there to the
north, beside the entrance to the gate near the
altar, stood the idol that had made the LORD so
jealous.
6 "Son of man," he said, "do you see what
they are doing? Do you see the detestable sins
the people of Israel are committing to drive me
from my Temple? But come, and you will see
even more detestable sins than these!" 7 Then he
brought me to the door of the Temple courtyard,
where I could see a hole in the wall. 8 He said to
me, "Now, son of man, dig into the wall." So I
dug into the wall and found a hidden doorway.
9 "Go in," he said, "and see the wicked and
detestable sins they are committing in there!"
10 So I went in and saw the walls engraved with
all kinds of crawling animals and detestable creatures. I also saw the various idols* worshiped
by the people of Israel. 11 Seventy leaders of Israel were standing there with Jaazaniah son of
Shaphan in the center. Each of them held an incense burner, from which a cloud of incense rose
above their heads.
12 Then the LORD said to me, "Son of man,
have you seen what the leaders of Israel are doing with their idols in dark rooms? They are saying, 'The LORD doesn't see us; he has deserted
our land!' " 13 Then the LORD added, "Come, and
I will show you even more detestable sins than
these!"
14 He brought me to the north gate of the
LORD's Temple, and some women were sitting
there, weeping for the god Tammuz. 15 "Have you
seen this?" he asked. "But I will show you even
more detestable sins than these!"
16 Then he brought me into the inner courtyard of the LORD's Temple. At the entrance to
the sanctuary, between the entry room and the
bronze altar, there were about twenty-five men
with their backs to the sanctuary of the LORD.
They were facing east, bowing low to the ground,
worshiping the sun!
17 "Have you seen this, son of man?" he asked.
"Is it nothing to the people of Judah that they
commit these detestable sins, leading the whole
nation into violence, thumbing their noses at me,
and provoking my anger? 18 Therefore, I will respond in fury. I will neither pity nor spare them.
And though they cry for mercy, I will not listen."

The Slaughter of Idolaters

9 Then the LORD thundered, "Bring on the
men appointed to punish the city! Tell
them to bring their weapons with them!"
2 Six men soon appeared from the upper gate that
faces north, each carrying a deadly weapon in his
hand. With them was a man dressed in linen,
who carried a writer's case at his side. They all

8:10 The Hebrew term (literally *round things*) probably alludes to dung.

sort or at least a hypostasis of his female side. Some scholars identify the Queen of Heaven, for whom cakes were made in Jerusalem (Jer 7:18; 44:19), with Asherah. **10–12:** Seventy men recognized as leaders of Israel were involved in clandestine worship of cult images engraved on walls. They claimed God could not see them and had left the land, but ironically, although the all-seeing God had not left, he was about to leave because of such idolatrous acts. **14:** The third scene moves to the entrance of the Temple's north gate, where women sat weeping for the god Tammuz, a Babylonian vegetation god who dies at the onset of the dry season and must be brought back to life to inaugurate the rains. Tammuz is often mentioned in poems and laments uttered by his wife, sister, and mother. The dry season (June/July), named after Tammuz, was when the ritual of weeping was generally undertaken. Accordingly it is thought that the third abomination was the worshiping of a Babylonian fertility deity by Judean women in the Temple. It is also possible that the women were using a Tammuz-like liturgy of mourning to grieve the departure or death of the LORD, which the elders had just announced. If this was their offense, their mistake was that the LORD may be absent but he was not dead. The fact that the women were carrying out their ritual in the sixth rather than the fourth month suggests the women were syncretistically incorporating Babylonian rituals into the worship of the LORD. Note that apart from the inner areas restricted to priests, women were not excluded from being in the Temple. The "court of the women" was only introduced in the later temple built by Herod the Great (40–4 BC). **16:** Whether these men understood themselves to be committing apostasy or whether they were in their minds legitimately incorporating solar symbolism into worship of the LORD is unclear. Their worship, however, is deemed spurious. **17–18:** God's response to all this spiritual and moral degeneration is anger leading to judgment. The time for pity and mercy has passed; God will no longer listen to their cries. These four scenes of cultic sin suggest that God is equally the covenant God of women and men. God demands covenant faithfulness, which expresses itself in purity of worship and life of all covenant partners. **9:1–11:** The slaughter of Jerusalem is brought about by the cultic sin in the previous chapter. **1–2:** The *six men* come from the north, just as the Babylonian army would have entered Judah from the

went into the Temple courtyard and stood beside
the bronze altar.
3 Then the glory of the God of Israel rose up
from between the cherubim, where it had rested,
and moved to the entrance of the Temple. And
the LORD called to the man dressed in linen who
was carrying the writer's case. 4 He said to him,
"Walk through the streets of Jerusalem and put
a mark on the foreheads of all who weep and sigh
because of the detestable sins being committed
in their city."
5 Then I heard the LORD say to the other men,
"Follow him through the city and kill everyone
whose forehead is not marked. Show no mercy;
have no pity! 6 Kill them all—old and young,
girls and women and little children. But do not
touch anyone with the mark. Begin right here at
the Temple." So they began by killing the seventy leaders.
7 "Defile the Temple!" the LORD commanded.
"Fill its courtyards with corpses. Go!" So they
went and began killing throughout the city.
8 While they were out killing, I was all alone.
I fell face down on the ground and cried out,
"O Sovereign LORD! Will your fury against Jerusalem wipe out everyone left in Israel?"
9 Then he said to me, "The sins of the people
of Israel and Judah are very, very great. The entire land is full of murder; the city is filled with
injustice. They are saying, 'The LORD doesn't see
it! The LORD has abandoned the land!' 10 So I will
not spare them or have any pity on them. I will
fully repay them for all they have done."
11 Then the man in linen clothing, who carried
the writer's case, reported back and said, "I have
done as you commanded."

The LORD's Glory Leaves the Temple

10 In my vision I saw what appeared to
be a throne of blue lapis lazuli above
the crystal surface over the heads
of the cherubim. 2 Then the LORD spoke to the
man in linen clothing and said, "Go between the
whirling wheels beneath the cherubim, and take
a handful of burning coals and scatter them over
the city." He did this as I watched.
3 The cherubim were standing at the south
end of the Temple when the man went in, and the
cloud of glory filled the inner courtyard. 4 Then
the glory of the LORD rose up from above the
cherubim and went over to the door of the Temple. The Temple was filled with this cloud of glory,
and the courtyard glowed brightly with the glory
of the LORD. 5 The moving wings of the cherubim sounded like the voice of God Almighty* and
could be heard even in the outer courtyard.
6 The LORD said to the man in linen clothing, "Go between the cherubim and take some
burning coals from between the wheels." So the
man went in and stood beside one of the wheels.
7 Then one of the cherubim reached out his hand
and took some live coals from the fire burning
among them. He put the coals into the hands
of the man in linen clothing, and the man took
them and went out. 8 (All the cherubim had what
looked like human hands under their wings.)
9 I looked, and each of the four cherubim had
a wheel beside him, and the wheels sparkled like
beryl. 10 All four wheels looked alike and were
made the same; each wheel had a second wheel
turning crosswise within it. 11 The cherubim
could move in any of the four directions they
faced, without turning as they moved. They went
straight in the direction they faced, never turning aside. 12 Both the cherubim and the wheels
were covered with eyes. The cherubim had eyes
all over their bodies, including their hands, their
backs, and their wings. 13 I heard someone refer
to the wheels as "the whirling wheels." 14 Each
of the four cherubim had four faces: the first was
the face of an ox,* the second was a human face,
the third was the face of a lion, and the fourth
was the face of an eagle.
15 Then the cherubim rose upward. These were
the same living beings I had seen beside the Kebar
River. 16 When the cherubim moved, the wheels
moved with them. When they lifted their wings
to fly, the wheels stayed beside them. 17 When
the cherubim stopped, the wheels stopped. When
they flew upward, the wheels rose up, for the
spirit of the living beings was in the wheels.

10:5 Hebrew *El-Shaddai.* **10:14** Hebrew *the face of a cherub;* compare 1:10.

north. **3–11:** God commands that a mark be put on the forehead of those *who weep and sigh* over the state of the city. Compare to the story from Exodus in which a mark on the doorpost protects the Israelites from God's plague against the Egyptians (Exod 12:23). **10:1–6:** The theme of judgment continues as the agent of deliverance becomes the agent of judgment. God directs the same *man in linen clothing* who saved select people in chapter 9 to take burning coals from the chariot throne and scatter them over the city. The purpose is to purify Jerusalem from its iniquity and impurity so that it can be reestablished at a later time (chaps. 40—48). **7–22:** The chariot throne is described again in great detail, reminding readers of the glory, holiness, and transcendence of the God who is bringing judgment on his rebellious people.

[18]Then the glory of the LORD moved out from the door of the Temple and hovered above the cherubim. [19]And as I watched, the cherubim flew with their wheels to the east gate of the LORD's Temple. And the glory of the God of Israel hovered above them.

[20]These were the same living beings I had seen beneath the God of Israel when I was by the Kebar River. I knew they were cherubim, [21]for each had four faces and four wings and what looked like human hands under their wings. [22]And their faces were just like the faces of the beings I had seen at the Kebar, and they traveled straight ahead, just as the others had.

Judgment on Israel's Leaders

11

Then the Spirit lifted me and brought me to the east gateway of the LORD's Temple, where I saw twenty-five prominent men of the city. Among them were Jaazaniah son of Azzur and Pelatiah son of Benaiah, who were leaders among the people.

[2]The Spirit said to me, "Son of man, these are the men who are planning evil and giving wicked counsel in this city. [3]They say to the people, 'Is it not a good time to build houses? This city is like an iron pot. We are safe inside it like meat in a pot.*' [4]Therefore, son of man, prophesy against them loudly and clearly."

[5]Then the Spirit of the LORD came upon me, and he told me to say, "This is what the LORD says to the people of Israel: I know what you are saying, for I know every thought that comes into your minds. [6]You have murdered many in this city and filled its streets with the dead.

[7]"Therefore, this is what the Sovereign LORD says: This city is an iron pot all right, but the pieces of meat are the victims of your injustice. As for you, I will soon drag you from this pot. [8]I will bring on you the sword of war you so greatly fear, says the Sovereign LORD. [9]I will drive you out of Jerusalem and hand you over to foreigners, who will carry out my judgments against you. [10]You will be slaughtered all the way to the borders of Israel. I will execute judgment on you, and you will know that I am the LORD. [11]No, this city will not be an iron pot for you, and you will not be like meat safe inside it. I will judge you even to the borders of Israel, [12]and you will know that I am the LORD. For you have refused to obey my decrees and regulations; instead, you have copied the standards of the nations around you."

[13]While I was still prophesying, Pelatiah son of Benaiah suddenly died. Then I fell face down on the ground and cried out, "O Sovereign LORD, are you going to kill everyone in Israel?"

Hope for Exiled Israel

[14]Then this message came to me from the LORD: [15]"Son of man, the people still left in Jerusalem are talking about you and your relatives and all the people of Israel who are in exile. They are saying, 'Those people are far away from the LORD, so now he has given their land to us!'

[16]"Therefore, tell the exiles, 'This is what the Sovereign LORD says: Although I have scattered you in the countries of the world, I will be a sanctuary to you during your time in exile. [17]I, the Sovereign LORD, will gather you back from the nations where you have been scattered, and I will give you the land of Israel once again.'

[18]"When the people return to their homeland, they will remove every trace of their vile images and detestable idols. [19]And I will give them singleness of heart and put a new spirit within them. I will take away their stony, stubborn heart and give them a tender, responsive heart,* [20]so they will obey my decrees and regulations. Then they will truly be my people, and I will be their God. [21]But as for those who long for vile images and

11:3 Hebrew *This city is the pot, and we are the meat.*
11:19 Hebrew *a heart of flesh.*

11:1–13: Ezekiel is shown twenty-five public officials involved in setting up schemes to uphold the city's defenses. This attitude ignored Jeremiah's counsel about the foolishness of resistance to Babylon and reflected the smug self-confidence of those left in Jerusalem. The condemnation of this group reveals that they had butchered many people; the dead were, figuratively, the meat in the pot of the city. The city would provide no protection for the wicked leaders. God's judgment would ultimately lead them to recognize his lordship. **13:** Ezekiel's question shows that he does not yet understand God's thinking. Ezekiel's reaction to Pelatiah's death makes it clear that he considers the remnant to be those in Jerusalem; the true remnant is among the exiles. **14–19:** The scene of despair is followed with a message of hope to the exiles, who had been written off by those remaining in Jerusalem. Though scattered and Temple-less, God assures them that he is their sanctuary, that is, that God's presence in the world, rather than the Temple's presence in Jerusalem, ensures their future. Moreover, God promises to gather them and give them back the land and the necessary inner resources to enable them to become God's faithful and obedient covenant people. **20:** *They will . . . . be my people, and I will be their God* is the traditional formulation for the covenant between

detestable idols, I will repay them fully for their
sins. I, the Sovereign LORD, have spoken!"

The LORD's Glory Leaves Jerusalem

22 Then the cherubim lifted their wings and rose
into the air with their wheels beside them, and the
glory of the God of Israel hovered above them.
23 Then the glory of the LORD went up from the
city and stopped above the mountain to the east.
24 Afterward the Spirit of God carried me back
again to Babylonia,* to the people in exile there.
And so ended the vision of my visit to Jerusalem.
25 And I told the exiles everything the LORD had
shown me.

Signs of the Coming Exile

12 Again a message came to me from the
LORD: 2 "Son of man, you live among
rebels who have eyes but refuse to
see. They have ears but refuse to hear. For they
are a rebellious people.
3 "So now, son of man, pretend you are being
sent into exile. Pack the few items an exile could
carry, and leave your home to go somewhere
else. Do this right in front of the people so they
can see you. For perhaps they will pay attention
to this, even though they are such rebels. 4 Bring
your baggage outside during the day so they
can watch you. Then in the evening, as they are
watching, leave your house as captives do when
they begin a long march to distant lands. 5 Dig a
hole through the wall while they are watching
and go out through it. 6 As they watch, lift your
pack to your shoulders and walk away into the
night. Cover your face so you cannot see the land
you are leaving. For I have made you a sign for
the people of Israel."
7 So I did as I was told. In broad daylight I
brought my pack outside, filled with the things I
might carry into exile. Then in the evening while
the people looked on, I dug through the wall with
my hands and went out into the night with my
pack on my shoulder.
8 The next morning this message came to me
from the LORD: 9 "Son of man, these rebels, the
people of Israel, have asked you what all this
means. 10 Say to them, 'This is what the Sovereign LORD says: These actions contain a message
for King Zedekiah in Jerusalem* and for all the
people of Israel.' 11 Explain that your actions are a
sign to show what will soon happen to them, for
they will be driven into exile as captives.
12 "Even Zedekiah will leave Jerusalem at night
through a hole in the wall, taking only what he
can carry with him. He will cover his face, and his
eyes will not see the land he is leaving. 13 Then I
will throw my net over him and capture him in
my snare. I will bring him to Babylon, the land
of the Babylonians,* though he will never see
it, and he will die there. 14 I will scatter his servants and warriors to the four winds and send
the sword after them. 15 And when I scatter them
among the nations, they will know that I am the
LORD. 16 But I will spare a few of them from death
by war, famine, or disease, so they can confess all
their detestable sins to their captors. Then they
will know that I am the LORD."
17 Then this message came to me from the
LORD: 18 "Son of man, tremble as you eat your
food. Shake with fear as you drink your water.
19 Tell the people, 'This is what the Sovereign
LORD says concerning those living in Israel and
Jerusalem: They will eat their food with trembling and sip their water in despair, for their land
will be stripped bare because of their violence.
20 The cities will be destroyed and the farmland
made desolate. Then you will know that I am the
LORD.'"

A New Proverb for Israel

21 Again a message came to me from the LORD:
22 "Son of man, you've heard that proverb they
quote in Israel: 'Time passes, and prophecies

11:24 Or *Chaldea.* **12:10** Hebrew *the prince in Jerusalem;* similarly in 12:12. **12:13** Or *Chaldeans.*

God and Israel/Judah. **22–25:** God's glory then leaves the city, and Ezekiel is returned to the exiles.

12:1–20 Exile Reenacted

Ezekiel's action will be seen by and later interpreted to his fellow captives, described as blind, deaf, and rebellious. Still, the fact that God gives Ezekiel a further message implies hope for the exiles, who may yet understand and repent. **5–7:** The wall he dug through was probably the wall of his home, though possibly it was a low retaining wall surrounding the captives' compound. Ezekiel's bemused neighbors might have wondered if this latest sign meant they would soon return home, but they discovered that the oracle concerned the capture, blinding, and exile of Zedekiah and the annihilation of his army.

12:21—14:11 True and False Prophecy

A new twist on an old proverb begins a section focusing on true and false prophecy. It begins with two familiar proverbs that reflect cynicism and unbelief regarding the prophets' words about the future. The

come to nothing.' 23 Tell the people, 'This is what the Sovereign LORD says: I will put an end to this proverb, and you will soon stop quoting it.' Now give them this new proverb to replace the old one: 'The time has come for every prophecy to be fulfilled!'

24 "There will be no more false visions and flattering predictions in Israel. 25 For I am the LORD! If I say it, it will happen. There will be no more delays, you rebels of Israel. I will fulfill my threat of destruction in your own lifetime. I, the Sovereign LORD, have spoken!"

26 Then this message came to me from the LORD: 27 "Son of man, the people of Israel are saying, 'He's talking about the distant future. His visions won't come true for a long, long time.' 28 Therefore, tell them, 'This is what the Sovereign LORD says: No more delay! I will now do everything I have threatened. I, the Sovereign LORD, have spoken!' "

Judgment against False Prophets

13 Then this message came to me from the LORD: 2 "Son of man, prophesy against the false prophets of Israel who are inventing their own prophecies. Say to them, 'Listen to the word of the LORD. 3 This is what the Sovereign LORD says: What sorrow awaits the false prophets who are following their own imaginations and have seen nothing at all!'

4 "O people of Israel, these prophets of yours are like jackals digging in the ruins. 5 They have done nothing to repair the breaks in the walls around the nation. They have not helped it to stand firm in battle on the day of the LORD. 6 Instead, they have told lies and made false predictions. They say, 'This message is from the LORD,' even though the LORD never sent them. And yet they expect him to fulfill their prophecies! 7 Can your visions be anything but false if you claim, 'This message is from the LORD,' when I have not even spoken to you?

8 "Therefore, this is what the Sovereign LORD says: Because what you say is false and your visions are a lie, I will stand against you, says the Sovereign LORD. 9 I will raise my fist against all the prophets who see false visions and make lying predictions, and they will be banished from the community of Israel. I will blot their names from Israel's record books, and they will never again set foot in their own land. Then you will know that I am the Sovereign LORD.

10 "This will happen because these evil prophets deceive my people by saying, 'All is peaceful' when there is no peace at all! It's as if the people have built a flimsy wall, and these prophets are trying to reinforce it by covering it with whitewash! 11 Tell these whitewashers that their wall will soon fall down. A heavy rainstorm will undermine it; great hailstones and mighty winds will knock it down. 12 And when the wall falls, the people will cry out, 'What happened to your whitewash?'

13 "Therefore, this is what the Sovereign LORD says: I will sweep away your whitewashed wall with a storm of indignation, with a great flood of anger, and with hailstones of fury. 14 I will break down your wall right to its foundation, and when it falls, it will crush you. Then you will know that I am the LORD. 15 At last my anger against the wall and those who covered it with whitewash will be satisfied. Then I will say to you: 'The wall and those who whitewashed it are both gone. 16 They were lying prophets who claimed peace would come to Jerusalem when there was no peace. I, the Sovereign LORD, have spoken!'

Judgment against False Women Prophets

17 "Now, son of man, speak out against the women who prophesy from their own imaginations.

---

proverbs are cleverly turned to remind the exiles of the truth of God's prophetic word. God's judgment was coming, and it was coming soon. **13:1–16:** Chapter 13 contains two sections that concern false prophets. The first group is judged for uttering delusions and lies to God's people by assuring them of peace when there is no peace. **17–23:** This is one of the few prophetic oracles addressed specifically to women (cf. Amos 4:1–3; Isa 3:16—4:1; 32:9–12). Moreover, it is the only oracle directed to women prophets. In Old Testament times, a small number of women are designated as prophets, though the nature of their ministries is varied and not always clearly defined: Miriam (Exod 15:20), Deborah (Judg 4:4; 5:7, 12), Huldah (2 Kgs 22:14–20; 2 Chr 34:22–28), Nodiah (Neh 6:14), and Isaiah's wife (Isa 8:3). Female prophets were well known in Mesopotamia, and their influence on Judean women in Babylon was most likely considerable. In this case, however, the methods and intentions of their prophetic work are deemed fraudulent. Indeed, commentators often appropriately identify these women as sorcerers, witches, charlatans, or practitioners of black magic. The incompatibility of magic and divination and true prophecy is seen in Deuteronomy 18, where improper and unauthorized methods of mediating the powers of life and death are delineated before the qualities of true prophesy are described. The *magic charms* and the *veils* were part of Mesopotamian magic arts. Ezekiel describes the intention of the magical acts as *ensnaring* peo-

[18]This is what the Sovereign LORD says: What
sorrow awaits you women who are ensnaring the
souls of my people, young and old alike. You tie
magic charms on their wrists and furnish them
with magic veils. Do you think you can trap others without bringing destruction on yourselves?
[19]You bring shame on me among my people for
a few handfuls of barley or a piece of bread. By
lying to my people who love to listen to lies, you
kill those who should not die, and you promise
life to those who should not live.
[20]"This is what the Sovereign LORD says: I
am against all your magic charms, which you use
to ensnare my people like birds. I will tear them
from your arms, setting my people free like birds
set free from a cage. [21]I will tear off the magic
veils and save my people from your grasp. They
will no longer be your victims. Then you will
know that I am the LORD. [22]You have discouraged the righteous with your lies, but I didn't
want them to be sad. And you have encouraged
the wicked by promising them life, even though
they continue in their sins. [23]Because of all this,
you will no longer talk of seeing visions that you
never saw, nor will you make predictions. For
I will rescue my people from your grasp. Then
you will know that I am the LORD."

The Idolatry of Israel's Leaders

14 Then some of the leaders of Israel visited me, and while they were sitting
with me, [2]this message came to me
from the LORD: [3]"Son of man, these leaders have
set up idols* in their hearts. They have embraced
things that will make them fall into sin. Why
should I listen to their requests? [4]Tell them, 'This
is what the Sovereign LORD says: The people of
Israel have set up idols in their hearts and fallen
into sin, and then they go to a prophet asking
for a message. So I, the LORD, will give them the
kind of answer their great idolatry deserves. [5]I
will do this to capture the minds and hearts of all
my people who have turned from me to worship
their detestable idols.'
[6]"Therefore, tell the people of Israel, 'This is
what the Sovereign LORD says: Repent and turn
away from your idols, and stop all your detestable sins. [7]I, the LORD, will answer all those, both
Israelites and foreigners, who reject me and set
up idols in their hearts and so fall into sin, and
who then come to a prophet asking for my advice. [8]I will turn against such people and make a
terrible example of them, eliminating them from
among my people. Then you will know that I am
the LORD.
[9]"'And if a prophet is deceived into giving a
message, it is because I, the LORD, have deceived
that prophet. I will lift my fist against such
prophets and cut them off from the community
of Israel. [10]False prophets and those who seek
their guidance will all be punished for their sins.
[11]In this way, the people of Israel will learn not
to stray from me, polluting themselves with sin.
They will be my people, and I will be their God.
I, the Sovereign LORD, have spoken!'"

14:3 The Hebrew term (literally *round things*) probably alludes to dung; also in 14:4, 5, 6, 7.

---

ple. The LORD's name was not to be called on in acts of divination. By so invoking the name and power of the LORD, they profaned his name. **19:** The women's actions became a source of power and income. They may have received the barley and bread as payment for services rendered (cf. 1 Sam 9:7). Their practices were unauthorized and their so-called prophetic ministry deemed to be false. **20–23:** God's response to these women was judgment. God would *tear* their bands *from* [their] *arms* and *tear off* their *veils*, which would free the souls they were trapping. Moreover, the women would no longer be able to prophesy. God's response to the victims, though, was deliverance. God calls them *my people* five times, suggesting his great compassion for those who are victims of deception, exploitation, and the occult. That many of the exiles were drawn to women who seemed to have divine knowledge and power over death and life is not surprising, because they lived with such uncertainty, instability, and fear. However, then as now, such practices are not value-neutral but rather exceedingly harmful. God has and continues to provide resources for the community of faith when it experiences times of confusion, pain, judgment, illness, death, prosperity, or blessing. Moreover, although this unique passage on women affirms the right of women to be prophets, it also warns that women are also capable of practicing illegitimate ministries, rooted not in God but in human ideas and pagan divination practices. **14:1–11:** Here, a group of leaders came to Ezekiel for a message from God. But the issue of their worship of idols alongside of their worship of the LORD was raised. The *idols in their hearts* is a reference to their consulting pagan diviners or a charge that other Judean prophets are false. The coarse term for *idols* (see translator's note on 14:3) demonstrates Ezekiel's disdain for such persons. These elders seemed to be blind to the fact that God demanded an exclusive allegiance from his covenant people. Repentance was required. Prophets who falsely spoke God's word to those who indulged in pagan practices are condemned alongside the idolatrous inquirers.

The Certainty of the LORD's Judgment

12 Then this message came to me from the LORD:
13 "Son of man, suppose the people of a country were to sin against me, and I lifted my fist
to crush them, cutting off their food supply and
sending a famine to destroy both people and animals. 14 Even if Noah, Daniel, and Job were there,
their righteousness would save no one but themselves, says the Sovereign LORD.

15 "Or suppose I were to send wild animals
to invade the country, kill the people, and make
the land too desolate and dangerous to pass
through. 16 As surely as I live, says the Sovereign LORD, even if those three men were there,
they wouldn't be able to save their own sons or
daughters. They alone would be saved, but the
land would be made desolate.

17 "Or suppose I were to bring war against the
land, and I sent enemy armies to destroy both
people and animals. 18 As surely as I live, says the
Sovereign LORD, even if those three men were
there, they wouldn't be able to save their own
sons or daughters. They alone would be saved.

19 "Or suppose I were to pour out my fury by
sending an epidemic into the land, and the disease killed people and animals alike. 20 As surely
as I live, says the Sovereign LORD, even if Noah,
Daniel, and Job were there, they wouldn't be able
to save their own sons or daughters. They alone
would be saved by their righteousness.

21 "Now this is what the Sovereign LORD says:
How terrible it will be when all four of these
dreadful punishments fall upon Jerusalem—war,
famine, wild animals, and disease—destroying
all her people and animals. 22 Yet there will be
survivors, and they will come here to join you
as exiles in Babylon. You will see with your own
eyes how wicked they are, and then you will
feel better about what I have done to Jerusalem.
23 When you meet them and see their behavior,
you will understand that these things are not being done to Israel without cause. I, the Sovereign
LORD, have spoken!"

Jerusalem—a Useless Vine

15 Then this message came to me from
the LORD: 2 "Son of man, how does
a grapevine compare to a tree? Is a
vine's wood as useful as the wood of a tree? 3 Can
its wood be used for making things, like pegs to
hang up pots and pans? 4 No, it can only be used
for fuel, and even as fuel, it burns too quickly.
5 Vines are useless both before and after being
put into the fire!

6 "And this is what the Sovereign LORD says:
The people of Jerusalem are like grapevines
growing among the trees of the forest. Since
they are useless, I have thrown them on the fire
to be burned. 7 And I will see to it that if they
escape from one fire, they will fall into another.
When I turn against them, you will know that I
am the LORD. 8 And I will make the land desolate
because my people have been unfaithful to me. I,
the Sovereign LORD, have spoken!"

Jerusalem—an Unfaithful Wife

16 Then another message came to me
from the LORD: 2 "Son of man, confront Jerusalem with her detestable
sins. 3 Give her this message from the Sovereign

14:12–15:8 A Righteous Few Cannot Save

The exiles' conviction that a righteous remnant would save Jerusalem from final destruction is shown to be out of line with a basic principle of justice, where not even the presence of righteous persons would save the land or their children from judgment. **14:13–23:** These verses show the "if . . . then" device, here *suppose I were to* . . . . Each person is responsible for his or her position before a righteous and just God. This principle of individual responsibility (cf. chap. 18) is important for women, who would now be judged on their merits and not on those of the men who controlled them. However, any who escaped the devastation of Jerusalem were not to be regarded as being saved by their righteousness. Rather, their unrighteous deeds and ways would demonstrate that God was fully justified in punishing Jerusalem. **15:1–8:** This short parable reiterates the message of the destruction of Jerusalem and attacks the exiles' optimism and false sense of security as the royal vine of God's planting (cf. Ps 80:9–12). God originally intended that the vine he had planted should produce fruit (cf. Isa 5:1–7). Ezekiel does not mention the fruit of the vine; it is as though its days of production are long gone. Instead, the uselessness of its wood is observed and its end declared (cf. John 15:1–6).

16:1–63 A Love Story Gone Wrong

God's judgment is communicated by means of a love story between God and Jerusalem that quickly goes awry. Ezekiel transforms the metaphor of the city as the wife of its patron god: The wife is not a benevolent goddess but the unfaithful human wife of a shamed and dishonored God. At the same time, Ezekiel builds on the metaphor of apostasy as adultery. In his attempt to shock his audience into a recognition of their situation in relation to God, Ezekiel explodes the metaphor of Jerusalem as wife to in-

LORD: You are nothing but a Canaanite! Your
father was an Amorite and your mother a Hittite. [4]On the day you were born, no one cared
about you. Your umbilical cord was not cut, and
you were never washed, rubbed with salt, and
wrapped in cloth. [5]No one had the slightest interest in you; no one pitied you or cared for you.
On the day you were born, you were unwanted,
dumped in a field and left to die.
[6]"But I came by and saw you there, helplessly kicking about in your own blood. As you
lay there, I said, 'Live!' [7]And I helped you to
thrive like a plant in the field. You grew up and
became a beautiful jewel. Your breasts became
full, and your body hair grew, but you were still
naked. [8]And when I passed by again, I saw that
you were old enough for love. So I wrapped my
cloak around you to cover your nakedness and
declared my marriage vows. I made a covenant
with you, says the Sovereign LORD, and you became mine.
[9]"Then I bathed you and washed off your
blood, and I rubbed fragrant oils into your skin.
[10]I gave you expensive clothing of fine linen and
silk, beautifully embroidered, and sandals made
of fine goatskin leather. [11]I gave you lovely jewelry, bracelets, beautiful necklaces, [12]a ring for
your nose, earrings for your ears, and a lovely
crown for your head. [13]And so you were adorned
with gold and silver. Your clothes were made of
fine linen and were beautifully embroidered. You
ate the finest foods—choice flour, honey, and olive oil—and became more beautiful than ever.
You looked like a queen, and so you were! [14]Your
fame soon spread throughout the world because
of your beauty. I dressed you in my splendor and
perfected your beauty, says the Sovereign LORD.
[15]"But you thought your fame and beauty
were your own. So you gave yourself as a prostitute to every man who came along. Your beauty
was theirs for the asking. [16]You used the lovely things I gave you to make shrines for idols,
where you played the prostitute. Unbelievable!
How could such a thing ever happen? [17]You took
the very jewels and gold and silver ornaments
I had given you and made statues of men and
worshiped them. This is adultery against me!
[18]You used the beautifully embroidered clothes
I gave you to dress your idols. Then you used
my special oil and my incense to worship them.
[19]Imagine it! You set before them as a sacrifice
the choice flour, olive oil, and honey I had given
you, says the Sovereign LORD.
[20]"Then you took your sons and daughters—

---

clude graphic and offensive references to the female body and a portrayal of God that when taken out of its metaphorical context, proves highly problematic. When these pictures of women are read out of their contexts, serious interpretive and theological problems occur. Ezekiel, however, intends that men and women identify themselves as the unfaithful lover of the God who throughout is assumed to be just and holy. God's rage is to be distinguished from human rage, which would be affected by pride, ego, and other aspects of sin. **4–6:** The description of Jerusalem as an abandoned newborn points to significant cultural differences between the world of the text and the world of readers. Postnatal care for a newborn child involved cutting the umbilical cord, bathing in clean water, rubbing in salt, and wrapping in cloth. The details regarding the neglectful state in which the baby was tossed out to die also point to ancient customs regarding legal rights and responsibilities for infants. **7–8:** The young woman grew sexually mature but remained naked. Signs of physical maturation were generally viewed positively in the ancient Near East. However, because menstruation was linked not only to fertility and blessing but also to impurity, its onset was viewed with ambivalence. The woman's vulnerability is noticed by her rescuer, who then spread a garment over her to symbolize the declaration of betrothal (cf. Ruth 3:9). **8–14:** The emphasis is on the husband's role as initiator, magnanimous provider, and enabler of his beloved. Although many brides in ancient times brought dowry items like gold, jewelry, textiles, and household utensils into a marriage, this foundling bride came naked. The hierarchical nature of this marriage reflects the broader patriarchal culture, but it also raises the expectation that the recipient of such gifts would respond in gratitude if not in kind. Mutuality in marriage was known in the Old Testament world (cf. the relationship between the lover and the beloved in Song of Songs). **15–34:** However, placing her confidence in her own beauty and forgetting her benevolent spouse, Jerusalem became a prostitute. Many of her acts of promiscuity involved a perversion of the gifts bestowed on her as the new bride by her loving husband. Perhaps the most perverse act of Jerusalem's religious promiscuity was sacrificing the children she had borne to the LORD. Here the figure of the mother, who is most often depicted positively as nurturer and caregiver in the Old Testament, slaughters her children as food for her lovers. Child sacrifice was practiced though never sanctioned in Israel and Judah. There is intense irony in the image of the once-rescued infant growing up to slaughter the children she bore to her rescuer. **23–29:** The metaphor shifts from religious to

the children you had borne to me—and sacrificed them to your gods. Was your prostitution
not enough? [21] Must you also slaughter my children by sacrificing them to idols? [22] In all your
years of adultery and detestable sin, you have
not once remembered the days long ago when
you lay naked in a field, kicking about in your
own blood.
[23] "What sorrow awaits you, says the Sovereign LORD. In addition to all your other wickedness, [24] you built a pagan shrine and put altars
to idols in every town square. [25] On every street
corner you defiled your beauty, offering your
body to every passerby in an endless stream of
prostitution. [26] Then you added lustful Egypt
to your lovers, provoking my anger with your
increasing promiscuity. [27] That is why I struck
you with my fist and reduced your boundaries.
I handed you over to your enemies, the Philistines, and even they were shocked by your lewd
conduct. [28] You have prostituted yourself with
the Assyrians, too. It seems you can never find
enough new lovers! And after your prostitution
there, you still were not satisfied. [29] You added to
your lovers by embracing Babylonia,* the land
of merchants, but you still weren't satisfied.
[30] "What a sick heart you have, says the Sovereign LORD, to do such things as these, acting
like a shameless prostitute. [31] You build your
pagan shrines on every street corner and your
altars to idols in every square. In fact, you have
been worse than a prostitute, so eager for sin that
you have not even demanded payment. [32] Yes,
you are an adulterous wife who takes in strangers instead of her own husband. [33] Prostitutes
charge for their services—but not you! You give
gifts to your lovers, bribing them to come and
have sex with you. [34] So you are the opposite of
other prostitutes. You pay your lovers instead of
their paying you!

Judgment on Jerusalem's Prostitution

[35] "Therefore, you prostitute, listen to this message from the LORD! [36] This is what the Sovereign LORD says: Because you have poured out
your lust and exposed yourself in prostitution
to all your lovers, and because you have worshiped detestable idols,* and because you have
slaughtered your children as sacrifices to your
gods, [37] this is what I am going to do. I will gather
together all your allies—the lovers with whom
you have sinned, both those you loved and those
you hated—and I will strip you naked in front of
them so they can stare at you. [38] I will punish you
for your murder and adultery. I will cover you
with blood in my jealous fury. [39] Then I will give
you to these many nations who are your lovers, and they will destroy you. They will knock
down your pagan shrines and the altars to your
idols. They will strip you and take your beautiful jewels, leaving you stark naked. [40] They will
band together in a mob to stone you and cut you
up with swords. [41] They will burn your homes
and punish you in front of many women. I will
stop your prostitution and end your payments to
your many lovers.
[42] "Then at last my fury against you will be
spent, and my jealous anger will subside. I will
be calm and will not be angry with you anymore.

16:29 Or *Chaldea*. **16:36** The Hebrew term (literally *round things*) probably alludes to dung.

political alliances with foreign nations. **30–34:** Israel is so eager to betray her husband that she pays her lovers to come to her. This probably refers to instances such as Ahaz's stripping the Temple of its wealth to bribe Tiglath-pileser (2 Kgs 16:8). **35–63:** In the honor-shame culture of the ancient world, an unfaithful wife brought dishonor to her husband. According to Middle Assyrian laws, a husband had the legal right to whip his unfaithful wife, to pull out her hair, to mutilate her ears or genitals, to tie her up and throw her into a river or from a tower, or to make her a slave. Ezekiel's metaphor assumes that the husband, who in this case is a righteous God and holy covenant partner, had the right to punish his wife. But although anger and vengeance were the expected responses to sexual violations in those cultures, neither the law nor the narratives attest to the kind of marital violence that is found in Ezekiel's extended metaphors (cf. Ezek 23). In Israel, punishment was based on compensation and penalty. Under such a system, capital punishment was reserved for crimes for which compensation was impossible (e.g., bringing someone back to life, restoring virginity, restoring the brokenness of adultery). The fact that adultery was such a crime makes Israel's eventual restoration all the more a miraculous and gracious act of God. **37–38:** Furthermore, the custom of stripping a woman as part of divorce proceedings is also attested (Hos 2:2–3). Thus the depiction of God's *fury* toward his wife is not unexpected in its context. Readers are expected to sympathize with the wronged divine husband. The penalties are for murder as well as adultery, a fact that may lessen in a small way the misogynist tone of the passage. **41:** The description of a female audience warns women against imitating Jerusalem's wantonness. **42:** In the end, God's fury and rage are satisfied. He is no longer shamed and promises to be angry no more. **43–58:** Ezekiel moves

43 But first, because you have not remembered your
youth but have angered me by doing all these evil
things, I will fully repay you for all of your sins,
says the Sovereign LORD. For you have added lewd
acts to all your detestable sins. 44 Everyone who
makes up proverbs will say of you, 'Like mother,
like daughter.' 45 For your mother loathed her husband and her children, and so do you. And you are
exactly like your sisters, for they despised their
husbands and their children. Truly your mother
was a Hittite and your father an Amorite.

46 "Your older sister was Samaria, who lived
with her daughters in the north. Your younger
sister was Sodom, who lived with her daughters
in the south. 47 But you have not merely sinned
as they did. You quickly surpassed them in corruption. 48 As surely as I live, says the Sovereign
LORD, Sodom and her daughters were never as
wicked as you and your daughters. 49 Sodom's
sins were pride, gluttony, and laziness, while the
poor and needy suffered outside her door. 50 She
was proud and committed detestable sins, so I
wiped her out, as you have seen.*

51 "Even Samaria did not commit half your
sins. You have done far more detestable things
than your sisters ever did. They seem righteous
compared to you. 52 Shame on you! Your sins are
so terrible that you make your sisters seem righteous, even virtuous.

53 "But someday I will restore the fortunes of
Sodom and Samaria, and I will restore you, too.
54 Then you will be truly ashamed of everything
you have done, for your sins make them feel
good in comparison. 55 Yes, your sisters, Sodom
and Samaria, and all their people will be restored,
and at that time you also will be restored. 56 In
your proud days you held Sodom in contempt.
57 But now your greater wickedness has been exposed to all the world, and you are the one who is
scorned—by Edom* and all her neighbors and by
Philistia. 58 This is your punishment for all your
lewdness and detestable sins, says the LORD.

59 "Now this is what the Sovereign LORD says:
I will give you what you deserve, for you have
taken your solemn vows lightly by breaking
your covenant. 60 Yet I will remember the covenant I made with you when you were young,
and I will establish an everlasting covenant with
you. 61 Then you will remember with shame all
the evil you have done. I will make your sisters,
Samaria and Sodom, to be your daughters, even
though they are not part of our covenant. 62 And I
will reaffirm my covenant with you, and you will
know that I am the LORD. 63 You will remember
your sins and cover your mouth in silent shame
when I forgive you of all that you have done. I,
the Sovereign LORD, have spoken!"

A Story of Two Eagles

17 Then this message came to me from
the LORD: 2 "Son of man, give this
riddle, and tell this story to the people

16:50 As in a few Hebrew manuscripts and Greek version; Masoretic Text reads *as I have seen.* **16:57** As in many Hebrew manuscripts and Syriac version; Masoretic Text reads *Aram.*

from a graphic depiction of Jerusalem's sin to a comparison built on the proverb "like mother, like daughter." Only a mother and sisters who bring dishonor to their roles as wives and mothers are named here. A more positive and literal casting of this proverb might include a consideration of honorable matriarchs like Sarah, Rebekah, or Deborah, who is named "a mother in Israel" (Judg 5:7). But Ezekiel uses the proverb to cast a negative light on Jerusalem as a daughter and mother. Even in restoration, Jerusalem will have to share her good fortune with Sodom and Samaria and their daughters. This shameful situation is regarded as further punishment for Jerusalem. **59–63:** Still, God promises to remember his covenant and establish an everlasting covenant with Jerusalem. Her sisters are not included in this covenant directly, though they will benefit from it in that they will be given to Jerusalem as daughters. By using these figures, Ezekiel intended to shock his predominantly male audience into listening to God's message about their infidelity to the covenant and their imminent punishment. The love story gone wrong explains the reasons for God's judgment on Jerusalem. To be sure, it raises important questions about God's character as God is presented as a compassionate rescuer, a deeply passionate and generous lover who responds to the wantonness of his wife with jealousy, anger, vengeance, and ultimately with promises of restoration. But these questions need to be studied with an appreciation for the text's genre and in light of the rest of Scripture.

17:1–18:32 A Riddle and a Proverb

The eagles represent Babylon and Egypt, and the vine is Zedekiah, who sought liberation from Babylon and looked to Egypt for help. This invites God's retribution. What seemed to Zedekiah a shrewd political solution to Judah's troubles, did not address the underlying moral and spiritual issues that were at the heart of Judah's problems. The message to the exiles, looking for a political solution to their troubles, was clear. **17:1–10:** The riddle is meant to be relayed to Israel in dialogue by Ezekiel. The LORD answers in another riddle (vv. 9–10) and explains the

of Israel. 3 Give them this message from the Sovereign LORD:

"A great eagle with broad wings and long
feathers,
covered with many-colored plumage,
came to Lebanon.
He seized the top of a cedar tree
4 and plucked off its highest branch.
He carried it away to a city filled with
merchants.
He planted it in a city of traders.
5 He also took a seedling from the land
and planted it in fertile soil.
He placed it beside a broad river,
where it could grow like a willow tree.
6 It took root there and
grew into a low, spreading vine.
Its branches turned up toward the eagle,
and its roots grew down into the ground.
It produced strong branches
and put out shoots.
7 But then another great eagle came
with broad wings and full plumage.
So the vine now sent its roots and branches
toward him for water,
8 even though it was already planted in good
soil
and had plenty of water
so it could grow into a splendid vine
and produce rich leaves and luscious fruit.
9 "So now the Sovereign LORD asks:
Will this vine grow and prosper?
No! I will pull it up, roots and all!
I will cut off its fruit
and let its leaves wither and die.
I will pull it up easily
without a strong arm or a large army.
10 But when the vine is transplanted,
will it thrive?
No, it will wither away
when the east wind blows against it.
It will die in the same good soil
where it had grown so well."

The Riddle Explained

11 Then this message came to me from the LORD:
12 "Say to these rebels of Israel: Don't you understand the meaning of this riddle of the eagles?
The king of Babylon came to Jerusalem, took
away her king and princes, and brought them to
Babylon. 13 He made a treaty with a member of
the royal family and forced him to take an oath
of loyalty. He also exiled Israel's most influential leaders, 14 so Israel would not become strong
again and revolt. Only by keeping her treaty
with Babylon could Israel survive.
15 "Nevertheless, this man of Israel's royal
family rebelled against Babylon, sending ambassadors to Egypt to request a great army and many
horses. Can Israel break her sworn treaties like
that and get away with it? 16 No! For as surely as
I live, says the Sovereign LORD, the king of Israel
will die in Babylon, the land of the king who put
him in power and whose treaty he disregarded
and broke. 17 Pharaoh and all his mighty army
will fail to help Israel when the king of Babylon
lays siege to Jerusalem again and destroys many
lives. 18 For the king of Israel disregarded his treaty and broke it after swearing to obey; therefore,
he will not escape.
19 "So this is what the Sovereign LORD says:
As surely as I live, I will punish him for breaking
my covenant and disregarding the solemn oath
he made in my name. 20 I will throw my net over
him and capture him in my snare. I will bring
him to Babylon and put him on trial for this
treason against me. 21 And all his best warriors*
will be killed in battle, and those who survive
will be scattered to the four winds. Then you will
know that I, the LORD, have spoken.
22 "This is what the Sovereign LORD says: I
will take a branch from the top of a tall cedar,
and I will plant it on the top of Israel's highest mountain. 23 It will become a majestic cedar,
sending forth its branches and producing seed.
Birds of every sort will nest in it, finding shelter
in the shade of its branches. 24 And all the trees
will know that it is I, the LORD, who cuts the tall
tree down and makes the short tree grow tall. It
is I who makes the green tree wither and gives
the dead tree new life. I, the LORD, have spoken,
and I will do what I said!"

The Justice of a Righteous God

18 Then another message came to me
from the LORD: 2 "Why do you quote
this proverb concerning the land of

17:21 Or *his fleeing warriors.* The meaning of the Hebrew is uncertain.

solution (vv. 11–24). **22–24:** In the epilogue, God becomes the great eagle and promises the continued existence of the Davidic line through a special shoot. God's final promise that what he has spoken, he will perform, is a word of hope for the community of faith who later recognized a messianic promise in these verses. **18:1–32:** A popular proverb encapsulating an attitude of fatalism is challenged.

Israel: 'The parents have eaten sour grapes, but their children's mouths pucker at the taste'? 3 As surely as I live, says the Sovereign LORD, you will not quote this proverb anymore in Israel. 4 For all people are mine to judge—both parents and children alike. And this is my rule: The person who sins is the one who will die.

5 "Suppose a certain man is righteous and does what is just and right. 6 He does not feast in the mountains before Israel's idols* or worship them. He does not commit adultery or have intercourse with a woman during her menstrual period. 7 He is a merciful creditor, not keeping the items given as security by poor debtors. He does not rob the poor but instead gives food to the hungry and provides clothes for the needy. 8 He grants loans without interest, stays away from injustice, is honest and fair when judging others, 9 and faithfully obeys my decrees and regulations. Anyone who does these things is just and will surely live, says the Sovereign LORD.

10 "But suppose that man has a son who grows up to be a robber or murderer and refuses to do what is right. 11 And that son does all the evil things his father would never do—he worships idols on the mountains, commits adultery, 12 oppresses the poor and helpless, steals from debtors by refusing to let them redeem their security, worships idols, commits detestable sins, 13 and lends money at excessive interest. Should such a sinful person live? No! He must die and must take full blame.

14 "But suppose that sinful son, in turn, has a son who sees his father's wickedness and decides against that kind of life. 15 This son refuses to worship idols on the mountains and does not commit adultery. 16 He does not exploit the poor, but instead is fair to debtors and does not rob them. He gives food to the hungry and provides clothes for the needy. 17 He helps the poor,* does not lend money at interest, and obeys all my regulations and decrees. Such a person will not die because of his father's sins; he will surely live. 18 But the father will die for his many sins—for being cruel, robbing people, and doing what was clearly wrong among his people.

19 " 'What?' you ask. 'Doesn't the child pay for the parent's sins?' No! For if the child does what is just and right and keeps my decrees, that child will surely live. 20 The person who sins is the one who will die. The child will not be punished for the parent's sins, and the parent will not be punished for the child's sins. Righteous people will be rewarded for their own righteous behavior, and wicked people will be punished for their own wickedness. 21 But if wicked people turn away from all their sins and begin to obey my decrees and do what is just and right, they will surely live and not die. 22 All their past sins will be forgotten, and they will live because of the righteous things they have done.

23 "Do you think that I like to see wicked people die? says the Sovereign LORD. Of course not! I want them to turn from their wicked ways and live. 24 However, if righteous people turn from their righteous behavior and start doing sinful things and act like other sinners, should they be allowed to live? No, of course not! All their righteous acts will be forgotten, and they will die for their sins.

25 "Yet you say, 'The Lord isn't doing what's right!' Listen to me, O people of Israel. Am I the one not doing what's right, or is it you? 26 When righteous people turn from their righteous behavior and start doing sinful things, they will die for it. Yes, they will die because of their sinful deeds. 27 And if wicked people turn from their wickedness, obey the law, and do what is just and right, they will save their lives. 28 They will live because they thought it over and decided to turn from their sins. Such people will not die. 29 And yet the people of Israel keep saying, 'The Lord

18:6 The Hebrew term (literally *round things*) probably alludes to dung; also in 18:12, 15. **18:17** Greek version reads *He refuses to do evil.*

Instead of placing the responsibility for God's present judgment on previous generations, Ezekiel declares that each person is responsible for his or her life. The various subjects of Ezekiel's exploration of individual responsibility are male, and the crimes are typically male (especially defiling another man's wife or approaching a menstruating woman). However, the principles are universal and inclusive. They are ultimately liberating for women, who must take responsibility for their spiritual and moral lives before God. Finally, although this passage repudiates the old proverb that allowed adult children to blame others for their circumstances, the proverb seen in its best light reminds parents of their responsibilities for teaching their children and their children's children the ways of God so that they will know how to live a righteous life before God. These verses also fall into the "if . . . then" (*suppose that* . . .) literary device, which is useful for presenting proverbial tenets. **21–24:** A new principle enters the debate: Repentance from evil ways will lead to salvation, but the reverse is also true. **30:** The same lesson holds: Each person is judged according to his or her own actions.

isn't doing what's right!' O people of Israel, it is you who are not doing what's right, not I.
30 "Therefore, I will judge each of you, O people of Israel, according to your actions, says the Sovereign LORD. Repent, and turn from your
sins. Don't let them destroy you! 31 Put all your
rebellion behind you, and find yourselves a new heart and a new spirit. For why should you die,
O people of Israel? 32 I don't want you to die, says
the Sovereign LORD. Turn back and live!

A Funeral Song for Israel's Kings

19 "Sing this funeral song for the princes of Israel:

2 "What is your mother?
  A lioness among lions!
She lay down among the young lions
  and reared her cubs.
3 She raised one of her cubs
  to become a strong young lion.
He learned to hunt and devour prey,
  and he became a man-eater.
4 Then the nations heard about him,
  and he was trapped in their pit.
They led him away with hooks
  to the land of Egypt.

5 "When the lioness saw
  that her hopes for him were gone,
she took another of her cubs
  and taught him to be a strong young lion.
6 He prowled among the other lions
  and stood out among them in his strength.
He learned to hunt and devour prey,
  and he, too, became a man-eater.
7 He demolished fortresses*
  and destroyed their towns and cities.
Their farms were desolated,
  and their crops were destroyed.
The land and its people trembled in fear
  when they heard him roar.
8 Then the armies of the nations attacked him,
  surrounding him from every direction.
They threw a net over him
  and captured him in their pit.
9 With hooks, they dragged him into a cage
  and brought him before the king of
    Babylon.
They held him in captivity,
  so his voice could never again be heard
  on the mountains of Israel.

10 "Your mother was like a vine
  planted by the water's edge.
It had lush, green foliage
  because of the abundant water.
11 Its branches became strong—

19:7 As in Greek version; Hebrew reads *He knew widows.*

19:1–14 The Lioness and the Vine

Following a chapter that focuses on fathers and children, this one features a mother imaged initially as a lioness and then as a vine. Although the chapter allows for positive reflection on the importance of mothers, it is a lament and ultimately leads readers to thoughtful reflection on pride, ambition, disappointment, sin, and judgment. In this, the first of Ezekiel's laments, there is considerable debate about the identity of the individual or entity mourned—that is, the *mother*. **2–9:** The first part features the lioness, extolled as a mother in her role as caregiver and educator of her cubs. She succeeded in raising two strong lions that learned (presumably from her) to tear the prey and devour people. Her role as an ambitious, perhaps controlling, yet effective trainer and teacher is underlined. **10–14:** The second part of the lament features the mother again, this time likened to a fruitful vine, growing strong and tall. The double references to the height of the vine ominously suggest the sin of pride. The association of women and pride is also made in Isaiah 3:16, where the women of Zion are called haughty, and in Ezekiel's description of Sodom and her daughters (16:49–58). The lamentation ends with images of death. The mother vine is left without life, and the death of the mother that is lamented in the funeral dirge has taken place. If readers look for close correspondence between symbol and reality to identify the lioness, her cubs, and the vine with historical figures, Hamutal, the wife of Josiah and mother of Jehoahaz and Zedekiah, is undoubtedly the strongest candidate for the mother figure (2 Kgs 24:18). Many interpreters, however, prefer to identify the mother as a collective entity such as Israel, Judah, its royal house, or Jerusalem. The view that the mother represents Judah collectively is supported by chapter 49, which may be the text that inspired this lament. If the cubs are to be identified as individuals, most commentators concur that the first cub is Jehoahaz. Difference of opinion exists, however, when it comes to identifying the second cub as Jehoiachin, in which case the vine may be identified as Nehushta, exiled with her son to Babylon (2 Kgs 24:12). On a positive note, this chapter calls attention to the importance of a mother's role in the formation of children. But the greatest hopes and dreams of the lioness and the vine for their progeny came to naught. This lament then underscores a common theme in Scripture concerning the impact of the failures and successes of

strong enough to be a ruler's scepter.
It grew very tall,
towering above all others.
It stood out because of its height
and its many lush branches.
[12] But the vine was uprooted in fury
and thrown down to the ground.
The desert wind dried up its fruit
and tore off its strong branches,
so that it withered
and was destroyed by fire.
[13] Now the vine is transplanted to the
wilderness,
where the ground is hard and dry.
[14] A fire has burst out from its branches
and devoured its fruit.
Its remaining limbs are not
strong enough to be a ruler's scepter.

"This is a funeral song, and it will be used in a
funeral."

The Rebellion of Israel

20 On August 14,* during the seventh
year of King Jehoiachin's captivity,
some of the leaders of Israel came to
request a message from the LORD. They sat down
in front of me to wait for his reply. [2]Then this
message came to me from the LORD: [3]"Son of
man, tell the leaders of Israel, 'This is what the
Sovereign LORD says: How dare you come to ask
me for a message? As surely as I live, says the
Sovereign LORD, I will tell you nothing!'
[4]"Son of man, bring charges against them and
condemn them. Make them realize how detestable the sins of their ancestors really were. [5]Give
them this message from the Sovereign LORD:
When I chose Israel—when I revealed myself to
the descendants of Jacob in Egypt—I took a solemn oath that I, the LORD, would be their God.
[6]I took a solemn oath that day that I would bring
them out of Egypt to a land I had discovered and
explored for them—a good land, a land flowing
with milk and honey, the best of all lands anywhere. [7]Then I said to them, 'Each of you, get rid
of the vile images you are so obsessed with. Do
not defile yourselves with the idols* of Egypt, for
I am the LORD your God.'
[8]"But they rebelled against me and would
not listen. They did not get rid of the vile images
they were obsessed with, or forsake the idols of
Egypt. Then I threatened to pour out my fury on
them to satisfy my anger while they were still in
Egypt. [9]But I didn't do it, for I acted to protect the
honor of my name. I would not allow shame to
be brought on my name among the surrounding
nations who saw me reveal myself by bringing
the Israelites out of Egypt. [10]So I brought them
out of Egypt and led them into the wilderness.
[11]There I gave them my decrees and regulations
so they could find life by keeping them. [12]And I
gave them my Sabbath days of rest as a sign between them and me. It was to remind them that I
am the LORD, who had set them apart to be holy.
[13]"But the people of Israel rebelled against
me, and they refused to obey my decrees there
in the wilderness. They wouldn't obey my regulations even though obedience would have given
them life. They also violated my Sabbath days.
So I threatened to pour out my fury on them,
and I made plans to utterly consume them in the
wilderness. [14]But again I held back in order to
protect the honor of my name before the nations
who had seen my power in bringing Israel out of
Egypt. [15]But I took a solemn oath against them
in the wilderness. I swore I would not bring them
into the land I had given them, a land flowing
with milk and honey, the most beautiful place on
earth. [16]For they had rejected my regulations, refused to follow my decrees, and violated my Sabbath days. Their hearts were given to their idols.
[17]Nevertheless, I took pity on them and held back
from destroying them in the wilderness.
[18]"Then I warned their children not to follow
in their parents' footsteps, defiling themselves
with their idols. [19]'I am the LORD your God,' I
told them. 'Follow my decrees, pay attention to

20:1 Hebrew *In the fifth month, on the tenth day,* of the ancient Hebrew lunar calendar. This day was August 14, 591 B.C.; also see note on 1:1. **20:7** The Hebrew term (literally *round things*) probably alludes to dung; also in 20:8, 16, 18, 24, 31, 39.

children on their parents. The lioness and the vine neglected teaching their children the ways of the righteous to the peril of their children and ultimately themselves. Finally, that the career that an ambitious mother viewed as successful led to the destruction of cities and the deaths of men reminds readers that women as well as men can be involved in encouraging the abuse and death of others.

20:1–44 Israel's History Revisited

The leaders who came to Ezekiel with a question to ask God were undoubtedly shocked by the long, grim rehearsal of Israel's history they were given. It was history recast to warn Ezekiel's contemporaries of coming judgment. The pattern of grace, rebellion, and restrained anger repeats itself. **23–26:** What fol-

my regulations, [20]and keep my Sabbath days holy, for they are a sign to remind you that I am the LORD your God.'

[21]"But their children, too, rebelled against me. They refused to keep my decrees and follow my regulations, even though obedience would have given them life. And they also violated my Sabbath days. So again I threatened to pour out my fury on them in the wilderness. [22]Nevertheless, I withdrew my judgment against them to protect the honor of my name before the nations that had seen my power in bringing them out of Egypt. [23]But I took a solemn oath against them in the wilderness. I swore I would scatter them among all the nations [24]because they did not obey my regulations. They scorned my decrees by violating my Sabbath days and longing for the idols of their ancestors. [25]I gave them over to worthless decrees and regulations that would not lead to life. [26]I let them pollute themselves* with the very gifts I had given them, and I allowed them to give their firstborn children as offerings to their gods—so I might devastate them and remind them that I alone am the LORD.

Judgment and Restoration

[27]"Therefore, son of man, give the people of Israel this message from the Sovereign LORD: Your ancestors continued to blaspheme and betray me, [28]for when I brought them into the land I had promised them, they offered sacrifices on every high hill and under every green tree they saw! They roused my fury as they offered up sacrifices to their gods. They brought their perfumes and incense and poured out their liquid offerings to them. [29]I said to them, 'What is this high place where you are going?' (This kind of pagan shrine has been called Bamah—'high place'—ever since.)

[30]"Therefore, give the people of Israel this message from the Sovereign LORD: Do you plan to pollute yourselves just as your ancestors did? Do you intend to keep prostituting yourselves by worshiping vile images? [31]For when you offer gifts to them and give your little children to be burned as sacrifices,* you continue to pollute yourselves with idols to this day. Should I allow you to ask for a message from me, O people of Israel? As surely as I live, says the Sovereign LORD, I will tell you nothing.

[32]"You say, 'We want to be like the nations all around us, who serve idols of wood and stone.' But what you have in mind will never happen. [33]As surely as I live, says the Sovereign LORD, I will rule over you with an iron fist in great anger and with awesome power. [34]And in anger I will reach out with my strong hand and powerful arm, and I will bring you back* from the lands where you are scattered. [35]I will bring you into the wilderness of the nations, and there I will judge you face to face. [36]I will judge you there just as I did your ancestors in the wilderness after bringing them out of Egypt, says the Sovereign LORD. [37]I will examine you carefully and hold you to the terms of the covenant. [38]I will purge you of all those who rebel and revolt against me. I will bring them out of the countries where they are in exile, but they will never enter the land of Israel. Then you will know that I am the LORD.

[39]"As for you, O people of Israel, this is what the Sovereign LORD says: Go right ahead and worship your idols, but sooner or later you will obey me and will stop bringing shame on my holy name by worshiping idols. [40]For on my holy mountain, the great mountain of Israel, says the Sovereign LORD, the people of Israel will someday worship me, and I will accept them. There I will require that you bring me all your offerings and choice gifts and sacrifices. [41]When I bring you home from exile, you will be like a pleasing sacrifice to me. And I will display my holiness through you as all the nations watch. [42]Then when I have brought you home to the land I

20:25-26 Or *I gave them worthless decrees and regulations. . . . I polluted them.* **20:31** Or *and make your little children pass through the fire.* **20:34** Greek version reads *I will welcome you.* Compare 2 Cor 6:17.

lows is a problematic statement that God gave them bad laws and rules that could not lead to life—most notably the sacrifice of firstborn. Many solutions to the theological problems raised by this text have been offered. One possibility is that Ezekiel is referring to a perverse twisting of the law that the firstborn belonged to the LORD, which was being used by God's covenant people to justify the practice of sacrificing children to the Canaanite god Molech. From the perspective of divine providence, Ezekiel could understand this "misunderstanding" or bad law as being part of God's larger plan to punish his rebellious people. **27–44:** Ezekiel's account of past sins continues with a description of the idolatry that took place upon entry into Canaan. Finally, Ezekiel's grim history reaches the present, and the elders are told that God will not give an answer because they have followed the pattern of rebellion of their forebears. In the end they are promised a new exodus, another wilderness experience, and a purging of the rebels that ultimately would create a people acknowledging the LORD and worshiping on his holy mountain.

promised with a solemn oath to give to your
ancestors, you will know that I am the LORD.
43 You will look back on all the ways you defiled
yourselves and will hate yourselves because of
the evil you have done. 44 You will know that I
am the LORD, O people of Israel, when I have
honored my name by treating you mercifully in
spite of your wickedness. I, the Sovereign LORD,
have spoken!"

Judgment against the Negev

45 *Then this message came to me from the
LORD: 46 "Son of man, turn and face the south*
and speak out against it; prophesy against the
brushlands of the Negev. 47 Tell the southern wilderness, 'This is what the Sovereign LORD says:
Hear the word of the LORD! I will set you on
fire, and every tree, both green and dry, will be
burned. The terrible flames will not be quenched
and will scorch everything from south to north.
48 And everyone in the world will see that I, the
LORD, have set this fire. It will not be put out.' "
49 Then I said, "O Sovereign LORD, they are
saying of me, 'He only talks in riddles!' "

The LORD's Sword of Judgment

21 1 *Then this message came to me
from the LORD: 2 "Son of man, turn
and face Jerusalem and prophesy
against Israel and her sanctuaries. 3 Tell her, 'This
is what the LORD says: I am your enemy, O Israel, and I am about to unsheath my sword to destroy your people—the righteous and the wicked
alike. 4 Yes, I will cut off both the righteous and
the wicked! I will draw my sword against everyone in the land from south to north. 5 Everyone
in the world will know that I am the LORD. My
sword is in my hand, and it will not return to its
sheath until its work is finished.'
6 "Son of man, groan before the people! Groan
before them with bitter anguish and a broken
heart. 7 When they ask why you are groaning,
tell them, 'I groan because of the terrifying news
I have heard. When it comes true, the boldest
heart will melt with fear; all strength will disappear. Every spirit will faint; strong knees will become as weak as water. And the Sovereign LORD
says: It is coming! It's on its way!' "

8 Then the LORD said to me, 9 "Son of man,
give the people this message from the LORD:

"A sword, a sword
is being sharpened and polished.
10 It is sharpened for terrible slaughter
and polished to flash like lightning!
Now will you laugh?
Those far stronger than you have fallen
beneath its power!*
11 Yes, the sword is now being sharpened and
polished;
it is being prepared for the executioner.

12 "Son of man, cry out and wail;
pound your thighs in anguish,
for that sword will slaughter my people and
their leaders—
everyone will die!
13 It will put them all to the test.
What chance do they have?*
says the Sovereign LORD.

14 "Son of man, prophesy to them
and clap your hands.
Then take the sword and brandish it twice,
even three times,
to symbolize the great massacre,
the great massacre facing them on every
side.
15 Let their hearts melt with terror,
for the sword glitters at every gate.
It flashes like lightning
and is polished for slaughter!
16 O sword, slash to the right,
then slash to the left,
wherever you will,
wherever you want.
17 I, too, will clap my hands,
and I will satisfy my fury.
I, the LORD, have spoken!"

20:45 Verses 20:45-49 are numbered 21:1-5 in Hebrew text. **20:46** Hebrew *toward Teman.* **21:1** Verses 21:1-32 are numbered 21:6-37 in Hebrew text. **21:10** The meaning of the Hebrew is uncertain. **21:13** The meaning of the Hebrew is uncertain.

20:45–21:32 The Sword

The Negev is the desert region of southern Judah from which spies were sent into Canaan (Num 13:17, 22) prior to the rebellion in the wilderness. The oracle in 21:1–5 might be a second version or explanation of 20:45–48, in answer to Ezekiel's complaint in v. 49. **21:1–32:** Here we find several oracles referring to a sword. **6–7:** Ezekiel is to respond to the report of God's destruction with grief and dismay to impress upon his audience the grim nature of the news. **8–17:** This sword will be used as an instrument of God's judgment against his people. Clapping and perhaps even a sword dance accompanied the words of this

Omens for Babylon's King
18 Then this message came to me from the LORD:
19 "Son of man, make a map and trace two routes
on it for the sword of Babylon's king to follow.
Put a signpost on the road that comes out of
Babylon where the road forks into two—20 one
road going to Ammon and its capital, Rabbah,
and the other to Judah and fortified Jerusalem.
21 The king of Babylon now stands at the fork,
uncertain whether to attack Jerusalem or Rabbah. He calls his magicians to look for omens.
They cast lots by shaking arrows from the quiver. They inspect the livers of animal sacrifices.
22 The omen in his right hand says, 'Jerusalem!'
With battering rams his soldiers will go against
the gates, shouting for the kill. They will put up
siege towers and build ramps against the walls.
23 The people of Jerusalem will think it is a false
omen, because of their treaty with the Babylonians. But the king of Babylon will remind the
people of their rebellion. Then he will attack and
capture them.
24 "Therefore, this is what the Sovereign LORD
says: Again and again you remind me of your sin
and your guilt. You don't even try to hide it! In
everything you do, your sins are obvious for all
to see. So now the time of your punishment has
come!
25 "O you corrupt and wicked prince of Israel,
your final day of reckoning is here! 26 This is
what the Sovereign LORD says:

"Take off your jeweled crown,
for the old order changes.
Now the lowly will be exalted,
and the mighty will be brought down.
27 Destruction! Destruction!
I will surely destroy the kingdom.
And it will not be restored until the one
appears
who has the right to judge it.
Then I will hand it over to him.

A Message for the Ammonites
28 "And now, son of man, prophesy concerning
the Ammonites and their mockery. Give them
this message from the Sovereign LORD:

"A sword, a sword
is drawn for your slaughter.
It is polished to destroy,
flashing like lightning!
29 Your prophets have given false visions,
and your fortune-tellers have told lies.
The sword will fall on the necks of the wicked
for whom the day of final reckoning has
come.

30 "Now return the sword to its sheath,
for in your own country,
the land of your birth,
I will pass judgment upon you.
31 I will pour out my fury on you
and blow on you with the fire of my anger.
I will hand you over to cruel men
who are skilled in destruction.
32 You will be fuel for the fire,
and your blood will be spilled in your own
land.
You will be utterly wiped out,
your memory lost to history,
for I, the LORD, have spoken!"

The Sins of Jerusalem
22 Now this message came to me from
the LORD: 2 "Son of man, are you
ready to judge Jerusalem? Are you
ready to judge this city of murderers? Publicly
denounce her detestable sins, 3 and give her this
message from the Sovereign LORD: O city of
murderers, doomed and damned—city of idols,*
filthy and foul—4 you are guilty because of the
blood you have shed. You are defiled because of
the idols you have made. Your day of destruction has come! You have reached the end of your
years. I will make you an object of mockery
throughout the world. 5 O infamous city, filled
with confusion, you will be mocked by people far
and near.
6 "Every leader in Israel who lives within your
walls is bent on murder. 7 Fathers and mothers
are treated with contempt. Foreigners are forced

22:3 The Hebrew term (literally *round things*) probably alludes to dung; also in 22:4.

---

dramatic and forceful oracle. **18–27:** The third oracle concerns the sword of Babylon's king. Jerusalem's fate and that of its prince, Zedekiah, is sealed. The Babylonian king will be the LORD's agent of destruction. **28–32:** Here the sword is brandished against the Ammonites, who had been spared earlier but now receive judgment, before the sword (probably referring to Babylon) returns to its sheath.

22:1–31 Jerusalem, the Guilty City

Three additional oracles center on Jerusalem (vv. 1–16). Ezekiel is asked to judge Jerusalem, *the city of murderers*. The catalogue of sins left no doubt that punishment was inevitable. Women are noted among the crime victims: Mothers (and fathers) are treated with contempt, strangers (possibly women)

to pay for protection. Orphans and widows are
wronged and oppressed among you. 8 You despise
my holy things and violate my Sabbath days of
rest. 9 People accuse others falsely and send them
to their death. You are filled with idol worshipers
and people who do obscene things. 10 Men sleep
with their fathers' wives and have intercourse
with women who are menstruating. 11 Within
your walls live men who commit adultery with
their neighbors' wives, who defile their daughters-in-law, or who rape their own sisters. 12 There
are hired murderers, loan racketeers, and extor-
tioners everywhere. They never even think of me
and my commands, says the Sovereign LORD.

13 "But now I clap my hands in indignation
over your dishonest gain and bloodshed. 14 How
strong and courageous will you be in my day of
reckoning? I, the LORD, have spoken, and I will do
what I said. 15 I will scatter you among the nations
and purge you of your wickedness. 16 And when I
have been dishonored among the nations because
of you,* you will know that I am the LORD."

The LORD's Refining Furnace

17 Then this message came to me from the LORD:
18 "Son of man, the people of Israel are the worthless slag that remains after silver is smelted. They
are the dross that is left over—a useless mixture
of copper, tin, iron, and lead. 19 So tell them, 'This
is what the Sovereign LORD says: Because you
are all worthless slag, I will bring you to my crucible in Jerusalem. 20 Just as copper, iron, lead, and
tin are melted down in a furnace, I will melt you
down in the heat of my fury. 21 I will gather you
together and blow the fire of my anger upon you,
22 and you will melt like silver in fierce heat. Then
you will know that I, the LORD, have poured out
my fury on you.' "

The Sins of Israel's Leaders

23 Again a message came to me from the LORD:
24 "Son of man, give the people of Israel this message: In the day of my indignation, you will be
like a polluted land, a land without rain. 25 Your
princes* plot conspiracies just as lions stalk their
prey. They devour innocent people, seizing treasures and extorting wealth. They make many
widows in the land. 26 Your priests have violated
my instructions and defiled my holy things. They
make no distinction between what is holy and
what is not. And they do not teach my people the
difference between what is ceremonially clean
and unclean. They disregard my Sabbath days so
that I am dishonored among them. 27 Your leaders
are like wolves who tear apart their victims. They
actually destroy people's lives for money! 28 And
your prophets cover up for them by announcing
false visions and making lying predictions. They
say, 'My message is from the Sovereign LORD,'
when the LORD hasn't spoken a single word to
them. 29 Even common people oppress the poor,
rob the needy, and deprive foreigners of justice.

30 "I looked for someone who might rebuild
the wall of righteousness that guards the land. I
searched for someone to stand in the gap in the
wall so I wouldn't have to destroy the land, but I
found no one. 31 So now I will pour out my fury
on them, consuming them with the fire of my
anger. I will heap on their heads the full penalty
for all their sins. I, the Sovereign LORD, have spoken!"

The Adultery of Two Sisters

23 This message came to me from the
LORD: 2 "Son of man, once there were
two sisters who were daughters of
the same mother. 3 They became prostitutes in
Egypt. Even as young girls, they allowed men to
fondle their breasts. 4 The older girl was named
Oholah, and her sister was Oholibah. I married
them, and they bore me sons and daughters. I am

22:16 Or *when you have been dishonored among the nations.*
22:25 As in Greek version; Hebrew reads *prophets.*

are cheated, widows and orphans are wronged. **10–11:** Moreover, women are victims of sexual violence. Menstruating women are ravished—a verb that suggests abuse is used instead of the expected euphemism for intercourse. Neighbors' wives, daughters-in-law, and sisters are also violated. These and other heinous sins lead to God's judgment. The attention that Ezekiel gives to women as the victims of crimes starkly contrasts with the extremely negative representations of women in other chapters. **17–22:** God's people are declared to be dross, *worthless slag.* They are to be thrown into a furnace, where they will experience God's wrath and come to know that their suffering comes from God. **23–31:** Jerusalem's princes, priests, and prophets are shown to be spiritually and morally bankrupt. Moreover, those whom they lead are also corrupt. God can find no one to *stand in the gap,* so judgment is inevitable. The blame for ruination is laid on the spiritually and morally corrupt individuals of Jerusalem.

23:1–49 The Story of Two Sisters

Like chapter 16, this is a long oracle viewing the city as a promiscuous female figure married to the LORD. And as such, it is replete with marital and

speaking of Samaria and Jerusalem, for Oholah
is Samaria and Oholibah is Jerusalem.
5 "Then Oholah lusted after other lovers instead of me, and she gave her love to the Assyrian officers. 6 They were all attractive young men,
captains and commanders dressed in handsome
blue, charioteers driving their horses. 7 And so
she prostituted herself with the most desirable
men of Assyria, worshiping their idols* and defiling herself. 8 For when she left Egypt, she did
not leave her spirit of prostitution behind. She
was still as lewd as in her youth, when the Egyptians slept with her, fondled her breasts, and used
her as a prostitute.
9 "And so I handed her over to her Assyrian lovers, whom she desired so much. 10 They
stripped her, took away her children as their
slaves, and then killed her. After she received her
punishment, her reputation was known to every
woman in the land.
11 "Yet even though Oholibah saw what had
happened to Oholah, her sister, she followed
right in her footsteps. And she was even more
depraved, abandoning herself to her lust and
prostitution. 12 She fawned over all the Assyrian officers—those captains and commanders in
handsome uniforms, those charioteers driving
their horses—all of them attractive young men.
13 I saw the way she was going, defiling herself
just like her older sister.
14 "Then she carried her prostitution even
further. She fell in love with pictures that were
painted on a wall—pictures of Babylonian*
military officers, outfitted in striking red uniforms. 15 Handsome belts encircled their waists,
and flowing turbans crowned their heads. They
were dressed like chariot officers from the land
of Babylonia.* 16 When she saw these paintings,
she longed to give herself to them, so she sent
messengers to Babylonia to invite them to come
to her. 17 So they came and committed adultery
with her, defiling her in the bed of love. After
being defiled, however, she rejected them in disgust.
18 "In the same way, I became disgusted with
Oholibah and rejected her, just as I had rejected
her sister, because she flaunted herself before
them and gave herself to satisfy their lusts. 19 Yet
she turned to even greater prostitution, remembering her youth when she was a prostitute in
Egypt. 20 She lusted after lovers with genitals as
large as a donkey's and emissions like those of a
horse. 21 And so, Oholibah, you relived your former days as a young girl in Egypt, when you first
allowed your breasts to be fondled.

The LORD's Judgment of Oholibah

22 "Therefore, Oholibah, this is what the Sovereign LORD says: I will send your lovers against
you from every direction—those very nations from which you turned away in disgust.
23 For the Babylonians will come with all the
Chaldeans from Pekod and Shoa and Koa. And
all the Assyrians will come with them—handsome young captains, commanders, chariot officers, and other high-ranking officers, all riding
their horses. 24 They will all come against you
from the north* with chariots, wagons, and a
great army prepared for attack. They will take
up positions on every side, surrounding you
with men armed with shields and helmets. And
I will hand you over to them for punishment
so they can do with you as they please. 25 I will
turn my jealous anger against you, and they
will deal harshly with you. They will cut off
your nose and ears, and any survivors will then
be slaughtered by the sword. Your children will
be taken away as captives, and everything that

23:7 The Hebrew term (literally *round things*) probably alludes to dung; also in 23:30, 37, 39, 49. **23:14** Or *Chaldean.* **23:15** Or *Chaldea;* also in 23:16. **23:24** As in Greek version; the meaning of the Hebrew is uncertain.

---

sexual images that are intentionally graphic, lewd, and offensive. **5–10:** Oholah's early sexual history is described in terms of the experience of the men who *used her as a prostitute*. When these verses are read through eyes sensitized to contemporary issues relating to the abuse and victimization of women, they read as a male perspective on child abuse or rape (note the absence of the female perspective). But we must remember the text's narrative purpose of shocking readers into an awareness of the long-standing unfaithfulness of Samaria and Jerusalem to their covenant LORD. In death, Oholah became proverbial among women for the ruinous effects of marital unfaithfulness. This is the story of Samaria, whose relationship with Assyria led to her demise in 722 BC, marking the end of the Northern Kingdom. **11–21:** Her sister Oholibah observed the demise of Oholah but did not learn from it. Her story is that of Jerusalem's political and religious history. **20:** The male genitals, usually referred to euphemistically in the Old Testament, are crudely likened to those of donkeys and horses. The coarse language is intended to disturb the reader whose response of aversion may not be unlike that of her divine lover, who observes Oholibah's wanton lifestyle and turns away in disgust. **22–35:** The message of divine judgment

is left will be burned. 26They will strip you of your beautiful clothes and jewels. 27In this way, I will put a stop to the lewdness and prostitution you brought from Egypt. You will never again cast longing eyes on those things or fondly remember your time in Egypt.

28"For this is what the Sovereign LORD says: I will surely hand you over to your enemies, to those you loathe, those you rejected. 29They will treat you with hatred and rob you of all you own, leaving you stark naked. The shame of your prostitution will be exposed to all the world. 30You brought all this on yourself by prostituting yourself to other nations, defiling yourself with all their idols. 31Because you have followed in your sister's footsteps, I will force you to drink the same cup of terror she drank.

32"Yes, this is what the Sovereign LORD says:

"You will drink from your sister's cup of
    terror,
  a cup that is large and deep.
It is filled to the brim
  with scorn and derision.
33 Drunkenness and anguish will fill you,
  for your cup is filled to the brim with
    distress and desolation,
  the same cup your sister Samaria drank.
34 You will drain that cup of terror
  to the very bottom.
Then you will smash it to pieces
  and beat your breast in anguish.
  I, the Sovereign LORD, have spoken!

35"And because you have forgotten me and turned your back on me, this is what the Sovereign LORD says: You must bear the consequences of all your lewdness and prostitution."

The LORD's Judgment on Both Sisters

36The LORD said to me, "Son of man, you must accuse Oholah and Oholibah of all their detestable sins. 37They have committed both adultery and murder—adultery by worshiping idols and murder by burning as sacrifices the children they bore to me. 38Furthermore, they have defiled my Temple and violated my Sabbath day! 39On the very day that they sacrificed their children to their idols, they boldly came into my Temple to worship! They came in and defiled my house.

40"You sisters sent messengers to distant lands to get men. Then when they arrived, you bathed yourselves, painted your eyelids, and put on your finest jewels for them. 41You sat with them on a beautifully embroidered couch and put my incense and my special oil on a table that was spread before you. 42From your room came the sound of many men carousing. They were lustful men and drunkards* from the wilderness, who put bracelets on your wrists and beautiful crowns on your heads. 43Then I said, 'If they really want to have sex with old worn-out prostitutes like these, let them!' 44And that is what they did. They had sex with Oholah and Oholibah, these shameless prostitutes. 45But righteous people will judge these sister cities for what they really are—adulterers and murderers.

46"Now this is what the Sovereign LORD says: Bring an army against them and hand them over to be terrorized and plundered. 47For their enemies will stone them and kill them with swords. They will butcher their sons and daughters and burn their homes. 48In this way, I will put an end to lewdness and idolatry in the land, and my judgment will be a warning to others not to fol-

23:42 Or *Sabeans.*

on Jerusalem comes four times and is no surprise to readers. **32–34:** The third judgment is a poetic lament that may have been a popular song adapted to convey again the message that Oholibah would end up like her sister. The image of a woman drinking from a cup that brings horror and desolation also recalls the ordeal of the suspected adulteress in Numbers 5:11–31. Unlike in Numbers, though, witnesses and evidence of infidelity are plentiful. The poem concludes with the grotesque picture of Oholibah draining the overflowing cup of intoxicating wine and then, desiring more, gnawing on the cup's broken pieces ("drink . . . and drain . . . and gnaw its shards," ESV). In her final moment, she will *beat* [her] *breasts in anguish* (often translated as "tear out"). This act starkly contrasts the earlier caressing of her breasts and her later longing for those experiences. It is a particularly violent image of self-hatred and grief. The cup of judgment was given because Jerusalem had rejected God. Jerusalem, to her peril, had failed to heed the many warnings about the importance of remembering the God of the covenant. **36–49:** The chapter closes with a general accusation of adultery and bloodshed against both sisters. The description of the sisters' allurement of their lovers is detailed. But beneath the actions of the literal adulteresses lies the cultic meaning, for the *incense* and *oil* set before their lovers belong to the LORD. Punishment is leveled against the sisters and the inhabitants of the cities the two sisters represent. **48:** *A warning to others:* Usually translated "to all women." This verse is an unexpected admonition to women that they take warning and not imitate the sisters' wantonness. This warning seems to shift the

low their wicked example. 49 You will be fully repaid for all your prostitution—your worship of idols. Yes, you will suffer the full penalty. Then you will know that I am the Sovereign LORD."

The Sign of the Cooking Pot

24 On January 15,* during the ninth year of King Jehoiachin's captivity, this message came to me from the LORD: 2 "Son of man, write down today's date, because on this very day the king of Babylon is beginning his attack against Jerusalem. 3 Then give these rebels an illustration with this message from the Sovereign LORD:

"Put a pot on the fire,
and pour in some water.
4 Fill it with choice pieces of meat—
the rump and the shoulder
and all the most tender cuts.
5 Use only the best sheep from the flock,
and heap fuel on the fire beneath the pot.
Bring the pot to a boil,
and cook the bones along with the meat.

6 "Now this is what the Sovereign LORD says:
What sorrow awaits Jerusalem,
the city of murderers!
She is a cooking pot
whose corruption can't be cleaned out.
Take the meat out in random order,
for no piece is better than another.
7 For the blood of her murders
is splashed on the rocks.
It isn't even spilled on the ground,
where the dust could cover it!
8 So I will splash her blood on a rock
for all to see,
an expression of my anger
and vengeance against her.

9 "This is what the Sovereign LORD says:
What sorrow awaits Jerusalem,
the city of murderers!
I myself will pile up the fuel beneath her.
10 Yes, heap on the wood!
Let the fire roar to make the pot boil.
Cook the meat with many spices,
and afterward burn the bones.
11 Now set the empty pot on the coals.
Heat it red hot!
Burn away the filth and corruption.
12 But it's hopeless;
the corruption can't be cleaned out.
So throw it into the fire.
13 Your impurity is your lewdness
and the corruption of your idolatry.
I tried to cleanse you,
but you refused.
So now you will remain in your filth
until my fury against you has been
satisfied.

14 "I, the LORD, have spoken! The time has come, and I won't hold back. I will not change my mind, and I will have no pity on you. You will be judged on the basis of all your wicked actions, says the Sovereign LORD."

24:1 Hebrew *On the tenth day of the tenth month,* of the ancient Hebrew lunar calendar. This event occurred on January 15, 588 B.C.; also see note on 1:1.

---

burden of the prophetic message from the house of Israel to individual women and their sexual mores. Both men and women are to learn from the hard lessons of Israel's persistent unfaithfulness, which led to disaster and death.

24:1–14 The Cooking Pot

This strong and climactic word of judgment comes as Nebuchadnezzar began his long siege of Jerusalem. The oracle apparently begins with a cooking song that has been likened to "Polly, put the kettle on." The cooking pot is Jerusalem. Continued references to blood assume knowledge of the Levitical laws about bleeding an animal killed for food. Not only did Jerusalemites not follow God's prescriptions but also sacrilegiously poured blood out on the bare rock, which may allude to the sacrifice of children at high places or to crimes involving bloodshed. God's response is to take vengeance on the city. **9–13:** The focus then shifts to God, who as chef takes over the cooking. God repeatedly attempts to purify the meat (the citizens of Jerusalem), but their diseases and lewd filthiness make them unclean. God then declares that opportunity for cleansing has passed and the city will be judged for her behavior. A reader cannot help but read the present text in light of the extended metaphors in which Jerusalem is personified as a whore (chaps. 16; 23). The proximity of chapter 23 has the effect of heightening the female images in this text. Jerusalem is a bloody city, unclean, diseased, and sexually defiled. Ezekiel declares that her punishment is not only imminent but also deserved. Jerusalem offers no hope for the exiles.

The Death of Ezekiel's Wife
15 Then this message came to me from the LORD:
16 "Son of man, with one blow I will take away
your dearest treasure. Yet you must not show
any sorrow at her death. Do not weep; let there
be no tears. 17 Groan silently, but let there be
no wailing at her grave. Do not uncover your
head or take off your sandals. Do not perform
the usual rituals of mourning or accept any food
brought to you by consoling friends."
18 So I proclaimed this to the people the next
morning, and in the evening my wife died. The
next morning I did everything I had been told to
do. 19 Then the people asked, "What does all this
mean? What are you trying to tell us?"
20 So I said to them, "A message came to me
from the LORD, 21 and I was told to give this
message to the people of Israel. This is what the
Sovereign LORD says: I will defile my Temple,
the source of your security and pride, the place
your heart delights in. Your sons and daughters
whom you left behind in Judea will be slaughtered by the sword. 22 Then you will do as Ezekiel
has done. You will not mourn in public or console yourselves by eating the food brought by
friends. 23 Your heads will remain covered, and
your sandals will not be taken off. You will not
mourn or weep, but you will waste away because
of your sins. You will mourn privately for all the
evil you have done. 24 Ezekiel is an example for
you; you will do just as he has done. And when
that time comes, you will know that I am the
Sovereign LORD."
25 Then the LORD said to me, "Son of man,
on the day I take away their stronghold—their
joy and glory, their heart's desire, their dearest
treasure—I will also take away their sons and
daughters. 26 And on that day a survivor from Jerusalem will come to you in Babylon and tell you
what has happened. 27 And when he arrives, your
voice will suddenly return so you can talk to him,
and you will be a symbol for these people. Then
they will know that I am the LORD."

A Message for Ammon
25 Then this message came to me from
the LORD: 2 "Son of man, turn and
face the land of Ammon and proph-
esy against its people. 3 Give the Ammonites
this message from the Sovereign LORD: Hear
the word of the Sovereign LORD! Because you
cheered when my Temple was defiled, mocked
Israel in her desolation, and laughed at Judah as
she went away into exile, 4 I will allow nomads
from the eastern deserts to overrun your country. They will set up their camps among you and
pitch their tents on your land. They will harvest
all your fruit and drink the milk from your livestock. 5 And I will turn the city of Rabbah into a
pasture for camels, and all the land of the Ammonites into a resting place for sheep and goats.
Then you will know that I am the LORD.
6 "This is what the Sovereign LORD says: Because you clapped and danced and cheered with
glee at the destruction of my people, 7 I will raise
my fist of judgment against you. I will give you
as plunder to many nations. I will cut you off
from being a nation and destroy you completely.
Then you will know that I am the LORD.

A Message for Moab
8 "This is what the Sovereign LORD says: Because
the people of Moab have said that Judah is just
like all the other nations, 9 I will open up their

24:15–27 The Death of Ezekiel's Wife

God's most difficult word to Ezekiel was news of his wife's imminent death. Ezekiel's wife is described as his *dearest treasure*, an expression implying that Ezekiel and his wife were close (1 Kgs 20:3–6; Lam 2:4; Song 5:16). Ezekiel's wife not only witnessed his sign acts but also probably supplied the materials used from her household goods (pots, an iron plate, a knife, baking supplies) and perhaps even instructed Ezekiel about baking bread and taught him the cooking song. **15–18:** Ezekiel's action draws upon priestly sanctity to symbolize the inability of God and the people of Judah to mourn the loss of Jerusalem when in exile. Priests may not come into contact with the dead, and the high priest may not mourn for the dead (Lev 21:1–12). **25–27:** Ezekiel's voice *will suddenly return*, signifying a change in Ezekiel's prophetic role. Now that judgment had come, Ezekiel could begin the work of reconstruction. The deaths of Ezekiel's wife and of the LORD's symbolic wife, Jerusalem, mark the virtual end of the use of feminine personification of Jerusalem in the book. Indeed, Jerusalem is never mentioned again by name.

25:1—32:32 Oracles against the Nations

This collection of oracles marks a dramatic shift in the focus of Ezekiel's message. Oracles of judgment against the enemies of God's people effectively delay the news of the fall of Jerusalem and provide a transition to the more positive news that follows. Oracles against Israel's most geographically immediate neighbors—Ammon, Moab, Edom, Philistia—are followed by a lengthy collection of oracles against Tyre and then Egypt.

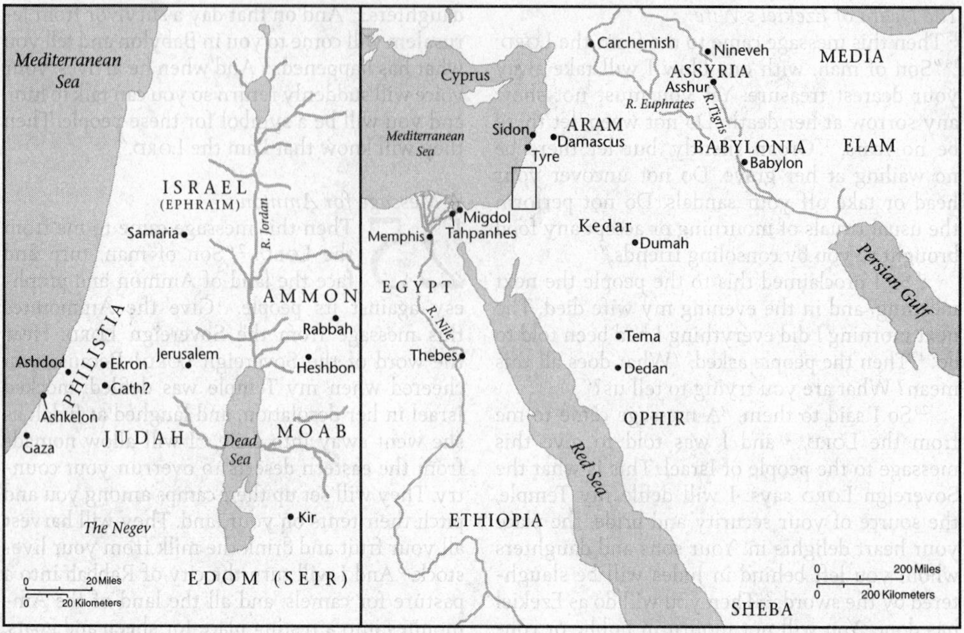

Places Mentioned in the Oracles against the Nations

eastern flank and wipe out their glorious frontier towns—Beth-jeshimoth, Baal-meon, and Kiriathaim. [10]And I will hand Moab over to nomads from the eastern deserts, just as I handed over Ammon. Yes, the Ammonites will no longer be counted among the nations. [11]In the same way, I will bring my judgment down on the Moabites. Then they will know that I am the LORD.

A Message for Edom

[12]"This is what the Sovereign LORD says: The people of Edom have sinned greatly by avenging themselves against the people of Judah. [13]Therefore, says the Sovereign LORD, I will raise my fist of judgment against Edom. I will wipe out its people and animals with the sword. I will make a wasteland of everything from Teman to Dedan. [14]I will accomplish this by the hand of my people of Israel. They will carry out my vengeance with anger, and Edom will know that this vengeance is from me. I, the Sovereign LORD, have spoken!

A Message for Philistia

[15]"This is what the Sovereign LORD says: The people of Philistia have acted against Judah out of bitter revenge and long-standing contempt. [16]Therefore, this is what the Sovereign LORD says: I will raise my fist of judgment against the land of the Philistines. I will wipe out the Kerethites and utterly destroy the people who live by the sea. [17]I will execute terrible vengeance against them to punish them for what they have done. And when I have inflicted my revenge, they will know that I am the LORD."

A Message for Tyre

26 On February 3, during the twelfth year of King Jehoiachin's captivity,* this message came to me from the LORD: [2]"Son of man, Tyre has rejoiced over the fall of Jerusalem, saying, 'Ha! She who was the gateway to the rich trade routes to the east has been broken, and I am the heir! Because she has been made desolate, I will become wealthy!'

[3]"Therefore, this is what the Sovereign LORD says: I am your enemy, O Tyre, and I will bring many nations against you, like the waves of the

26:1 Hebrew *In the eleventh year, on the first day of the month,* of the ancient Hebrew lunar calendar year. Since an element is missing in the date formula here, scholars have reconstructed this probable reading: *In the eleventh [month of the twelfth] year, on the first day of the month.* This reading would put this message on February 3, 585 B.C.; also see note on 1:1.

26:1—28:19 Oracles against Tyre. Why the oracles against Tyre are more extensive and more fierce than those against other nations is not clear. It speaks of their attitude to the fall of Israel but the greater con-

sea crashing against your shoreline. 4 They will
destroy the walls of Tyre and tear down its towers. I will scrape away its soil and make it a bare
rock! 5 It will be just a rock in the sea, a place for
fishermen to spread their nets, for I have spoken,
says the Sovereign LORD. Tyre will become the
prey of many nations, 6 and its mainland villages
will be destroyed by the sword. Then they will
know that I am the LORD.

7 "This is what the Sovereign LORD says: From
the north I will bring King Nebuchadnezzar* of
Babylon against Tyre. He is king of kings and
brings his horses, chariots, charioteers, and great
army. 8 First he will destroy your mainland villages. Then he will attack you by building a siege
wall, constructing a ramp, and raising a roof of
shields against you. 9 He will pound your walls
with battering rams and demolish your towers
with sledgehammers. 10 The hooves of his horses
will choke the city with dust, and the noise of the
charioteers and chariot wheels will shake your
walls as they storm through your broken gates.
11 His horsemen will trample through every
street in the city. They will butcher your people,
and your strong pillars will topple.

12 "They will plunder all your riches and merchandise and break down your walls. They will
destroy your lovely homes and dump your stones
and timbers and even your dust into the sea. 13 I
will stop the music of your songs. No more will
the sound of harps be heard among your people.
14 I will make your island a bare rock, a place for
fishermen to spread their nets. You will never
be rebuilt, for I, the LORD, have spoken. Yes, the
Sovereign LORD has spoken!

The Effect of Tyre's Destruction

15 "This is what the Sovereign LORD says to Tyre:
The whole coastline will tremble at the sound of
your fall, as the screams of the wounded echo in
the continuing slaughter. 16 All the seaport rulers will step down from their thrones and take
off their royal robes and beautiful clothing. They
will sit on the ground trembling with horror at
your destruction. 17 Then they will wail for you,
singing this funeral song:

"O famous island city,
once ruler of the sea,
how you have been destroyed!
Your people, with their naval power,
once spread fear around the world.
18 Now the coastlands tremble at your fall.
The islands are dismayed as you disappear.

19 "This is what the Sovereign LORD says: I
will make Tyre an uninhabited ruin, like many
others. I will bury you beneath the terrible
waves of enemy attack. Great seas will swallow
you. 20 I will send you to the pit to join those who
descended there long ago. Your city will lie in ruins, buried beneath the earth, like those in the
pit who have entered the world of the dead. You
will have no place of respect here in the land of
the living. 21 I will bring you to a terrible end, and
you will exist no more. You will be looked for,
but you will never again be found. I, the Sovereign LORD, have spoken!"

The End of Tyre's Glory

27 Then this message came to me from
the LORD: 2 "Son of man, sing a funeral song for Tyre, 3 that mighty
gateway to the sea, the trading center of the
world. Give Tyre this message from the Sovereign LORD:

"You boasted, O Tyre,
'My beauty is perfect!'
4 You extended your boundaries into the sea.
Your builders made your beauty perfect.
5 You were like a great ship
built of the finest cypress from Senir.*
They took a cedar from Lebanon
to make a mast for you.
6 They carved your oars
from the oaks of Bashan.
Your deck of pine from the coasts of Cyprus*
was inlaid with ivory.
7 Your sails were made of Egypt's finest linen,
and they flew as a banner above you.
You stood beneath blue and purple awnings
made bright with dyes from the coasts of
Elishah.
8 Your oarsmen came from Sidon and Arvad;
your helmsmen were skilled men from
Tyre itself.
9 Wise old craftsmen from Gebal did the
caulking.

26:7 Hebrew *Nebuchadrezzar,* a variant spelling of Nebuchadnezzar. **27:5** Or *Hermon.* **27:6** Hebrew *Kittim.*

centration is on their pride in their own status and achievements. **27:1–36:** Tyre is clearly presented as a great civilization, with a well-developed industrial and trading system. But as so often for Israel, pride in their own achievements and greed for more caused their downfall. Israel should take note. Present achievement will not prevent future disaster, and dependence on their own greatness will be fatal. It

Ships from every land came with goods to
barter for your trade.

10 "Men from distant Persia, Lydia, and Libya* served in your great army. They hung their
shields and helmets on your walls, giving you
great honor. 11 Men from Arvad and Helech stood
on your walls. Your towers were manned by men
from Gammad. Their shields hung on your walls,
completing your beauty.

12 "Tarshish sent merchants to buy your wares
in exchange for silver, iron, tin, and lead. 13 Merchants from Greece,* Tubal, and Meshech brought
slaves and articles of bronze to trade with you.

14 "From Beth-togarmah came riding horses,
chariot horses, and mules, all in exchange for
your goods. 15 Merchants came to you from Dedan.* Numerous coastlands were your captive
markets; they brought payment in ivory tusks
and ebony wood.

16 "Syria* sent merchants to buy your rich
variety of goods. They traded turquoise, purple
dyes, embroidery, fine linen, and jewelry of coral
and rubies. 17 Judah and Israel traded for your
wares, offering wheat from Minnith, figs,* honey, olive oil, and balm.

18 "Damascus sent merchants to buy your rich
variety of goods, bringing wine from Helbon and
white wool from Zahar. 19 Greeks from Uzal*
came to trade for your merchandise. Wrought
iron, cassia, and fragrant calamus were bartered
for your wares.

20 "Dedan sent merchants to trade their expensive saddle blankets with you. 21 The Arabians
and the princes of Kedar sent merchants to trade
lambs and rams and male goats in exchange for
your goods. 22 The merchants of Sheba and Raamah came with all kinds of spices, jewels, and
gold in exchange for your wares.

23 "Haran, Canneh, Eden, Sheba, Asshur, and
Kilmad came with their merchandise, too. 24 They
brought choice fabrics to trade—blue cloth, embroidery, and multicolored carpets rolled up and
bound with cords. 25 The ships of Tarshish were
your ocean caravans. Your island warehouse was
filled to the brim!

The Destruction of Tyre

26 "But look! Your oarsmen
have taken you into stormy seas!
A mighty eastern gale
has wrecked you in the heart of the sea!
27 Everything is lost—
your riches and wares,
your sailors and pilots,
your ship builders, merchants, and warriors.
On the day of your ruin,
everyone on board sinks into the depths of
the sea.
28 Your cities by the sea tremble
as your pilots cry out in terror.
29 All the oarsmen abandon their ships;
the sailors and pilots on shore come to
stand on the beach.
30 They cry aloud over you
and weep bitterly.
They throw dust on their heads
and roll in ashes.
31 They shave their heads in grief for you
and dress themselves in burlap.
They weep for you with bitter anguish
and deep mourning.
32 As they wail and mourn over you,
they sing this sad funeral song:
'Was there ever such a city as Tyre,
now silent at the bottom of the sea?
33 The merchandise you traded
satisfied the desires of many nations.
Kings at the ends of the earth
were enriched by your trade.
34 Now you are a wrecked ship,
broken at the bottom of the sea.
All your merchandise and crew
have gone down with you.
35 All who live along the coastlands
are appalled at your terrible fate.
Their kings are filled with horror
and look on with twisted faces.
36 The merchants among the nations
shake their heads at the sight of you,*
for you have come to a horrible end
and will exist no more.' "

A Message for Tyre's King

28 Then this message came to me from
the LORD: 2 "Son of man, give the
prince of Tyre this message from the
Sovereign LORD:

27:10 Hebrew *Paras, Lud, and Put.* **27:13** Hebrew *Javan.* **27:15** Greek version reads *Rhodes.* **27:16** Hebrew *Aram;* some manuscripts read *Edom.* **27:17** The meaning of the Hebrew is uncertain. **27:19** Hebrew *Vedan and Javan from Uzal.* The meaning of the Hebrew is uncertain. **27:36** Hebrew *hiss at you.*

is a warning that both women and men in today's world need to heed. **28:1–19:** Again pride is the focus. Like so many Israelite leaders, the king of Tyre started well, but power and riches went to his head. Societies as well as individuals again might heed this message.

"In your great pride you claim, 'I am a god!
I sit on a divine throne in the heart of the sea.'
But you are only a man and not a god,
though you boast that you are a god.
3 You regard yourself as wiser than Daniel
and think no secret is hidden from you.
4 With your wisdom and understanding you have amassed great wealth—
gold and silver for your treasuries.
5 Yes, your wisdom has made you very rich,
and your riches have made you very proud.
6 "Therefore, this is what the Sovereign LORD says:
Because you think you are as wise as a god,
7 I will now bring against you a foreign army,
the terror of the nations.
They will draw their swords against your marvelous wisdom
and defile your splendor!
8 They will bring you down to the pit,
and you will die in the heart of the sea,
pierced with many wounds.
9 Will you then boast, 'I am a god!'
to those who kill you?
To them you will be no god
but merely a man!
10 You will die like an outcast*
at the hands of foreigners.
I, the Sovereign LORD, have spoken!"

11 Then this further message came to me from
the LORD: 12 "Son of man, sing this funeral song
for the king of Tyre. Give him this message from
the Sovereign LORD:

"You were the model of perfection,
full of wisdom and exquisite in beauty.
13 You were in Eden,
the garden of God.
Your clothing was adorned with every precious stone*—
red carnelian, pale-green peridot, white moonstone,
blue-green beryl, onyx, green jasper,
blue lapis lazuli, turquoise, and emerald—
all beautifully crafted for you
and set in the finest gold.
They were given to you
on the day you were created.
14 I ordained and anointed you
as the mighty angelic guardian.*
You had access to the holy mountain of God
and walked among the stones of fire.
15 "You were blameless in all you did
from the day you were created
until the day evil was found in you.
16 Your rich commerce led you to violence,
and you sinned.
So I banished you in disgrace
from the mountain of God.
I expelled you, O mighty guardian,
from your place among the stones of fire.
17 Your heart was filled with pride
because of all your beauty.
Your wisdom was corrupted
by your love of splendor.
So I threw you to the ground
and exposed you to the curious gaze of kings.
18 You defiled your sanctuaries
with your many sins and your dishonest trade.
So I brought fire out from within you,
and it consumed you.
I reduced you to ashes on the ground
in the sight of all who were watching.
19 All who knew you are appalled at your fate.
You have come to a terrible end,
and you will exist no more."

A Message for Sidon

20 Then another message came to me from the
LORD: 21 "Son of man, turn and face the city of
Sidon and prophesy against it. 22 Give the people
of Sidon this message from the Sovereign LORD:

"I am your enemy, O Sidon,
and I will reveal my glory by what I do to you.
When I bring judgment against you
and reveal my holiness among you,
everyone watching will know
that I am the LORD.
23 I will send a plague against you,
and blood will be spilled in your streets.
The attack will come from every direction,

28:10 Hebrew *will die the death of the uncircumcised.*
28:13 The identification of some of these gemstones is uncertain. **28:14** Hebrew *guardian cherub;* similarly in 28:16.

28:20–24 The Message for Sidon. The theme of God's self-disclosure through judgment, made explicit here, is central to this collection. In addition, all the oracles serve to warn readers of the consequences of arrogance, selfishness, and vengeance. They also demonstrate the breadth of Ezekiel's prophetic ministry.

and your people will lie slaughtered within
your walls.
Then everyone will know
that I am the LORD.
24 No longer will Israel's scornful neighbors
prick and tear at her like briers and thorns.
For then they will know
that I am the Sovereign LORD.

Restoration for Israel

25 "This is what the Sovereign LORD says: The
people of Israel will again live in their own
land, the land I gave my servant Jacob. For I will
gather them from the distant lands where I have
scattered them. I will reveal to the nations of the
world my holiness among my people. 26 They will
live safely in Israel and build homes and plant
vineyards. And when I punish the neighboring
nations that treated them with contempt, they
will know that I am the LORD their God."

A Message for Egypt

29 On January 7,* during the tenth year
of King Jehoiachin's captivity, this
message came to me from the LORD:
2 "Son of man, turn and face Egypt and prophesy
against Pharaoh the king and all the people of
Egypt. 3 Give them this message from the Sovereign LORD:

"I am your enemy, O Pharaoh, king of
Egypt—
you great monster, lurking in the streams
of the Nile.
For you have said, 'The Nile River is mine;
I made it for myself.'
4 I will put hooks in your jaws
and drag you out on the land
with fish sticking to your scales.
5 I will leave you and all your fish
stranded in the wilderness to die.
You will lie unburied on the open ground,
for I have given you as food to the wild
animals and birds.
6 All the people of Egypt will know that I am
the LORD,
for to Israel you were just a staff made of
reeds.
7 When Israel leaned on you,
you splintered and broke
and stabbed her in the armpit.
When she put her weight on you, you gave
way,
and her back was thrown out of joint.

8 "Therefore, this is what the Sovereign LORD
says: I will bring an army against you, O Egypt,
and destroy both people and animals. 9 The land
of Egypt will become a desolate wasteland, and
the Egyptians will know that I am the LORD.

"Because you said, 'The Nile River is mine;
I made it,' 10 I am now the enemy of both you
and your river. I will make the land of Egypt a
totally desolate wasteland, from Migdol to Aswan, as far south as the border of Ethiopia.*
11 For forty years not a soul will pass that way,
neither people nor animals. It will be completely
uninhabited. 12 I will make Egypt desolate, and it
will be surrounded by other desolate nations. Its
cities will be empty and desolate for forty years,
surrounded by other ruined cities. I will scatter
the Egyptians to distant lands.

13 "But this is what the Sovereign LORD also
says: At the end of the forty years I will bring
the Egyptians home again from the nations to
which they have been scattered. 14 I will restore
the prosperity of Egypt and bring its people back
to the land of Pathros in southern Egypt from
which they came. But Egypt will remain an unimportant, minor kingdom. 15 It will be the lowliest of all the nations, never again great enough to
rise above its neighbors.

16 "Then Israel will no longer be tempted to
trust in Egypt for help. Egypt's shattered condition will remind Israel of how sinful she was to
trust Egypt in earlier days. Then Israel will know
that I am the Sovereign LORD."

Nebuchadnezzar to Conquer Egypt

17 On April 26, the first day of the new year,* during the twenty-seventh year of King Jehoiachin's
captivity, this message came to me from the
LORD: 18 "Son of man, the army of King Nebu-

29:1 Hebrew *On the twelfth day of the tenth month,* of the ancient Hebrew lunar calendar. This event occurred on January 7, 587 B.C.; also see note on 1:1. **29:10** Hebrew *from Migdol to Syene as far as the border of Cush.* **29:17** Hebrew *On the first day of the first month,* of the ancient Hebrew lunar calendar. This event occurred on April 26, 571 B.C.; also see note on 1:1.

28:25–26: Set between the oracles against the six nations and those against Egypt are words of promise for Israel. It was comforting for the exiles to be assured that God would judge their enemies, that God was sovereign over the nations and that through judgment, the nations would know the LORD.

29:1—30:26 Messages for Egypt. The same issues mentioned against Tyre and Sidon are raised in relation to Egypt: pride, dependence on their own

chadnezzar* of Babylon fought so hard against
Tyre that the warriors' heads were rubbed bare
and their shoulders were raw and blistered. Yet
Nebuchadnezzar and his army won no plunder
to compensate them for all their work. 19 Therefore, this is what the Sovereign LORD says: I will
give the land of Egypt to Nebuchadnezzar, king of
Babylon. He will carry off its wealth, plundering
everything it has so he can pay his army. 20 Yes, I
have given him the land of Egypt as a reward for
his work, says the Sovereign LORD, because he
was working for me when he destroyed Tyre.
21 "And the day will come when I will cause
the ancient glory of Israel to revive,* and then,
Ezekiel, your words will be respected. Then they
will know that I am the LORD."

A Sad Day for Egypt

30 This is another message that came
to me from the LORD: 2 "Son of man,
prophesy and give this message from
the Sovereign LORD:

"Weep and wail
for that day,
3 for the terrible day is almost here—
the day of the LORD!
It is a day of clouds and gloom,
a day of despair for the nations.
4 A sword will come against Egypt,
and those who are slaughtered will cover
the ground.
Its wealth will be carried away
and its foundations destroyed.
The land of Ethiopia* will be ravished.
5 Ethiopia, Libya, Lydia, all Arabia,*
and all their other allies
will be destroyed in that war.

6 "For this is what the LORD says:
All of Egypt's allies will fall,
and the pride of her power will end.
From Migdol to Aswan*
they will be slaughtered by the sword,
says the Sovereign LORD.
7 Egypt will be desolate,
surrounded by desolate nations,
and its cities will be in ruins,
surrounded by other ruined cities.
8 And the people of Egypt will know that I am
the LORD
when I have set Egypt on fire
and destroyed all their allies.
9 At that time I will send swift messengers in
ships
to terrify the complacent Ethiopians.
Great panic will come upon them
on that day of Egypt's certain destruction.
Watch for it!
It is sure to come!

10 "For this is what the Sovereign LORD says:
By the power of King Nebuchadnezzar* of
Babylon,
I will destroy the hordes of Egypt.
11 He and his armies—the most ruthless of all—
will be sent to demolish the land.
They will make war against Egypt
until slaughtered Egyptians cover the
ground.
12 I will dry up the Nile River
and sell the land to wicked men.
I will destroy the land of Egypt and
everything in it
by the hands of foreigners.
I, the LORD, have spoken!

13 "This is what the Sovereign LORD says:
I will smash the idols* of Egypt
and the images at Memphis.*
There will be no rulers left in Egypt;
terror will sweep the land.
14 I will destroy southern Egypt,*
set fire to Zoan,
and bring judgment against Thebes.*
15 I will pour out my fury on Pelusium,*
the strongest fortress of Egypt,
and I will stamp out

29:18 Hebrew *Nebuchadrezzar,* a variant spelling of Nebuchadnezzar; also in 29:19. **29:21** Hebrew *I will cause a horn to sprout for the house of Israel.* **30:4** Hebrew *Cush;* similarly in 30:9. **30:5** Hebrew *Cush, Put, Lud, all Arabia, Cub. Cub* is otherwise unknown and may be another spelling for *Lub* (Libya). **30:6** Hebrew *to Syene.* **30:10** Hebrew *Nebuchadrezzar,* a variant spelling of Nebuchadnezzar. **30:13a** The Hebrew term (literally *round things*) probably alludes to dung. **30:13b** Hebrew *Noph;* also in 30:16. **30:14a** Hebrew *Pathros.* **30:14b** Hebrew *No;* also in 30:15, 16. **30:15** Hebrew *Sin;* also in 30:16.

achievements, and acting against God and his people. **30:1–26:** These oracles contain little that pertains specifically to women, although cities and nations are gendered as feminine. In the descriptions of the impending devastations of the nations, women are mentioned as victims only in chapter 30. It is possible to interpret the reference to *its daughters* (v. 18b) as the women of Tahpanhes or all Egyptian women—although it could relate to "daughter" towns. The reason for Egypt's punishment, as for Israel's exile, was that they would recognize God's justice and acknowledge his sovereignty.

the hordes of Thebes.
16 Yes, I will set fire to all Egypt!
Pelusium will be racked with pain;
Thebes will be torn apart;
Memphis will live in constant terror.
17 The young men of Heliopolis and Bubastis*
will die in battle,
and the women* will be taken away as
slaves.
18 When I come to break the proud strength of
Egypt,
it will be a dark day for Tahpanhes, too.
A dark cloud will cover Tahpanhes,
and its daughters will be led away as
captives.
19 And so I will greatly punish Egypt,
and they will know that I am the LORD."

The Broken Arms of Pharaoh

20 On April 29,* during the eleventh year of King
Jehoiachin's captivity, this message came to me
from the LORD: 21 "Son of man, I have broken the
arm of Pharaoh, the king of Egypt. His arm has
not been put in a cast so that it may heal. Neither has it been bound up with a splint to make it
strong enough to hold a sword. 22 Therefore, this is
what the Sovereign LORD says: I am the enemy of
Pharaoh, the king of Egypt! I will break both of his
arms—the good arm along with the broken one—
and I will make his sword clatter to the ground. 23 I
will scatter the Egyptians to many lands throughout the world. 24 I will strengthen the arms of
Babylon's king and put my sword in his hand. But
I will break the arms of Pharaoh, king of Egypt,
and he will lie there mortally wounded, groaning
in pain. 25 I will strengthen the arms of the king of
Babylon, while the arms of Pharaoh fall useless to
his sides. And when I put my sword in the hand
of Babylon's king and he brings it against the land
of Egypt, Egypt will know that I am the LORD.
26 I will scatter the Egyptians among the nations,
dispersing them throughout the earth. Then they
will know that I am the LORD."

Egypt Compared to Fallen Assyria

31 On June 21,* during the eleventh
year of King Jehoiachin's captivity,
this message came to me from the
LORD: 2 "Son of man, give this message to Pharaoh, king of Egypt, and all his hordes:

"To whom would you compare your
greatness?
3 You are like mighty Assyria,
which was once like a cedar of Lebanon,
with beautiful branches that cast deep forest
shade
and with its top high among the clouds.
4 Deep springs watered it
and helped it to grow tall and luxuriant.
The water flowed around it like a river,
streaming to all the trees nearby.
5 This great tree towered high,
higher than all the other trees around it.
It prospered and grew long thick branches
because of all the water at its roots.
6 The birds nested in its branches,
and in its shade all the wild animals gave
birth.
All the great nations of the world
lived in its shadow.
7 It was strong and beautiful,
with wide-spreading branches,
for its roots went deep
into abundant water.
8 No other cedar in the garden of God
could rival it.
No cypress had branches to equal it;
no plane tree had boughs to compare.
No tree in the garden of God
came close to it in beauty.
9 Because I made this tree so beautiful,
and gave it such magnificent foliage,
it was the envy of all the other trees of
Eden,
the garden of God.

10 "Therefore, this is what the Sovereign LORD
says: Because Egypt* became proud and arrogant,
and because it set itself so high above the others,
with its top reaching to the clouds, 11 I will hand
it over to a mighty nation that will destroy it as
its wickedness deserves. I have already discarded
it. 12 A foreign army—the terror of the nations—
has cut it down and left it fallen on the ground.
Its branches are scattered across the mountains
and valleys and ravines of the land. All those
who lived in its shadow have gone away and left
it lying there.

30:17a Hebrew *of Awen and Pi-beseth.* **30:17b** Or *and her cities.* **30:20** Hebrew *On the seventh day of the first month,* of the ancient Hebrew lunar calendar. This event occurred on April 29, 587 B.C.; also see note on 1:1. **31:1** Hebrew *On the first day of the third month,* of the ancient Hebrew lunar calendar. This event occurred on June 21, 587 B.C.; also see note on 1:1. **31:10** Hebrew *you.*

31:1–18 Egypt and Assyria. Assyria and Egypt had both been seen as great powers in the world. Both viewed themselves as invincible. Neither were correct! The images and illustrations in these chapters wonderfully

13 "The birds roost on its fallen trunk,
and the wild animals lie among its branches.
14 Let the tree of no other nation
proudly exult in its own prosperity,
though it be higher than the clouds
and it be watered from the depths.
For all are doomed to die,
to go down to the depths of the earth.
They will land in the pit
along with everyone else on earth.

15 "This is what the Sovereign LORD says:
When Assyria went down to the grave,* I made
the deep springs mourn. I stopped its rivers and
dried up its abundant water. I clothed Lebanon in
black and caused the trees of the field to wilt. 16 I
made the nations shake with fear at the sound of
its fall, for I sent it down to the grave with all the
others who descend to the pit. And all the other
proud trees of Eden, the most beautiful and the
best of Lebanon, the ones whose roots went deep
into the water, took comfort to find it there with
them in the depths of the earth. 17 Its allies, too,
were all destroyed and had passed away. They
had gone down to the grave—all those nations
that had lived in its shade.
18 "O Egypt, to which of the trees of Eden will
you compare your strength and glory? You, too,
will be brought down to the depths with all these
other nations. You will lie there among the outcasts* who have died by the sword. This will be
the fate of Pharaoh and all his hordes. I, the Sovereign LORD, have spoken!"

A Warning for Pharaoh

32 On March 3,* during the twelfth
year of King Jehoiachin's captivity,
this message came to me from the
LORD: 2 "Son of man, mourn for Pharaoh, king of
Egypt, and give him this message:

"You think of yourself as a strong young lion
among the nations,
but you are really just a sea monster,
heaving around in your own rivers,
stirring up mud with your feet.
3 Therefore, this is what the Sovereign LORD says:
I will send many people
to catch you in my net
and haul you out of the water.
4 I will leave you stranded on the land to die.
All the birds of the heavens will land on you,
and the wild animals of the whole earth
will gorge themselves on you.
5 I will scatter your flesh on the hills
and fill the valleys with your bones.
6 I will drench the earth with your gushing blood
all the way to the mountains,
filling the ravines to the brim.
7 When I blot you out,
I will veil the heavens and darken the stars.
I will cover the sun with a cloud,
and the moon will not give you its light.
8 I will darken the bright stars overhead
and cover your land in darkness.
I, the Sovereign LORD, have spoken!

9 "I will disturb many hearts when I bring
news of your downfall to distant nations you
have never seen. 10 Yes, I will shock many lands,
and their kings will be terrified at your fate. They
will shudder in fear for their lives as I brandish
my sword before them on the day of your fall.
11 For this is what the Sovereign LORD says:

"The sword of the king of Babylon
will come against you.
12 I will destroy your hordes with the swords of mighty warriors—
the terror of the nations.
They will shatter the pride of Egypt,
and all its hordes will be destroyed.
13 I will destroy all your flocks and herds
that graze beside the streams.
Never again will people or animals
muddy those waters with their feet.
14 Then I will let the waters of Egypt become calm again,
and they will flow as smoothly as olive oil,
says the Sovereign LORD.
15 And when I destroy Egypt
and strip you of everything you own
and strike down all your people,
then you will know that I am the LORD.

31:15 Hebrew *to Sheol;* also in 31:16, 17. **31:18** Hebrew *among the uncircumcised.* **32:1** Hebrew *On the first day of the twelfth month,* of the ancient Hebrew lunar calendar. This event occurred on March 3, 585 B.C.; also see note on 1:1.

demonstrate Ezekiel's communication skills.

32:1–32: A further reference is made to women in the laments over Egypt. Although the NLT omits the reference, verse 16 mentions "the daughters of the nations" (ESV) mourning the death of Egypt. The picture of women from all nations cooperating to perform this universal mourning is truly remarkable.

[16] Yes, this is the funeral song
they will sing for Egypt.
Let all the nations mourn.
Let them mourn for Egypt and its hordes.
I, the Sovereign LORD, have spoken!"

Egypt Falls into the Pit
[17] On March 17,* during the twelfth year, another message came to me from the LORD: [18] "Son
of man, weep for the hordes of Egypt and for
the other mighty nations.* For I will send them
down to the world below in company with those
who descend to the pit. [19] Say to them,

'O Egypt, are you lovelier than the other
nations?
No! So go down to the pit and lie there
among the outcasts.*'

[20] The Egyptians will fall with the many who have
died by the sword, for the sword is drawn against
them. Egypt and its hordes will be dragged away
to their judgment. [21] Down in the grave* mighty
leaders will mockingly welcome Egypt and its
allies, saying, 'They have come down; they lie
among the outcasts, hordes slaughtered by the
sword.'

[22] "Assyria lies there surrounded by the
graves of its army, those who were slaughtered
by the sword. [23] Their graves are in the depths of
the pit, and they are surrounded by their allies.
They struck terror in the hearts of people everywhere, but now they have been slaughtered by
the sword.

[24] "Elam lies there surrounded by the graves
of all its hordes, those who were slaughtered
by the sword. They struck terror in the hearts
of people everywhere, but now they have descended as outcasts to the world below. Now
they lie in the pit and share the shame of those
who have gone before them. [25] They have a resting place among the slaughtered, surrounded by
the graves of all their hordes. Yes, they terrorized
the nations while they lived, but now they lie in
shame with others in the pit, all of them outcasts,
slaughtered by the sword.

[26] "Meshech and Tubal are there, surrounded by the graves of all their hordes. They once
struck terror in the hearts of people everywhere.
But now they are outcasts, all slaughtered by the
sword. [27] They are not buried in honor like their
fallen heroes, who went down to the grave* with
their weapons—their shields covering their bodies* and their swords beneath their heads. Their
guilt rests upon them because they brought terror to everyone while they were still alive.

[28] "You too, Egypt, will lie crushed and broken among the outcasts, all slaughtered by the
sword.

[29] "Edom is there with its kings and princes.
Mighty as they were, they also lie among those
slaughtered by the sword, with the outcasts who
have gone down to the pit.

[30] "All the princes of the north and the Sidonians are there with others who have died. Once
a terror, they have been put to shame. They lie
there as outcasts with others who were slaughtered by the sword. They share the shame of all
who have descended to the pit.

[31] "When Pharaoh and his entire army arrive,
he will take comfort that he is not alone in having
his hordes killed, says the Sovereign LORD. [32] Although I have caused his terror to fall upon all
the living, Pharaoh and his hordes will lie there
among the outcasts who were slaughtered by the
sword. I, the Sovereign LORD, have spoken!"

Ezekiel as Israel's Watchman
33 Once again a message came to me
from the LORD: [2] "Son of man, give
your people this message: 'When
I bring an army against a country, the people
of that land choose one of their own to be a
watchman. [3] When the watchman sees the enemy coming, he sounds the alarm to warn the
people. [4] Then if those who hear the alarm refuse
to take action, it is their own fault if they die.
[5] They heard the alarm but ignored it, so the responsibility is theirs. If they had listened to the
warning, they could have saved their lives. [6] But
if the watchman sees the enemy coming and
doesn't sound the alarm to warn the people, he

32:17 Hebrew *On the fifteenth day of the month,* presumably in the twelfth month of the ancient Hebrew lunar calendar (see 32:1). This would put this message at the end of King Jehoiachin's twelfth year of captivity, on March 17, 585 B.C.; also see note on 1:1. Greek version reads *On the fifteenth day of the first month,* which would put this message on April 27, 586 B.C., at the beginning of Jehoiachin's twelfth year. **32:18** The meaning of the Hebrew is uncertain. **32:19** Hebrew *the uncircumcised;* also in 32:21, 24, 25, 26, 28, 29, 30, 32. **32:21** Hebrew *in Sheol.* **32:27a** Hebrew *to Sheol.* **32:27b** The meaning of the Hebrew is uncertain.

33:1–33 Ezekiel, the Watchman

This new phase in Ezekiel's ministry of hope begins with his recommissioning as a watchman to warn Israel of potential judgment. This text is similar to part of Ezekiel's initial commissioning as a prophet (3:16–21), though his initial call to be a sentinel was private and this second one is public. **10–20:** What follows

is responsible for their captivity. They will die in their sins, but I will hold the watchman responsible for their deaths.'

7 "Now, son of man, I am making you a watchman for the people of Israel. Therefore, listen to what I say and warn them for me. 8 If I announce that some wicked people are sure to die and you fail to tell them to change their ways, then they will die in their sins, and I will hold you responsible for their deaths. 9 But if you warn them to repent and they don't repent, they will die in their sins, but you will have saved yourself.

The Watchman's Message

10 "Son of man, give the people of Israel this message: You are saying, 'Our sins are heavy upon us; we are wasting away! How can we survive?' 11 As surely as I live, says the Sovereign LORD, I take no pleasure in the death of wicked people. I only want them to turn from their wicked ways so they can live. Turn! Turn from your wickedness, O people of Israel! Why should you die?

12 "Son of man, give your people this message: The righteous behavior of righteous people will not save them if they turn to sin, nor will the wicked behavior of wicked people destroy them if they repent and turn from their sins. 13 When I tell righteous people that they will live, but then they sin, expecting their past righteousness to save them, then none of their righteous acts will be remembered. I will destroy them for their sins. 14 And suppose I tell some wicked people that they will surely die, but then they turn from their sins and do what is just and right. 15 For instance, they might give back a debtor's security, return what they have stolen, and obey my life-giving laws, no longer doing what is evil. If they do this, then they will surely live and not die. 16 None of their past sins will be brought up again, for they have done what is just and right, and they will surely live.

17 "Your people are saying, 'The Lord isn't doing what's right,' but it is they who are not doing what's right. 18 For again I say, when righteous people turn away from their righteous behavior and turn to evil, they will die. 19 But if wicked people turn from their wickedness and do what is just and right, they will live. 20 O people of Israel, you are saying, 'The Lord isn't doing what's right.' But I judge each of you according to your deeds."

Explanation of Jerusalem's Fall

21 On January 8,* during the twelfth year of our captivity, a survivor from Jerusalem came to me and said, "The city has fallen!" 22 The previous evening the LORD had taken hold of me and given me back my voice. So I was able to speak when this man arrived the next morning.

23 Then this message came to me from the LORD: 24 "Son of man, the scattered remnants of Judah living among the ruined cities keep saying, 'Abraham was only one man, yet he gained possession of the entire land. We are many; surely the land has been given to us as a possession.' 25 So tell these people, 'This is what the Sovereign LORD says: You eat meat with blood in it, you worship idols,* and you murder the innocent. Do you really think the land should be yours? 26 Murderers! Idolaters! Adulterers! Should the land belong to you?'

27 "Say to them, 'This is what the Sovereign LORD says: As surely as I live, those living in the ruins will die by the sword. And I will send wild animals to eat those living in the open fields. Those hiding in the forts and caves will die of disease. 28 I will completely destroy the land and demolish her pride. Her arrogant power will come to an end. The mountains of Israel will be so desolate that no one will even travel through them. 29 When I have completely destroyed the land because of their detestable sins, then they will know that I am the LORD.'

30 "Son of man, your people talk about you in

33:21 Hebrew *On the fifth day of the tenth month,* of the ancient Hebrew lunar calendar. This event occurred on January 8, 585 B.C.; also see note on 1:1. **33:25** The Hebrew term (literally *round things*) probably alludes to dung.

illustrates the watchman's task. The exiles' comment implied that some had taken Ezekiel's preaching to heart. But they were left with a feeling of despair, not understanding how God's justice worked. The divine response offers great hope. God offers life and forgiveness to the wicked if they repent. The hypothetical cases presented are reminiscent of 18:21–30. The notions of individual responsibility and divine justice tempered with mercy are affirmed. **21–33:** The fall of Jerusalem frees Ezekiel to speak. His first address is to those remaining in Jerusalem and using Abraham's actions to argue that they deserved the land left by those who had died or been taken into exile. However, their sins are exposed, including the defiling of one another's wives, and they are judged. Here Ezekiel alludes to Leviticus 26 to show that their sins preclude them from occupying the land at all. By leaving the last curse—exile (Lev 26:27–53)—unspoken, Ezekiel allows his audience to conclude that the people of Jerusalem will join the exiles, not vice versa. **30–33:** Ezekiel's second address also raises the issue of the people's hardened hearts. The exiles fi-

their houses and whisper about you at the doors.
They say to each other, 'Come on, let's go hear
the prophet tell us what the LORD is saying!' [31] So
my people come pretending to be sincere and sit
before you. They listen to your words, but they
have no intention of doing what you say. Their
mouths are full of lustful words, and their hearts
seek only after money. [32] You are very entertaining to them, like someone who sings love songs
with a beautiful voice or plays fine music on an
instrument. They hear what you say, but they
don't act on it! [33] But when all these terrible
things happen to them—as they certainly will—
then they will know a prophet has been among
them."

The Shepherds of Israel

34 Then this message came to me from
the LORD: [2] "Son of man, prophesy
against the shepherds, the leaders of
Israel. Give them this message from the Sovereign LORD: What sorrow awaits you shepherds
who feed yourselves instead of your flocks.
Shouldn't shepherds feed their sheep? [3] You
drink the milk, wear the wool, and butcher the
best animals, but you let your flocks starve. [4] You
have not taken care of the weak. You have not
tended the sick or bound up the injured. You have
not gone looking for those who have wandered
away and are lost. Instead, you have ruled them
with harshness and cruelty. [5] So my sheep have
been scattered without a shepherd, and they are
easy prey for any wild animal. [6] They have wandered through all the mountains and all the hills,
across the face of the earth, yet no one has gone
to search for them.

[7] "Therefore, you shepherds, hear the word of
the LORD: [8] As surely as I live, says the Sovereign
LORD, you abandoned my flock and left them to
be attacked by every wild animal. And though
you were my shepherds, you didn't search for
my sheep when they were lost. You took care of
yourselves and left the sheep to starve. [9] Therefore, you shepherds, hear the word of the LORD.
[10] This is what the Sovereign LORD says: I now
consider these shepherds my enemies, and I will
hold them responsible for what has happened to
my flock. I will take away their right to feed the
flock, and I will stop them from feeding themselves. I will rescue my flock from their mouths;
the sheep will no longer be their prey.

The Good Shepherd

[11] "For this is what the Sovereign LORD says: I
myself will search and find my sheep. [12] I will be
like a shepherd looking for his scattered flock. I
will find my sheep and rescue them from all the
places where they were scattered on that dark
and cloudy day. [13] I will bring them back home to
their own land of Israel from among the peoples
and nations. I will feed them on the mountains
of Israel and by the rivers and in all the places
where people live. [14] Yes, I will give them good
pastureland on the high hills of Israel. There
they will lie down in pleasant places and feed in
the lush pastures of the hills. [15] I myself will tend
my sheep and give them a place to lie down in
peace, says the Sovereign LORD. [16] I will search
for my lost ones who strayed away, and I will
bring them safely home again. I will bandage the
injured and strengthen the weak. But I will destroy those who are fat and powerful. I will feed
them, yes—feed them justice!

[17] "And as for you, my flock, this is what the

---

nally recognized him as a prophet, and he became quite popular as an entertainer rather than someone whose message they should take seriously.

34:1–31 Shepherds of Israel and a Covenant of Peace

Included in God's abused flock are the sick, the injured, the lost, and the neglected: They are all prey to wild beasts. God promises to deal with the shepherds (*the leaders of Israel*) and rescue his flock from them. This chapter declares the good news of a loving shepherd, the promise of new life, and future hope that lies beyond pain and suffering experienced in this life. These texts, which brought hope to African American slaves, continue to speak to women and men in the community of faith needing to hear God's words of hope and love. However, even among God's flock, there are those who abuse and greedily exploit other sheep. They will be judged, and God promises again to rescue the weak. God then appoints his servant prince David—meaning someone from David's line—as shepherd of his sheep. The idea of restoration in this chapter comes through even more clearly by comparing its imagery with that of Jeremiah 23, on which it seems to draw. To the exiles who were sheep without a shepherd, this message would have brought hope and comfort. It assured them that their future would be under the care of a loving shepherd God who would reestablish his covenant that promised peace, land, and a relationship with him. To Christian readers, Ezekiel's vision takes on more particularity if Jesus is identified as the Davidic prince, the *Good Shepherd* who came to seek, find, heal, and save the lost sheep and establish a new covenant and the new kingdom.

God's Concern for the Disenfranchised

God's concern for widows, orphans, slaves, women, sinners, and the dispossessed permeates the biblical story. God's self-description is "the great God, . . . who shows no partiality and cannot be bribed. He ensures that orphans and widows receive justice. He shows love to the foreigners living among you and gives them food and clothing" (Deut 10:17–18). The people who rightly reflect the image of this God do so by caring for these disenfranchised persons.

The prophets unrelentingly proclaim that Israel's failure to care for the dispossessed results in judgment and exile. Failing to practice mercy and justice (e.g., Amos 5:7; 6:12; Mic 6:1–12), Israel ground down the poor and needy (e.g., Jer 2:34; Ezek 22:29; Amos 2:6–7, cf. Job 24:9–14; Pss 37:14; 109:16).

The LORD's concern for the disenfranchised comes to fullest expression in the life of Jesus. Throughout his ministry Jesus welcomes, heals, and eats with prostitutes, tax collectors, sinners, and the unclean. He speaks with women and heals them without regard to impure status or ethnic background. He proclaims good news to the poor and freedom for prisoners (e.g., Luke 4:18). He provides food for the hungry and healing for foreigners. He instructs his followers to do likewise. This ministry comes to its climax in Jesus' death where God's self is identified with the disenfranchised.

These same concerns were clearly understood in the early church. Acts describes how the gathered community sold possessions to help those in need and responded to a concern about the neglect of Hebrew widows.

Throughout the Epistles, believers are called to continue to bear the image of their God in their practice of caring for those who have nothing (1 Cor 8—9). Moreover, it is clear that God's concern for the disenfranchised manifested itself in other ways: Paul's assertion that in Christ there is no longer Jew or Greek, slave or free, male or female (Gal 3:28; cf. Col 3:11); the household codes, which by addressing women, children, and slaves subvert the oppressive hierarchies of first-century culture (Eph 5:21—6:9; Col 3:18—4:1); the call for concern for laborers and the poor (Jas 1:27; 2:1–7, 14–17; 5:1–6; 1 Jn 3:17).

Descriptions of the new heaven and new earth as the place "filled with God's righteousness" (2 Pet 3:13) and where God will wipe away all tears (Rev 21:4) indicate that those who truly seek to hasten the coming of this kingdom will reflect the image of their God in their concern for the least as well.

Sovereign LORD says to his people: I will judge
between one animal of the flock and another,
separating the sheep from the goats. 18 Isn't it
enough for you to keep the best of the pastures
for yourselves? Must you also trample down the
rest? Isn't it enough for you to drink clear water
for yourselves? Must you also muddy the rest
with your feet? 19 Why must my flock eat what
you have trampled down and drink water you
have fouled?
20 "Therefore, this is what the Sovereign
LORD says: I will surely judge between the fat
sheep and the scrawny sheep. 21 For you fat sheep
pushed and butted and crowded my sick and
hungry flock until you scattered them to distant
lands. 22 So I will rescue my flock, and they will
no longer be abused. I will judge between one
animal of the flock and another. 23 And I will set
over them one shepherd, my servant David. He
will feed them and be a shepherd to them. 24 And
I, the LORD, will be their God, and my servant
David will be a prince among my people. I, the
LORD, have spoken!

The LORD's Covenant of Peace

25 "I will make a covenant of peace with my people and drive away the dangerous animals from
the land. Then they will be able to camp safely in
the wildest places and sleep in the woods without fear. 26 I will bless my people and their homes
around my holy hill. And in the proper season I
will send the showers they need. There will be
showers of blessing. 27 The orchards and fields of
my people will yield bumper crops, and everyone will live in safety. When I have broken their
chains of slavery and rescued them from those
who enslaved them, then they will know that I
am the LORD. 28 They will no longer be prey for
other nations, and wild animals will no longer
devour them. They will live in safety, and no one
will frighten them.
29 "And I will make their land famous for its

crops, so my people will never again suffer from
famines or the insults of foreign nations. 30 In this
way, they will know that I, the LORD their God,
am with them. And they will know that they, the
people of Israel, are my people, says the Sovereign LORD. 31 You are my flock, the sheep of my
pasture. You are my people, and I am your God.
I, the Sovereign LORD, have spoken!"

A Message for Edom

35 Again a message came to me from the
LORD: 2 "Son of man, turn and face
Mount Seir, and prophesy against its
people. 3 Give them this message from the Sovereign LORD:

"I am your enemy, O Mount Seir,
and I will raise my fist against you
to destroy you completely.
4 I will demolish your cities
and make you desolate.
Then you will know that I am the LORD.

5 "Your eternal hatred for the people of Israel
led you to butcher them when they were helpless, when I had already punished them for all
their sins. 6 As surely as I live, says the Sovereign
LORD, since you show no distaste for blood, I will
give you a bloodbath of your own. Your turn has
come! 7 I will make Mount Seir utterly desolate,
killing off all who try to escape and any who return. 8 I will fill your mountains with the dead.
Your hills, your valleys, and your ravines will be
filled with people slaughtered by the sword. 9 I
will make you desolate forever. Your cities will
never be rebuilt. Then you will know that I am
the LORD.

10 "For you said, 'The lands of Israel and
Judah will be ours. We will take possession of
them. What do we care that the LORD is there!'
11 Therefore, as surely as I live, says the Sovereign LORD, I will pay back your angry deeds with
my own. I will punish you for all your acts of
anger, envy, and hatred. And I will make myself
known to Israel* by what I do to you. 12 Then
you will know that I, the LORD, have heard every contemptuous word you spoke against the
mountains of Israel. For you said, 'They are desolate; they have been given to us as food to eat!'
13 In saying that, you boasted proudly against
me, and I have heard it all!

14 "This is what the Sovereign LORD says: The
whole world will rejoice when I make you desolate. 15 You rejoiced at the desolation of Israel's
territory. Now I will rejoice at yours! You will
be wiped out, you people of Mount Seir and all
who live in Edom! Then you will know that I am
the LORD.

Restoration for Israel

36 "Son of man, prophesy to Israel's
mountains. Give them this message:
O mountains of Israel, hear the word
of the LORD! 2 This is what the Sovereign LORD
says: Your enemies have taunted you, saying,
'Aha! Now the ancient heights belong to us!'
3 Therefore, son of man, give the mountains of
Israel this message from the Sovereign LORD:
Your enemies have attacked you from all directions, making you the property of many nations
and the object of much mocking and slander.
4 Therefore, O mountains of Israel, hear the
word of the Sovereign LORD. He speaks to the
hills and mountains, ravines and valleys, and to
ruined wastes and long-deserted cities that have
been destroyed and mocked by the surrounding
nations. 5 This is what the Sovereign LORD says:
My jealous anger burns against these nations,
especially Edom, because they have shown utter
contempt for me by gleefully taking my land for
themselves as plunder.

6 "Therefore, prophesy to the hills and mountains, the ravines and valleys of Israel. This is what
the Sovereign LORD says: I am furious that you
have suffered shame before the surrounding nations. 7 Therefore, this is what the Sovereign LORD
says: I have taken a solemn oath that those nations will soon have their own shame to endure.

35:11 Hebrew *to them;* Greek version reads *to you.*

35:1—36:38 Judgment and Restoration

This oracle of judgment against Mount Seir (Edom) at first sight seems misplaced in the midst of oracles of hope. With the prophecy to the mountains of Israel that follows (36:1–15), however, it provides a message of hope for the exiles. It confirms God's sovereignty over all nations and announces the judgment and removal of a persistent enemy standing in the way of God's plans to restore the land to Israel.

36:1–38 Restoration for Israel. This magnificent description of the restoration of the mountains provides a dramatic contrast to Ezekiel's earlier words about the coming desolation of Israel's mountains. Now that the devastation has happened, restoration is possible. This message would have undoubtedly encouraged the exiled captives; it can encourage later readers too. Ultimately it points to the eternal city of God. **2–5:** Before the exultant words of restoration, the LORD explains the problem of how the exile had

8 “But the mountains of Israel will produce
heavy crops of fruit for my people—for they will
be coming home again soon! 9 See, I care about
you, and I will pay attention to you. Your ground
will be plowed and your crops planted. 10 I will
greatly increase the population of Israel, and the
ruined cities will be rebuilt and filled with people. 11 I will increase not only the people, but also
your animals. O mountains of Israel, I will bring
people to live on you once again. I will make you
even more prosperous than you were before.
Then you will know that I am the LORD. 12 I will
cause my people to walk on you once again, and
you will be their territory. You will never again
rob them of their children.

13 “This is what the Sovereign LORD says: The
other nations taunt you, saying, ‘Israel is a land
that devours its own people and robs them of
their children!’ 14 But you will never again devour your people or rob them of their children,
says the Sovereign LORD. 15 I will not let you hear
those other nations insult you, and you will no
longer be mocked by them. You will not be a land
that causes its nation to fall, says the Sovereign
LORD.”

16 Then this further message came to me from
the LORD: 17 “Son of man, when the people of Israel were living in their own land, they defiled it
by the evil way they lived. To me their conduct
was as unclean as a woman’s menstrual cloth.
18 They polluted the land with murder and the
worship of idols,* so I poured out my fury on
them. 19 I scattered them to many lands to punish them for the evil way they had lived. 20 But
when they were scattered among the nations,
they brought shame on my holy name. For the
nations said, ‘These are the people of the LORD,
but he couldn’t keep them safe in his own land!’
21 Then I was concerned for my holy name, on
which my people brought shame among the nations.

22 “Therefore, give the people of Israel this
message from the Sovereign LORD: I am bringing you back, but not because you deserve it. I
am doing it to protect my holy name, on which
you brought shame while you were scattered
among the nations. 23 I will show how holy my
great name is—the name on which you brought
shame among the nations. And when I reveal my
holiness through you before their very eyes, says
the Sovereign LORD, then the nations will know
that I am the LORD. 24 For I will gather you up
from all the nations and bring you home again
to your land.

25 “Then I will sprinkle clean water on you,
and you will be clean. Your filth will be washed
away, and you will no longer worship idols. 26 And
I will give you a new heart, and I will put a new
spirit in you. I will take out your stony, stubborn
heart and give you a tender, responsive heart.*
27 And I will put my Spirit in you so that you
will follow my decrees and be careful to obey my
regulations.

28 “And you will live in Israel, the land I gave
your ancestors long ago. You will be my people,
and I will be your God. 29 I will cleanse you of
your filthy behavior. I will give you good crops
of grain, and I will send no more famines on
the land. 30 I will give you great harvests from
your fruit trees and fields, and never again will
the surrounding nations be able to scoff at your
land for its famines. 31 Then you will remember
your past sins and despise yourselves for all the
detestable things you did. 32 But remember, says
the Sovereign LORD, I am not doing this because
you deserve it. O my people of Israel, you should
be utterly ashamed of all you have done!

33 “This is what the Sovereign LORD says:
When I cleanse you from your sins, I will repopulate your cities, and the ruins will be rebuilt.
34 The fields that used to lie empty and desolate
in plain view of everyone will again be farmed.
35 And when I bring you back, people will say,

36:18 The Hebrew term (literally *round things*) probably alludes to dung; also in 36:25. **36:26** Hebrew *a heart of flesh.*

---

the effect of profaning his name before the nations. **13–21:** Within the initial rehearsal of Israel’s past sins, the LORD says that Israel’s behavior polluted the land and that their conduct (bloodshed and idolatry) was like the uncleanness of a woman in menstruation. This comparison of Israel’s crimes with a woman’s impurity is problematic since the involuntary pollution caused by menstruation is very different from the pollution caused by voluntary acts of murder and idolatry. Medieval Jewish expositors associated the image of an unclean woman with Ezekiel’s consequential metaphor of Jerusalem as God’s wife. One explanation is that God in his punishment of Israel is like a husband who puts his unclean wife away but then draws her near once she again becomes pure. **25–27:** As a means of vindicating his name, God proposes to cleanse his people, give them a new heart and spirit, and return them to an ancestral land abounding in fruitfulness. The people’s response would be recognition of their evil ways, personal remorse, and recognition of God’s lordship. The clear emphasis of this text is on God’s doing. God would act for the sake of his name so that Israel and indeed all nations would recognize him as LORD.

'This former wasteland is now like the Garden of Eden! The abandoned and ruined cities now have strong walls and are filled with people!' 36Then the surrounding nations that survive will know that I, the LORD, have rebuilt the ruins and replanted the wasteland. For I, the LORD, have spoken, and I will do what I say.

37"This is what the Sovereign LORD says: I am ready to hear Israel's prayers and to increase their numbers like a flock. 38They will be as numerous as the sacred flocks that fill Jerusalem's streets at the time of her festivals. The ruined cities will be crowded with people once more, and everyone will know that I am the LORD."

A Valley of Dry Bones

37 The LORD took hold of me, and I was carried away by the Spirit of the LORD to a valley filled with bones. 2He led me all around among the bones that covered the valley floor. They were scattered everywhere across the ground and were completely dried out. 3Then he asked me, "Son of man, can these bones become living people again?"

"O Sovereign LORD," I replied, "you alone know the answer to that."

4Then he said to me, "Speak a prophetic message to these bones and say, 'Dry bones, listen to the word of the LORD! 5This is what the Sovereign LORD says: Look! I am going to put breath into you and make you live again! 6I will put flesh and muscles on you and cover you with skin. I will put breath into you, and you will come to life. Then you will know that I am the LORD.'"

7So I spoke this message, just as he told me. Suddenly as I spoke, there was a rattling noise all across the valley. The bones of each body came together and attached themselves as complete skeletons. 8Then as I watched, muscles and flesh formed over the bones. Then skin formed to cover their bodies, but they still had no breath in them.

9Then he said to me, "Speak a prophetic message to the winds, son of man. Speak a prophetic message and say, 'This is what the Sovereign LORD says: Come, O breath, from the four winds! Breathe into these dead bodies so they may live again.'"

10So I spoke the message as he commanded me, and breath came into their bodies. They all came to life and stood up on their feet—a great army.

11Then he said to me, "Son of man, these bones represent the people of Israel. They are saying, 'We have become old, dry bones—all hope is gone. Our nation is finished.' 12Therefore, prophesy to them and say, 'This is what the Sovereign LORD says: O my people, I will open your graves of exile and cause you to rise again. Then I will bring you back to the land of Israel. 13When this happens, O my people, you will know that I am the LORD. 14I will put my Spirit in you, and you will live again and return home to your own land. Then you will know that I, the LORD, have spoken, and I have done what I said. Yes, the LORD has spoken!'"

Reunion of Israel and Judah

15Again a message came to me from the LORD: 16"Son of man, take a piece of wood and carve on it these words: 'This represents Judah and its allied tribes.' Then take another piece and carve these words on it: 'This represents Ephraim and the northern tribes of Israel.'* 17Now hold them together in your hand as if they were one piece of wood. 18When your people ask you what your actions mean, 19say to them, 'This is what the Sovereign LORD says: I will take Ephraim and the northern tribes and join them to Judah. I will make them one piece of wood in my hand.'

20"Then hold out the pieces of wood you have inscribed, so the people can see them. 21And give

37:16 Hebrew *This is Ephraim's wood, representing Joseph and all the house of Israel.*

37:1–28 Restoration of the House of Israel

Many have thought that the well-known vision of verses 1–14 should be interpreted literally as pointing to the idea of individual resurrection and life after death. It can also depict the return of the seemingly dead exiles to Israel, an interpretation that would accord well with other promises of return in Ezekiel. Clearly this text points to God as the giver of life, even to bones that are dead and dry. The text also restores hope to those who like the exiles experience life to be more like death. African American slaves found great encouragement in Ezekiel's message of new life beyond their present pilgrimage on earth. The identification of the bones as *the people of Israel* (v. 11) perhaps suggests that life and restoration is being offered to the long-dead remnants of the Northern and Southern Kingdoms or that Israel will be restored to its own land. **15–28:** The symbolic action of the two sticks shows the former Northern Kingdom and the Southern Kingdom reunited. The covenant formula—*I will be their God, and they will be my people*—appears twice, with slightly different phrasing (vv. 23, 27).

them this message from the Sovereign LORD: I
will gather the people of Israel from among the
nations. I will bring them home to their own
land from the places where they have been scattered. 22 I will unify them into one nation on the
mountains of Israel. One king will rule them all;
no longer will they be divided into two nations
or into two kingdoms. 23 They will never again
pollute themselves with their idols* and vile images and rebellion, for I will save them from their
sinful backsliding. I will cleanse them. Then they
will truly be my people, and I will be their God.

24 "My servant David will be their king, and
they will have only one shepherd. They will obey
my regulations and be careful to keep my decrees.
25 They will live in the land I gave my servant Jacob, the land where their ancestors lived. They
and their children and their grandchildren after
them will live there forever, generation after
generation. And my servant David will be their
prince forever. 26 And I will make a covenant of
peace with them, an everlasting covenant. I will
give them their land and increase their numbers,* and I will put my Temple among them
forever. 27 I will make my home among them. I
will be their God, and they will be my people.
28 And when my Temple is among them forever,
the nations will know that I am the LORD, who
makes Israel holy."

A Message for Gog

38 This is another message that came
to me from the LORD: 2 "Son of man,
turn and face Gog of the land of
Magog, the prince who rules over the nations
of Meshech and Tubal, and prophesy against
him. 3 Give him this message from the Sovereign LORD: Gog, I am your enemy! 4 I will turn
you around and put hooks in your jaws to lead
you out with your whole army—your horses
and charioteers in full armor and a great horde
armed with shields and swords. 5 Persia, Ethiopia, and Libya* will join you, too, with all their
weapons. 6 Gomer and all its armies will also join
you, along with the armies of Beth-togarmah
from the distant north, and many others.

7 "Get ready; be prepared! Keep all the armies
around you mobilized, and take command of
them. 8 A long time from now you will be called
into action. In the distant future you will swoop
down on the land of Israel, which will be enjoying peace after recovering from war and after its
people have returned from many lands to the
mountains of Israel. 9 You and all your allies—a
vast and awesome army—will roll down on them
like a storm and cover the land like a cloud.

10 "This is what the Sovereign LORD says: At
that time evil thoughts will come to your mind,
and you will devise a wicked scheme. 11 You will
say, 'Israel is an unprotected land filled with unwalled villages! I will march against her and destroy these people who live in such confidence!
12 I will go to those formerly desolate cities that
are now filled with people who have returned
from exile in many nations. I will capture vast
amounts of plunder, for the people are rich with
livestock and other possessions now. They think
the whole world revolves around them!' 13 But
Sheba and Dedan and the merchants of Tarshish
will ask, 'Do you really think the armies you
have gathered can rob them of silver and gold?
Do you think you can drive away their livestock
and seize their goods and carry off plunder?'

14 "Therefore, son of man, prophesy against
Gog. Give him this message from the Sovereign
LORD: When my people are living in peace in
their land, then you will rouse yourself.* 15 You
will come from your homeland in the distant
north with your vast cavalry and your mighty
army, 16 and you will attack my people Israel,
covering their land like a cloud. At that time in

37:23 The Hebrew term (literally *round things*) probably alludes to dung. **37:26** Hebrew reads *I will give them and increase their numbers;* Greek version lacks the entire phrase. **38:5** Hebrew *Paras, Cush, and Put.* **38:14** As in Greek version; Hebrew reads *then you will know.*

24–28: These verses refer again to Leviticus 26 indicating that Israel will get a fresh start with the LORD, gathered in the promised land under the leadership of God's servant David. Finally, this restoration will bring the nations to acknowledge that God sanctifies Israel. The Northern Kingdom had fallen in 722 BC, and it is difficult to understand how it might be seen as restored. Many Christians regard Jesus' coming as the inauguration of this messianic kingdom but suggest that the fulfillment is not completed. The concluding reference to God's sanctuary in the midst of his restored people looks ahead to the vision of the Temple in chapters 40—48.

38:1—39:29 Prophecies against Gog

These chapters have long been regarded as the most enigmatic and difficult in the book. Questions about placement, authorship, genre, meaning, and application abound. Who Gog refers to is uncertain but matters little; most interpreters have understood him to be a transnational symbol of evil (see 1 Chr 5; Rev 20:8). But although the battle takes on cosmic dimensions as God wages a great war against the forc-

the distant future, I will bring you against my land as everyone watches, and my holiness will be displayed by what happens to you, Gog. Then all the nations will know that I am the LORD.

17"This is what the Sovereign LORD asks: Are you the one I was talking about long ago, when I announced through Israel's prophets that in the future I would bring you against my people? 18But this is what the Sovereign LORD says: When Gog invades the land of Israel, my fury will boil over! 19In my jealousy and blazing anger, I promise a mighty shaking in the land of Israel on that day. 20All living things—the fish in the sea, the birds of the sky, the animals of the field, the small animals that scurry along the ground, and all the people on earth—will quake in terror at my presence. Mountains will be thrown down; cliffs will crumble; walls will fall to the earth. 21I will summon the sword against you on all the hills of Israel, says the Sovereign LORD. Your men will turn their swords against each other. 22I will punish you and your armies with disease and bloodshed; I will send torrential rain, hailstones, fire, and burning sulfur! 23In this way, I will show my greatness and holiness, and I will make myself known to all the nations of the world. Then they will know that I am the LORD.

The Slaughter of Gog's Hordes

39 "Son of man, prophesy against Gog. Give him this message from the Sovereign LORD: I am your enemy, O Gog, ruler of the nations of Meshech and Tubal. 2I will turn you around and drive you toward the mountains of Israel, bringing you from the distant north. 3I will knock the bow from your left hand and the arrows from your right hand, and I will leave you helpless. 4You and your army and your allies will all die on the mountains. I will feed you to the vultures and wild animals. 5You will fall in the open fields, for I have spoken, says the Sovereign LORD. 6And I will rain down fire on Magog and on all your allies who live safely on the coasts. Then they will know that I am the LORD.

7"In this way, I will make known my holy name among my people of Israel. I will not let anyone bring shame on it. And the nations, too, will know that I am the LORD, the Holy One of Israel. 8That day of judgment will come, says the Sovereign LORD. Everything will happen just as I have declared it.

9"Then the people in the towns of Israel will go out and pick up your small and large shields, bows and arrows, javelins and spears, and they will use them for fuel. There will be enough to last them seven years! 10They won't need to cut wood from the fields or forests, for these weapons will give them all the fuel they need. They will plunder those who planned to plunder them, and they will rob those who planned to rob them, says the Sovereign LORD.

11"And I will make a vast graveyard for Gog and his hordes in the Valley of the Travelers, east of the Dead Sea.* It will block the way of those who travel there, and they will change the name of the place to the Valley of Gog's Hordes. 12It will take seven months for the people of Israel to bury the bodies and cleanse the land. 13Everyone in Israel will help, for it will be a glorious victory for Israel when I demonstrate my glory on that day, says the Sovereign LORD.

14"After seven months, teams of men will be appointed to search the land for skeletons to bury, so the land will be made clean again. 15Whenever bones are found, a marker will be set up so the burial crews will take them to be buried in the Valley of Gog's Hordes. 16(There will be a town there named Hamonah, which means 'horde.') And so the land will finally be cleansed.

17"And now, son of man, this is what the Sovereign LORD says: Call all the birds and wild animals. Say to them: Gather together for my great sacrificial feast. Come from far and near to the mountains of Israel, and there eat flesh and drink blood! 18Eat the flesh of mighty men and drink the blood of princes as though they were rams, lambs, goats, and bulls—all fattened animals from Bashan! 19Gorge yourselves with flesh until you are glutted; drink blood until you are drunk. This is the sacrificial feast I have prepared for you. 20Feast at my banquet table—feast on horses and charioteers, on mighty men and all kinds of valiant warriors, says the Sovereign LORD.

21"In this way, I will demonstrate my glory to the nations. Everyone will see the punishment I have inflicted on them and the power of my fist when I strike. 22And from that time on the

39:11 Hebrew *the sea.*

es of evil, in the end the nations will know that God is the LORD who triumphs. **39:1–24:** The battle and its morbid aftermath are described vividly and symbolically. Dead bodies become food for birds and beasts. Earlier, the bones of Israel and Jacob had gone unburied. In the new land where God will dwell with Israel, however, purity demands the burial even of Gog's dead. When the great battle ends, God's glory

people of Israel will know that I am the LORD their God. [23]The nations will then know why Israel was sent away to exile—it was punishment for sin, for they were unfaithful to their God. Therefore, I turned away from them and let their enemies destroy them. [24]I turned my face away and punished them because of their defilement and their sins.

Restoration for God's People

[25]"So now, this is what the Sovereign LORD says: I will end the captivity of my people*; I will have mercy on all Israel, for I jealously guard my holy reputation! [26]They will accept responsibility for* their past shame and unfaithfulness after they come home to live in peace in their own land, with no one to bother them. [27]When I bring them home from the lands of their enemies, I will display my holiness among them for all the nations to see. [28]Then my people will know that I am the LORD their God, because I sent them away to exile and brought them home again. I will leave none of my people behind. [29]And I will never again turn my face from them, for I will pour out my Spirit upon the people of Israel. I, the Sovereign LORD, have spoken!"

The New Temple Area

40 On April 28,* during the twenty-fifth year of our captivity—fourteen years after the fall of Jerusalem—the LORD took hold of me. [2]In a vision from God he took me to the land of Israel and set me down on a very high mountain. From there I could see toward the south what appeared to be a city. [3]As he brought me nearer, I saw a man whose face shone like bronze standing beside a gateway entrance. He was holding in his hand a linen measuring cord and a measuring rod.

[4]He said to me, "Son of man, watch and listen. Pay close attention to everything I show you. You have been brought here so I can show you many things. Then you will return to the people of Israel and tell them everything you have seen."

The East Gateway

[5]I could see a wall completely surrounding the Temple area. The man took a measuring rod that was 10½ feet* long and measured the wall, and the wall was 10½ feet* thick and 10½ feet high.

[6]Then he went over to the eastern gateway. He climbed the steps and measured the threshold of the gateway; it was 10½ feet front to back.* [7]There were guard alcoves on each side built into the gateway passage. Each of these alcoves was 10½ feet square, with a distance between them of 8¾ feet* along the passage wall. The gateway's inner threshold, which led to the entry room at the inner end of the gateway passage, was 10½ feet front to back. [8]He also measured the entry room of the gateway.* [9]It was 14 feet* across, with supporting columns 3½ feet* thick. This entry room was at the inner end of the gateway structure, facing toward the Temple.

39:25 Hebrew *of Jacob.* **39:26** A few Hebrew manuscripts read *They will forget.* **40:1** Hebrew *At the beginning of the year, on the tenth day of the month,* of the ancient Hebrew lunar calendar. This event occurred on April 28, 573 B.C.; also see note on 1:1. **40:5a** Hebrew *6 long cubits* [3.2 meters], *each being a cubit* [18 inches or 45 centimeters] *and a handbreadth* [3 inches or 8 centimeters] *in length.* **40:5b** Hebrew *1 rod* [3.2 meters]; also in 40:5c, 7. **40:6** As in Greek version, which reads *1 rod* [3.2 meters] *deep;* Hebrew reads *1 rod deep, and 1 threshold, 1 rod deep.* **40:7** Hebrew *5 cubits* [2.7 meters]; also in 40:48. **40:8** Many Hebrew manuscripts add *which faced inward toward the Temple; it was 1 rod* [10.5 feet or 3.2 meters] *deep.* [9]*Then he measured the entry room of the gateway.* **40:9a** Hebrew *8 cubits* [4.2 meters]. **40:9b** Hebrew *2 cubits* [1.1 meters].

will be known among the nations. **25–29:** The holy and sovereign God reigns over all history and will ultimately triumph over evil. Readers of all periods can rejoice that God is in control of history and will ultimately *pour out* [his] *Spirit upon the people*. Such knowledge brings comfort and security.

40:1–48:35 The New Temple

Ezekiel concludes as it began, with a new vision of God. Initially God revealed his presence with the exiles in Babylon and the withdrawal of his presence from the Jerusalem Temple. To conclude, God returns to dwell in a new Temple among his restored people, now reestablished in the land. The final vision comes after twenty-five years of waiting, suffering, disappointment, and separation. It looks not to Israel's sinful past and present but to a happy future spent in God's presence. The last section portrays Ezekiel as a type of Moses leading his people in a new exodus to the new promised land, receiving new laws directly from God on a Sinai-like mountain and exercising a priestly role in the consecration of the new altar. Ezekiel's guided tour explores the new Temple complex, which begins at the wall outside the Temple area and gradually approaches the Temple. The dimensions of the various structures are carefully measured, and many of the fine architectural details noted. Ezekiel, trained as a priest but separated from the Temple for many years, was captivated by the symbolic significance of the various structures.

10 There were three guard alcoves on each
side of the gateway passage. Each had the same
measurements, and the dividing walls separating
them were also identical. 11 The man measured
the gateway entrance, which was 17½ feet*
wide at the opening and 22¾ feet* wide in the
gateway passage. 12 In front of each of the guard
alcoves was a 21-inch* curb. The alcoves themselves were 10½ feet* on each side.
13 Then he measured the entire width of the
gateway, measuring the distance between the
back walls of facing guard alcoves; this distance
was 43¾ feet.* 14 He measured the dividing
walls all along the inside of the gateway up to
the entry room of the gateway; this distance was
105 feet.* 15 The full length of the gateway passage was 87½ feet* from one end to the other.
16 There were recessed windows that narrowed
inward through the walls of the guard alcoves
and their dividing walls. There were also windows in the entry room. The surfaces of the dividing walls were decorated with carved palm
trees.

The Outer Courtyard

17 Then the man brought me through the gateway into the outer courtyard of the Temple.
A stone pavement ran along the walls of the
courtyard, and thirty rooms were built against
the walls, opening onto the pavement. 18 This
pavement flanked the gates and extended out
from the walls into the courtyard the same
distance as the gateway entrance. This was the
lower pavement. 19 Then the man measured
across the Temple's outer courtyard between
the outer and inner gateways; the distance was
175 feet.*

The North Gateway

20 The man measured the gateway on the north
just like the one on the east. 21 Here, too, there
were three guard alcoves on each side, with dividing walls and an entry room. All the measurements matched those of the east gateway.
The gateway passage was 87½ feet long and 43¾
feet wide between the back walls of facing guard
alcoves. 22 The windows, the entry room, and the
palm tree decorations were identical to those in
the east gateway. There were seven steps leading up to the gateway entrance, and the entry
room was at the inner end of the gateway passage. 23 Here on the north side, just as on the east,
there was another gateway leading to the Temple's inner courtyard directly opposite this outer
gateway. The distance between the two gateways
was 175 feet.

The South Gateway

24 Then the man took me around to the south
gateway and measured its various parts, and they
were exactly the same as in the others. 25 It had
windows along the walls as the others did, and
there was an entry room where the gateway passage opened into the outer courtyard. And like
the others, the gateway passage was 87½ feet
long and 43¾ feet wide between the back walls
of facing guard alcoves. 26 This gateway also had
a stairway of seven steps leading up to it, and
an entry room at the inner end, and palm tree
decorations along the dividing walls. 27 And here
again, directly opposite the outer gateway, was
another gateway that led into the inner courtyard. The distance between the two gateways
was 175 feet.

Gateways to the Inner Courtyard

28 Then the man took me to the south gateway
leading into the inner courtyard. He measured it,
and it had the same measurements as the other
gateways. 29 Its guard alcoves, dividing walls, and
entry room were the same size as those in the
others. It also had windows along its walls and in
the entry room. And like the others, the gateway
passage was 87½ feet long and 43¾ feet wide.
30 (The entry rooms of the gateways leading into
the inner courtyard were 14 feet* across and 43¾
feet wide.) 31 The entry room to the south gateway faced into the outer courtyard. It had palm
tree decorations on its columns, and there were
eight steps leading to its entrance.
32 Then he took me to the east gateway leading to the inner courtyard. He measured it, and
it had the same measurements as the other gateways. 33 Its guard alcoves, dividing walls, and
entry room were the same size as those of the
others, and there were windows along the walls
and in the entry room. The gateway passage
measured 87½ feet long and 43¾ feet wide. 34 Its
entry room faced into the outer courtyard. It had
palm tree decorations on its columns, and there
were eight steps leading to its entrance.
35 Then he took me around to the north gate-

40:11a Hebrew *10 cubits* [5.3 meters]. **40:11b** Hebrew *13 cubits* [6.9 meters]. **40:12a** Hebrew *1 cubit* [53 centimeters]. **40:12b** Hebrew *6 cubits* [3.2 meters]. **40:13** Hebrew *25 cubits* [13.3 meters]; also in 40:21, 25, 29, 30, 33, 36. **40:14** Hebrew *60 cubits* [31.8 meters]. Greek version reads *20 cubits* [35 feet or 10.6 meters]. The meaning of the Hebrew in this verse is uncertain. **40:15** Hebrew *50 cubits* [26.5 meters]; also in 40:21, 25, 29, 33, 36. **40:19** Hebrew *100 cubits* [53 meters]; also in 40:23, 27, 47. **40:30** As in 40:9, which reads *8 cubits* [14 feet or 4.2 meters]; here the Hebrew reads *5 cubits* [8¾ feet or 2.7 meters]. Some Hebrew manuscripts and the Greek version lack this entire verse.

way leading to the inner courtyard. He measured it, and it had the same measurements as the other gateways. [36]The guard alcoves, dividing walls, and entry room of this gateway had the same measurements as in the others and the same window arrangements. The gateway passage measured 87½ feet long and 43¾ feet wide. [37]Its entry room faced into the outer courtyard, and it had palm tree decorations on the columns. There were eight steps leading to its entrance.

Rooms for Preparing Sacrifices

[38]A door led from the entry room of one of the inner gateways into a side room, where the meat for sacrifices was washed. [39]On each side of this entry room were two tables, where the sacrificial animals were slaughtered for the burnt offerings, sin offerings, and guilt offerings. [40]Outside the entry room, on each side of the stairs going up to the north entrance, were two more tables. [41]So there were eight tables in all—four inside and four outside—where the sacrifices were cut up and prepared. [42]There were also four tables of finished stone for preparation of the burnt offerings, each 31½ inches square and 21 inches high.* On these tables were placed the butchering knives and other implements for slaughtering the sacrificial animals. [43]There were hooks, each 3 inches* long, fastened to the foyer walls. The sacrificial meat was laid on the tables.

Rooms for the Priests

[44]Inside the inner courtyard were two rooms,* one beside the north gateway, facing south, and the other beside the south* gateway, facing north. [45]And the man said to me, "The room beside the north inner gate is for the priests who supervise the Temple maintenance. [46]The room beside the south inner gate is for the priests in charge of the altar—the descendants of Zadok—for they alone of all the Levites may approach the LORD to minister to him."

The Inner Courtyard and Temple

[47]Then the man measured the inner courtyard, and it was a square, 175 feet wide and 175 feet across. The altar stood in the courtyard in front of the Temple. [48]Then he brought me to the entry room of the Temple. He measured the walls on either side of the opening to the entry room, and they were 8¾ feet thick. The entrance itself was 24½ feet wide, and the walls on each side of the entrance were an additional 5¼ feet long.* [49]The entry room was 35 feet* wide and 21 feet* deep. There were ten steps leading up to it, with a column on each side.

41 After that, the man brought me into the sanctuary of the Temple. He measured the walls on either side of its doorway, and they were 10½ feet* thick. [2]The doorway was 17½ feet* wide, and the walls on each side of it were 8¾ feet* long. The sanctuary itself was 70 feet long and 35 feet wide.*

[3]Then he went beyond the sanctuary into the inner room. He measured the walls on either side of its entrance, and they were 3½ feet* thick. The entrance was 10½ feet wide, and the walls on each side of the entrance were 12¼ feet* long. [4]The inner room of the sanctuary was 35 feet* long and 35 feet wide. "This," he told me, "is the Most Holy Place."

[5]Then he measured the wall of the Temple, and it was 10½ feet thick. There was a row of rooms along the outside wall; each room was 7 feet* wide. [6]These side rooms were built in three levels, one above the other, with thirty rooms on each level. The supports for these side rooms rested on exterior ledges on the Temple wall; they did not extend into the wall. [7]Each level was wider than the one below it, corresponding to the narrowing of the Temple wall as it rose higher. A stairway led up from the bottom level through the middle level to the top level.

[8]I saw that the Temple was built on a terrace, which provided a foundation for the side rooms. This terrace was 10½ feet* high. [9]The outer wall of the Temple's side rooms was 8¾ feet thick. This left an open area between these side rooms [10]and the row of rooms along the outer wall of the inner courtyard. This open area was 35 feet wide, and it went all the way around the Temple. [11]Two doors opened from the side rooms into the terrace yard, which was 8¾ feet wide. One door faced north and the other south.

[12]A large building stood on the west, facing

40:42 Hebrew *1½ cubits* [80 centimeters] *long and 1½ cubits wide and 1 cubit* [53 centimeters] *high.* **40:43** Hebrew *a handbreadth* [8 centimeters]. **40:44a** As in Greek version; Hebrew reads *rooms for singers.* **40:44b** As in Greek version; Hebrew reads *east.* **40:48** As in Greek version, which reads *The entrance was 14 cubits* [7.4 meters] *wide, and the walls of the entrance were 3 cubits* [1.6 meters] *on each side;* Hebrew lacks *14 cubits wide, and the walls of the entrance were.* **40:49a** Hebrew *20 cubits* [10.6 meters]. **40:49b** As in Greek version, which reads *12 cubits* [21 feet or 6.4 meters]; Hebrew reads *11 cubits* [19¼ feet or 5.8 meters]. **41:1** Hebrew *6 cubits* [3.2 meters]; also in 41:3, 5. **41:2a** Hebrew *10 cubits* [5.3 meters]. **41:2b** Hebrew *5 cubits* [2.7 meters]; also in 41:9, 11. **41:2c** Hebrew *40 cubits* [21.2 meters] *long and 20 cubits* [10.6 meters] *wide.* **41:3a** Hebrew *2 cubits* [1.1 meters]. **41:3b** Hebrew *7 cubits* [3.7 meters]. **41:4** Hebrew *20 cubits* [10.6 meters]; also in 41:4b, 10. **41:5** Hebrew *4 cubits* [2.1 meters]. **41:8** Hebrew *1 rod, 6 cubits* [3.2 meters].

the Temple courtyard. It was 122½ feet wide and 157½ feet long, and its walls were 8¾ feet* thick. 13 Then the man measured the Temple, and it was 175 feet* long. The courtyard around the building, including its walls, was an additional 175 feet in length. 14 The inner courtyard to the east of the Temple was also 175 feet wide. 15 The building to the west, including its two walls, was also 175 feet wide.

The sanctuary, the inner room, and the entry room of the Temple 16 were all paneled with wood, as were the frames of the recessed windows. The inner walls of the Temple were paneled with wood above and below the windows. 17 The space above the door leading into the inner room, and its walls inside and out, were also paneled. 18 All the walls were decorated with carvings of cherubim, each with two faces, and there was a carving of a palm tree between each of the cherubim. 19 One face—that of a man—looked toward the palm tree on one side. The other face—that of a young lion—looked toward the palm tree on the other side. The figures were carved all along the inside of the Temple, 20 from the floor to the top of the walls, including the outer wall of the sanctuary.

21 There were square columns at the entrance to the sanctuary, and the ones at the entrance of the Most Holy Place were similar. 22 There was an altar made of wood, 5¼ feet high and 3½ feet across.* Its corners, base, and sides were all made of wood. "This," the man told me, "is the table that stands in the LORD's presence."

23 Both the sanctuary and the Most Holy Place had double doorways, 24 each with two swinging doors. 25 The doors leading into the sanctuary were decorated with carved cherubim and palm trees, just as on the walls. And there was a wooden roof at the front of the entry room to the Temple. 26 On both sides of the entry room were recessed windows decorated with carved palm trees. The side rooms along the outside wall also had roofs.

Rooms for the Priests

42 Then the man led me out of the Temple courtyard by way of the north gateway. We entered the outer courtyard and came to a group of rooms against the north wall of the inner courtyard. 2 This structure, whose entrance opened toward the north, was 175 feet* long and 87½ feet* wide. 3 One block of rooms overlooked the 35-foot* width of the inner courtyard. Another block of rooms looked out onto the pavement of the outer courtyard. The two blocks were built three levels high and stood across from each other. 4 Between the two blocks of rooms ran a walkway 17½ feet* wide. It extended the entire 175 feet of the complex,* and all the doors faced north. 5 Each of the two upper levels of rooms was narrower than the one beneath it because the upper levels had to allow space for walkways in front of them. 6 Since there were three levels and they did not have supporting columns as in the courtyards, each of the upper levels was set back from the level beneath it. 7 There was an outer wall that separated the rooms from the outer courtyard; it was 87½ feet long. 8 This wall added length to the outer block of rooms, which extended for only 87½ feet, while the inner block—the rooms toward the Temple—extended for 175 feet. 9 There was an eastern entrance from the outer courtyard to these rooms.

10 On the south* side of the Temple there were two blocks of rooms just south of the inner courtyard between the Temple and the outer courtyard. These rooms were arranged just like the rooms on the north. 11 There was a walkway between the two blocks of rooms just like the complex on the north side of the Temple. This complex of rooms was the same length and width as the other one, and it had the same entrances and doors. The dimensions of each were identical. 12 So there was an entrance in the wall facing the doors of the inner block of rooms, and another on the east at the end of the interior walkway.

13 Then the man told me, "These rooms that overlook the Temple from the north and south are holy. Here the priests who offer sacrifices to the LORD will eat the most holy offerings. And because these rooms are holy, they will be used to store the sacred offerings—the grain offerings, sin offerings, and guilt offerings. 14 When the priests leave the sanctuary, they must not go directly to the outer courtyard. They must first take off the clothes they wore while ministering, because these clothes are holy. They must put on other clothes before entering the parts of the building complex open to the public."

15 When the man had finished measuring the

41:12 Hebrew *70 cubits* [37.1 meters] *wide and 90 cubits* [47.7 meters] *long, and its walls were 5 cubits* [2.7 meters] *thick.* **41:13** Hebrew *100 cubits* [53 meters]; also in 41:13b, 14, 15. **41:22** Hebrew *3 cubits* [1.6 meters] *high and 2 cubits* [1.1 meters] *across.* **42:2a** Hebrew *100 cubits* [53 meters]; also in 42:8. **42:2b** Hebrew *50 cubits* [26.5 meters]; also in 42:7, 8. **42:3** Hebrew *20-cubit* [10.6-meter]. **42:4a** Hebrew *10 cubits* [5.3 meters]. **42:4b** As in Greek and Syriac versions, which read *Its length was 100 cubits* [53 meters]; Hebrew reads *and a passage 1 cubit* [18 inches or 53 centimeters] *wide.* **42:10** As in Greek version; Hebrew reads *east.*

inside of the Temple area, he led me out through
the east gateway to measure the entire perim-
eter. 16 He measured the east side with his measuring rod, and it was 875 feet long.* 17 Then he
measured the north side, and it was also 875 feet.
18 The south side was also 875 feet, 19 and the west
side was also 875 feet. 20 So the area was 875 feet
on each side with a wall all around it to separate
what was holy from what was common.

The Lord's Glory Returns

43 After this, the man brought me back
around to the east gateway. 2 Suddenly, the glory of the God of Israel
appeared from the east. The sound of his coming
was like the roar of rushing waters, and the whole
landscape shone with his glory. 3 This vision was
just like the others I had seen, first by the Kebar
River and then when he came to destroy Jerusalem. I fell face down on the ground. 4 And the
glory of the Lord came into the Temple through
the east gateway.
5 Then the Spirit took me up and brought me
into the inner courtyard, and the glory of the
Lord filled the Temple. 6 And I heard someone
speaking to me from within the Temple, while
the man who had been measuring stood beside
me. 7 The Lord said to me, "Son of man, this is
the place of my throne and the place where I will
rest my feet. I will live here forever among the
people of Israel. They and their kings will not
defile my holy name any longer by their adulterous worship of other gods or by honoring the
relics of their kings who have died. 8 They put
their idol altars right next to mine with only
a wall between them and me. They defiled my
holy name by such detestable sin, so I consumed
them in my anger. 9 Now let them stop worshiping other gods and honoring the relics of their
kings, and I will live among them forever.
10 "Son of man, describe to the people of Israel the Temple I have shown you, so they will
be ashamed of all their sins. Let them study its
plan, 11 and they will be ashamed* of what they
have done. Describe to them all the specifications of the Temple—including its entrances and
exits—and everything else about it. Tell them
about its decrees and laws. Write down all these
specifications and decrees as they watch so they
will be sure to remember and follow them. 12 And
this is the basic law of the Temple: absolute holiness! The entire top of the mountain where the
Temple is built is holy. Yes, this is the basic law
of the Temple.

The Altar

13 "These are the measurements of the altar*:
There is a gutter all around the altar 21 inches
deep and 21 inches wide,* with a curb 9 inches*
wide around its edge. And this is the height* of
the altar: 14 From the gutter the altar rises 3½
feet* to a lower ledge that surrounds the altar
and is 21 inches* wide. From the lower ledge the
altar rises 7 feet* to the upper ledge that is also
21 inches wide. 15 The top of the altar, the hearth,
rises another 7 feet higher, with a horn rising up
from each of the four corners. 16 The top of the
altar is square, measuring 21 feet by 21 feet.*
17 The upper ledge also forms a square, measuring 24½ feet by 24½ feet,* with a 21-inch gutter
and a 10½-inch curb* all around the edge. There
are steps going up the east side of the altar."
18 Then he said to me, "Son of man, this is
what the Sovereign Lord says: These will be the
regulations for the burning of offerings and the
sprinkling of blood when the altar is built. 19 At
that time, the Levitical priests of the family of
Zadok, who minister before me, are to be given a

42:16 As in 45:2 and in Greek version at 42:17, which reads *500 cubits* [265 meters]; Hebrew reads *500 rods* [5,250 feet or 1,590 meters]; similarly in 42:17, 18, 19, 20. **43:11** As in Greek version; Hebrew reads *if they are ashamed.* **43:13a** Hebrew *measurements of the altar in long cubits, each being a cubit* [18 inches or 45 centimeters] *and a handbreadth* [3 inches or 8 centimeters] *in length.* **43:13b** Hebrew *a cubit* [53 centimeters] *deep and a cubit wide.* **43:13c** Hebrew *1 span* [23 centimeters]. **43:13d** As in Greek version; Hebrew reads *base.* **43:14a** Hebrew *2 cubits* [1.1 meters]. **43:14b** Hebrew *1 cubit* [53 centimeters]; also in 43:14d. **43:14c** Hebrew *4 cubits* [2.1 meters]; also in 43:15. **43:16** Hebrew *12 cubits* [6.4 meters] *long and 12 cubits wide.* **43:17a** Hebrew *14 cubits* [7.4 meters] *long and 14 cubits wide.* **43:17b** Hebrew *a gutter of 1 cubit* [53 centimeters] *and a curb of ½ a cubit* [27 centimeters].

43:1—48:35: When they reached the gate facing east, Ezekiel witnessed the glory of the Lord return to the Temple (43:1–4). God spoke to Ezekiel and announced that he would dwell with his people forever on the condition that they did not defile God's name by their *adulterous worship of other gods* (v. 7). This reference to prostitution is the only explicitly feminine image in this final section. It recalls Israel's former life, so dramatically imaged as an unfaithful wife in the first half of the book. References to women in general are noticeably absent from Ezekiel's vision of the future. **43:13–27:** The description of the new Temple contains the dimensions of an altar so large that steps had to be built into it. The purification of the altar with blood is analogous to the sprinkling of blood on the priests at their ordination (Exod 29:16), on the altar on Yom Kippur to make atonement for the people (Lev 16:18–19), and on the people to seal the

young bull for a sin offering, says the Sovereign LORD. [20]You will take some of its blood and smear it on the four horns of the altar, the four corners of the upper ledge, and the curb that runs around that ledge. This will cleanse and make atonement for the altar. [21]Then take the young bull for the sin offering and burn it at the appointed place outside the Temple area.

[22]"On the second day, sacrifice as a sin offering a young male goat that has no physical defects. Then cleanse and make atonement for the altar again, just as you did with the young bull. [23]When you have finished the cleansing ceremony, offer another young bull that has no defects and a perfect ram from the flock. [24]You are to present them to the LORD, and the priests are to sprinkle salt on them and offer them as a burnt offering to the LORD.

[25]"Every day for seven days a male goat, a young bull, and a ram from the flock will be sacrificed as a sin offering. None of these animals may have physical defects of any kind. [26]Do this each day for seven days to cleanse and make atonement for the altar, thus setting it apart for holy use. [27]On the eighth day, and on each day afterward, the priests will sacrifice on the altar the burnt offerings and peace offerings of the people. Then I will accept you. I, the Sovereign LORD, have spoken!"

The Prince, Levites, and Priests

44 Then the man brought me back to the east gateway in the outer wall of the Temple area, but it was closed. [2]And the LORD said to me, "This gate must remain closed; it will never again be opened. No one will ever open it and pass through, for the LORD, the God of Israel, has entered here. Therefore, it must always remain shut. [3]Only the prince himself may sit inside this gateway to feast in the LORD's presence. But he may come and go only through the entry room of the gateway."

[4]Then the man brought me through the north gateway to the front of the Temple. I looked and saw that the glory of the LORD filled the Temple of the LORD, and I fell face down on the ground.

[5]And the LORD said to me, "Son of man, take careful notice. Use your eyes and ears, and listen to everything I tell you about the regulations concerning the LORD's Temple. Take careful note of the procedures for using the Temple's entrances and exits. [6]And give these rebels, the people of Israel, this message from the Sovereign LORD: O people of Israel, enough of your detestable sins! [7]You have brought uncircumcised foreigners into my sanctuary—people who have no heart for God. In this way, you defiled my Temple even as you offered me my food, the fat and blood of sacrifices. In addition to all your other detestable sins, you have broken my covenant. [8]Instead of safeguarding my sacred rituals, you have hired foreigners to take charge of my sanctuary.

[9]"So this is what the Sovereign LORD says: No foreigners, including those who live among the people of Israel, will enter my sanctuary if they have not been circumcised and have not surrendered themselves to the LORD. [10]And the men of the tribe of Levi who abandoned me when Israel strayed away from me to worship idols* must bear the consequences of their unfaithfulness. [11]They may still be Temple guards and gatekeepers, and they may slaughter the animals brought for burnt offerings and be present to help the people. [12]But they encouraged my people to worship idols, causing Israel to fall into deep sin. So I have taken a solemn oath that they must bear the consequences for their sins, says the Sovereign LORD. [13]They may not approach me to minister as priests. They may not touch any of my holy things or the holy offerings, for they must bear the shame of all the detestable sins they have committed. [14]They are to serve as the Temple caretakers, taking charge of the maintenance work and performing general duties.

[15]"However, the Levitical priests of the family of Zadok continued to minister faithfully in the Temple when Israel abandoned me for idols. These men will serve as my ministers. They will stand in my presence and offer the fat and blood of the sacrifices, says the Sovereign LORD. [16]They alone will enter my sanctuary and approach my table to serve me. They will fulfill all my requirements.

[17]"When they enter the gateway to the inner

44:10 The Hebrew term (literally *round things*) probably alludes to dung; also in 44:12.

covenant (Exod 24:1–8). **44:1–31:** These further regulations apply only to men, since women were not allowed to enter the holy space. In the past, those who were *uncircumcised* (v. 7) had worked in the Temple (cf. 1 Kgs 11:4). But in the new Temple, they were excluded since they were not part of the community of faith. Even Levites are excluded from primary service to the LORD for their idolatrous behavior. The priestly duties were assigned to the male descendants of Zadok alone. These Levitical priests called to perform the holiest ministries were set apart and were to be kept clean, literally and ritually. **22:** The restrictions

courtyard, they must wear only linen clothing.
They must wear no wool while on duty in the
inner courtyard or in the Temple itself. [18] They
must wear linen turbans and linen undergarments. They must not wear anything that would
cause them to perspire. [19] When they return to
the outer courtyard where the people are, they
must take off the clothes they wear while ministering to me. They must leave them in the sacred rooms and put on other clothes so they do
not endanger anyone by transmitting holiness to
them through this clothing.
[20] "They must neither shave their heads nor
let their hair grow too long. Instead, they must
trim it regularly. [21] The priests must not drink
wine before entering the inner courtyard. [22] They
may choose their wives only from among the
virgins of Israel or the widows of the priests.
They may not marry other widows or divorced
women. [23] They will teach my people the difference between what is holy and what is common,
what is ceremonially clean and unclean.
[24] "They will serve as judges to resolve any
disagreements among my people. Their decisions
must be based on my regulations. And the priests
themselves must obey my instructions and decrees at all the sacred festivals, and see to it that
the Sabbaths are set apart as holy days.
[25] "A priest must not defile himself by being
in the presence of a dead person unless it is his
father, mother, child, brother, or unmarried sister. In such cases it is permitted. [26] Even then, he
can return to his Temple duties only after being
ceremonially cleansed and then waiting for sev-
en days. [27] The first day he returns to work and
enters the inner courtyard and the sanctuary, he
must offer a sin offering for himself, says the
Sovereign LORD.
[28] "The priests will not have any property or
possession of land, for I alone am their special
possession. [29] Their food will come from the gifts
and sacrifices brought to the Temple by the people—the grain offerings, the sin offerings, and
the guilt offerings. Whatever anyone sets apart*
for the LORD will belong to the priests. [30] The
first of the ripe fruits and all the gifts brought to
the LORD will go to the priests. The first samples
of each grain harvest and the first of your flour
must also be given to the priests so the LORD will
bless your homes. [31] The priests may not eat meat
from any bird or animal that dies a natural death
or that dies after being attacked by another animal.

Division of the Land

45 "When you divide the land among
the tribes of Israel, you must set
aside a section for the LORD as his
holy portion. This piece of land will be 8⅓ miles
long and 6⅔ miles wide.* The entire area will be
holy. [2] A section of this land, measuring 875 feet
by 875 feet,* will be set aside for the Temple. An
additional strip of land 87½ feet* wide is to be
left empty all around it. [3] Within the larger sacred area, measure out a portion of land 8⅓ miles
long and 3⅓ miles wide.* Within it the sanctuary of the Most Holy Place will be located. [4] This
area will be holy, set aside for the priests who
minister to the LORD in the sanctuary. They will
use it for their homes, and my Temple will be
located within it. [5] The strip of sacred land next
to it, also 8⅓ miles long and 3⅓ miles wide, will
be a living area for the Levites who work at the
Temple. It will be their possession and a place for
their towns.*
[6] "Adjacent to the larger sacred area will be a
section of land 8⅓ miles long and 1⅔ miles wide.*
This will be set aside for a city where anyone in
Israel can live.
[7] "Two special sections of land will be set apart
for the prince. One section will share a border
with the east side of the sacred lands and city,
and the second section will share a border on the
west side. Then the far eastern and western borders of the prince's lands will line up with the
eastern and western boundaries of the tribal areas. [8] These sections of land will be the prince's
allotment. Then my princes will no longer op-

44:29 The Hebrew term used here refers to the complete consecration of things or people to the LORD, either by destroying them or by giving them as an offering. **45:1** As in Greek version, which reads *25,000 cubits* [13.3 kilometers] *long and 20,000 cubits* [10.6 kilometers] *wide;* Hebrew reads *25,000 cubits long and 10,000 cubits* [3⅓ miles or 5.3 kilometers] *wide.* Compare 45:3, 5; 48:9. **45:2a** Hebrew *500 cubits* [265 meters] *by 500 cubits, a square.* **45:2b** Hebrew *50 cubits* [26.5 meters]. **45:3** Hebrew *25,000 cubits* [13.3 kilometers] *long and 10,000 cubits* [5.3 kilometers] *wide;* also in 45:5. **45:5** As in Greek version; Hebrew reads *They will have as their possession 20 rooms.* **45:6** Hebrew *25,000 cubits* [13.3 kilometers] *long and 5,000 cubits* [2.65 kilometers] *wide.*

about the kind of woman that a priest might marry must be seen in this context. **25–26:** Women are also mentioned in a list of family members whose death provided the only exception to the rule that priests could not enter a house where there was a dead body, which would defile him. **45:1–7:** The new community still needs structure. The organization of the Temple and the spiritual life of the community must be at the very center, thus the precise measurements dividing *the land among the tribes of Israel.* **8–12:** This time the

press and rob my people; they will assign the rest
of the land to the people, giving an allotment to
each tribe.

Rules for the Princes
[9]"For this is what the Sovereign LORD says:
Enough, you princes of Israel! Stop your violence and oppression and do what is just and
right. Quit robbing and cheating my people out
of their land. Stop expelling them from their
homes, says the Sovereign LORD. [10]Use only
honest weights and scales and honest measures,
both dry and liquid.* [11]The homer* will be your
standard unit for measuring volume. The ephah
and the bath* will each measure one-tenth of a
homer. [12]The standard unit for weight will be the
silver shekel.* One shekel will consist of twenty
gerahs, and sixty shekels will be equal to one
mina.*

Special Offerings and Celebrations
[13]"You must give this tax to the prince: one bushel of wheat or barley for every 60* you harvest,
[14]one percent of your olive oil,* [15]and one sheep
or goat for every 200 in your flocks in Israel.
These will be the grain offerings, burnt offerings,
and peace offerings that will make atonement
for the people who bring them, says the Sovereign LORD. [16]All the people of Israel must join
in bringing these offerings to the prince. [17]The
prince will be required to provide offerings that
are given at the religious festivals, the new moon
celebrations, the Sabbath days, and all other similar occasions. He will provide the sin offerings,
burnt offerings, grain offerings, liquid offerings,
and peace offerings to purify the people of Israel,
making them right with the LORD.*
[18]"This is what the Sovereign LORD says: In
early spring, on the first day of each new year,*
sacrifice a young bull with no defects to purify
the Temple. [19]The priest will take blood from this
sin offering and put it on the doorposts of the
Temple, the four corners of the upper ledge of
the altar, and the gateposts at the entrance to the
inner courtyard. [20]Do this also on the seventh
day of the new year for anyone who has sinned
through error or ignorance. In this way, you will
purify* the Temple.
[21]"On the fourteenth day of the first month,*
you must celebrate the Passover. This festival
will last for seven days. The bread you eat during that time must be made without yeast. [22]On
the day of Passover the prince will provide a
young bull as a sin offering for himself and the
people of Israel. [23]On each of the seven days of
the feast he will prepare a burnt offering to the
LORD, consisting of seven young bulls and seven
rams without defects. A male goat will also be
given each day for a sin offering. [24]The prince
will provide a basket of flour as a grain offering
and a gallon of olive oil* with each young bull
and ram.
[25]"During the seven days of the Festival of
Shelters, which occurs every year in early autumn,* the prince will provide these same sacrifices for the sin offering, the burnt offering,
and the grain offering, along with the required
olive oil.

46 "This is what the Sovereign LORD
says: The east gateway of the inner
courtyard will be closed during the
six workdays each week, but it will be open on
Sabbath days and the days of new moon celebrations. [2]The prince will enter the entry room of
the gateway from the outside. Then he will stand
by the gatepost while the priest offers his burnt
offering and peace offering. He will bow down

45:10 Hebrew *use honest scales, an honest ephah, and an honest bath.* **45:11a** The *homer* measures about 40 gallons or 182 liters. **45:11b** The *ephah* is a dry measure; the *bath* is a liquid measure. **45:12a** The *shekel* weighs about 0.4 ounces or 11 grams. **45:12b** Elsewhere the *mina* is equated to 50 shekels. **45:13** Hebrew *1/6 of an ephah from each homer of wheat and 1/6 of an ephah from each homer of barley.* **45:14** Hebrew *the portion of oil, measured by the bath, is 1/10 of a bath from each cor, which consists of 10 baths or 1 homer, for 10 baths are equivalent to a homer.* **45:17** Or *to make atonement for the people of Israel.* **45:18** Hebrew *On the first day of the first month,* of the Hebrew calendar. This day in the ancient Hebrew lunar calendar occurred in March or April. **45:20** Or *will make atonement for.* **45:21** This day in the ancient Hebrew lunar calendar occurred in late March, April, or early May. **45:24** Hebrew *an ephah* [20 quarts or 22 liters] *of flour . . . and a hin* [3.8 liters] *of olive oil.* **45:25** Hebrew *the festival which begins on the fifteenth day of the seventh month* (see Lev 23:34). This day in the ancient Hebrew lunar calendar occurred in late September, October, or early November.

princes (perhaps deliberately not called kings), are to behave as if they are servants of the people rather than the other way around. The LORD requires these princes of Israel to *do what is just and right.* **45:13—46:18:** The final chapters of the book contain a collection of additional laws about the development of the community. Of special interest are the inheritance laws for the prince, mandating that inheritance must pass on to his sons. Even gifts made to servants eventually would revert to the rightful male heirs. This system of inheritance was a continuation of what was normative in the ancient world (cf. the challenge of the daughters of Zelophehad, Num 27:1–11). Here, too, are laid out requirements to observe the holy days

in worship inside the gateway passage and then go back out the way he came. The gateway will not be closed until evening. [3]The common people will bow down and worship the LORD in front of this gateway on Sabbath days and the days of new moon celebrations.

[4]"Each Sabbath day the prince will present to the LORD a burnt offering of six lambs and one ram, all with no defects. [5]He will present a grain offering of a basket of choice flour to go with the ram and whatever amount of flour he chooses to go with each lamb, and he is to offer one gallon of olive oil* for each basket of flour. [6]At the new moon celebrations, he will bring one young bull, six lambs, and one ram, all with no defects. [7]With the young bull he must bring a basket of choice flour for a grain offering. With the ram he must bring another basket of flour. And with each lamb he is to bring whatever amount of flour he chooses to give. With each basket of flour he must offer one gallon of olive oil.

[8]"The prince must enter the gateway through the entry room, and he must leave the same way. [9]But when the people come in through the north gateway to worship the LORD during the religious festivals, they must leave by the south gateway. And those who entered through the south gateway must leave by the north gateway. They must never leave by the same gateway they came in, but must always use the opposite gateway. [10]The prince will enter and leave with the people on these occasions.

[11]"So at the special feasts and sacred festivals, the grain offering will be a basket of choice flour with each young bull, another basket of flour with each ram, and as much flour as the prince chooses to give with each lamb. Give one gallon of olive oil with each basket of flour. [12]When the prince offers a voluntary burnt offering or peace offering to the LORD, the east gateway to the inner courtyard will be opened for him, and he will offer his sacrifices as he does on Sabbath days. Then he will leave, and the gateway will be shut behind him.

[13]"Each morning you must sacrifice a one-year-old lamb with no defects as a burnt offering to the LORD. [14]With the lamb, a grain offering must also be given to the LORD—about three quarts of flour with a third of a gallon of olive oil* to moisten the choice flour. This will be a permanent law for you. [15]The lamb, the grain offering, and the olive oil must be given as a daily sacrifice every morning without fail.

[16]"This is what the Sovereign LORD says: If the prince gives a gift of land to one of his sons as his inheritance, it will belong to him and his descendants forever. [17]But if the prince gives a gift of land from his inheritance to one of his servants, the servant may keep it only until the Year of Jubilee, which comes every fiftieth year.* At that time the land will return to the prince. But when the prince gives gifts to his sons, those gifts will be permanent. [18]And the prince may never take anyone's property by force. If he gives property to his sons, it must be from his own land, for I do not want any of my people unjustly evicted from their property."

The Temple Kitchens

[19]In my vision, the man brought me through the entrance beside the gateway and led me to the sacred rooms assigned to the priests, which faced toward the north. He showed me a place at the extreme west end of these rooms. [20]He explained, "This is where the priests will cook the meat from the guilt offerings and sin offerings and bake the flour from the grain offerings into bread. They will do it here to avoid carrying the sacrifices through the outer courtyard and endangering the people by transmitting holiness to them."

[21]Then he brought me back to the outer courtyard and led me to each of its four corners. In each corner I saw an enclosure. [22]Each of these enclosures was 70 feet long and 52½ feet wide,* surrounded by walls. [23]Along the inside of these walls was a ledge of stone with fireplaces under the ledge all the way around. [24]The man said to me, "These are the kitchens to be used by the Temple assistants to boil the sacrifices offered by the people."

The River of Healing

47 In my vision, the man brought me back to the entrance of the Temple. There I saw a stream flowing east

46:5 Hebrew *an ephah* [20 quarts or 22 liters] *of choice flour . . . a hin* [3.8 liters] *of olive oil;* similarly in 46:7, 11. **46:14** Hebrew $^1/_6$ *of an ephah* [3.7 liters] *of flour with* $^1/_3$ *of a hin* [1.3 liters] *of olive oil.* **46:17** Hebrew *until the Year of Release;* see Lev 25:8-17. **46:22** Hebrew *40 cubits* [21.2 meters] *long and 30 cubits* [15.9 meters] *wide.*

(Passover, Sukkot). **46:19–24:** The sacred kitchen was separate lest the holiness of the offerings consecrate the worshipers. Other kitchens were located in the four corners of the outer courtyard, where the Levitical servers were to prepare the portions of the sacrifices and offerings that were going to be eaten by the worshipers. **47:1–12:** When Ezekiel was brought from the inner kitchen to the Temple entrance, he saw

from beneath the door of the Temple and passing
to the right of the altar on its south side. 2The
man brought me outside the wall through the
north gateway and led me around to the eastern
entrance. There I could see the water flowing out
through the south side of the east gateway.
3Measuring as he went, he took me along the
stream for 1,750 feet* and then led me across.
The water was up to my ankles. 4He measured
off another 1,750 feet and led me across again.
This time the water was up to my knees. After
another 1,750 feet, it was up to my waist. 5Then
he measured another 1,750 feet, and the river
was too deep to walk across. It was deep enough
to swim in, but too deep to walk through.
6He asked me, "Have you been watching, son
of man?" Then he led me back along the riverbank. 7When I returned, I was surprised by the
sight of many trees growing on both sides of the
river. 8Then he said to me, "This river flows east
through the desert into the valley of the Dead
Sea.* The waters of this stream will make the
salty waters of the Dead Sea fresh and pure.
9There will be swarms of living things wherever
the water of this river flows. Fish will abound in
the Dead Sea, for its waters will become fresh.
Life will flourish wherever this water flows.
10Fishermen will stand along the shores of the
Dead Sea. All the way from En-gedi to En-eglaim,
the shores will be covered with nets drying in the
sun. Fish of every kind will fill the Dead Sea, just
as they fill the Mediterranean.* 11But the marshes and swamps will not be purified; they will still
be salty. 12Fruit trees of all kinds will grow along
both sides of the river. The leaves of these trees
will never turn brown and fall, and there will always be fruit on their branches. There will be a
new crop every month, for they are watered by
the river flowing from the Temple. The fruit will
be for food and the leaves for healing."

Boundaries for the Land

13This is what the Sovereign LORD says: "Divide
the land in this way for the twelve tribes of Israel:
The descendants of Joseph will be given two shares
of land.* 14Otherwise each tribe will receive an
equal share. I took a solemn oath and swore that I
would give this land to your ancestors, and it will
now come to you as your possession.

15"These are the boundaries of the land:
The northern border will run from the
Mediterranean toward Hethlon, then on
through Lebo-hamath to Zedad; 16then it will
run to Berothah and Sibraim, which are on
the border between Damascus and Hamath,
and finally to Hazer-hatticon, on the border
of Hauran. 17So the northern border will run
from the Mediterranean to Hazar-enan, on
the border between Hamath to the north and
Damascus to the south.
18"The eastern border starts at a point
between Hauran and Damascus and runs
south along the Jordan River between Israel
and Gilead, past the Dead Sea* and as far
south as Tamar.* This will be the eastern
border.

47:3 Hebrew *1,000 cubits* [530 meters]; also in 47:4, 5. **47:8** Hebrew *the sea.* **47:10** Hebrew *the great sea;* also in 47:15, 17, 19, 20. **47:13** It was important to retain twelve portions of land. Since Levi had no portion, the descendants of Joseph's sons, Ephraim and Manasseh, received land as two tribes. **47:18a** Hebrew *the eastern sea.* **47:18b** As in Greek version; Hebrew reads *you will measure.*

water flowing down from the altar. The river brought life to everything in its path, even to the lifeless waters of the Dead Sea. Although the swamps and marshes continued to provide salt, the rest of the areas touched by the river produced trees bearing fruit for food and leaves bringing healing. Some commentators have interpreted this vision literally and tried to locate the source of this water on Mount Zion, but its meaning lies more correctly in its rich symbolism. The water, symbolizing God's presence, brings life, fruitfulness, and health to the Temple and to the entire area, including the wilderness. To the exiles, this vision brought hope. It promised that when God's presence was reestablished in the Temple, the blessings of new life would flow and transform the lives of those who encountered it (cf. Rev 22:2 and John 7:38). God desires to bless and renew his people, not because they deserve it or earn it but rather because of his gracious love. Some interpreters have seen implicit feminine images in the new Temple, which unlike the old Temple is fertile. This flow of water could be a counter to the unclean menstrual flow referred to so often in the first part of the book, or it can be seen as the rebuilt Temple's water breaking, giving birth to a new community of God. Water is used as an image of fertility elsewhere in the Old Testament, suggesting that feminine imagery is at least implicit in the image of the waters of life (Ezek 47; cf. Song 4:12–15; Pss 46:4; 87:1–7; Jer 31:12). **47:13—48:35:** The new city is not called Jerusalem or even the new Jerusalem, lest old associations with the unfaithful and unclean wife be made. Rather the new city is named *The LORD Is There* (48:35). Now the area of the new city is described as being perfectly symmetrical and accessible to all; God's presence makes it a holy city.

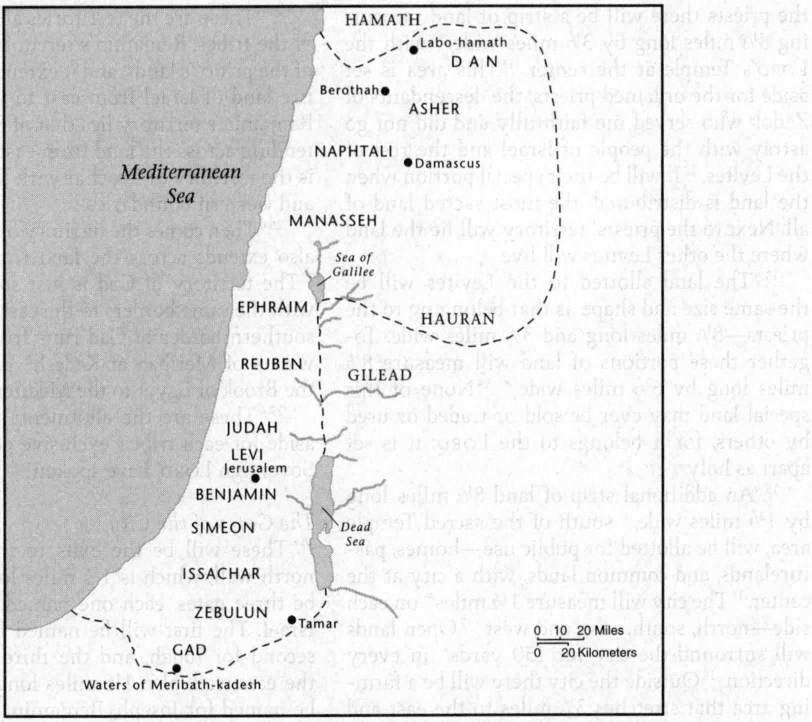

Tribal Territories in the Restored Israel

[19]"The southern border will go west from Tamar to the waters of Meribah at Kadesh* and then follow the course of the Brook of Egypt to the Mediterranean. This will be the southern border.

[20]"On the west side, the Mediterranean itself will be your border from the southern border to the point where the northern border begins, opposite Lebo-hamath.

[21]"Divide the land within these boundaries among the tribes of Israel. [22]Distribute the land as an allotment for yourselves and for the foreigners who have joined you and are raising their families among you. They will be like native-born Israelites to you and will receive an allotment among the tribes. [23]These foreigners are to be given land within the territory of the tribe with whom they now live. I, the Sovereign LORD, have spoken!

Division of the Land

48 "Here is the list of the tribes of Israel and the territory each is to receive. The territory of Dan is in the extreme north. Its boundary line follows the Hethlon road to Lebo-hamath and then runs on to Hazar-enan on the border of Damascus, with Hamath to the north. Dan's territory extends all the way across the land of Israel from east to west.

[2]"Asher's territory lies south of Dan's and also extends from east to west. [3]Naphtali's land lies south of Asher's, also extending from east to west. [4]Then comes Manasseh south of Naphtali, and its territory also extends from east to west. [5]South of Manasseh is Ephraim, [6]and then Reuben, [7]and then Judah, all of whose boundaries extend from east to west.

[8]"South of Judah is the land set aside for a special purpose. It will be 8⅓ miles* wide and will extend as far east and west as the tribal territories, with the Temple at the center.

[9]"The area set aside for the LORD's Temple will be 8⅓ miles long and 6⅔ miles wide.* [10]For

47:19 Hebrew *waters of Meribath-kadesh.* **48:8** Hebrew *25,000 cubits* [13.3 kilometers]. **48:9** As in one Greek manuscript and the Greek reading in 45:1: *25,000 cubits* [13.3 kilometers] *long and 20,000 cubits* [10.6 kilometers] *wide;* Hebrew reads *25,000 cubits long and 10,000 cubits* [3⅓ miles or 5.3 kilometers] *wide.* Similarly in 48:13b. Compare 45:1-5; 48:10-13.

the priests there will be a strip of land measuring 8⅓ miles long by 3⅓ miles wide,* with the
LORD's Temple at the center. 11 This area is set
aside for the ordained priests, the descendants of
Zadok who served me faithfully and did not go
astray with the people of Israel and the rest of
the Levites. 12 It will be their special portion when
the land is distributed, the most sacred land of
all. Next to the priests' territory will lie the land
where the other Levites will live.

13 "The land allotted to the Levites will be
the same size and shape as that belonging to the
priests—8⅓ miles long and 3⅓ miles wide. Together these portions of land will measure 8⅓
miles long by 6⅔ miles wide.* 14 None of this
special land may ever be sold or traded or used
by others, for it belongs to the LORD; it is set
apart as holy.

15 "An additional strip of land 8⅓ miles long
by 1⅔ miles wide,* south of the sacred Temple
area, will be allotted for public use—homes, pasturelands, and common lands, with a city at the
center. 16 The city will measure 1½ miles* on each
side—north, south, east, and west. 17 Open lands
will surround the city for 150 yards* in every
direction. 18 Outside the city there will be a farming area that stretches 3⅓ miles to the east and
3⅓ miles to the west* along the border of the
sacred area. This farmland will produce food for
the people working in the city. 19 Those who come
from the various tribes to work in the city may
farm it. 20 This entire area—including the sacred
lands and the city—is a square that measures 8⅓
miles* on each side.

21 "The areas that remain, to the east and to
the west of the sacred lands and the city, will belong to the prince. Each of these areas will be 8⅓
miles wide, extending in opposite directions to
the eastern and western borders of Israel, with
the sacred lands and the sanctuary of the Temple
in the center. 22 So the prince's land will include
everything between the territories allotted to Judah and Benjamin, except for the areas set aside
for the sacred lands and the city.

23 "These are the territories allotted to the rest
of the tribes. Benjamin's territory lies just south
of the prince's lands, and it extends across the entire land of Israel from east to west. 24 South of
Benjamin's territory lies that of Simeon, also extending across the land from east to west. 25 Next
is the territory of Issachar with the same eastern
and western boundaries.

26 "Then comes the territory of Zebulun, which
also extends across the land from east to west.
27 The territory of Gad is just south of Zebulun
with the same borders to the east and west. 28 The
southern border of Gad runs from Tamar to the
waters of Meribah at Kadesh* and then follows
the Brook of Egypt to the Mediterranean.*

29 "These are the allotments that will be set
aside for each tribe's exclusive possession. I, the
Sovereign LORD, have spoken!

The Gates of the City

30 "These will be the exits to the city: On the
north wall, which is 1½ miles long, 31 there will
be three gates, each one named after a tribe of
Israel. The first will be named for Reuben, the
second for Judah, and the third for Levi. 32 On
the east wall, also 1½ miles long, the gates will
be named for Joseph, Benjamin, and Dan. 33 The
south wall, also 1½ miles long, will have gates
named for Simeon, Issachar, and Zebulun. 34 And
on the west wall, also 1½ miles long, the gates
will be named for Gad, Asher, and Naphtali.

35 "The distance around the entire city will be
6 miles.* And from that day the name of the city
will be 'The LORD Is There.'* "

48:10 Hebrew *25,000 cubits* [13.3 kilometers] *long by 10,000 cubits* [5.3 kilometers] *wide;* also in 48:13a. **48:13** See note on 48:9. **48:15** Hebrew *25,000 cubits* [13.3 kilometers] *long by 5,000 cubits* [2.65 kilometers] *wide.* **48:16** Hebrew *4,500 cubits* [2.4 kilometers]; also in 48:30, 32, 33, 34. **48:17** Hebrew *250 cubits* [133 meters]. **48:18** Hebrew *10,000 cubits* [5.3 kilometers] *to the east and 10,000 cubits to the west.* **48:20** Hebrew *25,000 cubits* [13.3 kilometers]; also in 48:21. **48:28a** Hebrew *waters of Meribath-kadesh.* **48:28b** Hebrew *the great sea.* **48:35a** Hebrew *18,000 cubits* [9.6 kilometers]. **48:35b** Hebrew *Yahweh Shammah.*

DANIEL

INTRODUCTION

Daniel was not a typical prophet called to admonish God's people but a bureaucrat serving God in the hostile environment of pagan Babylon (modern Iraq). Thus in the Hebrew Bible, Daniel is grouped with the Writings rather than with the Prophets. The book's emphasis is apocalyptic, with strange dreams and visions of the future.

Two closely related languages are used: Hebrew (1:1—2:4; 8:1—12:13) and Aramaic (2:4—7:28). Aramaic, the official language of the Persian Empire, was more widely spoken, even as early as the eighth century BC (2 Kgs 18:26).

The book divides naturally into two parts: Daniel's youth and suffering in Babylon (chaps. 1—6), and Daniel's visions as an old man—visions about world history and the suffering of God's people (chaps. 7—12). Although the halves seem unrelated, there are definite signs of literary unity. The basics of chapter 2 reappear in chapter 7; the destruction "not by human hands" (2:34) parallels "not by human power" (8:25); and the indestructible kingdom (2:44) is paralleled in 7:27.

Although Daniel speaks in the third person in chapters 1—6 and in the first person in chapters 7—12, many interpreters assume the author to be a pious scribe who lived during a severe persecution of Jews by Antiochus Epiphanes (175–163 BC) but took the name of an ancient hero and set his tale in sixth-century Babylon. The arguments are complicated, but the book can still be read as a revelation from God to the exiled Daniel during the Babylonian and Persian empires. *—Joyce E. Winifred Every-Clayton*

1:1–21	Daniel, a Young Israelite in Babylon
2:1—6:28	Pagan Rulers Dream and Scheme in Babylon
7:1—12:3	Daniel Also Dreams in Babylon
12:4–13	Daniel, Receive Your Inheritance

✧

Daniel in Nebuchadnezzar's Court

1 During the third year of King Jehoiakim's reign in Judah,* King Nebuchadnezzar of Babylon came to Jerusalem and besieged it. [2]The Lord gave him victory over King Jehoiakim of Judah and permitted him to take some of the sacred objects from the Temple of God. So Nebuchadnezzar took them back to the land of Babylonia* and placed them in the treasure-house of his god.

[3]Then the king ordered Ashpenaz, his chief of staff, to bring to the palace some of the young men of Judah's royal family and other noble families, who had been brought to Babylon as captives. [4]"Select only strong, healthy, and good-looking young men," he said. "Make sure they are well versed in every branch of learning, are gifted with knowledge and good judgment, and are suited to serve in the royal palace. Train these young men in the language and literature of Babylon.*" [5]The king assigned them a daily ration of food and wine from his own kitchens. They were to be trained for three years, and then they would enter the royal service.

[6]Daniel, Hananiah, Mishael, and Azariah were four of the young men chosen, all from the tribe of Judah. [7]The chief of staff renamed them with these Babylonian names:

Daniel was called Belteshazzar.
Hananiah was called Shadrach.
Mishael was called Meshach.
Azariah was called Abednego.

[8]But Daniel was determined not to defile himself by eating the food and wine given to them by the king. He asked the chief of staff for permission not to eat these unacceptable foods. [9]Now God had given the chief of staff both respect and affection for Daniel. [10]But he responded, "I am afraid of my lord the king, who has ordered that you eat this food and wine. If you become pale and thin compared to the other youths your age, I am afraid the king will have me beheaded."

[11]Daniel spoke with the attendant who had been appointed by the chief of staff to look after Daniel, Hananiah, Mishael, and Azariah. [12]"Please test us for ten days on a diet of vegetables and water," Daniel said. [13]"At the end of the ten days, see how we look compared to the other young men who are eating the king's food. Then make your decision in light of what you see." [14]The attendant agreed to Daniel's suggestion and tested them for ten days.

[15]At the end of the ten days, Daniel and his three friends looked healthier and better nourished than the young men who had been eating the food assigned by the king. [16]So after that, the

1:1 This event occurred in 605 B.C., during the third year of Jehoiakim's reign (according to the calendar system in which the new year begins in the spring). **1:2** Hebrew *the land of Shinar.* **1:4** Or *of the Chaldeans.*

1:1–21 Daniel, a Young Israelite in Babylon

Details of the final turbulent years of Judah and of the collapse of Jerusalem appear in 2 Kings 24—25. **1:** This describes 605 BC, when Nebuchadnezzar invaded Syria, Palestine, and Egypt. **2:** The phrase *The Lord gave him victory over* introduces a theme of the book: God's rule over all, even powerful earthly rulers. **3–17:** It was common for a conqueror to take hostages and plunder back to his own god's treasury as a thank offering. So Daniel and three other *young men of Judah's royal family* moved to Babylon about eight years before the main group (Isa 39:7; Jer 25:11) and stayed there until 538 BC, the start of Cyrus's reign (Dan 1:21). The four gifted youths had three years of study and preparation in the royal court. They graduated with top grades in Babylonian *language and literature* (v. 4), *wisdom* (science) (v. 17) and *any matter requiring wisdom and balanced judgment* (v. 20), as well as in *visions and dreams* (v. 17). The young men's successes bear eloquent testimony to the dedication of unnamed parents and Israelite teachers. However, the main reason was that *God gave* [them] . . . *an unusual aptitude* (v. 17). **3, 9:** Ashpenaz was responsible for the selection process here just as Hegai was for the selection of Esther, another victim of the Babylonian invasion. The phrase *God had given the chief of staff . . . respect* parallels Esther 2:9 and Genesis 39:21. For Esther and Joseph, God's favor is presented as the secret of their survival and success in the pagan court. **7:** The change from Hebrew names, containing the name of God, to new names that may even use the names of pagan gods was common (2 Kgs 23:34; Gen 41:45; 43:32). So Daniel, meaning "God has judged," became Belteshazzar, meaning "protect the life of the king." This change may be to obliterate ethnic identity and speed up acculturation or just to aid pronunciation. **8:** Daniel's request for permission not to *defile himself* and to eat vegetarian food was because the king's food, consecrated to idols, could imply loyalty to idols. **11–21:** The Jews' stand against idolatry, their superior physical appearance, and intelligence undoubtedly called everyone's attention to them. They would not compromise with pagan culture where it opposed God's law. But nor were they fanatics, unwilling to benefit from secular education for fear of losing their faith.

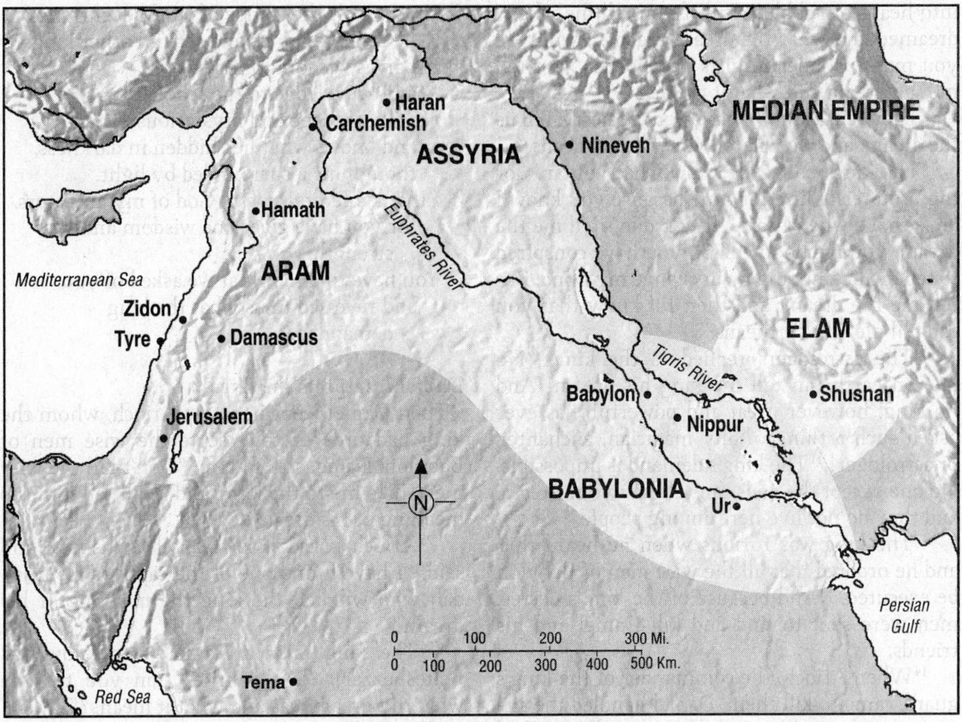

The Neo-Babylonian Empire

attendant fed them only vegetables instead of
the food and wine provided for the others.
[17]God gave these four young men an unusual
aptitude for understanding every aspect of literature and wisdom. And God gave Daniel the special ability to interpret the meanings of visions
and dreams.
[18]When the training period ordered by the
king was completed, the chief of staff brought all
the young men to King Nebuchadnezzar. [19]The
king talked with them, and no one impressed
him as much as Daniel, Hananiah, Mishael,
and Azariah. So they entered the royal service.
[20]Whenever the king consulted them in any matter requiring wisdom and balanced judgment, he
found them ten times more capable than any of
the magicians and enchanters in his entire kingdom.
[21]Daniel remained in the royal service until
the first year of the reign of King Cyrus.*

Nebuchadnezzar's Dream

2 One night during the second year of his
reign,* Nebuchadnezzar had such disturbing dreams that he couldn't sleep. [2]He
called in his magicians, enchanters, sorcerers, and
astrologers,* and he demanded that they tell him
what he had dreamed. As they stood before the
king, [3]he said, "I have had a dream that deeply
troubles me, and I must know what it means."
[4]Then the astrologers answered the king in
Aramaic,* "Long live the king! Tell us the dream,
and we will tell you what it means."
[5]But the king said to the astrologers, "I am
serious about this. If you don't tell me what my
dream was and what it means, you will be torn
limb from limb, and your houses will be turned

1:21 Cyrus began his reign (over Babylon) in 539 B.C.
2:1 The second year of Nebuchadnezzar's reign was 603 B.C.
2:2 Or *Chaldeans;* also in 2:4, 5, 10. **2:4** The original text from this point through chapter 7 is in Aramaic.

2:1–6:28 Pagan Rulers Dream and Scheme in Babylon

2:1–23 Nebuchadnezzar's Dream. Dreams, worry, insomnia, every possible type of astrologer, and a cruel demagogue in crisis making absurd demands are common today. Daniel's reaction is not uncommon either. He accepted the challenge, asked for prayer, and afterward expressed gratitude to God. **3–12:** The frustration of waking up and realizing he

into heaps of rubble! [6]But if you tell me what I
dreamed and what the dream means, I will give
you many wonderful gifts and honors. Just tell
me the dream and what it means!"
[7]They said again, "Please, Your Majesty. Tell us
the dream, and we will tell you what it means."
[8]The king replied, "I know what you are doing! You're stalling for time because you know I
am serious when I say, [9]'If you don't tell me the
dream, you are doomed.' So you have conspired
to tell me lies, hoping I will change my mind. But
tell me the dream, and then I'll know that you
can tell me what it means."
[10]The astrologers replied to the king, "No
one on earth can tell the king his dream! And
no king, however great and powerful, has ever
asked such a thing of any magician, enchanter,
or astrologer! [11]The king's demand is impossible.
No one except the gods can tell you your dream,
and they do not live here among people."
[12]The king was furious when he heard this,
and he ordered that all the wise men of Babylon
be executed. [13]And because of the king's decree,
men were sent to find and kill Daniel and his
friends.
[14]When Arioch, the commander of the king's
guard, came to kill them, Daniel handled the situation with wisdom and discretion. [15]He asked
Arioch, "Why has the king issued such a harsh
decree?" So Arioch told him all that had happened. [16]Daniel went at once to see the king and
requested more time to tell the king what the
dream meant.
[17]Then Daniel went home and told his friends
Hananiah, Mishael, and Azariah what had happened. [18]He urged them to ask the God of heaven
to show them his mercy by telling them the secret, so they would not be executed along with
the other wise men of Babylon. [19]That night the
secret was revealed to Daniel in a vision. Then
Daniel praised the God of heaven. [20]He said,

"Praise the name of God forever and ever,
for he has all wisdom and power.
[21] He controls the course of world events;
he removes kings and sets up other kings.
He gives wisdom to the wise
and knowledge to the scholars.
[22] He reveals deep and mysterious things
and knows what lies hidden in darkness,
though he is surrounded by light.
[23] I thank and praise you, God of my ancestors,
for you have given me wisdom and
strength.
You have told me what we asked of you
and revealed to us what the king
demanded."

Daniel Interprets the Dream

[24]Then Daniel went in to see Arioch, whom the
king had ordered to execute the wise men of
Babylon. Daniel said to him, "Don't kill the wise
men. Take me to the king, and I will tell him the
meaning of his dream."
[25]Arioch quickly took Daniel to the king and
said, "I have found one of the captives from Judah who will tell the king the meaning of his
dream!"
[26]The king said to Daniel (also known as
Belteshazzar), "Is this true? Can you tell me
what my dream was and what it means?"
[27]Daniel replied, "There are no wise men, enchanters, magicians, or fortune-tellers who can
reveal the king's secret. [28]But there is a God in
heaven who reveals secrets, and he has shown
King Nebuchadnezzar what will happen in the
future. Now I will tell you your dream and the
visions you saw as you lay on your bed.
[29]"While Your Majesty was sleeping, you
dreamed about coming events. He who reveals
secrets has shown you what is going to happen.
[30]And it is not because I am wiser than anyone
else that I know the secret of your dream, but
because God wants you to understand what was
in your heart.
[31]"In your vision, Your Majesty, you saw
standing before you a huge, shining statue of a
man. It was a frightening sight. [32]The head of the

---

had forgotten an important dream made the king dangerous, and his threats and promises increased the astrologers' tension and panic. **13–19:** Daniel's rational behavior—discreet questions and explanations—contrasts with the king's screaming petulance. **20–23:** Prayer (cf. Job 12:13, 15, 18, 22) is another theme of the book, and Daniel's dependence on God contrasts with the astrologers' complacent self-sufficiency.

2:24–45 Daniel Interprets. After prayer, action; and just as Joseph's God-given administrative ability saved Egyptians from death (Gen 41:55–56), so Daniel's God-given courage saved Babylonian seers from execution. This is an example of the fulfillment of God's promise to Abraham: "All the families on earth shall be blessed through you" (Gen 12:3). **28:** The dream is about the *future*, literally, "the end of days" used elsewhere of the messianic age (Isa 2:2; Jer 48:47). **31–35:** The statue, when struck by a rock, crashed to the ground, while the rock *became a great mountain*. The sharp contrast between carefully crafted but ultimately fragile manufactured objects and the raw

statue was made of fine gold. Its chest and arms
were silver, its belly and thighs were bronze, 33 its
legs were iron, and its feet were a combination of
iron and baked clay. 34 As you watched, a rock was
cut from a mountain, but not by human hands.
It struck the feet of iron and clay, smashing them
to bits. 35 The whole statue was crushed into
small pieces of iron, clay, bronze, silver, and gold.
Then the wind blew them away without a trace,
like chaff on a threshing floor. But the rock that
knocked the statue down became a great mountain that covered the whole earth.
36 "That was the dream. Now we will tell the
king what it means. 37 Your Majesty, you are the
greatest of kings. The God of heaven has given
you sovereignty, power, strength, and honor. 38 He
has made you the ruler over all the inhabited
world and has put even the wild animals and birds
under your control. You are the head of gold.
39 "But after your kingdom comes to an end,
another kingdom, inferior to yours, will rise to
take your place. After that kingdom has fallen,
yet a third kingdom, represented by bronze, will
rise to rule the world. 40 Following that kingdom,
there will be a fourth one, as strong as iron.
That kingdom will smash and crush all previous empires, just as iron smashes and crushes
everything it strikes. 41 The feet and toes you saw
were a combination of iron and baked clay, showing that this kingdom will be divided. Like iron
mixed with clay, it will have some of the strength
of iron. 42 But while some parts of it will be as
strong as iron, other parts will be as weak as clay.
43 This mixture of iron and clay also shows that
these kingdoms will try to strengthen themselves
by forming alliances with each other through intermarriage. But they will not hold together, just
as iron and clay do not mix.
44 "During the reigns of those kings, the God
of heaven will set up a kingdom that will never
be destroyed or conquered. It will crush all these
kingdoms into nothingness, and it will stand forever. 45 That is the meaning of the rock cut from
the mountain, though not by human hands, that
crushed to pieces the statue of iron, bronze, clay,
silver, and gold. The great God was showing the
king what will happen in the future. The dream
is true, and its meaning is certain."

Nebuchadnezzar Rewards Daniel

46 Then King Nebuchadnezzar threw himself
down before Daniel and worshiped him, and he
commanded his people to offer sacrifices and
burn sweet incense before him. 47 The king said to
Daniel, "Truly, your God is the greatest of gods,
the Lord over kings, a revealer of mysteries, for
you have been able to reveal this secret."
48 Then the king appointed Daniel to a high
position and gave him many valuable gifts. He
made Daniel ruler over the whole province of
Babylon, as well as chief over all his wise men.
49 At Daniel's request, the king appointed Shadrach, Meshach, and Abednego to be in charge of
all the affairs of the province of Babylon, while
Daniel remained in the king's court.

Nebuchadnezzar's Gold Statue

3 King Nebuchadnezzar made a gold statue
ninety feet tall and nine feet wide* and set
it up on the plain of Dura in the province
of Babylon. 2 Then he sent messages to the high
officers, officials, governors, advisers, treasurers,
judges, magistrates, and all the provincial officials
to come to the dedication of the statue he had set
up. 3 So all these officials* came and stood before
the statue King Nebuchadnezzar had set up.

3:1 Aramaic *60 cubits* [27 meters] *tall and 6 cubits* [2.7 meters] *wide.* **3:3** Aramaic *the high officers, officials, governors, advisers, treasurers, judges, magistrates, and all the provincial officials.*

simplicity, power, and solidity of that which comes from God is striking. **36–45:** Daniel's interpretation is that Nebuchadnezzar's glorious, worldwide reign will be succeeded by inferior ones until a divided strong/weak kingdom appears, which will also fall before the flying rock. Many understand the rock to refer to Christ. After Babylon came the Median kingdom, then the Persian and the Greek. Perhaps the list should read Medo-Persian, Greek, and Roman. Verse 44 suggests that the order is not necessarily chronological, for the rock destroyed all the kingdoms simultaneously and then grew in size and importance. Evidently a destructive but indestructible kingdom will succeed the kingdoms of this world. These kingdoms and their history are in the hands of the one true God, and only God can interpret that history.

2:46–49 Daniel Is Rewarded. Daniel accepted Nebuchadnezzar's *worship* (v. 46), in accordance with classic prophetic teaching (Isa 49:23; cf. Phil 2:10–11; Rev 21:24–26). It does not imply that Daniel or the king thought that he was a god.

3:1–18 Nebuchadnezzar's Gold Statue. His ego boosted by the dream, *Nebuchadnezzar made a gold statue* (v. 1). The phrase pulsates through the first half of the chapter. The statue was huge, strategically located, and to be worshiped by all. **2–6:** Names on the guest list appear in order of importance. The pomp of the dedication ceremony, complete with herald and

4 Then a herald shouted out, "People of all
races and nations and languages, listen to the
king's command! 5 When you hear the sound
of the horn, flute, zither, lyre, harp, pipes, and
other musical instruments,* bow to the ground
to worship King Nebuchadnezzar's gold statue.
6 Anyone who refuses to obey will immediately
be thrown into a blazing furnace."
7 So at the sound of the musical instruments,*
all the people, whatever their race or nation or
language, bowed to the ground and worshiped
the gold statue that King Nebuchadnezzar had
set up.
8 But some of the astrologers* went to the
king and informed on the Jews. 9 They said to
King Nebuchadnezzar, "Long live the king!
10 You issued a decree requiring all the people
to bow down and worship the gold statue when
they hear the sound of the horn, flute, zither,
lyre, harp, pipes, and other musical instruments.
11 That decree also states that those who refuse
to obey must be thrown into a blazing furnace.
12 But there are some Jews—Shadrach, Meshach,
and Abednego—whom you have put in charge
of the province of Babylon. They pay no attention to you, Your Majesty. They refuse to serve
your gods and do not worship the gold statue
you have set up."
13 Then Nebuchadnezzar flew into a rage and
ordered that Shadrach, Meshach, and Abednego
be brought before him. When they were brought
in, 14 Nebuchadnezzar said to them, "Is it true,
Shadrach, Meshach, and Abednego, that you
refuse to serve my gods or to worship the gold
statue I have set up? 15 I will give you one more
chance to bow down and worship the statue I
have made when you hear the sound of the musical instruments.* But if you refuse, you will be
thrown immediately into the blazing furnace.
And then what god will be able to rescue you
from my power?"
16 Shadrach, Meshach, and Abednego replied,
"O Nebuchadnezzar, we do not need to defend
ourselves before you. 17 If we are thrown into the
blazing furnace, the God whom we serve is able
to save us. He will rescue us from your power,
Your Majesty. 18 But even if he doesn't, we want
to make it clear to you, Your Majesty, that we
will never serve your gods or worship the gold
statue you have set up."

The Blazing Furnace

19 Nebuchadnezzar was so furious with Shadrach, Meshach, and Abednego that his face became distorted with rage. He commanded that
the furnace be heated seven times hotter than
usual. 20 Then he ordered some of the strongest
men of his army to bind Shadrach, Meshach,
and Abednego and throw them into the blazing
furnace. 21 So they tied them up and threw them
into the furnace, fully dressed in their pants, turbans, robes, and other garments. 22 And because
the king, in his anger, had demanded such a hot
fire in the furnace, the flames killed the soldiers
as they threw the three men in. 23 So Shadrach,
Meshach, and Abednego, securely tied, fell into
the roaring flames.
24 But suddenly, Nebuchadnezzar jumped up
in amazement and exclaimed to his advisers,
"Didn't we tie up three men and throw them into
the furnace?"
"Yes, Your Majesty, we certainly did," they
replied.
25 "Look!" Nebuchadnezzar shouted. "I see
four men, unbound, walking around in the fire
unharmed! And the fourth looks like a god*!"

3:5 The identification of some of these musical instruments is uncertain. **3:7** Aramaic *the horn, flute, zither, lyre, harp, and other musical instruments.* **3:8** Aramaic *Chaldeans.* **3:15** Aramaic *the horn, flute, zither, lyre, harp, pipes, and other musical instruments.* **3:25** Aramaic *like a son of the gods.*

an orchestra of instruments, was marred by the threat of dreadful punishment for any refusing to conform. **12:** This verse introduces the theme of anti-Semitism and reminds readers of Haman's accusation (Esth 3:8–9). Just when it seemed that Jews could survive in a pagan culture and even be a blessing there (cf. Esth 2:19–23), we discover that the astrologers are jealous of the Jews' promotion and able to convince a power-hungry Nebuchadnezzar. **13–18:** The irrational fury of the dictator who cannot cope with dissidents and kills even his supporters contrasts with the Jews' calm behavior, faith, and courage. No true Jew could worship this statue and so break the first two commandments (Exod 20:3–4). We see in the three friends no doubting of God but also no claiming immunity from suffering or fanaticism: just total faith in God's sovereign power to save, or not, as he wills. Nothing that God can do will make these men love him less.

3:19–30 Daniel's Friends Survive the Fiery Furnace. The verb *rescue* pulsates through the second half of this chapter (i.e., v. 28) and reappears in 6:14 (*save*); 6:16, 20; 12:1. The description of the fiery furnace is full of exaggeration, preparing the reader for the great miracle. Once again the demeanor of the king contrasts with that of God's people, quietly *walking around in the fire*, accompanied by a fourth person,

26 Then Nebuchadnezzar came as close as he
could to the door of the flaming furnace and
shouted: "Shadrach, Meshach, and Abednego,
servants of the Most High God, come out! Come
here!"

So Shadrach, Meshach, and Abednego stepped
out of the fire. 27 Then the high officers, officials,
governors, and advisers crowded around them
and saw that the fire had not touched them. Not
a hair on their heads was singed, and their clothing was not scorched. They didn't even smell of
smoke!

28 Then Nebuchadnezzar said, "Praise to the
God of Shadrach, Meshach, and Abednego! He
sent his angel to rescue his servants who trusted in him. They defied the king's command and
were willing to die rather than serve or worship any god except their own God. 29 Therefore, I make this decree: If any people, whatever
their race or nation or language, speak a word
against the God of Shadrach, Meshach, and
Abednego, they will be torn limb from limb,
and their houses will be turned into heaps of
rubble. There is no other god who can rescue
like this!"

30 Then the king promoted Shadrach, Meshach, and Abednego to even higher positions in
the province of Babylon.

Nebuchadnezzar's Dream about a Tree

4 1 *King Nebuchadnezzar sent this message
to the people of every race and nation and
language throughout the world:

"Peace and prosperity to you!

2 "I want you all to know about the
miraculous signs and wonders the Most High
God has performed for me.

3 How great are his signs,
how powerful his wonders!
His kingdom will last forever,
his rule through all generations.

4 *"I, Nebuchadnezzar, was living in my
palace in comfort and prosperity. 5 But one
night I had a dream that frightened me; I saw
visions that terrified me as I lay in my bed.
6 So I issued an order calling in all the wise
men of Babylon, so they could tell me what
my dream meant. 7 When all the magicians,
enchanters, astrologers,* and fortune-tellers
came in, I told them the dream, but they
could not tell me what it meant. 8 At last
Daniel came in before me, and I told him the
dream. (He was named Belteshazzar after my
god, and the spirit of the holy gods is in him.)

9 "I said to him, 'Belteshazzar, chief of the
magicians, I know that the spirit of the holy
gods is in you and that no mystery is too
great for you to solve. Now tell me what my
dream means.

10 " 'While I was lying in my bed, this is
what I dreamed. I saw a large tree in the
middle of the earth. 11 The tree grew very tall
and strong, reaching high into the heavens
for all the world to see. 12 It had fresh green
leaves, and it was loaded with fruit for all to
eat. Wild animals lived in its shade, and birds
nested in its branches. All the world was fed
from this tree.

13 " 'Then as I lay there dreaming, I saw a
messenger,* a holy one, coming down from
heaven. 14 The messenger shouted,

"Cut down the tree and lop off its
branches!
Shake off its leaves and scatter its fruit!
Chase the wild animals from its shade
and the birds from its branches.
15 But leave the stump and the roots in the
ground,
bound with a band of iron and bronze

4:1 Verses 4:1-3 are numbered 3:31-33 in Aramaic text.
4:4 Verses 4:4-37 are numbered 4:1-34 in Aramaic text.
4:7 Or *Chaldeans.* **4:13** Aramaic *a watcher;* also in 4:23.

perhaps an angel (Heb 1:14). **29:** The king's new decree is another example of dramatic parallel (cf. 2:5).

4:1–18 Nebuchadnezzar's Second Dream. God's sovereignty and human achievement (vv. 11, 20, 22, 30) are key themes in a chapter that highlights the struggle between divine and human greatness. The chapter is well structured: The king praises the Most High God, the king dreams, the dream is interpreted and fulfilled, and the king praises the Most High God. The conversion of the king does not appear in Babylonian court records, but the language used is general, merely a grandiose salutation with little religious significance. **4:** The palace description is in harmony with archaeological discoveries (cf. vv. 29–30). **10–15:** The enormous tree is a frequent theme in ancient literature (cf. Ezek 17; 31). The treetop touching the sky is reminiscent of Babel (Gen 11:1–9). **13, 17:** The language used of the *messenger* or "watchman," as some translations have it, is often used of angels (Job 5:1; 15:15). **15–16:** References to the strange illness, clinical lycanthropy (in which a person believes he is, or behaves like, an animal),

and surrounded by tender grass.
Now let him be drenched with the dew of
heaven,
and let him live with the wild animals
among the plants of the field.
16 For seven periods of time,
let him have the mind of a wild animal
instead of the mind of a human.
17 For this has been decreed by the
messengers*;
it is commanded by the holy ones,
so that everyone may know
that the Most High rules over the
kingdoms of the world.
He gives them to anyone he chooses—
even to the lowliest of people."

18 " 'Belteshazzar, that was the dream that
I, King Nebuchadnezzar, had. Now tell me
what it means, for none of the wise men of
my kingdom can do so. But you can tell me
because the spirit of the holy gods is in you.'

Daniel Explains the Dream

19 "Upon hearing this, Daniel (also known
as Belteshazzar) was overcome for a time,
frightened by the meaning of the dream. Then
the king said to him, 'Belteshazzar, don't be
alarmed by the dream and what it means.'

"Belteshazzar replied, 'I wish the events
foreshadowed in this dream would happen
to your enemies, my lord, and not to you!
20 The tree you saw was growing very tall and
strong, reaching high into the heavens for all
the world to see. 21 It had fresh green leaves
and was loaded with fruit for all to eat. Wild
animals lived in its shade, and birds nested in
its branches. 22 That tree, Your Majesty, is you.
For you have grown strong and great; your
greatness reaches up to heaven, and your rule
to the ends of the earth.

23 " 'Then you saw a messenger, a holy
one, coming down from heaven and saying,
"Cut down the tree and destroy it. But leave
the stump and the roots in the ground,
bound with a band of iron and bronze and
surrounded by tender grass. Let him be
drenched with the dew of heaven. Let him
live with the animals of the field for seven
periods of time."

24 " 'This is what the dream means, Your
Majesty, and what the Most High has
declared will happen to my lord the king.
25 You will be driven from human society,
and you will live in the fields with the wild
animals. You will eat grass like a cow, and
you will be drenched with the dew of heaven.
Seven periods of time will pass while you
live this way, until you learn that the Most
High rules over the kingdoms of the world
and gives them to anyone he chooses. 26 But
the stump and roots of the tree were left in
the ground. This means that you will receive
your kingdom back again when you have
learned that heaven rules.

27 " 'King Nebuchadnezzar, please accept
my advice. Stop sinning and do what is right.
Break from your wicked past and be merciful
to the poor. Perhaps then you will continue to
prosper.'

The Dream's Fulfillment

28 "But all these things did happen to King
Nebuchadnezzar. 29 Twelve months later he
was taking a walk on the flat roof of the royal
palace in Babylon. 30 As he looked out across
the city, he said, 'Look at this great city of
Babylon! By my own mighty power, I have
built this beautiful city as my royal residence
to display my majestic splendor.'

31 "While these words were still in his
mouth, a voice called down from heaven,
'O King Nebuchadnezzar, this message is for
you! You are no longer ruler of this kingdom.
32 You will be driven from human society. You
will live in the fields with the wild animals,
and you will eat grass like a cow. Seven
periods of time will pass while you live this
way, until you learn that the Most High rules
over the kingdoms of the world and gives
them to anyone he chooses.'

33 "That same hour the judgment was
fulfilled, and Nebuchadnezzar was driven
from human society. He ate grass like a cow,
and he was drenched with the dew of heaven.
He lived this way until his hair was as long as
eagles' feathers and his nails were like birds'
claws.

4:17 Aramaic *the watchers.*

occur in several later texts. **16, 25:** *Seven periods of time* is often interpreted as seven years, though it is perhaps better to see it as referring to an indefinite period of time (as in v. 26), where the duration of the period cannot be measured (cf. 7:25; 12:7).

4:19–37 Interpretation and Fulfillment. Nebuchadnezzar was terrified because he did not understand his dream; Daniel was terrified because he understood it only too well—it spoke of the end of an era. **33:** Nebuchadnezzar is *driven from human society*

Nebuchadnezzar Praises God

34 "After this time had passed, I,
Nebuchadnezzar, looked up to heaven. My
sanity returned, and I praised and worshiped
the Most High and honored the one who
lives forever.

His rule is everlasting,
and his kingdom is eternal.
35 All the people of the earth
are nothing compared to him.
He does as he pleases
among the angels of heaven
and among the people of the earth.
No one can stop him or say to him,
'What do you mean by doing these
things?'

36 "When my sanity returned to me, so
did my honor and glory and kingdom. My
advisers and nobles sought me out, and I was
restored as head of my kingdom, with even
greater honor than before.
37 "Now I, Nebuchadnezzar, praise and
glorify and honor the King of heaven. All
his acts are just and true, and he is able to
humble the proud."

The Writing on the Wall

5 Many years later King Belshazzar gave a
great feast for 1,000 of his nobles, and he
drank wine with them. 2 While Belshazzar
was drinking the wine, he gave orders to bring
in the gold and silver cups that his predecessor,*
Nebuchadnezzar, had taken from the Temple in
Jerusalem. He wanted to drink from them with
his nobles, his wives, and his concubines. 3 So they
brought these gold cups taken from the Temple,
the house of God in Jerusalem, and the king and
his nobles, his wives, and his concubines drank
from them. 4 While they drank from them they
praised their idols made of gold, silver, bronze,
iron, wood, and stone.
5 Suddenly, they saw the fingers of a human
hand writing on the plaster wall of the king's
palace, near the lampstand. The king himself saw
the hand as it wrote, 6 and his face turned pale
with fright. His knees knocked together in fear
and his legs gave way beneath him.
7 The king shouted for the enchanters, astrologers,* and fortune-tellers to be brought before him. He said to these wise men of Babylon,
"Whoever can read this writing and tell me what
it means will be dressed in purple robes of royal
honor and will have a gold chain placed around
his neck. He will become the third highest ruler
in the kingdom!"
8 But when all the king's wise men had come
in, none of them could read the writing or tell
him what it meant. 9 So the king grew even more
alarmed, and his face turned pale. His nobles, too,
were shaken.
10 But when the queen mother heard what was
happening, she hurried to the banquet hall. She
said to Belshazzar, "Long live the king! Don't be
so pale and frightened. 11 There is a man in your
kingdom who has within him the spirit of the
holy gods. During Nebuchadnezzar's reign, this
man was found to have insight, understanding,
and wisdom like that of the gods. Your predecessor, the king—your predecessor King Nebuchadnezzar—made him chief over all the magicians, enchanters, astrologers, and fortune-tellers
of Babylon. 12 This man Daniel, whom the king
named Belteshazzar, has exceptional ability and
is filled with divine knowledge and understanding. He can interpret dreams, explain riddles, and
solve difficult problems. Call for Daniel, and he
will tell you what the writing means."

5:2 Aramaic *father;* also in 5:11, 13, 18. **5:7** Or *Chaldeans;* also in 5:11.

---

and he eats *grass like a cow*, a huge contrast with the dignified Jewish vegetarians (chap. 1). **34–37:** Nebuchadnezzar is restored when he acknowledges God's universal sovereignty.

5:1–12 King Belshazzar's Vision. Given the grandeur of the Babylonian court—a large, if not always competent, staff, good food, gold images, orchestras, palaces, roof gardens—the reception room for one thousand guests is no surprise. Excavations have actually uncovered the huge palace throne room. Three of its walls were covered in white plaster, and the fourth had a design of blue enameled bricks. A magnificent setting for a magnificent party, comparable to that of Esther, but with women present (cf. Esth 1:9–12). The host, Belshazzar, dominates chapters 5—6; he was the oldest son of Nabonidus, the last Babylonian king. It would seem that, due to his father's many military exploits abroad, Belshazzar was a de facto ruler and therefore able to promise to make another *third highest ruler in the kingdom* (5:7, 16), after himself and Nabonidus. **5–9:** A spotlight focused on the plain white wall and "the palm of the hand which wrote" (5:5 lit.) there. The king was terrified and his advisers confused yet again. The almost photographic descriptions of royal emotions are a high point in the book. **10–12:** The queen mother's intervention resembles Pilate's wife's appearance (Matt 27:19).

Daniel Explains the Writing
[13] So Daniel was brought in before the king.
The king asked him, "Are you Daniel, one of
the exiles brought from Judah by my predecessor, King Nebuchadnezzar? [14] I have heard that
you have the spirit of the gods within you and
that you are filled with insight, understanding,
and wisdom. [15] My wise men and enchanters
have tried to read the words on the wall and
tell me their meaning, but they cannot do it. [16] I
am told that you can give interpretations and
solve difficult problems. If you can read these
words and tell me their meaning, you will be
clothed in purple robes of royal honor, and you
will have a gold chain placed around your neck.
You will become the third highest ruler in the
kingdom."
[17] Daniel answered the king, "Keep your gifts
or give them to someone else, but I will tell you
what the writing means. [18] Your Majesty, the
Most High God gave sovereignty, majesty, glory,
and honor to your predecessor, Nebuchadnezzar.
[19] He made him so great that people of all races
and nations and languages trembled before him in
fear. He killed those he wanted to kill and spared
those he wanted to spare. He honored those he
wanted to honor and disgraced those he wanted
to disgrace. [20] But when his heart and mind were
puffed up with arrogance, he was brought down
from his royal throne and stripped of his glory.
[21] He was driven from human society. He was
given the mind of a wild animal, and he lived
among the wild donkeys. He ate grass like a cow,
and he was drenched with the dew of heaven, until he learned that the Most High God rules over
the kingdoms of the world and appoints anyone
he desires to rule over them.
[22] "You are his successor,* O Belshazzar, and
you knew all this, yet you have not humbled
yourself. [23] For you have proudly defied the Lord
of heaven and have had these cups from his Temple brought before you. You and your nobles and
your wives and concubines have been drinking
wine from them while praising gods of silver,
gold, bronze, iron, wood, and stone—gods that
neither see nor hear nor know anything at all.
But you have not honored the God who gives
you the breath of life and controls your destiny!
[24] So God has sent this hand to write this message.
[25] "This is the message that was written:
MENE, MENE, TEKEL, and PARSIN. [26] This is what
these words mean:

Mene means 'numbered'—God has numbered
the days of your reign and has brought it
to an end.
[27] *Tekel* means 'weighed'—you have been
weighed on the balances and have not
measured up.
[28] *Parsin** means 'divided'—your kingdom has
been divided and given to the Medes and
Persians."

[29] Then at Belshazzar's command, Daniel was
dressed in purple robes, a gold chain was hung
around his neck, and he was proclaimed the third
highest ruler in the kingdom.
[30] That very night Belshazzar, the Babylonian* king, was killed.*
[31] *And Darius the Mede took over the kingdom at the age of sixty-two.

5:22 Aramaic *son.* **5:28** Aramaic *Peres,* the singular of *Parsin.* **5:30a** Or *Chaldean.* **5:30b** The Persians and Medes conquered Babylon in October 539 B.C. **5:31** Verse 5:31 is numbered 6:1 in Aramaic text.

5:13–31 Daniel's Explanation. Daniel's refusal of the promised gifts is similar to his refusal of luxury food. Faithful Jews did not need help from Gentiles (Esth 2:15). **18–24:** Just as in chapter 2, only God and his people can discern patterns of human history. Daniel's interpretation begins and ends with God: *God gave sovereignty, majesty . . . to Nebuchadnezzar* (v. 18); and *the God who gives you the breath of life . . . sent this hand* with a message (5:23–24). **25–28:** *Mene, Mene, Tekel, and Parsin* is literally "counted, counted, weighed, and divided." The concept of God weighing human actions is not uncommon (Job 31:6; 1 Sam 2:3). The scales show that, for all its apparent weight of glory, the Babylonian kingdom is weightless, a nothing in comparison with the truly weighty item, God's omnipotence (cf. 2 Cor 4:17).The details of dictators' methods and their tragic end have a contemporary ring. **31:** The party took place on the eve of the destruction of Babylon by the Medo-Persian army in 539 BC. Once again a historical detail confuses, for the leader of the invading army was Cyrus, not *Darius the Mede*. Possibly this is a reference to Darius I, the second successor to Cyrus as head of the Persian Empire.

There are different accounts of the fall of Babylon, and most agree about the basics. The ancient historian Xenophon, for example, reports that Cyrus and his troops diverted a stream to facilitate access to the city and that they entered it when the inhabitants were at an all-night drinking party. Belshazzar's end recalls Luke 12:16–21—fools are fools because they forget God (Ps 14:1), despise him (Dan 5:2), and do not repent as did Nebuchadnezzar (Dan 4:34–37).

Daniel in the Lions' Den

6 [1]*Darius the Mede decided to divide the
kingdom into 120 provinces, and he appointed a high officer to rule over each
province. [2]The king also chose Daniel and two
others as administrators to supervise the high
officers and protect the king's interests. [3]Daniel
soon proved himself more capable than all the
other administrators and high officers. Because
of Daniel's great ability, the king made plans to
place him over the entire empire.

[4]Then the other administrators and high officers began searching for some fault in the way
Daniel was handling government affairs, but they
couldn't find anything to criticize or condemn. He
was faithful, always responsible, and completely
trustworthy. [5]So they concluded, "Our only
chance of finding grounds for accusing Daniel will
be in connection with the rules of his religion."

[6]So the administrators and high officers went
to the king and said, "Long live King Darius!
[7]We are all in agreement—we administrators,
officials, high officers, advisers, and governors—
that the king should make a law that will be
strictly enforced. Give orders that for the next
thirty days any person who prays to anyone, divine or human—except to you, Your Majesty—
will be thrown into the den of lions. [8]And now,
Your Majesty, issue and sign this law so it cannot
be changed, an official law of the Medes and Persians that cannot be revoked." [9]So King Darius
signed the law.

[10]But when Daniel learned that the law had
been signed, he went home and knelt down as
usual in his upstairs room, with its windows
open toward Jerusalem. He prayed three times
a day, just as he had always done, giving thanks
to his God. [11]Then the officials went together to
Daniel's house and found him praying and asking for God's help. [12]So they went straight to the
king and reminded him about his law. "Did you
not sign a law that for the next thirty days any
person who prays to anyone, divine or human—
except to you, Your Majesty—will be thrown
into the den of lions?"

"Yes," the king replied, "that decision stands;
it is an official law of the Medes and Persians that
cannot be revoked."

[13]Then they told the king, "That man Daniel, one of the captives from Judah, is ignoring
you and your law. He still prays to his God three
times a day."

[14]Hearing this, the king was deeply troubled,
and he tried to think of a way to save Daniel. He
spent the rest of the day looking for a way to get
Daniel out of this predicament.

[15]In the evening the men went together to the
king and said, "Your Majesty, you know that according to the law of the Medes and the Persians,
no law that the king signs can be changed."

[16]So at last the king gave orders for Daniel to
be arrested and thrown into the den of lions. The
king said to him, "May your God, whom you
serve so faithfully, rescue you."

[17]A stone was brought and placed over the
mouth of the den. The king sealed the stone with
his own royal seal and the seals of his nobles,
so that no one could rescue Daniel. [18]Then the
king returned to his palace and spent the night
fasting. He refused his usual entertainment and
couldn't sleep at all that night.

[19]Very early the next morning, the king got

6:1 Verses 6:1-28 are numbered 6:2-29 in Aramaic text.

6:1–28 Daniel Survives the Den of Lions. Even under Darius, governor of the Medo-Persians, Daniel, now about eighty years old, remains at the top, as his *great ability* and *prospering* show. Several paired ideas give the theme for the chapter: the hope of and reality of God's rescue; the king's distress and subsequent joy; the decree of death for those who will not worship the king and then for those who will not worship Daniel's God—the dramatic inversions seem unending. **1–12:** The Medo-Persian Empire stretched from Libya, Egypt, and Turkey to the Indus River. It was ably administered, mainly by satraps, local governors; however, in chapter 3 (and in Esth 1:19; 8:8), the Persian bureaucracy ironically traps itself in its efficiency: The weak king is caught in the net of his unchangeable laws and lying lawyers. The contrast between a corrupt bureaucracy killing even its own people and Daniel's *faithful*[ness] and *trustworthy*[ness] is marked. **7:** The claim that the officials are *all in agreement* did not include Daniel, officially one of them. **10:** Daniel's *windows open toward Jerusalem* recalls the prayerful hope of Solomon (1 Kgs 8:41–43) and the tearful lament of exiles (Ps 137:4–6). His threefold praying recalls Psalm 55:17. **13:** The lying malice of the conspirators is evident in their description of the distinguished national figure as merely *one of the captives from Judah*. Similar disrespect for religious freedom, private and public, is common today, and the resulting conflicts of loyalty (Acts 5:29) bring intense suffering. **16–18:** The lions' den was not a modern-style cage but probably a deep pit, open cistern (Gen 37:24; Jer 38:6), or perhaps a long tunnel. The king's sleepless night recalls Xerxes' sleepless night before another miraculous intervention by God (Esth 6:1; cf. Ps 121:4). **19–23:** The episode suggests parallels between Daniel and Jesus

up and hurried out to the lions' den. 20 When
he got there, he called out in anguish, "Daniel,
servant of the living God! Was your God, whom
you serve so faithfully, able to rescue you from
the lions?"
21 Daniel answered, "Long live the king! 22 My
God sent his angel to shut the lions' mouths so
that they would not hurt me, for I have been
found innocent in his sight. And I have not
wronged you, Your Majesty."
23 The king was overjoyed and ordered that
Daniel be lifted from the den. Not a scratch was
found on him, for he had trusted in his God.
24 Then the king gave orders to arrest the men
who had maliciously accused Daniel. He had
them thrown into the lions' den, along with their
wives and children. The lions leaped on them and
tore them apart before they even hit the floor of
the den.
25 Then King Darius sent this message to the
people of every race and nation and language
throughout the world:

"Peace and prosperity to you!
26 "I decree that everyone throughout my
kingdom should tremble with fear before the
God of Daniel.

For he is the living God,
and he will endure forever.
His kingdom will never be destroyed,
and his rule will never end.
27 He rescues and saves his people;
he performs miraculous signs and
wonders
in the heavens and on earth.
He has rescued Daniel
from the power of the lions."

28 So Daniel prospered during the reign of
Darius and the reign of Cyrus the Persian.*

Daniel's Vision of Four Beasts

7 Earlier, during the first year of King Belshazzar's reign in Babylon,* Daniel had a
dream and saw visions as he lay in his bed.
He wrote down the dream, and this is what he
saw.
2 In my vision that night, I, Daniel, saw a
great storm churning the surface of a great sea,
with strong winds blowing from every direction.
3 Then four huge beasts came up out of the water,
each different from the others.
4 The first beast was like a lion with eagles'
wings. As I watched, its wings were pulled off,
and it was left standing with its two hind feet on

6:28 Or *of Darius, that is, the reign of Cyrus the Persian.*
7:1 The first year of Belshazzar's reign (who was co-regent with his father, Nabonidus) was 556 B.C. (or perhaps as late as 553 B.C.).

Christ, an innocent who also was trapped, interrogated, arrested (after prayer), condemned to a cruel death, buried in a sealed tomb—and miraculously delivered. Several reasons combined to guarantee Daniel's deliverance: God sent his angel and shut the lions' mouths (cf. Heb 11:33), and Daniel was *innocent in* [God's] *sight.* He had not wronged the king and he trusted God. This interweaving of God's sovereignty and human responsibility is a recurring biblical theme. **25–27:** Darius's doxology reminds us that throughout the Old Testament the chief function of miracles is to draw unbelievers to the God of Israel, with a view to their worshiping him (Exod 7:5; 8:10; 9:20; Josh 4:24; 1 Kgs 18:37; cf. John 9:1–4; 11:14–15).

7:1—12:3 Daniel Also Dreams in Babylon

7:1–28 The Vision of Four Beasts. Now Daniel *lay in his bed,* dreaming disturbing dreams—but while Nebuchadnezzar had broadcast his, Daniel kept the dream to himself (v. 28). Nebuchadnezzar needed an interpreter; Daniel's interpreter was on site. (Aramaic—an international language to deal with international questions—is used until v. 28, and there are clear parallels with chap. 2.) The content and symmetry of this chapter may be summarized:

human history judged—only some survive (vv. 2–12)
the goal of human history—"one like a son of man" rules (vv. 13–14)
human history judged—only the saints survive (vv. 15–25)
the end of human history—"the Most High" rules (vv. 26–27)

2: The *strong winds* contrast with the manufactured statue from chapter 2. The winds symbolize God's worldwide power, and the great sea symbolizes God's created world (Gen 1:6–7). As winds, sent by God, whip up the sea, so God stirs up human kingdoms (Dan 7:17; Isa 27:1; 51:9). **4–8:** The mysterious animals *like a lion . . . a bear . . . a leopard* and the horn with humanlike eyes recall the four-faced man, lion, ox, and eagle of Ezekiel 1:4–21. Both men lived in Babylon, and archaeological excavations reveal that Babylonians used such creatures as part of their decor. Because Daniel studied Babylonian sciences and culture and spent about sixty years of his

the ground, like a human being. And it was given
a human mind.
5 Then I saw a second beast, and it looked like
a bear. It was rearing up on one side, and it had
three ribs in its mouth between its teeth. And I
heard a voice saying to it, "Get up! Devour the
flesh of many people!"
6 Then the third of these strange beasts appeared, and it looked like a leopard. It had four
bird's wings on its back, and it had four heads.
Great authority was given to this beast.
7 Then in my vision that night, I saw a fourth
beast—terrifying, dreadful, and very strong. It
devoured and crushed its victims with huge iron
teeth and trampled their remains beneath its feet.
It was different from any of the other beasts, and
it had ten horns.
8 As I was looking at the horns, suddenly another small horn appeared among them. Three of
the first horns were torn out by the roots to make
room for it. This little horn had eyes like human
eyes and a mouth that was boasting arrogantly.

9 I watched as thrones were put in place
   and the Ancient One* sat down to judge.
His clothing was as white as snow,
   his hair like purest wool.
He sat on a fiery throne
   with wheels of blazing fire,
10 and a river of fire was pouring out,
   flowing from his presence.
Millions of angels ministered to him;
   many millions stood to attend him.
Then the court began its session,
   and the books were opened.

11 I continued to watch because I could hear
the little horn's boastful speech. I kept watching
until the fourth beast was killed and its body was
destroyed by fire. 12 The other three beasts had
their authority taken from them, but they were
allowed to live a while longer.*
13 As my vision continued that night, I saw
someone like a son of man* coming with the
clouds of heaven. He approached the Ancient
One and was led into his presence. 14 He was giv-
en authority, honor, and sovereignty over all the
nations of the world, so that people of every race
and nation and language would obey him. His
rule is eternal—it will never end. His kingdom
will never be destroyed.

The Vision Is Explained

15 I, Daniel, was troubled by all I had seen, and my
visions terrified me. 16 So I approached one of those
standing beside the throne and asked him what it
all meant. He explained it to me like this: 17 "These
four huge beasts represent four kingdoms that
will arise from the earth. 18 But in the end, the
holy people of the Most High will be given the
kingdom, and they will rule forever and ever."
19 Then I wanted to know the true meaning of

7:9 Aramaic *an Ancient of Days;* also in 7:13, 22.
7:12 Aramaic *for a season and a time.* **7:13** Or *like a Son of Man.*

---

life in Babylon, it is not surprising that God spoke through familiar things, in a cultural form that he understood. It is tempting to try to ascertain the precise relationship between different animals and different kingdoms, but it is not always possible or even helpful to do so. And it is easy to miss seeing the whole picture while wading through piles of wings, ribs, teeth, horns, and numbers. The key idea is that each animal is powerful, distinct, unique. The important thing is not that the first one is *like a lion* representing Babylon, but that it is stripped of its wings, unable to fly, powerless. The second animal is insatiable, *like a bear*; the third, *like a leopard* with four heads and four wings suggests many leaders and speed of movement. The fourth is terrifying in its cruelty. Different kingdoms mean different styles. **7–12:** The continuous rise and fall of empires that constitutes human history stops only when the last and most terrifying beast of all appears with iron teeth and the destructive possibilities implicit in ten horns. Then the *little horn*, probably a reference to a specific ruler (or on another level, the Antichrist [Rev 13:5–6]), with human eyes and boastful lips, will contend against God's people and even defeat them for a while. As in Revelation 5:1–5, the frightening clarity of his vision caused Daniel great sadness. **9–14:** After the cruel chaos of human history comes a vision of final judgment. Exodus 32:33, Isaiah 65:6, and Revelation 20:12 also refer to the *books*, God's file on human behavior. In this scene of majesty, purity, judgment, and power, the last, terrifying beast is consumed by fire, while others survive only *a while longer*. So human kingdoms end—and God's begins. **13–14:** *Son of man* often means an ordinary human being (Ps 8:4) or a prophet (Ezek 39:1). So when Jesus used this name of himself (Matt 25:31–32; 26:63–65), it may refer to Jesus' humanity. God, the *Ancient One*, grants to the one who comes *with the clouds of heaven* (Rev 1:7), all *authority, honor, and sovereignty* (cf. Matt 28:18–20). It is possible to see a fulfillment of Genesis 1:26, the perfect Son of Man exercising perfect dominion over all creation. **18:** *The holy people* are God's people of all ages and places, and their suffering is more than persecution. **19–25:** While this

the fourth beast, the one so different from the
others and so terrifying. It had devoured and
crushed its victims with iron teeth and bronze
claws, trampling their remains beneath its feet.
[20]I also asked about the ten horns on the fourth
beast's head and the little horn that came up afterward and destroyed three of the other horns.
This horn had seemed greater than the others,
and it had human eyes and a mouth that was
boasting arrogantly. [21]As I watched, this horn
was waging war against God's holy people and
was defeating them, [22]until the Ancient One—
the Most High—came and judged in favor of his
holy people. Then the time arrived for the holy
people to take over the kingdom.

[23]Then he said to me, "This fourth beast is the
fourth world power that will rule the earth. It will
be different from all the others. It will devour the
whole world, trampling and crushing everything
in its path. [24]Its ten horns are ten kings who will
rule that empire. Then another king will arise,
different from the other ten, who will subdue
three of them. [25]He will defy the Most High and
oppress the holy people of the Most High. He
will try to change their sacred festivals and laws,
and they will be placed under his control for a
time, times, and half a time.

[26]"But then the court will pass judgment, and
all his power will be taken away and completely
destroyed. [27]Then the sovereignty, power, and
greatness of all the kingdoms under heaven will
be given to the holy people of the Most High.
His kingdom will last forever, and all rulers will
serve and obey him."

[28]That was the end of the vision. I, Daniel,
was terrified by my thoughts and my face was
pale with fear, but I kept these things to myself.

Daniel's Vision of a Ram and Goat

8 [1]*During the third year of King Belshazzar's reign, I, Daniel, saw another vision,
following the one that had already appeared to me. [2]In this vision I was at the fortress
of Susa, in the province of Elam, standing beside
the Ulai River.*

[3]As I looked up, I saw a ram with two long
horns standing beside the river.* One of the
horns was longer than the other, even though it
had grown later than the other one. [4]The ram
butted everything out of his way to the west,
to the north, and to the south, and no one could
stand against him or help his victims. He did as
he pleased and became very great.

[5]While I was watching, suddenly a male goat
appeared from the west, crossing the land so
swiftly that he didn't even touch the ground. This
goat, which had one very large horn between its
eyes, [6]headed toward the two-horned ram that
I had seen standing beside the river, rushing at
him in a rage. [7]The goat charged furiously at the
ram and struck him, breaking off both his horns.
Now the ram was helpless, and the goat knocked
him down and trampled him. No one could rescue the ram from the goat's power.

[8]The goat became very powerful. But at the
height of his power, his large horn was broken
off. In the large horn's place grew four prominent horns pointing in the four directions of the
earth. [9]Then from one of the prominent horns
came a small horn whose power grew very great.
It extended toward the south and the east and

8:1 The original text from this point through chapter 12 is in Hebrew. See note at 2:4. **8:2** Or *the Ulai Gate;* also in 8:16. **8:3** Or *the gate;* also in 8:6.

tribulation can be interpreted as an apocalyptic attack from the Antichrist, it can also refer to a historic ruler who attempted to force the Jews to abandon their faith, a blasphemous tyrant whose goal is to *change . . . sacred festivals and laws*, or the calendar of Jewish holy days, and the moral teaching of the law of Moses. As for the *time, times and half a time*, "time" could be "year," suggesting the three-and-a-half-year persecution of Antiochus IV Epiphanes (see annotation on 8:2), but it can also be understood as a chronologically indefinite period.

8:1–14 Vision of a Ram and a Goat. The date given is approximately 544 BC, two years after chapter 7 and about seven years after the fall of Babylon. This chapter, written in Hebrew (Jewish language to deal with Jewish interests), differs from preceding ones in its precision about geographic location, the angel's name, and the names of the kingdoms. **2:** *I was at . . . Susa . . . beside the Ulai River* may suggest that Daniel did not live and work in Susa, Babylon's capital. Josephus registered how Daniel built himself "a tower at Ecbatana, in Media." Commenting on Daniel 8, the same writer concluded: "Indeed it so came to pass, that our nation suffered these things under Antiochus Epiphanes, according to Daniel's vision. . . . In the same manner Daniel also wrote concerning the Roman government, and that our country should be made desolate by them" (Josephus, *Antiquities of the Jews* 10.11.7). **3–25:** Historical detail is spelled out clearly: After the rapid advance of the ram (Persia, a kingdom whose mascot was a ram) comes the goat (Greece in general, v. 21), then the *large horn* of Alexander the Great, on whose sudden death the empire was divided among four generals (v. 22). **9–11:** The *small horn* (the "fierce king," v. 23), dominates,

toward the glorious land of Israel. 10 Its power
reached to the heavens, where it attacked the
heavenly army, throwing some of the heavenly
beings and some of the stars to the ground and
trampling them. 11 It even challenged the Commander of heaven's army by canceling the daily
sacrifices offered to him and by destroying his
Temple. 12 The army of heaven was restrained
from responding to this rebellion. So the daily
sacrifice was halted, and truth was overthrown.
The horn succeeded in everything it did.*

13 Then I heard two holy ones talking to each
other. One of them asked, "How long will the
events of this vision last? How long will the rebellion that causes desecration stop the daily sacrifices? How long will the Temple and heaven's
army be trampled on?"

14 The other replied, "It will take 2,300 evenings and mornings; then the Temple will be
made right again."

Gabriel Explains the Vision

15 As I, Daniel, was trying to understand the
meaning of this vision, someone who looked like
a man stood in front of me. 16 And I heard a human voice calling out from the Ulai River, "Gabriel, tell this man the meaning of his vision."

17 As Gabriel approached the place where I was
standing, I became so terrified that I fell with my
face to the ground. "Son of man," he said, "you
must understand that the events you have seen
in your vision relate to the time of the end."

18 While he was speaking, I fainted and lay
there with my face to the ground. But Gabriel
roused me with a touch and helped me to my
feet.

19 Then he said, "I am here to tell you what
will happen later in the time of wrath. What
you have seen pertains to the very end of time.
20 The two-horned ram represents the kings of
Media and Persia. 21 The shaggy male goat represents the king of Greece,* and the large horn
between his eyes represents the first king of the
Greek Empire. 22 The four prominent horns that
replaced the one large horn show that the Greek
Empire will break into four kingdoms, but none
as great as the first.

23 "At the end of their rule, when their sin
is at its height, a fierce king, a master of intrigue, will rise to power. 24 He will become very
strong, but not by his own power. He will cause
a shocking amount of destruction and succeed
in everything he does. He will destroy powerful leaders and devastate the holy people. 25 He
will be a master of deception and will become
arrogant; he will destroy many without warning. He will even take on the Prince of princes
in battle, but he will be broken, though not by
human power.

26 "This vision about the 2,300 evenings and
mornings* is true. But none of these things will
happen for a long time, so keep this vision a secret."

27 Then I, Daniel, was overcome and lay
sick for several days. Afterward I got up and
performed my duties for the king, but I was
greatly troubled by the vision and could not
understand it.

8:11-12 The meaning of the Hebrew for these verses is uncertain. **8:21** Hebrew *of Javan.* **8:26** Hebrew *about the evenings and mornings;* compare 8:14.

conquering all and extending his reach to the *glorious land of Israel* (cf. Jer 3:19), even reaching the heavens. The picture is of great arrogance (cf. Babel; Isa 14:12–15), of contempt even for the *Commander of heaven's army,* and of short-lived glory. **10–12, 24–25:** The emphasis falls on what the *small horn,* Antiochus IV, did: desecrating the Temple, taking away the burnt offering, overthrowing truth, and succeeding everywhere. The Temple was desecrated and destroyed on December 25, 167 BC. In the parallel verses 24–25, the emphasis falls on what happened to the small horn eventually: He became strong, succeeded in what he did, destroyed the powerful and the holy people, considered himself superior, but will eventually be destroyed, *though not by human power.* **14, 19, 26:** The timing for these dramatic events is indicated: *2,300 evenings and mornings* (v. 14); at *the very end of time* (v. 19); and not *for a long time* (v. 26). Many interpreters date this starting from Antiochus's campaign against Judah, which began in 171 BC, and ending with Judas Maccabeus's reconsecration of the Temple on December 25, 165 BC. This period is six years, three months, and twenty days, that is, twenty-three hundred days. Others understand mornings and evenings as years.

8:15–27 Gabriel's Explanation. The angel Gabriel interpreted this vision, warned about a delay in its fulfillment, and ordered Daniel to seal it (v. 26; contrast 12:4). **27:** Daniel's fear at what he saw was followed by a loss of consciousness (cf. 10:9; Rev 1:17) and by emotional exhaustion. The stress came from Daniel's vision of God's wrath, visible when proud nations rise meteorically and then crash, when God's sinful people bring disaster on themselves. Our world too is often beyond understanding, and contemplation of coming, deserved wrath is a sure recipe for stress unless, like Daniel, we can see beyond to the final, certain victory of God's people.

Daniel's Prayer for His People

9 It was the first year of the reign of Darius the Mede, the son of Ahasuerus, who became king of the Babylonians.* 2 During the first year of his reign, I, Daniel, learned from reading the word of the LORD, as revealed to Jeremiah the prophet, that Jerusalem must lie desolate for seventy years.* 3 So I turned to the Lord God and pleaded with him in prayer and fasting. I also wore rough burlap and sprinkled myself with ashes.

4 I prayed to the LORD my God and confessed:

"O Lord, you are a great and awesome God!
You always fulfill your covenant and keep
your promises of unfailing love to those who
love you and obey your commands. 5 But we
have sinned and done wrong. We have rebelled
against you and scorned your commands
and regulations. 6 We have refused to listen
to your servants the prophets, who spoke on
your authority to our kings and princes and
ancestors and to all the people of the land.

7 "Lord, you are in the right; but as you
see, our faces are covered with shame. This is
true of all of us, including the people of Judah
and Jerusalem and all Israel, scattered near
and far, wherever you have driven us because
of our disloyalty to you. 8 O LORD, we and
our kings, princes, and ancestors are covered
with shame because we have sinned against
you. 9 But the Lord our God is merciful and
forgiving, even though we have rebelled
against him. 10 We have not obeyed the
LORD our God, for we have not followed the
instructions he gave us through his servants
the prophets. 11 All Israel has disobeyed your
instruction and turned away, refusing to
listen to your voice.

"So now the solemn curses and judgments
written in the Law of Moses, the servant of
God, have been poured down on us because of
our sin. 12 You have kept your word and done
to us and our rulers exactly as you warned.
Never has there been such a disaster as
happened in Jerusalem. 13 Every curse written
against us in the Law of Moses has come true.
Yet we have refused to seek mercy from the
LORD our God by turning from our sins and
recognizing his truth. 14 Therefore, the LORD
has brought upon us the disaster he prepared.
The LORD our God was right to do all of these
things, for we did not obey him.

15 "O Lord our God, you brought lasting
honor to your name by rescuing your people
from Egypt in a great display of power. But
we have sinned and are full of wickedness.
16 In view of all your faithful mercies, Lord,
please turn your furious anger away from
your city Jerusalem, your holy mountain. All
the neighboring nations mock Jerusalem and
your people because of our sins and the sins
of our ancestors.

9:1 Or *the Chaldeans.* **9:2** See Jer 25:11-12; 29:10.

9:1–19 Daniel's Prayer. The date given is approximately 539 BC, and this chapter balances the preceding one. In chapter 8 a vision and an angel disclose the truth about the future. In chapter 9 the inspired Scriptures have already disclosed the truth about the future. In our generation, fascinated by dreams, visions, and futurology, it is necessary to give due importance to the written truth of God. The chapter structure carries a message, with the arithmetical references (seventy years, seventy sevens, seven sevens, sixty-two sevens) framing the long prayer and confession. It is possible to devote too much time and effort to counting up numbers and not enough to understanding the principles of divine judgment that the God of Israel—glorious, righteous, merciful and powerful—and the sin of Israel—blatant rebellion against God's law—cannot enjoy peaceful coexistence. **2–3:** Daniel began to study the prophetic Scriptures, an indication of their already recognized authority and status. Daniel found the reference to seventy years, calculated the sums, and realizing that the period was ending, turned to prayer, fasting, and reflection on the meaning of Scriptures for his generation (cf. Ezra 9:6–15; Neh 1:5–11; 9:6–37). **12–13:** Though the covenant-keeping God is a God of mercy in spite of sin, the holy God is a God of judgment and his judgments will be carried out. **15–19:** Instead of approaching God with a shopping list of requests, Daniel approaches him with another list:

your name . . . your people
your faithful mercies . . . your furious anger
your city . . . your holy mountain
your servant . . . your own sake . . . your desolate sanctuary
your eyes . . .

Daniel bases his requests entirely on God's own character and relationships, and God will respond to this (v. 23). **15–16:** Daniel invites God to repeat that unparalleled intervention in his people's history that was the Exodus from Egypt.

17 "O our God, hear your servant's prayer!
Listen as I plead. For your own sake, Lord,
smile again on your desolate sanctuary.
18 "O my God, lean down and listen to me.
Open your eyes and see our despair. See how
your city—the city that bears your name—
lies in ruins. We make this plea, not because
we deserve help, but because of your mercy.
19 "O Lord, hear. O Lord, forgive. O Lord,
listen and act! For your own sake, do not
delay, O my God, for your people and your
city bear your name."

Gabriel's Message about the Anointed One

20 I went on praying and confessing my sin and
the sin of my people, pleading with the LORD my
God for Jerusalem, his holy mountain. 21 As I was
praying, Gabriel, whom I had seen in the earlier
vision, came swiftly to me at the time of the evening sacrifice. 22 He explained to me, "Daniel, I
have come here to give you insight and understanding. 23 The moment you began praying, a
command was given. And now I am here to tell
you what it was, for you are very precious to
God. Listen carefully so that you can understand
the meaning of your vision.
24 "A period of seventy sets of seven* has
been decreed for your people and your holy city
to finish their rebellion, to put an end to their
sin, to atone for their guilt, to bring in everlasting righteousness, to confirm the prophetic vision, and to anoint the Most Holy Place.* 25 Now
listen and understand! Seven sets of seven plus
sixty-two sets of seven* will pass from the time
the command is given to rebuild Jerusalem until
a ruler—the Anointed One*—comes. Jerusalem
will be rebuilt with streets and strong defenses,*
despite the perilous times.
26 "After this period of sixty-two sets of sev-
en,* the Anointed One will be killed, appearing
to have accomplished nothing, and a ruler will
arise whose armies will destroy the city and the
Temple. The end will come with a flood, and war
and its miseries are decreed from that time to the
very end. 27 The ruler will make a treaty with the
people for a period of one set of seven,* but after
half this time, he will put an end to the sacrifices
and offerings. And as a climax to all his terrible
deeds,* he will set up a sacrilegious object that
causes desecration,* until the fate decreed for
this defiler is finally poured out on him."

Daniel's Vision of a Messenger

10 In the third year of the reign of King
Cyrus of Persia,* Daniel (also known
as Belteshazzar) had another vision.
He understood that the vision concerned events
certain to happen in the future—times of war
and great hardship.
2 When this vision came to me, I, Daniel, had

9:24a Hebrew *seventy sevens.* **9:24b** Or *the Most Holy One.* **9:25a** Hebrew *Seven sevens plus sixty-two sevens.* **9:25b** Or *an anointed one;* similarly in 9:26. Hebrew reads *a messiah.* **9:25c** Or *and a moat,* or *and trenches.* **9:26** Hebrew *After sixty-two sevens.* **9:27a** Hebrew *for one seven.* **9:27b** Hebrew *And on the wing of abominations;* the meaning of the Hebrew is uncertain. **9:27c** Hebrew *an abomination of desolation.* **10:1** The third year of Cyrus's reign was 536 B.C.

9:20–27 Gabriel's Message. 22–23: The words describing Gabriel's task stress that religious experience, even the ministry of angels, has an objective content that enables us to discern between truth and error. **24–27:** Jeremiah 25:8–10 (cf. Dan 9:2) gives precise details of the invasion to be headed up by Nebuchadnezzar and promises that the resulting servitude and exile will last seventy years. Then Babylon will be enslaved, and thus the Exile will end. But Daniel complicates the mathematics: (7 x 7) + (62 x 7) = 483, then we must add another 7, making a grand total of 490—Jeremiah's 70 has become 70 x 7 = 490. It is easy to get bogged down. Some say the arithmetic adds up to the date of the coming of Jesus, then to his death (9:26). This was followed, not long after, by the destruction of Jerusalem by invading Roman armies. Others note the change of tone in 9:26, where the Anointed One gives way to a different ruler, and they suggest an accompanying time interval. Many scholars again see this numbering of time as referring to the oppression by Antiochus IV. **26–27:** After the sixty-two sevens, which followed the seven sevens, comes a complete change. A further destructive ruler will be followed by *the end* and *the very end.* **27:** In his teaching about the end of all things, Jesus recalled the "sacrilegious object" that Daniel spoke about (Matt 24:15) and taught that it will immediately precede his second coming (Matt 24:3–35). On that basis the decreed end refers to the final, inglorious end of the enemy of God and of his people.

10:1—11:1 A Man Promises to Fight Princes. At this date (ca. 536 BC), some exiles had returned to Jerusalem with Zerubbabel (Ezra 1—2), but Daniel had continued to live in Babylon, his adopted home. Daniel's vision about a war dominates the beginning and end of this section, but as in chapter 9 the main thrust of the chapter is something else, this time not prayer but a glorious man who strengthens Daniel for the war to come. **2–3:** As at the beginning of his exile, Daniel fasts. Passover was celebrated on the

been in mourning for three whole weeks. 3 All
that time I had eaten no rich food. No meat or
wine crossed my lips, and I used no fragrant lotions until those three weeks had passed.
4 On April 23,* as I was standing on the bank
of the great Tigris River, 5 I looked up and saw a
man dressed in linen clothing, with a belt of pure
gold around his waist. 6 His body looked like a
precious gem. His face flashed like lightning, and
his eyes flamed like torches. His arms and feet
shone like polished bronze, and his voice roared
like a vast multitude of people.
7 Only I, Daniel, saw this vision. The men with
me saw nothing, but they were suddenly terrified and ran away to hide. 8 So I was left there
all alone to see this amazing vision. My strength
left me, my face grew deathly pale, and I felt very
weak. 9 Then I heard the man speak, and when I
heard the sound of his voice, I fainted and lay
there with my face to the ground.
10 Just then a hand touched me and lifted me,
still trembling, to my hands and knees. 11 And
the man said to me, "Daniel, you are very precious to God, so listen carefully to what I have
to say to you. Stand up, for I have been sent to
you." When he said this to me, I stood up, still
trembling.
12 Then he said, "Don't be afraid, Daniel. Since
the first day you began to pray for understanding
and to humble yourself before your God, your
request has been heard in heaven. I have come
in answer to your prayer. 13 But for twenty-one
days the spirit prince* of the kingdom of Persia
blocked my way. Then Michael, one of the archangels,* came to help me, and I left him there
with the spirit prince of the kingdom of Persia.*
14 Now I am here to explain what will happen to
your people in the future, for this vision concerns a time yet to come."
15 While he was speaking to me, I looked down
at the ground, unable to say a word. 16 Then the
one who looked like a man* touched my lips, and
I opened my mouth and began to speak. I said to
the one standing in front of me, "I am filled with
anguish because of the vision I have seen, my
lord, and I am very weak. 17 How can someone
like me, your servant, talk to you, my lord? My
strength is gone, and I can hardly breathe."
18 Then the one who looked like a man
touched me again, and I felt my strength returning. 19 "Don't be afraid," he said, "for you are
very precious to God. Peace! Be encouraged! Be
strong!"

As he spoke these words to me, I suddenly
felt stronger and said to him, "Please speak to
me, my lord, for you have strengthened me."
20 He replied, "Do you know why I have
come? Soon I must return to fight against the
spirit prince of the kingdom of Persia, and after
that the spirit prince of the kingdom of Greece*
will come. 21 Meanwhile, I will tell you what is
written in the Book of Truth. (No one helps me
against these spirit princes except Michael, your
spirit prince.* 11:1 I have been standing beside Michael* to support and strengthen him since the
first year of the reign of Darius the Mede.)

Kings of the South and North

11 2 "Now then, I will reveal the truth to
you. Three more Persian kings will
reign, to be succeeded by a fourth, far
richer than the others. He will use his wealth to

10:4 Hebrew *On the twenty-fourth day of the first month,* of the ancient Hebrew lunar calendar. This date in the book of Daniel can be cross-checked with dates in surviving Persian records and can be related accurately to our modern calendar. This event occurred on April 23, 536 B.C. **10:13a** Hebrew *the prince;* also in 10:13c, 20. **10:13b** Hebrew *the chief princes.* **10:13c** As in one Greek version; Hebrew reads *and I was left there with the kings of Persia.* The meaning of the Hebrew is uncertain. **10:16** As in most manuscripts of the Masoretic Text; one manuscript of the Masoretic Text and one Greek version read *Then something that looked like a human hand.* **10:20** Hebrew *of Javan.* **10:21** Hebrew *against these except Michael, your prince.* **11:1** Hebrew *him.*

fourteenth day of the first month, and the Festival of Unleavened Bread from the fifteenth through the twenty-first, so the vision of the great Deliverer was particularly appropriate for the time of year. Daniel's sadness may be related to his dismay that more Jews did not return to Jerusalem to rebuild the Temple and receive the blessings God had for them there. **4–9:** The location and content of the vision recall Ezekiel 1:1–28, and the description recurs in Revelation 1:12–16. Both texts record prostration before the glorious Son of Man (Rev 1:17). As with Daniel, Saul (Acts 9:7) fell to the ground, speechless, though his companions saw nothing. Daniel's companions fled.

10:19—11:1: The human touch and the assurance of God's love was just the encouragement Daniel needed to cope with the strange message of delay stemming from a spiritual battle (Eph 6:12; Rev 12:7) between spiritual beings: the demonic representatives of Persia and Greece and God's own representative, Michael. God will not stand on the sidelines forever. When his people are threatened he will enter the fray and engage in battle. Although much contemporary teaching on territorial spirits focuses on this section of Daniel, it is impossible to infer the existence of hierarchies of demons ruling over distinct geographical areas from this text. **10:21:** Unlike chapters 7 and 9,

stir up everyone to fight against the kingdom of Greece.*

3 “Then a mighty king will rise to power who will rule with great authority and accomplish everything he sets out to do. 4 But at the height of his power, his kingdom will be broken apart and divided into four parts. It will not be ruled by the king’s descendants, nor will the kingdom hold the authority it once had. For his empire will be uprooted and given to others.

5 “The king of the south will increase in power, but one of his own officials will become more powerful than he and will rule his kingdom with great strength.

6 “Some years later an alliance will be formed between the king of the north and the king of the south. The daughter of the king of the south will be given in marriage to the king of the north to secure the alliance, but she will lose her influence over him, and so will her father. She will be abandoned along with her supporters. 7 But when one of her relatives* becomes king of the south, he will raise an army and enter the fortress of the king of the north and defeat him. 8 When he returns to Egypt, he will carry back their idols with him, along with priceless articles of gold and silver. For some years afterward he will leave the king of the north alone.

9 “Later the king of the north will invade the realm of the king of the south but will soon return to his own land. 10 However, the sons of the king of the north will assemble a mighty army that will advance like a flood and carry the battle as far as the enemy’s fortress.

11 “Then, in a rage, the king of the south will rally against the vast forces assembled by the king of the north and will defeat them. 12 After the enemy army is swept away, the king of the south will be filled with pride and will execute many thousands of his enemies. But his success will be short lived.

13 “A few years later the king of the north will return with a fully equipped army far greater than before. 14 At that time there will be a general uprising against the king of the south. Violent men among your own people will join them in fulfillment of this vision, but they will not succeed. 15 Then the king of the north will come and lay siege to a fortified city and capture it. The best troops of the south will not be able to stand in the face of the onslaught.

16 “The king of the north will march onward unopposed; none will be able to stop him. He will pause in the glorious land of Israel,* intent on destroying it. 17 He will make plans to come with the might of his entire kingdom and will form an alliance with the king of the south. He will give him a daughter in marriage in order to overthrow the kingdom from within, but his plan will fail.

18 “After this, he will turn his attention to the coastland and conquer many cities. But a commander from another land will put an end to his insolence and cause him to retreat in shame. 19 He will take refuge in his own fortresses but will stumble and fall and be seen no more.

20 “His successor will send out a tax collector to maintain the royal splendor. But after a very brief reign, he will die, though not from anger or in battle.

21 “The next to come to power will be a despicable man who is not in line for royal succession. He will slip in when least expected and take over the kingdom by flattery and intrigue. 22 Before him great armies will be swept away, including a covenant prince. 23 With deceitful

11:2 Hebrew *of Javan.* **11:7** Hebrew *a branch from her roots.* **11:16** Hebrew *the glorious land.*

---

this chapter ends before we are told the final score, but not before we are reminded again of the Book of Truth (Exod 32:32).

11:2—12:3 Kings Go to War. 11:2–4: The three kings who succeeded Cyrus on the Persian throne were Cambyses, Smerdis, and Darius Hystaspis. The very rich fourth king was Xerxes, followed by the all-conquering Alexander the Great (336–323 BC), his sudden death, and the subsequent carving up of the empire into four parts in 301 BC. Historical records describe how, during the post-Persian period, two dynasties fought to control Palestine: the Ptolemaic, southern group, and the Seleucid, northern group. At times they did try to live at peace, but mostly it was war and more war. The Ptolemaic army was eventually defeated, and from 198 BC Seleucids ruled Palestine. But trouble began again when the Seleucid ruler Antiochus (196–187 BC) was routed by a [Roman] commander (11:18). His son, Seleucus IV, ruled from 187–175 BC, but we know little about him. **21–32:** The *despicable man* is Antiochus Epiphanes (175–163 BC), who through *flattery and intrigue* took over the kingdom. Antiochus Epiphanes’ reign of terror began when he rolled into Jerusalem; killed the *covenant prince* (possibly the high priest, Onias III); and bribed followers. He invaded Egypt on two occasions but was turned back; in 169 BC he spent his rage against the covenant people (11:30) in Jerusalem. First Maccabees in the Apocrypha also de-

promises, he will make various alliances. He will become strong despite having only a handful of followers. 24 Without warning he will enter the richest areas of the land. Then he will distribute among his followers the plunder and wealth of the rich—something his predecessors had never done. He will plot the overthrow of strongholds, but this will last for only a short while.

25 "Then he will stir up his courage and raise a great army against the king of the south. The king of the south will go to battle with a mighty army, but to no avail, for there will be plots against him. 26 His own household will cause his downfall. His army will be swept away, and many will be killed. 27 Seeking nothing but each other's harm, these kings will plot against each other at the conference table, attempting to deceive each other. But it will make no difference, for the end will come at the appointed time.

28 "The king of the north will then return home with great riches. On the way he will set himself against the people of the holy covenant, doing much damage before continuing his journey.

29 "Then at the appointed time he will once again invade the south, but this time the result will be different. 30 For warships from western coastlands* will scare him off, and he will withdraw and return home. But he will vent his anger against the people of the holy covenant and reward those who forsake the covenant.

31 "His army will take over the Temple fortress, pollute the sanctuary, put a stop to the daily sacrifices, and set up the sacrilegious object that causes desecration.* 32 He will flatter and win over those who have violated the covenant. But the people who know their God will be strong and will resist him.

33 "Wise leaders will give instruction to many, but these teachers will die by fire and sword, or they will be jailed and robbed. 34 During these persecutions, little help will arrive, and many who join them will not be sincere. 35 And some of the wise will fall victim to persecution. In this way, they will be refined and cleansed and made pure until the time of the end, for the appointed time is still to come.

36 "The king will do as he pleases, exalting himself and claiming to be greater than every god, even blaspheming the God of gods. He will succeed, but only until the time of wrath is completed. For what has been determined will surely take place. 37 He will have no respect for the gods of his ancestors, or for the god loved by women, or for any other god, for he will boast that he is greater than them all. 38 Instead of these, he will worship the god of fortresses—a god his ancestors never knew—and lavish on him gold, silver, precious stones, and expensive gifts. 39 Claiming this foreign god's help, he will attack the strongest fortresses. He will honor those who submit to him, appointing them to positions of authority and dividing the land among them as their reward.*

40 "Then at the time of the end, the king of the south will attack the king of the north. The king of the north will storm out with chariots, charioteers, and a vast navy. He will invade various lands and sweep through them like a flood. 41 He will enter the glorious land of Israel,* and many nations will fall, but Moab, Edom, and the best part of Ammon will escape. 42 He will conquer many countries, and even Egypt will not escape. 43 He will gain control over the gold, silver, and treasures of Egypt, and the Libyans and Ethiopians* will be his servants.

44 "But then news from the east and the north will alarm him, and he will set out in great anger to destroy and obliterate many. 45 He will stop between the glorious holy mountain and the sea and will pitch his royal tents. But while he is there, his time will suddenly run out, and no one will help him.

11:30 Hebrew *from Kittim.* **11:31** Hebrew *the abomination of desolation.* **11:39** Or *at a price.* **11:41** Hebrew *the glorious land.* **11:43** Hebrew *Cushites.*

scribes how many Jews fell at this time. **31–35:** The Temple was desecrated by an altar to the god Zeus (8:13; 9:27; 12:11). Some Jews capitulated but some resisted, sparking the Maccabean revolt (168 BC). The *little help* may refer to the Maccabees. It is real history, arranged marriages (vv. 6, 17) and all, and there for all to read in the history books. As noted in the introduction, many believe that the book of Daniel was written during Antiochus Epiphanes' reign and that claims about Daniel foretelling history are unfounded. No matter when the book was written, the message remains true: God's people will face war and oppression, but in the end, God will prevail. **36–45:** In a less specific way, these verses continue to describe Antiochus's reign, clarifying the reason for the name Epiphanes, meaning "God manifest," and promising that the disrespectful, self-exalting ruler will come to an inglorious and isolated end (v. 45). **40–45:** Many understand this section as (also) applying to the Antichrist, the ultimate arrogant, blasphemous small horn (chap. 7) before whom *many nations will fall,* though Edom, Moab, and Ammon, traditional enemies of God's people, will be spared. This ruler will set up camp in Jerusalem (v. 45), only

The Time of the End

12 "At that time Michael, the archangel* who stands guard over your nation, will arise. Then there will be a time of anguish greater than any since nations first came into existence. But at that time every one of your people whose name is written in the book will be rescued. 2 Many of those whose bodies lie dead and buried will rise up, some to everlasting life and some to shame and everlasting disgrace. 3 Those who are wise will shine as bright as the sky, and those who lead many to righteousness will shine like the stars forever. 4 But you, Daniel, keep this prophecy a secret; seal up the book until the time of the end, when many will rush here and there, and knowledge will increase."

5 Then I, Daniel, looked and saw two others standing on opposite banks of the river. 6 One of them asked the man dressed in linen, who was now standing above the river, "How long will it be until these shocking events are over?"

7 The man dressed in linen, who was standing above the river, raised both his hands toward heaven and took a solemn oath by the One who lives forever, saying, "It will go on for a time, times, and half a time. When the shattering of the holy people has finally come to an end, all these things will have happened."

8 I heard what he said, but I did not understand what he meant. So I asked, "How will all this finally end, my lord?"

9 But he said, "Go now, Daniel, for what I have said is kept secret and sealed until the time of the end. 10 Many will be purified, cleansed, and refined by these trials. But the wicked will continue in their wickedness, and none of them will understand. Only those who are wise will know what it means.

11 "From the time the daily sacrifice is stopped and the sacrilegious object that causes desecration* is set up to be worshiped, there will be 1,290 days. 12 And blessed are those who wait and remain until the end of the 1,335 days!

13 "As for you, go your way until the end. You will rest, and then at the end of the days, you will rise again to receive the inheritance set aside for you."

12:1 Hebrew *the great prince.* **12:11** Hebrew *the abomination of desolation.*

to find that the much promised *end* or *appointed time* (vv. 27, 35, 36) has finally arrived. **12:1:** However, rather than capitulate quietly, the arrogant king will inaugurate one last anguishing reign of terror (Matt 24:21). How to survive the dangerous times before God intervenes in history to bring about final victory for his people is an important theme of chapters 7—12. The secret? Keep the covenant, know God, resist the enemy, be wise, trust in God's protection, make sure your name is "written in the book" (12:1; Rev 20:12, 15). **2:** The final victory is nothing less than everlasting life after death (Isa 26:19), the final tragedy nothing less than everlasting shame and contempt (Isa 66:24; Matt 3:12).

12:4–13 Daniel, Receive Your Inheritance

The closing vision incorporates key elements of the whole book but with significant differences. **4:** The order to keep everything secret and sealed indicates that no more prophecies will be given and that what has been revealed is of great value and must be preserved (v. 9; contrast Rev 22:10). **5–7:** Two angels question the glorious man (10:5–6). Questioned, he swears by God himself, raising not the usual one hand (Deut 32:40) but both hands, showing the seriousness of the oath. **8:** However, neither the angels nor Daniel could calculate the "time, times, and half a time." Daniel wanted more details about the outcome but the man's lips were sealed. **9–10:** It is enough to know that the end will come; enough to know about the only options: *purified, cleansed, and refined* or *wicked*. **11–12:** Daniel seems to open up the subject of mathematical puzzles again, and for that reason many understand this verse to be a postscript. The foretold 1,290 days are about 3.5 years, but 1,335 days are 3.7 years, and commentators struggle to fit parts of history (past, present, or future) into these time frames. Nevertheless, the overall message is clear, having been repeated several times throughout the book: There is blessing for those who wait, for the end will surely come. **13:** The threefold, closing message to Daniel is almost another blessing: rest (death), resurrection, and reward. The message is a magnificent promise for the lifelong exile about whose family and descendants we know nothing. The God who has looked after Daniel will not forget him *at the end of the days*.

HOSEA

INTRODUCTION

Prostitution is an ugly word in any language, and an ugly reality in any culture. There are few places in the world where there is no sex trade. The overwhelming majority of prostitutes worldwide are female, both adults and children, and most suffer at the hands of the men who control them or use them. Few choose such a way of life voluntarily. Many are trafficked, especially the children; others are destitute and have no other means of feeding themselves or their children except by selling their bodies. Others need money to feed a drug habit. Whatever the complex of reasons in any particular case, prostitution always demeans and violates a human being made in the image of God. When that prostitution also betrays a marriage, its destructive power is magnified.

Hosea is a difficult book to read and perhaps especially difficult for women. It interweaves the personal history of Hosea and his family with Israel's relationship with God. Hosea's wife, Gomer, is not destitute; she has all the protection and provision of marriage to a man who keeps faith with her. She is no helpless victim of men or circumstance, deserving our pity. On the contrary, she deliberately chooses to embrace prostitution, leaving Hosea to take lovers, specifically in order to gain material luxuries. Appallingly, Gomer and her betrayal of Hosea becomes the parable for the betrayal of their covenant with God by the people of Israel. The LORD is presented as the husband and Israel as the wife in a marriage of grace. But, like Gomer, Israel has knowingly chosen prostitution, in this case by the worship of pagan gods. That worship is made all the more shocking by a reckless and simultaneous outward observance of allegiance to God, as if the two could be combined. Hosea's pain is a small reflection of God's pain at the unfaithfulness of his people.

Hosea was a prophet to the Northern Kingdom of Israel, in the mid-eighth century BC, at almost the same time as Amos, while Isaiah and Micah were prophesying to the smaller Southern Kingdom of Judah. King Jeroboam II of Israel (2 Kgs 14:23–29) was still on the throne as Hosea began his ministry. He had a long and prosperous reign, also winning back some territories that had been lost. But Jeroboam "did evil in the LORD's sight," specifically because he did not destroy the pagan shrines that his predecessors had set up, and he encouraged syncretism (combining different religions). After Jeroboam's death (753 BC), Israel, sometimes called "Ephraim" by Hosea, swiftly descended into political turmoil. A succession of rulers, violent coups and destructive alliances, and invasions by other nations led to the complete downfall of the kingdom in 723 BC. So Hosea is prophesying to his people in the final generation before Assyria conquered them, a fate from which they assumed confidently and totally mistakenly that the LORD would protect them.

Hosea, placed in our Bibles as the first of the Minor Prophets, is not always easy to interpret. Prophets would sometimes speak of something still future as if it were in the present—or even already in the past. For instance, in Hosea 1:2, where the LORD says to the prophet "Go and marry a prostitute," it is not clear whether Gomer was already engaged in prostitution (in which case the marriage would have been very shocking, and Hosea's credibility as a prophet destroyed at a stroke), or whether she had a reputation for being indiscreet, which spelled possible trouble in the future, or whether it is simply a statement of what was definitely going to happen. The book is also difficult to interpret because it is not always clear whether Hosea is speaking or the LORD, and because there are some textual uncertainties. Nonetheless, however difficult it is to study, there is no dispute that this short book rightly takes its place among the Scriptures. Indeed, there are several quotations and many echoes from Hosea in the New Testament. In particular, the metaphor of marriage to describe the relationship between God and his people is developed as the church is pictured as the bride of Christ (see, e.g., Eph 5:22–33; Rev 19:7).

Hosea weaves together the heartbreak of the LORD over his people's unfaithfulness, the inevitability of his severe judgment and punishment, and the message that superficial repentance is not acceptable—and yet there remains his yearning love, and finally his desire to see the errant wife restored to intimacy and commitment. Amid all the pain and horror, love and grace and mercy shine through. But this is no cheap grace. It is utterly costly to himself, pointing us to the supreme cost of love paid by our Lord Jesus Christ in his death on the cross to redeem us. And it is costly to us, too. In the words of the hymn "When I Survey the Wondrous Cross," "Love so amazing, so divine, demands my soul, my life, my all."

In much of today's world, promiscuity and marital unfaithfulness are endemic; Hosea's book highlights that everybody—guilty or innocent—caught up in such a relationship gets hurt. That flies in the face of libertarian values. In much of the modern church, professing Christians are as shallow in their commitment to God as the people of Israel were; Hosea's book warns us powerfully that only wholehearted and single-minded discipleship will do. That flies in the face of obsession with personal comfort and self-determination. There are especially severe condemnations of leaders who betray their people by leading them into error instead of challenging it; that, too, is a timeless word. —*Rosemary M. Dowsett*

1:1—3:5	Hosea's Family Tragedy
1:1	The Historical Setting
1:2—2:1	A Terrible Marriage—and a Glimmer of Hope
2:2–13	Israel the Prostitute
2:14–23	The LORD Will Win Her Back
3:1–5	The Cost of a New Beginning
4:1—11:11	Israel: Rebellious and Deluded
4:1–19	Priests and People: Sinners Together
5:1–15	The Consequences of Sin
6:1–11	The Outrage of Shallow Repentance
7:1–16	The Downward Spiral of Sin
8:1–14	The Inescapability of Judgment
9:1–17	The Inevitability of Exile
10:1–15	The Harvest of Wickedness
11:1–11	One Day in the Future
11:12—14:9	History and Hope
11:12—12:14	Learning from the Past
13:1–16	The Exclusiveness of God
14:1–9	A Final Plea

✧

1 The LORD gave this message to Hosea son
of Beeri during the years when Uzziah,
Jotham, Ahaz, and Hezekiah were kings of
Judah, and Jeroboam son of Jehoash* was king
of Israel.

Hosea's Wife and Children

[2]When the LORD first began speaking to Israel
through Hosea, he said to him, "Go and marry
a prostitute,* so that some of her children will
be conceived in prostitution. This will illustrate
how Israel has acted like a prostitute by turning
against the LORD and worshiping other gods."
[3]So Hosea married Gomer, the daughter of
Diblaim, and she became pregnant and gave Hosea a son. [4]And the LORD said, "Name the child
Jezreel, for I am about to punish King Jehu's
dynasty to avenge the murders he committed
at Jezreel. In fact, I will bring an end to Israel's
independence. [5]I will break its military power in
the Jezreel Valley."
[6]Soon Gomer became pregnant again and
gave birth to a daughter. And the LORD said to
Hosea, "Name your daughter Lo-ruhamah—
'Not loved'—for I will no longer show love to the
people of Israel or forgive them. [7]But I will show
love to the people of Judah. I will free them from
their enemies—not with weapons and armies or
horses and charioteers, but by my power as the
LORD their God."
[8]After Gomer had weaned Lo-ruhamah, she
again became pregnant and gave birth to a second son. [9]And the LORD said, "Name him Lo-
ammi—'Not my people'—for Israel is not my
people, and I am not their God.
[10]*"Yet the time will come when Israel's people will be like the sands of the seashore—too
many to count! Then, at the place where they
were told, 'You are not my people,' it will be said,
'You are children of the living God.' [11]Then the
people of Judah and Israel will unite together.
They will choose one leader for themselves, and
they will return from exile together. What a day
that will be—the day of Jezreel*—when God
will again plant his people in his land.
[2:1]*"In that day you will call your brothers
Ammi—'My people.' And you will call your sisters Ruhamah—'The ones I love.'

Charges against an Unfaithful Wife

2 [2]"But now bring charges against Israel—
your mother—
for she is no longer my wife,
and I am no longer her husband.
Tell her to remove the prostitute's makeup
from her face
and the clothing that exposes her breasts.

1:1 Hebrew *Joash,* a variant spelling of Jehoash. **1:2** Or *a promiscuous woman.* **1:10** Verses 1:10-11 are numbered 2:1-2 in Hebrew text. **1:11** *Jezreel* means "God plants." **2:1** Verses 2:1-23 are numbered 2:3-25 in Hebrew text.

1:1—3:5 Hosea's Family Tragedy

1:1 The Historical Setting. Hosea's prophetic ministry spanned several decades. King Uzziah ruled Judah 790–740 BC, and Hezekiah ruled 715–686 BC. Jeroboam II, king of Israel, died in 753 BC. So Hosea began not later than the end of Jeroboam's reign, and finished not sooner than the early years of Hezekiah's. The period is recorded in 2 Kings 15—20. *The LORD gave this message* underlines the divine authority with which Hosea spoke.

1:2—2:1 A Terrible Marriage—and a Glimmer of Hope. 1:2–3: It seems that God warned Hosea in advance that the marriage would be disastrous, but Hosea obeys without question. Then (as now) men expected to use prostitutes but not to marry one. Furthermore, men may father illegitimate children, but in most cultures they do not accept as their own a child conceived through their wife's adultery. Hosea is called to this terrible marriage in order to mirror Israel's unfaithfulness toward God. **4–5:** For Jehu's story, see 2 Kings 9:6—10:36. Jezreel was the place of Gideon's victory (see Judg 6:33—7:23) but also of Jehu's mass murder. So the name "Jezreel" paradoxically embraces both thanksgiving and shame, and the place of military triumph will become the place of military defeat. There is no hint of Gomer delighting in bearing children, the natural fruit of her sexual relationships. Pregnancy is most readily treasured in the context of mutual commitment. **6–7:** It is difficult to imagine a harsher name for a child than "Lo-ruhamah," *Not loved,* filled with rejection. For God who is Love to declare this in relation to his people Israel is shocking. **8–9:** In the same way, the next child's name "Lo-ammi," *Not my people,* is an appalling statement of dissociation, as God declares the covenant broken. **1:10—2:1:** Yet there is a glimmer of hope, the promise that one day the covenant will be restored, and God's family reconciled with himself and with one another. The New Testament refers directly to these verses in John 11:52; Romans 9:25–26; and 1 Peter 2:10.

2:2–13 Israel the Prostitute. Here the stories of Hosea and Gomer, and of Israel and God, are closely intertwined. **2:** This is probably referring to de facto separation rather than legal divorce, though Hosea

[3] Otherwise, I will strip her as naked
as she was on the day she was born.
I will leave her to die of thirst,
as in a dry and barren wilderness.
[4] And I will not love her children,
for they were conceived in prostitution.
[5] Their mother is a shameless prostitute
and became pregnant in a shameful way.
She said, 'I'll run after other lovers
and sell myself to them for food and water,
for clothing of wool and linen,
and for olive oil and drinks.'
[6] "For this reason I will fence her in with
thornbushes.
I will block her path with a wall
to make her lose her way.
[7] When she runs after her lovers,
she won't be able to catch them.
She will search for them
but not find them.
Then she will think,
'I might as well return to my husband,
for I was better off with him than I am
now.'
[8] She doesn't realize it was I who gave her
everything she has—
the grain, the new wine, the olive oil;
I even gave her silver and gold.
But she gave all my gifts to Baal.

[9] "But now I will take back the ripened grain
and new wine
I generously provided each harvest season.
I will take away the wool and linen clothing
I gave her to cover her nakedness.
[10] I will strip her naked in public,
while all her lovers look on.
No one will be able
to rescue her from my hands.
[11] I will put an end to her annual festivals,
her new moon celebrations, and her
Sabbath days—
all her appointed festivals.
[12] I will destroy her grapevines and fig trees,
things she claims her lovers gave her.
I will let them grow into tangled thickets,
where only wild animals will eat the
fruit.
[13] I will punish her for all those times
when she burned incense to her images of
Baal,
when she put on her earrings and jewels
and went out to look for her lovers
but forgot all about me,"
says the LORD.

The LORD's Love for Unfaithful Israel

[14] "But then I will win her back once again.
I will lead her into the desert
and speak tenderly to her there.
[15] I will return her vineyards to her
and transform the Valley of Trouble* into a
gateway of hope.
She will give herself to me there,
as she did long ago when she was young,

2:15 Hebrew *valley of Achor.*

certainly had grounds for divorcing Gomer. Challenge to abandon a sinful way of life must come first from within the family. Hosea, as an Israelite, had a parallel responsibility as a prophet to his own people. Gomer flaunts her sexuality through cosmetics and clothing; Christian women need to be careful not to do the same. **3–5:** Public humiliation of unfaithful women is still practiced in some cultures, often without corresponding penalties for men. Through childbearing, women are especially the guardians of life, and it is perhaps for this reason that most cultures treat male and female infidelity differently, and that the children of prostitution suffer so much. In Gomer's case, her excuse for taking lovers is to obtain food and clothing. In fact, under Israelite law (e.g., Exod 21:10–11), Hosea as husband would have been responsible for providing those, and there is no suggestion that he did not. **6–13:** Israel's lovers were the Baals, the pagan fertility gods. Rituals, some of them involving sexual acts, were designed to persuade the god to provide a good harvest, or live births among the flocks, or plenty of healthy babies. In sacrificing to the Baals and worshiping them, Israel was denying both the fact that the living God is the only true God, and that it is the LORD who is the true source of all that we need to sustain life and breath (v. 8). Indeed, God had not only given Israel what she needed, but much more besides: *I even gave her silver and gold. But she gave all my gifts to Baal.* What an outrageous insult! God's judgment will lead to the failure of the crops and flocks, and the futility of Baal worship will be exposed for what it is.

2:14–23 The LORD Will Win Her Back. 14–17: Here is love transformed! Not only does the wronged lover woo his unfaithful wife all over again, he blots out past sin and instead replaces it with hope, so that the relationship is more tender and intimate than it was before. The prostitute becomes a gladly loving, faithful, responsive wife. *The Valley of Trouble* recalls the sin of Achan (Josh 7) as the children of Israel entered the promised land. The image of God as perfect hus-

when I freed her from her captivity in
Egypt.
16 When that day comes," says the LORD,
"you will call me 'my husband'
instead of 'my master.'*
17 O Israel, I will wipe the many names of Baal
from your lips,
and you will never mention them again.
18 On that day I will make a covenant
with all the wild animals and the birds of
the sky
and the animals that scurry along the
ground
so they will not harm you.
I will remove all weapons of war from the
land,
all swords and bows,
so you can live unafraid
in peace and safety.
19 I will make you my wife forever,
showing you righteousness and justice,
unfailing love and compassion.
20 I will be faithful to you and make you mine,
and you will finally know me as the LORD.

21 "In that day, I will answer,"
says the LORD.
"I will answer the sky as it pleads for
clouds.
And the sky will answer the earth with
rain.
22 Then the earth will answer the thirsty cries
of the grain, the grapevines, and the olive
trees.
And they in turn will answer,
'Jezreel'—'God plants!'
23 At that time I will plant a crop of Israelites
and raise them for myself.
I will show love
to those I called 'Not loved.'*
And to those I called 'Not my people,'*
I will say, 'Now you are my people.'
And they will reply, 'You are our God!'"

Hosea's Wife Is Redeemed

3 Then the LORD said to me, "Go and love
your wife again, even though she* commits adultery with another lover. This will
illustrate that the LORD still loves Israel, even
though the people have turned to other gods and
love to worship them.*"
2 So I bought her back for fifteen pieces of silver* and five bushels of barley and a measure of
wine.* 3 Then I said to her, "You must live in my
house for many days and stop your prostitution.
During this time, you will not have sexual relations with anyone, not even with me.*"
4 This shows that Israel will go a long time
without a king or prince, and without sacrifices, sacred pillars, priests,* or even idols! 5 But
afterward the people will return and devote
themselves to the LORD their God and to David's descendant, their king.* In the last days,
they will tremble in awe of the LORD and of his
goodness.

2:16 Hebrew *'my baal.'* **2:23a** Hebrew *Lo-ruhamah;* see 1:6. **2:23b** Hebrew *Lo-ammi;* see 1:9. **3:1a** Or *Go and love a woman who.* **3:1b** Hebrew *love their raisin cakes.* **3:2a** Hebrew *15 shekels of silver,* about 6 ounces or 171 grams in weight. **3:2b** As in Greek version, which reads *a homer of barley and a wineskin full of wine;* Hebrew reads *a homer* [5 bushels or 182 liters] *of barley and a lethech* [2.5 bushels or 91 liters] *of barley.* **3:3** Or *and I will live with you.* **3:4** Hebrew *ephod,* the vest worn by the priest. **3:5** Hebrew *to David their king.*

band rather than "master" is doubly breathtaking, as Baal meant "master" in the fertility rites. **18–23:** The new covenant encompasses the whole of creation, as in Genesis 1 and 2. Hosea uses here the language of betrothal, suggesting a new beginning, with all its solemn commitment. The betrothal gifts are all the hallmarks of God's character: *righteousness and justice, unfailing love and compassion* and faithfulness. These are what God offers us when we enter into faithful covenant with him. The harmony between God and man is enlarged by harmony between humankind and environment. Gomer's children are renamed, symbolic of the radically changed marriage.

3:1–5 The Cost of a New Beginning. 1: Hosea returns to his own immediate situation. It seems that Gomer is living with another man, and actively adulterous. The LORD does not simply tell Hosea to bring her back, but to *love* her. Love involves putting the best interests of the other person first, however much that person may have hurt you and however vulnerable you may be to further hurt. **2:** Hosea has to buy back someone who already "belongs" to him, a powerful picture of Christ's redemption of us. The price paid here is probably that of redeeming a slave (see Exod 21:32), again echoing the cost of setting us free from the slavery of sin. **3–5:** Discipline includes deprivation of what lay at the heart of the sin, in this case (inappropriate) sexual activity. Can Gomer prove that she has had a change of heart? Part of Israel's discipline will be exile, loss of their monarchy and religious leaders, and separation from the Temple. *David's descendant, their king* points to the Lord Jesus Christ.

The Lord*'s Case against Israel*

4 [1]Hear the word of the LORD, O people of
Israel!
The LORD has brought charges against
you, saying:
"There is no faithfulness, no kindness,
no knowledge of God in your land.
2 You make vows and break them;
you kill and steal and commit adultery.
There is violence everywhere—
one murder after another.
3 That is why your land is in mourning,
and everyone is wasting away.
Even the wild animals, the birds of the sky,
and the fish of the sea are disappearing.

4 "Don't point your finger at someone else
and try to pass the blame!
My complaint, you priests,
is with you.*
5 So you will stumble in broad daylight,
and your false prophets will fall with you
in the night.
And I will destroy Israel, your mother.
6 My people are being destroyed
because they don't know me.
Since you priests refuse to know me,
I refuse to recognize you as my priests.
Since you have forgotten the laws of your
God,
I will forget to bless your children.
7 The more priests there are,
the more they sin against me.
They have exchanged the glory of God
for the shame of idols.*
8 "When the people bring their sin offerings,
the priests get fed.
So the priests are glad when the people sin!
9 'And what the priests do, the people also do.'
So now I will punish both priests and
people
for their wicked deeds.
10 They will eat and still be hungry.
They will play the prostitute and gain
nothing from it,
for they have deserted the LORD
11 to worship other gods.

"Wine has robbed my people
of their understanding.
12 They ask a piece of wood for advice!
They think a stick can tell them the future!
Longing after idols
has made them foolish.
They have played the prostitute,
serving other gods and deserting their God.
13 They offer sacrifices to idols on the
mountaintops.
They go up into the hills to burn incense
in the pleasant shade of oaks, poplars, and
terebinth trees.

"That is why your daughters turn to
prostitution,
and your daughters-in-law commit adultery.
14 But why should I punish them
for their prostitution and adultery?
For your men are doing the same thing,
sinning with whores and shrine prostitutes.
O foolish people! You refuse to understand,
so you will be destroyed.

4:4 Hebrew *Your people are like those with a complaint against the priests.* **4:7** As in Syriac version and an ancient Hebrew tradition; Masoretic Text reads *I will turn their glory into shame.*

4:1—11:11 Israel: Rebellious and Deluded

4:1–19 Priests and People: Sinners Together. 1–3: God's people should reflect the character of God: We are made in his image. Instead, there is no integrity (*faithfulness*), no care for others (*kindness*), and no genuine relationship with God (*knowledge*) evidenced by godly living (cf. 1 Jn 2:3–6). Human sin and ecological disaster are bound up with each other. Verses 1–2 touch on most of the Ten Commandments; no Israelite could claim ignorance of something so fundamental to his identity. **4–9:** The role of the priest was to act as intermediary between God and the people, helping the people draw near to God with true repentance, and representing God and his truth to the people. The role of the prophet was to be the mouthpiece of God's word, reminding the people of God's nature and demands, and declaring God's revelation for the present and the future. By contrast, Hosea says, these prophets were false and these priests encouraging sin for their own benefit. Their betrayal of God is deliberate (cf. *refuse* [v. 6], *forgotten* [v. 6]), and they have been at the heart of idol worship (v. 7). They are *wicked,* and their wickedness ensures that the people, too, are wicked. **10–14:** Shrines were commonly set up on hilltops and mountains, in the belief that worshipers would then be nearer the god they called on and that it would be easier for him to notice them. Often an altar would be placed in a grove of trees, and sometimes wood was carved for special reverence, or sticks were thrown for fortune-telling. Idolatry leads directly to cult prostitution and to general sexual immorality, involving both men and women, young and

15 "Though you, Israel, are a prostitute,
may Judah avoid such guilt.
Do not join the false worship at Gilgal or
Beth-aven,*
even though they take oaths there in the
LORD's name.
16 Israel is stubborn,
like a stubborn heifer.
So should the LORD feed her
like a lamb in a lush pasture?
17 Leave Israel* alone,
because she is married to idolatry.
18 When the rulers of Israel finish their
drinking,
off they go to find some prostitutes.
They love shame more than honor.*
19 So a mighty wind will sweep them away.
Their sacrifices to idols will bring them
shame.

The Failure of Israel's Leaders

5 1"Hear this, you priests.
Pay attention, you leaders of Israel.
Listen, you members of the royal family.
Judgment has been handed down against
you.
For you have led the people into a snare
by worshiping the idols at Mizpah and
Tabor.
2 You have dug a deep pit to trap them at
Acacia Grove.*
But I will settle with you for what you
have done.
3 I know what you are like, O Ephraim.
You cannot hide yourself from me,
O Israel.
You have left me as a prostitute leaves her
husband;
you are utterly defiled.
4 Your deeds won't let you return to your God.
You are a prostitute through and through,
and you do not know the LORD.

5 "The arrogance of Israel testifies against her;
Israel and Ephraim will stumble under
their load of guilt.
Judah, too, will fall with them.
6 When they come with their flocks and herds
to offer sacrifices to the LORD,
they will not find him,
because he has withdrawn from them.
7 They have betrayed the honor of the LORD,
bearing children that are not his.
Now their false religion will devour them
along with their wealth.*

8 "Sound the alarm in Gibeah!
Blow the trumpet in Ramah!
Raise the battle cry in Beth-aven*!
Lead on into battle, O warriors of
Benjamin!
9 One thing is certain, Israel*:
On your day of punishment,
you will become a heap of rubble.

10 "The leaders of Judah have become like
thieves.*
So I will pour my anger on them like a
waterfall.

4:15 *Beth-aven* means "house of wickedness"; it is being used as another name for Bethel, which means "house of God." **4:17** Hebrew *Ephraim,* referring to the northern kingdom of Israel. **4:18** As in Greek version; the meaning of the Hebrew is uncertain. **5:2** Hebrew *at Shittim.* The meaning of the Hebrew for this sentence is uncertain. **5:7** The meaning of the Hebrew is uncertain. **5:8** *Beth-aven* means "house of wickedness"; it is being used as another name for Bethel, which means "house of God." **5:9** Hebrew *Ephraim,* referring to the northern kingdom of Israel; also in 5:11, 12, 13, 14. **5:10** Hebrew *like those who move a boundary marker.*

old. **15–19:** Israel is in a worse state than Judah and will collapse before Judah. But Judah is warned not to join in Israel's sin and not to worship at her compromised shrines.

5:1–15 The Consequences of Sin. 1–2: Idolatry has not been the preserve of the ignorant poor; it is the priests and leaders and kings who have led the way. The very ones who should protect the people have led them towards inescapable disaster. They have behaved like hunters plotting to trap their prey (*snare, dug a deep pit to trap them*). They cannot escape God's anger. **3–9:** The people of both Israel and Judah share their leaders' guilt, for they cannot disentangle themselves from idolatry; it has become a way of life. Even when they bring costly sacrifices to the LORD, there is no genuine faith: He is simply one to worship alongside others. This fusion of religions is so offensive to God that he removes himself so that he cannot be found. Gibeah, Ramah, and Beth-aven were on the borders of Israel and Judah; verse 8 may refer to military skirmishes between the two or simply that both would face invaders and be conquered. **10–15:** Hosea uses a series of dramatic images to describe the fate of both Israel and Judah as God lets loose his judgment. The culmination is likening God to a lion in its prime, tearing them to pieces. Israel turns to Assyria for help, but that leads only to disaster. Only when they are completely desperate and hopeless will they begin to search for God with undivided hearts, facing up to their sin.

[11] The people of Israel will be crushed and
broken by my judgment
because they are determined to worship
idols.*
[12] I will destroy Israel as a moth consumes wool.
I will make Judah as weak as rotten wood.

[13] "When Israel and Judah saw how sick they
were,
Israel turned to Assyria—
to the great king there—
but he could neither help nor cure them.
[14] I will be like a lion to Israel,
like a strong young lion to Judah.
I will tear them to pieces!
I will carry them off,
and no one will be left to rescue them.
[15] Then I will return to my place
until they admit their guilt and turn to me.
For as soon as trouble comes,
they will earnestly search for me."

A Call to Repentance

6 [1]"Come, let us return to the LORD.
He has torn us to pieces;
now he will heal us.
He has injured us;
now he will bandage our wounds.
[2] In just a short time he will restore us,
so that we may live in his presence.
[3] Oh, that we might know the LORD!
Let us press on to know him.
He will respond to us as surely as the arrival
of dawn
or the coming of rains in early spring."

[4] "O Israel* and Judah,
what should I do with you?" asks the LORD.
"For your love vanishes like the morning mist
and disappears like dew in the sunlight.
[5] I sent my prophets to cut you to pieces—
to slaughter you with my words,
with judgments as inescapable as light.
[6] I want you to show love,*
not offer sacrifices.
I want you to know me*
more than I want burnt offerings.
[7] But like Adam,* you broke my covenant
and betrayed my trust.

[8] "Gilead is a city of sinners,
tracked with footprints of blood.
[9] Priests form bands of robbers,
waiting in ambush for their victims.
They murder travelers along the road to
Shechem
and practice every kind of sin.
[10] Yes, I have seen something horrible in
Ephraim and Israel:
My people are defiled by prostituting
themselves with other gods!

[11] "O Judah, a harvest of punishment is also
waiting for you,
though I wanted to restore the fortunes of
my people.

Israel's Love for Wickedness

7 [1]"I want to heal Israel,* but its sins are too
great.
Samaria is filled with liars.

5:11 Or *determined to follow human commands.* The meaning of the Hebrew is uncertain. **6:4** Hebrew *Ephraim,* referring to the northern kingdom of Israel. **6:6a** Greek version translates this Hebrew term as *to show mercy.* Compare Matt 9:13; 12:7. **6:6b** Hebrew *to know God.* **6:7** Or *But at Adam.* **7:1** Hebrew *Ephraim,* referring to the northern kingdom of Israel; also in 7:8, 11.

6:1–11 The Outrage of Shallow Repentance. 1–3: Israel and Judah apparently recognize that it is God himself who has caused their distress, but they do not acknowledge their guilt and thus their deserving judgment. They urge each other to *return to the LORD,* not out of love nor out of a cry for forgiveness, but because they would like their comfort to be restored. There is indeed a false confidence in God. Many centuries later, Archbishop Cranmer began a prayer in the Book of Common Prayer like this: "We do not presume to come to this thy table trusting in our own righteousness but in thy manifold and great mercies." There is to be humility and a recognition of needing the mercy of God when we approach him; our confidence rests solely in Christ, not in our returning. **4–7:** Israel and Judah's love is as ephemeral as morning mist or dew before the sunlight streams in. Words and ritual are easy. Love, intimacy, and trustworthiness are what God wants, and these flow only from a settled and wholehearted commitment. These are essential ingredients of a secure human marriage, too. **8–11:** The corrupt priests are at the forefront of appalling social violence. How could they possibly lead the people in spiritual integrity? Of course they couldn't! They continue to perform the sacrifices of their calling, but these are completely ineffectual while their sin is so blatant and while they also engage in Baal worship.

7:1–16 The Downward Spiral of Sin. 1–2: Despite everything, God longs to see Israel restored to himself. But, so deeply ingrained has addiction to sin be-

Thieves are on the inside
and bandits on the outside!
2 Its people don't realize
that I am watching them.
Their sinful deeds are all around them,
and I see them all.

3 "The people entertain the king with their wickedness,
and the princes laugh at their lies.
4 They are all adulterers,
always aflame with lust.
They are like an oven that is kept hot
while the baker is kneading the dough.
5 On royal holidays, the princes get drunk with wine,
carousing with those who mock them.
6 Their hearts are like an oven
blazing with intrigue.
Their plot smolders* through the night,
and in the morning it breaks out like a raging fire.
7 Burning like an oven,
they consume their leaders.
They kill their kings one after another,
and no one cries to me for help.

8 "The people of Israel mingle with godless foreigners,
making themselves as worthless as a half-baked cake!
9 Worshiping foreign gods has sapped their strength,
but they don't even know it.
Their hair is gray,
but they don't realize they're old and weak.
10 Their arrogance testifies against them,
yet they don't return to the LORD their God
or even try to find him.

11 "The people of Israel have become like silly, witless doves,
first calling to Egypt, then flying to Assyria for help.
12 But as they fly about,
I will throw my net over them
and bring them down like a bird from the sky.
I will punish them for all the evil they do.*

13 "What sorrow awaits those who have deserted me!
Let them die, for they have rebelled against me.
I wanted to redeem them,
but they have told lies about me.
14 They do not cry out to me with sincere hearts.
Instead, they sit on their couches and wail.
They cut themselves,* begging foreign gods
for grain and new wine,
and they turn away from me.
15 I trained them and made them strong,
yet now they plot evil against me.
16 They look everywhere except to the Most High.
They are as useless as a crooked bow.
Their leaders will be killed by their enemies
because of their insolence toward me.
Then the people of Egypt
will laugh at them.

Israel Harvests the Whirlwind

8 1"Sound the alarm!
The enemy descends like an eagle on the people of the LORD,
for they have broken my covenant
and revolted against my law.
2 Now Israel pleads with me,
'Help us, for you are our God!'
3 But it is too late.
The people of Israel have rejected what is good,
and now their enemies will chase after them.

7:6 Hebrew *Their baker sleeps.* **7:12** Hebrew *I will punish them because of what was reported against them in the assembly.* **7:14** As in Greek version; Hebrew reads *They gather together.*

come, there is no possibility of repentance. Indeed, the people do not even remember the existence of God, and that all is revealed to him. This same dreadful truth, that people can habituate themselves to sin to the point where repentance is impossible, is the basis of Romans 1:18—2:16. **3–7:** Israel has become so degenerate that sin has become entertaining. In today's world, how many films and TV programs present sin as funny? Hosea's vivid pictures show sin as a raging, destructive fire. In the course of thirty years, Israel had six kings, all murderers or murdered. **8–16:** In the context of growing instability, Israel tries to get help first from Egypt, then from Assyria, *godless foreigners* (v. 8). Such attempted alliances can only end in disaster. *I wanted to redeem them,* says God, but such is their rebellion, now *Let them die.*

8:1–14 The Inescapability of Judgment. 1: As Israel weakens through its self-induced chaos, Assyria is likened to an eagle about to pounce on its prey. **2–4:** In panic, Israel at last calls on God. *But it is too late.* Sin brings its inevitable consequences, and

4 The people have appointed kings without my
consent,
and princes without my knowledge.
By making idols for themselves from their
silver and gold,
they have brought about their own
destruction.

5 "O Samaria, I reject this calf—
this idol you have made.
My fury burns against you.
How long will you be incapable of
innocence?
6 This calf you worship, O Israel,
was crafted by your own hands!
It is not God!
Therefore, it must be smashed to bits.

7 "They have planted the wind
and will harvest the whirlwind.
The stalks of grain wither
and produce nothing to eat.
And even if there is any grain,
foreigners will eat it.
8 The people of Israel have been swallowed up;
they lie among the nations like an old
discarded pot.
9 Like a wild donkey looking for a mate,
they have gone up to Assyria.
The people of Israel* have sold themselves—
sold themselves to many lovers.
10 But though they have sold themselves to
many allies,
I will now gather them together for
judgment.
Then they will writhe
under the burden of the great king.

11 "Israel has built many altars to take away sin,
but these very altars became places for
sinning!
12 Even though I gave them all my laws,
they act as if those laws don't apply to
them.
13 The people of Israel love their rituals of
sacrifice,
but to me their sacrifices are all
meaningless.
I will hold my people accountable for their
sins,
and I will punish them.
They will return to Egypt.
14 Israel has forgotten its Maker and built great
palaces,
and Judah has fortified its cities.
Therefore, I will send down fire on their cities
and will burn up their fortresses."

Hosea Announces Israel's Punishment

9 1O people of Israel,
do not rejoice as other nations do.
For you have been unfaithful to your
God,
hiring yourselves out like prostitutes,
worshiping other gods on every threshing
floor.
2 So now your harvests will be too small to
feed you.
There will be no grapes for making new
wine.
3 You may no longer stay here in the LORD's
land.
Instead, you will return to Egypt,
and in Assyria you will eat food
that is ceremonially unclean.
4 There you will make no offerings of wine to
the LORD.
None of your sacrifices there will please
him.
They will be unclean, like food touched by a
person in mourning.
All who present such sacrifices will be
defiled.
They may eat this food themselves,
but they may not offer it to the LORD.

8:9 Hebrew *Ephraim,* referring to the northern kingdom of Israel; also in 8:11.

the people have nobody to blame but themselves for the fierce judgment about to fall on them. **5–6:** The calf is probably one of those erected by Jeroboam I (see 1 Kgs 12:26–30), echoing the gold calf of Exodus 32. **7–14:** Through disastrous political alliance (vv. 7–10) and corrupt religiosity (vv. 11–14), the people of Israel *have sold themselves* and must now render account. Worst of all, Israel has *forgotten its Maker* (v. 14), the LORD who is the very source of their identity, and instead put their faith in fortified cities and costly buildings. Total destruction is inescapable.

9:1–17 The Inevitability of Exile. 1–9: Famine will be followed inexorably by exile, and Israel will become a wasteland. Some will be taken captive by Egypt, some by Assyria, but there will be no freedom to retain their own distinctive ethnic identities. Even at this last stage, Israel refuses to believe the prophets' messages from God, persecuting them rather than believing them (cf. Matt 23:29–39). Gibeah (v. 9) was a byword for moral degradation (see Judg 19 and the story of the rape and murder of a concubine). *God will not forget,* says Hosea, even if society regarded

5 What then will you do on festival days?
How will you observe the LORD's festivals?
6 Even if you escape destruction from Assyria,
Egypt will conquer you, and Memphis*
will bury you.
Nettles will take over your treasures of silver;
thistles will invade your ruined homes.

7 The time of Israel's punishment has come;
the day of payment is here.
Soon Israel will know this all too well.
Because of your great sin and hostility,
you say, "The prophets are crazy
and the inspired men are fools!"
8 The prophet is a watchman over Israel* for
my God,
yet traps are laid for him wherever he
goes.
He faces hostility even in the house of God.
9 The things my people do are as depraved
as what they did in Gibeah long ago.
God will not forget.
He will surely punish them for their sins.

10 The LORD says, "O Israel, when I first found
you,
it was like finding fresh grapes in the
desert.
When I saw your ancestors,
it was like seeing the first ripe figs of the
season.
But then they deserted me for Baal-peor,
giving themselves to that shameful idol.
Soon they became vile,
as vile as the god they worshiped.
11 The glory of Israel will fly away like a bird,
for your children will not be born
or grow in the womb
or even be conceived.
12 Even if you do have children who grow up,
I will take them from you.
It will be a terrible day when I turn away
and leave you alone.
13 I have watched Israel become as beautiful as
Tyre.
But now Israel will bring out her children
for slaughter."
14 O LORD, what should I request for your
people?
I will ask for wombs that don't give birth
and breasts that give no milk.

15 The LORD says, "All their wickedness began
at Gilgal;
there I began to hate them.
I will drive them from my land
because of their evil actions.
I will love them no more
because all their leaders are rebels.
16 The people of Israel are struck down.
Their roots are dried up,
and they will bear no more fruit.
And if they give birth,
I will slaughter their beloved children."

17 My God will reject the people of Israel
because they will not listen or obey.
They will be wanderers,
homeless among the nations.

The LORD's Judgment against Israel

10 How prosperous Israel is—
a luxuriant vine loaded with fruit.
But the richer the people get,
the more pagan altars they build.
The more bountiful their harvests,
the more beautiful their sacred pillars.
2 The hearts of the people are fickle;
they are guilty and must be punished.
The LORD will break down their altars
and smash their sacred pillars.
3 Then they will say, "We have no king
because we didn't fear the LORD.
But even if we had a king,
what could he do for us anyway?"
4 They spout empty words
and make covenants they don't intend to
keep.
So injustice springs up among them
like poisonous weeds in a farmer's field.

9:6 Memphis was the capital of northern Egypt. **9:8** Hebrew *Ephraim,* referring to the northern kingdom of Israel; also in 9:11, 13, 16.

the woman as not worth bothering about. **10–17:** The LORD, the creator and giver of life, will make women infertile (v. 11) and destroy such children as survive (vv. 12, 16). Here is the most dreadful reversal of Genesis 1:28. People created in the image of the life-creating God will now only produce death. (Sexual promiscuity often leads to infertility.) Verse 13 may refer to child sacrifice, the ultimate atrocity of fertility rituals. With no continuity of children or homeland, the people of Israel have no future.

10:1–15 The Harvest of Wickedness. Hosea repeats the themes of preceding prophecies. Abundant harvest will give way to *thorns and thistles* (v. 8), parallel to the *poisonous weeds* (vv. 4, 13) of rampant injustice. The sovereign God will use pagan nations

[5] The people of Samaria tremble in fear
for what might happen to their calf idol at
Beth-aven.*
The people mourn and the priests wail,
because its glory will be stripped away.*
[6] This idol will be carted away to Assyria,
a gift to the great king there.
Ephraim will be ridiculed and Israel will be
shamed,
because its people have trusted in this idol.
[7] Samaria and its king will be cut off;
they will float away like driftwood on an
ocean wave.
[8] And the pagan shrines of Aven,* the place of
Israel's sin, will crumble.
Thorns and thistles will grow up around
their altars.
They will beg the mountains, "Bury us!"
and plead with the hills, "Fall on us!"

[9] The LORD says, "O Israel, ever since Gibeah,
there has been only sin and more sin!
You have made no progress whatsoever.
Was it not right that the wicked men of
Gibeah were attacked?
[10] Now whenever it fits my plan,
I will attack you, too.
I will call out the armies of the nations
to punish you for your multiplied sins.

[11] "Israel* is like a trained heifer treading out
the grain—
an easy job she loves.
But I will put a heavy yoke on her tender
neck.
I will force Judah to pull the plow
and Israel* to break up the hard ground.
[12] I said, 'Plant the good seeds of righteousness,
and you will harvest a crop of love.
Plow up the hard ground of your hearts,
for now is the time to seek the LORD,
that he may come
and shower righteousness upon you.'

[13] "But you have cultivated wickedness
and harvested a thriving crop of sins.
You have eaten the fruit of lies—
trusting in your military might,
believing that great armies
could make your nation safe.
[14] Now the terrors of war
will rise among your people.
All your fortifications will fall,
just as when Shalman destroyed Beth-
arbel.
Even mothers and children
were dashed to death there.
[15] You will share that fate, Bethel,
because of your great wickedness.
When the day of judgment dawns,
the king of Israel will be completely
destroyed.

The LORD's Love for Israel

11 [1] "When Israel was a child, I loved
him,
and I called my son out of Egypt.
[2] But the more I* called to him,
the farther he moved from me,
offering sacrifices to the images of Baal
and burning incense to idols.
[3] I myself taught Israel* how to walk,
leading him along by the hand.
But he doesn't know or even care
that it was I who took care of him.
[4] I led Israel along
with my ropes of kindness and love.
I lifted the yoke from his neck,
and I myself stooped to feed him.

[5] "But since my people refuse to return to me,
they will return to Egypt
and will be forced to serve Assyria.
[6] War will swirl through their cities;
their enemies will crash through their
gates.

10:5a *Beth-aven* means "house of wickedness"; it is being used as another name for Bethel, which means "house of God." **10:5b** Or *will be taken away into exile.* **10:8** *Aven* is a reference to Beth-aven; see 10:5a and the note there. **10:11a** Hebrew *Ephraim,* referring to the northern kingdom of Israel. **10:11b** Hebrew *Jacob.* The names "Jacob" and "Israel" are often interchanged throughout the Old Testament, referring sometimes to the individual patriarch and sometimes to the nation. **11:2** As in Greek version; Hebrew reads *they.* **11:3** Hebrew *Ephraim,* referring to the northern kingdom of Israel; also in 11:8, 9, 12.

to discipline his own people (v. 10). Only by sowing *the good seeds of righteousness* (v. 12) can Israel experience God's blessing.

11:1–11 One Day in the Future. With great poignancy, God likens himself to a father delighting in his child, helping him take his first few staggering steps and constantly watching over him to keep him from harm. Israel neither recognized nor cared about God's love for them. Pagan religion was much more attractive, demanding less. Yet, *how can I give you up?* is wrung from the very heart of God. One day, after exile, *I will bring them home again* (v. 11). The people with no future will in due time become a re-

They will destroy them,
trapping them in their own evil plans.
7 For my people are determined to desert me.
They call me the Most High,
but they don't truly honor me.

8 "Oh, how can I give you up, Israel?
How can I let you go?
How can I destroy you like Admah
or demolish you like Zeboiim?
My heart is torn within me,
and my compassion overflows.
9 No, I will not unleash my fierce anger.
I will not completely destroy Israel,
for I am God and not a mere mortal.
I am the Holy One living among you,
and I will not come to destroy.
10 For someday the people will follow me.
I, the LORD, will roar like a lion.
And when I roar,
my people will return trembling from the west.
11 Like a flock of birds, they will come from Egypt.
Trembling like doves, they will return from Assyria.
And I will bring them home again,"
says the LORD.

Charges against Israel and Judah

12* Israel surrounds me with lies and deceit,
but Judah still obeys God
and is faithful to the Holy One.*

12

1* The people of Israel* feed on the wind;
they chase after the east wind all day long.
They pile up lies and violence;
they are making an alliance with Assyria
while sending olive oil to buy support from Egypt.
2 Now the LORD is bringing charges against Judah.
He is about to punish Jacob* for all his deceitful ways,
and pay him back for all he has done.
3 Even in the womb,
Jacob struggled with his brother;
when he became a man,
he even fought with God.
4 Yes, he wrestled with the angel and won.
He wept and pleaded for a blessing from him.
There at Bethel he met God face to face,
and God spoke to him*—
5 the LORD God of Heaven's Armies,
the LORD is his name!
6 So now, come back to your God.
Act with love and justice,
and always depend on him.

7 But no, the people are like crafty merchants
selling from dishonest scales—
they love to cheat.
8 Israel boasts, "I am rich!
I've made a fortune all by myself!
No one has caught me cheating!
My record is spotless!"

9 "But I am the LORD your God,
who rescued you from slavery in Egypt.
And I will make you live in tents again,
as you do each year at the Festival of Shelters.*

11:12a Verse 11:12 is numbered 12:1 in Hebrew text. **11:12b** Or *and Judah is unruly against God, the faithful Holy One.* The meaning of the Hebrew is uncertain. **12:1a** Verses 12:1-14 are numbered 12:2-15 in Hebrew text. **12:1b** Hebrew *Ephraim,* referring to the northern kingdom of Israel; also in 12:8, 14. **12:2** *Jacob* sounds like the Hebrew word for "deceiver." **12:4** As in Greek and Syriac versions; Hebrew reads *to us.* **12:9** Hebrew *as in the days of your appointed feast.*

stored people. This has nothing to do with what they deserve, which is only permanent destruction. It is entirely to do with God's grace. Here is the gospel in Old Testament clothes.

11:12—14:9 History and Hope

11:12—12:14 Learning from the Past. Menahem, king of Israel from 752 to 742 BC, had already let Israel become a vassal state of Assyria in order to survive. Attempts to regain sovereignty under King Pekah in 735 led to Assyria annexing much of Israel. Hoshea, king from 732, tried to placate Assyria, but then double-crossed them by trying to forge a treaty with Egypt. This led directly to the final overthrow of Israel, with its people taken into exile. **12:2–8:** Jacob was a famous cheat (see Gen 27—30) who after an encounter with God became "Israel" and was considered to be a reformed character. Will Israel heed God's urgent call and *come back to your God* (12:6)? But with no willingness to encounter God as he is, Israel simply boasts that nobody can prove her cheating. **9–14:** God has constantly sent prophets to teach the people how to live and worship, and they have rejected them. Now nothing remains but the sentence of death because of their sin.

10 I sent my prophets to warn you
with many visions and parables."
11 But the people of Gilead are worthless
because of their idol worship.
And in Gilgal, too, they sacrifice bulls;
their altars are lined up like the heaps of
stone
along the edges of a plowed field.
12 Jacob fled to the land of Aram,
and there he* earned a wife by tending
sheep.
13 Then by a prophet
the LORD brought Jacob's descendants* out
of Egypt;
and by that prophet
they were protected.
14 But the people of Israel
have bitterly provoked the LORD,
so their Lord will now sentence them to death
in payment for their sins.

The LORD's Anger against Israel

13 1When the tribe of Ephraim spoke,
the people shook with fear,
for that tribe was important in
Israel.
But the people of Ephraim sinned by
worshiping Baal
and thus sealed their destruction.
2 Now they continue to sin by making silver
idols,
images shaped skillfully with human
hands.
"Sacrifice to these," they cry,
"and kiss the calf idols!"
3 Therefore, they will disappear like the
morning mist,
like dew in the morning sun,
like chaff blown by the wind,
like smoke from a chimney.

4 "I have been the LORD your God
ever since I brought you out of Egypt.
You must acknowledge no God but me,
for there is no other savior.
5 I took care of you in the wilderness,
in that dry and thirsty land.
6 But when you had eaten and were satisfied,
you became proud and forgot me.
7 So now I will attack you like a lion,
like a leopard that lurks along the road.
8 Like a bear whose cubs have been taken away,
I will tear out your heart.
I will devour you like a hungry lioness
and mangle you like a wild animal.

9 "You are about to be destroyed, O Israel—
yes, by me, your only helper.
10 Now where is* your king?
Let him save you!
Where are all the leaders of the land,
the king and the officials you demanded
of me?
11 In my anger I gave you kings,
and in my fury I took them away.

12 "Ephraim's guilt has been collected,
and his sin has been stored up for
punishment.
13 Pain has come to the people
like the pain of childbirth,
but they are like a child
who resists being born.
The moment of birth has arrived,
but they stay in the womb!

14 "Should I ransom them from the grave*?
Should I redeem them from death?
O death, bring on your terrors!
O grave, bring on your plagues!*
For I will not take pity on them.
15 Ephraim was the most fruitful of all his
brothers,
but the east wind—a blast from the
LORD—
will arise in the desert.
All their flowing springs will run dry,
and all their wells will disappear.
Every precious thing they own

12:12 Hebrew *Israel.* See note on 10:11b. **12:13** Hebrew *brought Israel.* See note on 10:11b. **13:10** As in Greek and Syriac versions and Latin Vulgate; Hebrew reads *I will be.* **13:14a** Hebrew *Sheol;* also in 13:14b. **13:14b** Greek version reads *O death, where is your punishment? / O grave* [Hades], *where is your sting?* Compare 1 Cor 15:55.

13:1–16 The Exclusiveness of God. The LORD now likens himself not to a loving father or to a loving husband but to a lion, a leopard, and a bear: all three feared as fierce animals, which tore people to pieces. The first two of the Ten Commandments make it crystal clear: *You must acknowledge no God but me, for there is no other savior* (v. 4). At the very heart of God's anger is idol worship: This is spiritual prostitution on a grand scale, for which violent destruction is the only possible outcome. God's agents of judgment will have no mercy, even on children and pregnant women. We rightly find this appalling. But it is a terrible truth we dare not ignore: God will not tolerate rivals. God is wrath as well as love.

will be plundered and carried away.
16*The people of Samaria
must bear the consequences of their guilt
because they rebelled against their God.
They will be killed by an invading army,
their little ones dashed to death against the ground,
their pregnant women ripped open by swords."

Healing for the Repentant

14 1*Return, O Israel, to the LORD your God,
for your sins have brought you down.
2 Bring your confessions, and return to the LORD.
Say to him,
"Forgive all our sins and graciously receive us,
so that we may offer you our praises.*
3 Assyria cannot save us,
nor can our warhorses.
Never again will we say to the idols we have made,
'You are our gods.'
No, in you alone
do the orphans find mercy."

4 The LORD says,
"Then I will heal you of your faithlessness;
my love will know no bounds,
for my anger will be gone forever.
5 I will be to Israel
like a refreshing dew from heaven.
Israel will blossom like the lily;
it will send roots deep into the soil
like the cedars in Lebanon.
6 Its branches will spread out like beautiful olive trees,
as fragrant as the cedars of Lebanon.
7 My people will again live under my shade.
They will flourish like grain and blossom like grapevines.
They will be as fragrant as the wines of Lebanon.
8 "O Israel,* stay away from idols!
I am the one who answers your prayers and cares for you.
I am like a tree that is always green;
all your fruit comes from me."
9 Let those who are wise understand these things.
Let those with discernment listen carefully.
The paths of the LORD are true and right,
and righteous people live by walking in them.
But in those paths sinners stumble and fall.

13:16 Verse 16 is numbered 14:1 in Hebrew text. **14:1** Verses 14:1-9 are numbered 14:2-10 in Hebrew text. **14:2** As in Greek and Syriac versions, which read *may repay the fruit of our lips;* Hebrew reads *may repay the bulls of our lips.* **14:8** Hebrew *Ephraim,* referring to the northern kingdom of Israel.

14:1–9 A Final Plea. 1–3: Shocked beyond words by the previous prophecy, it is hard to take in the final unfolding of the LORD's word through Hosea. God is wrath as well as love, love as well as wrath. Even now, Hosea pleads with his people to accept God's word and come to him with deep repentance. That involves a decisive break with all that they have trusted in and done, and a radically different future of life and worship. **4–8:** If the people do as Hosea says, the LORD will heal and restore and bless. It is as his people, with undivided love for him, that they will prosper and flourish and be content. **9:** Hosea, like all the prophets, has an unchanging word for all who will listen and learn. As the Lord Jesus Christ was to say centuries later, "Anyone with ears to hear should listen and understand!" (Matt 11:15).

JOEL

INTRODUCTION

Judah was in a sorry state. The people's faith had degenerated into mere duty. God hated seeing his people like this, so to reignite their faith, first he sent a disaster, then he sent the prophet Joel (meaning "the LORD is God") to interpret it. Dating is difficult, but the content (e.g., interest in Temple and cult but no mention of a king) suggests Joel lived around 500 BC. He says little about himself; what mattered was the "word of the LORD" that came to him. —*Gwynneth Marian Napier Raikes*

✧

1 The LORD gave this message to Joel son of Pethuel.

Mourning over the Locust Plague

2 Hear this, you leaders of the people.
Listen, all who live in the land.
In all your history,
has anything like this happened before?
3 Tell your children about it in the years to come,
and let your children tell their children.
Pass the story down from generation to generation.
4 After the cutting locusts finished eating the crops,
the swarming locusts took what was left!
After them came the hopping locusts,
and then the stripping locusts,* too!

5 Wake up, you drunkards, and weep!
Wail, all you wine-drinkers!
All the grapes are ruined,
and all your sweet wine is gone.
6 A vast army of locusts* has invaded my land,
a terrible army too numerous to count.
Its teeth are like lions' teeth,
its fangs like those of a lioness.
7 It has destroyed my grapevines
and ruined my fig trees,
stripping their bark and destroying it,
leaving the branches white and bare.
8 Weep like a bride dressed in black,
mourning the death of her husband.
9 For there is no grain or wine
to offer at the Temple of the LORD.
So the priests are in mourning.
The ministers of the LORD are weeping.
10 The fields are ruined,

1:4 The precise identification of the four kinds of locusts mentioned here is uncertain. **1:6** Hebrew *A nation.*

1:1–20 Responding to the Disaster

The disaster described was a severe locust plague, compounded by drought. **6–7:** Joel likens the swarming insects to invading armies. Behind the emphasis on *my land . . . my grapevines . . . my fig trees* is the truth that God cares and the encouragement to believe he will answer their prayers favorably. *Land* is feminine, leading to the imagery in verse 8. **7–12:** Humans and animals alike suffered, and the economy was ruined. No wonder that all *joy has dried up.* **5, 11, 13:** Joel especially encourages the drunkards,

the land is stripped bare.
The grain is destroyed,
the grapes have shriveled,
and the olive oil is gone.

11 Despair, all you farmers!
Wail, all you vine growers!
Weep, because the wheat and barley—
all the crops of the field—are ruined.
12 The grapevines have dried up,
and the fig trees have withered.
The pomegranate trees, palm trees, and apple trees—
all the fruit trees—have dried up.
And the people's joy has dried up with them.

13 Dress yourselves in burlap and weep, you priests!
Wail, you who serve before the altar!
Come, spend the night in burlap,
you ministers of my God.
For there is no grain or wine
to offer at the Temple of your God.
14 Announce a time of fasting;
call the people together for a solemn meeting.
Bring the leaders
and all the people of the land
into the Temple of the LORD your God,
and cry out to him there.
15 The day of the LORD is near,
the day when destruction comes from the Almighty.
How terrible that day will be!

16 Our food disappears before our very eyes.
No joyful celebrations are held in the house of our God.
17 The seeds die in the parched ground,
and the grain crops fail.
The barns stand empty,
and granaries are abandoned.
18 How the animals moan with hunger!
The herds of cattle wander about confused,
because they have no pasture.
The flocks of sheep and goats bleat in misery.
19 LORD, help us!
The fire has consumed the wilderness pastures,
and flames have burned up all the trees.
20 Even the wild animals cry out to you
because the streams have dried up,
and fire has consumed the wilderness pastures.

Locusts Invade like an Army

2 [1]Sound the alarm in Jerusalem*!
Raise the battle cry on my holy mountain!
Let everyone tremble in fear
because the day of the LORD is upon us.
2 It is a day of darkness and gloom,
a day of thick clouds and deep blackness.
Suddenly, like dawn spreading across the mountains,
a great and mighty army appears.

2:1 Hebrew *Zion;* also in 2:15, 23.

farmers, and priests to mourn. They would be particularly affected, as would the land itself. **13–15:** Joel wants to convince all the people to turn to God for help, for Joel saw beyond the immediate disaster to its spiritual and future significance. It was a sign of the coming *day of the LORD*. Joel's task was to shock the people into renewal: to help them see God's hand in their situation, to hear what God was saying, and to respond rightly. The LORD is not interested in mere external or emotional response. He seeks deep, heart-based response. Lamentation alone wasn't enough. Even the animals seek God's help; his people must do the same and turn to him in prayer, cry to him in repentance for help and mercy. Priests should set the example. **15:** Joel echoes Ezekiel 30:2–3 and Isaiah 13:6. There the *day of the LORD* threatened judgment for Judah's enemies. Here it warns of judgment for Judah, for the LORD is holy and demands holiness from his people. **16–20:** Years earlier, God promised that if they walked with him, he would make their land fruitful (e.g., Deut 11:13–17), but if they turned against him, their harvests would fail. The prophecy has become a reality. Their faith has degenerated into mere ritual, and they suffer the results of God's wrath, spiritually as well as physically.

Though not a priest, Joel identifies with God's people. He laments and prays. He recognizes this disaster as a sign of the far worse destruction from God that would fall on all who refused to take him seriously. Much later, Jesus Christ would repeat the warning (Mark 13:35–36). But even in such dark words of judgment, there is the light of hope.

2:1–17 Responding to the Day of the LORD

Chapter 2 begins with a warning: *The day of the LORD* is coming, of which the locusts are a forerunner. Both were days of inescapable *darkness and gloom* (cf.

Nothing like it has been seen before
or will ever be seen again.

3 Fire burns in front of them,
and flames follow after them.
Ahead of them the land lies
as beautiful as the Garden of Eden.
Behind them is nothing but desolation;
not one thing escapes.
4 They look like horses;
they charge forward like warhorses.*
5 Look at them as they leap along the mountaintops.
Listen to the noise they make—like the rumbling of chariots,
like the roar of fire sweeping across a field of stubble,
or like a mighty army moving into battle.

6 Fear grips all the people;
every face grows pale with terror.
7 The attackers march like warriors
and scale city walls like soldiers.
Straight forward they march,
never breaking rank.
8 They never jostle each other;
each moves in exactly the right position.
They break through defenses
without missing a step.
9 They swarm over the city
and run along its walls.
They enter all the houses,
climbing like thieves through the windows.
10 The earth quakes as they advance,
and the heavens tremble.
The sun and moon grow dark,
and the stars no longer shine.
11 The LORD is at the head of the column.
He leads them with a shout.
This is his mighty army,
and they follow his orders.
The day of the LORD is an awesome, terrible thing.
Who can possibly survive?

A Call to Repentance

12 That is why the LORD says,
"Turn to me now, while there is time.
Give me your hearts.
Come with fasting, weeping, and mourning.
13 Don't tear your clothing in your grief,
but tear your hearts instead."
Return to the LORD your God,
for he is merciful and compassionate,
slow to get angry and filled with unfailing love.
He is eager to relent and not punish.
14 Who knows? Perhaps he will give you a reprieve,
sending you a blessing instead of this curse.
Perhaps you will be able to offer grain and wine
to the LORD your God as before.

15 Blow the ram's horn in Jerusalem!
Announce a time of fasting;
call the people together
for a solemn meeting.
16 Gather all the people—
the elders, the children, and even the babies.
Call the bridegroom from his quarters
and the bride from her private room.
17 Let the priests, who minister in the LORD's presence,
stand and weep between the entry room to the Temple and the altar.
Let them pray, "Spare your people, LORD!
Don't let your special possession become an object of mockery.

2:4 Or *like charioteers.*

Exod 10:14–15; Zeph 1:15). **4–11:** Joel poetically portrays the invading army of locusts aggressively bent on destruction (cf. 1:6). People who heard them coming were terrified. The day of the LORD will be even more terrifying and destructive. The picture climaxes with the appearance of the army's commander: the LORD.

2:12–17 A Call to Repentance. Yet the situation could still change if Judah would respond rightly. For those who repent, the day brings good news of salvation. The first step is deep-seated, genuine repentance. Repentance will show itself outwardly in *fasting, weeping, and mourning,* but the inner (heart) response must come first. The basis of this hope of forgiveness is in God's character. The kindness of *the LORD your God* inclines him to grant a reprieve. **15–17:** So again Joel calls everyone to *a solemn meeting,* to urgent fasting and prayer. All, the aged and babies, even newlyweds, must participate, and again the priests must set the example. The remedy for dried-up faith doesn't change. The only way to deal with sin is by repentance. The only way to overcome failure is by prayer.

Don't let them become a joke for unbelieving
foreigners who say,
'Has the God of Israel left them?'"

The LORD's Promise of Restoration
18 Then the LORD will pity his people
and jealously guard the honor of his land.
19 The LORD will reply,
"Look! I am sending you grain and new wine
and olive oil,
enough to satisfy your needs.
You will no longer be an object of mockery
among the surrounding nations.
20 I will drive away these armies from the north.
I will send them into the parched
wastelands.
Those in the front will be driven into the
Dead Sea,
and those at the rear into the
Mediterranean.*
The stench of their rotting bodies will rise
over the land."

Surely the LORD has done great things!
21 Don't be afraid, my people.
Be glad now and rejoice,
for the LORD has done great things.
22 Don't be afraid, you animals of the field,
for the wilderness pastures will soon be
green.
The trees will again be filled with fruit;
fig trees and grapevines will be loaded
down once more.
23 Rejoice, you people of Jerusalem!
Rejoice in the LORD your God!
For the rain he sends demonstrates his
faithfulness.
Once more the autumn rains will come,
as well as the rains of spring.
24 The threshing floors will again be piled high
with grain,
and the presses will overflow with new
wine and olive oil.

25 The LORD says, "I will give you back what
you lost
to the swarming locusts, the hopping
locusts,
the stripping locusts, and the cutting locusts.*
It was I who sent this great destroying
army against you.
26 Once again you will have all the food you
want,
and you will praise the LORD your God,
who does these miracles for you.
Never again will my people be disgraced.
27 Then you will know that I am among my
people Israel,
that I am the LORD your God, and there is
no other.
Never again will my people be disgraced.

The LORD's Promise of His Spirit
28* "Then, after doing all those things,
I will pour out my Spirit upon all people.
Your sons and daughters will prophesy.

2:20 Hebrew *into the eastern sea, . . . into the western sea.* **2:25** The precise identification of the four kinds of locusts mentioned here is uncertain. **2:28** Verses 2:28-32 are numbered 3:1-5 in Hebrew text.

2:18–32 The LORD Responds to His Penitent People

Evidently Judah did repent and pray, for in response the LORD speaks directly (2:18—3:21). **18:** There are two faces to the LORD's steadfast covenant love: jealousy and pity. Both words convey an emotional involvement. His people, and even his land (see annotation on 1:6–7), may be full of deep emotion, but so is the LORD. Jealousy means he is exclusively committed to Judah and cannot tolerate anything less than Judah's exclusive commitment in return. Nor can he tolerate seeing his people humiliated (2:17; cf. Ps 79:4, 10). **19–26:** First God promises that the immediate future will be one of blessing. The LORD will restore locust-caused losses and will reverse the suffering of chapter 1. Prosperity will return. The next harvest will be plentiful, so land and animals need fear no more. Spiritual blessings will follow. Already the rains have started, and with them joy has returned. All this is a sign that the LORD has returned to his people and restored his covenant favor. **26–27:** But Joel knows how quickly God's people may again grow forgetful or complacent. Therefore land and people are called to remember that the LORD alone saves and to praise him. Therefore, Joel stresses that with prayer *never again will my people be disgraced.*

2:28–32 The LORD's Promise of His Spirit. More future blessings are promised. One day the LORD will pour out his Spirit *upon all people* (cf. Isa 44:3; Ezek 39:29; Zech 12:10). God's Spirit is active in creation and in equipping individuals for particular tasks (e.g., Judg 6:34; 1 Sam 10:10; Isa 61:1), but the Old Testament never said the Spirit is given to every believer. Now the LORD reveals that he wants this too. In Old Testament society, sons were often valued above daughters, older above younger, free above

Your old men will dream dreams,
and your young men will see visions.
29 In those days I will pour out my Spirit
even on servants—men and women alike.
30 And I will cause wonders in the heavens and on the earth—
blood and fire and columns of smoke.
31 The sun will become dark,
and the moon will turn blood red
before that great and terrible* day of the LORD arrives.
32 But everyone who calls on the name of the LORD
will be saved,
for some on Mount Zion in Jerusalem will escape,
just as the LORD has said.
These will be among the survivors
whom the LORD has called.

Judgment against Enemy Nations

3 1*"At the time of those events," says the LORD,
"when I restore the prosperity of Judah and Jerusalem,
2 I will gather the armies of the world
into the valley of Jehoshaphat.*
There I will judge them
for harming my people, my special possession,
for scattering my people among the nations,
and for dividing up my land.
3 They threw dice* to decide which of my people
would be their slaves.
They traded boys to obtain prostitutes
and sold girls for enough wine to get drunk.

4 "What do you have against me, Tyre and Sidon and you cities of Philistia? Are you trying to
take revenge on me? If you are, then watch out!
I will strike swiftly and pay you back for everything you have done. 5 You have taken my silver
and gold and all my precious treasures, and have
carried them off to your pagan temples. 6 You
have sold the people of Judah and Jerusalem to
the Greeks,* so they could take them far from
their homeland.
7 "But I will bring them back from all the places to which you sold them, and I will pay you
back for everything you have done. 8 I will sell
your sons and daughters to the people of Judah,
and they will sell them to the people of Arabia,*
a nation far away. I, the LORD, have spoken!"

9 Say to the nations far and wide:
"Get ready for war!
Call out your best warriors.
Let all your fighting men advance for the attack.
10 Hammer your plowshares into swords
and your pruning hooks into spears.
Train even your weaklings to be warriors.
11 Come quickly, all you nations everywhere.
Gather together in the valley."

And now, O LORD, call out your warriors!

12 "Let the nations be called to arms.
Let them march to the valley of Jehoshaphat.
There I, the LORD, will sit

2:31 Greek version reads *glorious.* **3:1** Verses 3:1-21 are numbered 4:1-21 in Hebrew text. **3:2** *Jehoshaphat* means "the LORD judges." **3:3** Hebrew *They cast lots.* **3:6** Hebrew *to the peoples of Javan.* **3:8** Hebrew *to the Sabeans.*

slave, and men above women. But when it comes to receiving and manifesting the Spirit, all distinctions are irrelevant. Acts 2:16–21 presents this prophecy as fulfilled at Pentecost. **31–32:** All this will happen on that *great and terrible day of the LORD*. First comes the pouring out of God's Spirit, then terrible signs in heaven and earth that God is bringing this world to an end (cf. Matt 24). But although salvation is offered to everyone, it will be received only by those who repent, believe, and pray: *everyone who calls on the name of the LORD*.

3:1–21 The LORD Restores His Penitent People

Joel describes the final triumph of justice and good over sin and evil. For a long time, Judah's neighbors had been abusing the nation. Child slavery was bad enough, but they were selling children solely for cheap pleasure. Now the LORD promises to judge them. **2–5:** Notice the repeated pronouns, *my people . . . my land . . . my precious treasures*, and the indignant question in God's voice. **4–8:** The Philistines are especially condemned because they had stolen the Temple treasures and sold God's covenant people into distant slavery (cf. Ezek 25:15—28:26). God will turn the tables so the punishment will fit the crime, and the mocking question of Joel 2:17 will be answered. History records that the Tyreans and Sidonians were enslaved in the mid-fourth century BC. **9–12:** There's a deliberate comparison between the summons to Jerusalem (1:14; 2:15) and that to Jehoshaphat. All are involved and must share responsibility; all must face the reality of God's wrath. **11–13:** Where Judah repented and the LORD responded with

to pronounce judgment on them all.
13 Swing the sickle,
for the harvest is ripe.*
Come, tread the grapes,
for the winepress is full.
The storage vats are overflowing
with the wickedness of these people."
14 Thousands upon thousands are waiting in the valley of decision.
There the day of the LORD will soon arrive.
15 The sun and moon will grow dark,
and the stars will no longer shine.
16 The LORD's voice will roar from Zion
and thunder from Jerusalem,
and the heavens and the earth will shake.
But the LORD will be a refuge for his people,
a strong fortress for the people of Israel.

Blessings for God's People

17 "Then you will know that I, the LORD your God,
live in Zion, my holy mountain.
Jerusalem will be holy forever,
and foreign armies will never conquer her again.
18 In that day the mountains will drip with sweet wine,
and the hills will flow with milk.
Water will fill the streambeds of Judah,
and a fountain will burst forth from the LORD's Temple,
watering the arid valley of acacias.*
19 But Egypt will become a wasteland
and Edom will become a wilderness,
because they attacked the people of Judah
and killed innocent people in their land.

20 "But Judah will be filled with people forever,
and Jerusalem will endure through all generations.
21 I will pardon my people's crimes,
which I have not yet pardoned;
and I, the LORD, will make my home
in Jerusalem* with my people."

3:13 Greek version reads *for the harvest time has come.* Compare Mark 4:29. **3:18** Hebrew *valley of Shittim.* **3:21** Hebrew *Zion.*

mercy (chap. 2), the nations remain arrogant, and the LORD brings down his warriors, presumably angels, to mete out judgment (cf. Zeph 3:8). **14–16:** By now Joel is speaking of all humanity. He again describes the day of the LORD until at last the nations realize they have been abusing not only God's people but also God (cf. Matt 25:45). So the valley of judgment becomes the valley of final decision—primarily God's decision, yet human decision too, because God's final decision about people is related to their final attitude to him.

3:17–21 Blessings for God's People. The day of the LORD holds terror only for God's enemies; those who trust him have nothing to fear. Better still, as he judges the nations, so the LORD will establish his people as citizens of a purified, holy, new Jerusalem, center of a glorious new world (cf. Rev 21:1—22:5). The LORD will live there among them and allow them to know him. The contrast of Judah's flowing streams and the fate of Egypt and Edom highlights the abundance of blessing. Again, it's a reversal of the devastation caused by the locusts. **21:** But much of this is yet to come. So Joel ends by reassuring those who still suffer that the LORD is always present and active on their behalf.

AMOS

INTRODUCTION

Amos, another of the twelve Minor Prophets, prophesied around 750 BC, two years before the earthquake that occurred toward the end of the reign of Jeroboam II (786–746 BC) and Uzziah (783–742 BC). Internal strife and external threats had returned after a time of peace and prosperity, which had brought relief from the constant warring with Judah and neighboring states.

Political strife, however, was not the only concern; social and economic conditions in Israel were also deteriorating. The international trade begun by the Omride dynasty (ninth century BC) had been continued by Jehu's dynasty and had brought prosperity to the upper classes at least. Israel exported agricultural products such as wheat, olive oil, and wine in exchange for luxury items like jewels, metal, and ivory. But at the same time, many peasants incurred debt, lost land and possessions, and were forced into debt slavery. The rich and powerful exploited the poor and weak through legal, if unethical, means. These lamentable consequences are also spoken of by other eighth-century prophets (Isa 5:8; Mic 2:2). The gap between rich and poor continued to widen in the eighth century BC, with increasingly luxurious lifestyle and conspicuous consumption for the wealthy and worsening living conditions for the poor. To this society Amos delivered his message.

The oracles were directed primarily to men, especially the wealthy and ruling class. But the attack on the rich women of Samaria shows that it was not just men who were the problem. Amos was the first prophet to have his oracles and visions collected into a book, although its authorship and date are much debated. A history of oral transmission and redaction of the oracles cannot be rejected, but the present structure of the book argues favorably for a single author, whether it is Amos or a later redactor.

Amos's concern for the poor and oppressed included women, but his focus was not on women per se. Modern readers, however, have benefited from recent research in such methods as social scientific and anthropological studies of preindustrial, agrarian societies, which help in the recovery of women's experience and women's voices from the pages of Amos.

The book of Amos addresses the social ills of eighth-century BC Israel but provides little information about the prophet. Amos 1:1 states that the prophet was a "shepherd from Tekoa" a town ten miles south of Jerusalem, on the border between arable land and the desert. The town was also known for its wise woman who reconciled Absalom to David (2 Sam 14:2). Amos was probably a large-scale sheep breeder, because the term "shepherd" is used in 2 Kings 3:4 to describe King Mesha of Moab. Amos also took "care of sycamore-fig trees" (Amos 7:14). The sycamore is a poor-quality fig that grows in the coastal plains and the Jordan Valley. Perhaps Amos's work took him outside of the hill country of Judah, and his business dealings with Israel revealed the abuses in the Northern Kingdom. His knowledge of international affairs and domestic conditions, as well as the language and structure of the book, suggests that Amos was not an ignorant, backwoods herdsman but one with a bright mind and a sensitive heart. —*Lai Ling Elizabeth Ngan*

1:1—2:3 Oracles against the Nations
2:4—6:14 Oracles against Judah and Israel
7:1—9:6 The Visions of Amos and Confrontation
9:7–15 Judgment and Hope

✧

1 This message was given to Amos, a shepherd from the town of Tekoa in Judah. He
received this message in visions two years
before the earthquake, when Uzziah was king of
Judah and Jeroboam II, the son of Jehoash,* was
king of Israel.
2 This is what he saw and heard:

"The LORD's voice will roar from Zion
and thunder from Jerusalem!
The lush pastures of the shepherds will dry up;
the grass on Mount Carmel will wither and
die."

God's Judgment on Israel's Neighbors

3 This is what the LORD says:

"The people of Damascus have sinned again
and again,*
and I will not let them go unpunished!
They beat down my people in Gilead
as grain is threshed with iron sledges.
4 So I will send down fire on King Hazael's
palace,
and the fortresses of King Ben-hadad will
be destroyed.
5 I will break down the gates of Damascus
and slaughter the people in the valley of
Aven.
I will destroy the ruler in Beth-eden,
and the people of Aram will go as captives
to Kir,"
says the LORD.

6 This is what the LORD says:

"The people of Gaza have sinned again and
again,
and I will not let them go unpunished!
They sent whole villages into exile,
selling them as slaves to Edom.
7 So I will send down fire on the walls of
Gaza,
and all its fortresses will be destroyed.
8 I will slaughter the people of Ashdod
and destroy the king of Ashkelon.
Then I will turn to attack Ekron,
and the few Philistines still left will be
killed,"
says the Sovereign LORD.

9 This is what the LORD says:

"The people of Tyre have sinned again and
again,

1:1 Hebrew *Joash,* a variant spelling of Jehoash. **1:3** Hebrew *have committed three sins, even four;* also in 1:6, 9, 11, 13.

1:1—2:3 Oracles against the Nations

Amos opened his indictments against the nations with an emphatic warning of the devastating effect of Yahweh's voice. Because the nations had exceeded the limit of offenses, God declared *I will not let them go unpunished.* The transgressions were not merely offenses but rebellions against Yahweh, and for these repeated rebellions, God would not hold back his voice.

1:3—2:3 Judgment on Neighboring Countries. In chapters 1—2, the prophet indicts eight nations: six non-Israelite nations for crimes against their neighbors, Judah for rejecting the Torah (*instruction*) of the LORD, and Israel for socioeconomic oppression against their own. **1:3–5:** The Syrians were accused of threshing Gilead with *iron sledges.* Second Samuel 12:31 uses the same phraseology to describe one form of punishment David exacted on the defeated Ammonites. In the Old Testament, iron evoked fear because of its association with weapons of brutality and torture from enemies, who used iron yokes, furnaces, chariots, and sharp threshing instruments (Deut 4:20; 28:48; Jer 28:14). **6–8:** The Philistines were indicted for wholesale deportation of communities, including young and old, male and female. Enslaving war captives was a common practice in the ancient world, but slave trading was different. What the Philistines did is comparable to events in Kosovo in 1999, when thousands of ethnic Albanians were forcibly removed from their homes in an attempt to displace and erase the memory of a people. **9–10:** The Phoenicians were also charged with wholesale slaving (cf. Joel 3:4–8; Ezek 27:13) made worse by not honoring covenant relationships formed by treaties.

and I will not let them go unpunished!
They broke their treaty of brotherhood with Israel,
selling whole villages as slaves to Edom.
10 So I will send down fire on the walls of Tyre,
and all its fortresses will be destroyed."

11 This is what the LORD says:

"The people of Edom have sinned again and again,
and I will not let them go unpunished!
They chased down their relatives, the Israelites, with swords,
showing them no mercy.
In their rage, they slashed them continually
and were unrelenting in their anger.
12 So I will send down fire on Teman,
and the fortresses of Bozrah will be destroyed."

13 This is what the LORD says:

"The people of Ammon have sinned again and again,
and I will not let them go unpunished!
When they attacked Gilead to extend their borders,
they ripped open pregnant women with their swords.
14 So I will send down fire on the walls of Rabbah,
and all its fortresses will be destroyed.
The battle will come upon them with shouts,
like a whirlwind in a mighty storm.
15 And their king* and his princes will go into exile together,"
says the LORD.

2 This is what the LORD says:

"The people of Moab have sinned again and again,*
and I will not let them go unpunished!
They desecrated the bones of Edom's king,
burning them to ashes.
2 So I will send down fire on the land of Moab,
and all the fortresses in Kerioth will be destroyed.
The people will fall in the noise of battle,
as the warriors shout and the ram's horn sounds.
3 And I will destroy their king
and slaughter all their princes,"
says the LORD.

God's Judgment on Judah and Israel

4 This is what the LORD says:

"The people of Judah have sinned again and again,
and I will not let them go unpunished!

1:15 Hebrew *malcam,* possibly referring to their god Molech.
2:1 Hebrew *have committed three sins, even four;* also in 2:4, 6.

11–12: If the Phoenicians were brothers by treaty, the Edomites were brothers by lineage (Gen 25:24–26). Yet Edom relentlessly *chased down their relatives . . . showing them no mercy.* The Hebrew word translated *mercy* is linked to the word "womb" (*rhm*). *Mercy* is a "womb feeling," an expression of tenderness and compassion toward the weak. **13–15:** The Ammonites likewise were indicted for ruthless slaughtering of women with the sword: *rip*[ping] *open pregnant women.* This horrific act of violence is not poetic exaggeration. In 2 Kings 8:12, Elisha wept for Hazael's future treatment of the Israelites. He will invade Israel and "dash their little children to the ground and rip open their pregnant women." Second Kings 15:16 reported that after Menahem son of Gadi seized the throne, he retaliated against Tappuach and the territory of Tirzah in the same way. Hosea 13:16 also pairs the dashing of the little ones with the ripping open of pregnant women as part of the horrors of war that will be inflicted on Samaria as just punishment from the LORD. This extreme brutality makes one recoil with disgust, but such violent crimes should be acknowledged for what they are and not relegated to a sociological phenomenon of war. Scholarly attempts to explain atrocities have tended to focus on the effect on the male population. Ripping open pregnant women should not be explained as an unfortunate result of eliminating the male line or of emasculating the fathers: The atrocity is perpetrated most directly on the woman. The unborn that is torn from the mother's womb is not always an unborn son; she may be an unborn daughter. Whatever the rationale for such barbarity, the woman is the one slaughtered. Ripping open pregnant women is the vicious murder of mothers and their children. **2:1–3:** Moab will be punished for its crimes against Edom, not Israel or Judah.

2:4—6:14 Oracles against Judah and Israel

The real target of Amos's preaching was Israel, here indicted for social injustice and for oppression and exploitation of the poor. The indictments against

They have rejected the instruction of the
LORD,
refusing to obey his decrees.
They have been led astray by the same lies
that deceived their ancestors.
5 So I will send down fire on Judah,
and all the fortresses of Jerusalem will be
destroyed."

6 This is what the LORD says:

"The people of Israel have sinned again and
again,
and I will not let them go unpunished!
They sell honorable people for silver
and poor people for a pair of sandals.
7 They trample helpless people in the dust
and shove the oppressed out of the way.
Both father and son sleep with the same
woman,
corrupting my holy name.
8 At their religious festivals,
they lounge in clothing their debtors put
up as security.
In the house of their gods,*
they drink wine bought with unjust fines.

9 "But as my people watched,
I destroyed the Amorites,
though they were as tall as cedars
and as strong as oaks.
I destroyed the fruit on their branches
and dug out their roots.
10 It was I who rescued you from Egypt
and led you through the desert for forty
years,
so you could possess the land of the
Amorites.
11 I chose some of your sons to be prophets
and others to be Nazirites.
Can you deny this, my people of Israel?"
asks the LORD.
12 "But you caused the Nazirites to sin by
making them drink wine,
and you commanded the prophets,
'Shut up!'

13 "So I will make you groan
like a wagon loaded down with sheaves of
grain.
14 Your fastest runners will not get away.
The strongest among you will become weak.
Even mighty warriors will be unable to save
themselves.
15 The archers will not stand their ground.
The swiftest runners won't be fast enough to
escape.
Even those riding horses won't be able to
save themselves.
16 On that day the most courageous of your
fighting men
will drop their weapons and run for their
lives,"
says the LORD.

2:8 Or *their God.*

Israel paralleled those against the other nations. They were accused of economic and territorial greed, of disregard for human life and decency. If God held other nations accountable for offenses against their neighbors, how much more would God hold Israel accountable for the same kind of offenses against their own? **2:4:** Israel was supposed to know God and his law. Their covenant relationship disallowed any claim of ignorance. **6–7a:** For the sake of economic and territorial greed, persons were sold for insignificant sums, the poor were treated with contempt, and justice was perverted. Debt slavery was common in the ancient Near East, and ancient Israel was no exception (cf. Exod 21:7; Lev 25:39–40; 2 Kgs 4:1–2; Neh 5:5). In a patriarchal society, a debtor who was forced to sell a dependent would more likely sell a daughter before a son. However, even when females had less worth in society, selling a child was not necessarily out of disregard for the daughter but out of desperate poverty. **7b:** Amos cites a specific abuse of women: *Both father and son sleep with the same woman.* The word translated here as *woman* refers to a virgin, a young woman of marriageable age or a high-ranking maidservant (Exod 2:5; 1 Sam 25:42; Esth 2:9; 4:4, 16). She was not necessarily a slave, nor a common or cultic prostitute. She was most likely a young female, dependent on and controlled by the males in her life. She represented a class of vulnerable and defenseless persons in society. The question remains as to what sort of sexual relations Amos was referring. There are prohibitions against father and son having sexual relations with each other's wife (Lev 18:8, 15), but the young woman's social status is not specified. Extramarital relations were not a problem for the man as long as they did not involve a woman who belonged to another male (Exod 21:7–11; Deut 15:12, 17). If the female was not designated, no property right was violated; then where was the offense? But the sexual exploitation of this young woman was a grave offense that profaned God's holy name. **9–11:** In contrast to Israel's treatment of the poor and defenseless, Amos presents God's gracious treatment when Israel was weak and oppressed. The imagery of God in this passage is

3 Listen to this message that the LORD has spoken against you, O people of Israel and Judah—against the entire family I rescued from Egypt:

2 "From among all the families on the earth,
I have been intimate with you alone.
That is why I must punish you
for all your sins."

Witnesses against Guilty Israel

3 Can two people walk together
without agreeing on the direction?
4 Does a lion ever roar in a thicket
without first finding a victim?
Does a young lion growl in its den
without first catching its prey?
5 Does a bird ever get caught in a trap
that has no bait?
Does a trap spring shut
when there's nothing to catch?
6 When the ram's horn blows a warning,
shouldn't the people be alarmed?
Does disaster come to a city
unless the LORD has planned it?

7 Indeed, the Sovereign LORD never does
anything
until he reveals his plans to his servants
the prophets.

8 The lion has roared—
so who isn't frightened?
The Sovereign LORD has spoken—
so who can refuse to proclaim his message?
9 Announce this to the leaders of Philistia*
and to the great ones of Egypt:
"Take your seats now on the hills around
Samaria,
and witness the chaos and oppression in
Israel."

10 "My people have forgotten how to do right,"
says the LORD.
"Their fortresses are filled with wealth
taken by theft and violence.
11 Therefore," says the Sovereign LORD,
"an enemy is coming!
He will surround them and shatter their
defenses.
Then he will plunder all their fortresses."

12 This is what the LORD says:

"A shepherd who tries to rescue a sheep from
a lion's mouth
will recover only two legs or a piece of an
ear.
So it will be for the Israelites in Samaria
lying on luxurious beds,
and for the people of Damascus reclining
on couches.*

13 "Now listen to this, and announce it
throughout all Israel,*" says the Lord, the LORD
God of Heaven's Armies.

14 "On the very day I punish Israel for its sins,
I will destroy the pagan altars at Bethel.
The horns of the altar will be cut off
and fall to the ground.
15 And I will destroy the beautiful homes of the
wealthy—

3:9 Hebrew *Ashdod.* **3:12** The meaning of the Hebrew in this sentence is uncertain. **3:13** Hebrew *the house of Jacob.* The names "Jacob" and "Israel" are often interchanged throughout the Old Testament, referring sometimes to the individual patriarch and sometimes to the nation.

not only of a warrior and savior but also of a mother who fiercely fought, protected, and provided for her brood, even though her children were callous and ungrateful. They even rejected God's provisions of prophets and Nazirites (Num 6:1–21). How unlike God the Israelites were! **3:1:** This verse and 4:1 and 5:1 begin with command to *listen* to the indictment from the LORD.

3:3–15 Witnesses against Guilty Israel. Amos provides a synopsis of Israel's sins and God's judgment. Most of the oracles here were directed toward the rich and powerful because they were responsible for the oppression and had the power to correct abuses. The accused here are Judah and Israel, whose behavior indicated that they had forgotten their covenant relationship with one another and with God. Private greed and ambition had replaced communal concern and welfare. Out of all the nations, God had entered into a relationship only with Israel; yet Israel did not act like one who knew God. Therefore God will punish them for all their iniquities. **9–11:** The prophet summoned the Philistines and Egyptians, enemies known for violence and oppression, to witness and be astounded by the tumults and oppressions in Samaria (cf. Ezek 45:9). The ruling class had grown rich and powerful through crimes against persons (*violence*) and property (*theft*). **11–12:** As a result of their moral and ethical offenses, Yahweh would destroy the nation. The social structures, which they saw as their security and the fruit of their exploitation, would be no more.

their winter mansions and their summer
houses, too—
all their palaces filled with ivory,"
says the LORD.

Israel's Failure to Learn

4 [1]Listen to me, you fat cows*
living in Samaria,
you women who oppress the poor
and crush the needy,
and who are always calling to your husbands,
"Bring us another drink!"
2 The Sovereign LORD has sworn this by his
holiness:
"The time will come when you will be led away
with hooks in your noses.
Every last one of you will be dragged away
like a fish on a hook!
3 You will be led out through the ruins of the
wall;
you will be thrown from your fortresses,*"
says the LORD.

4 "Go ahead and offer sacrifices to the idols at
Bethel.
Keep on disobeying at Gilgal.
Offer sacrifices each morning,
and bring your tithes every three days.
5 Present your bread made with yeast
as an offering of thanksgiving.
Then give your extra voluntary offerings
so you can brag about it everywhere!
This is the kind of thing you Israelites love
to do,"
says the Sovereign LORD.

6 "I brought hunger to every city
and famine to every town.
But still you would not return to me,"
says the LORD.

7 "I kept the rain from falling
when your crops needed it the most.
I sent rain on one town
but withheld it from another.
Rain fell on one field,
while another field withered away.
8 People staggered from town to town looking
for water,
but there was never enough.
But still you would not return to me,"
says the LORD.

9 "I struck your farms and vineyards with
blight and mildew.
Locusts devoured all your fig and olive
trees.
But still you would not return to me,"
says the LORD.

10 "I sent plagues on you
like the plagues I sent on Egypt long ago.
I killed your young men in war
and led all your horses away.*
The stench of death filled the air!
But still you would not return to me,"
says the LORD.

11 "I destroyed some of your cities,
as I destroyed* Sodom and Gomorrah.
Those of you who survived
were like charred sticks pulled from a fire.

4:1 Hebrew *you cows of Bashan.* **4:3** Or *thrown out toward Harmon,* possibly a reference to Mount Hermon. **4:10** Or *and slaughtered your captured horses.* **4:11** Hebrew *as when God destroyed.*

4:1–13 Israel's Failure to Learn. After the summary charges of 3:9–11, the oracles of 4:1, 5:1, and 6:1 focused on specific groups in Samaria. **1–3:** The first group was the *fat cows,* literally "cows of Bashan," a fertile Transjordanian region known for lush pastures and prized cattle (Deut 32:14; Ps 22:12). The Hebrew Bible and Ugaritic literature often use animal names as titles for leaders and dignitaries, and "cows of Bashan" refers to the wealthy women of the royal household and its officials. It may also be descriptive of these women's indulgent, pampered lifestyle rather than simply an insult. **1:** The wealthy women of Samaria were charged with the abuse and exploitation of the poor. They were oppressing the poor, crushing the needy, and asking their lords for *another drink.* The language suggests continuous action—their unquenchable demands for more were responsible for injustice and oppression in society. In Amos the frequent association of wine and excess feasting among the upper class suggests that the women were demanding wine and luxury items befitting their social status. These wealthy women, like others in patriarchal societies, were relegated to the domestic realm while their men dominated the public arena; but women were not without power or influence in their families and, indirectly, in society. The rich women were still in an advantaged position in comparison with women and men of lower socioeconomic status. They were dependent upon and controlled by their husbands, but the women were nevertheless responsible because they encouraged and participated in a lifestyle that perpetuated oppression. For Amos, the ethical implications of the covenant applied to women and men.

But still you would not return to me,"
says the LORD.

12 "Therefore, I will bring upon you all the
disasters I have announced.
Prepare to meet your God in judgment,
you people of Israel!"

13 For the LORD is the one who shaped the
mountains,
stirs up the winds, and reveals his thoughts
to mankind.
He turns the light of dawn into darkness
and treads on the heights of the earth.
The LORD God of Heaven's Armies is his
name!

A Call to Repentance

5 Listen, you people of Israel! Listen to this
funeral song I am singing:

2 "The virgin Israel has fallen,
never to rise again!
She lies abandoned on the ground,
with no one to help her up."

3 The Sovereign LORD says:

"When a city sends a thousand men to battle,
only a hundred will return.
When a town sends a hundred,
only ten will come back alive."

4 Now this is what the LORD says to the family of Israel:

"Come back to me and live!
5 Don't worship at the pagan altars at Bethel;
don't go to the shrines at Gilgal or
Beersheba.
For the people of Gilgal will be dragged off
into exile,
and the people of Bethel will be reduced to
nothing."

6 Come back to the LORD and live!
Otherwise, he will roar through Israel* like a
fire,
devouring you completely.
Your gods in Bethel
won't be able to quench the flames.
7 You twist justice, making it a bitter pill for
the oppressed.
You treat the righteous like dirt.

8 It is the LORD who created the stars,
the Pleiades and Orion.
He turns darkness into morning
and day into night.
He draws up water from the oceans
and pours it down as rain on the land.
The LORD is his name!
9 With blinding speed and power he destroys
the strong,
crushing all their defenses.

10 How you hate honest judges!
How you despise people who tell the truth!
11 You trample the poor,
stealing their grain through taxes and
unfair rent.
Therefore, though you build beautiful stone
houses,
you will never live in them.
Though you plant lush vineyards,
you will never drink wine from them.
12 For I know the vast number of your sins
and the depth of your rebellions.
You oppress good people by taking bribes
and deprive the poor of justice in the
courts.
13 So those who are smart keep their mouths shut,
for it is an evil time.

5:6 Hebrew *the house of Joseph.*

5:1–17 A Call to Repentance. Amos indicts Israel for its injustices and pleads with Israel to seek God in order to avoid disaster. **1–3:** A funeral lament directed at the house of Israel bemoans the fallen *virgin Israel*. This *virgin* is Samaria itself. The Old Testament frequently uses the feminine gender to denote cities. Jerusalem is called Daughter Zion, and the city of Abel-beth-maacah, "a mother in Israel" (2 Sam 20:19). Towns and villages surrounding a significant city were called its daughters. The Old Testament combines the feminine designation of cities with language of violence to present metaphorically the fallen city as a raped woman, whether it be Nineveh, Babylon, or Jerusalem, and here, Samaria. Samaria, like a raped woman, was ravished and abandoned, publicly violated and shamed on her own land but with no one to help. Where were her warriors and defenders? Had she been grievously wounded? Was she dead? Samaria will be punished because the Israelites were guilty. When the day of disaster comes, the capital city will no longer be an object of desire but an object of pity and contempt. The city, because of its idolatry and oppression, is dying. But this is a matter for deep mourning, and God longs that she may *come back to the LORD and live*.

14 Do what is good and run from evil
so that you may live!
Then the LORD God of Heaven's Armies will
be your helper,
just as you have claimed.
15 Hate evil and love what is good;
turn your courts into true halls of justice.
Perhaps even yet the LORD God of Heaven's
Armies
will have mercy on the remnant of his
people.*

16 Therefore, this is what the Lord, the LORD God of Heaven's Armies, says:

"There will be crying in all the public
squares
and mourning in every street.
Call for the farmers to weep with you,
and summon professional mourners to
wail.
17 There will be wailing in every vineyard,
for I will destroy them all,"
says the LORD.

Warning of Coming Judgment

18 What sorrow awaits you who say,
"If only the day of the LORD were here!"
You have no idea what you are wishing for.
That day will bring darkness, not light.
19 In that day you will be like a man who runs
from a lion—
only to meet a bear.
Escaping from the bear, he leans his hand
against a wall in his house—
and he's bitten by a snake.
20 Yes, the day of the LORD will be dark and
hopeless,
without a ray of joy or hope.
21 "I hate all your show and pretense—
the hypocrisy of your religious festivals
and solemn assemblies.
22 I will not accept your burnt offerings and
grain offerings.
I won't even notice all your choice peace
offerings.
23 Away with your noisy hymns of praise!
I will not listen to the music of your harps.
24 Instead, I want to see a mighty flood of
justice,
an endless river of righteous living.

25 "Was it to me you were bringing sacrifices
and offerings during the forty years in the wilderness, Israel? 26 No, you served your pagan
gods—Sakkuth your king god and Kaiwan your
star god—the images you made for yourselves.
27 So I will send you into exile, to a land east of
Damascus,*" says the LORD, whose name is the
God of Heaven's Armies.

6 1 What sorrow awaits you who lounge in
luxury in Jerusalem,*
and you who feel secure in Samaria!
You are famous and popular in Israel,
and people go to you for help.

5:15 Hebrew *the remnant of Joseph.* **5:26-27** Greek version reads *No, you carried your pagan gods—the shrine of Molech, the star of your god Rephan, and the images you made for yourselves. So I will send you into exile, to a land east of Damascus.* Compare Acts 7:43. **6:1** Hebrew *in Zion.*

5:18—6:14 Warning of Coming Judgment. Amos also challenged the Israelite belief in the day of the LORD. **5:18–20:** The Israelites looked forward eagerly to the day when God would fight for Israel and destroy their enemies, but Amos asked incredulously why they desired this day. It will not be a day of light and glory, as anticipated, but an inescapable day of darkness and gloom. **21–24:** What God desired of Israel was not extravagant rituals and manifold sacrifices but that *justice* and *righteous living* may permeate every aspect of society. Justice and righteousness are practical expressions of life together as the people of God. To establish justice and righteousness means the cessation of violence and robbery (cf. Ezek 45:9; Amos 3:9–11); it means to love good and hate evil and to correct what is crooked. God's desire for justice and righteousness is far from accomplished today. The people of God cannot be indifferent to the suffering that injustice and oppressions inflict. When taxation unfairly burdens the poor, when justice can be bought through highly paid lawyers, are these not exploitation and oppression? Nor can we claim ignorance when communication technology brings the needs of women and men around the world into our living rooms nightly. Neither can we feign powerlessness. Christians can work toward justice and righteousness by effecting structural changes in society, altering personal lifestyle choices, standing with the oppressed and needy, and promoting equality and dignity of all persons. What will God's people do to feed *the endless river of righteous living* (5:24)? **6:1–7:** This section consists of two woe oracles against the ruling house and leading citizens in Samaria. The prophet indicted them for their self-importance and false confidence, their violence and oppression without regard for consequence and their leisurely idleness and conspicuous consumption. **4–7:** Amos describes the Israelites' participation in

God's Call to Social Justice

Underlying God's call to social justice is the biblical teaching that because our just God created a good world, with adequate resources for all, God cares deeply about the welfare of the unique life-form created in his image (Gen 1:26–31; Ps 146).

In harmony with the New Testament teaching that faith without works is dead (Jas 2:14–16), the Old Testament connects doing justice with faith in God and unjust actions with unbelief (Prov 14:31; Jer 22:13–17). The repentant heart expresses its love for God by concern for the poor and oppressed (Ps 15), whereas ingrained injustice indicates a hardened heart that separates an individual and a nation from God (Isa 59:1–15). All of Scripture clearly links love of God with love for others (Ps 112; 1 Jn 3:16–17) and condemns the false piety of any who engage in outward religiosity while acting unjustly (Is 1:12–20; Amos 5:21–24; Luke 11:37–44).

The Old Testament prophets called God's people not only to turn to God and renounce personal sin but also to demonstrate a new inner heart for God by outward acts of compassion for the needy. In particular, Micah and Amos warned against the delusion that would think God's people exempt from God's call to pursue social righteousness, and they indicted Israel for tolerating personal and institutionalized legal and religious discrimination (Amos 5:11–15; Mic 3:9–12).

In the New Testament, Jesus explicitly connected discipleship with social concern (Luke 6:27–36) and cited compassion for the needy as one measure by which he would recognize his followers (Matt 25:31–46). One of the more somber biblical themes is that God's judgment will descend on individuals and nations who ignore social justice (Prov 22:8; Jer 5:20–29; Zech 7:8–14; Matt 23:23).

Rejecting any human notion that might makes right, the Bible places special emphasis on protecting the powerless, including orphans, aliens, and widows (Deut 24:17–21; 27:19; Jer 22:3; Jas 1:27). Throughout recorded history, women have been among the poorest of the poor, and Scripture teaches society's obligation to meet their basic needs.

The Bible contains significant examples of women who exemplify God's justice. The capable wife in Proverbs is a timeless role model who "opens her arms to the needy" (Prov 31:20). Tabitha was revered in the early church for "doing kind things for others and helping the poor" (Acts 9:36–41). Jesus' citation of the persistent widow who sued for justice encourages every powerless person facing unjust treatment (Luke 18: l–8).

Although women have most often been among the disadvantaged, nevertheless women as well as men are accountable to God for their response to God's call to social justice. Amos predicts doom for idle, rich women who "oppress the poor and crush the needy" (Amos 4:1–3). Sapphira and her husband were equally culpable for deceiving the faith community (Acts 5:1–11). Biblical justice rejects any special pleading that would in reality foster further discrimination against women by implying their inability to act as responsibly as men.

God's social ideal is a compassionate community in which all persons are equally valued as fellow image bearers.

2 But go over to Calneh
and see what happened there.
Then go to the great city of Hamath
and down to the Philistine city of Gath.
You are no better than they were,
and look at how they were destroyed.
3 You push away every thought of coming
disaster,
but your actions only bring the day of
judgment closer.
4 How terrible for you who sprawl on ivory
beds
and lounge on your couches,
eating the meat of tender lambs from the
flock
and of choice calves fattened in the stall.

the *mrzh* institution (*parties* or revelry; cf. Jer 16:5), a funerary association popular throughout the ancient Near East. The primary activity of the gathering was feasting, and the Israelite banqueting was clearly extravagant indeed. Reclining on couches and beds decorated with ivory inlay, the upper class of Samaria feasted on choice cuts of tender meat and improvised songs on musical instruments. Any meat was a rare luxury and they were overindulging in the most expensive lamb and veal while also lavishing wine and the finest oil on themselves. If this was a funerary association, how ironic that they did not see or

[5] You sing trivial songs to the sound of the harp
and fancy yourselves to be great musicians
like David.
[6] You drink wine by the bowlful
and perfume yourselves with fragrant
lotions.
You care nothing about the ruin of your
nation.*
[7] Therefore, you will be the first to be led away
as captives.
Suddenly, all your parties will end.

[8] The Sovereign LORD has sworn by his own
name, and this is what he, the LORD God of
Heaven's Armies, says:

"I despise the arrogance of Israel,*
and I hate their fortresses.
I will give this city
and everything in it to their enemies."

[9] (If there are ten men left in one house, they will
all die. [10] And when a relative who is responsible
to dispose of the dead* goes into the house to
carry out the bodies, he will ask the last survivor, "Is anyone else with you?" When the person
begins to swear, "No, by . . . ," he will interrupt
and say, "Stop! Don't even mention the name of
the LORD.")

[11] When the LORD gives the command,
homes both great and small will be
smashed to pieces.
[12] Can horses gallop over boulders?
Can oxen be used to plow them?
But that's how foolish you are when you turn
justice into poison
and the sweet fruit of righteousness into
bitterness.
[13] And you brag about your conquest of
Lo-debar.*
You boast, "Didn't we take Karnaim* by
our own strength?"

[14] "O people of Israel, I am about to bring an
enemy nation against you,"
says the LORD God of Heaven's Armies.
"They will oppress you throughout your
land—
from Lebo-hamath in the north
to the Arabah Valley in the south."

A Vision of Locusts

7 The Sovereign LORD showed me a vision.
I saw him preparing to send a vast swarm
of locusts over the land. This was after the
king's share had been harvested from the fields
and as the main crop was coming up. [2] In my vision the locusts ate every green plant in sight.
Then I said, "O Sovereign LORD, please forgive us
or we will not survive, for Israel* is so small."

6:6 Hebrew *of Joseph.* **6:8** Hebrew *Jacob.* See note on 3:13. **6:10** Or *to burn the dead.* The meaning of the Hebrew is uncertain. **6:13a** *Lo-debar* means "nothing." **6:13b** *Karnaim* means "horns," a term that symbolizes strength. **7:2** Hebrew *Jacob;* also in 7:5. See note on 3:13.

grieve over Israel's last gasps. **8–14:** God's judgment on the sinful nation was destruction. The themes of destruction and exile have reverberated throughout chapters 3—6. Just as the leading women will go into exile (4:2–3), so will the leading men (6:7) and the nation (5:27). Those who had regarded themselves as first will be the first to go into exile. Even the sanctuaries of Bethel and Gilgal and Beersheba will suffer the same fate. The destruction will affect everyone, rich or poor, male or female. The day will be so bitter that wailing and lamenting will be heard in all the squares and streets. Instead of celebrating the harvest of fields and vineyards, the farmers and the professional mourners will mourn (5:16–17).

Amos's oracles against the rich and powerful challenged the popular theology of eighth-century Israel by reversing its claims and expectations. Material wealth and prosperity were seen as indicators of blessings and right relation with God while being poor and afflicted was regarded as punishment for sin. Amos, however, called the poor righteous and the rich sinners. He scorned Israel for their fervent participation at cultic sites and their many offerings, as if sanctuaries could save. Amos urged them to seek God and not the house of God ("Bethel," 5:4–5). True worship requires integration of head, heart, and hand. Genuine worship of God and ethical behavior toward one's neighbor are inseparable (cf. Mic 6:8; Jas 1:27). While the Israelites claimed that God was with them, that they were in the right, Amos claimed that this could be reality only if they dedicated themselves wholly to seeking God and what God desires through a moral, ethical life (5:4–7, 14–15).

7:1—9:6 The Visions of Amos and Confrontation

In three separate visions, God shows Amos judgments that will befall Israel. **7:1–3:** The first vision relates an agricultural disaster in which locusts devour the newly sprouted crop that was planted after the king took the first crop. **4–6:** The second vision relates an ecological disaster in which fire devours the land and the water that supported the land (*the depths of the*

3 So the LORD relented from this plan. "I will
not do it," he said.

A Vision of Fire

4 Then the Sovereign LORD showed me another
vision. I saw him preparing to punish his people with a great fire. The fire had burned up the
depths of the sea and was devouring the entire
land. 5 Then I said, "O Sovereign LORD, please stop
or we will not survive, for Israel is so small."
6 Then the LORD relented from this plan, too.
"I will not do that either," said the Sovereign
LORD.

A Vision of a Plumb Line

7 Then he showed me another vision. I saw the
Lord standing beside a wall that had been built
using a plumb line. He was using a plumb line to
see if it was still straight. 8 And the LORD said to
me, "Amos, what do you see?"
I answered, "A plumb line."
And the Lord replied, "I will test my people
with this plumb line. I will no longer ignore all
their sins. 9 The pagan shrines of your ancestors*
will be ruined, and the temples of Israel will be
destroyed; I will bring the dynasty of King Jeroboam to a sudden end."

Amos and Amaziah

10 Then Amaziah, the priest of Bethel, sent a message to Jeroboam, king of Israel: "Amos is hatching a plot against you right here on your very
doorstep! What he is saying is intolerable. 11 He
is saying, 'Jeroboam will soon be killed, and the
people of Israel will be sent away into exile.' "
12 Then Amaziah sent orders to Amos: "Get
out of here, you prophet! Go on back to the land
of Judah, and earn your living by prophesying
there! 13 Don't bother us with your prophecies
here in Bethel. This is the king's sanctuary and
the national place of worship!"
14 But Amos replied, "I'm not a professional
prophet, and I was never trained to be one.* I'm
just a shepherd, and I take care of sycamore-fig
trees. 15 But the LORD called me away from my
flock and told me, 'Go and prophesy to my people in Israel.' 16 Now then, listen to this message
from the LORD:

"You say,
'Don't prophesy against Israel.
Stop preaching against my people.*'
17 But this is what the LORD says:
'Your wife will become a prostitute in this
city,
and your sons and daughters will be killed.
Your land will be divided up,
and you yourself will die in a foreign land.
And the people of Israel will certainly become
captives in exile,
far from their homeland.' "

A Vision of Ripe Fruit

8 Then the Sovereign LORD showed me another vision. In it I saw a basket filled with
ripe fruit. 2 "What do you see, Amos?" he
asked.
I replied, "A basket full of ripe fruit."
Then the LORD said, "Like this fruit, Israel is
ripe for punishment! I will not delay their punishment again. 3 In that day the singing in the
Temple will turn to wailing. Dead bodies will be
scattered everywhere. They will be carried out of

7:9 Hebrew *of Isaac.* **7:14** Or *I'm not a prophet nor the son of a prophet.* **7:16** Hebrew *against the house of Isaac.*

sea). Amos interceded in both cases, but his pleas only delayed judgment. **7–9:** In the third vision, God was standing by a wall. The word traditionally translated as *plumb line* is difficult to translate. A curious note is Amos's choice of word. Why did he use *anak*, an Akkadian loanword? It might indicate some kind of potential invasion by an enemy, leading to the destruction described in verse 9.

7:10–17 Encounter with Amaziah. Sandwiched between the third and fourth visions is Amaziah's confrontation with Amos. Amaziah challenged Amos's legitimacy to preach in the north and charged that his preaching was threatening the monarchy and social stability. Amos, however, countered the charge with the irresistible nature of the call of God. **16–17:** For his attempt to obstruct Amos's message, Amaziah was cursed with a fivefold curse, including a life of prostitution for his wife, a particularly harsh and degrading punishment for Amaziah because of the sanctity of the priesthood. Priests were strictly forbidden to marry prostitutes or divorced women (Lev 21:7–9, 13–15), and the daughter of a priest caught in adultery would be burned, not stoned (Lev 21:9). Like other women in war, Amaziah's wife would be victimized. Deprived of husband and children, her only means of survival was prostitution. She would bear a greater humiliation than other women, for she was the wife of the priest of Bethel.

8:1–14 Vision of Ripe Fruit. The fourth vision is based on a wordplay of *qayis*, "a basket of overripe fruit," and *qes*, "the final hour." The end has come because God will no longer overlook Israel's transgressions.

the city in silence. I, the Sovereign LORD, have spoken!"

4 Listen to this, you who rob the poor
and trample down the needy!
5 You can't wait for the Sabbath day to be over
and the religious festivals to end
so you can get back to cheating the
helpless.
You measure out grain with dishonest
measures
and cheat the buyer with dishonest scales.*
6 And you mix the grain you sell
with chaff swept from the floor.
Then you enslave poor people
for one piece of silver or a pair of sandals.

7 Now the LORD has sworn this oath
by his own name, the Pride of Israel*:
"I will never forget
the wicked things you have done!
8 The earth will tremble for your deeds,
and everyone will mourn.
The ground will rise like the Nile River at
floodtime;
it will heave up, then sink again.

9 "In that day," says the Sovereign LORD,
"I will make the sun go down at noon
and darken the earth while it is still day.
10 I will turn your celebrations into times of
mourning
and your singing into weeping.
You will wear funeral clothes
and shave your heads to show your
sorrow—
as if your only son had died.
How very bitter that day will be!

11 "The time is surely coming," says the
Sovereign LORD,
"when I will send a famine on the land—
not a famine of bread or water
but of hearing the words of the LORD.
12 People will stagger from sea to sea
and wander from border to border*
searching for the word of the LORD,
but they will not find it.
13 Beautiful girls and strong young men
will grow faint in that day,
thirsting for the LORD's word.
14 And those who swear by the shameful idols
of Samaria—
who take oaths in the name of the god of
Dan
and make vows in the name of the god of
Beersheba*—
they will all fall down,
never to rise again."

A Vision of God at the Altar

9 Then I saw a vision of the Lord standing
beside the altar. He said,

"Strike the tops of the Temple columns,
so that the foundation will shake.
Bring down the roof
on the heads of the people below.
I will kill with the sword those who survive.
No one will escape!

2 "Even if they dig down to the place of the
dead,*
I will reach down and pull them up.
Even if they climb up into the heavens,
I will bring them down.
3 Even if they hide at the very top of Mount
Carmel,
I will search them out and capture them.
Even if they hide at the bottom of the ocean,
I will send the sea serpent after them to
bite them.
4 Even if their enemies drive them into exile,
I will command the sword to kill them
there.
I am determined to bring disaster upon them
and not to help them."

5 The Lord, the LORD of Heaven's Armies,
touches the land and it melts,
and all its people mourn.
The ground rises like the Nile River at
floodtime,
and then it sinks again.
6 The LORD's home reaches up to the heavens,
while its foundation is on the earth.
He draws up water from the oceans

8:5 Hebrew *You make the ephah* [a unit for measuring grain] *small and the shekel* [a unit of weight] *great, and you deal falsely by using deceitful balances.* **8:7** Hebrew *the pride of Jacob.* See note on 3:13. **8:12** Hebrew *from north to east.* **8:14** Hebrew *the way of Beersheba.* **9:2** Hebrew *to Sheol.*

9:1–6 Vision of God at the Altar. The fifth vision confirmed that Yahweh's decision was final. The religious and political structures of Israel would be demolished (7:8–9; 8:3). Israel needed to be reminded of God's sovereignty and of Israel's own insignificance in light of that. Amos called into question Israel's arrogance and self-importance. They were no different from other people whom God moved at will.

and pours it down as rain on the land.
The LORD is his name!

7 "Are you Israelites more important to me
than the Ethiopians?*" asks the LORD.
"I brought Israel out of Egypt,
but I also brought the Philistines from
Crete*
and led the Arameans out of Kir.

8 "I, the Sovereign LORD,
am watching this sinful nation of Israel.
I will destroy it
from the face of the earth.
But I will never completely destroy the
family of Israel,*"
says the LORD.
9 "For I will give the command
and will shake Israel along with the other
nations
as grain is shaken in a sieve,
yet not one true kernel will be lost.
10 But all the sinners will die by the sword—
all those who say, 'Nothing bad will happen
to us.'

A Promise of Restoration

11 "In that day I will restore the fallen house* of
David.
I will repair its damaged walls.
From the ruins I will rebuild it
and restore its former glory.
12 And Israel will possess what is left of Edom
and all the nations I have called to be
mine.*"
The LORD has spoken,
and he will do these things.

13 "The time will come," says the LORD,
"when the grain and grapes will grow
faster
than they can be harvested.
Then the terraced vineyards on the hills of
Israel
will drip with sweet wine!
14 I will bring my exiled people of Israel
back from distant lands,
and they will rebuild their ruined cities
and live in them again.
They will plant vineyards and gardens;
they will eat their crops and drink their
wine.
15 I will firmly plant them there
in their own land.
They will never again be uprooted
from the land I have given them,"
says the LORD your God.

9:7a Hebrew *the Cushites?* **9:7b** Hebrew *Caphtor.* **9:8** Hebrew *the house of Jacob.* See note on 3:13. **9:11a** Or *kingdom;* Hebrew reads *tent.* **9:11b-12** Greek version reads *and restore its former glory, / so that the rest of humanity, including the Gentiles— / all those I have called to be mine—might seek me.* Compare Acts 15:16-17.

9:7–15 Judgment and Hope

Although the destruction from God was sure, God will not utterly destroy Israel. Hope was extended to the remnant. God will restore them to the golden age of the Davidic kingdom; their territory will expand; the land will respond with agricultural abundance; they will live in peace and security; and the gift of the land will be their permanent possession. **7:** If Yahweh can move the Arameans back to Kir, their place of origin (cf. 1:5; 2 Kgs 16:9), Yahweh can move the Israelites back to *their* place of origin. Israel's election brought responsibility, not immunity. God will punish the sinful nation.

OBADIAH

NTRODUCTION

The book is attributed to Obadiah, another of the Minor Prophets, whose name means "worshiper (or servant) of Yahweh." The time of composition is much debated, but evidence suggests the exilic period. First, Obadiah 11–14 likely alludes to the fall of Jerusalem (587 BC). Second, Obadiah 1–3 probably is dependent on Jeremiah 49:14–16, since Jeremiah speaks in the singular ("I have heard") as alone having received the word from the LORD, whereas Obadiah uses the plural ("we have heard"), grouping himself with the community that had heard Jeremiah's message. Third, Malachi's fifth-century BC description of Edom in ruins (Mal 1:2–5) makes it viable to link Obadiah 6–7 with the disaster Edom suffered at the hands of Babylonians (552 BC). The judgment on Edom as a whole lacks obvious historical reference and is cast in the context of an oracle against all nations.

Scripture presents Edom as sharing a common religious heritage with Israel, beginning with Esau. Deuteronomy 33:2, Judges 5:4, and Habakkuk 3:3 strikingly describe God's glory as proceeding from Edom. Deuteronomy 23:8 states that Edomites from the fourth generation may be admitted to the assembly of the LORD. The Bible mentions no idolatry in Edom until 2 Chronicles 25:5–24. Rather like Israel, then, Edomites apparently mixed worship of Yahweh and idols. Edom's religious affinity with Israel underscores the odious nature of its offenses.

Isaac's words of blessings to Jacob and Esau (Gen 27) are determinative of the future political relationship between Israel and Edom as one of dominion and vassalage. Edom was subjugated by David and gained independence under Jehoram in 845 BC (2 Kgs 8:20). Despite the mutual national hostility, Edomites provided a partial refuge to Judean fugitives after the fall of Jerusalem (Jer 40:11). —*Hyunhye Junia Pokrifka*

1	Title and Introduction
2–9	Judgment on Edom
10–14	Prohibitions for Edom
15–21	The Day of the LORD

This is the vision that the Sovereign LORD revealed to Obadiah concerning the land of Edom.

Edom's Judgment Announced

We have heard a message from the LORD
that an ambassador was sent to the nations
to say,
"Get ready, everyone!
Let's assemble our armies and attack
Edom!"

2 The LORD says to Edom,
"I will cut you down to size among the
nations;
you will be greatly despised.
3 You have been deceived by your own pride
because you live in a rock fortress
and make your home high in the
mountains.
'Who can ever reach us way up here?'
you ask boastfully.
4 But even if you soar as high as eagles
and build your nest among the stars,
I will bring you crashing down,"
says the LORD.

5 "If thieves came at night and robbed you
(what a disaster awaits you!),
they would not take everything.
Those who harvest grapes
always leave a few for the poor.
But your enemies will wipe you out
completely!
6 Every nook and cranny of Edom*
will be searched and looted.
Every treasure will be found and taken.
7 "All your allies will turn against you.
They will help to chase you from your land.
They will promise you peace
while plotting to deceive and destroy you.
Your trusted friends will set traps for you,
and you won't even know about it.
8 At that time not a single wise person
will be left in the whole land of Edom,"
says the LORD.
"For on the mountains of Edom
I will destroy everyone who has
understanding.
9 The mightiest warriors of Teman
will be terrified,
and everyone on the mountains of Edom
will be cut down in the slaughter.

Reasons for Edom's Punishment

10 "Because of the violence you did
to your close relatives in Israel,*
you will be filled with shame
and destroyed forever.
11 When they were invaded,
you stood aloof, refusing to help them.
Foreign invaders carried off their wealth
and cast lots to divide up Jerusalem,
but you acted like one of Israel's enemies.

12 "You should not have gloated
when they exiled your relatives to distant
lands.

6 Hebrew *Esau;* also in 8b, 9, 18, 19, 21. **10** Hebrew *your brother Jacob.* The names "Jacob" and "Israel" are often interchanged throughout the Old Testament, referring sometimes to the individual patriarch and sometimes to the nation.

1 Title and Introduction

The word *vision* generally refers to the revelation or word of God (1 Sam 3:1; Isa 1:1) often in visual form (cf. Isa 2:2; 13:1; Nah 1:1). A messenger urges the nations to rise up against Edom along with Israel and Judah (hereafter, Israel); hence, *Let's assemble our armies*.

2–9 Judgment on Edom

Obadiah assures us God will bring just retribution on the enemies of God's people, for vengeance belongs to the LORD (Deut 32:35; Rom 12:19). This should produce in women and men humility, forgiveness, and compassion rather than hypocritical vindictiveness or triumphalism when our adversaries or abusers (within and outside faith or family) undergo God's judgment, lest we ourselves be judged. **3:** Edom's pride is reminiscent of Israel's preexilic presumption of its inviolability. The divine favor and protection offered to Edom in Deuteronomy 2:3–6 and 23:6–7 may have contributed to its false sense of security. God's reproach comes in the light of Edom's arrogance and violent actions against Israel. **7:** That Edom is Israel's brother but sided with Israel's enemies (Obad 11) emphasizes Edom's treachery (cf. Amos 1:9–10)—by which Edom in turn will fall. Edom will be judged in the same manner as it abused Israel.

10–14 Prohibitions for Edom

12–14: The series of Hebrew imperatives should be rendered as prohibitions: "Do not gloat," and so on. As words of judgment (*You should not have . . .*), they are an indictment against Edom for its past actions; they are a straightforward series of prohibitions for Edom to abstain from further offense against Israel.

Sibling Rivalry

Sibling rivalry arose spontaneously in Cain after sin entered human relationships, and it has been with us ever since. Cain and Abel were seeking God's favor, so God's response to Cain reveals God's answer to sibling rivalry (Gen 4:7). God evaluates his people by what they do toward God and by how well they master sin. Scripture also illustrates God's prerogative to bestow favor as he wills, irrespective of human traditions. God chose Isaac over Ishmael, Jacob over Esau, Joseph over his brothers, Ephraim over Manasseh, and David over his brothers—in each case reversing the traditional hierarchy based on age. While the overriding of gender hierarchy is less frequent in Scripture, God also challenged it by giving Miriam a prominent role with her brothers, Aaron and Moses, and by directing that Zelophehad's daughters should inherit his land in the absence of sons (Num 27).

Scripture decries situations in which human choices increased sibling rivalry. The favoritism of Isaac and Rebekah fueled the rivalry between Jacob and Esau, and rather than learning from his experience, Jacob obviously favored Joseph. Prolonged antagonism between siblings was the result in both generations. Ungodly traditions, another source of sibling rivalry, produced Ishmael and led to early rivalry with Isaac that resulted in Ishmael's banishment. Evaluation by physical appearance led Samuel to favor David's older brothers and earned Samuel the LORD's rebuke for an ungodly standard. But the most common source of increased sibling rivalry in Scripture is polygamous marriage. No polygamous family in Scripture is portrayed as happy, and the sibling rivalry leading to rape, murder, and rebellion among David's children is one of the saddest examples of such rivalry.

A healthy pattern of sibling relationships emerges among Jesus' disciples, however. There is no indication of sibling rivalry even though two sets of brothers were among Jesus' twelve disciples. Andrew found Jesus first and brought his brother Peter to see Jesus. From that point we read much about Peter, including his being in the inner circle of three, but very little about Andrew. Although James and John were in Jesus' inner circle, John was closer to Jesus than was James.

Why, given these relationships, do we find no sibling rivalry among these brothers? Might it be that Jesus helped them to live by God's original instructions to Cain—to focus on pleasing God and mastering sin rather than on comparisons among themselves? When Peter compared himself with John after Jesus' resurrection, Jesus rebuked the comparison and called Peter to follow him (John 21:20–22). While acknowledging the inequities of the world and endeavoring to alleviate them, Scripture's instruction is to deal with sibling rivalry by shunning comparisons and instead focusing on mastering sin and pleasing God.

You should not have rejoiced
when the people of Judah suffered such misfortune.
You should not have spoken arrogantly
in that terrible time of trouble.
13 You should not have plundered the land of Israel
when they were suffering such calamity.
You should not have gloated over their destruction
when they were suffering such calamity.
You should not have seized their wealth
when they were suffering such calamity.
14 You should not have stood at the crossroads,
killing those who tried to escape.
You should not have captured the survivors
and handed them over in their terrible time of trouble.

Edom Destroyed, Israel Restored

15 "The day is near when I, the LORD,
will judge all godless nations!

The whole oracle is not only an antagonistic message of judgment against Edom but also an urgent warning and call to repentance for any nation that rejoices over the misfortune of its enemy (cf. Prov 24:17).

15–21 The Day of the LORD

In oracles about the day of the LORD, those nations that were familiar to Israel because of their geographical proximity and political relation serve as tangible examples of God's judgment. In Obadiah, Edom is the prime example of the fate of the nations. Thus Edom is not being singled out for God's judgment. As Israel was judged, so all nations will be judged. **15:** Justice will be done as Edom, along with the nations, receives just recompense according to its actions (cf. Joel 3:7). This last section addresses all Gentile nations, as well as Israel and Judah, whose final destiny

As you have done to Israel,
so it will be done to you.
All your evil deeds
will fall back on your own heads.
16 Just as you swallowed up my people
on my holy mountain,
so you and the surrounding nations
will swallow the punishment I pour out on
you.
Yes, all you nations will drink and stagger
and disappear from history.

17 "But Jerusalem* will become a refuge for
those who escape;
it will be a holy place.
And the people of Israel* will come back
to reclaim their inheritance.
18 The people of Israel will be a raging fire,
and Edom a field of dry stubble.
The descendants of Joseph will be a flame
roaring across the field, devouring
everything.
There will be no survivors in Edom.
I, the LORD, have spoken!

19 "Then my people living in the Negev
will occupy the mountains of Edom.
Those living in the foothills of Judah*
will possess the Philistine plains
and take over the fields of Ephraim and
Samaria.
And the people of Benjamin
will occupy the land of Gilead.
20 The exiles of Israel will return to their land
and occupy the Phoenician coast as far
north as Zarephath.
The captives from Jerusalem exiled in the
north*
will return home and resettle the towns of
the Negev.
21 Those who have been rescued* will go up to*
Mount Zion in Jerusalem
to rule over the mountains of Edom.
And the LORD himself will be king!"

17a Hebrew *Mount Zion.* **17b** Hebrew *house of Jacob;* also in 18. See note on 10. **19** Hebrew *the Shephelah.* **20** Hebrew *in Sepharad.* **21a** As in Greek and Syriac versions; Hebrew reads *Rescuers.* **21b** Or *from.*

is contrasted with that of the nations. **16:** *You* (plural) is best understood as referring to Israel and Judah. As *you . . . swallow the punishment* or drink the cup of God's wrath (cf. Jer 49:12; 25:15–26), so will all the nations, including Edom (Isa 51:22–23). **18:** The annihilation of Edom is an event cast in eschatological language. **19–20:** Note that there a distinction between national and individual destiny that allows the holy remnant in Edom and all nations to be saved (Amos 9:12; Zech 14:16). **21:** All high places or nations will be lowered and every proud heart will be humiliated, for the LORD alone will be exalted as king (Isa 2:1–5, 11; Mic 4:2–5).

JONAH

INTRODUCTION

Jonah, one of the twelve Minor Prophets, would seem to be the ultimate patriarchal book. Women never appear, the main characters are one man and his God, and even the backdrop is masculine: sailors on the high seas, a king and his court. Yet for all its masculine characteristics it transcends gender and implicitly attacks racism, sexism, agism and any -ism that questions God's full acceptance of all human beings and God's freedom to bestow good gifts on anyone. Recently scholarship has changed from arguing whether this is history or a type of parable to concentrate on its message and themes. Current concerns now revolve around the genre and tone of the book. Is it instruction or satire? Is it ironic or sympathetic?

The author writes with a purpose but is also an expert storyteller who delights in playing with words to create suspense and heighten the twists in the tale. Unfortunately much of the art is lost in translation. For example, a major key word in the book is *gadol,* "great." It occurs fourteen times, with many plays on its different nuances (great city, great storm, great fear, great fish). This is a story about a great nation but an even greater God who creates events to bring about salvation. Against this background the author mocks Jonah's great anger and great happiness as small-minded self-centeredness.

Perhaps one of the greatest skills of the narrator is to leave tantalizing gaps that require the reader's imagination and involvement in the plot. For many people, familiar with the story from Sunday school or sermons, these gaps are not readily obvious. Therefore the book, short as it is, repays careful rereading. One of the greatest enigmas of the book revolves around Jonah's behavior, and we receive little guidance until the end. Does he head for Joppa scared, rebellious, confused, or what? The omission of motive by the narrator creates space for us to fill the gap creatively and imaginatively. If we place ourselves in Jonah's shoes and ponder the enigma anew, God is free to pinpoint our fears, rebellions, or confusions and speak to us through the book.

Jonah seems to think that if the LORD is out there, he can go far enough down and in to escape the God of Israel—down to Joppa, into the ship, down into the hold, down into the sea (symbol of godless chaos), and even down into death (Sheol). He has yet to learn the truth of the psalmist that it is impossible to flee God's reach (Ps 139:8–10). He has also to discover, it seems, that God is preeminently a merciful God. In his utmost extremity he seems to have no concept that God might relent if he were to repent (Jon 1:6). Is this the ultimate in stubborn impenitence or a tragically faulty theology? Is the god he is running from not God at all?

The book gives no indication of either a date of composition or a date for the events, if they are historical. Second Kings 14:25 mentions a prophet named Jonah, son of Amittai, in the early eighth century BC, a time before Nineveh was a real threat to Israel; he may or may not be the same Jonah. Certain language and style factors suggest that the book was written in its current form after the Exile, but this does not help in dating its origin. It seems that the typically anonymous author has deliberately omitted the normal time reference "in the days of . . ." in order to create a timeless narrative, relevant to all. Thus the story is understandable with minimal background information. Nevertheless, it is a very Jewish tale. Gentile readers will need to recall the strict segregation that became an increasing part of Jewish life. This God-ordained separation was designed for Israel's protection, to lessen the temptation to apostasy and syncretism, to enable holiness. Yet the human tendency is so often to abuse and misuse God-given guidelines, to bend the rules, or apply them so rigidly that their purpose is defeated. Such legalistic application resulted in Ezra's banishment of foreign wives and Peter's reluctance to eat with Gentiles. Jonah, along with the stories of Ruth and Rahab, is part of the Old Testament's counterbalance. They remind us that God's guidelines exist because of our weakness, and we must not duck the hard task of rightly discerning when they are not applicable. Similarly, we need to recall that Nineveh was to Israel what Hitler was to the Jews and erase any notion that such divine punishment would be unjust.

The narrator's skills extend to a careful structuring of the book into two mirror halves. Many scholars wish to exclude chapter 2 as an ancient hymn of praise inserted into the book at a later stage. If so, the psalm has been extremely well integrated and is now so essential to the structure that it cannot be excluded or passed over.

What are we to make of Jonah? There are elements of caricature that support a pointed, satirical portrayal of Israel's self-righteous exclusivism. But such views overlook the positive aspects of chapters 2 and 3. So too do those views that write Jonah off as a petulant and rebellious prophet. Jonah is sullen and self-centered, but he can also be obedient. He knows that God is his salvation and hope, and if at times he acts from mixed motives does that not make him more human? Above all he is a person struggling to understand a God who is far bigger than he ever conceived. He is a finite human being caught in the tension between justice and mercy, the paradox of a sovereign God who gives way before prayer, the reality of a God who asks of us outrageous things.

The book is about God's staggering compassion on all people everywhere, even those who seem farthest from love. Our God delights to give gifts to those who, we think, are beyond the pale. But this is only one strand of a multifaceted message. The center is Jonah, representative of Israel and every reader and his or her relationship with God. Even God's saved people can harbor ingrained prejudices, legalistic attitudes, and unacknowledged self-centeredness. We can seek death rather than life, and work from a far-too-small picture of God. But God pursues us, ever offering a bigger perspective. We do not know if Jonah needed a fourth chance, but we can respond to the writer's invitation to examine our response. —*Elizabeth A. Harper*

1:1–17	The Consequences of Disobedience
2:1–10	Jonah's Monologue of Praise
3:1–10	The Consequences of Obedience
4:1–11	Jonah's Monologue of Complaint

Jonah Runs from the LORD

1 The LORD gave this message to Jonah son
of Amittai: 2 "Get up and go to the great
city of Nineveh. Announce my judgment
against it because I have seen how wicked its
people are."
3 But Jonah got up and went in the opposite
direction to get away from the LORD. He went
down to the port of Joppa, where he found a ship
leaving for Tarshish. He bought a ticket and went
on board, hoping to escape from the LORD by
sailing to Tarshish.
4 But the LORD hurled a powerful wind over
the sea, causing a violent storm that threatened
to break the ship apart. 5 Fearing for their lives, the
desperate sailors shouted to their gods for help and
threw the cargo overboard to lighten the ship.
But all this time Jonah was sound asleep down
in the hold. 6 So the captain went down after
him. "How can you sleep at a time like this?" he
shouted. "Get up and pray to your god! Maybe
he will pay attention to us and spare our lives."
7 Then the crew cast lots to see which of them
had offended the gods and caused the terrible
storm. When they did this, the lots identified Jonah as the culprit. 8 "Why has this awful storm
come down on us?" they demanded. "Who are
you? What is your line of work? What country
are you from? What is your nationality?"
9 Jonah answered, "I am a Hebrew, and I worship the LORD, the God of heaven, who made the
sea and the land."
10 The sailors were terrified when they heard
this, for he had already told them he was running
away from the LORD. "Oh, why did you do it?"
they groaned. 11 And since the storm was getting
worse all the time, they asked him, "What should
we do to you to stop this storm?"
12 "Throw me into the sea," Jonah said, "and it
will become calm again. I know that this terrible
storm is all my fault."
13 Instead, the sailors rowed even harder to
get the ship to the land. But the stormy sea was
too violent for them, and they couldn't make it.
14 Then they cried out to the LORD, Jonah's God.
"O LORD," they pleaded, "don't make us die for
this man's sin. And don't hold us responsible
for his death. O LORD, you have sent this storm
upon him for your own good reasons."
15 Then the sailors picked Jonah up and threw
him into the raging sea, and the storm stopped at
once! 16 The sailors were awestruck by the LORD's
great power, and they offered him a sacrifice and
vowed to serve him.
17 *Now the LORD had arranged for a great
fish to swallow Jonah. And Jonah was inside the
fish for three days and three nights.

Jonah's Prayer

2 1 *Then Jonah prayed to the LORD his God
from inside the fish. 2 He said,

"I cried out to the LORD in my great trouble,

1:17 Verse 1:17 is numbered 2:1 in Hebrew text. **2:1** Verses 2:1-10 are numbered 2:2-11 in Hebrew text.

1:1–17 The Consequences of Disobedience

The book commences as an oracle of judgment. *Nineveh*, capital of Assyria, is on the Tigris River. **3:** This illusion of prophecy quickly gives way to narrative. Reluctant prophets and patriarchs argued back (Abraham, Moses), but Jonah's mute disobedience is unique. Both *Joppa*, on the eastern coast of the Mediterranean, in Philistine territory, and *Tarshish*, either Tarsus in Turkey or Tartessus in Spain, were in *the opposite direction* from Nineveh. **4–14:** In response God does not gently woo Jonah back but actively pursues him, engaged in a policy of tough love. God even encourages Jonah in his downward and inward flight. But Jonah's disobedience has consequences for others. The sailors suffer, the cargo owners suffer, even the inanimate ship suffers (she is personified as "reckoning herself to be broken into pieces" [v. 4, author's translation]). Yet lest we despair, we should note that through Jonah's flight the sailors are brought to true fear of Yahweh. There is nothing God cannot redeem. **16:** Outsiders might be insiders—pagan sailors may worship more genuinely than Jonah. **17:** And even for Jonah, author of their misfortune, there is hope. Jonah has chosen, and Jonah has acted. Whatever the motives, Jonah has been in control of his life. But now that he has gone as far as he can, he finds his supposed control illusory. He has brought himself to the position where others now control his life. The self-absorbed subject becomes an object. But behind the sailors and *the great fish* is an even bigger subject who is at last free to act directly. It may not yet be apparent, but a turning point has been reached.

2:1–10 Jonah's Monologue of Praise

A psalm of praise is surprising at this point; many scholars regard it as a later addition. It fails to match either Jonah or his situation *inside the fish*. Yet in a text that delights in undermining readers' expectations, this psalm is quite plausible. Structurally chapter 2 balances chapter 4; both include statements about God's nature and the relationship between Jonah and God.

and he answered me.
I called to you from the land of the dead,*
and LORD, you heard me!
3 You threw me into the ocean depths,
and I sank down to the heart of the sea.
The mighty waters engulfed me;
I was buried beneath your wild and stormy waves.
4 Then I said, 'O LORD, you have driven me from your presence.
Yet I will look once more toward your holy Temple.'
5 "I sank beneath the waves,
and the waters closed over me.
Seaweed wrapped itself around my head.
6 I sank down to the very roots of the mountains.
I was imprisoned in the earth,
whose gates lock shut forever.
But you, O LORD my God,
snatched me from the jaws of death!
7 As my life was slipping away,
I remembered the LORD.
And my earnest prayer went out to you
in your holy Temple.
8 Those who worship false gods
turn their backs on all God's mercies.
9 But I will offer sacrifices to you with songs of praise,
and I will fulfill all my vows.
For my salvation comes from the LORD alone."

10 Then the LORD ordered the fish to spit Jonah out onto the beach.

Jonah Goes to Nineveh

3 Then the LORD spoke to Jonah a second time:
2 "Get up and go to the great city of Nineveh,
and deliver the message I have given you."
3 This time Jonah obeyed the LORD's command and went to Nineveh, a city so large that it
took three days to see it all.* 4 On the day Jonah
entered the city, he shouted to the crowds: "Forty
days from now Nineveh will be destroyed!" 5 The
people of Nineveh believed God's message, and
from the greatest to the least, they declared a fast
and put on burlap to show their sorrow.
6 When the king of Nineveh heard what Jonah
was saying, he stepped down from his throne and
took off his royal robes. He dressed himself in burlap and sat on a heap of ashes. 7 Then the king and
his nobles sent this decree throughout the city:

"No one, not even the animals from your
herds and flocks, may eat or drink anything
at all. 8 People and animals alike must wear
garments of mourning, and everyone must
pray earnestly to God. They must turn from
their evil ways and stop all their violence.
9 Who can tell? Perhaps even yet God will
change his mind and hold back his fierce
anger from destroying us."

2:2 Hebrew *from Sheol.* **3:3** Hebrew *a great city to God, of three days' journey.*

1–2: Jonah has been running from God, to the point where Sheol (*the land of the dead*) seems to be his only escape. God will not even allow him the luxury of death. In verse 1, the gender of the fish changes from 1:17 (2:1 in Heb.), where Jonah is swallowed into the inner parts or belly (*m'h,* a masculine noun) of a masculine fish *(dag)*. In verse 1 (v. 2 in Heb.) he prays from the belly *(m'h)* of a very feminine fish *(dagah)*. (Verse 10 [v. 11 in Heb.] returns to the masculine *dag.*) In verse 2 (v. 3 in Heb.) Jonah cries out again *from the land of the dead* (Heb., "from the belly of Sheol"); the word for belly is the feminine *beten,* a synonym with the added possible translation "womb." The image is incongruous. Sheol is the place of death, not birth, a barren womb (Prov 30:16) from which no one comes up (Job 7:9) and from whence none can praise God (Ps 6:5). Yet Jonah, who has sought death to escape God, discovers that death is his place of capture, his womb of rebirth. **7–9:** Having come near the death he sought and finding himself thankfully very much alive, Jonah is on the path to a proper understanding of God. He learns in a new way that the God who inhabits Israel's holy Temple is a God of rescue and salvation. His response is, as it can only be, praise, worship, and thanksgiving. Jonah's conversion and education have begun, but he has more lessons still to learn.

3:1–10 The Consequences of Obedience

The LORD never gives up on people. **1–2:** Mirroring chapter 1, this chapter begins with the call to Jonah, *Get up and go*. **3–4:** Jonah hastens, obediently it seems, to Nineveh, where almost immediately upon entering he begins to call out his message of doom. *On the day Jonah entered*: A trek of only one day into a city of *three days' journey* (translator's note) may not be eagerness in obedience but the bare minimum required to fulfill God's command. **6:** The *king,* as representative of the nation and the normal target for God's prophets, is left to hear the message secondhand. **7–9:** If, by God's grace, Jonah's disobedience brings pagan sailors to true fear, how much more does God use his obedience, eager or reluctant?

[10]When God saw what they had done and how they had put a stop to their evil ways, he changed his mind and did not carry out the destruction he had threatened.

Jonah's Anger at the LORD's Mercy

4 This change of plans greatly upset Jonah, and he became very angry. [2]So he complained to the LORD about it: "Didn't I say before I left home that you would do this, LORD? That is why I ran away to Tarshish! I knew that you are a merciful and compassionate God, slow to get angry and filled with unfailing love. You are eager to turn back from destroying people. [3]Just kill me now, LORD! I'd rather be dead than alive if what I predicted will not happen."

[4]The LORD replied, "Is it right for you to be angry about this?"

[5]Then Jonah went out to the east side of the city and made a shelter to sit under as he waited to see what would happen to the city. [6]And the LORD God arranged for a leafy plant to grow there, and soon it spread its broad leaves over Jonah's head, shading him from the sun. This eased his discomfort, and Jonah was very grateful for the plant.

[7]But God also arranged for a worm! The next morning at dawn the worm ate through the stem of the plant so that it withered away. [8]And as the sun grew hot, God arranged for a scorching east wind to blow on Jonah. The sun beat down on his head until he grew faint and wished to die. "Death is certainly better than living like this!" he exclaimed.

[9]Then God said to Jonah, "Is it right for you to be angry because the plant died?"

"Yes," Jonah retorted, "even angry enough to die!"

Such immediate response, such total repentance by the Ninevites, is little short of miraculous, and thus the storyteller springs the next surprise. Not even Israel in its best moments heeded the call of God's prophets so swiftly or so completely. The story begins to bite. The king's speech is a model of repentance. There is evidence of contrition, reform of lifestyle, and finally a proper humility before the sovereignty of God (Joel 2:14). For Jonah there is none of the scorn, derision, imprisonment, or even simple apathy that most prophets face. The extent of faith and remorse borders on the unbelievable. The thought of the renowned king of Nineveh in sackcloth, Job-like among the ashes, while whole herds of Ninevite cattle cease grazing to cry to the God of Israel is preposterous. The writer is not averse to playing up the story with a little hyperbole and plenty of puns (e.g., in Hebrew "evil" and "feed" sound similar, as do "decree" and "taste") to make the point and bring the story to its unexpected climax. **10:** In a fitting finale, the LORD, God of second chances, also repents of the *destruction* (lit., "evil": another key word in the book) intended. The author of Jonah is not afraid to attribute evil to God: the evil of the storm (1:7; 1:8) and the evil of planned destruction (3:10). Such evil is a fitting, just, and proper response to human evil. Jonah's disobedience endangers the lives of countless Ninevites who had in their turn created innumerable victims of their violence (v. 8). God is not oblivious to the evil of the world. The cries of the oppressed (so often feminine!) rise up to the LORD (1:1), and this story holds out for everyone hope of justice in this world. Yet paradoxically and thankfully the story also offers to all the assurance of a second chance, a new start.

4:1–11 Jonah's Monologue of Complaint

Jonah, sidelined in chapter 3, is the true center of the story. At last this enigmatic character will be revealed. Until now his motives have been masked, his actions ambiguous, his speech short and brusque. Nothing has prepared us for the sudden exposure of a deep, intense anger. **1:** *Very angry*: A vehement phrase; God's actions were, in Jonah's mind, a great evil. **2:** Only Jonah could turn the magnificent creed of Exodus (Exod 34:6; Ps 86:15; Joel 2:13) into a vindictive denunciation. **3:** What could be so bad as to provoke a death wish in Jonah? He has not been persecuted or ignored but has achieved a success the envy of any other prophet. Is he disgruntled because his reputation is tarnished—a false prophet whose word does not come true? Is he angry that God should show mercy on Gentiles, even on Israel's greatest oppressor? Does he feel let down, betrayed by an irrational God whose seemingly arbitrary mercy triumphs over justice and consistency? **5:** And what does he go out to see? Whether Nineveh will be destroyed? Or more subtly, how long the Ninevites will keep their change of heart—is repentance skin deep? Has God been conned? The author does not tell us, but the gap is worth pondering. In Jonah's shoes, what would make us so angry? **6–11:** Yet the God of third chances will not leave Jonah to his self-pity. So God seeks to engage him in conversation. Jonah, however, is not ready for dialogue. Therefore God must again resort to tough love to turn Jonah from his evil, as the Ninevites (and God) have turned from theirs. God appoints a *leafy plant* to shelter Jonah, which brought relief from Jonah's distress (Heb., "evil"). For the first time Jonah is happy. But God further appoints *a*

[10]Then the LORD said, "You feel sorry about the plant, though you did nothing to put it there. It came quickly and died quickly. [11]But Nineveh has more than 120,000 people living in spiritual darkness,* not to mention all the animals. Shouldn't I feel sorry for such a great city?"

4:11 Hebrew *people who don't know their right hand from their left.*

---

worm and an *east wind*. So at last taciturn Jonah is goaded into dialogue, and the full extent of his self-centeredness is revealed. Jonah is not interested in others, certainly not Gentile sailors and Ninevites. His concern is himself and occasionally his God. "I" and "me" occur twelve times in the few sentences he speaks, and even his praise in chapter 2 has twice as much "me" as "you." But God has caught him in a trap that will bring him face to face with his selfishness. He must either answer God's insistent question in the negative and confirm that God may do what God pleases, or he must answer (as God does) in the positive and confirm that it is right for God to be compassionate.

MICAH

INTRODUCTION

The primary message of the eighth-century BC prophetic books (Isaiah, Hosea, Amos, and Micah) is despair and outrage at perceived social disintegration with dire warnings of the consequences. But these books are not just doom and gloom. The world of everyday reality is contrasted with a world that could be; indeed, God willing, a world that will be in which all injustice will be righted, all aggression vanquished, and all oppressed released.

Micah's particular concern is the policies and practices (debt-inducing loans, land seizures, uncontrolled violence, extortionate prices) that cause poverty among the hard-working backbone of society. But he also criticizes the religious authorities for supporting the establishment and sees it all as a failure of true faith and true submission to Israel's savior, the LORD.

Micah is of particular interest to women for his championing of justice in the name of God for all people, including women and children. But he is also of interest for the extent of the female imagery used in his pregnant pictorial poetry. His imagery recognizes the good and bad in humanity, male and female, and overturns some common stereotypes.

Micah 1:1 suggests dates between 750 and 700 BC, but it is hard to date individual prophecies more specifically. The degree of generalization means any era can identify its own besetting sins and God's discipline through current events. Most scholars believe the core of Micah comes from this period, but the extent of this core is hotly debated.

Micah the prophet is, perhaps deliberately, an enigmatic figure. The focus is on the word of the LORD, not the servant. We learn most about Micah by examining his concerns. He feels deeply for ordinary people struggling to make ends meet, and fights strongly against any unjust structures and activities that tip people into poverty. He champions the cause of rural citizens (2:2) who ought to be self-sufficient contributors to the economy. He then moves on to the oppressed townsfolk who lose their hard-earned profits to extortion (3:11).

This was an unsettled time. The economic boom during King Uzziah's golden era resulted in a growing gap between poor and prosperous, accompanied by a disintegration of the traditional social order. International peace was shattered by renewed aggression from Assyria. Samaria's fall, 722 BC, sent shock waves through Judah as well as an influx of refugees to strain the economy. In 701 BC Assyria marched on Jerusalem, ravaging Micah's region, the Shephelah. Although Jerusalem survived, Judah was a smaller and poorer nation.

The status of women in ancient Israel is uncertain, although public society at least was male-dominated. Women's primary role was probably homemaking and childrearing in an extended family. This family was the only security; widows and childless women were particularly at their mercy (see Widows, 1 Tim 5; Singleness, 1 Cor 7). In the unsettled times women were doubtless even more vulnerable than men, often victims of rape and slavery through warfare (see Violence, Abuse and Oppression, Eccl 4). Micah recognizes women's vulnerability and in 2:9 singles out women for special mention. Nevertheless, it is likely that some women, especially those of wealth, had freedom, authority, and responsibility. Not all women were oppressed, and some were doubtless oppressors.

The book consists of a series of small, distinct, unconnected prophecies. (Some see chaps. 1—3 as original to the eighth century, with chaps. 4—5 as exilic, and chaps. 6—7 as a postexilic afterword.) For the prophet, forthtelling (God's perspective on the world as it is) and foretelling (God's intentions as a result) are interwoven in imaginative and provocative poetry. Attention to the rhetoric and poetry of Micah highlights how much literary poetic devices unite the book. There is a deliberate alternation of God's love-engendered judgment (or discipline) with reconciling restoration. This pattern occurs both within chapters and in the overall structure.

The book recognizes that our world is not as it should be, especially for women. Everyone with power, wealth, and authority (primarily men) is warned to take stock. Apathy, indifference, and a blinkered parochialism are as sinful as outright wickedness if they fail to prevent injustice. Such is God's love for all people, oppressed and oppressors, that this old world must be overturned and wealth, power, and authority redistributed, however painful such discipline may be. Only thus can a new world be born in which rich and poor, Israelite and Gentile, male and female might worship God equally. —*Elizabeth A. Harper*

1:1–16	Lament for a World Gone Wrong
2:1–13	Justice for Rural Citizens
3:1–12	Justice for Townspeople and Temple
4:1–13	A New World through New Birth
5:1–15	A New World through Reversal
6:1–16	Justice for YHWH
7:1–20	Second Lament for a World Gone Wrong

✧

1 The LORD gave this message to Micah of Moresheth during the years when Jotham, Ahaz, and Hezekiah were kings of Judah. The visions he saw concerned both Samaria and Jerusalem.

Grief over Samaria and Jerusalem

2 Attention! Let all the people of the world
listen!
Let the earth and everything in it hear.
The Sovereign LORD is making accusations
against you;
the Lord speaks from his holy Temple.
3 Look! The LORD is coming!
He leaves his throne in heaven
and tramples the heights of the earth.
4 The mountains melt beneath his feet
and flow into the valleys
like wax in a fire,
like water pouring down a hill.
5 And why is this happening?
Because of the rebellion of Israel*—
yes, the sins of the whole nation.
Who is to blame for Israel's rebellion?
Samaria, its capital city!

1:5 Hebrew *Jacob;* also in 1:5b. The names "Jacob" and "Israel" are often interchanged throughout the Old Testament, referring sometimes to the individual patriarch and sometimes to the nation.

1:1–16 Lament for a World Gone Wrong

Micah uses poetry and its attendant metaphors and imagery to announce his subversive, God-inspired protest against a world gone dreadfully wrong. **2:** His first image portrays Israel as a culpable defendant. **3–5:** The book opens with a theophany—an earth-shattering appearance of God—not to herald a glorious rescue, as might be expected, but to proclaim judgment and discipline. **5–6:** God's rebuke is directed first at the Northern Kingdom (Israel) typified by its capital, Samaria. For Micah, however, this is merely a preliminary warning for Judah and its capital, Jerusalem. Micah proclaims judgment, perhaps

Where is the center of idolatry in Judah?
In Jerusalem, its capital!

6 "So I, the LORD, will make the city of Samaria
a heap of ruins.
Her streets will be plowed up
for planting vineyards.
I will roll the stones of her walls into the
valley below,
exposing her foundations.
7 All her carved images will be smashed.
All her sacred treasures will be burned.
These things were bought with the money
earned by her prostitution,
and they will now be carried away
to pay prostitutes elsewhere."
8 Therefore, I will mourn and lament.
I will walk around barefoot and naked.
I will howl like a jackal
and moan like an owl.
9 For my people's wound
is too deep to heal.
It has reached into Judah,
even to the gates of Jerusalem.

10 Don't tell our enemies in Gath*;
don't weep at all.
You people in Beth-leaphrah,*
roll in the dust to show your despair.
11 You people in Shaphir,*
go as captives into exile—naked and
ashamed.
The people of Zaanan*
dare not come outside their walls.
The people of Beth-ezel* mourn,
for their house has no support.
12 The people of Maroth* anxiously wait for
relief,
but only bitterness awaits them
as the LORD's judgment reaches
even to the gates of Jerusalem.

13 Harness your chariot horses and flee,
you people of Lachish.*
You were the first city in Judah
to follow Israel in her rebellion,
and you led Jerusalem* into sin.
14 Send farewell gifts to Moresheth-gath*;
there is no hope of saving it.
The town of Aczib*
has deceived the kings of Israel.
15 O people of Mareshah,*
I will bring a conqueror to capture your
town.
And the leaders* of Israel
will go to Adullam.

16 Oh, people of Judah, shave your heads in
sorrow,

1:10a *Gath* sounds like the Hebrew term for "tell." **1:10b** *Beth-leaphrah* means "house of dust." **1:11a** *Shaphir* means "pleasant." **1:11b** *Zaanan* sounds like the Hebrew term for "come out." **1:11c** *Beth-ezel* means "adjoining house." **1:12** *Maroth* sounds like the Hebrew term for "bitter." **1:13a** *Lachish* sounds like the Hebrew term for "team of horses." **1:13b** Hebrew *the daughter of Zion.* **1:14a** *Moresheth* sounds like the Hebrew term for "gift" or "dowry." **1:14b** *Aczib* means "deception." **1:15a** *Mareshah* sounds like the Hebrew term for "conqueror." **1:15b** Hebrew *the glory.*

---

in the hope of provoking repentance (Jer 26:18–19). **7:** The images here are of Israel the prostitute. Today this metaphor seems harsh and disturbing, portraying unfaithfulness as a feminine vice and suggesting subconsciously an association between women and evil. From the context it is clear that Micah is using an image for idolatry. Prostitution, male as well as female, was likely to be linked in the prophet's mind with Canaanite fertility religions. The prophets, following Hosea, see the covenant relationship of Israel and God through the marriage metaphor. The LORD and Israel entered freely into this relationship (Josh 24:15–23) and undertook voluntarily the mutual obligations of loyalty, fidelity, and commitment. For the prophets, both parties are accountable, God (Mic 7:19–20) as well as Israel. We can see Israel's betrayal of God is everywhere apparent in injustice and religious compromise. The prophets' goal is to waken people to the hollowness of the marriage, that they may return to mutual love before it ends in divorce. (See sidebar, Micah's Feminine and Masculine Imagery.) **10–15:** Micah's opening ploy is a clever, humorous, attention-grabbing lament, full of untranslatable puns ("Tell it not in Telham; wail, O inhabitants of Whaleton") and the like. **16:** Yet underneath the black humor is heartfelt sorrow. Idolatry eventually brings destruction and often destroys the little people—the poor, the women, the children. The prophet laments in solidarity with them while provoking the complacent to fear and action. **16:** Judah remains personified as a woman—daughter, mother, mourner. There have been many debates as to the significance of feminine pronouns. Jerusalem and Judah may be "she" simply because the words for "city," "inhabitants," and "land" are feminine. This in turn may have led to villages being thought of as daughters to their mother cities. But each step in the process inevitably acquires deeper symbolism

Micah's Feminine and Masculine Imagery

Hebrew writers paint vivid word pictures but rarely stick long with one image. Micah is no exception. The prostituted feminine Samaria (1:7) is mirrored by the degenerate masculine Jacob (3:8) and the guilty masculine Israel (6:2). The nation in its injustice is likened not just to a prostitute but also to a butcher (3:2–3), a masculine aggressor (2:9), a bloodthirsty hunter (7:2), and a thornbush (7:4). Nor are all the feminine images negative. If Israel is a prostitute, she is also a bereaved mother (1:16) and a woman in the pangs of labor (3:10) bringing forth salvation for the nation (5:3). She is a sovereign ruler (4:8), an invincible female ox (4:13), and a beloved daughter destined for redemption in contrast to gloating masculine enemies destined for destruction (4:10–13).

Similarly, although the LORD is the humiliated husband, never the wronged wife, God is also shepherd (2:12), gentle teacher of peace (4:2), and compassionate gatherer of the afflicted (4:6; 7:19) who exhibits traditional masculine and feminine attributes. To discuss our relationship with God we have to use metaphors from our known world and culture. Micah's reality was a patriarchal society, and his metaphors reflect that. In his world, the image of Israel as an unfaithful wife would never have had the same shock value as it does in ours.

In a changed world and a different culture, certain metaphors, such as Micah's image of a prostitute, must be used with care, as they fail to communicate as intended. Our task is to find images that work in today's world, taking note of Micah's wide range of imagery—masculine, feminine, and neuter.

for the children you love will be snatched
away.
Make yourselves as bald as a vulture,
for your little ones will be exiled to distant
lands.

Judgment against Wealthy Oppressors

2 [1]What sorrow awaits you who lie awake
at night,
thinking up evil plans.
You rise at dawn and hurry to carry them out,
simply because you have the power to do so.
2 When you want a piece of land,
you find a way to seize it.
When you want someone's house,
you take it by fraud and violence.
You cheat a man of his property,
stealing his family's inheritance.

3 But this is what the LORD says:
"I will reward your evil with evil;
you won't be able to pull your neck out of
the noose.
You will no longer walk around proudly,
for it will be a terrible time."

4 In that day your enemies will make fun of
you
by singing this song of despair about you:
"We are finished,
completely ruined!
God has confiscated our land,

and significance. Did the designations stick because towns and villages were believed to provide stability, nurture, and community, just like women? We can only surmise. What is intriguing is the way Micah switches between masculine and feminine forms. In chapters 1 and 4 the majority of the words for "you" are feminine while in chapter 5 they are wholly masculine; however, neither is more positive or negative than the other. Perhaps it is part of his policy to have a mixture of images.

2:1–13 Justice for Rural Citizens

Having softened his audience with a witty lament, Micah now justifies his condemnation, graphically highlighting the evil they refuse to see. Here he speaks particularly for the villagers and small farmers of the countryside who have lost land, lodgings, and livelihood through violence or extortionate debt. The unjust risk being burned when the world gets turned upside down by the coming of God's justice. **1–4:** Typical of the prophets, Micah's justice envisages the punishment matching the crime. Those who seize fields shall lose land; those who plot evil will be the victims of an evil plot. For oppressed victims it may seem too little, too late. In pain we often long to make others suffer. But this is not God's way. Any punishment will be just, fair, and equal. **1:** Micah stresses that we are each accountable for our deeds.

taking it from us.
He has given our fields
to those who betrayed us.*"
5 Others will set your boundaries then,
and the LORD's people will have no say
in how the land is divided.

True and False Prophets
6 "Don't say such things,"
the people respond.*
"Don't prophesy like that.
Such disasters will never come our way!"
7 Should you talk that way, O family of
Israel?*
Will the LORD's Spirit have patience with
such behavior?
If you would do what is right,
you would find my words comforting.
8 Yet to this very hour
my people rise against me like an enemy!
You steal the shirts right off the backs
of those who trusted you,
making them as ragged as men
returning from battle.
9 You have evicted women from their pleasant
homes
and forever stripped their children of all
that God would give them.
10 Up! Begone!
This is no longer your land and home,
for you have filled it with sin
and ruined it completely.

11 Suppose a prophet full of lies would say to
you,
"I'll preach to you the joys of wine and
alcohol!"
That's just the kind of prophet you would
like!

Hope for Restoration
12 "Someday, O Israel, I will gather you;
I will gather the remnant who are left.
I will bring you together again like sheep in a
pen,
like a flock in its pasture.
Yes, your land will again
be filled with noisy crowds!
13 Your leader will break out
and lead you out of exile,
out through the gates of the enemy cities,
back to your own land.
Your king will lead you;
the LORD himself will guide you."

Judgment against Israel's Leaders
3 1 I said, "Listen, you leaders of Israel!
You are supposed to know right from
wrong,
2 but you are the very ones
who hate good and love evil.
You skin my people alive
and tear the flesh from their bones.
3 Yes, you eat my people's flesh,
strip off their skin,
and break their bones.
You chop them up
like meat for the cooking pot.
4 Then you beg the LORD for help in times of
trouble!
Do you really expect him to answer?

2:4 Or *to those who took us captive.* **2:6** Or *the prophets respond;* Hebrew reads *they prophesy.* **2:7** Hebrew *O house of Jacob?* See note on 1:5a.

2:6–11 True and False Prophets. His subversive message wins Micah no friends in high places. The chapter is punctuated by a terse argument between Micah and his opponents. They have no interest in truth. They don't want to hear Micah's message of judgment because they don't want to recognize the awfulness of their behavior. Micah's sarcasm is realistic. They really want to hear that God blesses those who indulge themselves! **9:** Micah particularly highlights the plight of women as casualties.

2:12–13 Hope for Restoration. God is not unaware of the injustice. The oppressed are to have hope. God may tarry, but the day of justice is coming—in this world, not the next. These verses are a rather startling juxtaposition to the previous judgment speeches. The verses are nuanced, however. Their ambiguity threatens exile while promising restoration. For the book, discipline and reconciliation go hand in hand. Judgment is not the last word. For the punished too there is a flame of hope.

3:1–12 Justice for Townspeople and Temple

Micah turns his attention to Jerusalem and the scandals within the sacred city. **1–3:** He commences a three-pronged attack on the unholy alliance of prophet, priest, and prince, who out of greed butcher the people. The image of butchery is among the most horrific in the book, used for its pure shock value. One can almost imagine the suffering crowds lapping it up and cheering Micah on. Micah's example affirms that it is right to be passionate about injustice, to fight for those who suffer. **5–7:** Such injustice and

After all the evil you have done,
he won't even look at you!"

5 This is what the LORD says:
"You false prophets are leading my people astray!
You promise peace for those who give you food,
but you declare war on those who refuse to feed you.
6 Now the night will close around you,
cutting off all your visions.
Darkness will cover you,
putting an end to your predictions.
The sun will set for you prophets,
and your day will come to an end.
7 Then you seers will be put to shame,
and you fortune-tellers will be disgraced.
And you will cover your faces
because there is no answer from God."

8 But as for me, I am filled with power—
with the Spirit of the LORD.
I am filled with justice and strength
to boldly declare Israel's sin and rebellion.
9 Listen to me, you leaders of Israel!
You hate justice and twist all that is right.
10 You are building Jerusalem
on a foundation of murder and corruption.
11 You rulers make decisions based on bribes;
you priests teach God's laws only for a price;
you prophets won't prophesy unless you are paid.
Yet all of you claim to depend on the LORD.
"No harm can come to us," you say,
"for the LORD is here among us."
12 Because of you, Mount Zion will be plowed
like an open field;
Jerusalem will be reduced to ruins!
A thicket will grow on the heights
where the Temple now stands.

The LORD's Future Reign

4 [1]In the last days, the mountain of the LORD's house
will be the highest of all—
the most important place on earth.
It will be raised above the other hills,
and people from all over the world will
stream there to worship.
2 People from many nations will come and say,
"Come, let us go up to the mountain of the LORD,
to the house of Jacob's God.
There he will teach us his ways,
and we will walk in his paths."
For the LORD's teaching will go out from Zion;
his word will go out from Jerusalem.
3 The LORD will mediate between peoples
and will settle disputes between strong
nations far away.
They will hammer their swords into plowshares
and their spears into pruning hooks.
Nation will no longer fight against nation,
nor train for war anymore.

---

oppression do not escape God's concern. It is not enough to to speak in God's name, to carry out the rituals, to trust in the LORD while practicing selfishness, complacency, and self-interest. In Micah justice comes before piety—justice is the true sign of piety. **8:** In all this, no self-effacing modesty prevents Micah from blowing his own trumpet. The lack of self-esteem that afflicts so many women (and men) does not inhibit Micah. He believes God has spoken to him personally, commissioned, and empowered him for a task. Micah's claim evidences a paradox. We must question our assurance, and yet we must also act boldly. Too often our motives are mixed, and we deceive ourselves into believing our views are God's views. Yet at the same time self-doubt, self-pity, and low self-esteem can be selfish excuses to avoid the tasks we are commissioned for. God's people are called to walk in the paradox of humility (6:8) and boldness. **12:** Micah, alone of the eighth-century prophets, dares to prophesy the fall of Jerusalem.

4:1–13 A New World through New Birth

At chapter 4 a remarkable change of direction occurs, so remarkable that many want to see this chapter as a later exilic addition. The book's juxtaposition of discipline and restoration is highlighted. God's judgment is not vengefully destructive purely for the sake of it. The world is torn down in order to build it up. Pain is a reality that in God's hands can become redemptive. So far Micah has proclaimed God's opinion of the world as it is, an opinion greatly at odds with the official view. This opinion will lead, Micah says, to the destruction of all that is rotten, even, if necessary, Jerusalem (3:12), but it will be replaced by a world as it should be. It is to this vision that the book turns. It is a vision of a new Zion that was already well known (Isa 2:2–4) but worth repeating, a vision in which the wrongs of the past are righted, force is forsaken, and freedom is forever.

4 Everyone will live in peace and prosperity,
enjoying their own grapevines and fig trees,
for there will be nothing to fear.
The LORD of Heaven's Armies
has made this promise!
5 Though the nations around us follow their idols,
we will follow the LORD our God forever and ever.

Israel's Return from Exile

6 "In that coming day," says the LORD,
"I will gather together those who are lame,
those who have been exiles,
and those whom I have filled with grief.
7 Those who are weak will survive as a remnant;
those who were exiles will become a strong nation.
Then I, the LORD, will rule from Jerusalem*
as their king forever."
8 As for you, Jerusalem,
the citadel of God's people,*
your royal might and power
will come back to you again.
The kingship will be restored
to my precious Jerusalem.

9 But why are you now screaming in terror?
Have you no king to lead you?
Have your wise people all died?
Pain has gripped you like a woman in childbirth.
10 Writhe and groan like a woman in labor,
you people of Jerusalem,*
for now you must leave this city
to live in the open country.
You will soon be sent in exile
to distant Babylon.
But the LORD will rescue you there;
he will redeem you from the grip of your enemies.

11 Now many nations have gathered against you.
"Let her be desecrated," they say.
"Let us see the destruction of Jerusalem.*"

4:7 Hebrew *Mount Zion.* **4:8** Hebrew *As for you, Migdal-eder, / the Ophel of the daughter of Zion.* **4:10** Hebrew *O daughter of Zion.* **4:11** Hebrew *of Zion.*

4:6–13 Israel's Return from Exile. In this new world many things are reversed and among them, it seems, the status of women. **6–7:** The lame, those driven away, and those cast off whom God restores are all feminine, although normally masculine forms are used (e.g., in Deut 30:4; Isa 11:12). The result is ambiguous. The feminine probably indicates that this is a metaphor for Israel personified now as a wounded woman. The Israelites no doubt thought of themselves as strong and masculine, but in exile they were to discover their weakness and vulnerability. Yet, in the new order, this weakness will be turned to strength. The fact that the lame and outcasts can be understood as a metaphor for Israel should not stop us from also taking them as a metaphor for suffering women. The ambiguity of the verse allows both meanings to hover on the horizon. Women, who in the old world have been weak, vulnerable, and wounded, will now be restored, made a strong nation, with God rather than man as their leader. **7–8:** This new, strong nation with power, dominion, and sovereignty remains in feminine form. It is Zion pictured as a woman in leadership who will bring good government over the land. In this chapter daughter Zion becomes a positive image that does not fit the stereotypical roles for women. **9–10:** God makes what may seem a sacrilegious confession: He admits to afflicting the people, bringing them evil or calamity. Faith in God is rarely a foolproof protection from harm. Once again Micah turns to feminine imagery, this time to prepare the people for the unimaginable—exile. Labor and childbirth have always been perceived with great fear and great joy. The pain and the danger of childbirth were even greater then than today, as the Bible honestly acknowledges (Gen 25:22; 35:17-19; Jer 4:31). To use the image was to paint a grim picture of the agony and fatalities of exile. Paradoxically, birth has also been a time of great happiness. Children are the enduring symbol of hope, of life, of future. And this too is captured in the prophet's image. Micah urges on Mother Zion (*Writhe*! Bring forth! Push!). Only through the pain can this new hope arise. No other image could capture this dual reality so completely (see Midwifery and Birthing Practices, Job 3; Childbearing and Rearing, Col 3; Birth Pain Imagery, John 16). **11–13:** It may be that the thought of a woman flailing in childbirth gave rise to the image on which this chapter closes—Jerusalem the threshing ox, or rather heifer, for Micah maintains the feminine forms. God commands Israel to break the mold, to break the expectations of others. She who once had to *leave* for *exile* (2:10) now is told to *rise up* and *trample*. Breaking stereotypes seems to be part of the new world order. In the new ideal, the land of God's promise (portrayed as a woman) has power, strength, and sovereignty. Once more the old things are turned upside down. Christians who claim to live in that long-awaited new order should not be surprised to see old stereotypes cast down.

12 But they do not know the LORD's thoughts
or understand his plan.
These nations don't know
that he is gathering them together
to be beaten and trampled
like sheaves of grain on a threshing floor.
13 "Rise up and crush the nations,
O Jerusalem!"*
says the LORD.
"For I will give you iron horns and bronze
hooves,
so you can trample many nations to pieces.
You will present their stolen riches to the
LORD,
their wealth to the LORD of all the earth."

5 1*Mobilize! Marshal your troops!
The enemy is laying siege to Jerusalem.
They will strike Israel's leader
in the face with a rod.

A Ruler from Bethlehem

2* But you, O Bethlehem Ephrathah,
are only a small village among all the
people of Judah.
Yet a ruler of Israel will come from you,
one whose origins are from the distant
past.
3 The people of Israel will be abandoned to
their enemies
until the woman in labor gives birth.
Then at last his fellow countrymen
will return from exile to their own land.
4 And he will stand to lead his flock with the
LORD's strength,
in the majesty of the name of the LORD his
God.
Then his people will live there undisturbed,
for he will be highly honored around the
world.
5 And he will be the source of peace.

When the Assyrians invade our land
and break through our defenses,
we will appoint seven rulers to watch over us,
eight princes to lead us.
6 They will rule Assyria with drawn swords
and enter the gates of the land of Nimrod.
He will rescue us from the Assyrians
when they pour over the borders to invade
our land.

The Remnant Purified

7 Then the remnant left in Israel*
will take their place among the nations.
They will be like dew sent by the LORD
or like rain falling on the grass,
which no one can hold back
and no one can restrain.
8 The remnant left in Israel
will take their place among the nations.
They will be like a lion among the animals of
the forest,
like a strong young lion among flocks of
sheep and goats,
pouncing and tearing as they go
with no rescuer in sight.
9 The people of Israel will stand up to their foes,
and all their enemies will be wiped out.

10 "In that day," says the LORD,
"I will slaughter your horses

4:13 Hebrew *"Rise up and thresh, O daughter of Zion."* **5:1** Verse 5:1 is numbered 4:14 in Hebrew text. **5:2** Verses 5:2-15 are numbered 5:1-14 in Hebrew text. **5:7** Hebrew *in Jacob;* also in 5:8. See note on 1:5a.

5:1–15 A New World through Reversal

This theme of contrast that so characterizes the new world continues. **1–2:** The humiliation of the current leadership is set against the new leadership that God will raise up. **2–6:** Under this new leader all will be reversed—the strong destroyed, the conquerors vanquished, the exiled restored. The superlatives Micah heaps on this new savior go beyond anything to which an ordinary mortal can aspire (cf. Matt 2:6).

7–15 The Purifying Remnant. The new age in this chapter seems to be much more violent and warlike than the one found in chapter 4. It is perhaps not surprising that we return to masculine imagery for Israel—not perhaps to its credit. **8–9:** Such imagery is difficult and seems to go against the Christian ideals of mercy and forgiveness. Revenge is a basic human desire, and forgiveness is more easily exhorted than executed. Often the only way to break the abuse of power is by rendering the oppressors powerless and conversely empowering those who have been oppressed. The danger, as we see played out on too many stages of the world, is that those so empowered become abusers of power in their turn. **10–15:** The chapter moves swiftly to the reassertion that power, wealth, and authority belong only to God. In the new world, horses and chariots will be destroyed, fortresses that demonstrate superiority and invincibility will be torn down, for no longer will we need protection. But above all false religion will be rooted out. The pseudo-gods, which seem to offer security and wealth without the need for submission to the LORD, will be unmasked as the human concoctions they are.

Women as Leaders

Leadership in the Old and New Testaments is based on the calling and spiritual gifting of God and the recognition of this by his people (Exod 3:10; 4:12; Judg 6:14, 34; 1 Sam 16:13; 18:6–7; Acts 6:3; Rom 12:3–8; 1 Pet 4:10).

The Bible accurately reflects the patriarchal background of the period, when leadership was predominantly male. But at the same time, it establishes principles that critique that situation. Miriam, a prophet, led the women in celebration and worship after the deliverance from Egypt. Five hundred years later she was included as one of the three great national leaders of the Exodus, when God said, *I sent Moses, Aaron, and Miriam to help you* (Mic 6:4; Exod 15:20–21). In the time of the judges, a married woman, Deborah, was already acknowledged as a prophet and a judge when she was called to summon Barak to lead the nation against the enemy. The text does not suggest that Barak was weak (Judg 4:4–9); he recognized that the LORD had chosen to speak through Deborah, and with spiritual insight he insisted that she should accompany him to battle.

There were several prophets in Judah, including Jeremiah, when the Book of the Law was found in the Temple. But Josiah, the king, turned to the married prophet Huldah, and on her authority the newly discovered book was recognized as the word of God to the nation (2 Kgs 22:11–20). Mordecai suggested that Esther had reached her unique position in order to save the nation, and she emerged with unusual authority, even for a queen (Esth 4:14; 8:7–8; 9:29).

God clearly called the first three women and overruled Esther's circumstances to use them as national leaders over both men and women. If they had refused, they would have disobeyed God.

Jesus also confronted contemporary culture. By word and action, he modeled servanthood (Matt 20:25–28; Luke 22:25–27; John 13:12–16). He treated women with the utmost respect, included them among his closest friends and followers, and finally, in a culture that rejected women as witnesses, called them to proclaim the news of his resurrection (Luke 24:5–11; see Women as Witnesses, Mark 16). His example influenced the early church as women and men worshiped, prayed, and worked together. Phoebe was a leader who helped Paul and served as a deacon in the church. Lydia, Priscilla, Phoebe, Apphia, and Nympha are mentioned as women of stature in the church, with homes large enough to accommodate the local congregation at a time when most homes were far too small. Women received the same spiritual gifts, including those of teaching and evangelism, as did men. These gifts were to be used for the strengthening of the churches (Eph 4:7–13; Acts 18:26). Junia, although thought to be a man (Junias) by some scholars, was described as an apostle, and other women worked alongside Paul as colleagues (Acts 1:14; 16:40; Rom 16:1–16; Phil 4:3; Col 4:15; Phlm 1–2).

The use of women as leaders even in the patriarchal societies of the Bible should make us critique our own culture. Women have shown that they possess gifts of leadership, but these are often undeveloped and lack public recognition in churches. Both women and men were created equally in the image of God and called to increase and have dominion over creation together (Gen 1:26–28). Jesus' example reinforced this. At Pentecost Joel's prophecy served to lay the foundation for the ministry of both women and men (Acts 2:17–18). Our task is to discover how God intends us to use these gifts in the redeemed community on earth.

and destroy your chariots.
11 I will tear down your walls
and demolish your defenses.
12 I will put an end to all witchcraft,
and there will be no more fortune-tellers.
13 I will destroy all your idols and sacred pillars,
so you will never again worship the work
of your own hands.
14 I will abolish your idol shrines with their
Asherah poles
and destroy your pagan cities.
15 I will pour out my vengeance
on all the nations that refuse to obey me."

The LORD's Case against Israel

6 Listen to what the LORD is saying:
"Stand up and state your case against me.
Let the mountains and hills be called to
witness your complaints.
2 And now, O mountains,
listen to the LORD's complaint!

He has a case against his people.
He will bring charges against Israel.

3 "O my people, what have I done to you?
What have I done to make you tired of me?
Answer me!
4 For I brought you out of Egypt
and redeemed you from slavery.
I sent Moses, Aaron, and Miriam to help you.
5 Don't you remember, my people,
how King Balak of Moab tried to have you cursed
and how Balaam son of Beor blessed you instead?
And remember your journey from Acacia Grove* to Gilgal,
when I, the LORD, did everything I could
to teach you about my faithfulness."

6 What can we bring to the LORD?
What kind of offerings should we give him?
Should we bow before God
with offerings of yearling calves?
7 Should we offer him thousands of rams
and ten thousand rivers of olive oil?
Should we sacrifice our firstborn children
to pay for our sins?
8 No, O people, the LORD has told you what is good,
and this is what he requires of you:
to do what is right, to love mercy,
and to walk humbly with your God.

Israel's Guilt and Punishment

9 Fear the LORD if you are wise!
His voice calls to everyone in Jerusalem:
"The armies of destruction are coming;
the LORD is sending them.*
10 What shall I say about the homes of the wicked
filled with treasures gained by cheating?
What about the disgusting practice
of measuring out grain with dishonest measures?*
11 How can I tolerate your merchants
who use dishonest scales and weights?
12 The rich among you have become wealthy
through extortion and violence.
Your citizens are so used to lying
that their tongues can no longer tell the truth.

6:5 Hebrew *Shittim.* **6:9** Hebrew *"Listen to the rod. / Who appointed it?"* **6:10** Hebrew *of using the short ephah?* The ephah was a unit for measuring grain.

6:1–16 Justice for the LORD

Chapter 6 is often considered a new and later section of the book. It starts with a new calling to order of the court of judgment. We return from the future of hope into the forlorn reality, a reality far removed from the justice and goodwill of God. Rather than the short, sharp shock of vivid metaphors, the prophet chooses this time an impassioned plea to shame the people into repentance. **3–8:** Recalling God's continuous salvation in the past, he questions in increasing hyperbole what might be a fitting response of gratitude. The answer, when it comes in verse 8, makes plain the current running throughout the book—what the LORD requires is not proper worship or sound doctrine or even great sacrifice but justice, humility, and *hesed,* the loving kindness, mercy, and faithfulness characteristic of God. Here, as always in the Old Testament, obedience to the commands and requirements of God is considered a response to the grace of God, not a prerequisite for it. **4–5:** God has already superabundantly demonstrated *hesed* for Israel. The LORD has already redeemed them, already brought them out of the Egypt of slavery, already settled them in a land of freedom. Among those mighty saving acts, says Micah, was the sending of Miriam. **4:** Micah alone of biblical writers thinks to include Miriam in the list of God's Exodus-ordained leaders (cf. Josh 24:5; 1 Sam 12:6; Ps 77:20; see Women as Leaders, sidebar). Yet her role and status as a leader of Israel was well-enough known to need no justification, explanation, or comment (unlike Balak, 6:5). As with most female biblical characters there is an elusiveness to Miriam. We are told that as a prophet she led the celebrations by the waters of salvation (Exod 15:20) but also that she instigated a rebellion against Moses and suffered for it (Num 12:1–15) before dying in the wilderness (Num 20:1). Micah accords her the honor of standing in her own right, unqualified by relationship to husband, father, or brother that was so typical of his male-dominated society. Once again Micah is not ashamed to ascribe God-given leadership and authority to women. **9–16:** *Hesed* is missing in the violent, greedy, deceitful streets of the city, and therefore God, out of *hesed* for the poor and oppressed, will reestablish it. Just to make sure that the point has not been missed, Micah provides details of the oppression and corruption that permeated Judean society. This time he concentrates on the merchants rather than the lawyers, leaders, and religious functionaries. They too will have the tables turned on them.

13 "Therefore, I will wound you!
I will bring you to ruin for all your sins.
14 You will eat but never have enough.
Your hunger pangs and emptiness will remain.
And though you try to save your money,
it will come to nothing in the end.
You will save a little,
but I will give it to those who conquer you.
15 You will plant crops
but not harvest them.
You will press your olives
but not get enough oil to anoint yourselves.
You will trample the grapes
but get no juice to make your wine.
16 You keep only the laws of evil King Omri;
you follow only the example of wicked King Ahab!
Therefore, I will make an example of you,
bringing you to complete ruin.
You will be treated with contempt,
mocked by all who see you."

Misery Turned to Hope

7 1How miserable I am!
I feel like the fruit picker after the harvest
who can find nothing to eat.
Not a cluster of grapes or a single early fig
can be found to satisfy my hunger.
2 The godly people have all disappeared;
not one honest person is left on the earth.
They are all murderers,
setting traps even for their own brothers.
3 Both their hands are equally skilled at doing evil!
Officials and judges alike demand bribes.
The people with influence get what they want,
and together they scheme to twist justice.
4 Even the best of them is like a brier;
the most honest is as dangerous as a hedge of thorns.
But your judgment day is coming swiftly now.
Your time of punishment is here, a time of confusion.
5 Don't trust anyone—
not your best friend or even your wife!
6 For the son despises his father.
The daughter defies her mother.
The daughter-in-law defies her mother-in-law.
Your enemies are right in your own household!

7 As for me, I look to the LORD for help.
I wait confidently for God to save me,
and my God will certainly hear me.
8 Do not gloat over me, my enemies!
For though I fall, I will rise again.
Though I sit in darkness,
the LORD will be my light.
9 I will be patient as the LORD punishes me,
for I have sinned against him.
But after that, he will take up my case
and give me justice for all I have suffered from my enemies.
The LORD will bring me into the light,
and I will see his righteousness.
10 Then my enemies will see that the LORD is on my side.
They will be ashamed that they taunted me, saying,
"So where is the LORD—
that God of yours?"
With my own eyes I will see their downfall;
they will be trampled like mud in the streets.

11 In that day, Israel, your cities will be rebuilt,
and your borders will be extended.
12 People from many lands will come and honor you—
from Assyria all the way to the towns of Egypt,
from Egypt all the way to the Euphrates River,*

7:12 Hebrew *the river.*

7:1–20 Second Lament for a World Gone Wrong

The book concludes as it began, with lament. Micah has so identified himself with his nation that this lament is the lament of exiled Israel. He, who until now has disowned Israel's leadership and distanced himself from his people, is now portrayed as one with them in the pain, punishment, and lament. It is because he is within, it is because he is a member, that Micah is qualified to speak out in such a judgmental way. **1:** This lament is turned inward almost in despair. The prophet collapses in feelings of failure and ostracism, the opposite of the fiery strength of 3:8. **2–6:** In a final but forlorn attempt to persuade he utters a personal lament for the decay of society. **7–9:** Micah may have felt a failure, but history saw things differently. Though nothing in the book suggests it, history would credit Micah with the salvation of Jerusalem (Jer 26:18–19). **10–13:** So often we have to walk in faith, trusting that God and history will vindicate our long and seemingly fruitless efforts at change.

and from distant seas and mountains.
13 But the land* will become empty and desolate
because of the wickedness of those who live
there.

The Lord's Compassion on Israel

14 O Lord, protect your people with your
shepherd's staff;
lead your flock, your special possession.
Though they live alone in a thicket
on the heights of Mount Carmel,*
let them graze in the fertile pastures of
Bashan and Gilead
as they did long ago.

15 "Yes," says the Lord,
"I will do mighty miracles for you,
like those I did when I rescued you
from slavery in Egypt."

16 All the nations of the world will stand
amazed
at what the Lord will do for you.
They will be embarrassed
at their feeble power.
They will cover their mouths in silent awe,
deaf to everything around them.
17 Like snakes crawling from their holes,
they will come out to meet the Lord our
God.
They will fear him greatly,
trembling in terror at his presence.

18 Where is another God like you,
who pardons the guilt of the remnant,
overlooking the sins of his special
people?
You will not stay angry with your people
forever,
because you delight in showing unfailing
love.
19 Once again you will have compassion on us.
You will trample our sins under your feet
and throw them into the depths of the
ocean!
20 You will show us your faithfulness and
unfailing love
as you promised to our ancestors Abraham
and Jacob long ago.

7:13 Or *earth.* **7:14** Or *surrounded by a fruitful land.*

7:14–20 The Lord's Compassion Revealed. Yet even in despair, Micah and Israel assert their faith in an absent God. The glimpse of hope of verse 8 is now reaffirmed. **16–20:** Micah's lament becomes a bold assertion of the majesty of God despite all appearances. A cynic might label it wishful thinking, foolhardy faith, but Judaism and Christianity together proclaim their faith in things not yet seen. God's light will shine in dark places, and women and men together will worship God in a world the same and yet so different from the one we now live in.

NAHUM

INTRODUCTION

The book of Nahum is largely a diatribe against the city of Nineveh, which was the capital city of the great Assyrian Empire. The Assyrians had increasingly dominated and oppressed a large section of the ancient Near East over the previous five hundred years. They were recognized throughout the region as cruel, violent, self-serving, and destructive, indicative of the whole empire. The city is situated on the banks of the Tigris River some 600-plus kilometers (360 miles) northeast of Jerusalem. The Northern Kingdom of Israel had fallen to Assyria in 722 BC; although Judah resisted and never came totally under Assyrian control, she was attacked and oppressed by her huge and powerful neighbor. She was forced to pay significant tribute to Assyria, and the fear that she also would be completely destroyed by the Assyrian army remained very real. Nahum's prophecy is quite violent, but it is written to encourage Judah and give hope that not only would she not be destroyed by Assyria but that Assyria herself would come under God's judgment and be destroyed. Powerful, oppressive godless nations do exist, but Nahum brings assurance that they will not last forever.

Chapter 3 speaks of the destruction of the great ancient Egyptian city of Thebes in 663 BC. We know that Nineveh itself was destroyed by the Babylonian alliance in 612 BC. Nahum's oracles therefore come between these two dates. Ashurbanipal was the Assyrian emperor from 669 to 633 BC, and Nahum's prophecies show assumptions concerning Assyria's power and her relationship with Judah that fit best within his reign, probably around 650 BC. —*Editors, Oxford University Press*

1:1	Introduction
1:2–15	First Oracle against Nineveh
2:1–13	Nineveh's Destruction Foretold
3:1–19	Desolation for Nineveh—Joy for Her Enemies

1 This message concerning Nineveh came as a vision to Nahum, who lived in Elkosh.

The LORD's Anger against Nineveh

2 The LORD is a jealous God,
filled with vengeance and rage.
He takes revenge on all who oppose him
and continues to rage against his enemies!
3 The LORD is slow to get angry, but his power
is great,
and he never lets the guilty go unpunished.
He displays his power in the whirlwind and
the storm.
The billowing clouds are the dust beneath
his feet.
4 At his command the oceans dry up,
and the rivers disappear.
The lush pastures of Bashan and Carmel fade,
and the green forests of Lebanon wither.
5 In his presence the mountains quake,
and the hills melt away;
the earth trembles,
and its people are destroyed.
6 Who can stand before his fierce anger?
Who can survive his burning fury?
His rage blazes forth like fire,
and the mountains crumble to dust in his
presence.

7 The LORD is good,
a strong refuge when trouble comes.
He is close to those who trust in him.
8 But he will sweep away his enemies
in an overwhelming flood.
He will pursue his foes
into the darkness of night.

9 Why are you scheming against the LORD?
He will destroy you with one blow;
he won't need to strike twice!
10 His enemies, tangled like thornbushes
and staggering like drunks,
will be burned up like dry stubble in a field.
11 Who is this wicked counselor of yours
who plots evil against the LORD?

12 This is what the LORD says:
"Though the Assyrians have many allies,
they will be destroyed and disappear.
O my people, I have punished you before,
but I will not punish you again.
13 Now I will break the yoke of bondage from
your neck
and tear off the chains of Assyrian
oppression."

14 And this is what the LORD says concerning
the Assyrians in Nineveh:
"You will have no more children to carry on
your name.
I will destroy all the idols in the temples of
your gods.

1:1 Introduction

Nahum follows the pattern found in many of the Old Testament prophetic books by mentioning briefly what the book is about, in this instance Nineveh, and who is responsible for it, here Nahum the Elkoshite. As we don't know where Elkosh is, and have no further information about Nahum, this does not help us as much as it would have helped the original readers. His oracle is described as a *vision*, which may mean that it came to him in a dream or angelic visit, but it could simply stress that it is a message from God. That is, it stands as the equivalent of "the word of the LORD" found at the beginning of other books in other translations.

1:2–15 First Oracle against Nineveh

The whole chapter is full of dramatic poetic imagery bringing the reader into the awesome presence of a great God who defies definition. This is not a comfortable read! In today's world we are often inclined only to emphasize what we see as the "nice" elements of God's character. However, none of the biblical writers, in the Old or the New Testaments, have any qualms about making it clear that God is not always "nice." He is powerful and strong and loving and good, but his passion for justice is beyond our imagination; he will take whatever action is necessary to make sure that justice will be served. He is also holy and cannot and will not allow that holiness to be compromised—in particular by sharing the allegiance of his followers with others. It is in this context that the descriptions of vengeance and wrath can be seen. For those, like Judah at that time, who are desperate for justice, this passage may be scary but it is also very satisfying. **2–8:** These verses form an incomplete acrostic. **3, 7, 10:** The prophet intersperses the positive aspects of God's character in the midst of this frightening picture of his determination to destroy evil. **12:** God's campaign against injustice has included action against the idolatry and injustices among his own people. That is not the focus of Nahum's prophecy. His concern is the need for the corrupt, violent, and destructive regime in Assyria to be shown for what it was, and because of what it was, to be shown to come under God's judgment. **14:** From Nahum's perspective the Assyrians *will have no more children to carry on your*

I am preparing a grave for you
because you are despicable!"

15*Look! A messenger is coming over the
mountains with good news!
He is bringing a message of peace.
Celebrate your festivals, O people of Judah,
and fulfill all your vows,
for your wicked enemies will never invade
your land again.
They will be completely destroyed!

The Fall of Nineveh

2
1*Your enemy is coming to crush you,
Nineveh.
Man the ramparts! Watch the roads!
Prepare your defenses! Call out your
forces!
2 Even though the destroyer has destroyed
Judah,
the LORD will restore its honor.
Israel's vine has been stripped of branches,
but he will restore its splendor.

3 Shields flash red in the sunlight!
See the scarlet uniforms of the valiant
troops!
Watch as their glittering chariots move into
position,
with a forest of spears waving above
them.*
4 The chariots race recklessly along the streets
and rush wildly through the squares.
They flash like firelight
and move as swiftly as lightning.
5 The king shouts to his officers;
they stumble in their haste,
rushing to the walls to set up their
defenses.
6 The river gates have been torn open!
The palace is about to collapse!
7 Nineveh's exile has been decreed,
and all the servant girls mourn its capture.
They moan like doves
and beat their breasts in sorrow.
8 Nineveh is like a leaking water reservoir!
The people are slipping away.
"Stop, stop!" someone shouts,
but no one even looks back.
9 Loot the silver!
Plunder the gold!
There's no end to Nineveh's treasures—
its vast, uncounted wealth.
10 Soon the city is plundered, empty, and
ruined.
Hearts melt and knees shake.
The people stand aghast,
their faces pale and trembling.

11 Where now is that great Nineveh,
that den filled with young lions?
It was a place where people—like lions and
their cubs—
walked freely and without fear.

1:15 Verse 1:15 is numbered 2:1 in Hebrew text. **2:1** Verses 2:1-13 are numbered 2:2-14 in Hebrew text. **2:3** Greek and Syriac versions read *into position, / the horses whipped into a frenzy.*

---

name ("didn't deserve to live") and therefore should not and would not live. This was not good news for Nineveh but for those who had suffered greatly from Assyria's aggression, the ensuing freedom was something to look forward to. It would be easy to condemn this kind of reveling in the prediction of destruction of another country, but those communities that are being destroyed by such evil regimes cannot help but be glad at the prospect of the end of such evil.

2:1–13 Nineveh's Destruction Foretold

A wonderful poetic description of Nineveh's end. Once the dreadful nature of the society has been grasped, the imagery can be seen more positively. As with Hitler's Germany, Amin's Uganda, and Mugabe's Zimbabwe, so much pain has been caused that the ensuing fall is a reason for joy. **1–5:** The picture is clear. The apparently invincible city is called upon to watch out. For the God of Israel, no human regime is unconquerable. The picture of flashing armor and glittering chariots reminds one of the war poetry of many nations where glorying in conquest is common. **6–12:** It is somewhat unusual that the lament for the city is also included. The regime was evil, but the servant girls, perhaps themselves captives from other nations including Judah, were nevertheless mourning at the destruction of the city that had given them employment. There is recognition that "better the devil you know than the one you don't." For some the security of the present, however dreadful, is less frightening than an unknown freedom. Both the strength and the wealth of the city are stressed, but neither will be enough to save them. Both will, like the people, flow away like the water from a leaking reservoir. This may not have happened yet, but Nahum has no doubt about it. Judah can be absolutely confident that Nineveh will be destroyed.

12 The lion tore up meat for his cubs
and strangled prey for his mate.
He filled his den with prey,
his caverns with his plunder.

13 "I am your enemy!"
says the LORD of Heaven's Armies.
"Your chariots will soon go up in smoke.
Your young men* will be killed in battle.
Never again will you plunder conquered nations.
The voices of your proud messengers will be heard no more."

The LORD's Judgment against Nineveh

3 1What sorrow awaits Nineveh,
the city of murder and lies!
She is crammed with wealth
and is never without victims.
2 Hear the crack of whips,
the rumble of wheels!
Horses' hooves pound,
and chariots clatter wildly.
3 See the flashing swords and glittering spears
as the charioteers charge past!
There are countless casualties,
heaps of bodies—
so many bodies that
people stumble over them.
4 All this because Nineveh,
the beautiful and faithless city,
mistress of deadly charms,
enticed the nations with her beauty.
She taught them all her magic,
enchanting people everywhere.

5 "I am your enemy!"
says the LORD of Heaven's Armies.
"And now I will lift your skirts
and show all the earth your nakedness and shame.
6 I will cover you with filth
and show the world how vile you really are.
7 All who see you will shrink back and say,
'Nineveh lies in ruins.
Where are the mourners?'
Does anyone regret your destruction?"

8 Are you any better than the city of Thebes,*
situated on the Nile River, surrounded by water?
She was protected by the river on all sides,
walled in by water.
9 Ethiopia* and the land of Egypt
gave unlimited assistance.
The nations of Put and Libya
were among her allies.
10 Yet Thebes fell,
and her people were led away as captives.
Her babies were dashed to death
against the stones of the streets.
Soldiers threw dice* to get Egyptian officers as servants.
All their leaders were bound in chains.

11 And you, Nineveh, will also stagger like a drunkard.
You will hide for fear of the attacking enemy.
12 All your fortresses will fall.
They will be devoured like the ripe figs
that fall into the mouths

2:13 Hebrew *young lions.* **3:8** Hebrew *No-amon;* also in 3:10. **3:9** Hebrew *Cush.* **3:10** Hebrew *They cast lots.*

3:1–19 Desolation for Nineveh—Joy for Her Enemies

Whereas chapter 2 reflects to some degree on the glory of war, chapter 3 concentrates more on the ugliness. There is no glory and no reveling in the heaps of dead bodies that *people stumble over* as they flee. **1–4:** The destruction is indeed terrible. **5–13:** Nineveh is portayed as a faithless prostitute who charmed other nations into leaving their own gods with no thought for their benefit but only to enrich herself. Many of the prophets describe Israel and Judah as acting as prostitutes, but here the parallel is with the north African city of Thebes. Thebes was also a proud city who charmed, then oppressed, surrounding nations. She was eventually humiliated and destroyed; Nahum envisages the same future for Nineveh. The behavior of such a prostitute is ugly, and the consequence of that behavior is equally ugly. Nahum is not here seeing the woman who is forced into prostitution because of desperate poverty or the oppression of others but the one who uses prostitution as a means of manipulation and oppression. He also is not suggesting that the sexual violation described here is to be viewed in any sense positively. The picture is meant to be horrific. The imagery is again varied. Nineveh is not only a shamed prostitute but a helpless drunkard incapable of standing, let alone fighting. The army troops are likened to weak women. The modern concept of competent female soldiers would have been completely outside of Nahum's experience or thinking. The image is not

of those who shake the trees.
13 Your troops will be as weak
and helpless as women.
The gates of your land will be opened wide to
the enemy
and set on fire and burned.
14 Get ready for the siege!
Store up water!
Strengthen the defenses!
Go into the pits to trample clay,
and pack it into molds,
making bricks to repair the walls.
15 But the fire will devour you;
the sword will cut you down.
The enemy will consume you like locusts,
devouring everything they see.
There will be no escape,
even if you multiply like swarming locusts.
16 Your merchants have multiplied
until they outnumber the stars.
But like a swarm of locusts,
they strip the land and fly away.
17 Your guards* and officials are also like
swarming locusts
that crowd together in the hedges on a cold
day.
But like locusts that fly away when the sun
comes up,
all of them will fly away and disappear.

18 Your shepherds are asleep, O Assyrian king;
your princes lie dead in the dust.
Your people are scattered across the
mountains
with no one to gather them together.
19 There is no healing for your wound;
your injury is fatal.
All who hear of your destruction
will clap their hands for joy.
Where can anyone be found
who has not suffered from your continual
cruelty?

3:17 Or *princes.*

intended to be a negative presentation of women but simply a way of indicating the helplessness of the army. **14–17:** A final challenge to Assyria. They are not encouraged to prepare to fight the oncoming armies; that would be fruitless. Rather the only thing they can do is get ready for the siege so the damage might be limited, but even that will prove useless. **18–19:** Nahum is one of only two biblical books that end with a question, and interestingly both of them relate to Nineveh. In Jonah, the other book, the question is quite positive. God rhetorically asks Jonah whether he ought to feel sorry for a great city that has been threatened by judgment but who has repented. Here in Nahum the question is also fairly rhetorical. Is there anyone at all who has not *suffered from* Nineveh's cruelty? The answer has already been presupposed! It is impossible to find anyone who will not rejoice at Nineveh's downfall. What a sad reflection on a dominant civilization, and what a challenge to modern regimes. Will the world be glad or sad if my society falls?

HABAKKUK

INTRODUCTION

In 1:1 and 3:1, Habakkuk is identified as a prophet, although regular aspects of prophetic books, like recorded sermons or calls to repentance, are missing here.

Habakkuk 1:6 indicates that the prophet was ministering in Judah while the Babylonians were dominant toward the end of the seventh century BC. His book presumably comes out of a historical situation in Judah, and the evidence points to a date around 609 to 598 BC when Jehoiakim reigned. Jehoiakim was extravagant with money, politically irresponsible, and repressive (see Jer 22:13–19; 26:20–23; 36:20–31), exacerbating the moral and religious crisis in Judah.

Habakkuk is a book for faithful people of any era who live in the time between the revelation of God's promises and their fulfillment. Most of the book is poetry, but in three very different genres: a dialogue between Habakkuk and the LORD (1:2—2:5), a series of five woes (2:6–20), and a prayer psalm complete with liturgical instructions (3:2–19). The overarching theme of the book is that regardless of present appearances, human violence will ultimately be defeated by divine violence. Many people today may question the continuing appropriateness of biblical images depicting God as violent. But when humans legitimately bemoan the lack of justice in society, God is aware and is responding.

Elements of Jeremiah's confessions (Jer 11:18—12:6; 15:10–21; 17:14–18; 18:18–23; 20:7–18) and the argumentative sounds of the Psalter's laments (e.g., Pss 44; 69) can be discerned in Habakkuk's complaint. Such agonizing occurs similarly in Job—how to understand the righteousness of God in an unjust world. Habakkuk was evidently thoughtful and sensitive, concerned about human suffering and helplessness before the powers of evil, and deeply troubled by God's apparent acquiescence in oppression. He shows us that it is acceptable to challenge and question God.

Habakkuk spoke for all oppressed who have no or little voice. Women especially feel and suffer the effects of injustice. Women and children are disproportionately victims of drug wars, gun violence, domestic violence, inequities in the workplace, sexual harassment, and the like. They can relate to the prophet's description of lack of control. —*Edwin C. Hostetter*

1:1–2:5 Dialogue
2:6–20 The Taunts
3:1–19 Habakkuk's Prayer

✧

1 This is the message that the prophet Habakkuk received in a vision.

Habakkuk's Complaint

2 How long, O LORD, must I call for help?
But you do not listen!
"Violence is everywhere!" I cry,
but you do not come to save.
3 Must I forever see these evil deeds?
Why must I watch all this misery?
Wherever I look,
I see destruction and violence.
I am surrounded by people
who love to argue and fight.
4 The law has become paralyzed,
and there is no justice in the courts.
The wicked far outnumber the righteous,
so that justice has become perverted.

The LORD's Reply

5 The LORD replied,

"Look around at the nations;
look and be amazed!*
For I am doing something in your own day,
something you wouldn't believe
even if someone told you about it.
6 I am raising up the Babylonians,*
a cruel and violent people.
They will march across the world
and conquer other lands.
7 They are notorious for their cruelty
and do whatever they like.
8 Their horses are swifter than cheetahs*
and fiercer than wolves at dusk.
Their charioteers charge from far away.
Like eagles, they swoop down to devour
their prey.

9 "On they come, all bent on violence.
Their hordes advance like a desert wind,
sweeping captives ahead of them like
sand.
10 They scoff at kings and princes
and scorn all their fortresses.
They simply pile ramps of earth
against their walls and capture them!
11 They sweep past like the wind
and are gone.
But they are deeply guilty,
for their own strength is their god."

Habakkuk's Second Complaint

12 O LORD my God, my Holy One, you who are
eternal—
surely you do not plan to wipe us out?

1:5 Greek version reads *Look, you mockers; / look and be amazed and die.* Compare Acts 13:41. **1:6** Or *Chaldeans.* **1:8** Or *leopards.*

1:1—2:5 Dialogue

1:2–4 Protesting Injustice. The strong in Judah, perpetrators of violence, oppress the weak. Habakkuk objects to this ill-treatment and the wrongs people endure from their fellow humans. He also rejects the arbitrary power of the administrators of the law and the suffering caused by perversion of justice. Judah has abandoned the righteous order intended by God for their society. Violence has become prevalent, and justice is warped. Why must one regard these things helplessly when the LORD could put a stop to it but does not? How long will the LORD remain silent, when the patience of those who pray is gradually being exhausted? The prophet does not doubt God's power to act; what agitates him is the lack of answer to his repeated cry. Habakkuk faces the dilemma of seemingly unanswered prayer that confronts believers in every age. The words of 1:2 can often be uttered by individuals, especially women and children, who suffer from domestic violence (see Violence, Abuse, and Oppression, Eccl 4; The Purpose and Value of Human Life, Rev 22). They may feel stuck in conditions of abuse without sensing either a divine or a human response to their pleas.

1:5–11 The LORD's Reply. God's response shows that the complaint has been heard. The LORD will act on the world stage according to his might and unsearchable wisdom. **6:** God will use Babylon to carry out his purposes. God, throughout history, has used the disciplinary and judicial activities of human instruments to accomplish his service. But the situation that troubled the prophet does not end. Instead, the Babylonians will bring more violence while they plunder the region, punishing for God the violence of those in Judah. **7–10:** The Babylonians themselves strive only to serve themselves: ransacking, confiscating, conquering, and pillaging. The LORD seems, by authorizing such workers, to be going in the wrong direction. Rather than peace, God ordains war; rather than security, violence. In place of life the LORD brings death. **9:** Among the countless captives are undoubtedly women and girls who will be raped by the enemy troops, pressed into servitude as prostitutes, or claimed as brides involuntarily. This is one of the sad features of wars.

1:12—2:1 Habakkuk's Objection. Habakkuk objects that violence within Judah should not be punished by worse Babylonian violence. **1:12–14:** The prophet

O LORD, our Rock, you have sent these
Babylonians to correct us,
to punish us for our many sins.
13 But you are pure and cannot stand the sight
of evil.
Will you wink at their treachery?
Should you be silent while the wicked
swallow up people more righteous than
they?

14 Are we only fish to be caught and killed?
Are we only sea creatures that have no
leader?
15 Must we be strung up on their hooks
and caught in their nets while they rejoice
and celebrate?
16 Then they will worship their nets
and burn incense in front of them.
"These nets are the gods who have made us
rich!"
they will claim.
17 Will you let them get away with this forever?
Will they succeed forever in their heartless
conquests?

2 [1]I will climb up to my watchtower
and stand at my guardpost.
There I will wait to see what the LORD
says
and how he* will answer my complaint.

The LORD's Second Reply
[2]Then the LORD said to me,

"Write my answer plainly on tablets,
so that a runner can carry the correct
message to others.
3 This vision is for a future time.
It describes the end, and it will be fulfilled.
If it seems slow in coming, wait patiently,
for it will surely take place.
It will not be delayed.

4 "Look at the proud!
They trust in themselves, and their lives
are crooked.
But the righteous will live by their
faithfulness to God.*
5 Wealth* is treacherous,
and the arrogant are never at rest.
They open their mouths as wide as the
grave,*
and like death, they are never satisfied.
In their greed they have gathered up many
nations
and swallowed many peoples.

6 "But soon their captives will taunt them.
They will mock them, saying,
'What sorrow awaits you thieves!

2:1 As in Syriac version; Hebrew reads *I*. **2:3b-4** Greek version reads *If the vision is delayed, wait patiently, / for it will surely come and not delay. / [4]I will take no pleasure in anyone who turns away. / But the righteous person will live by my faith.* Compare Rom 1:17; Gal 3:11; Heb 10:37-38. **2:5a** As in Dead Sea Scroll 1QpHab; other Hebrew manuscripts read *Wine*. **2:5b** Hebrew *as Sheol*.

both praises God and tries to hold God to account. We may compare how many women find themselves needing to appease men while trying to get them to stop their abuse. The analogy of the LORD as an abusive male is more than a little troubling. Habakkuk too seems truly and thoroughly perplexed by the LORD's actions or inactions. **13:** Why does the One with eyes too pure to behold evil choose this evil instrument to accomplish his will? How can the God of law and righteousness choose these means for the administration of justice? Can a God of overflowing life will that there be destruction and death before abundant living is granted? If so, it is an enigma in the working of God that defies human understanding. **1:14—2:1:** These laments (rather like the supplications in Pss 39; 88) do not end with an expression of confidence or trust in God, but more challenges. The change of mood from despair to assurance occurs later, among the woes and in the psalm.

2:2–5 The LORD's Second Reply. God does not explain his actions; rather, as the LORD of world history, he proclaims his will in a sovereign manner. When God sees fit, then he will fulfill his plan. **4–5:** Two extremes—the *proud* and the *righteous*—come into focus. The proud are vain, presumptuous, conceited persons, but the righteous fulfill the demands of relationship with God, people, and the earth. The LORD's final answer to the prophet's impatient complaint is that the proud will bear their punishment; the righteous will remain alive amid all their trials. Nevertheless, *faithfulness* brings together passive and active aspects—confidence and obedience toward God, whose deeds and ways remain beyond human comprehension. To have faith means to believe God's promise and to live in the light of it.

2:6–20 The Taunts

The series of consequences for the proud reinforce the promise given in verses 4–5 by showing that those relying on their own powers cannot sustain their self-contained lives or find any permanent satisfaction. The activities of the threatening forces that act for the

Now you will get what you deserve!
You've become rich by extortion,
but how much longer can this go on?'
7 Suddenly, your debtors will take action.
They will turn on you and take all you have,
while you stand trembling and helpless.
8 Because you have plundered many nations,
now all the survivors will plunder you.
You committed murder throughout the countryside
and filled the towns with violence.

9 "What sorrow awaits you who build big houses
with money gained dishonestly!
You believe your wealth will buy security,
putting your family's nest beyond the reach of danger.
10 But by the murders you committed,
you have shamed your name and forfeited your lives.
11 The very stones in the walls cry out against you,
and the beams in the ceilings echo the complaint.

12 "What sorrow awaits you who build cities
with money gained through murder and corruption!
13 Has not the LORD of Heaven's Armies promised
that the wealth of nations will turn to ashes?
They work so hard,
but all in vain!
14 For as the waters fill the sea,
the earth will be filled with an awareness
of the glory of the LORD.

15 "What sorrow awaits you who make your neighbors drunk!
You force your cup on them
so you can gloat over their shameful nakedness.
16 But soon it will be your turn to be disgraced.
Come, drink and be exposed!*
Drink from the cup of the LORD's judgment,
and all your glory will be turned to shame.
17 You cut down the forests of Lebanon.
Now you will be cut down.
You destroyed the wild animals,
so now their terror will be yours.
You committed murder throughout the countryside
and filled the towns with violence.

18 "What good is an idol carved by man,
or a cast image that deceives you?
How foolish to trust in your own creation—
a god that can't even talk!
19 What sorrow awaits you who say to wooden idols,
'Wake up and save us!'
To speechless stone images you say,

2:16 Dead Sea Scrolls and Greek and Syriac versions read *and stagger!*

LORD, the Babylonians, are temporary. God is at work in the world, and part of that working is judgment on all the proud and mighty. Habakkuk's five taunts confidently mock the oppressors, including the Babylonians, who will be penalized for their violence, since they achieved God's purpose in an excessive manner. It seems as if God must take some responsibility for that, since he picked them despite knowing their character. Nevertheless, the Babylonians would be held accountable for their behavior and would have to accept their punishment. God's use of their oppression does not take away their responsibility. **6–8:** The Babylonians will be mocked and scorned by those whom they have oppressed and humiliated. The *captives*, among them Judah, who had been subjugated by the Babylonians, will now mock. **9:** The exploiters seek to secure their valuables along with their households. This verse sounds quite similar to the modern phenomenon of gated communities that are meant to protect their inhabitants. The less fortunate are left to reside in deteriorating neighborhoods. **11:** There is hope that the suppressed voices will be heard. May they also gain full access to and participation in decision-making and power-brokering processes. **12–14:** They aim to create fame and glory by building—with blood. The attempts of human beings to gain glory for themselves by public works built on injustice are vain endeavors that will fall. Contrarily, *the earth will be filled with an awareness of the glory of the LORD*. **15–16:** The host of a party goes to excess and ensures that his guests become drunk and lose all inhibitions. The scene is reminiscent of reports from women sexually assaulted while under the influence of a date-rape drug. The whole stanza speaks about lack of respect and no restraint. **17:** This verse refers back to verse 8. The Babylonians destroyed humans, animals, forests, and other natural resources. Violence done to other nations will return upon the head of the violent and overwhelm them. **18–20:** Beside the LORD every divinity is born of human fantasy. God alone can uphold and guide. Habakkuk knows that idol worshipers rely not on the image but the de-

'Rise up and teach us!'
Can an idol tell you what to do?
They may be overlaid with gold and silver,
but they are lifeless inside.
20 But the LORD is in his holy Temple.
Let all the earth be silent before him."

Habakkuk's Prayer

3 This prayer was sung by the prophet Habakkuk*:

2 I have heard all about you, LORD.
I am filled with awe by your amazing works.
In this time of our deep need,
help us again as you did in years gone by.
And in your anger,
remember your mercy.

3 I see God moving across the deserts from Edom,*
the Holy One coming from Mount Paran.*
His brilliant splendor fills the heavens,
and the earth is filled with his praise.
4 His coming is as brilliant as the sunrise.
Rays of light flash from his hands,
where his awesome power is hidden.
5 Pestilence marches before him;
plague follows close behind.
6 When he stops, the earth shakes.
When he looks, the nations tremble.
He shatters the everlasting mountains
and levels the eternal hills.
He is the Eternal One!
7 I see the people of Cushan in distress,
and the nation of Midian trembling in terror.

8 Was it in anger, LORD, that you struck the rivers
and parted the sea?
Were you displeased with them?
No, you were sending your chariots of salvation!
9 You brandished your bow
and your quiver of arrows.
You split open the earth with flowing rivers.
10 The mountains watched and trembled.
Onward swept the raging waters.
The mighty deep cried out,
lifting its hands to the LORD.
11 The sun and moon stood still in the sky
as your brilliant arrows flew
and your glittering spear flashed.

12 You marched across the land in anger
and trampled the nations in your fury.
13 You went out to rescue your chosen people,
to save your anointed ones.
You crushed the heads of the wicked
and stripped their bones from head to toe.
14 With his own weapons,
you destroyed the chief of those
who rushed out like a whirlwind,

3:1 Hebrew adds *according to shigionoth,* probably indicating the musical setting for the prayer. **3:3a** Hebrew *Teman.* **3:3b** Hebrew adds *selah;* also in 3:9, 13. The meaning of this Hebrew term is uncertain; it is probably a musical or literary term.

ity represented by the image. The mockery, however, is part of an idol parody. It is a conscious and polemic negation of ascriptions of creative power to images and their gods. Yahweh, who is present for his people in his Temple, is to be feared and honored. God is ruled by holiness, says the prophet, even though he surely knew that God is also ruled by love.

3:1–19 Habakkuk's Prayer

Thus far God's judgment has operated through human violence; God was not directly involved. In this psalm, the LORD himself appears as a warrior conquering the earth, wreaking havoc in his path. The function of the hymn in Habakkuk is to give sufferers confidence that God can and will intervene to aid his people as he did in the past. **2:** *In your anger remember your mercy* signals a dreadful but compassionate LORD—before God's holy anger Habakkuk can only pray for mercy. **3–4:** God is depicted as a victorious storm god whose lightning brings destruction (see also vv. 9, 11). **5:** Pestilence and plague come in the military retinue. Pestilence is God's herald, while plague is God's rearguard. This may refer to ancient Canaanite views on the power of feared divinities that oppressed mortal human beings with epidemics. **6–7:** All nature and people along Yahweh's route are, like the prophet, profoundly upset. **8–15:** Yahweh's enemies are trampled and pierced, exterminated and overthrown. Habakkuk pictures Yahweh's granting release and salvation to his people in terms of a whirling tornado and a procession of war vehicles. God's *brilliant arrows* and *glittering spear* have terrified even the heavenly bodies in a blinding stream of light. The militarism depicted here more commonly characterizes the actions of men than of women. Yet the latter, counting civilians, suffer its consequences at least equally with the former. **10:** The Hebrew word for *trembled* frequently indicates labor. The moun-

thinking Israel would be easy prey.
15 You trampled the sea with your horses,
and the mighty waters piled high.

16 I trembled inside when I heard this;
my lips quivered with fear.
My legs gave way beneath me,*
and I shook in terror.
I will wait quietly for the coming day
when disaster will strike the people who
invade us.
17 Even though the fig trees have no blossoms,
and there are no grapes on the vines;
even though the olive crop fails,
and the fields lie empty and barren;
even though the flocks die in the fields,
and the cattle barns are empty,
18 yet I will rejoice in the LORD!
I will be joyful in the God of my salvation!
19 The Sovereign LORD is my strength!
He makes me as surefooted as a deer,*
able to tread upon the heights.

(For the choir director: This prayer is to be accompanied by stringed instruments.)

3:16 Hebrew *Decay entered my bones.* **3:19** Or *He gives me the speed of a deer.*

tains convulse as when a pregnant woman is in the pain of labor. **16:** With dismay Habakkuk hears the report and sees the execution of judgment, which will shake all humanity. The numbing situation of God's devouring and annihilating produces a terrible tension within the prophet. A trembling body accompanies the prophet's great inner shock and fear. **17–19:** From this shattering experience emerges an overflowing joy. Habakkuk ends with a trustful hope for the future. The theophany empowers the psalmist to find strength in God. Perhaps the image already used continues—although it involves pain, birthing brings great joy (see Birth Pain Imagery, John 16; Midwifery and Birthing Practices, Job 3).

Habakkuk's final affirmation is that nothing can steal his joy in the God of his salvation. It is not a question of mere human cheerfulness but of a deep calm arising from an inner harmony placed there by the LORD. Come what may, he and the faithful can rejoice and exult, because God is their salvation. Although God seemingly left Habakkuk alone in the world to deal with the problems of enduring evil and torture from another hand, the book gives a statement of faith that has few parallels in the Old Testament.

ZEPHANIAH

INTRODUCTION

The book of Zephaniah uses apocalyptic imagery, which often appears violent. Yet God sometimes works in destruction before renewal and purifying can begin. The prophet, Zephaniah son of Cushi, was descended from Hezekiah. The reference to Cushi either indicates the land of Zephaniah's birth in Africa ("Cush" is sometimes translated "Ethiopia") or the presence of Cushite people in Israel. If the prophet was of African descent, it reminds us of the place of all peoples in the work, salvation, and judgment of God (see Africans in Biblical History, 2 Kgs 19). In Zephaniah's text the whole known world faced judgment; those who had been exiled into regions of Africa would be among those God brought back to Israel.

Zephaniah's ministry, about 640 to 609 BC, was in Josiah's reign. Josiah was a reformer who took advantage of the Assyrians' declining power. Zephaniah condemned Judah's overall leadership, which had been corrupted by their embrace of other gods. The people had forgotten the law and intermingled worship of the LORD with worship of the gods of their captors. During Josiah's reign, however, one of the Deuteronomic scrolls was found, and Josiah began a program of religious renewal. Zephaniah's prophecies were spoken prior to this discovery. Interestingly, when the scroll was found, it was not Zephaniah who was consulted, but Huldah (2 Kgs 22:14–20). God's use of a woman to remind people how to apply and reinstate the divine law is significant. God did not make laws only for men; the law applies to all and can be interpreted by all those to whom God speaks.

In Zephaniah's prophecy, the "day of the LORD" took on great importance in the face of Judah's idolatry. The day of the LORD, when God pronounces judgment, is best known by most Christians from the New Testament passages of 1 Thessalonians 5:2 and 2 Peter 3:10. The message of Zephaniah is not only for past Israelites, it is relevant for all people living in idolatrous societies that have separated themselves from God's presence and plan. For women especially, the message of destruction and renewal can provide hope in the midst of unjust and burdensome situations. When the day of the LORD comes, the injustices of inequality, subjugation, and indifference to God will be destroyed.

Zephaniah lived in a time of turmoil for Israel and Judah. The Northern Kingdom (Israel) had been taken into captivity by the Assyrians, and in the Southern Kingdom (Judah) people had neglected the law and mingled worship of the LORD with that of other gods. Worship of some of these deities, creation goddesses such as Astarte, put women in charge of some idolatrous practices. But other idolatrous practices could cause them great grief. Their children could be sacrificed to Molech in a fiery ceremony. Women were abused sexually by the fertility rituals that worshipers engaged in. The modern embrace of the goddess must be tempered by the reality that even though the female form and person were worshiped, women were not treated justly in these societies. They were often chattels with few rights and many perils. —*Anthea D. Butler*

1:1–18 The Day of the LORD and the Following Destruction
2:1–15 Prophecies against the Nations and Jerusalem
3:1–20 Jerusalem's Rebellion and Redemption

✧

1 The LORD gave this message to Zephaniah
when Josiah son of Amon was king of Judah. Zephaniah was the son of Cushi, son of
Gedaliah, son of Amariah, son of Hezekiah.

Coming Judgment against Judah

2 "I will sweep away everything
from the face of the earth," says the LORD.
3 "I will sweep away people and animals alike.
I will sweep away the birds of the sky and
the fish in the sea.
I will reduce the wicked to heaps of rubble,*
and I will wipe humanity from the face of
the earth," says the LORD.
4 "I will crush Judah and Jerusalem with my fist
and destroy every last trace of their Baal
worship.
I will put an end to all the idolatrous priests,
so that even the memory of them will
disappear.
5 For they go up to their roofs
and bow down to the sun, moon, and stars.
They claim to follow the LORD,
but then they worship Molech,* too.
6 And I will destroy those who used to
worship me
but now no longer do.
They no longer ask for the LORD's guidance
or seek my blessings."
7 Stand in silence in the presence of the
Sovereign LORD,
for the awesome day of the LORD's
judgment is near.
The LORD has prepared his people for a great
slaughter
and has chosen their executioners.*
8 "On that day of judgment,"
says the LORD,
"I will punish the leaders and princes of
Judah
and all those following pagan customs.
9 Yes, I will punish those who participate in
pagan worship ceremonies,
and those who fill their masters' houses
with violence and deceit.
10 "On that day," says the LORD,
"a cry of alarm will come from the Fish
Gate

1:3 The meaning of the Hebrew is uncertain. **1:5** Hebrew *Malcam*, a variant spelling of Molech; or it could possibly mean *their king*. **1:7** Hebrew *has prepared a sacrifice and sanctified his guests*.

1:1–18 The Day of the LORD and the Following Destruction

The book begins by giving the genealogy of Zephaniah. This is a way to orient readers to the historical context, informing them that he is of the royal line, as well as from Cush, and showing that Zephaniah's messages from God cannot be separated from the circumstances of his birth or nationality. **2–6:** The theme of destruction is a stark beginning to these messages. God is doing destructive rather than creative work. The reversal of the created order through destruction suggests that there is an imbalance caused by worship of false gods. These times resemble our own, when Christians have embraced astrology and other religious means in order to enhance their spiritual experiences. Like their ancient counterparts, they have not sought the LORD in the matter of their worship practices. **4–6:** It is striking that the Israelites have taken to worshiping the gods of their oppressors, and even the LORD's priests participate in these idolatrous ceremonies. Some of these gods, which represent fertility, are invoked for creative or regenerative purposes. So when the creation is being destroyed, it may refer to the creations attempted by those who worship false gods. **5:** The seriousness of the idolatry is evident in the worship of Molech, to whom children were sacrificed in a fiery ceremony. **7–9:** In response the LORD will call for sacrifice, just as the Israelites have sacrificed to foreign gods. The sacrifice that God requires, however, is the sacrifice of those who have led the people astray. Those who have participated in the ceremonies, including royal officials and priests, will be punished. **10:** The text shifts to the effect that the destruction will have on Jerusalem. From the *Fish Gate*, where the fish markets were, to the *New Quarter*, the upper-class area where Huldah was reputed to have lived and that looked over the Temple, will come a *cry of alarm* from people, of all classes, who witness the destruction. **12–13:** The LORD will search Jerusa-

and echo throughout the New Quarter of the
city.*
And a great crash will sound from the hills.
11 Wail in sorrow, all you who live in the market
area,
for all the merchants and traders will be
destroyed.

12 "I will search with lanterns in Jerusalem's
darkest corners
to punish those who sit complacent in their
sins.
They think the LORD will do nothing to them,
either good or bad.
13 So their property will be plundered,
their homes will be ransacked.
They will build new homes
but never live in them.
They will plant vineyards
but never drink wine from them.

14 "That terrible day of the LORD is near.
Swiftly it comes—
a day of bitter tears,
a day when even strong men will cry out.
15 It will be a day when the LORD's anger is
poured out—
a day of terrible distress and anguish,
a day of ruin and desolation,
a day of darkness and gloom,
a day of clouds and blackness,
16 a day of trumpet calls and battle cries.
Down go the walled cities
and the strongest battlements!

17 "Because you have sinned against the LORD,
I will make you grope around like the
blind.
Your blood will be poured into the dust,
and your bodies will lie rotting on the
ground."

18 Your silver and gold will not save you
on that day of the LORD's anger.
For the whole land will be devoured
by the fire of his jealousy.
He will make a terrifying end
of all the people on earth.*

A Call to Repentance

2 1Gather together—yes, gather together,
you shameless nation.
2 Gather before judgment begins,
before your time to repent is blown away
like chaff.
Act now, before the fierce fury of the LORD
falls
and the terrible day of the LORD's anger
begins.
3 Seek the LORD, all who are humble,
and follow his commands.
Seek to do what is right
and to live humbly.
Perhaps even yet the LORD will protect
you—
protect you from his anger on that day of
destruction.

Judgment against Philistia

4 Gaza and Ashkelon will be abandoned,
Ashdod and Ekron torn down.
5 And what sorrow awaits you Philistines*

1:10 Or *the Second Quarter,* a newer section of Jerusalem. Hebrew reads *the Mishneh.* **1:18** Or *the people living in the land.* **2:5** Hebrew *Kerethites.*

lem with a lamp, so that no one will be able to hide from God's wrath. All the material goods that the Israelites have coveted will be destroyed. **14:** The destruction is emphasized by sound; the Hebrew word *qwl* (*cry*) emulates shrieking, a harsh sound of bitterness and wailing. Even the mighty will cry aloud at the destruction. **15:** Darkness, like a storm or an eclipse, will descend on the city. **16:** The trumpet, the ram's horn used to signify entrance into battle, will be used against God's people. The trumpet is also used in the New Testament as signaling the Lord's return (1 Cor 15:52) and indicates that the Lord's wrath and judgment are soon to come. Judgment will come upon the city, and the people will be ravaged. **18:** The whole earth will have felt the wrath of God's vengeance on unfaithful people. Zephaniah's focus is on Judah in particular.

2:1–15 Prophecies against the Nations

2:1–3 Call to Repentance. The theme of destruction is interrupted by a call to repentance. Those called to seek the LORD are the humble, perhaps the lower strata of society, which have not had the opportunity or the funds to engage in the sinful practices of those with too much money and time. The theme of the *day of the LORD* is mentioned again; those who seek the LORD will be hidden from the LORD's wrath on that day. The warning is strong, but there is a great hope for those who repent and turn from wickedness. **2–3:** In Hebrew, these verses start with words that begin in B, sounding an almost rhythmic beat.

2:4–7: Against Philistia. In the Hebrew text, each Philistine city has a punishment: Gaza, desertion; Ashke-

who live along the coast and in the land of
Canaan,
for this judgment is against you, too!
The LORD will destroy you
until not one of you is left.
6 The Philistine coast will become a wilderness
pasture,
a place of shepherd camps
and enclosures for sheep and goats.
7 The remnant of the tribe of Judah will
pasture there.
They will rest at night in the abandoned
houses in Ashkelon.
For the LORD their God will visit his people in
kindness
and restore their prosperity again.

Judgment against Moab and Ammon

8 "I have heard the taunts of the Moabites
and the insults of the Ammonites,
mocking my people
and invading their borders.
9 Now, as surely as I live,"
says the LORD of Heaven's Armies, the God
of Israel,
"Moab and Ammon will be destroyed—
destroyed as completely as Sodom and
Gomorrah.
Their land will become a place of stinging
nettles,
salt pits, and eternal desolation.
The remnant of my people will plunder them
and take their land."
10 They will receive the wages of their pride,
for they have scoffed at the people of the
LORD of Heaven's Armies.
11 The LORD will terrify them
as he destroys all the gods in the land.
Then nations around the world will worship
the LORD,
each in their own land.

Judgment against Ethiopia and Assyria

12 "You Ethiopians* will also be slaughtered
by my sword," says the LORD.

13 And the LORD will strike the lands of the
north with his fist,
destroying the land of Assyria.
He will make its great capital, Nineveh, a
desolate wasteland,
parched like a desert.
14 The proud city will become a pasture for
flocks and herds,
and all sorts of wild animals will settle
there.
The desert owl and screech owl will roost on
its ruined columns,
their calls echoing through the gaping
windows.
Rubble will block all the doorways,
and the cedar paneling will be exposed to
the weather.
15 This is the boisterous city,
once so secure.
"I am the greatest!" it boasted.
"No other city can compare with me!"
But now, look how it has become an utter ruin,
a haven for wild animals.
Everyone passing by will laugh in derision
and shake a defiant fist.

2:12 Hebrew *Cushites.*

lon, desolation; Ashdod, driven out; and Ekron, uprooted. These four cities are viewed as women, and they suffer abandonment, or desertion; spinsterhood, or desolation; divorce, or being driven out; and barrenness, or being uprooted (see Barrenness and Fertility, 1 Sam 1; Divorce, Ezra 10; Singleness, 1 Cor 7). For a woman of that time, any of these circumstances would diminish her status and jeopardize her ability to live. We may consider ourselves to be immune to such issues, but the pain of separation, loneliness, infertility, or abandonment continues to oppress women. What is unique in this passage is that the Philistine cities, not the Israelite cities, are being compared with women. Usually the prophets use this analogy for Israel.

2:8–11 Against Moab and Ammon. The focus of the LORD's attention widens. The prophet proclaims that the Moabites and the Ammonites will also face God's wrath. **9:** The Moabites and Ammonites are compared with Sodom and Gomorrah, the historically wicked cities that God destroyed. Because of their pride and sin, these nations will meet the same fate. Those who have lost possessions in Judah because of the wickedness of their kindred will have them restored. This allusion previews the theme of restoration to come in chapter 3.

2:12–15 Against Ethiopia and Assyria. Even the Ethiopians will be slain by the sword. Zephaniah recognizes that even his homeland will feel the wrath on the day of the LORD. Assyria, home to many gods that the Israelites worshiped and an especially vicious nation in its war against the Israelites, will have its prized city of canals, Nineveh, destroyed. The *city once so secure* and boastful would be destroyed so utterly that owls, ravens, and other creatures would take over the land.

Jerusalem's Rebellion and Redemption

3 [1]What sorrow awaits rebellious, polluted Jerusalem,
the city of violence and crime!
2 No one can tell it anything;
it refuses all correction.
It does not trust in the LORD
or draw near to its God.
3 Its leaders are like roaring lions
hunting for their victims.
Its judges are like ravenous wolves at evening time,
who by dawn have left no trace of their prey.
4 Its prophets are arrogant liars seeking their own gain.
Its priests defile the Temple by disobeying God's instructions.
5 But the LORD is still there in the city,
and he does no wrong.
Day by day he hands down justice,
and he does not fail.
But the wicked know no shame.
6 "I have wiped out many nations,
devastating their fortress walls and towers.
Their streets are now deserted;
their cities lie in silent ruin.
There are no survivors—
none at all.
7 I thought, 'Surely they will have reverence for me now!
Surely they will listen to my warnings.
Then I won't need to strike again,
destroying their homes.'
But no, they get up early
to continue their evil deeds.
8 Therefore, be patient," says the LORD.
"Soon I will stand and accuse these evil nations.
For I have decided to gather the kingdoms of the earth
and pour out my fiercest anger and fury on them.
All the earth will be devoured
by the fire of my jealousy.
9 "Then I will purify the speech of all people,
so that everyone can worship the LORD together.
10 My scattered people who live beyond the rivers of Ethiopia*
will come to present their offerings.
11 On that day you will no longer need to be ashamed,
for you will no longer be rebels against me.
I will remove all proud and arrogant people from among you.
There will be no more haughtiness on my holy mountain.
12 Those who are left will be the lowly and humble,
for it is they who trust in the name of the LORD.
13 The remnant of Israel will do no wrong;
they will never tell lies or deceive one another.
They will eat and sleep in safety,
and no one will make them afraid."
14 Sing, O daughter of Zion;
shout aloud, O Israel!

3:10 Hebrew *Cush.*

3:1–20 Jerusalem's Rebellion and Redemption

Chapter 3 switches the focus back to Jerusalem. Like other cities, Jerusalem and its inhabitants continue in their rebellion. **3–4:** Accepting no correction and not heeding God, the city's leaders are like roaring lions and evening wolves, beasts that stalk and devour prey. Even the prophets and priests subvert justice and attack those who are unable to defend themselves. Jerusalem's syncretism has taken them away from the truth given to them. Their behavior has become patterned on that of those who worship gods other than the LORD. **5–8:** Unlike Jerusalem's faithless residents, God is righteous and does no wrong. Every morning God's justice shines forth as a beacon to the unjust, but they continue in their practices without shame. God reminds Jerusalem of the destruction suffered by surrounding nations because of rebelliousness toward God. Yet Jerusalem takes no notice. God therefore resolves to bring witness (*stand and accuse*) against the nations and Jerusalem. **9–10:** Even in the midst of this destruction, God still creates. The corrupted speech of the people will be changed into pure speech that calls and serves the LORD. God will even reach far away, past Ethiopia, so that his scattered people in all lands can bring offerings to the LORD. **11–13:** Those who have been prideful and have worshiped other gods will be expelled. Those left will not need to feel shame and will not receive the punishments given to the rebels. The humble can find refuge and protection in the LORD's name. Those who remain after the destruction will be truthful and not lie about worshiping the LORD and then turning to other gods. Like sheep they will be comfortable and safe in their own pasture. **14–15:** Zephaniah calls Jerusalem to sing, shout, and rejoice, because the judgments that

Be glad and rejoice with all your heart,
O daughter of Jerusalem!
15 For the LORD will remove his hand of
judgment
and will disperse the armies of your enemy.
And the LORD himself, the King of Israel,
will live among you!
At last your troubles will be over,
and you will never again fear disaster.
16 On that day the announcement to Jerusalem
will be,
"Cheer up, Zion! Don't be afraid!
17 For the LORD your God is living among you.
He is a mighty savior.
He will take delight in you with gladness.
With his love, he will calm all your fears.*
He will rejoice over you with joyful songs."

18 "I will gather you who mourn for the
appointed festivals;
you will be disgraced no more.*
19 And I will deal severely with all who have
oppressed you.
I will save the weak and helpless ones;
I will bring together
those who were chased away.
I will give glory and fame to my former
exiles,
wherever they have been mocked and
shamed.
20 On that day I will gather you together
and bring you home again.
I will give you a good name, a name of
distinction,
among all the nations of the earth,
as I restore your fortunes before their very
eyes.
I, the LORD, have spoken!"

3:17 Or *He will be silent in his love.* Greek and Syriac versions read *He will renew you with his love.* **3:18** The meaning of the Hebrew for this verse is uncertain.

the LORD had pronounced have been taken away. Those who were enemies of the people of God, who worshiped the idols, have been cast out; God's presence is in the midst of the people. **16:** Zion should not fear nations that have plagued them in the past, nor be afraid of the LORD. **17–20:** Rather, their resolve should be strengthened because God is taking care of them. Their fear should be replaced by courageousness in the hope of the LORD's blessing. **17:** God's presence in Judah and Jerusalem is likened to a victorious warrior, a reminder not to fear the enemies surrounding them. The image of the warrior is also an image of salvation. The LORD has saved them from destruction because of their faithfulness. God rejoices over his righteous people with a renewed love. Where the noise of destruction once reigned, the voice of God singing loudly, as though at a festival or celebration, prevails. **19:** Any remaining oppressors will be dealt with and removed. Those who were oppressed, the lame, and the outcast will be brought back and their shame exchanged for praise and fame throughout the earth. **20:** The final verse brings in those who have been exiled, reuniting them with God's people. All that they have lost will be restored to them, and Israel will be restored to its former greatness in that region of the world. The blessings of God will restore the nation and its people.

HAGGAI

INTRODUCTION

Little is known about the prophet Haggai beyond the fact that he delivered four oracles to encourage the Jewish returnees from Babylon to rebuild the Jerusalem Temple and to restore their defiled relationships with God. We learn from Ezra 6:14 that the prophesying of Haggai and his contemporary Zechariah had prompted this remnant to rebuild the house of the LORD. These Jews had prospered, whereas previously they had suffered the loss of their material blessings (Hag 1:7–11). The restoration occurred during the second regnal year of the Persian emperor Darius I.

The history of the remnant of Jews (about forty-nine thousand) who returned to Palestine from the Babylonian captivity needs little repetition. Introductions to the historical books from 1 Samuel to Ezra and Nehemiah have told the story that forms the prelude to the prophecies of Haggai and Zechariah.

The first settlers to return from Babylon to Palestine were filled with dedication. Even before the foundation of the new Temple had been laid upon the old ruins, an altar was built and worship reinstituted (Ezra 3:1–6). While some rejoiced that praises were again being offered to God on the holy hill, others wept to compare the humble beginning with the grandeurs of the former Temple (Ezra 3:8–13). Before the walls could rise, the work was halted by the Persian king at the instigation of jealous neighboring peoples. Discouragement and despondency ensued.

In order to reestablish their revitalized faith in Jerusalem, priests and Levites had accompanied the returning band, expecting to build a strong community of faith with the Temple at its center. In that prospect the women might have found consolation, but this too had been wrenched from them. Somehow the original mission had been forgotten.

Women who are forced to relocate their families suffer especially in adjusting to a new environment. It is they who maintain the greatest attachment to the old country and to the old ways. They mourn what has been left behind and may experience severe depression as they try to find meaning in a new context. Often men have more opportunity to learn the language and to socialize with the population in the new environment. Women tend to be more isolated, lonely, and homesick. The hostility of the inhabitants was likely to be felt more keenly by the women. Having abandoned the work of rebuilding the Temple, the people had been left by God to their own devices. For sixteen years they had allowed the building materials to rot and rust while they entered, with great expectations, on a course designed to procure economic security and material comforts.

The book of Haggai responds to these feelings of displacement and the people's misplaced priorities by encouraging them to return their focus to God. Four prophecies are given and set in an editorial format. Haggai's message is one that the people of God, past and present, most need to hear and heed. When other concerns precede the priority of doing God's will, human effort amounts to little. The matters that greatly disturbed those sixth-century Jews were financial, but they were to learn that there were rewards greater than they could ever have expected in an obedience of faith (cf. Matt 6:31, 33). —*Richard Clark Kroeger Jr.*

✧

A Call to Rebuild the Temple

1 On August 29* of the second year of King Darius's reign, the LORD gave a message through the prophet Haggai to Zerubbabel son of Shealtiel, governor of Judah, and to Jeshua* son of Jehozadak, the high priest.

2 "This is what the LORD of Heaven's Armies says: The people are saying, 'The time has not yet come to rebuild the house of the LORD.' "

3 Then the LORD sent this message through the prophet Haggai: 4 "Why are you living in luxurious houses while my house lies in ruins? 5 This is what the LORD of Heaven's Armies says: Look at what's happening to you! 6 You have planted much but harvest little. You eat but are not satisfied. You drink but are still thirsty. You put on clothes but cannot keep warm. Your wages disappear as though you were putting them in pockets filled with holes!

7 "This is what the LORD of Heaven's Armies says: Look at what's happening to you! 8 Now go up into the hills, bring down timber, and rebuild my house. Then I will take pleasure in it and be honored, says the LORD. 9 You hoped for rich harvests, but they were poor. And when you brought your harvest home, I blew it away. Why? Because my house lies in ruins, says the LORD of Heaven's Armies, while all of you are busy building your own fine houses. 10 It's because of you that the heavens withhold the dew and the earth produces no crops. 11 I have called for a drought on your fields and hills—a drought to wither the grain and grapes and olive trees and all your other crops, a drought to starve you and your livestock and to ruin everything you have worked so hard to get."

Obedience to God's Call

12 Then Zerubbabel son of Shealtiel, and Jeshua son of Jehozadak, the high priest, and the whole remnant of God's people began to obey the message from the LORD their God. When they heard the words of the prophet Haggai, whom the LORD their God had sent, the people feared the LORD. 13 Then Haggai, the LORD's messenger, gave the people this message from the LORD: "I am with you, says the LORD!"

14 So the LORD sparked the enthusiasm of Zerubbabel son of Shealtiel, governor of Judah, and the enthusiasm of Jeshua son of Jehozadak,

1:1a Hebrew *On the first day of the sixth month,* of the ancient Hebrew lunar calendar. A number of dates in Haggai can be cross-checked with dates in surviving Persian records and related accurately to our modern calendar. This event occurred on August 29, 520 B.C. **1:1b** Hebrew *Joshua,* a variant spelling of Jeshua; also in 1:12, 14.

1:1–15 First Message: Consider How You Have Fared

In August 520 BC Haggai spoke to a forlorn people. **1:** *Zerubbabel,* the grandson of Jehoichin, the king of Judah exiled to Babylon in 597 BC (2 Kgs 24:8–17; 25:27–30), had returned to Judah with other exiles. **2–11:** There was an intention to rebuild the Temple at some point, but personal concerns took precedence. Those citizens of ancient Jerusalem had looked for much, but it had come to little. Their preoccupation with their houses had left the house of God still in ruins. What seemed to be natural calamities were disciplinary acts of God. **5–6:** These verses describe the futility of the people's efforts to establish economic security. **7–11:** God had blown away their resources, a devastating thought to Jews who had ventured back to the land of promise. They had understood themselves to be God's special emissaries sent to rebuild the Temple and to revive its worship. **8:** Rebuilding the Temple will set things right.

1:12–15 Obedience. Led by Zerubbabel and Jeshua, the people *obey the message from the LORD their God.* **12:** Haggai added words of interpretation and application to God's message. His hearers accepted his oracle as truly prophetic. **13:** *I am with you, says the LORD.* This is confirmation of their change of heart and willingness to obey. Immigrant women, far more isolated and lonely than their male counterparts as they settle into a strange environment, are given assurance of the companionship of the heavenly friend. **14:** Beyond mere human emotion, the Spirit of the LORD stirred up the spirits of the leaders and the remnant of the people. Throughout the return from exile, Hebrew women were respected as members of the covenant during times of obedience (cf. Neh 8:2–3) and debased during lapses of faith (Mal 2:11, 14–15).

the high priest, and the enthusiasm of the whole remnant of God's people. They began to work on the house of their God, the LORD of Heaven's Armies, [15]on September 21* of the second year of King Darius's reign.

The New Temple's Diminished Splendor

2 Then on October 17 of that same year,* the LORD sent another message through the prophet Haggai. [2]"Say this to Zerubbabel son of Shealtiel, governor of Judah, and to Jeshua* son of Jehozadak, the high priest, and to the remnant of God's people there in the land: [3]'Does anyone remember this house—this Temple—in its former splendor? How, in comparison, does it look to you now? It must seem like nothing at all! [4]But now the LORD says: Be strong, Zerubbabel. Be strong, Jeshua son of Jehozadak, the high priest. Be strong, all you people still left in the land. And now get to work, for I am with you, says the LORD of Heaven's Armies. [5]My Spirit remains among you, just as I promised when you came out of Egypt. So do not be afraid.'

[6]"For this is what the LORD of Heaven's Armies says: In just a little while I will again shake the heavens and the earth, the oceans and the dry land. [7]I will shake all the nations, and the treasures of all the nations will be brought to this Temple. I will fill this place with glory, says the LORD of Heaven's Armies. [8]The silver is mine, and the gold is mine, says the LORD of Heaven's Armies. [9]The future glory of this Temple will be greater than its past glory, says the LORD of Heaven's Armies. And in this place I will bring peace. I, the LORD of Heaven's Armies, have spoken!"

Blessings Promised for Obedience

[10]On December 18* of the second year of King Darius's reign, the LORD sent this message to the prophet Haggai: [11]"This is what the LORD of Heaven's Armies says. Ask the priests this question about the law: [12]'If one of you is carrying some meat from a holy sacrifice in his robes and his robe happens to brush against some bread or stew, wine or olive oil, or any other kind of food, will it also become holy?' "

The priests replied, "No."

[13]Then Haggai asked, "If someone becomes ceremonially unclean by touching a dead person and then touches any of these foods, will the food be defiled?"

And the priests answered, "Yes."

[14]Then Haggai responded, "That is how it is with this people and this nation, says the LORD.

1:15 Hebrew *on the twenty-fourth day of the sixth month,* of the ancient Hebrew lunar calendar. This event occurred on September 21, 520 B.C.; also see note on 1:1a. **2:1** Hebrew *on the twenty-first day of the seventh month,* of the ancient Hebrew lunar calendar. This event (in the second year of Darius's reign) occurred on October 17, 520 B.C.; also see note on 1:1a. **2:2** Hebrew *Joshua,* a variant spelling of Jeshua; also in 2:4. **2:10** Hebrew *On the twenty-fourth day of the ninth month,* of the ancient Hebrew lunar calendar (similarly in 2:18). This event occurred on December 18, 520 B.C.; also see note on 1:1a.

2:1–9 Second Message: Unexpected Blessing

Again God spoke through Haggai. **2–3:** People of the older generations, who in their youth had seen the glories of Solomon's Temple, were complaining that the structure and appointments of the new Temple are *like nothing* (cf. Ezra 3:12). Here God answers their complaint. Comparisons are odious, but here the comparison could be deadly. In light of the previous failures to further the work and the unfortunate consequences, this negative attitude could be disastrous. Many relocated people groups find meaning and perpetuation of their culture through their collective worship. Women in particular tend to preserve the language, culture, and spiritual values of the lands from which they came, usually within their houses of worship. **4–5:** But again God intervened through Haggai, calling on the whole host of Israelites to *be strong*. Three times God exhorts them and reminds the remnant at Jerusalem that he is with them. God links the promise here with the Mosaic covenant and its history. God first reminds Haggai and through him the people of his attribute as Immanuel ("God is with them"). **6–9:** The grousing of the older generations will suddenly cease in the face of Haggai's next overwhelming word *shake*. If the shaking of the earth at Sinai was God's answer, through Moses, to the complainers of that day, how much more will God's workings invest the second Temple with a greater glory? The earthquake of Sinai was a symbol of God's intentions for great change. One cannot escape the sense that Haggai anticipates glory and prosperity that were never literally realized even in the splendors of the Herodian structure.

2:10–19 Third Message: Holiness as Precursor to God's Blessing

Two months after the second message, Haggai received another word from God: for the priests of Israel to ensure ritual holiness. **14:** *Everything they do* refers to work on the Temple. *Everything they offer*

Everything they do and everything they offer is defiled by their sin. 15 Look at what was happening to you before you began to lay the foundation of the LORD's Temple. 16 When you hoped for a twenty-bushel crop, you harvested only ten. When you expected to draw fifty gallons from the winepress, you found only twenty. 17 I sent blight and mildew and hail to destroy everything you worked so hard to produce. Even so, you refused to return to me, says the LORD.

18 "Think about this eighteenth day of December, the day* when the foundation of the LORD's Temple was laid. Think carefully. 19 I am giving you a promise now while the seed is still in the barn.* You have not yet harvested your grain, and your grapevines, fig trees, pomegranates, and olive trees have not yet produced their crops. But from this day onward I will bless you."

Promises for Zerubbabel

20 On that same day, December 18,* the LORD sent this second message to Haggai: 21 "Tell Zerubbabel, the governor of Judah, that I am about to shake the heavens and the earth. 22 I will overthrow royal thrones and destroy the power of foreign kingdoms. I will overturn their chariots and riders. The horses will fall, and their riders will kill each other.

23 "But when this happens, says the LORD of Heaven's Armies, I will honor you, Zerubbabel son of Shealtiel, my servant. I will make you like a signet ring on my finger, says the LORD, for I have chosen you. I, the LORD of Heaven's Armies, have spoken!"

2:18 Or *On this eighteenth day of December, think about the day.* **2:19** Hebrew *Is the seed yet in the barn?* **2:20** Hebrew *On the twenty-fourth day of the [ninth] month;* see note on 2:10.

---

means Temple sacrifices. **15:** To the beginning of this verse some translations add "Consider what will come to pass from this day on." God is setting up a comparison between the future and the past. **16–17:** Before work on the Temple began, yields were low. **18–19:** Now that the people are rebuilding the Temple, there will be seed in their barns, and their grapevines, fig trees, pomegranates, and olive trees will be abundant producers. The conclusion of the third message is encouragement and *bless*[ing].

2:20–23 Fourth Message: Zerubbabel, a Kind of Messianic Figure

For the displaced and disheartened, there is a yet more glorious promise. God will give a charismatic leader who will bring God's people to a level of blessing and significance. **21:** *Zerubbabel* was of the Davidic line. (See annotation on 1:1.) **23:** The chosen people will be distinctive, for God's glory is as a *signet ring* especially designed for the hand of a ruler. Such a ring was pressed into hot wax by the king and left an impression of the image that had been carved into the ring. A document thus bore the seal and officially conveyed an unmistakable royal order. It was recognized for its authenticity and conveyed the official image to all peoples and nations. Thus, Zerubbabel and these chastened people were to become a sign of the working of God's love and power among the nations.

ZECHARIAH

INTRODUCTION

The Hebrew name Zechariah comprises two important words: "the LORD remembers" ("the LORD" is a single word in Hebrew). In essence, that is the theme of this book. The largest of the minor prophetic books, Zechariah is a great attestation that God cares about his people. The book continues to be an encouraging message to believers in every age.

The first verse of the book of Zechariah introduces the author as Zechariah, the son of Berechiah, the son of Iddo. Iddo was among the priestly families who returned from exile.

Most scholars agree that Zechariah wrote the first eight chapters, but there is considerable disagreement about chapters 9—14. The argument is that these later chapters contain a different vocabulary, style, and content. The historical setting of each section also appears to be different. For example, the Temple that is expected and encouraged in chapters 1—8 is a reality in chapters 9—14. Also, the Greeks are more evident on the world scene in chapters 9—14, as opposed to Persian dominance in chapters 1—8. In light of the most recent consensus—that the second part of Zechariah was written in the early fifth century BC—it is possible that the author wrote it late in his life. If he was a young man at the beginning of his ministry, this would account for the differences in style, vocabulary, and historical setting between the two sections of the book.

The evidence for authorship is not conclusive but whether it is of single or multiple authorship, the full book of Zechariah has been recognized as authentic prophecy from very early times by Jews and Christians alike. The text found in the Dead Sea Scrolls contains no seams, indicating multiple authorship. More than 30 percent of the Old Testament quotations in the passion narratives of the Gospels are from Zechariah 9—14 (cf. Zech 11:13 and Matt 27:9; Zech 13:7 and Mark 14:27; Zech 12:10 and John 19:37).

A unity of theology and purpose binds the book together. Both sections contain the following themes: the certainty of judgment (2:1–2; 14:6); the continuing divine covenant (8:8; 13:9); a glorious future under a messianic figure (3:8; 4:6; 9:6–7); concern for the renewal of Zion (2:5; 9:8; 14:11); the ultimate conversion of the nations (2:11; 8:22; 14:6); concern for leadership (4:9; 11:5); ingathering of exiles (8:7; 10:9–10); outpouring of the Spirit (4:6; 5:4; 12:10; 13:3); and, finally, expectation of peace and prosperity (8:6; 14:6–8). Both sections reveal the underlying tradition of the Mosaic law.

The prophecy of Zechariah concerns Judah under the Persian Empire. The first emperor of this regime, Cyrus, had allowed foreign captives, including the Jews of Babylon, to return to their homelands. He granted them a large measure of autonomy and allowed them freedom of religion. Approximately fifty thousand Jews returned from Babylon to Judah under the leadership of Sheshbazzar and Zerubbabel in 538 BC. The trip was assisted by the Persians, and the Temple vessels were restored (Ezra 1:3–11).

Although initially the returning exiles had been eager to work on the Temple, they had become discouraged by the hardships they faced from hostile neighbors and economic depression. The Samaritans even accused the Jews of planning a rebellion against the Persian government. Unsurprisingly, the Persians halted all attempts to rebuild the Temple. The return to the Jewish homeland had become a bitter disappointment.

In 520 BC, Haggai and Zechariah began to prophesy and encourage the people to rebuild the Temple. Haggai insisted that the Jews had used economic depression as an excuse for not finishing the work on the Temple. Zechariah promised that God's Spirit would assist them in the building effort (Zech 4:6). The Jews responded without delay, and in four years the Temple was completed (Ezra 6:14–17).

Zechariah reveals more about the Jewish community in Judah at the end of the sixth century BC. The eight night visions of Zechariah in the first eight chapters address particular concerns among the people. These range from issues of community security (chap. 2) to guilt feelings (chap. 3). Each vision promises divine assistance to meet the physical and spiritual needs of the people.

The oracles found in chapters 9—14 are of a different character from those in chapters 1—8 and probably reflect later circumstances. It appears that discouragement again plagued the Jewish community, this time in the early fifth century BC after the demise of Zerubbabel and Joshua. The apocalyptic oracles speak to a people disillusioned with their present situation and promises hope for the more distant future. —*Hannah Karajian Harrington*

1:1—8:23	Encouraging the Jewish Community
1:1–6	Introduction
1:7—6:15	Eight Night Visions
7:1–14	A Call to Justice and Mercy
8:1–23	Promised Blessings
9:1—14:21	Eschatological Oracles
9:1–17	The Messianic King
10:1—11:3	Restoration
11:4–17	The Good and Evil Shepherds
12:1—14:21	God's Final War

✧

A Call to Return to the LORD

1 In November* of the second year of King
Darius's reign, the LORD gave this message
to the prophet Zechariah son of Berekiah
and grandson of Iddo:
2 "I, the LORD, was very angry with your ancestors. 3 Therefore, say to the people, 'This is
what the LORD of Heaven's Armies says: Return
to me, and I will return to you, says the LORD of
Heaven's Armies.' 4 Don't be like your ancestors
who would not listen or pay attention when the
earlier prophets said to them, 'This is what the
LORD of Heaven's Armies says: Turn from your
evil ways, and stop all your evil practices.'
5 "Where are your ancestors now? They and
the prophets are long dead. 6 But everything I
said through my servants the prophets happened to your ancestors, just as I said. As a result, they repented and said, 'We have received
what we deserved from the LORD of Heaven's
Armies. He has done what he said he would
do.' "

1:1 Hebrew *In the eighth month.* A number of dates in Zechariah can be cross-checked with dates in surviving Persian records and related accurately to our modern calendar. This month of the ancient Hebrew lunar calendar occurred within the months of October and November 520 B.C.

1:1—8:23 Encouraging the Jewish Community

1:1–6 Introduction. God's love for his people, a central theme in Zechariah, is apparent in the introductory verses. **3:** God pleads with Israel and promises to meet his people halfway, as it were. He is more than willing to mend their broken relationship. The tone of the book is not accusatory but encouraging.

A Man among the Myrtle Trees

7 Three months later, on February 15,* the LORD
sent another message to the prophet Zechariah
son of Berekiah and grandson of Iddo.
8 In a vision during the night, I saw a man
sitting on a red horse that was standing among
some myrtle trees in a small valley. Behind him
were riders on red, brown, and white horses. 9 I
asked the angel who was talking with me, "My
lord, what do these horses mean?"
"I will show you," the angel replied.
10 The rider standing among the myrtle trees
then explained, "They are the ones the LORD has
sent out to patrol the earth."
11 Then the other riders reported to the angel
of the LORD, who was standing among the myrtle trees, "We have been patrolling the earth, and
the whole earth is at peace."
12 Upon hearing this, the angel of the LORD
prayed this prayer: "O LORD of Heaven's Armies,
for seventy years now you have been angry with
Jerusalem and the towns of Judah. How long until you again show mercy to them?" 13 And the
LORD spoke kind and comforting words to the
angel who talked with me.
14 Then the angel said to me, "Shout this message for all to hear: 'This is what the LORD of
Heaven's Armies says: My love for Jerusalem
and Mount Zion is passionate and strong. 15 But
I am very angry with the other nations that are
now enjoying peace and security. I was only a
little angry with my people, but the nations inflicted harm on them far beyond my intentions.
16 " 'Therefore, this is what the LORD says: I
have returned to show mercy to Jerusalem. My
Temple will be rebuilt, says the LORD of Heav-
en's Armies, and measurements will be taken for
the reconstruction of Jerusalem.*'
17 "Say this also: 'This is what the LORD of
Heaven's Armies says: The towns of Israel will
again overflow with prosperity, and the LORD
will again comfort Zion and choose Jerusalem as
his own.' "

Four Horns and Four Blacksmiths

18 *Then I looked up and saw four animal horns.
19 "What are these?" I asked the angel who was
talking with me.
He replied, "These horns represent the nations that scattered Judah, Israel, and Jerusalem."
20 Then the LORD showed me four blacksmiths.
21 "What are these men coming to do?" I asked.
The angel replied, "These four horns—these
nations—scattered and humbled Judah. Now
these blacksmiths have come to terrify those nations and throw them down and destroy them."

Future Prosperity of Jerusalem

2
1 *When I looked again, I saw a man with
a measuring line in his hand. 2 "Where are
you going?" I asked.
He replied, "I am going to measure Jerusalem, to see how wide and how long it is."
3 Then the angel who was with me went to
meet a second angel who was coming toward
him. 4 The other angel said, "Hurry, and say to
that young man, 'Jerusalem will someday be
so full of people and livestock that there won't
be room enough for everyone! Many will live
outside the city walls. 5 Then I, myself, will be a

1:7 Hebrew *On the twenty-fourth day of the eleventh month, the month of Shebat, in the second year of Darius.* This event occurred on February 15, 519 B.C.; also see note on 1:1. **1:16** Hebrew *and the measuring line will be stretched out over Jerusalem.* **1:18** Verses 1:18-21 are numbered 2:1-4 in Hebrew text. **2:1** Verses 2:1-13 are numbered 2:5-17 in Hebrew text.

1:7—6:15 Eight Night Visions. 1:7–17: In the first vision, that of the horses of the divine patrol, God is presented as a sort of universal watchman with a particular interest in Jerusalem. **12–15:** Zechariah's language personifies Jerusalem as a woman. Words such as *comforting* and *passionate* reveal the depth of personal emotion God feels. Other prophets describe God's intense feeling for Israel as a marriage relationship in which the husband, God, will not give up his wife, Israel, despite her unfaithfulness to him (Jer 3:1–14, 20–22; Ezek 16:8–14, 38, 60–63; Hos 11:8–9). **15:** God is angry that the nations he has used as a chastising agent against his people have punished them more than they had deserved. **16–17:** He promises to show compassion to the city in the future and enrich it.

1:18–21 The Second Vision. Horns are often used as symbols for kings or gods. **20:** *Blacksmiths* is probably too specific for the Hebrew word used. "Expert workers" might be a better translation. **21:** The blacksmiths will frighten Israel's enemies into submission.

2:1–13 The Third Vision. This speaks to the Jews' anxiety because of lack of protection from their enemies. The size of Judah in the early Persian period has been compared with that of Rhode Island, and some estimates of its population are well under ten thousand. Evidently the large group of Jewish exiles of the first return had dwindled considerably. In such a small, threatened community, many Jews no doubt questioned the wisdom of the Temple-building project. **5:** God encourages the Jews by promising to be

protective wall of fire around Jerusalem, says the
LORD. And I will be the glory inside the city!' "

The Exiles Are Called Home

6 The LORD says, "Come away! Flee from Babylon in the land of the north, for I have scattered
you to the four winds. 7 Come away, people of
Zion, you who are exiled in Babylon!"
8 After a period of glory, the LORD of Heaven's
Armies sent me* against the nations who plundered you. For he said, "Anyone who harms you
harms my most precious possession.* 9 I will
raise my fist to crush them, and their own slaves
will plunder them." Then you will know that the
LORD of Heaven's Armies has sent me.
10 The LORD says, "Shout and rejoice, O beautiful Jerusalem,* for I am coming to live among
you. 11 Many nations will join themselves to
the LORD on that day, and they, too, will be my
people. I will live among you, and you will know
that the LORD of Heaven's Armies sent me to
you. 12 The land of Judah will be the LORD's special possession in the holy land, and he will once
again choose Jerusalem to be his own city. 13 Be
silent before the LORD, all humanity, for he is
springing into action from his holy dwelling."

Cleansing for the High Priest

3 Then the angel showed me Jeshua* the
high priest standing before the angel of
the LORD. The Accuser, Satan,* was there
at the angel's right hand, making accusations
against Jeshua. 2 And the LORD said to Satan, "I,
the LORD, reject your accusations, Satan. Yes, the
LORD, who has chosen Jerusalem, rebukes you.
This man is like a burning stick that has been
snatched from the fire."
3 Jeshua's clothing was filthy as he stood there
before the angel. 4 So the angel said to the others standing there, "Take off his filthy clothes."
And turning to Jeshua he said, "See, I have taken
away your sins, and now I am giving you these
fine new clothes."
5 Then I said, "They should also place a clean
turban on his head." So they put a clean priestly turban on his head and dressed him in new
clothes while the angel of the LORD stood by.
6 Then the angel of the LORD spoke very solemnly to Jeshua and said, 7 "This is what the
LORD of Heaven's Armies says: If you follow my
ways and carefully serve me, then you will be
given authority over my Temple and its courtyards. I will let you walk among these others
standing here.
8 "Listen to me, O Jeshua the high priest, and
all you other priests. You are symbols of things
to come. Soon I am going to bring my servant,

2:8a The meaning of the Hebrew is uncertain. **2:8b** Hebrew *Anyone who touches you touches the pupil of his eye.* **2:10** Hebrew *O daughter of Zion.* **3:1a** Hebrew *Joshua,* a variant spelling of Jeshua; also in 3:3, 4, 6, 8, 9. **3:1b** Hebrew *The satan;* similarly in 3:2.

a *wall of fire* around Jerusalem and *glory* within it. Again Zechariah portrays God as jealously protective of his people. He is like fire, powerful and dangerous, ready to blaze hotly against any enemy of his people. God's glory (Heb., *kabod*) is the almost tangible evidence of the divine presence. To experience God's glory is to sense his presence. Ezekiel states that God's glory abandoned Jerusalem just before the city's destruction (Ezek 10:18–19; 11:22–24) but would return in the future (Ezek 32:3; 33:3; 43:2–5). Zechariah claims that divine glory will permeate Jerusalem and extend throughout the land of Israel (14:20–21). **8:** Israel is God's precious possession, in Hebrew the "apple of [God's] eye"(see translator's note). Whoever harms Israel harms, as it were, the very pupil of God's eye. This radical imagery emphasizes the preciousness of God's people to him. It is as if God cannot see the world without first seeing his people and their concerns. They are always in front of him. **10:** *O beautiful Jerusalem* translates literally as "daughter of Zion." In the ancient world daughters were dependent on their parents for financial support and for daily decision-making. They had the least independence of anyone in society. This is just what God wants of his people: their complete dependence on him. **11–13:** Laments will be turned into joy, for God is coming to dwell among his people. He will again choose Jerusalem as the site of his house.

3:1–10 The Fourth Vision. In Zechariah's fourth vision, Judah's problem is the torment of guilt. **1–3:** Jeshua the high priest officiates in the Temple in filthy robes, and Satan, like a prosecuting attorney, accuses him before God. However, God rebukes Satan and declares Jeshua to be innocent. The divine declaration of innocence is more than sufficient to nullify Satan's accusation. **3–5:** Jeshua's filthy clothing represents a deeper problem than physical uncleanness. Clothing is often a symbol for a person's moral condition (see Purity Laws Related to Women, Lev 15). In this case the filthiness of Jeshua's clothes represents his impurity and that of the people. First, there is the ritual impurity of a priest born and reared in a foreign land and thus unfit to serve in the Temple as the people's representative before God. Second, the people had been guilty of various sins. Replacing Jeshua's filthy clothes with clean garments symbolizes the change in his status before God and, by extension, the status

the Branch. [9]Now look at the jewel I have set before Jeshua, a single stone with seven facets.* I will engrave an inscription on it, says the LORD of Heaven's Armies, and I will remove the sins of this land in a single day.

[10]"And on that day, says the LORD of Heaven's Armies, each of you will invite your neighbor to sit with you peacefully under your own grapevine and fig tree."

A Lampstand and Two Olive Trees

4 Then the angel who had been talking with me returned and woke me, as though I had been asleep. [2]"What do you see now?" he asked.

I answered, "I see a solid gold lampstand with a bowl of oil on top of it. Around the bowl are seven lamps, each having seven spouts with wicks. [3]And I see two olive trees, one on each side of the bowl." [4]Then I asked the angel, "What are these, my lord? What do they mean?"

[5]"Don't you know?" the angel asked.

"No, my lord," I replied.

[6]Then he said to me, "This is what the LORD says to Zerubbabel: It is not by force nor by strength, but by my Spirit, says the LORD of Heaven's Armies. [7]Nothing, not even a mighty mountain, will stand in Zerubbabel's way; it will become a level plain before him! And when Zerubbabel sets the final stone of the Temple in place, the people will shout: 'May God bless it! May God bless it!'* "

[8]Then another message came to me from the LORD: [9]"Zerubbabel is the one who laid the foundation of this Temple, and he will complete it. Then you will know that the LORD of Heaven's Armies has sent me. [10]Do not despise these small beginnings, for the LORD rejoices to see the work begin, to see the plumb line in Zerubbabel's hand."

(The seven lamps* represent the eyes of the LORD that search all around the world.)

[11]Then I asked the angel, "What are these two olive trees on each side of the lampstand, [12]and what are the two olive branches that pour out golden oil through two gold tubes?"

[13]"Don't you know?" he asked.

"No, my lord," I replied.

[14]Then he said to me, "They represent the two heavenly beings who stand in the court of the Lord of all the earth."

A Flying Scroll

5 I looked up again and saw a scroll flying through the air.

[2]"What do you see?" the angel asked.

"I see a flying scroll," I replied. "It appears to be about 30 feet long and 15 feet wide.*"

[3]Then he said to me, "This scroll contains the curse that is going out over the entire land. One side of the scroll says that those who steal will be banished from the land; the other side says that those who swear falsely will be banished from the land. [4]And this is what the LORD of Heaven's Armies says: I am sending this curse into the house of every thief and into the house of everyone who swears falsely using my name. And my curse will remain in that house and completely destroy it—even its timbers and stones."

A Woman in a Basket

[5]Then the angel who was talking with me came forward and said, "Look up and see what's coming."

[6]"What is it?" I asked.

3:9 Hebrew *seven eyes.* **4:7** Hebrew *'Grace, grace to it.'* **4:10** Or *The seven facets* (see 3:9); Hebrew reads *These seven.* **5:2** Hebrew *20 cubits* [9 meters] *long and 10 cubits* [4.5 meters] *wide.*

---

of all of the returned exiles. **8–10:** Even though Israel has sinned, God has not totally rejected the people and never intended to do so (1:17; 2:12). Jeshua's purification is a symbol for that of the nation.

4:1–14 The Fifth Vision. In Zechariah's fifth vision, God promises strength to overcome opposition and rebuild the Temple. Through this vision God encouraged the people, represented by the lampstand, that the seeming mountain of opposition they faced would not be leveled by force but by his Spirit, represented by the oil and the light. **6–10:** The emphasis in this vision is on the oil representing God's Spirit as the agent of success (cf. Matt 25:1–12; 1 Jn 2:20, 27; Rev 4:5). **11–14:** When an individual was anointed, God conferred upon him the Holy Spirit, guaranteeing him support (1 Sam 16:13–14; 18:12), strength (Ps 89:21–25), and wisdom (Isa 11:1–4). The idea was that people became God's representatives empowered by his Spirit. The Spirit was poured on God's servants, even as the anointing oil was poured on the candidate for service (cf. Acts 2:17–18). In this vision the two leaders, symbolized by olive branches, are channels of God's Spirit to the community.

5:1–4 The Sixth Vision. The huge *flying scroll* condemns thieves and those who *swear falsely,* i.e., break their oaths. In this context this is may refer to those who steal from God by not keeping their promises to give money for the Temple restoration.

5:5–11 The Seventh Vision. In Zechariah's seventh

He replied, "It is a basket for measuring
grain,* and it's filled with the sins* of everyone
throughout the land."
7 Then the heavy lead cover was lifted off the
basket, and there was a woman sitting inside it.
8 The angel said, "The woman's name is Wickedness," and he pushed her back into the basket and
closed the heavy lid again.
9 Then I looked up and saw two women flying
toward us, gliding on the wind. They had wings
like a stork, and they picked up the basket and
flew into the sky.
10 "Where are they taking the basket?" I asked
the angel.
11 He replied, "To the land of Babylonia,*
where they will build a temple for the basket.
And when the temple is ready, they will set the
basket there on its pedestal."

Four Chariots

6 Then I looked up again and saw four chariots coming from between two bronze
mountains. 2 The first chariot was pulled
by red horses, the second by black horses, 3 the
third by white horses, and the fourth by powerful dappled-gray horses. 4 "And what are these,
my lord?" I asked the angel who was talking
with me.
5 The angel replied, "These are the four spirits* of heaven who stand before the Lord of all
the earth. They are going out to do his work.
6 The chariot with black horses is going north,
the chariot with white horses is going west,* and
the chariot with dappled-gray horses is going
south."
7 The powerful horses were eager to set out
to patrol the earth. And the LORD said, "Go and
patrol the earth!" So they left at once on their
patrol.
8 Then the LORD summoned me and said,
"Look, those who went north have vented the
anger of my Spirit* there in the land of the
north."

The Crowning of Jeshua

9 Then I received another message from the LORD:
10 "Heldai, Tobijah, and Jedaiah will bring gifts of
silver and gold from the Jews exiled in Babylon.
As soon as they arrive, meet them at the home of
Josiah son of Zephaniah. 11 Accept their gifts, and
make a crown* from the silver and gold. Then
put the crown on the head of Jeshua* son of Jehozadak, the high priest. 12 Tell him, 'This is what
the LORD of Heaven's Armies says: Here is the
man called the Branch. He will branch out from

5:6a Hebrew *an ephah* [20 quarts or 22 liters]; also in 5:7, 8, 9, 10, 11. **5:6b** As in Greek version; Hebrew reads *the appearance*. **5:11** Hebrew *the land of Shinar*. **6:5** Or *the four winds*. **6:6** Hebrew *is going after them*. **6:8** Hebrew *have given my Spirit rest*. **6:11a** As in Greek and Syriac versions; Hebrew reads *crowns*. **6:11b** Hebrew *Joshua*, a variant spelling of Jeshua.

vision he envisions a woman confined in a basket with a lid of lead. **7–8:** The interpreting angel explains that the woman represents *wickedness*. She may have looked like a fertility goddess or a genie in a jar. Like evil, she was hidden from sight but was a dangerous force difficult to contain. Several possibilities exist for this analogy: The impurity of menstruation is a common metaphor used by the prophets for sin; sin, especially idolatry, is sometimes described as prostitution, an evil often involving women (Hos 2:2; Jer 23:10; Ezek 16:15); or the woman in the basket might represent the foreign women with whom many Jews had wrongfully intermarried. Probably the answer to the female gender of wickedness in this vision is grammatical. The Hebrew word for wickedness is feminine and so must be represented by feminine pronouns, adjectives, and verbs. In any case, inherent female association with evil cannot be claimed on the basis of grammar, especially since the opposite of evil, righteousness *(tsedakah)*, is another feminine noun. **9:** Note that women are also the agents of sin's removal. **11:** The removal of the basket symbolizes the elimination of wickedness from Judean society. If the woman in the basket symbolizes a pagan goddess as the archrepresentative of evil, the symbolism of the shrine that is prepared for her in Babylon becomes clear. The transfer of the evil goddess, who represents the evil that had controlled Judah, to a shrine in Babylon is necessary for the countermovement of God to his Temple in Jerusalem. In order for Yahweh to move into his house, other gods had to move out.

6:1–15 The Eighth Vision. The final vision again pictures the LORD's horsemen riding out to do his work. **8:** The chariot patrol that goes north establishes the security of Judah on the international scene. It was from the north that Judah's enemies attacked (Jer 6:22), and it was from the north that Judah's exiles returned. **9–11:** The spiritual beings are paralleled on earth by those bringing gifts from the exiles in Babylon and by Jeshua who will be the one who ensures that the Temple is rebuilt. **11–13:** Zechariah sees Jeshua as combining the roles of king and priest, but this never actually happened. It may be that a speech directed at Zerubbabel, Judah's political leader, has been redirected to its religious leader.

where he is and build the Temple of the LORD. 13 Yes, he will build the Temple of the LORD. Then he will receive royal honor and will rule as king from his throne. He will also serve as priest from his throne,* and there will be perfect harmony between his two roles.'

14 "The crown will be a memorial in the Temple of the LORD to honor those who gave it—Heldai,* Tobijah, Jedaiah, and Josiah* son of Zephaniah."

15 People will come from distant lands to rebuild the Temple of the LORD. And when this happens, you will know that my messages have been from the LORD of Heaven's Armies. All this will happen if you carefully obey what the LORD your God says.

A Call to Justice and Mercy

7 On December 7* of the fourth year of King Darius's reign, another message came to Zechariah from the LORD. 2 The people of Bethel had sent Sharezer and Regemmelech,* along with their attendants, to seek the LORD's favor. 3 They were to ask this question of the prophets and the priests at the Temple of the LORD of Heaven's Armies: "Should we continue to mourn and fast each summer on the anniversary of the Temple's destruction,* as we have done for so many years?"

4 The LORD of Heaven's Armies sent me this message in reply: 5 "Say to all your people and your priests, 'During these seventy years of exile, when you fasted and mourned in the summer and in early autumn,* was it really for me that you were fasting? 6 And even now in your holy festivals, aren't you eating and drinking just to please yourselves? 7 Isn't this the same message the LORD proclaimed through the prophets in years past when Jerusalem and the towns of Judah were bustling with people, and the Negev and the foothills of Judah* were well populated?' "

8 Then this message came to Zechariah from the LORD: 9 "This is what the LORD of Heaven's Armies says: Judge fairly, and show mercy and kindness to one another. 10 Do not oppress widows, orphans, foreigners, and the poor. And do not scheme against each other.

11 "Your ancestors refused to listen to this message. They stubbornly turned away and put their fingers in their ears to keep from hearing. 12 They made their hearts as hard as stone, so they could not hear the instructions or the messages that the LORD of Heaven's Armies had sent them by his Spirit through the earlier prophets. That is why the LORD of Heaven's Armies was so angry with them.

13 "Since they refused to listen when I called to them, I would not listen when they called to me, says the LORD of Heaven's Armies. 14 As with a whirlwind, I scattered them among the distant nations, where they lived as strangers. Their land became so desolate that no one even traveled through it. They turned their pleasant land into a desert."

Promised Blessings for Jerusalem

8 Then another message came to me from the LORD of Heaven's Armies: 2 "This is what the LORD of Heaven's Armies says:

6:13 Or *There will be a priest by his throne.* **6:14a** As in Syriac version (compare 6:10); Hebrew reads *Helem.* **6:14b** As in Syriac version (compare 6:10); Hebrew reads *Hen.* **7:1** Hebrew *On the fourth day of the ninth month, the month of Kislev,* of the ancient Hebrew lunar calendar. This event occurred on December 7, 518 B.C.; also see note on 1:1. **7:2** Or *Bethel-sharezer had sent Regemmelech.* **7:3** Hebrew *mourn and fast in the fifth month.* The Temple had been destroyed in the fifth month of the ancient Hebrew lunar calendar (August 586 B.C.); see 2 Kgs 25:8. **7:5** Hebrew *fasted and mourned in the fifth and seventh months.* The fifth month of the ancient Hebrew lunar calendar usually occurs within the months of July and August. The seventh month usually occurs within the months of September and October; both the Day of Atonement and the Festival of Shelters were celebrated in the seventh month. **7:7** Hebrew *the Shephelah.*

7:1–14 A Call to Justice and Mercy. After the night visions, Zechariah's focus shifts to the matter of Israel's obligation to the covenant with God, that is, obedience to God's laws of justice and mercy. **8–10:** Through Zechariah God reminds the Jews, positively, to render true judgment and show kindness and, negatively, not to oppress other human beings or devise evil against them in any way. **9:** *Mercy and kindness* follow justice here, as they do in other passages (Deut 10:18; Mic 6:8). Indeed, there can be no kindness without justice. The word for mercy comes from the same root as the word for "womb." It signifies compassion, the epitome of which is seen in a mother toward her child. The Hebrew word for kindness means an attitude of love and also refers to loyalty and faithfulness. "Faithful love" may be a good translation of the term. **10:** The term for widow (Heb., *almanah*) refers particularly to a widow who has no means of financial support. **11–14:** The way in which one Israelite treats another directly affects the larger covenant relationship between God and Israel.

8:1–23 Promised Blessings. Chapters 1—8 conclude with God's promise that he will return to Jerusalem and cause it to flourish as never before. **4–5:** The elderly are living in peace and relaxation, and children

My love for Mount Zion is passionate and strong; I am consumed with passion for Jerusalem!

3 "And now the LORD says: I am returning to Mount Zion, and I will live in Jerusalem. Then Jerusalem will be called the Faithful City; the mountain of the LORD of Heaven's Armies will be called the Holy Mountain.

4 "This is what the LORD of Heaven's Armies says: Once again old men and women will walk Jerusalem's streets with their canes and will sit together in the city squares. 5 And the streets of the city will be filled with boys and girls at play.

6 "This is what the LORD of Heaven's Armies says: All this may seem impossible to you now, a small remnant of God's people. But is it impossible for me? says the LORD of Heaven's Armies.

7 "This is what the LORD of Heaven's Armies says: You can be sure that I will rescue my people from the east and from the west. 8 I will bring them home again to live safely in Jerusalem. They will be my people, and I will be faithful and just toward them as their God.

9 "This is what the LORD of Heaven's Armies says: Be strong and finish the task! Ever since the laying of the foundation of the Temple of the LORD of Heaven's Armies, you have heard what the prophets have been saying about completing the building. 10 Before the work on the Temple began, there were no jobs and no money to hire people or animals. No traveler was safe from the enemy, for there were enemies on all sides. I had turned everyone against each other.

11 "But now I will not treat the remnant of my people as I treated them before, says the LORD of Heaven's Armies. 12 For I am planting seeds of peace and prosperity among you. The grapevines will be heavy with fruit. The earth will produce its crops, and the heavens will release the dew. Once more I will cause the remnant in Judah and Israel to inherit these blessings. 13 Among the other nations, Judah and Israel became symbols of a cursed nation. But no longer! Now I will rescue you and make you both a symbol and a source of blessing. So don't be afraid. Be strong, and get on with rebuilding the Temple!

14 "For this is what the LORD of Heaven's Armies says: I was determined to punish you when your ancestors angered me, and I did not change my mind, says the LORD of Heaven's Armies. 15 But now I am determined to bless Jerusalem and the people of Judah. So don't be afraid. 16 But this is what you must do: Tell the truth to each other. Render verdicts in your courts that are just and that lead to peace. 17 Don't scheme against each other. Stop your love of telling lies that you swear are the truth. I hate all these things, says the LORD."

18 Here is another message that came to me from the LORD of Heaven's Armies. 19 "This is what the LORD of Heaven's Armies says: The traditional fasts and times of mourning you have kept in early summer, midsummer, autumn, and winter* are now ended. They will become festivals of joy and celebration for the people of Judah. So love truth and peace.

20 "This is what the LORD of Heaven's Armies says: People from nations and cities around the world will travel to Jerusalem. 21 The people of one city will say to the people of another, 'Come with us to Jerusalem to ask the LORD to bless us. Let's worship the LORD of Heaven's Armies. I'm determined to go.' 22 Many peoples and powerful nations will come to Jerusalem to seek the LORD of Heaven's Armies and to ask for his blessing.

23 "This is what the LORD of Heaven's Armies says: In those days ten men from different nations and languages of the world will clutch at

8:19 Hebrew *in the fourth, fifth, seventh, and tenth months.* The fourth month of the ancient Hebrew lunar calendar usually occurs within the months of June and July. The fifth month usually occurs within the months of July and August. The seventh month usually occurs within the months of September and October. The tenth month usually occurs within the months of December and January.

are not forced into labor but are allowed to play. **6:** In Zechariah's day, Jerusalem was not the happy place pictured here. Nevertheless, God rebukes in advance any lack of faith in Zechariah's audience regarding the divine promises. He challenges them that they are measuring difficulty on their scales rather than on his. The language reminds the reader of God's challenge to Sarah, who did not believe that she could bear a child at her advanced age: "Is anything too hard for the LORD?" (Gen 18:14; see also Jer 32:26). **7–8:** Not only will the citizens prosper but also God promises to bring the people of Judah back to Jerusalem from all over the world. **9–13:** The Jews were to be encouraged that although they were not enjoying these blessings at present, they were to be the sole link to Israel's glorious future. **20–23:** God promised to build up his future kingdom, which would attract even the Gentiles, upon their faithfulness.

9:1—14:21 Eschatological Oracles

Chapters 9—14 focus on the future of Israel. Unlike the first part of the book, the second part makes no direct reference to present circumstances. It consists of two eschatological oracles, chapters 9—11 and chapters 12—14.

the sleeve of one Jew. And they will say, 'Please let us walk with you, for we have heard that God is with you.' "

Judgment against Israel's Enemies

9 This is the message* from the LORD against the land of Aram* and the city of Damascus, for the eyes of humanity, including all the tribes of Israel, are on the LORD.

[2] Doom is certain for Hamath,
near Damascus,
and for the cities of Tyre and Sidon,
though they are so clever.
[3] Tyre has built a strong fortress
and has made silver and gold
as plentiful as dust in the streets!
[4] But now the Lord will strip away Tyre's
possessions
and hurl its fortifications into the sea,
and it will be burned to the ground.
[5] The city of Ashkelon will see Tyre fall
and will be filled with fear.
Gaza will shake with terror,
as will Ekron, for their hopes will be
dashed.
Gaza's king will be killed,
and Ashkelon will be deserted.
[6] Foreigners will occupy the city of Ashdod.
I will destroy the pride of the Philistines.
[7] I will grab the bloody meat from their
mouths
and snatch the detestable sacrifices from
their teeth.
Then the surviving Philistines will worship
our God
and become like a clan in Judah.*
The Philistines of Ekron will join my
people,
as the ancient Jebusites once did.
[8] I will guard my Temple
and protect it from invading armies.
I am watching closely to ensure
that no more foreign oppressors overrun
my people's land.

Zion's Coming King

[9] Rejoice, O people of Zion!*
Shout in triumph, O people of Jerusalem!
Look, your king is coming to you.
He is righteous and victorious,*
yet he is humble, riding on a donkey—
riding on a donkey's colt.
[10] I will remove the battle chariots from Israel*
and the warhorses from Jerusalem.
I will destroy all the weapons used in battle,
and your king will bring peace to the
nations.
His realm will stretch from sea to sea
and from the Euphrates River* to the ends
of the earth.*
[11] Because of the covenant I made with you,
sealed with blood,
I will free your prisoners
from death in a waterless dungeon.
[12] Come back to the place of safety,
all you prisoners who still have hope!
I promise this very day
that I will repay two blessings for each of
your troubles.
[13] Judah is my bow,
and Israel is my arrow.
Jerusalem* is my sword,
and like a warrior, I will brandish it against
the Greeks.*

[14] The LORD will appear above his people;
his arrows will fly like lightning!
The Sovereign LORD will sound the ram's
horn
and attack like a whirlwind from the
southern desert.
[15] The LORD of Heaven's Armies will protect his
people,

9:1a Hebrew *An Oracle: The message.* **9:1b** Hebrew *land of Hadrach.* **9:7** Hebrew *and will become a leader in Judah.* **9:9a** Hebrew *O daughter of Zion!* **9:9b** Hebrew *and is being vindicated.* **9:10a** Hebrew *Ephraim,* referring to the northern kingdom of Israel; also in 9:13. **9:10b** Hebrew *the river.* **9:10c** Or *the end of the land.* **9:13a** Hebrew *Zion.* **9:13b** Hebrew *the sons of Javan.*

9:1–17 The Messianic King. 1–8: God marches from north to south, defeating Judah's traditional enemies and taking up residence in Jerusalem. **9:** The *people of Zion,* literally "daughter of Zion," are told to rejoice and shout because a wonderful king is coming to greet them. When God intervenes during times of desperation, his people break forth in shouts of joy. **9–10:** The great king described here is like no other in history. He is triumphant but righteous; victorious but humble and gentle. Instead of riding a military horse, he rides on a lowly donkey. He brings world peace by destroying weapons of war. His reign will not be simply over Judah but will extend worldwide (cf. Ps 2:9; Isa 11:4; Zech 14:17; Rev 19:15). New Testament writers identify the coming king as Jesus (Matt 21:5; John 12:15). The triumphal entry of Jesus riding into Jerusalem on a donkey in the first century AD was hailed by crowds of Jews who expected in

and they will defeat their enemies by
hurling great stones.
They will shout in battle as though drunk
with wine.
They will be filled with blood like a bowl,
drenched with blood like the corners of the
altar.
16 On that day the LORD their God will rescue
his people,
just as a shepherd rescues his sheep.
They will sparkle in his land
like jewels in a crown.
17 How wonderful and beautiful they will be!
The young men will thrive on abundant
grain,
and the young women will flourish on new
wine.

The LORD Will Restore His People

10 1Ask the LORD for rain in the spring,
for he makes the storm clouds.
And he will send showers of rain
so every field becomes a lush pasture.
2 Household gods give worthless advice,
fortune-tellers predict only lies,
and interpreters of dreams pronounce
falsehoods that give no comfort.
So my people are wandering like lost sheep;
they are attacked because they have no
shepherd.

3 "My anger burns against your shepherds,
and I will punish these leaders.*
For the LORD of Heaven's Armies has arrived
to look after Judah, his flock.
He will make them strong and glorious,
like a proud warhorse in battle.
4 From Judah will come the cornerstone,
the tent peg,
the bow for battle,
and all the rulers.
5 They will be like mighty warriors in battle,
trampling their enemies in the mud under
their feet.
Since the LORD is with them as they fight,
they will overthrow even the enemy's
horsemen.

6 "I will strengthen Judah and save Israel*;
I will restore them because of my
compassion.
It will be as though I had never rejected them,
for I am the LORD their God, who will hear
their cries.
7 The people of Israel* will become like mighty
warriors,
and their hearts will be made happy as if
by wine.
Their children, too, will see it and be glad;
their hearts will rejoice in the LORD.
8 When I whistle to them, they will come
running,
for I have redeemed them.
From the few who are left,
they will grow as numerous as they were
before.
9 Though I have scattered them like seeds
among the nations,
they will still remember me in distant
lands.
They and their children will survive
and return again to Israel.
10 I will bring them back from Egypt
and gather them from Assyria.
I will resettle them in Gilead and Lebanon

10:3 Or *these male goats.* **10:6** Hebrew *save the house of Joseph.* **10:7** Hebrew *of Ephraim.*

Jesus the fulfillment of prophecy. **16–17:** On the day of national salvation, God promises that Israel will sparkle as *jewels in a crown.* Isaiah gives a similar description, "a splendid crown in the hand of God" (Isa 62:3). Israel will finally fulfill its mission as a priestly nation, a people who are holy before God (Exod 29:6).

10:1—11:3 Restoration. In the fifth century BC, the political situation was bleak for Judah. In response to the rise of the Greeks in the west, the Persians had increased military domination along the Mediterranean coast. Nevertheless, in God's master plan his people would overcome all of their enemies. **10:2–3:** Finding true leadership is a perennial problem for God's people. Jews in Zechariah's community were looking in the wrong places for guidance by resorting to diviners and household gods (see Household Gods, Jer 45). It was easy for false shepherds to lead the flock of Israel astray. Nevertheless, God is aware of every need, including the problem of deceivers, and he urges total reliance on him. He promises to make the lowly sheep like a *proud warhorse in battle.* **4:** Zechariah compares the messianic king with a cornerstone, the stone that is laid between two walls to hold them together. Both the Jewish Targums and the New Testament identify Zechariah's cornerstone with the Messiah. Peter accuses the Sanhedrin of rejecting the cornerstone when it rejected Jesus (Acts 4:11). First Peter also identifies Jesus as the cornerstone (1 Pet 2:6–7; cf. Ps 118:22; Isa 28:16). **6:** *Israel* is a reference to the Northern Kingdom.

until there is no more room for them all.
11 They will pass safely through the sea of distress,*
for the waves of the sea will be held back,
and the waters of the Nile will dry up.
The pride of Assyria will be crushed,
and the rule of Egypt will end.
12 By my power* I will make my people strong,
and by my authority they will go wherever they wish.
I, the LORD, have spoken!"

11 [1]Open your doors, Lebanon,
so that fire may devour your cedar forests.
2 Weep, you cypress trees, for all the ruined cedars;
the most majestic ones have fallen.
Weep, you oaks of Bashan,
for the thick forests have been cut down.
3 Listen to the wailing of the shepherds,
for their rich pastures are destroyed.
Hear the young lions roaring,
for their thickets in the Jordan Valley are ruined.

The Good and Evil Shepherds

[4]This is what the LORD my God says: "Go and
care for the flock that is intended for slaughter.
[5]The buyers slaughter their sheep without remorse. The sellers say, 'Praise the LORD! Now
I'm rich!' Even the shepherds have no compassion for them. [6]Likewise, I will no longer have
pity on the people of the land," says the LORD. "I
will let them fall into each other's hands and into
the hands of their king. They will turn the land
into a wilderness, and I will not rescue them."

[7]So I cared for the flock intended for slaughter—the flock that was oppressed. Then I took
two shepherd's staffs and named one Favor and
the other Union. [8]I got rid of their three evil
shepherds in a single month.

But I became impatient with these sheep, and
they hated me, too. [9]So I told them, "I won't be
your shepherd any longer. If you die, you die. If
you are killed, you are killed. And let those who
remain devour each other!"

[10]Then I took my staff called Favor and cut it
in two, showing that I had revoked the covenant
I had made with all the nations. [11]That was the
end of my covenant with them. The suffering
flock was watching me, and they knew that the
LORD was speaking through my actions.

[12]And I said to them, "If you like, give me
my wages, whatever I am worth; but only if you
want to." So they counted out for my wages thirty pieces of silver.

[13]And the LORD said to me, "Throw it to the
potter*"—this magnificent sum at which they
valued me! So I took the thirty coins and threw
them to the potter in the Temple of the LORD.

[14]Then I took my other staff, Union, and cut it
in two, showing that the bond of unity between
Judah and Israel was broken.

[15]Then the LORD said to me, "Go again and
play the part of a worthless shepherd. [16]This illustrates how I will give this nation a shepherd
who will not care for those who are dying, nor
look after the young,* nor heal the injured, nor
feed the healthy. Instead, this shepherd will eat
the meat of the fattest sheep and tear off their
hooves.

17 "What sorrow awaits this worthless shepherd
who abandons the flock!
The sword will cut his arm
and pierce his right eye.
His arm will become useless,
and his right eye completely blind."

Future Deliverance for Jerusalem

12 This* message concerning the fate of
Israel came from the LORD: "This message is from the LORD, who stretched
out the heavens, laid the foundations of the
earth, and formed the human spirit. [2]I will make
Jerusalem like an intoxicating drink that makes
the nearby nations stagger when they send their
armies to besiege Jerusalem and Judah. [3]On that
day I will make Jerusalem an immovable rock.

10:11 Or *the sea of Egypt,* referring to the Red Sea.
10:12 Hebrew *In the LORD.* **11:13** Syriac version reads *into the treasury;* also in 11:13b. Compare Matt 27:6-10.
11:16 Or *the scattered.* **12:1** Hebrew *An Oracle: This.*

11:4–17 The Good and Evil Shepherds. A prophet acts out the corrupt practices of Judah's leaders in order to expose and denounce them. Several overtones throughout the chapter remind Christians of Jesus. Jesus presents himself as the good shepherd who is truly concerned about the sheep (John 10:11); he is bought for thirty pieces of silver, which are later cast into the Temple (Matt 27:5); he breaks the exclusivity of the old covenant and gives the world a new one; and he is vindicated by the punishment of those who reject him. **5:** *The buyers* are Judah's leaders.

12:1—14:21 God's Final War. Zechariah's final oracle is a vivid description of the eschatological war against Judah. The nations of the world will eagerly muster troops for an expected easy victory over Je-

All the nations will gather against it to try to
move it, but they will only hurt themselves.
4"On that day," says the LORD, "I will cause
every horse to panic and every rider to lose his
nerve. I will watch over the people of Judah, but
I will blind all the horses of their enemies. 5And
the clans of Judah will say to themselves, 'The
people of Jerusalem have found strength in the
LORD of Heaven's Armies, their God.'
6"On that day I will make the clans of Judah
like a flame that sets a woodpile ablaze or like a
burning torch among sheaves of grain. They will
burn up all the neighboring nations right and
left, while the people living in Jerusalem remain
secure.
7"The LORD will give victory to the rest of
Judah first, before Jerusalem, so that the people
of Jerusalem and the royal line of David will not
have greater honor than the rest of Judah. 8On
that day the LORD will defend the people of Jerusalem; the weakest among them will be as mighty
as King David! And the royal descendants will be
like God, like the angel of the LORD who goes before them! 9For on that day I will begin to destroy
all the nations that come against Jerusalem.
10"Then I will pour out a spirit* of grace and
prayer on the family of David and on the people of Jerusalem. They will look on me whom
they have pierced and mourn for him as for an
only son. They will grieve bitterly for him as for
a firstborn son who has died. 11The sorrow and
mourning in Jerusalem on that day will be like
the great mourning for Hadad-rimmon in the
valley of Megiddo.
12"All Israel will mourn, each clan by itself,
and with the husbands separate from their wives.
The clan of David will mourn alone, as will the
clan of Nathan, 13the clan of Levi, and the clan of
Shimei. 14Each of the surviving clans from Judah
will mourn separately, and with the husbands
separate from their wives.

A Fountain of Cleansing

13 "On that day a fountain will be
opened for the dynasty of David and
for the people of Jerusalem, a fountain
to cleanse them from all their sins and impurity.
2"And on that day," says the LORD of Heav-
en's Armies, "I will erase idol worship throughout the land, so that even the names of the idols
will be forgotten. I will remove from the land
both the false prophets and the spirit of impurity that came with them. 3If anyone continues
to prophesy, his own father and mother will tell
him, 'You must die, for you have prophesied lies
in the name of the LORD.' And as he prophesies,
his own father and mother will stab him.
4"On that day people will be ashamed to
claim the prophetic gift. No one will pretend to
be a prophet by wearing prophet's clothes. 5He
will say, 'I'm no prophet; I'm a farmer. I began
working for a farmer as a boy.' 6And if someone asks, 'Then what about those wounds on
your chest?*' he will say, 'I was wounded at my
friends' house!'

The Scattering of the Sheep

7 "Awake, O sword, against my shepherd,
the man who is my partner,"
says the LORD of Heaven's Armies.
"Strike down the shepherd,
and the sheep will be scattered,
and I will turn against the lambs.
8 Two-thirds of the people in the land
will be cut off and die," says the LORD.
"But one-third will be left in the land.
9 I will bring that group through the fire
and make them pure.
I will refine them like silver
and purify them like gold.

12:10 Or *the Spirit.* **13:6** Hebrew *wounds between your hands?*

rusalem, but they will be destroyed by God. **12:3–4:** God can empower the weak who rely on him against strong opponents. Although Jerusalem appears weak on its own, God will, as in the days of Joshua, do most of the fighting, and the nations will have no chance against his weapons. In this battle God inflicts pain, panic, blindness, and madness on the attackers. **6:** *Like a burning torch among sheaves of grain,* they will be invincible. **10–11:** After the military victory, the Jews mourn over one who is *pierced.* The mourning is so intense that it brings about national repentance and purification. New Testament authors identify the pierced one with Jesus Christ (John 19:37). The phrase is used again in Revelation (Rev 1:7; cf. Matt 24:30). The person mourned might also refer to a member of the royal family. **12–14:** Women will be separated from men during this mourning period. The visitor to modern Jerusalem will be reminded of the custom of separate prayer at the Western (or Wailing) Wall, the only remaining wall of the second Temple courts. In accordance with rabbinic law, men pray on one side of the plaza and women on the other. The point is to reduce distraction while communicating with God.

13:1–9 Cleansing Fountain. After a national cleansing, God will renew his covenant with the people. **9:** As in any marriage covenant, the responsibility of both parties is emphasized. The reciprocal character

They will call on my name,
and I will answer them.
I will say, 'These are my people,'
and they will say, 'The LORD is our God.' "

The LORD Will Rule the Earth

14 Watch, for the day of the LORD is
coming when your possessions will
be plundered right in front of you! 2I
will gather all the nations to fight against Jerusalem. The city will be taken, the houses looted,
and the women raped. Half the population will
be taken into captivity, and the rest will be left
among the ruins of the city.
3Then the LORD will go out to fight against
those nations, as he has fought in times past. 4On
that day his feet will stand on the Mount of Olives, east of Jerusalem. And the Mount of Olives
will split apart, making a wide valley running
from east to west. Half the mountain will move
toward the north and half toward the south.
5You will flee through this valley, for it will reach
across to Azal.* Yes, you will flee as you did from
the earthquake in the days of King Uzziah of Judah. Then the LORD my God will come, and all
his holy ones with him.*
6On that day the sources of light will no longer shine,* 7yet there will be continuous day!
Only the LORD knows how this could happen.
There will be no normal day and night, for at
evening time it will still be light.
8On that day life-giving waters will flow out
from Jerusalem, half toward the Dead Sea and
half toward the Mediterranean,* flowing continuously in both summer and winter.
9And the LORD will be king over all the earth.
On that day there will be one LORD—his name
alone will be worshiped.
10All the land from Geba, north of Judah, to
Rimmon, south of Jerusalem, will become one
vast plain. But Jerusalem will be raised up in its
original place and will be inhabited all the way
from the Benjamin Gate over to the site of the
old gate, then to the Corner Gate, and from the
Tower of Hananel to the king's winepresses.
11And Jerusalem will be filled, safe at last, never
again to be cursed and destroyed.
12And the LORD will send a plague on all
the nations that fought against Jerusalem.
Their people will become like walking corpses,
their flesh rotting away. Their eyes will rot in
their sockets, and their tongues will rot in their
mouths. 13On that day they will be terrified,
stricken by the LORD with great panic. They will
fight their neighbors hand to hand. 14Judah, too,
will be fighting at Jerusalem. The wealth of all
the neighboring nations will be captured—great
quantities of gold and silver and fine clothing.
15This same plague will strike the horses, mules,
camels, donkeys, and all the other animals in the
enemy camps.
16In the end, the enemies of Jerusalem who
survive the plague will go up to Jerusalem each
year to worship the King, the LORD of Heaven's
Armies, and to celebrate the Festival of Shelters.
17Any nation in the world that refuses to come
to Jerusalem to worship the King, the LORD of
Heaven's Armies, will have no rain. 18If the people of Egypt refuse to attend the festival, the
LORD will punish them with the same plague
that he sends on the other nations who refuse
to go. 19Egypt and the other nations will all be
punished if they don't go to celebrate the Festival
of Shelters.
20On that day even the harness bells of the
horses will be inscribed with these words: HOLY
TO THE LORD. And the cooking pots in the Temple

14:5a The meaning of the Hebrew is uncertain. **14:5b** As in Greek version; Hebrew reads *with you.* **14:6** Hebrew *there will be no light, no cold or frost.* The meaning of the Hebrew is uncertain. **14:8** Hebrew *half toward the eastern sea and half toward the western sea.*

of the covenant is evident even in the syntax Zechariah uses. The pronouns are arranged in chiastic symmetry: *they . . . I . . . I . . . they.*

14:1–21 The LORD's Rule. Chapter 14 refers to the same eschatological battle described in the preceding chapters. However, this time the battle is presented from a different angle and its aftermath is included. **3–5:** The first scene is a shocking picture of God descending on the Mount of Olives, on the east side of Jerusalem. **6–8:** Changes in climate will be supernatural. Miraculously, water will flow out of Jerusalem, which has always depended on an outside water source. **9–16:** Jerusalem will become the capital of the world. Zechariah's emphasis on Jerusalem throughout the book reaches a climax in this final chapter. **16–19:** The survivors of the nations will be forced to come to Jerusalem to worship God and keep the Festival of Shelters *(Sukkot)*. Great joy, for the ingathering of the harvest as well as for the continuance of the covenant, was characteristic of the feast (Exod 23:16; 34:2; Lev 23:40; Deut 16:14–15; Neh 8:17). **20–21:** Jerusalem will be the epicenter of holiness in the eschatological kingdom. Holiness will extend outward from the Temple to encompass the city and land. Ordinary cooking pots in Jerusalem will become sacred and fit to contain sacrificial meat. Pots in the Temple will

of the LORD will be as sacred as the basins used
beside the altar. 21 In fact, every cooking pot in
Jerusalem and Judah will be holy to the LORD of
Heaven's Armies. All who come to worship will
be free to use any of these pots to boil their sacrifices. And on that day there will no longer be
traders* in the Temple of the LORD of Heaven's
Armies.

14:21 Hebrew *Canaanites.*

be as holy as those used at the altar. The biblical ideal that Israel would be a holy priesthood unto God and the land a center for divine activity will finally be realized.

MALACHI

INTRODUCTION

Malachi, the last of the Minor Prophets, concludes a collection that spans the history of Israel from the mid-eighth century BC through at least the fifth century BC. God's people had lost their status as nation-states, suffered conquest and exile, before the return of some to what was known as the province of Yehud in the satrapy Beyond the River. This province was ruled by a Persian-appointed governor from Jerusalem, where the LORD's Temple had been rebuilt with imperial sponsorship near the end of the sixth century.

The return from exile and the new Temple began to fulfill earlier promises of restoration after judgment. The book of Malachi reaffirms and supplements earlier eschatological prophecy, but its main purpose is to communicate God's word and will for the generations waiting for the LORD's coming. Through Malachi God urges repentance, obedience to the law, faithfulness within the covenant community, and the fear of the LORD.

Malachi's ministry and the composition of the book cannot be dated precisely. The rebuilt Temple, completed by 515 BC, had been in operation long enough for Malachi's audience to become disillusioned and cynical about worship there. A governor administered Persian rule and accepted tribute. Nehemiah held this office twice during the reign of Artaxerxes I (464–423 BC). Ezra taught and enforced covenant law in Jerusalem in the middle of the fifth century BC. Common concerns with Ezra and Nehemiah, including the issue of mixed marriages, suggest a time in the fifth century for Malachi's ministry.

Although the Persian emperor had contributed to the Temple building, the Jews worshiping there acknowledged the LORD as king. At the Temple they remembered their history and maintained their identity as the LORD's people. In Temple worship the Jews enjoyed more autonomy as a community than in any other area of life.

Six dispute speeches make up most of Malachi. Each speech has three basic parts: God makes an opening statement, either an announcement of good news or an accusation; then a question arising from the opening statement is attributed to the audience, and the question exposes the issues that may cause the audience to doubt or resist the divine word; finally, God answers the question with examples and instruction for living faithfully while waiting for the LORD's coming. —*Pamela J. Scalise*

1 This is the message* that the LORD gave to
Israel through the prophet Malachi.*

The LORD's Love for Israel
2 "I have always loved you," says the LORD.
But you retort, "Really? How have you loved
us?"
And the LORD replies, "This is how I showed
my love for you: I loved your ancestor Jacob,
3 but I rejected his brother, Esau, and devastated
his hill country. I turned Esau's inheritance into
a desert for jackals."
4 Esau's descendants in Edom may say, "We
have been shattered, but we will rebuild the ruins."
But the LORD of Heaven's Armies replies,
"They may try to rebuild, but I will demolish them again. Their country will be known as
'The Land of Wickedness,' and their people will
be called 'The People with Whom the LORD Is
Forever Angry.' 5 When you see the destruction
for yourselves, you will say, 'Truly, the LORD's
greatness reaches far beyond Israel's borders!' "

Unworthy Sacrifices
6 The LORD of Heaven's Armies says to the
priests: "A son honors his father, and a servant
respects his master. If I am your father and master, where are the honor and respect I deserve?
You have shown contempt for my name!
"But you ask, 'How have we ever shown contempt for your name?'
7 "You have shown contempt by offering defiled sacrifices on my altar.
"Then you ask, 'How have we defiled the sacrifices?*'
"You defile them by saying the altar of the
LORD deserves no respect. 8 When you give blind
animals as sacrifices, isn't that wrong? And isn't
it wrong to offer animals that are crippled and
diseased? Try giving gifts like that to your governor, and see how pleased he is!" says the LORD
of Heaven's Armies.

1:1a Hebrew *An Oracle: The message.* **1:1b** *Malachi* means "my messenger." **1:7** As in Greek version; Hebrew reads *defiled you?*

1:1 Superscription

The book gives no personal information about Malachi. Even his name sounds more like a title than a personal name. Malachi, "my messenger," does not fit the practice of a parent naming a son as a testimony (e.g., Gen 27—28). Rather, God is the one who sends messengers.

1:2–5 God's Love for Jacob

The first word in Malachi is a declaration of God's enduring love. God has loved Israel since before the birth of their ancestor, Jacob/Israel. **2–3:** The story of God's dealings with Esau and Jacob and the nations that came from them, Edom and Israel, shows the consequences of God's choice. Jacob is the bearer of the covenant and promises previously given to Abraham and Isaac (Gen 25:23; 28:13–15; Rom 9:10–13), but being loved and chosen did not give Jacob/Israel domestic security or political independence. Esau became wealthy and powerful in Edom; Jacob lived as a dependent in his father-in-law's household, far from the promised land. Jacob then went to Egypt, where his descendants became slaves, while Esau's descendants became chiefs in Edom. **3:** Malachi reports fulfillment of the judgments against Edom in Isaiah 34:6; Ezekiel 35:3–4; and Joel 3:19. God's choice of and love for Jacob is evident because Israel by God's grace had been brought back to its land and had rebuilt the capital city and Temple. **4–5:** When Edom tries to rebuild, however, God promises to thwart their efforts. Several bitter denunciations support the designation *wicked:* Edom had taken revenge and planned to devour Judah (Ezek 25:12–13; 35:1–15). The Edomites also were guilty of violence and shedding innocent blood (Joel 3:19). God's anger against Edom is just, and Malachi's audience will witness its effects.

1:6—2:9 The Priests Despise God's Name

God had chosen Jerusalem "as a dwelling for his name" (Deut 12:11). Priests ministered there in his name, responsible to live holy lives and carry out their duties so that that name would not be profaned. This second dispute speech accuses the priests of showing contempt for God by accepting forbidden animals for sacrifices. Women participated in worship at the Temple (see Women in Worship, Matt 28). Women sang in the Temple choir (Ezra 2:65; Neh 7:67) and may also have played in the orchestra (1 Chr 25:5–6). Certain offerings were specifically required of women (Lev 12:6; 15:29), and other sacrificial obligations fell on women and men (e.g., Lev 14, the purification of lepers). Women could make vows, including the Nazirite vow, although their fathers or husbands could cancel the vows (see Num). Vows typically included an offering, so free-will offerings must have been performed by women. **1:6:** Terminology suited to a patriarchal household, *father* and *master*, is applied to Temple life. **7–9:** The priests were privileged to bless the people, putting Yahweh's name upon them, but the priests' failure to honor

9 "Go ahead, beg God to be merciful to you!
But when you bring that kind of offering, why
should he show you any favor at all?" asks the
LORD of Heaven's Armies.
10 "How I wish one of you would shut the
Temple doors so that these worthless sacrifices
could not be offered! I am not pleased with you,"
says the LORD of Heaven's Armies, "and I will
not accept your offerings. 11 But my name is honored* by people of other nations from morning
till night. All around the world they offer* sweet
incense and pure offerings in honor of my name.
For my name is great among the nations," says
the LORD of Heaven's Armies.
12 "But you dishonor my name with your actions. By bringing contemptible food, you are
saying it's all right to defile the Lord's table.
13 You say, 'It's too hard to serve the LORD,' and
you turn up your noses at my commands," says
the LORD of Heaven's Armies. "Think of it! Animals that are stolen and crippled and sick are being presented as offerings! Should I accept from
you such offerings as these?" asks the LORD.
14 "Cursed is the cheat who promises to give a
fine ram from his flock but then sacrifices a defective one to the Lord. For I am a great king,"
says the LORD of Heaven's Armies, "and my
name is feared among the nations!

A Warning to the Priests

2 "Listen, you priests—this command is
for you! 2 Listen to me and make up your
minds to honor my name," says the LORD
of Heaven's Armies, "or I will bring a terrible
curse against you. I will curse even the blessings you receive. Indeed, I have already cursed
them, because you have not taken my warning
to heart. 3 I will punish your descendants and
splatter your faces with the manure from your
festival sacrifices, and I will throw you on the
manure pile. 4 Then at last you will know it was I
who sent you this warning so that my covenant
with the Levites can continue," says the LORD of
Heaven's Armies.
5 "The purpose of my covenant with the Levites was to bring life and peace, and that is what
I gave them. This required reverence from them,
and they greatly revered me and stood in awe
of my name. 6 They passed on to the people the
truth of the instructions they received from me.
They did not lie or cheat; they walked with me,
living good and righteous lives, and they turned
many from lives of sin.
7 "The words of a priest's lips should preserve
knowledge of God, and people should go to him
for instruction, for the priest is the messenger of
the LORD of Heaven's Armies. 8 But you priests
have left God's paths. Your instructions have
caused many to stumble into sin. You have corrupted the covenant I made with the Levites,"
says the LORD of Heaven's Armies. 9 "So I have
made you despised and humiliated in the eyes of
all the people. For you have not obeyed me but
have shown favoritism in the way you carry out
my instructions."

A Call to Faithfulness

10 Are we not all children of the same Father? Are
we not all created by the same God? Then why
do we betray each other, violating the covenant
of our ancestors?
11 Judah has been unfaithful, and a detestable

1:11a Or *will be honored.* **1:11b** Or *will offer.*

the name of the LORD made those blessing ineffectual. **10–11:** The Temple and its rituals constituted a gracious gift of access to the divine presence. God, however, remained free to shut the doors and, someday, to receive pure offerings everywhere. **13:** The priests saw their responsibilities as burdensome; the same Hebrew word is used elsewhere to refer only to hardship suffered under Egypt, Assyria, and Babylon (Exod 18:8; Num 20:14; Neh 9:32; Lam 3:5). **2:1–4:** Malachi presents this condemnation of the priests as a command to be heeded. The priests' faulty teaching and practice fostered falsehood, teaching the people that the LORD was less worthy of respect than the Persian-appointed governor. Whenever they accepted a blemished sacrifice in place of the perfect animal someone had vowed to give to God, they taught the people to cheat. And they destroyed the witness of Temple worship to the truth that the LORD's name is to be feared among the nations. There is opportunity for priests to repent and follow the model of Levi. **5–7:** God desired to preserve the priesthood. Malachi's profile of the ideal priest who reveres God's name, teaches the truth and turns many from iniquity condemns his priestly audience by comparison.

2:10–16 Faithlessness within the Covenant Community

Malachi condemns various marital transgressions as betrayal of the family of God. **10:** Malachi appeals again to the metaphor of the patriarchal household and to his audience's belief that members of the household ought to honor their father and not betray one another. The head of this household is the LORD. **11–12:** Malachi accuses *the men of Judah* of treachery in betraying their covenantal "father" and

thing has been done in Israel and in Jerusalem.
The men of Judah have defiled the LORD's beloved sanctuary by marrying women who worship idols. 12 May the LORD cut off from the
nation of Israel* every last man who has done
this and yet brings an offering to the LORD of
Heaven's Armies.
13 Here is another thing you do. You cover the
LORD's altar with tears, weeping and groaning
because he pays no attention to your offerings
and doesn't accept them with pleasure. 14 You
cry out, "Why doesn't the LORD accept my worship?" I'll tell you why! Because the LORD witnessed the vows you and your wife made when
you were young. But you have been unfaithful
to her, though she remained your faithful partner, the wife of your marriage vows.
15 Didn't the LORD make you one with your
wife? In body and spirit you are his.* And what
does he want? Godly children from your union.
So guard your heart; remain loyal to the wife
of your youth. 16 "For I hate divorce!" says the
LORD, the God of Israel. "To divorce your wife is
to overwhelm her with cruelty,*" says the LORD
of Heaven's Armies. "So guard your heart; do
not be unfaithful to your wife."
17 You have wearied the LORD with your
words.
"How have we wearied him?" you ask.
You have wearied him by saying that all who
do evil are good in the LORD's sight, and he is
pleased with them. You have wearied him by
asking, "Where is the God of justice?"

The Coming Day of Judgment

3 "Look! I am sending my messenger, and he
will prepare the way before me. Then the
Lord you are seeking will suddenly come

2:12 Hebrew *from the tents of Jacob.* The names "Jacob" and "Israel" are often interchanged throughout the Old Testament, referring sometimes to the individual patriarch and sometimes to the nation. **2:15** Or *Didn't the one LORD make us and preserve our life and breath?* or *Didn't the one LORD make her, both flesh and spirit?* The meaning of the Hebrew is uncertain. **2:16** Hebrew *to cover one's garment with violence.*

their covenantal family. If the LORD is the father of the Jewish husband, then the wife by analogy is a daughter of the deity she worships. Deuteronomy 7:3–4 forbids this type of intermarriage, as well as marrying one's daughters to Gentiles, because the children would learn to follow other gods. This kind of intermarriage damaged both individuals and the community. **13–16:** Malachi's second example of faithlessness is divorcing *the wife of your youth*. In the Old Testament a husband could divorce his wife by writing out and giving to her a bill of divorce (Deut 24:1–4; see Divorce, Ezra 10). **14:** The term *partner* is unique, a feminine noun from a verb meaning "unite, be joined." The masculine form of the noun denotes men who work together and have similar values (Ps 119:63; Prov 28:24; Song 1:7; Isa 1:23). This Hebrew word is an apt designation for a wife who has labored with her husband to build their family and to achieve shared goals of survival and sufficiency. *Your marriage vows*: This phrase is often translated by "covenant." Malachi uses the theology of the LORD's covenant with Israel to interpret marriage (see Marriage, Song 2). Although there are no marriage ceremonies in the Old Testament and marriage arrangements are never called covenants, the notion of marriage as a covenant has clear antecedents. In Deuteronomy 7:1–4 forbidden covenants between Israel and foreign nations parallel forbidden marriages between Israelites and non-Israelites. Marriage serves as a metaphor for the covenant relationship between the LORD and Israel (e.g., Hos 1—3). If the covenant is like a marriage, then a marriage could be like a covenant. **15:** The Old Testament associates *the wife of your youth* with the joys of mutual discovery and devotion (Prov 5:18; Jer 3:2). *Godly children* possibly refers to children of the husband and his Jewish first wife but also includes the whole of Israel, daughters and sons of the one God who created them as a people. **14, 16:** The LORD as witness speaks on behalf of the wife against the faithless husband. Divorcing one's Jewish wife to marry a woman who worships other gods is an act of violence, says God. It belongs to a category of malicious harm ranging from injustice created by false testimony to bloodshed. Violence leaves its mark on the perpetrator (see Violence, Abuse, and Oppression, Eccl 4), in this case likened to a stain on the husband's garment (see translator's note). Because a man might spread the corner of his garment over a woman as a gesture pledging marriage (Ruth 3:9; Ezek 16:8), the garment becomes a symbol of the relationship between husband and wife (Deut 22:30).

2:17—3:5 The Coming Day of Judgment

Malachi's audience has wearied the LORD with their doubts and complaints (2:17). Evil people appear to enjoy God's favor. Why doesn't God restore justice? **3:1–5:** The God of justice is indeed coming for judgment. The messenger of the covenant will prepare the way by purifying the priests. Then the divine judge will arrive to condemn those who are guilty according to the law. Priests who fear the Lord will be purified by teaching God's law and setting the people

to his Temple. The messenger of the covenant, whom you look for so eagerly, is surely coming," says the LORD of Heaven's Armies.

2 "But who will be able to endure it when he comes? Who will be able to stand and face him when he appears? For he will be like a blazing fire that refines metal, or like a strong soap that bleaches clothes. 3 He will sit like a refiner of silver, burning away the dross. He will purify the Levites, refining them like gold and silver, so that they may once again offer acceptable sacrifices to the LORD. 4 Then once more the LORD will accept the offerings brought to him by the people of Judah and Jerusalem, as he did in the past.

5 "At that time I will put you on trial. I am eager to witness against all sorcerers and adulterers and liars. I will speak against those who cheat employees of their wages, who oppress widows and orphans, or who deprive the foreigners living among you of justice, for these people do not fear me," says the LORD of Heaven's Armies.

A Call to Repentance

6 "I am the LORD, and I do not change. That is why you descendants of Jacob are not already destroyed. 7 Ever since the days of your ancestors, you have scorned my decrees and failed to obey them. Now return to me, and I will return to you," says the LORD of Heaven's Armies.

"But you ask, 'How can we return when we have never gone away?'

8 "Should people cheat God? Yet you have cheated me!

"But you ask, 'What do you mean? When did we ever cheat you?'

"You have cheated me of the tithes and offerings due to me. 9 You are under a curse, for your whole nation has been cheating me. 10 Bring all the tithes into the storehouse so there will be enough food in my Temple. If you do," says the LORD of Heaven's Armies, "I will open the windows of heaven for you. I will pour out a blessing so great you won't have enough room to take it in! Try it! Put me to the test! 11 Your crops will be abundant, for I will guard them from insects and disease.* Your grapes will not fall from the vine before they are ripe," says the LORD of Heaven's Armies. 12 "Then all nations will call you blessed, for your land will be such a delight," says the LORD of Heaven's Armies.

13 "You have said terrible things about me," says the LORD.

"But you say, 'What do you mean? What have we said against you?'

14 "You have said, 'What's the use of serving God? What have we gained by obeying his commands or by trying to show the LORD of Heaven's Armies that we are sorry for our sins? 15 From now on we will call the arrogant blessed. For those who do evil get rich, and those who dare God to punish them suffer no harm.' "

The LORD's Promise of Mercy

16 Then those who feared the LORD spoke with each other, and the LORD listened to what they

3:11 Hebrew *from the devourer.*

on the way to doing justice. The standard for the future judgment will be the law they already know and should obey. That law protects widows, orphans, day laborers, and aliens from oppression by the powerful. The law refutes the idea that God delights in evil.

3:6–12 How to Return to the LORD

Because the LORD doesn't change, Israel hasn't perished. Indeed, for as long as they had been turning away, God has loved them (1:2; cf. Hos 11:1–11). Because of this enduring fidelity God calls on them to repent and be restored to relationship with God (cf. Zech 1:3; Hos 14:1–8). **8:** When the people question, the response is severe but practical: *You have cheated me.* **9–10:** They must bring their full *tithes and offerings*. Offerings not only supported priests and Levites at the Temple, but also landless widows, orphans, and resident foreigners. Tithes were paid in grain, wine, and oil, and from flocks and herds. The spiritual purpose of tithing was to learn to fear the LORD and not transgress any divine commands. **10–12:** God's invitation to try him out is given in the context of the covenant. The nation stands under the curses of the covenant because the people have violated their covenant obligations. As a nation, Malachi's audience can prove God's faithfulness to the covenant by bringing the full tithe or 10 percent. If they do, curses on the crops will be turned back and bountiful blessings will be given, as listed in Deuteronomy 28:8–12. The covenant is not, however, a means for Israel to manipulate God to bless them. God's people have the opportunity to return because of God's unchanging mercy.

3:13—4:3 Choosing to Fear the LORD

The sixth dispute speech, like the fourth, is about the people's conversation. **3:14–15:** The people have been saying that either the LORD doesn't care about unrighteousness or lacks the power to do anything about it. **16:** A unique verse of narrative interrupts the speech

said. In his presence, a scroll of remembrance was
written to record the names of those who feared
him and always thought about the honor of his
name.
17 "They will be my people," says the LORD
of Heaven's Armies. "On the day when I act in
judgment, they will be my own special treasure.
I will spare them as a father spares an obedient
child. 18 Then you will again see the difference
between the righteous and the wicked, between
those who serve God and those who do not."

The Coming Day of Judgment

4 1 *The LORD of Heaven's Armies says, "The
day of judgment is coming, burning like a
furnace. On that day the arrogant and the
wicked will be burned up like straw. They will be
consumed—roots, branches, and all.
2 "But for you who fear my name, the Sun
of Righteousness will rise with healing in his
wings.* And you will go free, leaping with joy
like calves let out to pasture. 3 On the day when
I act, you will tread upon the wicked as if they
were dust under your feet," says the LORD of
Heaven's Armies.
4 "Remember to obey the Law of Moses, my
servant—all the decrees and regulations that I
gave him on Mount Sinai* for all Israel.
5 "Look, I am sending you the prophet Elijah
before the great and dreadful day of the LORD
arrives. 6 His preaching will turn the hearts of fathers to their children, and the hearts of children
to their fathers. Otherwise I will come and strike
the land with a curse."

4:1 Verses 4:1-6 are numbered 3:19-24 in Hebrew text.
4:2 Or *the sun of righteousness will rise with healing in its wings.* **4:4** Hebrew *Horeb,* another name for Sinai.

---

and describes a group who separated themselves from the rest of the audience. **17:** God acknowledges them as *my own special treasure* whom *I will spare*. The distinguishing feature of these people is that they fear the LORD. This fear is not panic at the prospect of punishment but a fitting response to God's holiness, power, and love. Malachi's audience in every generation can choose to follow the example of those who fear the LORD and receive the promise of healing and deliverance on the day that God acts. **4:1–3:** God describes the *day of judgment*, when the arrogant will be eliminated and the righteous spared.

4:4–6 Coda: Moses and Elijah

An admonition and a promise conclude Malachi and serve as a coda to the prophetic books. In Malachi, women and men who accept God's invitation to return and who fear the LORD keep the commands of the law. They accept as covenant obligations the statutes and ordinances that God gave at Horeb. **4:** As Joshua commanded Israel and David advised Solomon, so Malachi extends the admonition to remember the teaching *(torah)* of Moses to every generation of Israel waiting for the LORD's day.

THE

NEW TESTAMENT

MATTHEW

INTRODUCTION

Matthew's Gospel takes us leaping and dancing straight into the heart of the good news about the Lord Jesus Christ. A mere seventeen verses (1:1–17) provide the bridge between the Old Testament and the New. For centuries there had been an accumulating collection of God-breathed Scriptures, followed by a period of silent anticipation, puzzlement, or lethargy. Then, within a few short decades, the New Testament documents all came tumbling into life, marking the radical transition from the old dispensation to the new. It is not possible to date exactly when Matthew's Gospel took its place in that process, but it probably appeared in the AD 60s or possibly early 70s.

In the traditional belief of the church, traceable from early in the second century, Matthew, called by Jesus to leave his tax-collecting to become one of the original twelve disciples (9:9; 10:3), was the author. In this view, Matthew would have seen and heard firsthand most of what he writes about and would have had direct access to others, such as Mary, Jesus' mother, for further information.

Matthew seems to have written primarily for a Jewish audience, repeatedly and painstakingly showing how the events he records are the fulfillment of Old Testament prophecy and promise (e.g., 1:22; 2:17; 4:14). He regularly echoes or quotes from the Old Testament, drawing on many different parts of the Scriptures (e.g., Gen, Exod, Lev, Deut, Ps, Isa, Jer, Dan, Hos, Zech, and Mal—an extraordinary breadth of textual familiarity). He points to Jesus as the long-awaited Messiah and promised king of the Kingdom of Heaven. He frequently shows how familiar interpretations of the Old Testament were mistaken and that Jesus' teaching did not contradict the Scriptures but rather illuminated their true meaning. He writes about judgment in a style and language familiar to Jews from the prophets and intertestamental writings. He conveys Jesus' great love for his nation. He writes as a Jewish insider.

And yet, Matthew weaves throughout his Gospel some Gentile threads. It is Matthew, not Luke the Greek, who includes Gentiles and women in his prologue genealogy of Jesus. It is Matthew, not Luke, who tells us of the Gentile Magi coming to worship the infant Christ (2:1–12). It is Matthew who gives us the most familiar version of the Great Commission (28:16–20) with its resounding call to make disciples of *all* the nations. In many details, he hints at the universal scope of that great finale as he selects material for his biography. Yet here too Matthew is steadily asking his Jewish audience to revisit the way in which they had grown accustomed to understanding their Scriptures: "Look! Abraham's descendants, the Jewish nation, are called to bless and bring in the nations, to be a dynamic visual aid to help the Gentiles come to know and love and serve the living God!"

Matthew's theme of the kingdom would have resonated strongly with a Jewish reader or listener. From the days of David on, the kingdom had crumbled and had never been fully restored. Through civil war, exile, and occupation the dream had grown more precious, its realization apparently ever more elusive. By the time of Christ, first the Greek, then the Roman, imperial might had seemed to squeeze out the last drop of probability that the kingdom would be restored. At the same time, there were those who looked for it passion-ately, convinced that the Messiah would come and establish kingly rule over a freed and united kingdom.

It is against this background that Matthew's portrait of Jesus fits. At the outset Jesus is established as one descended from the royal line, great King David's greater Son, the one to whom, newborn, both the great and the humble come to pay homage. The Gospel is arranged around five major discourses on the theme of the kingdom, a kingdom far different from the sociopolitical aspirations of many Jews of the time, who were hoping to be freed from the Roman government. Jesus enters Jerusalem to the excited welcome by the crowds who name him their king; but they are dismayed that he does not make moves to evict the Romans. Tacked to the cross as the Lord hung dying was the label "This is Jesus, the King of the Jews"—mockery by the Roman soldiers. The irony was that such labels made claims too small, not too great. For the risen Christ's last command claims kingly authority over all the nations of the world, for time and eternity. Who is Jesus? An amazing King, declares Matthew.

Clearly none of the Gospels was written as a feminist tract, and it is inappropriate to judge them from such a framework. Nor were many of the questions that exercise us about the role of women in home, society, and church issues that Matthew could have dreamed of. Yet, given the male domination in the culture at that time and the entirely male worldview of most contemporary literature, the extraordinary thing is how Matthew draws attention to women as well as men in his Gospel. He is, of course, reflecting the radical way in which Jesus included women, dignifying them with value equal to that of men. This is evident in all four Gospels. But it is striking that Matthew did not edit out these statements as he selected material for his biography. He is able to summarize Jesus' thirty-three years in a few thousand words, and much had to be left out.

On the contrary, Matthew must have stunned many readers of the time by his inclusion of women in his introductory genealogy. That two of them (Rahab and Ruth) were not Jewish, and four of the five had at least questionable reputations, while the fifth claimed to have conceived and given birth while still a virgin, must have added to the shock for any alert reader or listener. Was Matthew out to shock? No. But, under the inspiration of the Holy Spirit, he draws attention, right from the start, to the fact that his Gospel is good news for *all* the human race, not just for men or the members of one group.

With the conclusion of the genealogy, Matthew introduces us to Mary. While some Christians have given her greater status than is warranted from Scripture, others, especially evangelical Protestants, have treated this remarkable woman with less respect than she deserves. Matthew tells us less than does Luke but more than either Mark or John. It is hard to see how anyone other than Mary could have been the source of much of the information contained in the opening chapters of Matthew and Luke's Gospels. The inclusion of the material, woven into the biographies on the same terms as everything else, indicates the highest value put on Mary's testimony, whether it came to Matthew directly or through others. This in itself is indicative of a lesson well learned from the Lord Jesus, for while he treated women with revolutionary respect, few men of his time would have been willing to trust a woman's word. Yet the Gospel writers depend on women's testimony for key events. Mary and Elizabeth must have told the story of the conception and birth of Jesus and of John the Baptist (Joseph, at least, and probably Zechariah, were long dead). But apart from John, we are told that it was the women who stayed close enough to witness the crucifixion, while the men slunk away; and it was the women who discovered the empty tomb and first met the risen Lord. By the time Matthew came to write his Gospel, he must have pondered the significance of God's sovereign dealings; he is without apology in asking us to stake our lives on the word of women. Why? Because God himself entrusts the key testimony to those breathtaking, world-changing events of his Son's birth, death, and resurrection to women!

There is another pervasive reason why Matthew's Gospel is good news for women. It is difficult to put ourselves into the shoes of first-century Jewish women. Yet the more we attempt to do that, the more liberating and extraordinary Christ's message is seen to be. Much of the religious life of Judaism revolved around the Temple and the synagogues. In both, women were tolerated but marginalized. In the Temple a woman could find a corner in which to pray, she could put her pennies in the collecting box, but with few exceptions (e.g., Anna the prophet in Luke 2:36–38) it was men who conducted the real business of Temple life and public worship. In the synagogue, women were seldom more than silent onlookers, if they were there at all.

Yet Matthew matter-of-factly shows Jesus breaking all the conventions. This teacher, unlike any self-respecting rabbi, scribe, or Pharisee, delights to teach women and children along with the men (14:21; 15:38). When the Twelve become impatient, almost certainly with women, Jesus is insistently welcoming and compassionate (19:13–15). He tackles the exploitative way in which many men treat women over divorce or as sex objects (5:27–32; 19:3–12). His teaching, the parables and stories he tells, the illustrations he uses, the way in which he teaches his disciples to pray to the Father in heaven, are as accessible to women as to men. Women listening to him must have been riveted by the sense of acceptance and inclusion they felt, the dignity bestowed, the courtesy extended. Here is a life of faith as open to them as to their fathers and husbands. Here is a life of faith wholly compatible with the domestic sphere and not dependent on the ritual that was largely the province of males.

Many contemporary preachers were urging armed resistance to throw off the Roman occupation: What hope could there be while their present political situation continued? By contrast, here was a man teaching transformed relationships, integrity, kindness, religion that engaged the heart and every part of everyday life. While the Romans excluded women, except by requiring them to give up their husbands and sons to violence and possible death, Jesus included them fully alongside their men, with a message that offered hope and change, even within the current political framework, and grounded in the practical realities of ordinary life. It is hard, from the standpoint of a modern Western woman with open access to so much information of every kind, to grasp quite how amazing this must have been to many of the women who heard Jesus or, later, heard or read Matthew's account.
—*Rosemary M. Dowsett*

1:1–17	Prologue: The Genealogy of Jesus
1:18—2:23	The Birth and Infancy of Jesus
3:1—4:25	Narrative: Preparation and the Beginnings of Public Ministry
5:1—7:29	First Discourse: Living the Life of the Kingdom
8:1—9:38	Narrative: Demonstrating the Life of the Kingdom
10:5–42	Second Discourse: The Mission of the Kingdom
11:1—12:50	Narrative: Opposition to the Kingdom
13:1–52	Third Discourse: Parables of the Kingdom
13:53—17:27	Narrative: The King Recognized, the King Rejected

18:1–35	Fourth Discourse: The Upside-Down Kingdom
19:1—23:39	Narrative: The King Must Die
24:1—25:46	Fifth Discourse: And the King Shall Come Again
26:1—28:20	Narrative: Tragedy—and Triumph!

✧

The Ancestors of Jesus the Messiah

1 This is a record of the ancestors of Jesus the Messiah, a descendant of David* and of Abraham:

2 Abraham was the father of Isaac.
Isaac was the father of Jacob.
Jacob was the father of Judah and his brothers.
3 Judah was the father of Perez and Zerah (whose mother was Tamar).
Perez was the father of Hezron.
Hezron was the father of Ram.*
4 Ram was the father of Amminadab.
Amminadab was the father of Nahshon.
Nahshon was the father of Salmon.
5 Salmon was the father of Boaz (whose mother was Rahab).
Boaz was the father of Obed (whose mother was Ruth).
Obed was the father of Jesse.
6 Jesse was the father of King David.
David was the father of Solomon (whose mother was Bathsheba, the widow of Uriah).
7 Solomon was the father of Rehoboam.
Rehoboam was the father of Abijah.
Abijah was the father of Asa.*
8 Asa was the father of Jehoshaphat.
Jehoshaphat was the father of Jehoram.*
Jehoram was the father* of Uzziah.
9 Uzziah was the father of Jotham.
Jotham was the father of Ahaz.
Ahaz was the father of Hezekiah.

1:1 Greek *Jesus the Messiah, son of David.* **1:3** Greek *Aram,* a variant spelling of Ram; also in 1:4. See 1 Chr 2:9-10. **1:7** Greek *Asaph,* a variant spelling of Asa; also in 1:8. See 1 Chr 3:10. **1:8a** Greek *Joram,* a variant spelling of Jehoram; also in 1:8b. See 1 Kgs 22:50 and note at 1 Chr 3:11. **1:8b** Or *ancestor;* also in 1:11.

1:1–17 Prologue: The Genealogy of Jesus

In biblical culture, as in many African and Asian cultures today, identity is often linked to birthplace and family relationships. Where filial piety or ancestor worship is practiced, genealogies are of the utmost importance. **2–16:** Jesus' family tree begins with *Abraham,* to demonstrate that Jesus is truly in the line of promise. It includes saint and sinner, illustrious king and obscure nobody. More intriguingly, it includes five women, five mothers, each of whom, in a beautiful way, is a sign of the grace of the gospel. **3:** Widowed *Tamar* (Gen 38) lured her father-in-law, Judah, to mistake her for a prostitute and impregnate her so that she might have the child she needed for identity and security. Under levirate law, Judah and his sons had sinned against her, and in this sense she was seeking what was hers by right. *Perez,* the firstborn twin of this incestuous union, is thus in the family tree of Jesus. **5:** *Rahab* was also a prostitute but became the mother of godly *Boaz.* She was a foreigner, a citizen in Jericho (Josh 2). Having risked her life to save the Israelite spies, she is spared the destruction that falls on her fellow citizens. In Hebrews 11 she is still referred to as "Rahab the prostitute" (Heb 11:31). Rahab became mother-in-law to *Ruth* the Moabitess (whose story is told in the book of Ruth). The story of the origin of the Moabites is one of the strangest in Scripture (Gen 19:30–38). In *Boaz* God provides Ruth with the kinsman-redeemer through whom the childless widow becomes a cherished wife and fruitful mother, the celebrated ancestor of King David—and Jesus. **6:** *Bathsheba,* the fourth woman in this extraordinary list (2 Sam 11—12), could be seen as the hapless victim of a society whose rules were heavily biased in favor of men. When David, full of lust, sends for her (2 Sam 11:4), she had no choice: A subject, especially a woman whose husband was away from home, had to obey the king. This is usually presented as adultery, implying mutual consent, but was probably closer to rape. Yet the God of grace brings a new future: a repentant David, a genuine marriage, a dearly loved son, Solomon. Out of sin and suffering God can bring transformed new life. Matthew, in including these women in the genealogy of Jesus, is celebrating the thread of God's grace in the Old Testament, how God turns tragedy into triumph. Women as well as men are of such immeasurable value to God that he will go to any lengths to give the grace of a new beginning with the slate of the past wiped clean. This is Matthew's first answer to the query: Who is this Jesus? He is the one who fits into the line of God's redeeming love, not ashamed to be identified with those who sin and those who have

[10] Hezekiah was the father of Manasseh.
Manasseh was the father of Amon.*
Amon was the father of Josiah.
[11] Josiah was the father of Jehoiachin* and his brothers (born at the time of the exile to Babylon).
[12] After the Babylonian exile:
Jehoiachin was the father of Shealtiel.
Shealtiel was the father of Zerubbabel.
[13] Zerubbabel was the father of Abiud.
Abiud was the father of Eliakim.
Eliakim was the father of Azor.
[14] Azor was the father of Zadok.
Zadok was the father of Akim.
Akim was the father of Eliud.
[15] Eliud was the father of Eleazar.
Eleazar was the father of Matthan.
Matthan was the father of Jacob.
[16] Jacob was the father of Joseph, the husband of Mary.
Mary gave birth to Jesus, who is called the Messiah.

[17] All those listed above include fourteen generations from Abraham to David, fourteen from David to the Babylonian exile, and fourteen from the Babylonian exile to the Messiah.

The Birth of Jesus the Messiah

[18] This is how Jesus the Messiah was born. His mother, Mary, was engaged to be married to Joseph. But before the marriage took place, while she was still a virgin, she became pregnant through the power of the Holy Spirit.
[19] Joseph, her fiancé, was a good man and did not want to disgrace her publicly, so he decided to break the engagement* quietly.
[20] As he considered this, an angel of the Lord appeared to him in a dream. "Joseph, son of David," the angel said, "do not be afraid to take Mary as your wife. For the child within her was conceived by the Holy Spirit.
[21] And she will have a son, and you are to name him Jesus,* for he will save his people from their sins."

[22] All of this occurred to fulfill the Lord's message through his prophet:

[23] "Look! The virgin will conceive a child!
She will give birth to a son,
and they will call him Immanuel,*
which means 'God is with us.' "

[24] When Joseph woke up, he did as the angel of the Lord commanded and took Mary as his wife.
[25] But he did not have sexual relations with

1:10 Greek *Amos,* a variant spelling of Amon; also in 1:10b. See 1 Chr 3:14. **1:11** Greek *Jeconiah,* a variant spelling of Jehoiachin; also in 1:12. See 2 Kgs 24:6 and note at 1 Chr 3:16. **1:19** Greek *to divorce her.* **1:21** *Jesus* means "The LORD saves." **1:23** Isa 7:14; 8:8, 10 (Greek version).

---

been sinned against. **17:** The genealogy is slightly adjusted, to make three neat blocks of *fourteen generations,* and it shows Jesus as a true Jew who could genuinely claim Abraham as his forefather.

1:18–2:23 The Birth and Infancy of Jesus

1:18–25 The Birth. 18: The fifth woman in the genealogy is *Mary*. Matthew does not relate the annunciation, the pregnancy, and birth. **19–25:** The account of *Joseph* explains God's dealings with the godly man who became Jesus' earthly father. **20:** Here and three other times (2:13, 19, 22) the Lord or his *angel* appears to Joseph *in a dream,* and each time Joseph does exactly what he is told. He protects Mary and the child she bears, the child of whom Joseph is not the father. Betrothal commonly lasted a year; it was a serious contract between two families and was designed to ensure that the first child born of the marriage was without doubt the child of the new husband. During the period of engagement, both young people would be watched closely by both families. Everybody knew the penalties for sexual misconduct, which could include being stoned to death. God's direct words to Joseph on four separate occasions must have given Joseph courage: to dare to trust God for an uncharted future, to dare to run the gauntlet of his family's almost certain outrage and the neighbors' gossip, to dare to cope with all the demands of travel and exile and danger on behalf of this child who was not his. How gracious God is! And God's grace gave Joseph grace: to marry Mary, to protect her, to live with her without seeking sexual consummation until after the birth of Jesus. Later, from their marriage, were to come at least four sons and several daughters (13:55–56). So Jesus is the son of Mary, born from her body, and the foster son of God-fearing Joseph: Jesus is fully human, fully Jewish, a precious firstborn, a child in a family. But miraculously, *the child . . . was conceived by the Holy Spirit*. From before birth he is declared to have a unique origin and a unique destiny. **21:** *Jesus* is the Greek spelling of the Hebrew name *Y'shua*, Joshua, meaning "The LORD saves," *for he will save his people from their sins*, a name and a future determined by God. Many a Christian mother dedicates her child to God from within her womb, recognizing that he or she is a gift from the Lord. But this child was not simply a gift from God. He was conceived through the Holy Spirit and singled out to be Savior and Messiah.

her until her son was born. And Joseph named him Jesus.

Visitors from the East

2 Jesus was born in Bethlehem in Judea, during the reign of King Herod. About that time some wise men* from eastern lands arrived in Jerusalem, asking, [2]"Where is the newborn king of the Jews? We saw his star as it rose,* and we have come to worship him."

[3]King Herod was deeply disturbed when he heard this, as was everyone in Jerusalem. [4]He called a meeting of the leading priests and teachers of religious law and asked, "Where is the Messiah supposed to be born?"

[5]"In Bethlehem in Judea," they said, "for this is what the prophet wrote:

[6] 'And you, O Bethlehem in the land of Judah,
are not least among the ruling cities* of Judah,
for a ruler will come from you
who will be the shepherd for my people Israel.'* "

[7]Then Herod called for a private meeting with the wise men, and he learned from them the time when the star first appeared. [8]Then he told them, "Go to Bethlehem and search carefully for the child. And when you find him, come back and tell me so that I can go and worship him, too!"

[9]After this interview the wise men went their way. And the star they had seen in the east guided them to Bethlehem. It went ahead of them and stopped over the place where the child was. [10]When they saw the star, they were filled with joy! [11]They entered the house and saw the child with his mother, Mary, and they bowed down and worshiped him. Then they opened their treasure chests and gave him gifts of gold, frankincense, and myrrh.

[12]When it was time to leave, they returned to their own country by another route, for God had warned them in a dream not to return to Herod.

The Escape to Egypt

[13]After the wise men were gone, an angel of the Lord appeared to Joseph in a dream. "Get up! Flee to Egypt with the child and his mother," the angel said. "Stay there until I tell you to return, because Herod is going to search for the child to kill him."

[14]That night Joseph left for Egypt with the child and Mary, his mother, [15]and they stayed there until Herod's death. This fulfilled what the Lord had spoken through the prophet: "I called my Son out of Egypt."*

[16]Herod was furious when he realized that the wise men had outwitted him. He sent soldiers to kill all the boys in and around Bethlehem who were two years old and under, based on the wise men's report of the star's first appearance. [17]Herod's brutal action fulfilled what God had spoken through the prophet Jeremiah:

[18] "A cry was heard in Ramah—
weeping and great mourning.
Rachel weeps for her children,
refusing to be comforted,
for they are dead."*

2:1 Or *royal astrologers;* Greek reads *magi;* also in 2:7, 16. **2:2** Or *star in the east.* **2:6a** Greek *the rulers.* **2:6b** Mic 5:2; 2 Sam 5:2. **2:15** Hos 11:1. **2:18** Jer 31:15.

2:1–12 The Visit from the Wise Men. How did Mary and Joseph feel as these educated foreigners poured their worship and their precious gifts at Jesus' feet? Did the Magi explain their coming as they had to Herod? Did they tell Mary why they believed her son to be "the king of the Jews"? Was this the first time that the parents linked that title to their child, special though they knew him to be? And in their turn, did Joseph and Mary tell the Magi how the angel of the Lord had spoken to each of them? **11:** The *gifts* have significance beyond their intrinsic worth: *gold* symbolizes royalty; *frankincense* means prayer and worship (Deut 33:10; Ps 141:2); *myrrh* was used to anoint the bodies of the dead (John 19:39).

2:13–15 The Flight to Egypt. No sooner had the wise men set off for home than the family was in danger. **13:** Once again, Joseph is guided by an *angel.* God's loving protection surrounds them. **15:** The scheming of the insecure puppet king, Herod, is powerless in the face of the authority over life and death, fulfilling the prophecy of old.

2:16–18 Herod's Slaughter. No doubt as Joseph and Mary heard of Herod's awful retribution on innocent families in Bethlehem, their hearts grew heavy. Those children died in the place of their son, as one day, and far more profoundly, he was to die in the place of all guilty humanity. It was further irony that they were safe in Egypt, the scene of another slaughter of the innocents, from which another baby, Moses, had escaped and later led his people to safety *out of Egypt* (v. 15).

The Return to Nazareth
19 When Herod died, an angel of the Lord appeared in a dream to Joseph in Egypt. 20 "Get up!"
the angel said. "Take the child and his mother
back to the land of Israel, because those who
were trying to kill the child are dead."
21 So Joseph got up and returned to the land of
Israel with Jesus and his mother. 22 But when he
learned that the new ruler of Judea was Herod's
son Archelaus, he was afraid to go there. Then,
after being warned in a dream, he left for the region of Galilee. 23 So the family went and lived
in a town called Nazareth. This fulfilled what
the prophets had said: "He will be called a Nazarene."

John the Baptist Prepares the Way
3 In those days John the Baptist came to the
Judean wilderness and began preaching.
His message was, 2 "Repent of your sins
and turn to God, for the Kingdom of Heaven is
near.*" 3 The prophet Isaiah was speaking about
John when he said,

"He is a voice shouting in the wilderness,
'Prepare the way for the LORD's coming!
Clear the road for him!' "*

4 John's clothes were woven from coarse camel
hair, and he wore a leather belt around his waist.
For food he ate locusts and wild honey. 5 People
from Jerusalem and from all of Judea and all over
the Jordan Valley went out to see and hear John.
6 And when they confessed their sins, he baptized
them in the Jordan River.
7 But when he saw many Pharisees and Sadducees coming to watch him baptize,* he denounced them. "You brood of snakes!" he exclaimed. "Who warned you to flee God's coming
wrath? 8 Prove by the way you live that you have
repented of your sins and turned to God. 9 Don't
just say to each other, 'We're safe, for we are
descendants of Abraham.' That means nothing,
for I tell you, God can create children of Abraham from these very stones. 10 Even now the ax
of God's judgment is poised, ready to sever the
roots of the trees. Yes, every tree that does not
produce good fruit will be chopped down and
thrown into the fire.
11 "I baptize with* water those who repent of
their sins and turn to God. But someone is coming soon who is greater than I am—so much
greater that I'm not worthy even to be his slave
and carry his sandals. He will baptize you with
the Holy Spirit and with fire.* 12 He is ready to
separate the chaff from the wheat with his winnowing fork. Then he will clean up the threshing
area, gathering the wheat into his barn but burning the chaff with never-ending fire."

The Baptism of Jesus
13 Then Jesus went from Galilee to the Jordan
River to be baptized by John. 14 But John tried to
talk him out of it. "I am the one who needs to
be baptized by you," he said, "so why are you
coming to me?"

3:2 Or *has come,* or *is coming soon.* **3:3** Isa 40:3 (Greek version). **3:7** Or *coming to be baptized.* **3:11a** Or *in.* **3:11b** Or *in the Holy Spirit and in fire.*

2:19–23 The Return. Twice more Joseph is guided through *a dream*, and the family treks north to settle in Nazareth. The vulnerable child, recognizable as to his true identity only by revelation responded to by faith, is kept safe by the sovereign power of the Father for the fulfillment of his special destiny as Savior, King of the Jews.

3:1—4:25 Narrative: Preparation and the Beginnings of Public Ministry

3:1–12 The Ministry of John the Baptist. Luke (3:23) tells us that Jesus was about thirty years old when he began his public ministry, and Jesus' cousin, John the Baptist, had preceded him. Matthew gives no explanation about John's background, as Luke does, but he presents John as an authentic Jewish prophet. **2:** *The Kingdom of Heaven is near*: A prophecy that God was about to restore Israel's sovereignty, for all the world to see, in contrast to their subjugation under Roman occupation. **7–12:** John's message is unpalatable: Asking his audience to repent and be baptized means treating them as pagans wishing to convert to Judaism, not as bona fide Jews. **9:** *Descendants of Abraham*: Brushing aside the importance of Jewish descent anticipates later acceptance of Gentiles into the Christian community. **11:** *Baptize you with the Holy Spirit*: Further anticipation of the inclusion of Jew and Gentile in the community. For all, including the properly religious, John preaches fearsome and imminent judgment, rather than the immediately comforting message of imminent deliverance from their political masters.

3:13–17 The Baptism of Jesus. We do not know how well John and Jesus knew one another, although their mothers knew that their lives would be intertwined. Nor do we know how much either mother talked to her son about the circumstances of his birth. By now each knows what he must do: Jesus has sought out

15 But Jesus said, "It should be done, for we
must carry out all that God requires.*" So John
agreed to baptize him.
16 After his baptism, as Jesus came up out of
the water, the heavens were opened* and he saw
the Spirit of God descending like a dove and settling on him. 17 And a voice from heaven said,
"This is my dearly loved Son, who brings me
great joy."

The Temptation of Jesus

4 Then Jesus was led by the Spirit into the
wilderness to be tempted there by the
devil. 2 For forty days and forty nights he
fasted and became very hungry.
3 During that time the devil* came and said to
him, "If you are the Son of God, tell these stones
to become loaves of bread."
4 But Jesus told him, "No! The Scriptures
say,

'People do not live by bread alone,
but by every word that comes from the
mouth of God.'* "

5 Then the devil took him to the holy city, Jerusalem, to the highest point of the Temple, 6 and
said, "If you are the Son of God, jump off! For
the Scriptures say,

'He will order his angels to protect you.
And they will hold you up with their hands
so you won't even hurt your foot on a
stone.'* "

7 Jesus responded, "The Scriptures also say,
'You must not test the LORD your God.'* "
8 Next the devil took him to the peak of a very
high mountain and showed him all the kingdoms
of the world and their glory. 9 "I will give it all to
you," he said, "if you will kneel down and worship me."
10 "Get out of here, Satan," Jesus told him.
"For the Scriptures say,

'You must worship the LORD your God
and serve only him.'* "

11 Then the devil went away, and angels came
and took care of Jesus.

The Ministry of Jesus Begins

12 When Jesus heard that John had been arrested,
he left Judea and returned to Galilee. 13 He went
first to Nazareth, then left there and moved to
Capernaum, beside the Sea of Galilee, in the region of Zebulun and Naphtali. 14 This fulfilled
what God said through the prophet Isaiah:

15 "In the land of Zebulun and of Naphtali,
beside the sea, beyond the Jordan River,
in Galilee where so many Gentiles live,
16 the people who sat in darkness
have seen a great light.
And for those who lived in the land where
death casts its shadow,
a light has shined."*

17 From then on Jesus began to preach, "Repent of your sins and turn to God, for the Kingdom of Heaven is near.*"

The First Disciples

18 One day as Jesus was walking along the shore
of the Sea of Galilee, he saw two brothers—Simon, also called Peter, and Andrew—throwing a
net into the water, for they fished for a living.
19 Jesus called out to them, "Come, follow me, and
I will show you how to fish for people!" 20 And
they left their nets at once and followed him.
21 A little farther up the shore he saw two
other brothers, James and John, sitting in a boat
with their father, Zebedee, repairing their nets.
And he called them to come, too. 22 They imme-

3:15 Or *for we must fulfill all righteousness.* **3:16** Some manuscripts read *opened to him.* **4:3** Greek *the tempter.* **4:4** Deut 8:3. **4:6** Ps 91:11-12. **4:7** Deut 6:16. **4:10** Deut 6:13. **4:15-16** Isa 9:1-2 (Greek version). **4:17** Or *has come,* or *is coming soon.*

John, and both realize that the moment has come for Jesus' ministry to begin. **16–17:** The visible *Spirit* and the *voice from heaven* show the Father's loving affirmation.

4:1–11 The Temptation of Jesus. Jesus' temptation in the wilderness is a deliberate echo of the experience of the children of Israel in the wilderness. **2:** They had been there for forty years, Jesus for *forty days*. **3–11:** They had been disobedient and unfaithful; Jesus remained utterly faithful. They had disregarded God's word; Jesus rebuffed Satan with it.

4:12–17 Beginning of Jesus' Ministry. 12: John is imprisoned. **13–17:** Jesus travels back to the north of the country to fulfill prophecy and to proclaim the same message as John had boldly declared.

4:18–22 Calling the First Disciples. Jesus' public ministry now begins. He gathers close associates, the Twelve, starting with *Peter* and *Andrew*, followed by *James* and *John*.

diately followed him, leaving the boat and their
father behind.

Crowds Follow Jesus

23 Jesus traveled throughout the region of Galilee,
teaching in the synagogues and announcing the
Good News about the Kingdom. And he healed
every kind of disease and illness. 24 News about
him spread as far as Syria, and people soon began
bringing to him all who were sick. And whatever
their sickness or disease, or if they were demon
possessed or epileptic or paralyzed—he healed
them all. 25 Large crowds followed him wherever
he went—people from Galilee, the Ten Towns,*
Jerusalem, from all over Judea, and from east of
the Jordan River.

The Sermon on the Mount

5 One day as he saw the crowds gathering,
Jesus went up on the mountainside and sat
down. His disciples gathered around him,
2 and he began to teach them.

The Beatitudes

3 "God blesses those who are poor and realize
their need for him,*
for the Kingdom of Heaven is theirs.
4 God blesses those who mourn,
for they will be comforted.
5 God blesses those who are humble,
for they will inherit the whole earth.
6 God blesses those who hunger and thirst for
justice,*
for they will be satisfied.
7 God blesses those who are merciful,
for they will be shown mercy.
8 God blesses those whose hearts are pure,
for they will see God.
9 God blesses those who work for peace,
for they will be called the children of
God.
10 God blesses those who are persecuted for
doing right,
for the Kingdom of Heaven is theirs.

11 "God blesses you when people mock you
and persecute you and lie about you* and say all
sorts of evil things against you because you are
my followers. 12 Be happy about it! Be very glad!
For a great reward awaits you in heaven. And remember, the ancient prophets were persecuted in
the same way.

4:25 Greek *Decapolis.* **5:3** Greek *poor in spirit.* **5:6** Or *for righteousness.* **5:11** Some manuscripts do not include *and lie about you.*

4:23–25 Growing Fame. Jesus, the newcomer, begins to draw crowds from many miles away, including *Syria* and *the Ten Towns,* which were Gentile territory. Word spreads quickly: His *teaching,* his preaching, his power to heal the *sick* and to deliver the *demon-possessed* mean he has authority.

5:1–7:29 First Discourse: Living the Life of the Kingdom

Jesus, in the Sermon on the Mount, the first great discourse, spells out in practical ways what the life of the kingdom looks like. The teaching may have taken place over many hours or more than one day, and a serious, sizable crowd stayed to hear. We assume that there were women and children as well as men among the crowd. The instruction is not for men only, nor is it only for the privileged few. It is rooted in the down-to-earth, everyday life and experience of old and young, male and female, educated and uneducated. A woman could say, "I can see how this relates to my life!" Prayer is quiet conversation in ordinary language in the privacy of one's own home (6:6–14). Principles are expressed in images of yeast and lamps, in keeping the moths out of the clothes closet. Images of the home, to be sure, but among Jesus' audience, it appeals especially to a woman's world. Perhaps Mary reared her son to help with domestic chores. He seems to be at home in the language of the kitchen.

5:1–12 The Beatitudes. Jesus sets the scene against the background of the Beatitudes, following the Old Testament formula (e.g., Ps 1:1, "O the joys . . ."; Prov 3:13, "Happy . . ."). None of the blessings is associated with being a strong man or with the characteristics of those who plotted to recapture Israel by violent overthrow of the Romans. The promise of the kingdom, future or present, is to those who exemplify what in the world's eyes might often be mistaken for weakness. There is nothing flabby about any of the qualities Jesus commends. On the contrary, it may take great strength of character to persist in making them our aim. Yet in many cultures these characteristics may be seen as more womanly than manly. **12:** Jesus' message, like that of *the ancient prophets,* would cause a storm of trouble, not least for those who would throw their lot in with him. He was challenging the Zealots' commitment to violence. He was an offensive menace to the religious leaders, challenging time-honored interpretations and the requirements to keep the law and to satisfy God. He upset the status quo for many ordinary folk, leading family members to leave their homes and follow him.

Teaching about Salt and Light
13 "You are the salt of the earth. But what good
is salt if it has lost its flavor? Can you make it
salty again? It will be thrown out and trampled
underfoot as worthless.
14 "You are the light of the world—like a city
on a hilltop that cannot be hidden. 15 No one lights
a lamp and then puts it under a basket. Instead,
a lamp is placed on a stand, where it gives light
to everyone in the house. 16 In the same way, let
your good deeds shine out for all to see, so that
everyone will praise your heavenly Father.

Teaching about the Law
17 "Don't misunderstand why I have come. I did
not come to abolish the law of Moses or the
writings of the prophets. No, I came to accomplish their purpose. 18 I tell you the truth, until
heaven and earth disappear, not even the smallest detail of God's law will disappear until its
purpose is achieved. 19 So if you ignore the least
commandment and teach others to do the same,
you will be called the least in the Kingdom of
Heaven. But anyone who obeys God's laws and
teaches them will be called great in the Kingdom
of Heaven.
20 "But I warn you—unless your righteousness is better than the righteousness of the
teachers of religious law and the Pharisees, you
will never enter the Kingdom of Heaven!

Teaching about Anger
21 "You have heard that our ancestors were told,
'You must not murder. If you commit murder,
you are subject to judgment.'* 22 But I say, if you
are even angry with someone,* you are subject
to judgment! If you call someone an idiot,* you
are in danger of being brought before the court.
And if you curse someone,* you are in danger of
the fires of hell.*
23 "So if you are presenting a sacrifice* at the
altar in the Temple and you suddenly remember
that someone has something against you, 24 leave
your sacrifice there at the altar. Go and be reconciled to that person. Then come and offer your
sacrifice to God.
25 "When you are on the way to court with
your adversary, settle your differences quickly.
Otherwise, your accuser may hand you over to
the judge, who will hand you over to an officer,
and you will be thrown into prison. 26 And if that
happens, you surely won't be free again until
you have paid the last penny.*

Teaching about Adultery
27 "You have heard the commandment that says,
'You must not commit adultery.'* 28 But I say,
anyone who even looks at a woman with lust
has already committed adultery with her in his
heart. 29 So if your eye—even your good eye*—
causes you to lust, gouge it out and throw it
away. It is better for you to lose one part of your
body than for your whole body to be thrown into
hell. 30 And if your hand—even your stronger
hand*—causes you to sin, cut it off and throw it
away. It is better for you to lose one part of your
body than for your whole body to be thrown into
hell.

Teaching about Divorce
31 "You have heard the law that says, 'A man can
divorce his wife by merely giving her a written
notice of divorce.'* 32 But I say that a man who
divorces his wife, unless she has been unfaithful, causes her to commit adultery. And anyone
who marries a divorced woman also commits
adultery.

Teaching about Vows
33 "You have also heard that our ancestors were
told, 'You must not break your vows; you must
carry out the vows you make to the LORD.'*
34 But I say, do not make any vows! Do not say,
'By heaven!' because heaven is God's throne.
35 And do not say, 'By the earth!' because the
earth is his footstool. And do not say, 'By Jerusa-

5:21 Exod 20:13; Deut 5:17. **5:22a** Some manuscripts add *without cause.* **5:22b** Greek uses an Aramaic term of contempt: *If you say to your brother, 'Raca.'* **5:22c** Greek *if you say, 'You fool.'* **5:22d** Greek *Gehenna;* also in 5:29, 30. **5:23** Greek *gift;* also in 5:24. **5:26** Greek *the last kodrantes* [i.e., quadrans]. **5:27** Exod 20:14; Deut 5:18. **5:29** Greek *your right eye.* **5:30** Greek *your right hand.* **5:31** Deut 24:1. **5:33** Num 30:2.

5:13–20 How Jesus' Followers Are to Live. 13–16: With religious, political, and community leaders all ranged against Jesus, his followers could expect opposition, especially since they were to live out their commitment to him openly. They must live lives of such transparent goodness that those looking on would be won over in spite of themselves. **17–20:** Yet contrary to accusation, Jesus was asking them to be more truly Jewish, not less so.

5:21–48 Six Illustrations of Commitment to Perfection. For the men and women gathered on the hillside, the application of the law to inner spirit and motivation, not just outward action, must have been breathtaking. **21–26:** *Murder* and anger. **27–30:** *Adultery* and *lust.* **31–32:** *Divorce.* **33–37:** *Vows* and

lem!' for Jerusalem is the city of the great King. 36 Do not even say, 'By my head!' for you can't turn one hair white or black. 37 Just say a simple, 'Yes, I will,' or 'No, I won't.' Anything beyond this is from the evil one.

Teaching about Revenge

38 "You have heard the law that says the punishment must match the injury: 'An eye for an eye, and a tooth for a tooth.'* 39 But I say, do not resist an evil person! If someone slaps you on the right cheek, offer the other cheek also. 40 If you are sued in court and your shirt is taken from you, give your coat, too. 41 If a soldier demands that you carry his gear for a mile,* carry it two miles. 42 Give to those who ask, and don't turn away from those who want to borrow.

Teaching about Love for Enemies

43 "You have heard the law that says, 'Love your neighbor'* and hate your enemy. 44 But I say, love your enemies!* Pray for those who persecute you! 45 In that way, you will be acting as true children of your Father in heaven. For he gives his sunlight to both the evil and the good, and he sends rain on the just and the unjust alike. 46 If you love only those who love you, what reward is there for that? Even corrupt tax collectors do that much. 47 If you are kind only to your friends,* how are you different from anyone else? Even pagans do that. 48 But you are to be perfect, even as your Father in heaven is perfect.

Teaching about Giving to the Needy

6 "Watch out! Don't do your good deeds publicly, to be admired by others, for you will lose the reward from your Father in heaven. 2 When you give to someone in need, don't do as the hypocrites do—blowing trumpets in the synagogues and streets to call attention to their acts of charity! I tell you the truth, they have received all the reward they will ever get. 3 But when you give to someone in need, don't let your left hand know what your right hand is doing. 4 Give your gifts in private, and your Father, who sees everything, will reward you.

Teaching about Prayer and Fasting

5 "When you pray, don't be like the hypocrites who love to pray publicly on street corners and in the synagogues where everyone can see them. I tell you the truth, that is all the reward they will ever get. 6 But when you pray, go away by yourself, shut the door behind you, and pray to your Father in private. Then your Father, who sees everything, will reward you.

7 "When you pray, don't babble on and on as people of other religions do. They think their prayers are answered merely by repeating their words again and again. 8 Don't be like them, for

5:38 Greek *the law that says: 'An eye for an eye and a tooth for a tooth.'* Exod 21:24; Lev 24:20; Deut 19:21. **5:41** Greek *milion* [4,854 feet or 1,478 meters]. **5:43** Lev 19:18. **5:44** Some manuscripts add *Bless those who curse you. Do good to those who hate you.* Compare Luke 6:27-28. **5:47** Greek *your brothers.*

---

truth-telling. **38–42:** Revenge. **43–47:** *Love your enemies.* **48:** Concluding exhortation: *You are to be perfect, even as your Father in heaven is perfect.* What lesser standard could meet the need? If you really want to see the restoration of the kingdom, it's not about kicking out the Romans, it's about living according to the mandate of the King. This teaching is shocking. How could anyone possibly meet such standards? Among modern Christians, the Sermon on the Mount is usually regarded as inspiring and comforting, but most of it is profoundly disturbing. A woman might be less likely than a man to commit murder, but she could certainly feel anger. She might not be able to take the initiative in divorce; but she could fantasize about someone else's spouse. She could not take refuge in her powerlessness in a patriarchal society, because sin bubbles up from the deepest recesses of human motivation, whether circumstance permits action or not.

6:1–18 Religious Observance: Charity, Prayer, Fasting. Public performance of *good deeds* is not acceptable. It may have seemed that Jesus' criticisms were directed toward men rather than women, because it would have been men *blowing trumpets* to announce their generosity; men who would *pray publicly;* men who would *look miserable* while they were fasting. Yet women, then as now, had ways of drawing attention to themselves when they wished for recognition of their virtues; quite as much as men, women could have sinful motives for their religious observances. Jesus' words would have challenged the integrity of anyone with ears to hear. But charity, prayer, and fasting were as open to women as to men and compatible with a more restricted, domestic life. It is estimated that the majority of secret believers in hostile contexts are women. What a comfort that, with or without the approval of those around for one's Christian faith, with or without access to a place of worship and public Christian life, a woman may find many quiet ways of being generous to those in need, of concentrating deep within on the Lord, and of praying in the simplest of words directly to her Father in heaven. **4, 6, 18:** *Your Father, who sees everything, will reward you.*

your Father knows exactly what you need even
before you ask him! 9 Pray like this:

Our Father in heaven,
may your name be kept holy.
10 May your Kingdom come soon.
May your will be done on earth,
as it is in heaven.
11 Give us today the food we need,*
12 and forgive us our sins,
as we have forgiven those who sin
against us.
13 And don't let us yield to temptation,*
but rescue us from the evil one.*

14 "If you forgive those who sin against you,
your heavenly Father will forgive you. 15 But if
you refuse to forgive others, your Father will not
forgive your sins.
16 "And when you fast, don't make it obvious,
as the hypocrites do, for they try to look miserable and disheveled so people will admire them
for their fasting. I tell you the truth, that is the
only reward they will ever get. 17 But when you
fast, comb your hair and wash your face. 18 Then
no one will notice that you are fasting, except
your Father, who knows what you do in private.
And your Father, who sees everything, will reward you.

Teaching about Money and Possessions

19 "Don't store up treasures here on earth, where
moths eat them and rust destroys them, and
where thieves break in and steal. 20 Store your
treasures in heaven, where moths and rust cannot destroy, and thieves do not break in and steal.
21 Wherever your treasure is, there the desires of
your heart will also be.
22 "Your eye is a lamp that provides light for
your body. When your eye is good, your whole
body is filled with light. 23 But when your eye is
bad, your whole body is filled with darkness. And
if the light you think you have is actually darkness, how deep that darkness is!
24 "No one can serve two masters. For you will
hate one and love the other; you will be devoted
to one and despise the other. You cannot serve
both God and money.
25 "That is why I tell you not to worry about
everyday life—whether you have enough food
and drink, or enough clothes to wear. Isn't life
more than food, and your body more than clothing? 26 Look at the birds. They don't plant or harvest or store food in barns, for your heavenly
Father feeds them. And aren't you far more valuable to him than they are? 27 Can all your worries
add a single moment to your life?
28 "And why worry about your clothing? Look
at the lilies of the field and how they grow. They
don't work or make their clothing, 29 yet Solomon
in all his glory was not dressed as beautifully as
they are. 30 And if God cares so wonderfully for
wildflowers that are here today and thrown into
the fire tomorrow, he will certainly care for you.
Why do you have so little faith?
31 "So don't worry about these things, saying,
'What will we eat? What will we drink? What will
we wear?' 32 These things dominate the thoughts
of unbelievers, but your heavenly Father already
knows all your needs. 33 Seek the Kingdom of
God* above all else, and live righteously, and he
will give you everything you need.
34 "So don't worry about tomorrow, for tomorrow will bring its own worries. Today's trouble is
enough for today.

Do Not Judge Others

7 "Do not judge others, and you will not be
judged. 2 For you will be treated as you treat
others.* The standard you use in judging is
the standard by which you will be judged.*
3 "And why worry about a speck in your
friend's eye* when you have a log in your own?
4 How can you think of saying to your friend,*
'Let me help you get rid of that speck in your
eye,' when you can't see past the log in your own
eye? 5 Hypocrite! First get rid of the log in your
own eye; then you will see well enough to deal
with the speck in your friend's eye.
6 "Don't waste what is holy on people who are

6:11 Or *Give us today our food for the day;* or *Give us today our food for tomorrow.* **6:13a** Or *And keep us from being tested.* **6:13b** Or *from evil.* Some manuscripts add *For yours is the kingdom and the power and the glory forever. Amen.* **6:33** Some manuscripts do not include *of God.* **7:2a** Or *For God will judge you as you judge others.* **7:2b** Or *The measure you give will be the measure you get back.* **7:3** Greek *your brother's eye;* also in 7:5. **7:4** Greek *your brother.*

6:19–34 Money, Possessions, and Worries. From here to the end of the sermon, with the exception of 7:22–27, every injunction, every illustration, is as inescapably directed to women as to men. Every principle is couched in language of home and garden: concern over food and drink and clothing, issues of values by which to live, straightforward dealings with God and with the people around one, recognition that it is all too easy to be critical of others while woefully deluded about ourselves.

7:1–29 The Behavior of True Disciples. 1–6: Judging

unholy.* Don't throw your pearls to pigs! They
will trample the pearls, then turn and attack you.

Effective Prayer
7 "Keep on asking, and you will receive what you
ask for. Keep on seeking, and you will find. Keep
on knocking, and the door will be opened to you.
8 For everyone who asks, receives. Everyone who
seeks, finds. And to everyone who knocks, the
door will be opened.
9 "You parents—if your children ask for a loaf
of bread, do you give them a stone instead? 10 Or
if they ask for a fish, do you give them a snake?
Of course not! 11 So if you sinful people know
how to give good gifts to your children, how
much more will your heavenly Father give good
gifts to those who ask him.

The Golden Rule
12 "Do to others whatever you would like them to
do to you. This is the essence of all that is taught
in the law and the prophets.

The Narrow Gate
13 "You can enter God's Kingdom only through
the narrow gate. The highway to hell* is broad,
and its gate is wide for the many who choose that
way. 14 But the gateway to life is very narrow and
the road is difficult, and only a few ever find it.

The Tree and Its Fruit
15 "Beware of false prophets who come disguised
as harmless sheep but are really vicious wolves.
16 You can identify them by their fruit, that is,
by the way they act. Can you pick grapes from
thornbushes, or figs from thistles? 17 A good tree
produces good fruit, and a bad tree produces bad
fruit. 18 A good tree can't produce bad fruit, and a
bad tree can't produce good fruit. 19 So every tree
that does not produce good fruit is chopped down
and thrown into the fire. 20 Yes, just as you can
identify a tree by its fruit, so you can identify
people by their actions.

True Disciples
21 "Not everyone who calls out to me, 'Lord!
Lord!' will enter the Kingdom of Heaven. Only
those who actually do the will of my Father in
heaven will enter. 22 On judgment day many will
say to me, 'Lord! Lord! We prophesied in your
name and cast out demons in your name and
performed many miracles in your name.' 23 But I
will reply, 'I never knew you. Get away from me,
you who break God's laws.'

Building on a Solid Foundation
24 "Anyone who listens to my teaching and follows it is wise, like a person who builds a house
on solid rock. 25 Though the rain comes in torrents and the floodwaters rise and the winds
beat against that house, it won't collapse because
it is built on bedrock. 26 But anyone who hears
my teaching and doesn't obey it is foolish, like a
person who builds a house on sand. 27 When the
rains and floods come and the winds beat against
that house, it will collapse with a mighty crash."
28 When Jesus had finished saying these
things, the crowds were amazed at his teaching,
29 for he taught with real authority—quite unlike
their teachers of religious law.

Jesus Heals a Man with Leprosy
8 Large crowds followed Jesus as he came
down the mountainside. 2 Suddenly, a man
with leprosy approached him and knelt be-

7:6 Greek *Don't give the sacred to dogs.* **7:13** Greek *The road that leads to destruction.*

oneself in preference to judging others. **7–11:** Praying effectively. **12:** The Golden Rule. **13–14:** *The narrow gate* is the difficult way. **16:** *Fruit . . . actions:* One's acts reveal what one truly is. **21–27:** Public ministry and house building were male preserves, but the principle could easily be illustrated in women's terms. The Master's lessons connect concretely with the daily realities of his audience's lives. This can be an example to copy as we try to communicate Christian truth today. **28–29:** Who is this Jesus? The one who *taught with real authority*. What did Jesus' mother, Mary, make of the reports that came back to her? Did she see the connection between the Beatitudes and the song she had sung before his birth (Luke 1:46–55)? Did she wonder how what was happening fulfilled the word of the angel of the Lord to Joseph, "you are to name him Jesus, for he will save his people from their sins" (1:21)?

8:1—9:38 Narrative: Demonstrating the Life of the Kingdom

Much of this section describes Jesus engaged in healing the sick, either in general terms or in thumbnail sketches of particular individuals.

8:1–4 Healing a Man with Leprosy. *Leprosy* made a person unclean; nevertheless, Jesus *touched* the man, which must have caused quite a stir. In some cultures females are much more tactile than men, though men may hug young children. In many cultures, for a man to touch a woman, other than those

fore him. "Lord," the man said, "if you are willing, you can heal me and make me clean."
[3]Jesus reached out and touched him. "I am
willing," he said. "Be healed!" And instantly the
leprosy disappeared. [4]Then Jesus said to him,
"Don't tell anyone about this. Instead, go to the
priest and let him examine you. Take along the
offering required in the law of Moses for those
who have been healed of leprosy.* This will be a
public testimony that you have been cleansed."

The Faith of a Roman Officer

[5]When Jesus returned to Capernaum, a Roman
officer* came and pleaded with him, [6]"Lord, my
young servant* lies in bed, paralyzed and in terrible pain."
[7]Jesus said, "I will come and heal him."
[8]But the officer said, "Lord, I am not worthy
to have you come into my home. Just say the
word from where you are, and my servant will
be healed. [9]I know this because I am under the
authority of my superior officers, and I have authority over my soldiers. I only need to say, 'Go,'
and they go, or 'Come,' and they come. And if I
say to my slaves, 'Do this,' they do it."
[10]When Jesus heard this, he was amazed.
Turning to those who were following him, he
said, "I tell you the truth, I haven't seen faith like
this in all Israel! [11]And I tell you this, that many
Gentiles will come from all over the world—
from east and west—and sit down with Abraham,
Isaac, and Jacob at the feast in the Kingdom of
Heaven. [12]But many Israelites—those for whom
the Kingdom was prepared—will be thrown into
outer darkness, where there will be weeping and
gnashing of teeth."
[13]Then Jesus said to the Roman officer, "Go
back home. Because you believed, it has happened." And the young servant was healed that
same hour.

Jesus Heals Many People

[14]When Jesus arrived at Peter's house, Peter's
mother-in-law was sick in bed with a high fever.
[15]But when Jesus touched her hand, the fever left
her. Then she got up and prepared a meal for him.
[16]That evening many demon-possessed people were brought to Jesus. He cast out the evil
spirits with a simple command, and he healed
all the sick. [17]This fulfilled the word of the Lord
through the prophet Isaiah, who said,

"He took our sicknesses
and removed our diseases."*

The Cost of Following Jesus

[18]When Jesus saw the crowd around him, he instructed his disciples to cross to the other side of
the lake.
[19]Then one of the teachers of religious law
said to him, "Teacher, I will follow you wherever
you go."

8:4 See Lev 14:2-32. **8:5** Greek *a centurion;* similarly in 8:8, 13. **8:6** Or *child;* also in 8:13. **8:17** Isa 53:4.

of his very closest family, would be scandalous. Yet all around the world, healing and compassionate touch are closely associated, perhaps explaining why many nurses, whose gentle touch is often crucial to patients' recovery, are women. Why is touch so important? Perhaps it communicates security and love, which is why abusive touch is experienced as betrayal. Jesus' touch is that of divine authority, not of magic; his authority was incontrovertible whether or not he touched the person being healed.

8:5–13 Healing the Officer's Servant. Healing was accomplished by word of command. The main point of the story is the officer's *faith* in Jesus' healing power. Jesus is clearly commending the officer's faith and recognition of the Lord's authority. Jesus' statement that some Gentiles will enter the kingdom while some Jews will be excluded must have been shocking, but Matthew is selecting teachings that lie behind the great conclusion of his Gospel.

8:14–17 Healing Peter's Mother-in-Law and Many Others. The family welcomed Jesus among them and recognized the honor of his company. **15:** *Prepared a meal*: Peter's mother-in-law must have been in charge of the domestic arrangements. A woman expecting guests would have to be quite sick before she would take to her bed. So the fever of which Jesus healed her may have been severe.

8:18–22 Cost of Being a Disciple. Jesus responds to an effusive volunteer by warning that discipleship strips away all other security; he responds to a cautious volunteer by demanding unconditional and immediate discipleship in terms that would have been shocking in that culture. For the first time in this Gospel, where there are a further twenty-nine occurrences, Jesus appears to lay claim to the title *Son of Man*, resonating with Old Testament content (Dan 7:13) that was used for the figure bringing in the end of the present era.

8:23–27 Stilling the Storm. This follows shortly after the first use of *Son of Man* and brings the response, *Even the winds and waves obey him!*

20 But Jesus replied, "Foxes have dens to live
in, and birds have nests, but the Son of Man* has
no place even to lay his head."
21 Another of his disciples said, "Lord, first let
me return home and bury my father."
22 But Jesus told him, "Follow me now. Let the
spiritually dead bury their own dead.*"

Jesus Calms the Storm

23 Then Jesus got into the boat and started across
the lake with his disciples. 24 Suddenly, a fierce
storm struck the lake, with waves breaking into
the boat. But Jesus was sleeping. 25 The disciples
went and woke him up, shouting, "Lord, save us!
We're going to drown!"
26 Jesus responded, "Why are you afraid? You
have so little faith!" Then he got up and rebuked
the wind and waves, and suddenly there was a
great calm.
27 The disciples were amazed. "Who is this
man?" they asked. "Even the winds and waves
obey him!"

Jesus Heals Two Demon-Possessed Men

28 When Jesus arrived on the other side of the
lake, in the region of the Gadarenes,* two men
who were possessed by demons met him. They
lived in a cemetery and were so violent that no
one could go through that area.
29 They began screaming at him, "Why are
you interfering with us, Son of God? Have you
come here to torture us before God's appointed
time?"
30 There happened to be a large herd of pigs
feeding in the distance. 31 So the demons begged,
"If you cast us out, send us into that herd of
pigs."
32 "All right, go!" Jesus commanded them. So
the demons came out of the men and entered the
pigs, and the whole herd plunged down the steep
hillside into the lake and drowned in the water.
33 The herdsmen fled to the nearby town, telling everyone what happened to the demon-possessed men. 34 Then the entire town came out to
meet Jesus, but they begged him to go away and
leave them alone.

Jesus Heals a Paralyzed Man

9 Jesus climbed into a boat and went back
across the lake to his own town. 2 Some
people brought to him a paralyzed man on
a mat. Seeing their faith, Jesus said to the paralyzed man, "Be encouraged, my child! Your sins
are forgiven."
3 But some of the teachers of religious law
said to themselves, "That's blasphemy! Does he
think he's God?"
4 Jesus knew* what they were thinking, so
he asked them, "Why do you have such evil
thoughts in your hearts? 5 Is it easier to say 'Your
sins are forgiven,' or 'Stand up and walk'? 6 So I
will prove to you that the Son of Man* has the
authority on earth to forgive sins." Then Jesus
turned to the paralyzed man and said, "Stand up,
pick up your mat, and go home!"
7 And the man jumped up and went home!
8 Fear swept through the crowd as they saw this
happen. And they praised God for sending a man
with such great authority.*

Jesus Calls Matthew

9 As Jesus was walking along, he saw a man named
Matthew sitting at his tax collector's booth. "Follow me and be my disciple," Jesus said to him. So
Matthew got up and followed him.
10 Later, Matthew invited Jesus and his disciples to his home as dinner guests, along with
many tax collectors and other disreputable sinners. 11 But when the Pharisees saw this, they
asked his disciples, "Why does your teacher eat
with such scum?*"
12 When Jesus heard this, he said, "Healthy
people don't need a doctor—sick people do."
13 Then he added, "Now go and learn the meaning of this Scripture: 'I want you to show mercy,
not offer sacrifices.'* For I have come to call not

8:20 "Son of Man" is a title Jesus used for himself. **8:22** Greek *Let the dead bury their own dead.* **8:28** Other manuscripts read *Gerasenes;* still others read *Gergesenes.* Compare Mark 5:1; Luke 8:26. **9:4** Some manuscripts read *saw.* **9:6** "Son of Man" is a title Jesus used for himself. **9:8** Greek *for giving such authority to human beings.* **9:11** Greek *with tax collectors and sinners?* **9:13** Hos 6:6 (Greek version).

8:28–33 Healing Two Demon-Possessed Men. Jesus demonstrates authority over the powers of darkness and the spirit world, and power to deal with sin and all its consequences. **29:** The demons recognize his true identity and call him *Son of God.*

9:1–8 Healing a Paralyzed Man. 3: The outraged *teachers of religious law* cannot recognize his true identity and the authority that flows from it, and they call him a blasphemer.

9:9–13 The Call of Matthew. *Tax collectors* were despised because they tended to extort the maximum payment they could get from the people and because they were collaborators with the occupying Roman government. It is the excluded who become the included. The *Pharisees* concede that Jesus is a *teacher* but think his powers are satanic in origin (v. 34).

those who think they are righteous, but those
who know they are sinners."

A Discussion about Fasting

14 One day the disciples of John the Baptist came
to Jesus and asked him, "Why don't your disciples fast* like we do and the Pharisees do?"

15 Jesus replied, "Do wedding guests mourn
while celebrating with the groom? Of course not.
But someday the groom will be taken away from
them, and then they will fast.

16 "Besides, who would patch old clothing with
new cloth? For the new patch would shrink and
rip away from the old cloth, leaving an even bigger tear than before.

17 "And no one puts new wine into old wineskins. For the old skins would burst from the
pressure, spilling the wine and ruining the skins.
New wine is stored in new wineskins so that
both are preserved."

Jesus Heals in Response to Faith

18 As Jesus was saying this, the leader of a synagogue came and knelt before him. "My daughter
has just died," he said, "but you can bring her
back to life again if you just come and lay your
hand on her."

19 So Jesus and his disciples got up and went
with him. 20 Just then a woman who had suffered
for twelve years with constant bleeding came up
behind him. She touched the fringe of his robe,
21 for she thought, "If I can just touch his robe, I
will be healed."

22 Jesus turned around, and when he saw her
he said, "Daughter, be encouraged! Your faith
has made you well." And the woman was healed
at that moment.

23 When Jesus arrived at the official's home,
he saw the noisy crowd and heard the funeral
music. 24 "Get out!" he told them. "The girl isn't
dead; she's only asleep." But the crowd laughed
at him. 25 After the crowd was put outside, however, Jesus went in and took the girl by the hand,
and she stood up! 26 The report of this miracle
swept through the entire countryside.

Jesus Heals the Blind

27 After Jesus left the girl's home, two blind men
followed along behind him, shouting, "Son of
David, have mercy on us!"

28 They went right into the house where he
was staying, and Jesus asked them, "Do you believe I can make you see?"

"Yes, Lord," they told him, "we do."

29 Then he touched their eyes and said, "Because of your faith, it will happen." 30 Then their
eyes were opened, and they could see! Jesus
sternly warned them, "Don't tell anyone about
this." 31 But instead, they went out and spread his
fame all over the region.

32 When they left, a demon-possessed man who
couldn't speak was brought to Jesus. 33 So Jesus cast
out the demon, and then the man began to speak.
The crowds were amazed. "Nothing like this has
ever happened in Israel!" they exclaimed.

34 But the Pharisees said, "He can cast out demons because he is empowered by the prince of
demons."

The Need for Workers

35 Jesus traveled through all the towns and villages of that area, teaching in the synagogues and

9:14 Some manuscripts read *fast often*.

9:14–26 Sayings about the Kingdom and Healings. 14–17: Jesus' presence is a new thing; old practices are no longer appropriate. **18–26:** These two intertwined healings show how Jesus reacts to the hemorrhaging woman and his touching of the dead child, offering challenges to misunderstandings about sin and uncleanness. **20–22:** Instructions originally given for protection and hygiene had become grounds of cruel rejection (see Menstruation, Gen 31). Sexual intercourse during a woman's menstruation is unwise, less because it is messy than because the woman's internal tissues are especially vulnerable at such a time to infection. God's instructions are compassionate and for the protection of women. But women had been treated as dirty and polluting during menstruation; should they so much as brush against a man at such a time they could be treated to a torrent of abuse and anger. Desperation and faith drive this woman to risk touching Jesus' cloak. Her *faith* is not misplaced. Instead of the rejection she must have experienced every day for those twelve long years, here is a loving welcome and total healing. The excluded finds herself among the included. **23–26:** Jesus is ambiguous about the little girl: She *isn't dead; she's only asleep*. Yet those gathered are sure that the child is dead: *The funeral music* is playing, and *the crowd laughed at* Jesus' assertion. But in raising the little girl Jesus graphically demonstrates that there is life beyond death, and he is Lord of it. Who is this Jesus? The one who holds power over life and death in his hands.

9:27–34 Two Blind Men and a Mute Man Healed. 27: *Son of David*, another title with Old Testament overtones and ambiguities: Is he one of David's innumerable descendants, or a specially anointed king,

announcing the Good News about the Kingdom.
And he healed every kind of disease and illness.
36 When he saw the crowds, he had compassion on
them because they were confused and helpless,
like sheep without a shepherd. 37 He said to his
disciples, "The harvest is great, but the workers
are few. 38 So pray to the Lord who is in charge of
the harvest; ask him to send more workers into
his fields."

Jesus Sends Out the Twelve Apostles

10 Jesus called his twelve disciples together and gave them authority to
cast out evil* spirits and to heal every
kind of disease and illness. 2 Here are the names
of the twelve apostles:

first, Simon (also called Peter),
then Andrew (Peter's brother),
James (son of Zebedee),
John (James's brother),
3 Philip,
Bartholomew,
Thomas,
Matthew (the tax collector),
James (son of Alphaeus),
Thaddaeus,*
4 Simon (the zealot*),
Judas Iscariot (who later betrayed him).

5 Jesus sent out the twelve apostles with these
instructions: "Don't go to the Gentiles or the
Samaritans, 6 but only to the people of Israel—
God's lost sheep. 7 Go and announce to them
that the Kingdom of Heaven is near.* 8 Heal the
sick, raise the dead, cure those with leprosy, and
cast out demons. Give as freely as you have received!

9 "Don't take any money in your money
belts—no gold, silver, or even copper coins.
10 Don't carry a traveler's bag with a change of
clothes and sandals or even a walking stick. Don't
hesitate to accept hospitality, because those who
work deserve to be fed.

11 "Whenever you enter a city or village,
search for a worthy person and stay in his home
until you leave town. 12 When you enter the
home, give it your blessing. 13 If it turns out to
be a worthy home, let your blessing stand; if it
is not, take back the blessing. 14 If any household or town refuses to welcome you or listen
to your message, shake its dust from your feet as
you leave. 15 I tell you the truth, the wicked cities
of Sodom and Gomorrah will be better off than
such a town on the judgment day.

16 "Look, I am sending you out as sheep among
wolves. So be as shrewd as snakes and harmless
as doves. 17 But beware! For you will be handed
over to the courts and will be flogged with whips
in the synagogues. 18 You will stand trial before
governors and kings because you are my followers. But this will be your opportunity to tell the

10:1 Greek *unclean.* **10:3** Other manuscripts read *Lebbaeus;* still others read *Lebbaeus who is called Thaddaeus.* **10:4** Greek *the Cananean,* an Aramaic term for Jewish nationalists. **10:7** Or *has come,* or *is coming soon.*

---

as was David? **34:** Again the religious authorities cannot recognize Jesus' true power.

9:35–38 The Need for Workers. 36–37: *Sheep without a shepherd*: Jesus' call for more *workers* is primarily for the benefit of the *crowds,* not for his own glory. This is an allusion to Ezekiel 34 and the failure of current religious leaders to fulfill their calling. Against that background, he insists that there is genuine spiritual responsiveness, if only there were those to harvest it.

10:1–42 Second Discourse: The Mission of the Kingdom

Jesus says the disciples must pray for the Lord to commission harvesters. Perhaps, as has happened frequently in the history of Christian mission, the disciples prayed and found themselves being called to be the answer. **1:** Jesus summons *the twelve disciples* and invests them with authority over sickness and demons. **2–4:** Matthew lists the names. They are, of course, all men. Some interpreters have used this in their argument that all Christian leadership must be vested in men (although they do not also insist that they must all be Jewish and that there must be twelve of them). It is extremely unlikely that Jesus is making such a point. He is using powerful symbolism, as have others before him: This group represents the twelve tribes of Israel but also the true spiritual Israel, the faithful remnant. **5–8:** God had promised (Ezek 34:11–31) to shepherd God's people. Jesus instructs the Twelve to go only to *the people of Israel. The Kingdom of Heaven is near . . . heal the sick, raise the dead, cure those with leprosy, and cast out demons,* the signs of the Lord's ministry. **9–42:** Jesus gives further instructions and warnings. The disciples can expect hostile responses and suffering. This is no promise of easy success. However plentiful the harvest may be, that may not be the dominant experience of the harvesters. They may be more aware of rejection, persecution, vulnerability, getting hurt, being frightened and hated, of families being set at loggerheads among themselves even to the extent of betrayal to death. **11–12:** There will be those who

rulers and other unbelievers about me.* 19 When
you are arrested, don't worry about how to respond or what to say. God will give you the right
words at the right time. 20 For it is not you who
will be speaking—it will be the Spirit of your Father speaking through you.
21 "A brother will betray his brother to death,
a father will betray his own child, and children
will rebel against their parents and cause them
to be killed. 22 And all nations will hate you because you are my followers.* But everyone who
endures to the end will be saved. 23 When you are
persecuted in one town, flee to the next. I tell you
the truth, the Son of Man* will return before
you have reached all the towns of Israel.
24 "Students* are not greater than their teacher, and slaves are not greater than their master.
25 Students are to be like their teacher, and slaves
are to be like their master. And since I, the master
of the household, have been called the prince of
demons,* the members of my household will be
called by even worse names!
26 "But don't be afraid of those who threaten
you. For the time is coming when everything
that is covered will be revealed, and all that is secret will be made known to all. 27 What I tell you
now in the darkness, shout abroad when daybreak comes. What I whisper in your ear, shout
from the housetops for all to hear!
28 "Don't be afraid of those who want to kill
your body; they cannot touch your soul. Fear
only God, who can destroy both soul and body in
hell.* 29 What is the price of two sparrows—one
copper coin*? But not a single sparrow can fall
to the ground without your Father knowing it.
30 And the very hairs on your head are all numbered. 31 So don't be afraid; you are more valuable
to God than a whole flock of sparrows.
32 "Everyone who acknowledges me publicly
here on earth, I will also acknowledge before my
Father in heaven. 33 But everyone who denies me
here on earth, I will also deny before my Father
in heaven.
34 "Don't imagine that I came to bring peace
to the earth! I came not to bring peace, but a
sword.
35 'I have come to set a man against his father,
a daughter against her mother,
and a daughter-in-law against her mother-in-law.
36 Your enemies will be right in your own household!'*
37 "If you love your father or mother more
than you love me, you are not worthy of being
mine; or if you love your son or daughter more
than me, you are not worthy of being mine. 38 If
you refuse to take up your cross and follow me,
you are not worthy of being mine. 39 If you cling
to your life, you will lose it; but if you give up
your life for me, you will find it.
40 "Anyone who receives you receives me,
and anyone who receives me receives the Father who sent me. 41 If you receive a prophet as
one who speaks for God,* you will be given the
same reward as a prophet. And if you receive
righteous people because of their righteousness,
you will be given a reward like theirs. 42 And if
you give even a cup of cold water to one of the
least of my followers, you will surely be rewarded."

Jesus and John the Baptist

11 When Jesus had finished giving these
instructions to his twelve disciples, he
went out to teach and preach in towns
throughout the region.

10:18 Or *But this will be your testimony against the rulers and other unbelievers.* **10:22** Greek *on account of my name.* **10:23** "Son of Man" is a title Jesus used for himself. **10:24** Or *Disciples.* **10:25** Greek *Beelzeboul;* other manuscripts read *Beezeboul;* Latin version reads *Beelzebub.* **10:28** Greek *Gehenna.* **10:29** Greek *one assarion* [i.e., one "as," a Roman coin equal to $^1/_{16}$ of a denarius]. **10:35-36** Mic 7:6. **10:41** Greek *receive a prophet in the name of a prophet.*

will welcome them and feed and house them. **19–20:** When they are hauled before the authorities, *the Spirit of your Father* will give them words to speak in self-defense. **32:** Jesus will be their advocate in heaven. **38:** Perhaps Jesus had experienced these oppressions much more than Matthew records up to this point, or perhaps he knows that from now on it will all steadily intensify. It is at this moment that Matthew first records Jesus speaking of the *cross.* If ever there had been a moment of romantic idealism in the heads of any of the disciples, it should surely have been banished now. It may have been twelve men who first received these awesome instructions, but many women have been commissioned too. They have experienced firsthand the suffering but also the promises Jesus spoke of that day, as they take up their crosses and follow.

11:1—12:50 Narrative: Opposition to the Kingdom

There is a world of difference between knowing in theory that suffering is part of following Christ and experiencing it.

[2]John the Baptist, who was in prison, heard about all the things the Messiah was doing. So he sent his disciples to ask Jesus, [3]"Are you the Messiah we've been expecting,* or should we keep looking for someone else?"

[4]Jesus told them, "Go back to John and tell him what you have heard and seen—[5]the blind see, the lame walk, the lepers are cured, the deaf hear, the dead are raised to life, and the Good News is being preached to the poor. [6]And tell him, 'God blesses those who do not turn away because of me.*' "

[7]As John's disciples were leaving, Jesus began talking about him to the crowds. "What kind of man did you go into the wilderness to see? Was he a weak reed, swayed by every breath of wind? [8]Or were you expecting to see a man dressed in expensive clothes? No, people with expensive clothes live in palaces. [9]Were you looking for a prophet? Yes, and he is more than a prophet. [10]John is the man to whom the Scriptures refer when they say,

'Look, I am sending my messenger ahead of you,
and he will prepare your way before you.'*

[11]"I tell you the truth, of all who have ever lived, none is greater than John the Baptist. Yet even the least person in the Kingdom of Heaven is greater than he is! [12]And from the time John the Baptist began preaching until now, the Kingdom of Heaven has been forcefully advancing,* and violent people are attacking it. [13]For before John came, all the prophets and the law of Moses looked forward to this present time. [14]And if you are willing to accept what I say, he is Elijah, the one the prophets said would come.* [15]Anyone with ears to hear should listen and understand!

[16]"To what can I compare this generation? It is like children playing a game in the public square. They complain to their friends,

[17]'We played wedding songs,
and you didn't dance,
so we played funeral songs,
and you didn't mourn.'

[18]For John didn't spend his time eating and drinking, and you say, 'He's possessed by a demon.' [19]The Son of Man,* on the other hand, feasts and drinks, and you say, 'He's a glutton and a drunkard, and a friend of tax collectors and other sinners!' But wisdom is shown to be right by its results."

Judgment for the Unbelievers

[20]Then Jesus began to denounce the towns where he had done so many of his miracles, because they hadn't repented of their sins and turned to God. [21]"What sorrow awaits you, Korazin and Bethsaida! For if the miracles I did in you had been done in wicked Tyre and Sidon, their people would have repented of their sins long ago, clothing themselves in burlap and throwing ashes on their heads to show their remorse. [22]I tell you, Tyre and Sidon will be better off on judgment day than you.

[23]"And you people of Capernaum, will you be honored in heaven? No, you will go down to the place of the dead.* For if the miracles I did for you had been done in wicked Sodom, it would

11:3 Greek *Are you the one who is coming?* **11:6** Or *who are not offended by me.* **11:10** Mal 3:1. **11:12** Or *the Kingdom of Heaven has suffered from violence.* **11:14** See Mal 4:5. **11:19** "Son of Man" is a title Jesus used for himself. **11:23** Greek *to Hades.*

11:1–19 Jesus and John. 2–3: John the Baptist, imprisoned and perhaps expecting a rather different unfolding of events once Jesus began his public ministry, begins to entertain doubts. Had he staked his life on the wrong person? Is Jesus only another forerunner, pointing to someone still to come? **4–6:** When tempted by Satan, Jesus hadn't argued but simply responded with Scripture (4:1–11). Now again he echoes God's word, this time the messianic prophecies in Isaiah 35:4–6 and Isaiah 61:1. **7–19:** If Jesus is who John says he is, why, the crowds wonder, hasn't he stepped in to free John from prison? This failure to meet their expectations makes them wary of John and Jesus. They have been happy to have him heal the sick and exorcise the demonized. But what about the rest of their agenda? Presuppositions can prevent us from recognizing the truth when it is in front of us. Jesus tells the crowds that they are right to believe that John is a prophet.

11:20–24 Judgment. Jesus says that failure to understand what is going on is not just unfortunate, it is profoundly culpable; and many of those communities that have seen and heard John, and now Jesus, can look forward only to the most fearful judgment. God had said in the past with the utmost clarity what he would do, and now he has done it or is doing it. **21–23:** They have had many privileges, they have seen *the miracles* that would even have brought the city of Sodom to repentance. But the people of *Korazin* and of *Bethsaida* and of *Capernaum* have chosen not to respond with the changed lives about which Jesus has so explicitly taught. They must live with the consequences. And the reference to *Sodom* reminds them that judgment brings destruction.

still be here today. 24 I tell you, even Sodom will
be better off on judgment day than you."

Jesus' Prayer of Thanksgiving

25 At that time Jesus prayed this prayer: "O Father, Lord of heaven and earth, thank you for
hiding these things from those who think themselves wise and clever, and for revealing them to
the childlike. 26 Yes, Father, it pleased you to do it
this way!

27 "My Father has entrusted everything to
me. No one truly knows the Son except the Father, and no one truly knows the Father except
the Son and those to whom the Son chooses to
reveal him."

28 Then Jesus said, "Come to me, all of you who
are weary and carry heavy burdens, and I will give
you rest. 29 Take my yoke upon you. Let me teach
you, because I am humble and gentle at heart, and
you will find rest for your souls. 30 For my yoke is
easy to bear, and the burden I give you is light."

A Discussion about the Sabbath

12 At about that time Jesus was walking
through some grainfields on the Sabbath. His disciples were hungry, so
they began breaking off some heads of grain and
eating them. 2 But some Pharisees saw them do it
and protested, "Look, your disciples are breaking
the law by harvesting grain on the Sabbath."

3 Jesus said to them, "Haven't you read in the
Scriptures what David did when he and his companions were hungry? 4 He went into the house
of God, and he and his companions broke the law
by eating the sacred loaves of bread that only the
priests are allowed to eat. 5 And haven't you read
in the law of Moses that the priests on duty in
the Temple may work on the Sabbath? 6 I tell you,
there is one here who is even greater than the
Temple! 7 But you would not have condemned
my innocent disciples if you knew the meaning
of this Scripture: 'I want you to show mercy, not
offer sacrifices.'* 8 For the Son of Man* is Lord,
even over the Sabbath!"

Jesus Heals on the Sabbath

9 Then Jesus went over to their synagogue,
10 where he noticed a man with a deformed hand.
The Pharisees asked Jesus, "Does the law permit
a person to work by healing on the Sabbath?"
(They were hoping he would say yes, so they
could bring charges against him.)

11 And he answered, "If you had a sheep that
fell into a well on the Sabbath, wouldn't you
work to pull it out? Of course you would. 12 And
how much more valuable is a person than a
sheep! Yes, the law permits a person to do good
on the Sabbath."

13 Then he said to the man, "Hold out your
hand." So the man held out his hand, and it was
restored, just like the other one! 14 Then the
Pharisees called a meeting to plot how to kill
Jesus.

Jesus, God's Chosen Servant

15 But Jesus knew what they were planning. So he
left that area, and many people followed him. He
healed all the sick among them, 16 but he warned
them not to reveal who he was. 17 This fulfilled
the prophecy of Isaiah concerning him:

18 "Look at my Servant, whom I have chosen.
He is my Beloved, who pleases me.
I will put my Spirit upon him,
and he will proclaim justice to the nations.
19 He will not fight or shout
or raise his voice in public.
20 He will not crush the weakest reed
or put out a flickering candle.
Finally he will cause justice to be
victorious.
21 And his name will be the hope
of all the world."*

Jesus and the Prince of Demons

22 Then a demon-possessed man, who was blind
and couldn't speak, was brought to Jesus. He
healed the man so that he could both speak and
see. 23 The crowd was amazed and asked, "Could it
be that Jesus is the Son of David, the Messiah?"

12:7 Hos 6:6 (Greek version). **12:8** "Son of Man" is a title Jesus used for himself. **12:18-21** Isa 42:1-4 (Greek version for 42:4).

11:25–30 Words of Thanksgiving and Comfort. 25–27: For the first time in Matthew, Jesus speaks directly with his *Father*. Who is Jesus? The one who exclusively completely knows, and is known by, the *Father* in *heaven*, God, from whom his authority comes. **28–30:** Words of comfort for those burdened by guilt.

12:1–14 Conflicts about the Sabbath. By word and act, Jesus claims that *the Son of Man is Lord, even over the Sabbath*, putting himself at the heart of what the law and worship are all about. **14:** As a result, the Pharisees determine to destroy Jesus.

12:15–45 Conflict with the Pharisees. 15–21: Matthew makes the connection between what is happening and messianic prophecy from the Old Testament.

24 But when the Pharisees heard about the miracle, they said, "No wonder he can cast out demons. He gets his power from Satan,* the prince of demons."

25 Jesus knew their thoughts and replied, "Any kingdom divided by civil war is doomed. A town or family splintered by feuding will fall apart. 26 And if Satan is casting out Satan, he is divided and fighting against himself. His own kingdom will not survive. 27 And if I am empowered by Satan, what about your own exorcists? They cast out demons, too, so they will condemn you for what you have said. 28 But if I am casting out demons by the Spirit of God, then the Kingdom of God has arrived among you. 29 For who is powerful enough to enter the house of a strong man like Satan and plunder his goods? Only someone even stronger—someone who could tie him up and then plunder his house.

30 "Anyone who isn't with me opposes me, and anyone who isn't working with me is actually working against me.

31 "So I tell you, every sin and blasphemy can be forgiven—except blasphemy against the Holy Spirit, which will never be forgiven. 32 Anyone who speaks against the Son of Man can be forgiven, but anyone who speaks against the Holy Spirit will never be forgiven, either in this world or in the world to come.

33 "A tree is identified by its fruit. If a tree is good, its fruit will be good. If a tree is bad, its fruit will be bad. 34 You brood of snakes! How could evil men like you speak what is good and right? For whatever is in your heart determines what you say. 35 A good person produces good things from the treasury of a good heart, and an evil person produces evil things from the treasury of an evil heart. 36 And I tell you this, you must give an account on judgment day for every idle word you speak. 37 The words you say will either acquit you or condemn you."

The Sign of Jonah

38 One day some teachers of religious law and Pharisees came to Jesus and said, "Teacher, we want you to show us a miraculous sign to prove your authority."

39 But Jesus replied, "Only an evil, adulterous generation would demand a miraculous sign; but the only sign I will give them is the sign of the prophet Jonah. 40 For as Jonah was in the belly of the great fish for three days and three nights, so will the Son of Man be in the heart of the earth for three days and three nights.

41 "The people of Nineveh will stand up against this generation on judgment day and condemn it, for they repented of their sins at the preaching of Jonah. Now someone greater than Jonah is here—but you refuse to repent. 42 The queen of Sheba* will also stand up against this generation on judgment day and condemn it, for she came from a distant land to hear the wisdom of Solomon. Now someone greater than Solomon is here—but you refuse to listen.

43 "When an evil* spirit leaves a person, it goes into the desert, seeking rest but finding none. 44 Then it says, 'I will return to the person I came from.' So it returns and finds its former home empty, swept, and in order. 45 Then the spirit finds seven other spirits more evil than itself, and they all enter the person and live there. And so that person is worse off than before. That will be the experience of this evil generation."

The True Family of Jesus

46 As Jesus was speaking to the crowd, his mother and brothers stood outside, asking to speak to him. 47 Someone told Jesus, "Your mother and your brothers are outside, and they want to speak to you."*

48 Jesus asked, "Who is my mother? Who are my brothers?" 49 Then he pointed to his disciples and said, "Look, these are my mother and brothers. 50 Anyone who does the will of my Father in heaven is my brother and sister and mother!"

12:24 Greek *Beelzeboul;* also in 12:27. Other manuscripts read *Beezeboul;* Latin version reads *Beelzebub.* **12:42** Greek *The queen of the south.* **12:43** Greek *unclean.* **12:47** Some manuscripts do not include verse 47. Compare Mark 3:32 and Luke 8:20.

24: *The Pharisees* insist that he is empowered by Satan. **25–45:** Jesus' explanation of the contradiction in the argument of the Pharisees leads to a larger point: Those who oppose the work of God are, whether they know it or not, doing the work of Satan.

12:46–50 Jesus' True Family. Into this hotbed of intrigue and danger come Mary and Jesus' brothers. Perhaps they had come to beg him to come home to safety, or they were afraid that they too would be in danger, or they had come to affirm their support. Whatever their motives, they undoubtedly were hurt or offended when he apparently played down their unique place in his life. And yet Jesus is saying something immensely important. It is the family of faith (to which we have access), rather than the family of his birth (to which we do not have access), who are his true family. Once more the excluded become the included.

Parable of the Farmer Scattering Seed

13 Later that same day Jesus left the
house and sat beside the lake. 2 A large
crowd soon gathered around him, so
he got into a boat. Then he sat there and taught
as the people stood on the shore. 3 He told many
stories in the form of parables, such as this one:
"Listen! A farmer went out to plant some
seeds. 4 As he scattered them across his field,
some seeds fell on a footpath, and the birds came
and ate them. 5 Other seeds fell on shallow soil
with underlying rock. The seeds sprouted quickly because the soil was shallow. 6 But the plants
soon wilted under the hot sun, and since they
didn't have deep roots, they died. 7 Other seeds
fell among thorns that grew up and choked out
the tender plants. 8 Still other seeds fell on fertile
soil, and they produced a crop that was thirty,
sixty, and even a hundred times as much as had
been planted! 9 Anyone with ears to hear should
listen and understand."

10 His disciples came and asked him, "Why do
you use parables when you talk to the people?"

11 He replied, "You are permitted to understand the secrets* of the Kingdom of Heaven,
but others are not. 12 To those who listen to my
teaching, more understanding will be given, and
they will have an abundance of knowledge. But
for those who are not listening, even what little
understanding they have will be taken away
from them. 13 That is why I use these parables,

For they look, but they don't really see.
They hear, but they don't really listen or
understand.

14 This fulfills the prophecy of Isaiah that says,

'When you hear what I say,
you will not understand.
When you see what I do,
you will not comprehend.
15 For the hearts of these people are hardened,
and their ears cannot hear,
and they have closed their eyes—
so their eyes cannot see,
and their ears cannot hear,
and their hearts cannot understand,
and they cannot turn to me
and let me heal them.'*

16 "But blessed are your eyes, because they
see; and your ears, because they hear. 17 I tell you
the truth, many prophets and righteous people
longed to see what you see, but they didn't see it.
And they longed to hear what you hear, but they
didn't hear it.

18 "Now listen to the explanation of the parable about the farmer planting seeds: 19 The
seed that fell on the footpath represents those
who hear the message about the Kingdom and
don't understand it. Then the evil one comes and
snatches away the seed that was planted in their
hearts. 20 The seed on the rocky soil represents
those who hear the message and immediately
receive it with joy. 21 But since they don't have
deep roots, they don't last long. They fall away
as soon as they have problems or are persecuted
for believing God's word. 22 The seed that fell
among the thorns represents those who hear
God's word, but all too quickly the message is
crowded out by the worries of this life and the
lure of wealth, so no fruit is produced. 23 The seed
that fell on good soil represents those who truly
hear and understand God's word and produce a
harvest of thirty, sixty, or even a hundred times
as much as had been planted!"

Parable of the Wheat and Weeds

24 Here is another story Jesus told: "The Kingdom of Heaven is like a farmer who planted good
seed in his field. 25 But that night as the workers
slept, his enemy came and planted weeds among
the wheat, then slipped away. 26 When the crop
began to grow and produce grain, the weeds also
grew.

27 "The farmer's workers went to him and said,
'Sir, the field where you planted that good seed is
full of weeds! Where did they come from?'

28 " 'An enemy has done this!' the farmer exclaimed.

" 'Should we pull out the weeds?' they
asked.

29 " 'No,' he replied, 'you'll uproot the wheat
if you do. 30 Let both grow together until the harvest. Then I will tell the harvesters to sort out the
weeds, tie them into bundles, and burn them, and
to put the wheat in the barn.' "

13:11 Greek *the mysteries.* **13:14-15** Isa 6:9-10 (Greek version).

13:1–52 Third Discourse: Parables of the Kingdom

Again Jesus teaches great crowds, which must have included women and children as well as men. Again he draws on themes familiar to them all. **1–43:** Parables of the kingdom growing secretly. Most of the parables revolve around the sowing of seed, but Matthew included a brief parable likening the Kingdom of Heaven to yeast mixed with flour until all is affected (v. 33).

Parable of the Mustard Seed
[31]Here is another illustration Jesus used: "The Kingdom of Heaven is like a mustard seed planted in a field. [32]It is the smallest of all seeds, but it becomes the largest of garden plants; it grows into a tree, and birds come and make nests in its branches."

Parable of the Yeast
[33]Jesus also used this illustration: "The Kingdom of Heaven is like the yeast a woman used in making bread. Even though she put only a little yeast in three measures of flour, it permeated every part of the dough."

[34]Jesus always used stories and illustrations like these when speaking to the crowds. In fact, he never spoke to them without using such parables. [35]This fulfilled what God had spoken through the prophet:

"I will speak to you in parables.
I will explain things hidden since the
creation of the world.*"

Parable of the Wheat and Weeds Explained
[36]Then, leaving the crowds outside, Jesus went into the house. His disciples said, "Please explain to us the story of the weeds in the field."

[37]Jesus replied, "The Son of Man* is the farmer who plants the good seed. [38]The field is the world, and the good seed represents the people of the Kingdom. The weeds are the people who belong to the evil one. [39]The enemy who planted the weeds among the wheat is the devil. The harvest is the end of the world,* and the harvesters are the angels.

[40]"Just as the weeds are sorted out and burned in the fire, so it will be at the end of the world. [41]The Son of Man will send his angels, and they will remove from his Kingdom everything that causes sin and all who do evil. [42]And the angels will throw them into the fiery furnace, where there will be weeping and gnashing of teeth. [43]Then the righteous will shine like the sun in their Father's Kingdom. Anyone with ears to hear should listen and understand!

Parables of the Hidden Treasure and the Pearl
[44]"The Kingdom of Heaven is like a treasure that a man discovered hidden in a field. In his excitement, he hid it again and sold everything he owned to get enough money to buy the field.

[45]"Again, the Kingdom of Heaven is like a merchant on the lookout for choice pearls. [46]When he discovered a pearl of great value, he sold everything he owned and bought it!

Parable of the Fishing Net
[47]"Again, the Kingdom of Heaven is like a fishing net that was thrown into the water and caught fish of every kind. [48]When the net was full, they dragged it up onto the shore, sat down, and sorted the good fish into crates, but threw the bad ones away. [49]That is the way it will be at the end of the world. The angels will come and separate the wicked people from the righteous, [50]throwing the wicked into the fiery furnace, where there will be weeping and gnashing of teeth. [51]Do you understand all these things?"

"Yes," they said, "we do."

[52]Then he added, "Every teacher of religious law who becomes a disciple in the Kingdom of Heaven is like a homeowner who brings from his storeroom new gems of truth as well as old."

Jesus Rejected at Nazareth
[53]When Jesus had finished telling these stories and illustrations, he left that part of the country. [54]He returned to Nazareth, his hometown. When he taught there in the synagogue, everyone was amazed and said, "Where does he get this wisdom and the power to do miracles?" [55]Then they scoffed, "He's just the carpenter's son, and we know Mary, his mother, and his brothers—James, Joseph,* Simon, and Judas. [56]All his sisters live right here among us. Where did he learn all these things?" [57]And they were deeply offended and refused to believe in him.

Then Jesus told them, "A prophet is honored

13:35 Some manuscripts do not include *of the world.* Ps 78:2. **13:37** "Son of Man" is a title Jesus used for himself. **13:39** Or *the age;* also in 13:40, 49. **13:55** Other manuscripts read *Joses;* still others read *John.*

After that, each time she made bread at home, did every woman who heard him recall his words? **44–52:** Parables of the kingdom as a thing of value that must be discovered or sorted out from among other things.

13:53—17:27 Narrative: The King Recognized and Rejected

13:53–58: For the people of Nazareth, the answer to the question who is Jesus was easy: He was Joseph and Mary's son, brother to four young men and to unnamed sisters. It was correct but incomplete, for it ruled out the possibility of anything more. Was Jesus' family proud of him, embarrassed by him, jealous of him, glad to see him leave? Did Mary remind him of what happened when he was born? Urge him to take care?

everywhere except in his own hometown and
among his own family." 58 And so he did only a
few miracles there because of their unbelief.

The Death of John the Baptist

14 When Herod Antipas, the ruler of
Galilee,* heard about Jesus, 2 he said
to his advisers, "This must be John
the Baptist raised from the dead! That is why he
can do such miracles."

3 For Herod had arrested and imprisoned John
as a favor to his wife Herodias (the former wife
of Herod's brother Philip). 4 John had been telling
Herod, "It is against God's law for you to marry her." 5 Herod wanted to kill John, but he was
afraid of a riot, because all the people believed
John was a prophet.

6 But at a birthday party for Herod, Herodias's
daughter performed a dance that greatly pleased
him, 7 so he promised with a vow to give her
anything she wanted. 8 At her mother's urging,
the girl said, "I want the head of John the Baptist on a tray!" 9 Then the king regretted what
he had said; but because of the vow he had made
in front of his guests, he issued the necessary
orders. 10 So John was beheaded in the prison,
11 and his head was brought on a tray and given
to the girl, who took it to her mother. 12 Later,
John's disciples came for his body and buried it.
Then they went and told Jesus what had happened.

Jesus Feeds Five Thousand

13 As soon as Jesus heard the news, he left in a
boat to a remote area to be alone. But the crowds
heard where he was headed and followed on foot
from many towns. 14 Jesus saw the huge crowd as
he stepped from the boat, and he had compassion
on them and healed their sick.

15 That evening the disciples came to him and
said, "This is a remote place, and it's already getting late. Send the crowds away so they can go to
the villages and buy food for themselves."

16 But Jesus said, "That isn't necessary—you
feed them."

17 "But we have only five loaves of bread and
two fish!" they answered.

18 "Bring them here," he said. 19 Then he told
the people to sit down on the grass. Jesus took
the five loaves and two fish, looked up toward
heaven, and blessed them. Then, breaking the
loaves into pieces, he gave the bread to the disciples, who distributed it to the people. 20 They all
ate as much as they wanted, and afterward, the
disciples picked up twelve baskets of leftovers.
21 About 5,000 men were fed that day, in addition
to all the women and children!

Jesus Walks on Water

22 Immediately after this, Jesus insisted that his
disciples get back into the boat and cross to the
other side of the lake, while he sent the people
home. 23 After sending them home, he went up
into the hills by himself to pray. Night fell while
he was there alone.

24 Meanwhile, the disciples were in trouble
far away from land, for a strong wind had risen,
and they were fighting heavy waves. 25 About
three o'clock in the morning* Jesus came toward them, walking on the water. 26 When the
disciples saw him walking on the water, they
were terrified. In their fear, they cried out, "It's
a ghost!"

27 But Jesus spoke to them at once. "Don't be
afraid," he said. "Take courage. I am here!*"

28 Then Peter called to him, "Lord, if it's really you, tell me to come to you, walking on the
water."

29 "Yes, come," Jesus said.

So Peter went over the side of the boat and
walked on the water toward Jesus. 30 But when
he saw the strong* wind and the waves, he was
terrified and began to sink. "Save me, Lord!" he
shouted.

31 Jesus immediately reached out and grabbed

14:1 Greek *Herod the tetrarch.* Herod Antipas was a son of King Herod and was ruler over Galilee. **14:25** Greek *In the fourth watch of the night.* **14:27** Or *The 'I AM' is here;* Greek reads *I am.* See Exod 3:14. **14:30** Some manuscripts do not include *strong.*

14:1–12 John's death. 1–2: Herod Antipas superstitiously feared that Jesus was John *raised from the dead.* **10:** *John was beheaded*: This was not the outcome Zechariah and Elizabeth had dreamed of, all those years ago, as they had held their baby in their arms. Did Mary, too, feel betrayed? Fear for her son must have come gnawing at her heart.

14:13–36 Jesus Feeds Five Thousand, Walks on Water, and His Disciples Begin to Recognize Him. **13–21:** On hearing of John's death, Jesus craved solitude, probably to grieve and pray. Instead he finds himself pursued by an enormous crowd of needy, hungry people. **22–36:** It was many hours before he could be alone and quiet, and he must have been emotionally and physically exhausted. And yet it is in the aftermath of these events and the storm that followed that the disciples take a giant step forward in acknowledging Jesus' true identity: *You really are the Son of God,* they say, and worship him.

him. "You have so little faith," Jesus said. "Why
did you doubt me?"
32 When they climbed back into the boat, the
wind stopped. 33 Then the disciples worshiped
him. "You really are the Son of God!" they exclaimed.
34 After they had crossed the lake, they landed
at Gennesaret. 35 When the people recognized
Jesus, the news of his arrival spread quickly
throughout the whole area, and soon people were
bringing all their sick to be healed. 36 They begged
him to let the sick touch at least the fringe of his
robe, and all who touched him were healed.

Jesus Teaches about Inner Purity

15 Some Pharisees and teachers of religious law now arrived from Jerusalem
to see Jesus. They asked him, 2 "Why
do your disciples disobey our age-old tradition?
For they ignore our tradition of ceremonial hand
washing before they eat."
3 Jesus replied, "And why do you, by your
traditions, violate the direct commandments of
God? 4 For instance, God says, 'Honor your father and mother,'* and 'Anyone who speaks disrespectfully of father or mother must be put to
death.'* 5 But you say it is all right for people to
say to their parents, 'Sorry, I can't help you. For
I have vowed to give to God what I would have
given to you.' 6 In this way, you say they don't
need to honor their parents.* And so you cancel
the word of God for the sake of your own tradition. 7 You hypocrites! Isaiah was right when he
prophesied about you, for he wrote,

8 'These people honor me with their lips,
but their hearts are far from me.
9 Their worship is a farce,
for they teach man-made ideas as
commands from God.'* "

10 Then Jesus called to the crowd to come and
hear. "Listen," he said, "and try to understand.
11 It's not what goes into your mouth that defiles
you; you are defiled by the words that come out
of your mouth."
12 Then the disciples came to him and asked,
"Do you realize you offended the Pharisees by
what you just said?"
13 Jesus replied, "Every plant not planted by
my heavenly Father will be uprooted, 14 so ignore
them. They are blind guides leading the blind,
and if one blind person guides another, they will
both fall into a ditch."
15 Then Peter said to Jesus, "Explain to us the
parable that says people aren't defiled by what
they eat."
16 "Don't you understand yet?" Jesus asked.
17 "Anything you eat passes through the stomach
and then goes into the sewer. 18 But the words you
speak come from the heart—that's what defiles
you. 19 For from the heart come evil thoughts,
murder, adultery, all sexual immorality, theft, lying, and slander. 20 These are what defile you. Eating with unwashed hands will never defile you."

The Faith of a Gentile Woman

21 Then Jesus left Galilee and went north to the
region of Tyre and Sidon. 22 A Gentile* woman
who lived there came to him, pleading, "Have
mercy on me, O Lord, Son of David! For my
daughter is possessed by a demon that torments
her severely."
23 But Jesus gave her no reply, not even a
word. Then his disciples urged him to send her
away. "Tell her to go away," they said. "She is
bothering us with all her begging."
24 Then Jesus said to the woman, "I was sent
only to help God's lost sheep—the people of Israel."

15:4a Exod 20:12; Deut 5:16. **15:4b** Exod 21:17 (Greek version); Lev 20:9 (Greek version). **15:6** Greek *their father;* other manuscripts read *their father or their mother.* **15:8-9** Isa 29:13 (Greek version). **15:22** Greek *Canaanite.*

15:1–20 Inner Purity. 1–9: By contrast, the *Pharisees,* sufficiently concerned to challenge Jesus to have walked for several days from Jerusalem to Gennesaret, are blind to his true identity because of their tenacious and sincerely held commitment to their religious system. **10–16:** A particular cultural form of worship may displace the one in whose honor the worship is undertaken. **17–20:** In many cultures, girls even more than boys are schooled to tight patterns of conformity from a very young age. Like the Pharisees, they may find Jesus' insistence on inner transformation rather than outward conformity profoundly disturbing before they discover its liberating power.

15:21–28 The Gentile Woman. Matthew does not tell us why Jesus then headed *north,* beyond the boundaries of Palestine. But like Elijah many centuries before, here Jesus encounters a woman in great distress and heals her precious child. **22:** The Canaanite woman, contemptuously labeled as a pagan and a foreigner by many Jews, nonetheless in simple but persistent faith has deep insight into his true identity—*Son of David* = king—and his authority over the powers of darkness. The disciples dismiss her as a nuisance: wrong race, wrong gender, perhaps. But the Lord draws her into the circle of his grace. The excluded takes her place among the included.

25 But she came and worshiped him, pleading
again, "Lord, help me!"
26 Jesus responded, "It isn't right to take food
from the children and throw it to the dogs."
27 She replied, "That's true, Lord, but even
dogs are allowed to eat the scraps that fall beneath their masters' table."
28 "Dear woman," Jesus said to her, "your
faith is great. Your request is granted." And her
daughter was instantly healed.

Jesus Heals Many People

29 Jesus returned to the Sea of Galilee and climbed
a hill and sat down. 30 A vast crowd brought to
him people who were lame, blind, crippled, those
who couldn't speak, and many others. They laid
them before Jesus, and he healed them all. 31 The
crowd was amazed! Those who hadn't been able
to speak were talking, the crippled were made
well, the lame were walking, and the blind could
see again! And they praised the God of Israel.

Jesus Feeds Four Thousand

32 Then Jesus called his disciples and told them, "I
feel sorry for these people. They have been here
with me for three days, and they have nothing
left to eat. I don't want to send them away hungry, or they will faint along the way."
33 The disciples replied, "Where would we get
enough food here in the wilderness for such a
huge crowd?"
34 Jesus asked, "How much bread do you
have?"

They replied, "Seven loaves, and a few small
fish."
35 So Jesus told all the people to sit down on
the ground. 36 Then he took the seven loaves and
the fish, thanked God for them, and broke them
into pieces. He gave them to the disciples, who
distributed the food to the crowd.
37 They all ate as much as they wanted. Afterward, the disciples picked up seven large baskets
of leftover food. 38 There were 4,000 men who
were fed that day, in addition to all the women
and children. 39 Then Jesus sent the people home,
and he got into a boat and crossed over to the
region of Magadan.

Leaders Demand a Miraculous Sign

16 One day the Pharisees and Sadducees
came to test Jesus, demanding that he
show them a miraculous sign from
heaven to prove his authority.
2 He replied, "You know the saying, 'Red sky
at night means fair weather tomorrow; 3 red sky
in the morning means foul weather all day.' You
know how to interpret the weather signs in the
sky, but you don't know how to interpret the
signs of the times!* 4 Only an evil, adulterous
generation would demand a miraculous sign, but
the only sign I will give them is the sign of the
prophet Jonah.*" Then Jesus left them and went
away.

Yeast of the Pharisees and Sadducees

5 Later, after they crossed to the other side of the
lake, the disciples discovered they had forgotten
to bring any bread. 6 "Watch out!" Jesus warned
them. "Beware of the yeast of the Pharisees and
Sadducees."
7 At this they began to argue with each other because they hadn't brought any bread. 8 Jesus knew
what they were saying, so he said, "You have so
little faith! Why are you arguing with each other
about having no bread? 9 Don't you understand
even yet? Don't you remember the 5,000 I fed
with five loaves, and the baskets of leftovers you
picked up? 10 Or the 4,000 I fed with seven loaves,
and the large baskets of leftovers you picked up?
11 Why can't you understand that I'm not talking
about bread? So again I say, 'Beware of the yeast
of the Pharisees and Sadducees.'"
12 Then at last they understood that he wasn't
speaking about the yeast in bread, but about the
deceptive teaching of the Pharisees and Sadducees.

Peter's Declaration about Jesus

13 When Jesus came to the region of Caesarea
Philippi, he asked his disciples, "Who do people
say that the Son of Man is?"*

16:2-3 Several manuscripts do not include any of the words in 16:2-3 after *He replied.* **16:4** Greek *the sign of Jonah.* **16:13** "Son of Man" is a title Jesus used for himself.

15:29–39 Healing and Feeding Miracles. Jesus had made a round trip of a hundred miles, perhaps, for one woman. Then he came back to the crowds beside Galilee, to heal, to love, to feed.

16:1–12 Warnings. The Pharisees try to discredit him, and Jesus presses the disciples to recognize the Pharisees' and Sadducees' teaching for the error that it was. **6:** *Yeast* was a sign of spoilage; grain contaminated with yeast was not fit for sacrifice (Lev 2:11).

16:13–20 Peter's Declaration. Caesarea Philippi was a city of religious pluralism, with temples to Baal, a great temple to Caesar, the headwaters of the Jordan (so important in Jewish history and identity); it also claimed to be the birthplace of the Greek god Pan.

14“Well,” they replied, “some say John the Baptist, some say Elijah, and others say Jeremiah or one of the other prophets.”

15Then he asked them, “But who do you say I am?”

16Simon Peter answered, “You are the Messiah,* the Son of the living God.”

17Jesus replied, “You are blessed, Simon son of John,* because my Father in heaven has revealed this to you. You did not learn this from any human being. 18Now I say to you that you are Peter (which means ‘rock’),* and upon this rock I will build my church, and all the powers of hell* will not conquer it. 19And I will give you the keys of the Kingdom of Heaven. Whatever you forbid* on earth will be forbidden in heaven, and whatever you permit* on earth will be permitted in heaven.”

20Then he sternly warned the disciples not to tell anyone that he was the Messiah.

Jesus Predicts His Death

21From then on Jesus* began to tell his disciples plainly that it was necessary for him to go to Jerusalem, and that he would suffer many terrible things at the hands of the elders, the leading priests, and the teachers of religious law. He would be killed, but on the third day he would be raised from the dead.

22But Peter took him aside and began to reprimand him* for saying such things. “Heaven forbid, Lord,” he said. “This will never happen to you!”

23Jesus turned to Peter and said, “Get away from me, Satan! You are a dangerous trap to me. You are seeing things merely from a human point of view, not from God’s.”

24Then Jesus said to his disciples, “If any of you wants to be my follower, you must turn from your selfish ways, take up your cross, and follow me. 25If you try to hang on to your life, you will lose it. But if you give up your life for my sake, you will save it. 26And what do you benefit if you gain the whole world but lose your own soul?* Is anything worth more than your soul? 27For the Son of Man will come with his angels in the glory of his Father and will judge all people according to their deeds. 28And I tell you the truth, some standing here right now will not die before they see the Son of Man coming in his Kingdom.”

The Transfiguration

17 Six days later Jesus took Peter and the two brothers, James and John, and led them up a high mountain to be alone. 2As the men watched, Jesus’ appearance was transformed so that his face shone like the sun, and his clothes became as white as light. 3Suddenly, Moses and Elijah appeared and began talking with Jesus.

4Peter exclaimed, “Lord, it’s wonderful for us to be here! If you want, I’ll make three shelters as memorials*—one for you, one for Moses, and one for Elijah.”

5But even as he spoke, a bright cloud overshadowed them, and a voice from the cloud said, “This is my dearly loved Son, who brings me great joy. Listen to him.” 6The disciples were terrified and fell face down on the ground.

7Then Jesus came over and touched them. “Get up,” he said. “Don’t be afraid.” 8And when they looked up, Moses and Elijah were gone, and they saw only Jesus.

9As they went back down the mountain, Jesus

16:16 Or *the Christ. Messiah* (a Hebrew term) and *Christ* (a Greek term) both mean “the anointed one.” **16:17** Greek *Simon bar-Jonah;* see John 1:42; 21:15-17. **16:18a** Greek *that you are Peter.* **16:18b** Greek *and the gates of Hades.* **16:19a** Or *bind,* or *lock.* **16:19b** Or *loose,* or *open.* **16:21** Some manuscripts read *Jesus the Messiah.* **16:22** Or *began to correct him.* **16:26** Or *your self?* also in 16:26b. **17:4** Greek *three tabernacles.*

15: Jesus forces the disciples to face up to his identity. **16:** Peter’s answer, *You are the Messiah, the Son of the living God,* refers to the one God of the Jews.

16:21–28 Prediction of the Passion. 21–23: This is the turning point of the Gospel. Everything else, from here to the end, weaves around the central theme of the cross. The King must die. **24–28:** Not only must the King die, but his subjects also must be willing to take up the cross. From now until Pentecost, the disciples will be walking into disaster. Any last vestiges of hope that they would be at the center of a triumphant, imminent restoration of Israel are swept away. They must have been shaken, probably tempted to abandon Jesus, and struggling over the price tag attached to staying with him.

17:1–13 The Transfiguration. Jesus in his tender grace takes Peter, James, and John to a high mountain where they see Jesus’ transfiguration. They see and hear that, in eternal terms, if not in earthly terms, Jesus has glory far beyond anything they could have dreamed of. They were right to look for a glorious king; but they were wrong, and their vision myopic, to look for that in terms of an insecure throne in a small and impoverished Mediterranean country. **3:** *Moses and Elijah* represent the teaching (“Torah”) and prophets of the Jewish people.

commanded them, "Don't tell anyone what you
have seen until the Son of Man* has been raised
from the dead."
10 Then his disciples asked him, "Why do the
teachers of religious law insist that Elijah must
return before the Messiah comes?*"
11 Jesus replied, "Elijah is indeed coming first
to get everything ready. 12 But I tell you, Elijah
has already come, but he wasn't recognized, and
they chose to abuse him. And in the same way
they will also make the Son of Man suffer."
13 Then the disciples realized he was talking about
John the Baptist.

Jesus Heals a Demon-Possessed Boy
14 At the foot of the mountain, a large crowd was
waiting for them. A man came and knelt before
Jesus and said, 15 "Lord, have mercy on my son.
He has seizures and suffers terribly. He often falls
into the fire or into the water. 16 So I brought him
to your disciples, but they couldn't heal him."
17 Jesus said, "You faithless and corrupt people! How long must I be with you? How long
must I put up with you? Bring the boy here to
me." 18 Then Jesus rebuked the demon in the boy,
and it left him. From that moment the boy was
well.
19 Afterward the disciples asked Jesus privately, "Why couldn't we cast out that demon?"
20 "You don't have enough faith," Jesus told
them. "I tell you the truth, if you had faith even
as small as a mustard seed, you could say to this
mountain, 'Move from here to there,' and it
would move. Nothing would be impossible.*"

Jesus Again Predicts His Death
22 After they gathered again in Galilee, Jesus told
them, "The Son of Man is going to be betrayed
into the hands of his enemies. 23 He will be killed,
but on the third day he will be raised from the
dead." And the disciples were filled with grief.

Payment of the Temple Tax
24 On their arrival in Capernaum, the collectors
of the Temple tax* came to Peter and asked him,
"Doesn't your teacher pay the Temple tax?"
25 "Yes, he does," Peter replied. Then he went
into the house.
But before he had a chance to speak, Jesus
asked him, "What do you think, Peter?* Do
kings tax their own people or the people they
have conquered?*"
26 "They tax the people they have conquered,"
Peter replied.
"Well, then," Jesus said, "the citizens are free!
27 However, we don't want to offend them, so go
down to the lake and throw in a line. Open the
mouth of the first fish you catch, and you will
find a large silver coin.* Take it and pay the tax
for both of us."

The Greatest in the Kingdom
18 About that time the disciples came to
Jesus and asked, "Who is greatest in
the Kingdom of Heaven?"
2 Jesus called a little child to him and put the
child among them. 3 Then he said, "I tell you the
truth, unless you turn from your sins and become like little children, you will never get into
the Kingdom of Heaven. 4 So anyone who be-

17:9 "Son of Man" is a title Jesus used for himself. **17:10** Greek *that Elijah must come first?* **17:20** Some manuscripts add verse 21, *But this kind of demon won't leave except by prayer and fasting.* Compare Mark 9:29. **17:24** Greek *the two-drachma [tax]*; also in 17:24b. See Exod 30:13-16; Neh 10:32-33. **17:25a** Greek *Simon?* **17:25b** Greek *their sons or others?* **17:27** Greek *a stater* [a Greek coin equivalent to four drachmas].

10–13: *Elijah* also prefigures *John the Baptist*.

17:14–20 [21] Healing a Demon-Possessed Boy. 20: *Mustard seed*: A very small seed that develops into a fairly large shrub. "Moving mountains," as its proverbial use suggests, is an exaggeration for rhetorical effect. Note: Verse 21 is not included in many manuscripts of Matthew. **22–23:** Another prediction of the passion.

17:24–27 Paying Taxes. What irony that the King of the whole earth should pay tax of any kind! That it should be the Temple tax is almost beyond belief, except that this King is the one who stands in the place of, is substitution for, his sinner subjects. Then it makes beautiful sense.

18:1–35 Fourth Discourse: The Upside-Down Kingdom

18:1–10 [11] True Greatness. Some cultures today have gravely distorted their children, encouraging them to become arrogant, manipulative, and selfish. But Jesus could use a small child, not to draw attention to childish innocence and purity, but because in his culture a child, though cherished, had the lowliest status. Children did not claim inflated rights but received what was given and were expected to be grateful, not grasping. This fundamental humility, Jesus says, is the childlike characteristic that should mark his disciples. Further, the humble disciple will gladly welcome and respect children and in so doing will be welcoming Christ. What a lovely affirmation of the

comes as humble as this little child is the greatest in the Kingdom of Heaven.

5 "And anyone who welcomes a little child like this on my behalf* is welcoming me. 6 But if you cause one of these little ones who trusts in me to fall into sin, it would be better for you to have a large millstone tied around your neck and be drowned in the depths of the sea.

7 "What sorrow awaits the world, because it tempts people to sin. Temptations are inevitable, but what sorrow awaits the person who does the tempting. 8 So if your hand or foot causes you to sin, cut it off and throw it away. It's better to enter eternal life with only one hand or one foot than to be thrown into eternal fire with both of your hands and feet. 9 And if your eye causes you to sin, gouge it out and throw it away. It's better to enter eternal life with only one eye than to have two eyes and be thrown into the fire of hell.*

10 "Beware that you don't look down on any of these little ones. For I tell you that in heaven their angels are always in the presence of my heavenly Father.*

Parable of the Lost Sheep

12 "If a man has a hundred sheep and one of them wanders away, what will he do? Won't he leave the ninety-nine others on the hills and go out to search for the one that is lost? 13 And if he finds it, I tell you the truth, he will rejoice over it more than over the ninety-nine that didn't wander away! 14 In the same way, it is not my heavenly Father's will that even one of these little ones should perish.

Correcting Another Believer

15 "If another believer* sins against you,* go privately and point out the offense. If the other person listens and confesses it, you have won that person back. 16 But if you are unsuccessful, take one or two others with you and go back again, so that everything you say may be confirmed by two or three witnesses. 17 If the person still refuses to listen, take your case to the church. Then if he or she won't accept the church's decision, treat that person as a pagan or a corrupt tax collector.

18 "I tell you the truth, whatever you forbid* on earth will be forbidden in heaven, and whatever you permit* on earth will be permitted in heaven.

19 "I also tell you this: If two of you agree here on earth concerning anything you ask, my Father in heaven will do it for you. 20 For where two or three gather together as my followers,* I am there among them."

Parable of the Unforgiving Debtor

21 Then Peter came to him and asked, "Lord, how often should I forgive someone* who sins against me? Seven times?"

22 "No, not seven times," Jesus replied, "but seventy times seven!*

23 "Therefore, the Kingdom of Heaven can be compared to a king who decided to bring his accounts up to date with servants who had borrowed money from him. 24 In the process, one of his debtors was brought in who owed him millions of dollars.* 25 He couldn't pay, so his master ordered that he be sold—along with his wife, his children, and everything he owned—to pay the debt.

26 "But the man fell down before his master and begged him, 'Please, be patient with me, and I will pay it all.' 27 Then his master was filled with pity for him, and he released him and forgave his debt.

28 "But when the man left the king, he went to a fellow servant who owed him a few thousand dollars.* He grabbed him by the throat and demanded instant payment.

29 "His fellow servant fell down before him and begged for a little more time. 'Be patient with me, and I will pay it,' he pleaded. 30 But his creditor wouldn't wait. He had the man arrested and put in prison until the debt could be paid in full.

18:5 Greek *in my name.* **18:9** Greek *the Gehenna of fire.* **18:10** Some manuscripts add verse 11, *And the Son of Man came to save those who are lost.* Compare Luke 19:10. **18:15a** Greek *If your brother.* **18:15b** Some manuscripts do not include *against you.* **18:18a** Or *bind,* or *lock.* **18:18b** Or *loose,* or *open.* **18:20** Greek *gather together in my name.* **18:21** Greek *my brother.* **18:22** Or *seventy-seven times.* **18:24** Greek *10,000 talents* [375 tons or 340 metric tons of silver]. **18:28** Greek *100 denarii.* A denarius was equivalent to a laborer's full day's wage.

dignity of child rearing, much of which falls to women (see Childbearing and Rearing, Col 3). Note: Verse 11 is not included in many manuscripts of Matthew.

18:12–14 Seeking the Lost. God cares so deeply that he hunts high and low for the least among his little ones.

18:15–35 True Forgiveness. 15–20: The world says, "Grab your revenge!" Even the law speaks of retaliation. Jesus says, instead show mercy, seek reconciliation, restore the sinner to fellowship, forgive over and over again. **21–35:** As we deal with hurt, we are humbled in the presence of our Father who has forgiven us so much.

31 "When some of the other servants saw this,
they were very upset. They went to the king
and told him everything that had happened.
32 Then the king called in the man he had forgiven and said, 'You evil servant! I forgave you
that tremendous debt because you pleaded with
me. 33 Shouldn't you have mercy on your fellow
servant, just as I had mercy on you?' 34 Then the
angry king sent the man to prison to be tortured
until he had paid his entire debt.
35 "That's what my heavenly Father will do to
you if you refuse to forgive your brothers and
sisters* from your heart."

Discussion about Divorce and Marriage

19 When Jesus had finished saying these
things, he left Galilee and went down
to the region of Judea east of the Jordan River. 2 Large crowds followed him there, and
he healed their sick.
3 Some Pharisees came and tried to trap him
with this question: "Should a man be allowed to
divorce his wife for just any reason?"
4 "Haven't you read the Scriptures?" Jesus
replied. "They record that from the beginning
'God made them male and female.'* 5 And he
said, 'This explains why a man leaves his father
and mother and is joined to his wife, and the two
are united into one.'* 6 Since they are no longer
two but one, let no one split apart what God has
joined together."
7 "Then why did Moses say in the law that a
man could give his wife a written notice of divorce and send her away?"* they asked.
8 Jesus replied, "Moses permitted divorce only
as a concession to your hard hearts, but it was
not what God had originally intended. 9 And I tell
you this, whoever divorces his wife and marries
someone else commits adultery—unless his wife
has been unfaithful.*"
10 Jesus' disciples then said to him, "If this is
the case, it is better not to marry!"
11 "Not everyone can accept this statement,"
Jesus said. "Only those whom God helps. 12 Some
are born as eunuchs, some have been made eunuchs by others, and some choose not to marry*
for the sake of the Kingdom of Heaven. Let anyone accept this who can."

Jesus Blesses the Children

13 One day some parents brought their children
to Jesus so he could lay his hands on them and
pray for them. But the disciples scolded the parents for bothering him.
14 But Jesus said, "Let the children come to
me. Don't stop them! For the Kingdom of Heav-
en belongs to those who are like these children."
15 And he placed his hands on their heads and
blessed them before he left.

The Rich Man

16 Someone came to Jesus with this question:
"Teacher,* what good deed must I do to have
eternal life?"

18:35 Greek *your brother.* **19:4** Gen 1:27; 5:2. **19:5** Gen 2:24. **19:7** See Deut 24:1. **19:9** Some manuscripts add *And anyone who marries a divorced woman commits adultery.* Compare Matt 5:32. **19:12** Greek *and some make themselves eunuchs.* **19:16** Some manuscripts read *Good Teacher.*

19:1–23:39 Narrative: The King Must Die

19:1–12 Divorce and Marriage. The Pharisees are bent on trapping Jesus, and the subject of divorce was a minefield (see Divorce, Ezra 10). Schools of Pharisees disagreed among themselves on the grounds, from the very strict to the very lax, for divorce. **4–6:** Jesus restates the creation principle (Gen 2:23–24): Marriage should be permanent, dissolved only by death; it is a profound union—two becoming one—of a man and woman equally; it is for mutual good; the woman is not to be at the mercy of her parents-in-law. This principle, rightly understood, gives great dignity and protection to women. **8–9:** Further, Moses' instructions (Deut 24:1), frequently used to justify a man divorcing a woman on trivial grounds, are a *concession*, an attempt to protect women from arbitrary divorce on the one hand or abusive captivity on the other. The law had become so twisted down through the centuries that a woman was a thing, a possession of her father, then her husband. She could not initiate divorce, however cruel her husband; she could not protect herself if her husband chose to evict her. Jesus is challenging this particular manifestation of male sin at the time and firmly asserting the preciousness of women in their Creator's sight. No wonder that the Pharisees were left speechless.

19:13–15 Blessing the Children. Despite Jesus' recent teaching, the disciples apparently see faith as a very adult thing and want to turn away little children too young to understand. There is more important adult business to attend to. Jesus' rebuke to the disciples and welcome to the children (mostly perhaps brought by their mothers) topples the men-women-children hierarchy. Each individual, male or female, old or young, Jew or Gentile, is profoundly valuable to the King.

19:16–30 The Rich Young Man. It is on the grounds of the character of God, not the status of the person, that there is entry to the Kingdom of Heaven. **23–24:**

17 "Why ask me about what is good?" Jesus
replied. "There is only One who is good. But to
answer your question—if you want to receive
eternal life, keep* the commandments."
18 "Which ones?" the man asked.
And Jesus replied: " 'You must not murder. You
must not commit adultery. You must not steal. You
must not testify falsely. 19 Honor your father and
mother. Love your neighbor as yourself.'* "
20 "I've obeyed all these commandments," the
young man replied. "What else must I do?"
21 Jesus told him, "If you want to be perfect, go
and sell all your possessions and give the money
to the poor, and you will have treasure in heaven.
Then come, follow me."
22 But when the young man heard this, he
went away sad, for he had many possessions.
23 Then Jesus said to his disciples, "I tell you
the truth, it is very hard for a rich person to enter the Kingdom of Heaven. 24 I'll say it again—it
is easier for a camel to go through the eye of a
needle than for a rich person to enter the Kingdom of God!"
25 The disciples were astounded. "Then who in
the world can be saved?" they asked.
26 Jesus looked at them intently and said,
"Humanly speaking, it is impossible. But with
God everything is possible."
27 Then Peter said to him, "We've given up everything to follow you. What will we get?"
28 Jesus replied, "I assure you that when the
world is made new* and the Son of Man* sits
upon his glorious throne, you who have been my
followers will also sit on twelve thrones, judging the twelve tribes of Israel. 29 And everyone
who has given up houses or brothers or sisters
or father or mother or children or property, for
my sake, will receive a hundred times as much in
return and will inherit eternal life. 30 But many
who are the greatest now will be least important
then, and those who seem least important now
will be the greatest then.*

Parable of the Vineyard Workers

20 "For the Kingdom of Heaven is like
the landowner who went out early one morning to hire workers for
his vineyard. 2 He agreed to pay the normal daily
wage* and sent them out to work.
3 "At nine o'clock in the morning he was passing through the marketplace and saw some people standing around doing nothing. 4 So he hired
them, telling them he would pay them whatever
was right at the end of the day. 5 So they went to
work in the vineyard. At noon and again at three
o'clock he did the same thing.
6 "At five o'clock that afternoon he was in
town again and saw some more people standing
around. He asked them, 'Why haven't you been
working today?'
7 "They replied, 'Because no one hired us.'
"The landowner told them, 'Then go out and
join the others in my vineyard.'
8 "That evening he told the foreman to call
the workers in and pay them, beginning with
the last workers first. 9 When those hired at five
o'clock were paid, each received a full day's wage.
10 When those hired first came to get their pay,
they assumed they would receive more. But
they, too, were paid a day's wage. 11 When they
received their pay, they protested to the owner,
12 'Those people worked only one hour, and yet
you've paid them just as much as you paid us
who worked all day in the scorching heat.'
13 "He answered one of them, 'Friend, I haven't
been unfair! Didn't you agree to work all day for
the usual wage? 14 Take your money and go. I
wanted to pay this last worker the same as you.
15 Is it against the law for me to do what I want
with my money? Should you be jealous because
I am kind to others?'
16 "So those who are last now will be first
then, and those who are first will be last."

Jesus Again Predicts His Death

17 As Jesus was going up to Jerusalem, he took
the twelve disciples aside privately and told them
what was going to happen to him. 18 "Listen," he
said, "we're going up to Jerusalem, where the
Son of Man* will be betrayed to the leading
priests and the teachers of religious law. They

19:17 Some manuscripts read *continue to keep.*
19:18-19 Exod 20:12-16; Deut 5:16-20; Lev 19:18.
19:28a Or *in the regeneration.* **19:28b** "Son of Man" is a title Jesus used for himself. **19:30** Greek *But many who are first will be last; and the last, first.* **20:2** Greek *a denarius,* the payment for a full day's labor; similarly in 20:9, 10, 13.
20:18 "Son of Man" is a title Jesus used for himself.

Indeed, so deeply ingrained is the belief that one's status, wealth, and attempts at morality can unlock heaven's door that these things become a hindrance.

20:1–16 The Workers in the Vineyard. The payment or reward is not calculated on the number of hours different workers have completed but on the generosity of the owner. The gift of eternal life does not come in incremental degrees based on the believer's length of service.

20:17–19 Another prediction of the passion.

will sentence him to die. 19 Then they will hand
him over to the Romans* to be mocked, flogged
with a whip, and crucified. But on the third day
he will be raised from the dead."

Jesus Teaches about Serving Others

20 Then the mother of James and John, the sons of
Zebedee, came to Jesus with her sons. She knelt
respectfully to ask a favor. 21 "What is your request?" he asked.

She replied, "In your Kingdom, please let my
two sons sit in places of honor next to you, one
on your right and the other on your left."

22 But Jesus answered by saying to them, "You
don't know what you are asking! Are you able to
drink from the bitter cup of suffering I am about
to drink?"

"Oh yes," they replied, "we are able!"

23 Jesus told them, "You will indeed drink from
my bitter cup. But I have no right to say who will
sit on my right or my left. My Father has prepared those places for the ones he has chosen."

24 When the ten other disciples heard what
James and John had asked, they were indignant.
25 But Jesus called them together and said, "You
know that the rulers in this world lord it over
their people, and officials flaunt their authority over those under them. 26 But among you it
will be different. Whoever wants to be a leader
among you must be your servant, 27 and whoever
wants to be first among you must become your
slave. 28 For even the Son of Man came not to be
served but to serve others and to give his life as a
ransom for many."

Jesus Heals Two Blind Men

29 As Jesus and the disciples left the town of Jericho,
a large crowd followed behind. 30 Two blind men
were sitting beside the road. When they heard that
Jesus was coming that way, they began shouting,
"Lord, Son of David, have mercy on us!"

31 "Be quiet!" the crowd yelled at them.

But they only shouted louder, "Lord, Son of
David, have mercy on us!"

32 When Jesus heard them, he stopped and
called, "What do you want me to do for you?"

33 "Lord," they said, "we want to see!" 34 Jesus
felt sorry for them and touched their eyes. Instantly they could see! Then they followed him.

Jesus' Triumphant Entry

21 As Jesus and the disciples approached
Jerusalem, they came to the town of
Bethphage on the Mount of Olives.
Jesus sent two of them on ahead. 2 "Go into the village over there," he said. "As soon as you enter it,
you will see a donkey tied there, with its colt beside
it. Untie them and bring them to me. 3 If anyone
asks what you are doing, just say, 'The Lord needs
them,' and he will immediately let you take them."

4 This took place to fulfill the prophecy that
said,

5 "Tell the people of Jerusalem,*
'Look, your King is coming to you.
He is humble, riding on a donkey—
riding on a donkey's colt.' "*

6 The two disciples did as Jesus commanded.
7 They brought the donkey and the colt to him
and threw their garments over the colt, and he
sat on it.*

8 Most of the crowd spread their garments on
the road ahead of him, and others cut branches

20:19 Greek *the Gentiles.* **21:5a** Greek *Tell the daughter of Zion.* Isa 62:11. **21:5b** Zech 9:9. **21:7** Greek *over them, and he sat on them.*

20:20–28 True Service. 20–21: *The mother of James and John* is eager to ensure the places of the highest honor for her sons. She may possibly have been Jesus' aunt, Mary's sister, Salome (cf. Matt 27:56; Mark 15:40; John 19:25). **22–23:** Jesus refuses her request: It is not his to grant, but his Father's. Jesus pulls the focus back to the cross and resurrection, now close at hand; there is no future glory, for him or for them, without deep suffering first. **24–28:** The reaction of the other disciples appears to be that of jealousy that James and John had put them at risk of taking a position inferior to theirs. They are still jockeying for positions in the hierarchy model. Jesus says that godly leadership is humble service, adopting the role of the slave who has no rights. Feminism that is assertive and domineering is as sinful, as much a product of the Fall, as any patriarchalism that it seeks to redress. Our sacrificial service does not save as Jesus' did; but his is the model from which flows spiritual fruitfulness and spiritual authority. It is as countercultural today as ever it was.

20:29–34 Healing Two Blind Men. The healing results in discipleship.

21:1–11 The Entry of the True King. It was not that Jesus was any the less a King for being a servant. **2–7:** Fulfilling Isaiah 62:11 and Zechariah 9:9, Jesus borrows a donkey and a colt and deliberately displays himself as the awaited Savior-King coming to Zion. Passover, the festival commemorating a historic deliverance, is only days away. It is a powerful symbol of salvation through the blood of a lamb shed in substitution for one's own.

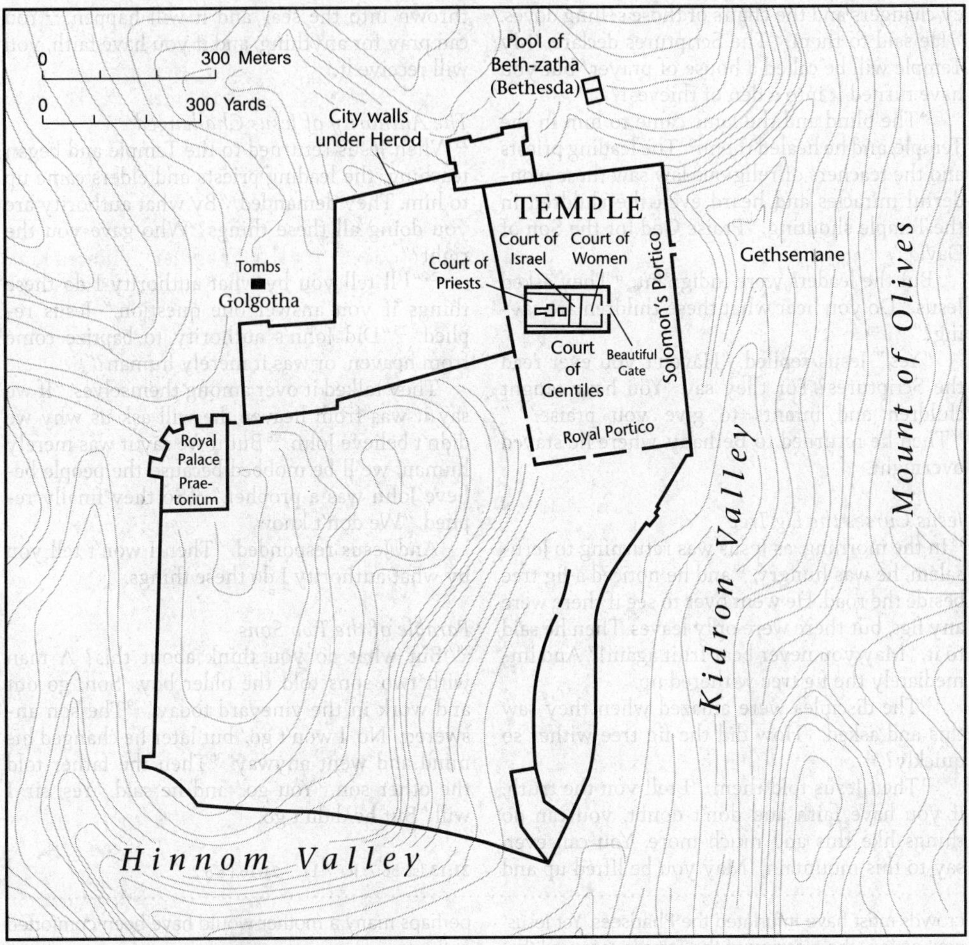

Jerusalem in the Time of Jesus

from the trees and spread them on the road.
[9]Jesus was in the center of the procession, and
the people all around him were shouting,

"Praise God* for the Son of David!
Blessings on the one who comes in the
name of the LORD!
Praise God in highest heaven!"*

[10]The entire city of Jerusalem was in an uproar as he entered. "Who is this?" they asked.

[11]And the crowds replied, "It's Jesus, the
prophet from Nazareth in Galilee."

Jesus Clears the Temple

[12]Jesus entered the Temple and began to drive
out all the people buying and selling animals for
sacrifice. He knocked over the tables of the mon-

21:9a Greek *Hosanna,* an exclamation of praise that literally means "save now"; also in 21:9b, 15. **21:9b** Pss 118:25-26; 148:1.

8: The crowds respond to symbol with symbol, cutting down palm branches as token that the one they greet is conquering hero, a King entering his rightful kingdom. **9:** As they shout, they identify him as the one who is to "Save now!" They echo the angel of the Lord (Matt 1:21). **10–11:** Yet, as others ask *Who is this?* they can only say *the prophet from Nazareth in Galilee*: true but inadequate. Down through the centuries, people have said, "Good man, great example, great teacher." That too is true but inadequate.

21:12–17 Clearing the Temple. The adulation of the

ey changers and the chairs of those selling doves. [13]He said to them, "The Scriptures declare, 'My Temple will be called a house of prayer,' but you have turned it into a den of thieves!"*

[14]The blind and the lame came to him in the Temple, and he healed them. [15]The leading priests and the teachers of religious law saw these wonderful miracles and heard even the children in the Temple shouting, "Praise God for the Son of David."

But the leaders were indignant. [16]They asked Jesus, "Do you hear what these children are saying?"

"Yes," Jesus replied. "Haven't you ever read the Scriptures? For they say, 'You have taught children and infants to give you praise.'* " [17]Then he returned to Bethany, where he stayed overnight.

Jesus Curses the Fig Tree

[18]In the morning, as Jesus was returning to Jerusalem, he was hungry, [19]and he noticed a fig tree beside the road. He went over to see if there were any figs, but there were only leaves. Then he said to it, "May you never bear fruit again!" And immediately the fig tree withered up.

[20]The disciples were amazed when they saw this and asked, "How did the fig tree wither so quickly?"

[21]Then Jesus told them, "I tell you the truth, if you have faith and don't doubt, you can do things like this and much more. You can even say to this mountain, 'May you be lifted up and thrown into the sea,' and it will happen. [22]You can pray for anything, and if you have faith, you will receive it."

The Authority of Jesus Challenged

[23]When Jesus returned to the Temple and began teaching, the leading priests and elders came up to him. They demanded, "By what authority are you doing all these things? Who gave you the right?"

[24]"I'll tell you by what authority I do these things if you answer one question," Jesus replied. [25]"Did John's authority to baptize come from heaven, or was it merely human?"

They talked it over among themselves. "If we say it was from heaven, he will ask us why we didn't believe John. [26]But if we say it was merely human, we'll be mobbed because the people believe John was a prophet." [27]So they finally replied, "We don't know."

And Jesus responded, "Then I won't tell you by what authority I do these things.

Parable of the Two Sons

[28]"But what do you think about this? A man with two sons told the older boy, 'Son, go out and work in the vineyard today.' [29]The son answered, 'No, I won't go,' but later he changed his mind and went anyway. [30]Then the father told the other son, 'You go,' and he said, 'Yes, sir, I will.' But he didn't go.

21:13 Isa 56:7; Jer 7:11. **21:16** Ps 8:2.

---

crowds must have infuriated the Pharisees. Yet Jesus' next action, the clearing of the Temple, ensured that the priests too were raging with anger against him. Jesus was tangling with their vested interests: The money changers and the dove sellers made the most of their monopoly, shamefully exploiting rather than serving travelers coming to the Temple to make their sacrifices. Excited bartering would make the place more like a street market than the place it was meant to be, a place of worship and awed encounter with God and a place of prayer for all nations (Isa 56:7). Abuse of power greatly angers God. **16–17:** The priests, the so-called experts, are, says Jesus, ignorant in comparison with the little children who sing "Hosanna." A tiny child may not be able to articulate his or her faith in adult terms, but even one so young as to be nursing at the breast can give beautiful praise to the Lord. Matthew has repeatedly recorded Jesus' great delight in young children. In a context where infant mortality was high and where in many parts of the Roman Empire unwanted infants—mostly girls—were left out to die (not normally practiced by Jews), perhaps many a mother would have been comforted at this.

21:18–22 The Fig Tree. In its context, this miracle is an acted parable expressing the failure of the religious leadership to produce the fruit that God desires of them.

21:23–27 True Authority. The chief priests are eager to trap Jesus by asking him about the source of his *authority*. If he answers, "God," he can be accused of blasphemy. But Jesus turns the tables on them.

21:28–32 The Two Sons. *Tax collectors and prostitutes* showed proper response to John's prophetic message. The *priests* would have been outraged at the suggestion that repentant prostitutes were more welcome than they. They despised prostitutes, blaming them for their lifestyle and conveniently overlooking the fact that men's demand for sexual gratification, or men's failure to provide for widows and desperately poor women, often drove them to the trade.

31 "Which of the two obeyed his father?"

They replied, "The first."*

Then Jesus explained his meaning: "I tell you the truth, corrupt tax collectors and prostitutes will get into the Kingdom of God before you do. 32 For John the Baptist came and showed you the right way to live, but you didn't believe him, while tax collectors and prostitutes did. And even when you saw this happening, you refused to believe him and repent of your sins.

Parable of the Evil Farmers

33 "Now listen to another story. A certain landowner planted a vineyard, built a wall around it, dug a pit for pressing out the grape juice, and built a lookout tower. Then he leased the vineyard to tenant farmers and moved to another country. 34 At the time of the grape harvest, he sent his servants to collect his share of the crop. 35 But the farmers grabbed his servants, beat one, killed one, and stoned another. 36 So the landowner sent a larger group of his servants to collect for him, but the results were the same.

37 "Finally, the owner sent his son, thinking, 'Surely they will respect my son.'

38 "But when the tenant farmers saw his son coming, they said to one another, 'Here comes the heir to this estate. Come on, let's kill him and get the estate for ourselves!' 39 So they grabbed him, dragged him out of the vineyard, and murdered him.

40 "When the owner of the vineyard returns," Jesus asked, "what do you think he will do to those farmers?"

41 The religious leaders replied, "He will put the wicked men to a horrible death and lease the vineyard to others who will give him his share of the crop after each harvest."

42 Then Jesus asked them, "Didn't you ever read this in the Scriptures?

'The stone that the builders rejected
has now become the cornerstone.
This is the LORD's doing,
and it is wonderful to see.'*

43 I tell you, the Kingdom of God will be taken away from you and given to a nation that will produce the proper fruit. 44 Anyone who stumbles over that stone will be broken to pieces, and it will crush anyone it falls on.*"

45 When the leading priests and Pharisees heard this parable, they realized he was telling the story against them—they were the wicked farmers. 46 They wanted to arrest him, but they were afraid of the crowds, who considered Jesus to be a prophet.

Parable of the Great Feast

22 Jesus also told them other parables. He said, 2 "The Kingdom of Heaven can be illustrated by the story of a king who prepared a great wedding feast for his son. 3 When the banquet was ready, he sent his servants to notify those who were invited. But they all refused to come!

4 "So he sent other servants to tell them, 'The feast has been prepared. The bulls and fattened cattle have been killed, and everything is ready. Come to the banquet!' 5 But the guests he had invited ignored them and went their own way, one to his farm, another to his business. 6 Others seized his messengers and insulted them and killed them.

7 "The king was furious, and he sent out his army to destroy the murderers and burn their town. 8 And he said to his servants, 'The wedding feast is ready, and the guests I invited aren't worthy of the honor. 9 Now go out to the street corners and invite everyone you see.' 10 So the servants brought in everyone they could find, good and bad alike, and the banquet hall was filled with guests.

11 "But when the king came in to meet the guests, he noticed a man who wasn't wearing the proper clothes for a wedding. 12 'Friend,' he asked, 'how is it that you are here without wedding clothes?' But the man had no reply. 13 Then the king said to his aides, 'Bind his hands and feet and throw him into the outer darkness, where there will be weeping and gnashing of teeth.'

14 "For many are called, but few are chosen."

21:29-31 Other manuscripts read *"The second."* In still other manuscripts the first son says "Yes" but does nothing, the second son says "No" but then repents and goes, and the answer to Jesus' question is that the second son obeyed his father. **21:42** Ps 118:22-23. **21:44** This verse is not included in some early manuscripts. Compare Luke 20:18.

21:33–46 The Vineyard Owner's Son. The parable is a scarcely veiled challenge: "You can kill me, but the Kingdom of God will be given instead to those you despise, the repentant ones, whatever their previous background."

22:1–14 The Wedding Feast. The priests and the Pharisees had ignored the invitation, "Repent, for the Kingdom of Heaven is at hand," brought by first John and then Jesus. So now the invitation has been given instead to those whom they would regard as unworthy.

Taxes for Caesar
[15]Then the Pharisees met together to plot how
to trap Jesus into saying something for which
he could be arrested. [16]They sent some of their
disciples, along with the supporters of Herod, to
meet with him. "Teacher," they said, "we know
how honest you are. You teach the way of God
truthfully. You are impartial and don't play favorites. [17]Now tell us what you think about this:
Is it right to pay taxes to Caesar or not?"
[18]But Jesus knew their evil motives. "You hypocrites!" he said. "Why are you trying to trap me?
[19]Here, show me the coin used for the tax." When
they handed him a Roman coin,* [20]he asked,
"Whose picture and title are stamped on it?"
[21]"Caesar's," they replied.
"Well, then," he said, "give to Caesar what
belongs to Caesar, and give to God what belongs
to God."
[22]His reply amazed them, and they went
away.

Discussion about Resurrection
[23]That same day Jesus was approached by some
Sadducees—religious leaders who say there is no
resurrection from the dead. They posed this question: [24]"Teacher, Moses said, 'If a man dies without children, his brother should marry the widow
and have a child who will carry on the brother's
name.'* [25]Well, suppose there were seven brothers. The oldest one married and then died without
children, so his brother married the widow. [26]But
the second brother also died, and the third brother married her. This continued with all seven of
them. [27]Last of all, the woman also died. [28]So tell
us, whose wife will she be in the resurrection? For
all seven were married to her."
[29]Jesus replied, "Your mistake is that you don't
know the Scriptures, and you don't know the
power of God. [30]For when the dead rise, they will
neither marry nor be given in marriage. In this
respect they will be like the angels in heaven.
[31]"But now, as to whether there will be a resurrection of the dead—haven't you ever read
about this in the Scriptures? Long after Abraham, Isaac, and Jacob had died, God said,* [32]'I am
the God of Abraham, the God of Isaac, and the
God of Jacob.'* So he is the God of the living,
not the dead."
[33]When the crowds heard him, they were astounded at his teaching.

The Most Important Commandment
[34]But when the Pharisees heard that he had silenced the Sadducees with his reply, they met
together to question him again. [35]One of them,
an expert in religious law, tried to trap him with
this question: [36]"Teacher, which is the most important commandment in the law of Moses?"
[37]Jesus replied, " 'You must love the LORD
your God with all your heart, all your soul, and
all your mind.'* [38]This is the first and greatest
commandment. [39]A second is equally important:
'Love your neighbor as yourself.'* [40]The entire
law and all the demands of the prophets are
based on these two commandments."

Whose Son Is the Messiah?
[41]Then, surrounded by the Pharisees, Jesus asked
them a question: [42]"What do you think about the
Messiah? Whose son is he?"
They replied, "He is the son of David."
[43]Jesus responded, "Then why does David,
speaking under the inspiration of the Spirit, call
the Messiah 'my Lord'? For David said,

[44]'The LORD said to my Lord,
Sit in the place of honor at my right hand
until I humble your enemies beneath your
feet.'*

[45]Since David called the Messiah 'my Lord,' how
can the Messiah be his son?"
[46]No one could answer him. And after that,
no one dared to ask him any more questions.

Jesus Criticizes the Religious Leaders
23 Then Jesus said to the crowds and to
his disciples, [2]"The teachers of religious law and the Pharisees are the

22:19 Greek *a denarius.* **22:24** Deut 25:5-6. **22:31** Greek *read about this? God said.* **22:32** Exod 3:6. **22:37** Deut 6:5. **22:39** Lev 19:18. **22:44** Ps 110:1.

22:15–46 Questions from the Pharisees and Sadducees. 15–22: Jesus exposes the wicked motives of the Pharisees and the Sadducees, cutting through their trick questions about paying taxes to the emperor. **23–33:** Another trick question, this time about the resurrection. **34–40:** This is the core of the commandments. **41–46:** Jesus asks a question in his turn that exposes the lack of understanding of the Scriptures of his opponents.

23:1–36 The Hypocrisy of the Religious Leaders. 1–12: Jesus tells the listeners that the scribes and Pharisees are hypocrites who do not practice what they preach. **13–36:** Jesus addresses the scribes and

official interpreters of the law of Moses.* [3]So practice and obey whatever they tell you, but don't follow their example. For they don't practice what they teach. [4]They crush people with unbearable religious demands and never lift a finger to ease the burden.

[5]"Everything they do is for show. On their arms they wear extra wide prayer boxes with Scripture verses inside, and they wear robes with extra long tassels.* [6]And they love to sit at the head table at banquets and in the seats of honor in the synagogues. [7]They love to receive respectful greetings as they walk in the marketplaces, and to be called 'Rabbi.'*

[8]"Don't let anyone call you 'Rabbi,' for you have only one teacher, and all of you are equal as brothers and sisters.* [9]And don't address anyone here on earth as 'Father,' for only God in heaven is your spiritual Father. [10]And don't let anyone call you 'Teacher,' for you have only one teacher, the Messiah. [11]The greatest among you must be a servant. [12]But those who exalt themselves will be humbled, and those who humble themselves will be exalted.

[13]"What sorrow awaits you teachers of religious law and you Pharisees. Hypocrites! For you shut the door of the Kingdom of Heaven in people's faces. You won't go in yourselves, and you don't let others enter either.*

[15]"What sorrow awaits you teachers of religious law and you Pharisees. Hypocrites! For you cross land and sea to make one convert, and then you turn that person into twice the child of hell* you yourselves are!

[16]"Blind guides! What sorrow awaits you! For you say that it means nothing to swear 'by God's Temple,' but that it is binding to swear 'by the gold in the Temple.' [17]Blind fools! Which is more important—the gold or the Temple that makes the gold sacred? [18]And you say that to swear 'by the altar' is not binding, but to swear 'by the gifts on the altar' is binding. [19]How blind! For which is more important—the gift on the altar or the altar that makes the gift sacred? [20]When you swear 'by the altar,' you are swearing by it and by everything on it. [21]And when you swear 'by the Temple,' you are swearing by it and by God, who lives in it. [22]And when you swear 'by heaven,' you are swearing by the throne of God and by God, who sits on the throne.

[23]"What sorrow awaits you teachers of religious law and you Pharisees. Hypocrites! For you are careful to tithe even the tiniest income from your herb gardens,* but you ignore the more important aspects of the law—justice, mercy, and faith. You should tithe, yes, but do not neglect the more important things. [24]Blind guides! You strain your water so you won't accidentally swallow a gnat, but you swallow a camel!*

[25]"What sorrow awaits you teachers of religious law and you Pharisees. Hypocrites! For you are so careful to clean the outside of the cup and the dish, but inside you are filthy—full of greed and self-indulgence! [26]You blind Pharisee! First wash the inside of the cup and the dish,* and then the outside will become clean, too.

[27]"What sorrow awaits you teachers of religious law and you Pharisees. Hypocrites! For you are like whitewashed tombs—beautiful on the outside but filled on the inside with dead people's bones and all sorts of impurity. [28]Outwardly you look like righteous people, but inwardly your hearts are filled with hypocrisy and lawlessness.

[29]"What sorrow awaits you teachers of religious law and you Pharisees. Hypocrites! For you build tombs for the prophets your ancestors killed, and you decorate the monuments of the godly people your ancestors destroyed. [30]Then you say, 'If we had lived in the days of our ancestors, we would never have joined them in killing the prophets.'

[31]"But in saying that, you testify against yourselves that you are indeed the descendants of those who murdered the prophets. [32]Go ahead

23:2 Greek *and the Pharisees sit in the seat of Moses.* **23:5** Greek *They enlarge their phylacteries and lengthen their tassels.* **23:7** *Rabbi,* from Aramaic, means "master" or "teacher." **23:8** Greek *brothers.* **23:13** Some manuscripts add verse 14, *What sorrow awaits you teachers of religious law and you Pharisees. Hypocrites! You shamelessly cheat widows out of their property and then pretend to be pious by making long prayers in public. Because of this, you will be severely punished.* Compare Mark 12:40 and Luke 20:47. **23:15** Greek *of Gehenna;* also in 23:33. **23:23** Greek *tithe the mint, the dill, and the cumin.* **23:24** See Lev 11:4, 23, where gnats and camels are both forbidden as food. **23:26** Some manuscripts do not include *and the dish.*

Pharisees again with a series of blistering charges. Repeatedly he calls them hypocrites. **13:** He batters them with their culpability not only in shutting themselves out of the kingdom but, even more damning, locking others out too. **23:** They have twisted God's law over and over again and totally missed the things that matter. **25–27:** They show religious rectitude on the outside, but God, who sees on the inside, sees only filth and sin. **29–33:** They set themselves up self-righteously, but their assured destination is hell.

and finish what your ancestors started. [33]Snakes!
Sons of vipers! How will you escape the judgment of hell?
[34]"Therefore, I am sending you prophets and
wise men and teachers of religious law. But you
will kill some by crucifixion, and you will flog
others with whips in your synagogues, chasing
them from city to city. [35]As a result, you will be
held responsible for the murder of all godly people of all time—from the murder of righteous
Abel to the murder of Zechariah son of Bara-
chiah, whom you killed in the Temple between
the sanctuary and the altar. [36]I tell you the truth,
this judgment will fall on this very generation.

Jesus Grieves over Jerusalem
[37]"O Jerusalem, Jerusalem, the city that kills the
prophets and stones God's messengers! How
often I have wanted to gather your children together as a hen protects her chicks beneath her
wings, but you wouldn't let me. [38]And now, look,
your house is abandoned and desolate.* [39]For I
tell you this, you will never see me again until
you say, 'Blessings on the one who comes in the
name of the LORD!'* "

Jesus Foretells the Future
24 As Jesus was leaving the Temple
grounds, his disciples pointed out to
him the various Temple buildings.
[2]But he responded, "Do you see all these buildings? I tell you the truth, they will be completely
demolished. Not one stone will be left on top of
another!"
[3]Later, Jesus sat on the Mount of Olives. His
disciples came to him privately and said, "Tell us,
when will all this happen? What sign will signal
your return and the end of the world?*"
[4]Jesus told them, "Don't let anyone mislead
you, [5]for many will come in my name, claiming,
'I am the Messiah.' They will deceive many. [6]And
you will hear of wars and threats of wars, but
don't panic. Yes, these things must take place, but
the end won't follow immediately. [7]Nation will
go to war against nation, and kingdom against
kingdom. There will be famines and earthquakes
in many parts of the world. [8]But all this is only
the first of the birth pains, with more to come.
[9]"Then you will be arrested, persecuted, and
killed. You will be hated all over the world because you are my followers.* [10]And many will
turn away from me and betray and hate each
other. [11]And many false prophets will appear and
will deceive many people. [12]Sin will be rampant
everywhere, and the love of many will grow cold.
[13]But the one who endures to the end will be
saved. [14]And the Good News about the Kingdom
will be preached throughout the whole world, so
that all nations* will hear it; and then the end
will come.
[15]"The day is coming when you will see
what Daniel the prophet spoke about—the sacrilegious object that causes desecration* standing in the Holy Place." (Reader, pay attention!)
[16]"Then those in Judea must flee to the hills.
[17]A person out on the deck of a roof must not
go down into the house to pack. [18]A person out
in the field must not return even to get a coat.
[19]How terrible it will be for pregnant women and
for nursing mothers in those days. [20]And pray
that your flight will not be in winter or on the
Sabbath. [21]For there will be greater anguish than
at any time since the world began. And it will
never be so great again. [22]In fact, unless that time
of calamity is shortened, not a single person will
survive. But it will be shortened for the sake of
God's chosen ones.
[23]"Then if anyone tells you, 'Look, here is the
Messiah,' or 'There he is,' don't believe it. [24]For
false messiahs and false prophets will rise up and

23:38 Some manuscripts do not include *and desolate.*
23:39 Ps 118:26. **24:3** Or *the age?* **24:9** Greek *on account of my name.* **24:14** Or *all peoples.* **24:15** Greek *the abomination of desolation.* See Dan 9:27; 11:31; 12:11.

23:37–39 Lament over Jerusalem. Jesus has effectively signed his death warrant. But it is not for himself that he grieves. He turns to the city and shares his heartache for all that lies ahead. He is a mother hen, spreading her wings so that her chicks may shelter beneath her when danger looms. It is a beautiful, tender, powerful image. But if the chicks won't come, what can she do? It is not only the King who will die.

24:1—25:46 Fifth Discourse: And the King Shall Come Again

24:1–41 Signs of the End. 1–3: Events were reaching a climax. Jesus foretells the destruction of the Temple, which would have horrified the disciples as well as the religious authorities. The disciples ask what signs will warn them of the end. *The end of the world,* or "end of [the present] age," indicates the end of the old order and beginning of the new, not the destruction of the universe. **4–28:** Jesus gives no timetable; rather, he speaks first of a lengthy period of suffering, of wars, and of natural disasters. He warns of those who will come claiming to be the returning Messiah and of many false prophets who will successfully deceive many people. **29–31:** But when he comes again, it will be no hidden event. Rather, the whole

perform great signs and wonders so as to deceive,
if possible, even God's chosen ones. 25 See, I have
warned you about this ahead of time.
26 "So if someone tells you, 'Look, the Messiah is out in the desert,' don't bother to go and
look. Or, 'Look, he is hiding here,' don't believe
it! 27 For as the lightning flashes in the east and
shines to the west, so it will be when the Son of
Man* comes. 28 Just as the gathering of vultures
shows there is a carcass nearby, so these signs indicate that the end is near.*
29 "Immediately after the anguish of those
days,

the sun will be darkened,
 the moon will give no light,
the stars will fall from the sky,
 and the powers in the heavens will be
  shaken.*

30 And then at last, the sign that the Son of Man
is coming will appear in the heavens, and there
will be deep mourning among all the peoples of
the earth. And they will see the Son of Man coming on the clouds of heaven with power and great
glory.* 31 And he will send out his angels with the
mighty blast of a trumpet, and they will gather
his chosen ones from all over the world*—from
the farthest ends of the earth and heaven.
32 "Now learn a lesson from the fig tree.
When its branches bud and its leaves begin to
sprout, you know that summer is near. 33 In the
same way, when you see all these things, you can
know his return is very near, right at the door. 34 I
tell you the truth, this generation* will not pass
from the scene until all these things take place.
35 Heaven and earth will disappear, but my words
will never disappear.
36 "However, no one knows the day or hour
when these things will happen, not even the
angels in heaven or the Son himself.* Only the
Father knows.
37 "When the Son of Man returns, it will be
like it was in Noah's day. 38 In those days before
the flood, the people were enjoying banquets and
parties and weddings right up to the time Noah
entered his boat. 39 People didn't realize what was
going to happen until the flood came and swept
them all away. That is the way it will be when the
Son of Man comes.
40 "Two men will be working together in the
field; one will be taken, the other left. 41 Two
women will be grinding flour at the mill; one will
be taken, the other left.
42 "So you, too, must keep watch! For you
don't know what day your Lord is coming. 43 Understand this: If a homeowner knew exactly when
a burglar was coming, he would keep watch and
not permit his house to be broken into. 44 You
also must be ready all the time, for the Son of
Man will come when least expected.
45 "A faithful, sensible servant is one to whom
the master can give the responsibility of managing
his other household servants and feeding them.
46 If the master returns and finds that the servant
has done a good job, there will be a reward. 47 I tell
you the truth, the master will put that servant in
charge of all he owns. 48 But what if the servant
is evil and thinks, 'My master won't be back for
a while,' 49 and he begins beating the other servants, partying, and getting drunk? 50 The master
will return unannounced and unexpected, 51 and
he will cut the servant to pieces and assign him a
place with the hypocrites. In that place there will
be weeping and gnashing of teeth.

Parable of the Ten Bridesmaids

25 "Then the Kingdom of Heaven will
be like ten bridesmaids* who took
their lamps and went to meet the
bridegroom. 2 Five of them were foolish, and five
were wise. 3 The five who were foolish didn't take
enough olive oil for their lamps, 4 but the other five were wise enough to take along extra oil.
5 When the bridegroom was delayed, they all became drowsy and fell asleep.

24:27 "Son of Man" is a title Jesus used for himself.
24:28 Greek *Wherever the carcass is, the vultures gather.*
24:29 See Isa 13:10; 34:4; Joel 2:10. **24:30** See Dan 7:13.
24:31 Greek *from the four winds.* **24:34** Or *this age,* or *this nation.* **24:36** Some manuscripts do not include *or the Son himself.* **25:1** Or *virgins;* also in 25:7, 11.

world from *east . . . to west* will see him in his glory. **32–41:** And yet there are signs that are seen in every generation, so that followers down through the centuries will always be ready and expectant, waiting for the King to return at any moment. **36:** The exact moment is known only to the Father.

24:42–51 Two Parables of Readiness. A *burglar* relies on surprise. *A faithful . . . servant* is ready for the master's return, but an *evil* servant will fall into bad ways and *the master will return unannounced* and punish him.

25:1–46 Parables of the Kingdom. 1–13 The Bridesmaids. Matthew has often shown the excluded becoming the included; here the reverse is true: Like the religious experts, some who are sure of their inclusion will find they are among the excluded.

6 "At midnight they were roused by the shout, 'Look, the bridegroom is coming! Come out and meet him!'

7 "All the bridesmaids got up and prepared their lamps. 8 Then the five foolish ones asked the others, 'Please give us some of your oil because our lamps are going out.'

9 "But the others replied, 'We don't have enough for all of us. Go to a shop and buy some for yourselves.'

10 "But while they were gone to buy oil, the bridegroom came. Then those who were ready went in with him to the marriage feast, and the door was locked. 11 Later, when the other five bridesmaids returned, they stood outside, calling, 'Lord! Lord! Open the door for us!'

12 "But he called back, 'Believe me, I don't know you!'

13 "So you, too, must keep watch! For you do not know the day or hour of my return.

Parable of the Three Servants

14 "Again, the Kingdom of Heaven can be illustrated by the story of a man going on a long trip. He called together his servants and entrusted his money to them while he was gone. 15 He gave five bags of silver* to one, two bags of silver to another, and one bag of silver to the last—dividing it in proportion to their abilities. He then left on his trip.

16 "The servant who received the five bags of silver began to invest the money and earned five more. 17 The servant with two bags of silver also went to work and earned two more. 18 But the servant who received the one bag of silver dug a hole in the ground and hid the master's money.

19 "After a long time their master returned from his trip and called them to give an account of how they had used his money. 20 The servant to whom he had entrusted the five bags of silver came forward with five more and said, 'Master, you gave me five bags of silver to invest, and I have earned five more.'

21 "The master was full of praise. 'Well done, my good and faithful servant. You have been faithful in handling this small amount, so now I will give you many more responsibilities. Let's celebrate together!*'

22 "The servant who had received the two bags of silver came forward and said, 'Master, you gave me two bags of silver to invest, and I have earned two more.'

23 "The master said, 'Well done, my good and faithful servant. You have been faithful in handling this small amount, so now I will give you many more responsibilities. Let's celebrate together!'

24 "Then the servant with the one bag of silver came and said, 'Master, I knew you were a harsh man, harvesting crops you didn't plant and gathering crops you didn't cultivate. 25 I was afraid I would lose your money, so I hid it in the earth. Look, here is your money back.'

26 "But the master replied, 'You wicked and lazy servant! If you knew I harvested crops I didn't plant and gathered crops I didn't cultivate, 27 why didn't you deposit my money in the bank? At least I could have gotten some interest on it.'

28 "Then he ordered, 'Take the money from this servant, and give it to the one with the ten bags of silver. 29 To those who use well what they are given, even more will be given, and they will have an abundance. But from those who do nothing, even what little they have will be taken away. 30 Now throw this useless servant into outer darkness, where there will be weeping and gnashing of teeth.'

The Final Judgment

31 "But when the Son of Man* comes in his glory, and all the angels with him, then he will sit upon his glorious throne. 32 All the nations* will be gathered in his presence, and he will separate the people as a shepherd separates the sheep from the goats. 33 He will place the sheep at his right hand and the goats at his left.

25:15 Greek *talents;* also throughout the story. A talent is equal to 75 pounds or 34 kilograms. **25:21** Greek *Enter into the joy of your master* [or *your Lord*]; also in 25:23. **25:31** "Son of Man" is a title Jesus used for himself. **25:32** Or *peoples.*

25:14–30 The Talents. The Master's return will be a moment of inescapable accountability and judgment. The parable highlights how God entrusts different gifts and resources to different people *in proportion to their abilities*. The question is not what we might have done in different circumstances or with someone else's opportunities but how we have used to the full what we do have for the benefit of the Lord.

25:31–46 The Judgment. *All the nations* of the world will see Jesus in his full glory and will be judged by him. Practical, compassionate goodness is as if done for the Lord. It is not that good works save us, but that those living out the reality of repentance echo the ministry of the Servant (Isa 61:1–2). Such mercy and kindness is open to old and young, male and female, rich and poor. That is the evidence that you belong in the kingdom. When the King returns, he will know where you belong for eternity.

34“Then the King will say to those on his
right, ‘Come, you who are blessed by my Father,
inherit the Kingdom prepared for you from the
creation of the world. 35For I was hungry, and you
fed me. I was thirsty, and you gave me a drink.
I was a stranger, and you invited me into your
home. 36I was naked, and you gave me clothing.
I was sick, and you cared for me. I was in prison,
and you visited me.’
37“Then these righteous ones will reply,
‘Lord, when did we ever see you hungry and
feed you? Or thirsty and give you something to
drink? 38Or a stranger and show you hospitality?
Or naked and give you clothing? 39When did we
ever see you sick or in prison and visit you?’
40“And the King will say, ‘I tell you the truth,
when you did it to one of the least of these my
brothers and sisters,* you were doing it to me!’
41“Then the King will turn to those on the left
and say, ‘Away with you, you cursed ones, into the
eternal fire prepared for the devil and his demons.*
42For I was hungry, and you didn’t feed me. I was
thirsty, and you didn’t give me a drink. 43I was a
stranger, and you didn’t invite me into your home.
I was naked, and you didn’t give me clothing. I was
sick and in prison, and you didn’t visit me.’
44“Then they will reply, ‘Lord, when did we
ever see you hungry or thirsty or a stranger or
naked or sick or in prison, and not help you?’
45“And he will answer, ‘I tell you the truth, when
you refused to help the least of these my brothers
and sisters, you were refusing to help me.’
46“And they will go away into eternal punishment, but the righteous will go into eternal
life.”

The Plot to Kill Jesus

26 When Jesus had finished saying all
these things, he said to his disciples,
2“As you know, Passover begins in
two days, and the Son of Man* will be handed
over to be crucified.”
3At that same time the leading priests and elders were meeting at the residence of Caiaphas, the
high priest, 4plotting how to capture Jesus secretly
and kill him. 5“But not during the Passover celebration,” they agreed, “or the people may riot.”

Jesus Anointed at Bethany

6Meanwhile, Jesus was in Bethany at the home
of Simon, a man who had previously had leprosy.
7While he was eating,* a woman came in with a
beautiful alabaster jar of expensive perfume and
poured it over his head.
8The disciples were indignant when they saw
this. “What a waste!” they said. 9“It could have
been sold for a high price and the money given
to the poor.”
10But Jesus, aware of this, replied, “Why criticize this woman for doing such a good thing to
me? 11You will always have the poor among you,
but you will not always have me. 12She has poured
this perfume on me to prepare my body for burial.
13I tell you the truth, wherever the Good News
is preached throughout the world, this woman’s
deed will be remembered and discussed.”

Judas Agrees to Betray Jesus

14Then Judas Iscariot, one of the twelve disciples,
went to the leading priests 15and asked, “How
much will you pay me to betray Jesus to you?”
And they gave him thirty pieces of silver. 16From
that time on, Judas began looking for an opportunity to betray Jesus.

The Last Supper

17On the first day of the Festival of Unleavened

25:40 Greek *my brothers.* **25:41** Greek *his angels.* **26:2** “Son of Man” is a title Jesus used for himself. **26:7** Or *reclining.*

26:1—28:20 Narrative: Tragedy—and Triumph!

26:1–5 The Plot to Kill Jesus. *Passover* was the focal point of the Jewish religious year, recalling God’s intervention to deliver his people from oppression (Exod 12). It had also become the focal point for nationalism. God who had delivered in the past must surely intervene again, and he had promised to do so through his Messiah. Many people believed that this year and this charismatic figure, Jesus, meant that now was the time. They were right. But the assumption that the Messiah would overthrow the Romans was wrong. **3–5:** Nonetheless the chief priests and religious leaders know they cannot wait a moment longer to get rid of Jesus.

26:6–13 Anointing. Jesus’ anointing—a sacred symbolic action—by an unnamed woman is especially poignant, since it was forbidden to anoint the body of an executed criminal. **12:** So Jesus says the act is *to prepare my body for burial*. Though he became sin for us, he was truly righteous and did not deserve to die a criminal’s death. Matthew does not tell us what prompted this woman’s extravagant gesture. She was probably lavishing on him her most costly possession. Jesus affirms the woman’s love and the accuracy of her intuition, promising she will be *remembered*.

26:14–16 Betrayal. The ointment was costly, but Jesus’ life can be bought with *thirty pieces of silver*, the price of a slave accidentally killed (Exod 21:32).

Bread, the disciples came to Jesus and asked,
“Where do you want us to prepare the Passover
meal for you?”
18 “As you go into the city,” he told them, “you
will see a certain man. Tell him, ‘The Teacher
says: My time has come, and I will eat the Passover meal with my disciples at your house.’ ”
19 So the disciples did as Jesus told them and prepared the Passover meal there.
20 When it was evening, Jesus sat down at the
table* with the twelve disciples.* 21 While they
were eating, he said, “I tell you the truth, one of
you will betray me.”
22 Greatly distressed, each one asked in turn,
“Am I the one, Lord?”
23 He replied, “One of you who has just eaten
from this bowl with me will betray me. 24 For the
Son of Man must die, as the Scriptures declared
long ago. But how terrible it will be for the one
who betrays him. It would be far better for that
man if he had never been born!”
25 Judas, the one who would betray him, also
asked, “Rabbi, am I the one?”
And Jesus told him, “You have said it.”
26 As they were eating, Jesus took some bread
and blessed it. Then he broke it in pieces and gave
it to the disciples, saying, “Take this and eat it,
for this is my body.”
27 And he took a cup of wine and gave thanks
to God for it. He gave it to them and said, “Each
of you drink from it, 28 for this is my blood,
which confirms the covenant* between God and
his people. It is poured out as a sacrifice to forgive the sins of many. 29 Mark my words—I will
not drink wine again until the day I drink it new
with you in my Father’s Kingdom.”
30 Then they sang a hymn and went out to the
Mount of Olives.

Jesus Predicts Peter’s Denial

31 On the way, Jesus told them, “Tonight all of
you will desert me. For the Scriptures say,

‘God will strike* the Shepherd,
and the sheep of the flock will be scattered.’

32 But after I have been raised from the dead, I
will go ahead of you to Galilee and meet you
there.”
33 Peter declared, “Even if everyone else deserts you, I will never desert you.”
34 Jesus replied, “I tell you the truth, Peter—
this very night, before the rooster crows, you
will deny three times that you even know me.”
35 “No!” Peter insisted. “Even if I have to die
with you, I will never deny you!” And all the
other disciples vowed the same.

Jesus Prays in Gethsemane

36 Then Jesus went with them to the olive grove
called Gethsemane, and he said, “Sit here while
I go over there to pray.” 37 He took Peter and
Zebedee’s two sons, James and John, and he became anguished and distressed. 38 He told them,
“My soul is crushed with grief to the point of
death. Stay here and keep watch with me.”
39 He went on a little farther and bowed with
his face to the ground, praying, “My Father! If
it is possible, let this cup of suffering be taken
away from me. Yet I want your will to be done,
not mine.”
40 Then he returned to the disciples and found
them asleep. He said to Peter, “Couldn’t you
watch with me even one hour? 41 Keep watch and
pray, so that you will not give in to temptation.
For the spirit is willing, but the body is weak!”
42 Then Jesus left them a second time and
prayed, “My Father! If this cup cannot be taken
away* unless I drink it, your will be done.” 43 When
he returned to them again, he found them sleeping, for they couldn’t keep their eyes open.
44 So he went to pray a third time, saying the
same things again. 45 Then he came to the disciples and said, “Go ahead and sleep. Have your
rest. But look—the time has come. The Son of
Man is betrayed into the hands of sinners. 46 Up,
let’s be going. Look, my betrayer is here!”

Jesus Is Betrayed and Arrested

47 And even as Jesus said this, Judas, one of the

26:20a Or *Jesus reclined.* **26:20b** Some manuscripts read *the Twelve.* **26:28** Some manuscripts read *the new covenant.* **26:31** Greek *I will strike.* Zech 13:7. **26:42** Greek *If this cannot pass.*

26:17–30 The Passover Meal. The meal is on the one hand completely in the shadow of betrayal and death, and on the other hand a triumphant reformulation of what it is all about. **28:** Jesus could not more explicitly state the reason for his death: *a sacrifice to forgive the sins of many*. The angel’s promise to Joseph (Matt 1:21) is about to be fulfilled.

26:31–56 Betrayal and Arrest. 31–35: In different ways all the disciples, not just Judas, betray Jesus. Even Peter, effusive to the last, will do so. **36–46:** Jesus faces his ordeal alone, even when surrounded by people. Only his *Father* stands by him, as he agonizes in prayer, and even his Father has no comforting word of reprieve. **47–56:** It is impossible to fathom the desolation of desertion by all his friends,

twelve disciples, arrived with a crowd of men
armed with swords and clubs. They had been
sent by the leading priests and elders of the
people. [48]The traitor, Judas, had given them a
prearranged signal: "You will know which one to
arrest when I greet him with a kiss." [49]So Judas
came straight to Jesus. "Greetings, Rabbi!" he
exclaimed and gave him the kiss.

[50]Jesus said, "My friend, go ahead and do
what you have come for."

Then the others grabbed Jesus and arrested
him. [51]But one of the men with Jesus pulled
out his sword and struck the high priest's slave,
slashing off his ear.

[52]"Put away your sword," Jesus told him.
"Those who use the sword will die by the sword.
[53]Don't you realize that I could ask my Father for
thousands* of angels to protect us, and he would
send them instantly? [54]But if I did, how would
the Scriptures be fulfilled that describe what
must happen now?"

[55]Then Jesus said to the crowd, "Am I some
dangerous revolutionary, that you come with
swords and clubs to arrest me? Why didn't you arrest me in the Temple? I was there teaching every
day. [56]But this is all happening to fulfill the words
of the prophets as recorded in the Scriptures." At
that point, all the disciples deserted him and fled.

Jesus before the Council

[57]Then the people who had arrested Jesus led him
to the home of Caiaphas, the high priest, where
the teachers of religious law and the elders had
gathered. [58]Meanwhile, Peter followed him at a
distance and came to the high priest's courtyard.
He went in and sat with the guards and waited to
see how it would all end.

[59]Inside, the leading priests and the entire high
council* were trying to find witnesses who would
lie about Jesus, so they could put him to death.
[60]But even though they found many who agreed
to give false witness, they could not use anyone's
testimony. Finally, two men came forward [61]who
declared, "This man said, 'I am able to destroy the
Temple of God and rebuild it in three days.' "

[62]Then the high priest stood up and said to
Jesus, "Well, aren't you going to answer these
charges? What do you have to say for yourself?"
[63]But Jesus remained silent. Then the high priest
said to him, "I demand in the name of the living
God—tell us if you are the Messiah, the Son of
God."

[64]Jesus replied, "You have said it. And in the
future you will see the Son of Man seated in the
place of power at God's right hand* and coming
on the clouds of heaven."*

[65]Then the high priest tore his clothing to
show his horror and said, "Blasphemy! Why do
we need other witnesses? You have all heard his
blasphemy. [66]What is your verdict?"

"Guilty!" they shouted. "He deserves to die!"

[67]Then they began to spit in Jesus' face and
beat him with their fists. And some slapped him,
[68]jeering, "Prophesy to us, you Messiah! Who
hit you that time?"

Peter Denies Jesus

[69]Meanwhile, Peter was sitting outside in the
courtyard. A servant girl came over and said to
him, "You were one of those with Jesus the Galilean."

[70]But Peter denied it in front of everyone. "I
don't know what you're talking about," he said.

[71]Later, out by the gate, another servant girl
noticed him and said to those standing around,
"This man was with Jesus of Nazareth.*"

[72]Again Peter denied it, this time with an
oath. "I don't even know the man," he said.

[73]A little later some of the other bystanders
came over to Peter and said, "You must be one of
them; we can tell by your Galilean accent."

[74]Peter swore, "A curse on me if I'm lying—
I don't know the man!" And immediately the
rooster crowed.

[75]Suddenly, Jesus' words flashed through Peter's mind: "Before the rooster crows, you will
deny three times that you even know me." And
he went away, weeping bitterly.

26:53 Greek *twelve legions.* **26:59** Greek *the Sanhedrin.* **26:64a** Greek *seated at the right hand of the power.* See Ps 110:1. **26:64b** See Dan 7:13. **26:71** Or *Jesus the Nazarene.*

---

the pain of having the crowds, over whom he had wept and mourned and for whom he had done so many compassionate acts, turn in abrupt fickleness from adulation to hatred. They come, a hostile army, prepared to fight to capture him. But there is no fight: Jesus gives himself up.

26:57–68 The Trial. There was no legitimate charge to be brought against Jesus. **59:** The *leading priests,* appointed guardians of truth and righteousness, deliberately seek false witnesses, purveyors of untruth and wickedness, to justify their unlawful actions. **62–66:** Finally it is that central question, Who is Jesus? addressed directly to Jesus by the *high priest,* that leads to the charge: *blasphemy.*

26:69–75 Peter's Denial. As Jesus foretold (v. 34), Peter too betrays him.

Judas Hangs Himself

27 Very early in the morning the leading priests and the elders of the people met again to lay plans for putting Jesus to death. 2 Then they bound him, led him away, and took him to Pilate, the Roman governor.

3 When Judas, who had betrayed him, realized that Jesus had been condemned to die, he was filled with remorse. So he took the thirty pieces of silver back to the leading priests and the elders. 4 "I have sinned," he declared, "for I have betrayed an innocent man."

"What do we care?" they retorted. "That's your problem."

5 Then Judas threw the silver coins down in the Temple and went out and hanged himself.

6 The leading priests picked up the coins. "It wouldn't be right to put this money in the Temple treasury," they said, "since it was payment for murder."* 7 After some discussion they finally decided to buy the potter's field, and they made it into a cemetery for foreigners. 8 That is why the field is still called the Field of Blood. 9 This fulfilled the prophecy of Jeremiah that says,

"They took* the thirty pieces of silver—
 the price at which he was valued by the
  people of Israel,
10 and purchased the potter's field,
 as the LORD directed."*

Jesus' Trial before Pilate

11 Now Jesus was standing before Pilate, the Roman governor. "Are you the king of the Jews?" the governor asked him.

Jesus replied, "You have said it."

12 But when the leading priests and the elders made their accusations against him, Jesus remained silent. 13 "Don't you hear all these charges they are bringing against you?" Pilate demanded. 14 But Jesus made no response to any of the charges, much to the governor's surprise.

15 Now it was the governor's custom each year during the Passover celebration to release one prisoner to the crowd—anyone they wanted. 16 This year there was a notorious prisoner, a man named Barabbas.* 17 As the crowds gathered before Pilate's house that morning, he asked them, "Which one do you want me to release to you—Barabbas, or Jesus who is called the Messiah?" 18 (He knew very well that the religious leaders had arrested Jesus out of envy.)

19 Just then, as Pilate was sitting on the judgment seat, his wife sent him this message: "Leave that innocent man alone. I suffered through a terrible nightmare about him last night."

20 Meanwhile, the leading priests and the elders persuaded the crowd to ask for Barabbas to be released and for Jesus to be put to death. 21 So the governor asked again, "Which of these two do you want me to release to you?"

The crowd shouted back, "Barabbas!"

22 Pilate responded, "Then what should I do with Jesus who is called the Messiah?"

They shouted back, "Crucify him!"

23 "Why?" Pilate demanded. "What crime has he committed?"

But the mob roared even louder, "Crucify him!"

24 Pilate saw that he wasn't getting anywhere and that a riot was developing. So he sent for a bowl of water and washed his hands before the crowd, saying, "I am innocent of this man's blood. The responsibility is yours!"

25 And all the people yelled back, "We will take responsibility for his death—we and our children!"*

26 So Pilate released Barabbas to them. He ordered Jesus flogged with a lead-tipped whip, then turned him over to the Roman soldiers to be crucified.

The Soldiers Mock Jesus

27 Some of the governor's soldiers took Jesus into

27:6 Greek *since it is the price for blood.* **27:9** Or *I took.* **27:9-10** Greek *as the LORD directed me.* Zech 11:12-13; Jer 32:6-9. **27:16** Some manuscripts read *Jesus Barabbas;* also in 27:17. **27:25** Greek *"His blood be on us and on our children."*

27:1–26 The Trial before Pilate. 1–2: Jesus is sent to Pilate. **3–10:** Judas's end. **11:** Pilate in turn asks, "Who are you?" The high priest had posed the question in Jewish religious terms: "Are you the Messiah?" (26:64); Pilate poses it in Gentile terms: *Are you the king of the Jews?* **17–24:** Shrewd enough to know that Jesus has been framed, Pilate nonetheless gives way to popular demand in order to prevent a riot. After all, he might pay with his life if there is an insurrection. His wife's dream may have filled him with superstitious dread, and he protests Jesus' innocence; he takes pains to show that he disclaims responsibility for Jesus' death. **25:** And the crowd's shout, *We will take responsibility for his death—we and our children* is more true than they know. Sadly, it has since been used to demonize Jews, but it is really meant to apply to all who, caught up in lynch-mob emotion, would connive at injustice.

27:27–31 Roman Mockery. Sentence passed, Jesus is fair game for abuse by the Roman soldiers. To them, holed up in a hostile foreign country, nervous be-

their headquarters* and called out the entire regiment. [28]They stripped him and put a scarlet robe on him. [29]They wove thorn branches into a crown and put it on his head, and they placed a reed stick in his right hand as a scepter. Then they knelt before him in mockery and taunted, "Hail! King of the Jews!" [30]And they spit on him and grabbed the stick and struck him on the head with it. [31]When they were finally tired of mocking him, they took off the robe and put his own clothes on him again. Then they led him away to be crucified.

The Crucifixion

[32]Along the way, they came across a man named Simon, who was from Cyrene,* and the soldiers forced him to carry Jesus' cross. [33]And they went out to a place called Golgotha (which means "Place of the Skull"). [34]The soldiers gave him wine mixed with bitter gall, but when he had tasted it, he refused to drink it.

[35]After they had nailed him to the cross, the soldiers gambled for his clothes by throwing dice.* [36]Then they sat around and kept guard as he hung there. [37]A sign was fastened above Jesus' head, announcing the charge against him. It read: "This is Jesus, the King of the Jews." [38]Two revolutionaries* were crucified with him, one on his right and one on his left.

[39]The people passing by shouted abuse, shaking their heads in mockery. [40]"Look at you now!" they yelled at him. "You said you were going to destroy the Temple and rebuild it in three days. Well then, if you are the Son of God, save yourself and come down from the cross!"

[41]The leading priests, the teachers of religious law, and the elders also mocked Jesus. [42]"He saved others," they scoffed, "but he can't save himself! So he is the King of Israel, is he? Let him come down from the cross right now, and we will believe in him! [43]He trusted God, so let God rescue him now if he wants him! For he said, 'I am the Son of God.' " [44]Even the revolutionaries who were crucified with him ridiculed him in the same way.

The Death of Jesus

[45]At noon, darkness fell across the whole land until three o'clock. [46]At about three o'clock, Jesus called out with a loud voice, *"Eli, Eli,* lema sabachthani?"* which means "My God, my God, why have you abandoned me?"*

[47]Some of the bystanders misunderstood and thought he was calling for the prophet Elijah. [48]One of them ran and filled a sponge with sour wine, holding it up to him on a reed stick so he could drink. [49]But the rest said, "Wait! Let's see whether Elijah comes to save him."*

[50]Then Jesus shouted out again, and he released his spirit. [51]At that moment the curtain in the sanctuary of the Temple was torn in two, from top to bottom. The earth shook, rocks split apart, [52]and tombs opened. The bodies of many godly men and women who had died were raised from the dead. [53]They left the cemetery after Jesus' resurrection, went into the holy city of Jerusalem, and appeared to many people.

[54]The Roman officer* and the other soldiers at the crucifixion were terrified by the earthquake and all that had happened. They said, "This man truly was the Son of God!"

[55]And many women who had come from Gali-

27:27 Or *into the Praetorium.* **27:32** *Cyrene* was a city in northern Africa. **27:35** Greek *by casting lots.* A few late manuscripts add *This fulfilled the word of the prophet: "They divided my garments among themselves and cast lots for my robe."* See Ps 22:18. **27:38** Or *criminals;* also in 27:44. **27:46a** Some manuscripts read *Eloi, Eloi.* **27:46b** Ps 22:1. **27:49** Some manuscripts add *And another took a spear and pierced his side, and out flowed water and blood.* Compare John 19:34. **27:54** Greek *The centurion.*

cause this was the most volatile point of the year, this is an opportunity for legalized violence, an occasion to open the valve on their pent-up emotions. Perhaps for them it was routine cruelty in a cruel age.

27:32–44 The Crucifixion. After brutal torture, Jesus is taken to Golgotha and crucified. **35–36:** Even in these last pain-wracked hours, shame is heaped on him. He is stripped. The soldiers gamble for his clothes, then settle down to watch until he dies. **37:** They contemptuously label him: *This is Jesus, the King of the Jews*. **39–44:** The *people*, the *priests*, and the *revolutionaries* dying alongside him mock and taunt.

27:45–56 The Death of Jesus. Yet at the moment of Jesus' death, the unnatural *darkness*, the earthquake, and the tearing of the great Temple *curtain*, symbolizing the opening up of access to God, brought transformed understanding. **54:** Gentiles, Romans at that, grasp who Jesus is: *This man truly was the Son of God!* **55–56:** It was the *women* who stayed with Jesus to the end. Matthew tells us they were *many*, though he names only three. *Mary (the mother of James and Joseph)* is probably Jesus' mother. Matthew tells us that these women had traveled with Jesus *to care for him*; perhaps even now they hoped to perform one last service for their loved one, though the bodies of the crucified were normally not returned to their

lee with Jesus to care for him were watching from
a distance. 56 Among them were Mary Magdalene,
Mary (the mother of James and Joseph), and the
mother of James and John, the sons of Zebedee.

The Burial of Jesus

57 As evening approached, Joseph, a rich man from
Arimathea who had become a follower of Jesus,
58 went to Pilate and asked for Jesus' body. And Pilate issued an order to release it to him. 59 Joseph
took the body and wrapped it in a long sheet of
clean linen cloth. 60 He placed it in his own new
tomb, which had been carved out of the rock. Then
he rolled a great stone across the entrance and left.
61 Both Mary Magdalene and the other Mary were
sitting across from the tomb and watching.

The Guard at the Tomb

62 The next day, on the Sabbath,* the leading
priests and Pharisees went to see Pilate. 63 They
told him, "Sir, we remember what that deceiver
once said while he was still alive: 'After three
days I will rise from the dead.' 64 So we request
that you seal the tomb until the third day. This
will prevent his disciples from coming and stealing his body and then telling everyone he was
raised from the dead! If that happens, we'll be
worse off than we were at first."

65 Pilate replied, "Take guards and secure it
the best you can." 66 So they sealed the tomb and
posted guards to protect it.

The Resurrection

28 Early on Sunday morning,* as the
new day was dawning, Mary Magdalene and the other Mary went out to
visit the tomb.

2 Suddenly there was a great earthquake! For
an angel of the Lord came down from heaven,
rolled aside the stone, and sat on it. 3 His face
shone like lightning, and his clothing was as
white as snow. 4 The guards shook with fear when
they saw him, and they fell into a dead faint.

5 Then the angel spoke to the women. "Don't be
afraid!" he said. "I know you are looking for Jesus,
who was crucified. 6 He isn't here! He is risen from
the dead, just as he said would happen. Come, see
where his body was lying. 7 And now, go quickly
and tell his disciples that he has risen from the dead,
and he is going ahead of you to Galilee. You will see
him there. Remember what I have told you."

8 The women ran quickly from the tomb. They
were very frightened but also filled with great
joy, and they rushed to give the disciples the angel's message. 9 And as they went, Jesus met them
and greeted them. And they ran to him, grasped
his feet, and worshiped him. 10 Then Jesus said to
them, "Don't be afraid! Go tell my brothers to
leave for Galilee, and they will see me there."

The Report of the Guard

11 As the women were on their way, some of the
guards went into the city and told the leading
priests what had happened. 12 A meeting with the
elders was called, and they decided to give the
soldiers a large bribe. 13 They told the soldiers,
"You must say, 'Jesus' disciples came during the
night while we were sleeping, and they stole
his body.' 14 If the governor hears about it, we'll
stand up for you so you won't get in trouble."
15 So the guards accepted the bribe and said what

27:62 Or *On the next day, which is after the Preparation.*
28:1 Greek *After the Sabbath, on the first day of the week.*

---

families but tossed into a common grave. What must Mary have felt as she watched her beloved son die? Moreover, watched him die in excruciating agony and utter disgrace? Could she even remotely begin to understand? Did she feel most of her life had been built around a lie, that she had been betrayed by God?

27:57–66 The Burial of Jesus. *Joseph*, a man of influence as well as wealth, obtains the body for dignified and proper burial, a tiny shaft of light on that bleak day. Did Mary help bathe the bloodied body, torn flesh of her flesh? **61:** At last there is nobody left but the two Marys. His mother is the only one to have been there from the very beginning to the very end.

28:1–15 The Risen Lord. As soon as the Sabbath is over, at dawn, the Marys return. **2–7:** The soldiers sent to guard the tomb are no match for divine intervention. A glorious *angel* tells the women not to be afraid: Just as he had promised, Jesus has risen from the dead. They are told to look for themselves to see that the tomb is empty and then to go and tell the disciples. **8–10:** As they turn to go, *frightened but also filled with great joy*, Jesus appears to them. Jesus' love for his mother is very tender at this point. So God entrusts to these women the key role of testimony to Jesus' death and resurrection. Every last detail must have been etched on Mary's mind and heart. God entrusted her with being the mother of his Son. Now he has entrusted her with that first revelation of Jesus' triumph over death and disaster. God has kept his word. Jesus is the one whom the angel said he would be: the Savior.

Women in Worship

The Old Testament originated in a world in which the male took the public role and the female, almost exclusively, the private role. Notable, however, is the presence of women who were fully recognized to be prophets (Miriam, Deborah, and Huldah); the openness of the office of Nazirite (an office comparable to the high priesthood in consecration) to women; and women bringing sacrifices without a male representing them.

Although it is true that there were no women priests in Israel, it should be remembered that the priestesses in the neighboring cults often were sacred prostitutes. Since the Old Testament was so inimical to the fertility cult, this alone might be considered a decisive factor in excluding women from the priesthood. Moreover, priesthood was considered a full-time vocation requiring such duties as the slaughtering of large animals. The periodic ritual uncleanness of women and the high value placed on the role of motherhood would also prevent women from participating in Israel's priesthood.

Simply because women were not required to appear three times a year at the sanctuary, as were men (Deut 16:16), does not exclude them from membership in the community. We must acknowledge that in that society it was natural that men sometimes represent women, but there are too many evidences of women participating fully and independently in the worship of Israel to suppose they were excluded from membership.

The data on the church at worship is scant in the New Testament. It must be noted, however, that Apollos seems to have been instructed by Priscilla and Aquila. Phoebe was a "deacon," a term used for Paul, Timothy, and many others. Paul takes for granted that women prophesy.

We find in some schools of ancient Judaism what seems a sharp antifeminist spirit, which is heard in such expressions as "the best way to destroy the law is to teach it to a woman" or the rabbinical prayer, "I thank you, Lord, that you have not made me . . . a woman." The more we learn of the social status of women in that culture the more astonishing is Jesus' relationship to women. His admonition to Martha that Mary had chosen the better part would hardly have merited the acclaim of the teachers of the law.

There is archaeological evidence from the third- and fourth-century frescoes that women may have functioned as clergy in the early church. The evidence is difficult to assess, but some see evidence that the hair of the person officiating at the altar has been removed, and there appear to be markings that show that someone scratched below the chin looking for a beard. Whether this is proof that there were female celebrants in the early church and that in a later period efforts were made to obscure or destroy such evidence is hard to determine. If the art of the early frescoes does indicate that women functioned as clergy, it would suggest that the early church did not see 1 Timothy 2:11–15 as universally applicable.

In the medieval period the governance of the church was strictly limited to a celibate male hierarchy. Women, however, did take a significant role in the monastic orders. During this period the rail at the altar became common; its purpose was to limit the proximity of women to the altar. Nevertheless, it must be said that a form of worship took place in devotional reading, study, writing, and singing. The apex of this activity may be seen in St. Teresa of Ávila (1515–82), whose actions and writings so influenced the church that she was beatified in 1614 by Pope Paul V and declared a doctor in the church in 1970 by Pope Paul VI.

they were told to say. Their story spread widely among the Jews, and they still tell it today.

The Great Commission

16 Then the eleven disciples left for Galilee, going to the mountain where Jesus had told them to go.
17 When they saw him, they worshiped him—but some of them doubted!
18 Jesus came and told his disciples, "I have been given all authority in heaven and on earth.

28:16–20 The Great Commission. Because Jesus is Savior, King, Messiah, and God's beloved Son, as Matthew has vividly shown, so *all authority in heaven and on earth* has been given to him. The King reigns. And because "King of the Jews," though true, is too small a title for the one who is King of the whole earth, it is now the whole earth, all the nations, all the peoples, who are to become *disciples*. It

19 Therefore, go and make disciples of all the nations,* baptizing them in the name of the Father and the Son and the Holy Spirit. 20 Teach these new disciples to obey all the commands I have given you. And be sure of this: I am with you always, even to the end of the age."

28:19 Or *all peoples.*

is now the Lord's people who are to go, *baptizing . . . in the name of the Father and the Son and the Holy Spirit* (in other words, with all the conjoint authority and equipping of the full Trinity, to every community of the globe, to declare the good news of the kingdom and to prepare for Jesus' promised return. And as they go they abide in grace: *Be sure of this: I am with you always, even to the end of the age.*

MARK

INTRODUCTION

The Gospel of Mark was probably written between AD 65 and AD 70. The only internal evidence for dating is Mark 13:14, which may be a reference to the siege of Jerusalem in 70. Toward the end of Nero's reign (AD 54–68) Christians in Rome suffered great persecution, and with the Jewish war of 66–70, their apocalyptic expectations surged. Both seem to be reflected in Mark—the Gospel for a suffering church. The text suggests it was written for a predominantly but not exclusively Gentile community. For one thing, it explains Jewish customs and beliefs, and contains many Latinisms. Suggested locations for Mark's community include Rome, Galilee, and Syria, or points east. The community's location must have been prominent enough that it was known and used in the writing of subsequent Gospels. John Chrysostom suggested Mark's Gospel might have originated in Egypt.

Ancient tradition associates Mark the evangelist with the John Mark of Acts in whose mother's home the Last Supper was said to have been held (see Acts 12:12, 25; 13:13; 15:37, 39; 1 Pet 5:13; Col 4:10; Phlm 24). Papias, who in the first half of the second century wrote the five-volume *Interpretation of the Lord's Sayings*, suggested that Mark was Peter's interpreter: "This also the Elder said: Mark, who became Peter's interpreter, wrote accurately, though not in order, all that he remembered of the things said and done by the Lord. For he had neither heard the Lord nor been one of his followers, but afterwards . . . he had followed Peter, who used to compose his discourses with a view to the need [of his hearers], but not as if he were composing a systematic account of the Lord's sayings. So Mark did nothing blameworthy in thus writing some things just as he remembered them; for he was careful of this one thing, to omit none of the things he had heard and to state no untruth therein."

Roughly one-fourth of the characters in Mark's narrative are women. In the Gospel's sixteen chapters, thirteen pericopes center around women (1:30–31; 3:31–35; 5:21–24, 35–43; 5:24–34; 6:3, 14–29; 7:24–30; 12:41–44; 14:3–9, 66–69; 15:40–41, 47; 16:1–8). Only five named women appear: Mary the mother of Jesus (6:3), Herodias (6:19), Mary of Magdala, Mary the mother of James and Joseph (see translator's note), and Salome (15:40, 47). Other women in the Gospel are designated in relation to men—Simon's mother-in-law (1:30); Jesus' mother and sisters (3:31–35; 6:3); Jairus's daughter (5:23); a widow (12:41–44); and a servant girl of the high priest (14:66–69)—or to their nationality (the Syro-Phoenician woman (7:24–30). Only the hemorrhaging woman (5:24–34) and the anointing woman (14:3–9) stand independently.

The enormous problem faced by Mark and the other Gospel writers was the question of why, if Jesus were the Messiah, he died as a criminal on a cross. The simplest answer is that is what happened; for Mark, however, three specific answers present themselves. First, Jesus' death was a result of his choice: He chooses to go to Jerusalem, even when his disciples fear that choice (10:32); he dies on a cross because he knows it is God's will for him (8:31; 9:31; 10:33); he goes his appointed way (14:21) to fulfill God's will for his messiahship. Second, Mark presents two conflicting views of religion in his Gospel: a rigid code of outward observance, and a flexible law of love, social responsibility, and mercy. The conflict between the two arises early in the narrative and culminates at 15:10.

Finally, that Jesus dies on a cross is consistent with the evangelist's view of discipleship. Mark apparently lives in and writes for a community that has experienced persecution or that is going through a difficult time. Pastorally Mark must make the connection between the suffering of his community and the suffering of Jesus. In short, Mark shapes his Gospel to be a word of encouragement and hope. In this divine human drama that begins with Israel's election, continues in the ministry of John the Baptist, and comes to a head in the life of Jesus of Nazareth, those who align themselves with God suffer but are ultimately vindicated by God, raised to new life. What is now going on is not what always will be. Mark's is preeminently the Gospel of hope for the suffering. —*Bonnie Bowman Thurston*

1:1–15	Prologue
1:16—6:6a	Ministry in and around Galilee
1:16–45	Typical Features of Jesus' Ministry
2:1—3:35	Opposition to Jesus
4:1–34	Teaching in Parables
4:35—5:43	Miracles
6:1–6a	Rejection
6:6b—8:21	Ministry around Capernaum
8:22—10:52	Journey to Jerusalem. Discipleship Teaching
11:1—16:8a	Ministry in and around Jerusalem
11:1–26	Triumphant Entry. Temple Teaching
11:27—12:44	Controversy in the Temple Precincts
13:1–36	Apocalyptic Discourse
14:1—16:8a	Passion and Resurrection
16:8b–20	The Gospel's Ending

✧

John the Baptist Prepares the Way

1 This is the Good News about Jesus the
Messiah, the Son of God.* It began 2 just as
the prophet Isaiah had written:

"Look, I am sending my messenger ahead of
you,
and he will prepare your way.*
3 He is a voice shouting in the wilderness,
'Prepare the way for the LORD's coming!
Clear the road for him!'* "

4 This messenger was John the Baptist. He was in
the wilderness and preached that people should
be baptized to show that they had repented of

1:1 Some manuscripts do not include *the Son of God.*
1:2 Mal 3:1. **1:3** Isa 40:3 (Greek version).

1:1–15 Prologue

Mark's prologue begins and ends with a focus on the gospel (1:1, 14–15) and within that frame alternates material about Jesus and John the Baptist (Jesus, 1:1; John, 1:2–8; Jesus, 1:9–13; John, 1:14; Jesus, 1:14–15). At the end of Mark's prologue, the heavenly word has been revealed: God has spoken, and Jesus has preached. Mark has attempted to communicate that the ministry of Jesus is about the inauguration of the reign of God. **1:** Generally accepted as the title and the main theme of this book, this verse gives the reader information that Jesus is Christ and Son of God. "The beginning of the good news (NRSV)" echoes the opening verse of Genesis, suggesting that with Jesus, God is making a new beginning. His story is the *Good News about Jesus,* a message of salvation. In short, the substance of Mark's Gospel is that Jesus is the *Messiah, the Son of God.* **2–4:** Immediately the reader is introduced to John the Baptist with a quotation conflating Malachi 3:1 and Isaiah 40:3. We are told that Jesus fulfills prophecy. John, as forerunner and proclaimer, is a prophetic figure reminiscent of Elijah. **5–6:** The wilderness locale reminds us that in Hebrew Scripture, the wilderness is the place where God prepares people for salvation and where

their sins and turned to God to be forgiven. 5 All
of Judea, including all the people of Jerusalem,
went out to see and hear John. And when they
confessed their sins, he baptized them in the Jordan River. 6 His clothes were woven from coarse
camel hair, and he wore a leather belt around his
waist. For food he ate locusts and wild honey.
7 John announced: "Someone is coming soon
who is greater than I am—so much greater that
I'm not even worthy to stoop down like a slave
and untie the straps of his sandals. 8 I baptize you
with* water, but he will baptize you with the
Holy Spirit!"

The Baptism and Temptation of Jesus

9 One day Jesus came from Nazareth in Galilee, and John baptized him in the Jordan River.
10 As Jesus came up out of the water, he saw the
heavens splitting apart and the Holy Spirit descending on him* like a dove. 11 And a voice from
heaven said, "You are my dearly loved Son, and
you bring me great joy."
12 The Spirit then compelled Jesus to go into
the wilderness, 13 where he was tempted by Satan
for forty days. He was out among the wild animals, and angels took care of him.
14 Later on, after John was arrested, Jesus
went into Galilee, where he preached God's Good
News.* 15 "The time promised by God has come
at last!" he announced. "The Kingdom of God is
near! Repent of your sins and believe the Good
News!"

The First Disciples

16 One day as Jesus was walking along the shore
of the Sea of Galilee, he saw Simon* and his
brother Andrew throwing a net into the water,
for they fished for a living. 17 Jesus called out to
them, "Come, follow me, and I will show you
how to fish for people!" 18 And they left their
nets at once and followed him.
19 A little farther up the shore Jesus saw
Zebedee's sons, James and John, in a boat repairing their nets. 20 He called them at once, and they
also followed him, leaving their father, Zebedee,
in the boat with the hired men.

Jesus Casts Out an Evil Spirit

21 Jesus and his companions went to the town
of Capernaum. When the Sabbath day came,
he went into the synagogue and began to teach.
22 The people were amazed at his teaching, for
he taught with real authority—quite unlike the
teachers of religious law.
23 Suddenly, a man in the synagogue who
was possessed by an evil* spirit began shout-

1:8 Or *in;* also in 1:8b. **1:10** Or *toward him,* or *into him.* **1:14** Some manuscripts read *the Good News of the Kingdom of God.* **1:16** *Simon* is called "Peter" in 3:16 and thereafter. **1:23** Greek *unclean;* also in 1:26, 27.

those expectations are fulfilled. John's message is that the Jews must repent; therefore equating God's chosen people with visible Israel is incorrect. Thus the Messiah is not to be a fulfiller of political expectations. **7–8:** John, alluding to Hebrew Scripture, has been presented as having prophetic authority, but he will stoop to do the work of a slave before the One who is coming. Already Mark's understanding is evident that for Jesus' disciples, authority comes via service. **9–11:** With the baptism of Jesus we learn more of his unique Sonship. This is the beginning of the ministry of Jesus, his commissioning by God. The theological problem is why Jesus was baptized. In Mark, Jesus' baptism carries with it something of the sign acts of the prophets in Hebrew Scripture. It expresses his solidarity with sinners (whom, the meaning of his name tells us, he came to save) and unifies Jesus with the new movement toward repentance. It solidifies his unity with the repentant, sets an example for his followers, sanctifies water, and reveals his divine nature (1:11). Here all three persons of the Trinity are present, the Son, the Spirit as dove, the Father as speaker. **12–13:** The temptation narrative is brief, perhaps because Mark views the whole ministry of Jesus as Jesus' temptation, his temptation to be a messiah in terms other than those of God. Moses and Elijah, who appear later on the mountain (9:2–4), spent "forty periods of time" in the wilderness. From the outset, Jesus is presented in the mode of the great leaders of Israel, of lawgivers and prophets. **14–15:** The evangelist's prologue is completed by proclaiming the gospel in miniature. History is dealt with summarily; the forerunner, John, is imprisoned and handed over (thus introducing the apocalyptic drama of preaching, being handed over, being martyred). Jesus' message is also presented with two indicatives (*the time . . . has come, the Kingdom of God is near*) and two imperatives (*repent of your sins, believe the Good News*), the two facts and the two acts that are required as a result. God's reign is revealed in the gift of a new relationship to God. Jesus' identity is now established, and God's presence is promised.

1:16–6:6a Ministry in and around Galilee

1:16–45 Typical Features of Jesus' Ministry. 16–20: The manner of this call emphasizes the radical nature of discipleship as Simon, Andrew, James, and John leave livelihood and family to follow Jesus. If verses 14–15 summarize the message of Jesus, verses

ing, [24]"Why are you interfering with us, Jesus of Nazareth? Have you come to destroy us? I know who you are—the Holy One of God!"

[25]Jesus cut him short. "Be quiet! Come out of the man," he ordered. [26]At that, the evil spirit screamed, threw the man into a convulsion, and then came out of him.

[27]Amazement gripped the audience, and they began to discuss what had happened. "What sort of new teaching is this?" they asked excitedly. "It has such authority! Even evil spirits obey his orders!" [28]The news about Jesus spread quickly throughout the entire region of Galilee.

Jesus Heals Many People

[29]After Jesus left the synagogue with James and John, they went to Simon and Andrew's home. [30]Now Simon's mother-in-law was sick in bed with a high fever. They told Jesus about her right away. [31]So he went to her bedside, took her by the hand, and helped her sit up. Then the fever left her, and she prepared a meal for them.

[32]That evening after sunset, many sick and demon-possessed people were brought to Jesus. [33]The whole town gathered at the door to watch. [34]So Jesus healed many people who were sick with various diseases, and he cast out many demons. But because the demons knew who he was, he did not allow them to speak.

Jesus Preaches in Galilee

[35]Before daybreak the next morning, Jesus got up and went out to an isolated place to pray. [36]Later Simon and the others went out to find him. [37]When they found him, they said, "Everyone is looking for you."

[38]But Jesus replied, "We must go on to other towns as well, and I will preach to them, too. That is why I came." [39]So he traveled throughout the region of Galilee, preaching in the synagogues and casting out demons.

Jesus Heals a Man with Leprosy

[40]A man with leprosy came and knelt in front of Jesus, begging to be healed. "If you are willing, you can heal me and make me clean," he said.

[41]Moved with compassion,* Jesus reached out and touched him. "I am willing," he said. "Be healed!" [42]Instantly the leprosy disappeared, and the man was healed. [43]Then Jesus sent him on his way with a stern warning: [44]"Don't tell anyone about this. Instead, go to the priest and let him examine you. Take along the offering required in the law of Moses for those who have been healed of leprosy.* This will be a public testimony that you have been cleansed."

[45]But the man went and spread the word, proclaiming to everyone what had happened. As a result, large crowds soon surrounded Jesus, and he couldn't publicly enter a town anywhere. He had to stay out in the secluded places, but people from everywhere kept coming to him.

Jesus Heals a Paralyzed Man

2 When Jesus returned to Capernaum several days later, the news spread quickly that he was back home. [2]Soon the house where he was staying was so packed with visitors that there was no more room, even outside the door. While he was preaching God's word to them, [3]four men arrived carrying a paralyzed man on

1:41 Some manuscripts read *Moved with anger.* **1:44** See Lev 14:2-32.

16–20 depict the appropriate response to it. **21–22:** "Teacher" is Mark's favorite designation for Jesus, although he presents fewer of his words than do the other evangelists. The *town of Capernaum* is established as his Galilean headquarters. In Jesus, people experience a new sort of authority. This causes problems because the religious authorities do not know its origin (*they* didn't authorize it). **23–28:** The exorcism introduces more apocalyptic elements as the spirit world recognizes Jesus' identity. Demons recognize Jesus and are commanded to be silent; the healed are enjoined not to reveal who healed them; the disciples are initially forbidden to make Jesus' messiahship public; and Jesus frequently withdraws to teach his disciples privately. The unfolding of the secret that he is the Messiah is introduced clearly. **29–34:** Mark's women are usually model disciples. Simon's mother-in-law begins to serve Jesus as soon as she is healed. Service or ministry *(diakonia)* is the prototypical act of discipleship. The healing of Peter's mother-in-law and other healings establish the fact that Jesus doesn't just talk; he is empowered to heal. **35–39:** Jesus withdraws for prayer. Thus the reader understands Jesus' ministry to be composed of calling disciples, teaching, healing, and prayer. **40–45:** As the healing of the leper demonstrates, these healing miracles are proof of Jesus' authority as a teacher. (Note that about half of the narrative in chapters 1—8 is healing miracles.)

2:1—3:35 Opposition to Jesus. 2:1–12: The paralytic is healed, but dissension ensues. Two great conflicts of the Gospel are prefigured as the Son of Man destroys the powers of evil, and the authority of Jesus faces the authorities of Judaism. In some ways the rest of the Gospel is the working out of these two

a mat. [4]They couldn't bring him to Jesus because
of the crowd, so they dug a hole through the roof
above his head. Then they lowered the man on
his mat, right down in front of Jesus. [5]Seeing
their faith, Jesus said to the paralyzed man, "My
child, your sins are forgiven."
[6]But some of the teachers of religious law
who were sitting there thought to themselves,
[7]"What is he saying? This is blasphemy! Only
God can forgive sins!"
[8]Jesus knew immediately what they were
thinking, so he asked them, "Why do you question this in your hearts? [9]Is it easier to say to the
paralyzed man 'Your sins are forgiven,' or 'Stand
up, pick up your mat, and walk'? [10]So I will prove
to you that the Son of Man* has the authority
on earth to forgive sins." Then Jesus turned to
the paralyzed man and said, [11]"Stand up, pick up
your mat, and go home!"
[12]And the man jumped up, grabbed his mat,
and walked out through the stunned onlookers. They were all amazed and praised God, exclaiming, "We've never seen anything like this
before!"

Jesus Calls Levi (Matthew)

[13]Then Jesus went out to the lakeshore again and
taught the crowds that were coming to him. [14]As
he walked along, he saw Levi son of Alphaeus
sitting at his tax collector's booth. "Follow me
and be my disciple," Jesus said to him. So Levi
got up and followed him.
[15]Later, Levi invited Jesus and his disciples to
his home as dinner guests, along with many tax
collectors and other disreputable sinners. (There
were many people of this kind among Jesus' followers.) [16]But when the teachers of religious law
who were Pharisees* saw him eating with tax
collectors and other sinners, they asked his disciples, "Why does he eat with such scum?*"
[17]When Jesus heard this, he told them,
"Healthy people don't need a doctor—sick people do. I have come to call not those who think
they are righteous, but those who know they are
sinners."

A Discussion about Fasting

[18]Once when John's disciples and the Pharisees
were fasting, some people came to Jesus and
asked, "Why don't your disciples fast like John's
disciples and the Pharisees do?"
[19]Jesus replied, "Do wedding guests fast while
celebrating with the groom? Of course not. They
can't fast while the groom is with them. [20]But
someday the groom will be taken away from
them, and then they will fast.
[21]"Besides, who would patch old clothing with
new cloth? For the new patch would shrink and
rip away from the old cloth, leaving an even bigger tear than before.
[22]"And no one puts new wine into old wineskins. For the wine would burst the wineskins,
and the wine and the skins would both be lost.
New wine calls for new wineskins."

A Discussion about the Sabbath

[23]One Sabbath day as Jesus was walking through
some grainfields, his disciples began breaking off
heads of grain to eat. [24]But the Pharisees said to
Jesus, "Look, why are they breaking the law by
harvesting grain on the Sabbath?"
[25]Jesus said to them, "Haven't you ever read
in the Scriptures what David did when he and his
companions were hungry? [26]He went into the
house of God (during the days when Abiathar was
high priest) and broke the law by eating the sacred
loaves of bread that only the priests are allowed to
eat. He also gave some to his companions."
[27]Then Jesus said to them, "The Sabbath was
made to meet the needs of people, and not people
to meet the requirements of the Sabbath. [28]So the
Son of Man is Lord, even over the Sabbath!"

Jesus Heals on the Sabbath

3 Jesus went into the synagogue again and
noticed a man with a deformed hand.
[2]Since it was the Sabbath, Jesus' enemies

2:10 "Son of Man" is a title Jesus used for himself.
2:16a Greek *the scribes of the Pharisees.* **2:16b** Greek *with tax collectors and sinners?*

strands of conflict. **13–17:** As Simon, Andrew, James, and John have left their livelihood and family to follow Jesus, Matthew now joins them. The Greek term *akoloutheo* (follow) is a technical word for discipleship, and Jesus' call emphasizes its radical nature and its transforming power. Here we also catch a glimpse of his williingness to include sinful individuals whom others find unacceptable. **18–22:** A discussion about fasting becomes a challenge to new patterns of belief and action, far removed from established religious norms. **23–28:** Jesus turns the legal concept of the Sabbath on its head. Sabbath legislation was established in recognition of the human need for rest rather than to prohibit the fulfillment of obtaining food or other resources for the hungry. **3:1–6:** The discussion of appropriate observance of the Sabbath now enters a more acute stage. Jesus infuriates the religious leaders not only by healing on the Sabbath but by defending his action with a logic that they are powerless to refute. The plot that will lead ultimately to Jesus'

watched him closely. If he healed the man's hand,
they planned to accuse him of working on the
Sabbath.
[3]Jesus said to the man with the deformed
hand, "Come and stand in front of everyone."
[4]Then he turned to his critics and asked, "Does
the law permit good deeds on the Sabbath, or is it
a day for doing evil? Is this a day to save life or to
destroy it?" But they wouldn't answer him.
[5]He looked around at them angrily and was
deeply saddened by their hard hearts. Then he
said to the man, "Hold out your hand." So the
man held out his hand, and it was restored! [6]At
once the Pharisees went away and met with the
supporters of Herod to plot how to kill Jesus.

Crowds Follow Jesus

[7]Jesus went out to the lake with his disciples, and
a large crowd followed him. They came from all
over Galilee, Judea, [8]Jerusalem, Idumea, from east
of the Jordan River, and even from as far north as
Tyre and Sidon. The news about his miracles had
spread far and wide, and vast numbers of people
came to see him.
[9]Jesus instructed his disciples to have a boat
ready so the crowd would not crush him. [10]He
had healed many people that day, so all the sick
people eagerly pushed forward to touch him.
[11]And whenever those possessed by evil* spirits
caught sight of him, the spirits would throw them
to the ground in front of him shrieking, "You are
the Son of God!" [12]But Jesus sternly commanded
the spirits not to reveal who he was.

Jesus Chooses the Twelve Apostles

[13]Afterward Jesus went up on a mountain and
called out the ones he wanted to go with him. And
they came to him. [14]Then he appointed twelve of
them and called them his apostles.* They were
to accompany him, and he would send them out
to preach, [15]giving them authority to cast out demons. [16]These are the twelve he chose:

Simon (whom he named Peter),
[17]James and John (the sons of Zebedee, but Jesus
nicknamed them "Sons of Thunder"*),
[18]Andrew,
Philip,
Bartholomew,
Matthew,
Thomas,
James (son of Alphaeus),
Thaddaeus,
Simon (the zealot*),
[19]Judas Iscariot (who later betrayed him).

Jesus and the Prince of Demons

[20]One time Jesus entered a house, and the crowds
began to gather again. Soon he and his disciples
couldn't even find time to eat. [21]When his family heard what was happening, they tried to take
him away. "He's out of his mind," they said.
[22]But the teachers of religious law who had
arrived from Jerusalem said, "He's possessed by
Satan,* the prince of demons. That's where he
gets the power to cast out demons."
[23]Jesus called them over and responded with
an illustration. "How can Satan cast out Satan?"
he asked. [24]"A kingdom divided by civil war will
collapse. [25]Similarly, a family splintered by feuding will fall apart. [26]And if Satan is divided and
fights against himself, how can he stand? He

3:11 Greek *unclean;* also in 3:30. **3:14** Some manuscripts do not include *and called them his apostles.* **3:17** Greek *whom he named Boanerges, which means Sons of Thunder.* **3:18** Greek *the Cananean,* an Aramaic term for Jewish nationalists. **3:22** Greek *Beelzeboul;* other manuscripts read *Beezeboul;* Latin version reads *Beelzebub.*

crucifixion begins to be hatched. **7–12:** Crowds flock to Jesus as they converge from various locations. The account moves steadily toward the Passion Narrative and is structured by means of geographical references that have theological significance: Galilee (1:14—6:13); beyond Galilee (6:14—8:26); Caesarea Philippi to Jerusalem (8:27—10:52); Jerusalem (11:1—16:8). Note that about half of Jesus' public ministry is in northern Palestine and half in the environs of Jerusalem. **13–19:** He chooses as regular companions *the ones he wanted to go with him,* those whom he will call *apostles.* Later we will learn the names of the women who regularly attended Jesus and traveled in his company. Mark 15:41 notes that there were *many other women who had come with him to Jerusalem,* indicating that the original circle of Galilean disciples included women (cf. Luke 8:1–3). Thus when Mark (4:10–34; 7:17; 9:28; and 10:10) describes the special instruction that Jesus gave to the disciples, women should probably be numbered among them. **20–21:** Jesus' family respond to reports of his popularity with unbelief. The presence of his mother is not recorded, but others of his kin have come to the conclusion that he is deranged. After the resurrection, they will become devoted followers (1 Cor 9:5; Gal 1:19; Epistle of James). **22–30:** As the jealousy grows more intense, the discussion centers on the spiritual power by which Jesus heals those who suffer from afflictions of the mind. Again, his logic proves irrefutable, and he sternly condemns those who confuse the power of God with the power of Satan. **31–34:** His mother comes for a visit accom-

would never survive. 27 Let me illustrate this further. Who is powerful enough to enter the house
of a strong man like Satan and plunder his goods?
Only someone even stronger—someone who
could tie him up and then plunder his house.
28 "I tell you the truth, all sin and blasphemy
can be forgiven, 29 but anyone who blasphemes
the Holy Spirit will never be forgiven. This is a
sin with eternal consequences." 30 He told them
this because they were saying, "He's possessed
by an evil spirit."

The True Family of Jesus

31 Then Jesus' mother and brothers came to see
him. They stood outside and sent word for him
to come out and talk with them. 32 There was a
crowd sitting around Jesus, and someone said,
"Your mother and your brothers* are outside
asking for you."
33 Jesus replied, "Who is my mother? Who are
my brothers?" 34 Then he looked at those around
him and said, "Look, these are my mother and
brothers. 35 Anyone who does God's will is my
brother and sister and mother."

Parable of the Farmer Scattering Seed

4 Once again Jesus began teaching by the
lakeshore. A very large crowd soon gathered around him, so he got into a boat. Then
he sat in the boat while all the people remained on
the shore. 2 He taught them by telling many stories in the form of parables, such as this one:
3 "Listen! A farmer went out to plant some
seed. 4 As he scattered it across his field, some of
the seed fell on a footpath, and the birds came
and ate it. 5 Other seed fell on shallow soil with
underlying rock. The seed sprouted quickly because the soil was shallow. 6 But the plant soon
wilted under the hot sun, and since it didn't have
deep roots, it died. 7 Other seed fell among thorns
that grew up and choked out the tender plants
so they produced no grain. 8 Still other seeds fell
on fertile soil, and they sprouted, grew, and produced a crop that was thirty, sixty, and even a
hundred times as much as had been planted!"
9 Then he said, "Anyone with ears to hear should
listen and understand."
10 Later, when Jesus was alone with the twelve
disciples and with the others who were gathered around, they asked him what the parables
meant.
11 He replied, "You are permitted to understand the secret* of the Kingdom of God. But
I use parables for everything I say to outsiders,
12 so that the Scriptures might be fulfilled:

'When they see what I do,
  they will learn nothing.
When they hear what I say,
  they will not understand.
Otherwise, they will turn to me
  and be forgiven.'*"

13 Then Jesus said to them, "If you can't understand the meaning of this parable, how will you
understand all the other parables? 14 The farmer
plants seed by taking God's word to others. 15 The
seed that fell on the footpath represents those
who hear the message, only to have Satan come
at once and take it away. 16 The seed on the rocky
soil represents those who hear the message and
immediately receive it with joy. 17 But since they
don't have deep roots, they don't last long. They
fall away as soon as they have problems or are persecuted for believing God's word. 18 The seed that
fell among the thorns represents others who hear
God's word, 19 but all too quickly the message is
crowded out by the worries of this life, the lure of
wealth, and the desire for other things, so no fruit
is produced. 20 And the seed that fell on good soil
represents those who hear and accept God's word
and produce a harvest of thirty, sixty, or even a
hundred times as much as had been planted!"

Parable of the Lamp

21 Then Jesus asked them, "Would anyone light a
lamp and then put it under a basket or under a

3:32 Some manuscripts add *and sisters.* **4:11** Greek *mystery.* **4:12** Isa 6:9-10 (Greek version).

panied by his siblings, and Jesus uses the opportunity to emphasize the family of faith that transcends the bounds of blood relationship. We begin to see the universality of the gospel.

4:1–34 Teaching in Parables. Chapters 4 and 13 are the largest blocks of Jesus' teaching in this Gospel. They form an inclusio around the active ministry of Jesus. Both chapters demonstrate Mark's compositional technique of giving a general teaching to a crowd and then a more detailed private instruction to the disciples. **1–9:** The first parable. **10–20:** As so often in the Gospel of Mark, the disciples fail to understand the meaning of Jesus' statements. In this they become a type of later adherents of Christ who must also puzzle out the thorny issues. **21–25:** The purpose of a lamp is to give light, and the purpose of a disciple is to let that which is within shine

bed? Of course not! A lamp is placed on a stand, where its light will shine. 22 For everything that is hidden will eventually be brought into the open, and every secret will be brought to light. 23 Anyone with ears to hear should listen and understand."

24 Then he added, "Pay close attention to what you hear. The closer you listen, the more understanding you will be given*—and you will receive even more. 25 To those who listen to my teaching, more understanding will be given. But for those who are not listening, even what little understanding they have will be taken away from them."

Parable of the Growing Seed

26 Jesus also said, "The Kingdom of God is like a farmer who scatters seed on the ground. 27 Night and day, while he's asleep or awake, the seed sprouts and grows, but he does not understand how it happens. 28 The earth produces the crops on its own. First a leaf blade pushes through, then the heads of wheat are formed, and finally the grain ripens. 29 And as soon as the grain is ready, the farmer comes and harvests it with a sickle, for the harvest time has come."

Parable of the Mustard Seed

30 Jesus said, "How can I describe the Kingdom of God? What story should I use to illustrate it? 31 It is like a mustard seed planted in the ground. It is the smallest of all seeds, 32 but it becomes the largest of all garden plants; it grows long branches, and birds can make nests in its shade."

33 Jesus used many similar stories and illustrations to teach the people as much as they could understand. 34 In fact, in his public ministry he never taught without using parables; but afterward, when he was alone with his disciples, he explained everything to them.

Jesus Calms the Storm

35 As evening came, Jesus said to his disciples, "Let's cross to the other side of the lake." 36 So they took Jesus in the boat and started out, leaving the crowds behind (although other boats followed). 37 But soon a fierce storm came up. High waves were breaking into the boat, and it began to fill with water.

38 Jesus was sleeping at the back of the boat with his head on a cushion. The disciples woke him up, shouting, "Teacher, don't you care that we're going to drown?"

39 When Jesus woke up, he rebuked the wind and said to the waves, "Silence! Be still!" Suddenly the wind stopped, and there was a great calm. 40 Then he asked them, "Why are you afraid? Do you still have no faith?"

41 The disciples were absolutely terrified. "Who is this man?" they asked each other. "Even the wind and waves obey him!"

Jesus Heals a Demon-Possessed Man

5 So they arrived at the other side of the lake, in the region of the Gerasenes.* 2 When Jesus climbed out of the boat, a man possessed by an evil* spirit came out from a cemetery to meet him. 3 This man lived among the

4:24 Or *The measure you give will be the measure you get back.* **5:1** Other manuscripts read *Gadarenes;* still others read *Gergesenes.* See Matt 8:28; Luke 8:26. **5:2** Greek *unclean;* also in 5:8, 13.

out. **26–29:** The agricultural enterprise begins with planting and ends with the harvest, but in between the two processes is the mysterious work of God. **30–33:** We are now given a third metaphor of plant growth. Palestinian mustard seed is very small indeed and yet produces a sizeable bush. It was a homely symbol that might prompt deep reflection. Mark voices an important pedagogical principle when he declares that Jesus taught people *as much as they were able to understand.* **34:** The statements about *the others who were gathered around* (v. 10) and *when he was alone with his disciples* make clear that Jesus' inner circle included more than twelve males. *His disciples* occurs forty-three times in Mark for Jesus' followers, suggesting that Mark is more interested in the larger issue of discipleship rather than of apostleship.

4:35—5:43 Miracles. The block of miracles in 4:35—5:43 is characteristic of Mark's compositional technique of gathering together units of material by genre. This miracle unit follows a parable unit (4:1–34). By having Jesus perform miracles, Mark demonstrates that he has the authority to teach as he did. In a sense, all four miracles—the stilling of the storm (4:35–41), the exorcism of the Gerasene demoniac (5:1–20), the healing of Jairus's daughter, and the healing of the woman with a hemorrhage (5:21–43)—are about fear. **4:35–39:** When Jesus stills the storm Mark attributes to him an authority the Old Testament gives only to God. The set of miracle stories shows the extent of Jesus' authority. He has authority over the natural world (the sea), over the spirit world (unclean spirits), over the human body (the hemorrhage), and over life and death (Jairus's daughter). Mark suggests that nothing in creation is outside the sphere of Jesus' authority (cf. Col 1:15–20). **5:1–20:** Here again Jesus confronts demons who acknowledge his identity,

burial caves and could no longer be restrained, even with a chain. [4]Whenever he was put into chains and shackles—as he often was—he snapped the chains from his wrists and smashed the shackles. No one was strong enough to subdue him. [5]Day and night he wandered among the burial caves and in the hills, howling and cutting himself with sharp stones.

[6]When Jesus was still some distance away, the man saw him, ran to meet him, and bowed low before him. [7]With a shriek, he screamed, "Why are you interfering with me, Jesus, Son of the Most High God? In the name of God, I beg you, don't torture me!" [8]For Jesus had already said to the spirit, "Come out of the man, you evil spirit."

[9]Then Jesus demanded, "What is your name?"

And he replied, "My name is Legion, because there are many of us inside this man." [10]Then the evil spirits begged him again and again not to send them to some distant place.

[11]There happened to be a large herd of pigs feeding on the hillside nearby. [12]"Send us into those pigs," the spirits begged. "Let us enter them."

[13]So Jesus gave them permission. The evil spirits came out of the man and entered the pigs, and the entire herd of about 2,000 pigs plunged down the steep hillside into the lake and drowned in the water.

[14]The herdsmen fled to the nearby town and the surrounding countryside, spreading the news as they ran. People rushed out to see what had happened. [15]A crowd soon gathered around Jesus, and they saw the man who had been possessed by the legion of demons. He was sitting there fully clothed and perfectly sane, and they were all afraid. [16]Then those who had seen what happened told the others about the demon-possessed man and the pigs. [17]And the crowd began pleading with Jesus to go away and leave them alone.

[18]As Jesus was getting into the boat, the man who had been demon possessed begged to go with him. [19]But Jesus said, "No, go home to your family, and tell them everything the Lord has done for you and how merciful he has been." [20]So the man started off to visit the Ten Towns* of that region and began to proclaim the great things Jesus had done for him; and everyone was amazed at what he told them.

Jesus Heals in Response to Faith

[21]Jesus got into the boat again and went back to the other side of the lake, where a large crowd gathered around him on the shore. [22]Then a leader of the local synagogue, whose name was Jairus, arrived. When he saw Jesus, he fell at his feet, [23]pleading fervently with him. "My little daughter is dying," he said. "Please come and lay your hands on her; heal her so she can live."

[24]Jesus went with him, and all the people followed, crowding around him. [25]A woman in the crowd had suffered for twelve years with constant bleeding. [26]She had suffered a great deal from many doctors, and over the years she had spent everything she had to pay them, but she had gotten no better. In fact, she had gotten worse. [27]She had heard about Jesus, so she came up behind him through the crowd and touched his robe. [28]For she thought to herself, "If I can

5:20 Greek *Decapolis.*

as they have done at 1:23, 34, and 3:11–12. They recognize him because he has contended with and overcome them in the wilderness (1:12–13). The story, however, focuses not on the destructive action of the demons but rather on the healing and resocialization of one whose terrifying conduct has rendered him totally rejected by his own community. **21–30:** Mark is particularly fond of the technique of intercalation, that is, a story-within-a-story construction. He begins the story of Jairus's daughter (5:21–24), interrupts it with the account of the hemorrhaging woman (5:25–34), and then returns to the original narrative (5:35–43). Mark uses this device repeatedly, and it effectively propels the reader toward Mark's central concern, Jesus' passion. He starts his journey at the desperate appeal of Jairus, whose daughter lies at death's door. She is just twelve years old, the age when many young girls begin to menstruate. As she hovers between life and death, Jesus interrupts one act of mercy to accomplish another. A woman with an issue of blood approaches him stealthily, pushing her way through the crowd. This woman is without a male relative to be her advocate, without financial resources, and subject to blood taboo. The Levitical restrictions on menstruating women (Lev 15:19–30) indicate that the woman would not only be considered unclean, she also would make anything she touched unclean. Her *constant bleeding* excluded her from normal social contact and religious or cultic activity. She has effectively been excluded from society for twelve years, precisely the time during which Jairus's daughter has been growing up. Unique in the healings in Mark, this woman takes the initiative to go to Jesus, ignoring the social custom that would have prevented her from speaking to a male in public and the cultic, blood taboos that would prevent

just touch his robe, I will be healed." [29]Immediately the bleeding stopped, and she could feel in her body that she had been healed of her terrible condition.

[30]Jesus realized at once that healing power had gone out from him, so he turned around in the crowd and asked, "Who touched my robe?"

[31]His disciples said to him, "Look at this crowd pressing around you. How can you ask, 'Who touched me?' "

[32]But he kept on looking around to see who had done it. [33]Then the frightened woman, trembling at the realization of what had happened to her, came and fell to her knees in front of him and told him what she had done. [34]And he said to her, "Daughter, your faith has made you well. Go in peace. Your suffering is over."

[35]While he was still speaking to her, messengers arrived from the home of Jairus, the leader of the synagogue. They told him, "Your daughter is dead. There's no use troubling the Teacher now."

[36]But Jesus overheard* them and said to Jairus, "Don't be afraid. Just have faith."

[37]Then Jesus stopped the crowd and wouldn't let anyone go with him except Peter, James, and John (the brother of James). [38]When they came to the home of the synagogue leader, Jesus saw much commotion and weeping and wailing. [39]He went inside and asked, "Why all this commotion and weeping? The child isn't dead; she's only asleep."

[40]The crowd laughed at him. But he made them all leave, and he took the girl's father and mother and his three disciples into the room where the girl was lying. [41]Holding her hand, he said to her, *"Talitha koum,"* which means "Little girl, get up!" [42]And the girl, who was twelve years old, immediately stood up and walked around! They were overwhelmed and totally amazed. [43]Jesus gave them strict orders not to tell anyone what had happened, and then he told them to give her something to eat.

Jesus Rejected at Nazareth

6 Jesus left that part of the country and returned with his disciples to Nazareth, his hometown. [2]The next Sabbath he began teaching in the synagogue, and many who heard him were amazed. They asked, "Where did he get all this wisdom and the power to perform such miracles?" [3]Then they scoffed, "He's just a carpenter, the son of Mary* and the brother of James, Joseph,* Judas, and Simon. And his sisters live right here among us." They were deeply offended and refused to believe in him.

[4]Then Jesus told them, "A prophet is honored everywhere except in his own hometown and among his relatives and his own family." [5]And because of their unbelief, he couldn't do any miracles among them except to place his hands on a few sick people and heal them. [6]And he was amazed at their unbelief.

Jesus Sends Out the Twelve Disciples

Then Jesus went from village to village, teaching the people. [7]And he called his twelve disciples together and began sending them out two by two,

5:36 Or *ignored.* **6:3a** Some manuscripts read *He's just the son of the carpenter and of Mary.* **6:3b** Most manuscripts read *Joses;* see Matt 13:55.

physical contact. **34:** Jesus responds verbally to her, acknowledging her existence. He calls her *Daughter*, establishing kinship within the family (cf. 3:31–35), and recognizes that her complete healing is because of her faith. He breaks social and religious custom to liberate a bound woman by restoring the wholeness of her body and consequently her social functioning. **36:** Jesus demands of Jairus the same faith that has made the hemorrhaging woman well. **37–43:** Women who make their career as professional mourners are already on duty. In contrast to the public wailing, Jesus respects the privacy of the family. He approaches the child quietly with only three of his closest followers and calls her to arise. *Talitha cumi* (*koum*, NLT), the actual Aramaic words that he speaks, are carefully recorded by Mark. This tendency to preserve important words of Jesus in the original Aramaic (3:17; 5:41; 7:11, 34; 14:36; 15:22, 34) suggests that this reflects the oral memory of Peter.

6:1–6a Rejection. Jesus gains no esteem or credence in his own hometown. As his fellow townsmen question his worth, they target the womenfolk in his family: his mother and his sisters. These women are accepted members of a community that viewed him as an ordinary carpenter. The very familiarity of hometown and family has obscured the presence of the Messiah.

6:6b—8:21 Ministry around Capernaum

In 6:6b–11 we see the Twelve sent out separately on individual missions. They are given instructions that will become the strategy for evangelism in the early church as the gospel was to spread across the known world. The homes in which they stayed were frequently hosted by women who became leaders in the house churches that developed to receive these missionaries and their message. **14–20:** In a

giving them authority to cast out evil* spirits. 8 He told them to take nothing for their journey except a walking stick—no food, no traveler's bag, no money.* 9 He allowed them to wear sandals but not to take a change of clothes.

10 "Wherever you go," he said, "stay in the same house until you leave town. 11 But if any place refuses to welcome you or listen to you, shake its dust from your feet as you leave to show that you have abandoned those people to their fate."

12 So the disciples went out, telling everyone they met to repent of their sins and turn to God. 13 And they cast out many demons and healed many sick people, anointing them with olive oil.

The Death of John the Baptist

14 Herod Antipas, the king, soon heard about Jesus, because everyone was talking about him. Some were saying,* "This must be John the Baptist raised from the dead. That is why he can do such miracles." 15 Others said, "He's the prophet Elijah." Still others said, "He's a prophet like the other great prophets of the past."

16 When Herod heard about Jesus, he said, "John, the man I beheaded, has come back from the dead."

17 For Herod had sent soldiers to arrest and imprison John as a favor to Herodias. She had been his brother Philip's wife, but Herod had married her. 18 John had been telling Herod, "It is against God's law for you to marry your brother's wife." 19 So Herodias bore a grudge against John and wanted to kill him. But without Herod's approval she was powerless, 20 for Herod respected John; and knowing that he was a good and holy man, he protected him. Herod was greatly disturbed whenever he talked with John, but even so, he liked to listen to him.

21 Herodias's chance finally came on Herod's birthday. He gave a party for his high government officials, army officers, and the leading citizens of Galilee. 22 Then his daughter, also named Herodias,* came in and performed a dance that greatly pleased Herod and his guests. "Ask me for anything you like," the king said to the girl, "and I will give it to you." 23 He even vowed, "I will give you whatever you ask, up to half my kingdom!"

24 She went out and asked her mother, "What should I ask for?"

Her mother told her, "Ask for the head of John the Baptist!"

25 So the girl hurried back to the king and told him, "I want the head of John the Baptist, right now, on a tray!"

26 Then the king deeply regretted what he had said; but because of the vows he had made in front of his guests, he couldn't refuse her. 27 So he immediately sent an executioner to the prison to cut off John's head and bring it to him. The soldier beheaded John in the prison, 28 brought his head on a tray, and gave it to the girl, who took it to her mother. 29 When John's disciples heard what had happened, they came to get his body and buried it in a tomb.

Jesus Feeds Five Thousand

30 The apostles returned to Jesus from their ministry tour and told him all they had done and taught. 31 Then Jesus said, "Let's go off by ourselves to a quiet place and rest awhile." He said this because there were so many people coming and going that Jesus and his apostles didn't even have time to eat.

32 So they left by boat for a quiet place, where they could be alone. 33 But many people recognized them and saw them leaving, and people from many towns ran ahead along the shore and got there ahead of them. 34 Jesus saw the huge crowd as he stepped from the boat, and he had compassion on them because they were like sheep without a shepherd. So he began teaching them many things.

35 Late in the afternoon his disciples came to him and said, "This is a remote place, and it's already getting late. 36 Send the crowds away so they can go to the nearby farms and villages and buy something to eat."

6:7 Greek *unclean.* **6:8** Greek *no copper coins in their money belts.* **6:14** Some manuscripts read *He was saying.* **6:22** Some manuscripts read *the daughter of Herodias herself.*

period of multiple convoluted sexual relationships (high rates of divorces, remarriages, extramarital affairs) among upper-class Jews, Herod Antipas had persuaded his brother Philip's wife to leave her husband for him. Their subsequent marriage was condemned by John the Baptist as a violation of the ethical standards of Israel (see Lev 18:16; 20:21). **21–29:** John the Baptist's moral stance costs him his life. Although Herod has found John's message compelling, the allure of the young dancer is greater. The mother and daughter's wrongful use of sexual enticement stands in marked contrast to the many women who seek out Jesus and value his message. **30–44:** The eagerness to hear Jesus exceeds the need of the crowd for food. His ministry is able to satisfy both spiritual and natural hunger. Mark's description of the grass as *green* indicates his interest in vivid, eye-witness touches (4:37; 5:5; 6:39;

37 But Jesus said, "You feed them."
"With what?" they asked. "We'd have to
work for months to earn enough money* to buy
food for all these people!"
38 "How much bread do you have?" he asked.
"Go and find out."
They came back and reported, "We have five
loaves of bread and two fish."
39 Then Jesus told the disciples to have the
people sit down in groups on the green grass. 40 So
they sat down in groups of fifty or a hundred.
41 Jesus took the five loaves and two fish,
looked up toward heaven, and blessed them.
Then, breaking the loaves into pieces, he kept
giving the bread to the disciples so they could
distribute it to the people. He also divided the
fish for everyone to share. 42 They all ate as much
as they wanted, 43 and afterward, the disciples
picked up twelve baskets of leftover bread and
fish. 44 A total of 5,000 men and their families
were fed from those loaves!

Jesus Walks on Water

45 Immediately after this, Jesus insisted that his
disciples get back into the boat and head across
the lake to Bethsaida, while he sent the people
home. 46 After telling everyone good-bye, he
went up into the hills by himself to pray.
47 Late that night, the disciples were in their
boat in the middle of the lake, and Jesus was alone
on land. 48 He saw that they were in serious trouble, rowing hard and struggling against the wind
and waves. About three o'clock in the morning*
Jesus came toward them, walking on the water.
He intended to go past them, 49 but when they
saw him walking on the water, they cried out in
terror, thinking he was a ghost. 50 They were all
terrified when they saw him.
But Jesus spoke to them at once. "Don't be
afraid," he said. "Take courage! I am here!*"
51 Then he climbed into the boat, and the wind
stopped. They were totally amazed, 52 for they
still didn't understand the significance of the
miracle of the loaves. Their hearts were too hard
to take it in.
53 After they had crossed the lake, they landed
at Gennesaret. They brought the boat to shore
54 and climbed out. The people recognized Jesus at
once, 55 and they ran throughout the whole area,
carrying sick people on mats to wherever they
heard he was. 56 Wherever he went—in villages,
cities, or the countryside—they brought the sick
out to the marketplaces. They begged him to let
the sick touch at least the fringe of his robe, and
all who touched him were healed.

Jesus Teaches about Inner Purity

7 One day some Pharisees and teachers of
religious law arrived from Jerusalem to see
Jesus. 2 They noticed that some of his disciples failed to follow the Jewish ritual of hand
washing before eating. 3 (The Jews, especially
the Pharisees, do not eat until they have poured
water over their cupped hands,* as required by
their ancient traditions. 4 Similarly, they don't eat
anything from the market until they immerse
their hands* in water. This is but one of many
traditions they have clung to—such as their ceremonial washing of cups, pitchers, and kettles.*)
5 So the Pharisees and teachers of religious
law asked him, "Why don't your disciples follow
our age-old tradition? They eat without first performing the hand-washing ceremony."
6 Jesus replied, "You hypocrites! Isaiah was
right when he prophesied about you, for he
wrote,

'These people honor me with their lips,
but their hearts are far from me.
7 Their worship is a farce,
for they teach man-made ideas as
commands from God.'*

8 For you ignore God's law and substitute your
own tradition."
9 Then he said, "You skillfully sidestep God's
law in order to hold on to your own tradition.

6:37 Greek *It would take 200 denarii.* A denarius was equivalent to a laborer's full day's wage. **6:48** Greek *About the fourth watch of the night.* **6:50** Or *The 'I AM' is here;* Greek reads *I am.* See Exod 3:14. **7:3** Greek *have washed with the fist.* **7:4a** Some manuscripts read *sprinkle themselves.* **7:4b** Some manuscripts add *and dining couches.* **7:7** Isa 29:13 (Greek version).

10:22). He has been an apt listener to those who told him stories of Jesus. **45–52:** Even when Jesus comes to them walking on the water, the disciples fail to understand the significance of what they are experiencing. **53–56:** The people seek to touch the fringe of Jesus' garment, as did the woman with the constant bleeding. Numbers 15:37–41 contains an instruction to wear tassels on one's garments as a reminder to observe all of the commandments of God (for Pharisaic observation, see Matt 23:5). **7:1–8:** Ancient sanitary custom had done much to preserve the lives and health of ancient Hebrews, but Jesus condemns a ritual that is empty of meaning. **9–23:** By a legal stratagem, it was possible to avoid providing for aging parents while appearing outwardly pious. Such devices violated the purposes of God's

10 For instance, Moses gave you this law from God: 'Honor your father and mother,'* and 'Anyone who speaks disrespectfully of father or mother must be put to death.'* 11 But you say it is all right for people to say to their parents, 'Sorry, I can't help you. For I have vowed to give to God what I would have given to you.'* 12 In this way, you let them disregard their needy parents. 13 And so you cancel the word of God in order to hand down your own tradition. And this is only one example among many others."

14 Then Jesus called to the crowd to come and hear. "All of you listen," he said, "and try to understand. 15 It's not what goes into your body that defiles you; you are defiled by what comes from your heart.*"

17 Then Jesus went into a house to get away from the crowd, and his disciples asked him what he meant by the parable he had just used. 18 "Don't you understand either?" he asked. "Can't you see that the food you put into your body cannot defile you? 19 Food doesn't go into your heart, but only passes through the stomach and then goes into the sewer." (By saying this, he declared that every kind of food is acceptable in God's eyes.)

20 And then he added, "It is what comes from inside that defiles you. 21 For from within, out of a person's heart, come evil thoughts, sexual immorality, theft, murder, 22 adultery, greed, wickedness, deceit, lustful desires, envy, slander, pride, and foolishness. 23 All these vile things come from within; they are what defile you."

The Faith of a Gentile Woman

24 Then Jesus left Galilee and went north to the region of Tyre.* He didn't want anyone to know which house he was staying in, but he couldn't keep it a secret. 25 Right away a woman who had heard about him came and fell at his feet. Her little girl was possessed by an evil* spirit, 26 and she begged him to cast out the demon from her daughter.

Since she was a Gentile, born in Syrian Phoenicia, 27 Jesus told her, "First I should feed the children—my own family, the Jews.* It isn't right to take food from the children and throw it to the dogs."

28 She replied, "That's true, Lord, but even the dogs under the table are allowed to eat the scraps from the children's plates."

29 "Good answer!" he said. "Now go home, for the demon has left your daughter." 30 And when she arrived home, she found her little girl lying quietly in bed, and the demon was gone.

Jesus Heals a Deaf Man

31 Jesus left Tyre and went up to Sidon before going back to the Sea of Galilee and the region of the Ten Towns.* 32 A deaf man with a speech impediment was brought to him, and the people begged Jesus to lay his hands on the man to heal him.

33 Jesus led him away from the crowd so they could be alone. He put his fingers into the man's ears. Then, spitting on his own fingers, he touched the man's tongue. 34 Looking up to heaven, he sighed and said, *"Ephphatha,"* which means, "Be opened!" 35 Instantly the man could hear perfectly, and his tongue was freed so he could speak plainly!

36 Jesus told the crowd not to tell anyone, but the more he told them not to, the more they spread the news. 37 They were completely amazed and said again and again, "Everything he does is wonderful. He even makes the deaf to hear and gives speech to those who cannot speak."

7:10a Exod 20:12; Deut 5:16. **7:10b** Exod 21:17 (Greek version); Lev 20:9 (Greek version). **7:11** Greek *'What I would have given to you is Corban' (that is, a gift).* **7:15** Some manuscripts add verse 16, *Anyone with ears to hear should listen and understand.* Compare 4:9, 23. **7:24** Some manuscripts add *and Sidon.* **7:25** Greek *unclean.* **7:27** Greek *Let the children eat first.* **7:31** Greek *Decapolis.*

law and corrupted the heart. **24–26:** Again Jesus is approached by a marginalized woman, a Gentile of Greek heritage and Syro-Phoenician by birth. There is an implied comparison in Mark between the way the religious officials have approached Jesus (7:1–23) and the woman's approach. Probably the single parent of a demon-possessed daughter, a triple liability, this woman throws herself at Jesus' feet with a request for her daughter. **27–30:** Jesus' response to her is troubling. But the woman persists, first agreeing with Jesus and addressing him as "Lord," the only time he is so addressed in Mark. Then she points out that when the children (the Jews) are fed, the dogs (Gentiles) get the leftovers. Jesus realizes the wisdom of the woman and in a long-distance exorcism frees her daughter from the demon. Mark probably preserved the story as part of his interest in the Gentile mission of the church. Here we see a sharp-witted Gentile woman, one who is altruistic, persistent, and inventive, and who does not hesitate to approach Jesus, and a Jesus who recognizes insights from outside the pale and acknowledges that faith can be found there too. **31–37:** Jesus enters the world of those cut off from normal communication by deafness and impaired speech. Despite his prohibition, the crowd is anxious to communicate the

Jesus Feeds Four Thousand
8 About this time another large crowd had
gathered, and the people ran out of food
again. Jesus called his disciples and told
them, [2]"I feel sorry for these people. They have
been here with me for three days, and they have
nothing left to eat. [3]If I send them home hungry,
they will faint along the way. For some of them
have come a long distance."
[4]His disciples replied, "How are we supposed
to find enough food to feed them out here in the
wilderness?"
[5]Jesus asked, "How much bread do you
have?"
"Seven loaves," they replied.
[6]So Jesus told all the people to sit down on the
ground. Then he took the seven loaves, thanked
God for them, and broke them into pieces. He
gave them to his disciples, who distributed the
bread to the crowd. [7]A few small fish were found,
too, so Jesus also blessed these and told the disciples to distribute them.
[8]They ate as much as they wanted. Afterward, the disciples picked up seven large baskets
of leftover food. [9]There were about 4,000 people
in the crowd that day, and Jesus sent them home
after they had eaten. [10]Immediately after this, he
got into a boat with his disciples and crossed over
to the region of Dalmanutha.

Pharisees Demand a Miraculous Sign
[11]When the Pharisees heard that Jesus had arrived, they came and started to argue with him.
Testing him, they demanded that he show them
a miraculous sign from heaven to prove his authority.
[12]When he heard this, he sighed deeply in his
spirit and said, "Why do these people keep demanding a miraculous sign? I tell you the truth, I
will not give this generation any such sign." [13]So
he got back into the boat and left them, and he
crossed to the other side of the lake.

Yeast of the Pharisees and Herod
[14]But the disciples had forgotten to bring any
food. They had only one loaf of bread with them
in the boat. [15]As they were crossing the lake,
Jesus warned them, "Watch out! Beware of the
yeast of the Pharisees and of Herod."
[16]At this they began to argue with each other
because they hadn't brought any bread. [17]Jesus
knew what they were saying, so he said, "Why
are you arguing about having no bread? Don't
you know or understand even yet? Are your
hearts too hard to take it in? [18]'You have eyes—
can't you see? You have ears—can't you hear?'*
Don't you remember anything at all? [19]When I
fed the 5,000 with five loaves of bread, how many
baskets of leftovers did you pick up afterward?"
"Twelve," they said.
[20]"And when I fed the 4,000 with seven
loaves, how many large baskets of leftovers did
you pick up?"
"Seven," they said.
[21]"Don't you understand yet?" he asked
them.

Jesus Heals a Blind Man
[22]When they arrived at Bethsaida, some people
brought a blind man to Jesus, and they begged
him to touch the man and heal him. [23]Jesus took
the blind man by the hand and led him out of
the village. Then, spitting on the man's eyes, he
laid his hands on him and asked, "Can you see
anything now?"
[24]The man looked around. "Yes," he said, "I

8:18 Jer 5:21.

news to those who can both hear and tell. **8:1–10:** Here we see the essential principle of fasting: the disregard of food in order to concentrate on the things of God. Nevertheless, Jesus is aware of the dangers of going without food for too protracted a period and makes appropriate provision. **11–21:** The male disciples misunderstand Jesus' person, mission, and message (9:32–33; 10:35–45), are sharp with their teacher (4:38; 5:31; 8:4; 14:4), and disobey him (7:36). For Mark, to follow Jesus is to be identified with the Lord and his passion. The disciples therefore are often depicted in the narrative as having a faulty or partial understanding of Jesus. Mark uses their inadequate Christology as an occasion to instruct his readers. The disciples' incomprehension helps our comprehension as Mark seeks to show how, in the life of discipleship, there is no shortcut around the cross. In Mark's Gospel, Jesus' women disciples seem to be the first to understand his message. These women disciples appear more positively than many of their male counterparts.

8:22—10:52 Journey to Jerusalem. Discipleship Teaching

Healing the blind man in 8:22–26 happens by degrees, leading some interpreters to suggest that when it comes to human regeneration, Jesus is not satisfied with second best; he works in human life until grace is complete. Many commentators divide Mark's Gospel at this point. The reader finds a body of material devoted primarily to discipleship and framed by

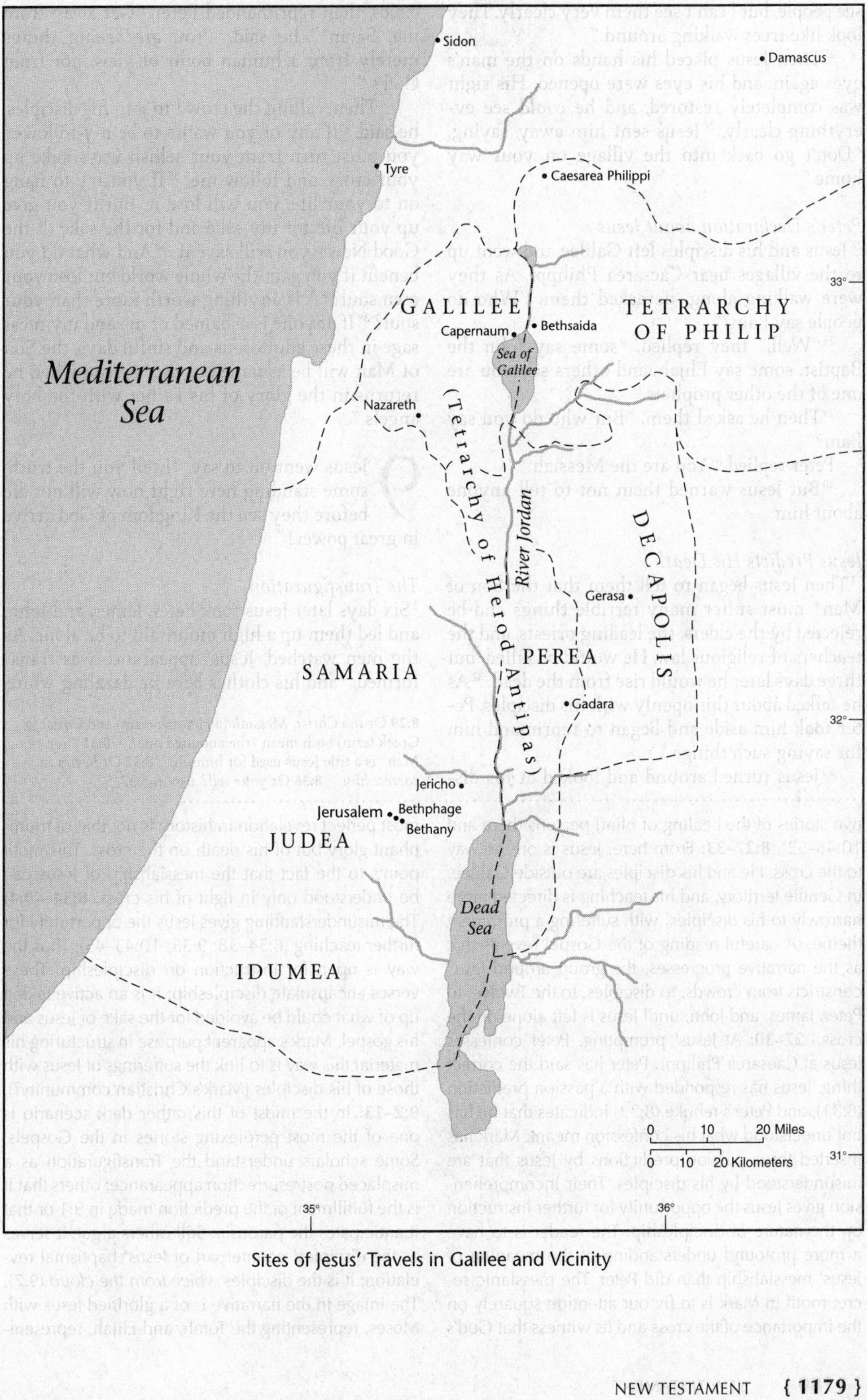

Sites of Jesus' Travels in Galilee and Vicinity

see people, but I can't see them very clearly. They
look like trees walking around."
25 Then Jesus placed his hands on the man's
eyes again, and his eyes were opened. His sight
was completely restored, and he could see everything clearly. 26 Jesus sent him away, saying,
"Don't go back into the village on your way
home."

Peter's Declaration about Jesus

27 Jesus and his disciples left Galilee and went up
to the villages near Caesarea Philippi. As they
were walking along, he asked them, "Who do
people say I am?"
28 "Well," they replied, "some say John the
Baptist, some say Elijah, and others say you are
one of the other prophets."
29 Then he asked them, "But who do you say
I am?"
Peter replied, "You are the Messiah.*"
30 But Jesus warned them not to tell anyone
about him.

Jesus Predicts His Death

31 Then Jesus began to tell them that the Son of
Man* must suffer many terrible things and be
rejected by the elders, the leading priests, and the
teachers of religious law. He would be killed, but
three days later he would rise from the dead. 32 As
he talked about this openly with his disciples, Peter took him aside and began to reprimand him
for saying such things.*
33 Jesus turned around and looked at his disciples, then reprimanded Peter. "Get away from
me, Satan!" he said. "You are seeing things
merely from a human point of view, not from
God's."
34 Then, calling the crowd to join his disciples,
he said, "If any of you wants to be my follower,
you must turn from your selfish ways, take up
your cross, and follow me. 35 If you try to hang
on to your life, you will lose it. But if you give
up your life for my sake and for the sake of the
Good News, you will save it. 36 And what do you
benefit if you gain the whole world but lose your
own soul?* 37 Is anything worth more than your
soul? 38 If anyone is ashamed of me and my message in these adulterous and sinful days, the Son
of Man will be ashamed of that person when he
returns in the glory of his Father with the holy
angels."

9 Jesus went on to say, "I tell you the truth,
some standing here right now will not die
before they see the Kingdom of God arrive
in great power!"

The Transfiguration

2 Six days later Jesus took Peter, James, and John,
and led them up a high mountain to be alone. As
the men watched, Jesus' appearance was transformed, 3 and his clothes became dazzling white,

8:29 Or *the Christ. Messiah* (a Hebrew term) and *Christ* (a Greek term) both mean "the anointed one." **8:31** "Son of Man" is a title Jesus used for himself. **8:32** Or *began to correct him.* **8:36** Or *your self?* also in 8:37.

two stories of the healing of blind persons (here and 10:46–52). **8:27–33:** From here, Jesus is on the way to the cross. He and his disciples are outside Galilee, in Gentile territory, and his teaching is directed more narrowly to his disciples, with suffering a prominent theme. (A careful reading of the Gospel reveals that as the narrative progresses, the group around Jesus constricts from crowds, to disciples, to the Twelve, to Peter, James, and John, until Jesus is left alone on the cross.) **27–30:** At Jesus' prompting, Peter confesses Jesus at Caesarea Philippi. Peter has said the correct thing; Jesus has responded with a passion prediction (8:31); and Peter's rebuke (8:32) indicates that he has not understood what his confession meant. Mark has inserted three passion predictions by Jesus that are misunderstood by his disciples. Their incomprehension gives Jesus the opportunity for further instruction on the nature of discipleship. The reader is to have a more profound understanding of the meaning of Jesus' messiahship than did Peter. The messianic secret motif in Mark is to fix our attention squarely on the importance of the cross and its witness that God's most perfect revelation in history is not that of triumphant glory but of his death on the cross. This motif points to the fact that the messiahship of Jesus can be understood only in light of his cross. **8:34—9:1:** The misunderstanding gives Jesus the opportunity for further teaching (8:34–38; 9:35; 10:43–45). Thus the way is open for instruction on discipleship. These verses encapsulate discipleship; it is an active taking up of what could be avoided for the sake of Jesus and his gospel. Mark's apparent purpose in structuring his material this way is to link the sufferings of Jesus with those of his disciples (Mark's Christian community?). **9:2–13:** In the midst of this rather dark scenario is one of the most perplexing stories in the Gospels. Some scholars understand the Transfiguration as a misplaced postresurrection appearance; others that it is the fulfillment of the prediction made in 9:1 or that it anticipates the parousia. Still others argue it serves as the disciples' counterpart of Jesus' baptismal revelation; it is the disciples' *voice from the cloud* (9:7). The image in the narrative is of a glorified Jesus with Moses, representing the Torah, and Elijah, represent-

far whiter than any earthly bleach could ever make them. 4 Then Elijah and Moses appeared and began talking with Jesus.

5 Peter exclaimed, "Rabbi, it's wonderful for us to be here! Let's make three shelters as memorials*—one for you, one for Moses, and one for Elijah." 6 He said this because he didn't really know what else to say, for they were all terrified.

7 Then a cloud overshadowed them, and a voice from the cloud said, "This is my dearly loved Son. Listen to him." 8 Suddenly, when they looked around, Moses and Elijah were gone, and they saw only Jesus with them.

9 As they went back down the mountain, he told them not to tell anyone what they had seen until the Son of Man* had risen from the dead. 10 So they kept it to themselves, but they often asked each other what he meant by "rising from the dead."

11 Then they asked him, "Why do the teachers of religious law insist that Elijah must return before the Messiah comes?*"

12 Jesus responded, "Elijah is indeed coming first to get everything ready. Yet why do the Scriptures say that the Son of Man must suffer greatly and be treated with utter contempt? 13 But I tell you, Elijah has already come, and they chose to abuse him, just as the Scriptures predicted."

Jesus Heals a Demon-Possessed Boy

14 When they returned to the other disciples, they saw a large crowd surrounding them, and some teachers of religious law were arguing with them. 15 When the crowd saw Jesus, they were overwhelmed with awe, and they ran to greet him.

16 "What is all this arguing about?" Jesus asked.

17 One of the men in the crowd spoke up and said, "Teacher, I brought my son so you could heal him. He is possessed by an evil spirit that won't let him talk. 18 And whenever this spirit seizes him, it throws him violently to the ground. Then he foams at the mouth and grinds his teeth and becomes rigid.* So I asked your disciples to cast out the evil spirit, but they couldn't do it."

19 Jesus said to them,* "You faithless people! How long must I be with you? How long must I put up with you? Bring the boy to me."

20 So they brought the boy. But when the evil spirit saw Jesus, it threw the child into a violent convulsion, and he fell to the ground, writhing and foaming at the mouth.

21 "How long has this been happening?" Jesus asked the boy's father.

He replied, "Since he was a little boy. 22 The spirit often throws him into the fire or into water, trying to kill him. Have mercy on us and help us, if you can."

23 "What do you mean, 'If I can'?" Jesus asked. "Anything is possible if a person believes."

24 The father instantly cried out, "I do believe, but help me overcome my unbelief!"

25 When Jesus saw that the crowd of onlookers was growing, he rebuked the evil* spirit. "Listen, you spirit that makes this boy unable to hear and speak," he said. "I command you to come out of this child and never enter him again!"

26 Then the spirit screamed and threw the boy into another violent convulsion and left him. The boy appeared to be dead. A murmur ran through the crowd as people said, "He's dead." 27 But Jesus took him by the hand and helped him to his feet, and he stood up.

28 Afterward, when Jesus was alone in the house with his disciples, they asked him, "Why couldn't we cast out that evil spirit?"

29 Jesus replied, "This kind can be cast out only by prayer.*"

Jesus Again Predicts His Death

30 Leaving that region, they traveled through Galilee. Jesus didn't want anyone to know he was there, 31 for he wanted to spend more time with his disciples and teach them. He said to them,

9:5 Greek *three tabernacles.* **9:9** "Son of Man" is a title Jesus used for himself. **9:11** Greek *that Elijah must come first?* **9:18** Or *becomes weak.* **9:19** Or *said to his disciples.* **9:25** Greek *unclean.* **9:29** Some manuscripts read *by prayer and fasting.*

---

ing the prophets, who in Jewish and Samaritan tradition were associated with the Messiah. Jesus' inner circle of Peter, James, and John is clearly told to "listen to *him*" (emphasis added). In Mark's narrative the event fits here after Peter's confession that Jesus is the Messiah, confirming its truth and, in the context of discipleship, showing what it means as Jesus is given precedence over the Law and the Prophets. **14–29:** The boy appears to have been afflicted with epilepsy. The word "demon," here translated as *evil spirit* was used in antiquity to refer not only to spiritual beings but also to human personality, moods, or to unusual forces. Even today we refer to epileptic *convulsions* as "seizures." **30–32:** The pattern in 8:27—10:1 is repeated twice in this section of the Gospel, which is preparing for the events of the passion by defining discipleship. A geographical reference (8:27; 9:30; 10:1) is followed by a passion prediction by Jesus

"The Son of Man is going to be betrayed into the hands of his enemies. He will be killed, but three days later he will rise from the dead." 32 They didn't understand what he was saying, however, and they were afraid to ask him what he meant.

The Greatest in the Kingdom

33 After they arrived at Capernaum and settled in a house, Jesus asked his disciples, "What were you discussing out on the road?" 34 But they didn't answer, because they had been arguing about which of them was the greatest. 35 He sat down, called the twelve disciples over to him, and said, "Whoever wants to be first must take last place and be the servant of everyone else."

36 Then he put a little child among them. Taking the child in his arms, he said to them, 37 "Anyone who welcomes a little child like this on my behalf* welcomes me, and anyone who welcomes me welcomes not only me but also my Father who sent me."

Using the Name of Jesus

38 John said to Jesus, "Teacher, we saw someone using your name to cast out demons, but we told him to stop because he wasn't in our group."

39 "Don't stop him!" Jesus said. "No one who performs a miracle in my name will soon be able to speak evil of me. 40 Anyone who is not against us is for us. 41 If anyone gives you even a cup of water because you belong to the Messiah, I tell you the truth, that person will surely be rewarded.

42 "But if you cause one of these little ones who trusts in me to fall into sin, it would be better for you to be thrown into the sea with a large millstone hung around your neck. 43 If your hand causes you to sin, cut it off. It's better to enter eternal life with only one hand than to go into the unquenchable fires of hell* with two hands.* 45 If your foot causes you to sin, cut it off. It's better to enter eternal life with only one foot than to be thrown into hell with two feet.* 47 And if your eye causes you to sin, gouge it out. It's better to enter the Kingdom of God with only one eye than to have two eyes and be thrown into hell, 48 'where the maggots never die and the fire never goes out.'*

49 "For everyone will be tested with fire.* 50 Salt is good for seasoning. But if it loses its flavor, how do you make it salty again? You must have the qualities of salt among yourselves and live in peace with each other."

Discussion about Divorce and Marriage

10 Then Jesus left Capernaum and went down to the region of Judea and into the area east of the Jordan River. Once again crowds gathered around him, and as usual he was teaching them.

2 Some Pharisees came and tried to trap him with this question: "Should a man be allowed to divorce his wife?"

3 Jesus answered them with a question: "What did Moses say in the law about divorce?"

4 "Well, he permitted it," they replied. "He said a man can give his wife a written notice of divorce and send her away."*

5 But Jesus responded, "He wrote this commandment only as a concession to your hard hearts. 6 But 'God made them male and female'* from the beginning of creation. 7 'This explains why a man leaves his father and mother and is joined to his wife,* 8 and the two are united into one.'* Since they are no longer two but one, 9 let no one split apart what God has joined together."

10 Later, when he was alone with his disciples in the house, they brought up the subject again. 11 He told them, "Whoever divorces his wife and

9:37 Greek *in my name.* **9:43a** Greek *Gehenna;* also in 9:45, 47. **9:43b** Some manuscripts add verse 44, *'where the maggots never die and the fire never goes out.'* See 9:48. **9:45** Some manuscripts add verse 46, *'where the maggots never die and the fire never goes out.'* See 9:48. **9:48** Isa 66:24. **9:49** Greek *salted with fire;* other manuscripts add *and every sacrifice will be salted with salt.* **10:4** See Deut 24:1. **10:6** Gen 1:27; 5:2. **10:7** Some manuscripts do not include *and is joined to his wife.* **10:7-8** Gen 2:24.

(8:31; 9:31; 10:33), which is again misunderstood by the disciples (8:32–33; 9:34; 10:42). **33–50:** Jesus respects the spiritual integrity of children and commends it for emulation. His strong condemnation of child abuse stands as an indication of his acute understanding of the harm that can be done to a young mind and soul. **10:1:** Here we have the last of the periodic summaries of Jesus' ministry (1:14–15, 21–22, 39; 2:13; 3:7–12; 5:21; 6:6, 12–13, 30–33, 53–56; 10:1). **2–8:** The discussion of divorce (see Divorce, Ezra 10) reflects a lively conflict in Judaism between the school of Shammai, which taught that divorce was to be sought only in response to infidelity (see Adultery, Exod 20), and that of Hillel, which was more lenient and allowed divorce for other reasons. The legal right to divorce is assumed (probably from Deut 24:1–3); what is at issue are the grounds for divorce. Jesus is more stringent than the rabbis; he appeals to what God wills, not to what the law allows. **5–9:** Jesus speaks a governing principle, not a law. Rather than ruling out divorce, he elevates marriage (see Marriage, Song 2). **10–12:** This reflects the situ-

marries someone else commits adultery against her. 12 And if a woman divorces her husband and marries someone else, she commits adultery."

Jesus Blesses the Children

13 One day some parents brought their children to Jesus so he could touch and bless them. But the disciples scolded the parents for bothering him.

14 When Jesus saw what was happening, he was angry with his disciples. He said to them, "Let the children come to me. Don't stop them! For the Kingdom of God belongs to those who are like these children. 15 I tell you the truth, anyone who doesn't receive the Kingdom of God like a child will never enter it." 16 Then he took the children in his arms and placed his hands on their heads and blessed them.

The Rich Man

17 As Jesus was starting out on his way to Jerusalem, a man came running up to him, knelt down, and asked, "Good Teacher, what must I do to inherit eternal life?"

18 "Why do you call me good?" Jesus asked. "Only God is truly good. 19 But to answer your question, you know the commandments: 'You must not murder. You must not commit adultery. You must not steal. You must not testify falsely. You must not cheat anyone. Honor your father and mother.'* "

20 "Teacher," the man replied, "I've obeyed all these commandments since I was young."

21 Looking at the man, Jesus felt genuine love for him. "There is still one thing you haven't done," he told him. "Go and sell all your possessions and give the money to the poor, and you will have treasure in heaven. Then come, follow me."

22 At this the man's face fell, and he went away sad, for he had many possessions.

23 Jesus looked around and said to his disciples, "How hard it is for the rich to enter the Kingdom of God!" 24 This amazed them. But Jesus said again, "Dear children, it is very hard* to enter the Kingdom of God. 25 In fact, it is easier for a camel to go through the eye of a needle than for a rich person to enter the Kingdom of God!"

26 The disciples were astounded. "Then who in the world can be saved?" they asked.

27 Jesus looked at them intently and said, "Humanly speaking, it is impossible. But not with God. Everything is possible with God."

28 Then Peter began to speak up. "We've given up everything to follow you," he said.

29 "Yes," Jesus replied, "and I assure you that everyone who has given up house or brothers or sisters or mother or father or children or property, for my sake and for the Good News, 30 will receive now in return a hundred times as many houses, brothers, sisters, mothers, children, and property—along with persecution. And in the world to come that person will have eternal life. 31 But many who are the greatest now will be least important then, and those who seem least important now will be the greatest then.*"

Jesus Again Predicts His Death

32 They were now on the way up to Jerusalem, and Jesus was walking ahead of them. The disciples were filled with awe, and the people following behind were overwhelmed with fear. Taking the twelve disciples aside, Jesus once more began to describe everything that was about to happen to him. 33 "Listen," he said, "we're going up to Jerusalem, where the Son of Man* will be betrayed to the leading priests and the teachers of religious law. They will sentence him to die and hand him over to the Romans.* 34 They will mock him, spit on him, flog him with a whip, and kill him, but after three days he will rise again."

10:19 Exod 20:12-16; Deut 5:16-20. **10:24** Some manuscripts read *very hard for those who trust in riches.* **10:31** Greek *But many who are first will be last; and the last, first.* **10:33a** "Son of Man" is a title Jesus used for himself. **10:33b** Greek *the Gentiles.*

ation of Mark's audience rather than Jesus' environment, since in Jewish Palestine women could not sue for divorce. **13–16:** Children are again recognized as full-fledged members of the Kingdom of God, granted full acceptance and respect. **17–31:** In this carefully constructed section of the Gospel, the story of the rich man parallels that of Peter's confession. Just as Jesus was interested in what Peter thought of him (8:29, *Who do you say that I am?*), here Jesus is interested in what this particular man needs to do to enter the kingdom. Some see the rich man as wrong in his priorities, his flattery and superficiality, but Jesus looks at him and presumably knows and loves him. Here is a man who has done the right things but who cannot accept the radical demands of discipleship. **32–45:** The penultimate unit in this section, the third passion prediction is sadly indicative that the male disciples, even those of the inner circle (James and John) still do not understand—neither Jesus as the suffering Messiah nor discipleship as a matter of ser-

Jesus Teaches about Serving Others
35 Then James and John, the sons of Zebedee, came
over and spoke to him. "Teacher," they said, "we
want you to do us a favor."
36 "What is your request?" he asked.
37 They replied, "When you sit on your glorious throne, we want to sit in places of honor
next to you, one on your right and the other on
your left."
38 But Jesus said to them, "You don't know
what you are asking! Are you able to drink from
the bitter cup of suffering I am about to drink?
Are you able to be baptized with the baptism of
suffering I must be baptized with?"
39 "Oh yes," they replied, "we are able!"
Then Jesus told them, "You will indeed drink
from my bitter cup and be baptized with my baptism of suffering. 40 But I have no right to say
who will sit on my right or my left. God has prepared those places for the ones he has chosen."
41 When the ten other disciples heard what
James and John had asked, they were indignant.
42 So Jesus called them together and said, "You
know that the rulers in this world lord it over
their people, and officials flaunt their authority over those under them. 43 But among you it
will be different. Whoever wants to be a leader
among you must be your servant, 44 and whoever
wants to be first among you must be the slave of
everyone else. 45 For even the Son of Man came
not to be served but to serve others and to give
his life as a ransom for many."

Jesus Heals Blind Bartimaeus
46 Then they reached Jericho, and as Jesus and his
disciples left town, a large crowd followed him. A
blind beggar named Bartimaeus (son of Timaeus)
was sitting beside the road. 47 When Bartimaeus
heard that Jesus of Nazareth was nearby, he began to shout, "Jesus, Son of David, have mercy
on me!"
48 "Be quiet!" many of the people yelled at
him.
But he only shouted louder, "Son of David,
have mercy on me!"
49 When Jesus heard him, he stopped and said,
"Tell him to come here."
So they called the blind man. "Cheer up,"
they said. "Come on, he's calling you!" 50 Bartimaeus threw aside his coat, jumped up, and came
to Jesus.
51 "What do you want me to do for you?"
Jesus asked.
"My rabbi,*" the blind man said, "I want to
see!"
52 And Jesus said to him, "Go, for your faith
has healed you." Instantly the man could see,
and he followed Jesus down the road.*

Jesus' Triumphant Entry
11 As Jesus and his disciples approached
Jerusalem, they came to the towns of
Bethphage and Bethany on the Mount
of Olives. Jesus sent two of them on ahead. 2 "Go
into that village over there," he told them. "As
soon as you enter it, you will see a young donkey tied there that no one has ever ridden. Untie
it and bring it here. 3 If anyone asks, 'What are
you doing?' just say, 'The Lord needs it and will
return it soon.'"
4 The two disciples left and found the colt
standing in the street, tied outside the front
door. 5 As they were untying it, some bystanders

10:51 Greek uses the Hebrew term *Rabboni*. **10:52** Or *on the way*.

---

vice rather than honor or prestige. The disciple must be like the master, who *came not to be served but to serve others and to give his life as a ransom for many.* **46–52:** The healing of blind Bartimaeus, shows us a man taking the initiative to be known by Jesus. This is the last healing miracle in the Gospel. The story illustrates Markan irony in that the blind man who uses a messianic title for Jesus *sees* more than the sighted, and the story picks up the theme of faith where it is least expected (cf. 7:24–30; 9:14–27). Jesus offers Bartimaeus three things that all people need: recognition, sight, and purpose. A nobody on the road of life has confessed Jesus and followed him. Discipleship has symbolically been understood. In the terms of the narrative it is time for Jesus to go on to Jerusalem and the violence awaiting him there.

11:1—16:8a Ministry in and around Jerusalem

Of the Gospel's sixteen chapters, the final six (11—16) relate the events of the last week of Jesus' life. Mark 11:1—14:9 chronicles Jesus' last week in Jerusalem. Mark 14:10—16:8 relates the passion and resurrection. Mark carefully keeps time with references that indicate the passing of the week (11:12, 20; 14:1, 12; 15:1, 42; 16:1). The day of the crucifixion is divided into Roman watches (15:1, 25, 33, 34, 42).

11:1–26 Triumphant Entry. Temple Teaching. The triumphant entry serves as prologue to the critical events that are to follow. **11:1–11:** Jesus enters Jerusalem and visits the Temple; a view of the Temple leads

demanded, "What are you doing, untying that colt?" [6]They said what Jesus had told them to say, and they were permitted to take it. [7]Then they brought the colt to Jesus and threw their garments over it, and he sat on it.

[8]Many in the crowd spread their garments on the road ahead of him, and others spread leafy branches they had cut in the fields. [9]Jesus was in the center of the procession, and the people all around him were shouting,

"Praise God!*
Blessings on the one who comes in the name of the LORD!
[10]Blessings on the coming Kingdom of our ancestor David!
Praise God in highest heaven!"*

[11]So Jesus came to Jerusalem and went into the Temple. After looking around carefully at everything, he left because it was late in the afternoon. Then he returned to Bethany with the twelve disciples.

Jesus Curses the Fig Tree

[12]The next morning as they were leaving Bethany, Jesus was hungry. [13]He noticed a fig tree in full leaf a little way off, so he went over to see if he could find any figs. But there were only leaves because it was too early in the season for fruit. [14]Then Jesus said to the tree, "May no one ever eat your fruit again!" And the disciples heard him say it.

Jesus Clears the Temple

[15]When they arrived back in Jerusalem, Jesus entered the Temple and began to drive out the people buying and selling animals for sacrifices. He knocked over the tables of the money changers and the chairs of those selling doves, [16]and he stopped everyone from using the Temple as a marketplace.* [17]He said to them, "The Scriptures declare, 'My Temple will be called a house of prayer for all nations,' but you have turned it into a den of thieves."*

[18]When the leading priests and teachers of religious law heard what Jesus had done, they began planning how to kill him. But they were afraid of him because the people were so amazed at his teaching.

[19]That evening Jesus and the disciples left* the city.

[20]The next morning as they passed by the fig tree he had cursed, the disciples noticed it had withered from the roots up. [21]Peter remembered what Jesus had said to the tree on the previous day and exclaimed, "Look, Rabbi! The fig tree you cursed has withered and died!"

[22]Then Jesus said to the disciples, "Have faith in God. [23]I tell you the truth, you can say to this mountain, 'May you be lifted up and thrown into the sea,' and it will happen. But you must really believe it will happen and have no doubt in your heart. [24]I tell you, you can pray for anything, and if you believe that you've received it, it will be yours. [25]But when you are praying, first forgive anyone you are holding a grudge against, so that your Father in heaven will forgive your sins, too.*"

11:9 Greek *Hosanna,* an exclamation of praise that literally means "save now"; also in 11:10. **11:9-10** Pss 118:25-26; 148:1. **11:16** Or *from carrying merchandise through the Temple.* **11:17** Isa 56:7; Jer 7:11. **11:19** Greek *they left;* other manuscripts read *he left.* **11:25** Some manuscripts add verse 26, *But if you refuse to forgive, your Father in heaven will not forgive your sins.* Compare Matt 6:15.

to the apocalyptic discourse (chap. 13). The symbol of the Temple and the conflict with Jewish authorities there dominates this section of Mark. **12–14:** This is the only miracle of destruction that Jesus performs and seems uncharacteristic of him, especially since figs were out of season. Immediately after the triumphant entry we encounter the curious lesson of the fig tree, another example of Markan intercalation. Jesus curses a tree that has no figs, cleanses the Temple (vv. 15–18), and uses the example of the fig tree in a teaching about faith and forgiveness (vv. 20–26). **15–19:** At this point the device of intercalation becomes extremely important, for the lesson is not about figs but about the Temple in Jerusalem. The first commentator on verses 12–26, Victor of Antioch in the fifth century, recognized that the fig tree was used to set forth the judgment that was about to fall on Jerusalem. While it is true that verses 17–18 set the stage for the following controversies, the point is that Jesus' Temple cleansing and his cursing the fig tree are powerful sign acts in the tradition of the prophets. Both presage the destruction of Jerusalem and the Temple. **20–26:** That the fig tree has *withered and died* represents what happens to the Temple. Jesus' injunction to *have faith in God* becomes the frame on which Mark hangs sayings on prayer and forgiveness. The teaching on prayer follows the destruction of the Temple because in the ancient world prayer was associated with a place. The question in the minds of Mark's readers might be: If there is no Temple, does God hear? Jesus responds that prayer is a matter of faith, of attitude, and not of geography.

The Authority of Jesus Challenged
27 Again they entered Jerusalem. As Jesus was
walking through the Temple area, the leading
priests, the teachers of religious law, and the
elders came up to him. 28 They demanded, "By
what authority are you doing all these things?
Who gave you the right to do them?"
29 "I'll tell you by what authority I do these
things if you answer one question," Jesus replied. 30 "Did John's authority to baptize come
from heaven, or was it merely human? Answer
me!"
31 They talked it over among themselves. "If
we say it was from heaven, he will ask why we
didn't believe John. 32 But do we dare say it was
merely human?" For they were afraid of what
the people would do, because everyone believed
that John was a prophet. 33 So they finally replied,
"We don't know."

And Jesus responded, "Then I won't tell you by what authority I do these things."

Parable of the Evil Farmers
12 Then Jesus began teaching them
with stories: "A man planted a vineyard. He built a wall around it, dug
a pit for pressing out the grape juice, and built
a lookout tower. Then he leased the vineyard to
tenant farmers and moved to another country.
2 At the time of the grape harvest, he sent one of
his servants to collect his share of the crop. 3 But
the farmers grabbed the servant, beat him up,
and sent him back empty-handed. 4 The owner
then sent another servant, but they insulted him
and beat him over the head. 5 The next servant
he sent was killed. Others he sent were either
beaten or killed, 6 until there was only one left—
his son whom he loved dearly. The owner finally
sent him, thinking, 'Surely they will respect my
son.'
7 "But the tenant farmers said to one another, 'Here comes the heir to this estate. Let's kill
him and get the estate for ourselves!' 8 So they
grabbed him and murdered him and threw his
body out of the vineyard.
9 "What do you suppose the owner of the
vineyard will do?" Jesus asked. "I'll tell you—
he will come and kill those farmers and lease the
vineyard to others. 10 Didn't you ever read this in
the Scriptures?

'The stone that the builders rejected
has now become the cornerstone.
11 This is the LORD's doing,
and it is wonderful to see.'* "

12 The religious leaders* wanted to arrest
Jesus because they realized he was telling the
story against them—they were the wicked farmers. But they were afraid of the crowd, so they
left him and went away.

Taxes for Caesar
13 Later the leaders sent some Pharisees and supporters of Herod to trap Jesus into saying something for which he could be arrested. 14 "Teacher,"
they said, "we know how honest you are. You are
impartial and don't play favorites. You teach the
way of God truthfully. Now tell us—is it right
to pay taxes to Caesar or not? 15 Should we pay
them, or shouldn't we?"

Jesus saw through their hypocrisy and said, "Why are you trying to trap me? Show me a Roman coin,* and I'll tell you."
16 When they
handed it to him, he asked, "Whose picture and
title are stamped on it?"

"Caesar's," they replied.

17 "Well, then," Jesus said, "give to Caesar
what belongs to Caesar, and give to God what
belongs to God."

His reply completely amazed them.

Discussion about Resurrection
18 Then Jesus was approached by some Sadducees—religious leaders who say there is no resurrection from the dead. They posed this question:
19 "Teacher, Moses gave us a law that if a man
dies, leaving a wife without children, his brother
should marry the widow and have a child who
will carry on the brother's name.* 20 Well, suppose
there were seven brothers. The oldest one married
and then died without children. 21 So the second
brother married the widow, but he also died without children. Then the third brother married her.
22 This continued with all seven of them, and still
there were no children. Last of all, the woman also
died. 23 So tell us, whose wife will she be in the resurrection? For all seven were married to her."

12:10-11 Ps 118:22-23. **12:12** Greek *They.* **12:15** Greek *a denarius.* **12:19** See Deut 25:5-6.

11:27—12:44 Controversy in the Temple Precincts. 11:27—12:12: In this series of conflict stories intended to demonstrate Jesus' superiority within Judaism, Jesus wins a debate with chief priests, scribes and elders. **12:13–17:** Pharisees and Herodians (enemies who have come together in the face of the threat that Jesus poses) question Jesus, but he foils their effort at entrapment and leaves them discomfited. **18–27:** Sadducees have no concern about a woman's status or the levirate law that was intended to protect the

24 Jesus replied, "Your mistake is that you
don't know the Scriptures, and you don't know
the power of God. 25 For when the dead rise,
they will neither marry nor be given in marriage. In this respect they will be like the angels
in heaven.

26 "But now, as to whether the dead will be
raised—haven't you ever read about this in the
writings of Moses, in the story of the burning
bush? Long after Abraham, Isaac, and Jacob had
died, God said to Moses,* 'I am the God of Abraham, the God of Isaac, and the God of Jacob.'*
27 So he is the God of the living, not the dead. You
have made a serious error."

The Most Important Commandment

28 One of the teachers of religious law was
standing there listening to the debate. He realized that Jesus had answered well, so he asked,
"Of all the commandments, which is the most
important?"

29 Jesus replied, "The most important commandment is this: 'Listen, O Israel! The LORD our
God is the one and only LORD. 30 And you must
love the LORD your God with all your heart, all
your soul, all your mind, and all your strength.'*
31 The second is equally important: 'Love your
neighbor as yourself.'* No other commandment
is greater than these."

32 The teacher of religious law replied, "Well
said, Teacher. You have spoken the truth by saying that there is only one God and no other.
33 And I know it is important to love him with
all my heart and all my understanding and all
my strength, and to love my neighbor as myself. This is more important than to offer all of
the burnt offerings and sacrifices required in the
law."

34 Realizing how much the man understood,
Jesus said to him, "You are not far from the
Kingdom of God." And after that, no one dared
to ask him any more questions.

Whose Son Is the Messiah?

35 Later, as Jesus was teaching the people in the
Temple, he asked, "Why do the teachers of religious law claim that the Messiah is the son of
David? 36 For David himself, speaking under the
inspiration of the Holy Spirit, said,

'The LORD said to my Lord,
Sit in the place of honor at my right hand
until I humble your enemies beneath your
feet.'*

37 Since David himself called the Messiah 'my
Lord,' how can the Messiah be his son?" The
large crowd listened to him with great delight.

38 Jesus also taught: "Beware of these teachers
of religious law! For they like to parade around
in flowing robes and receive respectful greetings
as they walk in the marketplaces. 39 And how they
love the seats of honor in the synagogues and the
head table at banquets. 40 Yet they shamelessly
cheat widows out of their property and then pretend to be pious by making long prayers in public. Because of this, they will be more severely
punished."

The Widow's Offering

41 Jesus sat down near the collection box in the
Temple and watched as the crowds dropped
in their money. Many rich people put in large
amounts. 42 Then a poor widow came and dropped
in two small coins.*

43 Jesus called his disciples to him and said,
"I tell you the truth, this poor widow has given
more than all the others who are making contributions. 44 For they gave a tiny part of their surplus, but she, poor as she is, has given everything
she had to live on."

12:26a Greek *in the story of the bush? God said to him.*
12:26b Exod 3:6. **12:29-30** Deut 6:4-5. **12:31** Lev 19:18.
12:36 Ps 110:1. **12:42** Greek *two lepta, which is a kodrantes* [i.e., a quadrans].

---

rights of widows. **28–34:** In the midst of the casuistry designed to subvert his teaching, Christ affirms the basic essentials of God's law. **35–40:** Jesus has condemned the scribes who *cheat widows out of their property.* Is the following pericope (12:44) praise for the widow or lament over a system that would lead her to give away her security? Should the religious establishment be supporting the widow? **41–44:** The widow, the one without legal protection or economic security, the one whose social vulnerability makes her a special object of God's concern, gives all she has to support the Temple and is commended by Jesus for doing so (see Widows, 1 Tim 5; God's Concern for the Disenfranchised, Ezek 34; God's Call to Social Justice, Amos 5). The usual reading of the text is that Mark is closing the conflictual Temple-teaching account with a contrast between outward religiosity and inward conviction. The next words of Jesus (13:2) predict the destruction of the Temple. The account does indicate that complete surrender to God is what counts, not outward ostentation, and it underlines Mark's understanding that discipleship implies such complete surrender. But while Jesus may have been moved by the widow's offering, he can hardly have approved of the religious system that explicitly or implicitly asked it of her.

Jesus Foretells the Future

13 As Jesus was leaving the Temple that day, one of his disciples said, "Teacher, look at these magnificent buildings! Look at the impressive stones in the walls."

[2] Jesus replied, "Yes, look at these great buildings. But they will be completely demolished. Not one stone will be left on top of another!"

[3] Later, Jesus sat on the Mount of Olives across the valley from the Temple. Peter, James, John, and Andrew came to him privately and asked him, [4] "Tell us, when will all this happen? What sign will show us that these things are about to be fulfilled?"

[5] Jesus replied, "Don't let anyone mislead you, [6] for many will come in my name, claiming, 'I am the Messiah.'* They will deceive many. [7] And you will hear of wars and threats of wars, but don't panic. Yes, these things must take place, but the end won't follow immediately. [8] Nation will go to war against nation, and kingdom against kingdom. There will be earthquakes in many parts of the world, as well as famines. But this is only the first of the birth pains, with more to come.

[9] "When these things begin to happen, watch out! You will be handed over to the local councils and beaten in the synagogues. You will stand trial before governors and kings because you are my followers. But this will be your opportunity to tell them about me.* [10] For the Good News must first be preached to all nations.* [11] But when you are arrested and stand trial, don't worry in advance about what to say. Just say what God tells you at that time, for it is not you who will be speaking, but the Holy Spirit.

[12] "A brother will betray his brother to death, a father will betray his own child, and children will rebel against their parents and cause them to be killed. [13] And everyone will hate you because you are my followers.* But the one who endures to the end will be saved.

[14] "The day is coming when you will see the sacrilegious object that causes desecration* standing where he* should not be." (Reader, pay attention!) "Then those in Judea must flee to the hills. [15] A person out on the deck of a roof must not go down into the house to pack. [16] A person out in the field must not return even to get a coat. [17] How terrible it will be for pregnant women and for nursing mothers in those days. [18] And pray that your flight will not be in winter. [19] For there will be greater anguish in those days than at any time since God created the world. And it will never be so great again. [20] In fact, unless the Lord shortens that time of calamity, not a single person will survive. But for the sake of his chosen ones he has shortened those days.

[21] "Then if anyone tells you, 'Look, here is the Messiah,' or 'There he is,' don't believe it. [22] For false messiahs and false prophets will rise up and perform signs and wonders so as to deceive, if possible, even God's chosen ones. [23] Watch out! I have warned you about this ahead of time!

[24] "At that time, after the anguish of those days,

the sun will be darkened,
  the moon will give no light,
[25] the stars will fall from the sky,
  and the powers in the heavens will be
    shaken.*

[26] Then everyone will see the Son of Man* coming on the clouds with great power and glory.* [27] And he will send out his angels to gather his chosen ones from all over the world*—from the farthest ends of the earth and heaven.

[28] "Now learn a lesson from the fig tree. When its branches bud and its leaves begin to sprout, you know that summer is near. [29] In the same way, when you see all these things taking place,

13:6 Greek *claiming, 'I am.'* **13:9** Or *But this will be your testimony against them.* **13:10** Or *all peoples.* **13:13** Greek *on account of my name.* **13:14a** Greek *the abomination of desolation.* See Dan 9:27; 11:31; 12:11. **13:14b** Or *it.* **13:24-25** See Isa 13:10; 34:4; Joel 2:10. **13:26a** "Son of Man" is a title Jesus used for himself. **13:26b** See Dan 7:13. **13:27** Greek *from the four winds.*

13:1–36 Apocalyptic Discourse. The placement of the material in chapter 13 is important (see annotation on 4:1–34). The narrative has moved rapidly toward the passion; the preceding conflict stories make it inevitable. The insertion of a speech into the narrative slows it down and gives special emphasis to the contents of the teaching. **1–14:** Much is puzzling: How is the reader to *pay attention* to the mysterious *sacrilegious object that causes desecration*? The word "apocalyptic" means "uncovering," and thus apocalypses uncover or reveal what will ultimately happen; their subject is eschatology. It sets forth the conviction that God's plans as foretold in Scripture will be fulfilled, specifically against the enemies of God's elect. **15–27:** Here is a profoundly sympathetic recognition that *pregnant women and . . . nursing mothers* are especially vulnerable in times of violence, war, and oppression. **28–36:** Note the reappearance of the metaphor of the fig tree in verse 28. One might also ask what the limits are on the Son's knowledge (v. 32) that bear closer examination than can be given here.

you can know that his return is very near, right
at the door. [30]I tell you the truth, this generation* will not pass from the scene before all these
things take place. [31]Heaven and earth will disappear, but my words will never disappear.
[32]"However, no one knows the day or hour
when these things will happen, not even the
angels in heaven or the Son himself. Only the
Father knows. [33]And since you don't know when
that time will come, be on guard! Stay alert*!
[34]"The coming of the Son of Man can be illustrated by the story of a man going on a long trip.
When he left home, he gave each of his slaves
instructions about the work they were to do, and
he told the gatekeeper to watch for his return.
[35]You, too, must keep watch! For you don't know
when the master of the household will return—
in the evening, at midnight, before dawn, or at
daybreak. [36]Don't let him find you sleeping when
he arrives without warning. [37]I say to everyone what I
say to everyone: Watch for him!"

Jesus Anointed at Bethany

14 It was now two days before Passover
and the Festival of Unleavened Bread.
The leading priests and the teachers
of religious law were still looking for an opportunity to capture Jesus secretly and kill him.
[2]"But not during the Passover celebration," they
agreed, "or the people may riot."
[3]Meanwhile, Jesus was in Bethany at the
home of Simon, a man who had previously had
leprosy. While he was eating,* a woman came in
with a beautiful alabaster jar of expensive perfume made from essence of nard. She broke open
the jar and poured the perfume over his head.
[4]Some of those at the table were indignant.
"Why waste such expensive perfume?" they
asked. [5]"It could have been sold for a year's wages* and the money given to the poor!" So they
scolded her harshly.
[6]But Jesus replied, "Leave her alone. Why
criticize her for doing such a good thing to me?
[7]You will always have the poor among you, and
you can help them whenever you want to. But
you will not always have me. [8]She has done what
she could and has anointed my body for burial
ahead of time. [9]I tell you the truth, wherever the
Good News is preached throughout the world,
this woman's deed will be remembered and discussed."

Judas Agrees to Betray Jesus

[10]Then Judas Iscariot, one of the twelve disciples,
went to the leading priests to arrange to betray
Jesus to them. [11]They were delighted when they
heard why he had come, and they promised to
give him money. So he began looking for an opportunity to betray Jesus.

The Last Supper

[12]On the first day of the Festival of Unleavened Bread, when the Passover lamb is sacrificed, Jesus' disciples asked him, "Where do you
want us to go to prepare the Passover meal for
you?"
[13]So Jesus sent two of them into Jerusalem
with these instructions: "As you go into the city,

13:30 Or *this age,* or *this nation.* **13:33** Some manuscripts add *and pray.* **14:3** Or *reclining.* **14:5** Greek *for 300 denarii.* A denarius was equivalent to a laborer's full day's wage.

14:1—16:8 Passion and Resurrection. 14:1–7: The Markan apocalypse is framed by stories of two anonymous and generous women who are contrasted to named and venal men: the scribes and Judas. In contrast to the plots against Jesus by men (vv. 1–2, 10–11), verses 3–9 narrate the extravagant love of a woman for him. (Note that vv. 1–11 show another example of intercalation.) It is one of the few stories recorded by all four evangelists. Jesus reclining at table indicates a festive occasion in the home of Simon the leper; Jesus' followers routinely met in private homes (1:29; 2:1, 15; 7:24; 9:33; 14:3, 15, 17). In this version, Jesus breaks cultural and religious taboos by keeping table fellowship with a leper (see Lev 13—14). Mark's wording suggests that the woman was one of the dinner guests or part of the household, another indication that the group around Jesus routinely included women. This woman anoints Jesus' head with an expensive perfume that represents a year's wages. Some of those with Jesus grumble about the waste involved in this anointing, indicating that they do not understand Jesus or what is imminent. In the history of Israel, anointing of the head signified selection for a special task, like priesthood or kingship. During the period of the United Kingdom, a primary function of the prophet was to anoint kings with oil. The woman's anointing is her symbolic confession that Jesus is Messiah, the anointed one. **8–9:** Mark's addition indicates that Jesus understood her action as prophetic of his crucifixion. Thus she is the first person in the Gospel to understand Jesus as the crucified Messiah, and she anticipates the spice-bearing women who are the first to go to the tomb and the first to receive the charge to declare the resurrection. **10–26:** The story of the Last Supper is all the more poignant because it begins with a grisly foreboding of what is to follow. **27–65:**

a man carrying a pitcher of water will meet you.
Follow him. [14]At the house he enters, say to the
owner, 'The Teacher asks: Where is the guest
room where I can eat the Passover meal with my
disciples?' [15]He will take you upstairs to a large
room that is already set up. That is where you
should prepare our meal." [16]So the two disciples
went into the city and found everything just as
Jesus had said, and they prepared the Passover
meal there.

[17]In the evening Jesus arrived with the twelve
disciples.* [18]As they were at the table* eating,
Jesus said, "I tell you the truth, one of you eating
with me here will betray me."

[19]Greatly distressed, each one asked in turn,
"Am I the one?"

[20]He replied, "It is one of you twelve who is
eating from this bowl with me. [21]For the Son of
Man* must die, as the Scriptures declared long
ago. But how terrible it will be for the one who
betrays him. It would be far better for that man
if he had never been born!"

[22]As they were eating, Jesus took some bread
and blessed it. Then he broke it in pieces and gave
it to the disciples, saying, "Take it, for this is my
body."

[23]And he took a cup of wine and gave thanks
to God for it. He gave it to them, and they all
drank from it. [24]And he said to them, "This is my
blood, which confirms the covenant* between
God and his people. It is poured out as a sacrifice
for many. [25]I tell you the truth, I will not drink
wine again until the day I drink it new in the
Kingdom of God."

[26]Then they sang a hymn and went out to the
Mount of Olives.

Jesus Predicts Peter's Denial

[27]On the way, Jesus told them, "All of you will
desert me. For the Scriptures say,

'God will strike* the Shepherd,
and the sheep will be scattered.'

[28]But after I am raised from the dead, I will go
ahead of you to Galilee and meet you there."

[29]Peter said to him, "Even if everyone else
deserts you, I never will."

[30]Jesus replied, "I tell you the truth, Peter—
this very night, before the rooster crows twice,
you will deny three times that you even know
me."

[31]"No!" Peter declared emphatically. "Even if
I have to die with you, I will never deny you!"
And all the others vowed the same.

Jesus Prays in Gethsemane

[32]They went to the olive grove called Gethsemane, and Jesus said, "Sit here while I go and
pray." [33]He took Peter, James, and John with him,
and he became deeply troubled and distressed.
[34]He told them, "My soul is crushed with grief
to the point of death. Stay here and keep watch
with me."

[35]He went on a little farther and fell to the
ground. He prayed that, if it were possible, the
awful hour awaiting him might pass him by.
[36]"Abba, Father,"* he cried out, "everything is
possible for you. Please take this cup of suffering
away from me. Yet I want your will to be done,
not mine."

[37]Then he returned and found the disciples
asleep. He said to Peter, "Simon, are you asleep?
Couldn't you watch with me even one hour?
[38]Keep watch and pray, so that you will not give
in to temptation. For the spirit is willing, but the
body is weak."

[39]Then Jesus left them again and prayed the
same prayer as before. [40]When he returned to
them again, he found them sleeping, for they
couldn't keep their eyes open. And they didn't
know what to say.

[41]When he returned to them the third time,
he said, "Go ahead and sleep. Have your rest. But
no—the time has come. The Son of Man is betrayed into the hands of sinners. [42]Up, let's be
going. Look, my betrayer is here!"

Jesus Is Betrayed and Arrested

[43]And immediately, even as Jesus said this, Judas,
one of the twelve disciples, arrived with a crowd
of men armed with swords and clubs. They had
been sent by the leading priests, the teachers of
religious law, and the elders. [44]The traitor, Judas, had given them a prearranged signal: "You
will know which one to arrest when I greet him
with a kiss. Then you can take him away under
guard." [45]As soon as they arrived, Judas walked
up to Jesus. "Rabbi!" he exclaimed, and gave him
the kiss.

[46]Then the others grabbed Jesus and arrest-

14:17 Greek *the Twelve.* **14:18** Or *As they reclined.*
14:21 "Son of Man" is a title Jesus used for himself.
14:24 Some manuscripts read *the new covenant.*
14:27 Greek *I will strike.* Zech 13:7. **14:36** *Abba* is an
Aramaic term for "father."

Mark's treatment of women in the Passion Narrative is fascinating. Whereas the named male disciples sleep when charged to watch (v. 37), betray Jesus (v. 43) and deny having known him (vv. 68, 70–71), women

ed him. 47 But one of the men with Jesus pulled out his sword and struck the high priest's slave, slashing off his ear.

48 Jesus asked them, "Am I some dangerous revolutionary, that you come with swords and clubs to arrest me? 49 Why didn't you arrest me in the Temple? I was there among you teaching every day. But these things are happening to fulfill what the Scriptures say about me."

50 Then all his disciples deserted him and ran away. 51 One young man following behind was clothed only in a long linen shirt. When the mob tried to grab him, 52 he slipped out of his shirt and ran away naked.

Jesus before the Council

53 They took Jesus to the high priest's home where the leading priests, the elders, and the teachers of religious law had gathered. 54 Meanwhile, Peter followed him at a distance and went right into the high priest's courtyard. There he sat with the guards, warming himself by the fire.

55 Inside, the leading priests and the entire high council* were trying to find evidence against Jesus, so they could put him to death. But they couldn't find any. 56 Many false witnesses spoke against him, but they contradicted each other. 57 Finally, some men stood up and gave this false testimony: 58 "We heard him say, 'I will destroy this Temple made with human hands, and in three days I will build another, made without human hands.' " 59 But even then they didn't get their stories straight!

60 Then the high priest stood up before the others and asked Jesus, "Well, aren't you going to answer these charges? What do you have to say for yourself?" 61 But Jesus was silent and made no reply. Then the high priest asked him, "Are you the Messiah, the Son of the Blessed One?"

62 Jesus said, "I AM.* And you will see the Son of Man seated in the place of power at God's right hand* and coming on the clouds of heaven.*"

63 Then the high priest tore his clothing to show his horror and said, "Why do we need other witnesses? 64 You have all heard his blasphemy. What is your verdict?"

"Guilty!" they all cried. "He deserves to die!"

65 Then some of them began to spit at him, and they blindfolded him and beat him with their fists. "Prophesy to us," they jeered. And the guards slapped him as they took him away.

Peter Denies Jesus

66 Meanwhile, Peter was in the courtyard below. One of the servant girls who worked for the high priest came by 67 and noticed Peter warming himself at the fire. She looked at him closely and said, "You were one of those with Jesus of Nazareth.*"

68 But Peter denied it. "I don't know what you're talking about," he said, and he went out into the entryway. Just then, a rooster crowed.*

69 When the servant girl saw him standing there, she began telling the others, "This man is definitely one of them!" 70 But Peter denied it again.

A little later some of the other bystanders confronted Peter and said, "You must be one of them, because you are a Galilean."

71 Peter swore, "A curse on me if I'm lying—I don't know this man you're talking about!" 72 And immediately the rooster crowed the second time.

Suddenly, Jesus' words flashed through Peter's mind: "Before the rooster crows twice, you will deny three times that you even know me." And he broke down and wept.

Jesus' Trial before Pilate

15 Very early in the morning the leading priests, the elders, and the teachers of religious law—the entire high council*—met to discuss their next step. They bound Jesus, led him away, and took him to Pilate, the Roman governor.

2 Pilate asked Jesus, "Are you the king of the Jews?"

Jesus replied, "You have said it."

3 Then the leading priests kept accusing him of many crimes, 4 and Pilate asked him, "Aren't you going to answer them? What about all these charges they are bringing against you?" 5 But Jesus said nothing, much to Pilate's surprise.

6 Now it was the governor's custom each year during the Passover celebration to release one prisoner—anyone the people requested. 7 One of the prisoners at that time was Barabbas, a revolutionary who had committed murder in an uprising. 8 The crowd went to Pilate and asked him to release a prisoner as usual.

14:55 Greek *the Sanhedrin.* **14:62a** Or *The 'I AM' is here;* or *I am the LORD.* See Exod 3:14. **14:62b** Greek *at the right hand of the power.* See Ps 110:1. **14:62c** See Dan 7:13. **14:67** Or *Jesus the Nazarene.* **14:68** Some manuscripts do not include *Just then, a rooster crowed.* **15:1** Greek *the Sanhedrin;* also in 15:43.

appear as astute bystanders and as loyal disciples. **66–72:** The servant girl of the high priest correctly identifies Peter as a follower of Jesus while he denies this identification. **15:1–15:** Although the trial was

9 "Would you like me to release to you this 'King of the Jews'?" Pilate asked. 10 (For he realized by now that the leading priests had arrested Jesus out of envy.) 11 But at this point the leading priests stirred up the crowd to demand the release of Barabbas instead of Jesus. 12 Pilate asked them, "Then what should I do with this man you call the king of the Jews?"

13 They shouted back, "Crucify him!"

14 "Why?" Pilate demanded. "What crime has he committed?"

But the mob roared even louder, "Crucify him!"

15 So to pacify the crowd, Pilate released Barabbas to them. He ordered Jesus flogged with a lead-tipped whip, then turned him over to the Roman soldiers to be crucified.

The Soldiers Mock Jesus

16 The soldiers took Jesus into the courtyard of the governor's headquarters (called the Praetorium) and called out the entire regiment. 17 They dressed him in a purple robe, and they wove thorn branches into a crown and put it on his head. 18 Then they saluted him and taunted, "Hail! King of the Jews!" 19 And they struck him on the head with a reed stick, spit on him, and dropped to their knees in mock worship. 20 When they were finally tired of mocking him, they took off the purple robe and put his own clothes on him again. Then they led him away to be crucified.

The Crucifixion

21 A passerby named Simon, who was from Cyrene,* was coming in from the countryside just then, and the soldiers forced him to carry Jesus' cross. (Simon was the father of Alexander and Rufus.) 22 And they brought Jesus to a place called Golgotha (which means "Place of the Skull"). 23 They offered him wine drugged with myrrh, but he refused it.

24 Then the soldiers nailed him to the cross. They divided his clothes and threw dice* to decide who would get each piece. 25 It was nine o'clock in the morning when they crucified him. 26 A sign announced the charge against him. It read, "The King of the Jews." 27 Two revolutionaries* were crucified with him, one on his right and one on his left.*

29 The people passing by shouted abuse, shaking their heads in mockery. "Ha! Look at you now!" they yelled at him. "You said you were going to destroy the Temple and rebuild it in three days. 30 Well then, save yourself and come down from the cross!"

31 The leading priests and teachers of religious law also mocked Jesus. "He saved others," they scoffed, "but he can't save himself! 32 Let this Messiah, this King of Israel, come down from the cross so we can see it and believe him!" Even the men who were crucified with Jesus ridiculed him.

The Death of Jesus

33 At noon, darkness fell across the whole land until three o'clock. 34 Then at three o'clock Jesus called out with a loud voice, *"Eloi, Eloi, lema sabachthani?"* which means "My God, my God, why have you abandoned me?"*

35 Some of the bystanders misunderstood and thought he was calling for the prophet Elijah. 36 One of them ran and filled a sponge with sour wine, holding it up to him on a reed stick so he could drink. "Wait!" he said. "Let's see whether Elijah comes to take him down!"

37 Then Jesus uttered another loud cry and breathed his last. 38 And the curtain in the sanctuary of the Temple was torn in two, from top to bottom.

39 When the Roman officer* who stood facing him* saw how he had died, he exclaimed, "This man truly was the Son of God!"

40 Some women were there, watching from a distance, including Mary Magdalene, Mary (the mother of James the younger and of Joseph*),

15:21 *Cyrene* was a city in northern Africa. **15:24** Greek *cast lots.* See Ps 22:18. **15:27a** Or *Two criminals.* **15:27b** Some manuscripts add verse 28, *And the Scripture was fulfilled that said, "He was counted among those who were rebels."* See Isa 53:12; also compare Luke 22:37. **15:34** Ps 22:1. **15:39a** Greek *the centurion;* similarly in 15:44, 45. **15:39b** Some manuscripts add *heard his cry and.* **15:40** Greek *Joses;* also in 15:47. See Matt 27:56.

conducted at night, word spread throughout Jerusalem to the women who came and stood along Jesus' path and attended his death. **16–39:** Simon of Cyrene appears to have been known to Mark's audience because he is identified as the father of Alexander and Rufus. **40–41:** At the crucifixion, no male disciples seem to be in attendance, but *Mary Magdalene, Mary (the mother of James the younger and of Joseph)*, and *Salome* are there, apparently with other women who *had been followers of Jesus and had cared for him while he was in Galilee*. The word "follow" (*akolutheo*) in verse 41 is a technical term and the exact word used for the responses of Andrew and Simon (1:18) and Levi (2:14) to Jesus. The word here translated as *cared for* (*diakoneo*) is probably more accurately rendered "ministered" or "served." It is the word used to describe the central aspect of Jesus' ministry and that which was required of all his disciples. At least

and Salome. 41 They had been followers of Jesus
and had cared for him while he was in Galilee.
Many other women who had come with him to
Jerusalem were also there.

The Burial of Jesus

42 This all happened on Friday, the day of preparation,* the day before the Sabbath. As evening approached, 43 Joseph of Arimathea took a risk and
went to Pilate and asked for Jesus' body. (Joseph
was an honored member of the high council, and
he was waiting for the Kingdom of God to come.)
44 Pilate couldn't believe that Jesus was already
dead, so he called for the Roman officer and
asked if he had died yet. 45 The officer confirmed
that Jesus was dead, so Pilate told Joseph he could
have the body. 46 Joseph bought a long sheet of
linen cloth. Then he took Jesus' body down from
the cross, wrapped it in the cloth, and laid it in a
tomb that had been carved out of the rock. Then
he rolled a stone in front of the entrance. 47 Mary
Magdalene and Mary the mother of Joseph saw
where Jesus' body was laid.

The Resurrection

16 Saturday evening, when the Sabbath ended, Mary Magdalene, Mary
the mother of James, and Salome
went out and purchased burial spices so they
could anoint Jesus' body. 2 Very early on Sunday morning,* just at sunrise, they went to
the tomb. 3 On the way they were asking each
other, "Who will roll away the stone for us
from the entrance to the tomb?" 4 But as they
arrived, they looked up and saw that the stone,
which was very large, had already been rolled
aside.

5 When they entered the tomb, they saw a
young man clothed in a white robe sitting on
the right side. The women were shocked, 6 but
the angel said, "Don't be alarmed. You are looking for Jesus of Nazareth,* who was crucified.
He isn't here! He is risen from the dead! Look,
this is where they laid his body. 7 Now go and tell
his disciples, including Peter, that Jesus is going
ahead of you to Galilee. You will see him there,
just as he told you before he died."

8 The women fled from the tomb, trembling
and bewildered, and they said nothing to anyone
because they were too frightened.*

15:42 Greek *It was the day of preparation.* **16:2** Greek *on the first day of the week;* also in 16:9. **16:6** Or *Jesus the Nazarene.* **16:8** The most reliable early manuscripts of the Gospel of Mark end at verse 8. Other manuscripts include various endings to the Gospel. A few include both the "shorter ending" and the "longer ending." The majority of manuscripts include the "longer ending" immediately after verse 8.

two technical terms related to discipleship are used of women in Mark's Gospel. Named women appear more prominently in the Passion Narrative than in any other section of the Gospel. Mark understands that discipleship is a matter of following, serving, and suffering, and in his Gospel women do all three. **42–47:** The faithful women disciples witness the crucifixion, follow to see where Jesus' body is, and set out early the first day of the week to anoint that body, thereby becoming the first witnesses to the resurrection and the first to be told to proclaim it. That Mary Magdalene and the other Mary witnessed the crucifixion, Jesus' death and the manner of his burial make them credible witnesses to the resurrection. In what may be the greatest Markan irony of all, the veracity of the resurrection is dependent on the witness of women (see Women as Witnesses, next page). The text of the Gospel as we have it suggests that the community for which Mark wrote also must have had strong women leaders. Some scholars have suggested it might have included some of the prominent women in the later chapters of the Gospel. **16:1–8a:** Mary Magdalene, Mary the mother of James, and Salome seem to parallel Jesus' inner circle of male disciples, Peter, James, and John. In the evangelist's scheme, we find that women are remarkably prominent. They are vital participants in the public ministry of Jesus, examples of his understanding of discipleship and witnesses—the crucial witnesses—of his death and resurrection As the narrative progresses they move from being passive recipients of miracles to active examples of discipleship, to being given the apostolic commission to *go, tell his disciples, including Peter*. For the women to be commanded to proclaim the resurrection is to place them firmly on this same path. No wonder they hesitate in silence before taking up the task! In fact, the rehabilitation of the Twelve and the male disciples depend on their accepting the testimony of women. Surely this is among Mark's most surprising understandings of the reign of God and the changes it will entail. **8a:** That the women *said nothing to anyone* forms an inverted inclusio with 1:45, where a leper who is charged not to speak begins to *proclaim . . . freely*. Here those charged to speak are initially silent, but only initially.

There is strong reason to think that these words were the intended conclusion of Mark's Gospel. The empty tomb is the signpost toward a new encounter with the risen Jesus. The angel has declared that Jesus is no longer dead, and the silence at the end suggests reverence in the face of the realization that the new day of God has dawned.

Women as Witnesses

Israel's jurisprudence relied heavily on witnesses and regarded testimony seriously. The law obligates witnesses to testify and requires at least two or three witnesses in any given case (Lev 5:1; Deut 19:15). The Decalogue (Ten Commandments) forbids perjury along with other serious transgressions such as idolatry, murder, adultery, and theft (Exod 20:16; Deut 5:20). Perjurers were subject to the *lex talionis* (the "eye for an eye" law), meaning that a perjurer might be put to death (Deut 19:16–21). Indeed, it became proverbial in Israel that "a false witness will not go unpunished, and a liar will be destroyed" (Prov 19:9).

The Old Testament records no instances of women giving legal testimony, but neither does it legislate against women being witnesses. This presumably reflects that in preexilic Israel, women's testimony was excluded not by law but in practice. In postexilic times, rabbinic codes make comprehensive but not categorical prohibitions against women's testimony.

In nonlegal contexts, women's testimony in religious confession and prophecy is common and accepted. Testimony to God's nature and deeds comes, for example, from Miriam (Exod 15:20–21), Deborah (Judg 5:1–31), Hannah (1 Sam 2:1–10), Huldah (2 Kgs 22:14–20), Mary (Luke 1:46–55), and Anna (Luke 2:36–38). Women also were competent to swear religious vows and oaths (Deut 29:9–15; 1 Sam 1:11; Jer 44:24–25).

Biblical and apocryphal writings record women giving eyewitness testimony to Jesus' resurrection. In Luke, disbelief is directed not against the gender of the witnesses but the content of their testimony: "But the story sounded like nonsense . . . so they didn't believe it" (Luke 24:11). In the longer ending of Mark, Jesus rebukes the apostles "because they refused to believe those who had seen him" (Mark 16:14)—a clear endorsement of the women's testimony.

Exceptions to the rabbinic prohibitions against women's testimony are intriguing when read against the Gospels, especially that of John. For example, the rabbis allowed the testimony of women to establish the fact of a man's death. Thus, Mary and Martha are qualified to testify to their brother Lazarus's death, and their dual witness to his death is crucial evidence that he was raised from the dead, not resuscitated from unconsciousness (John 11:1–44). Similarly, the women at Jesus' cross are eligible to provide multiple attestation to his death (John 19:25–30). Mary Magdalene's testimony serves to support that Jesus' body was not in the tomb, that it had not been removed, that it had not been resuscitated, and that his bodily appearances were not phantasms (John 20:1–18)—crucial evidence in support of the resurrection.

Paul's inherited list of resurrection witnesses does not include the women (1 Cor 15:5–8). Assuming that Paul knew about the women witnesses, why, when citing the list, would he either omit them or fail to add them? It has been argued that Paul excluded them because they were not credible witnesses. But if Paul were trying to maintain control over charismatic women leaders in the Corinthian church, it may be that he excluded them precisely because they were credible, and such credibility helped to invest the Corinthian women with authority and autonomy. Although Paul's letters do not record detailed cases of women acting as witnesses, his references to women as colleagues in his mission point to their active involvement in the witnessing of the earliest church (Rom 16:1–12; Phil 4:3).

[Shorter Ending of Mark]

Then they briefly reported all this to Peter and his companions. Afterward Jesus himself sent them out from east to west with the sacred and unfailing message of salvation that gives eternal life. Amen.

[Longer Ending of Mark]

9 After Jesus rose from the dead early on Sunday morning, the first person who saw him was Mary Magdalene, the woman from whom he had cast out seven demons. 10 She went to the disciples, who were grieving and weeping, and told

16:8b–20 The Gospel's Ending

Most scholars concur that 16:8a is the original ending of Mark. Ancient witnesses show no knowledge of Mark 16:8b–20, and its content, vocabulary, and style are distinctively non-Markan. So the narrative ends with the words *they were too frightened*. This ending has troubled some scholars, who have suggested variously that Mark might have been prevented from finishing the Gospel or that the real conclu-

them what had happened. [11]But when she told them that Jesus was alive and she had seen him, they didn't believe her.

[12]Afterward he appeared in a different form to two of his followers who were walking from Jerusalem into the country. [13]They rushed back to tell the others, but no one believed them.

[14]Still later he appeared to the eleven disciples as they were eating together. He rebuked them for their stubborn unbelief because they refused to believe those who had seen him after he had been raised from the dead.*

[15]And then he told them, "Go into all the world and preach the Good News to everyone. [16]Anyone who believes and is baptized will be saved. But anyone who refuses to believe will be condemned. [17]These miraculous signs will accompany those who believe: They will cast out demons in my name, and they will speak in new languages.* [18]They will be able to handle snakes with safety, and if they drink anything poisonous, it won't hurt them. They will be able to place their hands on the sick, and they will be healed."

[19]When the Lord Jesus had finished talking with them, he was taken up into heaven and sat down in the place of honor at God's right hand. [20]And the disciples went everywhere and preached, and the Lord worked through them, confirming what they said by many miraculous signs.

16:14 Some early manuscripts add: *And they excused themselves, saying, "This age of lawlessness and unbelief is under Satan, who does not permit God's truth and power to conquer the evil [unclean] spirits. Therefore, reveal your justice now." This is what they said to Christ. And Christ replied to them, "The period of years of Satan's power has been fulfilled, but other dreadful things will happen soon. And I was handed over to death for those who have sinned, so that they may return to the truth and sin no more, and so they may inherit the spiritual, incorruptible, and righteous glory in heaven."* **16:17** Or *new tongues;* some manuscripts do not include *new.*

sion was lost or destroyed or that it was suppressed. **8b:** The Shorter Ending is consistent with Mark's view of Jesus in the Gospel; faith has been generated by the word of Jesus, by message and not miracle. It also serves to illuminate Mark's view of discipleship. In his Gospel, no disciples, female or male, are perfect; all are in process. **9–20:** The Longer Ending of the Gospel shows us how fragile the message of Jesus is: Will the reader respond to it, proclaim it, or remain silently in fear? Mark's Gospel has depicted John the Baptist as having preached, been delivered up, and martyred. Jesus too preaches, is delivered up, and martyred. Disciples are not greater than their masters. They are to take up their crosses and follow, to lose their lives for the gospel (8:34–35), to be "last of all and servant of all" (9:35).

LUKE

INTRODUCTION

No book of the Bible is more dependent on the witness of women or more concerned with their welfare and work than the Gospel of Luke. The dating of the Third Gospel has ranged from AD 59 to the 70s or 80s.

Luke, a physician (2 Tim 4:11) and an associate of the apostle Paul (Col 4:14; Phlm 24), is the author of the Gospel of Luke and the Acts of the Apostles. Both books are addressed to Theophilus, perhaps a personal name or an honorific title. The addressee is also called "most honorable," a manner of address ordinarily reserved for high-ranking public officials (cf. Acts 23:26; 26:25). Some scholars have suggested that the two-part document was intended to present the activities of Jesus and his followers in an orderly and lucid fashion to those who might sit in judgment upon them. The presence of women during the interrogation of Paul (Acts 24:24; 25:23; 26:30, cf. Matt 27:19) and their interest in his defense are noted by Luke. A public official might well read with interest the careful delineation of the trial proceedings and charges brought against Jesus and Paul. But the treatise is aimed at other audiences as well, especially women. More were learning to read and were seeking stories that they could treasure.

Appropriately called a "Gospel of women," Luke's record recognizes the major role played by women in key salvation events. They are the major witnesses of the birth, crucifixion, burial, and resurrection of Jesus. They follow him on his mission trips, offer him care and concern, and interact with him in startling ways. Women, whether affluent and influential or poor and disadvantaged, are persons of great interest and importance to Luke. Step by step he builds the picture of women as followers, believers, transformed sinners, and credible witnesses in the remarkable narrative that he tells. It is not that women are emphasized at the expense of men or to the exclusion of men. Luke takes care to balance a story or a parable about a woman with one about a man or vice versa. Luke's equal stress on the part of women and men stands in contrast to other accounts and is therefore particularly noteworthy.

In writing his Gospel, Luke's purpose and method of composition are carefully defined. He wished to interview firsthand witnesses and to construct their concerted testimony into a "careful account." The witness of women is clear throughout, particularly that of Mary the mother of Jesus. She must have provided him with much of the information that fills the first two chapters. Only she or someone who knew her well would have been in a position to recount the details of her visit to Elizabeth, the dedication in the Temple, and the search for the adolescent Jesus.

The reader is led to suppose that Mary, who "kept all these things in her heart and thought about them often" (2:19, 51), had previously been reticent to divulge much of this information. Luke, the empathic Gentile, may have been the perfect auditor for whom she could review all that had passed and find in their integration a fuller and more satisfying meaning. —*Catherine Clark Kroeger*

1:1—2:52 The Birth and Childhood of Jesus
3:1—6:19 The Beginning of Jesus' Ministry
6:20—9:17 Good News for the Poor and Disadvantaged
9:18—19:27 On the Way to Jerusalem
19:28—22:46 Mounting Tensions in Jerusalem
22:47—23:56 Trial, Arrest, and Execution
24:1–53 The Disciples' Recognition of the Risen Jesus

✧

Introduction

1 Many people have set out to write accounts about the events that have been fulfilled among us. 2 They used the eyewitness reports circulating among us from the early disciples.* 3 Having carefully investigated everything from the beginning, I also have decided to write a careful account for you, most honorable Theophilus, 4 so you can be certain of the truth of everything you were taught.

The Birth of John the Baptist Foretold

5 When Herod was king of Judea, there was a Jewish priest named Zechariah. He was a member of the priestly order of Abijah, and his wife, Elizabeth, was also from the priestly line of Aaron. 6 Zechariah and Elizabeth were righteous in God's eyes, careful to obey all of the Lord's commandments and regulations. 7 They had no children because Elizabeth was unable to conceive, and they were both very old.

8 One day Zechariah was serving God in the Temple, for his order was on duty that week. 9 As was the custom of the priests, he was chosen by lot to enter the sanctuary of the Lord and burn incense. 10 While the incense was being burned, a great crowd stood outside, praying.

11 While Zechariah was in the sanctuary, an angel of the Lord appeared to him, standing to the right of the incense altar. 12 Zechariah was shaken and overwhelmed with fear when he saw him. 13 But the angel said, "Don't be afraid, Zechariah! God has heard your prayer. Your wife, Elizabeth, will give you a son, and you are to name him John. 14 You will have great joy and gladness, and many will rejoice at his birth, 15 for he will be great in the eyes of the Lord. He must never touch wine or other alcoholic drinks. He will be filled with the Holy Spirit, even before his birth.* 16 And he will turn many Israelites to the Lord their God. 17 He will be a man with the spirit and power of Elijah. He will prepare the people for the coming of the Lord. He will turn the hearts of the fathers to their children,* and he will cause those who are rebellious to accept the wisdom of the godly."

18 Zechariah said to the angel, "How can I be sure this will happen? I'm an old man now, and my wife is also well along in years."

19 Then the angel said, "I am Gabriel! I stand in the very presence of God. It was he who sent

1:2 Greek *from those who from the beginning were servants of the word.* **1:15** Or *even from birth.* **1:17** See Mal 4:5-6.

1:1—2:52 The Birth and Childhood of Jesus

1:1–4 Introduction. The author freely admits that others have made various attempts to recount the significant events and trends in the life of Jesus, but none has given the perspective that he seeks. As a methodical historian he interviews those best in a position to give him firsthand information.

1:5–25 The Birth of John the Baptist Foretold. The first announcement that the time has come at last for the birth of the Messiah is made in Jerusalem's Temple to a righteous priest as he performs his appointed duty. As the archangel Gabriel had appeared to Daniel "at the time of the evening sacrifice" (Dan 9:21), so now he appeared to Zechariah. The celestial being who foretold the rise and fall of mighty empires now communicates the preliminaries of a new stage in God's redemptive plan. The focus is an intensely personal one, on a pregnancy and the answered prayer of two devout people who longed not only for a child of their own but also for the deliverance of Israel. **14:** The archangel bursts into a song foretelling not only the joy that the parents will find in this child but also the gladness of those who will heed his message (vv. 13–17). He will come in the spirit of Elijah to turn an unready and unrepentant people back to the Lord. To this child is assigned the role of precursor for the anointed one. **18:** If Gabriel proclaims a time of divine fulfillment for God's plan, Zechariah sees that Elizabeth's biological time for conception and birth is long gone. Overwhelmed with amaze-

me to bring you this good news! [20]But now, since
you didn't believe what I said, you will be silent
and unable to speak until the child is born. For
my words will certainly be fulfilled at the proper
time."

[21]Meanwhile, the people were waiting for
Zechariah to come out of the sanctuary, wondering why he was taking so long. [22]When he finally
did come out, he couldn't speak to them. Then
they realized from his gestures and his silence
that he must have seen a vision in the sanctuary.

[23]When Zechariah's week of service in the
Temple was over, he returned home. [24]Soon afterward his wife, Elizabeth, became pregnant and
went into seclusion for five months. [25]"How kind
the Lord is!" she exclaimed. "He has taken away
my disgrace of having no children."

The Birth of Jesus Foretold

[26]In the sixth month of Elizabeth's pregnancy,
God sent the angel Gabriel to Nazareth, a village
in Galilee, [27]to a virgin named Mary. She was
engaged to be married to a man named Joseph,
a descendant of King David. [28]Gabriel appeared
to her and said, "Greetings, favored woman! The
Lord is with you!*"

[29]Confused and disturbed, Mary tried to
think what the angel could mean. [30]"Don't be
afraid, Mary," the angel told her, "for you have
found favor with God! [31]You will conceive and
give birth to a son, and you will name him Jesus.
[32]He will be very great and will be called the
Son of the Most High. The Lord God will give
him the throne of his ancestor David. [33]And he
will reign over Israel* forever; his Kingdom will
never end!"

[34]Mary asked the angel, "But how can this
happen? I am a virgin."

[35]The angel replied, "The Holy Spirit will
come upon you, and the power of the Most High
will overshadow you. So the baby to be born will
be holy, and he will be called the Son of God.
[36]What's more, your relative Elizabeth has become pregnant in her old age! People used to say
she was barren, but she has conceived a son and
is now in her sixth month. [37]For nothing is impossible with God.*"

[38]Mary responded, "I am the Lord's servant.
May everything you have said about me come
true." And then the angel left her.

1:28 Some manuscripts add *Blessed are you among women.* **1:33** Greek *over the house of Jacob.* **1:37** Some manuscripts read *For the word of God will never fail.*

ment, shock, hope and fear, he asks for a sign. His request bespeaks the many disappointments he must have known in his hope for a child. He dare not entertain another cruel hope. **20:** The sign of Zechariah's silence is not so much punishment for unbelief as it is confirmation of the promised event. During the remarkable pregnancies of his wife, Elizabeth, and her young protégé, Mary, the old man will be unable to offer advice, no matter how well intended. Zechariah's silence is also protection against the curiosity and concern of those who wait outside. He cannot communicate what must not yet be made public. **23–25:** Luke evinces a ready sympathy for Elizabeth's formerly devastating circumstance, the disgrace of barrenness (see Barrenness and Fertility, 1 Sam 1). She had failed at the most basic level in what is expected of her as a woman. In Luke's view of the kingdom of God, personal piety has far more relevance than reproductive capacity. Elizabeth delights in God, who has removed her humiliation, and in seclusion she ponders the working of God's power in her life. Better to savor in private her precious secret rather than to attempt explanations that no one would accept.

1:26–38 The Birth of Jesus Foretold. This time Gabriel comes neither to Daniel, prime minister of the vast Persian Empire, nor to the priestly Zechariah, but to a peasant girl in a city of dubious distinction. She is denoted a virgin *(parthenos)*. Although she is betrothed to Joseph, the engagement period was often a long one, and they are not yet living together. Mary has found favor *(charis)* with God, as did Noah (Gen 6:8) and Moses (Exod 33:12–13) when they were called to salvific tasks. After the promise comes a paean of praise, one that identifies Jesus as the Davidic Messiah and the Son of God. The coming One will bring in the unending kingdom of which Gabriel had spoken to Daniel. **34:** How can this be, since Mary has not yet experienced sexual congress with a man? Her response differs from that of Zechariah in that she requests clarification rather than a sign. She is, however, given a sign as well as an avenue for support during the months that would lie ahead. Just as Sarah was able to conceive in her old age (Gen 18:12–14), so too Elizabeth will discover that God can open the wombs of barren women. Mary is thus provided with a confidante with whom she can share the uncertainties, discomforts, and perplexities of incipient motherhood. Elizabeth, her cousin, has also been called to a mystifying and magnificent mission. **38:** Mary has been given an honest explanation and the opportunity to accept the mission or to decline it. This is not a matter of sexual exploitation but of a maiden consciously and willingly joining with the purpose of God to bring salvation to the world.

Mary Visits Elizabeth
39 A few days later Mary hurried to the hill country of Judea, to the town 40 where Zechariah lived.
She entered the house and greeted Elizabeth.
41 At the sound of Mary's greeting, Elizabeth's
child leaped within her, and Elizabeth was filled
with the Holy Spirit.
42 Elizabeth gave a glad cry and exclaimed to
Mary, "God has blessed you above all women,
and your child is blessed. 43 Why am I so honored, that the mother of my Lord should visit
me? 44 When I heard your greeting, the baby in
my womb jumped for joy. 45 You are blessed because you believed that the Lord would do what
he said."

The Magnificat: Mary's Song of Praise
46 Mary responded,

"Oh, how my soul praises the Lord.
47 How my spirit rejoices in God my Savior!
48 For he took notice of his lowly servant girl,
and from now on all generations will call
me blessed.
49 For the Mighty One is holy,
and he has done great things for me.
50 He shows mercy from generation to
generation
to all who fear him.
51 His mighty arm has done tremendous
things!
He has scattered the proud and haughty
ones.
52 He has brought down princes from their
thrones
and exalted the humble.
53 He has filled the hungry with good things
and sent the rich away with empty hands.
54 He has helped his servant Israel
and remembered to be merciful.
55 For he made this promise to our ancestors,
to Abraham and his children forever."

56 Mary stayed with Elizabeth about three
months and then went back to her own home.

The Birth of John the Baptist
57 When it was time for Elizabeth's baby to be
born, she gave birth to a son. 58 And when her
neighbors and relatives heard that the Lord had
been very merciful to her, everyone rejoiced with
her.

1:39–56 Mary Visits Elizabeth. In her sixth month of gestation, Elizabeth received her cousin Mary into her home. As the young woman called out her greeting, there came an exultant response from one yet unborn who was already attuned to intimations of the coming Messiah. **42:** Now a prophetic utterance rises to the lips of Elizabeth as she sings of a young mother's faith and courage. As a pregnant and unmarried woman, she had made her way to the home of a priestly couple distinguished by their scrupulous observance of the law. Surely she must have pondered how best to explain to them her situation, how to point to the angel's promise rather than her predicament. Beyond such immediate considerations lay the knowledge that a woman pregnant outside of wedlock could be stoned to death at worst, dishonored and disgraced at best. **46–56:** Each woman appears to have waited for the other to give full expression to the emotions that sweep through them. Elizabeth's recognition of Mary's faith has brought to expression what has been lying unsaid in the young mother's heart. The young mother-to-be bursts into a song that harks back to that of Hannah (1 Sam 2:1–10; see Women as Psalmists, Judg 5), but it is also reminiscent of certain of the psalms (Pss 33; 47; 48; 117; 135; 136). Mary's song requires readers to adopt a new set of values if they are to understand the significance of Luke's story. The kingdom belongs to those who are rich in faith but humble enough to see God's work in ordinary humanity. Pride and power become disqualifications for participation in the kingdom of God, and right attitude far outweighs the trappings of the establishment. The poor are filled, the rich are emptied, the despairing given hope, and the abject accorded a status of dignity. Mary will impart this concern for social justice to her children (see God's Call to Social Justice, Amos 5). Not only will Jesus sound the same notes, but James his brother will likewise insist on equality of treatment and respect for all persons. Jude, possibly another brother, will emphasize the fundamental justice of God. **56:** Elizabeth's special legacy to Mary is guidance on the path of faith. During their time together, the two work their way through delicate issues of faith and steadfastness against unbelievable odds. At the end of three months, Mary returns to Nazareth: perhaps because she has found the perspective that she had come to seek, perhaps because she is feeling well enough to travel after the nausea of the first trimester, perhaps to prevent an unnecessary burden on the household during the upcoming birth, perhaps to avoid difficult questions from meddlesome relatives.

1:57–80 The Birth of John the Baptist. 57: When the moment of birth comes, Elizabeth is surrounded with well-meaning friends, neighbors, and relatives. It is at such rites of passage that some women excel. Those well-experienced take charge, direct, and anticipate

[59]When the baby was eight days old, they all
came for the circumcision ceremony. They wanted to name him Zechariah, after his father. [60]But
Elizabeth said, "No! His name is John!"

[61]"What?" they exclaimed. "There is no one
in all your family by that name." [62]So they used
gestures to ask the baby's father what he wanted
to name him. [63]He motioned for a writing tablet,
and to everyone's surprise he wrote, "His name
is John." [64]Instantly Zechariah could speak again,
and he began praising God.

[65]Awe fell upon the whole neighborhood, and
the news of what had happened spread throughout the Judean hills. [66]Everyone who heard about
it reflected on these events and asked, "What will
this child turn out to be?" For the hand of the
Lord was surely upon him in a special way.

Zechariah's Prophecy

[67]Then his father, Zechariah, was filled with the
Holy Spirit and gave this prophecy:

[68] "Praise the Lord, the God of Israel,
because he has visited and redeemed his
people.
[69] He has sent us a mighty Savior*
from the royal line of his servant David,
[70] just as he promised
through his holy prophets long ago.
[71] Now we will be saved from our enemies
and from all who hate us.
[72] He has been merciful to our ancestors
by remembering his sacred covenant—
[73] the covenant he swore with an oath
to our ancestor Abraham.
[74] We have been rescued from our enemies
so we can serve God without fear,
[75] in holiness and righteousness
for as long as we live.

[76] "And you, my little son,
will be called the prophet of the Most High,
because you will prepare the way for the
Lord.
[77] You will tell his people how to find salvation
through forgiveness of their sins.
[78] Because of God's tender mercy,
the morning light from heaven is about to
break upon us,*
[79] to give light to those who sit in darkness and
in the shadow of death,
and to guide us to the path of peace."

[80]John grew up and became strong in spirit.
And he lived in the wilderness until he began his
public ministry to Israel.

The Birth of Jesus

2 At that time the Roman emperor, Augustus, decreed that a census should be tak-
en throughout the Roman Empire. [2](This
was the first census taken when Quirinius was
governor of Syria.) [3]All returned to their own
ancestral towns to register for this census. [4]And
because Joseph was a descendant of King David,
he had to go to Bethlehem in Judea, David's ancient home. He traveled there from the village
of Nazareth in Galilee. [5]He took with him Mary,
his fiancée, who was now obviously pregnant.

1:69 Greek *has raised up a horn of salvation for us.* **1:78** Or *the Morning Light from Heaven is about to visit us.*

all the needs before they are even felt. Those who had rejoiced with the mother and recognized the birth as the work of God's kindness (see Midwifery and Birthing Practices, Job 3) now become meddlesome as they insist on selecting the child's name. **61–65:** Officiously, the neighbors and kinsfolk carry the matter directly to Zechariah. No sooner has he penned a confirmation of the angel's instruction that his son be named John than the father's tongue is unloosed. He too bursts into a prophetic song, glorifying God for bringing salvation to Israel. The Third Gospel is rich in songs: those of hope and prophetic expectation, those of exaltation at the fulfillment of God's promises (1:42–45, 46–55, 68–79; 2:14, 29–32; 19:38), those of the angels (1:13–17, 30–33, 35–37; 2:14). There are as well snatches of prophetic poetry that become songs in Luke's handling of the material (3:4; 4:18–19). **67–80:** Hope has been kindled because a seemingly impossible birth has occurred, to parents who earnestly desire the consummation of God's promises for Israel. They recognize, however dimly, that they are to be agents in the development of that deliverance. Here we see birthing not merely as involving the realm of women, but rather as the focus of God's providence and provision for the world. It is the concern of a devout priest and of a mighty archangel. Bringing a child into the world is as significant a piece of work as is the administration of an empire, the defeat of an army, or the establishment of Temple worship. Luke's treatment of the birth narratives brings affirmation of the intrinsic dignity, honor, and significance of childbearing for all women (see Childbearing and Rearing, Col 3).

2:1–7 The Birth of Jesus. Mary's perceptions are the center of the telling of the miraculous birth of Jesus Christ. Luke tells us nothing of her betrothed's reaction to her news, as it was related by Matthew (Matt

6 And while they were there, the time came
for her baby to be born. 7 She gave birth to her
first child, a son. She wrapped him snugly in
strips of cloth and laid him in a manger, because
there was no lodging available for them.

The Shepherds and Angels

8 That night there were shepherds staying in
the fields nearby, guarding their flocks of sheep.
9 Suddenly, an angel of the Lord appeared among
them, and the radiance of the Lord's glory surrounded them. They were terrified, 10 but the angel reassured them. "Don't be afraid!" he said. "I
bring you good news that will bring great joy to
all people. 11 The Savior—yes, the Messiah, the
Lord—has been born today in Bethlehem, the
city of David! 12 And you will recognize him by
this sign: You will find a baby wrapped snugly in
strips of cloth, lying in a manger."
13 Suddenly, the angel was joined by a vast
host of others—the armies of heaven—praising
God and saying,

14 "Glory to God in highest heaven,
and peace on earth to those with whom
God is pleased."

15 When the angels had returned to heaven,
the shepherds said to each other, "Let's go to
Bethlehem! Let's see this thing that has happened, which the Lord has told us about."
16 They hurried to the village and found Mary
and Joseph. And there was the baby, lying in the
manger. 17 After seeing him, the shepherds told
everyone what had happened and what the angel had said to them about this child. 18 All who
heard the shepherds' story were astonished,
19 but Mary kept all these things in her heart and
thought about them often. 20 The shepherds went
back to their flocks, glorifying and praising God
for all they had heard and seen. It was just as the
angel had told them.

Jesus Is Presented in the Temple

21 Eight days later, when the baby was circumcised, he was named Jesus, the name given him
by the angel even before he was conceived.
22 Then it was time for their purification offering, as required by the law of Moses after the
birth of a child; so his parents took him to Jerusalem to present him to the Lord. 23 The law
of the Lord says, "If a woman's first child is a
boy, he must be dedicated to the LORD."* 24 So
they offered the sacrifice required in the law of
the Lord—"either a pair of turtledoves or two
young pigeons."*

2:23 Exod 13:2. **2:24** Lev 12:8.

1:18–22). **6–7:** The only accommodation available in Bethlehem is already occupied by animals. Thus the manger is readily at hand for use as a crib—safe, sturdy, and raised above the animals' hooves. The circumstances are those that prevail at the humblest of human births. As Mary has sung, she and her child take their position alongside the world's poor and unempowered (see God's Concern for the Disenfranchised, Ezek 34). The world's most momentous birth is also one of its lowliest and least pretentious. Jesus is born as a homeless person and will retain this identity in his adult life (9:58). There will be rejections of many sorts throughout Luke's Gospel (e.g., 2:7; 4:16–30; 5:21, 30; 6:11; 9:52–56; 10:12–16; 13:34). The event has not caught Joseph and Mary by surprise, however. The swaddling bands, linen strips that are absorbent and enveloping, have been carefully prepared.

2:8–20 The Shepherds and the Angels. Angels are again employed to announce the birth, not to the political or ecclesiastical establishment but to those who cared for the Temple flocks. Again there is singing, the giving of a sign, and joy promised to the world. Rather than the lordly wise men of Matthew's account, the visitants are simple folk of the field and fold. **19:** Just as Elizabeth had ruminated on all that God was doing, so Mary too keeps her counsel and ponders the revelation in her heart. Although her subsequent relations with her son will not always be harmonious, she retains a conviction of a divine purpose. The motif of her quiet contemplation will recur at 2:51.

2:21–24 Jesus Is Presented in the Temple. As faithful Jews, the parents observe not only the rite of circumcision for their infant son eight days after the birth but also after forty days the purification ritual of the mother from the pollution of childbirth. Until the beginning of the twentieth century, infection of puerperal fever was the scourge of new mothers. The purity laws of Israel did much to safeguard maternal health (see Purity Laws Related to Women, Lev 15). The ritual marking the end of the period required that Mary would bring a sacrifice to the Court of Women in the Temple. The couple can afford only two doves, as prescribed for the poor (2:24; Lev 12:8). One of the riddles with which Mary must wrestle is that of the exalted promises concerning her child and the impoverished circumstances attendant to the birth.

The Prophecy of Simeon
25At that time there was a man in Jerusalem
named Simeon. He was righteous and devout and
was eagerly waiting for the Messiah to come and
rescue Israel. The Holy Spirit was upon him 26and
had revealed to him that he would not die until
he had seen the Lord's Messiah. 27That day the
Spirit led him to the Temple. So when Mary and
Joseph came to present the baby Jesus to the Lord
as the law required, 28Simeon was there. He took
the child in his arms and praised God, saying,

29 "Sovereign Lord, now let your servant die in
 peace,
 as you have promised.
30 I have seen your salvation,
31 which you have prepared for all people.
32 He is a light to reveal God to the nations,
 and he is the glory of your people Israel!"

33Jesus' parents were amazed at what was being said about him. 34Then Simeon blessed them,
and he said to Mary, the baby's mother, "This
child is destined to cause many in Israel to fall,
but he will be a joy to many others. He has been
sent as a sign from God, but many will oppose
him. 35As a result, the deepest thoughts of many
hearts will be revealed. And a sword will pierce
your very soul."

The Prophecy of Anna
36Anna, a prophet, was also there in the Temple.
She was the daughter of Phanuel from the tribe
of Asher, and she was very old. Her husband died
when they had been married only seven years.
37Then she lived as a widow to the age of eighty-
four.* She never left the Temple but stayed there
day and night, worshiping God with fasting and
prayer. 38She came along just as Simeon was
talking with Mary and Joseph, and she began
praising God. She talked about the child to everyone who had been waiting expectantly for
God to rescue Jerusalem.

39When Jesus' parents had fulfilled all the requirements of the law of the Lord, they returned
home to Nazareth in Galilee. 40There the child
grew up healthy and strong. He was filled with
wisdom, and God's favor was on him.

Jesus Speaks with the Teachers
41Every year Jesus' parents went to Jerusalem for
the Passover festival. 42When Jesus was twelve
years old, they attended the festival as usual.
43After the celebration was over, they started
home to Nazareth, but Jesus stayed behind in
Jerusalem. His parents didn't miss him at first,
44because they assumed he was among the other
travelers. But when he didn't show up that evening, they started looking for him among their
relatives and friends.

45When they couldn't find him, they went
back to Jerusalem to search for him there.
46Three days later they finally discovered him in
the Temple, sitting among the religious teachers,
listening to them and asking questions. 47All who
heard him were amazed at his understanding and
his answers.

48His parents didn't know what to think.
"Son," his mother said to him, "why have you
done this to us? Your father and I have been
frantic, searching for you everywhere."
49"But why did you need to search?" he asked.

2:37 Or *She had been a widow for eighty-four years.*

2:25–35 The Prophecy of Simeon. Luke couples an aged man and woman, both of whom have prophetic insight, to discern the Messiah in the babe carried to the Temple by a humble and unprepossessing couple. Simeon not only thanks God for the advent of the child but also addresses Mary directly. Her anguish at the crucifixion is foretold with powerful insight. Simeon's song ends the round of hymns that have been sung during the birth narrative.

2:36–40 The Prophecy of Anna. Anna is specifically denoted as a prophet. As such, she will announce the arrival of the Messiah to all who await the redemption of Jerusalem. As the only prophet named in the birth narrative, she is both heir and precursor of women in prophetic ministry (Exod 15:20; Judg 4:4; 2 Kgs 22:14; Neh 6:14; Isa 8:3; Acts 21:9). While angels make the annunciation to Zechariah, Mary, and the shepherds, Anna makes the proclamation to the pious of the holy city.

2:41–52 Jesus Speaks with the Teachers. Mary's fear and anxiety are palpable throughout the narration of this event. Of all the stories that she may have told Luke about the childhood of Jesus, this may have been the one most sharply etched on her memory. Her young son as he approaches adolescence has traveled with her and Joseph to make his bar mitzvah in the Temple, to become a man in the eyes of the law. **48:** Her remark upon finding him indicates her dismay at his lack of consideration for her, while his response reveals that his overriding concern was to comply with the will of his heavenly Father. Although Jesus will return home with her, her son has set out on a journey that she cannot as yet fathom. Mary's understanding of Jesus' identity will advance slowly

"Didn't you know that I must be in my Father's
house?"* [50]But they didn't understand what he
meant.
[51]Then he returned to Nazareth with them
and was obedient to them. And his mother stored
all these things in her heart.
[52]Jesus grew in wisdom and in stature and in
favor with God and all the people.

John the Baptist Prepares the Way

3 It was now the fifteenth year of the reign
of Tiberius, the Roman emperor. Pontius
Pilate was governor over Judea; Herod Antipas was ruler* over Galilee; his brother Philip
was ruler* over Iturea and Traconitis; Lysanias
was ruler over Abilene. [2]Annas and Caiaphas
were the high priests. At this time a message
from God came to John son of Zechariah, who
was living in the wilderness. [3]Then John went
from place to place on both sides of the Jordan
River, preaching that people should be baptized
to show that they had repented of their sins and
turned to God to be forgiven. [4]Isaiah had spoken
of John when he said,

"He is a voice shouting in the wilderness,
'Prepare the way for the LORD's coming!
Clear the road for him!
[5] The valleys will be filled,
and the mountains and hills made level.
The curves will be straightened,
and the rough places made smooth.
[6] And then all people will see
the salvation sent from God.' "*

[7]When the crowds came to John for baptism,
he said, "You brood of snakes! Who warned you
to flee God's coming wrath? [8]Prove by the way
you live that you have repented of your sins
and turned to God. Don't just say to each other,
'We're safe, for we are descendants of Abraham.'
That means nothing, for I tell you, God can create children of Abraham from these very stones.
[9]Even now the ax of God's judgment is poised,
ready to sever the roots of the trees. Yes, every
tree that does not produce good fruit will be
chopped down and thrown into the fire."
[10]The crowds asked, "What should we do?"
[11]John replied, "If you have two shirts, give
one to the poor. If you have food, share it with
those who are hungry."
[12]Even corrupt tax collectors came to be baptized and asked, "Teacher, what should we do?"
[13]He replied, "Collect no more taxes than the
government requires."
[14]"What should we do?" asked some soldiers.
John replied, "Don't extort money or make
false accusations. And be content with your pay."
[15]Everyone was expecting the Messiah to
come soon, and they were eager to know whether
John might be the Messiah. [16]John answered their
questions by saying, "I baptize you with* water;
but someone is coming soon who is greater than
I am—so much greater that I'm not even worthy
to be his slave and untie the straps of his sandals.
He will baptize you with the Holy Spirit and with
fire.* [17]He is ready to separate the chaff from the

2:49 Or *"Didn't you realize that I should be involved with my Father's affairs?"* **3:1a** Greek *Herod was tetrarch.* Herod Antipas was a son of King Herod. **3:1b** Greek *tetrarch;* also in 3:1c. **3:4-6** Isa 40:3-5 (Greek version). **3:16a** Or *in.* **3:16b** Or *in the Holy Spirit and in fire.*

as she ponders these things in her heart. Until she stands at the foot of the cross, the relationship between mother and son will be an uneasy one. **51:** Jesus leaves the brilliant world of the Temple, where the disciples of Shammai and Hillel argue the intricacies of the law. He forsakes the intellectual excitement of Israel's finest schools to take up his father's trade in a humble village. He will adhere to the world of common people with real concerns and real needs.

3:1—6:19 The Beginning of Jesus' Ministry

3:1–20 John the Baptist Prepares the Way. Luke the historian identifies the historic period and location of the event with careful precision. John's ministry has beome a fulfillment of his father Zechariah's prophecy while Luke interprets his mission in terms of Isaiah's call to spiritual preparedness (Isa 40:3–5). The scathing words elicit concerns for social justice. He does not denounce the oppression of the Roman government but rather the attitudes and injustices of contemporary residents of Palestine. **8:** John insists that repentance must be proved *by the way you live.* Many an abused woman has been deceived by an offender who says that he is sorry and promises never to perpetrate abuse upon her again. Repentance needs to be demonstrated by practical and consistent behavior. Sometimes we are told that God uses women in ministry only when men are unavailable or unwilling to be used. John, however, is convinced that God can raise up folk to serve him according to his own choices. And often the biblical narrative tells us that choice has fallen upon women. **10–20:** Both John's sense of standing as heir of the prophetic tradition and his harsh message of coming judgment demand interpretation. How is he to be understood in light of an expectation of a coming Messiah?

wheat with his winnowing fork. Then he will
clean up the threshing area, gathering the wheat
into his barn but burning the chaff with never-
ending fire." 18 John used many such warnings as
he announced the Good News to the people.
19 John also publicly criticized Herod Antipas,
the ruler of Galilee,* for marrying Herodias, his
brother's wife, and for many other wrongs he
had done. 20 So Herod put John in prison, adding
this sin to his many others.

The Baptism of Jesus

21 One day when the crowds were being baptized,
Jesus himself was baptized. As he was praying,
the heavens opened, 22 and the Holy Spirit, in
bodily form, descended on him like a dove. And
a voice from heaven said, "You are my dearly
loved Son, and you bring me great joy.*"

The Ancestors of Jesus

23 Jesus was about thirty years old when he began
his public ministry.

Jesus was known as the son of Joseph.
Joseph was the son of Heli.
24 Heli was the son of Matthat.
Matthat was the son of Levi.
Levi was the son of Melki.
Melki was the son of Jannai.
Jannai was the son of Joseph.
25 Joseph was the son of Mattathias.
Mattathias was the son of Amos.
Amos was the son of Nahum.
Nahum was the son of Esli.
Esli was the son of Naggai.
26 Naggai was the son of Maath.
Maath was the son of Mattathias.
Mattathias was the son of Semein.
Semein was the son of Josech.
Josech was the son of Joda.
27 Joda was the son of Joanan.
Joanan was the son of Rhesa.
Rhesa was the son of Zerubbabel.
Zerubbabel was the son of Shealtiel.
Shealtiel was the son of Neri.
28 Neri was the son of Melki.
Melki was the son of Addi.
Addi was the son of Cosam.
Cosam was the son of Elmadam.
Elmadam was the son of Er.
29 Er was the son of Joshua.
Joshua was the son of Eliezer.
Eliezer was the son of Jorim.
Jorim was the son of Matthat.
Matthat was the son of Levi.
30 Levi was the son of Simeon.
Simeon was the son of Judah.
Judah was the son of Joseph.
Joseph was the son of Jonam.
Jonam was the son of Eliakim.
31 Eliakim was the son of Melea.
Melea was the son of Menna.
Menna was the son of Mattatha.
Mattatha was the son of Nathan.
Nathan was the son of David.
32 David was the son of Jesse.
Jesse was the son of Obed.
Obed was the son of Boaz.
Boaz was the son of Salmon.*
Salmon was the son of Nahshon.
33 Nahshon was the son of Amminadab.
Amminadab was the son of Admin.
Admin was the son of Arni.*
Arni was the son of Hezron.
Hezron was the son of Perez.
Perez was the son of Judah.
34 Judah was the son of Jacob.
Jacob was the son of Isaac.
Isaac was the son of Abraham.
Abraham was the son of Terah.
Terah was the son of Nahor.
35 Nahor was the son of Serug.
Serug was the son of Reu.
Reu was the son of Peleg.
Peleg was the son of Eber.
Eber was the son of Shelah.
36 Shelah was the son of Cainan.
Cainan was the son of Arphaxad.
Arphaxad was the son of Shem.
Shem was the son of Noah.
Noah was the son of Lamech.
37 Lamech was the son of Methuselah.
Methuselah was the son of Enoch.
Enoch was the son of Jared.

3:19 Greek *Herod the tetrarch.* **3:22** Some manuscripts read *my Son, and today I have become your Father.* **3:32** Greek *Sala,* a variant spelling of Salmon; also in 3:32b. See Ruth 4:22. **3:33** Some manuscripts read *Amminadab was the son of Aram. Arni* and *Aram* are alternate spellings of Ram. See 1 Chr 2:9-10.

3:21–22 The Baptism of Jesus. John's craggy lifestyle outside of ordinary human life stands in marked contrast to that of Jesus who mingles freely with humanity. Here Jesus comes with others to be baptized, identifying himself as a member of a multitude, while both Father and Spirit reveal his divine identity.

3:23–38 The Ancestors of Jesus. The perspective is less upon human begetting than it is upon a living faith that had been transmitted fron one generation to the next.

Jared was the son of Mahalalel.
Mahalalel was the son of Kenan.
38 Kenan was the son of Enosh.*
Enosh was the son of Seth.
Seth was the son of Adam.
Adam was the son of God.

The Temptation of Jesus

4 Then Jesus, full of the Holy Spirit, returned from the Jordan River. He was led
by the Spirit in the wilderness,* 2 where he
was tempted by the devil for forty days. Jesus ate
nothing all that time and became very hungry.
3 Then the devil said to him, "If you are the Son
of God, tell this stone to become a loaf of bread."
4 But Jesus told him, "No! The Scriptures say,
'People do not live by bread alone.'* "
5 Then the devil took him up and revealed to
him all the kingdoms of the world in a moment of
time. 6 "I will give you the glory of these kingdoms
and authority over them," the devil said, "because
they are mine to give to anyone I please. 7 I will
give it all to you if you will worship me."
8 Jesus replied, "The Scriptures say,

'You must worship the LORD your God
and serve only him.'* "

9 Then the devil took him to Jerusalem, to the
highest point of the Temple, and said, "If you are
the Son of God, jump off! 10 For the Scriptures say,

'He will order his angels to protect and guard
you.
11 And they will hold you up with their hands
so you won't even hurt your foot on a
stone.'* "

12 Jesus responded, "The Scriptures also say,
'You must not test the LORD your God.'* "
13 When the devil had finished tempting Jesus,
he left him until the next opportunity came.

Jesus Rejected at Nazareth

14 Then Jesus returned to Galilee, filled with the
Holy Spirit's power. Reports about him spread
quickly through the whole region. 15 He taught
regularly in their synagogues and was praised by
everyone.
16 When he came to the village of Nazareth,
his boyhood home, he went as usual to the synagogue on the Sabbath and stood up to read the
Scriptures. 17 The scroll of Isaiah the prophet was
handed to him. He unrolled the scroll and found
the place where this was written:

18 "The Spirit of the LORD is upon me,
for he has anointed me to bring Good
News to the poor.
He has sent me to proclaim that captives will
be released,
that the blind will see,
that the oppressed will be set free,
19 and that the time of the LORD's favor has
come.*"

20 He rolled up the scroll, handed it back to the
attendant, and sat down. All eyes in the synagogue looked at him intently. 21 Then he began to
speak to them. "The Scripture you've just heard
has been fulfilled this very day!"
22 Everyone spoke well of him and was amazed
by the gracious words that came from his lips.
"How can this be?" they asked. "Isn't this Joseph's son?"
23 Then he said, "You will undoubtedly quote
me this proverb: 'Physician, heal yourself'—
meaning, 'Do miracles here in your hometown
like those you did in Capernaum.' 24 But I tell
you the truth, no prophet is accepted in his own
hometown.
25 "Certainly there were many needy widows
in Israel in Elijah's time, when the heavens were
closed for three and a half years, and a severe
famine devastated the land. 26 Yet Elijah was not
sent to any of them. He was sent instead to a
foreigner—a widow of Zarephath in the land of

3:38 Greek *Enos*, a variant spelling of Enosh; also in 3:38b. See Gen 5:6. **4:1** Some manuscripts read *into the wilderness.* **4:4** Deut 8:3. **4:8** Deut 6:13. **4:10-11** Ps 91:11-12. **4:12** Deut 6:16. **4:18-19** Or *and to proclaim the acceptable year of the LORD.* Isa 61:1-2 (Greek version); 58:6.

4:1–13 The Temptation of Jesus. Neither immense political power nor intense bodily need can deflect Jesus from his divine calling. Nor is he led astray by the devil's clever manipulation of Scripture.

4:14–30 Jesus Rejected at Nazareth. Jesus returns after his baptismal and wilderness experience to proclaim his mission to those with the deepest needs. His mission is pointedly directed to reach the disadvantaged, the marginalized, and the oppressed. His townspeople can accept neither his messianic role nor its stated purpose. **26–27:** Naaman the Syrian was healed of his leprosy because of the witness of a young servant maid (2 Kgs 5:1–19), while the widow of Zarephath received the prophet Elijah into her home even when she did not have enough food for her child and herself. She understood that he was a prophet of God whose message she gladly received

Sidon. 27 And there were many lepers in Israel in
the time of the prophet Elisha, but the only one
healed was Naaman, a Syrian."
28 When they heard this, the people in the
synagogue were furious. 29 Jumping up, they
mobbed him and forced him to the edge of the
hill on which the town was built. They intended
to push him over the cliff, 30 but he passed right
through the crowd and went on his way.

Jesus Casts Out a Demon

31 Then Jesus went to Capernaum, a town in Galilee, and taught there in the synagogue every Sabbath day. 32 There, too, the people were amazed at
his teaching, for he spoke with authority.
33 Once when he was in the synagogue, a man
possessed by a demon—an evil* spirit—began
shouting at Jesus, 34 "Go away! Why are you interfering with us, Jesus of Nazareth? Have you
come to destroy us? I know who you are—the
Holy One of God!"
35 Jesus cut him short. "Be quiet! Come out of
the man," he ordered. At that, the demon threw
the man to the floor as the crowd watched; then
it came out of him without hurting him further.
36 Amazed, the people exclaimed, "What authority and power this man's words possess!
Even evil spirits obey him, and they flee at his
command!" 37 The news about Jesus spread
through every village in the entire region.

Jesus Heals Many People

38 After leaving the synagogue that day, Jesus
went to Simon's home, where he found Simon's mother-in-law very sick with a high fever.
"Please heal her," everyone begged. 39 Standing
at her bedside, he rebuked the fever, and it left
her. And she got up at once and prepared a meal
for them.
40 As the sun went down that evening, people throughout the village brought sick family
members to Jesus. No matter what their diseases
were, the touch of his hand healed every one.
41 Many were possessed by demons; and the demons came out at his command, shouting, "You
are the Son of God!" But because they knew he
was the Messiah, he rebuked them and refused
to let them speak.

Jesus Continues to Preach

42 Early the next morning Jesus went out to an
isolated place. The crowds searched everywhere
for him, and when they finally found him, they
begged him not to leave them. 43 But he replied,
"I must preach the Good News of the Kingdom
of God in other towns, too, because that is why
I was sent." 44 So he continued to travel around,
preaching in synagogues throughout Judea.*

The First Disciples

5 One day as Jesus was preaching on the
shore of the Sea of Galilee,* great crowds
pressed in on him to listen to the word of
God. 2 He noticed two empty boats at the water's edge, for the fishermen had left them and
were washing their nets. 3 Stepping into one of
the boats, Jesus asked Simon,* its owner, to push
it out into the water. So he sat in the boat and
taught the crowds from there.
4 When he had finished speaking, he said to
Simon, "Now go out where it is deeper, and let
down your nets to catch some fish."
5 "Master," Simon replied, "we worked hard
all last night and didn't catch a thing. But if you
say so, I'll let the nets down again." 6 And this
time their nets were so full of fish they began to
tear! 7 A shout for help brought their partners in
the other boat, and soon both boats were filled
with fish and on the verge of sinking.
8 When Simon Peter realized what had happened, he fell to his knees before Jesus and said,
"Oh, Lord, please leave me—I'm too much of a
sinner to be around you." 9 For he was awestruck
by the number of fish they had caught, as were
the others with him. 10 His partners, James and
John, the sons of Zebedee, were also amazed.

4:33 Greek *unclean;* also in 4:36. **4:44** Some manuscripts read *Galilee.* **5:1** Greek *Lake Gennesaret,* another name for the Sea of Galilee. **5:3** *Simon* is called "Peter" in 6:14 and thereafter.

(1 Kgs 17:24). Thus the impoverished Gentile widow stands as a witness against the unreceptive inhabitants of Nazareth.

4:31–36 Jesus Casts Out a Demon. Jesus finds a more hospitable climate in Capernaum and makes it his headquarters, becoming a regular participant in synagogue worship. He is willing to take on even the most difficult of human conditions and to bring healing.

4:38–44 Jesus Heals Many People. Luke the physician gives a detailed description of the *high fever* that rages within Peter's mother-in-law. Immediately upon her healing she rises to minister *(diakoneo)* to the guests. Here Luke begins the motif of women who are healed and enabled to minister to Jesus.

5:1–11 The First Disciples. Jesus steps into the commercial life of these fishermen to call them to another career and a higher calling.

Jesus replied to Simon, "Don't be afraid! From now on you'll be fishing for people!" [11]And as soon as they landed, they left everything and followed Jesus.

Jesus Heals a Man with Leprosy

[12]In one of the villages, Jesus met a man with an advanced case of leprosy. When the man saw Jesus, he bowed with his face to the ground, begging to be healed. "Lord," he said, "if you are willing, you can heal me and make me clean."

[13]Jesus reached out and touched him. "I am willing," he said. "Be healed!" And instantly the leprosy disappeared. [14]Then Jesus instructed him not to tell anyone what had happened. He said, "Go to the priest and let him examine you. Take along the offering required in the law of Moses for those who have been healed of leprosy.* This will be a public testimony that you have been cleansed."

[15]But despite Jesus' instructions, the report of his power spread even faster, and vast crowds came to hear him preach and to be healed of their diseases. [16]But Jesus often withdrew to the wilderness for prayer.

Jesus Heals a Paralyzed Man

[17]One day while Jesus was teaching, some Pharisees and teachers of religious law were sitting nearby. (It seemed that these men showed up from every village in all Galilee and Judea, as well as from Jerusalem.) And the Lord's healing power was strongly with Jesus.

[18]Some men came carrying a paralyzed man on a sleeping mat. They tried to take him inside to Jesus, [19]but they couldn't reach him because of the crowd. So they went up to the roof and took off some tiles. Then they lowered the sick man on his mat down into the crowd, right in front of Jesus. [20]Seeing their faith, Jesus said to the man, "Young man, your sins are forgiven."

[21]But the Pharisees and teachers of religious law said to themselves, "Who does he think he is? That's blasphemy! Only God can forgive sins!"

[22]Jesus knew what they were thinking, so he asked them, "Why do you question this in your hearts? [23]Is it easier to say 'Your sins are forgiven,' or 'Stand up and walk'? [24]So I will prove to you that the Son of Man* has the authority on earth to forgive sins." Then Jesus turned to the paralyzed man and said, "Stand up, pick up your mat, and go home!"

[25]And immediately, as everyone watched, the man jumped up, picked up his mat, and went home praising God. [26]Everyone was gripped with great wonder and awe, and they praised God, exclaiming, "We have seen amazing things today!"

Jesus Calls Levi (Matthew)

[27]Later, as Jesus left the town, he saw a tax collector named Levi sitting at his tax collector's booth. "Follow me and be my disciple," Jesus said to him. [28]So Levi got up, left everything, and followed him.

[29]Later, Levi held a banquet in his home with Jesus as the guest of honor. Many of Levi's fellow tax collectors and other guests also ate with them. [30]But the Pharisees and their teachers of religious law complained bitterly to Jesus' disciples, "Why do you eat and drink with such scum?*"

[31]Jesus answered them, "Healthy people don't need a doctor—sick people do. [32]I have come to call not those who think they are righteous, but those who know they are sinners and need to repent."

A Discussion about Fasting

[33]One day some people said to Jesus, "John the Baptist's disciples fast and pray regularly, and so do the disciples of the Pharisees. Why are your disciples always eating and drinking?"

5:14 See Lev 14:2-32. **5:24** "Son of Man" is a title Jesus used for himself. **5:30** Greek *with tax collectors and sinners?*

5:12–16 Jesus Heals a Man with Leprosy. Luke's is a Gospel of touch. Jesus touches and is touched by those whom we would not expect to find in such proximity to him. Here he reaches out to touch a man whom everyone else shuns.

5:17–26 Jesus Heals a Paralyzed Man. Jesus, seeing the faith of the friends who have brought him the paralyzed man, addresses the man's deepest need first. Then the man himself must have the faith to obey Jesus' command to stand up, pick up his mat, and go home.

5:27–31 Jesus Calls Levi (Matthew). Here Jesus invades the politically suspect world of those who collaborate with Roman oppressors and gather the tax money that supports the system. When he is condemned for violating the prohibition against eating with those outside observant Judaism (cf. Acts 11:3; Gal 2:2), he is able to express the radical purpose of his mission.

5:33–39 A Discussion about Fasting. Jesus is aware of the difficulty that many experience in moving to new forms of worship and practice. A new faith often brings new patterns.

[34]Jesus responded, "Do wedding guests fast
while celebrating with the groom? Of course not.
[35]But someday the groom will be taken away
from them, and then they will fast."
[36]Then Jesus gave them this illustration: "No
one tears a piece of cloth from a new garment
and uses it to patch an old garment. For then the
new garment would be ruined, and the new patch
wouldn't even match the old garment.
[37]"And no one puts new wine into old wineskins. For the new wine would burst the wineskins,
spilling the wine and ruining the skins. [38]New
wine must be stored in new wineskins. [39]But no
one who drinks the old wine seems to want the
new wine. 'The old is just fine,' they say."

A Discussion about the Sabbath

6 One Sabbath day as Jesus was walking
through some grainfields, his disciples
broke off heads of grain, rubbed off the
husks in their hands, and ate the grain. [2]But
some Pharisees said, "Why are you breaking the
law by harvesting grain on the Sabbath?"
[3]Jesus replied, "Haven't you read in the
Scriptures what David did when he and his companions were hungry? [4]He went into the house
of God and broke the law by eating the sacred
loaves of bread that only the priests can eat. He
also gave some to his companions." [5]And Jesus
added, "The Son of Man* is Lord, even over the
Sabbath."

Jesus Heals on the Sabbath

[6]On another Sabbath day, a man with a deformed
right hand was in the synagogue while Jesus was
teaching. [7]The teachers of religious law and the
Pharisees watched Jesus closely. If he healed the
man's hand, they planned to accuse him of working on the Sabbath.
[8]But Jesus knew their thoughts. He said to the
man with the deformed hand, "Come and stand
in front of everyone." So the man came forward.
[9]Then Jesus said to his critics, "I have a question
for you. Does the law permit good deeds on the
Sabbath, or is it a day for doing evil? Is this a day
to save life or to destroy it?"
[10]He looked around at them one by one and
then said to the man, "Hold out your hand." So
the man held out his hand, and it was restored!
[11]At this, the enemies of Jesus were wild with
rage and began to discuss what to do with him.

Jesus Chooses the Twelve Apostles

[12]One day soon afterward Jesus went up on a
mountain to pray, and he prayed to God all night.
[13]At daybreak he called together all of his disciples and chose twelve of them to be apostles.
Here are their names:

[14]Simon (whom he named Peter),
Andrew (Peter's brother),
James,
John,
Philip,
Bartholomew,
[15]Matthew,
Thomas,
James (son of Alphaeus),
Simon (who was called the zealot),
[16]Judas (son of James),
Judas Iscariot (who later betrayed him).

Crowds Follow Jesus

[17]When they came down from the mountain, the
disciples stood with Jesus on a large, level area,
surrounded by many of his followers and by the
crowds. There were people from all over Judea
and from Jerusalem and from as far north as the
seacoasts of Tyre and Sidon. [18]They had come to
hear him and to be healed of their diseases; and

6:5 "Son of Man" is a title Jesus used for himself.

6:1–5 A Discussion about the Sabbath. Provision for adequate rest is a basic human right. But other needs, such as that for nourishment, must also be respected. Jesus calls for a balance in understanding the purposes of God.

6:6–11 Jeals Heals on the Sabbath. Jesus sanctifies the Sabbath by doing *good* rather than *evil* and so glorifying God.

6:12–16 Jesus Chooses the Twelve Apostles. The apostles are identified carefully by name, for they will be appointed as witnesses of Jesus to carry his message into the world. Later women too will be identified (8:2–3) who will be the major witnesses to important salvation events.

6:17–19 Crowds Follow Jesus. The touch of Jesus is again emphasized. We will find that parents seek his touch for their infants (18:15). He allows a sinful woman and one with an issue of blood to touch him (7:39; 8:44–47). With his touch, he performs a healing on the ear of his captor (22:51). In each of these cases, there is an affirmation of solidarity and sympathy for those with desperate needs of body and soul. After he has risen from the grave, Jesus calls his disciples to touch him and thereby to discern for themselves the reality of his resurrection (24:39).

those troubled by evil* spirits were healed. 19 Everyone tried to touch him, because healing power
went out from him, and he healed everyone.

The Beatitudes

20 Then Jesus turned to his disciples and said,

"God blesses you who are poor,
for the Kingdom of God is yours.
21 God blesses you who are hungry now,
for you will be satisfied.
God blesses you who weep now,
for in due time you will laugh.

22 What blessings await you when people hate you
and exclude you and mock you and curse you as
evil because you follow the Son of Man. 23 When
that happens, be happy! Yes, leap for joy! For a
great reward awaits you in heaven. And remember, their ancestors treated the ancient prophets
that same way.

Sorrows Foretold

24 "What sorrow awaits you who are rich,
for you have your only happiness now.
25 What sorrow awaits you who are fat and
prosperous now,
for a time of awful hunger awaits you.
What sorrow awaits you who laugh now,
for your laughing will turn to mourning
and sorrow.
26 What sorrow awaits you who are praised by
the crowds,
for their ancestors also praised false
prophets.

Love for Enemies

27 "But to you who are willing to listen, I say, love
your enemies! Do good to those who hate you.
28 Bless those who curse you. Pray for those who
hurt you. 29 If someone slaps you on one cheek,
offer the other cheek also. If someone demands
your coat, offer your shirt also. 30 Give to anyone
who asks; and when things are taken away from
you, don't try to get them back. 31 Do to others as
you would like them to do to you.

32 "If you love only those who love you, why
should you get credit for that? Even sinners love
those who love them! 33 And if you do good only
to those who do good to you, why should you get
credit? Even sinners do that much! 34 And if you
lend money only to those who can repay you,
why should you get credit? Even sinners will
lend to other sinners for a full return.

35 "Love your enemies! Do good to them. Lend
to them without expecting to be repaid. Then
your reward from heaven will be very great, and
you will truly be acting as children of the Most
High, for he is kind to those who are unthankful
and wicked. 36 You must be compassionate, just as
your Father is compassionate.

Do Not Judge Others

37 "Do not judge others, and you will not be
judged. Do not condemn others, or it will all come
back against you. Forgive others, and you will be
forgiven. 38 Give, and you will receive. Your gift
will return to you in full—pressed down, shaken
together to make room for more, running over,
and poured into your lap. The amount you give
will determine the amount you get back.*"

39 Then Jesus gave the following illustration:
"Can one blind person lead another? Won't they
both fall into a ditch? 40 Students* are not greater
than their teacher. But the student who is fully
trained will become like the teacher.

41 "And why worry about a speck in your
friend's eye* when you have a log in your own?
42 How can you think of saying, 'Friend,* let me
help you get rid of that speck in your eye,' when
you can't see past the log in your own eye? Hypocrite! First get rid of the log in your own eye;
then you will see well enough to deal with the
speck in your friend's eye.

6:18 Greek *unclean.* **6:38** Or *The measure you give will be the measure you get back.* **6:40** Or *Disciples.* **6:41** Greek *your brother's eye;* also in 6:42. **6:42** Greek *Brother.*

6:20–9:17 Good News for the Poor and Disadvantaged

6:20–23 The Beatitudes. In Luke's shortened version of the Beatitudes, the blessing is not only for those with humble attitudes but also for those who are persecuted and rejected for their faith.

6:24–26 Sorrows Foretold. Prosperity and popularity are not extolled as marks of God's approval but rather as a cause for spiritual examination.

6:27–36 Love for Enemies. Some have understood this as an exhortation to endure abuse at the hands of another. Rather it is an instruction to return good for evil but not to enable further abuse to take place.

6:37–42 Do Not Judge Others. With the use of humor, Jesus demonstrates that judgmental attitudes should be replaced by charity. He gently lampoons our own failings that far exceed those of our friends.

The Tree and Its Fruit

43 "A good tree can't produce bad fruit, and a bad tree can't produce good fruit. 44 A tree is identified by its fruit. Figs are never gathered from thornbushes, and grapes are not picked from bramble bushes. 45 A good person produces good things from the treasury of a good heart, and an evil person produces evil things from the treasury of an evil heart. What you say flows from what is in your heart.

Building on a Solid Foundation

46 "So why do you keep calling me 'Lord, Lord!' when you don't do what I say? 47 I will show you what it's like when someone comes to me, listens to my teaching, and then follows it. 48 It is like a person building a house who digs deep and lays the foundation on solid rock. When the floodwaters rise and break against that house, it stands firm because it is well built. 49 But anyone who hears and doesn't obey is like a person who builds a house without a foundation. When the floods sweep down against that house, it will collapse into a heap of ruins."

The Faith of a Roman Officer

7 When Jesus had finished saying all this to the people, he returned to Capernaum. 2 At that time the highly valued slave of a Roman officer* was sick and near death. 3 When the officer heard about Jesus, he sent some respected Jewish elders to ask him to come and heal his slave. 4 So they earnestly begged Jesus to help the man. "If anyone deserves your help, he does," they said, 5 "for he loves the Jewish people and even built a synagogue for us."

6 So Jesus went with them. But just before they arrived at the house, the officer sent some friends to say, "Lord, don't trouble yourself by coming to my home, for I am not worthy of such an honor. 7 I am not even worthy to come and meet you. Just say the word from where you are, and my servant will be healed. 8 I know this because I am under the authority of my superior officers, and I have authority over my soldiers. I only need to say, 'Go,' and they go, or 'Come,' and they come. And if I say to my slaves, 'Do this,' they do it."

9 When Jesus heard this, he was amazed. Turning to the crowd that was following him, he said, "I tell you, I haven't seen faith like this in all Israel!" 10 And when the officer's friends returned to his house, they found the slave completely healed.

Jesus Raises a Widow's Son

11 Soon afterward Jesus went with his disciples to the village of Nain, and a large crowd followed him. 12 A funeral procession was coming out as he approached the village gate. The young man who had died was a widow's only son, and a large crowd from the village was with her. 13 When the Lord saw her, his heart overflowed with compassion. "Don't cry!" he said. 14 Then he walked over to the coffin and touched it, and the bearers stopped. "Young man," he said, "I tell you, get up." 15 Then the dead boy sat up and began to talk! And Jesus gave him back to his mother.

16 Great fear swept the crowd, and they praised God, saying, "A mighty prophet has risen among us," and "God has visited his people today." 17 And the news about Jesus spread throughout Judea and the surrounding countryside.

Jesus and John the Baptist

18 The disciples of John the Baptist told John about everything Jesus was doing. So John called for two of his disciples, 19 and he sent them to the

7:2 Greek *a centurion;* similarly in 7:6.

6:43–45 The Tree and Its Fruit. What flows from what is in the heart is not only indicative of our own attitude but also profoundly infuential on those around us.

6:46–49 Building on a Solid Foundation. As the last parable would speak to farmers, Jesus the carpenter now moves to sound concepts for building.

7:1–10 The Faith of a Roman Officer. Jesus uses the faith of a Gentile as an object lesson. More often women are used as spiritual examples.

7:11–17 Jesus Raises a Widow's Son. Jesus' sympathy is aroused by a mother who walks before the bier of her dead son. Jewish tradition required the female relatives to walk in front of the corpse in funeral processions. The custom was said to have been established as a reminder of Eve's defection in bringing death into the world. Just as women light the Sabbath candles because Eve brought darkness to humanity, so there is a reminder at this moment of deepest woe. Jesus stopped the funeral cortege and stretched out his hand to the figure on the bier. To touch the corpse would render him unclean for a week (Num 19:11). Jesus, however, is more concerned with alleviating the woman's grief than with his own impurity.

7:18–35 Jesus and John the Baptist. Jesus demonstrates that different lifestyles may be appropriate for the servants of God. John the Baptist lived on des-

Lord to ask him, "Are you the Messiah we've
been expecting,* or should we keep looking for
someone else?"
[20]John's two disciples found Jesus and said to
him, "John the Baptist sent us to ask, 'Are you
the Messiah we've been expecting, or should we
keep looking for someone else?' "
[21]At that very time, Jesus cured many people
of their diseases, illnesses, and evil spirits, and he
restored sight to many who were blind. [22]Then
he told John's disciples, "Go back to John and tell
him what you have seen and heard—the blind
see, the lame walk, the lepers are cured, the deaf
hear, the dead are raised to life, and the Good
News is being preached to the poor. [23]And tell
him, 'God blesses those who do not turn away
because of me.*' "
[24]After John's disciples left, Jesus began talking about him to the crowds. "What kind of man
did you go into the wilderness to see? Was he a
weak reed, swayed by every breath of wind? [25]Or
were you expecting to see a man dressed in expensive clothes? No, people who wear beautiful
clothes and live in luxury are found in palaces.
[26]Were you looking for a prophet? Yes, and he is
more than a prophet. [27]John is the man to whom
the Scriptures refer when they say,

'Look, I am sending my messenger ahead of
you,
and he will prepare your way before you.'*

[28]I tell you, of all who have ever lived, none is
greater than John. Yet even the least person in
the Kingdom of God is greater than he is!"
[29]When they heard this, all the people—even
the tax collectors—agreed that God's way was
right,* for they had been baptized by John. [30]But
the Pharisees and experts in religious law rejected God's plan for them, for they had refused
John's baptism.
[31]"To what can I compare the people of this
generation?" Jesus asked. "How can I describe
them? [32]They are like children playing a game
in the public square. They complain to their
friends,

'We played wedding songs,
and you didn't dance,
so we played funeral songs,
and you didn't weep.'

[33]For John the Baptist didn't spend his time eating
bread or drinking wine, and you say, 'He's possessed by a demon.' [34]The Son of Man,* on the
other hand, feasts and drinks, and you say, 'He's a
glutton and a drunkard, and a friend of tax collectors and other sinners!' [35]But wisdom is shown to
be right by the lives of those who follow it.*"

Jesus Anointed by a Sinful Woman

[36]One of the Pharisees asked Jesus to have dinner with him, so Jesus went to his home and sat
down to eat.* [37]When a certain immoral woman
from that city heard he was eating there, she
brought a beautiful alabaster jar filled with expensive perfume. [38]Then she knelt behind him at
his feet, weeping. Her tears fell on his feet, and
she wiped them off with her hair. Then she kept
kissing his feet and putting perfume on them.
[39]When the Pharisee who had invited him
saw this, he said to himself, "If this man were a
prophet, he would know what kind of woman is
touching him. She's a sinner!"
[40]Then Jesus answered his thoughts. "Simon," he said to the Pharisee, "I have something
to say to you."
"Go ahead, Teacher," Simon replied.
[41]Then Jesus told him this story: "A man
loaned money to two people—500 pieces of
silver* to one and 50 pieces to the other. [42]But
neither of them could repay him, so he kindly
forgave them both, canceling their debts. Who do
you suppose loved him more after that?"
[43]Simon answered, "I suppose the one for
whom he canceled the larger debt."

7:19 Greek *Are you the one who is coming?* Also in 7:20. **7:23** Or *who are not offended by me.* **7:27** Mal 3:1. **7:29** Or *praised God for his justice.* **7:34** "Son of Man" is a title Jesus used for himself. **7:35** Or *But wisdom is justified by all her children.* **7:36** Or *and reclined.* **7:41** Greek *500 denarii.* A denarius was equivalent to a laborer's full day's wage.

ert fare readily available to him, while Jesus joined rich and poor in their meals and in their homes. The wise can perceive the fundamental purposes even if there are wide varieties of practice among God's saints. Adaptation to a particular set of circumstances is often the most productive path in the Kingdom of Heaven. Wisdom, an abstraction, is personified as a mother whose children achieve their ends through varying routes along life's way.

7:36–50 Jesus Anointed by a Sinful Woman. Luke affords us here the clearest affirmation of Christ's acceptance of women with dubious sexual histories. The sinful woman is accepted while the judgmental stance of her critics is condemned. Jesus receives her ministrations and recognizes them as indicative of a profoundly altered attitude. Her act of devotion represents her best effort to express her newly awakened response to God's grace.

"That's right," Jesus said. 44 Then he turned to the woman and said to Simon, "Look at this woman kneeling here. When I entered your home, you didn't offer me water to wash the dust from my feet, but she has washed them with her tears and wiped them with her hair. 45 You didn't greet me with a kiss, but from the time I first came in, she has not stopped kissing my feet. 46 You neglected the courtesy of olive oil to anoint my head, but she has anointed my feet with rare perfume.

47 "I tell you, her sins—and they are many—have been forgiven, so she has shown me much love. But a person who is forgiven little shows only little love." 48 Then Jesus said to the woman, "Your sins are forgiven."

49 The men at the table said among themselves, "Who is this man, that he goes around forgiving sins?"

50 And Jesus said to the woman, "Your faith has saved you; go in peace."

Women Who Followed Jesus

8 Soon afterward Jesus began a tour of the nearby towns and villages, preaching and announcing the Good News about the Kingdom of God. He took his twelve disciples with him, 2 along with some women who had been cured of evil spirits and diseases. Among them were Mary Magdalene, from whom he had cast out seven demons; 3 Joanna, the wife of Chuza, Herod's business manager; Susanna; and many others who were contributing from their own resources to support Jesus and his disciples.

Parable of the Farmer Scattering Seed

4 One day Jesus told a story in the form of a parable to a large crowd that had gathered from many towns to hear him: 5 "A farmer went out to plant his seed. As he scattered it across his field, some seed fell on a footpath, where it was stepped on, and the birds ate it. 6 Other seed fell among rocks. It began to grow, but the plant soon wilted and died for lack of moisture. 7 Other seed fell among thorns that grew up with it and choked out the tender plants. 8 Still other seed fell on fertile soil. This seed grew and produced a crop that was a hundred times as much as had been planted!" When he had said this, he called out, "Anyone with ears to hear should listen and understand."

9 His disciples asked him what this parable meant. 10 He replied, "You are permitted to understand the secrets* of the Kingdom of God. But I use parables to teach the others so that the Scriptures might be fulfilled:

'When they look, they won't really see.
When they hear, they won't understand.'*

11 "This is the meaning of the parable: The seed is God's word. 12 The seeds that fell on the footpath represent those who hear the message, only to have the devil come and take it away from their hearts and prevent them from believing and being saved. 13 The seeds on the rocky soil represent those who hear the message and receive it with joy. But since they don't have deep roots, they believe for a while, then they fall away when they face temptation. 14 The seeds that fell among the thorns represent those who hear the message, but all too quickly the message is crowded out by the cares and riches and pleasures of this life. And so they never grow into

8:10a Greek *mysteries.* **8:10b** Isa 6:9 (Greek version).

8:1–3 Women Who Followed Jesus. In distinction to the listing of the male disciples in 6:12–19, here there is an abbreviated listing of named and identifiable women followers, persons healed of various diseases and afflictions. They had been given permission by their families to leave their homes and follow Jesus. Joanna, wife of Chuza, Herod's steward, despite her husband's prominent political position, travels with Jesus, supports his mission monetarily and is named as a witness of the resurrection. The most conspicuous of the group is Mary Magdalene. Contrary to popular supposition, she is never mentioned as a prostitute. Rather, she has borne a spiritual and mental affliction—that of possession by seven evil spirits. She has known the healing of Jesus and will assume the title "apostle to the apostles" as she is the first to see the risen Christ and to give testimony to the Easter event (Mark 16:9–10; John 20:1). Of Susanna we are told nothing more than her name, followed by the observation that many other women followed Jesus as well. These women traveled as part of the retinue of Jesus. Like the women who financed the Exodus (Exod 3:22; 11:2–3), these women provided much-needed resources for the ministry of Jesus. The names of these women will be given in the other Gospels as they stand watching the crucifixion (Matt 27:55–56; Mark 15:40–41; John 19:25), but Luke is careful to give us this information at the beginning of his ministry (see Women Disciples, next page).

8:4–15 Parable of the Farmer Scattering Seed. Here we are introduced to Jesus' method of telling commonplace stories with spiritual implications. To understand them takes serious reflection and interpretation.

Women Disciples

In the ancient world, teachers were seen as possessing superior knowledge that they would impart to disciples who gathered around them to learn from their life, words, and actions. Close relationships developed between teacher and learners over time as they committed themselves to one another and to their shared beliefs. Many teachers developed a peripatetic lifestyle, propagating their beliefs or philosophy in many places, assisted by their disciples.

By New Testament times discipling was a widely recognized method of teaching; Jesus used it to train the future leaders of his church. In the first century women usually had no part in organized education. Few were literate. Their education was confined to domestic and family matters. Thus the considerable evidence that women were followers of Jesus and played a significant part in the disciple band is in contrast to the accepted practices of the day.

The Greek verb meaning "to follow" is also a technical term for following someone as a disciple. It appears that the women mentioned in Luke 8:1–3 were Jesus' disciples who followed with him and his disciple band, and provided for Jesus from their resources.

At the end of the Gospel accounts we discover many women whose following (a continuous action, Mark 15:41) of Jesus had begun in Galilee and continued to Jerusalem and the cross. There they maintained their faithful vigil even though all others "deserted him and ran away" (Mark 14:50). The women watched where he was laid and prepared to anoint his body for burial, which was the customary way disciples demonstrated their final respect for their master (Matt 28:13; Mark 15:47—16:1).

Jesus welcomed many different women as learners (Mary of Bethany, Luke 10:39, 42) and encouraged them to engage with him in theological conversations (Martha, John 11:21–27; Canaanite woman, Matt 15:24–28; Samaritan woman, John 4:7–26). This was in contrast to the rabbinic practice of excluding women. Mary of Bethany was alone among his followers in her understanding that he was about to die (John 12:7). On the resurrection morning Jesus and the angelic messengers asked the women at the tomb to "remember" his previous instructions about their meeting in Galilee and commissioned them to remind the absent disciples of this arrangement when they conveyed the resurrection news (Matt 28:6–10; Mark 16:7; Luke 24:6–9). Being entrusted with that task indicated a divine endorsement of their role in sharing the good news and teaching others to obey Jesus' commands and placed them under the same obligation as the other disciples (Matt 28:19–20). Their access to the disciples, behind locked doors, on the day of resurrection shows their acceptance as welcome members of the disciple band (John 20:18–19).

The mention of the women's names in the Gospels probably indicates they were well known in the Christian community at the time of writing (Matt 27:56; 28:1; Mark 15:40–41; 16:1; Luke 8:2; 24:10; John 19:25; 20:1). It is possible that women were among the seventy Jesus sent in pairs to the towns of Galilee to prepare for his later visits by curing the sick, casting out demons, and announcing the coming kingdom (Luke 10:1–12, 17–20). The male disciples and Jesus had female relatives who were members of the disciple band. These included Jesus' mother and aunt (John 19:25), the mother of James and John (Matt 27:56), the mother of James the younger and Joseph (Mark 15:40), and the wife of Clopas (John 19:25; see also Luke 24:18). The believing wives of apostles and brothers of the Lord accompanied their husbands in traveling ministry two decades later (1 Cor 9:5).

In Acts the Greek word for "disciple" is used as a general term denoting all believers or members of the new Christian community. Acts nominates four individuals by the singular (Ananias, Acts 9:10; Timothy, Acts 16:1; Mnason, Acts 21:16; and Tabitha, Acts 9:36). All other occurrences are in the plural and include men and women living in Damascus, Jerusalem, Joppa, Antioch, Lystra, Derbe, Galatia and Phrygia, Ephesus, Tyre, and Caesarea. They took part in major church decisions (Acts 6:2), performed acts of service for others, and suffered persecution for their faith (Acts 9:1–2). Their service included charitable good works (Acts 9:36, 39), famine relief (Acts 11:29), providing spiritual and physical deliverance to Paul (Acts 9:17, 25; 14:20), and hospitality and advice concerning his well-being (Acts 19:30; 21:4, 16).

maturity. 15 And the seeds that fell on the good
soil represent honest, good-hearted people who
hear God's word, cling to it, and patiently produce a huge harvest.

Parable of the Lamp

16 "No one lights a lamp and then covers it with
a bowl or hides it under a bed. A lamp is placed
on a stand, where its light can be seen by all who
enter the house. 17 For all that is secret will eventually be brought into the open, and everything
that is concealed will be brought to light and
made known to all.

18 "So pay attention to how you hear. To those
who listen to my teaching, more understanding
will be given. But for those who are not listening, even what they think they understand will
be taken away from them."

The True Family of Jesus

19 Then Jesus' mother and brothers came to see
him, but they couldn't get to him because of the
crowd. 20 Someone told Jesus, "Your mother and
your brothers are outside, and they want to see
you."

21 Jesus replied, "My mother and my brothers
are all those who hear God's word and obey it."

Jesus Calms the Storm

22 One day Jesus said to his disciples, "Let's cross
to the other side of the lake." So they got into
a boat and started out. 23 As they sailed across,
Jesus settled down for a nap. But soon a fierce
storm came down on the lake. The boat was filling with water, and they were in real danger.

24 The disciples went and woke him up, shouting, "Master, Master, we're going to drown!"

When Jesus woke up, he rebuked the wind and
the raging waves. Suddenly the storm stopped
and all was calm. 25 Then he asked them, "Where
is your faith?"

The disciples were terrified and amazed. "Who
is this man?" they asked each other. "When he
gives a command, even the wind and waves obey
him!"

Jesus Heals a Demon-Possessed Man

26 So they arrived in the region of the Gerasenes,*
across the lake from Galilee. 27 As Jesus was
climbing out of the boat, a man who was possessed by demons came out to meet him. For a
long time he had been homeless and naked, living in a cemetery outside the town.

28 As soon as he saw Jesus, he shrieked and
fell down in front of him. Then he screamed,
"Why are you interfering with me, Jesus, Son
of the Most High God? Please, I beg you, don't
torture me!" 29 For Jesus had already commanded
the evil* spirit to come out of him. This spirit
had often taken control of the man. Even when
he was placed under guard and put in chains and
shackles, he simply broke them and rushed out
into the wilderness, completely under the demon's power.

30 Jesus demanded, "What is your name?"

"Legion," he replied, for he was filled with
many demons. 31 The demons kept begging Jesus
not to send them into the bottomless pit.*

32 There happened to be a large herd of pigs
feeding on the hillside nearby, and the demons
begged him to let them enter into the pigs.

So Jesus gave them permission. 33 Then the
demons came out of the man and entered the
pigs, and the entire herd plunged down the steep
hillside into the lake and drowned.

34 When the herdsmen saw it, they fled to the
nearby town and the surrounding countryside,
spreading the news as they ran. 35 People rushed
out to see what had happened. A crowd soon
gathered around Jesus, and they saw the man
who had been freed from the demons. He was
sitting at Jesus' feet, fully clothed and perfectly

8:26 Other manuscripts read *Gadarenes;* still others read *Gergesenes;* also in 8:37. See Matt 8:28; Mark 5:1. **8:29** Greek *unclean.* **8:31** Or *the abyss,* or *the underworld.*

8:16–18 Parable of the Lamp. Tending lamps was usually the domain of women, but here the emphasis is upon the quality of the light provided.

8:19–21 The True Family of Jesus. This pericope lets us see the rift that is growing between Jesus and his family. They have come to claim his time and his attention. They assume that he will send away the crowds and devote himself exclusively to them. Jesus maintains that those who are truly his family are those who prize the word of God and act on it. This reaction could not fail to have been a challenge to Mary in her role as mother of a son whom she could not understand.

8:22–25 Jesus Calms the Storm. As a violent storm sweeps down, the disciples puzzle over the identity of Jesus and his power over the forces of nature.

8:26–39 Jesus Heals a Demon-Possessed Man. The homeless and naked man among the tombs has been living a life that makes him more akin to animals than to other human beings. Now the townsfolk find him sitting at Jesus' feet, fully clothed and perfectly sane. He has been restored to full humanity.

sane, and they were all afraid. 36 Then those who
had seen what happened told the others how the
demon-possessed man had been healed. 37 And all
the people in the region of the Gerasenes begged
Jesus to go away and leave them alone, for a great
wave of fear swept over them.

So Jesus returned to the boat and left, crossing back to the other side of the lake. 38 The man
who had been freed from the demons begged to
go with him. But Jesus sent him home, saying,
39 "No, go back to your family, and tell them everything God has done for you." So he went all
through the town proclaiming the great things
Jesus had done for him.

Jesus Heals in Response to Faith

40 On the other side of the lake the crowds welcomed Jesus, because they had been waiting for
him. 41 Then a man named Jairus, a leader of the
local synagogue, came and fell at Jesus' feet,
pleading with him to come home with him. 42 His
only daughter,* who was about twelve years old,
was dying.

As Jesus went with him, he was surrounded
by the crowds. 43 A woman in the crowd had suffered for twelve years with constant bleeding,*
and she could find no cure. 44 Coming up behind
Jesus, she touched the fringe of his robe. Immediately, the bleeding stopped.

45 "Who touched me?" Jesus asked.

Everyone denied it, and Peter said, "Master,
this whole crowd is pressing up against you."

46 But Jesus said, "Someone deliberately
touched me, for I felt healing power go out from
me." 47 When the woman realized that she could
not stay hidden, she began to tremble and fell to
her knees in front of him. The whole crowd heard
her explain why she had touched him and that
she had been immediately healed. 48 "Daughter,"
he said to her, "your faith has made you well. Go
in peace."

49 While he was still speaking to her, a messenger arrived from the home of Jairus, the leader of
the synagogue. He told him, "Your daughter is
dead. There's no use troubling the Teacher now."

50 But when Jesus heard what had happened,
he said to Jairus, "Don't be afraid. Just have faith,
and she will be healed."

51 When they arrived at the house, Jesus
wouldn't let anyone go in with him except Peter,
John, James, and the little girl's father and mother. 52 The house was filled with people weeping
and wailing, but he said, "Stop the weeping! She
isn't dead; she's only asleep."

53 But the crowd laughed at him because they
all knew she had died. 54 Then Jesus took her by
the hand and said in a loud voice, "My child, get
up!" 55 And at that moment her life* returned,
and she immediately stood up! Then Jesus told
them to give her something to eat. 56 Her parents
were overwhelmed, but Jesus insisted that they
not tell anyone what had happened.

Jesus Sends Out the Twelve Disciples

9 One day Jesus called together his twelve
disciples* and gave them power and authority to cast out all demons and to heal
all diseases. 2 Then he sent them out to tell everyone about the Kingdom of God and to heal
the sick. 3 "Take nothing for your journey," he
instructed them. "Don't take a walking stick, a
traveler's bag, food, money,* or even a change

8:42 Or *His only child, a daughter.* **8:43** Some manuscripts add *having spent everything she had on doctors.* **8:55** Or *her spirit.* **9:1** Greek *the Twelve;* other manuscripts read *the twelve apostles.* **9:3** Or *silver coins.*

8:40–56 Jesus Heals in Response to Faith. In balance with the story of the healing of the male demoniac, Luke presents two episodes of Jesus' outreach to women in desperate straits. **41–42:** If at other points his position in the synagogue may have afforded Jairus some security, he must in this dire circumstance seek the aid of the controversial Jesus. **43–44:** Progress to Jairus's house is obstructed by a large crowd, however, and progress is further impeded by the presence of a woman afflicted with a flow of blood. In her extremity, she risks approaching Jesus to touch the *kraspedon,* the fringe of his prayer shawl, the holiest of his garments. Her discharge rendered her unclean according to Levitical law (Lev 15:19–33), and any whom she touched would also become unclean. Jesus shows no repugnance for the bodily function that is a recurrent feature of all women's experience. **52–53:** His entrance to the house is blocked by highly experienced professional mourners, women who led the family in expressions of grief at the time of death. Their unbelief stands in stark contrast to the faith of the woman who has been healed and the faith of Jairus's family. **54–55:** In defiance of the ritual prohibition against touching the dead, Jesus takes the girl's hand and commands, *My child, get up!* The astounded parents are bidden to provide her with nourishment—an intensely practical step to augment the mighty miracle.

9:1–6 Jesus Sends Out the Twelve Disciples. Here we find the missionary strategy established in the early church. One house in each community became the base to receive traveling evangelists and to gather those coming to hear their message.

of clothes. 4 Wherever you go, stay in the same
house until you leave town. 5 And if a town refuses to welcome you, shake its dust from your
feet as you leave to show that you have abandoned those people to their fate."
6 So they began their circuit of the villages,
preaching the Good News and healing the sick.

Herod's Confusion

7 When Herod Antipas, the ruler of Galilee,*
heard about everything Jesus was doing, he was
puzzled. Some were saying that John the Baptist
had been raised from the dead. 8 Others thought
Jesus was Elijah or one of the other prophets
risen from the dead.
9 "I beheaded John," Herod said, "so who is
this man about whom I hear such stories?" And
he kept trying to see him.

Jesus Feeds Five Thousand

10 When the apostles returned, they told Jesus everything they had done. Then he slipped quietly
away with them toward the town of Bethsaida.
11 But the crowds found out where he was going,
and they followed him. He welcomed them and
taught them about the Kingdom of God, and he
healed those who were sick.
12 Late in the afternoon the twelve disciples
came to him and said, "Send the crowds away to
the nearby villages and farms, so they can find
food and lodging for the night. There is nothing
to eat here in this remote place."
13 But Jesus said, "You feed them."
"But we have only five loaves of bread and two
fish," they answered. "Or are you expecting us to
go and buy enough food for this whole crowd?"
14 For there were about 5,000 men there.
Jesus replied, "Tell them to sit down in groups
of about fifty each." 15 So the people all sat down.
16 Jesus took the five loaves and two fish, looked up
toward heaven, and blessed them. Then, breaking
the loaves into pieces, he kept giving the bread
and fish to the disciples so they could distribute
it to the people. 17 They all ate as much as they
wanted, and afterward, the disciples picked up
twelve baskets of leftovers!

Peter's Declaration about Jesus

18 One day Jesus left the crowds to pray alone.
Only his disciples were with him, and he asked
them, "Who do people say I am?"
19 "Well," they replied, "some say John the
Baptist, some say Elijah, and others say you are
one of the other ancient prophets risen from the
dead."
20 Then he asked them, "But who do you say
I am?"
Peter replied, "You are the Messiah* sent
from God!"

Jesus Predicts His Death

21 Jesus warned his disciples not to tell anyone
who he was. 22 "The Son of Man* must suffer
many terrible things," he said. "He will be rejected by the elders, the leading priests, and the
teachers of religious law. He will be killed, but on
the third day he will be raised from the dead."
23 Then he said to the crowd, "If any of you
wants to be my follower, you must turn from
your selfish ways, take up your cross daily, and
follow me. 24 If you try to hang on to your life,
you will lose it. But if you give up your life for
my sake, you will save it. 25 And what do you
benefit if you gain the whole world but are yourself lost or destroyed? 26 If anyone is ashamed
of me and my message, the Son of Man will be
ashamed of that person when he returns in his
glory and in the glory of the Father and the holy
angels. 27 I tell you the truth, some standing here
right now will not die before they see the Kingdom of God."

The Transfiguration

28 About eight days later Jesus took Peter, John,
and James up on a mountain to pray. 29 And as
he was praying, the appearance of his face was
transformed, and his clothes became dazzling
white. 30 Suddenly, two men, Moses and Elijah,

9:7 Greek *Herod the tetrarch.* Herod Antipas was a son of King Herod and was ruler over Galilee. **9:20** Or *the Christ.* *Messiah* (a Hebrew term) and *Christ* (a Greek term) both mean "the anointed one." **9:22** "Son of Man" is a title Jesus used for himself.

9:7–9 Herod's Confusion. The power of John the Baptist's message will not leave Herod's mind (cf. Mark 6:20), and the presence and power of Jesus only add to the puzzle.

9:10–17 Jesus Feeds Five Thousand. According to Roman custom, only the adult males were enumerated, but the presence of women and children would have raised the number very considerably.

9:18—19:27 On the Way to Jerusalem

9:18–20 Peter's Declaration about Jesus. The designation of Messiah or Christ (anointed one) radically alters the disciples' growing understanding of Jesus.

9:21–27 Jesus Predicts His Death. To the disciples he points out his own coming death, but to the

appeared and began talking with Jesus. 31 They
were glorious to see. And they were speaking
about his exodus from this world, which was
about to be fulfilled in Jerusalem.
32 Peter and the others had fallen asleep. When
they woke up, they saw Jesus' glory and the two
men standing with him. 33 As Moses and Elijah
were starting to leave, Peter, not even knowing
what he was saying, blurted out, "Master, it's
wonderful for us to be here! Let's make three
shelters as memorials*—one for you, one for
Moses, and one for Elijah." 34 But even as he was
saying this, a cloud overshadowed them, and terror gripped them as the cloud covered them.
35 Then a voice from the cloud said, "This
is my Son, my Chosen One.* Listen to him."
36 When the voice finished, Jesus was there alone.
They didn't tell anyone at that time what they
had seen.

Jesus Heals a Demon-Possessed Boy

37 The next day, after they had come down the
mountain, a large crowd met Jesus. 38 A man in
the crowd called out to him, "Teacher, I beg you
to look at my son, my only child. 39 An evil spirit
keeps seizing him, making him scream. It throws
him into convulsions so that he foams at the
mouth. It batters him and hardly ever leaves him
alone. 40 I begged your disciples to cast out the
spirit, but they couldn't do it."
41 Jesus said, "You faithless and corrupt people! How long must I be with you and put up
with you?" Then he said to the man, "Bring your
son here."
42 As the boy came forward, the demon
knocked him to the ground and threw him into
a violent convulsion. But Jesus rebuked the evil*
spirit and healed the boy. Then he gave him back
to his father. 43 Awe gripped the people as they
saw this majestic display of God's power.

Jesus Again Predicts His Death

While everyone was marveling at everything he
was doing, Jesus said to his disciples, 44 "Listen to
me and remember what I say. The Son of Man
is going to be betrayed into the hands of his enemies." 45 But they didn't know what he meant.
Its significance was hidden from them, so they
couldn't understand it, and they were afraid to
ask him about it.

The Greatest in the Kingdom

46 Then his disciples began arguing about which
of them was the greatest. 47 But Jesus knew their
thoughts, so he brought a little child to his side.
48 Then he said to them, "Anyone who welcomes
a little child like this on my behalf* welcomes
me, and anyone who welcomes me also welcomes my Father who sent me. Whoever is the
least among you is the greatest."

Using the Name of Jesus

49 John said to Jesus, "Master, we saw someone
using your name to cast out demons, but we told
him to stop because he isn't in our group."
50 But Jesus said, "Don't stop him! Anyone
who is not against you is for you."

Opposition from Samaritans

51 As the time drew near for him to ascend to
heaven, Jesus resolutely set out for Jerusalem.
52 He sent messengers ahead to a Samaritan village to prepare for his arrival. 53 But the people of
the village did not welcome Jesus because he was
on his way to Jerusalem. 54 When James and John
saw this, they said to Jesus, "Lord, should we call
down fire from heaven to burn them up*?" 55 But

9:33 Greek *three tabernacles.* **9:35** Some manuscripts read *This is my dearly loved Son.* **9:42** Greek *unclean.* **9:48** Greek *in my name.* **9:54** Some manuscripts add *as Elijah did.*

---

crowd he points to the need to *give up your life for my sake*.

9:28–36 The Transfiguration. Moses and Elijah speak of Jesus' death as an *exodus from this world*, while the disciples seek to retain the presence of all three in shelters that they will construct.

9:37–43a Jesus Heals a Demon-Possessed Boy. Luke's detailed description appears to correspond to that of epilepsy. It is also indicative of the anguished state of the parent.

9:43b–45 Jesus Again Predicts His Death. This is the second of the threefold predictions of his death, so unsettling to the hearers that none dared ask for an explanation.

9:46–48 The Greatest in the Kingdom. The lust for power has brought dissension among the followers of Jesus and a total misunderstanding of the kingdom objectives. Lowliness produces true greatness.

9:49–50 Using the Name of Jesus. Those who toil in the name of Jesus are called to cooperation rather than confrontation.

9:51–56 Opposition from Samaritans. Jesus does not force his presence on anyone! It is the disciples who are rebuked rather than the Samaritans.

Jesus turned and rebuked them.* 56 So they went
on to another village.

The Cost of Following Jesus

57 As they were walking along, someone said to
Jesus, "I will follow you wherever you go."

58 But Jesus replied, "Foxes have dens to live
in, and birds have nests, but the Son of Man has
no place even to lay his head."

59 He said to another person, "Come, follow
me."

The man agreed, but he said, "Lord, first let
me return home and bury my father."

60 But Jesus told him, "Let the spiritually dead
bury their own dead!* Your duty is to go and
preach about the Kingdom of God."

61 Another said, "Yes, Lord, I will follow you,
but first let me say good-bye to my family."

62 But Jesus told him, "Anyone who puts a
hand to the plow and then looks back is not fit
for the Kingdom of God."

Jesus Sends Out His Disciples

10 The Lord now chose seventy-two*
other disciples and sent them ahead
in pairs to all the towns and places he
planned to visit. 2 These were his instructions to
them: "The harvest is great, but the workers are
few. So pray to the Lord who is in charge of the
harvest; ask him to send more workers into his
fields. 3 Now go, and remember that I am sending you out as lambs among wolves. 4 Don't take
any money with you, nor a traveler's bag, nor
an extra pair of sandals. And don't stop to greet
anyone on the road.

5 "Whenever you enter someone's home,
first say, 'May God's peace be on this house.' 6 If
those who live there are peaceful, the blessing
will stand; if they are not, the blessing will return to you. 7 Don't move around from home
to home. Stay in one place, eating and drinking
what they provide. Don't hesitate to accept hospitality, because those who work deserve their
pay.

8 "If you enter a town and it welcomes you,
eat whatever is set before you. 9 Heal the sick,
and tell them, 'The Kingdom of God is near you
now.' 10 But if a town refuses to welcome you, go
out into its streets and say, 11 'We wipe even the
dust of your town from our feet to show that
we have abandoned you to your fate. And know
this—the Kingdom of God is near!' 12 I assure
you, even wicked Sodom will be better off than
such a town on judgment day.

13 "What sorrow awaits you, Korazin and
Bethsaida! For if the miracles I did in you had
been done in wicked Tyre and Sidon, their people would have repented of their sins long ago,
clothing themselves in burlap and throwing ashes on their heads to show their remorse. 14 Yes,
Tyre and Sidon will be better off on judgment
day than you. 15 And you people of Capernaum,
will you be honored in heaven? No, you will go
down to the place of the dead.*"

16 Then he said to the disciples, "Anyone who
accepts your message is also accepting me. And
anyone who rejects you is rejecting me. And
anyone who rejects me is rejecting God, who
sent me."

17 When the seventy-two disciples returned,
they joyfully reported to him, "Lord, even the
demons obey us when we use your name!"

18 "Yes," he told them, "I saw Satan fall from
heaven like lightning! 19 Look, I have given you
authority over all the power of the enemy, and
you can walk among snakes and scorpions and
crush them. Nothing will injure you. 20 But don't

9:55 Some manuscripts add an expanded conclusion to verse 55 and an additional sentence in verse 56: *And he said, "You don't realize what your hearts are like. 56 For the Son of Man has not come to destroy people's lives, but to save them."* **9:60** Greek *Let the dead bury their own dead.* **10:1** Some manuscripts read *seventy;* also in 10:17. **10:15** Greek *to Hades.*

9:57–62 The Cost of Following Jesus. One man wishes to defer his commitment until after the death of his father, but following Jesus requires a self-renunciation that imposes difficulty upon all of his hearers.

10:1–20 Jesus Sends Out His Disciples. Ostensibly these are all men; deploying women to travel thus would have been too dangerous. In accounts of the early church we are made especially aware of the women who received traveling evangelists into their homes (Acts 16:15, 40; 18:2–3). More often than those of men, we are told the names of women in whose houses the early churches met (Acts 12:12; 16:13–15, 40; Rom 16:3–5; 1 Cor 16:19; Col 4:15). Theirs was the responsibility not only to provide food and housing for the itinerant missionary but also to assess the message that was brought (see 2 Jn; 3 Jn). This required that the women must be carefully taught and possess a strong understanding of the fundamentals of the gospel. If the visitor came with a faithful witness to Christ, the leaders were to aid in its dissemination within their communities (2 Jn 7–11; cf. 3 Jn 5–8).

rejoice because evil spirits obey you; rejoice because your names are registered in heaven."

Jesus' Prayer of Thanksgiving

21 At that same time Jesus was filled with the joy of the Holy Spirit, and he said, "O Father, Lord of heaven and earth, thank you for hiding these things from those who think themselves wise and clever, and for revealing them to the childlike. Yes, Father, it pleased you to do it this way.

22 "My Father has entrusted everything to me. No one truly knows the Son except the Father, and no one truly knows the Father except the Son and those to whom the Son chooses to reveal him."

23 Then when they were alone, he turned to the disciples and said, "Blessed are the eyes that see what you have seen. 24 I tell you, many prophets and kings longed to see what you see, but they didn't see it. And they longed to hear what you hear, but they didn't hear it."

The Most Important Commandment

25 One day an expert in religious law stood up to test Jesus by asking him this question: "Teacher, what should I do to inherit eternal life?"

26 Jesus replied, "What does the law of Moses say? How do you read it?"

27 The man answered, " 'You must love the LORD your God with all your heart, all your soul, all your strength, and all your mind.' And, 'Love your neighbor as yourself.' "*

28 "Right!" Jesus told him. "Do this and you will live!"

29 The man wanted to justify his actions, so he asked Jesus, "And who is my neighbor?"

Parable of the Good Samaritan

30 Jesus replied with a story: "A Jewish man was traveling from Jerusalem down to Jericho, and he was attacked by bandits. They stripped him of his clothes, beat him up, and left him half dead beside the road.

31 "By chance a priest came along. But when he saw the man lying there, he crossed to the other side of the road and passed him by. 32 A Temple assistant* walked over and looked at him lying there, but he also passed by on the other side.

33 "Then a despised Samaritan came along, and when he saw the man, he felt compassion for him. 34 Going over to him, the Samaritan soothed his wounds with olive oil and wine and bandaged them. Then he put the man on his own donkey and took him to an inn, where he took care of him. 35 The next day he handed the innkeeper two silver coins,* telling him, 'Take care of this man. If his bill runs higher than this, I'll pay you the next time I'm here.'

36 "Now which of these three would you say was a neighbor to the man who was attacked by bandits?" Jesus asked.

37 The man replied, "The one who showed him mercy."

Then Jesus said, "Yes, now go and do the same."

Jesus Visits Martha and Mary

38 As Jesus and the disciples continued on their way to Jerusalem, they came to a certain vil-

10:27 Deut 6:5; Lev 19:18. **10:32** Greek *A Levite.*
10:35 Greek *two denarii.* A denarius was equivalent to a laborer's full day's wage.

10:21–24 Jesus' Prayer of Thanksgiving. At the success of the disciples' mission, Jesus expresses his joy both to the Father and to his chosen disciples. God's promises have been fulfilled along the dusty roads of Palestine.

10:25–29 The Most Important Commandment. Loving God requires a commitment on a fourfold basis: *all your heart, all your soul, all your strength, and all your mind*. None must be neglected.

10:30–37 Parable of the Good Samaritan. In this story, one may find also a parallel to abused women in the condition of the victim. He has been deprived of his assets, abused, beaten, inflicted with serious bodily injury, stripped of dignity and basic human rights, and shunned by the religious establishment. Help comes from one outside the victim's own faith community, providing medical assistance, transportation to a safe location, shelter, and aftercare.

10:38–42 Jesus Visits Martha and Mary. The story before us presents a paradigm of the attitudes and activities of women who open their homes for gospel ministry. We find the sisters occupied with two different aspects of the total mission. Martha becomes overwhelmed by the arrangements that she has deemed necessary. *All these details* refers to much service *(diakonia)*. The pressure of these tasks did not permit Martha to learn from Jesus. Her strategy is to shame her sister into sharing the burden. Mary has seated herself at the feet of Jesus in the position of a learner (cf. Acts 22:3). In Jewish tradition, this was ordinarily not an option for women. A much-quoted proverb declared that it was better to give the Torah to be burned than to teach it to a woman. Luke will later demonstrate the importance of instructing women

lage where a woman named Martha welcomed him into her home. [39] Her sister, Mary, sat at the Lord's feet, listening to what he taught. [40] But Martha was distracted by the big dinner she was preparing. She came to Jesus and said, "Lord, doesn't it seem unfair to you that my sister just sits here while I do all the work? Tell her to come and help me."

[41] But the Lord said to her, "My dear Martha, you are worried and upset over all these details! [42] There is only one thing worth being concerned about. Mary has discovered it, and it will not be taken away from her."

Teaching about Prayer

11 Once Jesus was in a certain place praying. As he finished, one of his disciples came to him and said, "Lord, teach us to pray, just as John taught his disciples."

[2] Jesus said, "This is how you should pray:*

"Father, may your name be kept holy.
May your Kingdom come soon.
[3] Give us each day the food we need,*
[4] and forgive us our sins,
as we forgive those who sin against us.
And don't let us yield to temptation.*"

[5] Then, teaching them more about prayer, he used this story: "Suppose you went to a friend's house at midnight, wanting to borrow three loaves of bread. You say to him, [6] 'A friend of mine has just arrived for a visit, and I have nothing for him to eat.' [7] And suppose he calls out from his bedroom, 'Don't bother me. The door is locked for the night, and my family and I are all in bed. I can't help you.' [8] But I tell you this—though he won't do it for friendship's sake, if you keep knocking long enough, he will get up and give you whatever you need because of your shameless persistence.*

[9] "And so I tell you, keep on asking, and you will receive what you ask for. Keep on seeking, and you will find. Keep on knocking, and the door will be opened to you. [10] For everyone who asks, receives. Everyone who seeks, finds. And to everyone who knocks, the door will be opened.

[11] "You fathers—if your children ask* for a fish, do you give them a snake instead? [12] Or if they ask for an egg, do you give them a scorpion? Of course not! [13] So if you sinful people know how to give good gifts to your children, how much more will your heavenly Father give the Holy Spirit to those who ask him."

Jesus and the Prince of Demons

[14] One day Jesus cast out a demon from a man who couldn't speak, and when the demon was gone, the man began to speak. The crowds were amazed, [15] but some of them said, "No wonder he can cast out demons. He gets his power from Satan,* the prince of demons." [16] Others, trying to test Jesus, demanded that he show them a miraculous sign from heaven to prove his authority.

[17] He knew their thoughts, so he said, "Any kingdom divided by civil war is doomed. A family splintered by feuding will fall apart. [18] You say I am empowered by Satan. But if Satan is divided and fighting against himself, how can his kingdom survive? [19] And if I am empowered by Satan, what about your own exorcists? They cast out demons, too, so they will condemn you for what you have said. [20] But if I am casting out demons by the power of God,* then the Kingdom of God has arrived among you. [21] For when a strong man like Satan is fully armed and guards his palace, his possessions are safe—[22] until someone even stronger attacks and overpowers him, strips him of his weapons, and carries off his belongings.

[23] "Anyone who isn't with me opposes me, and anyone who isn't working with me is actually working against me.

[24] "When an evil* spirit leaves a person, it goes into the desert, searching for rest. But when it finds none, it says, 'I will return to the person I came from.' [25] So it returns and finds that its former home is all swept and in order. [26] Then the

11:2 Some manuscripts add additional phrases from the Lord's Prayer as it reads in Matt 6:9-13. **11:3** Or *Give us each day our food for the day;* or *Give us each day our food for tomorrow.* **11:4** Or *And keep us from being tested.* **11:8** Or *in order to avoid shame,* or *so his reputation won't be damaged.* **11:11** Some manuscripts add *for bread, do you give them a stone? Or [if they ask].* **11:15** Greek *Beelzeboul;* also in 11:18, 19. Other manuscripts read *Beezeboul;* Latin version reads *Beelzebub.* **11:20** Greek *by the finger of God.* **11:24** Greek *unclean.*

in order to make them faithful witnesses. The Third Evangelist's story is about fundamental priorities. A woman may find great satisfaction and much appreciation for her skill in the culinary arts. Nevertheless she is not ultimately defined by the excellence of the table she spreads but on spreading her heart open to God's Word (cf. 2 Cor 6:11).

11:1–13 Teaching about Prayer. Jesus opens to the disciples new vistas on prayer. It connects one with a loving Father but requires *shameless persistence.*

11:14–28 Jesus and the Prince of Demons. 17–26: Jesus gives a skillful response to those who are jealous of his ability to bring healing to those with men-

spirit finds seven other spirits more evil than itself, and they all enter the person and live there. And so that person is worse off than before."

[27]As he was speaking, a woman in the crowd called out, "God bless your mother—the womb from which you came, and the breasts that nursed you!"

[28]Jesus replied, "But even more blessed are all who hear the word of God and put it into practice."

The Sign of Jonah

[29]As the crowd pressed in on Jesus, he said, "This evil generation keeps asking me to show them a miraculous sign. But the only sign I will give them is the sign of Jonah. [30]What happened to him was a sign to the people of Nineveh that God had sent him. What happens to the Son of Man* will be a sign to these people that he was sent by God.

[31]"The queen of Sheba* will stand up against this generation on judgment day and condemn it, for she came from a distant land to hear the wisdom of Solomon. Now someone greater than Solomon is here—but you refuse to listen. [32]The people of Nineveh will also stand up against this generation on judgment day and condemn it, for they repented of their sins at the preaching of Jonah. Now someone greater than Jonah is here—but you refuse to repent.

Receiving the Light

[33]"No one lights a lamp and then hides it or puts it under a basket.* Instead, a lamp is placed on a stand, where its light can be seen by all who enter the house.

[34]"Your eye is a lamp that provides light for your body. When your eye is good, your whole body is filled with light. But when it is bad, your body is filled with darkness. [35]Make sure that the light you think you have is not actually darkness. [36]If you are filled with light, with no dark corners, then your whole life will be radiant, as though a floodlight were filling you with light."

Jesus Criticizes the Religious Leaders

[37]As Jesus was speaking, one of the Pharisees invited him home for a meal. So he went in and took his place at the table.* [38]His host was amazed to see that he sat down to eat without first performing the hand-washing ceremony required by Jewish custom. [39]Then the Lord said to him, "You Pharisees are so careful to clean the outside of the cup and the dish, but inside you are filthy—full of greed and wickedness! [40]Fools! Didn't God make the inside as well as

11:30 "Son of Man" is a title Jesus used for himself.
11:31 Greek *The queen of the south.* **11:33** Some manuscripts do not include *or puts it under a basket.*
11:37 Or *and reclined.*

---

tal afflictions. **27–28:** In this exchange, sexual identity is pitted against the spiritual identity of women. A woman from the crowd shouts out a blessing upon the womb and breasts that had produced and nourished so remarkable a son, a traditional form of praise for son and mother (cf. Gen 49:25). However, Jesus summons the crowd and his mother to move onto a higher plane. Though to this day many societies value women chiefly as childbearers, Jesus viewed them as total beings. Reproduction is not their highest calling. The childless woman is of equal value in God's economy (see Singleness, 1 Cor 7). Here Jesus affirms those who hear and obey his Word.

11:29–32 The Sign of Jonah. In balance to Jonah and the people of Nineveh, Jesus cites the queen of the south, apparently the queen of Sheba. She is thought to have hailed from the southernmost part of the known world on either the African or Arabian coast of the Red Sea. Powerful queens are historically attested in Yemen and in Ethiopia. Jesus maintained that her perception of Solomon's grandeur was a condemnation of those who could not perceive one greater than Solomon in their midst. To allude to her in this manner is a powerful statement about the significance of this woman and of all women of faith. They are respected for their initiative in searching for the truth, their courage, and their integrity.

11:33–36 Receiving the Light. It was the duty of women to fill the lamps with oil and to trim the wicks. A virtuous woman rose several times during the night to make sure that the lamp was burning properly (cf. Prov 31:18). The matter of spiritual clarity and illumination is even more of a challenge.

11:37–54 Jesus Criticizes the Religious Leaders. The condemnation of Jesus is characteristically directed toward *experts in religious law*. To ordinary sinners, he shows great respect and compassion. **49:** This is the only point in the New Testament at which personified Wisdom is given her own voice. Because God's message has not been heeded, a decision is made that prophets and apostles will be sent even though their lives may be at risk. Those who hear will gain insight, but those who resist the messengers must bear the guilt. Wisdom is set in direct antithesis to the male lawyers who *remove the key of knowledge* and hinder others from gaining admission to its halls.

the outside? 41 So clean the inside by giving gifts
to the poor, and you will be clean all over.
42 "What sorrow awaits you Pharisees! For
you are careful to tithe even the tiniest income
from your herb gardens,* but you ignore justice
and the love of God. You should tithe, yes, but do
not neglect the more important things.
43 "What sorrow awaits you Pharisees! For
you love to sit in the seats of honor in the synagogues and receive respectful greetings as you
walk in the marketplaces. 44 Yes, what sorrow
awaits you! For you are like hidden graves in a
field. People walk over them without knowing
the corruption they are stepping on."
45 "Teacher," said an expert in religious law,
"you have insulted us, too, in what you just
said."
46 "Yes," said Jesus, "what sorrow also awaits
you experts in religious law! For you crush people with unbearable religious demands, and you
never lift a finger to ease the burden. 47 What sorrow awaits you! For you build monuments for
the prophets your own ancestors killed long ago.
48 But in fact, you stand as witnesses who agree
with what your ancestors did. They killed the
prophets, and you join in their crime by building the monuments! 49 This is what God in his
wisdom said about you:* 'I will send prophets
and apostles to them, but they will kill some and
persecute the others.'
50 "As a result, this generation will be held responsible for the murder of all God's prophets
from the creation of the world—51 from the murder of Abel to the murder of Zechariah, who was
killed between the altar and the sanctuary. Yes, it
will certainly be charged against this generation.
52 "What sorrow awaits you experts in religious
law! For you remove the key to knowledge from
the people. You don't enter the Kingdom yourselves, and you prevent others from entering."
53 As Jesus was leaving, the teachers of religious law and the Pharisees became hostile
and tried to provoke him with many questions.
54 They wanted to trap him into saying something they could use against him.

A Warning against Hypocrisy

12 Meanwhile, the crowds grew until
thousands were milling about and
stepping on each other. Jesus turned
first to his disciples and warned them, "Beware of
the yeast of the Pharisees—their hypocrisy. 2 The
time is coming when everything that is covered
up will be revealed, and all that is secret will be
made known to all. 3 Whatever you have said
in the dark will be heard in the light, and what
you have whispered behind closed doors will be
shouted from the housetops for all to hear!
4 "Dear friends, don't be afraid of those who
want to kill your body; they cannot do any more
to you after that. 5 But I'll tell you whom to fear.
Fear God, who has the power to kill you and then
throw you into hell.* Yes, he's the one to fear.
6 "What is the price of five sparrows—two
copper coins*? Yet God does not forget a single
one of them. 7 And the very hairs on your head
are all numbered. So don't be afraid; you are
more valuable to God than a whole flock of sparrows.
8 "I tell you the truth, everyone who acknowledges me publicly here on earth, the Son
of Man* will also acknowledge in the presence
of God's angels. 9 But anyone who denies me
here on earth will be denied before God's angels.
10 Anyone who speaks against the Son of Man
can be forgiven, but anyone who blasphemes the
Holy Spirit will not be forgiven.
11 "And when you are brought to trial in the
synagogues and before rulers and authorities,
don't worry about how to defend yourself or
what to say, 12 for the Holy Spirit will teach you
at that time what needs to be said."

Parable of the Rich Fool

13 Then someone called from the crowd, "Teacher,
please tell my brother to divide our father's estate with me."
14 Jesus replied, "Friend, who made me a judge
over you to decide such things as that?" 15 Then
he said, "Beware! Guard against every kind of
greed. Life is not measured by how much you
own."
16 Then he told them a story: "A rich man had
a fertile farm that produced fine crops. 17 He said
to himself, 'What should I do? I don't have room

11:42 Greek *tithe the mint, the rue, and every herb.* **11:49** Greek *Therefore, the wisdom of God said.* **12:5** Greek *Gehenna.* **12:6** Greek *two assaria* [Roman coins equal to 1/16 of a denarius]. **12:8** "Son of Man" is a title Jesus used for himself.

12:1–11 A Warning against Hypocrisy. The metaphor of yeast would be well understood by women. It permeates every particle of the bread dough into which it is introduced. Just so hypocrisy contaminates every situation that it enters.

12:13–21 Parable of the Rich Fool. A squabble over a family inheritance is turned into the need for a *rich relationship with God.*

12:22–34 Teaching about Money and Possessions.

for all my crops.' 18 Then he said, 'I know! I'll tear
down my barns and build bigger ones. Then I'll
have room enough to store all my wheat and
other goods. 19 And I'll sit back and say to myself,
"My friend, you have enough stored away for
years to come. Now take it easy! Eat, drink, and
be merry!"'

20 "But God said to him, 'You fool! You will
die this very night. Then who will get everything
you worked for?'

21 "Yes, a person is a fool to store up earthly
wealth but not have a rich relationship with God."

Teaching about Money and Possessions

22 Then, turning to his disciples, Jesus said, "That is
why I tell you not to worry about everyday life—
whether you have enough food to eat or enough
clothes to wear. 23 For life is more than food, and
your body more than clothing. 24 Look at the ravens. They don't plant or harvest or store food in
barns, for God feeds them. And you are far more
valuable to him than any birds! 25 Can all your
worries add a single moment to your life? 26 And
if worry can't accomplish a little thing like that,
what's the use of worrying over bigger things?

27 "Look at the lilies and how they grow. They
don't work or make their clothing, yet Solomon
in all his glory was not dressed as beautifully
as they are. 28 And if God cares so wonderfully
for flowers that are here today and thrown into
the fire tomorrow, he will certainly care for you.
Why do you have so little faith?

29 "And don't be concerned about what to
eat and what to drink. Don't worry about such
things. 30 These things dominate the thoughts of
unbelievers all over the world, but your Father
already knows your needs. 31 Seek the Kingdom
of God above all else, and he will give you everything you need.

32 "So don't be afraid, little flock. For it gives
your Father great happiness to give you the
Kingdom.

33 "Sell your possessions and give to those in
need. This will store up treasure for you in heav-
en! And the purses of heaven never get old or
develop holes. Your treasure will be safe; no thief
can steal it and no moth can destroy it. 34 Wherever your treasure is, there the desires of your
heart will also be.

Be Ready for the Lord's Coming

35 "Be dressed for service and keep your lamps
burning, 36 as though you were waiting for your
master to return from the wedding feast. Then
you will be ready to open the door and let him
in the moment he arrives and knocks. 37 The servants who are ready and waiting for his return
will be rewarded. I tell you the truth, he himself
will seat them, put on an apron, and serve them
as they sit and eat! 38 He may come in the middle
of the night or just before dawn.* But whenever
he comes, he will reward the servants who are
ready.

39 "Understand this: If a homeowner knew exactly when a burglar was coming, he would not
permit his house to be broken into. 40 You also
must be ready all the time, for the Son of Man
will come when least expected."

41 Peter asked, "Lord, is that illustration just
for us or for everyone?"

42 And the Lord replied, "A faithful, sensible
servant is one to whom the master can give the
responsibility of managing his other household
servants and feeding them. 43 If the master returns and finds that the servant has done a good
job, there will be a reward. 44 I tell you the truth,
the master will put that servant in charge of all
he owns. 45 But what if the servant thinks, 'My
master won't be back for a while,' and he begins
beating the other servants, partying, and getting
drunk? 46 The master will return unannounced
and unexpected, and he will cut the servant in
pieces and banish him with the unfaithful.

47 "And a servant who knows what the master
wants, but isn't prepared and doesn't carry out
those instructions, will be severely punished.
48 But someone who does not know, and then
does something wrong, will be punished only
lightly. When someone has been given much,
much will be required in return; and when someone has been entrusted with much, even more
will be required.

Jesus Causes Division

49 "I have come to set the world on fire, and I wish
it were already burning! 50 I have a terrible baptism of suffering ahead of me, and I am under a

12:38 Greek *in the second or third watch.*

Conventionally it is a woman's duty to prepare food and clothing for her family, often a source of constant concern. An attitude of faith is far more beneficial to those around her.

12:35–48 Be Ready for the Lord's Coming. The endowment of wealth, learning or ability brings with it responsibility that cannot be disregarded.

12:49–59 Jesus Causes Division. Women often set great store by relationships and will sometimes sacrifice everything else to preserve them, even when

heavy burden until it is accomplished. [51]Do you think I have come to bring peace to the earth? No, I have come to divide people against each other! [52]From now on families will be split apart, three in favor of me, and two against—or two in favor and three against.

[53] 'Father will be divided against son
 and son against father;
mother against daughter
 and daughter against mother;
and mother-in-law against daughter-in-law
 and daughter-in-law against mother-in-law.'* "

[54]Then Jesus turned to the crowd and said, "When you see clouds beginning to form in the west, you say, 'Here comes a shower.' And you are right. [55]When the south wind blows, you say, 'Today will be a scorcher.' And it is. [56]You fools! You know how to interpret the weather signs of the earth and sky, but you don't know how to interpret the present times.

[57]"Why can't you decide for yourselves what is right? [58]When you are on the way to court with your accuser, try to settle the matter before you get there. Otherwise, your accuser may drag you before the judge, who will hand you over to an officer, who will throw you into prison. [59]And if that happens, you won't be free again until you have paid the very last penny.*"

A Call to Repentance

13 About this time Jesus was informed that Pilate had murdered some people from Galilee as they were offering sacrifices at the Temple. [2]"Do you think those Galileans were worse sinners than all the other people from Galilee?" Jesus asked. "Is that why they suffered? [3]Not at all! And you will perish, too, unless you repent of your sins and turn to God. [4]And what about the eighteen people who died when the tower in Siloam fell on them? Were they the worst sinners in Jerusalem? [5]No, and I tell you again that unless you repent, you will perish, too."

Parable of the Barren Fig Tree

[6]Then Jesus told this story: "A man planted a fig tree in his garden and came again and again to see if there was any fruit on it, but he was always disappointed. [7]Finally, he said to his gardener, 'I've waited three years, and there hasn't been a single fig! Cut it down. It's just taking up space in the garden.'

[8]"The gardener answered, 'Sir, give it one more chance. Leave it another year, and I'll give it special attention and plenty of fertilizer. [9]If we get figs next year, fine. If not, then you can cut it down.' "

Jesus Heals on the Sabbath

[10]One Sabbath day as Jesus was teaching in a synagogue, [11]he saw a woman who had been crippled by an evil spirit. She had been bent double for eighteen years and was unable to stand up straight. [12]When Jesus saw her, he called her over and said, "Dear woman, you are healed of your sickness!" [13]Then he touched her, and instantly she could stand straight. How she praised God!

[14]But the leader in charge of the synagogue was indignant that Jesus had healed her on the Sabbath day. "There are six days of the week for

12:53 Mic 7:6. **12:59** Greek *last lepton* [the smallest Jewish coin].

the ties are unhealthy. Jesus saw the family not as a fetish but as a union of persons who might have different values. Commitment of his followers must take precedence over domestic peace. Those who are willing to give first loyalty to the cause of Christ may encounter difficult circumstances and lack of understanding at home. He had come to bring fire upon the earth, a consuming passion that would stretch and strain families to the utmost.

13:1–5 A Call to Repentance. Disasters do not necessarily happen as a judgment but they can provide opportunity for serious reflection on one's lifestyle.

13:6–9 Parable of the Barren Fig Tree. Unlike Jesus cursing a barren fig tree (Mark 11:14), in this parable an unproductive tree is given opportunity and *special attention* in order for it to thrive. A second chance can produce remarkable results.

13:10–17 Jesus Heals on the Sabbath. This episode is recorded only in Luke and stands as a monument to the rights and dignity of women. For eighteen years the woman has been unable to stand upright, bent nearly double. Her affliction may have been *spondylitis ankylopoeitica*, or a severe case of osteoporosis, a condition that besets women more commonly than men. Marginalized women are objects of consistent concern to Jesus. He refers to her as *a daughter of Abraham* (thereby giving her value as a person of worth and dignity in the kingdom of God). His opponents, however, viewed her as less than human and unworthy of healing on the Sabbath. Jesus points out that on the Sabbath any of them would loose the tethers

working," he said to the crowd. "Come on those
days to be healed, not on the Sabbath."
[15] But the Lord replied, "You hypocrites! Each
of you works on the Sabbath day! Don't you
untie your ox or your donkey from its stall on
the Sabbath and lead it out for water? [16] This dear
woman, a daughter of Abraham, has been held in
bondage by Satan for eighteen years. Isn't it right
that she be released, even on the Sabbath?"
[17] This shamed his enemies, but all the people
rejoiced at the wonderful things he did.

Parable of the Mustard Seed

[18] Then Jesus said, "What is the Kingdom of God
like? How can I illustrate it? [19] It is like a tiny
mustard seed that a man planted in a garden; it
grows and becomes a tree, and the birds make
nests in its branches."

Parable of the Yeast

[20] He also asked, "What else is the Kingdom of
God like? [21] It is like the yeast a woman used in
making bread. Even though she put only a little
yeast in three measures of flour, it permeated every part of the dough."

The Narrow Door

[22] Jesus went through the towns and villages,
teaching as he went, always pressing on toward
Jerusalem. [23] Someone asked him, "Lord, will
only a few be saved?"
He replied, [24] "Work hard to enter the narrow door to God's Kingdom, for many will try
to enter but will fail. [25] When the master of the
house has locked the door, it will be too late. You
will stand outside knocking and pleading, 'Lord,
open the door for us!' But he will reply, 'I don't
know you or where you come from.' [26] Then you
will say, 'But we ate and drank with you, and you
taught in our streets.' [27] And he will reply, 'I tell
you, I don't know you or where you come from.
Get away from me, all you who do evil.'
[28] "There will be weeping and gnashing of
teeth, for you will see Abraham, Isaac, Jacob, and
all the prophets in the Kingdom of God, but you
will be thrown out. [29] And people will come from
all over the world—from east and west, north
and south—to take their places in the Kingdom
of God. [30] And note this: Some who seem least
important now will be the greatest then, and
some who are the greatest now will be least important then.*"

Jesus Grieves over Jerusalem

[31] At that time some Pharisees said to him, "Get
away from here if you want to live! Herod Antipas wants to kill you!"
[32] Jesus replied, "Go tell that fox that I will
keep on casting out demons and healing people
today and tomorrow; and the third day I will accomplish my purpose. [33] Yes, today, tomorrow,

13:30 Greek *Some are last who will be first, and some are first who will be last.*

---

of their livestock and lead them to water. How much more should this woman be loosed from her bonds on the Sabbath? As a liberated member of the covenant community, she may now stand erect and look people in the face. Those who must hide their faces in shame are they who would deny her this right.

13:18–19 Parable of the Mustard Seed. The wonder of growth is a recurring theme in Jesus' teaching.

13:20–21 Parable of the Yeast. In this text we can see Jesus' acute perception of the ordinary household tasks of women and his valuation of their labor. In balance with the parable of a man planting mustard seed is the parable of a woman kneading yeast into dough, thus affirming male and female participation as necessary to understand growth of the kingdom of God. Kneading the dough requires vigorous use of the hands, persistence, and sensitivity to the texture. Yeast, the leavening agent, is a living organism that does not always respond in precisely the same way. No two batches of dough are ever alike. Quantity of flour, temperature, and environment must all be controlled by the skilled breadmaker for the yeast to raise a mass to many times its weight. The parable suggests the influence and sensitivity of women in promoting the kingdom. Their hands-on ministry of positive nurture and practical outreach permeates society far beyond their numerical strength.

13:22–30 The Narrow Door. Importance in God's eyes may bear a very different face than in acceptable human circles.

13:31–35 Jesus Grieves over Jerusalem. In Hebrew Scriptures an image is developed of God as a mother bird protecting the young with her wings. The eagle bears her young on her wings as they learn to fly (Exod 19:4; Deut 32:11–12), though the more common figure is of God as a bird offering protective shelter under her wings (Pss 17:8; 36:7; 57:1; 61:4; 63:7; 91:4; cf. Ruth 2:12). All of these metaphors are those of loving nurturance, stability, and safety. Other maternal images are Deuteronomy 32:18; Isaiah 42:14; 49:15; 66:9, 13; Psalms 22:10–11 and 131:2–3 (see Images of God as Female, Deut 32).

and the next day I must proceed on my way. For it wouldn't do for a prophet of God to be killed except in Jerusalem!

34 "O Jerusalem, Jerusalem, the city that kills the prophets and stones God's messengers! How often I have wanted to gather your children together as a hen protects her chicks beneath her wings, but you wouldn't let me. 35 And now, look, your house is abandoned. And you will never see me again until you say, 'Blessings on the one who comes in the name of the LORD!'* "

Jesus Heals on the Sabbath

14 One Sabbath day Jesus went to eat dinner in the home of a leader of the Pharisees, and the people were watching him closely. 2 There was a man there whose arms and legs were swollen.* 3 Jesus asked the Pharisees and experts in religious law, "Is it permitted in the law to heal people on the Sabbath day, or not?" 4 When they refused to answer, Jesus touched the sick man and healed him and sent him away. 5 Then he turned to them and said, "Which of you doesn't work on the Sabbath? If your son* or your cow falls into a pit, don't you rush to get him out?" 6 Again they could not answer.

Jesus Teaches about Humility

7 When Jesus noticed that all who had come to the dinner were trying to sit in the seats of honor near the head of the table, he gave them this advice: 8 "When you are invited to a wedding feast, don't sit in the seat of honor. What if someone who is more distinguished than you has also been invited? 9 The host will come and say, 'Give this person your seat.' Then you will be embarrassed, and you will have to take whatever seat is left at the foot of the table!

10 "Instead, take the lowest place at the foot of the table. Then when your host sees you, he will come and say, 'Friend, we have a better place for you!' Then you will be honored in front of all the other guests. 11 For those who exalt themselves will be humbled, and those who humble themselves will be exalted."

12 Then he turned to his host. "When you put on a luncheon or a banquet," he said, "don't invite your friends, brothers, relatives, and rich neighbors. For they will invite you back, and that will be your only reward. 13 Instead, invite the poor, the crippled, the lame, and the blind. 14 Then at the resurrection of the righteous, God will reward you for inviting those who could not repay you."

Parable of the Great Feast

15 Hearing this, a man sitting at the table with Jesus exclaimed, "What a blessing it will be to attend a banquet* in the Kingdom of God!"

16 Jesus replied with this story: "A man prepared a great feast and sent out many invitations. 17 When the banquet was ready, he sent his servant to tell the guests, 'Come, the banquet is ready.' 18 But they all began making excuses. One said, 'I have just bought a field and must inspect it. Please excuse me.' 19 Another said, 'I have just bought five pairs of oxen, and I want to try them out. Please excuse me.' 20 Another said, 'I now have a wife, so I can't come.'

21 "The servant returned and told his master what they had said. His master was furious and said, 'Go quickly into the streets and alleys of the town and invite the poor, the crippled, the blind, and the lame.' 22 After the servant had done this, he reported, 'There is still room for more.' 23 So his master said, 'Go out into the country lanes and behind the hedges and urge anyone you find to come, so that the house will be full. 24 For none of those I first invited will get even the smallest taste of my banquet.' "

The Cost of Being a Disciple

25 A large crowd was following Jesus. He turned around and said to them, 26 "If you want to be my disciple, you must hate everyone else by comparison—your father and mother, wife and children, brothers and sisters—yes, even your own life. Otherwise, you cannot be my disciple.

13:35 Ps 118:26. **14:2** Or *who had dropsy.* **14:5** Some manuscripts read *donkey.* **14:15** Greek *to eat bread.*

14:1–6 Jesus Heals on the Sabbath. The dinner invitation appears to have been contrived to test out what Jesus would do about a man with dropsy. Again there is a miracle of touching, and legalism is again trumped by an appropriate recognition of God's purposes.

14:7–14 Jesus Teaches about Humility. The Pharisee's dinner party grows yet more uncomfortable as Jesus introduces new dynamics.

14:15–24 Parable of the Great Feast. The marginalized guests destined for the heavenly dinner party differ markedly from those whom the Pharisee had invited.

14:25–35 The Cost of Being a Disciple. Here Jesus uses the shrewd calculations of a building project and a military campaign as models to assess the cost of the heavenly calling.

27 And if you do not carry your own cross and
follow me, you cannot be my disciple.
28 "But don't begin until you count the cost.
For who would begin construction of a building
without first calculating the cost to see if there
is enough money to finish it? 29 Otherwise, you
might complete only the foundation before running out of money, and then everyone would
laugh at you. 30 They would say, 'There's the person who started that building and couldn't afford
to finish it!'
31 "Or what king would go to war against another king without first sitting down with his
counselors to discuss whether his army of 10,000
could defeat the 20,000 soldiers marching against
him? 32 And if he can't, he will send a delegation
to discuss terms of peace while the enemy is still
far away. 33 So you cannot become my disciple
without giving up everything you own.
34 "Salt is good for seasoning. But if it loses its
flavor, how do you make it salty again? 35 Flavor-
less salt is good neither for the soil nor for the
manure pile. It is thrown away. Anyone with ears
to hear should listen and understand!"

Parable of the Lost Sheep

15 Tax collectors and other notorious
sinners often came to listen to Jesus
teach. 2 This made the Pharisees and
teachers of religious law complain that he was
associating with such sinful people—even eating
with them!
3 So Jesus told them this story: 4 "If a man has
a hundred sheep and one of them gets lost, what
will he do? Won't he leave the ninety-nine others in the wilderness and go to search for the one
that is lost until he finds it? 5 And when he has
found it, he will joyfully carry it home on his
shoulders. 6 When he arrives, he will call together
his friends and neighbors, saying, 'Rejoice with
me because I have found my lost sheep.' 7 In the
same way, there is more joy in heaven over one
lost sinner who repents and returns to God than
over ninety-nine others who are righteous and
haven't strayed away!

Parable of the Lost Coin

8 "Or suppose a woman has ten silver coins* and
loses one. Won't she light a lamp and sweep the
entire house and search carefully until she finds
it? 9 And when she finds it, she will call in her
friends and neighbors and say, 'Rejoice with me
because I have found my lost coin.' 10 In the same
way, there is joy in the presence of God's angels
when even one sinner repents."

Parable of the Lost Son

11 To illustrate the point further, Jesus told them
this story: "A man had two sons. 12 The younger
son told his father, 'I want my share of your estate now before you die.' So his father agreed to
divide his wealth between his sons.
13 "A few days later this younger son packed
all his belongings and moved to a distant land,
and there he wasted all his money in wild living.
14 About the time his money ran out, a great famine swept over the land, and he began to starve.
15 He persuaded a local farmer to hire him, and
the man sent him into his fields to feed the pigs.
16 The young man became so hungry that even
the pods he was feeding the pigs looked good to
him. But no one gave him anything.
17 "When he finally came to his senses, he
said to himself, 'At home even the hired servants
have food enough to spare, and here I am dying
of hunger! 18 I will go home to my father and say,
"Father, I have sinned against both heaven and
you, 19 and I am no longer worthy of being called
your son. Please take me on as a hired servant."'
20 "So he returned home to his father. And
while he was still a long way off, his father saw

15:8 Greek *ten drachmas.* A drachma was the equivalent of a full day's wage.

15:1–7 Parable of the Lost Sheep. Although Jesus had a strong following among the common people, the three parables that follow are addressed to the religious leaders.

15:8–10 Parable of the Lost Coin. Grouped together are the parables of the lost sheep, the lost coin, and the lost son. Readers readily identify God in the figures of the seeking shepherd and of the waiting father. The image of God as housewife is more difficult for some readers to recognize. The woman is seeking a valuable coin that represents one-tenth of her dowry. Ordinarily the coins were sewn into a woman's headdress, thus becoming her adornment as well as her security against future adversity. The woman lights one of the tiny lamps that gave a flickering light and begins a more comprehensive search. With a broom, she sweeps the floor repeatedly until her diligent persistence is rewarded. In relief and joy she calls the good news to the other women of the neighborhood who hasten to join in the jubilation. Just so, Jesus insists, the angels rejoice before God at the reclamation of a sinner.

15:11–32 Parable of the Lost Son. There are two sinful sons, one loving father, but where is the mother?

him coming. Filled with love and compassion, he
ran to his son, embraced him, and kissed him.
21 His son said to him, 'Father, I have sinned
against both heaven and you, and I am no longer
worthy of being called your son.*'
22 "But his father said to the servants, 'Quick!
Bring the finest robe in the house and put it on
him. Get a ring for his finger and sandals for his
feet. 23 And kill the calf we have been fattening.
We must celebrate with a feast, 24 for this son of
mine was dead and has now returned to life. He
was lost, but now he is found.' So the party began.

25 "Meanwhile, the older son was in the fields
working. When he returned home, he heard
music and dancing in the house, 26 and he asked
one of the servants what was going on. 27 'Your
brother is back,' he was told, 'and your father has
killed the fattened calf. We are celebrating because of his safe return.'

28 "The older brother was angry and wouldn't
go in. His father came out and begged him, 29 but
he replied, 'All these years I've slaved for you and
never once refused to do a single thing you told
me to. And in all that time you never gave me
even one young goat for a feast with my friends.
30 Yet when this son of yours comes back after
squandering your money on prostitutes, you celebrate by killing the fattened calf!'

31 "His father said to him, 'Look, dear son, you
have always stayed by me, and everything I have
is yours. 32 We had to celebrate this happy day.
For your brother was dead and has come back to
life! He was lost, but now he is found!' "

Parable of the Shrewd Manager

16 Jesus told this story to his disciples:
"There was a certain rich man who
had a manager handling his affairs.
One day a report came that the manager was
wasting his employer's money. 2 So the employer
called him in and said, 'What's this I hear about
you? Get your report in order, because you are
going to be fired.'

3 "The manager thought to himself, 'Now
what? My boss has fired me. I don't have the
strength to dig ditches, and I'm too proud to beg.
4 Ah, I know how to ensure that I'll have plenty
of friends who will give me a home when I am
fired.'

5 "So he invited each person who owed money
to his employer to come and discuss the situation. He asked the first one, 'How much do you
owe him?' 6 The man replied, 'I owe him 800 gallons of olive oil.' So the manager told him, 'Take
the bill and quickly change it to 400 gallons.*'

7 " 'And how much do you owe my employer?'
he asked the next man. 'I owe him 1,000 bushels
of wheat,' was the reply. 'Here,' the manager said,
'take the bill and change it to 800 bushels.*'

8 "The rich man had to admire the dishonest
rascal for being so shrewd. And it is true that
the children of this world are more shrewd in
dealing with the world around them than are
the children of the light. 9 Here's the lesson: Use
your worldly resources to benefit others and
make friends. Then, when your earthly possessions are gone, they will welcome you to an
eternal home.*

10 "If you are faithful in little things, you will
be faithful in large ones. But if you are dishonest
in little things, you won't be honest with greater
responsibilities. 11 And if you are untrustworthy
about worldly wealth, who will trust you with
the true riches of heaven? 12 And if you are not
faithful with other people's things, why should
you be trusted with things of your own?

13 "No one can serve two masters. For you will
hate one and love the other; you will be devoted
to one and despise the other. You cannot serve
both God and money."

14 The Pharisees, who dearly loved their money, heard all this and scoffed at him. 15 Then he
said to them, "You like to appear righteous in
public, but God knows your hearts. What this
world honors is detestable in the sight of God.

16 "Until John the Baptist, the law of Moses
and the messages of the prophets were your
guides. But now the Good News of the Kingdom
of God is preached, and everyone is eager to get
in.* 17 But that doesn't mean that the law has lost
its force. It is easier for heaven and earth to disappear than for the smallest point of God's law
to be overturned.

18 "For example, a man who divorces his wife
and marries someone else commits adultery. And
anyone who marries a woman divorced from her
husband commits adultery."

15:21 Some manuscripts add *Please take me on as a hired servant.* **16:6** Greek *100 baths . . . 50 [baths].* **16:7** Greek *100 korous . . . 80 [korous].* **16:9** Or *you will be welcomed into eternal homes.* **16:16** Or *everyone is urged to enter in.*

16:1–17 Parable of the Shrewd Manager. In his work as a carpenter, Jesus had not been ignorant of business dealings nor of the spiritual implications that can be drawn.

16:18 Jesus and Divorce. In Luke's account we may discern in Jesus' teaching a desire to protect women against capricious divorce action that could leave them without protection (see Divorce, Ezra 10). A

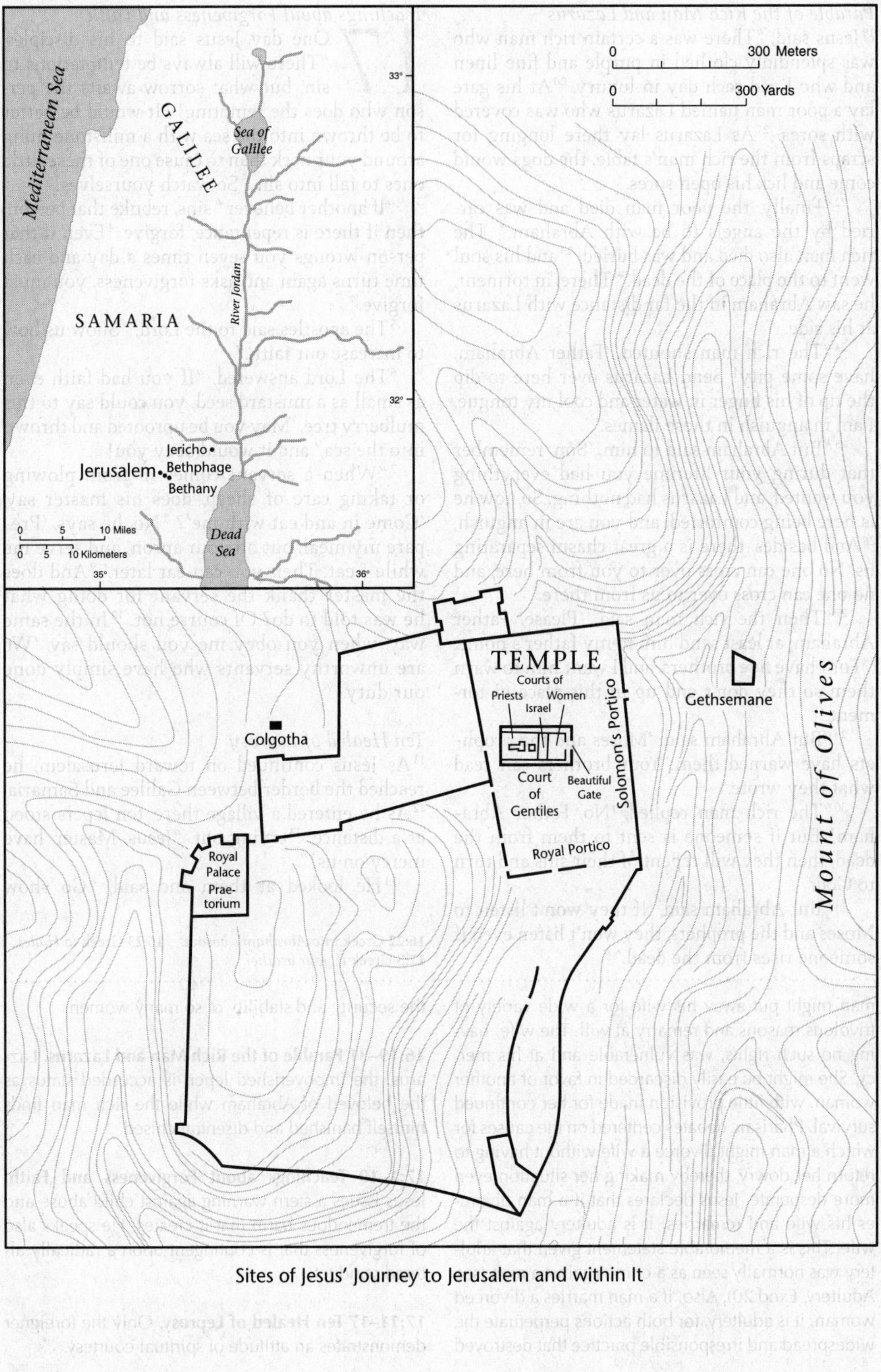

Sites of Jesus' Journey to Jerusalem and within It

Parable of the Rich Man and Lazarus

[19]Jesus said, "There was a certain rich man who was splendidly clothed in purple and fine linen and who lived each day in luxury. [20]At his gate lay a poor man named Lazarus who was covered with sores. [21]As Lazarus lay there longing for scraps from the rich man's table, the dogs would come and lick his open sores.

[22]"Finally, the poor man died and was carried by the angels to be with Abraham.* The rich man also died and was buried, [23]and his soul went to the place of the dead.* There, in torment, he saw Abraham in the far distance with Lazarus at his side.

[24]"The rich man shouted, 'Father Abraham, have some pity! Send Lazarus over here to dip the tip of his finger in water and cool my tongue. I am in anguish in these flames.'

[25]"But Abraham said to him, 'Son, remember that during your lifetime you had everything you wanted, and Lazarus had nothing. So now he is here being comforted, and you are in anguish. [26]And besides, there is a great chasm separating us. No one can cross over to you from here, and no one can cross over to us from there.'

[27]"Then the rich man said, 'Please, Father Abraham, at least send him to my father's home. [28]For I have five brothers, and I want him to warn them so they don't end up in this place of torment.'

[29]"But Abraham said, 'Moses and the prophets have warned them. Your brothers can read what they wrote.'

[30]"The rich man replied, 'No, Father Abraham! But if someone is sent to them from the dead, then they will repent of their sins and turn to God.'

[31]"But Abraham said, 'If they won't listen to Moses and the prophets, they won't listen even if someone rises from the dead.' "

Teachings about Forgiveness and Faith

17 One day Jesus said to his disciples, "There will always be temptations to sin, but what sorrow awaits the person who does the tempting! [2]It would be better to be thrown into the sea with a millstone hung around your neck than to cause one of these little ones to fall into sin. [3]So watch yourselves!

"If another believer* sins, rebuke that person; then if there is repentance, forgive. [4]Even if that person wrongs you seven times a day and each time turns again and asks forgiveness, you must forgive."

[5]The apostles said to the Lord, "Show us how to increase our faith."

[6]The Lord answered, "If you had faith even as small as a mustard seed, you could say to this mulberry tree, 'May you be uprooted and thrown into the sea,' and it would obey you!

[7]"When a servant comes in from plowing or taking care of sheep, does his master say, 'Come in and eat with me'? [8]No, he says, 'Prepare my meal, put on your apron, and serve me while I eat. Then you can eat later.' [9]And does the master thank the servant for doing what he was told to do? Of course not. [10]In the same way, when you obey me you should say, 'We are unworthy servants who have simply done our duty.' "

Ten Healed of Leprosy

[11]As Jesus continued on toward Jerusalem, he reached the border between Galilee and Samaria. [12]As he entered a village there, ten lepers stood at a distance, [13]crying out, "Jesus, Master, have mercy on us!"

[14]He looked at them and said, "Go show

16:22 Greek *into Abraham's bosom.* **16:23** Greek *to Hades.* **17:3** Greek *If your brother.*

---

man might put away his wife for a wide variety of frivolous reasons and remarry at will. The wife, having no such rights, was vulnerable and at his mercy. She might be easily discarded in favor of another woman, with little provision made for her continued survival. Pharisaic debates centered on the causes for which a man might divorce a wife without having to return her dowry, thereby making her situation even more desperate. Jesus declares that if a man divorces his wife and remarries, it is adultery against the wife. This is a memorable statement given that adultery was normally seen as a crime against a man (see Adultery, Exod 20). Also, if a man marries a divorced woman, it is adultery, for both actions perpetuate the widespread and irresponsible practice that destroyed the security and stability of so many women.

16:19–31 Parable of the Rich Man and Lazarus. Lazarus, the impoverished leper, is accorded status as the beloved of Abraham while the rich man finds himself banished and disenfranchised.

17:1–10 Teachings about Forgiveness and Faith. Jesus issues a stern warning against child abuse and the tremendous harm that it creates. He speaks also of forgiveness that is contingent upon a radically altered conduct.

17:11–17 Ten Healed of Leprosy. Only the foreigner demonstrates an attitude of spiritual courtesy.

yourselves to the priests."* And as they went,
they were cleansed of their leprosy.
15 One of them, when he saw that he was
healed, came back to Jesus, shouting, "Praise
God!" 16 He fell to the ground at Jesus' feet,
thanking him for what he had done. This man
was a Samaritan.
17 Jesus asked, "Didn't I heal ten men? Where
are the other nine? 18 Has no one returned to give
glory to God except this foreigner?" 19 And Jesus
said to the man, "Stand up and go. Your faith has
healed you.*"

The Coming of the Kingdom

20 One day the Pharisees asked Jesus, "When will
the Kingdom of God come?"
Jesus replied, "The Kingdom of God can't be
detected by visible signs.* 21 You won't be able to
say, 'Here it is!' or 'It's over there!' For the Kingdom of God is already among you.*"
22 Then he said to his disciples, "The time is
coming when you will long to see the day when
the Son of Man returns,* but you won't see it.
23 People will tell you, 'Look, there is the Son of
Man,' or 'Here he is,' but don't go out and follow
them. 24 For as the lightning flashes and lights up
the sky from one end to the other, so it will be
on the day when the Son of Man comes. 25 But
first the Son of Man must suffer terribly* and be
rejected by this generation.
26 "When the Son of Man returns, it will be
like it was in Noah's day. 27 In those days, the
people enjoyed banquets and parties and weddings right up to the time Noah entered his boat
and the flood came and destroyed them all.
28 "And the world will be as it was in the days
of Lot. People went about their daily business—
eating and drinking, buying and selling, farming and building—29 until the morning Lot left
Sodom. Then fire and burning sulfur rained
down from heaven and destroyed them all. 30 Yes,
it will be 'business as usual' right up to the day
when the Son of Man is revealed. 31 On that day
a person out on the deck of a roof must not go
down into the house to pack. A person out in the
field must not return home. 32 Remember what
happened to Lot's wife! 33 If you cling to your
life, you will lose it, and if you let your life go,
you will save it. 34 That night two people will be
asleep in one bed; one will be taken, the other
left. 35 Two women will be grinding flour together
at the mill; one will be taken, the other left.*"
37 "Where will this happen, Lord?"* the disciples asked.
Jesus replied, "Just as the gathering of vultures shows there is a carcass nearby, so these
signs indicate that the end is near."*

Parable of the Persistent Widow

18 One day Jesus told his disciples a story to show that they should always
pray and never give up. 2 "There was

17:14 See Lev 14:2-32. **17:19** Or *Your faith has saved you.* **17:20** Or *by your speculations.* **17:21** Or *is within you,* or *is in your grasp.* **17:22** Or *long for even one day with the Son of Man.* "Son of Man" is a title Jesus used for himself. **17:25** Or *suffer many things.* **17:35** Some manuscripts add verse 36, *Two men will be working in the field; one will be taken, the other left.* Compare Matt 24:40. **17:37a** Greek *"Where, Lord?"* **17:37b** Greek *"Wherever the carcass is, the vultures gather."*

17:20–37 The Coming of the Kingdom. 32: Lot's wife is an unusual instance in which Jesus employs a figure of a woman as a negative example in recalling the fate of Sodom and Gomorrah (Gen 19:15–28). Although the family had been commanded not to look back, she could not resist a last look at so much that had made her life meaningful. In this she evinced her willingness to cling to her attachment to the corrupt society she had known rather than to the commands of God. Lot's wife is here a symbol of the resistant and unbelieving soul, free to make her own decision but choosing an action that led to her death. Luke's Gospel gives women significance, but there is no idealization. **35:** Jesus shows sensitivity to the disparate work schedules of women and men. On the day of judgment, two men will be still sleeping while two women will be grinding grain, a task usually done early in the morning to prepare flour for the family's daily bread. The stone mill needed to crush the grain was heavy, and so the work was often shared by two women. Each would seize one of the wooden handles that protruded from the upper millstone and rotate it back and forth in rhythm. Believing and unbelieving women share common tasks until the final day when faith will make a clear distinction between them.

18:1–8 Parable of the Persistent Widow. The widow was a focus of particular concern in the Hebrew Scriptures (Exod 22:22–24; Pss 68:5; 146:9; Isa 1:17; Jer 7:6–7). The heroine of Jesus' parable is apparently threatened with dispossession, perhaps in payment of a debt (cf. 2 Kgs 4:1–7). She must seek to represent herself in her claim for what is rightfully hers, and she has pleaded in vain with the local judge, who *neither feared God nor cared about people.* He was a corrupt public official who withheld his power to dispense justice. At last the widow's persistence drives the judge to give her a fair hearing. The woman is rewarded not for her passive acquiescence but

a judge in a certain city," he said, "who neither
feared God nor cared about people. 3 A widow of
that city came to him repeatedly, saying, 'Give
me justice in this dispute with my enemy.' 4 The
judge ignored her for a while, but finally he said
to himself, 'I don't fear God or care about people,
5 but this woman is driving me crazy. I'm going
to see that she gets justice, because she is wearing me out with her constant requests!' "
6 Then the Lord said, "Learn a lesson from
this unjust judge. 7 Even he rendered a just decision in the end. So don't you think God will
surely give justice to his chosen people who cry
out to him day and night? Will he keep putting
them off? 8 I tell you, he will grant justice to
them quickly! But when the Son of Man* returns, how many will he find on the earth who
have faith?"

Parable of the Pharisee and Tax Collector

9 Then Jesus told this story to some who had
great confidence in their own righteousness and
scorned everyone else: 10 "Two men went to the
Temple to pray. One was a Pharisee, and the other
was a despised tax collector. 11 The Pharisee stood
by himself and prayed this prayer*: 'I thank you,
God, that I am not a sinner like everyone else.
For I don't cheat, I don't sin, and I don't commit
adultery. I'm certainly not like that tax collector!
12 I fast twice a week, and I give you a tenth of
my income.'
13 "But the tax collector stood at a distance
and dared not even lift his eyes to heaven as
he prayed. Instead, he beat his chest in sorrow,
saying, 'O God, be merciful to me, for I am a
sinner.' 14 I tell you, this sinner, not the Pharisee, returned home justified before God. For
those who exalt themselves will be humbled,
and those who humble themselves will be exalted."

Jesus Blesses the Children

15 One day some parents brought their little children to Jesus so he could touch and bless them.
But when the disciples saw this, they scolded the
parents for bothering him.
16 Then Jesus called for the children and said to
the disciples, "Let the children come to me. Don't
stop them! For the Kingdom of God belongs to
those who are like these children. 17 I tell you the
truth, anyone who doesn't receive the Kingdom
of God like a child will never enter it."

The Rich Man

18 Once a religious leader asked Jesus this question: "Good Teacher, what should I do to inherit
eternal life?"
19 "Why do you call me good?" Jesus asked
him. "Only God is truly good. 20 But to answer
your question, you know the commandments:
'You must not commit adultery. You must not
murder. You must not steal. You must not testify
falsely. Honor your father and mother.'* "
21 The man replied, "I've obeyed all these commandments since I was young."
22 When Jesus heard his answer, he said,
"There is still one thing you haven't done. Sell
all your possessions and give the money to the
poor, and you will have treasure in heaven. Then
come, follow me."
23 But when the man heard this he became
very sad, for he was very rich.
24 When Jesus saw this,* he said, "How hard
it is for the rich to enter the Kingdom of God!
25 In fact, it is easier for a camel to go through the
eye of a needle than for a rich person to enter the
Kingdom of God!"

18:8 "Son of Man" is a title Jesus used for himself.
18:11 Some manuscripts read *stood and prayed this prayer to himself.* **18:20** Exod 20:12-16; Deut 5:16-20. **18:24** Some manuscripts read *When Jesus saw how sad the man was.*

for her insistence on receiving justice. Her assertiveness is commended. Prayer too requires persistent assertiveness.

18:9–14 Parable of the Pharisee and Tax Collector. The prayer of the smug Pharisee emphasizes the absence of sinful conduct while the tax collector confesses his sin and begs for forgiveness.

18:15–17 Jesus Blesses the Children. The women and the children that they bring have been devalued by the callous reception of the disciples. Understandably the disciples felt that the intrusion of crying infants was disruptive of the orderly conduct of Jesus' mission. They are not only refused access to Jesus but rebuked as well. Running noses, sticky hands, and undergarments in need of change would not make them more attractive. The rebuke that the disciples issued cannot have been directed toward the infants but toward those who brought them. Few things are so painful to a mother as the feeling that she and her brood are unwanted. Jesus, however, insists that the children, as well as their caregivers, be brought to him and that they are of major importance. Despite the hardships and ignominy, mothers play a key role in building this kingdom and in instilling within their children attitudes of faith and receptivity.

18:18–30 The Rich Man. Jesus and his claims must be set ahead of financial and family values.

[26]Those who heard this said, "Then who in the world can be saved?"

[27]He replied, "What is impossible for people is possible with God."

[28]Peter said, "We've left our homes to follow you."

[29]"Yes," Jesus replied, "and I assure you that everyone who has given up house or wife or brothers or parents or children, for the sake of the Kingdom of God, [30]will be repaid many times over in this life, and will have eternal life in the world to come."

Jesus Again Predicts His Death

[31]Taking the twelve disciples aside, Jesus said, "Listen, we're going up to Jerusalem, where all the predictions of the prophets concerning the Son of Man will come true. [32]He will be handed over to the Romans,* and he will be mocked, treated shamefully, and spit upon. [33]They will flog him with a whip and kill him, but on the third day he will rise again."

[34]But they didn't understand any of this. The significance of his words was hidden from them, and they failed to grasp what he was talking about.

Jesus Heals a Blind Beggar

[35]As Jesus approached Jericho, a blind beggar was sitting beside the road. [36]When he heard the noise of a crowd going past, he asked what was happening. [37]They told him that Jesus the Nazarene* was going by. [38]So he began shouting, "Jesus, Son of David, have mercy on me!"

[39]"Be quiet!" the people in front yelled at him.

But he only shouted louder, "Son of David, have mercy on me!"

[40]When Jesus heard him, he stopped and ordered that the man be brought to him. As the man came near, Jesus asked him, [41]"What do you want me to do for you?"

"Lord," he said, "I want to see!"

[42]And Jesus said, "All right, receive your sight! Your faith has healed you." [43]Instantly the man could see, and he followed Jesus, praising God. And all who saw it praised God, too.

Jesus and Zacchaeus

19 Jesus entered Jericho and made his way through the town. [2]There was a man there named Zacchaeus. He was the chief tax collector in the region, and he had become very rich. [3]He tried to get a look at Jesus, but he was too short to see over the crowd. [4]So he ran ahead and climbed a sycamore-fig tree beside the road, for Jesus was going to pass that way.

[5]When Jesus came by, he looked up at Zacchaeus and called him by name. "Zacchaeus!" he said. "Quick, come down! I must be a guest in your home today."

[6]Zacchaeus quickly climbed down and took Jesus to his house in great excitement and joy. [7]But the people were displeased. "He has gone to be the guest of a notorious sinner," they grumbled.

[8]Meanwhile, Zacchaeus stood before the Lord and said, "I will give half my wealth to the poor, Lord, and if I have cheated people on their taxes, I will give them back four times as much!"

[9]Jesus responded, "Salvation has come to this home today, for this man has shown himself to be a true son of Abraham. [10]For the Son of Man* came to seek and save those who are lost."

Parable of the Ten Servants

[11]The crowd was listening to everything Jesus said. And because he was nearing Jerusalem, he told them a story to correct the impression that the Kingdom of God would begin right away. [12]He said, "A nobleman was called away to a distant empire to be crowned king and then return. [13]Before he left, he called together ten of his servants and divided among them ten pounds of silver,* saying, 'Invest this for me while I am gone.' [14]But his people hated him and sent a delegation after him to say, 'We do not want him to be our king.'

[15]"After he was crowned king, he returned and called in the servants to whom he had given the money. He wanted to find out what their

18:32 Greek *the Gentiles.* **18:37** Or *Jesus of Nazareth.*
19:10 "Son of Man" is a title Jesus used for himself.
19:13 Greek *ten minas;* one mina was worth about three months' wages.

18:31–34 Jesus Again Predicts His Death. This third prediction of Jesus' death is again misunderstood by the male disciples but will be comprehended by the women (24:8).

18:35–43 Jesus Heals a Blind Beggar. Again assertiveness is rewarded.

19:1–10 Jesus and Zacchaeus. Jesus enters the despised home of the chief tax gatherer and by this association demonstrates the essential purpose of his mission.

19:11–27 Parable of the Ten Servants. This parable speaks to women who far too frequently bury their God-given talents that ought properly to be developed.

profits were. 16 The first servant reported, 'Master, I invested your money and made ten times
the original amount!'
17 " 'Well done!' the king exclaimed. 'You are
a good servant. You have been faithful with the
little I entrusted to you, so you will be governor
of ten cities as your reward.'
18 "The next servant reported, 'Master, I invested your money and made five times the
original amount.'
19 " 'Well done!' the king said. 'You will be
governor over five cities.'
20 "But the third servant brought back only the
original amount of money and said, 'Master, I hid
your money and kept it safe. 21 I was afraid because
you are a hard man to deal with, taking what isn't
yours and harvesting crops you didn't plant.'
22 " 'You wicked servant!' the king roared.
'Your own words condemn you. If you knew that
I'm a hard man who takes what isn't mine and
harvests crops I didn't plant, 23 why didn't you
deposit my money in the bank? At least I could
have gotten some interest on it.'
24 "Then, turning to the others standing
nearby, the king ordered, 'Take the money from
this servant, and give it to the one who has ten
pounds.'
25 " 'But, master,' they said, 'he already has
ten pounds!'
26 " 'Yes,' the king replied, 'and to those who
use well what they are given, even more will
be given. But from those who do nothing, even
what little they have will be taken away. 27 And as
for these enemies of mine who didn't want me to
be their king—bring them in and execute them
right here in front of me.' "

Jesus' Triumphant Entry

28 After telling this story, Jesus went on toward
Jerusalem, walking ahead of his disciples. 29 As he
came to the towns of Bethphage and Bethany on
the Mount of Olives, he sent two disciples ahead.
30 "Go into that village over there," he told them.
"As you enter it, you will see a young donkey
tied there that no one has ever ridden. Untie it
and bring it here. 31 If anyone asks, 'Why are you
untying that colt?' just say, 'The Lord needs it.' "
32 So they went and found the colt, just as
Jesus had said. 33 And sure enough, as they were
untying it, the owners asked them, "Why are
you untying that colt?"
34 And the disciples simply replied, "The Lord
needs it." 35 So they brought the colt to Jesus and
threw their garments over it for him to ride on.
36 As he rode along, the crowds spread out
their garments on the road ahead of him. 37 When
he reached the place where the road started down
the Mount of Olives, all of his followers began
to shout and sing as they walked along, praising God for all the wonderful miracles they had
seen.

38 "Blessings on the King who comes in the
name of the LORD!
Peace in heaven, and glory in highest
heaven!"*

39 But some of the Pharisees among the crowd
said, "Teacher, rebuke your followers for saying
things like that!"
40 He replied, "If they kept quiet, the stones
along the road would burst into cheers!"

Jesus Weeps over Jerusalem

41 But as he came closer to Jerusalem and saw the
city ahead, he began to weep. 42 "How I wish today that you of all people would understand the
way to peace. But now it is too late, and peace is
hidden from your eyes. 43 Before long your enemies will build ramparts against your walls and
encircle you and close in on you from every side.
44 They will crush you into the ground, and your
children with you. Your enemies will not leave a
single stone in place, because you did not accept
your opportunity for salvation."

Jesus Clears the Temple

45 Then Jesus entered the Temple and began to
drive out the people selling animals for sacrifices.
46 He said to them, "The Scriptures declare, 'My
Temple will be a house of prayer,' but you have
turned it into a den of thieves."*

19:38 Pss 118:26; 148:1. **19:46** Isa 56:7; Jer 7:11.

19:28—22:46 Mounting Tensions in Jerusalem

19:28–40 Jesus' Triumphant Entry. The celebratory use of the Messianic psalms (Pss 118:26; 148:1) becomes the final outrage to the Pharisees.

19:41–44 Jesus Weeps over Jerusalem. The mourning over Jerusalem continues (cf. 13:31–35). Roman military might will overwhelm a city that has lost its spiritual vitality.

19:45–48 Jesus Clears the Temple. Jeremiah (Jer 7:11) had uttered a reproach to those who had robbed the first Temple of its spiritual significance. Jesus not only drove out the commercial interests but filled the rebuilt Temple with his own teaching and presence.

47 After that, he taught daily in the Temple,
but the leading priests, the teachers of religious
law, and the other leaders of the people began
planning how to kill him. 48 But they could think
of nothing, because all the people hung on every
word he said.

The Authority of Jesus Challenged

20 One day as Jesus was teaching the
people and preaching the Good News
in the Temple, the leading priests, the
teachers of religious law, and the elders came up
to him. 2 They demanded, "By what authority are
you doing all these things? Who gave you the
right?"
3 "Let me ask you a question first," he replied.
4 "Did John's authority to baptize come from
heaven, or was it merely human?"
5 They talked it over among themselves. "If
we say it was from heaven, he will ask why we
didn't believe John. 6 But if we say it was merely
human, the people will stone us because they are
convinced John was a prophet." 7 So they finally
replied that they didn't know.
8 And Jesus responded, "Then I won't tell you
by what authority I do these things."

Parable of the Evil Farmers

9 Now Jesus turned to the people again and told
them this story: "A man planted a vineyard, leased
it to tenant farmers, and moved to another country to live for several years. 10 At the time of the
grape harvest, he sent one of his servants to collect
his share of the crop. But the farmers attacked the
servant, beat him up, and sent him back empty-
handed. 11 So the owner sent another servant, but
they also insulted him, beat him up, and sent him
away empty-handed. 12 A third man was sent, and
they wounded him and chased him away.
13 " 'What will I do?' the owner asked himself.
'I know! I'll send my cherished son. Surely they
will respect him.'
14 "But when the tenant farmers saw his son,
they said to each other, 'Here comes the heir to
this estate. Let's kill him and get the estate for
ourselves!' 15 So they dragged him out of the
vineyard and murdered him.
"What do you suppose the owner of the vineyard will do to them?" Jesus asked. 16 "I'll tell
you—he will come and kill those farmers and
lease the vineyard to others."
"How terrible that such a thing should ever
happen," his listeners protested.
17 Jesus looked at them and said, "Then what
does this Scripture mean?

> 'The stone that the builders rejected
> has now become the cornerstone.'*

18 Everyone who stumbles over that stone will be
broken to pieces, and it will crush anyone it falls
on."
19 The teachers of religious law and the leading priests wanted to arrest Jesus immediately
because they realized he was telling the story
against them—they were the wicked farmers.
But they were afraid of the people's reaction.

Taxes for Caesar

20 Watching for their opportunity, the leaders sent
spies pretending to be honest men. They tried to
get Jesus to say something that could be reported
to the Roman governor so he would arrest Jesus.
21 "Teacher," they said, "we know that you speak
and teach what is right and are not influenced
by what others think. You teach the way of God
truthfully. 22 Now tell us—is it right for us to pay
taxes to Caesar or not?"
23 He saw through their trickery and said,
24 "Show me a Roman coin.* Whose picture and
title are stamped on it?"
"Caesar's," they replied.
25 "Well then," he said, "give to Caesar what
belongs to Caesar, and give to God what belongs
to God."
26 So they failed to trap him by what he said in
front of the people. Instead, they were amazed by
his answer, and they became silent.

Discussion about Resurrection

27 Then Jesus was approached by some Sadducees—religious leaders who say there is no resurrection from the dead. 28 They posed this question: "Teacher, Moses gave us a law that if a man

20:17 Ps 118:22. **20:24** Greek *a denarius.*

20:1–8 The Authority of Jesus Challenged. Jesus presents the religious establishment with yet another conundrum that they dare not solve.

20:9–19 Parable of the Evil Farmers. Jesus' enraged opponents understand the implications far better than do his followers.

20:20–26 Taxes for Caesar. Roman coins typically used portraiture for propagandistic purposes.

20:27–40 Discussion about Resurrection. The Sadducees have contrived a hypothetical case in which, according to the law of levirate marriage, a succession of brothers wed the widow of their deceased

dies, leaving a wife but no children, his brother should marry the widow and have a child who will carry on the brother's name.* [29]Well, suppose there were seven brothers. The oldest one married and then died without children. [30]So the second brother married the widow, but he also died. [31]Then the third brother married her. This continued with all seven of them, who died without children. [32]Finally, the woman also died. [33]So tell us, whose wife will she be in the resurrection? For all seven were married to her!"

[34]Jesus replied, "Marriage is for people here on earth. [35]But in the age to come, those worthy of being raised from the dead will neither marry nor be given in marriage. [36]And they will never die again. In this respect they will be like angels. They are children of God and children of the resurrection.

[37]"But now, as to whether the dead will be raised—even Moses proved this when he wrote about the burning bush. Long after Abraham, Isaac, and Jacob had died, he referred to the Lord* as 'the God of Abraham, the God of Isaac, and the God of Jacob.'* [38]So he is the God of the living, not the dead, for they are all alive to him."

[39]"Well said, Teacher!" remarked some of the teachers of religious law who were standing there. [40]And then no one dared to ask him any more questions.

Whose Son Is the Messiah?

[41]Then Jesus presented them with a question. "Why is it," he asked, "that the Messiah is said to be the son of David? [42]For David himself wrote in the book of Psalms:

'The LORD said to my Lord,
Sit in the place of honor at my right hand
[43] until I humble your enemies,
making them a footstool under your feet.'*

[44]Since David called the Messiah 'Lord,' how can the Messiah be his son?"

[45]Then, with the crowds listening, he turned to his disciples and said, [46]"Beware of these teachers of religious law! For they like to parade around in flowing robes and love to receive respectful greetings as they walk in the marketplaces. And how they love the seats of honor in the synagogues and the head table at banquets. [47]Yet they shamelessly cheat widows out of their property and then pretend to be pious by making long prayers in public. Because of this, they will be severely punished."

The Widow's Offering

21 While Jesus was in the Temple, he watched the rich people dropping their gifts in the collection box. [2]Then a poor widow came by and dropped in two small coins.*

[3]"I tell you the truth," Jesus said, "this poor widow has given more than all the rest of them. [4]For they have given a tiny part of their surplus, but she, poor as she is, has given everything she has."

Jesus Foretells the Future

[5]Some of his disciples began talking about the majestic stonework of the Temple and the memorial decorations on the walls. But Jesus said, [6]"The time is coming when all these things will be completely demolished. Not one stone will be left on top of another!"

[7]"Teacher," they asked, "when will all this happen? What sign will show us that these things are about to take place?"

[8]He replied, "Don't let anyone mislead you, for many will come in my name, claiming, 'I am the Messiah,'* and saying, 'The time has come!'

20:28 See Deut 25:5-6. **20:37a** Greek *when he wrote about the bush. He referred to the Lord.* **20:37b** Exod 3:6. **20:42-43** Ps 110:1. **21:2** Greek *two lepta* [the smallest of Jewish coins]. **21:8** Greek *claiming, 'I am.'*

---

brother (Deut 25:5; see Marriage, Song 2). Essentially the Sadducees view the woman as the property of her husband, with no autonomy. Jesus, however, perceives women as full persons here and hereafter, by no means the possession of another. He replies that the new relationships in heaven will no longer emphasize physical sexuality, marriage, or death. The spiritual bonding to God supersedes bonding in the flesh (cf. John 3:6).

20:41–47 Whose Son Is the Messiah? The theme of Jesus' concern for widows is a recurring one. He scathingly denounces their exploitation at the hands of the scribes.

21:1–4 The Widow's Offering. The gift is far beyond the widow's means. It is given not to gain recognition but to maintain the Temple and its services for all who desire to worship God. Again Jesus singles out a disadvantaged woman as a spiritual and practical model. She stands in direct contrast to the affluent who give only after their needs and gratification have been met.

21:4–38 Jesus Foretells the Future. The coming devastation will fall very heavily on *pregnant women and nursing mothers* (v. 23).

But don't believe them. 9 And when you hear of wars and insurrections, don't panic. Yes, these things must take place first, but the end won't follow immediately." 10 Then he added, "Nation will go to war against nation, and kingdom against kingdom. 11 There will be great earthquakes, and there will be famines and plagues in many lands, and there will be terrifying things and great miraculous signs from heaven.

12 "But before all this occurs, there will be a time of great persecution. You will be dragged into synagogues and prisons, and you will stand trial before kings and governors because you are my followers. 13 But this will be your opportunity to tell them about me.* 14 So don't worry in advance about how to answer the charges against you, 15 for I will give you the right words and such wisdom that none of your opponents will be able to reply or refute you! 16 Even those closest to you—your parents, brothers, relatives, and friends—will betray you. They will even kill some of you. 17 And everyone will hate you because you are my followers.* 18 But not a hair of your head will perish! 19 By standing firm, you will win your souls.

20 "And when you see Jerusalem surrounded by armies, then you will know that the time of its destruction has arrived. 21 Then those in Judea must flee to the hills. Those in Jerusalem must get out, and those out in the country should not return to the city. 22 For those will be days of God's vengeance, and the prophetic words of the Scriptures will be fulfilled. 23 How terrible it will be for pregnant women and for nursing mothers in those days. For there will be disaster in the land and great anger against this people. 24 They will be killed by the sword or sent away as captives to all the nations of the world. And Jerusalem will be trampled down by the Gentiles until the period of the Gentiles comes to an end.

25 "And there will be strange signs in the sun, moon, and stars. And here on earth the nations will be in turmoil, perplexed by the roaring seas and strange tides. 26 People will be terrified at what they see coming upon the earth, for the powers in the heavens will be shaken. 27 Then everyone will see the Son of Man* coming on a cloud with power and great glory.* 28 So when all these things begin to happen, stand and look up, for your salvation is near!"

29 Then he gave them this illustration: "Notice the fig tree, or any other tree. 30 When the leaves come out, you know without being told that summer is near. 31 In the same way, when you see all these things taking place, you can know that the Kingdom of God is near. 32 I tell you the truth, this generation will not pass from the scene until all these things have taken place. 33 Heaven and earth will disappear, but my words will never disappear.

34 "Watch out! Don't let your hearts be dulled by carousing and drunkenness, and by the worries of this life. Don't let that day catch you unaware, 35 like a trap. For that day will come upon everyone living on the earth. 36 Keep alert at all times. And pray that you might be strong enough to escape these coming horrors and stand before the Son of Man."

37 Every day Jesus went to the Temple to teach, and each evening he returned to spend the night on the Mount of Olives. 38 The crowds gathered at the Temple early each morning to hear him.

Judas Agrees to Betray Jesus

22 The Festival of Unleavened Bread, which is also called Passover, was approaching. 2 The leading priests and teachers of religious law were plotting how to kill Jesus, but they were afraid of the people's reaction.

3 Then Satan entered into Judas Iscariot, who was one of the twelve disciples, 4 and he went to the leading priests and captains of the Temple guard to discuss the best way to betray Jesus to them. 5 They were delighted, and they promised to give him money. 6 So he agreed and began looking for an opportunity to betray Jesus so they could arrest him when the crowds weren't around.

The Last Supper

7 Now the Festival of Unleavened Bread arrived, when the Passover lamb is sacrificed. 8 Jesus sent Peter and John ahead and said, "Go and prepare the Passover meal, so we can eat it together."

9 "Where do you want us to prepare it?" they asked him.

10 He replied, "As soon as you enter Jerusalem, a man carrying a pitcher of water will meet you. Follow him. At the house he enters, 11 say to the owner, 'The Teacher asks: Where is the guest room where I can eat the Passover meal with my disciples?' 12 He will take you upstairs to a large room that is already set up. That is

21:13 Or *This will be your testimony against them.*
21:17 Greek *on account of my name.* **21:27a** "Son of Man" is a title Jesus used for himself. **21:27b** See Dan 7:13.

22:1–6 Judas Agrees to Betray Jesus. The Temple guard is involved in the negotiation with Judas, and it is they who will actually make the arrest.

where you should prepare our meal." 13 They
went off to the city and found everything just
as Jesus had said, and they prepared the Passover meal there.
14 When the time came, Jesus and the apostles
sat down together at the table.* 15 Jesus said, "I
have been very eager to eat this Passover meal
with you before my suffering begins. 16 For I tell
you now that I won't eat this meal again until its
meaning is fulfilled in the Kingdom of God."
17 Then he took a cup of wine and gave thanks
to God for it. Then he said, "Take this and share
it among yourselves. 18 For I will not drink wine
again until the Kingdom of God has come."
19 He took some bread and gave thanks to God
for it. Then he broke it in pieces and gave it to
the disciples, saying, "This is my body, which is
given for you. Do this to remember me."
20 After supper he took another cup of wine and
said, "This cup is the new covenant between God
and his people—an agreement confirmed with my
blood, which is poured out as a sacrifice for you.*
21 "But here at this table, sitting among us as
a friend, is the man who will betray me. 22 For it
has been determined that the Son of Man* must
die. But what sorrow awaits the one who betrays
him." 23 The disciples began to ask each other
which of them would ever do such a thing.
24 Then they began to argue among themselves about who would be the greatest among
them. 25 Jesus told them, "In this world the kings
and great men lord it over their people, yet they
are called 'friends of the people.' 26 But among
you it will be different. Those who are the greatest among you should take the lowest rank,
and the leader should be like a servant. 27 Who
is more important, the one who sits at the table
or the one who serves? The one who sits at the
table, of course. But not here! For I am among
you as one who serves.
28 "You have stayed with me in my time of trial. 29 And just as my Father has granted me a Kingdom, I now grant you the right 30 to eat and drink
at my table in my Kingdom. And you will sit on
thrones, judging the twelve tribes of Israel.

Jesus Predicts Peter's Denial
31 "Simon, Simon, Satan has asked to sift each of
you like wheat. 32 But I have pleaded in prayer for
you, Simon, that your faith should not fail. So
when you have repented and turned to me again,
strengthen your brothers."
33 Peter said, "Lord, I am ready to go to prison
with you, and even to die with you."
34 But Jesus said, "Peter, let me tell you something. Before the rooster crows tomorrow morning, you will deny three times that you even
know me."
35 Then Jesus asked them, "When I sent you
out to preach the Good News and you did not
have money, a traveler's bag, or an extra pair of
sandals, did you need anything?"
"No," they replied.
36 "But now," he said, "take your money and a
traveler's bag. And if you don't have a sword, sell
your cloak and buy one! 37 For the time has come
for this prophecy about me to be fulfilled: 'He was
counted among the rebels.'* Yes, everything written about me by the prophets will come true."
38 "Look, Lord," they replied, "we have two
swords among us."
"That's enough," he said.

Jesus Prays on the Mount of Olives
39 Then, accompanied by the disciples, Jesus
left the upstairs room and went as usual to the
Mount of Olives. 40 There he told them, "Pray
that you will not give in to temptation."
41 He walked away, about a stone's throw, and
knelt down and prayed, 42 "Father, if you are willing, please take this cup of suffering away from
me. Yet I want your will to be done, not mine."
43 Then an angel from heaven appeared and
strengthened him. 44 He prayed more fervently,
and he was in such agony of spirit that his sweat
fell to the ground like great drops of blood.*

22:14 Or *reclined together.* **22:19-20** Some manuscripts do not include 22:19b-20, *which is given for you . . . which is poured out as a sacrifice for you.* **22:22** "Son of Man" is a title Jesus used for himself. **22:37** Isa 53:12. **22:43-44** Verses 43 and 44 are not included in many ancient manuscripts.

22:7–30 The Last Supper. 24–27: Even at the Last Supper the disciples are not immune from petty wrangling. Earlier they had argued over who held the foremost position among Christ's followers. As they anticipated the beginning of the kingdom, the potential for power began to pull them toward self-aggrandizement. Jesus' remark about kings of *this world* reveals that their thinking had taken a political turn. Jesus declares such manipulation of power and privilege to be antithetical to the values of the kingdom and to those who are truly great in God's eyes.

22:31–38 Jesus Predicts Peter's Denial. Jesus goes out anticipating the denial of Peter but buoyed by the claims of the prophets.

22:39–46 Jesus Prays on the Mount of Olives. The loneliness of Jesus and the lack of support from his friends has begun.

45 At last he stood up again and returned to
the disciples, only to find them asleep, exhausted
from grief. 46 "Why are you sleeping?" he asked
them. "Get up and pray, so that you will not give
in to temptation."

Jesus Is Betrayed and Arrested

47 But even as Jesus said this, a crowd approached,
led by Judas, one of the twelve disciples. Judas
walked over to Jesus to greet him with a kiss.
48 But Jesus said, "Judas, would you betray the
Son of Man with a kiss?"
49 When the other disciples saw what was
about to happen, they exclaimed, "Lord, should
we fight? We brought the swords!" 50 And one
of them struck at the high priest's slave, slashing
off his right ear.
51 But Jesus said, "No more of this." And he
touched the man's ear and healed him.
52 Then Jesus spoke to the leading priests, the
captains of the Temple guard, and the elders who
had come for him. "Am I some dangerous revolutionary," he asked, "that you come with swords
and clubs to arrest me? 53 Why didn't you arrest
me in the Temple? I was there every day. But
this is your moment, the time when the power
of darkness reigns."

Peter Denies Jesus

54 So they arrested him and led him to the high
priest's home. And Peter followed at a distance.
55 The guards lit a fire in the middle of the courtyard and sat around it, and Peter joined them
there. 56 A servant girl noticed him in the firelight
and began staring at him. Finally she said, "This
man was one of Jesus' followers!"
57 But Peter denied it. "Woman," he said, "I
don't even know him!"
58 After a while someone else looked at him
and said, "You must be one of them!"
"No, man, I'm not!" Peter retorted.
59 About an hour later someone else insisted,
"This must be one of them, because he is a Galilean, too."
60 But Peter said, "Man, I don't know what
you are talking about." And immediately, while
he was still speaking, the rooster crowed.
61 At that moment the Lord turned and looked
at Peter. Suddenly, the Lord's words flashed
through Peter's mind: "Before the rooster crows
tomorrow morning, you will deny three times
that you even know me." 62 And Peter left the
courtyard, weeping bitterly.
63 The guards in charge of Jesus began mocking
and beating him. 64 They blindfolded him and said,
"Prophesy to us! Who hit you that time?" 65 And
they hurled all sorts of terrible insults at him.

Jesus before the Council

66 At daybreak all the elders of the people assembled, including the leading priests and the teachers of religious law. Jesus was led before this high
council,* 67 and they said, "Tell us, are you the
Messiah?"
But he replied, "If I tell you, you won't believe me. 68 And if I ask you a question, you won't
answer. 69 But from now on the Son of Man will
be seated in the place of power at God's right
hand.*"
70 They all shouted, "So, are you claiming to
be the Son of God?"
And he replied, "You say that I am."
71 "Why do we need other witnesses?" they
said. "We ourselves heard him say it."

Jesus' Trial before Pilate

23 Then the entire council took Jesus to
Pilate, the Roman governor. 2 They
began to state their case: "This man
has been leading our people astray by telling

22:66 Greek *before their Sanhedrin*. **22:69** See Ps 110:1.

22:47–23:56 Trial, Arrest, and Execution

22:47–53 Jesus Is Betrayed and Arrested. Judas betrays with a kiss while Jesus heals with a touch.

22:54–63 Peter Denies Jesus. 56–57: The slave girl is one of the few female figures in Luke's Gospel who does not have a sympathetic attitude toward Jesus and his mission. She made up one of the large number of slaves owned by the priestly establishment. Perhaps wishing to demonstrate her importance as a clever informer in the high priest's service, she challenges Peter, who had hoped to escape notice in the midst of a crowd of bystanders. The quick-witted girl is the first one, after personal association has become so dangerous, to call Peter to an honest confession of his relationship to Jesus.

22:66–71 Jesus before the Council. Previously religious leaders had come out to observe his ministry, but now he stands in their midst at a hastily summoned meeting of the council.

23:1–25 Jesus' Trial before Pilate. Pilate understands perfectly well how to conduct a proper Roman interrogation and also how to use the event for his own political purposes.

them not to pay their taxes to the Roman government and by claiming he is the Messiah, a
king."
3 So Pilate asked him, "Are you the king of the
Jews?"
Jesus replied, "You have said it."
4 Pilate turned to the leading priests and to the
crowd and said, "I find nothing wrong with this
man!"
5 Then they became insistent. "But he is causing riots by his teaching wherever he goes—all
over Judea, from Galilee to Jerusalem!"
6 "Oh, is he a Galilean?" Pilate asked. 7 When
they said that he was, Pilate sent him to Herod
Antipas, because Galilee was under Herod's jurisdiction, and Herod happened to be in Jerusalem at the time.
8 Herod was delighted at the opportunity to
see Jesus, because he had heard about him and
had been hoping for a long time to see him perform a miracle. 9 He asked Jesus question after
question, but Jesus refused to answer. 10 Meanwhile, the leading priests and the teachers of
religious law stood there shouting their accusations. 11 Then Herod and his soldiers began mocking and ridiculing Jesus. Finally, they put a royal
robe on him and sent him back to Pilate. 12 (Herod
and Pilate, who had been enemies before, became
friends that day.)
13 Then Pilate called together the leading
priests and other religious leaders, along with
the people, 14 and he announced his verdict. "You
brought this man to me, accusing him of leading a revolt. I have examined him thoroughly on
this point in your presence and find him innocent. 15 Herod came to the same conclusion and
sent him back to us. Nothing this man has done
calls for the death penalty. 16 So I will have him
flogged, and then I will release him."*
18 Then a mighty roar rose from the crowd,
and with one voice they shouted, "Kill him,
and release Barabbas to us!" 19 (Barabbas was in
prison for taking part in an insurrection in Jerusalem against the government, and for murder.)
20 Pilate argued with them, because he wanted to
release Jesus. 21 But they kept shouting, "Crucify
him! Crucify him!"
22 For the third time he demanded, "Why?
What crime has he committed? I have found no
reason to sentence him to death. So I will have
him flogged, and then I will release him."
23 But the mob shouted louder and louder, demanding that Jesus be crucified, and their voices
prevailed. 24 So Pilate sentenced Jesus to die as
they demanded. 25 As they had requested, he
released Barabbas, the man in prison for insurrection and murder. But he turned Jesus over to
them to do as they wished.

The Crucifixion

26 As they led Jesus away, a man named Simon,
who was from Cyrene,* happened to be coming
in from the countryside. The soldiers seized him
and put the cross on him and made him carry it
behind Jesus. 27 A large crowd trailed behind, including many grief-stricken women. 28 But Jesus
turned and said to them, "Daughters of Jerusalem, don't weep for me, but weep for yourselves

23:16 Some manuscripts add verse 17, *Now it was necessary for him to release one prisoner to them during the Passover celebration.* Compare Matt 27:15; Mark 15:6; John 18:39.
23:26 *Cyrene* was a city in northern Africa.

23:26–43 The Crucifixion. 26–31: On the way to the cross a large crowd of people followed Jesus, including many women who mourned and lamented him. In the joyful Palm Sunday entry into Jerusalem, the children were prominent, but on Good Friday it is their mothers who line the way. They are determined to give Jesus the proper observances due him at his death. Roman law forbade women to prepare the body of an executed criminal for burial. If they will be denied access later, they will give Jesus his fitting funereal mourning as he walks past. The observance of rites of passage was usually entrusted to the hands of women. Women were the ones who washed the body for burial and wrapped it in grave clothes. It was they who raised their voices in lament as professional mourners and as those deeply devoted to the deceased. A funeral was not complete without the hands and voices of women. The spontaneously composed dirge was a form of literary expression in which women excelled. It is to this lament over his fate that Jesus responded. Jesus responds, not as to devout women bewailing his execution but as to *daughters of Jerusalem* who must soon face their impending fate. Already severely beaten and humiliated, he turns his attention to those who are even more marginalized than he. In his crisis, the disenfranchised, dehumanized, and disempowered Son of Man expresses his solidarity and sympathy with those who have come to mourn him. Luke makes Jesus a fellow sufferer with the women, willing to have them weep for themselves rather than for him. He too was deprived of justice even though the Roman governor declared him to be innocent of all the charges brought against him. It was precisely Jesus' sufferings that made this a supreme opportunity to address himself so clearly to the abuse of women and children. Surely this concern must be understood as encompassing a universal concern for violence

and for your children. 29 For the days are coming when they will say, 'Fortunate indeed are the
women who are childless, the wombs that have
not borne a child and the breasts that have never nursed.' 30 People will beg the mountains, 'Fall
on us,' and plead with the hills, 'Bury us.'* 31 For
if these things are done when the tree is green,
what will happen when it is dry?*"
32 Two others, both criminals, were led out to
be executed with him. 33 When they came to a
place called The Skull,* they nailed him to the
cross. And the criminals were also crucified—one
on his right and one on his left.
34 Jesus said, "Father, forgive them, for they
don't know what they are doing."* And the soldiers gambled for his clothes by throwing dice.*
35 The crowd watched and the leaders scoffed.
"He saved others," they said, "let him save himself if he is really God's Messiah, the Chosen
One." 36 The soldiers mocked him, too, by offering him a drink of sour wine. 37 They called out
to him, "If you are the King of the Jews, save
yourself!" 38 A sign was fastened above him with
these words: "This is the King of the Jews."
39 One of the criminals hanging beside him
scoffed, "So you're the Messiah, are you? Prove
it by saving yourself—and us, too, while you're
at it!"
40 But the other criminal protested, "Don't you
fear God even when you have been sentenced to
die? 41 We deserve to die for our crimes, but this
man hasn't done anything wrong." 42 Then he
said, "Jesus, remember me when you come into
your Kingdom."
43 And Jesus replied, "I assure you, today you
will be with me in paradise."

The Death of Jesus

44 By this time it was about noon, and darkness
fell across the whole land until three o'clock.
45 The light from the sun was gone. And suddenly, the curtain in the sanctuary of the Temple
was torn down the middle. 46 Then Jesus shouted,
"Father, I entrust my spirit into your hands!"*
And with those words he breathed his last.
47 When the Roman officer* overseeing the
execution saw what had happened, he worshiped
God and said, "Surely this man was innocent.*"
48 And when all the crowd that came to see the
crucifixion saw what had happened, they went
home in deep sorrow.* 49 But Jesus' friends, including the women who had followed him from
Galilee, stood at a distance watching.

The Burial of Jesus

50 Now there was a good and righteous man
named Joseph. He was a member of the Jewish
high council, 51 but he had not agreed with the
decision and actions of the other religious leaders. He was from the town of Arimathea in Judea,
and he was waiting for the Kingdom of God to
come. 52 He went to Pilate and asked for Jesus'
body. 53 Then he took the body down from the
cross and wrapped it in a long sheet of linen cloth
and laid it in a new tomb that had been carved
out of rock. 54 This was done late on Friday afternoon, the day of preparation,* as the Sabbath
was about to begin.
55 As his body was taken away, the women
from Galilee followed and saw the tomb where
his body was placed. 56 Then they went home and
prepared spices and ointments to anoint his body.
But by the time they were finished the Sabbath
had begun, so they rested as required by the law.

23:30 Hos 10:8. **23:31** Or *If these things are done to me, the living tree, what will happen to you, the dry tree?* **23:33** Sometimes rendered *Calvary,* which comes from the Latin word for "skull." **23:34a** This sentence is not included in many ancient manuscripts. **23:34b** Greek *by casting lots.* See Ps 22:18. **23:46** Ps 31:5. **23:47a** Greek *the centurion.* **23:47b** Or *righteous.* **23:48** Greek *went home beating their breasts.* **23:54** Greek *It was the day of preparation.*

---

against women and children, wherever and whenever it occurs (see Violence, Abuse, and Oppression, Eccl 4).

23:44–49 The Death of Jesus. Those who remain at the cross are identified as the *friends* of Jesus. They stand afar, unwilling witnesses of earth's greatest tragedy. The readily identified male disciples are no longer visible. Their place is taken by equally dedicated followers, the women who have accompanied Jesus from Galilee. We recognize in them the women followers of 8:2–3. The author does not name the women in this account as do the Gospels of Matthew (Matt 27:55–56) and Mark (Mark 15:40, 47). Luke will again give their names in his narrative of the resurrection. They will prove to be the major witnesses of the resurrection.

23:50–56 The Burial of Jesus. Although they are not allowed to assist in the removal of Jesus' body, the women *follow* along as Joseph of Arimathea and Nicodemus transport the corpse to its grave. Luke adds a point that will be an important corroborative witness to his story: They carefully observed the location of the tomb and *where his body was placed*. Their witness will be critical in the establishment of the facts concerning the raising of Christ from the dead.

The Resurrection

24 But very early on Sunday morning*
the women went to the tomb, taking
the spices they had prepared. 2They
found that the stone had been rolled away from
the entrance. 3So they went in, but they didn't
find the body of the Lord Jesus. 4As they stood
there puzzled, two men suddenly appeared to
them, clothed in dazzling robes.
5The women were terrified and bowed with
their faces to the ground. Then the men asked,
"Why are you looking among the dead for someone who is alive? 6He isn't here! He is risen from
the dead! Remember what he told you back in
Galilee, 7that the Son of Man* must be betrayed
into the hands of sinful men and be crucified, and
that he would rise again on the third day."
8Then they remembered that he had said this.
9So they rushed back from the tomb to tell his
eleven disciples—and everyone else—what had
happened. 10It was Mary Magdalene, Joanna,
Mary the mother of James, and several other
women who told the apostles what had happened. 11But the story sounded like nonsense
to the men, so they didn't believe it. 12However,
Peter jumped up and ran to the tomb to look.
Stooping, he peered in and saw the empty linen
wrappings; then he went home again, wondering
what had happened.

The Walk to Emmaus

13That same day two of Jesus' followers were
walking to the village of Emmaus, seven miles*
from Jerusalem. 14As they walked along they were
talking about everything that had happened. 15As
they talked and discussed these things, Jesus himself suddenly came and began walking with them.
16But God kept them from recognizing him.
17He asked them, "What are you discussing
so intently as you walk along?"
They stopped short, sadness written across
their faces. 18Then one of them, Cleopas, replied,
"You must be the only person in Jerusalem who
hasn't heard about all the things that have happened there the last few days."
19"What things?" Jesus asked.
"The things that happened to Jesus, the man
from Nazareth," they said. "He was a prophet
who did powerful miracles, and he was a mighty
teacher in the eyes of God and all the people.
20But our leading priests and other religious

24:1 Greek *But on the first day of the week, very early in the morning.* **24:7** "Son of Man" is a title Jesus used for himself. **24:13** Greek *60 stadia* [11.1 kilometers].

24:1–53 The Disciples' Recognition of the Risen Jesus

24:1–12 The Resurrection. Before sundown on the day of preparation, the women purchase spices that they will bring to the tomb at the dawning of the first day of the week.The women are obedient to the Jewish laws of the Sabbath but are willing to brave the Roman guard and the prohibition against women officiating at the burial of an executed criminal. They are also willing to take on the challenge of rolling back an exceedingly heavy stone that had been placed at the mouth of the tomb. The account becomes a succession of electrifying images impressed on the memories of the startled women. The records of the four resurrection accounts are not entirely congruent, a phenomenon that often occurs after a highly emotional, confusing, and terrifying event. There is agreement on the main points, and each individual recollection contributes to a wider picture than any of the narratives reflect. All of the accounts insist that women were the first witnesses of the risen Christ, and all contain the instruction that they were to proclaim the news to the male disciples. **24:7–8:** The angel reminds the women that Jesus has prepared them to be the witnesses of the resurrection. While they were still in Galilee, he had taught them of the necessity of his death and rising again on the third day. Then it was that the women remembered. Like the male disciples, they had apparently found Jesus' prophecies of his death too painful, and they had put them from their minds (cf. 9:21–22, 44–45; 18:31–34). Now, comprehending what it was that he had foretold, they hurry off to make their joyful announcement to the Eleven and to those gathered with them.

24:13–34 The Walk to Emmaus. This Cleopas may be the same person as Clopas whose wife observed the crucifixion (John 19:25). As he relates the report of the women and the corroboration of their story by the men who later visited the empty tomb, his skepticism shows through. At this point the stranger bursts in with a rebuke for the failure to accept the word of the women. Their testimony reveals the fulfillment of all that the prophets have foretold of God's design for human redemption through the death and resurrection of the Messiah. Jesus, the unidentified stranger, launches into a confirmation of the women's report by an exposition of the Scriptures concerning himself. The issue is one of God's promises, conveyed first by the ancient prophets and then by the terrified but faithful women. When the qualifications for an apostle are listed, it is clear that Jesus' women disciples possess the necessary qualifications (Acts 1:21–22).

leaders handed him over to be condemned to
death, and they crucified him. 21 We had hoped he
was the Messiah who had come to rescue Israel.
This all happened three days ago.
22 "Then some women from our group of his
followers were at his tomb early this morning,
and they came back with an amazing report.
23 They said his body was missing, and they had
seen angels who told them Jesus is alive! 24 Some
of our men ran out to see, and sure enough, his
body was gone, just as the women had said."
25 Then Jesus said to them, "You foolish people! You find it so hard to believe all that the
prophets wrote in the Scriptures. 26 Wasn't it
clearly predicted that the Messiah would have to
suffer all these things before entering his glory?"
27 Then Jesus took them through the writings of
Moses and all the prophets, explaining from all
the Scriptures the things concerning himself.
28 By this time they were nearing Emmaus
and the end of their journey. Jesus acted as if he
were going on, 29 but they begged him, "Stay the
night with us, since it is getting late." So he went
home with them. 30 As they sat down to eat,* he
took the bread and blessed it. Then he broke it
and gave it to them. 31 Suddenly, their eyes were
opened, and they recognized him. And at that
moment he disappeared!
32 They said to each other, "Didn't our hearts
burn within us as he talked with us on the road
and explained the Scriptures to us?" 33 And within
the hour they were on their way back to Jerusalem.
There they found the eleven disciples and the others who had gathered with them, 34 who said, "The
Lord has really risen! He appeared to Peter.*"

Jesus Appears to the Disciples

35 Then the two from Emmaus told their story
of how Jesus had appeared to them as they were
walking along the road, and how they had recognized him as he was breaking the bread. 36 And
just as they were telling about it, Jesus himself was suddenly standing there among them.
"Peace be with you," he said. 37 But the whole
group was startled and frightened, thinking they
were seeing a ghost!
38 "Why are you frightened?" he asked. "Why
are your hearts filled with doubt? 39 Look at my
hands. Look at my feet. You can see that it's really me. Touch me and make sure that I am not
a ghost, because ghosts don't have bodies, as you
see that I do." 40 As he spoke, he showed them his
hands and his feet.
41 Still they stood there in disbelief, filled with
joy and wonder. Then he asked them, "Do you have
anything here to eat?" 42 They gave him a piece of
broiled fish, 43 and he ate it as they watched.
44 Then he said, "When I was with you before, I
told you that everything written about me in the
law of Moses and the prophets and in the Psalms
must be fulfilled." 45 Then he opened their minds
to understand the Scriptures. 46 And he said, "Yes,
it was written long ago that the Messiah would
suffer and die and rise from the dead on the third
day. 47 It was also written that this message would
be proclaimed in the authority of his name to all
the nations,* beginning in Jerusalem: 'There is
forgiveness of sins for all who repent.' 48 You are
witnesses of all these things.
49 "And now I will send the Holy Spirit, just
as my Father promised. But stay here in the city
until the Holy Spirit comes and fills you with
power from heaven."

The Ascension

50 Then Jesus led them to Bethany, and lifting his
hands to heaven, he blessed them. 51 While he was
blessing them, he left them and was taken up to
heaven. 52 So they worshiped him and then returned
to Jerusalem filled with great joy. 53 And they spent
all of their time in the Temple, praising God.

24:30 Or *As they reclined.* **24:34** Greek *Simon.* **24:47** Or *all peoples.*

24:34–53 Jesus Appears to the Disciples. Jesus' resurrection appearance to Peter is also told in 1 Corinthians 15:5. In both of these accounts, we are given none of the sorts of details that are recounted in the women's encounter with the risen Christ in the garden, the exchange on the way to Emmaus, or the gathering of the disciples in Jerusalem. **35–40:** The men are still more reluctant to believe than the women at the tomb were. **41:** Their *joy and wonder* is more like Mary's faith than Zechariah's doubt at the beginning of the story (1:18–20, 28–38). **42–43:** Just as the Emmaus disciples recognized the Lord as he broke bread (vv. 30–32, 35) so now it is the partaking of food that convinces the disciples that the resurrected Jesus is indeed present with them. **44–48:** The post-resurrection teaching of Jesus centers on interpreting his ministry, death, and resurrection—as well as the future witness of his followers—in light of the ancient prophecies of the Messiah (cf. v. 27). **49–52:** The disciples must remain in the Holy City until the Holy Spirit empowers their ministry, for according to the prophecy of Isaiah (2:3), the proclamation of the gospel must begin at Jerusalem. After Christ's departure from earth, the disciples return to the Temple, coming full circle to the very location at which Luke begins the gospel story (1:8–23).

JOHN

INTRODUCTION

The Gospel of John gives an infinite view, before and behind, like standing between two full-length mirrors. The Gospel gives such an image of Jesus, in several senses. First, the Gospel writer (hereafter called John) literally takes infinity as the temporal scope of the story. The earthly life and ministry of Jesus are recounted, but the narrative is not limited to those years. John tells this story against the backdrop of the history of Israel, particularly Moses and the prophets. Thus the author keeps the historical past always in view. Beyond this, John also gazes continually toward prehistory: "In the beginning the Word already existed" (1:1). Before the creation, God's Word, God's self-revelation, already was.

The Gospel also addresses the problems that have arisen in the author's time, when the Gospel was being written, well after the crucifixion. It looks over that horizon, however, across geography and time, to speak to the modern reader. The story does not stop even there but maintains a continual awareness of the risen Christ, the Jesus who is eternally alive and lives for the eternal life of the believer.

This Gospel is multilayered in time and in meaning. Jesus' actions and teachings give an earthly account, a spiritual account, and a reflection on the impact of both on the current reader. For example, we are given a traditional account of Jesus conversing with the woman at the well. The larger subject of the story is the way in which any person might obtain eternal life (symbolized by "living water" [4:10]), thereby informing the modern reader that Jesus is the source. Each such narrative is punctuated by the use of double and triple meanings in the words. Although these terms are often evident in English, they are more striking in the original Greek. For example, in 4:11–14, the word for the source of water used by the woman means "artificial well" and emphasizes the seemingly still water into which one lowers a jar. However, the word used by Jesus means "spring," or running water, and symbolically, the Holy Spirit and eternal life. The multilevel nature of terms and of narratives makes this Gospel available to any reader, however theologically (un)sophisticated. But such a complex literary and theological style is the result of the author's long and deep incubation rather than of literary skill alone.

The Purpose of the Fourth Gospel

The totality of the Gospel, however complex, serves a single purpose. This purpose is announced in 1:12: "But to all who believed him and accepted him, [the Word] gave the right to become children of God." It is restated in 20:31 as the capstone of the narrative: "These [matters] are written so that you may continue to believe that Jesus is the Messiah, the Son of God, and that by believing in him you will have life by the power of his name." Becoming God's child is not like being given life through natural birth. It is a matter of birth from above, spiritual nurture, and an eternal heritage. The theme of birth is of central importance as a metaphor for the purpose of the book.

To accomplish this purpose, John builds and shapes the reader's knowledge of what does and does not constitute true faith and discipleship. In part this is done by contrasting the reactions of various characters with one another. In part it is done by a series of powerful literary devices, in particular ironies, misunderstandings, comments directed specifically to the reader and insider language, theological meanings known only to the community of the faithful. Often these four devices are combined, as in 11:49–53. The high priest explains why Jesus must die without realizing that he is stating God's purpose in it. The author then explains the real meaning to the reader, and the irony of the story becomes self-evident. A prominent insider term in John is that Jesus must be "lifted up." The faith community, unlike those in the story, know that the phrase refers to Jesus lifted up physically on the cross, and lifted up spiritually, since his death is inseparable from his glorification by God. The phrase also has another sense that transcends this distinction: lifted up in his resurrection. All of these literary devices contribute to the reader's sense of being an insider in the company of this great witness to Jesus and thus superior in faith to those who lack understanding. The reader thus is given ownership in the true faith.

Author, Date, Place of Writing, and Audience

The author is never named in the Gospel. The long-held traditional view is that the author was the Beloved Disciple, and that he was the apostle John. These assumptions are at least as old as the letters of the second-century bishop Irenaeus. A consensus about authorship no longer exists, however. Among the many views is that the author was a woman because of the treatment of women in the Gospel. In any case, the material in John bears traces of an eyewitness, such as its details of geography and conversation. For example, Jesus addresses his mother solely as "woman." Since these passages are unique in ancient Greek-language literature, the recorder of Jesus' words is unlikely to have invented this detail or made a mistake in this way.

It is virtually certain that chapter 21 was added later. John 21:20–23 answers a rumor that the Beloved Disciple would never die, implying that he had died by the time this chapter was written. The primary thematic element of John that is often thought to be indicative of a later date of composition is the characterization of Jesus' divinity. This high Christology is, however, the logical conclusion of such central elements as the author's opening statements of Jesus' true nature and the resurrection. The divine and human Jesus, the saving Christ, is the central revelation of Christianity. No matter when a particular christological phrase arrived in this Gospel, it cannot easily be dismissed.

This Gospel was probably written in its present form at the end of the first century, after a period of oral transmission or transmission in segments. The concern about the disciples' conflict with "the Jews," for example, echoes the most pressing concern of the Christian community in the 80s and 90s, when believers in Jesus were being thrown out of the synagogues and were becoming a distinct religious group. Other passages indicate that the Temple had been destroyed, dating the writing after AD 70. However, the author's concern with this event does not imply that Jesus never prophesied the destruction of the Temple (one possible implication of 2:19, "Destroy this temple, and . . . I will raise it up"). John's narrative reflects real disputes between Jesus and other Jews. However, this aspect of Jesus' ministry is highlighted all the more because of the circumstances of the Johannine community in the late first century, particularly the strife caused by their belief, voiced in the synagogues, that Jesus is divine.

The Gospel does not specify a place of writing. The way in which the locations are described, however, indicates that the writer knew Jerusalem in detail but the readers did not. Hence the readers are outside of Jerusalem. The translation in the text of certain Hebrew or Aramaic terms indicates that the audience spoke Greek or Latin but not Hebrew or Aramaic. A traditionally accepted place of origin is Ephesus in Asia Minor. The audience for which the author wrote was distinctive among Christians of the time. This is evidenced by John's high Christology, unique to this Gospel—the emphasis on the person of Jesus as the sole source of salvation. In addition, much of the material in John is different from that in the Synoptics, indicating a distinct set of traditions and sources.

Differences between John and the Synoptics

Over the centuries, readers have attempted to harmonize Matthew, Mark, and Luke with John. They cannot be harmonized because John differs in overall material, in the length and sequence of events, and especially in the nature of the Christ as preexistent Son of God rather than simply the one raised from the tomb. The need to reconcile the various Gospels is a modern problem and a misunderstanding of the nature of ancient writings. For the first-century writer or reader, differences do not imply that one or the other must be wrong or that the story must be fictional.

There are several reasons for this different attitude. History and the teachings of a great man or woman were passed down orally, but the keepers of the tradition—particularly the Jews—were extremely careful that the oral narrative be faithfully preserved. It was customary, however, for further traditions to be added to the old ones, even if they differed. Look, for example, at the two different yet complementary creation stories in Genesis 1 and Genesis 2. Also, with the passage of time, the communities that depended on these traditions placed the emphases differently to answer the new questions presented by their situation. Finally, as John 20:30 says, "Jesus did many other signs . . . which are not written in this book" (ESV). The tradition about Jesus that is preserved in John should be seen as complementary to that of the Synoptics. Each Gospel is a theological representation of the person and work of Christ. With this point of view, the reader can savor all of the Gospels as contributions to the question "Who is Jesus?"

The particular differences between John and the Synoptics include the following. Unlike the Synoptics, John's Christology renders belief in eternal life or other promises secondary to the person of Jesus. In John the appearance of the Son of God on earth, in mortal as well as resurrected form, is the evidence that the kingdom is already being realized for believers. This stance is alluded to in Luke, but it is everywhere in John.

In John, Jesus' ministry extends for three years as opposed to the one implied in the Synoptics. Also, in John, most of his ministry is conducted in and around Jerusalem rather than in Galilee. Unique to John are the designation of the miracles as "signs"; the "I am" statements of Jesus; places and people such as Cana, Nicodemus, the Samaritan woman, Lazarus, and the Beloved Disciple; the association of Jesus with the Paschal Lamb; and Mary Magdalene in the garden after the resurrection. Unlike Matthew and Luke, Mark and John contain no specific birth stories of Jesus but rather single-verse allusions (see Mark 1:7; 1:11; John 1:10; 1:45).

John contains no exorcisms, no mystical experiences such as the transfiguration, no Sermon on the Mount (Matthew) or on the plain (Luke), no explicit establishment of sacraments, and no messianic prophecies. The mother of Jesus is never named, and Jesus is never addressed by name by another person in the story. Most of the conversations and healings in John do not appear in the Synoptics, although all of the Gospels share the story of the passion. The command to love one another as Jesus has loved the believers is nowhere so prominent as in John. Love is the way in which the believers will be known.

Unlike the Synoptics, John contains no explicit reference to the Sadducees, the priestly party whose power was based in the Temple. However, the Pharisees (the legal experts) are prominent. Further, the crucifixion is blamed on the leading priests and Pharisees. John refers to "the Pharisees" eighteen times—sixteen of which show them driving the crucifixion and directly influencing those called "the Jews" against Jesus. The significance of this emphasis is twofold. First, it supports the assumption that the Gospel was written after the destruction of the Temple; then the base of the Sadducees' power was gone. At that time, the Pharisees had become the leaders of Judaism, reformulating Judaism around the law and the synagogue.

Second, John has made an explicit distinction between "the Jews" in general and "the Pharisees." If we include Nathanael ("an Israelite," ESV; "a genuine son of Israel," NLT) and Nicodemus ("a ruler of the Jews," ESV; "a Jewish religious leader," NLT), John has nine references to "the Jews" that show them believing in Jesus, and only nine or ten showing them against Jesus. Two other passages show "the Jews" in favor of the crucifixion, but only under the strong domination of the Pharisees. The rest of the references to "the Jews" show them asking neutral or challenging questions of Jesus—a time-honored manner of engaging in theological debate, preserved for us in the Talmud (Jewish law as it was later put into writing). Thus, unlike the Synoptics, John makes a strong distinction: Some particular leaders of the Jews determined to kill Jesus, but the Jews in general, including their customs and feasts, are affirmed.

John and Women

Commentaries on the Fourth Gospel as a document of significance for women tend to focus on Jesus' interactions with women. The major insights from this type of work have included the following. Women's inclusion in the narrative, especially in conversation with Jesus, bestows on them an importance beyond their status in the cultures of the first century. Each woman appears at a point in the narrative where the author is bringing Jesus' ministry to a new level. For example, the conversation with the Samaritan woman becomes the occasion for Jesus' revelation that he is the Messiah. Women are given a unique place in the Johannine community, as exemplary disciples and as full-fledged apostles. Mary Magdalene is the premier example. In Paul's letters (written several decades before John), the two criteria of apostleship are to have seen the risen Jesus and to have been sent to proclaim him. John 20:17–18 presents Mary Magdalene as the one person in John who most closely fits these criteria. Further, she makes the prototypical apostolic announcement of the resurrection: "I have seen the Lord."

Apart from these special roles given to women in John, it is probable that modern readers undervalue the traditional roles of women seen in John and in ancient Jewish society. Although women's sphere of action was usually the family, their role as the bearers of children—regarded by many as the means to immortality—was highly valued. In the Ten Commandments, father and mother are to be honored equally. The woman in the home also had a spiritual significance, one that is foreign to moderns. For example, as recorded in the Mishnah (an early, authoritative form of Jewish law expanding on the Pentateuch), Rabbi Phineas ben Hannah held that the woman in the home has an atoning force not inferior to the altar of sacrifice. Thus, what the Johannine community bestows upon women is not good exchanged for bad, but one type of honor given along with another.

There is yet deeper significance for women in John's Gospel. A closer look at the Gospel will lead to further conclusions in this domain. Suffice it to say here that Jesus takes on, in deeply symbolic fashion, the roles of birthing mother and midwife. (For the characteristics associated with these roles in the ancient Near East, see Midwifery and Birthing Practices, Job 3.) One striking example occurs in the raising of Lazarus, where Jesus employs the formula used by a midwife to bring to fruition a particularly difficult birth: "[Name], come forth!" Thus in 11:43, Jesus commands, "Lazarus, come out!" and a man is born again from above (by divine power) and from below as well (from the grave). The inclusion of such an image in the Gospel makes the allusion highly pointed, particularly in view of the importance of John's theme of new birth.

No greater affirmation of womanhood can be given than for Jesus to take on a role that in the first century is strictly the province of women—and to do so as a part of his essential nature, being one with the Creator. Such imagery is not new with John, however. Romans, written several decades earlier, has the whole creation "groaning as in the pains of childbirth" (Rom 8:22). In this text, the Holy Spirit is the midwife (Rom 8:26): "The Holy Spirit helps us" [i.e., to give birth; or, to be reborn] "in our weakness." This image of God would have been clear to the first-century reader. For the modern reader, it is especially significant in juxtaposition with what may appear to be John's exclusive characterization of God as Father.

Modern feminist theologies have much to offer. However, theological conclusions from the use of the feminine in John are left to the reader. The task here is to present, as faithfully as possible, the content of John and its meaning in its first-century cultural context.

The Structure of the Fourth Gospel

Most commentaries today divide John into four sections, plus a transition: the prologue (1:1–18), a testimony to Jesus' true identity; the book of signs (1:19—11.44); [a transitional section, 11:45—12:50]; the book of glory (13:1—20:31); and the epilogue (21:1–25). While this division is useful, it obscures structures that may indicate a point of connection with the Synoptics (to be discussed later). This structure is indicated in the outline.

The book of signs is named for the seven signs or mighty works of Jesus recorded therein. Other genres of John that are commonly discussed in commentaries are the seven "I am" statements of Jesus, a number of controversies with a group called "the Jews," and several one-to-one conversations between Jesus and a character in the narrative.

Another genre, however, has received far too little attention: the confession of faith in Jesus. The confession is defined here as any statement by one or more persons that Jesus demonstrates divine attributes such as performing miracles (signs) or any statement by the author that someone believed in Jesus (and thus must have confessed faith in him). Confessions can be seen as the skeleton of the narrative. The beginning and ending of John are confessions by the author. They are written specifically to propel the reader to confess Jesus as well. In between, the Fourth Gospel contains more than forty confessions by people in the story. These confessions represent the spectrum of belief, and cumulatively they form a paradigm of the purest type of confession.

Confessions are attributed to every group in the Gospel or their representatives. Almost all of the confessions are made by Jews, either called "Jews" in the immediate context or understood to be Jews, such as Jesus' disciples. This observation may seem to beg the question; nearly everyone in the Gospel is a Jew. The point is that in John, condemning the whole of "the Jews" is not the author's intent.

The confessions occur in systematic relationship to the signs, the one-to-one conversations, the controversies, and the "I am" statements. Before discussing the confessions, we trace several great sweeps of John's argument in these other aspects of the story. Among the signs, the changing of water to wine at Cana is the overall introduction of Jesus as Lord over all and as the real master of the wedding feast—that is, the marriage of God and God's people. The healing of the official's son and the healing of the invalid at the pool present Jesus as the healer of the present human condition. The next two signs, feeding the five thousand and walking on water, present Jesus as the Lord over nature and over earthly life. The healing of the man born blind and the raising of Lazarus demonstrate Jesus as the author of life (sight/blindness being considered a symbol of life). The "I am[s]" reveal Jesus metaphorically as the source of all things that are essential to human life—bread, light, security, life ("the resurrection and the life"; also the true vine, whose life flows out to its tendrils), and truth.

Further, the signs and the "I am[s]" interact with the controversies to create a series of larger images of Jesus' identity. Jesus' healing at the pool (the third sign) incites the first controversy. The controversy begins because the healing was on the Sabbath but continues because the Jews are angry that Jesus makes himself equal with God. Ironically the first three signs have shown that he is. The next controversy begins with the feeding of the five thousand. The theme of bread continues through the great controversy in which Jesus offers his flesh and blood for the life of the world. The section concludes when many disciples decide no longer to follow him, specifically because of the first "I am": "I am the bread of life."

"I am the light of the world" incites further controversy about Jesus' identity and particularly his origin (with the Father). The controversy escalates and ends abruptly with Jesus' answer to the Jews at 8:58: "Before Abraham was even born, I Am." Jesus has used the name of God by implication as his identity while also saying that his origins are even greater than the man regarded as the earthly father of the Jews. This self-revelation is intended as spiritual light given to those who are ready to receive it. John returns explicitly to the theme of light in the sixth sign, the healing of the man born blind. This section ends with a powerful argument in which Jesus accuses the Pharisees of spiritual blindness, the opposite of Jesus' nature, light (true revelation).

In chapter 10, the theme changes to that of the gate of the sheep and the good shepherd. These images are central to the next controversy, which strongly implies that the Jews who challenge him may not be of his and God's flock. The controversy ends with Jesus' declaration of the purpose of the signs (10:37–38): "If I am not doing the works of my Father, then do not believe me; but if I do them, even though you do not believe me, believe the works, that you may know and understand that the Father is in me and I am in the Father" (ESV).

The final sign is preceded by the fifth "I am": "I am the resurrection and the life." Upon the demonstration that this is so—the raising of Lazarus—the ultimate controversy occurs, wherein Jesus' opponents cease debating with him and plan his death, fearing the political implications of the large group of people who have seen and believed this sign. The final two "I am[s]" are reserved for the disciples in private and contribute to the disciples' corporate confession of faith. But all discussion is over; the disciples and the enemies of Jesus have set their differing courses.

The Meaning and Character of the Confessions in John

Confessions occur in every chapter except John 13—15 and John 17. The confession is defined broadly, in part so that this list will include the ones Jesus acknowledges as such. The disciples' confession in 16:29–31 is a good example: "From this [that Jesus knows everything] we believe that you came from God." Jesus answered them, "Do you finally believe?" Jesus immediately tells them that they are about to desert him, which might seem to negate their confession except that Jesus does not reject the confession per se. To understand the power and purpose of the confession genre, the various types of confession must be made clear. There are six types of confession defined as follows:

Direct type 1 consists of a quotation that ascribes a messianic title to Jesus or contains the words "I believe." The titles are usually "Christ," "Son of God," "King of Israel," "King of the Jews," or "the [or a] prophet."

Direct type 2 consists of a statement in which an individual is reported to have testified about Jesus. In Greek grammar, there is no formal difference between a direct quotation ("he said, 'X'") and an indirect one ("he said that . . ."). The major difference from direct type 1 is that type 2 is often stated to people other than Jesus.

Indirect type 1 consists of a collective subject ("the crowd," "the Jews," "the people," "the disciples") plus a statement that the subjects believed or the equivalent.

Indirect type 2 confessions are distinguished by the fact that the person or group who believed did not admit faith publicly because of fear, usually of the Jews. Note that sometimes the Jews hold back their testimony for fear of a subgroup of the Jews, "the Pharisees" (e.g., 12:42).

Ironic confessions are true statements indicating recognition of the extraordinary nature of Jesus' acts or person. However, they occur in the course of explaining why Jesus should be killed or in the argument over the sign on the cross that calls Jesus "the King of the Jews." John uses these ironies systematically and forcefully to proclaim a truth about Jesus.

Unique confessions are those in which Jesus confesses his messiahship (4:26) and the author looks back upon the Gospel and expresses belief (19:35; 21:24).

Considering the entire pattern of confessions, one particular literary structure becomes visible. In 6:68–69, Peter confesses that Jesus has "the words of eternal life" and is "the Holy One of God." The author has placed this statement and its immediate context at the virtual center of the presentation of Jesus' public ministry. Although verse numbers are not original to the text, verse counts yield a reasonable approximation of how much of the text occurs before and after the passage. In 1:19—11:57, there are 253 verses before the passage containing Peter's confession and 253 after it (through 11:44, 240 verses). This verse count supports the thesis that the author placed Peter's confession in a highly deliberate way.

The book of signs therefore bears a literary affinity with the Synoptics, which is of considerable interest to Bible scholars. In each of the Synoptics, Peter's confession is at the center of the book. Jesus' public ministry ends with it, and the Passion Narrative follows almost immediately. In John, Peter's confession occurs at the center also, but at the center of the book of signs only (that is, of John 1—11). In the immediate context (6:67–68), Peter is upheld, as in the Synoptics, as the one true believer. However, he is divided within himself, later denying Jesus three times. Further, Peter's confession is ultimately portrayed as inferior in John's theology to that of Martha (see 11:27).

Peter's confession in John further symbolizes division among the community. His confession immediately follows a unique statement: After Jesus had declared himself the bread of life, "many of his disciples turned away and deserted him" (6:66). Thus new and sharp division among the disciples is the occasion of Peter's confession. The divisions among the other characters in the narrative can be seen from the placement of the various types of confession. The direct type 1 confessions are about equally divided on either side of Peter's confession. However, the indirect types 1 and 2 occur almost exclusively after Peter's confession; almost all of them state explicitly that the believers represent one faction of a sharply divided group. The divisions reach their peak with the ironic confessions, all of which occur after Peter's confession. These statements, condemning Jesus for his acknowledged divine attributes and actions, represent a powerful spiritual division in the hearts of those who pronounce the worst condemnations. Thus the placement of Peter's confession ultimately makes Peter the symbol and signpost of division.

Could it be that John had read one or more of the Synoptics and is responding or completing the story by echoing their literary device of centering Peter's confession with this particular twist? Even if John is not intentionally commenting on the Synoptics, Peter's confession and the distribution of confessions around it ultimately render what constitutes the purest form of confession in John. The disciples are seen to represent the spectrum from outright betrayal (Judas) to belief, denial and return (Peter), all the way to a simple, loving presence with the person of Jesus (the Beloved Disciple at the Last Supper).

Another type of spectrum is represented in the pattern of confessions as well. After the prologue, John the Baptist's confessions (1:29, 34) provide a firm anchor by which other confessions may be judged. (Many scholars believe that the Johannine—John the apostle's—community was originally the followers of John the Baptist.) His confessions are matched only by that of Martha (11:27). Between 1:29 and 11:27, however, there is a general progression in the confessions. They begin with faith in Jesus occasioned by his works (seeing Nathanael under the fig tree; the changing of water to wine at Cana; the feeding of the five thousand). Then they begin to center on Jesus' promise of eternal life (Peter). Martha's confession is exemplary because she declares, "I have always believed you are the Messiah," so she believed before the resurrection of Lazarus. Hers is a faith in the person of Jesus; miracles and eternal life are neither the occasion nor the condition of her faith.

This crescendo of confessions is masterfully punctuated by the placement of the one-to-one conversations and the way in which they contrast with each other. These conversations also bring into high relief the role of women as disciples. In John, apart from John the Baptist's confessions, the women's confessions most consistently represent ideal statements of faith. For this reason, most of this commentary will dwell on the relationships among the conversations, particularly conversations with men versus women. Since exactly half of the conversations are with women, this analysis will provide some insight into the place of women among the Johannine community.

The Conversations in Relation to the Confessions

A conversation, in this essay, is a passage in which Jesus talks principally with one other person. Other people may be present but do not take part in the main conversation. An occasion and place are usually given. The person is usually named; one significant departure is when the mother of Jesus and the Samaritan woman are addressed, or referred to, by John, only as "woman." This is often read as a distancing or deprecating title. However, it bears one of John's pregnant double meanings; it is part of an extended reference to the object of Jesus' coming, the new birth of the people of God. Conversations may be distinguished from controversies; in the controversies, usually a question is posed and Jesus answers in what is essentially a monologue. In the conversation, however, a statement or question begins the section, followed by a series of misunderstandings by the other person. Through his statements combined with the misunderstandings, Jesus reveals to the reader something essential about himself.

It is therefore important to understand the Johannine concept of the believer as disciple. By this concept we may judge how closely each conversant approaches ideal discipleship. Discipleship is based upon love of Jesus and of one another—and upon service begotten of love, the peak of which is to lay down one's life for one's friend. Disciples are further appointed to continue Jesus' mission to the world.

While there are criteria for human response to Jesus, the variety of confessions shows also that human virtue does not determine eligibility for the love of God. In the Old Testament, Zion is given its place of honor despite its frequent unfaithfulness. The Samaritan woman is accepted even in her earthly unfaithful state. Think of the story of the woman caught in adultery (8:1–11). Or think of Peter: He is to become the shepherd for the Shepherd despite his periodic unfaithfulness (chap. 21). God will bless faithfulness wherever it is offered.

Conclusions

Several general statements may now be made about the theology of the Fourth Gospel. First, belief in Jesus Christ will produce divisions in the community of which the faithful are a part. John is particularly concerned to tell the faithful: Do not give up. God is with you, and Jesus Christ has already brought you to the door of the kingdom (that is, to himself).

Second, from the time of the earthly Jesus on, no temple or other physical location will be able to hold the Lord or be sufficient for true spiritual worship. The cleansing of the Temple, the discussion with the Samaritan woman, and the story of the man born blind being outcast from the synagogue all attest to this point. Similarly, ideal faith does not reside exclusively in any one ethnic or social group or stratum—Jews, Samaritans, Gentiles, men, women, faithful, sinful, well, or sick. All who believe in his name have the right to become the children of God.

Third, the Fourth Gospel is not anti-Semitic, since the full range of unbelief and belief in Jesus Christ is shown in Jews and non-Jews alike. It is also not nearly so exclusively male-dominated as it may seem on first glance. Women's roles in the Fourth Gospel as well as the feminine imagery used to describe Jesus show that the feminine response to God, as well as women's contributions to the community of the faithful, are to be greatly honored. Given the roles of Jesus' women disciples in John, bias against women's leadership in the church is not an appropriate response to John's Gospel. However, Jesus transcends the birth processes of men and women. The believer is to be born of God; next to that, human birth and human gender are secondary as a source of worth. Thus the spiritual potential of all humankind is affirmed, and this is the greatest reason to affirm the spiritual callings of all believers. —*Kamila A. Blessing*

1:1–18	Prologue
1:19—11:44	The Book of Signs
11:45—12:50	Transition: Physical and Symbolic
11:45–57	Final Plot to Kill Jesus
12:1–11	Jesus' Anointing
12:12–19	The Triumphant Entry into Jerusalem

12:20–36 Jesus' Prediction of His Death
12:37–50 Reaction and Response
13:1—20:31 The Book of Glory
13:1—17:26 Jesus Speaks with His Disciples
18:1—19:24 Jesus' Trial and Crucifixion
20:1–31 Jesus Returns to His Disciples
21:1–25 Epilogue: Jesus Appears to the Disciples

✧

Prologue: Christ, the Eternal Word

1 1 In the beginning the Word already
existed.
The Word was with God,
and the Word was God.
2 He existed in the beginning with God.
3 God created everything through him,
and nothing was created except through
him.
4 The Word gave life to everything that was
created,*
and his life brought light to everyone.
5 The light shines in the darkness,
and the darkness can never extinguish it.*

6 God sent a man, John the Baptist,* 7 to tell
about the light so that everyone might believe
because of his testimony. 8 John himself was not
the light; he was simply a witness to tell about the
light. 9 The one who is the true light, who gives
light to everyone, was coming into the world.
10 He came into the very world he created, but
the world didn't recognize him. 11 He came to his
own people, and even they rejected him. 12 But to
all who believed him and accepted him, he gave
the right to become children of God. 13 They are
reborn—not with a physical birth resulting from
human passion or plan, but a birth that comes
from God.
14 So the Word became human* and made his
home among us. He was full of unfailing love
and faithfulness.* And we have seen his glory,
the glory of the Father's one and only Son.
15 John testified about him when he shouted to
the crowds, "This is the one I was talking about
when I said, 'Someone is coming after me who is
far greater than I am, for he existed long before
me.' "
16 From his abundance we have all received
one gracious blessing after another.* 17 For the
law was given through Moses, but God's unfailing love and faithfulness came through Jesus
Christ. 18 No one has ever seen God. But the
unique One, who is himself God,* is near to the
Father's heart. He has revealed God to us.

The Testimony of John the Baptist

19 This was John's testimony when the Jewish
leaders sent priests and Temple assistants* from
Jerusalem to ask John, "Who are you?" 20 He
came right out and said, "I am not the Messiah."
21 "Well then, who are you?" they asked. "Are
you Elijah?"
"No," he replied.
"Are you the Prophet we are expecting?"*
"No."
22 "Then who are you? We need an answer
for those who sent us. What do you have to say
about yourself?"
23 John replied in the words of the prophet
Isaiah:

"I am a voice shouting in the wilderness,
'Clear the way for the LORD's coming!' "*

1:3-4 Or *and nothing that was created was created except through him. The Word gave life to everything.* **1:5** Or *and the darkness has not understood it.* **1:6** Greek *a man named John.* **1:14a** Greek *became flesh.* **1:14b** Or *grace and truth;* also in 1:17. **1:16** Or *received the grace of Christ rather than the grace of the law;* Greek reads *received grace upon grace.* **1:18** Some manuscripts read *But the one and only Son.* **1:19** Greek *and Levites.* **1:21** Greek *Are you the Prophet?* See Deut 18:15, 18; Mal 4:5-6. **1:23** Isa 40:3.

1:1–18 Prologue

In the beginning (v. 1) is a quotation of Gen 1:1. **14:** *Became human*, literally, "flesh" (see translator's note): "Flesh" meant the weakest aspects of human nature, what is mortal.

1:19—11:44 The Book of Signs

Sign (Greek *semeion*) is John's term for Jesus' miraculous acts, to emphasize their significance as well as their miraculous nature.

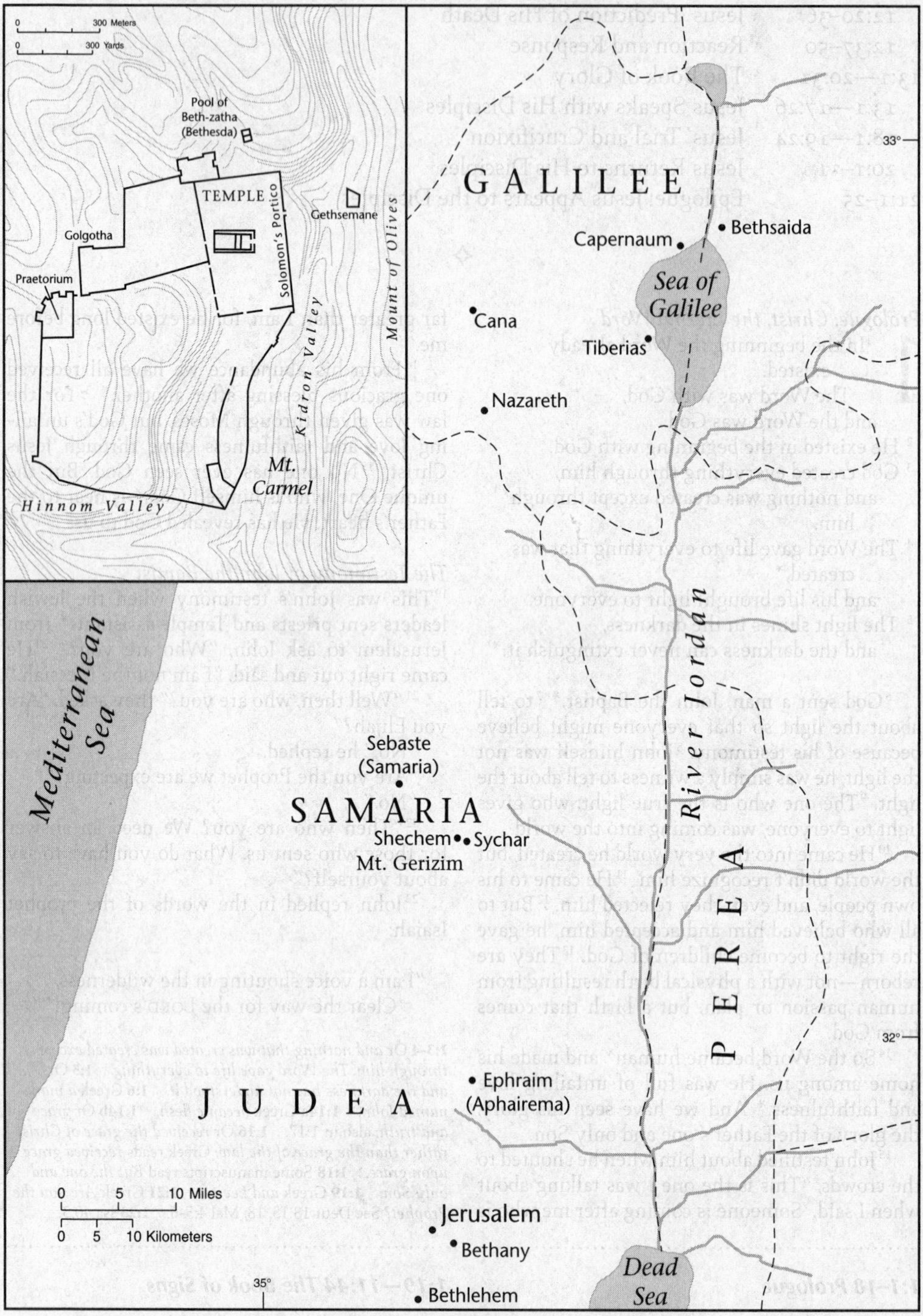

The Geography of the Gospel of John

24 Then the Pharisees who had been sent
25 asked him, "If you aren't the Messiah or Elijah or the Prophet, what right do you have to
baptize?"
26 John told them, "I baptize with* water, but
right here in the crowd is someone you do not
recognize. 27 Though his ministry follows mine,
I'm not even worthy to be his slave and untie the
straps of his sandal."
28 This encounter took place in Bethany, an
area east of the Jordan River, where John was
baptizing.

Jesus, the Lamb of God

29 The next day John saw Jesus coming toward
him and said, "Look! The Lamb of God who takes
away the sin of the world! 30 He is the one I was
talking about when I said, 'A man is coming after
me who is far greater than I am, for he existed
long before me.' 31 I did not recognize him as the
Messiah, but I have been baptizing with water so
that he might be revealed to Israel."
32 Then John testified, "I saw the Holy Spirit
descending like a dove from heaven and resting upon him. 33 I didn't know he was the one,
but when God sent me to baptize with water, he
told me, 'The one on whom you see the Spirit
descend and rest is the one who will baptize with
the Holy Spirit.' 34 I saw this happen to Jesus, so I
testify that he is the Chosen One of God.*"

The First Disciples

35 The following day John was again standing
with two of his disciples. 36 As Jesus walked by,
John looked at him and declared, "Look! There is
the Lamb of God!" 37 When John's two disciples
heard this, they followed Jesus.
38 Jesus looked around and saw them following. "What do you want?" he asked them.
They replied, "Rabbi" (which means "Teacher"), "where are you staying?"
39 "Come and see," he said. It was about four
o'clock in the afternoon when they went with
him to the place where he was staying, and they
remained with him the rest of the day.
40 Andrew, Simon Peter's brother, was one of
these men who heard what John said and then
followed Jesus. 41 Andrew went to find his brother, Simon, and told him, "We have found the
Messiah" (which means "Christ"*).
42 Then Andrew brought Simon to meet Jesus.
Looking intently at Simon, Jesus said, "Your
name is Simon, son of John—but you will be
called Cephas" (which means "Peter"*).
43 The next day Jesus decided to go to Galilee.
He found Philip and said to him, "Come, follow
me." 44 Philip was from Bethsaida, Andrew and
Peter's hometown.
45 Philip went to look for Nathanael and told
him, "We have found the very person Moses*
and the prophets wrote about! His name is Jesus,
the son of Joseph from Nazareth."
46 "Nazareth!" exclaimed Nathanael. "Can
anything good come from Nazareth?"
"Come and see for yourself," Philip replied.
47 As they approached, Jesus said, "Now here
is a genuine son of Israel—a man of complete
integrity."
48 "How do you know about me?" Nathanael
asked.
Jesus replied, "I could see you under the fig
tree before Philip found you."
49 Then Nathanael exclaimed, "Rabbi, you are
the Son of God—the King of Israel!"
50 Jesus asked him, "Do you believe this just
because I told you I had seen you under the
fig tree? You will see greater things than this."
51 Then he said, "I tell you the truth, you will all
see heaven open and the angels of God going up
and down on the Son of Man, the one who is the
stairway between heaven and earth.*"

The Wedding at Cana

2 The next day* there was a wedding celebration in the village of Cana in Galilee.
Jesus' mother was there, 2 and Jesus and
his disciples were also invited to the celebration.
3 The wine supply ran out during the festivities,

1:26 Or *in;* also in 1:31, 33. **1:34** Some manuscripts read *the Son of God.* **1:41** *Messiah* (a Hebrew term) and *Christ* (a Greek term) both mean "the anointed one." **1:42** The names *Cephas* (from Aramaic) and *Peter* (from Greek) both mean "rock." **1:45** Greek *Moses in the law.* **1:51** Greek *going up and down on the Son of Man;* see Gen 28:10-17. "Son of Man" is a title Jesus used for himself. **2:1** Greek *On the third day;* see 1:35, 43.

1:19–34 The Testimony of John the Baptist. 29: *Lamb of God*: The *lamb* was used in the Prophets to stand for a willing sacrificial victim (Isa 53:7; Jer 11:19).

1:35–51 Calling the First Disciples. 48–51: *Nathanael* is won over by Jesus' ability to tell that he was *under the fig tree,* where good Israelites rested (1 Kgs 4:25). Nathanael uses *Son of God* and *King of Israel* as synonyms, but the Gospel sees *Son of God* as meaning far more (3:16).

2:1–12 The Wedding at Cana. Note that the *wine* (symbolizing the messianic banquet, Mark 14:25) is a transformation of the *water* of *Jewish ceremonial washing.*

so Jesus' mother told him, "They have no more
wine."
4 "Dear woman, that's not our problem," Jesus
replied. "My time has not yet come."
5 But his mother told the servants, "Do whatever he tells you."
6 Standing nearby were six stone water jars,
used for Jewish ceremonial washing. Each could
hold twenty to thirty gallons.* 7 Jesus told the
servants, "Fill the jars with water." When the
jars had been filled, 8 he said, "Now dip some out,
and take it to the master of ceremonies." So the
servants followed his instructions.
9 When the master of ceremonies tasted the
water that was now wine, not knowing where it
had come from (though, of course, the servants
knew), he called the bridegroom over. 10 "A host
always serves the best wine first," he said. "Then,
when everyone has had a lot to drink, he brings
out the less expensive wine. But you have kept
the best until now!"
11 This miraculous sign at Cana in Galilee was
the first time Jesus revealed his glory. And his
disciples believed in him.

2:6 Greek *2 or 3 measures* [75 to 113 liters].

The passage says that when the wine provided by the host was gone, Jesus' mother "told him, 'They have no more wine.'" This statement of need without a direct request is a typical courteous form in which a Jewish woman of the time might ask a man for something (cf. 11:3). From this point in the story, however, almost all translations confuse Jesus' answer in one way or another, attempting a nearly impossible idiomatic translation. Literally what Jesus says is, "What [is that] to me and to you, woman? My hour has not come."

If the reader takes the first part of the reply literally, it makes sense. Jesus is a guest, and in that culture a guest is not called on for such things; it is a matter of honor for the groom's family to provide wine. One might dishonor them by presuming that they could not do so. Against this cultural backdrop, however, if Jesus does provide the wine, he must be the bridegroom. This is one of John's two-story stories, as may be seen in the use of *woman* and *my time*. Each term has at least two meanings, and John uses them with literary precision. They open for us an alternative reading, without denying that just given.

Let us take first the direct address, *woman*. John is uniquely marked by his direct address to the reader, and such direct address might occur anywhere in a narrative. Given that *woman* is a term that, by the end of the Gospel, means the true believer of either gender, it is possible that the author records Jesus speaking to his mother and, as the author, addresses all believers. If so, John is asking the believer a pointed and highly charged question: What *is* this to you and to me? Thereby he says, Notice this! "This" is the lack of wine and the miracle that is about to happen. The real question is, "What is the significance of these things in Jesus' life and in yours?" If you cannot answer, you have not understood; you are not an insider. The correct answer is: In this sign, I, Jesus, show you my identity. (Hence through this miracle, Jesus *revealed his glory. And his disciples believed in him*, 2:11.)

Such a communication to the reader is the more likely because of the phrase "my hour" (ESV), or *my time* (NLT). This phrase is used in only two ways in John. It refers to Jesus' ultimate purpose, his death and new birth for the sake of the believer's rebirth. It also refers to the woman's hour, the hour of giving birth. The latter, however, is a metaphor for Jesus' leaving (his death) and its effect on the disciples (16:21). This usage is further interpreted as the hour in which God will glorify Jesus and in which God is glorified. Jesus' glory will be ironically reflected in the sign over the cross, "the King of the Jews." However, the theme of glorification is most poignant in 12:27–28, the closest passage in John to the scene at Gethsemane. Jesus says, "Now my soul is deeply troubled. Should I pray, 'Father, save me from this hour'? But this is the very reason I came! Father, bring glory to your name." Thus the seemingly incongruous mention of his hour during the wedding at Cana is an example of familiar insiders' language. It tells us that Jesus' death and resurrection are the theological subject of the wedding story.

As the story goes on, Jesus' mother says, *Do whatever he tells you*—another word to characters in the story but also to the reader. Upon Jesus' command, the servants fill stone jars with water and present some of it to the master of the banquet. The master calls the bridegroom and says that, unlike everyone else, *you have kept the best until now*, that is, until the end (2:10). This is the end of the banquet and the end of the Gospel story, the crucifixion, and resurrection. The water and wine, usually assumed to be red wine, serve a double purpose. One of John's purposes in writing was to dispel the Gnostic heresy that Jesus seemed to be human but was solely spirit from the beginning. The water and wine are symbols of the genuine, earthly water and blood that are shed during earthly birth. They also foreshadow the blood and water that will flow from Jesus' earthly body on the cross. The presence of Jesus' mother, addressed as *woman*, reinforces the reader's association of the wedding at Cana with Jesus' natural birth, even while he is performing the first sign that will evidence his divinity. This complex of symbols thus affirms the incarnation. The Christian doctrine that Jesus is fully divine and fully human is strongly defended in these texts.

[12]After the wedding he went to Capernaum for a few days with his mother, his brothers, and his disciples.

Jesus Clears the Temple

[13]It was nearly time for the Jewish Passover celebration, so Jesus went to Jerusalem. [14]In the Temple area he saw merchants selling cattle, sheep, and doves for sacrifices; he also saw dealers at tables exchanging foreign money. [15]Jesus made a whip from some ropes and chased them all out of the Temple. He drove out the sheep and cattle, scattered the money changers' coins over the floor, and turned over their tables. [16]Then, going over to the people who sold doves, he told them, "Get these things out of here. Stop turning my Father's house into a marketplace!"

[17]Then his disciples remembered this prophecy from the Scriptures: "Passion for God's house will consume me."*

[18]But the Jewish leaders demanded, "What are you doing? If God gave you authority to do this, show us a miraculous sign to prove it."

[19]"All right," Jesus replied. "Destroy this temple, and in three days I will raise it up."

[20]"What!" they exclaimed. "It has taken forty-six years to build this Temple, and you can rebuild it in three days?" [21]But when Jesus said "this temple," he meant his own body. [22]After he was raised from the dead, his disciples remembered he had said this, and they believed both the Scriptures and what Jesus had said.

Jesus and Nicodemus

[23]Because of the miraculous signs Jesus did in Jerusalem at the Passover celebration, many began to trust in him. [24]But Jesus didn't trust them, because he knew human nature. [25]No one needed to tell him what mankind is really like.

3

There was a man named Nicodemus, a Jewish religious leader who was a Pharisee. [2]After dark one evening, he came to speak with Jesus. "Rabbi," he said, "we all know that God has sent you to teach us. Your miraculous signs are evidence that God is with you."

[3]Jesus replied, "I tell you the truth, unless you are born again,* you cannot see the Kingdom of God."

[4]"What do you mean?" exclaimed Nicodemus. "How can an old man go back into his mother's womb and be born again?"

[5]Jesus replied, "I assure you, no one can enter the Kingdom of God without being born of water and the Spirit.* [6]Humans can reproduce only human life, but the Holy Spirit gives birth to spiritual life.* [7]So don't be surprised when I say, 'You* must be born again.' [8]The wind blows wherever it wants. Just as you can hear the wind but can't tell where it comes from or where it is going, so you can't explain how people are born of the Spirit."

[9]"How are these things possible?" Nicodemus asked.

[10]Jesus replied, "You are a respected Jewish teacher, and yet you don't understand these things? [11]I assure you, we tell you what we know and have seen, and yet you won't believe our testimony. [12]But if you don't believe me when I tell you about earthly things, how can you possibly believe if I tell you about heavenly things? [13]No one has ever gone to heaven and returned. But the Son of Man* has come down from heaven. [14]And as Moses lifted up the bronze snake on a pole in the wilderness, so the Son of Man must be lifted up, [15]so that everyone who believes in him will have eternal life.*

[16]"For God loved the world so much that he

2:17 Or *"Concern for God's house will be my undoing."* Ps 69:9. **3:3** Or *born from above;* also in 3:7. **3:5** Or *and spirit.* The Greek word for *Spirit* can also be translated *wind;* see 3:8. **3:6** Greek *what is born of the Spirit is spirit.* **3:7** The Greek word for *you* is plural; also in 3:12. **3:13** Some manuscripts add *who lives in heaven.* "Son of Man" is a title Jesus used for himself. **3:15** Or *everyone who believes will have eternal life in him.*

2:13–25 Jesus at the Temple. In the other Gospels, this incident comes at the end of Jesus' ministry, when he enters Jerusalem, and it causes the priests to plan to kill him (Mark 11:18). In John's Gospel, however, the raising of Lazarus from the dead is the reason why the religious leaders try to have Jesus executed (John 11:53).

3:1–21 Jesus and Nicodemus. 1–2: The scene begins with Nicodemus coming to see Jesus *after dark,* an implicit contrast with the true followers who are drawn to the light (vv. 19–21). The seeker's faith is that *miraculous signs* mean *God is with you.* This in itself is not unacceptable. **3–5:** Jesus' reply introduces the major theme, being *born again,* "born from above," or both, and further that to *enter the Kingdom of God,* one must be *born of water and the Spirit.* Nicodemus misunderstands each of these statements, seeing only the material, reductionistic sense of Jesus' words. **14:** *Lifted up* is a reference to the crucifixion. Nicodemus appears only twice more: in 7:45–52 and 20:39–40. His faith does not bring others to Jesus; he will not endanger his life or status by acknowledging Jesus. He thus fails the criterion in 15:13 of giving one's life for a friend. Yet Nicodemus is a member of the most

gave his one and only Son, so that everyone who
believes in him will not perish but have eternal
life. 17 God sent his Son into the world not to judge
the world, but to save the world through him.

18 "There is no judgment against anyone who
believes in him. But anyone who does not believe
in him has already been judged for not believing
in God's one and only Son. 19 And the judgment
is based on this fact: God's light came into the
world, but people loved the darkness more than
the light, for their actions were evil. 20 All who
do evil hate the light and refuse to go near it for
fear their sins will be exposed. 21 But those who
do what is right come to the light so others can
see that they are doing what God wants.*"

John the Baptist Exalts Jesus

22 Then Jesus and his disciples left Jerusalem and
went into the Judean countryside. Jesus spent
some time with them there, baptizing people.

23 At this time John the Baptist was baptizing
at Aenon, near Salim, because there was plenty
of water there; and people kept coming to him
for baptism. 24 (This was before John was thrown
into prison.) 25 A debate broke out between John's
disciples and a certain Jew* over ceremonial
cleansing. 26 So John's disciples came to him and
said, "Rabbi, the man you met on the other side
of the Jordan River, the one you identified as the
Messiah, is also baptizing people. And everybody
is going to him instead of coming to us."

27 John replied, "No one can receive anything
unless God gives it from heaven. 28 You yourselves
know how plainly I told you, 'I am not the Messiah. I am only here to prepare the way for him.'
29 It is the bridegroom who marries the bride, and
the best man is simply glad to stand with him and
hear his vows. Therefore, I am filled with joy at
his success. 30 He must become greater and greater, and I must become less and less.

31 "He has come from above and is greater than
anyone else. We are of the earth, and we speak
of earthly things, but he has come from heaven
and is greater than anyone else.* 32 He testifies
about what he has seen and heard, but how few
believe what he tells them! 33 Anyone who accepts his testimony can affirm that God is true.
34 For he is sent by God. He speaks God's words,
for God gives him the Spirit without limit. 35 The
Father loves his Son and has put everything into
his hands. 36 And anyone who believes in God's
Son has eternal life. Anyone who doesn't obey
the Son will never experience eternal life but remains under God's angry judgment."

Jesus and the Samaritan Woman

4 Jesus* knew the Pharisees had heard that
he was baptizing and making more disciples than John 2 (though Jesus himself
didn't baptize them—his disciples did). 3 So he
left Judea and returned to Galilee.

4 He had to go through Samaria on the way.
5 Eventually he came to the Samaritan village of
Sychar, near the field that Jacob gave to his son
Joseph. 6 Jacob's well was there; and Jesus, tired
from the long walk, sat wearily beside the well
about noontime. 7 Soon a Samaritan woman
came to draw water, and Jesus said to her, "Please
give me a drink." 8 He was alone at the time because his disciples had gone into the village to
buy some food.

9 The woman was surprised, for Jews refuse to
have anything to do with Samaritans.* She said
to Jesus, "You are a Jew, and I am a Samaritan
woman. Why are you asking me for a drink?"

10 Jesus replied, "If you only knew the gift
God has for you and who you are speaking to,
you would ask me, and I would give you living
water."

11 "But sir, you don't have a rope or a bucket," she said, "and this well is very deep. Where
would you get this living water? 12 And besides,
do you think you're greater than our ancestor
Jacob, who gave us this well? How can you offer
better water than he and his sons and his animals
enjoyed?"

13 Jesus replied, "Anyone who drinks this wa-

3:21 Or *can see God at work in what he is doing.* **3:25** Some manuscripts read *some Jews.* **3:31** Some manuscripts do not include *and is greater than anyone else.* **4:1** Some manuscripts read *The Lord.* **4:9** Some manuscripts do not include this sentence.

acceptable and honored social group. He is named, male, a Jew, a Pharisee, and a ruler and a teacher of Israel.

3:22–36: Further testimony of John the Baptist.

4:1–42 Jesus and the Samaritan Woman. 1–15: The conversation revolves around a misunderstanding about water and the spirit. The woman, however, could not contrast more sharply with Nicodemus. She is thoroughly unworthy in the view of first-century Jews. A Jewish man did not engage in conversation with a woman to whom he was not related, a non-Jewish woman, anyone of disrepute, or any Samaritan. Thus her status is as low as it can be. The lack of a name further emphasizes her apparent unimportance. Throughout, the woman understands and responds to Jesus on the most material level.

ter will soon become thirsty again. [14]But those
who drink the water I give will never be thirsty
again. It becomes a fresh, bubbling spring within
them, giving them eternal life."
[15]"Please, sir," the woman said, "give me this
water! Then I'll never be thirsty again, and I
won't have to come here to get water."
[16]"Go and get your husband," Jesus told her.
[17]"I don't have a husband," the woman replied.
Jesus said, "You're right! You don't have a
husband—[18]for you have had five husbands, and
you aren't even married to the man you're living
with now. You certainly spoke the truth!"
[19]"Sir," the woman said, "you must be a
prophet. [20]So tell me, why is it that you Jews insist that Jerusalem is the only place of worship,
while we Samaritans claim it is here at Mount
Gerizim,* where our ancestors worshiped?"
[21]Jesus replied, "Believe me, dear woman, the
time is coming when it will no longer matter
whether you worship the Father on this mountain or in Jerusalem. [22]You Samaritans know very
little about the one you worship, while we Jews
know all about him, for salvation comes through
the Jews. [23]But the time is coming—indeed it's
here now—when true worshipers will worship
the Father in spirit and in truth. The Father is
looking for those who will worship him that way.
[24]For God is Spirit, so those who worship him
must worship in spirit and in truth."
[25]The woman said, "I know the Messiah is
coming—the one who is called Christ. When he
comes, he will explain everything to us."
[26]Then Jesus told her, "I AM the Messiah!"*
[27]Just then his disciples came back. They were
shocked to find him talking to a woman, but none
of them had the nerve to ask, "What do you want
with her?" or "Why are you talking to her?"
[28]The woman left her water jar beside the well and
ran back to the village, telling everyone, [29]"Come
and see a man who told me everything I ever did!
Could he possibly be the Messiah?" [30]So the people came streaming from the village to see him.
[31]Meanwhile, the disciples were urging Jesus,
"Rabbi, eat something."
[32]But Jesus replied, "I have a kind of food you
know nothing about."
[33]"Did someone bring him food while we
were gone?" the disciples asked each other.
[34]Then Jesus explained: "My nourishment
comes from doing the will of God, who sent me,
and from finishing his work. [35]You know the
saying, 'Four months between planting and harvest.' But I say, wake up and look around. The
fields are already ripe* for harvest. [36]The harvesters are paid good wages, and the fruit they
harvest is people brought to eternal life. What
joy awaits both the planter and the harvester
alike! [37]You know the saying, 'One plants and
another harvests.' And it's true. [38]I sent you to
harvest where you didn't plant; others had already done the work, and now you will get to
gather the harvest."

Many Samaritans Believe

[39]Many Samaritans from the village believed
in Jesus because the woman had said, "He told

4:20 Greek *on this mountain.* **4:26** Or *"The 'I AM' is here"*; or *"I am the LORD"*; Greek reads *"I am, the one speaking to you."* See Exod 3:14. **4:35** Greek *white.*

20–23: The subject then changes to a central point of contention between Jews and Samaritans: the place of true worship. Jesus responds that God will be worshiped neither in Jerusalem nor at the Samaritans' mountain, Gerizim. Rather, *the time is coming—indeed, it's here now—when true worshipers will worship the Father in spirit and in truth.* **26:** Literally this is, "I am, the one speaking to you," or "I am; the one speaking to you [is the 'I am']," using the name of God given to Moses (Exod 3:14). Thus the only pronouncement of Jesus' messiahship and an implicit identification of the Messiah with God is made to a woman, a non-Jew and a person of earthly disrepute, rather than to one of his own—because she is thirsty for that knowledge. **27–33:** Characteristically in John, the male disciples are passively present; they fail in persistence; they leave the tomb upon finding it empty; and they fail to speak their mind to Jesus. This woman may be regarded as one of the sowers whose planting the other disciples are to reap. In a powerful way, one that defies social convention, she carries out the functions of a true disciple. **39–42:** In contrast to Nicodemus, the Samaritan woman goes into the village and brings her fellow Samaritans to faith in Jesus. The Samaritans declare that they now believe because of Jesus rather than the woman's testimony alone. They alone call him *the Savior of the world.* The awareness of Jesus' true identity, within one person, then within the community, expands: Jesus is first a Jew, then Lord, greater than Jacob, prophet, Messiah, Christ, the "I am," and *Savior of the world.* In the structure of the narrative, the Samaritan woman has been used by the Lord to bring the reader along in faith. Thus this woman is fruitful for Christ, whereas Nicodemus is not. In this story, "well" refers to the female. In the Old Testament, the imagery of wells often refers to God's relationship with

me everything I ever did!" 40 When they came
out to see him, they begged him to stay in
their village. So he stayed for two days, 41 long
enough for many more to hear his message and
believe. 42 Then they said to the woman, "Now
we believe, not just because of what you told
us, but because we have heard him ourselves.
Now we know that he is indeed the Savior of
the world."

Jesus Heals an Official's Son

43 At the end of the two days, Jesus went on to
Galilee. 44 He himself had said that a prophet is
not honored in his own hometown. 45 Yet the
Galileans welcomed him, for they had been in
Jerusalem at the Passover celebration and had
seen everything he did there.

46 As he traveled through Galilee, he came to
Cana, where he had turned the water into wine.
There was a government official in nearby Capernaum whose son was very sick. 47 When he
heard that Jesus had come from Judea to Galilee,
he went and begged Jesus to come to Capernaum
to heal his son, who was about to die.

48 Jesus asked, "Will you never believe in me
unless you see miraculous signs and wonders?"

49 The official pleaded, "Lord, please come now
before my little boy dies."

50 Then Jesus told him, "Go back home. Your
son will live!" And the man believed what Jesus
said and started home.

51 While the man was on his way, some of his
servants met him with the news that his son was
alive and well. 52 He asked them when the boy
had begun to get better, and they replied, "Yesterday afternoon at one o'clock his fever suddenly disappeared!" 53 Then the father realized that
that was the very time Jesus had told him, "Your
son will live." And he and his entire household
believed in Jesus. 54 This was the second miraculous sign Jesus did in Galilee after coming from
Judea.

Jesus Heals a Lame Man

5 Afterward Jesus returned to Jerusalem for
one of the Jewish holy days. 2 Inside the
city, near the Sheep Gate, was the pool of
Bethesda,* with five covered porches. 3 Crowds
of sick people—blind, lame, or paralyzed—lay
on the porches.* 5 One of the men lying there
had been sick for thirty-eight years. 6 When
Jesus saw him and knew he had been ill for a
long time, he asked him, "Would you like to get
well?"

7 "I can't, sir," the sick man said, "for I have
no one to put me into the pool when the water bubbles up. Someone else always gets there
ahead of me."

8 Jesus told him, "Stand up, pick up your mat,
and walk!"

9 Instantly, the man was healed! He rolled up
his sleeping mat and began walking! But this
miracle happened on the Sabbath, 10 so the Jewish leaders objected. They said to the man who
was cured, "You can't work on the Sabbath!
The law doesn't allow you to carry that sleeping mat!"

11 But he replied, "The man who healed me
told me, 'Pick up your mat and walk.'"

12 "Who said such a thing as that?" they demanded.

13 The man didn't know, for Jesus had disappeared into the crowd. 14 But afterward Jesus
found him in the Temple and told him, "Now
you are well; so stop sinning, or something even
worse may happen to you." 15 Then the man went
and told the Jewish leaders that it was Jesus who
had healed him.

5:2 Other manuscripts read *Beth-zatha;* still others read *Bethsaida.* **5:3** Some manuscripts add an expanded conclusion to verse 3 and all of verse 4: *waiting for a certain movement of the water, 4 for an angel of the Lord came from time to time and stirred up the water. And the first person to step in after the water was stirred was healed of whatever disease he had.*

Israel (e.g., Prov 5:15–18; Song 4:12; Jer 2:1–15). Jesus' spring of living water (John 4:14) recalls God as "the fountain of living water" (Jer 2:13). Living water may also be construed as semen. (In ancient Jewish Palestinian culture, the male's semen was not considered to have greater value than the woman's equivalent contribution in procreation. It is Jesus' unique spiritual gift that is greater, and it is greater than the contribution of male and female alike.) In these terms, the Samaritan woman is a symbolic wife who brings to Jesus many offspring. Her disciple love for him is the love of the bride of Christ. Thus she is not only a woman, in the sense of being lowly. She is an active part of the rebirth by faith of God's new people. As a representative of the Samaritan community, she becomes a paradigm for any true disciple, man or woman.

4:43–54 Healing the Official's Son. This is an instance of "healing at a distance."

5:1–15 Healing a Lame Man. 6: *Would you like to get well?*—the question each person must answer not only about healing but about salvation.

Jesus Claims to Be the Son of God
[16] So the Jewish leaders began harassing* Jesus
for breaking the Sabbath rules. [17] But Jesus replied, "My Father is always working, and so am
I." [18] So the Jewish leaders tried all the harder to
find a way to kill him. For he not only broke the
Sabbath, he called God his Father, thereby making himself equal with God.
[19] So Jesus explained, "I tell you the truth, the
Son can do nothing by himself. He does only
what he sees the Father doing. Whatever the Father does, the Son also does. [20] For the Father loves
the Son and shows him everything he is doing.
In fact, the Father will show him how to do even
greater works than healing this man. Then you
will truly be astonished. [21] For just as the Father
gives life to those he raises from the dead, so the
Son gives life to anyone he wants. [22] In addition,
the Father judges no one. Instead, he has given
the Son absolute authority to judge, [23] so that everyone will honor the Son, just as they honor the
Father. Anyone who does not honor the Son is
certainly not honoring the Father who sent him.
[24] "I tell you the truth, those who listen to my
message and believe in God who sent me have
eternal life. They will never be condemned for
their sins, but they have already passed from
death into life.
[25] "And I assure you that the time is coming,
indeed it's here now, when the dead will hear my
voice—the voice of the Son of God. And those
who listen will live. [26] The Father has life in himself, and he has granted that same life-giving
power to his Son. [27] And he has given him authority to judge everyone because he is the Son
of Man.* [28] Don't be so surprised! Indeed, the
time is coming when all the dead in their graves
will hear the voice of God's Son, [29] and they will
rise again. Those who have done good will rise to
experience eternal life, and those who have continued in evil will rise to experience judgment.
[30] I can do nothing on my own. I judge as God
tells me. Therefore, my judgment is just, because
I carry out the will of the one who sent me, not
my own will.

Witnesses to Jesus
[31] "If I were to testify on my own behalf, my testimony would not be valid. [32] But someone else
is also testifying about me, and I assure you that
everything he says about me is true. [33] In fact,
you sent investigators to listen to John the Baptist, and his testimony about me was true. [34] Of
course, I have no need of human witnesses, but
I say these things so you might be saved. [35] John
was like a burning and shining lamp, and you
were excited for a while about his message. [36] But
I have a greater witness than John—my teachings and my miracles. The Father gave me these
works to accomplish, and they prove that he sent
me. [37] And the Father who sent me has testified
about me himself. You have never heard his
voice or seen him face to face, [38] and you do not
have his message in your hearts, because you do
not believe me—the one he sent to you.
[39] "You search the Scriptures because you
think they give you eternal life. But the Scriptures point to me! [40] Yet you refuse to come to
me to receive this life.
[41] "Your approval means nothing to me, [42] because I know you don't have God's love within
you. [43] For I have come to you in my Father's
name, and you have rejected me. Yet if others
come in their own name, you gladly welcome
them. [44] No wonder you can't believe! For you
gladly honor each other, but you don't care about
the honor that comes from the one who alone is
God.*
[45] "Yet it isn't I who will accuse you before
the Father. Moses will accuse you! Yes, Moses,
in whom you put your hopes. [46] If you really
believed Moses, you would believe me, because
he wrote about me. [47] But since you don't believe what he wrote, how will you believe what
I say?"

Jesus Feeds Five Thousand
6 After this, Jesus crossed over to the far side
of the Sea of Galilee, also known as the Sea
of Tiberias. [2] A huge crowd kept following
him wherever he went, because they saw his miraculous signs as he healed the sick. [3] Then Jesus
climbed a hill and sat down with his disciples
around him. [4] (It was nearly time for the Jewish
Passover celebration.) [5] Jesus soon saw a huge
crowd of people coming to look for him. Turning
to Philip, he asked, "Where can we buy bread to
feed all these people?" [6] He was testing Philip, for
he already knew what he was going to do.
[7] Philip replied, "Even if we worked for
months, we wouldn't have enough money* to
feed them!"

5:16 Or *persecuting.* **5:27** "Son of Man" is a title Jesus used for himself. **5:44** Some manuscripts read *from the only One.* **6:7** Greek *Two hundred denarii would not be enough.* A denarius was equivalent to a laborer's full day's wage.

5:16–47 Jesus as Son of God and the Testimony of John and the Scriptures. 19: The Son *does only what he sees the Father doing*: the basis of understanding the relationship of Father and Son.

8 Then Andrew, Simon Peter's brother, spoke up. 9 "There's a young boy here with five barley loaves and two fish. But what good is that with this huge crowd?"

10 "Tell everyone to sit down," Jesus said. So they all sat down on the grassy slopes. (The men alone numbered about 5,000.) 11 Then Jesus took the loaves, gave thanks to God, and distributed them to the people. Afterward he did the same with the fish. And they all ate as much as they wanted. 12 After everyone was full, Jesus told his disciples, "Now gather the leftovers, so that nothing is wasted." 13 So they picked up the pieces and filled twelve baskets with scraps left by the people who had eaten from the five barley loaves.

14 When the people saw him* do this miraculous sign, they exclaimed, "Surely, he is the Prophet we have been expecting!"* 15 When Jesus saw that they were ready to force him to be their king, he slipped away into the hills by himself.

Jesus Walks on Water

16 That evening Jesus' disciples went down to the shore to wait for him. 17 But as darkness fell and Jesus still hadn't come back, they got into the boat and headed across the lake toward Capernaum. 18 Soon a gale swept down upon them, and the sea grew very rough. 19 They had rowed three or four miles* when suddenly they saw Jesus walking on the water toward the boat. They were terrified, 20 but he called out to them, "Don't be afraid. I am here!*" 21 Then they were eager to let him in the boat, and immediately they arrived at their destination!

Jesus, the Bread of Life

22 The next day the crowd that had stayed on the far shore saw that the disciples had taken the only boat, and they realized Jesus had not gone with them. 23 Several boats from Tiberias landed near the place where the Lord had blessed the bread and the people had eaten. 24 So when the crowd saw that neither Jesus nor his disciples were there, they got into the boats and went across to Capernaum to look for him. 25 They found him on the other side of the lake and asked, "Rabbi, when did you get here?"

26 Jesus replied, "I tell you the truth, you want to be with me because I fed you, not because you understood the miraculous signs. 27 But don't be so concerned about perishable things like food. Spend your energy seeking the eternal life that the Son of Man* can give you. For God the Father has given me the seal of his approval."

28 They replied, "We want to perform God's works, too. What should we do?"

29 Jesus told them, "This is the only work God wants from you: Believe in the one he has sent."

30 They answered, "Show us a miraculous sign if you want us to believe in you. What can you do? 31 After all, our ancestors ate manna while they journeyed through the wilderness! The Scriptures say, 'Moses gave them bread from heaven to eat.'*"

32 Jesus said, "I tell you the truth, Moses didn't give you bread from heaven. My Father did. And now he offers you the true bread from heaven. 33 The true bread of God is the one who comes down from heaven and gives life to the world."

34 "Sir," they said, "give us that bread every day."

35 Jesus replied, "I am the bread of life. Whoever comes to me will never be hungry again. Whoever believes in me will never be thirsty. 36 But you haven't believed in me even though you have seen me. 37 However, those the Father has given me will come to me, and I will never reject them. 38 For I have come down from heaven to do the will of God who sent me, not to do my own will. 39 And this is the will of God, that I should not lose even one of all those he has given me, but that I should raise them up at the last day. 40 For it is my Father's will that all who see his Son and believe in him should have eternal life. I will raise them up at the last day."

41 Then the people* began to murmur in disagreement because he had said, "I am the bread that came down from heaven." 42 They said, "Isn't this Jesus, the son of Joseph? We know his father and mother. How can he say, 'I came down from heaven'?"

43 But Jesus replied, "Stop complaining about what I said. 44 For no one can come to me unless the Father who sent me draws them to me, and at the last day I will raise them up. 45 As it is written in the Scriptures,* 'They will all be taught by God.' Everyone who listens to the Father and learns from him comes to me. 46 (Not that anyone has ever seen the Father; only I, who was sent from God, have seen him.)

47 "I tell you the truth, anyone who believes has eternal life. 48 Yes, I am the bread of life! 49 Your ancestors ate manna in the wilderness, but they all died. 50 Anyone who eats the bread

6:14a Some manuscripts read *Jesus.* **6:14b** See Deut 18:15, 18; Mal 4:5-6. **6:19** Greek *25 or 30 stadia* [4.6 or 5.5 kilometers]. **6:20** Or *The 'I AM' is here;* Greek reads *I am.* See Exod 3:14. **6:27** "Son of Man" is a title Jesus used for himself. **6:31** Exod 16:4; Ps 78:24. **6:41** Greek *Jewish people;* also in 6:52. **6:45** Greek *in the prophets.* Isa 54:13.

from heaven, however, will never die. 51 I am the living bread that came down from heaven. Anyone who eats this bread will live forever; and this bread, which I will offer so the world may live, is my flesh."

52 Then the people began arguing with each other about what he meant. "How can this man give us his flesh to eat?" they asked.

53 So Jesus said again, "I tell you the truth, unless you eat the flesh of the Son of Man and drink his blood, you cannot have eternal life within you. 54 But anyone who eats my flesh and drinks my blood has eternal life, and I will raise that person at the last day. 55 For my flesh is true food, and my blood is true drink. 56 Anyone who eats my flesh and drinks my blood remains in me, and I in him. 57 I live because of the living Father who sent me; in the same way, anyone who feeds on me will live because of me. 58 I am the true bread that came down from heaven. Anyone who eats this bread will not die as your ancestors did (even though they ate the manna) but will live forever."

59 He said these things while he was teaching in the synagogue in Capernaum.

Many Disciples Desert Jesus

60 Many of his disciples said, "This is very hard to understand. How can anyone accept it?"

61 Jesus was aware that his disciples were complaining, so he said to them, "Does this offend you? 62 Then what will you think if you see the Son of Man ascend to heaven again? 63 The Spirit alone gives eternal life. Human effort accomplishes nothing. And the very words I have spoken to you are spirit and life. 64 But some of you do not believe me." (For Jesus knew from the beginning which ones didn't believe, and he knew who would betray him.) 65 Then he said, "That is why I said that people can't come to me unless the Father gives them to me."

66 At this point many of his disciples turned away and deserted him. 67 Then Jesus turned to the Twelve and asked, "Are you also going to leave?"

68 Simon Peter replied, "Lord, to whom would we go? You have the words that give eternal life. 69 We believe, and we know you are the Holy One of God.*"

70 Then Jesus said, "I chose the twelve of you, but one is a devil." 71 He was speaking of Judas, son of Simon Iscariot, one of the Twelve, who would later betray him.

Jesus and His Brothers

7 After this, Jesus traveled around Galilee. He wanted to stay out of Judea, where the Jewish leaders were plotting his death. 2 But soon it was time for the Jewish Festival of Shelters, 3 and Jesus' brothers said to him, "Leave here and go to Judea, where your followers can see your miracles! 4 You can't become famous if you hide like this! If you can do such wonderful things, show yourself to the world!" 5 For even his brothers didn't believe in him.

6 Jesus replied, "Now is not the right time for me to go, but you can go anytime. 7 The world can't hate you, but it does hate me because I accuse it of doing evil. 8 You go on. I'm not going* to this festival, because my time has not yet come." 9 After saying these things, Jesus remained in Galilee.

Jesus Teaches Openly at the Temple

10 But after his brothers left for the festival, Jesus also went, though secretly, staying out of public view. 11 The Jewish leaders tried to find him at the festival and kept asking if anyone had seen him. 12 There was a lot of grumbling about him among the crowds. Some argued, "He's a good man," but others said, "He's nothing but a fraud who deceives the people." 13 But no one had the courage to speak favorably about him in public, for they were afraid of getting in trouble with the Jewish leaders.

14 Then, midway through the festival, Jesus

6:69 Other manuscripts read *you are the Christ, the Holy One of God;* still others read *you are the Christ, the Son of God;* and still others read *you are the Christ, the Son of the living God.* **7:8** Some manuscripts read *not yet going.*

6:1–59 Feeding the Five Thousand. Walking on Water. The Bread of Life. 53–58: In John's gospel there is no account of the Last Supper (though Jesus and the disciples clearly are at supper [13:22–30]). But many commentators say that this account of Jesus' words, following the miracle of the feeding, serve as John's account of the importance of the Supper for Jesus' followers.

6:60–71 Some Disciples Leave. The difficulty for Jesus' followers who were observant Jews was that consuming blood was regarded as against God's law (Lev 17:15).

7:1–24 Jesus at the Festival of Shelters. This is Sukkoth, or the Feast of Booths (or Tabernacles), the Jewish harvest festival in the fall. It was called this because traditionally the harvesters built temporary shelters ("booths") in the fields while they were harvesting crops (Lev 23:42–43). Such shelters later were built for pilgrims returning to Jerusalem for the festival.

went up to the Temple and began to teach. [15]The people* were surprised when they heard him. "How does he know so much when he hasn't been trained?" they asked.

[16]So Jesus told them, "My message is not my own; it comes from God who sent me. [17]Anyone who wants to do the will of God will know whether my teaching is from God or is merely my own. [18]Those who speak for themselves want glory only for themselves, but a person who seeks to honor the one who sent him speaks truth, not lies. [19]Moses gave you the law, but none of you obeys it! In fact, you are trying to kill me."

[20]The crowd replied, "You're demon possessed! Who's trying to kill you?"

[21]Jesus replied, "I did one miracle on the Sabbath, and you were amazed. [22]But you work on the Sabbath, too, when you obey Moses' law of circumcision. (Actually, this tradition of circumcision began with the patriarchs, long before the law of Moses.) [23]For if the correct time for circumcising your son falls on the Sabbath, you go ahead and do it so as not to break the law of Moses. So why should you be angry with me for healing a man on the Sabbath? [24]Look beneath the surface so you can judge correctly."

Is Jesus the Messiah?

[25]Some of the people who lived in Jerusalem started to ask each other, "Isn't this the man they are trying to kill? [26]But here he is, speaking in public, and they say nothing to him. Could our leaders possibly believe that he is the Messiah? [27]But how could he be? For we know where this man comes from. When the Messiah comes, he will simply appear; no one will know where he comes from."

[28]While Jesus was teaching in the Temple, he called out, "Yes, you know me, and you know where I come from. But I'm not here on my own. The one who sent me is true, and you don't know him. [29]But I know him because I come from him, and he sent me to you." [30]Then the leaders tried to arrest him; but no one laid a hand on him, because his time* had not yet come.

[31]Many among the crowds at the Temple believed in him. "After all," they said, "would you expect the Messiah to do more miraculous signs than this man has done?"

[32]When the Pharisees heard that the crowds were whispering such things, they and the leading priests sent Temple guards to arrest Jesus. [33]But Jesus told them, "I will be with you only a little longer. Then I will return to the one who sent me. [34]You will search for me but not find me. And you cannot go where I am going."

[35]The Jewish leaders were puzzled by this statement. "Where is he planning to go?" they asked. "Is he thinking of leaving the country and going to the Jews in other lands?* Maybe he will even teach the Greeks! [36]What does he mean when he says, 'You will search for me but not find me,' and 'You cannot go where I am going'?"

Jesus Promises Living Water

[37]On the last day, the climax of the festival, Jesus stood and shouted to the crowds, "Anyone who is thirsty may come to me! [38]Anyone who believes in me may come and drink! For the Scriptures declare, 'Rivers of living water will flow from his heart.' "* [39](When he said "living water," he was speaking of the Spirit, who would be given to everyone believing in him. But the Spirit had not yet been given,* because Jesus had not yet entered into his glory.)

Division and Unbelief

[40]When the crowds heard him say this, some of them declared, "Surely this man is the Prophet we've been expecting."* [41]Others said, "He is the Messiah." Still others said, "But he can't be! Will the Messiah come from Galilee? [42]For the Scriptures clearly state that the Messiah will be born of the royal line of David, in Bethlehem, the village where King David was born."* [43]So the crowd was divided about him. [44]Some even wanted him arrested, but no one laid a hand on him.

[45]When the Temple guards returned without having arrested Jesus, the leading priests and Pharisees demanded, "Why didn't you bring him in?"

[46]"We have never heard anyone speak like this!" the guards responded.

7:15 Greek *Jewish people.* **7:30** Greek *his hour.* **7:35** Or *the Jews who live among the Greeks?* **7:37-38** Or *"Let anyone who is thirsty come to me and drink. [38]For the Scriptures declare, 'Rivers of living water will flow from the heart of anyone who believes in me.' "* **7:39** Some manuscripts read *But as yet there was no Spirit.* Still others read *But as yet there was no Holy Spirit.* **7:40** See Deut 18:15, 18; Mal 4:5-6. **7:42** See Mic 5:2.

7:25–53 Who Is Jesus? 37: *The last day*: The Festival of Shelters lasted for eight days (Lev 23:36); it was the time of year that the rainy season began. **38–39:** *Living water*: Running water, such as would have filled the stream beds during the rainy season.

47 "Have you been led astray, too?" the Pharisees mocked. 48 "Is there a single one of us rulers
or Pharisees who believes in him? 49 This foolish
crowd follows him, but they are ignorant of the
law. God's curse is on them!"
50 Then Nicodemus, the leader who had met
with Jesus earlier, spoke up. 51 "Is it legal to convict a man before he is given a hearing?" he
asked.
52 They replied, "Are you from Galilee, too?
Search the Scriptures and see for yourself—no
prophet ever comes* from Galilee!"

[The most ancient Greek manuscripts do not include John 7:53–8:11.]

53 Then the meeting broke up, and everybody
went home.

A Woman Caught in Adultery

8 Jesus returned to the Mount of Olives,
2 but early the next morning he was back
again at the Temple. A crowd soon gathered, and he sat down and taught them. 3 As he
was speaking, the teachers of religious law and
the Pharisees brought a woman who had been
caught in the act of adultery. They put her in
front of the crowd.
4 "Teacher," they said to Jesus, "this woman
was caught in the act of adultery. 5 The law of
Moses says to stone her. What do you say?"
6 They were trying to trap him into saying
something they could use against him, but Jesus
stooped down and wrote in the dust with his
finger. 7 They kept demanding an answer, so he
stood up again and said, "All right, but let the
one who has never sinned throw the first stone!"
8 Then he stooped down again and wrote in the
dust.
9 When the accusers heard this, they slipped
away one by one, beginning with the oldest, until only Jesus was left in the middle of the crowd
with the woman. 10 Then Jesus stood up again and
said to the woman, "Where are your accusers?
Didn't even one of them condemn you?"
11 "No, Lord," she said.
And Jesus said, "Neither do I. Go and sin no
more."

Jesus, the Light of the World

12 Jesus spoke to the people once more and said, "I
am the light of the world. If you follow me, you
won't have to walk in darkness, because you will
have the light that leads to life."
13 The Pharisees replied, "You are making
those claims about yourself! Such testimony is
not valid."
14 Jesus told them, "These claims are valid
even though I make them about myself. For I
know where I came from and where I am going,
but you don't know this about me. 15 You judge
me by human standards, but I do not judge anyone. 16 And if I did, my judgment would be correct in every respect because I am not alone. The
Father* who sent me is with me. 17 Your own
law says that if two people agree about something, their witness is accepted as fact.* 18 I am
one witness, and my Father who sent me is the
other."
19 "Where is your father?" they asked.
Jesus answered, "Since you don't know who
I am, you don't know who my Father is. If you
knew me, you would also know my Father."
20 Jesus made these statements while he was
teaching in the section of the Temple known as
the Treasury. But he was not arrested, because
his time* had not yet come.

The Unbelieving People Warned

21 Later Jesus said to them again, "I am going
away. You will search for me but will die in your
sin. You cannot come where I am going."
22 The people* asked, "Is he planning to commit suicide? What does he mean, 'You cannot
come where I am going'?"
23 Jesus continued, "You are from below; I am
from above. You belong to this world; I do not.
24 That is why I said that you will die in your sins;

7:52 Some manuscripts read *the prophet does not come.*
8:16 Some manuscripts read *The One.* **8:17** See Deut 19:15.
8:20 Greek *his hour.* **8:22** Greek *Jewish people;* also in 8:31, 48, 52, 57.

8:1–11 The Woman Caught Committing Adultery. This story is probably not originally part of John's Gospel. It fits better after Luke 21:38, and uses terms—*teachers of religious law*—that do not appear elsewhere in John. There is no reason, however, to regard it as unhistorical. The message, that we are to refrain from condemning others out of self-righteousness, is clearly one that Jesus taught.

8:12–20 The Light of the World. The contrast is between those who will not see the light and those who choose to walk by it. **13:** The *testimony* is that of a witness in a trial to a matter of fact. **19:** Jesus counters with testimony based on personal knowledge, on relationships, not on intellectual knowledge.

for unless you believe that I AM who I claim to
be,* you will die in your sins."
25 "Who are you?" they demanded.
Jesus replied, "The one I have always
claimed to be.* 26 I have much to say about you
and much to condemn, but I won't. For I say
only what I have heard from the one who sent
me, and he is completely truthful." 27 But they
still didn't understand that he was talking about
his Father.
28 So Jesus said, "When you have lifted up the
Son of Man on the cross, then you will understand that I AM he.* I do nothing on my own but
say only what the Father taught me. 29 And the
one who sent me is with me—he has not deserted me. For I always do what pleases him." 30 Then
many who heard him say these things believed
in him.

Jesus and Abraham

31 Jesus said to the people who believed in him,
"You are truly my disciples if you remain faithful to my teachings. 32 And you will know the
truth, and the truth will set you free."
33 "But we are descendants of Abraham," they
said. "We have never been slaves to anyone.
What do you mean, 'You will be set free'?"
34 Jesus replied, "I tell you the truth, everyone who sins is a slave of sin. 35 A slave is not a
permanent member of the family, but a son is
part of the family forever. 36 So if the Son sets
you free, you are truly free. 37 Yes, I realize that
you are descendants of Abraham. And yet some
of you are trying to kill me because there's no
room in your hearts for my message. 38 I am
telling you what I saw when I was with my Father. But you are following the advice of your
father."
39 "Our father is Abraham!" they declared.
"No," Jesus replied, "for if you were really
the children of Abraham, you would follow his
example.* 40 Instead, you are trying to kill me
because I told you the truth, which I heard from
God. Abraham never did such a thing. 41 No, you
are imitating your real father."
They replied, "We aren't illegitimate children! God himself is our true Father."
42 Jesus told them, "If God were your Father,
you would love me, because I have come to you
from God. I am not here on my own, but he sent
me. 43 Why can't you understand what I am saying? It's because you can't even hear me! 44 For
you are the children of your father the devil,
and you love to do the evil things he does. He
was a murderer from the beginning. He has always hated the truth, because there is no truth
in him. When he lies, it is consistent with his
character; for he is a liar and the father of lies.
45 So when I tell the truth, you just naturally
don't believe me! 46 Which of you can truthfully
accuse me of sin? And since I am telling you
the truth, why don't you believe me? 47 Anyone
who belongs to God listens gladly to the words
of God. But you don't listen because you don't
belong to God."
48 The people retorted, "You Samaritan devil!
Didn't we say all along that you were possessed
by a demon?"
49 "No," Jesus said, "I have no demon in me.
For I honor my Father—and you dishonor me.
50 And though I have no wish to glorify myself,
God is going to glorify me. He is the true judge.
51 I tell you the truth, anyone who obeys my
teaching will never die!"
52 The people said, "Now we know you are
possessed by a demon. Even Abraham and the
prophets died, but you say, 'Anyone who obeys
my teaching will never die!' 53 Are you greater
than our father Abraham? He died, and so did
the prophets. Who do you think you are?"
54 Jesus answered, "If I want glory for myself,
it doesn't count. But it is my Father who will
glorify me. You say, 'He is our God,*' 55 but you
don't even know him. I know him. If I said otherwise, I would be as great a liar as you! But I do
know him and obey him. 56 Your father Abraham
rejoiced as he looked forward to my coming. He
saw it and was glad."
57 The people said, "You aren't even fifty
years old. How can you say you have seen Abraham?*"
58 Jesus answered, "I tell you the truth, before
Abraham was even born, I AM!*" 59 At that point
they picked up stones to throw at him. But Jesus
was hidden from them and left the Temple.

8:24 Greek *unless you believe that I am.* See Exod 3:14.
8:25 Or *Why do I speak to you at all?* **8:28** Greek *When you have lifted up the Son of Man, then you will know that I am.* "Son of Man" is a title Jesus used for himself. **8:39** Some manuscripts read *if you are really the children of Abraham, follow his example.* **8:54** Some manuscripts read *your God.*
8:57 Some manuscripts read *How can you say Abraham has seen you?* **8:58** Or *before Abraham was even born, I have always been alive;* Greek reads *before Abraham was, I am.* See Exod 3:14.

8:21–58 Jesus and the Father. Jesus and Abraham. 28: *Lifted up*: The crucifixion is the final expression of Jesus' obedience. *I do nothing on my own*: Jesus' life and teaching are the expression of his Father's will. **58:** *I AM*: Once again Jesus refers to himself in terms that recall God's self-naming in Exodus 3:14.

Jesus Heals a Man Born Blind

9 As Jesus was walking along, he saw a man
who had been blind from birth. 2 “Rabbi,”
his disciples asked him, “why was this man
born blind? Was it because of his own sins or his
parents’ sins?”
3 “It was not because of his sins or his parents’
sins,” Jesus answered. “This happened so the
power of God could be seen in him. 4 We must
quickly carry out the tasks assigned us by the
one who sent us.* The night is coming, and then
no one can work. 5 But while I am here in the
world, I am the light of the world.”
6 Then he spit on the ground, made mud with
the saliva, and spread the mud over the blind
man’s eyes. 7 He told him, “Go wash yourself in
the pool of Siloam” (Siloam means “sent”). So
the man went and washed and came back seeing!
8 His neighbors and others who knew him as a
blind beggar asked each other, “Isn’t this the man
who used to sit and beg?” 9 Some said he was, and
others said, “No, he just looks like him!”
But the beggar kept saying, “Yes, I am the
same one!”
10 They asked, “Who healed you? What happened?”
11 He told them, “The man they call Jesus
made mud and spread it over my eyes and told
me, ‘Go to the pool of Siloam and wash yourself.’
So I went and washed, and now I can see!”
12 “Where is he now?” they asked.
“I don’t know,” he replied.
13 Then they took the man who had been blind
to the Pharisees, 14 because it was on the Sabbath
that Jesus had made the mud and healed him.
15 The Pharisees asked the man all about it. So he
told them, “He put the mud over my eyes, and
when I washed it away, I could see!”
16 Some of the Pharisees said, “This man Jesus
is not from God, for he is working on the Sabbath.” Others said, “But how could an ordinary
sinner do such miraculous signs?” So there was a
deep division of opinion among them.
17 Then the Pharisees again questioned the
man who had been blind and demanded, “What’s
your opinion about this man who healed you?”
The man replied, “I think he must be a
prophet.”
18 The Jewish leaders still refused to believe
the man had been blind and could now see, so
they called in his parents. 19 They asked them, “Is
this your son? Was he born blind? If so, how can
he now see?”
20 His parents replied, “We know this is our
son and that he was born blind, 21 but we don’t
know how he can see or who healed him. Ask
him. He is old enough to speak for himself.”
22 His parents said this because they were afraid
of the Jewish leaders, who had announced that
anyone saying Jesus was the Messiah would be
expelled from the synagogue. 23 That’s why they
said, “He is old enough. Ask him.”
24 So for the second time they called in the
man who had been blind and told him, “God
should get the glory for this,* because we know
this man Jesus is a sinner.”
25 “I don’t know whether he is a sinner,” the
man replied. “But I know this: I was blind, and
now I can see!”
26 “But what did he do?” they asked. “How did
he heal you?”
27 “Look!” the man exclaimed. “I told you
once. Didn’t you listen? Why do you want to
hear it again? Do you want to become his disciples, too?”
28 Then they cursed him and said, “You are
his disciple, but we are disciples of Moses! 29 We
know God spoke to Moses, but we don’t even
know where this man comes from.”
30 “Why, that’s very strange!” the man replied. “He healed my eyes, and yet you don’t
know where he comes from? 31 We know that God
doesn’t listen to sinners, but he is ready to hear
those who worship him and do his will. 32 Ever
since the world began, no one has been able to
open the eyes of someone born blind. 33 If this man
were not from God, he couldn’t have done it.”
34 “You were born a total sinner!” they answered. “Are you trying to teach us?” And they
threw him out of the synagogue.

Spiritual Blindness

35 When Jesus heard what had happened, he
found the man and asked, “Do you believe in the
Son of Man?*”

9:4 Other manuscripts read *I must quickly carry out the tasks assigned me by the one who sent me;* still others read *We must quickly carry out the tasks assigned us by the one who sent me.* **9:24** Or *Give glory to God, not to Jesus;* Greek reads *Give glory to God.* **9:35** Some manuscripts read *the Son of God?* “Son of Man” is a title Jesus used for himself.

9:1–41 Healing the Man Who Was Born Blind. 1–5: Jesus rejects *sins* (whether one’s own or one’s ancestors’) as the cause of suffering. *This happened so the power of God could be seen in him*: The stress is not on the cause of the man’s blindness, but on the *power of God* to change the situation. **5:** *I am the light of the world*: Recalling the Prologue: “The one . . . who gives light to everyone, was coming into the world” (1:9).

36 The man answered, "Who is he, sir? I want to believe in him."

37 "You have seen him," Jesus said, "and he is speaking to you!"

38 "Yes, Lord, I believe!" the man said. And he worshiped Jesus.

39 Then Jesus told him,* "I entered this world to render judgment—to give sight to the blind and to show those who think they see* that they are blind."

40 Some Pharisees who were standing nearby heard him and asked, "Are you saying we're blind?"

41 "If you were blind, you wouldn't be guilty," Jesus replied. "But you remain guilty because you claim you can see.

The Good Shepherd and His Sheep

10 "I tell you the truth, anyone who sneaks over the wall of a sheepfold, rather than going through the gate, must surely be a thief and a robber! 2 But the one who enters through the gate is the shepherd of the sheep. 3 The gatekeeper opens the gate for him, and the sheep recognize his voice and come to him. He calls his own sheep by name and leads them out. 4 After he has gathered his own flock, he walks ahead of them, and they follow him because they know his voice. 5 They won't follow a stranger; they will run from him because they don't know his voice."

6 Those who heard Jesus use this illustration didn't understand what he meant, 7 so he explained it to them: "I tell you the truth, I am the gate for the sheep. 8 All who came before me* were thieves and robbers. But the true sheep did not listen to them. 9 Yes, I am the gate. Those who come in through me will be saved.* They will come and go freely and will find good pastures. 10 The thief's purpose is to steal and kill and destroy. My purpose is to give them a rich and satisfying life.

11 "I am the good shepherd. The good shepherd sacrifices his life for the sheep. 12 A hired hand will run when he sees a wolf coming. He will abandon the sheep because they don't belong to him and he isn't their shepherd. And so the wolf attacks them and scatters the flock. 13 The hired hand runs away because he's working only for the money and doesn't really care about the sheep.

14 "I am the good shepherd; I know my own sheep, and they know me, 15 just as my Father knows me and I know the Father. So I sacrifice my life for the sheep. 16 I have other sheep, too, that are not in this sheepfold. I must bring them also. They will listen to my voice, and there will be one flock with one shepherd.

17 "The Father loves me because I sacrifice my life so I may take it back again. 18 No one can take my life from me. I sacrifice it voluntarily. For I have the authority to lay it down when I want to and also to take it up again. For this is what my Father has commanded."

19 When he said these things, the people* were again divided in their opinions about him. 20 Some said, "He's demon possessed and out of his mind. Why listen to a man like that?" 21 Others said, "This doesn't sound like a man possessed by a demon! Can a demon open the eyes of the blind?"

Jesus Claims to Be the Son of God

22 It was now winter, and Jesus was in Jerusalem at the time of Hanukkah, the Festival of Dedication. 23 He was in the Temple, walking through the section known as Solomon's Colonnade. 24 The people surrounded him and asked, "How long are you going to keep us in suspense? If you are the Messiah, tell us plainly."

9:38-39a Some manuscripts do not include *"Yes, Lord, I believe!" the man said. And he worshiped Jesus. Then Jesus told him.* **9:39b** Greek *those who see.* **10:8** Some manuscripts do not include *before me.* **10:9** Or *will find safety.* **10:19** Greek *Jewish people;* also in 10:24, 31.

39–41: The *judgment* lies in the exposure of those who are blind but *claim* that they *can see*, recalling Jesus' words to Nicodemus: "The judgment is based on this fact: God's light came into the world, but people loved the darkness more than the light" (3:19).

10:1–21 The Good Shepherd. There are two comparisons in this passage. **7:** *I am the gate* says that Jesus provides the way to salvation. **11:** *I am the good shepherd* is Jesus' claim that he *sacrifices his life for the sheep*, that he himself will die in order to save them from death. Both comparisons are based on the realities of sheepherding, in which sheep of a particular flock recognize their own shepherd, and they will go only where that shepherd leads them; they also rely on the shepherd to protect them from danger in the wilderness.

10:22–42 Jesus Is the Son of God. 22: *Hanukkah* or *the Festival of Dedication* commemorated the rededication of the Temple in 164 BC at the end of the Maccabean revolt against Antiochus Epiphanes IV, the Greek ruler who had stolen the Temple furnishings and desecrated it by sacrificing a pig on the altar. **24:** The occasion of the festival provided an opportunity to ask if Jesus was *the Messiah*, but the questioners

25 Jesus replied, "I have already told you, and
you don't believe me. The proof is the work I do
in my Father's name. 26 But you don't believe me
because you are not my sheep. 27 My sheep listen to my voice; I know them, and they follow
me. 28 I give them eternal life, and they will never
perish. No one can snatch them away from me,
29 for my Father has given them to me, and he is
more powerful than anyone else.* No one can
snatch them from the Father's hand. 30 The Father and I are one."

31 Once again the people picked up stones to
kill him. 32 Jesus said, "At my Father's direction I
have done many good works. For which one are
you going to stone me?"

33 They replied, "We're stoning you not for
any good work, but for blasphemy! You, a mere
man, claim to be God."

34 Jesus replied, "It is written in your own
Scriptures* that God said to certain leaders of the
people, 'I say, you are gods!'* 35 And you know
that the Scriptures cannot be altered. So if those
people who received God's message were called
'gods,' 36 why do you call it blasphemy when I
say, 'I am the Son of God'? After all, the Father
set me apart and sent me into the world. 37 Don't
believe me unless I carry out my Father's work.
38 But if I do his work, believe in the evidence of
the miraculous works I have done, even if you
don't believe me. Then you will know and understand that the Father is in me, and I am in
the Father."

39 Once again they tried to arrest him, but he
got away and left them. 40 He went beyond the
Jordan River near the place where John was first
baptizing and stayed there awhile. 41 And many
followed him. "John didn't perform miraculous
signs," they remarked to one another, "but everything he said about this man has come true."
42 And many who were there believed in Jesus.

The Raising of Lazarus

11 A man named Lazarus was sick. He
lived in Bethany with his sisters,
Mary and Martha. 2 This is the Mary
who later poured the expensive perfume on the
Lord's feet and wiped them with her hair.* Her
brother, Lazarus, was sick. 3 So the two sisters
sent a message to Jesus telling him, "Lord, your
dear friend is very sick."

4 But when Jesus heard about it he said, "Lazarus's sickness will not end in death. No, it happened for the glory of God so that the Son of God
will receive glory from this." 5 So although Jesus
loved Martha, Mary, and Lazarus, 6 he stayed
where he was for the next two days. 7 Finally, he
said to his disciples, "Let's go back to Judea."

8 But his disciples objected. "Rabbi," they
said, "only a few days ago the people* in Judea
were trying to stone you. Are you going there
again?"

9 Jesus replied, "There are twelve hours of
daylight every day. During the day people can
walk safely. They can see because they have the
light of this world. 10 But at night there is danger
of stumbling because they have no light." 11 Then
he said, "Our friend Lazarus has fallen asleep,
but now I will go and wake him up."

12 The disciples said, "Lord, if he is sleeping,
he will soon get better!" 13 They thought Jesus
meant Lazarus was simply sleeping, but Jesus
meant Lazarus had died.

14 So he told them plainly, "Lazarus is dead.
15 And for your sakes, I'm glad I wasn't there, for
now you will really believe. Come, let's go see
him."

16 Thomas, nicknamed the Twin,* said to his
fellow disciples, "Let's go, too—and die with
Jesus."

17 When Jesus arrived at Bethany, he was
told that Lazarus had already been in his grave
for four days. 18 Bethany was only a few miles*
down the road from Jerusalem, 19 and many of
the people had come to console Martha and
Mary in their loss. 20 When Martha got word that
Jesus was coming, she went to meet him. But
Mary stayed in the house. 21 Martha said to Jesus,
"Lord, if only you had been here, my brother
would not have died. 22 But even now I know that
God will give you whatever you ask."

23 Jesus told her, "Your brother will rise
again."

10:29 Other manuscripts read *for what my Father has given me is more powerful than anything;* still others read *for regarding that which my Father has given me, he is greater than all.* **10:34a** Greek *your own law.* **10:34b** Ps 82:6. **11:2** This incident is recorded in chapter 12. **11:8** Greek *Jewish people;* also in 11:19, 31, 33, 36, 45, 54. **11:16** Greek *Thomas, who was called Didymus.* **11:18** Greek *was about 15 stadia* [about 2.8 kilometers].

meant a leader who would restore Israel's independence, as the Maccabees had done. **37–38:** Jesus appeals not to a hunger for political independence, but to his efforts to *carry out* his *Father's work.* His sonship is not one of kingly appointment, but one of ministry, service, and complete identity with his Father.

11:1–44 The Raising of Lazarus. 25: *I am the resurrection and the life*: Even before his own death and resurrection, Jesus brings life out of death.

24 "Yes," Martha said, "he will rise when everyone else rises, at the last day."
25 Jesus told her, "I am the resurrection and
the life.* Anyone who believes in me will live,
even after dying. 26 Everyone who lives in me and
believes in me will never ever die. Do you believe
this, Martha?"
27 "Yes, Lord," she told him. "I have always
believed you are the Messiah, the Son of God,
the one who has come into the world from God."
28 Then she returned to Mary. She called Mary
aside from the mourners and told her, "The
Teacher is here and wants to see you." 29 So Mary
immediately went to him.
30 Jesus had stayed outside the village, at the
place where Martha met him. 31 When the people
who were at the house consoling Mary saw her
leave so hastily, they assumed she was going to
Lazarus's grave to weep. So they followed her
there. 32 When Mary arrived and saw Jesus, she
fell at his feet and said, "Lord, if only you had
been here, my brother would not have died."
33 When Jesus saw her weeping and saw the
other people wailing with her, a deep anger welled
up within him,* and he was deeply troubled.
34 "Where have you put him?" he asked them.
They told him, "Lord, come and see." 35 Then
Jesus wept. 36 The people who were standing
nearby said, "See how much he loved him!"
37 But some said, "This man healed a blind man.
Couldn't he have kept Lazarus from dying?"
38 Jesus was still angry as he arrived at the
tomb, a cave with a stone rolled across its entrance. 39 "Roll the stone aside," Jesus told them.
But Martha, the dead man's sister, protested,
"Lord, he has been dead for four days. The smell
will be terrible."
40 Jesus responded, "Didn't I tell you that
you would see God's glory if you believe?" 41 So
they rolled the stone aside. Then Jesus looked
up to heaven and said, "Father, thank you for
hearing me. 42 You always hear me, but I said it
out loud for the sake of all these people standing here, so that they will believe you sent me."
43 Then Jesus shouted, "Lazarus, come out!"
44 And the dead man came out, his hands and
feet bound in graveclothes, his face wrapped in
a headcloth. Jesus told them, "Unwrap him and
let him go!"

The Plot to Kill Jesus

45 Many of the people who were with Mary
believed in Jesus when they saw this happen.
46 But some went to the Pharisees and told them
what Jesus had done. 47 Then the leading priests
and Pharisees called the high council* together.
"What are we going to do?" they asked each
other. "This man certainly performs many miraculous signs. 48 If we allow him to go on like
this, soon everyone will believe in him. Then the
Roman army will come and destroy both our
Temple* and our nation."
49 Caiaphas, who was high priest at that time,*
said, "You don't know what you're talking about!
50 You don't realize that it's better for you that
one man should die for the people than for the
whole nation to be destroyed."
51 He did not say this on his own; as high priest
at that time he was led to prophesy that Jesus
would die for the entire nation. 52 And not only
for that nation, but to bring together and unite all
the children of God scattered around the world.
53 So from that time on, the Jewish leaders
began to plot Jesus' death. 54 As a result, Jesus
stopped his public ministry among the people
and left Jerusalem. He went to a place near the
wilderness, to the village of Ephraim, and stayed
there with his disciples.
55 It was now almost time for the Jewish Passover celebration, and many people from all over
the country arrived in Jerusalem several days early so they could go through the purification ceremony before Passover began. 56 They kept looking
for Jesus, but as they stood around in the Temple,
they said to each other, "What do you think? He
won't come for Passover, will he?" 57 Meanwhile,
the leading priests and Pharisees had publicly ordered that anyone seeing Jesus must report it immediately so they could arrest him.

Jesus Anointed at Bethany

12 Six days before the Passover celebration began, Jesus arrived in Bethany,
the home of Lazarus—the man he

11:25 Some manuscripts do not include *and the life.*
11:33 Or *he was angry in his spirit.* **11:47** Greek *the Sanhedrin.* **11:48** Or *our position;* Greek reads *our place.*
11:49 Greek *that year;* also in 11:51.

11:45—12:50 Transition: Physical and Symbolic

With the end of the Book of Signs, the narrative shifts to the events of Jesus' final week. This transitional section contains the scenes that flow from the ministry of Jesus and that anticipate his death and resurrection.

11:45–57 Final Plot to Kill Jesus. Note that the event that causes the plot to kill Jesus is the raising of Lazarus, not, as in the other Gospels, the cleansing of the Temple.

had raised from the dead. 2 A dinner was prepared
in Jesus' honor. Martha served, and Lazarus was
among those who ate* with him. 3 Then Mary
took a twelve-ounce jar* of expensive perfume
made from essence of nard, and she anointed
Jesus' feet with it, wiping his feet with her hair.
The house was filled with the fragrance.
4 But Judas Iscariot, the disciple who would
soon betray him, said, 5 "That perfume was
worth a year's wages.* It should have been sold
and the money given to the poor." 6 Not that he
cared for the poor—he was a thief, and since he
was in charge of the disciples' money, he often
stole some for himself.
7 Jesus replied, "Leave her alone. She did this
in preparation for my burial. 8 You will always
have the poor among you, but you will not always have me."
9 When all the people* heard of Jesus' arrival,
they flocked to see him and also to see Lazarus,
the man Jesus had raised from the dead. 10 Then
the leading priests decided to kill Lazarus, too,
11 for it was because of him that many of the
people had deserted them* and believed in
Jesus.

Jesus' Triumphant Entry

12 The next day, the news that Jesus was on the
way to Jerusalem swept through the city. A large
crowd of Passover visitors 13 took palm branches and went down the road to meet him. They
shouted,

"Praise God!*
Blessings on the one who comes in the name
of the LORD!
Hail to the King of Israel!"*

14 Jesus found a young donkey and rode on it, fulfilling the prophecy that said:

15 "Don't be afraid, people of Jerusalem.*
Look, your King is coming,
riding on a donkey's colt."*

16 His disciples didn't understand at the time
that this was a fulfillment of prophecy. But after
Jesus entered into his glory, they remembered
what had happened and realized that these things
had been written about him.
17 Many in the crowd had seen Jesus call Lazarus from the tomb, raising him from the dead,
and they were telling others* about it. 18 That was
the reason so many went out to meet him—because they had heard about this miraculous sign.
19 Then the Pharisees said to each other, "There's
nothing we can do. Look, everyone* has gone after him!"

Jesus Predicts His Death

20 Some Greeks who had come to Jerusalem for
the Passover celebration 21 paid a visit to Philip,
who was from Bethsaida in Galilee. They said,
"Sir, we want to meet Jesus." 22 Philip told Andrew about it, and they went together to ask
Jesus.
23 Jesus replied, "Now the time has come for
the Son of Man* to enter into his glory. 24 I tell
you the truth, unless a kernel of wheat is planted in the soil and dies, it remains alone. But its
death will produce many new kernels—a plentiful harvest of new lives. 25 Those who love their
life in this world will lose it. Those who care
nothing for their life in this world will keep it for
eternity. 26 Anyone who wants to be my disciple
must follow me, because my servants must be
where I am. And the Father will honor anyone
who serves me.
27 "Now my soul is deeply troubled. Should I
pray, 'Father, save me from this hour'? But this
is the very reason I came! 28 Father, bring glory
to your name."
Then a voice spoke from heaven, saying, "I
have already brought glory to my name, and I
will do so again." 29 When the crowd heard the
voice, some thought it was thunder, while others
declared an angel had spoken to him.

12:2 Or *who reclined.* **12:3** Greek *took 1 litra* [327 grams]. **12:5** Greek *worth 300 denarii.* A denarius was equivalent to a laborer's full day's wage. **12:9** Greek *Jewish people;* also in 12:11. **12:11** Or *had deserted their traditions;* Greek reads *had deserted.* **12:13a** Greek *Hosanna,* an exclamation of praise adapted from a Hebrew expression that means "save now." **12:13b** Ps 118:25-26; Zeph 3:15. **12:15a** Greek *daughter of Zion.* **12:15b** Zech 9:9. **12:17** Greek *were testifying.* **12:19** Greek *the world.* **12:23** "Son of Man" is a title Jesus used for himself.

12:1–11 Jesus' Anointing. Mary, the sister of Lazarus, anoints Jesus. This anticipates the care of Jesus' body by Nicodemus at the tomb (19:38–40); Jesus' washing the feet of his disciples (13:1–5); and the negative role of Judas.

12:12–19 The Triumphant Entry into Jerusalem. Jesus' popular appeal temporarily protects him from the authorities.

12:20–36 Jesus' Prediction of His Death. 23: *Glory:* For Jesus, the consummation of his role as Messiah and Son of God means death and resurrection. The cross is part of the glory.

[30]Then Jesus told them, "The voice was for
your benefit, not mine. [31]The time for judging
this world has come, when Satan, the ruler of
this world, will be cast out. [32]And when I am
lifted up from the earth, I will draw everyone to
myself." [33]He said this to indicate how he was
going to die.

[34]The crowd responded, "We understood from
Scripture* that the Messiah would live forever.
How can you say the Son of Man will die? Just
who is this Son of Man, anyway?"

[35]Jesus replied, "My light will shine for you
just a little longer. Walk in the light while you
can, so the darkness will not overtake you. Those
who walk in the darkness cannot see where they
are going. [36]Put your trust in the light while
there is still time; then you will become children
of the light."

After saying these things, Jesus went away
and was hidden from them.

The Unbelief of the People

[37]But despite all the miraculous signs Jesus had
done, most of the people still did not believe in
him. [38]This is exactly what Isaiah the prophet
had predicted:

"LORD, who has believed our message?
To whom has the LORD revealed his
powerful arm?"*

[39]But the people couldn't believe, for as Isaiah
also said,

[40] "The Lord has blinded their eyes
and hardened their hearts—
so that their eyes cannot see,
and their hearts cannot understand,
and they cannot turn to me
and have me heal them."*

[41]Isaiah was referring to Jesus when he said
this, because he saw the future and spoke of
the Messiah's glory. [42]Many people did believe
in him, however, including some of the Jewish
leaders. But they wouldn't admit it for fear that
the Pharisees would expel them from the synagogue. [43]For they loved human praise more than
the praise of God.

[44]Jesus shouted to the crowds, "If you trust
me, you are trusting not only me, but also God
who sent me. [45]For when you see me, you are
seeing the one who sent me. [46]I have come as a
light to shine in this dark world, so that all who
put their trust in me will no longer remain in the
dark. [47]I will not judge those who hear me but
don't obey me, for I have come to save the world
and not to judge it. [48]But all who reject me and
my message will be judged on the day of judgment by the truth I have spoken. [49]I don't speak
on my own authority. The Father who sent me
has commanded me what to say and how to say it.
[50]And I know his commands lead to eternal life;
so I say whatever the Father tells me to say."

Jesus Washes His Disciples' Feet

13 Before the Passover celebration, Jesus
knew that his hour had come to leave
this world and return to his Father.
He had loved his disciples during his ministry on
earth, and now he loved them to the very end.*
[2]It was time for supper, and the devil had already
prompted Judas,* son of Simon Iscariot, to betray Jesus. [3]Jesus knew that the Father had given
him authority over everything and that he had
come from God and would return to God. [4]So he
got up from the table, took off his robe, wrapped
a towel around his waist, [5]and poured water into
a basin. Then he began to wash the disciples' feet,
drying them with the towel he had around him.

[6]When Jesus came to Simon Peter, Peter said
to him, "Lord, are you going to wash my feet?"

[7]Jesus replied, "You don't understand now
what I am doing, but someday you will."

[8]"No," Peter protested, "you will never ever
wash my feet!"

Jesus replied, "Unless I wash you, you won't
belong to me."

[9]Simon Peter exclaimed, "Then wash my
hands and head as well, Lord, not just my feet!"

[10]Jesus replied, "A person who has bathed all
over does not need to wash, except for the feet,*
to be entirely clean. And you disciples are clean,
but not all of you." [11]For Jesus knew who would
betray him. That is what he meant when he said,
"Not all of you are clean."

12:34 Greek *from the law.* **12:38** Isa 53:1. **12:40** Isa 6:10.
13:1 Or *he showed them the full extent of his love.* **13:2** Or
the devil had already intended for Judas. **13:10** Some
manuscripts do not include *except for the feet.*

12:37–50 Reaction and Response. 46–48: Jesus again compares trusting him, and through him, God, to coming into the light rather than remaining in the dark. And rejecting him carries its own judgment, as does staying in the dark.

13:1—20:31 The Book of Glory

13:1—17:26 Jesus Speaks with His Disciples. 13:1–17: Jesus washes the feet of the disciples. **14:** The lesson that Jesus tries to teach: Serve each other.

[12]After washing their feet, he put on his robe again and sat down and asked, "Do you understand what I was doing? [13]You call me 'Teacher' and 'Lord,' and you are right, because that's what I am. [14]And since I, your Lord and Teacher, have washed your feet, you ought to wash each other's feet. [15]I have given you an example to follow. Do as I have done to you. [16]I tell you the truth, slaves are not greater than their master. Nor is the messenger more important than the one who sends the message. [17]Now that you know these things, God will bless you for doing them.

Jesus Predicts His Betrayal

[18]"I am not saying these things to all of you; I know the ones I have chosen. But this fulfills the Scripture that says, 'The one who eats my food has turned against me.'* [19]I tell you this beforehand, so that when it happens you will believe that I AM the Messiah.* [20]I tell you the truth, anyone who welcomes my messenger is welcoming me, and anyone who welcomes me is welcoming the Father who sent me."

[21]Now Jesus was deeply troubled,* and he exclaimed, "I tell you the truth, one of you will betray me!"

[22]The disciples looked at each other, wondering whom he could mean. [23]The disciple Jesus loved was sitting next to Jesus at the table.* [24]Simon Peter motioned to him to ask, "Who's he talking about?" [25]So that disciple leaned over to Jesus and asked, "Lord, who is it?"

[26]Jesus responded, "It is the one to whom I give the bread I dip in the bowl." And when he had dipped it, he gave it to Judas, son of Simon Iscariot. [27]When Judas had eaten the bread, Satan entered into him. Then Jesus told him, "Hurry and do what you're going to do." [28]None of the others at the table knew what Jesus meant. [29]Since Judas was their treasurer, some thought Jesus was telling him to go and pay for the food or to give some money to the poor. [30]So Judas left at once, going out into the night.

Jesus Predicts Peter's Denial

[31]As soon as Judas left the room, Jesus said, "The time has come for the Son of Man* to enter into his glory, and God will be glorified because of him. [32]And since God receives glory because of the Son,* he will soon give glory to the Son. [33]Dear children, I will be with you only a little longer. And as I told the Jewish leaders, you will search for me, but you can't come where I am going. [34]So now I am giving you a new commandment: Love each other. Just as I have loved you, you should love each other. [35]Your love for one another will prove to the world that you are my disciples."

[36]Simon Peter asked, "Lord, where are you going?"

And Jesus replied, "You can't go with me now, but you will follow me later."

[37]"But why can't I come now, Lord?" he asked. "I'm ready to die for you."

[38]Jesus answered, "Die for me? I tell you the truth, Peter—before the rooster crows tomorrow morning, you will deny three times that you even know me.

Jesus, the Way to the Father

14 "Don't let your hearts be troubled. Trust in God, and trust also in me. [2]There is more than enough room in my Father's home.* If this were not so, would I have told you that I am going to prepare a place for you?* [3]When everything is ready, I will come and get you, so that you will always be with me where I am. [4]And you know the way to where I am going."

[5]"No, we don't know, Lord," Thomas said. "We have no idea where you are going, so how can we know the way?"

[6]Jesus told him, "I am the way, the truth, and the life. No one can come to the Father except through me. [7]If you had really known me, you would know who my Father is.* From now on, you do know him and have seen him!"

[8]Philip said, "Lord, show us the Father, and we will be satisfied."

[9]Jesus replied, "Have I been with you all this

13:18 Ps 41:9. **13:19** Or *that the 'I AM' has come;* or *that I am the LORD;* Greek reads *that I am.* See Exod 3:14. **13:21** Greek *was troubled in his spirit.* **13:23** Greek *was reclining on Jesus' bosom.* The "disciple Jesus loved" was probably John. **13:31** "Son of Man" is a title Jesus used for himself. **13:32** Some manuscripts do not include *And since God receives glory because of the Son.* **14:2a** Or *There are many rooms in my Father's house.* **14:2b** Or *If this were not so, I would have told you that I am going to prepare a place for you.* Some manuscripts read *If this were not so, I would have told you. I am going to prepare a place for you.* **14:7** Some manuscripts read *If you have really known me, you will know who my Father is.*

13:18–38 Predictions of Betrayal and Denial. The betrayal of Judas is worse than the denial of Peter, but Jesus speaks of both at the same time as a warning to his followers about what it means to follow him.

14:1–14 The Way to the Father. 6: *I am the way, the truth, and the life*: For the follower of Jesus, acting, thinking, and life itself all depend on knowing Jesus and, through Jesus, God. **12–14:** To *ask for* something

time, Philip, and yet you still don't know who I am? Anyone who has seen me has seen the Father! So why are you asking me to show him to you? 10 Don't you believe that I am in the Father and the Father is in me? The words I speak are not my own, but my Father who lives in me does his work through me. 11 Just believe that I am in the Father and the Father is in me. Or at least believe because of the work you have seen me do.

12 "I tell you the truth, anyone who believes in me will do the same works I have done, and even greater works, because I am going to be with the Father. 13 You can ask for anything in my name, and I will do it, so that the Son can bring glory to the Father. 14 Yes, ask me for anything in my name, and I will do it!

Jesus Promises the Holy Spirit

15 "If you love me, obey* my commandments. 16 And I will ask the Father, and he will give you another Advocate,* who will never leave you. 17 He is the Holy Spirit, who leads into all truth. The world cannot receive him, because it isn't looking for him and doesn't recognize him. But you know him, because he lives with you now and later will be in you.* 18 No, I will not abandon you as orphans—I will come to you. 19 Soon the world will no longer see me, but you will see me. Since I live, you also will live. 20 When I am raised to life again, you will know that I am in my Father, and you are in me, and I am in you. 21 Those who accept my commandments and obey them are the ones who love me. And because they love me, my Father will love them. And I will love them and reveal myself to each of them."

22 Judas (not Judas Iscariot, but the other disciple with that name) said to him, "Lord, why are you going to reveal yourself only to us and not to the world at large?"

23 Jesus replied, "All who love me will do what I say. My Father will love them, and we will come and make our home with each of them. 24 Anyone who doesn't love me will not obey me. And remember, my words are not my own. What I am telling you is from the Father who sent me. 25 I am telling you these things now while I am still with you. 26 But when the Father sends the Advocate as my representative—that is, the Holy Spirit—he will teach you everything and will remind you of everything I have told you.

27 "I am leaving you with a gift—peace of mind and heart. And the peace I give is a gift the world cannot give. So don't be troubled or afraid. 28 Remember what I told you: I am going away, but I will come back to you again. If you really loved me, you would be happy that I am going to the Father, who is greater than I am. 29 I have told you these things before they happen so that when they do happen, you will believe.

30 "I don't have much more time to talk to you, because the ruler of this world approaches. He has no power over me, 31 but I will do what the Father requires of me, so that the world will know that I love the Father. Come, let's be going.

Jesus, the True Vine

15 "I am the true grapevine, and my Father is the gardener. 2 He cuts off every branch of mine that doesn't produce fruit, and he prunes the branches that do bear fruit so they will produce even more. 3 You have already been pruned and purified by the message I have given you. 4 Remain in me, and I will remain in you. For a branch cannot produce fruit if it is severed from the vine, and you cannot be fruitful unless you remain in me.

5 "Yes, I am the vine; you are the branches. Those who remain in me, and I in them, will produce much fruit. For apart from me you can do nothing. 6 Anyone who does not remain in me

14:15 Other manuscripts read *you will obey;* still others read *you should obey.* **14:16** Or *Comforter,* or *Encourager,* or *Counselor.* Greek reads *Paraclete;* also in 14:26. **14:17** Some manuscripts read *and is in you.*

---

in someone's *name* is to speak and ask in place of that person; to speak in the king's name is to speak in place of the king, as the king would speak. A follower asking "in Jesus' name" is asking as Jesus would ask—not for his or her own benefit, but on behalf of others.

14:15–31 The Promise of the Holy Spirit. 16: *Advocate*: The Greek word *parakletos* means "one who stands alongside" another. Depending on the context, it can mean one who speaks up in defense of someone ("advocate"), one who offers support ("encourager"), one who strengthens ("comforter"), or one who gives advice ("counselor"). **26:** Jesus promises a fuller revelation after his death and resurrection, one led by the Holy Spirit.

15:1–17 The True Vine. The comparison is that Jesus is the entire plant, of which his followers are individual branches. **5:** One life flows through him and them. **6:** The wood of the grapevine cannot be used for anything other than growing grapes: Its fibrous grain cannot be carved or shaped into utensils; it is not strong enough for building anything; and it cannot be woven like hemp. Dead grapevines can only be burned.

is thrown away like a useless branch and withers. Such branches are gathered into a pile to be burned. [7]But if you remain in me and my words remain in you, you may ask for anything you want, and it will be granted! [8]When you produce much fruit, you are my true disciples. This brings great glory to my Father.

[9]"I have loved you even as the Father has loved me. Remain in my love. [10]When you obey my commandments, you remain in my love, just as I obey my Father's commandments and remain in his love. [11]I have told you these things so that you will be filled with my joy. Yes, your joy will overflow! [12]This is my commandment: Love each other in the same way I have loved you. [13]There is no greater love than to lay down one's life for one's friends. [14]You are my friends if you do what I command. [15]I no longer call you slaves, because a master doesn't confide in his slaves. Now you are my friends, since I have told you everything the Father told me. [16]You didn't choose me. I chose you. I appointed you to go and produce lasting fruit, so that the Father will give you whatever you ask for, using my name. [17]This is my command: Love each other.

The World's Hatred

[18]"If the world hates you, remember that it hated me first. [19]The world would love you as one of its own if you belonged to it, but you are no longer part of the world. I chose you to come out of the world, so it hates you. [20]Do you remember what I told you? 'A slave is not greater than the master.' Since they persecuted me, naturally they will persecute you. And if they had listened to me, they would listen to you. [21]They will do all this to you because of me, for they have rejected the one who sent me. [22]They would not be guilty if I had not come and spoken to them. But now they have no excuse for their sin. [23]Anyone who hates me also hates my Father. [24]If I hadn't done such miraculous signs among them that no one else could do, they would not be guilty. But as it is, they have seen everything I did, yet they still hate me and my Father. [25]This fulfills what is written in their Scriptures*: 'They hated me without cause.'

[26]"But I will send you the Advocate*—the Spirit of truth. He will come to you from the Father and will testify all about me. [27]And you must also testify about me because you have been with me from the beginning of my ministry.

16 "I have told you these things so that you won't abandon your faith. [2]For you will be expelled from the synagogues, and the time is coming when those who kill you will think they are doing a holy service for God. [3]This is because they have never known the Father or me. [4]Yes, I'm telling you these things now, so that when they happen, you will remember my warning. I didn't tell you earlier because I was going to be with you for a while longer.

The Work of the Holy Spirit

[5]"But now I am going away to the one who sent me, and not one of you is asking where I am going. [6]Instead, you grieve because of what I've told you. [7]But in fact, it is best for you that I go away, because if I don't, the Advocate* won't come. If I do go away, then I will send him to you. [8]And when he comes, he will convict the world of its sin, and of God's righteousness, and of the coming judgment. [9]The world's sin is that it refuses to believe in me. [10]Righteousness is available because I go to the Father, and you will see me no more. [11]Judgment will come because the ruler of this world has already been judged.

[12]"There is so much more I want to tell you, but you can't bear it now. [13]When the Spirit of truth comes, he will guide you into all truth. He will not speak on his own but will tell you what he has heard. He will tell you about the future. [14]He will bring me glory by telling you whatever he receives from me. [15]All that belongs to the Father is mine; this is why I said, 'The Spirit will tell you whatever he receives from me.'

15:25 Greek *in their law.* Pss 35:19; 69:4. **15:26** Or *Comforter,* or *Encourager,* or *Counselor.* Greek reads *Paraclete.* **16:7** Or *Comforter,* or *Encourager,* or *Counselor.* Greek reads *Paraclete.*

15:18—16:4 Hatred and Persecution. 16:2: *Expelled from the synagogues*: This reflects the division between Judaism and Christianity that developed during the later part of the first century.

16:5–15 The Work of the Holy Spirit. The *Spirit of truth* will make clear *the world's sin*, or estrangement from God; God's *righteousness*, not simply the fact that God is just but that we can share in that righteousness; and *judgment*, the distinction and definition that must be made between the two. The *truth* is *what* [the Spirit] *has heard* and *whatever he receives from* Jesus Christ, but particularly his *glory*—his sacrifice on the cross and the vindication of his resurrection.

Birth Pain Imagery

Because of their intensity and the peril associated with them, yet the positive result that is hoped for, birth pains are a potent theological metaphor.

The intensity and the peril are in view in Genesis 35:16–18, the story of Rachel's death in childbirth. These aspects are also in view in many other passages (e.g., Jer 4:31; 30:12–15) where pain is a symbol for God's judgment. In 1 Enoch 62:4–6 (the books of 1 and 2 Enoch are late Jewish or early Christian writings; 1 Enoch is a collection of apocalyptic visions) and other passages the process of childbirth is the focus and the birth itself is omitted. The metaphor does not extend to birth: No metaphorical child is born to the kings and governors who are being judged; they have the intense pain and nothing more. This narrow focus is present also in some of the New Testament passages (Mark 13, surprisingly, and 1 Thes 5:3). It is important not to read in the birth event when the passage does not contain it.

Birth pains are not only intense and dangerous, however; they are also pains that cannot be prevented or relieved. The biblical authors capitalize on this aspect in passages such as Jeremiah 48:41 or Isaiah 13:4–8. Again, facets such as birth and hope are out of the picture; what is in view is the pain, ineffectuality, and humiliation. This is probably the background of Romans 8, where the frustration and pain is rather remarkably featured alongside not birth but adoption. When Paul feels labor pains for the Galatians "until Christ is fully developed," the birth is implied, but the metaphor mostly speaks about helplessness and frustration: "I don't know how . . . to help you" (Gal 4:19–20).

The biblical authors make use of one more aspect of labor pains: They are a type of pain that must run its course. This pain is not just sharp; it involves a period of time rather than a point in time. It recurs within that period of time, and once begun, there is no escape until it runs to completion. For the Scriptures, this is a perfect analogy for the eschaton: The onset of labor is not yet the end but the beginning of a process that must surely culminate (Mark 13:8).

From the curse in Genesis to the birth of the Holy One in Revelation, birth pains are an important image. In the Christian writings, such as Revelation, however, the image has been turned upside down. In the Prophets, the mighty God causes his enemies to swoon like women in labor. In Revelation 12, it is the enemy who seems mighty, while salvation arrives through the humility of labor pains and childbirth.

Sadness Will Be Turned to Joy
[16]"In a little while you won't see me anymore.
But a little while after that, you will see me
again."
[17]Some of the disciples asked each other,
"What does he mean when he says, 'In a little
while you won't see me, but then you will see
me,' and 'I am going to the Father'? [18]And what
does he mean by 'a little while'? We don't understand."
[19]Jesus realized they wanted to ask him about
it, so he said, "Are you asking yourselves what I
meant? I said in a little while you won't see me,
but a little while after that you will see me again.
[20]I tell you the truth, you will weep and mourn
over what is going to happen to me, but the world
will rejoice. You will grieve, but your grief will
suddenly turn to wonderful joy. [21]It will be like
a woman suffering the pains of labor. When her
child is born, her anguish gives way to joy because she has brought a new baby into the world.
[22]So you have sorrow now, but I will see you
again; then you will rejoice, and no one can rob
you of that joy. [23]At that time you won't need
to ask me for anything. I tell you the truth, you
will ask the Father directly, and he will grant your
request because you use my name. [24]You haven't
done this before. Ask, using my name, and you
will receive, and you will have abundant joy.
[25]"I have spoken of these matters in figures of
speech, but soon I will stop speaking figuratively
and will tell you plainly all about the Father.
[26]Then you will ask in my name. I'm not saying I will ask the Father on your behalf, [27]for the
Father himself loves you dearly because you love
me and believe that I came from God.* [28]Yes, I
came from the Father into the world, and now I
will leave the world and return to the Father."

16:27 Some manuscripts read *from the Father.*

16:16–33 Predictions of Trials. Jesus' Eventual Return. Although the manifestation of God's kingdom will not be immediate, in Jesus' death and resurrection it has been accomplished: *I have overcome the world.*

[29]Then his disciples said, "At last you are
speaking plainly and not figuratively. [30]Now
we understand that you know everything, and
there's no need to question you. From this we
believe that you came from God."
[31]Jesus asked, "Do you finally believe? [32]But
the time is coming—indeed it's here now—when
you will be scattered, each one going his own
way, leaving me alone. Yet I am not alone because
the Father is with me. [33]I have told you all this
so that you may have peace in me. Here on earth
you will have many trials and sorrows. But take
heart, because I have overcome the world."

The Prayer of Jesus

17 After saying all these things, Jesus
looked up to heaven and said, "Father,
the hour has come. Glorify your Son
so he can give glory back to you. [2]For you have
given him authority over everyone. He gives
eternal life to each one you have given him. [3]And
this is the way to have eternal life—to know you,
the only true God, and Jesus Christ, the one you
sent to earth. [4]I brought glory to you here on
earth by completing the work you gave me to do.
[5]Now, Father, bring me into the glory we shared
before the world began.
[6]"I have revealed you* to the ones you gave
me from this world. They were always yours.
You gave them to me, and they have kept your
word. [7]Now they know that everything I have
is a gift from you, [8]for I have passed on to them
the message you gave me. They accepted it and
know that I came from you, and they believe you
sent me.
[9]"My prayer is not for the world, but for
those you have given me, because they belong to
you. [10]All who are mine belong to you, and you
have given them to me, so they bring me glory.
[11]Now I am departing from the world; they are
staying in this world, but I am coming to you.
Holy Father, you have given me your name;*
now protect them by the power of your name so
that they will be united just as we are. [12]During
my time here, I protected them by the power of
the name you gave me.* I guarded them so that
not one was lost, except the one headed for destruction, as the Scriptures foretold.
[13]"Now I am coming to you. I told them many
things while I was with them in this world so
they would be filled with my joy. [14]I have given
them your word. And the world hates them because they do not belong to the world, just as I
do not belong to the world. [15]I'm not asking you
to take them out of the world, but to keep them
safe from the evil one. [16]They do not belong to
this world any more than I do. [17]Make them holy
by your truth; teach them your word, which is
truth. [18]Just as you sent me into the world, I am
sending them into the world. [19]And I give myself
as a holy sacrifice for them so they can be made
holy by your truth.
[20]"I am praying not only for these disciples
but also for all who will ever believe in me
through their message. [21]I pray that they will all
be one, just as you and I are one—as you are in
me, Father, and I am in you. And may they be in
us so that the world will believe you sent me.
[22]"I have given them the glory you gave me,
so they may be one as we are one. [23]I am in them
and you are in me. May they experience such
perfect unity that the world will know that you
sent me and that you love them as much as you
love me. [24]Father, I want these whom you have
given me to be with me where I am. Then they
can see all the glory you gave me because you
loved me even before the world began!
[25]"O righteous Father, the world doesn't
know you, but I do; and these disciples know you
sent me. [26]I have revealed you to them, and I will
continue to do so. Then your love for me will be
in them, and I will be in them."

Jesus Is Betrayed and Arrested

18 After saying these things, Jesus
crossed the Kidron Valley with his
disciples and entered a grove of olive
trees. [2]Judas, the betrayer, knew this place, because Jesus had often gone there with his disciples. [3]The leading priests and Pharisees had given
Judas a contingent of Roman soldiers and Temple guards to accompany him. Now with blazing

17:6 Greek *have revealed your name;* also in 17:26.
17:11 Some manuscripts read *you have given me these [disciples].* **17:12** Some manuscripts read *I protected those you gave me, by the power of your name.*

17:1–26 Jesus' Prayer to the Father. 1–5: *Father, . . . Glorify your Son so he can give glory back to you. . . . The glory we shared before the world began*: The *glory* is sacrificial love, which Jesus in this prayer portrays as the living reality of God from eternity. **22–23:** The *glory* of sacrificial love is Jesus' gift to his followers, so that they may live in the *unity* of God, a unity of *love*.

18:1—19:27 Jesus' Trial and Crucifixion. 18:1–14: Because Jesus is first to be accused of blasphemy against the Jewish religion, he is brought first to the Jewish authorities. *Annas* had been removed as high priest at Roman behest, but still exercised power through his son-in-law, *Caiaphas* (v. 13).

torches, lanterns, and weapons, they arrived at the olive grove.

[4] Jesus fully realized all that was going to happen to him, so he stepped forward to meet them. "Who are you looking for?" he asked.

[5] "Jesus the Nazarene,"* they replied.

"I AM he,"* Jesus said. (Judas, who betrayed him, was standing with them.) [6] As Jesus said "I AM he," they all drew back and fell to the ground! [7] Once more he asked them, "Who are you looking for?"

And again they replied, "Jesus the Nazarene."

[8] "I told you that I AM he," Jesus said. "And since I am the one you want, let these others go." [9] He did this to fulfill his own statement: "I did not lose a single one of those you have given me."*

[10] Then Simon Peter drew a sword and slashed off the right ear of Malchus, the high priest's slave. [11] But Jesus said to Peter, "Put your sword back into its sheath. Shall I not drink from the cup of suffering the Father has given me?"

Jesus at the High Priest's House

[12] So the soldiers, their commanding officer, and the Temple guards arrested Jesus and tied him up. [13] First they took him to Annas, the father-in-law of Caiaphas, the high priest at that time.* [14] Caiaphas was the one who had told the other Jewish leaders, "It's better that one man should die for the people."

Peter's First Denial

[15] Simon Peter followed Jesus, as did another of the disciples. That other disciple was acquainted with the high priest, so he was allowed to enter the high priest's courtyard with Jesus. [16] Peter had to stay outside the gate. Then the disciple who knew the high priest spoke to the woman watching at the gate, and she let Peter in. [17] The woman asked Peter, "You're not one of that man's disciples, are you?"

"No," he said, "I am not."

[18] Because it was cold, the household servants and the guards had made a charcoal fire. They stood around it, warming themselves, and Peter stood with them, warming himself.

The High Priest Questions Jesus

[19] Inside, the high priest began asking Jesus about his followers and what he had been teaching them. [20] Jesus replied, "Everyone knows what I teach. I have preached regularly in the synagogues and the Temple, where the people* gather. I have not spoken in secret. [21] Why are you asking me this question? Ask those who heard me. They know what I said."

[22] Then one of the Temple guards standing nearby slapped Jesus across the face. "Is that the way to answer the high priest?" he demanded.

[23] Jesus replied, "If I said anything wrong, you must prove it. But if I'm speaking the truth, why are you beating me?"

[24] Then Annas bound Jesus and sent him to Caiaphas, the high priest.

Peter's Second and Third Denials

[25] Meanwhile, as Simon Peter was standing by the fire warming himself, they asked him again, "You're not one of his disciples, are you?"

He denied it, saying, "No, I am not."

[26] But one of the household slaves of the high priest, a relative of the man whose ear Peter had cut off, asked, "Didn't I see you out there in the olive grove with Jesus?" [27] Again Peter denied it. And immediately a rooster crowed.

Jesus' Trial before Pilate

[28] Jesus' trial before Caiaphas ended in the early hours of the morning. Then he was taken to the headquarters of the Roman governor.* His accusers didn't go inside because it would defile them, and they wouldn't be allowed to celebrate the Passover. [29] So Pilate, the governor, went out to them and asked, "What is your charge against this man?"

18:5a Or *Jesus of Nazareth;* also in 18:7. **18:5b** Or *"The 'I AM' is here";* or *"I am the LORD";* Greek reads *I am;* also in 18:6, 8. See Exod 3:14. **18:9** See John 6:39 and 17:12. **18:13** Greek *that year.* **18:20** Greek *Jewish people;* also in 18:38. **18:28** Greek *to the Praetorium;* also in 18:33.

18:15–18 Peter's First Denial. 17: The *woman* asks Peter a question in a form that expects *"No"* for an answer—and she gets it.

18:19–24 Annas Questions Jesus. Annas tries to get Jesus to say something that will be self-incriminating, but Jesus refuses to fall into the trap. Jesus is sent to Caiaphas.

18:25–27 Peter's Second and Third Denials. The questioning becomes more pointed.

18:28—19:16a Jesus Is Tried before Pilate and Sentenced to Death. Jesus is brought to Pilate on an accusation of treason against Rome: claiming to be a king. (The Jewish death penalty is usually carried out by stoning; the Romans used crucifixion. The Jews would not have been allowed to carry out capital

30 "We wouldn't have handed him over to you
if he weren't a criminal!" they retorted.
31 "Then take him away and judge him by
your own law," Pilate told them.
"Only the Romans are permitted to execute
someone," the Jewish leaders replied. 32 (This fulfilled Jesus' prediction about the way he would
die.*)
33 Then Pilate went back into his headquarters
and called for Jesus to be brought to him. "Are
you the king of the Jews?" he asked him.
34 Jesus replied, "Is this your own question, or
did others tell you about me?"
35 "Am I a Jew?" Pilate retorted. "Your own
people and their leading priests brought you to
me for trial. Why? What have you done?"
36 Jesus answered, "My Kingdom is not an
earthly kingdom. If it were, my followers would
fight to keep me from being handed over to the
Jewish leaders. But my Kingdom is not of this
world."
37 Pilate said, "So you are a king?"
Jesus responded, "You say I am a king. Actually, I was born and came into the world to testify
to the truth. All who love the truth recognize
that what I say is true."
38 "What is truth?" Pilate asked. Then he went
out again to the people and told them, "He is not
guilty of any crime. 39 But you have a custom of
asking me to release one prisoner each year at
Passover. Would you like me to release this 'King
of the Jews'?"
40 But they shouted back, "No! Not this man.
We want Barabbas!" (Barabbas was a revolutionary.)

Jesus Sentenced to Death

19 Then Pilate had Jesus flogged with a
lead-tipped whip. 2 The soldiers wove
a crown of thorns and put it on his
head, and they put a purple robe on him. 3 "Hail!
King of the Jews!" they mocked, as they slapped
him across the face.
4 Pilate went outside again and said to the
people, "I am going to bring him out to you
now, but understand clearly that I find him not
guilty." 5 Then Jesus came out wearing the crown
of thorns and the purple robe. And Pilate said,
"Look, here is the man!"
6 When they saw him, the leading priests and
Temple guards began shouting, "Crucify him!
Crucify him!"
"Take him yourselves and crucify him," Pilate said. "I find him not guilty."
7 The Jewish leaders replied, "By our law he
ought to die because he called himself the Son
of God."
8 When Pilate heard this, he was more frightened than ever. 9 He took Jesus back into the
headquarters* again and asked him, "Where are
you from?" But Jesus gave no answer. 10 "Why
don't you talk to me?" Pilate demanded. "Don't
you realize that I have the power to release you
or crucify you?"
11 Then Jesus said, "You would have no power
over me at all unless it were given to you from
above. So the one who handed me over to you
has the greater sin."
12 Then Pilate tried to release him, but the
Jewish leaders shouted, "If you release this man,
you are no 'friend of Caesar.'* Anyone who declares himself a king is a rebel against Caesar."
13 When they said this, Pilate brought Jesus
out to them again. Then Pilate sat down on the
judgment seat on the platform that is called the
Stone Pavement (in Hebrew, *Gabbatha*). 14 It
was now about noon on the day of preparation
for the Passover. And Pilate said to the people,*
"Look, here is your king!"
15 "Away with him," they yelled. "Away with
him! Crucify him!"
"What? Crucify your king?" Pilate asked.
"We have no king but Caesar," the leading
priests shouted back.
16 Then Pilate turned Jesus over to them to be
crucified.

The Crucifixion

So they took Jesus away. 17 Carrying the cross by
himself, he went to the place called Place of the
Skull (in Hebrew, *Golgotha*). 18 There they nailed
him to the cross. Two others were crucified with
him, one on either side, with Jesus between them.
19 And Pilate posted a sign on the cross that read,
"Jesus of Nazareth,* the King of the Jews." 20 The
place where Jesus was crucified was near the city,

18:32 See John 12:32-33. **19:9** Greek *the Praetorium.*
19:12 "Friend of Caesar" is a technical term that refers to an ally of the emperor. **19:14** Greek *Jewish people;* also in 19:20.
19:19 Or *Jesus the Nazarene.*

punishment on their own.) **18:30:** The religious leaders are reluctant to specify a charge, since they do not wish to validate Roman rule publicly. But, in order to get what they want, they are going to have to do so (19:15). **19:13:** *Pilate sat down on the . . . Stone Pavement*: This is the signal that an official verdict will be passed. **15:** *"We have no king but Caesar"*: Pilate has gotten the religious leaders to acknowledge Roman rule. He hands Jesus over to the soldiers for crucifixion.

and the sign was written in Hebrew, Latin, and
Greek, so that many people could read it.
21 Then the leading priests objected and said to
Pilate, "Change it from 'The King of the Jews' to
'He said, I am King of the Jews.' "
22 Pilate replied, "No, what I have written, I
have written."
23 When the soldiers had crucified Jesus, they
divided his clothes among the four of them. They
also took his robe, but it was seamless, woven in
one piece from top to bottom. 24 So they said,
"Rather than tearing it apart, let's throw dice*
for it." This fulfilled the Scripture that says,
"They divided my garments among themselves
and threw dice for my clothing."* So that is what
they did.
25 Standing near the cross were Jesus' mother, and his mother's sister, Mary (the wife of
Clopas), and Mary Magdalene. 26 When Jesus saw
his mother standing there beside the disciple he
loved, he said to her, "Dear woman, here is your
son." 27 And he said to this disciple, "Here is your
mother." And from then on this disciple took her
into his home.

The Death of Jesus

28 Jesus knew that his mission was now finished,
and to fulfill Scripture he said, "I am thirsty."*
29 A jar of sour wine was sitting there, so they
soaked a sponge in it, put it on a hyssop branch,
and held it up to his lips. 30 When Jesus had tasted
it, he said, "It is finished!" Then he bowed his
head and released his spirit.
31 It was the day of preparation, and the Jewish leaders didn't want the bodies hanging there
the next day, which was the Sabbath (and a very
special Sabbath, because it was the Passover). So
they asked Pilate to hasten their deaths by ordering that their legs be broken. Then their bodies
could be taken down. 32 So the soldiers came and
broke the legs of the two men crucified with Jesus.
33 But when they came to Jesus, they saw that he
was already dead, so they didn't break his legs.
34 One of the soldiers, however, pierced his side
with a spear, and immediately blood and water
flowed out. 35 (This report is from an eyewitness

19:24a Greek *cast lots.* **19:24b** Ps 22:18. **19:28** See Pss 22:15; 69:21.

19:16b–37 Jesus Is Crucified and Dies. 25–27: *Jesus' mother*, three other women (including Mary Magdalene), and the *disciple he loved* stayed with Jesus at the cross. *Here is*, literally "Behold," a revelatory formula that doubles as prophetic pronouncement for the reader. To Jesus' mother and to the believer (the symbolic mother, the one who bears fruit for God), Jesus is saying: "Behold your Son, Jesus, on the cross." He reinforces this by a command to the disciple, including the reader, to behold his new mother: "Behold your mother, Jesus, on the cross, about to shed his blood for the new birth of the world." **30:** *Released his spirit*: The climax. **31:** *The day of preparation*: The day before Passover begins. Jesus is dying as the Passover lambs are being slaughtered. **34:** *Pierced his side . . . and immediately blood and water flowed out*: The mirror image, in a sense, of the miracle at Cana. The blood and water at his death are commonly taken as a reference to Jesus' natural birth as well as to his natural death, reinforcing the theological point already made. However, if this is birth imagery, it is that in the fullest sense (see Birth Pain Imagery, chap. 16). Jesus understood his death, its manner and its effect on the believer in this way (16:21–22): "When a woman is in labor, she has pain because her hour has come. But when her child is born, she no longer remembers the anguish because of the joy of having brought a human being into the world." The crucifixion is thus presented metaphorically as Jesus' going away to give birth to God's people. Like a woman in labor, he pours out his blood for the life of the world. **35:** The author stops the story to reinforce its importance. Jesus as birthgiver is made in the repetition of the imagery in the two incidents with Jesus' mother. This is symbolically the last birth in which the mother will experience anguish and pain—perhaps alluding to Isaiah 66:7–11, one of the most graphic prophecies of the new creation, and one of two passages, along with Psalm 22, in which God is described as midwife (see Midwifery and Birthing Practices, Job 3). It is also a promise that when the new creation is complete—for John's community, that means in the resurrection—it will be as it was before the Fall of humankind. Isaiah 66:7 says, "Before the birth pains even begin, Jerusalem gives birth to a son." The curse of painful birth will be reversed; God's people are freed from the effects of the Fall. Thus Jesus takes on the ultimate and most deeply honored role of the woman, that of birthgiver. He takes on and takes away the pain, the curse of disobedience to God, not only for women but also for the whole world. Since God is the author and presider over this death and birth (John 19:11), there my be further allusion: Psalm 22:9 says, "You [God] . . . brought me safely from my mother's womb and led me to trust you at my mother's breast." In Matthew 27:46 and Mark 15:34, Jesus on the cross quotes Psalm 22:1, "My God, my God, why have you forsaken me?" Matthew and Mark thus make Jesus the speaker of this psalm—the one who is brought forth from the womb by God. There are further complex quotes and allusions to Psalm

giving an accurate account. He speaks the truth so
that you also can believe.*) 36These things happened in fulfillment of the Scriptures that say,
"Not one of his bones will be broken,"* 37and
"They will look on the one they pierced."*

The Burial of Jesus

38Afterward Joseph of Arimathea, who had been
a secret disciple of Jesus (because he feared the
Jewish leaders), asked Pilate for permission to
take down Jesus' body. When Pilate gave permission, Joseph came and took the body away.
39With him came Nicodemus, the man who had
come to Jesus at night. He brought about seventy-five pounds* of perfumed ointment made
from myrrh and aloes. 40Following Jewish burial
custom, they wrapped Jesus' body with the spices
in long sheets of linen cloth. 41The place of crucifixion was near a garden, where there was a new
tomb, never used before. 42And so, because it was
the day of preparation for the Jewish Passover*
and since the tomb was close at hand, they laid
Jesus there.

The Resurrection

20 Early on Sunday morning,* while it
was still dark, Mary Magdalene came
to the tomb and found that the stone
had been rolled away from the entrance. 2She
ran and found Simon Peter and the other disciple, the one whom Jesus loved. She said, "They
have taken the Lord's body out of the tomb, and
we don't know where they have put him!"

3Peter and the other disciple started out for
the tomb. 4They were both running, but the
other disciple outran Peter and reached the tomb
first. 5He stooped and looked in and saw the linen
wrappings lying there, but he didn't go in. 6Then
Simon Peter arrived and went inside. He also noticed the linen wrappings lying there, 7while the
cloth that had covered Jesus' head was folded up
and lying apart from the other wrappings. 8Then
the disciple who had reached the tomb first also
went in, and he saw and believed—9for until
then they still hadn't understood the Scriptures
that said Jesus must rise from the dead. 10Then
they went home.

Jesus Appears to Mary Magdalene

11Mary was standing outside the tomb crying,
and as she wept, she stooped and looked in. 12She
saw two white-robed angels, one sitting at the
head and the other at the foot of the place where
the body of Jesus had been lying. 13"Dear woman, why are you crying?" the angels asked her.

"Because they have taken away my Lord,"
she replied, "and I don't know where they have
put him."

14She turned to leave and saw someone
standing there. It was Jesus, but she didn't recognize him. 15"Dear woman, why are you crying?"
Jesus asked her. "Who are you looking for?"

She thought he was the gardener. "Sir," she
said, "if you have taken him away, tell me where
you have put him, and I will go and get him."

16"Mary!" Jesus said.

She turned to him and cried out, "Rabboni!"
(which is Hebrew for "Teacher").

19:35 Some manuscripts read *can continue to believe.* **19:36** Exod 12:46; Num 9:12; Ps 34:20. **19:37** Zech 12:10. **19:39** Greek *100 litras* [32.7 kilograms]. **19:42** Greek *because of the Jewish day of preparation.* **20:1** Greek *On the first day of the week.*

22 in these three Gospels' accounts of the passion. For example, in John, Jesus' flow of blood and water alludes to Psalm 22:14, "My life is poured out like water." Thus John, perhaps having read these other Gospels, may be naming God as the midwife of the new creation birthed by Jesus on the cross and of Jesus, reborn from the tomb. God is midwife to the one who is simultaneously dying, giving birth, and about to be reborn. God is Father, but to limit God to the role of an earthly man is reductionistic, almost blasphemous: God is Creator. God therefore is also midwife and birthgiver, and these roles are far from incidental. Thus John punctuates the male images of Jesus and the Father with profound images of the feminine—the more powerful because of their placement at the beginning and end of Jesus' earthly ministry.

19:38–42 Jesus' Burial. The anointing and burial here are carried out by men: Joseph of Arimathea and Nicodemus.

20:1–31 Jesus Returns to His Disciples. The tomb is empty, and the *other disciple* (v. 3) believes in the resurrection and in Jesus as a result.

20:11–18 Jesus Appears to Mary Magdalene. Peter and the other disciple have left, but Mary still mourns outside the tomb. She is centered wholeheartedly on the person of Jesus, seeking his body. She will not desist, despite the other disciples' having left in confusion after seeing the empty tomb. She is blinded by her own tears, and mistakes the risen Lord for *the gardener*. **16–17:** At his voice, she recognizes him, thereby recalling the image of the Good Shepherd

17 "Don't cling to me," Jesus said, "for I haven't yet ascended to the Father. But go find my brothers and tell them, 'I am ascending to my Father and your Father, to my God and your God.' "

18 Mary Magdalene found the disciples and told them, "I have seen the Lord!" Then she gave them his message.

Jesus Appears to His Disciples

19 That Sunday evening* the disciples were meeting behind locked doors because they were afraid of the Jewish leaders. Suddenly, Jesus was standing there among them! "Peace be with you," he said. 20 As he spoke, he showed them the wounds in his hands and his side. They were filled with joy when they saw the Lord! 21 Again he said, "Peace be with you. As the Father has sent me, so I am sending you." 22 Then he breathed on them and said, "Receive the Holy Spirit. 23 If you forgive anyone's sins, they are forgiven. If you do not forgive them, they are not forgiven."

Jesus Appears to Thomas

24 One of the twelve disciples, Thomas (nicknamed the Twin),* was not with the others when Jesus came. 25 They told him, "We have seen the Lord!"

But he replied, "I won't believe it unless I see the nail wounds in his hands, put my fingers into them, and place my hand into the wound in his side."

26 Eight days later the disciples were together again, and this time Thomas was with them. The doors were locked; but suddenly, as before, Jesus was standing among them. "Peace be with you," he said. 27 Then he said to Thomas, "Put your finger here, and look at my hands. Put your hand into the wound in my side. Don't be faithless any longer. Believe!"

28 "My Lord and my God!" Thomas exclaimed.

29 Then Jesus told him, "You believe because you have seen me. Blessed are those who believe without seeing me."

Purpose of the Book

30 The disciples saw Jesus do many other miraculous signs in addition to the ones recorded in this book. 31 But these are written so that you may continue to believe* that Jesus is the Messiah,

20:19 Greek *In the evening of that day, the first day of the week.* **20:24** Greek *Thomas, who was called Didymus.* **20:31** Some manuscripts read *that you may believe.*

(10:1–5) whose voice the sheep know; he tells her, *"Don't cling to me"*: That is, do not try to retain the earthly relationship you had with me. **18:** She proceeds to feed his other sheep by proclaiming his resurrection. She thus becomes the first to be sent by Jesus to witness to the resurrection and the first to witness to the other disciples (see Women as Witnesses, Mark 16). For this reason, she is often called the apostle of the apostles. Where Martha is considered the model of ideal faith, Mary Magdalene is considered to be the model of Christian praxis.

20:19–23 Jesus Appears to the Disciples. The gift of *the Holy Spirit*, and the power of forgiveness, are imparted after the resurrection.

20:24–29 Jesus Appears to Thomas. Jesus' *wounds*—the entirety of his incarnate experience, in fact—are resurrected. John contrasts Thomas with the two women who have looked so long for Jesus without asking for any personal demonstration. **25:** Thomas, having missed the appearance of the risen Christ to the other disciples, declares, *"I won't believe it unless I see the nail wounds in his hands, put my fingers into them, and place my hand into the wound in his side."* This turns the paradigm of seeking Jesus upside down. Thomas has good reason to believe that Jesus is risen, but he puts a condition on his faith. The reader is thus predisposed by the author to recoil from Thomas's manner of expressing his faith. **27:** Nevertheless, Jesus accommodates Thomas, even using Thomas's words in granting his desire. Thus Jesus heals Thomas's petulantly expressed fear of disappointment and confirms his demand for a personal visitation. This is paradoxical; but with it, John has set in place everything that is required for his conclusion. **28–29:** This is the reason for Jesus' strangely formulated final word to Thomas: *You believe because you have seen me. Blessed are those who believe without seeing me.* The disciple who will not believe without a sign is not disconfirmed. Thomas's ultimate recognition of Jesus is in fact a model for the reader: *My Lord and my God!* John hopes that the reader will rise and say these resounding words along with Thomas, albeit without seeing signs beyond those that are written in this book.

20:30–31 The Purpose of the Book. The Gospel was written *so that you may continue to believe . . .* and *have life.* John wants the reader to believe all of the signs Jesus performs, including the resurrection. The reader's faith is to be based in large part upon the signs. Beyond this, John wants the reader to know Jesus' boundless love for the believer, even when, like Thomas, the believer is not perfect in faith. John wants the reader to confess Jesus even in the absence of signs. If this point is not made, Martha's reward of Lazarus's resurrection and the appearance to Mary Magdalene might seem to foster a dependence on

the Son of God, and that by believing in him you
will have life by the power of his name.

Epilogue: Jesus Appears to Seven Disciples

21 Later, Jesus appeared again to the
disciples beside the Sea of Galilee.*
This is how it happened. 2 Several of
the disciples were there—Simon Peter, Thomas
(nicknamed the Twin),* Nathanael from Cana in
Galilee, the sons of Zebedee, and two other disciples.
3 Simon Peter said, "I'm going fishing."
"We'll come, too," they all said. So they
went out in the boat, but they caught nothing
all night.
4 At dawn Jesus was standing on the beach, but
the disciples couldn't see who he was. 5 He called
out, "Fellows,* have you caught any fish?"
"No," they replied.
6 Then he said, "Throw out your net on the
right-hand side of the boat, and you'll get some!"
So they did, and they couldn't haul in the net because there were so many fish in it.
7 Then the disciple Jesus loved said to Peter,
"It's the Lord!" When Simon Peter heard that
it was the Lord, he put on his tunic (for he had
stripped for work), jumped into the water, and
headed to shore. 8 The others stayed with the boat
and pulled the loaded net to the shore, for they
were only about a hundred yards* from shore.
9 When they got there, they found breakfast
waiting for them—fish cooking over a charcoal
fire, and some bread.
10 "Bring some of the fish you've just caught,"
Jesus said. 11 So Simon Peter went aboard
and dragged the net to the shore. There were
153 large fish, and yet the net hadn't torn.
12 "Now come and have some breakfast!"
Jesus said. None of the disciples dared to ask
him, "Who are you?" They knew it was the Lord.
13 Then Jesus served them the bread and the fish.
14 This was the third time Jesus had appeared to
his disciples since he had been raised from the
dead.
15 After breakfast Jesus asked Simon Peter,
"Simon son of John, do you love me more than
these?*"
"Yes, Lord," Peter replied, "you know I love
you."
"Then feed my lambs," Jesus told him.
16 Jesus repeated the question: "Simon son of
John, do you love me?"
"Yes, Lord," Peter said, "you know I love
you."
"Then take care of my sheep," Jesus said.
17 A third time he asked him, "Simon son of
John, do you love me?"
Peter was hurt that Jesus asked the question a
third time. He said, "Lord, you know everything.
You know that I love you."
Jesus said, "Then feed my sheep.
18 "I tell you the truth, when you were young,
you were able to do as you liked; you dressed
yourself and went wherever you wanted to go.
But when you are old, you will stretch out your
hands, and others* will dress you and take you
where you don't want to go." 19 Jesus said this to
let him know by what kind of death he would
glorify God. Then Jesus told him, "Follow me."
20 Peter turned around and saw behind them
the disciple Jesus loved—the one who had leaned
over to Jesus during supper and asked, "Lord,
who will betray you?" 21 Peter asked Jesus, "What
about him, Lord?"
22 Jesus replied, "If I want him to remain
alive until I return, what is that to you? As for
you, follow me." 23 So the rumor spread among
the community of believers* that this disciple
wouldn't die. But that isn't what Jesus said at all.
He only said, "If I want him to remain alive until
I return, what is that to you?"
24 This disciple is the one who testifies to these
events and has recorded them here. And we know
that his account of these things is accurate.
25 Jesus also did many other things. If they
were all written down, I suppose the whole world
could not contain the books that would be written.

21:1 Greek *Sea of Tiberias,* another name for the Sea of Galilee. **21:2** Greek *Thomas, who was called Didymus.* **21:5** Greek *Children.* **21:8** Greek *200 cubits* [90 meters]. **21:15** Or *more than these others do?* **21:18** Some manuscripts read *and another one.* **21:23** Greek *the brothers.*

---

signs. In John's time, evidently this was becoming a problem for even the most ardent disciples.

21:1–25 Epilogue: Jesus Appears to the Disciples

This third appearance of the risen Lord comes in the midst of the disciples' ordinary daily life. **15–17:** In contrast to Mary Magdalene, Peter must be commanded three times to feed Jesus' sheep—after all of the opportunities for spontaneous imitation of the good shepherd, when the disciples had him to themselves, have passed.

ACTS

INTRODUCTION

Acts is an extraordinary, remarkably accurate historical record. It covers the period from around AD 33 to around AD 65, and it was probably written sometime in the early 70s or possibly a little later. But like a novel, Acts well repays reading straight through or at least in satisfying, long sections, so that the reader is immersed in the drama and the flow of the story. Reading disjointed snippets dulls our senses and leaves us unaware of how amazing is the tale that is unfolding.

This story, which spans a mere thirty years, takes us from the ascension of the Lord Jesus Christ into heaven to a point at which the fledgling church has turned the world upside down. It takes us from a small, dejected, and fearful band of disciples hidden behind locked doors in Jerusalem to many thousands of believers established in worshiping congregations throughout Palestine, Asia Minor, and Greece, and even as far away as Rome, the center of the great empire. It takes us from a group bewildered at the absence of their human companion and leader, Jesus, to a vast community confident in the constant presence of the Holy Spirit. And it takes us from a fundamentally monocultural Jewish sect to a multicultural predominantly Gentile religion.

It shows us, for example, how the churches to which the Epistles are addressed began and against what background; it tells us who Timothy was; and it describes the persecution experienced by congregations such as those to which Peter wrote. It is crucial in showing us how the church, led by the Holy Spirit, made those huge transitions. And it is crucial in establishing for us many important principles as we too seek to live for Jesus Christ in our diverse contexts. But most of all it is crucial in demonstrating that Jesus Christ, crucified, risen, and ascended, is the fulfillment of all past history and promise and the pivotal figure for all humanity in the present and the future.

At first glance it might seem that Luke is not interested in women, inside or outside the church. Certainly men—Peter, John, James, Philip, Barnabas, Paul, Festus, and Agrippa—stride through the story. Yet to conclude that Acts marginalizes women would be superficial judgment. In the world in which the events of Acts take place, and especially in the public world of debating in the marketplace or standing up and teaching in the synagogue, it could not be otherwise than that men hold the stage. In any case, Luke's primary purpose is not to provide an apologetic for women's equality in the church but to continue the "orderly account [begun in the Gospel] . . . so that you may know the truth concerning the things about which you have been instructed" (Luke 1:3–4, NRSV). The central concern of that account is to establish the identity and credentials of the Lord Jesus Christ and the reliability of the apostolic teaching about him.

Nonetheless, Luke repeatedly draws attention to the full involvement of women in the emerging Christian community. We encounter women praying (1:14; 12:12; 16:13) and prophesying (2:17; 21:9), coming to faith and being baptized (5:14; 8:12), and being persecuted alongside their menfolk (8:3; 9:2; 22:4). In the terrible story of Ananias and Sapphira (5:1–11), Luke makes clear that women are answerable to God in their own right and may not devolve responsibility on their husbands. Through the story of Tabitha (also known as

Dorcas, 9:36–42), we are left in no doubt that a godly woman can have a powerful testimony to the grace of God, affecting a whole community. In Priscilla (18:2, 26), we meet a woman discipling a man, recorded with approval. And in Lydia (16:14–15, 40) we are introduced to the first convert on the European mainland through Paul's ministry, who became the linchpin of the church at Philippi.

These records are neither sentimental nor apologetic but quietly matter-of-fact. Given the absence of parables and the limited number of encounters with individuals, in both of which many of the Gospel references to women appear, and given the focus of Acts (e.g., establishing the facts about Jesus through many public sermons, or describing pioneer evangelism into new areas, or explaining how God was insisting the church must be universal and not Jewish), our surprise should be at how much, not how little, is said specifically about women.

Many commentators have divided Acts into six main sections. Each section focuses on one key phase in the establishing and expansion of the church, and each concludes with a summary statement indicating progress for the Word of God and for the church. This simple outline is helpful and is therefore adopted here, though with fresh headings.

—*Rosemary M. Dowsett*

1:1—6:7	The Church Is Born: Beginnings in Jerusalem
6:8—9:31	Beyond Jerusalem: Persecution and the Scattering of God's People
9:32—12:24	Further Still: Bridgehead into the Gentile World
12:25—16:5	The Asian World: Good News for Gentiles
16:6—19:20	Across the Sea: The Gospel for Europe
19:21—28:31	At Great Cost: Rome at Last

✧

The Promise of the Holy Spirit

1 In my first book* I told you, Theophilus,
about everything Jesus began to do and
teach [2]until the day he was taken up to
heaven after giving his chosen apostles further
instructions through the Holy Spirit. [3]During
the forty days after his crucifixion, he appeared
to the apostles from time to time, and he proved
to them in many ways that he was actually alive.
And he talked to them about the Kingdom of
God.
[4]Once when he was eating with them, he
commanded them, "Do not leave Jerusalem until
the Father sends you the gift he promised, as I
told you before. [5]John baptized with* water, but
in just a few days you will be baptized with the
Holy Spirit."

The Ascension of Jesus

[6]So when the apostles were with Jesus, they kept
asking him, "Lord, has the time come for you to
free Israel and restore our kingdom?"
[7]He replied, "The Father alone has the au-

1:1 The reference is to the Gospel of Luke. **1:5** Or *in;* also in 1:5b.

1:1—6:7 The Church Is Born: Beginnings in Jerusalem

1:1–5 The Promise of the Holy Spirit. 1–2: Luke, the author, tells us that Acts is the sequel to his Gospel; but, whereas we have four Gospels, this is the only historical record of the birth and early growth of the church. It is crucial not only for the history of the church but also in setting the context for the Epistles that follow. **3–4:** Acts begins with a recapitulation of the final verses of Luke's Gospel, including the promise of the Holy Spirit, so soon to be given, and the anticipation of the worldwide mission of the church.

1:6–11 The Ascension of Jesus. Numerous Old Testament references to the outpouring of the Spirit were understood to be referring to the restoration of exiles to their land and a new beginning for Israel (e.g., Isa

thority to set those dates and times, and they are not for you to know. [8]But you will receive power when the Holy Spirit comes upon you. And you will be my witnesses, telling people about me everywhere—in Jerusalem, throughout Judea, in Samaria, and to the ends of the earth."

[9]After saying this, he was taken up into a cloud while they were watching, and they could no longer see him. [10]As they strained to see him rising into heaven, two white-robed men suddenly stood among them. [11]"Men of Galilee," they said, "why are you standing here staring into heaven? Jesus has been taken from you into heaven, but someday he will return from heaven in the same way you saw him go!"

Matthias Replaces Judas

[12]Then the apostles returned to Jerusalem from the Mount of Olives, a distance of half a mile.* [13]When they arrived, they went to the upstairs room of the house where they were staying.

Here are the names of those who were present: Peter, John, James, Andrew, Philip, Thomas, Bartholomew, Matthew, James (son of Alphaeus), Simon (the Zealot), and Judas (son of James). [14]They all met together and were constantly united in prayer, along with Mary the mother of Jesus, several other women, and the brothers of Jesus.

[15]During this time, when about 120 believers* were together in one place, Peter stood up and addressed them. [16]"Brothers," he said, "the Scriptures had to be fulfilled concerning Judas, who guided those who arrested Jesus. This was predicted long ago by the Holy Spirit, speaking through King David. [17]Judas was one of us and shared in the ministry with us."

[18](Judas had bought a field with the money he received for his treachery. Falling headfirst there, his body split open, spilling out all his intestines. [19]The news of his death spread to all the people of Jerusalem, and they gave the place the Aramaic name *Akeldama,* which means "Field of Blood.")

[20]Peter continued, "This was written in the book of Psalms, where it says, 'Let his home become desolate, with no one living in it.' It also says, 'Let someone else take his position.'*

[21]"So now we must choose a replacement for Judas from among the men who were with us the entire time we were traveling with the Lord Jesus—[22]from the time he was baptized by John until the day he was taken from us. Whoever is chosen will join us as a witness of Jesus' resurrection."

[23]So they nominated two men: Joseph called Barsabbas (also known as Justus) and Matthias. [24]Then they all prayed, "O Lord, you know every heart. Show us which of these men you have chosen [25]as an apostle to replace Judas in this ministry, for he has deserted us and gone where he belongs." [26]Then they cast lots, and Matthias was selected to become an apostle with the other eleven.

The Holy Spirit Comes

2 On the day of Pentecost* all the believers were meeting together in one place. [2]Suddenly, there was a sound from heaven like the roaring of a mighty windstorm, and it filled

1:12 Greek *a Sabbath day's journey.* **1:15** Greek *brothers.* **1:20** Pss 69:25; 109:8. **2:1** The Festival of Pentecost came 50 days after Passover (when Jesus was crucified).

32:12–20; Ezek 36:25–28). **9–10:** The King returns to heaven rather than arrives on earth. **14:** It is unclear whether it was only the Eleven together with the women who were constantly united in prayer or whether the 120 believers were also engaged in a sustained, prayerful watchfulness extending from the fortieth day since Passover to Pentecost, the fiftieth day. Contrary to common but not exclusive synagogue practice, it seems that the women joined the men for prayer, and over such a period some of them must have been also occupied with preparing food and caring for children and other domestic tasks.

1:12–26 Matthias Replaces Judas. Conscious of the symbolic importance of having twelve apostles to represent the whole of Israel, Peter urges the company, in the context of prayer, to appoint someone to take Judas's place. Here is an intriguing bringing together of Scripture (which must be fulfilled), divine sovereignty (God could overrule the outcome of the lot), and human responsibility (choosing two people who met the criteria). **21–22:** There were certainly women who met the criteria set out here (Luke 8:2–3), but for whatever reason, none of these made the short list.

2:1–13 The Holy Spirit Comes. Pentecost, also known as the Feast of Weeks, was a celebration and thanksgiving for the barley harvest (see Lev 23:16; Exod 34:22; Deut 16:9, 16) to be held fifty days after Passover. Many pilgrims, especially those of the Jewish diaspora, who came to Jerusalem for Passover stayed on for Pentecost as well, so that the city would have been crowded with men and women from far and wide, in a celebratory mood. This was the great party before heading home. *All the believers were meeting together in one place,* men and women, presumably

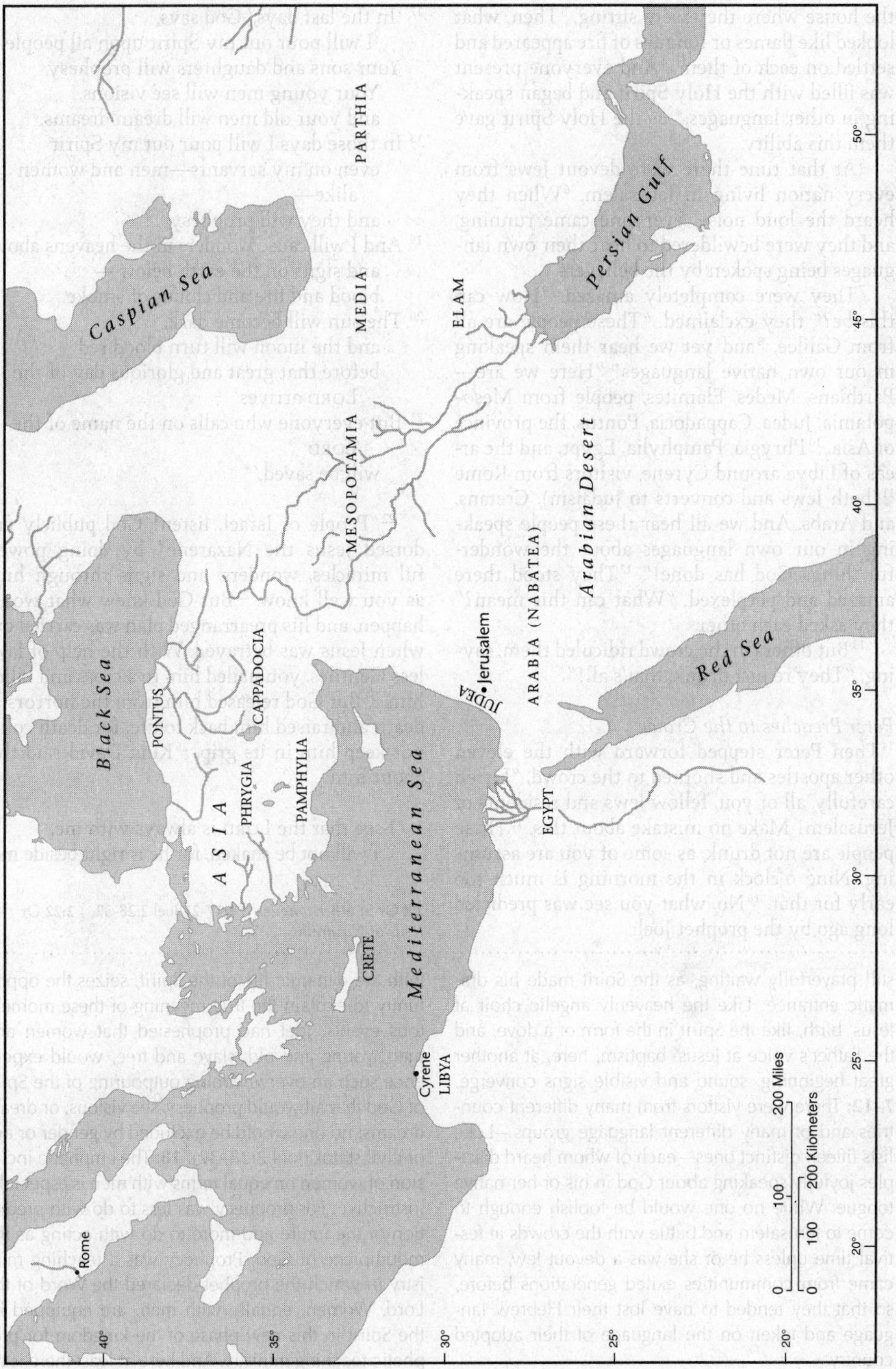

The Native Lands of Pentecost Pilgrims

the house where they were sitting. 3 Then, what
looked like flames or tongues of fire appeared and
settled on each of them. 4 And everyone present
was filled with the Holy Spirit and began speaking in other languages,* as the Holy Spirit gave
them this ability.

5 At that time there were devout Jews from
every nation living in Jerusalem. 6 When they
heard the loud noise, everyone came running,
and they were bewildered to hear their own languages being spoken by the believers.

7 They were completely amazed. "How can
this be?" they exclaimed. "These people are all
from Galilee, 8 and yet we hear them speaking
in our own native languages! 9 Here we are—
Parthians, Medes, Elamites, people from Mesopotamia, Judea, Cappadocia, Pontus, the province
of Asia, 10 Phrygia, Pamphylia, Egypt, and the areas of Libya around Cyrene, visitors from Rome
11 (both Jews and converts to Judaism), Cretans,
and Arabs. And we all hear these people speaking in our own languages about the wonderful things God has done!" 12 They stood there
amazed and perplexed. "What can this mean?"
they asked each other.

13 But others in the crowd ridiculed them, saying, "They're just drunk, that's all!"

Peter Preaches to the Crowd

14 Then Peter stepped forward with the eleven
other apostles and shouted to the crowd, "Listen
carefully, all of you, fellow Jews and residents of
Jerusalem! Make no mistake about this. 15 These
people are not drunk, as some of you are assuming. Nine o'clock in the morning is much too
early for that. 16 No, what you see was predicted
long ago by the prophet Joel:

17 'In the last days,' God says,
'I will pour out my Spirit upon all people.
Your sons and daughters will prophesy.
Your young men will see visions,
and your old men will dream dreams.
18 In those days I will pour out my Spirit
even on my servants—men and women alike—
and they will prophesy.
19 And I will cause wonders in the heavens above
and signs on the earth below—
blood and fire and clouds of smoke.
20 The sun will become dark,
and the moon will turn blood red
before that great and glorious day of the LORD arrives.
21 But everyone who calls on the name of the LORD
will be saved.'*

22 "People of Israel, listen! God publicly endorsed Jesus the Nazarene* by doing powerful miracles, wonders, and signs through him,
as you well know. 23 But God knew what would
happen, and his prearranged plan was carried out
when Jesus was betrayed. With the help of lawless Gentiles, you nailed him to a cross and killed
him. 24 But God released him from the horrors of
death and raised him back to life, for death could
not keep him in its grip. 25 King David said this
about him:

'I see that the LORD is always with me.
I will not be shaken, for he is right beside me.

2:4 Or *in other tongues.* **2:17-21** Joel 2:28-32. **2:22** Or *Jesus of Nazareth.*

still prayerfully waiting, as the Spirit made his dramatic entrance. Like the heavenly angelic choir at Jesus' birth, like the Spirit in the form of a dove, and the Father's voice at Jesus' baptism, here, at another great beginning, sound and visible signs converge. **7–12:** There were visitors from many different countries and of many different language groups—Luke lists fifteen distinct ones—each of whom heard disciples joyfully speaking about God in his or her native tongue. While no one would be foolish enough to come to Jerusalem and battle with the crowds at festival time unless he or she was a devout Jew, many came from communities exiled generations before, so that they tended to have lost their Hebrew language and taken on the language of their adopted country.

2:14–41 Peter Preaches to the Crowd. Peter, bold with the dynamic life of the Spirit, seizes the opportunity to explain the true meaning of these momentous events. Joel had prophesied that women and men, young and old, slave and free, would experience such an overwhelming outpouring of the Spirit of God that all would prophesy, see visions, or dream dreams; no one would be excluded by gender or age or civil status (Joel 2:28–32). **18:** The emphatic inclusion of women on equal terms with men is especially instructive. For prophecy was less to do with prediction of the future and more to do with acting as the mouthpiece of God. Prophecy was a teaching ministry in which the prophet declared the Word of the Lord. Women, equally with men, are equipped by the Spirit in this new phase of the kingdom for prophetic teaching ministry. And here at least there is no hint that this ministry must be exercised only among women, any more than men only among men.

26 No wonder my heart is glad,
and my tongue shouts his praises!
My body rests in hope.
27 For you will not leave my soul among the
dead*
or allow your Holy One to rot in the grave.
28 You have shown me the way of life,
and you will fill me with the joy of your
presence.'*

29 "Dear brothers, think about this! You can be
sure that the patriarch David wasn't referring to
himself, for he died and was buried, and his tomb
is still here among us. 30 But he was a prophet,
and he knew God had promised with an oath that
one of David's own descendants would sit on his
throne. 31 David was looking into the future and
speaking of the Messiah's resurrection. He was
saying that God would not leave him among the
dead or allow his body to rot in the grave.
32 "God raised Jesus from the dead, and we are
all witnesses of this. 33 Now he is exalted to the
place of highest honor in heaven, at God's right
hand. And the Father, as he had promised, gave
him the Holy Spirit to pour out upon us, just
as you see and hear today. 34 For David himself
never ascended into heaven, yet he said,

'The LORD said to my Lord,
"Sit in the place of honor at my right hand
35 until I humble your enemies,
making them a footstool under your feet."'*

36 "So let everyone in Israel know for certain
that God has made this Jesus, whom you crucified, to be both Lord and Messiah!"
37 Peter's words pierced their hearts, and they
said to him and to the other apostles, "Brothers,
what should we do?"
38 Peter replied, "Each of you must repent of
your sins and turn to God, and be baptized in the
name of Jesus Christ for the forgiveness of your
sins. Then you will receive the gift of the Holy
Spirit. 39 This promise is to you, and to your children, and even to the Gentiles*—all who have
been called by the Lord our God." 40 Then Peter
continued preaching for a long time, strongly
urging all his listeners, "Save yourselves from
this crooked generation!"
41 Those who believed what Peter said were
baptized and added to the church that day—
about 3,000 in all.

The Believers Form a Community
42 All the believers devoted themselves to the
apostles' teaching, and to fellowship, and to sharing in meals (including the Lord's Supper*), and
to prayer.
43 A deep sense of awe came over them all,
and the apostles performed many miraculous
signs and wonders. 44 And all the believers met
together in one place and shared everything they
had. 45 They sold their property and possessions
and shared the money with those in need. 46 They
worshiped together at the Temple each day, met
in homes for the Lord's Supper, and shared their
meals with great joy and generosity*—47 all the
while praising God and enjoying the goodwill of
all the people. And each day the Lord added to
their fellowship those who were being saved.

Peter Heals a Crippled Beggar
3 Peter and John went to the Temple one
afternoon to take part in the three o'clock
prayer service. 2 As they approached the
Temple, a man lame from birth was being carried
in. Each day he was put beside the Temple gate,
the one called the Beautiful Gate, so he could beg
from the people going into the Temple. 3 When
he saw Peter and John about to enter, he asked
them for some money.

2:27 Greek *in Hades;* also in 2:31. **2:25-28** Ps 16:8-11 (Greek version). **2:34-35** Ps 110:1. **2:39** Or *and to people far in the future;* Greek reads *and to those far away.* **2:42** Greek *the breaking of bread;* also in 2:46. **2:46** Or *and sincere hearts.*

2:42–47 The Believers Form a Community. Ordinary daily work came to a standstill. Pilgrims, unexpectedly delayed, would run out of funds. The apostles, possibly most of the 120, were from Galilee and therefore several days' journey from their homes. Day after day, thousands must be accommodated and fed in a culture in which hospitality was important. (How busy the women must have been! Did the prices in the market soar? How many jars of water did they have to carry every day?) The only possible solution was to pool resources, and it seems they did so gladly. All other affairs paled into insignificance.

3:1–11 Peter Heals a Crippled Beggar. Males with disabilities, along with women, were excluded from the Court of Israel on the grounds that nothing imperfect could pollute such a hallowed place; the crippled man was as close as he was permitted to go. The significance of his healing is deeper than we might think. Not only for the first time in more than forty years (4:22) could this man walk but now he could enter that inner sanctum of the Court of Israel and worship at the altar. The Lord Jesus gives access to the presence of God.

[4]Peter and John looked at him intently, and Peter said, "Look at us!" [5]The lame man looked at them eagerly, expecting some money. [6]But Peter said, "I don't have any silver or gold for you. But I'll give you what I have. In the name of Jesus Christ the Nazarene,* get up and* walk!"

[7]Then Peter took the lame man by the right hand and helped him up. And as he did, the man's feet and ankles were instantly healed and strengthened. [8]He jumped up, stood on his feet, and began to walk! Then, walking, leaping, and praising God, he went into the Temple with them.

[9]All the people saw him walking and heard him praising God. [10]When they realized he was the lame beggar they had seen so often at the Beautiful Gate, they were absolutely astounded! [11]They all rushed out in amazement to Solomon's Colonnade, where the man was holding tightly to Peter and John.

Peter Preaches in the Temple

[12]Peter saw his opportunity and addressed the crowd. "People of Israel," he said, "what is so surprising about this? And why stare at us as though we had made this man walk by our own power or godliness? [13]For it is the God of Abraham, Isaac, and Jacob—the God of all our ancestors—who has brought glory to his servant Jesus by doing this. This is the same Jesus whom you handed over and rejected before Pilate, despite Pilate's decision to release him. [14]You rejected this holy, righteous one and instead demanded the release of a murderer. [15]You killed the author of life, but God raised him from the dead. And we are witnesses of this fact!

[16]"Through faith in the name of Jesus, this man was healed—and you know how crippled he was before. Faith in Jesus' name has healed him before your very eyes.

[17]"Friends,* I realize that what you and your leaders did to Jesus was done in ignorance. [18]But God was fulfilling what all the prophets had foretold about the Messiah—that he must suffer these things. [19]Now repent of your sins and turn to God, so that your sins may be wiped away. [20]Then times of refreshment will come from the presence of the Lord, and he will again send you Jesus, your appointed Messiah. [21]For he must remain in heaven until the time for the final restoration of all things, as God promised long ago through his holy prophets. [22]Moses said, 'The LORD your God will raise up for you a Prophet like me from among your own people. Listen carefully to everything he tells you.'* [23]Then Moses said, 'Anyone who will not listen to that Prophet will be completely cut off from God's people.'*

[24]"Starting with Samuel, every prophet spoke about what is happening today. [25]You are the children of those prophets, and you are included in the covenant God promised to your ancestors. For God said to Abraham, 'Through your descendants* all the families on earth will be blessed.' [26]When God raised up his servant, Jesus, he sent him first to you people of Israel, to bless you by turning each of you back from your sinful ways."

Peter and John before the Council

4 While Peter and John were speaking to the people, they were confronted by the priests, the captain of the Temple guard, and some of the Sadducees. [2]These leaders were very disturbed that Peter and John were teaching the people that through Jesus there is a resurrection of the dead. [3]They arrested them and, since it was already evening, put them in jail until morning. [4]But many of the people who heard their message believed it, so the number of believers now totaled about 5,000 men, not counting women and children.*

[5]The next day the council of all the rulers and elders and teachers of religious law met in Jeru-

3:6a Or *Jesus Christ of Nazareth.* **3:6b** Some manuscripts do not include *get up and.* **3:17** Greek *Brothers.* **3:22** Deut 18:15. **3:23** Deut 18:19; Lev 23:29. **3:25** Greek *your seed;* see Gen 12:3; 22:18. **4:4** Greek *5,000 adult males.*

3:12–26 Peter Preaches in the Temple. Peter is by now back in the huge outer court, accessible to both men and women, Jews and Gentiles. He hastens to seize the opportunity to explain that it is not he but Jesus who has so wonderfully healed the man. Once again there is a massive response, though it is not clear whether the five thousand (4:4) are all fresh converts or whether this represents a running total.

4:1–22 Peter and John before the Council. For the first time since the resurrection, we are told of active hostility toward the apostles. Not surprisingly, it comes from the Temple authorities, dominated by the Sadducean party. The particular issue that raised their anger, Luke records, was that the apostles *were teaching the people that through Jesus there is a resurrection of the dead.* This was at the heart of their message. By contrast, the Sadducees denied the possibility of resurrection, so should many people come to believe what the apostles were saying, the Saddu-

salem. 6 Annas the high priest was there, along with Caiaphas, John, Alexander, and other relatives of the high priest. 7 They brought in the two disciples and demanded, "By what power, or in whose name, have you done this?"

8 Then Peter, filled with the Holy Spirit, said to them, "Rulers and elders of our people, 9 are we being questioned today because we've done a good deed for a crippled man? Do you want to know how he was healed? 10 Let me clearly state to all of you and to all the people of Israel that he was healed by the powerful name of Jesus Christ the Nazarene,* the man you crucified but whom God raised from the dead. 11 For Jesus is the one referred to in the Scriptures, where it says,

'The stone that you builders rejected
  has now become the cornerstone.'*

12 There is salvation in no one else! God has given no other name under heaven by which we must be saved."

13 The members of the council were amazed when they saw the boldness of Peter and John, for they could see that they were ordinary men with no special training in the Scriptures. They also recognized them as men who had been with Jesus. 14 But since they could see the man who had been healed standing right there among them, there was nothing the council could say. 15 So they ordered Peter and John out of the council chamber* and conferred among themselves.

16 "What should we do with these men?" they asked each other. "We can't deny that they have performed a miraculous sign, and everybody in Jerusalem knows about it. 17 But to keep them from spreading their propaganda any further, we must warn them not to speak to anyone in Jesus' name again." 18 So they called the apostles back in and commanded them never again to speak or teach in the name of Jesus.

19 But Peter and John replied, "Do you think God wants us to obey you rather than him? 20 We cannot stop telling about everything we have seen and heard."

21 The council then threatened them further, but they finally let them go because they didn't know how to punish them without starting a riot. For everyone was praising God 22 for this miraculous sign—the healing of a man who had been lame for more than forty years.

The Believers Pray for Courage

23 As soon as they were freed, Peter and John returned to the other believers and told them what the leading priests and elders had said. 24 When they heard the report, all the believers lifted their voices together in prayer to God: "O Sovereign Lord, Creator of heaven and earth, the sea, and everything in them—25 you spoke long ago by the Holy Spirit through our ancestor David, your servant, saying,

'Why were the nations so angry?
  Why did they waste their time with futile
    plans?
26 The kings of the earth prepared for battle;
  the rulers gathered together
against the LORD
  and against his Messiah.'*

27 "In fact, this has happened here in this very city! For Herod Antipas, Pontius Pilate the governor, the Gentiles, and the people of Israel were all united against Jesus, your holy servant, whom you anointed. 28 But everything they did was determined beforehand according to your will. 29 And now, O Lord, hear their threats, and give us, your servants, great boldness in preaching your word. 30 Stretch out your hand with healing power; may miraculous signs and wonders be done through the name of your holy servant Jesus."

31 After this prayer, the meeting place shook, and they were all filled with the Holy Spirit. Then they preached the word of God with boldness.

4:10 Or *Jesus Christ of Nazareth.* **4:11** Ps 118:22. **4:15** Greek *the Sanhedrin.* **4:25-26** Or *his anointed one;* or *his Christ.* Ps 2:1-2.

---

cees' credibility and power would be undermined. **16–21:** There was no legally sustainable charge; the lame man had been healed and, however briefly, the apostles were enjoying widespread popular support. Far from being cowed, Peter and John insist not only that the religious leaders were guilty of failing to see Jesus' divine credentials (v. 11) but also that salvation is exclusively to be found in Jesus Christ (v. 12). Only months before, Peter had denied all association with Jesus (Luke 22:54–62). Now, filled with the Holy Spirit, he throws down the gauntlet in the most unmistakable manner possible.

4:23–31 The Believers Pray for Courage. The response of the newborn church is united and decisive. They interpret the opposition as the fulfillment of prophecy (Ps 2:1–2), and they affirm their faith in the Lord as sovereign. They pray that they might witness boldly, while asking the Lord to perform unequivocal healings and signs to confirm their message.

The Believers Share Their Possessions
32 All the believers were united in heart and mind.
And they felt that what they owned was not their
own, so they shared everything they had. 33 The
apostles testified powerfully to the resurrection
of the Lord Jesus, and God's great blessing was
upon them all. 34 There were no needy people
among them, because those who owned land or
houses would sell them 35 and bring the money
to the apostles to give to those in need.
36 For instance, there was Joseph, the one the
apostles nicknamed Barnabas (which means
"Son of Encouragement"). He was from the tribe
of Levi and came from the island of Cyprus. 37 He
sold a field he owned and brought the money to
the apostles.

Ananias and Sapphira
5 But there was a certain man named Ananias who, with his wife, Sapphira, sold some
property. 2 He brought part of the money
to the apostles, claiming it was the full amount.
With his wife's consent, he kept the rest.
3 Then Peter said, "Ananias, why have you let
Satan fill your heart? You lied to the Holy Spirit,
and you kept some of the money for yourself.
4 The property was yours to sell or not sell, as
you wished. And after selling it, the money was
also yours to give away. How could you do a
thing like this? You weren't lying to us but to
God!"
5 As soon as Ananias heard these words, he
fell to the floor and died. Everyone who heard
about it was terrified. 6 Then some young men
got up, wrapped him in a sheet, and took him out
and buried him.
7 About three hours later his wife came in, not
knowing what had happened. 8 Peter asked her,
"Was this the price you and your husband received for your land?"
"Yes," she replied, "that was the price."
9 And Peter said, "How could the two of you
even think of conspiring to test the Spirit of the
Lord like this? The young men who buried your
husband are just outside the door, and they will
carry you out, too."
10 Instantly, she fell to the floor and died.
When the young men came in and saw that she
was dead, they carried her out and buried her beside her husband. 11 Great fear gripped the entire
church and everyone else who heard what had
happened.

The Apostles Heal Many
12 The apostles were performing many miraculous signs and wonders among the people. And
all the believers were meeting regularly at the
Temple in the area known as Solomon's Colonnade. 13 But no one else dared to join them, even
though all the people had high regard for them.
14 Yet more and more people believed and were
brought to the Lord—crowds of both men and

4:32–37 The Believers Share Their Possessions. Not only does the Holy Spirit shake the place where they are gathered—which in itself must have been an awesome experience—but their commitment to one another is profoundly reinforced, so that *what they owned was not their own,* that is, was available to the Christian community rather than just to the legal owners. This included revenue raised by the sale of property, both land and houses. It is important to note that this was not compulsory. Nor would it seem that it was total or universal: In 12:12 Luke (without need for explanation) refers to a private home belonging to an early believer. So this is not a charter for Marxist public ownership. Rather, it seems that under the compulsion of the Spirit different people sold property to meet the needs of the church as they arose. **36:** Barnabas was a member of the sizable Jewish community in Cyprus at that time. Among the thousands, Barnabas apparently stood out as an individual to the apostles, for it was they who gave him his nickname *Son of Encouragement.* He sold a field and gave the proceeds to the apostles for careful distribution.

5:1–11 Ananias and Sapphira. Luke deliberately contrasts the noble example of Barnabas with the actions of Ananias and Sapphira. They too sold property, but they gave only a part of the proceeds to the apostles. That in itself would not have mattered; Peter makes it clear that they had the right to sell or not to sell the property, just as they had the right to give or not to give the proceeds. What mattered was that they deliberately lied, saying they had handed over the full value when they had not done so. Judgment comes swiftly and dramatically: Perhaps it seems rather a horrifying punishment for telling a lie. But what is at stake is integrity and truthfulness within the young Christian community, hypocrisy about commitment and, as Peter puts it, the attempt to *lie[d] to the Holy Spirit.* **7:** Sapphira has to take full responsibility for her dishonesty. In a day when almost any wife could excuse herself on the grounds that she had no freedom to do other than obey her husband, Peter insists that she may not hide behind her husband's leadership. When it comes to moral and spiritual issues, a wife must put the Lord's requirements before her husband's.

5:12–16 The Apostles Heal Many. Luke is careful to note the inclusion of women, here recognizing the

women. [15]As a result of the apostles' work, sick people were brought out into the streets on beds and mats so that Peter's shadow might fall across some of them as he went by. [16]Crowds came from the villages around Jerusalem, bringing their sick and those possessed by evil* spirits, and they were all healed.

The Apostles Meet Opposition

[17]The high priest and his officials, who were Sadducees, were filled with jealousy. [18]They arrested the apostles and put them in the public jail. [19]But an angel of the Lord came at night, opened the gates of the jail, and brought them out. Then he told them, [20]"Go to the Temple and give the people this message of life!"

[21]So at daybreak the apostles entered the Temple, as they were told, and immediately began teaching.

When the high priest and his officials arrived, they convened the high council*—the full assembly of the elders of Israel. Then they sent for the apostles to be brought from the jail for trial. [22]But when the Temple guards went to the jail, the men were gone. So they returned to the council and reported, [23]"The jail was securely locked, with the guards standing outside, but when we opened the gates, no one was there!"

[24]When the captain of the Temple guard and the leading priests heard this, they were perplexed, wondering where it would all end. [25]Then someone arrived with startling news: "The men you put in jail are standing in the Temple, teaching the people!"

[26]The captain went with his Temple guards and arrested the apostles, but without violence, for they were afraid the people would stone them. [27]Then they brought the apostles before the high council, where the high priest confronted them. [28]"Didn't we tell you never again to teach in this man's name?" he demanded. "Instead, you have filled all Jerusalem with your teaching about him, and you want to make us responsible for his death!"

[29]But Peter and the apostles replied, "We must obey God rather than any human authority. [30]The God of our ancestors raised Jesus from the dead after you killed him by hanging him on a cross.* [31]Then God put him in the place of honor at his right hand as Prince and Savior. He did this so the people of Israel would repent of their sins and be forgiven. [32]We are witnesses of these things and so is the Holy Spirit, who is given by God to those who obey him."

[33]When they heard this, the high council was furious and decided to kill them. [34]But one member, a Pharisee named Gamaliel, who was an expert in religious law and respected by all the people, stood up and ordered that the men be sent outside the council chamber for a while. [35]Then he said to his colleagues, "Men of Israel, take care what you are planning to do to these men! [36]Some time ago there was that fellow Theudas, who pretended to be someone great. About 400 others joined him, but he was killed, and all his followers went their various ways. The whole movement came to nothing. [37]After him, at the time of the census, there was Judas of Galilee. He got people to follow him, but he was killed, too, and all his followers were scattered.

[38]"So my advice is, leave these men alone. Let

5:16 Greek *unclean.* **5:21** Greek *Sanhedrin;* also in 5:27, 41. **5:30** Greek *on a tree.*

---

crowds of both men and women who came to faith. Luke does not give us a time frame, but it seems that this time of consolidation and growth extended for quite some while.

5:17–42 The Apostles Meet Opposition. The Sadducees and the high priest, unable to contain themselves any longer, were filled with jealousy, perhaps because of the numbers who traveled from farther and farther afield to Jerusalem and flocked to hear the apostles. Sadducees were antisupernaturalists, so that the constant preaching about the resurrection of Jesus and the repeated healings, signs, and wonders taking place through the Christian community called in question everything for which they stood. Moreover, the Sadducees were powerful but not popular. No wonder they seethed with bitter jealousy. Luke does not tell us how many or specifically who are thrown into prison and subsequently released by an angel. **20:** The angel tells the apostles to go straight back to bold preaching in the Temple, that most public of places. No prudent pause or withdrawing to some secluded spot: The Holy Spirit seems to be pressing the apostles into increasingly deliberate confrontation with the religious authorities. **26:** When only a few hours later the apostles are brought before the council, Peter's preaching is again inflammatory. Without any doubt, Peter is accusing those whose calling it is to be spiritual leaders of being the greatest barrier to the people coming to salvation. Further, he is claiming that he and the apostles are the ones who are obedient to the Holy Spirit, not the high priest or the council or the religious bureaucracy. **34:** Had it not been for the intervention of Gamaliel—a Pharisee, and thus possibly less opposed to everything the apostles were teaching and doing, and a man highly respected—Peter and

them go. If they are planning and doing these things merely on their own, it will soon be overthrown. [39]But if it is from God, you will not be able to overthrow them. You may even find yourselves fighting against God!"

[40]The others accepted his advice. They called in the apostles and had them flogged. Then they ordered them never again to speak in the name of Jesus, and they let them go.

[41]The apostles left the high council rejoicing that God had counted them worthy to suffer disgrace for the name of Jesus.* [42]And every day, in the Temple and from house to house, they continued to teach and preach this message: "Jesus is the Messiah."

Seven Men Chosen to Serve

6 But as the believers* rapidly multiplied, there were rumblings of discontent. The Greek-speaking believers complained about the Hebrew-speaking believers, saying that their widows were being discriminated against in the daily distribution of food.

[2]So the Twelve called a meeting of all the believers. They said, "We apostles should spend our time teaching the word of God, not running a food program. [3]And so, brothers, select seven men who are well respected and are full of the Spirit and wisdom. We will give them this responsibility. [4]Then we apostles can spend our time in prayer and teaching the word."

[5]Everyone liked this idea, and they chose the following: Stephen (a man full of faith and the Holy Spirit), Philip, Procorus, Nicanor, Timon, Parmenas, and Nicolas of Antioch (an earlier convert to the Jewish faith). [6]These seven were presented to the apostles, who prayed for them as they laid their hands on them.

[7]So God's message continued to spread. The number of believers greatly increased in Jerusalem, and many of the Jewish priests were converted, too.

5:41 Greek *for the name.* **6:1** Greek *disciples;* also in 6:2, 7.

the others with him would surely have been killed. **38–39:** Gamaliel is not convinced about whether the Christians are right but is pragmatic enough to urge a wait-and-see policy. Moreover, for the council to kill them would be beyond their legal rights under the Roman administration, but if Peter and the rest were spearheading another nationalist uprising, the Romans would soon deal with them as they had former rebellions. **40:** Flogging was brutal (up to thirty-nine lashes, which could lay flesh open to the bone) but commonplace enough and within the rights of the Jewish authorities. **41:** Luke does not dwell on the apostles' injuries, focusing instead on the fact that they rejoiced that God had counted them worthy to suffer dishonor for the name of Jesus, a remarkable response that has been repeated in many places down through the years of church history. In fact, much of the New Testament reflects the fact that suffering is a normal part of discipleship, not an infrequent aberration. In this case, the apostles immediately return to teaching and preaching in the Temple, demonstrating what they had claimed: They must obey God rather than human authorities (4:19; 5:29).

6:1–7 Seven Men Chosen to Serve. Luke gives us no clue as to how these events were perceived by the ordinary believers. Some must have been fearful, but overall faith and morale must have been high because there continued to be a steady growth in numbers. In fact, the next difficulty came from within rather than outside the church. Judaism had a well-established tradition of caring for widows and other vulnerable members of society, even if the practice didn't always live up to the theory. And Jerusalem had more than its fair share of widows, since there was a custom for elderly Jews of the diaspora to return to the city at the heart of their faith and identity as they awaited death. If their wives outlived them, they were needy indeed, far from their families and friends and isolated in terms of supportive relationships. It seems that some of these women had come to faith in Jesus and were now part of the church. Probably they could be more easily overlooked because they would be less well known to the mainstream community. It is hard to be on the fringes. **2–4:** For the first time in Luke's record, we are given a glimpse of tension within the church, a sense of unfairness that some do better than others. The apostles see the grave potential of such resentment left to fester, and they do not brush off the needs of these women as only widows but insist that they themselves are called to prayer and teaching the Word. Their respect for these vulnerable women is such that only the best care is appropriate, and so seven men who are well respected and full of the Spirit and of wisdom are appointed. **5:** These men all have Greek names suggesting that they probably had strong links with the diaspora community and would thus be especially sympathetic advocates for the widows. The apostles see their ministry as so significant that Luke records for the first time formal appointment through prayer and laying on of hands. **7:** With the conversion of Jewish priests, it seems that some of the religious establishment was recognizing the truth of the apostolic message.

Stephen Is Arrested
8 Stephen, a man full of God's grace and power,
performed amazing miracles and signs among the
people. 9 But one day some men from the Synagogue of Freed Slaves, as it was called, started to
debate with him. They were Jews from Cyrene,
Alexandria, Cilicia, and the province of Asia.
10 None of them could stand against the wisdom
and the Spirit with which Stephen spoke.
11 So they persuaded some men to lie about
Stephen, saying, "We heard him blaspheme Moses, and even God." 12 This roused the people, the
elders, and the teachers of religious law. So they
arrested Stephen and brought him before the
high council.*
13 The lying witnesses said, "This man is always speaking against the holy Temple and
against the law of Moses. 14 We have heard him
say that this Jesus of Nazareth* will destroy the
Temple and change the customs Moses handed
down to us."
15 At this point everyone in the high council
stared at Stephen, because his face became as
bright as an angel's.

Stephen Addresses the Council
7 Then the high priest asked Stephen, "Are
these accusations true?"
2 This was Stephen's reply: "Brothers
and fathers, listen to me. Our glorious God appeared to our ancestor Abraham in Mesopotamia before he settled in Haran.* 3 God told him,
'Leave your native land and your relatives, and
come into the land that I will show you.'* 4 So
Abraham left the land of the Chaldeans and lived
in Haran until his father died. Then God brought
him here to the land where you now live.
5 "But God gave him no inheritance here, not
even one square foot of land. God did promise,
however, that eventually the whole land would
belong to Abraham and his descendants—even
though he had no children yet. 6 God also told
him that his descendants would live in a foreign
land, where they would be oppressed as slaves for
400 years. 7 'But I will punish the nation that enslaves them,' God said, 'and in the end they will
come out and worship me here in this place.'*
8 "God also gave Abraham the covenant of
circumcision at that time. So when Abraham became the father of Isaac, he circumcised him on
the eighth day. And the practice was continued
when Isaac became the father of Jacob, and when
Jacob became the father of the twelve patriarchs
of the Israelite nation.
9 "These patriarchs were jealous of their
brother Joseph, and they sold him to be a slave in
Egypt. But God was with him 10 and rescued him
from all his troubles. And God gave him favor
before Pharaoh, king of Egypt. God also gave Joseph unusual wisdom, so that Pharaoh appointed
him governor over all of Egypt and put him in
charge of the palace.
11 "But a famine came upon Egypt and Canaan. There was great misery, and our ancestors
ran out of food. 12 Jacob heard that there was still
grain in Egypt, so he sent his sons—our ancestors—to buy some. 13 The second time they went,
Joseph revealed his identity to his brothers,* and
they were introduced to Pharaoh. 14 Then Joseph

6:12 Greek *Sanhedrin;* also in 6:15. **6:14** Or *Jesus the Nazarene.* **7:2** *Mesopotamia* was the region now called Iraq. *Haran* was a city in what is now called Syria. **7:3** Gen 12:1. **7:5-7** Gen 12:7; 15:13-14; Exod 3:12. **7:13** Other manuscripts read *Joseph was recognized by his brothers.*

6:8—9:31 Beyond Jerusalem: Persecution and the Scattering of God's People

6:8–15: It is Stephen—one of the seven appointed to care for the widows, rather than one of the apostles—who becomes the first martyr in the church. Luke gives us a portrait of a remarkable, winsome, and godly man. He is also the first besides the apostles whom Luke specifically tells us *performed amazing miracles and signs.* **9:** Luke does not tell us why some men of the Synagogue of Freed Slaves should take this initiative. Stephen's name and appointment imply that he was not a native Hebrew but one who had been born in a Greek-speaking family somewhere in the dispersion. The Synagogue of Freed Slaves was a temple for those who, prior to coming to Jerusalem, had once been slaves (Jews within Palestine could not be enslaved). The mainstream Jewish community, conveniently overlooking its own history of exile, regarded them as inferior. Stephen may have been converted from among these Jews or he could easily have been identified with them, mistakenly or not. In their desire to be accepted by the Hebrews, the Freedmen would wish to make clear their disassociation from Stephen. Moreover, by discrediting the Christians they could curry favor with the Jewish leaders. **11:** Whether this is what lay behind their subsequent actions or not, they could lay charges against Stephen only by resorting to false witnesses. The trumped-up charges of these men ensured that Stephen was taken before the high priest and Sanhedrin.

7:1—8:1a Stephen Addresses the Council. Stephen's defense is a masterly review of Old Testament history that tellingly highlights the experience of slavery in Egypt and the frequent failure of God's people to

sent for his father, Jacob, and all his relatives to
come to Egypt, seventy-five persons in all. 15 So
Jacob went to Egypt. He died there, as did our
ancestors. 16 Their bodies were taken to Shechem
and buried in the tomb Abraham had bought for
a certain price from Hamor's sons in Shechem.
17 "As the time drew near when God would fulfill his promise to Abraham, the number of our
people in Egypt greatly increased. 18 But then a
new king came to the throne of Egypt who knew
nothing about Joseph. 19 This king exploited our
people and oppressed them, forcing parents to
abandon their newborn babies so they would die.
20 "At that time Moses was born—a beautiful child in God's eyes. His parents cared for him
at home for three months. 21 When they had to
abandon him, Pharaoh's daughter adopted him
and raised him as her own son. 22 Moses was
taught all the wisdom of the Egyptians, and he
was powerful in both speech and action.
23 "One day when Moses was forty years old,
he decided to visit his relatives, the people of Israel. 24 He saw an Egyptian mistreating an Israelite.
So Moses came to the man's defense and avenged
him, killing the Egyptian. 25 Moses assumed his
fellow Israelites would realize that God had sent
him to rescue them, but they didn't.
26 "The next day he visited them again and
saw two men of Israel fighting. He tried to be
a peacemaker. 'Men,' he said, 'you are brothers.
Why are you fighting each other?'
27 "But the man in the wrong pushed Moses
aside. 'Who made you a ruler and judge over us?'
he asked. 28 'Are you going to kill me as you killed
that Egyptian yesterday?' 29 When Moses heard
that, he fled the country and lived as a foreigner in
the land of Midian. There his two sons were born.
30 "Forty years later, in the desert near Mount
Sinai, an angel appeared to Moses in the flame
of a burning bush. 31 When Moses saw it, he was
amazed at the sight. As he went to take a closer
look, the voice of the LORD called out to him, 32 'I
am the God of your ancestors—the God of Abraham, Isaac, and Jacob.' Moses shook with terror
and did not dare to look.
33 "Then the LORD said to him, 'Take off your
sandals, for you are standing on holy ground. 34 I
have certainly seen the oppression of my people
in Egypt. I have heard their groans and have
come down to rescue them. Now go, for I am
sending you back to Egypt.'*
35 "So God sent back the same man his people
had previously rejected when they demanded,
'Who made you a ruler and judge over us?'
Through the angel who appeared to him in the
burning bush, God sent Moses to be their ruler
and savior. 36 And by means of many wonders
and miraculous signs, he led them out of Egypt,
through the Red Sea, and through the wilderness
for forty years.
37 "Moses himself told the people of Israel,
'God will raise up for you a Prophet like me
from among your own people.'* 38 Moses was
with our ancestors, the assembly of God's people
in the wilderness, when the angel spoke to him
at Mount Sinai. And there Moses received life-
giving words to pass on to us.*
39 "But our ancestors refused to listen to Moses. They rejected him and wanted to return to
Egypt. 40 They told Aaron, 'Make us some gods
who can lead us, for we don't know what has
become of this Moses, who brought us out of
Egypt.' 41 So they made an idol shaped like a calf,
and they sacrificed to it and celebrated over this
thing they had made. 42 Then God turned away
from them and abandoned them to serve the
stars of heaven as their gods! In the book of the
prophets it is written,

'Was it to me you were bringing sacrifices
  and offerings
during those forty years in the wilderness,
  Israel?
43 No, you carried your pagan gods—
  the shrine of Molech,
  the star of your god Rephan,
  and the images you made to worship them.
So I will send you into exile
  as far away as Babylon.'*

44 "Our ancestors carried the Tabernacle* with
them through the wilderness. It was constructed
according to the plan God had shown to Moses.
45 Years later, when Joshua led our ancestors in
battle against the nations that God drove out of
this land, the Tabernacle was taken with them
into their new territory. And it stayed there until
the time of King David.
46 "David found favor with God and asked for
the privilege of building a permanent Temple for
the God of Jacob.* 47 But it was Solomon who actually built it. 48 However, the Most High doesn't

7:31-34 Exod 3:5-10. **7:37** Deut 18:15. **7:38** Some manuscripts read *to you.* **7:42-43** Amos 5:25-27 (Greek version). **7:44** Greek *the tent of witness.* **7:46** Some manuscripts read *the house of Jacob.*

recognize what God was doing among them. **7:48:** Stephen is accused of dishonoring Moses; on the contrary, how much more did their forebears do just that. Stephen has been accused of speaking against

live in temples made by human hands. As the
prophet says,

49 'Heaven is my throne,
and the earth is my footstool.
Could you build me a temple as good as that?'
asks the LORD.
'Could you build me such a resting place?
50 Didn't my hands make both heaven and
earth?'*

51 "You stubborn people! You are heathen* at
heart and deaf to the truth. Must you forever resist
the Holy Spirit? That's what your ancestors did,
and so do you! 52 Name one prophet your ancestors
didn't persecute! They even killed the ones who
predicted the coming of the Righteous One—the
Messiah whom you betrayed and murdered. 53 You
deliberately disobeyed God's law, even though you
received it from the hands of angels."
54 The Jewish leaders were infuriated by Stephen's accusation, and they shook their fists at him
in rage.* 55 But Stephen, full of the Holy Spirit,
gazed steadily into heaven and saw the glory of
God, and he saw Jesus standing in the place of hon-
or at God's right hand. 56 And he told them, "Look, I
see the heavens opened and the Son of Man standing in the place of honor at God's right hand!"
57 Then they put their hands over their ears
and began shouting. They rushed at him 58 and
dragged him out of the city and began to stone
him. His accusers took off their coats and laid
them at the feet of a young man named Saul.*
59 As they stoned him, Stephen prayed, "Lord
Jesus, receive my spirit." 60 He fell to his knees,
shouting, "Lord, don't charge them with this
sin!" And with that, he died.

8 Saul was one of the witnesses, and he
agreed completely with the killing of Stephen.

Persecution Scatters the Believers

A great wave of persecution began that day,
sweeping over the church in Jerusalem; and
all the believers except the apostles were scattered through the regions of Judea and Samaria.
2 (Some devout men came and buried Stephen
with great mourning.) 3 But Saul was going everywhere to destroy the church. He went from
house to house, dragging out both men and
women to throw them into prison.

Philip Preaches in Samaria

4 But the believers who were scattered preached
the Good News about Jesus wherever they went.

7:49-50 Isa 66:1-2. **7:51** Greek *uncircumcised.* **7:54** Greek *they were grinding their teeth against him.* **7:58** *Saul* is later called Paul; see 13:9.

---

the Temple (6:13); on the contrary, *the Most High doesn't live in temples made by human hands.* **51, 53:** It would have been hard for Stephen to have been more provocative, but this is the provocation of the impassioned evangelist and apologist for truth rather than insult for insult's sake. **56:** The last straw is when Stephen claims to *see the heavens opened and the Son of Man standing in the place of honor at God's right hand.* The crowd would have picked up the allusion at once: Daniel spoke of the Son of Man as the one who would come with direct and eternal authority from God (Dan 7:13–14), and Jesus had frequently taken the title upon himself. Further, the position of standing indicated a judge declaring judgment. Stephen is saying, "God is judging you at this very moment, and it's not I who am found guilty!" **58–59:** The enraged crowd drags him outside the city walls and stones him, the traditional punishment for blasphemy. That they did so is the measure of their anger, for capital punishment could legally be sanctioned only by the Roman authorities, and there were severe penalties for those who took the law into their own hands. In the heat of anger we do not always stop to consider consequences. As he dies, Stephen echoes the Lord Jesus on the cross—*Lord Jesus, receive my spirit* (v. 59)—and prays that his murderers may be forgiven. **8:1a:** Stephen's death marks a critical turning point in the life of the church. That day severe and widespread persecution broke out, affecting the whole Christian community, not just the leaders, so that many disciples were scattered throughout Judea and Samaria. The attacks were spearheaded by Saul, who had witnessed approvingly Stephen's stoning.

8:1b–3 Persecution Scatters the Believers. It is highly significant that Luke tells us Saul arrested women and men; normally women would not have been imprisoned. Saul recognizes that women are as committed to the cause as men and that to stamp out the church must involve destroying everybody associated with it. If women were to be members of this new religion in their own right, so be it. They must take the full consequences—the responsibilities along with the privileges.

8:4–25 Philip Preaches in Samaria. Meanwhile, those who escaped proclaimed the Word wherever they traveled, a direct fulfillment of Matthew 28:19. That Philip, who like Stephen had been appointed to care for the Hellenist widows, was not a Palestinian

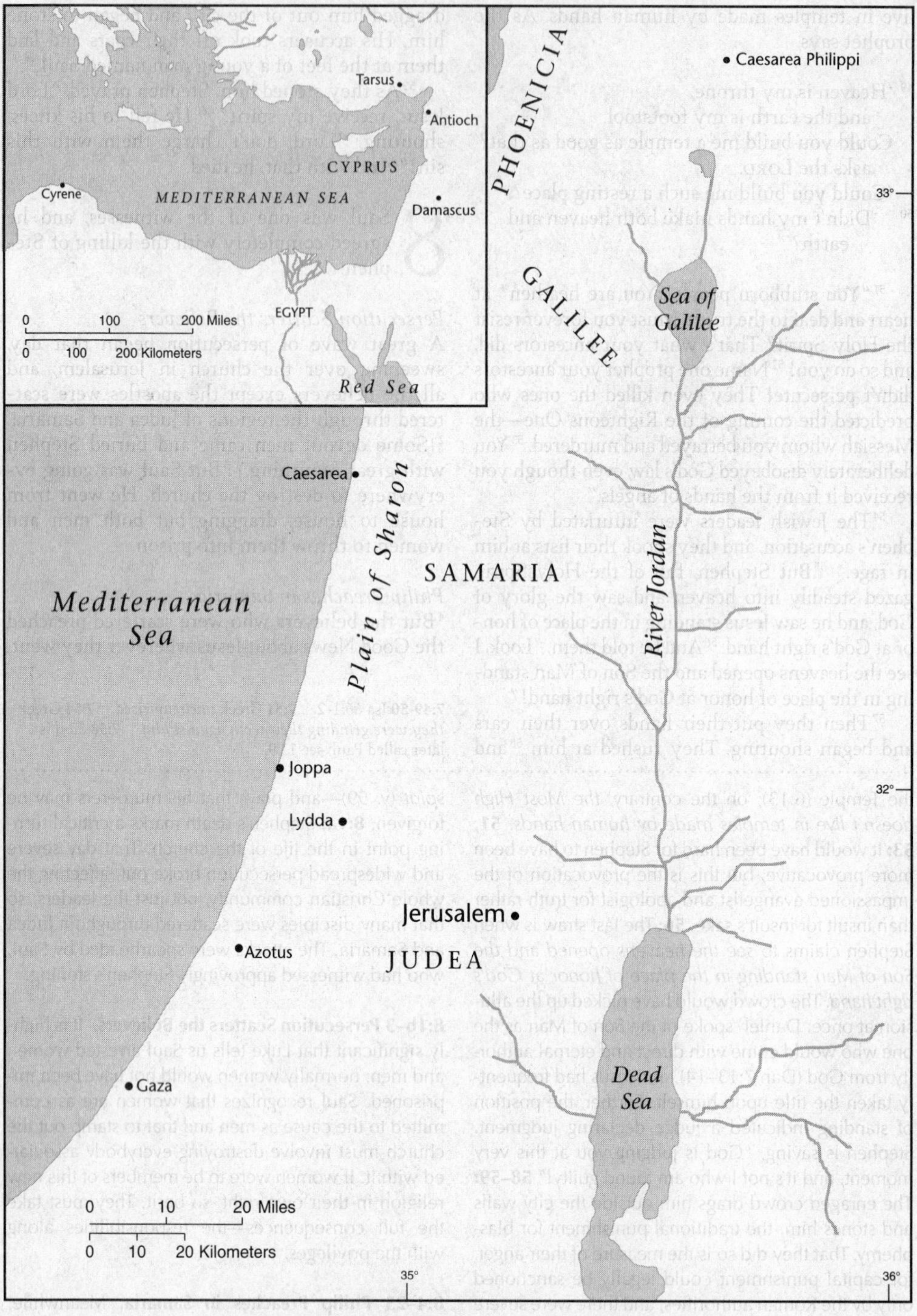

Sites of Early Christian Missionary Activities

5 Philip, for example, went to the city of Samaria and told the people there about the Messiah.
6 Crowds listened intently to Philip because they
were eager to hear his message and see the miraculous signs he did. 7 Many evil* spirits were
cast out, screaming as they left their victims.
And many who had been paralyzed or lame were
healed. 8 So there was great joy in that city.

9 A man named Simon had been a sorcerer
there for many years, amazing the people of Samaria and claiming to be someone great. 10 Everyone, from the least to the greatest, often spoke
of him as "the Great One—the Power of God."
11 They listened closely to him because for a long
time he had astounded them with his magic.

12 But now the people believed Philip's message of Good News concerning the Kingdom of
God and the name of Jesus Christ. As a result,
many men and women were baptized. 13 Then
Simon himself believed and was baptized. He
began following Philip wherever he went, and
he was amazed by the signs and great miracles
Philip performed.

14 When the apostles in Jerusalem heard that
the people of Samaria had accepted God's message, they sent Peter and John there. 15 As soon
as they arrived, they prayed for these new believers to receive the Holy Spirit. 16 The Holy
Spirit had not yet come upon any of them, for
they had only been baptized in the name of the
Lord Jesus. 17 Then Peter and John laid their
hands upon these believers, and they received
the Holy Spirit.

18 When Simon saw that the Spirit was given
when the apostles laid their hands on people, he
offered them money to buy this power. 19 "Let
me have this power, too," he exclaimed, "so that
when I lay my hands on people, they will receive
the Holy Spirit!"

20 But Peter replied, "May your money be destroyed with you for thinking God's gift can be
bought! 21 You can have no part in this, for your
heart is not right with God. 22 Repent of your
wickedness and pray to the Lord. Perhaps he will
forgive your evil thoughts, 23 for I can see that
you are full of bitter jealousy and are held captive by sin."

24 "Pray to the Lord for me," Simon exclaimed,
"that these terrible things you've said won't happen to me!"

25 After testifying and preaching the word of
the Lord in Samaria, Peter and John returned to
Jerusalem. And they stopped in many Samaritan
villages along the way to preach the Good News.

8:7 Greek *unclean.*

Jew probably made it easier for him to overcome prejudice and go to Samaria; and by the same token it might have made it easier for the Samaritans to listen to what he had to say. It is intriguing to wonder whether the Lord Jesus' encounter (John 4) with the woman at the well and the subsequent belief in him of "many Samaritans from the village" (John 4:39), perhaps three years previously, significantly affected their response now. **6:** Confronted with healings and deliverance from demons, the Samaritans responded joyfully, and both men and women are mentioned among those who were baptized. Luke frequently mentions the response of women, as do other early Christian writers. The heavy involvement of women becomes a major component in nascent Christianity. **14:** Word came back to the apostles in Jerusalem, and so improbable did it sound to them that Samaritans should come to true faith—moreover faith that had at its heart Jesus the Jew—that Peter and John are dispatched to Samaria. Had Philip in some way changed the message to make it more palatable to Samaritans? Luke does not suggest in any way that he had done so; instead, he writes positively about what had happened. But that must have been in the minds of the apostles, the more so because there was no evidence yet that the Samaritans had received the Holy Spirit. What was God doing? **19:** Could it be that God was determined that, despite this radical new departure, everybody must see the essential unity of the true church? Had the apostles not come, the Samaritans might have continued on their separatist way, refused to acknowledge the Jewishness of Jesus, and have sought to establish an independent Samaritan church. Had Peter and John not come, they and the Jerusalem church might have continued in their historic rejection of the Samaritans and refused to accept them as true brothers and sisters in Christ. In this event, the Holy Spirit is underlining their interdependence. If the Samaritans needed to acknowledge that Jesus was king of the Jews, the Jews needed to acknowledge that Jesus was king of the Samaritans and also of the Gentiles. The Holy Spirit is gently nudging them closer to the true meaning of the universal lordship of Christ. **18:** Peter's and John's decisive intervention underscores the profound difference between Simon's magic and the authentic work of the Spirit, that which cannot be bought either by money or technique. The Holy Spirit is truly the gift of God's grace. **25:** The Spirit is steadily reinforcing his lesson as Peter and John proclaim the good news in many Samaritan villages on their way back to Jerusalem.

Philip and the Ethiopian Eunuch
26 As for Philip, an angel of the Lord said to him,
"Go south* down the desert road that runs from
Jerusalem to Gaza." 27 So he started out, and he
met the treasurer of Ethiopia, a eunuch of great
authority under the Kandake, the queen of Ethiopia. The eunuch had gone to Jerusalem to worship, 28 and he was now returning. Seated in his
carriage, he was reading aloud from the book of
the prophet Isaiah.
29 The Holy Spirit said to Philip, "Go over and
walk along beside the carriage."
30 Philip ran over and heard the man reading
from the prophet Isaiah. Philip asked, "Do you
understand what you are reading?"
31 The man replied, "How can I, unless someone instructs me?" And he urged Philip to come
up into the carriage and sit with him.
32 The passage of Scripture he had been reading was this:

"He was led like a sheep to the slaughter.
  And as a lamb is silent before the shearers,
  he did not open his mouth.
33 He was humiliated and received no justice.
  Who can speak of his descendants?
  For his life was taken from the earth."*

34 The eunuch asked Philip, "Tell me, was the
prophet talking about himself or someone else?"
35 So beginning with this same Scripture, Philip
told him the Good News about Jesus.
36 As they rode along, they came to some water, and the eunuch said, "Look! There's some
water! Why can't I be baptized?"* 38 He ordered
the carriage to stop, and they went down into the
water, and Philip baptized him.
39 When they came up out of the water, the
Spirit of the Lord snatched Philip away. The eunuch never saw him again but went on his way
rejoicing. 40 Meanwhile, Philip found himself farther north at the town of Azotus. He preached
the Good News there and in every town along
the way until he came to Caesarea.

Saul's Conversion
9 Meanwhile, Saul was uttering threats
with every breath and was eager to kill
the Lord's followers.* So he went to the
high priest. 2 He requested letters addressed to
the synagogues in Damascus, asking for their
cooperation in the arrest of any followers of
the Way he found there. He wanted to bring
them—both men and women—back to Jerusalem in chains.

8:26 Or *Go at noon.* **8:32-33** Isa 53:7-8 (Greek version). **8:36** Some manuscripts add verse 37, *"You can," Philip answered, "if you believe with all your heart." And the eunuch replied, "I believe that Jesus Christ is the Son of God."* **9:1** Greek *disciples.*

8:26–40 Philip and the Ethiopian Eunuch. Philip is perhaps unexpectedly removed from the buzz of Samaria—where, it could be argued, there must be plenty of ongoing teaching to be done and where he would be sorely needed. He trudges down a desert road many miles away in obedience to an angel. There is no hint that Philip knew in advance why he must go; this is raw obedience, walking by faith and not by human reason. But what an amazing encounter the Spirit has organized! We know nothing about Philip's social status, but he is chosen by God to lead to faith one of the highest in the land from one of the great ancient kingdoms. **27:** The man in charge of the treasury of Ethiopia, undoubtedly a black African, probably came from Meroe, which is located in modern-day Sudan. He may have been a Jew, but as a eunuch he was more probably a Gentile Jewish proselyte or God-fearer. He must have been devout to have made the long and expensive journey to Jerusalem in order to worship, especially when few Jews would have anything to do with a castrated male. And he must have been wealthy in his own right to be traveling in a chariot, the Rolls-Royce of the day, and to possess his own scroll of Isaiah. **35:** It was not hard for Philip to start from Isaiah 53 and lead to Jesus Christ, and the Ethiopian is clearly prepared by the Holy Spirit to come to believing faith. We know no more about the Ethiopian eunuch, but it is possible that he was the first to take the gospel into Africa south beyond Alexandria. Philip is led by the Spirit up the coast through Azotus to Caesarea, the seat of the Roman governor of Judea and home to a large Roman garrison.

9:1–19a Saul's Conversion. Luke moves from the story of Philip to pick up the story of Saul. We are not told what became of the believers thrown into prison in Jerusalem, but it may well be that many of them, men and women, were flogged if not put to death. Now Saul turns his attention farther afield and asks the high priest for letters to the leaders of the synagogues in Damascus. These would less likely have been letters of introduction for Saul personally than letters urging the synagogue leaders to help in the hunt for Christians, again both men and women, and to arrange for their extradition to Jerusalem. Damascus in Syria, about 140 miles north of Jerusalem, had many thousands of Jewish inhabitants; perhaps as many as eighteen thousand were later to die in the Jewish revolt of AD 66. We do not know how the gos-

3 As he was approaching Damascus on this mission, a light from heaven suddenly shone down around him. 4 He fell to the ground and heard a voice saying to him, "Saul! Saul! Why are you persecuting me?"

5 "Who are you, lord?" Saul asked.

And the voice replied, "I am Jesus, the one you are persecuting! 6 Now get up and go into the city, and you will be told what you must do."

7 The men with Saul stood speechless, for they heard the sound of someone's voice but saw no one! 8 Saul picked himself up off the ground, but when he opened his eyes he was blind. So his companions led him by the hand to Damascus. 9 He remained there blind for three days and did not eat or drink.

10 Now there was a believer* in Damascus named Ananias. The Lord spoke to him in a vision, calling, "Ananias!"

"Yes, Lord!" he replied.

11 The Lord said, "Go over to Straight Street, to the house of Judas. When you get there, ask for a man from Tarsus named Saul. He is praying to me right now. 12 I have shown him a vision of a man named Ananias coming in and laying hands on him so he can see again."

13 "But Lord," exclaimed Ananias, "I've heard many people talk about the terrible things this man has done to the believers* in Jerusalem! 14 And he is authorized by the leading priests to arrest everyone who calls upon your name."

15 But the Lord said, "Go, for Saul is my chosen instrument to take my message to the Gentiles and to kings, as well as to the people of Israel. 16 And I will show him how much he must suffer for my name's sake."

17 So Ananias went and found Saul. He laid his hands on him and said, "Brother Saul, the Lord Jesus, who appeared to you on the road, has sent me so that you might regain your sight and be filled with the Holy Spirit." 18 Instantly something like scales fell from Saul's eyes, and he regained his sight. Then he got up and was baptized. 19 Afterward he ate some food and regained his strength.

Saul in Damascus and Jerusalem

Saul stayed with the believers* in Damascus for a few days. 20 And immediately he began preaching about Jesus in the synagogues, saying, "He is indeed the Son of God!"

21 All who heard him were amazed. "Isn't this the same man who caused such devastation among Jesus' followers in Jerusalem?" they asked. "And didn't he come here to arrest them and take them in chains to the leading priests?"

22 Saul's preaching became more and more powerful, and the Jews in Damascus couldn't refute his proofs that Jesus was indeed the Messiah. 23 After a while some of the Jews plotted together to kill him. 24 They were watching for him day and night at the city gate so they could murder him, but Saul was told about their plot. 25 So during the night, some of the other believers* lowered him in a large basket through an opening in the city wall.

26 When Saul arrived in Jerusalem, he tried to meet with the believers, but they were all afraid of him. They did not believe he had truly become a believer! 27 Then Barnabas brought him to the apostles and told them how Saul had seen the Lord on the way to Damascus and how the Lord had spoken to Saul. He also told them that Saul had preached boldly in the name of Jesus in Damascus.

9:10 Greek *disciple;* also in 9:26, 36. **9:13** Greek *God's holy people;* also in 9:32, 41. **9:19** Greek *disciples;* also in 9:26, 38. **9:25** Greek *his disciples.*

---

pel came to Damascus, but Luke tells us that disciples were established there (9:19). **3:** Centuries before, Moses had come face to face with the blazing glory of God in the burning bush and heard God speak directly to him (Exod 3). Now Saul too is overwhelmed by blazing light and God's direct Word. There can be no mistaking now the identity of Jesus. Saul's world is turned upside down. Blind, stunned, prayerfully fasting, he waits in Damascus for the Lord to show him what to do next. **10–18:** In visions, the Lord instructs Ananias to go to Saul and for Saul to expect Ananias. Ananias knows about Saul's reputation and his purpose for coming to Damascus, but the Lord insists that *Saul is my chosen instrument to take my message to the Gentiles and to kings, as well as to the people of Israel.* Ananias obeys and greets Saul with those memorable words, *Brother Saul*! Here is a glimpse into how radical a new life Ananias believed Saul's to be. The fanatical persecutor has been transformed into one of the family.

9:19b–31 Saul in Damascus and Jerusalem. Baptized, filled with the Spirit, and with sight restored, Saul immediately becomes as passionate an advocate for Jesus Christ as before he had been implacable enemy. Luke does not tell us how long Saul remained in Damascus, although Paul (Gal 1:17) tells us that after a brief period of reflection in Arabia he returned and spent three years in Damascus. This was long enough for him to attract quite a following as a Christian rabbi, but eventually his life is in danger and he escapes to Jerusalem. **27:** It is Barnabas, the "Son of

28 So Saul stayed with the apostles and went
all around Jerusalem with them, preaching boldly in the name of the Lord. 29 He debated with
some Greek-speaking Jews, but they tried to
murder him. 30 When the believers* heard about
this, they took him down to Caesarea and sent
him away to Tarsus, his hometown.
31 The church then had peace throughout
Judea, Galilee, and Samaria, and it became stronger as the believers lived in the fear of the Lord.
And with the encouragement of the Holy Spirit,
it also grew in numbers.

Peter Heals Aeneas and Raises Dorcas

32 Meanwhile, Peter traveled from place to place,
and he came down to visit the believers in the
town of Lydda. 33 There he met a man named Aeneas, who had been paralyzed and bedridden for
eight years. 34 Peter said to him, "Aeneas, Jesus
Christ heals you! Get up, and roll up your sleeping mat!" And he was healed instantly. 35 Then
the whole population of Lydda and Sharon saw
Aeneas walking around, and they turned to the
Lord.
36 There was a believer in Joppa named Tabitha
(which in Greek is Dorcas*). She was always doing kind things for others and helping the poor.
37 About this time she became ill and died. Her
body was washed for burial and laid in an upstairs room. 38 But the believers had heard that
Peter was nearby at Lydda, so they sent two men
to beg him, "Please come as soon as possible!"
39 So Peter returned with them; and as soon as
he arrived, they took him to the upstairs room.
The room was filled with widows who were
weeping and showing him the coats and other
clothes Dorcas had made for them. 40 But Peter
asked them all to leave the room; then he knelt
and prayed. Turning to the body he said, "Get up,
Tabitha." And she opened her eyes! When she
saw Peter, she sat up! 41 He gave her his hand and
helped her up. Then he called in the widows and
all the believers, and he presented her to them
alive.
42 The news spread through the whole town,
and many believed in the Lord. 43 And Peter
stayed a long time in Joppa, living with Simon,
a tanner of hides.

Cornelius Calls for Peter

10 In Caesarea there lived a Roman army
officer* named Cornelius, who was a
captain of the Italian Regiment. 2 He
was a devout, God-fearing man, as was everyone
in his household. He gave generously to the poor
and prayed regularly to God. 3 One afternoon

9:30 Greek *brothers.* **9:36** The names *Tabitha* in Aramaic and *Dorcas* in Greek both mean "gazelle." **10:1** Greek *a centurion;* similarly in 10:22.

Encouragement," who persuades the fearful apostles of the genuineness of Saul's conversion. **29:** This time threatened by the Hellenists, he is escorted to Caesarea to board a ship to Tarsus, his home city several hundred miles away to the north.

9:32—12:25 Further Still: Bridgehead into the Gentile World

9:32–43 Peter Heals Aeneas and Raises Dorcas. Peter, still the key leader in Jerusalem, apparently also visited groups of believers elsewhere. On such a journey he comes to Lydda, twenty miles northwest of Jerusalem, where Aeneas, bedridden for eight years, is healed through his ministry. The news traveled, and ten miles away in Joppa, when a greatly cherished disciple died, the believers immediately want Peter to come to them. It is hard to tell whether they hoped he would raise Tabitha from the dead or whether they wanted him to conduct the funeral. Perhaps the old Peter would have brushed off the request; after all, what value was a widow, especially a dead widow, in traditional culture (see Widows, 1 Tim 5)? But the Lord Jesus had demonstrated tender care for widows, and now Peter does too. **39:** Luke's portrait of Tabitha (also known as Dorcas, both mean "gazelle") is of a much-loved and compassionate woman, greatly mourned. She had already been prepared for burial, but Peter prays and then commands her to get up. We do not know whether some of the signs and wonders to which Luke refers earlier in his narrative included people being raised from the dead; this is the first specific account. **42:** As word spreads of this extraordinary event, *many believed in the Lord.* Peter makes it plain that the Lord, not Peter, has brought Tabitha back to life.

10:1–33 Cornelius Calls for Peter. Thirty miles farther north, in Caesarea, lived the Roman centurion Cornelius. As an army officer on active service, he was not entitled to be married, but the household to which Luke refers (10:2, 24; 11:14) could have included extended family, servants, and friends. Cornelius was a God-fearer rather than a proselyte (vv. 2, 28) but took his religion seriously and observed the Temple hours of prayer (v. 3). **3:** As with Saul and Ananias, the Lord appears in visions to Peter and Cornelius in order to ensure that they are brought together. Cornelius's vision is straightforward enough, terrifying though he found it to see and hear an angel.

Women and Philanthropy

Tabitha (or Dorcas; see translator's note) was one of the finest examples of a philanthropist that can be found in the Bible or in secular history and literature (9:36). First, she acted voluntarily. She was under no obligation to perform good deeds—her actions weren't dependent on a salary. Second, she took action. She went beyond the rhetoric of philanthropy. Third, she acted on behalf of the public within her reach, especially those often ignored by the church and government of her day, such as widows and their children. Finally, she concentrated on actions that produced good results for her constituents. Her philanthropic example was so powerful that God chose to intervene and allow her more years than at first expected. He moved through Peter to restore her to life so that her good works and acts of charity could continue and that her skills, energy, and caring spirit might be a blessing to many.

A dramatic example of mass philanthropy occurred during the wilderness wanderings of the children of Israel. God commanded that they build a tabernacle so that they would have visible, tangible evidence of God's continual presence. This story, told in Exodus 35—36, states that men and women came, all who were of a willing heart, and voluntarily gave offerings. Women parted with precious possessions, especially jewelry. The Israelites were so generous when moved by a worthwhile cause and when invited by God to participate in the project that they had to be restrained from giving. As the text states, "Their contributions were more than enough to complete the whole project" (Exod 36:7).

A few highlights, therefore, of philanthropic action by women can be noted. The author of Proverbs discussed a worthy woman and states that "she extends a helping hand to the poor and opens her arms to the needy" (Prov 31:20). As the story is told in 1 Kings 17, Elijah asked a widow of Zarephath for a loaf of bread before she prepared the last meal with the meager provisions she had. She complied, even though it seemed that she would use up her food supplies by making the loaf of bread, and her reward was that she and her son continued to have the basic food supply they needed, for as long as it was needed. An exceptional example of a philanthropic woman is the widow who gave her two mites as a Temple offering. She gave literally all she had! Jesus noted her generosity and sacrifice and lauded her philanthropic act (Luke 21:1–4).

Paul wrote in Galatians, "whenever we have the opportunity, we should do good to everyone—especially to those in the family of faith" (Gal 6:10). Women can be justifiably proud of the excellent examples of philanthropic action performed by their spiritual ancestors and emulate those actions for the glory of God and the benefit of humankind.

about three o'clock, he had a vision in which he
saw an angel of God coming toward him. "Cornelius!" the angel said.
4 Cornelius stared at him in terror. "What is
it, sir?" he asked the angel.

And the angel replied, "Your prayers and
gifts to the poor have been received by God as
an offering! 5 Now send some men to Joppa, and
summon a man named Simon Peter. 6 He is staying with Simon, a tanner who lives near the seashore."
7 As soon as the angel was gone, Cornelius
called two of his household servants and a devout soldier, one of his personal attendants. 8 He
told them what had happened and sent them off
to Joppa.

Peter Visits Cornelius

9 The next day as Cornelius's messengers were
nearing the town, Peter went up on the flat roof
to pray. It was about noon, 10 and he was hungry.
But while a meal was being prepared, he fell into
a trance. 11 He saw the sky open, and something
like a large sheet was let down by its four corners. 12 In the sheet were all sorts of animals, reptiles, and birds. 13 Then a voice said to him, "Get
up, Peter; kill and eat them."
14 "No, Lord," Peter declared. "I have never
eaten anything that our Jewish laws have declared impure and unclean.*"
15 But the voice spoke again: "Do not call

10:14 Greek *anything common and unclean.*

9: It would have been shocking, for every Jewish household knew and lived by the ancient food laws. Perhaps Peter thinks at first that the Lord is testing his resistance to temptation—whether hunger would make him justify disobedience. What a lot hinged on waiting for lunch! **19:** Cornelius's three messengers

something unclean if God has made it clean."
16 The same vision was repeated three times. Then
the sheet was suddenly pulled up to heaven.
17 Peter was very perplexed. What could the
vision mean? Just then the men sent by Cornelius found Simon's house. Standing outside the
gate, 18 they asked if a man named Simon Peter
was staying there.
19 Meanwhile, as Peter was puzzling over the
vision, the Holy Spirit said to him, "Three men
have come looking for you. 20 Get up, go downstairs, and go with them without hesitation.
Don't worry, for I have sent them."
21 So Peter went down and said, "I'm the man
you are looking for. Why have you come?"
22 They said, "We were sent by Cornelius, a
Roman officer. He is a devout and God-fearing
man, well respected by all the Jews. A holy angel
instructed him to summon you to his house so
that he can hear your message." 23 So Peter invited the men to stay for the night. The next day
he went with them, accompanied by some of the
brothers from Joppa.
24 They arrived in Caesarea the following day.
Cornelius was waiting for them and had called
together his relatives and close friends. 25 As Peter entered his home, Cornelius fell at his feet
and worshiped him. 26 But Peter pulled him up
and said, "Stand up! I'm a human being just like
you!" 27 So they talked together and went inside,
where many others were assembled.
28 Peter told them, "You know it is against our
laws for a Jewish man to enter a Gentile home
like this or to associate with you. But God has
shown me that I should no longer think of anyone as impure or unclean. 29 So I came without
objection as soon as I was sent for. Now tell me
why you sent for me."
30 Cornelius replied, "Four days ago I was
praying in my house about this same time, three
o'clock in the afternoon. Suddenly, a man in dazzling clothes was standing in front of me. 31 He
told me, 'Cornelius, your prayer has been heard,
and your gifts to the poor have been noticed by
God! 32 Now send messengers to Joppa, and summon a man named Simon Peter. He is staying in
the home of Simon, a tanner who lives near the
seashore.' 33 So I sent for you at once, and it was
good of you to come. Now we are all here, waiting before God to hear the message the Lord has
given you."

The Gentiles Hear the Good News

34 Then Peter replied, "I see very clearly that God
shows no favoritism. 35 In every nation he accepts
those who fear him and do what is right. 36 This
is the message of Good News for the people of
Israel—that there is peace with God through
Jesus Christ, who is Lord of all. 37 You know
what happened throughout Judea, beginning in
Galilee, after John began preaching his message
of baptism. 38 And you know that God anointed
Jesus of Nazareth with the Holy Spirit and with
power. Then Jesus went around doing good and
healing all who were oppressed by the devil, for
God was with him.
39 "And we apostles are witnesses of all he did
throughout Judea and in Jerusalem. They put
him to death by hanging him on a cross,* 40 but
God raised him to life on the third day. Then
God allowed him to appear, 41 not to the general
public,* but to us whom God had chosen in advance to be his witnesses. We were those who ate
and drank with him after he rose from the dead.
42 And he ordered us to preach everywhere and to
testify that Jesus is the one appointed by God to
be the judge of all—the living and the dead. 43 He
is the one all the prophets testified about, saying that everyone who believes in him will have
their sins forgiven through his name."

The Gentiles Receive the Holy Spirit

44 Even as Peter was saying these things, the Holy
Spirit fell upon all who were listening to the

10:39 Greek *on a tree.* **10:41** Greek *the people.*

quickly provide the first clue to understanding the vision, for the slaves and the soldier would have been Gentiles, not welcome to stay in a Jewish home. **28:** When they arrive in Caesarea, Luke records Peter's opening remarks, which must stand among the most gauche comments in Scripture: *You know it is against our laws for a Jewish man to enter a Gentile home like this or to associate with you. But God has shown me that I should no longer think of anyone as impure or unclean.* Yet, when Peter was later challenged over what happened next, he clearly realized that this was a defining moment.

10:34–43 The Gentiles Hear the Good News. The careful repetition of how God had dealt first with Cornelius, then with Peter, emphatically shows that this was no coincidence invested with meaning God had never intended. **36:** Peter's sermon is different from earlier ones: His audience is different, and he does not blame them for Jesus' death.

10:44–48 The Gentiles Receive the Holy Spirit. As Peter speaks, the Holy Spirit falls on them and they speak in tongues and praise God. If the Spirit has been so manifestly given in exactly the same way

message. 45 The Jewish believers* who came with
Peter were amazed that the gift of the Holy Spirit had been poured out on the Gentiles, too. 46 For
they heard them speaking in other tongues* and
praising God.

Then Peter asked, 47 "Can anyone object to
their being baptized, now that they have received
the Holy Spirit just as we did?" 48 So he gave orders for them to be baptized in the name of Jesus
Christ. Afterward Cornelius asked him to stay
with them for several days.

Peter Explains His Actions

11 Soon the news reached the apostles
and other believers* in Judea that
the Gentiles had received the word of
God. 2 But when Peter arrived back in Jerusalem,
the Jewish believers* criticized him. 3 "You entered the home of Gentiles* and even ate with
them!" they said.

4 Then Peter told them exactly what had happened. 5 "I was in the town of Joppa," he said,
"and while I was praying, I went into a trance
and saw a vision. Something like a large sheet
was let down by its four corners from the sky.
And it came right down to me. 6 When I looked
inside the sheet, I saw all sorts of tame and wild
animals, reptiles, and birds. 7 And I heard a voice
say, 'Get up, Peter; kill and eat them.'

8 " 'No, Lord,' I replied. 'I have never eaten
anything that our Jewish laws have declared impure or unclean.*'

9 "But the voice from heaven spoke again: 'Do
not call something unclean if God has made it
clean.' 10 This happened three times before the
sheet and all it contained was pulled back up to
heaven.

11 "Just then three men who had been sent
from Caesarea arrived at the house where we
were staying. 12 The Holy Spirit told me to go
with them and not to worry that they were Gentiles. These six brothers here accompanied me,
and we soon entered the home of the man who
had sent for us. 13 He told us how an angel had
appeared to him in his home and had told him,
'Send messengers to Joppa, and summon a man
named Simon Peter. 14 He will tell you how you
and everyone in your household can be saved!'

15 "As I began to speak," Peter continued, "the
Holy Spirit fell on them, just as he fell on us at
the beginning. 16 Then I thought of the Lord's
words when he said, 'John baptized with* water,
but you will be baptized with the Holy Spirit.'
17 And since God gave these Gentiles the same
gift he gave us when we believed in the Lord
Jesus Christ, who was I to stand in God's way?"

18 When the others heard this, they stopped
objecting and began praising God. They said,
"We can see that God has also given the Gentiles the privilege of repenting of their sins and
receiving eternal life."

The Church in Antioch of Syria

19 Meanwhile, the believers who had been scattered during the persecution after Stephen's
death traveled as far as Phoenicia, Cyprus, and
Antioch of Syria. They preached the word of
God, but only to Jews. 20 However, some of the
believers who went to Antioch from Cyprus and

10:45 Greek *The faithful ones of the circumcision.* **10:46** Or *in other languages.* **11:1** Greek *brothers.* **11:2** Greek *those of the circumcision.* **11:3** Greek *of uncircumcised men.* **11:8** Greek *anything common or unclean.* **11:16** Or *in;* also in 11:16b.

as he had come to the disciples at Pentecost, there can be no grounds for excluding them. Peter baptizes them. They are fully identified with the Christian community.

11:1–18 Peter Explains His Actions. Predictably, when Peter returns to Jerusalem, he is taken to task as to why he has entered the home of Gentiles and eaten with them. Patiently, step by step, Peter tells his story and Cornelius's story. We should not underestimate how painfully hard it must have been for many there to think outside of the categories of deeply rooted traditional Judaism. If circumcision was the sign of the covenant, how could the uncircumcised be included in God's promises? **18:** And if the Jews were God's chosen people, how could the Gentiles be numbered among the chosen, unless they submitted to circumcision and became as Jews? It was a huge psychological hurdle for them to say, *"God has also given the Gentiles the privilege of repenting of their sins and receiving eternal life."*

11:19–30 The Church in Antioch of Syria. The persistence of the orientation toward Jews rather than Gentiles was not an issue only in Jerusalem. The believers who scattered after Stephen's martyrdom went up the coast beyond Palestinian territory to Phoenicia, across to Cyprus, and far away up to Antioch, which was at the time the third largest city in the Roman world. **20–21:** Most concentrated on witnessing to Jews, but among those who went to Antioch were some men who came from Cyprus and from Cyrene, on the Mediterranean coast in modern-day Libya. We are not told why they went to Antioch rather than back home, but their background may well have made them more at home in the Greek-

Cyrene began preaching to the Gentiles* about
the Lord Jesus. 21 The power of the Lord was with
them, and a large number of these Gentiles believed and turned to the Lord.
22 When the church at Jerusalem heard what
had happened, they sent Barnabas to Antioch.
23 When he arrived and saw this evidence of
God's blessing, he was filled with joy, and he encouraged the believers to stay true to the Lord.
24 Barnabas was a good man, full of the Holy
Spirit and strong in faith. And many people were
brought to the Lord.
25 Then Barnabas went on to Tarsus to look
for Saul. 26 When he found him, he brought him
back to Antioch. Both of them stayed there with
the church for a full year, teaching large crowds
of people. (It was at Antioch that the believers*
were first called Christians.)
27 During this time some prophets traveled from Jerusalem to Antioch. 28 One of them
named Agabus stood up in one of the meetings
and predicted by the Spirit that a great famine
was coming upon the entire Roman world. (This
was fulfilled during the reign of Claudius.) 29 So
the believers in Antioch decided to send relief to
the brothers and sisters* in Judea, everyone giving as much as they could. 30 This they did, entrusting their gifts to Barnabas and Saul to take
to the elders of the church in Jerusalem.

James Is Killed and Peter Is Imprisoned

12 About that time King Herod Agrippa*
began to persecute some believers in
the church. 2 He had the apostle James
(John's brother) killed with a sword. 3 When Herod saw how much this pleased the Jewish people,
he also arrested Peter. (This took place during
the Passover celebration.*) 4 Then he imprisoned
him, placing him under the guard of four squads
of four soldiers each. Herod intended to bring
Peter out for public trial after the Passover. 5 But
while Peter was in prison, the church prayed
very earnestly for him.

Peter's Miraculous Escape from Prison

6 The night before Peter was to be placed on trial,
he was asleep, fastened with two chains between
two soldiers. Others stood guard at the prison
gate. 7 Suddenly, there was a bright light in the
cell, and an angel of the Lord stood before Peter. The angel struck him on the side to awaken
him and said, "Quick! Get up!" And the chains
fell off his wrists. 8 Then the angel told him, "Get
dressed and put on your sandals." And he did.
"Now put on your coat and follow me," the angel
ordered.
9 So Peter left the cell, following the angel. But
all the time he thought it was a vision. He didn't
realize it was actually happening. 10 They passed
the first and second guard posts and came to the
iron gate leading to the city, and this opened for
them all by itself. So they passed through and
started walking down the street, and then the angel suddenly left him.
11 Peter finally came to his senses. "It's really
true!" he said. "The Lord has sent his angel and
saved me from Herod and from what the Jewish
leaders* had planned to do to me!"
12 When he realized this, he went to the home
of Mary, the mother of John Mark, where many

11:20 Greek *the Hellenists* (i.e., those who speak Greek); other manuscripts read *the Greeks.* **11:26** Greek *disciples;* also in 11:29. **11:29** Greek *the brothers.* **12:1** Greek *Herod the king.* He was the nephew of Herod Antipas and a grandson of Herod the Great. **12:3** Greek *the days of unleavened bread.* **12:11** Or *the Jewish people.*

---

speaking communities than in the traditional Jewish synagogues. **22:** Perhaps fearful of what could go wrong with an ingathering of Gentiles far from the watchful eye of the apostles, the church in Jerusalem dispatched the trusted Barnabas to investigate. It was an inspired choice, for Barnabas appears to have had the humble flexibility that was more alert to what God might be doing, however unexpectedly, than that bound by expectation. He quickly realized help was needed and went to Tarsus to enlist Saul. **26:** Enriched and empowered by the full year of teaching and strategic planning, Christianity would increasingly be seen as a distinct faith rather than as merely a messianic sect within Judaism.

12:1–5 James Is Killed and Peter Imprisoned. When Barnabas and Saul arrive with a love gift from the believers in Antioch to the believers in Judea, they find themselves in a time of great trouble for the church in Jerusalem. King Herod (Agrippa I), himself part Jewish, unleashed persecution in order to curry favor with the Jews by his execution of James and the arrest of Peter. Herod was taking no chances, for he has Peter put in the charge of sixteen soldiers, two of them chained to him.

12:6–19 Peter's Miraculous Escape from Prison. Peter makes his way to the house of John Mark's mother, Mary. Apparently she is the leader of a house church. She must have been a wealthy and unusually fortunate woman, and probably a widow, to have a house in her name and with an outer gate. Despite the fact that the disciples were all earnestly praying for Peter's safety, they did not presume that he must be mirac-

were gathered for prayer. [13]He knocked at the door in the gate, and a servant girl named Rhoda came to open it. [14]When she recognized Peter's voice, she was so overjoyed that, instead of opening the door, she ran back inside and told everyone, "Peter is standing at the door!"

[15]"You're out of your mind!" they said. When she insisted, they decided, "It must be his angel."

[16]Meanwhile, Peter continued knocking. When they finally opened the door and saw him, they were amazed. [17]He motioned for them to quiet down and told them how the Lord had led him out of prison. "Tell James and the other brothers what happened," he said. And then he went to another place.

[18]At dawn there was a great commotion among the soldiers about what had happened to Peter. [19]Herod Agrippa ordered a thorough search for him. When he couldn't be found, Herod interrogated the guards and sentenced them to death. Afterward Herod left Judea to stay in Caesarea for a while.

The Death of Herod Agrippa

[20]Now Herod was very angry with the people of Tyre and Sidon. So they sent a delegation to make peace with him because their cities were dependent upon Herod's country for food. The delegates won the support of Blastus, Herod's personal assistant, [21]and an appointment with Herod was granted. When the day arrived, Herod put on his royal robes, sat on his throne, and made a speech to them. [22]The people gave him a great ovation, shouting, "It's the voice of a god, not of a man!"

[23]Instantly, an angel of the Lord struck Herod with a sickness, because he accepted the people's worship instead of giving the glory to God. So he was consumed with worms and died.

[24]Meanwhile, the word of God continued to spread, and there were many new believers.

[25]When Barnabas and Saul had finished their mission to Jerusalem, they returned,* taking John Mark with them.

Barnabas and Saul Are Commissioned

13 Among the prophets and teachers of the church at Antioch of Syria were Barnabas, Simeon (called "the black man"*), Lucius (from Cyrene), Manaen (the childhood companion of King Herod Antipas*), and Saul. [2]One day as these men were worshiping the Lord and fasting, the Holy Spirit said, "Dedicate Barnabas and Saul for the special work to which I have called them." [3]So after more fasting and prayer, the men laid their hands on them and sent them on their way.

Paul's First Missionary Journey

[4]So Barnabas and Saul were sent out by the Holy Spirit. They went down to the seaport of Seleucia and then sailed for the island of Cyprus. [5]There, in the town of Salamis, they went to the Jewish synagogues and preached the word of God. John Mark went with them as their assistant.

12:25 Or *mission, they returned to Jerusalem.* Other manuscripts read *mission, they returned from Jerusalem;* still others read *mission, they returned from Jerusalem to Antioch.* **13:1a** Greek *who was called Niger.* **13:1b** Greek *Herod the tetrarch.*

ulously delivered from prison. **13:** The maid Rhoda may have been little more than a child as the term *paidiske* can refer either to a child or a slave (for slave women in the New Testament, see Matt 26:69–71; Mark 14:66–69; Luke 22:55; John 18:17; Acts 2:18; 16:16–21). Whatever her age or status, she has been entrusted with the responsibility of guarding the door at a time of imminent danger to the church. With the delighted excitement of a surprised youngster, she tells of Peter's presence and yet is able to withstand the disbelief of the gathered Christians and to insist on the reality of her information. After testifying to what the Lord had done, Peter leaves, probably concerned for his friends' security.

12:20–25 The Death of Herod Agrippa. Shortly after executing the guards, Herod himself meets an ugly end because he allowed himself to be worshiped as a god. Such is God's jealousy for his glory.

13:1–16:5 The Asian World: Good News for Gentiles

13:1–3 Barnabas and Saul Are Commisioned. Barnabas and Saul returned to Antioch, taking John Mark with them. The apostles had never stirred far from Jerusalem, and despite Peter's experience with Cornelius they did not show any signs of seriously undertaking a mission to the Gentiles. But the Antioch church, by now well supplied with gifted leaders, is prompted by the Spirit to dedicate Paul and Barnabas for the mission of the church. The Lord had made clear at the time of Saul's conversion that he was to be an apostle to the Gentiles as well as to Jews.

13:4–12 Paul's First Missionary Journey. Together with John Mark, Saul (from now on called Paul, his Roman name) and Barnabas went first to Cyprus, Barnabas's home territory, working their way across

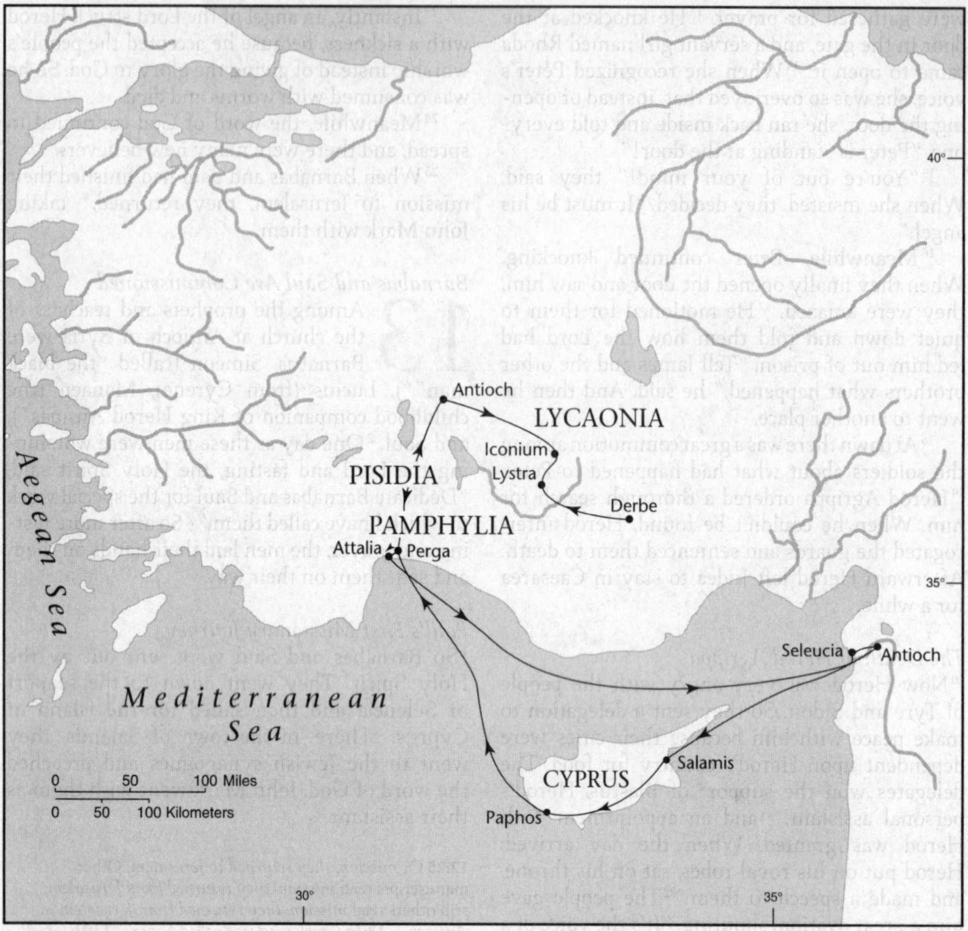

First Missionary Journey of Paul

6 Afterward they traveled from town to town
across the entire island until finally they reached
Paphos, where they met a Jewish sorcerer, a false
prophet named Bar-Jesus. 7 He had attached himself to the governor, Sergius Paulus, who was an
intelligent man. The governor invited Barnabas
and Saul to visit him, for he wanted to hear the
word of God. 8 But Elymas, the sorcerer (as his
name means in Greek), interfered and urged the
governor to pay no attention to what Barnabas
and Saul said. He was trying to keep the governor from believing.
9 Saul, also known as Paul, was filled with the
Holy Spirit, and he looked the sorcerer in the
eye. 10 Then he said, "You son of the devil, full
of every sort of deceit and fraud, and enemy of
all that is good! Will you never stop perverting
the true ways of the Lord? 11 Watch now, for the
Lord has laid his hand of punishment upon you,
and you will be struck blind. You will not see
the sunlight for some time." Instantly mist and
darkness came over the man's eyes, and he began
groping around begging for someone to take his
hand and lead him.
12 When the governor saw what had happened,
he became a believer, for he was astonished at the
teaching about the Lord.

Paul Preaches in Antioch of Pisidia
13 Paul and his companions then left Paphos by
ship for Pamphylia, landing at the port town of
Perga. There John Mark left them and returned

---

the island. Despite the opposition of a Jewish magician, doubtless afraid of losing his hold over people, the Word of God prevails and the proconsul comes to faith.

to Jerusalem. [14]But Paul and Barnabas traveled
inland to Antioch of Pisidia.*
On the Sabbath they went to the synagogue
for the services. [15]After the usual readings from
the books of Moses* and the prophets, those in
charge of the service sent them this message:
"Brothers, if you have any word of encouragement for the people, come and give it."
[16]So Paul stood, lifted his hand to quiet them,
and started speaking. "Men of Israel," he said,
"and you God-fearing Gentiles, listen to me.
[17]"The God of this nation of Israel chose our
ancestors and made them multiply and grow
strong during their stay in Egypt. Then with a
powerful arm he led them out of their slavery.
[18]He put up with them* through forty years
of wandering in the wilderness. [19]Then he destroyed seven nations in Canaan and gave their
land to Israel as an inheritance. [20]All this took
about 450 years.
"After that, God gave them judges to rule until the time of Samuel the prophet. [21]Then the
people begged for a king, and God gave them
Saul son of Kish, a man of the tribe of Benjamin,
who reigned for forty years. [22]But God removed
Saul and replaced him with David, a man about
whom God said, 'I have found David son of Jesse,
a man after my own heart. He will do everything
I want him to do.'*
[23]"And it is one of King David's descendants,
Jesus, who is God's promised Savior of Israel!
[24]Before he came, John the Baptist preached that
all the people of Israel needed to repent of their
sins and turn to God and be baptized. [25]As John
was finishing his ministry he asked, 'Do you
think I am the Messiah? No, I am not! But he is
coming soon—and I'm not even worthy to be his
slave and untie the sandals on his feet.'
[26]"Brothers—you sons of Abraham, and
also you God-fearing Gentiles—this message
of salvation has been sent to us! [27]The people
in Jerusalem and their leaders did not recognize
Jesus as the one the prophets had spoken about.
Instead, they condemned him, and in doing this
they fulfilled the prophets' words that are read
every Sabbath. [28]They found no legal reason to
execute him, but they asked Pilate to have him
killed anyway.
[29]"When they had done all that the prophecies said about him, they took him down from
the cross* and placed him in a tomb. [30]But God
raised him from the dead! [31]And over a period of
many days he appeared to those who had gone
with him from Galilee to Jerusalem. They are
now his witnesses to the people of Israel.
[32]"And now we are here to bring you this
Good News. The promise was made to our ancestors, [33]and God has now fulfilled it for us, their
descendants, by raising Jesus. This is what the
second psalm says about Jesus:

'You are my Son.
Today I have become your Father.*'

[34]For God had promised to raise him from the
dead, not leaving him to rot in the grave. He said,
'I will give you the sacred blessings I promised
to David.'* [35]Another psalm explains it more
fully: 'You will not allow your Holy One to rot
in the grave.'* [36]This is not a reference to David,
for after David had done the will of God in his
own generation, he died and was buried with his
ancestors, and his body decayed. [37]No, it was a
reference to someone else—someone whom God
raised and whose body did not decay.
[38]*"Brothers, listen! We are here to proclaim
that through this man Jesus there is forgiveness
for your sins. [39]Everyone who believes in him is
declared right with God—something the law of
Moses could never do. [40]Be careful! Don't let the
prophets' words apply to you. For they said,

[41]'Look, you mockers,
be amazed and die!
For I am doing something in your own day,
something you wouldn't believe
even if someone told you about it.'* "

[42]As Paul and Barnabas left the synagogue
that day, the people begged them to speak about
these things again the next week. [43]Many Jews
and devout converts to Judaism followed Paul

13:13-14 *Pamphylia* and *Pisidia* were districts in what is now Turkey. **13:15** Greek *from the law.* **13:18** Some manuscripts read *He cared for them;* compare Deut 1:31. **13:22** 1 Sam 13:14. **13:29** Greek *from the tree.* **13:33** Or *Today I reveal you as my Son.* Ps 2:7. **13:34** Isa 55:3. **13:35** Ps 16:10. **13:38** English translations divide verses 38 and 39 in various ways. **13:41** Hab 1:5 (Greek version).

13:13–52 Paul Preaches in Antioch of Pisidia. Paul, Barnabas, and John Mark return to the mainland, where John Mark leaves them to go back to Jerusalem. Luke does not tell us why John Mark left (was he concerned about his mother?), but Paul must have disapproved, because later (15:37–40) he and Barnabas disagreed so deeply about him that they parted company. However, for the moment Paul and Barnabas press on to Antioch in Pisidia, far inland in today's Turkey.

and Barnabas, and the two men urged them to continue to rely on the grace of God.

Paul Turns to the Gentiles

44 The following week almost the entire city turned out to hear them preach the word of the Lord. 45 But when some of the Jews saw the crowds, they were jealous; so they slandered Paul and argued against whatever he said.

46 Then Paul and Barnabas spoke out boldly and declared, "It was necessary that we first preach the word of God to you Jews. But since you have rejected it and judged yourselves unworthy of eternal life, we will offer it to the Gentiles. 47 For the Lord gave us this command when he said,

'I have made you a light to the Gentiles,
to bring salvation to the farthest corners of the earth.'* "

48 When the Gentiles heard this, they were very glad and thanked the Lord for his message; and all who were chosen for eternal life became believers. 49 So the Lord's message spread throughout that region.

50 Then the Jews stirred up the influential religious women and the leaders of the city, and they incited a mob against Paul and Barnabas and ran them out of town. 51 So they shook the dust from their feet as a sign of rejection and went to the town of Iconium. 52 And the believers* were filled with joy and with the Holy Spirit.

Paul and Barnabas in Iconium

14 The same thing happened in Iconium.* Paul and Barnabas went to the Jewish synagogue and preached with such power that a great number of both Jews and Greeks became believers. 2 Some of the Jews, however, spurned God's message and poisoned the minds of the Gentiles against Paul and Barnabas. 3 But the apostles stayed there a long time, preaching boldly about the grace of the Lord. And the Lord proved their message was true by giving them power to do miraculous signs and wonders. 4 But the people of the town were divided in their opinion about them. Some sided with the Jews, and some with the apostles.

5 Then a mob of Gentiles and Jews, along with their leaders, decided to attack and stone them. 6 When the apostles learned of it, they fled to the region of Lycaonia—to the towns of Lystra and Derbe and the surrounding area. 7 And there they preached the Good News.

Paul and Barnabas in Lystra and Derbe

8 While they were at Lystra, Paul and Barnabas came upon a man with crippled feet. He had been that way from birth, so he had never walked. He was sitting 9 and listening as Paul preached. Looking straight at him, Paul realized he had faith to be healed. 10 So Paul called to him in a loud voice, "Stand up!" And the man jumped to his feet and started walking.

11 When the crowd saw what Paul had done, they shouted in their local dialect, "These men are gods in human form!" 12 They decided that Barnabas was the Greek god Zeus and that Paul was Hermes, since he was the chief speaker. 13 Now the temple of Zeus was located just outside the town. So the priest of the temple and the crowd brought bulls and wreaths of flowers to

13:47 Isa 49:6. **13:52** Greek *the disciples.* **14:1** *Iconium,* as well as *Lystra* and *Derbe* (14:6), were towns in what is now Turkey.

13:44–52 Paul Turns to the Gentiles. Once more they first make their way to the synagogue, where as visitors they are courteously invited to speak. As with other recorded sermons to Jews, Paul first traces Jewish history, showing how Jesus is the fulfillment of the Old Testament law and prophets. Again there is an emphasis on the resurrection and on the need to respond in repentance and faith for the forgiveness of sins. **48:** Soon public opinion is polarized between those (especially Gentiles) who respond in faith and those (especially Jews) who reject them in great anger. Paul and Barnabas tell the crowds that since the Jews, who should hear first, have rejected the Word of the Lord, they are free to turn their attention to the Gentiles. This becomes the normal pattern of their ministry: to the Jews first, then to the Gentiles. **50:** The Jews incite civic leaders, including *influential religious women* to drive them out of the city. Ancient sources note that a number of wealthy and politically important women were interested in Judaism; thus the Jews successfully solicited their support in driving Paul and Barnabas out of the city.

14:1–7 Paul and Barnabas in Iconium. A similar pattern emerges at Iconium and Lystra, though in Iconium Jews and Greeks became believers, and it was some time before Paul and Barnabas were forced to flee.

14:8–20 Paul and Barnabas in Lystra and Derbe. In Lystra, following the healing of a cripple, the crowds misinterpret what is going on and try to worship Paul and Barnabas as a visitation of Zeus and Hermes. Such a misunderstanding could not have occurred when Paul and Barnabas were preaching to Jews, and the

the town gates, and they prepared to offer sacrifices to the apostles.
[14]But when the apostles Barnabas and Paul
heard what was happening, they tore their clothing in dismay and ran out among the people,
shouting, [15]"Friends,* why are you doing this?
We are merely human beings—just like you!
We have come to bring you the Good News that
you should turn from these worthless things
and turn to the living God, who made heaven
and earth, the sea, and everything in them. [16]In
the past he permitted all the nations to go their
own ways, [17]but he never left them without evidence of himself and his goodness. For instance,
he sends you rain and good crops and gives you
food and joyful hearts." [18]But even with these
words, Paul and Barnabas could scarcely restrain
the people from sacrificing to them.
[19]Then some Jews arrived from Antioch and
Iconium and won the crowds to their side. They
stoned Paul and dragged him out of town, thinking he was dead. [20]But as the believers* gathered
around him, he got up and went back into the
town. The next day he left with Barnabas for
Derbe.

Paul and Barnabas Return to Antioch of Syria
[21]After preaching the Good News in Derbe and
making many disciples, Paul and Barnabas returned to Lystra, Iconium, and Antioch of Pisidia, [22]where they strengthened the believers.
They encouraged them to continue in the faith,
reminding them that we must suffer many hardships to enter the Kingdom of God. [23]Paul and
Barnabas also appointed elders in every church.
With prayer and fasting, they turned the elders
over to the care of the Lord, in whom they had
put their trust. [24]Then they traveled back through
Pisidia to Pamphylia. [25]They preached the word
in Perga, then went down to Attalia.
[26]Finally, they returned by ship to Antioch
of Syria, where their journey had begun. The
believers there had entrusted them to the grace
of God to do the work they had now completed. [27]Upon arriving in Antioch, they called the
church together and reported everything God
had done through them and how he had opened
the door of faith to the Gentiles, too. [28]And they
stayed there with the believers for a long time.

The Council at Jerusalem
15 While Paul and Barnabas were at Antioch of Syria, some men from Judea
arrived and began to teach the believers*: "Unless you are circumcised as required by
the law of Moses, you cannot be saved." [2]Paul
and Barnabas disagreed with them, arguing vehemently. Finally, the church decided to send Paul
and Barnabas to Jerusalem, accompanied by some
local believers, to talk to the apostles and elders
about this question. [3]The church sent the delegates to Jerusalem, and they stopped along the
way in Phoenicia and Samaria to visit the believers. They told them—much to everyone's joy—
that the Gentiles, too, were being converted.
[4]When they arrived in Jerusalem, Barnabas
and Paul were welcomed by the whole church,
including the apostles and elders. They reported everything God had done through them. [5]But
then some of the believers who belonged to the
sect of the Pharisees stood up and insisted, "The
Gentile converts must be circumcised and required to follow the law of Moses."
[6]So the apostles and elders met together to
resolve this issue. [7]At the meeting, after a long
discussion, Peter stood and addressed them as
follows: "Brothers, you all know that God chose
me from among you some time ago to preach to
the Gentiles so that they could hear the Good
News and believe. [8]God knows people's hearts,
and he confirmed that he accepts Gentiles by giv-

14:15 Greek *Men.* **14:20** Greek *disciples;* also in 14:22, 28.
15:1 Greek *brothers;* also in 15:3, 23, 32, 33, 36, 40.

reality of reaching the pagan Gentile world perhaps registered more sharply than ever before. It is significant that here the preaching does not presuppose any familiarity with Jewish Scriptures and that the people are expressing themselves *in their local dialect.* There is both a language and a cultural problem.

14:21–28 Paul and Barnabas Return to Antioch of Syria. Despite being driven out of Lystra, after visiting Derbe, Paul and Barnabas retrace their steps through all the towns and cities where they have been—to strengthen those who have come to faith, to warn them of the inevitability of suffering, and to appoint *elders in every church.* Only after they have done all that they can to assure stability and growth in discipleship do they return to Antioch, reporting to the church that had sent them on their missionary journey.

15:1–21 The Council at Jerusalem. It was timely that they should be in Antioch then, for disciples came from Judea teaching that salvation was not possible without circumcision. Soon Paul and Barnabas and others are sent to Jerusalem where they are able to tell of all God had been doing among Jews and Gentiles alike. **5:** Certain Pharisees who had actually embraced the new faith try to insist that the Gentiles

ing them the Holy Spirit, just as he did to us.
9 He made no distinction between us and them,
for he cleansed their hearts through faith. 10 So
why are you now challenging God by burdening
the Gentile believers* with a yoke that neither
we nor our ancestors were able to bear? 11 We believe that we are all saved the same way, by the
undeserved grace of the Lord Jesus."

12 Everyone listened quietly as Barnabas and
Paul told about the miraculous signs and won-
ders God had done through them among the
Gentiles.

13 When they had finished, James stood and
said, "Brothers, listen to me. 14 Peter* has told
you about the time God first visited the Gentiles
to take from them a people for himself. 15 And
this conversion of Gentiles is exactly what the
prophets predicted. As it is written:

16 'Afterward I will return
and restore the fallen house* of David.
I will rebuild its ruins
and restore it,
17 so that the rest of humanity might seek the
Lord,
including the Gentiles—
all those I have called to be mine.
The Lord has spoken—
18 he who made these things known so long
ago.'*

19 "And so my judgment is that we should not
make it difficult for the Gentiles who are turning to God. 20 Instead, we should write and tell
them to abstain from eating food offered to idols,
from sexual immorality, from eating the meat of
strangled animals, and from consuming blood.
21 For these laws of Moses have been preached in
Jewish synagogues in every city on every Sabbath for many generations."

The Letter for Gentile Believers

22 Then the apostles and elders together with the
whole church in Jerusalem chose delegates, and
they sent them to Antioch of Syria with Paul
and Barnabas to report on this decision. The men
chosen were two of the church leaders*—Judas
(also called Barsabbas) and Silas. 23 This is the letter they took with them:

"This letter is from the apostles and elders,
your brothers in Jerusalem. It is written to
the Gentile believers in Antioch, Syria, and
Cilicia. Greetings!

24 "We understand that some men from
here have troubled you and upset you
with their teaching, but we did not send
them! 25 So we decided, having come to
complete agreement, to send you official
representatives, along with our beloved
Barnabas and Paul, 26 who have risked their
lives for the name of our Lord Jesus Christ.
27 We are sending Judas and Silas to confirm
what we have decided concerning your
question.

28 "For it seemed good to the Holy Spirit
and to us to lay no greater burden on
you than these few requirements: 29 You
must abstain from eating food offered to
idols, from consuming blood or the meat
of strangled animals, and from sexual
immorality. If you do this, you will do well.
Farewell."

30 The messengers went at once to Antioch,
where they called a general meeting of the believers and delivered the letter. 31 And there was
great joy throughout the church that day as they
read this encouraging message.

32 Then Judas and Silas, both being prophets,
spoke at length to the believers, encouraging
and strengthening their faith. 33 They stayed for
a while, and then the believers sent them back
to the church in Jerusalem with a blessing of
peace.* 35 Paul and Barnabas stayed in Antioch.

15:10 Greek *disciples.* **15:14** Greek *Symeon.* **15:16** Or *kingdom;* Greek reads *tent.* **15:16-18** Amos 9:11-12 (Greek version); Isa 45:21. **15:22** Greek *were leaders among the brothers.* **15:33** Some manuscripts add verse 34, *But Silas decided to stay there.*

must be circumcised and keep the law of Moses. **6–21:** After extensive debate between the apostles and elders, in turn Peter, Paul, and Barnabas, and finally James appeal to a combination of Scripture and events. They show how God is welcoming Gentiles into the church and that for Jew and Gentile alike the basis of salvation is not circumcision but *the undeserved grace of the Lord Jesus.* **13:** We now see James assuming the leadership of the Jerusalem group. He suggests that a handful of directives, which by tradition predated Mosaic law or Abraham and were believed to have been given to Noah (Gen 9:3–4), should be urged upon everyone.

15:22–35 The Letter for Gentile Believers. Keeping these directives was not for salvation but for basic upright living. This becomes the substance of a letter sent by the apostles to Antioch, conveyed not only by Paul and Barnabas but also by two senior leaders from Jerusalem.

They and many others taught and preached the
word of the Lord there.

Paul and Barnabas Separate
36 After some time Paul said to Barnabas, "Let's
go back and visit each city where we previously preached the word of the Lord, to see
how the new believers are doing." 37 Barnabas
agreed and wanted to take along John Mark.
38 But Paul disagreed strongly, since John Mark
had deserted them in Pamphylia and had not
continued with them in their work. 39 Their
disagreement was so sharp that they separated. Barnabas took John Mark with him and
sailed for Cyprus. 40 Paul chose Silas, and as he
left, the believers entrusted him to the Lord's
gracious care. 41 Then he traveled throughout
Syria and Cilicia, strengthening the churches
there.

Paul's Second Missionary Journey
16 Paul went first to Derbe and then
to Lystra, where there was a young
disciple named Timothy. His moth-
er was a Jewish believer, but his father was a
Greek. 2 Timothy was well thought of by the believers* in Lystra and Iconium, 3 so Paul wanted
him to join them on their journey. In deference
to the Jews of the area, he arranged for Timothy
to be circumcised before they left, for everyone
knew that his father was a Greek. 4 Then they
went from town to town, instructing the believers to follow the decisions made by the apostles
and elders in Jerusalem. 5 So the churches were
strengthened in their faith and grew larger every day.

A Call from Macedonia
6 Next Paul and Silas traveled through the area
of Phrygia and Galatia, because the Holy Spirit
had prevented them from preaching the word in
the province of Asia at that time. 7 Then coming
to the borders of Mysia, they headed north for
the province of Bithynia,* but again the Spirit of
Jesus did not allow them to go there. 8 So instead,
they went on through Mysia to the seaport of
Troas.
9 That night Paul had a vision: A man from
Macedonia in northern Greece was standing
there, pleading with him, "Come over to Macedonia and help us!" 10 So we* decided to leave for
Macedonia at once, having concluded that God
was calling us to preach the Good News there.

Lydia of Philippi Believes in Jesus
11 We boarded a boat at Troas and sailed straight
across to the island of Samothrace, and the next
day we landed at Neapolis. 12 From there we
reached Philippi, a major city of that district of
Macedonia and a Roman colony. And we stayed
there several days.
13 On the Sabbath we went a little way outside
the city to a riverbank, where we thought people
would be meeting for prayer, and we sat down to
speak with some women who had gathered there.
14 One of them was Lydia from Thyatira, a merchant of expensive purple cloth, who worshiped
God. As she listened to us, the Lord opened her
heart, and she accepted what Paul was saying.

16:2 Greek *brothers;* also in 16:40. **16:6-7** *Phrygia, Galatia, Asia, Mysia,* and *Bithynia* were all districts in what is now Turkey. **16:10** Luke, the writer of this book, here joined Paul and accompanied him on his journey.

15:36–41 Paul and Barnabas Separate. After the peaceful resolution of affairs in Jerusalem, Paul and Barnabas soon have such a bitter argument that they never work together again. Yet out of even this tragedy God brought blessing, for Paul teamed up with Silas, and Barnabas with John Mark, and all had effective ministry, revisiting and strengthening existing churches and planting new ones.

16:1–5 Paul's Second Missionary Journey. It was on such a journey, revisiting Lystra, that Paul recruits Timothy to travel with him and Silas. Luke tells us that Timothy's mother was a Jewish believer, but because his father was Greek, Paul has him circumcised—not as an issue of salvation (which would have repudiated the recent decision in Jerusalem) but in order to make him less offensive to Jews as they go to new areas, beginning with the synagogues, on their missionary journeys.

16:6—19:20 Across the Sea: The Gospel for Europe

16:6–10 A Call from Macedonia. Paul, Silas, and Timothy, shortly to be joined by Luke, had no liberty to preach as they traveled through Asia; puzzled, they found themselves at Troas. Troas was the major port linking Asia Minor and Macedonia, now northern Greece, and linking with the splendid Egnatian Way leading to Rome. The Holy Spirit convinces Paul through a vision that they should sail for Macedonia, and they disembark at Neapolis and proceed to the Roman colony of Philippi.

16:11–15 Lydia of Philippi Believes in Jesus. In his days as a Pharisee, possibly even from childhood, Paul would have been trained to say each day, "I thank you, Lord, that you did not create me a slave, a woman, or a Gentile." In the gentle humor of the

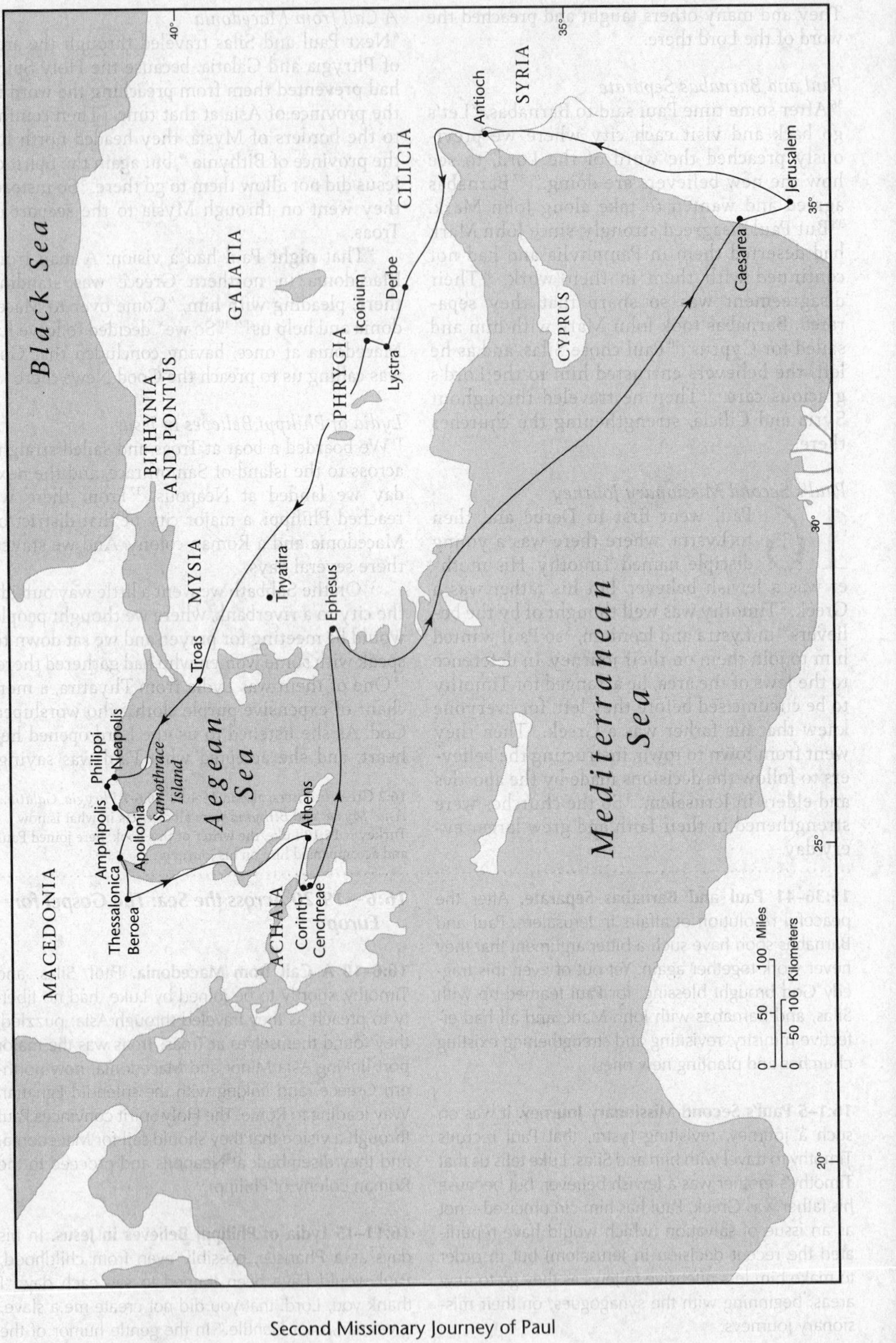

Second Missionary Journey of Paul

15 She was baptized along with other members of
her household, and she asked us to be her guests.
"If you agree that I am a true believer in the
Lord," she said, "come and stay at my home."
And she urged us until we agreed.

Paul and Silas in Prison

16 One day as we were going down to the place of
prayer, we met a demon-possessed slave girl. She
was a fortune-teller who earned a lot of money
for her masters. 17 She followed Paul and the rest
of us, shouting, "These men are servants of the
Most High God, and they have come to tell you
how to be saved."

18 This went on day after day until Paul got
so exasperated that he turned and said to the demon within her, "I command you in the name of
Jesus Christ to come out of her." And instantly
it left her.

19 Her masters' hopes of wealth were now
shattered, so they grabbed Paul and Silas and
dragged them before the authorities at the marketplace. 20 "The whole city is in an uproar because of these Jews!" they shouted to the city
officials. 21 "They are teaching customs that are
illegal for us Romans to practice."

22 A mob quickly formed against Paul and Silas, and the city officials ordered them stripped
and beaten with wooden rods. 23 They were severely beaten, and then they were thrown into
prison. The jailer was ordered to make sure they
didn't escape. 24 So the jailer put them into the
inner dungeon and clamped their feet in the
stocks.

25 Around midnight Paul and Silas were praying and singing hymns to God, and the other
prisoners were listening. 26 Suddenly, there was
a massive earthquake, and the prison was shaken
to its foundations. All the doors immediately
flew open, and the chains of every prisoner fell
off! 27 The jailer woke up to see the prison doors
wide open. He assumed the prisoners had escaped, so he drew his sword to kill himself. 28 But
Paul shouted to him, "Stop! Don't kill yourself!
We are all here!"

29 The jailer called for lights and ran to the
dungeon and fell down trembling before Paul
and Silas. 30 Then he brought them out and asked,
"Sirs, what must I do to be saved?"

31 They replied, "Believe in the Lord Jesus
and you will be saved, along with everyone in
your household." 32 And they shared the word of
the Lord with him and with all who lived in his
household. 33 Even at that hour of the night, the
jailer cared for them and washed their wounds.
Then he and everyone in his household were immediately baptized. 34 He brought them into his
house and set a meal before them, and he and
his entire household rejoiced because they all believed in God.

35 The next morning the city officials sent the
police to tell the jailer, "Let those men go!" 36 So
the jailer told Paul, "The city officials have said
you and Silas are free to leave. Go in peace."

Lord, the first three converts (as recorded by Luke) through Paul's ministry (in today's European mainland) were a woman, a slave girl, and a Gentile. There was no synagogue in Philippi, which probably means that the Jewish community was too small for there to be the requisite minimum of ten Jewish males. There is no mention of observant men at all. A group of women met by the river to pray, among them Lydia, *who worshiped God* and was spiritually alert. She was a native of Thyatira and by trade a dealer in purple cloth, a luxury fabric for which the dye was extracted not from plants but from shellfish. She may have been a widow or a married woman with an absent husband (see Marriage, Song 2), and there is no hint as to the size of her household. She urges Paul and the others to become her guests, and this would give them plenty of opportunity to make disciples of these new believers.

16:16–40 Paul and Silas in Prison. Soon afterward Paul and Silas met a demon-possessed slave girl and *command*[ed] the demon *to come out of her*. The disciples do not wish to accept testimony from a demonic source. The girl's exploitative owners are furious, for her supernatural powers have been lucrative for them, however distressing they may have been to her. They care nothing for her as a human being but only for her commercial value to them. They cunningly appeal to the magistrates, so that Paul and Silas are flogged and thrown into prison. Even here they bear witness to Jesus Christ through prayer and singing. **28:** The jailer assumes they all will have escaped. Rather than face execution for losing his prisoners, he is about to attempt suicide when Paul assures him that nobody has left. The jailer attributes this extraordinary turn of events to divine intervention and immediately asks for instruction in finding salvation. Soon he and his household are believing, baptized, and rejoicing. **35:** Perhaps superstitious about the earthquake, the magistrates are eager to be rid of Paul and Silas. But Paul reveals that, Jew notwithstanding, he is a Roman citizen, and the authorities apologize, afraid of retribution for the illegal treatment that they have accorded him. The disciples spend some more time with this new little church family before walking on to Thessalonica.

37 But Paul replied, "They have publicly beaten us without a trial and put us in prison—and we are Roman citizens. So now they want us to leave secretly? Certainly not! Let them come themselves to release us!"

38 When the police reported this, the city officials were alarmed to learn that Paul and Silas were Roman citizens. 39 So they came to the jail and apologized to them. Then they brought them out and begged them to leave the city. 40 When Paul and Silas left the prison, they returned to the home of Lydia. There they met with the believers and encouraged them once more. Then they left town.

Paul Preaches in Thessalonica

17 Paul and Silas then traveled through the towns of Amphipolis and Apollonia and came to Thessalonica, where there was a Jewish synagogue. 2 As was Paul's custom, he went to the synagogue service, and for three Sabbaths in a row he used the Scriptures to reason with the people. 3 He explained the prophecies and proved that the Messiah must suffer and rise from the dead. He said, "This Jesus I'm telling you about is the Messiah." 4 Some of the Jews who listened were persuaded and joined Paul and Silas, along with many God-fearing Greek men and quite a few prominent women.*

5 But some of the Jews were jealous, so they gathered some troublemakers from the marketplace to form a mob and start a riot. They attacked the home of Jason, searching for Paul and Silas so they could drag them out to the crowd.* 6 Not finding them there, they dragged out Jason and some of the other believers* instead and took them before the city council. "Paul and Silas have caused trouble all over the world," they shouted, "and now they are here disturbing our city, too. 7 And Jason has welcomed them into his home. They are all guilty of treason against Caesar, for they profess allegiance to another king, named Jesus."

8 The people of the city, as well as the city council, were thrown into turmoil by these reports. 9 So the officials forced Jason and the other believers to post bond, and then they released them.

Paul and Silas in Berea

10 That very night the believers sent Paul and Silas to Berea. When they arrived there, they went to the Jewish synagogue. 11 And the people of Berea were more open-minded than those in Thessalonica, and they listened eagerly to Paul's message. They searched the Scriptures day after day to see if Paul and Silas were teaching the truth. 12 As a result, many Jews believed, as did many of the prominent Greek women and men.

13 But when some Jews in Thessalonica learned that Paul was preaching the word of God in Berea, they went there and stirred up trouble. 14 The believers acted at once, sending Paul on to the coast, while Silas and Timothy remained behind. 15 Those escorting Paul went with him all the way to Athens; then they returned to Berea with instructions for Silas and Timothy to hurry and join him.

Paul Preaches in Athens

16 While Paul was waiting for them in Athens, he was deeply troubled by all the idols he saw ev-

17:4 Some manuscripts read *quite a few of the wives of the leading men.* **17:5** Or *the city council.* **17:6** Greek *brothers;* also in 17:10, 14.

17:1–9 Paul Preaches in Thessalonica. Paul and Silas were to spend only three weeks in Thessalonica, which makes the Thessalonian epistles all the more remarkable (e.g., 1 Thes 1:2–10). Jews and Gentiles, including *quite a few prominent women,* believed. Paul is able to captivate women by the message he brings. **7:** This time the charge brought against them by enraged Jews is one of sedition. They are accused of professsing *allegiance to another king, named Jesus,* in other words, a rival to the emperor.

17:10–15 Paul and Silas in Berea. Paul and Silas slip away to Berea, where the Jews were more receptive than those in Thessalonica. *They searched the Scriptures* for verification of the message. Once again Jews and Gentiles, including *many of the prominent Greek women and men,* come to faith before Paul has to move on for safety's sake, this time to Athens, several hundred miles to the south. Within the pluralism of the Greco-Roman world, women, especially wealthy women, had greater religious freedom than their Jewish sisters, and it may have been easier for them to convert even when their husbands did not. The Thessalonian and Berean women respond positively in contrast to the women of Pisidian Antioch.

17:16–34 Paul Preaches in Athens. Athens' greatest glory had faded, but it was still buzzing with philosophers and debaters—and idolatry. Paul is deeply distressed by the latter, but it became the stimulus for profound apologetics and preaching to the pagan world. Starting from the altar to the unknown god—the Athenians' attempt to cover all possibilities—Paul declares that their *Unknown God* is knowable and revealed in the God and Father of the Lord Jesus Christ, the one who made the world, who is close at

erywhere in the city. 17 He went to the synagogue to reason with the Jews and the God-fearing Gentiles, and he spoke daily in the public square to all who happened to be there.

18 He also had a debate with some of the Epicurean and Stoic philosophers. When he told them about Jesus and his resurrection, they said, "What's this babbler trying to say with these strange ideas he's picked up?" Others said, "He seems to be preaching about some foreign gods."

19 Then they took him to the high council of the city.* "Come and tell us about this new teaching," they said. 20 "You are saying some rather strange things, and we want to know what it's all about." 21 (It should be explained that all the Athenians as well as the foreigners in Athens seemed to spend all their time discussing the latest ideas.)

22 So Paul, standing before the council,* addressed them as follows: "Men of Athens, I notice that you are very religious in every way, 23 for as I was walking along I saw your many shrines. And one of your altars had this inscription on it: 'To an Unknown God.' This God, whom you worship without knowing, is the one I'm telling you about.

24 "He is the God who made the world and everything in it. Since he is Lord of heaven and earth, he doesn't live in man-made temples, 25 and human hands can't serve his needs—for he has no needs. He himself gives life and breath to everything, and he satisfies every need. 26 From one man* he created all the nations throughout the whole earth. He decided beforehand when they should rise and fall, and he determined their boundaries.

27 "His purpose was for the nations to seek after God and perhaps feel their way toward him and find him—though he is not far from any one of us. 28 For in him we live and move and exist. As some of your* own poets have said, 'We are his offspring.' 29 And since this is true, we shouldn't think of God as an idol designed by craftsmen from gold or silver or stone.

30 "God overlooked people's ignorance about these things in earlier times, but now he commands everyone everywhere to repent of their sins and turn to him. 31 For he has set a day for judging the world with justice by the man he has appointed, and he proved to everyone who this is by raising him from the dead."

32 When they heard Paul speak about the resurrection of the dead, some laughed in contempt, but others said, "We want to hear more about this later." 33 That ended Paul's discussion with them, 34 but some joined him and became believers. Among them were Dionysius, a member of the council,* a woman named Damaris, and others with them.

Paul Meets Priscilla and Aquila in Corinth

18 Then Paul left Athens and went to Corinth.* 2 There he became acquainted with a Jew named Aquila, born in Pontus, who had recently arrived from Italy with his wife, Priscilla. They had left Italy when Claudius Caesar deported all Jews from Rome. 3 Paul lived and worked with them, for they were tentmakers* just as he was.

4 Each Sabbath found Paul at the synagogue, trying to convince the Jews and Greeks alike. 5 And after Silas and Timothy came down from Macedonia, Paul spent all his time preaching the word. He testified to the Jews that Jesus was the Messiah. 6 But when they opposed and insulted him, Paul shook the dust from his clothes and said, "Your blood is upon your own heads—I am innocent. From now on I will go preach to the Gentiles."

7 Then he left and went to the home of Titius Justus, a Gentile who worshiped God and lived next door to the synagogue. 8 Crispus, the leader of the synagogue, and everyone in his household believed in the Lord. Many others in Corinth also heard Paul, became believers, and were baptized.

17:19 Or *the most learned society of philosophers in the city.* Greek reads *the Areopagus.* **17:22** Traditionally rendered *standing in the middle of Mars Hill;* Greek reads *standing in the middle of the Areopagus.* **17:26** Greek *From one;* other manuscripts read *From one blood.* **17:28** Some manuscripts read *our.* **17:34** Greek *an Areopagite.* **18:1** *Athens* and *Corinth* were major cities in Achaia, the region in the southern portion of the Greek peninsula. **18:3** Or *leatherworkers.*

hand and who will judge all humankind through the risen Jesus. Among those who come to believe are Dionysius and Damaris (v. 34).

18:1–17 Paul Meets Priscilla and Aquila in Corinth. Paul moves on to Corinth, where he stays with Aquila and Priscilla, Jewish believers recently expelled from Rome by the emperor Claudius and by trade tentmakers like Paul. Here Priscilla's name stands second, but in most of the other references to this couple her name comes first, apparently indicating that she was the more active of the two in Christian ministry. **8:** Initially Paul again tries to win a hearing at the synagogue, and some believe, including Crispus, that is, the person responsible for the synagogue services. Following a vision, Paul stays in Corinth for

9 One night the Lord spoke to Paul in a vision and told him, "Don't be afraid! Speak out!
Don't be silent! 10 For I am with you, and no one
will attack and harm you, for many people in this
city belong to me." 11 So Paul stayed there for the
next year and a half, teaching the word of God.
12 But when Gallio became governor of Achaia, some Jews rose up together against Paul and
brought him before the governor for judgment.
13 They accused Paul of "persuading people to
worship God in ways that are contrary to our
law."
14 But just as Paul started to make his defense, Gallio turned to Paul's accusers and said,
"Listen, you Jews, if this were a case involving
some wrongdoing or a serious crime, I would
have a reason to accept your case. 15 But since it is
merely a question of words and names and your
Jewish law, take care of it yourselves. I refuse to
judge such matters." 16 And he threw them out of
the courtroom.
17 The crowd* then grabbed Sosthenes, the
leader of the synagogue, and beat him right there
in the courtroom. But Gallio paid no attention.

Paul Returns to Antioch of Syria

18 Paul stayed in Corinth for some time after that,
then said good-bye to the brothers and sisters*
and went to nearby Cenchrea. There he shaved
his head according to Jewish custom, marking
the end of a vow. Then he set sail for Syria, taking Priscilla and Aquila with him.
19 They stopped first at the port of Ephesus,
where Paul left the others behind. While he was
there, he went to the synagogue to reason with
the Jews. 20 They asked him to stay longer, but
he declined. 21 As he left, however, he said, "I will
come back later,* God willing." Then he set sail
from Ephesus. 22 The next stop was at the port
of Caesarea. From there he went up and visited
the church at Jerusalem* and then went back to
Antioch.
23 After spending some time in Antioch, Paul
went back through Galatia and Phrygia, visiting
and strengthening all the believers.*

Apollos Instructed at Ephesus

24 Meanwhile, a Jew named Apollos, an eloquent
speaker who knew the Scriptures well, had arrived in Ephesus from Alexandria in Egypt.
25 He had been taught the way of the Lord, and
he taught others about Jesus with an enthusiastic spirit* and with accuracy. However, he knew
only about John's baptism. 26 When Priscilla and
Aquila heard him preaching boldly in the synagogue, they took him aside and explained the
way of God even more accurately.
27 Apollos had been thinking about going to
Achaia, and the brothers and sisters in Ephesus
encouraged him to go. They wrote to the believers in Achaia, asking them to welcome him. When
he arrived there, he proved to be of great benefit
to those who, by God's grace, had believed. 28 He
refuted the Jews with powerful arguments in
public debate. Using the Scriptures, he explained
to them that Jesus was the Messiah.

Paul's Third Missionary Journey

19 While Apollos was in Corinth, Paul
traveled through the interior regions
until he reached Ephesus, on the
coast, where he found several believers.* 2 "Did
you receive the Holy Spirit when you believed?"
he asked them.
"No," they replied, "we haven't even heard
that there is a Holy Spirit."
3 "Then what baptism did you experience?"
he asked.
And they replied, "The baptism of John."

18:17 Greek *Everyone;* other manuscripts read *All the Greeks.* **18:18** Greek *brothers;* also in 18:27. **18:21** Some manuscripts read *"I must by all means be at Jerusalem for the upcoming festival, but I will come back later."* **18:22** Greek *the church.* **18:23** Greek *disciples;* also in 18:27. **18:25** Or *with enthusiasm in the Spirit.* **19:1** Greek *disciples;* also in 19:9, 30.

eighteen months, as many Gentiles come to faith. **15:** The Jews try to accuse him to the proconsul of stepping outside the boundaries of Judaism and thus putting himself beyond the protection offered to Jews. Gallio dismisses the charge as petty squabbling over trivia and refuses to intervene.

18:18–23 Paul Returns to Antioch of Syria. Paul sails back to Asia Minor, taking Priscilla and Aquila with him. He leaves them at Ephesus, going to Jerusalem via Caesarea and then on to Antioch. It had been a long journey.

18:24–28 Apollos Instructed at Ephesus. In Ephesus, Priscilla and Aquila share the instructing of Apollos, an Alexandrian Jewish believer whose grasp of the faith had considerable gaps. It appears that there was no bar to Priscilla teaching a man.

19:1–20 Paul's Third Missionary Journey. When Paul comes to Ephesus, he finds more believers who have received the baptism of John but not of the Holy Spirit. As the church grew and sometimes small groups of new believers had to be left without well-instructed leadership, it was inevitable that occasionally teach-

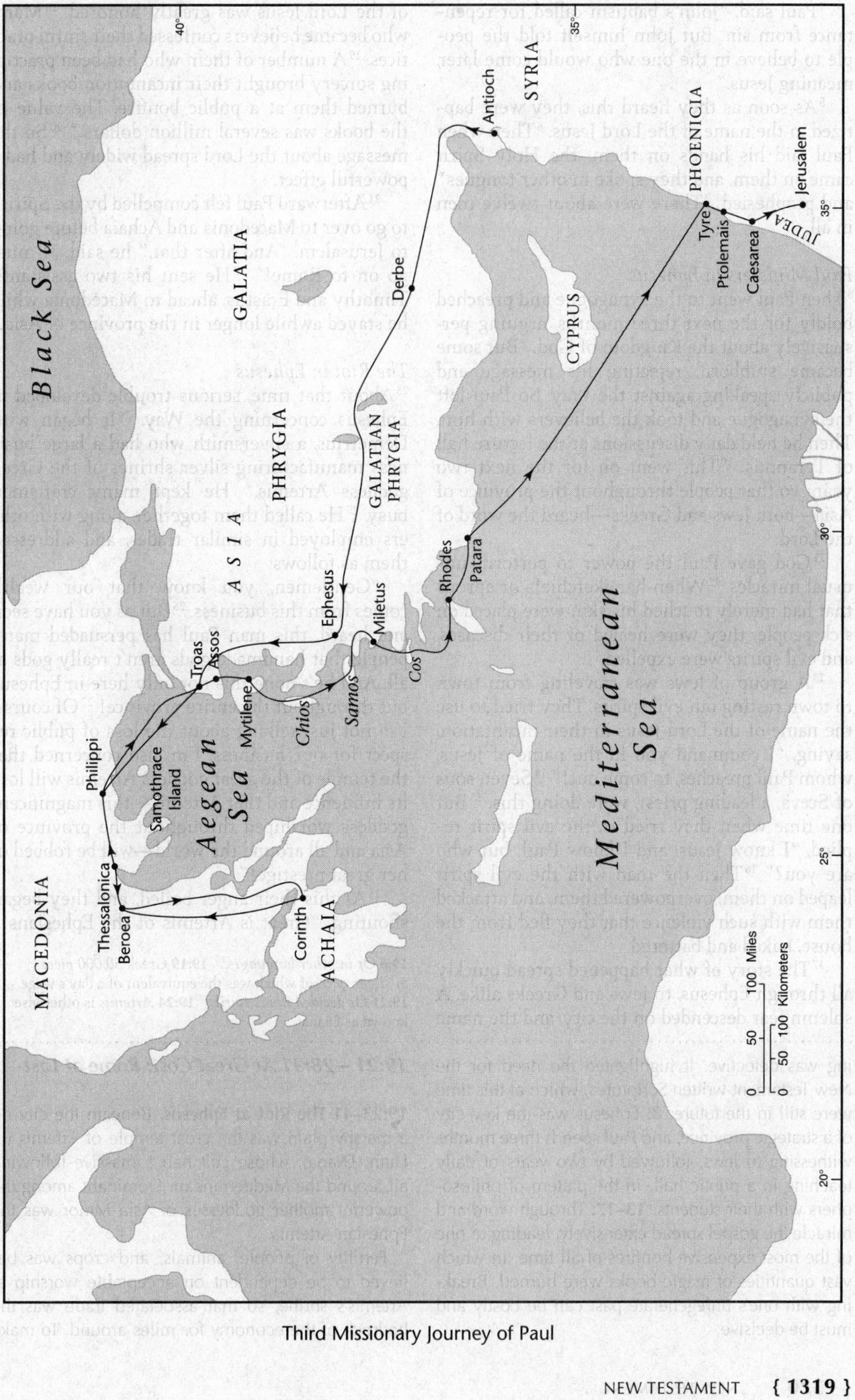

Third Missionary Journey of Paul

[4]Paul said, "John's baptism called for repentance from sin. But John himself told the people to believe in the one who would come later,
meaning Jesus."
[5]As soon as they heard this, they were baptized in the name of the Lord Jesus. [6]Then when
Paul laid his hands on them, the Holy Spirit
came on them, and they spoke in other tongues*
and prophesied. [7]There were about twelve men
in all.

Paul Ministers in Ephesus

[8]Then Paul went to the synagogue and preached
boldly for the next three months, arguing persuasively about the Kingdom of God. [9]But some
became stubborn, rejecting his message and
publicly speaking against the Way. So Paul left
the synagogue and took the believers with him.
Then he held daily discussions at the lecture hall
of Tyrannus. [10]This went on for the next two
years, so that people throughout the province of
Asia—both Jews and Greeks—heard the word of
the Lord.
[11]God gave Paul the power to perform unusual miracles. [12]When handkerchiefs or aprons
that had merely touched his skin were placed on
sick people, they were healed of their diseases,
and evil spirits were expelled.
[13]A group of Jews was traveling from town
to town casting out evil spirits. They tried to use
the name of the Lord Jesus in their incantation,
saying, "I command you in the name of Jesus,
whom Paul preaches, to come out!" [14]Seven sons
of Sceva, a leading priest, were doing this. [15]But
one time when they tried it, the evil spirit replied, "I know Jesus, and I know Paul, but who
are you?" [16]Then the man with the evil spirit
leaped on them, overpowered them, and attacked
them with such violence that they fled from the
house, naked and battered.
[17]The story of what happened spread quickly
all through Ephesus, to Jews and Greeks alike. A
solemn fear descended on the city, and the name
of the Lord Jesus was greatly honored. [18]Many
who became believers confessed their sinful practices. [19]A number of them who had been practicing sorcery brought their incantation books and
burned them at a public bonfire. The value of
the books was several million dollars.* [20]So the
message about the Lord spread widely and had a
powerful effect.
[21]Afterward Paul felt compelled by the Spirit*
to go over to Macedonia and Achaia before going
to Jerusalem. "And after that," he said, "I must
go on to Rome!" [22]He sent his two assistants,
Timothy and Erastus, ahead to Macedonia while
he stayed awhile longer in the province of Asia.

The Riot in Ephesus

[23]About that time, serious trouble developed in
Ephesus concerning the Way. [24]It began with
Demetrius, a silversmith who had a large business manufacturing silver shrines of the Greek
goddess Artemis.* He kept many craftsmen
busy. [25]He called them together, along with others employed in similar trades, and addressed
them as follows:
"Gentlemen, you know that our wealth
comes from this business. [26]But as you have seen
and heard, this man Paul has persuaded many
people that handmade gods aren't really gods at
all. And he's done this not only here in Ephesus
but throughout the entire province! [27]Of course,
I'm not just talking about the loss of public respect for our business. I'm also concerned that
the temple of the great goddess Artemis will lose
its influence and that Artemis—this magnificent
goddess worshiped throughout the province of
Asia and all around the world—will be robbed of
her great prestige!"
[28]At this their anger boiled, and they began
shouting, "Great is Artemis of the Ephesians!"

19:6 Or *in other languages.* **19:19** Greek *50,000 pieces of silver,* each of which was the equivalent of a day's wage. **19:21** Or *decided in his spirit.* **19:24** *Artemis* is otherwise known as Diana.

---

ing was defective. It highlighted the need for the New Testament written Scriptures, which at this time were still in the future. **8:** Ephesus was the key city of a strategic province, and Paul spends three months witnessing to Jews, followed by two years of daily teaching in a public hall, in the pattern of philosophers with their students. **13–17:** Through word and miracle the gospel spread extensively, leading to one of the most expensive bonfires of all time, in which vast quantities of magic books were burned. Breaking with one's unregenerate past can be costly and must be decisive.

19:21—28:31 At Great Cost: Rome at Last

19:23–41 The Riot at Ephesus. Beneath the city on a marshy plain was the great temple of Artemis (in Latin, Diana), whose cult had a massive following all around the Mediterranean. Dominant among the powerful mother goddesses of Asia Minor was the Ephesian Artemis.

Fertility of people, animals, and crops was believed to be dependent on acceptable worship at Artemis's shrine, so that associated trade was the bedrock of the economy for miles around. To make

29 Soon the whole city was filled with confusion.
Everyone rushed to the amphitheater, dragging
along Gaius and Aristarchus, who were Paul's
traveling companions from Macedonia. 30 Paul
wanted to go in, too, but the believers wouldn't
let him. 31 Some of the officials of the province,
friends of Paul, also sent a message to him, begging him not to risk his life by entering the amphitheater.
32 Inside, the people were all shouting, some
one thing and some another. Everything was in
confusion. In fact, most of them didn't even know
why they were there. 33 The Jews in the crowd
pushed Alexander forward and told him to explain the situation. He motioned for silence and
tried to speak. 34 But when the crowd realized he
was a Jew, they started shouting again and kept it
up for about two hours: "Great is Artemis of the
Ephesians! Great is Artemis of the Ephesians!"
35 At last the mayor was able to quiet them
down enough to speak. "Citizens of Ephesus,"
he said. "Everyone knows that Ephesus is the
official guardian of the temple of the great Artemis, whose image fell down to us from heaven.
36 Since this is an undeniable fact, you should
stay calm and not do anything rash. 37 You have
brought these men here, but they have stolen
nothing from the temple and have not spoken
against our goddess.
38 "If Demetrius and the craftsmen have a case
against them, the courts are in session and the
officials can hear the case at once. Let them make
formal charges. 39 And if there are complaints
about other matters, they can be settled in a legal
assembly. 40 I am afraid we are in danger of being
charged with rioting by the Roman government,
since there is no cause for all this commotion.
And if Rome demands an explanation, we won't
know what to say." 41 *Then he dismissed them,
and they dispersed.

Paul Goes to Macedonia and Greece

20 When the uproar was over, Paul sent
for the believers* and encouraged
them. Then he said good-bye and
left for Macedonia. 2 While there, he encouraged
the believers in all the towns he passed through.
Then he traveled down to Greece, 3 where he
stayed for three months. He was preparing to
sail back to Syria when he discovered a plot by
some Jews against his life, so he decided to return
through Macedonia.
4 Several men were traveling with him.
They were Sopater son of Pyrrhus from Berea;
Aristarchus and Secundus from Thessalonica;
Gaius from Derbe; Timothy; and Tychicus and
Trophimus from the province of Asia. 5 They
went on ahead and waited for us at Troas. 6 After
the Passover* ended, we boarded a ship at Philippi in Macedonia and five days later joined them
in Troas, where we stayed a week.

Paul's Final Visit to Troas

7 On the first day of the week, we gathered with
the local believers to share in the Lord's Supper.* Paul was preaching to them, and since he
was leaving the next day, he kept talking until
midnight. 8 The upstairs room where we met was
lighted with many flickering lamps. 9 As Paul
spoke on and on, a young man named Eutychus,
sitting on the windowsill, became very drowsy.
Finally, he fell sound asleep and dropped three
stories to his death below. 10 Paul went down,
bent over him, and took him into his arms.
"Don't worry," he said, "he's alive!" 11 Then they
all went back upstairs, shared in the Lord's Supper,* and ate together. Paul continued talking to

19:41 Some translations include verse 41 as part of verse 40. **20:1** Greek *disciples.* **20:6** Greek *the days of unleavened bread.* **20:7** Greek *to break bread.* **20:11** Greek *broke the bread.*

---

offerings to Diana was the closest to an insurance policy anyone could have. But Paul's preaching has been so effective that financial vested interests are severely challenged. **32:** The theater to which two of Paul's companions are dragged is an impressive structure, evidence of wealth generated by the Artemis cult. The town clerk quiets the mob by urging due procedure rather than mob rule, which can only bring down the wrath of the Roman authorities. Luke wants us to understand that opposition is because of the offense of the gospel and not because Paul and his friends wantonly flout the law.

20:1–6 Paul Goes to Macedonia and Greece. Among Paul's traveling companions is Timothy (see 19:22). To avoid a threat on his life, Paul takes the long land journey back to Philippi instead of sailing back toward Antioch in Syria.

20:7–12 Paul's Final Visit to Troas. Overpowered by weariness and the smokiness from the lamps, a lad named Eutychus falls asleep and crashes through the window to the courtyard three floors below. Paul brings him back to life and then *continue*[s] *talking to them.* One can't help wondering whether the women would not have been far too concerned about whether Eutychus was truly fully recovered than to have paid close attention to more apostolic discussion.

them until dawn, and then he left. [12] Meanwhile, the young man was taken home unhurt, and everyone was greatly relieved.

Paul Meets the Ephesian Elders

[13] Paul went by land to Assos, where he had arranged for us to join him, while we traveled by ship. [14] He joined us there, and we sailed together to Mitylene. [15] The next day we sailed past the island of Kios. The following day we crossed to the island of Samos, and* a day later we arrived at Miletus.

[16] Paul had decided to sail on past Ephesus, for he didn't want to spend any more time in the province of Asia. He was hurrying to get to Jerusalem, if possible, in time for the Festival of Pentecost. [17] But when we landed at Miletus, he sent a message to the elders of the church at Ephesus, asking them to come and meet him.

[18] When they arrived he declared, "You know that from the day I set foot in the province of Asia until now [19] I have done the Lord's work humbly and with many tears. I have endured the trials that came to me from the plots of the Jews. [20] I never shrank back from telling you what you needed to hear, either publicly or in your homes. [21] I have had one message for Jews and Greeks alike—the necessity of repenting from sin and turning to God, and of having faith in our Lord Jesus.

[22] "And now I am bound by the Spirit* to go to Jerusalem. I don't know what awaits me, [23] except that the Holy Spirit tells me in city after city that jail and suffering lie ahead. [24] But my life is worth nothing to me unless I use it for finishing the work assigned me by the Lord Jesus—the work of telling others the Good News about the wonderful grace of God.

[25] "And now I know that none of you to whom I have preached the Kingdom will ever see me again. [26] I declare today that I have been faithful. If anyone suffers eternal death, it's not my fault,* [27] for I didn't shrink from declaring all that God wants you to know.

[28] "So guard yourselves and God's people. Feed and shepherd God's flock—his church, purchased with his own blood*—over which the Holy Spirit has appointed you as elders.* [29] I know that false teachers, like vicious wolves, will come in among you after I leave, not sparing the flock. [30] Even some men from your own group will rise up and distort the truth in order to draw a following. [31] Watch out! Remember the three years I was with you—my constant watch and care over you night and day, and my many tears for you.

[32] "And now I entrust you to God and the message of his grace that is able to build you up and give you an inheritance with all those he has set apart for himself.

[33] "I have never coveted anyone's silver or gold or fine clothes. [34] You know that these hands of mine have worked to supply my own needs and even the needs of those who were with me. [35] And I have been a constant example of how you can help those in need by working hard. You should remember the words of the Lord Jesus: 'It is more blessed to give than to receive.' "

[36] When he had finished speaking, he knelt and prayed with them. [37] They all cried as they embraced and kissed him good-bye. [38] They were sad most of all because he had said that they would never see him again. Then they escorted him down to the ship.

Paul's Journey to Jerusalem

21 After saying farewell to the Ephesian elders, we sailed straight to the island of Cos. The next day we reached Rhodes and then went to Patara. [2] There we boarded a ship sailing for Phoenicia. [3] We sighted the island of Cyprus, passed it on our left, and landed at the harbor of Tyre, in Syria, where the ship was to unload its cargo.

[4] We went ashore, found the local believers,* and stayed with them a week. These believers prophesied through the Holy Spirit that Paul should not go on to Jerusalem. [5] When we returned to the ship at the end of the week, the entire congregation, including women* and children, left the city and came down to the shore with us. There we knelt, prayed, [6] and said our farewells. Then we went aboard, and they returned home.

[7] The next stop after leaving Tyre was Ptolemais, where we greeted the brothers and sisters*

20:15 Some manuscripts read *and having stayed at Trogyllium.* **20:22** Or *by my spirit,* or *by an inner compulsion;* Greek reads *by the spirit.* **20:26** Greek *I am innocent of the blood of all.* **20:28a** Or *with the blood of his own [Son].* **20:28b** Greek *overseers.* **21:4** Greek *disciples;* also in 21:16. **21:5** Or *wives.*

20:13–38 Paul Meets the Ephesian Elders. Here Paul delivers his moving farewell speech. Such speeches were customarily recorded following a well-established literary pattern, but that does not mean that Luke invents empty rhetoric. As with all the speeches and sermons in Acts, Luke gives us a summary, but one that carefully captures the essence of what was said. It is a poignant glimpse into the way Paul reflected on his missionary service.

and stayed for one day. [8]The next day we went on to Caesarea and stayed at the home of Philip the Evangelist, one of the seven men who had been chosen to distribute food. [9]He had four unmarried daughters who had the gift of prophecy.

[10]Several days later a man named Agabus, who also had the gift of prophecy, arrived from Judea. [11]He came over, took Paul's belt, and bound his own feet and hands with it. Then he said, "The Holy Spirit declares, 'So shall the owner of this belt be bound by the Jewish leaders in Jerusalem and turned over to the Gentiles.' " [12]When we heard this, we and the local believers all begged Paul not to go on to Jerusalem.

[13]But he said, "Why all this weeping? You are breaking my heart! I am ready not only to be jailed at Jerusalem but even to die for the sake of the Lord Jesus." [14]When it was clear that we couldn't persuade him, we gave up and said, "The Lord's will be done."

Paul Arrives at Jerusalem

[15]After this we packed our things and left for Jerusalem. [16]Some believers from Caesarea accompanied us, and they took us to the home of Mnason, a man originally from Cyprus and one of the early believers. [17]When we arrived, the brothers and sisters in Jerusalem welcomed us warmly.

[18]The next day Paul went with us to meet with James, and all the elders of the Jerusalem church were present. [19]After greeting them, Paul gave a detailed account of the things God had accomplished among the Gentiles through his ministry.

[20]After hearing this, they praised God. And then they said, "You know, dear brother, how many thousands of Jews have also believed, and they all follow the law of Moses very seriously. [21]But the Jewish believers here in Jerusalem have been told that you are teaching all the Jews who live among the Gentiles to turn their backs on the laws of Moses. They've heard that you teach them not to circumcise their children or follow other Jewish customs. [22]What should we do? They will certainly hear that you have come.

[23]"Here's what we want you to do. We have four men here who have completed their vow. [24]Go with them to the Temple and join them in the purification ceremony, paying for them to have their heads ritually shaved. Then everyone will know that the rumors are all false and that you yourself observe the Jewish laws.

[25]"As for the Gentile believers, they should do what we already told them in a letter: They should abstain from eating food offered to idols, from consuming blood or the meat of strangled animals, and from sexual immorality."

Paul Is Arrested

[26]So Paul went to the Temple the next day with the other men. They had already started the purification ritual, so he publicly announced the date when their vows would end and sacrifices would be offered for each of them.

[27]The seven days were almost ended when some Jews from the province of Asia saw Paul in the Temple and roused a mob against him. They grabbed him, [28]yelling, "Men of Israel, help us! This is the man who preaches against our people everywhere and tells everybody to disobey the Jewish laws. He speaks against the Temple—and even defiles this holy place by bringing in Gentiles.*" [29](For earlier that day they had seen him in the city with Trophimus, a Gentile from Ephe-

21:7 Greek *brothers;* also in 21:17. **21:28** Greek *Greeks.*

21:1–14 Paul's Journey to Jerusalem. Leaving the coast, they sail across the open sea to Tyre and then on to Caesarea. **9:** That Philip's daughters were all unmarried probably means that they were below marriageable age, that is, younger than sixteen. This is surely an example of the fulfillment of Joel's prophecy, quoted by Peter at Pentecost (2:17–18).

21:15–25 Paul Arrives at Jerusalem. The leaders of the Jerusalem church are still nervous about Jewish believers' perceptions of Gentile believers, especially the ongoing unhappiness that the latter practiced neither circumcision nor all the requirements of the Mosaic law. The council of Acts 15 had not settled the question decisively enough, at least for some of the rank-and-file Jewish Christians. Perhaps there were those who were willing to turn a blind eye to what happened far away but could not cope with the decision being implemented under their noses. There are sensitivities about what is appropriate in different cultural contexts and a struggle to discern what is acceptable cultural contextualization and what is syncretism, violating principles.

21:26–36 Paul Is Arrested. Paul is still a Jew, albeit a Christian Jew, and the leaders urge him to observe the rites of purification and to support four men who will also undertake them. This he is happy to do, apparently convinced that to do so does not compromise the gospel fundamental that salvation is by grace through faith, and not through circumcision or law keeping. However, some Jews stir up trouble, accusing Paul of disobeying Mosaic laws and of bringing Gentiles into areas of the Temple forbidden

sus,* and they assumed Paul had taken him into
the Temple.)
30 The whole city was rocked by these accusations, and a great riot followed. Paul was grabbed
and dragged out of the Temple, and immediately
the gates were closed behind him. 31 As they were
trying to kill him, word reached the commander
of the Roman regiment that all Jerusalem was
in an uproar. 32 He immediately called out his
soldiers and officers* and ran down among the
crowd. When the mob saw the commander and
the troops coming, they stopped beating Paul.
33 Then the commander arrested him and
ordered him bound with two chains. He asked
the crowd who he was and what he had done.
34 Some shouted one thing and some another.
Since he couldn't find out the truth in all the
uproar and confusion, he ordered that Paul
be taken to the fortress. 35 As Paul reached the
stairs, the mob grew so violent the soldiers had
to lift him to their shoulders to protect him.
36 And the crowd followed behind, shouting,
"Kill him, kill him!"

Paul Speaks to the Crowd

37 As Paul was about to be taken inside, he said to
the commander, "May I have a word with you?"
"Do you know Greek?" the commander asked,
surprised. 38 "Aren't you the Egyptian who led a
rebellion some time ago and took 4,000 members
of the Assassins out into the desert?"
39 "No," Paul replied, "I am a Jew and a citizen
of Tarsus in Cilicia, which is an important city.
Please, let me talk to these people." 40 The commander agreed, so Paul stood on the stairs and
motioned to the people to be quiet. Soon a deep
silence enveloped the crowd, and he addressed
them in their own language, Aramaic.*

22 "Brothers and esteemed fathers,"
Paul said, "listen to me as I offer my
defense." 2 When they heard him
speaking in their own language,* the silence was
even greater.
3 Then Paul said, "I am a Jew, born in Tarsus, a
city in Cilicia, and I was brought up and educated
here in Jerusalem under Gamaliel. As his student,
I was carefully trained in our Jewish laws and
customs. I became very zealous to honor God in
everything I did, just like all of you today. 4 And
I persecuted the followers of the Way, hounding
some to death, arresting both men and women
and throwing them in prison. 5 The high priest
and the whole council of elders can testify that
this is so. For I received letters from them to our
Jewish brothers in Damascus, authorizing me to
bring the Christians from there to Jerusalem, in
chains, to be punished.
6 "As I was on the road, approaching Damascus about noon, a very bright light from heaven
suddenly shone down around me. 7 I fell to the
ground and heard a voice saying to me, 'Saul,
Saul, why are you persecuting me?'
8 " 'Who are you, lord?' I asked.
"And the voice replied, 'I am Jesus the Nazarene,* the one you are persecuting.' 9 The people
with me saw the light but didn't understand the
voice speaking to me.
10 "I asked, 'What should I do, Lord?'
"And the Lord told me, 'Get up and go into
Damascus, and there you will be told everything
you are to do.'
11 "I was blinded by the intense light and had
to be led by the hand to Damascus by my companions. 12 A man named Ananias lived there.
He was a godly man, deeply devoted to the law,
and well regarded by all the Jews of Damascus.
13 He came and stood beside me and said, 'Brother
Saul, regain your sight.' And that very moment
I could see him!
14 "Then he told me, 'The God of our ancestors
has chosen you to know his will and to see the
Righteous One and hear him speak. 15 For you are
to be his witness, telling everyone what you have
seen and heard. 16 What are you waiting for? Get
up and be baptized. Have your sins washed away
by calling on the name of the Lord.'
17 "After I returned to Jerusalem, I was praying in the Temple and fell into a trance. 18 I saw
a vision of Jesus* saying to me, 'Hurry! Leave
Jerusalem, for the people here won't accept your
testimony about me.'
19 " 'But Lord,' I argued, 'they certainly know
that in every synagogue I imprisoned and beat
those who believed in you. 20 And I was in complete agreement when your witness Stephen was
killed. I stood by and kept the coats they took off
when they stoned him.'
21 "But the Lord said to me, 'Go, for I will send
you far away to the Gentiles!' "

21:29 Greek *Trophimus, the Ephesian.* **21:32** Greek *centurions.* **21:40** Or *Hebrew.* **22:2** Greek *in Aramaic,* or *in Hebrew.* **22:8** Or *Jesus of Nazareth.* **22:18** Greek *him.*

to them. **31–32:** Paul would probably have been torn limb from limb had it not been for the intervention of soldiers from the Roman fortress close by.

21:37—22:23 Paul Speaks to the Crowd. The commander of the fortress mistakenly assumes that Paul is a notorious wanted Egyptian assassin, but when

22 The crowd listened until Paul said that
word. Then they all began to shout, "Away with
such a fellow! He isn't fit to live!" 23 They yelled,
threw off their coats, and tossed handfuls of dust
into the air.

Paul Reveals His Roman Citizenship

24 The commander brought Paul inside and ordered him lashed with whips to make him confess his crime. He wanted to find out why the
crowd had become so furious. 25 When they tied
Paul down to lash him, Paul said to the officer*
standing there, "Is it legal for you to whip a Roman citizen who hasn't even been tried?"
26 When the officer heard this, he went to the
commander and asked, "What are you doing?
This man is a Roman citizen!"
27 So the commander went over and asked
Paul, "Tell me, are you a Roman citizen?"
"Yes, I certainly am," Paul replied.
28 "I am, too," the commander muttered, "and
it cost me plenty!"
Paul answered, "But I am a citizen by birth!"
29 The soldiers who were about to interrogate
Paul quickly withdrew when they heard he was a
Roman citizen, and the commander was frightened
because he had ordered him bound and whipped.

Paul before the High Council

30 The next day the commander ordered the leading priests into session with the Jewish high
council.* He wanted to find out what the trouble
was all about, so he released Paul to have him
stand before them.

23 Gazing intently at the high council,*
Paul began: "Brothers, I have always
lived before God with a clear conscience!"
2 Instantly Ananias the high priest commanded
those close to Paul to slap him on the mouth. 3 But
Paul said to him, "God will slap you, you corrupt
hypocrite!* What kind of judge are you to break
the law yourself by ordering me struck like that?"
4 Those standing near Paul said to him, "Do
you dare to insult God's high priest?"
5 "I'm sorry, brothers. I didn't realize he was the
high priest," Paul replied, "for the Scriptures say,
'You must not speak evil of any of your rulers.'* "
6 Paul realized that some members of the high
council were Sadducees and some were Pharisees, so he shouted, "Brothers, I am a Pharisee,
as were my ancestors! And I am on trial because
my hope is in the resurrection of the dead!"
7 This divided the council—the Pharisees
against the Sadducees—8 for the Sadducees say
there is no resurrection or angels or spirits, but the
Pharisees believe in all of these. 9 So there was a
great uproar. Some of the teachers of religious law
who were Pharisees jumped up and began to argue forcefully. "We see nothing wrong with him,"
they shouted. "Perhaps a spirit or an angel spoke
to him." 10 As the conflict grew more violent, the
commander was afraid they would tear Paul apart.
So he ordered his soldiers to go and rescue him by
force and take him back to the fortress.
11 That night the Lord appeared to Paul and
said, "Be encouraged, Paul. Just as you have been
a witness to me here in Jerusalem, you must
preach the Good News in Rome as well."

The Plan to Kill Paul

12 The next morning a group of Jews* got together and bound themselves with an oath not to eat

22:25 Greek *the centurion;* also in 22:26. **22:30** Greek *Sanhedrin.* **23:1** Greek *Sanhedrin;* also in 23:6, 15, 20, 28. **23:3** Greek *you whitewashed wall.* **23:5** Exod 22:28. **23:12** Greek *the Jews.*

Paul explains his identity the commander gives him permission to speak to the crowd. **22:22:** The crowd listens attentively—until Paul says that the Lord commissioned him to go to the Gentiles. Immediately an uproar breaks out again, so deep is the outrage that Paul should claim that God could possibly say such a thing. That God should be equally concerned for the Gentiles is as unacceptable to them as it had been to the Lord Jesus' audience in Nazareth (Luke 4:16–30). Paul touches a raw nerve, but he cannot and will not compromise on the universal lordship of Christ.

22:24–29 Paul Reveals His Roman Citizenship. Paul is whisked inside, where, following common custom, the commander orders him to be flogged. When Paul tells him that he is by birth a Roman citizen, the commander dare not proceed.

22:30—23:11 Paul before the High Council. The commander orders the Jewish council to assemble so that he can cross-examine them and Paul. **23:3:** When, contrary to Jewish law, the high priest orders Paul to be struck on the mouth while still unconvicted, Paul challenges him.

23:12–22 The Plan to Kill Paul. During Jewish festivals, there was a strong military presence that was not considered necessary during most times of the year. The conspirators intend to take advantage of diminished numbers of Roman soldiers to pluck the prisoner from them.

or drink until they had killed Paul. 13 There were more than forty of them in the conspiracy. 14 They went to the leading priests and elders and told them, "We have bound ourselves with an oath to eat nothing until we have killed Paul. 15 So you and the high council should ask the commander to bring Paul back to the council again. Pretend you want to examine his case more fully. We will kill him on the way."

16 But Paul's nephew—his sister's son—heard of their plan and went to the fortress and told Paul. 17 Paul called for one of the Roman officers* and said, "Take this young man to the commander. He has something important to tell him."

18 So the officer did, explaining, "Paul, the prisoner, called me over and asked me to bring this young man to you because he has something to tell you."

19 The commander took his hand, led him aside, and asked, "What is it you want to tell me?"

20 Paul's nephew told him, "Some Jews are going to ask you to bring Paul before the high council tomorrow, pretending they want to get some more information. 21 But don't do it! There are more than forty men hiding along the way ready to ambush him. They have vowed not to eat or drink anything until they have killed him. They are ready now, just waiting for your consent."

22 "Don't let anyone know you told me this," the commander warned the young man.

Paul Is Sent to Caesarea

23 Then the commander called two of his officers and ordered, "Get 200 soldiers ready to leave for Caesarea at nine o'clock tonight. Also take 200 spearmen and 70 mounted troops. 24 Provide horses for Paul to ride, and get him safely to Governor Felix." 25 Then he wrote this letter to the governor:

26 "From Claudius Lysias, to his Excellency, Governor Felix: Greetings!

27 "This man was seized by some Jews, and they were about to kill him when I arrived with the troops. When I learned that he was a Roman citizen, I removed him to safety. 28 Then I took him to their high council to try to learn the basis of the accusations against him. 29 I soon discovered the charge was something regarding their religious law—certainly nothing worthy of imprisonment or death. 30 But when I was informed of a plot to kill him, I immediately sent him on to you. I have told his accusers to bring their charges before you."

31 So that night, as ordered, the soldiers took Paul as far as Antipatris. 32 They returned to the fortress the next morning, while the mounted troops took him on to Caesarea. 33 When they arrived in Caesarea, they presented Paul and the letter to Governor Felix. 34 He read it and then asked Paul what province he was from. "Cilicia," Paul answered.

35 "I will hear your case myself when your accusers arrive," the governor told him. Then the governor ordered him kept in the prison at Herod's headquarters.*

Paul Appears before Felix

24 Five days later Ananias, the high priest, arrived with some of the Jewish elders and the lawyer* Tertullus, to present their case against Paul to the governor. 2 When Paul was called in, Tertullus presented the charges against Paul in the following address to the governor:

"You have provided a long period of peace for us Jews and with foresight have enacted reforms for us. 3 For all of this, Your Excellency, we are very grateful to you. 4 But I don't want to bore you, so please give me your attention for only a moment. 5 We have found this man to be a troublemaker who is constantly stirring up riots among the Jews all over the world. He is a ring-

23:17 Greek *centurions;* also in 23:23. **23:35** Greek *Herod's Praetorium.* **24:1** Greek *some elders and an orator.*

23:23–35 Paul Is Sent to Caesarea. The commander does not wish to risk being answerable for the death of a Roman citizen and hastens to shift the responsibility for his fate to someone else. He arranges for Paul to be taken with a formidable escort—nearly five hundred strong—to the much more secure garrison at Caesarea, where he can be turned over to the governor, Felix. The size of the escort reflects recognition of the desperate lengths to which the commander fears the Jewish leaders might go in order to murder Paul. At the time there were also bands of national dissidents who might attack a small Roman detachment.

24:1–27 Paul before Felix. The spokesman, Tertullus, begins with blatant flattery of Felix, who had been a corrupt governor. Tertullus then accuses Paul of being a political agitator, which would be of far more significance to the Roman authorities than religious squabbles. He also accuses Paul of profaning the

leader of the cult known as the Nazarenes. 6 Furthermore, he was trying to desecrate the Temple when we arrested him.* 8 You can find out the truth of our accusations by examining him yourself." 9 Then the other Jews chimed in, declaring that everything Tertullus said was true.

10 The governor then motioned for Paul to speak. Paul said, "I know, sir, that you have been a judge of Jewish affairs for many years, so I gladly present my defense before you. 11 You can quickly discover that I arrived in Jerusalem no more than twelve days ago to worship at the Temple. 12 My accusers never found me arguing with anyone in the Temple, nor stirring up a riot in any synagogue or on the streets of the city. 13 These men cannot prove the things they accuse me of doing.

14 "But I admit that I follow the Way, which they call a cult. I worship the God of our ancestors, and I firmly believe the Jewish law and everything written in the prophets. 15 I have the same hope in God that these men have, that he will raise both the righteous and the unrighteous. 16 Because of this, I always try to maintain a clear conscience before God and all people.

17 "After several years away, I returned to Jerusalem with money to aid my people and to offer sacrifices to God. 18 My accusers saw me in the Temple as I was completing a purification ceremony. There was no crowd around me and no rioting. 19 But some Jews from the province of Asia were there—and they ought to be here to bring charges if they have anything against me! 20 Ask these men here what crime the Jewish high council* found me guilty of, 21 except for the one time I shouted out, 'I am on trial before you today because I believe in the resurrection of the dead!' "

22 At that point Felix, who was quite familiar with the Way, adjourned the hearing and said, "Wait until Lysias, the garrison commander, arrives. Then I will decide the case." 23 He ordered an officer* to keep Paul in custody but to give him some freedom and allow his friends to visit him and take care of his needs.

24 A few days later Felix came back with his wife, Drusilla, who was Jewish. Sending for Paul, they listened as he told them about faith in Christ Jesus. 25 As he reasoned with them about righteousness and self-control and the coming day of judgment, Felix became frightened. "Go away for now," he replied. "When it is more convenient, I'll call for you again." 26 He also hoped that Paul would bribe him, so he sent for him quite often and talked with him.

27 After two years went by in this way, Felix was succeeded by Porcius Festus. And because Felix wanted to gain favor with the Jewish people, he left Paul in prison.

Paul Appears before Festus

25 Three days after Festus arrived in Caesarea to take over his new responsibilities, he left for Jerusalem, 2 where the leading priests and other Jewish leaders met with him and made their accusations against Paul. 3 They asked Festus as a favor to transfer Paul to Jerusalem (planning to ambush and kill him on the way). 4 But Festus replied that Paul was at Caesarea and he himself would be returning there soon. 5 So he said, "Those of you in authority can return with me. If Paul has done anything wrong, you can make your accusations."

6 About eight or ten days later Festus returned to Caesarea, and on the following day he took his seat in court and ordered that Paul be brought in. 7 When Paul arrived, the Jewish leaders from Jerusalem gathered around and made many serious accusations they couldn't prove.

8 Paul denied the charges. "I am not guilty of any crime against the Jewish laws or the Temple or the Roman government," he said.

24:6 Some manuscripts add an expanded conclusion to verse 6, all of verse 7, and an additional phrase in verse 8: *We would have judged him by our law, 7 but Lysias, the commander of the garrison, came and violently took him away from us, 8 commanding his accusers to come before you.* **24:20** Greek *Sanhedrin.* **24:23** Greek *a centurion.*

Temple; the Roman authorities, aware of the extreme sensitivities of the Jews in respect of their holy place, would be nervous of the destabilizing impact of such an act. **21:** Paul defends himself simply, claiming to have been scrupulous in every way during his visit to Jerusalem, doing nothing to cause offense or trouble. The only thing that he could be accused of was his *one time* mention: *I believe in the resurrection of the dead.* **23:** Felix remands Paul in custody but defers sentence. Permission is given for Paul to be cared for by his friends; they would bring him food and other necessities as well as keeping him company. This implies that Felix knows that Paul is not guilty, but ongoing imprisonment is the best guarantee of his safety.

25:1–22 Paul Appears before Festus. For two years Paul was left in prison, until Felix was replaced as governor by Porcius Festus. Within days the Jewish leaders in Jerusalem were urging Festus to transfer Paul there, since they hoped to be able to ambush and kill him. This is an extraordinary comment on the

9 Then Festus, wanting to please the Jews, asked him, "Are you willing to go to Jerusalem and stand trial before me there?" 10 But Paul replied, "No! This is the official Roman court, so I ought to be tried right here. You know very well I am not guilty of harming the Jews. 11 If I have done something worthy of death, I don't refuse to die. But if I am innocent, no one has a right to turn me over to these men to kill me. I appeal to Caesar!"

12 Festus conferred with his advisers and then replied, "Very well! You have appealed to Caesar, and to Caesar you will go!"

13 A few days later King Agrippa arrived with his sister, Bernice,* to pay their respects to Festus. 14 During their stay of several days, Festus discussed Paul's case with the king. "There is a prisoner here," he told him, "whose case was left for me by Felix. 15 When I was in Jerusalem, the leading priests and Jewish elders pressed charges against him and asked me to condemn him. 16 I pointed out to them that Roman law does not convict people without a trial. They must be given an opportunity to confront their accusers and defend themselves.

17 "When his accusers came here for the trial, I didn't delay. I called the case the very next day and ordered Paul brought in. 18 But the accusations made against him weren't any of the crimes I expected. 19 Instead, it was something about their religion and a dead man named Jesus, who Paul insists is alive. 20 I was at a loss to know how to investigate these things, so I asked him whether he would be willing to stand trial on these charges in Jerusalem. 21 But Paul appealed to have his case decided by the emperor. So I ordered that he be held in custody until I could arrange to send him to Caesar."

22 "I'd like to hear the man myself," Agrippa said.

And Festus replied, "You will—tomorrow!"

Paul Speaks to Agrippa

23 So the next day Agrippa and Bernice arrived at the auditorium with great pomp, accompanied by military officers and prominent men of the city. Festus ordered that Paul be brought in. 24 Then Festus said, "King Agrippa and all who are here, this is the man whose death is demanded by all the Jews, both here and in Jerusalem. 25 But in my opinion he has done nothing deserving death. However, since he appealed his case to the emperor, I have decided to send him to Rome.

26 "But what shall I write the emperor? For there is no clear charge against him. So I have brought him before all of you, and especially you, King Agrippa, so that after we examine him, I might have something to write. 27 For it makes no sense to send a prisoner to the emperor without specifying the charges against him!"

26 Then Agrippa said to Paul, "You may speak in your defense."

So Paul, gesturing with his hand, started his defense: 2 "I am fortunate, King Agrippa, that you are the one hearing my defense today against all these accusations made by the Jewish leaders, 3 for I know you are an expert on all Jewish customs and controversies. Now please listen to me patiently!

4 "As the Jewish leaders are well aware, I was given a thorough Jewish training from my earliest childhood among my own people and in Jerusalem. 5 If they would admit it, they know that I have been a member of the Pharisees, the strictest sect of our religion. 6 Now I am on trial because of my hope in the fulfillment of God's promise made to our ancestors. 7 In fact, that is why the twelve tribes of Israel zealously worship God night and day, and they share the same hope I have. Yet, Your Majesty, they accuse me for having this hope! 8 Why does it seem incredible to any of you that God can raise the dead?

9 "I used to believe that I ought to do everything I could to oppose the very name of Jesus the Nazarene.* 10 Indeed, I did just that in Jerusalem. Authorized by the leading priests, I caused many believers* there to be sent to prison. And I cast my vote against them when they were condemned to death. 11 Many times I had them punished in the synagogues to get them to curse Jesus.* I was so violently opposed to them that I even chased them down in foreign cities.

12 "One day I was on such a mission to Damascus, armed with the authority and commission of the leading priests. 13 About noon, Your

25:13 Greek *Agrippa the king and Bernice arrived.* **26:9** Or *Jesus of Nazareth.* **26:10** Greek *many of God's holy people.* **26:11** Greek *to blaspheme.*

festering sore Paul's survival was to them and probably a measure of his continuing influence despite his imprisonment. **9:** Festus is far too prudent to permit a Roman citizen to be lynched without good grounds. He offers Paul the chance to go to Jerusalem, but Paul instead appeals to his right to go before the emperor. Maybe during his long imprisonment he has concluded that this is the only way he will get to Rome. **14:** Festus asks Agrippa for advice, because the latter was conversant with Jewish and Roman law.

Majesty, as I was on the road, a light from heaven brighter than the sun shone down on me and my companions. 14 We all fell down, and I heard a voice saying to me in Aramaic,* 'Saul, Saul, why are you persecuting me? It is useless for you to fight against my will.*'

15 " 'Who are you, lord?' I asked.

"And the Lord replied, 'I am Jesus, the one you are persecuting. 16 Now get to your feet! For I have appeared to you to appoint you as my servant and witness. You are to tell the world what you have seen and what I will show you in the future. 17 And I will rescue you from both your own people and the Gentiles. Yes, I am sending you to the Gentiles 18 to open their eyes, so they may turn from darkness to light and from the power of Satan to God. Then they will receive forgiveness for their sins and be given a place among God's people, who are set apart by faith in me.'

19 "And so, King Agrippa, I obeyed that vision from heaven. 20 I preached first to those in Damascus, then in Jerusalem and throughout all Judea, and also to the Gentiles, that all must repent of their sins and turn to God—and prove they have changed by the good things they do. 21 Some Jews arrested me in the Temple for preaching this, and they tried to kill me. 22 But God has protected me right up to this present time so I can testify to everyone, from the least to the greatest. I teach nothing except what the prophets and Moses said would happen—23 that the Messiah would suffer and be the first to rise from the dead, and in this way announce God's light to Jews and Gentiles alike."

24 Suddenly, Festus shouted, "Paul, you are insane. Too much study has made you crazy!"

25 But Paul replied, "I am not insane, Most Excellent Festus. What I am saying is the sober truth. 26 And King Agrippa knows about these things. I speak boldly, for I am sure these events are all familiar to him, for they were not done in a corner! 27 King Agrippa, do you believe the prophets? I know you do—"

28 Agrippa interrupted him. "Do you think you can persuade me to become a Christian so quickly?"*

29 Paul replied, "Whether quickly or not, I pray to God that both you and everyone here in this audience might become the same as I am, except for these chains."

30 Then the king, the governor, Bernice, and all the others stood and left. 31 As they went out, they talked it over and agreed, "This man hasn't done anything to deserve death or imprisonment."

32 And Agrippa said to Festus, "He could have been set free if he hadn't appealed to Caesar."

Paul Sails for Rome

27 When the time came, we set sail for Italy. Paul and several other prisoners were placed in the custody of a Roman officer* named Julius, a captain of the Imperial Regiment. 2 Aristarchus, a Macedonian from Thessalonica, was also with us. We left on a ship whose home port was Adramyttium on the northwest coast of the province of Asia;* it was scheduled to make several stops at ports along the coast of the province.

3 The next day when we docked at Sidon, Julius was very kind to Paul and let him go ashore to visit with friends so they could provide for his needs. 4 Putting out to sea from there, we encountered strong headwinds that made it difficult to keep the ship on course, so we sailed north of Cyprus between the island and the mainland. 5 Keeping to the open sea, we passed along the coast of Cilicia and Pamphylia, landing at Myra, in the province of Lycia. 6 There the commanding officer found an Egyptian ship from Alexandria that was bound for Italy, and he put us on board.

7 We had several days of slow sailing, and after great difficulty we finally neared Cnidus. But the wind was against us, so we sailed across to Crete and along the sheltered coast of the island, past the cape of Salmone. 8 We struggled along the coast with great difficulty and finally arrived

26:14a Or *Hebrew.* **26:14b** Greek *It is hard for you to kick against the oxgoads.* **26:28** Or *"A little more, and your arguments would make me a Christian."* **27:1** Greek *centurion;* similarly in 27:6, 11, 31, 43. **27:2** *Asia* was a Roman province in what is now western Turkey.

25:23—26:32 Paul Speaks to Agrippa. Soon Paul is permitted to explain himself before Agrippa, Bernice, and Festus, and a large military and civic audience. **26:22:** Paul takes trouble to explain how Jesus is the key to the Scriptures' rightful meaning. **31–32:** Agrippa's evaluation is that Paul has done nothing justifying imprisonment under Roman law and could have been set free had he not already appealed to the emperor. Since he had, he must go to Rome. That is exactly where Paul wishes to go, and he believes God is sovereignly overruling his circumstances to take him there.

27:1–12 Paul Sails for Rome. Luke is among Paul's companions as they set sail for Italy. They are accompanied by other prisoners, all under the guard of an officer and his detachment of about eighty men. Sailing against the prevailing winds, they made slow progress.

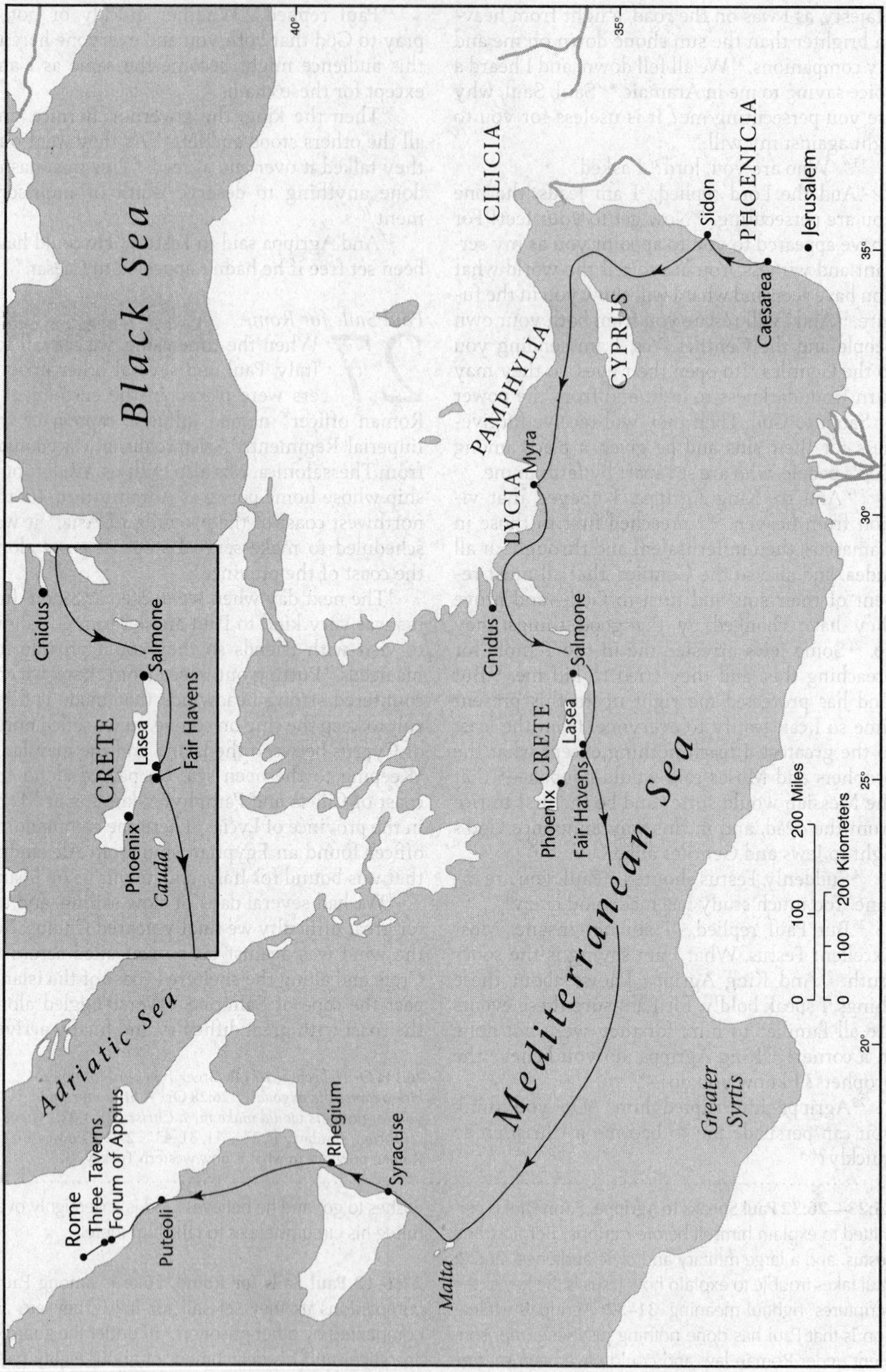

Paul's Journey to Rome

at Fair Havens, near the town of Lasea. 9 We had
lost a lot of time. The weather was becoming
dangerous for sea travel because it was so late
in the fall,* and Paul spoke to the ship's officers
about it.
10 "Men," he said, "I believe there is trouble
ahead if we go on—shipwreck, loss of cargo, and
danger to our lives as well." 11 But the officer
in charge of the prisoners listened more to the
ship's captain and the owner than to Paul. 12 And
since Fair Havens was an exposed harbor—
a poor place to spend the winter—most of the
crew wanted to go on to Phoenix, farther up the
coast of Crete, and spend the winter there. Phoenix was a good harbor with only a southwest and
northwest exposure.

The Storm at Sea

13 When a light wind began blowing from the
south, the sailors thought they could make it.
So they pulled up anchor and sailed close to
the shore of Crete. 14 But the weather changed
abruptly, and a wind of typhoon strength (called
a "northeaster") burst across the island and blew
us out to sea. 15 The sailors couldn't turn the ship
into the wind, so they gave up and let it run before the gale.
16 We sailed along the sheltered side of a small
island named Cauda,* where with great difficulty we hoisted aboard the lifeboat being towed
behind us. 17 Then the sailors bound ropes around
the hull of the ship to strengthen it. They were
afraid of being driven across to the sandbars of
Syrtis off the African coast, so they lowered the
sea anchor to slow the ship and were driven before the wind.
18 The next day, as gale-force winds continued
to batter the ship, the crew began throwing the
cargo overboard. 19 The following day they even
took some of the ship's gear and threw it overboard. 20 The terrible storm raged for many days,
blotting out the sun and the stars, until at last all
hope was gone.
21 No one had eaten for a long time. Finally,
Paul called the crew together and said, "Men,
you should have listened to me in the first place
and not left Crete. You would have avoided all
this damage and loss. 22 But take courage! None
of you will lose your lives, even though the ship
will go down. 23 For last night an angel of the God
to whom I belong and whom I serve stood beside me, 24 and he said, 'Don't be afraid, Paul, for
you will surely stand trial before Caesar! What's
more, God in his goodness has granted safety to
everyone sailing with you.' 25 So take courage!
For I believe God. It will be just as he said. 26 But
we will be shipwrecked on an island."

The Shipwreck

27 About midnight on the fourteenth night of the
storm, as we were being driven across the Sea of
Adria,* the sailors sensed land was near. 28 They
dropped a weighted line and found that the water
was 120 feet deep. But a little later they measured again and found it was only 90 feet deep.*
29 At this rate they were afraid we would soon be
driven against the rocks along the shore, so they
threw out four anchors from the back of the ship
and prayed for daylight.
30 Then the sailors tried to abandon the ship;
they lowered the lifeboat as though they were
going to put out anchors from the front of the
ship. 31 But Paul said to the commanding officer
and the soldiers, "You will all die unless the sailors stay aboard." 32 So the soldiers cut the ropes
to the lifeboat and let it drift away.
33 Just as day was dawning, Paul urged everyone to eat. "You have been so worried that you
haven't touched food for two weeks," he said.
34 "Please eat something now for your own good.
For not a hair of your heads will perish." 35 Then
he took some bread, gave thanks to God before
them all, and broke off a piece and ate it. 36 Then
everyone was encouraged and began to eat—37 all
276 of us who were on board. 38 After eating, the
crew lightened the ship further by throwing the
cargo of wheat overboard.
39 When morning dawned, they didn't recognize the coastline, but they saw a bay with a
beach and wondered if they could get to shore by
running the ship aground. 40 So they cut off the
anchors and left them in the sea. Then they lowered the rudders, raised the foresail, and headed

27:9 Greek *because the fast was now already gone by.* This fast was associated with the Day of Atonement (*Yom Kippur*), which occurred in late September or early October.
27:16 Some manuscripts read *Clauda.* **27:27** The *Sea of Adria* includes the central portion of the Mediterranean.
27:28 Greek *20 fathoms . . . 15 fathoms* [37 meters . . . 27 meters].

27:13–26 The Storm at Sea. The wiser course would have been to have wintered in Crete, but instead they are caught in a terrible storm. Despite throwing the cargo overboard to lighten the load, the crew and their passengers lose hope of surviving. The ship must have been large, for Luke tells us that there were 276 people on board.

27:27–44 The Shipwreck. Reassured in a dream, Paul is confident that he and his companions will survive

toward shore. 41 But they hit a shoal and ran the ship aground too soon. The bow of the ship stuck fast, while the stern was repeatedly smashed by the force of the waves and began to break apart.

42 The soldiers wanted to kill the prisoners to make sure they didn't swim ashore and escape. 43 But the commanding officer wanted to spare Paul, so he didn't let them carry out their plan. Then he ordered all who could swim to jump overboard first and make for land. 44 The others held on to planks or debris from the broken ship.* So everyone escaped safely to shore.

Paul on the Island of Malta

28 Once we were safe on shore, we learned that we were on the island of Malta. 2 The people of the island were very kind to us. It was cold and rainy, so they built a fire on the shore to welcome us.

3 As Paul gathered an armful of sticks and was laying them on the fire, a poisonous snake, driven out by the heat, bit him on the hand. 4 The people of the island saw it hanging from his hand and said to each other, "A murderer, no doubt! Though he escaped the sea, justice will not permit him to live." 5 But Paul shook off the snake into the fire and was unharmed. 6 The people waited for him to swell up or suddenly drop dead. But when they had waited a long time and saw that he wasn't harmed, they changed their minds and decided he was a god.

7 Near the shore where we landed was an estate belonging to Publius, the chief official of the island. He welcomed us and treated us kindly for three days. 8 As it happened, Publius's father was ill with fever and dysentery. Paul went in and prayed for him, and laying his hands on him, he healed him. 9 Then all the other sick people on the island came and were healed. 10 As a result we were showered with honors, and when the time came to sail, people supplied us with everything we would need for the trip.

Paul Arrives at Rome

11 It was three months after the shipwreck that we set sail on another ship that had wintered at the island—an Alexandrian ship with the twin gods* as its figurehead. 12 Our first stop was Syracuse,* where we stayed three days. 13 From there we sailed across to Rhegium.* A day later a south wind began blowing, so the following day we sailed up the coast to Puteoli. 14 There we found some believers,* who invited us to spend a week with them. And so we came to Rome.

15 The brothers and sisters* in Rome had heard we were coming, and they came to meet us at the Forum* on the Appian Way. Others joined us at The Three Taverns.* When Paul saw them, he was encouraged and thanked God.

16 When we arrived in Rome, Paul was permitted to have his own private lodging, though he was guarded by a soldier.

Paul Preaches at Rome under Guard

17 Three days after Paul's arrival, he called together the local Jewish leaders. He said to them, "Brothers, I was arrested in Jerusalem and handed over to the Roman government, even though I had done nothing against our people or the cus-

27:44 Or *or were helped by members of the ship's crew.*
28:11 The *twin gods* were the Roman gods Castor and Pollux.
28:12 *Syracuse* was on the island of Sicily. **28:13** *Rhegium* was on the southern tip of Italy. **28:14** Greek *brothers.*
28:15a Greek *brothers.* **28:15b** *The Forum* was about 43 miles (70 kilometers) from Rome. **28:15c** *The Three Taverns* was about 35 miles (57 kilometers) from Rome.

---

and reach dry land. He encourages the desperate men with his calm assurance. **44:** By the grace of God, not one person is drowned. Even on a calm voyage that would have been unusual; in these circumstances it is miraculous. Luke emphasizes the way in which God is protecting Paul in order that his Word might be fulfilled.

28:1–10 On Malta. After two terrifying weeks they run aground on Malta. Luke gives us a vivid description, complete with many specific details, about the final frightening days of the voyage and then the dramatic process of getting to shore. **5–6:** When Paul is bitten by a snake, those around him superstitiously assume this is judgment for wickedness: he should not have cheated death at sea. When Paul is none the worse for his snakebite, their superstition swings to the opposite extreme: he must be not a criminal but a god.

28:11–16 Paul Arrives at Rome. Paul and his companions sail past Sicily and come to the port of Puteoli, where they are able to spend a week with believers, an indication of the spread of the gospel to the Italian peninsula. Finally they come to Rome, the destination Paul has had his heart set on for so many years. Perhaps he might never have chosen to come through such painful suffering, but he is convinced that God has mercifully ordained his circumstances every step of the way.

28:17–31 Paul Preaches at Rome. Despite being called to take the gospel to the Gentiles, Paul never lost his great longing to see his own people come to

toms of our ancestors. [18]The Romans tried me
and wanted to release me, because they found
no cause for the death sentence. [19]But when the
Jewish leaders protested the decision, I felt it necessary to appeal to Caesar, even though I had no
desire to press charges against my own people.
[20]I asked you to come here today so we could get
acquainted and so I could explain to you that I
am bound with this chain because I believe that
the hope of Israel—the Messiah—has already
come."

[21]They replied, "We have had no letters from
Judea or reports against you from anyone who
has come here. [22]But we want to hear what you
believe, for the only thing we know about this
movement is that it is denounced everywhere."

[23]So a time was set, and on that day a large
number of people came to Paul's lodging. He explained and testified about the Kingdom of God
and tried to persuade them about Jesus from the
Scriptures. Using the law of Moses and the books
of the prophets, he spoke to them from morning until evening. [24]Some were persuaded by the
things he said, but others did not believe. [25]And
after they had argued back and forth among
themselves, they left with this final word from
Paul: "The Holy Spirit was right when he said to
your ancestors through Isaiah the prophet,

[26] 'Go and say to this people:
When you hear what I say,
 you will not understand.
When you see what I do,
 you will not comprehend.
[27] For the hearts of these people are hardened,
 and their ears cannot hear,
 and they have closed their eyes—
so their eyes cannot see,
 and their ears cannot hear,
 and their hearts cannot understand,
and they cannot turn to me
 and let me heal them.'*

[28]So I want you to know that this salvation from
God has also been offered to the Gentiles, and
they will accept it."*

[30]For the next two years, Paul lived in Rome
at his own expense.* He welcomed all who visited him, [31]boldly proclaiming the Kingdom of
God and teaching about the Lord Jesus Christ.
And no one tried to stop him.

28:26-27 Isa 6:9-10 (Greek version). **28:28** Some manuscripts add verse 29, *And when he had said these words, the Jews departed, greatly disagreeing with each other.* **28:30** Or *in his own rented quarters.*

faith in Christ. At once he gathers the Jewish leaders and insists that he is guilty of no offense against the Jews. His one great desire is to be able to convince them that Jesus is their Messiah and that truly he has risen from the dead. **30:** Luke's marvelous account ends on a triumphant note. For two years Paul had a full and fruitful ministry, without any problems from the Roman authorities. His desire to carry the gospel of Jesus, the risen Messiah, to the heart of the Gentile world is granted by the grace of God. Luke does not tell us the end of Paul's story. Perhaps in the mind of God it is of little significance, at least in the grand scheme of things. We may be curious, but we do not need to know. After all, we do not follow Paul but Jesus Christ, and it is Christ's death, not Paul's, that is the foundation of the church.

ROMANS

INTRODUCTION

No other epistle of Paul has had such an impact on the Christian faith throughout history. In a comprehensive way, the letter to the Romans addresses the concepts of sin, salvation, and sanctification. Paul's goal is to explain God's salvation plan in relation to Jews and Gentiles as groups, thereby strengthening and reassuring individual believers.

The epistle has relevance for women, especially in its explication of sin and forgiving grace. This good news is urgently needed by many women, some of whom are willing to accept abuse because they are under the delusion that they deserve punishment for some misdeed in their past. Romans tells of universal sin and the free offer of forgiveness through the atoning work of Christ. For women struggling under a load of guilt, how blessed is the affirmation that there is now no condemnation for those who believe! Paul offers profound insight into the reality of a life liberated from besetting sin. Each believer is summoned to utilize her or his gift in ministry to the body of Christ and to those outside of it (Rom 12). The letter ends with the most extensive list of Christian women known in the New Testament.

Throughout the centuries, women have been defined as daughters, wives, and mothers first—and as disciples second. Or perhaps more accurately, women have been told that their Christian behavior is best defined as being a good daughter, a good wife, a good mother. Romans challenges that position by requiring each woman to take seriously her call before God. Paul asserts that all believers, women and men, must first be disciples. That self-identity then informs the various roles a woman might play in her family group, including daughter, wife, and mother, but perhaps extending to church, community, and occupational leadership service.

There is no dispute concerning the authorship of this letter; all scholars agree that Paul composed it. This conclusion is based on the familiar style and language as well as the theology and ethics found in other works by the apostle.

It is likely that Paul wrote Romans from Corinth in about AD 57 to 58. This dating is supported by Acts 20:2–3, which says that Paul spent some time in Corinth before traveling to Jerusalem with a financial gift collected from his churches (1 Cor 16:1; 2 Cor 8—9). He wrote Romans before delivering this gift (Rom 15:25–28), in anticipation of coming to Rome and then going on to Spain.

Paul explains that he is writing to the church at Rome, addressing those from among the nations (1:5–6, 13; see also 6:17–22; 11:13; 15:14–21). Some interpreters argue that he is also speaking to Jewish believers in the church, citing the discussion about the place of Israel in God's salvation plan (esp. 9:1—11:16; 7:1). Romans 16 greets several Jewish believers who are in Rome. Probably they were among the many Jews and Jewish Christians who had been expelled by Claudius in AD 49 and returned to Rome after his death in 54. Paul met these expelled Jewish believers in other cities, most notably Priscilla and Aquila in Corinth and later Ephesus (Acts 18:2).

Aside from Romans 16, where Paul greets old friends, it is probable that Gentiles are his intended readers. Some of these Gentiles might have been sympathetic to and familiar with Judaism and the synagogue, where they would have become familiar with the Greek translation of the Jewish Bible (see Acts 10:1–2; 17:4; 18:7). A significant number of women converted to Judaism in this time, and their activities and enthusiastic adherence aroused literary comment.

While no one seriously questions that Paul wrote Romans, there is no consensus as to *why* he wrote it. Because he is not personally known to the Roman church, it is possible that he explains much about his mission and teachings by way of introducing himself. It is less likely that Paul wanted to write a summary of his theology, a sort of last will and testament. This theory does not explain the ethical instructions of Romans 14—15. Moreover, not all of his theology is addressed in Romans. For example, he does not speak on communion, on the makeup of the church, or on the second coming of Jesus Christ, each a crucial component of Paul's theology. It is important to keep in mind that this is not a sermon or systematic theology lecture but a well-composed and articulated letter, one directed to a particular church that Paul had not visited (1:8).

The problems faced by the Roman church seem to concern the relationship between Jews and Gentiles, especially as that relates to God's overall plan of salvation for humankind. There is no hint of a group stirring up discord, but there is evidence that the relationship between the law given to Moses and the work of Christ, especially as it pertains to Gentiles, was a live issue. This explains why Paul placed so much emphasis on the proper interpretation of the law (3:1—4:25), as well as the place of Gentiles and Israel in God's salvation plan (9:1—11:32).

There has been a tendency in the interpretation of this letter to minimize the historic situation of the Gentiles' grappling for a proper understanding of a right relationship with God through Christ, and the Jews' struggle for an understanding of Jesus' work as Messiah. Romans is often read as though it spoke primarily to the individual, answering the question "How can I be saved?" It is true that Romans 5—6 stresses individual responsibility to God in Christ, but that is done in a context of explaining how God, from the beginning of creation, has worked out his salvation plan. It has always been by faith that one is made right with God, and God has always desired that the Gentiles share in his love.

Rome at this time was the center of the Mediterranean world. The city included people from all parts of the empire and boasted about thirteen congregations. Later Christian tradition claims that Peter began the church there and that Paul was martyred there under Nero in the early sixties. No concrete evidence supports these claims, and it is possible that Roman Jews who were in Jerusalem for the first Christian Pentecost took their new faith with them when they returned to Rome.

There is concern about the last two chapters of the letter, as some ancient manuscript and commentary evidence indicates that certain writers knew only the first fourteen chapters of Romans. Marcion, a second-century heretic, was the first person to make a collection of several of Paul's letters, and his Romans letter was reported to end with 14:23. Irenaeus, Cyprian, and Tertullian, notable church fathers, do not quote from Romans 15—16 in their writings. But this argument from silence is not convincing proof that Romans was expanded, especially because all the Greek manuscripts of Romans contain the full text. Moreover, from a literary standpoint, Paul's argument in Romans 14 is clearly continued in Romans 15. Again, there is some speculation that Romans 16 was a personal letter intended to be sent to Ephesus. This theory is fueled by the fact that the oldest evidence of Romans (ca. AD 200) includes the doxology of 16:25–27 between 15:33 and 16:1, and then adds the rest of chapter 16. It is more likely, however, that the Jews whom Paul knew and greeted in this chapter had moved or returned to Rome. Thus it is best to view Romans as originally including sixteen chapters penned by Paul from Corinth to Rome. —*Lynn H. Cohick*

1:1–7	Greetings from Paul
1:8—2:16	Gentiles Sin against God
2:17—4:25	Jews Sin against God
5:1–21	Jesus Reconciles Believers to God
6:1—7:25	Sin and the Law Work against Faith
8:1–39	The Holy Spirit Indwells the Believer
9:1—11:36	Jews and Gentiles in God's Salvation Plan
12:1—15:13	Transformed Behavior for the Believer
15:14—16:27	Personal Greetings

✧

Greetings from Paul

1 This letter is from Paul, a slave of Christ
Jesus, chosen by God to be an apostle and
sent out to preach his Good News. 2 God
promised this Good News long ago through his
prophets in the holy Scriptures. 3 The Good News
is about his Son. In his earthly life he was born
into King David's family line, 4 and he was shown
to be* the Son of God when he was raised from
the dead by the power of the Holy Spirit.* He is
Jesus Christ our Lord. 5 Through Christ, God has
given us the privilege* and authority as apostles
to tell Gentiles everywhere what God has done
for them, so that they will believe and obey him,
bringing glory to his name.

6 And you are included among those Gentiles
who have been called to belong to Jesus Christ.
7 I am writing to all of you in Rome who are
loved by God and are called to be his own holy
people.

May God our Father and the Lord Jesus Christ
give you grace and peace.

God's Good News

8 Let me say first that I thank my God through
Jesus Christ for all of you, because your faith
in him is being talked about all over the world.
9 God knows how often I pray for you. Day and
night I bring you and your needs in prayer to
God, whom I serve with all my heart* by spreading the Good News about his Son.

10 One of the things I always pray for is the
opportunity, God willing, to come at last to see
you. 11 For I long to visit you so I can bring you
some spiritual gift that will help you grow strong
in the Lord. 12 When we get together, I want to
encourage you in your faith, but I also want to
be encouraged by yours.

13 I want you to know, dear brothers and sisters,* that I planned many times to visit you,
but I was prevented until now. I want to work

1:4a Or *and was designated.* **1:4b** Or *by the Spirit of holiness; or in the new realm of the Spirit.* **1:5** Or *the grace.* **1:9** Or *in my spirit.* **1:13** Greek *brothers.*

1:1–7 Greetings from Paul

Paul understands himself as a slave or servant belonging to Jesus. In the Greek translation of the Hebrew Bible, the Septuagint, done by Jews about two hundred years before the birth of Jesus, many prophets are described as slaves, such as Moses (2 Kgs 18:12), Joshua (Judg 2:8), and David (2 Sam 7:5). Paul also identifies himself as an apostle, chosen or set apart for God's special purpose (see also Gal 1:15). The phrase "set apart" reflects prophetic language, as in Isaiah 49:1 and Jeremiah 1:4–5. **2–4:** Paul understands the *Good News* to be the message of salvation. He asserts that the Messiah was foretold by the prophets, showing that God's plan was outlined in advance. Jesus was born a descendant of David, "as a man": here Paul juxtaposes the ideas of humanness (of David) and divine working (raised by God). Although Paul rarely talks about the earthly life of Jesus, he makes it clear that Jesus was completely human, and thus his resurrection stands as a signal of hope that all believers will likewise be raised. **7:** While Paul is called to be an apostle, those to whom he is writing are called to be God's own people, literally, "holy ones." God has called all his children to be holy.

among you and see spiritual fruit, just as I have
seen among other Gentiles. [14]For I have a great
sense of obligation to people in both the civi-
lized world and the rest of the world,* to the
educated and uneducated alike. [15]So I am eager
to come to you in Rome, too, to preach the Good
News.

[16]For I am not ashamed of this Good News
about Christ. It is the power of God at work, saving everyone who believes—the Jew first and also
the Gentile.* [17]This Good News tells us how God
makes us right in his sight. This is accomplished
from start to finish by faith. As the Scriptures
say, "It is through faith that a righteous person
has life."*

God's Anger at Sin

[18]But God shows his anger from heaven against
all sinful, wicked people who suppress the truth
by their wickedness.* [19]They know the truth
about God because he has made it obvious to
them. [20]For ever since the world was created,
people have seen the earth and sky. Through
everything God made, they can clearly see his
invisible qualities—his eternal power and divine
nature. So they have no excuse for not knowing
God.

[21]Yes, they knew God, but they wouldn't worship him as God or even give him thanks. And
they began to think up foolish ideas of what God
was like. As a result, their minds became dark
and confused. [22]Claiming to be wise, they instead
became utter fools. [23]And instead of worshiping
the glorious, ever-living God, they worshiped
idols made to look like mere people and birds and
animals and reptiles.

[24]So God abandoned them to do whatever
shameful things their hearts desired. As a result,
they did vile and degrading things with each other's bodies. [25]They traded the truth about God
for a lie. So they worshiped and served the things
God created instead of the Creator himself, who
is worthy of eternal praise! Amen. [26]That is why
God abandoned them to their shameful desires.
Even the women turned against the natural way
to have sex and instead indulged in sex with each
other. [27]And the men, instead of having normal
sexual relations with women, burned with lust
for each other. Men did shameful things with
other men, and as a result of this sin, they suffered within themselves the penalty they deserved.

[28]Since they thought it foolish to acknowledge God, he abandoned them to their foolish
thinking and let them do things that should
never be done. [29]Their lives became full of every kind of wickedness, sin, greed, hate, envy,
murder, quarreling, deception, malicious behavior, and gossip. [30]They are backstabbers, haters of God, insolent, proud, and boastful. They
invent new ways of sinning, and they disobey
their parents. [31]They refuse to understand,
break their promises, are heartless, and have no
mercy. [32]They know God's justice requires that
those who do these things deserve to die, yet
they do them anyway. Worse yet, they encourage others to do them, too.

1:14 Greek *to Greeks and barbarians.* **1:16** Greek *also the Greek.* **1:17** Or *"The righteous will live by faith."* Hab 2:4. **1:18** Or *who, by their wickedness, prevent the truth from being known.*

1:8–2:16 Gentiles Sin against God

1:8–17 God's Good News. 16: Why might one be ashamed? In 1 Corinthians 1:18–23 Paul states that the gospel is foolishness to Greeks and a stumbling block to the Jews. The Romans were heavily influenced by Greek thought and culture, so the allusion to Greek opinion is clever. Jesus' execution as a criminal was shameful by Roman standards and ridiculous to Greeks (Gentiles). It was so contrary to Jewish messianic expectation that many Jews also rejected Jesus as Messiah. **17:** The term "faith" in Paul's writings is critical. He is not speaking of a warm feeling or a set of principles. Rather, he is referring to God's objective work in raising Christ. It is Christ's faithfulness and God's righteousness that are important. Believers are to live on the basis of Jesus' faithfulness to God's purposes and promises. Because Jesus lived faithfully, believers live faithfully.

1:18–32 God's Anger at Sin. 18–25: Paul speaks of God's wrath as the flip side of salvation. He preaches salvation by faith, but he recognizes that humanity has turned from God to follow wickedness. "They" are Gentiles—that is, humanity prior to the calling of the Jewish people and those since who refuse to heed God's voice. Paul is describing the devolution of pagan religion, where humans choose to turn from God and follow their own sensual desires. **26–27:** The resultant sexual immorality includes homosexuality, which Paul decries as unnatural. Lesbianism seems to be directly addressed here by Paul, though a few scholars disagree with this reading of the Greek. **32:** The law is written on the human conscience, an innate sense possessed by all humans to determine right from wrong or to discover the natural law. Here Paul differs directly from Aristotle, who maintained that women were not endowed with a conscience.

God's Judgment of Sin

2 You may think you can condemn such people, but you are just as bad, and you have no excuse! When you say they are wicked and should be punished, you are condemning yourself, for you who judge others do these very same things. [2]And we know that God, in his justice, will punish anyone who does such things. [3]Since you judge others for doing these things, why do you think you can avoid God's judgment when you do the same things? [4]Don't you see how wonderfully kind, tolerant, and patient God is with you? Does this mean nothing to you? Can't you see that his kindness is intended to turn you from your sin?

[5]But because you are stubborn and refuse to turn from your sin, you are storing up terrible punishment for yourself. For a day of anger is coming, when God's righteous judgment will be revealed. [6]He will judge everyone according to what they have done. [7]He will give eternal life to those who keep on doing good, seeking after the glory and honor and immortality that God offers. [8]But he will pour out his anger and wrath on those who live for themselves, who refuse to obey the truth and instead live lives of wickedness. [9]There will be trouble and calamity for everyone who keeps on doing what is evil—for the Jew first and also for the Gentile.* [10]But there will be glory and honor and peace from God for all who do good—for the Jew first and also for the Gentile. [11]For God does not show favoritism.

[12]When the Gentiles sin, they will be destroyed, even though they never had God's written law. And the Jews, who do have God's law, will be judged by that law when they fail to obey it. [13]For merely listening to the law doesn't make us right with God. It is obeying the law that makes us right in his sight. [14]Even Gentiles, who do not have God's written law, show that they know his law when they instinctively obey it, even without having heard it. [15]They demonstrate that God's law is written in their hearts, for their own conscience and thoughts either accuse them or tell them they are doing right. [16]And this is the message I proclaim—that the day is coming when God, through Christ Jesus, will judge everyone's secret life.

The Jews and the Law

[17]You who call yourselves Jews are relying on God's law, and you boast about your special relationship with him. [18]You know what he wants; you know what is right because you have been taught his law. [19]You are convinced that you are a guide for the blind and a light for people who are lost in darkness. [20]You think you can instruct the ignorant and teach children the ways of God. For you are certain that God's law gives you complete knowledge and truth.

[21]Well then, if you teach others, why don't you teach yourself? You tell others not to steal, but do you steal? [22]You say it is wrong to commit adultery, but do you commit adultery? You condemn idolatry, but do you use items stolen from pagan temples?* [23]You are so proud of knowing the law, but you dishonor God by breaking it. [24]No wonder the Scriptures say, "The Gentiles blaspheme the name of God because of you."*

[25]The Jewish ceremony of circumcision has value only if you obey God's law. But if you

2:9 Greek *also for the Greek;* also in 2:10. **2:22** Greek *do you steal from temples?* **2:24** Isa 52:5 (Greek version).

2:1–16 God's Judgment of Sin. 1: Paul begins a diatribe, a method of argument common in the ancient world in which the writer engages a fictitious opponent in dialogue. The hypothetical Gentile is one who believes he or she has mastered the passions and thus despises those Gentiles who are ruled by their obsessions. Such critics do not realize that their judgmental attitude is just as hateful to God as the sins listed in Romans 1. **5–16:** God is described as the God of Jews and Gentiles. There is no distinction made in favor of Jews in the context of salvation. It is likely that Paul is arguing against the assumption that Jews will have some special benefit toward salvation. Instead, Gentiles will be judged on the revelation given them, as will the Jews. Because the Jews were given the law through Moses, they will be held to that standard. The Gentiles are accountable to the law of their conscience.

2:17—4:25 Jews Sin against God

2:17–29 The Jews and the Law. Paul turns from the proud Gentiles to the Jewish teacher of Gentiles as he introduces a new interlocutor. **17–27:** Some Jews believed that their circumcision protected them from God's wrath and that their obedience to the law was only secondary to their circumcision. Paul claims that circumcision is of no value if one's behavior does not match the obedience to the law that circumcision symbolizes. The law that the uncircumcised (Gentiles) followed is the law imprinted on their conscience, which supported the Mosaic law but was not identical to it. The lawbreaker is not a sinner who recognizes her or his sinfulness and repents, but rather is one who does not repent even in the face of the evidence against her or him. The one whom God will praise is the one who serves the Lord

don't obey God's law, you are no better off than
an uncircumcised Gentile. 26 And if the Gentiles
obey God's law, won't God declare them to be his
own people? 27 In fact, uncircumcised Gentiles
who keep God's law will condemn you Jews who
are circumcised and possess God's law but don't
obey it.
28 For you are not a true Jew just because you
were born of Jewish parents or because you have
gone through the ceremony of circumcision.
29 No, a true Jew is one whose heart is right with
God. And true circumcision is not merely obeying the letter of the law; rather, it is a change of
heart produced by God's Spirit. And a person
with a changed heart seeks praise* from God,
not from people.

God Remains Faithful

3 Then what's the advantage of being a Jew?
Is there any value in the ceremony of circumcision? 2 Yes, there are great benefits!
First of all, the Jews were entrusted with the
whole revelation of God.*
3 True, some of them were unfaithful; but just
because they were unfaithful, does that mean
God will be unfaithful? 4 Of course not! Even if
everyone else is a liar, God is true. As the Scriptures say about him,

"You will be proved right in what you say,
and you will win your case in court."*

5 "But," some might say, "our sinfulness
serves a good purpose, for it helps people see how
righteous God is. Isn't it unfair, then, for him to
punish us?" (This is merely a human point of
view.) 6 Of course not! If God were not entirely fair, how would he be qualified to judge the
world? 7 "But," someone might still argue, "how
can God condemn me as a sinner if my dishonesty highlights his truthfulness and brings him
more glory?" 8 And some people even slander us
by claiming that we say, "The more we sin, the
better it is!" Those who say such things deserve
to be condemned.

All People Are Sinners

9 Well then, should we conclude that we Jews are
better than others? No, not at all, for we have
already shown that all people, whether Jews or
Gentiles,* are under the power of sin. 10 As the
Scriptures say,

"No one is righteous—
not even one.
11 No one is truly wise;
no one is seeking God.
12 All have turned away;
all have become useless.
No one does good,
not a single one."*
13 "Their talk is foul, like the stench from an
open grave.
Their tongues are filled with lies."
"Snake venom drips from their lips."*
14 "Their mouths are full of cursing and
bitterness."*
15 "They rush to commit murder.
16 Destruction and misery always follow
them.
17 They don't know where to find peace."*
18 "They have no fear of God at all."*

19 Obviously, the law applies to those to whom
it was given, for its purpose is to keep people

2:29 Or *receives praise.* **3:2** Greek *the oracles of God.* **3:4** Ps 51:4 (Greek version). **3:9** Greek *or Greeks.* **3:10-12** Pss 14:1-3; 53:1-3 (Greek version). **3:13** Pss 5:9 (Greek version); 140:3. **3:14** Ps 10:7 (Greek version). **3:15-17** Isa 59:7-8. **3:18** Ps 36:1.

---

from a heart of obedience. **28–29:** This teaching was relevant to Paul because it allowed for the inclusion of Gentiles in the church, but today it may also be relevant to women. The rite of Jewish circumcision identified males as part of God's chosen ones, but there was no special rite that initiated women. In removing that male distinction of circumcision, Paul has leveled the ground not only between Jews and Gentiles but also between male and female.

3:1–8 God Remains Faithful. 3–7: The apostle refuses to entertain the notion that sin is acceptable because it shows God is right. Paul presupposes a moral perspective whereby a person longs to be holy before God. Yet his letters indicate that he meets people who would sooner justify their sin than consider its consequences for God's honor. **8:** The rumor that Paul advocated evil perhaps arose because he allowed Gentiles to enter the church as Gentiles (uncircumcised), hence as sinners in some people's eyes (see Gal 2:15).

3:9–20 All People Are Sinners. 9–18: Sin is more than the sum total of bad deeds done by humans; it is a force that has great influence over the earth for the present (see chaps. 5—6). Every human, Gentile and Jew, is sinful before God. **19–20:** The law brings knowledge of sin, not protection from it. The law is used by God to judge deeds but not to impute salvation. Jews and Gentiles are on equal footing, because

from having excuses, and to show that the entire world is guilty before God. [20] For no one can ever be made right with God by doing what the law commands. The law simply shows us how sinful we are.

Christ Took Our Punishment

[21] But now God has shown us a way to be made right with him without keeping the requirements of the law, as was promised in the writings of Moses* and the prophets long ago. [22] We are made right with God by placing our faith in Jesus Christ. And this is true for everyone who believes, no matter who we are.

[23] For everyone has sinned; we all fall short of God's glorious standard. [24] Yet God, with undeserved kindness, declares that we are righteous. He did this through Christ Jesus when he freed us from the penalty for our sins. [25] For God presented Jesus as the sacrifice for sin. People are made right with God when they believe that Jesus sacrificed his life, shedding his blood. This sacrifice shows that God was being fair when he held back and did not punish those who sinned in times past, [26] for he was looking ahead and including them in what he would do in this present time. God did this to demonstrate his righteousness, for he himself is fair and just, and he declares sinners to be right in his sight when they believe in Jesus.

[27] Can we boast, then, that we have done anything to be accepted by God? No, because our acquittal is not based on obeying the law. It is based on faith. [28] So we are made right with God through faith and not by obeying the law.

[29] After all, is God the God of the Jews only? Isn't he also the God of the Gentiles? Of course he is. [30] There is only one God, and he makes people right with himself only by faith, whether they are Jews or Gentiles.* [31] Well then, if we emphasize faith, does this mean that we can forget about the law? Of course not! In fact, only when we have faith do we truly fulfill the law.

The Faith of Abraham

4

Abraham was, humanly speaking, the founder of our Jewish nation. What did he discover about being made right with God? [2] If his good deeds had made him acceptable to God, he would have had something to boast about. But that was not God's way. [3] For the Scriptures tell us, "Abraham believed God, and God counted him as righteous because of his faith."*

[4] When people work, their wages are not a gift, but something they have earned. [5] But people are counted as righteous, not because of their work, but because of their faith in God who forgives sinners. [6] David also spoke of this when he described the happiness of those who are declared righteous without working for it:

[7] "Oh, what joy for those
whose disobedience is forgiven,
whose sins are put out of sight.
[8] Yes, what joy for those
whose record the LORD has cleared of sin."*

[9] Now, is this blessing only for the Jews, or is it also for uncircumcised Gentiles?* Well, we have been saying that Abraham was counted as righteous by God because of his faith. [10] But how did this happen? Was he counted as righteous only after he was circumcised, or was it before he was circumcised? Clearly, God accepted Abraham before he was circumcised!

3:21 Greek *in the law.* **3:30** Greek *whether they are circumcised or uncircumcised.* **4:3** Gen 15:6. **4:7-8** Ps 32:1-2 (Greek version). **4:9** Greek *is this blessing only for the circumcised, or is it also for the uncircumcised?*

the scales of justice are modified or personalized to reflect the person's background.

3:21–31 Christ Took Our Punishment. 21–22: Paul clarifies the place of the law in God's overall plan of salvation. The law served its purpose in pointing to God's work in the Messiah. **25:** How could the overlooking of previous sins reveal the justice of God? The term does not indicate forgiveness, only that God does not discipline Gentiles as he does his people, Israel. This is a delay of judgment, a display of God's mercy as he gives time and opportunity for all people to repent. **31:** Believers uphold the law, not as a means of salvation but because the law reveals God's holiness and moral expectations.

4:1–25 The Faith of Abraham. Abraham was one of the most important figures in Judaism at this time (see Gen 15:1—17:27). Many Jewish males defined themselves as sons of Abraham as a way of securing their relationship with God. It appears that some Gentiles in the early church were troubled because they were not technically children of Abraham. **2:** Although Abraham lived before the law of Moses and had only the covenant of circumcision, nothing that Abraham did earned him favor with God. He had faith in God, who justifies the ungodly. **10:** Abraham was declared righteous before he was circumcised, because salvation was a gift from God even in Abraham's time. **12:** Circumcision was never intended to save, but it was a distinction that separated those who believed

[11]Circumcision was a sign that Abraham already had faith and that God had already accepted him and declared him to be righteous—even before he was circumcised. So Abraham is the spiritual father of those who have faith but have not been circumcised. They are counted as righteous because of their faith. [12]And Abraham is also the spiritual father of those who have been circumcised, but only if they have the same kind of faith Abraham had before he was circumcised.

[13]Clearly, God's promise to give the whole earth to Abraham and his descendants was based not on his obedience to God's law, but on a right relationship with God that comes by faith. [14]If God's promise is only for those who obey the law, then faith is not necessary and the promise is pointless. [15]For the law always brings punishment on those who try to obey it. (The only way to avoid breaking the law is to have no law to break!)

[16]So the promise is received by faith. It is given as a free gift. And we are all certain to receive it, whether or not we live according to the law of Moses, if we have faith like Abraham's. For Abraham is the father of all who believe. [17]That is what the Scriptures mean when God told him, "I have made you the father of many nations."* This happened because Abraham believed in the God who brings the dead back to life and who creates new things out of nothing.

[18]Even when there was no reason for hope, Abraham kept hoping—believing that he would become the father of many nations. For God had said to him, "That's how many descendants you will have!"* [19]And Abraham's faith did not weaken, even though, at about 100 years of age, he figured his body was as good as dead—and so was Sarah's womb.

[20]Abraham never wavered in believing God's promise. In fact, his faith grew stronger, and in this he brought glory to God. [21]He was fully convinced that God is able to do whatever he promises. [22]And because of Abraham's faith, God counted him as righteous. [23]And when God counted him as righteous, it wasn't just for Abraham's benefit. It was recorded [24]for our benefit, too, assuring us that God will also count us as righteous if we believe in him, the one who raised Jesus our Lord from the dead. [25]He was handed over to die because of our sins, and he was raised to life to make us right with God.

Faith Brings Joy

5 Therefore, since we have been made right in God's sight by faith, we have peace with God because of what Jesus Christ our Lord has done for us. [2]Because of our faith, Christ has brought us into this place of undeserved privilege where we now stand, and we confidently and joyfully look forward to sharing God's glory.

[3]We can rejoice, too, when we run into problems and trials, for we know that they help us develop endurance. [4]And endurance develops strength of character, and character strengthens our confident hope of salvation. [5]And this hope will not lead to disappointment. For we know how dearly God loves us, because he has given us the Holy Spirit to fill our hearts with his love.

[6]When we were utterly helpless, Christ came at just the right time and died for us sinners. [7]Now, most people would not be willing to die for an upright person, though someone might perhaps be willing to die for a person who is especially good. [8]But God showed his great love for us by sending Christ to die for us while we were still sinners. [9]And since we have been made right in God's sight by the blood of Christ, he will certainly save us from God's condemnation. [10]For since our friendship with God was restored by

4:17 Gen 17:5. **4:18** Gen 15:5.

(ancient Israel) from those who did not. **13–14:** God's promise, not the contractual agreement (the law) established between Israel and God, has the power to save. **15:** There is no transgression without the law. That is, if there is no responsibility given there is no accountability. **16–18:** "Promise" is a key concept for Paul (see also Gal 3), here that God will give his free gift (salvation) to many peoples (nations) through Abraham (Gen 17). **23–25:** Paul mentions two distinctive aspects of Jesus' role in God's salvation plan: his death and his resurrection. The death of Jesus is what satisfies for the punishment of sin, and the resurrection is what establishes a believer as righteous before God.

5:1–21 Jesus Reconciles Believers to God

5:1–11 Faith Brings Joy. 1–2: Paul uses "we" now to mean Christians. Believers have peace and complete acceptance before God, because he has declared Jesus' death an acceptable substitution for human sinfulness. **3:** Paul rejoices in the situations of suffering brought about by his choice to live for God. This is a direct challenge to those who proclaim that an outwardly comfortable life, relatively free of suffering, marks a true, beloved disciple of the Lord. **5:** Suffering focuses attention on God's love, and hope is confirmed by the Holy Spirit. **9–11:** This is likely the final judgment when God will judge the secret

the death of his Son while we were still his enemies, we will certainly be saved through the life
of his Son. [11]So now we can rejoice in our wonderful new relationship with God because our
Lord Jesus Christ has made us friends of God.

Adam and Christ Contrasted

[12]When Adam sinned, sin entered the world.
Adam's sin brought death, so death spread to
everyone, for everyone sinned. [13]Yes, people
sinned even before the law was given. But it was
not counted as sin because there was not yet any
law to break. [14]Still, everyone died—from the
time of Adam to the time of Moses—even those
who did not disobey an explicit commandment
of God, as Adam did. Now Adam is a symbol, a
representation of Christ, who was yet to come.
[15]But there is a great difference between Adam's
sin and God's gracious gift. For the sin of this one
man, Adam, brought death to many. But even
greater is God's wonderful grace and his gift of
forgiveness to many through this other man,
Jesus Christ. [16]And the result of God's gracious
gift is very different from the result of that one
man's sin. For Adam's sin led to condemnation,
but God's free gift leads to our being made right
with God, even though we are guilty of many
sins. [17]For the sin of this one man, Adam, caused
death to rule over many. But even greater is
God's wonderful grace and his gift of righteousness, for all who receive it will live in triumph
over sin and death through this one man, Jesus
Christ.

[18]Yes, Adam's one sin brings condemnation
for everyone, but Christ's one act of righteousness brings a right relationship with God and
new life for everyone. [19]Because one person disobeyed God, many became sinners. But because
one other person obeyed God, many will be made
righteous.

[20]God's law was given so that all people could
see how sinful they were. But as people sinned
more and more, God's wonderful grace became
more abundant. [21]So just as sin ruled over all
people and brought them to death, now God's
wonderful grace rules instead, giving us right
standing with God and resulting in eternal life
through Jesus Christ our Lord.

Sin's Power Is Broken

6 Well then, should we keep on sinning so
that God can show us more and more of
his wonderful grace? [2]Of course not! Since
we have died to sin, how can we continue to live
in it? [3]Or have you forgotten that when we were
joined with Christ Jesus in baptism, we joined
him in his death? [4]For we died and were buried
with Christ by baptism. And just as Christ was
raised from the dead by the glorious power of the
Father, now we also may live new lives.

[5]Since we have been united with him in his
death, we will also be raised to life as he was.
[6]We know that our old sinful selves were crucified with Christ so that sin might lose its power in our lives. We are no longer slaves to sin.
[7]For when we died with Christ we were set free
from the power of sin. [8]And since we died with
Christ, we know we will also live with him. [9]We
are sure of this because Christ was raised from
the dead, and he will never die again. Death no
longer has any power over him. [10]When he died,
he died once to break the power of sin. But now
that he lives, he lives for the glory of God. [11]So
you also should consider yourselves to be dead
to the power of sin and alive to God through
Christ Jesus.

---

thoughts of all people. Jesus' death brings forgiveness of sins and thus reconciliation, and his resurrection confirms the hope of life eternal with God. Salvation does not mean only an escape from damnation but also offers a relationship with God through Jesus Christ.

5:12–21 Adam and Christ Contrasted. 12: Sin took root in this world when Adam sinned, and so every human consequently dies, because death is the natural outcome of sin. Here, as in 1 Corinthians 15:22, responsibility for the first sin is attributed to Adam rather than Eve (cf. 2 Cor 11:3; 1 Tim 2:14). Adam and Eve both, however, represent all subsequent *humans,* male and female, in their disobedience. **14:** Adam is identified as a transgressor using the same Greek word, *parabasis,* that is used for Eve in 1 Tim 2:14. **15–18:** Jesus' death on the cross and his resurrection reversed the process Adam set in motion. Jesus' gift of salvation breaks the vicious cycle and allows for righteous living. **20–21:** Adam's sin was not reversed by the law; in fact, the law served to increase the things that Israel could do wrong. Sin, while powerful enough to have death as its consequence, is no match for the power of God's grace shown in Jesus Christ.

6:1—7:25 Sin and the Law Work against Faith

6:1–14 Sin's Power Is Broken. 3–4: Baptism connects the believer with Jesus' death on the cross, and by killing the old self, which was in Adam, a believer is now "born from above" (John 3:3) and is a "new creation" (2 Cor 5:17). The faithfulness of God working

[12]Do not let sin control the way you live;*
do not give in to sinful desires. [13]Do not let any
part of your body become an instrument of
evil to serve sin. Instead, give yourselves completely to God, for you were dead, but now you
have new life. So use your whole body as an
instrument to do what is right for the glory of
God. [14]Sin is no longer your master, for you no
longer live under the requirements of the law.
Instead, you live under the freedom of God's
grace.
[15]Well then, since God's grace has set us free
from the law, does that mean we can go on sinning? Of course not! [16]Don't you realize that
you become the slave of whatever you choose
to obey? You can be a slave to sin, which leads
to death, or you can choose to obey God, which
leads to righteous living. [17]Thank God! Once you
were slaves of sin, but now you wholeheartedly
obey this teaching we have given you. [18]Now
you are free from your slavery to sin, and you
have become slaves to righteous living.
[19]Because of the weakness of your human
nature, I am using the illustration of slavery to
help you understand all this. Previously, you let
yourselves be slaves to impurity and lawlessness,
which led ever deeper into sin. Now you must
give yourselves to be slaves to righteous living
so that you will become holy.
[20]When you were slaves to sin, you were free
from the obligation to do right. [21]And what was
the result? You are now ashamed of the things
you used to do, things that end in eternal doom.
[22]But now you are free from the power of sin and
have become slaves of God. Now you do those
things that lead to holiness and result in eternal
life. [23]For the wages of sin is death, but the free
gift of God is eternal life through Christ Jesus
our Lord.

No Longer Bound to the Law

7 Now, dear brothers and sisters*—you who
are familiar with the law—don't you know
that the law applies only while a person is
living? [2]For example, when a woman marries,
the law binds her to her husband as long as he is
alive. But if he dies, the laws of marriage no longer apply to her. [3]So while her husband is alive,

6:12 Or *Do not let sin reign in your body, which is subject to death.* **7:1** Greek *brothers;* also in 7:4.

through the faith of the believer secures this new life. **12–14:** Paul urges believers to behave as members of the new reality of grace that Christ has brought. They now have the power to resist sin, as they have moved out of its sphere of influence.

6:15–23 Freedom to Obey God. Paul responds to those who would take advantage of God's grace. **16:** Each human is a slave to sin or to righteousness; there is no middle ground. In Christ, believers can live the life they have always wanted to, a life pleasing to God, outside the debilitating power of sin. **17–23:** Here we see slavery as a metaphor for bondage and for meaningful commitment. Paul may have been the son of former slaves. He may have been attached to the Synagogue of Freed Slaves, as those from Cilicia, his home province, spearheaded the persecution of Stephen (Acts 6—9). Freed slaves of Roman citizens received citizenship upon their manumission. Paul may well have thus inherited his citizenship (Acts 22:27–28). Many a freed slave advanced to positions of power and prominence. Thus Paul could see the degradation and dehumanization of slavery, but also the opportunities that it might bring for advancement and propagation of the gospel.

7:1–6 No Longer Bound to the Law. Although Paul is not engaged in a discussion of marriage per se, what he assumes about this institution is worth noting. He does not mention divorce, but assumes that a woman cannot live with another man other than her husband. In 1 Corinthians 7, Paul discusses marriage, and there he states that believers should not separate from each other, but that if they do, they should remain single or reunite with each other. A wife is bound to her husband as long as he lives and is free to remarry when he dies, though Paul asks that the second husband be a believer. On the surface, there seems little room for divorce and even less for remarriage after divorce (see Divorce, Ezra 10; Marriage, Song 2). This understanding has been used as a weapon against women trapped in abusive situations. A more careful reading of Paul's teachings on marriage, including Ephesians 5, and Peter's message (1 Pet 3), placed in the context of suffering in general in the New Testament, offers hope to those in abusive situations. It is clear that suffering at the hands of a husband or wife is not the kind of suffering that a disciple is called to endure. The wife is to love her husband (Titus 2:4). Paul and Peter make it clear that the husband is to love his wife, to treat her body as his own (Eph 5:25–33), and to honor it (1 Pet 3:7). Considering that these men wrote to real situations, it likely means that some husbands in the first century scorned their wives. But abuse is not acceptable in God's sight. Spousal abuse is not in the category of redemptive suffering. In the case of abuse, we might look to Jesus' words that divorce is allowed because of unfaithfulness.

she would be committing adultery if she married another man. But if her husband dies, she is free from that law and does not commit adultery when she remarries.

[4]So, my dear brothers and sisters, this is the point: You died to the power of the law when you died with Christ. And now you are united with the one who was raised from the dead. As a result, we can produce a harvest of good deeds for God. [5]When we were controlled by our old nature,* sinful desires were at work within us, and the law aroused these evil desires that produced a harvest of sinful deeds, resulting in death. [6]But now we have been released from the law, for we died to it and are no longer captive to its power. Now we can serve God, not in the old way of obeying the letter of the law, but in the new way of living in the Spirit.

God's Law Reveals Our Sin

[7]Well then, am I suggesting that the law of God is sinful? Of course not! In fact, it was the law that showed me my sin. I would never have known that coveting is wrong if the law had not said, "You must not covet."* [8]But sin used this command to arouse all kinds of covetous desires within me! If there were no law, sin would not have that power. [9]At one time I lived without understanding the law. But when I learned the command not to covet, for instance, the power of sin came to life, [10]and I died. So I discovered that the law's commands, which were supposed to bring life, brought spiritual death instead. [11]Sin took advantage of those commands and deceived me; it used the commands to kill me. [12]But still, the law itself is holy, and its commands are holy and right and good.

[13]But how can that be? Did the law, which is good, cause my death? Of course not! Sin used what was good to bring about my condemnation to death. So we can see how terrible sin really is. It uses God's good commands for its own evil purposes.

Struggling with Sin

[14]So the trouble is not with the law, for it is spiritual and good. The trouble is with me, for I am all too human, a slave to sin. [15]I don't really understand myself, for I want to do what is right, but I don't do it. Instead, I do what I hate. [16]But if I know that what I am doing is wrong, this shows that I agree that the law is good. [17]So I am not the one doing wrong; it is sin living in me that does it.

[18]And I know that nothing good lives in me, that is, in my sinful nature.* I want to do what is right, but I can't. [19]I want to do what is good, but I don't. I don't want to do what is wrong, but I do it anyway. [20]But if I do what I don't want to do, I am not really the one doing wrong; it is sin living in me that does it.

[21]I have discovered this principle of life—that when I want to do what is right, I inevitably do what is wrong. [22]I love God's law with all my heart. [23]But there is another power* within me that is at war with my mind. This power makes me a slave to the sin that is still within me. [24]Oh, what a miserable person I am! Who will free me from this life that is dominated by sin and death? [25]Thank God! The answer is in Jesus Christ our Lord. So you see how it is: In my mind I really want to obey God's law, but because of my sinful nature I am a slave to sin.

Life in the Spirit

8 So now there is no condemnation for those who belong to Christ Jesus. [2]And because you belong to him, the power* of the life-giving Spirit has freed you* from the power of sin that leads to death. [3]The law of Moses was unable to save us because of the weakness of our sinful nature.* So God did what the law could

7:5 Greek *When we were in the flesh.* **7:7** Exod 20:17; Deut 5:21. **7:18** Greek *my flesh;* also in 7:25. **7:23** Greek *law;* also in 7:23b. **8:2a** Greek *the law;* also in 8:2b. **8:2b** Some manuscripts read *me.* **8:3** Greek *our flesh;* similarly in 8:4, 5, 6, 7, 8, 9, 12.

7:7–13 God's Law Reveals Our Sin. Many commentators have understood Paul to be speaking biographically about his life before believing in Jesus as Savior. A better understanding is that Paul is using *I* as a representative of humanity before the coming of Jesus. He is writing a history of God's salvation work in the world, especially as it relates to Gentiles becoming part of God's people. He also uses *I* to represent all humans in 1 Corinthians 13 and Galatians 2:20.

7:14–25 Struggling with Sin. 22–23: Paul notes that nothing good dwells in him, but then exclaims that he loves God and desires good. We see the experience of a person who knows the law but has no power to put the law into practice. **24–25:** Paul, representing a seeker, cries out for help from this desperate situation. And he praises God that Jesus rescues those who call out to him.

8:1–39 The Holy Spirit Indwells the Believer

8:1–17 Life in the Spirit. 3–4: Our sinful nature, literally, "flesh," though powerless to resist sin, has

not do. He sent his own Son in a body like the
bodies we sinners have. And in that body God
declared an end to sin's control over us by giving
his Son as a sacrifice for our sins. [4]He did this
so that the just requirement of the law would be
fully satisfied for us, who no longer follow our
sinful nature but instead follow the Spirit.
[5]Those who are dominated by the sinful nature
think about sinful things, but those who are controlled by the Holy Spirit think about things that
please the Spirit. [6]So letting your sinful nature
control your mind leads to death. But letting the
Spirit control your mind leads to life and peace.
[7]For the sinful nature is always hostile to God.
It never did obey God's laws, and it never will.
[8]That's why those who are still under the control
of their sinful nature can never please God.
[9]But you are not controlled by your sinful
nature. You are controlled by the Spirit if you
have the Spirit of God living in you. (And remember that those who do not have the Spirit of
Christ living in them do not belong to him at all.)
[10]And Christ lives within you, so even though
your body will die because of sin, the Spirit gives
you life* because you have been made right with
God. [11]The Spirit of God, who raised Jesus from
the dead, lives in you. And just as God raised
Christ Jesus from the dead, he will give life to
your mortal bodies by this same Spirit living
within you.
[12]Therefore, dear brothers and sisters,* you
have no obligation to do what your sinful nature
urges you to do. [13]For if you live by its dictates,
you will die. But if through the power of the
Spirit you put to death the deeds of your sinful
nature,* you will live. [14]For all who are led by
the Spirit of God are children* of God.
[15]So you have not received a spirit that makes
you fearful slaves. Instead, you received God's
Spirit when he adopted you as his own children.*
Now we call him, "Abba, Father."* [16]For his Spirit joins with our spirit to affirm that we are God's
children. [17]And since we are his children, we are
his heirs. In fact, together with Christ we are
heirs of God's glory. But if we are to share his
glory, we must also share his suffering.

The Future Glory

[18]Yet what we suffer now is nothing compared
to the glory he will reveal to us later. [19]For all
creation is waiting eagerly for that future day
when God will reveal who his children really are.
[20]Against its will, all creation was subjected to
God's curse. But with eager hope, [21]the creation
looks forward to the day when it will join God's
children in glorious freedom from death and
decay. [22]For we know that all creation has been
groaning as in the pains of childbirth right up to
the present time. [23]And we believers also groan,
even though we have the Holy Spirit within us
as a foretaste of future glory, for we long for our
bodies to be released from sin and suffering. We,
too, wait with eager hope for the day when God
will give us our full rights as his adopted children,* including the new bodies he has promised
us. [24]We were given this hope when we were
saved. (If we already have something, we don't
need to hope* for it. [25]But if we look forward to
something we don't yet have, we must wait patiently and confidently.)
[26]And the Holy Spirit helps us in our weakness. For example, we don't know what God
wants us to pray for. But the Holy Spirit prays
for us with groanings that cannot be expressed
in words. [27]And the Father who knows all hearts

8:10 Or *your spirit is alive.* **8:12** Greek *brothers;* also in 8:29. **8:13** Greek *deeds of the body.* **8:14** Greek *sons;* also in 8:19. **8:15a** Greek *you received a spirit of sonship.* **8:15b** *Abba* is an Aramaic term for "father." **8:23** Greek *wait anxiously for sonship.* **8:24** Some manuscripts read *wait.*

---

been condemned by Christ's work on the cross. Jesus was able to fulfill all the just requirements of the law, and so believers too fulfill them in Christ, following the Spirit. **5–11:** There is a marked contrast made between the sinful nature and the Spirit. "In the Spirit" means living by faith in the power and reality of God's perfect gift of salvation. It means recognizing that the power of sin has been defeated in one's life. Paul's ethics are deceptively easy; he asks that believers listen to the Holy Spirit. **15:** The cry uttered in the Spirit, "Abba, Father," is confirmation to believers that they belong to God. The Aramaic word *Abba* was thought to mean "daddy," suggesting a new intimacy that Jesus brought; however, further study has suggested that Jesus did not introduce this new use of Abba. It is Aramaic for "father."

8:18–30 The Future Glory. 19–21: The earth itself was damaged in the Fall and is itself longing for the end of sin's control. In this we can see Paul's appreciation for the magnitude of Christ's redemptive work. **22–25:** He suggests that the earth is going through just what each believer goes through—waiting, groaning as in childbirth. In both cases, it is waiting for God to make all things new. **26–27:** The Romans' feeble prayers are magnified by the Spirit, who presents their needs to God in an effective way. They are not abandoned children but are cared for even beyond what words can express.

knows what the Spirit is saying, for the Spirit
pleads for us believers* in harmony with God's
own will. 28 And we know that God causes everything to work together* for the good of those
who love God and are called according to his purpose for them. 29 For God knew his people in advance, and he chose them to become like his Son,
so that his Son would be the firstborn* among
many brothers and sisters. 30 And having chosen
them, he called them to come to him. And having
called them, he gave them right standing with
himself. And having given them right standing,
he gave them his glory.

Nothing Can Separate Us from God's Love

31 What shall we say about such wonderful things
as these? If God is for us, who can ever be against
us? 32 Since he did not spare even his own Son
but gave him up for us all, won't he also give us
everything else? 33 Who dares accuse us whom
God has chosen for his own? No one—for God
himself has given us right standing with himself. 34 Who then will condemn us? No one—for
Christ Jesus died for us and was raised to life for
us, and he is sitting in the place of honor at God's
right hand, pleading for us.

35 Can anything ever separate us from Christ's
love? Does it mean he no longer loves us if we
have trouble or calamity, or are persecuted, or
hungry, or destitute, or in danger, or threatened with death? 36 (As the Scriptures say, "For
your sake we are killed every day; we are being
slaughtered like sheep."*) 37 No, despite all these
things, overwhelming victory is ours through
Christ, who loved us.

38 And I am convinced that nothing can ever
separate us from God's love. Neither death nor
life, neither angels nor demons,* neither our
fears for today nor our worries about tomorrow—not even the powers of hell can separate
us from God's love. 39 No power in the sky above
or in the earth below—indeed, nothing in all creation will ever be able to separate us from the
love of God that is revealed in Christ Jesus our
Lord.

God's Selection of Israel

9 With Christ as my witness, I speak with
utter truthfulness. My conscience and the
Holy Spirit confirm it. 2 My heart is filled
with bitter sorrow and unending grief 3 for my
people, my Jewish brothers and sisters.* I would
be willing to be forever cursed—cut off from
Christ!—if that would save them. 4 They are the
people of Israel, chosen to be God's adopted children.* God revealed his glory to them. He made
covenants with them and gave them his law. He
gave them the privilege of worshiping him and
receiving his wonderful promises. 5 Abraham,
Isaac, and Jacob are their ancestors, and Christ
himself was an Israelite as far as his human nature is concerned. And he is God, the one who
rules over everything and is worthy of eternal
praise! Amen.*

6 Well then, has God failed to fulfill his promise to Israel? No, for not all who are born into
the nation of Israel are truly members of God's
people! 7 Being descendants of Abraham doesn't
make them truly Abraham's children. For the
Scriptures say, "Isaac is the son through whom
your descendants will be counted,"* though
Abraham had other children, too. 8 This means
that Abraham's physical descendants are not
necessarily children of God. Only the children
of the promise are considered to be Abraham's
children. 9 For God had promised, "I will return
about this time next year, and Sarah will have
a son."*

8:27 Greek *for God's holy people.* **8:28** Some manuscripts read *And we know that everything works together.* **8:29** Or *would be supreme.* **8:36** Ps 44:22. **8:38** Greek *nor rulers.* **9:3** Greek *my brothers.* **9:4** Greek *chosen for sonship.* **9:5** Or *May God, the one who rules over everything, be praised forever. Amen.* **9:7** Gen 21:12. **9:9** Gen 18:10, 14.

8:31–39 Nothing Can Separate Us from God's Love. Those who love God will triumph ultimately, because God will work out his purpose. **38:** The love of Jesus Christ will conquer all the perils faced by humanity, including the ultimate one, death.

9:1—11:36 Jews and Gentiles in God's Salvation Plan

9:1–29 God's Selection of Israel. 1–5: One of Paul's deepest hurts is that not all of his people, the Jews, have taken advantage of God's gift. He is even willing to give up his salvation for their sake. He acknowledges that the Jews of his day are recipients of such wonders from God, including being claimed by God, rescued gloriously from Egypt, given the law, the Temple, and the prophets' promises, which are fulfilled in the Messiah. This completes the question raised in Romans 3:1, the advantage of being a Jew. **6–10:** Paul argues that not all those who call themselves Jews are truly chosen. He points to Abraham's sons, Isaac and Ishmael, noting that only through Isaac do God's promises come (Gen 21:1–7). Sarah learned firsthand the dangers of trying to manufacture God's will by giving her slave, Hagar, to Abraham to have a child for her. Ishmael was born, and dissension

10 This son was our ancestor Isaac. When
he married Rebekah, she gave birth to twins.*
11 But before they were born, before they had
done anything good or bad, she received a message from God. (This message shows that God
chooses people according to his own purposes;
12 he calls people, but not according to their good
or bad works.) She was told, "Your older son
will serve your younger son."* 13 In the words
of the Scriptures, "I loved Jacob, but I rejected
Esau."*

14 Are we saying, then, that God was unfair?
Of course not! 15 For God said to Moses,

"I will show mercy to anyone I choose,
and I will show compassion to anyone I
choose."*

16 So it is God who decides to show mercy. We can
neither choose it nor work for it.

17 For the Scriptures say that God told Pharaoh, "I have appointed you for the very purpose
of displaying my power in you and to spread my
fame throughout the earth."* 18 So you see, God
chooses to show mercy to some, and he chooses
to harden the hearts of others so they refuse to
listen.

19 Well then, you might say, "Why does God
blame people for not responding? Haven't they
simply done what he makes them do?"

20 No, don't say that. Who are you, a mere
human being, to argue with God? Should the
thing that was created say to the one who created it, "Why have you made me like this?"
21 When a potter makes jars out of clay, doesn't
he have a right to use the same lump of clay
to make one jar for decoration and another to
throw garbage into? 22 In the same way, even
though God has the right to show his anger
and his power, he is very patient with those on
whom his anger falls, who are destined for destruction. 23 He does this to make the riches of
his glory shine even brighter on those to whom
he shows mercy, who were prepared in advance
for glory. 24 And we are among those whom he
selected, both from the Jews and from the Gentiles.

25 Concerning the Gentiles, God says in the
prophecy of Hosea,

"Those who were not my people,
I will now call my people.
And I will love those
whom I did not love before."*

26 And,

"Then, at the place where they were told,
'You are not my people,'
there they will be called
'children of the living God.' "*

27 And concerning Israel, Isaiah the prophet cried
out,

"Though the people of Israel are as numerous
as the sand of the seashore,
only a remnant will be saved.
28 For the LORD will carry out his sentence upon
the earth
quickly and with finality."*

29 And Isaiah said the same thing in another
place:

"If the LORD of Heaven's Armies
had not spared a few of our children,
we would have been wiped out like Sodom,
destroyed like Gomorrah."*

9:10 Greek *she conceived children through this one man.* **9:12** Gen 25:23. **9:13** Mal 1:2-3. **9:15** Exod 33:19. **9:17** Exod 9:16 (Greek version). **9:25** Hos 2:23. **9:26** Greek *sons of the living God.* Hos 1:10. **9:27-28** Isa 10:22-23 (Greek version). **9:29** Isa 1:9.

---

settled upon their house (Gen 16:1–16; 21:8–21). **11–13:** One of Rebekah's twin sons was chosen by God even before he was born. God explained that the struggle she felt in her womb would continue during the two sons' lives, and that the younger one (Jacob/Israel, Gen 32:28) would be served by the elder (Esau). In these examples, the fathers (Abraham and Isaac) and the mothers (Sarah and Rebekah) are given equal billing. It was more common in the ancient world to note just the father, but Paul's point can be made only using Sarah (not Hagar) and Rebekah (see Gen 24—27). God chose these women to further his purpose and to show that Israel is called by God, not because of anything Israel did or would do. **17–18:** Pharaoh, the god-king of the Egyptians, was given his kingdom by God so that God could show the Egyptians and the Hebrews that God is more powerful than the Egyptian gods, including the pharaoh. In Exodus 7, Pharaoh turned from God and hardened himself against God's plan. God, knowing the pharaoh's response, is said to have hardened Pharaoh's heart. The Lord forewarned Moses and Aaron of Pharaoh's response so that they would not become disheartened. The point is that God is sovereign over history, and no human has the right to argue with God on how God proceeds with his plan.

Israel's Unbelief

30 What does all this mean? Even though the Gentiles were not trying to follow God's standards,
they were made right with God. And it was by
faith that this took place. 31 But the people of Israel,
who tried so hard to get right with God by keeping
the law, never succeeded. 32 Why not? Because they
were trying to get right with God by keeping the
law* instead of by trusting in him. They stumbled
over the great rock in their path. 33 God warned
them of this in the Scriptures when he said,

"I am placing a stone in Jerusalem* that
makes people stumble,
a rock that makes them fall.
But anyone who trusts in him
will never be disgraced."*

10 Dear brothers and sisters,* the longing of my heart and my prayer to
God is for the people of Israel to be
saved. 2 I know what enthusiasm they have for
God, but it is misdirected zeal. 3 For they don't
understand God's way of making people right
with himself. Refusing to accept God's way, they
cling to their own way of getting right with God
by trying to keep the law. 4 For Christ has already
accomplished the purpose for which the law was
given.* As a result, all who believe in him are
made right with God.

Salvation Is for Everyone

5 For Moses writes that the law's way of making a
person right with God requires obedience to all of
its commands.* 6 But faith's way of getting right
with God says, "Don't say in your heart, 'Who
will go up to heaven?' (to bring Christ down to
earth). 7 And don't say, 'Who will go down to the
place of the dead?' (to bring Christ back to life
again)." 8 In fact, it says,

"The message is very close at hand;
it is on your lips and in your heart."*

And that message is the very message about faith
that we preach: 9 If you confess with your mouth
that Jesus is Lord and believe in your heart that
God raised him from the dead, you will be saved.
10 For it is by believing in your heart that you
are made right with God, and it is by confessing with your mouth that you are saved. 11 As
the Scriptures tell us, "Anyone who trusts in
him will never be disgraced."* 12 Jew and Gentile* are the same in this respect. They have the
same Lord, who gives generously to all who call
on him. 13 For "Everyone who calls on the name
of the LORD will be saved."*
14 But how can they call on him to save them
unless they believe in him? And how can they
believe in him if they have never heard about
him? And how can they hear about him unless
someone tells them? 15 And how will anyone go
and tell them without being sent? That is why
the Scriptures say, "How beautiful are the feet of
messengers who bring good news!"*
16 But not everyone welcomes the Good
News, for Isaiah the prophet said, "LORD, who
has believed our message?"* 17 So faith comes
from hearing, that is, hearing the Good News
about Christ. 18 But I ask, have the people of
Israel actually heard the message? Yes, they
have:

"The message has gone throughout the earth,
and the words to all the world."*

9:32 Greek *by works.* **9:33a** Greek *in Zion.* **9:33b** Isa 8:14; 28:16 (Greek version). **10:1** Greek *Brothers.* **10:4** Or *For Christ is the end of the law.* **10:5** See Lev 18:5. **10:6-8** Deut 30:12-14. **10:11** Isa 28:16 (Greek version). **10:12** Greek *and Greek.* **10:13** Joel 2:32. **10:15** Isa 52:7. **10:16** Isa 53:1. **10:18** Ps 19:4.

9:30—10:4 Israel's Unbelief. 30: God's plan of salvation is by faith alone. Gentiles are invited, even though in their history they did not strive for a close relationship with the one true God. **9:31—10:3:** Israel, though it had advantages over Gentiles, was tripped up over its understanding of faith.

10:5–21 Salvation Is for Everyone. 11–13: Christ's death and resurrection ended the separation of Jew and Gentile and fulfilled the law, so that all people might be made right before God **14–21:** A series of questions serves to highlight the disobedience of Israel to God's message, a pattern seen in the prophets, especially Isaiah. Paul notes that a person cannot call on someone in whom she or he has no belief. Lack of belief may stem from not hearing about Christ. **14–15:** This passage is often used as a missionary call. This is perhaps part of Paul's intention because he was an apostle (similar to a missionary) to the Gentiles. But those Gentiles Paul sought lived in cities also inhabited by Jews, and many of those Gentiles heard the message of the one true God from the synagogue. It would be inaccurate to label Paul as a cross-cultural missionary. It is important to keep in mind Paul's original question: Why isn't *all Israel* saved if this Jesus is the Jewish Messiah? Isaiah's experience helps to answer the question: He was sent but not believed (v. 20). **16–18:** Paul supposes that Israel has heard about Christ; he notes that not all have obeyed the good news, but that "they" (the

[19] But I ask, did the people of Israel really understand? Yes, they did, for even in the time of Moses, God said,

"I will rouse your jealousy through people
who are not even a nation.
I will provoke your anger through the
foolish Gentiles."*

[20] And later Isaiah spoke boldly for God, saying,

"I was found by people who were not looking
for me.
I showed myself to those who were not
asking for me."*

[21] But regarding Israel, God said,

"All day long I opened my arms to them,
but they were disobedient and rebellious."*

God's Mercy on Israel

11 I ask, then, has God rejected his own people, the nation of Israel? Of course not! I myself am an Israelite, a descendant of Abraham and a member of the tribe of Benjamin.

[2] No, God has not rejected his own people, whom he chose from the very beginning. Do you realize what the Scriptures say about this? Elijah the prophet complained to God about the people of Israel and said, [3] "LORD, they have killed your prophets and torn down your altars. I am the only one left, and now they are trying to kill me, too."*

[4] And do you remember God's reply? He said, "No, I have 7,000 others who have never bowed down to Baal!"*

[5] It is the same today, for a few of the people of Israel* have remained faithful because of God's grace—his undeserved kindness in choosing them. [6] And since it is through God's kindness, then it is not by their good works. For in that case, God's grace would not be what it really is—free and undeserved.

[7] So this is the situation: Most of the people of Israel have not found the favor of God they are looking for so earnestly. A few have—the ones God has chosen—but the hearts of the rest were hardened. [8] As the Scriptures say,

"God has put them into a deep sleep.
To this day he has shut their eyes so they do
not see,
and closed their ears so they do not hear."*

[9] Likewise, David said,

"Let their bountiful table become a snare,
a trap that makes them think all is well.
Let their blessings cause them to stumble,
and let them get what they deserve.
[10] Let their eyes go blind so they cannot see,
and let their backs be bent forever."*

[11] Did God's people stumble and fall beyond recovery? Of course not! They were disobedient, so God made salvation available to the Gentiles. But he wanted his own people to become jealous and claim it for themselves. [12] Now if the Gentiles were enriched because the people of Israel turned down God's offer of salvation, think how much greater a blessing the world will share when they finally accept it.

[13] I am saying all this especially for you Gentiles. God has appointed me as the apostle to the Gentiles. I stress this, [14] for I want somehow to make the people of Israel jealous of what you Gentiles have, so I might save some of them. [15] For since their rejection meant that God offered salvation to the rest of the world, their acceptance will be even more wonderful. It will be life for those who were dead! [16] And since Abraham and the other patriarchs were holy, their descendants will also be holy—just as the entire batch of dough is holy because the portion given

10:19 Deut 32:21. **10:20** Isa 65:1 (Greek version). **10:21** Isa 65:2 (Greek version). **11:3** 1 Kgs 19:10, 14. **11:4** 1 Kgs 19:18. **11:5** Greek *for a remnant.* **11:8** Isa 29:10; Deut 29:4. **11:9-10** Ps 69:22-23 (Greek version).

Jews) have indeed heard. **19–21:** Israel has the potential to understand what God is doing in Christ because the prophets have predicted as much: The nations will turn to God. But Israel has not accepted God's offer of salvation in Christ.

11:1–24 God's Mercy on Israel. 1–6: God has been faithful to Israel and has consistently desired a relationship based on faith. The idea of a faithful remnant is developed to explain how God has dealt with Israel. There have always been those, like Elijah, who have followed God by faith, and Paul includes himself in that number. God works through grace, accepting people not based on their deeds but because of God's mercy. **11–24:** The analogy of an olive tree with branches broken off and others grafted in is a visual lesson for the Gentile believers that their inclusion into God's family is completely by grace. Paul stresses that Israel can be reattached to the olive tree and hopes that his ministry might save some Jews.

as an offering is holy. For if the roots of the tree
are holy, the branches will be, too.
17 But some of these branches from Abraham's tree—some of the people of Israel—have
been broken off. And you Gentiles, who were
branches from a wild olive tree, have been grafted in. So now you also receive the blessing God
has promised Abraham and his children, sharing
in the rich nourishment from the root of God's
special olive tree. 18 But you must not brag about
being grafted in to replace the branches that were
broken off. You are just a branch, not the root.
19 "Well," you may say, "those branches were
broken off to make room for me." 20 Yes, but
remember—those branches were broken off
because they didn't believe in Christ, and you
are there because you do believe. So don't think
highly of yourself, but fear what could happen.
21 For if God did not spare the original branches,
he won't* spare you either.
22 Notice how God is both kind and severe. He
is severe toward those who disobeyed, but kind
to you if you continue to trust in his kindness.
But if you stop trusting, you also will be cut
off. 23 And if the people of Israel turn from their
unbelief, they will be grafted in again, for God
has the power to graft them back into the tree.
24 You, by nature, were a branch cut from a wild
olive tree. So if God was willing to do something
contrary to nature by grafting you into his cultivated tree, he will be far more eager to graft the
original branches back into the tree where they
belong.

God's Mercy Is for Everyone

25 I want you to understand this mystery, dear
brothers and sisters,* so that you will not feel
proud about yourselves. Some of the people of
Israel have hard hearts, but this will last only until the full number of Gentiles comes to Christ.
26 And so all Israel will be saved. As the Scriptures say,

"The one who rescues will come from
Jerusalem,*
and he will turn Israel* away from
ungodliness.
27 And this is my covenant with them,
that I will take away their sins."*

28 Many of the people of Israel are now enemies of the Good News, and this benefits you
Gentiles. Yet they are still the people he loves
because he chose their ancestors Abraham, Isaac,
and Jacob. 29 For God's gifts and his call can never
be withdrawn. 30 Once, you Gentiles were rebels against God, but when the people of Israel
rebelled against him, God was merciful to you
instead. 31 Now they are the rebels, and God's
mercy has come to you so that they, too, will
share* in God's mercy. 32 For God has imprisoned
everyone in disobedience so he could have mercy
on everyone.
33 Oh, how great are God's riches and wisdom
and knowledge! How impossible it is for us to
understand his decisions and his ways!

34 For who can know the LORD's thoughts?
Who knows enough to give him advice?*
35 And who has given him so much
that he needs to pay it back?*

36 For everything comes from him and exists
by his power and is intended for his glory. All
glory to him forever! Amen.

A Living Sacrifice to God

12 And so, dear brothers and sisters,* I
plead with you to give your bodies
to God because of all he has done for
you. Let them be a living and holy sacrifice—the
kind he will find acceptable. This is truly the way
to worship him.* 2 Don't copy the behavior and

11:21 Some manuscripts read *perhaps he won't.* **11:25** Greek *brothers.* **11:26a** Greek *from Zion.* **11:26b** Greek *Jacob.* **11:26-27** Isa 59:20-21; 27:9 (Greek version). **11:31** Other manuscripts read *will now share;* still others read *will someday share.* **11:34** Isa 40:13 (Greek version). **11:35** See Job 41:11. **12:1a** Greek *brothers.* **12:1b** Or *This is your spiritual worship;* or *This is your reasonable service.*

11:25–36 God's Mercy Is for Everyone. 25–27: Paul expresses his belief that Israel is hardened or has turned from God. During this time, many Gentiles will come into a saving relationship with God through Jesus. This is a *mystery,* a word Paul uses elsewhere in speaking about the wonderful plan of salvation, the inclusion of Gentiles in Israel as one large family. This does not suppose that in this family, every individual member will be saved. The phrase *all Israel* is likely parallel in meaning to the "full number" of Gentiles. **28–32:** Both Jews and Gentiles have chosen sin, but God has chosen to use such disobedience to show his mercy. **33–36:** Joy springs from knowing that God is acting mercifully to all.

12:1—15:13 Transformed Behavior for the Believer

12:1–21 A Living Sacrifice to God. The Jews still offered sacrifices at the Jerusalem Temple, and pagans

customs of this world, but let God transform
you into a new person by changing the way you
think. Then you will learn to know God's will for
you, which is good and pleasing and perfect.
3 Because of the privilege and authority* God
has given me, I give each of you this warning:
Don't think you are better than you really are.
Be honest in your evaluation of yourselves, measuring yourselves by the faith God has given us.*
4 Just as our bodies have many parts and each
part has a special function, 5 so it is with Christ's
body. We are many parts of one body, and we all
belong to each other.

6 In his grace, God has given us different gifts
for doing certain things well. So if God has given
you the ability to prophesy, speak out with as
much faith as God has given you. 7 If your gift
is serving others, serve them well. If you are a
teacher, teach well. 8 If your gift is to encourage
others, be encouraging. If it is giving, give generously. If God has given you leadership ability, take the responsibility seriously. And if you
have a gift for showing kindness to others, do it
gladly.

9 Don't just pretend to love others. Really love
them. Hate what is wrong. Hold tightly to what is
good. 10 Love each other with genuine affection,*
and take delight in honoring each other. 11 Never
be lazy, but work hard and serve the Lord enthusiastically.* 12 Rejoice in our confident hope. Be
patient in trouble, and keep on praying. 13 When
God's people are in need, be ready to help them.
Always be eager to practice hospitality.

14 Bless those who persecute you. Don't curse
them; pray that God will bless them. 15 Be happy
with those who are happy, and weep with those
who weep. 16 Live in harmony with each other.
Don't be too proud to enjoy the company of ordinary people. And don't think you know it all!

17 Never pay back evil with more evil. Do
things in such a way that everyone can see you
are honorable. 18 Do all that you can to live in
peace with everyone.

19 Dear friends, never take revenge. Leave that
to the righteous anger of God. For the Scriptures
say,

> "I will take revenge;
> I will pay them back,"*
> says the LORD.

20 Instead,

> "If your enemies are hungry, feed them.
> If they are thirsty, give them something to drink.
> In doing this, you will heap
> burning coals of shame on their heads."*

21 Don't let evil conquer you, but conquer evil by
doing good.

Respect for Authority

13 Everyone must submit to governing
authorities. For all authority comes
from God, and those in positions of
authority have been placed there by God. 2 So
anyone who rebels against authority is rebelling

12:3a Or *Because of the grace;* compare 1:5. **12:3b** Or *by the faith God has given you;* or *by the standard of our God-given faith.* **12:10** Greek *with brotherly love.* **12:11** Or *but serve the Lord with a zealous spirit;* or *but let the Spirit excite you as you serve the Lord.* **12:19** Deut 32:35. **12:20** Prov 25:21-22.

---

continued to offer sacrifices in their various temples, so the image of animal sacrifice is a real one for the Romans. A living sacrifice, however, is a contradiction in terms. A believer is to be a living sacrifice, one who turns her mind completely to the will of God and thus knows what is good and perfect in God's sight. **6–8:** God determines the role for each believer to play in the church, and there are no small parts. The gifts listed here are not to be seen as exclusive, for Paul lists other gifts elsewhere; rather, they are examples of how God might prepare a person to be used in the church. Nor are the gifts related to one's gender; there are no female gifts and no male gifts. Within the church, there is functional equality (Gal 3:28). **9–21:** Genuine love hates evil and seeks good. Hating evil does not mean that one can take revenge, nor does one have the luxury of hating one's enemy. Instead, the believer is to own God's perspective on what is ethical and exemplary and what is unjust and wicked.

13:1–7 Respect for Authority. In Palestine, many Jews thought that Rome was evil. Their assumption was that the Messiah would overthrow Rome and set up God's political rule on earth. The anti-Roman sentiment was based in part on a belief that a pagan empire should not rule the people of God. Paul does not sanction such beliefs, for he does not believe that Christians must be politically self-determining. The higher love of God is demonstrated when the civil laws of the larger community are practiced. Paul defines what he means by being subject to authorities when he discourages disobeying current laws set up by the government. He assumes that the government will keep the community peace and allow Christians the same freedoms the Jews enjoyed in the empire (cf. 1 Thes 4:9–12).

against what God has instituted, and they will be punished. [3]For the authorities do not strike fear in people who are doing right, but in those who are doing wrong. Would you like to live without fear of the authorities? Do what is right, and they will honor you. [4]The authorities are God's servants, sent for your good. But if you are doing wrong, of course you should be afraid, for they have the power to punish you. They are God's servants, sent for the very purpose of punishing those who do what is wrong. [5]So you must submit to them, not only to avoid punishment, but also to keep a clear conscience.

[6]Pay your taxes, too, for these same reasons. For government workers need to be paid. They are serving God in what they do. [7]Give to everyone what you owe them: Pay your taxes and government fees to those who collect them, and give respect and honor to those who are in authority.

Love Fulfills God's Requirements

[8]Owe nothing to anyone—except for your obligation to love one another. If you love your neighbor, you will fulfill the requirements of God's law. [9]For the commandments say, "You must not commit adultery. You must not murder. You must not steal. You must not covet."* These—and other such commandments—are summed up in this one commandment: "Love your neighbor as yourself."* [10]Love does no wrong to others, so love fulfills the requirements of God's law.

[11]This is all the more urgent, for you know how late it is; time is running out. Wake up, for our salvation is nearer now than when we first believed. [12]The night is almost gone; the day of salvation will soon be here. So remove your dark deeds like dirty clothes, and put on the shining armor of right living. [13]Because we belong to the day, we must live decent lives for all to see. Don't participate in the darkness of wild parties and drunkenness, or in sexual promiscuity and immoral living, or in quarreling and jealousy. [14]Instead, clothe yourself with the presence of the Lord Jesus Christ. And don't let yourself think about ways to indulge your evil desires.

The Danger of Criticism

14 Accept other believers who are weak in faith, and don't argue with them about what they think is right or wrong. [2]For instance, one person believes it's all right to eat anything. But another believer with a sensitive conscience will eat only vegetables. [3]Those who feel free to eat anything must not look down on those who don't. And those who don't eat certain foods must not condemn those who do, for God has accepted them. [4]Who are you to condemn someone else's servants? Their own master will judge whether they stand or fall. And with the Lord's help, they will stand and receive his approval.

[5]In the same way, some think one day is more

13:9a Exod 20:13-15, 17. **13:9b** Lev 19:18.

Does Paul then advocate peace at any price with the government? Paul is never willing to give an inch when it comes to a correct and clear understanding of the gospel. He is willing to accept all manner of beatings if they are done because he is a Christian. Yet he demands respect as a Roman citizen and will not accept mistreatment if people are against him personally. He insists on an escort out of Philippi because he is a Roman citizen (Acts 16:37). He forcefully requests to see Caesar (hoping to present the gospel to him) because he is a Roman citizen (Acts 22:25–29; 25:11–12).

This teaching is especially important for women. If a woman is persecuted because she is a Christian, then God will be glorified by her obedience. But she need not accept punishment or poor treatment *because* she is a woman. No believer is called to be insulted in her person, although a believer might be called to give her life for the sake of God. Specifically, no man (husband) has the right to discipline a woman (wife). Domestic violence is never acceptable and can never be excused based on a false notion that a woman is suffering for Christ in such a situation.

13:8–14 Love Fulfills God's Requirements. At the second coming, Christ will judge the world and reward all according to their deeds and will embrace those who by faith have accepted his work on the cross for their sins.

14:1–23 The Danger of Criticism. 1–4: Paul uses the phrase *weak in faith* to connote a believer who is following the food laws and Sabbath practices closely, rather than someone who is behaving sinfully. He encourages believers not to judge other believers on incidental matters of practice that are not sinful but are based on local custom or interpretation of the Jewish law. **5–6:** It is likely that Paul is speaking of the Sabbath that Jewish believers or those Gentiles who connected themselves with the synagogue set aside as holy. Gentiles might not think any day of the week more special, as their background would not include such convictions. It might also be that some in Rome

holy than another day, while others think every
day is alike. You should each be fully convinced
that whichever day you choose is acceptable.
6 Those who worship the Lord on a special day do
it to honor him. Those who eat any kind of food
do so to honor the Lord, since they give thanks to
God before eating. And those who refuse to eat
certain foods also want to please the Lord and give
thanks to God. 7 For we don't live for ourselves or
die for ourselves. 8 If we live, it's to honor the Lord.
And if we die, it's to honor the Lord. So whether
we live or die, we belong to the Lord. 9 Christ died
and rose again for this very purpose—to be Lord
both of the living and of the dead.
10 So why do you condemn another believer*?
Why do you look down on another believer? Remember, we will all stand before the judgment
seat of God. 11 For the Scriptures say,

" 'As surely as I live,' says the LORD,
'every knee will bend to me,
and every tongue will confess and give
praise to God.*' "

12 Yes, each of us will give a personal account to
God. 13 So let's stop condemning each other. Decide instead to live in such a way that you will
not cause another believer to stumble and fall.
14 I know and am convinced on the authority
of the Lord Jesus that no food, in and of itself, is
wrong to eat. But if someone believes it is wrong,
then for that person it is wrong. 15 And if another
believer is distressed by what you eat, you are
not acting in love if you eat it. Don't let your eating ruin someone for whom Christ died. 16 Then
you will not be criticized for doing something
you believe is good. 17 For the Kingdom of God is
not a matter of what we eat or drink, but of living
a life of goodness and peace and joy in the Holy
Spirit. 18 If you serve Christ with this attitude,
you will please God, and others will approve of
you, too. 19 So then, let us aim for harmony in the
church and try to build each other up.
20 Don't tear apart the work of God over what
you eat. Remember, all foods are acceptable, but
it is wrong to eat something if it makes another
person stumble. 21 It is better not to eat meat or
drink wine or do anything else if it might cause
another believer to stumble. 22 You may believe
there's nothing wrong with what you are doing,
but keep it between yourself and God. Blessed
are those who don't feel guilty for doing something they have decided is right. 23 But if you
have doubts about whether or not you should eat
something, you are sinning if you go ahead and
do it. For you are not following your convictions.
If you do anything you believe is not right, you
are sinning.

Living to Please Others

15 We who are strong must be considerate of those who are sensitive about
things like this. We must not just
please ourselves. 2 We should help others do what
is right and build them up in the Lord. 3 For even
Christ didn't live to please himself. As the Scriptures say, "The insults of those who insult you,
O God, have fallen on me."* 4 Such things were
written in the Scriptures long ago to teach us.
And the Scriptures give us hope and encouragement as we wait patiently for God's promises to
be fulfilled.
5 May God, who gives this patience and encouragement, help you live in complete harmony with each other, as is fitting for followers of
Christ Jesus. 6 Then all of you can join together
with one voice, giving praise and glory to God,
the Father of our Lord Jesus Christ.

14:10 Greek *your brother;* also in 14:10b, 13, 15, 21.
14:11 Or *confess allegiance to God.* Isa 49:18; 45:23 (Greek version). **15:3** Greek *who insult you have fallen on me.* Ps 69:9.

---

are meeting on Sunday, the Lord's day (1 Cor 16:2), though little is known about early Christian worship habits. Paul is revolutionary in declaring that Gentiles do not have to follow the same requirements before God as did Jews. **14–15:** Some connected meat with idol worship and sacrifice. Most people in the ancient world rarely ate meat because it was so expensive. But during a festival for the city and state gods and goddesses, the wealthy patrons of the city would sponsor meals that often included meat. Moreover, since much of the meat sold at markets had been previously sacrificed in a pagan temple, some believers thought that eating it would tarnish them or their witness (see 1 Cor 8:10; also Mark 2:23–28; 7:18–19; Acts 10). **16–23:** If believers use their freedom to eat meat but cause pain to another believer by so eating, the good has been rendered bad. God is most pleased with believers who consider others before their own legitimate privileges.

15:1–13 Living to Please Others. Paul identifies himself with those who are strong, those who can eat meat with a clean conscience. The primary responsibility is not to make the weak strong but to accept them as they are and respect them for their love of Christ. The goal of a strong believer is to build up the body, not challenge a weak believer's faith on a particular issue. **7–8:** All believers are exhorted to accept

[7]Therefore, accept each other just as Christ
has accepted you so that God will be given glory.
[8]Remember that Christ came as a servant to the
Jews* to show that God is true to the promises
he made to their ancestors. [9]He also came so
that the Gentiles might give glory to God for his
mercies to them. That is what the psalmist meant
when he wrote:

"For this, I will praise you among the
Gentiles;
I will sing praises to your name."*

[10]And in another place it is written,

"Rejoice with his people,
you Gentiles."*

[11]And yet again,

"Praise the LORD, all you Gentiles.
Praise him, all you people of the earth."*

[12]And in another place Isaiah said,

"The heir to David's throne* will come,
and he will rule over the Gentiles.
They will place their hope on him."*

[13]I pray that God, the source of hope, will fill
you completely with joy and peace because you
trust in him. Then you will overflow with confident hope through the power of the Holy Spirit.

Paul's Reason for Writing

[14]I am fully convinced, my dear brothers and sisters,* that you are full of goodness. You know
these things so well you can teach each other all
about them. [15]Even so, I have been bold enough
to write about some of these points, knowing that
all you need is this reminder. For by God's grace,
[16]I am a special messenger from Christ Jesus to
you Gentiles. I bring you the Good News so that
I might present you as an acceptable offering to
God, made holy by the Holy Spirit. [17]So I have
reason to be enthusiastic about all Christ Jesus
has done through me in my service to God. [18]Yet
I dare not boast about anything except what
Christ has done through me, bringing the Gentiles to God by my message and by the way I
worked among them. [19]They were convinced by
the power of miraculous signs and wonders and
by the power of God's Spirit.* In this way, I have
fully presented the Good News of Christ from
Jerusalem all the way to Illyricum.*
[20]My ambition has always been to preach the
Good News where the name of Christ has never been heard, rather than where a church has
already been started by someone else. [21]I have
been following the plan spoken of in the Scriptures, where it says,

"Those who have never been told about him
will see,
and those who have never heard of him
will understand."*

[22]In fact, my visit to you has been delayed so long
because I have been preaching in these places.

Paul's Travel Plans

[23]But now I have finished my work in these regions, and after all these long years of waiting, I
am eager to visit you. [24]I am planning to go to
Spain, and when I do, I will stop off in Rome.

15:8 Greek *servant of circumcision.* **15:9** Ps 18:49. **15:10** Deut 32:43. **15:11** Ps 117:1. **15:12a** Greek *The root of Jesse.* David was the son of Jesse. **15:12b** Isa 11:10 (Greek version). **15:14** Greek *brothers;* also in 15:30. **15:19a** Other manuscripts read *the Spirit;* still others read *the Holy Spirit.* **15:19b** *Illyricum* was a region northeast of Italy. **15:21** Isa 52:15 (Greek version).

one another, or literally, welcome them as neighbors. This message might have special relevance for women, who traditionally are responsible for the hospitality of the family and the church. The servant Jesus declared that when anyone helps another, it is as though that person were helping him (Matt 10:40–42). This model of servanthood casts a holy light on deeds that society tends to devalue. It encourages women, the typical servers, to recognize the incredible value their deeds have in God's kingdom.

15:14—16:27 Personal Greetings

15:14–22 Paul's Reason for Writing. 20–22: Paul defines his mission from God as that of preaching to Gentiles, especially those who have not yet heard the gospel. He will not boast about another's ministry and claim it for his own. His preaching in other regions has been accomplished, and thus he is free to journey to Rome.

15:23–33 Paul's Travel Plans. 30–32: He recognizes that he will be in some danger personally when he takes the offering to the poor saints in Jerusalem. He requests that the Romans pray for his safety and that his offering is acceptable to the believers in Jerusalem.

And after I have enjoyed your fellowship for a
little while, you can provide for my journey.
[25]But before I come, I must go to Jerusalem
to take a gift to the believers* there. [26]For you
see, the believers in Macedonia and Achaia* have
eagerly taken up an offering for the poor among
the believers in Jerusalem. [27]They were glad to
do this because they feel they owe a real debt
to them. Since the Gentiles received the spiritual
blessings of the Good News from the believers
in Jerusalem, they feel the least they can do in
return is to help them financially. [28]As soon as
I have delivered this money and completed this
good deed of theirs, I will come to see you on my
way to Spain. [29]And I am sure that when I come,
Christ will richly bless our time together.
[30]Dear brothers and sisters, I urge you in
the name of our Lord Jesus Christ to join in my
struggle by praying to God for me. Do this because of your love for me, given to you by the
Holy Spirit. [31]Pray that I will be rescued from
those in Judea who refuse to obey God. Pray also
that the believers there will be willing to accept
the donation* I am taking to Jerusalem. [32]Then,
by the will of God, I will be able to come to you
with a joyful heart, and we will be an encouragement to each other.
[33]And now may God, who gives us his peace,
be with you all. Amen.*

Paul Greets His Friends

16 I commend to you our sister Phoebe, who is a deacon in the church in
Cenchrea. [2]Welcome her in the Lord
as one who is worthy of honor among God's people. Help her in whatever she needs, for she has
been helpful to many, and especially to me.
[3]Give my greetings to Priscilla and Aquila,
my co-workers in the ministry of Christ Jesus.

15:25 Greek *God's holy people;* also in 15:26, 31. **15:26** *Macedonia* and *Achaia* were the northern and southern regions of Greece. **15:31** Greek *the ministry;* other manuscripts read *the gift.* **15:33** Some manuscripts do not include *Amen.* One very early manuscript places 16:25-27 here.

16:1–16 Paul Greets His Friends. The greetings constitute a remarkable attestation of the involvement of Christian women in the church. We are given not only their names but also their ministries. **1–2:** As with other emissaries unknown to a congregation, Phoebe is sent with a letter of commendation (cf. Acts 18:20; 2 Cor 3:1). These letters gave not only the name of the person being sent but also the qualifications for ministry (cf. 1 Cor 4:17; Phil 2:19–30). She is introduced to the Romans as a deacon *(diakonos)* (cf. Acts 18:27; Phil 2:29; 3 Jn 10–12). Many English translations change the Greek term to the feminine "deaconess," but Paul is not making any functional distinction based on Phoebe's gender. Thus she carries the same responsibilities and authority as anyone else who shares that title. Paul identifies himself as a *diakonos* (1 Cor 3:5; 2 Cor 3:6; Eph 3:7; Phil 1:1) as well as Timothy (1 Thes 3:2; 1 Tim 4:7), Tychicus (Eph 6:21; Col 4:7), Apollos (1 Cor 3:5), and Epaphras (Col 1:7). Christ too is a *diakonos* (Rom 15:8; Gal 2:17). The term is often translated correctly as "servant" or "minister" because it carries the meaning of someone serving or ministering to a ruler. As such, it would be correct to identify Phoebe as a minister in the Cenchrean church, located about nine miles from Corinth.

Phoebe has come to Rome on the business of the church. There is speculation that this may have been to raise support for the projected visit to Spain, as the word *propempo* is one used for promotion of a missionary endeavor (Acts 20:38; 21:5). Phoebe appears to have traveled independently and may have been able to make important contacts and to secure official permissions that would be necessary for the expedition to Spain.

Paul describes Phoebe as one who has helped him, calling her his benefactor *(prostatis).* The literal meaning is "one who presides" or "a woman who is set over others." This noun is found only here in the New Testament, but the masculine form *(prostates)* is employed by some to denote the person presiding at Communion. Paul uses the verbal form of the word in several places, certainly a help in determining the meaning here. In 1 Thessalonians 5:12, the Thessalonians are encouraged to respect those who are over them in the Lord, and in Romans 12:8, Paul uses the participial form to describe the gift of leadership. The term also carries with it a sense of caring or giving aid, though in Paul's use supervisory leadership is emphasized. In the Pastoral Epistles, the word is used of church officials who preside over the congregation (1 Tim 3:4–5; 5:17). **3–4:** Although Paul has never visited Rome, he is able to send greetings to named individuals whom he has known elsewhere in his travels. The significant contribution of Priscilla and Aquila to the advancement of the gospel is noted. Priscilla's name is mentioned first here (as in Acts 18:18, 26 and 2 Tim 4:19; though in Acts 18:2 and 1 Cor 16:19 Aquila's name comes first). In the ancient world, the first named in a pair carried the greater honor. Thus it is likely that Priscilla was gifted as a teacher and speaker, yet both share equally in their ministry. After sojourns in Corinth and Ephesus, they are back in Rome, leading a house church. They are "co-workers" of Paul; this term *(synergos)* is used by Paul to describe himself and many of his

Paul's Greetings to Female Colleagues

Paul's greetings to female colleagues usually occur toward the end of his letters. His typical closings include hortatory remarks, greetings, a wish of peace, and a benediction. In Hellenistic letters the purpose of greetings was emotional expression. Greeting forms include the writer greeting someone, asking the addressee to greet someone, or relaying a third party's greetings. In these letters a greeting verb is followed by an indication of the one greeting; the person greeted is named, and elaborating phrases emphasize some aspect of the greeting. Paul's letters follow this format.

Paul greets or mentions the following women co-workers in his letters: Apphia (Phlm 2), Euodia and Syntyche (Phil 4:2), Junia (Rom 16:7), Mary (Rom 16:6), Nympha (Col 4:15), Phoebe (Rom 16:1), Prisca (Rom 16:3; 1 Cor 16:19), and Tryphena and Tryphosa (Rom 16:12). Euodia and Syntyche and Prisca are called "fellow workers"; Junia is called an apostle and "countryman"; Mary, Tryphena, and Tryphosa, "hard workers"; and Phoebe, a deacon. These are the same terms Paul uses for his male associates. Other women greeted in passing include Persis (Rom 16:12), Rufus's mother (Rom 16:13), Julia, Nereus's sister, and Olympas (Rom 16:15). Whenever greetings are to the "brethren" or to a church community, women are included.

Three women Paul greets are of special interest as leaders in their churches: Phoebe, Junia, and Nympha. Romans 16:1–2 uses two technical phrases in connection with Phoebe—"deacon of the church" and "helper of many." Although the meaning of deacon is not self-evident, it was a church office (see Phil 1:1; 1 Tim 3:8, 13). "Helper of many" is the equivalent of the Latin *patrona*, a word used here in the New Testament but found in the Septuagint and in contemporary inscriptions for patronesses. Evidence strongly supports the idea that the person in Romans 16:7 is Junia, a female, not Junias, a male (see translator's note for 16:7a). No commentator until Aegidius of Rome (1245–1316) took this person to be male. While the term apostle is not defined, a missionary couple (like Prisca and Aquila) are "outstanding among the apostles," and thus a woman is clearly called an apostle. Nympha (Col 4:15) seems to have been a householder who provided a church with a place to meet and thus, like Chloe in Corinth (1 Cor 1:11), was probably the leader of a house church.

Paul's greetings to his female associates indicate that he worked with and valued the contributions of women to Christian mission, that he used the same technical terminology in relation to them that he did with his male associates, and that he numbered women among his friends, supporters, and fellow workers.

4 In fact, they once risked their lives for me. I
am thankful to them, and so are all the Gentile
churches. 5 Also give my greetings to the church
that meets in their home.

Greet my dear friend Epenetus. He was the
first person from the province of Asia to become
a follower of Christ. 6 Give my greetings to Mary,
who has worked so hard for your benefit. 7 Greet
Andronicus and Junia,* my fellow Jews,* who
were in prison with me. They are highly respect-

16:7a *Junia* is a feminine name. Some late manuscripts accent the word so it reads *Junias,* a masculine name; still others read *Julia* (feminine). **16:7b** Or *compatriots;* also in 16:21.

colleagues, including Urbanus (Rom 16:9), Timothy (Rom 16:21; 1 Thes 3:2), Tychicus (Col 4:7), Philemon (Phlm 1), Euodias and Syntyche (Phil 4:3), Mark, Aristarchus, Demas and Luke (Phlm 24), and members of the household of Stephanas (1 Cor 16:15–16). To such, says Paul, the church ought to be subject (1 Cor 16:16). **6:** Paul describes Mary as working "so hard," using the same term that he applies to himself (1 Cor 15:10; Gal 4:11; Phil 2:16; Col 1:29; 1 Tim 4:10). 1 Timothy 5:17 offers the injunction *Elders who do their work well should be respected and paid well, especially those who work hard at both preaching and teaching*. Other examples of the verb as indicating labor for the gospel may be found at John 4:38, 1 Corinthians 16:16, and 1 Thessalonians 5:12. Each time that the verb is used in Romans 16, it is applied to a woman: Mary, Tryphena, Tryphosa, and Persis. **7:** The name Junia is a Latin one and follows a specific, common pattern in transliterating it into Greek. The male form of this name in Latin is Junius (Gk., *Iounios*), while the female form in Latin is Junia (Gk., *Iounia*). In the fourth century, the name "Junia" was acknowledged as referring to a woman by no less a figure than John Chrysostom, the Patriarch of Constantinople.

Later church leaders, uncomfortable with a woman apostle who had leadership within the church, changed her name and created one that is unknown

ed among the apostles and became followers of Christ before I did. 8 Greet Ampliatus, my dear friend in the Lord. 9 Greet Urbanus, our co-worker in Christ, and my dear friend Stachys.

10 Greet Apelles, a good man whom Christ approves. And give my greetings to the believers from the household of Aristobulus. 11 Greet Herodion, my fellow Jew.* Greet the Lord's people from the household of Narcissus. 12 Give my greetings to Tryphena and Tryphosa, the Lord's workers, and to dear Persis, who has worked so hard for the Lord. 13 Greet Rufus, whom the Lord picked out to be his very own; and also his dear mother, who has been a mother to me.

14 Give my greetings to Asyncritus, Phlegon, Hermes, Patrobas, Hermas, and the brothers and sisters* who meet with them. 15 Give my greetings to Philologus, Julia, Nereus and his sister, and to Olympas and all the believers* who meet with them. 16 Greet each other in Christian love.* All the churches of Christ send you their greetings.

Paul's Final Instructions

17 And now I make one more appeal, my dear brothers and sisters. Watch out for people who cause divisions and upset people's faith by teaching things contrary to what you have been taught. Stay away from them. 18 Such people are not serving Christ our Lord; they are serving their own personal interests. By smooth talk and glowing words they deceive innocent people. 19 But everyone knows that you are obedient to the Lord. This makes me very happy. I want you to be wise in doing right and to stay innocent of any wrong. 20 The God of peace will soon crush Satan under your feet. May the grace of our Lord Jesus* be with you.

21 Timothy, my fellow worker, sends you his greetings, as do Lucius, Jason, and Sosipater, my fellow Jews.

22 I, Tertius, the one writing this letter for Paul, send my greetings, too, as one of the Lord's followers.

23 Gaius says hello to you. He is my host and also serves as host to the whole church. Erastus, the city treasurer, sends you his greetings, and so does our brother Quartus.*

25 Now all glory to God, who is able to make you strong, just as my Good News says. This message about Jesus Christ has revealed his plan for you Gentiles, a plan kept secret from the beginning of time. 26 But now as the prophets* foretold and as the eternal God has commanded, this message is made known to all Gentiles everywhere, so that they too might believe and obey him. 27 All glory to the only wise God, through Jesus Christ, forever. Amen.

16:11 Or *compatriot.* **16:14** Greek *brothers;* also in 16:17. **16:15** Greek *all of God's holy people.* **16:16** Greek *with a sacred kiss.* **16:20** Some manuscripts read *Lord Jesus Christ.* **16:23** Some manuscripts add verse 24, *May the grace of our Lord Jesus Christ be with you all. Amen.* Still others add this sentence after verse 27. **16:26** Greek *the prophetic writings.*

---

in Greek sources—Junias. The name is nowhere attested in any inscription, public monument, graffito, or literary document.

Junia and Andronicus are notable among the apostles. The term *apostle* as used in the New Testament could refer to the Twelve, but Paul explains his qualification as one who had seen Jesus (1 Cor 9:1; cf. Rom 1:1; 1 Cor 1:1; 9:1–2; 15:9; 2 Cor 1:1; 12:11; Gal 1:1; Eph 1:1; Col 1:1; 1 Tim 1:1; 2 Tim 1:1; Titus 1:1). Acts 1:21–22 also suggests that another criterion for an apostle was someone who had followed Jesus in his earthly ministry. Such a person was qualified, Peter explains, to be a *witness of Jesus' resurrection*. Others called apostles include Barnabas (Acts 14:14), James the Lord's brother (Gal 1:19), Matthias (Acts 1:26), Epaphroditus (Phil 2:25), and unnamed brothers or sisters (2 Cor 8:23). There is no reason to assume the gift/call of apostleship should be restricted to males. Junia is a clear example that it was not. She and Andronicus may have planted the gospel in Rome much as Paul did in Corinth. **12–15:** Besides Tryphena, Tryphosa, Persis, and Julia, there are two unnamed women. These are the sister of Nereus and the mother of Rufus. Of Rufus we may perhaps read in Mark 15:21, but the object of Paul's greeting is now in Rome. In a previous location his mother has shown a kindness and concern for Paul that cause him to consider her as a mother to him. The ministry of mothering those who are not of a woman's own blood is one that God has blessed throughout the ages.

16:17–27 Paul's Final Instructions. 22: Tertius identifies himself as the writer of the letter. It was quite common to use scribes to write letters or take dictation. Paul hints at this same procedure in Galatians 6:11 and 1 Corinthians 16:21, where he seems to be distinguishing his handwriting from that of the scribe. **25–27:** The mystery of how God in Christ will save Gentiles has been revealed and completed. Even the prophets attest to this mystery, resting as it does on the wisdom of God and the faith of the people in Jesus Christ.

1 CORINTHIANS

INTRODUCTION

First Corinthians is one of the earliest New Testament documents and attests to the skill of the apostle Paul in addressing a multiplicity of church problems. The audience appears to have consisted of a mix of Jews, Greeks, and other subject peoples of the Roman Empire. Some converts had little status, education, or illustrious family background, while others maintained an exalted opinion of themselves and their spiritual gifts. Snobbery in various forms was rampant. Far from the purity often thought to have existed in the early church, we are confronted with the reality of divisions, depravity, debauchery, and rancor.

Formerly some of the congregation had been idol worshipers and had exhibited a dissolute, promiscuous lifestyle. Addressed to a community in the midst of profound social, political, and philosophical change, the letter contains directives to this diverse congregation, all of whom had come to faith in Christ amid difficult circumstances. Mutual accommodation required new patterns and new understandings of one another.

First Corinthians, almost universally regarded as Pauline, is the prime example of an occasional epistle, written in response to specific inquiries. There is considerable debate as to whether the letter as it now stands is a cohesive document or whether it is two or more different communications combined into one treatise. Although it lacks a sustained argument, the letter is not the patchwork that it may at first seem. The theme most consistently running through this epistle is an appeal to respect the unity of the church and to preserve it from doctrinal and moral corruption.

The adherents of Chloe ("some members of Chloe's household" [1:11]) had reported animosities and factions in the church. "Chloe's people" probably indicates a worshiping community with a female leader. A number of New Testament house churches appear to have been led by women (Acts 12:5–17; 16:40; Col 4:15; Rom 16:3–5; 1 Cor 1:11; 16:19; 2 Jn). Under this leadership, the group had taken the responsibility to inform the apostle of troubling factors and to solicit his help. Here we may gain a glimpse of the significant, if often unheralded, roles that women played in the early church. The initiative of a woman lies behind the letter's composition.

Paul's response deals primarily with issues of particular interest to women. The emphasis is on the social and relational aspects of the life of the congregation. Peace making, an endeavor often espoused by women, is of major importance in the letter. Slavery, prostitution, and social responsibility are given consideration, along with cultic activities that held a special attraction for women. Intimate issues concerning women, such as concepts of body, sexuality, puberty, marriage, divorce, feminine attire and conduct, foods and household management, come to the fore.

There are indications that the apostle is responding to messages and inquiries that have been sent to him at Ephesus. At points, usually in rebuttal, he quotes directly from his informants. They appear to have asked about several issues, though the letter may also include responses to other groups within the Corinthian congregation. —*Catherine Clark Kroeger*

✧

Greetings from Paul

1 This letter is from Paul, chosen by the will
of God to be an apostle of Christ Jesus, and
from our brother Sosthenes.
2 I am writing to God's church in Corinth,*
to you who have been called by God to be his
own holy people. He made you holy by means
of Christ Jesus,* just as he did for all people everywhere who call on the name of our Lord Jesus
Christ, their Lord and ours.
3 May God our Father and the Lord Jesus
Christ give you grace and peace.

Paul Gives Thanks to God

4 I always thank my God for you and for the
gracious gifts he has given you, now that you
belong to Christ Jesus. 5 Through him, God has
enriched your church in every way—with all of
your eloquent words and all of your knowledge.
6 This confirms that what I told you about Christ
is true. 7 Now you have every spiritual gift you
need as you eagerly wait for the return of our
Lord Jesus Christ. 8 He will keep you strong to
the end so that you will be free from all blame
on the day when our Lord Jesus Christ returns.
9 God will do this, for he is faithful to do what
he says, and he has invited you into partnership
with his Son, Jesus Christ our Lord.

1:2a *Corinth* was the capital city of Achaia, the southern region of the Greek peninsula. **1:2b** Or *because you belong to Christ Jesus.*

1:1—4:21 Laying Out the Issues

1:1–9 Loving and Affirming Greeting. 2: In view of the manifold problems facing the congregation, the term *holy* is surprising. Yet the Greek *hagiazo* ("make holy") is used throughout the epistle of some unlikely people. A recurring theme will be the need for unity and purity within the body of believers.

Divisions in the Church

[10]I appeal to you, dear brothers and sisters,* by the authority of our Lord Jesus Christ, to live in harmony with each other. Let there be no divisions in the church. Rather, be of one mind, united in thought and purpose. [11]For some members of Chloe's household have told me about your quarrels, my dear brothers and sisters. [12]Some of you are saying, "I am a follower of Paul." Others are saying, "I follow Apollos," or "I follow Peter,*" or "I follow only Christ."

[13]Has Christ been divided into factions? Was I, Paul, crucified for you? Were any of you baptized in the name of Paul? Of course not! [14]I thank God that I did not baptize any of you except Crispus and Gaius, [15]for now no one can say they were baptized in my name. [16](Oh yes, I also baptized the household of Stephanas, but I don't remember baptizing anyone else.) [17]For Christ didn't send me to baptize, but to preach the Good News—and not with clever speech, for fear that the cross of Christ would lose its power.

The Wisdom of God

[18]The message of the cross is foolish to those who are headed for destruction! But we who are being saved know it is the very power of God. [19]As the Scriptures say,

> "I will destroy the wisdom of the wise
> and discard the intelligence of the
> intelligent."*

[20]So where does this leave the philosophers, the scholars, and the world's brilliant debaters? God has made the wisdom of this world look foolish. [21]Since God in his wisdom saw to it that the world would never know him through human wisdom, he has used our foolish preaching to save those who believe. [22]It is foolish to the Jews, who ask for signs from heaven. And it is foolish to the Greeks, who seek human wisdom. [23]So when we preach that Christ was crucified, the Jews are offended and the Gentiles say it's all nonsense.

[24]But to those called by God to salvation, both Jews and Gentiles,* Christ is the power of God and the wisdom of God. [25]This foolish plan of God is wiser than the wisest of human plans, and God's weakness is stronger than the greatest of human strength.

[26]Remember, dear brothers and sisters, that few of you were wise in the world's eyes or powerful or wealthy* when God called you. [27]Instead, God chose things the world considers foolish in order to shame those who think they are wise. And he chose things that are powerless to shame those who are powerful. [28]God chose things despised by the world,* things counted as nothing at all, and used them to bring to nothing what the world considers important. [29]As a result, no one can ever boast in the presence of God.

[30]God has united you with Christ Jesus. For our benefit God made him to be wisdom itself. Christ made us right with God; he made us pure and holy, and he freed us from sin. [31]Therefore, as the Scriptures say, "If you want to boast, boast only about the LORD."*

1:10 Greek *brothers;* also in 1:11, 26. **1:12** Greek *Cephas.* **1:19** Isa 29:14. **1:24** Greek *and Greeks.* **1:26** Or *high born.* **1:28** Or *God chose those who are low born.* **1:31** Jer 9:24.

1:10–17 Divided Loyalties. 11: Chloe's people have sought him out and look to him for mediation. Apparently they consider him to be the individual who could most effectively bring unity into their divided midst. **12:** The congregation is divided among factions, dependent on human personality rather than the Holy Spirit's guidance. Those who followed Apollos must have been swayed by the brilliance of the Alexandrian school (Acts 18:24); the adherents of Peter were probably from a Jewish background (Gal 2:7–8); those who maintained that they were of Christ's party appear to have been as factious as the rest. They seem to have adopted a spirituality that placed little importance on matters of everyday life or the human condition. Such individuals displayed complacency toward the sins of the flesh and negativity toward the resurrection of the physical body.

1:18–31 The Centrality of Christ Crucified. 20: The Athenian Academy had influenced some of the Corinthian Christians, but Paul argues that there is more than one way of knowing and more than one way of perceiving the mind of God. **26:** Women's insights and perspectives are not necessarily the same as those of men, but they may afford significant access to truth. While privileged males had been schooled in certain methods of intellectual inquiry, Paul offers a more universal avenue. The majority of the Corinthian congregation lacked the social, political, and financial resources necessary to have command of these esoteric thought processes. Gender further disbarred most women from a comprehension of the academy. **28–30:** The entry to God's truth is open to the poor, the uneducated, even those without superior mental endowment. To the humble seeker, Christ is made wisdom from God. Wisdom is not an abstraction and is bestowed on those open to receive it.

Paul's Message of Wisdom

2 When I first came to you, dear brothers
and sisters,* I didn't use lofty words and
impressive wisdom to tell you God's secret
plan.* 2 For I decided that while I was with you I
would forget everything except Jesus Christ, the
one who was crucified. 3 I came to you in weakness—timid and trembling. 4 And my message
and my preaching were very plain. Rather than
using clever and persuasive speeches, I relied
only on the power of the Holy Spirit. 5 I did this
so you would trust not in human wisdom but in
the power of God.

6 Yet when I am among mature believers, I do
speak with words of wisdom, but not the kind
of wisdom that belongs to this world or to the
rulers of this world, who are soon forgotten.
7 No, the wisdom we speak of is the mystery of
God*—his plan that was previously hidden, even
though he made it for our ultimate glory before
the world began. 8 But the rulers of this world
have not understood it; if they had, they would
not have crucified our glorious Lord. 9 That is
what the Scriptures mean when they say,

"No eye has seen, no ear has heard,
and no mind has imagined
what God has prepared
for those who love him."*

10 But* it was to us that God revealed these
things by his Spirit. For his Spirit searches out
everything and shows us God's deep secrets.
11 No one can know a person's thoughts except
that person's own spirit, and no one can know
God's thoughts except God's own Spirit. 12 And
we have received God's Spirit (not the world's
spirit), so we can know the wonderful things God
has freely given us.

13 When we tell you these things, we do not use
words that come from human wisdom. Instead,
we speak words given to us by the Spirit, using
the Spirit's words to explain spiritual truths.*
14 But people who aren't spiritual* can't receive
these truths from God's Spirit. It all sounds foolish to them and they can't understand it, for only
those who are spiritual can understand what the
Spirit means. 15 Those who are spiritual can evaluate all things, but they themselves cannot be
evaluated by others. 16 For,

"Who can know the LORD's thoughts?
Who knows enough to teach him?"*

But we understand these things, for we have the
mind of Christ.

Paul and Apollos, Servants of Christ

3 Dear brothers and sisters,* when I was
with you I couldn't talk to you as I would
to spiritual people.* I had to talk as though
you belonged to this world or as though you
were infants in the Christian life.* 2 I had to feed
you with milk, not with solid food, because you

2:1a Greek *brothers.* **2:1b** Greek *God's mystery;* other manuscripts read *God's testimony.* **2:7** Greek *But we speak God's wisdom in a mystery.* **2:9** Isa 64:4. **2:10** Some manuscripts read *For.* **2:13** Or *explaining spiritual truths in spiritual language,* or *explaining spiritual truths to spiritual people.* **2:14** Or *who don't have the Spirit;* or *who have only physical life.* **2:16** Isa 40:13 (Greek version). **3:1a** Greek *Brothers.* **3:1b** Or *to people who have the Spirit.* **3:1c** Greek *in Christ.*

2:1–16 God's Power in Weakness and Simplicity. 3: Paul's mission strategy had taken him to Athens, the intellectual capital of the ancient world, to Ephesus, the religious capital, to Rome, the political capital, and to Corinth, the commercial capital. He had dared to come to Corinth to assert the seemingly ridiculous claims of the gospel. His address would focus on straightforward promulgation of the gospel's content, without the highly polished rhetoric that composed so large a part of Greek education. **4:** God's wisdom is more profound than the brightest of human ideas. Here we have not a repudiation of higher education but recognition that the Holy Spirit's power is mightier. Though well trained in the rabbinic and philosophical traditions of his world, Paul acknowledges that spiritual perceptions are communicated by other paths. Individuals denied an opportunity to be schooled in the niceties of a theological education might be empowered by calling, conviction, and commitment. **13:** The ancient insistence upon rhetorical form as more important than substance placed women at a serious disadvantage in terms of communication. Their manner of expression betrayed their lack of formal education and of contact with the cultural bastions of ancient society. Yet theirs was the promise of enrichment in knowledge and in utterance.

3:1–23 The Folly and Immaturity of Personality Cults. 2: Breast *milk* was sometimes given to initiates of the mystery cults, and Paul depicts himself as wet nurse for infants too immature to be nourished with table food (cf. 1 Thes 2:7; for image of Paul as birthing mother, see Gal 4:19; Phlm 10). The nursing relationship between mother and child is one of tenderness and deep intimacy. But in order to grow adequately and develop into maturity, an infant must be weaned onto stronger food. As a mother, Paul must make har-

weren't ready for anything stronger. And you
still aren't ready, [3]for you are still controlled by
your sinful nature. You are jealous of one another
and quarrel with each other. Doesn't that prove
you are controlled by your sinful nature? Aren't
you living like people of the world? [4]When one
of you says, "I am a follower of Paul," and another says, "I follow Apollos," aren't you acting
just like people of the world?

[5]After all, who is Apollos? Who is Paul? We
are only God's servants through whom you believed the Good News. Each of us did the work
the Lord gave us. [6]I planted the seed in your
hearts, and Apollos watered it, but it was God
who made it grow. [7]It's not important who does
the planting, or who does the watering. What's
important is that God makes the seed grow. [8]The
one who plants and the one who waters work together with the same purpose. And both will be
rewarded for their own hard work. [9]For we are
both God's workers. And you are God's field. You
are God's building.

[10]Because of God's grace to me, I have laid the
foundation like an expert builder. Now others are
building on it. But whoever is building on this
foundation must be very careful. [11]For no one
can lay any foundation other than the one we
already have—Jesus Christ.

[12]Anyone who builds on that foundation may
use a variety of materials—gold, silver, jewels,
wood, hay, or straw. [13]But on the judgment day,
fire will reveal what kind of work each builder
has done. The fire will show if a person's work
has any value. [14]If the work survives, that builder
will receive a reward. [15]But if the work is burned
up, the builder will suffer great loss. The builder
will be saved, but like someone barely escaping
through a wall of flames.

[16]Don't you realize that all of you together
are the temple of God and that the Spirit of God
lives in* you? [17]God will destroy anyone who
destroys this temple. For God's temple is holy,
and you are that temple.

[18]Stop deceiving yourselves. If you think you
are wise by this world's standards, you need to
become a fool to be truly wise. [19]For the wisdom
of this world is foolishness to God. As the Scriptures say,

"He traps the wise
in the snare of their own cleverness."*

[20]And again,

"The LORD knows the thoughts of the wise;
he knows they are worthless."*

[21]So don't boast about following a particular
human leader. For everything belongs to you—
[22]whether Paul or Apollos or Peter,* or the world,
or life and death, or the present and the future.
Everything belongs to you, [23]and you belong to
Christ, and Christ belongs to God.

Paul's Relationship with the Corinthians

4 So look at Apollos and me as mere servants
of Christ who have been put in charge of
explaining God's mysteries. [2]Now, a person who is put in charge as a manager must be
faithful. [3]As for me, it matters very little how
I might be evaluated by you or by any human
authority. I don't even trust my own judgment
on this point. [4]My conscience is clear, but that
doesn't prove I'm right. It is the Lord himself
who will examine me and decide.

[5]So don't make judgments about anyone
ahead of time—before the Lord returns. For he

3:16 Or *among.* **3:19** Job 5:13. **3:20** Ps 94:11. **3:22** Greek *Cephas.*

mony among squabbling children who each prefer dependence on their own leader. **5:** Women who feel inadequate tend to gravitate to a dominant personality whom they consider more knowledgeable than themselves. For some, it is easier to accept the work of a recognized leader than to think seriously for oneself. The objective, however, is not to take pride in following the deductions of another but in reaching one's own conclusion by mature reasoning. **16:** After a long image about building, the thought of believers as the temple of God is introduced, but in the plural. The use of the plural *all of you* (Gk., *hymin*) indicates that Paul is not speaking of the individual believers' bodies (as in 6:19) but of the corporate body, the church: We are together the temple of God, and God dwells among us. Though women were excluded from worship in some of the most important Greco-Roman temples, they not only have access to but also are part of the temple of God. Factionalism threatens the temple of God.

4:1–21 Buffoons for Christ's Sake. 1: Paul and his ministry appear to have been disparaged by some of the factions attached to other leaders. Although he had first brought the gospel to their city, Paul's relationship with the Corinthians had not always been harmonious. If he was revered by some, he had been repudiated by others. At some point he had been treated shabbily by them, and on at least one of Paul's visits, he was rejected (2 Cor 2:1).

will bring our darkest secrets to light and will
reveal our private motives. Then God will give to
each one whatever praise is due.
[6]Dear brothers and sisters,* I have used Apollos and myself to illustrate what I've been saying. If you pay attention to what I have quoted
from the Scriptures,* you won't be proud of one
of your leaders at the expense of another. [7]For
what gives you the right to make such a judgment? What do you have that God hasn't given
you? And if everything you have is from God,
why boast as though it were not a gift?
[8]You think you already have everything you
need. You think you are already rich. You have
begun to reign in God's kingdom without us! I
wish you really were reigning already, for then
we would be reigning with you. [9]Instead, I sometimes think God has put us apostles on display,
like prisoners of war at the end of a victor's parade, condemned to die. We have become a spec-
tacle to the entire world—to people and angels
alike.
[10]Our dedication to Christ makes us look
like fools, but you claim to be so wise in Christ!
We are weak, but you are so powerful! You are
honored, but we are ridiculed. [11]Even now we go
hungry and thirsty, and we don't have enough
clothes to keep warm. We are often beaten and
have no home. [12]We work wearily with our own
hands to earn our living. We bless those who
curse us. We are patient with those who abuse
us. [13]We appeal gently when evil things are said
about us. Yet we are treated like the world's garbage, like everybody's trash—right up to the
present moment.
[14]I am not writing these things to shame you,
but to warn you as my beloved children. [15]For
even if you had ten thousand others to teach you
about Christ, you have only one spiritual father.
For I became your father in Christ Jesus when I
preached the Good News to you. [16]So I urge you
to imitate me.
[17]That's why I have sent Timothy, my beloved and faithful child in the Lord. He will remind you of how I follow Christ Jesus, just as I
teach in all the churches wherever I go.
[18]Some of you have become arrogant, thinking I will not visit you again. [19]But I will come—
and soon—if the Lord lets me, and then I'll find
out whether these arrogant people just give
pretentious speeches or whether they really
have God's power. [20]For the Kingdom of God is
not just a lot of talk; it is living by God's power.
[21]Which do you choose? Should I come with a
rod to punish you, or should I come with love
and a gentle spirit?

Paul Condemns Spiritual Pride

5 I can hardly believe the report about the
sexual immorality going on among you—
something that even pagans don't do. I am
told that a man in your church is living in sin
with his stepmother.* [2]You are so proud of your-

4:6a Greek *Brothers.* **4:6b** Or *If you learn not to go beyond "what is written."* **5:1** Greek *his father's wife.*

9–13: Paul writes poignantly of his marginalization and personal sacrifice. He notes that he and Apollos are being treated like "scum," literally the sweat and dirt that was scraped off the bodies of athletes after competition (*treated like the world's garbage . . . everybody's trash*, v. 13). **10:** Paul and Apollos have become a theater to the world. Paul has become a clown for Christ's sake, ridiculed and disgraced as a buffoon. He has taken on the persona of a *mimetes*, a low-class character or fool in the farcical mime that was much in vogue at this period. Paul exhorts his followers to adopt a similar stance as fellow actors on the stage. Even though the role of actor was forbidden for respectable women, in the church they might play a role for the advancement of the gospel. Paul-the-fool is for them father and mother, able to nurture gently or to admonish sternly.

5:1—7:40 Sexual Matters

5:1–8 Dealing with Abuse. 1: Paul considered the private sexual conduct of an individual to be the business of the believing community. In the case of known immorality in the Corinthian church, he demands that the congregation take responsibility for what they had so complacently accepted. There is a shocking case of incest: A man makes no secret of the affair that he is carrying on with his father's wife. The case is one that Paul maintains would fill even the pagans with horror. The text does not tell us whether the Corinthian man was having an affair with his mother or with a subsequent wife of his father. She may have been a girl, for brides were usually between the ages of ten and fourteen. Only the man is condemned, whether because the woman was not within the fold of the church or she was too young and powerless to prevent what was happening. In that case, she would be vulnerable and must be regarded as a victim rather than an accomplice. It seems unlikely that this was a marriage with the father's widow, since Roman law forbade that. The Hebrew Scriptures also prohibited such unions (Lev 18:7–8; 20:11; Deut 22:30). **2:** By contrast, the Corinthian Christians view the situation with complacency. They take pride in their permis-

selves, but you should be mourning in sorrow
and shame. And you should remove this man
from your fellowship.
3 Even though I am not with you in person, I
am with you in the Spirit.* And as though I were
there, I have already passed judgment on this
man 4 in the name of the Lord Jesus. You must
call a meeting of the church.* I will be present
with you in spirit, and so will the power of our
Lord Jesus. 5 Then you must throw this man out
and hand him over to Satan so that his sinful nature will be destroyed* and he himself* will be
saved on the day the Lord* returns.
6 Your boasting about this is terrible. Don't
you realize that this sin is like a little yeast that
spreads through the whole batch of dough? 7 Get
rid of the old "yeast" by removing this wicked
person from among you. Then you will be like
a fresh batch of dough made without yeast,
which is what you really are. Christ, our Passover Lamb, has been sacrificed for us.* 8 So let us
celebrate the festival, not with the old bread* of
wickedness and evil, but with the new bread* of
sincerity and truth.
9 When I wrote to you before, I told you not to
associate with people who indulge in sexual sin.
10 But I wasn't talking about unbelievers who indulge in sexual sin, or are greedy, or cheat people,
or worship idols. You would have to leave this
world to avoid people like that. 11 I meant that you
are not to associate with anyone who claims to be
a believer* yet indulges in sexual sin, or is greedy,
or worships idols, or is abusive, or is a drunkard, or
cheats people. Don't even eat with such people.
12 It isn't my responsibility to judge outsiders,
but it certainly is your responsibility to judge
those inside the church who are sinning. 13 God
will judge those on the outside; but as the Scriptures say, "You must remove the evil person
from among you."*

Avoiding Lawsuits with Christians

6 When one of you has a dispute with another believer, how dare you file a lawsuit
and ask a secular court to decide the matter instead of taking it to other believers*! 2 Don't
you realize that someday we believers will judge
the world? And since you are going to judge the
world, can't you decide even these little things
among yourselves? 3 Don't you realize that we

5:3 Or *in spirit.* **5:4** Or *In the name of the Lord Jesus, you must call a meeting of the church.* **5:5a** Or *so that his body will be destroyed;* Greek reads *for the destruction of the flesh.* **5:5b** Greek *and the spirit.* **5:5c** Other manuscripts read *the Lord Jesus;* still others read *our Lord Jesus Christ.* **5:7** Greek *has been sacrificed.* **5:8a** Greek *not with old leaven.* **5:8b** Greek *but with unleavened [bread].* **5:11** Greek *a brother.* **5:13** Deut 17:7. **6:1** Greek *God's holy people;* also in 6:2.

sive attitude, "proud of themselves" when they ought to be devastated by this infraction of God's law. Their acceptance has perpetuated the problem. **5:** Paul lays the responsibility for restoring purity on the offending church member and on the body of believers who have countenanced the conduct. They must neither ignore the outrage nor condone it by their tolerance. The faith community should treat the individual redemptively but repudiate the behavior. The offender is not entitled to full fellowship until he repents and lives a transformed life. It is the duty of the church to deal with the abuse, to exclude the offender from full fellowship until he has a chance to reconsider and amend his ways. **6–7:** The misconduct of one has polluted the covenant community like the pervasive action of yeast. All have been permeated and betrayed. Here the apostle refers to the duties of women at Passover. Before the preparation of the meal and the baking of unleavened bread, there must be intensive housecleaning that is to this day incumbent on Jewish women. They must sweep and scour the house to make sure that even the tiniest speck of yeast has been ferreted out and removed.

5:9–13 Maintaining Standards of Sexual Purity. **9–11:** The apostle's twin concerns are for the unity and purity of the church, and he condemns all that may threaten it. Those who display serious breaches of Christian behavior are not to be tolerated at table fellowship. The vice lists contain some of the disqualifying offenses. Many are components of crimes against women. Idolatrous worship frequently required women to engage in ritual prostitution, fertility rites, and sexual surrender. Verbal abuse is specifically condemned, as is sexual immorality, substance abuse, and rape. Here translated as one who *cheats people*, Greek *harpax* is the technical word for a rapist (see also 6:10). Rape, even in marriage, is a horrendous crime that leaves severe trauma. **13:** While Jesus had dealt with overly judgmental Pharisees, Paul addresses those who were willing to countenance any sort of misconduct within the church. He spells out the sorts of behaviors that are not acceptable, for the most part involving abuse, sexual manipulation, and exploitation. Upon these the church must act; what lies outside must be left to God.

6:1–8 Excursus on Going to Law Before Unbelievers. **1:** Members were going to civil courts of law to have their internal disputes settled. The church must find a suitable judge to arbitrate disputes without appealing

will judge angels? So you should surely be able to
resolve ordinary disputes in this life. 4 If you have
legal disputes about such matters, why go to outside judges who are not respected by the church?
5 I am saying this to shame you. Isn't there anyone in all the church who is wise enough to decide these issues? 6 But instead, one believer* sues
another—right in front of unbelievers!
7 Even to have such lawsuits with one another
is a defeat for you. Why not just accept the injustice and leave it at that? Why not let yourselves
be cheated? 8 Instead, you yourselves are the
ones who do wrong and cheat even your fellow
believers.*
9 Don't you realize that those who do wrong
will not inherit the Kingdom of God? Don't fool
yourselves. Those who indulge in sexual sin, or
who worship idols, or commit adultery, or are
male prostitutes, or practice homosexuality, 10 or
are thieves, or greedy people, or drunkards, or are
abusive, or cheat people—none of these will inherit the Kingdom of God. 11 Some of you were
once like that. But you were cleansed; you were
made holy; you were made right with God by
calling on the name of the Lord Jesus Christ and
by the Spirit of our God.

Avoiding Sexual Sin

12 You say, "I am allowed to do anything"—
but not everything is good for you. And even
though "I am allowed to do anything," I must
not become a slave to anything. 13 You say, "Food
was made for the stomach, and the stomach for
food." (This is true, though someday God will
do away with both of them.) But you can't say
that our bodies were made for sexual immorality.
They were made for the Lord, and the Lord cares
about our bodies. 14 And God will raise us from
the dead by his power, just as he raised our Lord
from the dead.
15 Don't you realize that your bodies are actually parts of Christ? Should a man take his body,
which is part of Christ, and join it to a prostitute? Never! 16 And don't you realize that if a
man joins himself to a prostitute, he becomes
one body with her? For the Scriptures say, "The
two are united into one."* 17 But the person who
is joined to the Lord is one spirit with him.
18 Run from sexual sin! No other sin so clearly
affects the body as this one does. For sexual im-

6:6 Greek *one brother.* **6:8** Greek *even the brothers.*
6:16 Gen 2:24.

---

to those outside the faith. **5:** Paul's use of the indefinite *tis* (*anyone*) indicates that a wise person of either gender might be used as arbitrator (a tradition known in early Israel; cf. Judg 4—5). The role of peacemaker is often congenial to women (cf. 1 Sam 25:14–22). Furthermore, there was hope that a woman would more easily obtain justice within the church rather than in a secular legal system, where female litigants had fewer rights.

6:9–20 The Transforming and Purifying Power of Christ. 9: As in the Old Testament covenant community, certain behaviors jeopardized the welfare of the group (cf. Lev 18; 20). For the most part, these are sexual misdemeanors. Paul's diatribe employs vocabulary that denotes the agents who do these deeds—though their identity will change. First come those who are sexually immoral. The Greek word *pornoi* refers to prostitutes of both genders and to those who engage in other sorts of sexual impropriety. Then follows the mention of idolaters and adulterers, an association often made in Hebrew literature. Throughout the Bible there are repeated condemnations of adultery and fornication, but seldom is there a mention of homosexual acts. **11:** Those whose deeds have been unacceptable in the community may find a new identity, however, as those who are washed and sanctified and justified. Regardless of their past, they are joyfully received as part of God's new family.

6:12–14 Of Liberty and Its Loss. 12: Here there appears to be a quotation in vogue among the dissidents: *"I am allowed to do anything."* Paul takes up the saying and executes a play on words. The Greek *existi* is usually translated as "it is permitted" or "it is lawful." It may also be rendered as "it is right, possible, fitting, or permitted." Paul argues that though all things may be licit, they do not benefit the church or even his well-being.

6:15–18 The Bonding Power of Sex. 15: The body and its parts are given for appropriate use. In order to promote health and proper functioning, these uses must be respected. The body (involving the physical, emotional, and spiritual nature) had never been designed for impurity, obscenity, fornication, or adultery. The personality is intended for God and can only thus know its ultimate fulfillment. Other paths mean prostitution of the soul. The body, no less than the soul, of a believer is bound to God in a covenantal relationship. **16:** When Paul speaks of being joined to a prostitute, he uses the Greek word *kollao* (also used in Matt 19:5, a Septuagintal rendering of Gen 2:24). The term means in the first instance to glue or cement something but also to bind one thing, element, or person to another, to join fast, to unite, or to bond indissolubly. **18:** The implication is that sexual sin inflicts upon oneself a spiritual, psychological, or even physical injury. This returns to the thread taken up by

morality is a sin against your own body. [19] Don't
you realize that your body is the temple of the
Holy Spirit, who lives in you and was given to
you by God? You do not belong to yourself, [20] for
God bought you with a high price. So you must
honor God with your body.

Instruction on Marriage

7 Now regarding the questions you asked in
your letter. Yes, it is good to abstain from
sexual relations.* [2] But because there is so
much sexual immorality, each man should have
his own wife, and each woman should have her
own husband.
[3] The husband should fulfill his wife's sexual
needs, and the wife should fulfill her husband's
needs. [4] The wife gives authority over her body
to her husband, and the husband gives authority
over his body to his wife.
[5] Do not deprive each other of sexual relations, unless you both agree to refrain from
sexual intimacy for a limited time so you can
give yourselves more completely to prayer. Afterward, you should come together again so that
Satan won't be able to tempt you because of your
lack of self-control. [6] I say this as a concession,
not as a command. [7] But I wish everyone were
single, just as I am. Yet each person has a special
gift from God, of one kind or another.
[8] So I say to those who aren't married and to
widows—it's better to stay unmarried, just as I
am. [9] But if they can't control themselves, they
should go ahead and marry. It's better to marry
than to burn with lust.
[10] But for those who are married, I have a
command that comes not from me, but from the
Lord.* A wife must not leave her husband. [11] But
if she does leave him, let her remain single or
else be reconciled to him. And the husband must
not leave his wife.
[12] Now, I will speak to the rest of you, though
I do not have a direct command from the Lord. If
a Christian man* has a wife who is not a believer
and she is willing to continue living with him, he
must not leave her. [13] And if a Christian woman
has a husband who is not a believer and he is
willing to continue living with her, she must not
leave him. [14] For the Christian wife brings holi-

7:1 Or *to live a celibate life;* Greek reads *It is good for a man not to touch a woman.* **7:10** See Matt 5:32; 19:9; Mark 10:11-12; Luke 16:18. **7:12** Greek *a brother.*

Paul's question, *Should a man take his body, which is part of Christ, and join it to a prostitute?* (v. 15). Perhaps the answer is found in the previous comment that a little leaven exerts its influence on the mass of dough. An ungodly sexual union on the part of one member affects all. Sexuality, according to Paul, lies far closer to our spirituality than we might imagine. The powerful bonding force may join us to another appropriately or inappropriately. Such union can do great harm to the other, but it can also do great harm to ourselves. We have come to realize that one person's sexual conduct can put a whole society at risk.

6:19–20 The Body as the Temple of the Spirit. 19: A recurring motif is that of the body: body as representing the personality, body as representing the believing community, body as the temple of the Holy Spirit. Sexual expression must first glorify God and then respect the unity of the covenant community.

7:1–40 Marriage, Singleness, Divorce, and Widowhood. 3–4: The apostle has some remarkable things to say about legitimate sexual union, including equality in the marriage bed. Sex is an integral part of marriage between believers, and no one is to deprive anybody in this respect. This entails not only sharing one's body but also the right to have one's body respected. In sexual union, believers are to be considerate of one another. **5:** The injunction not to defraud one's partner has often been interpreted to justify inappropriate demands on a woman's body. Practices that are repugnant to one member of the union constitute a deprivation of a meaningful and satisfying experience. According to 1 Thessalonians 4:3–6, sexual expression must be made in holiness and honor, without violation or exploitation. **7:** Paul maintains that it is a gift to be married and a gift to be single, and sex is basic to marriage. Only mutual consent might, for a time, remit the obligation of each partner to meet the other's sexual need. If sex is power, it also demands responsibility. Neither partner is to deny the other its joy and fulfillment. Paul understood sex as a drive that is not to be denied but recognized and channeled in meaningful ways. **8:** Paul's permission to remain unmarried stood in direct opposition to the demands of the Roman state. Cicero tells of a fine that was imposed on the celibate. Widowers were allowed six months before they were expected to remarry, and widows were given an eighteen-month respite from marriage, but Paul encouraged marriage only when there was a true yearning for conjugal union. **12:** Paul's concern is one of relationship not only to an unbelieving spouse but also to a community of faith. In this case, the issue is not that of having divorced a believer but of an individual coming to Christ after the marriage. **14:** The unbelieving spouse is recognized as a legitimate appendage to the faith community; and the children,

Singleness

How do we live in society? How do we ensure that life continues into future generations? These two questions are as relevant today as they were in Old and New Testament times. They encompass issues such as the public and permanent commitment of a man and a woman to each other (see Marriage, Song 2), sexual intercourse and procreation, as well as the outworking of one's service to the Lord. Traditionally singleness has been an umbrella term to indicate either no or a yet-to-occur lifelong commitment to one person of the opposite sex and therefore by implication a celibate and childless life. Nevertheless, the boundaries are quickly stretched in instances of widowhood, nonconsummation of marriage, and deliberate abstinence from sexual intercourse within marriage (generally for a limited period of time and motivated by a spiritual impulse, 1 Cor 7:5).

At the core of the discussion lies the question of uncompromising, loving commitment, attested to throughout the Bible as being fundamental to the growth and dignity of the person. Unworthy commitment is degrading to the person and dishonoring to God, however, and Scripture presents a hierarchical order in which God is to be loved above all (Exod 20:3) and in which commitment to a spouse may mirror but not supersede this heavenly relationship (2 Cor 11:2; Rev 21:2). Marriage is the norm in human life, yet Scripture does not affirm it as necessarily better. Old and New Testament examples of singleness include Jeremiah (Jer 16:2), John the Baptist, and Jesus; Paul too declares his singleness and sees this as a gift from God through whose grace it is maintained (1 Cor 7:7–8). The exalted status of these men in biblical terms has inspired many since to embrace the same state.

Scripture affirms the life so completely committed to God that commitment to another would risk introducing a diversion and distraction (Luke 17:27–30; 1 Cor 7:28). Singleness is portrayed as a positive choice of joyous, willed, and willing obedience that ultimately liberates the bearer both emotionally and practically (1 Cor 7:32–35). Single people can be dedicated totally to the kingdom of God and widely able to practice the command to love their neighbor. It is unfortunate that lived examples of undivided devotion to and service for the Lord have all too easily been both awkwardly lived and scorned. Often single people find the privilege of their singleness deprecated and the outworking of Jesus' teaching emphasizing the need to value a relationship with him above all others (Matt 19:29; Luke 14:26–27) considered at best only second best and at worst unattainable or undesirable. Those who actively choose singleness are accompanied by those challenged to accept the state through force of circumstance (Matt 19:12). Within Christianity these are often women, due to both longevity of life and faith commitment; these women nevertheless have throughout the centuries radiated the truth of God's Word through their lives, witness, work, and achievements.

For some, however, singleness remains an unwelcome position in which pain may well outweigh the pleasure of privilege. As so often in Scripture, ultimate reassurance is found in eschatological hope: Those of the life to come "will neither marry nor be given in marriage" (Luke 20:35). Human wholeness and completeness, epitomized on earth by the single Jesus, will be expressed once again through singleness in heaven.

ness to her marriage, and the Christian husband*
brings holiness to his marriage. Otherwise, your
children would not be holy, but now they are
holy. 15 (But if the husband or wife who isn't a
believer insists on leaving, let them go. In such
cases the Christian husband or wife* is no longer
bound to the other, for God has called you*
to live in peace.) 16 Don't you wives realize that
your husbands might be saved because of you?
And don't you husbands realize that your wives
might be saved because of you?
17 Each of you should continue to live in whatever
situation the Lord has placed you, and remain
as you were when God first called you. This
is my rule for all the churches. 18 For instance, a

7:14 Greek *the brother.* **7:15a** Greek *the brother or sister.* **7:15b** Some manuscripts read *us.*

apparently being reared in the nurture and admonition of the Lord, are considered holy, as the Corinthians are considered holy. **15:** This might, however, place unwelcome constrictions on the unbelieving spouse. Christian commitment of necessity infringes on the ordering of the household and might rouse the ire of an unsympathetic spouse. If the unbelieving partner cannot accept the spiritual values of the believer, he or she may leave the marriage without any onus being placed on the remaining partner. The be-

man who was circumcised before he became a
believer should not try to reverse it. And the
man who was uncircumcised when he became a
believer should not be circumcised now. [19] For it
makes no difference whether or not a man has
been circumcised. The important thing is to keep
God's commandments.
[20] Yes, each of you should remain as you were
when God called you. [21] Are you a slave? Don't
let that worry you—but if you get a chance to
be free, take it. [22] And remember, if you were a
slave when the Lord called you, you are now free
in the Lord. And if you were free when the Lord
called you, you are now a slave of Christ. [23] God
paid a high price for you, so don't be enslaved
by the world.* [24] Each of you, dear brothers and
sisters,* should remain as you were when God
first called you.
[25] Now regarding your question about the
young women who are not yet married. I do not
have a command from the Lord for them. But the
Lord in his mercy has given me wisdom that can
be trusted, and I will share it with you. [26] Because
of the present crisis,* I think it is best to remain
as you are. [27] If you have a wife, do not seek to
end the marriage. If you do not have a wife, do
not seek to get married. [28] But if you do get married, it is not a sin. And if a young woman gets
married, it is not a sin. However, those who get
married at this time will have troubles, and I am
trying to spare you those problems.
[29] But let me say this, dear brothers and sisters: The time that remains is very short. So
from now on, those with wives should not focus only on their marriage. [30] Those who weep
or who rejoice or who buy things should not be
absorbed by their weeping or their joy or their
possessions. [31] Those who use the things of the
world should not become attached to them. For
this world as we know it will soon pass away.
[32] I want you to be free from the concerns of
this life. An unmarried man can spend his time
doing the Lord's work and thinking how to please
him. [33] But a married man has to think about his
earthly responsibilities and how to please his
wife. [34] His interests are divided. In the same way,
a woman who is no longer married or has never
been married can be devoted to the Lord and holy
in body and in spirit. But a married woman has
to think about her earthly responsibilities and
how to please her husband. [35] I am saying this for
your benefit, not to place restrictions on you. I
want you to do whatever will help you serve the
Lord best, with as few distractions as possible.
[36] But if a man thinks that he's treating his fiancée improperly and will inevitably give in to
his passion, let him marry her as he wishes. It
is not a sin. [37] But if he has decided firmly not to
marry and there is no urgency and he can control
his passion, he does well not to marry. [38] So the
person who marries his fiancée does well, and the
person who doesn't marry does even better.
[39] A wife is bound to her husband as long as
he lives. If her husband dies, she is free to marry anyone she wishes, but only if he loves the
Lord.* [40] But in my opinion it would be better for
her to stay single, and I think I am giving you
counsel from God's Spirit when I say this.

7:23 Greek *don't become slaves of people.* **7:24** Greek *brothers;* also in 7:29. **7:26** Or *the pressures of life.* **7:39** Greek *but only in the Lord.*

liever is not obligated to hold the spouse in the marriage or in the confines of the believing community.

7:21–23 Excursus on Slavery. 21: In the main, it is best to remain in the condition where one first made a commitment to Christ, whether married or single. This is expanded with the recommendation that those who came to Christ as slaves should not now seek their freedom. Yet Paul, who was free, maintains that he enslaved himself to all in order to win all. In his thinking, the metaphor of slavery has positive and negative aspects. Slavery under the Romans sometimes offered excellent prospects for education, a trade, career advancement, and promotion to a responsible position.

7:24–40 Return to Discussion of Marriage. 32: In Paul's view, freedom from the obligations of marriage was freedom to serve Christ. Nevertheless, he defended the right of the apostles to be married and to travel with their wives and specifically mentions Peter in this regard (9:5). **36–38:** Paul argues that people have the right to remain single. Some scholars have maintained that here he addresses the plight of daughters who were married off at far too young an age. The Greek may be understood either as speaking against marriage or against a father giving a young girl in a marriage for which she was not willing or ready. The young woman usually was married to a much older man whom she did not know and did not want. Then the text gives the woman a chance to marry, if she wishes, once she has passed through puberty. This was far more humane than forcing marriage on an immature girl. Even Aristotle remarked that fewer young mothers would die in childbirth if they were allowed to pass through puberty before marriage. And the Spartans refused to marry off their daughters when they were "too young or unready."

Food Sacrificed to Idols

8 Now regarding your question about food
that has been offered to idols. Yes, we know
that "we all have knowledge" about this issue. But while knowledge makes us feel important, it is love that strengthens the church. [2]Any-
one who claims to know all the answers doesn't
really know very much. [3]But the person who
loves God is the one whom God recognizes.*
[4]So, what about eating meat that has been offered to idols? Well, we all know that an idol is
not really a god and that there is only one God.
[5]There may be so-called gods both in heaven
and on earth, and some people actually worship
many gods and many lords. [6]But we know that
there is only one God, the Father, who created
everything, and we live for him. And there is
only one Lord, Jesus Christ, through whom God
made everything and through whom we have
been given life.
[7]However, not all believers know this. Some
are accustomed to thinking of idols as being real,
so when they eat food that has been offered to
idols, they think of it as the worship of real gods,
and their weak consciences are violated. [8]It's true
that we can't win God's approval by what we eat.
We don't lose anything if we don't eat it, and we
don't gain anything if we do.
[9]But you must be careful so that your freedom
does not cause others with a weaker conscience
to stumble. [10]For if others see you—with your
"superior knowledge"—eating in the temple of
an idol, won't they be encouraged to violate their
conscience by eating food that has been offered
to an idol? [11]So because of your superior knowledge, a weak believer* for whom Christ died will
be destroyed. [12]And when you sin against other
believers* by encouraging them to do something
they believe is wrong, you are sinning against
Christ. [13]So if what I eat causes another believer
to sin, I will never eat meat again as long as I
live—for I don't want to cause another believer
to stumble.

Paul Gives Up His Rights

9 Am I not as free as anyone else? Am I not
an apostle? Haven't I seen Jesus our Lord
with my own eyes? Isn't it because of
my work that you belong to the Lord? [2]Even if
others think I am not an apostle, I certainly am
to you. You yourselves are proof that I am the
Lord's apostle.
[3]This is my answer to those who question my
authority.* [4]Don't we have the right to live in
your homes and share your meals? [5]Don't we
have the right to bring a Christian wife with us
as the other apostles and the Lord's brothers do,
and as Peter* does? [6]Or is it only Barnabas and I
who have to work to support ourselves?
[7]What soldier has to pay his own expenses?
What farmer plants a vineyard and doesn't have
the right to eat some of its fruit? What shepherd cares for a flock of sheep and isn't allowed
to drink some of the milk? [8]Am I expressing
merely a human opinion, or does the law say the
same thing? [9]For the law of Moses says, "You

8:3 Some manuscripts read *the person who loves has full knowledge.* **8:11** Greek *brother;* also in 8:13. **8:12** Greek *brothers.* **9:3** Greek *those who examine me.* **9:5** Greek *Cephas.*

8:1—11:1 Ethical Matters

8:1–13 Avoidance of Stumbling Blocks. 1: Former idol worshipers found themselves at an unexpected juncture because animal sacrifice was a major component of Greek religion as well as opportunity for socialization. Meat was not a staple of the ordinary diet, and sacrifice provided an opportunity for enjoying a meal of roasted flesh. Excavations of the temple of Dionysos at Corinth reveal the remains of several private rooms for the accommodation of small dinner parties. **4:** Paul agrees that an idol has no reality as a deity, but the conscience of other believers is another matter. In essence the question is whether offense should be given to old friends, who may feel snubbed by Christians' refusal to attend their banquets, or whether instead to offend believers who were struggling to break free from a strong bond with the old cult. **10:** What are others to think if they see a Christian participating in a feast in the idol's temple? For socially disadvantaged women, this convivial setting may have been the most difficult aspect of the old religion to renounce. **13:** In this case, the first loyalty must be to the body of Christ and to the sensitivities of its members. Nothing should be done to confuse or impede those coming to faith in Christ. Even if their enlightenment enabled some to attend a sacrifice without a twinge of religious conscience, this was not the path of a love that built up others in their faith.

9:1–27 The Identity and Rights of an Apostle. 4–5: If Paul chooses to be self-supporting, that is his right. It is also his right to travel with a wife, as do Peter and the other disciples. The early church retained a memory of these traveling husband-wife teams, and especially of the devotion of Peter to his wife, even at the moment of her martyrdom. The wives were involved in ministry and were said by Clement of Alexandria to have gained entrance to the secluded quarters of

must not muzzle an ox to keep it from eating as it treads out the grain."* Was God thinking only about oxen when he said this? [10] Wasn't he actually speaking to us? Yes, it was written for us, so that the one who plows and the one who threshes the grain might both expect a share of the harvest.

[11] Since we have planted spiritual seed among you, aren't we entitled to a harvest of physical food and drink? [12] If you support others who preach to you, shouldn't we have an even greater right to be supported? But we have never used this right. We would rather put up with anything than be an obstacle to the Good News about Christ.

[13] Don't you realize that those who work in the temple get their meals from the offerings brought to the temple? And those who serve at the altar get a share of the sacrificial offerings. [14] In the same way, the Lord ordered that those who preach the Good News should be supported by those who benefit from it. [15] Yet I have never used any of these rights. And I am not writing this to suggest that I want to start now. In fact, I would rather die than lose my right to boast about preaching without charge. [16] Yet preaching the Good News is not something I can boast about. I am compelled by God to do it. How terrible for me if I didn't preach the Good News!

[17] If I were doing this on my own initiative, I would deserve payment. But I have no choice, for God has given me this sacred trust. [18] What then is my pay? It is the opportunity to preach the Good News without charging anyone. That's why I never demand my rights when I preach the Good News.

[19] Even though I am a free man with no master, I have become a slave to all people to bring many to Christ. [20] When I was with the Jews, I lived like a Jew to bring the Jews to Christ. When I was with those who follow the Jewish law, I too lived under that law. Even though I am not subject to the law, I did this so I could bring to Christ those who are under the law. [21] When I am with the Gentiles who do not follow the Jewish law,* I too live apart from that law so I can bring them to Christ. But I do not ignore the law of God; I obey the law of Christ.

[22] When I am with those who are weak, I share their weakness, for I want to bring the weak to Christ. Yes, I try to find common ground with everyone, doing everything I can to save some. [23] I do everything to spread the Good News and share in its blessings.

[24] Don't you realize that in a race everyone runs, but only one person gets the prize? So run to win! [25] All athletes are disciplined in their training. They do it to win a prize that will fade away, but we do it for an eternal prize. [26] So I run with purpose in every step. I am not just shadowboxing. [27] I discipline my body like an athlete, training it to do what it should. Otherwise, I fear that after preaching to others I myself might be disqualified.

Lessons from Israel's Idolatry

10 I don't want you to forget, dear brothers and sisters,* about our ancestors in the wilderness long ago. All of them were guided by a cloud that moved ahead of them, and all of them walked through the sea on dry ground. [2] In the cloud and in the sea, all of them were baptized as followers of Moses. [3] All of them ate the same spiritual food, [4] and all of them drank the same spiritual water. For they drank from the spiritual rock that traveled with them, and that rock was Christ. [5] Yet God was not pleased with most of them, and their bodies were scattered in the wilderness.

9:9 Deut 25:4. **9:21** Greek *those without the law.*
10:1 Greek *brothers.*

---

women. **16–18:** Paul expresses a compulsion to proclaim the gospel by word and deed. He must not only preach Christ but must do so in a way that is freely available to all. No financial expectation is placed upon his hearers. **19–23:** Rather than adopting a libertarian stance, Paul curtails his liberty in order to gain others for Christ. He will move among varying cultures and traditions in order to win persons of every sort and condition. He is willing to adopt their culture and their modes of expression. **24–27:** The chapter ends with an athletic image that might have appealed to the city that hosted the Isthmian Games every second year. The bodies of athletes were subjected to enormous discipline. Paul maintains that he behaves likewise, specifically beating and enslaving his body for his own race (*I discipline my body like an athlete*). The prize for Paul's training is not the laurel wreath, however, but approval with God.

10:1—11:1 Idolatry, Allegory, and Application. 10:1: Storytelling has always been a domain in which women excel. Whether as mothers, nurses, or household attendants, women preserved the ancient myths and gave them new life in the telling. Plato remarked that by their stories nursemaids shaped the souls of their charges. Thus we see a potential that had particular significance for women. By their selection and interpretation of Bible stories, mothers and nurses influ-

6 These things happened as a warning to us, so that we would not crave evil things as they did, 7 or worship idols as some of them did. As the Scriptures say, "The people celebrated with feasting and drinking, and they indulged in pagan revelry."* 8 And we must not engage in sexual immorality as some of them did, causing 23,000 of them to die in one day.

9 Nor should we put Christ* to the test, as some of them did and then died from snakebites. 10 And don't grumble as some of them did, and then were destroyed by the angel of death. 11 These things happened to them as examples for us. They were written down to warn us who live at the end of the age.

12 If you think you are standing strong, be careful not to fall. 13 The temptations in your life are no different from what others experience. And God is faithful. He will not allow the temptation to be more than you can stand. When you are tempted, he will show you a way out so that you can endure.

14 So, my dear friends, flee from the worship of idols. 15 You are reasonable people. Decide for yourselves if what I am saying is true. 16 When we bless the cup at the Lord's Table, aren't we sharing in the blood of Christ? And when we break the bread, aren't we sharing in the body of Christ? 17 And though we are many, we all eat from one loaf of bread, showing that we are one body. 18 Think about the people of Israel. Weren't they united by eating the sacrifices at the altar?

19 What am I trying to say? Am I saying that food offered to idols has some significance, or that idols are real gods? 20 No, not at all. I am saying that these sacrifices are offered to demons, not to God. And I don't want you to participate with demons. 21 You cannot drink from the cup of the Lord and from the cup of demons, too. You cannot eat at the Lord's Table and at the table of demons, too. 22 What? Do we dare to rouse the Lord's jealousy? Do you think we are stronger than he is?

23 You say, "I am allowed to do anything"*—but not everything is good for you. You say, "I am allowed to do anything"—but not everything is beneficial. 24 Don't be concerned for your own good but for the good of others.

25 So you may eat any meat that is sold in the marketplace without raising questions of conscience. 26 For "the earth is the LORD's, and everything in it."*

27 If someone who isn't a believer asks you home for dinner, accept the invitation if you want to. Eat whatever is offered to you without raising questions of conscience. 28 (But suppose someone tells you, "This meat was offered to an idol." Don't eat it, out of consideration for the conscience of the one who told you. 29 It might not be a matter of conscience for you, but it is for the other person.) For why should my freedom be limited by what someone else thinks? 30 If I can thank God for the food and enjoy it, why should I be condemned for eating it?

31 So whether you eat or drink, or whatever you do, do it all for the glory of God. 32 Don't give offense to Jews or Gentiles* or the church of God. 33 I, too, try to please everyone in everything I do.

10:7 Exod 32:6. **10:9** Some manuscripts read *the Lord.* **10:23** Greek *All things are lawful;* also in 10:23b. **10:26** Ps 24:1. **10:32** Greek *or Greeks.*

enced spiritual formation of the young. **6:** Just so we may observe Paul's shaping of an ancient story. His objective is to warn against idolatry, but he stops to allegorize other wilderness experiences of Israel. The Exodus events were intended as examples (Gk., *typoi*) to present-day Christians to warn them against yielding to their lusts. The Israelites going astray after idols prefigured the defections of Corinthian converts, especially the worship of idols and those practices that accompanied pagan rites—feasting, promiscuity, and sacred prostitution. **8:** He moves to the story of the seduction of Israelite men by Moabite cult prostitutes (Num 25:1–3; 31:16) and then to those who were afflicted by serpent bites because of their murmuring and complaining (Num 21:5–6). **11:** Likewise those who complained of the demands of Christ on their lives were guilty of tempting Christ. Renunciation of pagan ways was not easy. **16–17:** Here for the first time, the word *body* implies the church, the body of believers. Table fellowship was not possible with Christ and with false gods. Although the latter had no reality, those at their banquets venerated them as a living and powerful presence. Participation in the ritual feast, whether pagan or Christian, is an act of worship. **17:** The importance of sharing a common meal will recur. Breaking of bread is part of the Eucharist, but also part of congregational meals. Ties are formed, joys and concerns shared, needs understood, and discussion of aspirations promoted. Such fellowship remains one of the major sources of the bonding and development of the church as the body of Christ. **32:** Like a parent arbitrating between bickering children, Paul has addressed the dissidents who are weak and who are strong. It is important for each group to understand what he says to the other so that they may understand their respective concerns and viewpoint. They are free as Paul is free, but freedom must be a blessing rather than a stumbling block to others.

I don't just do what is best for me; I do what is best for others so that many may be saved. 11:1 And you should imitate me, just as I imitate Christ.

Instructions for Public Worship

11 2 I am so glad that you always keep me in your thoughts, and that you are following the teachings I passed on to you. 3 But there is one thing I want you to know: The head of every man is Christ, the head of woman is man, and the head of Christ is God.*
4 A man dishonors his head* if he covers his head while praying or prophesying. 5 But a woman dishonors her head* if she prays or prophesies without a covering on her head, for this is the same as shaving her head. 6 Yes, if she refuses to wear a head covering, she should cut off all her hair! But since it is shameful for a woman to have her hair cut or her head shaved, she should wear a covering.*

11:3 Or *to know: The source of every man is Christ, the source of woman is man, and the source of Christ is God.* Or *to know: Every man is responsible to Christ, a woman is responsible to her husband, and Christ is responsible to God.* **11:4** Or *dishonors Christ.* **11:5** Or *dishonors her husband.* **11:6** Or *should have long hair.*

11:2—14:40 Worship and Congregational Life

11:2–16 Male and Female Together in Christ. 2–6: We are first told that Christ is *head of every man.* This would have great relevance for the new Christian, torn between loyalty to family and to Christ. In the Roman legal system, only the oldest male agnate (whether father, grandfather, or even great-grandfather) was the recognized person (i.e., head) of the family. As such he made domestic, financial, and legal decisions for the family. He arranged marriages and also made religious choices for the family, expecting those under his control to participate in the worship of the ancestors and to make the appropriate offerings. This control, known as "patria potestas," was not only onerous but in many instances stifling. The Greek system, though less stringent than the Roman, still deprived grown children of full personhood. Thus Christ as head is good news for those who struggled with pagan ways. We must understand that the Greek and Latin words for "head" frequently indicated "source" or "beginning." Tiberius calls Augustus "your head and a father of the people," while Esau is "head and progenitor" of the Edomites. Men might look to Christ as their source and progenitor in the new birth, and their essential loyalty belonged to him. The text follows the initial statement with a concomitant concept: that man is head of woman. The Greek word *kephale* did not ordinarily imply a metaphor of authority; more often it had the sense of source or point of beginning. This refers in part to Eve being drawn from Adam (11:8, 12), but it also serves to define the status of a married woman. In some forms of marriage in the Roman Empire, a woman passed under the patria potestas of her husband's family, but more frequently she remained under the structures of her own. In either case a woman's ability to serve Christ was restricted. A wife who was transferred into her husband's family assumed the legal status of a daughter in relationship to him. As the text proceeds, it will offer the believing wife greater status than the subordinate role of daughter. The final part of the statement declares that the head of Christ is God. It is theologically consistent to understand the Father as Source, sending forth the Son, the Son as source of every man, and man as source of woman. **4:** The thought shifts to propriety of dress in worship. The directions to men are often overlooked, but they are important. In the religions known to have existed at Corinth, especially in Dionysiac celebrations, the exchange of male and female garments was a ritual act. Men in the cult of Cybele castrated themselves to become she priests. For women too, donning male personae was a part of worship. Philosophers such as Epictetus addressed deeper problems of sexual identity: "Therefore we ought to preserve the marks God has given us; we ought not to give them up, nor, as far as we can prevent it, confuse the sexes which have been thus distinguished." In a similar vein, Paul calls for Christians to assume the gender that nature had assigned them. **5:** Arrangement of the hair and its covering were paramount issues for the status and respectability of women. The apostle decries the practice of a woman praying or prophesying with her head uncovered (Gk., *akatakalyptos*). Since the word "veil" is not used in the passage, there is much scholarly debate as to whether this is a denunciation of a praying or prophesying woman's unveiled head or of her unbound hair. Both were considered dangerous and out of order. By the New Testament era, in some Jewish circles divorce was obligatory for a woman who appeared unveiled in the street. For a woman so to appear was a disgrace to her husband, her family, and herself. Greeks viewed a woman's uncovered hair with the same distaste. Unbound hair was a characteristic of female worshipers of Dionysos, those uncontrolled creatures called maenads, or "mad ones." Chapter 14:23 may refer to such ritual madness, for there are other indications that the members of the congregation who had previously been led astray by idols carried with them remnants of the Dionysiac cult. These include eating food sacrificed to idols, returning to the idol's temple for ceremonial feasts,

[7]A man should not wear anything on his head
when worshiping, for man is made in God's image and reflects God's glory. And woman reflects
man's glory. [8]For the first man didn't come from
woman, but the first woman came from man.
[9]And man was not made for woman, but woman
was made for man. [10]For this reason, and because
the angels are watching, a woman should wear
a covering on her head to show she is under authority.*
[11]But among the Lord's people, women are not
independent of men, and men are not independent of women. [12]For although the first woman
came from man, every other man was born from
a woman, and everything comes from God.
[13]Judge for yourselves. Is it right for a woman
to pray to God in public without covering her
head? [14]Isn't it obvious that it's disgraceful for
a man to have long hair? [15]And isn't long hair a
woman's pride and joy? For it has been given to
her as a covering. [16]But if anyone wants to argue
about this, I simply say that we have no other
custom than this, and neither do God's other
churches.

Order at the Lord's Supper

[17]But in the following instructions, I cannot
praise you. For it sounds as if more harm than
good is done when you meet together. [18]First, I
hear that there are divisions among you when
you meet as a church, and to some extent I believe it. [19]But, of course, there must be divisions
among you so that you who have God's approval
will be recognized!
[20]When you meet together, you are not really
interested in the Lord's Supper. [21]For some of
you hurry to eat your own meal without sharing
with others. As a result, some go hungry while
others get drunk. [22]What? Don't you have your
own homes for eating and drinking? Or do you
really want to disgrace God's church and shame
the poor? What am I supposed to say? Do you
want me to praise you? Well, I certainly will not
praise you for this!
[23]For I pass on to you what I received from the
Lord himself. On the night when he was betrayed,
the Lord Jesus took some bread [24]and gave thanks

11:10 Greek *should have an authority on her head.*

and ritual intoxication. Lack of appropriate headgear bespoke not only moral looseness but also marital renunciation. As such, it constituted blatant disregard for accepted social convention. **7:** That woman is called "the glory of man" is not a diminution of her glory, for she is equally made in the image of God (Gen 1:27; 5:2–3). Glory augments the reputation, wealth, or status of another (cf. 2 Cor 3:7–11, 18). Paul declares that the Thessalonians were his "glory and joy" (1 Thes 2:20), surely not a pejorative term. They are the fulfillment of his aspirations, and his pride and happiness in them know no bounds. **8:** While the Greek myths maintained that woman was created of inferior substance and was incapable of true grandeur in her soul, Genesis tells of woman drawn from man's side, bone of his bone and flesh of his flesh. She was endowed with the same spiritual aspirations, the same emotions, a capacity for the same moral virtues. She was worthy to be bound to man, his soul mate and complement. **9:** Woman was given to complete and fulfill man, to minister to his aloneness (Gen 2:18). The typical Greek view was that the gods had created womankind as a deliberate curse upon men. The Genesis account tells of woman as a blessed gift created *for man*. The Greek term *dia* (for the benefit) is often used to designate an objective of ministry (4:10; 9:10 [twice], 23; 2 Cor 2:10; 4:11, 15). Christ was made poor for our sakes (2 Cor 8:9; see also John 12:30); Paul proclaimed himself a slave *for Jesus' sake* (2 Cor 4:5). **10:** The *angeloi*, perhaps messengers or talebearers who would report the proceedings of Christian worship to outsiders, might well misconstrue the situation. Just as Paul in 1 Corinthians 8:10 and 14:23 asks what outsiders might think, so here too he calls for propriety. A more literal translation could be that a woman "should have an authority on her head." Again using the root of *existemi* (see annotation on 6:12), Paul may be affirming that women have the power of choice about their own dress and deportment. **11–12:** The apostle began the passage, as does Genesis, with a statement of God's being and of the relationality within the Godhead. Humanity as male and female draws its reality and meaning from a reflection of God's being. Man's aloneness had been "not good," and so woman was created as partner and companion. Thus it is that Paul sets forth the interdependence of man and woman and their need for one another.

11:17–34 The Integrity of the Body Destroyed. 17–19: The common meal has proved blessed and distressing. The words begin with a reproof for lack of the fellowship that constitutes the nature of communion. It is intended as a sacred tryst of penitents who together experience the joy of forgiven sin and an assurance of pardon. **20–22:** Instead the gathering is characterized by gluttony, drunkenness, and callous insensitivity. The poor leave hungry and humiliated, while the affluent are gorged, inebriated, and unable to recognize another's need. **23–25:** In this account of the institution of the Lord's Supper we are given words of the earthly Jesus that are not found in the

to God for it. Then he broke it in pieces and said,
"This is my body, which is given for you.* Do this
to remember me." 25 In the same way, he took the
cup of wine after supper, saying, "This cup is the
new covenant between God and his people—an
agreement confirmed with my blood. Do this to
remember me as often as you drink it." 26 For every
time you eat this bread and drink this cup, you are
announcing the Lord's death until he comes again.
27 So anyone who eats this bread or drinks this
cup of the Lord unworthily is guilty of sinning
against* the body and blood of the Lord. 28 That is
why you should examine yourself before eating
the bread and drinking the cup. 29 For if you eat the
bread or drink the cup without honoring the body
of Christ,* you are eating and drinking God's
judgment upon yourself. 30 That is why many of
you are weak and sick and some have even died.
31 But if we would examine ourselves, we
would not be judged by God in this way. 32 Yet
when we are judged by the Lord, we are being
disciplined so that we will not be condemned
along with the world.
33 So, my dear brothers and sisters,* when
you gather for the Lord's Supper, wait for each
other. 34 If you are really hungry, eat at home
so you won't bring judgment upon yourselves
when you meet together. I'll give you instructions about the other matters after I arrive.

Spiritual Gifts

12 Now, dear brothers and sisters,* regarding your question about the special abilities the Spirit gives us. I don't
want you to misunderstand this. 2 You know that
when you were still pagans, you were led astray
and swept along in worshiping speechless idols.
3 So I want you to know that no one speaking by
the Spirit of God will curse Jesus, and no one can
say Jesus is Lord, except by the Holy Spirit.
4 There are different kinds of spiritual gifts, but
the same Spirit is the source of them all. 5 There
are different kinds of service, but we serve the
same Lord. 6 God works in different ways, but it
is the same God who does the work in all of us.
7 A spiritual gift is given to each of us so we
can help each other. 8 To one person the Spirit
gives the ability to give wise advice*; to another
the same Spirit gives a message of special knowledge.* 9 The same Spirit gives great faith to another, and to someone else the one Spirit gives
the gift of healing. 10 He gives one person the
power to perform miracles, and another the ability to prophesy. He gives someone else the ability
to discern whether a message is from the Spirit of
God or from another spirit. Still another person
is given the ability to speak in unknown languages,* while another is given the ability to interpret
what is being said. 11 It is the one and only Spirit
who distributes all these gifts. He alone decides
which gift each person should have.

One Body with Many Parts

12 The human body has many parts, but the many
parts make up one whole body. So it is with the
body of Christ. 13 Some of us are Jews, some are
Gentiles,* some are slaves, and some are free.
But we have all been baptized into one body by
one Spirit, and we all share the same Spirit.*
14 Yes, the body has many different parts, not
just one part. 15 If the foot says, "I am not a part
of the body because I am not a hand," that does
not make it any less a part of the body. 16 And if
the ear says, "I am not part of the body because
I am not an eye," would that make it any less a
part of the body? 17 If the whole body were an
eye, how would you hear? Or if your whole body
were an ear, how would you smell anything?
18 But our bodies have many parts, and God has
put each part just where he wants it. 19 How strange
a body would be if it had only one part! 20 Yes, there
are many parts, but only one body. 21 The eye can
never say to the hand, "I don't need you." The head
can't say to the feet, "I don't need you."
22 In fact, some parts of the body that seem
weakest and least important are actually the most

11:24 Greek *which is for you;* other manuscripts read *which is broken for you.* **11:27** Or *is responsible for.* **11:29** Greek *the body;* other manuscripts read *the Lord's body.* **11:33** Greek *brothers.* **12:1** Greek *brothers.* **12:8a** Or *gives a word of wisdom.* **12:8b** Or *gives a word of knowledge.* **12:10** Or *in various tongues;* also in 12:28, 30. **12:13a** Greek *some are Greeks.* **12:13b** Greek *we were all given one Spirit to drink.*

Gospels. The only other instance is in his observation that it is more blessed to give than to receive (Acts 20:35). **33:** One cannot worthily partake of the Eucharist without a concern for others.

12:1–31 Harmonizing the Spiritual Gifts. 1: If some have utilized their economic resources to embarrass others, the use of spiritual gifts is no less of a problem. The owners of certain gifts disparage those who have different gifts. **2:** Here we find acknowledgement of the raw paganism from which some of the congregation had come. **12–21:** Paul maintained that believers were a *body*, each part interdependent with the others. No gift or member is dispensable, though the functions differ. Interdependence of the head appears as a bodily member that cannot do

necessary. 23 And the parts we regard as less honorable are those we clothe with the greatest care.
So we carefully protect those parts that should
not be seen, 24 while the more honorable parts do
not require this special care. So God has put the
body together such that extra honor and care are
given to those parts that have less dignity. 25 This
makes for harmony among the members, so that
all the members care for each other. 26 If one part
suffers, all the parts suffer with it, and if one part
is honored, all the parts are glad.
27 All of you together are Christ's body, and
each of you is a part of it. 28 Here are some of the
parts God has appointed for the church:

first are apostles,
second are prophets,
third are teachers,
then those who do miracles,
those who have the gift of healing,
those who can help others,
those who have the gift of leadership,
those who speak in unknown languages.

29 Are we all apostles? Are we all prophets?
Are we all teachers? Do we all have the power to
do miracles? 30 Do we all have the gift of healing?
Do we all have the ability to speak in unknown
languages? Do we all have the ability to interpret
unknown languages? Of course not! 31 So you
should earnestly desire the most helpful gifts.

But now let me show you a way of life that
is best of all.

Love Is the Greatest

13 If I could speak all the languages of
earth and of angels, but didn't love
others, I would only be a noisy gong
or a clanging cymbal. 2 If I had the gift of prophecy, and if I understood all of God's secret plans
and possessed all knowledge, and if I had such
faith that I could move mountains, but didn't
love others, I would be nothing. 3 If I gave everything I have to the poor and even sacrificed my
body, I could boast about it;* but if I didn't love
others, I would have gained nothing.
4 Love is patient and kind. Love is not jealous
or boastful or proud 5 or rude. It does not demand
its own way. It is not irritable, and it keeps no record of being wronged. 6 It does not rejoice about
injustice but rejoices whenever the truth wins out.
7 Love never gives up, never loses faith, is always
hopeful, and endures through every circumstance.
8 Prophecy and speaking in unknown languages* and special knowledge will become useless. But love will last forever! 9 Now our knowledge is partial and incomplete, and even the gift
of prophecy reveals only part of the whole picture! 10 But when the time of perfection comes,
these partial things will become useless.
11 When I was a child, I spoke and thought and
reasoned as a child. But when I grew up, I put
away childish things. 12 Now we see things im-
perfectly, like puzzling reflections in a mirror, but
then we will see everything with perfect clarity.*
All that I know now is partial and incomplete,
but then I will know everything completely, just
as God now knows me completely.
13 Three things will last forever—faith, hope,
and love—and the greatest of these is love.

Tongues and Prophecy

14 Let love be your highest goal! But
you should also desire the special
abilities the Spirit gives—especially

13:3 Some manuscripts read *sacrificed my body to be burned.* **13:8** Or *in tongues.* **13:12** Greek *see face to face.*

without the foot. Relationality, not dominance, is stressed. **23:** Then comes another of Paul's surprising statements about sex: The genitals are worthy of the most profound honor and respect. Private parts were called *aidoia*, "shameful members," although the term also implied a shame that led to modesty. *Aidos*, the root word, implied both shame and reverence. **24:** New meaning is given to those parts of the body that distinguish a woman's gender identity. The bodily members that remain hidden are intended not only for sexual distinction but also for delight, intimacy, communion, and the engendering of human life. These organs play a major role in God's purposes of covenant and communion.

13:1–13 The Superiority of Love. 1: In the midst of his efforts to heal bitter altercations and rivalries, Paul bursts into an unparalleled paean in praise of *love*. Love might resolve the specific abuses that vexed the Corinthian church. **2:** Charismatic gifts are useful to build and uplift the church, but none can compare with the gift of love. Love is more to be prized than the accoutrements of mystery religion: the gongs and cymbals, the acquisition of arcane knowledge, the mystic mirrors, the comprehension of mysteries. **13:** This magnificent treatise is placed at the climax of the argument for the unity and purity of the Corinthian congregation. All that precedes has been buildup, all that follows a winding down.

14:1–40 The Orderly Conduct of Worship. 3: The first concern is that of the need to convey meaning in

the ability to prophesy. 2 For if you have the ability to speak in tongues,* you will be talking only to God, since people won't be able to understand you. You will be speaking by the power of the Spirit,* but it will all be mysterious. 3 But one who prophesies strengthens others, encourages them, and comforts them. 4 A person who speaks in tongues is strengthened personally, but one who speaks a word of prophecy strengthens the entire church.

5 I wish you could all speak in tongues, but even more I wish you could all prophesy. For prophecy is greater than speaking in tongues, unless someone interprets what you are saying so that the whole church will be strengthened.

6 Dear brothers and sisters,* if I should come to you speaking in an unknown language,* how would that help you? But if I bring you a revelation or some special knowledge or prophecy or teaching, that will be helpful. 7 Even lifeless instruments like the flute or the harp must play the notes clearly, or no one will recognize the melody. 8 And if the bugler doesn't sound a clear call, how will the soldiers know they are being called to battle?

9 It's the same for you. If you speak to people in words they don't understand, how will they know what you are saying? You might as well be talking into empty space.

10 There are many different languages in the world, and every language has meaning. 11 But if I don't understand a language, I will be a foreigner to someone who speaks it, and the one who speaks it will be a foreigner to me. 12 And the same is true for you. Since you are so eager to have the special abilities the Spirit gives, seek those that will strengthen the whole church.

13 So anyone who speaks in tongues should pray also for the ability to interpret what has been said. 14 For if I pray in tongues, my spirit is praying, but I don't understand what I am saying.

15 Well then, what shall I do? I will pray in the spirit,* and I will also pray in words I understand. I will sing in the spirit, and I will also sing in words I understand. 16 For if you praise God only in the spirit, how can those who don't understand you praise God along with you? How can they join you in giving thanks when they don't understand what you are saying? 17 You will be giving thanks very well, but it won't strengthen the people who hear you.

18 I thank God that I speak in tongues more than any of you. 19 But in a church meeting I would rather speak five understandable words to help others than ten thousand words in an unknown language.

20 Dear brothers and sisters, don't be childish in your understanding of these things. Be innocent as babies when it comes to evil, but be mature in understanding matters of this kind. 21 It is written in the Scriptures*:

"I will speak to my own people
 through strange languages
 and through the lips of foreigners.
But even then, they will not listen to me,"*
 says the LORD.

22 So you see that speaking in tongues is a sign, not for believers, but for unbelievers. Prophecy, however, is for the benefit of believers, not unbelievers. 23 Even so, if unbelievers or people who don't understand these things come into your church meeting and hear everyone

14:2a Or *in unknown languages;* also in 14:4, 5, 13, 14, 18, 22, 26, 27, 28, 39. **14:2b** Or *speaking in your spirit.* **14:6a** Greek *brothers;* also in 14:20, 26, 39. **14:6b** Or *in tongues;* also in 14:19, 23. **14:15** Or *in the Spirit;* also in 14:15b, 16. **14:21a** Greek *in the law.* **14:21b** Isa 28:11-12.

worship. While *tongues* are frequently an accompaniment of ecstatic devotion, communication through prophecy is more necessary. Prophesying is here defined as speech that is intended to build up, comfort, and exhort. This definition is useful in understanding other New Testament references to women as prophets (Luke 2:36–38; Acts 2:17–18; 21:9; 1 Cor 11:4, 13). **6–11:** Paul differentiates between nonintelligible speech, frequently designated in this chapter by the Greek verb *laleo,* and meaningful speech (*lego*). The word used in the prohibition for women (v. 34) is *laleo,* a term used by Aristophanes for the frivolous chatter of women. **13–14:** The apostle places a far higher valuation on meaningful speech than on glossolalia, and insists that all ecstatic utterance should be interpreted so that all may be edified. **23:** In pagan orgiastic worship, women in particular were swept along into an altered state of consciousness. Dionysos was known as "the lord of the loud cry, the mad exciter of women." Their abandoned state of mind led to raving and uncontrolled actions, as well as to ceremonial cries known as ululation. Even in more orderly cults, the cries of women were part of the ritual at properly appointed moments. At Corinth, in a temple used primarily by women, a series of plaques have been excavated. One is dedicated to the sacred shouts of women. In this vein, Paul asks whether observers might not consider the Corinthian congregation to be mad—probably a reference to the ritual madness of these cults rather than to insanity. **26–27:** Only one person

speaking in an unknown language, they will
think you are crazy. 24 But if all of you are prophesying, and unbelievers or people who don't understand these things come into your meeting,
they will be convicted of sin and judged by what
you say. 25 As they listen, their secret thoughts
will be exposed, and they will fall to their knees
and worship God, declaring, "God is truly here
among you."

A Call to Orderly Worship

26 Well, my brothers and sisters, let's summarize.
When you meet together, one will sing, another
will teach, another will tell some special revelation God has given, one will speak in tongues, and
another will interpret what is said. But everything
that is done must strengthen all of you.

27 No more than two or three should speak
in tongues. They must speak one at a time, and
someone must interpret what they say. 28 But if
no one is present who can interpret, they must
be silent in your church meeting and speak in
tongues to God privately.

29 Let two or three people prophesy, and let
the others evaluate what is said. 30 But if someone is prophesying and another person receives
a revelation from the Lord, the one who is speaking must stop. 31 In this way, all who prophesy
will have a turn to speak, one after the other,
so that everyone will learn and be encouraged.
32 Remember that people who prophesy are in
control of their spirit and can take turns. 33 For
God is not a God of disorder but of peace, as in all
the meetings of God's holy people.*

34 Women should be silent during the church
meetings. It is not proper for them to speak. They
should be submissive, just as the law says. 35 If
they have any questions, they should ask their
husbands at home, for it is improper for women
to speak in church meetings.*

36 Or do you think God's word originated
with you Corinthians? Are you the only ones to
whom it was given? 37 If you claim to be a prophet
or think you are spiritual, you should recognize
that what I am saying is a command from the
Lord himself. 38 But if you do not recognize this,
you yourself will not be recognized.*

39 So, my dear brothers and sisters, be eager to
prophesy, and don't forbid speaking in tongues.
40 But be sure that everything is done properly
and in order.

The Resurrection of Christ

15 Let me now remind you, dear brothers and sisters,* of the Good News I
preached to you before. You welcomed
it then, and you still stand firm in it. 2 It is this
Good News that saves you if you continue to believe the message I told you—unless, of course,
you believed something that was never true in
the first place.*

3 I passed on to you what was most important
and what had also been passed on to me. Christ

14:33 The phrase *as in all the meetings of God's holy people* could instead be joined to the beginning of 14:34.
14:35 Some manuscripts place verses 34-35 after 14:40.
14:38 Some manuscripts read *If you are ignorant of this, stay in your ignorance.* **15:1** Greek *brothers;* also in 15:31, 50, 58.
15:2 Or *unless you never believed it in the first place.*

may speak at a time, and others must be allowed to take their turn. **28:** A person who speaks in tongues must be silent if there is no interpreter. **30:** A person who is prophesying must desist (lit., "be silent") if another wishes a turn. **34:** Some have suggested that this referred to interrupting the service by asking questions at inappropriate times, others that women were buzzing with their private conversations when they should instead have attended to the Word of God. If the women found the material difficult to understand, they might have a profitable conversation with their husbands at home, where there was frequently little communication between marital partners. Women are enjoined to silence in exactly the same way as the one who has no interpreter (v. 27) and the one who must yield a turn at prophesying to another (v. 28). All are given the right to prophesy (v. 30), so that it does not seem to be a prohibition against contributing a message of spiritual significance to the service of worship. Rather, it is a prohibition against a disruption of some sort. It is possible that the injunction is meant to curb the ululations that women had been taught were their contribution to ritual. A command for submission (Gk., *hypotasso*) had been issued to ecstatic prophets as part of an instruction to allow only one person to speak at a time. In the same manner, women are instructed to be submissive—again implying restraint, responsibility, and responsiveness to the worshiping community. In the ancient Near East, silence and submission denoted willingness to heed and obey the divine voice. **35:** Many scholars have argued that verses 34–35 are an interpolation, perhaps a gloss, appearing sometimes in its current location and sometimes after verse 40; 14:36 continues the argument of 14:33.

15:1–58 Resurrection and Immortality

The discussion begins with the events of Christ's passion and moves on to his resurrection appearances

died for our sins, just as the Scriptures said. 4 He was buried, and he was raised from the dead on the third day, just as the Scriptures said. 5 He was seen by Peter* and then by the Twelve. 6 After that, he was seen by more than 500 of his followers* at one time, most of whom are still alive, though some have died. 7 Then he was seen by James and later by all the apostles. 8 Last of all, as though I had been born at the wrong time, I also saw him. 9 For I am the least of all the apostles. In fact, I'm not even worthy to be called an apostle after the way I persecuted God's church.

10 But whatever I am now, it is all because God poured out his special favor on me—and not without results. For I have worked harder than any of the other apostles; yet it was not I but God who was working through me by his grace. 11 So it makes no difference whether I preach or they preach, for we all preach the same message you have already believed.

The Resurrection of the Dead

12 But tell me this—since we preach that Christ rose from the dead, why are some of you saying there will be no resurrection of the dead? 13 For if there is no resurrection of the dead, then Christ has not been raised either. 14 And if Christ has not been raised, then all our preaching is useless, and your faith is useless. 15 And we apostles would all be lying about God—for we have said that God raised Christ from the grave. But that can't be true if there is no resurrection of the dead. 16 And if there is no resurrection of the dead, then Christ has not been raised. 17 And if Christ has not been raised, then your faith is useless and you are still guilty of your sins. 18 In that case, all who have died believing in Christ are lost! 19 And if our hope in Christ is only for this life, we are more to be pitied than anyone in the world.

20 But in fact, Christ has been raised from the dead. He is the first of a great harvest of all who have died.

21 So you see, just as death came into the world through a man, now the resurrection from the dead has begun through another man. 22 Just as everyone dies because we all belong to Adam, everyone who belongs to Christ will be given new life. 23 But there is an order to this resurrection: Christ was raised as the first of the harvest; then all who belong to Christ will be raised when he comes back.

24 After that the end will come, when he will turn the Kingdom over to God the Father, having destroyed every ruler and authority and power. 25 For Christ must reign until he humbles all his enemies beneath his feet. 26 And the last enemy to be destroyed is death. 27 For the Scriptures say, "God has put all things under his authority."* (Of course, when it says "all things are under his authority," that does not include God himself, who gave Christ his authority.) 28 Then, when all things are under his authority, the Son will put himself under God's authority, so that God, who gave his Son authority over all things, will be utterly supreme over everything everywhere.

29 If the dead will not be raised, what point is there in people being baptized for those who are dead? Why do it unless the dead will someday rise again?

30 And why should we ourselves risk our lives hour by hour? 31 For I swear, dear brothers and sisters, that I face death daily. This is as certain as my pride in what Christ Jesus our Lord has done in you. 32 And what value was there in fighting wild beasts—those people of Ephesus*—if there will be no resurrection from the dead? And if there is no resurrection, "Let's feast and drink, for tomorrow we die!"* 33 Don't be fooled by those who say such things, for "bad company corrupts good character." 34 Think carefully about what is right, and stop sinning. For to your shame I say that some of you don't know God at all.

The Resurrection Body

35 But someone may ask, "How will the dead be raised? What kind of bodies will they have?" 36 What a foolish question! When you put a seed

15:5 Greek *Cephas.* **15:6** Greek *the brothers.* **15:27** Ps 8:6. **15:32a** Greek *fighting wild beasts in Ephesus.* **15:32b** Isa 22:13.

(vv. 3–8). The mention of his encounter with Mary Magdalene and the other women is conspicuously absent, while two of the noted appearances are undocumented elsewhere in Scripture: the appearance to James and to five hundred at once. The references are to the witness of leaders of the church (Peter and James and the Twelve). These are the very ones whose Corinthian followers now claim an inappropriate authority. **22:** Those who hold Eve accountable for initiating the sin leading to the Fall should notice the statement that in Adam all die (cf. Rom 5:12–14). The biblical account is evenhanded in its attribution of responsibility for humanity's original sin. Paul's point is not to dwell on the effects of sin but rather to insist on the promised results of Christ's resurrection. **33:** Paul's willingness to accept even prostitutes is perhaps demonstrated by his quotation here of a snippet from a play about a famous courtesan, Menander's *Thais* (218). **36:** Against those who would deny the validity of the resurrection, Paul

into the ground, it doesn't grow into a plant unless it dies first. 37 And what you put in the ground is not the plant that will grow, but only a bare seed of wheat or whatever you are planting. 38 Then God gives it the new body he wants it to have. A different plant grows from each kind of seed. 39 Similarly there are different kinds of flesh—one kind for humans, another for animals, another for birds, and another for fish.

40 There are also bodies in the heavens and bodies on the earth. The glory of the heavenly bodies is different from the glory of the earthly bodies. 41 The sun has one kind of glory, while the moon and stars each have another kind. And even the stars differ from each other in their glory.

42 It is the same way with the resurrection of the dead. Our earthly bodies are planted in the ground when we die, but they will be raised to live forever. 43 Our bodies are buried in brokenness, but they will be raised in glory. They are buried in weakness, but they will be raised in strength. 44 They are buried as natural human bodies, but they will be raised as spiritual bodies. For just as there are natural bodies, there are also spiritual bodies.

45 The Scriptures tell us, "The first man, Adam, became a living person."* But the last Adam—that is, Christ—is a life-giving Spirit. 46 What comes first is the natural body, then the spiritual body comes later. 47 Adam, the first man, was made from the dust of the earth, while Christ, the second man, came from heaven. 48 Earthly people are like the earthly man, and heavenly people are like the heavenly man. 49 Just as we are now like the earthly man, we will someday be like* the heavenly man.

50 What I am saying, dear brothers and sisters, is that our physical bodies cannot inherit the Kingdom of God. These dying bodies cannot inherit what will last forever.

51 But let me reveal to you a wonderful secret. We will not all die, but we will all be transformed! 52 It will happen in a moment, in the blink of an eye, when the last trumpet is blown. For when the trumpet sounds, those who have died will be raised to live forever. And we who are living will also be transformed. 53 For our dying bodies must be transformed into bodies that will never die; our mortal bodies must be transformed into immortal bodies.

54 Then, when our dying bodies have been transformed into bodies that will never die,* this Scripture will be fulfilled:

"Death is swallowed up in victory.*
55 O death, where is your victory?
O death, where is your sting?*"

56 For sin is the sting that results in death, and the law gives sin its power. 57 But thank God! He gives us victory over sin and death through our Lord Jesus Christ.

58 So, my dear brothers and sisters, be strong and immovable. Always work enthusiastically for the Lord, for you know that nothing you do for the Lord is ever useless.

The Collection for Jerusalem

16 Now regarding your question about the money being collected for God's people in Jerusalem. You should follow the same procedure I gave to the churches in Galatia. 2 On the first day of each week, you should each put aside a portion of the money you have earned. Don't wait until I get there and then try to collect it all at once. 3 When I come, I will write letters of recommendation for the messengers you choose to deliver your gift to Jerusalem. 4 And if it seems appropriate for me to go along, they can travel with me.

Paul's Final Instructions

5 I am coming to visit you after I have been to Macedonia,* for I am planning to travel through Macedonia. 6 Perhaps I will stay awhile with you, possibly all winter, and then you can send me on my way to my next destination. 7 This time I

15:45 Gen 2:7. **15:49** Some manuscripts read *let us be like.* **15:54a** Some manuscripts add *and our mortal bodies have been transformed into immortal bodies.* **15:54b** Isa 25:8. **15:55** Hos 13:14 (Greek version). **16:5** *Macedonia* was in the northern region of Greece.

argues for the body as seed for the immortal vehicle of the soul. Greek philosophers viewed the body as a tomb and prison. In the same vein, Gnostics despised their corporeal existence and longed to be liberated from all that chained them to this world. They hated their material bodies no less than do many contemporary women. But Paul affirms a glorious existence in the transformed bodies that spring from the old. **53:** Ultimately the body is linked to Paul's concept of immortality. The soul after death is not disembodied but clothed anew.

16:1–24 Closing Instructions

The conclusion is conciliatory. If Paul has previously been harsh, he now speaks of his visit and suggests a plan of systematic giving so that a contribution may be ready for Jerusalem at his coming (vv. 1–2).

don't want to make just a short visit and then go
right on. I want to come and stay awhile, if the
Lord will let me. 8 In the meantime, I will be staying here at Ephesus until the Festival of Pentecost. 9 There is a wide-open door for a great work
here, although many oppose me.
10 When Timothy comes, don't intimidate
him. He is doing the Lord's work, just as I am.
11 Don't let anyone treat him with contempt.
Send him on his way with your blessing when
he returns to me. I expect him to come with the
other believers.*
12 Now about our brother Apollos—I urged
him to visit you with the other believers, but he
was not willing to go right now. He will see you
later when he has the opportunity.
13 Be on guard. Stand firm in the faith. Be courageous.* Be strong. 14 And do everything with
love.
15 You know that Stephanas and his household were the first of the harvest of believers
in Greece,* and they are spending their lives in
service to God's people. I urge you, dear brothers
and sisters,* 16 to submit to them and others like
them who serve with such devotion. 17 I am very
glad that Stephanas, Fortunatus, and Achaicus
have come here. They have been providing the
help you weren't here to give me. 18 They have
been a wonderful encouragement to me, as they
have been to you. You must show your appreciation to all who serve so well.

Paul's Final Greetings

19 The churches here in the province of Asia* send
greetings in the Lord, as do Aquila and Priscilla*
and all the others who gather in their home for
church meetings. 20 All the brothers and sisters
here send greetings to you. Greet each other
with Christian love.*
21 Here is my greeting in my own handwriting—Paul.
22 If anyone does not love the Lord, that person is cursed. Our Lord, come!*
23 May the grace of the Lord Jesus be with
you.
24 My love to all of you in Christ Jesus.*

16:11 Greek *with the brothers;* also in 16:12. **16:13** Greek *Be men.* **16:15a** Greek *in Achaia,* the southern region of the Greek peninsula. **16:15b** Greek *brothers;* also in 16:20. **16:19a** *Asia* was a Roman province in what is now western Turkey. **16:19b** Greek *Prisca.* **16:20** Greek *with a sacred kiss.* **16:22** From Aramaic, *Marana tha.* Some manuscripts read *Maran atha,* "Our Lord has come." **16:24** Some manuscripts add *Amen.*

19: Among those who send greetings are *Aquila,* here named first, and *Priscilla,* whom he regarded as fellow laborers (Rom 16:3) and to whom he asks the Corinthians to be subject. **20:** By heeding the patterns that Paul and his associates have instilled, the Corinthians may grow from fractious children into those mature in the faith. His love remains with even the most difficult of them.

2 CORINTHIANS

INTRODUCTION

The book of 2 Corinthians is in many ways Paul's most personal letter. Written to the congregation already known to us from 1 Corinthians, this letter has less to do with the struggles experienced by that group than with Paul's understanding of his ministry, particularly as that ministry is the subject of criticism. Some readers treasure 2 Corinthians because Paul speaks eloquently of strength in weakness; others find it difficult to accept what they see as Paul's forward and overbearing manner. It may be argued that 2 Corinthians presents a feminine side of Paul, a Paul who is openly emotional, who rejects games of spiritual one-upmanship, who talks about his feelings and concerns. Yet the personality who emerges from these pages is no weakling. Paul proclaims that in his weakness God's power is demonstrated, but he does not use his weakness as an excuse to do nothing. Rather, in 2 Corinthians Paul remains engaged in ministry, even as he refuses to let ministry become a vehicle for vaunting human achievement.

Paul wrote to the Corinthians more than twice: references to a previous letter (1 Cor 5:9) and a tearful letter (2 Cor 2:4) point to a complicated history. Too, it is difficult to reconcile the conciliatory, joyful tone of 2 Corinthians 1—2 with the angry outbursts of 10—13. The shift in subject of 8—9, which deal with the offering for the church at Jerusalem, seems to fit uneasily with what has gone before, and some scholars see a possible interpolation in 6:14—7:1. Paul may need to speak sternly (chaps. 10—13), but the church finally listens to him, and the end of the story is the confident thanksgiving at the end of chapter 9. It is painful to imagine the alternate scenario for 2 Corinthians. After a humiliating visit from Paul, a tearful letter from him, and reconciliation with the apostle, the church fell back into old ways, and Paul was forced to write an even more scathing letter, with uncertain results.

Difficult though this scenario may be, it is not uncharacteristic of the ebb and flow of church life, of spiritual highs and divisive squabbles. We must admit that we read Paul's Corinthian correspondence without knowing whether the apostle was finally successful in keeping his beloved congregation loyal to himself.

The letter (or letters, if edited) clearly comes after 1 Corinthians and from somewhere far enough away from Corinth that Paul could not travel there on a whim, but near enough to keep up a complicated correspondence. The place of writing was likely Macedonia (see 2:13); the date, the mid- to late 50s.

The focused attention given to the collection for Jerusalem (chaps. 8—9) clues us in to the economic dynamics that underlie this letter. The apparent wealth of some of the Corinthian church's members, including some of its women, also signals us to other social dynamics underlying 2 Corinthians. In the cities of the Roman Empire, social status was determined by a number of factors—wealth, gender, occupational prestige, family, religion, liberty or servitude, and so forth. An individual's overall social status was in a sense the sum of the varying places he or she fell within these hierarchies. Some individuals would occupy strikingly different positions on different scales: a slave with a high-status occupation, for example, or a female head of a well-to-do household. Such status inconsistency, as sociologists call it, may have contributed to a heightened concern about status and social role.

The history of Paul's relationships with the Corinthian church, as we can reconstruct it from the letters and Acts, is complicated. Acts 18:8 attests, and the letters confirm, that Paul founded the church in Corinth, spending a year and a half there according to Acts 18:11. The first piece of Corinthian correspondence of which we have knowledge is that letter described in 1 Corinthians 5:9, in which Paul warns the church not to allow immorality among its membership. Apparently this directive was misunderstood by some members of the congregation, and Paul mentions the previous letter by way of correcting them. Our 1 Corinthians, then, is the second piece of correspondence from Paul to the Corinthian congregation; it is prompted by written communication from the church (1 Cor 7:1) and messengers to Paul from Chloe (1 Cor 1:11). Paul then visited Corinth, but the visit did not go well, and Paul wrote a tearful letter rather than returning to risk such pain again (2 Cor 2:1–4, 9; some scholars think that the tearful letter is 2 Cor 10—13). This letter had its desired effect, as reported by Titus (7:6–9); thus the beginning of our 2 Corinthians reflects Paul's great joy and relief at his *comfort* in being reconciled with the Corinthians.

Much of the letter deals with various questions regarding Paul's ministry. His means of support has been questioned as have his motives in taking up a collection from his Gentile congregations for the church in Jerusalem. The disciplinary measures he has advised for his Corinthian congregation have not met with universal support, and other preachers of the gospel have come to Corinth with great shows of spiritual prowess, undermining Paul's message and his authority. Second Corinthians addresses all of these issues, as Paul defends and continues to proclaim his gospel. —*Sandra Hack Polaski*

1:1–11	Salutation and Thanksgiving
1:12—7:16	Paul's Ministry
1:12—2:13	Issues of Past Concern
2:14—5:21	Paul Describes His Ministry
6:1–13	A Call for Reconciliation
6:14—7:1	A Call for Separation
7:2–16	Paul's Confidence in the Corinthians
8:1—9:15	The Offering for Jerusalem
8:1–15	Appeal for the Offering
8:16—9:5	Approved Co-Workers
9:6–15	Results of Generous Giving
10:1—13:10	Paul's Response to His Opponents
10:1–18	Paul Lays Out His Claim
11:1—12:10	The Fool's Speech
12:11—13:10	Summary Appeal and Warnings
13:11–14	Final Greetings and Benediction

Greetings from Paul

1 This letter is from Paul, chosen by the will
of God to be an apostle of Christ Jesus, and
from our brother Timothy.
I am writing to God's church in Corinth and
to all of his holy people throughout Greece.*
2May God our Father and the Lord Jesus
Christ give you grace and peace.

God Offers Comfort to All

3All praise to God, the Father of our Lord Jesus
Christ. God is our merciful Father and the source
of all comfort. 4He comforts us in all our troubles so that we can comfort others. When they
are troubled, we will be able to give them the
same comfort God has given us. 5For the more
we suffer for Christ, the more God will shower
us with his comfort through Christ. 6Even when
we are weighed down with troubles, it is for your
comfort and salvation! For when we ourselves
are comforted, we will certainly comfort you.
Then you can patiently endure the same things
we suffer. 7We are confident that as you share in
our sufferings, you will also share in the comfort
God gives us.
8We think you ought to know, dear brothers
and sisters,* about the trouble we went through
in the province of Asia. We were crushed and
overwhelmed beyond our ability to endure, and
we thought we would never live through it.
9In fact, we expected to die. But as a result, we
stopped relying on ourselves and learned to rely
only on God, who raises the dead. 10And he did
rescue us from mortal danger, and he will rescue
us again. We have placed our confidence in him,
and he will continue to rescue us. 11And you are
helping us by praying for us. Then many people
will give thanks because God has graciously answered so many prayers for our safety.

Paul's Change of Plans

12We can say with confidence and a clear conscience that we have lived with a God-given
holiness* and sincerity in all our dealings. We
have depended on God's grace, not on our own
human wisdom. That is how we have conducted
ourselves before the world, and especially toward
you. 13Our letters have been straightforward,
and there is nothing written between the lines
and nothing you can't understand. I hope someday you will fully understand us, 14even if you
don't understand us now. Then on the day when
the Lord Jesus* returns, you will be proud of us
in the same way we are proud of you.
15Since I was so sure of your understanding
and trust, I wanted to give you a double blessing by visiting you twice—16first on my way
to Macedonia and again when I returned from
Macedonia.* Then you could send me on my
way to Judea.
17You may be asking why I changed my plan.
Do you think I make my plans carelessly? Do
you think I am like people of the world who say
"Yes" when they really mean "No"? 18As surely
as God is faithful, our word to you does not waver between "Yes" and "No." 19For Jesus Christ,
the Son of God, does not waver between "Yes"
and "No." He is the one whom Silas,* Timothy,
and I preached to you, and as God's ultimate

1:1 Greek *Achaia,* the southern region of the Greek peninsula. **1:8** Greek *brothers.* **1:12** Some manuscripts read *honesty.* **1:14** Some manuscripts read *our Lord Jesus.* **1:16** *Macedonia* was in the northern region of Greece. **1:19** Greek *Silvanus.*

1:1–11 Salutation and Thanksgiving

The opening section of ancient letters followed a set pattern: the names of the sender and receiver, greetings and some form of thanksgiving to God for the sender's or receiver's health, safe travel in a recent journey and so forth. Paul follows this familiar formula but in every respect makes it reflect Christ. **3:** As is typical in Paul's letters, the thanksgiving is also a clue to the letter's important themes. Paul speaks forthrightly of affliction, reminds his readers of God's consolation, and emphasizes that divine consolation has as its end the shared comfort of the community. **3–7:** The incessant repetition of the language of *comfort* or "consolation" may seem to some readers a bit cloying. **8:** But here the tone changes drastically. Paul makes it clear to his readers that this is no shallow theology but an expression of deep joy arising from the experience of deep suffering. In speaking of God's consolation Paul speaks of what he knows.

1:12—7:16 Paul's Ministry

1:12—2:13 Issues of Past Concern. 1:14: Paul's delight and pride in the new believers is a recurring theme with twenty occurrences in this letter. Yet the boasting or pride that Paul expresses here is positive. This is boasting in its best sense and constitutes the news Paul longs to tell about the Corinthian church, but he continues to chide them that another kind of boasting is divisive and dangerous. **17:** When the first of two planned visits went badly, however, Paul canceled his return trip, writing instead an anguished letter to express his outrage and insist on congregational discipline. At the writing of the current letter, Paul has received word of the results of that previous

Depression

It should not surprise readers to find that many great people in the Bible experienced depression. Scripture never shrinks from pointing to a God "who encourages those who are discouraged" (2 Cor 7:6). Nonetheless, depression tends to deaden the sense of God's presence for even the most committed Christian. This could be why we are often told the sadder details of many lives in Scripture, which contains an extraordinary mass of evidence that God notices and cares about even the most private, complicated pain. For example, we read how Rebekah's daughters-in-law "made life miserable" (Gen 26:35); Michal, though first lady, was spurned (2 Sam 6:23); Leah felt fruitful but unloved, while Rachel felt loved but was unfruitful (Gen 29:31); a woman Jesus healed had been bent over for eighteen years (Luke 13:11). We find ourselves learning from women who overcame depressive situations from positions of powerlessness. Esther refused political oppression; Ruth and Naomi exploited family connections to escape poverty; Rahab, through faith, went from prostitute to honored ancestor of Jesus.

Jesus' words in Luke 6:21 indicate that for some people depression is part of life; depression is not inconsistent with faith. This does not, however, mean there is nothing a depressed woman can do about it. She can seek and accept professional help and reach out to offer support to others. She can talk about her feelings with friends and become alert to depression-prone situations. She can read psalms (Pss 22, 31, 42, 56, 69) and practice trust in God and challenge negative thinking (Phil 4:8). She can tackle depression arising from poor diet and poor physical fitness.

She can anticipate the "future and . . . hope" (Jer 29:11; Rom 5:3–5) and take heart from Jesus' attitude. He did not condemn Mary of Bethany when grief and resentment and disbelief hindered her from coming to meet him (John 11:20, 33). He did not refuse the silent prayer of the woman who touched him for her healing after twelve years of suffering (Luke 8:43–48).

"Yes," he always does what he says. [20] For all of
God's promises have been fulfilled in Christ with
a resounding "Yes!" And through Christ, our
"Amen" (which means "Yes") ascends to God for
his glory.

[21] It is God who enables us, along with you, to
stand firm for Christ. He has commissioned us,
[22] and he has identified us as his own by placing
the Holy Spirit in our hearts as the first installment that guarantees everything he has promised us.

[23] Now I call upon God as my witness that I
am telling the truth. The reason I didn't return to
Corinth was to spare you from a severe rebuke.
[24] But that does not mean we want to dominate
you by telling you how to put your faith into
practice. We want to work together with you so
you will be full of joy, for it is by your own faith
that you stand firm.

2 So I decided that I would not bring you
grief with another painful visit. [2] For if I
cause you grief, who will make me glad?
Certainly not someone I have grieved. [3] That is
why I wrote to you as I did, so that when I do
come, I won't be grieved by the very ones who
ought to give me the greatest joy. Surely you all
know that my joy comes from your being joyful. [4] I wrote that letter in great anguish, with a
troubled heart and many tears. I didn't want to
grieve you, but I wanted to let you know how
much love I have for you.

Forgiveness for the Sinner

[5] I am not overstating it when I say that the man
who caused all the trouble hurt all of you more
than he hurt me. [6] Most of you opposed him, and
that was punishment enough. [7] Now, however, it
is time to forgive and comfort him. Otherwise he

communication. With relief he reminds them that even church discipline should be restrained when it has served its purpose, so that consolation may abound. **23:** Paul writes openly of his feelings in having to discipline the Corinthian church, and the parental nature of his love is evident. He caused them pain by his disciplinary action—today we might call it tough love—and their pain grieved him deeply; yet he is glad that their pain led to reform and reconciliation, so he cannot say that he regrets having been its cause. He is not ashamed to let his feelings be known or to admit that he avoided unpleasant and unproductive conflict. **2:4–5:** He reminds them that his love for them remains constant. He is not even willing that the church member whose action precipitated the crisis be permanently exiled from the community; he encourages them to welcome this repentant brother.

may be overcome by discouragement. 8So I urge
you now to reaffirm your love for him.
9I wrote to you as I did to test you and see
if you would fully comply with my instructions.
10When you forgive this man, I forgive him, too.
And when I forgive whatever needs to be forgiven, I do so with Christ's authority for your
benefit, 11so that Satan will not outsmart us. For
we are familiar with his evil schemes.
12When I came to the city of Troas to preach
the Good News of Christ, the Lord opened a door
of opportunity for me. 13But I had no peace of
mind because my dear brother Titus hadn't yet
arrived with a report from you. So I said good-
bye and went on to Macedonia to find him.

Ministers of the New Covenant

14But thank God! He has made us his captives and
continues to lead us along in Christ's triumphal
procession. Now he uses us to spread the knowledge of Christ everywhere, like a sweet perfume.
15Our lives are a Christ-like fragrance rising up to
God. But this fragrance is perceived differently by
those who are being saved and by those who are
perishing. 16To those who are perishing, we are a
dreadful smell of death and doom. But to those
who are being saved, we are a life-giving perfume.
And who is adequate for such a task as this?
17You see, we are not like the many hucksters* who preach for personal profit. We preach
the word of God with sincerity and with Christ's
authority, knowing that God is watching us.

3 Are we beginning to praise ourselves again?
Are we like others, who need to bring you
letters of recommendation, or who ask you
to write such letters on their behalf? Surely not!
2The only letter of recommendation we need is
you yourselves. Your lives are a letter written in
our* hearts; everyone can read it and recognize
our good work among you. 3Clearly, you are
a letter from Christ showing the result of our
ministry among you. This "letter" is written not
with pen and ink, but with the Spirit of the living
God. It is carved not on tablets of stone, but on
human hearts.
4We are confident of all this because of our
great trust in God through Christ. 5It is not that
we think we are qualified to do anything on our
own. Our qualification comes from God. 6He has
enabled us to be ministers of his new covenant.
This is a covenant not of written laws, but of the
Spirit. The old written covenant ends in death;
but under the new covenant, the Spirit gives
life.

The Glory of the New Covenant

7The old way,* with laws etched in stone, led to
death, though it began with such glory that the
people of Israel could not bear to look at Moses'
face. For his face shone with the glory of God,

2:17 Some manuscripts read *the rest of the hucksters.*
3:2 Some manuscripts read *your.* **3:7** Or *ministry;* also in 3:8, 9, 10, 11, 12.

2:14—5:21 Paul Describes His Ministry. 2:14: Paul abruptly interrupts his narrative (it will resume in 7:5) to reflect theologically on the ministry in which he is engaged. First comes a military metaphor, that of a victory procession—although it is not clear whether those of *us* who are being led are soldiers of the victorious Christ or his prisoners. **15:** The most vivid part of the metaphor is the olfactory image: the smell of incense that permeates the scene, sweetly fragrant to the victors but a putrid reminder to the prisoners of their defeat and, quite likely, approaching death. Smells often recall emotions to us, and the fragrance that to one person is the family holiday dinner or the beloved's cologne is to another person a reminder of painful past events. Similarly those who proclaim God's message are likely to be treated rudely by those who reject the message, even as they are welcomed by those who are glad to hear the word. **17:** Focus on the proclaimers leads Paul to a related topic and a different metaphor. Those who are worthy to proclaim Christ, he says, are persons of sincerity like himself, not *hucksters* out to make a profit. Here we see a hint of one of the recurring themes of 2 Corinthians: Paul's contrast between himself and the rival preachers, whom he later describes as "false apostles" or (sarcastically) *"super apostles"* (11:5). **3:1:** Apparently these rivals, eager to ingratiate themselves to the Corinthians at Paul's expense, made a great deal of their glowing letters of recommendation, perhaps even from the Jerusalem church. The early church, functioning as small and scattered cells throughout the far-flung Roman Empire, relied on such letters to distinguish true preachers of the gospel, who deserved hospitality, from hucksters or worse. **2–3:** For Paul and the Corinthian congregation, though, the requirement of written credentials was ridiculous. Paul was the church's founder! If the Corinthians needed credentials, they should look to themselves; their Christian existence was Paul's letter of recommendation.

3:7–18 The Glory of the New Covenant. 7: The comparison between stone tablets and living hearts leads Paul to the deeper theological significance of his metaphor, and he reminds the Corinthians that

even though the brightness was already fading away. [8]Shouldn't we expect far greater glory under the new way, now that the Holy Spirit is giving life? [9]If the old way, which brings condemnation, was glorious, how much more glorious is the new way, which makes us right with God! [10]In fact, that first glory was not glorious at all compared with the overwhelming glory of the new way. [11]So if the old way, which has been replaced, was glorious, how much more glorious is the new, which remains forever!

[12]Since this new way gives us such confidence, we can be very bold. [13]We are not like Moses, who put a veil over his face so the people of Israel would not see the glory, even though it was destined to fade away. [14]But the people's minds were hardened, and to this day whenever the old covenant is being read, the same veil covers their minds so they cannot understand the truth. And this veil can be removed only by believing in Christ. [15]Yes, even today when they read Moses' writings, their hearts are covered with that veil, and they do not understand.

[16]But whenever someone turns to the Lord, the veil is taken away. [17]For the Lord is the Spirit, and wherever the Spirit of the Lord is, there is freedom. [18]So all of us who have had that veil removed can see and reflect the glory of the Lord. And the Lord—who is the Spirit—makes us more and more like him as we are changed into his glorious image.

Treasure in Fragile Clay Jars

4 Therefore, since God in his mercy has given us this new way,* we never give up. [2]We reject all shameful deeds and underhanded methods. We don't try to trick anyone or distort the word of God. We tell the truth before God, and all who are honest know this.

[3]If the Good News we preach is hidden behind a veil, it is hidden only from people who are perishing. [4]Satan, who is the god of this world, has blinded the minds of those who don't believe. They are unable to see the glorious light of the Good News. They don't understand this message about the glory of Christ, who is the exact likeness of God.

[5]You see, we don't go around preaching about ourselves. We preach that Jesus Christ is Lord, and we ourselves are your servants for Jesus' sake. [6]For God, who said, "Let there be light in the darkness," has made this light shine in our hearts so we could know the glory of God that is seen in the face of Jesus Christ.

[7]We now have this light shining in our hearts, but we ourselves are like fragile clay jars containing this great treasure.* This makes it clear that our great power is from God, not from ourselves.

[8]We are pressed on every side by troubles, but we are not crushed. We are perplexed, but not driven to despair. [9]We are hunted down, but never abandoned by God. We get knocked down, but we are not destroyed. [10]Through suffering, our bodies continue to share in the death of Jesus so that the life of Jesus may also be seen in our bodies.

[11]Yes, we live under constant danger of death because we serve Jesus, so that the life of Jesus will be evident in our dying bodies. [12]So we live in the face of death, but this has resulted in eternal life for you.

[13]But we continue to preach because we have the same kind of faith the psalmist had when he said, "I believed in God, so I spoke."* [14]We know that God, who raised the Lord Jesus,* will also raise us with Jesus and present us to himself together with you. [15]All of this is for your ben-

4:1 Or *ministry.* **4:7** Greek *We now have this treasure in clay jars.* **4:13** Ps 116:10. **4:14** Some manuscripts read *who raised Jesus.*

---

he is involved in the ministry of a new, life-giving covenant. He develops this idea with the account in Exodus 34:29–35 of Moses' shining face and the veil he used to cover his face. **16:** Paul is distressed that his Jewish brothers and sisters fail to see the fullness of God's glory—that shocking, scandalous glory that has made divine grace available even to Gentiles.

4:1—5:15 A New Covenant Ministry. 4:2: This remarkable gift of divine glory requires complete openness on the part of its ministers: They are to veil nothing. Paul ties together the theological insight, that God gives the ability to recognize the truth of the gospel, with the ministerial insight, that it is the responsibility of those who proclaim the gospel to do so openly and without deceit. **7:** Here we see the first development of the strength-in-weakness theme that is so important in this epistle. Paul will fall prey neither to the temptation to self-aggrandizement nor to the tendency to understate God's power. **11:** Indeed, the life of the apostle is not an easy one. On three separate occasions in 2 Corinthians Paul recites a résumé of sorts, each time focusing not on his accomplishments but on his sufferings and hardships. In this first list, Paul uses antitheses, paradoxes, and wordplay to emphasize the reality of the hardship he faces and the depth of the hope that sustains him.

efit. And as God's grace reaches more and more people, there will be great thanksgiving, and God will receive more and more glory.

[16] That is why we never give up. Though our bodies are dying, our spirits are* being renewed every day. [17] For our present troubles are small and won't last very long. Yet they produce for us a glory that vastly outweighs them and will last forever! [18] So we don't look at the troubles we can see now; rather, we fix our gaze on things that cannot be seen. For the things we see now will soon be gone, but the things we cannot see will last forever.

New Bodies

5 For we know that when this earthly tent we live in is taken down (that is, when we die and leave this earthly body), we will have a house in heaven, an eternal body made for us by God himself and not by human hands. [2] We grow weary in our present bodies, and we long to put on our heavenly bodies like new clothing. [3] For we will put on heavenly bodies; we will not be spirits without bodies.* [4] While we live in these earthly bodies, we groan and sigh, but it's not that we want to die and get rid of these bodies that clothe us. Rather, we want to put on our new bodies so that these dying bodies will be swallowed up by life. [5] God himself has prepared us for this, and as a guarantee he has given us his Holy Spirit.

[6] So we are always confident, even though we know that as long as we live in these bodies we are not at home with the Lord. [7] For we live by believing and not by seeing. [8] Yes, we are fully confident, and we would rather be away from these earthly bodies, for then we will be at home with the Lord. [9] So whether we are here in this body or away from this body, our goal is to please him. [10] For we must all stand before Christ to be judged. We will each receive whatever we deserve for the good or evil we have done in this earthly body.

We Are God's Ambassadors

[11] Because we understand our fearful responsibility to the Lord, we work hard to persuade others. God knows we are sincere, and I hope you know this, too. [12] Are we commending ourselves to you again? No, we are giving you a reason to be proud of us,* so you can answer those who brag about having a spectacular ministry rather than having a sincere heart. [13] If it seems we are crazy, it is to bring glory to God. And if we are in our right minds, it is for your benefit. [14] Either way, Christ's love controls us.* Since we believe that Christ died for all, we also believe that we have all died to our old life.* [15] He died for everyone so that those who receive his new life will no longer live for themselves. Instead, they will live for Christ, who died and was raised for them.

4:16 Greek *our inner being is.* **5:3** Greek *we will not be naked.* **5:12** Some manuscripts read *proud of yourselves.* **5:14a** Or *urges us on.* **5:14b** Greek *Since one died for all, then all died.*

Again, the underlying contrast is that of death and life. **17:** At the same time, he is developing an image suggested by a wordplay: the Hebrew *kabod,* meaning "weight" and "glory." Although Paul is writing in Greek, the idea of weight of glory suggests a helpful concept to him: The burdens we now bear are a sort of strength training to prepare us for the wonderful weight of divine glory to be given to us one day. **18:** We should not let the fact that Paul speaks almost offhandedly of the mortal dangers he has faced distract us from the reality of those dangers. There is no reason to think Paul exaggerates when he says that he has faced life-threatening situations in his ministry and that his physical suffering and material deprivation have been serious. Yet Paul mentions such experiences on the way to speaking of the surpassing greatness of God's grace. **5:1–5:** He is constantly on guard against the religious-philosophical view popular in the Greco-Roman world, that the body and things of this world are evil and should be cast away. Paul's theology, rooted deeply in a concept of a good creation, rejected such notions, even as he recognized the power of sin in the material world and longed for the transformation of the physical body, so prone to suffering. The metaphors of clothing and the house suggest protection for the individual, and Paul mixes them in developing his argument. **6–9:** It may be disconcerting to read of Paul seemingly taking earthly life so lightly, speaking of it as nothing more than a rather interesting journey from which he will be glad to return *home.* While Paul is still engaged in active ministry, he has reached a state of peace and confidence. **14–15:** Indeed, Paul offers in this context a most interesting interpretation of the meaning of salvation. *Christ died for all,* but he does not follow with the conclusion we might expect, namely, that no one else has to die. Rather, he makes the opposite, surprising statement: *we have all died.* Death is no less a fact of human life than it ever was—except for those who are in Christ, that most difficult and frightful experience is already behind us, accomplished in Christ for us. Thus we are freed from life lived under the shadow of death to live not for ourselves but for Christ.

16 So we have stopped evaluating others from a human point of view. At one time we thought of Christ merely from a human point of view. How differently we know him now! 17 This means that anyone who belongs to Christ has become a new person. The old life is gone; a new life has begun!

18 And all of this is a gift from God, who brought us back to himself through Christ. And God has given us this task of reconciling people to him. 19 For God was in Christ, reconciling the world to himself, no longer counting people's sins against them. And he gave us this wonderful message of reconciliation. 20 So we are Christ's ambassadors; God is making his appeal through us. We speak for Christ when we plead, "Come back to God!" 21 For God made Christ, who never sinned, to be the offering for our sin,* so that we could be made right with God through Christ.

6 As God's partners,* we beg you not to accept this marvelous gift of God's kindness and then ignore it. 2 For God says,

"At just the right time, I heard you.
On the day of salvation, I helped you."*

Indeed, the "right time" is now. Today is the day of salvation.

Paul's Hardships

3 We live in such a way that no one will stumble because of us, and no one will find fault with our ministry. 4 In everything we do, we show that we are true ministers of God. We patiently endure troubles and hardships and calamities of every kind. 5 We have been beaten, been put in prison, faced angry mobs, worked to exhaustion, endured sleepless nights, and gone without food. 6 We prove ourselves by our purity, our understanding, our patience, our kindness, by the Holy Spirit within us,* and by our sincere love. 7 We faithfully preach the truth. God's power is working in us. We use the weapons of righteousness in the right hand for attack and the left hand for defense. 8 We serve God whether people honor us or despise us, whether they slander us or praise us. We are honest, but they call us impostors. 9 We are ignored, even though we are well known. We live close to death, but we are still alive. We have been beaten, but we have not been killed. 10 Our hearts ache, but we always have joy. We are poor, but we give spiritual riches to others. We own nothing, and yet we have everything.

11 Oh, dear Corinthian friends! We have spoken honestly with you, and our hearts are open to you. 12 There is no lack of love on our part, but you have withheld your love from us. 13 I am asking you to respond as if you were my own children. Open your hearts to us!

The Temple of the Living God

14 Don't team up with those who are unbelievers. How can righteousness be a partner with wickedness? How can light live with darkness? 15 What harmony can there be between Christ and the devil*? How can a believer be a partner with an unbeliever? 16 And what union can there be between God's temple and idols? For we are the temple of the living God. As God said:

"I will live in them
and walk among them.
I will be their God,

5:21 Or *to become sin itself.* **6:1** Or *As we work together.* **6:2** Isa 49:8 (Greek version). **6:6** Or *by our holiness of spirit.* **6:15** Greek *Beliar;* various other manuscripts render this proper name of the devil as *Belian, Beliab,* or *Belial.*

5:16–21 New Creation. 17: This renewal includes the believer's becoming a part of the divine work of reconciliation. The intimate, relationship-focused notion of reconciliation is a way of imaging God's work to which many women can relate. True reconciliation cannot be coerced; it requires willingness to become involved in the life of the other, to see things from the other's point of view. And, as many women and men can attest, reconciliation is arduous work. Yet we are made reconcilers by none other than the one who reconciled us; we speak not on our own behalf but that of Christ.

6:1–13 A Call for Reconciliation. 4–10: Paul has made himself and his co-workers examples of reconciling messengers; now he enlarges his message of reconciliation with his second list of experiences. It is an odd sort of appeal if we imagine that Paul is inviting his readers to share his ministry—who would willingly choose such a life?

6:14—7:1 A Call for Separation. 14: The Corinthian believers were converts from various Greco-Roman religions; their culture tended to encourage individuals to construct religion from various sources. In 1 Corinthians we learn that some of them found it hard to leave old religious practices and beliefs behind. **18:** The promise is originally made to David (2 Sam 7:14); Paul expands it, changing the original "you shall be my son" to *you will be my sons*

and they will be my people.*
17 Therefore, come out from among unbelievers,
and separate yourselves from them, says
the LORD.
Don't touch their filthy things,
and I will welcome you.*
18 And I will be your Father,
and you will be my sons and daughters,
says the LORD Almighty.*"

7 Because we have these promises, dear
friends, let us cleanse ourselves from everything that can defile our body or spirit.
And let us work toward complete holiness because we fear God.

2 Please open your hearts to us. We have not
done wrong to anyone, nor led anyone astray,
nor taken advantage of anyone. 3 I'm not saying
this to condemn you. I said before that you are in
our hearts, and we live or die together with you.
4 I have the highest confidence in you, and I take
great pride in you. You have greatly encouraged
me and made me happy despite all our troubles.

Paul's Joy at the Church's Repentance

5 When we arrived in Macedonia, there was no rest
for us. We faced conflict from every direction, with
battles on the outside and fear on the inside. 6 But
God, who encourages those who are discouraged,
encouraged us by the arrival of Titus. 7 His presence was a joy, but so was the news he brought of
the encouragement he received from you. When
he told us how much you long to see me, and how
sorry you are for what happened, and how loyal
you are to me, I was filled with joy!

8 I am not sorry that I sent that severe letter to
you, though I was sorry at first, for I know it was
painful to you for a little while. 9 Now I am glad
I sent it, not because it hurt you, but because the
pain caused you to repent and change your ways.
It was the kind of sorrow God wants his people
to have, so you were not harmed by us in any
way. 10 For the kind of sorrow God wants us to
experience leads us away from sin and results in
salvation. There's no regret for that kind of sorrow. But worldly sorrow, which lacks repentance,
results in spiritual death.
11 Just see what this godly sorrow produced
in you! Such earnestness, such concern to clear
yourselves, such indignation, such alarm, such
longing to see me, such zeal, and such a readiness to punish wrong. You showed that you have
done everything necessary to make things right.
12 My purpose, then, was not to write about who
did the wrong or who was wronged. I wrote to
you so that in the sight of God you could see for
yourselves how loyal you are to us. 13 We have
been greatly encouraged by this.

In addition to our own encouragement, we
were especially delighted to see how happy Titus was about the way all of you welcomed
him and set his mind* at ease. 14 I had told him
how proud I was of you—and you didn't disappoint me. I have always told you the truth, and
now my boasting to Titus has also proved true!
15 Now he cares for you more than ever when he
remembers the way all of you obeyed him and
welcomed him with such fear and deep respect.
16 I am very happy now because I have complete
confidence in you.

A Call to Generous Giving

8 Now I want you to know, dear brothers and
sisters,* what God in his kindness has done
through the churches in Macedonia. 2 They
are being tested by many troubles, and they are
very poor. But they are also filled with abundant
joy, which has overflowed in rich generosity.

3 For I can testify that they gave not only what
they could afford, but far more. And they did it
of their own free will. 4 They begged us again and
again for the privilege of sharing in the gift for
the believers* in Jerusalem. 5 They even did more
than we had hoped, for their first action was to

6:16 Lev 26:12; Ezek 37:27. **6:17** Isa 52:11; Ezek 20:34 (Greek version). **6:18** 2 Sam 7:14. **7:13** Greek *his spirit.* **8:1** Greek *brothers.* **8:4** Greek *for God's holy people.*

and daughters, emphasizing that the promise is to all believers.

7:2–16 Paul's Confidence in the Corinthians. 5: Paul resumes the story he left in 2:13. The consolation language of the thanksgiving recurs, again with the reminder that Paul's comfort is great because his suffering has been great as well. **8:** His grief was caused by the pain the church felt, even though he knew that discipline was the right thing to do. It is important to Paul that the Corinthians know the emotions he experienced and recognize that he did not enjoy causing them to grieve—traits that are often described as feminine. **16:** The language is exuberant, even exaggerated; Paul's relief at his reconciliation with his beloved congregation spills out in his complete confidence in them.

8:1–9:15 The Offering for Jerusalem

8:1–15: Appeal for the Offering. 6–7: Paul demonstrates that he is not squeamish about this practical

give themselves to the Lord and to us, just as God
wanted them to do.

6 So we have urged Titus, who encouraged
your giving in the first place, to return to you
and encourage you to finish this ministry of giving. 7 Since you excel in so many ways—in your
faith, your gifted speakers, your knowledge, your
enthusiasm, and your love from us*—I want you
to excel also in this gracious act of giving.

8 I am not commanding you to do this. But I
am testing how genuine your love is by comparing it with the eagerness of the other churches.

9 You know the generous grace of our Lord
Jesus Christ. Though he was rich, yet for your
sakes he became poor, so that by his poverty he
could make you rich.

10 Here is my advice: It would be good for
you to finish what you started a year ago. Last
year you were the first who wanted to give, and
you were the first to begin doing it. 11 Now you
should finish what you started. Let the eagerness you showed in the beginning be matched
now by your giving. Give in proportion to what
you have. 12 Whatever you give is acceptable if
you give it eagerly. And give according to what
you have, not what you don't have. 13 Of course, I
don't mean your giving should make life easy for
others and hard for yourselves. I only mean that
there should be some equality. 14 Right now you
have plenty and can help those who are in need.
Later, they will have plenty and can share with
you when you need it. In this way, things will be
equal. 15 As the Scriptures say,

"Those who gathered a lot had nothing left
over,
and those who gathered only a little had
enough."*

Titus and His Companions

16 But thank God! He has given Titus the same
enthusiasm for you that I have. 17 Titus welcomed
our request that he visit you again. In fact, he
himself was very eager to go and see you. 18 We
are also sending another brother with Titus. All
the churches praise him as a preacher of the
Good News. 19 He was appointed by the churches to accompany us as we take the offering to
Jerusalem*—a service that glorifies the Lord and
shows our eagerness to help.

20 We are traveling together to guard against
any criticism for the way we are handling this
generous gift. 21 We are careful to be honorable
before the Lord, but we also want everyone else
to see that we are honorable.

22 We are also sending with them another of
our brothers who has proven himself many times
and has shown on many occasions how eager he
is. He is now even more enthusiastic because
of his great confidence in you. 23 If anyone asks
about Titus, say that he is my partner who works
with me to help you. And the brothers with him
have been sent by the churches,* and they bring
honor to Christ. 24 So show them your love, and
prove to all the churches that our boasting about
you is justified.

The Collection for Christians in Jerusalem

9 I really don't need to write to you about
this ministry of giving for the believers in
Jerusalem.* 2 For I know how eager you are
to help, and I have been boasting to the churches

8:7 Some manuscripts read *your love for us.* **8:15** Exod 16:18. **8:19** See 1 Cor 16:3-4. **8:23** Greek *are apostles of the churches.* **9:1** Greek *about the offering for God's holy people.*

---

matter of ministry. Nor does he treat it as something beneath his purview as an apostle; rather, he addresses the subject squarely as a theological issue. He refers to the offering as a *charis* ("grace") translated variously as "service," "gracious work," "act of grace," "generous undertaking," but here as *gracious act of giving.* **10:** Throughout his ministry, Paul promoted the collection of an offering for the church at Jerusalem, to whom he refers as the "saints." Understandably this practice raised a number of questions. As Paul's letters and the book of Acts demonstrate, relationships between Jews and Gentiles, even between Jewish Christians and Gentile Christians, were frequently strained. Gentiles of modest means, and those who experienced ostracism and persecution for their expression of Christian faith, may well have hesitated to contribute to a fund for persecuted Jewish Christians in far-off Jerusalem.

8:16—9:5 Approved Co-Workers. 8:20: Others wondered whether Paul took some of these funds for his use, and such speculation seems to have been encouraged by some of Paul's rivals. The subject of money must be handled carefully. **22–23:** Paul recognizes that the trustworthiness of his ministry requires forthrightness in handling financial matters, and he recites the credentials of his co-workers who will see to the transfer of funds. While we frequently think of Paul working alone in ministry, texts such as this one reveal the depth of his reliance on others. Taking Paul as a ministry model should not cause us to neglect our cooperation with partners in ministry or denigrate the value of their service. **9:2:** Again Paul

in Macedonia that you in Greece* were ready to
send an offering a year ago. In fact, it was your
enthusiasm that stirred up many of the Macedonian believers to begin giving.
3 But I am sending these brothers to be sure
you really are ready, as I have been telling them,
and that your money is all collected. I don't want
to be wrong in my boasting about you. 4 We
would be embarrassed—not to mention your
own embarrassment—if some Macedonian believers came with me and found that you weren't
ready after all I had told them! 5 So I thought I
should send these brothers ahead of me to make
sure the gift you promised is ready. But I want it
to be a willing gift, not one given grudgingly.
6 Remember this—a farmer who plants only
a few seeds will get a small crop. But the one
who plants generously will get a generous crop.
7 You must each decide in your heart how much
to give. And don't give reluctantly or in response
to pressure. "For God loves a person who gives
cheerfully."* 8 And God will generously provide
all you need. Then you will always have everything you need and plenty left over to share with
others. 9 As the Scriptures say,

"They share freely and give generously to
the poor.
Their good deeds will be remembered
forever."*

10 For God is the one who provides seed for the
farmer and then bread to eat. In the same way, he
will provide and increase your resources and then
produce a great harvest of generosity* in you.
11 Yes, you will be enriched in every way so
that you can always be generous. And when we
take your gifts to those who need them, they will
thank God. 12 So two good things will result from
this ministry of giving—the needs of the believers in Jerusalem* will be met, and they will joyfully express their thanks to God.
13 As a result of your ministry, they will give
glory to God. For your generosity to them and to
all believers will prove that you are obedient to
the Good News of Christ. 14 And they will pray
for you with deep affection because of the overflowing grace God has given to you. 15 Thank God
for this gift* too wonderful for words!

Paul Defends His Authority

10 Now I, Paul, appeal to you with the
gentleness and kindness of Christ—
though I realize you think I am timid
in person and bold only when I write from far
away. 2 Well, I am begging you now so that when
I come I won't have to be bold with those who
think we act from human motives.
3 We are human, but we don't wage war as humans do. 4 *We use God's mighty weapons, not
worldly weapons, to knock down the strongholds
of human reasoning and to destroy false arguments. 5 We destroy every proud obstacle that
keeps people from knowing God. We capture their

9:2 Greek *in Achaia,* the southern region of the Greek peninsula. *Macedonia* was in the northern region of Greece. **9:7** See footnote on Prov 22:8. **9:9** Ps 112:9. **9:10** Greek *righteousness.* **9:12** Greek *of God's holy people.* **9:15** Greek *his gift.* **10:4** English translations divide verses 4 and 5 in various ways.

---

speaks of boasting in its positive sense, with a suggestion of the familial relationship between himself and the Corinthian congregation. He has spoken of them in such glowing terms that their failure to do what he has promised would reflect badly not just on themselves but on him as well, as when children fail to meet the expectations of their parents. Paul walks a thin line between encouragement and coercion, so eager is he for the Corinthians to do what he has asked. He uses every tool of persuasion, including comparing them with others, appealing to the Corinthians' heightened sense of status consciousness; yet he continues to insist that the offering is voluntary.

9:6–15 Results of Generous Giving. 13: The voluntary nature of the Corinthians' gift has theological ramifications. Their freewill offering is a fitting response to God's blessings freely offered to them. Paul makes it clear that financial matters are not a subject apart from theological reflection. Rather, stewardship and generosity are themes intimately related to gratitude and thanksgiving for the abundance of the divine blessing. The act of giving increases fellowship among members and between churches, with the ultimate result being glory to God.

10:1—13:10 Paul's Response to His Opponents

10:1–18 Paul Lays Out His Claim. 2: Beginning in chapter 10 Paul's tone shifts markedly. Perhaps Paul has received new information as chapters 1—9 were being dictated, and he shifts his tone to address the changed situation. It is possible that the complexity of the Corinthian situation, inaccessible to us centuries later, justified to Paul the writing of a letter that praised (some of?) his recipients' renewed loyalty to him and castigated those who remained his opponents. While we cannot reconstruct the situation with certainty, we can sense the outrage the apostle

rebellious thoughts and teach them to obey Christ.
6 And after you have become fully obedient, we
will punish everyone who remains disobedient.
7 Look at the obvious facts.* Those who say
they belong to Christ must recognize that we belong to Christ as much as they do. 8 I may seem
to be boasting too much about the authority
given to us by the Lord. But our authority builds
you up; it doesn't tear you down. So I will not be
ashamed of using my authority.
9 I'm not trying to frighten you by my letters. 10 For some say, "Paul's letters are demanding and forceful, but in person he is weak, and his
speeches are worthless!" 11 Those people should
realize that our actions when we arrive in person
will be as forceful as what we say in our letters
from far away.
12 Oh, don't worry; we wouldn't dare say that
we are as wonderful as these other men who
tell you how important they are! But they are
only comparing themselves with each other, using themselves as the standard of measurement.
How ignorant!
13 We will not boast about things done outside
our area of authority. We will boast only about
what has happened within the boundaries of
the work God has given us, which includes our
working with you. 14 We are not reaching beyond
these boundaries when we claim authority over
you, as if we had never visited you. For we were
the first to travel all the way to Corinth with the
Good News of Christ.
15 Nor do we boast and claim credit for the
work someone else has done. Instead, we hope
that your faith will grow so that the boundaries
of our work among you will be extended. 16 Then
we will be able to go and preach the Good News
in other places far beyond you, where no one else
is working. Then there will be no question of our
boasting about work done in someone else's territory. 17 As the Scriptures say, "If you want to
boast, boast only about the LORD."*
18 When people commend themselves, it
doesn't count for much. The important thing is
for the Lord to commend them.

Paul and the False Apostles

11 I hope you will put up with a little
more of my foolishness. Please bear
with me. 2 For I am jealous for you
with the jealousy of God himself. I promised you
as a pure bride* to one husband—Christ. 3 But
I fear that somehow your pure and undivided
devotion to Christ will be corrupted, just as Eve
was deceived by the cunning ways of the serpent.
4 You happily put up with whatever anyone tells
you, even if they preach a different Jesus than
the one we preach, or a different kind of Spirit
than the one you received, or a different kind of
gospel than the one you believed.
5 But I don't consider myself inferior in any
way to these "super apostles" who teach such
things. 6 I may be unskilled as a speaker, but I'm
not lacking in knowledge. We have made this
clear to you in every possible way.

10:7 Or *You look at things only on the basis of appearance.*
10:17 Jer 9:24. **11:2** Greek *a virgin.*

---

expresses in these chapters. **10:** According to Paul, his opponents insinuate that he is a cowardly bully, threatening from afar what he cannot carry out in their presence. **12:** Paul, ever self-confident, is loath to admit that his opponents even have a case. But as it becomes increasingly clear in these chapters, he does have to contend with rivals who put on a better show than he does and openly cast aspersions on him by comparison. Paul does not dignify their charges with a direct reply but denounces their methods, charging that their tactics of self-commendation are *ignorant*. **13–15:** Paul will limit his boasting to the strengths God has given him and seek to work within the limits God has imposed. His words are a powerful reminder that our responsibility lies in cultivating the gifts we have.

11:1—12:10 The Fool's Speech. 11:1: Paul begins an extraordinary protestation by asking his readers to indulge him in *foolishness*. What he reveals about himself in the following verses, often termed "the fool's speech," has been found helpful by Christians through the ages who have experienced similar struggles. **2:** Paul opens this section with a metaphor that trades on a pair of stereotypes: the virgin bride and the sinful Eve. Paul images himself as father of the bride, eager to present her to her husband chaste and unviolated. **3:** By contrast, he points to the story of Eve's deception by the serpent, perhaps alluding to the later Jewish tradition that the serpent's seduction was of a sexual nature and neglecting to mention Adam's culpability. Women readers may be uncomfortable with the use of these stereotypes, which reduce women's identity to their sexual status. Nonetheless it is important to notice that Paul is not speaking merely of the women in the Corinthian congregation, as if he were singling them out as particularly prone to deception. Rather, he encourages the entire congregation, men and women, to identify themselves in these female metaphors. The sexual imagery, while blunt, is apt in the context of Paul's concern about his opponents, whom he sees

[7]Was I wrong when I humbled myself and honored you by preaching God's Good News to you without expecting anything in return? [8]I "robbed" other churches by accepting their contributions so I could serve you at no cost. [9]And when I was with you and didn't have enough to live on, I did not become a financial burden to anyone. For the brothers who came from Macedonia brought me all that I needed. I have never been a burden to you, and I never will be. [10]As surely as the truth of Christ is in me, no one in all of Greece* will ever stop me from boasting about this. [11]Why? Because I don't love you? God knows that I do.

[12]But I will continue doing what I have always done. This will undercut those who are looking for an opportunity to boast that their work is just like ours. [13]These people are false apostles. They are deceitful workers who disguise themselves as apostles of Christ. [14]But I am not surprised! Even Satan disguises himself as an angel of light. [15]So it is no wonder that his servants also disguise themselves as servants of righteousness. In the end they will get the punishment their wicked deeds deserve.

Paul's Many Trials

[16]Again I say, don't think that I am a fool to talk like this. But even if you do, listen to me, as you would to a foolish person, while I also boast a little. [17]Such boasting is not from the Lord, but I am acting like a fool. [18]And since others boast about their human achievements, I will, too. [19]After all, you think you are so wise, but you enjoy putting up with fools! [20]You put up with it when someone enslaves you, takes everything you have, takes advantage of you, takes control of everything, and slaps you in the face. [21]I'm ashamed to say that we've been too "weak" to do that!

But whatever they dare to boast about—I'm talking like a fool again—I dare to boast about it, too. [22]Are they Hebrews? So am I. Are they Israelites? So am I. Are they descendants of Abraham? So am I. [23]Are they servants of Christ? I know I sound like a madman, but I have served him far more! I have worked harder, been put in prison more often, been whipped times without number, and faced death again and again. [24]Five different times the Jewish leaders gave me thirty-nine lashes. [25]Three times I was beaten with rods. Once I was stoned. Three times I was shipwrecked. Once I spent a whole night and a day adrift at sea. [26]I have traveled on many long journeys. I have faced danger from rivers and from robbers. I have faced danger from my own people, the Jews, as well as from the Gentiles. I have faced danger in the cities, in the deserts, and on the seas. And I have faced danger from men who claim to be believers but are not.* [27]I have worked hard and long, enduring many sleepless nights. I have been hungry and thirsty and have often gone without food. I have shivered in the cold, without enough clothing to keep me warm. [28]Then, besides all this, I have the daily burden of my concern for all the churches. [29]Who is weak without my feeling that weakness? Who is led astray, and I do not burn with anger?

[30]If I must boast, I would rather boast about the things that show how weak I am. [31]God, the Father of our Lord Jesus, who is worthy of eternal praise, knows I am not lying. [32]When I was in

11:10 Greek *Achaia,* the southern region of the Greek peninsula. **11:26** Greek *from false brothers.*

---

as seducing the Corinthians' hearts and minds. **7–8:** His refusal to be supported by the Corinthians (who likely would have misunderstood any acceptance of support as a signal of a patron-client relationship) has been interpreted as a lack of love for them; his opponents may have pointed to his many tribulations as evidence that God has not given divine support and protection to his ministry. **13–14:** Paul is angered by these deceptions and levels harsh countercharges at his opponents, as *false apostles,* implying that they are in league with Satan. **19–20:** Again, this indictment from Paul sounds strikingly like a description of modern church situations. Not only are leaders who abuse their power a problem in the congregation; just as problematic are members who allow themselves to be taken advantage of, who are unwilling to challenge their spiritual leaders on grounds of mistreatment, who accept suffering within the congregation either as deserved or as an appropriate mirror of Christ's suffering. Paul categorically rejects the acceptance of abuse from leaders of the congregation as Christian suffering. Such suffering, he says, is not to be tolerated, no matter how spiritually strong the leaders might seem. **23–26:** Almost casually Paul rattles off the list of calamities that have befallen him; some of these we are familiar with from stories in Acts, but in other cases this list is our only indication of the extent of Paul's tribulations. These dangerous, frightening, and often humiliating experiences Paul lists as a badge of honor, not omitting the fact that in all these life-threatening circumstances his concern is not only for himself but also for his churches. **30–32:** The culminating story paints a comically pathetic scene: Paul escaping from Damascus by huddling in a basket as it is lowered down the city wall by his friends. The Corinthians would have known well

Damascus, the governor under King Aretas kept guards at the city gates to catch me. [33]I had to be lowered in a basket through a window in the city wall to escape from him.

Paul's Vision and His Thorn in the Flesh

12 This boasting will do no good, but I must go on. I will reluctantly tell about visions and revelations from the Lord. [2]I* was caught up to the third heaven fourteen years ago. Whether I was in my body or out of my body, I don't know—only God knows. [3]Yes, only God knows whether I was in my body or outside my body. But I do know [4]that I was caught up* to paradise and heard things so astounding that they cannot be expressed in words, things no human is allowed to tell.

[5]That experience is worth boasting about, but I'm not going to do it. I will boast only about my weaknesses. [6]If I wanted to boast, I would be no fool in doing so, because I would be telling the truth. But I won't do it, because I don't want anyone to give me credit beyond what they can see in my life or hear in my message, [7]even though I have received such wonderful revelations from God. So to keep me from becoming proud, I was given a thorn in my flesh, a messenger from Satan to torment me and keep me from becoming proud.

[8]Three different times I begged the Lord to take it away. [9]Each time he said, "My grace is all you need. My power works best in weakness." So now I am glad to boast about my weaknesses, so that the power of Christ can work through me. [10]That's why I take pleasure in my weaknesses, and in the insults, hardships, persecutions, and troubles that I suffer for Christ. For when I am weak, then I am strong.

Paul's Concern for the Corinthians

[11]You have made me act like a fool—boasting like this.* You ought to be writing commenda-

12:2 Greek *I know a man in Christ who.* **12:3-4** Greek *But I know such a man, [4]that he was caught up.* **12:11** Some manuscripts do not include *boasting like this.*

the Roman practices of war against walled cities and how the first soldier to accomplish the risky feat of scaling the wall of a besieged town was treated with special honor. Paul is the comic anti-hero, descending the wall by the power of others in order to scurry away. By making such an experience his *boast*, Paul drastically redefines apostolic honor. **12:1–2:** Presumably Paul's rivals have demonstrated their spiritual prowess by speaking extensively of their visions and special revelations. Once again, Paul is apparently torn by opposite impulses: He too has had ecstatic religious experiences but he does not find it appropriate to use these experiences as proof of his apostleship. The circumlocution he employs, "I know a person in Christ" (see translator's note), is patently transparent; he is speaking of himself but in such a way as to avoid at least the baldest form of self-aggrandizement. It is worth noting that Paul does think of ecstatic visions and revelations as valid spiritual experiences. He does not consider it appropriate to use such experiences as a yardstick of one's spiritual maturity or to compare such experiences or lack of them with those of others. **7:** *Was given*: Does Paul mean "given by God"? It is not clear. *Thorn in the flesh*: The phrase is even more unclear. What was the nature of Paul's *thorn*? *Skolops* means something that is sharp and pointed, and the word can denote anything from a fishhook to a stake. This is Paul's only direct reference to it. Paul does not directly charge God with being the source of his torment; he refers to it as *a messenger of Satan* (Gk., *angelos* can also mean "angel"). Yet God is responsible for the negative answer to Paul's prayer that the thorn be removed. Paul well mirrors our experiences with evil and suffering; while we are uneasy about accusing God of being suffering's cause, we find to our dismay that God says no to our earnest pleas for removal of the suffering. Perhaps it is instructive, however, that we do not have a more specific definition of Paul's thorn in the flesh. Over the centuries countless Christians have each found their varied sufferings mirrored in Paul's description of his thorn and heard the divine response as words spoken directly to them. **9–10:** The Lord's answer does not explain suffering or remove its source but provides assurance of divine presence and care in the midst of suffering. Human weakness is a fact of life, but it need not engender helplessness. Oppression is real, but this is not a divine counsel to accept oppression passively. God does not tell Paul—and us—to quiet down and be content with weakness; rather, God offers the remarkable revelation that divine power dwells within human weakness. The cross is a paradoxical symbol of a paradoxical faith: In human terms it can mean only defeat, humiliation and suffering, but transformed by Christ it represents victory and life. Paul is not one who passively receives abuse or tolerates injustice. He lashes out at his rivals, defends his reputation, and brooks no compromise with sin. Yet he is able to continue to fight these battles because he knows that God's strength is at work in his weakness. Thus he can say *when I am weak, then I am strong*. Perhaps women, who were often perceived as weak, could take particular encouragement from this thought.

tions for me, for I am not at all inferior to these "super apostles," even though I am nothing at all. [12]When I was with you, I certainly gave you proof that I am an apostle. For I patiently did many signs and wonders and miracles among you. [13]The only thing I failed to do, which I do in the other churches, was to become a financial burden to you. Please forgive me for this wrong!

[14]Now I am coming to you for the third time, and I will not be a burden to you. I don't want what you have—I want you. After all, children don't provide for their parents. Rather, parents provide for their children. [15]I will gladly spend myself and all I have for you, even though it seems that the more I love you, the less you love me.

[16]Some of you admit I was not a burden to you. But others still think I was sneaky and took advantage of you by trickery. [17]But how? Did any of the men I sent to you take advantage of you? [18]When I urged Titus to visit you and sent our other brother with him, did Titus take advantage of you? No! For we have the same spirit and walk in each other's steps, doing things the same way.

[19]Perhaps you think we're saying these things just to defend ourselves. No, we tell you this as Christ's servants, and with God as our witness. Everything we do, dear friends, is to strengthen you. [20]For I am afraid that when I come I won't like what I find, and you won't like my response. I am afraid that I will find quarreling, jealousy, anger, selfishness, slander, gossip, arrogance, and disorderly behavior. [21]Yes, I am afraid that when I come again, God will humble me in your presence. And I will be grieved because many of you have not given up your old sins. You have not repented of your impurity, sexual immorality, and eagerness for lustful pleasure.

Paul's Final Advice

13 This is the third time I am coming to visit you (and as the Scriptures say, "The facts of every case must be established by the testimony of two or three witnesses"*). [2]I have already warned those who had been sinning when I was there on my second visit. Now I again warn them and all others, just as I did before, that next time I will not spare them.

[3]I will give you all the proof you want that Christ speaks through me. Christ is not weak when he deals with you; he is powerful among you. [4]Although he was crucified in weakness, he now lives by the power of God. We, too, are weak, just as Christ was, but when we deal with you we will be alive with him and will have God's power.

[5]Examine yourselves to see if your faith is genuine. Test yourselves. Surely you know that Jesus Christ is among you*; if not, you have failed the test of genuine faith. [6]As you test yourselves, I hope you will recognize that we have not failed the test of apostolic authority.

[7]We pray to God that you will not do what is wrong by refusing our correction. I hope we won't need to demonstrate our authority when we arrive. Do the right thing before we come—even if that makes it look like we have failed to demonstrate our authority. [8]For we cannot oppose the truth, but must always stand for the truth. [9]We are glad to seem weak if it helps show that you are actually strong. We pray that you will become mature.

[10]I am writing this to you before I come, hoping that I won't need to deal severely with you when I do come. For I want to use the authority the Lord has given me to strengthen you, not to tear you down.

Paul's Final Greetings

[11]Dear brothers and sisters,* I close my letter with these last words: Be joyful. Grow to ma-

13:1 Deut 19:15. **13:5** Or *in you.* **13:11** Greek *Brothers.*

12:11—13:10 Summary Appeal and Warnings. 12:11: Paul prepares to sum up his letter by reminding the Corinthians that he has been forced to say what he has said to them by the tactics of the *super apostles* and by the Corinthians' obstinacy to hear the voices of reason. **14:** Again he defends his practice of not accepting support from them, which must have been a major obstacle to some members of the congregation, by appealing to a metaphor implied and stated throughout this letter: Paul as the parent, the Corinthians as *my own children* (cf. 6:13). **20:** He longs for them to love one another as family. Familial affection does not, however, obviate the need for discipline. Indeed, moral failures are more serious within familial bonds than among business associates. **13:2:** Perhaps with the *painful visit* (2:1) still in mind, Paul warns that he will discipline the congregation when he returns, if he finds sin still among them.

13:11–14 Final Greetings and Benediction

Paul's farewell is accompanied by a list of brief exhortations. The word usually translated "farewell" or "goodbye" in this context is the word Paul uses more

turity. Encourage each other. Live in harmony
and peace. Then the God of love and peace will
be with you.
12 Greet each other with Christian love.* 13 All
of God's people here send you their greetings.
14 *May the grace of the Lord Jesus Christ, the
love of God, and the fellowship of the Holy Spirit
be with you all.

13:12 Greek *with a sacred kiss.* **13:14** Some English translations include verse 13 as part of verse 12, and then verse 14 becomes verse 13.

---

commonly to mean "rejoice." Even as he closes this often-stern letter, Paul wants his last word to be not one of scolding but one of encouragement. **14:** The brief benediction, trinitarian in form, with which Paul closes this letter has long been a favorite of preachers and worship leaders. Perhaps we should learn, when we hear it at the close of our worship services, to recognize it as coming from 2 Corinthians and be reminded that this gifted, troubled, beloved congregation has much to teach us as well.

GALATIANS

INTRODUCTION

During his career as a missionary in the urban centers of the eastern Roman Empire, Paul of Tarsus had an experience familiar to numerous Christian workers since: He fell ill in the middle of a crucial missionary effort. As a result of his poor health, Paul spent some time with a group of pagan Celts (also called Gauls) in what is now north-central Turkey and preached Christ to them. They responded by placing their trust in God's Messiah Jesus, and the communities of new believers experienced the joy and miracle-working power of the Holy Spirit.

Not long after he moved on to a new mission station, Paul learned that other teachers had come into the Galatian churches. These people had begun to teach the new believers that in addition to trusting Christ it was necessary for them to be circumcised, to participate in the religious observances of the Jewish calendar, and to observe the biblical food laws. Since Paul had taught them that the God of Israel had sent the Messiah, the new converts naturally wanted to obey the God to whom they now belonged. If God's Torah said that the men of every family had to be circumcised, these eager new believers were ready to schedule themselves for surgery.

The letter before us is Paul's response to this situation. Apparently unable to come in person, he does the next best thing: He entrusts a written communication to a messenger, perhaps one of his associates, whom he instructs to read the letter to the believers gathered for worship. —*Kristen Plinke Bentley and Sharyn Dowd*

1:1–5	Opening of the Letter
1:6–10	The Galatians' Defection
1:11—2:21	The Divine Origin of the Good News
3:1—5:12	Paul Presents His Arguments
3:1–18	Claiming the Inheritance of Faith
3:19—4:11	The Law as a Substitute Teacher
4:12–20	The Personal Appeal of a Mother
4:21—5:1	Born Free
5:2–12	A Direct Assault on Circumcision
5:13—6:10	The Way of Life in the Spirit
6:11–18	Closing of the Letter

Greetings from Paul

1 This letter is from Paul, an apostle. I was
not appointed by any group of people or
any human authority, but by Jesus Christ
himself and by God the Father, who raised Jesus
from the dead.
[2]All the brothers and sisters* here join me in
sending this letter to the churches of Galatia.
[3]May God our Father and the Lord Jesus
Christ* give you grace and peace. [4]Jesus gave his
life for our sins, just as God our Father planned,
in order to rescue us from this evil world in
which we live. [5]All glory to God forever and
ever! Amen.

There Is Only One Good News

[6]I am shocked that you are turning away so soon
from God, who called you to himself through the
loving mercy of Christ.* You are following a different way that pretends to be the Good News
[7]but is not the Good News at all. You are being
fooled by those who deliberately twist the truth
concerning Christ.
[8]Let God's curse fall on anyone, including us
or even an angel from heaven, who preaches a
different kind of Good News than the one we
preached to you. [9]I say again what we have said
before: If anyone preaches any other Good News
than the one you welcomed, let that person be
cursed.
[10]Obviously, I'm not trying to win the approval of people, but of God. If pleasing people
were my goal, I would not be Christ's servant.

Paul's Message Comes from Christ

[11]Dear brothers and sisters, I want you to understand that the gospel message I preach is not
based on mere human reasoning. [12]I received
my message from no human source, and no one
taught me. Instead, I received it by direct revelation from Jesus Christ.*

1:2 Greek *brothers;* also in 1:11. **1:3** Some manuscripts read *God the Father and our Lord Jesus Christ.* **1:6** Some manuscripts read *through loving mercy.* **1:12** Or *by the revelation of Jesus Christ.*

1:1–5 Opening of the Letter

Paul begins all his letters with a formula common to letter writers in antiquity: Sender to recipient(s), greetings! For the usual greetings Paul substitutes *grace and peace*, important concepts in his preaching. At the beginning of this letter Paul makes it clear that the good news that he had brought to the Galatians was not a new human way of being religious but a word from God. He stresses that he is an apostle, or missionary or emissary, from God. **1:** The Greek word *anthropos*, meaning "human being," contrasts to the divine being, God. It does not mean "male" in contrast to female. Another Greek word, *aner*, means "man," "male," or "husband," but that word is not used here. **2:** Similarly, when Paul refers to his associates or to believers in general as *adelphoi* ("brothers"), he does not intend to exclude women believers. That is why our text translates *adelphoi* as *brothers and sisters* (1:2; 4:12, 28, 31; 5:11; 6:1). **3–4:** The *grace and peace* offered to the Galatians come not from Paul but from *God our Father* and from *the Lord Jesus Christ*, whose death *for our sins* had the purpose not merely of forgiveness but of freedom from *this evil world*. Paul implies a contrast with the age to come, or the reign of God, in which the corrupt values and standards of the present world will be overturned.

1:6–10 The Galatians' Defection

The other Pauline letters preserved in the New Testament include an expression of thanksgiving for the faithfulness of the recipients immediately after the letter opening. In writing to the Galatians, however, Paul sees little cause for thanksgiving. The One who called the Galatian believers was not Paul but God, and it is God whom they have deserted by turning to a gospel that is not good news. How could it be, when human efforts are being substituted for the free gift (grace) available in Christ? This theme appears again in 5:4. **10:** Paul's disclaimer serves as a transition into his account of his call. His primary obligation is to God. The problem with conforming to human or cultural expectations is not only that it is impossible to please all of the people all of the time but also that such a posture rules out the possibility of being the slave (Gk., *doulos*) of Christ, "whom to serve is perfect freedom" (Augustine).

1:11—2:21 The Divine Origin of the Good News

In dealing with the situation in the Galatian churches, Paul emphasizes that the good news that he proclaimed was a *revelation* (Gk., *apokalypsis*) directly from God (v. 12)—not a private religious experience but a lifting of the veil that obscures the purposes of God from humans caught in the *evil world* that is rapidly coming to a close. God has done a new and unexpected thing in the death and resurrection of Jesus that cannot be comprehended in the traditional categories used by the teachers who supplanted Paul in Galatia.

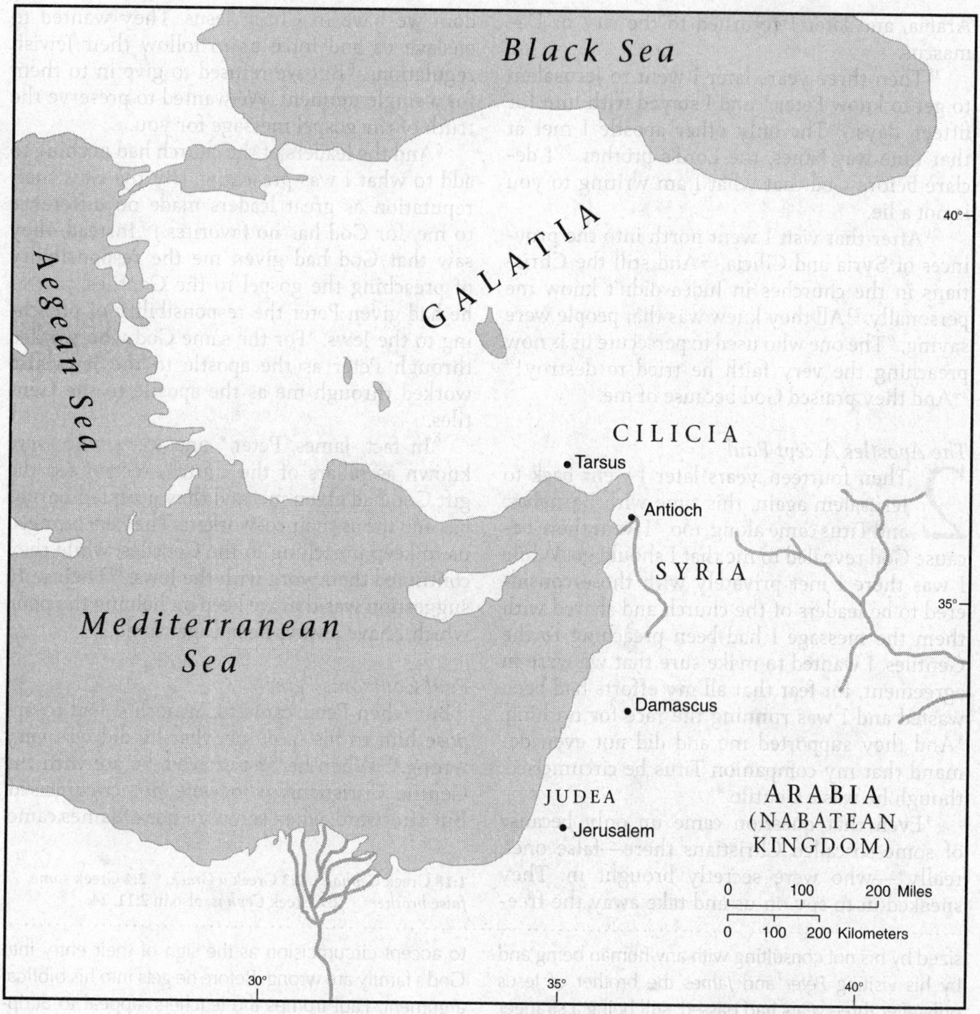

Paul's Journeys in Asia Minor

[13]You know what I was like when I followed the Jewish religion—how I violently persecuted God's church. I did my best to destroy it. [14]I was far ahead of my fellow Jews in my zeal for the traditions of my ancestors.

[15]But even before I was born, God chose me and called me by his marvelous grace. Then it pleased him [16]to reveal his Son to me* so that I would proclaim the Good News about Jesus to the Gentiles.

When this happened, I did not rush out to consult with any human being.* [17]Nor did I go up to Jerusalem to consult with those who were apostles before I was. Instead, I went away into

1:16a Or *in me.* **1:16b** Greek *with flesh and blood.*

1:13—2:10 Autobiographical Statement. Paul is not dependent on the Jerusalem church for the authority of his mission, but the original Christian community had given full approval to his preaching. **1:15–16:** By this testimony Paul echoes the Old Testament prophets (Jer 1:4–5; Isa 49:1–6) and dates God's gracious call prior to his, Paul's, circumcision, because the call was prior to his birth. Keeping the focus on the God of Israel, Paul reports the experience that changed his life as an apocalyptic act by God, who *reveal*[ed] *his Son to me so that I would proclaim the Good News about Jesus to the Gentiles.* His mission to pagan Galatia began at that moment and was initiated by God. **17–24:** Paul's independence of human authorities is empha-

Arabia, and later I returned to the city of Damascus.
[18]Then three years later I went to Jerusalem
to get to know Peter,* and I stayed with him for
fifteen days. [19]The only other apostle I met at
that time was James, the Lord's brother. [20]I declare before God that what I am writing to you
is not a lie.
[21]After that visit I went north into the provinces of Syria and Cilicia. [22]And still the Christians in the churches in Judea didn't know me
personally. [23]All they knew was that people were
saying, "The one who used to persecute us is now
preaching the very faith he tried to destroy!"
[24]And they praised God because of me.

The Apostles Accept Paul

2 Then fourteen years later I went back to
Jerusalem again, this time with Barnabas;
and Titus came along, too. [2]I went there because God revealed to me that I should go. While
I was there I met privately with those considered to be leaders of the church and shared with
them the message I had been preaching to the
Gentiles. I wanted to make sure that we were in
agreement, for fear that all my efforts had been
wasted and I was running the race for nothing.
[3]And they supported me and did not even demand that my companion Titus be circumcised,
though he was a Gentile.*
[4]Even that question came up only because
of some so-called Christians there—false ones,
really*—who were secretly brought in. They
sneaked in to spy on us and take away the freedom we have in Christ Jesus. They wanted to
enslave us and force us to follow their Jewish
regulations. [5]But we refused to give in to them
for a single moment. We wanted to preserve the
truth of the gospel message for you.
[6]And the leaders of the church had nothing to
add to what I was preaching. (By the way, their
reputation as great leaders made no difference
to me, for God has no favorites.) [7]Instead, they
saw that God had given me the responsibility
of preaching the gospel to the Gentiles, just as
he had given Peter the responsibility of preaching to the Jews. [8]For the same God who worked
through Peter as the apostle to the Jews also
worked through me as the apostle to the Gentiles.
[9]In fact, James, Peter,* and John, who were
known as pillars of the church, recognized the
gift God had given me, and they accepted Barnabas and me as their co-workers. They encouraged
us to keep preaching to the Gentiles, while they
continued their work with the Jews. [10]Their only
suggestion was that we keep on helping the poor,
which I have always been eager to do.

Paul Confronts Peter

[11]But when Peter came to Antioch, I had to oppose him to his face, for what he did was very
wrong. [12]When he first arrived, he ate with the
Gentile Christians, who were not circumcised.
But afterward, when some friends of James came,

1:18 Greek *Cephas.* **2:3** Greek *a Greek.* **2:4** Greek *some false brothers.* **2:9** Greek *Cephas;* also in 2:11, 14.

---

sized by his not consulting with any human being and by his visiting *Peter* and *James* the brother of Jesus only after three years had passed, still being a stranger to the Jerusalem church in general. **2:2:** When it became necessary to consult with Jerusalem, Paul did not go because he was summoned but in response to a revelation. It was God's idea that the church should be unified, and Paul remained committed to that unity throughout his ministry. **3:** Paul insists that his gospel came directly from God and had the approval of the apostles in Jerusalem, who acknowledged Titus, an uncircumcised believer, as a full member of the community of Messiah Jesus. **4:** These teachers apparently emphasize the importance of descent from Abraham for membership in the covenant people. They argue that this status is available to Gentiles only through the circumcision of males; and they have good scriptural backing for their claim. In addition, Jesus is not recorded as saying anything about circumcision. That means that Paul has to find some way to persuade the Galatian believers that the teachers who are urging them to accept circumcision as the sign of their entry into God's family are wrong. Before he gets into his biblical argument, Paul trumps the teachers' appeal to Scripture by claiming that the good news that he preached in Galatia came to him by revelation from the Author of Scripture. **9:** Four times in his account of this consultation Paul refers to the acknowledged leaders of the Jerusalem church (2:2, 6 [twice], 9), and in the fourth instance he names *Peter*, *James,* and *John* and calls them *pillars*. This must be a response to the teachers' claim that they represent the views of the Jerusalem leaders and Paul does not. For Paul, the meeting in Jerusalem confirmed what he already knew: That which God had done in Christ had changed everything, including God's definition of the covenant community.

2:11–21 Paul Confronts Peter. 12–13: The issue is not mere table fellowship, in the sense of sitting beside someone unpleasant at the church potluck dinner. When people in antiquity ate together, they ate the same food, and in Antioch it was obviously not fully

Peter wouldn't eat with the Gentiles anymore. He was afraid of criticism from these people who insisted on the necessity of circumcision. [13]As a result, other Jewish Christians followed Peter's hypocrisy, and even Barnabas was led astray by their hypocrisy.

[14]When I saw that they were not following the truth of the gospel message, I said to Peter in front of all the others, "Since you, a Jew by birth, have discarded the Jewish laws and are living like a Gentile, why are you now trying to make these Gentiles follow the Jewish traditions?

[15]"You and I are Jews by birth, not 'sinners' like the Gentiles. [16]Yet we know that a person is made right with God by faith in Jesus Christ, not by obeying the law. And we have believed in Christ Jesus, so that we might be made right with God because of our faith in Christ, not because we have obeyed the law. For no one will ever be made right with God by obeying the law."*

[17]But suppose we seek to be made right with God through faith in Christ and then we are found guilty because we have abandoned the law. Would that mean Christ has led us into sin? Absolutely not! [18]Rather, I am a sinner if I rebuild the old system of law I already tore down. [19]For when I tried to keep the law, it condemned me. So I died to the law—I stopped trying to meet all its requirements—so that I might live for God. [20]My old self has been crucified with Christ.* It

2:16 Some translators hold that the quotation extends through verse 14; others through verse 16; and still others through verse 21. **2:20** Some English translations put this sentence in verse 19.

kosher food. But Peter, Paul, Barnabas, and the other Jewish believers were in the habit of eating the same food the Gentiles ate when they met together because God had done a new thing by bringing them into one body in Christ. When Peter and the other Jews kept themselves separate because they feared censure from representatives of the Jerusalem church, they were denying that Jesus' death on the cross was enough to bring them together. Furthermore, they were in effect saying to the Gentile believers that if they wanted to continue to share meals, the Gentiles would have to learn to cook and keep kosher. They were saying, "Do it our way or you aren't part of God's people." It is clear that the Jewish *friends of James* are guilty of the same offense as the teachers now disturbing the Galatian churches. That is why Paul relates the incident in Antioch. It is the climax of his account of how he came to preach good news to the Gentiles and what that good news means for Jewish believers in Christ. It means that God has changed the rules and it is the old guard who has to change to get in step with God, not the Gentiles who have to change to line up with the old rules. **15–16:** Paul allows his speech to Peter to slide imperceptibly into a speech addressed to the Jewish teachers now influencing the Galatians. Including himself, Peter, and the teachers with the pronoun *we,* Paul assumes that all Jewish Christians would agree that Jesus' death and resurrection make it possible for human beings to be in right relationship with God. That is what makes them different from Jews who do not believe in Jesus. But Paul draws a conclusion from this that makes his preaching and his practice more radical: Because of Jesus' faithful death in response to God's will, Gentiles can be included in the covenant people without Torah observance (*obeying the law*). For Paul, the good news is that Jesus was faithful and obedient, even to "death on a cross" (Phil 2:8), and that faithfulness is the source of our relationship with God, whether we are Jews or Gentiles. But no human being, Jew or Gentile, is put right with God by Torah observance. The corollary is that Torah observance cannot and must not separate Jewish and Gentile believers in Christ, at the table or anywhere else, because, as Paul will go on to say in Galatians 3:28, *you are all one in Christ Jesus*. **17–18:** The teachers in Galatia are concerned about the possible consequences of destroying the connection between law keeping and relationship with God. What will motivate people to live moral lives if they are told that trusting Christ's faithfulness is all that matters? In response to the accusation that he has made Christ a promoter of sinful behavior, Paul exclaims, *Absolutely not!* On the contrary, Paul says, if he were to try to add anything to God's straightforward, law-free gospel, that would make him a sinner. Then he goes on to explain why there is no going back and no need to go back. **19–20:** Paul, a former Torah-observant Jew, has, by trusting Christ, died to the Torah in order to live in relationship with God, and he regards it as better than a fair trade. The teachers would not agree that God's Torah could be separated from relationship with God, but Paul has identified with the crucified Christ in such a way that he can say, *My old self has been crucified with Christ.* Paul's law-free gospel is not the lawless message that the teachers accuse him of preaching (see 5:13—6:10). The faithful and obedient Christ who lives within and through Paul empowers Paul's faithful obedience to God. The gracious gift of Torah to the people of Israel, symbolized by circumcision of the males of Israel, has been universalized into the gracious gift of the indwelling Christ to all human beings, Jews and Gentiles, females as well as males. From Paul's point of view, to add anything to this gift would be to act as though Christ's self-giving death were unnecessary, and that Paul is not willing to do.

is no longer I who live, but Christ lives in me. So
I live in this earthly body by trusting in the Son
of God, who loved me and gave himself for me.
21 I do not treat the grace of God as meaningless.
For if keeping the law could make us right with
God, then there was no need for Christ to die.

The Law and Faith in Christ

3 Oh, foolish Galatians! Who has cast an
evil spell on you? For the meaning of Jesus
Christ's death was made as clear to you as
if you had seen a picture of his death on the cross.
2 Let me ask you this one question: Did you receive the Holy Spirit by obeying the law of Moses? Of course not! You received the Spirit because you believed the message you heard about
Christ. 3 How foolish can you be? After starting
your Christian lives in the Spirit, why are you
now trying to become perfect by your own human effort? 4 Have you experienced* so much for
nothing? Surely it was not in vain, was it?

5 I ask you again, does God give you the Holy
Spirit and work miracles among you because you
obey the law? Of course not! It is because you
believe the message you heard about Christ.

6 In the same way, "Abraham believed God,
and God counted him as righteous because of his
faith."* 7 The real children of Abraham, then, are
those who put their faith in God.

8 What's more, the Scriptures looked forward
to this time when God would declare the Gentiles to be righteous because of their faith. God
proclaimed this good news to Abraham long ago
when he said, "All nations will be blessed through
you."* 9 So all who put their faith in Christ share
the same blessing Abraham received because of
his faith.

10 But those who depend on the law to make
them right with God are under his curse, for the
Scriptures say, "Cursed is everyone who does
not observe and obey all the commands that
are written in God's Book of the Law."* 11 So it
is clear that no one can be made right with God
by trying to keep the law. For the Scriptures say,
"It is through faith that a righteous person has
life."* 12 This way of faith is very different from
the way of law, which says, "It is through obeying the law that a person has life."*

13 But Christ has rescued us from the curse
pronounced by the law. When he was hung on
the cross, he took upon himself the curse for our
wrongdoing. For it is written in the Scriptures,
"Cursed is everyone who is hung on a tree."*
14 Through Christ Jesus, God has blessed the

3:4 Or *Have you suffered.* **3:6** Gen 15:6. **3:8** Gen 12:3; 18:18; 22:18. **3:10** Deut 27:26. **3:11** Hab 2:4. **3:12** Lev 18:5. **3:13** Deut 21:23 (Greek version).

3:1—5:12 Paul Presents His Arguments

3:1–18 Claiming the Inheritance of Faith. Paul's first task is to show that faith in Christ is the full story, not merely the prologue to something else. There are three parts to this argument. Paul first calls the Galatians to focus on their spiritual experience (vv. 1–5); then he appeals to Scripture and the historical example of Abraham (vv. 6–14); finally he argues from common legal practice (vv. 15–18). **1:** He confronts them with a series of stinging questions, accusing them of being *foolish*. It is clear from the context that Paul does not consider the Galatian converts to be slow to grasp an intellectual concept or an important facet of belief. Rather, he is accusing them of abandoning something of which they once were convinced—their authentic experience with God's Holy Spirit. The teachers have used their superior ability to quote Scripture to intimidate the Galatians into doubting their own experience. Paul will have none of it. The believers' faith relationship with Christ is the whole truth of the gospel. They are part of the new thing God has done through Jesus Christ. Not only is circumcision unnecessary for the Galatian believers because they already have been made part of God's new covenant people, but also undergoing circumcision would undercut the core of the message of God's gracious gift. **2:** Evidently Paul had overestimated the Galatians' grasp of the good news he had preached to them. Yet they were eyewitnesses to their own conversion, and he cannot believe that they are prepared to deny the powerful spiritual experience that they had then. He wants them to remember that their birth in the Spirit had nothing to do with the works of the law. **6–9:** Because of their faith response to what God has done in Christ, they are Abraham's true descendants even without circumcision. They are children of Abraham, who was given a right relationship with God on the basis of his trustful response to God. Like Abraham (Gen 12:3), they had turned to God from other beliefs and responded in trust, and therefore had been declared righteous. Similarly God has acted to accept the Gentiles on the basis of faith. **10:** Getting involved with Torah involves hidden costs for the Galatians. If they are going to live a life centered on the law, then according to what Torah teaches, they are under a curse, because *Cursed is everyone who does not observe and obey all these commands that are written in God's Book of the Law* (Deut 27:26). **13:** As one who hangs *on a tree* (or cross), Jesus was also under a Torah curse (Deut 21:23), but by his faithful death for

Gentiles with the same blessing he promised to Abraham, so that we who are believers might receive the promised* Holy Spirit through faith.

The Law and God's Promise

15 Dear brothers and sisters,* here's an example from everyday life. Just as no one can set aside or amend an irrevocable agreement, so it is in this case. 16 God gave the promises to Abraham and his child.* And notice that the Scripture doesn't say "to his children,*" as if it meant many descendants. Rather, it says "to his child"—and that, of course, means Christ. 17 This is what I am trying to say: The agreement God made with Abraham could not be canceled 430 years later when God gave the law to Moses. God would be breaking his promise. 18 For if the inheritance could be received by keeping the law, then it would not be the result of accepting God's promise. But God graciously gave it to Abraham as a promise.

19 Why, then, was the law given? It was given alongside the promise to show people their sins. But the law was designed to last only until the coming of the child who was promised. God gave his law through angels to Moses, who was the mediator between God and the people. 20 Now a mediator is helpful if more than one party must reach an agreement. But God, who is one, did not use a mediator when he gave his promise to Abraham.

21 Is there a conflict, then, between God's law and God's promises?* Absolutely not! If the law could give us new life, we could be made right with God by obeying it. 22 But the Scriptures declare that we are all prisoners of sin, so we receive God's promise of freedom only by believing in Jesus Christ.

God's Children through Faith

23 Before the way of faith in Christ was available to us, we were placed under guard by the law. We were kept in protective custody, so to speak, until the way of faith was revealed.

24 Let me put it another way. The law was our guardian until Christ came; it protected us until we could be made right with God through faith. 25 And now that the way of faith has come, we no longer need the law as our guardian.

26 For you are all children* of God through faith in Christ Jesus. 27 And all who have been united with Christ in baptism have put on Christ, like putting on new clothes.* 28 There is no longer Jew or Gentile,* slave or free, male and female. For you are all one in Christ Jesus. 29 And now that you belong to Christ, you are the

3:14 Some manuscripts read *the blessing of the.* **3:15** Greek *Brothers.* **3:16a** Greek *seed;* also in 3:16c, 19. See notes on Gen 12:7 and 13:15. **3:16b** Greek *seeds.* **3:21** Some manuscripts read *and the promises?* **3:26** Greek *sons.* **3:27** Greek *have put on Christ.* **3:28** Greek *Jew or Greek.*

us (cf. Gal 1:4; 3:20), he initiated a new kind of living, one that is redeemed from the curse. **14:** Turning from the negative (curse) and returning to the positive (blessing), Paul reminds the Galatians that the purpose of Christ's death was to extend the blessing of Abraham to the Gentiles. Identifying with his Gentile converts, Paul, the circumcised descendant of Abraham, uses the first person plural: *so that we . . . might receive the promised Holy Spirit through faith*. He makes it clear that his Jewishness does not make him any more a descendant of Abraham than the most recent convert from paganism to Christ. As people who are already part of the covenant with Abraham because of their Abraham-like trust, the Galatian believers have no need to consider circumcision. What can they gain if they already have everything? **17:** In case the Galatian believers are worried that the covenant of faith established through Abraham and guaranteed through Christ is invalidated by their failure to observe circumcision and food laws, Paul refers to the common legal practice of the time. He explains that God's covenant, like a will, is not annulled through something that comes later. Since the law came later than the promise to Abraham, the promise is still valid. The Galatians, like all Gentile believers in Christ, have been gratuitously included within the covenant alongside Abraham's descendants. Therefore they have no reason to worry about their rightful claim to the inheritance of faith.

3:19—4:11 The Law as a Substitute Teacher. 3:19–24: Paul continues his argument using questions the Galatians might have at this point: *Why . . . was the law given?* and *Is there a conflict . . . between God's law and God's promises?* Within God's plan for creation, the law had played a necessary role as a teacher during the interim period before God's promised fulfillment of time. As generations of people waited for God to fulfill the promise, they needed to know how to live; also, the law served to show people their sinfulness. **26–29:** New believers took off their old clothes when entering the waters of baptism and put on new garments after coming up out of the waters. This symbolized the reality that the believers had cast off their old lives and were now new creations in Christ, alive to a new kind of existence. As the act that marked a person's entrance into this new covenant community, baptism was a unifying act. Unlike circumcision, which involved only males, this sign of membership was one that touched all human

true children* of Abraham. You are his heirs, and
God's promise to Abraham belongs to you.

4 Think of it this way. If a father dies and
leaves an inheritance for his young children, those children are not much better
off than slaves until they grow up, even though
they actually own everything their father had.
2They have to obey their guardians until they
reach whatever age their father set. 3And that's
the way it was with us before Christ came. We
were like children; we were slaves to the basic
spiritual principles* of this world.
4But when the right time came, God sent his
Son, born of a woman, subject to the law. 5God
sent him to buy freedom for us who were slaves
to the law, so that he could adopt us as his very
own children.* 6And because we* are his children, God has sent the Spirit of his Son into our
hearts, prompting us to call out, "Abba, Father."*
7Now you are no longer a slave but God's own
child.* And since you are his child, God has made
you his heir.

Paul's Concern for the Galatians

8Before you Gentiles knew God, you were slaves
to so-called gods that do not even exist. 9So now
that you know God (or should I say, now that
God knows you), why do you want to go back
again and become slaves once more to the weak
and useless spiritual principles of this world?
10You are trying to earn favor with God by observing certain days or months or seasons or
years. 11I fear for you. Perhaps all my hard work
with you was for nothing. 12Dear brothers and
sisters,* I plead with you to live as I do in freedom from these things, for I have become like
you Gentiles—free from those laws.

You did not mistreat me when I first preached
to you. 13Surely you remember that I was sick
when I first brought you the Good News. 14But
even though my condition tempted you to reject me, you did not despise me or turn me away.
No, you took me in and cared for me as though
I were an angel from God or even Christ Jesus
himself. 15Where is that joyful and grateful spirit
you felt then? I am sure you would have taken
out your own eyes and given them to me if it had
been possible. 16Have I now become your enemy
because I am telling you the truth?

17Those false teachers are so eager to win your
favor, but their intentions are not good. They are
trying to shut you off from me so that you will
pay attention only to them. 18If someone is eager
to do good things for you, that's all right; but let
them do it all the time, not just when I'm with
you.

19Oh, my dear children! I feel as if I'm going through labor pains for you again, and they
will continue until Christ is fully developed in
your lives. 20I wish I were with you right now
so I could change my tone. But at this distance I
don't know how else to help you.

3:29 Greek *seed.* **4:3** Or *powers;* also in 4:9. **4:5** Greek *sons;* also in 4:6. **4:6a** Greek *you.* **4:6b** *Abba* is an Aramaic term for "father." **4:7** Greek *son;* also in 4:7b. **4:12** Greek *brothers;* also in 4:28, 31.

---

beings, leaving its mark on men and women, who, because they have been baptized into Christ, *are all one in Christ Jesus*. Since they are all one person, their former claims based on race, gender, or station in life no longer matter. **4:1–7:** The interim time of the law is now past. Christ's coming, *born of a woman* and *subject to the law*, marks the fulfillment of God's time. This is good news for the Jews and Gentiles in Paul's time and for all people of our time. Previously, people were waiting under guardians, either as minor heirs or as slaves. Now all are living in a new time and a new situation. Through Christ a new family is being born in the world, a community in which all people, despite their former distinctions, may join together in crying out, "Abba!" to the one Father who is like no other.

4:12–20 The Personal Appeal of a Mother. 19: Paul uses the Greek word *odino*, which is correctly translated "to endure birth pangs" or "to labor in childbirth," to describe how he suffers for the Galatians' mature growth in Christ (see Birth Pain Imagery, John 16). Since he is male, it would have made more sense for Paul to have referred to himself as a father to the Galatians; he describes himself as a father to other believers in 1 Corinthians 4:14–15 and Philemon 10. Yet that would not have served his purpose; begetting a child is a wholly different experience from giving birth to a child. Birthing a child involves a passage of time, a hidden promise, and a suffering in anticipation of new life in the future, none of which are part of the experience of begetting. While his reference to himself as the mother of the Galatians is odd, it is one with which the Galatians could agree. After all, they remember their close relationship with Paul. He is calling the Galatians to remember their spiritual birth (cf. 3:1–5) while communicating that his work as an apostle is set within the larger framework of God's work in bringing forth the reign of God in the midst of this present evil age. Although Paul is experiencing the labor pains, it is Christ who is being formed in the whole community of believers.

Abraham's Two Children
21 Tell me, you who want to live under the law,
do you know what the law actually says? 22 The
Scriptures say that Abraham had two sons, one
from his slave wife and one from his freeborn
wife.* 23 The son of the slave wife was born in a
human attempt to bring about the fulfillment of
God's promise. But the son of the freeborn wife
was born as God's own fulfillment of his promise.

24 These two women serve as an illustration
of God's two covenants. The first woman, Hagar,
represents Mount Sinai where people received
the law that enslaved them. 25 And now Jerusalem is just like Mount Sinai in Arabia,* because
she and her children live in slavery to the law.
26 But the other woman, Sarah, represents the
heavenly Jerusalem. She is the free woman, and
she is our mother. 27 As Isaiah said,

"Rejoice, O childless woman,
you who have never given birth!
Break into a joyful shout,
you who have never been in labor!
For the desolate woman now has more
children
than the woman who lives with her
husband!"*

28 And you, dear brothers and sisters, are children of the promise, just like Isaac. 29 But you are
now being persecuted by those who want you to
keep the law, just as Ishmael, the child born by
human effort, persecuted Isaac, the child born by
the power of the Spirit.
30 But what do the Scriptures say about that?
"Get rid of the slave and her son, for the son of
the slave woman will not share the inheritance
with the free woman's son."* 31 So, dear brothers and sisters, we are not children of the slave
woman; we are children of the free woman.

Freedom in Christ
5 So Christ has truly set us free. Now make
sure that you stay free, and don't get tied
up again in slavery to the law.

2 Listen! I, Paul, tell you this: If you are counting on circumcision to make you right with God,
then Christ will be of no benefit to you. 3 I'll say
it again. If you are trying to find favor with God
by being circumcised, you must obey every regulation in the whole law of Moses. 4 For if you
are trying to make yourselves right with God
by keeping the law, you have been cut off from
Christ! You have fallen away from God's grace.

5 But we who live by the Spirit eagerly wait
to receive by faith the righteousness God has
promised to us. 6 For when we place our faith in
Christ Jesus, there is no benefit in being circumcised or being uncircumcised. What is important
is faith expressing itself in love.

7 You were running the race so well. Who
has held you back from following the truth? 8 It
certainly isn't God, for he is the one who called
you to freedom. 9 This false teaching is like a little yeast that spreads through the whole batch

4:22 See Gen 16:15; 21:2-3. **4:25** Greek *And Hagar, which is Mount Sinai in Arabia, is now like Jerusalem;* other manuscripts read *And Mount Sinai in Arabia is now like Jerusalem.* **4:27** Isa 54:1. **4:30** Gen 21:10.

4:21—5:1 Born Free. 4:21: Paul continues using birth language while challenging those whom he addresses as *you who want to live under the law*. Again he turns to the figure of Abraham (see also 3:6–18), now tracing the Galatians' spiritual lineage to their mother, rather than to their father, Abraham. He uses parts of the stories of Abraham, Hagar, and Sarah (Gen 16:1—17:15; 21:1–21). Though Paul compares a free woman with a slave woman in this section, he is not making a judgment about historical women or encouraging the mistreatment of slaves or children. Neither is he condoning slavery by writing about a slave. He contrasts the free woman with the slave woman in order to contrast the covenant of God's promise and faith in Christ with the Mosaic covenant. For rhetorical purposes he associates freedom with the former and slavery with the latter. **28–30:** By telling the Gentile Galatians that they are the children of the *freeborn wife,* Paul is rejecting the position of the teachers that Jews trace their lineage to Sarah and Gentiles to Hagar. He is also reminding his listeners that the source of their spiritual experience was "believing what you heard" not "works of the law" (3:2), the "Spirit" and not the "flesh" (3:3, ESV). Those who teach the Galatian believers otherwise are guilty of "persecuting" those who were *born by the power of the Spirit,* and Torah tells the believers what they must do to those teachers: Get rid of them (cf. Gen 21:10). The Gentile converts' birth was to a new creation (cf. Gal 6:15). Their birth waters were the waters of baptism and God's free outpouring of the Spirit on the Gentile converts. They began their relationship with the Spirit rather than with the law, and Paul hopes that they will no longer deny their true birth mother.

5:2–12 A Direct Assault on Circumcision. 2: Once males undergo circumcision, they are doing more than cutting off a piece of flesh; they are also obligating themselves to the Mosaic covenant and cut-

of dough! [10]I am trusting the Lord to keep you from believing false teachings. God will judge that person, whoever he is, who has been confusing you.

[11]Dear brothers and sisters,* if I were still preaching that you must be circumcised—as some say I do—why am I still being persecuted? If I were no longer preaching salvation through the cross of Christ, no one would be offended. [12]I just wish that those troublemakers who want to mutilate you by circumcision would mutilate themselves.*

[13]For you have been called to live in freedom, my brothers and sisters. But don't use your freedom to satisfy your sinful nature. Instead, use your freedom to serve one another in love. [14]For the whole law can be summed up in this one command: "Love your neighbor as yourself."* [15]But if you are always biting and devouring one another, watch out! Beware of destroying one another.

Living by the Spirit's Power

[16]So I say, let the Holy Spirit guide your lives. Then you won't be doing what your sinful nature craves. [17]The sinful nature wants to do evil, which is just the opposite of what the Spirit wants. And the Spirit gives us desires that are the opposite of what the sinful nature desires. These two forces are constantly fighting each other, so you are not free to carry out your good intentions. [18]But when you are directed by the Spirit, you are not under obligation to the law of Moses.

[19]When you follow the desires of your sinful nature, the results are very clear: sexual immorality, impurity, lustful pleasures, [20]idolatry, sorcery, hostility, quarreling, jealousy, outbursts of anger, selfish ambition, dissension, division, [21]envy, drunkenness, wild parties, and other sins like these. Let me tell you again, as I have before, that anyone living that sort of life will not inherit the Kingdom of God.

[22]But the Holy Spirit produces this kind of fruit in our lives: love, joy, peace, patience, kindness, goodness, faithfulness, [23]gentleness, and self-control. There is no law against these things!

[24]Those who belong to Christ Jesus have nailed the passions and desires of their sinful nature to his cross and crucified them there. [25]Since we are living by the Spirit, let us follow the Spirit's leading in every part of our lives. [26]Let us not become conceited, or provoke one another, or be jealous of one another.

5:11 Greek *Brothers;* similarly in 5:13. **5:12** Or *castrate themselves,* or *cut themselves off from you;* Greek reads *cut themselves off.* **5:14** Lev 19:18.

ting themselves off from the covenant of Christ. **12:** He ends with a graphic exclamation that he wishes those who support circumcision "would cut themselves off" or "castrate themselves." No doubt Paul wished those teachers would cut themselves off from the Galatian communities rather than mislead new believers.

5:13—6:10 The Way of Life in the Spirit

5:13–14: Paul has contrasted freedom (positive) with slavery (negative). In preparation for his exhortations about community life in 5:16—6:10, he now redefines the freedom to which the Galatian believers have been called as a positive kind of servitude based on and empowered by love. Paul reminds those who are so concerned about the law that the classic summary of all that Torah teaches about human relationships is "Love your neighbor as yourself" (Lev 19:18; Matt 22:39–40; Mark 12:31; Luke 10:27–28; Rom 13:8–10; Jas 2:8). The opposite of serving one another through love and loving the neighbor as oneself is allowing freedom to become license for self-gratification. **16:** *Doing what your sinful nature craves* means engaging in behavior patterns that destroy the community, that is, refusing to serve and love the neighbor. To *let the Holy Spirit guide your lives* is to live in ways that build up the Christian community. **19–21:** People who choose these paths demonstrate that they care nothing for the communal life of God's realm. **22–23:** By contrast, the life of the Spirit flowing through each individual Christian produces the *fruit* or virtues listed in our lives, which enhance the communal life of those who are *all one . . . in Christ Jesus* (3:28). The lists are framed by Paul's repetitive insistence that Torah cannot produce but does endorse the Spirit-led life and by the exhortation to the Galatian believers to conduct their lives in this way. The vices are the result of human ambition while the fruit is the natural result of the life of the vine flowing through its attached branches (cf. John 15:1–17). The vices denounced and the virtues praised here are the same behaviors that were regarded as vicious and virtuous by general agreement among pagan and Jewish moralists of Paul's time. The lifestyle prescribed by Torah and achieved by the Stoic sage by dint of considerable effort and self-control Paul claimed for the Christian as a gift from the indwelling Spirit of Christ. **6:1–10:** After a few final admonitions pointedly directed against those who *think* they are *important,* Paul moves to the closing section of his letter.

We Harvest What We Plant

6 Dear brothers and sisters, if another believer* is overcome by some sin, you who
are godly* should gently and humbly
help that person back onto the right path. And
be careful not to fall into the same temptation
yourself. 2 Share each other's burdens, and in this
way obey the law of Christ. 3 If you think you
are too important to help someone, you are only
fooling yourself. You are not that important.
4 Pay careful attention to your own work, for
then you will get the satisfaction of a job well
done, and you won't need to compare yourself to
anyone else. 5 For we are each responsible for our
own conduct.
6 Those who are taught the word of God
should provide for their teachers, sharing all
good things with them.
7 Don't be misled—you cannot mock the justice of God. You will always harvest what you
plant. 8 Those who live only to satisfy their own
sinful nature will harvest decay and death from
that sinful nature. But those who live to please
the Spirit will harvest everlasting life from the
Spirit. 9 So let's not get tired of doing what is
good. At just the right time we will reap a harvest of blessing if we don't give up. 10 Therefore,
whenever we have the opportunity, we should
do good to everyone—especially to those in the
family of faith.

Paul's Final Advice

11 NOTICE WHAT LARGE LETTERS I USE AS I WRITE
THESE CLOSING WORDS IN MY OWN HANDWRITING.
12 Those who are trying to force you to be circumcised want to look good to others. They don't
want to be persecuted for teaching that the cross
of Christ alone can save. 13 And even those who
advocate circumcision don't keep the whole law
themselves. They only want you to be circumcised so they can boast about it and claim you as
their disciples.
14 As for me, may I never boast about anything except the cross of our Lord Jesus Christ.
Because of that cross,* my interest in this world
has been crucified, and the world's interest in
me has also died. 15 It doesn't matter whether
we have been circumcised or not. What counts
is whether we have been transformed into a new
creation. 16 May God's peace and mercy be upon
all who live by this principle; they are the new
people of God.*
17 From now on, don't let anyone trouble me
with these things. For I bear on my body the
scars that show I belong to Jesus.
18 Dear brothers and sisters,* may the grace of
our Lord Jesus Christ be with your spirit. Amen.

6:1a Greek *Brothers, if a man.* **6:1b** Greek *spiritual.*
6:14 Or *Because of him.* **6:16** Greek *this principle, and upon the Israel of God.* **6:18** Greek *Brothers.*

6:11–18 The Closing of the Letter

In this short final section, Paul calls attention to his personal signature, which appears in larger letters than those of the secretary who has written the letter. He takes a few parting shots at the teachers, re-emphasizing the nonimportance of circumcision, and then he ends as he began, with a blessing of *peace* and *grace* for the believers in Galatia.

EPHESIANS

INTRODUCTION

Ephesians is written as a letter, yet it differs from Paul's other letters in that he does not deal here with detailed local church issues, as in 1 Corinthians. There are no names of individuals, as in Romans, and there does not seem to have been an immediately obvious situation he was writing to as there was in Philemon, a letter of recommendation, or in Philippians, a thank-you letter. The writing is therefore of broader interest and application. Paul adapts the letter form for his own use, to communicate this Christian content to its recipients.

Acts 19:1–20 and Acts 20:31 tell of Paul's visits to Ephesus and his three-year ministry among the Christians there. His close links with that church make it remarkable that he makes no personal references to individuals. Along with the fact that the words "in Ephesus" (Eph 1:1) are not found in the earliest and best manuscripts, it is not possible to say with certainty that the letter is directed to the Ephesian church in particular. Some think that the letter "to the church at Laodicea" (Col 4:16) could be the letter of the Ephesians. It may be that the words "in Ephesus" were inserted later in a manuscript in Ephesus to show that the letter had been originally circulated among the churches of Asia Minor, of which Ephesus was a major one.

The letter shows that Paul is keenly aware of the cultural and religious backgrounds of the readers. It seems likely that most of them had been converted from Gentile beginnings (Eph 2:11; 3:1), and even if they had encountered Judaism they would have been widely influenced by prevailing Hellenistic philosophies and pagan religions. Even to Gentiles Paul freely quotes and expounds the Hebrew Scriptures as part of their new heritage that is fulfilled in Jesus, the Messiah, who unites Jew and Gentile in himself (2:17–19). Paul writes to encourage (6:22) the recently planted Gentile church and to build it up.

Paul writes this letter not to a church pastor or leaders but to "brothers and sisters" (6:23) and "God's holy people" (1:1). The expectation is that all who belong to Christ—men, women, and children—are being equally addressed. This is true of Scripture as a whole. While human history shows that theology has often traditionally been more the domain of male scholars, pastors, or teachers, the Bible makes no such distinction between men and women. Both have equal access before God to his Word, and therefore men and women have the responsibility to read, understand, and pass on to others its riches.

The writer calls himself Paul. Some scholars have maintained that this is a later follower of Paul, writing with his authority and expanding on the letter of Colossians. This view seeks to make sense of the apparent lack of some features in Paul's undisputed letters (such as writing to specific people with specific needs) and a lack of some of the topics (such as justification by faith) that are found in the Pauline letters. And for many commentators it does not detract from the authority of the letter within the New Testament canon.

It is a normal human experience, however, that people write on different topics, with different words, to different people. It is also difficult to see why Paul's name should have been associated with the letter from such an early time if he were not the actual writer. During the letter there are hints that Paul was writing from prison (Acts records that Paul was detained in Jerusalem, Caesarea, and Rome), as a direct result of his preaching to the Gentiles (3:1; 4:1; 6:20).

There is a remarkable similarity between Ephesians and Colossians. Much of the wording and structure are the same, yet obviously not as a simple matter of copying. It is likely that Paul was writing the two letters around the same time, to differing groups, which may account for the similarities and the differences. —*Claire M. Powell*

✧

Greetings from Paul

1 This letter is from Paul, chosen by the will
of God to be an apostle of Christ Jesus.
I am writing to God's holy people in Ephesus,* who are faithful followers of Christ Jesus.
2 May God our Father and the Lord Jesus
Christ give you grace and peace.

Spiritual Blessings

3 All praise to God, the Father of our Lord Jesus
Christ, who has blessed us with every spiritual
blessing in the heavenly realms because we are
united with Christ. 4 Even before he made the
world, God loved us and chose us in Christ to be
holy and without fault in his eyes. 5 God decided
in advance to adopt us into his own family by
bringing us to himself through Jesus Christ. This
is what he wanted to do, and it gave him great

1:1 The most ancient manuscripts do not include *in Ephesus.*

1:1–2 Paul's Introduction

Paul was the apostle to the Gentiles. In the New Testament apostle is used in three distinct ways: to describe the Twelve, who were symbolically patterned on the twelve tribes of Israel to denote continuity and fulfillment in the Christian church; to describe some of the early Christian workers such as Barnabas and Paul; and to describe more broadly the function of someone sent to proclaim Christ. The last category may be likened to a missionary. Most apostles in the New Testament are men. There is no indication that this confers greater propensity to leadership for men or that all apostles must always be men. It may be descriptive of what was culturally more acceptable for those days. Even against such prevailing patriarchal culture, Junia (Rom 16:7) is most likely a woman apostle of the missionary kind, commended for her prominence, probably in the hard work she and Andronicus were doing.

1:3–23 Praise of God and Prayer for the Believers

God is not only intimately known as Father to Christians but also is described as the *Father of our Lord Jesus Christ* (v. 3). This is not a literal male fathering; rather, it means the closeness of relationship that has always been true within the Godhead. Since Paul is writing to all the believers, it is an encouragement and reminder that *every spiritual blessing* is accessible to men and women. The highest mysteries or blessings of Christianity are not only for a few. All believers, young and old, male and female, Jew and Gentile, are blessed with every spiritual blessing that heaven affords, and this has been in the mind of God from all eternity. **4:** So also is God's great plan for Christians, that they should be holy. In many countries and cultures it is more acceptable for men to be less holy in their morals than are women. Sometimes standards in sexual ethics are harsher for women than for men. Women are often required to be virgins at marriage, for example, whereas men are not. Scripture requires the same high ethical standards and purity for men and women. Holiness means being set apart for God, being acceptable to God, and also living a life worthy of God. **5:** Paul describes the purpose of God for each believer as *huiothesia* (adoption). The purpose of adoption under Roman law was to perpetuate the family line, whereas the Jewish idea, which is the

pleasure. [6]So we praise God for the glorious
grace he has poured out on us who belong to his
dear Son.* [7]He is so rich in kindness and grace
that he purchased our freedom with the blood of
his Son and forgave our sins. [8]He has showered
his kindness on us, along with all wisdom and
understanding.
[9]God has now revealed to us his mysterious
plan regarding Christ, a plan to fulfill his own
good pleasure. [10]And this is the plan: At the right
time he will bring everything together under the
authority of Christ—everything in heaven and
on earth. [11]Furthermore, because we are united
with Christ, we have received an inheritance
from God,* for he chose us in advance, and he
makes everything work out according to his
plan.
[12]God's purpose was that we Jews who were
the first to trust in Christ would bring praise and
glory to God. [13]And now you Gentiles have also
heard the truth, the Good News that God saves
you. And when you believed in Christ, he identified you as his own* by giving you the Holy
Spirit, whom he promised long ago. [14]The Spirit
is God's guarantee that he will give us the inheritance he promised and that he has purchased
us to be his own people. He did this so we would
praise and glorify him.

Paul's Prayer for Spiritual Wisdom

[15]Ever since I first heard of your strong faith in
the Lord Jesus and your love for God's people
everywhere,* [16]I have not stopped thanking God
for you. I pray for you constantly, [17]asking God,
the glorious Father of our Lord Jesus Christ, to
give you spiritual wisdom* and insight so that
you might grow in your knowledge of God. [18]I
pray that your hearts will be flooded with light
so that you can understand the confident hope
he has given to those he called—his holy people
who are his rich and glorious inheritance.*
[19]I also pray that you will understand the incredible greatness of God's power for us who believe him. This is the same mighty power [20]that
raised Christ from the dead and seated him in the
place of honor at God's right hand in the heavenly realms. [21]Now he is far above any ruler or authority or power or leader or anything else—not
only in this world but also in the world to come.
[22]God has put all things under the authority of
Christ and has made him head over all things for
the benefit of the church. [23]And the church is his
body; it is made full and complete by Christ, who
fills all things everywhere with himself.

Made Alive with Christ

2 Once you were dead because of your disobedience and your many sins. [2]You used
to live in sin, just like the rest of the world,
obeying the devil—the commander of the powers in the unseen world.* He is the spirit at work
in the hearts of those who refuse to obey God.
[3]All of us used to live that way, following the

1:6 Greek *to us in the beloved.* **1:11** Or *we have become God's inheritance.* **1:13** Or *he put his seal on you.* **1:15** Some manuscripts read *your faithfulness to the Lord Jesus and to God's people everywhere.* **1:17** Or *to give you the Spirit of wisdom.* **1:18** Or *called, and the rich and glorious inheritance he has given to his holy people.* **2:2** Greek *obeying the commander of the power of the air.*

background here, was for the benefit of the child: to confer the full rights and privileges of the family. The rights and privileges normally accorded to adopted sons in those days are likened to the closeness of relationship God is willing to bestow on all who follow him. **9:** Paul excites his readers with the greatness of all that Christ has done on their behalf. There is a strong message that Christians have always been known by God and that belonging to Christ has always been their destiny. This is always something that Christians see in retrospect, whereas before people become Christians it is always true that "whosoever will, may come." The New Testament consistently teaches the parallel truths of our free choice of God and his predestination of us. **11–18:** In many countries inheritance is something that passes through the male line. This is not true of the biblical inheritance. It is given to all those, women and men, who are children of the living God, and it is something that Paul prays that the believers will increasingly come to appreciate and understand its greatness. **19–23:** The power of Christ is of cosmic dimensions. To sit at God's right hand is the place of ultimate power and authority. This is further described as being above every *ruler, authority, power,* and dominion, past and future. Many of the words used here would ring bells within the religious milieu of Asia Minor; Christ is greater than any local magic, religious rite, prevailing philosophy, or spiritual power. Goddess worship was important in personal religion and in the social fabric. Acts 19:24 shows the silversmith Demetrius being fearful of the gospel because it would affect his business at Ephesus if people no longer bought silver idols of Artemis. In Acts 19 there is no attempt by Paul to replace goddess worship with a male God. The maleness of Christ is never referred to in Scripture as important in terms of salvation or leadership. His humanity, that which is common to men and women, is the key to his identification with and salvation of human beings.

passionate desires and inclinations of our sinful nature. By our very nature we were subject to God's anger, just like everyone else.

4 But God is so rich in mercy, and he loved us so much, 5 that even though we were dead because of our sins, he gave us life when he raised Christ from the dead. (It is only by God's grace that you have been saved!) 6 For he raised us from the dead along with Christ and seated us with him in the heavenly realms because we are united with Christ Jesus. 7 So God can point to us in all future ages as examples of the incredible wealth of his grace and kindness toward us, as shown in all he has done for us who are united with Christ Jesus.

8 God saved you by his grace when you believed. And you can't take credit for this; it is a gift from God. 9 Salvation is not a reward for the good things we have done, so none of us can boast about it. 10 For we are God's masterpiece. He has created us anew in Christ Jesus, so we can do the good things he planned for us long ago.

Oneness and Peace in Christ

11 Don't forget that you Gentiles used to be outsiders. You were called "uncircumcised heathens" by the Jews, who were proud of their circumcision, even though it affected only their bodies and not their hearts. 12 In those days you were living apart from Christ. You were excluded from citizenship among the people of Israel, and you did not know the covenant promises God had made to them. You lived in this world without God and without hope. 13 But now you have been united with Christ Jesus. Once you were far away from God, but now you have been brought near to him through the blood of Christ.

14 For Christ himself has brought peace to us. He united Jews and Gentiles into one people when, in his own body on the cross, he broke down the wall of hostility that separated us. 15 He did this by ending the system of law with its commandments and regulations. He made peace between Jews and Gentiles by creating in himself one new people from the two groups. 16 Together as one body, Christ reconciled both groups to God by means of his death on the cross, and our hostility toward each other was put to death.

17 He brought this Good News of peace to you Gentiles who were far away from him, and peace to the Jews who were near. 18 Now all of us can come to the Father through the same Holy Spirit because of what Christ has done for us.

A Temple for the Lord

19 So now you Gentiles are no longer strangers and foreigners. You are citizens along with all of God's holy people. You are members of God's family. 20 Together, we are his house, built on the foundation of the apostles and the prophets. And the cornerstone is Christ Jesus himself. 21 We are carefully joined together in him, becoming a holy temple for the Lord. 22 Through him you Gentiles are also being made part of this dwelling where God lives by his Spirit.

2:1—3:21 What God Has Done for Gentile Christians

Paul reminds the believers of their former life in unbelief, which he describes in the strongest terms: They were once dead in sin but are now alive in Christ. It is also important to remember that it is God who creates each individual. Genesis 1 records God's verdict on the initial creation of men and women as equally "very good." Throughout subsequent history men and women's dealings together have tended to engender the idea that women are somehow not quite as good as men. This is not a scriptural understanding. We are what God has made us, equally capable of good works that are to characterize our Christian walk. **11:** Circumcision was the sign of the covenant of God with the Jewish people, from the time of Abraham on. It denoted being part of the chosen people and therefore belonging to and being accepted by God. It was a sign in the flesh of what was to be a spiritual reality. Circumcision was only ever done to males, never to females. Boys were to be circumcised at eight days old, but no cutting was ever advocated for girls. It is that which was done to the flesh of Jesus in his sacrificial death that is the mark of belonging and the uniting factor of Christians, rather than circumcision. Women were no less part of God's covenant people. **14–15:** Paul addresses the Gentile believers and explains how Jews and Gentiles are now one in Christ. By doing this there is now *one new people*. When Paul speaks of the *two groups* at this point he is not thinking of men and women but of Jew and Gentile, who are to become one. **19:** *Members of God's family* are those who are in the same house, which is another way of expressing being part of the family rather than a stranger. Although Paul couches his teaching in theoretical terms, this would have had practical implications in the way believers would treat and welcome one another within the church. The local church should always show in word and in action the family belonging and inclusive welcome that the gospel proclaims. No one should ever feel

God's Mysterious Plan Revealed

3 When I think of all this, I, Paul, a prisoner
of Christ Jesus for the benefit of you Gentiles* . . . [2]assuming, by the way, that you
know God gave me the special responsibility of
extending his grace to you Gentiles. [3]As I briefly
wrote earlier, God himself revealed his mysterious plan to me. [4]As you read what I have written,
you will understand my insight into this plan
regarding Christ. [5]God did not reveal it to previous generations, but now by his Spirit he has
revealed it to his holy apostles and prophets.
[6]And this is God's plan: Both Gentiles and
Jews who believe the Good News share equally
in the riches inherited by God's children. Both
are part of the same body, and both enjoy the
promise of blessings because they belong to
Christ Jesus.* [7]By God's grace and mighty power, I have been given the privilege of serving him
by spreading this Good News.
[8]Though I am the least deserving of all God's
people, he graciously gave me the privilege of
telling the Gentiles about the endless treasures
available to them in Christ. [9]I was chosen to
explain to everyone* this mysterious plan that
God, the Creator of all things, had kept secret
from the beginning.
[10]God's purpose in all this was to use the
church to display his wisdom in its rich variety to
all the unseen rulers and authorities in the heavenly places. [11]This was his eternal plan, which he
carried out through Christ Jesus our Lord.
[12]Because of Christ and our faith in him,* we
can now come boldly and confidently into God's
presence. [13]So please don't lose heart because of
my trials here. I am suffering for you, so you
should feel honored.

Paul's Prayer for Spiritual Growth

[14]When I think of all this, I fall to my knees and
pray to the Father,* [15]the Creator of everything
in heaven and on earth.* [16]I pray that from his
glorious, unlimited resources he will empower
you with inner strength through his Spirit.
[17]Then Christ will make his home in your hearts
as you trust in him. Your roots will grow down
into God's love and keep you strong. [18]And may
you have the power to understand, as all God's
people should, how wide, how long, how high,
and how deep his love is. [19]May you experience
the love of Christ, though it is too great to understand fully. Then you will be made complete
with all the fullness of life and power that comes
from God.
[20]Now all glory to God, who is able, through
his mighty power at work within us, to accomplish infinitely more than we might ask or
think. [21]Glory to him in the church and in Christ
Jesus through all generations forever and ever!
Amen.

Unity in the Body

4 Therefore I, a prisoner for serving the
Lord, beg you to lead a life worthy of your
calling, for you have been called by God.
[2]Always be humble and gentle. Be patient with
each other, making allowance for each other's
faults because of your love. [3]Make every effort

3:1 Paul resumes this thought in verse 14: "When I think of all this, I fall to my knees and pray to the Father." **3:6** Or *because they are united with Christ Jesus.* **3:9** Some manuscripts do not include *to everyone.* **3:12** Or *Because of Christ's faithfulness.* **3:14** Some manuscripts read *the Father of our Lord Jesus Christ.* **3:15** Or *from whom every family in heaven and on earth takes its name.*

like an outsider. **3:7:** Paul describes himself as a "servant," using the Greek word *diakonos*. This word can be descriptive of an official function in the church (Rom 16:1, Phoebe; Phil 1:1) or it can mean a servile attitude. It is not always easy to distinguish between these meanings. Here it would seem to be less of an official designation and more of an explanation of the allegiance Paul has to the gospel of Christ and serving God through his ministry. **14–15:** Paul prefaces his prayer for the believers with an understanding of the greatness of the One to whom he is praying.

4:1–16 Gifts and Graces in the Church

Paul uses his situation of imprisonment for the Lord as a spur to the believers' evidence of service. This serves as an introduction to the second section of the letter, which focuses on the practical and ethical outworking of life and lifestyle of the believer. In Paul's writings there is no doctrine that cannot be put into practice, and there is no ethical command that does not rest clearly on theological and christological argument. The two are gloriously interwoven in Ephesians. Yet Paul introduces an *amen* (so be it) at the end of chapter 3 to draw his doxology to a close, and he begins chapter 4 with an injunction to holy living because of all he has said in the first three chapters. **2:** Humility, gentleness, and patience are often virtues more associated with women than with men, and in many societies they are expected of women but not of men. It may be more of a comment on our cultures that some aspects of godliness are not usually considered masculine, and a reminder of the biblical view that men, just as much as women, are required to be *humble*, *gentle*, and *patient*, just as also to be "kind . . . tenderhearted . . . forgiving" (see v. 32).

to keep yourselves united in the Spirit, binding
yourselves together with peace. 4 For there is one
body and one Spirit, just as you have been called
to one glorious hope for the future. 5 There is
one Lord, one faith, one baptism, 6 and one God
and Father, who is over all and in all and living
through all.
7 However, he has given each one of us a special gift* through the generosity of Christ. 8 That
is why the Scriptures say,

"When he ascended to the heights,
he led a crowd of captives
and gave gifts to his people."*

9 Notice that it says "he ascended." This clearly
means that Christ also descended to our lowly
world.* 10 And the same one who descended is
the one who ascended higher than all the heavens, so that he might fill the entire universe with
himself.
11 Now these are the gifts Christ gave to the
church: the apostles, the prophets, the evangelists,
and the pastors and teachers. 12 Their responsibility is to equip God's people to do his work and
build up the church, the body of Christ. 13 This
will continue until we all come to such unity in
our faith and knowledge of God's Son that we
will be mature in the Lord, measuring up to the
full and complete standard of Christ.
14 Then we will no longer be immature like
children. We won't be tossed and blown about
by every wind of new teaching. We will not be
influenced when people try to trick us with lies
so clever they sound like the truth. 15 Instead, we
will speak the truth in love, growing in every
way more and more like Christ, who is the head
of his body, the church. 16 He makes the whole
body fit together perfectly. As each part does its
own special work, it helps the other parts grow,
so that the whole body is healthy and growing
and full of love.

Living as Children of Light

17 With the Lord's authority I say this: Live no
longer as the Gentiles do, for they are hopelessly confused. 18 Their minds are full of darkness;
they wander far from the life God gives because
they have closed their minds and hardened their
hearts against him. 19 They have no sense of
shame. They live for lustful pleasure and eagerly
practice every kind of impurity.
20 But that isn't what you learned about Christ.
21 Since you have heard about Jesus and have
learned the truth that comes from him, 22 throw
off your old sinful nature and your former way
of life, which is corrupted by lust and deception.
23 Instead, let the Spirit renew your thoughts and
attitudes. 24 Put on your new nature, created to be
like God—truly righteous and holy.
25 So stop telling lies. Let us tell our neighbors
the truth, for we are all parts of the same body.
26 And "don't sin by letting anger control you."*
Don't let the sun go down while you are still angry, 27 for anger gives a foothold to the devil.
28 If you are a thief, quit stealing. Instead, use
your hands for good hard work, and then give
generously to others in need. 29 Don't use foul
or abusive language. Let everything you say be
good and helpful, so that your words will be an
encouragement to those who hear them.
30 And do not bring sorrow to God's Holy
Spirit by the way you live. Remember, he has

4:7 Greek *a grace.* **4:8** Ps 68:18. **4:9** Or *to the lowest parts of the earth.* **4:26** Ps 4:4.

3–6: The physical expression of unity in Christ is not to do with circumcision but baptism, which is inclusive of men and women, Jew and Gentile. **8:** The allusion is to Psalm 68:18, a psalm that probably had associations with the Jewish festival of Pentecost and hence the link with gifts for the church. **12:** Within the unity of the church Christ gives gifts to his people, for the building up of the church, which is described as *the body of Christ.* The list is not exhaustive. Because many of these functions are seen to be done by men in Scripture and in the church, the image they conjure up when reading them is that these are gifts for men, not women, and many people have therefore a mental image of men as the personification of these gifts. However, there is no such delineation of the gifts in Ephesians, and in a context speaking so much in terms of unity of the body and grace given to each of us, the thought that such gifts would be for men only would be distinctly out of place. **16:** God's gifts are for all members of the church, and the church can grow properly only when *each part does its own special work,* and each member is encouraged to use and develop her or his God-given gifts.

4:17—5:14 Exhortation to Practical Godly Living

Christians are those who have a new life, continually clothing themselves with a new self. This does not refer to conversion but to the ethical dimension of holiness that should characterize believers' lives and set them apart from others. Christians will be marked out by their loving kindness, truthfulness, control of anger, honest hard work, and wholesome talk.

Fatherhood

One of the most intimate metaphors for God in Scripture is that of father. It is found eight times in Ephesians. The problem with human language is that it often conjures up images in our minds. Father has many human images associated with it. For some people, the father figure is someone good and kind and close—the type of image that is properly associated with God's fatherhood. Others have had bad experiences of earthly fatherhood. This can influence their view of God, who becomes one to be wrongly feared, not trusted, or even hated. The problem lies in the fact that the word "father" is initially an analogy, born of what we know of human fatherhood.

Not everything associated with a human father is transferable to God. The major obstacle of the image is that all human fathers, by definition, are male. Yet this is not true of God as Father. Maleness is a human characteristic, created by God to image him along with femaleness. But it cannot be said that God is either male or female. To characterize God with the attributes of human fathers is not warranted according to Scripture. Deuteronomy 4:16 expressly forbids the people of Israel from making idols in the form of male or female, animals, or any other created thing, knowing that to do such a thing would be to reduce God to human form. God is the Creator, and human beings image God; God does not image us.

"Parent" might be an appropriate way of thinking of God as Father, since God's parental love and commitment are the point, not maleness or femaleness. The Hebrew word *ab* ("father") is also capable of such a meaning and is a more inclusive term than the more narrowly restricted word for mother.

identified you as his own,* guaranteeing that
you will be saved on the day of redemption.
31 Get rid of all bitterness, rage, anger, harsh
words, and slander, as well as all types of evil
behavior. 32 Instead, be kind to each other, tenderhearted, forgiving one another, just as God
through Christ has forgiven you.

Living in the Light

5 Imitate God, therefore, in everything you
do, because you are his dear children. 2 Live
a life filled with love, following the example of Christ. He loved us* and offered himself as
a sacrifice for us, a pleasing aroma to God.
3 Let there be no sexual immorality, impurity,
or greed among you. Such sins have no place
among God's people. 4 Obscene stories, foolish
talk, and coarse jokes—these are not for you.
Instead, let there be thankfulness to God. 5 You
can be sure that no immoral, impure, or greedy
person will inherit the Kingdom of Christ and of
God. For a greedy person is an idolater, worshiping the things of this world.
6 Don't be fooled by those who try to excuse these sins, for the anger of God will fall
on all who disobey him. 7 Don't participate in
the things these people do. 8 For once you were
full of darkness, but now you have light from
the Lord. So live as people of light! 9 For this
light within you produces only what is good
and right and true.
10 Carefully determine what pleases the Lord.
11 Take no part in the worthless deeds of evil and
darkness; instead, expose them. 12 It is shameful
even to talk about the things that ungodly people
do in secret. 13 But their evil intentions will be
exposed when the light shines on them, 14 for the

4:30 Or *has put his seal on you.* **5:2** Some manuscripts read *loved you.*

5:1: They are to be imitators of God in the same way that children imitate (we get the English word "mimic" from the Greek here) their parents. The familiar parental image in Scripture for God is that of Father. Here, however, that is not specified, and the natural image is of children imitating father and mother. Also, Christ and his model of self-giving sacrifice are to be the catalyst to holy living that is acceptable to God. **3–4:** Fornication and impurity are to be outside the believers' experience and even their talking and thinking. Here Paul is speaking about sexual immorality outside of marriage, particularly of adultery (see Adultery, Exod 20). In those days it probably also included the specific idea of prostitution. Such things are still prevalent and are forbidden to Christians. While many people may think that sexual sins are practiced more by men than women or that men may tend more to temptation in the area of sexual ethics, Paul makes no such distinction and is probably more realistic. Such injunctions are applicable to men and women alike.

light makes everything visible. This is why it is
said,

"Awake, O sleeper,
rise up from the dead,
and Christ will give you light."

Living by the Spirit's Power

[15] So be careful how you live. Don't live like fools,
but like those who are wise. [16] Make the most of
every opportunity in these evil days. [17] Don't act
thoughtlessly, but understand what the Lord
wants you to do. [18] Don't be drunk with wine,
because that will ruin your life. Instead, be filled
with the Holy Spirit, [19] singing psalms and hymns
and spiritual songs among yourselves, and making music to the Lord in your hearts. [20] And give
thanks for everything to God the Father in the
name of our Lord Jesus Christ.

Spirit-Guided Relationships: Wives and Husbands

[21] And further, submit to one another out of reverence for Christ.
[22] For wives, this means submit to your husbands as to the Lord. [23] For a husband is the head
of his wife as Christ is the head of the church.
He is the Savior of his body, the church. [24] As the
church submits to Christ, so you wives should
submit to your husbands in everything.
[25] For husbands, this means love your wives,
just as Christ loved the church. He gave up his
life for her [26] to make her holy and clean, washed
by the cleansing of God's word.* [27] He did this to
present her to himself as a glorious church without a spot or wrinkle or any other blemish. Instead, she will be holy and without fault. [28] In the

5:26 Greek *washed by water with the word.*

5:15—6:9 Mutual Respect and Submission in Various Relationships

Drunkenness (although not drinking of alcohol per se) is a foolish waste and is contrasted with the wisdom of the continual infilling of the Spirit (5:18–21). The command to *be filled with the Holy Spirit* (the present tense implying continuous action) is followed by five dependent participles: speaking in psalms, singing, making music, giving thanks, and submitting to one another. **5:22:** Referring to the submission of wives to their husbands, this verse does not begin a new section, contra many of the Bible versions. In fact, this verse does not have a main verb or even participle of its own, relying instead on the participle "submitting" (v. 21). So it reads more like "be filled with the Spirit . . . submitting to one another out of reverence for Christ; wives, to your husbands, as to the Lord." This shows that the injunction to wives is not separate from the injunction to mutual submission of all believers within the body of Christ but flows from it. Paul is not requiring submission from wives only and therefore relegating them to a subordinate place. Paul prefaces the injunctions to husbands and wives with the command to submit to one another. He continues by outlining what this will mean for wives and what it will mean for husbands. The command to submit to one another applies to the entire section: wives and husbands, children and fathers, slaves and masters. The form of this list of ethical injunctions was termed *Haustafel*, or "household code," by Martin Luther. It may have been a recognized form in pre-Christian literature, and it appears elsewhere in the New Testament (Col 3:18—4:1; 1 Pet 2:17—3:9; 1 Tim 2:8–15; 6:1–10; Titus 2:1–10; some being incomplete sets, others dealing with the whole range of relationships). It may be that the most vulnerable or easily exploited of the relationships are mentioned first, and in comparison with pre-Christian sources, it is remarkable that these often lesser-valued people are addressed with greater dignity within the body of Christ. The command to submit is clear within marriage, but a different word, *hypakouo* (obey), is used for children to parents and slaves to masters. This word for obedience is used only once in reference to marriage, when in 1 Peter 3:6 Sarah is said to have "obeyed" Abraham. Scripture does not mandate that a wife give unquestioning obedience to a husband any more than a husband give unquestioning obedience to a wife. The submission Paul is requiring is not something enforced but embraced voluntarily, out of love for Christ and for one another. Giving way to others or compromising our needs or wishes is something that is necessary to make a relationship work and is eventually a mark of strength, not of weakness. The relationship advocated is not one of doormat to exploiter but of equals giving in at appropriate times to each other in love. **23:** The husband is not commanded to be head but is described in metaphorical terms as *head of his wife*. *Head* has been explained as ruler, supreme, governor, boss, derivation, or source. The word is capable of these meanings, but it does not make sense that Paul should be using all possible meanings of the word here. The context is the parallel not of the glorious ruling of Christ but of his self-giving sacrifice. What the husband stands for when described as head is the caring, giving, sacrificial love that is like Christ. **28:** While Paul urges husbands to love their wives, he is not rigidly dictating that wives submit and husbands love. Obviously both do both, and this is further descriptive of what it means to submit to one

Hierarchy and Equality in the Home

The Bible presents two contrasting pictures of the male-female relationship in marriage. The first appears in Genesis 1 and 2 as a relationship of mutuality in equality; the second emerges in Genesis 3 when, as a consequence of the Fall, the creational model of equality is overturned by sin and replaced by a hierarchical order. Readers can trace the degeneration of the marital relationship through the mutual blaming in Genesis 3, the advent of polygamy in Genesis 4, and the shift to a view of the wife as one more possession to be owned, used, and replaced if the owner wishes.

In the Old Testament individual women exercised political, religious, and familial authority in ways that challenged the prevailing patterns of hierarchy: Deborah served primarily as a judge and prophet within Israel and secondarily as the wife of Lappidoth (Judg 4:4—5:31); Abigail, wife of the wealthy Nabal, received God's approval and David's praise when she authoritatively overruled her husband's decisions and independently acted to reverse them in order to save him and their entire household from destruction (1 Sam 25); Huldah, a prophet in Jerusalem and the wife of a Temple officer, spoke out forcefully when the high priest consulted her about the nation's fate. Because of her forthright denunciation of religious corruption in Judah, King Josiah instituted major changes in the nation (2 Kgs 22:11—23:25); The Song of Songs describes the sexual equality of husband and wife throughout the poem. Both the husband and wife display deference and care for the other's desires; neither one manipulates nor dominates the other. The Song elaborates the "one flesh" relationship of Genesis 2:24–25.

Whereas the Old Testament patterns emerge indirectly through the narratives, the New Testament addresses the issue of marital relationships directly. The two clearest teaching passages are found in 1 Corinthians 7 and Ephesians 5:21–32.

In 1 Corinthians 7:3–5, the apostle Paul clearly states that both wife and husband have expectations that the other should meet. This is the only passage in the New Testament that discusses the authority one spouse has over the other, and Paul is careful to state symmetrically that the exercise of authority is always reciprocal in the marital relationship. Both husband and wife have the same rights over each other.

Paul also teaches mutual decision-making in 1 Corinthians 7:5: Neither one is to impose his or her decision as spiritual leader over the other. Decision-making is based on consensual partnership. The context (1 Cor 6:13–20) establishes that the "body" is God's temple, to be used for his honor, and thus encompasses much more than sexuality.

This becomes clearer in Ephesians 5:21–32 in which husbands, when they love their wives as their own bodies, image the love of Christ for his church. The mutual concern for the fulfillment of one's spouse (in sexual relations as well as the larger marriage) pictures the union of Christ and the church, and this is precisely the teaching of Ephesians 5.

Ephesians 5:22 is widely used to support a doctrine of hierarchy in Christian marriage, and the paragraphing in many Bibles enhances that interpretation by splitting verse 22 from its immediate context. Textually, this is indefensible because verse 22 does not contain a verb but infers it from Ephesians 5:21, in which submission is enjoined on all believers. Verse 21, in turn, continues the instructions of verses 15–20, which describe the visible evidences of being filled with the Spirit of God. This hinge verse sets down the principle of submission, which Paul then explores in 5:22—6:9, describing what it looks like for wives, for husbands, for children, for fathers, for slaves, and for masters. In particular, a wife's submission to her husband is to be "as to the Lord": She has only one Lord (Christ), but her devotion to her husband is to be of the same quality as her devotion to God. A husband shows his love for his wife by following Christ's example of humility and self-sacrifice (clearly forms of submission). There is no hint in this passage that a husband exercises power or authority over his wife.

same way, husbands ought to love their wives as
they love their own bodies. For a man who loves
his wife actually shows love for himself. [29]No
one hates his own body but feeds and cares for it,
just as Christ cares for the church. [30]And we are
members of his body.
[31]As the Scriptures say, "A man leaves his father and mother and is joined to his wife, and the
two are united into one."* [32]This is a great mystery, but it is an illustration of the way Christ
and the church are one. [33]So again I say, each
man must love his wife as he loves himself, and
the wife must respect her husband.

Children and Parents

6 Children, obey your parents because you
belong to the Lord,* for this is the right
thing to do. [2]"Honor your father and
mother." This is the first commandment with a
promise: [3]If you honor your father and mother,
"things will go well for you, and you will have a
long life on the earth."*
[4]Fathers, do not provoke your children to
anger by the way you treat them. Rather, bring
them up with the discipline and instruction that
comes from the Lord.

Slaves and Masters

[5]Slaves, obey your earthly masters with deep
respect and fear. Serve them sincerely as you
would serve Christ. [6]Try to please them all the
time, not just when they are watching you. As
slaves of Christ, do the will of God with all your
heart. [7]Work with enthusiasm, as though you
were working for the Lord rather than for people. [8]Remember that the Lord will reward each
one of us for the good we do, whether we are
slaves or free.
[9]Masters, treat your slaves in the same way.
Don't threaten them; remember, you both have
the same Master in heaven, and he has no favorites.

The Whole Armor of God

[10]A final word: Be strong in the Lord and in
his mighty power. [11]Put on all of God's armor
so that you will be able to stand firm against
all strategies of the devil. [12]For we* are not
fighting against flesh-and-blood enemies, but

5:31 Gen 2:24. **6:1** Or *Children, obey your parents who belong to the Lord;* some manuscripts read simply *Children, obey your parents.* **6:2-3** Exod 20:12; Deut 5:16. **6:12** Some manuscripts read *you.*

---

another (v. 21). Perhaps Paul exhorts each to behave in ways they found difficult. The sacrificial nature of love is the parallel between the husband and Christ. In quoting Genesis 2:24, Paul appears to be advocating the creation of a new family unit at marriage, with the forsaking of the old family ties (see Marriage, Song 2). This does not mean an abandoning of wider family responsibilities, but in some cultures where the wife is forced to leave her family and become a virtual slave in the husband's family, this may have some force. Nowhere is the husband called upon to be Christ to the wife. It is the loving intimacy of marriage that is a suitable parallel to the love of Christ and the church. These verses cut across the human tendency to selfishness and ambition within marriage and extol the workable virtues of self-sacrifice, mutual submission, care, and love that are the foundations for any successful marriage. Human love within marriage is something possible for non-Christians, since marriage is part of God's will for creation as a whole. But the sort of sacrificial love seen in Christ is not possible on our own. It is no mistake that these injunctions are under the general command of needing to be filled with the Spirit. **6:1–2:** Paul quotes from the Mosaic Decalogue the commandment with the promise attached of the blessing that comes from obedience and that is passed through the generations to come. **4:** Paul seems to expect fathers to take an active role in bringing up children. It is probably a Western preoccupation with the value of monetary rewards in the workplace over against the devalued role of parenthood that has often relegated looking after the children as purely the woman's task. There is warrant for the responsibility of both parents in that the normal pattern God shows for family units is of wife, husband, and children, not absent fathering (see Parental Influence, Josh 4). However, this verse is not advocating that it is the father's sole job to discipline and instruct children, rather than mothers. (In single-parent families this may be impossible.) Paul is dealing with a problem the fathers may specifically have had. He is encouraging them to take a more active part. **10–18:** After addressing family matters, Paul's final instruction is that believers should *be strong.* Roman weaponry was the most feared and the most powerful in the ancient world. Military armament was not without allure to women, for the Roman satirist Juvenal ridiculed women who donned the outfits of gladiators and entered the arena. Paul, however, calls his hearers not to masquerade in military trappings but to take up the weapons of the Spirit. Powerless women might equip themselves with spiritual armor that made them more than a match for the political and military might of Rome. As valiant warriors in the army of Christ, they might press on to a victory of which they were in the end assured.

against evil rulers and authorities of the unseen world, against mighty powers in this dark world, and against evil spirits in the heavenly places.

[13]Therefore, put on every piece of God's armor so you will be able to resist the enemy in the time of evil. Then after the battle you will still be standing firm. [14]Stand your ground, putting on the belt of truth and the body armor of God's righteousness. [15]For shoes, put on the peace that comes from the Good News so that you will be fully prepared.* [16]In addition to all of these, hold up the shield of faith to stop the fiery arrows of the devil.* [17]Put on salvation as your helmet, and take the sword of the Spirit, which is the word of God.

[18]Pray in the Spirit at all times and on every occasion. Stay alert and be persistent in your prayers for all believers everywhere.*

[19]And pray for me, too. Ask God to give me the right words so I can boldly explain God's mysterious plan that the Good News is for Jews and Gentiles alike.* [20]I am in chains now, still preaching this message as God's ambassador. So pray that I will keep on speaking boldly for him, as I should.

Final Greetings

[21]To bring you up to date, Tychicus will give you a full report about what I am doing and how I am getting along. He is a beloved brother and faithful helper in the Lord's work. [22]I have sent him to you for this very purpose—to let you know how we are doing and to encourage you.

[23]Peace be with you, dear brothers and sisters,* and may God the Father and the Lord Jesus Christ give you love with faithfulness. [24]May God's grace be eternally upon all who love our Lord Jesus Christ.

6:15 Or *For shoes, put on the readiness to preach the Good News of peace with God.* **6:16** Greek *the evil one.* **6:18** Greek *all of God's holy people.* **6:19** Greek *explain the mystery of the Good News;* some manuscripts read simply *explain the mystery.* **6:23** Greek *brothers.*

6:10–24 Final Encouragement and Blessing

In his closing, Paul is not describing Tychicus as a church leader but referring to his faithfulness of service in all that he does.

PHILIPPIANS

INTRODUCTION

In one of his homilies on Paul's letter to the Philippians, the early Greek bishop and theologian John Chrysostom remarked in reference to Euodia and Syntyche, the two co-workers of Paul mentioned in Philippians 4:2–3, "It appears to me that these women were the heads of the church at Philippi" (Homily 13). What is interesting is that the allusion is made so matter-of-factly. Chrysostom displays no indication that anyone would think of disputing his remark. Though the narrative of Paul's encounter with Lydia and the women gathered at the place of prayer outside the gates of Philippi (Acts 16:11–15, 40) does not mention Euodia and Syntyche by name, it does indicate that the first converts in Philippi consisted of the household of Lydia.

That women predominated in the community at Philippi seems to have been more or less taken for granted by most scholars, at least implicitly. This approach may have contributed to the relative lack of interest in Philippians in comparison with Romans, Galatians, and 1 and 2 Corinthians, as well as to the tendency to view the disputes hinted at in Philippians 2:1–5 as minor faults, the kind of disagreements one might find in any Ladies' Altar Society. Paul's use of the example of the Christ who was obedient unto death (Phil 2) indicates that his purpose in writing to the Philippians had more to do with encouraging them to stand fast in the face of threatened persecution than with exhorting them to practice humility in minor everyday matters. —*Veronica Koperski*

1:1–2	Salutation
1:3–26	Prologue
1:3–11	*Koinonia* in the Gospel from the Beginning
1:12–26	Contrast Between Paul and Unworthy Leaders
1:27—4:4	Body of the Letter
1:27–2:5	Encouragement to Unity
2:6–11	Example of Christ
2:12–16	Encouragement to Obey
2:17–18	Encouragement to Rejoice Despite Difficulties
2:19–24	Praise of Timothy
2:25–30	Praise of Epaphroditus
3:1–2	Caution against Judaizers
3:3–14	Example of Paul
3:15–17	Call to Imitate Paul and Positive Leaders
3:18–19	Examples of Those Who "Walk" Differently from Paul
3:20–21	The Glorified Body in the Resurrection
4:1–4	Encouragement to Agreement between Two Women Leaders
4:5–20	Epilogue
4:5–13	Exhortation with Paul as Model
4:14–20	*Koinonia* in the Gospel from the Beginning
4:21–23	Salutation and Benediction

Greetings from Paul

1 This letter is from Paul and Timothy, slaves of Christ Jesus.

I am writing to all of God's holy people in Philippi who belong to Christ Jesus, including the elders* and deacons.

[2] May God our Father and the Lord Jesus Christ give you grace and peace.

Paul's Thanksgiving and Prayer

[3] Every time I think of you, I give thanks to my God. [4] Whenever I pray, I make my requests for all of you with joy, [5] for you have been my partners in spreading the Good News about Christ from the time you first heard it until now. [6] And I am certain that God, who began the good work within you, will continue his work until it is finally finished on the day when Christ Jesus returns.

[7] So it is right that I should feel as I do about all of you, for you have a special place in my heart. You share with me the special favor of God, both in my imprisonment and in defending and confirming the truth of the Good News. [8] God knows how much I love you and long for you with the tender compassion of Christ Jesus.

[9] I pray that your love will overflow more and more, and that you will keep on growing in knowledge and understanding. [10] For I want you to understand what really matters, so that you may live pure and blameless lives until the day of Christ's return. [11] May you always be filled with the fruit of your salvation—the righteous character produced in your life by Jesus Christ*—for this will bring much glory and praise to God.

Paul's Joy That Christ Is Preached

[12] And I want you to know, my dear brothers and sisters,* that everything that has happened to me here has helped to spread the Good News. [13] For everyone here, including the whole palace guard,* knows that I am in chains because of Christ. [14] And because of my imprisonment, most of the believers* here have gained confidence and boldly speak God's message* without fear.

[15] It's true that some are preaching out of jealousy and rivalry. But others preach about Christ with pure motives. [16] They preach because they love me, for they know I have been appointed to defend the Good News. [17] Those others do not have pure motives as they preach about Christ.

1:1 Or *overseers;* or *bishops.* **1:11** Greek *with the fruit of righteousness through Jesus Christ.* **1:12** Greek *brothers.* **1:13** Greek *including all the Praetorium.* **1:14a** Greek *brothers in the Lord.* **1:14b** Some manuscripts read *speak the message.*

1:1–2 Salutation

If we regard Philippians as all of a piece and also take into account the remarks in 2 Corinthians 8:1–9 and 2 Corinthians 11:9, which refer to the Philippians, it is clear that Paul is writing to a community for which he has a high regard. If, additionally, we take the reference to Euodia and Syntyche (Phil 4:2–3) together with the narrative of the encounter with Lydia and the other women at prayer (Acts 16), this was a community in which women most likely were a sizable portion, if not a majority, of the community. It was one in which they exercised considerable influence as well.

1:3–26 Prologue

1:3–11 *Koinonia* in the Gospel from the Beginning. 3: Paul's high regard for the Philippian Christians is further apparent in the positive description of them evidenced in the opening thanksgiving of the letter as well as in the consistently courteous terms of address employed throughout. Nowhere in the epistle does Paul claim the title of apostle, father, or mother to the community; the authority by virtue of which he exhorts them is based on mutual affection in Christ. **5:** The esteem in which Paul holds the Philippians is demonstrated throughout the letter in connection with the terminology of *koinonia*, a Greek word that is difficult to translate, often rendered "fellowship" or "partnership." Paul sometimes emphasizes the aspect of financial sharing when using *koinonia*, but its full meaning cannot be restricted to financial considerations. **6:** A recurring theme is that of spiritual growth (cf. 1:25; 2:13; 3:12). As in plant life, the process is the work of God who can be trusted to bring the living organism to full fruition (1:11). **7–8:** Paul is not ashamed to express affection toward those who have stood with him so fully in adversity and in the propagation of the gospel. **9–10:** This community that he regards so highly and loves so well is in danger and in need of his loving support. There is dissension. Paul counters with a prayer for deepened love toward one another, along with knowledge and understanding of God's ways. Pettiness can be overcome by a profundity that produces abundant fruit.

1:12–26 Contrast between Paul and Unworthy Leaders. 12–19: Although reports of his imprisonment might create serious demoralization in Philippi, Paul himself sees within the adversity a remarkable expansion of opportunity for proclamation of the gospel. Even the select members of the imperial guard become objects of evangelism. **19:** The apos-

They preach with selfish ambition, not sincerely,
intending to make my chains more painful to me.
[18] But that doesn't matter. Whether their motives
are false or genuine, the message about Christ is
being preached either way, so I rejoice. And I will
continue to rejoice. [19] For I know that as you pray
for me and the Spirit of Jesus Christ helps me,
this will lead to my deliverance.

Paul's Life for Christ

[20] For I fully expect and hope that I will never be
ashamed, but that I will continue to be bold for
Christ, as I have been in the past. And I trust that
my life will bring honor to Christ, whether I live
or die. [21] For to me, living means living for Christ,
and dying is even better. [22] But if I live, I can do
more fruitful work for Christ. So I really don't
know which is better. [23] I'm torn between two
desires: I long to go and be with Christ, which
would be far better for me. [24] But for your sakes,
it is better that I continue to live.

[25] Knowing this, I am convinced that I will remain alive so I can continue to help all of you
grow and experience the joy of your faith. [26] And
when I come to you again, you will have even
more reason to take pride in Christ Jesus because
of what he is doing through me.

Live as Citizens of Heaven

[27] Above all, you must live as citizens of heaven,
conducting yourselves in a manner worthy of
the Good News about Christ. Then, whether I
come and see you again or only hear about you,
I will know that you are standing together with
one spirit and one purpose, fighting together for
the faith, which is the Good News. [28] Don't be
intimidated in any way by your enemies. This
will be a sign to them that they are going to be
destroyed, but that you are going to be saved,
even by God himself. [29] For you have been giv-
en not only the privilege of trusting in Christ
but also the privilege of suffering for him. [30] We
are in this struggle together. You have seen my
struggle in the past, and you know that I am still
in the midst of it.

Have the Attitude of Christ

2 Is there any encouragement from belonging to Christ? Any comfort from his love?
Any fellowship together in the Spirit? Are
your hearts tender and compassionate? [2] Then
make me truly happy by agreeing wholeheartedly with each other, loving one another, and
working together with one mind and purpose.

[3] Don't be selfish; don't try to impress others. Be humble, thinking of others as better than
yourselves. [4] Don't look out only for your own
interests, but take an interest in others, too.

[5] You must have the same attitude that Christ
Jesus had.

---

tles, the Jewish Christians, or someone who already has the faith shares it with the Gentiles, and they in turn share at least their material wealth with those who had given them spiritual riches. Thus whenever Paul employs the term *koinonia* or one of its cognates with emphasis on the financial aspect, the prior spiritual benefit that grounds the obligation to render such financial assistance must always be kept in mind. **20–26:** The prospect of imminent martyrdom has sharpened Paul's perspective in thinking through objectives of both life and death. Cause for rejoicing may be found, whether in the apostle's death or in his release from prison. In no way should either obstruct the radiant quality of the Philippians' faith.

1:27—4:4 Body of the Letter

1:27—2:5 Encouragement to Unity. 1:27–28: Paul, a citizen of Rome, now finds himself its prisoner. Though frequently considered enemies of the state, Christians are called to model citizenship in both heavenly and earthly realms. **29–30:** Suffering should not be an end in itself, nor should a Christian voluntarily submit to abuse at the hands of another unless it furthers the cause of Christ. **2:1:** *Fellowship* (*koinonia*) is something one is called to or shares in by virtue of being Christian. It is used in connection with the Christians' relation with Jesus Christ (1 Cor 1:9), with the gospel (1 Cor 9:23; Phil 1:5; 4:15), with faith (Phlm 7), with suffering and consolation (2 Cor 1:7; Phil 3:10), with grace (Phil 1:7), with the Eucharist (1 Cor 10:14–22), and with the Holy Spirit (2 Cor 13:13; Phil 2:1). In many of the occurrences of *koinonia* terminology, monetary factors appear to be at best implicit. **2:** The entreaty at the beginning of chapter 2, as well as the specific counsels in verses 2–4, imply that some sort of disagreement was disturbing the harmony of the Christian community at Philippi; the reference to the disagreement between Euodia and Syntyche (4:2) reinforces this conclusion. **3–4:** Dissension is usually built upon one's desire to get one's own way, but the kingdom of God is built by the desire to see others thrive. An attitude of humility strives for harmony, avoids selfishness and conceit, and looks to the interest of others. It is unseemly for believers to allow discord among themselves because they have been made one in Christ. **5:** A literal rendering might be "This think in you which also in Christ Jesus," or as we read in this translation *you must have the same attitude that Christ Jesus*

Faith Development

Faith is a concept present throughout the Bible, from the first family (Heb 11:4) to the saints who are "maintaining their faith in Jesus" (Rev 14:12). In the Old Testament God's faithfulness is a continuing theme (Deut 7:9), and the men and women who hoped and trusted in him were considered to have faith (Pss 26:1; 42:5). His great promise was that "the righteous . . . live by their faithfulness" (Hab 2:4). In the New Testament the basic meaning of faith is that of trust or confidence in God; God in Christ initiated and developed the faith of God's people (Heb 12:2).

Growth in faith involves growth in knowing and experiencing God, relying on the Son for salvation, believing God's promises, and finding daily strength to obey his will through the power of the Holy Spirit.

Jesus Nurtured His Followers' Faith

Jesus desired to nurture faith among his hearers. He selected men and women who formed a group of learners committed to close, personal, long-term relationships with him and with one another. At his call they left home, family, employment, and their communities (Luke 5:10–11; 9:58), met different people, and faced conflict with the religious authority figures (Mark 2:23; 7:1–13; Luke 19:39). Jesus structured their experiences so that their relationships and active involvements forced them into critical reflection concerning their beliefs and values, and led them to relate to him with increasing faith.

Matthew's Gospel gives insight into three distinct stages of faith that Jesus identified among those he encountered. First was the "little faith" of his disciples. Jesus drew attention to their need for faith development when they feared the storm even though he was with them; when Peter began to sink and doubted Jesus' calling; when they missed the spiritual dimensions of his teaching because they were too busy discussing food; and when they failed to use his imparted authority to heal and deliver (Matt 8:26; 10:1; 14:31; 16:8; 17:20). The second level of faith was described as "small as a mustard seed." This does not appear to be very different from little faith, but its identifying characteristic is believing prayer in the face of humanly impossible situations (Matt 17:21; 21:21). The third level and highest commendation for "great faith" was reserved for two Gentiles—a Roman centurion and a Canaanite woman (Matt 8:10; 15:28). By praising them Jesus demonstrated that faith in God is greater than observing the law.

The event with the greatest impact on the faith of Jesus' followers was the crisis precipitated by his death and resurrection (Matt 28:17). When it was obvious that their master would no longer be present among them, they were forced to accept responsibility for their lives, beliefs, commitments, and values.

Faith Nurture in the Early Church

Acts and the Epistles record how the early faith communities took up the task of bringing others to a growing faith relationship with Christ. They taught that faith is a trusting relationship with God as Father, Son, and Spirit and expresses itself in action within a person's daily life and in a continuing struggle between flesh and Spirit (John 20:31; Jas 2:14–17; Rom 5—8). They carried their message across the Roman Empire; they planted and taught new churches so that the different members would use their spiritual gifts to build up Christ's body and develop faith (Eph 4:11–16). Then all received spiritual nourishment to bring about a maturity that enabled them to share the faith with neighbors and succeeding generations (Heb 5:11–14; 2 Tim 2:2). Women may indeed have had a special part to play in faith nurturing, as Lois and Eunice did with Timothy (2 Tim 1:5).

6 Though he was God,*
he did not think of equality with God
as something to cling to.
7 Instead, he gave up his divine privileges*;
he took the humble position of a slave*
and was born as a human being.
When he appeared in human form,*
8 he humbled himself in obedience to God
and died a criminal's death on a cross.

9 Therefore, God elevated him to the place of
highest honor
and gave him the name above all other
names,
10 that at the name of Jesus every knee should
bow,
in heaven and on earth and under the
earth,
11 and every tongue confess that Jesus Christ
is Lord,
to the glory of God the Father.

Shine Brightly for Christ

12 Dear friends, you always followed my instructions when I was with you. And now that I am
away, it is even more important. Work hard to
show the results of your salvation, obeying God
with deep reverence and fear. 13 For God is working in you, giving you the desire and the power
to do what pleases him.
14 Do everything without complaining and
arguing, 15 so that no one can criticize you. Live
clean, innocent lives as children of God, shining like bright lights in a world full of crooked
and perverse people. 16 Hold firmly to the word
of life; then, on the day of Christ's return, I will
be proud that I did not run the race in vain and
that my work was not useless. 17 But I will rejoice
even if I lose my life, pouring it out like a liquid
offering to God,* just like your faithful service
is an offering to God. And I want all of you to
share that joy. 18 Yes, you should rejoice, and I
will share your joy.

Paul Commends Timothy

19 If the Lord Jesus is willing, I hope to send Timothy to you soon for a visit. Then he can cheer
me up by telling me how you are getting along.
20 I have no one else like Timothy, who genuinely
cares about your welfare. 21 All the others care
only for themselves and not for what matters to
Jesus Christ. 22 But you know how Timothy has
proved himself. Like a son with his father, he has
served with me in preaching the Good News. 23 I
hope to send him to you just as soon as I find out
what is going to happen to me here. 24 And I have
confidence from the Lord that I myself will come
to see you soon.

Paul Commends Epaphroditus

25 Meanwhile, I thought I should send Epaphroditus back to you. He is a true brother, co-worker,

2:6 Or *Being in the form of God.* **2:7a** Greek *he emptied himself.* **2:7b** Or *the form of a slave.* **2:7c** Some English translations put this phrase in verse 8. **2:17** Greek *I will rejoice even if I am to be poured out as a liquid offering.*

---

had. The Greek verb *phroneo* ("to think"), which is used in the first part of the verse, is also used twice in verse 2; it refers more to an inward disposition encompassing the will and emotions than simply to an intellectual attitude. This suggests that those who are one in Christ are being called to put on his attitude no matter what it costs, and not only when it concerns relations with each other.

2:6–11 Example of Christ. Paul depicts the kind of attitude, or thinking, that Christ had, which led him to be obedient even to death on a cross. Paul can exhort the Philippian Christians, and more particularly the women among them, to follow Christ's example of self-emptying because in becoming members of the Christian community the women of Philippi have become leaders in that community as well.

2:12–16 Encouragement to Obey. The immediately ensuing charge to put into action God's saving work is a further appeal, as in 1:27–28, to stand fast in their obedience to God in this situation of threatened persecution, even if this requires obedience unto death. The use of the sublime example of Christ makes more sense if the exhortation is to remain steadfast under threat of persecution and death rather than to improve community relations.

2:17–18 Encouragement to Rejoice Despite Difficulties. This is a Paul who is contemplating his death and who is yet filled with joy, which will be complete if they will listen to him. He is not just asking them to do something difficult. He has discovered that the way of the cross leads to joy.

2:19–24 Praise of Timothy. Mentoring involves not only loving instruction but also sending forth the advisee for independent ministry. Here it is clear that the mentor cares deeply for the advisee and is deeply dependent on him.

2:25–30 Praise of Epaphroditus. Ever since its beginning, Christianity has understood the importance of communication between faith communities, with

and fellow soldier. And he was your messenger to help me in my need. [26]I am sending him because he has been longing to see you, and he was very distressed that you heard he was ill. [27]And he certainly was ill; in fact, he almost died. But God had mercy on him—and also on me, so that I would not have one sorrow after another.

[28]So I am all the more anxious to send him back to you, for I know you will be glad to see him, and then I will not be so worried about you. [29]Welcome him with Christian love* and with great joy, and give him the honor that people like him deserve. [30]For he risked his life for the work of Christ, and he was at the point of death while doing for me what you couldn't do from far away.

The Priceless Value of Knowing Christ

3 Whatever happens, my dear brothers and sisters,* rejoice in the Lord. I never get tired of telling you these things, and I do it to safeguard your faith.

[2]Watch out for those dogs, those people who do evil, those mutilators who say you must be circumcised to be saved. [3]For we who worship by the Spirit of God* are the ones who are truly circumcised. We rely on what Christ Jesus has done for us. We put no confidence in human effort, [4]though I could have confidence in my own effort if anyone could. Indeed, if others have reason for confidence in their own efforts, I have even more!

[5]I was circumcised when I was eight days old. I am a pure-blooded citizen of Israel and a member of the tribe of Benjamin—a real Hebrew if there ever was one! I was a member of the Pharisees, who demand the strictest obedience to the Jewish law. [6]I was so zealous that I harshly persecuted the church. And as for righteousness, I obeyed the law without fault.

[7]I once thought these things were valuable, but now I consider them worthless because of what Christ has done. [8]Yes, everything else is worthless when compared with the infinite value of knowing Christ Jesus my Lord. For his sake I have discarded everything else, counting it all as garbage, so that I could gain Christ [9]and become one with him. I no longer count on my own righteousness through obeying the law; rather, I become righteous through faith in Christ.* For God's way of making us right with himself depends on faith. [10]I want to know Christ and experience the mighty power that raised him from the dead. I want to suffer with him, sharing in his death, [11]so that one way or another I will experience the resurrection from the dead!

Pressing toward the Goal

[12]I don't mean to say that I have already achieved these things or that I have already reached perfection. But I press on to possess that perfection for which Christ Jesus first possessed me. [13]No, dear brothers and sisters, I have not achieved it,* but I focus on this one thing: Forgetting the past and looking forward to what lies ahead, [14]I press on to reach the end of the race and receive the heavenly prize for which God, through Christ Jesus, is calling us.

[15]Let all who are spiritually mature agree on

2:29 Greek *in the Lord.* **3:1** Greek *brothers;* also in 3:13, 17. **3:3** Some manuscripts read *worship God in spirit;* one early manuscript reads *worship in spirit.* **3:9** Or *through the faithfulness of Christ.* **3:13** Some manuscripts read *not yet achieved it.*

---

each offering information, inspiration, encouragement, and instruction to another.

3:1–2 Caution against Judaizers. The harsh threefold warning to beware of outside agitators who advocate circumcision may also be related to the threat of persecution and death. Since the Jews enjoyed a protected status within the Roman Empire, some in the Philippian community (perhaps Euodia or Syntyche) may have felt that identifying themselves as Jewish in the eyes of the Roman authorities by adopting Jewish identity markers such as circumcision would serve to deflect the threatened persecution. Or Paul might have been concerned that some might be considering such a solution, which he adamantly opposed.

3:3–14 Example of Paul. 3–6: Although his own Jewish credentials are impeccable, they could not bring a personal knowledge of God's Son to a searching soul. **7–11:** Paul is so centered on the overwhelming *gain* of knowing Christ Jesus his Lord that he is not interested in any other gain. Everything else is cheerfully acknowledged as wothless from his new perspective. In 2:1 Paul has presumed the community's *koinonia* in the Spirit; in 3:8–11 he defines his knowledge of Christ as knowing the power of Christ's resurrection and the *koinonia* of his sufferings. This twofold knowledge of Christ is all that Paul desires, and for it he gladly gives up everything else. **12–14:** Like all other Christians, Paul is honest that he is still in the growing stage—a model to all those who acknowledge their imperfections and keep moving on.

3:15–17 Call to Imitate Paul and Positive Leaders. Paul asks the community to join in imitating his example, but the example he has just offered (vv. 7–11)

these things. If you disagree on some point, I
believe God will make it plain to you. 16 But we
must hold on to the progress we have already
made.
17 Dear brothers and sisters, pattern your lives
after mine, and learn from those who follow our
example. 18 For I have told you often before, and
I say it again with tears in my eyes, that there
are many whose conduct shows they are really
enemies of the cross of Christ. 19 They are headed
for destruction. Their god is their appetite, they
brag about shameful things, and they think only
about this life here on earth. 20 But we are citizens of heaven, where the Lord Jesus Christ lives.
And we are eagerly waiting for him to return as
our Savior. 21 He will take our weak mortal bodies and change them into glorious bodies like his
own, using the same power with which he will
bring everything under his control.

4 Therefore, my dear brothers and sisters,*
stay true to the Lord. I love you and long
to see you, dear friends, for you are my joy
and the crown I receive for my work.

Words of Encouragement

2 Now I appeal to Euodia and Syntyche. Please,
because you belong to the Lord, settle your disagreement. 3 And I ask you, my true partner,*
to help these two women, for they worked hard
with me in telling others the Good News. They
worked along with Clement and the rest of my
co-workers, whose names are written in the
Book of Life.
4 Always be full of joy in the Lord. I say it
again—rejoice! 5 Let everyone see that you are
considerate in all you do. Remember, the Lord is
coming soon.
6 Don't worry about anything; instead, pray
about everything. Tell God what you need, and
thank him for all he has done. 7 Then you will experience God's peace, which exceeds anything we
can understand. His peace will guard your hearts
and minds as you live in Christ Jesus.
8 And now, dear brothers and sisters, one final thing. Fix your thoughts on what is true,
and honorable, and right, and pure, and lovely,
and admirable. Think about things that are
excellent and worthy of praise. 9 Keep putting
into practice all you learned and received from
me—everything you heard from me and saw
me doing. Then the God of peace will be with
you.

4:1 Greek *brothers;* also in 4:8. **4:3** Or *loyal Syzygus.*

is that of suffering the loss of all things other than the knowledge of Christ Jesus suffering and risen, a self-emptying that imitates the example of the one he confesses as "my Lord" (v. 8; cf. 2:11).

3:18–19 Examples of Those Who "Walk" Differently from Paul. Even in the early days of the church there were dissidents both inside and outside the faith community.

3:20–21 The Glorious Body in the Resurrection. The joy to which the Philippian Christians are exhorted throughout the letter is the joy that comes from following Christ, even in the way of the cross that leads to death, but beyond that, to the glorious transformation in which Christ will transform their lowly bodies to be conformed to the body of his glory.

4:1–4 Encouragement to Agreement between Two Women Leaders. 2: The importance of *Euodia* and *Syntyche* is recognized by a growing number of modern scholars. Some hold that *Euodia* and *Syntyche* were prominent in the church at Philippi, probably among the *episkopoi* ("elders") and *diakonoi* ("deacons") of 1:1. These commentators suggest that their dispute might have posed a threat to the unity of the church. But Paul is not saying in 2:1–5, "Be nice to each other because you are Christians." He is not addressing a merely human institution. *Euodia* and *Syntyche* have labored with him in the gospel. If all he desired were for them to get along, he would not have to plead by virtue of all they hold most sacred as well as by virtue of their affection for him. **3:** All of this suggests that from the beginning—and consistently throughout their relationship—the Philippian Christians have shared with Paul the missionary labor of the gospel in addition to assisting him monetarily from their limited financial resources.

4:5–20 Epilogue

4:5–13 Exhortation with Paul as Model. 5–8: Here Paul turns again to the attitude he had at 2:6–11. He lays before them not only serenity of mind but a grand vista of all that is good and true and beautiful within human experience. **9:** The exhortation to imitate Paul is repeated, but what they have learned and heard and seen in Paul is not simply a model of the virtues in 4:8, which could be found in any upright pagan. Paul was a person who would stand up to Peter in arguing for freedom from Jewish ritual law, yet he would be solicitous to remind the Gentile Christians to care for the material needs of the poor Christians in Jerusalem. He was a person who would

Paul's Thanks for Their Gifts
[10] How I praise the Lord that you are concerned
about me again. I know you have always been
concerned for me, but you didn't have the
chance to help me. [11] Not that I was ever in
need, for I have learned how to be content with
whatever I have. [12] I know how to live on almost
nothing or with everything. I have learned the
secret of living in every situation, whether it
is with a full stomach or empty, with plenty
or little. [13] For I can do everything through
Christ,* who gives me strength. [14] Even so, you
have done well to share with me in my present
difficulty.
[15] As you know, you Philippians were the only
ones who gave me financial help when I first
brought you the Good News and then traveled
on from Macedonia. No other church did this.
[16] Even when I was in Thessalonica you sent help
more than once. [17] I don't say this because I want
a gift from you. Rather, I want you to receive a
reward for your kindness.
[18] At the moment I have all I need—and more!
I am generously supplied with the gifts you sent
me with Epaphroditus. They are a sweet-smelling
sacrifice that is acceptable and pleasing to God.
[19] And this same God who takes care of me will
supply all your needs from his glorious riches,
which have been given to us in Christ Jesus.
[20] Now all glory to God our Father forever and
ever! Amen.

Paul's Final Greetings
[21] Give my greetings to each of God's holy people—all who belong to Christ Jesus. The brothers
who are with me send you their greetings. [22] And
all the rest of God's people send you greetings,
too, especially those in Caesar's household.
[23] May the grace of the Lord Jesus Christ be
with your spirit.

4:13 Greek *through the one.*

speak out for Christ even when perceiving himself as a less than imposing speaker, who would accept the consequences of his speaking out without bitterness, who was willing to be a fool for Christ's sake, and who refused to glory except in the cross of Christ. Could he ask less of those who were so dear to him, especially when he had already begun to experience the joy that was the result? Could he wish for them anything less? **10–13:** Here we are given another glimpse of the affectionate relationship that had been established between Paul and this supportive community.

4:14–20 *Koinonia* in the Gospel from the Beginning. As far as the financial aspect of *koinonia* is concerned, the letter is unusual because Paul indicates that he has accepted financial help from this community, not from any other, from the beginning of their relationship, sharing with Paul the labor of spreading the gospel as well as assisting him monetarily throughout their relationship. Paul's exhortation to the Christians in Philippi can thus be viewed as an invitation to enter into a special intimacy that allows him to reveal even the state of his personal finances.

4:21–23 Salutation and Benediction

The letter closes with mutual greetings. Those in Caesar's household are slaves of the emperor in Rome or the colonies.

COLOSSIANS

INTRODUCTION

The biblical text cites Paul as the author of Colossians. The many similarities between Colossians and Philemon, which is generally agreed to be Pauline, provide evidence in favor of Pauline authorship. It seems likely that Paul, in prison, wrote Colossians, Philemon, and Ephesians at about the same time; he asked Tychicus, accompanied by Onesimus, to take them to Ephesus and then to Colosse. He hoped that the runaway slave Onesimus would reconcile with his master in Colosse (Col 4:7–9; Phlm 10–21). Paul was probably in Rome but may have been in Caesarea or Ephesus. If he was in Rome, then the date is in the mid-fifties to early sixties. Many of his supporters are with him as he writes.

Paul has never been to Colosse (Col 1:4, 7–9; 2:1). Although of waning importance, this small city was nonetheless cosmopolitan, home to varied cultural and religious expressions. The largely Gentile church at Colosse (1:21, 27; 2:13) had received the gospel from Epaphras (1:7–8; 4:12–13), who shares Paul's imprisonment (Phlm 23). Paul thanks God for these brothers and sisters in Christ: They have faith and love for the saints, they heard and comprehended the grace of God, and the gospel is bearing fruit among them. —*Shirley A. Decker-Lucke*

1:1–2	Opening: Authors and Audience
1:3–14	Thanksgiving and Prayer
1:15–23	The Person and Work of Christ
1:24—2:5	Paul's Struggles for the Church
2:6–23	Warnings to Live in Christ
3:1—4:6	Implications of Being in Christ
4:7–18	Closing: Greetings and Instructions

✧

Greetings from Paul

1 This letter is from Paul, chosen by the will
of God to be an apostle of Christ Jesus, and
from our brother Timothy.
2 We are writing to God's holy people in the
city of Colosse, who are faithful brothers and sisters* in Christ.
May God our Father give you grace and
peace.

Paul's Thanksgiving and Prayer

3 We always pray for you, and we give thanks to
God, the Father of our Lord Jesus Christ. 4 For we
have heard of your faith in Christ Jesus and your
love for all of God's people, 5 which come from
your confident hope of what God has reserved
for you in heaven. You have had this expectation
ever since you first heard the truth of the Good
News.
6 This same Good News that came to you is
going out all over the world. It is bearing fruit
everywhere by changing lives, just as it changed
your lives from the day you first heard and understood the truth about God's wonderful grace.
7 You learned about the Good News from
Epaphras, our beloved co-worker. He is Christ's
faithful servant, and he is helping us on your behalf.* 8 He has told us about the love for others
that the Holy Spirit has given you.
9 So we have not stopped praying for you since
we first heard about you. We ask God to give you
complete knowledge of his will and to give you
spiritual wisdom and understanding. 10 Then the
way you live will always honor and please the
Lord, and your lives will produce every kind of
good fruit. All the while, you will grow as you
learn to know God better and better.
11 We also pray that you will be strengthened
with all his glorious power so you will have all
the endurance and patience you need. May you
be filled with joy,* 12 always thanking the Father.
He has enabled you to share in the inheritance
that belongs to his people, who live in the light.
13 For he has rescued us from the kingdom of
darkness and transferred us into the Kingdom of
his dear Son, 14 who purchased our freedom* and
forgave our sins.

Christ Is Supreme

15 Christ is the visible image of the invisible
God.
He existed before anything was created and
is supreme over all creation,*

1:2 Greek *faithful brothers.* **1:7** Or *he is ministering on your behalf;* some manuscripts read *he is ministering on our behalf.* **1:11** Or *all the patience and endurance you need with joy.* **1:14** Some manuscripts add *with his blood.* **1:15** Or *He is the firstborn of all creation.*

1:1–2 Opening: Authors and Audience

This opening follows the standard ancient letter style by identifying the author and audience.

1:3–14 Thanksgiving and Prayer

A thanksgiving to God or the gods was a standard element in ancient letters. Paul incorporates this element in his letter (vv. 3–4), and expresses his thankfulness for the faith of the saints in Colosse, based as it is upon a hope that centers in Christ. **6:** The Greek wording literally speaks of the gospel as growing and bearing fruit. It is working transformation throughout the world as well as among the Colossian Christians. This expansive description easily includes children, women, and men as those for whom Paul is thankful. **7–8:** Epaphras first taught them the word of the truth. He is a *diakonos*, a *servant* or minister (the same term that is used of Phoebe, Rom 16:1). **9–10:** Paul's prayer is that they may be given an *understanding* of God's will for their lives and that it may have outreach into the lives of others. **11–12:** The embracing of the Gentiles, who were considered unclean and were excluded from the innermost places of the Temple, would have had significant parallels for Jewish and Gentile women, who had also been considered unclean and who were also excluded from those most holy places of the Temple. Thus, women are included in Paul's prayer that the Colossians will be strengthened with God's power, enabled to share the inheritance (women's inclusion could not be taken for granted in the first-century world). Men and women alike are given God's power so that they can live lives that please God and can be free from the power of darkness. Women living in Roman cities, which were known to be dangerous after dark, would likely have been particularly fearful of the dangers presented by literal darkness. This image of being rescued from the power of darkness and brought into a kingdom would have struck a deep chord with women.

1:15–23 The Person and Work of Christ

The hymn in verses 15–20, whether written by Paul or adopted by him from an earlier source, sets before the Colossians the person of Christ. In it Christ is presented as the image (*eikon*) of God. In 3:10, the Colossian women, children, and men are told that their new selves are being renewed according to the image (*eikon*) of God. Even though the Old Testament describes God in predominately adult male terms,

16 for through him God created everything
in the heavenly realms and on earth.
He made the things we can see
and the things we can't see—
such as thrones, kingdoms, rulers, and
authorities in the unseen world.
Everything was created through him and
for him.
17 He existed before anything else,
and he holds all creation together.
18 Christ is also the head of the church,
which is his body.
He is the beginning,
supreme over all who rise from the dead.*
So he is first in everything.
19 For God in all his fullness
was pleased to live in Christ,
20 and through him God reconciled
everything to himself.
He made peace with everything in heaven
and on earth
by means of Christ's blood on the cross.

21 This includes you who were once far away
from God. You were his enemies, separated from
him by your evil thoughts and actions. 22 Yet now
he has reconciled you to himself through the
death of Christ in his physical body. As a result,
he has brought you into his own presence, and
you are holy and blameless as you stand before
him without a single fault.
23 But you must continue to believe this truth
and stand firmly in it. Don't drift away from
the assurance you received when you heard the
Good News. The Good News has been preached
all over the world, and I, Paul, have been appointed as God's servant to proclaim it.

Paul's Work for the Church

24 I am glad when I suffer for you in my body,
for I am participating in the sufferings of Christ
that continue for his body, the church. 25 God has
given me the responsibility of serving his church
by proclaiming his entire message to you. 26 This
message was kept secret for centuries and generations past, but now it has been revealed to God's
people. 27 For God wanted them to know that the
riches and glory of Christ are for you Gentiles,
too. And this is the secret: Christ lives in you.
This gives you assurance of sharing his glory.
28 So we tell others about Christ, warning everyone and teaching everyone with all the wisdom
God has given us. We want to present them to God,
perfect* in their relationship to Christ. 29 That's
why I work and struggle so hard, depending on
Christ's mighty power that works within me.

2 I want you to know how much I have agonized for you and for the church at Laodicea, and for many other believers who
have never met me personally. 2 I want them to
be encouraged and knit together by strong ties
of love. I want them to have complete confidence
that they understand God's mysterious plan,
which is Christ himself. 3 In him lie hidden all
the treasures of wisdom and knowledge.
4 I am telling you this so no one will deceive
you with well-crafted arguments. 5 For though

1:18 Or *the firstborn from the dead.* **1:28** Or *mature.*

women and children are now able to be God's image, to represent or be like God, to be revealers of God's glory and goodness. **21–22:** Paul uses a rhetorical form common in New Testament letters, "you were once . . . but now you are," to show the transformation and reconciliation that Christ has brought about. Children, women, and men are presented as *holy, blameless,* and irreproachable (*anenkletos*, a judicial word). The culture was invested in keeping and presenting women as blameless before and after marriage. Women were in many ways the keepers of the family's honor, and those women who were not able to maintain irreproachable conduct and reputation would bring shame on themselves and their families. Girls and women would have especially understood the importance and relief at being found blameless and irreproachable, free from shame. **23:** Paul warns these Christians (whom he does not know personally) against the false religions and the syncretism by which they are tempted. His primary way of attacking this heresy is by insisting on the centrality and all-sufficiency of Christ in Christian belief.

1:24—2:5 Paul's Struggles for the Church

Paul describes his suffering and sacrifices on behalf of the Colossians (1:24–25). He is accepting submission and self-sacrifice for himself and holding it up as an honorable concern. Submission was more strongly urged upon the women, children, and slaves of the New Testament culture than on free males (see the household code, 3:18—4:1). Yet here Paul voluntarily humbles himself and holds that humility is an honorable position. **2:4:** The Colossians do not need false traditions, ceremonies, or practices to help them become complete in Christ because they are already complete. As Paul writes these warnings against false teachings, he must have been aware that in other Christian communities some women had seemed to be particularly susceptible to false teaching (1 Cor 14:34; 1 Tim 5:11–

I am far away from you, my heart is with you.
And I rejoice that you are living as you should
and that your faith in Christ is strong.

Freedom from Rules and New Life in Christ

[6]And now, just as you accepted Christ Jesus as
your Lord, you must continue to follow him.
[7]Let your roots grow down into him, and let
your lives be built on him. Then your faith will
grow strong in the truth you were taught, and
you will overflow with thankfulness.

[8]Don't let anyone capture you with empty
philosophies and high-sounding nonsense that
come from human thinking and from the spiritual powers* of this world, rather than from
Christ. [9]For in Christ lives all the fullness of God
in a human body.* [10]So you also are complete
through your union with Christ, who is the head
over every ruler and authority.

[11]When you came to Christ, you were "circumcised," but not by a physical procedure.
Christ performed a spiritual circumcision—the
cutting away of your sinful nature.* [12]For you
were buried with Christ when you were baptized. And with him you were raised to new life
because you trusted the mighty power of God,
who raised Christ from the dead.

[13]You were dead because of your sins and because your sinful nature was not yet cut away.
Then God made you alive with Christ, for he forgave all our sins. [14]He canceled the record of the
charges against us and took it away by nailing
it to the cross. [15]In this way, he disarmed* the
spiritual rulers and authorities. He shamed them
publicly by his victory over them on the cross.

[16]So don't let anyone condemn you for what
you eat or drink, or for not celebrating certain
holy days or new moon ceremonies or Sabbaths.
[17]For these rules are only shadows of the reality
yet to come. And Christ himself is that reality.
[18]Don't let anyone condemn you by insisting
on pious self-denial or the worship of angels,*
saying they have had visions about these things.
Their sinful minds have made them proud, [19]and
they are not connected to Christ, the head of
the body. For he holds the whole body together
with its joints and ligaments, and it grows as God
nourishes it.

[20]You have died with Christ, and he has set
you free from the spiritual powers of this world.

2:8 Or *the spiritual principles;* also in 2:20. **2:9** Or *in him dwells all the completeness of the Godhead bodily.*
2:11 Greek *the cutting away of the body of the flesh.*
2:15 Or *he stripped off.* **2:18** Or *or worshiping with angels.*

---

13). This vulnerability could be because women in general received less teaching, were less familiar with the Old Testament, and were less educated in rhetoric and discriminating, logical thinking.

2:6–23 Warnings to Live in Christ

Women are told not to let anyone condemn or disqualify them. No one in the Colossian congregation is allowed to accept passively what others determine to be proper spirituality; women can be free from these false teachings and are responsible to live their lives in Christ Jesus. **11–13:** One wonders how the use of circumcision as an identifying mark would have impacted women of Colosse. Although Jewish women would have often heard this term used in a broad way and would have understood themselves as included among the chosen people of the circumcision (Gen 17:10–14), only males carried this mark (Gen 17:23–27). Circumcised individuals were not allowed into the gymnasium. Some Jews even had the equivalent of plastic surgery to remove the evidence of circumcision. Most Gentile women would have been unfamiliar with circumcision among their family members. It is hard to imagine that this image would have been an inspiring one for the women and girls of the Christian community at Colosse—or for the uncircumcised men and boys. Nonetheless, the explanation that all Christians were now granted a "spiritual circumcision," the cutting away of their sinful nature, and therefore needed no external representation of this status, must have fallen on grateful ears. For Christians the external representation of this death to the flesh and rebirth through faith is baptism, in which all believers can fully participate, regardless of gender. **18:** The Colossians have nonetheless been taken in by false teachings and have adopted a number of unnecessary religious practices. They were treating peripheral issues—ceremonies, the worship of angels, visions, and self-denial—as the focus of their belief instead of Christ. Paul describes the false teachings and warns the Colossians against them. It seems likely that a syncretism of various beliefs and practices was taking place. We can see Judaism reflected in references to circumcision and the Sabbath (vv. 11–13, 16), and Greco-Roman concerns reflected in the mentions of *knowledge, philosophies,* and *severe bodily discipline* (vv. 3, 8, 23). Possible allusions to dualism, astrology, Gnosticism, asceticism, and pagan mystery religions can also be seen (vv. 16, 18, 20–21, 23). **19:** Here Paul gives us an insight into his understanding of the function of the head in relationship to the rest of the body: It provides connection, communication, support, and strength. As in Ephesians 4:15–16, the head causes the body to grow and to build itself up in

So why do you keep on following the rules of
the world, such as, [21]"Don't handle! Don't taste!
Don't touch!"? [22]Such rules are mere human
teachings about things that deteriorate as we
use them. [23]These rules may seem wise because
they require strong devotion, pious self-denial,
and severe bodily discipline. But they provide no
help in conquering a person's evil desires.

Living the New Life

3 Since you have been raised to new life with
Christ, set your sights on the realities of
heaven, where Christ sits in the place of
honor at God's right hand. [2]Think about the
things of heaven, not the things of earth. [3]For
you died to this life, and your real life is hidden
with Christ in God. [4]And when Christ, who is
your* life, is revealed to the whole world, you
will share in all his glory.

[5]So put to death the sinful, earthly things
lurking within you. Have nothing to do with
sexual immorality, impurity, lust, and evil desires. Don't be greedy, for a greedy person is an
idolater, worshiping the things of this world.
[6]Because of these sins, the anger of God is coming.* [7]You used to do these things when your life
was still part of this world. [8]But now is the time
to get rid of anger, rage, malicious behavior, slander, and dirty language. [9]Don't lie to each other,
for you have stripped off your old sinful nature
and all its wicked deeds. [10]Put on your new nature, and be renewed as you learn to know your
Creator and become like him. [11]In this new life,
it doesn't matter if you are a Jew or a Gentile,*
circumcised or uncircumcised, barbaric, uncivilized,* slave, or free. Christ is all that matters,
and he lives in all of us.

[12]Since God chose you to be the holy people
he loves, you must clothe yourselves with tenderhearted mercy, kindness, humility, gentleness, and

3:4 Some manuscripts read *our.* **3:6** Some manuscripts read *is coming on all who disobey him.* **3:11a** Greek *a Greek.* **3:11b** Greek *Barbarian, Scythian.*

---

love. **20–23:** The Colossian Christians no longer need to submit to the rules of this world: "Don't handle, don't eat, don't touch." Women can now handle, taste, and touch, but more noteworthy is that women—often the object that was unclean and not to be touched (Lev 12; 15:1–33)—are now freed from this status.

3:1—4:6 Implications of Being in Christ

Paul's instruction for how to live one's life is tied to his emphasis that the Colossians are now fully in Christ. Their life is to be lived in a certain way, not because it will fulfill some religious obligation but because people who belong to Christ are people of a high morality. The Colossians are to have a realized eschatology: That is, they are to live lives that claim the reality of Christ's presence. They can and must act with a morality and compassion and conscientiousness that reflect their chosen status. **4:** To be in a public (or *revealed*) position of honor or glory would be an unusual and perhaps uncomfortable experience for women. Any grasping of this sort of position for themselves would be dishonorable in their culture. Now, however, Christ has won honor for women, and they (and men as well) must receive it. Women's honorable status in the community would have been earned through following the roles prescribed by their culture; stepping out of their domestic roles into any sort of public arena would have brought shame upon themselves and their families. They also would have been accustomed to having their honor protected by others; the men in their families would have been careful to do this. For women of this culture, passively accepting Christ's work on their behalf may have been easier than it was for the men of the first-century world and easier than it is for Christian women, children, and men today. **10:** With minds set on things above, the Colossians are to put to death immoral practices of the old nature, strip off negative attitudes, and clothe themselves with a new self that is being continually renewed in Christ. **11:** This description of this renewed self may disappoint those women who love the assertions of Galatians 3:28, "There is no longer Jew or Gentile, slave or free, male and female. For you are all one in Christ Jesus" (see 1 Cor 12:13, which also leaves this out). This omission is due far more to Paul's concerns to customize his message to the need of his immediate audience than it is to any lack of commitment to women's full inclusion in the body of Christ. In Galatians, Paul is likely responding to a Jewish prayer, "Oh God, thank you that I am not a Greek or a slave or a woman." Here in Colossians, however, Paul is more concerned with the unity in Christ of people from a variety of cultural backgrounds, Jewish and non-Jewish alike. **12–16:** Now Christian women are to clothe themselves with love as well as a brand new nature (v. 10). As a public sign of a woman's status and priorities, clothes needed to be chosen carefully (see 1 Tim 2:8–10 for an example of women who were clothing themselves with the wrong priorities; see also 1 Cor 11:5–6, 13; Jas 2:2–3; 1 Pet 3:3); now their first priority is being clothed in Christian love. Their freedom in Christ does not, however, mean a freedom from responsibility. They are told to *teach and coun-*

Childbearing and Rearing

In many places of the world, it is tradition immediately after birth to lay the newborn baby on the mother's breast: flesh on flesh, enveloped in love, warmth, and hope. A mother gazing tenderly upon her child, the fruit of sexual pleasure with her beloved, is a portrait of God looking lovingly upon creation (Gen 1:31). The intimacy of the ideal mother-child relationship resembles the love God has for us, children born of human desire but fashioned in the likeness of our Creator God. Jesus uses the analogy of a mother hen, who gathers the chicks and protects them under her wings, to refer to his love for the children of Jerusalem (Matt 23:37; Luke 13:34).

These word pictures rekindle within women shared emotional experiences of love, intimacy, protection, and survival. They raise the central themes of parenthood, of dependency and bonding, of resemblance and likeness, of closeness and nurture, and of the human need to be loved.

Scripture instructs mothers and fathers to love their children and to provide for their temporal and spiritual needs (1 Tim 5:8). The Judeo-Christian heritage has always taught that children are a gift from God. From the presentation of Samuel at the Tabernacle by Hannah (1 Sam 1:28) to Christ's words, "Let the children come to me" (Mark 10:14), Christian teaching holds a high view of children. The concepts of new life and new birth in Christ reinforce the notion that children and parenting are special motifs in the experience of Christians.

But parenting is far from easy. There is more to rearing children than feeding and housing them. Children need to be instructed and disciplined (Eph 6:4). In Deuteronomy 11:18–19 we read: "commit yourselves wholeheartedly to these words of mine. . . . Teach them to your children. Talk about them when you are at home and when you are on the road, when you are going to bed and when you are getting up." As Christian parents, we should never tire of telling our children the story of God's love and forgiveness, of miracles and commandments, of the Great Commission, and our collective call to compassion.

patience. 13 Make allowance for each other's faults,
and forgive anyone who offends you. Remember,
the Lord forgave you, so you must forgive others.
14 Above all, clothe yourselves with love, which
binds us all together in perfect harmony. 15 And
let the peace that comes from Christ rule in your
hearts. For as members of one body you are called
to live in peace. And always be thankful.
16 Let the message about Christ, in all its richness, fill your lives. Teach and counsel each other
with all the wisdom he gives. Sing psalms and
hymns and spiritual songs to God with thankful
hearts. 17 And whatever you do or say, do it as a
representative of the Lord Jesus, giving thanks
through him to God the Father.

Instructions for Christian Households

18 Wives, submit to your husbands, as is fitting
for those who belong to the Lord.
19 Husbands, love your wives and never treat
them harshly.
20 Children, always obey your parents, for this
pleases the Lord. 21 Fathers, do not aggravate your
children, or they will become discouraged.

sel each other, that is, to do the same sort of integral work that Paul and his co-workers did (Col 1:28; cf. 1 Thes 5:12; Titus 3:10). **17:** For women, who lived largely in the private, unseen world of small children, cooking utensils, and dirty laundry, the all-inclusive assertion that everything they did in word or deed could be done in Jesus' name would have given an added value to their lives and their ability to honor and please God.

3:18—4:1: Household Code. Such a code is a listing of moral obligations necessary to maintain order within the household. Similar codes can be found in Hellenistic and Jewish writings, as well as elsewhere in the New Testament (Eph 5:22—6:9; cf. 1 Tim 2:8–15; 6:1; Titus 2:1–10; 1 Pet 2:8—3:7). The code contains three pairs of reciprocal obligations that are motivated by the need to do all things in the name of the Lord. **3:18–19:** In the first pair wives are to *submit*, "be subject" (Gk., *hypotassesthe* plural reflexive imperative) to their husbands. This verb communicates a mutual submission arrangement in Ephesians 5:21; Paul did not use "obey" (*hypakouo*), which is found in the instructions to children and slaves (Col 3:20, 22), and this instruction to wives is balanced by the instruction that husbands *love* (*agapao*, Christian love) their wives and not make themselves a bitter taste in their wives' mouths (the verb *pikraino*, "to make a sharp or bitter taste," here is reflexive). **20–21:** The second pair of obligations is that children

22 Slaves, obey your earthly masters in everything you do. Try to please them all the time, not just when they are watching you. Serve them sincerely because of your reverent fear of the Lord. 23 Work willingly at whatever you do, as though you were working for the Lord rather than for people. 24 Remember that the Lord will give you an inheritance as your reward, and that the Master you are serving is Christ.* 25 But if you do what is wrong, you will be paid back for the wrong you have done. For God has no favorites.

4 Masters, be just and fair to your slaves. Remember that you also have a Master—in heaven.

An Encouragement for Prayer

2 Devote yourselves to prayer with an alert mind and a thankful heart. 3 Pray for us, too, that God will give us many opportunities to speak about his mysterious plan concerning Christ. That is why I am here in chains. 4 Pray that I will proclaim this message as clearly as I should.

5 Live wisely among those who are not believers, and make the most of every opportunity. 6 Let your conversation be gracious and attractive* so that you will have the right response for everyone.

Paul's Final Instructions and Greetings

7 Tychicus will give you a full report about how I am getting along. He is a beloved brother and faithful helper who serves with me in the Lord's work. 8 I have sent him to you for this very purpose—to let you know how we are doing and to encourage you. 9 I am also sending Onesimus, a faithful and beloved brother, one of your own

3:24 Or *and serve Christ as your Master.* **4:6** Greek *and seasoned with salt.*

---

obey both parents, and that fathers refrain from provoking their children (cf. Eph 6:1). No differentiation is made between girls or young children of both sexes, who would have been primarily within the sphere of mothers, and older boys, who were more likely to come within the sphere of their fathers. Children are addressed directly, as members of the community with the ability to hear and the responsibility to respond to these words; parents are not intermediaries between Paul's words and the children. The warning to fathers is a limitation to the standard father's role, which allowed for the customary beating of their children, and it indicates a sense of a father's complicity in family conflicts. **22–23:** In the third pair of obligations, the slaves receive noticeably lengthier instructions than do the masters (4:1), perhaps in light of the Colossians' familiarity with the situation of the runaway slave Onesimus. **4:1:** Paul does not directly challenge the social code of his time. He tells masters to treat their slaves justly, keeping their Master in heaven in mind, but he does not overturn the institution of slavery. For Paul, protecting the cause of Christ was always more important than trying to change or improve the secular culture.

4:2–6: Paul asks Christians to pray and to live their lives *wisely*, aware that outsiders would be watching their actions and listening to their speech. Believers needed to be conscientious, since many outsiders viewed Christians with great skepticism; for example, rumors that they practiced cannibalism and incestuous drunken orgies were widespread. When women in the early church sometimes broke from the customary behavior for women of that time, they could attract people to Christianity, or they could lead outsiders to draw the wrong conclusions. They needed to appear moral and upstanding by the broader society's cultural standards, but they were also required to exercise their freedom in Christ, practice their call by Christ (through Paul), evangelize, pray, resist false teachers, become strong in God, and perhaps even challenge some of those cultural norms. The early Christians would have felt acutely the tension between wanting to stand up and speak out for Christ and the need to avoid attracting the wrong kind of attention. The Roman Empire was quick to quash any movement perceived as a threat to its rule and interests. Modern women have the same sort of tensions. Many of us live lives that are different from those lives modeled for us by our mothers and grandmothers. We are in the workplace or homeschooling, we are pastors or church leaders, we are facing evolving issues as mothers, wives, and women in the twenty-first century. In our desire to be godly women, we want to follow the Bible's instructions in faith and practice, but there are often widely varying contemporary understandings of what that means. We want to be in this world enough to be able to relate to it and bring a Christian presence to it, and we also want to uphold Christian understandings of what it means to be a godly woman, without being needlessly constrained by outdated or misinformed social understandings of that concept. And we need to strike this balance in a way that does not give outsiders any reason to criticize our faith.

4:7–18 Closing: Greetings and Instructions

In closing his letter, Paul sends personal greetings and instructions to individuals at Colosse. **15:** Of

people. He and Tychicus will tell you everything
that's happening here.
10 Aristarchus, who is in prison with me, sends
you his greetings, and so does Mark, Barnabas's
cousin. As you were instructed before, make
Mark welcome if he comes your way. 11 Jesus
(the one we call Justus) also sends his greetings.
These are the only Jewish believers among my
co-workers; they are working with me here for
the Kingdom of God. And what a comfort they
have been!
12 Epaphras, a member of your own fellowship and a servant of Christ Jesus, sends you his
greetings. He always prays earnestly for you,
asking God to make you strong and perfect, fully
confident that you are following the whole will
of God. 13 I can assure you that he prays hard for
you and also for the believers in Laodicea and
Hierapolis.
14 Luke, the beloved doctor, sends his greetings,
and so does Demas. 15 Please give my greetings
to our brothers and sisters* at Laodicea, and to
Nympha and the church that meets in her house.
16 After you have read this letter, pass it on to
the church at Laodicea so they can read it, too.
And you should read the letter I wrote to them.
17 And say to Archippus, "Be sure to carry out
the ministry the Lord gave you."
18 HERE IS MY GREETING IN MY OWN HAND-
WRITING—PAUL.

Remember my chains.
May God's grace be with you.

4:15 Greek *brothers.*

most interest to us is Paul's greeting to *Nympha and the church that meets in her house.* While it is hard to be sure what Nympha's role in this church would have been, as the named host and owner of a house large enough for the church (most homes would have been very small) she would have been at the least a respected member and patron of the church. Given the prominence of her name in association with this house church, she is most likely its leader.

1 THESSALONIANS

INTRODUCTION

The first epistle to the church at Thessalonica claims Pauline authorship. The internal evidence of vocabulary, style, and theology supports this claim. Paul wrote the letter from Corinth either in AD 50 or 51. It represents the earliest of the Pauline Epistles and contains many of Paul's characteristic teaching emphases. Thus it provides insight into the lives, faith, and sufferings of some of the first Christians. First Thessalonians encourages believers to stand firm in the midst of life's trials. We must remain faithful and live with the expectation that Christ will return at any moment. This promised event is developed most fully in this epistle as well as in 2 Thessalonians.

Thessalonica stood as the largest and most important city in the Roman province and geographical area of Macedonia, that is, northern Greece. It was a free (self-governing) city and the capital of the province. It served as a commercial, transportation, and seaport city, due to its location on the important east-west road called the Ignatian Way and on the Thermaic Gulf at the head of the Aegean Sea. Cassandra, a general of Alexander the Great, founded the city in 315 BC. He named the city for his wife, Thessalonica, the daughter of Philip of Macedon and the half-sister of Alexander. The modern Greek city of Salonika is built on the same location as Thessalonica and reflects the ancient name.

Acts 17:1–9 relates Paul's initial ministry in Thessalonica. As was his custom, the apostle started his work in the Jewish synagogue. A good number of Jews, devout Greeks (Gentiles), and leading women responded to this ministry (Acts 17:4). Women enjoyed a higher status in Macedonia and Asia Minor than elsewhere. They held extensive economic rights, including the right over their dowry. They could buy, own, and sell goods and property. Women's degree of freedom and opportunity depended on their rank in society. Women of the poorer classes experienced fewer privileges. The prominent women who became charter members of the church at Thessalonica were possibly wealthy landowners, since the primary source of wealth was land. They probably enjoyed a high measure of political power and social prestige. Paul did not name any of these women in 1 Thessalonians. The rhetorically skilled orators and writers of that time tried to avoid mentioning the names of living, honorable, socially prominent women unless the circumstances warranted it. They would more likely mention by name women connected to their opponents, dead women, or women of questionable reputation.

Paul's success in Thessalonica provoked hostility among unbelieving Jews. Consequently, they started a riot, hauled some believers before the city authorities, and charged them with disloyalty to Caesar. The apostle realized it was time to leave in order to avoid bringing additional hardship on the Thessalonian believers. These Christians suffered persecution from the beginning of their commitment to Jesus Christ. The apostle wanted to encourage the Thessalonian believers as they faced intense persecution. He responded to criticism against his motives in Christian service by explaining how he had conducted his ministry in Thessalonica. The death of some members in the congregation led to questions about how they would participate in the coming return of Christ. Paul answered these questions and gave the church instructions about relating to fellow believers, God's will, and the healthy use of spiritual gifts. —*Sharon H. Gritz*

1:1–10	Greeting and Thanksgiving for the Thessalonians
2:1–12	Paul's Defense of His Thessalonian Ministry
2:13—3:13	Paul's Relationship to the Thessalonians
2:13–16	Thanksgiving for the Thessalonians' Endurance of Persecution
2:17–20	Paul's Desire to Visit
3:1–5	Paul's Willingness to Send Timothy
3:6–10	Paul's Joy and Thanksgiving for the Thessalonians' Progress
3:11–13	Paul's Prayer for the Thessalonians' Spiritual Growth
4:1—5:22	Doctrinal and Ethical Exhortations
4:1–12	Instructions about the Christian Life
4:13—5:11	Instructions about the Return of the Lord
5:12–22	Instructions about Life in the Church
5:23–28	Conclusion: Prayer, Requests, and Benediction

✧

Greetings from Paul

1 This letter is from Paul, Silas,* and Timothy.
We are writing to the church in Thessalonica, to you who belong to God the Father and
the Lord Jesus Christ.
May God give you grace and peace.

The Faith of the Thessalonian Believers

2 We always thank God for all of you and pray for
you constantly. 3 As we pray to our God and Father about you, we think of your faithful work,
your loving deeds, and the enduring hope you
have because of our Lord Jesus Christ.
4 We know, dear brothers and sisters,* that
God loves you and has chosen you to be his own
people. 5 For when we brought you the Good
News, it was not only with words but also with
power, for the Holy Spirit gave you full assurance* that what we said was true. And you know
of our concern for you from the way we lived
when we were with you. 6 So you received the
message with joy from the Holy Spirit in spite of
the severe suffering it brought you. In this way,
you imitated both us and the Lord. 7 As a result,
you have become an example to all the believers in Greece—throughout both Macedonia and
Achaia.*
8 And now the word of the Lord is ringing out
from you to people everywhere, even beyond
Macedonia and Achaia, for wherever we go we
find people telling us about your faith in God. We
don't need to tell them about it, 9 for they keep
talking about the wonderful welcome you gave
us and how you turned away from idols to serve
the living and true God. 10 And they speak of how

1:1 Greek *Silvanus,* the Greek form of the name. **1:4** Greek *brothers.* **1:5** Or *with the power of the Holy Spirit, so you can have full assurance.* **1:7** *Macedonia* and *Achaia* were the northern and southern regions of Greece.

1:1–10 Greeting and Thanksgiving for the Thessalonians

At the time of writing Silas and Timothy had just returned to Paul in Corinth from a mission to Macedonia (Acts 18:5).

1:2–10 Thanksgiving for the Thessalonians. 2–3: Timothy's good report about the Thessalonian church prompted the apostle to write this letter. Paul and his missionary associates expressed gratitude for what these readers were doing for Christ and for the Christian virtues that produced such effort. **4:** The apostle addressed the Thessalonians as brothers and sisters more than twenty times in 1 and 2 Thessalonians. **7:** Despite severe suffering, the response of the Thessalonians provided a model for all believers in Greece and in every place. This should encourage women living in the twenty-first century who suffer in any way as a result of their commitment to Jesus Christ. Women can influence others for God despite the obstacles placed in their path. **8–9:** The Thessalonians sounded forth the word of the Lord as an echo continues ringing out from a brass instrument. The fact that Paul described the Thessalonian believers as turning to God from idols indicates that most of these converts came from Gentile rather than Jewish backgrounds. **10:** The Lord's return is more than a doctrine; it is a promise. It has more than future implications. The second coming has a vital influence on how we conduct ourselves. We must live moral and holy lives, ever watchful for the return of our Lord.

you are looking forward to the coming of God's
Son from heaven—Jesus, whom God raised from
the dead. He is the one who has rescued us from
the terrors of the coming judgment.

Paul Remembers His Visit

2 You yourselves know, dear brothers and
sisters,* that our visit to you was not a
failure. 2 You know how badly we had been
treated at Philippi just before we came to you
and how much we suffered there. Yet our God
gave us the courage to declare his Good News to
you boldly, in spite of great opposition. 3 So you
can see we were not preaching with any deceit or
impure motives or trickery.

4 For we speak as messengers approved by
God to be entrusted with the Good News. Our
purpose is to please God, not people. He alone
examines the motives of our hearts. 5 Never once
did we try to win you with flattery, as you well
know. And God is our witness that we were not
pretending to be your friends just to get your
money! 6 As for human praise, we have never
sought it from you or anyone else.
7 As apostles of Christ we certainly had a right
to make some demands of you, but instead we
were like children* among you. Or we were like
a mother feeding and caring for her own children. 8 We loved you so much that we shared
with you not only God's Good News but our
own lives, too.

9 Don't you remember, dear brothers and sisters, how hard we worked among you? Night and
day we toiled to earn a living so that we would
not be a burden to any of you as we preached
God's Good News to you. 10 You yourselves are
our witnesses—and so is God—that we were devout and honest and faultless toward all of you
believers. 11 And you know that we treated each
of you as a father treats his own children. 12 We
pleaded with you, encouraged you, and urged
you to live your lives in a way that God would
consider worthy. For he called you to share in his
Kingdom and glory.

2:1 Greek *brothers;* also in 2:9, 14, 17. **2:7** Some manuscripts read *we were gentle.*

2:1–12 Paul's Defense of His Thessalonian Ministry

Paul had encountered great difficulties while serving in Thessalonica, yet he refused to quit or even be discouraged. As a result, his Thessalonian ministry achieved great success. **3:** Now the apostle appears to be defending himself against various charges brought by the Jews concerning his motives, actions, and general behavior. They had forced him to leave Thessalonica prematurely. Since his departure the Jews had apparently carried on a slander campaign against him. Paul insisted that he had pure motives. His preaching was free from error, motivated by unmixed reasons, untainted by trickery or deceit. He contrasted his motives and methods with those of pagan priests, exorcists, magicians, prophets, and philosophers. These pagans employed all kinds of tricks to take advantage of the gullible, but Paul did not work in this way. He refused to accept money from a church to which he was ministering at the time, a practice that further distinguished him from pagan teachers, who charged all the trade would bear. He supported himself by manual labor and offerings from other churches. **7:** Paul compared himself to a gentle nursing mother and to a caring father (v. 11). Christians need fatherly teaching and encouragement as well as motherly care. By using the female imagery to speak of his relationship to converts, Paul recalled the Old Testament metaphor of the divine maternal care of God's people. The Scriptures refer to God as a nursing mother to express the comfort and tender care that God gives (Isa 66:13). A nursing mother provides a natural source of nourishment for her child, one designed by the Creator God. A mother's milk provides important antibodies to protect the newborn child against infectious diseases. Breast-feeding creates a special bond between a mother and her baby. Nursing requires a mother's special commitment to her child by making physical and time demands on her. Through this unique relationship a child receives not only physical nourishment but also spiritual nurture. In showing her infant love, gentleness, and caring through breast-feeding, a mother models God's love, compassion, and concern for those created in the divine image. This beautiful maternal metaphor shows how believers should serve others, seeing them, as it were, through a mother's eyes and feeling for them as from a mother's heart. **9:** Paul's defense of his Thessalonian ministry provides a good manual for Christian ministers—women and men—especially those who endure hardship for the Lord. Women, as well as men, should conduct their ministries with integrity. Their motivation should always be to please and serve God, not themselves or their personal agendas. Where churches do not provide financial support for women in ministry, Paul's example offers guidance. Some women ministers may have to serve in a volunteer capacity, supporting themselves in bivocational service. Women can serve God in every occupation.

[13]Therefore, we never stop thanking God that
when you received his message from us, you
didn't think of our words as mere human ideas.
You accepted what we said as the very word of
God—which, of course, it is. And this word continues to work in you who believe.
[14]And then, dear brothers and sisters, you suffered persecution from your own countrymen.
In this way, you imitated the believers in God's
churches in Judea who, because of their belief in
Christ Jesus, suffered from their own people, the
Jews. [15]For some of the Jews killed the prophets,
and some even killed the Lord Jesus. Now they
have persecuted us, too. They fail to please God
and work against all humanity [16]as they try to
keep us from preaching the Good News of salvation to the Gentiles. By doing this, they continue
to pile up their sins. But the anger of God has
caught up with them at last.

Timothy's Good Report about the Church

[17]Dear brothers and sisters, after we were separated from you for a little while (though our hearts
never left you), we tried very hard to come back
because of our intense longing to see you again.
[18]We wanted very much to come to you, and I,
Paul, tried again and again, but Satan prevented
us. [19]After all, what gives us hope and joy, and
what will be our proud reward and crown as we
stand before our Lord Jesus when he returns? It
is you! [20]Yes, you are our pride and joy.

3 Finally, when we could stand it no longer,
we decided to stay alone in Athens, [2]and we
sent Timothy to visit you. He is our brother
and God's co-worker* in proclaiming the Good
News of Christ. We sent him to strengthen you,
to encourage you in your faith, [3]and to keep you
from being shaken by the troubles you were going through. But you know that we are destined
for such troubles. [4]Even while we were with you,
we warned you that troubles would soon come—
and they did, as you well know. [5]That is why,
when I could bear it no longer, I sent Timothy to
find out whether your faith was still strong. I was
afraid that the tempter had gotten the best of you
and that our work had been useless.
[6]But now Timothy has just returned, bring-

3:2 Other manuscripts read *and God's servant;* still others read *and a co-worker,* or *and a servant and co-worker for God,* or *and God's servant and our co-worker.*

2:13–3:13 Paul's Relationship to the Thessalonians

2:13–16 Thanksgiving for the Thessalonians' Endurance of Persecution. 14: Willingness to suffer for one's faith indicates its genuineness. In their suffering the Gentile majority in the Thessalonian church was following the example of Jewish Christians in Judea, who were being persecuted by their fellow Jews. **15:** As Paul thought about how *some* Jews helped to bring about the death of Jesus and then persecuted his followers in Palestine and abroad, he launched into the harshest attack on them in any of his letters. He echoed the approach of Old Testament prophets who denounced their people for departing from God's ways. **16:** Here Paul denounces those who would prevent him from proclaiming the gospel. How often women have been barred from this calling!

2:17–20 Paul's Desire to Visit. In a climactic way the apostle expressed his affection for the Thessalonians. These believers were his hope, joy, and crown of boasting before the Lord. Paul was describing his spiritual children. Women—as mothers, grandmothers, aunts, or other family relationships—know the intense pride children bring in who they are as well as in their accomplishments. Children can be a mother's hope, joy, and crown of boasting. Do we feel the same way toward our children in the faith? All women can participate in the spiritual birth and development of others. God calls all of us to make disciples.

3:1–5 Paul's Willingness to Send Timothy. 1: *Stay alone* implies a sense of abandonment. Paul felt that the Thessalonians had a need greater than his own. He was willing to do without his beloved co-worker, Timothy. God calls believers to put the needs of others above their own. Women, who already tend to practice self-denial, can set a clear example for the world by ordering their priorities according to God's Word. **5:** Greatly distressed by the intensity of the persecution that the Thessalonians faced, Paul sent Timothy to find out what was happening and to instruct the church further. Timothy could quietly return to the city because he was not as well known to the authorities as Paul. The apostle had told the Thessalonian Christians that they would suffer persecution. He was indicating that suffering represents a normal part of Christian experience. Most believers will experience some form of suffering, whether mild or severe, because of their commitment to Jesus Christ. Women possess no exemption in this matter.

3:6–10 Paul's Joy and Thanksgiving for the Thessalonians' Progress. 6–8: Timothy's return with a report

ing us good news about your faith and love. He
reports that you always remember our visit with
joy and that you want to see us as much as we
want to see you. [7]So we have been greatly encouraged in the midst of our troubles and suffering, dear brothers and sisters,* because you
have remained strong in your faith. [8]It gives us
new life to know that you are standing firm in
the Lord.

[9]How we thank God for you! Because of you
we have great joy as we enter God's presence.
[10]Night and day we pray earnestly for you, asking God to let us see you again to fill the gaps in
your faith.

[11]May God our Father and our Lord Jesus
bring us to you very soon. [12]And may the Lord
make your love for one another and for all people
grow and overflow, just as our love for you overflows. [13]May he, as a result, make your hearts
strong, blameless, and holy as you stand before
God our Father when our Lord Jesus comes again
with all his holy people. Amen.

Live to Please God

4 Finally, dear brothers and sisters,* we urge
you in the name of the Lord Jesus to live in
a way that pleases God, as we have taught
you. You live this way already, and we encourage you to do so even more. [2]For you remember
what we taught you by the authority of the Lord
Jesus.

[3]God's will is for you to be holy, so stay away
from all sexual sin. [4]Then each of you will control his own body* and live in holiness and hon-
or—[5]not in lustful passion like the pagans who
do not know God and his ways. [6]Never harm or
cheat a Christian brother in this matter by violating his wife,* for the Lord avenges all such sins,
as we have solemnly warned you before. [7]God
has called us to live holy lives, not impure lives.

3:7 Greek *brothers.* **4:1** Greek *brothers;* also in 4:10, 13. **4:4** Or *will know how to take a wife for himself;* or *will learn to live with his own wife;* Greek reads *will know how to possess his own vessel.* **4:6** Greek *Never harm or cheat a brother in this matter.*

of the Thessalonians' steadfastness rejuvenated Paul. He could say he now really lived since he had the certainty his readers would continue to stand firm in the Lord. Paul's attitude toward these converts reflects that of a mother for her children. He felt such a sense of oneness with the Thessalonians that he felt renewed as mothers really live when they know with certainty that their children are doing what they should be doing. Their achievements bring encouragement and renewal.

3:11–13 Paul's Prayer for the Thessalonians' Spiritual Growth. 11–13: Prayer has increasingly become an important area of ministry for women. These intercessory prayer efforts require time, commitment, perseverance, and strength because the struggle is not against enemies of flesh and blood (Eph 6:12). Women have made a difference in the lives of their family members, in their country, and in the spread of the gospel by approaching God's throne of grace boldly on behalf of others. Prayer unleashes God's power. It changes people according to the divine will. Women prayer warriors have greatly affected the kingdom of God.

4:1—5:22 Doctrinal and Ethical Exhortations

4:1–12 Instructions about the Christian Life. 1: God's will for his people is their sanctification, the process of being made holy or set apart, dedicated to God and God's purposes. Sanctification results in a changed lifestyle for believers. God sets Christians apart at their conversion. They live out that dedication in holiness as the Holy Sprit works to conform them to the image of Jesus Christ. **3:** Sanctification involves not only believers' spiritual lives but also their physical and sexual lives. Sexual laxity characterized life in the first-century Roman Empire, especially in Greece. Many of the pagan cults featured inappropriate sexual expression in their practices, including sacred prostitution and lewd gestures as a part of worship. Some pagan religions taught that ritual coitus promoted fertility and blessing. The prevailing sexual laxity that Paul witnessed throughout the Roman Empire caused him to remind his readers that sexual purity represents the will of God. Sexual holiness gives value to God's gift of sex. It prevents the treatment of women and men as sex objects. **4:** *Control his own body* literally means "possess his own vessel." This expression has been interpreted as referring either to taking a wife or to controlling the body, particularly the male sexual organ. Paul desired that this vessel be honored, not dishonored and degraded. One could interpret this as the apostle's warning against relating to one's wife in a lustful manner. **6:** Living a sanctified life involves abstaining from any sort of sexual immorality, whether this involves the abuse of a wife in the passion of lust or the defrauding of a Christian brother through an adulterous relationship with his wife. Paul was warning the men among his readers that misconduct in marriage is just as much a sin as the offense of adultery. **7–8:** Paul made it clear that God had not called believers to trifle with sexual

8 Therefore, anyone who refuses to live by these
rules is not disobeying human teaching but is rejecting God, who gives his Holy Spirit to you.
9 But we don't need to write to you about the
importance of loving each other,* for God himself has taught you to love one another. 10 Indeed,
you already show your love for all the believers* throughout Macedonia. Even so, dear brothers and sisters, we urge you to love them even
more.
11 Make it your goal to live a quiet life, minding your own business and working with your
hands, just as we instructed you before. 12 Then
people who are not Christians will respect the
way you live, and you will not need to depend
on others.

The Hope of the Resurrection

13 And now, dear brothers and sisters, we want
you to know what will happen to the believers
who have died* so you will not grieve like people
who have no hope. 14 For since we believe that
Jesus died and was raised to life again, we also
believe that when Jesus returns, God will bring
back with him the believers who have died.
15 We tell you this directly from the Lord: We
who are still living when the Lord returns will
not meet him ahead of those who have died.*
16 For the Lord himself will come down from
heaven with a commanding shout, with the voice
of the archangel, and with the trumpet call of
God. First, the Christians who have died* will
rise from their graves. 17 Then, together with
them, we who are still alive and remain on the
earth will be caught up in the clouds to meet the
Lord in the air. Then we will be with the Lord
forever. 18 So encourage each other with these
words.

5 Now concerning how and when all this
will happen, dear brothers and sisters,* we
don't really need to write you. 2 For you
know quite well that the day of the Lord's return
will come unexpectedly, like a thief in the night.
3 When people are saying, "Everything is peaceful and secure," then disaster will fall on them
as suddenly as a pregnant woman's labor pains
begin. And there will be no escape.
4 But you aren't in the dark about these things,

4:9 Greek *about brotherly love.* **4:10** Greek *the brothers.* **4:13** Greek *those who have fallen asleep;* also in 4:14. **4:15** Greek *those who have fallen asleep.* **4:16** Greek *the dead in Christ.* **5:1** Greek *brothers;* also in 5:4, 12, 14, 25, 26, 27.

impurity but to live a holy life. **9–10:** In addition to maintaining moral purity, the Thessalonians needed to deepen their love for one another. They were already loving their fellow believers, yet all Christians in regard to Christian virtues can do even more. **11:** Paul insisted on the necessity of work. In doing so he dignified manual labor, something upper-class Greeks and Romans despised. Evidently some people in the church had quit their jobs, possibly in anticipation of an imminent return of the Lord. The result was excessive excitement, meddling in the affairs of others, and dependence on others for support. Meddling in the affairs of others as busybodies brings to mind the stereotype of gossiping women. Gossip has a destructive force; it destroys unity and trust and endangers relationships. Women as well as men must learn to control their tongues.

4:13—5:11 Instructions about the Return of the Lord. 4:13: As did many of the early Christians, the Thessalonians naively assumed that Christ would return during their lifetime. When some of their fellow believers died, they became concerned that these would miss some of the benefits of Christ's return. Paul reassured his readers that, far from being at a disadvantage, the Christian dead would take precedence over living Christians. At the return of Christ, the dead would rise first and go to meet the Lord. The dead would then be joined in the Lord's presence by living believers. **15:** The event when the Christian living will be caught up with the dead in Christ to meet the descending Lord in the air is sometimes called the "rapture" because the Latin verb *rapere* means "caught up." **17:** Secular Greek writings sometimes used the word translated *meet* (*parousia*) to describe how the people of a city would go out to meet a visiting king or general and accompany him back to their city in festal procession. This word has come to refer to Christ's return. Whatever the particular events connected with the Lord's return, the parousia will result in unending fellowship between Christ and his people. **5:1:** Believers in Thessalonica were asking, "When will the Lord return?" Paul indicated that they did not need additional instruction about the timing of the return. For most human beings that event would occur suddenly, unexpectedly, like the coming of a thief. **3:** To make vivid the sudden, unexpected disaster that will come upon non-Christians engaged in their daily, ordinary pursuits, Paul used an analogy. The onset of labor points to the inevitable birth to follow. This image indicates that unbelievers will have no possible escape from God's judgment when the Lord returns. It conveys the urgency of being ready or prepared. Mothers know the sudden pain and helplessness when labor takes them by surprise. They have no opportunity to change their

dear brothers and sisters, and you won't be surprised when the day of the Lord comes like a
thief.* 5 For you are all children of the light and
of the day; we don't belong to darkness and night.
6 So be on your guard, not asleep like the others.
Stay alert and be clearheaded. 7 Night is the time
when people sleep and drinkers get drunk. 8 But
let us who live in the light be clearheaded, protected by the armor of faith and love, and wearing
as our helmet the confidence of our salvation.
9 For God chose to save us through our Lord
Jesus Christ, not to pour out his anger on us.
10 Christ died for us so that, whether we are dead
or alive when he returns, we can live with him
forever. 11 So encourage each other and build each
other up, just as you are already doing.

Paul's Final Advice

12 Dear brothers and sisters, honor those who
are your leaders in the Lord's work. They work
hard among you and give you spiritual guidance.
13 Show them great respect and wholehearted
love because of their work. And live peacefully
with each other.
14 Brothers and sisters, we urge you to warn
those who are lazy. Encourage those who are
timid. Take tender care of those who are weak.
Be patient with everyone.
15 See that no one pays back evil for evil, but
always try to do good to each other and to all
people.
16 Always be joyful. 17 Never stop praying.
18 Be thankful in all circumstances, for this is
God's will for you who belong to Christ Jesus.
19 Do not stifle the Holy Spirit. 20 Do not scoff
at prophecies, 21 but test everything that is said.
Hold on to what is good. 22 Stay away from every
kind of evil.

Paul's Final Greetings

23 Now may the God of peace make you holy in
every way, and may your whole spirit and soul
and body be kept blameless until our Lord Jesus
Christ comes again. 24 God will make this happen,
for he who calls you is faithful.
25 Dear brothers and sisters, pray for us.
26 Greet all the brothers and sisters with
Christian love.*
27 I command you in the name of the Lord to
read this letter to all the brothers and sisters.
28 May the grace of our Lord Jesus Christ be
with you.

5:4 Some manuscripts read *comes upon you as if you were thieves.* **5:26** Greek *with a holy kiss.*

minds. **4–11:** Believers should prepare for the Lord's return by disciplined, godly living supported by attitudes of faith, love, and hope. Paul wanted to discourage rationalistic speculation about the time of the parousia. He insisted that watching for Jesus' return involved consistent living in obedience to the Lord's commands.

5:12–22 Instructions about Life in the Church. 12: The apostle did not give any clues to indicate the extent to which women participated in activities in the church in Thessalonica. He named neither male nor female leaders but directed all of his readers to acknowledge God's sovereignty and providence by expressing thanks in all circumstances. **19:** He urged the Thessalonians to accept the gifts of the Spirit with an openness characterized by a discerning evaluation of the gift. All of us should beware stifling the gift of the Spirit in those whom God has called.

5:23–28 Conclusion: Prayer, Requests, and Benediction

Paul concluded his letter with a prayer for the consecration of his readers and a reminder of God's faithfulness in directing their sanctification. He requested prayer for himself and urged his friends to greet one another with the holy kiss of warmth and love. The kiss symbolized the bond that unites believers. Paul's benediction focused on his favorite concept—grace.

2 THESSALONIANS

INTRODUCTION

Second Thessalonians is unusual in containing both apocalyptic material and recommendations for social improvements. Ordinarily apocalyptic literature focuses on the dire straits in which a society finds itself and predicts that the situation will get worse until God's final intervention. Women view apocalyptic literature with particular discomfort because it describes hostility that will be directed against them (Dan 11:37; Rev 12:13–17) and foretells dangers to which they, as nurturers and caregivers, are particularly vulnerable. War, famine, and natural disasters exact a horrible toll on women and on all that they hold dear. Jesus expressed the deepest fears of women as he walked the way of sorrows (Luke 23:27–31).

Upper-class, well-educated women had responded enthusiastically to Paul and Silas's original mission to Thessalonica (Acts 17:4) and were a significant part of the body of believers, so it is appropriate that anxieties common to women should be addressed. The city, located on the main road that stretched from east to west in the Roman Empire, had become the locus of persecution for Christians. As the afflictions worsened, it was natural to assume that the end of the world was at hand. The sufferers considered themselves powerless to do anything except to await deliverance from God.

In this epistle, the message is one of encouragement and common sense for those who are obsessed by the imminence of Christ's second coming. The result is fear, frustration, and dysfunction. Paul calls them to calmness of spirit, to orderly and constructive conduct, and to faithful discharge of duty. —*Janet Nasambu Kassilly*

1:1–4	Comfort for the Thessalonians
1:5–12	God Will Set All Things Right
2:1–12	Implications of the Second Coming
2:13—3:15	Positive Faith for Here and Now
3:16–18	Closing Greetings

Greetings from Paul

1 This letter is from Paul, Silas,* and Timothy.
We are writing to the church in Thessalonica, to you who belong to God our Father and
the Lord Jesus Christ.
2 May God our Father* and the Lord Jesus
Christ give you grace and peace.

Encouragement during Persecution

3 Dear brothers and sisters,* we can't help but
thank God for you, because your faith is flourishing and your love for one another is growing. 4 We proudly tell God's other churches about
your endurance and faithfulness in all the persecutions and hardships you are suffering. 5 And
God will use this persecution to show his justice
and to make you worthy of his Kingdom, for
which you are suffering. 6 In his justice he will
pay back those who persecute you.
7 And God will provide rest for you who are
being persecuted and also for us when the Lord
Jesus appears from heaven. He will come with his
mighty angels, 8 in flaming fire, bringing judgment
on those who don't know God and on those who
refuse to obey the Good News of our Lord Jesus.
9 They will be punished with eternal destruction,
forever separated from the Lord and from his glorious power. 10 When he comes on that day, he will
receive glory from his holy people—praise from
all who believe. And this includes you, for you believed what we told you about him.
11 So we keep on praying for you, asking our

1:1 Greek *Silvanus,* the Greek form of the name. **1:2** Some manuscripts read *God the Father.* **1:3** Greek *Brothers.*

1:1–4 Comfort for the Thessalonians

The ascription speaks of *Silas* and *Timothy*, with *Paul* sharing in the composition. Dual authorship is ascribed in several epistles, but triple authorship appears unique to the Thessalonian letters (cf. 1 Thes 1:1). Timothy, perhaps in company with Silas, delivered the first letter to the church at Thessalonica (1 Thes 3:2, 6). They appear to have joined Paul in composing a second treatise shortly after their return to Corinth in AD 51 or 52. Whether in writing, traveling, tent making, or proclaiming the gospel, Paul is usually found as part of a team in which there is lively interaction. **2–3:** Through the *grace* of Christ we know the *peace* of God and the power of new life that restores broken harmonies. **4:** The Thessalonians' Christian witness has advanced even beyond their excellent showing from the last time Paul wrote. He stresses the strong relationship between their faith and their lives. The ensuing fusion results in a correspondingly greater consideration for each other. The apostle is proud of their endurance and faithfulness during persecutions. Their faith gives them power to endure.

1:5–12 God Will Set All Things Right

Paul comforts the Thessalonians by pointing out how the righteous judgment of God shows itself. There will be everlasting reward for their faith and patience in their suffering for the gospel, along with punishment for their persecutors. The Thessalonians' faith has been strengthened rather than weakened by adversity; they have been given power to endure all the ills that befall them. This is the surest indicator that there is a just God who cares for his people. He is nearer to them in affliction than in prosperity, thus giving proof of where his final judgment will fall between them and their persecutors. **7–9:** God has pledged that however much evil seems to triumph, victory would be theirs. Furthermore, by these hardships they are being fitted for full citizenship as redeemed saints in Christ's kingdom. When the day of the Lord comes, the humble and faithful who have borne the assaults of the world will find that worldly judgments are overturned. God's justice, of which even now they have proof, will vindicate those who have kept faith. God's justice, like his wrath (Rom 1:18), is inherent in the nature of a moral universe. Because God is the ruler of that universe, retribution for sin is a part of life, either here or in the hereafter (Luke 16:25). Here the emphasis is on the final vindication of goodness and the punishment of evil. This is consolation for women, who so often suffer injustice without being able to defend themselves. The mention of flaming fire recalls the appearance of God at Sinai (Deut 33:2; Exod 3:2; Isa 66:15). Christ's glory, which is at present hidden from the mass of humankind, though glimpsed by faithful Christians, will become manifest. Those who do not know God are presumably pagans. They will be punished because they have willfully disregarded the knowledge of God that they did possess. Humankind is judged on its response to the light that it is given (John 3:18–19). **10:** The apostle gives a word of comfort for any despondent Thessalonian—and women are particularly susceptible to despondency. Through all their stumbling and falling, their sense of unworthiness was the surest proof that they were still Christ's people and that they would take their place among his folk on his day. **11–12:** Their example of Christian behavior will be a testimony to the Lord on his day. He will be glorified in them, and they will be glorified in him. To be known as Christ's people at his coming will be to share in the honor paid to him.

God to enable you to live a life worthy of his
call. May he give you the power to accomplish
all the good things your faith prompts you to do.
[12]Then the name of our Lord Jesus will be honored because of the way you live, and you will
be honored along with him. This is all made possible because of the grace of our God and Lord,
Jesus Christ.*

Events prior to the Lord's Second Coming

2 Now, dear brothers and sisters,* let us
clarify some things about the coming of
our Lord Jesus Christ and how we will be
gathered to meet him. [2]Don't be so easily shak-
en or alarmed by those who say that the day of
the Lord has already begun. Don't believe them,
even if they claim to have had a spiritual vision, a
revelation, or a letter supposedly from us. [3]Don't
be fooled by what they say. For that day will not
come until there is a great rebellion against God
and the man of lawlessness* is revealed—the
one who brings destruction.* [4]He will exalt himself and defy everything that people call god and
every object of worship. He will even sit in the
temple of God, claiming that he himself is God.
[5]Don't you remember that I told you about
all this when I was with you? [6]And you know
what is holding him back, for he can be revealed
only when his time comes. [7]For this lawlessness
is already at work secretly, and it will remain secret until the one who is holding it back steps out
of the way. [8]Then the man of lawlessness will be
revealed, but the Lord Jesus will kill him with
the breath of his mouth and destroy him by the
splendor of his coming.

[9]This man will come to do the work of Satan
with counterfeit power and signs and miracles.
[10]He will use every kind of evil deception to fool
those on their way to destruction, because they
refuse to love and accept the truth that would
save them. [11]So God will cause them to be greatly
deceived, and they will believe these lies. [12]Then
they will be condemned for enjoying evil rather
than believing the truth.

Believers Should Stand Firm

[13]As for us, we can't help but thank God for you,
dear brothers and sisters loved by the Lord. We

1:12 Or *of our God and our Lord Jesus Christ.* **2:1** Greek *brothers;* also in 2:13, 15. **2:3a** Some manuscripts read *the man of sin.* **2:3b** Greek *the son of destruction.*

2:1–12 Implications of the Second Coming

Excitement and unrest seem to have grown in Thessalonica since Paul's first letter. Talk about the second advent and judgment appear to have unsettled Christians' minds and habits. They have been misled by what has been said by others and from a fraudulent letter that purported to be from the apostolic team. The problem of false prophets and false missives was a real one in the early church, and women and men who were leaders of house churches had to discern what documents and what teachers they would receive as genuine (Acts 12:12–17; 2 Jn 7–11; see 3 Jn). **3–4:** Therefore Paul deals with the signs that must precede the end. Before the last day, the man of lawlessness, who is at present held in restraint, must appear in the world as the antithesis of all goodness, yet he is likely to be mistaken for Christ. Until then, it is futile to talk as if the end of the world were already upon them. The apocalypse will not be realized unless the rebellion comes first. God has a fixed order for the final events. The word *rebellion* (lit., "apostasy") refers to one of the unnatural portents and manifestations that precede the end of the world. It will take the form of a widespread and violent defiance of the authority of God. Along with it will come *the man of lawlessness,* a man of sin whose character is the essence of evil. In the description are traits of ancient tyrants (e.g., Antiochus Epiphanes, Caligula, Nero). **5–6:** Paul holds before the readers the certainty of the Lord's coming and what it will entail. At the Lord's advent, he had already told them, believers who are still alive will be gathered to meet him and the resurrected saints in the air (1 Thes 4:15–17). **7–12:** The result of rejecting God's truth will be moral and spiritual death as humankind falls under the evil spell and forfeits its chance of salvation. The two traditional aspects of Antichrist—the demonic and the human—remind us that evil, like God's mercy that is new every morning, is the same in principle throughout the ages. It is a force of darkness calling mortals to its service and binding them fast in its chains. Evil as an abstraction must always be incarnated in human personalities. Evil is in all of us. Only when the evil in humankind is overcome, when Antichrist is vanquished by Christ, will God's kingly rule be complete. Whether it comes quickly, as the early church believed, or whether slowly by the spread of the gospel, it is an act of God alone.

2:13—3:15 Positive Faith for Here and Now

Christ loved the Thessalonians, and God chose them for salvation (2:13–14). He has honored them by choosing them to be first in his new order of creation and therefore an offering to himself. He chose them from the beginning, for their knowledge and experience of his loving grace had its roots in the mind and

Paul's Use of Feminine Imagery

It is a little-known fact that Paul uses maternal imagery quite often. Female images surface in descriptions of Christ, calling, eschatological deliverance, and ministry especially. Paul weaves Old Testament female personifications of divine wisdom into his Christology (see Images of God as Female, Deut 32). The apostle uses birth imagery to describe his call (Gal 1:15; 1 Cor 15:8; see Birth Pain Imagery, John 16). And in his descriptions of eschatological deliverance, all creation groans, waiting to give birth—an image of eschatological hope (Rom 8:22; cf. Isa 13:8). Believers likewise groan, awaiting not their birth but their adoption (Rom 8:23).

Paul compares himself with a woman in labor, a conventional metaphor signifying anguish and anticipation (Gal 4:19). It is a second labor for Paul; he awaits not the believers' birth but for Christ to be formed in his "dear children."

In describing his apostolic leadership, Paul refers to himself as a wet nurse (1 Thes 2:7–8; cf. Num 11:12). He did not stop at giving the Thessalonians the gospel but shared with them his very substance (1 Thes 2:8), as a nurse does when she gives milk from her breast. This nursing image is one of three familial figures that Paul employs in succession in order to clarify his motivations and style of ministry. Apostles are unassuming and guileless like infants (1Thes 2:7), tender and self-giving like women who nurse (1 Thes 2:7–8), and directive like fathers who instruct and encourage (1 Thes 2:11). Together, these familial figures reinforce ministry as connectedness.

The nursing image, axiomatic in antiquity for nurture and affection, radicalizes ministry by locating authority outside customary expectations. Ecclesiastical authority is redefined as intimate relationality: In contrast to professional codes of conduct, Paul expresses his feelings of deep attachment and tenderness toward the Thessalonians. Imagery of nursing an infant further reconceptualizes ecclesiastical authority as self-giving vulnerability rather than demands for the rights of office. In the eyes of the world, this Christlike style of ministry (Phil 2:5–8) is too often devalued and ridiculed (1 Cor 4:9–13). Chastising the Corinthians for being too spiritually immature to be weaned, Paul likens his task to a mother's, who diligently works to wean her child from milk to solid food (1 Cor 3:2).

The early church was aware of female images for ministry. In the Priscilla catacombs in Rome, an ancient fresco depicts a woman suckling an infant; nearby, a bishop appoints a woman with similar features to ministry. The third-century artist may have been drawing upon Paul's infant/nurse imagery to memorialize the nurturing, relational, self-giving style of the decedent's ministry, a style that Paul daringly advocates for all who minister.

are always thankful that God chose you to be
among the first* to experience salvation—a salvation that came through the Spirit who makes
you holy and through your belief in the truth.
14 He called you to salvation when we told you
the Good News; now you can share in the glory
of our Lord Jesus Christ.
15 With all these things in mind, dear brothers
and sisters, stand firm and keep a strong grip on
the teaching we passed on to you both in person
and by letter.
16 Now may our Lord Jesus Christ himself and
God our Father, who loved us and by his grace
gave us eternal comfort and a wonderful hope,
17 comfort you and strengthen you in every good
thing you do and say.

Paul's Request for Prayer

3 Finally, dear brothers and sisters,* we ask
you to pray for us. Pray that the Lord's
message will spread rapidly and be honored
wherever it goes, just as when it came to you.
2 Pray, too, that we will be rescued from wicked

2:13 Some manuscripts read *chose you from the very beginning.* **3:1** Greek *brothers;* also in 3:6, 13.

intention of God from before the world was made. **2:15–17:** Order must be restored in a community that should be living and working soberly and prayerfully so that when the Lord comes, he should not find them off course. Instead, they were behaving like a ship that had been insecurely anchored, had broken from its moorings, and was blown here and there by every rumor or chance remark that the end of the world has come. There is no reason to think that the end of the world is upon them (cf. Matt 24:26–27; Luke 17:23–24). The concern must be for the spiritual readiness of the people. **3:1:** The Lord's message is spoken of as if it were almost an independent spiritual force not relying on the eloquence and physical powers of the

and evil people, for not everyone is a believer.
3 But the Lord is faithful; he will strengthen you
and guard you from the evil one.* 4 And we are
confident in the Lord that you are doing and will
continue to do the things we commanded you.
5 May the Lord lead your hearts into a full understanding and expression of the love of God and
the patient endurance that comes from Christ.

An Exhortation to Proper Living

6 And now, dear brothers and sisters, we give you
this command in the name of our Lord Jesus
Christ: Stay away from all believers* who live
idle lives and don't follow the tradition they received* from us. 7 For you know that you ought
to imitate us. We were not idle when we were
with you. 8 We never accepted food from anyone
without paying for it. We worked hard day and
night so we would not be a burden to any of you.
9 We certainly had the right to ask you to feed us,
but we wanted to give you an example to follow.
10 Even while we were with you, we gave you this
command: "Those unwilling to work will not get
to eat."
11 Yet we hear that some of you are living idle
lives, refusing to work and meddling in other
people's business. 12 We command such people
and urge them in the name of the Lord Jesus
Christ to settle down and work to earn their own
living. 13 As for the rest of you, dear brothers and
sisters, never get tired of doing good.
14 Take note of those who refuse to obey what
we say in this letter. Stay away from them so
they will be ashamed. 15 Don't think of them as
enemies, but warn them as you would a brother
or sister.*

Paul's Final Greetings

16 Now may the Lord of peace himself give you
his peace at all times and in every situation. The
Lord be with you all.
17 HERE IS MY GREETING IN MY OWN HANDWRIT-
ING—PAUL. I DO THIS IN ALL MY LETTERS TO PROVE
THEY ARE FROM ME.
18 May the grace of our Lord Jesus Christ be
with you all.

3:3 Or *from evil.* **3:6a** Greek *from every brother.* **3:6b** Some manuscripts read *you received.* **3:15** Greek *as a brother.*

missionaries. In an expression used only of the honor due to God or Christ, Paul speaks of the gospel's triumph or glory. **2–5:** The Thessalonians should pray that the apostles may be delivered from perverse or *wicked and evil people*. It was just such local thugs who had been stirred up by opponents to Paul while he was in Thessalonica (Acts 17:5). The Greek word (*atopos*) literally means "having no place or position" (i.e., in society). These ruffians stand in direct contrast to the upper-class women who were incited to hostility against Paul in Antioch of Pisidia (Acts 13:50). But here Paul's methods and message were warmly received by women. **6–15:** Paul had had occasion in his first letter to caution the converts gently about the danger of allowing advent expectations to unsettle them. Some were reluctant to carry on their ordinary work, for they felt the time was short, and others felt unready to meet their Lord. While their endeavors might have seemed profitless in view of the Lord's immediate return, it also provided a theological pretext for idleness. Since Christians were willing to share with others of the faith, the situation lent itself to serious exploitation by those who were indisposed to honest labor. **11–12:** The Greek word *hesychia*, sometimes applied to women's silence (1 Tim 2:11–12), means to refrain from *meddling in other people's business* and to tend to one's own affairs. In 1 Thessalonians 4:11, the same sense is found in the verbal form *hesychazein*. The adjectival *hesychios* means a "quiet and peaceable life" (1 Tim 2:2). Perhaps its use here can help us to understand women's *hesychia* in 1 Timothy 2:11–12: Rather than indicating that women may not speak, it may mean that they should avoid idleness, mind their own business, and behave in a discreet fashion. **14:** Hence the stern injunction treated in threefold manner. First Paul cites his example of independence and self-support. He further appeals to the loafers to go back to their jobs. If these admonitions fail, he instructs the congregation to have nothing to do with the offending members, so that they will be ashamed. The rule of the Thessalonians was that people were "to do their work quietly and to earn their own living."

3:16–18 Closing Greetings

The letter ends with Paul's own autograph, and a prayer that God's grace might be with them all—with mourners, with the distraught, with the victims of persecution, with those who need him most.

1 TIMOTHY

INTRODUCTION

The best way to approach this epistle is to follow the admonition of 1 Timothy itself: These sacred things are not to be understood by clever human arguments or by endless disputations (6:3–5). They can be apprehended only by faith. The first element of faith is to trust the Lord with the outcome. The reader must allow the epistle to speak for itself and be open to the Word of God, whatever it might say. With this approach, we find a high degree of contemporary relevance in the epistle. Specifically, we find there an approach to women that is astonishingly modern for its time. We also find the Holy Spirit at work as we contemplate the basis of the instruction contained in the letter: Honoring the Lord is the index of our understanding and our behavior, and anything less falls short of Christianity. As in 4:6–10, "We have set [our] hope [entirely] upon God, the living One who is Deliverer of all people" (translations within quotation marks are author's unless otherwise noted; quotations from the NLT in the annotations are in italics).

Authorship

There are several arguments concerning the authorship of 1 Timothy. First, some interpreters maintain that the chronology of the letter does not fit with the account of Paul's journeys in Acts. Second, the Pastoral Epistles contain genuinely Pauline ideas and concerns, but differ in style and vocabulary from the generally accepted letters of Paul. Possibly a disciple of Paul wrote the letter in his name—a common and accepted practice in the ancient Near East. Countering this argument, Paul's letters contain a quantity of *hapax legomenoi* (Gk., "things said once")—terms that occur only once in the Bible. Thus vocabulary alone is not determinative.

Concerning style, 1 Timothy is less emotional than Paul generally is when confronted with a "different gospel." (See Gal 1:6—3:1, where Paul berates the Galatians for following a nongospel message.) Also, in 1 Timothy, Paul does not, as usual, explicitly contrast the law (of Moses) with the working of the Holy Spirit. However, that message is very much present in the letter. See, for instance, the contrast drawn between faith-engendered behavior (4:4–6) and the pseudo-ascetic practices upheld in the "different teaching" (1:4–5; 4:1–3). Paul's personal investment (and his strong feelings) are evident in his determination to come personally to deal with the issues (3:14–15).

Finally, certain elements in the letter seem to be dated later than the mid-first century when Paul wrote his letters. On the other hand, the same "late" doctrines discussed here were already current in Paul's time.

The history of the interpretation of the Pastoral Epistles has been significantly one of reading into the text the cultural expectations of the interpreter. In particular, assumptions about the terms and ideas in the letters contribute to a discussion about their authorship that has no real resolution. The letters are usually assumed to decree women's silence and subjection, for all of the church and for all time. A careful reading reveals a more thoughtful and supportive attitude toward women, slaves, and others than is sometimes supposed.

Occasion

The occasion of the letter is twofold. It instructs Timothy to center his ministry upon the Holy Scriptures and our ransom by Jesus Christ, and to govern his own behavior through godliness (lit., "worshipfulness of life"), love, and a good conscience. And it conveys unequivocally that, despite Timothy's youth, Paul's full authority stands behind him.

The express purpose of the letter is to explain "how people must conduct themselves in the household of God" (3:15) as they must respond to those who deviate from the standards of the gospel both in doctrine and behavior.

Paul counsels Timothy to preserve peaceful relations with the Ephesian pagans, and in the church to read the Scriptures, preach, and teach (4:13–16). Overall, Timothy must fight the good fight to guard the deposit of faith that has been entrusted to him (6:20). In his own time, the Lord will appear again and reveal to all the truth of the gospel (6:14–16).

Structure

The outline shows the organization of the epistle. We suggest reading the entire letter and then rereading in sequence all of the sections here labeled "instructions to Timothy" as a guide to Christian ministry. —*Kamila A. Blessing*

1:1–2	Greeting
1:3–7	Initial Instructions to Timothy
1:8–11	The Law and Its Proper Use
1:12–17	Paul's Conversion and God's Mercy
1:18–20	Instructions to Timothy; Two Blasphemers
2:1—6:2	Conduct in the House of the Lord: The Roles of Various Groups in the Church
2:1–8	Paul Commands Prayer for All People
2:9–15	The Role of Women in the Church
3:1–7	The Role of the Overseer (Elder)
3:8–13	The Role of the "Servant" (Deacon)
3:14–16	Paul's Intent to Visit and a Doxology
4:1–3	Heresy and Hypocrisy Foretold
4:4—5:2	Instructions to Timothy: The Role of the Minister
5:3–16	The Role of Widows; Who Should Support Them
5:17–20	The Role of Elders
5:21–25	Instructions to Timothy on Appointing Officers of the Church
6:1–2	The Role of Believing Slaves; Behavior toward Their Masters
6:3–21a	Recapitulation of the Problem, Focusing on the Problem of Money
6:3–10	Of False Teachers; of Money and Its Place in the Life of the Believer
6:11–21a	Final Instructions to Timothy
6:21b	Closing

Greetings from Paul

1 This letter is from Paul, an apostle of Christ
Jesus, appointed by the command of God
our Savior and Christ Jesus, who gives us
hope.
[2] I am writing to Timothy, my true son in the
faith.
May God the Father and Christ Jesus our
Lord give you grace, mercy, and peace.

Warnings against False Teachings

[3] When I left for Macedonia, I urged you to stay
there in Ephesus and stop those whose teaching is
contrary to the truth. [4] Don't let them waste their
time in endless discussion of myths and spiritual
pedigrees. These things only lead to meaningless
speculations,* which don't help people live a life
of faith in God.*
[5] The purpose of my instruction is that all
believers would be filled with love that comes
from a pure heart, a clear conscience, and genuine
faith. [6] But some people have missed this whole
point. They have turned away from these things
and spend their time in meaningless discussions.
[7] They want to be known as teachers of the law of
Moses, but they don't know what they are talking
about, even though they speak so confidently.
[8] We know that the law is good when used
correctly. [9] For the law was not intended for
people who do what is right. It is for people who
are lawless and rebellious, who are ungodly and
sinful, who consider nothing sacred and defile
what is holy, who kill their father or mother or
commit other murders. [10] The law is for people
who are sexually immoral, or who practice homosexuality, or are slave traders,* liars, promise
breakers, or who do anything else that contradicts the wholesome teaching [11] that comes from
the glorious Good News entrusted to me by our
blessed God.

1:4a Greek *in myths and endless genealogies, which cause speculation.* **1:4b** Greek *a stewardship of God in faith.* **1:10** Or *kidnappers.*

1:1–2 Greeting

First Timothy and the other Pastoral Epistles (2 Tim and Titus) are addressed to individuals and center upon the communal life and pastoral care of churches founded by Paul. *Appointed by the command of God*: Only in the Pastoral Epistles does the writer use this phrase; it emphasizes that God's own authority is behind the instruction given here. *Timothy, my true son in the faith*: The Greek implies a genetic relationship, albeit by the Spirit rather than the flesh. Apparently Paul met and converted Timothy in the Greek city of Lystra on his second missionary journey. Timothy accompanied Paul to various cities and participated in his third (and last recorded) missionary journey. He was still with Paul in Rome before Paul's execution by Roman authorities. Some scholars argue that Paul must have left Rome and continued his missionary work, passing through Macedonia again and commissioning Timothy to Ephesus. However, Paul passed through Ephesus and Macedonia several times during the three journeys. **2:** *Grace, mercy, and peace*: Only in the Pastorals is *mercy* included; it implies that Timothy (or any minister) is in need of God's care in light of the authority conferred upon him.

1:3–7 Initial Instructions to Timothy

The text gives no indication when exactly Paul sent Timothy to "remain" in Ephesus, or whether Timothy did in fact remain there permanently. The specific problem Timothy is to counteract is the "different teaching" (*teaching . . . contrary to the truth*) by some who are preaching celibacy and abstinence from certain foods as "law" (4:3). **4–5:** *Myths and spiritual pedigrees* ("genealogies"): The false teachers used tales of the ancestors to justify their "biblical" morality and practices. Many scholars consider the false doctrine to have been a very early form of Gnosticism ("knowledge": cf. 6:20). The system included many elaborate tales filled with ancient pagan myths and distortions of biblical narratives. The true message is that God loves his people despite their sins, while calling them to a pure heart and good conscience. The latter message is easily accessible to those who read the text and take it seriously. **6–7:** *Meaningless discussions* ("empty talking"): As in some modern churches, members are claiming stature for themselves by teaching without having studied the Bible or life in Christ. Some of the believers at Ephesus have not understood law or gospel.

1:8–11 The Law and Its Proper Use

8: *The law is good*: The law of Moses, or the "law of Christ" (Gal 6:2) or both. The goodness of the law, despite the fact that it reveals evildoing, is typically Pauline; see Rom 7:11–12; Gal 3:21. **9–10:** *Sexually immoral*: The Greek term is *pornois* (sexually immoral ones; related to English "pornography"). *Who practice homosexuality*: The Greek term, *arsenokoitais,* cannot mean "homosexuals" as a name for people. There was no such terminology in any language, until an article published in 1869 by a Hungarian physician. The physician was appealing for the decriminalization of homosexuality by observing that

Paul's Gratitude for God's Mercy

12 I thank Christ Jesus our Lord, who has given me strength to do his work. He considered me trustworthy and appointed me to serve him, 13 even though I used to blaspheme the name of Christ. In my insolence, I persecuted his people. But God had mercy on me because I did it in ignorance and unbelief. 14 Oh, how generous and gracious our Lord was! He filled me with the faith and love that come from Christ Jesus.

15 This is a trustworthy saying, and everyone should accept it: "Christ Jesus came into the world to save sinners"—and I am the worst of them all. 16 But God had mercy on me so that Christ Jesus could use me as a prime example of his great patience with even the worst sinners. Then others will realize that they, too, can believe in him and receive eternal life. 17 All honor and glory to God forever and ever! He is the eternal King, the unseen one who never dies; he alone is God. Amen.

Timothy's Responsibility

18 Timothy, my son, here are my instructions for you, based on the prophetic words spoken about you earlier. May they help you fight well in the Lord's battles. 19 Cling to your faith in Christ, and keep your conscience clear. For some people have deliberately violated their consciences; as a result, their faith has been shipwrecked. 20 Hymenaeus and Alexander are two examples. I threw them out and handed them over to Satan so they might learn not to blaspheme God.

Instructions about Worship

2 I urge you, first of all, to pray for all people. Ask God to help them; intercede on their behalf, and give thanks for them. 2 Pray this way for kings and all who are in authority so that we can live peaceful and quiet lives marked by godliness and dignity. 3 This is good and pleases God our Savior, 4 who wants everyone to be saved and to understand the truth. 5 For there is only one God and one Mediator who can reconcile God and humanity—the man Christ Jesus. 6 He gave his life to purchase freedom for everyone. This is the message God gave to the world at just the right time. 7 And I have been chosen as a preacher and apostle to teach the Gentiles this message about faith and truth. I'm not exaggerating—just telling the truth.

some people have a different sexual orientation by birth. In contrast, ancient Greek and Jewish thought addressed homosexual actions, not persons. Paul refers here to people who engage in same-sex behaviors (Gk., lit., "male having relations with male"). Although the ancients were aware that people differed in their preferences, they assumed that anyone might engage in any sexual behavior. What makes the behavior abominable to Paul beyond the already-mentioned sexual immorality is that it was part of a pagan ritual or rite of passage. *Liars . . . promise breakers*: "Liars" and "perjurers" are different; the latter break the ninth commandment (Deut 5:20), "Do not testify falsely against your neighbor."

1:12–17 Paul's Conversion and God's Mercy

Paul says, literally, "I was a blasphemer (Gk., *blasphemon*) and persecutor and insolent one . . . ignorant, having acted outside of faith [in Christ]." (See the accounts of Paul's conversion experience in Acts 9:1–19; 22:3–16; 26:9–18.) **16:** *As a prime example* (Gk., *hypotyposis*, "type," "prototype"): Greek *typos* and words derived from it signify more than a pattern to be learned intellectually. The term implies that God's loving-kindness is communicated directly into the soul by the power of the Holy Spirit. Hence Paul expects his churches to receive that love and faith through his testimony combined with the direct action of the Spirit.

1:18–20 Instructions to Timothy; Two Blasphemers

I . . . handed them over to Satan: Paul sent them out of the church because they were unreachable with the word of faith (cf. 1 Cor 5:1–5).

2:1—6:2 Conduct in the House of the Lord: Roles of Various Groups in the Church

2:1–8 Paul Commands Prayer for All People. 1: *To pray*: Literally, "to offer supplications, prayers, intercessions, thanksgivings." This phrase is a literary device to indicate the importance of prayer generally. However, the last position in a Greek sentence or list conveys the importance of that word. Here we see Paul's characteristic emphasis on thanksgiving (*eucharistia*) as a necessary part of all prayer (1:12; 4:4–5; cf. Rom 14:6; Eph 5:18–20, lit., "be filled with the Spirit . . . always and in everything giving thanks . . . to God"). For all people *he gave his life to purchase freedom for everyone* (v. 6): The universality is intentional. See 4:10: ". . . God, who is the Savior of all people, and particularly of all believers" (cf. 1 John 2:2; Rom 3:29). Paul's reason in 1 Timothy as elsewhere is that there is one God and Creator of all. The one Creator is the reason that Paul is permitted to preach Jesus Christ to the Gentiles (pagans), whom traditional Jews looked down upon (2:5–7).

[8]In every place of worship, I want men to
pray with holy hands lifted up to God, free from
anger and controversy.
[9]And I want women to be modest in their
appearance.* They should wear decent and appropriate clothing and not draw attention to
themselves by the way they fix their hair or by
wearing gold or pearls or expensive clothes. [10]For
women who claim to be devoted to God should
make themselves attractive by the good things
they do.
[11]Women should learn quietly and submissively. [12]I do not let women teach men or have
authority over them.* Let them listen quietly.
[13]For God made Adam first, and afterward he
made Eve. [14]And it was not Adam who was deceived by Satan. The woman was deceived, and
sin was the result. [15]But women will be saved
through childbearing,* assuming they continue
to live in faith, love, holiness, and modesty.

2:9 Or *to pray in modest apparel.* **2:12** Or *teach men or usurp their authority.* **2:15** Or *will be saved by accepting their role as mothers,* or *will be saved by the birth of the Child.*

2:9–15 The Role of Women in the Church. 9–10: Riches do not accord a person a place of prominence in the church, but rather good deeds as an expression of God's love. This situation is complicated by the presence of a substantial wealthy membership. Some wealthy women have evidently tried to lord it over others with the "different" message, attempting to gain authority by flaunting their wealth and social standing. **11–12:** *Learn quietly and submissively . . . listen quietly*: "Quietly" and "silence" are both *hesychia* in Greek. The term represents the way in which all people in Jewish (and Christian) culture were to learn (also see annotation on 2 Thes 3:11–12). The same Greek word is used in verse 2, "live peaceful and quiet lives." It is a prescription for the entire church so that they can survive in a city that is the world headquarters for worship of the pagan goddess Artemis (see Acts 19:21–41). It is also a prescription for individuals in the church to maintain peace among themselves (see, e.g., v. 8, they are all to remain "free from anger and controversy"). *Submissively* (Gk., *hypotage*) refers not simply to a lower position but to obedience foremost to the Lord, the overcoming of a certain resistance to the demands of gospel living (as in 2 Cor 9:13), and further, integration of the person into the entire Christian fellowship. *Hypotage* stands in opposition to mandated submission as in 2 Corinthians 11:20, *katadouloi*, (to be made) slaves. Contrast Ephesians 5:21, "submit to one another out of reverence for Christ," which uses a term related to *hypotage*. Some of the other terms used to describe the godly woman are also used to describe the godly overseer ("sensible," Gk., *sophrona*). A related term is used for women; both are based on *sophia*, "wisdom." Both the women and the overseers are to be modest (Gk. root word *kosmios*). The reader will benefit from understanding two general aspects of Paul's reasoning. First, a characteristic of every epistle is "contingency" alongside "coherence." Coherence represents the message of Jesus Christ crucified for our salvation. It never varies. This gospel is the index of all behavior (see 4:6). In writing for contingency, Paul is giving a command for a specific situation. As in 1 Timothy, he may advocate commonly accepted behavior (thus keeping the gospel's ideal of peace with one's neighbor). However, the opposite command might be given to another church, or to the same church in a different situation—whatever brings the church into better alignment with the gospel. Paul now addresses the behavior of women believers at a worship service that was less than orderly. He advises decorous silence (see 1 Cor 14:34). Earlier in the same epistle, at 1 Corinthians 11:5, he writes, "A woman dishonors her head (husband) if she prays or prophesies without a covering on her head." Here are two opposite commands, contingent upon the specific situation. In 1 Corinthians 11, Paul assumes that women will prophesy in the context of a Christian gathering. Likewise in 1 Timothy, Paul assumes that women will learn—highly unusual for his time. Thus in the end, Paul accords women more than usual honor. As to women teaching, Paul refers in Philippians 4:3 to women who have joined him as evangelists (cf. Rom 16:1–3). The command that women not teach is contingent upon the situation in Ephesus. It is not a requirement of the gospel. **13–14:** The plain text of Genesis presents the *adam* as an androgynous creature. The transition from a single kind of being to two genders of the species is made explicit in the King James' literal translation of Genesis 1:27: "So God created man in his *own* image, in the image of God created he *him*; male and female created he *them*." Ancient Jewish interpreters sometimes reinterpreted the story, while Gnostic storytellers distorted the narrative to tell of Eve as life-giver and instructor of Adam. A few scholars offer an alternative translation of verse 12, interpreting it as a prohibition against this type of doctrine, that is, "I do not allow a woman to teach that she is the originator of man." To understand Paul's use of the Old Testament we must see that (1) faith in Jesus Christ is the invariable element, and (2) Paul is deliberately attending to the pastoral care of the congregation in that context and is doing so using a technique (the proof text) that is accepted in his time. **15:** *But women will be saved through*

Leaders in the Church

3 This is a trustworthy saying: "If someone
aspires to be an elder,* he desires an honorable position." 2 So an elder must be a man
whose life is above reproach. He must be faithful to his wife.* He must exercise self-control,
live wisely, and have a good reputation. He must
enjoy having guests in his home, and he must be
able to teach. 3 He must not be a heavy drinker*
or be violent. He must be gentle, not quarrelsome, and not love money. 4 He must manage his
own family well, having children who respect
and obey him. 5 For if a man cannot manage his
own household, how can he take care of God's
church?
6 An elder must not be a new believer, because
he might become proud, and the devil would
cause him to fall.* 7 Also, people outside the
church must speak well of him so that he will not
be disgraced and fall into the devil's trap.
8 In the same way, deacons must be well respected and have integrity. They must not be
heavy drinkers or dishonest with money. 9 They
must be committed to the mystery of the faith
now revealed and must live with a clear conscience. 10 Before they are appointed as deacons,
let them be closely examined. If they pass the
test, then let them serve as deacons.
11 In the same way, their wives* must be respected and must not slander others. They must
exercise self-control and be faithful in everything they do.
12 A deacon must be faithful to his wife, and

3:1 Or *an overseer, or a bishop;* also in 3:2, 6. **3:2** Or *must have only one wife,* or *must be married only once;* Greek reads *must be the husband of one wife;* also in 3:12. **3:3** Greek *must not drink too much wine;* similarly in 3:8. **3:6** Or *he might fall into the same judgment as the devil.* **3:11** Or *the women deacons.* The Greek word can be translated *women* or *wives.*

childbearing: If Paul means that childbearing in itself can save the woman, salvation becomes a merely human act. Various scholars interpret the verse (lit., "saved through *the* childbearing") to mean: (1) Women are saved through *the birth*, that is, of Jesus Christ. The notion enjoys some popularity and goes back to the second-century bishop Irenaeus. (2) *Faith, love, holiness, and modesty* (as the verse continues) will bring her closer to God and thus help to preserve her through the often-fatal bearing of children. The latter view implies that the Christian will participate in the reversal of the curse of Eve (Gen 3:15)—even before the second coming.

3:1–7 The Role of the Overseer (Elder). 1–2: *Elder* (or overseer, or bishop, see translator's note): Understanding of the leadership of (supposed) bishops, priests, and deacons depends upon a modern interpretation of the three Greek terms. First, Paul writes instruction for those who are eager for the *episcope* (episcopate). The episcopate is simply the role of *episcopoi*, literally, overseers (3:1ff.). He also instructs *presbyteroi* (elders, 5:17ff.) and *diakonoi* (servants, 3:8ff.). All of these roles were common in the ancient household. They were only later seen as offices of the church. Were the people so designated ordained? Most likely, they did receive the laying on of hands with prayer, like the first *diakonos* Stephen (Acts 6:5–6). However, this process of communal affirmation was the established custom for any commissioning. In Acts 6, it was employed literally to commission Stephen to wait on tables (be a servant) for the needy Greek-speaking believers. The answer here is that the terms represent both the earliest church with its family-like roles, and the later church whose roles had taken on a new organizational meaning. The two separate sections about elders (*presbyteroi*) may indicate a later revision of the text addressing eldership as an office as well as a familial role to which respect was due. **3:2:** *He must be faithful to his wife*: Literally, be "a one-woman man." This text has been used to "prove" that bishops must be male. Its point, however, is that the overseer not have multiple wives or be divorced and remarried. Ancient Jewish law permitted Israelite men to have more than one wife. The practice of polygamy among Hebrew men continued until it was abolished by the code of Justinian in AD 565. The text does not address the issue of whether women can be overseers.

3:8–13 The Role of the "Servant" (Deacon). 8: *In the same way, deacons*: Greek *diakonos* is used in Ephesians 3:7 and Colossians 1:23, 25 of Paul as "minister"; Paul is certainly not a deacon in the modern sense. See also 4:6, of Timothy: "If you explain these things to the brothers and sisters, you will be a worthy servant [*diakonos*] of Christ Jesus." **11:** *In the same way, their wives*: In Greek, "women likewise." Greek has no separate term for "wife." Many interpreters say that Paul is instructing the wives of the deacons, and that view may be correct. On the other hand, Phoebe was a woman deacon (Rom 16:1–3); and since the instructions to servants/deacons parallel so closely those of overseers (deacons likewise [ESV]), we might expect instructions to the wives of the overseers. The latter might imply that in this community (or in Paul's experience) there were women deacons but not women overseers.

he must manage his children and household well.
13 Those who do well as deacons will be rewarded
with respect from others and will have increased
confidence in their faith in Christ Jesus.

The Truths of Our Faith

14 I am writing these things to you now, even
though I hope to be with you soon, 15 so that if
I am delayed, you will know how people must
conduct themselves in the household of God.
This is the church of the living God, which is the
pillar and foundation of the truth.

16 Without question, this is the great mystery
of our faith*:

Christ* was revealed in a human body
  and vindicated by the Spirit.*
He was seen by angels
  and announced to the nations.
He was believed in throughout the world
  and taken to heaven in glory.

Warnings against False Teachers

4 Now the Holy Spirit tells us clearly that
in the last times some will turn away from
the true faith; they will follow deceptive
spirits and teachings that come from demons.
2 These people are hypocrites and liars, and their
consciences are dead.*

3 They will say it is wrong to be married and
wrong to eat certain foods. But God created those
foods to be eaten with thanks by faithful people
who know the truth. 4 Since everything God created is good, we should not reject any of it but
receive it with thanks. 5 For we know it is made
acceptable* by the word of God and prayer.

A Good Servant of Christ Jesus

6 If you explain these things to the brothers and
sisters,* Timothy, you will be a worthy servant
of Christ Jesus, one who is nourished by the message of faith and the good teaching you have followed. 7 Do not waste time arguing over godless
ideas and old wives' tales. Instead, train yourself to be godly. 8 "Physical training is good, but
training for godliness is much better, promising
benefits in this life and in the life to come." 9 This
is a trustworthy saying, and everyone should accept it. 10 This is why we work hard and continue
to struggle,* for our hope is in the living God,
who is the Savior of all people and particularly
of all believers.

11 Teach these things and insist that everyone
learn them. 12 Don't let anyone think less of you
because you are young. Be an example to all believers in what you say, in the way you live, in
your love, your faith, and your purity. 13 Until I
get there, focus on reading the Scriptures to the
church, encouraging the believers, and teaching
them.

14 Do not neglect the spiritual gift you received
through the prophecy spoken over you when
the elders of the church laid their hands on you.
15 Give your complete attention to these matters.
Throw yourself into your tasks so that everyone
will see your progress. 16 Keep a close watch on
how you live and on your teaching. Stay true to
what is right for the sake of your own salvation
and the salvation of those who hear you.

3:16a Or *of godliness.* **3:16b** Greek *He who;* other manuscripts read *God.* **3:16c** Or *in his spirit.* **4:2** Greek *are seared.* **4:5** Or *made holy.* **4:6** Greek *brothers.* **4:10** Some manuscripts read *continue to suffer.*

3:14–16 Paul's Intent to Visit and a Doxology. 14: *I am writing these things to you now.* Paul himself is sending these instructions, whether or not a disciple or a scribe is transmitting the message (cf. Gal 6:11).

4:1–3 Heresy and Hypocrisy Foretold. Although we often romanticize conditions in the early church, within it were inevitably some false teachers. These people preached prohibition of marriage and certain foods in imitation of some philosophical groups or of the Jews, but in doing so to the Christians, they misrepresented the gospel.

4:4—5:2 Instructions to Timothy: The Role of the Minister. 4:4–5: *Everything God created is good,* even holy, for us as long as we receive it with thanksgiving to God. The false teachings do not honor the Lord. The emphasis on thanksgiving is typical of Paul (see, e.g., Phil 4:6; cf. Col 4:2). **7:** *Old wives' tales*: Timothy is being warned against heeding the false teaching mentioned in 4:1–3, although he must be aware of it. Likewise, genealogies and other things that are not Christ-centered do not contribute to the spiritual life of a minister of the gospel. **12:** *Be an example to all believers*: Here again we have Greek *typos* for "example." See annotation on 1:16. **13–14:** The tasks set before the godly minister are the public reading of Scripture, preaching, and teaching. The instruction in verse 14 applies to all of us: *Do not neglect the spiritual gift you received through the prophecy spoken over you when the elders of the church laid their hands on you.* **16:** *Your teaching*: The Greek says "the teaching"—the gospel. It is only by holding onto the gospel that he can deliver those who hear his preaching and teaching. This is Timothy's part in God's plan for our deliverance.

Advice about Widows, Elders, and Slaves

5 Never speak harshly to an older man,* but
appeal to him respectfully as you would to
your own father. Talk to younger men as
you would to your own brothers. 2 Treat older
women as you would your mother, and treat
younger women with all purity as you would
your own sisters.

3 Take care of* any widow who has no one else
to care for her. 4 But if she has children or grandchildren, their first responsibility is to show godliness at home and repay their parents by taking
care of them. This is something that pleases God.

5 Now a true widow, a woman who is truly
alone in this world, has placed her hope in God.
She prays night and day, asking God for his help.
6 But the widow who lives only for pleasure is
spiritually dead even while she lives. 7 Give these
instructions to the church so that no one will be
open to criticism.

8 But those who won't care for their relatives,
especially those in their own household, have denied the true faith. Such people are worse than
unbelievers.

9 A widow who is put on the list for support
must be a woman who is at least sixty years old
and was faithful to her husband.* 10 She must be
well respected by everyone because of the good
she has done. Has she brought up her children
well? Has she been kind to strangers and served
other believers humbly?* Has she helped those
who are in trouble? Has she always been ready to
do good?

11 The younger widows should not be on the
list, because their physical desires will overpower
their devotion to Christ and they will want to remarry. 12 Then they would be guilty of breaking
their previous pledge. 13 And if they are on the
list, they will learn to be lazy and will spend their
time gossiping from house to house, meddling in
other people's business and talking about things
they shouldn't. 14 So I advise these younger
widows to marry again, have children, and take
care of their own homes. Then the enemy will
not be able to say anything against them. 15 For
I am afraid that some of them have already gone
astray and now follow Satan.

16 If a woman who is a believer has relatives who
are widows, she must take care of them and not put
the responsibility on the church. Then the church
can care for the widows who are truly alone.

17 Elders who do their work well should be
respected and paid well,* especially those who
work hard at both preaching and teaching. 18 For
the Scripture says, "You must not muzzle an ox
to keep it from eating as it treads out the grain."

5:1 Or *an elder.* **5:3** Or *Honor.* **5:9** Greek *was the wife of one husband.* **5:10** Greek *and washed the feet of God's holy people?* **5:17** Greek *should be worthy of double honor.*

5:1–2: Chapter 5 begins with instruction on the way Timothy should relate to a *presbyteros* and to a *presbytera,* taken to mean "old man" and "old woman"; could they instead be male and female elders of the church, in the sense of an official capacity? Compare verses 17–18: The elders are to be paid and given social honor. The Eastern Orthodox have a quasi-official role called "presbytera"—the official role and title of the wife of the priest. Her consent is required for his ordination; they share (differently) in the upholding of the office of priest. This custom also is an attempt to honor, in an Orthodox way, the customs of the first century. While we should not read back from modern customs to the church of Paul's time, we should look for the origins of the modern customs in the words of the epistle and thus gain insight into their possible meaning.

5:3–16 The Role of Widows; Who Should Support Them. 3–4: The worth of aged women is here affirmed as well as their right to receive support from those whom they have served long and selflessly. **5:** The early church often called widows "the altar of God" because of their dedicated prayer ministry. **9–10, 16:** Here is a remarkable testimonial to the often unnoticed and undervalued services performed by women both to their families and to the church. The list of caring actions regularly to be performed by the "real widows" has suggested to many that in Ephesus, "real widow" was a formal ministry or office. Clearly any woman whose husband has died is literally, a real widow. In any case, it is the ones who have no other means of support and also conduct these ministries whom the church is to support. **11–14:** Elsewhere Paul enjoins people to remain unmarried if they are able because of the shortness of time before the return of the Lord (1 Cor 7:25–40). He does have the return of the Lord in mind in 1 Timothy (6:13–16). **15:** Some of the widows used their visits to others for gossip rather than in service of the gospel. **16:** Women as well as men were expected to shoulder appropriate responsibility for the support of relations who were widows.

5:17–20 The Role of Elders. 17–18: Elders should be paid in accordance with Old Testament law (the quotations are from Lev 19:13; Deut 24:14).

Widows

The legal status of widows varied widely in biblical cultures. In Hebrew tradition widowhood was a misfortune and even disgraceful (Ruth 1:20–21). A widow could return to her family only if her bride price were repaid. She was expected to await levirate marriage or public refusal (Deut 25:5–10). Little provision was made for widows; as a consequence, God is viewed as their protector (Ps 68:5) who will "heed their cry" (Exod 22:23; Deut 10:18; Ps 146:9) and bring them justice. The covenant code links relationship to God with response to the poor and oppressed (see Exod 22:21–22; Deut 10:18; 14:28–29).

Prohibitions against oppressing widows and provisions for them include that every three years a widow should receive a portion of the produce tithe (Deut 14:28–29); that her garment is not taken in pledge (Deut 24:17–18); that she be invited to public festal meals (Deut 16:11, 14) and be allowed to glean vineyards and fields (Deut 24:19–24; cf. Ruth). Since according to Genesis 38:14, 19 widows wore special clothing, ignorance was no excuse for noncompliance with regulations. Women's status was lower than men's, and widows were the lowest women.

The widow's legal status improved in the Roman Empire. Roman widows functioned as independent, legal parties if their finances allowed. They could inherit from husbands and manage their own property. Augustan marriage laws encouraged younger widows to remarry; those under fifty who did not do so within a specified period were debarred from inheritance. Later, perhaps due to Christian influence, second marriages were discouraged and once-marrieds were honored.

In the New Testament, Paul mentions widows (1 Cor 7:8, 39–40; Rom 7:1, 3) and generally prefers they not remarry. In Mark, widows demonstrate Jesus' advocacy for the oppressed. The tradition in Luke contains extensive material on widows in the Gospel (Luke 2:36–38; 4:25–26; 7:11–17; 18:1–8) and Acts (Acts 6:1–7; 9:36–43). The longest New Testament passage on widows is 1 Timothy 5:3–16, which defines membership in and duties of the order of widows in the church. In James, true religion is evidenced by care of widows (Jas 1:27), echoing Jesus' teaching (Mark 12:38–44; Luke 20:46–47) and traditional teaching that caring for widows serves God (Hos 6:6; Matt 9:13; 25:40). In Revelation 18:7 the widow is used figuratively in contrast to the harlot of Babylon, who mistakenly thinks she will escape the humbling of widowhood.

While the widow generally was relegated to low social, economic, and legal positions in the Roman world, the New Testament offers the possibility of status for the widow that includes specific, constructive duties and privileges within the Christian community and claim to benevolence from it.

And in another place, "Those who work deserve
their pay!"*
19 Do not listen to an accusation against an
elder unless it is confirmed by two or three witnesses. 20 Those who sin should be reprimanded
in front of the whole church; this will serve as a
strong warning to others.
21 I solemnly command you in the presence of
God and Christ Jesus and the highest angels to
obey these instructions without taking sides or
showing favoritism to anyone.
22 Never be in a hurry about appointing a
church leader.* Do not share in the sins of others.
Keep yourself pure.
23 Don't drink only water. You ought to drink
a little wine for the sake of your stomach because
you are sick so often.
24 Remember, the sins of some people are obvious, leading them to certain judgment. But there
are others whose sins will not be revealed until
later. 25 In the same way, the good deeds of some
people are obvious. And the good deeds done in
secret will someday come to light.

6 All slaves should show full respect for
their masters so they will not bring shame
on the name of God and his teaching. 2 If

5:18 Deut 25:4; Luke 10:7. **5:22** Greek *about the laying on of hands.*

5:21–25 Instructions to Timothy on Appointing Officers of the Church. 22: *Never be in a hurry about appointing a church leader*: Test the person and be careful of his or her character and actions before conferring authority.

6:1–2 The Role of Believing Slaves; Behavior toward Their Masters. 1–2: In 1:10, Paul condemns slave traders along with the worst moral offenders. He cannot, therefore, be defending the institution of slavery here. Rather he enjoins appropriate conduct

the masters are believers, that is no excuse for
being disrespectful. Those slaves should work all
the harder because their efforts are helping other
believers* who are well loved.

False Teaching and True Riches

Teach these things, Timothy, and encourage everyone to obey them. 3Some people may contradict our teaching, but these are the wholesome
teachings of the Lord Jesus Christ. These teachings promote a godly life. 4Anyone who teaches
something different is arrogant and lacks understanding. Such a person has an unhealthy desire
to quibble over the meaning of words. This stirs
up arguments ending in jealousy, division, slander,
and evil suspicions. 5These people always cause
trouble. Their minds are corrupt, and they have
turned their backs on the truth. To them, a show
of godliness is just a way to become wealthy.

6Yet true godliness with contentment is itself
great wealth. 7After all, we brought nothing with
us when we came into the world, and we can't take
anything with us when we leave it. 8So if we have
enough food and clothing, let us be content.

9But people who long to be rich fall into
temptation and are trapped by many foolish and
harmful desires that plunge them into ruin and
destruction. 10For the love of money is the root
of all kinds of evil. And some people, craving
money, have wandered from the true faith and
pierced themselves with many sorrows.

Paul's Final Instructions

11But you, Timothy, are a man of God; so run
from all these evil things. Pursue righteousness
and a godly life, along with faith, love, perseverance, and gentleness. 12Fight the good fight for
the true faith. Hold tightly to the eternal life
to which God has called you, which you have
confessed so well before many witnesses. 13And
I charge you before God, who gives life to all,
and before Christ Jesus, who gave a good testimony before Pontius Pilate, 14that you obey
this command without wavering. Then no one
can find fault with you from now until our Lord
Jesus Christ comes again. 15For at just the right
time Christ will be revealed from heaven by the
blessed and only almighty God, the King of all
kings and Lord of all lords. 16He alone can never
die, and he lives in light so brilliant that no human can approach him. No human eye has ever
seen him, nor ever will. All honor and power to
him forever! Amen.

17Teach those who are rich in this world not to
be proud and not to trust in their money, which
is so unreliable. Their trust should be in God,
who richly gives us all we need for our enjoyment. 18Tell them to use their money to do good.
They should be rich in good works and generous to those in need, always being ready to share
with others. 19By doing this they will be storing
up their treasure as a good foundation for the
future so that they may experience true life.

20Timothy, guard what God has entrusted to
you. Avoid godless, foolish discussions with those
who oppose you with their so-called knowledge.
21Some people have wandered from the faith by
following such foolishness.

May God's grace be with you all.

6:2 Greek *brothers.*

---

within a difficult social system.

6:3–21a Recapitulation of the Problem, Focusing on the Problem of Money

6:3–10 Of False Teachers; of Money and Its Place in the Life of the Believer. 7: This is an ancient philosophical aphorism.

6:11–21a Final Instructions to Timothy. 12: *Fight the good fight*: Clearly Paul does not mean to engage in angry words or blows; these things are forbidden throughout 1 Timothy (see vv. 20–21a). **17–19:** Paul counsels the wealthy not to put their hope in earthly gain but to use their riches to do good works. Thus they will lay up for themselves treasure in heaven (cf. Luke 12:16–21). **20–21:** This is the last warning about the wrong pattern of belief and behavior that recurs so frequently in the epistle (1:3–4, 6–7; 4:1–3; 6:3–5, 20–21). Timothy is to guard against *foolish discussions . . . so-called knowledge* (Gk., *gnosis*), referring again to myths and false teaching of all kinds. The type of false teaching may have been an early form of Gnosticism.

6:21b Closing

May God's grace be with you all. The word *you* is plural, showing that the letter is addressed to the entire church. Paul is upholding before all the church the authority and the specific instructions he has given to Timothy.

2 TIMOTHY

INTRODUCTION

Timothy and his situation, his youth, and his shyness have often been remarked upon. Without making these characteristics central in interpreting the letters, it adds to the poignancy of the book if we remember that like many of us, Timothy seems to have sometimes felt himself in over his head. That Timothy's leadership was questioned helps to make these books particularly relevant to those who feel their calling doubted. In our era it is not always because of youth but because of gender. The book of 2 Timothy may discuss women's issues far less specifically or directly than does 1 Timothy, but the overall situation speaks to women. Paul's encouragements and exhortations will therefore speak to those whose situations thus resonate with that of his original reader. It is worth noting that features in 2 Timothy such as the frequent digressions about people as well as the more typical closing greetings and personal requests (like that for a cloak) make the letter's authenticity all the more probable. —*Conrad Gempf*

✧

Greetings from Paul

1 This letter is from Paul, chosen by the will
of God to be an apostle of Christ Jesus. I
have been sent out to tell others about the
life he has promised through faith in Christ
Jesus.
[2] I am writing to Timothy, my dear son.
May God the Father and Christ Jesus our
Lord give you grace, mercy, and peace.

Encouragement to Be Faithful

[3] Timothy, I thank God for you—the God I serve
with a clear conscience, just as my ancestors did.
Night and day I constantly remember you in my
prayers. [4] I long to see you again, for I remember
your tears as we parted. And I will be filled with
joy when we are together again.
[5] I remember your genuine faith, for you
share the faith that first filled your grandmother
Lois and your mother, Eunice. And I know that
same faith continues strong in you. [6] This is why
I remind you to fan into flames the spiritual gift
God gave you when I laid my hands on you. [7] For
God has not given us a spirit of fear and timidity,
but of power, love, and self-discipline.
[8] So never be ashamed to tell others about our
Lord. And don't be ashamed of me, either, even
though I'm in prison for him. With the strength
God gives you, be ready to suffer with me for
the sake of the Good News. [9] For God saved us
and called us to live a holy life. He did this, not
because we deserved it, but because that was
his plan from before the beginning of time—to
show us his grace through Christ Jesus. [10] And
now he has made all of this plain to us by the appearing of Christ Jesus, our Savior. He broke the
power of death and illuminated the way to life
and immortality through the Good News. [11] And
God chose me to be a preacher, an apostle, and a
teacher of this Good News.
[12] That is why I am suffering here in prison.
But I am not ashamed of it, for I know the one
in whom I trust, and I am sure that he is able to
guard what I have entrusted to him* until the
day of his return.
[13] Hold on to the pattern of wholesome teaching you learned from me—a pattern shaped by
the faith and love that you have in Christ Jesus.
[14] Through the power of the Holy Spirit who lives
within us, carefully guard the precious truth that
has been entrusted to you.
[15] As you know, everyone from the province
of Asia has deserted me—even Phygelus and
Hermogenes.
[16] May the Lord show special kindness to
Onesiphorus and all his family because he often visited and encouraged me. He was never
ashamed of me because I was in chains. [17] When

1:12 Or *what has been entrusted to me.*

1:1–5 Greetings, Gratitude, and Grounding

Paul's opening stresses personal elements, calling Timothy *my dear son* and focusing on their respective backgrounds. In this late letter of Paul, it is refreshing to see an acknowledgment that true faith can be in continuity with one's upbringing. Although he regards Timothy as his spiritual son, Timothy's relationship to and debt of gratitude to his *mother* and *grandmother* are not negated. **3:** *Ancestors*: Paul uses a vague term instead of referring directly to his own parents; this may be deliberate: Paul's pedigree is not bad, but Timothy's family is much more spiritually connected—it is not a set of traditions handed down for generations but a living faith shared by particular close family members.

1:6–18 Attitude toward Paul and the Gospel

Paul wants Timothy to realize that he is not on his own and by implication that Paul, in his sufferings, can draw comfort from Timothy's companionship. **7:** It appears that Timothy was not as assertive as Paul might have liked him to be. English does not have an exact equivalent for *deilia* (*timidity*), which is found only here in the New Testament. It is somewhere between cowardice and timidity: inaction through lack of confidence. Timothy is being challenged into positive action, but he is not being accused of cowardice. The remedy is God-given *power, love, and self-discipline*. **12–14:** The "shame" of being a prisoner points to a real burden borne by the apostle and his friends (see also 2:8, 14). Our culture is much less driven by concerns of honor and shame than was Paul's, yet it's easy to imagine the embarrassment of a spiritual adviser with a criminal record. Within the space of a few short sentences, Paul exhorts Timothy to *carefully guard the precious truth*, having affirmed that God "is able to guard." From that grace and in the knowledge of God's actions on our behalf, we, like Timothy, are to take our security, courage, and boldness. **15–18:** These verses are only the first of several sections mentioning people who deserted Paul as well as some of the few who stood by him. *Phygelus and Hermogenes* (neither mentioned elsewhere in the New Testament) are blameworthy in their turning away. But finding and visiting the imprisoned Paul showed some bravery on *Onesiphorus*['s] part, bravery that Paul would like Timothy to emulate.

he came to Rome, he searched everywhere until
he found me. 18 May the Lord show him special
kindness on the day of Christ's return. And you
know very well how helpful he was in Ephesus.

A Good Soldier of Christ Jesus

2 Timothy, my dear son, be strong through
the grace that God gives you in Christ Jesus.
2 You have heard me teach things that have
been confirmed by many reliable witnesses. Now
teach these truths to other trustworthy people
who will be able to pass them on to others.
3 Endure suffering along with me, as a good
soldier of Christ Jesus. 4 Soldiers don't get tied up
in the affairs of civilian life, for then they cannot please the officer who enlisted them. 5 And
athletes cannot win the prize unless they follow
the rules. 6 And hardworking farmers should be
the first to enjoy the fruit of their labor. 7 Think
about what I am saying. The Lord will help you
understand all these things.
8 Always remember that Jesus Christ, a descendant of King David, was raised from the
dead. This is the Good News I preach. 9 And because I preach this Good News, I am suffering
and have been chained like a criminal. But the
word of God cannot be chained. 10 So I am willing to endure anything if it will bring salvation
and eternal glory in Christ Jesus to those God
has chosen.
11 This is a trustworthy saying:

If we die with him,
  we will also live with him.
12 If we endure hardship,
  we will reign with him.
If we deny him,
  he will deny us.
13 If we are unfaithful,
  he remains faithful,
  for he cannot deny who he is.

14 Remind everyone about these things, and
command them in God's presence to stop fighting over words. Such arguments are useless, and
they can ruin those who hear them.

An Approved Worker

15 Work hard so you can present yourself to God
and receive his approval. Be a good worker, one
who does not need to be ashamed and who correctly explains the word of truth. 16 Avoid worthless, foolish talk that only leads to more godless
behavior. 17 This kind of talk spreads like cancer,*
as in the case of Hymenaeus and Philetus. 18 They
have left the path of truth, claiming that the resurrection of the dead has already occurred; in
this way, they have turned some people away
from the faith.
19 But God's truth stands firm like a foundation stone with this inscription: "The LORD
knows those who are his,"* and "All who belong
to the LORD must turn away from evil."*
20 In a wealthy home some utensils are made
of gold and silver, and some are made of wood

2:17 Greek *gangrene.* **2:19a** Num 16:5. **2:19b** See Isa 52:11.

2:1–13 Endurance and Good Teaching

Paul calls for the strength to spread the good news, to teach others who in turn will *pass* the truth *on* v. 2). **4–6:** The task involves sharing, and that may entail disappointing and hurtful relationships as well as those that bear fruit. The way is illustrated by three short metaphors. Ministry is to be done single-mindedly, as a soldier must concentrate on one task; it is to be done according to the rules, as with the athlete; but it is to be done with the certainty of outcome, as with the farmer. **9:** Paul has already mentioned his imprisonment (1:8). **11–13:** This series of pairs may be quotations from a hymn rather than Paul's composition. The initial two pairs take the form: If we do X, *we* will attain Y. The first concerns becoming a Christian; the second is about living as a Christian. The next two take the form: If we do X, *he* will do Y. These are about things going wrong. The second part of each pair is about God's response to these failures. Note that "If we lack faith" [author's translation] is not coupled with the reciprocal "God will lack faith in us." Quite the opposite: "If we lack faith, he remains faithful—for he cannot deny himself" [author's translation]. Once within the relationship the dealings are not strictly reciprocal: We will be human and therefore fail, but he will be divine and constant.

2:14–26 The Dangers of Wrangling over Words

2:14–18: It is not merely quarrels over *worthless, foolish talk* that Timothy seeks to avoid. Others concern such fundamental matters as the doctrine of the resurrection. From Jesus' resurrection and the phenomenon of Pentecost, it is easy to see how people could think that the resurrection had already taken place. Parts of Paul's writings could be so construed (see 2 Cor 5:17). As well as *Hymenaeus* and *Philetus*, some of the Corinthians and Thessalonians succumbed to this error (1 Cor 15; 2 Thes 2:2). **20–21:** The large house here

and clay. The expensive utensils are used for special occasions, and the cheap ones are for everyday use. 21 If you keep yourself pure, you will be
a special utensil for honorable use. Your life will
be clean, and you will be ready for the Master to
use you for every good work.
22 Run from anything that stimulates youthful lusts. Instead, pursue righteous living, faithfulness, love, and peace. Enjoy the companionship
of those who call on the Lord with pure hearts.
23 Again I say, don't get involved in foolish,
ignorant arguments that only start fights. 24 A
servant of the Lord must not quarrel but must be
kind to everyone, be able to teach, and be patient
with difficult people. 25 Gently instruct those who
oppose the truth. Perhaps God will change those
people's hearts, and they will learn the truth.
26 Then they will come to their senses and escape
from the devil's trap. For they have been held
captive by him to do whatever he wants.

The Dangers of the Last Days

3 You should know this, Timothy, that in the
last days there will be very difficult times.
2 For people will love only themselves and
their money. They will be boastful and proud,
scoffing at God, disobedient to their parents, and
ungrateful. They will consider nothing sacred.
3 They will be unloving and unforgiving; they
will slander others and have no self-control.
They will be cruel and hate what is good. 4 They
will betray their friends, be reckless, be puffed up
with pride, and love pleasure rather than God.
5 They will act religious, but they will reject the
power that could make them godly. Stay away
from people like that!
6 They are the kind who work their way into
people's homes and win the confidence of* vulnerable women who are burdened with the guilt
of sin and controlled by various desires. 7 (Such
women are forever following new teachings, but
they are never able to understand the truth.)
8 These teachers oppose the truth just as Jannes
and Jambres opposed Moses. They have depraved
minds and a counterfeit faith. 9 But they won't
get away with this for long. Someday everyone
will recognize what fools they are, just as with
Jannes and Jambres.

Paul's Charge to Timothy

10 But you, Timothy, certainly know what I teach,
and how I live, and what my purpose in life is.
You know my faith, my patience, my love, and
my endurance. 11 You know how much persecution and suffering I have endured. You know all
about how I was persecuted in Antioch, Iconium,

3:6 Greek *and take captive.*

stands for the church, and the different articles the different people or perhaps teachers. One should strive to be numbered with the useful, *special utensils.*

3:1–9 The Last Days: Unteachable Listeners and Deceitful Teachers

The day of the Lord had not yet come, but Paul did not think it was far away. Timothy is living in the *last days* and is told to avoid the people who err. Paul's description still applies: We and our culture are people of the last days—the messianic age. **2–5:** A few specific sinful deeds are mentioned, but the list of vices is mostly about wrong attitudes. These people *love themselves, money,* and pleasure rather than God. They maintain a pretense of godliness but *reject the power* to truly become godly. **6–7:** The false teachers insinuate themselves into private homes (cf. 1 Tim 5:13; Titus 1:11) and ensnare women unsophisticated in theological discourse and gullible in their eagerness to learn (cf. 1 Tim 2:11 as a countering measure). While some women are being victimized, others are assuming leadership roles in the heresy (1 Tim 2:12; 4:7; 5:13–15). The victims are also portrayed in a negative light. These *vulnerable women* are not only sinful and swayed by desires but also apparently incapable of learning, despite being instructed. We need only to note that later in the letter Paul sends his greetings to Priscilla, who was not only instructed and arrived at the truth but also was able to instruct (Acts 18:26). **8–9:** But the female victims are not the main focus of the passage. The caricature is of one type of gullible person in Ephesus who might be susceptible to such evil teachers. The women are not brought up as a topic in their own right but as the beginning of the explanation for the surprising advice to ignore them. *Jannes and Jambres,* the Egyptian magicians (the traditional names for Pharaoh's magicians, Exod 7:11; 9:11), coupled with the reputation of Ephesus for interest in magic (Acts 19:19), has led some scholars to speculate that the description of verse 7 refers to these people's cravings for religious and occult novelties.

3:10—4:8 Paul's Example and Charge to Timothy

The extended section starts and ends with Paul's example, but the middle part contains imperatives for Timothy. The contrast is between those whose folly will be found out by their intended students and Paul's teaching of and example to Timothy.

and Lystra—but the Lord rescued me from all of it. 12 Yes, and everyone who wants to live a godly life in Christ Jesus will suffer persecution. 13 But evil people and impostors will flourish. They will deceive others and will themselves be deceived.

14 But you must remain faithful to the things you have been taught. You know they are true, for you know you can trust those who taught you. 15 You have been taught the holy Scriptures from childhood, and they have given you the wisdom to receive the salvation that comes by trusting in Christ Jesus. 16 All Scripture is inspired by God and is useful to teach us what is true and to make us realize what is wrong in our lives. It corrects us when we are wrong and teaches us to do what is right. 17 God uses it to prepare and equip his people to do every good work.

4 I solemnly urge you in the presence of God and Christ Jesus, who will someday judge the living and the dead when he appears to set up his Kingdom: 2 Preach the word of God. Be prepared, whether the time is favorable or not. Patiently correct, rebuke, and encourage your people with good teaching.

3 For a time is coming when people will no longer listen to sound and wholesome teaching. They will follow their own desires and will look for teachers who will tell them whatever their itching ears want to hear. 4 They will reject the truth and chase after myths.

5 But you should keep a clear mind in every situation. Don't be afraid of suffering for the Lord. Work at telling others the Good News, and fully carry out the ministry God has given you.

6 As for me, my life has already been poured out as an offering to God. The time of my death is near. 7 I have fought the good fight, I have finished the race, and I have remained faithful. 8 And now the prize awaits me—the crown of righteousness, which the Lord, the righteous Judge, will give me on the day of his return. And the prize is not just for me but for all who eagerly look forward to his appearing.

Paul's Final Words

9 Timothy, please come as soon as you can. 10 Demas has deserted me because he loves the things of this life and has gone to Thessalonica. Crescens has gone to Galatia, and Titus has gone to Dalmatia. 11 Only Luke is with me. Bring Mark with you when you come, for he will be helpful to me in my ministry. 12 I sent Tychicus to Ephesus. 13 When you come, be sure to bring the coat I left with Carpus at Troas. Also bring my books, and especially my papers.*

14 Alexander the coppersmith did me much harm, but the Lord will judge him for what he has done. 15 Be careful of him, for he fought against everything we said.

16 The first time I was brought before the judge, no one came with me. Everyone abandoned me. May it not be counted against them. 17 But the Lord stood with me and gave me strength so that

4:13 Greek *especially the parchments.*

3:11: It is likely that Paul mentions *Antioch, Iconium, and Lystra* (cf. Acts 13—14) because Timothy is from Lystra, where their history together began. **16:** Good teaching is one obvious remedy for bad teaching. The inspiration and usefulness of Scripture represents another strong antidote. Paul has in mind what we think of as the Old Testament (see 1 Tim 5:18; 2 Pet 3:15–16 for hints, however, of a possible authority for Christian teaching). During the transition from oral to written teaching, those who could hear the living witness of the apostles were particularly favored. But Paul could no longer travel. Aware that he has finished his race, Paul reminds Timothy of the lasting influence of Scripture. **4:1–2:** Paul invokes an official-sounding formula. This is not one friend asking a favor of another but a matter of the utmost gravity: proclamation, persistence, patience, bearing witness, convincing, and rebuking. **6–8:** Paul is metaphorically passing on the torch to Timothy. He is being *poured out* (cf. Phil 2:17) and his time has come. It is Timothy's perseverance that Paul is trying to influence. This is a good model for our communication: Talking, even talking about ourselves, can be others-directed as well.

4:9–22 Final Greetings, Personal Details, and Logistics

The letter turns to personal greetings (vv. 10–14). *Titus*: The man to whom the epistle was written. *Mark* and *Luke*: The Gospels authors. *Crescens* is otherwise unknown, but *Demas* is mentioned elsewhere (Col 4:14; Phlm 24), always alongside Luke. His desertion is disappointing, but it may only be temporary; Paul also once regarded Mark as a deserter (Acts 15:37–38). *Tychicus* is mentioned elsewhere (Eph 6:21, cf. Col 4:7). *Carpus* is unknown. *Alexander*: Most likely the Alexander of 1 Timothy 1:20 (but not Acts 19:33–34). The *books* and *papers* are likely the Old Testament Scriptures, Paul's notes, and perhaps even his copies of some letters. **16–17:** This may refer to a preliminary hearing during the present imprisonment or the first of his Roman imprisonments (cf. Acts 28).

I might preach the Good News in its entirety for
all the Gentiles to hear. And he rescued me from
certain death.* [18]Yes, and the Lord will deliver
me from every evil attack and will bring me safely into his heavenly Kingdom. All glory to God
forever and ever! Amen.

Paul's Final Greetings

[19]Give my greetings to Priscilla and Aquila and
those living in the household of Onesiphorus.
[20]Erastus stayed at Corinth, and I left Trophimus
sick at Miletus.
[21]Do your best to get here before winter.
Eubulus sends you greetings, and so do Pudens,
Linus, Claudia, and all the brothers and sisters.*
[22]May the Lord be with your spirit. And may
his grace be with all of you.

4:17 Greek *from the mouth of a lion.* **4:21** Greek *brothers.*

19–20: *Priscilla* and her husband are mentioned in Romans 16:3–4; *Erastus* in Romans 16:23 and Acts 19:22; and *Trophimus* in Acts 20:4; 21:29.

TITUS

INTRODUCTION

The letter to Titus has been described as a preliminary draft of 1 Timothy. It addresses the same concerns and situations, uses the same vocabulary, and adopts a similar tone. Like 1 and 2 Timothy, its dominant theme is combating the behavior and doctrines of false teachers. While 1 Timothy specifies the proper conduct for a church already established, Titus differs in giving instructions for installing officers in one or more congregations.

Authorship and date have been vigorously debated, as have been the identity and location of the person addressed. The letter bears the name of the apostle Paul and is addressed to Titus in Crete. Lively speculation notwithstanding, we are better served to study the letter on its own terms (see Introduction to 1 Timothy).

In the distant past Crete had afforded women a high social position. Wall paintings show richly adorned women participating equally with men in diverse areas of life, including athletic, social, and cultic activities. Many of the earliest religious representations are those of female deities. Important shrines of archaic goddesses still attracted the devotion of many in the New Testament period. The Cretans had a proprietary attitude toward many forms of religious expression practiced throughout the Mediterranean world. On Crete, tradition said, the gods of the Greeks had their origin and from there their cults had spread. Even the Ephesian goddess Artemis was called "the Cretan lady of Ephesus."

The Cretans' forebears had long before dominated the Mediterranean world, and remnants of their civilization were still visible in the landscape. Athenians extolled Theseus, who freed them from vassaldom to Crete, as their greatest king. Despite the passage of many centuries, mainlanders still harbored feelings of hostility toward the denizens of the island. The presence of Jewish communities in Crete is well attested from the first century BC until the fifth century AD. Josephus, who was married to a Cretan Jewish woman, implies that they were easily misled (*Antiquities* 17.327; *Jewish Wars* 2.103). Religious currents, pagan and Jewish, rendered Crete a particular challenge to the early church. The deviant doctrines addressed in the letter resemble those described in 1 and 2 Timothy. Based especially on the reference of 1 Timothy 6:20 to "what is falsely called knowledge" (ESV), the heresy is thought to be an early form of Gnosticism. Like the Cretans, Gnostics claimed a deeper knowledge of religious realities than others had. Both groups shared a predilection for powerful female figures and for stories of divine beginnings. —*Catherine Clark Kroeger*

1:1–16 Organizing to Meet the Opposition
2:1–15 Applying Sound Doctrine to the Household of God
3:1–15 Advice for Christian Living

Greetings from Paul

1 This letter is from Paul, a slave of God and
an apostle of Jesus Christ. I have been sent
to proclaim faith to* those God has chosen
and to teach them to know the truth that shows
them how to live godly lives. 2 This truth gives
them confidence that they have eternal life,
which God—who does not lie—promised them
before the world began. 3 And now at just the
right time he has revealed this message, which
we announce to everyone. It is by the command
of God our Savior that I have been entrusted
with this work for him.

4 I am writing to Titus, my true son in the
faith that we share.

May God the Father and Christ Jesus our Savior give you grace and peace.

Titus's Work in Crete

5 I left you on the island of Crete so you could
complete our work there and appoint elders in
each town as I instructed you. 6 An elder must live
a blameless life. He must be faithful to his wife,*
and his children must be believers who don't have
a reputation for being wild or rebellious. 7 An elder* is a manager of God's household, so he must
live a blameless life. He must not be arrogant or
quick-tempered; he must not be a heavy drinker,*
violent, or dishonest with money.

8 Rather, he must enjoy having guests in his
home, and he must love what is good. He must
live wisely and be just. He must live a devout and
disciplined life. 9 He must have a strong belief in
the trustworthy message he was taught; then he
will be able to encourage others with wholesome
teaching and show those who oppose it where
they are wrong.

10 For there are many rebellious people who
engage in useless talk and deceive others. This is
especially true of those who insist on circumcision for salvation. 11 They must be silenced, because they are turning whole families away from
the truth by their false teaching. And they do it
only for money. 12 Even one of their own men, a
prophet from Crete, has said about them, "The
people of Crete are all liars, cruel animals, and
lazy gluttons."* 13 This is true. So reprimand

1:1 Or *to strengthen the faith of.* **1:6** Or *must have only one wife,* or *must be married only once;* Greek reads *must be the husband of one wife.* **1:7a** Or *An overseer,* or *A bishop.* **1:7b** Greek *must not drink too much wine.* **1:12** This quotation is from Epimenides of Knossos.

1:1–16 Organizing to Meet the Opposition

Elsewhere in the New Testament *Titus* is identified as a close Greek associate of Paul (Gal 2:1–3) who made a missionary trip to Dalmatia (2 Tim 4:10) and demonstrated administrative skills in the service of the Corinthian congregation (2 Cor 2:13; 7:6–16; 8:6, 16–23; 12:18). Church difficulties required Titus to remain in Crete (as Timothy had remained at Ephesus; 1 Tim 1:3–4) to resolve problems by appointing elders to oversee churches and repudiate error. **6:** The stipulation that an *elder* must be the husband of only one wife (see translator's note) may address Jewish polygamy. Even middle-class Jews could legitimately marry more than one nondivorced woman, a practice that continued until it was prohibited under the code of Justinian. The intention of the specification appears not to be the exclusion of women or of unmarried men but rather the restriction of a marital pattern that was unacceptable in a church including Jews and Gentiles. Elders must create peace and harmony in their homes. The elders' children should not be *rebellious,* the adjectival opposite of the verb "submit." The word implies disorderly conduct and failure to fulfill responsibilities. **7:** An elder must not be arrogant, disposed to anger or alcohol, and must not be a batterer. *Violent* means literally, "one who beats or rains blows on another." The instruction is repeated in 1 Timothy 3:3; elders and bishops must abstain from all violence, whether in the home or in the broader society. **9:** Christian leaders must understand Christian truth in order both to instruct the faithful and to rebuke opponents, countering heresy as it appears in the Cretan congregations. **10:** The troublemakers are described as *rebellious,* just as earlier Titus was urged not to choose elders with rebellious children. They are full of *useless talk* and an erring mind-set—two characteristics of incipient Gnosticism. Here, however, those subscribing to a false doctrine are *especially . . . those who insist on circumcision,* a clear indication that they were Jews or had at least imbibed Jewish teaching. **11:** Titus is to silence those who brought disruptive and deviant doctrine (cf. 1 Tim 1:3–4, 20; 2:12). Entire households are being led astray, indicating the involvement of women. In 2 Timothy 3:6–7 women are targets in the heretics' invasion of private homes. This was a known cult strategy, notably among the priests of Cybele, who gained female adherents by insinuating themselves into the domestic sphere. As the younger widows of Ephesus went from house to house "talking about things they shouldn't" (1 Tim 5:13), here the opponents are teaching for sordid gain. **12–13:** Cretans were reputed to be the only people who did not consider dishonest gain a disgrace. The Roman author Juvenal mentions women who paid handsomely for the visits of religious charlatans. The couplet about Cretans derives from an oracle of the seventh-century BC sage Epimenides.

them sternly to make them strong in the faith.
[14]They must stop listening to Jewish myths and
the commands of people who have turned away
from the truth.
[15]Everything is pure to those whose hearts
are pure. But nothing is pure to those who are
corrupt and unbelieving, because their minds
and consciences are corrupted. [16]Such people
claim they know God, but they deny him by the
way they live. They are detestable and disobedient, worthless for doing anything good.

Promote Right Teaching

2 As for you, Titus, promote the kind of
living that reflects wholesome teaching.
[2]Teach the older men to exercise self-control, to be worthy of respect, and to live wisely.
They must have sound faith and be filled with
love and patience.
[3]Similarly, teach the older women to live in
a way that honors God. They must not slander others or be heavy drinkers.* Instead, they
should teach others what is good. [4]These older
women must train the younger women to love
their husbands and their children, [5]to live wisely
and be pure, to work in their homes,* to do good,
and to be submissive to their husbands. Then
they will not bring shame on the word of God.
[6]In the same way, encourage the young men
to live wisely. [7]And you yourself must be an
example to them by doing good works of every

2:3 Greek *be enslaved to much wine.* **2:5** Some manuscripts read *to care for their homes.*

Though a native of Crete, he denounced certain aspects of his society. The original hexameter was quoted extensively, principally to repudiate the Cretan insistence that Zeus was not only dead but also lay buried on their island—his tomb served as a tourist attraction. The theological implications of the god's demise struck at the heart of Greek religion and aroused widespread outrage. The continued propensity to distort established dogma posed a threat to the Christian community. **14:** The theme of error springing from Judaism is reintroduced, not this time as bondage to the law but rather as *listening to Jewish myths*: not stories from the biblical canon, for which the writer has the profoundest respect, but later Gnostic accounts subverting the early stories of Genesis for its theology. Gnostic elements, including myth, are present but have not coalesced into the theological formulations that would follow. "Myths" are part of the false doctrine in 1 Timothy, where they are called "old wives' tales" (1 Tim 4:7; cf. 1 Tim 1:4). Women were often the storytellers of antiquity, and ancient authors regarded some of their renditions as scurrilous because of the unfavorable light in which they cast the gods. Retelling brought revision and often a very different perspective from that of the original author: 1 Timothy 2:12–14 may represent an effort to control such a deviation in the Adam and Eve story. These storytelling women needed to be reclaimed to the sound teaching of the canonical Scriptures. **15–16:** Right thinking about God brings right conduct.

2:1–15 Applying Sound Doctrine to the Household of God

Titus is to teach elders to be temperate, serious, prudent, and sound in faith, in love, and in endurance (v. 2). An elder is sometimes understood to be an *older* or "mature man" in the congregation, but the letter emphasizes throughout the preparation of officers to strengthen the church during a time of storm. **3:** If *presbytes* is best understood as a church officer, then the term *presbytis* is best understood not simply as an *older* "woman" but as a "female presbyter." The lifestyles of these women must be appropriate for serving the Lord (lit., "worthy of the priesthood"), indicating they must be fit for special function within the church. The ensuing qualification list is comparable to that for elders and bishops. Just as all elders should counter opposition with sound teaching, female elders must disseminate good doctrine. **4–5:** These verses offer a touching description of mentoring young women by those who have learned much from life. Elizabeth gave such mentoring to Mary as she anticipated a birth that would not be understood. Naomi mentored Ruth as she entered an alien society and found her way through social and economic distress to the blessings of a loving marriage and children. Young wives reared in a pagan background may well have lacked family support as they struggled to adjust to marriage, care for children, and cope with household management. Mature women in positions of Christian leadership could help them and inculcate moral qualities as well. They could teach the temperate use of alcohol; its abuse was rampant among frustrated pagan women. Chastity was an important virtue in a world in which women were thought not to have a developed conscience and to be incurably lustful. *Submissive* indicates orderly and responsible conduct toward their husbands. If these young women were leaders in the church, the obligation to fulfill all domestic duties would be the more necessary so that no shame would be brought to the Word of God. **6:** "Young man" and "young/er men" are sometimes designations for a deacon or junior official (cf. Acts 5:6, 10). If the old and young men are official church leaders, it is likely that the old and young women

Menopause

Mention of menopause in the Bible is usually in connection with the inability to bear children. Sarah's laughter at the announcement that she will bear a son in her old age is provoked by the fact that she "had stopped having a woman's periods" (Gen 18:11, Anchor Bible). The miracle of Sarah's conception is echoed in Elizabeth's pregnancy, which is offered to Mary as a sign of God's ability to initiate Mary's miraculous pregnancy: "Your relative Elizabeth has become pregnant in her old age" (Luke 1:36). When Sarah asks, "How could a worn-out woman like me enjoy such pleasure?" (Gen 18:12) there is also the intimation that there has also been the cessation of pleasurable sexual activity.

In the story of Ruth, Naomi is more questionably menopausal. Her address to her daughters-in-law suggests an improbable scenario: "even if it were possible, and I were to get married tonight and bear sons" (Ruth 1:12–13). Her deferral of her kinswoman's claim to marriage to Boaz suggests that she is at least perimenopausal; she is rewarded for her generosity of spirit when she vicariously bears a child through Ruth.

Menopause was not the end of a woman's "productive" life, however. Given the restrictions the Levitical law placed on women (menstruation was a time of ritual uncleanness), menopause would have signaled an era of enlarged personal freedoms for older women within the worshiping community.

In the New Testament, "older women," probably post- or perimenopausal, are given a specific role in teaching younger women in the church (Titus 2:3–4). There is also an ethic of care for senior widows, the church perpetuating the dying Christ's concern for the care of his mother in caring for widowed women.

In the New Testament, interest in women's reproductive capacity is replaced with an interest in their spiritual fruitfulness. Priscilla teaches in her home without any hint given of her age; since no children are mentioned, it might be possible that Priscilla is either postmenopausal or, in Old Testament terminology, barren. Yet she is fruitful in her ministry. Under the new covenant, women are to be valued not for their reproductive capacity but for their ability to "produce every kind of good fruit" (Col 1:10).

Contemporary secular authors have written about menopause and postmenopause as a time when women are no longer defined in society by their sexual attractiveness and can be valued for other attributes. Christian women find their worth throughout their lives in the knowledge that they have been created lovingly and are embraced by God's love from conception to death. They can see menopause as marking the commencement of a new season of maturity and serenity and be secure in the promise, "The godly will flourish like palm trees. . . . In old age they will still produce fruit; they will remain vital and green" (Ps 92:12, 14).

kind. Let everything you do reflect the integrity
and seriousness of your teaching. 8 Teach the
truth so that your teaching can't be criticized.
Then those who oppose us will be ashamed and
have nothing bad to say about us.
9 Slaves must always obey their masters and
do their best to please them. They must not talk
back 10 or steal, but must show themselves to be
entirely trustworthy and good. Then they will
make the teaching about God our Savior attractive in every way.
11 For the grace of God has been revealed,

are as well, whose conduct should be worthy of the priesthood and who teach what is good. Titus appears to be a young officer like Timothy, called to be a model to the congregation (1 Tim 4:12; 5:1; cf. Titus 2:15). **9–10:** Detractors alleged that Christianity appealed principally to slaves, women, and children. Church leaders came from those groups, and at least one pope was a former slave. Slaves were part of the Roman *familia* and sometimes were entrusted with positions of financial, political, and administrative importance. As Christians they should continue to show respect, rather than opposition, even if vested with greater churchly responsibility than their earthly masters. The honesty of Christian slaves and their eagerness to please should be powerful ornaments for the gospel. Three times in this section appropriate behavior is enjoined to demonstrate the legitimacy of the gospel. Verses 5 and 8 seek to silence opposition, but only in reference to slaves is there a positive emphasis on evangelism. **11–15:** The radiantly trans-

bringing salvation to all people. 12 And we are instructed to turn from godless living and sinful pleasures. We should live in this evil world with wisdom, righteousness, and devotion to God, 13 while we look forward with hope to that wonderful day when the glory of our great God and Savior, Jesus Christ, will be revealed. 14 He gave his life to free us from every kind of sin, to cleanse us, and to make us his very own people, totally committed to doing good deeds.

15 You must teach these things and encourage the believers to do them. You have the authority to correct them when necessary, so don't let anyone disregard what you say.

Do What Is Good

3 Remind the believers to submit to the government and its officers. They should be obedient, always ready to do what is good. 2 They must not slander anyone and must avoid quarreling. Instead, they should be gentle and show true humility to everyone.

3 Once we, too, were foolish and disobedient. We were misled and became slaves to many lusts and pleasures. Our lives were full of evil and envy, and we hated each other.

4 But—"When God our Savior revealed his kindness and love, 5 he saved us, not because of the righteous things we had done, but because of his mercy. He washed away our sins, giving us a new birth and new life through the Holy Spirit.* 6 He generously poured out the Spirit upon us through Jesus Christ our Savior. 7 Because of his grace he declared us righteous and gave us confidence that we will inherit eternal life." 8 This is a trustworthy saying, and I want you to insist on these teachings so that all who trust in God will devote themselves to doing good. These teachings are good and beneficial for everyone.

9 Do not get involved in foolish discussions about spiritual pedigrees* or in quarrels and fights about obedience to Jewish laws. These things are useless and a waste of time. 10 If people are causing divisions among you, give a first and second warning. After that, have nothing more to do with them. 11 For people like that have turned away from the truth, and their own sins condemn them.

Paul's Final Remarks and Greetings

12 I am planning to send either Artemas or Tychicus to you. As soon as one of them arrives, do your best to meet me at Nicopolis, for I have decided to stay there for the winter. 13 Do everything you can to help Zenas the lawyer and Apollos with their trip. See that they are given everything they need. 14 Our people must learn to do good by meeting the urgent needs of others; then they will not be unproductive.

15 Everybody here sends greetings. Please give my greetings to the believers—all who love us.

May God's grace be with you all.

3:5 Greek *He saved us through the washing of regeneration and renewing of the Holy Spirit.* **3:9** Or *spiritual genealogies.*

formed lifestyle of believers must command respect throughout the world.

3:1–15 Advice for Christian Living

All believers must show exemplary conduct, responsible citizenship, and gentleness (vv. 1–3). Christianity's best apologetic is the constructive and Christlike attitude of its adherents. **3–8:** A thumbnail sketch of the conversion and transformation of human beings into trophies of God's grace. **9–11:** The description of the false teachers is suggestive of later Gnostic traditions, which often included elaborate genealogies of celestial beings (cf. 1 Tim 1:4), engaged in specious arguments, debated precepts of Jewish law, and tore at the fabric of revealed truth. After appropriate and conscientious efforts at their reconstruction, it is best to let anyone *causing divisions* (*hairetikos*, the Gk. word from which we get "heretic") go his or her way. **12–15:** The letter closes with instructions for Paul's companions. All are to seek to excel in good works so that their labors may not be fruitless. Error may beset the church, but those who are faithful bring truth and righteousness to troubled congregations in Crete.

PHILEMON

INTRODUCTION

The letter to Philemon is the shortest and most personal of the thirteen epistles attributed to Paul, and its authorship is undisputed. Differing opinions exist, however, regarding the location of sender and recipient. If Apphia is the wife of Philemon and Archippus the son, then the letter is a rather graceful effort to intrude into the life of a family whose home is the meeting place for a local church. The letter demonstrates considerable effort in its address to a delicate situation. The matter is further complicated because Onesimus bears the missive.

The traditional view of the letter's circumstances is that Paul, imprisoned in Rome, has found solace in the ministrations of Onesimus, whom he has led to faith in Christ. The apostle faces an ethical dilemma: Although he finds Onesimus helpful, he recognizes that Philemon, as master of the slave, has a prior claim on him. The honorable course is to reveal the circumstances and to throw himself and Onesimus on the kindness of the letter's recipients.

Paul wrote his letter in a society dependent on slavery. It was one part of a larger patriarchal system in which the basic unit was the household. Within the Hellenistic household there were three primary sets of relationships: master-slave, husband-wife, and father-child. Their proper management had, since the time of Aristotle (*Politics* 1.2.1–14a; 1.5.1–2), been considered essential to the order of society. In contemporary thought, the quality of life in a household depended on the master. In Christian tradition, however, the wife was responsible for managing the household (1 Tim 5:14; cf. Prov 31:15–21).

The reintroduction of Onesimus will disrupt the balance of established relationships, probably with particular implications for Apphia. Hers would have been the responsibility to manage a household stretched by the inclusion of a worshiping community. Now she is asked to receive back a disruptive member of the family, for slaves were considered part of the Roman *familia.* The relationship between mistress and household slaves was frequently a close one; literary evidence reveals that much of a slave's treatment lay in the hands of the mistress. In the case of Onesimus, a breach of trust must be overcome. Onesimus's malfeasance has betrayed the administration of an orderly household, and wounds remain.

Onesimus appears to have continued in ministry, for he was sent with Tychicus to the Colossians as an emissary and fellow citizen (Col 4:9). If Onesimus was a slave, then we see at work a policy of openness and mutuality in reestablishing a relationship. The transformation of his character and life demands that he be received on equal footing, empowered to serve in the bonds of the gospel. His new identity has made him a full person, worthy of respect and of acceptance in the body of Christ. —*Kristen Plinke Bentley*

1–3	Salutation and Greetings
4–7	Prayer
8–22	Body of Letter
23–25	Conclusion

Greetings from Paul
This letter is from Paul, a prisoner for preaching
the Good News about Christ Jesus, and from our
brother Timothy.
I am writing to Philemon, our beloved co-
worker, [2]and to our sister Apphia, and to our
fellow soldier Archippus, and to the church that
meets in your* house.
[3]May God our Father and the Lord Jesus
Christ give you grace and peace.

Paul's Thanksgiving and Prayer
[4]I always thank my God when I pray for you,
Philemon, [5]because I keep hearing about your
faith in the Lord Jesus and your love for all of
God's people. [6]And I am praying that you will
put into action the generosity that comes from
your faith as you understand and experience all
the good things we have in Christ. [7]Your love
has given me much joy and comfort, my brother,
for your kindness has often refreshed the hearts
of God's people.

Paul's Appeal for Onesimus
[8]That is why I am boldly asking a favor of you.
I could demand it in the name of Christ because
it is the right thing for you to do. [9]But because
of our love, I prefer simply to ask you. Consider
this as a request from me—Paul, an old man
and now also a prisoner for the sake of Christ
Jesus.*
[10]I appeal to you to show kindness to my
child, Onesimus. I became his father in the faith
while here in prison. [11]Onesimus* hasn't been of
much use to you in the past, but now he is very
useful to both of us. [12]I am sending him back to
you, and with him comes my own heart.
[13]I wanted to keep him here with me while I
am in these chains for preaching the Good News,
and he would have helped me on your behalf.
[14]But I didn't want to do anything without your
consent. I wanted you to help because you were
willing, not because you were forced. [15]It seems
you lost Onesimus for a little while so that you
could have him back forever. [16]He is no longer
like a slave to you. He is more than a slave, for
he is a beloved brother, especially to me. Now he
will mean much more to you, both as a man and
as a brother in the Lord.
[17]So if you consider me your partner, welcome him as you would welcome me. [18]If he has
wronged you in any way or owes you anything,
charge it to me. [19]I, PAUL, WRITE THIS WITH MY
OWN HAND: I WILL REPAY IT. AND I WON'T MEN-
TION THAT YOU OWE ME YOUR VERY SOUL!
[20]Yes, my brother, please do me this favor* for
the Lord's sake. Give me this encouragement in
Christ.
[21]I am confident as I write this letter that you
will do what I ask and even more! [22]One more
thing—please prepare a guest room for me, for

2 Throughout this letter, *you* and *your* are singular except in verses 3, 22, and 25. **9** Or *a prisoner of Christ Jesus.* **11** *Onesimus* means "useful." **20** Greek *onaimen*, a play on the name Onesimus.

1–3 Greetings from Paul

The letter's opening uses the customary formula for ancient letters: sender to recipient, followed by greetings. **2:** *To the church that meets in your house*: The content is a personal matter but also one intended for the congregation.

4–7 Paul's Thanksgiving and Prayer

This praise is intended to focus attention on the recipient and to secure a favorable response. **7:** The word *splanchna* (*hearts*) could refer to any of the affections or internal organs, including the womb (see vv. 12, 20).

8–22 Paul's Appeal for Onesimus

Paul bases his appeal on love rather than insisting on what is appropriate. **10:** Literally, "birthed in bonds," feminine imagery. **11:** Slave terminology asserts that Onesimus is different now than in the past. Onesimus's name, which means "useful," becomes part of a wordplay employing standard terms for bad slaves ("useless," *achreston*) and for good slaves ("useful," *euchreston*). **12:** Onesimus is described as Paul's *splanchna*. **15:** *Have him back forever*: Even if Onesimus is returned to minister to Paul, he will remain part of Philemon's family. Freed slaves continued to have a familial relationship and might derive from the former owner use of the family name, Roman citizenship, support in legal matters, and bonds of affection. **15, 17–19:** Paul's words may imply that there has been ill treatment on both sides. Onesimus's wrongs and injuries Paul asks to have charged to him. **20:** *Onaimen* (*favor*) comes from the same stem as the name Onesimus, again a subtle form of encouragement to do the right thing in a difficult circumstance. Slave and master must be useful in Christ's service. *Give me this encouragement* (or "refresh my heart"): The term *splanchna* reappears here. The recurrence is intentional, drawing Onesimus into the

I am hoping that God will answer your prayers and let me return to you soon.

Paul's Final Greetings

[23] Epaphras, my fellow prisoner in Christ Jesus, sends you his greetings. [24] So do Mark, Aristarchus, Demas, and Luke, my co-workers.

[25] May the grace of the Lord Jesus Christ be with your spirit.

---

family circle of hospitality and acceptance. **22:** *Prepare a guest room for me*: The guest room reminds the family of the hospitality gladly afforded the apostle and now requested for Onesimus.

23–25 Paul's Final Greetings

Demas (2 Tim 4:10) and *Mark* (Acts 15:37–39): Two individuals with whom relationships were not always harmonious.

HEBREWS

INTRODUCTION

Hebrews is a carefully composed, formal text whose oratorical style resembles a tract or written sermon. Its ending suggests a letter even though it lacks the usual opening salutation. The author described the work as a "brief exhortation" (13:22), rooting this urgent sermon-letter in life and addressing believers who discovered that adverse circumstances over which they exercised no control could affect them. Hebrews reflects the writer's sensitive pastoral response to people in danger of relinquishing their Christian commitment. Wanting to strengthen the hearers so that they could stand firm in their faith, the author issued five warnings dealing with the danger of neglecting the salvation in Christ as a result of unbelief, apostasy, or compromise.

Hebrews is anonymous, and we can only speculate about who its author was. Its Greek language and style have high literary qualities, indicating some degree of education, especially in the art of rhetoric. This and other internal evidence suggest that the writer was a highly educated, Hellenistic, Jewish Christian who possessed a pastor's heart. Scholars have suggested Paul, Barnabas, Luke, Apollos, Priscilla, and others as the author. Why do some scholars believe Priscilla wrote this book, when no other New Testament book is attributed to a woman? Priscilla, like the writer of Hebrews, belonged to Paul's immediate circle and was Timothy's colleague. She did not know Jesus from direct experience but received his teachings from others. Hebrews also expresses a marked sympathy for women (11:11, 31, 35). Its account of Sarah emphasizes her faith as she faced the challenges of a child in her old age (11:11). In contrast, the account in Genesis refers to her laughter of unbelief at the promise of a son (Gen 18:11–15). Some scholars have suggested a team effort by Priscilla and her husband, Aquila, since the author(s) moved easily from a first person singular to a first person plural. Also, the writing team or person knew about the persecution of believers in Rome. They served as leaders in the community addressed by the letter, knowing well its members' lack of spiritual maturity. Knowledgeable in Jewish Scriptures, they wrote of the Tabernacle ritual but gave no hint of familiarity with Temple procedure. The New Testament does not record Priscilla and Aquila as traveling to Jerusalem. If Priscilla was the main or only author, scribes may have suppressed this because of their prejudice against women.

The Greek title, "To the Hebrews," appeared in some early manuscripts but not necessarily in the original text. The frequent appeals to the Old Testament, the assumption that the readers knew Jewish ritual, and the warnings against returning to Judaism suggest the author wrote to Jewish Christians. These believers had endured public abuse, imprisonment, and the looting of their property, but they had not yet been called on to die for their faith. They hesitated to separate themselves decisively from Judaism, which enjoyed the protection of Roman law, because total commitment to the Christian way would bring risks. Instead of pressing ahead, they were inclined to come to a full stop in their spiritual progress, if not to slip back to a stage they had left. The epistle also implies the recipients were Hellenistic. All of the Old Testament quotations follow the Septuagint, the Greek translation of the Hebrew Scriptures. Their knowledge of Israel's sacrificial ritual seems derived from their reading of the Old Testament and not from firsthand contact with the

Temple services. The words "you ought to be teaching others" (5:12) may indicate the author addressed a group within a church rather than the whole fellowship. The author probably addressed comparatively well-educated Jewish Christians somewhere in the Mediterranean dispersion.

Clement of Rome quoted Hebrews authoritatively in AD 95. Consequently any date between 60 and 95 for its composition is possible. Most evidence points to a time of writing prior to 70. The description of the persecution endured (10:32–34) points to that under the emperor Claudius. The persecution predicted (12:4) implies the intensity of persecution during the reign of Nero in 64. Nor does the epistle mention the destruction of the Temple in 70, an event of great importance to Jewish Christians. The writer's imminent expectation of the parousia (the second coming, 10:25, 36–39) and the reference to Timothy's release from prison (13:23) also point to a relatively early date.

During this period Christians in Rome and probably in other cities appear to have met in house churches. Even though many Gentiles had embraced Christianity, some groups continued to reflect their Jewish background. The remains of buildings of several stories dating to the second and third centuries indicate what characterized early house churches in Rome. Shops apparently occupied the ground floors, while prosperous families lived in the upper levels. For example, the house of Priscilla and Aquila must have served as a workshop, residence, and meeting place (Rom 16:3–5). The multiplicity of house churches throughout large cities suggests why the early church had problems with disunity. Hebrews gives evidence of tension between the readers and those currently recognized as leaders. The writer wanted to bring the two groups together and did not want the members of the house church to regard themselves as an autonomous fellowship or to isolate themselves from other household groups. These Jewish Christians were also experiencing persecution from Jews and Gentiles, tempting them to return to the Jewish community. The writer reminded them of the basis of their faith—Jesus Christ. For the author of Hebrews, Judaism alone is insufficient.

Hebrews represents a practical response to an urgent situation. The readers stood on the verge of taking action that would deny the Christian faith. Indeed, some had already left. Among those who remained, some had lost confidence in the effectiveness of their convictions. They might have questioned whether the past event of Jesus' sacrificial death had continuing efficacy. They had retreated from the bold commitment they had shown on first becoming believers, when they had endured public abuse, imprisonment, and loss of property. Attraction to traditions conflicting with the Word of God caused unresolved tension between the community and its leaders. The writer proposed to stop this return to Judaism—or perhaps to a heretical, gnosticizing Judaism influenced by Hellenistic ideas—by presenting the sufficiency and superiority of Christ. Christianity alone offered superior benefits and promises. All other religions lacked hope, failed to lead to a deeper knowledge of God, and could not provide the power for holy living. Whether the delay of the parousia, social ostracism and impending persecution, neglect of fellowship, listening to heretical teachers, a general fading of enthusiasm, or erosion of confidence caused the problems, the author wrote to warn readers against apostasy and to bring them back into the community of the faithful. —*Sharon H. Gritz*

1:1—4:13 The Superiority of Christ's Person
1:1–3 The Superiority of Christ in the Revelation of God
1:4—2:18 The Superiority of Christ to Angels
3:1—4:13 The Superiority of Christ to Moses and Joshua
4:14—10:18 The Superiority of Christ's Work
4:14—7:28 The Superior Priesthood Demonstrated in Christ
8:1–13 The Superior Covenant Introduced by Christ
9:1—10:18 The Superior Sacrifice Offered by Christ
10:19—12:29 The Superiority of Christ's Power
10:19–39 An Appeal for Endurance
11:1–40 The Encouragement of Faith
12:1–13 The Experience of Discipline
12:14–29 A Warning against Rejecting God
13:1–17 Final Exhortations
13:18–25 Benediction and Conclusion

✧

Jesus Christ Is God's Son

1 Long ago God spoke many times and in
many ways to our ancestors through the
prophets. 2 And now in these final days, he
has spoken to us through his Son. God promised everything to the Son as an inheritance, and
through the Son he created the universe. 3 The
Son radiates God's own glory and expresses the
very character of God, and he sustains everything
by the mighty power of his command. When he
had cleansed us from our sins, he sat down in the
place of honor at the right hand of the majestic
God in heaven. 4 This shows that the Son is far
greater than the angels, just as the name God
gave him is greater than their names.

The Son Is Greater Than the Angels

5 For God never said to any angel what he said
to Jesus:

"You are my Son.
Today I have become your Father.*"

God also said,

"I will be his Father,
and he will be my Son."*

1:5a Or *Today I reveal you as my Son.* Ps 2:7. **1:5b** 2 Sam 7:14.

1:1—4:13 The Superiority of Christ's Person

The prologue establishes the theme of Hebrews: the superiority of Christ.

1:1–3 The Superiority of Christ in the Revelation of God. 1: God has revealed himself to human beings in a variety of ways in the past, most clearly through the prophets. **2:** The revelation through Christ has superiority and finality. *In these final days*: In Jesus the new age, the messianic age, has appeared. **3:** In quality and quantity God had no more revelation to give other than what he had given in Jesus. Jesus Christ reveals what God is like. What an encouragement for women! The Gospels show Jesus as the friend of women who dared to talk with them in public. He risked his reputation and theirs by allowing them to travel as part of his group of disciples. He met their needs, revealed great spiritual truths to them, and respected their work and their thinking. God cares for women as Jesus did. Women should want to know this God.

1:4—2:18 The Superiority of Christ to Angels. 1:4–14: Seven quotations from the Old Testament show the authority of Scripture to prove to Jewish Christians the superiority of Christ to the angels. The quotations are seen christologically: Passages that referred to God or Israel's king are applied to Christ. Jews regarded *angels* highly, as God's intermediaries in conveying the law to Moses. **6:** The

[6]And when he brought his supreme* Son into the world, God said,*

"Let all of God's angels worship him."*

[7]Regarding the angels, he says,

"He sends his angels like the winds,
his servants like flames of fire."*

[8]But to the Son he says,

"Your throne, O God, endures forever and ever.
You rule with a scepter of justice.
[9] You love justice and hate evil.
Therefore, O God, your God has anointed you,
pouring out the oil of joy on you more than on anyone else."*

[10]He also says to the Son,

"In the beginning, Lord, you laid the foundation of the earth
and made the heavens with your hands.
[11] They will perish, but you remain forever.
They will wear out like old clothing.
[12] You will fold them up like a cloak
and discard them like old clothing.
But you are always the same;
you will live forever."*

[13]And God never said to any of the angels,

"Sit in the place of honor at my right hand
until I humble your enemies,
making them a footstool under your feet."*

[14]Therefore, angels are only servants—spirits sent to care for people who will inherit salvation.

A Warning against Drifting Away

2 So we must listen very carefully to the
truth we have heard, or we may drift away
from it. [2]For the message God delivered
through angels has always stood firm, and every
violation of the law and every act of disobedience was punished. [3]So what makes us think we
can escape if we ignore this great salvation that
was first announced by the Lord Jesus himself
and then delivered to us by those who heard him
speak? [4]And God confirmed the message by giving signs and wonders and various miracles and
gifts of the Holy Spirit whenever he chose.

Jesus, the Man

[5]And furthermore, it is not angels who will control the future world we are talking about. [6]For
in one place the Scriptures say,

"What are mere mortals that you should think about them,
or a son of man* that you should care for him?
[7] Yet you made them only a little lower than the angels
and crowned them with glory and honor.*
[8] You gave them authority over all things."*

1:6a Or *firstborn.* **1:6b** Or *when he again brings his supreme Son* [or *firstborn Son*] *into the world, God will say.* **1:6c** Deut 32:43. **1:7** Ps 104:4 (Greek version). **1:8-9** Ps 45:6-7. **1:10-12** Ps 102:25-27. **1:13** Ps 110:1. **2:6** Or *the Son of Man.* **2:7** Some manuscripts add *You gave them charge of everything you made.* **2:6-8** Ps 8:4-6 (Greek version).

writer identifies Jesus as *the Son* and the Creator who received *worship* from the angels. **7–14:** *Angels* are God's *servants*, created beings, *spirits* who minister to believers. Jesus, superior over angels, is our main focus.

2:1–4 A Warning against Rejecting Christ's Superiority. The writer cautions against drifting away from the superior gospel of Christ. **2–3:** If *the message* the angels declared (the Mosaic law) led to the punishment of its violators, how much greater will be the punishment for those who neglect the great salvation declared through the Lord? The Old Testament does not speak of angels in connection with the giving of the law, but the New Testament mentions their presence (Acts 7:38, 53; Gal 3:19). Intertestamental and rabbinical Judaism did also. Women have greater opportunities now than in any preceding age in terms of education, employment, and achievement. The demands of their lives could cause them to neglect their spiritual needs. Women should heed the warning not to neglect the great salvation found in Jesus Christ.

2:5–18 The Reason for Christ's Incarnation. The nature of the work Jesus came to accomplish required the incarnation. The transcendent Son of God became a human being liable to death in order to achieve for women and men their glorious destiny designed by God. **6–8:** The writer quotes from Psalm 8, which usually is not seen as referring to

Now when it says "all things," it means nothing
is left out. But we have not yet seen all things put
under their authority. [9]What we do see is Jesus,
who was given a position "a little lower than the
angels"; and because he suffered death for us,
he is now "crowned with glory and honor." Yes,
by God's grace, Jesus tasted death for everyone.
[10]God, for whom and through whom everything
was made, chose to bring many children into glory. And it was only right that he should make
Jesus, through his suffering, a perfect leader, fit
to bring them into their salvation.
[11]So now Jesus and the ones he makes holy
have the same Father. That is why Jesus is not
ashamed to call them his brothers and sisters.*
[12]For he said to God,

"I will proclaim your name to my brothers
and sisters.
I will praise you among your assembled
people."*

[13]He also said,

"I will put my trust in him,"
that is, "I and the children God has
given me."*

[14]Because God's children are human beings—made of flesh and blood—the Son also
became flesh and blood. For only as a human
being could he die, and only by dying could
he break the power of the devil, who had* the
power of death. [15]Only in this way could he set
free all who have lived their lives as slaves to
the fear of dying.
[16]We also know that the Son did not come to
help angels; he came to help the descendants of
Abraham. [17]Therefore, it was necessary for him
to be made in every respect like us, his brothers
and sisters,* so that he could be our merciful and
faithful High Priest before God. Then he could
offer a sacrifice that would take away the sins of
the people. [18]Since he himself has gone through
suffering and testing, he is able to help us when
we are being tested.

Jesus Is Greater Than Moses

3 And so, dear brothers and sisters who belong to God and* are partners with those
called to heaven, think carefully about this
Jesus whom we declare to be God's messenger*
and High Priest. [2]For he was faithful to God,
who appointed him, just as Moses served faithfully when he was entrusted with God's entire*
house.
[3]But Jesus deserves far more glory than Moses, just as a person who builds a house deserves
more praise than the house itself. [4]For every
house has a builder, but the one who built everything is God.
[5]Moses was certainly faithful in God's house
as a servant. His work was an illustration of the
truths God would reveal later. [6]But Christ, as the

2:11 Greek *brothers;* also in 2:12. **2:12** Ps 22:22. **2:13** Isa 8:17-18. **2:14** Or *has.* **2:17** Greek *like the brothers.* **3:1a** Greek *And so, holy brothers who.* **3:1b** Greek *God's apostle.* **3:2** Some manuscripts do not include *entire.*

---

the Messiah. In the original context it referred to humanity rather than to an individual. The Greek text, however, reveals that the writer uses the singular *son of man* to refer to the sovereign Christ. **9–10:** Christ's condescension—to be made for a brief while *lower than the angels*—set in motion a sequence of events in which his ultimate exaltation first required the abasement and humiliation associated with his *death*. His coronation and investiture with priestly glory and splendor provide assurance that the power of sin and death has been nullified and that humanity will one day fully realize its intended glory. The concept of the Messiah suffering would have been abhorrent to some Jews, yet God made his great and glorious Son *perfect* through *suffering*. **11–15:** The portrayal of Jesus as champion (12:2) offers a word of comfort and encouragement to these Christians in crisis, helping them to look beyond their immediate trouble to the triumph that already had been secured for them. Because Jesus was in every respect perfectly and completely human, he can act on people's behalf as their high priest, fully able to understand their needs, sufferings, and temptations. Jesus understands and helps women and men in times of testing and temptation. He is their champion. **17:** As *High Priest*, Jesus has made a *sacrifice* for *the sins of the people*, which satisfies God's justice and turns away his wrath against sin. The Christian use of "atoning sacrifice" does not include the pagan idea of bribing a deity to appease his wrath. Although God's holiness and opposition to all evil demand a sacrifice, his love leads him to provide the means of atonement.

3:1—4:13 The Superiority of Christ to Moses and Joshua. 3:1–6: Moses and Jesus were faithful to God in fulfilling their respective offices. **2:** House, household, the people of God. **3–5:** Jesus is worthy of greater honor than Moses because he was the builder of the house. **6:** Faithful sonship is superior to faith-

Son, is in charge of God's entire house. And we
are God's house, if we keep our courage and remain confident in our hope in Christ.*
7 That is why the Holy Spirit says,

"Today when you hear his voice,
8 don't harden your hearts
as Israel did when they rebelled,
when they tested me in the wilderness.
9 There your ancestors tested and tried my
patience,
even though they saw my miracles for
forty years.
10 So I was angry with them, and I said,
'Their hearts always turn away from me.
They refuse to do what I tell them.'
11 So in my anger I took an oath:
'They will never enter my place of rest.' "*

12 Be careful then, dear brothers and sisters.*
Make sure that your own hearts are not evil and
unbelieving, turning you away from the living
God. 13 You must warn each other every day,
while it is still "today," so that none of you will
be deceived by sin and hardened against God.
14 For if we are faithful to the end, trusting God
just as firmly as when we first believed, we will
share in all that belongs to Christ. 15 Remember
what it says:

"Today when you hear his voice,
don't harden your hearts
as Israel did when they rebelled."*

16 And who was it who rebelled against God,
even though they heard his voice? Wasn't it the
people Moses led out of Egypt? 17 And who made
God angry for forty years? Wasn't it the people
who sinned, whose corpses lay in the wilderness?
18 And to whom was God speaking when he took
an oath that they would never enter his rest?
Wasn't it the people who disobeyed him? 19 So
we see that because of their unbelief they were
not able to enter his rest.

Promised Rest for God's People

4 God's promise of entering his rest still
stands, so we ought to tremble with fear
that some of you might fail to experience
it. 2 For this good news—that God has prepared
this rest—has been announced to us just as it
was to them. But it did them no good because
they didn't share the faith of those who listened
to God.* 3 For only we who believe can enter his
rest. As for the others, God said,

"In my anger I took an oath:
'They will never enter my place of rest,' "*

even though this rest has been ready since he
made the world. 4 We know it is ready because
of the place in the Scriptures where it mentions
the seventh day: "On the seventh day God rested

3:6 Some manuscripts add *faithful to the end.* **3:7-11** Ps 95:7-11. **3:12** Greek *brothers.* **3:15** Ps 95:7-8. **4:2** Some manuscripts read *they didn't combine what they heard with faith.* **4:3** Ps 95:11.

ful servanthood; therefore the readers should remain loyal to Christ rather than returning to their Jewish faith.

3:7–19 A Warning against Unbelief. A second warning about the danger of refusing to believe God's Word, and a serious call to persevering discipleship, quotes Psalm 95. Both Christians and ancient Israelites were people whose pilgrimage was almost over and who were on the verge of attaining what God had promised. Despite their miraculous deliverance from Egypt, the Israelites grumbled against God and continued in disobedience. Refusing to acknowledge God's presence and voice, they forfeited the possibility of entrance into his rest and failed to attain the goal of their redemption. The writer cautions readers that if they also harden their hearts, refuse to believe, turn away from the living God, sin, fail to persevere to the end, rebel, and disobey, a worse thing will happen to them. They will not enter God's ultimate rest. **7, 13:** *Today*: A fresh moment of biography and history, conditioned always by the response of obedience or disobedience, of faith or unbelief. **8:** To *harden the heart* is to disobey God and act in accordance with one's own desires. **12:** *Turning . . . away*: Like drifting away (2:1), it is the temptation of apostasy, willful rejection of the Christian faith. Jewish believers could have said that they believed in the same God as Christians, so returning to Jewish practice did not mean rejecting God. But God's highest revelation was Jesus Christ. The letter does not say whether those who apostatized were genuine Christians but focuses only on the practical result. The readers are to encourage one another so that none of them might be hardened by the deceitfulness of sin. Such exhortation is often the role of mothers, who have to teach their children about the deceitfulness of sin and train them not to allow the world's attractions to deceive them lest their hearts harden to God's call.

4:1–10 A Comparison of Christ's Rest and Joshua's Rest. If the ancient Israelites, with all their advantag-

from all his work."* [5]But in the other passage
God said, "They will never enter my place of
rest."*
[6]So God's rest is there for people to enter, but
those who first heard this good news failed to enter because they disobeyed God. [7]So God set another time for entering his rest, and that time is
today. God announced this through David much
later in the words already quoted:

"Today when you hear his voice,
don't harden your hearts."*

[8]Now if Joshua had succeeded in giving them
this rest, God would not have spoken about another day of rest still to come. [9]So there is a special rest* still waiting for the people of God. [10]For
all who have entered into God's rest have rested
from their labors, just as God did after creating
the world. [11]So let us do our best to enter that
rest. But if we disobey God, as the people of Israel did, we will fall.
[12]For the word of God is alive and powerful.
It is sharper than the sharpest two-edged sword,
cutting between soul and spirit, between joint
and marrow. It exposes our innermost thoughts
and desires. [13]Nothing in all creation is hidden
from God. Everything is naked and exposed before his eyes, and he is the one to whom we are
accountable.

Christ Is Our High Priest

[14]So then, since we have a great High Priest who
has entered heaven, Jesus the Son of God, let us
hold firmly to what we believe. [15]This High Priest
of ours understands our weaknesses, for he faced
all of the same testings we do, yet he did not sin.
[16]So let us come boldly to the throne of our gracious God. There we will receive his mercy, and we
will find grace to help us when we need it most.

5 Every high priest is a man chosen to represent other people in their dealings with
God. He presents their gifts to God and offers sacrifices for their sins. [2]And he is able to
deal gently with ignorant and wayward people
because he himself is subject to the same weaknesses. [3]That is why he must offer sacrifices for
his own sins as well as theirs.
[4]And no one can become a high priest simply because he wants such an honor. He must be
called by God for this work, just as Aaron was.
[5]That is why Christ did not honor himself by assuming he could become High Priest. No, he was
chosen by God, who said to him,

"You are my Son.
Today I have become your Father.*"

4:4 Gen 2:2. **4:5** Ps 95:11. **4:7** Ps 95:7-8. **4:9** Or *a Sabbath rest.* **5:5** Or *Today I reveal you as my Son.* Ps 2:7.

---

es, failed to enter the *rest*, believers must beware lest they too fail to enter the blessing. The writer tempers the warning by the encouragement that God has not revoked the promise of entering his rest. The failure of the Exodus generation to enter the promised rest did not nullify the reality and accessibility of that rest for future generations. There is a far better rest than that eventually found in Canaan by the believing Israelites. **10:** Christians inherit this rest, a state of completion and harmony when God's people have rested from their labors, a wonderful promise for believing women who find their household labors repetitive and unending.

4:11–13 An Exhortation to Enter Christ's Rest. 11: We believers must *do our best to enter* God's rest through faith in his word of promise and obedient response to the voice of God in Scripture. **12:** The Word of God indicates every way in which God speaks, especially the word that came through Jesus Christ. God's message came in the text of Scriptures cited in 3:7—4:11, among others—not the incarnate Word, Jesus. *Alive and powerful*: God's revelation is dynamic. *Two-edged sword*: God's Word penetrates the innermost recesses of one's being. **13:** *Naked and exposed*: One can hide no secrets from God. *Accountable* is a legal term: The Word of God passes judgment on one's thoughts and motives. Only as people know this word can they obey it. Saturating themselves in the Scriptures will enable them to respond to the God who loves them.

4:14—10:18 The Superiority of Christ's Work

4:14—7:28 The Superior Priesthood Demonstrated in Christ. 4:14–16: Jesus, the great High Priest, understands our weaknesses through being tempted, yet he did not sin. He can stand before God but also stand alongside men and women. This dual role, being the bridge between God and human beings, is what it means to be High Priest. Knowing that Jesus is our High Priest should motivate us to hold fast to our confession as Christians and approach God boldly for help in time of need. Those who pray effect a great difference in their lives and in the lives of those for whom they intercede. **5:1–5:** Aaron and Jesus did not exalt themselves to the office of high priest: God chose

6 And in another passage God said to him,

"You are a priest forever in the order of
Melchizedek."*

7 While Jesus was here on earth, he offered
prayers and pleadings, with a loud cry and tears,
to the one who could rescue him from death. And
God heard his prayers because of his deep reverence for God. 8 Even though Jesus was God's Son,
he learned obedience from the things he suffered. 9 In this way, God qualified him as a perfect
High Priest, and he became the source of eternal
salvation for all those who obey him. 10 And God
designated him to be a High Priest in the order
of Melchizedek.

A Call to Spiritual Growth

11 There is much more we would like to say about
this, but it is difficult to explain, especially since
you are spiritually dull and don't seem to listen.
12 You have been believers so long now that you
ought to be teaching others. Instead, you need
someone to teach you again the basic things
about God's word.* You are like babies who need
milk and cannot eat solid food. 13 For someone
who lives on milk is still an infant and doesn't
know how to do what is right. 14 Solid food is
for those who are mature, who through training have the skill to recognize the difference between right and wrong.

6 So let us stop going over the basic teachings about Christ again and again. Let us
go on instead and become mature in our
understanding. Surely we don't need to start
again with the fundamental importance of repenting from evil deeds* and placing our faith in
God. 2 You don't need further instruction about
baptisms, the laying on of hands, the resurrection of the dead, and eternal judgment. 3 And so,
God willing, we will move forward to further
understanding.

4 For it is impossible to bring back to repentance those who were once enlightened—those
who have experienced the good things of heaven
and shared in the Holy Spirit, 5 who have tasted
the goodness of the word of God and the power
of the age to come—6 and who then turn away
from God. It is impossible to bring such people
back to repentance; by rejecting the Son of God,
they themselves are nailing him to the cross once
again and holding him up to public shame.

5:6 Ps 110:4. **5:12** Or *about the oracles of God.* **6:1** Greek *from dead works.*

them. **6–10:** *The order of Melchizedek* (see 7:1–10): As the first priest mentioned in Scripture, Melchizedek is the archetype of all priesthood, which validates Jesus' priesthood as different from and superior to the Levitical priesthood. Christ was without sin, and God summoned him to be a priest forever. This rendered the Aaronic institution obsolete. Christ's high-priestly offering culminated in his suffering death in perfect obedience to God's revealed will. Christian salvation is eternal because it is based on the sacrifice of Christ, which was once for all, never to be repeated, and forever valid. **9:** *For all those who obey him*: Not that believers earn their salvation by obedience but believers respond in obedience to the call to trust Christ for salvation. They express their Christian faith through obedience in daily life.

5:11—6:20 The Warning against Falling Away. 5:11–14: The believers appear unwilling to accept the deeper implications of faith and obedience. **12:** *Basic things*: Elementary religious teaching, as symbolized by *milk,* an image well understood by mothers of infants. *God's word* probably refers to divine revelation in general. These Christians had departed from the boldness and mature commitment they had shown earlier. Later (see 6:9) the author indicates he believes these believers possess maturity and wants to shame them into assuming responsibilities of a spiritually mature group of Christians in a hostile society.

6:1–3 Exhortation to Move Forward. The six beliefs or practices—*repenting,* having *faith in God, baptisms, laying on of hands, resurrection,* and *judgment*—could be either Jewish or Christian. If they refer to Jewish rituals, the writer is pleading with the recipients to leave Jewish teachings and practices, which were prepared for Christianity, and move on to Christian maturity. If they refer to Christian teachings, the author's plea remains the same: press forward in the faith. *Instruction about baptisms* (note the plural) might refer to purification ceremonies in most religions of that day, including Judaism. Christian converts had to be taught the true meaning of Christian baptism, a single act, as well as the right approach to the various ablutions they encountered. *Laying on of hands* might mean the giving of blessing for Jews and the conferring of specific gifts for Christians. *Resurrection of the dead* and *eternal judgment* relate to the future.

6:4–8 Warning against Apostasy. 4–5: *Once enlightened; experienced the good things of heaven; shared in the Holy Spirit; tasted the goodness of the word of God*: All ways of describing those who seem to have professed Christ. **6:** *Turn away*: Commit apostasy.

7 When the ground soaks up the falling rain
and bears a good crop for the farmer, it has God's
blessing. 8 But if a field bears thorns and thistles,
it is useless. The farmer will soon condemn that
field and burn it.
9 Dear friends, even though we are talking this
way, we really don't believe it applies to you. We
are confident that you are meant for better things,
things that come with salvation. 10 For God is not
unjust. He will not forget how hard you have
worked for him and how you have shown your
love to him by caring for other believers,* as you
still do. 11 Our great desire is that you will keep
on loving others as long as life lasts, in order to
make certain that what you hope for will come
true. 12 Then you will not become spiritually dull
and indifferent. Instead, you will follow the example of those who are going to inherit God's
promises because of their faith and endurance.

God's Promises Bring Hope

13 For example, there was God's promise to Abraham. Since there was no one greater to swear by,
God took an oath in his own name, saying:

14 "I will certainly bless you,
and I will multiply your descendants
beyond number."*

15 Then Abraham waited patiently, and he received what God had promised.
16 Now when people take an oath, they call on
someone greater than themselves to hold them
to it. And without any question that oath is binding. 17 God also bound himself with an oath, so
that those who received the promise could be
perfectly sure that he would never change his
mind. 18 So God has given both his promise and
his oath. These two things are unchangeable because it is impossible for God to lie. Therefore, we
who have fled to him for refuge can have great
confidence as we hold to the hope that lies before
us. 19 This hope is a strong and trustworthy anchor for our souls. It leads us through the curtain
into God's inner sanctuary. 20 Jesus has already
gone in there for us. He has become our eternal
High Priest in the order of Melchizedek.

Melchizedek Is Greater Than Abraham

7 This Melchizedek was king of the city of
Salem and also a priest of God Most High.
When Abraham was returning home after
winning a great battle against the kings, Melchizedek met him and blessed him. 2 Then Abraham took a tenth of all he had captured in battle
and gave it to Melchizedek. The name Melchizedek means "king of justice," and king of Salem
means "king of peace." 3 There is no record of his
father or mother or any of his ancestors—no beginning or end to his life. He remains a priest
forever, resembling the Son of God.
4 Consider then how great this Melchizedek

6:10 Greek *for God's holy people.* **6:14** Gen 22:17.

6:9–12 Confidence in Perseverance. Recognizing the severity of the warnings, the writer asserts confidently that they will persevere in their faith, as demonstrated by their previous compassion and love for others. They have not earned their salvation by their good works, but their service to others gives evidence of God's work in them. Many women have servant hearts; they delight in serving family members and others. They must not confuse these good works with the necessity of faith.

6:13–20 A Reminder of God's Unchangeable Purpose. After exposing the danger of spiritual immaturity, the writer affirms the reliability of God's word of promise to the Christian community. **13–15:** The promise for Abraham (Gen 22:15–18) has its ultimate fulfillment in Christ and the church. **17–20:** God's *promise* and *oath* are *unchangeable* and confirm his purpose: God would fulfill his promise. Salvation through the high-priestly ministry of Jesus is certain because God guaranteed it. Believers have a steadfast hope because through his sacrificial death Jesus has entered the presence of God on behalf of his people and has made it possible for them to approach God in priestly service. The *inner sanctuary* behind *the curtain*: In the Temple, the curtain divided the holiest place, where the ark of God was kept, from the rest of the Tabernacle. It symbolized the barrier keeping sinful human beings away from the presence of God. Only the chief priest, a man, could ever pass that curtain and then only on the Day of Atonement. But Jesus' death split the curtain into two and made the way open for his followers, including women, to enter into God's presence.

7:1–10 The Melchizedek Order of Christ's Priesthood. Melchizedek was the mysterious figure described in Genesis 14:18–20. **1–2:** The author implies that righteousness comes through his kind of priesthood. *Salem*, probably an ancient name for Jerusalem, means "peace." This implies that peace with God comes through this kind of priesthood. The author shows Melchizedek's superiority to Abraham by indicating that Melchizedek *blessed* Abraham and received tribute from him. **3:** *No record of his father or mother*: The point is not that Melchizedek had no

was. Even Abraham, the great patriarch of Israel,
recognized this by giving him a tenth of what
he had taken in battle. [5] Now the law of Moses
required that the priests, who are descendants
of Levi, must collect a tithe from the rest of
the people of Israel,* who are also descendants
of Abraham. [6] But Melchizedek, who was not a
descendant of Levi, collected a tenth from Abraham. And Melchizedek placed a blessing upon
Abraham, the one who had already received the
promises of God. [7] And without question, the
person who has the power to give a blessing is
greater than the one who is blessed.

[8] The priests who collect tithes are men who
die, so Melchizedek is greater than they are, because we are told that he lives on. [9] In addition,
we might even say that these Levites—the ones
who collect the tithe—paid a tithe to Melchizedek
when their ancestor Abraham paid a tithe to him.
[10] For although Levi wasn't born yet, the seed
from which he came was in Abraham's body
when Melchizedek collected the tithe from him.

[11] So if the priesthood of Levi, on which the
law was based, could have achieved the perfection God intended, why did God need to establish a different priesthood, with a priest in the
order of Melchizedek instead of the order of Levi
and Aaron?*

[12] And if the priesthood is changed, the law
must also be changed to permit it. [13] For the priest
we are talking about belongs to a different tribe,
whose members have never served at the altar
as priests. [14] What I mean is, our Lord came from
the tribe of Judah, and Moses never mentioned
priests coming from that tribe.

Jesus Is like Melchizedek

[15] This change has been made very clear since
a different priest, who is like Melchizedek, has
appeared. [16] Jesus became a priest, not by meeting the physical requirement of belonging to the
tribe of Levi, but by the power of a life that cannot be destroyed. [17] And the psalmist pointed this
out when he prophesied,

"You are a priest forever in the order of
Melchizedek."*

[18] Yes, the old requirement about the priesthood
was set aside because it was weak and useless.
[19] For the law never made anything perfect. But
now we have confidence in a better hope, through
which we draw near to God.

[20] This new system was established with a solemn oath. Aaron's descendants became priests
without such an oath, [21] but there was an oath
regarding Jesus. For God said to him,

"The LORD has taken an oath and will not
break his vow:
'You are a priest forever.' "*

[22] Because of this oath, Jesus is the one who guarantees this better covenant with God.

[23] There were many priests under the old system, for death prevented them from remaining
in office. [24] But because Jesus lives forever, his
priesthood lasts forever. [25] Therefore he is able,

7:5 Greek *from their brothers.* **7:11** Greek *the order of Aaron?* **7:17** Ps 110:4. **7:21** Ps 110:4.

parents but rather that the absence of the record is significant. The people of antiquity put much emphasis on a priest's genealogy. After the Exile, certain priests whose genealogy could not be established were excluded from the priesthood as unclean (Neh 7:64). **5–10:** Melchizedek's superiority to Abraham, the founder of the Israelites, also made him superior to the latter's descendants, including Levi, the father of the priestly tribe. In these ways Melchizedek prefigured the messianic priest, Christ. He served as a precedent for a superior priesthood, the one to which Christ belongs. His position stood apart from the line of descent, and his ordination was apart from law. This royal priestly figure with no parentage, successor, beginning, or end of life evoked the notion of a priest who continues in this office forever.

7:11–28 The Superiority of Christ's Priesthood. There is need for a new priesthood, new law, and new covenant because the Levitical system did not provide perfection. Jewish Christians were tempted to return to Judaism, perhaps thinking that the law and the covenant were best for them. The writer rejects and tries to correct this belief, appealing to Melchizedek to prove that Jesus' priesthood was different from and superior to the Levitical priesthood. The old priesthood, that of sacrifices and covenant, had been replaced by the new priest and the new covenant he secured with his sacrifice. The Melchizedek Christology primarily proves the effectiveness of the Son's eternal priesthood. Christ's singular offering of himself put an end to Levitical sacrifice. His continual access to the presence of God makes his priesthood effective and perpetual. Evidently the members of the house church doubt the ability of God to act decisively in the present on their behalf. The writer shows the reality of God's final action in Jesus and of Christ's present ability to help them. Women who face discouragement need this reminder.

once and forever, to save* those who come to
God through him. He lives forever to intercede
with God on their behalf.
26 He is the kind of high priest we need because he is holy and blameless, unstained by sin.
He has been set apart from sinners and has been
given the highest place of honor in heaven.*
27 Unlike those other high priests, he does not
need to offer sacrifices every day. They did this
for their own sins first and then for the sins of
the people. But Jesus did this once for all when
he offered himself as the sacrifice for the people's sins. 28 The law appointed high priests who
were limited by human weakness. But after the
law was given, God appointed his Son with an
oath, and his Son has been made the perfect High
Priest forever.

Christ Is Our High Priest

8 Here is the main point: We have a High
Priest who sat down in the place of hon-
or beside the throne of the majestic God
in heaven. 2 There he ministers in the heavenly
Tabernacle,* the true place of worship that was
built by the Lord and not by human hands.
3 And since every high priest is required to
offer gifts and sacrifices, our High Priest must
make an offering, too. 4 If he were here on earth,
he would not even be a priest, since there already
are priests who offer the gifts required by the
law. 5 They serve in a system of worship that is
only a copy, a shadow of the real one in heaven.
For when Moses was getting ready to build the
Tabernacle, God gave him this warning: "Be sure
that you make everything according to the pattern I have shown you here on the mountain."*
6 But now Jesus, our High Priest, has been given
a ministry that is far superior to the old priesthood,
for he is the one who mediates for us a far better
covenant with God, based on better promises.
7 If the first covenant had been faultless, there
would have been no need for a second covenant
to replace it. 8 But when God found fault with the
people, he said:

"The day is coming, says the LORD,
when I will make a new covenant
with the people of Israel and Judah.
9 This covenant will not be like the one
I made with their ancestors
when I took them by the hand
and led them out of the land of Egypt.
They did not remain faithful to my covenant,
so I turned my back on them, says the LORD.
10 But this is the new covenant I will make
with the people of Israel on that day,* says
the LORD:
I will put my laws in their minds,
and I will write them on their hearts.
I will be their God,
and they will be my people.
11 And they will not need to teach their
neighbors,
nor will they need to teach their relatives,*
saying, 'You should know the LORD.'
For everyone, from the least to the greatest,
will know me already.
12 And I will forgive their wickedness,
and I will never again remember their
sins."*

13 When God speaks of a "new" covenant, it
means he has made the first one obsolete. It is
now out of date and will soon disappear.

Old Rules about Worship

9 That first covenant between God and Israel had regulations for worship and a place
of worship here on earth. 2 There were two
rooms in that Tabernacle.* In the first room were
a lampstand, a table, and sacred loaves of bread on
the table. This room was called the Holy Place.
3 Then there was a curtain, and behind the curtain was the second room* called the Most Holy

7:25 Or *is able to save completely.* **7:26** Or *has been exalted higher than the heavens.* **8:2** Or *tent;* also in 8:5. **8:5** Exod 25:40; 26:30. **8:10** Greek *after those days.* **8:11** Greek *their brother.* **8:8-12** Jer 31:31-34. **9:2** Or *tent;* also in 9:11, 21. **9:3** Greek *second tent.*

8:1–13 The Superior Covenant Introduced by Christ. 1–5: The earthly Aaronic priesthood served as a *copy,* a sketch and a *shadow* pointing to Christ. Jesus entered the *heavenly Tabernacle,* the *true place of worship,* where he has unrestricted access to God's eternal presence. This shows the eternal superiority of his priestly service to the ministry of the Levitical high priest. **6:** The author describes Jesus as *the one who mediates for us a far better covenant.* A mediator is a legal representative who arbitrates between two parties. Christ mediates between God and people, establishing the new covenant. **8–12:** Jeremiah 31:31–34 says the new covenant provides forgiveness of sins by an inward and personal relationship with God open to all. Everyone can know God through the new covenant in Jesus Christ. There is no longer any place for the old covenant.

9:1—10:18 The Superior Sacrifice Offered by Christ. 9:1–14: The author shows the superiority of the new covenant by pointing to the way of worship in the old one. He focuses not on the Temple but on the

Place. [4]In that room were a gold incense altar and a wooden chest called the Ark of the Covenant, which was covered with gold on all sides. Inside the Ark were a gold jar containing manna, Aaron's staff that sprouted leaves, and the stone tablets of the covenant. [5]Above the Ark were the cherubim of divine glory, whose wings stretched out over the Ark's cover, the place of atonement. But we cannot explain these things in detail now.

[6]When these things were all in place, the priests regularly entered the first room* as they performed their religious duties. [7]But only the high priest ever entered the Most Holy Place, and only once a year. And he always offered blood for his own sins and for the sins the people had committed in ignorance. [8]By these regulations the Holy Spirit revealed that the entrance to the Most Holy Place was not freely open as long as the Tabernacle* and the system it represented were still in use.

[9]This is an illustration pointing to the present time. For the gifts and sacrifices that the priests offer are not able to cleanse the consciences of the people who bring them. [10]For that old system deals only with food and drink and various cleansing ceremonies—physical regulations that were in effect only until a better system could be established.

Christ Is the Perfect Sacrifice

[11]So Christ has now become the High Priest over all the good things that have come.* He has entered that greater, more perfect Tabernacle in heaven, which was not made by human hands and is not part of this created world. [12]With his own blood—not the blood of goats and calves—he entered the Most Holy Place once for all time and secured our redemption forever.

[13]Under the old system, the blood of goats and bulls and the ashes of a young cow could cleanse people's bodies from ceremonial impurity. [14]Just think how much more the blood of Christ will purify our consciences from sinful deeds* so that we can worship the living God. For by the power of the eternal Spirit, Christ offered himself to God as a perfect sacrifice for our sins. [15]That is why he is the one who mediates a new covenant between God and people, so that all who are called can receive the eternal inheritance God has promised them. For Christ died to set them free from the penalty of the sins they had committed under that first covenant.

[16]Now when someone leaves a will,* it is necessary to prove that the person who made it is dead.* [17]The will goes into effect only after the person's death. While the person who made it is still alive, the will cannot be put into effect.

[18]That is why even the first covenant was put into effect with the blood of an animal. [19]For after Moses had read each of God's commandments to all the people, he took the blood of calves and goats,* along with water, and sprinkled both the book of God's law and all the people, using hyssop branches and scarlet wool. [20]Then he said, "This blood confirms the covenant God has made

9:6 Greek *first tent.* **9:8** Or *the first room;* Greek reads *the first tent.* **9:11** Some manuscripts read *that are about to come.* **9:14** Greek *from dead works.* **9:16a** Or *covenant;* also in 9:17. **9:16b** Or *Now when someone makes a covenant, it is necessary to ratify it with the death of a sacrifice.* **9:19** Some manuscripts do not include *and goats.*

---

long-vanished Tabernacle. Only Jews near Jerusalem had access to the Temple, but the Scriptures told all Jews everywhere about the Tabernacle. **1–10:** The old sanctuary consisted of a system of barriers between the worshiper and God. The cultic provisions allowed the people to approach God only through their representatives, the priests and the high priest. Only the high priest could enter the rear compartment, and then *only once a year* under strictly prescribed conditions. He must never enter without the sacrificial *blood.* The setup and use of the Tabernacle reflected the ineffectiveness of the old covenant, which centered on external matters, such as *food, drink,* and ceremonial washings. Under the old covenant it was necessary to repeat sacrifices that were never adequate to remove sin, cleanse the conscience, and achieve an unbroken relationship with God. **11–14:** But when Christ came and acted as the High Priest and the perfect sacrifice, he purified and made perfect the conscience of believers. *He entered the Most Holy Place* and offered his *blood,* thereby securing eternal *redemption.*

9:15–28 A Sacrifice That Removes Sin. 15–23: Christ's death put the new covenant into effect, just as the death of the testator puts a will into effect. His death on the cross is the sacrifice of the new covenant corresponding to the animal sacrifices prescribed under the old covenant. All sacrificial blood is powerful, but Christ's blood is the most powerful because it achieved decisive purification and the removal of every barrier to the enjoyment of God. **24–28:** But unlike all previous sacrifices, which needed to be repeated, Christ's sacrifice was once for all. Christ deals with sin now, *at the end of the age,* and *will come again . . . to bring salvation.*

with you."* 21 And in the same way, he sprinkled blood on the Tabernacle and on everything used for worship. 22 In fact, according to the law of Moses, nearly everything was purified with blood. For without the shedding of blood, there is no forgiveness.

23 That is why the Tabernacle and everything in it, which were copies of things in heaven, had to be purified by the blood of animals. But the real things in heaven had to be purified with far better sacrifices than the blood of animals.

24 For Christ did not enter into a holy place made with human hands, which was only a copy of the true one in heaven. He entered into heaven itself to appear now before God on our behalf. 25 And he did not enter heaven to offer himself again and again, like the high priest here on earth who enters the Most Holy Place year after year with the blood of an animal. 26 If that had been necessary, Christ would have had to die again and again, ever since the world began. But now, once for all time, he has appeared at the end of the age* to remove sin by his own death as a sacrifice.

27 And just as each person is destined to die once and after that comes judgment, 28 so also Christ died once for all time as a sacrifice to take away the sins of many people. He will come again, not to deal with our sins, but to bring salvation to all who are eagerly waiting for him.

Christ's Sacrifice Once for All

10 The old system under the law of Moses was only a shadow, a dim preview of the good things to come, not the good things themselves. The sacrifices under that system were repeated again and again, year after year, but they were never able to provide perfect cleansing for those who came to worship. 2 If they could have provided perfect cleansing, the sacrifices would have stopped, for the worshipers would have been purified once for all time, and their feelings of guilt would have disappeared.

3 But instead, those sacrifices actually reminded them of their sins year after year. 4 For it is not possible for the blood of bulls and goats to take away sins. 5 That is why, when Christ* came into the world, he said to God,

"You did not want animal sacrifices or sin
offerings.
But you have given me a body to offer.
6 You were not pleased with burnt offerings
or other offerings for sin.
7 Then I said, 'Look, I have come to do your
will, O God—
as is written about me in the Scriptures.' "*

8 First, Christ said, "You did not want animal sacrifices or sin offerings or burnt offerings or other offerings for sin, nor were you pleased with them" (though they are required by the law of Moses). 9 Then he said, "Look, I have come to do your will." He cancels the first covenant in order to put the second into effect. 10 For God's will was for us to be made holy by the sacrifice of the body of Jesus Christ, once for all time.

11 Under the old covenant, the priest stands and ministers before the altar day after day, offering the same sacrifices again and again, which can never take away sins. 12 But our High Priest offered himself to God as a single sacrifice for sins, good for all time. Then he sat down in the place of honor at God's right hand. 13 There he waits until his enemies are humbled and made a footstool under his feet. 14 For by that one offering he forever made perfect those who are being made holy.

15 And the Holy Spirit also testifies that this is so. For he says,

16 "This is the new covenant I will make
with my people on that day,* says the
LORD:
I will put my laws in their hearts,
and I will write them on their minds."*

9:20 Exod 24:8. **9:26** Greek *the ages.* **10:5** Greek *he;* also in 10:8. **10:5-7** Ps 40:6-8 (Greek version). **10:16a** Greek *after those days.* **10:16b** Jer 31:33a.

10:1–18 A Voluntary, Unrepeatable Sacrifice. 1–4: A summary concerning the failure of the law, Christ's final sacrifice, and the forgiveness of sins: Sacrifices under the law were unable to provide forgiveness. **5–7:** Psalm 40:6–8, seen christologically, presents the words of the psalm as being spoken by Christ to God at the time of the incarnation. **8–14:** Christ's bodily existence identifies him with humanity, so his sacrificial death made possible the participation of others in his consecration to the service of God. Jesus' self-offering as a once-for-all sacrifice abolished the Levitical sacrificial system. His sufficient sacrifice in conformity to the will of God effectively removed obstacles to fellowship with him for the worshiping community. **15–18:** Jesus' saving action was performed in history, but it possesses a validity that transcends history.

17 Then he says,

"I will never again remember
their sins and lawless deeds."*

18 And when sins have been forgiven, there is no
need to offer any more sacrifices.

A Call to Persevere
19 And so, dear brothers and sisters,* we can boldly enter heaven's Most Holy Place because of the
blood of Jesus. 20 By his death,* Jesus opened a
new and life-giving way through the curtain
into the Most Holy Place. 21 And since we have
a great High Priest who rules over God's house,
22 let us go right into the presence of God with
sincere hearts fully trusting him. For our guilty
consciences have been sprinkled with Christ's
blood to make us clean, and our bodies have been
washed with pure water.
23 Let us hold tightly without wavering to the
hope we affirm, for God can be trusted to keep
his promise. 24 Let us think of ways to motivate
one another to acts of love and good works. 25 And
let us not neglect our meeting together, as some
people do, but encourage one another, especially
now that the day of his return is drawing near.
26 Dear friends, if we deliberately continue
sinning after we have received knowledge of the
truth, there is no longer any sacrifice that will
cover these sins. 27 There is only the terrible expectation of God's judgment and the raging fire
that will consume his enemies. 28 For anyone
who refused to obey the law of Moses was put to
death without mercy on the testimony of two or
three witnesses. 29 Just think how much worse the
punishment will be for those who have trampled
on the Son of God, and have treated the blood of
the covenant, which made us holy, as if it were
common and unholy, and have insulted and disdained the Holy Spirit who brings God's mercy
to us. 30 For we know the one who said,

"I will take revenge.
I will pay them back."*

He also said,

"The LORD will judge his own people."*

31 It is a terrible thing to fall into the hands of the
living God.
32 Think back on those early days when you
first learned about Christ.* Remember how you
remained faithful even though it meant terrible
suffering. 33 Sometimes you were exposed to
public ridicule and were beaten, and sometimes
you helped others who were suffering the same
things. 34 You suffered along with those who
were thrown into jail, and when all you owned
was taken from you, you accepted it with joy.
You knew there were better things waiting for
you that will last forever.
35 So do not throw away this confident trust in
the Lord. Remember the great reward it brings
you! 36 Patient endurance is what you need now,
so that you will continue to do God's will. Then
you will receive all that he has promised.

37 "For in just a little while,
the Coming One will come and not delay.
38 And my righteous ones will live by faith.*
But I will take no pleasure in anyone who
turns away."*

10:17 Jer 31:34b. **10:19** Greek *brothers.* **10:20** Greek *Through his flesh.* **10:30a** Deut 32:35. **10:30b** Deut 32:36. **10:32** Greek *when you were first enlightened.* **10:38** Or *my righteous ones will live by their faithfulness;* Greek reads *my righteous one will live by faith.* **10:37-38** Hab 2:3-4.

10:19—12:29 The Superiority of Christ's Power
This begins the ethical section.

10:19–39 An Appeal for Endurance. 19–25: Christ's deeds should stir his people to action. The believing community gained benefits from Christ's sacrifice. **19:** All believers, male and female, can now enter the *Most Holy Place*. **22:** *Consciences . . . sprinkled*: The cleansing effect of the blood of Christ on the inmost being; *bodies . . . water,* baptism. **23–25:** Act responsibly; do not waver in commitment to Christ. *Motivate one another*: Many women serve as effective role models in this way.

10:26–31 Fearing the Living God. If an individual rejects the sacrifice of Christ, there is no other one who can provide forgiveness for sins. The result can only be judgment, punishment, and death. **26:** *Deliberately continue sinning*: Not backsliding but rejecting the message of the gospel. **29:** *Trampl*[ing] *on the Son of God*: Not only rejecting Christ but also despising him. Insolent self-assertion disregards the respect due to others, in this case to the Holy Spirit.

10:32–39 Considering Past Experiences and Future Reward. The readers will recognize their peril, and will demonstrate faithfulness and steadfast endurance consistent with their relationship with God through Christ and the goal set before them.

[39]But we are not like those who turn away from God to their own destruction. We are the faithful ones, whose souls will be saved.

Great Examples of Faith

11 Faith is the confidence that what we hope for will actually happen; it gives us assurance about things we cannot see. [2]Through their faith, the people in days of old earned a good reputation.

[3]By faith we understand that the entire universe was formed at God's command, that what we now see did not come from anything that can be seen.

[4]It was by faith that Abel brought a more acceptable offering to God than Cain did. Abel's offering gave evidence that he was a righteous man, and God showed his approval of his gifts. Although Abel is long dead, he still speaks to us by his example of faith.

[5]It was by faith that Enoch was taken up to heaven without dying—"he disappeared, because God took him."* For before he was taken up, he was known as a person who pleased God. [6]And it is impossible to please God without faith. Anyone who wants to come to him must believe that God exists and that he rewards those who sincerely seek him.

[7]It was by faith that Noah built a large boat to save his family from the flood. He obeyed God, who warned him about things that had never happened before. By his faith Noah condemned the rest of the world, and he received the righteousness that comes by faith.

[8]It was by faith that Abraham obeyed when God called him to leave home and go to another land that God would give him as his inheritance. He went without knowing where he was going. [9]And even when he reached the land God promised him, he lived there by faith—for he was like a foreigner, living in tents. And so did Isaac and Jacob, who inherited the same promise. [10]Abraham was confidently looking forward to a city with eternal foundations, a city designed and built by God.

[11]It was by faith that even Sarah was able to have a child, though she was barren and was too old. She believed* that God would keep his promise. [12]And so a whole nation came from this one man who was as good as dead—a nation with so many people that, like the stars in the sky and the sand on the seashore, there is no way to count them.

[13]All these people died still believing what God had promised them. They did not receive what was promised, but they saw it all from a distance and welcomed it. They agreed that they were foreigners and nomads here on earth. [14]Obviously people who say such things are looking forward to a country they can call their own. [15]If they had longed for the country they came from, they could have gone back. [16]But they were looking for a better place, a heavenly homeland. That is why God is not ashamed to be called their God, for he has prepared a city for them.

[17]It was by faith that Abraham offered Isaac as a sacrifice when God was testing him. Abraham, who had received God's promises, was ready to sacrifice his only son, Isaac, [18]even though God had told him, "Isaac is the son through whom your descendants will be counted."* [19]Abraham reasoned that if Isaac died, God was able to bring him back to life again. And in a sense, Abraham did receive his son back from the dead.

[20]It was by faith that Isaac promised blessings for the future to his sons, Jacob and Esau.

[21]It was by faith that Jacob, when he was old and dying, blessed each of Joseph's sons and bowed in worship as he leaned on his staff.

[22]It was by faith that Joseph, when he was about to die, said confidently that the people of Israel would leave Egypt. He even commanded

11:5 Gen 5:24. **11:11** Or *It was by faith that he [Abraham] was able to have a child, even though Sarah was barren and he was too old. He believed.* **11:18** Gen 21:12.

11:1–40 The Encouragement of Faith. 1–3: Faith is defined as confidence and assurance: trust in what God has promised and perseverance as a result. **4–40:** The author illustrates faith and encourages readers in their walk of faith by listing Old Testament heroes and heroines who lived in faithfulness to God. In these examples we see faith as active obedience. Each champion of faith worked out his or her faith in different ways. Although the majority of these faithful were men, the author includes references to Sarah, Moses' parents, Rahab, and women in general. **11:** Although Sarah laughed when first hearing that she was to have a child, her disbelief evidently turned to faith long before the birth of her son, Isaac (Gen 18:12). Like her husband, Abraham, Sarah had to believe that the God who made promises would honor his word, despite how impossible it must have seemed to her as a woman long past childbearing years. Sarah shared not only her husband's challenges and disappointments but also his dreams and blessings. She stood by his side through good and bad decisions, adversities and blessings, in youth and old age. The New Testament describes Sarah as one of the holy women of old because she

them to take his bones with them when they
left.

23 It was by faith that Moses' parents hid him
for three months when he was born. They saw
that God had given them an unusual child, and
they were not afraid to disobey the king's command.

24 It was by faith that Moses, when he grew up,
refused to be called the son of Pharaoh's daughter. 25 He chose to share the oppression of God's
people instead of enjoying the fleeting pleasures
of sin. 26 He thought it was better to suffer for
the sake of Christ than to own the treasures of
Egypt, for he was looking ahead to his great reward. 27 It was by faith that Moses left the land
of Egypt, not fearing the king's anger. He kept
right on going because he kept his eyes on the
one who is invisible. 28 It was by faith that Moses commanded the people of Israel to keep the
Passover and to sprinkle blood on the doorposts
so that the angel of death would not kill their
firstborn sons.

29 It was by faith that the people of Israel went
right through the Red Sea as though they were
on dry ground. But when the Egyptians tried to
follow, they were all drowned.

30 It was by faith that the people of Israel
marched around Jericho for seven days, and the
walls came crashing down.

31 It was by faith that Rahab the prostitute
was not destroyed with the people in her city
who refused to obey God. For she had given a
friendly welcome to the spies.

32 How much more do I need to say? It would
take too long to recount the stories of the faith of
Gideon, Barak, Samson, Jephthah, David, Samuel, and all the prophets. 33 By faith these people
overthrew kingdoms, ruled with justice, and received what God had promised them. They shut
the mouths of lions, 34 quenched the flames of
fire, and escaped death by the edge of the sword.
Their weakness was turned to strength. They became strong in battle and put whole armies to
flight. 35 Women received their loved ones back
again from death.

But others were tortured, refusing to turn
from God in order to be set free. They placed
their hope in a better life after the resurrection.
36 Some were jeered at, and their backs were cut
open with whips. Others were chained in prisons. 37 Some died by stoning, some were sawed
in half,* and others were killed with the sword.
Some went about wearing skins of sheep and
goats, destitute and oppressed and mistreated.
38 They were too good for this world, wandering
over deserts and mountains, hiding in caves and
holes in the ground.

39 All these people earned a good reputation
because of their faith, yet none of them received
all that God had promised. 40 For God had something better in mind for us, so that they would
not reach perfection without us.

God's Discipline Proves His Love

12 Therefore, since we are surrounded
by such a huge crowd of witnesses to
the life of faith, let us strip off every
weight that slows us down, especially the sin that
so easily trips us up. And let us run with endurance the race God has set before us. 2 We do this

11:37 Some manuscripts add *some were tested.*

willingly cooperated with her husband and with God (1 Pet 3:5). **23:** Moses' mother, Jochebed, emerged as a fearless and focused woman of faith. She circumvented the Egyptian edict to destroy her baby and cleverly protected her son. She acted as a caring and resourceful mother despite the evil around her. God saw her heart, heard her prayers, and intervened on her behalf. **31:** Rahab, the Gentile prostitute, demonstrates that God does not restrict faith to those of acceptable race, background, or gender. A prostitute initially seems an unlikely example of faith, yet Jews and Christians highly regard Rahab. James mentions her as an example to follow because her faith was not without works (Jas 2:25). Matthew lists her in the genealogy of the Lord as the wife of Salmon (Matt 1:5). Although Rahab came from a pagan people, she acted decisively out of her deep convictions about God, about whom she must have heard from the Hebrew spies. She risked her life for God's people. Rahab exercised her faith. **35:** Women who received their loved ones by resurrection included the widow of Zarephath and the Shunammite woman (1 Kgs 17; 2 Kgs 4). All these figures of faith, male and female, possessed a strong future hope. They never saw the full working out of God's promises. Faith enables believers to endure suffering, even martyrdom. The capacity to endure suffering and death presupposes a relationship to the unseen world. **35–40:** The summary verses speak of people whose circumstances of poverty and persecution singled them out as undesirable from the viewpoint of the world. The writer of Hebrews, however, exclaims that the world was not worthy of them. They were the people of God and recipients of his blessings.

12:1–13 The Experience of Discipline. 1–3: The athletic metaphor compares the Christian life with a race. Contemporary women may be able to relate to

by keeping our eyes on Jesus, the champion who
initiates and perfects our faith.* Because of the
joy* awaiting him, he endured the cross, disregarding its shame. Now he is seated in the place
of honor beside God's throne. 3 Think of all the
hostility he endured from sinful people;* then
you won't become weary and give up. 4 After all,
you have not yet given your lives in your struggle against sin.

5 And have you forgotten the encouraging
words God spoke to you as his children?* He
said,

"My child,* don't make light of the LORD's
discipline,
and don't give up when he corrects you.
6 For the LORD disciplines those he loves,
and he punishes each one he accepts as his
child."*

7 As you endure this divine discipline, remember
that God is treating you as his own children. Who
ever heard of a child who is never disciplined by
its father? 8 If God doesn't discipline you as he
does all of his children, it means that you are illegitimate and are not really his children at all.
9 Since we respected our earthly fathers who disciplined us, shouldn't we submit even more to
the discipline of the Father of our spirits, and live
forever?*

10 For our earthly fathers disciplined us for
a few years, doing the best they knew how. But
God's discipline is always good for us, so that we
might share in his holiness. 11 No discipline is enjoyable while it is happening—it's painful! But
afterward there will be a peaceful harvest of right
living for those who are trained in this way.

12 So take a new grip with your tired hands
and strengthen your weak knees. 13 Mark out a
straight path for your feet so that those who are
weak and lame will not fall but become strong.

A Call to Listen to God

14 Work at living in peace with everyone, and
work at living a holy life, for those who are not
holy will not see the Lord. 15 Look after each other so that none of you fails to receive the grace of
God. Watch out that no poisonous root of bitterness grows up to trouble you, corrupting many.
16 Make sure that no one is immoral or godless
like Esau, who traded his birthright as the firstborn son for a single meal. 17 You know that afterward, when he wanted his father's blessing, he
was rejected. It was too late for repentance, even
though he begged with bitter tears.

18 You have not come to a physical mountain,*

12:2a Or *Jesus, the originator and perfecter of our faith.* **12:2b** Or *Instead of the joy.* **12:3** Some manuscripts read *Think of how people hurt themselves by opposing him.* **12:5a** Greek *sons;* also in 12:7, 8. **12:5b** Greek *son;* also in 12:6, 7. **12:5-6** Prov 3:11-12 (Greek version). **12:9** Or *and really live?* **12:18** Greek *to something that can be touched.*

---

this image better than their first-century counterparts since many of them participate in sports or fitness activity. **1:** The runners, believers, find themselves surrounded by a *huge crowd of witnesses*, the champions of faith. *Witnesses* are those who have testified to the faith, not those who are onlookers to our lives. Christians can compete in the race of life well only by laying aside every impediment that hinders them from putting forth their best effort and running with perseverance. **2:** Believers should turn from the models of faithfulness in Israel's past to Jesus *who initiates and perfects* their faith. Like the readers, Jesus faced conflict in a hostile environment, enduring the abject humiliation of crucifixion. **3:** Believers must fix their gaze on Jesus and show responsible commitment in difficulty. Jesus offers a model for Christians whenever they are tempted to be disheartened by opposition.

12:4–13 The Purpose of God. For believers, the cross transforms all affliction. The Savior, who suffered, will not lead his followers into meaningless trials. **5–6:** To help readers perceive the significance of their hardships, Proverbs 3:11–12 demonstrates the essential and integral relationship between sufferings and a filial relationship with God. **7–13:** Sufferings are corrective—and disciplinary when God makes them a means for maturing his children spiritually—helping them to participate in his holiness. When the community of faith experiences unpleasantness, pain, and adversity because they are Christians, they should recognize in these sufferings the pledge of the Father's love. Difficulties come to everybody, but are easier to bear when accepted as meaningful.

12:14–29 A Warning against Rejecting God. 14–21: Careless disregard for the blessings of the new covenant exposes these Jewish Christians to the threat of apostasy. Therefore the writer calls them to pursue peace and holiness as an expression of Christian maturity, urging them to be vigilant lest anyone fail to *receive the grace of God*. Esau exemplifies an immoral, godless person who had contempt for his spiritual privileges. Imagery of two mountains represents the old and new covenants to show the differences. *Mount Sinai* symbolized the law, the sacrificial system, and the Aaronic priesthood. The threatening judgment and fear are connected with the giving of

to a place of flaming fire, darkness, gloom, and
whirlwind, as the Israelites did at Mount Sinai.
19 For they heard an awesome trumpet blast and
a voice so terrible that they begged God to stop
speaking. 20 They staggered back under God's
command: "If even an animal touches the mountain, it must be stoned to death."* 21 Moses himself was so frightened at the sight that he said, "I
am terrified and trembling."*

22 No, you have come to Mount Zion, to the
city of the living God, the heavenly Jerusalem,
and to countless thousands of angels in a joyful
gathering. 23 You have come to the assembly of
God's firstborn children, whose names are written in heaven. You have come to God himself,
who is the judge over all things. You have come
to the spirits of the righteous ones in heaven who
have now been made perfect. 24 You have come to
Jesus, the one who mediates the new covenant
between God and people, and to the sprinkled
blood, which speaks of forgiveness instead of
crying out for vengeance like the blood of Abel.

25 Be careful that you do not refuse to listen to
the One who is speaking. For if the people of Israel
did not escape when they refused to listen to Moses, the earthly messenger, we will certainly not
escape if we reject the One who speaks to us from
heaven! 26 When God spoke from Mount Sinai
his voice shook the earth, but now he makes another promise: "Once again I will shake not only
the earth but the heavens also."* 27 This means
that all of creation will be shaken and removed, so
that only unshakable things will remain.

28 Since we are receiving a Kingdom that is
unshakable, let us be thankful and please God
by worshiping him with holy fear and awe. 29 For
our God is a devouring fire.

Concluding Words

13 Keep on loving each other as brothers and sisters.* 2 Don't forget to show
hospitality to strangers, for some who
have done this have entertained angels without
realizing it! 3 Remember those in prison, as if
you were there yourself. Remember also those
being mistreated, as if you felt their pain in your
own bodies.

4 Give honor to marriage, and remain faithful to one another in marriage. God will surely
judge people who are immoral and those who
commit adultery.

5 Don't love money; be satisfied with what
you have. For God has said,

"I will never fail you.
I will never abandon you."*

6 So we can say with confidence,

"The LORD is my helper,
so I will have no fear.
What can mere people do to me?"*

12:20 Exod 19:13. **12:21** Deut 9:19. **12:26** Hag 2:6.
13:1 Greek *Continue in brotherly love.* **13:5** Deut 31:6, 8.
13:6 Ps 118:6.

the law at Mount Sinai (see Exod 19—20; Deut 5). These things created an atmosphere of dread and confusion, and show the distance that separated the worshipers from God under the old covenant. **22–24:** By contrast, believers have *come to Mount Zion*. The images describe the realization of the eschatological hopes of God's people under the old and new covenants. God can be approached in the new covenant. Christians meet him in joyful assembly, together with angels, the faithful men and women of God, and Jesus. **25–29:** The frank awareness of the awesome character of God's holiness deepens the worship experience.

13:1–17 Final Exhortations

13:1–3 Exhortations for Social Life. Believers cannot restrict worship to praise and prayer. Instead, worship infuses every aspect of life with service to God. It means *loving each other*, showing *hospitality to strangers*, and aiding *those in prison* and *those being mistreated*. If itinerant missionaries had had only public inns, characterized by filth and immorality, to stay in, rather than the hospitality of Christian homes, the spread of the faith would have been hampered. Although conditions differ now, people still respond to the warmth and intimacy of a home. Many women today embrace the ministry of hospitality, opening their homes and offering their creative talents to the Lord.

13:4–6 Exhortations for Home Life. Believers should honor marriage; God takes the marriage covenant seriously (see Marriage, Song 2), affirming the significance and responsibility of the wife and the husband. The exhortation to honor marriage refers primarily to sexual immorality and unfaithfulness, but might also be against sexual asceticism that viewed marriage as a lesser state than celibacy. Believers should also be wary of the dangers of materialism. Dependence on material things can become idolatry, undermining dependence on God, who never fails or forsakes us.

7 Remember your leaders who taught you the word of God. Think of all the good that has come from their lives, and follow the example of their faith.

8 Jesus Christ is the same yesterday, today, and forever. 9 So do not be attracted by strange, new ideas. Your strength comes from God's grace, not from rules about food, which don't help those who follow them.

10 We have an altar from which the priests in the Tabernacle* have no right to eat. 11 Under the old system, the high priest brought the blood of animals into the Holy Place as a sacrifice for sin, and the bodies of the animals were burned outside the camp. 12 So also Jesus suffered and died outside the city gates to make his people holy by means of his own blood. 13 So let us go out to him, outside the camp, and bear the disgrace he bore. 14 For this world is not our permanent home; we are looking forward to a home yet to come.

15 Therefore, let us offer through Jesus a continual sacrifice of praise to God, proclaiming our allegiance to his name. 16 And don't forget to do good and to share with those in need. These are the sacrifices that please God.

17 Obey your spiritual leaders, and do what they say. Their work is to watch over your souls, and they are accountable to God. Give them reason to do this with joy and not with sorrow. That would certainly not be for your benefit.

18 Pray for us, for our conscience is clear and we want to live honorably in everything we do. 19 And especially pray that I will be able to come back to you soon.

20 Now may the God of peace—
who brought up from the dead our Lord Jesus,
the great Shepherd of the sheep,
and ratified an eternal covenant with his blood—
21 may he equip you with all you need
for doing his will.
May he produce in you,*
through the power of Jesus Christ,
every good thing that is pleasing to him.
All glory to him forever and ever! Amen.

22 I urge you, dear brothers and sisters,* to pay attention to what I have written in this brief exhortation.

23 I want you to know that our brother Timothy has been released from jail. If he comes here soon, I will bring him with me to see you.

24 Greet all your leaders and all the believers there.* The believers from Italy send you their greetings.

25 May God's grace be with you all.

13:10 Or *tent.* **13:21** Some manuscripts read *in us.*
13:22 Greek *brothers.* **13:24** Greek *all of God's holy people.*

13:7–17 Exhortations for Religious Life. 7: Believers should treat their spiritual leaders with respect, following their examples of faith. Those with authority must also accept responsibility for their actions. **8–10:** The followers of Jesus Christ can rely on him and base their conduct on the certainty of his unchanging nature. **11–17:** Jesus suffered in order to sanctify his people. Jesus' death *outside the city gates* of Jerusalem symbolized the rejection of the Jewish authorities. The readers should leave the security of ancestral belief and go outside to Jesus regardless of the difficulties this decision might involve.

13:18–25 Benediction and Conclusion

The author asks readers for their prayers. **20–22:** He in turn prays that God might enable them to do his will in all things. **23–25:** He gives information about Timothy and sends greetings to the rest of the church, suggesting that this letter was sent not to a whole church but to a particular group.

JAMES

INTRODUCTION

James is a difficult book to classify. It is almost, but not quite, a letter; there is an opening greeting but no closing benediction. It is almost, but not quite, a sermon; there is much advice but no structured argument. It is almost, but not quite, a wisdom treatise, like the book of Proverbs; but there is too much personal involvement for that. It consists of a series of thoughts and recommendations that are related but not systematically organized, explaining what is involved in living a Christian life. James's conviction that Christian faith is meaningless without a practical outworking comes across strongly. The focus moves from subject to subject apparently as different ideas came to mind. At every stage, however, the concern is with how those who are servants (or slaves) "of God and of the Lord Jesus Christ" (Jas 1:1) should think and behave and live. James is not unconcerned with doctrine—the practical life of which he speaks stems from clear belief—but his primary concern is with what that belief means in the nitty-gritty of everyday life. There are parallels to this in the teaching of Jesus. Note the many echoes of the Sermon on the Mount found within the book of James (Matt 5:12 in Jas 1:2, Matt 5:48 in Jas 1:4, Matt 7:7 in Jas 1:5, Matt 7:11 in Jas 1:17, and Matt 5:22 in Jas 1:19 are just a few of the examples from Jas 1). James seems to have taken that sermon to heart.

James may have had specific situations of persecution (1:2) or favoritism (2:1) in mind, but his thoughts would apply across the board. Cetainly James's focus on the importance of down-to-earth, everyday behavior would have been especially relevant to those who saw themselves as of little account. As James pours out encouragement and challenge to his Christian family—the all-embracing "brothers" involves men, women and children—those, perhaps particularly women, who were engulfed by domestic responsibilities would have been reassured that any service they might give to God was far from irrelevant or worthless.

Because James jumps from one idea to another it is hard to produce a sequential outline, but the following structure gives some idea of his particular interests. He addresses Christians' attitude to problems (1:2–4, 12–15; 5:7–11), attitude to possessions (1:9–11, 16–18; 4:1–10, 13–16; 5:1–6), and attitude to people (2:1–16; 5:19–20). He also emphasizes listening and doing (1:19–27; 2:17–27; 4:17), wisdom (1:5–8; 3:1–2, 13–18), and speech (3:2–12; 4:11–12; 5:12–18). —*Mary J. Evans*

1:1–27	Introduction to the Christian Life
2:1–26	Status in Christ
3:1—4:10	Use and Misuse of Speech
4:11—5:20	Reprise and Redevelopment

Greetings from James

1 This letter is from James, a slave of God and
of the Lord Jesus Christ.
I am writing to the "twelve tribes"—
Jewish believers scattered abroad.
Greetings!

Faith and Endurance

[2] Dear brothers and sisters,* when troubles come
your way, consider it an opportunity for great joy.
[3] For you know that when your faith is tested, your
endurance has a chance to grow. [4] So let it grow, for
when your endurance is fully developed, you will
be perfect and complete, needing nothing.
[5] If you need wisdom, ask our generous God,
and he will give it to you. He will not rebuke
you for asking. [6] But when you ask him, be sure
that your faith is in God alone. Do not waver,
for a person with divided loyalty is as unsettled
as a wave of the sea that is blown and tossed by
the wind. [7] Such people should not expect to receive anything from the Lord. [8] Their loyalty is
divided between God and the world, and they are
unstable in everything they do.
[9] Believers who are* poor have something to
boast about, for God has honored them. [10] And
those who are rich should boast that God has
humbled them. They will fade away like a little
flower in the field. [11] The hot sun rises and the
grass withers; the little flower droops and falls,
and its beauty fades away. In the same way, the
rich will fade away with all of their achievements.
[12] God blesses those who patiently endure
testing and temptation. Afterward they will receive the crown of life that God has promised to
those who love him. [13] And remember, when you
are being tempted, do not say, "God is tempting
me." God is never tempted to do wrong,* and he
never tempts anyone else. [14] Temptation comes
from our own desires, which entice us and drag
us away. [15] These desires give birth to sinful actions. And when sin is allowed to grow, it gives
birth to death.

1:2 Greek *brothers;* also in 1:16, 19. **1:9** Greek *The brother who is.* **1:13** Or *God should not be put to a test by evil people.*

1:1–27 Introduction to the Christian Life

1:1 Introductory Greeting. We cannot be sure of who this James is, although traditionally the book has been ascribed to Jesus' brother James. There is also little clue to the recipients. It is addressed to *the "twelve tribes"—Jewish believers scattered abroad* ("in the dispersion"), which may indicate an intended Jewish readership but is just as likely to be a symbolic way of referring to Christians throughout the world. The NLT text combines both in the assumption that it refers to Jewish Christians.

1:2–18 Faith and Endurance. Beginning here, chapter 1 contains seven separate paragraphs, each dealing with what appears to be a separate topic. However, there is enough link between them to justify the conclusion that the chapter is not a collection of isolated thoughts but was composed at the same time. **2–4:** James begins by speaking of the trials that he assumes all Christians will face. Trials are not to be seen as a failure of faith or even as an unexpected intrusion. Rather, they are to be welcomed as a God-given means of strengthening faith and bringing maturity. Patient endurance or steadfastness is a positive Christian quality, and the cultivation of this characteristic will enable any trial to have a positive effect on Christians' spiritual lives. **5–8:** In this context, James probably refers to the kind of wisdom needed to understand the reason for whatever trials Christians face. God does want them to understand, but spiritual discernment based on trust in God's sovereignty is needed. This kind of wisdom comes from God alone. There is no assurance here that if only people have the right kind of faith, then their every request will be granted, or even a promise that they will never remain in the dark over any issue. **9–11:** James's readers need to have the right attitude to status as well as to problems. The danger of assuming that Christians should expect riches and that riches must mean God's blessing was as real as the danger of assuming that Christians should not face trials. The poor Christians, including the believing women who had little public recognition or personal wealth, should be glad that they have abundant wealth and status in Christ, regardless of any material possessions. And any rich Christians, including the wealthy businessmen who might have expected their status to carry over into the church, should be glad that their salvation is not dependent on passing possessions. **12–15:** The temptation James has first in mind is probably to underestimate one's status in Christ or to overestimate one's status in the world. Women throughout the world have been prone to the temptation to denigrate themselves and should perhaps take special note of James's words. It is often assumed that excessive humility is a sign of spirituality and comes from God. This is quite wrong. To underestimate the significance of life and status in Christ, to assume that although we have that life and status we are still insignificant nobodies, is as likely to lead to spiritual death as the assumption that human

16 So don't be misled, my dear brothers and
sisters. 17 Whatever is good and perfect comes
down to us from God our Father, who created all
the lights in the heavens.* He never changes or
casts a shifting shadow.* 18 He chose to give birth
to us by giving us his true word. And we, out of
all creation, became his prized possession.*

Listening and Doing

19 Understand this, my dear brothers and sisters:
You must all be quick to listen, slow to speak,
and slow to get angry. 20 Human anger* does
not produce the righteousness* God desires.
21 So get rid of all the filth and evil in your lives,
and humbly accept the word God has planted in
your hearts, for it has the power to save your
souls.
22 But don't just listen to God's word. You
must do what it says. Otherwise, you are only
fooling yourselves. 23 For if you listen to the word
and don't obey, it is like glancing at your face in a
mirror. 24 You see yourself, walk away, and forget
what you look like. 25 But if you look carefully
into the perfect law that sets you free, and if you
do what it says and don't forget what you heard,
then God will bless you for doing it.
26 If you claim to be religious but don't control
your tongue, you are fooling yourself, and your
religion is worthless. 27 Pure and genuine religion
in the sight of God the Father means caring for
orphans and widows in their distress and refusing to let the world corrupt you.

A Warning against Prejudice

2 My dear brothers and sisters,* how can
you claim to have faith in our glorious
Lord Jesus Christ if you favor some people
over others?
2 For example, suppose someone comes into
your meeting* dressed in fancy clothes and expensive jewelry, and another comes in who is
poor and dressed in dirty clothes. 3 If you give
special attention and a good seat to the rich
person, but you say to the poor one, "You can
stand over there, or else sit on the floor"—well,
4 doesn't this discrimination show that your
judgments are guided by evil motives?
5 Listen to me, dear brothers and sisters. Hasn't
God chosen the poor in this world to be rich in
faith? Aren't they the ones who will inherit the

1:17a Greek *from above, from the Father of lights.* **1:17b** Some manuscripts read *He never changes, as a shifting shadow does.* **1:18** Greek *we became a kind of firstfruit of his creatures.* **1:20a** Greek *A man's anger.* **1:20b** Or *the justice.* **2:1** Greek *brothers;* also in 2:5, 14. **2:2** Greek *your synagogue.*

status does have spiritual significance. James can in no way be seen as encouraging women or men to a self-deprecation that fails to acknowledge the power of the work of Christ's Spirit within them. **16–18:** Far from tempting people into evil of any kind, God gives only good gifts. Therefore, *whatever is good and perfect,* whether it comes from the wealthy or the poor, is inspired by and reflects God, who is the parent of all believers. The reference to God as *our Father* in verse 17 is paralleled by the reference to mothering, (the language used is that of giving birth), in verse 18, and it is hard to see this parallel as anything other than deliberate. The family likeness, illustrated by such characteristics as generosity (v. 17), the ability to listen and the lack of anger (vv. 19–20), is brought about through *the word God has planted* in the believer (v. 21).

1:19–27 Listening and Doing. Hearing the *word* is important. The *perfect law that sets you free* cannot be understood without hearing about it. But to have an intellectual appreciation of gospel truth and to think that that makes you into a Christian is self-deception. That kind of knowledge is no more lasting than your reflection in a mirror after you have moved on. Real blessing comes from knowing the gospel and living it out—which means ongoing moral purity, concern for the poor, and control of speech and temper.

2:1–26 Status in Christ

In James 2, the issue of right and wrong attitudes that was introduced in James 1 is further developed.

2:1–13 Warning against Prejudice. A wrong attitude toward possessions and status can be reflected in a wrong attitude toward those who have possessions and status. To show favoritism to people just because they have status in the world is to negate the significance of faith in Jesus Christ. To organize the seating in a way that gives special importance to people because of their wealth or their education or maybe their gender is to imply that these factors take priority over the work of Christ. The contrast that James introduces, between the tawdry shoddiness of worldly wealth and Christ as the *glorious Lord,* shows just how bad this kind of behavior was. James has no doubt that to show partiality because of wealth—as opposed to caring for rich and poor alike—is sin. It breaks God's law and is just as serious as committing adultery or murder. If Christians make judgments on the basis of worldly criteria, then they will be placed under such merciless judgment. There is a strong

Kingdom he promised to those who love him? 6 But you dishonor the poor! Isn't it the rich who oppress you and drag you into court? 7 Aren't they the ones who slander Jesus Christ, whose noble name* you bear?

8 Yes indeed, it is good when you obey the royal law as found in the Scriptures: "Love your neighbor as yourself."* 9 But if you favor some people over others, you are committing a sin. You are guilty of breaking the law.

10 For the person who keeps all of the laws except one is as guilty as a person who has broken all of God's laws. 11 For the same God who said, "You must not commit adultery," also said, "You must not murder."* So if you murder someone but do not commit adultery, you have still broken the law.

12 So whatever you say or whatever you do, remember that you will be judged by the law that sets you free. 13 There will be no mercy for those who have not shown mercy to others. But if you have been merciful, God will be merciful when he judges you.

Faith without Good Deeds Is Dead

14 What good is it, dear brothers and sisters, if you say you have faith but don't show it by your actions? Can that kind of faith save anyone? 15 Suppose you see a brother or sister who has no food or clothing, 16 and you say, "Good-bye and have a good day; stay warm and eat well"—but then you don't give that person any food or clothing. What good does that do?

17 So you see, faith by itself isn't enough. Unless it produces good deeds, it is dead and useless.

18 Now someone may argue, "Some people have faith; others have good deeds." But I say, "How can you show me your faith if you don't have good deeds? I will show you my faith by my good deeds."

19 You say you have faith, for you believe that there is one God.* Good for you! Even the demons believe this, and they tremble in terror. 20 How foolish! Can't you see that faith without good deeds is useless?

21 Don't you remember that our ancestor Abraham was shown to be right with God by his actions when he offered his son Isaac on the altar? 22 You see, his faith and his actions worked together. His actions made his faith complete. 23 And so it happened just as the Scriptures say: "Abraham believed God, and God counted him as righteous because of his faith."* He was even called the friend of God.* 24 So you see, we are shown to be right with God by what we do, not by faith alone.

25 Rahab the prostitute is another example. She was shown to be right with God by her actions when she hid those messengers and sent them safely away by a different road. 26 Just as the body is dead without breath,* so also faith is dead without good works.

2:7 Greek *slander the noble name.* **2:8** Lev 19:18. **2:11** Exod 20:13-14; Deut 5:17-18. **2:19** Some manuscripts read *that God is one;* see Deut 6:4. **2:23a** Gen 15:6. **2:23b** See Isa 41:8. **2:26** Or *without spirit.*

---

warning here to any who pay too much attention to external factors like fashion, jewelry, or hairstyle when they make judgments about people. Two additional arguments are given in support of James's position. First, the poor have been chosen by God to receive faith, and therefore to dishonor the poor is to dishonor God (v. 5). Second, those who come from the higher social strata have caused many problems for the young churches, and therefore to honor them does not make sense (vv. 6–7).

2:14–26 Faith without Good Deeds Is Dead. 14–16: Christians must not only have a loving attitude to rich and poor alike but also must show loving actions, making sure that the material needs of all are met. Sympathizing with the poor is not much better than despising them if it doesn't lead to helpful action. **17–26:** James's development of this thought has sometimes been seen as controversial. His statements *Our ancestor Abraham was shown to be right with God by his actions* and *His actions made his faith complete* are seen as being in direct contradiction to Paul's statement "We are made right with God through faith and not by obeying the law" (Rom 3:28), or his argument in Romans 4 that Abraham was justified by faith and not by works. However, a closer examination reveals that Paul and James are using the words for faith and for works in different senses. For James, faith is intellectual assent to certain truths, whereas for Paul it is personal belief and commitment. For Paul works are acts of obedience to specific laws, whereas for James they are acts of love and kindness. James and Paul come to the same position via different routes. Both target the necessity of faith in action. This kind of worked-out faith was demonstrated by Abraham, the high-reputation, righteous father of the nation, and by Rahab, the foreign prostitute. Maybe James is subtly pressing home his previous point that it is not whether one is on the top of the pile or the bottom that counts for men or for women but a worked-out faith in Jesus Christ.

Controlling the Tongue

3 Dear brothers and sisters,* not many of
you should become teachers in the church,
for we who teach will be judged more
strictly. 2 Indeed, we all make many mistakes.
For if we could control our tongues, we would be
perfect and could also control ourselves in every
other way.
3 We can make a large horse go wherever we
want by means of a small bit in its mouth. 4 And
a small rudder makes a huge ship turn wherever
the pilot chooses to go, even though the winds
are strong. 5 In the same way, the tongue is a
small thing that makes grand speeches.
But a tiny spark can set a great forest on fire.
6 And the tongue is a flame of fire. It is a whole
world of wickedness, corrupting your entire
body. It can set your whole life on fire, for it is
set on fire by hell itself.*
7 People can tame all kinds of animals, birds,
reptiles, and fish, 8 but no one can tame the
tongue. It is restless and evil, full of deadly poison.
9 Sometimes it praises our Lord and Father, and
sometimes it curses those who have been made
in the image of God. 10 And so blessing and cursing come pouring out of the same mouth. Surely,
my brothers and sisters, this is not right! 11 Does a
spring of water bubble out with both fresh water
and bitter water? 12 Does a fig tree produce olives,
or a grapevine produce figs? No, and you can't
draw fresh water from a salty spring.*

True Wisdom Comes from God

13 If you are wise and understand God's ways,
prove it by living an honorable life, doing good
works with the humility that comes from wisdom. 14 But if you are bitterly jealous and there
is selfish ambition in your heart, don't cover up
the truth with boasting and lying. 15 For jealousy
and selfishness are not God's kind of wisdom.
Such things are earthly, unspiritual, and demonic. 16 For wherever there is jealousy and selfish
ambition, there you will find disorder and evil of
every kind.
17 But the wisdom from above is first of all
pure. It is also peace loving, gentle at all times,
and willing to yield to others. It is full of mercy
and good deeds. It shows no favoritism and is always sincere. 18 And those who are peacemakers
will plant seeds of peace and reap a harvest of
righteousness.*

Drawing Close to God

4 What is causing the quarrels and fights
among you? Don't they come from the
evil desires at war within you? 2 You want
what you don't have, so you scheme and kill to
get it. You are jealous of what others have, but
you can't get it, so you fight and wage war to

3:1 Greek *brothers;* also in 3:10. **3:6** Or *for it will burn in hell* (Greek *Gehenna*). **3:12** Greek *from salt.* **3:18** Or *of good things,* or *of justice.*

3:1—4:10 The Use and Misuse of Speech

3:1–12 Controlling the Tongue. It seems unlikely that James wrote with Christian women particularly in mind. However, it is interesting to note how closely the topics relate to the lives of women. Conversation, which tends to be especially important to women, is picked out as the key area in which the believer can stand or fall. If Christians avoid letting their speech get out of control, then they can be confident of success in their attempt to live Christian lives. **1–2:** A link with the previous concern about status is provided by the initial warning for would-be teachers. James is not suggesting that teaching is unnecessary or bad. However, he warns teachers and taught alike against placing too much dependence on the reliability of any human teacher and points out that whatever status the role of teacher might bring may be outweighed by the spiritual accountability involved. **3–12:** The abundance of dynamic images—horses, ships, fire, animal taming—brings out the importance that James places on this question of how speech is used. It is vital that the family likeness to God *our Lord and Father* (v. 9) is shown in this area. It is not appropriate for Christians to participate in cursing, lying, thoughtlessness, unkind gossip, bragging, or aggressive disputation.

3:13–18 Godly Wisdom. 3: The sins of the tongue have their origin in self-seeking covetousness. Godly talk is different. Never being able to admit to a mistake or willing to lose an argument is by no means a sign of strength, and the threatening, do-not-dare-to-contradict-me approach is not a sign of wisdom. Destroying other people by aggressive and wounding words or using prayer as a means of trying to blackmail God into acceding to selfish demands is spiritual adultery (4:4), a betrayal of all that life in Christ implies.

4:1–10 Drawing Close to God. The previous thoughts are somewhat daunting, and it is as if James, as his thoughts move on, suddenly realizes that it might sound as if what God requires is impossible. So in verses 6–9 James refocuses: God's empowering and God's willingness to help come into focus. Because God *gives us even more grace,* the devil can be defeated. Will power is involved, the believer must actively resist, but God's grace makes successful resistance possible.

take it away from them. Yet you don't have what you want because you don't ask God for it. 3 And even when you ask, you don't get it because your motives are all wrong—you want only what will give you pleasure.

4 You adulterers!* Don't you realize that friendship with the world makes you an enemy of God? I say it again: If you want to be a friend of the world, you make yourself an enemy of God. 5 What do you think the Scriptures mean when they say that the spirit God has placed within us is filled with envy?* 6 But he gives us even more grace to stand against such evil desires. As the Scriptures say,

"God opposes the proud
but favors the humble."*

7 So humble yourselves before God. Resist the devil, and he will flee from you. 8 Come close to God, and God will come close to you. Wash your hands, you sinners; purify your hearts, for your loyalty is divided between God and the world. 9 Let there be tears for what you have done. Let there be sorrow and deep grief. Let there be sadness instead of laughter, and gloom instead of joy. 10 Humble yourselves before the Lord, and he will lift you up in honor.

Warning against Judging Others

11 Don't speak evil against each other, dear brothers and sisters.* If you criticize and judge each other, then you are criticizing and judging God's law. But your job is to obey the law, not to judge whether it applies to you. 12 God alone, who gave the law, is the Judge. He alone has the power to save or to destroy. So what right do you have to judge your neighbor?

Warning about Self-Confidence

13 Look here, you who say, "Today or tomorrow we are going to a certain town and will stay there a year. We will do business there and make a profit." 14 How do you know what your life will be like tomorrow? Your life is like the morning fog—it's here a little while, then it's gone. 15 What you ought to say is, "If the Lord wants us to, we will live and do this or that." 16 Otherwise you are boasting about your own plans, and all such boasting is evil.

17 Remember, it is sin to know what you ought to do and then not do it.

Warning to the Rich

5 Look here, you rich people: Weep and groan with anguish because of all the terrible troubles ahead of you. 2 Your wealth is rotting away, and your fine clothes are moth-eaten rags. 3 Your gold and silver have become worthless. The very wealth you were counting on will eat away your flesh like fire. This treasure you have accumulated will stand as evidence against you on the day of judgment. 4 For listen! Hear the cries of the field workers whom you have cheated of their pay. The wages you held back cry out against you. The cries of those who harvest your fields have reached the ears of the LORD of Heaven's Armies.

5 You have spent your years on earth in luxury, satisfying your every desire. You have fattened yourselves for the day of slaughter. 6 You have condemned and killed innocent people,* who do not resist you.*

Patience and Endurance

7 Dear brothers and sisters,* be patient as you

4:4 Greek *You adulteresses!* **4:5** Or *that God longs jealously for the human spirit he has placed within us?* or *that the Holy Spirit, whom God has placed within us, opposes our envy?* **4:6** Prov 3:34 (Greek version). **4:11** Greek *brothers.* **5:6a** Or *killed the Righteous One.* **5:6b** Or *Don't they resist you?* or *Doesn't God oppose you?* or *Aren't they now accusing you before God?* **5:7** Greek *brothers;* also in 5:9, 10, 12, 19.

4:11—5:20 Reprise and Redevelopment

4:11–12 Against Judging Others. To speak *evil against each other*, like having the wrong approach to status, is to put oneself in the place of a judge, not only of the individual involved but also of the law. Usurping the divine role in this way is presented as a serious matter.

4:13–17 About Self-Confidence. To spend one's time seeking after worldly rewards is to ignore the fact that what counts are the values of heaven. James is not suggesting that business activities are wrong, but to see moneymaking as an end in itself and to forget the transience of human values and even human life is foolish.

5:1–6 Warning to the Rich. It is not impossible to be both godly and rich, but the suspicion creeps in that those on top of the ladder are likely to have gotten there by treading on those who remain below, deliberately or not. James's words should come home with particular force to those of us who live surrounded by the luxuries of Western society.

5:7–12 Patience and Endurance. It may appear that worldly status and worldly possessions are what count in life, but believers should not doubt that *the*

wait for the Lord's return. Consider the farmers
who patiently wait for the rains in the fall and
in the spring. They eagerly look for the valuable
harvest to ripen. 8 You, too, must be patient. Take
courage, for the coming of the Lord is near.
9 Don't grumble about each other, brothers
and sisters, or you will be judged. For look—the
Judge is standing at the door!
10 For examples of patience in suffering, dear
brothers and sisters, look at the prophets who
spoke in the name of the Lord. 11 We give great
honor to those who endure under suffering. For
instance, you know about Job, a man of great endurance. You can see how the Lord was kind to
him at the end, for the Lord is full of tenderness
and mercy.
12 But most of all, my brothers and sisters,
never take an oath, by heaven or earth or anything else. Just say a simple yes or no, so that you
will not sin and be condemned.

The Power of Prayer

13 Are any of you suffering hardships? You
should pray. Are any of you happy? You should
sing praises. 14 Are any of you sick? You should
call for the elders of the church to come and pray
over you, anointing you with oil in the name of
the Lord. 15 Such a prayer offered in faith will
heal the sick, and the Lord will make you well.
And if you have committed any sins, you will
be forgiven.
16 Confess your sins to each other and pray
for each other so that you may be healed. The
earnest prayer of a righteous person has great
power and produces wonderful results. 17 Elijah
was as human as we are, and yet when he prayed
earnestly that no rain would fall, none fell for
three and a half years! 18 Then, when he prayed
again, the sky sent down rain and the earth began to yield its crops.

Restore Wandering Believers

19 My dear brothers and sisters, if someone
among you wanders away from the truth and
is brought back, 20 you can be sure that whoever
brings the sinner back will save that person
from death and bring about the forgiveness of
many sins.

---

coming of the Lord is near. Expectant steadfastness, involving endurance through the trials of life with hope and patience in suffering, is the attitude that Christians should cultivate; following Job's example, speech and actions must be related. There should be no need to back up speech with rash oaths of any kind. One's word should be surety enough. James is not making a specific point about the necessity of refusing to swear an oath in a court but about the vital importance of keeping one's word. He is not condemning the speaking out of an oath as such but against the kind of unreliability that might make an oath necessary.

5:13–18 The Power of Prayer. The tongue can be misused, but there are also right uses such as prayer, praise, and confession. Wrong prayer will be ineffective, but there should be no misunderstanding about this; right prayer, stemming from right motives and in line with the will of God, is powerful. James may be speaking of physical and spiritual healing, but his reference to the need for confession of sins and his earlier calls to endurance warn *against* the assumption that Christians can expect all physical ailments to be automatically removed.

5:19–20 Restore the Wandering Believers. The loving attitude that leads people to take action and provide for material needs should also lead to action in providing for the needs of the spiritually poor. Helping another person to return to a full, applied knowledge of the truth is about the greatest thing that a woman or a man can do. James is content to bring his recommendations to a close on that point.

1 PETER

INTRODUCTION

This epistle deals with the faith, comportment, and courage of believers enduring persecution or the threat of it. The occasion may have been the persecution under the emperor Nero (ca. AD 64–68). How widely this may have spread throughout other parts of the Roman Empire is not known, but local persecutions occurred sporadically in Asia Minor.

The letter claims to be from "Peter, an apostle of Jesus Christ" (1 Pet 1:1), "an elder and a witness to the sufferings of Christ" (5:1). The early church unhesitatingly identified 1 Peter as written by the apostle himself. Eusebius described the church's recognition of 1 Peter as being equal to the "recognized letters" of Paul (*Ecclesiastical History* 3.25). Papias (AD 60–135) mentions 1 Peter and its composition in Rome (*Ecclesiastical History* 2.15). Clement of Rome (AD 30–101), the *Didache*, and Polycarp (AD 69–156) quote from every chapter. Second Peter 3:1 refers to 1 Peter. Irenaeus (AD 130–200) quotes from 1 Peter by name (*Against Heresies* 4.9.2). Some modern critics, however, have questioned Peter's authorship. They point out that the historical situation appears to be later than the persecution of Nero during which Peter was presumably martyred. The Greek is literate, the recipients are apparently Gentiles living in areas associated with the apostle Paul, and the concerns expressed are close to those identified with Paul.

Although Peter was described as having "no special training" (Acts 4:13), he was not necessarily illiterate. By law Jews were taught to read Scripture, write, and work out mathematical sums (Mishnah, *Aboth* 5:2; Josephus, *Against Apion* 2.25). Galilee, Peter's home province, was known to be bilingual (Matt 26:73; Greek and Aramaic). Fishermen such as Peter were middle-class business people who would need to use koine, or common, Greek as a trade language.

Peter's encounter with Jews from Pontus, Cappadocia, and Asia (Acts 2:9) may have involved continuing communication, as the same locations are also mentioned in 1 Peter 1:1. Paul is not known to have visited the provinces of Bithynia (Acts 16:6–7), Pontus, or Cappadocia.

The epistle shows knowledge of Mark, John, James, Paul, Luke, Matthew, and Jesus. It touches on motifs known to be concerns of Peter, such as rejected stones (1 Pet 2:4, 7–8; Mark 12:10; Acts 4:11), silver as not being important (1 Pet 1:18; 3:3; Acts 3:6), prophecy (1 Pet 1:10–12; Acts 2:16, 30; 10:43), God as impartial judge (1 Pet 1:17; Acts 10:34, 42), Peter as witness (1 Pet 5:1; Acts 2:32), baptism (1 Pet 3:21; Acts 2:38), service (1 Pet 4:10–11; Acts 6:2–4), sin (1 Pet 1:18; Acts 2:40), and salvation for the household (1 Pet 3:20; Acts 2:39). The attitudes expressed are often those exhibited by Peter in the Gospels and the book of Acts.

In these 105 verses are more than 130 New Testament and 60 Old Testament quotations and allusions. In addition, 63 words occur that are unique in the New Testament, which abounds in metaphors and similes. Because of the multiplicity of topics discussed and the inclusion of a doxology, some readers have failed to see clear arrangement and progression in the letter. Nevertheless, the progression of the letter can be outlined. Recipients of the letter are encouraged to "live in reverent fear" during the time of their exile (1:17) as they remember the good news (1:3–25), and grow in their salvation (2:1—5:11). A primary motif is that of the people of God as a family. In the initial spread of Christianity, the home became the platform for propagating the new faith in communities. Here family, friends, and neighbors gathered to hear the message of the traveling evangelist, to worship, and to discuss what they had heard. Interested persons who became part of the faith community not only observed the family from the outside but also were incorporated into its interior life. One might view the treatise as a discussion of the birth, development, character, relationships, and conduct of the household of faith. —*Catherine Clark Kroeger* and *Aida Besançon Spencer*

1:1–2	Greeting
1:3–25	Remember the Good News Announced to You
1:3–12	Giving Birth to the Heirs of Promise
1:13–25	Becoming Proactive Family Members
2:1—5:11	Growing in Salvation
2:1–3	Feeding the New Child
2:4–10	Integration into a Kinship Structure
2:11–17	Submission Silences Critics outside the Household
2:18—3:12	Submission Silences Critics within the Household
3:13—4:19	The Household Making Sense of Suffering
5:1–11	Humility within the Household
5:12–14	Greetings among Christ's Family

✧

Greetings from Peter

1 This letter is from Peter, an apostle of Jesus
Christ.
I am writing to God's chosen people
who are living as foreigners in the provinces of
Pontus, Galatia, Cappadocia, Asia, and Bithynia.*
2 God the Father knew you and chose you long
ago, and his Spirit has made you holy. As a result,
you have obeyed him and have been cleansed by
the blood of Jesus Christ.
May God give you more and more grace and
peace.

The Hope of Eternal Life

3 All praise to God, the Father of our Lord Jesus
Christ. It is by his great mercy that we have been
born again, because God raised Jesus Christ from

1:1 *Pontus, Galatia, Cappadocia, Asia,* and *Bithynia* were Roman provinces in what is now Turkey.

1:1–2 Greeting

The writer is identified as an *apostle*. As one of the Twelve (Luke 6:13–14), Peter had insisted on a replacement for Judas. He specified that such an individual must have accompanied the original twelve apostles from the time that John baptized Jesus until he ascended (Acts 1:21–22), so that they could testify to firsthand knowledge of the risen Christ (1 Cor 9:2). The readers are Christians who had not seen Jesus. Although Jewish believers lived in these provinces (Acts 2:5–9), Gentiles appear to be Peter's focus. *Foreigners*: Either a metaphor referring to the Christian life in the world or resident aliens deprived of full status as citizens. Thousands of displaced persons lived in Asia Minor; family identity is critically important to the disenfranchised (see God's Concern for the Disenfranchised, Ezek 34).

1:3–25 Remember the Good News Announced to You

1:3–12 Giving Birth to the Heirs of Promise. Birth imagery recurs throughout the letter; we enter fami-

the dead. Now we live with great expectation,
4 and we have a priceless inheritance—an inheritance that is kept in heaven for you, pure and
undefiled, beyond the reach of change and decay.
5 And through your faith, God is protecting you
by his power until you receive this salvation,
which is ready to be revealed on the last day for
all to see.

6 So be truly glad.* There is wonderful joy
ahead, even though you have to endure many
trials for a little while. 7 These trials will show
that your faith is genuine. It is being tested as
fire tests and purifies gold—though your faith
is far more precious than mere gold. So when
your faith remains strong through many trials, it
will bring you much praise and glory and honor
on the day when Jesus Christ is revealed to the
whole world.

8 You love him even though you have never
seen him. Though you do not see him now, you
trust him; and you rejoice with a glorious, inexpressible joy. 9 The reward for trusting him will
be the salvation of your souls.

10 This salvation was something even the
prophets wanted to know more about when they
prophesied about this gracious salvation prepared
for you. 11 They wondered what time or situation the Spirit of Christ within them was talking about when he told them in advance about
Christ's suffering and his great glory afterward.
12 They were told that their messages were
not for themselves, but for you. And now this
Good News has been announced to you by those
who preached in the power of the Holy Spirit
sent from heaven. It is all so wonderful that even
the angels are eagerly watching these things
happen.

A Call to Holy Living

13 So think clearly and exercise self-control.
Look forward to the gracious salvation that will
come to you when Jesus Christ is revealed to the
world. 14 So you must live as God's obedient children. Don't slip back into your old ways of living to satisfy your own desires. You didn't know
any better then. 15 But now you must be holy in
everything you do, just as God who chose you is
holy. 16 For the Scriptures say, "You must be holy
because I am holy."*

17 And remember that the heavenly Father to
whom you pray has no favorites. He will judge
or reward you according to what you do. So you
must live in reverent fear of him during your
time as "foreigners in the land." 18 For you know
that God paid a ransom to save you from the
empty life you inherited from your ancestors.
And the ransom he paid was not mere gold or
silver. 19 It was the precious blood of Christ, the
sinless, spotless Lamb of God. 20 God chose him
as your ransom long before the world began,
but he has now revealed him to you in these last
days.

21 Through Christ you have come to trust in
God. And you have placed your faith and hope in
God because he raised Christ from the dead and
gave him great glory.

22 You were cleansed from your sins when you
obeyed the truth, so now you must show sincere
love to each other as brothers and sisters.* Love
each other deeply with all your heart.*

23 For you have been born again, but not to a

1:6 Or *So you are truly glad.* **1:16** Lev 11:44-45; 19:2; 20:7. **1:22a** Greek *must have brotherly love.* **1:22b** Some manuscripts read *with a pure heart.*

---

lies only by birth or adoption. **3–4:** *Born again*: The word mainly used of a mother "bearing a child" but also for the father's act of begetting. *Great expectation . . . priceless inheritance*: God has given new birth, a maternal gift, with an imperishable inheritance, bequeathed by a father. Both represent familial continuity. Such *expectation* contrasts with high infant mortality in the ancient world, where parents often remained emotionally detached from a newborn until it was clear that the child would survive. God's *inheritance* never decays and is always untainted. It cannot be lost, for it is *kept in heaven*. **5–7:** Children must be protected and guided until they can responsibly use what has been preserved for them. The child matures through training; Christians' faith is *tested* by *trials* so that it becomes durable, persisting until Jesus' return. **8–12:** Peter now understands the necessity of the Messiah's agony and death, a comprehension denied to *prophets* and *angels*. The ultimate revelation had come to those who heard and heeded the *Good News*.

1:13–25 Becoming Proactive Family Members. 13: *Think clearly . . . self-control*: Literally, "belt up the garments of your minds." **14:** Parent-child vocabulary reminds believers that they must be holy as God is holy, for the child is identified by her resemblance to the parent. **17–20:** The metaphor of a heavenly Father is reintroduced as the impartial judge. This had been a hard lesson for Peter to learn. As a devout Jew and a fisherman, Peter had been required to separate unclean from clean fish. By stages he learned that Samaritans and Gentiles could participate in the blessing of faith in Christ and that no one should be called unclean. Under pressure, Peter stopped eating with Gentiles but eventually defended Paul's and

life that will quickly end. Your new life will last
forever because it comes from the eternal, living
word of God. 24 As the Scriptures say,

"People are like grass;
their beauty is like a flower in the field.
The grass withers and the flower fades.
25 But the word of the Lord remains
forever."*

And that word is the Good News that was
preached to you.

2 So get rid of all evil behavior. Be done with
all deceit, hypocrisy, jealousy, and all unkind speech. 2 Like newborn babies, you
must crave pure spiritual milk so that you will
grow into a full experience of salvation. Cry out
for this nourishment, 3 now that you have had a
taste of the Lord's kindness.

Living Stones for God's House

4 You are coming to Christ, who is the living
cornerstone of God's temple. He was rejected
by people, but he was chosen by God for great
honor.

5 And you are living stones that God is building into his spiritual temple. What's more, you
are his holy priests.* Through the mediation of
Jesus Christ, you offer spiritual sacrifices that
please God. 6 As the Scriptures say,

"I am placing a cornerstone in Jerusalem,*
chosen for great honor,
and anyone who trusts in him
will never be disgraced."*

7 Yes, you who trust him recognize the honor God
has given him. But for those who reject him,

"The stone that the builders rejected
has now become the cornerstone."*

8 And,

"He is the stone that makes people stumble,
the rock that makes them fall."*

1:24-25 Isa 40:6-8. **2:5** Greek *holy priesthood.* **2:6a** Greek *in Zion.* **2:6b** Isa 28:16 (Greek version). **2:7** Ps 118:22. **2:8** Isa 8:14.

Barnabas's ministry to Gentiles. Though the addressees live as strangers away from their home, in danger of being treated unjustly, the Father is impartial; and freedom depends on an imperishable ransom. **23–25:** The believers have been *born again . . . through the eternal, living word of God.* As God created the world by a word, now again there is creation for every believer by God's message. Unlike the Roman Empire, in which a victim of persecution could be denied status and legal rights, one can never be deprived of the rebirth. Quoting Isaiah 40:6–8, the writer makes the point that we safely rely upon the word of an eternal God.

2:1—5:11 Growing in Salvation

2:1–3 Feeding the New Child. While some newborns begin to nurse naturally, others have no idea how or where to satisfy their hunger. They turn away from the breast, crying because their basic need is unsatisfied. Usually resistance stops once they have tasted milk. Peter, who apparently had observed the nursing process, insisted that those who had tasted of Christ's grace should thirst after it (Ps 34:8). A newborn wants nothing so much as nourishment: an apt metaphor for the ravenous desire of a new believer for the Word of God and for assimilating that Word into one's life. With astonishing frequency the infant demands more feedings. Ingesting the will and Word of God is an ongoing process that must become a frequent practice. By implication, God is portrayed as a nursing mother, an image used in the Old Testament (Isa 49:15; Ps 131:2; see Images of God as Female, Deut 32).

2:4–10 Integration into a Kinship Structure. A newborn was not automatically accepted as part of the family. There was a formal ceremony in which the baby was laid on the floor in full view of assembled kinfolk. The father, in official recognition of the new arrival as his child, would take up the baby. Then followed reception into the larger family, clan, and tribe. **4–8:** The newborn believer was similarly integrated into a *spiritual temple* (or "house"). Coming to Christ is like being made part of a divinely constructed edifice. The *stones* are large, costly, polished marble, like those in the Temple in Jerusalem (Isa 28:16). The cornerstone of this marvelous edifice was a stone that had previously been left in the quarry (Ps 118:22; Luke 20:17) but now was placed in the position of greatest honor. Peter (whose name ["rock"] is *petros* rather than *lithos*, as here), contemplated the eternal stone (*lithos*) that could not be moved or vacillate as he had done (Isa 8:14–15). While the picture of a nursing infant is individual, the collective body of stones is communal. **9:** The metaphor changes to that of priests within the temple. Each is given a specific assignment, but all work together to conduct

They stumble because they do not obey God's
word, and so they meet the fate that was planned
for them.
9 But you are not like that, for you are a chosen
people. You are royal priests,* a holy nation, God's
very own possession. As a result, you can show
others the goodness of God, for he called you out
of the darkness into his wonderful light.

10 "Once you had no identity as a people;
now you are God's people.
Once you received no mercy;
now you have received God's mercy."*

11 Dear friends, I warn you as "temporary
residents and foreigners" to keep away from
worldly desires that wage war against your very
souls. 12 Be careful to live properly among your
unbelieving neighbors. Then even if they accuse
you of doing wrong, they will see your honorable behavior, and they will give honor to God
when he judges the world.*

Respecting People in Authority

13 For the Lord's sake, respect all human authority—whether the king as head of state, 14 or the
officials he has appointed. For the king has sent
them to punish those who do wrong and to hon-
or those who do right.
15 It is God's will that your honorable lives
should silence those ignorant people who make
foolish accusations against you. 16 For you are
free, yet you are God's slaves, so don't use your
freedom as an excuse to do evil. 17 Respect everyone, and love your Christian brothers and sisters.* Fear God, and respect the king.

Slaves

18 You who are slaves must accept the authority of your masters with all respect.* Do what
they tell you—not only if they are kind and reasonable, but even if they are cruel. 19 For God is
pleased with you when you do what you know
is right and patiently endure unfair treatment.
20 Of course, you get no credit for being patient if
you are beaten for doing wrong. But if you suffer for doing good and endure it patiently, God is
pleased with you.
21 For God called you to do good, even if it
means suffering, just as Christ suffered* for you.

2:9 Greek *a royal priesthood.* **2:10** Hos 1:6, 9; 2:23. **2:12** Or *on the day of visitation.* **2:17** Greek *love the brotherhood.* **2:18** Or *because you fear God.* **2:21** Some manuscripts read *died.*

---

worship of God. The new identity of this priesthood is spelled out in a dramatic list drawn from Exodus 19:4–6. *People* (lit., "race") highlights direct descendants; *nation* emphasizes common people as opposed to leaders. However, the descendants are *chosen*; the common people are God's *possession*. Though of obscure status, they hold a *royal* post. Unlike the hereditary priesthood of Aaron and Phinehas, these believers, once outside Israel, are of holy stock and have a share with the people of God in worship and mission. Priestly functions are no longer divided by gender, birth, race, or physical characteristics (e.g., Exod 28:1; Lev 21:17–21; 22:4–13). **10:** See Hosea 2:23.

2:11–17 Submission Silences Critics outside the Household. 11–12: These *temporary residents and foreigners* should not seek to establish rights of citizenship in a country that indulges passions of the flesh. Instead they should strive after good conduct so that nonbelievers might glorify God from having observed believers' good actions. *See*: A word also used in Greek mystery religion for a vision that brought knowledge; those seeing Christian behavior gain practical knowledge of their religion. **13–17:** Believers are to live honorably among the Gentiles. Two centuries earlier, two thousand Jewish families had been deported from Babylonia to Asia Minor, where they would serve as a stabilizing influence on restive local populations (Josephus, *Antiquities* 12.150). Jews were known for their law-abiding lifestyle, one that the new people of God also needed to demonstrate. *Respect*: Literally, "place oneself under"; the word can mean "honor," "love," "fear," "ally oneself with," or "be loyal to." In view of Peter's insistence that obedience must be yielded to God rather than to human beings (Acts 4:19; 5:29), we do not construe the term as requiring absolute obedience. Rather, it calls for compliance with the structures necessary for the peaceful functioning of society and carrying out all rightful obligations of citizenship. **15:** *Silence*: Literally, "muzzle," as one muzzles a dog to stop its barking. If Christians do good, their critics can find little basis for accusations.

2:18—3:7 Submission Silences Critics within the Household. These directives were addressed to persons being persecuted for their faith. Ancient philosophers maintained that the welfare of the political state depended on proper order within the household, a state in microcosm. The conduct of slaves, wives, and children was therefore of paramount concern, especially in situations where the faith and lifestyle of Christians were considered to be damaging to the state and to society. Their conduct will provide an apologetic for Christianity. **2:18–20:** Household

He is your example, and you must follow in his steps.

22 He never sinned,
nor ever deceived anyone.*
23 He did not retaliate when he was insulted,
nor threaten revenge when he suffered.
He left his case in the hands of God,
who always judges fairly.
24 He personally carried our sins
in his body on the cross
so that we can be dead to sin
and live for what is right.
By his wounds
you are healed.
25 Once you were like sheep
who wandered away.
But now you have turned to your Shepherd,
the Guardian of your souls.

Wives

3 In the same way, you wives must accept the
authority of your husbands. Then, even if
some refuse to obey the Good News, your
godly lives will speak to them without any words.
They will be won over 2 by observing your pure
and reverent lives.
3 Don't be concerned about the outward
beauty of fancy hairstyles, expensive jewelry, or
beautiful clothes. 4 You should clothe yourselves
instead with the beauty that comes from within,
the unfading beauty of a gentle and quiet spirit,
which is so precious to God. 5 This is how the
holy women of old made themselves beautiful.
They trusted God and accepted the authority of
their husbands. 6 For instance, Sarah obeyed her
husband, Abraham, and called him her master.
You are her daughters when you do what is right
without fear of what your husbands might do.

Husbands

7 In the same way, you husbands must give honor
to your wives. Treat your wife with understanding as you live together. She may be weaker than
you are, but she is your equal partner in God's
gift of new life. Treat her as you should so your
prayers will not be hindered.

2:22 Isa 53:9.

slaves were in part responsible for the harmony and cooperation necessary within the household. **21–25:** The writer differentiates between constructive behavior that should be expected from Christian slaves and the abuse that they might suffer in consequence of professing their faith. Unlike other New Testament instructions to slaves, there is no accompanying caution offered to Christian masters, perhaps reflecting a social situation that included slaves within the church but not the wealthier slave owners. **3:1–6:** *In the same way*, . . . wives should honor their husbands so that *they will be won over*, a financial metaphor, Literally, "they may gain a profit." The husbands, unconvinced of Christ's claims, are debits on a financial sheet. The purpose of the wives' loyalty and responsible conduct is redemptive. In an age of promiscuity, sexual purity was a quality to be noted and prized. A husband had a right to his wife's fidelity, respect, and propriety. These are tools to bring him to Christ. **3–5:** *Quiet* bespeaks a state of calm, restraint at the proper time, respect, and affirmation, emblematic of true beauty as opposed to *outward beauty*. **6:** *Master*: Literally, "lord" (*kyrios*), a common deferential mode of address (e.g., "sir," John 12:21). Sarah, like Christ, committed no sin, obeyed Abraham (e.g., Gen 12:11–13), agreeing to protect him, and instead, placed her hopes in God, while Abraham, like the unbelieving husband in 3:1, showed lack of obedience to God's promise (Gen 12:2–3). **7:** As a deterrent to possible abusive behavior on the part of believing husbands, a new set of instructions outlines the norm for Christian family living. *In the same way*: Echoing verse 1 and connecting the submission of the husband to that of the wife, the household slaves, and the more general earlier commands. *Weaker*: Literally, "weaker vessel," denoting an implement of any kind, such as a utensil, furniture, or equipment. Elsewhere in the New Testament, Paul is called a "chosen vessel" (Acts 9:15), and those who have matured in Christian virtues are vessels "to honor" (2 Tim 2:20–21). The image means that husbands should take into consideration that women generally possess less physical strength than do men. Husbands must, nevertheless, honor their spouses as joint heirs, to receive an inheritance and manage it. The concept of a woman as joint heir with her husband was a radical one in Jewish and Roman society. According to rabbinic tradition, sons inherited and daughters received maintenance (Mishnah, *Ketuboth* 4:6). A Roman woman upon marriage sank to the legal status of her husband's daughter and could claim only a daughter's inheritance—half that of a son. Here women are presented as *equal partner*[s] *in God's gift of new life*, equal in the sight of God and of the believing community. The husband who affirmed his wife in honor and equality would find power in his prayers. Abuse or degradation of his wife would bring an obstruction. Significantly, New Testament calls for wifely submission are always accompanied with specific directives to prevent abuse on the part of the husband (Eph 5:28–29; Col 3:19).

All Christians

8 Finally, all of you should be of one mind. Sympathize with each other. Love each other as brothers and sisters.* Be tenderhearted, and keep a humble attitude. 9 Don't repay evil for evil. Don't retaliate with insults when people insult you. Instead, pay them back with a blessing. That is what God has called you to do, and he will bless you for it. 10 For the Scriptures say,

"If you want to enjoy life
and see many happy days,
keep your tongue from speaking evil
and your lips from telling lies.
11 Turn away from evil and do good.
Search for peace, and work to maintain it.
12 The eyes of the Lord watch over those who do right,
and his ears are open to their prayers.
But the Lord turns his face
against those who do evil."*

Suffering for Doing Good

13 Now, who will want to harm you if you are eager to do good? 14 But even if you suffer for doing what is right, God will reward you for it. So don't worry or be afraid of their threats. 15 Instead, you must worship Christ as Lord of your life. And if someone asks about your Christian hope, always be ready to explain it. 16 But do this in a gentle and respectful way.* Keep your conscience clear. Then if people speak against you, they will be ashamed when they see what a good life you live because you belong to Christ. 17 Remember, it is better to suffer for doing good, if that is what God wants, than to suffer for doing wrong!

18 Christ suffered* for our sins once for all time. He never sinned, but he died for sinners to bring you safely home to God. He suffered physical death, but he was raised to life in the Spirit.*

19 So he went and preached to the spirits in prison—20 those who disobeyed God long ago when God waited patiently while Noah was building his boat. Only eight people were saved from drowning in that terrible flood.* 21 And that water is a picture of baptism, which now saves you, not by removing dirt from your body, but as a response to God from* a clean conscience. It is effective because of the resurrection of Jesus Christ.

22 Now Christ has gone to heaven. He is seated in the place of honor next to God, and all the angels and authorities and powers accept his authority.

Living for God

4 So then, since Christ suffered physical pain, you must arm yourselves with the same attitude he had, and be ready to suffer, too. For if you have suffered physically for

3:8 Greek *Show brotherly love.* **3:10-12** Ps 34:12-16.
3:16 Some English translations put this sentence in verse 15.
3:18a Some manuscripts read *died.* **3:18b** Or *in spirit.*
3:20 Greek *saved through water.* **3:21** Or *as an appeal to God for.*

3:8–12 Summary of Teaching. The call for endurance under persecution must not be misapplied to other situations. This passage has been woefully misinterpreted in a way that has been destructive to many Christian homes.

3:13—4:19 The Household Making Sense of Suffering. 3:13–18: Believers are called to faith rather than fear while sanctifying *Christ as Lord.* When the opportunity arises for persecuted believers to give a defense of their faith, they must be ready. *Your Christian hope*: The second person plural shows that this hope is the community's. Being in Christian community is another key for arresting fear. **16:** Outwardly Christians are *gentle* and *respectful,* while inwardly they maintain a good conscience in the knowledge that they have not sinned. **17–18:** In the foregoing chapters, the example and sufferings of Christ have been mentioned. Here we see voluntary suffering to promote a righteous cause. In similar cases believers may be called on to suffer if they are to remain faithful to Christ. On August 28, 1963, Martin Luther King Jr. said to those who had labored for racial justice, "You have been veterans of creative suffering. Continue to work with the faith that unearned suffering is redemptive." Suffering was a necessary corollary to advancing a righteous cause. The conduct of the sufferers must be irreproachable, or the power of witness is diminished. Here the example of Christ is paramount. Though wronged and vilified in his arrest and trial, he did not reciprocate but remained silent and respectful. Christ provides the example for the correct reason to suffer, not because of sin but *for . . . sins.* He remained righteous while bringing sinners to God. **19–22:** Those sinners included people back to the time of Noah, who now have the chance to participate in the baptism that Noah and his family experienced by undergoing the flood. Christ now dwells in *heaven* where his *authority* has been established by his death and resurrection. **4:1–6:** The example of Christ has been given so that readers might *arm yourselves with the same attitude.* They were not to defend themselves with the weapons of earthly warfare but with those supplied by Christ. All forms

Christ, you have finished with sin.* [2]You won't
spend the rest of your lives chasing your own
desires, but you will be anxious to do the will
of God. [3]You have had enough in the past of the
evil things that godless people enjoy—their immorality and lust, their feasting and drunkenness and wild parties, and their terrible worship
of idols.
[4]Of course, your former friends are surprised
when you no longer plunge into the flood of wild
and destructive things they do. So they slander
you. [5]But remember that they will have to face
God, who will judge everyone, both the living
and the dead. [6]That is why the Good News was
preached to those who are now dead*—so although they were destined to die like all people,*
they now live forever with God in the Spirit.*
[7]The end of the world is coming soon. Therefore, be earnest and disciplined in your prayers.
[8]Most important of all, continue to show deep
love for each other, for love covers a multitude
of sins. [9]Cheerfully share your home with those
who need a meal or a place to stay.
[10]God has given each of you a gift from his
great variety of spiritual gifts. Use them well
to serve one another. [11]Do you have the gift of
speaking? Then speak as though God himself
were speaking through you. Do you have the
gift of helping others? Do it with all the strength
and energy that God supplies. Then everything
you do will bring glory to God through Jesus
Christ. All glory and power to him forever and
ever! Amen.

Suffering for Being a Christian

[12]Dear friends, don't be surprised at the fiery
trials you are going through, as if something
strange were happening to you. [13]Instead, be
very glad—for these trials make you partners
with Christ in his suffering, so that you will have
the wonderful joy of seeing his glory when it is
revealed to all the world.
[14]So be happy when you are insulted for being a Christian,* for then the glorious Spirit of
God* rests upon you.* [15]If you suffer, however,
it must not be for murder, stealing, making trouble, or prying into other people's affairs. [16]But
it is no shame to suffer for being a Christian.
Praise God for the privilege of being called by
his name! [17]For the time has come for judgment,
and it must begin with God's household. And
if judgment begins with us, what terrible fate
awaits those who have never obeyed God's Good
News? [18]And also,

"If the righteous are barely saved,
  what will happen to godless sinners?"*

[19]So if you are suffering in a manner that pleases
God, keep on doing what is right, and trust your
lives to the God who created you, for he will
never fail you.

Advice for Elders and Young Men

5 And now, a word to you who are elders in
the churches. I, too, am an elder and a witness to the sufferings of Christ. And I, too,

4:1 Or *For the one* [or *One*] *who has suffered physically has finished with sin.* **4:6a** Greek *preached even to the dead.* **4:6b** Or *so although people had judged them worthy of death.* **4:6c** Or *in spirit.* **4:14a** Greek *for the name of Christ.* **4:14b** Or *for the glory of God, which is his Spirit.* **4:14c** Some manuscripts add *On their part he is blasphemed, but on your part he is glorified.* **4:18** Prov 11:31 (Greek version).

of licentiousness, debauchery, and idolatry must be abandoned. Promiscuity, *drunkenness* (*komoi*, a technical word for rites involving excessive use of wine), and idolatry were basic components of paganism. **7–11:** What should believers do, since the time of judgment is near? They should be *earnest and disciplined*, having a sound mind, showing self-control, being temperate. God's help is indispensable in the end times, especially during this time of persecution. An individual's relationship with God should be coupled with relationships to human beings, involving love and hospitality, qualities that enable the ministry of others. Hospitality was imperative to shelter traveling missionaries exposed to imminent danger and to afford them the opportunity of proclaiming the gospel in a community. The distribution of gifts within the family is according to God's choice, but the exercise of them is the responsibility of the faithful steward of the household regardless of gender (cf. Rom 12:6–8; 1 Cor 12; Eph 4:11–12). **12–19:** Christians are not to rejoice in all sufferings but only when they are *partners with Christ in his suffering*. They may be vilified for bearing the name of Christ. The mere name of Christian would later become sufficient grounds for a death sentence. Believers would suffer "as Christians" and thereby glorify God because of that name. The suffering that remains steadfast under persecution is that which glorifies God.

5:1–11 Humility within the Household. 1–4: This is a touching mandate for feeding the flock of God. As Peter had been urged to feed the sheep (John 21:15–17), the command is now passed on to others. **2:** They are to serve without compulsion or in the hope of financial gain. **3:** Neither are they to *lord it over* those in their care (cf. 2 Cor 1:24). The

will share in his glory when he is revealed to the whole world. As a fellow elder, I appeal to you:
2 Care for the flock that God has entrusted to you. Watch over it willingly, not grudgingly—not for what you will get out of it, but because you are eager to serve God.
3 Don't lord it over the people assigned to your care, but lead them by your own good example.
4 And when the Great Shepherd appears, you will receive a crown of never-ending glory and honor.

5 In the same way, you younger men must accept the authority of the elders. And all of you, serve each other in humility, for

"God opposes the proud
  but favors the humble."*

6 So humble yourselves under the mighty power of God, and at the right time he will lift you up in honor.
7 Give all your worries and cares to God, for he cares about you.

8 Stay alert! Watch out for your great enemy, the devil. He prowls around like a roaring lion, looking for someone to devour.
9 Stand firm against him, and be strong in your faith. Remember that your Christian brothers and sisters* all over the world are going through the same kind of suffering you are.

10 In his kindness God called you to share in his eternal glory by means of Christ Jesus. So after you have suffered a little while, he will restore, support, and strengthen you, and he will place you on a firm foundation.
11 All power to him forever! Amen.

Peter's Final Greetings

12 I have written and sent this short letter to you with the help of Silas,* whom I commend to you as a faithful brother. My purpose in writing is to encourage you and assure you that what you are experiencing is truly part of God's grace for you. Stand firm in this grace.

13 Your sister church here in Babylon* sends you greetings, and so does my son Mark.
14 Greet each other with Christian love.*

Peace be with all of you who are in Christ.

5:5 Prov 3:34 (Greek version). **5:9** Greek *your brothers.* **5:12** Greek *Silvanus.* **5:13** Greek *The elect one in Babylon.* Babylon was probably symbolic for Rome. **5:14** Greek *with a kiss of love.*

term occurs also in Matthew 20:25 and Mark 10:42 as Jesus announces that exercising such power over others is unacceptable among his followers. **5–10:** The exhortation to those who are *younger* to *humble* themselves, accepting instruction and guidance, leads naturally to the thought that all members of the community should *serve each other in humility*. *All power*, after all, is God's alone.

5:12–14 Greetings among Christ's Family

Silas was the name of one of Paul's companions (Acts 15:22; 2 Cor 1:19). **13:** *Sister church*: Literally, "the elect one" (see translator's note), which could be a specific individual woman. The woman's name may have been withheld to protect her identity in a dangerous environment. Yet she may have wished to send a message to those among whom she had ministered and to encourage them in their time of tribulation to remember the Lord. The affection that Peter expresses here, as for Mark, may be understood to be for his wife, whose mother Jesus had healed (Mark 1:30–31). Paul speaks of the pair traveling together in a gospel ministry (1 Cor 9:5). Clement of Alexandria described their union as "blessed" and their feelings toward each other as "consummate" (Eusebius, *Ecclesiastical History* 3.30). As she was led away to martyrdom, Peter shouted out to her, "My dear, remember the Lord." *Babylon*: Probably a code name for Rome. *Mark* was another of Paul's companions (Phlm 24).

2 PETER

INTRODUCTION

Second Peter shares with other New Testament writings a conviction that eschatology and ethics are of a piece, that behavior in the present is conditioned by expectation of what is to come. Like other early Christian writings, it connects sexual continence and eschatological expectation (e.g., 1 Cor 7; Luke 20:34–36). The early church considered that sexuality would be excluded from the new age (e.g., Mark 12:25). Consequently, those who looked forward to the new heaven and the new earth regarded sexual restraint in this age as critical. Early Christianity thought that exercising self-control in the present was directly related to the future judgment (Acts 24:25). Second Peter does not present a positive description of sexuality. Rather, we find a denigrating of the false teachers' enslavement to debauched sexuality and a polemical use of Scriptures that refer to sexual immorality. The letter's denunciation of licentiousness and extolling of sexual purity is typical of Christian writings with an eschatological focus (cf. 1 Thes 4:4–7; Rev 14:4).

The message of the letter is bluntly simple, devoid of many early Christian concerns. It does not discuss, for instance, the cross of Christ and his resurrection, the process of becoming a Christian, such as we might find in the Gospels, or the new identity given believers, as we find in Paul. Nor does it address communal worship, community responsibilities, how the church relates to the *polis*, or Christian household concerns, including the matter of sex within marriage. It focuses solely on calling its hearers back to a particular aspect of the faith. The author considers his message so important that he intends his letter to be a constant reminder (2 Pet 1:12). The dissenting view—that there will be no judgment and that Christ will not come again—has gained significant ground among the readers. Those teaching this view are part of the community to which the letter is addressed, sharing common meals with the readers of the letter (2:13). Being at a distance, the author has only his words with which to challenge his readers, who may be young in the faith (2:18), with a message that is at odds with the false teachers, at odds with common sense, and at odds with his readers' desires.

The message is at odds with the false teachers because while they say that Jesus will not return, the author claims he will, and while they say that enjoying the pleasures of the body is a good, the author claims that such is self-indulgence (2:13) and will lead only to destruction. The message is also at odds with common sense, for the expectation that Jesus would appear again has begun to appear nonsensical. Some in the community scoff at the idea that Christ will come, saying that since the first generation of believers has died, it is folly to hope for Christ's return (3:4). The false teachers say that things will go on as they are indefinitely. The author retorts that God has already demonstrated that God creates and destroys (3:5–6). Moreover, what appears to humans like a delay is not so in the divine agenda (3:8). God's slowness about bringing the end is connected to God's compassion, for God hopes that all would turn to God before the time of judgment (3:9; cf. 3:15). Furthermore, the message is contrary to the natural desires of the readers. The false teachers deny that there is a coming judgment and so encourage believers to yield to their natural passions; the author warns that God will come to judge the behavior of all, including believers. God will destroy those who have behaved unrighteously (3:7).

Second Peter is often characterized as being a letter and a last will and testament. One strategy the author uses to increase the value placed on Peter's authority is to present Peter's exhortation as a deathbed speech. Within Hellenistic Judaism there was a tradition of patriarchs on the verge of death giving ethical advice to their descendants (e.g., *Testaments of the Twelve Patriarchs*). Often the patriarchs' advice is based on their unique vision of heavenly things (e.g., *Testament of Naphtali*, 5; *Testament of Joseph*, 19).

The Letter's Strategy: Emphasizing Peter's Authority

The daunting challenge of turning his addressees away from the persuasive arguments of the false teachers requires the author to be strategic. The most obvious strategy he uses, as he tries to convince his readers that Jesus will return at the judgment and that upright behavior matters, is to appeal to Peter's authority. Scholars debate whether Peter the apostle actually wrote the letter. For various reasons, including the letter's highblown language and the late date implied by referring to Paul's letters as Scripture (3:16), many consider 2 Peter to be pseudonymous. A significant number of scholars regard the letter as written in Peter's name in order to convey to a particular community that its message accords with Peter's views. The issue of authorship is not overly important, however. Second Peter's authority rests on its being in the Christian canon. It should be recognized, furthermore, that whether or not Peter wrote the letter, the letter's message is grounded on the apostle's authoritative knowledge. This fact is seen even more clearly if we accept what many take to be the best explanation for the similarities between the epistle of Jude and 2 Peter (e.g., Jude 4 and 2 Pet 2:1–3; Jude 5 and 2 Pet 2:5; Jude 6–7 and 2 Pet 2:4, 6; Jude 8–9 and 2 Pet 2:10–11). Most scholars hold that 2 Peter is dependent on Jude. When the author of 2 Peter used Jude in composing his letter, he reshaped the material to focus on Peter's credibility and unimpeachable apostolic credentials. The message that Jesus will come at the judgment is reliable because it comes from the apostle Peter.

The author claims that he, Simon Peter, is the one capable of reminding his readers of the truth. He focuses on the danger of forgetting (1:9) and the importance of remembering. The readers must never forget that they have been privileged to receive a faith equal to that of the apostle Peter (1:1): One that knows that the Lord Jesus Christ will return at the day of judgment and that in the meantime believers in Christ must live righteously. The letter invokes Peter's authority to underscore the importance of this. The faithful must hold onto this conviction; lack of certainty about this matter leads to immoral living and ultimately to damnation. The letter does not indicate that currently the readers are living immorally. It is rather a warning to people the author thinks are relatively stable (3:17) but who are being adversely influenced by false teachers. Unlike Paul's first letter to Corinth, this one is not addressed to people who are currently behaving badly. It is more like Paul's Galatian letter, in which the focus is on helping Christians maintain right belief in the face of an alternate gospel. The author's strategy is to denounce the false teachers as deviants from the true faith. —*L. Ann Jervis*

1:1–2 Salutation
1:3–11 Homily on Godliness
1:12–21 Authority of Peter
2:1–22 Denunciation of the False Teachers
3:1–13 The Message of the Letter
3:15–18 Conclusion

✧

Greetings from Peter

1 This letter is from Simon* Peter, a slave
and apostle of Jesus Christ.
I am writing to you who share the same
precious faith we have. This faith was given to
you because of the justice and fairness* of Jesus
Christ, our God and Savior.
2 May God give you more and more grace and
peace as you grow in your knowledge of God and
Jesus our Lord.

Growing in Faith

3 By his divine power, God has given us everything we need for living a godly life. We have received all of this by coming to know him, the one
who called us to himself by means of his marvelous glory and excellence. 4 And because of his
glory and excellence, he has given us great and
precious promises. These are the promises that
enable you to share his divine nature and escape
the world's corruption caused by human desires.
5 In view of all this, make every effort to respond to God's promises. Supplement your faith
with a generous provision of moral excellence,
and moral excellence with knowledge, 6 and
knowledge with self-control, and self-control
with patient endurance, and patient endurance
with godliness, 7 and godliness with brotherly
affection, and brotherly affection with love for
everyone.
8 The more you grow like this, the more productive and useful you will be in your knowledge of our Lord Jesus Christ. 9 But those who
fail to develop in this way are shortsighted or
blind, forgetting that they have been cleansed
from their old sins.
10 So, dear brothers and sisters,* work hard to
prove that you really are among those God has
called and chosen. Do these things, and you will

1:1a Greek *Symeon.* **1:1b** Or *to you in the righteousness.*
1:10 Greek *brothers.*

1:1–2 Salutation

Second Peter is ostensibly a letter, beginning with a salutation in which the sender identifies himself, followed by the name of the recipients and a wish for grace and peace. This is standard letter form.

1:3–11 Homily on Godliness

The book does not contain a normal letter body, including a thanksgiving section (e.g., 1 Cor 1: 4–9). The book moves directly from the epistolary salutation to a sermon on godliness. **3:** Readers must remember that they are the ones who have true knowledge and the capacity for *everything we need for living a godly life*. The author affirms that the readers know nothing less than God who has called them to share in God's *glory and excellence*. **4:** The power inherent in Jesus is that believers may approach God's character and may *share* in the *divine nature*. **5–7:** In the Hellenistic world, passion did not refer exclusively to sexual passion. Desire or passion was part of human nature and a trap from which we must be freed. The problem with passion is that one makes one's happiness or peace dependent on achieving or receiving what one desires, whether it be money, position, or another person. Passion was understood to be a cruel master of humankind. The solution to this human dilemma was to find the means by which to eradicate the passions. The Jewish thinker Philo advocated circumcision for "the excision of pleasure and all passions" (*On the Migration of Abraham*, 92). The Stoic philosopher Epictetus offered a way of life based on the understanding that "freedom is not acquired by satisfying yourself with what you desire, but by destroying your desire" (*Arrian's Discourses,* 4.1.175). The writer of 2 Peter claims that to escape slavery to the passions, we must *respond to God's promises* so that that we are capable of *moral excellence, knowledge, self-control, patient endurance, godliness, brotherly affection*, and *love*. There is no talk of the Spirit helping believers with their passions; the focus is on correct convictions. **9:** Believers are privileged to share in God's nature and so to live

never fall away. 11 Then God will give you a grand entrance into the eternal Kingdom of our Lord and Savior Jesus Christ.

Paying Attention to Scripture

12 Therefore, I will always remind you about these things—even though you already know them and are standing firm in the truth you have been taught. 13 And it is only right that I should keep on reminding you as long as I live.* 14 For our Lord Jesus Christ has shown me that I must soon leave this earthly life,* 15 so I will work hard to make sure you always remember these things after I am gone.

16 For we were not making up clever stories when we told you about the powerful coming of our Lord Jesus Christ. We saw his majestic splendor with our own eyes 17 when he received honor and glory from God the Father. The voice from the majestic glory of God said to him, "This is my dearly loved Son, who brings me great joy."* 18 We ourselves heard that voice from heaven when we were with him on the holy mountain.

19 Because of that experience, we have even greater confidence in the message proclaimed by the prophets. You must pay close attention to what they wrote, for their words are like a lamp shining in a dark place—until the Day dawns, and Christ the Morning Star shines* in your hearts. 20 Above all, you must realize that no prophecy in Scripture ever came from the prophet's own understanding,* 21 or from human initiative. No, those prophets were moved by the Holy Spirit, and they spoke from God.

The Danger of False Teachers

2 But there were also false prophets in Israel, just as there will be false teachers among you. They will cleverly teach destructive heresies and even deny the Master who bought them. In this way, they will bring sudden destruction on themselves. 2 Many will follow their evil teaching and shameful immorality. And because of these teachers, the way of truth will be slandered. 3 In their greed they will make up clever lies to get hold of your money. But God condemned them long ago, and their destruction will not be delayed.

4 For God did not spare even the angels who sinned. He threw them into hell,* in gloomy pits of darkness,* where they are being held until the day of judgment. 5 And God did not spare the ancient world— except for Noah and the seven others in his family. Noah warned the world of God's righteous judgment. So God protected Noah when he destroyed the world of ungodly people with a vast flood. 6 Later, God condemned the cities of Sodom and Gomorrah and turned them into heaps of ashes. He made them an example of what will happen to ungodly people. 7 But God also rescued Lot out of Sodom because he was a righteous man who was sick of the shameful immorality of the wicked people around him. 8 Yes, Lot was a righteous man who was tormented in his soul by the wickedness he saw and heard day after day. 9 So you see, the Lord knows how to rescue godly people from their trials, even while keeping the wicked under punishment until the day of final judgment. 10 He is especially hard on those who follow their own twisted sexual desire, and who despise authority.

These people are proud and arrogant, daring even to scoff at supernatural beings* without so

1:13 Greek *as long as I am in this tent* [or *tabernacle*]. **1:14** Greek *I must soon put off my tent* [or *tabernacle*]. **1:17** Matt 17:5; Mark 9:7; Luke 9:35. **1:19** Or *rises.* **1:20** Or *is a matter of one's own interpretation.* **2:4a** Greek *Tartarus.* **2:4b** Some manuscripts read *in chains of gloom.* **2:10** Greek *at glorious ones,* which are probably evil angels.

cleansed from their old sins. Proper knowledge will result in proper action. **10–11:** And proper action will result in a more secure calling and election and certainty of *entrance* into Christ's *eternal Kingdom*.

1:12–21 Authority of Peter

Peter's admission that he is dying (vv. 13–15) is a way of offering a last will and testament to other Christians. **16–21:** Peter sees not only the majesty of God's Son and hears God's declaration of Jesus as Son, but also he knows how this event is connected to the future hope. He is the one moved by the Holy Spirit to correctly interpret writings, such as Paul's. **16–18:** The message concerns *the powerful coming of our Lord Jesus Christ*. The basis of Peter's authority is that he was a spectator of Christ's majesty, particularly at the transfiguration. **19:** Consequently, the prophetic word that he gives in the letter is firm; it is the only reliable guide. **20–21:** These verses refer to the prophets in the Old Testament. Moved by the Holy Spirit, they spoke from God: God's appointment of a Son was prophesied in the Old Testament (e.g., Ps 2).

2:1–22 Denunciation of the False Teachers

False teaching leads to immorality. **4–10a:** The author vividly describes God's judgmental activities in the past. The abilities promised above (1:5–7) exclude debauchery and are antithetical to being focused on and enslaved to bodily desires. **10b–22:** A severe depiction of the immorality that follows such false

much as trembling. [11]But the angels, who are
far greater in power and strength, do not dare
to bring from the Lord* a charge of blasphemy
against those supernatural beings.
[12]These false teachers are like unthinking
animals, creatures of instinct, born to be caught
and destroyed. They scoff at things they do not
understand, and like animals, they will be destroyed. [13]Their destruction is their reward for
the harm they have done. They love to indulge
in evil pleasures in broad daylight. They are a
disgrace and a stain among you. They delight in
deception* even as they eat with you in your
fellowship meals. [14]They commit adultery with
their eyes, and their desire for sin is never satisfied. They lure unstable people into sin, and
they are well trained in greed. They live under
God's curse. [15]They have wandered off the right
road and followed the footsteps of Balaam son
of Beor,* who loved to earn money by doing
wrong. [16]But Balaam was stopped from his mad
course when his donkey rebuked him with a human voice.
[17]These people are as useless as dried-up
springs or as mist blown away by the wind.
They are doomed to blackest darkness. [18]They
brag about themselves with empty, foolish
boasting. With an appeal to twisted sexual desires, they lure back into sin those who have
barely escaped from a lifestyle of deception.
[19]They promise freedom, but they themselves
are slaves of sin and corruption. For you are
a slave to whatever controls you. [20]And when
people escape from the wickedness of the world
by knowing our Lord and Savior Jesus Christ
and then get tangled up and enslaved by sin
again, they are worse off than before. [21]It would
be better if they had never known the way to
righteousness than to know it and then reject
the command they were given to live a holy life.
[22]They prove the truth of this proverb: "A dog
returns to its vomit."* And another says, "A
washed pig returns to the mud."

The Day of the Lord Is Coming

3 This is my second letter to you, dear
friends, and in both of them I have tried
to stimulate your wholesome thinking and
refresh your memory. [2]I want you to remember
what the holy prophets said long ago and what
our Lord and Savior commanded through your
apostles.
[3]Most importantly, I want to remind you that
in the last days scoffers will come, mocking the
truth and following their own desires. [4]They will
say, "What happened to the promise that Jesus is
coming again? From before the times of our ancestors, everything has remained the same since
the world was first created."
[5]They deliberately forget that God made the
heavens by the word of his command, and he
brought the earth out from the water and surrounded it with water. [6]Then he used the water
to destroy the ancient world with a mighty flood.
[7]And by the same word, the present heavens and
earth have been stored up for fire. They are being kept for the day of judgment, when ungodly
people will be destroyed.
[8]But you must not forget this one thing,
dear friends: A day is like a thousand years to
the Lord, and a thousand years is like a day. [9]The
Lord isn't really being slow about his promise,
as some people think. No, he is being patient
for your sake. He does not want anyone to be
destroyed, but wants everyone to repent. [10]But
the day of the Lord will come as unexpectedly as
a thief. Then the heavens will pass away with a
terrible noise, and the very elements themselves
will disappear in fire, and the earth and everything on it will be found to deserve judgment.*
[11]Since everything around us is going to be
destroyed like this, what holy and godly lives you

2:11 Other manuscripts read *to the Lord;* still others do not include this phrase at all. **2:13** Some manuscripts read *in fellowship meals.* **2:15** Some manuscripts read *Bosor.* **2:22** Prov 26:11. **3:10** Other manuscripts read *will be burned up;* still others read *will be found destroyed.*

teaching. **20–21:** The writer strongly implies that scriptural prophecy supports his view and that he therefore is a spiritually gifted interpreter of prophecy. Presumably the image of God shared by the author and his readers, unlike the image presented in the Greco-Roman pantheon, is that God is asexual. Becoming like God entails sexual continence.

3:1–14 The Message of the Letter

The author refers to *the holy prophets* and the Savior's words mediated *through your apostles* about the coming of Jesus (v. 2). This implies possible dissension over whether Peter or the false teachers were the correct interpreters of the Old Testament. **5–7:** The creation, the *flood,* and the coming *day of judgment* all testify to God's control. A proper understanding of God includes regarding God as Creator and Judge. **8–10:** Judgment is held back by God's mercy. The faithful have received a promise that Jesus will return in concert with the judgment of God on unrighteousness. **11–14:** The Greek word *parousia* (coming, *looking forward*) that is used to describe the return of Christ (e.g., 2 Thes 2:8) refers

should live, [12]looking forward to the day of God
and hurrying it along. On that day, he will set
the heavens on fire, and the elements will melt
away in the flames. [13]But we are looking forward
to the new heavens and new earth he has promised, a world filled with God's righteousness.

[14]And so, dear friends, while you are waiting
for these things to happen, make every effort to
be found living peaceful lives that are pure and
blameless in his sight.

[15]And remember, our Lord's patience gives
people time to be saved. This is what our beloved
brother Paul also wrote to you with the wisdom
God gave him—[16]speaking of these things in all
of his letters. Some of his comments are hard
to understand, and those who are ignorant and
unstable have twisted his letters to mean something quite different, just as they do with other
parts of Scripture. And this will result in their
destruction.

Peter's Final Words

[17]I am warning you ahead of time, dear friends.
Be on guard so that you will not be carried away
by the errors of these wicked people and lose
your own secure footing. [18]Rather, you must
grow in the grace and knowledge of our Lord and
Savior Jesus Christ.

All glory to him, both now and forever!
Amen.

---

here to *the day of God*. The coming of Jesus means the coming day of God, the inescapable judgment. Jesus will return at the day of God; unrighteousness will be judged and destroyed; and a new heaven and a new earth full of righteousness will be established. This conviction is critical because it is integrally related to right conduct: The faithful can escape the corruption of the world and behave in a holy and godly manner. The author seeks to persuade his readers that attachment to the world as it is is equivalent to writing one's death warrant. The gift of God to those who believe, however, is the possibility of escaping the world's fate.

3:15–18 Conclusion

The author describes Paul's letters as confirming his viewpoint (vv. 15–16). Furthermore, the writings of Paul, which the author and his audience regard as Scripture, refer to Jesus as God's Son and connect his Sonship to his coming in power at the end (1 Thes 1:10; 1 Cor 15:23–28). Paul's letters, however, were a bone of contention. **17–18:** The writing closes with a warning and a doxology (cf. Rom 16:27).

1 JOHN

INTRODUCTION

Living in the light and love of the Lord Jesus Christ is the challenge of 1 John. The author touches on great central themes of Christian theology and ethics, such as sin, faith, forgiveness, and love, which remain as relevant for our times as for that of the author. Who was this writer and what do we know of the circumstances for which the author wrote? While we will examine some possible answers to these questions, the historical setting, the recipients and the structure of 1 John provide an not only an intriguing challenge for scholars but still remain a mystery.

The Gospel of John, 1 John, 2 John, 3 John, and the Revelation of John all mention this name in their titles. Did the same author write them all? In what order were they written? For whom were they written, and why? Debate continues over whether the same author wrote the Gospel and the letters; opposing views argue over similarities and differences in style, language, and concepts. But there is general agreement that the Gospel and the letters have some relationship, with similar themes and styles of writing.

Early church fathers and theologians Polycarp (himself a disciple of John), Irenaeus, Justin Martyr, Tertullian, and Clement of Alexandria all supported the view that the apostle John was the author of the Gospel. There is still support today for this view. Some scholars think that there may have been a first draft of the Gospel (with John the apostle as the author) and that after his death, his followers published a final version in Ephesus around AD 85. These scholars think that 1 John was written after the first draft but before the final version of the Gospel.

First John does not reveal anything about its author, but 1:1–4 strongly suggests the author was an eyewitness to the events. Second John and 3 John, by contrast, state that they are from the elder (2 Jn 1; 3 Jn 1). Debate continues as to whether the same author wrote all three letters or whether there were two authors. It seems reasonable to hold that the apostle John was responsible for the Fourth Gospel regardless of whether he completed an initial draft and his followers the final version, and that a John known as the elder wrote 2 John and 3 John, and also may have written 1 John.

Early traditions indicate that the apostle John planted churches in Ephesus. These may have been house churches, communities, or fellowships, but they were people who accepted him in some sense as their leader. Irenaeus (AD 130–200) wrote that John was a leading figure in Asia Minor and that many traveled to Ephesus to learn from him. Tradition holds that the church in Ephesus preserved the Johannine writings, including the Gospel and the letters.

There were several groups in this community. First, there were Jewish Christians, some totally committed to the teachings of John, and others, while believing in Jesus, found it hard to accept him as Messiah and had strong loyalty to the Jewish law. They accepted the humanity of Jesus and show similarities to a group known as the Ebionites, who emphasized keeping the Jewish law; some also denied the deity of Christ.

Second, there were Hellenistic Christians and also some Jewish Christians who lived in a Hellenistic environment. Hellenistic dualism and some pre-Gnostic ideas may have influenced them. Their difficulty would have been accepting the humanity of Jesus Christ. Thus there were groups having too low a view of Jesus Christ, emphasizing his humanity, and others who had too high a view of Jesus Christ and saw mainly his deity.

The third group, the opponents or secessionists, were those who had once embraced the teaching of John but clashed with John and perhaps with others in the community over matters of belief and behavior. It became impossible for them to remain within the Johannine community, and they had left (1 Jn 2:19).

The letters help trace the development of this community. Second John reveals that the divisions in the community had deepened and that more people had left it. Many had gone out into the world, especially those who did not confess that Jesus Christ had come in the flesh (2 Jn 7). Third John indicates that there were threats from someone named Diotrephes, who refused to acknowledge the authority of the leadership and expelled believers from the community. The community disappeared, leaving no records or heritage.

This first letter (1 Jn) recognizes and addresses the problems that have arisen in the community. John lays down the true teaching and defends it against the claims of his opponents, the secessionists. He emphasizes the reality and importance of the incarnation of Jesus Christ, the humanity of Jesus, the reality of sin and the need to confess it, forgiveness found through Jesus Christ and his death, and the commandment to love. He is concerned that the believers have right doctrine and behave ethically. His letter is a call to the community to discern truth from falsehood, to walk worthy of the gospel in their behavior, and to remember the incarnation of Jesus Christ.

First John is referred to as a letter or epistle, but it lacks some of the elements of a letter. Some scholars consider the lack of an address, greetings, and conclusion as indicating that it is more akin to a pamphlet, brochure, or tract for wide distribution. Yet there is a tone of endearment and closeness characteristic of letters. The comments here adopt the traditional convention of referring to 1 John as a letter or epistle.

First John contains parallels to the Fourth Gospel; in particular, the prologue in the Gospel and the introduction to 1 John have common themes of light, life, and the incarnation of Jesus Christ. The ending of the Gospel parallels the ending of the letter (Jn 21; cf. 1 Jn 5:14–21). Probably John had a draft of the Gospel, and some of what he wrote presupposes knowledge of it.

First John does not have an obvious structure. There is one natural division, however, occurring at 1 John 3:11, which separates the letter into two halves. These are closely linked with light and love, key concerns in both. The first half concentrates on the difference between those who live in the light and those who live in darkness. The second half focuses on the quality of Christian life in the community. —*Margaret A. Motion*

1:1–4	Prologue: The Word of Life Revealed
1:5—3:10	God Is Light: Walk in the Light
1:5—2:2	Walking in Light or Walking in Darkness
2:3–11	Three Tests of Authentic Living
2:12–17	Staying Strong through Knowing the Father
2:18–27	Warning against Antichrists
2:28—3:10	Children of God or Children of the Devil
3:11—5:13	God Is Love: Consequences for the Children of God
3:11–24	Children of God Love One Another

✧

Introduction

1 We proclaim to you the one who existed
from the beginning,* whom we have heard
and seen. We saw him with our own eyes
and touched him with our own hands. He is the
Word of life. 2 This one who is life itself was revealed to us, and we have seen him. And now we
testify and proclaim to you that he is the one
who is eternal life. He was with the Father, and
then he was revealed to us. 3 We proclaim to you
what we ourselves have actually seen and heard
so that you may have fellowship with us. And
our fellowship is with the Father and with his
Son, Jesus Christ. 4 We are writing these things
so that you may fully share our joy.*

Living in the Light

5 This is the message we heard from Jesus* and
now declare to you: God is light, and there is no
darkness in him at all. 6 So we are lying if we say we
have fellowship with God but go on living in spiritual darkness; we are not practicing the truth. 7 But
if we are living in the light, as God is in the light,
then we have fellowship with each other, and the
blood of Jesus, his Son, cleanses us from all sin.
8 If we claim we have no sin, we are only fooling ourselves and not living in the truth. 9 But if
we confess our sins to him, he is faithful and just
to forgive us our sins and to cleanse us from all
wickedness. 10 If we claim we have not sinned, we
are calling God a liar and showing that his word
has no place in our hearts.

1:1 Greek *What was from the beginning.* **1:4** Or *so that our joy may be complete;* some manuscripts read *your joy.* **1:5** Greek *from him.*

1:1–4 Prologue: The Word of Life Revealed

We have heard . . . saw him . . . touched him: John attempts to convey the reality of Jesus' entry into this world and human history. He experienced the word of life through his senses, showing that ordinary people may also experience it. **2:** *Life* (eternal life) was with God (see Prologue to John's Gospel, 1:1–17) and came into the world. **3:** *Fellowship* (Gk. *koinonia*, what is held "in common") expresses intimate human relationship that is generous, participatory, and shared. It has two dimensions: human fellowship among Christian believers of the community, and fellowship with the Father and his Son Jesus Christ.

1:5—3:10 God Is Light: Walk in the Light

1:5—2:2 Walking in Light or Walking in Darkness. Right thinking about God intertwines theology and ethics. **1:5:** A form of Hebrew parallelism, in which the second line may reinforce the idea of the first line, be part of a development or express the contrast to the first line. *God is light* is reinforced by *there is no darkness in* [God] *at all*. *Living in spiritual darkness* parallels *living in the light*. God as light is a concept rooted in the Old Testament. Moses experienced God in the burning bush, and God's presence was as fire for guidance during travel in the desert (Ex 3:2–4; cf. Ex 13). God's light eliminates the darkness physically and spiritually (Ps 18:28). Light is God's character (Ps 27:1). See also John's gospel, which refers to Jesus as the light shining in the darkness (John 1:5) and contains Jesus' claim, "I am the light of the world" (9:5). In 1 John 1:5 the statement is *God is light*. For some early Gnostic followers, light was a metaphor for God. John is giving a positive message to the Christians still in the community, but at the same time he is setting up a defense of his teaching and a framework in which to refute the false teaching. **6–10:** This passage has six clauses, three negative, probably referring to the Gnostics, and three positive challenges for the Johannine community to abide by. *If we say . . . spiritual darkness*: Choosing sin (darkness) rather than truth or light; John may be condemning outsiders for their lying and deceptive behavior. *In the light, as God is in the light*: Habitually living in God's way results in *fellowship* with one another and cleansing from *sin* through *the blood of Jesus*. *If we claim we have no sin . . . if we confess our sins*: John's opponents said that everyday living was related to this world and separated from God; therefore sin, being of the world, did not affect their

2 My dear children, I am writing this to you
so that you will not sin. But if anyone does
sin, we have an advocate who pleads our
case before the Father. He is Jesus Christ, the one
who is truly righteous. 2 He himself is the sacrifice that atones for our sins—and not only our
sins but the sins of all the world.

3 And we can be sure that we know him if we
obey his commandments. 4 If someone claims, "I
know God," but doesn't obey God's commandments, that person is a liar and is not living in
the truth. 5 But those who obey God's word truly
show how completely they love him. That is how
we know we are living in him. 6 Those who say
they live in God should live their lives as Jesus
did.

A New Commandment

7 Dear friends, I am not writing a new commandment for you; rather it is an old one you have
had from the very beginning. This old commandment—to love one another—is the same
message you heard before. 8 Yet it is also new.
Jesus lived the truth of this commandment, and
you also are living it. For the darkness is disappearing, and the true light is already shining.

9 If anyone claims, "I am living in the light,"
but hates a Christian brother or sister,* that
person is still living in darkness. 10 Anyone who
loves another brother or sister* is living in the
light and does not cause others to stumble. 11 But
anyone who hates another brother or sister is
still living and walking in darkness. Such a person does not know the way to go, having been
blinded by the darkness.

12 I am writing to you who are God's children
because your sins have been forgiven
through Jesus.*
13 I am writing to you who are mature in the
faith*
because you know Christ, who existed
from the beginning.
I am writing to you who are young in the faith
because you have won your battle with the
evil one.
14 I have written to you who are God's children
because you know the Father.
I have written to you who are mature in the
faith
because you know Christ, who existed
from the beginning.
I have written to you who are young in the
faith
because you are strong.
God's word lives in your hearts,
and you have won your battle with the evil
one.

Do Not Love This World

15 Do not love this world nor the things it offers you, for when you love the world, you do

2:9 Greek *hates his brother;* similarly in 2:11. **2:10** Greek *loves his brother.* **2:12** Greek *through his name.* **2:13** Or *to you fathers;* also in 2:14.

relationship with God. John intensifies his response: *not living in the truth*. On the other hand, *if we confess* God is *faithful and just to forgive*. *If we claim we have not sinned*: It seems the opponents are claiming they have never sinned. John responds that *his word* is not in these people, probably a reference to Jesus. **2:1–2:** John turns to the members of the community who have remained, acknowledging the possibility that members of the community have sinned. He assures his community that there is an *advocate* (or "counselor") for the times when they sin. The *sacrifice that atones*: in Greek, *hilasmos*, a sacrifice made to placate an angry person. Sin is covered, the sins of the whole world, not just of an elite group.

2:3–11 Three Tests of Authentic Living in the Light of God. Three statements test the authenticity of a person's Christian life, each building on what has gone before. *I know God, I live in God, I am living in the light*: The truth of these claims depends on the person's life. **3–4:** Knowing God must result in obedience is the first test. Disobedience reveals that the person is a liar and that the *truth* (Christ) does not exist in that person's life. **6–8:** *Live in God . . . live . . . as Jesus did*: The second test of an authentic Christian life, a two-way indwelling, the Christian indwelling in God and God indwelling the Christian. **7–11:** *Love one another*: The third test, an old and a new commandment that the Old Testament expresses and that Jesus Christ demonstrated by laying down his life, the supreme example of love. His truth and light illuminate what is right conduct toward a brother or sister.

2:12–17 Staying Strong through Knowing the Father. John gives the community praise and reassurance. **12–14:** *Children . . . mature . . . young*: Family terms of endearment refering to the whole community, male and female. *Mature*: Greek "fathers" but meaning mature adults, male *and* female. They provide a foundation for the young people in the community. **15–17:** Warnings against loving the world and a list of three things that may lead the believer astray: *physical pleasure*, *craving* for possessions, and *pride* in riches.

not have the love of the Father in you. [16]For the
world offers only a craving for physical pleasure,
a craving for everything we see, and pride in our
achievements and possessions. These are not
from the Father, but are from this world. [17]And
this world is fading away, along with everything
that people crave. But anyone who does what
pleases God will live forever.

Warning about Antichrists

[18]Dear children, the last hour is here. You have
heard that the Antichrist is coming, and already
many such antichrists have appeared. From this
we know that the last hour has come. [19]These
people left our churches, but they never really
belonged with us; otherwise they would have
stayed with us. When they left, it proved that
they did not belong with us.

[20]But you are not like that, for the Holy One
has given you his Spirit,* and all of you know
the truth. [21]So I am writing to you not because
you don't know the truth but because you know
the difference between truth and lies. [22]And who
is a liar? Anyone who says that Jesus is not the
Christ.* Anyone who denies the Father and
the Son is an antichrist.* [23]Anyone who denies
the Son doesn't have the Father, either. But anyone
who acknowledges the Son has the Father also.

[24]So you must remain faithful to what you
have been taught from the beginning. If you do,
you will remain in fellowship with the Son and
with the Father. [25]And in this fellowship we enjoy the eternal life he promised us.

[26]I am writing these things to warn you
about those who want to lead you astray. [27]But
you have received the Holy Spirit,* and he lives
within you, so you don't need anyone to teach
you what is true. For the Spirit* teaches you everything you need to know, and what he teaches
is true—it is not a lie. So just as he has taught
you, remain in fellowship with Christ.

Living as Children of God

[28]And now, dear children, remain in fellowship
with Christ so that when he returns, you will be
full of courage and not shrink back from him in
shame.

[29]Since we know that Christ is righteous, we
also know that all who do what is right are God's
children.

3 See how very much our Father loves us,
for he calls us his children, and that is what
we are! But the people who belong to this
world don't recognize that we are God's children
because they don't know him. [2]Dear friends, we
are already God's children, but he has not yet
shown us what we will be like when Christ appears. But we do know that we will be like him,
for we will see him as he really is. [3]And all who
have this eager expectation will keep themselves
pure, just as he is pure.

[4]Everyone who sins is breaking God's law, for
all sin is contrary to the law of God. [5]And you

2:20 Greek *But you have an anointing from the Holy One.* **2:22a** Or *not the Messiah.* **2:22b** Or *the antichrist.* **2:27a** Greek *the anointing from him.* **2:27b** Greek *the anointing.*

2:18–27 Warning against Antichrists. The thought of going astray by loving the world reminds John of those who have left the community, the *antichrists*. **18:** *The last hour*: Description of the end of the age, the eschaton. **22–23:** The first error of the antichrists or opponents is the denial that Jesus is the Christ (see also 1 John 4:1–6). In denying the Son, the opponents also denied the Father. **20, 26–27:** Quite possibly they were claiming spiritual authority as they propounded their beliefs, and hence John reminds the community that *the Holy One* has anointed them (*given you his Spirit*), giving them knowledge and discernment.

2:28—3:10 Children of God or Children of the Devil. This passage highlights the contrast between those who do right (2:28—3:3) and those who sin (3:4–6). **2:28:** *When he returns*: Two phrases in Greek, "when he is revealed" and "at his coming," continuing the eschatological theme: when Christ will be unveiled before the world and when Christ will judge. **29:** John reassures the believers that they will have no sense of shame if they abide in Christ. **3:1–3:** Knowing God's righteousness will lead them to imitate his righteousness in their daily living, and they may have confidence at his coming. The believers will see the reflection of his righteousness in their behavior and will see how through abiding in him their lives have been shaped into conformity with his. **4–10:** This passage reflects the tensions between sin and doing what is right, between being *children of the devil* and *children of God*. John accents the positive by negative examples. Those who sin are guilty of lawlessness. Christians do not sin because God's *life* (Greek "seed") abides in them and because they *have been born into God's family*. Does this mean perfection is demanded? Not at all; John writes this passage in the present continuous tense. The sense is that of continuing to sin or an ongoing habit of sin. Habitual sin has no place in the life of the believer. The presence of Christ in the believer enables this to become reality. Finally, how you live reveals what you are. Those

know that Jesus came to take away our sins, and
there is no sin in him. 6 Anyone who continues
to live in him will not sin. But anyone who keeps
on sinning does not know him or understand
who he is.
7 Dear children, don't let anyone deceive
you about this: When people do what is right,
it shows that they are righteous, even as Christ
is righteous. 8 But when people keep on sinning,
it shows that they belong to the devil, who has
been sinning since the beginning. But the Son
of God came to destroy the works of the devil.
9 Those who have been born into God's family
do not make a practice of sinning, because God's
life* is in them. So they can't keep on sinning,
because they are children of God. 10 So now we
can tell who are children of God and who are
children of the devil. Anyone who does not live
righteously and does not love other believers*
does not belong to God.

Love One Another

11 This is the message you have heard from the
beginning: We should love one another. 12 We
must not be like Cain, who belonged to the evil
one and killed his brother. And why did he kill
him? Because Cain had been doing what was
evil, and his brother had been doing what was
righteous. 13 So don't be surprised, dear brothers
and sisters,* if the world hates you.
14 If we love our Christian brothers and sisters,* it proves that we have passed from death
to life. But a person who has no love is still dead.
15 Anyone who hates another brother or sister*
is really a murderer at heart. And you know that
murderers don't have eternal life within them.
16 We know what real love is because Jesus
gave up his life for us. So we also ought to give
up our lives for our brothers and sisters. 17 If
someone has enough money to live well and sees
a brother or sister* in need but shows no compassion—how can God's love be in that person?
18 Dear children, let's not merely say that we
love each other; let us show the truth by our actions. 19 Our actions will show that we belong to
the truth, so we will be confident when we stand
before God. 20 Even if we feel guilty, God is greater than our feelings, and he knows everything.
21 Dear friends, if we don't feel guilty, we can
come to God with bold confidence. 22 And we will
receive from him whatever we ask because we
obey him and do the things that please him.
23 And this is his commandment: We must believe in the name of his Son, Jesus Christ, and love
one another, just as he commanded us. 24 Those who
obey God's commandments remain in fellowship
with him, and he with them. And we know he lives
in us because the Spirit he gave us lives in us.

Discerning False Prophets

4 Dear friends, do not believe everyone who
claims to speak by the Spirit. You must test
them to see if the spirit they have comes
from God. For there are many false prophets in

3:9 Greek *because his seed.* **3:10** Greek *does not love his brother.* **3:13** Greek *brothers.* **3:14** Greek *the brothers;* similarly in 3:16. **3:15** Greek *hates his brother.* **3:17** Greek *sees his brother.*

who do not do what is right are not from God; nor are those who do not love their brothers and sisters (*other believers*).

3:11—5:13 God Is Love: Consequences for the Children of God

3:11–24 Children of God Love One Another. The letter seems to divide at this point in almost equal halves, closely linked, with love and light as major themes. **12–13:** *Cain* becomes a negative example; his actions were consistent with those of *the evil one*. Cain's envy and jealousy of his brother and his righteous deeds are compared with that of *the world* toward the righteousness of the believers as they love one another. **16–17:** Christ's *love* in laying down *his life* for us is the supreme example. It reflects God's heart for the poor and needy. To see a brother or sister in need and to refuse help is not showing the love of God. Something is set aside that is personally valued and is precious. Christ did this by setting aside his own life. John challenges the community to set aside that which is precious and valued in order to help the needy. **19:** Believers will know that they belong to the truth by the evidence of their obedience to this command to love. **20:** This is reassurance for times of self-doubt. **23–24:** John links this obedience to faith or belief in the true nature, the *name*, of God's *Son, Jesus Christ*. The Spirit enables the believer to abide in Christ and to live ethically in love.

4:1–6 Children of God Discern the Spirits. The opponents had left the community but were obviously still giving it some trouble by claiming spiritual authority for their beliefs and teaching. Advice to the community on how to discern the spirits would be natural. **1–3:** John warns of the need to recognize the spirits and gives the necessary test: Every spirit that confesses that Jesus Christ has come in *a real body* ("the flesh") is from God, and every spirit that does not so confess is not. The test acknowledges the incarnation, the deity of Jesus Christ and his messiahship.

the world. 2 This is how we know if they have
the Spirit of God: If a person claiming to be a
prophet* acknowledges that Jesus Christ came
in a real body, that person has the Spirit of God.
3 But if someone claims to be a prophet and does
not acknowledge the truth about Jesus, that person is not from God. Such a person has the spirit
of the Antichrist, which you heard is coming into
the world and indeed is already here.

4 But you belong to God, my dear children.
You have already won a victory over those people, because the Spirit who lives in you is greater
than the spirit who lives in the world. 5 Those
people belong to this world, so they speak from
the world's viewpoint, and the world listens to
them. 6 But we belong to God, and those who
know God listen to us. If they do not belong to
God, they do not listen to us. That is how we
know if someone has the Spirit of truth or the
spirit of deception.

Loving One Another

7 Dear friends, let us continue to love one another,
for love comes from God. Anyone who loves is a
child of God and knows God. 8 But anyone who
does not love does not know God, for God is love.

9 God showed how much he loved us by sending his one and only Son into the world so that
we might have eternal life through him. 10 This
is real love—not that we loved God, but that he
loved us and sent his Son as a sacrifice to take
away our sins.

11 Dear friends, since God loved us that much,
we surely ought to love each other. 12 No one has
ever seen God. But if we love each other, God
lives in us, and his love is brought to full expression in us.

13 And God has given us his Spirit as proof
that we live in him and he in us. 14 Furthermore,
we have seen with our own eyes and now testify
that the Father sent his Son to be the Savior of
the world. 15 All who confess that Jesus is the Son
of God have God living in them, and they live in
God. 16 We know how much God loves us, and we
have put our trust in his love.

God is love, and all who live in love live in
God, and God lives in them. 17 And as we live in
God, our love grows more perfect. So we will not
be afraid on the day of judgment, but we can face
him with confidence because we live like Jesus
here in this world.

18 Such love has no fear, because perfect love
expels all fear. If we are afraid, it is for fear of
punishment, and this shows that we have not
fully experienced his perfect love. 19 We love each
other* because he loved us first.

20 If someone says, "I love God," but hates
a Christian brother or sister,* that person is a
liar; for if we don't love people we can see, how
can we love God, whom we cannot see? 21 And
he has given us this command: Those who love
God must also love their Christian brothers and
sisters.*

Faith in the Son of God

5 Everyone who believes that Jesus is the
Christ* has become a child of God. And everyone who loves the Father loves his children, too. 2 We know we love God's children if we

4:2 Greek *If a spirit;* similarly in 4:3. **4:19** Greek *We love.* Other manuscripts read *We love God;* still others read *We love him.* **4:20** Greek *hates his brother.* **4:21** Greek *The one who loves God must also love his brother.* **5:1** Or *the Messiah.*

The struggle to come to terms with the humanity and deity of Christ occupied the early church for many years and was not finally settled until the Council of Chalcedon (AD 451), which affirmed and built on the work of the Councils of Nicea (325) and Constantinople (381). **4–6:** The believers have conquered the opponents because of the abiding of Christ within them. Those outside the community are described as being *in the world.* John condemns their teaching as associated with the darkness of the world in contrast to the light of the truth. The test of right teaching has become the validation of claims to the Spirit's inspiration or authority.

4:7–21 Children of God Love because God First Loved. John explains the origin and motivation for love. **7–8:** *Love comes from God,* and the true believer demonstrates this in life. Failure to love invalidates the claim to know God. **9–12:** Love is revealed by God through his only Son as the atoning sacrifice for our sins. God took the initiative. Our response should be *to love each other.* **13–21:** God's love is the basis for our love of one another. The first response to God's love is the confession that the Father has sent his Son as the Savior of the world. The second is obedience to the command to love one another. The result is assurance that we need not fear punishment. Those who do not love their brothers and sisters who are visible cannot love God whom they have not seen.

5:1–5 Children of God Conquer the World. 1–2: John interprets loving God in human terms, using the analogy of the family. Friendship with parents involves accepting and loving their children. Women in present-day society demonstrate this very well as

love God and obey his commandments. [3] Loving God means keeping his commandments, and his commandments are not burdensome. [4] For every child of God defeats this evil world, and we achieve this victory through our faith. [5] And who can win this battle against the world? Only those who believe that Jesus is the Son of God.

[6] And Jesus Christ was revealed as God's Son by his baptism in water and by shedding his blood on the cross*—not by water only, but by water and blood. And the Spirit, who is truth, confirms it with his testimony. [7] So we have these three witnesses*—[8] the Spirit, the water, and the blood—and all three agree. [9] Since we believe human testimony, surely we can believe the greater testimony that comes from God. And God has testified about his Son. [10] All who believe in the Son of God know in their hearts that this testimony is true. Those who don't believe this are actually calling God a liar because they don't believe what God has testified about his Son.

[11] And this is what God has testified: He has given us eternal life, and this life is in his Son. [12] Whoever has the Son has life; whoever does not have God's Son does not have life.

Conclusion

[13] I have written this to you who believe in the name of the Son of God, so that you may know you have eternal life. [14] And we are confident that he hears us whenever we ask for anything that pleases him. [15] And since we know he hears us when we make our requests, we also know that he will give us what we ask for.

[16] If you see a Christian brother or sister* sinning in a way that does not lead to death, you should pray, and God will give that person life. But there is a sin that leads to death, and I am not saying you should pray for those who commit it. [17] All wicked actions are sin, but not every sin leads to death.

[18] We know that God's children do not make a practice of sinning, for God's Son holds them securely, and the evil one cannot touch them. [19] We know that we are children of God and that the world around us is under the control of the evil one.

[20] And we know that the Son of God has come, and he has given us understanding so that we can know the true God.* And now we live in fellowship with the true God because we live in fellowship with his Son, Jesus Christ. He is the only true God, and he is eternal life.

[21] Dear children, keep away from anything that might take God's place in your hearts.*

5:6 Greek *This is he who came by water and blood.* **5:7** A few very late manuscripts add *in heaven—the Father, the Word, and the Holy Spirit, and these three are one. And we have three witnesses on earth.* **5:16** Greek *a brother.* **5:20** Greek *the one who is true.* **5:21** Greek *keep yourselves from idols.*

they show practical love and concern for the children of others. **3–5:** The person born of God is the one who believes that Jesus is the Christ. The believer is being shaped in this world by God and overcomes it by not accepting its standards and not being controlled by it.

5:6–13 The Testimony of God to His Son. These verses concern the witness to the Son to establish his validity. **6–7:** Most scholars understand *water* as a reference to the baptism of Jesus and *blood* as a reference to his death. John Calvin applied both terms to the death of Christ, when blood and water flowed as his side was pierced. Both explanations show the humanity of Jesus in his death, a counter to the rejection of the humanity of Christ held by the opponents of the community. **8–13:** According to Judaism, three witnesses made for creditable evidence. A further witness is the testimony of God, an inner testimony of eternal life, established by the Spirit in the hearts of believers.

5:14–21 Final Words

It is unclear whether these verses were original or added later. Since they repeat previous themes, they were most likely points that John wished to emphasize and added as afterthoughts. **14–15:** This is not a promise but rather an indication of what a brother or sister ought to pray for. **16:** Prayer is for a brother or sister who is *sinning in a way that does not lead to death*. The answer is: *God will give that person life*. But *sin that leads to death* probably refers to unconfessed sin outside of the community. John has already shown how sin inside the community may be confessed and forgiven. Those outside the community, denying the fact of sin in their lives, do not have the means for confession and forgiveness. Those within the community have the light of Christ to show them the truth, bring about conviction of sin, and deal with it.

2 JOHN

INTRODUCTION

This book, 2 John, has often been regarded an outline for 1 John, although it could just as easily be its summary. Commentators often determine the sequence of Johannine writings according to what seems to make sense. Thus 1 John is an extension of 2 John if the circumstances, which in 2 John had been a threat, have become reality in all churches of the "elder."

There has been much debate about the author of Johannine literature, as well as about the date and the recipients. Some scholars argue for a date in the late second century because of arguments against Gnosticism that they see in the letter. This would preclude John the apostle as the author and gives no other clues for author or audience. Others (including these comments) believe that these works have a common apostolic author and could have been written between 80 and 95. In all of these works pastoral and leadership problems developed as churches became older.

Comparing 2 John and 3 John, which are similar in language, style, and approach, and which deal with the issue of itinerant teachers, will illuminate both letters and their meanings for readers today.

Almost nothing definitive can be claimed about the setting of 2 John. However, a leader in Asia Minor, around Ephesus, could be the recipient (see the circle of churches [Rev 2–4], in which a man named John was the elder). John the apostle would still be a living witness of the old commandment, but his churches now had new leaders, several of whom may have been women. Churches usually met in homes, and there is evidence that the egalitarian character of the early Christians attracted influential women. They opened their homes to the church when they became Christians, and naturally they served in them. The New Testament testifies to several such women: for example, Apphia (Phlm 2), Prisca (1 Cor 16:19; Rom 16:3), and Nympha (Col 4:15), who by faithful service may have become overseers.

Itinerant preaching and teaching was a popular profession even in the secular realm. Christians used it, sometimes in the context of their secular work of trading, to spread the gospel. Hospitality to people who traveled and evangelized was important and a natural duty of a house-church leader. Such hospitality became more challenging as the church grew bigger and older. Knowing who was a true teacher required spiritual discernment, and 2 John is an introduction to the subject from one of the last authentic authorities. The elder, if he was John, was too old now to visit his churches regularly, but it seemed he was to make one more visit because difficulties with false teachers had increased.

Gnostic tendencies in some leaders created strife in the church. Those who "deny that Jesus Christ came in a real body" (2 John 7) are, as in all Johannine literature, the primary false teachers and false teaching. This developed out of the dualism of body and spirit that was posited in the ever-present Hellenistic religion and philosophy. Historical findings show that women were often attracted to ecstatic spirituality in their homes and promoted it there. Against such hyperspirituality, our author demands obedience to the double commandment that "we have had from the beginning" (5): Christ's commandment of love and truth. A person who has the spirit and the truth knows the Father; a person who doesn't is a deceiver. —*Ksenija Magda*

1–3 Greetings
4–11 The Concern: Love and Truth
12–13 Announcement and Final Greetings

✧

Greetings
This letter is from John, the elder.*
I am writing to the chosen lady and to her
children,* whom I love in the truth—as does everyone else who knows the truth—2 because the
truth lives in us and will be with us forever.
3 Grace, mercy, and peace, which come from
God the Father and from Jesus Christ—the Son
of the Father—will continue to be with us who
live in truth and love.

Live in the Truth
4 How happy I was to meet some of your children
and find them living according to the truth, just
as the Father commanded.
5 I am writing to remind you, dear friends,*
that we should love one another. This is not a new
commandment, but one we have had from the beginning. 6 Love means doing what God has commanded us, and he has commanded us to love one
another, just as you heard from the beginning.
7 I say this because many deceivers have gone
out into the world. They deny that Jesus Christ
came* in a real body. Such a person is a deceiver
and an antichrist. 8 Watch out that you do not
lose what we* have worked so hard to achieve.
Be diligent so that you receive your full reward.
9 Anyone who wanders away from this teaching
has no relationship with God. But anyone who
remains in the teaching of Christ has a relationship with both the Father and the Son.
10 If anyone comes to your meeting and does
not teach the truth about Christ, don't invite
that person into your home or give any kind of
encouragement. 11 Anyone who encourages such
people becomes a partner in their evil work.

1a Greek *From the elder.* **1b** Or *the church God has chosen and its members.* **5** Greek *I urge you, lady.* **7** Or *will come.* **8** Some manuscripts read *you.*

1–3 Greetings

The title, *chosen lady* (v. 1), is intriguing, but the lady's identity is disputed. Many interpreters think this is a poetic description of the church. There is, however, no parallel or logical explanation for that interpretation. Some think that *eklekte* (Gk. "chosen") as well as *kyria* ("lady") could be proper names. *Kyria* could also be a title of respect for the lady of the house (where there was no male head, or *kyrios*) or possibly the house where the church met; *eklekte* could be an honorary title meaning everything up to "ordained." For these reasons as well as for the parallelism with 3 John, which is undoubtedly a personal letter, it is safe to assume that 2 John is written to a female church leader. **2–3:** *Truth and love*: Words directly or indirectly present in every verse. The balance of love and truth is an important imperative, especially in women's ministries today, as it was for the elect lady. Those who would serve others must not let tenderness lead them to shade the need for truth.

4–11 The Concern: Love and Truth

Johannine literature emphasizes the importance of the incarnation (v. 7). For these churches it was a starting point. The emphasis on Jesus' body is important for God's saving work, and it also rescues believers from a Platonic spirituality in which spirit and body are strictly divorced and the body is declared evil. *Deceiver . . . antichrist*: Possibly the elder has one false teacher in mind. The author clearly identifies the risks and hopes that the leader will understand what is at stake. **10–11:** The elder asks for a revolutionary act of dissociation from the deceiver, showing that even greeting him means having a part in his *evil work*. (See Jude and 2 Pet 2 for possible insight into this evil.)

Conclusion
[12]I have much more to say to you, but I don't want to do it with paper and ink. For I hope to visit you soon and talk with you face to face. Then our joy will be complete.

[13]Greetings from the children of your sister,* chosen by God.

13 Or *from the members of your sister church.*

12–13 Announcement and Final Greetings

The announcement of the *visit* (v. 12) connects to 3 John 13. **13:** *Children of your sister, chosen by God*: Traditionally John's home church, but possibly believers in John's neighborhood who are led by the lady's relative, or the children of the lady's sister, who also is a Christian.

3 JOHN

INTRODUCTION

Nobody has ever doubted that 3 John is a personal letter to a prominent Christian, Gaius. The parallel with 2 John in structure and language, as well as the announcement of a visit by the elder, gives grounds enough to think of 2 John as a personal letter also. Accordingly, the final greetings in both letters show parallel familiarity. As Gaius is greeted by present friends in 3 John, so the "children of your sister" may be the lady's relatives who are close to the elder and thus a unifying factor between her and the elder.

As is the case in 2 John, nothing in 3 John indicates the place or date of origin. As shown in the introduction to 2 John, these comments assume that John the apostle is the author and Ephesus a possible place of origin. The impetus for writing, however, is clear: One of the leaders in the churches, Diotrephes, is fighting for authority and challenging the elder, the old overseer of several churches in the area. Diotrephes has refused hospitality to itinerant teachers sent by the elder and is stirring up the church against his emissaries. Gaius, a prominent member in the church in this town but not necessarily in the same house-church, has proven faithful (3 Jn 1–3) and is trustworthy to accept this recommendation of Demetrius, a traveling teacher (3 Jn 12).

Close to the end of first century, orthodoxy was not yet well defined, the churches lacked the Bible in a written form, and the first-generation apostles were no longer living. Even guidelines such as the second-century church practice manual, the *Didache,* with all its practical advice, did not yet exist. "Those who do good prove that they are God's children, and those who do evil prove that they do not know God" (11) suggests that the church leaders should be helping members discern between right and wrong leaders. Diotrephes' love of being first and his malicious gossiping and unfriendliness toward brothers and sisters are therefore as easily identified, as is Gaius's loving faithfulness.

In both 2 John and 3 John, leaders are being instructed on how to discern the teachers who can contribute to the well-being of their church. In 2 John the lady is warned against accepting false teachers too willingly; here Diotrephes doesn't accept the true ones. We may see them acting wrongly along typical gender lines, ontological or sociological in origin. The lady is accepting, caring, and challenged by creativity and spirituality; Diotrephes is strict, orthodox, and stern. While she may sometimes lack the needed strictness, orthodoxy, and sternness (perhaps through lack of learning opportunity and experience), he lacks openness, acceptance, and caring (perhaps because of pride in his knowledge).

The need for both female and male leadership strengths becomes evident in the elder's guidelines for true teachers. They include orthodoxy and moral values as well as affection and acceptance of others, especially co-workers in Christ. In 3 John, Diotrephes' character is lacking. His strict orthodoxy seems to produce moral inadequacies common to heretic teachers: They question apostolic authority, gossip, create enmities among churches, and lack love (cf. Jude; 2 Pet 2). —*Ksenija Magda*

1 Address
2–8 Praise for Gaius's Faithfulness
9–11 Against Diotrephes
12 Recommendation for Demetrius
13–15 Announcement and Greetings

✧

Greetings
This letter is from John, the elder.*
I am writing to Gaius, my dear friend, whom
I love in the truth.
[2]Dear friend, I hope all is well with you and
that you are as healthy in body as you are strong
in spirit. [3]Some of the traveling teachers* recently returned and made me very happy by
telling me about your faithfulness and that you
are living according to the truth. [4]I could have
no greater joy than to hear that my children are
following the truth.

Caring for the Lord's Workers
[5]Dear friend, you are being faithful to God
when you care for the traveling teachers who
pass through, even though they are strangers
to you. [6]They have told the church here of your
loving friendship. Please continue providing for
such teachers in a manner that pleases God. [7]For
they are traveling for the Lord,* and they accept
nothing from people who are not believers.* [8]So
we ourselves should support them so that we can
be their partners as they teach the truth.

[9]I wrote to the church about this, but Diotrephes, who loves to be the leader, refuses to
have anything to do with us. [10]When I come, I
will report some of the things he is doing and the
evil accusations he is making against us. Not only
does he refuse to welcome the traveling teachers,
he also tells others not to help them. And when
they do help, he puts them out of the church.
[11]Dear friend, don't let this bad example influence you. Follow only what is good. Remember that those who do good prove that they are
God's children, and those who do evil prove that
they do not know God.*
[12]Everyone speaks highly of Demetrius, as
does the truth itself. We ourselves can say the
same for him, and you know we speak the truth.

Conclusion
[13]I have much more to say to you, but I don't

1 Greek *From the elder.* **3** Greek *the brothers;* also in verses 5 and 10. **7a** Greek *They went out on behalf of the Name.* **7b** Greek *from Gentiles.* **11** Greek *they have not seen God.*

1 Address

The introductory greeting is short but affectionate. In a setting where his authority is challenged, the elder appreciates faithful people like Gaius. *Dear friend*: The favorite address in this letter, occurs four times in only fifteen verses.

2–8 Praise for Gaius's Faithfulness

The elder praises Gaius (v. 2). Gaius's *spirit* is so well that one can only wish him bodily health to match. **3–6:** He lives *according to the truth*, and others testify to that fact. Both *truth* and *loving friendship* are evident in his life, especially in the way he treats real *teachers* of the gospel, accepting and equipping them for their ministry even under opposition. Thus Gaius takes part in their ministry, just as the one who welcomes the deceiver in 2 John participates in his evil deeds.

9–11 Against Diotrephes

Gaius is a well-balanced Christian, in contrast to Diotrephes. **11:** Although the elder does not rebuke Diotrephes' ideas directly, the comment *those who do evil prove that they do not know God* shows what the elder thinks of this bad example. Diotrephes is close to being labeled false.

12 Recommendation for Demetrius

John indicates the occasion for writing this letter. Demetrius is coming to Gaius's church or town, and the elder wants to prevent unpleasant circumstances that occurred earlier, when the elder sent his letter of recommendation to the church directly. Demetrius should be accepted on the basis of a threefold testimony: from everybody; from the truth, meaning the Christ; and the elder and his co-workers. Gaius knows that the elder and his testimony are truthful at all times.

want to write it with pen and ink. [14] For I hope
to see you soon, and then we will talk face to
face.
[15] *Peace be with you.
Your friends here send you their greetings.
Please give my personal greetings to each of our
friends there.

15 Some English translations combine verses 14 and 15 into verse 14.

13–15 Announcement and Greetings

The announcement of the visit is not a main issue of the letter, as it seems to be in 2 John. Presumably the elder has to travel to his churches to reestablish doctrine and his authority. **15:** The letter ends with *peace* and *greetings* from friends to friends, leaving us with the feeling that regardless of the nasty situation, the elder's authority still means something to a larger circle of people.

JUDE

INTRODUCTION

The epistle is ascribed to "Jude, a slave of Jesus Christ and a brother of James." References in the church fathers as well as internal evidence supports that most likely this was Jude, the brother of James, head of the Jerusalem church, and the brother of Jesus (Matt 13:55). The author was familiar with Palestinian, apocalyptic, and Old Testament literature. The vocabulary, although fairly extensive, would not have been beyond the rhetorical skills expected of a traveling Jewish preacher.

Even less can be said about the destination of the letter. Syria, Asia Minor, or Egypt are possibilities. The readers were largely Jewish Christians struggling with the problems of a Gentile environment. Although some scholars suggest Gnosticism as the nature of the heresy reflected in the epistle, more likely it is antinomianism—the idea that Christians were free in Christ not to abide by laws or rules, an idea also reflected in the Corinthian letters and Revelation.

Equally little is known about the date of the epistle, which may be as early as the 50s or as late as the 90s. The character of the epistle is that of Palestinian apocalyptic Jewish Christianity. The author's accomplished use of exegesis is more like that found in the Qumran literature than in diaspora Judaism. He uses apocalyptic material like 1 Enoch and the account of Moses' death, and he shows a strong dependence on the Hebrew Bible rather than on the Greek Septuagint, the version widely used in the diaspora. Jude also uses a triplet style showing a concern for coherence and textual discourse. —*Rebecca Skaggs*

1–2 Introduction
3–4 Purpose
5–16 The Body of the Letter
17–23 Relation to the Community
24–25 Conclusion

✧

Greetings from Jude
This letter is from Jude, a slave of Jesus Christ
and a brother of James.
I am writing to all who have been called by
God the Father, who loves you and keeps you
safe in the care of Jesus Christ.*
2 May God give you more and more mercy,
peace, and love.

The Danger of False Teachers
3 Dear friends, I had been eagerly planning to
write to you about the salvation we all share.
But now I find that I must write about something else, urging you to defend the faith that
God has entrusted once for all time to his holy
people. 4 I say this because some ungodly people
have wormed their way into your churches, saying that God's marvelous grace allows us to live
immoral lives. The condemnation of such people
was recorded long ago, for they have denied our
only Master and Lord, Jesus Christ.
5 So I want to remind you, though you already know these things, that Jesus* first rescued the nation of Israel from Egypt, but later
he destroyed those who did not remain faithful.
6 And I remind you of the angels who did not
stay within the limits of authority God gave
them but left the place where they belonged.
God has kept them securely chained in prisons of
darkness, waiting for the great day of judgment.
7 And don't forget Sodom and Gomorrah and
their neighboring towns, which were filled with
immorality and every kind of sexual perversion.
Those cities were destroyed by fire and serve as a
warning of the eternal fire of God's judgment.
8 In the same way, these people—who claim
authority from their dreams—live immoral lives,
defy authority, and scoff at supernatural beings.*

1 Or *keeps you for Jesus Christ.* **5** As in the best manuscripts; various other manuscripts read *[the] Lord,* or *God,* or *Christ;* one reads *God Christ.* **8** Greek *at glorious ones,* which are probably evil angels.

1–2 Introduction

The author cites as his authority that he is a slave of Jesus Christ and a brother of James. If he was the brother of Jesus, it is particularly interesting that he uses *slave* rather than "brother." Perhaps we can see his alignment of himself with his call to service rather than a reliance on his personal status. The content of Jude's blessing, a usual component of Jewish and Christian letters, is unique because he excludes the concept of grace, common to most Christian forms, but includes *love*. The use of *love* in this context is not found in any Jewish examples, and only one Christian example of blessing includes it. Love, mercy, and peace make up the major themes of the epistle.

3–4 Purpose

Jude establishes the epistle's dual purpose: *to write to you about the salvation we all share* and an appeal to defend the truth of the Good News. When he refers to salvation, Jude probably refers to the corporate nature of Christianity, perhaps in contrast to the opponents who are causing strife within the community. The second phrase can be translated to indicate the emphasis on an aggressive posture; *to defend*, literally, "contend for," is a figure taken from the athletic games. **4:** Jude proceeds to describe the opponents in vivid terms: They *have wormed their way into your churches*, they are already condemned, and they are *ungodly people* who misuse the kindness of *God's marvelous grace*. Although he continues to describe and denounce these opponents, they are deceptive and will be condemned by God because of their denial of the authority of Jesus and even God. The deception of the opponents is graphically captured in the figure of having *wormed their way* in. The connotation is of secret or illegal entry into the community with wrong intentions. Jude further describes the opponents' condemnation by using examples from apocalyptic and Old Testament literature.

5–16 The Body of the Letter

Jude proceeds in his usual style of triplets. Three Old Testament examples (vv. 5–7) illustrate his point that those who challenge God's authority will be punished: the Exodus, the fallen angels, and Sodom and Gomorrah. All of these vivid illustrations would have been familiar to his readers. In the Exodus, the unbelievers were destroyed; the angels were exiled from heaven and are kept in chains until the judgment; Sodom and Gomorrah were subjected to *eternal fire*. **8:** Jude applies these examples to his opponents. *Immoral lives* can be interpreted several ways but most likely has to do with sexual immorality. *Defy*[ing] *authority* is reflected in all three examples and probably here, as in verse 4, implies not necessarily a christological heresy but behavior that rejects the laws of God. The third category is vague—*supernatural beings* (see translator's note for "glorious ones") could refer to angels, as in the Dead Sea Scrolls. If so, this would most likely relate to a rejection of their role in Judaism as guardians of the law of Moses. Evidently these people were not only practicing their refusal to follow the law but also teaching it, basing their authority on their dreams or prophetic visions, a common practice in apocalyptic Judaism and early Christian-

[9]But even Michael, one of the mightiest of the
angels,* did not dare accuse the devil of blasphemy, but simply said, "The Lord rebuke you!"
(This took place when Michael was arguing with
the devil about Moses' body.) [10]But these people
scoff at things they do not understand. Like
unthinking animals, they do whatever their instincts tell them, and so they bring about their
own destruction. [11]What sorrow awaits them!
For they follow in the footsteps of Cain, who
killed his brother. Like Balaam, they deceive
people for money. And like Korah, they perish in
their rebellion.
[12]When these people eat with you in your fellowship meals commemorating the Lord's love,
they are like dangerous reefs that can shipwreck
you.* They are like shameless shepherds who
care only for themselves. They are like clouds
blowing over the land without giving any rain.
They are like trees in autumn that are doubly
dead, for they bear no fruit and have been pulled
up by the roots. [13]They are like wild waves of
the sea, churning up the foam of their shameful deeds. They are like wandering stars, doomed
forever to blackest darkness.
[14]Enoch, who lived in the seventh generation
after Adam, prophesied about these people. He
said, "Listen! The Lord is coming with countless
thousands of his holy ones [15]to execute judgment on the people of the world. He will convict
every person of all the ungodly things they have
done and for all the insults that ungodly sinners
have spoken against him."*
[16]These people are grumblers and complainers, living only to satisfy their desires. They brag
loudly about themselves, and they flatter others
to get what they want.

A Call to Remain Faithful

[17]But you, my dear friends, must remember what
the apostles of our Lord Jesus Christ said. [18]They
told you that in the last times there would be

9 Greek *Michael, the archangel.* **12** Or *they are contaminants among you;* or *they are stains.* **14-15** The quotation comes from intertestamental literature: Enoch 1:9.

---

ity as well as paganism. **9–10:** Jude cites an example to illustrate a different point. Michael, a leading figure in apocalyptic literature, demonstrates that judgment belongs to God. Even Michael does not revile Satan in the dispute; this authority belongs to God. In contrast, the false teachers in the community *scoff at things they do not understand.* Out of this ignorance, they behave like irrational animals. The irony is remarkable—the teachers claim spiritual insight from revelations but merely follow basic instincts like animals. **11:** Jude cites three more Old Testament examples to describe the false teachers and their coming condemnation. Like Cain, the teachers are godless, self-seeking, hostile to authority, a challenge to God's authority; they finally bring about the death of others (Gen 4:1–16). Like Balaam, they are greedy and lead people astray to benefit themselves (Num 31:16; Deut 23:3–5; but see also Num 22—23). And like Korah, they rebel against God's authority (Num 16). These examples underscore the problems of greed, a rejection of God's authority, and an attempt to lead the people astray. The heretics have plunged into the error of Balaam, the mercenary prophet who wanted to accept the wages of King Balak to curse the Israelites in their wilderness journey. God forbids Balaam to accompany Balak's messengers back to Moab, but when the messengers return with offers of still higher economic gain, Balaam begs to be allowed to go to Balak. Balaam is warned that he must proclaim only the oracles of God. Once in Moab, Balaam blesses Israel; God will not allow him to curse them. Still eager to earn a reward, Balaam turns to another path to wreak havoc on the Israelites. The women of Moab are instructed to inveigle the men into union with cultic prostitutes (Num 31:16; 25:1–2; see also Rev 2:14). Israel became involved in the worship of Baal of Peor, in eating meat offered to the god, and in ritual promiscuity. The error of Balaam involved the manipulation of women for the sake of his financial advantage. **12–13:** Six similies are used to describe the heresy; images from each of the four regions of the physical world: air, earth, sea, and heavens (or space). All of them emphasize emptiness and futility, probably referring to the false teachers' vain words and arrogance. All of them illustrate nature gone awry—clouds without rain, trees without fruit, wandering stars. The noncanonical book 1 Enoch is reflected here where even nature becomes chaotic when it does not follow God's laws. It is implied that as disaster results from lawless nature, so disaster will result from the behavior of the false teachers. **14–16:** Jude now quotes directly from 1 Enoch 1:9. This does not necessarily mean that he considered 1 Enoch part of the canon. He uses it to set the situation into an eschatological context. The opponents may be currently rejecting God's authority, but the Lord is eventually coming to execute judgment on all. Verses 15–16 echo the sins mentioned earlier, but here Jude directly relates them to speech.

17–23 Relation to the Community

The tone of the letter changes in verses 17–19. Jude urges the *dear friends* to remember the Old Testament

scoffers whose purpose in life is to satisfy their ungodly desires. [19]These people are the ones who are creating divisions among you. They follow their natural instincts because they do not have God's Spirit in them.

[20]But you, dear friends, must build each other up in your most holy faith, pray in the power of the Holy Spirit,* [21]and await the mercy of our Lord Jesus Christ, who will bring you eternal life. In this way, you will keep yourselves safe in God's love.

[22]And you must show mercy to* those whose faith is wavering. [23]Rescue others by snatching them from the flames of judgment. Show mercy to still others,* but do so with great caution, hating the sins that contaminate their lives.*

A Prayer of Praise

[24]Now all glory to God, who is able to keep you from falling away and will bring you with great joy into his glorious presence without a single fault. [25]All glory to him who alone is God, our Savior through Jesus Christ our Lord. All glory, majesty, power, and authority are his before all time, and in the present, and beyond all time! Amen.

20 Greek *pray in the Holy Spirit.* **22** Some manuscripts read *must reprove.* **22-23a** Some manuscripts have only two categories of people: (1) those whose faith is wavering and therefore need to be snatched from the flames of judgment, and (2) those who need to be shown mercy. **23b** Greek *with fear, hating even the clothing stained by the flesh.*

prophecy and the words of the apostles. The word for *you* is emphatic. His readers stand in marked contrast to the lawless behavior of the opponents. Jude admonishes his readers to build themselves up in the faith, pray in the Holy Spirit (perhaps in contrast to the false revelations of the opponents), keep themselves in the love of God, wait for the mercy of the Lord, and have mercy for others.

24–25 Conclusion

The letter concludes with a traditional doxology adapted by Jude. The reference to *keep* completes Jude's emphasis on this concept throughout the epistle. Just as God is able to *keep* the wicked for destruction, he is able to *keep* his faithful ones from the dangers of the false teachers. The result of being kept is to be able to stand in God's glory with rejoicing. These terms suggest an eschatological connotation and emphasize the final result of salvation. Jude underscores the sovereignty of God in his community in marked contrast to the views of the false teachers.

REVELATION

INTRODUCTION

The book of Revelation has long been viewed as a book of mystery and intrigue, full of mythical beasts, bloodthirsty battles, and seemingly inexplicable events. Some readers cannot understand what it is saying and so dismiss it as irrelevant to their life and faith, viewing it as a mistaken entry in Scripture, as did Martin Luther. Others love its rich imagery and powerful reassurances. However Revelation strikes an individual, it is impossible to be neutral toward it, which is part of its purpose. The book seeks to encourage people of all eras, genders, and nationalities to respond to the message of Jesus Christ. There can be no neutrality in the battles portrayed between good and evil—everyone is either a faithful witness for Christ or against him.

The authorship of Revelation is traditionally ascribed to John the apostle, the son of Zebedee. Another suggestion attributes it to John the elder, known to the churches of Asia Minor; still another, that the text is the product of a school of John that ascribed it to its founder in order to add weight to its authority. There are arguments for and against each of these views. But the work is the revelation of Jesus Christ, and it carries such an overwhelming message that the human intermediary is secondary.

What can be discerned about this skillful writer, however, is important. He describes himself as John, a prophet, never as an apostle. He was well acquainted with and had a degree of authority over the churches in Asia Minor to whom he writes. He had been exiled to Patmos by the Roman authorities for his witness to the Christian faith. During the early AD 90s, the emperor Domitian (90–95) tried to enforce emperor worship, causing conflict between the ruling authorities and the Christian community and leading to persecution. It was at this time that John received a series of visions that he recorded for encouraging the churches, which were also suffering from the infiltration of heretical teachings that threatened to undermine their consistency of witness in an already precarious situation. Although the message addresses the immediate needs of the seven churches, its wider message of hope and reassurance of the victory of Christ over all is relevant for Christians of all eras.

Two of the puzzling questions asked of Revelation are how it is to be interpreted and to what genre it belongs. Four traditional methods or approaches are generally proposed. The *preterist* (past-historical) approach interprets the book as relating only to the circumstances of the first-century readers. The *futurist* method finds its meaning in relating the whole text to the end times of history when all the prophecies will be fulfilled. The *poetic* or *symbolic* approach emphasizes the images and attempts to interpret their meaning in terms of values relevant to all eras; the *historical* method proposes an interpretation based on viewing the prophecies of Revelation as relating to historical events through the ages from the early church to the second coming. Each view has drawbacks and weaknesses, so a more effective approach is to use the most helpful aspect of each.

The answer to the question of genre is found within the book. The first word claims that it is an apocalypse (a "revealing" or "unveiling"), and one does not have to read far before it becomes clear that this apocalyptic piece of writing refers to the end times. At the same time it claims to be a prophecy and its writer a prophet, and its qualifications as a letter are also found within the opening paragraphs. On a most basic level Revelation is a letter to all churches that is simultaneously prophetic and apocalyptic.

Does Revelation have particular relevance to women, their faith and life? At first glance some women may reject it as a bloodthirsty, military, male-dominated book, but closer examination demonstrates that the book has at its heart the image of a faithful, pure woman who personifies the church in all its glory. The basic message of Revelation applies equally to women and men. It is a call for Christians to be faithful to Christ, to continue their witness even though they may suffer for it, some to the point of death. Reassurance is given that God is in control, however persistent evil may appear, and that ultimately God will bring about judgment and vindicate his people. Unbelievers and waverers are constantly encouraged to repent so that they too will share in the good things of God. Revelation begins by addressing the failings of the church but ends gloriously with the marriage of the purified church to the Lamb. —*Keren E. Morrell*

1:1–3	Introduction and Blessing on Readers
1:4—3:22	Letters to the Seven Churches
4:1–11	Heavenly Vision of God Enthroned
5:1—6:17	The First Six of the Seven Seals
5:1–14	The Lamb That Was Slain Can Open the Seals
6:1–8	Four Seals of Destruction: Conquest, Slaughter, Famine, Disease
6:9–17	Two (of Three) Seals of Judgment: Martyrdom and Oppression
7:1–17	Interlude: Marking God's Own
8:1–5	Seventh Seal
8:6—9:21	The First Six Trumpets
8:6–13	Four Trumpets of Destruction
9:1–21	Two (Out of Three) Trumpets of Woe
10:1—11:13	Interlude. John Is Commissioned to Be a Prophet. Two Prophetic Witnesses Are Martyred
11:14–19	Seventh Trumpet (Third of Woe): God's Kingdom Begins
12:1–17	The Woman, the Child, and the Dragon
12:18—13:18	The Two Beasts
14:1–20	Seven Visions: Salvation for the Blessed, Judgment for the Evil
15:1—16:21	Seven Bowls of Wrath; Plagues Like Those in Egypt
17:1—18:24	The Fall of Babylon
19:1–10	Song of Praise to God
19:11–21	Conquest of Evil by the Heavenly Host
20:1–10	Defeat of Satan
20:11–15	The Final Judgment
21:1—22:5	The New Jerusalem
21:1–8	The New Creation
21:9–27	The Heavenly City (the Bride)
22:1–5	The River and Tree of Life
22:6–21	Concluding Warnings and Assurances

✧

Prologue

1 This is a revelation from* Jesus Christ,
which God gave him to show his servants
the events that must soon* take place. He
sent an angel to present this revelation to his servant John, 2 who faithfully reported everything
he saw. This is his report of the word of God and
the testimony of Jesus Christ.
3 God blesses the one who reads the words of
this prophecy to the church, and he blesses all
who listen to its message and obey what it says,
for the time is near.

John's Greeting to the Seven Churches

4 This letter is from John to the seven churches in
the province of Asia.*

Grace and peace to you from the one who is,
who always was, and who is still to come; from
the sevenfold Spirit* before his throne; 5 and
from Jesus Christ. He is the faithful witness to
these things, the first to rise from the dead, and
the ruler of all the kings of the world.

All glory to him who loves us and has freed
us from our sins by shedding his blood for us.
6 He has made us a Kingdom of priests for God
his Father. All glory and power to him forever
and ever! Amen.

7 Look! He comes with the clouds of heaven.
And everyone will see him—
even those who pierced him.
And all the nations of the world
will mourn for him.
Yes! Amen!

8 "I am the Alpha and the Omega—the beginning and the end,"* says the Lord God. "I am the
one who is, who always was, and who is still to
come—the Almighty One."

Vision of the Son of Man

9 I, John, am your brother and your partner in
suffering and in God's Kingdom and in the patient endurance to which Jesus calls us. I was
exiled to the island of Patmos for preaching the
word of God and for my testimony about Jesus.
10 It was the Lord's Day, and I was worshiping in
the Spirit.* Suddenly, I heard behind me a loud
voice like a trumpet blast. 11 It said, "Write in
a book* everything you see, and send it to the
seven churches in the cities of Ephesus, Smyrna,
Pergamum, Thyatira, Sardis, Philadelphia, and
Laodicea."
12 When I turned to see who was speaking to
me, I saw seven gold lampstands. 13 And stand-

1:1a Or *of.* **1:1b** Or *suddenly,* or *quickly.* **1:4a** *Asia* was a Roman province in what is now western Turkey. **1:4b** Greek *the seven spirits.* **1:8** Greek *I am the Alpha and the Omega,* referring to the first and last letters of the Greek alphabet. **1:10** Or *in spirit.* **1:11** Or *on a scroll.*

1:1–3 Introduction and Blessing on Readers

The title states that the book is *a revelation from Jesus Christ . . . to . . . his servants,* reminiscent of prophetic books (cf. Isa 1:1). The motto briefly describes what *must soon take place.* **3:** *God blesses* all who read, hear, and heed the prophecies. A similar blessing rounds off the book (22:7).

1:4–3:22 Letters to the Seven Churches in Asia Minor

Although addressed to *seven churches,* Revelation is intended for the whole of Christianity. It is a message for all who love Christ, freed from sin by his blood, to remain faithful to him. The inclusive nature is evident. All who are faithful witnesses are redeemed priests serving God. Gender is irrelevant, and trying to make it an issue only causes grief to those who then feel excluded from part of God's plan for his people. All are priests because of Christ's blood and not because of social favoritism, gender, race, position, or wealth (cf. 1 Pet 2:9). The text carries a matter-of-fact warning that there will be a time of distress and judgment when Christ returns and all will see Christ in his glory.

1:4–8 Greeting to the Churches. 4–5: The greeting follows the format of many New Testament letters (e.g., Eph 1:2). **8:** God sets out his credentials. He is eternal, in all times and places. This is one of the themes that weaves through the text to enrich and give continuity to the whole.

1:9–20 John's Vision of Christ. The description of the sender of the messages to the seven churches links the introduction to the seven letters. **10–11:** John falls into an ecstatic state in which the earthly fades away and the spiritual comes into clear focus. He hears and sees incredible sights and sounds that he is instructed to record and send to the seven churches. John, with his senses heightened by his worship on the *Lord's Day,* had a vision in which he not only saw and heard amazing things but also took part and interacted with the characters. **12–16:** John describes his vision of Christ using imagery from the Old Testament. Each aspect of the figure points to an aspect of Christ's character. *Seven gold lampstands* represent the seven churches and mean that Christ is present with his church. *Robe . . . gold sash*: The figure is dressed in priestly and royal

ing in the middle of the lampstands was someone like the Son of Man.* He was wearing a
long robe with a gold sash across his chest. 14 His
head and his hair were white like wool, as white
as snow. And his eyes were like flames of fire.
15 His feet were like polished bronze refined in
a furnace, and his voice thundered like mighty
ocean waves. 16 He held seven stars in his right
hand, and a sharp two-edged sword came from
his mouth. And his face was like the sun in all
its brilliance.

17 When I saw him, I fell at his feet as if I were
dead. But he laid his right hand on me and said,
"Don't be afraid! I am the First and the Last. 18 I
am the living one. I died, but look—I am alive
forever and ever! And I hold the keys of death
and the grave.*

19 "Write down what you have seen—both
the things that are now happening and the things
that will happen.* 20 This is the meaning of the
mystery of the seven stars you saw in my right
hand and the seven gold lampstands: The seven
stars are the angels* of the seven churches, and
the seven lampstands are the seven churches.

The Message to the Church in Ephesus

2 "Write this letter to the angel* of the
church in Ephesus. This is the message
from the one who holds the seven stars
in his right hand, the one who walks among the
seven gold lampstands:

2 "I know all the things you do. I have seen
your hard work and your patient endurance. I
know you don't tolerate evil people. You have
examined the claims of those who say they
are apostles but are not. You have discovered
they are liars. 3 You have patiently suffered
for me without quitting.

4 "But I have this complaint against you.
You don't love me or each other as you did at
first!* 5 Look how far you have fallen! Turn
back to me and do the works you did at first.
If you don't repent, I will come and remove
your lampstand from its place among the
churches. 6 But this is in your favor: You hate
the evil deeds of the Nicolaitans, just as I do.

7 "Anyone with ears to hear must listen
to the Spirit and understand what he is
saying to the churches. To everyone who is
victorious I will give fruit from the tree of life
in the paradise of God.

1:13 Or *like a son of man.* See Dan 7:13. "Son of Man" is a title Jesus used for himself. **1:18** Greek *and Hades.* **1:19** Or *what you have seen and what they mean—the things that have already begun to happen.* **1:20** Or *the messengers.* **2:1** Or *the messenger;* also in 2:8, 12, 18. **2:4** Greek *You have lost your first love.*

---

clothing, demonstrating his function as mediator between God and his people. *His head and his hair were white,* indicating wisdom; *his eyes were like flames of fire,* indicating piercing spiritual insight. *His feet* cannot be shaken, and his thunderous voice blots out all other sounds. *Seven stars* represent angels and his authority over supernatural beings. *A sharp two-edged sword* denotes the ability to bring judgment and peace with a word discerning the thoughts of the heart (cf. Heb 4:12). **17–20:** John's senses are overloaded and he is rendered unconscious. Jesus reassures him with a touch. Here we have the familiar, compassionate Jesus of the Gospels; his heavenly, holy appearance may inspire awe, but he is still the same. After calming John's fears, Jesus assures him of Christ's supremacy over all things, including death, because he has conquered death and is alive. Jesus instructs John to record all he sees. The remainder of Revelation is this record.

2:1—3:22 Letters to the Seven Churches. These letters introduce the main theme of Revelation: a call to a life of faithful witness to Christ, resulting in eternal reward; failure to heed the call, and a lack of repentance, resulting in punishment. Although they are aimed at specific situations in the first century, these letters can also be used as an encouragement for all Christians in all eras to remain faithful to Christ. The failings represented by the seven churches are reflected in many situations through the ages; the command to listen to what the Spirit of God says and the call to repentance are as relevant today as they have ever been. The letters follow the same format: They begin with the sender; each uses a different description of Christ from the vision of chapter 1; each is addressed to the angel of the church who represents the church in heaven. Each church is first commended for the positive areas of its life and worship, and then reprimanded for its failings. The exceptions are the churches of Smyrna and Philadelphia, for which there is nothing but praise. Then comes a call to repent, with promise of reward for those who do and punishment for those who do not.

2:1–7 Message to the Church in Ephesus. Ephesus was known as the center for the worship of Diana, the fertility goddess, and the emperor cult. It had a strong Jewish community from which Paul launched his mission into Asia. **2–3:** This community is commended for vigilance against heretics and for suffering steadfastly under persection. **4–5:** They have held on to the truth, but they have followed it so rigidly that they have forgotten love, the first prin-

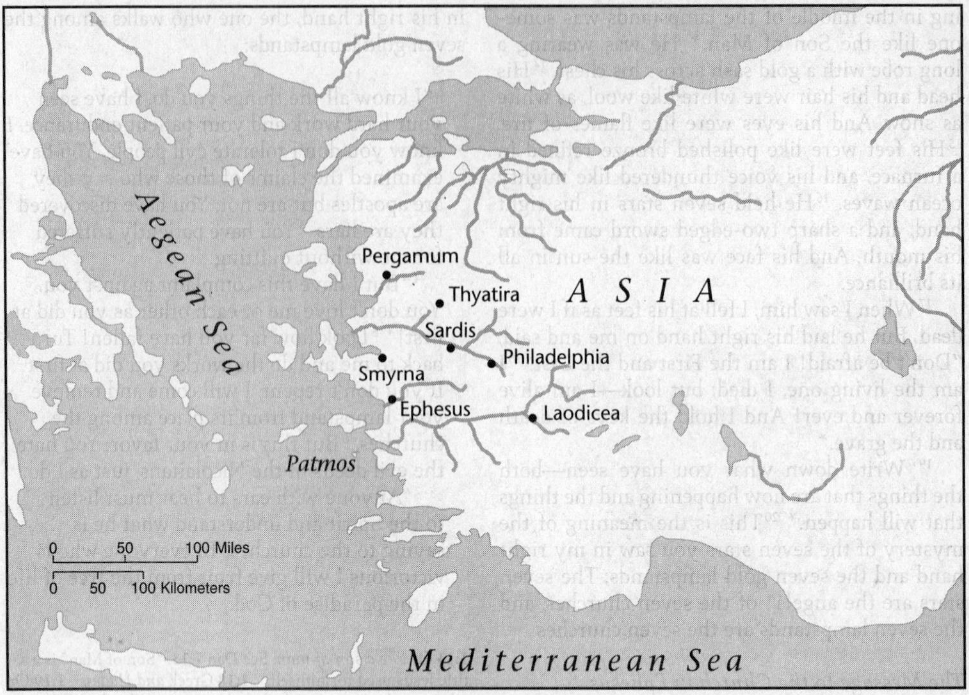

The Seven Churches

The Message to the Church in Smyrna
8"Write this letter to the angel of the church in
Smyrna. This is the message from the one who
is the First and the Last, who was dead but is now
alive:
9"I know about your suffering and your
poverty—but you are rich! I know the
blasphemy of those opposing you. They say
they are Jews, but they are not, because their
synagogue belongs to Satan. 10Don't be afraid
of what you are about to suffer. The devil
will throw some of you into prison to test
you. You will suffer for ten days. But if you
remain faithful even when facing death, I will
give you the crown of life.
11"Anyone with ears to hear must listen to
the Spirit and understand what he is saying
to the churches. Whoever is victorious will
not be harmed by the second death.

ciple of Christian faith. Their passion for rooting out those in error has overtaken their passion for Christ. **6:** *Nicolaitans*: The word means "conquerors of the people," presumably referring to a group whose beliefs had "conquered" certain individuals, but what specifically those mistaken beliefs are is no longer known. **7:** *Anyone with ears to hear*: The traditional rendering—"he who has ears to hear"—with its use of the male pronoun may obscure the fact that the message is applicable to the whole church and not only to men.

2:8–11 Message to the Church in Smyrna. The community at Smyrna also found itself in the midst of a large Jewish community and a center dedicated to the emperor cult. **9–10:** These Christians are highly commended for their faithfulness in the face of adversity, and nothing negative is found against them. Their faithfulness has, however, had repercussions on their financial status. In a city renowned for its wealth, these Christians are materially poor. In order to prosper, trade workers had to belong to the city guilds, membership that included participating in the worship of the guilds' patron gods. Without such membership one could not work or earn a living. The church had the second problem of no longer coming under the protection previously afforded to Christians as a Jewish sect. The Romans insisted that conquered peoples take on Roman religion, which included paying homage and making sacrifices to the emperor as god. Judaism was exempt from this, and Jews were allowed to continue practicing their

The Message to the Church in Pergamum
12 "Write this letter to the angel of the church
in Pergamum. This is the message from the one
with the sharp two-edged sword:

13 "I know that you live in the city where
Satan has his throne, yet you have remained
loyal to me. You refused to deny me even
when Antipas, my faithful witness, was
martyred among you there in Satan's city.
14 "But I have a few complaints against you.
You tolerate some among you whose teaching
is like that of Balaam, who showed Balak how
to trip up the people of Israel. He taught them
to sin by eating food offered to idols and by
committing sexual sin. 15 In a similar way, you
have some Nicolaitans among you who follow
the same teaching. 16 Repent of your sin, or I
will come to you suddenly and fight against
them with the sword of my mouth.
17 "Anyone with ears to hear must listen to
the Spirit and understand what he is saying to
the churches. To everyone who is victorious
I will give some of the manna that has been
hidden away in heaven. And I will give to each
one a white stone, and on the stone will be
engraved a new name that no one understands
except the one who receives it.

The Message to the Church in Thyatira
18 "Write this letter to the angel of the church in
Thyatira. This is the message from the Son of
God, whose eyes are like flames of fire, whose
feet are like polished bronze:

19 "I know all the things you do. I have seen
your love, your faith, your service, and
your patient endurance. And I can see your
constant improvement in all these things.
20 "But I have this complaint against you.
You are permitting that woman—that Jezebel
who calls herself a prophet—to lead my
servants astray. She teaches them to commit
sexual sin and to eat food offered to idols.
21 I gave her time to repent, but she does not
want to turn away from her immorality.
22 "Therefore, I will throw her on a bed of
suffering,* and those who commit adultery
with her will suffer greatly unless they
repent and turn away from her evil deeds.
23 I will strike her children dead. Then all the
churches will know that I am the one who
searches out the thoughts and intentions of
every person. And I will give to each of you
whatever you deserve.
24 "But I also have a message for the rest of
you in Thyatira who have not followed this
false teaching ('deeper truths,' as they call
them—depths of Satan, actually). I will ask
nothing more of you 25 except that you hold
tightly to what you have until I come. 26 To all
who are victorious, who obey me to the very
end,

To them I will give authority over all the
nations.
27 They will rule the nations with an iron rod
and smash them like clay pots.*

28 They will have the same authority I
received from my Father, and I will also give
them the morning star!

2:22 Greek *a bed.* **2:26-27** Ps 2:8-9 (Greek Version).

religion. The Jewish community may have stirred up trouble for the Christians and drawn the Romans' attention to their noncompliance to the religious laws. The church at Smyrna was about to undergo persecution and was called to remain faithful, even if that meant martyrdom. In doing so it would receive great rewards from Christ.

2:12–17 Message to the Church in Pergamum. Pergamum was yet another center for emperor worship and also had temples dedicated to Zeus and Asclepius, both of whom bore the title of savior and took the serpent as their symbol. **13–14:** Praised for its faithful witness, even after the execution of one of the congregation, the church at Pergamum still is rebuked. *Balaam*, who at the instigation of Balak the king of Moab (Num 22; 25:1–3; 31:7–18) led the Israelites into error, had become synonymous with a teacher who leads the people of God into infidelity. **15:** Adherence to the *Nicolaitans'* teaching meant compromising with society, not remaining exclusively faithful to Christ.

2:18–29 Message to the Church in Thyatira. This is the longest of the letters but follows the same format as the others. **20–23:** This congregation's promising record has been spoiled by its toleration of the teachings of a false prophet. *Jezebel*, the wife of King Ahab (2 Kgs 9:22), had become symbolic of someone who encouraged false beliefs and worship. Some in the church had been drawn into her web of deceit and sin; all had sinned by tolerating these errors and allowing them to flourish. The teachings of this *Jezebel*, like the harlot of Babylon (Rev 17), involved Christians in spiritual idolatry.

29"Anyone with ears to hear must listen to
the Spirit and understand what he is saying
to the churches.

The Message to the Church in Sardis

3 "Write this letter to the angel* of the
church in Sardis. This is the message from
the one who has the sevenfold Spirit* of
God and the seven stars:

"I know all the things you do, and that you
have a reputation for being alive—but you
are dead. 2Wake up! Strengthen what little
remains, for even what is left is almost dead.
I find that your actions do not meet the
requirements of my God. 3Go back to what
you heard and believed at first; hold to it
firmly. Repent and turn to me again. If you
don't wake up, I will come to you suddenly, as
unexpected as a thief.
4"Yet there are some in the church in
Sardis who have not soiled their clothes
with evil. They will walk with me in white,
for they are worthy. 5All who are victorious
will be clothed in white. I will never erase
their names from the Book of Life, but I will
announce before my Father and his angels
that they are mine.
6"Anyone with ears to hear must listen to
the Spirit and understand what he is saying
to the churches.

The Message to the Church in Philadelphia

7"Write this letter to the angel of the church in
Philadelphia.

This is the message from the one who is holy
and true,
the one who has the key of David.
What he opens, no one can close;
and what he closes, no one can open:*

8"I know all the things you do, and I have
opened a door for you that no one can close.
You have little strength, yet you obeyed my
word and did not deny me. 9Look, I will force
those who belong to Satan's synagogue—
those liars who say they are Jews but are
not—to come and bow down at your feet.
They will acknowledge that you are the ones
I love.
10"Because you have obeyed my command
to persevere, I will protect you from the
great time of testing that will come upon the
whole world to test those who belong to this
world. 11I am coming soon.* Hold on to what
you have, so that no one will take away your
crown. 12All who are victorious will become
pillars in the Temple of my God, and they
will never have to leave it. And I will write
on them the name of my God, and they will
be citizens in the city of my God—the new
Jerusalem that comes down from heaven
from my God. And I will also write on them
my new name.
13"Anyone with ears to hear must listen to
the Spirit and understand what he is saying
to the churches.

3:1a Or *the messenger;* also in 3:7, 14. **3:1b** Greek *the seven spirits.* **3:7** Isa 22:22. **3:11** Or *suddenly,* or *quickly.*

3:1–6 Message to the Church in Sardis. Sardis was a commercial city on the major trade route through Asia Minor. During its history it had twice fallen to enemies through complacency. Instead of keeping watch at night, the city had slept. Public buildings had been started but never completed. John spiritualizes these themes to demonstrate the faults of the church, which appeared to be a thriving community but was spiritually lifeless. It is called to rouse from its slumber and apathy before it is overtaken by the sleep of death from which it will never awake. The church's deeds for Christ have been incomplete and substandard. It has not finished what it started, and it has failed to prepare for Christ's return. If the church wakes, shakes itself out of apathy, and repents, then it too will be among those commended and rewarded. If not, then Christ will appear when they least expect it and attack them with his full fury.

3:7–13 Message to the Church in Philadelphia. Like the church at Smyrna, the congregation at Philadelphia is praised by Christ, who holds the keys to unlock the future. This community has remained faithful to Christ even though it is powerless in the face of opposition. But the church is reassured by the fact that Christ alone is in control of all that happens to them. Christ has put an open doorway in front of them through which he alone gives access, and they are given entry because of their faithful witness. The encouragements to hold fast and patiently endure form the backbone of the message to the churches, not just in the seven letters but also throughout Revelation. The main theme that undergirds the visions and revelations is a plea to remain faithful and not to be led astray by fear of persecution, apathy, lack of love, or the seductions of false teaching.

The Message to the Church in Laodicea
14 "Write this letter to the angel of the church in
Laodicea. This is the message from the one who
is the Amen—the faithful and true witness, the
beginning* of God's new creation:

15 "I know all the things you do, that you are
neither hot nor cold. I wish that you were
one or the other! 16 But since you are like
lukewarm water, neither hot nor cold, I will
spit you out of my mouth! 17 You say, 'I am
rich. I have everything I want. I don't need
a thing!' And you don't realize that you are
wretched and miserable and poor and blind
and naked. 18 So I advise you to buy gold from
me—gold that has been purified by fire. Then
you will be rich. Also buy white garments
from me so you will not be shamed by your
nakedness, and ointment for your eyes so you
will be able to see. 19 I correct and discipline
everyone I love. So be diligent and turn from
your indifference.

20 "Look! I stand at the door and knock. If
you hear my voice and open the door, I will
come in, and we will share a meal together
as friends. 21 Those who are victorious will
sit with me on my throne, just as I was
victorious and sat with my Father on his
throne.

22 "Anyone with ears to hear must listen to
the Spirit and understand what he is saying
to the churches."

Worship in Heaven
4 Then as I looked, I saw a door standing
open in heaven, and the same voice I had
heard before spoke to me like a trumpet
blast. The voice said, "Come up here, and I will
show you what must happen after this." 2 And
instantly I was in the Spirit,* and I saw a throne
in heaven and someone sitting on it. 3 The one
sitting on the throne was as brilliant as gemstones—like jasper and carnelian. And the glow
of an emerald circled his throne like a rainbow.
4 Twenty-four thrones surrounded him, and
twenty-four elders sat on them. They were all
clothed in white and had gold crowns on their
heads. 5 From the throne came flashes of lightning and the rumble of thunder. And in front
of the throne were seven torches with burning
flames. This is the sevenfold Spirit* of God. 6 In
front of the throne was a shiny sea of glass, sparkling like crystal.

In the center and around the throne were four
living beings, each covered with eyes, front and

3:14 Or *the ruler,* or *the source.* **4:2** Or *in spirit.* **4:5** Greek *They are the seven spirits.*

3:14–22 Message to the Church in Laodicea. *Laodicea* was a prosperous commercial city known for its clothing industry, ophthalmic medical center, and banking activities. **15–16:** Here the *hot* medicinal waters of Hierapolis (for healing) and the *cold* (refreshing) water of Colossae met, but the mixture of the two waters produced lukewarm, nauseating water that was not fit to drink. The spiritual condition of the church is reflected in this unhealthy water supply. The lukewarm state of the church meant it could offer neither healing nor refreshment. As such it was fit only to be spit out. **17–18:** The self-reliant, *rich,* complacent atmosphere of the city had permeated the Christian community, causing it to lose its distinctiveness and witness. Christ, however, offers a remedy if the church will repent and accept it. They think of themselves as rich but are in spiritual poverty; to this Christ offers what they cannot buy. They are spiritually blind in a city with ophthalmic experts; Christ offers *ointment* to soothe the eyes and help them see. They have no clothing in a city famous for its garment industry; Christ provides *white garments* to wear. Christ is the answer to their failings. **20–21:** They are urged to *hear* [Christ's] *voice* and not to rely on their wealth. Christ waits for them to respond and accept his remedy, but he does not force it on them. The Laodiceans are given a choice—to welcome his help or not. To those who *open the door* to Christ, the gateway into the Father's presence will be opened.

4:1–11 Heavenly Vision of God Enthroned

Having set the scene on earth by commenting on seven specific churches, the vision moves on to set the stage where the scenes in the heavenly realm will be played out. This realm is unlike anything experienced by John on earth, but the two realms are linked by worship of the One on the throne. The realms, running parallel, from time to time overlap so that the scenes played out in one affect the other. **1:** The way for John into this world is through *a door standing open in heaven* through which the familiar voice invites him. **2–8:** At first the impression of the throne room is that of a cold, stark, and frightening place. A *throne, flashes of lightning and the rumble of thunder* emanating from it, stands in the center surrounded by *twenty-four elders* constantly worshiping the figure on the throne. They are accompanied by *four living beings* that also worship and sing. In the foreground is a *sea of glass,* smooth and cold to the touch. On the throne is a figure described in terms of precious stones—cold, rigid, hard stone.

back. [7]The first of these living beings was like a
lion; the second was like an ox; the third had a
human face; and the fourth was like an eagle in
flight. [8]Each of these living beings had six wings,
and their wings were covered all over with eyes,
inside and out. Day after day and night after
night they keep on saying,

"Holy, holy, holy is the Lord God, the
Almighty—
the one who always was, who is, and who is
still to come."

[9]Whenever the living beings give glory and hon-
or and thanks to the one sitting on the throne
(the one who lives forever and ever), [10]the twenty-four elders fall down and worship the one
sitting on the throne (the one who lives forever
and ever). And they lay their crowns before the
throne and say,

[11]"You are worthy, O Lord our God,
to receive glory and honor and power.
For you created all things,
and they exist because you created what
you pleased."

The Lamb Opens the Scroll

5 Then I saw a scroll* in the right hand of the
one who was sitting on the throne. There
was writing on the inside and the outside
of the scroll, and it was sealed with seven seals.
[2]And I saw a strong angel, who shouted with a
loud voice: "Who is worthy to break the seals on
this scroll and open it?" [3]But no one in heaven or
on earth or under the earth was able to open the
scroll and read it.
[4]Then I began to weep bitterly because no
one was found worthy to open the scroll and
read it. [5]But one of the twenty-four elders said
to me, "Stop weeping! Look, the Lion of the tribe
of Judah, the heir to David's throne,* has won
the victory. He is worthy to open the scroll and
its seven seals."
[6]Then I saw a Lamb that looked as if it had
been slaughtered, but it was now standing between the throne and the four living beings and
among the twenty-four elders. He had seven
horns and seven eyes, which represent the sevenfold Spirit* of God that is sent out into every
part of the earth. [7]He stepped forward and took
the scroll from the right hand of the one sitting
on the throne. [8]And when he took the scroll, the
four living beings and the twenty-four elders fell
down before the Lamb. Each one had a harp, and
they held gold bowls filled with incense, which
are the prayers of God's people. [9]And they sang a
new song with these words:

"You are worthy to take the scroll
and break its seals and open it.
For you were slaughtered, and your blood has
ransomed people for God
from every tribe and language and people
and nation.
[10]And you have caused them to become

5:1 Or *book;* also in 5:2, 3, 4, 5, 7, 8, 9. **5:5** Greek *the root of David.* See Isa 11:10. **5:6** Greek *which are the seven spirits.*

The images seem frightening and unwelcoming. But for first-century readers such semiprecious stones convey not coldness or stonelike qualities but the reflection of light. Brilliant light everywhere reflects off every surface, and radiant light emanates from the One on the throne. **9–11:** Here we are introduced to some of the heavenly characters who repeatedly contribute to the worship in heaven. *Twenty-four elders,* to represent the twelve tribes of Israel and the twelve apostles, act as royal priests in leading the worship. The *living beings,* supreme representatives of their kind, are covered with eyes; nothing goes unnoticed by these eyes, which are forever awake and vigilant. Both groups sing constantly in praise and worship of God.

5:1–6:17 The First Six of the Seven Seals

5:1–14 The Lamb That Was Slain Can Open the Seals. **1–3:** A *scroll* contained information or instruction. The *right hand* was the hand of strength. *Seals* served to verify the sender and prevent unauthorized readers of a scroll. *To break the seals* meant that one was authorized to proclaim the contents of the scroll. **4–6:** *Lion of the tribe of Judah* recalls King David and is a way of referring to the Messiah; it also (like the American eagle) was a national symbol of strength. **6:** The *Lamb that looked as if it had been slaughtered* refers to the crucified Christ. John's readers, familiar with the Old Testament, would understand the allusion to the Passover lamb (Exod 12), Isaiah's lamb led to the slaughter (Isa 53:7), and the traditional names for the Jewish Messiah. They know beyond a doubt that this is Jesus. Christ's conquering through the cross is the event on which all else hangs, without which there could be no revelation, no future. **7–10:** As the Lamb takes the scroll he is worshiped by the creatures and elders in the same manner as the One

a Kingdom of priests for our God.
And they will reign* on the earth."

11 Then I looked again, and I heard the voices
of thousands and millions of angels around the
throne and of the living beings and the elders.
12 And they sang in a mighty chorus:

"Worthy is the Lamb who was slaughtered—
to receive power and riches
and wisdom and strength
and honor and glory and blessing."

13 And then I heard every creature in heaven
and on earth and under the earth and in the sea.
They sang:

"Blessing and honor and glory and power
belong to the one sitting on the throne
and to the Lamb forever and ever."

14 And the four living beings said, "Amen!"
And the twenty-four elders fell down and worshiped the Lamb.

The Lamb Breaks the First Six Seals

6 As I watched, the Lamb broke the first of
the seven seals on the scroll.* Then I heard
one of the four living beings say with a
voice like thunder, "Come!" 2 I looked up and saw
a white horse standing there. Its rider carried a
bow, and a crown was placed on his head. He rode
out to win many battles and gain the victory.

3 When the Lamb broke the second seal, I
heard the second living being say, "Come!"
4 Then another horse appeared, a red one. Its rider was given a mighty sword and the authority
to take peace from the earth. And there was war
and slaughter everywhere.

5 When the Lamb broke the third seal, I heard
the third living being say, "Come!" I looked up
and saw a black horse, and its rider was holding
a pair of scales in his hand. 6 And I heard a voice
from among the four living beings say, "A loaf
of wheat bread or three loaves of barley will cost
a day's pay.* And don't waste* the olive oil and
wine."

7 When the Lamb broke the fourth seal, I heard
the fourth living being say, "Come!" 8 I looked up
and saw a horse whose color was pale green. Its
rider was named Death, and his companion was
the Grave.* These two were given authority over
one-fourth of the earth, to kill with the sword
and famine and disease* and wild animals.

9 When the Lamb broke the fifth seal, I saw
under the altar the souls of all who had been martyred for the word of God and for being faithful
in their testimony. 10 They shouted to the Lord
and said, "O Sovereign Lord, holy and true, how
long before you judge the people who belong to
this world and avenge our blood for what they

5:10 Some manuscripts read *they are reigning.* **6:1** Or *book.* **6:6a** Greek *A choinix* [1 quart or 1 liter] *of wheat for a denarius, and 3 choinix of barley for a denarius.* A denarius was equivalent to a laborer's full day's wage. **6:6b** Or *harm.* **6:8a** Greek *was Hades.* **6:8b** Greek *death.*

---

on the throne. **11–14:** The Lamb is equal; it is his due. It is worth noting here that John's later attempts to worship an angel were rejected. If worship of the Lamb were erroneous, then rebuke would have followed. Angels and all creatures in heaven and earth acknowledge the supremacy of the Lamb and worship him (cf. Phil 2:9–11). The one slain out of self-sacrifice regains his rightful position.

6:1–8 Four Seals of Destruction: Conquest, Slaughter, Famine, Disease. The opening of the seven seals inaugurates the first of three septets of disasters that rain down against the earth, its inhabitants, and the enemies of God. Each septet is divided into an initial quartet of related plagues, followed by three more. The first quartet introduces the four horsemen of the apocalypse who with permission—all that happens is permitted and under the control of God—destroy a quarter of the earth. They recall the horses in Zechariah 1:8; 6:2–8, sent by God to punish the nations who oppress his people. Although they mark the onset of destruction, the horsemen also emphasize the continued desire of God to be merciful, to persuade those remaining, by whatever means, to repentance through the witness of the church. **2:** The first, *white horse* is ridden by a divine and royal personage. His mission is to conquer. **4:** The rider of the second horse, *red* (the color of blood and the dragon; see 12:3), removes all peace from the earth through war. **5:** The third horse is *black* (the color of darkness and of rotted vegetation) and represents famine. This famine is partial; it affects the immediate harvest, but not those food products requiring advance preparation. **8:** The fourth horse, *pale green* (the color of decomposing flesh) is ridden by *Death*, and *the Grave* follows close behind.

6:9–17 Two (of Three) Seals of Judgment: Martyrdom and Oppression. 9–11: The opening of the fifth seal indicates a shift in emphasis. The cry of the innocent for vengeance is characteristic of apocalyptic writing, but this will take place only after the allocated number of martyrs has been reached. Theirs is a plea for public justice rather than personal revenge: that

have done to us?" 11 Then a white robe was given
to each of them. And they were told to rest a little longer until the full number of their brothers
and sisters*—their fellow servants of Jesus who
were to be martyred—had joined them.
12 I watched as the Lamb broke the sixth seal,
and there was a great earthquake. The sun became as dark as black cloth, and the moon became as red as blood. 13 Then the stars of the sky
fell to the earth like green figs falling from a tree
shaken by a strong wind. 14 The sky was rolled up
like a scroll, and all of the mountains and islands
were moved from their places.
15 Then everyone—the kings of the earth,
the rulers, the generals, the wealthy, the powerful, and every slave and free person—all hid
themselves in the caves and among the rocks of
the mountains. 16 And they cried to the mountains and the rocks, "Fall on us and hide us from
the face of the one who sits on the throne and
from the wrath of the Lamb. 17 For the great day
of their wrath has come, and who is able to survive?"

God's People Will Be Preserved

7 Then I saw four angels standing at the four
corners of the earth, holding back the four
winds so they did not blow on the earth or
the sea, or even on any tree. 2 And I saw another
angel coming up from the east, carrying the seal
of the living God. And he shouted to those four
angels, who had been given power to harm land
and sea, 3 "Wait! Don't harm the land or the sea
or the trees until we have placed the seal of God
on the foreheads of his servants."
4 And I heard how many were marked with
the seal of God—144,000 were sealed from all
the tribes of Israel:

5 from Judah 12,000
from Reuben 12,000
from Gad 12,000
6 from Asher 12,000
from Naphtali 12,000
from Manasseh 12,000
7 from Simeon 12,000
from Levi 12,000
from Issachar 12,000
8 from Zebulun 12,000
from Joseph 12,000
from Benjamin 12,000

Praise from the Great Crowd

9 After this I saw a vast crowd, too great to count,
from every nation and tribe and people and language, standing in front of the throne and before

6:11 Greek *their brothers.*

their faithfulness to Christ be recognized while those responsible suffer public humiliation (see the fate of the harlot, 17:15—19:2). In the meantime the martyrs are instructed to wait and rest. **12–17:** The sixth seal unleashes *the wrath of the Lamb* on the earth in an act that plunges the world back into precreation chaos to clear the way for a new order. But before this can happen, people must recognize God. Everyone runs to hide from the devastation, but there is no escape. The people see who has initiated the destruction; they are terrified but do not repent.

7:1–17 Interlude. Marking God's Own

Before the final scroll is opened the scene changes while the question *Who is able to survive?* (6:17) is considered. **1–8:** The answer: the servants of God sealed with his mark, the sign of ownership and protection. Until these *144,000* are *sealed,* the disasters are delayed, and *four angels* assigned to hold back the winds that would do dreadful damage to the earth. In the Old Testament the blood of the Passover lamb on the doorframes protected the Israelites from the angel of death (Exod 12:12–13). Later, those who worship the beast are sealed with a counterfeit mark (Rev 13:16–18). Notice the different use of seals within this section. The seals on the scroll are the type made of wax bearing the name, mark, or crest of the sender. Such a seal is to be broken only by the person authorized. The second, a seal in terms of a mark, denotes ownership. The number of those to be sealed includes twelve thousand from each of the tribes of Israel (7:4–8). But the list does not correspond to traditional lists; instead, it represents the faithful remnant of Israel or believers in Christ and is symbolic of all those under God's protection. **9–17:** The scene shifts again, looking forward. Again a *vast crowd,* the faithful who have come through the terrible *tribulation,* for which John is preparing the seven churches, worships the Lamb. In 5:13 the multitude celebrated the payment of their ransom; here they celebrate their place around the throne. The *Lamb* is the *Shepherd* leading his flock into eternal life where *God will wipe every tear from their eyes* (see 21:4). They will drink *life-giving water,* in contrast to worshipers of the beast, who are given blood to drink (16:4–9). The theme of endurance and assurance from the second and sixth letters reassures the faithful that there is a place for them in eternity even though dreadful times are inevitable.

the Lamb. They were clothed in white robes and
held palm branches in their hands. 10 And they
were shouting with a great roar,

"Salvation comes from our God who sits on
the throne
and from the Lamb!"

11 And all the angels were standing around the
throne and around the elders and the four living
beings. And they fell before the throne with their
faces to the ground and worshiped God. 12 They
sang,

"Amen! Blessing and glory and wisdom
and thanksgiving and honor
and power and strength belong to our God
forever and ever! Amen."

13 Then one of the twenty-four elders asked
me, "Who are these who are clothed in white?
Where did they come from?"

14 And I said to him, "Sir, you are the one who
knows."

Then he said to me, "These are the ones
who died in* the great tribulation.* They have
washed their robes in the blood of the Lamb and
made them white.

15 "That is why they stand in front of God's
throne
and serve him day and night in his
Temple.
And he who sits on the throne
will give them shelter.
16 They will never again be hungry or thirsty;
they will never be scorched by the heat of
the sun.
17 For the Lamb on the throne*
will be their Shepherd.
He will lead them to springs of life-giving
water.
And God will wipe every tear from their
eyes."

The Lamb Breaks the Seventh Seal

8 When the Lamb broke the seventh seal on
the scroll,* there was silence throughout
heaven for about half an hour. 2 I saw the
seven angels who stand before God, and they
were given seven trumpets.

3 Then another angel with a gold incense
burner came and stood at the altar. And a great
amount of incense was given to him to mix with
the prayers of God's people as an offering on the
gold altar before the throne. 4 The smoke of the
incense, mixed with the prayers of God's holy
people, ascended up to God from the altar where
the angel had poured them out. 5 Then the angel
filled the incense burner with fire from the altar
and threw it down upon the earth; and thunder
crashed, lightning flashed, and there was a terrible earthquake.

The First Four Trumpets

6 Then the seven angels with the seven trumpets
prepared to blow their mighty blasts.

7 The first angel blew his trumpet, and hail
and fire mixed with blood were thrown down on

7:14a Greek *who came out of.* **7:14b** Or *the great suffering.*
7:17 Greek *on the center of the throne.* **8:1** Or *book.*

8:1–5 The Seventh Seal

The vision returns to the opening of the seventh and final seal. **2:** Something unexpected happens: *There was silence*, which is as important as the noise and action of the previous scenes. The silence, instead of the expected contents of the scroll, keeps readers in suspense. Additionally, silence serves a worshipful function, a Sabbath pause that gives an opportunity for the prayers of the saints to be heard as they raise to God a fragrant offering. In response (see 6:9–10) the censer filled with fire is flung at the earth as a prelude to divine judgment. Each septet of disasters concludes with demonstrations of God's holiness modeled on Mount Sinai (Exod 19:16–17; see also Rev 11:19; 16:18; 4:5). During this silence seven trumpets are handed to the archangels to announce and warn of the impending plagues (cf. Exod 8—12) and as a call to repentance.

8:6—9:21 The First Six Trumpets

8:6–13 Four Trumpets of Destruction. Trumpets are warnings and calls to action. The first four trumpet calls form a distinct group resulting in plagues that destroy a third of the earth through ecological disasters. The first destroys vegetation essential for the production of oxygen and the sustaining of animal life. With the second, one third of the sea creatures and ships are destroyed by the tidal waves produced by an enormous fireball and, possibly, by the melting of the ice cap and pollution. The third trumpet announces the fall of a great star from heaven. This fall poisons one third of the water supply, making it unsuitable for drinking. Thus another vital resource essential for survival is devastated. The final trumpet darkens the skies, reducing the amount of light and warmth necessary for a healthy life to penetrate the atmosphere. By the end of these plagues, the whole

the earth. One-third of the earth was set on fire,
one-third of the trees were burned, and all the
green grass was burned.
8 Then the second angel blew his trumpet, and
a great mountain of fire was thrown into the sea.
One-third of the water in the sea became blood,
9 one-third of all things living in the sea died,
and one-third of all the ships on the sea were
destroyed.
10 Then the third angel blew his trumpet,
and a great star fell from the sky, burning like
a torch. It fell on one-third of the rivers and on
the springs of water. 11 The name of the star was
Bitterness.* It made one-third of the water bitter,
and many people died from drinking the bitter
water.
12 Then the fourth angel blew his trumpet, and
one-third of the sun was struck, and one-third of
the moon, and one-third of the stars, and they
became dark. And one-third of the day was dark,
and also one-third of the night.
13 Then I looked, and I heard a single eagle
crying loudly as it flew through the air, "Terror,
terror, terror to all who belong to this world because of what will happen when the last three
angels blow their trumpets."

The Fifth Trumpet Brings the First Terror

9 Then the fifth angel blew his trumpet, and I
saw a star that had fallen to earth from the
sky, and he was given the key to the shaft of
the bottomless pit.* 2 When he opened it, smoke
poured out as though from a huge furnace, and
the sunlight and air turned dark from the smoke.
3 Then locusts came from the smoke and descended on the earth, and they were given power
to sting like scorpions. 4 They were told not to
harm the grass or plants or trees, but only the
people who did not have the seal of God on their
foreheads. 5 They were told not to kill them but
to torture them for five months with pain like
the pain of a scorpion sting. 6 In those days people will seek death but will not find it. They will
long to die, but death will flee from them!
7 The locusts looked like horses prepared for
battle. They had what looked like gold crowns on
their heads, and their faces looked like human
faces. 8 They had hair like women's hair and teeth
like the teeth of a lion. 9 They wore armor made
of iron, and their wings roared like an army of
chariots rushing into battle. 10 They had tails that
stung like scorpions, and for five months they
had the power to torment people. 11 Their king
is the angel from the bottomless pit; his name in
Hebrew is *Abaddon*, and in Greek, *Apollyon*—
the Destroyer.
12 The first terror is past, but look, two more
terrors are coming!

The Sixth Trumpet Brings the Second Terror

13 Then the sixth angel blew his trumpet, and I
heard a voice speaking from the four horns of
the gold altar that stands in the presence of God.
14 And the voice said to the sixth angel who held
the trumpet, "Release the four angels who are
bound at the great Euphrates River." 15 Then the
four angels who had been prepared for this hour
and day and month and year were turned loose
to kill one-third of all the people on earth. 16 I
heard the size of their army, which was 200 million mounted troops.

8:11 Greek *Wormwood.* **9:1** Or *the abyss,* or *the underworld;* also in 9:11.

ecosystem is seriously damaged, and a situation reminiscent of precreation chaos is emerging.

9:1–21 Two (Out of Three) Trumpets of Woe. An eagle announces (8:13) three times that *terror* (or "woe"—Gk., *ouai*, an exclamation of distress, like "Alas!"), worse than anything experienced so far, will afflict the earth. The first four trumpets announced judgments that attacked the world's resources; the fifth through seventh trumpets involve demonic activity. **1–11:** The fifth trumpet unlocks the bottomless pit, the place of evil spirits (see Luke 8:31, where the spirits in the swine are sent to the abyss). Thick, black smoke blocks out the light and heat of the sun and makes the air unbreathable. *Locusts* (Exod 10:21–23; Joel 2:1–11) emerge to torture those not sealed by God. They were not to harm the vegetation, an unusual behavior for locusts, which normally ravage the countryside and crops. This torture is the first woe announced by the eagle; two more are to follow. **12–21:** The angel with the sixth trumpet releases the four angels, who wreak havoc by bringing about the destruction of one third of humankind. They release a great army with a terrifying appearance that kills with fiery, dragonlike breath. The incredible aspect of this episode is not the monstrous creatures or the deaths of so many but the fact that the survivors still refuse to repent. They are so hardened against God that no amount of torture, discomfort, or terrifying experiences can move them to repentance. The objective is to bring them to repentance so that they do not suffer the eternal second death (20:14), but still they continue to worship demonic forces rather than recognize the living God.

17 And in my vision, I saw the horses and the riders sitting on them. The riders wore armor that was fiery red and dark blue and yellow. The horses had heads like lions, and fire and smoke and burning sulfur billowed from their mouths. 18 One-third of all the people on earth were killed by these three plagues—by the fire and smoke and burning sulfur that came from the mouths of the horses. 19 Their power was in their mouths and in their tails. For their tails had heads like snakes, with the power to injure people.

20 But the people who did not die in these plagues still refused to repent of their evil deeds and turn to God. They continued to worship demons and idols made of gold, silver, bronze, stone, and wood—idols that can neither see nor hear nor walk! 21 And they did not repent of their murders or their witchcraft or their sexual immorality or their thefts.

The Angel and the Small Scroll

10 Then I saw another mighty angel coming down from heaven, surrounded by a cloud, with a rainbow over his head. His face shone like the sun, and his feet were like pillars of fire. 2 And in his hand was a small scroll* that had been opened. He stood with his right foot on the sea and his left foot on the land. 3 And he gave a great shout like the roar of a lion. And when he shouted, the seven thunders answered.

4 When the seven thunders spoke, I was about to write. But I heard a voice from heaven saying, "Keep secret* what the seven thunders said, and do not write it down."

5 Then the angel I saw standing on the sea and on the land raised his right hand toward heaven. 6 He swore an oath in the name of the one who lives forever and ever, who created the heavens and everything in them, the earth and everything in it, and the sea and everything in it. He said, "There will be no more delay. 7 When the seventh angel blows his trumpet, God's mysterious plan will be fulfilled. It will happen just as he announced it to his servants the prophets."

8 Then the voice from heaven spoke to me again: "Go and take the open scroll from the hand of the angel who is standing on the sea and on the land."

9 So I went to the angel and told him to give me the small scroll. "Yes, take it and eat it," he said. "It will be sweet as honey in your mouth, but it will turn sour in your stomach!" 10 So I took the small scroll from the hand of the angel, and I ate it! It was sweet in my mouth, but when I swallowed it, it turned sour in my stomach.

11 Then I was told, "You must prophesy again about many peoples, nations, languages, and kings."

The Two Witnesses

11 Then I was given a measuring stick, and I was told, "Go and measure the Temple of God and the altar, and count the number of worshipers. 2 But do not measure the outer courtyard, for it has been turned over to the nations. They will trample the holy city for 42 months. 3 And I will give power to my two witnesses, and they will be clothed in burlap and will prophesy during those 1,260 days."

4 These two prophets are the two olive trees and the two lampstands that stand before the

10:2 Or *book;* also in 10:8, 9, 10. **10:4** Greek *Seal up.*

10:1—11:13 Interlude. John Is Commissioned to Be a Prophet. Two Prophetic Witnesses Are Martyred

10:1–11: The prophetic word of God is presented to John in the form of a *scroll.* He is to imitate Ezekiel's action (Ezek 2:8—3:11) and *eat* the scroll, taking in, digesting, and understanding the words. The anticipation of God's justice is *sweet.* But as the reality sets in, it becomes *sour,* for John can see the consequences of the words he must prophesy. They, like the gospel, will bring salvation for some and harsh judgment to others. In contrast to the scroll in Revelation 5, this scroll is open; the contents are not secret but are available to all. **11:1–13:** Following this comes the episode of two witnesses of Christ whose words and actions cause repentance. But first John must *measure the Temple,* to calculate how many worship God and determine what part of the Temple will be preserved and what part destroyed. Measuring tools were used to symbolize the boundaries between good and evil; here the lines between the two groups are being drawn up, and the divide between them grows. The *outer courtyard* is the domain of the Gentiles; in the restored Temple there will be no need for this, because all will be God's people. Those who identify themselves primarily with unbelievers cannot be counted among the worshipers. The *two witnesses,* two being the minimum number necessary for valid witness, represent the witness of the church in the world. Their role is to prophesy and bring the peoples to repentance. To this end they spend 1,260 days, the same amount of time the unbelievers trample the holy city (i.e., forty-two months of thirty days) prophesying and are given miraculous powers in order to help and protect them and give weight to their arguments. After the allotted period of

Lord of all the earth. 5If anyone tries to harm
them, fire flashes from their mouths and consumes their enemies. This is how anyone who
tries to harm them must die. 6They have power
to shut the sky so that no rain will fall for as
long as they prophesy. And they have the power
to turn the rivers and oceans into blood, and to
strike the earth with every kind of plague as often as they wish.

7When they complete their testimony, the
beast that comes up out of the bottomless pit*
will declare war against them, and he will conquer them and kill them. 8And their bodies will lie
in the main street of Jerusalem,* the city that is
figuratively called "Sodom" and "Egypt," the city
where their Lord was crucified. 9And for three and
a half days, all peoples, tribes, languages, and nations will stare at their bodies. No one will be allowed to bury them. 10All the people who belong
to this world will gloat over them and give presents to each other to celebrate the death of the two
prophets who had tormented them.

11But after three and a half days, God breathed
life into them, and they stood up! Terror struck
all who were staring at them. 12Then a loud voice
from heaven called to the two prophets, "Come
up here!" And they rose to heaven in a cloud as
their enemies watched.

13At the same time there was a terrible earthquake that destroyed a tenth of the city. Seven
thousand people died in that earthquake, and everyone else was terrified and gave glory to the
God of heaven.

14The second terror is past, but look, the third
terror is coming quickly.

The Seventh Trumpet Brings the Third Terror

15Then the seventh angel blew his trumpet, and
there were loud voices shouting in heaven:

"The world has now become the Kingdom of
our Lord and of his Christ,*
and he will reign forever and ever."

16The twenty-four elders sitting on their thrones
before God fell with their faces to the ground and
worshiped him. 17And they said,

"We give thanks to you, Lord God, the
Almighty,
the one who is and who always was,
for now you have assumed your great
power
and have begun to reign.
18The nations were filled with wrath,
but now the time of your wrath has
come.
It is time to judge the dead
and reward your servants the prophets,
as well as your holy people,
and all who fear your name,
from the least to the greatest.
It is time to destroy
all who have caused destruction on the
earth."

19Then, in heaven, the Temple of God was
opened and the Ark of his covenant could be seen
inside the Temple. Lightning flashed, thunder
crashed and roared, and there was an earthquake
and a terrible hailstorm.

The Woman and the Dragon

12 Then I witnessed in heaven an event
of great significance. I saw a woman
clothed with the sun, with the moon

11:7 Or *the abyss,* or *the underworld.* **11:8** Greek *the great city.* **11:15** Or *his Messiah.*

witness, *the beast*, the enemy of God, emerges from the bottomless pit to kill the two witnesses, possibly referring to a time of persecution resulting in martyrdoms. Echoing the resurrection of Jesus, the two witnesses are restored to life, to the horror and amazement of the onlookers. Those who had been publicly slain for their witness are publicly vindicated and rewarded by ascending to heaven. At their resurrection a tenth of the watching city is destroyed in a mighty earthquake, reminiscent of those that shook the earth at Jesus' death and resurrection (Matt 27:51–54; 28:2), again adding to the similarities between Jesus and his witnesses. At this point, shaken to the core, the people finally repent. The faithful witnesses, rather than the dreadful plagues, bring repentance.

11:14–19 Seventh Trumpet (Third of Woe): God's Kingdom Begins

The stage is set for the final woe (12:13—13:18). But first the final trumpet call instigates a liturgical interlude in which the words and songs look ahead to the future but speak as though it is already accomplished. This reassures believers in the seven churches and all about to undergo persecution. They can look forward to a time when the kingdom of God is established and they will receive their hard-earned reward. Access to the holiest part of the temple of God is available to all (compare this with the opening of the earthly Most Holy Place at Christ's death, Matt 27:51–52).

beneath her feet, and a crown of twelve stars on
her head. 2 She was pregnant, and she cried out
because of her labor pains and the agony of giving birth.
3 Then I witnessed in heaven another significant event. I saw a large red dragon with seven
heads and ten horns, with seven crowns on his
heads. 4 His tail swept away one-third of the stars
in the sky, and he threw them to the earth. He
stood in front of the woman as she was about to
give birth, ready to devour her baby as soon as
it was born.
5 She gave birth to a son who was to rule
all nations with an iron rod. And her child was
snatched away from the dragon and was caught
up to God and to his throne. 6 And the woman
fled into the wilderness, where God had prepared
a place to care for her for 1,260 days.
7 Then there was war in heaven. Michael
and his angels fought against the dragon and
his angels. 8 And the dragon lost the battle, and
he and his angels were forced out of heaven.
9 This great dragon—the ancient serpent called
the devil, or Satan, the one deceiving the whole
world—was thrown down to the earth with all
his angels.
10 Then I heard a loud voice shouting across
the heavens,

"It has come at last—
salvation and power
and the Kingdom of our God,
and the authority of his Christ.*
For the accuser of our brothers and sisters*
has been thrown down to earth—
the one who accuses them
before our God day and night.
11 And they have defeated him by the blood of
the Lamb
and by their testimony.
And they did not love their lives so much
that they were afraid to die.
12 Therefore, rejoice, O heavens!
And you who live in the heavens, rejoice!
But terror will come on the earth and the sea,
for the devil has come down to you in great
anger,
knowing that he has little time."

13 When the dragon realized that he had been
thrown down to the earth, he pursued the woman
who had given birth to the male child. 14 But she
was given two wings like those of a great eagle
so she could fly to the place prepared for her in
the wilderness. There she would be cared for and
protected from the dragon* for a time, times, and
half a time.
15 Then the dragon tried to drown the woman
with a flood of water that flowed from his mouth.

12:10a Or *his Messiah.* **12:10b** Greek *brothers.*
12:14 Greek *the serpent;* also in 12:15. See 12:9.

12:1–17 The Woman, the Child, and the Dragon

The venue has moved to the earth, where a *woman,* portrayed as a queen of heaven, is about to give birth. The woman, most obviously, represents Mary the mother of Jesus, here pictured as a woman glorified, with her role as mother bearing eternal significance. Mary, in turn, embodies all the faithful in Israel who have looked forward to the birth of the Messiah: She represents the ideal Israel as personified in the Old Testament image of a faithful wife or bride of Yahweh who gives birth to the Messiah (the Messiah comes from the faithful line of Israel). On a third level the woman represents the church, which, as a continuation of the Old Testament picture, becomes the faithful bride of Christ. The woman is about to give birth, the most vulnerable time for any woman. **3–4:** In the moments prior to the birth a *red dragon*—the age-old enemy of people, the one who tempted them to sin—aims to destroy the one who would seek to destroy him. The woman cannot get up and save herself and her child. She is in the hands of God, just as Israel and the church depend on God for survival and protection. **5–6:** Without midwife or protector, the woman gives birth. What chance of survival do she and her child have? What chance does the infant church—weak, few in number, and vulnerable—have in the face of evil persecution? But just as with the woman, God gives a place of safety and nourishment to the church if it remains faithful to the end. On one level the dragon wishes to kill the child, Jesus, so that God's plans will be thwarted; on another, the dragon wants to destroy the church and its witness by temptations, persecution, and any other means. The child is snatched away to safety, but the mother is left at the dragon's mercy. Exhausted and sore after childbirth, she nevertheless flees to the wilderness, where God has prepared a safe place for her to recover and rest. **7–17:** The pursuit of the woman is delayed while the dragon and his angels go into battle with the archangel Michael and his forces. Michael is victorious, and the dragon is exiled to earth, resuming pursuit of the woman. Again she is protected. Failing once more to harm the woman, the dragon turns on the rest of her children, the church, in a twofold attack of persecution and deception.

16 But the earth helped her by opening its mouth
and swallowing the river that gushed out from
the mouth of the dragon. 17 And the dragon was
angry at the woman and declared war against the
rest of her children—all who keep God's commandments and maintain their testimony for
Jesus.
18 Then the dragon took his stand* on the
shore beside the sea.

The Beast out of the Sea

13 Then I saw a beast rising up out of
the sea. It had seven heads and ten
horns, with ten crowns on its horns.
And written on each head were names that blasphemed God. 2 This beast looked like a leopard,
but it had the feet of a bear and the mouth of
a lion! And the dragon gave the beast his own
power and throne and great authority.
3 I saw that one of the heads of the beast
seemed wounded beyond recovery—but the fatal
wound was healed! The whole world marveled
at this miracle and gave allegiance to the beast.
4 They worshiped the dragon for giving the beast
such power, and they also worshiped the beast.
"Who is as great as the beast?" they exclaimed.
"Who is able to fight against him?"
5 Then the beast was allowed to speak great
blasphemies against God. And he was given authority to do whatever he wanted for forty-two
months. 6 And he spoke terrible words of blasphemy against God, slandering his name and his
dwelling—that is, those who dwell in heaven.*
7 And the beast was allowed to wage war against
God's holy people and to conquer them. And he
was given authority to rule over every tribe and
people and language and nation. 8 And all the
people who belong to this world worshiped the
beast. They are the ones whose names were not
written in the Book of Life before the world was
made—the Book that belongs to the Lamb who
was slaughtered.*

9 Anyone with ears to hear
should listen and understand.
10 Anyone who is destined for prison
will be taken to prison.
Anyone destined to die by the sword
will die by the sword.

This means that God's holy people must endure
persecution patiently and remain faithful.

The Beast out of the Earth

11 Then I saw another beast come up out of the
earth. He had two horns like those of a lamb,
but he spoke with the voice of a dragon. 12 He
exercised all the authority of the first beast.

12:18 Greek *Then he took his stand;* some manuscripts read *Then I took my stand.* Some translations put this entire sentence into 13:1. **13:6** Some manuscripts read *and his dwelling and all who dwell in heaven.* **13:8** Or *not written in the Book of Life that belongs to the Lamb who was slaughtered before the world was made.*

12:18—13:18 The Two Beasts

Two horrific beasts join with the dragon to form an unholy trinity in direct opposition to God and the Lamb.

13:1–10 The Beast from the Sea. 1–2: The first *beast,* a conglomeration of the four beasts of Daniel's vision (Dan 7), emerges from *the sea,* the birthplace of chaos. In Daniel the beasts represent earthly empires; John's beast is often identified with the Roman Empire, which persecuted the church of God. The dragon's *authority, power,* and *throne* given to the beast represent the empire's claim to godlike status, a parody of the true rule of Jesus (Rev 5). **3–4:** The beast's fatal wound—perhaps a reference to the assassination of Julius Caesar—has been miraculously healed. All those not belonging to God are taken in by the counterfeit. **5–10:** God allows the beast to blaspheme for the same amount of time that the two witnesses prophesied (11:3). The beast's prophecies are the opposite of the message of the witnesses. The dragon, having been banished from heaven, establishes his own kingdom, a parody of God's kingdom. This counterfeit kingdom is so good a copy that many people are taken in by it. Only those who have remained faithful to Christ can see it for what it is.

13:11–18 The Beast from the Earth. 11–15: This beast is far more appealing than the last; it looks like *a lamb* in a direct parody of the Lamb of God. But when it speaks, it shows its true character, *the voice of a dragon.* It is a wolf in sheep's clothing (see Matt 7:15). It leads the inhabitants of earth away from the worship of the true God by performing miracles—perhaps a reference to practices in Roman idol worship. Refusal to worship the emperor is a capital offense. Idols have an evil force at work behind them. To take part in the emperor cult meant to worship the evil behind the image. In this parody of the divine Trinity the second beast could equally be the counterfeit of Christ, with the appearance of the Lamb, or of the Holy Spirit, who leads people to follow Christ and performs signs and wonders through God's people. **16–18:** All

And he required all the earth and its people to
worship the first beast, whose fatal wound had
been healed. 13 He did astounding miracles, even
making fire flash down to earth from the sky
while everyone was watching. 14 And with all the
miracles he was allowed to perform on behalf
of the first beast, he deceived all the people who
belong to this world. He ordered the people to
make a great statue of the first beast, who was
fatally wounded and then came back to life. 15 He
was then permitted to give life to this statue so
that it could speak. Then the statue of the beast
commanded that anyone refusing to worship it
must die.

16 He required everyone—small and great,
rich and poor, free and slave—to be given a mark
on the right hand or on the forehead. 17 And no
one could buy or sell anything without that
mark, which was either the name of the beast or
the number representing his name. 18 Wisdom
is needed here. Let the one with understanding
solve the meaning of the number of the beast, for
it is the number of a man.* His number is 666.*

The Lamb and the 144,000

14 Then I saw the Lamb standing on
Mount Zion, and with him were
144,000 who had his name and his
Father's name written on their foreheads. 2 And
I heard a sound from heaven like the roar of
mighty ocean waves or the rolling of loud thunder. It was like the sound of many harpists playing together.

3 This great choir sang a wonderful new song
in front of the throne of God and before the four
living beings and the twenty-four elders. No one
could learn this song except the 144,000 who had
been redeemed from the earth. 4 They have kept
themselves as pure as virgins,* following the
Lamb wherever he goes. They have been purchased from among the people on the earth as a
special offering* to God and to the Lamb. 5 They
have told no lies; they are without blame.

The Three Angels

6 And I saw another angel flying through the sky,
carrying the eternal Good News to proclaim to
the people who belong to this world—to every
nation, tribe, language, and people. 7 "Fear God,"
he shouted. "Give glory to him. For the time has
come when he will sit as judge. Worship him
who made the heavens, the earth, the sea, and all
the springs of water."

8 Then another angel followed him through
the sky, shouting, "Babylon is fallen—that great
city is fallen—because she made all the nations
of the world drink the wine of her passionate immorality."

9 Then a third angel followed them, shouting,
"Anyone who worships the beast and his statue
or who accepts his mark on the forehead or on
the hand 10 must drink the wine of God's anger. It
has been poured full strength into God's cup of
wrath. And they will be tormented with fire and
burning sulfur in the presence of the holy angels
and the Lamb. 11 The smoke of their torment will
rise forever and ever, and they will have no relief
day or night, for they have worshiped the beast
and his statue and have accepted the mark of his
name."

13:18a Or *of humanity.* **13:18b** Some manuscripts read *616.* **14:4a** Greek *They are virgins who have not defiled themselves with women.* **14:4b** Greek *as firstfruits.*

those who worship the beast will be marked with its sign, a counterfeit of the seal with which the saints of God are marked. *The number of the beast . . . 666*: Probably Nero, whose name and title in Hebrew letters total 666 in conventional number values; more generally it means radical incompleteness, 6 falling short of 7, or any human being (created on the sixth day) trying to usurp God's status.

14:1–20 Seven Visions: Salvation for the Blessed, Judgment for the Evil

The setting changes to the gathering of the forces of the Lamb.

14:1–5 First Vision. The Lamb on Mount Zion surrounded by the saved. The Lamb and his followers are waiting for the battle to commence. While they wait they sing a song of redemption known only to themselves. **4:** *As pure as virgins*: The Greek reads "who have not defiled themselves with women" (see translator's note). This imagery is derived from the practice of Israelite soldiers in holy war (1 Sam 21:5; see Lev 15).

14:6–7 Second Vision. The eternal gospel of judgment. The judgment is *Good News* because it means the manifestation of God's justice.

14:8 Third Vision. The fall of Babylon. *Babylon* is the symbol of the idolatry of empire, the political power opposed to God.

14:9–11 Fourth Vision. Judgment of the followers of the beast. The rejection of the powers of evil opposed to God will last *forever and ever.*

12 This means that God's holy people must
endure persecution patiently, obeying his commands and maintaining their faith in Jesus.
13 And I heard a voice from heaven saying,
"Write this down: Blessed are those who die
in the Lord from now on. Yes, says the Spirit,
they are blessed indeed, for they will rest from
their hard work; for their good deeds follow
them!"

The Harvest of the Earth

14 Then I saw a white cloud, and seated on the
cloud was someone like the Son of Man.* He
had a gold crown on his head and a sharp sickle
in his hand.
15 Then another angel came from the Temple
and shouted to the one sitting on the cloud,
"Swing the sickle, for the time of harvest has
come; the crop on earth is ripe." 16 So the one sitting on the cloud swung his sickle over the earth,
and the whole earth was harvested.
17 After that, another angel came from the
Temple in heaven, and he also had a sharp
sickle. 18 Then another angel, who had power
to destroy with fire, came from the altar. He
shouted to the angel with the sharp sickle,
"Swing your sickle now to gather the clusters
of grapes from the vines of the earth, for they
are ripe for judgment." 19 So the angel swung
his sickle over the earth and loaded the grapes
into the great winepress of God's wrath. 20 The
grapes were trampled in the winepress outside
the city, and blood flowed from the winepress
in a stream about 180 miles* long and as high
as a horse's bridle.

The Song of Moses and of the Lamb

15 Then I saw in heaven another marvelous event of great significance.
Seven angels were holding the seven
last plagues, which would bring God's wrath to
completion. 2 I saw before me what seemed to be
a glass sea mixed with fire. And on it stood all the
people who had been victorious over the beast
and his statue and the number representing his
name. They were all holding harps that God had
given them. 3 And they were singing the song of
Moses, the servant of God, and the song of the
Lamb:

"Great and marvelous are your works,
O Lord God, the Almighty.
Just and true are your ways,
O King of the nations.*
4 Who will not fear you, Lord,
and glorify your name?
For you alone are holy.
All nations will come and worship before
you,
for your righteous deeds have been
revealed."

The Seven Bowls of the Seven Plagues

5 Then I looked and saw that the Temple in heav-
en, God's Tabernacle, was thrown wide open.
6 The seven angels who were holding the seven
plagues came out of the Temple. They were

14:14 Or *like a son of man.* See Dan 7:13. "Son of Man" is a title Jesus used for himself. **14:20** Greek *1,600 stadia* [296 kilometers]. **15:3** Some manuscripts read *King of the ages.*

14:12–13 Fifth Vision. The endurance of the saints and the blessed resting from their labors.

14:14–16 Sixth Vision. The ingathering of the blessed. The wheat (not stated but implied) symbolizes the blessed.

14:17–20 Seventh Vision. The winepress of God's wrath. *Grapes* or wine symbolize the idolatrous. The *blood* flowing for *1,600 stadia* (see translator's note) symbolizes complete coverage of the earth (4 is "all directions" on earth, so 4 x 4 is "completely, in all directions," strengthened by a multiple of 10, meaning "fully").

15:1—16:21 Seven Bowls of Wrath; Plagues Like Those in Egypt

The final seven disasters arrive. The previous two sets have caused partial destruction; these seven cause the total destruction brought about by the full wrath of God.

15:1–4 The Song of Moses and of the Lamb. There is a glimpse of heaven, looking toward the defeat of the beast, and showing the victorious army singing and worshiping God.

15:5—16:21 Seven Bowls of Seven Plagues. 15:5: *The Temple in heaven* is now open to all, recalling the rending of the Temple curtain at the crucifixion (Matt 27:51). In the Old Testament, when the Lord was present in the Temple no one could enter because of his holiness (Isa 6:4). The pattern of these seven plagues follows those of the seven trumpets with the theme of the retribution and punishment of the beast's followers. **16:1–9:** The first four plagues are based on the plagues of Egypt (Exod 7:14—10:29).

clothed in spotless white linen* with gold sashes
across their chests. [7]Then one of the four living
beings handed each of the seven angels a gold
bowl filled with the wrath of God, who lives forever and ever. [8]The Temple was filled with smoke
from God's glory and power. No one could enter
the Temple until the seven angels had completed
pouring out the seven plagues.

16 Then I heard a mighty voice from the
Temple say to the seven angels, "Go
your ways and pour out on the earth
the seven bowls containing God's wrath."
[2]So the first angel left the Temple and poured
out his bowl on the earth, and horrible, malignant sores broke out on everyone who had the
mark of the beast and who worshiped his statue.
[3]Then the second angel poured out his bowl
on the sea, and it became like the blood of a
corpse. And everything in the sea died.
[4]Then the third angel poured out his bowl on
the rivers and springs, and they became blood.
[5]And I heard the angel who had authority over
all water saying,

"You are just, O Holy One, who is and who
always was,
because you have sent these judgments.
[6] Since they shed the blood
of your holy people and your prophets,
you have given them blood to drink.
It is their just reward."

[7]And I heard a voice from the altar,* saying,

"Yes, O Lord God, the Almighty,
your judgments are true and just."

[8]Then the fourth angel poured out his bowl
on the sun, causing it to scorch everyone with its
fire. [9]Everyone was burned by this blast of heat,
and they cursed the name of God, who had control over all these plagues. They did not repent of
their sins and turn to God and give him glory.

[10]Then the fifth angel poured out his bowl
on the throne of the beast, and his kingdom was
plunged into darkness. His subjects ground their
teeth in anguish, [11]and they cursed the God of
heaven for their pains and sores. But they did not
repent of their evil deeds and turn to God.
[12]Then the sixth angel poured out his bowl on
the great Euphrates River, and it dried up so that
the kings from the east could march their armies
toward the west without hindrance. [13]And I saw
three evil* spirits that looked like frogs leap from
the mouths of the dragon, the beast, and the false
prophet. [14]They are demonic spirits who work
miracles and go out to all the rulers of the world
to gather them for battle against the Lord on that
great judgment day of God the Almighty.

[15]"Look, I will come as unexpectedly as a
thief! Blessed are all who are watching for
me, who keep their clothing ready so they
will not have to walk around naked and
ashamed."

[16]And the demonic spirits gathered all the
rulers and their armies to a place with the Hebrew name *Armageddon*.*
[17]Then the seventh angel poured out his bowl
into the air. And a mighty shout came from the
throne in the Temple, saying, "It is finished!"
[18]Then the thunder crashed and rolled, and lightning flashed. And a great earthquake struck—
the worst since people were placed on the earth.
[19]The great city of Babylon split into three sections, and the cities of many nations fell into
heaps of rubble. So God remembered all of Babylon's sins, and he made her drink the cup that
was filled with the wine of his fierce wrath. [20]And
every island disappeared, and all the mountains
were leveled. [21]There was a terrible hailstorm,
and hailstones weighing as much as seventy-five

15:6 Other manuscripts read *white stone;* still others read *white [garments] made of linen.* **16:7** Greek *I heard the altar.* **16:13** Greek *unclean.* **16:16** Or *Harmagedon.*

These plagues represent elements of nature and are an attack on the followers of the beast, but the effect this time is destruction. Those who shed the blood of the martyrs now only have blood to drink—a fitting punishment. **10–21:** The last three bowls of wrath target the forces of deception rather than individuals. The fifth strikes the heart of the beast's authority as its center of its worship is destroyed. With the sixth bowl the river Euphrates (the starting point for the invasion of Palestine in the Old Testament) dries up in readiness for the invasion of the kings from the east. At this point evil spirits from the dragon assemble the unbelieving kings for battle. **15:** No one knows the time, the hour, or the day when Christ will return (see Matt 24:44), so the church must remain faithful, awake, alert, and on guard. **17–21:** With the pouring out of the contents of the seventh bowl God, in an announcement reminiscent of Jesus' cry from the cross (John 19:30), states *It is finished!* The final plague is unleashed on the earth, its inhabitants, and the demonic forces.

pounds* fell from the sky onto the people below. They cursed God because of the terrible plague of the hailstorm.

The Great Prostitute

17 One of the seven angels who had poured out the seven bowls came over and spoke to me. "Come with me," he said, "and I will show you the judgment that is going to come on the great prostitute, who rules over many waters. 2 The kings of the world have committed adultery with her, and the people who belong to this world have been made drunk by the wine of her immorality."

3 So the angel took me in the Spirit* into the wilderness. There I saw a woman sitting on a scarlet beast that had seven heads and ten horns, and blasphemies against God were written all over it. 4 The woman wore purple and scarlet clothing and beautiful jewelry made of gold and precious gems and pearls. In her hand she held a gold goblet full of obscenities and the impurities of her immorality. 5 A mysterious name was written on her forehead: "Babylon the Great, Mother of All Prostitutes and Obscenities in the World." 6 I could see that she was drunk—drunk with the blood of God's holy people who were witnesses for Jesus. I stared at her in complete amazement.

7 "Why are you so amazed?" the angel asked. "I will tell you the mystery of this woman and of the beast with seven heads and ten horns on which she sits. 8 The beast you saw was once alive but isn't now. And yet he will soon come up out of the bottomless pit* and go to eternal destruction. And the people who belong to this world, whose names were not written in the Book of Life before the world was made, will be amazed at the reappearance of this beast who had died.

9 "This calls for a mind with understanding: The seven heads of the beast represent the seven hills where the woman rules. They also represent seven kings. 10 Five kings have already fallen, the sixth now reigns, and the seventh is yet to come, but his reign will be brief.

11 "The scarlet beast that was, but is no longer, is the eighth king. He is like the other seven, and he, too, is headed for destruction. 12 The ten horns of the beast are ten kings who have not yet risen to power. They will be appointed to their kingdoms for one brief moment to reign with the beast. 13 They will all agree to give him their power and authority. 14 Together they will go to war against the Lamb, but the Lamb will defeat them because he is Lord of all lords and King of all kings. And his called and chosen and faithful ones will be with him."

15 Then the angel said to me, "The waters where the prostitute is ruling represent masses of people of every nation and language. 16 The scarlet beast and his ten horns all hate the prostitute. They will strip her naked, eat her flesh, and burn her remains with fire. 17 For God has put a plan into their minds, a plan that will carry out his purposes. They will agree to give their authority to the scarlet beast, and so the words of God will be fulfilled. 18 And this woman you saw in your vision represents the great city that rules over the kings of the world."

16:21 Greek *1 talent* [34 kilograms]. **17:3** Or *in spirit.* **17:8** Or *the abyss,* or *the underworld.*

17:1—18:24 The Fall of Babylon

17:1–18 Babylon the Prostitute. The prostitute is not based on a particular woman and is not intended to portray women in a negative light. Instead, she is based on the Old Testament image of unfaithfulness to God symbolized as an unfaithful wife who prostitutes herself (Hos 1—3). She is the opposite of the virtuous mother and bride who represent the faithful church. The prostitute pictures the seductive power that leads people away from Christ and into partnership with the dragon. But her activities also undermine the core of society, for her behavior damages marriage and family. Those who collude with her are equally to blame: She used her seductive ways, but no one forced them into intimacy with her. The harlot and the dragon are in league with each other. They aim to corrupt and seduce the faithful while blinding the whole of humanity to truth with deception and lies about wealth and power. **7–14:** There have been many interpretations about the *seven kings*. Some commentators have taken them to be various Roman emperors, while others have thought of them in terms of modern tyrannical leaders (e.g., Adolf Hitler). The important fact is that these rulers hand over their authority to the beast. They become his subjects and join together against the Lamb. What an encouragement for the believers in the first century to be told that even though times are bleak, they and not society are on the winning side because their leader is the King of Kings and Lord of Lords. **15–18:** The final destruction of the harlot is brought about by those who used her. Those she had seduced now turn on her. There was never love or respect but only lust for power, wealth, and pleasure. They take all she has and leave her naked and humiliated. Then they kill and burn her. God uses the harlot's clients as the instrument of her destruction (cf. Jer 41:30–31; Ezek 23:1–27).

The Fall of Babylon

18 After all this I saw another angel come
down from heaven with great authority, and the earth grew bright with his
splendor. 2 He gave a mighty shout:

"Babylon is fallen—that great city is fallen!
She has become a home for demons.
She is a hideout for every foul* spirit,
a hideout for every foul vulture
and every foul and dreadful animal.*
3 For all the nations have fallen*
because of the wine of her passionate
immorality.
The kings of the world
have committed adultery with her.
Because of her desires for extravagant
luxury,
the merchants of the world have grown
rich."

4 Then I heard another voice calling from heaven,

"Come away from her, my people.
Do not take part in her sins,
or you will be punished with her.
5 For her sins are piled as high as heaven,
and God remembers her evil deeds.
6 Do to her as she has done to others.
Double her penalty* for all her evil deeds.
She brewed a cup of terror for others,
so brew twice as much* for her.
7 She glorified herself and lived in luxury,
so match it now with torment and sorrow.
She boasted in her heart,
'I am queen on my throne.
I am no helpless widow,
and I have no reason to mourn.'
8 Therefore, these plagues will overtake her in
a single day—
death and mourning and famine.
She will be completely consumed by fire,
for the Lord God who judges her is
mighty."

9 And the kings of the world who committed
adultery with her and enjoyed her great luxury
will mourn for her as they see the smoke rising
from her charred remains. 10 They will stand at
a distance, terrified by her great torment. They
will cry out,

"How terrible, how terrible for you,
O Babylon, you great city!
In a single moment
God's judgment came on you."

11 The merchants of the world will weep and
mourn for her, for there is no one left to buy their
goods. 12 She bought great quantities of gold, silver, jewels, and pearls; fine linen, purple, silk,
and scarlet cloth; things made of fragrant thyine
wood, ivory goods, and objects made of expensive wood; and bronze, iron, and marble. 13 She
also bought cinnamon, spice, incense, myrrh,
frankincense, wine, olive oil, fine flour, wheat,
cattle, sheep, horses, chariots, and bodies—that
is, human slaves.

14 "The fancy things you loved so much
are gone," they cry.
"All your luxuries and splendor
are gone forever,
never to be yours again."

15 The merchants who became wealthy by
selling her these things will stand at a distance,
terrified by her great torment. They will weep
and cry out,

16 "How terrible, how terrible for that great
city!
She was clothed in finest purple and scarlet
linens,
decked out with gold and precious stones
and pearls!
17 In a single moment
all the wealth of the city is gone!"

And all the captains of the merchant ships and
their passengers and sailors and crews will stand
at a distance. 18 They will cry out as they watch
the smoke ascend, and they will say, "Where is

18:2a Greek *unclean;* also in each of the two following phrases. **18:2b** Some manuscripts condense the last two lines to read *a hideout for every foul [unclean] and dreadful vulture.* **18:3** Some manuscripts read *have drunk.* **18:6a** Or *Give her an equal penalty.* **18:6b** Or *brew just as much.*

18:1–24 The Song of Triumph. Now that Babylon is destroyed, a song of triumph echoes from the heavens. The great city that affected everyone's life and livelihood is left in ruins. This ruination affects the city but also all who slept with her. With the city destroyed so too is the trade, the means of earning a living. **2–9:** The voice of triumph from heaven contrasts with the voices of lament and wailing from those who used the harlot to become wealthy and powerful or to gain power and prestige. **4–8:** A *voice* from *heaven* instructs the faithful to leave the city so that they are not caught up in the destruction.

there another city as great as this?" 19 And they
will weep and throw dust on their heads to show
their grief. And they will cry out,

"How terrible, how terrible for that great city!
The shipowners became wealthy
by transporting her great wealth on the seas.
In a single moment it is all gone."

20 Rejoice over her fate, O heaven
and people of God and apostles and
prophets!
For at last God has judged her
for your sakes.

21 Then a mighty angel picked up a boulder
the size of a huge millstone. He threw it into the
ocean and shouted,

"Just like this, the great city Babylon
will be thrown down with violence
and will never be found again.
22 The sound of harps, singers, flutes, and trumpets
will never be heard in you again.
No craftsmen and no trades
will ever be found in you again.
The sound of the mill
will never be heard in you again.
23 The light of a lamp
will never shine in you again.
The happy voices of brides and grooms
will never be heard in you again.
For your merchants were the greatest in the
world,
and you deceived the nations with your
sorceries.
24 In your* streets flowed the blood of the
prophets and of God's holy people
and the blood of people slaughtered all over
the world."

Songs of Victory in Heaven

19 After this, I heard what sounded like a
vast crowd in heaven shouting,

"Praise the LORD!*
Salvation and glory and power belong to
our God.
2 His judgments are true and just.
He has punished the great prostitute
who corrupted the earth with her immorality.
He has avenged the murder of his
servants."

3 And again their voices rang out:

"Praise the LORD!
The smoke from that city ascends forever
and ever!"

4 Then the twenty-four elders and the four
living beings fell down and worshiped God,
who was sitting on the throne. They cried out,
"Amen! Praise the LORD!"
5 And from the throne came a voice that said,

"Praise our God,
all his servants,
all who fear him,
from the least to the greatest."

6 Then I heard again what sounded like the
shout of a vast crowd or the roar of mighty ocean
waves or the crash of loud thunder:

"Praise the LORD!
For the Lord our God,* the Almighty,
reigns.
7 Let us be glad and rejoice,
and let us give honor to him.
For the time has come for the wedding feast
of the Lamb,
and his bride has prepared herself.
8 She has been given the finest of pure white
linen to wear."
For the fine linen represents the good deeds
of God's holy people.

18:24 Greek *her.* **19:1** Greek *Hallelujah;* also in 19:3, 4, 6. *Hallelujah* is the transliteration of a Hebrew term that means "Praise the LORD." **19:6** Some manuscripts read *the Lord God.*

20: All this destruction has come about because the saints stood firm against wickedness even to death. Now God has avenged the saints' cry for vengeance (6:10).

19:1–10 Song of Praise to God

Heaven resounds with the sound of worship. The familiar characters of previous liturgical scenes are present. **7–10:** The worship turns into rejoicing over the forthcoming *wedding feast of the Lamb.* The *bride,* the church, has *prepared herself* by remaining faithful to him and not allowing herself to be corrupted or tainted by idolatrous ideas or ways. Her love for the Lamb was so great that she would forego all the attractions of the world to remain loyal to him. Her bridal gown is made from the most costly of materials—the righteous deeds of the saints—and as such

[9] And the angel said to me, "Write this: Blessed are those who are invited to the wedding feast of the Lamb." And he added, "These are true words that come from God."

[10] Then I fell down at his feet to worship him, but he said, "No, don't worship me. I am a servant of God, just like you and your brothers and sisters* who testify about their faith in Jesus. Worship only God. For the essence of prophecy is to give a clear witness for Jesus.*"

The Rider on the White Horse

[11] Then I saw heaven opened, and a white horse was standing there. Its rider was named Faithful and True, for he judges fairly and wages a righteous war. [12] His eyes were like flames of fire, and on his head were many crowns. A name was written on him that no one understood except himself. [13] He wore a robe dipped in blood, and his title was the Word of God. [14] The armies of heaven, dressed in the finest of pure white linen, followed him on white horses. [15] From his mouth came a sharp sword to strike down the nations. He will rule them with an iron rod. He will release the fierce wrath of God, the Almighty, like juice flowing from a winepress. [16] On his robe at his thigh* was written this title: King of all kings and Lord of all lords.

[17] Then I saw an angel standing in the sun, shouting to the vultures flying high in the sky: "Come! Gather together for the great banquet God has prepared. [18] Come and eat the flesh of kings, generals, and strong warriors; of horses and their riders; and of all humanity, both free and slave, small and great."

[19] Then I saw the beast and the kings of the world and their armies gathered together to fight against the one sitting on the horse and his army. [20] And the beast was captured, and with him the false prophet who did mighty miracles on behalf of the beast—miracles that deceived all who had accepted the mark of the beast and who worshiped his statue. Both the beast and his false prophet were thrown alive into the fiery lake of burning sulfur. [21] Their entire army was killed by the sharp sword that came from the mouth of the one riding the white horse. And the vultures all gorged themselves on the dead bodies.

The Thousand Years

20 Then I saw an angel coming down from heaven with the key to the bottomless pit* and a heavy chain in his hand. [2] He seized the dragon—that old serpent, who is the devil, Satan—and bound him in chains for a thousand years. [3] The angel threw him into the bottomless pit, which he then shut and locked so Satan could not deceive the nations anymore until the thousand years were finished. Afterward he must be released for a little while.

[4] Then I saw thrones, and the people sitting on them had been given the authority to judge. And I saw the souls of those who had been beheaded for their testimony about Jesus and for proclaiming the word of God. They had not worshiped the beast or his statue, nor accepted his mark on their forehead or their hands. They all came to life again, and they reigned with Christ for a thousand years.

[5] This is the first resurrection. (The rest of the dead did not come back to life until the thousand years had ended.) [6] Blessed and holy are those

19:10a Greek *brothers.* **19:10b** Or *is the message confirmed by Jesus.* **19:16** Or *On his robe and thigh.* **20:1** Or *the abyss, or the underworld;* also in 20:3.

is pure, uncorrupted, and beautiful. **9:** The church is the bride, but at the same time the saints are invited guests at the *wedding feast.* **10:** Overcome, John falls at the angel's feet in worship. The angel rebukes him, for the angel is a fellow servant of God, and only God is worthy to be worshiped.

19:11–21 Conquest of Evil by the Heavenly Host

The rider, *Faithful and True,* clearly represents Jesus (vv. 11–16). *Heaven* is *opened* so that everyone on earth will see his arrival (see Matt 24:23–27). **17–18:** In readiness for the ensuing battle, an angel gathers all the carrion birds together. No one will be left to bury the dead, so their bodies will be left to the scavengers. Contrast this with the wedding supper of the Lamb to which the saints are invited. **19–21:** The beast and the ruler of earth go into battle against the white rider and his army. The battle is not described, almost as if it is over before it begins. *The sharp sword* in the mouth of the rider is the word that "exposes . . . innermost thoughts" (Heb 4:12).

20:1–10 Defeat of Satan

With the beast and the false prophet languishing in the lake of fire, the third part of the unholy alliance, the *dragon,* is seized and *bound . . . for a thousand years.* **4–6:** Christ reigns with his faithful followers, those who had been martyred and those who refused to worship the beast. Only the dead in Christ are resurrected at this point. Later, all those who have died come alive to be judged.

who share in the first resurrection. For them the
second death holds no power, but they will be
priests of God and of Christ and will reign with
him a thousand years.

The Defeat of Satan

7 When the thousand years come to an end, Satan
will be let out of his prison. 8 He will go out to
deceive the nations—called Gog and Magog—in
every corner of the earth. He will gather them
together for battle—a mighty army, as number-
less as sand along the seashore. 9 And I saw them
as they went up on the broad plain of the earth
and surrounded God's people and the beloved
city. But fire from heaven came down on the attacking armies and consumed them.
10 Then the devil, who had deceived them, was
thrown into the fiery lake of burning sulfur, joining the beast and the false prophet. There they
will be tormented day and night forever and ever.

The Final Judgment

11 And I saw a great white throne and the one sitting on it. The earth and sky fled from his presence, but they found no place to hide. 12 I saw the
dead, both great and small, standing before God's
throne. And the books were opened, including
the Book of Life. And the dead were judged according to what they had done, as recorded in
the books. 13 The sea gave up its dead, and death
and the grave* gave up their dead. And all were
judged according to their deeds. 14 Then death and
the grave were thrown into the lake of fire. This
lake of fire is the second death. 15 And anyone
whose name was not found recorded in the Book
of Life was thrown into the lake of fire.

The New Jerusalem

21 Then I saw a new heaven and a new
earth, for the old heaven and the old
earth had disappeared. And the sea
was also gone. 2 And I saw the holy city, the new
Jerusalem, coming down from God out of heaven
like a bride beautifully dressed for her husband.
3 I heard a loud shout from the throne, saying,
"Look, God's home is now among his people! He
will live with them, and they will be his people.
God himself will be with them.* 4 He will wipe
every tear from their eyes, and there will be no
more death or sorrow or crying or pain. All these
things are gone forever."
5 And the one sitting on the throne said,
"Look, I am making everything new!" And then
he said to me, "Write this down, for what I tell
you is trustworthy and true." 6 And he also said,
"It is finished! I am the Alpha and the Omega—
the Beginning and the End. To all who are thirsty
I will give freely from the springs of the water of
life. 7 All who are victorious will inherit all these
blessings, and I will be their God, and they will
be my children.
8 "But cowards, unbelievers, the corrupt, murderers, the immoral, those who practice witchcraft, idol worshipers, and all liars—their fate
is in the fiery lake of burning sulfur. This is the
second death."
9 Then one of the seven angels who held the
seven bowls containing the seven last plagues
came and said to me, "Come with me! I will
show you the bride, the wife of the Lamb."

20:13 Greek *and Hades;* also in 20:14. **21:3** Some manuscripts read *God himself will be with them, their God.*

7–10: After the thousand years Satan is released and allowed to deceive the nations, gathering them again for battle. They surround the camp of the saints but are defeated. Satan is thrown into the *lake of fire*, to be tormented for eternity.

20:11–15 The Final Judgment

All the dead have now been raised and stand before *God's throne* (v. 12). Heaven and earth no longer exist, so there is nowhere to hide from God's presence. It appears that the dead are judged by their works rather than upon their acceptance of Christ, though in the deeper meaning of the book the *deeds* may in fact indicate where the person's faith in fact lay. **14–15:** *Death and the grave* are the last enemies to be destroyed. Now there is no death. Just as at the beginning of creation there was no death, so now with the new creation death does not exist. Death was the punishment for sin. With no sin there is no death.

21:1—22:5 The New Jerusalem

21:1–8 The New Creation. *A new heaven and a new earth* are created. *The new Jerusalem* descends from heaven like a beautiful bride dressed for her husband. God will now live with his people as he had planned from the beginning of creation. Then his plan had been spoiled through rebellion and sin. God had given people freedom of choice, but they used it to reject him. All those in this new creation have already chosen him freely. Paradise has been restored. There are no tears, death, mourning, crying, or pain. All those things that came into being as a result of sin no longer exist. Heaven and earth are beginning all over again.

21:9–27 The Heavenly City (the Bride). Contrast this new Jerusalem with the city of Babylon, which

10 So he took me in the Spirit* to a great, high
mountain, and he showed me the holy city, Jerusalem, descending out of heaven from God. 11 It
shone with the glory of God and sparkled like a
precious stone—like jasper as clear as crystal.
12 The city wall was broad and high, with twelve
gates guarded by twelve angels. And the names
of the twelve tribes of Israel were written on the
gates. 13 There were three gates on each side—east,
north, south, and west. 14 The wall of the city had
twelve foundation stones, and on them were written the names of the twelve apostles of the Lamb.
15 The angel who talked to me held in his hand
a gold measuring stick to measure the city, its
gates, and its wall. 16 When he measured it, he
found it was a square, as wide as it was long. In
fact, its length and width and height were each
1,400 miles.* 17 Then he measured the walls and
found them to be 216 feet thick* (according to
the human standard used by the angel).
18 The wall was made of jasper, and the city
was pure gold, as clear as glass. 19 The wall of the
city was built on foundation stones inlaid with
twelve precious stones:* the first was jasper, the
second sapphire, the third agate, the fourth emerald, 20 the fifth onyx, the sixth carnelian, the
seventh chrysolite, the eighth beryl, the ninth
topaz, the tenth chrysoprase, the eleventh jacinth, the twelfth amethyst.
21 The twelve gates were made of pearls—each
gate from a single pearl! And the main street was
pure gold, as clear as glass.
22 I saw no temple in the city, for the Lord God
Almighty and the Lamb are its temple. 23 And the
city has no need of sun or moon, for the glory
of God illuminates the city, and the Lamb is its
light. 24 The nations will walk in its light, and the
kings of the world will enter the city in all their
glory. 25 Its gates will never be closed at the end
of day because there is no night there. 26 And all
the nations will bring their glory and honor into
the city. 27 Nothing evil* will be allowed to enter,
nor anyone who practices shameful idolatry and
dishonesty—but only those whose names are
written in the Lamb's Book of Life.

22 Then the angel showed me a river
with the water of life, clear as crystal, flowing from the throne of God
and of the Lamb. 2 It flowed down the center of
the main street. On each side of the river grew a
tree of life, bearing twelve crops of fruit,* with a
fresh crop each month. The leaves were used for
medicine to heal the nations.
3 No longer will there be a curse upon anything. For the throne of God and of the Lamb
will be there, and his servants will worship him.
4 And they will see his face, and his name will
be written on their foreheads. 5 And there will be
no night there—no need for lamps or sun—for
the Lord God will shine on them. And they will
reign forever and ever.
6 Then the angel said to me, "Everything you
have heard and seen is trustworthy and true. The
Lord God, who inspires his prophets,* has sent his
angel to tell his servants what will happen soon.*"

Jesus Is Coming

7 "Look, I am coming soon! Blessed are those
who obey the words of prophecy written in
this book.*"

21:10 Or *in spirit.* **21:16** Greek *12,000 stadia* [2,220 kilometers]. **21:17** Greek *144 cubits* [65 meters]. **21:19** The identification of some of these gemstones is uncertain. **21:27** Or *ceremonially unclean.* **22:2** Or *twelve kinds of fruit.* **22:6a** Or *The Lord, the God of the spirits of the prophets.* **22:6b** Or *suddenly,* or *quickly;* also in 22:7, 12, 20. **22:7** Or *scroll;* also in 22:9, 10, 18, 19.

sought power and authority by aligning itself with the beast. **22–23:** No special place of worship is necessary, for God is with his people, and his presence means that sources of light are no longer needed. **25–27:** The *gates* of the city are always open to those whose names are in *the Lamb's Book of Life* but closed to any unclean thing or person. The punishment of unbelievers is separation from God.

22:1–5 The River and Tree of Life. John is shown the *river . . . of life* flowing *from the throne of God.* All life comes from God. The river is surrounded by fruit trees with different fruit for each month. God meets all the needs of the new community: food, water, light.

22:6–21 Concluding Warnings and Assurances

John is returned to his own time and instructed to proclaim the revelation to as many people as possible. Time is running out. The events John saw in the visions are soon to take place, and Christ is soon to return. The book of Revelation begins and ends with a blessing on those who remain faithful to God and heed the message contained in it. A final warning is given to anyone who might be tempted to alter the messages contained within the book. Jesus is the originator of all the visions and his words are trustworthy and true. Revelation ends with a benediction reminiscent of those in New Testament letters. The Bible brings us full circle. It begins with creation and ends with the new creation. The end is the beginning.

The Purpose and Value of Human Life

The biblical teaching about God creating us in the divine image points toward the answer to our human quest for purpose. It reminds us that God graciously gives purpose to our lives. But the Bible also speaks to our longing for a sense of value. The good news is that God likewise graciously bestows value on us.

Every human being has value and is to be seen as a person of value. In contrast to many contemporary outlooks, however, the Scriptures ground this evaluation neither in society nor in the human person but squarely in God. The Bible opens with the ringing statement, "In the beginning God created the heavens and the earth" (Gen 1:1), an assertion that finds echo in the Apostles' Creed, which rightly commences with the words, "I believe in God the Father Almighty, Creator of heaven and earth." We could conclude that the term "Creator" capsulates the fundamental relationship between God and the world. To confess God as Creator is to acknowledge that everything owes its existence and being to, and everyone derives her existence and being from, the God of the Bible: "For in him we live and move and exist" (Acts 17:28).

To acknowledge God as Creator is to set forth a theological foundation for understanding and affirming value. If God is Creator, then questions of value must be approached from the perspective of the divine Valuer. If God is Creator, God alone ultimately determines what value is. Furthermore, as the one who values truly, God is the standard for value. And this God calls us to value after the manner by which our Creator values.

What does God value? The first answer must be "all creation." God values everything God made. Consequently, God calls us to view all creatures as valuable. But in acknowledging the value of creation, we must avoid falling into the widely held idea that we are the ones who determine this value. The value of anything does not arise from its utility for us. Nor are other creatures valuable merely insofar as they serve our ends. Instead, all creatures are valuable because God values them. And the loving Creator desires that we—as those created in the divine image—show God's loving character toward all by valuing them after the divine pattern.

Although God values all creation, God places special value on humans. Jesus pointed to this special value when he encouraged his disciples to trust in the gracious heavenly Father rather than to worry about the cares of physical life: "Look at the birds. They don't plant or harvest or store food in barns, for your heavenly Father feeds them. And aren't you far more valuable to him than they are?" (Matt 6:26). God values every human being.

We must note, however, that this assertion brings us again to the theological foundation of value. Contrary to the human-centered appeals widely espoused today, humans do not possess intrinsic value. The basis of our value does not lie in ourselves, in anything we might possess, or even in anything we might do or accomplish. Rather, because we are God's creation, whatever value we have is derived value. Our value arises solely from the gracious judgment of the divine Valuer who values us. As a result, we can never dictate the value of any human, not even ourselves. Instead, God calls us to value one another and ourselves as God does.

8 I, John, am the one who heard and saw all
these things. And when I heard and saw them, I
fell down to worship at the feet of the angel who
showed them to me. 9 But he said, "No, don't worship me. I am a servant of God, just like you and
your brothers the prophets, as well as all who obey
what is written in this book. Worship only God!"
10 Then he instructed me, "Do not seal up the
prophetic words in this book, for the time is near.
11 Let the one who is doing harm continue to do
harm; let the one who is vile continue to be vile;
let the one who is righteous continue to live righteously; let the one who is holy continue to be
holy."

12 "Look, I am coming soon, bringing my
reward with me to repay all people according
to their deeds. 13 I am the Alpha and the
Omega, the First and the Last, the Beginning
and the End."

14 Blessed are those who wash their robes.
They will be permitted to enter through the
gates of the city and eat the fruit from the tree
of life. 15 Outside the city are the dogs—the sorcerers, the sexually immoral, the murderers, the
idol worshipers, and all who love to live a lie.

16 "I, Jesus, have sent my angel to give you

this message for the churches. I am both the source of David and the heir to his throne.* I am the bright morning star."

17 The Spirit and the bride say, "Come." Let
anyone who hears this say, "Come." Let anyone who is thirsty come. Let anyone who desires drink freely from the water of life. 18 And
I solemnly declare to everyone who hears the
words of prophecy written in this book: If anyone adds anything to what is written here, God
will add to that person the plagues described
in this book. 19 And if anyone removes any of
the words from this book of prophecy, God will
remove that person's share in the tree of life
and in the holy city that are described in this
book.
20 He who is the faithful witness to all these
things says, "Yes, I am coming soon!"
Amen! Come, Lord Jesus!
21 May the grace of the Lord Jesus be with
God's holy people.*

22:16 Greek *I am the root and offspring of David.*
22:21 Other manuscripts read *be with all;* still others read *be with all of God's holy people.* Some manuscripts add *Amen.*

THE GEOGRAPHY OF THE BIBLE

The geographical territory encompassed by the Bible (if one includes all identifiable places that are mentioned) includes most countries that border the Mediterranean Sea as well as those to its east. The majority of the narratives of the Hebrew Bible and the Apocrypha, as well as the Gospels in the New Testament, are set in that subregion of the Middle East known as the Levant and now governed by Lebanon, Syria, Jordan, Israel, and the Palestinian Authority. Egypt to the southwest and Mesopotamia (largely modern Iraq) and Persia (Iran) to the northeast are also part of the biblical landscape.

In Mesopotamia—the Greek term for the region between the Euphrates and Tigris Rivers—as in Egypt, urban civilization developed by the fourth millennium BC in the river valleys that provided the essential water for a region where rainfall was at best seasonal and at worst, especially in the case of Egypt, insufficient for agriculture. The regular summer flooding of the Nile Valley enabled the early and continuous existence of a remarkably long-lasting culture in Egypt, which because of its proximity to the Middle East was an important player in that region's history, and the locale for a number of key episodes in biblical narrative, most notably the Exodus. In Mesopotamia the inhabitants had harnessed the two rivers to provide, by means of an elaborate irrigation system, sufficient water for agriculture as well as for consumption. The several successive imperial powers that originated in Mesopotamia were able to use this productive region as a base for expansion, especially to the west, over which they exercised control throughout most of the first millennium BC, until the Hellenistic period.

Although surrounded by vast deserts, there is a narrow stretch of land where agriculture can flourish that extends from the Nile Valley around to the Persian Gulf. The western part of this "fertile crescent," the Levant, has the same environment as much of the rest of the region adjacent to the Mediterranean, which today—as for the last several millennia—is characterized by almost ideal growing conditions for grapes and olives and for raising sheep and goats; grains and legumes and other fruits can also be grown in much of the region. Its climate is moderate, without excessively high or low temperatures for the most part, and with abundant rainfall that occurs mainly during the winter months. Jerusalem, for example, receives on average about 550 mm (22 in) of rain annually, most of it falling between November and February, with January being the rainiest month. Higher elevations to the north receive still more rainfall, and the southern and easternmost regions considerably less.

Within the Levant itself, the primary focus of biblical narratives, there is a wide variety of environments, the result of the geological substructure of the region, which presents dramatic changes in a relatively small area. Moving from west to east, the Mediterranean coast is occupied by a coastal plain that is about 25 km (15 mi) wide in the south but narrows as one moves north. It is interrupted by Mount Carmel, which juts into it, and this plain virtually disappears in northern Israel and Lebanon. The coast itself has several excellent harbors in the north from which the Canaanites and their successors the Phoenicians conducted a flourishing maritime trade. Farther south, the coast is relatively even, and there are few natural harbors. Phoenician influence eventually extended to such port cities as Acco, Dor, Joppa, and Ashkelon, and in the late first century Herod the Great constructed an impressive artificial harbor at Caesarea. Along the coastal plain was a major route, known as "the way of the sea" (Isa 9:1, NRSV), used by traders and by armies of conquest between Egypt and Damascus. This route ran to the point where the coast narrows below Mount Carmel, from which passes led from the coastal plain to the Jezreel (Esdraelon) Valley; from there, several routes could be taken to the northeast.

Adjacent to the coastal plain in the south is an uplift of smaller, gentler hills called "the Shephelah" ("lowland"). As the natural western boundary of the kingdom of Judah in the Iron Age, and of other entities in the same region before and after, it was protected by a number of important cities, including Lachish and Gezer. The Shephelah forms the foothills of the mountainous region immediately to its east. This is the "hill country" of the biblical writers, with higher elevations to the north. For example, Jerusalem, about 55 km (35 mi) east of the Mediterranean, is 760 m (2,500 ft) above sea level, and many mountains in northern Galilee have elevations of over 1,000 m (3,300 ft). The highest peak in the region is Mount Hermon, which is 2,800 m (9,200 ft) high and for that reason is snow-covered year-round. The hill country is the setting for many of the key locales in biblical narrative, including the relatively inaccessible sites of Jerusalem, the capital of the kingdom of Judah (later Judea), and Samaria, the capital of the Northern Kingdom of Israel and later of the province with the same name. This central mountainous ridge is bisected by the broad, fertile Jezreel Valley, the major route to the interior and hence the location of a number of important ancient cities, including Jokneam, Megiddo, Taanach, Ibleam, and Jezreel. Mount Tabor rises from the floor of the Jezreel Valley in splendid isolation to an elevation of 588 m (1,929 ft) above sea level. The village of Nazareth, home of Jesus, is in the hills immediately north of the valley.

To the north of the Jezreel Valley lies Galilee. Because of its abundant springs, Galilee was dotted by settlements from prehistoric times, but it plays little role in biblical narratives until the end of the first millennium BC, when it is the setting both for some of the campaigns of the Maccabees and, in the early first century AD, of the ministry of Jesus in the Gospels.

Just east of this central mountainous region is the Rift Valley. This major depression in the earth's crust extends from southern Turkey into East Africa; in Israel and Jordan it is almost entirely below sea level. Included in it are the Huleh Basin in northern Galilee, 70 m (230 ft) above sea level, where the site of Hazor was a major fortified city from early in the second millennium BC until its destruction by the Assyrians in 732 BC. Some 20 km (12 mi) south of Lake Huleh is the Sea of Chinnereth, or the Sea of Galilee (also called the Sea of Tiberias), a large lake about 20 km (12 mi) long that fills the valley. It lies 210 m (700 ft) below sea level, and is fed by the Jordan River, which flows into it from the north. It is habitat to nearly two dozen species of fish, and the fishing industry has been an important part of the local economy since prehistoric times. Many of the events narrated in the Gospels are set in the many towns and cities near the lake, and the region was a center of resistance against the Romans during the First Jewish Revolt of AD 66–73.

The Jordan River continues its flow south from the Sea of Galilee 105 km (65 mi) to the Dead Sea. The valley itself is about 20 km (12 mi) wide and is entirely below sea level, with a semitropical climate that produces lush vegetation, even though because of its low elevation it receives relatively little rain. Important cities in the valley include Beth-shan (later Scythopolis) in the north and Jericho in the south. The valley was an important subsidiary route, especially during the Roman period, when Jews often avoided the district controlled by the Samaritans between Galilee and Judea.

The Dead Sea, lying 400 m (1,300 ft) below sea level, is the lowest point on the land mass of the earth. Because of evaporation due to high temperatures (a record 51° C [124° F] was measured here), the composition of the water is about 25 percent salt and other minerals, making organic life impossible and giving this lake its ancient name, "the salt sea" (Num 34:3, 12; "Dead Sea," NRSV/NLT). The desolate region that surrounds it is the narrative setting for the legendary cities of Sodom and Gomorrah. On its western shore are Qumran, where the Dead Sea Scrolls were found, and Masada, a palace constructed by Herod that was the last Jewish outpost to be captured in the First Jewish Revolt.

East of the Rift Valley there is a rapid rise to the relatively level Transjordanian plateau to the east, with the elevation of modern Amman (ancient Rabbah, later Philadelphia) at ca. 820 m (2,700 ft) about average. This region too receives sufficient rainfall to sustain agriculture and moreover is watered by two tributaries of the Jordan, the Yarmuk and the Jabbok, and by the Arnon, which flows into the Dead Sea. The northern part of the plateau, biblical Bashan, was famous for its cattle and for its oak forests, and in the Hellenistic and Roman periods was the location of several of the cities of the Decapolis. Traversing the Transjordanian plateau from south to north is a major route, called in the Bible the "King's Highway" (Num 20:17, NRSV), used throughout antiquity as a conduit for the incense and spice trade from Arabia to Damascus. East of the plateau is a vast desert region, a continuation of the Arabian desert that extends northward to the Euphrates Valley, and thus limits the Fertile Crescent on both east and west. Apart from a few oases, especially Tadmor (later Palmyra) northeast of Damascus, this desert was essentially uninhabited in historic times.

South of the hill country of Judah lies the Negev, a region of limited rainfall and hence marginal agriculture. The city of Beersheba is located in the extreme northern Negev, just south of the Judean hill country. The Negev merges into the Sinai peninsula, which is formed by the two northern arms of the Red Sea, separating the Sinai from the North African desert to its west and the Arabian desert to its east.

The small size of this region is out of proportion to its importance in ancient times and to the importance of the biblical texts, which are set in it. West of the Jordan, the traditional boundaries of ancient Israel were Dan in the north and Beersheba in the south, separated by a distance of about 240 km (150 mi). Between these two cities, and between the Mediterranean and the Rift Valley, is a region with an area approximately the same as that of the state of Vermont. From another perspective, Jerusalem is about 55 km (35 mi) east of the Mediterranean and 25 km (16 mi) west of the Dead Sea. In the right conditions, both bodies of water are visible from Jerusalem's hills.

CULTURAL CONTEXTS:
The Ancient Near East and Ancient Israel to the Mid-First Millennium BC

BEGINNINGS

By the time Israel appeared on the stage of the ancient Near East, civilization and the patterns of empires and of the larger shared culture of the Levant were already well established. Before the end of the fourth millennium BC, full urbanization had developed in the great river valleys of Egypt and Mesopotamia. The development of sophisticated technology to exploit the flooding of the Nile and to channel the waters of the Euphrates and Tigris enabled the production of regular food supplies and led to regional hegemonies. In Egypt, oriented about the south-to-north direction of the Nile's flow, this culminated in the unification of Upper (southern) and Lower (northern) Egypt, at the onset of the Early Dynastic Period toward the end of the fourth millennium. In southern Mesopotamia the kings of Sumer ruled that region from a succession of dominant city-states beginning at about the same time.

The stages that had preceded urbanization are prehistoric in the sense that they antedate the development of writing. Archaeologists have been able to trace the slow, and often independent, progress from hunter-gatherer economies throughout the Near East to stable cultures that relied on domesticated crops and animals for their sustenance. Dependable supplies of food led to increases of population and ultimately competition for resources. These factors combined to necessitate specialization of tasks, centralized control, and record keeping. For these purposes writing was invented, again toward the end of the fourth millennium and, once introduced, was widely adopted in different systems in Egypt and Mesopotamia. By 3000 BC, then, written history may be said to have begun.

The result of nearly two centuries of discovery, excavation, and decipherment of ancient texts is that a detailed chronology of the ancient Near East has been established. While there are occasional gaps in the sequence of rulers for Egypt and for the various Mesopotamian city-states, those sequences are relatively complete. For regions peripheral to the centers of power the historical record is more spotty but still substantial. Allowing for minor scholarly disagreements, the chronology is secure and is the framework for the history of the entire ancient Near East, including Israel. Although there remain some small groups of undeciphered texts, including a few in what is apparently the Philistine language, and although much of cuneiform literature is still underground, it is unlikely that new discoveries will require substantial revision of our current understanding of the essential chronology of the ancient Near East.

Nor is the knowledge of the historical record restricted to kings and princes. Hundreds of thousands of nonelite texts have been found. These are not great myths and royal inscriptions but mundane business and commercial records that shed valuable light on the lives of ordinary men and women, and have begun to make possible a reconstruction of the social world of the ancient Near East.

Ancient cultures were as intrigued as we are by beginnings, and they constructed elaborate myths to explain their own prehistory. The establishment of the natural and social orders is typically presented in these myths as the work of a deity, usually the principal god or goddess of the political entity in which they were written. Both Egyptian and Mesopotamian literatures have a large number of such creation myths, many features of which have parallels in biblical traditions. Like their more powerful neighbors to the southwest and northeast, the ancient Israelites had their own accounts of origins, some of which were ultimately collected and edited in the book of Genesis. The early chapters of Genesis deal with prehistory and are largely mythical. In these Israelite expressions of the origins of the world, of society, and of civilization, the principal agent is the god of Israel. And, although intended as the prologue to a larger historical narrative, they are not historical in any modern sense; that is, they do not accurately represent what the archaeological record shows to have taken place, whether in terms of chronology, or the origin of species, or a universal flood.

Egypt and Mesopotamia have their own complex histories during the third millennium, now relatively well known thanks to textual and archaeological data. In the Levant this is the period known as the Early Bronze Age, when northern Syria was largely in the orbit of Mesopotamia, and Egypt exercised direct control over Palestine. For complex reasons not fully understood, toward the end of the third millennium Egypt experienced some internal disruption, reflected in the decline of city-states in Palestine but not in Syria farther to the north. By 2000 BC, however, centralized control had been reestablished, and the textual and artifactual evidence is abundant. Trade flourished, as is indicated by both the archaeological record and commercial and diplomatic correspondence among larger urban centers, and between them and Mesopotamia and Egypt. The Levant was spanned by a cultural continuum, with Syria and northern Canaan being more closely linked with Mesopotamia, and southern Canaan with Egypt. Canaan itself had a relatively homogeneous culture, and its inhabitants, especially in rural and village settings, went about their lives with relatively few changes despite the struggles of the urban centers with each other. From as far back as the end of the fourth millennium, and into the first, there appears to have been continuity of population whose patterns of material culture develop rather than being replaced by successive waves of invaders, as earlier historical reconstructions suggested.

It is in this larger context that Israel placed its own beginnings, centered on the lives of four generations of ancestors, the families of Abraham and Sarah, of Isaac and Rebekah, and of Jacob and Leah, Rachel, Bilhah, and Zilpah, and their offspring.

THE HISTORICITY OF THE ANCESTRAL NARRATIVES IN GENESIS

In the biblical account of the origins of Israel, narratives concerning Israel's ancestors in Genesis 12–50 follow the mythic material in chapters 1–11. The chronology of the narratives themselves is set in the early second millennium BC, but there are no direct connections between the biblical traditions and nonbiblical sources. No person or event known from Egyptian, Mesopotamian, or other sources is even mentioned in the biblical narrative.

At the relatively few points where the Bible does name rulers (as in Gen 14; 20:2; 26:8), none of them is found in any nonbiblical sources. Moreover, at many points in the narrative the Bible is tantalizingly vague. If the biblical writers had just named, for example, the pharaoh who took Sarah into his house (Gen 12:15), or the pharaoh in whose court Joseph rose to power (Gen 41), we would at least know *when* the biblical writers thought those events took place and could thus correlate them with Egyptian chronology.

The biblical narratives themselves are the result of a lengthy and complicated process of formation, transmission, and editing. Although the reconstruction of that process is hypothetical, there is no doubt that the process itself has caused the inclusion of a large number of anachronisms. These reflect the times when the transmission and editing took place rather than the times in which the narratives are presumably set.

As a result of these factors, not surprisingly, scholars are divided on the question of historicity, with proposed dates for the ancestors of Israel, if in fact they even existed, spanning the entire second millennium BC. A cautious positive assessment would be at best a convergence of possibilities. Allowing for anachronisms, the data are not inconsistent with the Middle to Late Bronze Ages (ca. 2000–1200), with some clues pointing to earlier rather than later in that time span. These clues are admittedly indirect, and include the forms of personal names used and the identification of the god of the ancestors as El (see Exod 6:3), also known in texts from Ugarit in northwest Syria as the head of the Canaanite pantheon. The account of Joseph's elevation to a position of prominence in the Egyptian court is not incompatible with the rise to power of the Hyksos, the Fifteenth Dynasty rulers of Semitic origin who controlled much of Lower Egypt at the end of the Middle Bronze Age (ca. 1650–1550).

Yet most of the details of the lives of the ancestors of Israel, both as pastoral seminomads and as periodically migrating to Egypt, fit not only the mid-second millennium but other times as well. Biblical writings probably do preserve some authentic historical memories, but these have been so refracted by the processes of transmission and the idealization of the ancestors that it is impossible to designate any of the individuals mentioned in Genesis as historical or to establish anything resembling a precise chronology.

THE HISTORICITY OF THE EXODUS FROM EGYPT

As with the ancestral narratives in Genesis, there is no direct connection between biblical traditions and other ancient sources. Egyptian records contain no mention of the major individuals and events of the narrative in Exodus 1–15: Moses, Aaron, the plagues, and the defeat of the Egyptian army at the sea are completely absent from the extensive documentation we have for ancient Egypt. Again, the biblical sources are frustratingly unspecific. Neither the pharaoh "who did not know Joseph" (Exod 1:8, NRSV) nor the pharaoh of the Exodus itself (Exod 5–15) is named. The only precise detail in the narrative is the store cities named in Exodus 1:11, but both their precise location and the dates when they were founded and occupied are uncertain, and their inclusion could also be anachronistic. In addition, biblical chronology is both vague and inconsistent. Moreover, as with the ancestral narratives in Genesis 12–50, the narrative has been shaped by centuries of transmission and redaction. Finally, although the importance of the Exodus is evident from the amount of space devoted to the generation of the Exodus (the books of Exodus through Deuteronomy), the narrative framework was supplemented by the attachment of large chunks of legal and ritual material from subsequent periods. Once again, then, it is hardly surprising that scholars have divergent views about the date and even the historicity of the Exodus and of its principal characters. And, again, we do best to speak of a convergence of probabilities based on indirect evidence.

The first fixed datum, one of great importance, is a victory stele of Pharaoh Merneptah (1213–1203). In it he claims to have defeated various enemies in Canaan, including the identifiable cities of Gezer, Yanoam, and Ashkelon, and in the same geographical region, a group identified as Israel. Whether the victory celebrated on the stela is as complete as claimed, it is clear that by the end of the thirteenth century the Egyptians knew of the existence of a geopolitical entity called Israel in the land of Canaan. Thus, the Exodus, or some movement of Hebrews out of Egypt, and their entry into Canaan, where they formed at least part of the group that called itself Israel, must have occurred before that date.

The biblical narrative is composite, and when critically analyzed suggests that what the Bible presents as a single episode may in fact have been several, and that more than one group of "Hebrews" eventually moved from Egypt to Palestine, probably entering it at several different places. Yet admittedly most of the details of the account of the forced labor of the Hebrews and of the glimpses of the Egyptian court that we get in the narratives would fit almost any period in ancient Egyptian history.

A majority of modern scholars, but by no means all, date the central episode, associated with Moses, to the thirteenth century, during the reign of Rameses II (1279–1213). An earlier date, toward the beginning of the Late Bronze Age, would link the Exodus with the expulsion of the Hyksos Dynasties from Egypt in the mid-sixteenth century and better fits the chronology in the biblical text, which dates the Exodus to 480 years prior to the construction of the Solomonic Temple in the mid-tenth century (1 Kgs 6:1). This correlation was first proposed by the first-century AD historian Josephus and has many modern adherents. Among the arguments against it is the absence of any mention of Israel in the land of Canaan before the Merneptah inscription. This is especially true in the case of the Amarna Letters, which are diplomatic correspondence from the fourteenth century between the Egyptian court and the rulers of city-states in Canaan. Furthermore, the biblical accounts of the period after the entry into the land found in the books of Joshua and Judges contain no hint of Egyptian presence in the land, although both archaeological and written sources indicate that it was significant throughout the Late Bronze Age. It thus seems more probable to most current scholars that the Exodus took place during the thirteenth century BC.

That some exodus took place is a responsible inference, given the persistence of the Exodus tradition in the Bible and its presence in the earliest biblical poetry (notably Exod 15), and some smaller details, such as the Egyptian names of Moses, Aaron, and Phinehas. The event must have involved fewer people than the exaggerated biblical numbers (see Exod 12:37) indicate, and may have constituted little more than the escape of a relatively small group of Hebrews from forced labor in the eastern Nile delta. Given the lack of historical data it is impossible to say more.

That group, whatever its size, interpreted its escape as the direct intervention of the deity Yahweh on its behalf, to be celebrated in hymns and magnified in importance as it was told and retold. When the group eventually entered Canaan, at a time when there was no centralized power to oppose it, it joined with others and eventually became the twelve-tribe confederation of Israel.

THE EARLY HISTORY OF ISRAEL IN THE LAND OF CANAAN

Perhaps no period in the history of Israel is more controversial than the first two centuries of the Iron Age. The beginning and end of this era are framed by two synchronisms: the mention of Israel in the Merneptah Stele in the late thirteenth century , and the campaign of the pharaoh Shishak in Palestine in 925, an event documented both in Egyptian sources and in the Bible. During the intervening three centuries, according to the chronology accepted by the majority of scholars, Israel developed from a loose confederation of tribes into a relatively stable dynastic monarchy. But of the principal events and individuals that figure in biblical narratives, none occur in other sources. Once more, a historical reconstruction must be inferential.

One reconstruction of the beginning of this period that was dominant from the early to the mid-twentieth century is that of conquest. The book of Joshua describes how the large group of Israelites crossed the Jordan under the leadership of Joshua and in a series of swift and relentless campaigns defeated the kings of the major Canaanite cities and annihilated most of the indigenous population. This view seemed to be confirmed by the presence of destruction layers at key sites, all dated to the very end of the Late Bronze Age.

Reexcavation of many of those sites and more refined ceramic chronology, however, made it clear that some of the sites had not in fact been occupied at that time, and that the destructions were not all contemporaneous. Moreover, the opening chapters of the book of Judges presented a very different picture. While some Israelite tribes were apparently successful in defeating their Canaanite neighbors, many others coexisted alongside them. This is apparently confirmed even in the book of Joshua, where such Canaanite groups as the family of Rahab (Josh 6:25) and the Gibeonites (Josh 9) were incorporated into Israel. Thus the conquest model has largely been abandoned by scholars, but no other reconstruction has gained general acceptance.

One plausible scenario is to combine elements of various models to suggest that Israel as we know it emerged in the land of Canaan and was made up of diverse groups. One of these was the Exodus group, whose allegiance to the god who had brought them out of Egypt, Yahweh, would become the central religious tenet of the confederation. They were joined by others, some who were apparently their kin who had never gone down to Egypt, and some who may have been Canaanites disaffected from the centers of power. These disparate elements united in a confederation or league, whose primary principles of sole worship of Yahweh and mutual support were expressed in a social compact or covenant. The elements are called tribes, and they are associated with specific subregions in the land. While the number of twelve tribes is constant, both the names of the tribes and the territories with which they were associated shifted in response to historical vicissitudes. The religious symbol of the confederation was a movable shrine, the Ark of the Covenant, which seems to have been based at different tribal centers at different times. The confederation was decentralized, with no overarching authority, and the tribes were relatively independent. In time of crisis, however, tribes were expected to come to the assistance of a beleaguered member, as in the very ancient poem in Judges 5, or to punish one of their own for breach of the compact, as in the account of the Benjaminite war in Judges 19–21. In situations like these a volunteer militia was mustered.

This reconstruction takes into account a variety of biblical data that are admittedly embedded in a later historical work, the Deuteronomistic History. It also incorporates recent archaeological evidence, including both significant elements of cultural continuity between the Late Bronze Age and the Iron Age, and the proliferation of small rural settlements in the hill country both west and east of the Jordan. Not all of these settlements would have been Israelite, nor would tribal territory necessarily entail complete control. A number of urban centers remained outside the confederation, and Israel did not achieve total control of the promised land until the end of the eleventh century.

At the beginning of the Iron Age (ca. 1200 BC), shortly after the likely date for the Exodus, another group had arrived in Canaan. These were the Philistines, one component of the "Sea Peoples" well documented in Egyptian sources and in the archaeological record. Of Aegean origin, they had repeatedly failed in their attempts to invade Egypt, and one or more of these Sea Peoples, including the Philistines, settled in Canaan. According to the biblical account, they formed a pentapolis in the five cities of Gaza, Ashkelon, Ashdod, Gath, and Ekron, and four of these cities that have been securely identified (Gath is the exception) show a remarkably homogenous material culture at this time.

The biblical account, in Judges 13–16 and in 1 and 2 Samuel, and the archaeological record are in considerable agreement. The Philistines had a superior technology, especially in metallurgy (see 1 Sam 13:20) and military hardware, and a professional standing army. By the mid-eleventh century they had considerably expanded their territory to the north and east, and their presence is evident at important centers beyond it, including Beth-shan in the Jordan Valley, and at military outposts in the heart of Judah, the dominant southern tribe, and in the north as well. The Philistines and the Israelites were thus on a collision course, both vying for control of the same region, and Israel's survival was at stake.

THE UNITED MONARCHY (CA. 1020–928 BC)

The emergence of Israel as a nation-state is part of a larger pattern of the development of regional geopolitical and ethnic entities throughout the region, such as those of the Edomites, Moabites, and Ammonites in Transjordan, the Arameans in Damascus and other centers in central and northern Syria, and the Phoenicians in Tyre. In the case of Israel, there was a particular stimulus. At least in part because of the Philistine threat, toward the end of the eleventh century Israel profoundly changed its form of government from a loose confederation of tribes to a monarchy. The first ruler, Saul, seems to have been more a military chief than a full-fledged king. Despite initial successes, he was unable to check the Philistine advance and died in a battle with them deep in Israel's territory in the Jezreel Valley. He was succeeded by a former commander in his army, David, who moved swiftly to contain the Philistines within their original territory and to unite Israel around himself and a newly chosen capital, Jerusalem.

Biblical historians describe additional military successes, which enabled David, and his son and successor Solomon, to subject kingdoms adjacent to Israel to vassal status, including the Edomites, the Moabites, the Ammonites in Transjordan, and the Arameans in Damascus. Whether the extent of the territory controlled by David and Solomon is as large as biblical sources suggest is questionable. Clearly the biblical historians have magnified the period of the United Monarchy, the reigns of David and Solomon, viewing them in many respects as an ideal age, made possible by divine grant. Underlying the sometimes hyperbolic biblical accounts, however, is authentic historical memory of increasing centralized control and concomitant administrative complexity, a picture indirectly confirmed by the archaeological record. When textual and archaeological data are added to the synchronisms between the Israelite monarchy and those of its neighbors, beginning in the tenth century, there is little doubt that the outlines of the biblical narrative are essentially correct.

The most important of these synchronisms comes just after the death of Solomon. The Egyptian pharaoh Shishak (Sheshonq I) undertook a campaign in western Asia in 925, a date based on established Egyptian chronology. Mentioned in 1 Kings 14:25–26 (cf. 2 Chr 12:2–9), this campaign is further documented in Egyptian sources and is confirmed by destruction layers at key cities in Israel. This synchronism is the basis for the chronology of the first three kings of Israel, Saul (ca. 1025–1005), David (1005–965), and Solomon (968–928, allowing for a coregency with David at the beginning of his reign).

The biblical account of the reigns of these three kings, found in 1 and 2 Samuel and 1 Kings 1–11, is shaped by theological concerns and also displays a pervading interest in the characters of the narrative—the tragically inadequate Saul, the heroic David, the ambitious but flawed Solomon—and in the intrigues of the royal court. But it is also significantly different from narratives about earlier periods in Israel's history. Divine intervention is minimal, with most events taking place largely on the human plane. Moreover, a careful reading of the biblical text discloses a myriad of archival and other details that can be correlated with the archaeological record and are consistent with the framework of events presupposed by the narrative. Thus, the skepticism of some modern historians, who argue that the biblical accounts of the United Monarchy are fictional retroversions from a later time, seems unwarranted.

David also seems to have initiated the transformation of the monarchy into a dynastic kingship, which, consistent with other Near Eastern models, was promulgated as the result of divine choice. With the establishment of the monarchy came social and religious innovation. The older structures of the decentralized premonarchic confederation were now coopted by royal institutions. The Ark of the Covenant was enshrined in the Temple in Jerusalem built by Solomon, providing in effect divine sanction for the monarchy. Priests became royal appointees, and there was a growing movement toward centralization of worship in the capital. Yet this centralized administration formed a kind of overlay, a veneer, on the social systems of the nation as a whole. Individuals still identified themselves as members of a family, clan, and tribe, and disputes between them were usually settled at the local level. Apart from the requirement of paying taxes and providing personnel for royal projects and for the army, life in the villages probably proceeded much as it had for centuries.

The establishment of the monarchy, however, had entailed the formation of an elite, wealthy class. Life in the capital of Jerusalem and, after the split of the kingdom into two, in the northern capital of Samaria as well, was characterized by conspicuous consumption. This is evident in the accounts of Solomon's court (1 Kgs 4:22–28; 10:14–22), and in the description of the Temple and royal palace complex he constructed (1 Kgs 6–7). That the extravagances documented in these accounts are not entirely an exaggeration is evident from archaeological data at Samaria, and at royal cities such as Megiddo, Hazor, Gezer, and Dan. With the concentration of political power in the hands of a ruling aristocracy came abuse. One of the constants of the biblical traditions is opposition to the exploitation of the poorer classes. This opposition was frequently expressed in prophetic rebukes of the aristocracy, as in the admittedly legendary traditions concerning Elijah (2 Kgs 20), and in the books of the prophets themselves. While their own relationship to the centers of power was not always antagonistic, prophets such as Amos, Isaiah, and Micah in the eighth century and Jeremiah in the late seventh to early sixth centuries were harsh in their denunciation of social injustice. In a sense they were conservatives, even perhaps reactionaries, insisting that the older premonarchic tradition of covenant was still binding, a tradition that commanded not only exclusive worship of Yahweh but also fair treatment of every Israelite.

THE DIVIDED MONARCHIES (CA. 928 TO THE LATE SEVENTH CENTURY BC)

The union of north and south had been fragile, even during the United Monarchy, and it disintegrated at Solomon's death. The reason implied in 1 Kings 12 is the northerners' anger at the cost of the extravagances of the capital, and this must have been at least part of the motivation. Solomon's son and successor Rehoboam was unable to gain the allegiance of the ten northern tribes, who seceded and formed a separate kingdom. This inaugurates the period of the Divided Monarchy, the two kingdoms of Israel in the north and Judah in the south. The dynasty that David had established remained in power in Judah for nearly four centuries, while Israel was ruled by a succession of royal families, many of whose rulers came to power in military coups. The parts were less than their sum had been, and the two kingdoms had mixed relations, sometimes friendly, sometimes hostile. Neither was able to control effectively the regions that bordered them, and the Davidic empire, such as it was, ceased to exist.

Changes on the larger international scene would increasingly affect these two kingdoms. Pressure from a revived Egypt is already evident in the above-mentioned campaign of Shishak to the north in 925. Meanwhile, in northern Mesopotamia, the kingdom of Assyria had consolidated its control over Babylon in the south and adjacent regions to the north and east, and by the ninth century was poised to expand into the Levant. At this point the fairly complete Assyrian annals enable the construction of a relatively exact chronology and provide numerous synchronisms with biblical texts. Beginning with Ahab, king of Israel in the mid-ninth century, many of the rulers of both Israel and Judah are mentioned in Assyrian sources, an indication of the growing Assyrian interest in the region and a coincidence of ominous significance.

For the Assyrians were establishing an empire, a process that reached its zenith with the Assyrian king Esarhaddon's subjugation of Egypt in 671. They accomplished this by virtue of a technologically sophisticated army, which in relatively rapid advance overwhelmed the smaller kingdoms of Syria and Palestine, usually incorporating their territories into the empire as provinces and deporting the elite of their populations to other regions. By the late eighth century this subjugation was virtually complete. The Syrian kingdoms had been taken, including that of the Arameans in Damascus in 732. In 722 Samaria fell, its ruling class was exiled to Assyria, and the Northern Kingdom of Israel became an Assyrian province. Judah's territory was curtailed, and in part because of the remote location of Jerusalem, was allowed to exist in vassal status. Toward the end of the eighth century the Judean king Hezekiah attempted to reassert Judean independence but was ruthlessly quashed by the Assyrian king Sennacherib in a campaign (701), which is well documented in both biblical and Assyrian sources. Jerusalem avoided destruction only by payment of a heavy tribute, and the Davidic dynasty survived.

Beginning with Amos and Hosea in the mid-eighth century, the prophets, and the later authors of the Deuteronomistic History (Josh–2 Kgs), interpreted these events as a deserved punishment inflicted by Yahweh on his rebellious people. For them, the repeated experiences of attack, siege, and exile were ultimately caused not by the inexorable progress of the Assyrian armies but by divine agency, imposing the fulfillment of the curses attached to the covenant.

THE END OF THE KINGDOM OF JUDAH (LATE SEVENTH TO EARLY SIXTH CENTURIES BC)

By the late seventh century the Assyrian Empire was overextended; it was unable to prevent first independence and eventual overthrow by a resurgent Babylonia to its south. The Babylonians captured the Assyrian capital of Nineveh in 612 and in effect took over the Assyrian Empire. In the initial years, Egypt and Judah attempted to take advantage of the transfer of power by reasserting their independence. This was the time of the reign of the Judean king Josiah (640–609), whom biblical sources compare to David and whose accomplishments are magnified like those of his illustrious predecessor. While it seems likely that Judah was able to reestablish control over some of the territory to the north and west that had been under direct Assyrian rule, its autonomy, such as it was, was short-lived. After Josiah's death in battle at Megiddo in 609, in a failed attempt to prevent the Egyptians from moving north to reinforce the tottering Assyrians, Judah was again reduced to the status of a vassal, first to Egypt, and then, by the end of the seventh century, to Babylon. Caught between two greater powers, the Judean kings Jehoiakim and Zedekiah successively allied themselves with Egypt, which proved to be the weaker partner. Under Nebuchadrezzar (or Nebuchadnezzar) II, the Babylonians laid siege to Jerusalem in 597 and 586, in the second instance destroying the city and ending the Davidic dynasty.

It was the end of an era. Despite the extravagant propaganda of the royal establishment, neither the Davidic dynasty nor its capital city were impregnable. Jerusalem was destroyed, its dynastic Temple burned, and its population decimated by death and exile. Autonomous control of the promised land became only a memory. And despite partial restoration later in the sixth century, exile in Babylon forever transformed the religion of Judah-Judaism. From this point on, a significant proportion of Jews would be living outside the promised land, without king, Temple, or priesthood.

CULTURAL CONTEXTS:
THE PERSIAN AND HELLENISTIC PERIODS

THE PERSIAN PERIOD (539–333 BC)

The Babylonian exile and the period of Persian domination that followed was a time of great transformation for Judean institutions, religious practices, and culture, but it was equally a time in which the fundamental continuity with preexilic traditions was reaffirmed and secured. When Nebuchadnezzar put down the rebellion of Judah in 586 BC, he exiled to Babylonia a portion of the population, including the ruling class and the skilled artisans. Most, however, remained in Judah, where a subsistence economy was soon reestablished. Although the system of regular sacrifices at the Temple was disrupted, the ruined Temple remained a focus for religious observances. The book of Lamentations may preserve liturgical poems used on days commemorating the destruction of Jerusalem and its Temple. Little is known about the circumstances of those who went into exile, although it appears that the exiles were settled in a number of local communities in Babylonia, where they were able to oversee their own internal and cultural affairs under the leadership of Jewish elders and prophets (see Ezek; Isa 40–55).

The conquest of Babylon by the Persian king Cyrus the Great in 539 BC brought significant changes. In keeping with his policy of respecting the various deities worshiped throughout the empire, a decree by Cyrus in 538 (see Ezra 1:1–4; 6:1–5) authorized the rebuilding of the Temple in Jerusalem and the return of the Temple vessels captured by Nebuchadnezzar. In addition, Cyrus allowed any of the exiles who wished to return to Judah to do so. Within the exilic community in Babylon the anonymous prophet known as "Second Isaiah" (Isa 40–55) strongly supported Cyrus and urged the exiles to return to Judah. Although historical sources are few and not always easy to interpret, it appears that only a small minority of the exiles and their descendants returned to Judah, most choosing to remain in Babylonia. This latter group became the nucleus of a large and highly significant Jewish diaspora community (Jews of "the dispersion," that is, living outside Palestine), which strongly influenced the development of Judaism and Jewish culture during the following centuries.

Despite the decree of Cyrus, the Temple in Jerusalem was not rebuilt until 520–515 BC. The reasons for the delay were various. Persian control over the western territories may actually have been tentative until after the Persians conquered Egypt in 525. The economy of Yehud (the name by which the Persian province of Judah was known) was weak, and there appears to have been friction between the population that had remained in the land and the small but powerful group who returned from exile with the authorization and financial backing of the Persian king. Conflicts with the neighboring territories of Samaria and Geshur and Ammon in Transjordan also complicated the situation. Within the Bible the prophetic books of Haggai and Zechariah and portions of Ezra 1–6 refer to this period, but these sources have to be read and interpreted critically, for they are neither consistent with one another nor easy to understand on their own terms. At least during the early part of Persian rule the governors of Judah appear to have been prominent Jews from the diaspora community, one of whom, Zerubbabel, was actually a member of the Davidic royal family. The province of Yehud itself was very small, consisting of Jerusalem and the territory surrounding it within a radius of about 24–32 km (15–20 mi).

Once the Temple was rebuilt, it became the nucleus of the restored community, and consequently a focus of conflict (Isa 56–66; Mal). The high priestly family, which had also returned from the diaspora, became very powerful, and at least on occasion was in conflict with the governor appointed by the Persian king. Although the details are often not clear, there appears to have been continuing conflict during the fifth century between those Jews whose ancestors had been in exile and those whose ancestors had remained in the land. Those who returned from the diaspora styled themselves the "children of the exile" and referred rather contemptuously to the rest as "people of the land," as though their very status as Jews was in question. In fact, the question of the limits of the community was one of the most contentious issues of the period, reflected both in the controversy over mixed marriages between Jewish men and ethnically foreign women (Ezra 10; Neh 13) and also in conflicts within the Jewish community over who had the right to claim the traditional identity as descendants of "Abraham" and "Israel" (see Isa 63:16 and more generally "Third Isaiah," Isa 56–66). Although the conflicts between various contending groups in early Persian period Yehud are largely cast in religious terms, there is no question that they were also in part socioeconomic (see Neh 5). All of these conflicts and efforts toward redefinition of the community, however, took place within the reality of Persian imperial control. Thus it is not by accident that the two most prominent figures involved in various reforms of mid-fifth century Yehud, Ezra and Nehemiah, were diaspora Jews of high standing, carrying out tasks that had been specifically authorized by the Persian kings.

Because this was a period of self-conscious reconstruction, it was also a time of immense literary activity, as traditional materials were collected, revised, and edited, and new works composed. Although much of the Pentateuch may have existed in various forms during the time of the monarchy, it was probably reworked during the Persian period into something close to its final form. Indeed, some have suggested that this revision may have been undertaken under the sponsorship of the Persian government, reflecting Persia's interest in achieving stability throughout its empire by means of religious and legal reforms in the provinces. Although a history of Israel and Judah known as the Deuteronomistic History (Deuteronomy through 2 Kings) had been composed during the latter years of the monarchy and updated during the Exile, a new version of that history, 1–2 Chronicles, was prepared during the Persian period (ca. 350 BC). It clearly reflects the concerns of the postexilic community, focusing almost exclusively on the history of Judah and giving particular emphasis to the institution of the Temple. The books of Ezra and Nehemiah interpret events from the decree of Cyrus in 538 until the late fifth century.

In addition to the prophetic books composed at this time (Isa 56–66, Hag, Zech, Mal, and perhaps Joel), there is evidence that the texts of older prophets were also edited and reinterpreted. Psalmody had been an important element of worship at the First Temple, but appears to have taken on an even more significant role in the Second Temple. Although the expansion and revision of the book of Psalms may have continued until well into the Hellenistic or even Roman period, an important shaping of the Psalter, perhaps including its division into five "books," was part of Persian period activity. Wisdom writing, too, flourished during this time. The book of Job, parts of the book of Proverbs, and perhaps Ecclesiastes were likely composed then.

THE HELLENISTIC PERIOD (333–63 BC)

The westward expansion of the Persian Empire into the area of Asia Minor had brought it into conflict with Greece, since many of the cities of Asia Minor that came under Persian control had been founded and populated by Greeks. Twice the Persians had even invaded the Greek mainland but were defeated on both occasions. Eventually, Philip of Macedon developed a plan to free the Greek cities of Asia Minor from Persian domination. Although he died before he could undertake the campaign, it was taken up by his son Alexander the Great in 334 BC. Alexander, however, did not stop with the accomplishment of that initial goal. In 333 he continued down the Phoenician coast, subduing any city that resisted, conquered Egypt, then turned to the Persian heartland, defeating Darius III, the last Persian emperor, in 331. Alexander continued his conquest into the eastern reaches of the Persian Empire before returning in 324 to Babylon, which he apparently intended to establish as the capital of the empire he now controlled. He died in 323, however, before he could successfully organize his enormous territory. After Alexander's death, his generals fought for control of portions of the empire. By 301 an agreement gave Egypt to Ptolemy, and Mesopotamia and Syria-Palestine to Seleucus. Ptolemy, however, occupied Palestine and southern Syria. Through a series of five wars extending over more than a hundred years, the Ptolemaic kings managed to hold onto their Palestinian territory, finally losing it to the Seleucids in 198 BC.

Jerusalem had surrendered to Alexander in 333 and was relatively undisturbed by the events of his conquest. Samaria, too, surrendered, but rebelled in 332 and was severely punished, its inhabitants killed or sold into slavery, and the city refounded as a Macedonian military colony. Documents belonging to a group of Samaritans who fled and were later tracked down and killed by Alexander's troops have been excavated from the Wadi Daliyeh in the Jordan Valley. In contrast to the relatively settled conditions following Alexander's conquest, however, the dispute between the Ptolemies and the Seleucids over control of Palestine had serious consequences for Jerusalem and Judea. Not only did the wars sometimes affect Judean territory, but the nation's leaders had to make difficult choices concerning which power to support. The conflict between pro-Ptolemaic and pro-Seleucid factions within the Judean community was a significant factor in internal politics during the third century BC.

Although the high priest was the primary representative of the Judeans, the Ptolemaic system of government and taxation had significant effects on the power structure of the country. The Ptolemies considered their territories primarily as a source of revenue. Rather than collecting funds directly, they employed "tax farmers," often local persons who bought the right to collect taxes for a specified area. Their profit was the difference between the amount they raised and the amount they had pledged to the government. Some of these positions were quite lucrative. Moreover, the Ptolemies also engaged prominent landowners to keep the peace as the heads of locally organized military villages. The Jewish historian Josephus preserves a long account of the Tobiad family, which served the Ptolemaic government in both capacities. From his lively narrative one has a sense not only of the power and wealth such positions could afford but also of the dangers and conflict they often entailed.

Culturally, the most significant effect of Ptolemaic rule was the establishment of a large Jewish diaspora community in Egypt, centered in the new city of Alexandria, founded by Alexander the Great. Jews had often migrated to Egypt during times of economic or political trouble (see Jer 42–44). In the fifth century a Jewish military colony in the service of the Persian army was established at Elephantine (near modern Aswan). They had their own temple, though they remained in correspondence with Jerusalem concerning various religious matters, including the proper celebration of Passover and assistance in securing Persian permission for the rebuilding of the Elephantine temple after it was destroyed by local Egyptians. The various Aramaic documents found there (letters, contracts, marriage documents, records of legal disputes, etc.) provide an important glimpse into the daily life of this Jewish community in Egypt. Among the papyri was a copy of the book of Ahikar, a legendary story about an official in the Assyrian court at the time of Sennacherib and Esarhaddon (late eighth to early seventh century). Although the story was not Jewish in origin, it became popular among the Jews. The book of Tobit in the Apocrypha makes reference to Ahikar, even calling him Tobit's nephew (Tob 1:21–22).

The Hellenistic-era Egyptian diaspora, however, was much larger and more influential than the previous small communities of Jews living in Egypt. Its origins are not clear, but during the initial Ptolemaic conquest of Palestine, Ptolemy I apparently captured Jerusalem and took many prisoners back to Egypt, where they settled. Later many other Jews migrated there, presumably for economic reasons. The community continued to grow, both in numbers and in prosperity, until in the Roman period the Jewish population numbered in the hundreds of thousands, including many wealthy and prominent families.

By the middle of the third century BC, the Jewish community in Egypt had translated the books of the Torah (Genesis–Deuteronomy) into Greek, and over the next century or so, the other books of the Hebrew Bible were also translated. A legendary account of this project is contained in the Letter of Aristeas. According to that narrative, the impetus for the project came from the king himself, Ptolemy II Philadelphus (285–246 BC), who wished to have a copy for the library of Alexandria. Seventy-two Jewish translators were brought to Egypt from Jerusalem for the task; hence the translation came to be known as the Septuagint, from the Greek word for "seventy." Scholars largely reject this account as unhistorical and maintain that the translation was undertaken for the religious needs of a Jewish community that no longer understood Hebrew.

In addition to the translation of the Scriptures, the Jewish diaspora in Egypt produced a rich and varied literature in Greek. One should not assume, however, that every Jewish writing in Greek originated in Alexandria, for during the Hellenistic period Greek became the most important international language. Educated Jews in Palestine and in the eastern diaspora were nearly as likely to speak Greek as their counterparts in Egypt. Nevertheless, Alexandria remained unparalleled in the richness of its intellectual culture.

Throughout the Hellenistic world the increasing contact between different ethnic groups led to a new self-consciousness within communities about their own historical traditions and how these traditions related to those of other peoples. Thus historiographical writing, from the scholarly to the popular, became an important type of literary activity. In the late third century BC, an Alexandrian Jew named Demetrius investigated the chronologies of the biblical tradition, attempting to explain apparent contradictions and logical inconsistencies. A more entertaining work is Eupolemus's *Concerning the Kings in Judea*. A friend of Judas Maccabeus (see p. 1576), Eupolemus retold the biblical narrative with many embellishments and legendary details in an attempt to glorify Israel's traditions and accomplishments. In Eupolemus's history Moses appears as a culture-bringer, the inventor of the alphabet, which the Phoenicians and the Greeks later borrowed. Eupolemus particularly emphasizes the power and influence of the Israelite kingdom under David and Solomon, as well as the splendor of the Solomonic Temple. Not only was the Temple decorated with gifts from the kings of Tyre and Egypt, but Solomon reciprocated, sending a golden pillar to the temple of Zeus in Tyre.

The tendency to make connections between one's own traditions and those of other ethnic groups and to claim priority in the arts of civilization is reflected in the highly legendary history written in the second century BC by an anonymous Samaritan. He identifies Enoch with Greek Atlas and claims that Abraham was the inventor of astrology, which he taught to the Egyptians when he sojourned there. A similar tendency is evident in the work of Artapanus in whose history Moses becomes the inventor of the technologies basic to civilization. Moreover, this Moses serves as a general in the Egyptian army, organizes Egyptian religion, and comes to be treated virtually as a god by the Egyptians, who identify him with Hermes (the Greek equivalent of the Egyptian god Thoth). The interest of Egyptian Jews in the biblical figure of Joseph is reflected in the romance *Joseph and Asenath,* which tells the story of Joseph's marriage to the Egyptian noblewoman Asenath. She is depicted as a model convert to Judaism, and the story depicts some of the complications that attended Jewish-Gentile relations in Hellenistic Egypt.

Jewish poetic works composed in Greek also reflect a blending of cultural traditions. The Hellenistic genre of poetry praising cities and countries is represented in the work of Theodotus and Philo the epic poet, who wrote poems about Shechem and Jerusalem, respectively. Even more ambitious was the work of Ezekiel the tragedian, whose play *The Exodus* retold the account of Exodus 1–15 in a style influenced by the Greek dramatists Aeschylus and Euripedes.

Greek philosophy, too, left its imprint on Hellenistic Jewish culture. As late as the second century BC an Alexandrian Jew named Aristobulus produced a philosophical commentary on the Torah in which he claimed that the law of Moses anticipated many of the fundamental tenets of Greek philosophy and that the Greek philosophers Pythagoras, Socrates, and Plato derived their ideas from the Jewish law. Written toward the end of the Hellenistic period, the Wisdom of Solomon continues the biblical tradition of wisdom books like Proverbs but incorporates many elements of Greek rhetoric, philosophy, and literary style.

Less is known about the Jews of the eastern diaspora who remained under Seleucid control than about the Jews of Egypt and Palestine, but it appears that peoples of various ethnic groups had access to economic and political advancement within the Seleucid Empire. Several writings from this time—Tobit, Daniel 1–6, and Esther—suggest something of the outlook of Jews in the eastern diaspora. Written originally in Hebrew or Aramaic and later enlarged when they were translated into Greek, these books are works of fiction, edifying entertainments that tell the stories of Jews who achieved high status in foreign courts, were threatened by jealous rivals, and yet succeeded in securing personal power and the good will of the king. Though the stories are all set in the pre-Hellenistic period (Tobit in the Assyrian Empire, Daniel in the Babylonian exile, and Esther in the Persian court), they were probably written during the Seleucid period. While they acknowledge that faithful Jews may be vulnerable because of their religion, on the whole these are optimistic stories with a positive view of the Gentile kings.

The eastern diaspora was also the conduit for important religious developments that arose from the contact between Judaism and the religions of Babylon and Persia. This influence is most clearly seen in the development of apocalyptic literature. Parts of the pseudepigraphical book of 1 Enoch composed in the third century BC reflect astronomical lore and traditions about antediluvian sages that derive from Babylonian sources. Although it is more difficult to trace the path of influence in its earliest stages, the dualistic religious beliefs of Persian Zoroastrianism almost certainly contributed to the development of Jewish apocalyptic thought and to some of the ideas of the sectarians at Qumran.

The eventual triumph of the Seleucid kingdom over the Ptolemies in the fifth Syrian war (198 BC) obviously had a greater significance for the Jews of Judea than for those of Egypt. The Seleucid ruler Antiochus III treated the Judeans generously in appreciation for the support he received from the pro-Seleucid faction, granting an allowance for the Temple and various tax concessions, as well as confirming the Judeans' right to live "according to the laws of their country." Although relations began well, the difference in the way the Seleucid Empire governed its territories set the stage for a terrible conflict. Unlike the Ptolemaic system of centralized government administered with the cooperation of local leaders, the Seleucid regime was more decentralized. It derived some unity, however, from a network of Greek cities established throughout the empire. These were not necessarily ethnically Greek but were cities that had received a charter to organize as a polis, the Greek form of city government. Cultural prestige and economic advantages often led the leadership of Near Eastern cities to request such a charter.

The events leading up to the conflict between Judea and the Seleucid king Antiochus IV Epiphanes (175–164 BC) are complex and not fully understood. In part they involved a struggle for succession to the high priesthood and the attempts of various contenders to secure the support of the king by paying him large sums of money. The first of the contenders, Jason, also paid to have Jerusalem established as a Greek polis, Antioch at Jerusalem. Neither of these acts in itself seems to have aroused much opposition in Jerusalem. The conflict was not a cultural conflict between Judaism and Hellenism, for Palestinian Jews had already incorporated significant elements of Hellenistic culture, which they considered quite compatible with their religious identity.

The crisis was sparked by the attempt by another contender, Menelaus, to buy the office of high priest. When he promised the king more than he could pay, he attempted to raise the money by taking golden vessels from the Temple. At this, a riot broke out in Jerusalem. Subsequent fighting between the forces of Jason and Menelaus convinced Antiochus that Judea was in revolt, and he retook the city and plundered the Temple, either in 169 or 168. Sometime later there were further disturbances, and Antiochus sent Syrian troops, which remained garrisoned in Jerusalem. Whether the status of Jerusalem at this point was a polis or a military colony is uncertain, but in either case in 167 the Temple was reorganized to accommodate the religious needs of the Syrian troops. A dedication was made to Zeus Olympius, the Greek name for the Syrian god Baal Shamem, and an altar established for sacrifice. Though Menelaus continued to preside as high priest, most Jews considered these actions to have profaned the Temple. In addition, the traditional practice of Judaism was suppressed by Antiochus, perhaps with the cooperation of Menelaus. Since religious persecution was virtually unknown in antiquity, it is difficult to know how Antiochus understood this repression and what he hoped to accomplish by it. Its actual result was to ignite the resistance known as the Maccabean revolt.

The Hasmoneans, Mattathias and his sons Judas Maccabeus, Jonathan, Simon, John, and Eleazar, were the leaders of the revolt. Although Judas managed to retake control of the Temple in 164 (its rededication being the occasion for the institution of the festival of

Hanukkah), it was not until 142 that the last of the Seleucid army was expelled and actual independence was secured by Simon. From then until the Roman conquest of Judea in 63 BC the small kingdom was ruled by the Hasmonean family, which in addition to ruling as kings also assumed the office of high priest.

Religious and cultural life in Judea during the Seleucid and Hasmonean periods was rich and varied, with a remarkable quantity of literature produced in Hebrew, Aramaic, and to some extent in Greek. The Apocryphal/Deuterocanonical book of Sirach (Ecclesiasticus), Jesus Ben Sira's book of wisdom teachings, was probably composed in Hebrew about 180 BC. Though largely traditional, it embodies several innovations: Ben Sira's identification of wisdom with the law of Moses, his praise of the contemporary high priest Simon II, and his own explicit claim to authorship. Ben Sira disapproved of apocalyptic speculation, but the crisis under Antiochus IV produced an upsurge in apocalyptic writings, not only Daniel 7–12 but also 1 Enoch 83–90 and the Testament of Moses. After the establishment of the Hasmonean monarchy, a supporter of the dynasty composed an account of the war in Hebrew (1 Maccabees [Apocrypha]), modeling it after the earlier books of Kings and Chronicles. An Egyptian Jewish writer, Jason of Cyrene, also wrote a history of the war in Greek (2 Maccabees [Apocrypha]), which was strongly influenced by forms of Hellenistic history writing.

Our knowledge of the literature of this time has been greatly increased by the discovery of the Dead Sea Scrolls at Qumran. Although this library was the property of a sectarian religious group related to the Essenes, it contained many Hebrew and Aramaic texts that were not sectarian compositions. Several of these scrolls contain noncanonical psalms, blessings, and other liturgical material. There are also many examples of what is called "the rewritten Bible," fairly free retellings of parts of the biblical story, embellished with new narrative episodes, prayers, and other elements (e.g., Jubilees, the Genesis Apocryphon, the Apocryphon of Joshua). Some texts elaborate on the apocalyptic elements of the books of Ezekiel and Daniel or place apocalyptic pronouncements in the mouths of other biblical figures, such as Levi, Qahat, and Amram. A number of texts, often having to do with matters of religious law, purport to be discourses of Moses. Perhaps the most remarkable document is the Temple Scroll, which apparently takes the form of an address by God to Moses. Although it incorporates material from the books of Exodus through Deuteronomy, it also contains much new material, including detailed instructions for building the Temple.

These documents and others pertaining to the Qumran sect itself help to clarify a number of issues of religious controversy that shaped the period of Hasmonean rule. The Temple and the Torah were central institutions for Judaism, which made them focal points for conflict. The Qumran scrolls show that conflict over the proper calendar (i.e., a solar or lunar calendar) for the conduct of Temple sacrifices was a major issue dividing the Qumran Essenes from their rivals, the Pharisees. Though the Hasmoneans were not always on good terms with the Pharisees, they adopted the lunar calendar favored by them. Many other writings from Qumran also elaborate their understanding of disputed issues such as purity, marriage, and Sabbath observance, concerning which they were at odds with the Pharisees. Although the Qumran community did not compose apocalypses (i.e., reports of revelatory visions), they were strongly influenced by apocalyptic ideas and considered themselves to be living in the last times, just before God would intervene to restore proper order to the world. They supported their ideas in part by writing commentaries (*pesharim*) on biblical texts, which they read as referring to themselves and their opponents.

In general, the Hellenistic period presents a picture of Judaism that is much more diverse than is often imagined. Not only did Jews live in a vast range of lands from Egypt to Parthia, they also creatively adapted many elements from the varied Hellenistic cultures of these lands. Nevertheless, important symbols and institutions, including the Temple in Jerusalem, the scriptures, and common religious practices based in the Torah, provided a sense of unity and common identity.

CULTURAL CONTEXTS:
THE ROMAN PERIOD

The Roman conquest of Judea in 63 BC was part of a centuries-long expansion of the power of Rome. The destruction of Carthage in North Africa in 146 BC concluded the Punic Wars and secured the western Mediterranean, and the destruction of Corinth in the same year demonstrated Rome's control of Greece. In the next century, a series of conflicts with the successors of Alexander the Great in Asia and Egypt brought Roman rule to the entire eastern Mediterranean. The events that led to the replacement of the Roman republic by autocratic rule culminated with the installation of Julius Caesar's nephew Octavian (later Augustus) as the first emperor in 27 BC, and included the conquest of Egypt. The Mediterranean was now, as it has aptly been called, "a Roman lake."

Within the Roman Empire, especially in the east, client states were allowed considerable autonomy as long as their rulers maintained order and paid tribute to Rome. In Judea, Herod the Great, king of Judea from 37 to 4 BC, succeeded on both counts, and with Roman sanction his control eventually extended to all of the region west of the Jordan and over much of Transjordan. His successors were not so adept, and direct Roman rule of Judea itself began in AD 6. Thus began an uneasy détente between a series of Roman governors and the leaders of the Jewish community, based in the Temple in Jerusalem. This broke down during the First Jewish Revolt (66–73), prompting the Roman destruction of Jerusalem in 70. A brief resurgence of Jewish nationalism in the Second Jewish Revolt (132–135) was easily crushed, and Jerusalem became Aelia Capitolina, a fully Hellenized city from which Jews were banned.

This is the historical setting for the life of Jesus and the development of earliest Christianity, one of several "Judaisms" that coexisted in Palestine before AD 70. For most of them the Temple was the primary place of worship and the locus of authority in religious and intracommunity issues. The priesthood in the Temple was hereditary, but from the time of Herod onward the high priest was appointed by a ruler or governor. The high priest was head of a council, called the Sanhedrin, which had jurisdiction in religious and, to a limited extent, in civic matters. Other groups that comprised Judaism, with boundaries not always sharply drawn, included the Sadducees, members of the priesthood whose social status was aristocratic and whose views conservative. The Pharisees were a lay movement concerned with observance of the Torah and hence with its interpretation, often through local houses of assembly; these "synagogues," however, did not supplant the Temple as the place of sacrifice and pilgrimage. The Pharisees were forerunners of the rabbinic Judaism that developed after the Temple's destruction in 70. Outside of these groups, but still part of the broad spectrum of Judaism, were the Essenes, who had seceded from the Temple-based priesthood during the early Hasmonean period (mid-first century BC), and the Samaritans, whose rejection of the Jerusalem Temple as the proper place for sacrificial worship had crystallized by the same time.

Cultural Contexts: The Roman Period

WITHIN THE ROMAN EMPIRE

Readers encounter two different cultural spaces within the New Testament: the village economy of agriculture and fishing in the Galilee, and the mobile economy of merchants and tradesmen in the urban centers of the empire. The first, the village economy, forms the context of Jesus' ministry and of the itinerant disciples who formulated the collections of sayings, stories, and miracles that underlie the Gospels. The second, the merchant economy, constitutes the world of Paul's missions as well as that of countless unknown disciples like those responsible for bringing the gospel message to Rome around AD 41. This larger, urban world is that of the epistles and the book of Acts. It is also evident in the expansions and reformulations of Mark and "Q" that are found in Matthew and Luke. Both the village agriculturists and the traveling merchants view from below a third cultural space: that of the wealthy, educated elite who are responsible for most of the architectural, artistic, literary, legal, philosophical, and religious remains that represent the Roman world and its influence within Western history and culture.

The predominance of this third, elite world in its cultural influence creates a problem for historians. We must be cautious in using the productions of an elite minority to describe the religious or social world of ordinary people in ancient societies. Anthropologists, for instance, make a distinction between the high tradition of sacred texts, temple rites, and the learned commentary upon them that centers upon the great urban cultural milieu, and the humbler, smaller traditions of religious belief, story, and practice that villagers hand on to one another. The story of the young Jesus remaining in the Temple to debate the teachers (Luke 2:41–52) exemplifies this distinction. For the Galilean peasants, religious devotion is focused on, and expressed in, the act of pilgrimage to Jerusalem for Passover. For the religious elite, it consists of learned interpretation of the sacred texts. The thousands of papyri that have been found in the dry climate of Egypt are yielding new insights into the lives of ordinary people in ancient times. Scholars can also study texts for nonelite forms of storytelling, popular belief, and everyday life; these aspects of experience are reflected in novels, in expansions of the biblical text in the Targums (Aramaic paraphrases of the Hebrew Bible), in Jewish and Christian apocryphal writings, and within the New Testament itself, as well as in the remains of material culture recovered by archaeologists.

Roman rule constituted the overarching political reality for both the village agricultural society in the Gospels and the urban context of Acts and the epistles. Its most immediate impact within Palestine was the accession of the Idumean Herod as king. Rome, not the Jewish populace, established the terms of Herodian rule. Herod's massive building projects—including the city of Caesarea, his own mausoleum at Herodion, and the Temple complex in Jerusalem—followed Greek and Roman models. Further consequences of Herod's rule included the severing of ties between tenant farmers and landholders who were no longer local patrons (see Mark 12:1–9). The pressure on the tax system to meet Roman demands and to finance Herod's building projects must have been considerable; this, and the possibilities for corruption and extortion inherent in the system itself, resulted in the cultural disdain reflected in the phrase "tax collector and sinner" (Luke 15:1–2; Matt 18:17 uses the alternative, equally dismissive, "tax collector and Gentile"). The presence of Roman soldiers might mean that goods and services were extorted at random from the local populace (Matt 5:41), but retired centurions might also be valuable local patrons (Luke 7:1–10). Physicians who were attached to the army units could also serve the populace on the side (Mark 5:26).

Most of Galilee seems to have been a prosperous region of small landholders and grazing herds of sheep and goats. Families in the villages where Jesus preached were largely self-sufficient. Craftsmen, such as Jesus himself, may have worked in the cities that were being built in the region, like Tiberias and Sepphoris. Even the rebellion against Rome, which zealots in Judea ignited in AD 66, had a short life in Galilee. Within a year its populace had given up and returned to everyday life. Further evidence for the general prosperity of the region emerges when one turns to the occupation of Jesus' core disciples, Peter, James, and John (Mark 1:16–20). The fishing industry around the Sea of Galilee was a flourishing one, as the archaeological remains of extensive harbor installations indicate. Fishing involved families or partners who owned the boats working with hired hands. Fish was salted, dried, smoked, or pickled and packed in jars for export. Thus Jesus and his disciples were neither naïve isolated pastoralists nor poor peasants, but were engaged in economic enterprises crucial to Galilee's place in the larger world.

For Jerusalem, a city whose chief economic asset was its Temple, the crowds of pilgrims at major feasts and the massive new complex of buildings were both an economic boon and a source of civic pride. The major cities in the eastern Mediterranean, such as Antioch, Ephesus, Philippi, Corinth, and Thessalonica, also enjoyed increased prosperity as a consequence of Roman rule and the growing numbers of travelers on land and sea. Without the possibility of such routine travel, the Christian mission could not have taken place. It was also furthered by the existence of Jewish communities in those cities, which provided an initial network (e.g., see Acts 13:5; 14:1). Many of the peoples incorporated into the Roman Empire, Jew and non-Jew alike, would have shared positive sentiments toward its authority (see Rom 13:1–7; 1 Pet 2:13–17).

On the other hand, civic discord, rioting, and full-scale rebellion against Roman rule remained real possibilities. Alexandria in Egypt had a large Jewish population that included highly educated, cultured, and wealthy individuals like the philosopher and exegete Philo of Alexandria (d. ca. AD 50). Yet non-Jewish residents rioted in AD 41 when the Jewish elite sought the same citizenship rights as the citizen descendants of the Greek founders. Despite the appeals of a delegation of prominent Jewish Alexandrians, the emperor Claudius refused to grant their request and threatened severe punishment if further civil discord occurred. Claudius also expelled members of Rome's Jewish community for "rioting at the name of Chrestus," presumably local discord occasioned by Christian missionaries (see Acts 18:1–2). Nero, in 65, executed a number of the new sect of undesirables, the Christians—including, according to tradition, Peter and Paul—as scapegoats for a fire that destroyed blocks of wooden tenements in Rome. Nero became the focus of anti-Roman sentiment, the demonic persecutor of faithful Christians in later generations (see Rev 13:1–18).

Despite the counsel of moderate voices and the opposition of Agrippa, zealous leaders led Palestinian Jews to revolt against Rome in 66; by August of 70 Titus led Roman troops in burning and destroying the Temple. Christians living in Jerusalem appear to have fled the city prior to its fall. Jews living in the diaspora did not support the rebellion; this did not keep the Romans from penalizing all Jews after the defeat. The Romans forced Jews who once paid a tax to support the Temple (see Matt 17:24–27) to pay instead an increased tax to the temple of Jupiter Capitolinus in Rome.

THE TYPICAL ROMAN CITY

A brief tour of Caesarea Maritima, the residence of the Roman governor of Judea (Acts

8:40; 9:30; 10:1, 24; 11:11; 12:19–23; 18:22; 21:8; 23:23; 25:1–13), reveals the outline of an ancient city from the perspective of the rich. It was originally a small military settlement dating from the mid-third century BC; Augustus gave it to Herod, who built a magnificent city of some eight thousand acres and a harbor to rival that of Alexandria. Two breakwaters created a sheltered harbor of forty acres. An area with a temple on a raised mound, dedicated to Rome and Augustus, faces the harbor at the south end of the forum that runs along the harborside. To the south of the city, a theater faces the sea, although the structure that has been unearthed is a later, rebuilt one. Among the discoveries there is a stone with an inscription referring to Pontius Pilate as prefect. There is also a large amphitheater similar to the Colosseum and a large racecourse (hippodrome).

An aqueduct supplied the city with water from springs on Mount Carmel, and an elaborate sewer system under the city drained away waste. Walkways were decorated with mosaics, and promenades were lined with columns. Herod presumably spared no expense on his showcase; builders used imported marbles from Italy and Egypt and pink granite from Aswan. There were warehouses facing the harbor to store the goods that passed through the city from extensive maritime trade, which reached as far as south Asia. The residents of Palestine did not have to journey to Alexandria, Corinth, or Rome to see the world's riches on display for a wealthy elite.

Capernaum on the northern shore of the Sea of Galilee was the base for Jesus' preaching activities around Galilee. It lay on the Via Maris, the road that connected Caesarea and Ptolemais (Acco) on the coast with Damascus in Syria. Even if they never visited the new city of Caesarea, the traffic along the highway between the coast and Damascus would have alerted Jesus and his contemporaries to the cultural realities of Greco-Roman cities. Two other city foundations within Galilee itself, Sepphoris and Tiberias, contributed to the growth of urbanization. Herod Antipas, tetrarch of Galilee and Perea from 4 BC to AD 39, resided at Sepphoris, a mere 7 km (4 mi) from Nazareth, until he moved to the newly built Tiberias on the lake in AD 19–20. The term *tekton* used for Joseph and his sons (Mark 6:3; Matt 13:55) is usually translated "carpenter," but there is no reason to assume that Jesus and his family were restricted to the carpenter's shop of a village. They are just as likely to have been employed in the building that occurred in Sepphoris and Tiberias. Jesus' view of the rich could have been shaped by such experiences, and his followers probably included some connected to the Herodian court (see Luke 8:3).

STATUS AND SOCIAL CLASS IN THE CITY

The artisans, manual laborers, and merchants who lived in a typical Roman city had little time for the pleasures of the city's main streets. Long days in cramped and often dark shops would have been more typical of Paul's life as a tentmaker, for instance (Acts 18:3; 2 Cor 6:5; 11:27). This trade involved creating the awnings, made of a rough, thick fabric like sailcloth, that provided cover from the sun in theaters and the forum, and in front of the booths from which goods were sold. When crowds thronged the city for a festival, such as the biennial Isthmian games outside Corinth in honor of Poseidon, there would be no shortage of work for tentmakers.

The members of the wealthy elite and the educated scribes, Pharisees (or philosophers who were attached to them) despised such lowly occupations, as well as those who collected the taxes. The tensions between rich and poor that were evident in Corinth (1 Cor 11:17–34) show how difficult it could be to cross social divisions of class and status. Those in whose homes the community assembled would have thought it their right to provide a feast for the others who were from their own group; as for the rest—artisans who had to work from dawn to dusk as well as slave members of the community—they should be glad for the meager rations provided for them. Similarly, the letter of James (2:1–13) excoriates Christians for showing deference to a rich man, giving him a comfortable seat and asking the poor to squat on the floor in the assembly. Although Paul's letters lack the sharp attacks on wealth found in the teaching of Jesus or in the letter of James, Paul does attack the privileges of social superiority to one's fellows when they surface in the Christian community.

Although most Christians did not belong to the local civic elite (1 Cor 1:26–30), a few individuals associated with the Corinthian church could claim such status. Acts 18:8 refers to Crispus (1 Cor 1:14) as *archisynagogos,* a title that he may have been accorded as a benefactor, perhaps by contributing funds for a synagogue building. Women can appear as patronesses and *archisynagogoi* as well. Paul recommends Phoebe, a deaconess from the Corinthian port city Cenchrea (Rom 16:1–2). Such recommendations were a common letter form in the ancient world, in which patronage relationships were essential to success. Gaius (1 Cor 1:14) was wealthy enough to host all the Christians in Corinth at once (Rom 16:23).

Paul also conveys greetings from a certain Erastus, who is *oikonomos* of Corinth, the only convert who is known to have held a civic office. A pavement from the area between the north market and the theater bears an inscription stating that one Erastus paved the area at his own expense in return for the office of *aedile* (one of the four magistrates who governed the city, and particularly the public officers in charge of the streets). Since the name is an unusual one (no other instances are known), scholars think it possible that it was the same person. The term that Paul uses is not the Greek equivalent for *aedile,* so it may therefore represent a lesser position in the municipal government that was an intermediate step on the way to becoming a magistrate.

Since Corinth had been refounded as a Roman colony under Julius Caesar less than a century before, and therefore would have had no long-entrenched ruling class, the opportunities it could offer for civic advancement may have encouraged competition. For other cities, the ranks of citizens—those enrolled who could hold various public offices—were strictly limited to a particular group of aristocratic families. Other residents, no matter how wealthy or influential, were excluded. Jews who sought to be included on the citizen rolls of Alexandria were rebuffed. Since Roman citizens and the Greek citizens of Alexandria were exempt from poll taxes levied by the Roman state, this status carried some economic advantage. Most Jews who were laborers and artisans would not have been eligible for enrollment in any case. Whether Jewish families succeeded in joining the citizen elite elsewhere in the diaspora is less clear. Luke has Paul claim to be a citizen of Tarsus (Acts 21:39), but this may be mistaken or imprecise.

LITERACY AND EDUCATION

Scholars remain divided over how to assess the extent of literacy in the Greco-Roman period. Portraits showing girls holding the stylus and wax tablet of the student suggest that among the elite some level of education extended to women, but on the evidence of documentary papyri, far fewer women than men were able to sign their names, and women who were able to write often pointed out that fact explicitly. The cities and larger villages of Egypt had teachers who drilled children in the rudiments of reading and writing Greek as well as the study of classic texts. Further education would require sending each young person, accompanied by a family slave, off to Alexandria in search of a suitable tutor.

Even among those who could read, the difficulty of deciphering texts in which all the letters were run together (the standard way in which ancient texts are written) often made it preferable to listen to a slave who was trained to read such texts aloud. We can deduce which texts were most in demand by studying the literary papyri. Homeric texts are by far the most frequently found, with considerable numbers of texts by Demosthenes, Euripides, and Hesiod as well. Technical manuals on such subjects as medicine and astrology also show up in papyri fragments. Among the papyri that have been discovered are some that were orders to and from a book dealer in Oxyrhynchus: Outgoing orders seek dialogues of Plato and works of Homer, Menander, Euripides, and Aristophanes. The dealer acknowledges receipt of treatises on such edifying subjects as "On Training," "On Marriage," "On Freedom from Pain," "On the Uses of Parents," "On the Uses of Domestic Slaves," and Book 3 of a work by Poseidonios, *On Persuasion*. Apparently this dealer's clientele read for self-improvement or practical purposes as much as for entertainment or philosophical enlightenment.

The requirements of reading Torah may have made basic schooling even more necessary for Jewish boys, for whom the Bible would replace Homer as the text. Assimilated Jews in cities like Tarsus and Alexandria, however, saw to it that their sons received instruction in the classics as well. Philo defends the practice of sending Jewish students on to more advanced instruction in arithmetic, geometry, music, and philosophy at the equivalent of a secondary school, the gymnasium. Educational centers like Alexandria and Tarsus had numerous schools of rhetoric to further a young man's ability to take his place in public affairs by training him to speak fluently and write persuasively. Although Paul insists that eloquence ("wisdom") is not needed to communicate the truth of the gospel (1 Cor 1:17) and disclaims any use of such methods (1 Cor 2:4; 2 Cor 11:6), both his opponents (2 Cor 10:10) and contemporary scholars notice a high degree of rhetorical art in his letters. Even his refusal to engage in the sort of rhetorical discourse that would please his audience exhibits familiarity with such arts (see the "fool's speech," 2 Cor 11:1—12:13).

It is more difficult to assess the kind of education received by boys growing up in the Galilean towns and villages. In an oral society, persons can be highly skilled and even have extensive cultural knowledge, such as Jesus' knowledge of Scripture, without being able to read or write. Luke 4:16 presumes that Jesus was literate, though Luke may be speaking from the perspective of an urban class that assumes literate habits as a normal part of education. The Jewish historian Josephus writing in the AD 90s makes no such assumption. Weekly Torah study can be accomplished orally: "He [Moses] appointed the Law to be most excellent and a necessary form of instructions, ordaining that it be heard not once or twice or several times, but that every week men should quit their other occupations and assemble to listen to the Law and obtain a thorough and accurate knowledge of it."

The first-century AD synagogue building at Gamla in the Golan lacks the elaborate religious features of later synagogues like that at Capernaum. It consists of a central nave created by two rows of columns and four levels of stone benches set in steps along the walls. Without the ritual bath attached to the complex there would be nothing to distinguish it from an ordinary assembly hall. There is no evidence of a Torah shrine built into the walls, of a fixed elevated podium from which Torah was read, or of a seat of honor near the center; presumably Torah reading and instruction took place in the central area. The architectural space of the synagogue could serve a variety of community functions, from teaching and worship to legal proceedings and social gathering.

Another form of education required by Jesus and his disciples involves skills specific to their individual trades. Measuring, counting, and recording skills necessary to building or running a fishing business could have been taught on an apprentice basis. Tax collectors had to keep records of persons and amounts. Officials in the local Jewish community also had to collect the annual half-shekel paid to the Temple by all Jewish males (Exod 30:11–16; Matt 17:24–27). Such practical skills must have been taught, but little evidence of the process survives. Though not considered "education" by the literate, rhetorically trained elite of the Greco-Roman cities or by the literate scribes learned in Jewish Torah, such skills would distinguish Jesus and his disciples from others in their villages.

RELIGION, ASTROLOGY, AND MAGIC

When Herod the Great built Caesarea Maritima, he placed the temple to Rome and Augustus in a prominent place. The city was dedicated to the emperor; its civic life would include festive sacrifices in the ruler's honor. Herod's renovations to the Jerusalem Temple and his expansions of its surroundings were planned to enhance the prestige of the city. Other cities also had famous shrines and festivals that drew visitors from abroad. Acts 19:21–40 tells a story of a riot at Ephesus that occurred when those who sold silver models of its famous temple to the goddess Artemis (Diana) claimed that the effectiveness of Paul's preaching had cut into their business.

Christianity did not deliver the death blow to the established civic worship that Luke seems to suggest. Most of his readers lived in cities, and they could easily witness the ongoing enthusiasm for sacrifices and festivals. What individual residents actually believed about the gods was not an issue; their participation, not their internal assent, was the key, and that participation (or lack of it) was observed by the authorities. To join in sacrifices honoring the Roman emperor, for example, demonstrated that the city and its populace were loyal subjects of the empire. Jews refused to participate in these events, and this refusal often brought on them accusations of "hatred of humanity." At Alexandria some argued that Jews could never be admitted to the citizen rolls because they did not worship the city's gods. Nevertheless, through long-tolerated practice, Jews were not often persecuted for this failure to participate in civic rituals. When Christians who were not of Jewish origin began to withdraw from such public activities, however, it caused comment, suspicion, and even persecution. A story like that of Paul's deeds in Ephesus, leading some to abandon the worship of Artemis, would have highlighted the superiority of Christ to one of Asia Minor's most famous religious shrines and might increase Christian resolve to remain separate. Not all Christians would choose persecution, however. Some clearly followed the lead of educated pagans, who often did not believe in the real existence of the gods or in their myths. They would join public religious activities as required by their social status or civic office, as a social bond rather than as a religious profession. When faced with Christians who obstinately refused to participate, magistrates had no qualms about sentencing them to exile or death.

Astrologers, diviners, and magicians could be visited in the marketplace. Although such activities were frowned upon by those higher in the social scale, the large number of horoscopes, amulets, and magic spells recovered shows that these methods of making decisions, predicting the future, and bringing good luck (or guarding against bad) continued to be popular. Astrologers to the upper classes justified their practices with a philosophical veneer based on Stoic physical doctrines explaining the relations between earthly and heavenly bodies by means of an all-pervading "rational spirit." Christian insistence that the glorified and exalted Christ is above all the demonic powers and planetary forces (see Col 2:8–23; Eph 1:15–2:2; 6:12) did little to curb popular enthusiasm for these beliefs and practices. Biblical texts show up in Christian magical amulets. Jesus' exorcisms led to accusations that his powers were a consequence of an alliance with the leader of the demonic world (Mark 3:22–30), and Acts describes conflicts between Christian missionaries and local magicians (8:4–25; 13:4–12).

PHILOSOPHY AS HEALING THE SOUL

Unlike the monotheistic faith of Jews and Christians, which placed a high premium on hearing, interpreting, and acting on divine revelation preserved in sacred texts, Greco-Roman religions did not produce texts, legal and ethical codes, or theological doctrines. Those who sought teaching about the divine and its relationship to the observable cosmos, or moral guidance and advice about how to live a good life, turned to philosophy. Formal study of the philosophical systems that emerged from the schools of classical and Hellenistic Athens—especially Platonism, Stoicism, and Epicureanism—could be pursued only by the elite, who had the leisure time to devote to them. Luke's tale of Paul's visit to Athens (Acts 17:16–31) shows its first-century reputation as a destination for intellectuals, not the powerful center of commerce and art that it had been.

More ordinary citizens learned what they knew of philosophy from anthologies of moralistic tales, treatises on how to cope with various problems in life, public discourses offered by itinerant philosophical preachers, and the like. The philosopher-teacher saw himself as a physician for the soul. Under his guidance, people might be converted from the mindless, destructive pursuit of the passions, from fears about a future they could not control, even from superstitious belief in the gods. Some treatises, like Plutarch's "Advice on Marriage" even recommend that the young husband share his knowledge with his wife. Such knowledge will protect her against the passion for luxuries, foolish behavior, and talk common among women. If she knows something of Plato, Xenophon, and astronomy, she will not be taken in by the common practices of magic or witchcraft. Such treatises also presume that in the properly ordered household the husband governs the life of his wife, his children, and his slaves in accordance with a reason that has been schooled by philosophical instruction. Similar kinds of assumptions appear in sections of the New Testament often referred to as "household codes" (Col 3:18–4:1; Eph 5:21–6:9; 1 Pet 2:18–3:7). They also inform the descriptions of requirements for leadership (1 Tim 3:1–11), including those that exclude women from teaching or supervising men (1 Tim 2:9–15; 1 Cor 14:34–36).

Scholars have become particularly interested in a movement of rough-spoken, anti-establishment street preachers called Cynics, from the Greek word for dog, originally a derogatory name that referred to their unrefined public behavior. Claiming as their inspiration Socrates, the impoverished stonemason who went about Athens challenging all its citizens, representatives of this movement could be found in the public marketplaces. They rejected the comforts that could be offered by wealthy patrons and lived on as little as possible. They were known for sharp sayings intended to wound an opponent, not persuasive speeches to soothe one into agreement. If the harsh medicine worked, the hearer might convert to a philosophical way of life. If not, he might become angry, even murderously so, as had Socrates' opponents. Some scholars think that this movement provides the best ancient analogy for the itinerant mission of Jesus and his disciples, as depicted in the Gospels. Others have proposed that Paul's description of himself as the solicitous nurse or the father to his fledgling converts (1 Thes 2:1–12) is analogous to the Cynics' relationship to their own followers. Although these cultural models may not have dictated the content of early Christian preaching, they provide a context for understanding what missionaries like Paul were doing in the cities that they visited, and how they would have appeared to their first hearers.

Timeline

DATE	PERIOD	EGYPT
Ca. 3300–2000 BC	EARLY BRONZE AGE	
3300–3100	Early Bronze I	Earliest forms of writing
3100–2700	Early Bronze II	Political unification; Early Dynastic period
2700–2300	Early Bronze III	Old Kingdom; Dynasties 3–5
2300–2000	Early Bronze IV	First Intermediate Period
Ca. 2000–1550 BC	MIDDLE BRONZE AGE	
2000–1650	Middle Bronze I–II	Middle Kingdom; Dynasties 11–12
1650–1550	Middle Bronze III	Second Intermediate/ Hyksos Period
Ca. 1550–1200 BC	LATE BRONZE AGE	New Kingdom; Dynasties 18–19: Thutmose III (1479–1425), Akenhaten (1352–1336), Seti I (1294–1279), Rameses II (1279–1213), Merneptah (1213–1203); Sea Peoples (groups including Philistines) invasions begin
Ca. 1200–586 BC	IRON AGE	
Ca. 1200–1025	Iron I	Rameses III (1184–1153)[1]
Ca. 1025–586	Iron II	
Ca. 1025–928	Iron IIA	
Ca. 928–722	Iron IIB	Shishak I invades Palestine (925)

1. For a more complete list of rulers, see "Chronological Table of Rulers," p. 1592.

SYRIA-PALESTINE		MESOPOTAMIA, ASIA MINOR
		Earliest forms of writing; Full urbanization; Sumerian culture develops
In Egyptian sphere		High point of Sumerian culture
Flourishing city-states		Sargon of Akkad; Naram-Sin of Akkad; Gudea of Lagash
Decline/abandonment of city-states		Third Dynasty of Ur
Revival of urbanism; Invention of alphabet		Amorite kingdoms: Shamshi-Adad of Assyria (ca. 1813–1781); Hammurapi of Babylon (ca. 1792–1750); Rise of Hittites
In Egyptian sphere; Rise of Mitanni in north; Ugarit flourishes		
Exodus of the Hebrews from Egypt;		Hittites challenge Egypt for control of Syria
Collapse of city-states		Hittite empire collapses; Trojan War
Israel emerges in Canaan; Philistines settle on SW coast; Small city-states develop in Phoenicia, Syria, Transjordan		Resurgence of Assyria: Tiglath-pileser I (1114–1076)
United Monarchy in Israel: Saul (1025–1005); David (1005–965); Solomon (968–928)		
Divided Monarchy:		
JUDAH:	ISRAEL:	
Rehoboam (928–911)	Jeroboam I (928–907) Omri (882–871); Capital at Samaria Ahab (873–852)	Rise of Neo-Assyrian Empire Shalmaneser III (858–824); Battle of Qarqar (853)
Jehoshaphat (867–846)	Prophet Elijah (mid-ninth century) Prophet Elisha (mid- to late ninth century)	
Athaliah (842–836)	Jehu (842–814)	
Jehoash (836–798)	Jehoash (800–788) Jeroboam II (788–747) Prophet Amos (mid-eighth century)	Adad-nirari III (811–783)
	Prophet Hosea (mid-eighth century)	Tiglath-pileser III (745–727); Assyrian conquest of the Levant
Ahaz (743/735–727/715)	Hoshea (732–722)	Shalmaneser V (727–722) Samaria captured (722)

Timeline

DATE	PERIOD	EGYPT
Ca. 722–586	Iron IIC	Egypt conquered by Assyria (671) Psammetichus I (664–610) Neco II (610–595)
Ca. 586–539	NEO-BABYLONIAN	
		GREECE AND ROME
539–332	PERSIAN	Greeks repel Persian invasions Peloponnesian War (431–404)
332–63	HELLENISTIC	Alexander the Great (336–323); Defeats Persians at Issus (332); Occupies the Levant and Egypt Rome gains control over Greece (ca. 188–146); Sack of Carthage and Corinth (146)
63 BC–AD 330	ROMAN	Julius Caesar named dictator (49); assassinated (44) Octavian (Augustus) defeats Antony at Actium (31); (Emperor 27 BC–AD 14) Tiberius (AD 14–37) Gaius (Caligula) (37–41) Claudius (41–54) Nero (54–68) Vespasian (69–79) Titus (79–81) Domitian (81–96) Nerva (96–98) Trajan (98–117) Hadrian (117–138)

SYRIA-PALESTINE	MESOPOTAMIA
JUDAH: Prophet Isaiah (late eighth to early seventh centuries) Prophet Micah (late eighth century) Hezekiah (727/715–698/687) Manasseh (698/687–642) Josiah (639–609) Prophet Zephaniah (late seventh century) Prophet Jeremiah (late seventh to early sixth centuries) Jehoahaz (609) Jehoiakim (608–598) Jehoiachin (597) Prophet Ezekiel (early sixth century) Zedekiah (597–586); Capture of Jerusalem (586)	Sargon II (722–705) Sennacherib (705–681); Attack on Judah and seige of Jerusalem (701) Esar-haddon (681–669) Ashurbanipal (669–627) Rise of Babylon Assyrian capital of Nineveh captured (612) Nebuchadrezzar II (604–562) of Babylon Nabonidus (556–539)
EASTERN MEDITERRANEAN	
Some exiles return from Babylon (538) Second Temple built (520–515) Prophet Haggai (520); Prophet Zechariah (520–518) Nehemiah governor of Judah (ca. 445–430) Mission of Ezra the scribe (mid-fifth [or early fourth] century)	Cyrus II (the Great) (559–530); Capture of Babylon Cambyses (530–522); Capture of Egypt (525) Darius I (522–486) Xerxes I (486–465) Artaxerxes I (465–424) Artaxerxes II (405–359)
Seleucus I (312/311–281) controls Syria and Mesopotamia Ptolemy I (323–282) controls Egypt, Palestine, Phoenicia Antiochus III (223–187) gains control of southern Syria, Phoenicia, and Judea from Ptolemy IV (202–198) Ben Sira (Sirach) (early second century) Antiochus IV Epiphanes (175–164) Revolt of the Maccabees (167–164) HASMONEAN RULE OF JUDEA (165–37): John Hyrcanus (135–104); Alexander Janneus (103–76); Salome Alexandra (76–67)	
Pompey conquers the Levant (66–62); Enters Jerusalem (63) Herod the Great king of Judea (37–4); Rebuilds Second Temple (Herod) Antipas (4 BC–AD 39) Life of Jesus of Nazareth (ca. 4 BC–AD 30) Pontius Pilate governor of Judea (26–36) (Herod) Agrippa I (39–44) Missionary activity of Paul (mid-first century) (Herod) Agrippa II (53–93) First Jewish Revolt in Judea against Rome (66–73); Jerusalem is captured (70) Jewish revolts in Egypt, Libya, Cyprus (115–118) Second Jewish Revolt in Judea against Rome (132–135)	

Chronological Table of Rulers

DATE	EGYPT	ASSYRIA	BABYLONIA
1300 BC	DYNASTY 19 (1295–1186):		
	Seti I (1294–1279)		
	Rameses II (1279–1213)		
	Merneptah (1213–1203)		
1200			
	DYNASTY 20 (1186–1069)		
		Tiglath-pileser I (1114–1076)	
	DYNASTY 21 (1069–945)		
1000			
	DYNASTIES 22–24 (945–715):		
	Shoshenq I (**Shishak**) (945–924)		
		Shalmaneser III (858–824)	
		Shamshi-Adad V (824–811)	
	DYNASTY 25 (780–656):		
800		Adad-nirari III (811–783)	
		Shalmaneser IV (783–773)	
		Ashur-dan III (773–755)	
		Ashur-nirari V (755–745)	
		Tiglath-pileser III (Pul) (745–727)	**Marduk-apal-iddina II (Merodach-baladan)** (721–710, 703)
		Shalmaneser V (727–722)	
		Sargon II (722–705)	
700		**Sennacherib** (705–681)	
	Taharqa (**Tirhakah**) (690–664)	**Esar-haddon** (681–669)	
		Ashurbanipal (669–627)	
		Ashur-etil-ilani (627–612)	
	DYNASTY 26 (664–525):	Sin-shum-lishir (627–612)	Nabo-polassar (625–605)
		Sin-shar-ishkun (627–612)	**Nebuchadrezzar II (Nebuchadnezzar)** (605–562)
	Psammetichus I (664–610)	Ashur-uballit II (612–609)	
	Neco II (610–595)		**Amel-Marduk (Evil-merodach)** (562–560)
	Psammetichus II (595–589)		
	Apries (**Hophra**) (589–570)		Neriglissar (560–556)
	Amasis II (570–526)		Labashi-Marduk (556)
	Psammetichus III (526–525)		**Nabonidus** (556–539)
			Belshazzar (coregent 553–543)
400			
325 BC			

Chronological Table of Rulers

Note: Names in boldface occur in the Bible. Overlapping dates indicate coregencies. Date ranges are reigns, not life spans.

1. The data are inconsistent for the dates of the reigns of Ahaz, Hezekiah, and Manasseh.

DATE	PERSIA	ISRAEL	
1300 BC			
1200			
		UNITED MONARCHY:	
		Saul (1025–1005); **David** (1005–965);	
1000		**Solomon (Yedidiah)** (968–928)	
		DIVIDED MONARCHY:	
		JUDAH:	ISRAEL:
		Rehoboam (928–911)	**Jeroboam I** (928–907)
		Abijam (Abijah) (911–908)	**Nadab** (907–906)
		Asa (908–867)	**Baasha** (906–883)
		Jehoshaphat (870–846)	**Elah** (883–882); **Zimri** (882)
			Omri (882–871)
			Ahab (873–852)
		Jehoram (Joram) (851–843)	**Ahaziah** (852–851)
		Ahaziah (Jehoahaz) (843–842)	**Jehoram (Joram)** (851–842)
		Athaliah (842–836)	**Jehu** (842–814)
800		**Jehoash** (Joash) (836–798)	**Jehoahaz** (817–800)
		Amaziah (798–769)	**Jehoash (Joash)** (800–784)
		Azariah (Uzziah) (785–733)	**Jeroboam II** (788–747)
			Zechariah (747); **Shallum** (747)
			Menahem (747–737)
			Pekahiah (737–735)
		Jotham (759–743)	**Pekah** (735–732)
		Ahaz (743/735–727/715)[1]	**Hoshea** (732–722)
		Hezekiah (727/715–698/687)[1]	
700			
		Manasseh (698/687–642)[1]	
		Amon (641–640)	
		Josiah (640–609)	
		Jehoahaz (Shallum) (609)	
		Jehoiakim (Eliakim) (608–598)	
		Jehoiachin (Jeconiah, etc.) (597)	
		Zedekiah (Mattaniah) (597–586)	
	Cyrus II (559–530)		
	Cambyses (530–522)		
	Darius I (522–486)		
	Xerxes I (**Ahasuerus**) (486–465)		
	Artaxerxes I (465–424)		
	Darius II (423–405)		
400	Artaxerxes II (405–359)		
	Artaxerxes III (359–338)		
	Artaxerxes IV (338–336)		
	Darius III (336–330)		
325 BC			

Chronological Table of Rulers

DATE	EGYPT	SYRIA
	HELLENISTIC PERIOD	**Alexander** (the Great) (336–323)
300 BC	Ptolemy I Soter (305–282)	**Seleucus I Nicator** (305–281)
	Ptolemy II Philadelphus (285–246)	Antiochus I Soter (281–261)
		Antiochus II Theos (261–246)
	Ptolemy III Euergetes (246–221)	Seleucus II Callinicus (246–225)
	Ptolemy IV Philopator (221–204)	Seleucus III Soter Ceraunos (225–223)
	Ptolemy V Epiphanes (204–180); Cleopatra I (180–176)	**Antiochus III** (the Great) (223–187)
		Seleucus IV Philopator (187–175)
		Antiochus IV Epiphanes (175–164)
	Ptolemy VI Philometor (180–145); **Cleopatra** II (175–116)	**Antiochus V Eupator** (164–162)
		Demetrius I Soter (162–150)
	Ptolemy VII Neos Philopator (145)	**Alexander Epiphanes** (Balas) (150–145)
	Ptolemy VIII Euergetes II Physcon (170–116)	**Demetrius** II Nicator (145–141 and 129–125)
		Antiochus VI Epiphanes (145–142)
		Trypho (142–138)
		Antiochus VII Sidetes (138–129)
		Cleopatra Thea (126–121)
		Antiochus VIII Grypus (125–121 and 121–96)
	Cleopatra III (116–101)	Seleucus V (125)
	Ptolemy IX Soter II (116–107 and 88–80)	Antiochus IX Cyzicenus (115–95)
100 BC	Ptolemy X Alexander I (107–88)	Seleucus VI (95)
		Antiochus X Eusebes (95–83)
		Antiochus XI Philadelphus (95)
	Cleopatra Berenice (101–88)	Demetrius III Eukairos (95–88)
		Philip I Epiphanes Philadelphus (95–84)
	Ptolemy XI Alexander II (80)	Antiochus XII Dionysus Epiphanes (87–84)
		Philip II (67–66)
	Ptolemy XII Auletes (80–59 and 55–51)	Antiochus XIII Asiaticus (69–68 and 65–64)
50 BC	Cleopatra VII (51–30)	
	Ptolemy XIII (51–47)	
	Ptolemy XIV (47–44)	
		ROMAN EMPIRE
		ROMAN EMPERORS:
		Octavian (**Augustus**) (27 BC–AD 14)
AD 25		**Tiberius** (14–37)
		Gaius Caligula (37–41)
AD 50		**Claudius** (41–54)
		Nero (54–68)
		Galba (68–69); Otho (69); Vitellius (69)
		Vespasian (69–79)
		Titus (79–81)
AD 100		Domitian (81–96)
		Nerva (96–98)
		Trajan (98–117)
		Hadrian (117–138)

DATE	PALESTINE	
300 BC		
	HASMONEAN RULERS	
	[Mattathias d. 166]	
	Judas Maccabeus, son of Mattathias (165–160)	
	Jonathan, son of Mattathias (160–142)	
	Simon, son of Mattathias (142–135)	
	John Hyrcanus I, son of Simon (135–104)	
	Judah Aristobulus I , son of John Hyrcanus (104–103)	
	Alexander Janneus, son of John Hyrcanus (103–76)	
100 BC		
	Salome Alexandra, wife of Alexander Jannaeus (76–67)	
	Aristobulus II, son of Alexander Jannaeus and Salome Alexandra (67–63)	
	Hyrcanus II, son of Alexander Jannaeus and Salome Alexandra (63–40)	
	Mattathias Antigonus, son of Aristobulus II (40–37)	
50 BC		
	HERODIAN DYNASTY	
	Herod the Great, king of the Jews (37–4)	
	Herod Archelaus, son of Herod the Great, ethnarch of Judea, Samaria, Idumea (4 BC–AD 6)	ROMAN GOVERNORS OF JUDEA
	Herod Antipas, son of Herod the Great, tetrarch of Galilee and Perea (4 BC–AD 39)	Coponius (AD 6–8) M. Ambivius (9–12)
AD 25	Herod **Philip,** son of Herod the Great, tetrarch of Batanea, Trachonitis, Auranitis (4 BC–AD 34)	Annius Rufus (12–15) Valerius Gratus (15–26) **Pontius Pilate** (26–36)
	Herod Agrippa I, grandson of Herod the Great, king of Batanea, Trachonitis, Aurantis (37–44) and of Judea, Galilee, and Perea (41–44)	Marcellus (36–37) Marullus (37–41)[2] Cuspius Fadus (44–46) Tiberius Julius Alexander (46–48)
AD 50		Ventidius Cumanus (48–52)
	Herod **Agrippa** II, son of Herod Agrippa I, king of Chalcis (50–53), king of Batanea, Trachonitis, Auranitis, Galilee, Perea (53–ca. 93)	M. Antonius **Felix** (52–60?) **Porcius Festus** (60?–62) Clodius Albinus (62–64) Gessius Florus (64–66)
AD 100		

2. In 41 Judea was made part of the kingdom of Herod Agrippa I, grandson of Herod the Great (see Herodian Dynasty, above). At his death in 44 it became a province again.

GLOSSARY

A

Abaddon (Heb "place of destruction") the realm of the dead (Job 26:6; Prov 15:11; Ps 88:10–12; Rev 9:11)

Abba (Aram "father") the word Jesus (Mark 14:36) and the early church (Rom 8:15) used to address God

accession the act of taking one's place as a ruler

acrostic a literary device in which the first letter of each line of poetry occurs according to a predetermined pattern. In the poetry of the Hebrew Bible all acrostics are alphabetical: The individual lines of a poem (or occasionally small groups of lines) begin with the twenty-two letters of the Hebrew alphabet in order. (This would be equivalent to the first line of an English poem beginning with A, the second with B, etc.) The acrostic form, besides giving the esthetic pleasure of a pattern, may have been intended to make memorization easier. It may also have been intended as a way of expressing completeness: in Lamentations, for instance, the acrostic format of the individual chapters might have been used to express the completeness of the outpouring of grief. The following poems in the Bible are acrostics: Pss 9–10, 25, 34, 37, 111, 112, 119, 145; Prov 31:10–31; Lam 1, 2, 3, 4 (Lam 5 is not an acrostic but preserves part of the form by having twenty-two lines, the number of letters in the Hebrew alphabet); Nah 1:2–8 (or 9) (incomplete). In the Hebrew text of Sirach, 51:13–30 is acrostic.

AD *anno domini* "in the year of the Lord"

Adar the twelfth month (February/March) in the Jewish year. In order to bring the lunar calendar into alignment with the solar year, a leap year, in which there are two months of Adar, occurs seven times during each nineteen-year cycle of years.

Adonai (Heb "my Lord") a divine title and the word generally substituted for **YHWH** when the Bible is read aloud

Ahikar an ancient Near Eastern story of a prime minister to the king of Assyria, who is betrayed by an ungrateful nephew but ultimately vindicated. It is alluded to in Tob 1:21–22.

Akedah (Heb "binding") the story of the binding of Isaac (Gen 22)

Akkadian the language of Assyria and Babylonia. Akkadian is a Semitic language related to Hebrew, and is written in cuneiform, wedge-shaped writing.

allegory an extended comparison that directly describes one reality while indirectly describing something entirely different. An allegory as a narrative uses action, setting, and characters to point symbolically to something else.

alleluia a Greek and Latin form of a Hebrew phrase that means "Praise the Lord." See **hallelujah**.

Amarna Letters diplomatic correspondence from the reigns of the Egyptian pharaohs Amenophis III and Akhenaten, written in **Akkadian** cuneiform, that provide information about **Canaan** in the fourteenth century BC.

Ammon, Ammonites the territory and its inhabitants east of the Jordan River

Amorites according to the Bible, one of the native nations of Canaan. Amorites are attested in other ancient Near Eastern documents from the third millennium BC and on as residents of Syria who migrated to Mesopotamia and other areas. Their language was related to Hebrew.

amphictyony a social organization in ancient Greece in which groups were united around a central sanctuary and serviced this sanctuary on a rotating basis. Some scholars think that a similar system existed in Israel in premonarchic times.

anachronism an element in a story that is out of place because it did not exist at the time in which the story is set. Anachronisms can be valuable clues to when a narrative was written.

Anat a Canaanite goddess often depicted as a warrior

anoint touch or rub with oil. Anointing was a sign that a person or thing was dedicated to God. See also **messiah**.

anthropomorphic (Gk "human form") language that presents God in human or human-like terms

antithesis the contrast of ideas through closely contrasted words

antithetic parallelism two parallel lines related to one another by opposition or contrast

aphorism a short, memorable saying

apocalypse (Gk *apokalypsis*, "removal of the veil, revelation") a literary genre in which an angel or other heavenly being communicates to a human being the divine plan for history, especially the end of time

apocalyptic having the character of an apocalypse

Apocrypha (Gk "hidden things") a group of about twenty mostly Jewish works, many of which were included in the **Septuagint**, but which are not included in the Jewish or Protestant canons of the Bible. Most of these works are canonical for Roman Catholics; a few more are canonical for Orthodox Christians. See **deuterocanon**.

apodictic law law stated absolutely, as in the Decalogue's "you shall not," rather than casuistically, "if a person. . . ." See **casuistic law**.

apologia (Gk "explanation") a defense of one's actions or beliefs, usually in a formal speech or written document

apostasy abandoning a set of beliefs, or the position of having abandoned them

apostle (Gk "one who is sent") a delegate or representative. In the New Testament, an apostle was one who had known Jesus and could witness to the resurrection (Acts 1:21–22), or a preacher of the gospel who had been called by God (1 Cor 12:28; Rom 16:7).

apostrophe an address to an absent person or personified entity

Aramaic a Semitic language used widely in the Near East during the Persian period, although it developed earlier. It became the ordinary language of Jews and was used by Jesus. An Aramaic translation of the Hebrew Bible is called a **Targum**.

Aramaism the use in another language of a word or grammatical form derived from Aramaic

Arameans a Semitic people living in Syria from the second millennium BC on. Damascus was a principal city of the Arameans.

Ark of the Covenant the chest in the Tabernacle or Temple that contained the text or tablets of the covenant, and that served as part of the throne of the LORD

Armageddon the traditional site of the final battle between good and evil (Rev 16:6), possibly derived from Megiddo, a strategically located site where many battles occurred

Asherah (pl. Asherim) Canaanite goddess, wife or consort of **El**. Her sacred symbol, a pole or tree, was the object of prophetic condemnation.

Assyria a Mesopotamian world power in the second and first millennia BC. Its capital cities included Ashur and Nineveh. The Assyrian Empire conquered the Northern Kingdom of Israel in 722 BC and exiled its people. The Assyrians were well-known for their massive building projects and for their cruelty in war.

Astarte the Canaanite goddess of love and fertility

atbash a form of code in Hebrew in which the last letter of the alphabet is substituted for the first, the next-to-last for the second, and so on: *alep* becomes *taw*, *bet* becomes *shin*, *gimel* becomes *resh*, etc. (In English, A would become Z, B would become Y, etc.) In Jer 25:26; 51:41, Babylon (b-b-l) is written Sheshach (sh-sh-k).

atonement expiation for sin, or reparation for an injury committed against another

Atrahasis hero of the Mesopotamian epic named for him, who survives the god Enlil's efforts to destroy humankind by a flood. See also **Gilgamesh**.

B

Baal ("master," "lord," "husband") the chief god of Canaanite religion, a storm god

Babylonia a Mesopotamian world power. It often competed against Assyria, which it conquered in 612 BC. Its major city was Babylon (Akk "gate of the gods"); its main god became Marduk. Babylonia destroyed Jerusalem in 586, and was conquered by the Persian king **Cyrus** the Great in 539.

Babylonian Exile the forced relocation of some of the population of Judah, especially the elite, after the conquest by Babylonia in the early sixth century BC. The Exile ended with the permitted return to the land under **Cyrus** in 538 BC.

Babylonian Talmud see **Talmud**

ban (Heb *herem*) the dedication or sacrifice of war booty (including people) to the deity

baptism ritual purification by immersion in water, used by Christians as an initiation into the community

BC Before Christ

BCE Before the Common Era, equivalent to BC

Beelzebul (also Baalzebul, Baalzebub, Beelzebub) the ruler of the demons (Matt 12:24–27). It is based on the Hebrew *Baalzebul,* "Baal the exalted," a title of the Phoenician god at Ekron (2 Kgs 1:2–18), changed probably as a derogatory name into Baalzebub, "lord of flies."

Behemoth a mythical beast in Job 40:15–24 who represents violent forces in the world

Bel (Akk "master," cognate to **Baal**) title of **Marduk**

berit (Heb "treaty, contract, covenant") a term that may be used of a legal agreement between two individuals, groups, or nations, or between God and Israel (see **covenant**)

bicolon unit of Hebrew poetry composed of two *cola,* or lines (sometimes called a *distich)*

Binding (of Isaac) see **Akedah**

Book of the Covenant see **Covenant Collection**

Booths, Festival of (Heb *Sukkot*) the autumn harvest festival, also called the Festival of Shelters), so named because the harvesters lived in the fields in makeshift tents or booths, also called tabernacles or shelters

bulla a clay seal with the impression of a signet ring or other symbol of authority

C

Cairo Geniza the storeroom (see **geniza**) of a synagogue in Old Cairo in which were discovered many thousands of fragments of texts, including a portion of the book of Sirach (Ecclesiasticus) in Hebrew

Cambyses son of **Cyrus** and king of Persia 529–522 BC. He conquered Egypt in 525.

Canaan in Mesopotamian and Egyptian documents and in some biblical texts, a name for the region that became biblical Israel. Also a grandson of Noah.

canon (Gk "measuring rod") the rule by which something is determined to belong (or not belong) to a category. Christian tradition uses the word for the official list of the books that make up the Bible.

canonical criticism the interpretation of a biblical text based upon its final form, rather than viewing it as an assemblage of preexisting units

casuistic law (also called "case law") the form of law dealing with the treatment of specific cases. It is frequently in the form of "if/when . . . then" formulae. Most ancient Near Eastern law collections are formulated this way.

CE Common Era, equivalent to AD

ceramic typology dating different levels of an archaeological site by classifying the pieces of pottery found in them according to the approximate eras in which they were made

chaos complete lack of order. In ancient Near Eastern mythology, chaos was sometimes personified as divine beings who had to be conquered by other gods in order to establish an orderly, habitable universe.

charismatic (Gk "gifted, graced") characterized

by the ability to influence or lead others; personally magnetic; talented

Chemosh the chief god of **Moab**

cherubim mythical, composite creatures with body parts from various animals; they often had wings and human heads. They were commonly guardians of temples and palaces in the ancient Near East.

chiasm, chiasmus (from Gk *chi,* the letter that resembles an "X") inverting the second pair of terms in a parallel structure, so that the corresponding terms, if laid out in a square, would form an X. The resultant pattern is ABBA, ABCBA, ABCCBA, and so forth.

Christ (Gk "anointed") the translation of Heb *mashiah,* "messiah." In the New Testament and in general usage, "Christ" always refers to Jesus of Nazareth.

Christology the theological doctrines concerning the nature of Christ

chronicle an account of events in the order in which they occurred

Chronicler the name for the unknown author of the books of Chronicles; sometimes also applied to the author of Ezra and Nehemiah

church fathers see **patristic writers**

circumcision the removal of the foreskin of the penis

Cisjordan (Lat "this side of Jordan") the region west of the Jordan River

citadel a stronghold or fortress, whether standing alone or serving as the inner fortification of a city

cities of refuge six Levitical cities, three on the east side of the Jordan, three on the west side, set apart as refuges for persons who had committed unintentional murder

clan a social unit, composed of several families considered to be descended from a common ancestor; several clans constituted a tribe

clean a state of ritual purity

climax (Gk "ladder") a series of clauses in which each succeeding clause repeats the important term from the previous clause, each clause in turn making a more important point

codex a manuscript of separate pages, bound along one edge. Modern books are a development of the codex.

colon (pl. *cola*) a single line of poetry (also known as a *stich*)

colophon (Gk "summit," by extension "finishing touch") a notice, usually found at the end of an ancient text, giving information about details such as authorship

concordance a word index to a given text, listing each occurrence of a given word along with its context

concubine a woman who is the sexual partner of a man, and is legally recognized as such, but who does not have the full status of a wife

consecrate to make or declare sacred or set aside for God

corvée forced labor for the state

cosmology an account of the origins of the cosmos

cosmos (Gk "order, regularity") the created world of order, stability, relative permanence; the opposite of chaos

Council of Trent the twenty-ninth ecumenical council of the Roman Catholic Church (1545–63), held after the Protestant Reformation had begun. Among other decisions, it defined the books that are included in the Catholic canon of Scripture.

covenant (Heb *berit*) a contract or treaty. Some covenants have specific conditions or treaty stipulations, while others are covenants of grant; often used of the relationship between God and Israel.

Covenant Code another term for **Covenant Collection**

Covenant Collection an ancient set of laws (Exod 20:19—23:33), which details the terms of the covenant between God and Israel

cult rituals and religious practices at a place of worship. The cult of the Jerusalem Temple means the religious practices carried out there, with no judgment about their value.

cult prostitute one available for sexual intercourse with worshipers at the temple of a god

Cyrus Cylinder an Akkadian inscription describing the conquest of Babylon by **Cyrus**

Cyrus king of Persia (559–530 BC). He defeated Media in 550 and conquered most of the ancient Near East, including **Babylonia**, allowing the Jewish exiles in Babylonia to return to Judah in 538.

D

D according to the **Documentary Hypothesis**, the Deuteronomic source, which covers almost the entire book of Deuteronomy

Davidic dynasty the direct descendants of King David, who ruled in Jerusalem from the tenth to the early sixth centuries BC

Day of Atonement (Heb **Yom Kippur**) the tenth day of the seventh month in the fall, a day of fasting and repentance

Day of the Lord the time mentioned in many prophetic books when God will appear as a warrior, sometimes fighting against Israel, sometimes against Israel's enemies

Dead Sea Scrolls a group of manuscripts found beginning in 1947 in caves near the Dead Sea, at Wadi Qumran. The scrolls were probably the library of an Essene settlement that flourished at the site from the second century BC until it was destroyed by the Romans in AD 68. The library included Hebrew manuscripts of biblical books older than those previously known, and other scrolls regulating the life of the community that shed light on the variety of Jewish belief and practice in the Roman period.

Decalogue (Gk "ten words") a traditional name for the list of ten commandments in Exod 20:1–17, Deut 5:6–21

defective spelling the form of a word in the Hebrew text that is missing one or more optional vowel letters

defilement a state of ritual impurity caused by contact with a corpse or other impure object. Priestly literature in the Torah is especially concerned with defilement and removing defilement.

deuterocanon, deuterocanonical (Gk "second canon") those books or portions of books not included in the Jewish or Protestant canons but accepted as canonical by some Christian churches (Roman Catholic and Orthodox) because they were included in the **Septuagint**. The NRSV places notices within the Apocryphal/Deuterocanonical Books explaining which ones are accepted by which groups.

Deutero-Isaiah see **Second Isaiah**

Deuteronomistic pertaining to the editor(s) of the history comprised in the books of Joshua, Judges, Samuel, and Kings, as prefaced by the book of Deuteronomy. The term is also applied to the style of these books, reflecting concern for such matters as obedience to the laws given in Deuteronomy, centralized worship in Jerusalem, and support for the **Davidic dynasty**.

Deuteronomistic History the account in the books Deuteronomy, Joshua, Judges, Samuel, and Kings, that presents the history of Israel in the promised land, interpreting it a partial failure to keep the covenant faithfully, and the consequences of that failure. These books show significant theological and linguistic similarities, suggesting that they have a common editor or editors.

diaspora (Gk "dispersal") the scattering of Jews from the promised land Israel, and hence any Jews living outside Israel. Also **dispersion**.

diatribe an argument against a position, or one critical of a person or group. Diatribe often includes an imagined dialogue between opposing viewpoints.

Didache (Gk "teaching") an early Christian writing, dating from around AD 150 but including earlier materials. It consists of moral exhortation, a manual of church order, and guidance for community life. It is valuable for providing insight into the concerns of early Christian communities, and contains material similar to that in the **Pastoral Epistles**.

disciple a follower, an adherent of a particular teaching

dispersion see **diaspora**

divination the effort to learn about the present or the future, by consulting mediums, interpreting omens, and the like

divine warrior God in the role of leader of the heavenly armies, usually seen as fighting for Israel. See also **holy war**.

Documentary Hypothesis a theory about the formation of the first five books of the Bible, Genesis through Deuteronomy. The hypothesis holds that there are four traditions underlying these books, naming them after a chief characteristic of each: "J" or the "Yahwist" ("J" from the German spelling "Jahweh") uses the divine name "YHWH" (the LORD) consistently and contains much of the oldest material; "E" or the "Elohist" uses the divine name "Elohim" (God) fairly consistently and contains traditions from the Northern Kingdom of Israel; "P" or the "Priestly" writer is concerned largely with legal codes and matters of religious practice; and "D" or the "Deuteronomist" represents the traditions gathered mostly in Deuteronomy.

doxology (Gk "word of glory") a prayer of praise to God, or one glorifying God

dualism the religious or philosophical view that reality consists of two basic elements, often seen as "good" and "evil"

dynasty a ruling family; when a leader dies, the next leader is always chosen from among the family members

E

E according to the **Documentary Hypothesis**, the Elohist source, which in Genesis refers to God as *elohim*. It is generally thought to have originated in the Northern Kingdom of Israel.

Edom, Edomites the territory and people to the southeast and south of Judah, first attested in late second-millennium BC texts. Edom is identified in Genesis 36 with Esau, Jacob's brother. The enmity between these brothers and between Judah and Edom mirror each other. Edom was later called **Idumea**.

El a Canaanite deity popular in the second millennium BC. In the texts from Ugarit, he is a significant deity, but is often depicted as old and is largely supplanted by **Baal**.

Elephantine Papyri Aramaic documents, mostly from the fifth century BC, found on the island of Elephantine, near Syene (modern Aswan) in Egypt. The papyri show that among those who inhabited the colony on Elephantine were Jews who kept up religious observances, such as Passover, and had their own temple.

elohim the Hebrew word usually translated "God," though its plural form is sometimes also translated "gods." It is originally a common noun (a god), though it is often used as a proper noun for the God of Israel, even though it is a plural form.

Elohist the presumed author of the **E** source according to the **Documentary Hypothesis**

encomium a formal speech praising someone, as in a funeral oration

Enuma Elish a Babylonian text in which the god Marduk becomes king of the gods after creating the cosmos from the body of the goddess of the deep, Tiamat, whom Marduk defeated

epiphany (Gk "manifestation, appearance") usually the appearance of a god or divine being in a form that can be seen by human beings

ephod (1) the linen apron worn by priests in the Temple; (2) a device used to divine the will of God. The second kind of ephod was carried in priestly garments, which may explain why the same word can be used for both.

Ephraim son of Joseph, for whom the most important tribe of the **Northern Kingdom** is named

Epicureans a Greek philosophical school, founded by Epicurus (341–270 BC), who taught that human beings naturally seek pleasure, and that the best way to achieve this pursuit was in moderation, since moderation permits the longest possible life of pleasure-seeking

Epiphanes a title, "[God] made manifest," adopted by Antiochus IV, the ruler of the part of the Greek Empire that included Judea during the second century BC. He was the king who forced pagan worship to occur in the Jerusalem Temple, thus provoking the revolt of the Maccabees.

epistle a letter, sometimes intended for public reading and therefore written according to a particular literary form

epithet a word or phrase that characterizes a person or thing, and that can often be used by itself to refer to the person

eschatological, eschatology (Gk *eschata,* "last things") a concern with the end time, or the end of the world as we know it, whether that involves a new historical era radically discontinuous from this one, or an entirely new cosmos after the destruction of the current one

Essenes a communal society in Judaism from the second century BC to the first century AD whose members lived apart in communities that were similar in some respects to later monastic groups. It is generally agreed that the **Dead Sea Scrolls** were collected and preserved by an Essene community.

etiology (Gk *aition,* "cause") an explanation for a name, an event, a custom or ritual, or a natural phenomenon. An etiological story is one that posits a particular cause (not necessarily correctly) for something.

Eucharist a ritual or service of thanksgiving, centering on the sharing of bread and wine, based on the final meal Jesus shared with his followers before his trial and crucifixion; also called Communion, the Lord's Supper, and the Mass

euphemism the substitution of an inoffensive word for one that is too explicit or impolite

evangelist (from Gk *euangelion,* "good news") the author of a gospel

exegesis (Gk "lead into") the explanation or interpretation of the meaning of a written text

exhortation urging a particular course of action or behavior by argument or advice

exile the forced removal of a people from its land, and the community in which they lived in the foreign land. The Israelites of the Northern Kingdom were exiled by the Assyrians in the late eighth century BC, and the Judeans were exiled by the Babylonians in the early sixth century. Specifically, "the Exile" is the period from 586 to 538 BC, when much of the population of Judah was deported from Judah to Babylon. See **Babylonian Exile**.

F

fable an illustrative story in which animals or plants have speaking parts

Fertile Crescent the agriculturally fertile areas of the Near East and Mesopotamia, forming an arc through the modern countries of Israel, Palestine, Jordan, Lebanon, Syria, and Iraq

festival scrolls the five short books that are read on five holy days in the Jewish calendar: Song of Songs on Passover, Ruth on the Festival of Weeks, Lamentations on 9 Ab (the date of the Temple's destruction), Ecclesiastes on the Festival of Shelters, and Esther on Purim

First Temple the Temple in Jerusalem built by King Solomon in the tenth century BC and destroyed by the Babylonians in 586 BC

form criticism the interpretation of a text with particular attention to its genre and structure and to the original setting (***Sitz im Leben***) out of which it arose

Former Prophets the name in the Hebrew Bible for the first part of the longer section called "the Prophets." The Former Prophets are the books of Joshua, Judges, Samuel, and Kings.

G

Galilee the northernmost geographical area of Israel

Gehenna originally the valley of (the son of) Hinnom, a place outside of Jerusalem where children were burned as sacrificial offerings. Its associations with burning and evil developed into the image of a place of fiery punishment.

gematria (Heb *gimatriya,* likely from Gk *geometria*) a procedure for interpreting a word or phrase by its numerical value. Hebrew letters may represent numbers (*alef* = 1; *bet* = 2, etc.), and the letters of a word or phrase are added up and equated with other words having the same total.

genealogy a list or history of the ancestors of an individual or group

geniza a storeroom in a synagogue used for keeping old books and objects, especially those too sacred to be discarded. See also **Cairo Geniza**.

genre a form of literature with particular characteristics

Gentile a non-Jew

Gilgamesh the Mesopotamian epic, whose hero, Gilgamesh, travels the world in search of immortality. Among the characters he encounters is Utnapishtim, whose tale of the flood has parallels with the biblical account of Noah.

glean to gather or collect, usually by hand, grain, fruit, or vegetables left behind by reapers

Gnosticism (from Gk *gnosis,* "knowledge") a philosophy that regards spirit and matter as opposites. According to Gnostic teaching, human beings are spirits trapped or imprisoned in matter; the material world is an illusion or the work of an inferior, even demonic, divine being; and the purpose of life is to learn how to free oneself from material things (including the body) and attain eternal life in the spiritual realm. This is accomplished by learning specialized or secret knowledge about the nature of reality; it is from this emphasis on knowledge that Gnosticism gets its name.

Greek Bible a general term for the variety of ancient translations of the Hebrew Bible into Greek in antiquity, including the **Septuagint** and the translations of Aquila, **Symmachus,** and **Theodotion**

H

H see **Holiness Code**

Hades the abode of the dead in Greek religion, used in the New Testament as the general name for the place where souls go after death

hallelujah a Hebrew acclamation, "Praise Yah!" It is frequent in the Psalms.

Hanukkah see **Hasmonean Revolt**

Hammurabi (or **Hammurapi**) king of Babylon in the eighteenth century BC, responsible for the formulation of a legal collection (the Code [or Laws] of Hammurabi) that is one of the earliest collections of case law

Hasmonean the dynasty descended from the Maccabee brothers. It ruled Judea from 135 to 36 BC; the last Hasmonean was overthrown by Herod the Great.

Hasmonean Revolt the uprising led by the family of Mattathias Heshmon against the **Seleucid** ruler Antiochus IV Epiphanes beginning in 166 BC, particularly by Mattathias's son Judah (or Judas) Maccabeus ("the hammer"), which succeeded in liberating Jerusalem and the surrounding territory from Seleucid rule in 164. When the Temple, which had been desecrated by Antiochus, was retaken by the Jews it was rededicated, an event commemorated in the festival of Hanukkah ("dedication").

Hebrew Bible a term used to refer to what Christians call the (Protestant) Old Testament. Although the two terms refer to the same body of writings, the order of books in the Hebrew Bible (that is, the Jewish Bible) differs from that found in the Old Testament.

Hellenism the spread of Greek culture, politics, and language around the Mediterranean in the period after the conquests of Alexander the Great (d. 323 BC)

Hellenistic Greek-speaking or influenced by Greek culture after the time of Alexander

Hellenize bring under the influence of Greek language and culture

herem see **ban**

hermeneutics (Gk "interpretation") the theory and practice of interpretation

Herodian followers and members of the court of Herod the Great and his sons (late first century BC to late first century AD)

Hexapla the compendium of six Bible versions (in columns: 1. Hebrew, 2. Hebrew transliterated into Greek, 3. Greek [Aquila], 4. Greek [**Symmachus**], 5. **Septuagint**, 6. Greek [**Theodotion**]) compiled by the early Christian scholar Origen (d. 254). The original was lost, but quotations from and translations of it have survived.

Hexateuch (Gk "six scrolls") a scholarly grouping of the first six books in the Bible, Genesis through Joshua. See **Pentateuch, Tetrateuch**

high places shrines, usually on a hill or a raised platform, where worship, especially sacrifices, took place

higher criticism the effort to distinguish among the sources of biblical documents, and to trace them back to their origins; distinguished from "lower criticism" or textual criticism, which is concerned with establishing the most accurate text in its final form. See **Documentary Hypothesis; synoptic problem**.

historical-critical method interpreting a text by trying to understand its original setting and audience, and what it would have meant when it was originally written or spoken. This method uses the tools of historical research to understand the conditions of the past, and critical tools to understand the traditions and developments that lie behind the surface of the text. It is also a general term that includes such methods as form criticism and redaction criticism.

Holiness Code the ritual and ethical laws in Leviticus 17–26, named from the repeated exhortation to the Israelites to be holy. The authors of this group of laws were affiliated with the Priestly school, and also wrote small sections dispersed throughout the first four books of the Bible; the entire work is also called the Holiness Collection, and is abbreviated H.

Holiness Collection see **Holiness Code**

holocaust a sacrifice entirely consumed by fire, a whole burnt offering

holy war battles conducted under divine guidance in which the LORD fought for Israel in the role of **divine warrior**

homily a sermon

hortatory characteristic of writing or speech that aims at changing the behavior of the hearers or inspiring them to a particular course of action

hosanna a Hebrew word, meaning "Save!" used as a cry of acclamation

household code a list of rules or prescribed behaviors for the members of an extended family and their servants living under one roof

Hyksos rulers in Egypt of Semitic origin in the mid-second millennium BC

hyperbole exaggeration for effect

hypostatization speaking of an abstract quality as if it were an object or a living being. See also **personification**.

hyssop a shrub related to mint. It was used as a medicine and because of its leafy branches, for ritual sprinkling of water or blood.

I

idolatry the worship of anything other than what the worshiper defines as the true God

Idumea later name for **Edom**, a kingdom located south of Judah, between the Dead Sea and the Mediterranean

Ignatius, Letters of early Christian writings of instruction. The author, Ignatius, bishop of Antioch in the late first century AD, wrote them (seven are known to have survived) on his way to martyrdom in Rome. They are largely concerned with overcoming divisions in local churches, combating false teaching, and conducting one's life properly.

impurity a ritual state which prevented an individual from participating in religious rituals (see **defilement**)

incarnation (Lat "enfleshment") the belief that a divine being has become human in some form

inclusio the use of the same word or phrase at the end of a passage as appeared at the beginning, thus rounding off or completing it. Also called inclusion, frame, and envelope structure.

incubation the practice of sleeping in a particular place, or in contact with particular things (animal skins, the ground) in order to induce dreams that might provide divine guidance

inspiration the belief that the words uttered by a human being are really the words of a divine being. In the ancient world, prophets and oracles were thought to be inspired. In Christian tradition, the notion of inspiration was eventually applied to the whole Bible.

intercalation adding a day or month to a calendar to compensate for the inexact fit between the solar year and the daily or lunar cycle. In the Jewish calendar, an extra month (a repetition of **Adar**) is intercalated in seven years of the nineteen-year cycle.

interpolation an insertion of material into a previously existent text

irony (adj., ironic) a characteristic of literature in which the reader or listener knows more than the characters about the situation in the story. By extension, an ironic aspect of a story, situation, or fact is one that from the outside looks very different than it does from the inside. Irony thus becomes a rhetorical technique in which the author's literal meaning differs from the author's intended meaning.

Ishtar Mesopotamian goddess of fertility and war

Isis Egyptian goddess, wife of Osiris, the god of vegetation and hence of regeneration

Israel the name for both the union of twelve tribal groups, of which David and Solomon were kings, and for the northern section of this kingdom, which split off after the death of Solomon and began a separate political existence under Jeroboam (1 Kgs 12). See **Northern Kingdom**, **Southern Kingdom**.

J

J (from Jahvist, German for Yahwist) according to the **Documentary Hypothesis**, the document or source that uses the divine name (see **YHWH**). J is usually understood to be the earliest source, and to have been written in Judah. It frequently depicts God in very anthropomorphic terms.

Jerome (ca. AD 340–420) Christian theologian and translator. He translated the Bible into Latin, in the case of the Old Testament directly from the Hebrew. His version became known as the Vulgate ("common") because it was commonly used in western Christianity. With the Protestant Reformation, its authority was questioned, but was reaffirmed by the Roman Catholic Church at the **Council of Trent**.

Joseph and Aseneth (also spelled Asenath) a Jewish novel written in Greek in the first century BC or the first century AD about Joseph's life in Egypt; his marriage to Asenath, the daughter of an Egyptian priest (see Gen 41:45); her conversion to faith in Joseph's God; and their triumph over a plot to kill them.

Josephus a Jewish historian who lived from about AD 37 to about AD 100. Four of his works, all written in Greek, have survived: *The Jewish War,* an account of the rebellion against Rome in AD 66–70, with background information starting at about 200 BC; *The Antiquities of the Jews,* a complete history from the creation up to the point where *The Jewish War* begins; *Against Apion,* a defense of Judaism; and an autobiography, the *Life*.

jubilee (Heb *yovel,* perhaps "ram" from the sounding of the ram's horn to mark the beginning of the observance) the year of release for slaves and return of ancestral lands to their original owners (or descendants of the owners), to occur every fifty years (after seven sabbaths of years). It is a cornerstone of Priestly ideology, but it is uncertain if it was ever practiced.

Jubilees, book of a retelling, attributed to Moses, of much of Genesis and Exodus and representing itself as a hidden revelation from the Angel of the Presence. It was most likely written in the second century BC in Judea. The book gets its name from its concern with cycles of time. Jubilees was apparently considered authoritative by the Qumran community.

Judah the major tribal group of the Southern Kingdom, named for one of the sons of Jacob. After the death of Solomon in the late tenth century BC, the kingdom was divided into two, with Judah in the south and Israel in the north. The capital of Judah was Jerusalem.

Judea the Roman name for **Judah**

K

kere see ***qere***

Ketubim (also Kethubim, Ketuvim) The Writings, the third division of the Hebrew Bible

ketib ("what is written"; also *ketiv*) the biblical text in its written form, in contrast, in certain cases, to the way it is to be read aloud (***qere***)

kosher (Heb "fit" or "proper") a general term used in postbiblical texts for dietary laws; usually applied to food, but also to other ritual objects and practices

L

lament a poem of grief or mourning (see also **qinah**)

Latter Prophets the canonical division of **Nevi'im** that includes the books of Isaiah, Jeremiah, Ezekiel, and the Twelve **Minor Prophets**

law the usual English translation of Hebrew *torah,* which more generally means "teaching, instruction." *Torah* is also the name for the first five books of the Hebrew Bible, Genesis through Deuteronomy.

lectionary a list of readings of Scripture passages for sabbaths and holy days (in Judaism) or Sundays and holy days (in Christianity). Christian lectionaries also sometimes include readings for weekdays. Lectionaries are partly designed to read certain portions of the Bible—for instance, the Torah, in Jewish lectionaries, or the first three Gospels, in many Christian lectionaries—completely through, in order, over a lectionary cycle of a year or several years. In addition, in Christian lectionaries important seasons (for instance, Christmas or Easter) have their own specific readings outside the continuous readings. In the synagogue, the Torah reading is followed by what is called a Haftarah reading (*haphtarah* is Hebrew for "conclusion, completion") from one of the prophets; in addition, the **festival scrolls** are read on five holy days.

legate an official representative

legend a popular story, sometimes exaggerated or romanticized, about a holy or important person or place

Leviathan a monster of the sea in Canaanite mythology, who is defeated by Baal. It is sometimes identified with the crocodile (Job 41:1) and represents the forces of watery chaos which must be overcome at creation (Ps 74:1–17) and that will be finally defeated at the end of time (Isa 27:1). In the book of Revelation, the dragon, the enemy of God, is identified with the sea (17:1, 3), and in the new creation there is no more sea (21:1).

levirate marriage (from Lat *levir,* "husband's brother") the provision that if a man died without an heir to carry on his name, his brother would marry the widow and the first son she bore would be regarded as the dead brother's heir

lex talionis (Lat "law [of retribution] in kind") punishment fitting the crime; see **talion**

lingua franca a common tongue or shared language that enables people with different native languages to converse, carry on commercial relationships, etc. In the Persian period **Aramaic** replaced Akkadian as a lingua franca around the Near East; during the Hellenistic period Greek did the same for the lands surrounding the eastern Mediterranean.

littoral a region along the shore of a large body of water

liturgy the form or ritual for communal, public worship

lower criticism or **textual criticism** see **higher criticism**

LXX the roman numeral 70, the standard abbreviation for the **Septuagint**

M

Maat Egyptian goddess of reason and order; her name literally means "truth"

malediction curse; opposite of benediction, "blessing"

manumission release from servitude

Marduk chief god of Babylon; according to ***Enuma Elish,*** he formed the cosmos from the corpse of **Tiamat**, goddess of the deep

martyr (Gk "witness") a person who demonstrates loyalty by remaining faithful to his or her religion even when being threatened with death or being killed

Masorah (Heb "tradition") the system of markings (vowel signs, marginal notes, cantillation and accent marks, etc.) that were added to the consonantal Hebrew text by scribal scholars (**Masoretes**) in the early Middle Ages

Masorete a scholar of the scribal schools that in the early Middle Ages established the basic Hebrew text for the Bible, fixed its accepted pronunciation, and ensured its accurate copying and transmission by a system of markings (**Masorah**)

Masoretic Text the text of the Hebrew Bible, established by Jewish scholars (**Masoretes**). The text consists of the Hebrew consonants, vowel signs, accent markings, and other notes. Texts derived from this effort date from ca. AD 900 to AD 1000. The Masoretic Text is the only complete form of the Hebrew Bible that has survived, though individual manuscripts of books are among the **Dead Sea Scrolls**.

matrilineal tracing descent through female ancestors; see **patrilineal**

matzah unleavened bread, associated with **Passover**, but also used with certain sacrifices.

Megillot Heb "scrolls," or more specifically the five **festival scrolls**

merism a figure of speech in which opposing terms, e.g., "good and bad," are combined to convey the idea of including both terms and everything in between

Merneptah Stele an Egyptian inscribed stone that includes the first mention of Israel outside the Bible. It celebrates victories of Pharaoh Merneptah (ca. 1200 BC) in Canaan.

Merodach a Hebrew version of **Marduk,** chief god of Babylon

Mesha Stele (also called the Moabite Stone) a monument dating from about 830 BC with engraved text celebrating the reign of King Mesha of **Moab** (2 Kgs 3:4–5). Besides an account of the dealings of Mesha with the descendants of Omri, king of the Northern Kingdom of Israel, the text mentions the god of Moab, Chemosh, and the favor that Chemosh has shown to Mesha in contrast to his predecessors in allowing Mesha to reclaim territory from Israel. It also contains a reference to the ***herem*** or ban.

Mesopotamia (Gk "between the rivers") the area between the Tigris and Euphrates rivers

messiah (Heb *mashiah,* "anointed [one]") a title for a king or other servant or agent of God (priest, prophet, or even the non-Israelite Cyrus in Isa 45:1). In the Hebrew Bible, *mashiah* never refers to the future ideal king. Later the term came to be used of the expected savior of the Jewish people, and was taken over by Christians to refer to Jesus, whom they believed to be the messiah (Gk *christos,* "anointed"). See also **Christ**.

metaphor a direct comparison between two things

mezuzah (Heb "doorpost") a parchment on which are written the paragraphs of the **Shema**

midrash, midrashic (Heb *derash* "inquire") interpretation that finds meanings in a text that are other than, or go beyond, the "plain sense" (see ***peshat***)

Milcom the principal god of the **Ammonites**; also called **Molech**

Minor Prophets (so-called because compared to the Major Prophets, Isaiah, Jeremiah, and Ezekiel, they are much shorter) the books from Hosea through Malachi; in the Hebrew Bible they are treated as one collection, "The Book of the Twelve."

Mishnah (Heb "oral instruction," from *shanah* "repeat") the compilation of oral law and rabbinic commentary, edited ca. AD 200, that is the basis of the **Talmud**

Moab, Moabites the territory and its inhabitants east of the Dead Sea

Moabite Stone see **Mesha Stele**

Molech a Canaanite god whose worship according to the biblical writers included child sacrifice

Mot the **Canaan**ite god of death

motif an image or character type that recurs throughout a literary work

mystery in the New Testament, a divine truth that is kept hidden or secret by God until the right moment for it to be revealed

mystery religion any one of various religious groups in the Greek and Roman empires which practiced secret rites of initiation. Mystery religions taught that the real meaning of life could not be learned without divine guidance and that such guidance was available in their secret teachings and practices. These secret rites were themselves known as "mysteries," and had the sense of a revelation from the divine realm that is similar to some of the New Testament uses of "mystery."

N

narrative a connected, orderly account of an incident, or a longer account including many incidents. Narratives can be historical, fictional, legendary, mythical, or a combination of types.

Nebi'im see **Nevi'im**

necromancy the practice of divination by communication with the dead, who were presumed to have knowledge of the future

Negeb, Negev the region south of the central hill country of Israel

Nevi'im (also Nebi'im) the Prophets, the second division of the Hebrew Bible, subdivided into the **Former Prophets** and the **Latter Prophets**

new moon the beginning of any month in the Jewish calendar

Northern Kingdom the political assembly of tribal groups that split off from the kingdom of Israel after Solomon's death. This newly formed kingdom was itself called Israel, and in some texts also **Ephraim**, after its largest tribe.

novel a fictional work in prose. Ancient novels were often **romances**

O

obelisk a four-sided stone shaft, usually tapered and topped with a pyramid, characteristic of ancient Egypt

Old Latin the Latin translation of the Bible based on the Greek text, the **Septuagint**. The Old Latin version was replaced by the Vulgate, the Latin translation by **Jerome**.

oracle (usually translates Heb *masa,'* lit "burden") a statement uttered by a prophet or other sacred person, purporting to be the words of a deity

oracular having the qualities of an oracle or sacred speech

Oral Torah a synonym for the **Mishnah** and **Talmud**. According to traditional rabbinic belief, the Oral Law was given to Moses on Mount Sinai along with the written law, the Torah. It was committed to writing by the rabbis in the first millennium AD.

ordination a formal ceremony and process by which certain members of the community are set apart for religious service, for instance as priests

oxymoron (Gk "clever-foolish") combining two terms that appear contradictory

P

P according to the **Documentary Hypothesis**, the Priestly source in the Pentateuch, comprised of both narratives and laws. It is concerned, among other things, with laws and regulations, ritual practices, the proper conduct of the Temple worship, holiness and purity, and genealogies.

Palestine a name first used by the fifth-century BC historian Herodotus and adopted by the Romans in the designation *Provincia Syria Palaestina* ("Syro-Palestinian Province"), which replaced *Provincia Judaea* ("Judean Province") after AD 135. The word is derived from the term translated "**Philistine**," and the Latin spelling of "Philistine," and the Roman designation was probably intended as a derogation of Jewish claims to the territory.

parable a statement or story that uses figurative or imaginative language to evoke a reality that lies beyond the literal level of the story of statement. A parable makes its point by analogy, or the comparison of a known fact, situation, or experience with one that is less familiar.

parenesis moral exhortation

parallelism a characteristic feature of biblical Hebrew poetry in which the second line of a unit in some way echoes the meaning or grammatical structure of the first line. This can take the form of a repetition of the meaning, or of a statement of opposites, or of a further statement that serves to extend or modify the first line in some way.

parousia (Gk "coming") the second coming of Christ; the expected return of the **messiah** at the end of the age or the end of the world

Paschal pertaining to the **Passover** (ultimately from Gk *pascha,* derived from Heb *pesah*)

Passover (Heb *pesah*) the festival that commemorates the Exodus of the Israelites from Egypt

Pastoral Epistles or **Pastoral Letters** a term used for three letters attributed to Paul, 1 and 2 Timothy, and Titus

patriarchs the ancestors of Israel: Abraham, Isaac, and Jacob

patrilineal tracing one's descent through male ancestors; see also **matrilineal**

patristic writers theologians of the early Christian centuries, including Clement, Irenaeus, Origen, and Jerome

penitential psalms Psalms 6, 32, 38, 51, 102, 130, and 143, used in Christian services of repentance from the earliest times

Pentapolis the five cities of the **Philistines**: Ashdod, Ashkelon, Ekron, Gath, Gaza

Pentateuch (Gk "five scrolls") the first five books of the Bible, Genesis through Deuteronomy; the Torah

Pentecost see **Weeks, Festival of**

pericope a selection from a book

periphrasis, periphrastic the use of more words than necessary to express a thought

Persian period the era from 539 to 333 BC, from Cyrus until Alexander

personification representing an idea, a value, or other abstract thought as a person

Pesah see **Passover**

peshat (Heb "simple") the "plain sense" or "contextual sense" of a text, often contrasted with *derash,* the homiletical meaning

pesher (pl. *pesharim;* "interpretation") a type of commentary on the Bible in the **Dead Sea Scrolls** in which the biblical text is understood to be fulfilled in the interpreter's time

Peshitta (Syriac, "simple") the name of the Syriac translation of the Bible (called "simple" because it was a plain translation from Hebrew, not a translation with textual apparatus like the **Syrohexapla**). The Peshitta contains books of the Bible translated by Jews for Jewish worshipers who spoke Syriac, but it was taken over and completed (including a New Testament) by Syriac-speaking Christians.

Pharisees a Jewish sect in the first century AD, according to Josephus and the New Testament. The Pharisees were concerned to extend Jewish practice into all areas of life, and followed the tradition of interpretation (**Oral Torah**) associated with the schools of Hillel and Shammai. They were opponents of the more conservative **Sadducees**, who did not accept their traditions of oral law.

Philistines a group of the **Sea Peoples**, who invaded and settled in on the southeastern coast of the Mediterranean in the late second millennium BC, having been repulsed in an invasion of Egypt (ca. 1190 BC). The five major Philistine cities (the **Pentapolis**) were Ashkelon, Ashdod, Ekron, Gath, and Gaza.

Philo a Hellenistic Jewish philosopher and interpreter of Scripture, who lived in Alexandria, Egypt, from about 20 BC to AD 50. He wrote works in philosophy, scriptural interpretation, and history. In Philo's view, the best insights of Greek philosophy could be found in the Bible by means of allegorical interpretation. He influenced Jewish writers like the author of the Wisdom of Solomon and Christian theologians such as Clement, Origen, and Ambrose.

Phoenicians the people who lived in the area north of Israel, in part of what is present-day Lebanon. Their chief cities were Tyre and Sidon. The Phoenicians were known throughout the eastern Mediterranean region as merchants, and for producing a reddish-purple dye, from which they apparently got their name (*phoinix* is the Gk word for the color of the dye).

phylacteries (Gk *phulakterion,* "amulet," from *phulax,* "guard") small black leather boxes containing biblical passages (Exod 13:1–10, 13:11–16; Deut 6:4–9, 11:13–21), worn during prayer on the head and on the left arm. Also called "tefillin."

Platonism a philosophy derived from the teaching of Plato, saying that there is a profound difference, even an opposition, between the realm of matter and the realm of spirit, and that the world of sense experience is essentially an illusion, deriving what reality it has from a correspondence with a true, ultimately real world of Forms

pogrom an officially encouraged, organized massacre of a minority group

polemic, polemical (Gk *polemos,* "war") an argument or debate in the form of an attack on one's opponent or on the opposing position. Polemical speech is characterized by verbal attacks, exaggerated language, and sometimes violent imagery

Polycarp, Letter of an early second-century AD Christian letter of instruction, written by Polycarp, bishop of Smyrna, and addressed to the church of Philippi

potsherd a broken piece of pottery. Examination of such pieces allows archaeologists to date the different levels of a site according to the type of pottery represented at a given level.

primogeniture the social tradition by which the eldest son inherits a father's title or the bulk of the father's property

proem a short introduction or preface to a literary text

prophet (Gk *prophetes,* "speak out" or "speak forth") the **Septuagint** translation of *nabi'* ("one who is called"), the standard Heb term for prophet. Synonyms include "seer," "man of God," and "visionary."

prophetic lawsuit (Heb *rib*) a literary form in the prophets and elsewhere in which the people are accused of breaking their covenant with God

Prophets, The (Heb **Nevi'im**) the second division of the **Hebrew Bible**

pseudepigrapha (Gk "writings with false attributions of authorship") a diverse group of Jewish or Christian religious writings that are not included in the books of the Hebrew Bible, the New Testament, or the Apocrypha. These writings date from about 250 BC to AD 200, and some of them are quoted from or alluded to in the Bible.

pseudonymous written or published under a false name. Pseudonymous writing in antiquity is often attributed to someone much better known than the actual writer, in order to give the text the benefit of the presumed authority of the famous person.

Ptolemies the rulers of Egypt and its surrounding areas after the breakup of the Greek Empire of Alexander the Great, following his death in 323 BC

Purim the festival that commemorates the delivery of the Jews in Persia from destruction, as recounted in the book of Esther

Q

Q see **synoptic problem**

qere ("what is read") in the **Masoretic Text**, a word as it should be pronounced, in contrast to what is written (*ketib*) in the main text

qinah meter a metrical pattern consisting of a line with three stresses followed by a line with two stresses; it is primarily used in psalms of lament or complaint, and in the book of Lamentations

Qumran community the settlement near Wadi Qumran at the Dead Sea, most likely composed of Essenes. The Qumran group was a sectarian Jewish community that kept its own practices in opposition to the established community in Jerusalem and Judea; the library of this group was discovered beginning in 1947 and is known as the **Dead Sea Scrolls**.

R

rabbi (Aram "teacher") a Jewish religious leader who studies the **Torah** and its associated commentaries, particularly the **Talmud**, and offers his own teaching based on that study

reader-response criticism analyzing a text by looking at the relationship between the text and its reader, including the clues within the text that guide the reader in drawing meaning from it

redaction criticism the study of how already existing textual units—narratives of incidents, laws, proverbs, or other isolatable pieces that can be disentangled by **source criticism**—were combined into larger texts by the activities of editors, called **redactors**

redactor an editor who works with already existing units to combine them into larger wholes

resident alien a foreigner with legal rights living in Israel or an Israelite residing in the territory of another tribe

revelation (Lat "remove the veil," translating Gk *apokalypsis*) belief or insight granted to a human being by a deity or heavenly being

rhetoric (Gk *rhetor*, "speaker, orator") the art or study of persuasive speech or writing

Roman period the period of Roman rule in Judea, beginning in 63 BC

romance a popular storytelling technique in the ancient Mediterranean world that recounted the situation of young lovers and how they overcame obstacles to their marriage. In early Christianity the form was modified to tell the stories of early converts and martyrs and the obstacles to their faith.

Rule of the Community one of the Dead Sea Scrolls (1QS) that sets out the arrangements under which the community functioned and those that they held up as an ideal: holding property in common; eating, blessing, and advising one another in unity; preparing for the end time; and training new members of the community in their responsibilities

S

sackcloth rough cloth, often made from animal hair. A garment made of sackcloth is uncomfortable and is worn to indicate penitence or grief.

Sadducees a Jewish sect in the first century AD, according to Josephus and the New Testament. They held to a strict application of Torah and to maintaining Temple worship according to its mandate. They were opposed to the **Pharisees** in not accepting the traditions of oral law, and they were also opposed to the political activists who wished to rebel against Roman rule, fearing that any rebellion would bring an end to the limited autonomy under which they could maintain Temple worship.

saga popular narrative account of prehistory or events of the distant past. Sagas often involve stories of the ancestors of a group or the founders of a country.

Samaritan Pentateuch a Hebrew text of the first five books of the Bible used by the **Samaritans**. This text differs from the **Masoretic Text** at many points. Some of these disagreements reflect Samaritan beliefs, but others are supported by the **Dead Sea Scrolls** and reflect an alternate textual tradition.

Samaritans the descendants of the population of Samaria (the capital of the **Northern Kingdom** of Israel) after the Assyrían invasion of that kingdom and the deportation of its inhabitants in 722 BC. The Samaritans regard themselves as descended from the Jewish remnant after the deportation, but the returning exiles from the Southern Kingdom of Judah (after the **Babylonian Exile** in the early sixth century) did not regard them as Jews, seeing them rather as descendants of foreigners who had been settled there after the Jewish population had been removed. Therefore, beginning with Ezra and Nehemiah, the leadership forbade intermarriage between Samaritans and Jews. The Samaritans maintained worship (with a temple on Mount Gerizim) and the **Pentateuch** (but not the rest of the Bible), although their calendar is not the same as the Jewish calendar.

Sanhedrin (ultimately from Gk *synedria* from *syn-* and *hedra*, "with seat," i.e., "council") the religious court, whose membership was drawn from the Jewish ruling classes, that held ruling authority over the territory of Palestine under the Roman Empire. The Sanhedrin was responsible for census-taking and taxation as well as for acting as a court that would decide cases on its own and also, after preliminary determination, send cases on to the Roman governors. "Sanhedrin" is also the title of a tractate of the **Mishnah** dealing with law courts in general.

scribe in general, one who could write, especially official documents, and take down dictation for letters, legal proceedings, etc. In the New Testament, a scribe was a lawyer, one who was expert in the requirements and meaning of Jewish law, especially the **Torah**.

scroll a long strip of parchment (treated leather) or papyrus (reeds split, moistened, and pressed together), on which a text was written in columns. The scroll was read by unrolling one side while rolling up the other, to expose successive columns of text.

Sea Peoples remnants of the Mycenean or Aegean civilizations, which collapsed toward the end of the second millennium BC. Some of these people sailed eastward on the Mediterranean and attacked those living along the coast; they were repulsed from Egypt and settled in southwest Canaan. The biblical **Philistines** are among the Sea Peoples.

Second Isaiah, also **Deutero-Isaiah**, the general term for chapters 40–55 of the book of Isaiah. These chapters are primarily concerned with the events leading up to the decree of the Persian king Cyrus in 538 BC permitting the exiles to return to Judah from Babylon and rebuild Jerusalem and the Temple. See also **Third Isaiah**.

Second Temple the Temple constructed beginning ca. 515 BC by the returning exiles, and continued and expanded over the course of time, until its destruction by the Romans in AD 70

sect a religious grouping that emphasizes strict adherence to particular teachings and excludes those who do not conform

seder (Heb "order") the ritual meal and recitation of Passover. Also, the major divisions of the **Mishnah** (pl. *sedarim*).

Seleucids the rulers of Syria and its surrounding areas after the breakup of the Greek Empire of Alexander the Great, following his death. The Seleucid ruler Antiochus IV "Epiphanes" desecrated the Temple in 167 BC, leading to the Maccabean revolt and the rededication of the Temple in 164 BC, an event commemorated in the festival of Hanukkah.

Septuagint the ancient Greek translation of the Hebrew Scriptures. The Septuagint was translated over a lengthy period beginning probably in the third century BC. Traditionally there were seventy-two translators, a number that was rounded off to seventy and, in roman numerals, used as the abbreviation for this translation (LXX). The Septuagint was prepared for the use of Jews who lived in the **diaspora** whose main language was Greek. It is important for several reasons: it translated a version of the Hebrew text that is older than the **Masoretic Text**; it contains additional works, grouped in NRSV as the Apocryphal/Deuterocanonical Books, most of which were originally written in Greek; and it was the Old Testament of early Christians.

Shavuot see **Weeks, Festival of**

Shema the first word, used as a title, of the exhortation "Hear, O Israel, the LORD is our God, the LORD alone" (Deut 6:4); also the name of perhaps the most important and best-known prayer in Judaism, comprised of Deut 6:4–9; 11:13–21; and Num 15:37–41

Sheol the underworld or abode of the dead

Shephelah the foothills leading to the central hill country of the land of Israel

shofar, also **shophar**, the ram's horn for ceremonial use. In ancient Israel it was sounded to announce the anointing of a king or as a summons to war or to sound an alarm; today, in the synagogue, it is sounded on the High Holy Days.

signet ring a ring bearing a personal seal, used to make an indentation in clay as a sign of authenticity of authorship

simile a comparison, using "like" or "as" rather than, as in metaphor, linking two things directly

Sitz im Leben (Ger "setting in life") in **form criticism**, the original context in which a specific genre or form was used

sorites a philosophical argument in the form of linked propositions. The second part of each proposition forms the first part of the next, and the series therefore becomes an extended chain of reasoning.

source criticism the effort to discover the sources or documents behind a text and to explore how the sources were combined into larger units. See **Documentary Hypothesis**.

Southern Kingdom see **Judah**

Stoics Greek philosophers in the Hellenistic and Roman periods, who taught that emotions should be strictly controlled by reason

Sukkot see **Booths, Festival of**

Sumer a civilization that ruled southern Mesopotamia from the late fourth millennium to the early second millennium BC. The Sumerians developed cuneiform writing, which involved using a wedge-shaped reed to press marks into wet clay; the clay was then baked.

suzerain the lord or ruler to whom loyalty is due in a covenant relationship

Symmachus a second-century AD translator of the Bible into Greek, whose translation was included in Origen's **Hexapla** (a compendium of six Bible versions)

synagogue (Gk "coming together with") an assembly; a congregation. For Jews who were too distant from the Temple to worship at it, and for all Jews after the final destruction of the Temple by the Romans in AD 70, the synagogue became the only form of worship. Services consisted of prayer, song, and study of the sacred text.

syncretism the incorporation into one religion of practices and teachings derived from another, or the effort to combine two different religious traditions into a third, composite religion

synonymous parallelism a type of **parallelism** where the second line or **colon** of a **bicolon** echoes the meaning of the first in different terms

Synoptic Gospels Matthew, Mark, and Luke. "Synoptic" means "view together," and is applied to these writings because they, unlike John, can be readily compared.

synoptic problem the observation that in many passages Matthew and Luke repeat with only minor changes what Mark says, yet in other passages they do not follow Mark, or include stories or sayings that Mark does not have, yet match each other very closely. According to the most widely held theory, Matthew and Luke relied on Mark and on another document (now lost) that contained mostly sayings of Jesus; this second document is referred to as "Q" (from the German word "Quelle," meaning "source"). In addition, Matthew and Luke each had their own sources.

Syriac an eastern form of **Aramaic** that was the language of some Jews and of some eastern Christian communities in the early centuries AD. It is the language of the **Peshitta**.

Syrohexapla (or Syriac hexapla) a Syriac translation of the Septuagint text that provides textual evidence about the nature of the Septuagint. Although the Hexapla was translated in the seventh century AD, it is based upon a **Septuagint** text dating from as early as the third century AD.

T

Tabernacle the portable sanctuary used by the Israelites during their wanderings in the wilderness

Tabernacles, Feast of see **Booths, Festival of**

tablet a slab, typically of clay, with a smoothed surface that can be inscribed with a text

talion (Lat *talio*, "in kind" from *talis*, "like," "such like") a punishment that is of the same kind as the crime, exacting an equivalent penalty, such as an equal economic loss for theft, or death for murder, or "an eye for an eye." Talion is well attested in Mesopotamian law, and in some biblical legal collections.

Talmud (Heb "teaching") the title of the two great collections of rabbinic teaching, the Jerusalem Talmud (also called the Palestinian Talmud or the Talmud of the Land of Israel) and the Babylonian Talmud. The Talmuds were compiled beginning after AD 200. They consist of comments on, and extensions of, the Mishnah in order to apply Jewish teaching to everyday life, but they also include information on a wide range of topics. The two centers of rabbinic study (the land of Israel and Babylonia) were in contact with each other and the commentary therefore reflected a common effort; later, especially with the completion of the Talmud in Israel (ca. AD 400), the Babylonian effort continued to refine and extend the applications, and it was the Talmud developed in Babylonia (completion after AD 500) that was distributed worldwide, under the auspices of the academies that continued to work in Babylon until the beginning of the second millennium AD.

Tanakh an acronym formed from the beginning letters of the three divisions of the **Hebrew Bible**: Torah, Nevi'im, Ketubim

Targum translation of the Hebrew Bible into **Aramaic**. The Targums are important for textual criticism of the Hebrew text, since they provide evidence about it at a stage earlier than that of the **Masoretic Text**.

tel (Heb), **tell** (Arab) a mound formed by repeated construction, occupation, and destruction of buildings on a particular site

Temple the central place of worship for Israelite religion in Jerusalem, referring either to the **First Temple** or the **Second Temple**

Tetragrammaton (Gk "four letters") the divine name, **YHWH**

Tetrateuch the first four books of the Bible, Genesis through Numbers, regarded by some scholars as an edited collection to which Deuteronomy was then attached. See **Pentateuch**.

textual criticism the effort to establish, by scholarly assessment of manuscript copies and other sources, an accurate version of a text; also called "lower criticism"

theocracy a form of government by God (or a god), usually through a priestly order. Israel was a theocracy from the time of Moses until the monarchy began with Saul.

theodicy the theological effort to justify the goodness of God in the face of suffering

Theodotion (ca. second century AD) a translator of the Hebrew Bible into Greek and reviser of the Septuagint

theophany (Gk "appearance of god") the temporary appearance or manifestation of a divine being in a form that can be apprehended by the human senses

Third Isaiah, also **Trito-Isaiah**, the scholarly term for chapters 56–66 of the book of Isaiah, which are primarily concerned with the life of the returned exiles in the province of Yehud (the Persian name for Judah) after 538 BC. Some scholars doubt the separate existence of Third Isaiah; others maintain that it is not the product of one author, but a collection of diverse oracles by different members of a "school of Isaiah" collected during the **Persian period**. See also **Second Isaiah**.

Thomas, Gospel of an early collection of sayings attributed to Jesus. It contains no miracle stories and no account of Jesus' deeds, his birth, death, or resurrection. Some of the sayings resemble those in the canonical Gospels, but others reflect **Gnosticism**.

thresh to beat gathered stalks of grain in order to separate the grain from the stems and husks. A threshing floor, a flat area used for threshing grain, was often built on a hilltop to catch the breeze necessary for **winnowing**.

threshing floor see **thresh**

Tiamat goddess of the deep and mother of the Babylonian pantheon; she is sometimes portrayed as a dragon

Torah (Heb "teaching, instruction") the first division of the Hebrew Bible, consisting of Genesis through Deuteronomy. The word (and hence the title) is sometimes translated "law," but this translation is misleading since the five books contain much more than law codes and regulations.

tradition criticism the investigation of the development of a text from its earliest stages (oral or original source documents) to the latest (canonical) stage

Transjordan the region east of the Jordan River

transmission history an account, usually inferred, of how a text came down to the present from its originator. Steps in transmission history can include oral transmission, redaction, manuscript copying, and scribal emendation.

Trito-Isaiah see **Third Isaiah**

Twelve, Book of the see **Minor Prophets**

typology (Gk *tupos*) the raised design on a seal for imprinting in wax, then by extension a pattern or model) understanding persons or events, especially in the New Testament, by referring them to earlier biblical precursors.

U

Ugarit city on the Mediterranean coast (Ras-Shamra in present-day Syria), source of an important collection of Canaanite myths and other texts from the second half of the second millennium BC in a language called Ugaritic, which was related to Hebrew

unclean A state of ritual impurity, which required cleansing. A person's being unclean did not mean she or he had committed a sin. Some substances are permanently unclean and cannot be made ritually pure.

unleavened bread (Heb *matzah,* pl. *matzot*)

bread made without yeast; also the Festival of Unleavened Bread associated with **Passover**.

Urim and Thummim a method of **divination** used to discover God's response to "yes" or "no" questions

V

vassal the underlord in a covenant relationship, who is granted power and control over people in a particular area in return for loyalty to the **suzerain**

Vassal Treaty of Esarhaddon an Assyrian treaty document from the reign of the Assyrian king Esarhaddon (681–669 BC), with parallels to parts of Deuteronomy

Vulgate *see* **Jerome**

W

wadi (Arab) a stream bed or valley that is dry for part of the year; an arroyo or gulch

Weeks, Festival of (Heb *Shavuot*; "Pentecost," Gk for "fiftieth" [day]) the spring harvest, occurring according to Priestly texts fifty days (seven full weeks) after Passover

winnow to separate grain from its husks (called chaff) after it has been threshed. The threshed grain is placed in a wide, flat basket and tossed repeatedly into the air, allowing a breeze to blow away the lighter chaff while the grain drops back down into the basket.

wisdom literature Job, Proverbs, and Ecclesiastes in the Hebrew Bible, Sirach and Wisdom in the Apocrypha, and some Psalms. Wisdom literature is concerned with insight, instruction, meditation of the meaning of life, and moral exhortation. It does not generally concern itself with key events in Israel's history, such as the Exodus; central teachings, such as the covenant; or focal institutions, such as the Davidic monarchy, prophecy, or the Temple.

Writings the third division of the **Hebrew Bible**

Y

Yahweh see **YHWH**

Yehud designation of the province of Judea during Persian times

YHWH (sometimes also YHVH) the name of God, which in Jewish tradition is conventionally unpronounced; moden scholars use the conventional pronunciation "Yahweh." The name is represented in the **Masoretic Text** by the Hebrew letters *yod-he-vav-he* and the vowels for the title *Adonai*, "my Lord." In most English translations, following an ancient substitution, YHWH is represented by the word LORD written in capital and small capital letters. The original vocalization and meaning of this name is uncertain, though it is connected to the verb *h-y-h*, "be" or "become," most likely in a causative sense, "he who causes to be."

Yom Kippur see **Day of Atonement**

Z

Zealot a member of a Jewish revolutionary movement during the Roman occupation of Palestine in the first century AD

ziggurat a temple-tower in ancient Mesopotamia. Ziggurats are presumed to represent a mount, on the top of which the earthly and divine realms merged.

Zion the name of the fortified hill within Jerusalem and thus, by extension, an alternative name for Jerusalem itself, especially in bibilical poetry

INDEX OF WOMEN

To the reader: This index makes no attempt to list every woman mentioned in the Bible. Rather, it includes those who are portrayed as having an active role in the story of God's relationship with his people or those from whom readers can learn about the lives of women at the time or in modern days. Women named in genealogies, greeted in letters, or mentioned in passing should not be considered less important because all we know about each one is her name.

Unnamed women are listed in one of two ways:

1 The most common way of referring to them in the notes and other modern resources. This is often a familial relationship or a place name, e.g., Manoah's wife or the Shunammite woman.

2 A descriptor of their situation or story, e.g., Girl Possessed by a Demon or Widow Aided by Elisha.

Small Caps indicate that the word or name has its own entry.

Scripture references include complete stories, not just the specific verses in which the woman is named or mentioned. While the primary purpose of the index is as a reference tool, it can also be used as a study or reading guide, allowing the reader to explore previously unknown stories.

✧

A

ABIGAIL, wife of Nabal, and afterwards of David
1 Sam 25
27:3
30:5

ABISHAG, ministers to David, cause of breach between Solomon and Adonijah
1 Kgs 1:1–4
2:13–25

ACSAH, won in marriage by Othniel
Josh 15:16–19
Judg 1:12–15

ANNA, A prophet
Luke 2:36–38

ATHALIAH, seized the throne of Judah through murder
2 Kgs 8:26
11
2 Chr 22—23

B

BATHSHEBA, wife of Uriah, taken by David
2 Sam 11:1—12:25
1 Kgs 1
2:13–22

BELOVED/BRIDE, *see* YOUNG WOMAN

BELSHAZZAR'S MOTHER, advised her son to consult Daniel
Dan 5:10–12

BILHAH, Rachel's servant
Gen 29:29
30:3–7
35:22

C

CHOSEN LADY, recipient of the Second Letter of John
2 Jn 1

COZBI, a Midianite woman slain by Phinehas for leading Israel into apostasy
Num 25:6–18

D

DAVID'S CONCUBINES, political pawns between David and Absalom
2 Sam 15:16
16:21–22

DEBORAH, a judge in Israel
Judg 4—5

DELILAH, seduced and betrayed Samson
Judg 16

DINAH, Jacob's daughter, raped by Shechem
Gen 30:21
34

DORCAS, *see* TABITHA

E

ELI'S DAUGHTER-IN-LAW, died in childbirth from sorrow
1 Sam 4:19–22

ELIZABETH, mother of John the Baptist
Luke 1

ESTHER, became queen of Persia and saved the Jewish people from genocide
Esth 1—10

EUODIA, a source of discord in the church in Philippi, with SYNTYCHE
Phil 4:2

EVE, the first woman
Gen 2:21—4:2
2 Cor 11:3
1 Tim 2:13

EZEKIEL'S WIFE, her death was used by God as a message
Ezek 24:15–27

G

GOMER, the prostitute wife of Hosea
Hos 1:2–8
3:1–3

GIRL POSSESSED BY A DEMON, healed by Paul
Acts 16:16–18

H

HADASSAH, another name for Esther
Esth 2:7

HAGAR, Sarai's (Sarah) servant; mother of Ishmael
Gen 16
21:8–21
Gal 4:24–25

HANNAH, barren woman blessed by God; Samuel's mother
1 Sam 1—2

HERODIAS
Herod's wife; plans the death of John the Baptist
Matt 14:2–12
Mark 6:17–29
Herodias' daughter; danced for Herod
Matt 14:6–11
Mark 6:22–28

HOGLAH, one of Zelophehad's Daughters

HULDAH, Prophet during King Josiah's reign
2 Kgs 22:14–20
2 Chr 34:14–28

I

ISAIAH'S WIFE, called a "prophetess" in many translations
Isa 8:3

J

JAEL, kills Sisera, a Canaanite general
Judg 4:17–22

JAIRUS' DAUGHTER, daughter of a synagogue leader; healed by Jesus
Matt 9:23–26
Mark 5:22, 35–42
Luke 8:41–42, 49–55

JEHOSHEBA, rescues the infant Joash from Athaliah
2 Kgs 11:2

JEPHTHAH'S DAUGHTER, sacrificed by her father
Judg 11:29–40

JEROBOAM'S WIFE, consults a prophet about her son
1 Kgs 14:1–18

JEZEBEL
wife of King Ahab; promoted the worship of Baal
1 Kgs 16:31
18:4
19:1–2
21
2 Kgs 9:10, 30–37
a supposed prophetess, probably metaphorical
Rev 2:20–23

JOANNA, One of Jesus' disciples
Luke 8:1–3
24:1–10

JOB'S WIFE, urges Job to curse God
Job 2:9–10

JOCHEBED, mother of Moses
Exod 2:1–3, 8–10
6:20
Num 26:59

JUNIA, imprisoned for her faith
Rom 16:7

L

LEAH, one of Jacob's wives; RACHEL'S sister
Gen 29:16–26
29:31–35
30:9–21
31:4–18
33:1–7

LEVITE'S CONCUBINE, raped and murdered in the town of Gibeah
Judg 19

LOT'S DAUGHTERS, offered to the men of Sodom; had intercourse with their father
Gen 19:6–8
19:30–38

LOT'S WIFE, turned into a pillar of salt
Gen 19:26

LYDIA, A merchant converted by Paul
Acts 16:13–15, 40

M

MAHLAH, one of ZELOPHEHAD'S DAUGHTERS

MANOAH'S WIFE, visited by an angel; Samson's mother
Judg 13
Judg 14:3–4

MARA, the name Naomi gives herself
Ruth 1:20

MARTHA, friend and disciple of Jesus (*see also* MARY)
Luke 10:38–42
John 11:1–44
12:2

MARY
mother of Jesus
Matt 1:16–25
2:11–15
Luke 1:25–56
2:1–24, 27–33, 39
2:41–51
John 19:25–27
Acts 1:14
friend and disciple of Jesus (*see also* MARTHA)
Luke 10:38–42
John 11:1–44
12:3–8
mother of James and Joseph (or "the other Mary")
Matt 27:56
27:61
28:1
Mark 15:40–41, 47
16:1–8
Luke 24:1–10
wife of Clopas
John 19:25
hosted a prayer gathering, mother of John Mark
Acts 12:12

MARY MAGDALENE, a member of Jesus' inner circle of disciples
Matt 27:56
27:61
28:1
Mark 15:40–41, 47
16:1–11
Luke 8:1–3
24:1–10
John 19:25
20:1–18

MEDIUM OF ENDOR, summoned Samuel's spirit for Saul
1 Sam 28:4–25

MERAB, Saul's daughter
1 Sam 14:49
18:17–19

MICAH'S MOTHER, cast coins into an idol
Judg 17:1–5

MICHAL, Saul's daughter given to David in marriage
1 Sam 14:49
1 Sam 18:20–29
1 Sam 19:11–18
1 Sam 25:44
2 Sam 3:13–16
2 Sam 6:16–23
1 Chr 15:29

MILCAH, one of ZELOPHEHAD'S DAUGHTERS

MIRIAM, a leader of the Exodus; Moses' sister
Exod 2:1–8
Exod 15:20–21
Num 12:1–15
Num 20:1
Mic 6:4

MOTHERS IN SOLOMON'S COURT, dispute over an infant
1 Kgs 3:16–28

N

NAAMAN'S WIFE'S MAID, an Israelite in Aram
2 Kgs 5:1–4

NAOMI, an Israelite widow; See also RUTH
Ruth 1—4

NOAH, one of ZELOPHEHAD'S DAUGHTERS

NYMPHA, hosted a house church; greeted by Paul
Col 4:15

O

OHOLAH, Samaria personified as a woman; *see also* OHOLIBAH
Ezek 23:1–10
23:36–49

OHOLIBAH, Jerusalem personified as a woman; *see also* OHOLAH
Ezek 23:1–4
23:11–49

ORPAH, Naomi's daughter-in-law
Ruth 1:4–14

P

PENINNAH, HANNAH'S co-wife
1 Sam 1:1–7

PETER'S MOTHER-IN-LAW, healed by Jesus
Matt 8:14–15
Mark 1:29–31
Luke 4:38–39

PETER'S WIFE, accompanied Peter on his travels
1 Cor 9:5

PHARAOH'S DAUGHTER, adopted Moses
Exod 2:5–10

PHOEBE, a deacon in the early church
Rom 16:1

PILATE'S WIFE, told Pilate to release Jesus
Matt 27:19

POTIPHAR'S WIFE, attempted to seduce Joseph
Gen 39:6–19

PRISCILLA, a believer in Corinth; with Aquila, hosted Paul
Acts 18:2–3
18:18
18:26

PUAH, a Hebrew midwife in Egypt, with Shiphrah
Exod 1:15–21

Q

QUEEN OF SHEBA, visited Solomon in Jerusalem
1 Kgs 10:1–13
2 Chr 9:1–12

R

RACHEL, Jacob's favorite wife; Leah's sister
Gen 29:9–31
30:1–8
30:14–24
31:4–19, 30–35
48:7

RAHAB, a prostitute in Jericho
Josh 2
Josh 6:17, 22–25
Matt 1:5
Heb 11:31
Jas 2:25

REBEKAH, Isaac's wife; helped Jacob steal his brother's blessing
Gen 24
25:20–26
26:7–11
27:1–17, 41–46

REUEL'S DAUGHTERS, women of Midian helped by Moses; *see also* Zipporah
Exod 2:15–20

RHODA, a servant girl
Acts 12:13–16

RIZPAH, tended the corpses of her executed sons
2 Sam 3:7
21:8–14

RUTH, Naomi's devoted daughter-in-law
Ruth 1—4
Matt 1:5

S

SALOME, mother of the apostles James and John
Mark 15:40–41
16:1–8
see Herodias for Herod's daughter

SAMARITAN MOTHER IN FAMINE, killed and ate her own son
2 Kgs 6:24–30

SAMARITAN WOMAN AT THE WELL, conversed with Jesus
John 4:1–42

SAPPHIRA, a believer who lied about her assets
Acts 5:1–11

SARAH, a mother of the faith; Abraham's wife; *see also* Sarai
Gen 17:15–19
18:1–15
20:1–18
21:1–10
23
Isa 51:1–2
Heb 11:11
1 Pet 3:5–6

SARAI, Abram's wife; *see also* Sarah
Gen 11:29–31
12:10–20
16:1–6
17:15

SERVANT GIRL(S) IN THE COURTYARD, accused Peter of being a follower of Jesus
Matt 26:69–74
Mark 14:66–72
Luke 22:54–60
John 18:16–18

SHALLUM'S DAUGHTERS, helped rebuild the Jerusalem wall
Neh 3:12

SHEERAH, built two towns
1 Chr 7:24

SHIPHRAH, a Hebrew midwife in Egypt, with Puah
Exod 1:15–21

SHUNAMMITE WOMAN, hosted Elisha in her home
2 Kgs 4:8–37
8:1–6

SUSANNA, one of Jesus' disciples
Luke 8:1–3

SYNTYCHE, a source of discord in the church in Philippi, with Euodia
Phil 4:2

SYRO-PHOENICIAN WOMAN, Gentile healed by Jesus after asking for "scraps that fall" from the table
Matt 15:21–28
Mark 7:24–30

T

TABITHA, a charitable woman raised from death by Peter
Acts 9:36–41

TAMAR
Judah's daughter-in-law; tricked him into fathering a child
Gen 38:6–30
daughter of David; raped by her half-brother
2 Sam 13:1–22

TEKOA, WOMAN FROM, convinced David to speak with Absalom
2 Sam 14:1–21

THEBEZ, WOMAN OF, killed Abimelech
Judg 9:50–54

TIRZAH, one of Zelophehad's Daughters

V

VASHTI, queen of Persia
Esth 1

W

WIDOW AIDED BY ELISHA, saved from debt
2 Kgs 4:1–7

WIDOW GIVING AN OFFERING IN THE TEMPLE, poor woman giving her "two small coins"
Mark 12:41–44
Luke 21:1–4

WIDOW OF ZAREPHATH, hosted Elijah; her oil and flour never ran out
1 Kgs 17:8–24

WISE WOMAN OF ABEL, negotiates with Joab
2 Sam 20:14–22

WOMAN CAUGHT IN ADULTERY, saved from stoning by Jesus
John 8:1–11

WOMAN HEALED ON THE SABBATH, healed by Jesus
Luke 13:10–17

WOMAN OF EN-ROGEL, saved David's life
2 Sam 17:17–20

WOMAN WHO ANNOINTED JESUS' FEET, forgiven by Jesus; often misidentified as MARY MAGDALENE
Luke 7:36–50

WOMAN WITH CONSTANT BLEEDING, healed by touching Jesus' cloak
Matt 9:20–22
Mark 5:25–34
Luke 8:43–48

Y

YOUNG WOMAN, the female member of a pair of lovers; sometimes referred to as the Bride or Beloved
Song 1—8

Z

ZELOPHEHAD'S DAUGHTERS, won inheritance rights
Num 26:33
27:1–8
38:1–12
Josh 17:3–6

ZERESH, a Persian woman; Haman's wife
Esth 5:9–14
6:13

ZILPAH, handmaid to LEAH and mother of two of Jacob's sons
Gen 29:24
30:9–13

ZIPPORAH, Moses' wife; *see also* REUEL'S DAUGHTERS
Exod 2:21–22
4:20–26
18:2–6

NLT DICTIONARY/CONCORDANCE

A

AARON

First high priest of Israel; elder brother and spokesman of Moses (Exod 4:14-31; 7:1-2); confronted Pharaoh with Moses (Exod 5–12); held up Moses' hands during battle (Exod 17:8-15); led Israel while Moses was absent (Exod 24:14); priestly clothing and accessories (Exod 28); his ordination (Exod 29; Lev 8); his failure with the gold calf (Exod 32; Acts 7:40); spoke against Moses, then interceded on behalf of sister, Miriam (Num 12:1-16); helped stop the plague (Num 16:45-48); priesthood confirmed (Num 17; Heb 5:1-4); failed at Meribah and was denied entry to Promised Land (Num 20:1-13); died (Num 20:22-29; 33:38-39).

ABANDON, ABANDONED, ABANDONS (v)

to desert or forsake

Josh 1:5	will not fail you or **a** you.
Josh 24:16	We would never **a** the LORD
Ezra 9:9	God did not **a** us in our slavery.
Neh 9:31	completely or **a** them forever.
Ps 22:1	why have you **a-ed** me?
Ps 37:25	never seen the godly **a-ed**
Ps 37:28	he will never **a** the godly.
Prov 15:10	Whoever **a-s** the right path
Matt 27:46	why have you **a-ed** me?
John 16:1	you won't **a** your faith.
Rom 1:24	So God **a-ed** them to do
Rom 1:28	**a-ed** them to their foolish
2 Cor 4:9	down, but never **a-ed** by God.
Heb 13:5	I will never **a** you.

ABASED (KJV)

Ezek 21:26	mighty will be *brought down.*
Matt 23:12	themselves will be *humbled*
Phil 4:12	how to *live on almost nothing*

ABEL

Son of Adam and Eve, brother of Cain (Gen 4:1-2); his offering accepted (Gen 4:4; Heb 11:4); murdered by Cain (Gen 4:8; Matt 23:35; Luke 11:51; Heb 12:24; 1 Jn 3:11-12; Jude 1:11); replaced by Seth (Gen 4:25).

ABHOR (v)

to hate or loathe

Ps 119:163	I hate and **a** all falsehood,

ABIDE(TH), ABIDING (KJV)

Luke 2:8	shepherds *staying* in the fields
John 12:46	no longer *remain* in the dark
John 15:4	be fruitful unless you *remain*

ABILITY, ABILITIES (n)

talent, aptitude, or skill

Exod 35:34	the **a** to teach their skills
Dan 6:3	because of Daniel's great **a,**
Acts 2:4	Spirit gave them this **a.**
1 Cor 12:1	special **a-ies** the Spirit gives
1 Cor 14:1	special **a-ies** the Spirit gives—
1 Cor 14:12	special **a-ies** the Spirit gives,
2 Cor 1:8	beyond our **a** to endure,

ABLE (adj)

marked by power, intelligence, competence, skill, giftedness

Deut 16:17	must give as they are **a,**
Dan 3:17	whom we serve is **a** to save
Rom 8:39	ever be **a** to separate us from
Rom 16:25	to God, who is **a** to
Eph 3:20	all glory to God, who is **a,**
Eph 6:13	you will be **a** to resist
2 Tim 1:12	that he is **a** to guard
2 Tim 2:24	be **a** to teach, and
Jude 1:24	to God, who is **a** to keep

ABOLISH (v)

to destroy; to annul

Matt 5:17	did not come to **a** the law

ABOUND(ED) (KJV)

Prov 28:20	person will *get a rich reward*
Matt 24:12	Sin will *be rampant everywhere*
Rom 5:15	*even greater* is God's wonderful grace
Rom 5:20	grace *became more abundant*
2 Cor 8:7	*excel* also in this gracious act

ABOVE (adv or prep)
in a higher position, superior
Ps 95:3 a great King **a** all gods.
Ps 99:2 exalted **a** all the nations.
Luke 12:31 Seek the Kingdom of God **a** all
Eph 1:21 far **a** any ruler or authority
Phil 2:9 the name **a** all other names,
1 Tim 3:2 a man whose life is **a** reproach.
Jas 3:17 wisdom from **a** is first of all pure.

ABRAHAM (ABRAM)
Father of the nation of Israel (Isa 51:2; John 8:37-59); friend of God (Isa 41:8); father of all people of faith (Gen 12–25; Rom 4; Heb 11); made covenant with the LORD (Gen 12:1-3; 13:14-17; 15:12-21; 22:15-18; 50:24; Exod 2:24; 32:13; Lev 26:42; 2 Kgs 13:23; 1 Chr 13:23; 16:16; Neh 9:8; Ps 105:9; Luke 1:73; Acts 3:25; Gal 3:17-20; Heb 6:13); descendant of Terah from Ur (Gen 11:27-31); husband of Sarah (Sarai) (Gen 11:29); called to leave home (Gen 12:1-9; Acts 7:2-4; Heb 11:8-10); went to Egypt and deceived the Pharaoh (Gen 12:10-20); chose Canaan over the Jordan Plain (Gen 13); rescued Lot from enemies (Gen 14:11-16); blessed by Melchizedek (Gen 14:18-24; Heb 7:1); covenant restated by God (Gen 15); faith counted as righteousness (Gen 15:6; Rom 4:3; Gal 3:6-9; Jas 2:21-23); given son (Ishmael) by Hagar (Gen 16); circumcision commanded (Gen 17; Rom 4:9-12); name changed to "Abraham" (Gen 17:5; Neh 9:7); son promised to Sarah (Gen 17:16; 18:10); welcomed heavenly visitor (Gen 18:1-15); bargained to save Sodom and Gomorrah (Gen 18:16-33); deceived Abimelech (Gen 20); named as a prophet (Gen 20:7); given son (Isaac) by Sarah (Gen 21:1-7; Heb 11:11-12); sent Hagar and Ishmael away (Gen 21:9-14; Gal 4:21-31); offered Isaac as test (Gen 22:1-19; Heb 11:17-19; Jas 2:21); secured burial ground for Sarah (Gen 23); found a wife for Isaac (Gen 24); descendants through wife Keturah (Gen 25:1-6); died (Gen 25:7-11).

ABSTAIN (v)
to refrain from, forgo
Exod 19:15 then **a** from having sexual intercourse.
Acts 15:20 **a** from eating food offered to idols,

ABUNDANCE (n)
great quantity, affluence; more than ample
Job 36:31 giving them food in **a.**
Ps 66:12 a place of great **a.**
Jer 31:14 The priests will enjoy **a,**
Matt 13:12 have an **a** of knowledge.
Matt 25:29 they will have an **a.**
John 1:16 From his **a** we have all

ABUNDANT (adj)
marked by great plenty, abounding
Deut 28:11 livestock, and **a** crops.
Ps 68:9 You sent **a** rain, O God
Jer 31:12 good gifts—the **a** crops
John 16:24 you will have **a** joy.
2 Cor 8:2 are also filled with **a** joy,

ABUSE (n)
strong condemnation or disapproval
Mark 15:29 shouted **a,** shaking their heads

ABUSE (v)
to injure or damage physically or verbally
1 Cor 4:12 patient with those who **a** us.

ABUSIVE (adj)
using harsh, insulting language; characterized by wrong or improper use or action
1 Cor 5:11 worships idols, or is **a,**
1 Cor 6:10 drunkards, or are **a,** or
Eph 4:29 use foul or **a** language.

ABYSS (KJV)
Luke 8:31 send them into the *bottomless pit*
Rev 9:1 the shaft of the *bottomless pit*
Rev 9:11 the angel from the *bottomless pit*

ACACIA (n)
several species of shrubs and trees, some of which are found in the Holy Land, yielding highly durable wood
Exod 25:10 make an Ark of **a** wood
Exod 27:1 **a** wood, construct a square altar
Josh 2:1 the Israelite camp at **A** Grove.

ACCEPT, ACCEPTED, ACCEPTS (v)
to receive willingly
Gen 4:4 The LORD **a-ed** Abel
Gen 4:7 be **a-ed** if you do what is right.
Deut 16:19 Never **a** a bribe, for bribes
Job 42:8 I will **a** his prayer
Job 42:9 the LORD **a-ed** Job's prayer.
Eccl 5:18 to **a** their lot in life.
Luke 4:24 no prophet is **a-ed** in his
Luke 10:16 who **a-s** your message
John 1:12 believed him and **a-ed** him,
John 17:8 They **a-ed** it and know that
Rom 11:12 when they finally **a** it.
Gal 2:9 they **a-ed** Barnabas and me
Col 2:6 just as you **a-ed** Christ Jesus
1 Tim 1:15 everyone should **a** it:
1 Tim 4:9 everyone should **a** it.
Jas 1:21 **a** the word God has planted

ACCEPTABLE (adj)
capable or worthy of being accepted; welcome, pleasing, favorable
Mark 7:19 every kind of food is **a**

Rom 4:2 had made him **a** to God,
Rom 12:1 the kind he will find **a.**
Rom 14:20 all foods are **a,** but it is
2 Cor 8:12 is **a** if you give it eagerly.
1 Tim 4:5 made **a** by the word of God

ACCIDENTALLY (adv)
unintentionally, by mistake
Josh 20:9 who **a** killed another person
Matt 23:24 so you won't **a** swallow a gnat,

ACCOMPLISH, ACCOMPLISHES (v)
perform, do to completion
Eccl 2:11 to **a,** it was all so meaningless
Isa 55:11 fruit. It will **a** all I want it to,
Matt 5:17 No, I came to **a** their purpose.
John 6:63 Human effort **a-es** nothing.
Eph 3:20 within us, to **a** infinitely more
2 Thes 1:11 power to **a** all the good things

ACCOUNT (n)
description of facts, conditions, or events; a report
Gen 2:4 This is the **a** of the creation
Gen 5:1 written **a** of the descendants
Gen 6:9 the **a** of Noah and his family.
Gen 10:1 This is the **a** of the families
Gen 37:2 This is the **a** of Jacob and
Rom 14:12 give a personal **a** to God.

ACCOUNTABLE (adj)
subject to giving an account; answerable
Heb 4:13 the one to whom we are **a.**
Heb 13:17 and they are **a** to God.

ACCURATE (adj)
conforming exactly to truth or to a standard; free from error, correct
Lev 19:36 and weights must be **a.**
Deut 25:13 You must use **a** scales
Prov 11:1 delights in **a** weights.
Prov 22:21 take an **a** report to those
John 21:24 account of these things is **a.**

ACCURSED (KJV)
Deut 21:23 anyone who is hung is *cursed*
Josh 6:18 things *set apart for destruction*
1 Cor 12:3 will *curse* Jesus, and no one
Gal 1:9 let that person be *cursed*

ACCUSATION, ACCUSATIONS (n)
a charge of wrongdoing, often false
Ps 4:2 will you make groundless **a-s?**
Luke 3:14 extort money or make false **a-s.**
1 Tim 5:19 Do not listen to an **a**

ACCUSE, ACCUSED, ACCUSES, ACCUSING (v)
to charge with fault or offense; to blame
Job 22:4 **a-s** you and brings judgment
Ps 27:12 For they **a** me of things
Dan 6:5 grounds for **a-ing** Daniel
Luke 23:14 **a-ing** him of leading a revolt.
John 5:45 it isn't I who will **a**
John 7:7 because I **a** it of doing evil.
John 8:46 can truthfully **a** me of sin?
Acts 18:13 **a-d** Paul of "persuading
Rom 2:15 and thoughts either **a** them
Rom 8:33 Who dares **a** us whom God
Rev 12:10 who **a-s** them before our God

ACCUSER, ACCUSERS (n)
one who charges another of wrongdoing
Deut 19:18 If the **a** has brought false
Isa 50:8 Where are my **a-s?**
Luke 12:58 the way to court with your **a,**
Rev 12:10 the **a** of our brothers

ACKNOWLEDGE, ACKNOWLEDGES (v)
to express a gratitude of debt; to recognize as valid; to confess (wrongdoing)
Jer 3:13 Only **a** your guilt. Admit
Matt 10:32 Everyone who **a-s** me
Luke 12:8 Son of Man will also **a**
Rom 1:28 thought it foolish to **a** God,
1 Jn 2:23 anyone who **a-s** the Son
1 Jn 4:3 and does not **a** the truth

ACQUAINTED (v)
to make familiar; to know firsthand
Isa 53:3 sorrows, **a** with deepest grief.
Acts 18:2 **a** with a Jew named Aquila,

ACQUIT, ACQUITTING (v)
to free from the penalty of a guilty action; (used theologically) to justify or make right with God
2 Chr 6:23 **A** the innocent because of
Prov 17:15 **A-ing** the guilty and

ACT (v)
to behave; to take action or do something
Ps 119:126 it is time for you to **a,**
Eccl 6:8 how to **a** in front of others?

ACTION, ACTIONS (n)
a thing done, deed; an exercise of will
Jer 4:18 Your own **a-s** have brought
Phlm 1:6 put into **a** the generosity
Rev 3:2 **a-s** do not meet the requirements

ACTIVITY (n)
a pursuit in which a person is active; quality or state of being active

Eccl 3:1 for every **a** under heaven.

ADAM
First man (Gen 1:26–2:25; Rom 5:14; 1 Tim 2:13-14); son of God (Luke 3:38); sinned (Gen 3:1-19; Hos 6:7; Rom 5:12-21); descendants of (Gen 5); died (Gen 5:5; 1 Cor 15:22-49).

ADD, ADDED (v)
to make or serve as an addition
Deut 4:2 Do not **a** to or subtract from
Deut 12:32 You must not **a** anything to
Prov 30:6 Do not **a** to his words,
Eccl 3:14 Nothing can be **a-ed** to it
Matt 6:27 worries **a** a single moment
Luke 12:25 worries **a** a single moment
Acts 2:47 each day the Lord **a-ed** to their
Rev 22:18 God will **a** to that person

ADEQUATE (adj)
suitable for a task; suitable
2 Cor 2:16 who is **a** for such a task as this?

ADMIT (v)
to acknowledge, confess
Hos 5:15 until they **a** their guilt
John 12:42 But they wouldn't **a** it

ADMINISTRATOR
Num 3:32 chief **a** over all the Levites
Isa 37:2 sent Eliakim the palace **a**

ADMONISH(ED) (KJV)
Eccl 12:12 give you *some further advice*
Jer 42:19 Don't forget this *warning* I
2 Thes 3:15 *warn* them as you would
Heb 8:5 God *gave* him this *warning*

ADMONITION (KJV)
1 Cor 10:11 written down *to warn us*
Eph 6:4 *instruction* that comes from the Lord
Titus 3:10 a first and second *warning*

ADOPT, ADOPTED (v)
to take another's child into one's own family
Rom 8:15 when he **a-ed** you as his own
Rom 8:23 rights as his **a-ed** children,
Rom 9:4 to be God's **a-ed** children.
Gal 4:5 so that he could **a** us as
Eph 1:5 decided in advance to **a** us

ADULTERER, ADULTERERS (n)
one who commits adultery
Job 24:15 The **a** waits for the twilight,
Jas 4:4 You **a-s**! Don't you realize

ADULTEROUS (adj)
prone to adultery or idolatry
Mark 8:38 in these **a** and sinful days,

ADULTERY (n)
unlawful sexual relations between a married and an unmarried person; symbolic of idolatry
Exod 20:14 You must not commit **a.**
Deut 5:18 You must not commit **a.**
Prov 6:32 who commits **a** is an utter fool,
Matt 5:27 You must not commit **a.**
Matt 19:18 You must not commit **a.**
Mark 10:11 someone else commits **a**
Luke 18:20 You must not commit **a.**
John 8:4 caught in the act of **a.**
1 Cor 6:9 **a,** or are male prostitutes,

ADVANTAGE (n)
benefit; upper hand
Exod 17:11 in his hand, the Israelites had the **a.**
Lev 25:17 not taking **a** of each other.
Rom 3:1 Then what's the **a** of being a Jew?
Rom 7:11 Sin took **a** of those commands
2 Cor 7:2 astray, nor taken **a** of anyone.

ADVERSARY, ADVERSARIES (n)
enemy, opponent
2 Sam 19:22 Why have you become my **a**
Esth 7:6 Haman is our **a** and our enemy.
Ps 89:23 beat down his **a-ies** before him
Matt 5:25 on the way to court with your **a,**

ADVERSITY (n)
affliction, misfortune, woe
Job 36:15 gets their attention through **a.**
Isa 30:20 gave you **a** for food and suffering

ADVICE (n)
recommendation regarding a decision or course of conduct; counsel
1 Kgs 12:8 rejected the **a** of
2 Chr 10:8 rejected the **a** of
Prov 12:5 **a** of the wicked is
Prov 12:26 godly give good **a** to their
Prov 15:22 Plans go wrong for lack of **a;**
Isa 44:25 I cause the wise to give bad **a,**
Rom 11:34 enough to give him **a?**

ADVISE (v)
to give advice; to counsel
Ps 32:8 I will **a** you and watch over
1 Tim 5:14 I **a** these younger widows
Rev 3:18 I **a** you to buy gold from me—

ADVISERS (n)
one who gives advice; counselor

1 Sam 28:23	his **a** joined the woman in
1 Kgs 12:14	counsel of his younger **a.**
Esth 1:13	consulted with his wise **a,**
Prov 11:14	safety in having many **a.**
Prov 29:12	all his **a** will be wicked.

ADVOCATE (n)
one who pleads the cause of another; defender
see also HOLY SPIRIT, COUNSELOR

Job 16:19	My **a** is there on high.
John 14:16	he will give you another **A,**
John 14:26	the Father sends the **A**
John 15:26	I will send you the **A**—
John 16:7	if I don't, the **A** won't come.
1 Jn 2:1	an **a** who pleads our case

AFFECTION (n)
tender attachment; a positive feeling

Rom 12:10	each other with genuine **a,**
2 Pet 1:7	godliness with brotherly **a,**

AFFIRM (v)
to validate; to confirm

John 3:33	can **a** that God is true.
Rom 8:16	**a** that we are God's children.
Heb 10:23	hope we **a,** for God can

AFFLICT, AFFLICTED (v)
relating to, characterized by, or given to persistent suffering or anguish

Deut 28:61	LORD will **a** you
1 Sam 5:12	were **a-ed** with tumors;

AFFORD (v)
to have enough money or other assets for

Lev 5:7	cannot **a** to bring a sheep,
2 Cor 8:3	they could **a,** but far more.

AFRAID (adj)
fearful or apprehensive about an unwanted or uncertain situation

Gen 3:10	I was **a** because I was naked.
Gen 26:24	Do not be **a,** for I am
Exod 3:6	he was **a** to look at God.
Deut 1:21	Don't be **a!**
Deut 20:1	your own, do not be **a.**
Ps 23:4	I will not be **a,** for you are
Isa 10:24	do not be **a** of the Assyrians
Isa 41:10	Don't be **a,** for I am
Isa 43:1	Do not be **a,** for I have
Matt 8:26	Why are you **a?**
Matt 10:31	So don't be **a;**
Mark 5:36	Don't be **a.**
John 14:27	don't be troubled or **a.**
2 Tim 4:5	Don't be **a** of suffering
1 Pet 3:14	don't worry or be **a**

AFRESH (adv)
from a fresh beginning; anew, again

Lam 3:23	his mercies begin **a** each

AGAINST (prep)
in opposition or hostility to; contrary to

Ps 41:9	has turned **a** me.
Ps 78:19	even spoke **a** God himself,
Matt 6:12	those who sin **a** us.
Matt 10:35	to set a man **a** his father,
Matt 12:30	actually working **a** me.
Acts 26:14	for you to fight **a** my will.
Rom 11:30	Gentiles were rebels **a** God,
1 Cor 8:12	you are sinning **a** Christ.
1 Pet 5:9	Stand firm **a** him,

AGED (adj)
showing the effects or characteristics of increasing age

Job 12:12	Wisdom belongs to the **a,**
Prov 17:6	crowning glory of the **a;**

AGES (n)
long period of time; a generation; a measure of history, geology, or culture

Prov 8:23	I was appointed in **a** past,
Jer 23:40	infamous throughout the **a.**
Eph 2:7	in all future **a** as examples

AGGRAVATE (v)
to cause anger by persistent goading; to produce inflammation in

Col 3:21	do not **a** your children,

AGONY (n)
extreme pain and suffering

Ps 6:2	Lord, for my bones are in **a.**
Luke 22:44	he was in such **a** of spirit that

AGREE, AGREED, AGREEING (v)
to admit, concede

Matt 18:19	If two of you **a** here on
Luke 7:29	**a-d** that God's way was right,
Rom 7:16	that I **a** that the law is good.
Phil 2:2	make me truly happy by **a-ing**

AID (v)
to give assistance

Acts 24:17	with money to **a** my people

AIM (v)
to direct to or toward a specified object or goal

Rom 14:19	**a** for harmony in the church

AIR (n)
empty space, nothingness; atmosphere

1 Thes 4:17	meet the Lord in the **a.**

ALABASTER (adj)
a compact, fine-textured, usually white and translucent plaster often carved into vases and ornaments
Matt 26:7 with a beautiful **a** jar
Mark 14:3 with a beautiful **a** jar
Luke 7:37 she brought a beautiful **a** jar

ALARM (n)
a signal that warns or alerts
Num 10:9 sound the **a** with the trumpets.
2 Cor 7:11 such indignation, such **a,**

ALCOHOL (n)
drink (as wine or beer) containing ethanol
Prov 20:1 **a** leads to brawls.
Isa 5:22 boast about all the **a** they

ALCOHOLIC (adj)
containing alcohol
Num 6:3 give up wine and other **a**

ALERT (adj)
quick to perceive and act
Isa 21:7 the watchman be fully **a.**
Mark 13:33 be on guard! Stay **a!**
1 Pet 5:8 Stay **a!** Watch out for

ALIEN (KJV)
Exod 18:3 a *foreigner* in a foreign
Job 19:15 I am like a *foreigner* to them
Eph 2:12 were *excluded from citizenship*

ALIENATED (KJV)
Ezek 48:14 traded or *used by others*
Eph 4:18 *wander far from* the life God
Col 1:21 were *once far away from God*

ALIVE (adj)
animate, having life; active; aware
Gen 45:7 keep you and your families **a**
Ps 41:2 them and keeps them **a.**
Luke 24:23 Jesus is **a!**
Acts 1:3 ways that he was actually **a.**
Rom 6:11 the power of sin and **a** to God
Rev 2:8 who was dead but is now **a:**

ALLELUIA (KJV)
Rev 19:1 shouting, *"Praise the Lord!*
Rev 19:3 rang out: *"Praise the Lord!*
Rev 19:4 "Amen! *Praise the Lord!"*
Rev 19:6 *"Praise the Lord!* For the Lord

ALLOTMENT, ALLOTMENTS (n)
share, portion, provision
Num 18:21 Instead of an **a** of land, I will
Josh 13:32 These are the **a-s** Moses had
Jer 13:25 your **a,** the portion I have assigned

ALLOWANCE (n)
the act of admitting or conceding; permission
Eph 4:2 **a** for each other's faults

ALLOW, ALLOWED (v)
to admit or concede; to permit
1 Cor 6:12 though "I am **a-ed** to
1 Cor 10:23 I am **a-ed** to do anything
2 Cor 12:4 no human is **a-ed** to tell.

ALMIGHTY (n)
having absolute power over all; God
see also (HEAVEN'S) ARMIES
Gen 17:1 I am El-Shaddai—'God **A.'**
Exod 6:3 as El-Shaddai—'God **A'**—
Ruth 1:20 **A** has made life very bitter
Job 6:14 without any fear of the **A.**
Job 33:4 breath of the **A** gives me life.
Ps 91:1 rest in the shadow of the **A.**
Rev 4:8 the **A**—the one who always was,
Rev 15:3 O Lord God, the **A.**
Rev 19:6 our God, the **A,** reigns.

ALONE (adj)
isolated or solitary; solely or exclusively; without aid or support
John 5:44 the one who **a** is God.

ALONGSIDE (adv)
at the side; in parallel position, close by
Gal 3:19 It was given **a** the promise

ALPHA (n)
first letter of Greek alphabet; figurative of beginning or first one
Rev 1:8 I am the **A** and the Omega—
Rev 21:6 I am the **A** and the Omega—
Rev 22:13 I am the **A** and the Omega,

ALTAR, ALTARS (n)
high places of worship on which sacrifices are offered or incense is burned
Gen 8:20 Noah built an **a** to the LORD,
Gen 12:7 Abram built an **a** there
Gen 22:9 Abraham built an **a** and
Gen 26:25 Isaac built an **a** there
Exod 30:1 make another **a** of acacia
Exod 37:25 incense **a** of acacia wood.
Josh 8:30 Joshua built an **a** to the LORD,
Josh 22:10 a large and imposing **a.**
1 Sam 7:17 Samuel built an **a** to the
2 Chr 4:1 made a bronze **a** 30 feet long,
2 Chr 4:19 Temple of God: the gold **a;**
2 Chr 32:12 only at the **a** at the Temple

2 Chr 33:16	restored the **a** of the LORD
Ezra 3:2	rebuilding the **a** of the God
Isa 6:6	coal he had taken from the **a**
Matt 5:23	presenting a sacrifice at the **a**
Acts 17:23	your **a-s** had this inscription
Heb 13:10	an **a** from which the priests
Rev 6:9	I saw under the **a** the souls

ALTERED (v)
to make change or become different; to modify

John 10:35	the Scriptures cannot be **a.**

ALWAYS (adv)
at all times; forever, perpetually

1 Kgs 2:4	will **a** sit on the throne
Ps 16:8	the LORD is **a** with me.
Ps 52:8	will **a** trust in God's unfailing
Ps 102:27	But you are **a** the same;
Ps 106:3	and **a** do what is right.
Prov 23:7	They are **a** thinking about
Isa 16:5	He will **a** do what is just
Matt 28:20	I am with you **a,** even to
Mark 14:7	You will **a** have the poor
John 12:8	you will not **a** have me.
1 Pet 3:15	**a** be ready to explain it.

AMAZED (v)
to fill with wonder, astound

Matt 7:28	were **a** at his teaching
Mark 7:37	They were completely **a** and
Mark 10:24	This **a** them. But Jesus
Luke 2:33	Jesus' parents were **a** at
Acts 2:7	They were completely **a.**

AMAZING (adj)
causing amazement, great wonder, or surprise

1 Chr 16:24	about the **a** things he does.
Ps 96:3	about the **a** things he does.
Ps 126:2	What **a** things the LORD has

AMBASSADOR, AMBASSADORS (n)
an authorized representative or messenger

2 Cor 5:20	So we are Christ's **a-s;**
Eph 6:20	this message as God's **a.**

AMBITION (n)
aspiration to achieve a particular goal, good or bad

Gal 5:20	anger, selfish **a,** dissension,
Phil 1:17	They preach with selfish **a,**
Jas 3:14	there is selfish **a** in your heart,

ANCESTOR, ANCESTORS (n)
one from whom a person is descended; forefather

Exod 3:15	God of your **a-s**—the God of
Deut 19:14	markers your **a-s** set up
Isa 9:7	throne of his **a** David for all
Isa 43:27	your first **a** sinned against me;
Mark 11:10	Kingdom of our **a** David!
Luke 1:32	the throne of his **a** David.
Rom 9:5	Abraham, Isaac, and Jacob are their **a-s,**
Gal 1:14	for the traditions of my **a-s.**
Heb 1:1	to our **a-s** through the prophets.

ANCHOR (n)
a reliable or principal support; mainstay

Heb 6:19	trustworthy **a** for our souls.

ANCIENT (adj)
having the qualities of age or long existence; old

Dan 7:22	until the **A** One—the Most High—
Mark 7:3	required by their **a** traditions.

ANDREW
One of the 12 disciples; listed second (Matt 10:2; Luke 6:14) and fourth (Mark 3:18; 13:3; Acts 1:13); came from Bethsaida (John 1:44); brother of Simon Peter (Matt 4:18); former fisherman (Mark 1:16); follower of John the Baptist who introduced Peter to Jesus (John 1:40-44).

ANGEL, ANGELS (n)
human or superhuman agent or messenger of God

Exod 23:20	I am sending an **a**
2 Sam 24:16	and said to the death **a,**
Ps 91:11	will order his **a-s** to protect
Matt 4:6	will order his **a-s** to protect
Matt 28:2	an **a** of the Lord came down
Luke 1:26	God sent the **a** Gabriel
Luke 2:9	an **a** of the Lord appeared
Luke 20:36	they will be like **a-s.**
Acts 12:7	The **a** struck him on the side
1 Cor 6:3	we will judge **a-s?**
2 Cor 11:14	disguises himself as an **a**
Gal 1:8	or even an **a** from heaven,
Heb 1:6	all of God's **a-s** worship him.
Heb 2:7	a little lower than the **a-s**
Heb 13:2	entertained **a-s** without
1 Pet 1:12	the **a-s** are eagerly watching
2 Pet 2:4	even the **a-s** who sinned.
Jude 1:6	I remind you of the **a-s**

ANGELIC (adj)
having or displaying characteristics of an angel

2 Sam 22:11	on a mighty **a** being, he flew,
Ps 18:10	on a mighty **a** being, he flew,

ANGER (n)
a strong feeling of displeasure

Exod 34:6	slow to **a** and filled with
Num 14:18	slow to **a** and filled with
Deut 9:19	furious **a** of the LORD,
Deut 29:28	In great **a** and fury

2 Kgs 22:13	LORD's great **a** is burning
Ps 30:5	his **a** lasts only a moment,
Ps 78:38	Many times he held back his **a**
Rom 1:18	God shows his **a** from heaven
Rom 2:5	a day of **a** is coming,
Eph 4:26	by letting **a** control you.
1 Thes 5:9	pour out his **a** on us.
Jas 1:20	Human **a** does not produce
Rev 14:10	the wine of God's **a.**

ANGRY (adj)

feeling or showing anger; wrathful

Exod 32:11	so **a** with your own people
Neh 9:17	merciful, slow to become **a,**
Ps 103:8	merciful, slow to get **a**
Prov 22:24	Don't befriend **a** people
Jonah 4:2	slow to get **a** and filled
Matt 5:22	if you are even **a** with
Mark 10:14	he was **a** with his disciples.
John 3:36	under God's **a** judgment.
Acts 4:25	Why were the nations so **a?**
Jas 1:19	to speak, and slow to get **a.**

ANGUISH (n)

extreme pain, distress, or anxiety

Isa 53:11	by his **a,** he will be satisfied.
Zeph 1:15	of terrible distress and **a,**
Matt 24:21	greater **a** than at any time
Luke 16:24	I am in **a** in these flames.
Rev 16:10	ground their teeth in **a,**

ANIMAL, ANIMALS (n)

any of a kingdom of living things that typically differ from plants

Gen 1:24	livestock, small **a-s** that scurry
Gen 6:19	a pair of every kind of **a**—
Gen 7:8	all the various kinds of **a-s**—
Deut 14:4	These are the **a-s** you may eat:
1 Kgs 4:33	**a-s,** birds, small creatures,
Job 12:7	ask the **a-s,** and they will teach
Ps 73:22	like a senseless **a** to you.
Isa 43:20	The wild **a-s** in the fields

ANNIHILATED (v)

to cause to cease to exist; to kill

Esth 3:13	and **a** on a single day.

ANNOUNCE, ANNOUNCED, ANNOUNCING (v)

to proclaim; to tell news

Jer 51:10	let us **a** in Jerusalem
Matt 9:35	and **a-ing** the Good News
Mark 15:26	**a-ed** the charge against him.
Acts 26:23	**a** God's light to Jews and
Rev 10:7	as he **a-d** it to his servants the prophets.

ANNUAL (adj)

occurring or happening every year or once a year

Exod 30:10	a regular, **a** event
Judg 21:19	the **a** festival of the LORD
1 Sam 1:21	their **a** trip to offer a sacrifice
1 Sam 20:6	for an **a** family sacrifice.
2 Chr 8:13	the three **a** festivals—

ANOINT, ANOINTED, ANOINTING (v)

to smear or rub with oil; used for healing or consecration to sacred duty; used for grooming or burial; figurative for divine appointment

see also ANOINTED ONE

Exod 30:26	oil to **a** the Tabernacle,
Exod 30:30	**A** Aaron and his sons
Lev 8:12	**a-ing** him and making him holy
1 Sam 15:1	told me to **a** you as king
2 Sam 2:4	David and **a-ed** him king over
2 Sam 23:1	man **a-ed** by the God of Jacob,
Ps 23:5	honor me by **a-ing** my head
Ps 92:10	You have **a-ed** me with
Isa 61:1	the LORD has **a-ed** me
Dan 9:24	and to **a** the Most Holy Place.
Acts 10:38	you know that God **a-ed** Jesus
Heb 1:9	your God has **a-ed** you,
Jas 5:14	over you, **a-ing** you with oil

ANOINTED ONE (n)

one chosen by divine election

see also MESSIAH

1 Sam 2:10	the strength of his **a."**
1 Sam 26:9	attacking the LORD's **a?**
Ps 132:17	my **a** will be a light for
Isa 45:1	the LORD says to Cyrus, his **a**
Dan 9:25	a ruler—the **A**—comes.

ANSWER, ANSWERED (v)

to reply to a question; to solve a problem

Ps 6:9	the LORD will **a** my prayer.
Ps 34:4	LORD, and he **a-ed** me.
Jonah 2:2	trouble, and he **a-ed** me.

ANTICHRIST, ANTICHRISTS (n)

opponent of Christ; the personification of evil

1 Jn 2:18	heard that the **A** is coming,
1 Jn 2:18	many such **a-s** have appeared.
1 Jn 4:3	has the spirit of the **A,**
2 Jn 1:7	deceiver and an **a.**

ANTS (n)

any of a family of colonial hymenopterous insects

Prov 6:6	from the **a,** you lazybones.

ANXIETY, CARE(S) (KJV)

Ps 139:23	know my *anxious thoughts*
Phil 4:6	Don't *worry* about anything

1 Pet 5:7	your *worries and cares* to God,

APOSTLE, APOSTLES (n)
messengers or "sent ones"; generally but not exclusively applied to the original twelve followers of Christ and to Paul

Mark 3:14	and called them his **a-s.**
Acts 1:26	selected to become an **a**
Acts 5:2	part of the money to the **a-s,**
Acts 8:18	**a-s** laid their hands on
Rom 11:13	the **a** to the Gentiles.
1 Cor 9:1	Am I not an **a?**
1 Cor 9:2	I am the Lord's **a.**
1 Cor 12:28	first are **a-s,** second are,
2 Cor 12:12	I am an **a.**
Eph 2:20	on the foundation of the **a-s**
Eph 4:11	the **a-s,** the prophets,
2 Tim 1:11	to be a preacher, an **a,**
Rev 21:14	of the twelve **a-s** of the Lamb.

APPEAR, APPEARED, APPEARING, APPEARS (v)
to come out of hiding and show up in public view; to make one's presence known

Gen 1:9	so dry ground may **a.**
Num 14:10	presence of the LORD **a-ed**
Deut 33:16	**a-ed** in the burning bush.
Mal 3:2	and face him when he **a-s?**
Matt 1:20	angel of the Lord **a-ed** to him
Matt 24:30	will **a** in the heavens,
Luke 2:9	angel of the Lord **a-ed** among
Luke 16:15	You like to **a** righteous
Phil 2:7	When he **a-ed** in human form,
2 Thes 1:7	the Lord Jesus **a-s** from
2 Tim 1:10	by the **a-ing** of Christ Jesus,
2 Tim 4:1	**a-s** to set up his Kingdom:
Heb 9:24	**a** now before God on our
Heb 9:26	**a-ed** at the end of the age
1 Pet 5:4	when the Great Shepherd **a-s,**
1 Jn 3:2	will be like when Christ **a-s.**

APPEARANCE (n)
external show; the outward or visible aspect

Isa 53:2	or majestic about his **a,**

APPETITE (n)
the desire to eat; an inherent craving

Prov 13:2	have an **a** for violence.
Prov 16:26	good for workers to have an **a;**
Phil 3:19	Their god is their **a,**

APPLES (n)
the fleshy, usually rounded, red, yellow, or green edible fruit of a tree

Prov 25:11	golden **a** in a silver basket.

APPLY (v)
to bring into action; to put to use especially for some practical purpose

Prov 22:17	**a** your heart to my instruction.

APPOINT, APPOINTED, APPOINTING (v)
to ordain or designate; to name officially

Deut 1:15	**a-ed** them to serve as judges
2 Sam 7:11	the time I **a-ed** judges to rule
Prov 8:23	I was **a-ed** in ages past,
John 15:16	I chose you. I **a-ed** you
Rom 11:13	God has **a-ed** me as the
1 Tim 5:22	about **a-ing** a church leader.
Titus 1:5	work there and **a** elders

APPOINTED (adj)
marked by being fixed or set officially

Exod 23:15	annually at the **a** time
Lev 23:2	the LORD's **a** festivals,
Dan 11:27	come at the **a** time.
Matt 8:29	before God's **a** time?"
Acts 3:20	Jesus, your **a** Messiah.

APPRECIATE (v)
to value or admire highly

Prov 28:23	people **a** honest criticism

APPRECIATION (n)
an expression of admiration, approval, or gratitude

1 Cor 16:18	must show your **a** to all

APPROACH (v)
to draw closer to; to come very near to

1 Tim 6:16	no human can **a** him.

APPROPRIATE (adj)
especially suitable or compatible; fitting

Deut 25:2	lashes **a** to the crime.
1 Tim 2:9	wear decent and **a** clothing

APPROVAL (n)
an act or instance of approving

Ps 90:17	LORD our God show us his **a**
John 6:27	the seal of his **a.**
Rom 14:4	stand and receive his **a.**
1 Cor 11:19	you who have God's **a**
2 Tim 2:15	and receive his **a.**
Heb 11:4	God showed his **a** of his gifts.

APPROVE, APPROVED, APPROVES (v)
to have or express a favorable opinion of; to attest

Gen 7:2	animal I have **a-ed** for eating
Prov 12:2	LORD **a-s** of those who
Rom 14:18	and others will **a** of you,
Rom 16:10	a good man whom Christ **a-s.**
1 Thes 2:4	speak as messengers **a-ed**

ARARAT (n)
a mountain on the far east border of modern Turkey; the mountain Noah's ark rested on after the Flood
Gen 8:4 to rest on the mountains of **A.**

ARCHANGEL, ARCHANGELS (n)
a leader and chief angel; biblically designated as Michael
Dan 10:13 one of the **a-s,** came to help
Dan 12:1 At that time Michael, the **a**
1 Thes 4:16 with the voice of the **a,**

ARCHER (n)
one who uses a bow and arrow
Prov 26:10 an **a** who shoots at random.

ARCHITECT (n)
a person who designs buildings and advises in their construction; a person who designs and guides a plan or undertaking
Prov 8:30 I was the **a** at his side.

ARGUE, ARGUING (v)
to contend or disagree in words; to dispute
Job 13:8 Will you **a** God's case
Job 40:2 to **a** with the Almighty?
Prov 25:9 **a-ing** with your neighbor,
Isa 45:9 those who **a** with their Creator.
Rom 14:1 and don't **a** with them
1 Cor 11:16 anyone wants to **a**

ARGUMENT, ARGUMENTS (n)
the act or process of arguing; discourse intended to persuade
Job 32:3 to answer Job's **a-s.**
Job 36:3 I will present profound **a-s**
Prov 26:17 in someone else's **a**
1 Tim 6:4 This stirs up **a-s**
2 Tim 2:14 Such **a-s** are useless,

ARK (n)
commonly, a portable wooden chest, box, or coffer; specifically, of Noah, a ship the size of a light cruiser; of the Covenant, a sacred housing for the Law of Moses
Exod 25:21 inside the **A** the stone
Deut 10:5 tablets in the **A** of the
1 Kgs 8:9 Nothing was in the **A** except
1 Chr 13:9 his hand to steady the **A.**
Rev 11:19 the **A** of his covenant

ARM, ARMS (n)
upper limb of the body; extension or projection of; lineage; figurative of power or might
Num 11:23 Has my **a** lost its power?
Deut 4:34 a powerful **a,** and terrifying
Deut 7:19 strong hand and powerful **a**
Deut 33:27 everlasting **a-s** are under
Ps 44:3 it was not their own strong **a**
Ps 98:1 his holy **a** has shown
Isa 40:11 carry the lambs in his **a-s,**
Isa 65:2 opened my **a-s** to a rebellious
Jer 27:5 powerful **a** I made the earth
Mark 10:16 took the children in his **a-s**
1 Pet 4:1 you must **a** yourselves with

ARMAGEDDON (n)
the gathering place for the final battle between God's forces and Satan's forces associated with Christ's second coming
Rev 16:16 with the Hebrew name **A.**

ARMOR (n)
weapons of war or self-defense; figurative of spiritual resources
Ps 91:4 are your **a** and protection.
Isa 59:17 righteousness as his body **a**
Jer 46:4 and prepare your **a.**
Rom 13:12 put on the shining **a**
Eph 6:11 Put on all of God's **a**
Eph 6:13 put on every piece of God's **a**
1 Thes 5:8 protected by the **a** of faith

ARMY, ARMIES (n)
large band of men organized and armed for war; any large multitude devoted to a cause
Ps 33:16 best-equipped **a** cannot save
Ps 84:12 LORD of Heaven's **A-ies,**
Isa 6:3 LORD of Heaven's **A-ies!**
Isa 45:13 LORD of Heaven's **A-ies,**
Isa 51:15 the LORD of Heaven's **A-ies.**
Joel 2:2 great and mighty **a** appears.
Joel 2:5 like a mighty **a** moving into
Joel 2:11 This is his mighty **a,**
Hag 1:5 LORD of Heaven's **A-ies** says:
Zech 8:6 LORD of Heaven's **A-ies** says:
Rev 19:14 The **a-ies** of heaven,
Rev 19:19 the horse and his **a.**

AROMA (n)
a distinctive, pervasive, and usually pleasant or savory smell; a distinctive quality or atmosphere
Gen 8:21 LORD was pleased with the **a**
Exod 29:18 it is a pleasing **a,**
Lev 3:16 a special gift of food, a pleasing **a**
Eph 5:2 a pleasing **a** to God.

ARREST, ARRESTED, ARRESTING (v)
to take or keep in custody by authority of law
Dan 6:16 orders for Daniel to be **a-ed**
Matt 10:19 When you are **a-ed,** don't
Mark 14:44 **a** when I greet him with a kiss.
Mark 14:49 Why didn't you **a** me in the Temple?

Luke 20:20 so he would **a** Jesus.
Acts 22:4 to death, **a-ing** both men

ARROGANCE (n)
a feeling or an impression of superiority manifested in an overbearing manner or presumptuous claims
1 Sam 2:3 Don't speak with such **a!**
Prov 8:13 I hate pride and **a,**
Isa 16:6 its pride and **a** and rage.
2 Cor 12:20 slander, gossip, **a,**

ARROGANT (adj)
exaggerating or disposed to exaggerate one's own worth or importance in an overbearing manner
Ps 31:23 harshly punishes the **a.**
Ps 119:78 upon the **a** people who lied
1 Tim 6:4 is **a** and lacks understanding.
Titus 1:7 not be **a** or quick-tempered;

ARROW, ARROWS (n)
a missile weapon shot from a bow and usually having a slender shaft, a pointed head, and feathers at the butt
Ps 64:3 their bitter words like **a-s.**
Ps 64:7 with his **a-s,** suddenly striking
Ps 91:5 the **a** that flies in the day.
Ps 127:4 like **a-s** in a warrior's hands.
Eph 6:16 the fiery **a-s** of the devil.

ASCEND, ASCENDED (v)
to go or move up
Ps 68:18 When you **a-ed** to the heights,
Isa 14:13 I will **a** to heaven
John 6:62 Son of Man **a** to heaven again?
John 20:17 I haven't yet **a-ed** to the Father.
Acts 2:34 never **a-ed** into heaven,
Eph 4:8 When he **a-ed** to the heights,

ASHAMED (adj)
feeling shame, guilt, or disgrace
Ps 69:6 be **a** because of me,
Jer 31:19 I was thoroughly **a** of all I did
Jer 48:13 were **a** of their gold calf
Mark 8:38 If anyone is **a** of me
Luke 9:26 If anyone is **a** of me
Rom 1:16 I am not **a** of this Good News
2 Tim 1:8 So never be **a** to tell others
2 Tim 2:15 who does not need to be **a**

ASHES (n)
burnt residue or remains of the dead, or anything ruined; denotes grief, repentance, or humiliation
Job 42:6 sit in dust and **a**
Matt 11:21 throwing **a** on their heads

ASK, ASKED, ASKING, ASKS (v)
to seek information; to call on for an answer; to make a request
1 Sam 10:22 So they **a-ed** the LORD,
Prov 18:6 they are **a-ing** for a beating.
Isa 8:19 Let's **a** the mediums
Matt 7:7 **a-ing,** and you will receive
Luke 6:30 Give to anyone who **a-s;**
Luke 11:9 will receive what you **a** for.
John 17:15 I'm not **a-ing** you to take them
Eph 3:20 more than we might **a** or
Phlm 1:21 do what I **a** and even more!
1 Jn 5:14 whenever we **a** for anything

ASLEEP (adj)
state of bodily rest; figurative for physical death or spiritual dullness
see also DIE, SLEEP
Judg 4:21 Sisera fell **a** from exhaustion,
1 Kgs 18:27 away on a trip, or is **a** and
Matt 9:24 isn't dead; she's only **a.**"
Matt 26:40 disciples and found them **a.**
John 11:11 Lazarus has fallen **a,** but
1 Thes 5:6 be on your guard, not **a** like

ASSEMBLY (n)
a company of persons gathered for deliberation and legislation, worship, or entertainment
Ps 35:18 in front of the great **a.**
Ps 149:1 praises in the **a** of the faithful.

ASSIGN, ASSIGNED (v)
to transfer (property) to another, especially in trust or for the benefit of creditors; to appoint to a duty or task
Gen 47:11 So Joseph **a-ed** the best land
Deut 32:8 the Most High **a-ed** lands
Josh 13:14 Moses did not **a** any allotment

ASSOCIATE (v)
to join as a partner, friend, or companion; to keep company with
Prov 13:20 **a** with fools and get in
Prov 22:24 or **a** with hot-tempered
Prov 24:21 Don't **a** with rebels,
Acts 10:28 like this or to **a** with you.
1 Cor 5:9 not to **a** with people who
1 Cor 5:11 are not to **a** with anyone

ASSURANCE (n)
the act or action of giving confidence to or making sure or certain
Col 1:27 This gives you **a** of sharing
1 Thes 1:5 full **a** that what we said

ASSURE (v)
to make certain or reassure

Mark 10:29 I **a** you that everyone who has
Luke 23:43 I **a** you, today you will be with
John 3:5 I **a** you, no one can enter
John 5:25 I **a** you that the time is coming,

ASTRAY (adv)
off the right path or route; in error, away from what is desirable or proper
Prov 20:1 Those led **a** by drink
Isa 47:10 'knowledge' have led you **a,**
Jer 50:6 shepherds have led them **a**
1 Jn 2:26 who want to lead you **a.**

ASTROLOGERS (n)
one who studies the stars and planets to foresee or foretell future events by their positions and aspects
Isa 47:13 all your **a,** those stargazers
Dan 2:2 enchanters, sorcerers, and **a,**

ATE (v)
to partake of food
see also EAT
Gen 3:6 some of the fruit and **a** it.
Ezek 3:3 And when I **a** it, it tasted as
Matt 15:37 **a** as much as they wanted.
Rev 10:10 I **a** it! It was sweet

ATHLETE, ATHLETES (n)
a person who is trained or skilled in exercises, sports, or games requiring physical strength, agility, or stamina
Ps 19:5 like a great **a** eager to run
1 Cor 9:25 All **a-s** are disciplined
1 Cor 9:27 body like an **a,** training it
2 Tim 2:5 **a-s** cannot win the prize unless

ATONE, ATONES (v)
to supply satisfaction for; to make amends; to reconcile
see also FORGIVE
Dan 9:24 their sin, to **a** for their guilt,
1 Jn 2:2 sacrifice that **a-s** for our sins—

ATONEMENT (n)
reconciliation; reparation for an offense or injury; cleansing
see also FORGIVENESS
Exod 25:17 cover—the place of **a**—
Lev 23:27 Day of **A** on the tenth day
2 Chr 29:24 to make **a** for the sins
Prov 16:6 faithfulness make **a** for sin.

ATTACK, ATTACKED (v)
to set upon or work against forcefully; to assail with unfriendly or bitter words
1 Sam 17:48 Goliath moved closer to **a,**
Joel 3:19 they **a-ed** the people of Judah
Zech 10:2 **a-ed** because they have no
2 Tim 4:18 deliver me from every evil **a**

ATTENTION (n)
the act or state of applying the mind to an object or thought
Exod 23:13 Pay close **a** to all my
Prov 4:20 pay **a** to what I say.
Prov 5:1 My son, pay **a** to my wisdom;
Acts 18:17 Gallio paid no **a.**
1 Tim 4:15 Give your complete **a** to

ATTITUDE, ATTITUDES (n)
a mental position with regard to a fact or state; a feeling or emotion toward a fact or state
Eph 4:23 your thoughts and **a-s.**
Phil 2:5 have the same **a** that Christ
1 Pet 3:8 keep a humble **a.**
1 Pet 4:1 with the same **a** he had,

ATTRACT, ATTRACTED (v)
to pull to or draw toward oneself or itself; to draw by appeal to natural or excited interest, emotion, or aesthetic sense
Isa 53:2 nothing to **a** us to him.
Heb 13:9 **a-ed** by strange, new ideas.

ATTRACTIVE (adj)
arousing interest or pleasure; having the power to attract
Prov 19:22 Loyalty makes a person **a.**
Col 4:6 conversation be gracious and **a**
1 Tim 2:10 make themselves **a** by the
Titus 2:10 God our Savior **a** in every

AUTHORITY, AUTHORITIES (n)
the right to govern; the freedom or ability to act; one entrusted with the right to govern
Matt 28:18 been given all **a** in heaven
Luke 10:19 have given you **a** over
John 5:22 absolute **a** to judge,
Acts 1:7 **a** to set those dates and times,
Rom 13:1 submit to governing **a-ies.**
Rom 13:1 For all **a** comes from God,
Rom 13:2 anyone who rebels against **a**
Rom 13:3 without fear of the **a-ies?**
1 Cor 4:3 by any human **a.**
1 Cor 15:24 ruler and **a** and power.
Eph 1:22 things under the **a** of Christ
Eph 3:10 all the unseen rulers and **a-ies**
Eph 6:12 against evil rulers and **a-ies**
Col 2:10 every ruler and **a.**
Col 2:15 the spiritual rulers and **a-ies.**
1 Tim 2:2 all who are in **a** so that
Titus 2:15 You have the **a** to correct
1 Pet 2:18 accept the **a** of your masters

1 Pet 3:1 accept the **a** of your husbands.
1 Pet 3:22 the angels and **a-ies** and
1 Pet 5:5 accept the **a** of the elders.
Jude 1:6 the limits of **a** God gave them

AVENGE, AVENGES (v)
to take revenge or punish
Deut 32:43 **a** the blood of his servants;
1 Thes 4:6 the Lord **a-s** all such sins,
Rev 6:10 **a** our blood for what they

AVENGER (n)
one who seeks revenge or to punish an evildoer
Num 35:27 **a** finds him outside the city

AVOID, AVOIDING (v)
to keep away from; to depart or withdraw from
Prov 4:24 **A** all perverse talk;
Prov 14:16 are cautious and **a** danger;
Prov 16:6 By fearing the LORD, people **a**
Prov 20:3 **A-ing** a fight is a mark
Eccl 7:18 fears God will **a** both
Rom 2:3 think you can **a** God's

AWAKE (v)
to cease sleeping; to become aroused or active again
see also WAKE
Ps 17:15 When I **a,** I will see
Eph 5:14 "**A,** O sleeper, rise up

AWARE (adj)
having or showing realization, perception, or knowledge
Exod 34:29 he wasn't **a** that

AWARENESS (n)
the state of realization or perception
Hab 2:14 filled with an **a** of the glory

AWAY (adv)
in another direction; by a long distance or interval
1 Thes 4:3 stay **a** from all sexual sin.
2 Tim 3:5 Stay **a** from people like that!
1 Pet 2:11 keep **a** from worldly desires

AWE (n)
an emotion variously combining dread, respect, and wonder that is inspired by authority or the sacred
see also FEAR, REVERENCE
1 Kgs 3:28 people were in **a** of the king,
Ps 119:120 I stand in **a** of your
Luke 5:26 with great wonder and **a,**
Acts 2:43 sense of **a** came over them
Heb 12:28 holy fear and **a.**

AWESOME (adj)
characterized by reverential fear; expressive of or inspiring awe
see also MARVELOUS, WONDERFUL
Exod 34:10 the **a** power I will display
Deut 7:21 a great and **a** God.
2 Sam 7:23 You performed **a** miracles
Neh 1:5 the great and **a** God
Job 10:16 display your **a** power
Ps 47:2 Most High is **a.**
Ps 65:5 answer our prayers with **a**
Ps 99:3 your great and **a** name.
Ps 106:22 such **a** deeds at the Red Sea.
Ps 131:1 too **a** for me to grasp.
Dan 9:4 a great and **a** God!

AX (n)
a cutting tool that is used especially for felling trees and chopping and splitting wood
2 Kgs 6:6 Then the **a** head floated
Prov 25:18 hitting them with an **a,**

B

BAAL (n)
a fertility and nature god of the Canaanites and Phoenicians
1 Kgs 18:25 said to the prophets of **B,**
1 Kgs 19:18 bowed down to **B** or kissed
Rom 11:4 have never bowed down to **B!**

BABY, BABIES (n)
infant child; youngest of a group; figurative of new or immature Christians
Exod 2:7 women to nurse the **b** for you?
Luke 1:44 **b** in my womb jumped for
Luke 2:12 find a **b** wrapped snugly
Luke 2:16 the **b,** lying in the manger.
Acts 7:19 abandon their newborn **b-ies**
1 Cor 14:20 Be innocent as **b-ies** when
1 Pet 2:2 Like newborn **b-ies,** you must

BABYLON (n)
capital city of the Babylonian Empire; a city devoted to materialism and sensual pleasure; biblical writers used as model of paganism and idolatry
Ps 137:1 Beside the rivers of **B,** we sat
Jer 29:10 will be in **B** for seventy years.
Jer 51:37 **B** will become a heap of ruins,
Rev 14:8 shouting, "**B** is fallen—

BACKSLIDERS, BACKSLIDING (KJV)
Prov 14:14 *Backsliders* get what they deserve
Jer 3:22 I will heal your *wayward* hearts
Jer 31:22 wander, my *wayward* daughter
Hos 14:4 heal you of your *faithlessness*

BAD (adj)
poor, inadequate; morally objectionable; disagreeable, unpleasant

Job 2:10 — of God and never anything **b**?
Eccl 12:14 — thing, whether good or **b**.
Isa 45:7 — good times and **b** times.

BALAAM
Pagan prophet, summoned to curse the Israelites but instead blessed them (Num 22–24; also Deut 23:3-5; 2 Pet 2:15-16; Jude 1:11; Rev 2:14); died (Num 31:8; Josh 13:22).

BALANCES (n)
an instrument for weighing; a means of judging or deciding
see also SCALES

Dan 5:27 — you have been weighed on the **b**

BALD (adj)
lacking a natural or usual covering (as of hair or vegetation); bare, unadorned

Mic 1:16 — yourselves as **b** as a vulture,

BALDY (n)
a derogatory nickname for someone who is bald

2 Kgs 2:23 — "Go away, **b**!" they chanted.

BANNER (n)
a piece of cloth attached by one edge to a staff and used by a leader as his emblem

Exod 17:15 — "the LORD is my **b**").
Isa 11:10 — will be a **b** of salvation

BANQUET, BANQUETS (n)
a sumptuous feast, especially a ceremonious meal in honor of a person, occasion, or achievement

Song 2:4 — He escorts me to the **b** hall;
Matt 24:38 — enjoying **b-s** and parties

BAPTISM, BAPTISMS (n)
a Christian ordinance; a washing with water to demonstrate cleansing from sin, linked with repentance and admission into the community of faith; figurative of an ordeal or initiation

Matt 3:16 — After his **b**, as Jesus came up
Luke 3:7 — crowds came to John for **b**,
Acts 19:3 — what **b** did you experience?
Rom 6:3 — joined with Christ Jesus in **b**,
Gal 3:27 — united with Christ in **b**
Eph 4:5 — one Lord, one faith, one **b**,
Heb 6:2 — further instruction about **b-s**,
1 Pet 3:21 — that water is a picture of **b**,

BAPTIST (n)
one who baptizes

Matt 11:11 — greater than John the **B**.
Mark 1:4 — messenger was John the **B**.

BAPTIZE, BAPTIZED, BAPTIZING (v)
to engage in the ordinance of baptism (see above)
see also WASH

Matt 3:13 — River to be **b-d** by John.
Matt 28:19 — of all the nations, **b-ing**
Mark 1:4 — that people should be **b-d**
Mark 1:8 — will **b** you with the Holy Spirit!
Mark 10:38 — suffering I must be **b-d** with?
Luke 3:3 — that people should be **b-d**
Luke 3:16 — I **b** you with water;
Luke 3:21 — Jesus himself was **b-d**.
John 1:28 — where John was **b-ing**.
John 1:31 — I have been **b-ing** with water
John 1:33 — is the one who will **b** with
John 3:22 — with them there, **b-ing** people.
John 3:26 — is also **b-ing** people.
John 4:1 — was **b-ing** and making more
John 4:2 — Jesus himself didn't **b** them—
John 10:40 — where John was first **b-ing**
Acts 1:5 — be **b-d** with the Holy Spirit.
Acts 1:22 — time he was **b-d** by John
Acts 2:41 — **b-d** and added to the church
Acts 8:12 — and women were **b-d**.
Acts 8:38 — water, and Philip **b-d** him.
Acts 11:16 — will be **b-d** with the Holy
Acts 16:15 — She was **b-d** along with
Acts 16:33 — were immediately **b-d**.
Acts 19:5 — **b-d** in the name of the Lord
1 Cor 1:13 — you **b-d** in the name of Paul?
1 Cor 1:14 — I did not **b** any of you
1 Cor 1:16 — **b-d** the household of
1 Cor 10:2 — were **b-d** as followers
1 Cor 15:29 — **b-d** for those who are dead?
Col 2:12 — when you were **b-d**.

BARN (n)
a usually large building for the storage of farm products, feed, animals, and/or equipment

Matt 13:30 — the wheat in the **b**.

BARREN (adj)
unproductive, unfruitful, especially in childbearing

Heb 11:11 — she was **b** and was too old.

BASKET (n)
a receptacle made of interwoven material; any of various lightweight, usually wood, containers

Exod 2:3 — she got a **b** made of papyrus
Acts 9:25 — lowered him in a large **b**
2 Cor 11:33 — in a **b** through a window

BARNABAS
Levite believer from Cyprus, generous giver of prop-

erty (Acts 4:36-37); encourager of Paul (Acts 9:26-29); missionary with Paul (Acts 11:22-30; 12:25; 13:1-3); at Jerusalem council (Acts 15:1-2, 12); disagreed with Paul over John Mark (Acts 15:36-40; *see also* 1 Cor 9:6; Col 4:10).

BATCH (n)
the quantity baked at one time
Rom 11:16 the entire **b** of dough is holy
1 Cor 5:6 through the whole **b** of dough?
1 Cor 5:7 like a fresh **b** of dough
Gal 5:9 through the whole **b** of dough!

BATH (n)
a washing or soaking (as in water or steam) of all or part of the body
2 Sam 11:2 unusual beauty taking a **b.**

BATHED (v)
to take a bath; to give a bath to
John 13:10 A person who has **b** all over

BATHSHEBA
Committed adultery with King David, widow of Uriah the Hittite(2 Sam 11–12); mother of Solomon, her second son with David (1 Kgs 1–2; 1 Chr 3:5).

BATTLE, BATTLES (n)
a combat between two persons; a general encounter between armies, ships of war, aircraft; an extended contest, struggle, or controversy
1 Sam 17:47 This is the LORD's **b,**
1 Sam 18:17 the LORD's **b-s.**
1 Sam 25:28 the LORD's **b-s.**
2 Kgs 14:8 Come and meet me in **b!**
2 Chr 32:8 to fight our **b-s** for us!
Ps 24:8 LORD, invincible in **b.**
Rev 16:14 gather them for **b** against
Rev 20:8 gather them together for **b**—

BEAR (v)
to carry or support; to give as testimony; to give birth to or produce
see also BORN
Gen 4:13 too great for me to **b!**
Ps 38:4 too heavy to **b.**
John 15:2 branches that do **b** fruit
Heb 13:13 and **b** the disgrace he bore.

BEAR, BEARS (n)
a large heavy mammal with shaggy hair, rudimentary tail, and plantigrade feet
2 Kgs 2:24 Then two **b-s** came out
Isa 11:7 cow will graze near the **b.**
Dan 7:5 it looked like a **b.**

BEARD, BEARDS (n)
the hair that grows on a man's face often excluding the mustache
Lev 19:27 or trim your **b-s.**
Isa 50:6 who pulled out my **b.**

BEAST, BEASTS (n)
devilish creature(s) ravishing the earth during the Tribulation; animals, as distinguished from plants or humans; a contemptible person
Dan 7:3 Then four huge **b-s** came up
Dan 7:6 authority was given to this **b.**
1 Cor 15:32 fighting wild **b-s**—those
Rev 13:18 number of the **b,** for it is
Rev 16:2 had the mark of the **b**
Rev 19:20 accepted the mark of the **b**

BEATEN (v)
to be stricken repeatedly so as to inflict pain
see also FLOGGED, WHIPPED
Acts 16:23 They were severely **b,**
2 Cor 11:25 Three times I was **b**
1 Pet 2:20 if you are **b** for doing wrong.

BEAUTIFUL (adj)
lovely, handsome, or pleasing to the eye; excellent
Gen 2:9 trees that were **b**
Gen 6:2 sons of God saw the **b**
Prov 11:22 A **b** woman who lacks
Eccl 3:11 everything **b** for its own time.
Isa 53:2 was nothing **b** or majestic
Lam 2:15 the city called 'Most **B**
Acts 3:2 the one called the **B** Gate,
Rom 10:15 How **b** are the feet of

BEAUTY (n)
a particularly graceful, ornamental, or excellent quality; the quality in a person or thing that gives pleasure to the senses
2 Sam 11:2 a woman of unusual **b**
Ps 50:2 the perfection of **b,** God shines
Prov 31:30 and **b** does not last;
Isa 28:1 but its glorious **b** will fade
Jas 1:11 and its **b** fades away.
1 Pet 1:24 their **b** is like a flower
1 Pet 3:4 **b** of a gentle and quiet spirit,

BED (n)
a piece of furniture on or in which to lie and sleep; a place for sleeping
Deut 6:7 when you are going to **b**
Song 3:1 as I lay in **b,** I yearned
Luke 17:34 will be asleep in one **b;**

BEDROCK (n)
the solid rock underlying loosely arranged surface materials (as soil)
Matt 7:25 it is built on **b.**

BEG, BEGGED, BEGGING (v)
to ask for charity or mercy; to ask earnestly for
Ps 37:25 their children **b-ging** for bread.
Ps 80:14 Come back, we **b** you,
Mal 1:9 Go ahead, **b** God to
2 Cor 12:8 different times I **b-ged** the Lord

BEGINNING (n)
the point at which something starts; the first part; the origin, source
Gen 1:1 In the **b** God created
John 1:1 In the **b** the Word already
Rom 16:25 secret from the **b** of time.
1 Jn 1:1 one who existed from the **b,**
Rev 21:6 the **B** and the End.
Rev 22:13 the **B** and the End.

BEHEMOTH (n)
Hebrew word that could mean elephant, crocodile, hippopotamus, water buffalo, or mythological monster; a mighty animal created as an example of the power of God
Job 40:15 a look at **B,** which I made,

BELIEF (n)
the content of one's conviction on a matter; confidence in or reliance upon the truth of a matter
1 Thes 2:14 because of their **b** in Christ
2 Thes 2:13 through your **b** in the truth.
Titus 1:9 **b** in the trustworthy message

BELIEVE, BELIEVED, BELIEVES, BELIEVING (v)
to trust in; to hold a firm conviction about; to accept as true, genuine, or real
see also FAITH, TRUST
Gen 15:6 Abram **b-d** the Lord,
Prov 14:15 simpletons **b** everything
Isa 53:1 Who has **b-d** our message?
Matt 27:42 we will **b** in him!
Mark 9:23 is possible if a person **b-s.**
Mark 9:24 I do **b,** but help me
Mark 15:32 we can see it and **b** him!
Luke 8:12 prevent them from **b-ing**
Luke 24:25 You find it so hard to **b**
John 1:7 so that everyone might **b**
John 1:12 all who **b-d** him and accepted
John 3:16 everyone who **b-s** in him
John 4:41 hear his message and **b.**
John 5:38 because you do not **b** me—
John 6:69 We **b,** and we know you are
John 7:5 his brothers didn't **b** in him.
John 7:39 to everyone **b-ing** in him.
John 9:35 asked, "Do you **b** in the Son
John 9:38 Yes, Lord, I **b!**
John 10:37 Don't **b** me unless
John 11:25 Anyone who **b-s** in me
John 11:27 **b-d** you are the Messiah,
John 11:40 see God's glory if you **b?**
John 12:37 did not **b** in him.
John 12:38 who has **b-d** our message?
John 13:19 you will **b** that I Am
John 14:11 Or at least **b** because of the
John 14:12 anyone who **b-s** in me
John 16:30 **b** that you came from God.
John 17:21 world will **b** you sent me.
John 19:35 so that you also can **b.**
John 20:8 and he saw and **b-d**—
John 20:29 **b** because you have seen
John 20:31 and that by **b-ing** in him
Acts 10:43 that everyone who **b-s** in him
Acts 13:8 keep the governor from **b-ing.**
Acts 16:31 **B** in the Lord Jesus and
Acts 19:4 **b** in the one who would come
Acts 26:27 do you **b** the prophets?
Acts 27:25 For I **b** God. I will be just
Rom 1:16 saving everyone who **b-s**—
Rom 3:22 for everyone who **b-s,** no
Rom 3:25 **b** that Jesus sacrificed his life,
Rom 4:3 tell us, "Abraham **b-d** God,
Rom 4:20 never wavered in **b-ing** God's
Rom 10:9 **b** in your heart that God
Rom 10:10 For it is by **b-ing** in your heart
Rom 10:14 unless they **b** in him?
Rom 14:23 anything you **b** is not right,
Rom 16:26 they too might **b** and obey
1 Cor 1:21 to save those who **b.**
1 Cor 15:2 **b-d** something that was never
2 Cor 5:7 by **b-ing** and not by seeing.
2 Cor 5:14 Since we **b** that Christ
Gal 3:2 because you **b-d** the message
Gal 3:6 same way, "Abraham **b-d** God,
Eph 2:8 his grace when you **b-d.**
Col 1:23 continue to **b** this truth
1 Thes 4:14 For since we **b** that Jesus
2 Thes 2:11 and they will **b** these lies.
2 Thes 2:12 enjoying evil rather than **b-ing**
1 Tim 3:16 He was **b-d** in throughout the
Heb 3:14 firmly as when we first **b-d,**
Heb 11:6 must **b** that God exists
Heb 11:13 still **b-ing** what God had
Jas 2:19 you **b** that there is one God.
1 Jn 3:23 We must **b** in the name
1 Jn 4:1 friends, do not **b** everyone
1 Jn 5:1 Everyone who **b-s** that Jesus is
1 Jn 5:10 All who **b** in the Son

BELIEVER, BELIEVERS (n)
one who accepts something as true, genuine, or real; one who trusts in or has a firm conviction about
Matt 18:15 If another **b** sins
Acts 2:44 all the **b-s** met together
Acts 4:32 All the **b-s** were united
Acts 6:1 as the **b-s** rapidly multiplied,
Acts 6:7 number of **b-s** greatly increased
Acts 13:48 for eternal life became **b-s.**
Acts 14:22 they strengthened the **b-s.**
Acts 15:2 accompanied by some local **b-s,**
Acts 15:23 to the Gentile **b-s** in Antioch,
Acts 15:32 to the **b-s,** encouraging
Acts 16:15 I am a true **b** in the Lord,
Acts 20:2 there, he encouraged the **b-s**
Acts 21:25 As for the Gentile **b-s,**
Rom 8:27 the Spirit pleads for us **b-s**
Rom 14:13 cause another **b** to stumble
Rom 14:15 if another **b** is distressed
Rom 14:21 cause another **b** to stumble.
Rom 15:27 the **b-s** in Jerusalem,
1 Cor 6:2 someday we **b-s** will judge
1 Cor 10:27 who isn't a **b** asks you
1 Cor 14:22 tongues is a sign, not for **b-s,**
2 Cor 6:15 can a **b** be a partner with an
2 Cor 11:26 claim to be **b-s** but are not.
Col 4:5 among those who are not **b-s,**
2 Thes 3:6 away from all **b-s** who live idle
1 Tim 3:6 An elder must not be a new **b,**
1 Tim 4:12 Be an example to all **b-s**
1 Tim 5:16 a woman who is a **b**
1 Jn 3:10 and does not love other **b-s**

BELITTLE (v)
to cause (a person or thing) to seem little or less; to speak slightingly of
Prov 11:12 foolish to **b** one's neighbor;
Prov 14:21 a sin to **b** one's neighbor;

BELLY (n)
abdomen; the stomach and its adjuncts
Gen 3:14 crawl on your **b,** groveling
Dan 2:32 its **b** and thighs were bronze,
Matt 12:40 in the **b** of the great fish

BELONG, BELONGED, BELONGS (v)
to be the property of a person or thing
Lev 25:55 people of Israel **b** to me.
Lev 27:30 **b-s** to the LORD and
Ps 22:28 royal power **b-s** to the LORD.
John 8:47 Anyone who **b-s** to God
John 15:19 if you **b-ed** to it, but you
Rom 1:6 called to **b** to Jesus
Rom 12:5 we all **b** to each other.
2 Cor 10:7 who say they **b** to Christ
Gal 5:24 Those who **b** to Christ
1 Thes 5:5 we don't **b** to darkness
2 Tim 2:19 All who **b** to the LORD
1 Pet 3:16 because you **b** to Christ.
1 Jn 4:6 If they do not **b** to God,

BELOVED (adj)
dearly loved; dear to the heart
Ps 60:5 rescue your **b** people.
Matt 12:18 He is my **B,** who pleases me.
1 Cor 4:14 as my **b** children.
1 Cor 4:17 Timothy, my **b** and faithful
Eph 6:21 a **b** brother and faithful helper
Col 1:7 Epaphras, our **b** co-worker.
Col 4:9 a faithful and **b** brother,
Col 4:14 Luke, the **b** doctor,
Phlm 1:1 to Philemon, our **b** co-worker,
Phlm 1:16 he is a **b** brother,
2 Pet 3:15 our **b** brother Paul also wrote
Rev 20:9 God's people and the **b** city.

BENEFICIAL (adj)
conferring benefits; conducive to personal or social well-being
Titus 3:8 good and **b** for everyone.

BENEFIT, BENEFITS (n)
advantages or blessings; something that promotes well-being
Prov 12:14 Wise words bring many **b-s,**
Acts 18:27 he proved to be of great **b** to
2 Cor 4:15 this is for your **b.**

BENEFIT, BENEFITS (v)
to be useful or profitable to; to favor (another) or gain (for oneself)
Job 36:28 and everyone **b-s.**
Prov 9:12 you will be the one to **b.**
Luke 9:25 what do you **b** if you gain
1 Cor 9:14 by those who **b** from it.

BENJAMIN
Second son of Jacob and Rachel, the youngest of Jacob's 12 sons; never knew his mother (Gen 35:16-20); taken to Egypt against Jacob's wishes (Gen 43:3-17); gave his name to a tribe of Israel; his tribe was blessed (Gen 49:27; Deut 33:12), numbered (Num 1:36-37), allotted land and cities (Josh 18:11-28); civil war nearly wiped them out (Judg 20–21); 12,000 will be marked by God (Rev 7:8).

BESEECH(ING), BESOUGHT (KJV)
Deut 3:23 I *pleaded with* the LORD
Ps 118:25 *LORD, please* give us success
Jon 1:14 *pleaded,* "don't make us die
Matt 8:5 came and *pleaded with* him
2 Cor 12:8 *begged* the Lord to take it away

BESIDE (prep)
by the side of
Ps 16:8 he is right **b** me.
Ps 109:31 he stands **b** the needy,

BEST (adj)
excelling all others
Ps 122:9 seek what is **b** for you,
1 Cor 12:31 life that is **b** of all.
Heb 4:11 do our **b** to enter that rest.

BESTOWED (KJV)
Isa 63:7 he has *granted* according

BETHLEHEM (n)
a city about five miles south of Jerusalem in the hill country of Judah; the ancestral home of King David and the birthplace of Jesus Christ
Ruth 1:19 When they came to **B,**
1 Sam 16:1 go to **B.** Find a man named
2 Sam 23:15 the well by the gate in **B.**
Mic 5:2 **B** Ephrathah, are only a small
Matt 2:1 Jesus was born in **B** in Judea,
Matt 2:6 you, O **B** in the land of Judah,

BETRAY, BETRAYED (v)
to turn your back on a friend; to deliver to an enemy by treachery; to lead astray, seduce
Num 5:6 men or women—**b** the LORD
Deut 32:51 both of you **b-ed** me
Jer 38:22 They have **b-ed** and misled
Mal 2:10 Then why do we **b** each other,
Matt 10:21 A brother will **b** his brother
Matt 24:10 and **b** and hate each other.
Matt 26:21 one of you will **b** me.
Matt 27:4 I have **b-ed** an innocent man.
Luke 6:16 (who later **b-ed** him).
John 18:5 Judas, who **b-ed** him,

BETRAYER (n)
one who violates a trust or loyalty
Matt 26:46 Look, my **b** is here!
John 18:2 Judas, the **b,** knew this place,

BETTER (adj)
more attractive, favorable, or commendable; more advantageous or effective
Ps 63:3 unfailing love is **b** than life
Matt 5:20 unless your righteousness is **b**
Phil 1:21 and dying is even **b.**

BEWARE (v)
to take heed or be careful
Mark 8:15 **B** of the yeast of the Pharisees

BIRD, BIRDS (n)
any of a class of warm-blooded vertebrates distinguished by having the body more or less completely covered with feathers and the forelimbs modified as wings
Prov 27:8 **b** that strays from its nest.
Eccl 10:20 **b** might deliver your
Matt 8:20 and **b-s** have nests,
Luke 9:58 and **b-s** have nests,

BIRTH (n)
the emergence of a new individual from the body of its parent; beginning, start
Gen 25:24 the time came to give **b,**
Ps 58:3 even from **b** they have lied
Matt 24:8 only the first of the **b** pains,
John 3:6 Spirit gives **b** to spiritual life.
Titus 3:5 giving us a new **b** and new life
Jas 1:15 it gives **b** to death.

BIRTHRIGHT (KJV)
Gen 25:31 your *rights as the firstborn son*
1 Chr 5:1 *birthright* was given to the
Heb 12:16 *birthright as the firstborn son*

BITTER (adj)
expressive of severe pain, grief, or regret; distasteful
Exod 12:8 eat it along with **b** salad greens
Prov 27:7 **b** food tastes sweet to the
Prov 30:23 a **b** woman who finally gets
Jas 3:11 both fresh water and **b** water?

BITTERNESS (n)
an intense or severe expression or feeling of pain, grief, or regret; exhibiting intense animosity
Prov 14:10 Each heart knows its own **b,**
Prov 17:25 **b** to the one who gave them
Rom 3:14 full of cursing and **b.**
Eph 4:31 Get rid of all **b,** rage,

BLACK (adj)
of the color black; very dark in color
Zech 6:6 The chariot with **b** horses
Rev 6:5 I looked up and saw a **b** horse,

BLAME (n)
an expression of disapproval or reproach; responsibility for something believed to deserve censure
1 Cor 1:8 free from all **b** on the day
Rev 14:5 they are without **b.**

BLAMELESS (adj)
characterized by being free from sin and fault
see also INTEGRITY, RIGHTEOUS
Gen 6:9 only **b** person living on earth
Job 1:8 **b**—a man of complete integrity.

Ps 18:23 I am **b** before God;
Prov 13:6 guards the path of the **b,**
Prov 29:10 The bloodthirsty hate **b**
Phil 1:10 live pure and **b** lives
Col 1:22 and you are holy and **b**
1 Thes 5:23 kept **b** until our Lord
Titus 1:6 must live a **b** life.
2 Pet 3:14 pure and **b** in his sight.

BLASPHEME, BLASPHEMED, BLASPHEMES, BLASPHEMING (v)
to dishonor or revile God; to speak of or address with irreverence
Lev 24:11 son of an Israelite woman **b-ed**
Lev 24:16 Anyone who **b-s** the Name
Num 15:30 have **b-ed** the LORD,
Isa 52:5 My name is **b-ed** all day long.
Dan 11:36 even **b-ing** the God of gods.
Mark 3:29 who **b-s** the Holy Spirit
Luke 12:10 who **b-s** the Holy Spirit
Acts 6:11 We heard him **b** Moses,
Rom 2:24 Gentiles **b** the name of God
1 Tim 1:13 to **b** the name of Christ.
1 Tim 1:20 learn not to **b** God.
Rev 13:1 were names that **b-ed** God.

BLASPHEMER (n)
one who dishonors or reviles God; one who speaks or addresses with irreverence
Lev 24:14 Take the **b** outside the camp,
Lev 24:23 took the **b** outside the camp

BLASPHEMOUS (adj)
impiously irreverent; profane
2 Kgs 19:6 by this **b** speech against me
Isa 37:6 by this **b** speech against me

BLASPHEMY, BLASPHEMIES (n)
the words or actions that dishonor God; the act of insulting or showing contempt or lack of reverence for God
Neh 9:18 They committed terrible **b-ies.**
Mark 3:28 all sin and **b** can be forgiven,
Mark 14:64 You have all heard his **b.**
John 10:33 for any good work, but for **b!**
2 Pet 2:11 a charge of **b** against those
Rev 13:5 speak great **b-ies** against God.
Rev 13:6 words of **b** against God,
Rev 17:3 and **b-ies** against God were

BLESS, BLESSED, BLESSES (v)
to confer prosperity or happiness upon; to honor in worship; to offer approval or encouragement; to bring pleasure or divine favor
Gen 1:22 Then God **b-ed** them,
Gen 12:3 I will **b** those who **b** you
Gen 22:18 of the earth will be **b-ed**—
Ps 16:7 I will **b** the LORD who guides
Prov 31:28 Her children stand and **b**
Matt 5:3 God **b-es** those who are poor
Matt 5:7 **b-es** those who are merciful,
Matt 5:9 God **b-es** those who work for
Matt 5:11 God **b-es** you when people
Jas 1:12 God **b-es** those who patiently
Rev 22:7 **B-ed** are those who obey
Rev 22:14 **B-ed** are those who wash

BLESSING, BLESSINGS (n)
happiness; praise; divine favor or heavenly reward; the antidote to cursings
Josh 8:34 **b-s** and curses Moses
Prov 13:21 **b-s** reward the righteous.
John 12:13 **B-s** on the one who comes in
Acts 4:33 God's great **b** was upon them
Acts 11:23 evidence of God's **b,**
Rom 15:27 spiritual **b-s** of the Good
Eph 3:6 both enjoy the promise of **b-s**
Rev 7:12 **B** and glory and wisdom

BLIND (adj)
sightless; lacking spiritual discernment
Matt 11:5 the **b** see, the lame walk,
Matt 15:14 **b** guides leading the **b,**
Mark 10:46 **b** beggar named
Luke 6:39 Can one **b** person lead

BLINDED (v)
to withhold light from; to be without sight
John 12:40 The Lord has **b** their eyes
2 Cor 4:4 god of this world, has **b** the

BLINK (n)
glimpse, glance; a usually involuntary shutting and opening of the eye
1 Cor 15:52 moment, in the **b** of an eye,

BLOOD (n)
fluid in the circulatory system; signifies human life; kinfolk; of animals, used in priestly sacrifices; of Christ, effective for the forgiveness of sins; on hands or head, symbolic of guilt
Exod 12:13 When I see the **b,** I will pass
Deut 12:23 But never consume the **b,**
Isa 1:11 no pleasure from the **b** of bulls
Mark 14:24 my **b,** which confirms the
John 6:53 and drink his **b,** you cannot
Acts 15:20 and from consuming **b.**
1 Cor 11:25 confirmed with my **b.**
Eph 1:7 with the **b** of his Son
Eph 2:13 through the **b** of Christ.
Heb 9:7 offered **b** for his own sins
Heb 9:20 This **b** confirms the covenant

1 Pet 1:2 cleansed by the **b** of Jesus
1 Pet 1:19 the precious **b** of Christ,
1 Jn 1:7 the **b** of Jesus, his Son, cleanses
Rev 1:5 by shedding his **b** for us.
Rev 5:9 your **b** has ransomed people
Rev 7:14 in the **b** of the Lamb
Rev 12:11 by the **b** of the Lamb
Rev 19:13 He wore a robe dipped in **b,**

BLOT (v)
to wipeout, destroy; to erase or cover up
Ps 51:1 **b** out the stain of my sins.
Isa 43:25 I alone—will **b** out your sins

BOAST, BOASTED, BOASTING (v)
to puff oneself up in speech, brag
Isa 20:5 **b-ed** of their allies in Egypt!
Jer 9:23 the wise **b** in their wisdom,
Rom 2:17 **b** about your special
1 Cor 1:31 **b, b** only about the Lord.
2 Cor 8:24 our **b-ing** about you is justified.
2 Cor 10:13 We will **b** only about
Gal 6:14 **b** about anything except
Eph 2:9 none of us can **b** about it.
Jas 1:9 have something to **b** about,
Jas 4:16 **b-ing** about your own plans,

BOASTFUL (adj)
bragging, overproud, vainglorious
Ps 12:3 and silence their **b** tongues.
1 Cor 13:4 Love is not jealous or **b** or proud

BOAT, BOATS (n)
a small vessel for travel on water; ship
Gen 6:14 Build a large **b** from cypress
Luke 5:3 Stepping into one of the **b-s,**

BOAZ
1. Family redeemer and husband of the widow Ruth; ancestor of David in the family line of Jesus (Ruth 2–4; especially 4:1-10, 18-21; *see also* 1 Chr 2:12-15; Matt 1:5; Luke 3:23).
2. Pillar's name at front of the Jerusalem Temple (1 Kgs 7:15-22).

BODILY (adj)
of or relating to the body
Col 2:23 and severe **b** discipline.

BODY, BODIES (n)
one's physical essence; a corpse; a group of people
see also FLESH
Job 19:26 in my **b** I will see God!
Ps 49:14 Their **b-ies** will rot in the grave,
Isa 26:19 their **b-ies** will rise again!
Matt 26:41 willing, but the **b** is weak!
Mark 14:22 Take it, for this is my **b.**
Rom 12:4 our **b-ies** have many parts
1 Cor 6:15 that your **b-ies** are actually
1 Cor 6:19 that your **b** is the temple
1 Cor 6:20 honor God with your **b.**
1 Cor 11:24 my **b,** which is given for
1 Cor 12:13 into one **b** by one Spirit,
1 Cor 15:44 be raised as spiritual **b-ies.**
2 Cor 5:1 eternal **b** made for us by God
2 Cor 5:2 to put on our heavenly **b-ies**
2 Cor 5:4 so that these dying **b-ies** will
Eph 1:23 the church is his **b;**
Eph 3:6 Both are part of the same **b,**
Eph 5:28 love their own **b-ies.**
Eph 5:30 are members of his **b.**
Col 1:24 for his **b,** the church.

BOLD (adj)
fearless before danger; self-assured, confident; prominent
2 Sam 7:27 been **b** enough to pray
1 Chr 17:25 been **b** enough to pray
Phil 1:20 continue to be **b** for Christ,

BOLDLY (adv)
showing a fearless, daring spirit
Acts 26:26 I speak **b,** for I am sure
Eph 3:12 **b** and confidently into God's
Heb 4:16 let us come **b** to the throne
Heb 10:19 **b** enter heaven's Most Holy

BOLDNESS (n)
fearlessness before danger; self-assurance; confidence; prominence
Acts 4:13 they saw the **b** of Peter
Acts 4:29 give us, your servants, great **b**

BONE, BONES (n)
one of the hard parts of the skeleton
Gen 2:23 This one is **b** from my **b,**
Ps 22:14 all my **b-s** are out of joint.
Ps 22:17 I can count all my **b-s.**
Ezek 37:1 a valley filled with **b-s.**
John 19:36 Not one of his **b-s** will be

BOOK, BOOKS (n)
a long written or printed literary composition; written records, register, or accounting
Josh 1:8 Study this **B** of Instruction
Ps 69:28 names from the **B** of Life;
Ps 139:16 recorded in your **b.**
Eccl 12:12 for writing **b-s** is endless,
Dan 7:10 and the **b-s** were opened.
Dan 12:1 name is written in the **b**
John 21:25 could not contain the **b-s**
Phil 4:3 are written in the **B** of Life.

Rev 3:5 names from the **B** of Life,
Rev 20:12 including the **B** of Life.
Rev 20:12 as recorded in the **b-s.**
Rev 21:27 in the Lamb's **B** of Life.

BORN (v)
to give birth to or produce; to be productive; spiritually, to renew or confirm a commitment of faith
see also BEAR
Ps 51:5 For I was **b** a sinner—
Eccl 3:2 time to be **b** and a time to die.
Isa 9:6 For a child is **b** to us,
Luke 2:11 the Lord—has been **b** today
John 3:3 unless you are **b** again,
John 3:7 You must be **b** again.
1 Pet 1:3 we have been **b** again,
1 Pet 1:23 you have been **b** again,

BORROWER, BORROWERS (n)
one who takes with the implied or expressed intention of returning the same; to borrow (money) with the intention of returning the same plus interest
Prov 22:7 the **b** is servant to the lender.
Isa 24:2 lenders and **b-s,** bankers and

BOSS (n)
one who directs or supervises workers
Eccl 10:4 If your **b** is angry at you,
Luke 16:3 Now what? My **b** has fired me

BOTTOMLESS (adj)
unfathomable; boundless, unlimited
Luke 8:31 into the **b** pit.
Rev 9:1 shaft of the **b** pit.
Rev 9:11 the angel from the **b** pit;
Rev 11:7 up out of the **b** pit
Rev 17:8 up out of the **b** pit
Rev 20:1 the key to the **b** pit
Rev 20:3 into the **b** pit,

BOUGHT (v)
to purchase; to obtain by way of sacrifice or expenditure
see also BUY
Job 28:15 It cannot be **b** with gold.
1 Cor 6:20 God **b** you with a high price.
2 Pet 2:1 the Master who **b** them.

BOUND (v)
to confine, restrain, or restrict as if with bonds; to put under an obligation
Acts 20:22 now I am **b** by the Spirit
Rev 20:2 and **b** him in chains

BOUNDARY (n)
border, limit; dividing line
Num 34:3 The southern **b** will begin
Prov 22:28 moving the ancient **b** markers

BOUNTIFUL (adj)
given or provided abundantly; generous
Ps 65:11 year with a **b** harvest;
Ps 68:10 with a **b** harvest, O God,

BOUNTY (n)
crop yield; generosity
Deut 33:16 gifts of the earth and its **b,**

BOW, BOWED, BOWS (v)
to bend the head, body, or knee in reverence, submission, or shame
Gen 47:31 Jacob **b-ed** humbly
Deut 5:9 You must not **b** down to them
1 Kgs 1:16 Bathsheba **b-ed** down before
1 Kgs 19:18 never **b-ed** down to Baal
2 Chr 29:29 everyone with him **b-ed** down
2 Chr 29:30 and **b-ed** down in worship.
Esth 3:2 would **b** down before Haman
Ps 72:9 nomads will **b** before him;
Ps 95:6 let us worship and **b** down.
Isa 44:15 an idol and **b-s** down in front
Mic 6:6 Should we **b** before God
Rom 11:4 never **b-ed** down to Baal!
Phil 2:10 every knee should **b,** in heaven

BOWL (n)
a concave vessel often used for holding food or liquids
Prov 15:17 A **b** of vegetables with
Luke 8:16 covers it with a **b** or hides

BOY, BOYS (n)
a male child from birth to puberty
Gen 21:17 God has heard the **b** crying
Gen 22:12 Don't lay a hand on the **b!**
Exod 1:18 you allowed the **b-s** to live?
1 Sam 2:11 the **b** served the LORD
1 Sam 3:8 who was calling the **b.**
Matt 17:18 rebuked the demon in the **b,**

BRAG (v)
to talk boastfully
Prov 27:1 Don't **b** about tomorrow,
Amos 4:5 so you can **b** about it
2 Cor 5:12 you can answer those who **b**

BRANCH, BRANCHES (n)
limb of a (family) tree; part of a complex body (of knowledge); figurative of offspring and of disciples (of Christ and his disciples)
Isa 4:2 the **b** of the LORD will be beautiful
Dan 4:21 nested in its **b-es.**
Zech 3:8 bring my servant, the **B.**

Matt 13:32	make nests in its **b-es.**"
John 15:2	**b** of mine that doesn't
John 15:4	a **b** cannot produce fruit if
John 15:5	you are the **b-es.**
Rom 11:20	those **b-es** were broken off
Rom 11:21	not spare the original **b-es,**

BREAD (n)
basic staple in diet of ancient Israel, usually baked using flour or meal; signifies livelihood
see also FOOD

Exod 23:15	Festival of Unleavened **B.**
Prov 20:17	Stolen **b** tastes sweet,
Mark 14:22	Jesus took some **b** and
Luke 4:3	stone to become a loaf of **b.**
Luke 9:13	only five loaves of **b**
John 6:48	Yes, I am the **b** of life!
John 6:51	I am the living **b**
1 Cor 10:16	when we break the **b,**
1 Cor 11:23	the Lord Jesus took some **b**
1 Cor 11:26	eat this **b** and drink

BREAK, BREAKING (v)
to fracture; to shatter; to violate or transgress; to burst forth; to separate into parts
see also BROKE

Lev 26:15	and if you **b** my covenant
Prov 25:15	soft speech can **b** bones.
Matt 5:33	You must not **b** your vows;
1 Cor 10:16	And when we **b** the bread,
1 Jn 3:4	who sins is **b-ing** God's law,

BREAKFAST (n)
first meal of the day, especially taken in the morning

Prov 31:15	to prepare **b** for her

BREATH (n)
air inhaled and exhaled in breathing; a spoken sound, utterance; a slight indication, suggestion

Gen 2:7	He breathed the **b** of life
Exod 15:8	At the blast of your **b,**
Ps 18:15	at the blast of your **b,**
Ps 144:4	we are like a **b** of air;

BREATHED (v)
to inhale and exhale freely; to blow softly

Gen 2:7	He **b** the breath of life
Mark 15:37	and **b** his last.
John 20:22	Then he **b** on them

BREVITY (n)
shortness of duration

Ps 90:12	to realize the **b** of life,

BRIBE (n)
something that serves to induce or influence

Deut 16:19	Never accept a **b,**

BRIBERY (n)
the act or practice of giving or taking a bribe

Job 15:34	homes, enriched through **b,**

BRICKS (n)
units for building or paving, made of mud and often a binding agent such as straw; in the ancient world bricks were baked or sun dried

Gen 11:3	Let's make **b** and harden
Exod 5:7	any more straw for making **b.**
Exod 5:13	Meet your daily quota of **b,**
Isa 9:10	the broken **b** of our ruins
Nah 3:14	making **b** to repair the walls.

BRIDE (n)
a woman just married or about to be married

2 Cor 11:2	as a pure **b** to one husband—
Rev 19:7	**b** has prepared herself.
Rev 21:2	like a **b** beautifully dressed
Rev 21:9	the **b,** the wife of the Lamb.
Rev 22:17	Spirit and the **b** say, "Come."

BRIDEGROOM (n)
a man just married or about to be married

Ps 19:5	like a radiant **b** after
Matt 25:1	and went to meet the **b.**
Matt 25:5	When the **b** was delayed,

BRIDESMAIDS (n)
women attendants of a bride

Matt 25:1	will be like ten **b** who

BRIDLE (n)
the headgear consisting of a bit and reigns with which a horse or other animal is governed

Prov 26:3	a donkey with a **b,** and a fool

BRIGHTNESS (n)
the quality or state of being bright; luminance; radiance

Ps 18:12	shielded the **b** around him
Isa 24:23	the **b** of the sun will fade,

BRILLIANT (adj)
very bright, glittering; striking, distinctive

Hab 3:4	His coming is as **b** as
1 Tim 6:16	he lives in light so **b** that

BROAD (adj)
extending far and wide; spacious

Matt 7:13	highway to hell is **b,**

BROKE, BROKEN (v)
see also BREAK

Josh 9:20	if we **b** our oath.
1 Kgs 19:10	have **b-n** their covenant
Ps 34:20	not one of them is **b-n!**
Ps 51:17	not reject a **b-n** and repentant
Eccl 4:12	braided cord is not easily **b-n.**
Eccl 12:6	the golden bowl is **b-n.**
Matt 26:26	Then he **b** it in pieces
Mark 14:22	Then he **b** it in pieces
Luke 20:18	stone will be **b-n** to pieces,
John 19:36	of his bones will be **b-n,**
Rom 11:20	those branches were **b-n** off
1 Cor 11:24	Then he **b** it in pieces
2 Tim 1:10	He **b** the power of death
Jas 2:10	who has **b-n** all of God's laws.

BROKENHEARTED (n)
those who are overcome by grief or despair

Ps 34:18	The LORD is close to the **b;**
Ps 109:16	he hounded the **b** to death.
Ps 147:3	He heals the **b** and

BROTHER, BROTHERS (n)
male family members with the same parents; kinsmen in the extended family, church, or nation; co-workers in ministry; fellow believers, followers, or friends in Christ

Ps 133:1	**b-s** live together in harmony!
Prov 18:24	friend sticks closer than a **b.**
Prov 27:10	to ask your **b** for assistance.
Mark 3:33	Who are my **b-s?**
Mark 10:29	given up house or **b-s** or
John 7:5	even his **b-s** didn't believe
Heb 2:11	ashamed to call them his **b-s**
Heb 13:1	each other as **b-s** and sisters.
Jas 2:15	you see a **b** or sister
Jas 4:11	against each other, dear **b-s**
1 Pet 1:22	each other as **b-s** and sisters.
1 Pet 3:8	Love each other as **b-s** and
1 Jn 2:9	a Christian **b** or sister,
1 Jn 3:16	for our **b-s** and sisters.
1 Jn 3:17	sees a **b** or sister in need
1 Jn 4:20	hates a Christian **b** or sister,
1 Jn 4:21	love their Christian **b-s** and
Rev 12:10	the accuser of our **b-s** and

BROTHERLY (adj)
natural or becoming to brothers; affectionate

2 Pet 1:7	godliness with **b** affection,

BROUGHT (v)
to carry, lead, or otherwise cause something to move toward an end

Jer 40:2	has **b** this disaster on this land,
Rom 5:12	Adam's sin **b** death, so death
Eph 2:17	He **b** this Good News

BUILD, BUILDING, BUILDS, BUILT (v)
to erect or construct; to edify or encourage; to increase, enlarge

Gen 6:14	**B** a large boat from cypress
1 Kgs 6:14	Solomon finished **b-ing** the
Neh 4:17	who were **b-ing** the wall.
Ps 127:1	Unless the LORD **b-s** a house,
Prov 14:1	A wise woman **b-s** her home,
Prov 16:12	his rule is **b-t** on justice.
Hag 1:9	**b-ing** your own fine houses.
Matt 7:24	who **b-s** a house on solid rock
Matt 16:18	rock I will **b** my church,
Rom 14:19	try to **b** each other up.
1 Cor 3:10	Now others are **b-ing** on it.
1 Cor 3:12	Anyone who **b-s** on that
2 Cor 10:8	But our authority **b-s** you up;
Eph 2:20	**b-t** on the foundation of the
Eph 4:12	work and **b** up the church,
Col 2:7	let your lives be **b-t** on him.
1 Thes 5:11	and **b** each other up, just as
Heb 3:3	as a person who **b-s** a house
1 Pet 2:5	God is **b-ing** into his spiritual
Jude 1:20	friends, must **b** each other up

BUILDER, BUILDERS (n)
one who builds

Ps 118:22	The stone that the **b-s** rejected
Mark 12:10	stone that the **b-s** rejected
Acts 4:11	The stone that you **b-s** rejected
1 Cor 3:10	foundation like an expert **b.**
1 Cor 3:14	that **b** will receive a reward.
Heb 3:4	For every house has a **b,**
1 Pet 2:7	The stone that the **b-s** rejected

BUILDING (n)
a walled structure built for permanent use; figurative of the Church

1 Cor 3:9	You are God's **b.**

BULL, BULLS (n)
a male, adult, uncastrated bovine

Lev 4:3	a young **b** with no defects.
Heb 10:4	the blood of **b-s** and goats

BURDEN, BURDENS (n)
a (usually) heavy load to be borne—physically, emotionally, or spiritually

Ps 38:4	a **b** too heavy to bear.
Matt 11:28	weary and carry heavy **b-s,**
Matt 11:30	the **b** I give you is light.
Acts 15:28	to lay no greater **b** on you
2 Cor 11:9	a financial **b** to anyone.
2 Cor 11:28	the daily **b** of my concern
2 Cor 12:14	I will not be a **b** to you.
Gal 6:2	Share each other's **b-s,**
1 Thes 2:9	so that we would not be a **b**

2 Thes 3:8 so we would not be a **b**

BURDENED (v)
to load; to oppress
Isa 43:23 I have not **b** and wearied you
Isa 43:24 Instead, you have **b** me
2 Tim 3:6 are **b** with the guilt of sin

BURGLAR (n)
one who enters a building with the intent to commit a crime
Luke 12:39 when a **b** was coming,

BURLAP (n)
a coarse, heavy, plain-woven fabric usually of jute or hemp used for bagging and wrapping
Dan 9:3 I also wore rough **b**
Matt 11:21 clothing themselves in **b**

BURN, BURNED, BURNING (v)
to consume by fire; to be emotionally excited or agitated; to produce or undergo discomfort or pain
see also BURNING, BURNT
Exod 27:20 keep the lamps **b-ing**
Lev 6:9 must be kept **b-ing** all night.
Deut 7:5 Asherah poles and **b** their idols.
Ps 79:5 will your jealousy **b** like fire?
Isa 30:27 far away, **b-ing** with anger,
Jer 23:29 Does not my word **b** like fire?
Luke 24:32 "Didn't our hearts **b** within us
Rom 1:27 **b-ed** with lust for each other.
1 Cor 7:9 to marry than to **b** with lust.

BURNER, BURNERS (n)
the part of a fuel-burning device where the flame or heat is produced
Lev 16:12 an incense **b** with burning coals
Num 16:6 prepare your incense **b-s.**

BURNING (adj)
being on fire
see also BURN, BURNT
Prov 25:22 heap **b** coals of shame
Rom 12:20 heap **b** coals of shame
Rev 19:20 fiery lake of **b** sulfur.

BURNISHED (adj)
shiny or lustrous from rubbing; polished
1 Kgs 7:45 these things of **b** bronze
Ezek 1:7 shone like **b** bronze.

BURNT (adj)
marked by alteration or destruction by fire
see also BURN
Gen 22:2 sacrifice him as a **b** offering
Exod 18:12 brought a **b** offering
Lev 1:3 present as a **b** offering
Josh 8:31 they presented **b** offerings
Judg 6:26 Sacrifice the bull as a **b**
Judg 13:16 a **b** offering as a sacrifice
1 Kgs 3:4 sacrificed 1,000 **b** offerings.
Ezra 3:2 to sacrifice **b** offerings

BURY, BURIED (v)
to deposit in the earth or in a tomb; figurative of denying oneself and submitting to Christ
Deut 34:6 The LORD **b-ied** him
Ruth 1:17 and there I will be **b-ied.**
Mark 6:29 get his body and **b-ied** it in
Luke 9:60 dead **b** their own dead!
Luke 23:30 plead with the hills, '**B** us.'
Rom 6:4 and were **b-ied** with Christ
1 Cor 15:4 **b-ied,** and he was raised
Col 2:12 For you were **b-ied** with Christ

BUSH (n)
a low, densely branched shrub
Exod 3:2 fire from the middle of a **b.**
Mark 12:26 story of the burning **b?**
Luke 20:37 wrote about the burning **b.**
Acts 7:35 him in the burning **b,**

BUSINESS (n)
economic dealings; affair or matter
Gen 40:8 Interpreting dreams is God's **b,**
Ps 112:5 conduct their **b** fairly.
1 Thes 4:11 minding your own **b** and
2 Thes 3:11 meddling in other people's **b.**
1 Tim 5:13 meddling in other people's **b**

BUSY (adj)
engaged in action; occupied
1 Kgs 20:40 I was **b** doing something
Eccl 11:6 keep **b** all afternoon,
Hag 1:9 **b** building your own fine houses.

BUY, BUYS (v)
to purchase; to redeem; to hire, bribe
see also BOUGHT
Prov 31:16 to inspect a field and **b-s** it;
Gal 4:5 sent him to **b** freedom for us
Rev 13:17 no one could **b** or sell

C

CAESAR (n)
a title applied to several emperors of the Roman Empire
Matt 22:21 to **C** what belongs to **C,**

CALF (n)
the young of a domestic cow

Exod 32:4 it into the shape of a **c.**
Luke 15:23 kill the **c** we have been
Acts 7:41 made an idol shaped like a **c,**

CALL, CALLED, CALLING, CALLS (v)
to make a request or demand; to designate or name
see also CHOSE, CHOSEN
Gen 2:23 She will be **c-ed** 'woman,'
1 Kgs 18:24 **c** on the name of your god,
2 Kgs 5:11 leprosy and **c** on the name
2 Chr 7:14 who are **c-ed** by my name
Ps 147:4 stars and **c-s** them all by name.
Isa 40:26 **c-ing** each by its name.
Isa 45:3 the one who **c-s** you by name.
Isa 56:7 Temple will be **c-ed** a house of
Hos 11:1 I **c-ed** my son out of Egypt.
Joel 2:32 everyone who **c-s** on the name
Matt 2:15 I **c-ed** my Son out of Egypt.
Matt 9:13 I have come to **c** not those
Matt 22:14 many are **c-ed,** but few are
Matt 22:43 **c** the Messiah 'my Lord'?
Mark 2:17 I have come to **c** not those
Mark 10:49 Come on, he's **c-ing** you!
Luke 1:32 **c-ed** the Son of the Most High.
Luke 23:15 this man has done **c-s**
Acts 2:21 everyone who **c-s** on the name
Acts 2:39 have been **c-ed** by the Lord
Acts 9:14 arrest everyone who **c-s** upon
Acts 22:16 sins washed away by **c-ing** on
Rom 1:6 **c-ed** to belong to Jesus
Rom 8:28 **c-ed** according to his purpose
Rom 10:12 to all who **c** on him.
Rom 10:13 Everyone who **c-s** on the
Rom 11:29 **c** can never be withdrawn.
1 Cor 1:2 who have been **c-ed** by God
1 Cor 1:2 **c** on the name of our Lord
1 Cor 1:24 **c-ed** by God to salvation,
1 Cor 7:17 when God first **c-ed** you.
Gal 1:6 so soon from God, who **c-ed**
Gal 5:13 been **c-ed** to live in freedom,
Eph 1:18 to those he **c-ed**—his holy
Col 3:15 you are **c-ed** to live in peace.
1 Thes 2:12 **c-ed** you to share in his
1 Thes 4:7 God has **c-ed** us to live holy
1 Thes 5:24 he who **c-s** you is faithful.
2 Tim 2:22 those who **c** on the Lord
Heb 9:15 all who are **c-ed** can receive
1 Pet 2:9 he **c-ed** you out of the darkness
1 Pet 3:9 what God has **c-ed** you to do,
1 Pet 5:10 God **c-ed** you to share in his
2 Pet 1:10 are among those God has **c-ed**

CALLING (n)
a strong inner impulse toward a particular course of action; an occupation or vocation
Eph 4:1 to lead a life worthy of your **c,**

CALM (v)
to make still; to free from agitation, excitement, or disturbance
Zeph 3:17 he will **c** all your fears.

CALVARY (KJV)
Luke 23:33 place called *The Skull,*

CAME (v)
to originate or proceed from
see also COME
John 1:17 faithfulness **c** through Jesus
Heb 7:14 our Lord **c** from the tribe of

CAMEL (n)
either of two large ruminant mammals used as draft and saddle animals in desert regions especially of Africa and Asia
Matt 19:24 easier for a **c** to go through
Matt 23:24 but you swallow a **c!**

CANAAN (n)
region along the Mediterranean Sea taken and settled by the Israelites
Num 33:51 Jordan River into the land of **C,**
1 Chr 16:18 **C** as your special possession.
Ps 105:11 **C** as your special possession.
Acts 13:19 destroyed seven nations in **C**

CANCEL, CANCELED (v)
to destroy the force, effectiveness, or validty of; to annul
Deut 15:1 year you must **c** the debts
Matt 15:6 so you **c** the word of God
Col 2:14 **c-ed** the record of the charges

CANDLE (n)
a usually molded or dipped mass of wax or tallow containing a wick that may be burned
Isa 42:3 or put out a flickering **c.**
Matt 12:20 or put out a flickering **c.**

CANDLESTICK(S) (KJV)
Exod 25:31 Make a *lampstand* of pure,
Dan 5:5 palace, near the *lampstand.*
Matt 5:15 a lamp is placed on a *stand*
Heb 9:2 a *lampstand,* a table, and
Rev 1:12 I saw seven gold *lampstands*

CANOPY (n)
a cover (as of cloth) fixed or carried above a person of high rank or a sacred object; a protective covering
2 Kgs 16:18 he also removed the **c** that
Isa 4:5 He will provide a **c** of cloud
Isa 51:16 stretched out the sky like a **c**
Jer 43:10 spread his royal **c** over them.

CAPSTONE, HEADSTONE (KJV)
Ps 118:22 become the *cornerstone*
Zech 4:7 the *final stone* of the Temple
Matt 21:42 now become the *cornerstone.*
Luke 20:17 now become the *cornerstone.*

CAPTIVE (adj)
(people) taken and held against their will
Prov 5:22 is held **c** by his own sins;
Acts 8:23 and are held **c** by sin.
2 Tim 2:26 they have been held **c**

CAPTIVES (n)
prisoners
Ps 68:18 you led a crowd of **c.**
Isa 60:11 led as **c** in a victory
Isa 61:1 that **c** will be released
Luke 4:18 that **c** will be released,

CAPTIVITY (n)
imprisonment, exile; subjection or subservience
Deut 28:41 they will be led away into **c.**

CAPTURE, CAPTURED (v)
an act of catching, winning, or gaining control by force, stratagem, or guile
1 Sam 4:11 The Ark of God was **c-ed,**
2 Sam 5:7 David **c-ed** the fortress of Zion,
Song 4:9 You have **c-ed** my heart,
2 Cor 10:5 We **c** their rebellious
Col 2:8 **c** you with empty philosophies

CARCASS (n)
a dead body; corpse
Judg 14:9 honey from the **c** of the lion.
Matt 24:28 vultures shows there is a **c**

CARE, CARED, CARES, CARING (v)
to feel interest or concern; to attend to or provide for the needs, operation, or treatment of
Deut 1:31 LORD your God **c-d** for you
Ps 8:4 human beings that you should **c**
Ps 37:17 LORD takes **c** of the godly.
Ps 65:9 take **c** of the earth and
Ps 116:15 **c-s** deeply when his loved
Ps 138:6 is great, he **c-s** for the humble,
Prov 12:10 godly **c** for their animals,
Prov 27:23 into **c-ing** for your herds,
Isa 53:8 **c-d** that he died without
Jer 23:2 Instead of **c-ing** for my flock
Matt 6:30 if God **c-s** so wonderfully for
Matt 25:36 sick, and you **c-d** for me.
Luke 10:34 an inn, where he took **c** of
John 10:13 really **c** about the sheep.
John 12:25 who **c** nothing for their life
John 21:16 Then take **c** of my sheep,
Eph 5:29 just as Christ **c-s** for the church.
Phil 2:21 others **c** only for themselves
1 Thes 2:7 **c-ing** for her own children.
1 Tim 5:14 take **c** of their own homes.
1 Tim 5:16 she must take **c** of them and
Heb 2:6 that you should **c** for him?
1 Pet 5:2 **C** for the flock that God
1 Pet 5:7 and cares to God, for he **c-s**

CAREFUL (adj)
marked by wary caution; meticulous
Exod 34:12 **c** never to make a treaty
Lev 18:4 and be **c** to obey my decrees,
Lev 22:2 be very **c** with the sacred gifts
Lev 26:3 are **c** to obey my commands,
Deut 4:9 But watch out! Be **c** never to
Deut 6:3 and be **c** to obey.
Deut 8:1 Be **c** to obey all the commands
Deut 12:1 **c** to obey when you live in
Deut 12:28 Be **c** to obey all my
Josh 1:7 and very courageous. Be **c**
Josh 23:11 be very **c** to love the LORD
2 Kgs 21:8 Israelites will be **c** to obey
1 Cor 8:9 be **c** so that your freedom
1 Cor 10:12 strong, be **c** not to fall.
Eph 5:15 So be **c** how you live.

CAREFULLY (adv)
scrupulously attentive
Deut 11:13 **c** obey all the commands
2 Kgs 18:6 he **c** obeyed all the commands
Prov 5:1 to my wisdom; listen **c**
1 Cor 15:34 **c** about what is right, and stop
Heb 2:1 must listen very **c** to the truth
Heb 3:1 think **c** about this Jesus

CARNAL(LY) (KJV)
Rom 7:14 *all too human,* a slave to sin
Rom 8:6 letting your *sinful nature* control
1 Cor 3:3 still *controlled by your sinful nature*
2 Cor 10:4 not *worldly* weapons

CAROUSE, CAROUSING (v)
to drink liquor freely or excessively
Prov 23:20 Do not **c** with drunkards
Luke 21:34 your hearts be dulled by **c-ing**

CARPENTER (n)
a worker who builds or repairs wooden structures or their structural parts
Matt 13:55 He's just the **c**'s son,
Mark 6:3 He's just a **c,** the son of Mary

CARRY, CARRIED, CARRIES (v)
to transport or convey; to sustain the weight of; to bring to a successful end

Exod 19:4	how I **c-ied** you on eagles'
Lev 16:22	will **c** all the people's sins
Deut 32:11	to take them up and **c-ied**
Ps 68:19	For each day he **c-ies** us in his
Ps 103:20	ones who **c** out his plans,
Isa 40:11	**c** the lambs in his arms,
Isa 53:4	it was our weaknesses he **c-ied;**
Isa 63:9	He lifted them up and **c-ied**
Luke 14:27	do not **c** your own cross
Col 4:17	Be sure to **c** out the ministry
1 Pet 2:24	He personally **c-ied** our sins
2 Pet 3:17	not be **c-ied** away by the errors

CAST, CASTING (v)
to toss (dice); to drive out

Lev 16:8	He is to **c** sacred lots to
Matt 10:1	authority to **c** out evil spirits
Matt 12:26	if Satan is **c-ing** out Satan,

CATCH (v)
to entangle; to seize and hold firmly
see also CAUGHT

Luke 5:4	let down your nets to **c** some fish.

CATTLE (n)
bovine animals on a farm or ranch

Ps 50:10	I own the **c** on a thousand

CAUGHT (v)
to get entangled; to seize and hold firmly
see also CATCH

Gen 22:13	saw a ram **c** by its horns
Prov 6:2	and are **c** by what you said—
2 Cor 12:2	I was **c** up to the third heaven
1 Thes 4:17	will be **c** up in the clouds

CAUTION (n)
prudent forethought to minimize risk; precaution; warning

Jude 1:23	with great **c,** hating the sins

CEASE (v)
to come to an end; to discontinue

Lam 3:22	His mercies never **c.**

CELEBRATE, CELEBRATED, CELEBRATING (v)
to perform (a sacrament or ceremony) publicly and with appropriate rites; to observe a notable occasion with festivities

Exod 10:9	together in **c-ing** a festival
Exod 12:47	Israel must **c** this Passover
Exod 13:5	You must **c** this event in this
Exod 23:14	**c** three festivals in my
Exod 34:18	**c** the Festival of Unleavened
Exod 34:22	**c** the Festival of the Final
Num 9:2	**c** the Passover at the
Deut 16:1	your God, **c** the Passover
2 Sam 6:21	so I **c** before the LORD.
2 Kgs 23:21	**c** the Passover to the LORD
2 Chr 30:1	Jerusalem to **c** the Passover.
2 Chr 30:13	**c** the Festival of Unleavened
2 Chr 30:23	**c-d** joyfully for another
Neh 8:12	to **c** with great joy
Esth 8:15	people of Susa **c-d** the new
Esth 9:19	villages **c** an annual festival
Esth 9:21	to **c** an annual festival
Matt 25:21	Let's **c** together!
Luke 15:23	We must **c** with a feast,
Luke 15:32	We had to **c** this happy day.
John 18:28	to **c** the Passover.
Col 2:16	for not **c-ing** certain holy days
Rev 11:10	to **c** the death of the two prophets

CELEBRATION, CELEBRATIONS (n)
a party or festival in honor of a religious ceremony or holiday; the observation of a notable occasion with festivities

Num 9:3	regulations concerning this **c.**
2 Sam 6:12	City of David with a great **c.**
Esth 8:17	had a great **c** and declared
Jer 31:13	young—will join in the **c.**
Joel 1:16	No joyful **c-s** are held in the
Zech 8:19	**c** for the people of Judah.
John 11:55	for the Jewish Passover **c,**

CELIBATE (adj)
characterized by abstaining from marriage and sexual relations

1 Cor 7:1	it is good to live a **c** life.

CENSUS (n)
count of population, sometimes including assessment of property value

2 Sam 24:1	to harm them by taking a **c.**
Luke 2:1	that a **c** should be taken

CENTURION (KJV)

Matt 8:5	*Roman officer* came and
Luke 7:2	slave of a *Roman officer* was sick
Acts 10:1	*Roman army officer* named Cornelius

CEPHAS (n)
rock; Aramaic name of Simon Peter, given to him by Christ

John 1:42	called C" (which means

CEREMONIAL (adj)
marked by, involved in, or belonging to ceremony; stressing careful attention to form and detail

Lev 14:2	seeking **c** purification from a
John 2:6	used for Jewish **c** washing.

John 3:25 Jew over **c** cleansing.
Heb 9:13 bodies from **c** impurity.

CEREMONIALLY (adv)
in accordance with law and custom
Lev 4:12 the camp that is **c** clean,
Lev 6:11 to a place that is **c** clean.
Lev 10:14 eaten in any place that is **c** clean.
Lev 12:2 she will be **c** unclean for seven
Lev 13:3 pronounce the person **c** unclean.
Lev 15:13 water, and he will be **c** clean.
Lev 15:33 intercourse with a woman who is **c** unclean
Lev 21:1 **c** unclean by touching
Lev 22:3 any of your descendants is **c**
Num 5:2 who has become **c** unclean by
Num 9:6 the men had been **c** defiled
Num 18:11 your family who is **c** clean
Num 19:7 **c** unclean until evening.
Num 19:18 someone who is **c** clean must
Deut 12:22 whether **c** clean or unclean,
Deut 14:7 so they are **c** unclean for you.
1 Sam 20:26 made David **c** unclean.

CEREMONY, CEREMONIES (n)
a formal act or series of acts prescribed by ritual, protocol, or convention
Exod 12:25 continue to observe this **c.**
Exod 12:26 ask, 'What does this **c** mean?'
Neh 12:27 to assist in the **c-ies.**
Acts 24:18 completing a purification **c.**
Heb 9:10 and various cleansing **c-ies**—

CERTAIN (adj)
assured in mind or action; dependable, reliable; known or proved to be true, indisputable
Josh 23:13 know for **c** that the LORD
Eccl 7:14 nothing is **c** in this life.
Luke 1:4 so you can be **c** of the truth
Phil 1:6 **c** that God, who began the good work
Heb 6:11 to make **c** that what you hope

CHAFF (n)
the seed coverings and other debris separated from the seed in threshing grain; something comparatively worthless
Ps 1:4 **c,** scattered by the wind.
Ps 35:5 Blow them away like **c** in the
Dan 2:35 like **c** on a threshing floor.
Matt 3:12 separate the **c** from the

CHAIN, CHAINS (n)
metal links or rings connected to one another and used for various purposes
Prov 1:9 a **c** of honor around your neck.
Acts 26:29 as I am, except for these **c-s.**"
Eph 6:20 I am in **c-s** now, still preaching
Col 4:18 Remember my **c-s.**
2 Tim 1:16 because I was in **c-s.**

CHAINED (v)
to fasten, bind, or connect with or as with a chain; to obstruct
2 Tim 2:9 the word of God cannot be **c.**
Jude 1:6 **c** in prisons of darkness,

CHALLENGE (v)
to put to a test or trial; to dispute with
Jer 49:19 like me, and who can **c** me?

CHANCE (n)
something that happens unpredictably without discernible human intention or cause, luck; a situation favoring some purpose, opportunity
1 Sam 18:21 another **c** to see him killed
Eccl 9:11 all decided by **c,** by being
Jer 15:6 giving you another **c.**
Phil 4:10 didn't have the **c** to help

CHANGE, CHANGED, CHANGES (v)
to make different or transform; to shift, exchange, or transfer
Exod 32:14 the LORD **c-d** his mind about
1 Sam 10:6 be **c-d** into a different person.
1 Sam 15:29 human that he should **c**
Ps 93:5 Your royal laws cannot be **c-d.**
Isa 14:27 who can **c** his plans?
Jer 33:25 than I would **c** my laws
Jonah 3:9 even yet God will **c** his mind
Mal 3:6 I am the LORD, and I do not **c.**
2 Cor 3:18 we are **c-d** into his glorious
Heb 6:17 he would never **c** his mind.
Jas 1:17 never **c-s** or casts a shifting

CHARACTER (n)
moral excellence and firmness; main or essential nature
Rom 5:4 develops strength of **c,**
1 Cor 15:33 corrupts good **c.**
Heb 1:3 expresses the very **c** of God,

CHARGE, CHARGES (n)
management, supervision; obligation, requirement; a formal assertion of illegality or statement of complaint
Deut 19:18 brought false **c-s** against
Ps 8:6 gave them **c** of everything you
Prov 23:11 bring their **c-s** against you.
Isa 50:8 dare to bring **c-s** against me
Mic 6:2 will bring **c-s** against Israel.
1 Cor 4:1 in **c** of explaining God's
1 Cor 4:2 in **c** as a manager must be

CHARGE, CHARGED, CHARGING (v)
to impose a financial burden on; to command, instruct, or exhort with authority
Ps 119:4 **c-d** us to keep your commandments
1 Cor 9:18 the Good News without **c-ing**
Phlm 1:18 owes you anything, **c** it to me.

CHARIOT, CHARIOTS (n)
a two-wheeled horse-drawn battle car of ancient times used also in processions and races
2 Kgs 2:11 suddenly a **c** of fire appeared,
2 Kgs 6:17 with horses and **c-s** of fire.
Ps 20:7 boast of their **c-s** and horses,
Ps 68:17 thousands of **c-s**, the LORD came
Ps 104:3 You make the clouds your **c;**

CHARITY (KJV)
1 Cor 8:1 *love* that strengthens the church
1 Cor 13:1 but didn't *love* others, I would
Col 3:14 clothe yourselves with *love,*
1 Tim 4:12 in your *love,* your faith, and
2 Pet 1:7 with *love* for everyone

CHARM (n)
something worn about the person to ward off evil or ensure good fortune; a trait that fascinates, allures, or delights
Prov 17:8 A bribe is like a lucky **c;**
Prov 31:30 **C** is deceptive, and beauty

CHASTE (KJV)
2 Cor 11:2 a *pure* bride to one husband—
Titus 2:5 to live wisely and be *pure*
1 Pet 3:2 *pure* and reverent lives

CHASTEN(ED) (KJV)
Ps 6:1 or *discipline* me in your rage
Prov 19:18 *Discipline* your children
1 Cor 11:32 *being disciplined* so that we
Heb 12:11 No *discipline* is enjoyable
Rev 3:19 I correct and *discipline*

CHEAT, CHEATED, CHEATING, CHEATS (v)
to deprive of something valuable by deceit or fraud; to practice fraud or trickery
Gen 31:7 he has **c-ed** me, changing my
1 Sam 12:3 Have I ever **c-ed** any of you?
1 Sam 12:4 have never **c-ed** or oppressed
Amos 8:5 get back to **c-ing** the helpless.
Mal 3:8 You have **c-ed** me of the tithes
Mark 10:19 You must not **c** anyone.
Mark 12:40 they shamelessly **c** widows
1 Cor 5:10 are greedy, or **c** people,
1 Cor 5:11 is a drunkard, or **c-s** people.
1 Cor 6:7 not let yourselves be **c-ed?**
1 Cor 6:8 who do wrong and **c** even
1 Cor 6:10 abusive, or **c** people—

CHEEK (n)
the fleshy side of the face below the eye and above and to the side of the mouth
Matt 5:39 slaps you on the right **c,**
Luke 6:29 offer the other **c** also.

CHEERFUL (adj)
full of good spirits; merry, ungrudging
Prov 15:30 A **c** look brings joy
Prov 17:22 A **c** heart is good medicine,

CHEERFULLY (adv)
marked by or suggestive of lighthearted ease of mind and spirit; cheerily, gladly
2 Cor 9:7 loves a person who gives **c.**
1 Pet 4:9 **C** share your home with those

CHEERS (v)
to instill with hope, joy, hilarity, or comfort
Prov 12:25 encouraging word **c** a person

CHERISH (v)
to hold dear; to feel or show affection for
Ps 102:14 **c** even the dust in her streets.
Prov 19:8 people who **c** understanding

CHERUBIM (n)
winged angelic beings, often associated with worship and praise of God
Gen 3:24 God stationed mighty **c** to the
Exod 25:19 Mold the **c** on each end
1 Sam 4:4 enthroned between the **c.**
1 Kgs 6:23 He made two **c** of wild olive
Isa 37:16 between the mighty **c!**
Ezek 10:1 over the heads of the **c.**

CHEST (n)
a wooden box or container; the trunk or rib cage of the human body
Exod 25:10 a sacred **c** 45 inches long,
2 Kgs 12:9 a hole in the lid of a large **c**
Zech 13:6 those wounds on your **c?**
Rev 1:13 with a gold sash across his **c.**

CHESTPIECE (n)
a breastplate attached to the front of an ephod worn by the high priest
Exod 28:15 make a **c** to be worn for

CHILD, CHILDREN (n)
an unborn or recently born person; a young person between infancy and youth, not yet of age; offspring or descendants
see also SON(S)

Exod 20:5 family is affected—even **c-ren**
Deut 24:16 sins of their **c-ren,** nor **c-ren**
Deut 32:46 as a command to your **c-ren**
1 Kgs 3:26 Give her the **c**—please do
Job 1:5 Perhaps my **c-ren** have sinned
Ps 8:2 have taught **c-ren** and infants
Prov 20:7 blessed are their **c-ren** who
Prov 23:13 discipline your **c-ren.**
Prov 29:15 To discipline a **c** produces
Prov 31:28 Her **c-ren** stand and bless
Isa 7:14 The virgin will conceive a **c!**
Isa 9:6 For a **c** is born to us,
Isa 54:13 I will teach all your **c-ren,**
Mal 4:6 hearts of **c-ren** to their fathers.
Matt 1:23 The virgin will conceive a **c!**
Matt 5:9 will be called the **c-ren** of God.
Matt 18:3 and become like little **c-ren,**
Mark 9:37 welcomes a little **c** like this
Mark 10:14 Let the **c-ren** come to me.
Mark 10:16 took the **c-ren** in his arms
Luke 1:42 and your **c** is blessed.
Luke 6:35 as **c-ren** of the Most High,
Luke 18:15 their little **c-ren** to Jesus
John 1:12 to become **c-ren** of God.
John 12:36 become **c-ren** of the light.
Acts 2:39 to your **c-ren,** and even to the
Rom 9:26 called '**c-ren** of the living God.'
1 Cor 13:11 and reasoned as a **c.**
Gal 3:26 you are all **c-ren** of God
Eph 3:6 riches inherited by God's **c-ren.**
Eph 6:1 **C-ren,** obey your parents
Eph 6:4 not provoke your **c-ren** to anger
Col 3:21 do not aggravate your **c-ren,**
1 Tim 3:4 having **c-ren** who respect and
1 Tim 3:12 manage his **c-ren** and
1 Tim 5:10 brought up her **c-ren** well?
Heb 12:7 treating you as his own **c-ren.**
1 Jn 4:7 who loves is a **c** of God
1 Jn 5:4 every **c** of God defeats this evil
1 Jn 5:18 God's **c-ren** do not make a

CHILDISH (adj)
of, relating to, or befitting a child; marked by or suggestive of immaturity
1 Cor 13:11 I put away **c** things.
1 Cor 14:20 brothers and sisters, don't be **c**

CHILDLESS (adj)
a person characterized by lack of children; barren
Ps 113:9 He gives the **c** woman a family,
Isa 54:1 Sing, O **c** woman, you who
Gal 4:27 Rejoice, O **c** woman, you who

CHILDLIKE (adj)
resembling, suggesting, or appropriate to a child; marked by innocence, trust, and ingenuousness
Ps 116:6 protects those of **c** faith;
Matt 11:25 revealing them to the **c.**

CHOOSE, CHOOSES (v)
to decide; to have a preference for; to select freely and after consideration
see also CALL, CHOSE
Deut 30:19 Oh, that you would **c** life, so
Josh 24:15 **c** today whom you will serve.
Eccl 10:2 A wise person **c-s** the right road;
Jer 27:5 things of mine to anyone I **c.**
Dan 4:25 gives them to anyone he **c-s.**
John 15:16 You didn't **c** me. I chose you.
Rom 9:11 God **c-s** people according to
Rom 9:18 he **c-s** to harden the hearts of

CHOSE, CHOSEN (v)
to decide; to have a preference for
see also CALL, CHOOSE, CHOSEN
Matt 22:14 called, but few are **c-n.**
John 15:16 You didn't choose me. I **c** you.
Rom 1:1 **c-n** by God to be an apostle
Rom 8:29 **c** them to become like his
1 Cor 1:1 Paul, **c-n** by the will of God
1 Cor 1:27 **c** things that are powerless
Eph 1:4 loved us and **c** us in Christ
Eph 1:11 God, for he **c** us in advance,
2 Thes 2:13 thankful that God **c** you
1 Pet 1:15 as God who **c** you is holy.
2 Pet 1:10 God has called and **c-n.**

CHOSEN (adj)
selected or marked for special favor or privilege
see also CALLED
1 Chr 16:22 Do not touch my **c** people,
Isa 41:8 my **c** one, descended from Abraham
Mark 13:20 for the sake of his **c** ones
Luke 23:35 God's Messiah, the **C** One.
John 1:34 that he is the **C** One of God.
1 Pet 1:1 writing to God's **c** people
1 Pet 2:9 for you are a **c** people.

CHRIST (n)
Son of God, Messiah, Anointed One
see also JESUS, MESSIAH
John 1:17 faithfulness came through Jesus **C.**
Rom 1:4 He is Jesus **C** our Lord.
Rom 3:22 by placing our faith in Jesus **C.**
Rom 5:1 Jesus **C** our Lord has done
Rom 5:6 **C** came at just the right time
Rom 5:11 **C** has made us friends of God.
Rom 6:4 as **C** was raised from the dead
Rom 6:23 eternal life through **C** Jesus
Rom 7:4 when you died with **C.**
Rom 8:1 who belong to **C** Jesus.
Rom 8:34 **C** Jesus died for us and

Rom 8:35 separate us from **C**'s love?
Rom 14:9 **C** died and rose again for this
Rom 15:5 fitting for followers of **C** Jesus.
Rom 15:20 where the name of **C** has never
1 Cor 1:2 the name of our Lord Jesus **C**,
1 Cor 1:13 Has **C** been divided into
1 Cor 1:17 cross of **C** would lose its power.
1 Cor 1:23 preach that **C** was crucified,
1 Cor 1:30 God has united you with **C**
1 Cor 5:7 **C**, our Passover Lamb,
1 Cor 6:15 his body, which is part of **C**,
1 Cor 8:12 you are sinning against **C**.
1 Cor 9:19 to bring many to **C**.
1 Cor 10:4 that rock was **C**.
1 Cor 10:9 Nor should we put **C** to the test,
1 Cor 11:3 and the head of **C** is God.
1 Cor 12:27 you together are **C**'s body,
1 Cor 15:3 **C** died for our sins,
2 Cor 1:5 the more we suffer for **C**, the
2 Cor 3:3 you are a letter from **C**
2 Cor 3:14 removed only by believing in **C**.
2 Cor 5:10 stand before **C** to be judged.
2 Cor 5:14 **C**'s love controls us.
2 Cor 5:20 we are **C**'s ambassadors;
Gal 1:7 twist the truth concerning **C**.
Gal 2:4 the freedom we have in **C** Jesus.
Gal 2:21 need for **C** to die.
Gal 3:13 But **C** has rescued us
Gal 4:19 continue until **C** is fully developed
Gal 5:4 you have been cut off from **C**!
Gal 5:24 Those who belong to **C** Jesus
Eph 1:3 because we are united with **C**.
Eph 1:10 under the authority of **C**—
Eph 1:20 that raised **C** from the dead
Eph 2:10 created us anew in **C** Jesus,
Eph 2:20 the cornerstone is **C** Jesus
Eph 4:7 through the generosity of **C**.
Eph 4:32 God through **C** has forgiven you.
Eph 5:21 out of reverence for **C**.
Eph 5:23 head of his wife as **C** is
Eph 5:25 wives, just as **C** loved the
Phil 1:21 living means living for **C**,
Phil 1:23 with **C**, which would be far better
Phil 1:29 the privilege of trusting in **C**
Phil 2:5 same attitude that **C** Jesus had.
Phil 3:18 enemies of the cross of **C**.
Col 1:22 through the death of **C**
Col 2:2 mysterious plan, which is **C**
Col 2:6 accepted **C** Jesus as your Lord,
Col 2:13 God made you alive with **C**,
Col 3:1 raised to new life with **C**,
Col 3:3 life is hidden with **C** in God.
Col 3:15 peace that comes from **C**
1 Thes 5:9 through our Lord Jesus **C**,
1 Tim 1:15 **C** Jesus came into the world
1 Tim 2:5 humanity—the man **C** Jesus.
2 Tim 1:10 by the appearing of **C** Jesus,
2 Tim 2:3 as a good soldier of **C** Jesus.
2 Tim 2:10 eternal glory in **C** Jesus
2 Tim 3:12 a godly life in **C** Jesus will
2 Tim 3:15 by trusting in **C** Jesus.
2 Tim 4:1 of God and **C** Jesus, who will
Titus 2:13 and Savior, Jesus **C**, will be
Heb 3:14 share in all that belongs to **C**.
Heb 6:1 teachings about **C** again and
Heb 9:14 the blood of **C** will purify
Heb 9:28 **C** died once for all time
Heb 10:10 body of Jesus **C**, once for all
Heb 13:8 Jesus **C** is the same yesterday,
1 Pet 1:11 the Spirit of **C** within them
1 Pet 1:19 blood of **C**, the sinless,
1 Pet 2:21 just as **C** suffered for you.
1 Pet 3:15 you must worship **C** as Lord
1 Pet 4:13 partners with **C** in his suffering,
2 Pet 1:16 coming of our Lord Jesus **C**.
1 Jn 2:1 He is Jesus **C**, the one who is
1 Jn 2:22 says that Jesus is not the **C**.
1 Jn 4:2 that Jesus **C** came in a real
1 Jn 5:1 Jesus is the **C** has become
1 Jn 5:20 fellowship with his Son, Jesus **C**.
Rev 1:1 from Jesus **C**, which God gave
Rev 1:5 his throne; and from Jesus **C**.
Rev 20:4 and they reigned with **C** for
Rev 20:6 God and of **C** and will reign

CHRISTIAN, CHRISTIANS (n)
one who professes belief in and follows the teachings of Jesus Christ; believer
Acts 11:26 believers were first called **C-s**.
Acts 26:28 persuade me to become a **C**
Gal 2:4 some so-called **C-s**
1 Thes 4:12 people who are not **C-s**
1 Pet 4:14 insulted for being a **C**,
1 Pet 4:16 to suffer for being a **C**.
1 Pet 5:9 your **C** brothers and sisters

CHURCH, CHURCHES (n)
"assembly" or "called ones"; the body of believers gathered to worship Jesus (not the building in which they meet)
Matt 16:18 this rock I will build my **c**,
Matt 18:17 take your case to the **c**.
Acts 16:5 the **c-es** were strengthened
Acts 20:28 shepherd God's flock—his **c**,
1 Cor 15:9 way I persecuted God's **c**.
Gal 1:13 I violently persecuted God's **c**.
Eph 5:23 Christ is the head of the **c**.
Col 1:18 head of the **c**, which is his
Col 1:24 continue for his body, the **c**.
2 Thes 1:4 tell God's other **c-es** about your
Rev 1:20 angels of the seven **c-es**,

CIRCUMCISE, CIRCUMCISED, CIRCUMCISING (v)
to cut off the foreskin of a male child
Gen 17:10 among you must be **c-d.**
Gen 17:12 **c-d** on the eighth day after his
Josh 5:3 made flint knives and **c-d**
John 7:23 correct time for **c-ing** your son
Acts 21:21 not to **c** their children
Rom 4:11 even before he was **c-d.**
1 Cor 7:19 or not a man has been **c-d.**

CIRCUMCISION (n)
the condition of being circumcised; the ceremony signifying Israel's covenant with God; act symbolic of cleansing
Rom 2:25 **c** has value only if you obey
Rom 2:29 true **c** is not merely
Gal 5:2 If you are counting on **c** to make

CIRCUMSTANCES (n)
conditions, facts, or events accompanying, conditioning, or determining another
1 Thes 5:18 Be thankful in all **c,** for this

CITIZEN, CITIZENS (n)
a person owing allegiance to and deriving protection from a sovereign state
Acts 22:28 But I am a **c** by birth!
Eph 2:19 You are **c-s** along with
Phil 3:20 But we are **c-s** of heaven,

CITIZENSHIP (n)
the status of being a citizen; membership in a community
Eph 2:12 excluded from **c** among

CLAIM, CLAIMS (v)
to assert in the face of possible contradiction; to take as the rightful owner
Eccl 8:17 no matter what they **c.**
Song 7:10 and he **c-s** me as his own.
Isa 62:4 delights in you and will **c** you
Jas 1:26 **c** to be religious but don't
1 Jn 1:10 If we **c** we have not sinned,
1 Jn 2:9 If anyone **c-s,** "I am living in

CLAP, CLAPPED (v)
to strike (the hands) together repeatedly usually in applause
2 Kgs 11:12 everyone **c-ped** their hands
Ps 47:1 everyone! **C** your hands!
Ps 98:8 Let the rivers **c** their hands
Isa 55:12 trees of the field will **c**
Nah 3:19 hear of your destruction will **c**

CLAY (n)
an earthy material that is pliable when moist but hard when fired and is used for brick, tile, and pottery
Isa 45:9 Does the **c** dispute with the one
Isa 64:8 **c,** and you are the potter.
Lam 4:2 are now treated like pots of **c**
Dan 2:33 of iron and baked **c.**
Rom 9:21 to use the same lump of **c**
2 Cor 4:7 **c** jars containing this great
2 Tim 2:20 are made of wood and **c.**

CLEAN (adj)
unadulterated, pure; without guilt or moral corruption; without ceremonial defilement
see also PURE
Lev 10:10 unclean and what is **c.**
Ps 51:2 Wash me **c** from my guilt.
Ps 51:7 and I will be **c;** wash me,
Ps 51:10 Create in me a **c** heart, O God.
John 13:10 you disciples are **c,** but not all
Acts 10:15 if God has made it **c.**
2 Tim 2:21 Your life will be **c,**

CLEANSE, CLEANSED, CLEANSES (v)
to make clean, pure, holy
see also PURIFY, WASH
Ps 19:12 **C** me from these hidden
Prov 20:9 Who can say, "I have **c-d** my
Jer 4:14 O Jerusalem, **c** your heart
Acts 15:9 he **c-d** their hearts through
1 Cor 6:11 were **c-d;** you were made holy;
2 Cor 7:1 let us **c** ourselves from
Titus 2:14 **c** us, and to make us his
Heb 1:3 he had **c-d** us from our sins,
Heb 9:13 of a young cow could **c**
1 Pet 1:2 and have been **c-d** by the blood
1 Pet 1:22 You were **c-d** from your sins
2 Pet 1:9 that they have been **c-d**
1 Jn 1:7 blood of Jesus, his Son, **c-s** us
1 Jn 1:9 to **c** us from all wickedness.

CLEAR, CLEARED (v)
to free from what obstructs or is unneeded
Ps 32:2 whose record the LORD has **c-ed**
John 1:23 **C** the way for the Lord's coming!
Rom 4:8 whose record the LORD has **c-ed**

CLEARHEADED (adj)
having or showing a clear understanding; able to think clearly
1 Thes 5:6 Stay alert and be **c.**

CLEVER (adj)
mentally quick and resourceful; marked by wit or ingenuity
Job 15:5 are based on **c** deception.

Isa 5:21	and think themselves so **c.**
Eph 4:14	so **c** they sound like the truth.
2 Pet 1:16	we were not making up **c** stories

CLEVERNESS (n)
the state of being mentally quick and resourceful; showing wit or ingenuity

1 Cor 3:19	in the snare of their own **c.**

CLING (v)
to adhere as if glued firmly; to hold or hold on tightly or tenaciously

Deut 10:20	worship him and **c** to him.
Deut 13:4	listen to his voice, and **c** to
Matt 10:39	If you **c** to your life,
Luke 8:15	who hear God's word, **c** to it,
John 20:17	"Don't **c** to me," Jesus
Phil 2:6	as something to **c** to.

CLOSE, CLOSED, CLOSES (v)
to draw near; to contract, fold, swing, or slide so as to leave no opening

Gen 7:16	Then the Lord **c-d** the door
Prov 28:27	who **c** their eyes to poverty
Isa 22:22	no one will be able to **c** them;
Acts 28:27	and they have **c-d** their eyes—
Rev 3:7	what he **c-s,** no one can open:
Rev 21:25	Its gates will never be **c-d**

CLOSE, CLOSER (adv)
being near in time, space, effect, or degree

Exod 3:5	Do not come any **c-r,**
Ps 34:18	is **c** to the brokenhearted;
Ps 148:14	of Israel who are **c** to him.
Prov 18:24	sticks **c-r** than a brother.
Isa 40:11	in his arms, holding them **c**

CLOTHED (v)
to dress; to endow especially with power or a quality

Ps 30:11	mourning and **c** me with joy,
Prov 31:25	She is **c** with strength
Rev 7:9	They were **c** in white robes
Rev 7:13	these who are **c** in white?

CLOTHES (n)
cloth articles of personal use that can be worn and washed

Deut 8:4	years your **c** didn't wear out,
Isa 50:9	old **c** that have been eaten by
Matt 6:25	food and drink, or enough **c**
Matt 27:35	soldiers gambled for his **c**
John 19:23	they divided his **c** among
Gal 3:27	like putting on new **c.**

CLOTHING (n)
garments in general; covering

Gen 3:21	God made **c** from animal skins
Deut 22:5	must not put on men's **c,**
Ps 22:18	and throw dice for my **c.**
Matt 6:28	And why worry about your **c?**
1 Tim 6:8	food and **c,** let us be content.

CLOUD, CLOUDS (n)
a visible mass of particles of condensed vapor suspended in the atmosphere

1 Kgs 18:44	I saw a little **c** about the
Ps 68:4	praises to him who rides the **c-s.**
Ps 108:4	faithfulness reaches to the **c-s.**
Isa 19:1	Egypt, riding on a swift **c.**
Dan 7:13	coming with the **c-s** of heaven.
Mark 13:26	coming on the **c-s** with great
Luke 21:27	Son of Man coming on a **c**
1 Thes 4:17	up in the **c-s** to meet the Lord
Rev 1:7	comes with the **c-s** of heaven.
Rev 14:14	I saw a white **c,** and seated on

COALS (n)
a piece of glowing carbon or charred wood; ember

Prov 25:22	heap burning **c** of shame
Rom 12:20	heap burning **c** of shame

COARSE (adj)
crude or unrefined in taste, manners, or language; harsh, raucous, or rough in tone

Eph 5:4	**c** jokes—these are not for you.

COAT (n)
an outer garment worn on the upper body

Matt 5:40	give your **c,** too.
Luke 6:29	your **c,** offer your shirt

COIN, COINS (n)
a usually flat piece of metal issued by governmental authority as money

Mark 12:15	Show me a Roman **c,**
Mark 12:42	dropped in two small **c-s.**
Luke 12:6	sparrows—two copper **c-s?**
Luke 15:8	woman has ten silver **c-s**

COLLAPSE (v)
to cave or fall in or give way

Matt 7:25	it won't **c** because it is built
Luke 6:49	it will **c** into a heap of ruins.

COLLECTED (v)
to bring together into one body or place

Hos 13:12	Ephraim's guilt has been **c,**
1 Cor 16:1	about the money being **c**

COLT (n)
a young male animal of the horse family

Zech 9:9	riding on a donkey's **c.**

COME, COMES, COMING (v)
to originate, arise; to move or journey to a vicinity with a specified purpose; to happen, occur
see also CAME

Ps 121:1	does my help **c** from there?
Prov 12:21	No harm **c-s** to the godly,
1 Thes 3:13	our Lord Jesus **c-s** again
Heb 9:28	He will **c** again,
Heb 13:7	good that has **c** from their
Jas 5:8	for the **c-ing** of the Lord
Rev 7:10	Salvation **c-s** from our God

COMFORT (n)
consolation in time of trouble or worry; solace

Gen 24:67	she was a special **c** to him
Job 10:20	I may have a moment of **c**
Ps 94:19	your **c** gave me renewed hope
Zech 10:2	falsehoods that give no **c.**
2 Cor 1:5	shower us with his **c**
2 Cor 1:7	share in the **c** God gives us.
Col 4:11	And what a **c** they have been!

COMFORT, COMFORTED, COMFORTS (v)
to give strength and hope to; to console

Gen 37:35	he refused to be **c-ed.**
Ruth 2:13	You have **c-ed** me by speaking
Job 2:11	traveled from their homes to **c**
Job 42:11	consoled him and **c-ed** him
Ps 69:20	one would turn and **c** me.
Ps 86:17	O LORD, help and **c** me.
Ps 119:50	it **c-s** me in all my troubles.
Ps 119:52	O LORD, they **c** me.
Isa 40:1	**C, c** my people,
Isa 49:13	the LORD has **c-ed** his people
Isa 51:3	The LORD will **c** Israel again
Isa 51:12	yes I, am the one who **c-s** you.
Isa 51:19	Who is left to **c** you?
Isa 52:9	the LORD has **c-ed** his people.
Isa 61:1	to **c** the brokenhearted
Isa 66:13	as a mother **c-s** her child.
Lam 1:2	there is no one left to **c** her.
Lam 1:17	but no one **c-s** her.
Zech 1:17	the LORD will again **c** Zion
Matt 5:4	mourn, for they will be **c-ed.**
1 Cor 14:3	encourages them, and **c-s**
2 Cor 1:4	He **c-s** us in all our troubles
2 Cor 1:4	so that we can **c** others.
2 Cor 1:6	when we ourselves are **c-ed,**
2 Cor 1:6	we will certainly **c** you.
2 Cor 2:7	forgive and **c** him.

COMFORTER (KJV)

John 14:16	another *Advocate,* who will
John 14:26	sends the *Advocate* as my
John 15:26	the *Advocate*—the Spirit of
John 16:7	if I don't, the *Advocate* won't

COMMAND, COMMANDS (n)
an order given; religious instruction
see also COMMANDMENT

Exod 20:6	who love me and obey my **c-s.**
Exod 24:12	the instructions and **c-s**
Lev 22:31	keep all my **c-s**
Num 15:39	and obey all the **c-s**
Deut 4:2	or subtract from these **c-s**
Deut 6:6	wholeheartedly to these **c-s**
Deut 7:9	who love him and obey his **c-s.**
Deut 8:1	Be careful to obey all the **c-s**
Deut 11:1	decrees, regulations, and **c-s.**
Deut 11:27	if you obey the **c-s** of the
Deut 28:1	keep all his **c-s** that I am giving
Deut 32:46	as a **c** to your children
Josh 1:9	my **c**—be strong and
1 Kgs 8:58	obey all the **c-s,** decrees,
1 Kgs 8:61	obey his decrees and **c-s,**
1 Chr 28:7	if he continues to obey my **c-s**
Neh 1:5	who love him and obey his **c-s,**
Job 36:10	**c-s** that they turn from evil.
Ps 33:9	It appeared at his **c.**
Ps 78:7	and obeying his **c-s.**
Ps 103:20	listening for each of his **c-s.**
Ps 112:1	and delight in obeying his **c-s.**
Ps 119:32	I will pursue your **c-s,**
Ps 119:47	How I delight in your **c-s!**
Ps 119:73	the sense to follow your **c-s.**
Ps 119:96	your **c-s** have no limit.
Ps 119:127	I love your **c-s** more than
Ps 119:143	I find joy in your **c-s.**
Ps 119:172	all your **c-s** are right.
Ps 119:176	I have not forgotten your **c-s.**
Prov 3:1	Store my **c-s** in your heart.
Prov 6:23	For their **c** is a lamp
Eccl 12:13	Fear God and obey his **c-s,**
Isa 48:18	you had listened to my **c-s!**
Dan 9:4	who love you and obey your **c-s.**
Matt 28:20	disciples to obey all the **c-s**
John 15:17	my **c:** Love each other.
Acts 17:30	he **c-s** everyone everywhere to
Rom 7:8	sin used this **c** to arouse
Rom 7:9	I learned the **c** not to covet,
Rom 7:12	law itself is holy, and its **c-s** are
1 Cor 14:37	saying is a **c** from the Lord
Gal 5:14	summed up in this one **c:**
2 Thes 3:6	we give you this **c**
2 Pet 2:21	reject the **c** they were given

COMMAND, COMMANDED, COMMANDING (v)
to issue a charge or directive

Gen 7:5	everything as the LORD **c-ed**
Exod 7:6	did just as the LORD had **c-ed**
Exod 19:7	everything the LORD had **c-ed**
Deut 6:1	your God **c-ed** me to teach

Deut 6:24 our God **c-ed** us to obey
Deut 15:11 why I am **c-ing** you to share
John 15:14 my friends if you do what I **c.**
2 Tim 2:14 **c** them in God's presence
2 Pet 3:2 Savior **c-ed** through your
1 Jn 3:23 just as he **c-ed** us.
2 Jn 1:4 just as the Father **c-ed.**

COMMANDER (n)
one in an official position of command or control
Eph 2:2 **c** of the powers in the unseen

COMMANDMENT, COMMANDMENTS (n)
a gracious provision of God's law or covenant, obeyed as an act of love and devotion
see also COMMAND
Exod 34:28 Ten **C-s**—on the stone
Deut 4:13 his covenant—the Ten **C-s**
Deut 10:4 LORD wrote the Ten **C-s** on
Ps 103:18 of those who obey his **c-s!**
Ps 111:7 all his **c-s** are trustworthy.
Ps 111:10 who obey his **c-s** will grow
Ps 119:93 I will never forget your **c-s,**
Prov 19:16 the **c-s** and keep your life;
Matt 5:19 if you ignore the least **c**
Matt 19:17 eternal life, keep the **c-s.**
Matt 22:36 the most important **c**
Matt 22:38 the first and greatest **c.**
Mark 10:19 you know the **c-s:**
Mark 12:28 **c-s,** which is the most
Luke 18:20 you know the **c-s:**
John 13:34 a new **c:** Love each other.
John 14:15 If you love me, obey my **c-s.**
Rom 13:9 in this one **c:** "Love your
1 Cor 7:19 is to keep God's **c-s.**
Eph 2:15 law with its **c-s** and regulations.
Eph 6:2 the first **c** with a promise:
Heb 9:19 had read each of God's **c-s**
1 Jn 2:3 know him if we obey his **c-s.**
1 Jn 3:24 Those who obey God's **c-s**
1 Jn 5:3 God means keeping his **c-s,**
Rev 12:17 who keep God's **c-s** and

COMMEND, COMMENDING (v)
to entrust for care or preservation; to praise
Rom 16:1 I **c** to you our sister Phoebe,
2 Cor 5:12 Are we **c-ing** ourselves to you
2 Cor 10:18 When people **c** themselves,

COMMENDATIONS (n)
a praiseworthy citation
2 Cor 12:11 ought to be writing **c** for me,

COMMIT, COMMITS, COMMITTED, COMMITTING (v)
to carry into action deliberately, perpetrate; to obligate or pledge oneself
Deut 30:20 **c-ting** yourself firmly to him.
2 Chr 16:9 hearts are fully **c-ted** to him.
2 Chr 17:6 deeply **c-ted** to the ways
Prov 6:32 the man who **c-s** adultery
Prov 29:22 a hot-tempered person **c-s**
Matt 5:28 has already **c-ted** adultery
Matt 5:32 causes her to **c** adultery.
Matt 19:9 someone else **c-s** adultery—
Mark 10:11 someone else **c-s** adultery
Mark 10:19 You must not **c** adultery.
Luke 16:18 her husband **c-s** adultery.
Rom 13:9 You must not **c** adultery.
Titus 2:14 totally **c-ted** to doing good
Jas 2:11 You must not **c** adultery,
Rev 18:3 world have **c-ted** adultery with
Rev 18:9 the world who **c-ted** adultery

COMMON (adj)
characterized by a lack of privilege or special status; belonging to or shared by two or more individuals or things or all members of a group
Lev 10:10 what is sacred and what is **c,**
1 Cor 9:22 I try to find **c** ground with

COMMUNITY (n)
a unified body of individuals
Num 20:1 whole **c** of Israel arrived

COMPANION , COMPANIONS (n)
a close friend or fellow participant
Ps 55:13 my **c** and close friend.
Ps 55:20 As for my **c,** he betrayed his
Prov 16:29 mislead their **c-s,** leading

COMPANY (n)
association with another, fellowship; companions, associates
Prov 21:16 end up in the **c** of the dead.
Prov 24:1 or desire their **c.**
Rom 12:16 to enjoy the **c** of ordinary
1 Cor 15:33 for "bad **c** corrupts good

COMPASSION (n)
sympathy, usually granted because of unusual or distressing circumstances
Exod 34:6 The God of **c** and mercy!
Ps 51:1 Because of your great **c,**
Ps 86:15 a God of **c** and mercy, slow to
Ps 145:9 He showers **c** on all
Isa 49:13 and will have **c** on them
Isa 63:15 your mercy and **c** now?
Lam 3:32 brings grief, he also shows **c**

Hos 2:19 unfailing love and **c.**
Mic 7:19 you will have **c** on us.
Zech 10:6 because of my **c.**
Mark 1:41 Moved with **c,** Jesus reached
Mark 6:34 and he had **c** on them
Luke 15:20 with love and **c,** he ran to
Rom 9:15 show **c** to anyone I choose.

COMPASSIONATE (adj)
having or showing compassion; sympathetic
Ps 103:13 tender and **c** to those who
Ps 112:4 They are generous, **c,**
Ps 145:8 is merciful and **c,** slow to
Joel 2:13 he is merciful and **c,** slow to
Luke 6:36 You must be **c,** just as your
Phil 2:1 Are your hearts tender and **c?**

COMPELLED (v)
to drive or urge forcefully or irresistibly
1 Cor 9:16 I am **c** by God to do it.

COMPENSATION (n)
something that constitutes an equivalent or recompense
Prov 6:35 He will accept no **c,**

COMPLACENCY (n)
self-satisfaction especially when accompanied by unawareness of actual dangers or deficiencies
Prov 1:32 destroyed by their own **c.**
Isa 32:11 throw off your **c.**

COMPLACENT (adj)
self-satisfied; unconcerned
Jer 49:31 attack that **c** nation,
Zeph 1:12 who sit **c** in their sins.

COMPLAINED, COMPLAINING (v)
to express grief, pain, or discontent; to make a formal accusation or charge
Exod 15:24 the people **c** and turned
Num 14:2 in the wilderness!" they **c.**
Num 14:29 Because you **c** against me,
John 6:43 Jesus replied, "Stop **c-ing**
Phil 2:14 Do everything without **c-ing**

COMPLAINERS (n)
one who complains
Jude 1:16 grumblers and **c,** living only

COMPLAINT (n)
a formal allegation against a party
Mic 6:2 listen to the LORD's **c!**

COMPLETE (adj)
having all necessary parts, elements, or steps
Eph 4:13 full and **c** standard of Christ.
Jas 2:22 made his faith **c.**
2 Jn 1:12 joy will be **c.**

COMPREHEND (v)
to grasp the nature, significance, or meaning of
Matt 13:14 I do, you will not **c.**

COMPREHENSION (n)
the act or action of grasping with the intellect; understanding
Ps 147:5 is beyond **c!**

CONCEAL, CONCEALED (v)
to prevent disclosure or recognition of; to place out of sight
Prov 25:2 God's privilege to **c**
Prov 28:13 People who **c** their sins will
Luke 8:17 everything that is **c-ed** will be

CONCEIT (n)
excessive appreciation of one's own worth or virtue
Ps 36:2 In their blind **c,** they cannot

CONCEITED (adj)
having or showing an excessively high opinion of oneself
Gal 5:26 us not become **c,** or provoke

CONCEIVE, CONCEIVED (v)
to become pregnant; to devise or imagine
Gen 29:31 Rachel could not **c.**
Ps 7:14 The wicked **c** evil; they are
Matt 1:20 was **c-d** by the Holy Spirit.
Luke 1:7 Elizabeth was unable to **c,**
Luke 1:31 You will **c** and give birth

CONCERN, CONCERNS (n)
affair or business; an uneasy state of blended interest, uncertainty, and apprehension
Job 19:4 that is my **c,** not yours.
1 Cor 7:32 free from the **c-s** of this life.
2 Cor 7:11 such **c** to clear yourselves,
2 Cor 11:28 the daily burden of my **c**

CONCERN, CONCERNED (v)
to involve; to be a care, trouble, or distress to
1 Sam 23:21 someone is **c-ed** about me!
Ps 131:1 I don't **c** myself with matters
1 Cor 10:24 be **c-ed** for your own good
Phil 4:10 have always been **c-ed** for me,

CONCUBINE, CONCUBINES (n)
a woman living in a man's household, though not married; of lower family status than the wife
Judg 19:1 in Judah to be his **c.**

2 Sam 3:7 one of his father's **c-s,**
2 Sam 5:13 David married more **c-s** and
2 Sam 16:22 sex with his father's **c-s.**
2 Sam 21:11 what Rizpah, Saul's **c,** had
1 Chr 1:32 Keturah, Abraham's **c,**
1 Chr 7:13 of Jacob's **c** Bilhah.

CONDEMN, CONDEMNED, CONDEMNING, CONDEMNS (v)
to declare guilty; to sentence or doom
Job 15:6 Your own mouth **c-s** you, not I.
Job 40:8 my justice and **c** me just to
Ps 37:33 or let the godly be **c-ed**
Ps 102:20 to release those **c-ed** to die.
Prov 12:2 **c-s** those who plan wickedness.
Prov 17:15 guilty and **c-ing** the innocent—
Isa 53:8 Unjustly **c-ed,** he was led away.
Matt 12:7 not have **c-ed** my innocent
Matt 12:37 acquit you or **c** you.
Matt 12:41 on judgment day and **c** it,
Matt 27:3 Jesus had been **c-ed** to die,
Luke 11:31 on judgment day and **c** it,
John 8:10 even one of them **c** you?
Rom 2:1 think you can **c** such people,
Rom 2:1 you are **c-ing** yourself,
Rom 3:7 how can God **c** me as a sinner
Rom 3:8 deserve to be **c-ed.**
Rom 8:34 Who then will **c** us? No one—
Rom 14:3 foods must not **c** those who
Rom 14:13 So let's stop **c-ing** each other.
1 Cor 4:9 a victor's parade, **c-ed** to die.
2 Cor 7:3 saying this to **c** you.
Col 2:16 So don't let anyone **c** you
Jas 5:6 You have **c-ed** and killed
Jas 5:12 not sin and be **c-ed.**

CONDEMNATION (n)
conviction of guilt; censure or blame
Rom 5:9 save us from God's **c.**
Rom 5:18 Adam's one sin brings **c**
Rom 7:13 bring about my **c** to death.
Rom 8:1 there is no **c** for those who
2 Cor 3:9 which brings **c,** was glorious,

CONDUCT (n)
a mode or standard of personal behavior especially as based on moral principles
Prov 20:11 act, whether their **c** is pure,
Jer 32:19 You see the **c** of all people,
Gal 6:5 responsible for our own **c.**

CONDUCT, CONDUCTED, CONDUCTING (v)
to cause (oneself) to act or behave in a particular and controlled manner; to direct or take part in the management or operation of
Exod 18:20 them how to **c** their lives.
Ps 112:5 lend money generously and **c**
2 Cor 1:12 how we have **c-ed** ourselves
Phil 1:27 of heaven, **c-ing** yourselves in a
1 Tim 3:15 **c** themselves in the

CONFESS, CONFESSED, CONFESSES, CONFESSING (v)
to admit or acknowledge (sin or faith)
1 Sam 7:6 **c-ed** that they had sinned
Ezra 10:11 So now **c** your sin to
Ps 32:3 I refused to **c** my sin,
Ps 32:5 Finally, I **c-ed** all my sins
Ps 38:18 But I **c** my sins;
Ps 66:18 If I had not **c-ed** the sin in my
Dan 9:4 to the LORD my God and **c-ed:**
Dan 9:20 praying and **c-ing** my sin
Matt 18:15 **c-es** it, you have won
Mark 1:5 And when they **c-ed** their sins,
Rom 10:10 by **c-ing** with your mouth
Rom 14:11 every tongue will **c** and give
Phil 2:11 and every tongue **c** that Jesus
1 Tim 6:12 which you have **c-ed** so well
Jas 5:16 **C** your sins to each other
1 Jn 1:9 But if we **c** our sins to him,

CONFESSION, CONFESSIONS (n)
a disclosure of one's sins; a formal statement of religious beliefs
Ezra 10:1 and made this **c,** weeping
Hos 14:2 your **c-s,** and return

CONFIDENCE (n)
faith or belief that one will act in a right, proper, or effective way; a feeling or consciousness of one's powers; a quality or state of being certain
Ps 146:3 Don't put your **c** in powerful
Isa 30:15 In quietness and **c** is your
2 Cor 8:22 of his great **c** in you.
Phil 1:14 believers here have gained **c**
Phil 2:24 And I have **c** from the Lord
Phil 3:4 I could have **c** in my own
Col 2:2 want them to have complete **c**
1 Thes 5:8 as our helmet the **c** of our
Titus 1:2 This truth gives them **c**
Heb 11:1 Faith is the **c** that what we
2 Pet 1:19 we have even greater **c**
1 Jn 4:17 but we can face him with **c**

CONFIDENT (adj)
full of conviction, certain; trustful
Ps 27:13 Yet I am **c** I will see the
Ps 57:7 My heart is **c** in you, O God;
2 Cor 3:4 We are **c** of all this
Eph 1:18 can understand the **c** hope
Col 1:5 **c** hope of what God has reserved
Col 4:12 fully **c** that you are following

2 Thes 3:4 And we are **c** in the Lord
Heb 3:6 keep our courage and remain **c**

CONFIDENTLY (adv)
acting with confidence
Ps 112:7 they **c** trust the LORD
Rom 5:2 we **c** and joyfully look forward
Eph 3:12 boldly and **c** into God's

CONFIRM, CONFIRMED, CONFIRMING, CONFIRMS (v)
to strengthen; to remove doubt by authoritative statement or action
Gen 6:18 I will **c** my covenant with you.
Gen 9:17 sign of the covenant I am **c-ing**
Gen 17:21 will be **c-ed** with Isaac,
Heb 9:20 This blood **c-s** the covenant

CONFLICT (n)
fight, battle, war
Prov 13:10 Pride leads to **c;**
Prov 17:1 filled with feasting—and **c.**
Gal 3:21 Is there a **c,** then, between

CONFUSED (v)
to confound, stupify, perplex
Gen 11:9 where the Lord **c** the people

CONFUSED (adj)
the state of being confounded, stupified, perplexed
Matt 9:36 they were **c** and helpless,
Rom 1:21 their minds became dark and **c.**

CONGRATULATE (v)
to express pleasure to (a person) on the occasion of success or good fortune
2 Sam 19:7 go out there and **c** your troops,

CONGREGATION (n)
an assembly or gathering (not church)
Ps 107:32 exalt him publicly before the **c**

CONQUER, CONQUERED, CONQUERING (v)
to gain or acquire by force of arms
see also OVERCOME
Gen 22:17 descendants will **c** the cities
Num 13:30 We can certainly **c** it!
Prov 16:32 than to **c** a city.
Dan 2:44 never be destroyed or **c-ed.**
Matt 16:18 of hell will not **c** it.
Rom 12:21 Don't let evil **c** you,
Col 2:23 no help in **c-ing** a person's evil

CONQUEROR (n)
one who subdues, defeats, or vanquishes
Mic 1:15 I will bring a **c** to capture

CONSCIENCE, CONSCIENCES (n)
one's moral sensitivity or scruples
2 Sam 24:10 census, David's **c** began to
Acts 24:16 maintain a clear **c** before God
Rom 14:2 with a sensitive **c** will eat
1 Cor 8:7 their weak **c-s** are violated.
1 Cor 8:10 to violate their **c** by eating
1 Cor 10:25 raising questions of **c.**
1 Tim 1:5 a clear **c,** and genuine faith.
1 Tim 1:19 and keep your **c** clear.
Titus 1:15 minds and **c-s** are corrupted.
Heb 9:9 are not able to cleanse the **c-s**
Heb 9:14 will purify our **c-s** from sinful
Heb 10:22 guilty **c-s** have been sprinkled
Heb 13:18 for our **c** is clear
1 Pet 3:16 Keep your **c** clear.
1 Pet 3:21 to God from a clean **c.**

CONSCIENTIOUS (adj)
scrupulous, meticulous, careful
2 Chr 29:34 been more **c** about purifying

CONSECRATE, CONSECRATED (v)
to devote irrevocably to God by a solemn ceremony; to make or declare sacred
see also DEDICATE, DEVOTE, ORDAINED
Exod 40:9 all its furnishings to **c** them
Lev 19:24 the entire crop must be **c-d**
2 Chr 29:31 you have **c-d** yourselves

CONSIDER (v)
to think about carefully; to come to judge or classify; to regard
Job 37:14 Stop and **c** the wonderful
Rom 6:11 **c** yourselves to be dead
Jas 1:2 troubles come your way, **c** it

CONSIDERATE (adj)
thoughtful of the rights and feelings of others
Phil 4:5 see that you are **c** in all you

CONSOLE, CONSOLING (v)
to alleviate the grief or sense of loss; to offer just reward
John 11:19 come to **c** Martha and Mary
John 11:31 at the house **c-ing** Mary

CONSTANT (adj)
marked by steadfast faithfulness; continually occurring or recurring
Ps 119:98 they are my **c** guide.
Prov 27:15 is as annoying as **c** dripping
Luke 18:5 with her **c** requests!

CONSTRUCT (v)
to build

1 Kgs 6:1 he began to **c** the Temple

CONSULT (v)
to ask the advice or opinion of; to confer
Gal 1:16 rush out to **c** with any human

CONSUME, CONSUMED (v)
to engage fully, engross
Ps 69:9 Passion for your house has **c-d**
John 2:17 Passion for God's house will **c**

CONTAIN (v)
to keep within limits; to restrain or control
1 Kgs 8:27 heavens cannot **c** you.
John 21:25 world could not **c** the books

CONTAMINATE (v)
to soil, corrupt, or infect
Jude 1:23 the sins that **c** their lives.

CONTEMPT (n)
the state of despising; displaying disgust, scorn, or disdain
Gen 25:34 showed **c** for his rights
Ps 119:51 The proud hold me in utter **c**,
Prov 18:3 scandalous behavior brings **c.**
Mal 1:6 ever shown **c** for your name?

CONTENT, CONTENTED (adj)
feeling or showing satisfaction with one's possessions, status, or situation; pleased
Josh 7:7 If only we had been **c**
1 Kgs 4:20 They were very **c-ed,**
Prov 13:25 godly eat to their hearts' **c,**
Luke 3:14 And be **c** with your pay.
Phil 4:11 I have learned how to be **c**
1 Tim 6:8 food and clothing, let us be **c.**

CONTENTMENT (n)
the quality or state of being contented
1 Tim 6:6 godliness with **c** is

CONTINUAL (adj)
continuing indefinitely in time
Prov 15:15 life is a **c** feast.

CONTINUALLY (adv)
in continual or steadily recurring manner
1 Chr 16:11 **c** seek him.

CONTINUE, CONTINUED, CONTINUES (v)
to maintain without interruption a condition, course, or action
Ps 100:5 unfailing love **c-s** forever,
Jer 32:20 have **c-d** to do
Acts 13:43 **c** to rely on
Acts 14:22 encouraged them to **c**
Rom 11:22 if you **c** to trust in
Col 1:23 But you must **c** to believe
Col 2:6 you must **c** to follow
1 Tim 2:15 assuming they **c** to live in
1 Jn 3:6 who **c-s** to live in him
Rev 22:11 **c** to be holy.

CONTRACT (n)
a binding agreement between two or more persons or parties
Exod 21:8 who broke the **c** with her.

CONTRIBUTIONS (n)
a payment imposed by authorities for a special purpose; the act of giving to a common fund or store
Mark 12:43 who are making **c.**

CONTRITE (adj)
feeling or showing sorrow or remorse for a sin
see also HUMBLE, REPENTANT
Isa 66:2 have humble and **c** hearts,

CONTROL, CONTROLS (v)
to exercise restraining or directing influence over; to rule
Job 37:15 know how God **c-s** the storm
Rom 6:12 Do not let sin **c**
Rom 8:6 letting the Spirit **c** your mind
Rom 8:8 still under the **c** of
1 Cor 7:9 they can't **c** themselves,
1 Cor 7:37 and he can **c** his passion,
2 Cor 5:14 Christ's love **c-s** us.
Jas 1:26 but don't **c** your tongue,
Jas 3:2 could also **c** ourselves
2 Pet 2:19 a slave to whatever **c-s** you.

CONTROVERSY, CONTROVERSIES (n)
a dispute or quarrel
Acts 26:3 customs and **c-ies.**
1 Tim 2:8 from anger and **c.**

CONVERTED (v)
to bring over from one belief, view, or party to another
Acts 6:7 priests were **c,** too.
Acts 15:3 the Gentiles, too, were being **c.**

CONVICT, CONVICTED (v)
to find or prove guilty of an offense
Prov 24:25 for those who **c** the guilty;
John 7:51 Is it legal to **c** a man
John 16:8 he will **c** the world of
1 Cor 14:24 they will be **c-ed** of sin
Jude 1:15 He will **c** every person

CONVICTIONS (n)
strongly held beliefs or principles
Rom 14:23 you are not following your **c.**

CONVINCE, CONVINCED (v)
to persuade to a belief, consent, or course of action
Exod 4:31 people of Israel were **c-d**
Acts 18:4 to **c** the Jews and Greeks
Rom 2:19 are **c-d** that you are a guide
Rom 8:38 I am **c-d** that nothing
Rom 14:14 I know and am **c-d**
Rom 15:14 I am fully **c-d,**
Phil 1:25 I am **c-d** that I will

COPY (n)
an imitation or reproduction of an original work; a duplicate
Heb 8:5 that is only a **c,**
Heb 9:24 was only a **c** of

COPY (v)
to duplicate; to model oneself on
Deut 17:18 he must **c** for himself
Rom 12:2 Don't **c** the behavior and

CORD (n)
a long, slender, flexible material usually consisting of several strands woven together
Eccl 4:12 for a triple-braided **c**

CORNERSTONE (n)
a stone forming a corner or angle in a wall; foundation
Ps 118:22 now become the **c.**
Mark 12:10 now become the **c.**
Acts 4:11 now become the **c.**
Eph 2:20 And the **c** is Christ
1 Pet 2:7 now become the **c.**

CORRECT, CORRECTED, CORRECTING, CORRECTS (v)
to set right with remedies, revisions, or reforms
Job 5:17 joy of those **c-ed** by God!
Ps 141:5 If they **c** me,
Prov 3:12 For the Lord **c-s** those
Prov 9:8 don't bother **c-ing** mockers;
Prov 19:25 if you **c** the wise,
Jer 5:3 refused to be **c-ed.**
Jer 10:24 Do not **c** me in anger,
2 Tim 3:16 It **c-s** us when we
2 Tim 4:2 Patiently **c,** rebuke,
Titus 2:15 the authority to **c** them
Heb 12:5 give up when he **c-s** you.

CORRECTION (n)
a rebuke or punishment; the action of making right
Prov 10:17 those who ignore **c**
Prov 12:1 it is stupid to hate **c.**
Prov 15:5 learns from **c** is wise.
Prov 15:10 whoever hates **c** will die.
Prov 15:32 if you listen to **c,**
Zeph 3:2 it refuses all **c.**

CORRUPT (adj)
morally degenerate and perverted; depraved
Gen 6:11 the earth had become **c**
Ps 14:1 They are **c,**
Ps 14:3 all have become **c.**
Prov 19:28 A **c** witness
Luke 9:41 faithless and **c** people!

CORRUPT, CORRUPTED, CORRUPTS (v)
to change from good to bad, physically or morally
Eccl 7:7 and bribes **c** the heart.
1 Cor 15:33 bad company **c-s** good
Titus 1:15 and consciences are **c-ed.**
Jas 1:27 let the world **c** you.

CORRUPTION (n)
impairment of integrity, virtue, or moral principle; depravity, decay
2 Pet 1:4 the world's **c** caused
2 Pet 2:19 slaves of sin and **c.**

CORRUPTLY (adv)
marked by moral perversion and degeneracy
Deut 32:5 they have acted **c**

COST (n)
loss or penalty incurred especially in gaining something; price
Num 16:38 sinned at the **c** of their lives,
Luke 14:28 calculating the **c**

COST (v)
to require effort, suffering, or loss
Prov 7:23 it would **c** him his life.
Rev 6:6 barley will **c** a day's pay.

COUNCIL (n)
a group elected or appointed as an advisory or legislative body
Acts 17:19 to the high **c** of the city.
Acts 17:22 standing before the **c,**
Acts 17:34 a member of the **c,**

COUNSEL (n)
advice; policy, plan, or action
Ps 37:30 godly offer good **c;**
Ps 73:24 guide me with your **c,**
Ps 107:11 scorning the **c** of the
Prov 27:9 The heartfelt **c** of a friend
1 Cor 7:40 I am giving you **c**

COUNSEL (v)
to advise
Col 3:16 Teach and **c** each other

COUNSELOR (n)
one who gives advice or wisdom
see also ADVOCATE, HOLY SPIRIT
Isa 9:6 Wonderful **C,** Mighty God,

COUNT, COUNTED, COUNTING, COUNTS (v)
to number; to consider
Gen 15:6 and the LORD **c-ed** him as
Ps 22:17 I can **c** all my bones.
Ps 130:5 yes, I am **c-ing** on him.
Ps 147:4 He **c-s** the stars
Prov 20:25 and only later **c-ing** the cost.
Acts 5:41 **c-ed** them worthy to suffer
Rom 4:9 Abraham was **c-ed** as righteous
Rom 4:24 that God will also **c** us
Rom 5:13 it was not **c-ed** as sin
2 Cor 5:19 no longer **c-ing** people's sins
Gal 3:6 and God **c-ed** him as righteous
Jas 2:23 and God **c-ed** him as righteous

COUNTENANCE (KJV)
Gen 4:6 Why do you *look* so dejected
Num 6:26 LORD *show you his favor*
1 Sam 16:7 Don't judge by his *appearance*
Prov 15:13 glad heart makes a happy *face*
Luke 9:29 *appearance of his face* was transformed

COURAGE (n)
mental or moral strength
Judg 5:21 March on with **c,** my soul!
2 Chr 15:8 he took **c** and removed
Dan 11:25 stir up his **c** and raise a
Mark 6:50 Take **c!** I am here!
Acts 27:22 But take **c!**
Heb 3:6 if we keep our **c**
Jas 5:8 Take **c,** for the coming
1 Jn 2:28 be full of **c** and not shrink

COURAGEOUS (adj)
having or characterized by courage; brave
Deut 31:6 So be strong and **c!**
Josh 1:6 Be strong and **c,**
2 Sam 10:12 Be **c!** Let us fight
2 Chr 32:7 Be strong and **c!**
Ps 31:24 be strong and **c,**
1 Cor 16:13 Be **c.** Be strong.

COURT, COURTS (n)
a place for the administration of justice; an open space enclosed by buildings
Ps 82:1 presides over heaven's **c;**
Ps 84:10 single day in your **c-s**
Ps 96:8 come into his **c-s.**
Ps 100:4 go into his **c-s**
Prov 22:22 exploit the needy in **c.**
Prov 25:8 to go to **c.**
Isa 3:13 takes his place in **c**
Amos 5:15 **c-s** into true halls of justice.
Zech 8:16 verdicts in your **c-s**
Matt 5:25 are on the way to **c**

COURTROOM (n)
a room in which a court of law is held
Eccl 3:16 evil in the **c.**

COURTYARD (n)
enclosed area adjacent to a building
Exod 27:9 make the **c** for the Tabernacle,
Exod 27:18 the entire **c** will be 150 feet long
Matt 26:69 sitting outside in the **c.**

COVENANT, COVENANTS (n)
a mutual agreement or contract (between persons, between nations, or between God and humanity) with conditions and consequences spelled out
see also PROMISE, VOW
Gen 9:9 hereby confirm my **c**
Gen 17:2 I will make a **c** with you,
Exod 19:5 and keep my **c,**
Deut 4:13 He proclaimed his **c**—
Judg 2:1 never break my **c**
1 Kgs 8:21 which contains the **c**
2 Kgs 23:2 Book of the **C** that had been
2 Chr 6:14 You keep your **c**
Neh 1:5 keeps his **c** of unfailing love
Ps 105:8 stands by his **c**—
Prov 2:17 and ignores the **c**
Isa 61:8 an everlasting **c** with them.
Jer 31:31 make a new **c** with the people
Hos 10:4 make **c-s** they don't intend
Mal 3:1 messenger of the **c,**
Mark 14:24 confirms the **c** between God
Luke 22:20 new **c** between God and his
Rom 9:4 He made **c-s** with them
1 Cor 11:25 new **c** between God and his
2 Cor 3:6 under the new **c,**
Heb 8:6 a far better **c** with God,
Heb 9:15 mediates a new **c** between
Heb 12:24 the new **c** between God and

COVER (n)
something that is placed over or about another thing; lid or top piece
Exod 25:17 make the Ark's **c**—
Exod 25:21 put the atonement **c**
Lev 16:2 the atonement **c.**

COVER, COVERED, COVERS (v)
to hide from sight or knowledge; to lay or spread something over; to lie over

Gen 3:7	to **c** themselves.
Exod 33:22	and **c** you with my hand
Job 29:14	Righteousness **c-ed** me
Ps 85:2	you **c-ed** all their sins.
Ps 91:4	He will **c** you with
Isa 6:2	they **c-ed** their faces,
Matt 10:26	everything that is **c-ed**
1 Cor 11:4	if he **c-s** his head while
2 Cor 3:15	their hearts are **c-ed**
Jas 3:14	don't **c** up the truth
1 Pet 4:8	love **c-s** a multitude of sins.

COVERING (n)
something that covers or conceals

1 Cor 11:5	without a **c** on her head,
1 Cor 11:15	given to her as a **c.**

COVET, COVETED, COVETING (v)
to inordinately desire unjust gain or another's property
see also DESIRE

Exod 20:17	not **c** your neighbor's wife,
Exod 34:24	so no one will **c** and conquer
Deut 7:25	must not **c** the silver or gold
Acts 20:33	**c-ed** anyone's silver or gold
Rom 7:7	known that **c-ing** is wrong
Rom 13:9	You must not **c.**

COWARDS (n)
one who shows disgraceful fear or timidity

Rev 21:8	But **c,** unbelievers, the

COWS (n)
the mature female of cattle

Gen 41:2	he saw seven fat, healthy **c**

CRAFTSMAN, CRAFTSMEN (n)
a worker who practices a trade or handicraft

Isa 45:16	All **c-en** who make idols
Jer 10:3	and a **c** carves an idol.

CRAFTSMANSHIP (n)
the product of a craftsman that demonstrates his skill

Ps 19:1	the skies display his **c.**

CRAVE, CRAVED, CRAVES (v)
to want greatly; to yearn for

Num 11:4	began to **c** the good things
Num 11:34	people who had **c-d** meat
Ps 78:18	the foods they **c-d.**
Ps 78:29	gave them what they **c-d.**
Prov 31:4	should not **c** alcohol.
Gal 5:16	your sinful nature **c-s.**
1 Pet 2:2	**c** pure spiritual milk
1 Jn 2:17	everything that people **c.**

CRAVING (n)
an intense, urgent, or abnormal desire or longing

Ps 78:30	they satisfied their **c,**
Prov 10:3	satisfy the **c** of the wicked.
1 Jn 2:16	world offers only a **c**

CREATE, CREATED, CREATING (v)
to bring into being; to form, make, or produce
see also FORMED, MADE, MAKE

Gen 1:1	God **c-d** the heavens
Gen 1:27	male and female he **c-d** them;
Gen 6:7	human race I have **c-d** from
Ps 51:10	**C** in me a clean heart
Ps 104:30	life is **c-d,** and you renew
Prov 8:22	before he **c-d** anything else.
Isa 43:1	the LORD who **c-d** you.
Isa 43:7	I who **c-d** them.
Isa 45:8	I, the LORD, **c-d** them.
Isa 54:16	I have **c-d** the blacksmith
Isa 65:17	I am **c-ing** new heavens and
John 1:3	**c-d** everything through him,
Rom 1:20	since the world was **c-d,**
Rom 1:25	served the things God **c-d**
Rom 9:20	the thing that was **c-d** say
Eph 2:10	He has **c-d** us anew
Eph 2:15	by **c-ing** in himself
Eph 4:24	**c-d** to be like God—
Col 1:16	Everything was **c-d** through
1 Tim 4:3	But God **c-d** those foods
Heb 1:2	through the Son he **c-d**
1 Pet 4:19	to the God who **c-d** you,
Rev 4:11	For you **c-d** all things,
Rev 10:6	who **c-d** the heavens

CREATION (n)
something that is created; the world; the act of bringing the world into existence

Gen 2:3	from all his work of **c.**
Mark 10:6	from the beginning of **c.**
Rom 8:19	For all **c** is waiting
Rom 8:39	nothing in all **c** will ever
Gal 6:15	into a new **c.**
Col 1:17	holds all **c** together.
Heb 12:27	all of **c** will be shaken
Jas 1:18	we, out of all **c,**
Rev 3:14	of God's new **c:**

CREATOR (n)
maker; one who creates
see also MAKER

Gen 14:19	God Most High, **C** of heaven
Job 40:19	only its **C** can threaten
Eccl 12:1	to forget your **C.**

Isa 40:28	the **C** of all the earth.
Isa 45:9	argue with their **C.**
Isa 51:13	the LORD, your **C,**
Jer 51:19	He is the **C** of everything
Rom 1:25	instead of the **C** himself,
Eph 3:9	the **C** of all things,
Eph 3:15	the **C** of everything

CREATURE, CREATURES (n)
something created either animate or inanimate

Lev 17:14	the life of any **c** is in
Ps 104:24	full of your **c-s.**

CREDIT (n)
honor, recognition, or acknowledgment

Luke 6:33	should you get **c?**
1 Pet 2:20	no **c** for being patient

CRETE (n)
an island in the Mediterranean Sea

Acts 27:12	up the coast of **C,**
Titus 1:12	The people of **C** are all liars,

CRIME, CRIMES (n)
a grave offense; criminal activity

Deut 22:26	no **c** worthy of death
Judg 19:30	Such a horrible **c** has
1 Sam 20:1	What is my **c?** How have I
Job 31:11	lust is a shameful sin, a **c**
Ps 52:1	about your **c-s,** great warrior?
Luke 11:48	join in their **c** by
Luke 23:41	deserve to die for our **c-s,**

CRIMINAL, CRIMINALS (n)
one who has broken the law

Ps 59:2	Rescue me from these **c-s;**
Isa 53:9	he was buried like a **c;**
Luke 23:32	Two others, both **c-s,**

CRIMSON (n)
any of several deep purplish reds

Isa 1:18	Though they are red like **c,**

CRIPPLED (adj)
lame, physically disabled

2 Sam 9:3	He is **c** in both feet.
Luke 14:13	invite the poor, the **c,** the lame,
Acts 14:8	came upon a man with **c** feet.

CRITIC (n)
one who expresses an opinion on a matter involving a judgment of its value, truth, righteousness, beauty, or technique

Job 40:2	You are God's **c,** but do you

CRITICISM (n)
a critical observation or remark; critique

Prov 15:31	listen to constructive **c,**
Prov 25:12	valid **c** is like a gold
Prov 28:23	people appreciate honest **c**
Prov 29:1	refuses to accept **c**
2 Cor 8:20	guard against any **c**

CRITICIZE, CRITICIZED, CRITICIZING (v)
to find fault with; to point out the faults of

Job 34:29	who can **c** him?
Eccl 7:5	be **c-d** by a wise person
Rom 14:16	not be **c-d** for doing
Phil 2:15	no one can **c** you.
Titus 2:8	teaching can't be **c-d.**
Jas 4:11	**c-ing** and judging God's law.

CROOKED (adj)
not straight, twisted; dishonest, evil

Ps 125:5	those who turn to **c** ways,
Prov 5:6	staggers down a **c** trail
Prov 8:8	nothing devious or **c** in it.
Prov 10:9	those who follow **c** paths
Prov 21:8	The guilty walk a **c** path;
Eccl 7:13	what he has made **c?**
Isa 59:8	have mapped out **c** roads,

CROP, CROPS (n)
the product or yield after a harvest

Exod 23:16	bring me the first **c-s**
Prov 28:3	that destroys the **c-s.**
Hos 10:12	harvest a **c** of love.
Matt 13:8	they produced a **c** that was
Matt 21:41	his share of the **c**

CROSS (n)
an upright post used as an instrument of death in ancient times; the means by which atonement was made between God and humanity

Mark 8:34	take up your **c,**
Luke 9:23	take up your **c** daily,
Acts 2:23	you nailed him to a **c**
Acts 5:30	hanging him on a **c.**
1 Cor 1:18	message of the **c** is
Gal 3:1	death on the **c.**
Gal 6:12	that the **c** of Christ alone
Phil 2:8	criminal's death on a **c.**
Col 1:20	Christ's blood on the **c.**
Heb 12:2	he endured the **c,**
1 Pet 2:24	his body on the **c**

CROSSED (v)
to fold one (arm) over the other

Gen 48:14	But Jacob **c** his arms

CROSSROADS (n)
the place of intersection of two or more roads
Jer 6:16 Stop at the **c** and look

CROUCHING (v)
to lie close to the ground with the legs bent
Gen 4:7 Sin is **c** at the door,

CROW, CROWED, CROWS (v)
to make the loud shrill sound characteristic of a rooster
Matt 26:34 before the rooster **c-s,**
Matt 26:74 the rooster **c-ed.**

CROWD, CROWDS (n)
a large number of persons especially when collected together
Exod 23:2 by the **c** to twist justice.
Matt 9:36 When he saw the **c-s,**
Heb 12:1 such a huge **c** of witnesses
Rev 19:1 like a vast **c** in heaven

CROWDED (v)
to push or force
Mark 4:19 the message is **c** out

CROWN, CROWNS (n)
top of the head; a cap or headdress worn by victors, priests, or royalty
Prov 16:31 Gray hair is a **c** of glory;
Song 3:11 He wears the **c** his mother
Isa 61:3 will give a **c** of beauty
Isa 62:3 a splendid **c** in the hand
Zech 9:16 like jewels in a **c.**
Matt 27:29 thorn branches into a **c**
Mark 15:17 thorn branches into a **c**
John 19:2 wove a **c** of thorns
John 19:5 wearing the **c** of thorns
Phil 4:1 and the **c** I receive
1 Thes 2:19 our proud reward and **c**
Jas 1:12 will receive the **c** of life
Rev 2:10 will give you the **c** of life.
Rev 3:11 take away your **c.**
Rev 4:4 had gold **c-s** on their heads.
Rev 4:10 lay their **c-s** before the throne
Rev 12:3 with seven **c-s** on his heads.
Rev 14:14 He had a gold **c** on his head
Rev 19:12 on his head were many **c-s.**

CROWNED, CROWNS (v)
to place a crown on the head of; to bless or adorn
Ps 8:5 and **c-ed** them with
Ps 149:4 he **c-s** the humble
Prov 14:18 are **c-ed** with knowledge.
Isa 51:11 **c-ed** with everlasting joy.
Heb 2:7 and **c-ed** them with
Heb 2:9 **c-ed** with glory and honor.

CRUCIFIXION (n)
the execution or death of a person on a cross
Matt 23:34 you will kill some by **c,**
John 19:41 The place of **c** was near

CRUCIFY, CRUCIFIED (v)
to execute or nail to the cross; to put to death
Matt 26:2 handed over to be **c-ied.**
Matt 27:22 "**C** him!"
Matt 27:44 who were **c-ied** with him
Mark 15:13 "**C** him!"
Mark 15:27 revolutionaries were **c-ied**
Mark 15:32 who were **c-ied** with Jesus
Mark 16:6 who was **c-ied.**
Luke 23:21 "**C** him! **C** him!"
Luke 23:23 that Jesus be **c-ied,**
Luke 23:33 criminals were also **c-ied**—
Luke 24:20 and they **c-ied** him.
John 19:6 "**C** him! **C** him!"
John 19:10 to release you or **c** you?
John 19:20 where Jesus was **c-ied**
John 19:32 the two men **c-ied** with Jesus.
Acts 4:10 the man you **c-ied**
Rom 6:6 were **c-ied** with Christ
1 Cor 1:13 Was I, Paul, **c-ied** for you?
1 Cor 1:23 preach that Christ was **c-ied,**
1 Cor 2:8 would not have **c-ied**
2 Cor 13:4 he was **c-ied** in weakness,
Gal 5:24 and **c-ied** them there.
Rev 11:8 where their Lord was **c-ied.**

CRUEL (adj)
disposed to inflict pain or suffering; devoid of human feelings
2 Tim 3:3 They will be **c** and hate
1 Pet 2:18 even if they are **c.**

CRUELTY (n)
the quality or state of being cruel; inhuman treatment
Prov 11:17 your **c** will destroy you.

CRUSH, CRUSHED (v)
to squeeze or force by pressure so as to alter or destroy; to oppress or burden grievously
Ps 34:18 whose spirits are **c-ed.**
Prov 31:8 justice for those being **c-ed.**
Isa 42:3 will not **c** the weakest reed
Isa 42:13 and **c** all his enemies.
Isa 53:5 **c-ed** for our sins.
Matt 26:38 My soul is **c-ed** with grief
Luke 10:19 scorpions and **c** them.
Rom 16:20 will soon **c** Satan
2 Cor 1:8 were **c-ed** and overwhelmed
2 Cor 4:8 but we are not **c-ed.**

CRY, CRIES (n)
entreaty, appeal; an inarticulate utterance of distress, rage, or pain

Exod 2:23	their **c** rose up to God.
Ps 5:2	Listen to my **c** for help,
Ps 34:15	open to their **c-ies** for help.
Ps 40:1	and heard my **c.**
Ps 142:6	Hear my **c,** for I am
Prov 21:13	to the **c-ies** of the poor

CRY, CRIED (v)
to shout; to beg or beseech; to shed tears often noisily

Exod 14:10	They **c-ied** out to the LORD,
Josh 24:7	When your ancestors **c-ied** out
Judg 3:9	people of Israel **c-ied** out
Judg 4:3	people of Israel **c-ied** out
Judg 6:6	Then the Israelites **c-ied** out
Judg 10:12	you **c-ied** out to me
Ps 18:6	in my distress I **c-ied** out
Eccl 3:4	A time to **c** and a time
Lam 2:18	**C** aloud before the LORD,
Hab 2:11	walls **c** out against you,

CULTIVATE (v)
to foster the growth of; to encourage

Job 4:8	plant trouble and **c** evil

CUP (n)
a drinking vessel; figurative of human vessel; token of tangible consolation, salvation of Christ, wrath of God, drunkenness, or fate

Ps 23:5	My **c** overflows
Matt 26:39	let this **c** of suffering
Matt 26:42	If this **c** cannot be
Mark 10:39	drink from my bitter **c**
Mark 14:23	And he took a **c** of wine
Mark 14:36	take this **c** of suffering
Luke 22:20	This **c** is the new covenant
John 18:11	from the **c** of suffering
1 Cor 10:16	When we bless the **c**
1 Cor 10:21	from the **c** of the Lord
1 Cor 11:25	took the **c** of wine after
1 Cor 11:25	This **c** is the new covenant

CUP-BEARER (n)
one who tasted and served wine to a king

Gen 40:1	Pharaoh's chief **c**
Neh 1:11	I was the king's **c.**

CURE (n)
recovery or relief from a disease; a complete or permanent solution

Jer 30:15	wound that has no **c?**
Luke 8:43	she could find no **c.**

CURE, CURED (v)
to restore to health, soundness, or normality

Isa 30:26	and **c** the wounds
Matt 11:5	the lepers are **c-d,**
John 5:10	said to the man who was **c-d,**

CURSE, CURSES, CURSING (n)
a condemnation or judgment

Num 5:23	priest will write these **c-s**
Josh 8:34	blessings and **c-s** Moses had
Rom 3:14	full of **c-ing** and bitterness.
Rom 8:20	was subjected to God's **c.**
Gal 3:10	right with God are under his **c,**
Gal 3:13	the **c** for our wrongdoing.
Jas 3:10	and **c-ing** come pouring out
Rev 22:3	No longer will there be a **c**

CURSE, CURSES(v)
to pronounce a sentence; to afflict; to call upon a supernatural power to bring injury upon; to utter profane language against

Gen 8:21	will never again **c** the ground
Gen 12:3	**c** those who treat you
Prov 3:33	**c-s** the house of the wicked,
Matt 5:22	And if you **c** someone,
Rom 12:14	Don't **c** them;
1 Cor 12:3	will **c** Jesus, and no one
Jas 3:9	and sometimes it **c-s** those who

CURSED (adj)
being under or deserving a curse

Gen 3:17	the ground is **c** because
Deut 21:23	anyone who is hung is **c**
Deut 27:16	**C** is anyone who dishonors
Deut 27:18	**C** is anyone who leads
Deut 27:20	**C** is anyone who has sexual
Deut 27:24	**C** is anyone who attacks a
Deut 27:26	**C** is anyone who does not
Prov 28:27	poverty will be **c.**
Gal 3:10	**C** is everyone who does not
Gal 3:13	**C** is everyone who is hung

CURTAIN (n)
a hanging screen usually capable of being drawn back or up

Isa 40:22	the heavens like a **c**
Mark 15:38	And the **c** in the sanctuary

CUT OFF (v)
separated; isolated

Gen 17:14	fails to be circumcised will be **c**
Ps 31:22	"I am **c** from the Lord!"
Prov 21:28	false witness will be **c,** but a
Ezek 21:4	will **c** both the righteous
Hos 10:7	Samaria and its king will be **c**
Zech 13:8	in the land will be **c** and die

Rom 9:3 **c** from Christ!—if that
Gal 5:4 the law, you have been **c**

D

DAILY (adv)
every day
Deut 17:19 read it **d** as long as he
Acts 17:17 spoke **d** in the public square

DAN
1. First son of Jacob and Bilhah (Gen 30:3-6), who gave his name to a tribe of Israel; his tribe was blessed (Gen 49:16-17; Deut 33:22), numbered (Num 1:39), allotted land and cities (Josh 19:40-47); took the town of Laish and renamed it Dan (Judg 18).
2. Town at the northern boundary of Israel (Judg 20:1), earlier known as Laish; captured and renamed by Danites (Josh 19:47); became a center for idolatry (1 Kgs 12:28-30); attacked by Ben-hadad (1 Kgs 15:20).

DANCE, DANCING (n)
a series of rhythmic bodily movements usually performed to music
Ps 30:11 into joyful **d-ing.**
Mark 6:22 a **d** that greatly pleased

DANCE, DANCED (v)
to move in a rhythmic manner, usually to music
2 Sam 6:14 David **d-d** before the LORD
Eccl 3:4 and a time to **d.**
Matt 11:17 and you didn't **d,**

DANGER (n)
harm or damage
Ps 57:1 until the **d** passes by.
Prov 22:3 prudent person foresees **d**
Matt 5:22 in **d** of being brought
Rom 8:35 or in **d,** or threatened
2 Cor 1:10 did rescue us from mortal **d,**
2 Cor 11:26 I have faced **d** from rivers

DANGEROUS (adj)
able or likely to inflict injury or harm
Prov 29:25 Fearing people is a **d** trap,

DANIEL
1. Prophet of Judah (southern kingdom), exiled to Babylon; also called "Belteshazzar" (Dan 1:6-7); refused food of the Babylonian court (Dan 1:8-17); interpreted dreams (Dan 2) and writing on a wall (Dan 5:12-29); survived in lion's den (Dan 6:1-23); recorded visions (Dan 7–12); identified as a hero of renown (Ezek 14:14, 20; 28:3).
2. Son of David (1 Chr 3:1), also called "Kileab" (2 Sam 3:3).

DARK, DARKEST (adj)
devoid or partially devoid of light; wholly or partially black
Exod 20:21 approached the **d** cloud
Ps 23:4 walk through the **d-est** valley,
Song 1:6 because I am **d**—
Song 5:10 My lover is **d** and dazzling,
Joel 2:31 The sun will become **d,**
Acts 2:20 The sun will become **d,**
2 Pet 1:19 lamp shining in a **d** place—

DARKENED (v)
to make dark
Matt 24:29 the sun will be **d,**

DARKNESS (n)
the state of being devoid of light; nightfall; in spiritual terms, secret, closed, blinded, or evil; place of punishment (hell)
Gen 1:2 and **d** covered the deep waters.
Gen 1:4 the light from the **d.**
Ps 18:28 my God, lights up my **d.**
Matt 4:16 people who sat in **d**
Luke 23:44 it was about noon, and **d** fell
John 1:5 light shines in the **d,**
John 3:19 people loved the **d** more
John 12:35 the **d** will not overtake
2 Cor 4:6 Let there be light in the **d,**
2 Cor 6:14 can light live with **d?**
Eph 5:8 once you were full of **d,**
Eph 5:11 deeds of evil and **d;**
1 Pet 2:9 called you out of the **d**
1 Jn 1:5 there is no **d** in him at all.
1 Jn 2:9 is still living in **d.**
Jude 1:6 chained in prisons of **d,**

DARLING (n)
a dearly loved person
Song 2:10 Rise up, my **d!**
Jer 31:20 my son, my **d** child?" says

DAUGHTER, DAUGHTERS (n)
the female offspring or adopted offspring of parents
Gen 19:36 Lot's **d-s** became pregnant
Num 36:10 The **d-s** of Zelophehad
Judg 11:40 the fate of Jephthah's **d.**
Esth 2:7 raised her as his own **d.**
Joel 2:28 sons and **d-s** will prophesy.
Mark 5:34 said to her, "**D,** your faith
Mark 7:29 the demon has left your **d.**

DAVID
King of Israel (united kingdom); son of Jesse, in the family line of Jesus (Ruth 4:17-22; Matt 1:1; Luke 3:31); anointed king (1 Sam 16:1-13); skillful musician to Saul (1 Sam 16:14-23; 18:10); David and Goliath

(1 Sam 17); faithful friendship with Jonathan (1 Sam 18:1-4); envied by Saul; loved by the people (1 Sam 18:5-16); married Michal (1 Sam 18:17-30); wives and children (2 Sam 3:2-5; 5:13-16; 1 Chr 3:1-9); fled from Saul (1 Sam 19–23); ate used "Bread of the Presence" (1 Sam 21:1-6; Matt 12:3-4); dealings with the Philistines (1 Sam 21:10-14; 27–30); spared Saul twice (1 Sam 22–24; 26); married widow Abigail (1 Sam 25:2-42); lamented death of Saul and Jonathan (2 Sam 1); contended with Saul's dynasty (2 Sam 2–4); anointed king of Judah (2 Sam 2:1-7); lamented Abner's death (2 Sam 3:31-39); made king over all Israel (2 Sam 5:1-5); victories over the Philistines (2 Sam 5:17-25; 21:15-22; 1 Chr 14:8-17; 20:4-8); made Jerusalem the royal city (2 Sam 5:6-16); moved Ark to Jerusalem (2 Sam 6); eternal covenant with God (2 Sam 7; 1 Chr 17); showed loyal love to Mephibosheth (2 Sam 9); committed adultery with Bathsheba (2 Sam 11–12; Pss 32; 51); plotted Uriah's death (2 Sam 11:14-25); rebuked by Nathan (2 Sam 12:1-12); repented of affair and intrigue (2 Sam 12:13); rebellion and death of Absalom (2 Sam 14–18); lamented Absalom's death (2 Sam 18:33–19:8); rebellion and death of Sheba (2 Sam 20); judged for taking census (2 Sam 24:1-25); made Solomon next king (1 Kgs 1:28–2:9); final words to Solomon (1 Kgs 2:1-9); died (1 Kgs 2:10-12); preparations for the Temple (1 Chr 22–29).

DAWN (n)
first appearance of light in the morning followed by sunrise

Exod 14:24	But just before **d** the LORD
Ps 37:6	radiate like the **d,** and the
Prov 4:18	gleam of **d,** which shines ever
Prov 31:15	gets up before **d** to prepare
Amos 4:13	the light of **d** into darkness
Acts 20:11	talking to them until **d,**

DAWNS (v)
to begin to grow light as the sun rises

Hos 10:15	day of judgment **d,** the king
2 Pet 1:19	until the Day **d,** and Christ

DAY, DAYS (n)
the time of light between one night and the next; a specified time or period; a 24-hour time period

Gen 1:5	called the light "**d**" and the
Gen 2:2	On the seventh **d** God had
Exod 16:30	any food on the seventh **d.**
Lev 23:28	it is the **D** of Atonement,
Josh 1:8	Meditate on it **d** and night so
2 Kgs 7:9	This is a **d** of good news,
Ps 23:6	all the **d-s** of my life,
Ps 84:10	A single **d** in your
Ps 118:24	This is the **d** the LORD has
Isa 13:9	coming—the terrible **d** of his
Jer 46:10	this is the **d** of the LORD,
Jer 50:31	Your **d** of reckoning
Hos 3:5	In the last **d-s,** they will
Joel 1:15	How terrible that **d** will be!
Joel 2:31	great and terrible **d** of the
Amos 5:20	Yes, the **d** of the LORD
Zeph 1:14	That terrible **d** of the
Zech 14:1	Watch, for the **d** of the LORD
Zech 14:7	there will be continuous **d!**
Mal 4:5	great and dreadful **d** of the
Matt 24:38	In those **d-s** before the
Luke 11:3	Give us each **d** the food we
Acts 2:17	'In the last **d-s,**' God says,
Rom 14:5	some think one **d** is more holy
1 Cor 5:5	be saved on the **d** the Lord
2 Cor 4:16	renewed every **d.**
1 Thes 5:2	the **d** of the Lord's return
1 Thes 5:4	surprised when the **d** of the
2 Thes 2:2	say that the **d** of the Lord
2 Tim 3:1	in the last **d-s** there will be
Heb 1:2	now in these final **d-s,** he has
2 Pet 3:3	in the last **d-s** scoffers will
2 Pet 3:10	But the **d** of the Lord
Rev 16:14	that great judgment **d** of God

DAZZLING (adj)
characterized by shining brilliantly or arousing admiration

Job 37:22	is clothed in **d** splendor.
Song 5:10	My lover is dark and **d,**
Mark 9:3	his clothes became **d** white,

DEACON, DEACONS (n)
a servant; an officer of the church
see also ELDERS

Phil 1:1	the elders and **d-s.**
1 Tim 3:8	**d-s** must be well respected
1 Tim 3:10	they are appointed as **d-s,**
1 Tim 3:12	A **d** must be faithful
1 Tim 3:13	Those who do well as **d-s**

DEAD (n)
Those who have died (physically or spiritually)

Matt 8:22	the spiritually **d** bury their
Luke 24:46	rise from the **d** on the third
1 Cor 15:29	If the **d** will not be raised
Rev 20:12	I saw the **d,** both great and

DEAD (adj)
without (physical or spiritual) life; fatal; useless; unresponsive

Rom 6:11	be **d** to the power of sin
Eph 2:1	Once you were **d** because of
Jas 2:17	good deeds, it is **d** and useless.
1 Pet 2:24	that we can be **d** to sin and
Rev 2:8	Last, who was **d** but is now

DEAF (adj)
lacking or deficient in the sense of hearing
Ps 94:9 Is he **d**—the one who made

DEAR (adj)
highly valued; precious
1 Cor 10:14 my **d** friends, flee from
2 Cor 7:1 these promises, **d** friends,
Eph 5:1 you are his **d** children.
2 Tim 1:2 to Timothy, my **d** son.
Jas 1:16 don't be misled, my **d** brothers
1 Jn 4:4 to God, my **d** children.
3 Jn 1:1 to Gaius, my **d** friend, whom I
Jude 1:20 But you, **d** friends, must

DEATH (n)
the cessation of (physical or spiritual) life; personification and consequence of evil
Exod 21:12 must be put to **d.**
Ruth 1:17 anything but **d** to separate
Prov 11:19 evil people find **d.**
Prov 14:12 it ends in **d.**
Prov 23:14 save them from **d.**
Song 8:6 love is as strong as **d,**
Isa 38:17 have rescued me from **d**
Acts 2:24 for **d** could not keep him
Rom 5:12 brought **d,** so **d** spread to
Rom 6:23 the wages of sin is **d,**
Rom 7:24 dominated by sin and **d?**
1 Cor 15:21 see, just as **d** came into the
1 Cor 15:26 enemy to be destroyed is **d.**
2 Cor 3:6 written covenant ends in **d;**
Gal 3:1 the meaning of Jesus Christ's **d**
2 Tim 1:10 power of **d** and illuminated
Heb 2:14 who had the power of **d.**
Heb 9:17 after the person's **d.**
1 Jn 5:16 there is a sin that leads to **d,**
Rev 2:11 by the second **d.**
Rev 20:6 them the second **d** holds no
Rev 20:14 of fire is the second **d.**
Rev 21:4 be no more **d** or sorrow or
Rev 21:8 This is the second **d.**

DEBATERS (n)
one who contends or argues
1 Cor 1:20 world's brilliant **d?**

DEBAUCHERY (KJV)
Rom 13:13 promiscuity and *immoral living*
2 Cor 12:21 *eagerness for lustful pleasure*
Gal 5:19 impurity, *lustful pleasures*
1 Pet 4:3 their *immorality* and lust, their

DEBT, DEBTS (n)
what is owing; sense of obligation
Deut 15:1 cancel the **d-s** of everyone
Deut 15:3 This release from **d,** however,
Deut 15:9 year for canceling **d-s** is close
1 Sam 22:2 trouble or in **d** or who were
2 Kgs 4:7 pay your **d-s,** and
Neh 10:31 will cancel all **d-s** owed to us.
Prov 22:26 another person's **d** or put up
Matt 18:25 to pay the **d.**
Matt 18:27 and forgave his **d.**
Matt 18:30 in prison until the **d** could
Matt 18:32 you that tremendous **d**
Luke 7:42 canceling their **d-s.**
Luke 7:43 canceled the larger **d.**

DEBTORS (n)
those who owe a debt
Hab 2:7 Suddenly, your **d** will take

DECAY (n)
a wasting or wearing away
Rom 8:21 freedom from death and **d.**
1 Pet 1:4 the reach of change and **d.**

DECAY, DECAYED (v)
to undergo decomposition
Job 19:26 my body has **d-ed,** yet in my
Acts 13:37 whose body did not **d.**

DECEIT (n)
fraud; trickery; lying
Mark 7:22 greed, wickedness, **d,** lustful
Acts 13:10 of every sort of **d** and fraud,
1 Pet 2:1 done with all **d,** hypocrisy,

DECEITFUL (adj)
not honest; misleading, deceptive
Isa 59:13 planning our **d** lies.
2 Cor 11:13 They are **d** workers who

DECEIVE, DECEIVED, DECEIVES, DECEIVING (v)
to lead astray; to cause to accept as true what is false
Gen 3:13 "The serpent **d-d** me," she
Prov 10:31 the tongue that **d-s** will be
Prov 14:8 but fools **d** themselves.
Prov 26:24 but they're **d-ing** you.
Matt 24:24 so as to **d,** if possible, even
Mark 13:6 They will **d** many.
Rom 7:11 those commands and **d-d** me;
Rom 16:18 they **d** innocent people.
1 Cor 3:18 Stop **d-ing** yourselves.
2 Cor 11:3 as Eve was **d-d** by the cunning
Col 2:4 so no one will **d** you with
1 Tim 2:14 The woman was **d-d,** and sin
2 Tim 3:13 They will **d** others and will
2 Tim 3:13 will themselves be **d-d.**
Heb 3:13 you will be **d-d** by sin

Rev 20:3 Satan could not **d** the nations
Rev 20:10 devil, who had **d-d** them, was

DECEIVER, DECEIVERS (n)
one who leads astray; one who causes another to accept as true what is false
Ps 101:7 will not allow **d-s** to serve in
Matt 27:63 remember what that **d** once said
2 Jn 1:7 because many **d-s** have gone
2 Jn 1:7 Such a person is a **d** and an

DECENT (adj)
conforming to the standards of propriety or morality; modest
1 Tim 2:9 should wear **d** and appropriate

DECEPTION (n)
something that deceives; trick; the act of deceiving
Isa 28:15 refuge made of lies and **d.**
Dan 8:25 He will be a master of **d**
Rom 1:29 quarreling, **d,** malicious
Eph 4:22 corrupted by lust and **d.**
2 Thes 2:10 kind of evil **d** to fool those
1 Jn 4:6 truth or spirit of **d.**

DECEPTIVE (adj)
tending or having power to deceive; misleading
Prov 31:30 Charm is **d,** and beauty
1 Tim 4:1 will follow **d** spirits and

DECIDE, DECIDED, DECIDES (v)
to make a final choice or judgment about; to select as a course of action
1 Sam 14:7 whatever you **d.**
Job 14:5 You have **d-d** the length of
Ps 75:7 he **d-s** who will rise and
Rom 14:13 **D** instead to live
Rom 14:22 they have **d-d** is right.
1 Cor 2:2 For I **d-d** that while I
1 Cor 6:2 can't you **d** even these
1 Cor 12:11 He alone **d-s** which gift
2 Cor 9:7 You must each **d** in your heart

DECISION, DECISIONS (n)
a determination arrived at after consideration; conclusion
Joel 3:14 waiting in the valley of **d.**
Mic 3:11 You rulers make **d-s** based on
Rom 11:33 to understand his **d-s** and his

DECLARE, DECLARED, DECLARING (v)
to make known formally, officially, or explicitly; to state emphatically, affirm; to make evident, show
Deut 25:1 and the judges **d** that one is
Ps 71:8 praising you; I **d** your glory
Ps 92:15 They will **d,** "The LORD

Prov 31:31 deeds publicly **d** her praise.
Dan 4:24 what the Most High has **d-d**
Mark 7:19 saying this, he **d-d** that every
Acts 20:27 didn't shrink from **d-ing** all
Rom 4:6 who are **d-d** righteous without
Heb 3:1 Jesus whom we **d** to be God's

DECREE, DECREES (n)
an order usually having the force of law; a foreordaining will
Exod 15:25 them the following **d**
Exod 15:26 and keeping all his **d-s,** then I
Exod 18:20 Teach them God's **d-s,**
Lev 18:4 to obey my **d-s,** for I am the
Num 15:15 to the same **d-s.**
Deut 4:1 to these **d-s** and regulations
1 Kgs 3:3 and followed all the **d-s** of his
1 Chr 16:17 it to Jacob as a **d,**
Ps 2:7 proclaims the LORD's **d:**
Ps 119:12 LORD; teach me your **d-s.**
Ps 119:54 Your **d-s** have
Ps 148:6 His **d** will never be

DECREED (v)
to determine or order judicially; to command by or as if by decree
Dan 9:24 sets of seven has been **d**
Luke 2:1 Augustus, **d** that a census

DEDICATE, DEDICATED (v)
to devote to the worship of a divine being; to set apart to a definite use
see also CONSECRATE, DEVOTE, ORDAINED
Exod 13:2 **D** to me every firstborn
Num 6:9 the hair they have **d-d** will be
Num 6:18 the hair that had been **d-d**
Num 18:6 a gift to you, **d-d** to the LORD
1 Kgs 8:63 Israel **d-d** the Temple
Neh 3:1 which they **d-d,** and the Tower
Luke 2:23 he must be **d-d** to the LORD.

DEDICATION (n)
an act or rite of dedicating to a diving being or to sacred use
John 10:22 the Festival of **D.**

DEED, DEEDS (n)
a signed instrument containing some legal transfer, bargain, or contract; a usually illustrious act or action; feat, exploit
see also WORKS
Ps 45:4 perform awe-inspiring **d-s!**
Ps 66:3 awesome are your **d-s!**
Ps 71:24 your righteous **d-s** all day
Ps 88:12 your wonderful **d-s?**
Ps 96:3 his glorious **d-s** among the

Ps 105:2 his wonderful **d-s.**
Prov 31:31 Let her **d-s** publicly declare
Isa 64:6 our righteous **d-s,** they are
Jer 32:10 and sealed the **d** of purchase
Matt 5:16 let your good **d-s** shine out for
Rom 4:2 If his good **d-s** had made him
2 Cor 9:9 Their good **d-s** will be
Col 3:9 all its wicked **d-s.**
Jas 2:18 my faith by my good **d-s.**
Jas 2:20 without good **d-s** is useless?

DEEP, DEEPER (adj)
extending far downward from some surface or area; situated well within the boundaries; difficult to penetrate or comprehend
Gen 1:2 covered the **d** waters.
Rom 6:19 which led ever **d-er** into sin.
1 Cor 2:10 shows us God's **d** secrets.

DEEPLY (adv)
in an intense, profound manner
Ps 116:15 The LORD cares **d**
Isa 66:11 Drink **d** of her glory

DEER (n)
a mammal with usually brownish fur and antlers borne by the males
Ps 42:1 As the **d** longs for streams of

DEFEAT (n)
an overthrow especially of an army in battle; loss, destruction
Ps 25:2 enemies rejoice in my **d.**
1 Cor 6:7 with one another is a **d**

DEFEAT, DEFEATED, DEFEATS (v)
to destroy; to win victory over
Ps 129:2 they have never **d-d** me.
1 Jn 5:4 child of God **d-s** this evil
Rev 12:11 And they have **d-d** him by the
Rev 17:14 the Lamb will **d** them

DEFEND, DEFENDING, DEFENDS (v)
to maintain or support in the face of argument or hostile criticism; to drive danger or attack away from
Deut 33:7 strength to **d** their cause;
Ps 10:14 You **d** the orphans.
Ps 34:7 he surrounds and **d-s** all who
Ps 72:4 Help him to **d** the poor,
Ps 106:8 saved them—to **d** the honor of
Phil 1:7 and in **d-ing** and confirming
Phil 1:16 been appointed to **d** the Good
Jude 1:3 urging you to **d** the faith

DEFENDER (n)
one who guards and protects
Ps 68:5 the fatherless, **d** of widows—
Prov 22:23 the LORD is their **d.**
Isa 51:22 your God and **D,** says:

DEFENSE (n)
the act of defending
Ps 35:23 Rise to my **d!**

DEFILE, DEFILED, DEFILING (v)
to make unclean—either physically, sexually, ethically, or ceremonially
Num 6:7 must not **d** themselves,
Num 15:39 desires and **d-ing** yourselves,
Ezek 23:7 idols and **d-ing** herself.
Ezek 44:7 In this way, you **d-d** my Temple
Matt 15:11 you are **d-d** by the words
Mark 7:23 they are what **d** you.
Acts 21:28 even **d-s** this holy place
2 Cor 7:1 that can **d** our body or

DEFLECTS (v)
to turn aside; deviate
Prov 15:1 A gentle answer **d** anger,

DEFY, DEFIED, DEFYING (v)
to challenge to combat, dare; to disregard
1 Sam 17:10 I **d** the armies of Israel
1 Sam 17:45 whom you have **d-ied.**
Isa 37:23 Whom have you been **d-ing**

DELAY (n)
the state of being delayed; putting off; wait
Rev 10:6 There will be no more **d.**

DELAY, DELAYED (v)
to put off; to postpone
Eccl 5:4 don't **d** in following through,
Matt 25:5 the bridegroom was **d-ed,**
Heb 10:37 will come and not **d.**

DELIBERATE (adj)
characterized by awareness of the consequences
Ps 19:13 servant from **d** sins!

DELICACIES (n)
indulgences; something pleasing to eat that is considered rare or luxurious
Ps 141:4 share in the **d** of those who
Prov 23:6 don't desire their **d.**

DELIGHT, DELIGHTS (n)
source of great pleasure; joy
Ps 36:8 your river of **d-s.**
Ps 40:6 You take no **d** in sacrifices
Ps 119:111 they are my heart's **d.**
Prov 8:30 I was his constant **d,**

Isa 58:13	and speak of it with **d**
Jer 15:16	my joy and my heart's **d,**
Mal 3:12	your land will be such a **d,**
Mark 12:37	to him with great **d.**

DELIGHT, DELIGHTED, DELIGHTING, DELIGHTS (v)

to enjoy

Exod 4:14	He will be **d-ed** to see you.
2 Sam 22:20	because he **d-s** in me.
Ps 1:2	But they **d** in the law of
Ps 18:19	he rescued me because he **d-s**
Ps 27:4	**d-ing** in the LORD's
Ps 37:4	Take **d** in the LORD,
Ps 119:70	I **d** in your instructions.
Prov 3:12	a child in whom he **d-s.**
Prov 11:1	he **d-s** in accurate weights.
Prov 11:20	he **d-s** in those with integrity.
Song 8:10	he is **d-ed** with what he sees.
Isa 11:3	He will **d** in obeying
Isa 65:19	and **d** in my people.
Isa 66:3	**d-ing** in their detestable sins—
Jer 9:24	I **d** in these things.

DELIGHTFUL (adj)

highly pleasing

Prov 3:17	guide you down **d** paths;
Song 2:3	sit in his **d** shade and taste

DELIVER (v)

to save, liberate, set free from

Ps 82:4	**d** them from the grasp of evil
2 Tim 4:18	**d** me from every evil attack

DELIVERANCE (n)

freedom from harm, salvation

Esth 4:14	**d** and relief for the Jews will arise
Isa 51:1	"Listen to me, all who hope for **d**
Phil 1:19	this will lead to my **d.**

DEMON-POSSESSED (adj)

characterized by the possession or control of demons

Matt 4:24	if they were **d** or epileptic
Matt 8:16	That evening many **d** people
Matt 8:33	happened to the **d** men.
Matt 9:32	When they left, a **d** man who
Matt 12:22	Then a **d** man, who was
Mark 1:32	many sick and **d** people were
Mark 5:16	about the **d** man and
Luke 8:36	others how the **d** man had

DEMON, DEMONS (n)

an agent of the Devil; an evil spirit

Deut 32:17	They offered sacrifices to **d-s,**
Matt 8:31	So the **d-s** begged, "If you cast
Matt 9:34	by the prince of **d-s.**
Matt 11:18	He's possessed by a **d.**
Matt 12:24	he can cast out **d-s.**
Matt 12:28	if I am casting out **d-s** by the
Matt 17:18	Jesus rebuked the **d**
Mark 1:34	But because the **d-s** knew who
Mark 5:15	by the legion of **d-s.**
Mark 5:18	been **d** possessed begged
Mark 7:29	the **d** has left your daughter.
Mark 9:38	to cast out **d-s,** but we told
Mark 16:9	cast out seven **d-s.**
Mark 16:17	will cast out **d-s** in my name,
Luke 4:33	possessed by a **d**—an evil
Luke 7:33	He's possessed by a **d.**
Luke 8:2	he had cast out seven **d-s;**
Luke 8:30	with many **d-s.**
Luke 8:33	Then the **d-s** came out of the
Luke 8:38	freed from the **d-s** begged
Luke 9:49	to cast out **d-s,** but we told
Luke 10:17	Lord, even the **d-s** obey us
Luke 11:14	Jesus cast out a **d** from
Luke 11:19	They cast out **d-s,** too, so they
Luke 11:20	casting out **d-s** by the power
John 8:49	Jesus said, "I have no **d** in me.
John 10:21	possessed by a **d!**
Rom 8:38	neither angels nor **d-s,**
1 Cor 10:20	to participate with **d-s.**
1 Cor 10:21	the cup of **d-s,** too.
1 Cor 10:21	the table of **d-s,** too.
1 Tim 4:1	teachings that come from **d-s.**
Rev 9:20	to worship **d-s** and idols made
Rev 18:2	become a home for **d-s.**

DEMONIC (adj)

of, relating to, or suggestive of a demon

Jas 3:15	unspiritual, and **d.**
Rev 16:14	They are **d** spirits who work

DEMONSTRATE (v)

to show clearly

Ezek 39:21	**d** my glory to the nations.
Rom 3:26	to **d** his righteousness,

DEN (n)

the lair of a wild, usually predatory, animal; a center of secret activity

Dan 6:16	thrown into the **d** of lions.
Matt 21:13	into a **d** of thieves!

DENY, DENIED, DENIES (v)

to disavow or refuse to accept as true; to refuse to grant

Exod 23:6	you must not **d** justice to the
Deut 27:19	is anyone who **d-ies** justice
Prov 30:9	I may **d** you and say,
Matt 10:33	everyone who **d-ies** me
Matt 26:35	I will never **d** you!

Matt 26:70 But Peter **d-ied** it
Luke 12:9 anyone who **d-ies** me
Luke 22:34 you will **d** three times
John 18:25 He **d-ied** it, saying,
Acts 4:16 We can't **d** that they
1 Tim 5:8 have **d-ied** the true faith.
2 Tim 2:12 **d** him, he will **d** us.
Titus 1:16 **d** him by the way they live.
2 Pet 2:1 and even **d** the Master who
1 Jn 2:22 Anyone who **d-ies** the Father
1 Jn 2:23 Anyone who **d-ies** the Son
Jude 1:4 they have **d-ied** our only Master
Rev 3:8 and did not **d** me.

DEPEND (v)
to place reliance or trust
Prov 3:5 do not **d** on your own
Jer 49:11 widows, too, can **d** on me
Gal 3:10 But those who **d** on the law

DEPOSIT (v)
to place especially for safekeeping
Matt 25:27 why didn't you **d** my money in

DEPRAVED (adj)
characterized by moral corruption or evil; perverted
2 Tim 3:8 They have **d** minds and

DEPRESSION (n)
a state of feeling sad; dejection
Ps 143:7 answer me, for my **d** deepens.

DEPRIVE (v)
to withhold something from; to remove
Isa 10:2 They **d** the poor
1 Cor 7:5 Do not **d** each other of

DEPTHS (n)
a deep place in a body of water; the quality of being deep
Ps 130:1 From the **d** of despair,
Mic 7:19 them into the **d** of the ocean!

DESCENDANT, DESCENDANTS (n)
those who came or originated from; offspring, children
see also OFFSPRING, SON(S)
Gen 12:7 give this land to your **d-s.**
Gen 13:16 will give you so many **d-s** that,
Gen 17:9 You and all your **d-s** have this
Deut 30:19 you and your **d-s** might live!
Isa 53:8 he died without **d-s,** that his
Isa 53:10 he will have many **d-s.**
Jer 23:5 I will raise up a righteous **d**
Matt 1:1 the Messiah, a **d** of David and
Acts 3:25 Through your **d-s** all the
Rom 4:18 That's how many **d-s** you will
Rom 9:8 Abraham's physical **d-s** are not

DESCEND, DESCENDED, DESCENDING (v)
to pass from a higher place or level to a lower one
Matt 3:16 Spirit of God **d-ing** like a dove
Mark 1:10 the Holy Spirit **d-ing** on him
Eph 4:9 that Christ also **d-ed** to our

DESECRATE, DESECRATED (v)
to profane something holy or treat it with contempt
Neh 13:18 Sabbath to be **d-d** in this way!
Isa 56:6 and do not **d** the Sabbath day

DESECRATION (n)
violation of something sacred; profanation; blasphemy
Dan 11:31 object that causes **d.**
Dan 12:11 object that causes **d** is set
Matt 24:15 causes **d** standing in the

DESERT, DESERTS (n)
arid land with usually sparse vegetation
see also WILDERNESS
Prov 21:19 better to live alone in the **d**
Isa 32:2 like streams of water in the **d**
Isa 43:20 giving them water in the **d.**
2 Cor 11:26 cities, in the **d-s,** and on the

DESERTED (v)
to abandon
Matt 26:56 all the disciples **d** him and
2 Tim 1:15 of Asia has **d** me—even

DESERVE, DESERVED, DESERVES (v)
to be worthy, fit, or suitable for some reward or requital; to merit
Judg 9:16 the honor he **d-s** for all he
2 Sam 12:5 do such a thing **d-s** to die!
Neh 9:33 gave us only what we **d-d.**
Ps 103:10 with us, as we **d.**
Prov 14:14 Backsliders get what they **d;**
Dan 9:18 not because we **d** help,
Zech 1:6 received what we **d-d** from the
Luke 7:4 If anyone **d-s** your help,
Acts 26:31 done anything to **d** death or
Rom 3:8 who say such things **d** to be
Rom 11:9 get what they **d.**
2 Cor 11:15 their wicked deeds **d.**
1 Tim 5:18 Those who work **d** their pay!
Heb 3:3 But Jesus **d-s** far more

DESIRABLE (adj)
attractive; worth seeking or doing
Ps 19:10 They are more **d** than gold,

DUST (n)
specks or clumps of earthy matter; ground or earth

Gen 2:7	man from the **d** of the ground.
Gen 3:19	were made from **d**, and to **d**
Ps 22:15	laid me in the **d** and left me
Eccl 3:20	they return to **d.**
Matt 10:14	shake its **d** from your feet
1 Cor 15:47	from the **d** of the earth,

DUTY, DUTIES (n)
moral or legal obligation; assigned service or task

Eccl 8:3	to avoid doing your **d,**
Eccl 12:13	is everyone's **d.**
Dan 8:27	performed my **d-ies** for the

DWELLING (n)
a shelter (as a house) in which one lives; residence
see also HOME, HOUSE

Exod 15:17	your own **d,** the sanctuary,
Eph 2:22	made part of this **d** where God

DWELLS (v)
to stay for a time; to live as a resident
see also LIVE(S)

Ps 26:8	glorious presence **d.**

DYING (v)
see also DIE

John 11:25	even after **d.**
2 Cor 4:16	our bodies are **d,** our spirits
Phil 1:21	for Christ, and **d** is even

DYNASTY (n)
a succession of rulers of the same line of descent
see also HOUSE

2 Sam 3:1	Saul's **d** became weaker and
1 Chr 17:17	your servant a lasting **d!**

E

EAGER (adj)
marked by enthusiastic or impatient desire or interest

Rom 15:23	I am **e** to visit you.
1 Cor 14:39	sisters, be **e** to prophesy,
1 Pet 5:2	because you are **e** to serve

EAGERLY (adv)
in an enthusiastic or impatient manner

Rom 8:19	creation is waiting **e** for that

EAGERNESS (n)
the state or quality of enthusiasm for a desire or interest

Ps 119:36	Give me an **e** for your laws

EAGLE, EAGLES (n)
any of various large diurnal birds of prey noted for their strength, size, keenness of vision, and powers of flight

Deut 32:11	Like an **e** that rouses her chicks
Isa 40:31	soar high on wings like **e-s.**
Rev 4:7	was like an **e** in flight.
Rev 12:14	wings like those of a great **e**

EARN, EARNED (v)
to receive as return for effort or work done

2 Thes 3:12	**e** their own living.
Heb 11:2	**e-ed** a good reputation.

EARNEST (adj)
characterized by or proceeding from an intense and serious state of mind; ardent or fervent

Jas 5:16	The **e** prayer of a righteous
1 Pet 4:7	be **e** and disciplined

EARNESTLY (adv)
in a manner that is intense and serious; fervently

2 Chr 15:15	they **e** sought after God,
Col 4:12	He always prays **e** for you,

EARNINGS (n)
pay; wages

Prov 31:16	with her **e** she plants a vineyard.

EARRING, EARRINGS (n)
an ornament for the ear and especially the earlobe

Exod 35:22	gold—brooches, **e-s,** rings
Prov 25:12	valid criticism is like a gold **e**

EARS (n)
the external organ for hearing, expressing the entire faculty of understanding

Prov 2:2	Tune your **e** to wisdom,
Eccl 5:1	**e** open and your mouth shut.
2 Tim 4:3	whatever their itching **e** want

EARTH (n)
The ground; the planet on which we live

Gen 1:1	created the heavens and the **e.**
Gen 7:24	floodwaters covered the **e**
Gen 14:19	Creator of heaven and **e.**
Job 26:7	and hangs the **e** on nothing.
Job 38:4	I laid the foundations of the **e?**
Ps 24:1	The **e** is the Lord's, and
Ps 108:5	your glory shine over all the **e.**
Prov 8:23	first, before the **e** began.
Prov 8:26	had made the **e** and fields
Isa 6:3	whole **e** is filled with his glory!
Isa 40:22	God sits above the circle of the **e.**
Isa 44:23	O depths of the **e!**
Isa 55:9	higher than the **e,** so my ways

Isa 65:17 new heavens and a new **e,**
Isa 66:1 and the **e** is my footstool.
Jer 23:24 in all the heavens and **e?**
Hab 2:20 Let all the **e** be silent
Matt 5:18 until heaven and **e** disappear,
Matt 5:35 do not say, 'By the **e**!'
Matt 6:10 your will be done on **e,**
Matt 16:19 Whatever you forbid on **e**
Matt 28:18 in heaven and on **e.**
Luke 2:14 and peace on **e**
Acts 4:24 Creator of heaven and **e,**
Acts 7:49 the **e** is my footstool.
Rom 8:39 or in the **e** below—
1 Cor 10:26 the **e** is the Lord's,
Eph 3:15 in heaven and on **e.**
Phil 2:10 in heaven and on **e** and under
Col 3:2 not the things of **e.**
Heb 1:10 laid the foundation of the **e**
2 Pet 3:13 and new **e** he has promised,
Rev 20:11 The **e** and sky fled
Rev 21:1 a new heaven and a new **e,**
Rev 21:1 the old **e** had disappeared.

EARTHLY (adj)
belonging to the earth; mundane or worldly; temporal or temporary; human
Rom 1:3 In his **e** life he was born
Col 3:5 put to death the sinful, **e** things

EARTHQUAKE, EARTHQUAKES (n)
a shaking or trembling of the earth
Matt 24:7 There will be famines and **e-s**
Matt 28:2 there was a great **e!**
Rev 6:12 there was a great **e.**

EAST (n)
the general direction of the sunrise
Gen 2:8 a garden in Eden in the **e,**
Ps 103:12 far from us as the **e** is from

EASTERN (adj)
coming from the east
Matt 2:1 wise men from **e** lands arrived

EASY (adj)
causing or involving little difficulty or discomfort
Matt 11:30 For my yoke is **e** to bear,

EAT, EATEN, EATING, EATS (v)
to ingest, chew, and swallow in turn
see also ATE
Gen 2:16 You may freely **e** the fruit
Gen 3:11 Have you **e-en** from the tree
Deut 14:4 the animals you may **e:**
Isa 65:25 The lion will **e** hay
Jer 31:29 parents have **e-en** sour grapes,
Matt 26:26 Take this and **e** it,
Luke 15:2 sinful people—even **e-ing** with
John 6:52 give us his flesh to **e?**
John 6:54 anyone who **e-s** my flesh and
Acts 10:13 "Get up, Peter; kill and **e** them.
Acts 10:14 I have never **e-en** anything
Rom 14:15 Don't let your **e-ing** ruin
1 Cor 8:4 So, what about **e-ing** meat that
1 Cor 8:10 **e-ing** in the temple of an idol,
1 Cor 10:31 So whether you **e** or drink,
1 Cor 11:26 every time you **e** this bread
1 Cor 11:27 anyone who **e-s** this bread or

EDEN (n)
the garden where Adam and Eve first lived
Gen 2:8 a garden in **E** in the east,
Ezek 28:13 in **E,** the garden of God.

EDIFY, EDIFYING (KJV)
1 Cor 10:23 but not everything is *beneficial*
1 Cor 14:5 will be *strengthened*
1 Cor 14:17 won't *strengthen* the people
Eph 4:12 work and *build up* the church,

EFFORT, EFFORTS (n)
conscious exertion of power; hard work; a serious attempt
2 Chr 31:21 **e-s** to follow God's laws
Ps 90:17 make our **e-s** successful.
Gal 3:3 by your own human **e?**
Eph 4:3 Make every **e** to keep
2 Pet 1:5 make every **e** to respond
2 Pet 3:14 make every **e** to be found

EGYPT (n)
the country in the northeast corner of Africa that extended from the Mediterranean Sea on the north to the Nile River on the south
Gen 46:6 his entire family went to **E—**
Exod 3:11 people of Israel out of **E?**
Exod 12:40 Israel had lived in **E**
Hos 11:1 I called my son out of **E.**
Matt 2:15 I called my Son out of **E.**
Heb 11:27 Moses left the land of **E,**

ELDER, ELDERS (n)
older, wise man; ruling body of decision makers invested with authority by virtue of their age, character, or experience
see also DEACONS
Acts 14:23 appointed **e-s** in every church.
Acts 15:2 talk to the apostles and **e-s**
Acts 20:17 a message to the **e-s** of the
Acts 20:28 appointed you as **e-s.**
Phil 1:1 including the **e-s** and deacons.
1 Tim 3:1 aspires to be an **e,** he desires

1 Tim 3:2	**e** must be a man whose life is
1 Tim 4:14	**e-s** of the church laid their
1 Tim 5:19	against an **e** unless it is
Titus 1:6	An **e** must live a blameless life.
Titus 1:7	An **e** is a manager of God's
Jas 5:14	call for the **e-s** of the church
1 Pet 5:1	a word to you who are **e-s**
1 Pet 5:1	I, too, am an **e** and a witness
1 Pet 5:5	the authority of the **e-s.**
2 Jn 1:1	letter is from John, the **e.**
3 Jn 1:1	letter is from John, the **e.**
Rev 4:10	the twenty-four **e-s** fall down

ELDERLY (n)
people of advanced age

Lev 19:32	the **e,** and show respect

ELECT (KJV)

Isa 42:1	*chosen one,* who pleases me
Matt 24:31	gather his *chosen ones* from all
Rom 8:33	*us whom God has chosen* for
Col 3:12	*chose* you to be the holy people
2 Tim 2:10	Jesus to *those God has chosen*

ELEMENTS (n)
any of four substances air, water, fire, and earth

2 Pet 3:10	the very **e** themselves
2 Pet 3:12	the **e** will melt away

ELIJAH
Powerful prophet in Israel (northern kingdom); proclaimed drought (1 Kgs 17:1; Jas 5:17); hid and was fed by ravens (1 Kgs 17:2-6); performed miracles for widow (1 Kgs 17:8-24; Luke 4:25); proclaimed truth to King Ahab (1 Kgs 18:1-15); defeated Baal and his prophets on Mount Carmel (1 Kgs 18:16-40); brought rain (1 Kgs 18:41-46; Jas 5:17); ran for his life (1 Kgs 19:3); served by angels (1 Kgs 19:1-9); given assurance by God (1 Kgs 19:9-18); put mantle on Elisha (1 Kgs 19:19-21); condemned by Ahab (1 Kgs 21:17-29); whirlwind and fire took him into heaven (2 Kgs 2:11); return prophesied and expected (Mal 4:5-6; Matt 11:14; Luke 1:17; John 1:25); compared to John the Baptist (Matt 17:9-13; Mark 9:9-13; Luke 1:17); appeared at Jesus' Transfiguration (Matt 17:1-8; Mark 9:1-8).

ELISHA
Powerful prophet in Israel (northern kingdom) who replaced Elijah (1 Kgs 19:16-21); inherited Elijah's cloak (2 Kgs 2:1-18); asked for double measure of spirit (2 Kgs 2:9); witnessed Elijah's departure (2 Kgs 2:11-12); healed bad water (2 Kgs 2:19-22); cursed 42 mockers (2 Kgs 2:23-25); prophesied victory over Moab (2 Kgs 3:11-27); provided abundant oil for widow (2 Kgs 4:1-7); raised child to life (2 Kgs 4:32-37); made stew edible (2 Kgs 4:38-41); fed a multitude with few loaves (2 Kgs 4:42-44); healed Naaman's leprosy (2 Kgs 5:14-15); made an ax head float (2 Kgs 6:1-7); prophesied the availability of food (2 Kgs 7:1); prophesied death of Ben-hadad (2 Kgs 8:7-15); died (2 Kgs 13:20); bones produced miracle after death (2 Kgs 13:21).

ELIZABETH
Mother of John the Baptist, cousin of Mary the mother of Jesus (Luke 1:5-66).

EMBARRASSED (v)
to become anxiously self-conscious

Luke 14:9	you will be **e,** and you will

EMBARRASSMENT (n)
the state of being anxiously self-conscious

2 Cor 9:4	not to mention your own **e**—

EMPLOYER (n)
one who provides with a job that pays wages

Luke 16:5	owed money to his **e** to come

EMPOWER, EMPOWERED (v)
to give official authority or legal power to; to enable

Luke 11:18	You say I am **e-ed** by Satan.
Eph 3:16	resources he will **e** you with

EMPTINESS (n)
a void; containing nothing

Job 15:31	for **e** will be their only
Isa 40:17	nothing—mere **e** and froth

EMPTY (adj)
containing nothing; having no purpose or result; destitute of effect or force

Gen 1:2	formless and **e,** and darkness
Deut 32:47	not **e** words—they are your life!
Job 26:7	the northern sky over **e** space
Isa 45:18	not to be a place of **e** chaos.
Jer 4:23	and it was **e** and formless.
Luke 1:53	the rich away with **e** hands.
1 Cor 14:9	be talking into **e** space.
1 Pet 1:18	to save you from the **e** life
2 Pet 2:18	with **e,** foolish boasting.

EMPTY-HANDED (adj)
having, bringing, or gaining nothing

Eccl 5:15	as naked and **e** as on the day

ENABLE, ENABLED (v)
to make possible, provide an opportunity for

2 Cor 3:6	**e-ed** us to be ministers of his
2 Thes 1:11	to **e** you to live a life worthy
2 Pet 1:4	**e** you to share his divine

ENCOURAGE, ENCOURAGED, ENCOURAGES, ENCOURAGING (v)
to inspire with courage or hope; to spur on
Isa 41:7 The carver **e-s** the goldsmith,
Acts 11:23 and he **e-d** the believers
Acts 15:32 length to the believers, **e-ing**
Acts 20:1 sent for the believers and **e-d**
Acts 28:15 he was **e-d** and thanked God.
Rom 1:12 I also want to be **e-d** by yours.
Rom 12:8 your gift is to **e** others,
1 Cor 8:12 other believers by **e-ing**
1 Cor 14:3 strengthens others, **e-s** them,
2 Cor 7:6 who **e-s** those who are
2 Cor 7:6 **e-d** us by the arrival of Titus.
2 Cor 7:13 have been greatly **e-d** by this.
Eph 6:22 how we are doing and to **e**
Col 4:8 how we are doing and to **e** you.
1 Thes 2:12 pleaded with you, **e-d** you,
1 Thes 3:2 to strengthen you, to **e** you
1 Thes 3:7 we have been greatly **e-d** in
1 Thes 5:11 So **e** each other and build
1 Thes 5:14 **E** those who are timid.
Titus 1:9 he will be able to **e** others
Heb 12:5 you forgotten the **e-ing** words
1 Pet 5:12 purpose in writing is to **e** you
2 Jn 1:11 Anyone who **e-s** such people

ENCOURAGEMENT (n)
the act of encouraging; the state of being encouraged
Rom 15:5 who gives this patience and **e,**
1 Cor 16:18 a wonderful **e** to me,
2 Cor 7:13 In addition to our own **e,**
Eph 4:29 an **e** to those who hear them.
Phil 2:1 any **e** from belonging to Christ?
Phlm 1:20 Give me this **e** in Christ.

END, ENDS (n)
the point where something ceases to exist; death and destruction; the goal or result toward which some action or agent is heading
Ps 65:8 live at the **e-s** of the earth stand
Eccl 3:11 work from beginning to **e.**
Isa 30:8 stand until the **e** of time
Isa 49:6 bring my salvation to the **e-s**
Matt 24:13 the one who endures to the **e**
Matt 24:14 and then the **e** will come.
Matt 24:31 farthest **e-s** of the earth
1 Cor 15:24 After that the **e** will come,
Phil 3:14 press on to reach the **e** of
Rev 21:6 the Beginning and the **E.**
Rev 22:13 the Beginning and the **E.**

END, ENDING, ENDS (v)
to come to an end; to die
1 Sam 12:23 sin against the LORD by **e-ing**
Prov 14:12 but it **e-s** in death.
Prov 14:13 the laughter **e-s,** the grief
Prov 29:23 Pride **e-s** in humiliation,
Isa 9:7 its peace will never **e.**
Eph 2:15 by **e-ing** the system of law

ENDANGER (v)
to bring into danger or peril
Prov 22:25 be like them and **e** your soul.

ENDLESS (adj)
being or seeming to be without end
Eccl 12:12 writing books is **e,**
Amos 5:24 an **e** river of righteous
Eph 3:8 the **e** treasures available

ENDURANCE (n)
the ability to withstand hardship or adversity
see also PERSEVERANCE
Rom 5:3 they help us develop **e.**
Col 1:11 have all the **e** and patience
2 Thes 1:4 your **e** and faithfulness
Heb 12:1 let us run with **e** the race
Jas 1:3 your faith is tested, your **e**
2 Pet 1:6 self-control with patient **e,**
Rev 1:9 in the patient **e** to which Jesus

ENDURE, ENDURED, ENDURES, ENDURING (v)
to withstand, suffer, or persevere
see also PERSEVERE
Ps 89:2 Your faithfulness is as **e-ing** as
Ps 136:1 faithful love **e-s** forever.
Matt 10:22 everyone who **e-s** to the end
Mark 13:13 one who **e-s** to the end
1 Cor 13:7 **e-s** through every
2 Cor 1:6 Then you can patiently **e**
2 Cor 6:4 patiently **e** troubles and
2 Tim 2:3 **E** suffering along with me,
2 Tim 2:12 If we **e** hardship,
2 Tim 3:11 suffering I have **e-d.**
Heb 12:2 he **e-d** the cross,
Heb 12:3 hostility he **e-d** from sinful
Heb 12:7 As you **e** this divine discipline,
Jas 1:12 who patiently **e** testing and
Jas 5:11 those who **e** under suffering.
1 Pet 2:19 patiently **e** unfair treatment.
Rev 13:10 must **e** persecution patiently

ENEMY, ENEMIES (n)
foe—personal, national, or spiritual
Ps 23:5 the presence of my **e-ies.**
Ps 62:7 rock where no **e** can reach me.
Prov 16:7 even their **e-ies** are at peace
Prov 24:17 rejoice when your **e-ies** fall;
Prov 25:21 If your **e-ies** are hungry,
Prov 27:6 than many kisses from an **e.**

Isa 51:13 fear the anger of your **e-ies?**
Isa 59:18 repay his **e-ies** for their evil
Matt 5:44 love your **e-ies!** Pray for those
Luke 6:35 Love your **e-ies!** Do good to
Luke 10:19 over all the power of the **e,**
Rom 5:10 while we were still his **e-ies,**
Rom 12:20 If your **e-ies** are hungry,
1 Cor 15:25 until he humbles all his **e-ies**
1 Cor 15:26 the last **e** to be destroyed
Phil 3:18 they are really **e-ies** of the cross
Jas 4:4 makes you an **e** of God?
1 Pet 5:8 Watch out for your great **e,**

ENERGY (n)
vigorous exertion of power; effort
Ezra 5:8 with great **e** and success.
John 6:27 your **e** seeking the eternal

ENGAGED (adj)
pledged to be married; betrothed
Matt 1:18 His mother, Mary, was **e** to

ENGAGEMENT (n)
a pledge to marry; betrothal
Matt 1:19 to break the **e** quietly.

ENJOY, ENJOYED, ENJOYING (v)
to have a good time; to experience; to take pleasure in
see also HAPPY, JOY
Deut 6:2 you will **e** a long life.
Neh 9:25 grew fat and **e-ed** themselves
Eccl 5:19 good health to **e** it.
Eccl 5:20 so busy **e-ing** life that
Eccl 8:15 eat, drink, and **e** life.
2 Tim 2:6 the first to **e** the fruit
Heb 11:25 **e-ing** the fleeting pleasures
1 Pet 3:10 If you want to **e** life

ENJOYABLE (adj)
of or relating to having a good time; pleasurable
Heb 12:11 No discipline is **e** while

ENJOYMENT (n)
an attitude, circumstance, or favorable response to a stimulus that tends to make one gratified or happy; delight; joy
1 Tim 6:17 all we need for our **e.**

ENQUIRE (KJV)
1 Sam 28:7 a medium, so I can go and *ask*
2 Kgs 1:2 the god of Ekron, to *ask*

ENRICH, ENRICHED (v)
to make rich or richer; to enhance
Prov 31:11 she will greatly **e** his life.
2 Cor 9:11 you will be **e-ed** in every way

ENSLAVE, ENSLAVED (v)
to reduce to slavery; to subjugate
Gal 2:4 wanted to **e** us and force us
2 Pet 2:20 get tangled up and **e-d** by sin

ENSURE (v)
to make sure, certain, or safe; to guarantee
Prov 31:8 **e** justice for those being crushed.

ENTER, ENTERED, ENTERING, ENTERS (v)
to go or come in
Ps 100:4 **E** his gates with thanksgiving
Matt 5:20 you will never **e** the Kingdom
Matt 7:13 **e** God's Kingdom only
Matt 19:23 rich person to **e** the
Mark 9:43 **e** eternal life with only
Mark 10:23 for the rich to **e** the
Luke 11:52 prevent others from **e-ing.**
Luke 13:24 Work hard to **e** the narrow
Luke 18:17 like a child will never **e** it.
John 3:5 no one can **e** the Kingdom
John 10:2 who **e-s** through the gate
Rom 5:12 When Adam sinned, sin **e-ed**
Heb 3:11 will never **e** my place of rest.
Heb 4:1 God's promise of **e-ing** his rest
Heb 4:11 do our best to **e** that rest.
Heb 9:12 of goats and calves—he **e-ed**

ENTERTAIN, ENTERTAINS (v)
to provide entertainment for; to amuse
Ps 45:8 music of strings **e-s** you.
Hos 7:3 The people **e** the king

ENTERTAINMENT (n)
amusement or diversion provided especially by performers
Dan 6:18 refused his usual **e**

ENTHRONED (v)
to seat ceremonially on a throne or in a place associated with power and authority
1 Sam 4:4 **e** between the cherubim.
2 Kgs 19:15 **e** between the mighty
1 Chr 13:6 **e** between the cherubim.
Ps 22:3 you are holy, **e** on the praises
Ps 113:5 God, who is **e** on high?
Isa 37:16 God of Israel, you are **e**

ENTHUSIASM (n)
strong excitement of feeling; zeal, fervor, passion
Neh 4:6 the people had worked with **e.**
Prov 19:2 **E** without knowledge
Rom 10:2 I know what **e** they have
2 Cor 8:7 your **e,** and your love
2 Cor 8:16 Titus the same **e** for you
2 Cor 9:2 your **e** that stirred up

Eph 6:7 Work with **e,** as though

ENTHUSIASTIC (adj)
filled with or marked by zeal, fervor, or passion
Ps 45:15 a joyful and **e** procession
Acts 18:25 about Jesus with an **e** spirit
Rom 15:17 I have reason to be **e** about

ENTICE, ENTICED, ENTICES (v)
to tempt; to lure
Deut 13:6 someone secretly **e-s** you—
Job 31:27 secretly **e-d** in my heart
Prov 1:10 if sinners **e** you, turn your back
Prov 7:21 and **e-d** him with her flattery.
Jas 1:14 our own desires, which **e** us

ENTRUST, ENTRUSTED (v)
to commit to another with confidence
Ps 31:5 I **e** my spirit into your hand.
Luke 12:48 has been **e-ed** with much,
Luke 23:46 I **e** my spirit into your
Acts 15:40 left, the believers **e-ed** him
Acts 20:32 And now I **e** you to God
Rom 3:2 Jews were **e-ed** with the whole
1 Thes 2:4 to be **e-ed** with the Good News.
1 Tim 1:11 Good News **e-ed** to me
2 Tim 1:14 truth that has been **e-ed** to you.
1 Pet 5:2 flock that God has **e-ed** to you.

ENVY (n)
discontent or resentment because of another's success, advantages, or superiority
see also JEALOUSY
Mark 7:22 lustful desires, **e,** slander,
Rom 1:29 sin, greed, hate, **e,** murder,
Gal 5:21 **e,** drunkenness, wild parties,
Titus 3:3 full of evil and **e,** and we hated
Jas 4:5 within us is filled with **e?**

ENVY (v)
to feel or show envy; to begrudge
Prov 3:31 Don't **e** violent people
Prov 24:1 Don't **e** evil people

EPILEPTIC (adj)
relating to, affected with, or having characteristics of epilepsy
Matt 4:24 were demon-possessed or **e** or

EQUAL (adj)
like in quantity, quality, nature, or status
John 5:18 making himself **e** with God.
2 Cor 8:14 In this way, things will be **e.**

EQUIP (v)
to prepare; to furnish for service or action
Eph 4:12 to **e** God's people to do
2 Tim 3:17 to prepare and **e** his people
Heb 13:21 **e** you with all you need

ERASE (v)
to blot out, cause to disappear
Ps 34:16 **e** their memory from the earth.
Rev 3:5 **e** their names from the Book

ESCAPE (n)
evasion of something undesirable
1 Thes 5:3 there will be no **e.**

ESCAPE, ESCAPED, ESCAPING (v)
to avoid; to get free of or break away from
Ps 89:48 can **e** the power of the grave.
Ps 139:7 I can never **e** from your Spirit!
Matt 23:33 will you **e** the judgment
1 Cor 3:15 barely **e-ing** through a wall of
Heb 2:3 think we can **e** if we ignore
Heb 12:25 we will certainly not **e** if we
2 Pet 2:18 those who have barely **e-d**
2 Pet 2:20 **e** from the wickedness

ESTABLISH, ESTABLISHED (v)
to institute permanently; to set up; to bring into existence
1 Kgs 9:5 **e** the throne of your dynasty
Ps 89:4 I will **e** your descendants as kings
Prov 8:28 when he **e-ed** springs
Isa 16:5 God will **e** one of David's

ESTEEM (n)
the regard in which one is held; worth; value
2 Chr 18:1 great riches and high **e,**
Prov 22:1 being held in high **e** is better

ESTHER
Jewish exile who became queen of Persia, also known as "Hadassah" (Esth 1:1); cousin of Mordecai (Esth 2:7); brought into king's harem (Esth 2:8-9); crowned queen (Esth 2:17); agreed to help Jews (Esth 4:14-17); invited king to a banquet (Esth 5:1-8); revealed Haman's plan (Esth 7:3-6); rescued the Jews (Esth 8:8); established Festival of Purim (Esth 9:18-32).

ETERNAL (adj)
having infinite duration; valid or existing at all times
see also EVERLASTING, FOREVER
Gen 9:16 will remember the **e** covenant
Exod 3:15 my **e** name, my name to
Lev 24:8 a requirement of the **e**
Num 18:19 an **e** and unbreakable
Ps 119:142 Your justice is **e,**
Jer 50:5 with an **e** covenant
Dan 4:34 and his kingdom is **e.**

Dan 7:14 His rule is **e**—
Matt 18:8 better to enter **e** life with
Matt 19:16 must I do to have **e** life?
Matt 25:41 into the **e** fire prepared
Matt 25:46 away into **e** punishment,
Mark 3:29 a sin with **e** consequences.
Luke 10:25 should I do to inherit **e** life?
Luke 18:18 should I do to inherit **e** life?
John 3:15 in him will have **e** life.
John 3:16 not perish but have **e** life.
John 3:36 believes in God's Son has **e**
John 5:29 will rise to experience **e** life,
John 5:39 you think they give you **e** life.
John 6:68 the words that give **e** life.
John 12:50 his commands lead to **e** life;
John 17:2 He gives **e** life prepared for
Rom 1:20 **e** power and divine nature
Rom 5:21 resulting in **e** life through
Rom 6:23 free gift of God is **e** life
Rom 9:5 is worthy of **e** praise! Amen.
Rom 16:26 the **e** God has commanded,
Eph 3:11 This was his **e** plan,
2 Thes 1:9 punished with **e** destruction,
1 Tim 6:12 Hold tightly to the **e** life
Titus 3:7 we will inherit **e** life.
Heb 5:9 source of **e** salvation
Heb 9:15 **e** inheritance God has
Heb 13:20 an **e** covenant with his blood—
1 Pet 1:23 from the **e**, living word
1 Pet 5:10 to share in his **e** glory
1 Jn 1:2 he is the one who is **e** life.
1 Jn 2:25 we enjoy the **e** life he
1 Jn 5:20 and he is **e** life.
Jude 1:7 the **e** fire of God's judgment.
Jude 1:21 who will bring you **e** life.

ETERNALLY (adv)
in an endless, infinite manner
Eph 6:24 May God's grace be **e** upon all

ETERNITY (n)
immortality; infinite time
Eccl 3:11 has planted **e** in the human
Isa 57:15 who lives in **e**, the Holy One,
John 12:25 will keep it for **e**.

EUNUCH, EUNUCHS (n)
male attendant, often castrated, implying singular devotion to a master
Isa 56:4 I will bless those **e-s** who keep
Matt 19:12 some have been made **e-s** by
Acts 8:27 The **e** had gone to Jerusalem

EVALUATE, EVALUATED (v)
to determine the significance, worth, or value of
1 Cor 2:15 Those who are spiritual can **e**
1 Cor 2:15 cannot be **e-d** by others.
1 Cor 4:3 **e-d** by you or by any human
1 Cor 14:29 let the others **e** what is said.

EVALUATION (n)
the determination of the significance, worth, or value of
Rom 12:3 in your **e** of yourselves,

EVANGELIST, EVANGELISTS (n)
preacher of the gospel
Acts 21:8 Philip the **E**, one of the seven
Eph 4:11 apostles, the prophets, the **e-s**,

EVE
First woman and mother of all people; created from Adam's rib (Gen 2:21-23; 1 Tim 2:13); deceived by the serpent (Gen 3:1-13; 2 Cor 11:3); named "Eve" by Adam (Gen 3:20); cursed with painful childbirth (Gen 3:16; 4:1); descendants of (Gen 5).

EVENING (n)
the latter part and close of the day
Gen 1:5 **e** passed and morning came,

EVER-LIVING (adj)
eternal; immortal
Rom 1:23 the glorious, **e** God,

EVER (adv)
always; at any time
Exod 15:18 will reign forever and **e**!
Ps 145:1 praise your name forever and **e**.
Dan 7:18 they will rule forever and **e**.
John 1:18 No one has **e** seen God.
Phil 4:20 forever and **e**! Amen.
2 Tim 4:18 glory to God forever and **e**!
Heb 1:8 endures forever and **e**.
1 Pet 4:11 to him forever and **e**! Amen.
1 Jn 4:12 No one has **e** seen God.
Rev 1:6 to him forever and **e**! Amen.
Rev 1:18 I am alive forever and **e**!
Rev 22:5 they will reign forever and **e**.

EVERLASTING (adj)
continuing indefinitely
see also ETERNAL, FOREVER
Gen 17:7 This is the **e** covenant:
Gen 48:4 as an **e** possession.
2 Sam 23:5 made an **e** covenant with
Ps 139:24 lead me along the path of **e** life.
Isa 9:6 God, **E** Father, Prince of Peace.
Isa 35:10 crowned with **e** joy.
Isa 40:28 The LORD is the **e** God,
Isa 54:8 But with **e** love
Isa 55:3 an **e** covenant with you.

Isa 60:19	God will be your **e** light,
Isa 60:20	the LORD will be your **e** light.
Isa 61:7	and **e** joy will be yours.
Isa 61:8	an **e** covenant with them.
Jer 10:10	the living God and the **e** King!
Jer 31:3	with an **e** love.
Ezek 16:60	establish an **e** covenant with
Dan 4:34	His rule is **e,**
Dan 9:24	to bring in **e** righteousness,
Dan 12:2	to **e** life and some to shame
Gal 6:8	will harvest **e** life from the

EVERYTHING (n)
all that exists; all that relates to the subject

Ps 145:17	is righteous in **e** he does;
Matt 6:6	your Father, who sees **e,**
Mark 12:44	has given **e** she had to live on.
Acts 2:44	and shared **e** they had.
2 Cor 1:22	**e** he has promised
2 Cor 6:10	and yet we have **e.**
Heb 13:18	to live honorably in **e** we do.

EVIDENCE (n)
an outward sign; proof

Acts 11:23	**e** of God's blessing,
Heb 11:4	**e** that he was a righteous man,

EVIL (adj)
bad, sinful, or morally reprehensible; of the devil

Gen 6:5	was consistently and totally **e.**
Exod 32:22	know how **e** these people
Ps 51:4	what is **e** in your sight.
Ps 140:8	not let **e** people have their way.
Prov 15:26	The LORD detests **e** plans,
Matt 6:13	rescue us from the **e** one.
Matt 12:45	spirits more **e** than itself,
Matt 15:19	from the heart come **e**
Mark 7:21	heart, come **e** thoughts,
Luke 11:24	When an **e** spirit leaves
John 17:15	them safe from the **e** one.
Acts 19:13	casting out **e** spirits.
Rom 2:9	keeps on doing what is **e**—
Rom 13:14	to indulge your **e** desires.
1 Cor 5:13	remove the **e** person from
Eph 5:16	in these **e** days.
Col 3:5	lust, and **e** desires.
2 Thes 3:3	guard you from the **e** one.
1 Tim 6:4	slander, and **e** suspicions.
2 Tim 3:13	**e** people and impostors
1 Jn 2:13	your battle with the **e** one.
1 Jn 3:12	who belonged to the **e** one
1 Jn 5:18	the **e** one cannot touch

EVIL (n)
something that brings sorrow, distress, or misfortune

Gen 2:9	the knowledge of good and **e.**
Gen 3:5	knowing both good and **e.**
Judg 6:1	The Israelites did **e**
Ps 5:5	for you hate all who do **e.**
Ps 14:4	those who do **e** never learn?
Ps 34:13	tongue from speaking **e**
Ps 37:27	Turn from **e** and do good,
Ps 45:7	You love justice and hate **e.**
Ps 53:4	those who do **e** never learn?
Ps 92:15	There is no **e** in him!
Ps 101:4	and stay away from every **e.**
Ps 125:5	with those who do **e.**
Prov 6:18	a heart that plots **e,**
Prov 8:13	fear the LORD will hate **e.**
Prov 11:27	search for **e,** it will find you!
Prov 13:6	but the **e** are misled by sin.
Prov 17:13	repay good with **e, e** will
Prov 20:30	cleanses away **e;** such
Isa 5:20	those who say that **e** is good
Isa 13:11	punish the world for its **e**
Jer 23:14	who are doing **e** so that
Hab 1:13	cannot stand the sight of **e.**
Mal 3:15	those who do **e** get rich,
Matt 5:45	to both the **e** and the good,
Luke 13:27	all you who do **e.**
John 3:20	All who do **e** hate the light
Rom 12:21	Don't let **e** conquer you,
1 Cor 14:20	babies when it comes to **e,**
1 Thes 5:15	no one pays back **e** for **e,**
1 Thes 5:22	away from every kind of **e.**
1 Tim 6:10	the root of all kinds of **e.**
2 Tim 2:19	must turn away from **e.**
Heb 1:9	You love justice and hate **e.**
Jas 1:21	get rid of all the filth and **e**
Jas 3:8	It is restless and **e,**
1 Pet 2:16	as an excuse to do **e.**
1 Pet 3:9	Don't repay **e** for **e.**
1 Pet 3:11	Turn away from **e** and do
3 Jn 1:11	those who do **e** prove that they

EVILDOERS (n)
one who does evil

Ps 92:7	like weeds and **e** flourish,
Ps 92:9	perish; all **e** will be scattered.
Ps 94:16	will stand up for me against **e?**
Prov 21:15	it terrifies **e.**
Prov 24:19	Don't fret because of **e;**

EVIL-MINDED (adj)
having an evil disposition or evil thoughts

Ps 119:115	out of my life, you **e** people,

EXALT, EXALTED, EXALTING, EXALTS (v)
to elevate; to glorify; to raise in rank or power
see also GLORIFY, HONOR

Exod 15:2	and I will **e** him!
2 Sam 22:47	of my salvation, be **e-ed!**

Neh 9:5 be **e-ed** above all blessing
Job 36:7 kings and **e-s** them forever.
Ps 18:46 God of my salvation be **e-ed!**
Ps 30:1 I will **e** you, LORD,
Ps 92:8 O LORD, will be **e-ed** forever.
Ps 97:9 you are **e-ed** far above all gods.
Ps 107:32 Let them **e** him publicly
Ps 145:1 I will **e** you, my God and King,
Dan 11:36 as he pleases, **e-ing** himself
Luke 14:11 those who **e** themselves will
Acts 2:33 is **e-ed** to the place of highest
2 Thes 2:4 He will **e** himself

EXAMINE, EXAMINED, EXAMINES, EXAMINING (v)
to test the condition of; to inspect closely
1 Chr 29:17 you **e** our hearts
Ps 11:4 **e-ing** every person on earth.
Ps 11:5 The LORD **e-s** both
Ps 17:3 **e-d** my heart in the night.
Ps 139:1 LORD, you have **e-d** my heart
Prov 5:21 **e-ing** every path he takes.
Prov 21:2 the LORD **e-s** their heart.
Jer 11:20 you **e** the deepest thoughts
Jer 17:10 and **e** secret motives.
Lam 3:40 let us test and **e** our ways.
1 Cor 4:4 Lord himself who will **e**
1 Cor 11:28 you should **e** yourself
2 Cor 13:5 **E** yourselves to see
1 Thes 2:4 He alone **e-s** the motives

EXAMPLE, EXAMPLES (n)
one that serves as a pattern to be or not to be imitated
John 13:15 given you an **e** to
1 Cor 10:11 happened to them as **e-s** for
2 Thes 3:9 give you an **e** to follow.
Titus 2:7 **e** to them by doing good
Heb 13:7 and follow the **e** of their faith.
Jas 5:10 For **e-s** of patience in suffering,
1 Pet 2:21 He is your **e,** and you must

EXCEEDS (v)
to be greater than or superior to
Phil 4:7 **e** anything we can understand.

EXCEL (v)
to surpass in accomplishment or achievement
2 Cor 8:7 **e** also in this gracious act of

EXCELLENCE (n)
something that gives especial worth or value
2 Pet 1:5 generous provision of moral **e,**

EXCELLENT (adj)
very good of its kind; superior
Phil 4:8 Think about things that are **e**

EXCHANGE (n)
the act of giving or taking one thing for another
Lev 17:11 blood, given in **e** for a life,

EXCHANGED (v)
to part with for a substitute
Job 28:19 cannot be **e** for it.
Jer 2:11 have **e** their glorious God
Hos 4:7 They have **e** the glory of God

EXCUSE (n)
the apology or justification offered
John 15:22 they have no **e** for their sin.
Rom 1:20 no **e** for not knowing God.
Rom 2:1 and you have no **e!**
1 Pet 2:16 your freedom as an **e**

EXCUSE (v)
to overlook, justify, or make an apology for
Exod 34:7 But I do not **e** the guilty.
Eph 5:6 those who try to **e** these sins,

EXECUTED (v)
to put to death
Num 35:16 the murderer must be **e.**
Deut 21:22 and is **e** and hung on a tree,

EXECUTION (n)
a putting to death especially as a legal penalty
Num 35:31 murder and subject to **e;**

EXHAUST (v)
to consume entirely
Isa 7:13 you **e** the patience of my God

EXHAUSTION (n)
fatigue, tiredness, collapse
2 Cor 6:5 worked to **e,** endured

EXHORT(ATION) (KJV)
Rom 12:8 If your gift is to *encourage*
1 Thes 2:3 not *preaching* with any deceit
Heb 3:13 You must *warn* each other

EXILE, EXILES (n)
the state of forced absence from one's country or home; a person who is in exile
2 Kgs 25:11 took as **e-s** the rest of
2 Kgs 25:21 sent into **e** from their land.
Ezra 2:1 the Jewish **e-s** of the provinces
Jer 52:27 sent into **e** from their land.

EXILED (v)
to banish or expel
2 Kgs 17:6 of Israel were **e** to Assyria.
2 Kgs 17:23 So Israel was **e** from their land

EXISTS (v)
to have real being whether material or spiritual
Heb 11:6 must believe that God **e**

EXORCISTS (n)
one who expels evil spirits
Luke 11:19 what about your own **e**?

EXPELLED, EXPELS (v)
to force to leave
Ezek 28:16 I **e** you, O mighty guardian,
1 Jn 4:18 perfect love **e-s** all fear.

EXPENSES (n)
financial costs
1 Cor 9:7 has to pay his own **e**?

EXPENSIVE (adj)
involving high cost
Mark 14:3 alabaster jar of **e** perfume
Luke 7:25 a man dressed in **e** clothes?
John 12:3 a twelve-ounce jar of **e** perfume
1 Tim 2:9 gold or pearls or **e** clothes.

EXPERIENCE (v)
to learn by or have direct observation or participation
Deut 28:2 You will **e** all these blessings
Eph 3:19 May you **e** the love of Christ,

EXPLAIN, EXPLAINED, EXPLAINS (v)
to make plain or understandable; to give the reason or cause
Gen 2:24 This **e-s** why a man leaves his
Neh 8:8 and clearly **e-ed** the meaning
Matt 19:5 This **e-s** why a man leaves his
Acts 17:3 He **e-ed** the prophecies
Acts 18:28 **e-ed** to them that Jesus was
Eph 6:19 **e** God's mysterious plan
2 Tim 2:15 correctly **e-s** the word of
1 Pet 3:15 always be ready to **e** it.

EXPLOIT (v)
to make use of meanly or unfairly for one's own advantage
Exod 22:22 not **e** a widow or an orphan.
Prov 22:22 or **e** the needy in court.

EXPLOITED (n)
one unfairly used for another's advantage
Isa 11:4 fair decisions for the **e.**

EXPLORE (v)
to investigate, study, or analyze
Num 13:2 Send out men to **e** the land
Num 32:8 to **e** the land.

EXPOSE, EXPOSED, EXPOSES, EXPOSING (v)
to make known; to display
Prov 20:27 **e-ing** every hidden motive.
Lam 4:22 your many sins will be **e-d.**
John 3:20 fear their sins will be **e-d.**
Eph 5:11 instead, **e** them.
Heb 4:12 It **e-s** our innermost thoughts
Heb 4:13 naked and **e-d** before his eyes,

EXTENDS (v)
to stretch out to the fullest length; to proffer
Ps 119:90 faithfulness **e** to every
Prov 31:20 She **e** a helping hand

EXTINGUISH (v)
to cause to cease burning
John 1:5 the darkness can never **e** it.

EXTOL(LED) (KJV)
Ps 30:1 will *exalt* you, Lord, for you
Ps 66:17 to him for help, *praising* him
Ps 68:4 *Sing loud praises* to him who
Isa 52:13 he will be *highly exalted*

EXTORTION (n)
the act or practice of obtaining money or property by illegal power
Lev 6:4 or the money you took by **e,**

EXTREME
Josh 15:21 of Edom in the **e** south
Ezek 46:19 a place at the **e** west end
Ezek 48:1 Dan is in the **e** north

EXTREMES (n)
something situated at or marking one end or the other of a range
Eccl 7:18 will avoid both **e.**

EXULT (v)
to be extremely joyful; to rejoice
Ps 89:16 They **e** in your righteousness.

EYE, EYES (n)
organ of (physical and spiritual) sight
Exod 21:24 an **e** for an **e,**
Deut 16:19 bribes blind the **e-s** of
Job 36:7 never takes his **e-s** off the
Ps 119:18 Open my **e-s** to see
Ps 119:37 Turn my **e-s** from worthless
Ps 123:1 I lift my **e-s** to you,
Prov 4:25 and fix your **e-s** on what
Matt 5:29 **e**—causes you to lust,
Matt 5:38 An **e** for an **e,**
Matt 6:22 When your **e** is good,
1 Cor 2:9 when they say, "No **e** has seen,

Heb 12:2	by keeping our **e-s** on Jesus,	
2 Pet 1:16	with our own **e-s**	
Rev 21:4	wipe every tear from their **e-s,**	

EYELIDS (n)
the movable fold of skin and muscle that closes over the eyeball

2 Kgs 9:30 — painted her **e** and fixed her hair

EYEWITNESS (n)
one who sees an occurrence or object

Luke 1:2 — They used the **e** reports

EZEKIEL
Prophet of Judah (southern kingdom) and priest (Ezek 1:3); exiled to Babylon near the Kebar River (Ezek 3:15).

EZRA
Postexilic priestly reformer in time of Artaxerxes (Ezra 7; 10; Neh 8; 12); descendant of Seraiah (Ezra 7:1); skillful, learned teacher of the Law (Ezra 7:6); determined to study and obey the Law (Ezra 7:10); served as priest (Ezra 7:11); restored Temple and its worship (Ezra 7–8); corrected pagan intermarriage (Ezra 9–10); dedicated Jerusalem's repaired walls (Neh 12).

F

FACE (n)
in or into direct contact or confrontation (as in "face to face"); countenance; presence; the front part of the head

Gen 32:30 — I have seen God **f** to **f,**
Exod 33:11 — speak to Moses **f** to **f,**
Exod 34:29 — his **f** had become radiant
Num 12:8 — I speak to him **f** to **f,**
Deut 31:17 — hiding my **f** from them,
Judg 6:22 — angel of the LORD **f** to **f!**
2 Chr 7:14 — and seek my **f** and turn from
Ps 4:6 — Let your **f** smile on us,
Ps 17:15 — I will see you **f** to **f**
Ps 67:1 — May his **f** smile with favor
Luke 9:29 — appearance of his **f** was
2 Cor 3:7 — For his **f** shone with the glory
Rev 1:16 — And his **f** was like the sun
Rev 22:4 — they will see his **f,**

FACE, FACED, FACING (v)
to confront; to be confronted by

Ps 112:8 — **f** their foes triumphantly.
Ps 116:6 — I was **f-ing** death, and he saved
2 Cor 6:5 — **f-d** angry mobs,

FADE, FADING (v)
to lose freshness, strength, or vitality

Isa 40:7 — and the flowers **f**
1 Cor 9:25 — to win a prize that will **f**
2 Cor 3:7 — brightness was already **f-ing**
2 Cor 3:13 — it was destined to **f** away.
Jas 1:11 — the rich will **f** away
1 Jn 2:17 — this world is **f-ing** away,

FAIL, FAILED, FAILS (v)
to disappoint; to fall short; to weaken; to miss performing an expected service; to be unsuccessful

Num 23:19 — spoken and **f-ed** to act?
Deut 31:6 — He will neither **f** you
Josh 23:14 — Not a single one has **f-ed!**
1 Kgs 8:56 — Not one word has **f-ed**
Ps 77:8 — his promises permanently **f-ed?**
Luke 13:24 — try to enter but will **f.**
Luke 22:32 — faith should not **f.**
Rom 9:6 — has God **f-ed** to fulfill his promise
2 Cor 13:5 — if not, you have **f-ed** the test
2 Cor 13:6 — we have not **f-ed** the test
Heb 12:15 — none of you **f-s** to receive
Heb 13:5 — I will never **f** you.
1 Pet 4:19 — he will never **f** you.

FAINT (adj)
lacking strength or vigor

Jonah 4:8 — grew **f** and wished to die.

FAINT (v)
to become weak or lose courage in body or spirit

Isa 40:31 — will walk and not **f.**

FAIR (adj)
free from self-interest, prejudice, or favoritism; beautiful

Prov 1:3 — do what is right, just, and **f.**
Song 2:13 — away with me, my **f** one!
Isa 11:4 — make **f** decisions for the
Rom 3:25 — God was being **f** when he
Rom 3:26 — he himself is **f** and just,
Col 4:1 — be just and **f** to your slaves.

FAIRNESS (n)
the quality of being free from self-interest, prejudice, or favoritism

Ps 9:8 — rule the nations with **f.**
Ps 98:9 — and the nations with **f.**
Ps 99:4 — you have established **f.**
Isa 9:7 — will rule with **f** and justice

FAITH (n)
reliance, loyalty, or complete trust in God; a system of religious beliefs
see also BELIEVE, FAITHLESS, TRUST

Exod 14:31 — They put their **f** in the LORD
Isa 7:9 — Unless your **f** is firm,

Matt 9:2	Seeing their **f,** Jesus said
Matt 9:29	Because of your **f,** it will
Matt 15:28	your **f** is great.
Matt 17:20	**f** even as small as a mustard
Matt 21:22	if you have **f,** you will receive
Mark 10:52	for your **f** has healed you.
Luke 5:20	Seeing their **f,** Jesus said
Luke 7:50	Your **f** has saved you;
Luke 8:48	your **f** has made you well.
Luke 12:28	Why do you have so little **f?**
Luke 17:6	**f** even as small as a mustard
Luke 18:8	find on the earth who have **f?**
John 16:1	won't abandon your **f.**
Acts 6:5	full of **f** and the Holy Spirit
Acts 14:9	he had **f** to be healed.
Acts 14:27	opened the door of **f** to the
Acts 16:5	strengthened in their **f** and
Acts 24:24	told them about **f** in Christ
Rom 1:8	**f** in him is being talked about
Rom 1:12	to encourage you in your **f,**
Rom 1:17	from start to finish by **f.**
Rom 1:17	through **f** that a righteous
Rom 3:28	right with God through **f**
Rom 3:30	right with himself only by **f,**
Rom 3:31	only when we have **f**
Rom 4:5	because of their **f** in God
Rom 4:9	righteous because of his **f.**
Rom 4:12	same kind of **f** Abraham had
Rom 4:13	with God that comes by **f.**
Rom 4:14	then **f** is not necessary
Rom 4:16	the promise is received by **f.**
Rom 4:16	if we have **f** like Abraham's.
Rom 4:19	Abraham's **f** did not weaken,
Rom 4:20	In fact, his **f** grew stronger,
Rom 5:1	made right in God's sight by **f,**
Rom 5:2	Because of our **f,** Christ has
Rom 10:8	message about **f** that we preach:
Rom 10:17	So **f** comes from hearing,
Rom 12:6	speak out with as much **f** as
Rom 14:1	believers who are weak in **f,**
1 Cor 12:9	gives great **f** to another,
1 Cor 13:13	**f,** hope, and love—
1 Cor 15:14	and your **f** is useless.
1 Cor 16:13	Stand firm in the **f.**
2 Cor 1:24	put your **f** into practice.
2 Cor 13:5	failed the test of genuine **f.**
Gal 1:23	the very **f** he tried to destroy!
Gal 3:9	all who put their **f** in Christ
Gal 3:11	**f** that a righteous person
Gal 3:12	This way of **f** is very different
Gal 3:14	Holy Spirit through **f.**
Gal 3:23	way of **f** in Christ was available
Gal 3:24	made right with God through **f.**
Gal 3:25	the way of **f** has come,
Gal 3:26	of God through **f** in Christ
Gal 5:5	eagerly wait to receive by **f**
Eph 1:15	of your strong **f** in the Lord
Eph 4:5	one Lord, one **f,** one baptism,
Eph 6:16	hold up the shield of **f**
Phil 1:25	experience the joy of your **f.**
Phil 3:9	righteous through **f** in Christ.
Col 1:4	have heard of your **f** in Christ
1 Thes 1:8	telling us about your **f** in God.
1 Thes 3:5	your **f** was still strong.
1 Thes 3:10	fill the gaps in your **f.**
2 Thes 1:3	because your **f** is flourishing
1 Tim 1:4	live a life of **f** in God.
1 Tim 1:19	Cling to your **f** in Christ,
1 Tim 3:9	mystery of the **f** now
1 Tim 4:1	will turn away from the true **f;**
1 Tim 6:10	have wandered from the true **f**
1 Tim 6:12	good fight for the true **f.**
2 Tim 1:5	remember your genuine **f,**
2 Tim 2:18	away from the **f.**
2 Tim 3:10	You know my **f,** my patience,
Titus 1:1	have been sent to proclaim **f**
Titus 1:13	make them strong in the **f.**
Titus 2:2	must have sound **f** and be filled
Phlm 1:5	about your **f** in the Lord
Phlm 1:6	that comes from your **f**
Heb 4:2	they didn't share the **f**
Heb 6:1	and placing our **f** in God.
Heb 6:12	their **f** and endurance.
Heb 10:38	righteous ones will live by **f.**
Heb 11:5	It was by **f** that Enoch
Heb 11:7	It was by **f** that Noah
Heb 11:8	It was by **f** that Abraham
Heb 11:23	It was by **f** that Moses' parents
Heb 11:29	It was by **f** that the people
Heb 12:2	initiates and perfects our **f.**
Jas 1:3	when your **f** is tested,
Jas 2:5	this world to be rich in **f?**
Jas 2:14	Can that kind of **f** save anyone?
Jas 2:17	**f** by itself isn't enough.
Jas 2:18	Some people have **f;**
Jas 2:20	**f** without good deeds
Jas 2:22	made his **f** complete.
Jas 2:24	what we do, not by **f** alone.
Jas 2:26	so also **f** is dead without good
Jas 5:15	prayer offered in **f** will heal
1 Pet 1:21	have placed your **f** and hope
2 Pet 1:1	the same precious **f** we have.
Jude 1:3	defend the **f** that God
Jude 1:20	in your most holy **f,**

FAITHFUL (adj)

firm in adherence, utterly loyal

see also LOYAL, TRUSTWORTHY, UNFAILING

Deut 7:9	He is the **f** God who keeps his
1 Sam 2:9	will protect his **f** ones,
1 Sam 20:14	me with the **f** love of the
2 Sam 22:26	you show yourself **f;** to those

1 Kgs 8:61 you be completely **f** to the
1 Kgs 15:14 remained completely **f** to
2 Kgs 20:3 have always been **f** to you
Ps 18:25 you show yourself **f**;
Ps 71:22 because you are **f** to your
Ps 89:8 You are entirely **f**.
Ps 89:49 to David with a **f** pledge.
Ps 143:1 you are **f** and righteous.
Isa 38:3 have always been **f** to you and
Hos 11:12 God and is **f** to the Holy One.
Zech 8:3 be called the **F** City;
Zech 8:8 I will be **f** and just toward
Matt 24:45 A **f**, sensible servant is one
Matt 25:21 You have been **f** in handling
Matt 25:23 my good and **f** servant.
Luke 12:42 Lord replied, "A **f**, sensible
Luke 16:10 If you are **f** in little things,
1 Cor 4:17 my beloved and **f** child in the
2 Cor 1:18 as God is **f**, our word to you
Eph 1:1 who are **f** followers of Christ
Phil 2:17 just like your **f** service is
Col 4:7 brother and **f** helper who
Col 4:9 Onesimus, a **f** and beloved
1 Thes 1:3 we think of your **f** work,
1 Thes 5:24 for he who calls you is **f**.
2 Thes 3:3 But the Lord is **f**; he will
1 Tim 3:2 He must be **f** to his wife.
1 Tim 3:11 and be **f** in everything they
1 Tim 5:9 old and was **f** to her husband.
2 Tim 4:7 I have remained **f**.
Heb 2:17 merciful and **f** High Priest
Heb 3:2 For he was **f** to God, who
Heb 8:9 They did not remain **f** to my
Heb 13:4 marriage, and remain **f** to one
1 Jn 1:9 to him, he is **f** and just to
Rev 1:5 He is the **f** witness to these
Rev 2:10 But if you remain **f** even when
Rev 3:14 is the Amen—the **f** and true
Rev 17:14 chosen and **f** ones will be

FAITHFUL (n)
those who practice faith
Ps 149:1 assembly of the **f**.
Ps 149:5 Let the **f** rejoice that he

FAITHFULLY (adv)
in a manner that is firm, regular, and steady
Deut 7:12 regulations and **f** obey them,
1 Kgs 8:25 and **f** follow me
2 Chr 32:1 Hezekiah had **f** carried out
Neh 13:14 all that I have **f** done for
Isa 61:8 I will **f** reward my people for

FAITHFULNESS (n)
the quality of steadfast loyalty or firm adherence to promises
Exod 34:6 unfailing love and **f**.
Ps 25:10 with unfailing love and **f**
Ps 36:5 your **f** reaches beyond
Ps 57:10 Your **f** reaches to the clouds.
Ps 92:2 your **f** in the evening,
Ps 100:5 **f** continues to each
Prov 14:22 unfailing love and **f**.
Prov 16:6 love and **f** make atonement
Prov 20:28 love and **f** protect the king;
Isa 38:18 no longer hope in your **f**.
Lam 3:23 Great is his **f**;
Gal 5:22 kindness, goodness, **f**,
Eph 6:23 give you love with **f**.
2 Thes 1:4 your endurance and **f**
2 Tim 2:22 pursue righteous living, **f**,

FAITHLESS (adj)
disloyal; lacking trust
Ps 78:57 and were as **f** as their parents.
Jer 3:8 I divorced **f** Israel because
Jer 3:11 Even **f** Israel is less guilty than
Jer 3:12 Israel, my **f** people, come home
Matt 17:17 You **f** and corrupt people!
Mark 9:19 You **f** people!
John 20:27 Don't be **f** any longer.

FALL, FALLEN, FALLING (v)
to collapse; to drop down (wounded or dead); to become lower in degree or level; to come by assignment or inheritance; to descend; to stumble or stray (morally)
2 Sam 1:19 the mighty heroes have **f-en**!
Ps 37:24 they will never **f**,
Ps 69:9 who insult you have **f-en** on
Prov 10:8 babbling fools **f** flat on their
Prov 24:17 when your enemies **f**;
Isa 14:12 How you are **f-en** from heaven,
Matt 13:21 They **f** away as soon as
Luke 10:18 I saw Satan **f** from heaven
Rom 3:23 we all **f** short of God's glorious
Rom 14:13 believer to stumble and **f**.
Gal 5:4 **f-en** away from God's grace.
2 Pet 1:10 and you will never **f** away.
Jude 1:24 to keep you from **f-ing** away

FALSE (adj)
intentionally untrue; dishonest; misleading; unwise; faithless
Prov 12:17 a **f** witness tells lies.
Isa 44:25 I expose the **f** prophets as
Matt 24:11 And many **f** prophets will
Mark 13:22 For **f** messiahs and **f** prophets
2 Cor 11:13 These people are **f** apostles.
Titus 1:11 by their **f** teaching.
2 Pet 2:1 were also **f** prophets in Israel,
1 Jn 4:1 many **f** prophets in the world.
Rev 16:13 and the **f** prophet.

Rev 19:20	beast and his **f** prophet were
Rev 20:10	the beast and the **f** prophet.

FALSEHOOD (n)
a lie; the practice of lying

Ps 119:163	hate and abhor all **f,**

FALSELY (adv)
in an untrue, deceptive, or misleading manner

Exod 20:16	must not testify **f** against
Mark 10:19	You must not testify **f.**

FAME (n)
popular acclaim

Exod 9:16	spread my **f** throughout the earth.
Ps 49:12	but their **f** will not last.
Ps 102:12	Your **f** will endure
Isa 66:19	heard of my **f** or seen my glory.

FAMILY, FAMILIES (n)
a household unit of related people, as in a clan
see also HOUSEHOLD

Josh 24:15	my **f,** we will serve the LORD.
Ps 68:6	God places the lonely in **f-ies;**
Mark 3:25	a **f** splintered by feuding
Luke 9:61	let me say good-bye to my **f.**
Luke 12:52	**f-ies** will be split apart,
Gal 6:10	to those in the **f** of faith.
Eph 2:19	members of God's **f.**
1 Tim 3:4	manage his own **f** well,
Titus 1:11	whole **f-ies** away from the truth
1 Jn 3:9	have been born into God's **f**

FAMINE (n)
extreme scarcity of food

Gen 12:10	a severe **f** struck the land
Gen 26:1	A severe **f** now struck the
Gen 41:30	seven years of **f** so great
Ruth 1:1	a severe **f** came upon the land.
1 Kgs 18:2	the **f** had become very
Amos 8:11	I will send a **f** on the land—

FAMOUS (adj)
widely known; honored for achievement

Gen 11:4	This will make us **f**
Gen 12:2	bless you and make you **f,**
Isa 63:12	making himself **f** forever?

FANCY (adj)
not plain; ornamental

1 Pet 3:3	outward beauty of **f** hairstyles,

FANTASIES (n)
unrealistic or improbable mental images

Prov 12:11	who chases **f** has no sense.

FAR (adv)
at a considerable distance in space or degree

Ps 22:19	Lord, do not stay **f** away!
Ezek 11:15	are **f** away from the Lord
Eph 2:13	you were **f** away from God,
Col 1:21	were once **f** away from God

FARMER (n)
one who cultivates crops or raises animals for food

Isa 28:24	Does a **f** always plow and
Isa 55:10	producing seed for the **f**
Matt 13:18	the parable about the **f** planting
2 Cor 9:6	a **f** who plants only a few seeds
2 Cor 9:10	seed for the **f** and then bread

FARTHEST (adj)
most distant, especially in space or time

Acts 13:47	bring salvation to the **f** corners

FAST, FASTING (v)
to abstain from food

Ps 35:13	denied myself by **f-ing** for
Matt 6:16	when you **f,** don't make it
Acts 13:2	worshiping the Lord and **f-ing,**

FASTING (n)
the practice of abstaining, usually from food

Joel 2:12	Come with **f-ing,** weeping,
Acts 14:23	prayer and **f-ing,** they turned

FATE (n)
an inevitable and often adverse outcome or end

Prov 1:19	the **f** of all who are greedy
Eccl 9:3	suffers the same **f.**
1 Pet 2:8	the **f** that was planned for them.

FATHER, FATHERS (n)
male parent; ancestor(s); characteristic of a mentor or provider relationship; name and role for God in relation to the children he fosters/adopts; originator or creator
see also PARENT

Gen 2:24	a man leaves his **f** and mother
Gen 17:4	make you the **f** of a multitude
Exod 20:12	Honor your **f** and mother.
Exod 21:15	Anyone who strikes **f** or
Deut 32:6	he your **F** who created you?
2 Sam 7:14	I will be his **f,** and he
Ps 2:7	Today I have become your **F.**
Ps 89:26	You are my **F,** my God,
Prov 10:1	wise child brings joy to a **f;**
Prov 23:22	Listen to your **f,** who gave you
Isa 9:6	Everlasting **F,** Prince of Peace.
Isa 63:16	you would still be our **F.**
Jer 3:19	forward to your calling me '**F,**'
Ezek 22:10	sleep with their **f-s'** wives

Mal 2:10 children of the same **F**?
Mal 4:6 will turn the hearts of **f-s**
Matt 5:16 will praise your heavenly **F.**
Matt 6:9 Our **F** in heaven, may your
Matt 6:14 heavenly **F** will forgive
Matt 10:37 If you love your **f** or mother
Matt 11:27 no one truly knows the **F**
Matt 15:4 Honor your **f** and mother,
Matt 16:27 in the glory of his **F**
Matt 19:5 a man leaves his **f** and mother
Matt 19:29 or **f** or mother or children
Matt 23:9 is your spiritual **F.**
Luke 1:17 hearts of the **f-s** to their
Luke 9:59 return home and bury my **f.**"
John 4:21 you worship the **F** on this
John 5:17 My **F** is always working,
John 5:20 For the **F** loves the Son
John 6:44 come to me unless the **F**
John 6:65 unless the **F** gives them
John 8:19 you don't know who my **F** is.
John 8:41 God himself is our true **F.**
John 10:38 understand that the **F** is in me,
John 14:6 come to the **F** except through
John 14:21 love me, my **F** will love
John 15:8 brings great glory to my **F.**
John 15:23 also hates my **F.**
John 20:17 ascending to my **F** and
Acts 13:33 Today I have become your **F.**
Rom 4:11 Abraham is the spiritual **f**
Rom 4:16 Abraham is the **f** of all who
Rom 8:15 we call him, "Abba, **F.**"
2 Cor 6:18 I will be your **F,** and you
Eph 5:31 man leaves his **f** and mother
Eph 6:2 Honor your **f** and mother.
Eph 6:4 **F-s,** do not provoke
Phil 2:11 to the glory of God the **F.**
Col 3:21 **F-s,** do not aggravate
Heb 12:7 is never disciplined by its **f**?
Heb 12:9 earthly **f-s** who disciplined
1 Jn 1:3 fellowship is with the **F** and
1 Jn 2:15 the love of the **F** in you.
1 Jn 2:22 who denies the **F** and the Son
1 Jn 3:1 See how very much our **F** loves
Rev 3:21 sat with my **F** on his throne.

FATHERLESS (adj)
without a father; orphaned
see also ORPHAN
Ps 68:5 Father to the **f,** defender of

FATTENING (v)
to feed (as a stock animal) and make fat for slaughter
Luke 15:23 calf we have been **f.**

FAULT (n)
lack or error; moral weakness less serious than a vice
1 Sam 29:3 never found a single **f** in
Prov 17:9 when a **f** is forgiven,
Acts 20:26 eternal death, it's not my **f,**
2 Cor 6:3 no one will find **f** with our
Eph 5:27 she will be holy and without **f.**
Jude 1:24 without a single **f.**

FAULTLESS (adj)
having no fault; irreproachable
1 Thes 2:10 honest and **f** toward all of you

FAVOR, FAVORS (n)
gracious kindness; approval from a superior; a special privilege or right granted or conceded
see also GRACE
Gen 6:8 Noah found **f** with the LORD.
Exod 34:9 if it is true that I have found **f**
1 Sam 2:26 and grew in **f** with the LORD
Prov 3:4 you will find **f** with both God
Prov 18:22 receives **f** from the LORD.
Prov 19:6 Many seek **f-s** from a ruler;
Zech 11:7 named one **F** and the other
Luke 1:30 you have found **f** with God!
Luke 2:40 and God's **f** was on him.
Luke 2:52 and in **f** with God
Luke 4:19 the time of the LORD's **f**
Rom 11:7 have not found the **f** of God
Phil 1:7 with me the special **f** of God,

FAVOR, FAVORING (v)
to show partiality toward
Lev 19:15 justice in legal matters by **f-ing**
Jas 2:9 But if you **f** some people over

FAVORITE (adj)
specially favored or liked
Gen 27:4 Prepare my **f** dish,

FAVORITES (n)
persons specially loved, trusted, or provided with favors
see also PARTIALITY
Job 32:21 I won't play **f**
Matt 22:16 and don't play **f.**
Gal 2:6 for God has no **f.**
Eph 6:9 he has no **f.**
Col 3:25 For God has no **f.**

FAVORITISM (n)
the showing of special favor; partiality
see also DISCRIMINATION, PARTIALITY
Prov 24:23 **f** when passing judgment.
Mal 2:9 **f** in the way you carry out
Acts 10:34 that God shows no **f.**
Rom 2:11 God does not show **f.**
Jas 3:17 It shows no **f** and is always

FEAR, FEARS (n)
dread or alarm in facing danger; profound reverence and awe
2 Sam 23:3 who rules in the **f** of God,
Ps 2:11 Serve the LORD with reverent **f,**
Ps 34:4 freed me from all my **f-s.**
Prov 1:33 untroubled by **f** of harm.
Heb 13:6 will have no **f.**

FEAR, FEARED, FEARING, FEARS (v)
to have reverential awe of God; to be afraid or apprehensive
Deut 6:13 You must **f** the LORD your
Deut 8:6 walking in his ways and **f-ing**
Deut 13:4 your God and **f** him alone.
Deut 31:12 learn to **f** the LORD your God
Josh 4:24 might **f** the LORD your God
1 Sam 12:14 if you **f** and worship
2 Chr 26:5 taught him to **f** God.
Neh 5:15 But because I **f-ed** God,
Neh 7:2 a faithful man who **f-ed** God
Job 1:1 He **f-ed** God and stayed
Job 1:8 **f-s** God and stays away from
Ps 34:7 and defends all who **f** him.
Ps 46:2 not **f** when earthquakes come
Ps 61:5 for those who **f** your name.
Ps 76:7 you are greatly **f-ed!**
Ps 103:17 with those who **f** him.
Ps 128:1 joyful are those who **f** the
Prov 8:13 All who **f** the LORD will
Prov 28:14 those who **f** to do wrong,
Prov 31:30 a woman who **f-s** the LORD
Isa 25:3 nations will **f** you.
Jer 2:19 your God and not to **f** him.
Mal 3:16 those who **f-ed** the LORD spoke
Mal 4:2 for you who **f** my name,
2 Cor 7:1 because we **f** God.
Rev 11:18 and all who **f** your name,

FEARFUL (adj)
very great—used as an intensive
2 Cor 5:11 our **f** responsibility to the Lord,

FEAST (n)
an elaborate meal; banquet
Ps 23:5 You prepare a **f** for me
Prov 15:15 life is a continual **f.**
Luke 15:29 goat for a **f** with my friends.

FEAST, FEASTING (v)
to enjoy a good meal
Esth 9:17 a day of **f-ing** and gladness.
Prov 17:1 a house filled with **f-ing**—and
Prov 23:20 or **f** with gluttons,
Isa 22:13 You **f** on meat and drink wine.

FED (v)
to give food to
see also FEED
Deut 8:16 He **f** you with manna
Ezek 3:2 mouth, and he **f** me the scroll.
John 6:26 want to be with me because I **f**

FEED, FEEDS (v)
to give food to; to eat; to provide something essential to the development, sustenance, maintenance, or operation of
see also FED
Prov 15:14 while the fool **f-s** on trash.
Prov 22:9 because they **f** the poor.
Jer 50:19 own land, to **f** in the fields
Matt 6:26 your heavenly Father **f-s** them.
Matt 14:16 necessary—you **f** them."
Matt 25:42 and you didn't **f** me.
John 6:57 anyone who **f-s** on me will live
John 21:15 "Then **f** my lambs,"
John 21:17 "Then **f** my sheep."
Rom 12:20 enemies are hungry, **f** them.

FEEL (v)
to perceive by physical sensation
Ps 115:7 have hands but cannot **f,**

FEET (n)
see also FOOT
Ps 22:16 pierced my hands and **f.**
Ps 40:2 He set my **f** on solid ground
Ps 73:2 My **f** were slipping,
Ps 119:105 a lamp to guide my **f**
Isa 52:7 are the **f** of the messenger
Matt 10:14 shake its dust from your **f**
Luke 24:39 Look at my **f.**
John 13:5 began to wash the disciples' **f,**
John 13:14 wash each other's **f.**
Rom 10:15 beautiful are the **f** of
Rom 16:20 crush Satan under your **f.**
1 Cor 15:25 his enemies beneath his **f.**
Heb 1:13 a footstool under your **f.**
Heb 12:13 a straight path for your **f**

FELLOWSHIP (n)
friendship; association; company; partnership
Gen 5:24 walking in close **f** with God.
1 Cor 5:2 remove this man from your **f.**
2 Cor 13:14 and the **f** of the Holy Spirit
1 Jn 1:3 you may have **f** with us.
1 Jn 1:3 our **f** is with the Father and
1 Jn 1:6 we say we have **f** with God but
1 Jn 2:27 remain in **f** with Christ.

FEMALE (adj)
of, relating to, or being a woman

Gen 1:27 male and **f** he created them.
Gen 5:2 He created them male and **f**,
Mark 10:6 God made them male and **f**
Gal 3:28 slave or free, male and **f**.

FERTILE (adj)
capable of sustaining abundant growth; productive
Mark 4:8 other seeds fell on **f** soil,

FESTIVAL, FESTIVALS (n)
a time of celebration marked by special observances
Lev 23:2 the LORD's appointed **f-s**,
Isa 30:29 at the holy **f-s**.
Amos 5:21 religious **f-s** and solemn
Zech 14:18 of Egypt refuse to attend the **f**,
1 Cor 5:8 let us celebrate the **f**,

FESTIVE (adj)
joyful, happy
Isa 61:3 **f** praise instead of despair.

FEVER (n)
a rise of body temperature above the normal
Job 30:30 my bones burn with **f**.
Matt 8:14 sick in bed with a high **f**.
Luke 4:38 very sick with a high **f**.
John 4:52 his **f** suddenly disappeared!
Acts 28:8 was ill with **f** and dysentery.

FEW (adj)
not many; a low number of
Prov 17:27 wise person uses **f** words;
Matt 9:37 is great, but the workers are **f**.
Matt 22:14 many are called, but **f** are

FIANCÉE (n)
a woman engaged to be married
1 Cor 7:36 treating his **f** improperly

FIELD, FIELDS (n)
an open land area free of woods and buildings; an area of cleared land used for cultivation
Lev 19:9 along the edges of your **f-s**,
Ruth 2:2 into the harvest **f-s** to pick
Isa 40:6 the flowers in a **f**.
Matt 6:28 Look at the lilies of the **f**
Matt 13:44 discovered hidden in a **f**.
Luke 2:8 staying in the **f-s** nearby,
John 4:35 The **f-s** are already ripe
1 Cor 3:9 And you are God's **f**.
1 Pet 1:24 like a flower in the **f**.

FIERY (adj)
consisting of fire
Eph 6:16 stop the **f** arrows of the devil.

FIG, FIGS (n)
an oblong or pear-shaped syconium fruit of a tree of the mulberry family; a fruit-producing plant which could be either a tall tree or a low-spreading shrub
Gen 3:7 they sewed **f** leaves together
Judg 9:10 they said to the **f** tree,
Prov 27:18 workers who tend a **f** tree
Mic 4:4 grapevines and **f** trees,
Zech 3:10 grapevine and **f** tree.
Matt 21:19 a **f** tree beside the road.
Luke 13:6 man planted a **f** tree in his
Jas 3:12 Does a **f** tree produce olives,
Jas 3:12 or a grapevine produce **f-s**?

FIGHT, FIGHTS (n)
a hostile encounter; a struggle for a goal or an objective
Prov 15:18 hot-tempered person starts **f-s**;
Prov 20:3 Avoiding a **f** is a mark of
Prov 29:22 An angry person starts **f-s**;
2 Tim 4:7 fought the good **f**,
Jas 4:1 causing the quarrels and **f-s**

FIGHT, FIGHTING, FIGHTS (v)
to actively oppose or combat, as with weapons; to gain by struggle
see also FOUGHT
Exod 14:14 LORD himself will **f** for you.
Josh 23:10 LORD your God **f-s** for you,
1 Sam 17:32 I'll go **f** him!
1 Sam 25:28 are **f-ing** the LORD's battles.
Neh 4:20 our God will **f** for us!
Ps 35:1 **F** those who **f** against me.
Prov 28:25 Greed causes **f-ing**;
Isa 49:25 I will **f** those who **f** you,
1 Cor 15:32 value was there in **f-ing** wild
Phil 1:27 one purpose, **f-ing** together for
1 Tim 6:12 **F** the good fight
Jas 4:2 so you **f** and wage war

FILL, FILLED, FILLS (v)
to occupy the whole of; to supply fully; to spread through
Gen 1:28 **F** the earth and govern it.
Exod 34:6 **f-ed** with unfailing love
1 Kgs 8:11 presence of the LORD **f-ed**
Ps 81:10 and I will **f** it with good things.
Ps 107:9 the thirsty and **f-s** the hungry
Ps 119:64 unfailing love **f-s** the earth;
Ps 123:3 have had our **f** of contempt.
Isa 6:3 earth is **f-ed** with his glory!
Joel 2:13 and **f-ed** with unfailing love.
Jonah 4:2 and **f-ed** with unfailing love.
Hag 2:7 I will **f** this place with glory,
Luke 1:15 be **f-ed** with the Holy Spirit,
Luke 1:41 was **f-ed** with the Holy Spirit.

Luke 1:67 **f-ed** with the Holy Spirit
Luke 2:40 He was **f-ed** with wisdom,
Luke 24:49 Holy Spirit comes and **f-s**
Acts 2:4 was **f-ed** with the Holy Spirit
Acts 2:28 you will **f** me with the joy
Acts 4:8 **f-ed** with the Holy Spirit,
Acts 4:31 all **f-ed** with the Holy Spirit.
Acts 9:17 be **f-ed** with the Holy Spirit.
Acts 13:9 was **f-ed** with the Holy Spirit,
Rom 5:5 Holy Spirit to **f** our hearts
Rom 15:13 **f** you completely with joy
Eph 1:23 by Christ, who **f-s** all things
Eph 5:18 be **f-ed** with the Holy Spirit,
Col 3:16 in all its richness, **f** your lives.

FILTH (n)
moral corruption or defilement
Isa 4:4 wash the **f** from beautiful Zion

FILTHY (adj)
covered with, containing, or characterized by foul or putrid matter or moral corruption
Isa 6:5 I have **f** lips, and I live
Isa 64:6 they are nothing but **f** rags.
Zech 3:4 Take off his **f** clothes.
2 Cor 6:17 Don't touch their **f** things,

FINANCIAL (adj)
relating to money
2 Cor 11:9 did not become a **f** burden

FIND, FINDS (v)
to attain or reach (a goal or conclusion); to discover by searching or effort; to experience
see also FOUND
1 Chr 28:9 seek him, you will **f** him.
Job 23:3 knew where to **f** God,
Prov 3:13 the person who **f-s** wisdom,
Prov 8:17 who search will surely **f** me.
Prov 8:35 For whoever **f-s** me **f-s** life
Prov 11:27 you will **f** favor;
Prov 31:10 Who can **f** a virtuous and
Isa 55:6 while you can **f** him.
Jer 6:16 will **f** rest for your souls.
Matt 7:7 seeking, and you will **f**.
Matt 7:8 Everyone who seeks, **f-s**.
Matt 10:39 your life for me, you will **f** it.
Luke 11:9 and you will **f**.
Luke 11:10 Everyone who seeks, **f-s**.
Luke 15:4 that is lost until he **f-s** it?
Luke 15:8 search carefully until she **f-s** it?

FINEST (adj)
superior in kind, quality, or appearance
Isa 55:2 will enjoy the **f** food.
Jer 3:19 the **f** possession in the world.

FINGER, FINGERS (n)
any of the five terminating members of the hand; figurative for the power of God
Exod 8:19 This is the **f** of God!
Exod 31:18 written by the **f** of God.
Deut 9:10 had written with his own **f**
Luke 16:24 dip the tip of his **f** in water
John 8:6 wrote in the dust with his **f**.
John 20:25 in his hands, put my **f-s** into

FINISH (n)
the end
Rom 1:17 from start to **f** by faith.

FINISH, FINISHED, FINISHING (v)
to bring to completion; to bring to an end
Gen 2:2 had **f-ed** his work of creation,
John 4:34 and from **f-ing** his work.
John 19:30 he said, "It is **f-ed**!"
Acts 20:24 I use it for **f-ing** the work
2 Cor 8:11 Now you should **f** what you
2 Tim 4:7 I have **f-ed** the race,
Rev 20:3 the thousand years were **f-ed**.

FIRE, FIRES (n)
hot flame and burning light; symbolic of hell; severe trial or ordeal
Exod 3:2 **f** from the middle of a bush.
Exod 13:21 at night with a pillar of **f**.
Dan 3:25 walking around in the **f**
Matt 3:11 the Holy Spirit and with **f**.
Matt 5:22 are in danger of the **f-s** of hell.
Matt 18:8 be thrown into eternal **f**
Mark 9:43 the unquenchable **f-s** of hell
Mark 9:49 be tested with **f**.
Luke 3:16 with the Holy Spirit and with **f**.
Acts 2:3 tongues of **f** appeared and
1 Cor 3:13 The **f** will show
Heb 12:29 God is a devouring **f**.
Jas 3:6 it is set on **f** by hell itself.

FIRM (adj)
securely or solidly fixed in place; not weak or uncertain
Isa 7:9 Unless your faith is **f**,
2 Cor 1:21 to stand **f** for Christ.
2 Cor 1:24 own faith that you stand **f**.
Eph 6:13 will still be standing **f**.
1 Thes 3:8 you are standing **f** in the Lord.
2 Thes 2:15 brothers and sisters, stand **f**
1 Pet 5:9 Stand **f** against him,

FIRMAMENT (KJV)
Gen 1:7 *space* to separate the waters
Ps 19:1 *skies* display his craftsmanship
Ezek 1:22 surface like the *sky*, glittering

Dan 12:3	will shine as bright as the *sky*

FIRST (adj)
preceding all others in time, order, or importance

Gen 1:5	came, marking the **f** day.
Isa 44:6	I am the **F** and the Last;
Isa 48:12	God, the **F** and the Last.
Matt 22:38	the **f** and greatest
Mark 9:35	wants to be **f** must take last
Mark 13:10	Good News must **f** be
Rom 1:16	Jew **f** and also the Gentile.
Rom 2:9	Jew **f** and also for the Gentile.
1 Cor 15:45	The **f** man, Adam,
Eph 6:2	the **f** commandment with a
1 Tim 2:13	God made Adam **f**,
Heb 10:9	He cancels the **f** covenant
1 Jn 4:19	because he loved us **f**.
Rev 1:17	I am the **F** and the Last.
Rev 22:13	and the Omega, the **F** and the

FIRSTBEGOTTEN (KJV)

Heb 1:6	his *supreme Son* into the world

FIRSTBORN (adj)
eldest; the most prominent; the rightful heir

Exod 11:5	All the **f** sons will die
Exod 34:20	buy back every **f** son.
Ps 89:27	I will make him my **f** son,
Mic 6:7	sacrifice our **f** children to pay
Heb 12:23	assembly of God's **f** children

FIRSTBORN (n)
the eldest offspring; one possessing special rights of inheritance

Gen 25:34	for his rights as the **f**.
Exod 13:2	every **f** among the Israelites.
Exod 34:19	The **f** of every animal

FIRSTFRUITS (KJV)

Exod 23:16	the *first crops* of your harvest
Exod 23:19	bring the *very best* of
Lev 2:14	*first portion* of your harvest
Lev 23:10	you harvest its *first crops*,
Num 28:26	the *first* of your new grain
Rev 14:4	as a *special offering* to God

FISH(n)
any of numerous cold-blooded aquatic vertebrates

Jonah 1:17	had arranged for a great **f**
Matt 12:40	in the belly of the great **f**
Luke 9:13	loaves of bread and two **f**,
John 6:9	five barley loaves and two **f**.

FISH, FISHED, FISHING (v)
to attempt to catch fish

Mark 1:16	for they **f-ed** for a living.
Mark 1:17	how to **f** for people!
Luke 5:10	you'll be **f-ing** for people!

FISHERMEN (n)

Ezek 26:5	a rock in the sea, a place for **f**

FISHERS (KJV)
those who fish for a living

Isa 19:8	*fishermen* will lament for lack of work
Jer 16:16	*fishermen* who will catch
Matt 4:19	*how to fish* for people

FLAME, FLAMES (n)
a state of blazing combustion; burning zeal or passion

Isa 5:24	and dry grass shrivels in the **f**,
1 Cor 3:15	escaping through a wall of **f-s**.
2 Tim 1:6	fan into **f-s** the spiritual gift
Rev 1:14	his eyes were like **f-s** of fire.

FLAMING (adj)
blazing; intense

Isa 4:5	and smoke and **f** fire at night,
2 Thes 1:8	in **f** fire, bringing judgment on
Heb 12:18	to a place of **f** fire, darkness,

FLASHED (v)
to break forth in or like a sudden flame; to give off light suddenly

1 Kgs 18:38	the fire of the LORD **f** down
Dan 10:6	His face **f** like lightning,

FLATTER (v)
to praise excessively out of self-interest

Job 32:21	or try to **f** anyone.
Prov 29:5	To **f** friends is
Dan 11:32	He will **f** and win over those
Jude 1:16	**f** others to get what they want.

FLATTERING (adj)
characterized by excessive praise out of self-interest

Ps 12:2	speaking with **f** lips
Ps 12:3	cut off their **f** lips
Prov 26:28	and **f** words cause ruin.

FLATTERY (n)
insincere or excessive praise

Job 32:22	For if I tried **f**, my Creator
Ps 5:9	tongues are filled with **f**.
Prov 28:23	criticism far more than **f**.
1 Thes 2:5	try to win you with **f**,

FLEE (v)
to run away; to shun

1 Cor 10:14	**f** from the worship of idols.
Jas 4:7	and he will **f** from you.

FLEECE (n)
the wool obtained from a sheep at one shearing
Judg 6:37 If the **f** is wet with dew

FLEETING (adj)
passing swiftly
Ps 39:4 how **f** my life is.

FLESH (n)
the meaty part of animal and human bodies
see also BODY, HUMAN
Gen 2:23 and **f** from my **f**!
John 6:51 so the world may live, is my **f.**
1 Cor 15:39 different kinds of **f**—

FLIGHT (n)
an act or instance of running away
Deut 32:30 put ten thousand to **f,**

FLIRTING (v)
to behave amorously without serious intent
Isa 3:16 **f** with her eyes,

FLOCK, FLOCKS (n)
a group of animals assembled or herded together; a group under the guidance of a leader
Isa 40:11 feed his **f** like a shepherd.
Jer 10:21 and their **f-s** are scattered.
Jer 31:10 as a shepherd does his **f.**
Zech 11:17 who abandons the **f**!
Matt 26:31 the **f** will be scattered.
Luke 2:8 guarding their **f-s** of sheep.
Luke 12:32 don't be afraid, little **f.**
John 10:16 one **f** with one shepherd.
Acts 20:28 shepherd God's **f**—

FLOGGED (v)
to beat with a rod or whip
Deut 25:2 is sentenced to be **f,**
John 19:1 Pilate had Jesus **f**
Acts 5:40 and had them **f.**

FLOOD, FLOODS (n)
a rising and overflowing of a body of water; the destruction of the world by water during the time of Noah
Gen 7:7 the boat to escape the **f**—
Prov 27:4 cruel, and wrath is like a **f,**
Matt 24:38 In those days before the **f,**
Luke 6:49 the **f-s** sweep down against
2 Pet 2:5 ungodly people with a vast **f.**

FLOUR (n)
a product consisting of finely milled wheat
Lev 2:1 must consist of choice **f.**
Num 7:13 **f** moistened with olive oil.
Luke 17:35 grinding **f** together at the mill;

FLOURISH, FLOURISHING (v)
to grow luxuriantly; to prosper or thrive
Ps 72:7 all the godly **f** during his reign.
Ps 92:7 and evildoers **f,** they will be
Ps 92:12 the godly will **f** like palm trees
Prov 14:11 the tent of the godly will **f.**
Prov 28:28 meet disaster, the godly **f.**
Isa 35:7 reeds and rushes will **f**
2 Thes 1:3 your faith is **f-ing**

FLOW, FLOWING, FLOWS (v)
to proceed smoothly and readily; to abound
Exod 3:8 **f-ing** with milk and honey—
Exod 33:3 land that **f-s** with milk and
Num 13:27 **f-ing** with milk and honey.
Josh 5:6 **f-ing** with milk and honey.
Ps 119:171 Let praise **f** from my lips,
Jer 32:22 **f-ing** with milk and honey.
Lam 1:16 tears **f** down my cheeks.
John 7:38 living water will **f** from his
Rev 22:1 **f-ing** from the throne of God

FLOWER, FLOWERS (n)
the blossom of a plant
Job 14:2 We blossom like a **f** and then
Isa 40:6 as quickly as the **f-s** in a field.
Isa 40:7 **f-s** fade beneath the breath
Jas 1:10 like a little **f** in the field.

FOCUS (v)
to concentrate attention or effort
1 Tim 4:13 **f** on reading the Scriptures

FOES (n)
adversary, opponent, or enemy
Ps 112:8 face their **f** triumphantly.

FOLLOW, FOLLOWED, FOLLOWING, FOLLOWS (v)
to pursue or run after; to imitate; to obey
Deut 1:36 because he has **f-ed** the LORD
Deut 5:32 **f-ing** his instructions
Josh 14:14 he wholeheartedly **f-ed** the
1 Kgs 3:3 loved the LORD and **f-ed**
2 Chr 10:14 and **f-ed** the counsel
Prov 4:27 feet from **f-ing** evil.
Prov 10:9 those who **f** crooked paths
Isa 57:2 For those who **f** godly paths
Isa 65:2 But they **f** their own evil paths
Matt 4:20 at once and **f-ed** him.
Matt 7:24 listens to my teaching and **f-s**
Matt 8:19 I will **f** you wherever you go.
Matt 8:22 **F** me now. Let the
Matt 9:9 got up and **f-ed** him.
Matt 16:24 take up your cross, and **f**
Matt 19:27 given up everything to **f** you.

Matt 26:58 Meanwhile, Peter **f-ed** him
Mark 1:17 Come, **f** me, and I will show
Luke 9:23 your cross daily, and **f** me.
Luke 17:23 go out and **f** them.
Luke 18:43 **f-ed** Jesus, praising God.
John 8:12 If you **f** me, you won't have to
John 10:4 they **f** him because they know
John 10:27 know them, and they **f** me.
John 12:26 to be my disciple must **f** me,
John 21:19 Jesus told him, "**F** me."
1 Cor 1:12 or "I **f** only Christ."
1 Cor 4:17 of how I **f** Christ Jesus,
Gal 5:7 you back from **f-ing** the truth?
Gal 5:25 **f** the Spirit's leading
Phil 2:12 always **f-ed** my instructions
Phil 3:17 those who **f** our example.
2 Thes 3:6 and don't **f** the tradition
1 Pet 2:21 must **f** in his steps.
Rev 14:4 as virgins, **f-ing** the Lamb

FOLLOWER, FOLLOWERS (n)
one who follows the teachings of another; a disciple
1 Kgs 18:3 was a devoted **f** of the LORD.
Matt 10:42 one of the least of my **f-s,**
Matt 18:20 together as my **f-s,** I am there
Acts 9:21 Jesus' **f-s** in Jerusalem?

FOLLY (KJV)
Prov 14:18 clothed with *foolishness*
Prov 26:11 a fool repeats his *foolishness*
Eccl 2:13 is better than *foolishness*
Isa 9:17 they all speak *foolishness*
2 Tim 3:9 recognize what *fools* they are

FOOD (n)
something that nourishes, sustains, or supplies energy and vitality
see also BREAD
Lev 11:2 the ones you may use for **f.**
Prov 25:21 hungry, give them **f** to eat.
Isa 58:7 Share your **f** with the hungry,
Dan 1:8 defile himself by eating the **f**
Matt 6:11 today the **f** we need,
Matt 6:25 Isn't life more than **f,**
Mark 7:19 every kind of **f** is acceptable
John 6:55 my flesh is true **f,** and my
John 13:18 eats my **f** has turned against
Acts 15:20 abstain from eating **f**
Rom 14:6 kind of **f** do so to honor
1 Tim 6:8 have enough **f** and clothing,
Jas 2:15 who has no **f** or clothing,

FOOL, FOOLS (n)
one deficient in intellectual, practical, or moral sense
1 Sam 25:25 He is a **f,** just as his name
Ps 14:1 Only **f-s** say in their hearts,
Prov 6:32 commits adultery is an utter **f,**
Prov 10:8 babbling **f-s** fall flat on
Prov 10:23 wrong is fun for a **f,**
Prov 17:7 are not fitting for a **f;**
Prov 17:16 to pay tuition to educate a **f,**
Prov 26:1 associated with **f-s** than snow
Prov 26:7 A proverb in the mouth of a **f**
Prov 29:11 **F-s** vent their anger,
Prov 29:20 more hope for a **f** than for
Rom 1:22 became utter **f-s.**
1 Cor 3:18 need to become a **f** to be
2 Cor 11:21 I'm talking like a **f** again—
Eph 5:15 Don't live like **f-s,**
2 Tim 3:9 recognize what **f-s** they are,

FOOL, FOOLED, FOOLING (v)
to trick or deceive
Ps 119:118 are only **f-ing** themselves.
Jer 7:4 don't be **f-ed** by those who
1 Cor 15:33 Don't be **f-ed** by those who
Gal 6:3 you are only **f-ing** yourself.
Eph 5:6 Don't be **f-ed** by those who try
2 Thes 2:3 Don't be **f-ed** by what they say.
Jas 1:22 are only **f-ing** yourselves.
Jas 1:26 you are **f-ing** yourself,
1 Jn 1:8 we are only **f-ing** ourselves

FOOLISH (adj)
lacking in sense, judgment, or discretion; irreverent
Prov 26:4 the **f** arguments of fools,
Prov 26:17 else's argument is as **f**
Rom 1:28 abandoned them to their **f**
1 Cor 1:18 the cross is **f** to those who
1 Cor 1:27 world considers **f** in order to
1 Cor 2:14 It all sounds **f** to them
Eph 5:4 Obscene stories, **f** talk,
1 Tim 6:20 Avoid godless, **f** discussions
Titus 3:9 not get involved in **f** discussions

FOOLISHNESS (n)
aimless behavior befitting a fool
Prov 19:3 ruin their lives by their own **f**
Prov 22:15 heart is filled with **f,**
Eccl 10:1 so a little **f** spoils great
Mark 7:22 envy, slander, pride, and **f.**

FOOT (n)
the end of the leg upon which an individual stands
see also FEET
Josh 1:3 Wherever you set **f,**
Matt 18:8 with only one hand or one **f**
Luke 4:11 won't even hurt your **f**
1 Cor 12:15 If the **f** says,
Rev 10:2 and his left **f** on the land.

FOOTHOLD (n)
a strategic position enabling further advance or advantage
Eph 4:27 anger gives a **f** to the devil.

FOOTSTOOL (n)
a low stool used to support the feet
Ps 110:1 making them a **f** under
Isa 66:1 throne, and the earth is my **f.**
Matt 5:35 the earth is his **f.**
Acts 7:49 the earth is my **f.**
Heb 1:13 making them a **f** under
Heb 10:13 and made a **f** under

FORBID, FORBIDDEN (v)
to command against
Matt 16:19 Whatever you **f** on earth
Matt 16:19 will be **f-den** in heaven,
Matt 18:18 whatever you **f** on earth
1 Cor 14:39 don't **f** speaking in

FORCE (n)
violence, compulsion, or constraint exerted upon or against a person or thing
Zech 4:6 is not by **f** nor by strength,

FORCE, FORCED (v)
to compel by physical, moral, or intellectual means
Matt 27:32 soldiers **f-d** him to carry
John 6:15 were ready to **f** him to be

FORCEFUL (adj)
possessing or filled with force; effective
2 Cor 10:10 letters are demanding and **f,**

(FORE)FATHERS (KJV)
Exod 10:6 *ancestors* seen a plague like
Num 11:12 swore to give their *ancestors*
Jer 11:10 the sins of their *forefathers*
Matt 23:32 what your *ancestors* started

FOREHEAD, FOREHEADS (n)
the part of the face above the eyes
Exod 13:9 on your hand or your **f.**
Deut 6:8 wear them on your **f**
1 Sam 17:49 hit the Philistine in the **f.**
Rev 9:4 seal of God on their **f-s.**
Rev 13:16 right hand or on the **f.**
Rev 14:1 written on their **f-s.**

FOREIGN (adj)
related to or dealing with other nations; pagan
see also STRANGE
2 Chr 14:3 He removed the **f** altars and
2 Chr 33:15 also removed the **f** gods and
Isa 28:11 through **f** oppressors

FOREIGNER, FOREIGNERS (n)
nonresident, alien, or sojourner
see also STRANGER
Exod 22:21 not mistreat or oppress **f-s**
Exod 23:9 must not oppress **f-s.**
Lev 24:22 to the **f-s** living among you.
Neh 9:2 separated themselves from all **f-s**
Ps 119:19 I am only a **f** in the land
Hos 7:8 mingle with godless **f-s,**
Luke 17:18 glory to God except this **f?**
1 Cor 14:11 I will be a **f** to someone
Eph 2:19 no longer strangers and **f-s.**
1 Pet 1:1 living as **f-s** in the provinces
1 Pet 2:11 temporary residents and **f-s**

FOREKNOW, FOREKNEW, FOREKNOWLEDGE (KJV)
Acts 2:23 God *knew what would happen*
Rom 8:29 God *knew* his people *in advance*
Rom 11:2 whom he *chose from the very beginning*
1 Pet 1:2 Father *knew you and chose you*

FOREORDAINED (KJV)
1 Pet 1:20 *chose* him *as* your ransom

FORESKIN (n)
flap of skin covering the tip of the penis
Gen 17:11 cut off the flesh of your **f** as
Exod 4:25 touched his feet with the **f** and
Lev 12:3 boy's **f** must be circumcised.

FORETASTE (n)
a small anticipatory sample
Rom 8:23 as a **f** of future glory,

FORETOLD (v)
to tell beforehand; to predict
Rom 16:26 as the prophets **f**

FOREVER (adv)
for a limitless time; continually
see also ETERNAL, EVERLASTING
Gen 3:22 they will live **f!**
Gen 17:8 be their possession **f,**
2 Sam 7:26 name be honored **f**
1 Chr 17:24 be established and honored **f**
1 Chr 29:10 be praised **f** and ever!
Ezra 9:12 prosperity to your children **f.**
Ps 9:7 the LORD reigns **f,**
Ps 21:4 of his life stretch on **f.**
Ps 28:9 in your arms **f.**
Ps 37:28 keep them safe **f,**
Ps 61:8 sing praises to your name **f**
Ps 73:26 he is mine **f.**
Ps 79:13 will thank you **f** and ever,

Ps 86:12 glory to your name **f**,
Ps 92:8 will be exalted **f**.
Ps 100:5 unfailing love continues **f**,
Ps 103:17 the LORD remains **f** with
Ps 107:1 faithful love endures **f**.
Ps 110:4 are a priest **f**
Ps 111:8 They are **f** true,
Ps 112:9 be remembered **f**.
Ps 119:152 laws will last **f**.
Ps 146:6 every promise **f**.
Isa 32:17 and confidence **f**.
Isa 51:6 but my salvation lasts **f**.
Isa 60:15 make you beautiful **f**,
Isa 63:12 making himself famous **f**?
Jer 25:5 you and your ancestors **f**.
Dan 2:44 and it will stand **f**.
Dan 4:3 kingdom will last **f**, his rule
Dan 7:27 kingdom will last **f**,
John 6:51 eats this bread will live **f**;
1 Cor 13:8 But love will last **f**!
1 Cor 13:13 Three things will last **f**—
1 Cor 15:42 will be raised to live **f**.
1 Cor 15:50 inherit what will last **f**.
2 Cor 4:17 and will last **f**!
2 Cor 4:18 cannot see will last **f**.
1 Thes 4:17 will be with the Lord **f**.
2 Thes 1:9 destruction, **f** separated
Heb 5:6 a priest **f** in the order
Heb 7:17 a priest **f** in the order
Heb 7:24 Jesus lives **f**,
Heb 9:12 secured our redemption **f**.
Heb 13:8 yesterday, today, and **f**.
1 Pet 1:25 word of the Lord remains **f**.
1 Jn 2:17 will live **f**.
Rev 22:5 they will reign **f** and ever.

FORGAVE (v)
to pardon or acquit of guilt
see also FORGIVE

Ps 78:38 was merciful and **f** their sins
Luke 7:42 so he kindly **f** them both,
Eph 1:7 his Son and **f** our sins.
Col 1:14 our freedom and **f** our sins.
Col 2:13 with Christ, for he **f** all our

FORGET, FORGETTING (v)
to slip from remembrance; to disregard intentionally; to cease from remembering
see also FORGOT

Deut 4:9 careful never to **f**
Ps 78:7 hope anew on God, not **f-ting**
Ps 119:16 and not **f** your word.
Prov 3:1 My child, never **f**
Eccl 12:1 cause you to **f** your Creator.
Jer 2:32 a young woman **f** her jewelry?
Luke 12:6 God does not **f** a single one
Rom 3:31 we can **f** about the law?
Phil 3:13 **F-ting** the past and looking
Heb 13:16 And don't **f** to do good
Jas 1:24 walk away, and **f**
Jas 1:25 and don't **f** what you heard,
2 Pet 1:9 **f-ting** that they have been
2 Pet 3:8 must not **f** this one thing,

FORGIVE, FORGIVEN, FORGIVES, FORGIVING (v)
to pardon or acquit of sins
see also ATONE, FORGAVE

Gen 50:17 Please **f** your brothers
Exod 23:21 he will not **f** your rebellion.
Exod 34:7 I **f** iniquity, rebellion,
Exod 34:9 but please **f** our iniquity and
Num 14:18 **f-ting** every kind of sin
Num 14:19 just as you have **f-n** them
1 Sam 3:14 never be **f-n** by sacrifices
1 Kgs 8:34 hear from heaven and **f**
Ps 65:3 by our sins, you **f** them all.
Ps 79:9 Save us and **f** our sins
Ps 86:5 so good, so ready to **f**,
Ps 103:3 He **f-s** all my sins
Prov 17:9 when a fault is **f-n**,
Isa 22:14 you will never be **f-n** for this
Isa 38:17 and **f-n** all my sins.
Isa 55:7 for he will **f** generously.
Jer 31:34 I will **f** their wickedness,
Dan 9:19 O Lord, hear. O Lord, **f**.
Hos 14:2 **F** all our sins and
Matt 6:12 and **f** us our sins,
Matt 6:14 If you **f** those who sin
Matt 6:15 if you refuse to **f** others,
Matt 9:6 authority on earth to **f** sins.
Matt 18:21 how often should I **f**
Matt 26:28 to **f** the sins of many.
Mark 2:7 Only God can **f** sins!
Mark 2:10 authority on earth to **f** sins.
Mark 3:29 will never be **f-n**.
Mark 11:25 first **f** anyone you are
Mark 11:25 will **f** your sins,
Luke 5:21 Only God can **f** sins!
Luke 5:24 authority on earth to **f** sins.
Luke 6:37 **F** others, and you will be
Luke 7:47 a person who is **f-n** little
Luke 7:49 he goes around **f-ing** sins?
Luke 11:4 **f** us our sins, as we
Luke 17:3 if there is repentance, **f**.
Luke 17:4 asks forgiveness, you must **f**.
Luke 23:34 Father, **f** them,
John 20:23 If you **f** anyone's sins,
Acts 5:31 repent of their sins and be **f-n**.
Acts 8:22 Perhaps he will **f** your evil
Rom 4:5 faith in God who **f-s** sinners.
Rom 4:7 whose disobedience is **f-n**,

2 Cor 2:7 time to **f** and comfort
2 Cor 2:10 When you **f** this man,
Col 3:13 so you must **f** others.
Heb 8:12 I will **f** their wickedness,
1 Jn 1:9 is faithful and just to **f** us

FORGIVENESS (n)
aquittal or pardon of sins
see also ATONEMENT, MERCY
Neh 9:17 you are a God of **f,**
Luke 24:47 There is **f** of sins for all
Acts 13:38 this man Jesus there is **f**
Rom 5:15 his gift of **f** to many
Heb 9:22 of blood, there is no **f.**
Jas 5:20 bring about the **f** of many sins.

FORGOT, FORGOTTEN (v)
see also FORGET
Deut 32:18 **f** the God who had given
Ps 44:20 If we had **f-ten** the name
Ps 78:11 They **f** what he had done—
Ps 106:13 how quickly they **f**
Ps 119:176 not **f-ten** your commands.
Isa 17:10 You have **f-ten** the Rock
Isa 51:13 Yet you have **f-ten** the LORD,
Hos 8:14 Israel has **f-ten** its Maker

FORMED (v)
to create, fashion, or give shape to something
see also CREATE(D), MADE, MAKE
Gen 2:7 the LORD God **f** the man
Gen 2:19 LORD God **f** from the ground
Ps 94:9 the one who **f** your eyes?
Isa 49:5 the one who **f** me
Jer 1:5 knew you before I **f** you
Heb 11:3 universe was **f** at God's

FORMLESS (adj)
lacking order or arrangement; having no physical existence
Gen 1:2 The earth was **f** and empty,
Jer 4:23 and it was empty and **f.**

FORNICATION (KJV)
Isa 23:17 *be a prostitute* to all kingdoms
Matt 19:9 wife has been *unfaithful*
1 Cor 5:1 *sexual immorality* going on
1 Cor 6:18 *sexual immorality* is a sin
Jude 1:7 were filled with *immorality*

FORSAKE (v)
to renounce or turn away from entirely
1 Chr 28:9 But if you **f** him, he will
Job 28:28 to **f** evil is real understanding.

FORTRESS (n)
a fortified place; a place of security or survival
see also REFUGE
2 Sam 22:2 my **f,** and my savior;
Ps 27:1 The LORD is my **f,**
Ps 71:3 my rock and my **f.**
Ps 144:2 and my **f,** my tower of safety,
Prov 18:10 LORD is a strong **f;**
Zeph 3:6 devastating their **f** walls and

FORTUNE-TELLER, FORTUNE-TELLERS (n)
one who professes to foretell future events
Jer 29:8 your prophets and **f-s** who are
Acts 16:16 She was a **f** who earned a lot

FORTUNE-TELLING (n)
the act of one foretelling future events by occultic means
Lev 19:26 not practice **f** or witchcraft.

FORTY (adj)
the number 40
Gen 7:4 for **f** days and **f** nights,
Exod 16:35 Israel ate manna for **f** years
Exod 24:18 **f** days and **f** nights.
Num 14:34 wilderness for **f** years—
Matt 4:2 For **f** days and **f** nights
Acts 1:3 the **f** days after his crucifixion,
Acts 13:18 **f** years of wandering

FOUGHT (v)
see also FIGHT
Gen 32:28 because you have **f** with God
Josh 10:14 Surely the LORD **f** for Israel
2 Tim 4:7 I have **f** the good fight,

FOUND (v)
see also FIND
2 Kgs 22:8 I have **f** the Book of the Law
2 Kgs 23:24 Hilkiah the priest had **f**
2 Chr 15:15 after God, and they **f**
Luke 15:6 I have **f** my lost sheep.
Luke 15:9 because I have **f** my lost coin.
Luke 15:24 but now he is **f.**
Jas 2:8 the royal law as **f** in the
Rev 5:4 because no one was **f** worthy

FOUNDATION (n)
basis upon which something is built, supported, or added to; substructure
Prov 1:7 Fear of the LORD is the **f**
Prov 9:10 the LORD is the **f** of wisdom.
Isa 28:16 placing a **f** stone in Jerusalem,
Luke 6:49 a house without a **f.**
Eph 2:20 built on the **f** of the apostles
1 Tim 3:15 pillar and **f** of the truth.

2 Tim 2:19 stands firm like a **f** stone
Heb 1:10 you laid the **f** of the earth

FOUNTAIN (n)
source; spring of water
Isa 12:3 from the **f** of salvation!
Zech 13:1 a **f** to cleanse them

FOXES (n)
any of various carnivorous mammals of the dog family with shorter legs, pointed muzzles, and long bushy tails
Song 2:15 Catch all the **f,** those little **f,**
Luke 9:58 **F** have dens to live in,

FRAGRANCE (n)
a sweet or delicate odor
see also PERFUME
2 Cor 2:15 are a Christ-like **f** rising up

FRANKINCENSE (n)
an aromatic gum resin obtained from the Boswellia tree
Matt 2:11 gifts of gold, **f,** and myrrh.

FRAUD (n)
an act of deceiving or misrepresenting; trickery
Lev 6:2 you steal or commit **f,**
Acts 13:10 every sort of deceit and **f,**

FREE (adj)
not bound, confined, or detained by force; without restraint, inhibition, or cost; possessing the rights of citizenship
John 8:32 the truth will set you **f.**
John 8:36 sets you **f,** you are truly **f.**
Rom 6:7 we were set **f** from the power
Rom 6:18 you are **f** from your slavery
Gal 3:28 slave or **f,** male and female.
Jas 1:25 the perfect law that sets you **f,**
1 Pet 2:16 For you are **f,** yet

FREED, FREES (v)
to relieve or rid of what restrains, confines, restricts, or embarrasses
Ps 116:16 **f-d** me from my chains.
Ps 146:7 The Lord **f-s** the prisoners.
Isa 61:1 prisoners will be **f-d.**
Rom 3:24 he **f-d** us from the penalty
1 Cor 1:30 and he **f-d** us from sin.
Rev 1:5 and has **f-d** us from our sins

FREEDOM (n)
liberation from slavery, restraint, or the power of another
Ps 119:45 I will walk in **f,** for I have
2 Cor 3:17 the Lord is, there is **f.**
Gal 2:4 the **f** we have in Christ
Gal 4:5 sent him to buy **f** for us
Gal 5:13 don't use your **f** to satisfy
Eph 1:7 purchased our **f** with the blood
1 Pet 2:16 don't use your **f** as an excuse

FRIEND, FRIENDS (n)
intimate associate; a favored companion
Prov 16:28 separates the best of **f-s.**
Prov 17:9 on it separates close **f-s.**
Prov 20:6 will say they are loyal **f-s,**
Prov 27:6 Wounds from a sincere **f** are
Prov 28:7 with wild **f-s** bring shame
Prov 29:5 To flatter **f-s** is to lay a trap
Isa 41:8 from Abraham my **f,**
Zech 13:6 was wounded at my **f-s'** house!
John 11:3 Lord, your dear **f** is very sick.
John 15:13 one's life for one's **f-s.**
John 15:14 You are my **f-s** if you do
John 15:15 Now you are my **f-s,**
John 19:12 you are no '**f** of Caesar.'
Jas 2:23 even called the **f** of God.
Jas 4:4 want to be a **f** of the world,

FRIENDSHIP (n)
association of familiarity and companionship
Prov 3:32 he offers his **f** to the godly.
Rom 5:10 since our **f** with God was
Jas 4:4 you realize that **f** with the world

FRIGHTENED (v)
to terrify; to make afraid
Heb 12:21 was so **f** at the sight

FRINGE (n)
the edge; the threads hanging from cut or raveled edges
Matt 9:20 touched the **f** of his robe,

FROGS (n)
a leaping aquatic amphibian with smooth moist skin, long hind legs, and webbed feet
Exod 8:2 I will send a plague of **f**
Rev 16:13 spirits that looked like **f**

FRUIT (n)
a product of plant growth; product or result
Ps 1:3 bearing **f** each season.
Isa 11:1 new Branch bearing **f** from
Dan 4:12 loaded with **f** for all to eat.
Matt 3:10 not produce good **f** will be
Matt 7:20 can identify a tree by its **f,**
Matt 12:33 is bad, its **f** will be bad.
John 15:2 that doesn't produce **f,**
John 15:16 go and produce lasting **f,**

Gal 5:22 produces this kind of **f**
Phil 1:11 the **f** of your salvation—
2 Tim 2:6 first to enjoy the **f**
Rev 22:2 bearing twelve crops of **f,**

FRUITFUL (adj)
bearing fruit (product of a tree or plant); abundant (at producing work or in bearing children)
Gen 1:22 Be **f** and multiply.
Gen 9:1 Be **f** and multiply.
Gen 35:11 Be **f** and multiply.
Ps 128:3 will be like a **f** grapevine,
Jer 2:7 brought you into a **f** land
Phil 1:22 do more **f** work for Christ.

FRUSTRATES (v)
to impede or obstruct; to make invalid or with no effect
Ps 33:10 The LORD **f** the plans

FULFILL, FULFILLED, FULFILLS (v)
to complete or perform as promised; to measure up or satisfy
Ps 57:2 to God who will **f** his purpose
Dan 9:4 You always **f** your covenant
Matt 2:15 This **f-ed** what the Lord had
Matt 2:23 This **f-ed** what the prophets
Matt 13:35 **f-ed** what God had spoken
Matt 27:9 This **f-ed** the prophecy of
Luke 4:21 has been **f-ed** this very day!
Luke 24:44 Psalms must be **f-ed.**
John 18:9 this to **f** his own statement:
John 19:28 and to **f** Scripture he said,
Acts 1:16 Scriptures had to be **f-ed**
Rom 3:31 do we truly **f** the law.
Rom 13:8 you will **f** the requirements
Rom 13:10 love **f-s** the requirements
Eph 1:9 to **f** his own good pleasure.

FULFILLMENT (n)
the act of bringing to completion as promised
John 19:36 happened in **f** of the Scriptures

FULL (adj)
possessing or containing a great amount
Deut 34:9 was **f** of the spirit of wisdom,
Luke 4:1 Then Jesus, **f** of the Holy Spirit,
Acts 6:3 **f** of the Spirit and wisdom.
Acts 6:5 Stephen (a man **f** of faith and
Acts 7:55 Stephen, **f** of the Holy Spirit,
Acts 11:24 man, **f** of the Holy Spirit

FULLNESS (n)
the quality or state of containing all that is wanted, needed, or possible
Eph 3:19 with all the **f** of life and
Col 1:19 God in all his **f** was pleased
Col 2:9 lives all the **f** of God

FUN (n)
providing entertainment, amusement, or enjoyment
Prov 10:23 Doing wrong is **f** for a fool,
Prov 14:9 Fools make **f** of guilt,

FUNDAMENTAL (adj)
primary; basic; central
Heb 6:1 the **f** importance of repenting

FUNERAL (adj)
of, relating to, or constituting the observances held for a dead person
2 Sam 1:17 David composed a **f** song
Luke 7:32 so we played **f** songs,

FUNERALS (n)
the observances held for a dead person
Eccl 7:2 Better to spend your time at **f**

FURIOUS (adj)
exhibiting or goaded by anger
Judg 14:19 But Samson was **f**
2 Sam 12:5 David was **f.**
Jer 21:5 You have made me **f!**

FURNACE (n)
an enclosed structure in which heat is produced
Dan 3:6 be thrown into a blazing **f.**
Matt 13:42 throw them into the fiery **f,**

FURY (n)
wrath; fierceness; rage
Exod 15:7 You unleash your blazing **f;**
Deut 29:28 In great anger and **f**
Ps 7:6 against the **f** of my enemies!
Jer 32:37 will scatter them in my **f.**
Zeph 2:2 the fierce **f** of the Lord.

FUTILITY
the state of having no hope of success
Job 7:3 months of **f**, long and weary

FUTURE (adj)
existing or occurring at a later time
Deut 29:15 also with the **f** generations
Rom 8:19 waiting eagerly for that **f** day
Eph 2:7 can point to us in all **f** ages
Heb 2:5 will control the **f** world

FUTURE (n)
time that is to come; what is going to happen
Num 24:14 do to your people in the **f.**
Ps 31:15 My **f** is in your hands.

Ps 37:37	a wonderful **f** awaits those
Isa 42:9	tell you the **f** before it happens.
Isa 46:10	can tell you the **f** before it
Jer 29:11	to give you a **f** and a hope.
Jer 31:17	There is hope for your **f,**

G

GABRIEL

Angel who stands in God's presence; seen in Daniel's visions (Dan 8:16-18; 9:21); announced birth of John the Baptist (Luke 1:11-20); announced birth of Jesus (Luke 1:26-28).

GAIN (n)

winnings or profits

Isa 56:11	intent on personal **g.**

GAIN, GAINED, GAINS (v)

to acquire or win; to profit or increase

Prov 3:13	one who **g-s** understanding.
Prov 11:16	gracious woman **g-s** respect,
Mark 8:36	**g** the whole world but lose
Luke 9:25	**g** the whole world but are
1 Cor 13:3	I would have **g-ed** nothing.

GALILEE (n)

a Roman province of Palestine during the time of Jesus

Isa 9:1	a time in the future when **G**
Matt 4:15	beyond the Jordan River, in **G**
Matt 26:32	I will go ahead of you to **G**
Matt 28:10	my brothers to leave for **G,**

GARBAGE (n)

food waste; discarded or useless material

1 Cor 4:13	treated like the world's **g,**
Phil 3:8	counting it all as **g,**

GARDEN (n)

a planted area where fruits, vegetables, and flowers are cultivated

Gen 2:8	God planted a **g** in Eden
Gen 2:15	God placed the man in the **G**
1 Kgs 4:25	had its own home and **g.**
Song 4:12	my private **g,** my treasure,
Isa 58:11	will be like a well-watered **g,**
Jer 31:12	life will be like a watered **g,**
Ezek 28:13	in Eden, the **g** of God.

GARDENER (n)

one who takes care of a garden

John 15:1	my Father is the **g.**
John 20:15	She thought he was the **g.**

GARMENT, GARMENTS (n)

an article of clothing

Exod 28:2	Make sacred **g-s** for Aaron
Lev 16:23	he must take off the linen **g-s**
Lev 16:24	put on his regular **g-s,** and go
Ps 102:26	You will change them like a **g**
John 19:24	divided my **g-s** among

GATE, GATES (n)

opening in a (city) wall or fence, consisting of a door and protected by defensive structures (as towers); the place of judicial decisions, town criers, and marketplace trade; entrance

Esth 6:10	sits at the **g** of the palace.
Ps 24:7	Open up, ancient **g-s!**
Ps 100:4	his **g-s** with thanksgiving;
Isa 62:10	Go out through the **g-s!**
Matt 7:13	only through the narrow **g.**
John 10:1	going through the **g,**
John 10:2	who enters through the **g**
John 10:7	I am the **g** for the sheep.
Heb 13:12	died outside the city **g-s**
Rev 21:21	**g-s** were made of pearls—
Rev 21:21	each **g** from a single pearl!

GATEKEEPER (n)

one who guards or tends a gate

Ps 84:10	a **g** in the house of my God

GATHER, GATHERED, GATHERING (v)

to bring together; to reap or harvest; to assemble

Exod 16:18	Those who **g-ed** a lot
Jer 23:3	will **g** together the remnant
Zech 14:2	I will **g** all the nations
Matt 24:31	they will **g** his chosen ones
Matt 25:26	**g-ed** crops I didn't cultivate,
Matt 25:32	the nations will be **g-ed** in his
Mark 13:27	to **g** his chosen ones
Luke 3:17	**g-ing** the wheat into his barn
Luke 13:34	wanted to **g** your children
2 Cor 8:15	say, "Those who **g-ed** a lot
2 Thes 2:1	we will be **g-ed** to meet him.
Rev 16:16	demonic spirits **g-ed** all

GAVE (v)

to suffer the loss of

see also GIVE

John 3:16	he **g** his one and only Son,
Rom 8:32	**g** him up for us all,
Gal 2:20	loved me and **g** himself for me.
1 Tim 2:6	He **g** his life to purchase

GENERATION, GENERATIONS (n)

the whole body of individuals born about the same time (nation or racial group); the period of time dur-

ing which those individuals lived (also, age or era); offspring
Gen 17:7 after you, from **g** to **g.**
Exod 20:6 love for a thousand **g-s**
Num 32:13 the entire **g** that sinned
Judg 2:10 After that **g** died,
1 Chr 16:15 to a thousand **g-s.**
Ps 71:18 your power to this new **g,**
Ps 100:5 continues to each **g.**
Ps 102:12 endure to every **g.**
Ps 102:18 recorded for future **g-s,**
Ps 105:8 to a thousand **g-s.**
Ps 119:90 extends to every **g,**
Ps 145:4 Let each **g** tell its children
Ps 146:10 throughout the **g-s.**
Prov 27:24 not be passed to the next **g.**
Isa 41:4 summoning each new **g**
Lam 5:19 continues from **g** to **g.**
Joel 1:3 the story down from **g** to **g.**
Matt 12:39 Only an evil, adulterous **g**
Mark 13:30 this **g** will not pass
Luke 1:48 all **g-s** will call me blessed.
Luke 11:29 This evil **g** keeps asking me
Acts 2:40 from this crooked **g!**
Eph 3:5 not reveal it to previous **g-s,**
Eph 3:21 all **g-s** forever and ever!

GENEROSITY (n)
the quality or fact of being magnanimous, kindly, or openhanded; abundance
Acts 2:46 meals with great joy and **g**—
2 Cor 9:10 a great harvest of **g** in you.
Eph 4:7 through the **g** of Christ.
Phlm 1:6 put into action the **g** that

GENEROUS (adj)
magnanimous, kindly; liberal in giving; abundant
Deut 15:8 Instead, be **g** and lend
Ps 37:26 godly always give **g** loans to
2 Cor 9:6 will get a **g** crop.
1 Tim 6:18 **g** to those in need,

GENTILE, GENTILES (n)
non-Jewish individuals or nations, often connoting heathens or pagans
see also NATION(S)
Isa 49:6 make you a light to the **G-s,**
Luke 21:24 period of the **G-s** comes
Acts 10:45 out on the **G-s,** too.
Acts 14:27 faith to the **G-s,** too.
Acts 15:14 God first visited the **G-s**
Acts 21:25 As for the **G** believers,
Acts 28:28 also been offered to the **G-s,**
Rom 1:16 Jews first and also the **G.**
Rom 2:9 Jews first and also for the **G.**
Rom 3:9 people, whether Jews or **G-s,**
Rom 3:29 God of the **G-s?**
Rom 10:12 Jew and **G** are the same
Rom 11:11 available to the **G-s.**
Rom 15:9 the **G-s** might give glory
Rom 15:27 **G-s** received the spiritual
Gal 2:2 preaching to the **G-s.**
Gal 2:8 apostle to the **G-s.**
Gal 2:9 keep preaching to the **G-s,**
Gal 3:8 God would declare the **G-s**
Gal 3:14 blessed the **G-s** with the same
Gal 3:28 no longer Jew or **G,** slave or
Eph 3:8 the privilege of telling the **G-s**
Col 3:11 a Jew or a **G,** circumcised or

GENTLE (adj)
kind; mild-mannered; soft
1 Kgs 19:12 sound of a **g** whisper.
Prov 15:1 A **g** answer deflects anger,
Prov 15:4 **G** words are a tree of life;
Matt 11:29 am humble and **g** at heart,
1 Cor 4:21 love and a **g** spirit?
Eph 4:2 be humble and **g.** Be patient
1 Tim 3:3 must be **g,** not quarrelsome,
Titus 3:2 be **g** and show true humility
Jas 3:17 **g** at all times,

GENTLENESS (n)
mildness of manners or disposition
Gal 5:23 **g,** and self-control.
Col 3:12 kindness, humility, **g,** and
1 Tim 6:11 perseverance, and **g.**

GENUINE (adj)
actual, true, authentic, sincere
John 1:47 here is a **g** son of Israel—
2 Cor 8:8 I am testing how **g** your love
Phil 1:18 motives are false or **g,**
2 Tim 1:5 I remember your **g** faith,

GETHSEMANE (n)
the garden where Jesus often went for prayer, rest, or fellowship; the site where Judas betrayed Jesus before the crucifixion
Matt 26:36 to the olive grove called **G,**
Mark 14:32 to the olive grove called **G,**

GHOST, GHOSTS (n)
the soul of a dead person believed to appear to the living in bodily likeness
Luke 24:39 I am not a **g,** because **g-s**

GIDEON
Judge of Israel, also called "Jerub-baal" (Judg 6–8; 7:1; Heb 11:32); called by angel of the LORD (Judg 6:11-16); cut down Baal's altar (Judg 6:25-32); used fleece for guidance (Judg 6:36-40); led Israel against Midian-

ite oppressors (Judg 7:1–8:21); refused kingship (Judg 8:22-23); made an ephod (Judg 8:24-28); died (Judg 8:29-35).

GIFT, GIFTS (n)
a present from people to people (often a bribe); a sacrifice from people to God; anything given voluntarily or at no cost; that which is given from God, enabling or empowering his people
Prov 18:16 Giving a **g** can open doors;
Matt 2:11 and gave him **g-s** of gold,
Luke 11:13 how to give good **g-s** to your
Rom 4:16 given as a free **g.**
Rom 5:15 and God's gracious **g.**
Rom 6:23 free **g** of God is eternal
Rom 11:29 For God's **g-s** and his call
1 Cor 12:4 kinds of spiritual **g-s,**
1 Cor 12:7 A spiritual **g** is given
1 Cor 12:31 the most helpful **g-s.**
2 Cor 9:5 I want it to be a willing **g,**
2 Cor 9:15 Thank God for this **g**
Gal 2:9 recognized the **g** God had
Eph 2:8 it is a **g** from God.
Eph 4:8 and gave **g-s** to his people.
2 Tim 1:6 the spiritual **g** God gave you
Heb 2:4 **g-s** of the Holy Spirit
1 Pet 3:7 equal partner in God's **g**
1 Pet 4:10 of spiritual **g-s.**

GIRL (n)
a female child from birth to adulthood
2 Kgs 5:2 was a young **g** who had been
Mark 5:41 which means "Little **g**, get up!"

GIVE, GIVEN, GIVES, GIVING (v)
to grant, bestow, convey, offer, provide, or designate; to yield or produce; to suffer the loss of (life)
Exod 30:15 poor must not **g** less.
1 Sam 1:28 **g-ing** him to the LORD,
Ps 112:9 share freely and **g** generously
Ps 119:130 your word **g-s** light,
Prov 21:26 the godly love to **g!**
Prov 23:26 O my son, **g** me your heart.
Isa 9:6 a son is **g-n** to us.
Matt 7:11 heavenly Father **g** good gifts
Matt 16:19 And I will **g** you the keys
Matt 22:30 marry nor be **g-n** in marriage.
Mark 6:7 by two, **g-ing** them authority
Luke 11:13 know how to **g** good gifts to
Luke 14:33 my disciple without **g-ing** up
Luke 22:19 body, which is **g-n** for you.
John 1:17 the law was **g-n** through Moses,
John 5:21 so the Son **g-s** life to anyone
John 13:34 So now I am **g-ing** you a new
John 14:27 And the peace I **g** is a gift
Acts 5:32 Spirit, who is **g-n** by God
Acts 14:3 was true by **g-ing** them power
Acts 15:8 by **g-ing** them the Holy Spirit
Acts 20:35 is more blessed to **g** than to
Rom 2:7 He will **g** eternal life
Rom 5:5 because he has **g-n** us the Holy
Rom 8:32 won't he also **g** us everything
Rom 10:12 Lord, who **g-s** generously
Rom 12:8 is giving, **g** generously.
Rom 14:12 each of us will **g** a personal
1 Cor 9:17 God has **g-n** me this sacred
1 Cor 11:24 body, which is **g-n** for you.
1 Cor 15:57 thank God! He **g-s** us victory
2 Cor 3:6 the Spirit **g-s** life.
2 Cor 8:6 this ministry of **g-ing.**
2 Cor 9:7 how much to **g.**
Eph 4:7 he has **g-n** each one of us
Eph 4:28 and then **g** generously to
1 Thes 4:8 rejecting God, who **g-s**
1 Tim 6:17 God, who richly **g-s** us all we
1 Jn 4:13 And God has **g-n** us his Spirit

GLAD (adj)
joyful or happy, often with shouts
Ps 16:9 my heart is **g**, and I rejoice.
Ps 32:11 LORD and be **g**, all you who
Ps 69:32 at work and be **g.**
Ps 97:1 coastlands be **g.**
Ps 104:15 wine to make them **g,**
Ps 118:24 will rejoice and be **g** in it.
Prov 10:8 The wise are **g** to be
Prov 27:11 make my heart **g.**
Isa 35:1 and desert will be **g**
Zeph 3:14 O Israel! Be **g** and rejoice
Matt 5:12 Be very **g!**
John 11:15 for your sakes, I'm **g** I wasn't
Acts 13:48 they were very **g**
1 Cor 12:26 the parts are **g.**
2 Cor 2:2 will make me **g?**
Rev 19:7 Let us be **g** and rejoice,

GLADNESS (n)
the quality or state of joy or delight; happiness
Ps 40:16 with joy and **g** in you.
Ps 90:15 Give us **g** in proportion to
Isa 35:10 filled with joy and **g.**
Jer 48:33 Joy and **g** are gone
Zeph 3:17 in you with **g.**

GLEAMING (adj)
shining with or as if with moderate brightness
Ezek 1:27 he looked like **g** amber,

GLORIFY, GLORIFIED, GLORIFIES, GLORIFYING (v)
to bestow honor or praise (as in worship); to magnify
see also EXALT, HONOR

Ps 147:12 **G** the LORD, O Jerusalem!
Isa 26:8 desire is to **g** your name.
Isa 42:12 the whole world **g** the LORD;
Dan 4:37 praise and **g** and honor the
Luke 2:20 flocks, **g-ing** and praising
John 8:50 no wish to **g** myself, God is
John 13:31 God will be **g-ied**
John 17:1 **G** your Son so
John 21:19 of death he would **g** God.
2 Cor 8:19 a service that **g-ies** the Lord
Eph 1:14 would praise and **g** him.
Rev 15:4 you, Lord, and **g** your name?

GLORIOUS (adj)
possessing or deserving special honor; splendid or magnificent
Exod 15:6 O LORD, is **g** in power.
Exod 33:18 show me your **g** presence.
Deut 32:3 the LORD; how **g** is our God!
1 Chr 16:28 the LORD is **g** and strong.
Neh 9:5 prayed: "May your **g** name be
Job 37:5 God's voice is **g** in the
Ps 45:3 You are so **g**, so majestic!
Ps 76:4 You are **g** and more majestic
Ps 96:3 Publish his **g** deeds among the
Ps 149:9 This is the **g** privilege of
Isa 55:5 of Israel, have made you **g**.
Isa 63:15 from your holy, **g** home,
Dan 8:9 east and toward the **g** land of
Dan 11:45 between the **g** holy mountain
Matt 19:28 sits upon his **g** throne,
Acts 2:20 that great and **g** day of the
Acts 7:2 Our **g** God appeared to
Rom 1:23 worshiping the **g**, ever-living
Rom 3:23 of God's **g** standard.
Rom 8:21 children in **g** freedom from
2 Cor 3:9 how much more **g** is the new
2 Cor 3:10 first glory was not **g** at all
2 Cor 3:18 into his **g** image.
Eph 1:6 God for the **g** grace he has
Eph 1:17 asking God, the **g** Father of
Eph 3:16 that from his **g**, unlimited
Eph 5:27 himself as a **g** church without
Phil 3:21 them into **g** bodies like his
Phil 4:19 from his **g** riches, which have
Col 1:11 with all his **g** power so you
Jas 2:1 faith in our **g** Lord Jesus
1 Pet 1:8 with a **g**, inexpressible joy.
1 Pet 4:14 for then the **g** Spirit of God
Jude 1:24 into his **g** presence without a

GLORY (n)
honor bestowed; splendor or magnificence; a distinguishing quality, asset, or attribute
Exod 16:10 awesome **g** of the LORD
Num 14:21 filled with the LORD's **g**,
Josh 7:19 My son, give **g** to the LORD,
1 Sam 4:21 said, "Israel's **g** is gone."
Ps 8:5 them with **g** and honor.
Ps 19:1 proclaim the **g** of God.
Ps 29:1 LORD for his **g** and strength.
Ps 44:8 O God, we give **g** to you
Ps 57:11 May your **g** shine over all the
Ps 71:8 I declare your **g** all day
Ps 86:12 I will give **g** to your name
Ps 108:5 May your **g** shine over all the
Ps 145:12 the majesty and **g** of your
Prov 16:31 is a crown of **g**; it is gained
Isa 6:3 earth is filled with his **g**!
Isa 24:16 songs that give **g** to the
Isa 35:2 display his **g**, the splendor
Isa 42:8 not give my **g** to anyone else,
Isa 48:11 not share my **g** with idols!
Isa 66:11 Drink deeply of her **g** even
Isa 66:19 they will declare my **g** to the
Ezek 44:4 saw that the **g** of the LORD
Matt 16:27 angels in the **g** of his Father
Matt 25:31 comes in his **g**, and all the
Mark 13:26 great power and **g**.
Luke 2:14 **G** to God in highest heaven,
Luke 9:26 and in the **g** of the Father
Luke 9:32 they saw Jesus' **g** and the two
Luke 21:27 power and great **g**.
John 1:14 have seen his **g**, the **g** of
John 7:39 not yet entered into his **g**.
John 11:40 you would see God's **g** if
John 12:23 enter into his **g**.
John 12:41 the Messiah's **g**.
John 14:13 the Son can bring **g** to the
John 16:14 will bring me **g** by telling
John 17:22 given them the **g** you gave
Acts 3:13 who has brought **g** to his
Rom 2:7 seeking after the **g** and honor
Rom 2:10 there will be **g** and honor and
Rom 3:7 and brings him more **g**?
Rom 4:20 in this he brought **g** to God.
Rom 8:17 heirs of God's **g**.
Rom 8:18 compared to the **g** he will
Rom 8:30 gave them his **g**.
Rom 9:4 God revealed his **g** to them.
Rom 9:23 riches of his **g** shine even
Rom 9:23 in advance for **g**.
Rom 15:6 giving praise and **g** to God,
Rom 15:9 Gentiles might give **g** to God
Rom 16:27 All **g** to the only wise God
1 Cor 2:7 for our ultimate **g** before the
1 Cor 10:31 all for the **g** of God.
1 Cor 15:43 will be raised in **g**.
2 Cor 1:20 to God for his **g**.
2 Cor 3:7 shone with the **g** of God, even
2 Cor 3:10 In fact, that first **g** was not
2 Cor 4:4 about the **g** of Christ, who is

2 Cor 4:17 for us a **g** that vastly
Eph 1:12 bring praise and **g** to God.
Phil 1:11 will bring much **g** and praise
Phil 2:11 is Lord, to the **g** of God the
Phil 4:20 Now all **g** to God our
1 Thes 2:12 Kingdom and **g.**
2 Thes 2:14 share in the **g** of our Lord
1 Tim 1:17 All honor and **g** to God
1 Tim 3:16 to heaven in **g.**
2 Tim 4:18 All **g** to God forever
Titus 2:13 when the **g** of our great God
Heb 1:3 God's own **g** and expresses the
Heb 2:9 crowned with **g** and honor.
Heb 3:3 far more **g** than Moses, just
1 Pet 1:7 much praise and **g** and honor
1 Pet 1:21 gave him great **g.**
1 Pet 5:4 of never-ending **g** and honor.
2 Pet 1:3 means of his marvelous **g** and
2 Pet 1:17 from the majestic **g** of God
Jude 1:25 All **g,** majesty, power,
Rev 4:9 beings give **g** and honor and
Rev 4:11 God, to receive **g** and honor
Rev 5:12 honor and **g** and blessing.
Rev 5:13 and honor and **g** and power
Rev 11:13 terrified and gave **g** to the
Rev 16:9 God and give him **g.**
Rev 21:11 shone with the **g** of God and
Rev 21:23 for the **g** of God
Rev 21:26 will bring their **g** and honor

GLUTTON, GLUTTONS (n)
one given habitually to greedy and voracious eating and drinking
Prov 23:20 or feast with **g-s,**
Matt 11:19 He's a **g** and a drunkard,
Titus 1:12 cruel animals, and lazy **g-s.**

GNASHING (v)
to grate or grind one's teeth together as an expression of hatred, scorn, or utter despair
Matt 8:12 be weeping and **g** of teeth.

GNAT, GNATS (n)
any of various small usually biting dipteran flies
Exod 8:16 swarms of **g-s** throughout the
Matt 23:24 swallow a **g,** but you swallow

GOAL (n)
the end toward which effort is directed; aim
1 Cor 14:1 be your highest **g!**
2 Cor 5:9 our **g** is to please him.
1 Thes 4:11 Make it your **g** to live a

GOAT, GOATS (n)
any of various hollow-horned ruminant mammals with backwardly arching horns, a short tail, and usually straight hair
Gen 15:9 a three-year-old female **g,**
Gen 30:32 all the sheep and **g-s** that are
Gen 37:31 killed a young **g** and dipped
Lev 16:9 sin offering the **g** chosen by
Num 7:16 and a male **g** for a sin
Num 7:17 rams, five male **g-s,** and five
Isa 11:6 with the baby **g.**
Dan 8:5 a male **g** appeared from the
Matt 25:32 the sheep from the **g-s.**
Heb 10:4 blood of bulls and **g-s**

GOD, GODS (n)
eternal, infinite Spirit; Creator, Redeemer, sovereign Lord; impotent pagan diety; image of pagan diety (made of wood, metal, or stone)
see also IDOL(S)
Gen 1:1 In the beginning **G** created
Gen 1:27 In the image of **G** he created
Gen 3:1 Did **G** really say you must not
Gen 6:2 The sons of **G** saw the
Gen 14:18 a priest of **G** Most High,
Gen 17:1 El-Shaddai—'**G** Almighty.'
Gen 22:12 I know that you truly fear **G.**
Gen 50:20 **G** intended it all for good.
Exod 20:5 am a jealous **G** who will not
Exod 22:28 must not dishonor **G** or curse
Exod 32:4 these are the **g-s** who brought
Exod 34:6 The **G** of compassion
Deut 6:4 LORD is our **G,** the LORD
Deut 23:5 LORD your **G** loves you.
Deut 32:16 by worshiping foreign **g-s;** they
Deut 32:39 There is no other **g** but me!
Deut 33:27 The eternal **G** is
Josh 24:19 a holy and jealous **G.**
1 Kgs 8:23 there is no **G** like you
1 Kgs 18:21 if Baal is **G,** then follow
2 Kgs 19:15 You alone are **G** of all
Ezra 9:9 unfailing love our **G** did not
Neh 1:5 awesome **G** who keeps
Ps 19:1 proclaim the glory of **G.**
Ps 22:1 My **G,** my **G,** why have
Ps 42:2 I thirst for **G,** the living **G.**
Ps 42:8 praying to **G** who gives
Ps 51:10 a clean heart, O **G.**
Ps 82:6 say, 'You are **g-s;** you are all
Ps 100:3 the LORD is **G!**
Ps 139:23 Search me, O **G,** and know
Prov 24:12 For **G** understands all
Eccl 12:13 conclusion: Fear **G** and obey
Isa 9:6 Mighty **G,** Everlasting Father,
Isa 43:10 I alone am **G.**
Dan 6:16 May your **G,** whom you
Jonah 4:2 compassionate **G,** slow to
Mic 6:8 walk humbly with your **G.**

Mic 7:18 Where is another **G** like you,
Nah 1:2 a jealous **G,** filled with
Mark 2:7 Only **G** can forgive
Mark 3:35 Anyone who does **G**'s will is
Mark 15:34 My **G,** my **G,** why
Luke 2:14 Glory to **G** in highest
Luke 10:9 The Kingdom of **G** is near
Luke 16:13 cannot serve both **G** and
Luke 20:38 So he is the **G** of the living,
John 1:1 Word was with **G**
John 1:18 One, who is himself **G,** is near
John 1:29 The Lamb of **G** who
John 3:16 For **G** loved the world so
John 10:34 I say, you are **g-s**!
John 14:1 Trust in **G,** and trust also
Acts 5:29 We must obey **G** rather than
Acts 12:24 word of **G** continued to
Acts 19:26 aren't really **g-s** at all.
Rom 1:16 the power of **G** at work,
Rom 3:23 short of **G**'s glorious
Rom 5:1 have peace with **G** because
Rom 5:5 know how dearly **G** loves us,
Rom 6:23 free gift of **G** is eternal
Rom 8:17 are heirs of **G**'s glory.
Rom 12:2 learn to know **G**'s will for you,
1 Cor 1:18 the very power of **G.**
1 Cor 1:25 foolish plan of **G** is wiser
1 Cor 6:20 you must honor **G** with your
1 Cor 14:33 not a **G** of disorder but
2 Cor 10:4 We use **G**'s mighty weapons,
Gal 3:6 believed **G,** and **G** counted him
Eph 2:10 For we are **G**'s masterpiece.
Eph 5:1 Imitate **G,** therefore, in
Phil 2:6 equality with **G** as something
Phil 4:7 you will experience **G**'s peace,
Col 2:9 the fullness of **G** in a human
1 Thes 5:18 for this is **G**'s will
1 Tim 2:5 is only one **G** and one
Titus 1:2 **G**—who does not lie—
Heb 6:18 is impossible for **G** to lie.
Heb 7:19 we draw near to **G.**
Heb 11:6 believe that **G** exists
Jas 2:19 there is one **G.**
Jas 2:23 Abraham believed **G,** and **G**
Jas 4:8 Come close to **G,** and **G**
1 Pet 2:15 It is **G**'s will that your
1 Pet 5:5 for "**G** opposes the proud
1 Jn 1:5 declare to you: **G** is light,
1 Jn 4:21 Those who love **G** must also
Rev 19:6 the Lord our **G,** the Almighty,
Rev 21:23 glory of **G** illuminates the

GOD-BREATHED (KJV)

2 Tim 3:16 Scripture is *inspired by God*

GOD-FEARING (adj)

having a reverent feeling toward God; devout

Acts 10:2 was a devout, **G** man,
Acts 10:22 is a devout and **G** man,
Acts 13:26 and also you **G** Gentiles—this
Acts 17:4 along with many **G** Greek men
Acts 17:17 Jews and the **G** Gentiles,

GODDESS (n)

a female god

Acts 19:27 of the great **g** Artemis will

GODLESS (adj)

not acknowledging a deity or divine law

see also UNGODLY

Job 20:5 joy of the **g** has been only
Hos 7:8 mingle with **g** foreigners,
1 Tim 6:20 Avoid **g,** foolish
2 Tim 2:16 to more **g** behavior.
Titus 2:12 to turn from **g** living and
1 Pet 4:3 things that **g** people enjoy—
1 Pet 4:18 will happen to **g** sinners?

GODLINESS (n)

devotion to God; piety

see also RIGHTEOUSNESS

Prov 16:8 Better to have little, with **g,**
1 Tim 4:8 but training for **g** is much
1 Tim 5:4 to show **g** at home
1 Tim 6:6 Yet true **g** with contentment

GODLY (adj)

marked by or showing reverence for God and devotion to worship

see also RIGHTEOUS, UPRIGHT

Ps 31:23 LORD, all you **g** ones!
Ps 34:9 LORD, you his **g** people,
Prov 16:31 by living a **g** life.
Prov 23:24 The father of **g** children has
Acts 22:12 He was a **g** man, deeply
Gal 6:1 you who are **g** should gently
1 Tim 6:3 promote a **g** life.
2 Tim 3:12 to live a **g** life in Christ
Titus 1:1 how to live **g** lives.
2 Pet 2:9 how to rescue **g** people from
2 Pet 3:11 what holy and **g** lives you

GODLY (n)

people who are righteous or devout

Ps 1:5 no place among the **g.**
Ps 37:21 but the **g** are generous givers.
Ps 37:30 The **g** offer good counsel;
Ps 68:3 But let the **g** rejoice.
Ps 118:20 LORD, and the **g** enter there.
Prov 3:32 friendship to the **g.**
Prov 10:11 The words of the **g** are a

Prov 10:20 The words of the **g** are like
Prov 10:28 The hopes of the **g** result in
Prov 11:5 The **g** are directed by
Prov 11:28 But the **g** flourish like
Prov 13:9 The life of the **g** is full of
Prov 20:7 The **g** walk with
Prov 21:15 Justice is a joy to the **g**,
Prov 28:1 the **g** are as bold as lions.

GOLD (n)
a valuable yellow malleable metal especially used in coins and jewelry
1 Kgs 20:3 Your silver and **g** are mine,
Ps 19:10 more desirable than **g**,
Ps 119:127 even the finest **g**.
Prov 3:14 are better than **g**.
Matt 2:11 gifts of **g**, frankincense,
Rev 3:18 advise you to buy **g** from me—

GOLGOTHA (n)
a hill just outside Jerusalem; the place where Jesus was crucified
Matt 27:33 a place called **G**
Mark 15:22 a place called **G**
John 19:17 (in Hebrew, **G**).

GOLIATH
Great Philistine warrior killed by David (1 Sam 17:4, 8, 23; 21:9; 22:10; 2 Sam 21:19; 1 Chr 20:5).

GOMORRAH (n)
one of the five "cities of the plain" located in the Valley of Siddim; God destroyed this city by fire for its extreme wickedness
Gen 19:24 on Sodom and **G**.
Matt 10:15 and **G** will be better
2 Pet 2:6 of Sodom and **G** and turned
Jude 1:7 forget Sodom and **G** and their

GOOD (adj)
kind; profitable; excellent; fitting or appropriate; morally right
Gen 1:4 that the light was **g**.
Gen 1:31 it was very **g**!
Gen 2:18 It is not **g** for the man to
2 Chr 7:3 He is **g**! His faithful
2 Chr 31:20 was pleasing and **g** in the
Ps 34:8 see that the LORD is **g**.
Ps 119:68 You are **g** and do only
Eccl 7:20 earth is always **g** and never
Isa 5:20 that evil is **g** and **g** is
Isa 45:7 I send **g** times and
Mic 6:8 told you what is **g**, and this is
Matt 5:29 eye—even your **g** eye—causes
Matt 19:17 is only One who is **g**.
Matt 22:10 they could find, **g** and bad
Matt 25:21 Well done, my **g** and
Mark 3:4 the law permit **g** deeds on the
Mark 10:18 God is truly **g**.
Luke 6:45 person produces **g** things from
Luke 6:45 treasury of a **g** heart,
Luke 8:15 seeds that fell on the **g** soil
Luke 14:34 Salt is **g** for seasoning.
Luke 18:19 God is truly **g**.
Luke 19:17 You are a **g** servant.
John 10:11 I am the **g** shepherd.
Rom 7:12 and right and **g**.
Rom 7:16 that the law is **g**.
Rom 7:18 know that nothing **g** lives in
Rom 7:19 do what is **g**, but I don't.
Rom 12:2 you, which is **g** and pleasing
Rom 12:9 Hold tightly to what is **g**.
1 Cor 6:12 not everything is **g** for you.
1 Cor 7:1 Yes, it is **g** to abstain
1 Cor 15:33 corrupts **g** character.
Gal 6:9 doing what is **g**.
Eph 2:10 so we can do the **g** things he
Phil 1:6 who began the **g** work within
1 Thes 5:21 Hold on to what is **g**.
1 Tim 4:4 everything God created is **g**,
1 Tim 6:12 Fight the **g** fight
2 Tim 3:17 people to do every **g** work.
2 Tim 4:7 I have fought the **g** fight,
Titus 3:8 These teachings are **g**
Heb 10:24 of love and **g** works.
Heb 12:10 is always **g** for us,
Jas 2:8 indeed, it is **g** when you obey

GOOD (n)
something that is excellent, profitable, or morally right; advancement of prosperity or well-being; something useful or beneficial
Gen 2:9 the knowledge of **g** and evil.
Gen 3:22 knowing both **g** and evil.
Gen 50:20 God intended it all for **g**.
1 Sam 26:23 reward for doing **g** and for
Ps 14:1 not one of them does **g**!
Ps 53:3 No one does **g**, not a single
Prov 3:27 Do not withhold **g** from those
Prov 11:27 If you search for **g**, you will
Prov 31:12 She brings him **g**, not harm,
Isa 55:2 does you no **g**?
Jer 13:23 you start doing **g**, for you
Jer 32:39 for their own **g** and for the
Matt 5:45 evil and the **g**, and he sends
Rom 3:12 No one does **g**, not a single
Rom 8:28 together for the **g** of those
Rom 13:4 sent for your **g**.
1 Cor 10:24 but for the **g** of others.
Gal 6:10 we should do **g** to everyone—
Eph 6:8 each one of us for the **g** we do,
1 Tim 5:10 because of the **g** she has

Heb 13:16 forget to do **g** and to share
1 Pet 2:20 suffer for doing **g** and endure
1 Pet 3:17 suffer for doing **g**, if that

GOODNESS (n)
the beneficial quality of something; kindness
Ps 145:7 the story of your wonderful **g**;
Isa 63:7 in his great **g** to Israel,
Rom 14:17 a life of **g** and peace and joy
Rom 15:14 that you are full of **g**.

GOSPEL (KJV)
Mark 1:1 the *Good News* about Jesus
Luke 4:18 anointed me to bring *Good News*
Rom 1:16 not ashamed of this *Good News*
Rom 10:15 feet of messengers who bring *good news*
Gal 3:8 proclaimed this *good news*

GOSSIP (n)
rumor or report revealing personal or sensational facts about others
Prov 16:28 of strife; **g** separates the
Prov 26:20 disappear when **g** stops.
2 Cor 12:20 slander, **g**, arrogance,

GOSSIP, GOSSIPING (v)
to relate rumors or reports about others
Ps 15:3 who refuse to **g** or harm their
1 Tim 5:13 spend their time **g-ing**

GOVERN (v)
to exercise continuous sovereign authority over; to control or rule
Gen 1:16 larger one to **g** the day,
Gen 1:28 the earth and **g** it.
Gen 49:16 Dan will **g** his people, like
Job 34:17 Could God **g** if he hated
Ps 67:4 because you **g** the nations

GOVERNMENT (n)
the organization or agency through which a political unit exercises authority
Isa 9:6 The **g** will rest on his
Rom 13:6 For **g** workers need
Titus 3:1 to submit to the **g** and its

GRACE (n)
God's free and unmerited favor toward sinful humanity
see also FAVOR
Acts 6:8 full of God's **g** and power,
Acts 14:3 about the **g** of the Lord.
Acts 15:11 by the undeserved **g** of the
Acts 20:32 message of his **g** that is able
Rom 5:15 is God's wonderful **g** and his
Rom 5:21 now God's wonderful **g** rules
Rom 6:1 of his wonderful **g**?
Rom 11:5 of God's **g**—his undeserved
Rom 12:6 In his **g**, God has given us
1 Cor 3:10 Because of God's **g** to me,
1 Cor 16:23 May the **g** of the Lord
2 Cor 4:15 And as God's **g** reaches more
2 Cor 9:14 of the overflowing **g** God has
Gal 1:15 by his marvelous **g**.
Gal 2:21 do not treat the **g** of God as
Gal 5:4 away from God's **g**.
Eph 1:7 in kindness and **g** that he
Eph 2:5 only by God's **g** that you have
Eph 2:7 wealth of his **g** and kindness
Eph 2:8 saved you by his **g** when you
Eph 3:2 of extending his **g** to you
Eph 3:7 By God's **g** and mighty
Phil 4:23 May the **g** of the Lord
2 Thes 1:12 because of the **g** of our God
2 Thes 2:16 and by his **g** gave us eternal
1 Tim 1:2 Lord give you **g**, mercy,
2 Tim 1:9 show us his **g** through Christ
2 Tim 2:1 strong through the **g** that God
2 Tim 4:22 And may his **g** be with all of
Titus 2:11 For the **g** of God has
Titus 3:7 Because of his **g** he declared
Titus 3:15 May God's **g** be with you
Heb 4:16 and we will find **g** to help us
Heb 12:15 to receive the **g** of God.
Heb 13:9 comes from God's **g**, not from
Heb 13:25 May God's **g** be with you all.
Jas 4:6 gives us even more **g** to stand
1 Pet 5:12 Stand firm in this **g**.
2 Pet 3:18 grow in the **g** and knowledge
Rev 22:21 May the **g** of the Lord

GRACIOUS (adj)
abounding in grace and kindness; merciful, compassionate
2 Kgs 13:23 the LORD was **g** and merciful
Ps 145:13 he is **g** in all he
Prov 11:16 A **g** woman gains
John 1:16 received one **g** blessing after
2 Cor 8:7 also in this **g** act of giving.
Col 4:6 your conversation be **g** and
1 Tim 1:14 generous and **g** our Lord was!
1 Pet 1:10 about this **g** salvation
1 Pet 1:13 to the **g** salvation that will

GRAFTED (v)
to unite a shoot or bud with a growing plant so they grow as one
Rom 11:18 not brag about being **g** in to

GRANDCHILDREN (n)
the child of one's son or daughter
1 Tim 5:4 children or **g**, their first

GRANDMOTHER (n)
the mother of one's father or mother
2 Tim 1:5 first filled your **g** Lois and

GRANT (n)
property transferred by deed or writing
Josh 14:3 already given a **g** of land to

GRANT, GRANTED (v)
to permit as a right, privilege, or favor; to consent to carry out for a person
Prov 10:24 of the godly will be **g-ed.**
Isa 26:12 LORD, you will **g** us peace;
Matt 15:28 Your request is **g-ed.**" And her
John 15:7 and it will be **g-ed!**

GRAPES (n)
a smooth-skinned juicy greenish-white to deep red or purple berry
Gen 40:10 it produced clusters of ripe **g**
Lev 19:10 not pick up the **g** that fall
Num 6:3 not eat **g** or raisins
Num 13:23 single cluster of **g** so large
Deut 32:32 Their **g** are poison
Job 15:33 a vine whose **g** are harvested
Isa 5:4 expected sweet **g**, why did
Isa 63:3 my enemies as if they were **g**
Matt 7:16 **g** from thornbushes, or figs
Rev 14:19 **g** into the great winepress

GRAPEVINE (n)
the vine on which grapes grow
Ps 128:3 a fruitful **g**, flourishing
Isa 36:16 from your own **g** and fig tree
John 15:1 am the true **g**, and my Father

GRASS (n)
green plants that grow from the ground and are suitable for grazing animals
Isa 40:6 people are like the **g.**
1 Pet 1:24 The **g** withers and

GRAVE, GRAVES (n)
burial place; euphemism for Hades, hell, or Sheol
Ps 5:9 from an open **g.**
Ps 49:15 power of the **g.**
John 5:28 dead in their **g-s** will hear the
Acts 2:27 rot in the **g.**
Rom 3:13 from an open **g.**
Rev 20:13 death and the **g** gave up their

GRAVECLOTHES (n)
strips of cloth wrapped around a corpse in preparation for burial
John 11:44 and feet bound in **g**, his face

GREAT, GREATER, GREATEST (adj)
huge; remarkable in magnitude, degree, or effectiveness
Deut 10:17 He is the **g** God, the mighty
2 Sam 24:14 his mercy is **g.**
Ps 107:8 LORD for his **g** love and for
Ps 147:5 How **g** is our LORD!
Dan 9:4 you are a **g** and awesome God!
Matt 12:41 someone **g-er** than Jonah is
Matt 12:42 **g-er** than Solomon
Matt 19:30 who are the **g-est** now will be
Matt 22:38 first and **g-est** commandment.
John 3:30 He must become **g-er**
John 15:13 There is no **g-er** love than to
1 Cor 13:13 and the **g-est** of these is love.
Rev 20:11 I saw a **g** white throne and

GREED (n)
a selfish and excessive desire for more of something (as money) than is needed
Prov 15:27 **G** brings grief
Rom 1:29 of wickedness, sin, **g**, hate,
2 Pet 2:3 In their **g** they will make up
2 Pet 2:14 well trained in **g.**

GREEDY (adj)
having or showing a selfish desire for wealth and possessions
1 Sam 8:3 for they were **g** for money.
Prov 1:19 all who are **g** for money;
Prov 21:26 people are always **g**
1 Cor 6:10 are thieves, or **g** people,
Eph 5:5 For a **g** person is an
Col 3:5 Don't be **g**, for a **g**

GREEKS (n)
natives or inhabitants of Greece
1 Cor 1:22 And it is foolish to the **G,**

GREEN (adj)
of the color green; pleasantly alluring
Ps 23:2 lets me rest in **g** meadows;

GREET (v)
to address with expressions of kind wishes upon meeting or arrival
Rom 16:16 **G** each other in Christian
1 Cor 16:20 **G** each other with
2 Cor 13:12 **G** each other with
1 Thes 5:26 **G** all the brothers
1 Pet 5:14 **G** each other with

GREW (v)
to increase; to develop in maturity
see also GROW
Luke 1:80 John **g** up and became

Luke 2:52 Jesus **g** in wisdom
Acts 9:31 Spirit, it also **g** in numbers.
Acts 16:5 faith and **g** larger every day.

GRIEF (n)
deep and poignant distress due to bereavement; a cause of suffering
Job 16:5 take away your **g.**
Ps 10:14 the trouble and **g** they cause.
Prov 10:1 a foolish child brings **g** to a
Prov 15:27 Greed brings **g** to the
John 16:20 your **g** will suddenly turn
Rom 9:2 sorrow and unending **g**

GRIEVE, GRIEVED (v)
to feel, show, or cause distress, vexation, sorrow, or regret
Eccl 3:4 A time to **g** and a time
Isa 63:10 rebelled against him and **g-d**
Lam 3:20 time, as I **g** over my loss.
1 Thes 4:13 so you will not **g** like people

GROAN, GROANING, GROANINGS (n)
a deep moan indicative of pain, grief, or annoyance
Exod 2:24 God heard their **g-ing**, and he
Ps 90:9 ending our years with a **g.**
Rom 8:26 for us with **g-ings** that cannot

GROAN, GROANING (v)
to utter a deep moan indicative of pain, grief, or annoyance
Job 35:9 They **g** beneath the power
Rom 8:22 creation has been **g-ing** as
Rom 8:23 believers also **g**, even though
2 Cor 5:4 bodies, we **g** and sigh,

GROUND (n)
soil, earth, or territory
Gen 1:10 called the dry **g** "land" and
Gen 3:17 the **g** is cursed because of you.
Gen 4:2 Cain cultivated the **g.**
Gen 4:10 cries out to me from the **g!**
Exod 3:5 standing on holy **g.**
Exod 15:19 sea on dry **g!**
Isa 53:2 like a root in dry **g.**
Matt 10:29 fall to the **g** without your

GROW, GROWING, GROWS (v)
to become; to spring up and develop to maturity
see also GREW
Isa 40:31 run and not **g** weary.
1 Cor 3:6 God who made it **g.**
Eph 4:16 is healthy and **g-ing** and full of
Phil 1:25 all of you **g** and experience
Col 2:19 it **g-s** as God nourishes it.
2 Thes 1:3 one another is **g-ing.**

Jas 1:15 when sin is allowed to **g,**
2 Pet 3:18 Rather, you must **g** in the

GRUDGE (n)
a feeling of deep-seated resentment or ill will
Mark 11:25 you are holding a **g** against,

GRUMBLE (v)
to mutter in discontent
1 Cor 10:10 And don't **g** as some
Jas 5:9 Don't **g** about each other

GRUMBLERS (n)
those who mutter in discontent
Jude 1:16 people are **g** and complainers,

GUARANTEE (n)
an assurance for the fulfillment of a condition
2 Cor 5:5 and as a **g** he has given us

GUARANTEED, GUARANTEEING, GUARANTEES (v)
to assure that some agreement or condition will be fulfilled; to give security for
Ps 111:9 He has **g** his covenant
2 Cor 1:22 first installment that **g-s**
Eph 4:30 **g-ing** that you will be saved
Heb 7:22 is the one who **g-s** this better

GUARD (adj)
defensively watchful; alert
2 Pet 3:17 Be on **g** so that you

GUARD, GUARDING, GUARDS (v)
to protect by watchful attention; to watch over
see also KEEP
Prov 4:23 **G** your heart
Prov 7:2 as you **g** your own eyes.
Prov 24:12 He who **g-s** your soul knows
Luke 2:8 fields nearby, **g-ing** their flocks
Phil 4:7 His peace will **g** your hearts
2 Thes 3:3 and **g** you from

GUARDIAN (n)
one caring for another person or the property of another
Gen 4:9 Am I my brother's **g?**
Gal 3:25 the law as our **g.**
1 Pet 2:25 your Shepherd, the **G** of your

GUIDANCE (n)
direction or counsel provided by another person
2 Chr 26:5 as the king sought **g** from
Prov 24:6 go to war without wise **g;**
Prov 29:18 do not accept divine **g,**

GUIDE, GUIDED, GUIDES, GUIDING (v)
to direct, supervise, or influence usually to a particular end
Exod 13:21 He **g-d** them during the
Exod 15:13 In your might, you **g** them
Deut 1:33 **g-ing** you with a pillar of fire
Job 10:10 **g-d** my conception and formed
Ps 16:7 bless the LORD who **g-s** me;
Ps 23:3 He **g-s** me along
Ps 32:8 I will **g** you along
Ps 139:10 your hand will **g** me,
John 16:13 he will **g** you into all
Gal 5:16 let the Holy Spirit **g** your lives.
Jas 2:4 are **g-d** by evil motives?

GUIDES (n)
those who lead or direct another's way
Matt 23:16 Blind **g!** What sorrow
Matt 23:24 Blind **g!** You strain

GUILT (n)
the state or feeling of one who has committed an offense
Job 6:29 Stop assuming my **g**, for I
Ps 32:2 the LORD has cleared of **g,**
Ps 38:4 My **g** overwhelms me—
Ps 51:2 Wash me clean from my **g.**
Isa 6:7 Now your **g** is removed,
Dan 9:24 atone for their **g,** to bring

GUILTY (adj)
justly chargeable with wrongdoing
Lev 19:17 not be held **g** for their sin.
Rom 3:19 entire world is **g** before God.
1 Cor 11:27 **g** of sinning against
1 Jn 3:20 if we feel **g,** God is greater
1 Jn 3:21 we don't feel **g,** we can come

H

HAGAR
Sarah's Egyptian servant and rival, mother of Ishmael (Gen 16); sent away by Abraham, son's cries heard by God (Gen 21:9-21); Paul's analogy using Hagar and Sarah (Gal 4:24-25).

HAIL (n)
precipitation in the form of small balls of ice and snow
Exod 9:19 die when the **h** falls.
Ps 18:12 rained down **h** and
Rev 8:7 his trumpet, and **h** and fire

HAIR, HAIRS (n)
a slender threadlike outgrowth of the skin of an animal or human
Lev 19:27 Do not trim off the **h** on your
2 Sam 18:9 his **h** got caught in the tree.
Matt 10:30 And the very **h-s** on your head
1 Cor 11:6 to have her **h** cut or her head
1 Cor 11:14 man to have long **h?**
1 Cor 11:15 And isn't long **h** a woman's
Rev 1:14 His head and his **h** were white

HAIRSTYLES (n)
a way of wearing the hair
1 Pet 3:3 outward beauty of fancy **h,**

HAIRY (adj)
covered with hair
Gen 27:11 Esau, is a **h** man, and my skin

HALF, HALVES (n)
either of two equal parts that compose something
Gen 15:17 between the **h-ves** of the carcasses.
Exod 30:13 (This payment is **h** a shekel,
1 Kgs 3:25 to one woman and **h** to the
1 Kgs 10:7 not heard the **h** of it!
Esth 5:3 if it is **h** the kingdom!
Jer 34:18 between its **h-ves** to solemnize
Dan 7:25 a time, times, and **h** a time.
Mark 6:23 ask, up to **h** my kingdom!

HALLELUJAH (KJV)
Rev 19:1 shouting, *"Praise the Lord!*
Rev 19:3 rang out: *"Praise the Lord!*
Rev 19:4 "Amen! *Praise the Lord!"*
Rev 19:6 *"Praise the Lord!* For the Lord

HALLOW(ED) (KJV)
Exod 20:11 Sabbath day and *set it apart as holy*
Lev 25:10 *Set* this year *apart as holy*
1 Kgs 9:3 *set* this Temple *apart to be holy*
Matt 6:9 *may* your name *be kept holy*

HAND, HANDS (n)
the end of the arm that serves as a grasping and handling tool for humans; symbolic of power
Gen 47:29 Put your **h** under my
Exod 15:6 Your right **h,** O LORD,
Exod 29:10 will lay their **h-s** on its head.
Exod 33:22 cover you with my **h** until
1 Kgs 13:4 king's **h** became paralyzed
Ps 22:16 have pierced my **h-s** and feet.
Ps 24:4 those whose **h-s** and hearts
Ps 32:4 your **h** of discipline
Ps 44:3 It was your right **h** and
Ps 63:4 my **h-s** to you in prayer.
Ps 75:8 a cup in his **h** that is full
Ps 110:1 at my right **h** until I humble
Ps 137:5 let my right **h** forget how to
Ps 145:16 you open your **h,** you satisfy
Isa 40:12 the oceans in his **h?**

Isa 41:13 by your right **h**—I, the LORD
Isa 55:12 will clap their **h-s!**
Isa 64:8 formed by your **h.**
Dan 10:10 Just then a **h** touched me
Matt 5:30 And if your **h**—even your
Matt 6:3 don't let your left **h** know what
Matt 18:8 with only one **h** or one foot
Matt 26:64 at God's right **h** and coming
Mark 12:36 at my right **h** until I humble
Acts 6:6 they laid their **h-s** on them.
Acts 7:55 at God's right **h.**
Acts 8:18 laid their **h-s** on people,
Acts 13:3 men laid their **h-s** on them
Acts 19:6 Paul laid his **h-s** on them,
Acts 28:8 and laying his **h-s** on him,
1 Thes 4:11 working with your **h-s,**
1 Tim 2:8 pray with holy **h-s** lifted up
1 Tim 4:14 church laid their **h-s** on you.
2 Tim 1:6 when I laid my **h-s** on you.
Heb 1:13 at my right **h** until I humble
Rev 13:16 mark on the right **h** or on the

HANDED (v)
to yield control of
Rom 4:25 He was **h** over to die
1 Tim 1:20 them out and **h** them over

HANDFUL (n)
a small quantity or number
Eccl 4:6 to have one **h** with quietness

HANDSOME (adj)
having a pleasing and unusually impressive appearance; beautiful
Gen 39:6 Joseph was a very **h** and
1 Sam 16:12 dark and **h,** with beautiful
2 Sam 14:25 as the most **h** man in all Israel.
1 Kgs 1:6 he was very **h.**
Ezek 23:6 commanders dressed in **h** blue,

HANGED, HANGING, HANGS (v)
to suspend; to execute (on a tree or gallows)
see also HUNG
Job 26:7 **h-s** the earth on nothing.
Matt 27:5 went out and **h-ed** himself.
Acts 10:39 death by **h-ing** him on a cross,

HAPPINESS (n)
a state of well-being and contentment; joy
Deut 24:5 **h** to the wife he has married.
Job 7:7 never again feel **h.**
Job 9:25 a glimpse of **h.**
Ps 86:4 Give me **h,** O LORD,
Ps 119:35 that is where my **h** is found.
Eccl 8:15 **h** along with all the hard work
Isa 65:18 Jerusalem as a place of **h.**
Luke 6:24 you have your only **h** now.

HAPPY (adj)
expressing, reflecting, or suggestive of happiness
see also BLESSED
Deut 16:14 festival will be a **h** time
Ps 113:9 making her a **h** mother.
Prov 15:13 A glad heart makes a **h** face;
Prov 15:15 for the **h** heart, life is
Prov 23:25 she who gave you birth be **h.**
Eccl 9:7 drink your wine with a **h** heart,
Zech 10:7 will be made **h** as if by wine.
Rom 12:15 Be **h** with those who are **h,**
Phil 2:2 make me truly **h** by agreeing
Jas 5:13 Are any of you **h?**

HARBOR (n)
a part of a body of water where ships dock; a place of security and comfort
Ps 107:30 brought them safely into **h!**

HARD (adj)
lacking in responsiveness, unfeeling; demanding the exertion of energy
Rom 11:25 of Israel have **h** hearts,
Rev 2:2 I have seen your **h** work and

HARD, HARDER (adv)
with great or utmost effort or energy
Prov 13:4 those who work **h**
Acts 20:35 in need by working **h.**
Rom 16:12 has worked so **h**
1 Cor 15:10 worked **h-er** than any of
2 Cor 11:23 worked **h-er,** been put in
1 Thes 5:12 They work **h** among you
2 Thes 3:8 We worked **h** day and night

HARD-HEARTED (adj)
lacking in sympathetic understanding; unfeeling
Deut 15:7 do not be **h** or tightfisted

HARDEN, HARDENED (v)
to make callous or unfeeling
Exod 4:21 But I will **h** his heart
Exod 10:20 LORD **h-ed** Pharaoh's heart
Ps 95:8 Don't **h** your hearts as Israel did
Isa 6:10 **H** the hearts of these people.
Matt 13:15 hearts of these people are **h-ed,**
John 12:40 and **h-ed** their hearts—
Eph 4:18 minds and **h-ed** their hearts
Heb 3:8 don't **h** your hearts as Israel did

HARDSHIPS (n)
things that cause or entail suffering or privation
Acts 14:22 must suffer many **h** to enter
2 Cor 6:4 troubles and **h** and calamities

2 Thes 1:4 and **h** you are suffering.
Jas 5:13 Are any of you suffering **h?**

HARLOT (KJV)
Gen 38:15 thought she was a *prostitute*
Josh 2:1 a *prostitute* named Rahab
Hos 4:15 you, Israel, are a *prostitute*
Matt 21:31 *prostitutes* will get into the Kingdom
Rev 17:5 Mother of All *Prostitutes* and

HARM (n)
physical or mental damage; injury, hurt
Ps 37:8 it only leads to **h.**
Prov 3:29 Don't plot **h** against your
Prov 19:23 and protection from **h.**
Prov 31:12 brings him good, not **h,** all
1 Cor 11:17 more **h** than good is done

HARM, HARMED, HARMS (v)
to injure or hurt
Ps 121:6 sun will not **h** you by day,
Jer 10:5 they can neither **h** you nor do
Zech 2:8 who **h-s** you **h-s** my most
Rev 2:11 will not be **h-ed** by the second

HARMLESS (adj)
lacking capacity or intent to injure
Matt 10:16 shrewd as snakes and **h** as

HARMONY (n)
tranquility; agreement; unity
Zech 6:13 will be perfect **h** between his
Rom 12:16 Live in **h** with each other.
Rom 14:19 aim for **h** in the church
Rom 15:5 live in complete **h** with each
1 Cor 12:25 This makes for **h**
2 Cor 6:15 What **h** can there be
2 Cor 13:11 Live in **h** and peace.
Col 3:14 together in perfect **h.**

HARP, HARPS (n)
a plucked stringed instrument
Gen 4:21 all who play the **h** and flute.
1 Sam 16:23 would play the **h.**
Ps 33:2 on the ten-stringed **h.**
Ps 98:5 with the **h** and melodious song,
Ps 137:2 our **h-s,** hanging them
Ps 144:9 a ten-stringed **h.**
Ps 147:7 praises to our God with a **h.**
Ps 150:3 praise him with the lyre and **h!**
Rev 5:8 Each one had a **h,** and they

HARSH (adj)
causing a disagreeable reaction; unduly exacting
Prov 15:1 **h** words make tempers flare.
Eph 4:31 rage, anger, **h** words,

HARVEST, HARVESTS (n)
the time or fruit of reaping or gathering in a crop—physically or spiritually
Deut 16:15 blesses you with bountiful **h-s**
Matt 9:37 The **h** is great, but
John 4:35 fields are already ripe for **h.**
1 Cor 15:23 raised as the first of the **h;**
2 Cor 9:10 great **h** of generosity
Gal 6:9 we will reap a **h** of blessing
Heb 12:11 peaceful **h** of right living
Jas 3:18 reap a **h** of righteousness.
Rev 14:15 the time of **h** has come;

HARVEST, HARVESTS (v)
to gather in (a crop); to reap
Gen 8:22 there will be planting and **h,**
Job 4:8 and cultivate evil will **h**
Prov 10:5 wise youth **h-s** in the summer,
Gal 6:8 sinful nature will **h** decay and

HARVESTER, HARVESTERS (n)
one who gathers in (a crop)
Ruth 2:3 to gather grain behind the **h-s.**
John 4:36 planter and the **h** alike!

HASTE (n)
rash or headlong action; swiftness
Prov 19:2 **h** makes mistakes.

HASTY (adj)
done or made in a hurry; impatient; speedy
Prov 21:5 **h** shortcuts lead to poverty.
Eccl 5:2 don't be **h** in bringing matters

HATE, HATED, HATES, HATING (v)
to feel extreme enmity toward; to have a strong aversion to
Ps 45:7 love justice and **h** evil.
Prov 1:22 you fools **h** knowledge?
Prov 6:16 six things the Lord **h-s**—
Prov 13:5 The godly **h** lies;
Prov 15:27 those who **h** bribes will live.
Prov 26:28 A lying tongue **h-s** its victims,
Prov 28:16 but one who **h-s** corruption
Mal 2:16 "For I **h** divorce!"
Matt 5:43 and **h** your enemy.
Matt 24:9 be **h-d** all over the world
Luke 6:22 when people **h** you
John 3:20 All who do evil **h** the light
John 15:18 remember that it **h-d** me
2 Tim 3:3 be cruel and **h** what is good.
Heb 1:9 You love justice and **h** evil.
1 Jn 2:9 **h-s** a Christian brother or sister,
1 Jn 4:20 **h-s** a Christian brother or
Jude 1:23 **h-ing** the sins that contaminate

HATERS (n)
one who feels or expresses enmity or aversion

Rom 1:30	are backstabbers, **h** of God,

HATRED (n)
strong emotional aversion

Lev 19:17	Do not nurse **h** in your heart
Prov 26:24	People may cover their **h**

HAUGHTY (adj)
blatantly and disdainfully proud

Prov 6:17	**h** eyes, a lying tongue,
Prov 21:24	are proud and **h;** they act

HAY (n)
herbage and especially grass mowed and cured for fodder

1 Cor 3:12	jewels, wood, **h,** or straw.

HEAD, HEADS (n)
top part of the body that contains the brain; one in charge; person, individual

Gen 3:15	He will strike your **h,** and
Lev 26:13	walk with your **h-s** held high.
Ps 22:7	shake their **h-s,** saying,
Ps 23:5	by anointing my **h** with oil.
Ps 133:2	over Aaron's **h,** that ran
Prov 25:22	coals of shame on their **h-s,**
Matt 27:39	shaking their **h-s** in mockery.
John 19:2	thorns and put it on his **h,**
Acts 18:6	your own **h-s**—I am innocent.
Rom 12:20	coals of shame on their **h-s.**
Eph 1:22	and has made him **h** over all
Eph 5:23	as Christ is the **h** of the
Rev 4:4	crowns on their **h-s.**
Rev 14:14	He had a gold crown on his **h**
Rev 19:12	on his **h** were many crowns.

HEADCLOTH (n)
portion of burial garb covering the head and face

John 11:44	wrapped in a **h.**

HEAL, HEALED, HEALING, HEALS (v)
to mend, cure, make whole; to restore to health

Gen 20:17	and God **h-ed** Abimelech,
Exod 15:26	I am the LORD who **h-s** you.
Num 12:13	I beg you, please **h** her!
Deut 32:39	one who wounds and **h-s;**
2 Chr 30:20	prayer and **h-ed** the people.
Job 5:18	his hands also **h.**
Ps 6:2	**H** me, LORD,
Ps 103:3	and **h-s** all my diseases.
Ps 107:20	his word and **h-ed** them,
Prov 3:8	will have **h-ing** for your body
Prov 13:17	messenger brings **h-ing.**
Isa 6:10	and turn to me for **h-ing.**
Isa 30:26	LORD begins to **h** his people
Isa 57:18	but I will **h** them anyway!
Isa 57:19	the LORD, who **h-s** them.
Jer 8:18	My grief is beyond **h-ing;**
Jer 17:14	O LORD, if you **h** me, I will
Jer 17:14	I will be truly **h-ed;**
Jer 30:13	No medicine can **h** you.
Hos 6:1	now he will **h** us.
Hos 7:1	I want to **h** Israel, but its
Hos 14:4	Then I will **h** you of your
Zech 11:16	nor **h** the injured,
Mal 4:2	with **h-ing** in his wings.
Matt 4:23	And he **h-ed** every kind
Matt 8:7	will come and **h** him.
Matt 8:16	and he **h-ed** all the sick.
Matt 9:35	he **h-ed** every kind of disease
Matt 10:8	**H** the sick, raise the
Matt 15:30	Jesus, and he **h-ed** them all.
Matt 17:16	they couldn't **h** him.
Mark 1:34	So Jesus **h-ed** many people
Mark 3:2	If he **h-ed** the man's
Mark 3:10	He had **h-ed** many people
Mark 5:28	touch his robe, I will be **h-ed.**
Mark 6:5	sick people and **h** them.
Mark 6:13	and **h-ed** many sick
Mark 6:56	who touched him were **h-ed.**
Mark 10:52	your faith has **h-ed** you.
Luke 4:23	Physician, **h** yourself
Luke 4:40	his hand **h-ed** every one.
Luke 6:7	If he **h-ed** the man's
Luke 8:50	faith, and she will be **h-ed.**
Luke 10:9	**H** the sick, and tell them
Luke 13:14	indignant that Jesus had **h-ed**
Luke 14:3	**h** people on the Sabbath
Luke 14:4	the sick man and **h-ed** him
Luke 17:19	Your faith has **h-ed** you.
Luke 18:42	Your faith has **h-ed** you.
Luke 22:51	man's ear and **h-ed** him.
John 4:47	to Capernaum to **h** his son,
John 7:23	angry with me for **h-ing** a man
John 12:40	and have me **h** them.
Acts 3:16	this man was **h-ed**—
Acts 4:9	to know how he was **h-ed?**
Acts 4:14	see the man who had been **h-ed**
Acts 4:22	sign—the **h-ing** of a man
Acts 8:7	or lame were **h-ed.**
Acts 9:34	Jesus Christ **h-s** you! Get up,
Acts 10:38	and **h-ing** all who were
Acts 28:8	his hands on him, he **h-ed**
Acts 28:27	turn to me and let me **h**
1 Cor 12:28	the gift of **h-ing,**
1 Cor 12:30	have the gift of **h-ing?**
Jas 5:16	so that you may be **h-ed.**
1 Pet 2:24	By his wounds you are **h-ed.**
Rev 13:3	fatal wound was **h-ed!**
Rev 13:12	wound had been **h-ed.**

HEALING (adj)
marked by restoring to original purity or integrity
Luke 6:19 **h** power went out from him,
Acts 4:30 your hand with **h** power;

HEALTH (n)
the general condition of the body
Ps 38:3 my **h** is broken because of
Ps 38:7 and my **h** is broken.
Prov 15:30 makes for good **h.**
Isa 38:16 You restore my **h**
Jer 30:17 I will give you back your **h**

HEALTHY, HEALTHIER (adj)
enjoying good health and vigor of body, mind, or spirit
Ps 73:4 bodies are so **h** and strong.
Prov 16:24 the soul and **h** for the body.
Dan 1:15 friends looked **h-ier** and better
Zech 11:16 nor feed the **h.** Instead,
Matt 9:12 he said, "**H** people don't need
Mark 2:17 **H** people don't need
Luke 5:31 answered them, "**H** people
Eph 4:16 whole body is **h** and growing
3 Jn 1:2 that you are as **h** in body as

HEAP (v)
to pile in great quantity; to load heavily
Prov 25:22 You will **h** burning coals of
Rom 12:20 you will **h** burning coals of

HEAR, HEARD, HEARING (v)
to perceive sound; to listen with attention; to be informed of; to take testimony from and make a legal decision
see also LISTEN
Gen 3:8 and his wife **h-d** the LORD God
Exod 2:24 God **h-d** their groaning,
Deut 1:16 judges, 'You must **h** the cases
Josh 7:9 people living in the land **h**
1 Kgs 8:30 May you **h** the humble
2 Chr 7:14 I will **h** from heaven and will
Neh 1:11 O LORD, please **h** my prayer!
Ps 5:1 O LORD, **h** me as I pray;
Ps 89:1 Young and old will **h** of your
Isa 29:18 the deaf will **h** words read
Isa 30:21 own ears will **h** him.
Isa 40:28 Have you never **h-d**?
Isa 59:1 too deaf to **h** you call.
Dan 10:12 has been **h-d** in heaven.
Matt 5:21 have **h-d** that our ancestors
Matt 5:43 You have **h-d** the law
Matt 11:5 cured, the deaf **h,** the dead
Matt 13:14 When you **h** what I say,
Mark 4:12 When they **h** what I say,
Luke 7:22 cured, the deaf **h,** the dead
John 8:26 what I have **h-d** from the one
Acts 2:6 When they **h-d** the loud noise,
Acts 13:7 he wanted to **h** the word of
Rom 10:14 how can they **h** about him
Rom 10:17 faith comes from **h-ing,**
1 Cor 2:9 no ear has **h-d,** and no mind
1 Cor 12:17 how would you **h?**
Heb 3:7 Today when you **h** his voice,
2 Jn 1:6 just as you **h-d** from the
Rev 3:20 If you **h** my voice and
Rev 22:8 I, John, am the one who **h-d**

HEART, HEARTS (n)
figuratively, the seat of emotions, thoughts, and intentions; personality, disposition; courage; love, affection; central or most vital part of something
Gen 6:6 It broke his **h.**
Exod 4:21 will harden his **h** so he
Exod 35:21 All whose **h-s** were stirred
Deut 6:5 LORD your God with all your **h,**
Deut 9:10 from the **h** of the fire
Deut 20:3 Do not lose **h** or panic
Deut 28:65 will cause your **h** to tremble,
Josh 22:5 with all your **h** and all your
Josh 23:14 Deep in your **h-s** you know
1 Sam 1:15 pouring out my **h**
1 Sam 10:9 God gave him a new **h,**
1 Sam 12:20 the LORD with all your **h,**
1 Sam 13:14 a man after his own **h.**
1 Sam 16:7 but the LORD looks at the **h.**
1 Kgs 8:48 with their whole **h** and soul
1 Kgs 11:2 turn your **h-s** to their gods.
1 Kgs 11:3 turn his **h** away from the LORD.
1 Kgs 14:8 followed me with all his **h**
2 Kgs 23:3 with all his **h** and soul.
1 Chr 22:19 God with all your **h** and soul.
2 Chr 6:38 with their whole **h** and soul
2 Chr 22:9 sought the LORD with all his **h.**
2 Chr 34:31 with all his **h** and soul.
Ezra 1:5 stirred the **h-s** of the priests
Job 4:5 trouble strikes, you lose **h.**
Ps 9:1 praise you, LORD, with all my **h;**
Ps 14:1 say in their **h-s,** "There is no
Ps 19:14 meditation of my **h**
Ps 24:4 whose hands and **h-s** are pure,
Ps 27:8 my **h** responds, "LORD,
Ps 36:1 within their **h-s.** They have no
Ps 42:11 Why is my **h** so sad?
Ps 45:1 Beautiful words stir my **h.**
Ps 51:10 Create in me a clean **h,** O God.
Ps 57:7 my **h** is confident.
Ps 73:7 everything their **h-s** could ever
Ps 73:26 the strength of my **h;**
Ps 108:1 with all my **h!**
Ps 111:1 thank the LORD with all my **h**
Ps 119:2 with all their **h-s.**

Ps 119:11 hidden your word in my **h,**
Ps 119:58 With all my **h** I want your
Ps 119:145 I pray with all my **h;**
Ps 139:23 and know my **h;** test me and
Prov 3:3 deep within your **h.**
Prov 4:23 Guard your **h** above all else,
Prov 13:12 deferred makes the **h** sick,
Prov 14:30 A peaceful **h** leads to a
Prov 15:13 a broken **h** crushes the
Prov 15:30 look brings joy to the **h;**
Prov 17:22 A cheerful **h** is good
Prov 20:9 have cleansed my **h;** I am pure
Prov 23:15 wise, my own **h** will rejoice!
Prov 27:23 and put your **h** into caring
Song 4:9 captured my **h,** my treasure,
Song 5:2 I slept, but my **h** was awake,
Song 5:4 and my **h** thrilled within me.
Song 8:6 like a seal over your **h,**
Isa 1:5 and your **h** is sick.
Isa 6:10 Harden the **h-s** of these people.
Isa 42:4 or lose **h** until justice
Jer 3:15 shepherds after my own **h,**
Jer 3:22 your wayward **h-s.**
Jer 9:26 have uncircumcised **h-s.**
Jer 20:9 burns in my **h** like a fire.
Jer 32:39 will give them one **h** and one
Ezek 44:7 who have no **h** for God.
Joel 2:12 Give me your **h-s.** Come with
Matt 5:8 those whose **h-s** are pure,
Matt 5:28 adultery with her in his **h.**
Matt 11:29 I am humble and gentle at **h,**
Matt 12:34 whatever is in your **h**
Matt 15:19 For from the **h** come evil
Matt 18:35 and sisters from your **h.**
Matt 22:37 God with all your **h,** all your
Mark 11:23 have no doubt in your **h.**
Mark 12:30 God with all your **h,** all your
Mark 12:33 love him with all my **h** and
Luke 6:45 treasury of a good **h,**
Luke 10:27 God with all your **h,** all your
Luke 12:34 desires of your **h** will also
Luke 24:38 Why are your **h-s** filled with
John 5:38 your **h-s,** because you do not
Acts 1:24 you know every **h.** Show us
Acts 4:32 were united in **h** and mind.
Acts 8:21 this, for your **h** is not right
Acts 15:8 God knows people's **h-s,** and
Acts 16:14 Lord opened her **h,** and she
Acts 28:27 hear, and their **h-s** cannot
Rom 1:9 with all my **h** by spreading
Rom 2:15 written in their **h-s,** for their
Rom 2:29 changed **h** seeks praise
Rom 10:9 believe in your **h** that God
2 Cor 2:4 with a troubled **h** and many
2 Cor 7:2 Please open your **h-s** to us.
2 Cor 9:7 decide in your **h** how much to
Eph 1:18 I pray that your **h-s** will be
Eph 3:13 don't lose **h** because of my
Eph 5:19 music to the Lord in your **h-s.**
Eph 6:6 of God with all your **h.**
Phil 1:7 place in my **h.** You share with
1 Tim 1:5 comes from a pure **h,** a clear

HEARTLESS (adj)
lacking feeling; cruel
Rom 1:31 promises, are **h,** and have no

HEATHEN, HEATHENS (n)
one who does not worship the true God; uncivilized; without religion
Acts 7:51 You are **h** at heart and deaf to
Eph 2:11 called "uncircumcised **h-s**" by

HEAVEN, HEAVENS (n)
sky and stars above; God's dwelling place; abode of eternal bliss
Deut 30:12 is not kept in **h,** so distant
Job 41:11 Everything under **h** is mine.
Ps 18:16 down from **h** and rescued me;
Ps 71:19 to the highest **h-s.** You have
Ps 108:4 than the **h-s.** Your faithfulness
Matt 11:25 Father, Lord of **h** and earth,
Matt 24:30 appear in the **h-s,** and there
Rom 10:6 go up to **h?**' (to bring Christ
2 Cor 12:2 to the third **h** fourteen years
Heb 9:24 He entered into **h** itself to

HEAVENLY (adj)
celestial; of or pertaining to God in the highest
Ps 29:1 the Lord, you **h** beings;

HEIR, HEIRS (n)
one who succeeds to a hereditary title; one who inherits
see also INHERIT(ANCE)
Isa 11:10 In that day the **h** to David's
Rom 8:17 with Christ we are **h-s** of God's

HELL (n)
abode of the dead; place of punishment; personification of evil; lowest place one can go
see also UNDERWORLD
Matt 5:22 of the fires of **h.**
Matt 16:18 all the powers of **h** will not
Matt 23:33 judgment of **h?**
Mark 9:43 fires of **h** with two hands.
Luke 12:5 throw you into **h.**
Jas 3:6 on fire by **h** itself.
2 Pet 2:4 threw them into **h,** in gloomy

HELMET (n)
any of various protective head coverings usually made of hard metal
Isa 59:17 and placed the **h** of salvation
Eph 6:17 salvation as your **h,** and take

HELP (n)
aid, assistance
2 Sam 22:36 your **h** has made me great.
Ps 30:2 I cried to you for **h,** and you
Ps 33:20 He is our **h** and our shield.
Ps 108:12 for all human **h** is useless.
Isa 30:18 wait for his **h.**
Isa 38:14 looking to heaven for **h.** I am
Phil 4:16 you sent **h** more than once.

HELP, HELPED, HELPING, HELPS (v)
to give assistance or support; to rescue or save
Exod 23:5 Instead, stop and **h.**
Deut 2:36 our God also **h-ed** us conquer
1 Sam 7:12 the LORD has **h-ed** us!
Ps 46:1 always ready to **h** in times of
Ps 72:12 he will **h** the oppressed,
Ps 145:14 The LORD **h-s** the fallen
Prov 11:4 Riches won't **h** on the
Prov 14:31 their Maker, but **h-ing** the poor
Prov 19:17 If you **h** the poor,
Isa 41:10 strengthen you and **h** you.
Isa 44:10 that cannot **h** him one bit?
Jer 51:9 We would have **h-ed** her if we
Lam 4:16 he no longer **h-s** them.
Mark 9:24 but **h** me overcome
Acts 9:36 for others and **h-ing** the poor.
Acts 16:9 to Macedonia and **h** us!
Rom 12:13 be ready to **h** them.
1 Cor 12:28 those who can **h** others,
2 Cor 6:2 salvation, I **h-ed** you.
Gal 6:1 and humbly **h** that person back
1 Tim 5:10 Has she **h-ed** those who
2 Tim 2:7 Lord will **h** you understand
Heb 10:33 you **h-ed** others who
1 Pet 4:11 the gift of **h-ing** others?

HELPER (n)
one who gives aid; co-worker
Gen 2:18 I will make a **h** who is just
Ps 70:5 You are my **h** and my savior;
Ps 115:9 He is your **h** and your shield.
Heb 13:6 The LORD is my **h,** so I will

HELPFUL (adj)
of service or assistance; useful
Job 22:2 Can even a wise person be **h**
Prov 10:32 the godly speak **h** words,
1 Cor 12:31 desire the most **h** gifts.
Eph 4:29 be good and **h,** so that your

HELPLESS (adj)
without any aid, comfort, protection, or chance of success
Ps 9:12 cares for the **h.** He does not
Ps 10:12 not ignore the **h!**
Ps 34:2 let all who are **h** take heart.
Ps 35:10 Who else protects the **h**
Amos 2:7 They trample **h** people in the
Matt 9:36 confused and **h,** like sheep
Rom 5:6 were utterly **h,** Christ came

HEN (n)
a female chicken especially over a year old
Matt 23:37 together as a **h** protects her
Luke 13:34 together as a **h** protects her

HEROD
1. Herod the Great, ruler of Palestine at birth of John the Baptist and Jesus (Luke 1:5); tried to kill baby Jesus (Matt 2:1-18); died (Matt 2:19).
2. Herod Antipas, tetrarch of Galilee (Luke 3:1), son of Herod the Great; arrested and beheaded John the Baptist (Matt 14:1-12; Mark 1:14; 6:14-29; Luke 3:19-20; 9:7-9); tried Jesus (Luke 23:7-15).
3. Herod Agrippa I, grandson of Herod the Great; killed the apostle James (Acts 12:1-2); arrested Peter (Acts 12:3-19); died (Acts 12:21-23).
4. Herod Agrippa II, great grandson of Herod the Great; spoke at Paul's trial (Acts 25–26).

HEROES (n)
greatly admired persons
Ps 16:3 in the land are my true **h!**

HEZEKIAH
King of Judah (southern kingdom) (2 Kgs 18–20; 2 Chr 29–32); reformed the Temple and its worship (2 Chr 29:20-36); offered effective prayer during war against Assyria (2 Kgs 19:14-19; 2 Chr 32:1-23; Isa 36:14-20); became sick but was healed (2 Kgs 20:1-11; 2 Chr 32:24-26; Isa 38:1-22); showed kingdom's treasures to Babylonians (2 Kgs 20:12-19; 2 Chr 32:31; Isa 39); died (2 Kgs 20:20-21; 2 Chr 32:32-33).

HID, HIDDEN (v)
to remain out of sight; unrevealed
see also HIDE
Ps 119:11 I have **h-den** your word
Matt 13:35 explain things **h-den** since the
Matt 13:44 discovered **h-den** in a field.
Matt 13:44 he **h** it again and
Matt 25:25 your money, so I **h** it in the
Mark 4:22 that is **h-den** will eventually be
1 Cor 2:7 was previously **h-den,** even
Col 3:3 real life is **h-den** with Christ in
Heb 11:23 that Moses' parents **h** him

HIDE, HIDING (v)
to shield; to seek protection; to put or remain out of sight
see also HID
Deut 31:17 abandon them, **h-ing** my face
1 Sam 10:22 "He is **h-ing** among the
Ps 27:5 he will **h** me in his
Ps 57:1 I will **h** beneath the shadow
Ps 143:9 run to you to **h** me.
Jer 16:17 cannot hope to **h** from me.
Matt 11:25 thank you for **h-ing** these

HIGH, HIGHER, HIGHEST (adj)
foremost in rank, dignity, or standing; having large extension upward; of greater degree or value than average, usual, or expected
Gen 14:18 of God Most **H,** brought Abram
Gen 14:22 LORD, God Most **H,** Creator of
Ps 113:4 glory is **h-er** than the heavens.
Isa 14:14 be like the Most **H.**
Dan 4:17 that the Most **H** rules over
Mark 5:7 Son of the Most **H** God?
Phil 2:9 the place of **h-est** honor and
Heb 7:1 a priest of God Most **H.**

HIGHLIGHTS (v)
to throw a strong light on
Rom 3:7 sinner if my dishonesty **h** his

HIGHWAY (n)
a main direct road
Isa 40:3 Make a straight **h** through the
Matt 7:13 The **h** to hell is broad

HILLS (n)
a usually rounded natural elevation of land lower than a mountain
1 Kgs 20:23 are gods of the **h;**
Ps 50:10 the cattle on a thousand **h.**
Isa 40:4 mountains and **h.** Straighten
Hos 10:8 plead with the **h,** "Fall on
Matt 24:16 Judea must flee to the **h.**
Luke 3:5 mountains and **h** made level.
Luke 23:30 plead with the **h,** 'Bury us.'
Rev 17:9 the seven **h** where the woman

HILLTOP (n)
the highest part of a hill
Matt 5:14 a city on a **h** that cannot be

HINDER, HINDERED (v)
to delay, impede, or prevent action
1 Sam 14:6 for nothing can **h** the LORD.
1 Pet 3:7 will not be **h-ed.**

HIRE (v)
to engage the personal services of for pay
Luke 15:15 a local farmer to **h** him,

HOARD, HOARDING (v)
to keep something to oneself
Prov 11:26 those who **h** their grain,
Eccl 5:13 **H-ing** riches harms

HOLD, HOLDING, HOLDS (v)
to keep under restraint; to have or maintain in the grasp; to keep from falling or moving; to have in the mind or express as a judgment, opinion, or belief; to maintain control of
2 Kgs 4:16 you will be **h-ing** a son in
Ps 3:3 the one who **h-s** my head high.
Ps 37:24 for the LORD **h-s** them by the
Ps 39:1 I will **h** my tongue when
Ps 63:8 right hand **h-s** me securely.
Prov 27:16 **h** something with greased
Isa 40:11 **h-ing** them close to his heart.
Isa 48:9 name, I will **h** back my anger
Matt 4:6 And they will **h** you up with
Mark 11:25 forgive anyone you are **h-ing**
Col 1:17 and he **h-s** all creation
Col 2:19 For he **h-s** the whole body
Heb 4:14 God, let us **h** firmly to what
Heb 10:23 Let us **h** tightly without

HOLINESS (n)
sanctity or purity
Exod 15:11 glorious in **h,** awesome in
Deut 32:51 to demonstrate my **h** to the
Ps 29:2 the splendor of his **h.**
Luke 1:75 in **h** and righteousness for
1 Cor 7:14 wife brings **h** to her
2 Cor 1:12 a God-given **h** and sincerity
1 Thes 4:4 and live in **h** and honor—
1 Tim 2:15 faith, love, **h,** and modesty.
Heb 12:10 share in his **h.**

HOLY (adj)
consecrated or set aside for sacred use (as opposed to pagan or common use); standing apart from sin and evil; characteristic of God, especially the third person of the Trinity
see also PURE
Gen 2:3 and declared it **h,** because it
Exod 3:5 are standing on **h** ground.
Exod 19:6 priests, my **h** nation.
Exod 26:33 separate the **H** Place
Exod 29:37 'be absolutely **h,**
Exod 30:10 LORD's most **h** altar.
Exod 31:13 the LORD, who makes you **h.**
Lev 11:45 you must be **h** because I am
Lev 19:8 for defiling what is **h** to the

Lev 20:7 set yourselves apart to be **h,**
Lev 20:26 You must be **h** because I,
Lev 21:12 for he has been made **h** by the
Lev 22:32 the LORD who makes you **h.**
Lev 27:9 LORD will be considered **h.**
Deut 5:12 by keeping it **h,** as the LORD
Josh 5:15 where you are standing is **h.**
Josh 24:19 he is a **h** and jealous God.
1 Chr 16:35 we can thank your **h** name
Neh 11:1 in Jerusalem, the **h** city.
Ps 22:3 Yet you are **h,** enthroned on
Ps 30:4 Praise his **h** name.
Ps 99:3 Your name is **h!**
Ps 105:3 Exult in his **h** name; rejoice,
Ps 111:9 What a **h,** awe-inspiring name
Prov 9:10 of the **H** One results in good
Isa 6:3 to each other, "**H, h, h**
Isa 40:25 my equal?" asks the **H** One.
Isa 54:5 your Redeemer, the **H** One of
Isa 66:20 them to my **h** mountain in
Dan 7:18 But in the end, the **h** people
Dan 9:24 anoint the Most **H** Place.
Zech 14:5 and all his **h** ones with him.
Matt 24:15 standing in the **H** Place.
Mark 1:24 you are—the **H** One of God
Luke 1:35 baby to be born will be **h,**
Luke 1:49 Mighty One is **h,** and he has
Luke 4:34 you are—the **H** One of God
Luke 11:2 may your name be kept **h.**
John 6:69 you are the **H** One of God!"
John 17:17 Make them **h** by your
Acts 13:35 not allow your **H** One to rot
Rom 7:12 the law itself is **h,** and its
Rom 14:5 day is more **h** than another
Rom 15:16 made **h** by the **H** Spirit.
1 Cor 1:2 be his own **h** people.
1 Cor 1:30 made us pure and **h,**
1 Cor 3:17 God's temple is **h,** and you
1 Cor 6:11 you were made **h;** you were
1 Cor 7:14 children would not be **h,** but
Eph 1:4 in Christ to be **h** and without
Eph 2:21 becoming a **h** temple for
Eph 4:24 righteous and **h.**
Eph 5:26 to make her **h** and clean,
Col 1:22 and you are **h** and blameless
1 Thes 3:13 blameless, and **h** as you
1 Thes 4:7 called us to live **h** lives,
1 Thes 5:23 make you **h** in every
2 Thes 1:10 from his **h** people—praise
1 Tim 2:8 to pray with **h** hands lifted
2 Tim 1:9 called us to live a **h** life.
2 Tim 3:15 taught the **h** Scriptures from
Heb 2:11 ones he makes **h** have the same
Heb 10:14 those who are being made **h.**
Heb 10:19 heaven's Most **H** Place
Heb 10:29 which made us **h,** as if it
Heb 13:12 make his people **h** by means
1 Pet 1:16 You must be **h** because I am
1 Pet 2:5 you are his **h** priests.
1 Pet 2:9 priests, a **h** nation, God's
1 Pet 3:5 is how the **h** women of old
2 Pet 1:18 on the **h** mountain.
2 Pet 2:21 to live a **h** life.
2 Pet 3:11 like this, what **h** and godly
Rev 3:7 one who is **h** and true,
Rev 4:8 on saying, "**H, h, h** is
Rev 15:4 you alone are **h.** All nations
Rev 20:6 Blessed and **h** are those who
Rev 22:11 continue to be **h.**

HOLY GHOST (KJV)

Matt 1:18 the power of the *Holy Spirit*
Matt 3:11 baptize you with the *Holy Spirit*
Matt 28:19 the Son and the *Holy Spirit*
Luke 3:22 *Holy Spirit,* in bodily form,
1 Jn 5:7-8 three witnesses—the *Spirit*

HOLY SPIRIT

the third person of the Holy Trinity
see ADVOCATE, COUNSELOR
Luke 11:13 give the **H** to those
2 Cor 5:5 he has given us his **H.**
Eph 1:13 **H,** whom he promised
Eph 4:30 sorrow to God's **H**
1 Thes 4:8 gives his **H** to you

HOME (n)

one's place of residence; place of origin, destiny, or comfort; family-style social unit
see also DWELLING, HOUSE
Deut 11:19 when you are at **h** and
1 Chr 16:43 turned and went **h** to bless
Ps 46:4 God, the sacred **h** of the Most
Prov 3:33 but he blesses the **h** of the
Prov 27:8 person who strays from **h**
Matt 10:11 stay in his **h** until you leave
Luke 10:7 move around from **h**
Luke 19:9 has come to this **h** today,
John 14:2 in my Father's **h.** If this
John 14:23 make our **h** with each
Acts 16:15 come and stay at my **h.**
Rom 16:5 meets in their **h.** Greet my
Eph 3:17 will make his **h** in your
1 Tim 5:4 show godliness at **h**
Heb 13:14 not our permanent **h;** we are
1 Pet 4:9 share your **h** with those who

HOMELAND (n)

area set aside to be a state for a people of a particular national, cultural, or racial origin
2 Sam 7:10 And I will provide a **h** for my

HOMETOWN (n)
the city or town where one was born or grew up
Matt 13:57 in his own **h** and among his
Luke 4:24 is accepted in his own **h.**
John 4:44 is not honored in his own **h.**

HOMOSEXUALITY (n)
erotic activity with another of the same sex
1 Cor 6:9 prostitutes, or practice **h,**
1 Tim 1:10 or who practice **h,** or are

HONEST (adj)
truthful; genuine; reputable; marked by integrity
Exod 18:21 some capable, **h** men
2 Kgs 12:15 were **h** and trustworthy
Ps 37:37 those who are **h** and good,
Prov 12:17 An **h** witness tells
Prov 28:6 Better to be poor and **h** than
Jer 5:1 even one just and **h** person,
Matt 22:16 we know how **h** you are.
1 Thes 2:10 devout and **h** and faultless

HONESTY (n)
fairness and straightforwardness of conduct; sincerity
Ps 51:6 But you desire **h** from the
Prov 11:5 are directed by **h;** the wicked
Jer 5:3 searching for **h.** You struck

HONEY (n)
a sweet liquid substance produced by bees; symbolic of abundance or delight in God's word
Exod 3:8 with milk and **h**—the land
1 Sam 14:26 They didn't dare touch the **h**
Ps 19:10 sweeter than **h,** even **h**
Ps 119:103 they are sweeter than **h.**
Isa 7:15 eating yogurt and **h.**
Rev 10:9 be sweet as **h** in your mouth,

HONEYCOMB (n)
a mass of hexagonal wax cells in a honeybee nest that stores honey
Song 5:1 and eat **h** with my honey.

HONOR, HONORS (n)
having a renowned reputation or social standing; physical or spiritual blessing (from God); a showing of merited respect
Ps 8:5 crowned them with glory and **h.**
Ps 104:1 are robed with **h** and majesty.
Prov 3:35 The wise inherit **h,** but fools
Prov 15:33 humility precedes **h.**
Prov 25:27 not good to seek **h-s**
Isa 53:12 I will give him the **h-s** of a
Isa 55:13 will bring great **h** to the
Luke 14:8 don't sit in the seat of **h.**
Eph 1:20 the place of **h** at God's right
Heb 13:4 Give **h** to marriage,
1 Pet 2:6 chosen for great **h,** and
1 Pet 2:12 they will give **h** to God when
1 Pet 3:7 husbands must give **h** to
2 Pet 1:17 when he received **h** and glory
Rev 4:9 give glory and **h** and thanks
Rev 19:7 and let us give **h** to him.

HONOR, HONORED, HONORING, HONORS (v)
of God, to reverence his majesty; of man, to respect or esteem; to confer honor upon
Exod 20:12 **H** your father and mother.
1 Kgs 8:43 Temple I have built **h-s**
Neh 1:11 who delight in **h-ing** you.
Ps 29:1 **H** the Lord, you
Ps 45:11 **h** him, for he is your Lord.
Ps 46:10 I will be **h-ed** by every nation.
Ps 47:9 He is highly **h-ed** everywhere.
Prov 14:31 helping the poor **h-s** him.
Isa 66:5 the Lord be **h-ed!**
Matt 15:4 God says, '**H** your father and
Mark 6:4 A prophet is **h-ed** everywhere
Luke 16:15 What this world **h-s**
John 5:23 that everyone will **h** the Son,
John 12:26 the Father will **h** anyone who
Rom 12:10 delight in **h-ing** each other.
Rom 13:3 and they will **h** you.
1 Cor 6:20 So you must **h** God with your
1 Cor 12:26 if one part is **h-ed,** all the
Eph 6:2 **H** your father and mother
Col 1:10 the way you live will always **h**
1 Thes 5:12 and sisters, **h** those who are
2 Thes 1:12 be **h-ed** along with him.
Titus 2:3 a way that **h-s** God.

HONORABLE (adj)
characterized by integrity; upright
Rom 12:17 everyone can see you are **h.**
2 Cor 8:21 to see that we are **h.**
Phil 4:8 is true, and **h,** and right,
1 Pet 2:12 will see your **h** behavior,

HOOKS (n)
a pole bearing a curved blade for pruning plants
Isa 2:4 into pruning **h.** Nation will
Joel 3:10 your pruning **h** into spears.
Mic 4:3 into pruning **h.** Nation will

HOPE, HOPES (n)
confident trust with the expectation of fulfillment
1 Sam 9:20 focus of all Israel's **h-s.**
Job 31:16 crushed the **h-s** of widows?
Ps 10:17 Lord, you know the **h-s** of the
Ps 42:5 I will put my **h** in God!
Ps 112:10 slink away, their **h-s** thwarted.

Ps 119:49 to me; it is my only **h.**
Ps 119:74 I have put my **h** in your word.
Prov 10:24 the **h-s** of the godly will be
Prov 13:12 **H** deferred makes the heart
Zech 9:12 prisoners who still have **h!**
Rom 5:4 our confident **h** of salvation.
Rom 8:20 curse. But with eager **h,**
Rom 12:12 Rejoice in our confident **h.**
Rom 15:4 give us **h** and encouragement
Rom 15:13 God, the source of **h,** will
1 Cor 13:13 faith, **h,** and love—
1 Cor 15:19 And if our **h** in Christ is
Eph 2:12 without God and without **h.**
1 Thes 1:3 and the enduring **h** you have
1 Tim 4:10 struggle, for our **h** is in the
Heb 10:23 wavering to the **h** we affirm,
1 Pet 3:15 about your Christian **h,**

HOPE (v)
to desire with expectation of obtainment
Rom 8:24 don't need to **h** for it.

HOPEFUL (adj)
full of or inclined to hope
1 Cor 13:7 is always **h,** and endures

HORN, HORNS (n)
a bony material arising from the head of many animals; a projection on the four corners of the altar in the tabernacle and Temple; a symbol of power and might
Exod 19:13 when the ram's **h** sounds a
Exod 27:2 so that the **h-s** and altar are
Judg 7:19 blew the rams' **h-s** and broke
Dan 7:8 This little **h** had eyes
Dan 7:24 Its ten **h-s** are ten kings
Amos 2:2 and the ram's **h** sounds.
Zech 9:14 sound the ram's **h** and attack
Rev 5:6 He had seven **h-s** and seven
Rev 12:3 heads and ten **h-s,** with seven
Rev 13:1 heads and ten **h-s,** with ten
Rev 17:3 and ten **h-s,** and blasphemies

HORROR (n)
painful and intense fear, dread, or aversion
Jer 2:12 shrink back in **h** and dismay,

HORSE (n)
a large solid-hoofed herbivorous mammal often used for working or riding
Ps 147:10 strength of a **h** or in human
Prov 26:3 Guide a **h** with a
Zech 1:8 on a red **h** that was standing
Rev 6:2 saw a white **h** standing there.
Rev 6:4 Then another **h** appeared,
Rev 6:5 saw a black **h,** and its rider
Rev 6:8 and saw a **h** whose color was
Rev 19:11 and a white **h** was standing

HOSANNA (KJV)
Matt 21:9 *Praise God* in highest heaven!
Matt 21:15 *Praise God* for the Son of David
Mark 11:9 *Praise God!* Blessings on the
Mark 11:10 *Praise God* in highest heaven
John 12:13 *Praise God!* Blessings on the

HOSPITALITY (n)
generous and cordial treatment, reception, or disposition
Matt 25:38 and show you **h?**
Luke 10:7 Don't hesitate to accept **h,**
Rom 12:13 be eager to practice **h.**

HOSTILE (adj)
openly opposed or resisting
Rom 8:7 nature is always **h** to God.

HOSTILITY (n)
deep-seated ill will; enmity
Gen 3:15 I will cause **h** between you
Lev 26:28 I will give full vent to my **h.**
Gal 5:20 sorcery, **h,** quarreling,
Eph 2:14 the wall of **h** that separated
Eph 2:16 our **h** toward each other was
Heb 12:3 of all the **h** he endured from

HOUR (n)
a (short) unit or passage of time; moment
John 12:27 save me from this **h**'?
John 13:1 knew that his **h** had come
John 17:1 Father, the **h** has come.

HOUSE, HOUSES (n)
living quarters; a family including ancestors, descendants, and kindred extended family unit, including ancestors and descendants
see also DWELLING, DYNASTY, HOME, TEMPLE
Exod 12:22 doorframes of your **h-s.**
Exod 12:27 he passed over the **h-s** of the
Exod 20:17 your neighbor's **h.**
2 Sam 7:11 he will make a **h** for you—
Ps 23:6 live in the **h** of the LORD
Ps 27:4 to live in the **h** of the LORD
Ps 69:9 for your **h** has consumed me,
Ps 127:1 Unless the LORD builds a **h,**
Isa 54:2 Enlarge your **h;** build an
Amos 5:11 beautiful stone **h-s,** you will
Matt 7:24 who builds a **h** on solid rock.
Matt 19:29 given up **h-s** or brothers or
Mark 11:17 be called a **h** of prayer for
John 2:17 for God's **h** will consume me.

HOUSEHOLD (n)
a social unit composed of those living together in the same dwelling; family
see also FAMILY
Exod 12:3 one animal for each **h.**
Acts 16:31 everyone in your **h.**
1 Tim 3:5 manage his own **h,**
1 Tim 3:12 children and **h** well.
1 Tim 3:15 themselves in the **h** of God.
1 Pet 4:17 begin with God's **h.**

HOUSETOPS (n)
roof
Matt 10:27 shout from the **h** for all to

HUMAN (adj)
of, relating to, or characteristic of men and women collectively; mortal; finite
see also FLESH
Gen 1:26 Let us make **h** beings in our
Gen 3:22 Look, the **h** beings have
Gen 9:6 If anyone takes a **h** life,
Ps 9:20 they are merely **h.**
Ps 33:13 sees the whole **h** race.
Ps 89:47 futile this **h** existence!
John 1:14 So the Word became **h**
John 2:24 because he knew **h** nature.
John 8:15 judge me by **h** standards,
Rom 6:19 weakness of your **h** nature,
1 Cor 2:5 trust not in **h** wisdom but in
1 Cor 2:13 come from **h** wisdom.
2 Cor 3:3 of stone, but on **h** hearts.
2 Cor 10:3 We are **h,** but we
Gal 3:3 by your own **h** effort?
Col 2:9 of God in a **h** body.
1 Thes 2:13 words as mere **h** ideas.
Heb 7:28 limited by **h** weakness.
2 Pet 1:21 or from **h** initiative.

HUMAN, HUMANS (n)
a homo sapien; mankind
Gen 6:3 Spirit will not put up with **h-s**
Isa 2:22 trust in mere **h-s.** They are as
Jer 17:5 trust in mere **h-s,** who rely on

HUMANITY (n)
the quality or state of being human; the human race
Job 14:1 How frail is **h!** How short
Zech 2:13 Be silent before the Lord, all **h,**

HUMBLE (adj)
not proud or haughty; can imply lower social or economic status; meek or gentle
Num 12:3 Moses was very **h**—
Ps 138:6 cares for the **h,** but he keeps
Ps 149:4 he crowns the **h** with victory.
Zech 9:9 yet he is **h,** riding on a
Matt 5:5 those who are **h,**
Matt 11:29 I am **h** and gentle at
Matt 21:5 He is **h,** riding on a
Eph 4:2 Always be **h** and gentle.
Phil 2:3 Be **h,** thinking of
Jas 4:6 but favors the **h.**
1 Pet 3:8 and keep a **h** attitude.

HUMBLE, HUMBLED, HUMBLES (v)
to not think too highly of oneself; to bring low or prostrate
Isa 26:5 He **h-s** the proud and
Luke 14:11 themselves will be **h-d,**
Luke 18:14 will be **h-d,** and those who
2 Cor 11:7 wrong when I **h-d** myself
Phil 2:8 he **h-d** himself in obedience
Jas 1:10 that God has **h-d** them.
Jas 4:10 **H** yourselves before the Lord,
1 Pet 5:6 So **h** yourselves under

HUMBLY (adv)
in an unhaughty, unproud manner; in an insignificant or unpretentious manner
Zeph 2:3 and to live **h.** Perhaps even
Acts 20:19 I have done the Lord's work **h**
1 Tim 5:10 served other believers **h?**

HUMILIATE, HUMILIATED (v)
to shame or mortify
Deut 21:14 for you have **h-ed** her.
2 Sam 22:28 watch the proud and **h**
Ps 18:27 but you **h** the proud

HUMILIATION (n)
shame, mortification, disgrace, dishonor
Job 19:5 using my **h** as evidence
Ps 44:15 the constant **h;** shame is
Prov 29:23 ends in **h,** while humility

HUMILITY (n)
show of meekness; quality of being humble
Prov 11:2 but with **h** comes wisdom.
Prov 15:33 **h** precedes honor.
Prov 22:4 True **h** and fear
Col 3:12 kindness, **h,** gentleness,
Jas 3:13 works with the **h** that comes
1 Pet 5:5 each other in **h,** for "God

HUNDRED (n)
the number 100
Matt 13:8 and even a **h** times as much as
Luke 8:8 that was a **h** times as much as

HUNG (v)
to suspend

see also HANG
Deut 21:23 anyone who is **h** is cursed
Luke 19:48 all the people **h** on every word
Gal 3:13 When he was **h** on the cross,

HUNGER (n)
a craving or urgent need for food
Ps 145:16 you satisfy the **h** and thirst

HUNGRY (adj)
feeling a strong desire for food; a craving for anything
Prov 25:21 If your enemies are **h,**
Matt 15:32 to send them away **h,**
Matt 25:35 For I was **h,** and you fed me.
Luke 1:53 He has filled the **h** with good
Luke 6:21 you who are **h** now, for you
John 6:35 never be **h** again.
Rom 8:35 or are persecuted, or **h,** or
Rom 12:20 enemies are **h,** feed them.
Rev 7:16 never again be **h** or thirsty;

HUNT, HUNTED (v)
to pursue with intent to capture
Ps 119:86 from those who **h** me
2 Cor 4:9 We are **h-ed** down,

HURT, HURTING, HURTS (v)
to wound, injure, or damage
1 Chr 16:22 and do not **h** my prophets.
Ps 15:4 promises even when it **h-s.**
Eccl 8:9 the power to **h** each other.
Lam 3:33 he does not enjoy **h-ing** people
Matt 4:6 you won't even **h** your foot on
Mark 16:18 it won't **h** them.

HUSBAND, HUSBANDS (n)
male partner in a marriage; head of family; protector and provider; figurative of Christ
Ruth 1:8 kindness to your **h-s** and to me.
Prov 12:4 is a crown for her **h,**
Prov 31:28 Her **h** praises her:
Jer 3:20 wife who leaves her **h.**
Rom 7:2 binds her to her **h** as long as
1 Cor 7:3 The **h** should fulfill
1 Cor 7:10 not leave her **h.**
1 Cor 7:39 is bound to her **h** as long as
2 Cor 11:2 bride to one **h**—Christ.
Gal 4:27 lives with her **h!**
Eph 5:22 submit to your **h-s** as to the
Eph 5:23 For a **h** is the head
Eph 5:25 For **h-s,** this means
Eph 5:28 same way, **h-s** ought to love
Col 3:18 submit to your **h-s,** as is
Col 3:19 **H-s,** love your
1 Tim 5:9 faithful to her **h.**
Titus 2:4 to love their **h-s** and their
1 Pet 3:1 the authority of your **h-s.**
1 Pet 3:7 same way, you **h-s** must give

HYMN, HYMNS (n)
a song of praise to God
Ps 40:3 to sing, a **h** of praise to our
Matt 26:30 they sang a **h** and went out
Mark 14:26 they sang a **h** and went out
Acts 16:25 praying and singing **h-s**
Eph 5:19 psalms and **h-s** and spiritual
Col 3:16 psalms and **h-s** and spiritual

HYPOCRISY (n)
feigning to be what one is not; pretense of piety
Matt 23:28 your hearts are filled with **h**
Mark 12:15 saw through their **h**
Gal 2:13 followed Peter's **h,** and even
Gal 2:13 led astray by their **h.**
1 Pet 2:1 all deceit, **h,** jealousy,

HYPOCRITE, HYPOCRITES (n)
a person who portrays a false appearance of religion; a pretender
Matt 6:16 make it obvious, as the **h-s**
Matt 7:5 **H!** First get rid of the log
Matt 23:13 and you Pharisees. **H-s!**
Luke 6:42 the log in your own eye? **H!**
Luke 13:15 Lord replied, "You **h-s!**
1 Tim 4:2 These people are **h-s** and liars,

HYSSOP (n)
an aromatic shrub of the species of marjoram and a member of the mint family that has clusters of yellow flowers
Exod 12:22 Brush the **h** across the
John 19:29 put it on a **h** branch, and held it

I

IDEAS (n)
formulated thoughts or opinions; notions or concepts
Ps 73:20 you will laugh at their silly **i**
Ps 81:12 living according to their own **i.**

IDENTIFY, IDENTIFIED (v)
to establish the distinguishing character or personality of; to relate to in solidarity
Matt 7:16 You can **i** them by their fruit,
Matt 12:33 A tree is **i-ied** by its fruit.
Eph 1:13 believed in Christ, he **i-ied** you

IDLE (adj)
not employed or useful for work; inactive, lazy
2 Thes 3:6 believers who live **i** lives
2 Thes 3:7 not **i** when we were with you.
2 Thes 3:11 you are living **i** lives,

IDLENESS (n)
a state of unemployment, inactivity, or laziness
Prov 19:15 but **i** leaves them hungry.
Eccl 10:18 **i** leads to a leaky house.

IDOL, IDOLS (n)
a representation or symbol of a false god
Exod 20:4 make for yourself an **i**
Deut 27:15 who carves or casts an **i**
1 Sam 15:23 as bad as worshiping **i-s.**
Isa 40:19 Can he be compared to an **i**
Isa 44:9 who worship **i-s** don't know
Isa 44:15 makes an **i** and bows down
Isa 44:17 and makes his god: a carved **i!**
Isa 44:19 who made the **i** never stops to
Hab 2:18 What good is an **i** carved
Acts 15:20 eating food offered to **i-s,**
Rom 1:23 worshiped **i-s** made to look
1 Cor 6:9 or who worship **i-s,** or commit
1 Cor 8:1 has been offered to **i-s.**
1 Cor 8:4 an **i** is not really a god
Rev 2:14 sin by eating food offered to **i-s**

IDOLATER (n)
worshiper of idols; one who worships an undeserving object blindly
Eph 5:5 a greedy person is an **i,**
Col 3:5 a greedy person is an **i,**

IDOLATRY (n)
the worship of a physical object as a god; immoderate attachment or devotion to something
Gal 5:20 pleasures, **i,** sorcery,

IGNORANT (adj)
resulting from or showing lack of knowledge, comprehension, or intelligence; unaware, uninformed
Job 38:2 questions my wisdom with such **i**
Heb 5:2 with **i** and wayward people
1 Pet 2:15 lives should silence those **i**
2 Pet 3:16 are **i** and unstable have twisted

IGNORE (v)
to refuse to take notice of
Ps 9:12 He does not **i** the cries of
Ps 9:17 all the nations who **i** God.
Ps 10:12 Do not **i** the helpless!
Prov 13:18 If you **i** criticism,
Heb 2:3 if we **i** this great salvation

ILL-TEMPERED (adj)
having a cross or surly disposition; quarrelsome
1 Sam 25:17 He's so **i** that no

ILLEGITIMATE (adj)
not recognized as lawful offspring
Heb 12:8 means that you are **i** and

ILLUMINATES (v)
to supply or brighten with light
Rev 21:23 the glory of God **i** the city,

IMAGE (n)
a God-given likeness or reflection; a tangible or visible representation
Gen 1:26 make human beings in our **i,**
Gen 1:27 human beings in his own **i.**
Gen 9:6 made human beings in his own **i.**
Col 1:15 Christ is the visible **i** of the
Jas 3:9 made in the **i** of God.

IMAGINE, IMAGINED (v)
to form a mental image of; to suppose or guess
Gen 6:5 **i-d** was consistently and totally
Job 37:5 can't even **i** the greatness
1 Cor 2:9 no mind has **i-ed** what God has

IMITATE, IMITATED (v)
to follow as a pattern, model, or example; to resemble; to mimic
1 Cor 4:16 I urge you to **i** me.
1 Cor 11:1 should **i** me, just as I **i**
1 Thes 1:6 you **i-d** both us and the Lord
1 Thes 2:14 you **i-d** the believers
2 Thes 3:7 that you ought to **i** us.

IMMANUEL
Hebrew name meaning "God is with us"
Isa 7:14 to a son and will call him **I**
Isa 8:8 one end to the other, O **I.**
Matt 1:23 a son, and they will call him **I,**

IMMATURE (adj)
lacking complete growth, development, or maturity
Eph 4:14 no longer be **i** like children.

IMMORAL (adj)
characterized by conflicting with traditionally (biblically) held moral principles; sinful or impure
Prov 2:16 save you from the **i** woman,
Prov 6:24 keep you from the **i** woman,
Prov 22:14 an **i** woman is a dangerous
Luke 7:37 a certain **i** woman from
Rom 13:13 promiscuity and **i** living,
Eph 5:5 be sure that no **i,** impure,
1 Tim 1:10 people who are sexually **i,**
Jude 1:4 grace allows us to live **i** lives.
Rev 22:15 the sorcerers, the sexually **i,**

IMMORALITY (n)
the quality or state of being immoral; an immoral act or practice

Matt 15:19 all sexual **i,** theft, lying,
Acts 15:29 animals, and from sexual **i.**
1 Cor 6:13 made for sexual **i.**
1 Cor 6:18 **i** is a sin against
1 Cor 7:2 there is so much sexual **i,**
Gal 5:19 very clear: sexual **i,** impurity,
2 Pet 2:7 who was sick of the shameful **i**
Jude 1:7 towns, which were filled with **i**

IMMORTAL (adj)
exempt from death; imperishable
1 Cor 15:53 transformed into **i** bodies.

IMMORTALITY (n)
unending existence; lasting fame
Rom 2:7 and honor and **i**
2 Tim 1:10 the way to life and **i**

IMMOVABLE (adj)
incapable of being moved; steadfast, unyielding
1 Cor 15:58 be strong and **i.** Always work

IMPALED (v)
to torture or kill by fixing on a sharp stake
Esth 7:10 they **i** Haman on the pole

IMPARTIAL (adj)
not partial or biased; treating all equally
Deut 1:17 and **i** in your judgments.
Matt 22:16 **i** and don't play favorites.

IMPATIENT (adj)
restless or short of temper especially under irritation, delay, or opposition
Zech 11:8 I became **i** with these sheep,

IMPORTANT (adj)
marked by or indicative of significant worth or consequence
Matt 23:23 ignore the more **i** aspects of
Matt 23:23 do not neglect the more **i**
Mark 12:29 The most **i** commandment
Mark 12:33 I know it is **i** to love him
1 Cor 7:19 The **i** thing is to keep God's
1 Cor 15:3 what was most **i** and what
Gal 5:6 What is **i** is faith expressing

IMPOSSIBLE (adj)
incapable of being or occurring
Zech 8:6 this may seem **i** to you now,
Luke 1:37 For nothing is **i** with God.
Heb 6:4 it is **i** to bring back
Heb 11:6 it is **i** to please God

IMPOSTORS (n)
those who assume false identity or title for the purpose of deception
2 Cor 6:8 are honest, but they call us **i.**
2 Tim 3:13 evil people and **i** will flourish.

IMPRESS, IMPRESSED (v)
to gain the admiration or interest of
Dan 1:19 **i-ed** him as much as Daniel,
Phil 2:3 don't try to **i** others. Be humble

IMPRESSION (n)
an often indistinct or imprecise notion or remembrance
Luke 19:11 correct the **i** that the Kingdom

IMPRESSIVE (adj)
having the power to excite attention, awe, or admiration
Ps 107:24 his **i** works on the deepest seas.

IMPURE (adj)
ritually unclean; lewd, unchaste
Acts 11:8 have declared **i** or unclean.
Eph 5:5 no immoral, **i,** or greedy person
1 Thes 2:3 with any deceit or **i** motives
1 Thes 4:7 live holy lives, not **i** lives.

IMPURITY, IMPURITIES (n)
something that is impure or makes something else impure; the quality or state of being impure
Prov 25:4 Remove the **i-ies** from silver,
Gal 5:19 clear: sexual immorality, **i,**
Col 3:5 to do with sexual immorality, **i,**

INCENSE (n)
material used to produce a fragrant odor when burned
Exod 30:1 acacia wood for burning **i.**
Exod 30:38 Anyone who makes **i**
Exod 40:5 Place the gold **i** altar
Ps 141:2 Accept my prayer as **i** offered
Heb 9:4 In that room were a gold **i** altar
Rev 5:8 held gold bowls filled with **i,**
Rev 8:3 great amount of **i** was given
Rev 8:4 smoke of the **i,** mixed with the

INCORRUPTIBLE (KJV)
1 Cor 15:52 will be raised *to live forever.*
1 Pet 1:4 *beyond the reach of* change and *decay.*

INCREASE, INCREASED, INCREASES (v)
to become progressively greater (as in size, amount, number, or intensity)
1 Sam 2:10 he **i-s** the strength of his anointed
Ps 62:10 if your wealth **i-s,** don't
Luke 17:5 Show us how to **i** our faith.

Acts 6:7 — number of believers greatly **i-d**

INCREDIBLE (adj)

too extraordinary and improbable to be believed; amazing, extraordinary

Acts 26:8 — does it seem **i** to any of you
Eph 2:7 — examples of the **i** wealth of

INCURABLE (adj)

unlikely to be changed or corrected

Jer 30:12 — Your injury is **i**—a terrible

INDEPENDENT (adj)

not requiring or relying on others; not subject to control by others

1 Cor 11:11 — women are not **i** of men,
1 Cor 11:11 — men are not **i** of women.

INDULGE, INDULGED, INDULGES (v)

to take unrestrained pleasure in

Rom 1:26 — **i-d** in sex with each other.
Rom 13:14 — ways to **i** your evil desires.
1 Cor 5:9 — people who **i** in sexual sin.
1 Cor 5:11 — claims to be a believer yet **i-s**

INEXPRESSIBLE (adj)

not capable of being expressed; indescribable

1 Pet 1:8 — rejoice with a glorious, **i** joy.

INFANTS (n)

a child in the first period of (physical or spiritual) life

Ps 8:2 — and **i** to tell of your strength,
Matt 21:16 — and **i** to give you praise.
1 Cor 3:1 — were **i** in the Christian life.

INFINITE (adj)

subject to no limitation or external determination

Phil 3:8 — compared with the **i** value

INFLUENCE, INFLUENCED (v)

to sway; to affect or modify

Luke 20:21 — **i-d** by what others think.
3 Jn 1:11 — bad example **i** you.

INFLUENTIAL (adj)

exerting or possessing the power or capacity of causing an effect in indirect ways

Ruth 2:1 — there was a wealthy and **i** man

INHERIT, INHERITED (v)

to receive as a legacy or promise; to take possession as a rightful heir

Matt 5:5 — they will **i** the whole earth.
Matt 25:34 — **i** the Kingdom prepared
Mark 10:17 — I do to **i** eternal life?
1 Cor 6:9 — will not **i** the Kingdom
Eph 3:6 — share equally in the riches **i-ed**
Eph 5:5 — impure, or greedy person will **i**
Rev 21:7 — All who are victorious will **i**

INHERITANCE (n)

the acquisition of a possession, condition, or trait from past generations; something that is or may be inherited

Ps 16:6 — What a wonderful **i**!
Ps 33:12 — people he has chosen as his **i.**
Ps 61:5 — an **i** reserved for those who
Gal 4:30 — will not share the **i**
Eph 1:14 — give us the **i** he promised
Col 3:24 — give you an **i** as your reward,
Heb 9:15 — receive the eternal **i** God has

INIQUITY, INIQUITIES (KJV)

Ps 51:9 — Remove the stain of my *guilt*
Isa 6:7 — your *guilt* is removed,
Isa 53:6 — laid on him the *sins* of us all.
1 Cor 13:6 — not rejoice about *injustice*
Rev 18:5 — God remembers her *evil deeds*

INJURE, INJURED (v)

to do an injustice to; to harm or impair

Prov 8:36 — who miss me **i** themselves.
Ezek 34:16 — I will bandage the **i-ed** and
Zech 11:16 — nor heal the **i-ed,** nor feed

INJUSTICE (n)

unfairness; wrongs

1 Cor 6:7 — accept the **i** and leave it
1 Cor 13:6 — It does not rejoice about **i**

INK (n)

a colored, usually liquid, material for writing and printing

2 Cor 3:3 — is written not with pen and **i,**

INNOCENCE (n)

freedom from guilt or sin through being unacquainted with evil; blamelessness

Gen 20:5 — I acted in complete **i**!
2 Sam 22:25 — He has seen my **i.**
Hos 8:5 — will you be incapable of **i?**

INNOCENT (adj)

regarded as righteous; free from guilt or sin; unaware or ignorant

Job 13:18 — I will be proved **i.**
Job 34:5 — Job also said, 'I am **i,**
Ps 7:8 — for I am **i,** O Most High!
Ps 26:1 — Declare me **i,** O LORD, for I
Ps 143:2 — no one is **i** before you.
Matt 27:4 — I have betrayed an **i** man.
Matt 27:24 — I am **i** of this man's blood.

Rom 16:18 they deceive **i** people.

INQUIRE (v)
to ask about or look into
Deut 12:30 Do not **i** about their gods,
Deut 32:7 **I** of your elders
1 Chr 21:30 to go there to **i** of God

INSIGHT (n)
the power or act of seeing into a situation; discernment
Ps 19:8 are clear, giving **i** for living.
Prov 7:4 make **i** a beloved member
Eph 1:17 and **i** so that you might grow

INSOLENCE (n)
the quality or state of being overbearing or impudent
1 Tim 1:13 In my **i,** I persecuted his people.

INSPECT (v)
to view closely in critical appraisal
Prov 31:16 She goes to **i** a field

INSPIRATION (n)
guidance by divine influence
Matt 22:43 under the **i** of the Spirit

INSPIRED (adj)
Influenced, moved; guided or created by divine influence
2 Tim 3:16 All Scripture is **i** by God

INSTINCT, INSTINCTS (n)
a natural or inherent aptitude, impulse, or capacity
2 Pet 2:12 creatures of **i,** born to be caught
Jude 1:10 whatever their **i-s** tell them,
Jude 1:19 They follow their natural **i-s**

INSTITUTED (v)
to originate and get established; to set going
Rom 13:2 against what God has **i,**

INSTRUCT, INSTRUCTED, INSTRUCTS (v)
to provide with authoritative information or advice; to teach, train, or direct
Exod 4:12 I will **i** you in what to say.
Deut 2:1 just as the LORD had **i-ed** me,
Deut 4:36 so he could **i** you.
Josh 11:9 chariots, as the LORD had **i-ed.**
Josh 11:23 as the LORD had **i-ed** Moses.
Ps 105:22 He could **i** the king's aides
Prov 9:9 **I** the wise, and they will be
Prov 10:8 The wise are glad to be **i-ed,**
Prov 21:11 if you **i** the wise,
Acts 8:31 unless someone **i-s** me?
2 Tim 2:25 Gently **i** those who oppose
Titus 2:12 **i-ed** to turn from godless living

INSTRUCTION, INSTRUCTIONS (n)
a command or principle intended especially as a general rule of action; an order; directions; the action, practice, or profession of teaching
see also COMMANDMENT(S), LAW(S)
Exod 34:32 Moses gave them all the **i-s**
Deut 31:11 you must read this Book of **I**
Josh 1:7 Be careful to obey all the **i-s**
Josh 1:8 Study this Book of **I**
Ps 19:7 The **i-s** of the LORD are perfect,
Ps 40:8 **i-s** are written on my heart.
Ps 119:97 Oh, how I love your **i-s!**
Prov 4:13 Take hold of my **i-s;**
Prov 7:2 Guard my **i-s** as you guard
Prov 8:33 Listen to my **i** and be wise.
Prov 23:12 Commit yourself to **i;**
Isa 40:14 need **i** about what is good?
Jer 31:33 put my **i-s** deep within
Zech 7:12 they could not hear the **i-s**
1 Tim 1:5 purpose of my **i** is that all
1 Tim 1:18 here are my **i-s** for you,

INSTRUMENT, INSTRUMENTS (n)
a device used to produce music; one used by another as a means or aid; a means whereby something is achieved, performed, or furthered
Dan 3:7 at the sound of the musical **i-s,**
Hab 3:19 accompanied by stringed **i-s.)**
Acts 9:15 Saul is my chosen **i**
Rom 6:13 part of your body become an **i**

INSULT, INSULTS (n)
a gross indignity
Job 20:3 I've had to endure your **i-s,**
Ps 69:7 For I endure **i-s** for your sake;
Ps 69:9 the **i-s** of those who insult you
Ps 69:20 Their **i-s** have broken my heart,
Prov 9:7 will get an **i** in return.
Prov 22:10 and **i-s** will disappear.
Rom 15:3 The **i-s** of those who insult you,
2 Cor 12:10 and in the **i-s,** hardships,
Jude 1:15 all the **i-s** that ungodly sinners

INSULT, INSULTED (v)
to treat with insolence, indignity, or contempt
Prov 12:16 stays calm when **i-ed.**
Prov 20:20 **i** your father or mother,
Prov 30:9 and thus **i** God's holy name.
Heb 10:29 have **i-ed** and disdained
1 Pet 2:23 not retaliate when he was **i-ed,**
1 Pet 3:9 insults when people **i** you.
1 Pet 4:14 be happy when you are **i-ed**

INTEGRITY (n)
honesty; without compromise or corruption
Job 2:3 a man of complete **i.**
Job 2:9 still trying to maintain your **i?**
Job 27:5 I will defend my **i** until I die.
Ps 25:21 May **i** and honesty protect me,
Ps 26:11 I live with **i.** So redeem
Ps 111:8 faithfully and with **i.**
Ps 119:1 Joyful are people of **i,**
Prov 2:7 shield to those who walk with **i.**
Prov 10:9 People with **i** walk safely,
Titus 2:7 you do reflect the **i**

INTELLIGENCE (n)
the ability to learn or understand; mental acuteness
Isa 29:14 the **i** of the intelligent will
1 Cor 1:19 the **i** of the intelligent.

INTELLIGENT (adj)
having or indicating a high or satisfactory degree of mental capacity
Job 32:8 that makes them **i.**
Prov 17:28 mouths shut, they seem **i.**

INTERCEDE, INTERCEDED (v)
to mediate or plead another's case for justice or mercy
Isa 53:12 of many and **i-d** for rebels.
1 Tim 2:1 **i** on their behalf, and
Heb 7:25 lives forever to **i** with God

INTEREST, INTERESTS (n)
a charge for borrowed money; the profit in goods or money that is made on invested capital; a feeling that accompanies or causes special attention to an object
Lev 25:36 Do not charge **i** or make a profit
Deut 23:20 You may charge **i** to foreigners,
Deut 23:20 not charge **i** to Israelites,
Neh 5:10 stop this business of charging **i.**
Ps 15:5 lend money without charging **i,**
Prov 28:8 Income from charging high **i**
Matt 25:27 I could have gotten some **i**
1 Cor 7:34 His **i-s** are divided.
Phil 2:4 look out only for your own **i-s,**

INTERMARRY, INTERMARRYING (v)
to marry across a group boundaries
Deut 7:3 You must not **i** with them.
Ezra 9:14 **i-ing** with people who

INTERPRET, INTERPRETS (v)
to explain; to translate
Gen 41:15 a dream you can **i** it.
Matt 16:3 how to **i** the weather
1 Cor 12:30 to **i** unknown languages?
1 Cor 14:5 unless someone **i-s** what you
1 Cor 14:13 **i** what has been said.
1 Cor 14:26 another will **i** what is said.
1 Cor 14:27 must **i** what they say.
1 Cor 14:28 is present who can **i,**

INTIMIDATED (v)
to make timid or fearful
Phil 1:28 Don't be **i** in any way

INVADED (v)
to enter for conquest or plunder
2 Kgs 17:5 king of Assyria **i** the entire
2 Kgs 24:1 Nebuchadnezzar of Babylon **i**

INVENT (v)
to devise by thinking; to find or discover
Rom 1:30 They **i** new ways of sinning,

INVISIBLE (adj)
hidden; imperceptible
Rom 1:20 see his **i** qualities—
Col 1:15 visible image of the **i** God.
Heb 11:27 his eyes on the one who is **i.**

INVITATION (n)
an often formal request to be present or participate
1 Cor 10:27 accept the **i** if you want to.

INVITE, INVITED (v)
to request the presence or participation of; to welcome
Matt 25:35 a stranger, and you **i-d** me
Luke 14:12 For they will **i** you back,
Rev 19:9 Blessed are those who are **i-d**

IRON (n)
metal used in instruments of war, farming, and building; symbolic of strength for both security and destruction
Ps 2:9 break them with an **i** rod
Prov 27:17 As **i** sharpens **i,** so
Dan 2:33 its legs were **i,** and its feet
Rev 2:27 rule the nations with an **i** rod
Rev 12:5 nations with an **i** rod.
Rev 19:15 rule them with an **i** rod.

IRRITABLE (adj)
easily exasperated or excited
1 Cor 13:5 It is not **i,** and it keeps

ISAAC
Patriarch, son of Abraham; promised by God (Gen 17:16-22; 18:14); born (Gen 21:1-7; 1 Chr 1:28; Acts 7:8); recipient of divine covenant (Gen 17:21; 26:2-5); offered to God by Abraham (Gen 22:1-19; Heb 11:17-19); took Rebekah as wife (Gen 24:67); inherited wealth (Gen 25:5); prayed for wife to have children (Gen 25:20-21); father of twins, Esau and Jacob (Gen

25:24; 1 Chr 1:34); preferred Esau (Gen 25:28); dealings with Abimelech (Gen 26:1-31); tricked into blessing Jacob (Gen 27:1-29); died (Gen 35:27-29); father of a nation (Deut 29:13; Rom 9:7, 10); often mentioned in NT (Luke 3:34; Gal 4:28; Heb 11:9, 17-20; Jas 2:21).

ISAIAH

Prophet of Judah (southern kingdom) who prophesied during the reigns of four consecutive kings (Isa 1:1); called by God in a vision (Isa 6); prophesied Immanuel's coming (Isa 7–11); prophesied to Hezekiah (2 Kgs 19–20; Isa 36–38); recorded history of kings (2 Chr 26:22; 32:32); often quoted in NT (Matt 3:3; 4:14; 8:17; 12:17; 13:14; 15:7; Luke 4:17; John 12:38; Acts 8:28; 28:25; Rom 9:27; 10:16, 20).

ISLAND (n)

small tract of land surrounded by water

Rev 1:9	I was exiled to the **i** of Patmos
Rev 16:20	And every **i** disappeared,

ISRAEL

1. Another name for Jacob (Gen 32:28)
2. The united kingdom of Israel, including all twelve tribes, as ruled by Saul, David, and Solomon.
3. The northern kingdom of Israel, including the ten northern tribes, in contrast to Judah (southern kingdom) (*see* 2 Sam 19:41-43).

Exod 3:9	cry of the people of **I** has
Exod 12:37	**I** left Rameses and started
Exod 16:1	**I** set out from Elim
Exod 28:29	**I** on the sacred chestpiece
Exod 31:16	**I** must keep the Sabbath day
Exod 39:42	**I** followed all of the LORD's
Lev 25:55	the people of **I** belong to me.
Num 6:23	**I** with this special blessing:
Num 9:17	**I** would break camp and follow
Num 20:22	community of **I** left Kadesh
Num 27:12	I have given the people of **I.**
Num 35:10	instructions to the people of **I.**
Deut 10:12	**I,** what does the LORD your
Josh 21:3	**I** gave the Levites the following
Judg 17:6	In those days **I** had no king;
1 Sam 3:20	And all **I,** from Dan
1 Sam 4:21	said, "**I**'s glory is gone."
1 Sam 15:26	rejected you as king of **I.**
1 Sam 18:16	all **I** and Judah loved David
2 Sam 14:25	handsome man in all **I.**
1 Kgs 1:35	him to be ruler over **I**
1 Kgs 12:1	**I** had gathered to make him king.
1 Kgs 19:18	preserve 7,000 others in **I**
2 Kgs 17:24	replacing the people of **I.**
1 Chr 11:4	and all **I** went to Jerusalem
1 Chr 21:1	Satan rose up against **I**
2 Chr 9:8	Because God loves **I**
Ps 73:1	Truly God is good to **I,**
Ps 98:3	to love and be faithful to **I.**
Isa 44:6	says—**I**'s King and Redeemer,
Isa 44:21	you are my servant, O **I.**
Jer 2:3	In those days **I** was holy
Jer 31:2	give rest to the people of **I.**
Jer 31:9	For I am **I**'s father,
Jer 31:31	covenant with the people of **I**
Ezek 3:17	as a watchman for **I.**
Hos 1:10	**I**'s people will be like the sands
Hos 3:1	LORD still loves **I,** even though
Amos 4:12	in judgment, you people of **I!**
Amos 8:2	Like this fruit, **I** is ripe
Mic 5:2	a ruler of **I** will come from you,
Mal 1:5	far beyond **I**'s borders!
Matt 2:6	the shepherd for my people **I.**
Matt 10:6	people of **I**—God's lost sheep.
Matt 15:24	lost sheep—the people of **I.**
Mark 12:29	Listen, O **I!**
Acts 1:6	time come for you to free **I**
Acts 9:15	as well as to the people of **I.**
Rom 9:4	**I,** chosen to be God's adopted
Rom 9:6	**I** are truly members of God's
Rom 9:27	**I** are as numerous as the sand
Rom 9:31	**I,** who tried so hard to get
Rom 10:1	the people of **I** to be saved.
Rom 11:7	**I** have not found the favor
Rom 11:26	And so all **I** will be saved.
Eph 2:12	citizenship among the people of **I,**
Phil 3:5	a pure-blooded citizen of **I** and
Heb 8:8	covenant with the people of **I**
Rev 7:4	sealed from all the tribes of **I:**
Rev 21:12	**I** were written on the gates.

ISRAELITE, ISRAELITES (n)

members of the nation of Israel

see also JEW(S)

Exod 1:7	the **I-s,** had many children
Exod 16:12	heard the **I-s'** complaints.
Lev 25:46	never treat your fellow **I-s** this
Num 10:12	**I-s** set out from the wilderness
Josh 1:2	lead these people, the **I-s,**
Josh 7:1	was very angry with the **I-s.**
Judg 2:7	**I-s** served the LORD throughout
Judg 3:12	**I-s** did evil in the LORD's sight,
Judg 6:1	**I-s** did evil in the LORD's sight.
Judg 10:16	**I-s** put aside their foreign
Rom 11:1	I myself am an **I,** a descendant
2 Cor 11:22	Are they **I-s**? So am I.

ITALY (n)

a long boot-shaped country that juts into the Mediterranean Sea

Acts 27:1	we set sail for **I.**
Heb 13:24	believers from **I** send

J

JACOB

Patriarch, son of Isaac, grandson of Abraham; younger twin son of Issac and Rebekah (Gen 25:23–35:26; 48–49); also known as "Israel" (Gen 32:28); favored by Rebekah (Gen 25:28); bought Esau's birthright for a meal (Gen 25:29-34); deceived Isaac to receive his blessing (Gen 27:1-29); fled from Esau (Gen 27:41-45); married inside of clan (Gen 28:1-5); Jacob's ladder (Gen 28:12); covenant extended to Jacob in a dream (Gen 28:13-15); wives and concubines, Rachel favored (Gen 29:1-30); children (Gen 29:31–30:24; 35:16-26); prospered at his uncle Laban's expense (Gen 30:25-43); fled from Laban (Gen 31); name changed to "Israel" (Gen 32:22-32); reconciled with Esau (Gen 33); favored Rachel's oldest son Joseph (Gen 37:3); overwhelmed by loss of Joseph (Gen 37:33-35); migrated to Egypt (Gen 46:5-7); blessed Joseph's sons (Gen 48); blessed his own sons (Gen 49:1-28); died (Gen 49:33); buried (Gen 50:1-14); often mentioned in NT (John 4:5-6, 12; Acts 7:8-15; Rom 9:13; Heb 11:20-21).

see ISRAEL

JAMES

1. One of the 12 disciples, brother of John, son of Zebedee (Matt 10:2; Mark 3:17); called by Jesus (Matt 4:21; Luke 5:10); zealous for the Lord (Luke 9:54); wanted honor (Mark 10:35-45); witnessed the Transfiguration (Matt 17:1-9; Mark 9:2-8; Luke 9:28-36); killed by Herod Agrippa I (Acts 12:2).
2. One of the 12 disciples, son of Alphaeus (Matt 10:3; Mark 3:18; Luke 6:15); called "the younger" (Mark 15:40).
3. Half-brother of Jesus (Matt 13:55; Mark 6:3; Luke 24:10; 1 Cor 15:7; Gal 1:19; 2:9, 12), brother of Jude (Jude 1:1); leader of Jerusalem Council (Acts 15:13; 21:18); with select group before Pentecost (Acts 1:13); wrote letter (Jas 1:1).
4. Father of the apostle Judas, not Iscariot (Luke 6:16).
5. Son of a certain Mary, perhaps the same as the "son of Alphaeus" (Matt 27:56).

JAR, JARS (n)

an open container, typically made of clay in the ancient world

John 12:3	**j** of expensive perfume
John 19:29	A **j** of sour wine was
2 Cor 4:7	like fragile clay **j-s** containing

JAVELIN (n)

a light spear thrown as a weapon of war or in hunting

1 Sam 17:45	sword, spear, and **j**, but I

JAWBONE (n)

either of two bony structures that border the mouth

Judg 15:15	**j** of a recently killed donkey.

JEALOUS (adj)

intolerant of rivalry or unfaithfulness; hostile toward a rival

Exod 20:5	am a **j** God who will not
Exod 34:14	whose very name is **J**,
Prov 6:34	**j** husband will be furious,
Nah 1:2	a **j** God, filled with vengeance
Rom 11:14	**j** of what you Gentiles have,
1 Cor 13:4	Love is not **j** or boastful
Gal 5:26	provoke one another, or be **j**
Jas 3:14	if you are bitterly **j** and there is

JEALOUSY (n)

a jealous feeling, disposition, or attitude

Prov 27:4	but **j** is even more dangerous.
Rom 10:19	I will rouse your **j**
Rom 13:13	or in quarreling and **j**.
1 Cor 10:22	dare to rouse the Lord's **j**?
2 Cor 11:2	you with the **j** of God
Gal 5:20	**j**, outbursts of anger,
1 Tim 6:4	arguments ending in **j**,
1 Pet 2:1	with all deceit, hypocrisy, **j**,

JEERED, JEERS (v)

to scoff; to taunt

Job 27:23	**j-s** at them and mocks them.
Heb 11:36	Some were **j-ed** at,

JEHOVAH (KJV)

Exod 6:3	did not reveal my name, *Yahweh*, to them
Ps 83:18	you alone are called *the* LORD
Isa 12:2	The LORD *GOD* is my strength
Isa 26:4	the LORD *GOD* is the eternal

JEREMIAH

Prophet of Judah (southern kingdom) from Anathoth (Jer 11:18-23); never married (Jer 16:2); put in stocks (Jer 20:1-6); threatened by priests and prophets (Jer 26:8); brought death to false prophet (Jer 28:16-17); writings burned (Jer 36); imprisoned in dungeon (Jer 37:15); removed from the dungeon by King Zedekiah (Jer 37:21); lowered into cistern (Jer 38:1-6); set free by invaders (Jer 39:11–40:6); taken to Egypt (Jer 43); mentioned in NT (Matt 2:17; 27:9).

JERICHO (n)

a city in the plain of the Jordan Valley at the foot of the ascent to the Judean mountains

Num 22:1	across from **J**.
Josh 3:16	near the town of **J**.
Josh 5:10	at Gilgal on the plains of **J**,

Luke 10:30	from Jerusalem down to **J**,
Heb 11:30	around **J** for seven days,

JERUSALEM (n)

sacred city and well-known capital of Palestine during Bible times

Josh 10:1	Adoni-zedek, king of **J**, heard
Josh 15:8	where the city of **J** is located.
Judg 1:8	attacked **J** and captured it,
2 Sam 5:5	**J** he reigned over all Israel
2 Sam 11:1	David stayed behind in **J**.
1 Kgs 9:15	terraces, the wall of **J**,
1 Kgs 10:26	and some near him in **J**.
1 Kgs 14:25	came up and attacked **J**.
2 Kgs 8:17	he reigned in **J** eight years.
2 Kgs 12:1	He reigned in **J** forty years.
2 Kgs 14:2	reigned in **J** twenty-nine years.
2 Kgs 15:2	he reigned in **J** fifty-two years.
2 Kgs 16:2	he reigned in **J** sixteen years.
2 Kgs 18:2	reigned in **J** twenty-nine years.
2 Kgs 19:31	will spread out from **J**,
2 Kgs 21:12	I will bring such disaster on **J**
2 Kgs 22:1	reigned in **J** thirty-one years.
2 Kgs 23:31	he reigned in **J** three months.
2 Kgs 24:8	he reigned in **J** three months.
2 Kgs 24:14	Nebuchadnezzar took all of **J**
2 Kgs 24:20	anger against the people of **J**
2 Kgs 25:9	and all the houses of **J**.
1 Chr 21:16	reaching out over **J**.
2 Chr 3:1	the Temple of the LORD in **J**
2 Chr 9:1	she came to **J** to test him
2 Chr 20:15	all you people of Judah and **J**!
2 Chr 29:8	has fallen upon Judah and **J**.
2 Chr 36:19	tore down the walls of **J**,
Ezra 2:1	but now they returned to **J**
Ezra 4:12	came here to **J** from Babylon
Ezra 6:12	who has chosen the city of **J**
Ezra 9:9	a protective wall in Judah and **J**.
Neh 1:3	The wall of **J** has been torn
Neh 3:8	They left out a section of **J**
Neh 11:1	of the people were living in **J**,
Neh 12:43	joy of the people of **J** could be
Ps 9:11	the LORD who reigns in **J**.
Ps 51:18	rebuild the walls of **J**.
Ps 74:2	remember **J**, your home here
Ps 79:1	made **J** a heap of ruins.
Ps 87:2	He loves the city of **J** more than
Ps 102:13	arise and have mercy on **J**—
Ps 122:2	standing inside your gates, O **J**.
Ps 122:6	Pray for peace in **J**.
Ps 125:2	**J**, so the LORD surrounds
Ps 128:5	May you see **J** prosper
Ps 137:3	Sing us one of those songs of **J**!
Ps 137:5	If I forget you, O **J**,
Ps 147:2	The LORD is rebuilding **J**
Ps 147:12	Glorify the LORD, O **J**!

Isa 1:1	saw concerning Judah and **J**.
Isa 3:1	take away from **J** and Judah
Isa 4:3	who survive the destruction of **J**
Isa 27:13	return to **J** to worship the LORD
Isa 31:5	will hover over **J** and protect it
Isa 40:2	Speak tenderly to **J**.
Isa 51:11	They will enter **J** singing,
Isa 52:1	clothes, O holy city of **J**,
Isa 52:8	see the LORD returning to **J**.
Isa 62:7	makes **J** the pride of the earth.
Jer 2:2	Go and shout this message to **J**.
Jer 4:5	to Judah, and broadcast to **J**!
Jer 6:6	ramps against the walls of **J**.
Jer 9:11	will make **J** into a heap of ruins,
Jer 23:14	prophets of **J** are even worse!
Jer 26:18	**J** will be reduced to ruins!
Jer 39:1	came with his army to besiege **J**.
Jer 51:50	think about your home in **J**.
Lam 1:7	**J** remembers her ancient splendor.
Dan 6:10	windows open toward **J**.
Dan 9:2	**J** must lie desolate for seventy
Dan 9:12	a disaster as happened in **J**.
Dan 9:25	command is given to rebuild **J**
Joel 3:16	from Zion and thunder from **J**,
Amos 2:5	fortresses of **J** will be destroyed.
Obad 1:11	and cast lots to divide up **J**,
Mic 4:2	his word will go out from **J**.
Zeph 3:16	the announcement to **J** will be,
Zech 1:17	Zion and choose **J** as his own.
Zech 2:4	**J** will someday be so full
Zech 8:8	home again to live safely in **J**.
Zech 8:22	nations will come to **J** to seek
Zech 9:10	and the warhorses from **J**.
Zech 12:10	and on the people of **J**.
Zech 14:8	waters will flow out from **J**,
Matt 20:18	going up to **J**, where the Son
Matt 21:10	city of **J** was in an uproar
Matt 23:37	**J**, the city that kills the
Mark 10:33	going up to **J**, where the Son
Luke 2:22	parents took him to **J**
Luke 2:41	Jesus' parents went to **J**
Luke 4:9	Then the devil took him to **J**,
Luke 9:31	about to be fulfilled in **J**.
Luke 13:34	O **J**, **J**, the city that kills
Luke 18:31	to **J**, where all the predictions
Luke 21:20	you see **J** surrounded
Luke 24:47	nations, beginning in **J**:
Acts 1:8	about me everywhere—in **J**,
Acts 6:7	believers greatly increased in **J**,
Acts 20:22	bound by the Spirit to go to **J**.
Acts 23:11	a witness to me here in **J**,
Rom 9:33	I am placing a stone in **J**
Rom 11:26	rescues will come from **J**,
Rom 15:19	from **J** all the way to Illyricum.
Gal 4:25	**J** is just like Mount Sinai
Gal 4:26	represents the heavenly **J**.

Heb 12:22	living God, the heavenly **J,**
Rev 21:10	he showed me the holy city, **J,**

JESUS
see also CHRIST, MESSIAH
Family line (Matt 1:1-17; Luke 3:23-38); birth announced (Matt 1:18-25; Luke 1:26-38); born in Bethlehem (Luke 2:1-20); circumcised, officially named, and presented at Temple (Luke 2:21-40); visited by Magi (Matt 2:1-12); escape to and return from Egypt (Matt 2:13-23); amazed the Temple scholars (Luke 2:41-50); summary of youth (Luke 2:51-52); baptized by John (Matt 3:13-17; Mark 1:9-11; Luke 3:21-22; John 1:32-34); tempted by Satan (Matt 4:1-11; Mark 1:12-13; Luke 4:1-13); ministered in Galilee (Matt 4:12–18:35; Mark 1:14–9:50); transfigured on a mountain (Matt 17:1-13; Mark 9:2-13; Luke 9:28-36; 2 Pet 1:16-18); triumphal entry (Matt 21:1-11; Mark 11:1-11; Luke 19:28-44; John 12:12-19); the Last Supper (Matt 26:17-35; Mark 14:12-31; Luke 22:7-38; John 13–17); betrayed and tried (Matt 26:36–27:31; Mark 14:32–15:20; Luke 22:39–23:25; John 18:1–19:16); crucified, died, and was buried (Matt 27:32-66; Mark 15:21-47; Luke 23:26-56; John 19:17-42); rose again and appeared to followers (Matt 28; Mark 16; Luke 24; John 20–21; Acts 1:1-11; 7:55-56; 9:3-6; 1 Cor 15:1-8; Rev 1:1-20); ascended to heaven (Mark 16:19; Luke 24:50-53; John 1:51; Acts 1:9; Eph 4:8).

JEW, JEWS (n)
a name applied first to the people living in the southern kingdom of Judah; broadly, a descendant of Abraham
see also ISRAELITE(S)

Esth 3:13	property of the **J-s** would be
Zech 8:23	clutch at the sleeve of one **J.**
Matt 2:2	the newborn king of the **J-s?**
John 19:3	Hail! King of the **J-s!**
Acts 20:21	message for **J-s** and Greeks
Acts 21:39	I am a **J** and a citizen of
Rom 1:16	everyone who believes—the **J**
Rom 2:28	you are not a true **J**
Rom 9:24	from the **J-s** and from
Rom 10:12	**J** and Gentile are the same
1 Cor 9:20	with the **J-s,** I lived like a **J**
1 Cor 12:13	**J-s,** some are Gentiles,
Gal 2:8	Peter as the apostle to the **J-s**
Gal 2:14	**J** by birth, have discarded
Gal 3:28	There is no longer **J** or Gentile,
Eph 3:6	Gentiles and **J-s** who believe
Col 3:11	**J** or a Gentile, circumcised or

JEWEL, JEWELS (n)
a precious stone; gem

Prov 3:22	They are like **j-s** on a necklace.
Song 4:9	with a single **j** of your necklace.
Isa 61:10	or a bride with her **j-s.**
Zech 9:16	in his land like **j-s** in a crown.
1 Cor 3:12	gold, silver, **j-s,** wood, hay,

JEWELRY (n)
objects of precious metal worn for personal adornment

Prov 25:12	earring or other gold **j.**
Jer 2:32	a young woman forget her **j?**
Ezek 16:11	I gave you lovely **j,** bracelets,

JEWISH (adj)
of, relating to, or characteristic of the Jews

Esth 2:5	a **J** man in the fortress of Susa
John 3:10	You are a respected **J** teacher,

JEZEBEL
Queen of Israel (northern kingdom), daughter of Ethbaal, king of Sidon; evil, influential wife of King Ahab (1 Kgs 21:25); Baal worshiper (1 Kgs 16:31-33); tried to kill all the LORD's prophets (1 Kgs 18:4, 13); vowed to kill Elijah (1 Kgs 19:1-2); arranged murder to get vineyard for Ahab (1 Kgs 21:1-16); death foretold and fulfilled (1 Kgs 21:23; 2 Kgs 9:10, 30-37).

JOB
Man who feared God and had integrity (Job 1:1-5); slandered and attacked by Satan (Job 1:6–2:10); debated suffering with his "friends" (Job 3–37); enlightened by vision of the LORD (Job 38–41); restored to peace and prosperity (Job 42); example of righteousness (Ezek 14:14, 20); example of endurance in suffering (Jas 5:11).

JOHN
1. The Baptist, son of Zechariah and Elizabeth (Luke 1:5-25, 57-80); called to prepare the way for the Messiah (Isa 40:3-5; Luke 3:1-6; John 1:19-28); called to preach and baptize (Matt 3:1-12; Mark 1:1-8); preached repentance (Luke 3:7-20); baptized Jesus (Matt 3:13-17; Luke 3:21-22); confirmed Jesus' ministry (Matt 3:11-12; Mark 1:7-8; Luke 3:15-18; John 3:22-36; 5:33); ministry compared to Elijah (Mal 4:5; Matt 11:11-19; Mark 9:11-13; Luke 7:24-35); arrested and beheaded by Herod Antipas (Matt 14:1-12; Mark 6:14-29; Luke 9:7-9).
2. One of the 12 disciples, brother of James, son of Zebedee (Matt 10:2; Mark 3:17); witnessed the Transfiguration (Matt 17:1-9; Mark 9:2-8; Luke 9:28-36); inner circle of Jesus' followers (Matt 17:1; Mark 5:37; 9:2; 13:3; Luke 8:51; 9:28; Gal 2:9); with Peter, healed a man and was arrested (Acts 3–4); with Peter, rebuked sorcerer (Acts 8:14-25); wrote fourth Gospel (John 13:23-25; *see also* 20:2; 21:20-25), letters of John (the "elder," 2 Jn 1:1; 3 Jn 1:1), and Revelation (the "servant," Rev 1:1, 9; 22:8).
3. *See* MARK, also known as John Mark.

JOIN, JOINED, JOINS (v)

to put or bring into close association or relationship; to take part in a collective activity

Ps 26:5	I refuse to **j** in with the wicked.
Dan 11:34	who **j** them will not be sincere.
Zech 2:11	will **j** themselves to the LORD
Matt 19:6	what God has **j-ed** together.
Mark 10:9	what God has **j-ed** together.
Rom 6:3	**j-ed** with Christ Jesus in baptism,
Rom 8:16	his Spirit **j-s** with our spirit
Rom 15:30	**j** in my struggle by praying
1 Cor 6:16	if a man **j-s** himself to
Eph 2:21	carefully **j-ed** together in him,

JOINT (n)

the point of contact between bone and the parts surrounding and supporting it

Ps 22:14	all my bones are out of **j.**
Heb 4:12	between **j** and marrow.

JOKE, JOKES (n)

something said or done to provoke laughter

Ps 44:14	made us the butt of their **j-s;**
Ps 89:41	he has become a **j** to his
Eph 5:4	coarse **j-s**—these are not

JOKING (v)

to jest; to kid

Gen 19:14	men thought he was only **j.**
Prov 26:19	and then says, "I was only **j.**"

JONAH

Prophet of Israel (northern kingdom), in the days of Jeroboam II (2 Kgs 14:25); swallowed by great fish (Jonah 1:17); survived and then preached to Nineveh (Jon 3); mentioned by Jesus as a sign (Matt 12:39-41; 16:4; Luke 11:29-32).

JORDAN (n)

the longest and most important river in Palestine

Josh 4:22	crossed the **J** on dry ground.
Matt 3:6	them in the **J** River.
Matt 4:15	sea, beyond the **J** River, in
Mark 1:9	him in the **J** River.

JOSEPH

1. Oldest son of Jacob and Rachel (Gen 30:24); loved by Jacob—hated by brothers (Gen 37:3-4); dreamer of dreams (Gen 37:5-11); captured to be killed, but sold into slavery (Gen 37:20, 27-28); faithfully served Egyptian master (Gen 39:3); wrongfully accused and imprisoned (Gen 39); interpreted dreams of royal staff (Gen 40); interpreted dreams of Pharaoh, then ruled Egypt (Gen 41:4-44); prepared Egypt for famine (Gen 41:46-57); tested brothers, revealed identity, and reconciled with them (Gen 42–45); brought his father Jacob and family to Egypt (Gen 46–47); sons, Ephraim and Manasseh, blessed by Jacob (Gen 48); Joseph blessed by Jacob (Gen 49:22-26; Deut 33:13-17); reassured his brothers (Gen 50:15-21); died (Gen 50:22-26; Heb 11:22); remembered as one chosen and helped by God (Acts 7:9-18); 12,000 descendants will be marked by God (Rev 7:8).

2. Husband of Mary the mother of Jesus; accepted supernatural pregnancy of Mary (Matt 1:16-25); had no relations with Mary until birth of Jesus (Matt 1:25); was present at birth and dedication of Jesus (Luke 2:4-38); fled to Egypt, then Nazareth (Matt 2:13-22); ancestor of David in the family line of Jesus (Luke 3:23); Jesus called his son (Luke 4:22; John 1:45; 6:42).

JOSHUA

Son of Nun, who led Israel into Promised Land (Acts 7:45; Heb 4:8); commanded by Moses to fight Amalek (Exod 17:8-16); assistant to Moses (Exod 24:13); explored Canaan (Num 13:8); demonstrated faith in his report (Num 14:6-9); allowed to enter Promised Land (Num 14:30; Deut 1:38); became Israel's leader after Moses (Num 27:18-23; Deut 31:1-18); went with Moses up the mountain of God (Exod 24:13); assumed command (Josh 1); sent spies to Jericho (Josh 2); led Israel across the Jordan (Josh 3–4); established memorial stones (Josh 4); circumcised the people (Josh 5:2-9); conquered Jericho (Josh 6) and Ai (Josh 7–8); uncovered Achan's sin (Josh 7:10-26); made pact with the Gibeonites (Josh 9); sun stood still (Josh 10:1-15); conquered southern Canaan (Josh 10:28-43); conquered northern Canaan (Josh 11–12); divided the land (Josh 13–22); gave final words to Israel (Josh 23); made covenant at Shechem (Josh 8:30-35; 24:1-28); died (Josh 24:29-30).

JOURNEY (n)

an act or instance of traveling from one place to another

Judg 18:6	LORD is watching over your **j.**
Ezra 8:21	give us a safe **j**
Rom 15:24	provide for my **j.**

JOY, JOYS (n)

the emotion evoked by well-being, success, or good fortune

Deut 16:15	be a time of great **j** for all.
1 Sam 18:6	danced for **j** with tambourines
1 Chr 16:27	and **j** fill his dwelling.
1 Chr 29:22	with great **j** that day.
Ezra 3:12	however, were shouting for **j.**
Neh 8:10	**j** of the LORD is your strength!
Neh 8:17	they were all filled with great **j!**
Esth 9:22	and their mourning into **j.**
Job 3:22	with **j** when they finally die,
Job 8:21	your lips with shouts of **j.**

Ps 1:1 **j-s** of those who do not follow
Ps 2:12 **j** for all who take refuge in him!
Ps 9:2 filled with **j** because of you.
Ps 19:8 bringing **j** to the heart.
Ps 21:1 He shouts with **j**
Ps 28:7 my heart is filled with **j.**
Ps 30:11 and clothed me with **j,**
Ps 32:2 what **j** for those whose record
Ps 33:12 **j** for the nation whose God
Ps 41:1 **j-s** of those who are kind
Ps 42:4 singing for **j** and giving thanks
Ps 45:7 pouring out the oil of **j** on you
Ps 46:4 A river brings **j** to the city
Ps 51:12 to me the **j** of your salvation,
Ps 65:8 you inspire shouts of **j.**
Ps 65:13 They all shout and sing for **j!**
Ps 71:23 I will shout for **j** and sing
Ps 92:4 I sing for **j** because of what
Ps 98:4 in praise and sing for **j!**
Ps 105:43 his people out of Egypt with **j,**
Ps 106:5 Let me rejoice in the **j**
Ps 119:92 hadn't sustained me with **j,**
Ps 126:2 laughter, and we sang for **j.**
Ps 132:9 loyal servants sing for **j.**
Ps 132:16 servants will sing for **j.**
Ps 145:7 **j** about your righteousness.
Prov 10:1 A wise child brings **j**
Prov 11:10 **j** when the wicked die.
Prov 14:10 no one else can fully share its **j.**
Prov 15:20 Sensible children bring **j** to
Prov 21:15 Justice is a **j** to the godly,
Prov 23:25 your father and mother **j!**
Prov 29:6 righteous escape, shouting for **j.**
Isa 12:6 shout his praise with **j!**
Isa 16:9 no more shouts of **j** over your
Isa 16:10 gone the **j** of harvest.
Isa 26:19 will rise up and sing for **j!**
Isa 35:10 crowned with everlasting **j.**
Isa 42:11 Let the people of Sela sing for **j;**
Isa 49:13 Sing for **j,** O heavens!
Isa 51:11 filled with **j** and gladness.
Isa 52:8 watchmen shout and sing with **j,**
Isa 56:7 fill them with **j** in my house
Isa 60:15 beautiful forever, a **j** to all
Isa 61:7 everlasting **j** will be yours.
Isa 65:14 My servants will sing for **j,** but
Jer 31:13 young women will dance for **j,**
Jer 31:13 turn their mourning into **j.**
Jer 33:11 the sounds of **j** and laughter.
Jer 48:33 treads the grapes with shouts of **j.**
Jer 49:25 a city of **j,** will be forsaken!
Joel 1:12 the people's **j** has dried up
Matt 2:10 they were filled with **j!**
Matt 28:8 but also filled with great **j,**
Mark 1:11 Son, and you bring me great **j.**
Mark 4:16 receive it with **j.**
Luke 1:14 have great **j** and gladness,
Luke 1:44 in my womb jumped for **j.**
Luke 2:10 bring great **j** to all people.
Luke 6:23 be happy! Yes, leap for **j!**
Luke 10:21 with the **j** of the Holy Spirit,
Luke 24:41 filled with **j** and wonder.
John 15:11 you will be filled with my **j.**
John 16:20 turn to wonderful **j.**
John 16:24 and you will have abundant **j.**
John 20:20 **j** when they saw the Lord!
Acts 2:28 you will fill me with the **j**
Acts 2:46 their meals with great **j**
Acts 11:23 he was filled with **j,**
Acts 13:52 believers were filled with **j**
Acts 15:3 much to everyone's **j**—
Rom 14:17 and **j** in the Holy Spirit.
Rom 15:13 with **j** and peace because
2 Cor 1:24 so you will be full of **j,**
2 Cor 2:3 ought to give me the greatest **j.**
2 Cor 2:3 **j** comes from your being joyful.
2 Cor 6:10 but we always have **j.**
2 Cor 7:7 I was filled with **j!**
Gal 5:22 fruit in our lives: love, **j,** peace,
Phil 1:4 requests for all of you with **j,**
Phil 1:25 experience the **j** of your faith.
Phil 4:1 you are my **j** and the crown
1 Thes 1:6 received the message with **j**
1 Thes 2:19 what gives us hope and **j,**
1 Thes 2:20 Yes, you are our pride and **j.**
1 Thes 3:9 we have great **j**
2 Tim 1:4 with **j** when we are together
Heb 10:34 you accepted it with **j.**
Heb 12:2 Because of the **j** awaiting him,
Heb 13:17 reason to do this with **j**
Jas 1:2 it an opportunity for great **j.**
1 Pet 1:8 a glorious, inexpressible **j.**
1 Pet 4:13 the wonderful **j** of seeing his
1 Jn 1:4 you may fully share our **j.**

JOYFUL (adj)
characterized by gladness or delight
Ps 30:11 my mourning into **j** dancing.
Ps 66:1 Shout **j** praises to God, all the
Ps 98:6 a **j** symphony before the LORD,
Ps 137:3 insisted on a **j** hymn:
Rom 15:32 come to you with a **j** heart,
Gal 4:15 that **j** and grateful spirit
Gal 4:27 Break into a **j** shout, you who
1 Thes 5:16 Always be **j.**
Heb 12:22 angels in a **j** gathering.

JOYOUS (adj)
characterized by gladness or delight
2 Chr 29:30 offered **j** praise and bowed
Neh 12:43 were offered on that **j** day,
Isa 61:3 for ashes, a **j** blessing instead

Jer 33:11 with the **j** songs of people

JUBILEE (n)
a year of celebration, emancipation, and restoration
Lev 25:11 fiftieth year will be a **j**

JUDAH
1. Fourth son of Jacob and Leah (Gen 29:35), who gave his name to a tribe of Israel; interceded for Joseph (Gen 37:26-27); failed to uphold daughter-in-law Tamar's rights (Gen 38:1-30); offered himself as slave and ransom (Gen 44:18-34); given the family birthright by Jacob (Gen 49:3-10); his tribe was numbered (Num 1:26-27), allotted land and cities (Josh 15:1-63), led the conquest of Canaan (Judg 1:2); 12,000 will be marked by God (Rev 7:7).
2. The southern kingdom of Judah, including the tribes of Judah and Benjamin, in contrast to Israel (northern kingdom) (*see* 2 Sam 12:8).

JUDAISM (n)
the cultural, social, and religious beliefs and practices of the Jews
Acts 13:43 converts to **J** followed Paul

JUDAS
1. One of the 12 disciples, also known as "Iscariot" (Mark 3:19; Luke 6:16); criticized Mary (John 12:3-6); foretold as betrayer (John 6:70-71; 13:21-30); made deal for 30 pieces of silver (Matt 26:14-15; *see also* Mark 14:10); identified as a thief (John 12:6); entered by Satan (Luke 22:3; John 13:27); betrayed Jesus with kiss (Mark 14:43-45); had remorse and committed suicide (Matt 27:3-10; Acts 1:18); his position refilled (Acts 1:20-26).
2. One of the 12 disciples, son of James, likely also called Thaddaeus (Matt 10:3; Mark 3:18), not Iscariot (John 14:22); *see also* Luke 6:16; Acts 1:13.
3. Brother of James and half-brother of Jesus, also known as "Jude" (Matt 13:55; Mark 6:3; Jude 1:1).

JUDEA (n)
the Greco-Roman name for the land of Judah
Matt 2:1 was born in Bethlehem in **J,**
Matt 24:16 in **J** must flee to the hills.
Luke 3:1 Pilate was governor over **J;**
Acts 1:8 throughout **J,** in Samaria,
Acts 9:31 had peace throughout **J,**
1 Thes 2:14 in God's churches in **J**

JUDGE, JUDGES (n)
a public official authorized to decide issues brought before a court; one of a cycle of charismatic deliverers of ancient Israel
Deut 17:12 to reject the verdict of the **j**
Judg 2:16 LORD raised up **j-s** to rescue
Judg 2:18 the LORD raised up a **j**
1 Sam 7:6 Samuel became Israel's **j.**)
1 Sam 7:15 continued as Israel's **j**
Ps 50:6 God himself will be the **j.**
Isa 33:22 the LORD is our **j,** our lawgiver,
Acts 7:35 you a ruler and **j** over us?
Acts 10:42 **j** of all—the living and
Rev 14:7 he will sit as **j.**

JUDGE, JUDGED, JUDGES, JUDGING (v)
to form an evaluation of; to decide as a judge; to govern or rule; to punish or condemn; to form a negative opinion about
1 Sam 16:7 Don't **j** by his appearance or
1 Sam 24:12 the LORD **j** between us.
2 Chr 19:7 **j** with integrity, for the LORD
Ps 7:8 The LORD **j-s** the nations.
Ps 9:4 For you have **j-d** in my favor;
Ps 9:8 He will **j** the world
Ps 82:8 Rise up, O God, and **j** the earth,
Ps 96:10 He will **j** all peoples fairly.
Ps 96:13 will **j** the world with justice,
Prov 16:10 he must never **j** unfairly.
Prov 29:14 If a king **j-s** the poor fairly,
Isa 11:3 He will not **j** by appearance
Isa 66:16 He will **j** the earth,
Matt 7:1 Do not **j** others, and you
Matt 16:27 will **j** all people according
Matt 19:28 thrones, **j-ing** the twelve
John 3:18 been **j-d** for not believing
John 5:22 the Father **j-s** no one.
John 5:22 absolute authority to **j,**
John 5:27 authority to **j** everyone
John 5:30 I **j** as God tells me.
John 12:31 time for **j-ing** this world
John 12:47 not **j** those who hear me
Acts 17:31 he has set a day for **j-ing**
Rom 2:16 Jesus, will **j** everyone's secret
Rom 3:6 be qualified to **j** the world?
1 Cor 6:2 we believers will **j** the world?
1 Cor 11:31 we would not be **j-d**
2 Cor 5:10 stand before Christ to be **j-d.**
2 Tim 4:1 Jesus, who will someday **j**
Heb 10:30 The LORD will **j** his own
Heb 13:4 **j** people who are immoral
Jas 2:13 will be merciful when he **j-s**
Jas 3:1 we who teach will be **j-d** more
Jas 4:11 criticizing and **j-ing** God's law.
Jas 4:12 So what right do you have to **j**
1 Pet 1:17 He will **j** or reward you
1 Pet 2:23 God, who always **j-s** fairly.
Rev 19:11 **j-s** fairly and wages a righteous
Rev 20:4 given the authority to **j.**
Rev 20:12 the dead were **j-d** according to

JUDGMENT, JUDGMENTS (n)

a ruling or decision by a ruler, a judge, or an individual; the process of forming an opinion or evalution by discerning and comparing

see also JUSTICE

Deut 1:17	impartial in your **j-s.**
1 Sam 3:13	warned him that **j** is coming
Ps 1:5	be condemned at the time of **j.**
Ps 37:13	he sees their day of **j** coming.
Ps 51:4	your **j** against me is just.
Prov 4:1	Pay attention and learn good **j,**
Prov 4:7	else you do, develop good **j.**
Prov 9:10	results in good **j.**
Isa 3:14	comes forward to pronounce **j**
Jer 11:20	you make righteous **j-s,**
Jer 25:31	His cry of **j** will reach
Dan 9:11	curses and **j-s** written in
Hos 6:5	with **j-s** as inescapable as light.
Joel 3:12	LORD, will sit to pronounce **j**
Matt 5:21	murder, you are subject to **j.**
Matt 11:24	will be better off on **j** day
Matt 12:36	on **j** day for every idle word
Matt 12:41	this generation on **j** day
John 5:30	**j** is just, because I carry out
John 8:16	if I did, my **j** would be correct
John 16:8	and of the coming **j.**
Acts 24:25	coming day of **j,**
1 Cor 4:3	I don't even trust my own **j**
1 Cor 4:5	don't make **j-s** about anyone
1 Cor 11:29	eating and drinking God's **j**
2 Thes 1:8	**j** on those who don't know
Heb 9:27	and after that comes **j,**
1 Pet 4:17	And if **j** begins with us,
2 Pet 2:9	until the day of final **j.**
2 Pet 3:7	being kept for the day of **j,**
Jude 1:6	waiting for the great day of **j.**
Rev 16:7	your **j-s** are true and just.

JUST (adj)

conforming to a standard of correctness; faithful to the original design; honest, fair, upright

see also RIGHT, RIGHTEOUS

Gen 18:19	by doing what is right and **j.**
Deut 32:4	Everything he does is **j**
2 Sam 8:15	did what was **j** and right
Neh 9:13	and instructions that were **j,**
Job 37:23	he is **j** and righteous,
Ps 33:5	loves whatever is **j** and good;
Ps 92:15	The LORD is **j!** He is
Ps 119:121	I have done what is **j**
Prov 1:3	do what is right, **j,** and fair.
Prov 2:9	will understand what is right, **j,**
Prov 12:5	The plans of the godly are **j;**
Isa 16:5	He will always do what is **j**
Isa 59:8	or what it means to be **j**
Jer 22:3	Be fair-minded and **j.**
Ezek 18:5	and does what is **j** and right.
Dan 4:37	All his acts are **j** and true,
Matt 5:45	rain on the **j** and the unjust
1 Jn 1:9	he is faithful and **j** to forgive
Rev 15:3	**J** and true are your ways,
Rev 16:5	You are **j,** O Holy One,
Rev 16:7	your judgments are true and **j.**
Rev 19:2	His judgments are true and **j.**

JUSTICE (n)

the administration of law that determines what is right, based on principles of equity and correctness, and rewards accordingly; the quality of being just, impartial, or fair

see also JUDGMENT, RIGHTEOUSNESS

Exod 23:2	by the crowd to twist **j.**
Lev 19:15	Do not twist **j** in legal matters
Deut 16:19	never twist **j** or show partiality
Deut 32:36	LORD will give **j** to his
1 Sam 8:3	bribes and perverted **j.**
1 Kgs 3:11	governing my people with **j**
1 Kgs 7:7	Hall of **J,** where he sat to hear
2 Chr 9:8	so you can rule with **j**
Job 8:3	Does God twist **j?**
Job 19:7	I protest, but there is no **j.**
Job 31:6	weigh me on the scales of **j,**
Job 34:17	God govern if he hated **j?**
Ps 9:8	He will judge the world with **j**
Ps 10:18	You will bring **j** to the orphans
Ps 36:6	your **j** like the ocean depths.
Ps 45:4	defending truth, humility, and **j.**
Ps 45:7	You love **j** and hate evil.
Ps 72:1	Give your love of **j** to the king,
Ps 82:3	Give **j** to the poor
Ps 96:13	He will judge the world with **j,**
Ps 98:9	**j,** and the nations with fairness.
Ps 99:4	You have acted with **j**
Ps 103:6	**j** to all who are treated
Ps 146:7	He gives **j** to the oppressed
Prov 16:12	his rule is built on **j.**
Prov 19:28	makes a mockery of **j;**
Prov 29:26	but **j** comes from the LORD.
Prov 31:9	and see that they get **j.**
Isa 1:17	Seek **j.** Help the oppressed.
Isa 1:27	Zion will be restored by **j;**
Isa 5:16	will be exalted by his **j.**
Isa 10:2	They deprive the poor of **j**
Isa 28:17	with the measuring line of **j**
Isa 33:5	make Jerusalem his home of **j**
Isa 42:1	He will bring **j** to the nations.
Isa 51:4	my **j** will become a light
Isa 59:9	there is no **j** among us,
Isa 59:14	**j** is nowhere to be found.
Isa 61:8	I, the LORD, love **j.**
Jer 4:2	you could do so with truth, **j,**
Jer 9:24	who brings **j** and righteousness

Jer 21:12	Give **j** each morning
Jer 30:11	discipline you, but with **j;**
Lam 3:36	if they twist **j** in the courts—
Hos 2:19	righteousness and **j,**
Amos 5:7	You twist **j,** making it a bitter
Amos 5:15	courts into true halls of **j.**
Amos 6:12	when you turn **j** into poison
Mic 3:8	I am filled with **j** and strength
Hab 1:4	there is no **j** in the courts.
Zeph 3:5	Day by day he hands down **j,**
Mal 2:17	Where is the God of **j?**
Matt 5:6	who hunger and thirst for **j,**
Matt 12:18	proclaim **j** to the nations.
Matt 23:23	aspects of the law—**j,**
Luke 11:42	ignore **j** and the love of God.
Luke 18:3	Give me **j** in this dispute
Acts 8:33	humiliated and received no **j.**
Acts 17:31	**j** by the man he has appointed
Rom 2:2	God, in his **j,** will punish
2 Thes 1:5	persecution to show his **j**
2 Thes 1:6	In his **j** he will pay back
Heb 1:8	You rule with a scepter of **j.**
Heb 7:2	Melchizedek means "king of **j,**"
Heb 11:33	ruled with **j,** and received

JUSTIFY, JUSTIFIED (v)

to prove to be just, right, or reasonable; to acquit or absolve

see also RIGHT, RIGHTEOUS

Luke 10:29	wanted to **j** his actions,
Luke 18:14	returned home **j-ied**
2 Cor 8:24	boasting about you is **j-ied.**

K

KEEP, KEEPING, KEEPS, KEPT (v)

to be faithful to; to have in control; to refrain from granting, giving, or allowing; to cause to remain in a given place, situation, or condition; to refrain from revealing; to maintain or preserve

see also GUARD, OBEY, PROTECT

Exod 12:42	the LORD **k-pt** his promise
Exod 20:8	Sabbath day by **k-ing** it holy.
Exod 31:13	Be careful to **k** my Sabbath
Deut 5:12	Sabbath day by **k-ing** it holy,
Deut 7:8	**k-ing** the oath he had sworn
Deut 7:9	God who **k-s** his covenant for a
Deut 7:12	your God will **k** his covenant
2 Chr 6:14	You **k** your covenant
2 Chr 34:31	to obey the LORD by **k-ing**
Neh 1:5	God who **k-s** his covenant of
Ps 15:4	**k** their promises even when
Ps 116:14	I will **k** my promises to
Ps 119:100	**k-pt** your commandments.
Ps 121:7	The LORD **k-s** you from
Ps 130:3	LORD, if you **k-pt** a record of
Ps 146:6	He **k-s** every promise
Prov 10:19	and **k** your mouth
Prov 15:3	**k-ing** his eye on
Prov 21:23	your tongue and **k**
Eccl 3:6	A time to **k** and a time to
John 17:6	and they have **k-pt** your word.
Acts 2:24	death could not **k** him in its
Rom 10:3	by trying to **k** the law.
Rom 14:22	**k** it between yourself
1 Cor 1:8	He will **k** you strong
1 Cor 7:19	**k** God's commandments.
1 Cor 13:5	it **k-s** no record
Eph 4:3	effort to **k** yourselves united
1 Tim 5:22	**K** yourself pure.
2 Tim 4:5	But you should **k** a clear mind
Heb 11:27	going because he **k-pt** his eyes
Jas 2:10	the person who **k-s** all of the
1 Pet 1:4	**k-pt** in heaven for you, pure
1 Jn 5:3	**k-ing** his commandments,
Jude 1:21	**k** yourselves safe in God's love.
Rev 12:17	**k** God's commandments

KEY, KEYS (n)

instrument that opens (or locks) doors or gates; symbolic of authority, power, and control

Matt 16:19	the **k-s** of the Kingdom
Rev 1:18	And I hold the **k-s** of death and
Rev 20:1	with the **k** to the bottomless

KILL, KILLED, KILLING, KILLS (v)

to take or deprive of life

Gen 4:8	Abel, and **k-ed** him.
Exod 2:12	Moses **k-ed** the Egyptian
Exod 21:12	assaults and **k-s** another
Lev 24:21	whoever **k-s** another person
2 Sam 2:26	always be **k-ing** each other?
Neh 9:26	they **k-ed** your prophets
Job 13:15	God might **k** me, but I
Ps 44:22	for your sake we are **k-ed**
Prov 6:17	hands that **k** the innocent,
Eccl 3:3	A time to **k** and a time to
Matt 10:28	who want to **k** your body;
Matt 16:21	He would be **k-ed,**
Mark 10:34	flog him with a whip, and **k**
Luke 11:48	They **k-ed** the prophets,
Acts 3:15	You **k-ed** the author
Rom 8:36	For your sake we are **k-ed**
1 Tim 1:9	who **k** their father or mother
1 Jn 3:12	evil one and **k-ed** his brother.

KIND (adj)

affectionate, loving; of a sympathetic or helping nature; gentle

Luke 6:35	for he is **k** to those who are
1 Cor 13:4	is patient and **k.** Love is not
Eph 4:32	Instead, be **k** to each other,

2 Tim 2:24 — but must be **k** to everyone,

KIND, KINDS (n)
nature, family, type, or category

Gen 1:12 — and trees of the same **k.**
1 Cor 12:4 — different **k-s** of spiritual gifts,
1 Tim 6:10 — root of all **k-s** of evil.

KINDNESS (n)
a kind deed; affection; the quality or state of being kind

Ps 106:7 — his many acts of **k** to them.
Rom 2:4 — his **k** is intended to turn you
Rom 3:24 — with undeserved **k,** declares
Rom 12:8 — gift for showing **k** to others,
2 Cor 6:1 — marvelous gift of God's **k**
2 Cor 8:1 — God in his **k** has done through
2 Cor 10:1 — gentleness and **k** of Christ—
Gal 5:22 — peace, patience, **k,** goodness,
Eph 2:7 — his grace and **k** toward us,
Col 3:12 — mercy, **k,** humility,
Titus 3:4 — revealed his **k** and love,
1 Pet 2:3 — a taste of the Lord's **k.**

KING, KINGS (n)
a sovereign ruler (often God); chief among competitors

Deut 17:14 — We should select a **k** to rule
Judg 17:6 — In those days Israel had no **k;**
1 Sam 8:5 — Give us a **k** to judge us
1 Sam 11:15 — they made Saul **k.**
2 Sam 2:4 — and anointed him **k** over the
2 Kgs 19:15 — of all the **k-s** of the earth.
Ps 44:4 — You are my **K** and my God.
Ps 68:32 — to God, you **k-s** of the earth.
Ps 72:11 — All **k-s** will bow
Ps 97:1 — The LORD is **k!**
Isa 32:1 — a righteous **k** is coming!
Isa 37:16 — of all the **k-s** of the earth.
Dan 2:21 — he removes **k-s** and sets
Dan 4:17 — Most High rules over the **k-s**
Dan 4:37 — and honor the **K** of heaven.
Dan 7:24 — Its ten horns are ten **k-s**
Zeph 3:8 — to gather the **k-s** of the earth
Zech 9:9 — Look, your **k** is coming to you.
Matt 27:11 — Are you the **k** of the Jews?
John 1:49 — Son of God—the **K** of Israel!
John 12:13 — Hail to the **K** of Israel!
Acts 17:7 — to another **k,** named Jesus.
1 Tim 1:17 — is the eternal **K,** the unseen
1 Tim 6:15 — the **K** of all **k-s** and
1 Pet 2:13 — the **k** as head of state,
Rev 1:5 — of all the **k-s** of the world.
Rev 17:14 — all lords and **K** of all **k-s.**
Rev 19:16 — **K** of all **k-s** and Lord

KINGDOM (n)
rule or realm; dominion of a king

Exod 19:6 — will be my **k** of priests,
1 Kgs 11:31 — to tear the **k** from the hand
1 Chr 28:7 — make his **k** last forever.
Ps 145:11 — glory of your **k;**
Matt 3:2 — for the **K** of Heaven is near.
Matt 4:23 — Good News about the **K.**
Matt 5:10 — right, for the **K** of Heaven is
Matt 5:19 — great in the **K** of Heaven.
Matt 6:10 — May your **K** come soon.
Matt 7:21 — will enter the **K** of Heaven.
Matt 8:12 — for whom the **K** was prepared—
Matt 10:7 — them that the **K** of Heaven is
Matt 11:12 — until now, the **K** of Heaven
Matt 12:26 — His own **k** will not
Matt 13:11 — secrets of the **K** of Heaven,
Matt 13:38 — represents the people of the **K.**
Matt 13:43 — their Father's **K.** Anyone with
Matt 13:45 — Again, the **K** of Heaven is
Matt 13:52 — a disciple in the **K** of Heaven
Matt 16:28 — Son of Man coming in his **K.**
Matt 18:4 — greatest in the **K** of Heaven.
Matt 19:12 — sake of the **K** of Heaven.
Matt 19:23 — to enter the **K** of Heaven.
Matt 20:1 — For the **K** of Heaven is
Matt 21:43 — I tell you, the **K** of God will
Matt 23:13 — shut the door of the **K** of Heaven
Matt 24:14 — Good News about the **K** will be
Matt 25:34 — inherit the **K** prepared for
Mark 3:24 — A **k** divided by
Mark 4:11 — secret of the **K** of God.
Mark 4:30 — I describe the **K** of God?
Mark 9:1 — they see the **K** of God arrive
Mark 10:15 — doesn't receive the **K** of God
Mark 10:24 — to enter the **K** of God.
Mark 11:10 — on the coming **K** of our
Mark 13:8 — and **k** against **k.**
Mark 15:43 — waiting for the **K** of God to
Luke 4:43 — Good News of the **K** of God in
Luke 7:28 — least person in the **K** of God
Luke 8:10 — secrets of the **K** of God.
Luke 9:11 — taught them about the **K** of God,
Luke 9:60 — preach about the **K** of God.
Luke 10:9 — tell them, 'The **K** of God is
Luke 10:11 — know this—the **K** of God is
Luke 11:17 — he said, "Any **k** divided
Luke 11:20 — the **K** of God has arrived
Luke 12:31 — Seek the **K** of God
Luke 13:18 — What is the **K** of God like?
Luke 14:15 — a banquet in the **K** of God!
Luke 17:20 — When will the **K** of God
Luke 17:21 — For the **K** of God is
Luke 18:24 — to enter the **K** of God!
Luke 18:29 — for the sake of the **K** of God,
Luke 21:10 — and **k** against **k.**

Luke 22:16 fulfilled in the **K** of God.
Luke 22:29 granted me a **K,** I now grant
Luke 23:42 come into your **K.**
John 3:3 you cannot see the **K** of God.
John 3:5 no one can enter the **K** of God
John 18:36 But my **K** is not of
Acts 1:3 talked to them about the **K** of God.
Acts 1:6 restore our **k?**
Acts 8:12 News concerning the **K** of God
Acts 19:8 about the **K** of God.
Acts 28:23 testified about the **K** of God
Rom 14:17 For the **K** of God is
1 Cor 4:20 For the **K** of God is
1 Cor 6:10 will inherit the **K** of God.
1 Cor 15:24 will turn the **K** over to God
1 Cor 15:50 cannot inherit the **K** of God.
Gal 5:21 will not inherit the **K** of God.
Eph 5:5 will inherit the **K** of Christ
Col 4:11 with me here for the **K** of God.
1 Thes 2:12 to share in his **K** and glory.
2 Thes 1:5 worthy of his **K,** for which
2 Tim 4:18 his heavenly **K.** All glory to
Heb 12:28 we are receiving a **K** that is
Jas 2:5 inherit the **K** he promised to
2 Pet 1:11 into the eternal **K** of our
Rev 1:6 made us a **K** of priests for
Rev 5:10 to become a **K** of priests for
Rev 11:15 now become the **K** of our Lord
Rev 12:10 power and the **K** of our God,
Rev 16:10 **k** was plunged into darkness.

KINSMAN-REDEEMER (KJV)
Ruth 3:9 my *family redeemer*
Ruth 3:12 of your *family redeemers*
Ruth 4:1 the *family redeemer* he had

KISS, KISSES (n)
a greeting or caress with the lips; an expression of affection
Prov 27:6 better than many **k-es** from an
Song 7:9 May your **k-es** be as
Mark 14:45 and gave him the **k.**
Luke 22:48 the Son of Man with a **k?**

KISS, KISSING (v)
to caress with the lips
Song 1:2 **K** me and **k** me again,
Song 8:1 Then I could **k** you no matter
Luke 7:38 Then she kept **k-ing** his feet

KNEE, KNEES (n)
the joint in the middle part of the leg; when bent, symbolic of submission or defeat
Isa 35:3 those who have weak **k-s.**
Isa 45:23 Every **k** will bend to me,
Luke 5:8 he fell to his **k-s** before Jesus
Rom 14:11 every **k** will bend to me,
Eph 3:14 I fall to my **k-s** and pray to
Phil 2:10 at the name of Jesus every **k**
Heb 12:12 strengthen your weak **k-s.**

KNEEL, KNELT (v)
to bend the knee; to fall or rest on the knees; usually a gesture of submission, defeat, or reverence
2 Chr 6:13 then he **k-lt** in front of
Ps 95:6 Let us **k** before the LORD
Dan 6:10 went home and **k-lt** down
Matt 8:2 approached him and **k-lt**
Matt 9:18 came and **k-lt** before him.
Matt 17:14 came and **k-lt** before Jesus
Matt 27:29 **k-lt** before him in mockery
Luke 22:41 stone's throw, and **k-lt** down
Acts 20:36 speaking, he **k-lt** and prayed
Acts 21:5 There we **k-lt,** prayed,

KNEW (v)
to be familiar with
see also KNOW
Matt 7:23 reply, 'I never **k** you.
John 2:24 because he **k** human nature.
John 19:28 Jesus **k** that his mission
Acts 2:23 But God **k** what would
Rom 1:21 Yes, they **k** God,
Rom 8:29 God **k** his people in advance,
1 Pet 1:2 God the Father **k** you and

KNIT (v)
to link firmly or closely
Ps 139:13 **k** me together in my mother's
Col 2:2 encouraged and **k** together by

KNOCK, KNOCKING, KNOCKS (v)
to strike sharply
Matt 7:7 Keep on **k-ing,** and the door
Matt 7:8 to everyone who **k-s,** the door
Luke 11:9 Keep on **k-ing,** and the door
Rev 3:20 I stand at the door and **k.**

KNOW, KNOWING, KNOWN, KNOWS (v)
to be intimately familiar with; to discern, recognize, regard, acknowledge, pay heed to, approve, learn
see also KNEW
Gen 3:5 like God, **k-ing** both good and
Gen 3:22 like us, **k-ing** both good and
Gen 22:12 for now I **k** that you truly
Exod 6:7 Then you will **k** that I am the
Deut 18:21 How will we **k** whether or not
Deut 29:29 God has secrets **k-n** to no
Josh 23:14 Deep in your hearts you **k** that
Job 19:25 for me, I **k** that my Redeemer
Ps 9:10 Those who **k** your name trust
Ps 19:2 after night they make him **k-n.**

Ps 44:21 for he **k-s** the secrets of
Ps 46:10 Be still, and **k** that I am
Ps 94:10 doesn't he also **k** what you
Ps 94:11 The LORD **k-s** people's thoughts;
Ps 103:14 For he **k-s** how weak we are;
Ps 119:168 you **k** everything I do.
Ps 139:2 You **k** when I sit
Ps 139:23 O God, and **k** my heart;
Isa 12:4 Let them **k** how mighty
Jer 9:24 that they truly **k** me and
Jer 31:34 will **k** me already,
Dan 11:32 the people who **k** their God
Matt 6:3 don't let your left hand **k** what
Matt 10:29 without your Father **k-ing** it.
Matt 11:27 no one truly **k-s** the Father
Mark 12:24 you don't **k** the Scriptures,
Luke 11:13 if you sinful people **k** how to
Luke 13:25 will reply, 'I don't **k** you
Luke 16:15 but God **k-s** your hearts.
Luke 23:34 they don't **k** what they are
John 3:11 you what we **k** and have seen,
John 4:42 Now we **k** that he
John 6:69 we **k** you are the Holy One
John 7:28 Yes, you **k** me, and you
John 8:14 For I **k** where I came
John 8:32 And you will **k** the truth,
John 10:4 because they **k** his voice.
John 10:27 I **k** them, and they follow
John 13:17 Now that you **k** these things,
John 14:7 If you had really **k-n** me,
John 16:30 we understand that you **k**
John 17:23 the world will **k** that you sent
John 21:15 Peter replied, "you **k** I love
Acts 1:24 O Lord, you **k** every heart.
Rom 1:19 They **k** the truth
Rom 7:18 And I **k** that nothing good
Rom 8:26 we don't **k** what God wants us
Rom 8:27 the Father who **k-s** all hearts
Rom 11:34 For who can **k** the LORD's
Rom 12:16 And don't think you **k** it all!
Rom 16:26 message is made **k-n** to all
1 Cor 2:11 no one can **k** God's thoughts
1 Cor 13:12 All that I **k** now is partial
2 Cor 4:6 so we could **k** the glory of
Gal 4:9 now that you **k** God (or should
Phil 3:10 I want to **k** Christ and
Col 1:10 you learn to **k** God better and
1 Thes 3:3 But you **k** that we
1 Thes 5:2 For you **k** quite well
2 Thes 1:8 on those who don't **k** God
1 Tim 1:7 but they don't **k** what they
1 Tim 3:15 you will **k** how people must
2 Tim 1:12 I **k** the one in whom I trust,
2 Tim 2:19 The LORD **k-s** those who are
Heb 8:11 greatest, will **k** me already.
Heb 11:8 without **k-ing** where he
Jas 1:3 For you **k** that when your faith
Jas 4:14 How do you **k** what your life
Jas 4:17 it is sin to **k** what you ought
1 Pet 2:19 do what you **k** is right and
2 Pet 2:21 they had never **k-n** the way to
1 Jn 2:3 we can be sure that we **k** him
1 Jn 2:4 claims, "I **k** God," but
1 Jn 2:5 is how we **k** we are living in
1 Jn 2:11 person does not **k** the way to
1 Jn 2:29 Since we **k** that Christ
1 Jn 3:1 they don't **k** him.
1 Jn 3:2 But we do **k** that we will be
1 Jn 3:24 And we **k** he lives in us
1 Jn 4:6 is how we **k** if someone has
1 Jn 4:7 is a child of God and **k-s** God.
1 Jn 4:8 does not **k** God, for God
1 Jn 5:13 you may **k** you have eternal
1 Jn 5:15 And since we **k** he hears us
1 Jn 5:20 And we **k** that the Son of
Rev 3:15 I **k** all the things you do,

KNOWLEDGE (n)

the fact or condition of being aware of something, of having information, or of being learned; information, wisdom

Gen 2:9 the tree of the **k** of good and
Gen 2:17 the tree of the **k** of good and
Prov 1:7 foundation of true **k,** but fools
Prov 2:6 From his mouth come **k** and
Prov 3:20 By his **k** the deep
Prov 8:10 **k** rather than pure gold.
Prov 14:6 **k** comes easily to those with
Prov 18:15 Their ears are open for **k.**
Isa 11:2 the Spirit of **k** and the fear
Luke 11:52 remove the key to **k** from
Rom 2:20 gives you complete **k**
1 Cor 12:8 gives a message of special **k.**
1 Cor 13:2 and possessed all **k,**
1 Cor 13:9 Now our **k** is partial
2 Cor 2:14 to spread the **k** of Christ
Eph 1:17 grow in your **k** of God.
Eph 4:13 our faith and **k** of God's Son
Phil 1:9 will keep on growing in **k** and
Col 1:9 to give you complete **k** of his
Col 2:3 treasures of wisdom and **k.**
Heb 10:26 we have received **k** of the
2 Pet 1:5 and moral excellence with **k,**
2 Pet 1:8 **k** of our Lord Jesus Christ.
2 Pet 3:18 the grace and **k** of our Lord

L

LABOR (adj)

of or relating to manual labor; of or relating to the physical activities of giving birth

1 Kgs 12:4 Lighten the harsh **l** demands

Gal 4:19 I'm going through **l** pains for

LABOR (n)
work that produces goods and services; the physical activities of giving birth
Ps 128:2 enjoy the fruit of your **l.**
Isa 54:1 you who have never been in **l.**
Gal 4:27 have never been in **l!**

LACK (n)
the fact or state of being wanting or deficient; absence
Prov 5:23 die for **l** of self-control;
Prov 15:22 go wrong for **l** of advice;
1 Cor 7:5 because of your **l** of self-control.

LACK, LACKED, LACKING (v)
to be deficient, missing, or short; to have need of something
Deut 2:7 and you have **l-ed** nothing.
Deut 28:48 naked, and **l-ing** in everything.
Neh 9:21 and they **l-ed** nothing.
Prov 28:27 the poor will **l** nothing,

LAID (v)
to place or set down
see also LAY
Isa 53:6 Yet the LORD **l** on him the
Acts 6:6 as they **l** their hands on them.
Acts 8:18 the apostles **l** their hands on
1 Tim 4:14 elders of the church **l** their
2 Tim 1:6 when I **l** my hands on

LAKE (n)
a considerable inland body of standing water
Matt 8:24 a fierce storm struck the **l,**
Luke 8:33 into the **l** and drowned.
John 6:25 on the other side of the **l**
Rev 19:20 into the fiery **l** of burning
Rev 20:14 This **l** of fire is

LAKESHORE (n)
the land bordering a lake
Mark 4:1 Jesus began teaching by the **l.**

LAMB, LAMBS (n)
a young sheep that is less than one year old
Exod 12:21 pick out a **l** or young goat
Isa 53:7 He was led like a **l** to the
Mark 14:12 the Passover **l** is sacrificed,
Luke 10:3 out as **l-s** among wolves.
John 1:29 and said, "Look! The **L** of God
John 21:15 "Then feed my **l-s,"** Jesus
Acts 8:32 And as a **l** is silent before
1 Pet 1:19 sinless, spotless **L** of God.
Rev 5:6 Then I saw a **L** that looked as
Rev 5:12 Worthy is the **L** who was
Rev 7:14 robes in the blood of the **L**
Rev 15:3 the song of the **L:**
Rev 17:14 to war against the **L,** but the
Rev 19:9 to the wedding feast of the **L.**
Rev 21:23 and the **L** is its light.

LAME (adj)
having a disabled body part as to impair freedom of movement
Isa 33:23 Even the **l** will take
Isa 35:6 The **l** will leap like a
Matt 11:5 blind see, the **l** walk,
Matt 15:31 the **l** were walking,
Luke 14:21 the blind, and the **l.**
Heb 12:13 weak and **l** will not fall

LAMP, LAMPS (n)
a source of intellectual or spiritual illumination; any of various devices for producing light
2 Sam 22:29 O LORD, you are my **l.**
Ps 18:28 You light a **l** for me.
Ps 119:105 Your word is a **l** to guide my
Prov 6:23 For their command is a **l**
Prov 31:18 her **l** burns late
Matt 6:22 Your eye is a **l** that
Matt 25:1 who took their **l-s**
Matt 25:7 got up and prepared their **l-s.**
Luke 8:16 No one lights a **l** and then
Luke 12:35 and keep your **l-s** burning,
Rev 22:5 no need for **l-s** or sun—for the

LAMPSTAND, LAMPSTANDS (n)
a support that holds a lamp
Exod 25:31 Make the entire **l** and its
2 Chr 4:7 cast ten gold **l-s** according to
Zech 4:2 a solid gold **l** with a bowl of
Zech 4:11 on each side of the **l,**
Heb 9:2 In the first room were a **l,**
Rev 1:12 I saw seven gold **l-s.**
Rev 1:20 the seven gold **l-s:**
Rev 2:5 and remove your **l** from its

LAND (n)
the solid part of the surface of the earth; a portion of the earth's solid surface distinguishable by boundaries or ownership
Gen 1:10 the dry ground "**l**" and the
Gen 15:18 I have given this **l** to your
Exod 6:8 you into the **l** I swore to
Deut 8:7 you into a good **l** of flowing
Ps 37:11 will possess the **l** and will

LANGUAGE, LANGUAGES (n)
means of communication peculiar to a certain people; a special language gift given by the Holy Spirit
see also TONGUE(S)

Gen 11:9 the people with different **l-s.**
Isa 28:11 speak a strange **l!**
Mark 16:17 they will speak in new **l-s.**
Acts 2:4 speaking in other **l-s,** as the
1 Cor 12:28 speak in unknown **l-s.**
1 Cor 12:30 to interpret unknown **l-s?**
1 Cor 13:8 in unknown **l-s** and special
1 Cor 14:19 in an unknown **l.**
Eph 4:29 or abusive **l.** Let everything
Col 3:8 slander, and dirty **l.**
Rev 5:9 every tribe and **l** and people
Rev 7:9 and tribe and people and **l,**
Rev 14:6 nation, tribe, **l,** and people.

LAP (v)
to take in food or drink with the tongue
Judg 7:5 and **l** it up with their tongues

LASCIVIOUSNESS (KJV)
Mark 7:22 deceit, *lustful desires,* envy,
2 Cor 12:21 and *eagerness for lustful pleasure*
Gal 5:19 impurity, *lustful pleasures*
Eph 4:19 They live for *lustful pleasure*
1 Pet 4:3 their *immorality* and lust,

LAST, LASTING (adj)
following all the rest; being the only remaining; belonging to the final stage; of or relating to being continuous in time; existing or continuing a long while
Prov 10:25 have a **l-ing** foundation.
Matt 20:16 who are **l** now will be first
John 15:16 to go and produce **l-ing** fruit,
Acts 2:17 'In the **l** days,' God says,
1 Cor 15:26 And the **l** enemy to be
1 Cor 15:52 **l** trumpet is blown.
2 Tim 3:1 that in the **l** days there will
2 Pet 3:3 that in the **l** days scoffers
Jude 1:18 you that in the **l** times there
Rev 1:17 I am the First and the **L.**
Rev 22:13 the Omega, the First and the **L,**

LAST (n)
the one who is at or endures to the end
Isa 41:4 First and the **L.** I alone
Isa 44:6 First and the **L;** there is no
Isa 48:12 God, the First and the **L.**

LAST, LASTS (v)
to continue in time
Ps 30:5 For his anger **l** only a moment,
1 Cor 13:13 **l** forever—faith, hope, and

LAUGH, LAUGHED, LAUGHS (v)
to show mirth or joy or to despise or mock something with a chuckle or explosive vocal sound
Gen 17:17 **l-ed** to himself in disbelief.
Gen 18:12 So she **l-ed** silently to herself
Ps 2:4 one who rules in heaven **l-s.**
Ps 37:13 the LORD just **l-s,** for he sees
Ps 59:8 But LORD, you **l** at them.
Prov 31:25 and she **l-s** without fear of
Eccl 3:4 and a time to **l.** A time to
Luke 6:21 for in due time you will **l.**
Luke 6:25 awaits you who **l** now,

LAUGHTER (n)
a chuckle or explosive vocal sound; cause for merriment
Gen 21:6 God has brought me **l.**
Ps 126:2 We were filled with **l,** and we
Eccl 2:2 So I said, "**L** is silly.
Jer 7:34 happy singing and **l** in the
Jas 4:9 instead of **l,** and gloom

LAVER(S) (KJV)
Exod 30:18 Make a bronze *washbasin*
Lev 8:11 *washbasin* and its stand,
1 Kgs 7:38 ten smaller bronze *basins*
2 Chr 4:14 carts holding the *basins*

LAVISH (v)
to expend or bestow with profusion
Exod 34:7 I **l** unfailing love

LAW, LAWS (n)
words of Moses; a binding decree; a universal principle; governing authority
see also COMMANDMENT(S), INSTRUCTION(S), REGULATIONS, TEACHING(S)
2 Chr 17:9 the Book of the **L**
Ps 1:2 delight in the **l** of the LORD,
Ps 93:5 Your royal **l-s** cannot be
Ps 119:14 rejoiced in your **l-s** as much as
Ps 119:36 for your **l-s** rather than a love
Ps 119:125 I will understand your **l-s.**
Ps 119:152 days that your **l-s** will last
Matt 5:17 to abolish the **l** of Moses or
Matt 5:19 who obeys God's **l-s**
Matt 22:40 The entire **l** and all the
Matt 23:23 of the **l**—justice, mercy,
Mark 7:8 ignore God's **l** and substitute
Luke 11:52 experts in religious **l!**
Luke 23:56 rested as required by the **l.**
Luke 24:44 written about me in the **l**
John 1:17 For the **l** was given
Rom 2:12 be judged by that **l** when they
Rom 2:15 that God's **l** is written in
Rom 2:20 that God's **l** gives you
Rom 2:25 if you don't obey God's **l,**
Rom 3:19 Obviously, the **l** applies to
Rom 3:21 requirements of the **l,** as was
Rom 3:28 not by obeying the **l.**

Rom 4:13	his obedience to God's **l,**
Rom 4:16	according to the **l** of Moses,
Rom 5:13	was not yet any **l** to break.
Rom 6:15	has set us free from the **l,**
Rom 7:4	power of the **l** when you died
Rom 7:5	the **l** aroused these evil desires
Rom 7:8	If there were no **l,** sin would
Rom 7:12	But still, the **l** itself is
Rom 7:22	I love God's **l** with all my
Rom 7:25	I really want to obey God's **l,**
Rom 8:3	did what the **l** could not do.
Rom 8:4	requirement of the **l** would be
Rom 8:7	did obey God's **l-s,** and it
Rom 9:4	gave them his **l.** He gave them
Rom 9:31	with God by keeping the **l,**
Rom 10:4	for which the **l** was given.
Rom 13:10	requirements of God's **l.**
1 Cor 9:9	For the **l** of Moses
1 Cor 9:21	I obey the **l** of Christ.
2 Cor 3:6	not of written **l-s,** but of the
Gal 2:16	by obeying the **l.** And we have
Gal 2:19	So I died to the **l**—I stopped
Gal 3:2	by obeying the **l** of Moses?
Gal 3:5	because you obey the **l?**
Gal 3:11	by trying to keep the **l.**
Gal 3:19	But the **l** was designed
Gal 3:21	If the **l** could give us
Gal 3:23	placed under guard by the **l.**
Gal 4:21	live under the **l,** do you know
Gal 5:3	in the whole **l** of Moses.
Gal 5:14	the whole **l** can be summed
Gal 6:2	this way obey the **l** of Christ.
Eph 2:15	the system of **l** with its
Phil 3:6	I obeyed the **l** without fault.
1 Tim 1:8	know that the **l** is good when
Heb 10:1	under the **l** of Moses
Jas 1:25	into the perfect **l** that sets
Jas 2:8	obey the royal **l** as found in
Jas 2:10	all of the **l-s** except one is as

LAWGIVER (n)

one who gives a code of laws to a people

Isa 33:22	is our judge, our **l,** and our

LAWLESS (adj)

not regulated by law; not restrained or controlled by law; unruly

Acts 2:23	the help of **l** Gentiles,
Heb 10:17	their sins and **l** deeds.

LAWLESSNESS (n)

the quality or state of not being restrained or controlled by law

2 Thes 2:3	the man of **l** is revealed—
2 Thes 2:7	For this **l** is already
2 Thes 2:8	Then the man of **l** will be

LAWSUITS (n)

an act or instance of suing

1 Cor 6:7	Even to have such **l** with one

LAY, LAYING (v)

to put or set down

see also LAID

Exod 29:10	his sons will **l** their hands
Lev 1:4	**L** your hand on
Lev 4:15	must then **l** their hands on
Num 8:10	of Israel must **l** their hands
Num 27:18	in him, and **l** your hands on
Acts 8:19	so that when I **l** my hands on
Heb 6:2	the **l-ing** on of hands,
Rev 4:10	And they **l** their crowns

LAZINESS (n)

a disinclination to activity or exertion

Prov 31:27	suffers nothing from **l.**
Ezek 16:49	gluttony, and **l,** while the

LAZY (adj)

disinclined to activity or exertion; not energetic or vigorous

Prov 12:27	**L** people don't
Prov 20:4	Those too **l** to plow in the
Rom 12:11	Never be **l,** but work
1 Tim 5:13	they will learn to be **l**
Titus 1:12	animals, and **l** gluttons.

LAZYBONES (n)

a lazy person

Prov 6:6	from the ants, you **l.**

LEAD, LEADING, LEADS (v)

to guide by direction or example; to go at the head of; to result in

see also LED

Deut 27:18	anyone who **l-s** a blind
Deut 31:2	no longer able to **l** you.
Josh 1:6	one who will **l** these people
2 Chr 1:10	knowledge to **l** them
Ps 25:9	He **l-s** the humble in
Ps 73:24	with your counsel, **l-ing** me to a
Prov 6:22	counsel will **l** you.
Prov 14:30	A peaceful heart **l-s** to a
Prov 19:23	Fear of the LORD **l-s** to life,
Isa 11:6	little child will **l** them all.
Matt 15:14	blind guides **l-ing** the blind,
John 10:3	by name and **l-s** them out.
Rom 6:16	to sin, which **l-s** to death,
Rom 6:22	things that **l** to holiness and
1 Tim 5:24	**l-ing** them to certain judgment.
Rev 7:17	He will **l** them to

LEADER, LEADERS (n)
a person who has commanding authority or influence; chief among others
1 Sam 13:14 to be the **l** of his people,
Prov 17:26 to flog **l-s** for being honest.
Jer 51:46 **l-s** fight against each other.
Matt 20:26 a **l** among you must be
Mark 10:43 a **l** among you must be
Luke 22:26 **l** should be like a servant.
Acts 13:27 Jerusalem and their **l-s** did not
1 Thes 5:12 who are your **l-s** in the Lord's
Heb 13:7 Remember your **l-s** who taught
Heb 13:17 Obey your spiritual **l-s,** and do
3 Jn 1:9 to be the **l,** refuses to have

LEADERSHIP (n)
the office or position of a leader; capacity to lead
Num 33:1 under the **l** of Moses
1 Cor 12:28 those who have the gift of **l,**

LEAP, LEAPED (v)
to spring from (or as if from) the ground
Isa 35:6 The lame will **l** like a deer,
Luke 1:41 Elizabeth's child **l-ed** within

LEARN, LEARNED, LEARNS (v)
to come to know or realize; to acquire knowledge, skill, or behavioral tendency
Deut 4:10 Then they will **l** to fear me
Deut 5:1 so you may **l** them and obey
Prov 9:9 and they will **l** even more.
Prov 18:15 are always ready to **l.**
Isa 1:17 **L** to do good.
Isa 26:9 will people **l** what is right.
Isa 29:13 man-made rules **l-ed** by rote.
Matt 2:7 and he **l-ed** from them the time
John 6:45 listens to the Father and **l-s**
Phil 4:9 all you **l-ed** and received from
Phil 4:11 have **l-ed** how to be content
Col 1:10 grow as you **l** to know God
1 Tim 2:11 Women should **l** quietly and
2 Tim 1:13 teaching you **l-ed** from me—
Heb 5:8 he **l-ed** obedience from the

LEAST (adj)
lowest in importance or position
Matt 19:30 will be **l** important then,
Mark 10:31 will be **l** important then,

LEATHER (adj)
of or relating to animal skin dressed for use
2 Kgs 1:8 he wore a **l** belt around his
Matt 3:4 he wore a **l** belt around his

LEAVEN (KJV)
Exod 12:20 anything made with *yeast*
Exod 13:7 any *yeast* at all found within
Matt 13:33 of Heaven is like the *yeast*
Matt 16:6 the *yeast* of the Pharisees
1 Cor 5:6 this sin is like a little *yeast*

LED (v)
to guide by direction or example
see also LEAD
Ps 68:18 the heights, you **l** a crowd of
Isa 53:7 He was **l** like a lamb
Jer 11:19 like a lamb being **l** to the
Luke 4:1 He was **l** by the Spirit
Acts 8:32 He was **l** like a sheep
Rom 8:14 all who are **l** by the Spirit
Eph 4:8 the heights, he **l** a crowd of

LEFT (adj)
of, relating to, situated on, or being the side of the body in which the heart is mostly located
Matt 6:3 don't let your **l** hand know

LEFT (n)
the location or direction of the left side
Josh 1:7 or to the **l.** Then you will be
Josh 23:6 either to the right or to the **l.**
Isa 30:21 to the right or to the **l.**
Matt 25:33 and the goats at his **l.**
Matt 25:41 those on the **l** and say, 'Away

LEFT (v)
to depart from; to allow to remain
Isa 53:6 We have **l** God's paths
Ezek 34:8 and **l** the sheep to starve.

LEFTOVERS (n)
something that remains unused or unconsumed
Matt 14:20 picked up twelve baskets of **l.**

LEGION (n)
a very large number; multitude
Mark 5:9 My name is **L,** because there

LEND, LENDING (v)
to give for temporary use on condition that the same or its equivalent be returned
Lev 25:37 interest on money you **l**
Deut 15:8 and **l** them whatever
Ps 15:5 Those who **l** money without
Prov 19:17 you are **l-ing** to the LORD—
Luke 6:34 Even sinners will **l** to other

LENDER, LENDERS (n)
one who loans to another
Exod 22:25 as a money **l** would.
Prov 22:7 borrower is servant to the **l.**
Isa 24:2 and sellers, **l-s** and borrowers,

LENGTHENS (v)
to make longer; to extend
Prov 10:27 of the LORD **l** one's life,

LEPERS (n)
one who suffers from a severe contagious skin and nerve disease
Matt 11:5 lame walk, the **l** are cured,
Luke 17:12 ten **l** stood at a distance,

LEPROSY (n)
a chronic infectious disease affecting the skin and peripheral nerves which causes loss of sensation, paralysis, and deformities
Num 12:10 as white as snow from **l.**
2 Kgs 5:1 he suffered from **l.**
2 Kgs 7:3 four men with **l** sitting at
2 Chr 26:21 King Uzziah had **l** until the

LESSON (n)
something learned by study or experience; an instructive example
Lev 26:23 to learn the **l** and continue
Prov 6:6 Take a **l** from the ants,

LETTER, LETTERS (n)
a piece of written communication
Deut 24:1 he writes her a **l** of divorce,
2 Cor 3:2 Your lives are a **l** written in
2 Cor 10:10 Paul's **l-s** are demanding
2 Thes 3:14 obey what we say in this **l.**
2 Pet 3:16 have twisted his **l-s** to mean

LEVEL (v)
to make flat
Isa 40:4 valleys, and **l** the mountains

LEVI
1. Third son of Jacob and Leah (Gen 29:34), who gave his name to a tribe of Israel; violently avenged his sister Dinah (Gen 34); cursed for his violent temper (Gen 49:5-7); his tribe was blessed (Deut 33:8-11), chosen for priestly service (Num 3–4), numbered (Num 3:39; 26:62), allotted cities, but not land (Josh 13:14; *see also* Num 18:21-32); 12,000 will be marked by God (Rev 7:7).
2. *See* MATTHEW, also known as Levi.

LEVIATHAN (n)
a sea monster represented as a cruel enemy defeated by God
Job 41:1 Can you catch **L** with a hook
Ps 74:14 crushed the heads of **L** and
Isa 27:1 and punish **L,** the swiftly

LEWDNESS
that which lacks legal or moral restraints; sexual obscenity or vulgarity
Ezek 23:27 stop to the **l** and prostitution
Ezek 24:13 impurity is your **l** and

LIAR, LIARS (n)
a person who deceives by telling untruths or falsehoods
Ps 63:11 while **l-s** will be silenced.
Ps 116:11 These people are all **l-s!**
Prov 17:4 **l-s** pay close attention to
Prov 29:12 pays attention to **l-s,** all his
Prov 30:6 expose you as a **l.**
Isa 57:4 of sinners and **l-s!**
John 8:44 a **l** and the father of lies.
Rom 3:4 else is a **l,** God is true.
1 Tim 1:10 are slave traders, **l-s,** promise
Titus 1:12 are all **l-s,** cruel animals,
1 Jn 1:10 calling God a **l** and showing
1 Jn 2:4 that person is a **l** and is not
1 Jn 4:20 that person is a **l;** for if we
1 Jn 5:10 calling God a **l** because they
Rev 3:9 synagogue—those **l-s** who say
Rev 21:8 and all **l-s**—their fate is in

LIBERATORS (n)
one who frees or sets at liberty
Neh 9:27 you sent them **l** who rescued

LICK (v)
to draw the tongue over
Isa 49:23 before you and **l** the dust

LIE, LIES (n)
an untrue or inaccurate statement; something that misleads or deceives
Ps 7:14 give birth to **l-s.**
Ps 24:4 and never tell **l-s.**
Ps 34:13 lips from telling **l-s!**
Prov 12:17 a false witness tells **l-s.**
Prov 30:8 never to tell a **l.**
John 8:44 the father of **l-s.**
Rom 1:25 about God for a **l.**
Rom 3:13 filled with **l-s.**
Eph 4:14 to trick us with **l-s** so clever
Eph 4:25 So stop telling **l-s.**
2 Thes 2:11 they will believe these **l-s.**
1 Pet 3:10 and your lips from telling **l-s.**
2 Pet 2:3 make up clever **l-s** to get hold
1 Jn 2:21 between truth and **l-s.**
Rev 14:5 They have told no **l-s;**

LIE, LIED, LIES (v)
to make an untrue statement with intent to deceive; to create a false or misleading impression

see also LYING
Lev 6:3 lost property and **l** about it,
Job 31:5 Have I **l-d** to anyone or
Ps 58:3 even from birth they have **l-d**
Ps 89:35 in my holiness I cannot **l**:
Prov 24:28 don't **l** about them.
Prov 26:19 who **l-s** to a friend
Jer 7:9 commit adultery, **l**, and burn
Matt 5:11 persecute you and **l**
Col 3:9 Don't **l** to each other,
Titus 1:2 God—who does not **l**

LIFE (n)
the quality that distinguishes a vital and functional being from a dead body; period from birth to death; a way or manner of living; spiritual existence transcending death; salvation
see also LIVES
Gen 1:30 everything that has **l**.
Gen 2:7 He breathed the breath of **l**
Gen 2:9 the tree of **l** and the tree of
Gen 9:5 who takes another person's **l**.
Gen 9:6 a human **l**, that person's **l**
Exod 21:23 the injury: a **l** for a **l**,
Num 35:31 payment for the **l** of someone
Deut 19:21 be **l** for **l**, eye for eye,
Deut 30:19 choice between **l** and death,
Deut 32:39 kills and gives **l**; I am the
1 Sam 2:6 both death and **l**; he brings
Ps 23:6 the days of my **l**, and I will
Ps 69:28 the Book of **L**; don't let them
Ps 91:16 with a long **l** and give them
Ps 139:24 the path of everlasting **l**.
Prov 3:2 your **l** will be satisfying.
Prov 6:26 will cost you your **l**.
Prov 13:3 have a long **l**; opening your
Prov 15:4 Gentle words are a tree of **l**;
Prov 21:21 will find **l**, righteousness,
Prov 28:16 will have a long **l**.
Isa 53:8 that his **l** was cut short in
Isa 55:3 you will find **l**. I will make
Lam 3:58 you have redeemed my **l**.
Dan 12:2 to everlasting **l** and some to
Matt 7:14 But the gateway to **l** is very
Matt 18:8 to enter eternal **l** with only
Matt 20:28 and to give his **l** as a ransom
Mark 8:35 to hang on to your **l**,
Mark 10:45 and to give his **l** as a ransom
Luke 6:9 a day to save **l** or to destroy
Luke 9:24 give up your **l** for my sake,
Luke 12:25 single moment to your **l**?
John 1:4 The Word gave **l** to everything
John 3:15 will have eternal **l**.
John 4:14 giving them eternal **l**.
John 5:24 passed from death into **l**.
John 5:39 they give you eternal **l**.
John 6:27 the eternal **l** that the Son of
John 6:35 I am the bread of **l**.
John 6:47 who believes has eternal **l**.
John 6:53 have eternal **l** within you.
John 6:68 the words that give eternal **l**.
John 10:10 a rich and satisfying **l**.
John 10:15 So I sacrifice my **l** for the
John 10:28 give them eternal **l**, and they
John 12:25 nothing for their **l** in this
John 14:6 the truth, and the **l**.
John 17:2 He gives eternal **l** to each
John 20:31 you will have **l** by the power
Acts 3:15 You killed the author of **l**,
Rom 1:17 a righteous person has **l**.
Rom 2:7 will give eternal **l** to those
Rom 4:25 he was raised to **l** to make us
Rom 5:10 be saved through the **l** of his
Rom 5:18 God and new **l** for everyone.
Rom 5:21 in eternal **l** through Jesus
Rom 6:13 now you have new **l**.
Rom 6:22 result in eternal **l**.
Rom 6:23 is eternal **l** through Christ
Rom 8:6 mind leads to **l** and peace.
Rom 8:11 he will give **l** to your mortal
Rom 8:38 death nor **l**, neither angels
2 Cor 3:6 the Spirit gives **l**.
2 Cor 4:10 so that the **l** of Jesus may
Gal 3:11 a righteous person has **l**.
Gal 3:21 give us new **l**, we could be
Gal 6:8 harvest everlasting **l** from
Eph 2:5 he gave us **l** when he raised
Eph 4:1 to lead a **l** worthy of your
Phil 2:16 Hold firmly to the word of **l**;
Phil 4:3 written in the Book of **L**.
Col 3:3 and your real **l** is hidden
1 Tim 1:16 and receive eternal **l**.
1 Tim 4:8 and in the **l** to come.
1 Tim 6:19 may experience true **l**.
2 Tim 1:9 called us to live a holy **l**.
2 Tim 3:12 to live a godly **l** in Christ
Titus 3:5 new **l** through the Holy Spirit.
Heb 7:16 power of a **l** that cannot be
Jas 1:12 the crown of **l** that God has
1 Pet 3:7 God's gift of new **l**.
1 Pet 3:10 want to enjoy **l** and see many
1 Pet 3:16 see what a good **l** you live
2 Pet 1:3 for living a godly **l**.
1 Jn 1:1 He is the Word of **l**.
1 Jn 3:14 have passed from death to **l**.
1 Jn 3:16 gave up his **l** for us.
1 Jn 5:20 God, and he is eternal **l**.
Jude 1:21 bring you eternal **l**.
Rev 3:5 names from the Book of **L**,
Rev 13:8 in the Book of **L** before the
Rev 17:8 in the Book of **L** before the
Rev 20:12 the Book of **L**. And the dead

Rev 21:27 in the Lamb's Book of **L.**
Rev 22:1 with the water of **l,** clear as
Rev 22:2 a tree of **l,** bearing twelve
Rev 22:14 eat the fruit from the tree of **l.**
Rev 22:17 from the water of **l.**
Rev 22:19 in the tree of **l** and in the

LIFE-GIVING (adj)
giving or having power to give life and spirit; invigorating
Prov 10:11 the godly are a **l** fountain;
Prov 16:22 Discretion is a **l** fountain to
Rom 8:2 the power of the **l** Spirit has
1 Cor 15:45 Christ—is a **l** Spirit.
2 Cor 2:16 we are a **l** perfume.
Rev 7:17 to springs of **l** water.

LIFETIME (n)
the duration of the existence of a living being or thing
Ps 30:5 his favor lasts a **l!**
Ps 39:5 My entire **l** is just a
Luke 16:25 that during your **l** you had

LIFT, LIFTED, LIFTING, LIFTS (v)
to raise from a lower to a higher position; to raise in rank or condition
Lev 23:11 the priest will **l** it up
1 Sam 2:7 some down and **l-s** others up.
Neh 8:6 as they **l-ed** their hands.
Ps 28:2 I **l** my hands toward your holy
Ps 63:4 **l-ing** up my hands to you in prayer.
Ps 89:13 Your right hand is **l-ed** high in
Ps 113:7 He **l-s** the poor from the dust
Ps 123:1 I **l** my eyes to you, O God
Ps 134:2 **L** up holy hands
Lam 1:9 no one to **l** her out.
Lam 3:41 Let us **l** our hearts and
John 3:14 Son of Man must be **l-ed** up,
John 8:28 When you have **l-ed** up the Son
John 12:32 And when I am **l-ed** up
1 Tim 2:8 holy hands **l-ed** up to God,
Jas 4:10 he will **l** you up in honor.
1 Pet 5:6 he will **l** you up in honor.

LIGHT, LIGHTS (n)
daylight; brightness; illumination; celestial body; spiritual enlightenment; exposure to the truth and justice
Gen 1:3 "Let there be **l,**" and there
Gen 1:14 said, "Let **l-s** appear in the sky
Exod 13:21 and he provided **l** at night
Job 38:19 Where does **l** come from,
Ps 27:1 The Lord is my **l** and my
Ps 56:13 in your life-giving **l.**
Ps 119:105 my feet and a **l** for my path.
Ps 132:17 will be a **l** for my people.
Ps 139:12 Darkness and **l** are the
Isa 2:5 us walk in the **l** of the Lord!
Isa 42:6 you will be a **l** to guide the
Isa 45:7 I create the **l** and make the
Isa 49:6 make you a **l** to the Gentiles,
Matt 5:14 You are the **l** of the world—
Luke 2:32 He is a **l** to reveal God to
Luke 11:33 its **l** can be seen by all
John 1:4 life brought **l** to everyone.
John 1:9 who is the true **l,** who gives
John 3:20 All who do evil hate the **l**
John 3:21 come to the **l** so others can
John 8:12 I am the **l** of the world.
John 9:5 I am the **l** of the world.
John 12:46 I have come as a **l** to shine
Acts 13:47 made you a **l** to the Gentiles,
2 Cor 4:6 said, "Let there be **l** in the
2 Cor 6:14 can **l** live with darkness?
2 Cor 11:14 as an angel of **l.**
Eph 1:18 be flooded with **l** so that you
Eph 5:8 live as people of **l!**
Phil 2:15 like bright **l-s** in a world
1 Thes 5:5 children of the **l** and of the
1 Tim 6:16 he lives in **l** so brilliant
1 Pet 2:9 into his wonderful **l.**
1 Jn 1:5 God is **l,** and there is
1 Jn 1:7 living in the **l,** as God is in
1 Jn 2:9 I am living in the **l,**
Rev 21:23 city, and the Lamb is its **l.**

LIGHT, LIGHTS (v)
to brighten; to ignite something
Ps 18:28 The Lord, my God, **l-s** up my
Luke 8:16 No one **l-s** a lamp and

LIGHTNING (n)
the flashing of light produced by a discharge of atmospheric electricity
Exod 9:23 **l** flashed toward the earth.
Exod 20:18 saw the flashes of **l** and the
Dan 10:6 face flashed like **l,** and his
Matt 24:27 For as the **l** flashes in the
Matt 28:3 face shone like **l,** and his
Luke 10:18 from heaven like **l!**
Rev 4:5 came flashes of **l** and the

LIKE (prep)
similar in appearance, character, quality
Gen 1:26 to be **l** us. They will
Ps 86:8 No pagan god is **l** you, O Lord.
Isa 14:14 and be **l** the Most High.
Luke 13:18 Kingdom of God **l?**
Rom 8:3 Son in a body **l** the bodies we
Rom 8:29 to become **l** his Son,

LIKENESS (n)
copy; resemblance; appearance

2 Cor 4:4 is the exact **l** of God.

LINEN (adj)
made of flax
Lev 16:4 **l** undergarments worn next to
Prov 31:24 makes belted **l** garments
Mark 15:46 a long sheet of **l** cloth.
John 20:6 noticed the **l** wrappings lying

LINEN (n)
cloth made of flax and noted for its strength, coolness, and luster
Prov 31:22 dresses in fine **l** and purple
Rev 15:6 in spotless white **l** with gold
Rev 19:8 of pure white **l** to wear.

LION, LIONS (n)
a wild beast with a threatening roar; symbolic of a strong and fierce enemy
Isa 11:7 The **l** will eat hay like a cow.
Isa 65:25 The **l** will eat hay like a cow.
Dan 6:7 thrown into the den of **l-s.**
Dan 7:4 was like a **l** with eagles'
1 Pet 5:8 like a roaring **l,** looking for
Rev 5:5 Look, the **L** of the tribe of

LIPS (n)
the fleshy, muscular folds that surround the mouth; symbolic of speech
Ps 140:3 drips from their **l.**
Prov 12:22 The LORD detests lying **l,**
Isa 6:5 I have filthy **l,** and I live
Matt 15:8 honor me with their **l,**
Rom 3:13 venom drips from their **l.**
1 Pet 3:10 evil and your **l** from telling

LISTEN, LISTENED, LISTENING (v)
to hear something with thoughtful attention
see also HEAR
Deut 6:4 **L,** O Israel! The LORD
Deut 18:15 You must **l** to him.
1 Sam 3:9 LORD, your servant is **l-ing.**
Neh 8:3 All the people **l-ed** closely to
Ps 95:7 If only you would **l** to his voice
Prov 12:15 but the wise **l** to others.
Prov 18:13 Spouting off before **l-ing** to
Isa 6:9 to this people, '**L** carefully,
Dan 9:6 We have refused to **l** to your
Mark 9:7 dearly loved Son. **L** to him.
Luke 10:39 the Lord's feet, **l-ing** to
Luke 16:31 If they won't **l** to Moses and
John 10:27 My sheep **l** to my
John 15:20 And if they had **l-ed** to me,
Rom 2:13 For merely **l-ing** to the law
1 Tim 2:12 Let them **l** quietly.
Jas 1:19 be quick to **l,** slow to speak,
1 Jn 4:6 they do not **l** to us.
Rev 1:3 he blesses all who **l** to its
Rev 2:7 to hear must **l** to the Spirit

LIVE, LIVED, LIVES, LIVING (v)
to be alive or come to life; to endure a period of time (a life span); to attain eternal life; to dwell; to subsist; to continue alive; to conduct or pass one's life
see also DWELLS
Gen 3:22 Then they will **l** forever!
Exod 20:12 Then you will **l** a long, full
Lev 26:11 I will **l** among you,
Deut 6:2 as long as you **l.**
Deut 8:3 that people do not **l** by bread
Job 14:14 Can the dead **l** again?
Job 19:25 that my Redeemer **l-s,** and he
Ps 23:6 and I will **l** in the house of
Ps 37:3 Then you will **l** safely in the
Ps 61:4 Let me **l** forever in your
Ps 104:33 as long as I **l.** I will praise
Prov 21:19 It's better to **l** alone in the
Isa 33:14 Who can **l** with this
Isa 45:18 He made the world to be **l-d** in,
Amos 5:6 to the LORD and **l!**
Hab 2:4 the righteous will **l** by their
Zech 2:11 I will **l** among you,
Matt 4:4 People do not **l** by bread
John 14:19 Since I **l,** you also will **l.**
Acts 17:28 For in him we **l** and move
Rom 2:8 on those who **l** for themselves,
Rom 6:10 he **l-s,** he **l-s** for the glory
Rom 8:11 same Spirit **l-ing** within you.
Rom 13:13 we must **l** decent lives
Rom 14:7 For we don't **l** for ourselves
1 Cor 3:16 Spirit of God **l-s** in you?
2 Cor 5:7 For we **l** by believing
2 Cor 6:16 said: "I will **l** in them and
Gal 2:20 no longer I who **l,** but Christ
Gal 5:25 Since we are **l-ing** by the Spirit,
Col 1:19 was pleased to **l** in Christ,
Col 2:5 you are **l-ing** as you should
1 Thes 4:11 your goal to **l** a quiet life,
1 Thes 5:13 And **l** peacefully with
1 Tim 2:2 so that we can **l** peaceful and
1 Tim 4:16 close watch on how you **l**
2 Tim 3:12 who wants to **l** a godly life
Heb 10:38 righteous ones will **l** by faith.
Heb 12:14 and work at **l-ing** a holy life,
1 Pet 1:17 So you must **l** in reverent
1 Jn 1:7 But if we are **l-ing** in the light,
1 Jn 4:16 God, and God **l-s** in them.

LIVES (n)
way or manner of living
see also LIFE
Exod 23:26 I will give you long, full **l.**

1 Thes 2:8 — but our own **l,** too.
1 Tim 2:2 — and quiet **l** marked by
1 Pet 3:2 — pure and reverent **l.**
1 Pet 4:2 — rest of your **l** chasing your

LIVING (adj)
having life; active, functioning
Gen 2:7 — man became a **l** person.
Gen 6:17 — destroy every **l** thing that
Jer 2:13 — the fountain of **l** water.
Matt 22:32 — God of the **l,** not the dead.
John 4:10 — would give you **l** water.
John 6:51 — I am the **l** bread that came
Rom 12:1 — Let them be a **l** and holy
Heb 10:31 — the hands of the **l** God.
Rev 1:18 — I am the **l** one.

LIVING (n)
conduct or manner of life
Phil 1:21 — to me, **l** means living for
2 Tim 2:22 — righteous **l,** faithfulness,

LOAF, LOAVES (n)
a shaped or molded mass of bread
Mark 6:41 — took the five **l-ves** and two fish,
Mark 8:6 — the seven **l-ves,** thanked God
Luke 11:5 — to borrow three **l-ves** of bread.
1 Cor 10:17 — all eat from one **l** of bread,

LOAN, LOANS (n)
money lent at interest
Deut 15:2 — must cancel the **l-s** they have
Deut 15:9 — refuse someone a **l**
Deut 24:6 — as security for a **l,** for the
Ps 37:26 — give generous **l-s** to others,

LOANED (v)
to give for temporary use
Luke 7:41 — A man **l** money to two

LOCKED (v)
to fasten in or out or to make secure or inaccessible by means of locks
Job 38:10 — For I **l** it behind barred
John 20:26 — doors were **l;** but suddenly,

LOCUSTS (n)
a short-horned grasshopper
Exod 10:4 — a swarm of **l** on your country.
Joel 2:25 — and the cutting **l.** It was I
Matt 3:4 — he ate **l** and wild honey.
Rev 9:3 — Then **l** came from

LODGING (n)
a temporary place to stay
Luke 2:7 — there was no **l** available for

LOFTY (adj)
elevated in character, spirit, and status; rising to a great height
Isa 6:1 — sitting on a **l** throne,
Isa 57:15 — The high and **l** one who lives

LOG (n)
a usually bulky piece or length of a tree
Matt 7:3 — you have a **l** in your own?
Luke 6:41 — you have a **l** in your own?

LONG (adj)
extending over a considerable time or space
Deut 5:33 — will live **l** and prosperous
1 Cor 11:14 — man to have **l** hair?
Eph 3:18 — how wide, how **l,** how high,

LONG, LONGING, LONGS (v)
to feel a strong desire or craving; to yearn
Job 7:2 — a worker who **l-s** for the shade,
Ps 42:1 — As the deer **l-s** for streams of
Ps 42:1 — of water, so I **l** for you,
Ps 63:1 — my whole body **l-s** for you in
Ps 119:131 — **l-ing** for your commands.
Luke 16:21 — lay there **l-ing** for scraps from
Phil 1:8 — I love you and **l** for you with
Phil 2:26 — he has been **l-ing** to see you,

LONGING (n)
a strong desire especially for something unattainable; craving
Rom 10:1 — the **l** of my heart and
2 Cor 7:11 — such alarm, such **l** to see me,
1 Thes 2:17 — of our intense **l** to see you

LONGSUFFERING (KJV)
Exod 34:6 — I am *slow to anger* and filled
Num 14:18 — LORD is *slow to anger*
Ps 86:15 — mercy, *slow to get angry*
Gal 5:22 — love, joy, peace, *patience,*
Eph 4:2 — Be *patient* with each other

LOOK (n)
glance
Prov 15:30 — A cheerful **l** brings joy to

LOOK, LOOKED, LOOKING, LOOKS (v)
to direct the eyes; to examine; to see; to make sure or take care (that something is done); to regard with contempt; to seem; to search
Gen 19:17 — And don't **l** back or
Gen 19:26 — But Lot's wife **l-ed** back as she
Exod 3:6 — was afraid to **l** at God.
1 Sam 6:19 — they **l-ed** into the Ark
1 Sam 16:7 — LORD **l-s** at the heart.
Ps 34:5 — Those who **l** to him for

Ps 113:6 He stoops to **l** down on heaven
Ps 123:2 We keep **l-ing** to the LORD
Isa 65:1 but no one was **l-ing** for me.
Dan 10:5 I **l-ed** up and saw a man
Hab 3:6 When he **l-s,** the nations
Zech 12:10 They will **l** on me
Matt 5:28 who even **l-s** at a woman
Mark 16:6 You are **l-ing** for Jesus
Luke 9:62 plow and then **l-s** back is not
Luke 22:61 turned and **l-ed** at Peter.
John 4:23 The Father is **l-ing** for those
John 17:1 Jesus **l-ed** up to heaven
Rom 14:10 Why do you **l** down
Phil 2:4 Don't **l** out only
Heb 11:16 they were **l-ing** for a better
Jas 1:25 But if you **l** carefully into
2 Pet 3:12 **l-ing** forward to the day
Rev 5:6 I saw a Lamb that **l-ed** as if it

LOOSE (adv)
in an unrigidly fastened or unsecure manner
Isa 33:23 sails hang **l** on broken masts

LORD (n)
traditionally rendered, Jehovah (Hebrew *Yahweh*); the sovereign God Almighty
see also YAHWEH
Gen 2:4 When the **L** God made
Gen 4:4 The **L** accepted Abel
Gen 15:6 Abram believed the **L,** and
Gen 22:14 the **L** will provide
Gen 31:49 May the **L** keep watch
Exod 6:2 I am Yahweh—'the **L.**'
Exod 15:26 I am the **L** who heals you.
Exod 40:34 the glory of the **L** filled
Lev 20:26 because I, the **L,** am holy.
Lev 23:4 these are the **L**'s appointed
Num 6:24 May the **L** bless you and
Num 14:18 The **L** is slow to anger
Num 14:21 filled with the **L**'s glory,
Num 14:41 disobeying the **L**'s orders
Deut 5:9 I, the **L** your God, am a jealous
Deut 6:5 love the **L** your God with all
Deut 6:18 good in the **L**'s sight,
Deut 10:13 obey the **L**'s commands
Deut 10:20 must fear the **L** your God
Deut 11:1 must love the **L** your God
Deut 29:29 The **L** our God has secrets
Deut 30:20 obey the **L,** you will live
Josh 23:11 to love the **L** your God.
2 Sam 22:2 sang: "The **L** is my rock,
2 Sam 22:31 All the **L**'s promises prove
2 Kgs 22:2 pleasing in the **L**'s sight
2 Kgs 22:8 Law in the **L**'s Temple!
1 Chr 17:1 Ark of the **L**'s Covenant is
2 Chr 16:9 The eyes of the **L** search
Neh 9:6 You alone are the **L.**
Job 38:1 Then the **L** answered Job
Ps 1:6 For the **L** watches over
Ps 12:6 The **L**'s promises are pure,
Ps 18:30 All the **L**'s promises prove
Ps 23:1 The **L** is my shepherd;
Ps 24:1 The earth is the **L**'s,
Ps 34:3 tell of the **L**'s greatness;
Ps 34:8 see that the **L** is good.
Ps 89:1 sing of the **L**'s unfailing love
Ps 92:13 to the **L**'s own house.
Ps 95:6 kneel before the **L** our maker,
Ps 97:1 The **L** is king!
Ps 99:5 Exalt the **L** our God!
Ps 100:5 For the **L** is good.
Ps 107:1 thanks to the **L,** for he is
Ps 118:8 better to take refuge in the **L**
Ps 118:23 This is the **L**'s doing,
Ps 121:2 help comes from the **L,** who
Ps 145:3 Great is the **L!**
Ps 145:17 The **L** is righteous
Ps 146:7 The **L** frees the prisoners.
Ps 147:11 No, the **L**'s delight is
Prov 3:5 Trust in the **L** with all your
Prov 3:9 Honor the **L** with your
Prov 3:11 reject the **L**'s discipline,
Prov 12:22 The **L** detests lying
Prov 15:33 Fear of the **L**
Prov 19:21 the **L**'s purpose will prevail.
Prov 21:2 the **L** examines their heart.
Prov 31:30 a woman who fears the **L** will
Isa 6:3 holy is the **L** of Heaven's
Isa 24:14 praise the **L**'s majesty.
Isa 30:9 to the **L**'s instructions.
Isa 42:8 I am the **L**; that is my name!
Isa 43:11 I, am the **L,** and there is
Isa 49:4 leave it all in the **L**'s hand;
Isa 53:6 Yet the **L** laid on him
Isa 53:10 was the **L**'s good plan
Isa 55:13 honor to the **L**'s name;
Isa 61:2 time of the **L**'s favor
Isa 66:15 See, the **L** is coming
Jer 8:7 do not know the **L**'s laws.
Jer 17:10 But I, the **L,** search all
Jer 31:11 For the **L** has redeemed
Jer 48:10 to do the **L**'s work,
Jer 51:7 cup in the **L**'s hands,
Ezek 7:19 day of the **L**'s anger.
Ezek 44:4 the glory of the **L** filled
Joel 1:15 The day of the **L** is near,
Joel 3:18 from the **L**'s Temple, watering
Jonah 2:9 salvation comes from the **L**
Mic 4:1 mountain of the **L**'s house
Mic 6:2 listen to the **L**'s complaint!
Nah 1:2 The **L** is a jealous God,
Nah 1:7 The **L** is good, a strong

Hab 2:16	cup of the **L**'s judgment,
Zeph 2:3	yet the **L** will protect
Matt 3:3	way for the **L**'s coming!
Matt 4:7	not test the **L** your God.
Matt 4:10	must worship the **L** your God
Matt 22:37	must love the **L** your God
Mark 1:3	way for the **L**'s coming!
Mark 12:11	This is the **L**'s doing,
John 1:23	way for the **L**'s coming!
Acts 2:21	name of the **L** will be saved.
Rom 10:13	name of the **L** will be saved.
Rom 11:34	can know the **L**'s thoughts?
1 Cor 10:26	the earth is the **L**'s,
Heb 12:5	of the **L**'s discipline,

LORD, LORDS (n)

honored one or a superior; master (to a slave); king or ruler; God or Jesus

see also LORD

Deut 10:17	of gods and **L** of **l-s**.
Neh 4:14	Remember the **L**, who is
Isa 6:1	I saw the **L**. He was sitting
Dan 9:19	O **L**, listen and act!
Matt 12:8	Son of Man is **L**, even
Luke 1:38	I am the **L**'s servant.
Acts 10:36	Christ, who is **L** of all.
Acts 16:31	Believe in the **L** Jesus
Rom 10:9	that Jesus is **L** and believe
1 Cor 8:6	only one **L**, Jesus Christ,
1 Cor 11:26	announcing the **L**'s death
1 Cor 12:3	say Jesus is **L**, except
Eph 4:5	There is one **L**, one faith,
Phil 2:11	Jesus Christ is **L**,
Col 2:6	Jesus as your **L**, you must
1 Thes 5:2	day of the **L**'s return
1 Tim 6:15	kings and **L** of all **l-s**.
Jas 5:8	the coming of the **L** is near.
1 Pet 2:3	taste of the **L**'s kindness.
1 Pet 3:15	worship Christ as **L** of
Rev 4:8	holy, holy is the **L** God,
Rev 4:11	are worthy, O **L** our God,
Rev 19:16	kings and **L** of all **l-s**.
Rev 22:20	Amen! Come, **L** Jesus!

LOSE, LOSES (v)

to fail to keep, sustain, or maintain; to damn

Matt 10:39	cling to your life, you will **l**
Mark 8:36	whole world but **l** your own
Luke 15:8	silver coins and **l-s** one.
Luke 17:33	cling to your life, you will **l**
John 6:39	I should not **l** even one of
2 Jn 1:8	you do not **l** what we have

LOSS (n)

the act of losing possession; deprivation

1 Cor 3:15	the builder will suffer great **l**.

LOST (adj)

no longer possessed or known; lacking assurance of eternal salvation

Jer 50:6	have been **l** sheep.
Ezek 34:16	will search for my **l** ones
Luke 15:4	and one of them gets **l**,
Luke 15:6	I have found my **l** sheep.
Luke 15:9	have found my **l** coin.
Luke 15:24	He was **l**, but now he

LOTS (n)

small stones or other devices used for making choices, much like throwing dice or drawing straws

Josh 18:10	Joshua cast sacred **l** in the
Obad 1:11	wealth and cast **l** to divide
Acts 1:26	they cast **l**, and Matthias was

LOUD (adj)

marked by intensity or volume of sound

Isa 54:1	Break into **l** and joyful song,

LOVE (n)

the ultimate expression of God's loyalty, purity, and mercy extended toward his people—to be reflected in human relationships of brotherly concern, marital fidelity, and adoration of God; a beloved person

Gen 24:12	unfailing **l** to my master,
Gen 32:10	unfailing **l** and faithfulness
Gen 34:3	he fell in **l** with her, and he
Gen 39:21	showed him his faithful **l**.
Exod 20:6	unfailing **l** for a thousand
Exod 34:6	filled with unfailing **l** and
Num 14:18	with unfailing **l**, forgiving
Num 14:19	unfailing **l**, please pardon
Deut 5:10	unfailing **l** for a thousand
Deut 7:9	his unfailing **l** on those who
Deut 10:15	the objects of his **l**.
Deut 10:18	He shows **l** to the
Deut 10:19	must show **l** to foreigners,
Judg 16:4	Samson fell in **l** with a woman
1 Sam 18:20	had fallen in **l** with David,
1 Kgs 8:23	and show unfailing **l** to all
1 Kgs 10:9	LORD's eternal **l** for Israel,
1 Chr 16:41	for "his faithful **l** endures
1 Chr 29:18	See to it that their **l**
2 Chr 5:13	His faithful **l** endures
2 Chr 20:21	faithful **l** endures forever!
Ezra 3:11	His faithful **l** for Israel
Job 37:13	to show his unfailing **l**.
Ps 6:4	because of your unfailing **l**.
Ps 13:5	I trust in your unfailing **l**.
Ps 18:50	you show unfailing **l** to your
Ps 21:7	The unfailing **l** of the
Ps 23:6	and unfailing **l** will pursue
Ps 25:6	and unfailing **l**, which you
Ps 25:10	leads with unfailing **l** and

Ps 26:3 of your unfailing **l**, and I
Ps 31:7 in your unfailing **l**, for you
Ps 31:16 your unfailing **l**, rescue me.
Ps 32:10 but unfailing **l** surrounds
Ps 33:5 the unfailing **l** of the
Ps 33:18 who rely on his unfailing **l**.
Ps 33:22 your unfailing **l** surround us,
Ps 36:5 Your unfailing **l**, O Lord, is
Ps 36:10 Pour out your unfailing **l** on
Ps 40:10 of your unfailing **l** and
Ps 40:11 Let your unfailing **l** and
Ps 42:8 his unfailing **l** upon me,
Ps 48:9 on your unfailing **l** as we
Ps 51:1 your unfailing **l**. Because of
Ps 57:3 send forth his unfailing **l** and
Ps 57:10 For your unfailing **l** is as
Ps 59:10 In his unfailing **l**, my God
Ps 59:16 your unfailing **l**. For you
Ps 59:17 shows me unfailing **l**.
Ps 62:12 unfailing **l**, O Lord, is yours.
Ps 66:20 his unfailing **l** from me.
Ps 69:16 Lord, for your unfailing **l** is
Ps 77:8 his unfailing **l** gone forever?
Ps 85:7 us your unfailing **l**, O Lord,
Ps 86:5 full of unfailing **l** for all
Ps 86:15 filled with unfailing **l** and
Ps 88:11 your unfailing **l**?
Ps 89:1 Lord's unfailing **l** forever!
Ps 89:14 Unfailing **l** and truth
Ps 89:49 is your unfailing **l**?
Ps 90:14 with your unfailing **l**, so we
Ps 92:2 your unfailing **l** in the
Ps 100:5 His unfailing **l** continues
Ps 101:1 sing of your **l** and justice,
Ps 103:4 crowns me with **l** and tender
Ps 103:11 his unfailing **l** toward those
Ps 103:17 But the **l** of the Lord
Ps 106:1 His faithful **l** endures
Ps 106:45 because of his unfailing **l**.
Ps 107:31 for his great **l** and for the
Ps 107:43 the faithful **l** of the Lord.
Ps 108:4 your unfailing **l** is higher
Ps 109:26 because of your unfailing **l**.
Ps 115:1 for your unfailing **l** and
Ps 118:1 His faithful **l** endures
Ps 119:41 give me your unfailing **l**,
Ps 119:76 let your unfailing **l** comfort
Ps 119:124 deal with me in unfailing **l**,
Ps 130:7 Lord there is unfailing **l**.
Ps 138:2 unfailing **l** and faithfulness;
Ps 143:12 your unfailing **l**, silence all
Ps 147:11 hope in his unfailing **l**.
Prov 5:19 be captivated by her **l**.
Prov 14:22 will receive unfailing **l** and
Prov 16:6 Unfailing **l** and
Prov 20:28 is made secure through **l**.
Prov 21:21 and unfailing **l** will find
Prov 27:5 better than hidden **l**!
Song 1:4 We praise your **l** even more
Song 1:7 Tell me, my **l**, where are you
Song 1:16 so handsome, my **l**, pleasing
Song 2:7 not to awaken **l** until the
Song 2:17 to me, my **l**, like a gazelle
Song 3:4 I found my **l**!
Song 4:10 Your **l** delights me,
Song 4:16 your garden, my **l**; taste its
Song 5:5 door for my **l**, and my hands
Song 5:8 tell him I am weak with **l**.
Song 7:6 How pleasing, my **l**, how full
Song 7:12 will give you my **l**.
Song 8:4 not to awaken **l** until the
Song 8:7 cannot quench **l**, nor can
Song 8:6 for **l** is as strong as death
Song 8:14 Come away, my **l**!
Isa 55:3 the unfailing **l** I promised to
Isa 63:7 Lord's unfailing **l**.
Isa 63:9 In his **l** and mercy he
Jer 2:25 I'm in **l** with these
Jer 9:24 demonstrates unfailing **l** and
Jer 16:5 taken away my unfailing **l**
Jer 31:3 with an everlasting **l**.
Jer 33:11 His faithful **l** endures
Lam 3:22 The faithful **l** of the
Lam 3:32 the greatness of his unfailing **l**.
Dan 9:4 of unfailing **l** to those who
Hos 1:7 I will show **l** to the people
Hos 2:19 and justice, unfailing **l** and
Hos 2:23 I will show **l** to those I
Hos 6:4 For your **l** vanishes like the
Hos 6:6 want you to show **l**, not offer
Hos 11:4 my ropes of kindness and **l**.
Hos 12:6 Act with **l** and justice,
Joel 2:13 filled with unfailing **l**.
Jonah 4:2 filled with unfailing **l**.
Zeph 3:17 With his **l**, he will
Zech 8:17 Stop your **l** of telling
Mark 10:21 Jesus felt genuine **l** for him.
John 5:42 have God's **l** within you.
John 15:9 Remain in my **l**.
John 15:10 remain in his **l**.
John 15:13 is no greater **l** than to lay
John 17:26 Then your **l** for me will
Rom 5:5 fill our hearts with his **l**.
Rom 5:8 showed his great **l** for us by
Rom 8:35 us from Christ's **l**?
Rom 8:39 us from the **l** of God that is
Rom 13:10 **L** does no wrong
Rom 13:10 to others, so **l** fulfills the
Rom 14:15 not acting in **l** if you eat
Rom 15:30 because of your **l** for me,
1 Cor 4:21 I come with **l** and a gentle
1 Cor 8:1 it is **l** that strengthens the

1 Cor 13:13	faith, hope, and **l**—and the
1 Cor 13:13	the greatest of these is **l.**
2 Cor 2:4	know how much **l** I have for
2 Cor 2:8	to reaffirm your **l** for him.
2 Cor 5:14	Either way, Christ's **l** controls
2 Cor 8:7	and your **l** from us—I want
2 Cor 8:24	show them your **l,** and prove
Gal 5:22	**l,** joy, peace, patience,
Eph 1:15	Jesus and your **l** for God's
Eph 3:17	down into God's **l** and keep
Eph 3:18	how deep his **l** is.
Eph 4:15	the truth in **l,** growing in
Eph 5:2	filled with **l,** following the
Eph 6:23	give you **l** with faithfulness.
Phil 1:9	that your **l** will overflow
Col 1:4	Jesus and your **l** for all of
Col 1:8	told us about the **l** for others
Col 2:2	strong ties of **l.**
1 Thes 3:6	your faith and **l.**
1 Thes 3:12	the Lord make your **l** for one
1 Thes 5:13	and wholehearted **l** because of
2 Thes 3:5	expression of the **l** of God
1 Tim 1:5	be filled with **l** that comes
1 Tim 2:15	in faith, **l,** holiness,
1 Tim 4:12	live, in your **l,** your faith,
1 Tim 6:10	For the **l** of money is the
1 Tim 6:11	with faith, **l,** perseverance,
2 Tim 1:7	but of power, **l,** and
2 Tim 1:13	the faith and **l** that you have
2 Tim 2:22	living, faithfulness, **l,** and
2 Tim 3:10	my patience, my **l,** and my
Titus 2:2	filled with **l** and patience.
Titus 3:4	revealed his kindness and **l,**
Heb 10:24	to acts of **l** and good works.
1 Pet 4:8	for **l** covers a multitude
1 Pet 5:14	with Christian **l.**
1 Jn 3:14	who has no **l** is still dead.
1 Jn 3:16	know what real **l** is because
1 Jn 4:7	for **l** comes from God.
1 Jn 4:8	for God is **l.**
1 Jn 4:10	This is real **l**—not that we
1 Jn 4:16	put our trust in his **l.**
1 Jn 4:16	God is **l,** and all who
1 Jn 4:17	live in God, our **l** grows more
1 Jn 4:18	because perfect **l** expels all
Jude 1:12	commemorating the Lord's **l,**
Jude 1:21	safe in God's **l.**
Rev 2:19	have seen your **l,** your faith,

LOVE, LOVED, LOVES, LOVING (v)
to hold dear; to feel a lover's passion, devotion, or tenderness for; to feel affection or experience desire; to like or desire actively

Gen 22:2	Isaac, whom you **l** so much—
Gen 29:32	my husband will **l** me.
Exod 21:5	may declare, 'I **l** my master,
Lev 19:34	as you **l** yourself.
Deut 4:37	Because he **l-d** your ancestors,
Deut 6:5	And you must **l** the LORD your
Deut 7:8	that the LORD **l-s** you, and he
Deut 7:13	He will **l** you and
Deut 11:13	and if you **l** the LORD your
Deut 13:3	if you truly **l** him with all
Deut 15:16	because he **l-s** you and
Deut 21:15	son of the wife he does not **l.**
Deut 23:5	LORD your God **l-s** you.
Deut 30:6	that you will **l** him with all
Deut 30:16	to **l** the LORD
Deut 30:20	this choice by **l-ing** the LORD
Deut 30:20	And if you **l** and obey the
Deut 33:3	Indeed, he **l-s** his people;
Josh 23:11	be very careful to **l** the LORD
Judg 14:16	said, "You don't **l** me;
Judg 16:15	tell me, 'I **l** you,' when you
1 Sam 18:1	for Jonathan **l-d** David.
2 Sam 12:24	The LORD **l-d** the child
2 Sam 19:6	You seem to **l** those who hate
1 Kgs 3:3	Solomon **l-d** the LORD and
1 Kgs 11:1	Solomon **l-d** many foreign
2 Chr 2:11	the LORD **l-s** his people
2 Chr 19:2	the wicked and **l** those who
Neh 1:5	with those who **l** him and obey
Neh 13:26	**l-d** him and made him king
Ps 11:5	those who **l** violence.
Ps 11:7	righteous LORD **l-s** justice.
Ps 18:1	I **l** you, LORD;
Ps 26:8	I **l** your sanctuary,
Ps 36:10	on those who **l** you;
Ps 40:16	those who **l** your salvation
Ps 44:3	helped them, for you **l-d** them.
Ps 45:7	You **l** justice and
Ps 52:3	You **l** evil more
Ps 52:4	You **l** to destroy
Ps 70:4	those who **l** your salvation
Ps 78:68	Mount Zion, which he **l-d.**
Ps 89:28	I will **l** him and be
Ps 89:33	I will never stop **l-ing** him nor
Ps 91:14	rescue those who **l** me.
Ps 97:10	You who **l** the LORD,
Ps 98:3	his promise to **l** and be
Ps 119:48	I honor and **l** your commands.
Ps 119:97	how I **l** your instructions!
Ps 119:113	but I **l** your instructions.
Ps 119:119	no wonder I **l** to obey your
Ps 119:127	I **l** your commands more
Ps 119:140	that is why I **l** them so much.
Ps 122:6	May all who **l** this city
Ps 145:20	all those who **l** him, but he
Ps 146:8	The LORD **l-s** the godly.
Prov 3:12	corrects those he **l-s,** just as
Prov 8:17	**l** all who **l** me.
Prov 8:21	Those who **l** me inherit

Prov 8:36	All who hate me **l** death.
Prov 9:8	and they will **l** you.
Prov 12:1	you must **l** discipline; it is
Prov 15:17	with someone you **l** is better
Prov 17:19	Anyone who **l-s** to quarrel
Prov 18:21	those who **l** to talk
Prov 19:8	wisdom is to **l** oneself;
Prov 21:17	Those who **l** pleasure
Prov 22:11	Whoever **l-s** a pure
Prov 30:19	how a man **l-s** a woman.
Eccl 3:8	A time to **l** and a time
Eccl 9:9	the woman you **l** through all
Song 1:3	the young women **l** you!
Song 3:2	search for the one I **l.**
Song 3:3	Have you seen the one I **l?**
Isa 1:23	All of them **l** bribes and
Isa 56:6	serve him and **l** his name, who
Isa 61:8	I, the LORD, **l** justice.
Jer 2:2	long ago, how you **l-d** me and
Jer 8:2	my people have **l-d,** served,
Jer 31:20	to punish him, but I still **l** him,
Hos 2:1	Ruhamah—'The ones I **l.'**
Hos 2:4	I will not **l** her children,
Hos 2:23	to those I called 'Not **l-d.'**
Hos 9:15	I will **l** them no
Hos 11:1	was a child, I **l-d** him, and I
Hos 12:7	scales—they **l** to cheat.
Amos 4:5	you Israelites **l** to do," says
Amos 5:15	Hate evil and **l** what is good;
Mic 6:8	is right, to **l** mercy, and to
Mal 1:2	"I have always **l-d** you," says
Matt 5:43	that says, '**L** your neighbor'
Matt 5:44	But I say, **l** your enemies!
Matt 5:46	If you **l** only those
Matt 6:24	hate one and **l** the other;
Matt 10:37	If you **l** your father or
Matt 19:19	**L** your neighbor
Matt 22:37	You must **l** the LORD your
Mark 12:6	his son whom he **l-d** dearly.
Mark 12:30	you must **l** the LORD your
Mark 12:33	it is important to **l** him with
Mark 12:33	and to **l** my neighbor as
Luke 6:27	I say, **l** your enemies!
Luke 6:32	If you **l** only those who
Luke 6:35	**L** your enemies!
Luke 10:27	You must **l** the LORD your
Luke 10:27	And, '**L** your neighbor
Luke 16:13	hate one and **l** the other;
John 3:16	For God **l-d** the world so
John 3:35	The Father **l-s** his Son
John 5:20	For the Father **l-s** the Son and
John 8:42	you would **l** me, because I
John 10:17	The Father **l-s** me because I
John 11:36	See how much he **l-d** him!
John 12:25	Those who **l** their life
John 12:43	For they **l-d** human praise more
John 13:1	He had **l-d** his disciples during
John 13:34	**L** each other. Just as I have
John 13:34	as I have **l-d** you, you should
John 14:21	are the ones who **l** me.
John 14:28	If you really **l-d** me, you
John 14:31	know that I **l** the Father.
John 17:23	and that you **l** them as much
John 17:24	gave me because you **l-d** me
John 19:26	beside the disciple he **l-d,**
John 20:2	one whom Jesus **l-d.**
John 21:15	do you **l** me more than
John 21:16	son of John, do you **l** me?
John 21:20	the disciple Jesus **l-d**—the one
Rom 8:28	of those who **l** God and are
Rom 8:37	through Christ, who **l-d** us.
Rom 9:13	Scriptures, "I **l-d** Jacob, but I
Rom 9:25	And I will **l** those whom I did
Rom 12:10	**L** each other with genuine
1 Cor 2:9	for those who **l** him.
1 Cor 13:2	but didn't **l** others, I would
1 Cor 16:22	anyone does not **l** the Lord,
2 Cor 9:7	For God **l-s** a person
2 Cor 12:15	the more I **l** you, the less
Gal 2:20	of God, who **l-d** me and gave
Eph 1:4	God **l-d** us and chose us
Eph 2:4	mercy, and he **l-d** us so much,
Eph 5:25	this means **l** your wives, just
Eph 5:25	just as Christ **l-d** the church.
Eph 5:28	their wives as they **l** their own
Eph 5:28	a man who **l-s** his wife actually
Eph 5:33	love his wife as he **l-s** himself,
Phil 1:16	preach because they **l** me,
Phil 2:2	each other, **l-ing** one another,
1 Thes 1:4	God **l-s** you and has chosen
1 Thes 4:10	urge you to **l** them even
2 Thes 2:10	they refuse to **l** and accept
2 Thes 2:16	our Father, who **l-d** us and
1 Tim 3:3	and not **l** money.
1 Tim 6:2	believers who are well **l-d.**
2 Tim 3:2	people will **l** only themselves
Titus 1:8	and he must **l** what is good.
Titus 2:4	women to **l** their husbands
Titus 3:15	believers—all who **l** us.
Heb 12:6	disciplines those he **l-s,**
Heb 13:1	Keep on **l-ing** each other as
Heb 13:5	Don't **l** money;
Jas 2:5	to those who **l** him?
1 Pet 1:8	You **l** him even though
1 Pet 2:17	Respect everyone, and **l** your
1 Pet 3:8	**L** each other as brothers
2 Pet 2:15	**l-d** to earn money by doing
1 Jn 2:5	how completely they **l** him.
1 Jn 2:10	Anyone who **l-s** another
1 Jn 3:1	very much our Father **l-s** us,
1 Jn 3:14	If we **l** our Christian
1 Jn 4:9	how much he **l-d** us by sending

1 Jn 4:10 not that we **l-d** God, but that
1 Jn 4:11 since God **l-d** us that much,
1 Jn 4:11 surely ought to **l** each other.
1 Jn 4:19 We **l** each other because he **l-d**
1 Jn 4:20 someone says, "I **l** God," but
1 Jn 4:20 how can we **l** God, whom we
1 Jn 5:1 everyone who **l-s** the Father
Jude 1:1 God the Father, who **l-s** you and
Rev 1:5 glory to him who **l-s** us and has
Rev 2:4 You don't **l** me or each other
Rev 3:9 you are the ones I **l**.
Rev 3:19 discipline everyone I **l**.
Rev 12:11 they did not **l** their lives so
Rev 22:15 and all who **l** to live a lie.

LOVE, LOVED, LOVING (adj)
of or relating to a strong affection for another; affectionate, painstaking
Ps 88:18 my companions and **l-d** ones.
Ps 127:2 gives rest to his **l-d** ones.
Ezek 33:32 who sings **l** songs with a
Mark 1:11 are my dearly **l-d** Son, and you
Mark 9:7 is my dearly **l-d** Son.
1 Thes 1:3 work, your **l-ing** deeds, and the

LOVELY (adj)
eliciting love by moral or ideal worth; beautiful
Phil 4:8 pure, and **l**, and admirable.

LOVER, LOVERS (n)
one who loves; two persons in love with each other; a person with whom one has sexual relations
Ps 99:4 Mighty King, **l** of justice,
Song 2:9 My **l** is like a
Song 5:2 I heard my **l** knocking and
Ezek 16:33 gifts to your **l-s**, bribing them
Ezek 16:39 who are your **l-s**, and they will
Hos 2:5 run after other **l-s** and sell

LOVINGKINDNESS (KJV)
Ps 25:6 *unfailing love*, which you have
Ps 40:11 Let your *unfailing love* and
Ps 63:3 *unfailing love* is better than life
Ps 143:8 *unfailing love* each morning
Isa 63:7 according to his *mercy and love*

LOWER, LOWEST (adj)
of lesser position, rank, or order
Ps 8:5 only a little **l** than God and
Luke 14:10 Instead, take the **l-est** place at
Heb 2:7 them only a little **l** than the

LOWLY (adj)
humble in manner or spirit; of or relating to a low social or economic rank
Ps 37:11 The **l** will possess

Ezek 21:26 Now the **l** will be

LOYAL (adj)
unswerving in allegiance; faithful
see also FAITHFUL, TRUSTWORTHY
1 Sam 26:23 and for being **l**,
2 Sam 2:6 May the LORD be **l** to you in
1 Chr 12:33 and completely **l** to David.
Ps 31:23 those who are **l** to him,
Ps 51:10 Renew a **l** spirit within
Prov 17:17 A friend is always **l**, and a
Prov 20:6 say they are **l** friends,

LOYALTY, LOYALTIES (n)
the quality or state or an instance of being loyal
Judg 8:35 Nor did they show any **l** to
Ps 119:113 I hate those with divided **l-ies**,
Prov 19:22 **L** makes a person

LUKE
The beloved doctor (Col 4:14); faithful co-worker of Paul (2 Tim 4:11; Phlm 1:23-24); noted fact-gatherer and writer of the third Gospel and the book of Acts.

LURE (n)
enticement, appeal, attraction
Mark 4:19 the **l** of wealth,

LURE (v)
to draw with a hint of pleasure or gain
2 Pet 2:18 they **l** back into sin those

LUST, LUSTS (n)
unbridled sexual desire; an intense longing
1 Cor 7:9 than to burn with **l**.
Eph 4:22 corrupted by **l** and deception.
Col 3:5 immorality, impurity, **l**, and
2 Tim 2:22 stimulates youthful **l-s**.
Titus 3:3 to many **l-s** and pleasures.

LUST, LUSTED (v)
to have an intense (sexual) desire
Prov 6:25 Don't **l** for her
Ezek 23:5 Then Oholah **l-ed** after other

LUSTFUL (adj)
excited by lust; lecherous
Mark 7:22 deceit, **l** desires, envy,
Gal 5:19 impurity, **l** pleasures,
Eph 4:19 They live for **l** pleasure and

LUXURY (n)
a condition of abundance or great ease and comfort
Prov 21:17 those who love wine and **l**
Jas 5:5 your years on earth in **l**,

LYING (adj)
marked by or containing falsehoods; false
Prov 6:17 haughty eyes, a **l** tongue,
Prov 12:22 The LORD detests **l** lips,
Prov 21:6 Wealth created by a **l** tongue
Prov 26:28 A **l** tongue hates

LYING (v)
to make an untrue statement with the intent to decieve
see also LIE
Mic 6:12 are so used to **l** that their
Matt 15:19 immorality, theft, **l,** and
Acts 5:4 You weren't **l** to us but
1 Cor 15:15 would all be **l** about God—

M

MACEDONIA (n)
a mountainous country north of Greece in the Balkan Peninsula
Acts 16:9 A man from **M** in northern

MAD (adj)
insane; carried away by intense anger
Deut 28:34 You will go **m** because of

MADE (v)
to create, prepare, or fashion; to bring about
see also CREATE(D), FORMED, MAKE
Gen 1:7 God **m** this space to separate
Gen 1:16 He also **m** the stars.
Gen 1:25 **m** all sorts of wild animals,
Gen 1:31 God looked over all he had **m,**
Gen 2:4 LORD God **m** the earth and
Gen 2:22 LORD God **m** a woman
Gen 6:6 LORD was sorry he had ever **m**
Gen 9:6 God **m** human beings in his
Exod 20:11 the LORD **m** the heavens,
Deut 32:6 Has he not **m** you and
2 Chr 2:12 **m** the heavens and
Job 10:9 that you **m** me from dust—
Ps 95:5 sea belongs to him, for he **m** it.
Ps 115:15 who **m** heaven and earth.
Prov 22:2 The LORD **m** them both.
Eccl 3:11 God has **m** everything
Isa 27:11 the one who **m** them will
Isa 43:7 I have **m** them for my glory.
Isa 57:16 all the souls I have **m.**
Jer 51:15 The LORD **m** the earth
Jonah 1:9 God of heaven, who **m** the sea
Matt 19:4 **m** them male and female.
Matt 19:28 when the world is **m** new
1 Cor 11:9 man was not **m** for woman,
2 Cor 5:1 an eternal body **m** for us by
1 Tim 2:13 For God **m** Adam first,
Heb 4:3 since he **m** the world.
Rev 13:8 before the world was **m**—
Rev 14:7 him who **m** the heavens,

MAGIC (adj)
having seemingly supernatural qualities or powers
Ezek 13:20 all your **m** charms,

MAGICIANS (n)
ones skilled in extraordinary power or influence seemingly from a supernatural source; sorcerers
Exod 7:11 Egyptian **m** did the same
Dan 2:2 called in his **m,** enchanters,

MAGNIFICENT (adj)
grand or lavish; strikingly beautiful or impressive
Num 14:19 In keeping with your **m,**
1 Chr 22:5 must be a **m** structure,
Ps 48:2 It is high and **m;**
Isa 63:14 and gained a **m** reputation.

MAJESTIC (adj)
having or exhibiting majesty; grand, stately
Ps 8:1 your **m** name fills the earth!
Ps 29:4 the voice of the LORD is **m.**
Ps 145:5 I will meditate on your **m,**
Isa 53:2 nothing beautiful or **m** about
Heb 1:3 hand of the **m** God in heaven.
Heb 8:1 the throne of the **m** God
2 Pet 1:16 saw his **m** splendor with our
2 Pet 1:17 from the **m** glory of God

MAJESTY (n)
greatness or splendor of quality or character; sovereign power, authority, or dignity
Exod 15:7 In the greatness of your **m,**
1 Chr 16:27 and **m** surround him;
Job 40:10 splendor, your honor and **m.**
Ps 21:5 with splendor and **m.**
Ps 68:34 His **m** shines down on Israel;
Ps 93:1 is king! He is robed in **m.**
Ps 145:12 about the **m** and glory of
Isa 2:10 and the glory of his **m.**
Isa 26:10 no notice of the LORD's **m.**
Jude 1:25 All glory, **m,** power, and

MAKE, MAKES, MAKING (v)
to create, prepare, or fashion; to force; to bring about; to render
see also CREATE(D), FORMED, MADE
Gen 1:26 Let us **m** human beings in our
Gen 2:18 will **m** a helper who is just
Exod 4:11 Who **m-s** a person's mouth?
Exod 25:40 you **m** everything
Lev 16:34 **m-ing** them right with the
Ps 19:7 **m-ing** wise the simple.

Ps 139:14 **m-ing** me so wonderfully
Prov 13:12 Hope deferred **m-s** the heart
Isa 8:14 stone that **m-s** people stumble,
Isa 29:16 "He didn't **m** me"?
Isa 44:10 fool would **m** his own god—
Jer 18:4 he was **m-ing** did not turn out
Jer 23:16 **m-ing** up everything they say.
Jer 31:31 when I will **m** a new covenant
Matt 28:19 **m** disciples of all
John 5:18 **m-ing** himself equal with God.
Rom 14:20 it **m-s** another person stumble.
1 Cor 3:7 that God **m-s** the seed grow.
Heb 8:5 you **m** everything according to
1 Pet 2:8 stone that **m-s** people stumble,

MAKER (n)
one who makes; God
see also CREATOR
Ps 95:6 before the LORD our **m,**
Ps 149:2 Israel, rejoice in your **M.**
Prov 17:5 mock the poor insult their **M;**
Isa 45:9 clay pot argue with its **m?**
Hos 8:14 Israel has forgotten its **M**

MALE (adj)
of, relating to, or being of the masculine sex
Gen 1:27 **m** and female he created them.
Matt 19:4 God made them **m** and female.
Gal 3:28 slave or free, **m** and female.

MALICIOUS (adj)
given to, marked by, or arising from a desire to cause pain, injury, or distress to another
Rom 1:29 deception, **m** behavior,
Col 3:8 of anger, rage, **m** behavior,

MAMMON (KJV)
Matt 6:24 serve both God and *money*
Luke 16:9 *worldly resources* to benefit
Luke 16:11 untrustworthy about *worldly wealth,*

MAN (n)
an adult male human; individual, person
Gen 2:7 the **m** from the dust
Gen 2:15 the **m** in the Garden
Gen 2:18 for the **m** to be alone.
Gen 2:23 she was taken from '**m.**'
Gen 2:25 **m** and his wife were both
Gen 3:9 God called to the **m,** "Where
Isa 53:3 rejected—a **m** of sorrows,
1 Cor 11:3 of every **m** is Christ,
1 Cor 11:3 the head of woman is **m,**
1 Cor 15:45 The first **m,** Adam,
Eph 5:31 A **m** leaves his father and
1 Tim 2:5 the **m** Christ Jesus.

MAN-MADE (adj)
manufactured, created, or constructed by human beings
Matt 15:9 teach **m** ideas as commands

MANAGE, MANAGING (v)
to handle or direct with a degree of skill
Luke 12:42 of **m-ing** his other household
1 Tim 3:4 **m** his own family well,
1 Tim 3:12 he must **m** his children

MANAGER (n)
a person who conducts business or household affairs
Luke 16:1 a **m** handling his affairs.
1 Cor 4:2 as a **m** must be faithful.
Titus 1:7 a **m** of God's household,

MANGER (n)
a trough or open box in a stable designed to hold feed for livestock
Luke 2:7 cloth and laid him in a **m,**
Luke 2:12 strips of cloth, lying in a **m.**

MANNA (n)
miraculous supply of food given to Israel in the wilderness; symbolic of spiritual nourishment
Exod 16:31 Israelites called the food **m.**
Deut 8:16 He fed you with **m** in the
John 6:49 Your ancestors ate **m** in the
Rev 2:17 some of the **m** that has been

MANNER (n)
a mode of procedure or way of acting
Phil 1:27 a **m** worthy of the Good News

MANSIONS (n)
very large houses
Isa 5:9 beautiful **m** will be empty.
Amos 3:15 their winter **m** and their

MARANATHA (KJV)
1 Cor 16:22 *Our Lord, come!*

MARCH (v)
to move along steadily usually with a rhythmic stride and in step with others; to advance or proceed
Josh 6:4 you are to **m** around the town
Isa 42:13 The LORD will **m** forth

MARK
Son of Mary of Jerusalem (Acts 12:12); traveled with Barnabas and Paul (Acts 12:25; 13:5); returned to Jerusalem (Acts 13:13); went to Cyprus with Barnabas (Acts 15:37-39); in Paul's greetings (Col 4:10; 2 Tim 4:11; Phlm 1:24); Peter's "son" (1 Pet 5:13).

MARK (n)
an impression (as a scratch, scar, or stain) made on something; a distinguishing trait or quality

Gen 4:15 LORD put a **m** on Cain
Rev 13:16 given a **m** on the right hand or

MARKETPLACE, MARKETPLACES (n)
an open square or place in town where markets or public sales are held

Matt 23:7 as they walk in the **m-s,**
John 2:16 my Father's house into a **m!**

MARRIAGE (adj)
of or relating to marriage

Gen 49:4 you defiled my **m** couch.
Mal 2:14 the wife of your **m** vows.

MARRIAGE (n)
the state of being lawfully united to a person of the opposite sex as husband or wife; an act of marrying

Matt 22:30 marry nor be given in **m.**
Rom 7:2 laws of **m** no longer apply
1 Cor 7:14 brings holiness to her **m,**
1 Cor 7:27 do not seek to end the **m.**
Heb 13:4 Give honor to **m,** and remain

MARRY, MARRIED, MARRIES, MARRYING (v)
to take a spouse according to law or custom

Exod 21:10 who has **m-ied** a slave wife
Deut 24:4 first husband may not **m** her
Deut 24:5 newly **m-ied** man must not be
Deut 25:5 husband's brother should **m**
Ezra 10:10 By **m-ing** pagan women,
Hos 1:2 Go and **m** a prostitute, so that
Matt 1:18 to be **m-ied** to Joseph.
Matt 19:9 divorces his wife and **m-ies**
Matt 22:30 will neither **m** nor be given
Mark 12:23 all seven were **m-ied** to her.
Luke 16:18 his wife and **m-ies** someone
Rom 7:2 when a woman **m-ies,** the law
1 Cor 7:9 better to **m** than to burn
1 Cor 7:28 if you do get **m-ied,** it is not
1 Cor 7:33 a **m-ied** man has to think
1 Tim 5:14 these younger widows to **m**

MARTYRED (v)
to put to death for adhering to a belief, faith, or profession

Rev 6:9 who had been **m** for the word

MARVELING (v)
to become filled with surprise, wonder, or amazed curiosity

Luke 9:43 everyone was **m** at

MARVELOUS (adj)
astonishing; miraculous, supernatural

Ps 9:1 tell of all the **m** things
Rev 15:1 heaven another **m** event
Rev 15:3 Great and **m** are your works,

MARY
1. Mother of Jesus, the foretold virgin (Matt 1:16-25; Luke 1:26-38); psalmist of the Magnificat (Luke 1:46-56); gave birth in Bethlehem (Luke 2:5-20); at first sign (miracle) of Jesus (John 2:1-5); at the cross (John 19:25-27); Jesus assigned her care to John (John 19:25-27); in upper room after the ascension (Acts 1:14).
2. Mary Magdalene, former demoniac, supporter of Jesus (Luke 8:1-3); at the cross and Jesus' burial (Matt 27:55-61; Mark 15:40-47; John 19:25); saw angel after resurrection (Matt 28:1-10; Mark 16:1-9; Luke 24:10); saw Jesus after resurrection (John 20:1-18).
3. Sister of Martha and Lazarus (Luke 10:38-42; John 11; 12:1-8).
4. Mother of James and Joseph (Matt 27:56; Mark 15:40, 47; 16:1).
5. Mother of John Mark (Acts 12:12).
6. A woman in Rome greeted by Paul (Rom 16:6).

MASTER, MASTERS (n)
one in authority or leadership; employer; teacher; lord or Lord

Jer 3:14 the LORD, "for I am your **m.**
Matt 10:24 are not greater than their **m.**
Luke 16:13 No one can serve two **m-s.**
Rom 6:14 Sin is no longer your **m,**
Eph 6:5 obey your earthly **m-s** with
Col 3:22 Slaves, obey your earthly **m-s**
1 Tim 6:1 full respect for their **m-s**
1 Tim 6:2 If the **m-s** are believers,
2 Tim 2:21 ready for the **M** to use you
Titus 2:9 always obey their **m-s** and do
1 Pet 2:18 the authority of your **m-s**
2 Pet 2:1 deny the **M** who bought them.
Jude 1:4 denied our only **M** and Lord,

MAT (n)
a large thick pad or cushion

Mark 2:9 pick up your **m,** and walk'?
Acts 9:34 and roll up your sleeping **m!**

MATTHEW
One of the 12 disciples (Matt 10:3; Mark 3:18; Luke 6:15; Acts 1:13); former tax collector who followed Jesus (Matt 9:9-10); also known as "Levi" (Mark 2:14).

MATURE (adj)
of or relating to a condition of full development or to attaining a desired or final state

1 Cor 2:6 I am among **m** believers,

1 Cor 14:20	but be **m** in understanding
2 Cor 13:9	that you will become **m.**
Eph 4:13	we will be **m** in the Lord,
Phil 3:15	all who are spiritually **m** agree
Heb 6:1	**m** in our understanding.
1 Jn 2:13	who are **m** in the faith

MATURITY (n)
the quality or state of being fully developed

Luke 8:14	so they never grow into **m.**
2 Cor 13:11	Grow to **m.** Encourage each

MEADOWS (n)
a grassy land area

Ps 23:2	He lets me rest in green **m;**

MEAL, MEALS (n)
a portion of food eaten usually at designated times in the day to satisfy appetite; an act or time of eating

Matt 26:18	I will eat the Passover **m**
Heb 12:16	firstborn son for a single **m.**
Jude 1:12	in your fellowship **m-s**

MEAN-SPIRITED (adj)
exhibiting or characterized by meanness of spirit

Deut 15:9	not be **m** and refuse someone

MEAN, MEANS (v)
to serve or intend to convey, show, or indicate

Gen 41:16	God can tell you what it **m-s**
Rom 3:3	that **m** God will be unfaithful?

MEANING (n)
the thing that is conveyed especially by language

Neh 8:8	and clearly explained the **m**

MEANINGLESS (adj)
having no meaning; lacking any significance

Eccl 1:2	**m,"** says the Teacher,
Eccl 8:14	not all that is **m** in our world.
1 Tim 1:6	their time in **m** discussions.

MEASURE, MEASURED, MEASURING (v)
to gauge or regulate the specific dimensions of; to have a specified measurement; to regulate by a standard

Ps 145:3	No one can **m** his greatness.
Isa 40:28	No one can **m** the depths
Jer 31:37	heavens cannot be **m-d** and
Ezek 45:3	area, **m** out a portion of land
Dan 5:27	balances and have not **m-d** up.
Zech 2:2	I am going to **m** Jerusalem,
Luke 12:15	Life is not **m-d** by how much
Eph 4:13	mature in the Lord, **m-ing** up
Rev 11:1	Go and **m** the Temple

MEASURES (n)
instruments or utensils for measuring; a system of standard units of measure

Deut 25:14	must use full and honest **m.**
Prov 20:10	unequal **m**—the LORD detests

MEAT (n)
animal tissue considered especially as food

Rom 14:21	better not to eat **m** or drink
1 Cor 8:13	sin, I will never eat **m** again
1 Cor 10:25	may eat any **m** that is sold

MEDDLING (v)
to interest oneself in what is not one's concern; to interfere without right or propriety

2 Thes 3:11	refusing to work and **m** in
1 Tim 5:13	**m** in other people's

MEDIATE, MEDIATES (v)
to act as an intermediary agent in bringing, effecting, or communicating; to interpose

Job 16:21	to **m** between God and me,
Isa 2:4	LORD will **m** between nations
Heb 8:6	the one who **m-s** for us a far
Heb 9:15	who **m-s** a new covenant
Heb 12:24	Jesus, the one who **m-s**

MEDIATOR (n)
one who mediates

Job 9:33	If only there were a **m** between
1 Tim 2:5	one God and one **M** who can

MEDICINE (n)
a substance or preparation used in treating disease; something that affects well-being

Prov 17:22	A cheerful heart is good **m,**
Jer 8:22	Is there no **m** in Gilead?
Rev 22:2	The leaves were used for **m**

MEDITATE, MEDITATING (v)
to contemplate, reflect, or ponder
see also *PONDER*, THINK

Gen 24:63	**m-ing** in the fields,
Ps 1:2	**m-ing** on it day and night.
Ps 48:9	O God, we **m** on your unfailing
Ps 63:6	**m-ing** on you through the night.
Ps 119:23	but I will **m** on your decrees.
Ps 119:27	**m** on your wonderful deeds.
Ps 119:48	I **m** on your decrees.
Ps 145:5	I will **m** on your majestic,

MEDITATION (n)
the act or process of meditating

Ps 19:14	words of my mouth and the **m**

MEDIUMS (n)
psychics; those through whom it is thought the dead communicate with the living
Lev 20:27 who act as **m** or who consult

MELCHIZEDEK
King of Salem, priest of God Most High (Gen 14:18); blessed Abram and accepted his tithe (Gen 14:19-20); associated with mysterious priesthood (Ps 110:4; Heb 7:11).

MELODIOUS (adj)
having a pleasant melody
Ps 98:5 the harp and **m** song,

MELODY (n)
a sweet succession or arrangement of sounds
Ps 92:3 harp and the **m** of the lyre.

MELT, MELTS (v)
to dissolve or disintegrate; to disappear as if by dissolving
Jer 9:7 **m** them down in a crucible
Amos 9:5 touches the land and it **m-s,**

MEMBERS (n)
the individuals composing a group; parts of a whole
see also PARTS
Eph 5:30 And we are **m** of his body.
Col 3:15 For as **m** of one body

MERCIFUL (adj)
compassionate; forgiving
Deut 4:31 your God is a **m** God;
Ps 78:38 Yet he was **m** and forgave
Dan 4:27 and be **m** to the poor.
Dan 9:9 our God is **m** and forgiving,
Matt 5:7 God blesses those who are **m,**
Luke 1:54 and remembered to be **m.**
Heb 2:17 **m** and faithful High Priest
Jas 2:13 God will be **m** when he judges

MERCY, MERCIES (n)
a blessing that is an act of divine favor or compassion; withholding of the punishment or judgment our sins deserve
see also COMPASSION, FORGIVENESS
Exod 34:6 God of compassion and **m!**
2 Sam 24:14 for his **m** is great.
Neh 9:27 In your great **m,** you sent
Job 41:3 beg you for **m** or implore
Ps 28:6 he has heard my cry for **m.**
Ps 103:4 me with love and tender **m-ies.**
Ps 119:77 with your tender **m-ies** so I
Ps 119:156 how great is your **m;**
Isa 14:1 LORD will have **m** on
Isa 49:10 LORD in his **m** will lead
Isa 60:10 I will now have **m** on you
Lam 3:22 His **m-ies** never cease.
Lam 3:23 **m-ies** begin afresh each morning.
Dan 9:18 because of your **m.**
Jonah 2:8 their backs on all God's **m-ies.**
Mic 6:8 do what is right, to love **m,**
Matt 5:7 for they will be shown **m.**
Matt 9:13 I want you to show **m,**
Matt 18:33 just as I had **m** on you?
Matt 23:23 law—justice, **m,** and faith.
Rom 9:15 I will show **m** to anyone
Rom 9:18 God chooses to show **m**
Rom 11:32 have **m** on everyone.
2 Cor 4:1 God in his **m** has given us
Gal 1:6 through the loving **m** of Christ.
Eph 2:4 But God is so rich in **m,** and
1 Tim 1:13 But God had **m** on me
Titus 3:5 but because of his **m.**
Heb 4:16 we will receive his **m,**
Heb 10:29 who brings God's **m** to us.
Jas 2:13 will be no **m** for those
Jas 3:17 It is full of **m** and good
1 Pet 1:3 by his great **m** that we
Jude 1:22 show **m** to those whose faith

MERCYSEAT (KJV)
Heb 9:5 the *Ark's cover, the place of atonement.*

MESSAGE (n)
a communication in writing, in speech, or by signals; an underlying theme or idea
Isa 53:1 Who has believed our **m?**
Isa 62:11 LORD has sent this **m**
John 12:38 who has believed our **m?**
Acts 5:20 give the people this **m** of life!
Acts 10:36 This is the **m** of Good News
Rom 10:16 who has believed our **m?**
1 Cor 1:18 The **m** of the cross
2 Cor 5:19 wonderful **m** of reconciliation.
Titus 1:9 belief in the trustworthy **m**
2 Pet 1:19 confidence in the **m** proclaimed

MESSENGER, MESSENGERS (n)
one who bears a message or does an errand
Prov 13:17 a reliable **m** brings healing.
Prov 25:13 Trustworthy **m-s** refresh like
Isa 52:7 feet of the **m** who brings good
Isa 66:19 who survive to be **m-s** to the
Mal 3:1 my **m,** and he will prepare
Matt 11:10 am sending my **m** ahead
Rom 10:15 feet of **m-s** who bring good
Rom 15:16 a special **m** from Christ
2 Cor 12:7 **m** from Satan to torment
Phil 2:25 he was your **m** to help me
1 Thes 2:4 speak as **m-s** approved by God

Heb 3:1 to be God's **m** and High Priest.

MESSIAH, MESSIAHS (n)
the one anointed by God to deliver His people and establish His kingdom
see also CHRIST, JESUS
Matt 24:24 false **m-s** and false
Mark 13:22 false **m-s** and false
John 1:41 him, "We have found the **M**"
John 4:25 I know the **M** is coming—

METHUSELAH
The oldest man, who lived 969 years; the son of Enoch, who never died (Gen 5:21-24); the father of Lamech (Gen 5:25-27).

MICHAEL
Ruling angel (Jude 1:9; Rev 12:7); great defender-prince in the visions of Daniel (Dan 10:13, 21; 11:1; 12:1).

MIDNIGHT (n)
the middle of the night
Exod 12:29 at **m**, the Lord struck down
Acts 16:25 Around **m** Paul and Silas were

MIDWIVES (n)
those who assist women in childbirth
Exod 1:17 because the **m** feared God,

MIGHT (n)
the power, energy, or intensity of which one is capable
Josh 9:9 heard of the **m** of the LORD
2 Sam 6:14 the LORD with all his **m,**
Ps 54:1 Defend me with your **m.**
Isa 11:2 the Spirit of counsel and **m,**
Isa 63:15 and the **m** you used to show

MIGHTY, MIGHTIER, MIGHTIEST (adj)
powerful; great or imposing in size or extent
Gen 49:24 hands of the **M** One of Jacob,
Deut 10:17 God, the **m** and awesome
Deut 34:12 With **m** power, Moses
2 Sam 23:8 David's **m-iest** warriors.
2 Chr 20:6 You are powerful and **m;**
Neh 9:32 and **m** and awesome God,
Job 9:4 For God is so wise and so **m.**
Job 36:5 He is **m** in both power and
Ps 24:8 LORD, strong and **m;**
Ps 47:5 ascended with a **m** shout.
Ps 50:1 LORD, the **M** One, is God,
Ps 71:16 I will praise your **m** deeds,
Ps 77:12 thinking about your **m** works.
Ps 89:27 son, the **m-iest** king on earth.
Ps 93:4 **m-ier** than the violent raging
Ps 93:4 LORD above is **m-ier** than these!
Ps 95:4 and the **m-iest** mountains.
Ps 145:4 children of your **m** acts;
Ps 145:12 will tell about your **m** deeds
Ps 150:2 Praise him for his **m** works;
Prov 24:5 wise are **m-ier** than the strong,
Isa 9:6 Wonderful Counselor, **M** God,
Isa 60:16 your Redeemer, the **M** One of
Zeph 3:17 He is a **m** savior.
Eph 1:19 This is the same **m** power
Eph 6:10 in the Lord and in his **m**
Heb 1:3 sustains everything by the **m**
1 Pet 5:6 yourselves under the **m**
Jude 1:9 Michael, one of the **m-iest** of the angels,

MILE (n)
In the Roman Empire, a unit of distance equal to 5280 feet
Matt 5:41 gear for a **m,** carry it two

MILK (n)
from goats, cows, or sheep, used for food and drink; figurative of abundant produce, prosperity, spiritual food, or salvation
Exod 3:8 flowing with **m** and honey—
1 Cor 3:2 feed you with **m,** not with
1 Pet 2:2 must crave pure spiritual **m**

MILLSTONE (n)
either of two circular stones used for grinding
Luke 17:2 into the sea with a **m** hung

MIND, MINDS (n)
the part of humans that engages in conscious thinking, feeling, and decision making; in the Bible, mind is akin to the heart, not the brain
Num 23:19 he does not change his **m.**
1 Sam 15:29 nor will he change his **m,**
Mark 12:30 all your soul, all your **m,**
Luke 24:45 opened their **m-s**
Acts 4:32 were united in heart and **m.**
Rom 8:6 Spirit control your **m**
1 Cor 1:10 be of one **m,** united in
1 Cor 2:9 heard, and no **m** has imagined
2 Cor 4:4 has blinded the **m-s** of those
Col 2:18 sinful **m-s** have made them
2 Tim 4:5 clear **m** in every situation.
Heb 8:10 I will put my laws in their **m-s,**
Heb 10:16 I will write them on their **m-s.**

MINDING (v)
to be concerned about
1 Thes 4:11 live a quiet life, **m** your own

MINISTERS (n)
agent; one who serves or assists another of higher rank
2 Cor 3:6 to be **m** of his new covenant.

MINISTRY (n)
exercise of one's gifts and resources
2 Cor 9:12 from this **m** of giving—
2 Cor 9:13 As a result of your **m,** they
Heb 8:6 a **m** that is far superior to

MIRACLE, MIRACLES (n)
an extraordinary event manifesting divine intervention in human affairs
Exod 3:20 performing all kinds of **m-s**
Exod 7:9 demand, 'Show me a **m.'**
Deut 13:1 they promise you signs or **m-s,**
Job 9:10 He performs countless **m-s.**
Ps 105:5 he has performed, his **m-s,**
Ps 106:2 the glorious **m-s** of the LORD?
Jer 32:19 and do great and mighty **m-s.**
Matt 7:22 and performed many **m-s**
Matt 13:54 and the power to do **m-s?**
Mark 6:2 power to perform such **m-s?**
Mark 9:39 No one who performs a **m**
Luke 19:37 wonderful **m-s** they had
Luke 23:8 to see him perform a **m.**
John 7:21 I did one **m** on the Sabbath,
Acts 2:22 by doing powerful **m-s,**
Acts 8:13 **m-s** Philip performed.
Acts 19:11 to perform unusual **m-s.**
1 Cor 12:28 those who do **m-s,** those
2 Cor 12:12 and **m-s** among you.
Gal 3:5 and work **m-s** among you
Heb 2:4 and various **m-s** and gifts of

MIRACULOUS (adj)
working or able to work miracles; supernatural
Ps 106:7 the LORD's **m** deeds.
Matt 12:39 would demand a **m**
John 9:16 sinner do such **m** signs?
John 12:37 despite all the **m** signs Jesus
John 20:30 do many other **m** signs
Acts 2:43 performed many **m** signs
Acts 4:16 have performed a **m** sign,
Rom 15:19 of **m** signs and wonders

MIRROR (n)
a polished or smooth surface (as of glass) that forms images by reflection
1 Cor 13:12 puzzling reflections in a **m,**
Jas 1:23 glancing at your face in a **m.**

MISERABLE (adj)
being in a pitiable state of distress or unhappiness
Rom 7:24 Oh, what a **m** person I am!

MISERY (n)
a state of suffering or discomfort; a state of great unhappiness and emotional distress
Judg 10:16 And he was grieved by their **m.**
Rom 3:16 Destruction and **m** always

MISFORTUNE (n)
bad luck; a distressing or unfortunate incident or event
Prov 17:5 who rejoice at the **m** of others
Obad 1:12 Judah suffered such **m.**

MISLEAD, MISLED (v)
to lead astray; to deceive
Prov 13:6 the evil are **m-ed** by sin.
Prov 16:29 **m** their companions,
Matt 24:4 Don't let anyone **m** you,
Gal 6:7 Don't be **m-ed**—you cannot
Jas 1:16 So don't be **m-ed,** my dear

MISTREAT, MISTREATED (v)
to treat badly; to abuse
Exod 22:21 You must not **m** or oppress
Prov 19:26 Children who **m** their father
Heb 13:3 those being **m-ed,** as if you

MISUSE (v)
to use incorrectly; to mistreat or abuse
Exod 20:7 must not **m** the name of
Deut 5:11 must not **m** the name of
Ps 139:20 your enemies **m** your name.

MOCK, MOCKED, MOCKS (v)
to treat with contempt or ridicule; to mimic in sport or derision
Job 11:3 When you **m** God, shouldn't
Ps 22:7 Everyone who sees me **m-s** me.
Ps 89:51 Your enemies have **m-ed** me,
Prov 3:34 The LORD **m-s** the mockers
Prov 30:17 The eye that **m-s** a father and
Mic 6:16 with contempt, **m-ed** by all
Matt 5:11 blesses you when people **m**
Matt 27:41 the elders also **m-ed** Jesus.
Mark 10:34 They will **m** him, spit on
Luke 6:22 and exclude you and **m** you
Gal 6:7 cannot **m** the justice of God.

MOCKER, MOCKERS (n)
one who mocks
Ps 1:1 sinners, or join in with **m-s.**
Prov 3:34 The LORD mocks the **m-s**
Prov 9:7 Anyone who rebukes a **m** will
Prov 20:1 Wine produces **m-s;** alcohol

MOCKERY (n)
a subject of laughter, derision, or sport; insulting or contemptuous action or speech
1 Kgs 9:7 object of **m** and ridicule
Isa 50:6 not hide my face from **m** and
Joel 2:17 become an object of **m.**

Matt 27:29 in **m** and taunted,

MODEL (n)
an example for imitation or emulation
Ezek 28:12 were the **m** of perfection,

MODESTY (n)
propriety in dress, speech, or conduct; freedom from conceit or vanity
1 Tim 2:15 faith, love, holiness, and **m.**

MOLTEN (adj)
made by melting and casting
Exod 34:17 not make any gods of **m** metal

MOMENT (n)
a comparatively brief period of time; instant
Ps 30:5 lasts only a **m,** but his favor
Prov 11:18 get rich for the **m,**
Isa 54:7 For a brief **m** I abandoned you,
Isa 66:8 come forth in a mere **m?**
Matt 6:27 your worries add a single **m**
Gal 2:5 give in to them for a single **m.**

MONEY (n)
officially coined currency
see also POSSESSIONS, RICHES, TREASURE(S), WEALTH
2 Chr 24:10 gladly brought their **m** and
Eccl 5:10 who love **m** will never have
Matt 6:24 serve both God and **m.**
Luke 3:14 Don't extort **m** or make false
1 Tim 3:3 and not love **m.**
1 Tim 6:10 love of **m** is the root of all
1 Tim 6:17 and not to trust in their **m,**
1 Jn 3:17 If someone has enough **m**

MONTH, MONTHS (n)
a measure of time corresponding nearly to the period of the moon's revolution and amounting to approximately 4 weeks or 30 days
Ezek 47:12 will be a new crop every **m,**
Gal 4:10 certain days or **m-s** or seasons
Rev 11:2 trample the holy city for 42 **m-s.**
Rev 13:5 he wanted for forty-two **m-s.**
Rev 22:2 fruit, with a fresh crop each **m.**

MOON (n)
a celestial body that orbits the earth
Josh 10:13 and the **m** stayed in place
Ps 121:6 harm you by day, nor the **m** at
Ps 148:3 Praise him, sun and **m!**
Joel 2:31 the **m** will turn blood red
Hab 3:11 The sun and **m** stood still
Matt 24:29 the **m** will give no light,
Acts 2:20 the **m** will turn blood red
Col 2:16 or new **m** ceremonies
Rev 21:23 city has no need of sun or **m,**

MORE (adv)
to a greater or higher degree
Ps 73:25 I desire you **m** than anything
1 Pet 1:2 give you **m** and **m** grace

MORNING (n)
the time from sunrise to noon
Gen 1:5 evening passed and **m** came,
Ps 5:3 Listen to my voice in the **m,**
Lam 3:23 mercies begin afresh each **m.**

MORNING STAR (n)
a bright planet (Venus) seen in the eastern sky before or at sunrise
2 Pet 1:19 and Christ the **M** shines
Rev 2:28 give them the **m!**
Rev 22:16 I am the bright **m.**

MORTAL (adj)
subject to death
Gen 6:3 for they are only **m** flesh.
Rom 8:11 will give life to your **m** bodies
1 Cor 15:53 our **m** bodies must be

MORTALS (n)
human beings
Ps 8:4 mere **m** that you should think
Ps 144:3 mere **m** that you should think

MOSES
Deliverer of Israel from Egypt, lawgiver, servant of God; "drawn out" of the Nile, raised in Pharaoh's house (Exod 2:1-10); killed an Egyptian and fled to Midian (Exod 2:11-15; Acts 7:24); married Zipporah and had a child (Exod 2:16-22); saw the LORD at the burning bush (Exod 3:1–4:17); returned to Egypt (Exod 4:18-31); conflict with Pharaoh and the 10 plagues (Exod 5–11); brother of Aaron and Miriam (1 Chr 6:3); Passover and the Exodus (Exod 12–14; 1 Cor 10:2); song of salvation and praise (Exod 15:1-21; Rev 15:3); heavenly provisions (Exod 15:22–17:7); raised arms to defeat enemies (Exod 17:8-16); delegated judgeships (Exod 18); received the law at Sinai (Exod 19–23; John 1:17; Heb 12:21); received Tabernacle plans (Exod 25–31); broke tablets at gold calf incident (Exod 32); received new tablets (Exod 33–34); face glowed with the LORD's glory (Exod 34:29-35; 2 Cor 3:13-15); directed the building of the Tabernacle (Exod 35–40); anointed Tabernacle and Aaronic priesthood (Lev 8–9); opposed by Aaron and Miriam, interceded for sister (Num 12); interceded for Israel when they refused to enter Canaan (Num 14:11-25); Korah's rebellion (Num 16); water at Meribah (Num 20:1-13); denied entrance to Promised

Land (Num 20:12; Deut 1:37; 3:23-28); bronze snake healed (Num 21:4-9; John 3:14); succeeded by Joshua (Num 27:12-23; Deut 31:1-8); received additional laws (Num 28–30); gave concluding messages to Israel (Deut 1–33); gave final blessings to the tribes (Deut 33; *see also* Gen 49); died and was exalted (Deut 34; Heb 3:2); wrote a psalm (Ps 90); recorded book of the law (Ezra 3:2; Neh 13:1; Luke 24:44); appeared with Elijah at the Transfiguration (Luke 9:30).

MOTHER (n)
a female parent; a woman in authority
see also PARENT

Gen 2:24	a man leaves his father and **m**
Gen 3:20	she would be the **m** of all who
Exod 20:12	Honor your father and **m.**
Deut 21:18	not obey his father or **m,**
Judg 5:7	Deborah arose as a **m**
Prov 10:1	brings grief to a **m.**
Prov 23:22	don't despise your **m**
Isa 66:13	as a **m** comforts her child.
Matt 10:35	a daughter against her **m,**
Matt 10:37	father or **m** more than you
Matt 12:48	Who is my **m?**
Mark 10:19	Honor your father and **m.**
John 19:27	disciple, "Here is your **m.**"
Eph 5:31	A man leaves his father and **m**
Eph 6:2	Honor your father and **m.**

MOTHER-IN-LAW (n)
the mother of one's spouse

Ruth 2:19	Ruth told her **m** about the man
Matt 10:35	daughter-in-law against her **m.**

MOTHS (n)
insects whose larvae eat wool, fur, or feathers

Matt 6:19	on earth, where **m** eat them

MOTIVES (n)
something (as a need or desire) that causes a person to act

1 Chr 29:17	all this with good **m,**
Ps 26:2	Test my **m** and my heart.
Prov 16:2	LORD examines their **m.**
Jer 17:10	hearts and examine secret **m.**
1 Cor 4:5	will reveal our private **m.**
Phil 1:18	Whether their **m** are false or
1 Thes 2:3	with any deceit or impure **m**
1 Thes 2:4	He alone examines the **m** of
Jas 4:3	your **m** are all wrong—

MOUNT (n)
a high hill; mountain

Exod 17:6	on the rock at **M** Sinai
Exod 19:18	**M** Sinai was covered with smoke
Zech 14:4	the **M** of Olives will split
Matt 24:3	Jesus sat on the **M** of Olives
Luke 22:39	as usual to the **M** of Olives

MOUNTAIN, MOUNTAINS (n)
a landmass that projects conspicuously above its surroundings and is higher than a hill

Exod 24:18	on the **m** forty days
Deut 5:4	At the **m** the LORD
Ps 36:6	is like the mighty **m-s,**
Ps 121:1	I look up to the **m-s**—
Isa 14:13	preside on the **m** of the gods
Matt 17:20	say to this **m,** 'Move
Mark 9:2	led them up a high **m**
Mark 9:9	went back down the **m,**
Luke 23:30	beg the **m-s,** 'Fall on us,'
1 Cor 13:2	faith that I could move **m-s,**
2 Pet 1:18	with him on the holy **m.**
Rev 6:16	they cried to the **m-s** and

MOUNTAINTOPS (n)
the summits of mountains

Isa 42:11	shout praises from the **m!**

MOURN (v)
to feel or express grief or sorrow

Gen 50:11	watched them **m**
Zech 12:10	have pierced and **m** for him
Matt 5:4	God blesses those who **m,**

MOURNING (n)
the act of sorrowing; a period of time during which signs of grief are shown

Ps 30:11	my clothes of **m** and clothed
Isa 60:20	Your days of **m** will come to
Isa 61:3	instead of **m,** festive praise
Jer 31:13	I will turn their **m** into joy.
Zech 8:19	times of **m** you have kept

MOUTH, MOUTHS (n)
the natural opening through which food passes into the body of an animal; voice, speech

Ps 10:7	Their **m-s** are full of cursing,
Ps 19:14	words of my **m** and
Prov 13:3	opening your **m** can ruin
Isa 51:16	have put my words in your **m**
Isa 53:7	he did not open his **m.**
Isa 59:3	and your **m** spews corruption.
Jer 31:29	their children's **m-s** pucker
Matt 4:4	word that comes from the **m**
Rom 3:14	Their **m-s** are full of cursing
Rom 10:9	**m** that Jesus is Lord
Rev 2:16	with the sword of my **m.**

MOVE, MOVED, MOVES, MOVING (v)
to change the place or position of; to go from one place to another in continuous motion; to carry on one's life

or activities in a specified environment; to stir the emotions or passions of; to prompt to the doing of something
Exod 35:21 and whose spirits were **m-d**
Deut 19:14 steal anyone's land by **m-ing**
Deut 23:14 LORD your God **m-s** around
Prov 4:15 Turn away and keep **m-ing.**
Prov 23:10 cheat your neighbor by **m-ing**
Isa 54:10 For the mountains may **m**
Acts 17:28 For in him we live and **m**
1 Cor 13:2 faith that I could **m**
2 Pet 1:21 were **m-d** by the Holy Spirit,

MUD (n)
soft, wet earth
Ps 40:2 pit of despair, out of the **m**
John 9:6 spread the **m** over the blind

MUDDYING (v)
to soil or stain with or as if with mud
Prov 25:26 a fountain or **m** a spring.

MULTIPLY, MULTIPLIED (v)
to increase greatly in extent or number
Gen 1:22 Be fruitful and **m.**
Acts 6:1 the believers rapidly **m-ied,**

MULTITUDE (n)
a great number
1 Pet 4:8 love covers a **m** of sins.

MURDER (n)
the personal, intentional killing of another person
Matt 5:21 If you commit **m,**
Rom 1:29 hate, envy, **m,** quarreling,

MURDER, MURDERED, MURDERS (v)
to kill (a human being) unlawf[illegible]
tated malice
Gen 9:5 **m-s** [illegible]
Exod 20:13 You [illegible]
Deut 5:17 You [illegible]
Matt 23:31 who **m**[illegible]
Acts 7:52 whom [illegible]
Rom 13:9 You mu[illegible]
Jas 2:11 You mu[illegible]

MURDERER, MURI[illegible]
one who commits the c[illegible]
Num 35:16 **m** must be[illegible]
Ps 5:6 LORD detes[illegible]
Ps 26:9 condemn m[illegible]
Ps 59:2 save me fro[illegible] **m-s.**
Ezek 18:10 a robber or **m** and refuses
1 Jn 3:15 brother or sister is really a **m**
Rev 21:8 the corrupt, **m-s,** the immoral,

Rev 22:15 the sexually immoral, the **m-s,**

MUSIC (n)
vocal, instrumental, or mechanical sounds having rhythm, melody, or harmony
Judg 5:3 I will make **m** to the LORD,
1 Chr 6:31 lead the **m** at the house of
Neh 12:27 and with the **m** of cymbals,
Ps 45:8 the **m** of strings entertains
Amos 5:23 to the **m** of your harps.
Eph 5:19 and making **m** to the Lord

MUSICAL (adj)
of or relating to music
1 Chr 23:5 praise the LORD with the **m**
2 Chr 23:13 with **m** instruments
Neh 12:36 the **m** instruments
Dan 3:5 and other **m** instruments,
Dan 3:15 of the **m** instruments.

MUSICIAN, MUSICIANS (n)
a composer, conductor, or performer of music; instrumentalist
1 Chr 6:33 Heman the **m** was from
1 Chr 9:33 **m-s,** all prominent Levites,
1 Chr 15:16 were singers and **m-s** to sing
1 Chr 15:19 The **m-s** Heman, Asaph,
2 Chr 9:11 lyres and harps for the **m-s.**
2 Chr 34:12 were skilled **m-s,**
2 Chr 35:15 **m-s,** descendants of

MUSTARD (n)
a plant whose seeds are used as a condiment and for oil; in Jesus' time, the smallest seed known
Matt 13:31 is like [illegible] seed planted
Matt 17[illegible] a **m** seed,
[illegible] seed planted
[illegible]u must be
[illegible]ring for the mouth of an
[illegible]ting
[illegible]an ox
[illegible]n ox
[illegible]rom a stiff-branched tree with
[illegible] flowers and plum-like fruit
Song 1:13 My lover is like a sachet of **m**
Matt 2:11 gold, frankincense, and **m.**
Mark 15:23 wine drugged with **m,**
John 19:39 ointment made from **m** and
Rev 18:13 incense, **m,** frankincense,

MYSTERIOUS (adj)
exciting wonder, curiosity, or surprise while baffling efforts to comprehend or identify; of, relating to, or constituting mystery
1 Cor 14:2 Spirit, but it will all be **m.**
Eph 1:9 now revealed to us his **m** plan
Eph 3:3 revealed his **m** plan to me.
Eph 6:19 explain God's **m** plan that the
Col 2:2 they understand God's **m** plan,
Col 4:3 about his **m** plan concerning
Rev 10:7 God's **m** plan will be fulfilled.

MYSTERY, MYSTERIES (n)
something not understood or beyond understanding; a religious truth that one can know only by revelation and cannot fully understand
see also SECRET(S)
Dan 4:9 and that no **m** is too great
Rom 11:25 to understand this **m,**
1 Cor 2:7 speak of is the **m** of God—
1 Cor 4:1 explaining God's **m-ies.**
1 Tim 3:9 to the **m** of the faith
1 Tim 3:16 the great **m** of our faith:
Rev 1:20 the **m** of the seven stars
Rev 17:7 tell you the **m** of this woman

MYTHS (n)
a popular belief or tradition that has grown up around something or someone
1 Tim 1:4 in endless discussion of **m**
2 Tim 4:4 and chase after **m.**
Titus 1:14 listening to Jewish **m**

N

NAILED, NAILING (v)
to fasten with or as if with a nail
Matt 27:35 had **n** him to the cross,
Mark 15:24 soldiers **n** him to the
Acts 2:23 you **n** him to a cross
Col 2:14 away by **n-ing** it to the cross.
Heb 6:6 are **n-ing** him to the cross

NAKED (adj)
not covered by clothing; nude
Gen 2:25 man and his wife were both **n,**
Job 1:21 and I will be **n** when I leave.
Eccl 5:15 the end of our lives as **n**

NAME, NAMES (n)
a word or phrase that constitutes the distinctive designation of a person or thing; reputation
see also REPUTATION
Gen 2:19 the man chose a **n** for each
Exod 3:15 my **n** to remember
Exod 28:9 on them the **n-s** of the tribes
Exod 34:14 whose very **n** is Jealous,
Lev 24:11 blasphemed the **N**
Deut 18:5 minister in the LORD's **n**
Deut 28:58 awesome **n** of the LORD
1 Chr 17:8 will make your **n** as famous
2 Chr 7:14 called by my **n** will humble
Ps 8:1 your majestic **n** fills the earth!
Ps 23:3 paths, bringing honor to his **n.**
Ps 34:3 let us exalt his **n** together.
Ps 66:2 Sing about the glory of his **n!**
Ps 103:1 I will praise his holy **n.**
Ps 138:2 I praise your **n** for your
Ps 147:4 stars and calls them all by **n.**
Isa 40:26 calling each by its **n.**
Isa 42:8 I am the LORD; that is my **n!**
Jer 15:16 I bear your **n,** O LORD
Dan 12:1 people whose **n** is written in
Joel 2:32 calls on the **n** of the LORD
Mic 5:4 majesty of the **n** of the LORD
Zech 14:9 one LORD—his **n** alone
Mal 1:6 shown contempt for my **n!**
Matt 24:5 come in my **n,** claiming, 'I am
Matt 28:19 baptizing them in the **n** of
Luke 10:20 your **n-s** are registered
Luke 11:2 may your **n** be kept holy.
John 16:24 Ask, using my **n,** and you
Acts 2:21 calls on the **n** of the LORD
Acts 4:12 no other **n** under heaven
Rom 10:13 calls on the **n** of the LORD
Phil 2:9 gave him the **n** above all
Phil 2:10 that at the **n** of Jesus every
Phil 4:3 whose **n-s** are written in the Book of Life.
Heb 12:23 **n-s** are written in heaven.
Jas 5:14 with oil in the **n** of the Lord.
Rev 2:17 stone will be engraved a new **n**
Rev 3:5 erase their **n-s** from the Book
Rev 3:12 write on them the **n**
Rev 20:15 whose **n** was not found
Rev 21:27 **n-s** are written in the Lamb's

NAME (v)
to give a name to; to call
Matt 1:21 you are to **n** him Jesus,

NARROW (adj)
of slender width
Matt 7:13 only through the **n** gate.
Matt 7:14 the gateway to life is very **n**

NATION, NATIONS (n)
group of people defined by geography or ethnicity
see also GENTILE(S), PEOPLE(S)
Gen 12:2 I will make you into a great **n.**
Gen 17:4 father of a multitude of **n-s!**
Gen 17:16 the mother of many **n-s.**

Gen 25:23 will become two **n-s.**
Gen 28:3 and become many **n-s!**
Exod 19:6 of priests, my holy **n.**
Deut 15:6 You will rule many **n-s,** but
Deut 28:10 the **n-s** of the world will see
Ps 2:8 you the **n-s** as your inheritance,
Ps 22:28 He rules all the **n-s.**
Ps 46:10 I will be honored by every **n.**
Ps 66:7 every movement of the **n-s;**
Ps 68:30 Scatter the **n-s** that delight in
Ps 87:6 the LORD registers the **n-s,**
Ps 99:2 exalted above all the **n-s.**
Ps 113:4 LORD is high above the **n-s;**
Prov 14:34 Godliness makes a **n** great,
Isa 11:10 The **n-s** will rally to him,
Isa 34:1 listen, O **n-s** of the earth.
Isa 40:15 for all the **n-s** of the world
Isa 42:1 He will bring justice to the **n-s.**
Isa 52:15 And he will startle many **n-s.**
Isa 56:7 a house of prayer for all **n-s.**
Isa 60:12 the **n-s** that refuse to serve
Isa 66:8 Has a **n** ever been born in a
Ezek 37:22 divided into two **n-s** or into
Joel 3:2 my people among the **n-s,**
Amos 9:12 **n-s** I have called to be mine.
Mic 4:3 disputes between strong **n-s**
Mic 5:7 take their place among the **n-s.**
Zeph 3:8 stand and accuse these evil **n-s.**
Hag 2:7 I will shake all the **n-s,**
Zech 8:13 Among the other **n-s,** Judah
Zech 12:2 makes the nearby **n-s** stagger
Matt 12:18 proclaim justice to the **n-s.**
Matt 24:14 so that all **n-s** will hear it;
Matt 28:19 make disciples of all the **n-s,**
Mark 11:17 house of prayer for all **n-s,**
Acts 4:25 Why were the **n-s** so angry?
Gal 3:8 All **n-s** will be blessed through
1 Pet 2:9 royal priests, a holy **n,**
Rev 5:9 language and people and **n.**
Rev 14:6 to every **n,** tribe, language,
Rev 21:24 The **n-s** will walk in its light,
Rev 22:2 for medicine to heal the **n-s.**

NATIVITY (KJV)
Gen 11:28 the land of his *birth*
Jer 46:16 to the land of our *birth.*

NATURAL (adj)
having a physical existence as contrasted with one that is spiritual
1 Cor 15:44 as there are **n** bodies,

NATURE (n)
inherent character or essence
Rom 1:20 eternal power and divine **n.**
Rom 8:4 follow our sinful **n**
Rom 8:7 For the sinful **n** is always
Gal 5:19 the desires of your sinful **n,**
Gal 5:24 desires of their sinful **n** to
2 Pet 1:4 share his divine **n** and escape

NAZARENE, NAZARENES (n)
a native or resident of Nazareth; an early name given to followers of Jesus
Matt 2:23 He will be called a **N.**
Acts 24:5 of the cult known as the **N-s.**
Acts 26:9 the very name of Jesus the **N.**

NAZARETH (n)
a town of lower Galilee where Jesus spent his boyhood years
Matt 4:13 He went first to **N,**
Mark 14:67 those with Jesus of **N.**
Mark 16:6 looking for Jesus of **N,** who
John 1:46 anything good come from **N?**

NAZIRITE (n)
a person consecrated to God by a vow to avoid drinking wine, cutting the hair, and being defiled by the presence of a corpse
Num 6:2 take the special vow of a **N,**
Judg 13:7 be dedicated to God as a **N**

NECK (n)
the part of the body that connects the head and the torso
Prov 6:21 Tie them around your **n.**
Matt 18:6 millstone tied around your **n**

NECKLACE (n)
an ornament worn around the neck
Prov 3:22 They are like jewels on a **n.**

NEED, NEEDS (n)
a condition requiring supply or relief; poverty; obligation; a lack of something requisite, desirable, or useful
1 Kgs 8:59 according to each day's **n-s.**
Ps 79:8 quickly meet our **n-s,**
Ps 112:9 give generously to those in **n.**
Prov 11:26 who sells in time of **n.**
Prov 30:8 just enough to satisfy my **n-s.**
Matt 6:2 give to someone in **n,**
Acts 2:45 the money with those in **n.**
Acts 20:35 you can help those in **n** by
Rom 12:13 God's people are in **n,**
1 Cor 7:3 fulfill his wife's sexual **n-s,**
Eph 4:28 give generously to others in **n.**
Phil 4:19 supply all your **n-s** from his
Titus 3:14 by meeting the urgent **n-s**

NEED, NEEDED, NEEDING (v)
to require; to be necessary; to be in want

Ps 34:9 — fear him will have all they **n.**
Ps 119:75 — disciplined me because I **n-ed**
Phil 4:6 — Tell God what you **n,** and
Heb 4:16 — grace to help us when we **n** it
Jas 1:4 — complete, **n-ing** nothing.
Jas 1:5 — If you **n** wisdom, ask our

NEEDLE (n)
a small slender instrument that has an eye for thread at one end and is used for sewing
Matt 19:24 — go through the eye of a **n**

NEEDY (adj)
poverty-stricken; marked by want of affection, attention, or emotional support
1 Sam 2:8 — **n** from the garbage dump.
Ps 9:18 — the **n** will not be ignored
Ps 68:10 — you provided for your **n**
Ps 69:33 — LORD hears the cries of the **n;**
Prov 22:22 — or exploit the **n** in court.
Prov 31:20 — opens her arms to the **n.**

NEGLECT (v)
to disregard; to overlook; to ignore
Deut 12:19 — careful never to **n** the Levites
Deut 14:27 — And do not **n** the Levites
Ezra 4:22 — and don't **n** this matter,
Neh 10:39 — together not to **n** the Temple
Luke 11:42 — do not **n** the more important
1 Tim 4:14 — Do not **n** the spiritual

NEHEMIAH
Cupbearer of the Persian king Artaxerxes (Neh 1:11); governor of Israel (Neh 5:14; 8:9); prayed for restoration (1:4); king commissioned him to rebuild Jerusalem's walls (Neh 2:8); rebuilt walls over opposition (Neh 2:9–6:19); reestablished worship (Neh 8:1-18); prayer of praise and confession (Neh 9); dedicated wall of Jerusalem (Neh 12:27-43).

NEIGHBOR, NEIGHBORS (n)
one living or located near another; fellow man
Lev 19:18 — but love your **n** as yourself.
Ps 15:3 — to gossip or harm their **n-s**
Prov 24:28 — your **n-s** without cause;
Prov 27:10 — better to go to a **n** than
Jer 31:34 — not need to teach their **n-s,**
Mark 12:31 — Love your **n** as yourself.
Luke 10:29 — And who is my **n?**
Rom 13:8 — If you love your **n,** you will
Gal 5:14 — Love your **n** as yourself.
Eph 4:25 — Let us tell our **n-s** the truth,
Heb 8:11 — not need to teach their **n-s,**
Jas 2:8 — Love your **n** as yourself.

NET, NETS (n)
a meshed fabric made of ropes used for catching fish, birds, insects, or other animals
Ps 66:11 — You captured us in your **n**
Ps 141:10 — wicked fall into their own **n-s,**
Hab 1:15 — caught in their **n-s** while they
Matt 4:20 — they left their **n-s** at once and
Matt 13:47 — is like a fishing **n** that was
John 21:6 — Throw out your **n** on the

NEVER (adv)
at no time; not in any degree; not under any condition
1 Chr 29:18 — their love for you **n** changes.
Ps 89:33 — But I will **n** stop loving him
Ps 111:3 — His righteousness **n** fails.
John 14:16 — who will **n** leave you.
Rom 11:29 — his call can **n** be withdrawn.
Rom 12:11 — **N** be lazy, but work hard
1 Cor 15:2 — something that was **n** true

NEVER-ENDING (adj)
unceasing
1 Chr 16:17 — of Israel as a **n** covenant:
Ps 105:10 — of Israel as a **n** covenant:
Luke 3:17 — burning the chaff with **n** fire.

NEW (adj)
fresh; original; different than before; unfamiliar
Ps 98:1 — Sing a **n** song to the LORD,
Jer 31:31 — I will make a **n** covenant with
Ezek 36:26 — I will give you a **n** heart,
Mark 16:17 — will speak in **n** languages.
Luke 22:20 — cup is the **n** covenant
Rom 6:4 — we also may live **n** lives.
Rom 12:2 — you into a **n** person
1 Cor 11:25 — cup is the **n** covenant
2 Cor 3:6 — but under the **n** covenant,
2 Cor 5:17 — is gone; a **n** life has begun!
Gal 6:15 — into a **n** creation.
Eph 4:24 — Put on your **n** nature,
Col 3:10 — Put on your **n** nature,
Heb 8:8 — when I will make a **n** covenant
Heb 9:15 — mediates a **n** covenant
Heb 12:24 — the **n** covenant
2 Pet 3:13 — **n** heavens and **n** earth he
Rev 2:17 — a **n** name that no one
Rev 21:1 — **n** heaven and a **n** earth,

NEWBORN (adj)
recently born
1 Pet 2:2 — Like **n** babies, you must crave

NEWS (n)
a report of recent events; "Good News": the Gospel of Jesus Christ
Isa 40:9 — of good **n,** shout from the

Matt 4:23 the Good **N** about
Mark 1:15 sins and believe the Good **N**!
Luke 4:43 I must preach the Good **N**
Acts 13:32 to bring you this Good **N.**
Acts 14:21 preaching the Good **N**
Rom 1:16 not ashamed of this Good **N**
Rom 10:17 the Good **N** about Christ.
Rom 15:16 I bring you the Good **N**
Rom 16:25 just as my Good **N** says.
1 Cor 1:17 to preach the Good **N**—
1 Cor 9:12 an obstacle to the Good **N**
1 Cor 9:16 preach the Good **N**!
1 Cor 9:23 to spread the Good **N**
1 Cor 15:1 the Good **N** I preached
2 Cor 4:4 glorious light of the Good **N.**
2 Cor 9:13 obedient to the Good **N**
2 Cor 11:7 preaching God's Good **N**
Gal 1:7 is not the Good **N** at all.
Eph 6:15 comes from the Good **N**
Phil 1:27 worthy of the Good **N**
Col 1:5 heard the truth of the Good **N.**
Col 1:23 Good **N** has been preached
1 Thes 2:4 entrusted with the Good **N.**
2 Thes 1:8 obey the Good **N** of our Lord
2 Tim 1:10 through the Good **N.**
2 Tim 4:5 telling others the Good **N,**
Rev 14:6 the eternal Good **N**

NIGHT, NIGHTS (n)
period of darkness between sunset and sunrise; figurative of suffering and sorrow or the reign of sin and immorality
Gen 1:16 smaller one to govern the **n.**
Exod 13:21 provided light at **n**
Job 35:10 who gives songs in the **n?**
Ps 1:2 meditating on it day and **n.**
Ps 19:2 **n** after **n** they make him
Ps 77:6 my **n-s** were filled with joyful
Jonah 1:17 for three days and three **n-s.**
Matt 4:2 days and forty **n-s** he fasted
Matt 12:40 for three days and three **n-s.**
Luke 2:8 That **n** there were shepherds
2 Cor 6:5 endured sleepless **n-s,** and
1 Thes 5:2 like a thief in the **n.**
1 Thes 5:5 belong to darkness and **n.**
Rev 21:25 there is no **n** there.

NINETY-NINE (n)
the number 99
Matt 18:13 than over the **n** that didn't
Luke 15:7 to God than over **n** others

NOAH
Builder of great boat, survivor of the Flood (Gen 6–9; Matt 24:37-38; Luke 17:26-27; Heb 11:7; 1 Pet 3:20; 2 Pet 2:5); family line (Gen 5:25-32); found favor with God (Gen 6:8); enacted covenant between God and all creatures (Gen 9:1-17); made wine and became drunk (Gen 9:18-23); gave blessings and curse to descendants (Gen 9:24-27); considered righteous (Ezek 14:14, 20).

NONSENSE (n)
words or language having no meaning or intelligible ideas; things of no importance or value
Luke 24:11 sounded like **n** to the men,
1 Cor 1:23 the Gentiles say it's all **n.**
Col 2:8 high-sounding **n** that come

NOOSE (n)
a loop with a slipknot that binds closer the more it is drawn
Job 41:1 or put a **n** around its jaw?

NORMAL (adj)
occurring naturally
Rom 1:27 **n** sexual relations with women,

NOSTRILS (n)
the external openings of the nose
Gen 2:7 breath of life into the man's **n,**

NOTES (n)
melody, song; tones
1 Cor 14:7 harp must play the **n** clearly,

NOTHING (pron)
not any thing
Neh 9:21 wilderness, and they lacked **n.**
Eccl 5:5 better to say **n** than to make
Jas 1:4 and complete, needing **n.**

NOTICE (n)
a warning or intimation of something; announcement
Matt 5:31 a written **n** of divorce.

NOTICED (v)
to treat with attention
Job 1:8 Satan, "Have you **n** my servant
Job 2:3 Satan, "Have you **n** my servant

NOTORIOUS (adj)
generally known and talked of; famous
Hab 1:7 They are **n** for their cruelty

NOURISHMENT (n)
food, nutriment; sustenance
John 4:34 my **n** comes from doing the
Rom 11:17 in the rich **n** from the root

NUMBERED (v)
to restrict to a definite number
Ps 39:4 Remind me that my days are **n**—

Matt 10:30 hairs on your head are all **n**.

NUMEROUS (adj)
consisting of great numbers; many
Ps 40:5 plans for us are too **n** to list.

O

OATH (n)
an appeal to God to witness the truth of some statement
Ps 95:11 in my anger I took an **o:**
Ps 110:4 LORD has taken an **o**
Ezek 20:42 I promised with a solemn **o**
Heb 6:16 people take an **o,** they call
Heb 7:20 established with a solemn **o.**
Heb 7:21 was an **o** regarding Jesus.
Jas 5:12 never take an **o,** by heaven

OBEDIENCE (n)
an act or instance of obeying; the quality or state of being obedient
Judg 2:17 who had walked in **o** to the
1 Sam 15:22 **O** is better than sacrifice,
Phil 2:8 humbled himself in **o** to God
Heb 5:8 learned **o** from the things he

OBEDIENT (adj)
submissive to authority; willing to obey
Luke 2:51 with them and was **o** to them.
Rom 16:19 that you are **o** to the Lord.
2 Cor 9:13 that you are **o** to the Good
2 Cor 10:6 you have become fully **o,**
1 Pet 1:14 as God's **o** children.

OBEY, OBEYED, OBEYING, OBEYS (v)
to follow the commands or guidance of; to conform to or comply with
see also KEEP
Gen 22:18 because you have **o-ed** me.
Exod 20:6 love me and **o** my commands.
Lev 18:4 be careful to **o** my decrees,
Lev 25:18 decrees and **o** my regulations.
Deut 4:2 Just **o** the commands of the
Deut 5:27 we will listen and **o.**
Deut 6:17 diligently **o** the commands of
Deut 6:25 when we **o** all the commands
Deut 11:1 and **o** all his requirements,
Deut 11:22 Be careful to **o** all these
Deut 13:4 **O** his commands, listen to his
Deut 26:16 to **o** them wholeheartedly.
Deut 28:1 If you fully **o** the LORD
Deut 30:2 if you **o** with all your heart
Deut 30:12 so we can hear it and **o?**
Deut 30:20 love and **o** the LORD,
Josh 1:7 to **o** all the instructions Moses
Josh 22:5 all his ways, **o** his commands,
1 Sam 7:3 to **o** only the LORD;
1 Kgs 8:61 May you always **o** his decrees
2 Kgs 17:13 **O** my commands and
2 Kgs 18:6 **o-ed** all the commands
2 Kgs 23:3 pledged to **o** the LORD
Neh 1:5 love him and **o** his commands,
Job 36:11 they listen and **o** God,
Ps 111:10 All who **o** his commandments
Ps 119:17 I may live and **o** your word.
Ps 119:129 No wonder I **o** them!
Eccl 8:2 **O** the king since you vowed
Eccl 12:13 and **o** his commands,
Isa 11:3 delight in **o-ing** the LORD.
Jer 32:33 not receive instruction or **o.**
Jer 42:6 For if we **o** him, everything
Jer 43:4 refused to **o** the LORD's
Dan 9:4 love you and **o** your commands.
Dan 9:10 We have not **o-ed** the LORD
Jonah 3:3 This time Jonah **o-ed** the LORD's
Mic 5:15 nations that refuse to **o** me.
Matt 5:19 anyone who **o-s** God's laws
Matt 8:27 the winds and waves **o** him!
Matt 19:20 **o-ed** all these commandments,
Matt 28:20 to **o** all the commands
Luke 8:21 hear God's word and **o** it.
John 3:36 who doesn't **o** the Son
John 8:51 anyone who **o-s** my teaching
John 14:15 **o** my commandments.
Acts 4:19 to **o** you rather than him?
Acts 5:29 We must **o** God rather than
Rom 1:5 believe and **o** him,
Rom 2:27 possess God's law but don't **o**
Rom 3:28 and not by **o-ing** the law.
Rom 6:16 of whatever you choose to **o?**
Rom 6:17 wholeheartedly **o** this
Rom 15:31 in Judea who refuse to **o** God.
2 Cor 10:5 teach them to **o** Christ.
Gal 2:16 Christ, not by **o-ing** the law.
Gal 3:2 by **o-ing** the law of Moses?
Gal 3:10 and **o** all the commands
Eph 2:2 who refuse to **o** God.
Eph 6:1 Children, **o** your parents
Eph 6:5 Slaves, **o** your earthly masters
2 Thes 3:14 who refuse to **o** what we
1 Tim 3:4 who respect and **o** him.
Titus 2:9 Slaves must always **o** their
Heb 11:8 that Abraham **o-ed** when God
Heb 11:31 who refused to **o** God.
Jas 2:8 good when you **o** the royal law
1 Pet 1:2 you have **o-ed** him and have
1 Pet 1:22 when you **o-ed** the truth,
1 Pet 2:8 they do not **o** God's word,
1 Jn 3:22 because we **o** him and do
Rev 22:7 Blessed are those who **o** the

OBLIGATION (n)
something one is bound to do; duty, responsibility
Rom 1:14 a great sense of **o** to people
Rom 8:12 no **o** to do what your sinful
Rom 13:8 except for your **o** to love one

OBSERVE, OBSERVES (v)
to notice or consider; to keep or comply with; to watch carefully
Exod 12:24 descendants must **o** forever.
Lev 25:2 the land itself must **o** a Sabbath
Deut 5:12 **O** the Sabbath day by keeping
Deut 16:13 **o** the Festival of Shelters
Ps 33:14 From his throne he **o-s** all who
Acts 21:24 **o** the Jewish laws.
Gal 3:10 everyone who does not **o**

OBSOLETE (adj)
no longer in use or no longer useful
Heb 8:13 he has made the first one **o.**

OBSTINATE (adj)
unreasonably persistent; stubborn
Isa 48:4 how stubborn and **o** you are
Ezek 3:8 as **o** and hard-hearted as

OCCUPY (v)
to take or hold possession or control of; to reside in as an owner or tenant
Deut 1:8 Go in and **o** it, for it is
Deut 4:14 are about to enter and **o.**

OFFEND, OFFENDED, OFFENDS (v)
to violate, wrong, insult, or hurt; to cause difficulty, discomfort, or injury
Ps 139:24 anything in me that **o-s** you,
1 Cor 1:23 the Jews are **o-ed** and the
Gal 5:11 Christ, no one would be **o-ed.**
Col 3:13 forgive anyone who **o-s** you.

OFFENSE, OFFENSES (n)
a cause or occasion of sin; the act of displeasing
Isa 44:22 I have scattered your **o-s**
Matt 18:15 and point out the **o.**
1 Cor 10:32 Don't give **o** to Jews or

OFFER, OFFERED, OFFERING (v)
to present for acceptance as an act of worship or devotion; to sacrifice
Ps 4:5 **O** sacrifices in the right spirit,
Ps 116:12 What can I **o** the LORD
Mic 6:7 Should we **o** him thousands of
1 Cor 10:20 sacrifices are **o-ed** to demons,
Eph 5:2 He loved us and **o-ed** himself
Heb 7:27 when he **o-ed** himself
Heb 9:14 Christ **o-ed** himself to God
Heb 9:25 to **o** himself again and again,
Heb 10:11 **o-ing** the same sacrifices again
Heb 11:17 that Abraham **o-ed** Isaac
Heb 13:15 let us **o** through Jesus
Jas 5:15 a prayer **o-ed** in faith will heal

OFFERING, OFFERINGS (n)
a sacrifice ceremonially offered as a part of worship; a contribution to the support of a church
Gen 22:8 a sheep for the burnt **o,**
1 Sam 13:9 Bring me the burnt **o**
1 Sam 15:22 burnt **o-s** and sacrifices
Ps 40:6 no delight in sacrifices or **o-s.**
Ps 141:2 hands as an evening **o.**
Isa 53:10 his life is made an **o** for sin,
Hos 6:6 more than I want burnt **o-s.**
Mal 3:8 of the tithes and **o-s**
Mark 12:33 all of the burnt **o-s**
Rom 15:26 taken up an **o** for the poor
Phil 2:17 faithful service is an **o**
Heb 10:5 animal sacrifices or sin **o-s.**
Heb 10:14 that one **o** he forever made
Heb 11:4 Abel's **o** gave evidence that he

OFFICER (n)
one who holds a position of authority or command in the armed forces
Matt 8:5 a Roman **o** came and pleaded
Luke 7:2 slave of a Roman **o** was sick
Acts 10:1 army **o** named Cornelius,
Acts 27:1 a Roman **o** named Julius,

OFFSPRING (n)
children or descendants
see also DESCENDANT(S)
Gen 3:15 between your **o** and her **o**
Acts 17:28 said, 'We are his **o.**'

OIL (n)
liquid produced from olives used in biblical times for lamp fuel, anointing, and dressing wounds; often symbolic of the Holy Spirit
Exod 29:7 anointing **o** over his head.
Exod 30:25 to make a holy anointing **o.**
1 Sam 10:1 **o** and poured it over Saul's
1 Sam 16:13 **o** he had brought and
Ps 23:5 anointing my head with **o.**
Ps 133:2 as precious as the anointing **o**
Heb 1:9 pouring out the **o** of joy

OINTMENT, OINTMENTS (n)
a salve for application to the skin
Isa 1:6 any soothing **o-s** or bandages.
Rev 3:18 and **o** for your eyes so you

OLD, OLDER (adj)
dating from the remote past; advanced in years or age
1 Kgs 12:8 rejected the advice of the **o-er**
2 Cor 3:11 So if the **o** way, which
1 Tim 5:2 Treat **o-er** women as you would
Titus 2:2 Teach the **o-er** men to exercise

OLIVE, OLIVES (n)
a Mediterranean evergreen tree with berries that ripen black; the berries of an olive tree
Gen 8:11 evening with a fresh **o** leaf
Jer 11:16 a thriving **o** tree, beautiful
Zech 4:3 And I see two **o** trees,
Zech 14:4 the Mount of **O-s** will split
Matt 24:3 Jesus sat on the Mount of **O-s.**
Rom 11:17 of God's special **o** tree.
Rom 11:24 cut from a wild **o** tree.
Jas 3:12 Does a fig tree produce **o-s,** or
Rev 11:4 prophets are the two **o** trees

OMEGA (n)
the last letter of the Greek alphabet
Rev 1:8 I am the Alpha and the **O**—
Rev 21:6 I am the Alpha and the **O**—
Rev 22:13 I am the Alpha and the **O,**

ONE (adj)
being a single unit or thing; being in agreement or union
2 Chr 30:12 giving them all **o** heart
Phil 2:2 working together with **o** mind

ONE (n)
a single person or thing
Gen 2:24 the two are united into **o.**
Jas 2:10 all of the laws except **o**

ONIONS (n)
a plant with a large pungent, edible bulb
Num 11:5 melons, leeks, **o,** and garlic

OPEN-MINDED (adj)
receptive to arguments or ideas
Acts 17:11 people of Berea were more **o**

OPENED (v)
to spread out; to unfold
Isa 65:2 All day long I **o** my arms
Rom 10:21 All day long I **o** my arms

OPINIONS (n)
a view, judgment, or appraisal formed in the mind about a particular matter
1 Kgs 18:21 hobbling between two **o?**

OPPONENTS (n)
those who take an opposite position; adversaries
Prov 18:18 disputes between powerful **o.**

OPPORTUNITY (n)
a favorable circumstance or advantage
2 Cor 11:12 looking for an **o** to boast
Gal 6:10 have the **o,** we should do good
Col 4:5 make the most of every **o.**

OPPOSE, OPPOSED, OPPOSES (v)
to set oneself against or opposite someone or something; to resist
Exod 23:22 **o** those who **o** you.
Ps 8:2 enemies and all who **o** you.
Ps 35:1 **o** those who **o** me.
Acts 26:11 was so violently **o-d** to them
Gal 2:11 I had to **o** him to his face,
1 Tim 6:20 with those who **o**
2 Tim 2:25 instruct those who **o**
Titus 1:9 show those who **o** it
Titus 2:8 who **o** us will be ashamed
Jas 4:6 God **o-s** the proud but favors
1 Pet 5:5 God **o-s** the proud but favors

OPPRESS, OPPRESSES, OPPRESSING (v)
to crush or burden by abuse of power or authority
Exod 22:21 not mistreat or **o** foreigners
Prov 22:16 gets ahead by **o-ing** the poor
Prov 28:16 no understanding will **o**
Isa 3:5 People will **o** each other—
Isa 58:3 you keep **o-ing** your workers.
Ezek 18:12 **o-es** the poor and helpless,
Dan 7:25 defy the Most High and **o** the
Amos 5:12 **o** good people by taking
Zech 7:10 Do not **o** widows, orphans,
Jas 2:6 the rich who **o** you and drag

OPPRESSED (n)
those subject to the abuse of another's power or authority
Ps 9:9 a shelter for the **o,** a refuge
Ps 14:6 frustrate the plans of the **o,**
Ps 82:3 uphold the rights of the **o**
Ps 146:7 He gives justice to the **o**
Prov 31:5 not give justice to the **o.**
Isa 1:17 Seek justice. Help the **o.**
Amos 2:7 shove the **o** out of the way.
Luke 4:18 that the **o** will be set free,

OPPRESSION (n)
unjust or cruel exercise of power or authority
Judg 2:18 burdened by **o** and suffering.
Ps 72:14 redeem them from **o** and
Ps 119:134 Ransom me from the **o** of
Isa 58:9 Remove the heavy yoke of **o.**

Heb 11:25 chose to share the **o** of God's

OPPRESSORS (n)
those who abuse power or authority to crush or burden others
Ps 72:4 and to crush their **o.**
Eccl 4:1 The **o** have great power,
Jer 22:3 rescue them from their **o.**

ORDAINED (v)
to appoint someone to a specific duty or office
see also CONSECRATE(D), DEDICATE(D)
Ezek 28:14 I **o** and anointed you

ORDER, ORDERS (n)
a rank, class, or special group in a community or society; a command
Ps 110:4 in the **o** of Melchizedek.
Joel 2:11 they follow his **o-s.**
Mark 1:27 spirits obey his **o-s!**
Heb 5:10 in the **o** of Melchizedek.

ORDER (v)
to command
Ps 91:11 For he will **o** his angels
Matt 4:6 He will **o** his angels

ORPHAN, ORPHANS (n)
a child deprived by death of one or usually both parents
see also FATHERLESS
Exod 22:22 not exploit a widow or an **o.**
Deut 10:18 **o-s** and widows receive
Deut 24:17 among you and to **o-s,**
Deut 24:19 **o-s,** and widows.
Ps 10:14 in you. You defend the **o-s.**
Ps 82:3 justice to the poor and the **o;**
Prov 23:10 the land of defenseless **o-s.**
John 14:18 will not abandon you as **o-s**—
Jas 1:27 caring for **o-s** and widows in

OUTSIDE (prep)
located on the outer side of
1 Tim 3:7 Also, people **o** the church

OUTSMART (v)
to get the better of; to outwit
2 Cor 2:11 Satan will not **o** us.

OUTWARD, OUTWARDLY (adj or adv)
superficial, having to do with external appearance or circumstance only
1 Sam 16:7 People judge by **o** appearance,
Matt 23:28 **o-ly** you look like righteous
1 Pet 3:3 concerned about the **o** beauty

OUTWEIGHS (v)
to exceed in weight, value, or importance
2 Cor 4:17 glory that vastly **o** them and

OVERCOME (v)
to get the better of; to overwhelm
see also CONQUER, VICTORIOUS, VICTORY
Ps 119:133 will not be **o** by evil.
Mark 9:24 but help me **o** my unbelief!
John 16:33 because I have **o** the world.
2 Cor 2:7 may be **o** by discouragement.

OVERFLOW, OVERFLOWED, OVERFLOWS (v)
to fill a space to capacity and spread beyond its limits; to flow over bounds
Ps 23:5 My cup **o-s** with blessings.
Ps 65:11 even the hard pathways **o** with
Prov 3:10 vats will **o** with good wine.
John 15:11 Yes, your joy will **o!**
Rom 15:13 you will **o** with confident
2 Cor 8:2 joy, which has **o-ed** in rich
Phil 1:9 I pray that your love will **o**
Col 2:7 you will **o** with thankfulness.

OVERJOYED (adj)
feeling great joy
Dan 6:23 The king was **o** and ordered
Acts 12:14 she was so **o** that,

OVERLOOKING (v)
to look past; to ignore or excuse
Prov 19:11 they earn respect by **o** wrongs.
Mic 7:18 **o** the sins of his special people?

OVERSEER(S) (KJV)
2 Chr 2:18 and 3,600 as *foremen*
Neh 11:22 *chief officer* of the Levites
Prov 6:7 or *governor* or ruler to make
Acts 20:28 appointed you as *elders*
1 Tim 3:1 an *elder* must be a man whose
1 Pet 2:25 Shepherd, the *Guardian* of

OVERSHADOW (v)
to cast a shadow over
Luke 1:35 power of the Most High will **o**

OVERWHELMED, OVERWHELMING, OVERWHELMS (v)
to overpower in thought or feeling; to submerge; to overthrow
2 Sam 22:5 waves of death **o-ed** me;
Job 19:27 I am **o-ed** at the thought!
Ps 38:4 My guilt **o-s** me—it is
Ps 65:3 we are **o-ed** by our sins,
Ps 90:7 we are **o-ed** by your fury.

Isa 61:10 I am **o-ed** with joy in
Mark 9:15 they were **o-ed** with awe,
2 Cor 1:8 We were crushed and **o-ed**
2 Cor 3:10 with the **o-ing** glory

OWE (v)
to be under obligation to pay or repay in return for something received
Rom 13:7 Give to everyone what you **o**
Phlm 1:19 that you **o** me your very soul!

OWN (adj)
belonging to oneself or itself
Luke 18:9 in their **o** righteousness
1 Cor 13:5 does not demand its **o** way.
Titus 2:14 to make us his very **o** people,

OWN (v)
to have or hold as property
Gen 28:4 May you **o** this land

OX, OXEN (n)
a domestic bovine mammal
Deut 25:4 not muzzle an **o** to keep it
1 Kgs 7:25 base of twelve bronze **o-en,**
1 Kgs 19:20 Elisha left the **o-en**
Isa 1:3 **o** knows its owner, and a
Ezek 1:10 the face of an **o** on the left
1 Cor 9:9 not muzzle an **o** to keep it
1 Tim 5:18 not muzzle an **o** to keep it
Rev 4:7 the second was like an **o;**

PACT (n)
an agreement or covenant between two or more parties
1 Sam 23:18 renewed their solemn **p** before

PAGAN (adj)
of or relating to a pagan
1 Sam 17:26 Who is this **p** Philistine

PAGAN, PAGANS (n)
a follower of a false god or religion; one who delights in sensual pleasures and material goods
Ps 106:35 they mingled among the **p-s**
Isa 2:6 have made alliances with **p-s.**
Matt 5:47 Even **p-s** do that.
Matt 18:17 treat that person as a **p**
1 Cor 5:1 something that even **p-s** don't
1 Cor 12:2 when you were still **p-s**, you

PAID (v)
to render payment or due return
see also PAY
1 Cor 7:23 God **p** a high price for you,
Col 3:25 be **p** back for the wrong
1 Tim 5:17 should be respected and **p**

PAIN, PAINS (n)
physical, mental, or emotional suffering; the spasms of childbirth
Job 6:10 Despite the **p,** I have not
Ps 73:14 every morning brings me **p.**
Jer 4:19 my heart—I writhe in **p!**
Matt 24:8 only the first of the birth **p-s,**
John 16:21 suffering the **p-s** of labor.
Rom 8:22 in the **p-s** of childbirth
Gal 4:19 going through labor **p-s** for
1 Thes 5:3 woman's labor **p-s** begin.
Heb 13:3 as if you felt their **p** in your
Rev 21:4 death or sorrow or crying or **p.**

PAINFUL (adj)
feeling or giving pain
Gen 5:29 the **p** labor of farming
Prov 17:21 **p** to be the parent of a fool;
2 Cor 2:1 grief with another **p** visit.
Heb 12:11 while it is happening—it's **p!**

PALACE, PALACES (n)
the official residence of a chief of state (as a monarch or president)
2 Sam 7:2 living in a beautiful cedar **p,**
Jer 22:6 concerning Judah's royal **p:**
Matt 11:8 expensive clothes live in **p-s.**
Luke 7:25 live in luxury are found in **p-s.**

PALM, PALMS (n)
a long feathery leaf from any of various mostly tropical or subtropical trees; the part of the human hand between the base of the fingers and wrist
Isa 49:16 on the **p-s** of my hands.
John 12:13 took **p** branches and went
Rev 7:9 and held **p** branches

PAMPERED (v)
to treat with extreme or excessive care and attention
Prov 29:21 A servant **p** from childhood

PANIC (n)
a sudden unreasoning terror often accompanied by mass flight
1 Sam 14:15 Suddenly, **p** broke out
Zech 14:13 by the LORD with great **p.**

PANIC (v)
to be affected with panic
Deut 20:3 Do not lose heart or **p**
Mark 13:7 threats of wars, but don't **p.**

PAPERS (n)
a piece of paper containing writing or print; documents

Jer 32:16	had given the **p** to Baruch,
2 Tim 4:13	books, and especially my **p.**

PARABLE, PARABLES (n)
a brief narrative story told with earthly analogies to illustrate a spiritual truth

Ps 78:2	I will speak to you in a **p.**
Matt 13:35	I will speak to you in **p-s.**
Luke 8:10	I use **p-s** to teach the

PARADE (n)
a public procession

1 Cor 4:9	at the end of a victor's **p,**

PARADISE (n)
an intermediate place where the souls of the righteous await resurrection and the final judgment

Luke 23:43	you will be with me in **p.**
2 Cor 12:4	that I was caught up to **p**

PARALYZED (adj)
characterized by the inability to move

Matt 9:2	Jesus said to the **p** man,
Mark 2:3	men arrived carrying a **p** man
John 5:3	blind, lame, or **p**—

PARDON, PARDONED (v)
to allow (an offense) to pass without punishment; to forgive

Num 14:19	**p** the sins of this people,
Deut 29:20	LORD will never **p** such
2 Kgs 5:18	may the LORD **p** me
2 Chr 30:18	LORD, who is good, **p**
Isa 40:2	gone and her sins are **p-ed.**
Jer 5:7	How can I **p** you?
Joel 3:21	I will **p** my people's crimes,
Joel 3:21	which I have not yet **p-ed;**

PARENT, PARENTS (n)
one who produces and cares for offspring
see also FATHER, MOTHER

Exod 20:5	I lay the sins of the **p-s** upon
Prov 13:1	child accepts a **p's** discipline;
Jer 31:29	**p-s** have eaten sour grapes,
Ezek 18:19	child pay for the **p's** sins?
Matt 10:21	will rebel against their **p-s**
Rom 1:30	and they disobey their **p-s.**
Eph 6:1	Children, obey your **p-s**
Col 3:20	always obey your **p-s,**

PART, PARTS (n)
portion or segment; role
see also MEMBER(S)

Rom 12:5	We are many **p-s** of one body,
1 Cor 6:15	are actually **p-s** of Christ?
1 Cor 12:18	each **p** just where he wants
1 Cor 12:28	**p-s** God has appointed for
Gal 5:25	leading in every **p** of our
Eph 4:25	we are all **p-s** of the same body.

PARTIAL (adj)
inclined to favor one party more than the other; of or relating to a part rather than the whole

Lev 19:15	or being **p** to the rich
1 Cor 13:10	**p** things will become

PARTIALITY (n)
the quality or state of being partial
see also FAVORITES, FAVORITISM

Deut 10:17	God, who shows no **p** and
Deut 16:19	twist justice or show **p.**
2 Chr 19:7	perverted justice, **p,**

PARTICIPATE (v)
to have a part or share in something; to take part

1 Cor 10:20	to **p** with demons.
Eph 5:7	**p** in the things these people

PARTNER, PARTNERS (n)
a person with whom one shares an intimate relationship; one associated with another, especially in action

Mal 2:14	she remained your faithful **p,**
2 Cor 6:14	can righteousness be a **p**
Phil 1:5	**p-s** in spreading the Good
1 Pet 3:7	but she is your equal **p** in
1 Pet 4:13	trials make you **p-s** with
3 Jn 1:8	be their **p-s** as they teach
Rev 1:9	your **p** in suffering and in God's Kingdom

PARTNERSHIP (n)
the state of being a partner

1 Cor 1:9	into **p** with his Son,

PARTY, PARTIES (n)
a social gathering

Luke 15:24	So the **p** began.
Rom 13:13	of wild **p-ies** and drunkenness,
1 Pet 4:3	drunkenness and wild **p-ies,**

PASS, PASSED (v)
to move, proceed, go; to go away; to move past

Exod 12:13	the blood, I will **p** over you.
Exod 33:22	my hand until I have **p-ed**
1 Kgs 19:11	there, the LORD **p-ed**
1 Cor 7:31	it will soon **p** away.
2 Pet 3:10	the heavens will **p** away

PASSION, PASSIONS (n)
intense, driving, or overmastering feeling or conviction; ardent affection; sexual desire

Isa 59:17	himself in a cloak of divine **p.**
Zech 8:2	with **p** for Jerusalem!
1 Cor 7:37	he can control his **p,** he does
Gal 5:24	Jesus have nailed the **p-s**
1 Thes 4:5	lustful **p** like the pagans

PASSIONATE (adj)
capable of, affected by, or expressing intense feeling

2 Kgs 19:31	**p** commitment of the LORD
Isa 9:7	**p** commitment of the LORD
Isa 37:32	**p** commitment of the LORD
Zech 1:14	Mount Zion is **p** and strong.
Zech 8:2	Mount Zion is **p** and strong;

PASSOVER (n)
a festival that commemorated the Hebrew departure from Egypt in haste

Num 9:2	celebrate the **P**
Deut 16:1	celebrate the **P** each year
Ezra 6:19	returned exiles celebrated **P.**
Mark 14:12	**P** lamb is sacrificed,
Heb 11:28	to keep the **P** and to sprinkle

PASTORS (n)
spiritual overseers

Eph 4:11	and the **p** and teachers.

PASTURE, PASTURES (n)
land or a plot of land used for grazing

Ps 100:3	his people, the sheep of his **p.**
John 10:9	freely and will find good **p-s.**

PATH, PATHS (n)
course, route; a way of life, conduct, or thought

1 Kgs 8:36	follow the right **p,**
Ps 23:3	He guides me along right **p-s,**
Ps 27:11	Lead me along the right **p,**
Prov 2:13	to walk down dark **p-s.**
Prov 3:6	show you which **p** to take.
Prov 5:21	examining every **p** he takes.
Prov 8:20	in **p-s** of justice.
Prov 14:12	a **p** before each person that
Isa 48:17	leads you along the **p-s**
Hos 14:9	**p-s** of the LORD are true
2 Tim 2:18	have left the **p** of truth,
Heb 12:13	Mark out a straight **p**

PATHWAY (n)
path, course

Ps 32:8	along the best **p** for your life.

PATIENCE (n)
the power or capacity to endure without complaint something difficult or disagreeable; forbearance, longsuffering

Rom 15:5	May God, who gives this **p**
Gal 5:22	joy, peace, **p,** kindness,
Col 1:11	endurance and **p** you need.
Col 3:12	humility, gentleness, and **p.**
2 Tim 3:10	my faith, my **p,** my love,
Titus 2:2	and be filled with love and **p.**
Jas 5:10	examples of **p** in suffering,
2 Pet 3:15	Lord's **p** gives people time

PATIENT (adj)
bearing pains or trials calmly or without complaint; steadfast despite opposition, difficulty, or adversity; not hasty or impetuous

Rom 2:4	and **p** God is with you?
Rom 12:12	Be **p** in trouble,
1 Cor 4:12	We are **p** with those who
1 Cor 13:4	Love is **p** and kind.
1 Thes 5:14	Be **p** with everyone.
Jas 5:8	You, too, must be **p.**

PATIENTLY (adv)
in a patient manner

Ps 40:1	I waited **p** for the LORD
1 Pet 3:20	God waited **p** while Noah
Rev 14:12	endure persecution **p,**

PATTERN (n)
a form or model proposed for imitation

Exod 25:40	according to the **p**
Exod 26:30	the **p** you were shown
2 Tim 1:13	Hold on to the **p**
Heb 8:5	according to the **p**

PAUL
Pharisee and Roman citizen (Acts 22:3); from city of Tarsus (Acts 9:11; Phil 3:5); became apostle (Gal 1) to the Gentiles (Rom 11:13); also known as "Saul" (Acts 7:58; 13:9); supported stoning of Stephen (Acts 8:1); attacked early Christians (Acts 8:1-3; 9:1-2; Gal 1:13); converted on road to Damascus (Acts 9:1-9; 22:6-16; 26:12-18); preached in Damascus (Acts 9:20-22); escaped over the wall in basket (Acts 9:23-25); escaped to Jerusalem, then on to Tarsus (Acts 9:26-30); saw visions in Arabia (Gal 1:17); with Barnabas in Antioch (Acts 11:22-26); sent to Jerusalem (Acts 11:27-30); first missionary journey: Cyprus and Galatia (Acts 13–14); advocate for Gentile believers (Acts 15:1-5); testified at Jerusalem Council (Acts 15:12); split with Barnabas over John Mark (Acts 15:36-41); second missionary journey with Silas: northern and southern Greece, western Asia (Acts 15:36–18:22); received call to Macedonia (Acts 16:6-10); Philippi, Thessalonica, Berea (Acts 16–17); Athens, Corinth (Acts 17–18); third missionary journey: returned to northern and south-

ern Greece, western Asia (Acts 18:23–21:14); Corinth, Ephesus, Macedonia, Troas—to Jerusalem (Acts 18–21); farewell to Ephesian elders (Acts 20:13-38); journey to Rome (Acts 21–28); falsely arrested and in hands of mob (Acts 21:26–22:21); saved by Roman custody (Acts 22:22-29; 23:10); before the Jewish high council (Acts 23:1-11); relocated to Caesarea (Acts 23:12-35); trial before Felix (Acts 24); appealed to Caesar before Festus (Acts 25:1-12), before Herod Agrippa (Acts 25:13–26:32); sailed to Rome, was shipwrecked (Acts 27); arrived in Rome (Acts 28); pattern of self-denial (1 Cor 9); his gospel message (Rom 1–5; Gal 3–6); catalog of trials (2 Cor 11:22-33); his goal (Phil 3:7-15); last known written words (2 Tim 4); intervened for returning slave (Phlm 1:8-22); wrote letters: Romans through Philemon (see the first verse of each book).

PAVEMENT (n)
a surface covered firmly and solidly with material (as asphalt or concrete)
John 19:13 that is called the Stone **P**

PAY (n)
something paid for a purpose and especially as a salary or wage
1 Tim 5:18 who work deserve their **p!**

PAY, PAYS (v)
to suffer the consequences of an act; to requite according to what is deserved; to make due return to for services or goods rendered
see also PAID
Exod 22:3 A thief who is caught must **p**
Deut 32:35 I will **p** them back.
Ps 137:8 Happy is the one who **p-s** you
Matt 22:17 to **p** taxes to Caesar or not?
Rom 12:19 I will **p** them back,
1 Thes 5:15 no one **p-s** back evil
2 Thes 1:6 he will **p** back those who

PAYMENT (n)
the act of paying; something that is paid
Deut 15:2 must not demand **p**
Deut 27:25 anyone who accepts **p**
Hos 9:7 the day of **p** is here.

PEACE (n)
a state of tranquility or quiet; a pact or agreement to end hostilities between those who have been at war or in a state of enmity; harmony in personal relations, especially with God; a state of security or order within a community; freedom from disquieting or oppressive thoughts or emotions
Exod 20:24 and **p** offerings, your sheep
Lev 26:6 I will give you **p** in the land,
Num 6:26 his favor and give you his **p.**
Deut 20:10 offer its people terms for **p.**
1 Sam 7:14 there was **p** between Israel
1 Kgs 5:4 God has given me **p** on every
1 Chr 22:9 a son who will be a man of **p.**
2 Chr 14:7 has given us **p** on every side.
Job 3:26 I have no **p,** no quietness.
Job 25:2 He enforces **p** in the heavens.
Ps 34:14 Search for **p,** and work to
Ps 37:37 awaits those who love **p.**
Ps 120:7 I search for **p;** but when I
Ps 147:14 He sends **p** across your nation
Prov 12:20 hearts that are planning **p!**
Eccl 3:8 for war and a time for **p.**
Isa 9:6 Everlasting Father, Prince of **P.**
Isa 32:17 righteousness will bring **p.**
Isa 48:22 there is no **p** for the wicked,
Isa 52:7 good news of **p** and salvation,
Jer 6:14 give assurances of **p** when
Jer 46:27 return to a life of **p** and quiet,
Ezek 34:25 I will make a covenant of **p**
Zech 8:19 So love truth and **p.**
Matt 5:9 blesses those who work for **p,**
Mark 9:50 live in **p** with each other.
Luke 1:79 guide us to the path of **p.**
John 16:33 you may have **p** in me.
Rom 5:1 by faith, we have **p** with God
Rom 8:6 your mind leads to life and **p.**
1 Cor 14:33 God of disorder but of **p,**
Gal 5:22 love, joy, **p,** patience,
Eph 2:14 Christ himself has brought **p**
Eph 2:15 made **p** between Jews and
Eph 2:17 Good News of **p** to you Gentiles
Eph 6:15 put on the **p** that comes from
Phil 4:7 experience God's **p,**
1 Thes 5:23 God of **p** make you holy
2 Thes 3:16 Lord of **p** himself give you
2 Tim 2:22 faithfulness, love, and **p.**
Heb 13:20 the God of **p**—who brought
Jas 3:17 It is also **p** loving, gentle
1 Pet 3:11 Search for **p,** and work to

PEACEFUL (adj)
quiet, tranquil; devoid of violence or force; of or relating to a state or time of peace
Ps 23:2 leads me beside **p** streams.
Prov 14:30 A **p** heart leads to a healthy
1 Thes 5:3 Everything is **p** and secure,
1 Tim 2:2 we can live **p** and quiet lives
Heb 12:11 a **p** harvest of right living
2 Pet 3:14 effort to be found living **p**

PEACEMAKER, PEACEMAKERS (n)
one who makes peace especially by reconciling parties at variance
Acts 7:26 He tried to be a **p.**
Jas 3:18 **p-s** will plant seeds of peace

PEARL, PEARLS (n)
a white translucent jewel created within certain species of mollusks

Matt 7:6	throw your **p-s** to pigs!
Matt 13:45	on the lookout for choice **p-s.**
1 Tim 2:9	or by wearing gold or **p-s**
Rev 21:21	were made of **p-s—**
Rev 21:21	each gate from a single **p!**

PENALTY (n)
disadvantage, loss, or hardship due to some action

Job 34:36	you deserve the maximum **p**
Rom 3:24	freed us from the **p**

PENNY (n)
the smallest monetary unit

Matt 5:26	you have paid the last **p.**
Luke 12:59	paid the very last **p.**

PENTECOST (n)
a Jewish feast celebrated on the 50th day after the Feast of Unleavened Bread; the day God sent the Holy Spirit after Christ's resurrection

Acts 2:1	the day of **P** all the believers
Acts 20:16	in time for the Festival of **P.**
1 Cor 16:8	until the Festival of **P.**

PEOPLE, PEOPLES (n)
human beings making up a group or assembly or linked by a common interest; clan or nation; humanity
see also NATION(S)

Exod 5:1	says: Let my **p** go
Exod 8:23	between my **p** and your **p.**
Exod 19:5	among all the **p-s** on earth;
Exod 19:8	all the **p** responded together,
Exod 33:13	nation is your very own **p.**
Lev 26:12	and you will be my **p.**
Num 14:11	How long will these **p**
Deut 7:6	you are a holy **p,** who belong
Deut 14:1	are the **p** of the LORD
Deut 32:9	For the **p** of Israel belong
Deut 33:29	**p** saved by the LORD?
Ruth 1:16	Your **p** will be my **p,**
2 Chr 7:20	uproot the **p** from this land
Neh 1:10	The **p** you rescued by your
Neh 8:1	the **p** assembled with a unified
Ps 33:12	whose **p** he has chosen
Ps 53:6	When God restores his **p,**
Ps 94:14	will not reject his **p;**
Ps 96:10	He will judge all **p-s** fairly.
Ps 135:14	will give justice to his **p**
Isa 2:2	**p** from all over the world
Isa 6:10	Harden the hearts of these **p.**
Isa 40:1	Comfort, comfort my **p,**
Isa 49:13	LORD has comforted his **p**
Isa 52:6	I will reveal my name to my **p,**
Isa 53:8	for the rebellion of my **p.**
Isa 55:4	my power among the **p-s.**
Jer 2:11	Yet my **p** have exchanged their
Jer 2:32	my **p** have forgotten me.
Jer 7:16	Pray no more for these **p,**
Jer 32:27	of all the **p-s** of the world.
Dan 8:24	and devastate the holy **p.**
Dan 9:24	decreed for your **p**
Hos 1:10	You are not my **p,**
Hos 2:23	Now you are my **p.**
Mic 4:1	**p** from all over the world
Mic 4:3	LORD will mediate between **p-s**
Matt 4:19	show you how to fish for **p!**
Mark 7:6	**p** honor me with their lips,
Mark 8:27	Who do **p** say I am?
Luke 1:68	visited and redeemed his **p.**
John 11:50	should die for the **p**
John 18:14	should die for the **p.**
Rom 9:25	Those who were not my **p,**
Rom 11:1	**p,** the nation of Israel?
2 Cor 6:16	and they will be my **p.**
Gal 6:16	they are the new **p** of God.
Eph 1:14	purchased us to be his own **p.**
Eph 1:18	he called—his holy **p**
Eph 2:15	creating in himself one new **p**
Eph 4:8	and gave gifts to his **p.**
2 Tim 2:2	trustworthy **p** who will
2 Tim 3:17	and equip his **p** to do every
Titus 2:11	bringing salvation to all **p.**
Titus 2:14	make us his very own **p,**
Heb 4:9	waiting for the **p** of God.
1 Pet 2:9	for you are a chosen **p.**
1 Pet 2:10	now you are God's **p.**
Rev 5:8	prayers of God's **p.**
Rev 10:11	again about many **p-s,**
Rev 18:4	from her, my **p.**
Rev 19:8	of God's holy **p.**
Rev 21:3	home is now among his **p!**

PERFECT (adj)
being entirely without fault or defect; corresponding to an ideal standard or abstract concept; mature, pure, complete

Deut 32:4	the Rock; his deeds are **p.**
Ps 19:7	instructions of the LORD are **p,**
Ps 119:138	laws are **p** and completely
Matt 5:48	you are to be **p,** even as
John 17:23	experience such **p** unity
Gal 3:3	become **p** by your
Col 4:12	God to make you strong and **p,**
Heb 2:10	suffering, a **p** leader,
Heb 5:9	as a **p** High Priest,
Heb 7:19	law never made anything **p.**
Heb 9:11	greater, more **p** Tabernacle
Heb 9:14	as a **p** sacrifice for our sins.
Heb 10:14	he forever made **p** those

Heb 12:23 who have now been made **p.**
Jas 1:25 look carefully into the **p** law
1 Jn 4:18 because **p** love expels all fear.

PERFECT, PERFECTED, PERFECTS (v)
to bring to final form; to refine or improve
Ezek 16:14 splendor and **p-ed** your beauty,
Heb 12:2 champion who initiates and **p-s**

PERFECTION (n)
flawlessness; maturity; an exemplification of supreme excellence
Job 37:16 with wonderful **p** and skill?
Ps 50:2 Mount Zion, the **p** of beauty,
1 Cor 13:10 when the time of **p** comes,
Phil 3:12 I have already reached **p.**
Heb 7:11 achieved the **p** God intended,
Heb 11:40 not reach **p** without us.

PERFORM, PERFORMED, PERFORMING (v)
to carry out; to do
Exod 3:20 **p-ing** all kinds of miracles
2 Sam 7:23 You **p-ed** awesome miracles
John 10:41 John didn't **p** miraculous

PERFUME (n)
a substance that emits a pleasant odor
Eccl 7:1 more valuable than costly **p.**
Mark 14:3 poured the **p** over his head.
2 Cor 2:14 everywhere, like a sweet **p.**
2 Cor 2:16 saved, we are a life-giving **p.**

PERISH, PERISHING (v)
to become destroyed or ruined physically or spiritually; to die
see also DESTROY, DIE
Ps 102:26 They will **p,** but you remain
John 3:16 believes in him will not **p** but
John 10:28 they will never **p.**
2 Cor 2:15 by those who are **p-ing.**
2 Cor 4:3 from people who are **p-ing.**
Jude 1:11 they **p** in their rebellion.

PERMANENT (n)
continuing or enduring without fundamental or marked change; lasting
Num 25:13 a **p** right to the priesthood,

PERMIT, PERMITTED (v)
to consent to; to authorize; to make possible
Matt 16:19 whatever you **p** on earth
Matt 18:18 whatever you **p** on earth
Matt 19:8 "Moses **p-ted** divorce

PERPLEXED (adj)
unable to grasp something clearly; puzzled
Luke 21:25 **p** by the roaring seas and
2 Cor 4:8 **p,** but not driven to despair.

PERSECUTE, PERSECUTED, PERSECUTING (v)
to harass or punish in a manner designed to injure, grieve, or afflict; to cause to suffer because of belief
Ps 140:12 help those they **p;**
Matt 5:10 blesses those who are **p-d**
Matt 5:11 when people mock you and **p**
Matt 5:12 prophets were **p-d**
Matt 5:44 Pray for those who **p** you!
Matt 13:21 **p-d** for believing God's
John 15:20 they **p-d** me, naturally they will **p** you.
Acts 9:4 Why are you **p-ing** me?
Rom 8:35 or are **p-d,** or hungry,
Rom 12:14 Bless those who **p** you.
1 Cor 15:9 the way I **p-d** God's church.
2 Thes 1:7 for you who are being **p-d**

PERSECUTION, PERSECUTIONS (n)
the condition of being persecuted, harassed, or annoyed
Mark 10:30 along with **p.**
2 Cor 12:10 insults, hardships, **p-s,**
2 Thes 1:4 all the **p-s** and hardships
2 Thes 1:5 God will use this **p** to show
2 Tim 3:11 You know how much **p** and
2 Tim 3:12 in Christ Jesus will suffer **p.**
Rev 13:10 must endure **p** patiently

PERSECUTORS (n)
those who persecute
Ps 142:6 Rescue me from my **p,**

PERSEVERANCE (n)
enduring hardships with patience; steadfastness
see also ENDURANCE
1 Tim 6:11 along with faith, love, **p,** and

PERSEVERE (v)
to persist in a state, enterprise, or undertaking in spite of opposition or discouragement
see also ENDURE
Rev 3:10 obeyed my command to **p,**

PERSISTENCE (n)
the action, quality, or state of continuing resolutely in the face of obstacles
Luke 11:8 because of your shameless **p.**

PERSON (n)
human, individual
Ps 119:9 How can a young **p** stay pure?
2 Cor 5:17 to Christ has become a new **p.**
Heb 9:27 just as each **p** is destined to die

PERSUADE, PERSUADED (v)
to move by argument or entreaty to a belief, position, or course of action

Prov 25:15	Patience can **p** a prince,
Acts 19:26	Paul has **p-d** many people
Acts 28:23	tried to **p** them about Jesus
Acts 28:24	were **p-d** by the things he

PERSUASIVE (adj)
tending to persuade

Prov 16:21	and pleasant words are **p.**
Prov 16:23	the words of the wise are **p.**
1 Cor 2:4	clever and **p** speeches,

PERVERSE (adj)
corrupt; improper, incorrect; perverted

Lev 18:23	This is a **p** act.
Lev 20:12	They have committed a **p** act
Phil 2:15	a world full of crooked and **p**

PERVERT, PERVERTED (v)
to cause to turn aside or away from what is good, true, or morally right; to corrupt

1 Sam 8:3	bribes and **p-ed** justice.
Prov 17:23	secret bribes to **p** the course

PETER
Leader of the twelve disciples, also known as "Simon son of John" (John 21:17) and "Cephas" (John 1:42); called to "fish for people" (Matt 4:18-20; Mark 1:16-20; Luke 5:1-11; *see also* John 21:3); mother-in-law healed (Matt 8:14-15; Mark 1:29-31; Luke 4:38-39); called to preach (Mark 1:36-39); brother of Andrew (Matt 10:2; Mark 3:16; Luke 6:14; Acts 1:13); present at raising of the dead (Mark 5:37; Luke 8:51); walked on water (Matt 14:22-33; Mark 6:45-52; John 6:15-21); identified Jesus as the Christ (Matt 16:13-20; Mark 8:27-30; Luke 9:18-20; *see also* John 6:68-69); rebuked by Jesus for lack of heavenly perspective (Matt 16:21-23; Mark 8:32-33; *see also* John 13:6-11); witnessed the Transfiguration (Matt 16:28–17:8; Mark 9:1-13; Luke 9:28-36; 2 Pet 1:16-20); noticed the withered fig tree (Mark 11:21; *see also* Matt 21:20); his denial predicted by Jesus (Matt 26:31-35; Mark 14:27-31; Luke 22:31-34; John 13:36-38); in Gethsemane (Matt 26:36-46; Mark 14:32-42; Luke 22:39-46); cut off ear of Malchus (Matt 26:51; Mark 14:47; Luke 22:50); denied Jesus—then wept (Matt 26:69-75; Mark 14:66-72; Luke 22:54-62; John 18:15-27); visited empty tomb (Luke 24:12; John 20:1-10; *see also* Matt 28:1-8); saw Jesus (Luke 24:34; 1 Cor 15:5); told by Jesus to shepherd his flock (John 21:15-19); in upper room before Pentecost (Acts 1:13); preached at Pentecost (Acts 2); performed miracles (Acts 3:1-10; 5:14-16; 9:32-43); preached at Temple (Acts 3:11-26); preached before Jewish high council (Acts 4:1-22); prophesied death of Ananias and Sapphira (Acts 5:1-11); preached again before Jewish high council (Acts 5:29-32); rebuked power seeker (Acts 8:14-25); healed sick (Acts 9:32-34); raised dead (Acts 9:36-43); introduced Gentiles to gospel (Acts 10–11); rescued by angel from prison (Acts 12:3-19); preached grace at Jerusalem Council (Acts 15); became pillar of the church (Gal 2:9); was correctable (Gal 2:14); wrote letters (1 Pet 1:1; 2 Pet 1:1); had believing wife (1 Cor 9:5).

PHARAOH (n)
the ruler of the ancient Egyptians

Gen 12:15	praises to **P**, their king,
Gen 41:14	went in and stood before **P.**
Exod 14:4	to display my glory through **P**
Exod 14:17	will be displayed through **P**

PHARISEE, PHARISEES (n)
a religious and political party in Palestine in New Testament times known for strict observance of rites and ceremonies of the written law and for insistence on the validity of their own oral traditions concerning the law

Matt 5:20	**P-s,** you will never enter
Matt 16:6	of the yeast of the **P-s**
Matt 23:13	and you **P-s.** Hypocrites!
John 3:1	religious leader who was a **P.**
Acts 23:6	**P,** as were my ancestors!

PHILIP
1. One of the twelve disciples (Matt 10:3; Mark 3:18; Luke 6:14; John 1:43-48; 12:21-22; 14:8; Acts 1:13).
2. Deacon and evangelist (Acts 6:5; Acts 8:5-25); with the Ethiopian eunuch (Acts 8:26-40); hosted Paul in Caesarea (Acts 21:8-9).
3. Son of Herod the Great and Cleopatra of Jerusalem, half-brother of Antipas and Archelaus; tetrarch of the regions north of Galilee (Luke 3:1).
4. Son of Herod the Great and Mariamne; first husband of Herodias, who left him for Herod Antipas (Matt 14:3; Mark 6:17). (He also was half-brother to Archelaus and Antipas.)

PHILISTINE, PHILISTINES (n)
a native or inhabitant of ancient Philistia

Judg 16:20	"Samson! The P-s have come
1 Sam 4:1	was at war with the **P-s.**
1 Sam 17:1	**P-s** now mustered their
1 Sam 17:26	get for killing this **P**
1 Sam 31:1	the **P-s** attacked Israel,

PHILOSOPHERS (n)
persons who seeks wisdom or enlightenment

1 Cor 1:20	leave the **p,** the scholars,

PHILOSOPHIES (n)
theories underlying or regarding a sphere of activity or thought
Col 2:8 capture you with empty **p**

PHYSICAL (adj)
having material existence; of or relating to the body
John 1:13 reborn—not with a **p** birth
Col 1:22 of Christ in his **p** body.
1 Tim 4:8 **P** training is good, but
1 Tim 5:11 **p** desires will overpower
1 Jn 2:16 a craving for **p** pleasure

PICTURE (n)
a representation, image, or copy
1 Pet 3:21 water is a **p** of baptism,

PIERCE, PIERCED (v)
to make a hole through; to stab
Exod 21:6 and publicly **p** his ear
Ps 22:16 have **p-d** my hands and feet.
Zech 12:10 me whom they have **p-d**
Luke 2:35 sword will **p** your very soul.
John 19:37 look on the one they **p-d.**
Rev 1:7 even those who **p-d** him.

PIG, PIGS (n)
a wild or domestic swine
Matt 7:6 Don't throw your pearls to **p-s!**
Mark 5:11 a large herd of **p-s** feeding
Luke 15:15 his fields to feed the **p-s.**
2 Pet 2:22 washed **p** returns to the mud.

PIGEONS (n)
any of the family of birds with a stout body, rather short legs, and smooth and compact plumage
Lev 5:11 turtledoves or two young **p,**
Luke 2:24 turtledoves or two young **p.**

PILATE
The procurator (Roman governor) in Palestine at the time of the crucifixion of Christ (Luke 3:1). "Pontius" was his family name; he questioned Jesus found him innocent; later, influenced by the Jewish leaders, he sentenced him to execution (Matt 27; Mark 15; Luke 23; John 18–19).

PILGRIMS (KJV)
Heb 11:13 *nomads* here on earth
1 Pet 2:11 as "temporary residents and *foreigners*"

PILLAR, PILLARS (n)
a column or shaft standing alone as a monument or supporting a superstructure; miraculous cloud by day and fire by night; memorial pile of stones; a supporting, integral, or upstanding member of a group
Gen 19:26 she turned into a **p** of salt.
Exod 13:21 night with a **p** of fire.
Exod 24:4 set up twelve **p-s,** one for
Deut 1:33 by night and a **p** of cloud by
Judg 16:26 my hands against the **p-s**
Gal 2:9 known as **p-s** of the church,
1 Tim 3:15 **p** and foundation of
Rev 3:12 victorious will become **p-s**

PINIONS (n)
the tips of a bird's wings
Deut 32:11 carried them safely on his **p.**

PIOUS (adj)
marked by or showing reverence for God and devotion to worship; religious
Isa 58:2 Yet they act so **p!**
Col 2:18 insisting on **p** self-denial
Col 2:23 strong devotion, **p** self-denial,

PIT (n)
a hole, shaft, or cavity in the ground; a place or situation of misery, futility, or degradation
Ps 40:2 me out of the **p** of despair,
Luke 14:5 or your cow falls into a **p,**

PITCH (n)
a black or dark sticky substance
Exod 2:3 waterproofed it with tar and **p.**

PITIED (v)
to feel pity for
1 Cor 15:19 we are more to be **p** than

PITY (n)
sympathetic sorrow for one suffering, distressed, or unhappy
Judg 2:18 For the LORD took **p** on
Ps 17:10 They are without **p.**
Ps 69:20 would show some **p;**
Ps 72:13 He feels **p** for the weak
Isa 27:11 show them no **p** or mercy.
Hos 13:14 I will not take **p** on them.

PLAGUE, PLAGUES (n)
a disastrous evil, affliction, or epidemic of infectious disease, issued by God in judgment
2 Chr 6:28 or a **p** or crop disease
Luke 21:11 will be famines and **p-s**
Rev 21:9 the seven last **p-s** came
Rev 22:18 add to that person the **p-s**

PLAGUED (v)
to smite, infest, or afflict with disease, calamity, or natural evil
Ps 73:5 they're not **p** with problems

PLAN, PLANS (n)
a detailed formulation of a program of action; goal, aim
see also PURPOSE
Ps 2:1 waste their time with futile **p-s?**
Ps 33:10 frustrates the **p-s** of the
Ps 40:5 **p-s** for us are too numerous
Isa 30:1 You make **p-s** that are contrary
Isa 32:6 and make evil **p-s.**
Jer 29:11 I know the **p-s** I have for you
Acts 2:23 his prearranged **p** was carried
Acts 4:25 waste their time with futile **p-s?**
Acts 7:44 according to the **p** God had
Rom 16:25 **p** kept secret from
Eph 3:9 this mysterious **p** that God,
Eph 3:11 This was his eternal **p,**
2 Tim 1:9 **p** from before the beginning

PLANNED, PLANNING (v)
to devise or project the realization or achievement of
Prov 12:20 hearts that are **p-ning** peace!
Isa 25:1 You **p-ed** them long ago,
Jer 23:20 has finished all he has **p-ed.**
Eph 2:10 do the good things he **p-ed**

PLANT (n)
a young tree, vine, shrub, or herb planted or suitable for planting
Matt 15:13 **p** not planted by
1 Cor 15:36 it doesn't grow into a **p**

PLANT, PLANTED, PLANTING, PLANTS (v)
to put or set (seeds or plants) in the ground for growth; to establish or settle
Gen 2:8 the LORD God **p-ed** a garden
Gen 8:22 there will be **p-ing** and harvest,
Ps 1:3 like trees **p-ed** along the riverbank,
Ps 126:5 who **p** in tears will harvest
Prov 22:8 who **p** injustice will harvest
Prov 31:16 earnings she **p-s** a vineyard.
Hos 10:12 **P** the good seeds
Amos 9:15 I will firmly **p** them there
Matt 6:26 They don't **p** or harvest or
Matt 13:3 A farmer went out to **p** some
Matt 13:18 about the farmer **p-ing**
1 Cor 3:6 **p-ed** the seed in your hearts,
1 Cor 3:7 who does the **p-ing,**
1 Cor 9:7 What farmer **p-s** a vineyard
1 Cor 15:42 earthly bodies are **p-ed**
2 Cor 9:6 a farmer who **p-s** only a few
Jas 1:21 accept the word God has **p-ed**
Jas 3:18 will **p** seeds of peace

PLANTER (n)
one who cultivates plants
John 4:36 What joy awaits both the **p** and

PLAY, PLAYED (v)
to perform music; to engage in sport or recreation
1 Sam 16:23 David would **p** the harp.
Ps 87:7 The people will **p** flutes
Ps 137:5 forget how to **p** the harp.
Isa 11:8 baby will **p** safely near the hole
Luke 7:32 so we **p-ed** funeral songs,

PLEA, PLEAS (n)
an earnest entreaty; appeal
1 Kgs 8:28 prayer and my **p,** O LORD
Ps 102:17 He will not reject their **p-s.**

PLEAD, PLEADING, PLEADS (v)
to entreat or appeal earnestly; to argue a case or cause
Job 9:15 I could only **p** for mercy.
Lam 3:56 Listen to my **p-ing!**
Hos 10:8 and **p** with the hills,
Acts 16:9 **p-ing** with him, "Come over
Rom 8:27 the Spirit **p-s** for us
Rom 8:34 right hand, **p-ing** for us.
2 Cor 5:20 speak for Christ when we **p,**

PLEASANT (adj)
having qualities that tend to give pleasure; agreeable
Gen 49:15 and how **p** the land,
Ps 16:6 given me is a **p** land.
Prov 16:21 and **p** words are persuasive.
Isa 5:7 of Judah are his **p** garden.

PLEASE, PLEASED, PLEASES (v)
to make glad; to satisfy; to like or wish; to be the will or pleasure of
Deut 12:25 doing what **p-s** the LORD.
Ps 135:6 The LORD does whatever **p-s**
Prov 16:7 people's lives **p** the LORD,
Isa 42:1 my chosen one, who **p-s** me.
Matt 12:18 my Beloved, who **p-s** me.
Luke 2:14 those with whom God is **p-d.**
Luke 10:21 Yes, Father, it **p-d** you to do
John 8:29 I always do what **p-s** him.
Rom 8:8 sinful nature can never **p** God.
Rom 14:18 this attitude, you will **p** God,
2 Cor 5:9 our goal is to **p** him.
Gal 6:8 live to **p** the Spirit will harvest
Eph 5:10 determine what **p-s** the
Phil 2:13 power to do what **p-s** him.
Col 1:10 always honor and **p** the Lord,
Col 1:19 God in all his fullness was **p-d**
1 Thes 2:4 Our purpose is to **p** God,
1 Thes 2:15 They fail to **p** God
1 Tim 2:3 is good and **p-s** God our
1 Tim 5:4 is something that **p-s** God.
Heb 10:6 not **p-d** with burnt offerings
Heb 11:6 to **p** God without faith.
Heb 13:16 sacrifices that **p** God.

1 Pet 2:19	God is **p-d** with you when
1 Jn 2:17	does what **p-s** God will live
Rev 4:11	you created what you **p-d.**

PLEASING (adj)
giving pleasure; agreeable

Lev 1:9	a special gift, a **p** aroma
Ps 19:14	of my heart be **p** to you,
Ps 104:34	my thoughts be **p** to him,
Eccl 7:26	who are **p** to God will escape
Rom 12:2	is good and **p** and perfect.
Phil 4:18	is acceptable and **p** to God.

PLEASURE, PLEASURES (n)
desire, inclination; a source of delight or joy; sensual gratification

Ps 5:4	you take no **p** in wickedness;
Ps 16:3	I take **p** in them!
Ps 16:11	the **p-s** of living with you
Isa 1:11	I get no **p** from the blood of
Luke 8:14	cares and riches and **p-s**
Eph 1:9	a plan to fulfill his own good **p.**
1 Tim 5:6	widow who lives only for **p**
2 Tim 3:4	and love **p** rather than God.
Titus 2:12	living and sinful **p-s.**
Titus 3:3	slaves to many lusts and **p-s.**
Heb 11:25	the fleeting **p-s** of sin.
Jas 4:3	only what will give you **p.**

PLEDGE (n)
a binding promise or agreement to do or forbear

1 Tim 5:12	breaking their previous **p.**

PLENTY (n)
the full or more-than-adequate amount or supply

Ps 17:14	May their children have **p,**
Prov 12:11	A hard worker has **p** of food,
2 Cor 8:14	now you have **p** and can help
2 Cor 9:8	**p** left over to share with others.

PLOT, PLOTS (v)
to plan or contrive especially secretly; to scheme

Prov 3:29	**p** harm against your neighbor
Prov 6:14	perverted hearts **p** evil,
Prov 6:18	a heart that **p-s** evil,

PLOWS (v)
to turn, break up, or work with a plow

1 Cor 9:10	the one who **p** and the one

PLOWSHARES (n)
a part of a plow that cuts the furrow

Isa 2:4	hammer their swords into **p**
Joel 3:10	Hammer your **p** into swords
Mic 4:3	hammer their swords into **p**

PLUNDER (v)
to take by force (as in war)

Matt 12:29	like Satan and **p** his goods?

PLUNGE (v)
to cause to enter a state or course of action usually suddenly, unexpectedly, or violently; to act with reckless haste

1 Tim 6:9	desires that **p** them into ruin
1 Pet 4:4	no longer **p** into the flood of

POINT (n)
a particular place; a particular step, stage, or degree in development

Matt 4:5	the highest **p** of the Temple,
Matt 26:38	grief to the **p** of death.

POINT (v)
to indicate the fact or probability of something specified

John 5:39	But the Scriptures **p** to me!

POISON (n)
a substance that usually kills, injures, or impairs an organism; something destructive or harmful

2 Kgs 4:40	there's **p** in this stew!
Jas 3:8	and evil, full of deadly **p.**

POISONOUS (adj)
destructive, harmful; venomous

Mark 16:18	**p,** it won't hurt them.

POLISHED (adj)
smooth or glossy; burnished

Dan 10:6	feet shone like **p** bronze,
Rev 1:15	feet were like **p** bronze refined
Rev 2:18	feet are like **p** bronze:

POLLUTE, POLLUTES, POLLUTING (v)
to make ceremonially, physically, or morally impure

Num 35:33	for murder **p-s** the land.
Prov 25:26	it's like **p-ing** a fountain
Isa 41:24	who choose you **p** themselves.

POMEGRANATES (n)
red fruit about the size of an orange with a thick, leathery skin and many tartish seeds

Exod 28:33	Make **p** out of blue, purple,
Song 4:3	Your cheeks are like rosy **p**

PONDER, PONDERED (v)
to think or consider especially quietly, soberly, and deeply
see also MEDITATE

Ps 111:2	delight in him should **p**
Ps 119:59	I **p-ed** the direction of my life,

Ps 143:5	I **p** all your great works

POOR (adj)
characterized by poverty or insufficient resources; humble

Deut 15:4	should be no **p** among you,
Deut 15:11	some in the land who are **p.**
Deut 24:12	If your neighbor is **p**
1 Sam 2:7	The LORD makes some **p**
Ps 35:10	protects the helpless and **p**
Prov 10:4	Lazy people are soon **p;**
Prov 13:7	Some who are **p** pretend
Prov 22:2	rich and **p** have this
Mark 12:42	Then a **p** widow came and
2 Cor 8:9	for your sakes he became **p,**
Jas 2:2	another comes in who is **p**

POOR (n)
those characterized by poverty or insufficient resources

Lev 19:10	Leave them for the **p**
Job 5:16	at last the **p** have hope,
Ps 41:1	those who are kind to the **p!**
Ps 82:3	Give justice to the **p** and the
Prov 14:21	those who help the **p.**
Prov 17:5	mock the **p** insult
Prov 21:13	cries of the **p** will be ignored
Prov 22:22	Don't rob the **p** just because
Prov 28:27	Whoever gives to the **p** will
Prov 31:20	helping hand to the **p**
Isa 3:14	things stolen from the **p.**
Isa 14:30	I will feed the **p** in my pasture;
Isa 32:7	They lie to convict the **p,**
Isa 61:1	to bring good news to the **p.**
Jer 22:16	help to the **p** and needy,
Amos 4:1	who oppress the **p** and crush
Amos 5:11	trample the **p,** stealing their
Zech 7:10	foreigners, and the **p.**
Matt 11:5	is being preached to the **p.**
Matt 19:21	and give the money to the **p,**
Mark 14:7	You will always have the **p**
Luke 4:18	to bring Good News to the **p.**
Luke 14:13	Instead, invite the **p,** the
John 12:8	You will always have the **p**
Rom 15:26	an offering for the **p** among
Jas 2:6	you dishonor the **p!**

PORTIONS (n)
an often limited part set off or abstracted from a whole; share

Num 18:29	give to the LORD the best **p**

POSITION (n)
social or official rank or status; job

Ps 109:8	let someone else take his **p.**
Acts 1:20	Let someone else take his **p.**
1 Tim 3:1	he desires an honorable **p.**

POSSESS, POSSESSED (v)
to seize, gain, or take (control of); to own
see also INHERIT

Ps 37:11	The lowly will **p** the land
Ps 37:29	The godly will **p** the land
John 7:20	You're demon **p-ed!**
John 8:48	you were **p-ed** by a demon?
John 8:52	you are **p-ed** by a demon.
John 10:20	He's demon **p-ed** and out
John 10:21	like a man **p-ed** by a demon!
Phil 3:12	press on to **p** that perfection

POSSESSION, POSSESSIONS (n)
something owned, occupied, or controlled
see also INHERITANCE, RICHES, TREASURE(S), WEALTH

Exod 6:8	as your very own **p.**
Deut 4:20	and his special **p,**
Deut 32:9	is his special **p.**
Zech 2:12	the LORD's special **p**
Matt 19:21	sell all your **p-s** and
Mark 10:22	for he had many **p-s.**
1 Pet 2:9	God's very own **p.**

POSSIBLE (adj)
being within the limits of ability, capacity, or realization

Matt 19:26	with God everything is **p.**
Matt 26:39	**p,** let this cup of suffering
Mark 9:23	Anything is **p** if a person
Mark 10:27	Everything is **p** with God.
Mark 14:35	if it were **p,** the awful hour
Heb 10:4	it is not **p** for the blood

POTTER (n)
one who makes pottery

Isa 29:16	**p** who made me is stupid"?
Isa 64:8	the clay, and you are the **p.**
Zech 11:13	threw them to the **p**
Matt 27:7	to buy the **p's** field,
Rom 9:21	a **p** makes jars out of clay,

POUR, POURED, POURING, POURS (v)
to move or come continuously; to supply or produce freely

Ps 42:8	LORD **p-s** his unfailing love
Ps 45:7	**p-ing** out the oil of joy on
Isa 32:15	Spirit is **p-ed** out on us
Isa 44:3	I will **p** out my Spirit
Ezek 39:29	I will **p** out my Spirit
Joel 2:28	I will **p** out my Spirit
Zech 12:10	I will **p** out a spirit of
Mal 3:10	I will **p** out a blessing
Luke 22:20	blood, which is **p-ed** out

Acts 2:17 I will **p** out my Spirit
Acts 2:33 the Holy Spirit to **p** out
Acts 10:45 Holy Spirit had been **p-ed**
Eph 1:6 grace he has **p-ed** out on us
Phil 2:17 **p-ing** it out like a liquid
Titus 3:6 generously **p-ed** out the Spirit

POVERTY (n)
the state of one who lacks money or material possessions
Prov 6:11 **p** will pounce on you like
Prov 13:18 end in **p** and disgrace;
Prov 21:5 hasty shortcuts lead to **p.**
Prov 24:34 **p** will pounce on you like
Prov 31:7 drink to forget their **p**
2 Cor 8:9 by his **p** he could make you
Rev 2:9 your suffering and your **p**—

POWER, POWERS (n)
ability to act or produce an effect; possession of control, authority, or influence over others; physical might; mental or moral efficacy; a controlling group
see also STRENGTH
Exod 15:6 LORD, is glorious in **p.**
Deut 8:18 one who gives you **p** to be
Ps 89:7 angelic **p-s** stand in awe
Isa 40:26 great **p** and incomparable
Jer 9:23 the powerful boast in their **p,**
Mic 3:8 I am filled with **p**—
Matt 16:18 all the **p-s** of hell will not
Matt 22:29 don't know the **p** of God.
Luke 1:35 the **p** of the Most High will
Luke 4:14 the Holy Spirit's **p.**
Luke 9:1 gave them **p** and authority
Luke 10:19 over all the **p** of the enemy,
Luke 11:20 demons by the **p** of God,
Acts 1:8 receive **p** when the Holy Spirit
Rom 1:16 the **p** of God at work,
Rom 1:20 his eternal **p** and divine
Rom 6:9 Death no longer has any **p** over
Rom 7:23 another **p** within me that is
Rom 8:38 not even the **p-s** of hell can
Rom 15:13 the **p** of the Holy Spirit.
1 Cor 1:18 is the very **p** of God.
1 Cor 6:14 from the dead by his **p,**
1 Cor 15:24 ruler and authority and **p.**
2 Cor 4:7 our great **p** is from God,
2 Cor 13:4 now lives by the **p** of God.
Eph 6:10 Lord and in his mighty **p.**
Phil 3:10 and experience the mighty **p**
Col 1:11 with all his glorious **p**
Col 1:29 on Christ's mighty **p**
1 Thes 1:5 words but also with **p,**
2 Tim 1:7 but of **p,** love, and
2 Tim 3:5 reject the **p** that could make
Heb 2:14 break the **p** of the devil,
Jas 5:16 righteous person has great **p**
1 Pet 1:5 is protecting you by his **p**
1 Pet 3:22 **p-s** accept his authority.
1 Pet 4:11 All glory and **p** to him
2 Pet 1:3 **p,** God has given us everything
Jude 1:25 **p,** and authority are his
Rev 4:11 receive glory and honor and **p.**
Rev 5:12 receive **p** and riches and
Rev 19:1 glory and **p** belong to our God.
Rev 20:6 the second death holds no **p,**

POWERFUL (adj)
having great power, prestige, or influence
Exod 6:6 will redeem you with a **p** arm
Deut 5:15 strong hand and **p** arm.
Job 25:2 God is **p** and dreadful.
Ps 29:4 the LORD is **p;**
Ps 136:12 strong hand and **p** arm.
Jer 9:23 the **p** boast in their power,
Jer 27:5 my great strength and **p** arm
Luke 24:19 who did **p** miracles,
1 Cor 1:27 to shame those who are **p.**

POWERLESS (adj)
devoid of strength or resources; lacking the authority or capacity to act
Num 24:13 would be **p** to do anything
1 Cor 1:27 things that are **p** to shame

PRACTICE, PRACTICING (v)
to do or perform often, habitually, or customarily; to carry out, apply
Lev 19:26 Do not **p** fortune-telling
Matt 23:3 they don't **p** what they teach.
Rom 12:13 eager to **p** hospitality.
Phil 4:9 putting into **p** all you learned
1 Jn 1:6 we are not **p-ing** the truth.
1 Jn 5:18 not make a **p** of sinning,

PRAISE, PRAISES (n)
worship; commendation; value, merit
Deut 26:19 **p,** honor, and renown.
2 Sam 22:4 LORD, who is worthy of **p,**
2 Chr 29:30 So they offered joyous **p**
Ps 7:17 I will sing **p** to the name
Ps 18:49 I will sing **p-s** to your name.
Ps 34:1 will constantly speak his **p-s.**
Ps 65:1 What mighty **p,** O God,
Ps 81:1 Sing **p-s** to God,
Ps 100:4 into his courts with **p.**
Ps 108:1 your **p-s** with all my heart!
Ps 145:3 He is most worthy of **p!**
Ps 149:6 Let the **p-s** of God be in
John 12:43 loved human **p** more than
Rom 2:29 heart seeks **p** from God,
Rom 15:9 will sing **p-s** to your name.

1 Thes 2:6 As for human **p,**
2 Thes 1:10 his holy people—**p** from all
Jas 5:13 You should sing **p-s.**

PRAISE, PRAISED, PRAISES, PRAISING (v)
to worship, commend, or give honor to
Exod 15:2 and I will **p** him—
1 Chr 16:35 name and rejoice and **p** you.
2 Chr 5:13 together in unison to **p** and
2 Chr 20:21 **p-ing** him for his holy
Neh 9:5 Stand up and **p** the LORD
Ps 9:1 I will **p** you, LORD,
Ps 12:8 evil is **p-d** throughout the land.
Ps 34:1 I will **p** the LORD
Ps 42:5 I will **p** him again—
Ps 45:17 nations will **p** you forever
Ps 51:15 my mouth may **p** you.
Ps 63:3 how I **p** you!
Ps 71:8 I can never stop **p-ing** you;
Ps 71:14 I will **p** you more and
Ps 74:21 and needy **p** your name.
Ps 89:5 angels will **p** you for your
Ps 96:2 LORD; **p** his name.
Ps 102:18 not yet born will **p** the
Ps 104:1 all that I am **p** the
Ps 115:18 But we can **p** the LORD
Ps 135:20 LORD, **p** the LORD!
Ps 144:1 **P** the LORD, who is
Ps 148:13 Let them all **p** the name
Ps 150:2 **p** his unequaled greatness!
Prov 27:2 Let someone else **p** you,
Prov 27:21 person is tested by being **p-d.**
Isa 63:7 I will **p** the LORD
Dan 2:19 Daniel **p-d** the God of heaven.
Dan 2:20 He said, "**P** the name
Dan 4:34 **p-d** and worshiped the Most
Matt 5:16 will **p** your heavenly Father.
Mark 11:9 were shouting, "**P** God!
Luke 1:46 how my soul **p-s** the Lord.
Luke 2:13 armies of heaven—**p-ing** God
Luke 2:20 glorifying and **p-ing** God for
Luke 18:43 all who saw it **p-d** God, too.
Luke 19:37 **p-ing** God for all the wonderful
Acts 2:47 all the while **p-ing** God
Acts 10:46 in other tongues and **p-ing** God
1 Cor 14:16 if you **p** God only in
Gal 1:24 they **p-d** God because of me.
Eph 1:6 we **p** God for the glorious
Jas 3:9 Sometimes it **p-s** our Lord
Rev 19:1 heaven shouting, "**P** the LORD!

PRAY, PRAYED, PRAYING, PRAYS (v)
to address God with adoration, confession, supplication, or thanksgiving; to intercede
Gen 24:45 I had finished **p-ing** in my
1 Sam 1:12 she was **p-ing** to the LORD,
2 Chr 7:14 humble themselves and **p** and
2 Chr 30:18 King Hezekiah **p-ed** for
Neh 4:9 we **p-ed** to our God and
Job 42:8 servant Job will **p** for you,
Job 42:10 When Job **p-ed** for his friends,
Ps 5:2 I **p** to no one but you.
Ps 32:6 all the godly **p** to you
Ps 34:6 In my desperation I **p-ed,**
Dan 6:10 He **p-ed** three times a day,
Dan 9:4 I **p-ed** to the LORD
Jonah 2:1 Jonah **p-ed** to the LORD
Matt 6:5 When you **p,** don't be like
Matt 6:9 **P** like this: Our Father in
Matt 26:39 face to the ground, **p-ing,**
Mark 11:24 you can **p** for anything,
Mark 11:25 when you are **p-ing,** first
Luke 3:21 **p-ing,** the heavens opened,
Luke 9:29 he was **p-ing,** the appearance
Luke 11:1 teach us to **p,** just as John
Luke 22:41 and knelt down and **p-ed,**
John 17:20 I am **p-ing** not only for these
Acts 6:6 apostles, who **p-ed** for them
Acts 9:11 He is **p-ing** to me right now.
Acts 16:25 Paul and Silas were **p-ing**
Rom 8:26 the Holy Spirit **p-s** for us
Rom 12:12 and keep on **p-ing.**
Rom 15:30 join in my struggle by **p-ing**
1 Cor 14:14 For if I **p** in tongues,
1 Cor 14:14 my spirit is **p-ing,**
2 Cor 13:9 We **p** that you will become
Eph 1:18 I **p** that your hearts will be
Eph 3:16 I **p** that from his glorious,
Phil 4:6 instead, **p** about everything.
1 Thes 1:3 As we **p** to our God and
1 Thes 5:17 Never stop **p-ing.**
2 Thes 1:11 we keep on **p-ing** for you,
1 Tim 2:8 to **p** with holy hands
Jas 5:13 You should **p.**
Jas 5:16 **p** for each other so that
Jude 1:20 **p** in the power of the Holy

PRAYER, PRAYERS (n)
conversation with God—in praise, thanksgiving, or intercession
2 Chr 30:27 God heard their **p** from
Ps 4:1 mercy on me and hear my **p.**
Ps 17:1 Pay attention to my **p,**
Ps 20:5 LORD answer all your **p-s.**
Ps 86:6 Listen closely to my **p,**
Prov 15:8 in the **p-s** of the upright.
Isa 1:15 Though you offer many **p-s,**
Isa 56:7 will be called a house of **p**
Matt 11:25 Jesus prayed this **p:**
John 17:9 My **p** is not for the world,
Acts 1:14 were constantly united in **p,**
Acts 4:31 After this **p,** the meeting

Acts 6:4 can spend our time in **p**
Acts 10:31 your **p** has been heard,
Acts 13:3 So after more fasting and **p,**
Eph 6:18 persistent in your **p-s** for all
Col 4:2 Devote yourselves to **p** with an
1 Pet 3:7 your **p-s** will not be hindered.
1 Pet 3:12 ears are open to their **p-s.**
Rev 5:8 are the **p-s** of God's people.

PREACH, PREACHED, PREACHES, PREACHING (v)
to deliver a sermon; to exhort an idea or course of action
see also PROCLAIM, TEACH
Luke 9:6 **p-ing** the Good News and
Luke 9:60 go and **p** about the Kingdom
Acts 5:42 teach and **p** this message:
Acts 9:20 he began **p-ing** about Jesus
Acts 16:10 to **p** the Good News
Acts 18:5 all his time **p-ing** the word.
Rom 1:15 to **p** the Good News.
1 Cor 2:4 my message and my **p-ing**
1 Cor 9:27 I fear that after **p-ing** to
1 Cor 15:1 Good News I **p-ed** to you
2 Cor 4:5 We **p** that Jesus Christ is Lord,
2 Cor 11:4 Jesus than the one we **p,**
Gal 1:8 **p-es** a different kind of Good
Gal 1:8 than the one we **p-ed** to you.
Gal 1:9 **p-es** any other Good News
Gal 5:11 no longer **p-ing** salvation
Phil 1:18 Christ is being **p-ed** either way,
Col 1:23 Good News has been **p-ed** all
1 Tim 5:17 work hard at both **p-ing** and
2 Tim 4:17 might **p** the Good News
1 Pet 1:25 Good News that was **p-ed** to
1 Pet 3:19 went and **p-ed** to the spirits

PREACHER (n)
one who delivers sermons or proclaims the gospel
1 Tim 2:7 chosen as a **p** and apostle
2 Tim 1:11 God chose me to be a **p,**

PRECEPT(S) (KJV)
Ps 119:15 study your *commandments*
Ps 119:159 I love your *commandments,*
Mark 10:5 this *commandment* only as a
Heb 9:19 each of God's *commandments*

PRECIOUS (adj)
of great value or high price; highly esteemed or cherished
Prov 31:10 She is more **p** than rubies.
Isa 28:16 It is a **p** cornerstone
1 Pet 1:19 was the **p** blood of Christ,
2 Pet 1:4 great and **p** promises.

PREDICTED (v)
to declare or indicate in advance; to foretell
Isa 43:12 First I **p** your rescue,
John 12:38 the prophet had **p:**
Acts 7:52 **p** the coming of

PREDICTIONS (n)
something that is predicted; forecast
Isa 44:26 I carry out the **p** of my
Jer 28:9 Only when his **p** come true

PREGNANCY (n)
the condition of being pregnant
Gen 3:16 sharpen the pain of your **p,**

PREGNANT (adj)
containing a developing unborn offspring within the body
Gen 11:30 was unable to become **p**
Matt 24:19 How terrible it will be for **p**
1 Thes 5:3 as a **p** woman's labor

PREPARE, PREPARED (v)
to make ready beforehand for some purpose, use, or activity; to get ready
Exod 23:20 to the place I have **p-d** for
Ps 23:5 You **p** a feast for me
Zeph 1:7 LORD has **p-d** his people
Mal 3:1 he will **p** the way before me.
Matt 3:3 '**P** the way for the Lord's
Matt 25:34 inherit the Kingdom **p-d**
John 14:2 I am going to **p** a place
1 Cor 2:9 has **p-d** for those who love
2 Cor 5:5 God himself has **p-d** us for
2 Tim 4:2 the word of God. Be **p-d,**

PRESBYTERY (KJV)
1 Tim 4:14 *elders of the church* laid their hands

PRESENCE (n)
company; nearness; (symbolic of) God-with-us
Exod 25:30 Bread of the **P** on the table
1 Sam 6:20 in the **p** of the LORD,
Ps 15:1 enter your **p** on your holy hill?
Ps 21:6 given him the joy of your **p.**
Ps 23:5 in the **p** of my enemies.
Ps 31:20 in the shelter of your **p,**
Ps 89:15 walk in the light of your **p,**
Ps 114:7 at the **p** of the God of Jacob.
Ps 139:7 never get away from your **p!**
Isa 53:2 grew up in the LORD's **p**
Jer 5:22 tremble in my **p?**
Matt 18:10 always in the **p** of my heavenly
1 Thes 3:9 joy as we enter God's **p.**

PRESENT (adj)
being in view or at hand; now existing or in progress
Lev 16:2 I myself am **p** in the cloud
1 Cor 7:26 Because of the **p** crisis,

PRESENT, PRESENTED, PRESENTING (v)
to give or bestow formally
Gen 28:22 I will **p** to God a tenth
Matt 5:23 you are **p-ing** a sacrifice
Rom 3:25 **p-ed** Jesus as the sacrifice
Rom 15:19 fully **p-ed** the Good News
Eph 5:27 did this to **p** her to himself
2 Tim 2:15 Work hard so you can **p**

PRESERVE, PRESERVES (v)
to keep safe from injury, harm, or destruction
see also SAVE
Gen 45:5 ahead of you to **p** your lives.
Deut 33:12 **p-s** them from every harm.
1 Kgs 19:18 I will **p** 7,000 others
Jer 10:12 he **p-s** it by his wisdom.

PRESS (v)
to follow through (a course of action)
Phil 3:12 I **p** on to possess that
Phil 3:14 I **p** on to reach the end

PRESSURE (n)
the burden of physical or mental distress
Prov 24:10 **p**, your strength is too small.

PRETEND, PRETENDED (v)
to give a false appearance of being, possessing, or performing
1 Sam 21:13 So he **p-ed** to be insane,
Zech 13:4 No one will **p** to be a prophet
Rom 12:9 Don't just **p** to love

PRETENSE (n)
professed rather than real intention or purpose
Amos 5:21 I hate all your show and **p**—

PREVAIL, PREVAILS (v)
to triumph
Prov 19:21 LORD's purpose will **p.**
Isa 42:4 lose heart until justice **p-s**

PRICE (n)
the quantity of one thing that is exchanged or demanded in barter or sale for another
Job 28:18 **p** of wisdom is far above
1 Cor 6:20 bought you with a high **p.**

PRIDE (n)
inordinate self-esteem or conceit; disdainful behavior or treatment of others
Ps 101:5 will not endure conceit and **p.**
Prov 6:3 Now swallow your **p;**
Prov 8:13 I hate **p** and arrogance,
Mark 7:22 envy, slander, **p,** and
1 Jn 2:16 **p** in our achievements and

PRIEST, PRIESTS (n)
one authorized to perform the sacred rites of sacrifice and worship; a mediator between God and humans
Exod 19:6 will be my kingdom of **p-s,**
Ps 110:4 You are a **p** forever
Mal 1:6 Armies says to the **p-s:**
Heb 4:14 since we have a great High **P**
Heb 5:6 You are a **p** forever
Heb 6:20 our eternal High **P**
Heb 8:1 a High **P** who sat down
1 Pet 2:5 you are his holy **p-s.**
1 Pet 2:9 You are royal **p-s,**
Rev 5:10 Kingdom of **p-s** for our God.
Rev 20:6 but they will be **p-s** of God

PRIESTHOOD (n)
the office, dignity, or character of a priest
Heb 7:24 his **p** lasts forever.

PRINCE, PRINCES (n)
a son of a king; the ruler of a principality or state; a man of high rank or high standing in his class or profession
Ps 118:9 LORD than to trust in **p-s.**
Prov 25:15 Patience can persuade a **p,**
Isa 9:6 Everlasting Father, **P** of Peace.
Ezek 34:24 David will be a **p** among
Dan 8:25 take on the **P** of **p-s**
Matt 10:25 called the **p** of demons,
Luke 11:15 the **p** of demons.
Acts 5:31 at his right hand as **P** and

PRINCESS (n)
the daughter of a king; a woman having sovereign power
Ps 45:13 The bride, a **p,** looks glorious

PRINCIPLE, PRINCIPLES (n)
a comprehensive and fundamental law, doctrine, or assumption
Gal 4:9 spiritual **p-s** of this world?
Gal 6:16 all who live by this **p;**

PRISON, PRISONS (n)
a state of confinement or captivity; jail
Ps 142:7 Bring me out of **p**
Isa 42:7 will free the captives from **p,**
Matt 25:36 I was in **p,** and you visited
2 Cor 11:23 been put in **p** more often,
Heb 11:36 were chained in **p-s.**

Heb 13:3 Remember those in **p,**
1 Pet 3:19 preached to the spirits in **p**—
Jude 1:6 chained in **p-s** of darkness,
Rev 20:7 Satan will be let out of his **p.**

PRISONER, PRISONERS (n)
a person deprived of liberty and kept under involuntary restraint, confinement, or custody
Ps 79:11 to the moaning of the **p-s.**
Ps 146:7 The LORD frees the **p-s.**
Zech 9:12 you **p-s** who still have hope!
Gal 3:22 we are all **p-s** of sin,
Eph 3:1 I, Paul, a **p** of Christ Jesus

PRIVATE, PRIVATELY (adj)
secret, not to be seen by others
Matt 6:4 Give your gifts in **p,** and
Matt 6:6 and pray to your Father in **p.**
Matt 18:15 go **p-ly** and point out the
1 Cor 4:5 and will reveal our **p** motives.

PRIVILEGE (n)
a right or immunity held as a peculiar benefit, advantage, or favor
Prov 25:2 God's **p** to conceal things
Rom 5:2 into this place of undeserved **p**
2 Cor 8:4 for the **p** of sharing in

PRIZE (n)
something offered or striven for in competitions or in contests
1 Cor 9:24 one person gets the **p?**
1 Cor 9:25 we do it for an eternal **p.**
Phil 3:14 heavenly **p** for which God,
2 Tim 2:5 cannot win the **p** unless
2 Tim 4:8 **p** awaits me—the crown

PRIZE (v)
to value highly, esteem
Prov 4:8 If you **p** wisdom,

PROBLEMS (n)
sources of perplexity, distress, or vexation
Matt 13:21 as soon as they have **p**
Rom 5:3 we run into **p** and trials,

PROCESSION (n)
a group of individuals moving along in an orderly often and ceremonial way
Ps 68:24 O God—the **p** of my God
2 Cor 2:14 in Christ's triumphal **p.**

PROCLAIM, PROCLAIMING, PROCLAIMS (v)
to declare publicly
see also PREACH
Lev 25:10 a time to **p** freedom
Deut 32:3 I will **p** the name of
1 Chr 16:8 and **p** his greatness.
Ps 2:7 king **p-s** the LORD's decree:
Ps 50:6 heavens **p** his justice,
Ps 97:6 heavens **p** his righteousness;
Ps 145:4 let them **p** your power.
Isa 61:1 to **p** that captives will be
Acts 28:31 **p-ing** the Kingdom of God
Col 1:25 **p-ing** his entire message to you.
1 Thes 3:2 in **p-ing** the Good News
Titus 1:1 I have been sent to **p** faith
1 Jn 1:1 **p** to you the one who existed

PRODUCE, PRODUCES (v)
to yield, make, or manufacture
Prov 3:9 best part of everything you **p.**
Isa 55:11 and it always **p-s** fruit.
Matt 7:18 good tree can't **p** bad fruit,
Luke 3:9 tree that does not **p** good fruit
John 15:8 When you **p** much fruit,
John 15:16 to go and **p** lasting fruit,
Rom 7:4 **p** a harvest of good deeds
Eph 5:9 light within you **p-s** only what
Col 1:10 lives will **p** every kind of good
Jas 2:17 Unless it **p-s** good deeds, it is

PRODUCTIVE (adj)
yielding results, benefits, or profits
2 Pet 1:8 the more **p** and useful you will

PROFANING (v)
to treat (something sacred) with abuse, irreverence, or contempt
Neh 13:17 Why are you **p** the Sabbath

PROFESSIONAL (adj)
of, relating to, or characteristic of a profession
Amos 7:14 I'm not a **p** prophet,

PROFIT (n)
gain, benefit, or usefulness
Prov 14:23 Work brings **p,** but
2 Cor 2:17 who preach for personal **p.**

PROFITABLE (adj)
yielding advantageous returns or results
Prov 31:18 her dealings are **p;**

PROGRESS (n)
a forward or onward movement (as to an objective or goal)
Phil 3:16 hold on to the **p** we have
1 Tim 4:15 everyone will see your **p.**

PROLONG (v)
to lengthen in time, extent, scope, or range

Ps 85:5 Will you **p** your wrath to all

PROMISCUITY (n)
sexual excesses
see also IMMORALITY
Rom 13:13 **p** and immoral living,

PROMISCUOUS (adj)
not restricted to one sexual partner
Prov 23:27 a **p** woman is as dangerous

PROMISE, PROMISES (n)
a declaration that one will do or refrain from doing something specified
see also COVENANT, VOW
2 Sam 7:25 a **p** that will last forever.
Neh 5:13 If you fail to keep your **p,**
Ps 91:4 faithful **p-s** are your armor
Ps 116:14 keep my **p-s** to the LORD
Ps 145:13 LORD always keeps his **p-s;**
Ps 146:6 He keeps every **p** forever.
Rom 4:20 in believing God's **p.**
Rom 9:4 receiving his wonderful **p-s.**
Rom 15:4 patiently for God's **p-s** to be
2 Cor 1:20 **p-s** have been fulfilled
2 Cor 7:1 Because we have these **p-s,**
Eph 2:12 covenant **p-s** God had made
Heb 6:13 God's **p** to Abraham.
Heb 8:6 based on better **p-s.**
Heb 10:23 be trusted to keep his **p.**
Heb 11:11 that God would keep his **p.**
2 Pet 3:4 **p** that Jesus is coming again?
2 Pet 3:9 being slow about his **p,**

PROMISED, PROMISES, PROMISING (v)
to pledge to do, bring about, or provide
Exod 3:17 I have **p-d** to rescue you
Deut 15:6 bless you as he has **p-d.**
Josh 23:15 the good things he **p-d,**
Luke 24:49 as my Father **p-d.**
Acts 1:4 sends you the gift he **p-d,**
Rom 4:21 able to do whatever he **p-s.**
Gal 3:14 blessing he **p-d** to Abraham,
1 Tim 4:8 **p-ing** benefits in this life
Titus 1:2 God—who does not lie—**p-d**
Heb 10:36 receive all that he has **p-d.**
Jas 1:12 of life that God has **p-d**
Jas 2:5 inherit the Kingdom he **p-d**
2 Pet 3:13 new earth he has **p-d,**
1 Jn 2:25 eternal life he **p-d** us.

PROMOTE (v)
to further; to advance
Titus 2:1 **p** the kind of living that

PRONOUNCE (v)
to declare officially or ceremoniously
1 Chr 23:13 to **p** blessings in his name

PROOF (n)
something that induces certainty or establishes validity
John 10:25 The **p** is the work I do

PROPERTY (n)
a piece of real estate owned or possessed
Acts 5:1 wife, Sapphira, sold some **p.**

PROPHECY, PROPHECIES (n)
the spoken or written word from God; may forthtell (consoling or corrective) and/or foretell (predicative)
Matt 13:14 fulfills the **p** of Isaiah
Acts 13:29 all that the **p-ies** said about
Acts 17:3 **p-ies** and proved that the Messiah
Acts 21:9 who had the gift of **p.**
Acts 21:10 who also had the gift of **p,**
1 Cor 13:2 If I had the gift of **p,**
1 Cor 13:9 gift of **p** reveals only part
1 Cor 14:6 knowledge or **p** or teaching,
Rev 22:18 words of **p** written in

PROPHESY, PROPHESIED, PROPHESIES, PROPHESYING (v)
to issue a prophecy
Num 11:25 upon them, they **p-ied.**
1 Sam 19:24 day and all night, **p-ing** in
Isa 42:9 Everything I **p-ied** has come true,
Joel 2:28 sons and daughters will **p.**
Matt 7:22 We **p-ied** in your name and
Acts 2:17 sons and daughters will **p.**
Acts 19:6 in other tongues and **p-ied.**
Rom 12:6 the ability to **p,**
1 Cor 11:4 head while praying or **p-ing.**
1 Cor 12:10 the ability to **p.**
1 Cor 14:1 the ability to **p.**
1 Cor 14:3 one who **p-ies** strengthens
1 Cor 14:39 be eager to **p,**

PROPHET, PROPHETS (n)
an interpreter of the times and people's hearts; one who issues divinely inspired revelations
Exod 7:1 Aaron, will be your **p.**
Exod 15:20 Miriam the **p,** Aaron's
Deut 13:1 there are **p-s** among you
Deut 18:18 I will raise up a **p** like you
1 Sam 9:9 **p-s** used to be called seers.
1 Kgs 18:36 Elijah the **p** walked up to
2 Kgs 5:8 a true **p** here in Israel.
2 Kgs 6:12 Elisha, the **p** in Israel,
Isa 44:26 the predictions of my **p-s!**
Hos 9:7 you say, "The **p-s** are crazy

Amos 7:14 I'm not a professional **p,**
Hab 1:1 that the **p** Habakkuk received
Zech 7:12 through the earlier **p-s.**
Mal 4:5 the **p** Elijah before the great
Matt 5:17 or the writings of the **p-s.**
Matt 7:12 in the law and the **p-s.**
Matt 10:41 the same reward as a **p.**
Matt 11:9 Yes, and he is more than a **p.**
Matt 12:39 sign of the **p** Jonah.
Matt 23:37 the city that kills the **p-s**
Matt 26:56 fulfill the words of the **p-s**
Luke 4:24 no **p** is accepted in his own
Luke 7:16 A mighty **p** has risen
Luke 11:49 will send **p-s** and apostles
Luke 24:19 **p** who did powerful
Luke 24:25 all that the **p-s** wrote in
Luke 24:44 law of Moses and the **p-s**
John 1:21 you the **P** we are expecting?
Acts 7:37 a **P** like me from among your
Acts 10:43 all the **p-s** testified about,
Acts 13:1 Among the **p-s** and teachers
Rom 1:2 long ago through his **p-s**
Rom 3:21 Moses and the **p-s** long ago.
Rom 11:3 they have killed your **p-s**
1 Cor 12:28 second are **p-s,** third are
1 Cor 14:37 If you claim to be a **p** or
Eph 2:20 of the apostles and the **p-s.**
Eph 3:5 to his holy apostles and **p-s.**
Eph 4:11 the apostles, the **p-s,** the
1 Pet 1:10 the **p-s** wanted to know
2 Pet 1:19 proclaimed by the **p-s.**
2 Pet 1:21 those **p-s** were moved by
2 Pet 3:2 what the holy **p-s** said long
Rev 11:10 death of the two **p-s** who
Rev 18:20 God and apostles and **p-s!**

PROPHETIC (adj)
of, relating to, or characteristic of a prophet or prophecy
Ezek 37:4 **p** message to these bones
Dan 9:24 to confirm the **p** vision,
1 Tim 1:18 based on the **p** words

PROPITIATION (KJV)
Rom 3:25 Jesus as the *sacrifice* for sin
1 Jn 2:2 the *sacrifice that atones*
1 Jn 4:10 *sacrifice to take away* our sins

PROSELYTE(S) (KJV)
Matt 23:15 and sea to make one *convert*
Acts 2:11 Jews and *converts to Judaism*
Acts 6:5 *convert to the Jewish faith*
Acts 13:43 devout *converts to Judaism*

PROSPER, PROSPERS (v)
to achieve economic success; to become strong and flourishing
Deut 28:63 pleasure in causing you to **p**
Ps 37:3 safely in the land and **p.**
Ps 73:3 **p** despite their wickedness.
Prov 16:20 listen to instruction will **p;**
Prov 17:9 Love **p-s** when a fault is forgiven,
Prov 19:8 cherish understanding will **p.**
Isa 53:10 LORD's good plan will **p**
Isa 55:11 it will **p** everywhere I send it.
Dan 4:27 then you will continue to **p.**

PROSPERITY (n)
the condition of being successful or thriving
Gen 41:29 will be a period of great **p**
Deut 28:11 LORD will give you **p**
Deut 30:15 life and death, between **p**
1 Sam 25:6 Peace and **p** to you,
Ps 41:2 He gives them **p** in the land
Prov 21:5 and hard work lead to **p,**
Prov 28:25 trusting the LORD leads to **p.**
Jer 33:6 give it **p** and true peace.
Mic 4:4 will live in peace and **p,**

PROSPEROUS (adj)
marked by success or economic well-being; flourishing
Deut 5:33 live long and **p** lives
Ps 30:6 When I was **p,** I said,
Ps 34:12 a life that is long and **p?**
Ps 128:2 How joyful and **p** you will be!
Ps 132:15 bless this city and make it **p;**
Jer 12:1 Why are the wicked so **p?**

PROSTITUTE, PROSTITUTES (n)
a person who engages in promiscuous sexual relations, especially for money
Josh 6:17 Rahab the **p** and
Prov 6:26 a **p** will bring you to poverty,
Prov 29:3 hangs around with **p-s,**
Ezek 16:15 as a **p** to every man
Ezek 23:3 They became **p-s** in Egypt.
Matt 21:31 **p-s** will get into the
Luke 15:30 your money on **p-s,**
1 Cor 6:16 if a man joins himself to a **p,**
Rev 17:1 going to come on the great **p,**

PROSTITUTING (v)
to devote to corrupt or unworthy purposes
Ezek 20:30 **p** yourselves by worshiping

PROSTITUTION (n)
the act or practice of engaging in promiscuous sexual relations especially for money
Lev 20:6 who commit spiritual **p** by
Hos 3:3 days and stop your **p.**

PROTECT, PROTECTED, PROTECTING, PROTECTS (v)

to cover or shield from exposure, injury, damage, or destruction; to defend

see also KEEP

Gen 15:1	for I will **p** you,
Num 6:24	bless you and **p** you.
Josh 6:17	for she **p-ed** our spies.
1 Sam 2:9	He will **p** his faithful ones,
Ps 23:4	your staff **p** and comfort me.
Ps 27:1	fortress, **p-ing** me from danger,
Ps 41:2	LORD **p-s** them and keeps
Ps 116:6	LORD **p-s** those of childlike
Ps 127:1	Unless the LORD **p-s** a city,
Ps 145:20	LORD **p-s** all those who love
Ps 146:9	LORD **p-s** the foreigners
Prov 2:8	**p-s** those who are faithful
Isa 31:5	like a bird **p-ing** its nest.
Isa 57:1	God is **p-ing** them from the
John 17:11	now **p** them by the power of
Acts 26:22	But God has **p-ed** me
Gal 3:24	**p-ed** us until we could be
1 Pet 1:5	God is **p-ing** you by his power
Rev 3:10	I will **p** you from the great

PROTECTION (n)

the act of protecting; the state of being protected

see also REFUGE

2 Sam 22:3	my rock, in whom I find **p.**
2 Sam 22:31	look to him for **p.**
Ps 5:11	Spread your **p** over them,
Ps 31:2	Be my rock of **p,**
Ps 71:1	I have come to you for **p;**
Ps 91:4	promises are your armor and **p.**
Prov 19:23	security and **p** from harm.

PROTECTIVE (adj)

of or relating to protection or defense

Ezra 9:9	He has given us a **p** wall

PROUD (adj)

having or displaying excessive self-esteem

Ps 5:5	**p** may not stand in your
Prov 21:4	Haughty eyes, a **p** heart,
Rom 1:30	haters of God, insolent, **p,**
1 Cor 13:4	not jealous or boastful or **p**
1 Tim 3:6	he might become **p,**
1 Tim 6:17	rich in this world not to be **p**
2 Tim 3:2	They will be boastful and **p,**

PROUD (n)

those having or displaying excessive self-esteem

Prov 16:5	LORD detests the **p;**
Dan 4:37	he is able to humble the **p.**
Jas 4:6	God opposes the **p** but favors
1 Pet 5:5	God opposes the **p** but favors

PROVE, PROVED, PROVING (v)

to test or establish the truth, validity, or genuineness of

Ps 51:4	**p-d** right in what you say,
Isa 44:25	thus **p-ing** them to be fools.
John 13:35	love for one another will **p**
Acts 1:3	he **p-d** to them in many ways
Acts 17:3	**p-d** that the Messiah
Acts 17:31	**p-d** to everyone who this is
Acts 26:20	**p** they have changed by
Rom 3:4	**p-d** right in what you say,

PROVIDE, PROVIDED, PROVIDES (v)

to furnish or supply, implying foresight in making provision for the future

Gen 22:8	God will **p** a sheep
Gen 22:14	means "the LORD will **p**"
Ps 68:10	O God, you **p-d** for your needy
Isa 4:5	the LORD will **p** shade
Jer 5:28	refuse to **p** justice to orphans
Ezek 18:7	and **p-s** clothes for the needy.
2 Cor 9:8	God will generously **p** all you
2 Cor 9:10	he will **p** and increase your

PROVOKE (v)

to incite to anger; to stir up purposely

Eph 6:4	do not **p** your children to anger

PROWLS (v)

to roam over in a predatory manner

1 Pet 5:8	**p** around like a roaring lion,

PRUDENT (adj)

marked by wisdom or judiciousness; discreet

Prov 14:8	**p** understand where they are
Prov 14:18	the **p** are crowned with
Prov 22:3	A **p** person foresees danger

PRUNES (v)

to cut back or off for better shape or more fruitful growth

John 15:2	and he **p** the branches

PRUNING HOOKS (n)

a pole bearing a curved blade for pruning plants

Isa 2:4	their spears into **p.**
Joel 3:10	your **p** into spears.

PSALMS (n)

a sacred song or poem used in worship

Ps 95:2	Let us sing **p** of praise
Eph 5:19	singing **p** and hymns and
Col 3:16	Sing **p** and hymns and spiritual

PSYCHICS (n)
those who claim to have sensitivity to knowledge and forces that lie outside the normal human experience

Deut 18:11 function as mediums or **p,**
2 Kgs 21:6 with mediums and **p.**
2 Kgs 23:24 rid of the mediums and **p,**

PUBLICAN(S) (KJV)

Matt 5:46 Even *corrupt tax collectors*
Matt 9:10 with many *tax collectors*
Matt 10:3 Matthew (the *tax collector*),
Luke 5:30 and drink with *such scum?*
Luke 18:11 not like that *tax collector*

PUNISH, PUNISHED, PUNISHES, PUNISHING (v)
to impose a penalty to fit the crime: from corrective measures (fines or scolding) and corporal punishment (spanking or whipping) to capital punishment and eternal damnation

Gen 15:14 But I will **p** the nation
1 Kgs 8:32 **P** the guilty as they deserve.
Prov 11:21 people will surely be **p-ed,**
Jer 25:14 I will **p** them in proportion
Lam 3:39 when we are **p-ed** for our sins?
Mark 12:40 will be more severely **p-ed.**
Acts 7:7 But I will **p** the nation
Rom 2:2 God, in his justice, will **p**
Rom 13:4 they have the power to **p** you.
Rom 13:4 the very purpose of **p-ing**
2 Thes 1:9 **p-ed** with eternal destruction,
Heb 2:2 act of disobedience was **p-ed.**
Heb 12:6 he **p-es** each one he accepts
1 Pet 2:14 sent them to **p** those who
Rev 19:2 has **p-ed** the great prostitute

PUNISHMENT (n)
suffering, pain, or loss that serves as retribution

Isa 53:4 troubles were a **p** from God,
Jer 2:19 will bring its own **p.**
Jer 4:18 This **p** is bitter, piercing
Hos 5:9 On your day of **p,** you will
Matt 25:46 will go away into eternal **p,**
Rom 13:5 not only to avoid **p,** but also
2 Pet 2:9 keeping the wicked under **p**

PURCHASE, PURCHASED (v)
to gain or acquire; to buy
see also REDEEM

Acts 20:28 **p-d** with his own blood—
Eph 1:7 **p-d** our freedom with the
Eph 1:14 **p-d** us to be his own people.
Col 1:14 who **p-d** our freedom
1 Tim 2:6 gave his life to **p** freedom
Rev 14:4 have been **p-d** from among

PURE (adj)
free of contamination or impurities; ritually clean; guileless; faultless; guiltless; chaste
see also CLEAN, HOLY

Ps 19:9 Reverence for the LORD is **p,**
Prov 20:9 I am **p** and free
Matt 5:8 those whose hearts are **p,**
1 Cor 1:30 he made us **p** and holy,
Phil 4:8 right, and **p,** and lovely,
1 Tim 5:22 Keep yourself **p.**
2 Tim 2:21 If you keep yourself **p,**
Titus 1:15 Everything is **p** to those
Titus 2:5 to live wisely and be **p,**
Jas 1:27 **P** and genuine religion
1 Pet 3:2 your **p** and reverent
2 Pet 3:14 are **p** and blameless
1 Jn 3:3 will keep themselves **p,** just as

PURIFICATION (n)
the act or an instance of purifying or of being purified

Lev 16:30 offerings of **p** will be made
Acts 21:24 join them in the **p** ceremony,

PURIFY, PURIFIED (v)
to make pure or remove (physical or moral) blemishes; to make ritually clean
see also CLEANSE

Exod 30:10 offering made to **p** the people
Exod 30:15 given to the LORD to **p**
Num 25:13 **p-ied** the people of Israel,
1 Chr 15:12 You must **p** yourselves and
2 Chr 30:17 had not **p-ied** themselves,
Neh 12:30 Levites first **p-ied** themselves;
Isa 52:11 and **p** yourselves,
John 15:3 pruned and **p-ied** by the
Heb 9:14 Christ will **p** our consciences
Heb 9:22 was **p-ied** with blood.
Jas 4:8 you sinners; **p** your hearts,

PURIM (n)
a Jewish holiday in commemoration of the deliverance of the Jews from the massacre plotted by Haman

Esth 9:26 this celebration is called **P,**

PURITY (n)
the quality or state of being pure

Job 14:4 Who can bring **p** out of an
Ps 86:11 Grant me **p** of heart,
2 Cor 6:6 by our **p,** our understanding,
1 Tim 4:12 love, your faith, and your **p.**
1 Tim 5:2 younger women with all **p**

PURPLE (adj)
of the color purple; symbolic of royalty and wealth

Prov 31:22 fine linen and **p** gowns.
Mark 15:17 They dressed him in a **p** robe,

Acts 16:14 merchant of expensive **p** cloth,

PURPOSE, PURPOSES (n)
something set up as an object or end to be attained; resolution, determination
see also PLAN
Exod 9:16 I have spared you for a **p**—
Prov 19:21 the LORD's **p** will prevail.
Rom 8:28 according to his **p** for them.
Rom 9:11 according to his own **p-s;**
Rom 9:17 for the very **p** of displaying
1 Cor 3:8 with the same **p.**
1 Cor 9:26 I run with **p** in every step.
Phil 2:2 together with one mind and **p.**

PURSUE, PURSUES (v)
to follow in order to overtake, capture, kill, or defeat; to seek
Ps 23:6 unfailing love will **p** me
Ps 119:32 I will **p** your commands,
Prov 15:9 those who **p** godliness.
Prov 21:21 Whoever **p-s** righteousness
1 Tim 6:11 **P** righteousness and a godly
2 Tim 2:22 Instead, **p** righteous living,

Q

QUAIL (n)
in Palestine, a migrating bird that arrives in droves along the shores of the Mediterranean Sea
Exod 16:13 vast numbers of **q** flew
Num 11:31 there were **q** flying

QUAKE (v)
to shake or vibrate
Ps 99:1 the whole earth **q!**

QUALIFICATION (n)
a condition or standard that must be complied with (as for the attainment of a privilege)
2 Cor 3:5 Our **q** comes from God.

QUALIFIED (adj)
to declare competent or adequate
2 Cor 3:5 not that we think we are **q**

QUALITIES (n)
distinguishing attributes; characteristics; nature
Rom 1:20 clearly see his invisible **q**—

QUARREL, QUARRELS (n)
a usually verbal conflict between antagonists
Prov 10:12 Hatred stirs up **q-s,**
Prov 17:14 Starting a **q** is like opening
Prov 26:20 **q-s** disappear when gossip
Prov 30:33 anger causes **q-s.**
Titus 3:9 **q-s** and fights about
Jas 4:1 causing the **q-s** and fights

QUARREL, QUARRELING (v)
to find fault; to contend or dispute actively
Exod 21:18 "Now suppose two men **q,**
Prov 17:19 Anyone who loves to **q** loves
Prov 20:3 fools insist on **q-ing.**
Isa 58:4 keep on fighting and **q-ing?**
Rom 13:13 or in **q-ing** and jealousy.
1 Cor 3:3 and **q** with each other.
2 Cor 12:20 will find **q-ing,** jealousy,

QUARRELSOME (adj)
apt or disposed to quarrel in an often petty manner; contentious
Prov 19:13 **q** wife is as annoying as
Prov 21:9 than with a **q** wife in a lovely
Prov 26:21 A **q** person starts fights
1 Tim 3:3 He must be gentle, not **q,**

QUEEN (n)
the wife or widow of a king; a female monarch
1 Kgs 10:1 **q** of Sheba heard
Ps 45:9 your right side stands the **q,**
Matt 12:42 The **q** of Sheba will

QUENCH (v)
to put out or extinguish
Song 8:7 Many waters cannot **q** love,

QUICK (KJV)
Heb 4:12 word of God is *alive* and
1 Pet 4:5 the *living* and the dead.

QUICKEN (KJV)
Ps 80:18 *Revive* us so we can call on
Ps 119:37 *give* me *life* through your
Rom 8:11 he will *give life* to your mortal

QUIET (adj)
calm; gentle; peaceful, still; free from noise
Prov 11:12 a sensible person keeps **q.**
Eccl 3:7 A time to be **q** and a time
Eccl 9:17 to hear the **q** words of a wise
Luke 19:40 If they kept **q,** the stones
1 Thes 4:11 to live a **q** life,
1 Tim 2:2 peaceful and **q** lives marked

QUIETNESS (n)
the state of being quiet; calmness; stillness
Eccl 4:6 one handful with **q** than two
Isa 30:15 **q** and confidence is
Isa 32:17 it will bring **q** and confidence

QUIT, QUITTING (v)
to cease action; to give up
Prov 23:4 wise enough to know when to **q.**
Eccl 10:4 boss is angry at you, don't **q!**
Rev 2:3 suffered for me without **q-ting.**

QUIVER (n)
a case for carrying or holding arrows
Ps 127:5 joyful is the man whose **q** is

R

RABBI (n)
a title of honor and respect given by the Jews to a teacher of the Law
Matt 23:8 anyone call you '**R,**'
John 3:2 "**R,**" he said, "we all know

RACE (n)
an athletic contest; an ethnic classification
Ps 19:5 athlete eager to run the **r.**
Eccl 9:11 doesn't always win the **r,**
Dan 7:14 people of every **r** and nation
1 Cor 9:24 that in a **r** everyone runs,
Gal 2:2 running the **r** for nothing.
Gal 5:7 were running the **r** so well.
2 Tim 4:7 I have finished the **r,**
Heb 12:1 run with endurance the **r** God

RACE (v)
to go, move, or function at top speed or out of control
Prov 6:18 feet that **r** to do wrong,

RADIANCE (n)
the quality or state of being radiant
Isa 60:3 will come to see your **r.**
Luke 2:9 and the **r** of the Lord's

RADIANT (adj)
vividly bright and shining; marked by or expressive of love, confidence, or happiness
Exod 34:29 face had become **r** because
Ps 34:5 help will be **r** with joy;
Ps 80:1 display your **r** glory

RADIATES (v)
to spread abroad or around as if from a center; to shine brightly
Heb 1:3 The Son **r** God's own glory

RAGE (n)
violent and uncontrolled anger
Isa 14:6 with endless blows of **r**
Col 3:8 rid of anger, **r,** malicious

RAGING (adj)
violent, wild
Ps 42:7 tumult of the **r** seas as your
Ps 65:7 You quieted the **r** oceans

RAGS (n)
clothes usually in poor or ragged condition
Isa 64:6 are nothing but filthy **r.**

RAIMENT (KJV)
Exod 12:35 *clothing* and articles of silver
Deut 8:4 your *clothes* didn't wear out
Luke 9:29 his *clothes* became dazzling

RAIN, RAINS (n)
water falling in drops from the sky
Deut 11:14 will send the **r-s** in their
1 Kgs 17:1 no dew or **r** during the next
1 Kgs 18:1 that I will soon send **r!**
Prov 16:15 refreshes like a spring **r.**
Matt 5:45 and he sends **r** on the just
Jas 5:17 earnestly that no **r** would fall,
Jude 1:12 land without giving any **r.**

RAIN (v)
to fall as water in drops from the clouds
Gen 7:4 And it will **r** for forty days

RAINBOW (n)
an arch of colors in the sky caused by light passing through moisture in the air
Gen 9:13 I have placed my **r** in the

RAISE, RAISED (v)
to recall from death
see also RESURRECTION
Judg 2:16 the Lord **r-d** up judges
Luke 7:22 the dead are **r-d** to life,
John 6:39 that I should **r** them up
Acts 2:32 God **r-d** Jesus from the dead,
Acts 24:15 that he will **r** both the
Rom 1:4 he was **r-d** from the dead
Rom 6:5 we will also be **r-d** to life
Rom 10:9 God **r-d** him from the dead,
1 Cor 15:4 he was **r-d** from the dead
Phil 3:10 mighty power that **r-d** him
1 Thes 4:14 died and was **r-d** to life
1 Pet 1:3 because God **r-d** Jesus Christ

RALLY (v)
to join in a common cause
Isa 11:10 The nations will **r** to him,

RAM, RAMS (n)
a male sheep
Gen 22:13 he took the **r** and sacrificed

1 Sam 15:22 offering the fat of **r-s.**
Dan 8:3 I saw a **r** with two long
Mic 6:7 him thousands of **r-s** and ten

RANSOM (n)
price paid or demanded to release someone or something from captivity
Matt 20:28 his life as a **r** for many.
Mark 10:45 his life as a **r** for many.
1 Pet 1:18 that God paid a **r** to save

RANSOM, RANSOMED (v)
to deliver especially from sin or its penalty; to free from captivity or punishment by paying a price
see also REDEEM(ED)
Ps 44:26 Help us! **R** us because of
Ps 71:23 for you have **r-ed** me.
Isa 35:10 have been **r-ed** by the LORD
Hos 13:14 Should I **r** them from
Rev 5:9 your blood has **r-ed** people

RAVEN, RAVENS (n)
a large, black, corvine bird
Gen 8:7 and released a **r.** The bird
1 Kgs 17:6 The **r-s** brought him bread and
Job 38:41 provides food for the **r-s**
Ps 147:9 feeds the young **r-s** when they
Luke 12:24 Look at the **r-s.** They don't

READ, READING, READS (v)
to receive and interpret letters or symbols by sight
Deut 17:19 with him and **r** it daily
Josh 8:34 Joshua then **r** to them
2 Kgs 23:2 There the king **r** to them
Acts 8:28 carriage, he was **r-ing** aloud
2 Cor 3:2 everyone can **r** it and
1 Tim 4:13 focus on **r-ing** the Scriptures
Rev 1:3 the one who **r-s** the words of

READY (adj)
prepared mentally or physically for some experience or action
1 Tim 6:18 always being **r** to share
1 Pet 3:15 always be **r** to explain

REAL (adj)
not artificial, fraudulent, or illusory; genuine
1 Kgs 3:26 who was the **r** mother of
1 Jn 4:2 Christ came in a **r** body,

REALITY (n)
a real event, entity, or state of affairs
Col 2:17 shadows of the **r** yet to come.

REALIZATION (n)
the state of being fully aware of
Mark 5:33 trembling at the **r** of what

REALIZE, REALIZED, REALIZING (v)
to be fully aware of; to conceive vividly as real
2 Chr 33:13 Manasseh finally **r-d** that
Job 38:18 Do you **r** the extent of
Ps 64:9 and **r** all the amazing things
Song 6:12 Before I **r-d** it, my strong
Isa 61:9 Everyone will **r** that they are
Heb 13:2 angels without **r-ing** it!
Jas 4:4 Don't you **r** that friendship

REALMS (n)
kingdoms; spheres, domains
Eph 1:3 in the heavenly **r** because we
Eph 2:6 in the heavenly **r** because we

REAP (v)
to harvest or gather; to obtain
see also HARVEST, GATHER
Gal 6:9 will **r** a harvest of blessing
Jas 3:18 **r** a harvest of righteousness.

REAPERS (KJV)
Ruth 2:3 grain behind the *harvesters*
2 Kgs 4:18 working with the *harvesters*
Matt 13:30 the *harvesters* to sort out
Matt 13:39 the *harvesters* are the angels

REBEL, REBELLED, REBELLING, REBELS (v)
to oppose or disobey one in authority or control
Num 14:9 Do not **r** against the
Num 27:14 of Israel **r-led,** you failed to
1 Sam 12:14 if you do not **r** against the
Ps 78:56 testing and **r-ling** against God
Isa 63:10 But they **r-led** against him
Matt 10:21 children will **r** against their
Rom 13:2 So anyone who **r-s** against

REBELLION (n)
opposition to one in authority or dominance; defiance
Exod 34:7 forgive iniquity, **r,** and sin.
Ps 32:5 I will confess my **r** to the
Ps 39:8 Rescue me from my **r.**
Ps 51:3 I recognize my **r;** it haunts
Isa 53:5 was pierced for our **r,**
Isa 53:8 for the **r** of my people.
Dan 9:24 to finish their **r,** to put an
2 Thes 2:3 is a great **r** against God

REBELLIOUS (adj)
given to or engaged in rebellion
Isa 65:2 opened my arms to a **r** people.
Luke 1:17 those who are **r** to accept
Rom 10:21 were disobedient and **r.**
1 Tim 1:9 people who are lawless and **r,**

Titus 1:6 reputation for being wild or **r.**

REBELS (n)
those who rebel or participate in a rebellion
Ps 51:13 will teach your ways to **r,**
Isa 53:12 He was counted among the **r.**
Luke 22:37 was counted among the **r.**
Rom 11:30 Gentiles were **r** against God,
Rom 11:31 they are the **r,** and God's

REBUILD, REBUILT (v)
to reconstruct; to restore to a previous state
Ezra 5:2 again to **r** the Temple of God
Neh 2:17 Let us **r** the wall of
Ps 102:16 the LORD will **r** Jerusalem.
Amos 9:14 and they will **r** their ruined
Zech 1:16 My Temple will be **r-t,** says the
Acts 15:16 I will **r** its ruins and

REBUKE (n)
an expression of strong disapproval; reprimand
see also CORRECT, DISCIPLINE
Prov 17:10 A single **r** does more for
Prov 27:5 An open **r** is better than

REBUKE, REBUKED (v)
to criticize sharply; to reprimand
Prov 30:6 or he may **r** you and expose
Mark 16:14 He **r-d** them for their
Luke 17:3 believer sins, **r** that person;
2 Tim 4:2 Patiently correct, **r,** and
Jas 1:5 He will not **r** you for asking.

RECEIVE, RECEIVED, RECEIVES (v)
to acquire or take possession of; to welcome
Matt 7:8 For everyone who asks, **r-s.**
Matt 19:17 you want to **r** eternal life,
John 20:22 said, "**R** the Holy Spirit.
Acts 1:8 But you will **r** power when the
Acts 2:38 Then you will **r** the gift of
Acts 8:17 they **r-d** the Holy Spirit.
Acts 10:47 they have **r-d** the Holy
Acts 19:2 Did you **r** the Holy Spirit
Rom 8:15 Instead, you **r-d** God's Spirit
1 Tim 1:16 in him and **r** eternal life.
Rev 4:11 our God, to **r** glory and honor

RECKONING (n)
a settling of accounts
Jer 51:18 On the day of **r** they will all

RECOGNIZE, RECOGNIZED (v)
to admit as being lord or sovereign; to acknowledge or take notice of in some definite way; to perceive to be something or someone previously known
1 Chr 16:28 of the world, **r** the LORD,
Ps 96:7 of the world, **r** the LORD;
Jer 24:7 give them hearts that **r** me
Hos 4:6 refuse to **r** you as my priests.
John 1:26 is someone you do not **r.**
1 Cor 14:38 But if you do not **r** this,
1 Cor 14:38 yourself will not be **r-d.**
2 Cor 3:2 read it and **r** our good work

RECOMMEND (v)
to endorse; to advise
Eccl 8:15 So I **r** having fun, because

RECOMMENDATION (n)
something that expresses commendation
2 Cor 3:1 to bring you letters of **r,**

RECONCILED, RECONCILING (v)
to restore to friendship or harmony, especially between God and human beings
2 Cor 5:18 task of **r-ing** people to him.
Eph 2:16 Christ **r-d** both groups to God
Col 1:20 God **r-d** everything to himself.
Col 1:22 now he has **r-d** you to himself

RECONCILIATION (n)
the action of reconciling; the state of being reconciled
Prov 14:9 acknowledge it and seek **r.**
2 Cor 5:19 this wonderful message of **r.**

RECORD (n)
an official body of known or recorded facts about someone
1 Cor 13:5 keeps no **r** of being wronged.
Col 2:14 canceled the **r** of the charges

RECORDED (v)
to set down in writing
John 20:30 to the ones **r** in this book.

RED (adj)
of the color red
Exod 15:4 are drowned in the **R** Sea.
Ps 106:9 He commanded the **R** Sea to
Prov 23:31 wine, seeing how **r** it is,
Isa 1:18 they are **r** like crimson,
Isa 63:1 with his clothing stained **r?**

REDEDICATE (v)
to devote or commit oneself or one's possessions again
Num 6:12 They must **r** themselves to

REDEEM, REDEEMED, REDEEMS (v)
to buy back; to save by payment of a ransom; to free from the consequences of sin
see also PURCHASE, RANSOM, RESCUE
Exod 6:6 I will **r** you with a powerful

2 Sam 7:23 have you **r-ed** from slavery
Ps 34:22 the LORD will **r** those
Ps 49:15 God will **r** my life.
Ps 74:2 the tribe you **r-ed** as your own
Ps 103:4 He **r-s** me from death and
Ps 107:2 Has the LORD **r-ed** you?
Ps 130:8 He himself will **r** Israel from
Isa 35:9 Only the **r-ed** will walk
Isa 63:9 love and mercy he **r-ed** them.
Hos 7:13 I wanted to **r** them, but they

REDEEMER (n)
one who frees or delivers another from difficulty, danger, or bondage, usually by the payment of a ransom price
Ruth 3:9 for you are my family **r.**
Ruth 4:14 has now provided a **r** for
Job 19:25 I know that my **R** lives,
Ps 19:14 LORD, my rock and my **r.**
Prov 23:11 For their **R** is strong;
Isa 44:6 Israel's King and **R,** the LORD
Isa 48:17 your **R,** the Holy One of Israel:
Isa 59:20 The **R** will come to Jerusalem

REDEMPTION (n)
the act, process, or an instance of redeeming
Ps 130:7 love. His **r** overflows.
Eph 4:30 be saved on the day of **r.**
Heb 9:12 and secured our **r** forever.

REEDS (n)
any of various tall grasses that grow in wet places
Exod 2:5 basket among the **r,**
Isa 35:7 **r** and rushes will flourish
Isa 58:5 bowing your heads like **r**
Ezek 29:6 a staff made of **r**

REFINE, REFINED (v)
to remove impurities from metal; figurative of purifying God's people of sin
Isa 48:10 I have **r-d** you in the furnace
Zech 13:9 I will **r** them like silver

REFINER (n)
someone or something that refines
Mal 3:3 will sit like a **r** of silver,

REFLECT, REFLECTS (v)
to make manifest or apparent; to think quietly and calmly
Ps 119:5 consistently **r** your decrees!
Ps 119:15 and **r** on your ways.
Prov 27:19 the heart **r-s** the real person.
Isa 44:19 never stops to **r,** "Why, it's
Titus 2:7 Let everything you do **r** the

REFRESH, REFRESHED, REFRESHES, REFRESHING (v)
to restore strength and animation to; to replenish, arouse, or stimulate
Prov 9:17 Stolen water is **r-ing;** food
Prov 11:25 will themselves be **r-ed.**
Prov 16:15 favor **r-es** like a spring rain.
Phlm 1:7 has often **r-ed** the hearts

REFUGE (n)
shelter or protection from danger or distress
see also FORTRESS, PROTECTION, SHELTER
Deut 33:27 eternal God is your **r,**
2 Sam 22:3 He is my **r,** my savior,
Ps 2:12 for all who take **r** in him!
Ps 5:11 But let all who take **r** in you
Ps 17:7 those who seek **r** from their
Ps 34:8 those who take **r** in him!
Ps 46:1 God is our **r** and strength,
Ps 91:2 He alone is my **r,** my place

REFUSE, REFUSED, REFUSING (v)
to show or express unwillingness to do or comply with
Lev 26:15 and **r-ing** to obey
Num 14:22 tested me by **r-ing** to listen to
Josh 24:15 But if you **r** to serve the
Prov 13:19 fools **r** to turn from evil
Eccl 11:10 So **r** to worry, and keep
Luke 15:29 never once **r-d** to do a single
Rom 14:6 And those who **r** to eat
2 Thes 2:10 because they **r** to love
2 Thes 3:14 of those who **r** to obey
Heb 12:25 escape when they **r-d** to listen

REFUTE (v)
to prove wrong by argument or evidence
Luke 21:15 be able to reply or **r** you!
Acts 9:22 couldn't **r** his proofs that

REGARDED (v)
to consider and appraise
Ps 106:31 has been **r** as a righteous

REGENERATION (KJV)
Matt 19:28 world is *made new* and the
Titus 3:5 giving us a *new birth* and new

REGISTERED (v)
to make or secure official entry of in a register
Luke 10:20 your names are **r** in heaven.

REGRET (v)
to be very sorry for
Nah 3:7 Does anyone **r** your destruction?

REGULAR (adj)
formed, built, arranged, or ordered according to some established rule, law, principle, or type
2 Kgs 25:30 gave him a **r** food allowance

REGULATIONS (n)
authoritative rules dealing with details or procedure
see also LAW(S)
Exod 21:1 These are the **r** you must
Deut 33:10 They teach your **r** to Jacob;
Ps 119:30 determined to live by your **r.**
Ps 119:43 for your **r** are my only hope.
Ps 119:120 I stand in awe of your **r.**
Ps 119:164 because all your **r** are just.
Ps 119:175 and may your **r** help me.

REIGN, REIGNED, REIGNING, REIGNS (v)
to possess or exercise sovereign power; to rule
Exod 15:18 The LORD will **r** forever
Ps 9:7 But the LORD **r-s** forever,
Ps 29:10 LORD **r-s** as king forever.
Ps 96:10 The LORD **r-s!**
Ps 146:10 The LORD will **r** forever.
Isa 52:7 that the God of Israel **r-s!**
1 Cor 4:8 we would be **r-ing** with you.
1 Cor 15:25 For Christ must **r** until he
Rev 5:10 And they will **r** on the earth.
Rev 11:15 and he will **r** forever
Rev 19:6 our God, the Almighty, **r-s.**
Rev 20:4 and they **r-ed** with Christ
Rev 22:5 And they will **r** forever

REIGNS (n)
the time during which one (as a sovereign) rules
Dan 2:44 During the **r** of those kings,

REJECT, REJECTED, REJECTING, REJECTS (v)
to refuse to accept, consider, submit to, or take for some purpose, or use; to refuse to hear, receive, or admit
1 Sam 8:7 me they are **r-ing,** not you.
Ps 51:17 not **r** a broken and repentant
Ps 118:22 stone that the builders **r-ed**
Prov 3:11 My child, don't **r** the LORD's
Mal 1:3 but I **r-ed** his brother,
Matt 21:42 stone that the builders **r-ed**
Luke 10:16 who **r-s** me is **r-ing** God,
John 6:37 I will never **r** them.
John 12:48 But all who **r** me and my
Rom 9:13 loved Jacob, but I **r-ed** Esau.
1 Thes 4:8 teaching but is **r-ing** God,
1 Tim 4:4 we should not **r** any of it
2 Tim 3:5 but they will **r** the power
Heb 6:6 by **r-ing** the Son of God, they
1 Pet 2:4 He was **r-ed** by people,
1 Pet 2:7 stone that the builders **r-ed**

REJECTION (n)
the action of rejecting
Rom 11:15 For since their **r** meant that

REJOICE, REJOICED, REJOICES, REJOICING (v)
to feel joy or great delight; to gladden
1 Chr 16:31 glad, and the earth **r!**
1 Chr 29:17 **r** when you find integrity
Esth 8:17 decree arrived, the Jews **r-d**
Ps 5:11 who take refuge in you **r;**
Ps 13:5 I will **r** because you
Ps 35:9 I will **r** in the LORD.
Ps 48:2 the whole earth **r-s** to see it!
Ps 58:10 The godly will **r** when they
Ps 66:6 There we **r-d** in him.
Ps 68:4 LORD—**r** in his presence!
Ps 119:14 I have **r-d** in your laws
Ps 119:162 I **r** in your word like one
Prov 8:31 I **r-d** with the human family!
Prov 17:5 who **r** at the misfortune
Prov 29:2 in authority, the people **r.**
Isa 9:3 and its people will **r.**
Isa 35:1 wasteland will **r** and blossom
Isa 62:5 **r** over you as a bridegroom **r-s**
Jer 51:48 the heavens and earth will **r,**
Lam 4:21 Are you **r-ing** in the land
Hab 1:15 while they **r** and celebrate?
Zeph 3:17 He will **r** over you
Zech 2:10 Shout and **r,** O beautiful
Luke 1:14 and many will **r** at his birth,
Luke 1:47 How my spirit **r-s** in God my
Luke 1:58 everyone **r-d** with her.
Luke 10:20 But don't **r** because evil
Luke 13:17 but all the people **r-d** at the
Acts 5:41 high council **r-ing** that God
Acts 16:34 his entire household **r-d**
1 Cor 13:6 **r** about injustice but **r-s**
Phil 2:18 you should **r,** and I will
Phil 3:1 and sisters, **r** in the Lord.
Phil 4:4 I say it again—**r!**
Col 2:5 I **r** that you are living as
Rev 19:7 Let us be glad and **r,** and

RELATIONSHIP (n)
a state of affairs existing between those having relations or dealings
Rom 5:11 our wonderful new **r** with God
2 Jn 1:9 teaching has no **r** with God.

RELATIVES (n)
a person connected with another by blood or affinity
Lev 19:17 your heart for any of your **r.**
Mark 6:4 among his **r** and his own
Luke 21:16 parents, brothers, **r,** and
1 Tim 5:8 who won't care for their **r,**

RELEASE (n)
relief or deliverance from restraint, sorrow, suffering, or trouble

Deut 31:10	the Year of **R,** during the
Job 14:14	eagerly await the **r** of death.

RELEASED (v)
to set free from restraint, confinement, or servitude

Isa 61:1	that captives will be **r**
Matt 18:27	and he **r** him and forgave
Matt 27:50	and he **r** his spirit.
Luke 4:18	that captives will be **r,**
John 19:30	his head and **r** his spirit.
Rom 7:6	we have been **r** from the law,
Rom 8:23	bodies to be **r** from sin and

RELENT, RELENTED (v)
to become less severe, harsh, or strict; to give in

Ps 106:45	**r-ed** because of his unfailing
Joel 2:13	eager to **r** and not punish.

RELIABLE (adj)
dependable

1 Chr 9:22	they were **r** men.
Prov 13:17	but a **r** messenger brings
Prov 20:6	find one who is truly **r?**
2 Tim 2:2	by many **r** witnesses.

RELIEF (n)
removal or lightening of something oppressive, painful, or distressing

Gen 5:29	he bring us **r** from our work
Ps 94:13	You give them **r** from troubled

RELIEVED, RELIEVING (v)
to free from a burden; to discharge the bladder or bowels

1 Kgs 18:27	or is **r-ing** himself.
Acts 20:12	and everyone was greatly **r-d.**

RELIGION, RELIGIONS (n)
a personal set or institutionalized system of religious attitudes, beliefs, and practices; the service and worship of God or the supernatural

Matt 6:7	as people of other **r-s** do.
Acts 25:19	something about their **r** and
Acts 26:5	the strictest sect of our **r.**
Gal 1:13	I followed the Jewish **r**—
Jas 1:26	and your **r** is worthless.

RELIGIOUS (adj)
relating to or manifesting faithful devotion to God or a god

Luke 11:46	with unbearable **r** demands,
Acts 13:50	the influential **r** women and
Jas 1:26	you claim to be **r** but don't

RELY, RELIED, RELIES (v)
to be dependent

2 Chr 16:8	time you **r-ied** on the LORD,
Ps 22:8	one who **r-ies** on the LORD?
Ps 33:18	those who **r** on his unfailing
Prov 11:7	for they **r** on their own feeble
Isa 50:10	the LORD and **r** on your God.
2 Cor 1:9	and learned to **r** only on God,

REMAIN, REMAINED, REMAINS (v)
to stay in the same place or with the same person or group; to continue unchanged

2 Kgs 18:6	He **r-ed** faithful to the LORD
John 15:7	But if you **r** in me and my
John 15:9	loved me. **R** in my love.
Rom 11:5	of Israel have **r-ed** faithful
2 Tim 2:13	unfaithful, he **r-s** faithful,
2 Tim 3:14	But you must **r** faithful
2 Tim 4:7	and I have **r-ed** faithful.
Heb 7:3	He **r-s** a priest forever,
Heb 10:32	how you **r-ed** faithful even
Heb 13:4	and **r** faithful to one another
1 Pet 1:25	word of the Lord **r-s**
1 Jn 2:27	**r** in fellowship with Christ.

REMARRY, REMARRIES (v)
to marry again after divorce or being widowed

Rom 7:3	commit adultery when she **r-ies.**
1 Tim 5:11	Christ and they will want to **r.**

REMEMBER, REMEMBERED, REMEMBERING, REMEMBERS (v)
to bring to mind or think of again; to keep in mind for attention or consideration; to retain in the memory

Gen 9:15	I will **r** my covenant with
Exod 2:24	**r-ed** his covenant promise
1 Chr 16:12	**R** the wonders he has
Ps 49:13	though they are **r-ed** as being
Ps 103:14	he **r-s** we are only dust.
Ps 106:45	**r-ed** his covenant with them
Ps 111:5	he always **r-s** his covenant.
Ps 136:23	He **r-ed** us in our weakness.
Jer 31:34	never again **r** their sins.
Jer 32:20	things still **r-ed** to this day!
Hab 3:2	in your anger, **r** your mercy.
Matt 26:13	will be **r-ed** and discussed.
Luke 1:72	**r-ing** his sacred covenant—
Luke 22:19	Do this to **r** me.
1 Cor 11:24	Do this to **r** me.
2 Tim 2:8	Always **r** that Jesus
Heb 8:12	never again **r** their sins.
2 Pet 1:15	you always **r** these things

REMIND, REMINDING (v)
to cause to remember

John 14:26	will **r** you of everything

2 Pet 1:12 I will always **r** you about
2 Pet 1:13 keep on **r-ing** you as long

REMINDER, REMINDERS (n)
something that causes to remember
Deut 6:8 them on your forehead as **r-s.**
Prov 7:3 Tie them on your fingers as a **r.**

REMISSION (KJV)
Matt 26:28 as a sacrifice *to forgive*
Acts 10:43 sins *forgiven* through his
Rom 3:25 he *held back and did not punish*
Heb 9:22 blood, there is no *forgiveness*

REMNANT (n)
a usually small part, member, or trace remaining; the few people left who gathered together after God scattered them into exile
Ezra 9:8 few of us to survive as a **r.**
Isa 6:13 a tenth—a **r**—survive,
Isa 11:11 to bring back the **r** of his
Jer 23:3 gather together the **r** of my
Zech 8:12 will cause the **r** in Judah

REMOVE, REMOVED (v)
to get rid of; to eliminate
Ps 103:12 He has **r-d** our sins as far
Isa 6:7 Now your guilt is **r-d,** and your
1 Cor 5:13 You must **r** the evil person

RENEW, RENEWED, RENEWS (v)
to restore to freshness, vigor, or perfection; to make new spiritually
Ps 23:3 He **r-s** my strength.
Ps 51:10 **R** a loyal spirit within me.
Isa 57:10 Desire gave you **r-ed** strength,
Eph 4:23 let the Spirit **r** your thoughts
Col 3:10 be **r-ed** as you learn to know

RENOWN (KJV)
Gen 6:4 the *heroes* and famous warriors
Isa 14:20 will never again *receive honor*
Ezek 16:14 *fame* soon spread
Ezek 39:13 a *glorious victory* for Israel

REPAY, REPAYS (v)
to give or inflict in return or requital; to pay back (money)
Ps 62:12 Surely you **r** all people
Prov 17:13 If you **r** good with evil,
Prov 19:17 and he will **r** you!
Jer 51:6 he will **r** her in full.
Jer 51:56 he always **r-s** in full.
Luke 6:34 to those who can **r** you,
Luke 7:42 neither of them could **r** him,
1 Tim 5:4 **r** their parents by taking

1 Pet 3:9 Don't **r** evil for evil.

REPENT, REPENTED, REPENTING, REPENTS (v)
to turn from sin and change one's heart and behavior; to feel regret and contrition
Matt 3:2 **R** of your sins and turn
Matt 3:8 that you have **r-ed** of your sins
Matt 4:17 began to preach, "**R** of your
Matt 11:21 people would have **r-ed** of
Luke 3:8 that you have **r-ed** of your sins
Luke 15:7 sinner who **r-s** and returns
Luke 15:10 when even one sinner **r-s.**
Acts 2:38 you must **r** of your sins
Acts 17:30 everywhere to **r** of their sins
Acts 20:21 necessity of **r-ing** from sin
Heb 6:1 importance of **r-ing** from evil
2 Pet 3:9 but wants everyone to **r.**
Rev 2:5 If you don't **r,** I will come

REPENTANCE (n)
a turning away from sin, disobedience, or rebellion, and a turning back to God
1 Kgs 8:47 to you in **r** and pray,
Job 42:6 dust and ashes to show my **r.**
Luke 17:3 if there is **r,** forgive.
2 Cor 7:10 sorrow, which lacks **r,**

REPENTANT (adj)
penitent; expressive of repentance
see also CONTRITE
Ps 51:17 a broken and **r** heart, O God.

REPORT (n)
a usually detailed account or statement
Luke 16:2 Get your **r** in order,

REPRESENTATIVE (n)
one that represents another as an agent or delegate usually being invested with the authority of the principal
Col 3:17 do it as a **r** of the Lord

REPRIMAND, REPRIMANDED (v)
to reprove sharply or censure formally
see also CORRECT, REBUKE
1 Tim 5:20 sin should be **r-ed** in front
Titus 1:13 So **r** them sternly to make

REPROACH (n)
a cause or occasion of blame, discredit, or disgrace
1 Tim 3:2 man whose life is above **r.**

REPUTATION (n)
overall quality or character as seen or judged by people in general

see also NAME

Ps 109:21	the sake of your own **r**!
Prov 3:4	you will earn a good **r.**
Prov 22:1	Choose a good **r** over great
Eccl 7:1	A good **r** is more valuable
1 Tim 3:2	wisely, and have a good **r.**
Heb 11:39	good **r** because of their

REQUIRE, REQUIRED, REQUIRES (v)

to demand as necessary or essential; to feel or be obliged

Ps 40:6	you don't **r** burnt offerings
Mic 6:8	this is what he **r-s** of you:
Luke 12:48	much will be **r-d** in return;
Luke 23:56	they rested as **r-d** by the law.
Rom 1:32	God's justice **r-s** that those
Heb 8:3	high priest is **r-d** to offer

REQUIREMENTS (n)

something required; condition

Rom 13:8	will fulfill the **r** of God's
Rom 13:10	love fulfills the **r** of God's

RESCUE, RESCUED, RESCUES, RESCUING (v)

to save or deliver

see also REDEEM, SAVE

2 Kgs 13:5	someone to **r** the Israelites
Ps 9:14	rejoice that you have **r-d** me.
Ps 17:7	mighty power you **r** those who
Ps 22:8	let the LORD **r** him!
Ps 31:2	listen to me; **r** me quickly.
Ps 37:39	The LORD **r-s** the godly;
Ps 37:40	LORD helps them, **r-ing** them
Ps 68:20	The Sovereign LORD **r-s** us
Ps 72:12	He will **r** the poor when
Ps 145:19	cries for help and **r-s** them.
Prov 11:8	godly are **r-d** from trouble,
Isa 56:1	coming soon to **r** you and
Dan 6:27	He **r-s** and saves his people;
Zech 8:7	that I will **r** my people from
Matt 6:13	but **r** us from the evil one.
Rom 11:26	The one who **r-s** will come
2 Cor 1:10	And he did **r** us from mortal
Gal 1:4	in order to **r** us from this
Gal 3:13	But Christ has **r-d** us from the
Col 1:13	For he has **r-d** us from the
1 Thes 1:10	the one who has **r-d** us
2 Pet 2:9	knows how to **r** godly people

RESCUER (n)

one who frees from confinement, danger, or evil

Judg 3:9	raised up a **r** to save them.
Judg 3:15	raised up a **r** to save them.
Ps 144:2	my tower of safety, my **r.**

RESIST (v)

to withstand the force or effect of; to counteract or defeat

Dan 11:32	will be strong and will **r** him.
Matt 5:39	do not **r** an evil person!
Jas 4:7	**R** the devil, and he will flee

RESPECT (n)

a high or special regard; esteem

see also AWE, REVERENCE

Prov 11:16	A gracious woman gains **r,**
Mal 1:6	the honor and **r** I deserve?
Titus 2:2	be worthy of **r,** and to live

RESPECT, RESPECTED (v)

to consider worthy of high regard; to esteem

Eph 5:33	the wife must **r** her husband.
1 Tim 3:4	children who **r** and obey him.
1 Tim 3:8	deacons must be well **r-ed**
1 Tim 3:11	their wives must be **r-ed**
1 Tim 5:17	work well should be **r-ed**
1 Pet 2:17	Fear God, and **r** the king.

RESPECTFUL (adj)

marked by or showing respect or deference

1 Pet 3:16	a gentle and **r** way.

RESPONSIBILITY (n)

moral, legal, or mental accountability

1 Cor 5:12	certainly is your **r** to judge
1 Tim 5:16	not put the **r** on the church.

RESPONSIBLE (adj)

marked by or involving responsibility or accountability; liable to be called to account as the primary cause, motive, or agent

Exod 32:34	hold them **r** for their sins.
Num 1:53	The Levites are **r** to stand
Ezek 33:6	he is **r** for their captivity.
Jonah 1:14	And don't hold us **r** for his
Gal 6:5	For we are each **r** for our own

REST (n)

freedom from activity or labor; peace of mind or spirit; repose, sleep

see also SABBATH

Exod 31:15	day of complete **r,** a holy
Exod 33:14	and I will give you **r**—
Ps 91:1	Most High will find **r** in the
Ps 127:2	for God gives **r** to his loved
Jer 6:16	you will find **r** for your
Matt 11:28	and I will give you **r.**
2 Thes 1:7	God will provide **r** for you
Heb 4:3	even though this **r** has been
Heb 4:9	a special **r** still waiting
Heb 4:10	who have entered into God's **r**

REST, RESTED, RESTING, RESTS (v)
to sit or lie on; to cease from action or motion; to take relief or respite

Gen 2:2	of creation, so he **r-ed** from all
Ps 16:9	My body **r-s** in safety.
Ps 23:2	He lets me **r** in green
Isa 11:2	Spirit of the LORD will **r**
Isa 30:15	and **r-ing** in me will you
John 1:32	from heaven and **r-ing** upon
Heb 4:4	seventh day God **r-ed** from all
Rev 14:13	will **r** from their hard work;

RESTITUTION (n)
a making good of or giving an equivalent for some injury

Lev 6:5	You must make **r** by paying
Num 5:8	relatives to whom **r** can be

RESTLESS (adj)
continuously moving

Isa 57:20	are like the **r** sea, which is

RESTORE, RESTORED, RESTORES, RESTORING (v)
to give back, return; to renew

Ps 14:7	When the LORD **r-s** his people,
Ps 30:2	and you **r-d** my health.
Isa 58:11	dry and **r-ing** your strength.
Jer 30:3	when I will **r** the fortunes of
Jer 30:18	from captivity and **r** their
Jer 31:18	Turn me again to you and **r**
Hos 6:2	a short time he will **r** us,
Nah 2:2	but he will **r** its splendor.
Rom 5:10	friendship with God was **r-d**
1 Pet 5:10	will **r**, support, and strengthen

RESURRECTION (n)
the state of one risen from the dead; the rising again to life of all the human dead before the final judgment
see also RAISE, RISE

Matt 27:53	cemetery after Jesus' **r**,
Mark 12:23	will she be in the **r**?
Luke 20:36	children of the **r**.
John 11:25	I am the **r** and the life.
Acts 1:22	as a witness of Jesus' **r**.
Acts 2:31	speaking of the Messiah's **r**.
Acts 4:2	there is a **r** of the dead.
Acts 4:33	powerfully to the **r** of
Acts 17:32	Paul speak about the **r** of
1 Cor 15:13	if there is no **r** of the
1 Cor 15:42	way with the **r** of the dead.
Phil 3:11	experience the **r** from the
2 Tim 2:18	claiming that the **r** of the
Heb 6:2	of hands, the **r** of the dead,
Heb 11:35	a better life after the **r**.
1 Pet 3:21	because of the **r** of Jesus
Rev 20:5	This is the first **r**.

RETALIATE (v)
to repay (as an injury) in kind; to get revenge

1 Pet 2:23	He did not **r** when he

RETURN, RETURNED, RETURNING, RETURNS (v)
to go or come back again; to go back in thought, practice, or condition; to repent

2 Sam 12:23	but he cannot **r** to me.
2 Chr 30:9	if you **r** to the LORD,
Neh 1:9	But if you **r** to me and obey
Ps 35:13	my prayers **r-ed** unanswered.
Ps 51:13	and they will **r** to you.
Ps 126:6	they sing as they **r** with the
Isa 52:8	the LORD **r-ing** to Jerusalem.
Jer 24:7	for they will **r** to me
Hos 6:1	let us **r** to the LORD.
Amos 4:6	you would not **r** to me,
Matt 24:46	If the master **r-s** and finds

REVEAL, REVEALED (v)
to make known through divine inspiration; to make (something secret or hidden) publicly or generally known; to display

Exod 6:3	did not **r** my name, Yahweh,
Deut 29:29	all that he has **r-ed** to us,
Isa 40:5	the LORD will be **r-ed**,
Isa 53:1	the LORD **r-ed** his powerful
Matt 10:26	is covered will be **r-ed**,
Matt 11:27	Son chooses to **r** him.
Luke 2:32	He is a light to **r** God
John 12:38	the LORD **r-ed** his powerful
John 14:21	love them and **r** myself
John 17:6	I have **r-ed** you to the
Rom 8:18	glory he will **r** to us
Rom 16:25	Christ has **r-ed** his plan
1 Cor 2:10	that God **r-ed** these things
Gal 1:16	to **r** his Son to me so that
Gal 2:2	because God **r-ed** to me
Eph 3:3	himself **r-ed** his mysterious
Col 1:26	it has been **r-ed** to God's
2 Thes 2:3	man of lawlessness is **r-ed**
Titus 2:13	Christ, will be **r-ed**.
Heb 9:8	the Holy Spirit **r-ed** that
1 Pet 1:7	when Jesus Christ is **r-ed**

REVELATION, REVELATIONS (n)
something that is revealed by God to humans; an act of revealing or communicating divine truth

1 Cor 14:6	bring you a **r** or some
1 Cor 14:30	person receives a **r** from
2 Cor 12:1	visions and **r-s** from the
2 Cor 12:7	wonderful **r-s** from God.
Gal 1:12	by direct **r** from Jesus

Rev 1:1 This is a **r** from Jesus

REVELRY (n)
noisy partying or merrymaking
Exod 32:6 they indulged in pagan **r.**
1 Cor 10:7 they indulged in pagan **r.**

REVENGE (n)
an act or instance of retaliating in order to get even
Lev 19:18 Do not seek **r** or bear
Num 31:3 war of **r** against Midian.
Deut 32:35 I will take **r;** I will
Josh 20:3 relatives seeking **r** for
Judg 20:10 will take **r** on Gibeah
Isa 34:8 day of the LORD's **r,**
Heb 10:30 I will take **r.** I will

REVERENCE (n)
profound, adoring, awed respect
see also AWE, FEAR, RESPECT
Lev 19:30 of rest, and show **r** toward
Job 15:4 fear of God, no **r** for him?
Job 37:24 who are wise show him **r.**
Eph 5:21 another out of **r** for Christ.
Heb 5:7 of his deep **r** for God.

REVERENT (adj)
expressing or characterized by reverence; worshipful
Col 3:22 because of your **r** fear
1 Pet 1:17 must live in **r** fear
1 Pet 3:2 your pure and **r** lives.

REVIVE, REVIVES, REVIVING (v)
to become active or flourishing again; to restore from a depressed, inactive, or unused state
Ps 19:7 are perfect, **r-ing** the soul.
Ps 85:6 Won't you **r** us again,
Ps 119:25 lie in the dust; **r** me
Ps 119:50 Your promise **r-s** me;
Prov 25:13 They **r** the spirit of

REVOLUTIONARIES (n)
those who engage in a revolution
Mark 15:27 Two **r** were crucified with

REWARD, REWARDS (n)
something that is given in return for good or evil done or received or that is offered or given for some service or attainment
Gen 15:1 and your **r** will be
1 Sam 26:23 gives his own **r** for doing
Prov 12:14 and hard work brings **r-s.**
Isa 49:4 I will trust God for my **r.**
Matt 5:12 For a great **r** awaits you
Matt 6:5 all the **r** they will ever
Luke 6:23 For a great **r** awaits you
Luke 6:35 your **r** from heaven will
Phil 4:17 you to receive a **r** for your
1 Thes 2:19 be our proud **r** and crown
Heb 10:35 the great **r** it brings you!
1 Pet 1:9 The **r** for trusting him

REWARD, REWARDED, REWARDS (v)
to give a reward to or for; to recompense
2 Sam 22:21 The LORD **r-ed** me for
Prov 13:21 while blessings **r** the
Prov 25:22 the LORD will **r** you.
Jer 31:16 for I will **r** you," says
Matt 6:18 sees everything, will **r** you.
Luke 12:37 for his return will be **r-ed.**
Luke 14:14 God will **r** you for
1 Cor 3:8 both will be **r-ed** for their
Eph 6:8 the Lord will **r** each one
1 Tim 3:13 will be **r-ed** with respect
Heb 11:6 that he **r-s** those who
Rev 11:18 the dead and **r** your servants

RICH (adj)
having abundant possessions and especially material wealth
Job 34:19 no more attention to the **r**
Ps 49:16 the wicked grow **r** and
Prov 10:4 poor; hard workers get **r.**
Prov 11:18 Evil people get **r** for
Prov 13:7 are poor pretend to be **r;**
Prov 21:17 and luxury will never be **r.**
Prov 22:2 The **r** and poor have this
Prov 23:4 yourself out trying to get **r.**
Prov 28:6 than to be dishonest and **r.**
Prov 28:22 Greedy people try to get **r**
Eccl 5:12 But the **r** seldom get a
Isa 53:9 put in a **r** man's grave.
Matt 19:23 hard for a **r** person to enter
Luke 1:53 and sent the **r** away with
Luke 6:24 you who are **r,** for you have
Luke 16:1 was a certain **r** man who had
Luke 21:1 watched the **r** people
2 Cor 8:9 Though he was **r,** yet for your
1 Tim 6:9 who long to be **r** fall into
1 Tim 6:17 who are **r** in this world
Jas 1:10 those who are **r** should boast
Jas 2:3 seat to the **r** person, but you
Jas 5:1 Look here, you **r** people:

RICHES (n)
things that make one rich; wealth
see also MONEY, POSSESSIONS, TREASURE(S), WEALTH
2 Chr 1:11 ask for wealth, **r,** fame,
Ps 49:6 wealth and boast of great **r.**
Prov 27:24 for **r** don't last forever,
Eccl 5:13 Hoarding **r** harms the

Jer 9:23 rich boast in their **r.**
Luke 8:14 cares and **r** and pleasures
Rom 11:33 great are God's **r** and
2 Cor 6:10 give spiritual **r** to others.
Col 1:27 know that the **r** and glory

RIDER (n)
one who sits and travels on the back of an animal
Rev 6:2 Its **r** carried a bow, and a
Rev 19:11 Its **r** was named Faithful and

RIDICULED, RIDICULING (v)
to make fun of
2 Kgs 19:22 you been defying and **r-ing?**
1 Cor 4:10 are honored, but we are **r.**

RIDING (v)
to sit and travel on the back of an animal that one directs
Zech 9:9 is humble, **r** on a donkey—
Matt 21:5 is humble, **r** on a donkey—

RIGHT (adj)
being in accordance with what is good, just, or proper; being in a correct or proper state; located opposite of left; acting or judging in accordance with truth or fact
see also JUST, JUSTIFY, RIGHTEOUS, UPRIGHT
Gen 4:7 do what is **r,** then watch out!
Gen 18:19 by doing what is **r** and just.
Exod 15:26 do what is **r** in his sight,
Num 25:13 making them **r** with me.
Deut 6:18 Do what is **r** and good
Deut 25:1 that one is **r** and the other
Josh 1:7 either to the **r** or to the
Judg 17:6 whatever seemed **r** in their
1 Sam 12:23 what is good and **r.**
1 Kgs 3:9 difference between **r** and
2 Chr 12:6 The Lord is **r** in doing
Ps 19:8 Lord are **r,** bringing joy
Ps 24:5 have a **r** relationship with
Ps 25:8 does what is **r;** he shows the
Ps 37:30 they teach **r** from wrong.
Ps 64:10 do what is **r** will praise him.
Ps 71:2 do what is **r.** Turn your ear
Ps 84:11 from those who do what is **r.**
Ps 97:11 on those whose hearts are **r.**
Ps 106:3 and always do what is **r.**
Ps 119:144 laws are always **r;** help me
Prov 1:3 do what is **r,** just, and fair.
Prov 2:13 men turn from the **r** way
Prov 14:2 who follow the **r** path
Prov 14:12 person that seems **r,** but
Prov 15:21 stays on the **r** path.
Prov 15:23 to say the **r** thing at the
Prov 18:17 in court sounds **r**—until
Eccl 8:5 and a way to do what is **r,**
Eccl 9:11 being in the **r** place at the
Isa 7:15 choose what is **r** and reject
Isa 16:5 be eager to do what is **r.**
Isa 26:7 who does what is **r,** and you
Jer 23:5 is just and **r** throughout the
Ezek 18:5 and does what is just and **r.**
Ezek 18:21 and do what is just and **r,**
Hos 14:9 are true and **r,** and righteous
Mic 3:1 to know **r** from wrong,
Mic 6:8 do what is **r,** to love mercy,
Zeph 2:3 to do what is **r** and to live
Matt 6:3 hand know what your **r** hand
Matt 22:44 of honor at my **r** hand until
Acts 2:34 the place of honor at my **r** hand
Acts 7:55 honor at God's **r** hand.
Acts 13:39 is declared **r** with God—
Rom 1:17 God makes us **r** in his sight.
Rom 2:13 doesn't make us **r** with God.
Rom 3:4 will be proved **r** in what you
Rom 3:20 ever be made **r** with God by
Rom 3:22 We are made **r** with God by
Rom 3:28 So we are made **r** with God
Rom 3:30 makes people **r** with himself
Rom 4:13 but on a **r** relationship with
Rom 4:25 life to make us **r** with God.
Rom 5:1 we have been made **r** in God's
Rom 5:16 being made **r** with God,
Rom 6:13 to do what is **r** for the glory
Rom 8:10 have been made **r** with God.
Rom 8:30 given them **r** standing,
Rom 9:30 they were made **r** with God.
Rom 10:3 way of getting **r** with God by
Rom 10:10 you are made **r** with God,
1 Cor 6:11 you were made **r** with God
2 Cor 3:9 which makes us **r** with God!
2 Cor 5:21 be made **r** with God
Gal 2:16 person is made **r** with God by
Gal 2:17 to be made **r** with God through
Gal 2:21 law could make us **r** with God,
Gal 3:11 can be made **r** with God by
Gal 3:21 could be made **r** with God by
Gal 3:24 could be made **r** with God
Gal 5:4 to make yourselves **r** with God
Eph 5:9 what is good and **r** and true.
Phil 4:8 honorable, and **r,** and pure,
2 Tim 3:16 teaches us to do what is **r.**
Heb 2:10 it was only **r** that he should
Heb 12:11 harvest of **r** living for those
Jas 2:24 are shown to be **r** with God by
1 Jn 2:29 who do what is **r** are God's

RIGHT, RIGHTS (n)
correct or moral behavior; something to which one has a just claim
Job 27:2 has taken away my **r-s,** by
Ps 25:9 in doing **r,** teaching them his

Ps 34:15 those who do **r;** his ears are
Ps 82:3 the **r-s** of the oppressed
Prov 29:7 about the **r-s** of the poor;
Isa 1:17 Fight for the **r-s** of widows.
Isa 10:2 and deny the **r-s** of the needy
Lam 3:35 others of their **r-s** in
Matt 5:10 for doing **r,** for the Kingdom
John 1:12 he gave the **r** to become
Rom 9:21 he have a **r** to use the same
1 Cor 9:4 have the **r** to live in your
1 Pet 3:12 those who do **r,** and his ears

RIGHTEOUS (adj)
acting in accord with divine or moral law; free from guilt or sin; morally right or justifiable
see also JUST, JUSTIFY, RIGHT, UPRIGHT
Gen 6:9 Noah was a **r** man, the only
Gen 15:6 counted him as **r** because of
Gen 18:23 sweep away both the **r** and
Ps 7:8 Declare me **r,** O LORD, for
Ps 17:15 Because I am **r,** I will see
Ps 106:31 regarded as a **r** man ever
Ps 119:7 I learn your **r** regulations,
Ps 119:137 O LORD, you are **r,**
Ps 145:17 The LORD is **r** in everything
Prov 4:18 The way of the **r** is like the
Prov 9:9 Teach the **r,** and they
Prov 29:6 but the **r** escape, shouting
Isa 26:2 to all who are **r;** allow the
Isa 42:21 Because he is **r,** the LORD
Isa 64:6 we display our **r** deeds,
Jer 11:20 you make **r** judgments, and
Jer 23:5 raise up a **r** descendant from
Ezek 3:20 None of their **r** acts will be
Amos 5:24 river of **r** living.
Hab 2:4 But the **r** will live
Mal 3:18 between the **r** and the wicked,
Matt 9:13 think they are **r,** but those
Matt 13:43 Then the **r** will shine
Matt 25:37 Then these **r** ones will
Luke 1:6 and Elizabeth were **r** in God's
Luke 16:15 like to appear **r** in public,
Rom 1:17 faith that a **r** person has
Rom 3:5 people see how **r** God is.
Rom 3:10 No one is **r**—not even one.
Rom 4:3 counted him as **r** because of
Rom 4:6 who are declared **r** without
Rom 4:22 God counted him as **r.**
Rom 6:19 be slaves to **r** living so that
Gal 3:6 counted him as **r** because of
Eph 4:24 like God—truly **r** and holy.
Phil 1:11 salvation—the **r** character
2 Tim 2:22 Instead, pursue **r** living,
Titus 3:7 he declared us **r** and gave us
Jas 2:23 counted him as **r** because of
Jas 5:16 prayer of a **r** person has
1 Jn 2:1 the one who is truly **r.**
1 Jn 3:7 that they are **r,** even as

RIGHTEOUSNESS (n)
the state or quality of being righteous
see also GODLINESS, JUSTICE
Ps 36:6 Your **r** is like the mighty
Ps 71:15 tell everyone about your **r.**
Ps 85:10 **R** and peace have kissed!
Ps 98:2 has revealed his **r** to every
Ps 111:3 His **r** never fails.
Prov 21:21 Whoever pursues **r** and
Isa 11:5 He will wear **r** like a belt
Isa 42:6 you to demonstrate my **r.**
Isa 45:8 so salvation and **r** can sprout
Isa 56:1 to display my **r** among you.
Isa 59:17 He put on **r** as his body
Jer 9:24 brings justice and **r** to the
Jer 23:6 LORD Is Our **R.**
Hos 10:12 come and shower **r** upon
Mic 7:9 and I will see his **r.**
Mal 4:2 the Sun of **R** will rise
Matt 5:20 unless your **r** is better
John 16:8 and of God's **r,** and of the
Acts 24:25 about **r** and self-control
Rom 3:26 to demonstrate his **r,** for he
Rom 5:18 one act of **r** brings a right
2 Cor 6:7 the weapons of **r** in the
Eph 6:14 the body armor of God's **r.**
Phil 3:6 And as for **r,** I obeyed the
2 Tim 4:8 the crown of **r,** which
Heb 11:7 he received the **r** that comes
Jas 3:18 and reap a harvest of **r.**
2 Pet 3:13 filled with God's **r.**

RIPE (adj)
fully grown and developed
John 4:35 are already **r** for harvest.
Rev 14:15 the crop on earth is **r.**

RISE, RISEN, RISES (v)
to ascend or extend above other objects; to return from death; to assume an upright position
see also RESURRECTION
Num 24:17 A star will **r** from Jacob;
Isa 26:19 bodies will **r** again!
Mal 4:2 of Righteousness will **r** with
Matt 22:30 when the dead **r,** they will
Matt 27:63 I will **r** from the dead.
Matt 28:6 He is **r-n** from the dead,
Mark 8:31 later he would **r** from the
Mark 16:6 He is **r-n** from the dead!
Luke 18:33 day he will **r** again.
Luke 24:34 The Lord has really **r-n!**
John 5:29 and they will **r** again.
John 11:24 when everyone else **r-s,** at

John 20:9 said Jesus must **r** from the
Acts 17:3 must suffer and **r** from the
1 Thes 4:16 have died will **r** from

RIVER (n)
a natural stream of water; large or overwhelming quantities
Isa 66:12 give Jerusalem a **r** of peace
Ezek 47:8 "This **r** flows east through
Amos 5:24 an endless **r** of righteous
Rev 22:1 showed me a **r** with the water

RIVERBANK (n)
the ground serving as an edge of a river
Ps 1:3 along the **r,** bearing fruit

ROAD (n)
an open way for vehicles, persons, and animals; a route or way to an end, conclusion, or circumstance
Ps 25:4 point out the **r** for me to
Prov 22:5 treacherous **r;** whoever values
Isa 35:8 And a great **r** will go through
Matt 3:3 Clear the **r** for him!

ROARING (adj)
making or characterized by a sound resembling a roar
1 Pet 5:8 around like a **r** lion, looking

ROB (v)
to steal from by force
Ezek 22:29 oppress the poor, **r** the needy,

ROBBERS (n)
one who steals usually by violence or threat
John 10:8 before me were thieves and **r.**

ROBBERY (n)
the act or practice of stealing by violence or threat
Isa 61:8 I hate **r** and wrongdoing.

ROBE (n)
a long, flowing outer garment
Gen 37:3 for Joseph—a beautiful **r.**
Isa 6:1 the train of his **r** filled the

ROBED (v)
clothed or covered with or as if with a robe
Ps 93:1 LORD is **r** in majesty

ROCK (n)
a stone; a cliff; foundation, support; refuge
Exod 17:6 Moses struck the **r** as he was
Num 20:8 speak to the **r** over there,
Deut 32:13 honey from the **r** and olive
2 Sam 22:2 LORD is my **r,** my
Ps 18:2 God is my **r,** in whom I
Ps 19:14 LORD, my **r** and my redeemer.
Ps 61:2 to the towering **r** of safety,
Ps 62:7 my refuge, a **r** where no enemy
Ps 92:15 He is my **r!**
Isa 26:4 GOD is the eternal **R.**
Matt 7:24 builds a house on solid **r.**
Matt 16:18 upon this **r** I will build
Rom 9:33 stumble, a **r** that makes them
1 Cor 10:4 and that **r** was Christ.
1 Pet 2:8 stumble, the **r** that makes

ROD, RODS (n)
a straight, slender stick used as a walking stick, a club or weapon, a shepherd's crook, a paddling stick, a royal scepter, or a measuring stick; figurative of divine authority
see also STAFF
2 Sam 7:14 him with the **r,** like any
Ps 2:9 will break them with an iron **r**
Ps 23:4 Your **r** and your staff
Prov 13:24 spare the **r** of discipline
2 Cor 11:25 times I was beaten with **r-s.**
Rev 2:27 the nations with an iron **r**
Rev 12:5 rule all nations with an iron **r.**
Rev 19:15 rule them with an iron **r.**

ROMAN (adj)
of or relating to Rome or the people of Rome
Acts 16:37 and we are **R** citizens.
Acts 22:25 you to whip a **R** citizen

ROMAN OFFICER (n)
a person of some authority in the Roman military
Matt 8:5 a **R** came and pleaded
Luke 23:47 the **R** overseeing the execution
Acts 10:22 sent by Cornelius, a **R**

ROMAN SOLDIERS (n)
those actively involved in the Roman military
Mark 15:15 over to the **R** to be crucified
John 18:3 given Judas a contingent of **R**

ROOSTER (n)
an adult male domestic chicken
Matt 26:34 before the **r** crows, you will

ROOT, ROOTS (n)
the part of a plant usually found underground ; something that is an origin or source (as of a condition or quality)
Isa 11:1 bearing fruit from the old **r.**
Isa 53:2 green shoot, like a **r** in dry
Matt 3:10 to sever the **r-s** of the trees.
Matt 13:21 don't have deep **r-s,** they
Eph 3:17 Your **r-s** will grow down
1 Tim 6:10 money is the **r** of all kinds

Jude 1:12 have been pulled up by the **r-s.**

ROPE, ROPES (n)
a large stout cord of strands twisted or braided together
Josh 2:18 this scarlet **r** hanging from
Prov 5:22 they are **r-s** that catch
Hos 11:4 with my **r-s** of kindness

ROT (v)
to undergo decomposition
Ps 16:10 holy one to **r** in the grave.
Acts 2:27 Holy One to **r** in the grave.
Acts 13:35 Holy One to **r** in the grave.

ROYAL (adj)
of, relating to, or subject to the crown
Ps 93:5 Your **r** laws cannot be
Isa 63:1 this in **r** robes, marching
Jas 2:8 you obey the **r** law as found
1 Pet 2:9 You are **r** priests,

RUDDER (n)
an underwater blade that steers a boat or ship
Jas 3:4 a small **r** makes a huge ship

RUDE (adj)
offensive in manner or action
1 Cor 13:5 or **r.** It does not demand

RUIN (n)
physical, moral, economic, or social collapse
Eccl 4:5 idle hands, leading them to **r.**
1 Tim 6:9 them into **r** and destruction.

RUIN, RUINED, RUINING, RUINS (v)
to damage irreparably; to subject to frustration, failure, or disaster
Prov 19:3 People **r** their lives by
Prov 19:18 you will **r** their lives.
Prov 22:23 He will **r** anyone who **r-s**
Isa 3:14 You have **r-ed** Israel,
Matt 9:17 the wine and **r-ing** the skins.
2 Tim 2:14 they can **r** those who hear

RULE, RULES (n)
a prescribed guide for conduct or action
Isa 29:13 but man-made **r-s** learned by
2 Tim 2:5 unless they follow the **r-s.**
Heb 13:9 not from **r-s** about food,

RULE, RULED, RULES (v)
to exert control, direction, or influence on; to exercise authority or power over
Gen 3:16 but he will **r** over you.
Ps 2:4 But the one who **r-s** in heaven
Ps 11:4 LORD still **r-s** from heaven.
Ps 55:19 God, who has **r-d** forever,
Ps 66:7 great power he **r-s** forever.
Ps 89:9 You **r** the oceans.
Ps 103:19 there he **r-s** over everything.
Prov 17:2 wise servant will **r** over the
Isa 9:7 He will **r** with fairness
Isa 40:10 He will **r** with a powerful
Jer 23:5 a King who **r-s** with wisdom.
Zech 6:13 honor and will **r** as king
Rom 5:21 as sin **r-d** over all people
Rom 15:12 come, and he will **r** over
Col 3:15 comes from Christ **r** in your
Rev 19:15 He will **r** them with

RULER, RULERS (n)
person with authority; tribal chief; prince or king; city magistrate; powerful spiritual beings; God himself
Judg 8:22 to Gideon, "Be our **r!**
1 Sam 10:1 to be the **r** over Israel,
Prov 19:6 favors from a **r;** everyone is
Prov 23:1 with a **r,** pay attention to
Jer 30:21 have their own **r** again,
Dan 7:27 all **r-s** will serve and obey him.
Dan 9:25 until a **r**—the Anointed One—
Mic 5:2 a **r** of Israel will come from
Matt 2:6 for a **r** will come from
Matt 20:25 that the **r-s** in this world
John 12:31 when Satan, the **r** of this
1 Cor 2:6 or to the **r-s** of this world,
Eph 1:21 far above any **r** or authority
Eph 3:10 the unseen **r-s** and authorities
Eph 6:12 but against evil **r-s** and
Col 1:16 as thrones, kingdoms, **r-s,** and
Col 2:15 disarmed the spiritual **r-s** and
Rev 1:5 and the **r** of all the kings

RUMORS (n)
a statement or report without known authority for its truth
Exod 23:1 must not pass along false **r.**
Prov 18:8 **R** are dainty morsels that
Jer 51:46 For **r** will keep coming year

RUN, RUNNING (v)
to go faster than a walk; to flee
Ps 19:5 athlete eager to **r** the race.
Prov 4:12 when you **r,** you won't
Isa 40:31 will **r** and not grow weary.
1 Cor 9:26 So I **r** with purpose in
Gal 2:2 and I was **r-ning** the race for
Gal 5:7 You were **r-ning** the race so
Phil 2:16 that I did not **r** the race in
1 Tim 6:11 so **r** from all these evil
2 Tim 2:22 **R** from anything that
Heb 12:1 let us **r** with endurance

RUNNER (n)
a messenger
Hab 2:2 so that a **r** can carry

RUST (n)
the reddish brittle coating formed on iron
Matt 6:19 them and **r** destroys them,

RUTH
Moabitess (Ruth 1:4); widowed daughter-in-law of Naomi (Ruth 1:18); later married Boaz (Ruth 4:10); ancestor of David and Jesus (Ruth 4:13, 21-22; Matt 1:5).

RUTHLESS (adj)
having no pity; cruel
Prov 11:16 gains respect, but **r** men gain
Isa 25:3 **r** nations will fear you.

S

SABAOTH (KJV)
Rom 9:29 the LORD of *Heaven's Armies*
Jas 5:4 the LORD of *Heaven's Armies*

SABBATH, SABBATHS (n)
cessation of activity; a holy day set aside to honor God through rest and worship
see also REST
Exod 20:8 to observe the **S** day by
Exod 31:14 must keep the **S** day, for it
Lev 25:2 must observe a **S** rest before
Deut 5:12 Observe the **S** day by
2 Chr 2:4 and evening, on the **S-s,**
Isa 56:2 who honor my **S** days of rest
Isa 56:6 do not desecrate the **S** day
Isa 58:13 Honor the **S** in everything
Matt 12:1 some grainfields on the **S.**
Luke 13:10 One **S** day as Jesus was
Col 2:16 new moon ceremonies or **S-s.**

SACKCLOTH (KJV)
Gen 37:34 dressed himself in *burlap.*
Esth 4:1 put on *burlap* and ashes,
Job 16:15 I wear *burlap* to show my grief
Ps 30:11 my *clothes of mourning* and
Luke 10:13 *burlap* and throwing ashes

SACRED (adj)
dedicated or set apart for the service or worship of a deity; entitled to reverence and respect
Lev 10:13 eat it in a **s** place, for
Num 4:15 and all the **s** articles.
2 Tim 3:2 They will consider nothing **s.**

SACRIFICE, SACRIFICES (n)
worship or atonement offering; something given up or lost
Exod 12:27 It is the Passover **s** to the
1 Sam 15:22 Obedience is better than **s,**
Ps 40:6 no delight in **s-s** or offerings.
Ps 51:16 do not desire a **s,** or I would
Ps 51:17 The **s** you desire is
Ps 107:22 offer **s-s** of thanksgiving
Prov 15:8 LORD detests the **s** of
Hos 6:6 to show love, not offer **s-s.**
Matt 9:13 to show mercy, not offer **s-s.**
Rom 3:25 Jesus as the **s** for sin.
Rom 8:3 Son as a **s** for our sins.
Rom 12:1 a living and holy **s**—the
Eph 5:2 himself as a **s** for us,
Heb 5:3 he must offer **s-s** for his own
Heb 7:27 need to offer **s-s** every day.
Heb 9:28 time as a **s** to take away
Heb 10:5 did not want animal **s-s** or sin
Heb 10:10 holy by the **s** of the body of
Heb 13:15 Jesus a continual **s** of praise
Heb 13:16 These are the **s-s** that please
1 Pet 2:5 offer spiritual **s-s** that please
1 Jn 2:2 himself is the **s** that atones
1 Jn 4:10 his Son as a **s** to take away

SACRIFICE, SACRIFICED, SACRIFICES (v)
to suffer loss of, give up, renounce, injure, kill, or destroy, especially for an ideal, belief, or end
Gen 22:2 Go and **s** him as a
John 10:11 good shepherd **s-s** his life
John 10:15 I **s** my life for the sheep.
1 Cor 5:7 Lamb, has been **s-d** for us.
1 Cor 13:3 poor and even **s-d** my body,

SACRILEGIOUS (adj)
of, relating to, or characterized by a violation of or gross irreverence toward something holy or sacred
Dan 11:31 and set up the **s** object that
Dan 12:11 stopped and the **s** object that
Matt 24:15 about—the **s** object that
Mark 13:14 will see the **s** object that

SAD (adj)
affected with or expressive of grief or unhappiness
Ps 42:5 Why is my heart so **s?**
Luke 18:23 **s,** for he was very rich.

SADDUCEES (n)
members of a Jewish faction that rejected doctrines not in the law (as resurrection, retribution in a future life, and the existence of angels)
Matt 16:6 yeast of the Pharisees and **S.**
Mark 12:18 **S**—religious leaders
Acts 23:8 for the **S** say there is no

SADNESS (n)
grief or unhappiness
Ps 31:10 my years are shortened by **s.**
Eccl 7:3 **s** has a refining influence
Jas 4:9 **s** instead of laughter

SAFE (adj)
free from harm or risk; secure from threat of danger, harm, or loss
Deut 29:19 I am **s,** even though I am
1 Sam 30:23 has kept us **s** and helped
Ps 4:8 O LORD, will keep me **s.**
Ps 28:8 He is a **s** fortress for his
Prov 2:11 will keep you **s.**
Prov 4:26 stay on the **s** path.
Prov 18:10 run to him and are **s.**
Prov 28:26 who walks in wisdom is **s.**
John 17:15 keep them **s** from the evil

SAFETY (n)
the condition of being safe from undergoing or causing hurt, injury, or loss
Deut 33:12 and live in **s** beside him.
2 Sam 23:5 ensure my **s** and success.
Ps 16:9 My body rests in **s.**
Ps 59:16 my refuge, a place of **s**
Prov 11:14 is **s** in having many advisers.
Prov 29:25 trusting the LORD means **s.**
Hos 2:18 live unafraid in peace and **s.**

SAINTS (KJV)
Ps 34:9 you his *godly people,* for
Ps 97:10 the lives of his *godly people*
Dan 7:18 *holy people* of the Most High
Rom 8:27 Spirit pleads for *us believers*
1 Cor 6:2 *we believers* will judge the

SAKE (n)
personal or social welfare, safety, or benefit; the good, advantage, or enhancement of some entity
Rom 8:36 say, "For your **s** we are
2 Tim 1:8 for the **s** of the Good News
Heb 11:26 to suffer for the **s** of Christ

SALT (n)
the mineral sodium chloride used mainly for seasoning and as a preservative
Gen 19:26 she turned into a pillar of **s.**
Matt 5:13 You are the **s** of the earth.

SALVATION (n)
deliverance from the power and effects of sin, danger, or difficulty by God's intervention
see also SAVE
2 Sam 22:47 Rock of my **s,** be exalted!
2 Chr 6:41 be clothed with **s;** may your
Ps 18:46 God of my **s** be exalted!
Ps 27:1 light and my **s**—so why should
Ps 40:16 love your **s** repeatedly shout,
Ps 51:12 joy of your **s,** and make me
Ps 62:2 rock and my **s,** my fortress
Ps 69:13 my prayer with your sure **s.**
Ps 74:12 ages past, bringing **s** to
Ps 85:4 us again, O God of our **s.**
Ps 89:26 and the Rock of my **s.**
Ps 91:16 long life and give them my **s.**
Ps 95:1 joyfully to the Rock of our **s.**
Isa 25:9 rejoice in the **s** he brings!
Isa 26:18 We have not given **s** to the
Isa 33:6 rich store of **s,** wisdom,
Isa 45:8 wide so **s** and righteousness
Isa 45:22 the world look to me for **s!**
Isa 49:6 will bring my **s** to the ends
Isa 51:6 but my **s** lasts forever.
Isa 52:7 of peace and **s,** the news that
Isa 59:17 the helmet of **s** on his head.
Isa 62:1 dawn, and her **s** blazes like
Lam 3:26 wait quietly for **s** from the
Jonah 2:9 For my **s** comes from the
Luke 1:77 to find **s** through forgiveness
Luke 2:30 I have seen your **s,**
Luke 3:6 will see the **s** sent from
Luke 21:28 up, for your **s** is near!
John 4:22 him, for **s** comes through the
Acts 13:26 this message of **s** has been
Acts 13:47 Gentiles, to bring **s** to the
Acts 28:28 know that this **s** from God
Rom 11:11 so God made **s** available to
Rom 13:11 for our **s** is nearer now
2 Cor 6:2 the day of **s,** I helped you.
2 Cor 7:10 from sin and results in **s.**
Eph 6:17 Put on **s** as your helmet,
Phil 2:12 show the results of your **s,**
2 Thes 2:13 to experience **s**—a **s**
Titus 2:11 bringing **s** to all people.
Heb 2:3 if we ignore this great **s** that
Heb 5:9 source of eternal **s** for all
Heb 9:28 but to bring **s** to all who
1 Pet 1:9 will be the **s** of your souls.
1 Pet 1:13 to the gracious **s** that will
1 Pet 2:2 into a full experience of **s.**
Rev 7:10 a great roar, "**S** comes from

SAMARIA (n)
the capital city of the northern kingdom of Israel; a region in the uplands of central Palestine between Galilee and Judea
1 Kgs 16:24 hill now known as **S** from
2 Kgs 17:6 Hoshea's reign, **S** fell,
John 4:4 to go through **S** on the way.

SAMARITAN (n or adj)
a native or inhabitant of Samaria
Luke 10:33 a despised **S** came along,
Luke 17:16 man was a **S.**
John 4:5 he came to the **S** village of
John 4:7 a **S** woman came to draw

SAMSON
Judge of Israel from tribe of Dan; defeated oppressing Philistines (Judg 14–15); killed lion with bare hands (Judg 14:6); set 300 fox tails on fire (Judg 15:4); killed 1,000 men (Judg 15:15); carried large gates to top of hill (Judg 16:3); seduced and deceived by Delilah (Judg 16:1-22); died as he destroyed many Philistines (Judg 16:23-31).

SAMUEL
Judge and prophet of Israel (Heb 11:32); prophet's birth and dedication (1 Sam 1); raised by Eli in the Temple (1 Sam 2:11, 18-21); called as a prophet (1 Sam 3); served as judge over Israel (1 Sam 7:15); warned Israel of the tyranny of kingship (1 Sam 8:10-18); anointed Saul (1 Sam 10:1); rejected Saul (1 Sam 15:23); anointed David (1 Sam 16:13); protected David from Saul (1 Sam 19:18-24); died (1 Sam 25:1); ghost of Samuel rebuked Saul (1 Sam 28:14-19).

SANCTIFY, SANCTIFIED (KJV)
Gen 2:3 and *declared it holy*
Exod 31:13 Lord, who *makes you holy*
Deut 5:12 Sabbath day by *keeping it holy*
John 17:19 myself as a *holy sacrifice*
Heb 10:10 for us to *be made holy* by

SANCTUARY (n)
a holy place set apart for worship of God or refuge from danger
see also TABERNACLE, TEMPLE
Exod 25:8 build me a holy **s** so I can
Lev 19:30 show reverence toward my **s.**
Ps 27:5 he will hide me in his **s.**
Ps 63:2 you in your **s** and gazed upon
Ps 68:35 God is awesome in his **s.**
Ps 150:1 Praise God in his **s;** praise
Heb 6:19 curtain into God's inner **s.**

SAND (n)
fine grains of rock that are worn away by wind and rain
Gen 22:17 in the sky and the **s** on
Matt 7:26 who builds a house on **s.**

SANDAL, SANDALS (n)
a shoe consisting of a sole strapped to the foot
Exod 3:5 Take off your **s-s,** for you are
Exod 12:11 wear your **s-s,** and carry
Deut 25:9 elders, pull his **s** from his
Josh 5:15 Take off your **s-s,** for the
Ruth 4:7 to remove his **s** and hand it
Matt 3:11 his slave and carry his **s-s.**

SANG (v)
to produce musical tones by means of the voice
see also SING
Exod 15:1 people of Israel **s** this
Exod 15:21 And Miriam **s** this song:
Num 21:17 the Israelites **s** this song:
Judg 5:1 son of Abinoam **s** this song:
2 Sam 22:1 David **s** this song to
Ezra 3:11 and thanks, they **s** this song
Job 38:7 morning stars **s** together and
Ps 106:12 Then they **s** his praise.
Matt 26:30 Then they **s** a hymn
Rev 5:9 And they **s** a new song
Rev 5:13 They **s:** "Blessing and
Rev 14:3 great choir **s** a wonderful

SAPS (v)
to gradually diminish the supply or intensity of
Prov 17:22 broken spirit **s** a person's

SARAH (SARAI)
Wife of Abraham (Abram) (Gen 11:30-31); was infertile (Gen 11:30; Rom 4:19) and very beautiful (Gen 12:11); with Abraham, deceived Pharaoh (Gen 12:10-20); dealings with Hagar and Ishmael (Gen 16); name changed (Gen 17:15); Isaac promised (Gen 18:10-15; Rom 9:9); example of faith (Heb 11:11); with Abraham, deceived Abimelech (Gen 20); Isaac born (Gen 21:1-7); Hagar and Ishmael sent away (Gen 21:8-21); died and was buried (Gen 23); Paul's analogy using Sarah and Hagar (Gal 4:25-26).

SARDIS (n)
the capital city of Lydia in the province of Asia, in western Asia Minor (modern Turkey)
Rev 3:1 the angel of the church in **S.**

SAT (v)
to place (the buttocks) on or in a seat
see also SIT
Dan 7:9 and the Ancient One **s** down to
Mark 16:19 into heaven and **s** down in
Heb 8:1 High Priest who **s** down in the
Heb 10:12 Then he **s** down in the

SATAN (n)
"adversary" of God and man; the personal name of the devil
see also DEVIL
Job 1:6 and the Accuser, **S,** came with
Zech 3:2 your accusations, **S.** Yes,

Matt 12:26 if **S** is casting out **S,** he
Matt 16:23 Get away from me, **S!**
Mark 4:15 only to have **S** come at once
Luke 10:18 told them, "I saw **S** fall from
Luke 22:3 Then **S** entered into Judas
Rom 16:20 soon crush **S** under your
1 Cor 5:5 him over to **S** so that his
2 Cor 11:14 Even **S** disguises himself as
2 Cor 12:7 from **S** to torment
1 Tim 1:20 them over to **S** so they might
Rev 12:9 the devil, or **S,** the one
Rev 20:2 is the devil, **S**—and bound
Rev 20:7 come to an end, **S** will be let

SATISFY, SATISFIED, SATISFIES, SATISFYING (v)
to make happy; to gratify to the full
Josh 22:33 Israelites were **s-ied** and
Ps 17:14 But **s** the hunger of your
Ps 17:15 you face to face and be **s-ied.**
Ps 22:26 poor will eat and be **s-ied.**
Ps 63:5 You **s** me more than the richest
Ps 105:40 quail; he **s-ied** their hunger
Ps 107:9 he **s-ies** the thirsty and fills
Ps 145:16 your hand, you **s** the hunger
Ps 147:14 and **s-ies** your hunger with the
Prov 5:19 Let her breasts **s** you always.
Prov 30:8 just enough to **s** my needs.
Prov 30:15 that are never **s-ied**—no, four
Isa 9:12 LORD's anger will not be **s-ied.**
Mic 7:1 be found to **s** my hunger.
Luke 6:21 now, for you will be **s-ied.**
Heb 13:5 be **s-ied** with what you have.
Jas 5:5 luxury, **s-ing** your every desire.

SAUL
1. First king of Israel (united kingdom), from tribe of Benjamin (1 Sam 9–11); anointed by Samuel (1 Sam 10:1); made unlawful sacrifices (1 Sam 13:1-14); warrior in battles (1 Sam 13:15–14:52); rejected as king (1 Sam 15:26); troubled by evil spirit (1 Sam 16:14-23); resentful of David and tried to kill him (1 Sam 18:5–19:22); gave Michal as wife to David (1 Sam 18:17-30); hunted David (1 Sam 22–24; 26); had priests at Nob killed (1 Sam 22:6-23); consulted medium at Endor, rebuked by Samuel's ghost (1 Sam 28:3-25); wounded in battle, then killed himself (1 Sam 31:4-6; *see also* 2 Sam 1:4-16); body desecrated, burned, and buried (1 Sam 31:12-13).
2. *See* PAUL, also known as Saul.

SAVE, SAVED, SAVES, SAVING (v)
to rescue or deliver from danger or harm; to deliver from sin; to preserve or guard from injury, destruction, or loss; to maintain or preserve
see also PRESERVE, RESCUE, SALVATION
2 Sam 22:3 the power that **s-s** me,
1 Chr 16:23 good news that he **s-s.**
Ps 7:10 is my shield, **s-ing** those whose
Ps 18:48 you **s** me from violent
Ps 22:8 let the LORD **s** him!
Ps 25:5 you are the God who **s-s** me.
Ps 33:16 army cannot **s** a king, nor
Ps 34:6 LORD listened; he **s-d** me
Ps 44:6 not count on my sword to **s**
Ps 68:20 Our God is a God who **s-s!**
Ps 109:31 the needy, ready to **s** them
Ps 116:6 death, and he **s-d** me.
Prov 2:16 Wisdom will **s** you from
Prov 10:2 right living can **s** your
Isa 25:9 trusted in him, and he **s-d** us!
Isa 30:15 resting in me will you be **s-d.**
Isa 35:4 He is coming to **s** you.
Isa 59:1 arm is not too weak to **s**
Isa 63:1 who has the power to **s!**
Jer 4:14 your heart that you may be **s-d.**
Jer 17:14 if you **s** me, I will
Jer 51:9 nothing can **s** her now.
Dan 3:17 we serve is able to **s** us.
Joel 2:32 name of the LORD will be **s-d,**
Mic 7:7 wait confidently for God to **s**
Zeph 1:18 gold will not **s** you
Matt 1:21 he will **s** his people
Matt 16:25 my sake, you will **s** it.
Matt 24:13 to the end will be **s-d.**
Luke 17:33 life go, you will **s** it.
Luke 19:10 seek and **s** those who are
John 10:9 in through me will be **s-d.**
John 12:47 I have come to **s** the world
Acts 2:21 name of the LORD will be **s-d.**
Acts 4:12 by which we must be **s-d.**
Acts 15:11 we are all **s-d** the same way,
Acts 16:30 what must I do to be **s-d?**
Rom 1:16 God at work, **s-ing** everyone
Rom 5:9 he will certainly **s** us from
Rom 10:9 the dead, you will be **s-d.**
Rom 10:13 of the LORD will be **s-d.**
1 Cor 1:18 we who are being **s-d** know
1 Cor 5:5 himself will be **s-d** on the
1 Cor 7:16 wives might be **s-d** because
1 Cor 10:33 so that many may be **s-d.**
1 Cor 15:2 this Good News that **s-s**
Eph 1:13 Good News that God **s-s** you.
1 Thes 5:9 God chose to **s** us through
1 Tim 1:15 the world to **s** sinners
1 Tim 2:4 wants everyone to be **s-d** and
1 Tim 2:15 women will be **s-d** through
2 Tim 1:9 For God **s-d** us and called
Titus 3:5 he **s-d** us, not because of the
Heb 7:25 and forever, to **s** those who
Jas 5:20 sinner back will **s** that person
2 Pet 3:15 gives people time to be **s-d.**

SAVING (adj)
of or relating to delivering or rescuing
Ps 40:10 faithfulness and **s** power.
Ps 67:2 the earth, your **s** power
Ps 69:29 God, by your **s** power.
Ps 71:15 proclaim your **s** power,
Ps 98:1 has shown his **s** power!

SAVIOR (n)
one who delivers from trouble, sin, or judgment
2 Sam 22:2 my fortress, and my **s;**
Ps 38:22 help me, O LORD my **s.**
Ps 40:17 You are my helper and my **s.**
Ps 106:21 They forgot God, their **s,**
Isa 43:11 and there is no other **S.**
Isa 45:21 a righteous God and **S.**
Isa 49:26 the LORD, am your **S** and
Isa 62:11 Look, your **S** is coming.
Jer 14:8 Hope of Israel, our **S** in
Hos 13:4 for there is no other **s.**
Zeph 3:17 He is a mighty **s.**
Luke 1:47 rejoices in God my **S!**
Luke 1:69 He has sent us a mighty **S**
John 4:42 he is indeed the **S** of the
Acts 5:31 right hand as Prince and **S.**
Acts 13:23 God's promised **S** of Israel!
Eph 5:23 He is the **S** of his body,
1 Tim 2:3 good and pleases God our **S,**
1 Tim 4:10 who is the **S** of all people
Titus 2:10 about God our **S** attractive
Titus 3:4 When God our **S** revealed his
2 Pet 3:2 Lord and **S** commanded
1 Jn 4:14 Son to be the **S** of the world.

SAVOUR (KJV)
2 Cor 2:16 a dreadful *smell* of death
Eph 5:2 for us, a pleasing *aroma* to God

SAW (v)
to percieve using the eye
see also SEE
Ps 139:16 You **s** me before I was born.

SCALES (n)
the outer covering of fish or reptiles; an instrument for weighing
see also BALANCES
Lev 11:9 fins and **s,** whether taken
Lev 19:36 Your **s** and weights
Deut 25:13 must use accurate **s** when you
Prov 11:1 use of dishonest **s,** but he
Rev 6:5 a pair of **s** in his hand.

SCAPEGOAT (n)
a goat upon whose head the sins of the people are symbolically placed, after which he is sent into the wilderness on the Day of Atonement
Lev 16:10 other goat, the **s** chosen by

SCARLET (adj)
of the color of any various bright reds
Josh 2:21 leaving the **s** rope hanging
Isa 1:18 sins are like **s,** I will make
Matt 27:28 and put a **s** robe on him.

SCARS (n)
marks left (as in the skin) by the healing of injured tissue
Gal 6:17 on my body the **s** that show

SCATTER, SCATTERED (v)
to separate and go in various directions; to disperse
Deut 4:27 the LORD will **s** you
Neh 1:8 to me, I will **s** you among
Isa 11:12 will gather the **s-ed** people
Jer 9:16 I will **s** them around
Jer 30:11 where I have **s-ed** you, but I
Jer 31:10 LORD, who **s-ed** his people,
Ezek 34:21 flock until you **s-ed** them to
Zech 2:6 for I have **s-ed** you to the four
Zech 10:9 Though I have **s-ed** them like
Zech 13:7 sheep will be **s-ed,** and I will
Matt 26:31 of the flock will be **s-ed.**
John 11:52 children of God **s-ed** around
Acts 8:4 were **s-ed** preached the Good
Jas 1:1 Jewish believers **s-ed** abroad.

SCEPTER (n)
the official staff of a ruler, symbolizing his authority and power
Gen 49:10 The **s** will not depart from
Num 24:17 a **s** will emerge from Israel.
Heb 1:8 rule with a **s** of justice.

SCHEME (v)
to make crafty or secret plans
Zech 8:17 Don't **s** against each

SCHEMERS (n)
those who plot or scheme
Job 5:12 He frustrates the plans of **s**
Prov 14:17 things, and **s** are hated.

SCHEMES (n)
crafty or secret plans
Job 5:13 cunning **s-s** are thwarted.
Ps 37:7 or fret about their wicked **s-s.**
Ps 140:8 let their evil **s-s** succeed,
Prov 13:11 from get-rich-quick **s-s**
2 Cor 2:11 familiar with his evil **s-s.**

SCOFF (v)
to show contempt by derisive acts or language; to mock

Lam 2:15	They **s** and insult
1 Thes 5:20	Do not **s** at prophecies,
2 Pet 2:12	They **s** at things they do not
Jude 1:8	defy authority, and **s** at

SCOFFERS (n)
those who scoff

2 Pet 3:3	the last days **s** will come,

SCORN (n)
open dislike, disrespect, or derision often mixed with indignation

Ps 109:25	they shake their heads in **s.**
Isa 51:7	not be afraid of people's **s,**

SCORN, SCORNED (v)
to reject or dismiss as contemptible or unworthy

Ps 22:6	I am **s-ed** and despised by all!
Ps 119:22	Don't let them **s** and insult
Prov 9:12	If you **s** wisdom, you will
Jer 6:10	They **s** the word of the LORD.

SCORNFUL (adj)
full of scorn; contemptuous

Ezek 28:24	will Israel's **s** neighbors

SCORPION (n)
a small crawling animal with eight legs, two sets of pincers, and a tail with a poisonous stinger

Luke 11:12	give them a **s?** Of course
Rev 9:5	pain of a **s** sting.

SCRIPTURE, SCRIPTURES (n)
the law; the writings of Moses; the entire collection of sacred books

Matt 21:16	you ever read the **S-s?**
Matt 22:29	you don't know the **S-s,**
Luke 24:27	from all the **S-s** the things
Luke 24:45	to understand the **S-s.**
John 2:22	believed both the **S-s** and
John 5:39	You search the **S-s** because
John 7:42	the **S-s** clearly state that
John 10:35	know that the **S-s** cannot
Acts 8:32	The passage of **S** he had
1 Cor 4:6	quoted from the **S-s,** you won't
1 Tim 4:13	focus on reading the **S-s** to
2 Tim 3:16	All **S** is inspired by God
Heb 10:7	written about me in the **S-s.**
2 Pet 1:20	no prophecy in **S** ever came
2 Pet 3:16	do with other parts of **S.**

SCROLL (n)
a roll (as of papyrus, leather, or parchment) for writing a document

Isa 34:4	disappear like a rolled-up **s.**
Ezek 3:1	giving you—eat this **s!**
Rev 6:14	sky was rolled up like a **s,**
Rev 10:8	take the open **s** from the hand

SEA, SEAS (n)
a great body of salt water that covers much of the earth; a large basic used in the Temple

Exod 14:16	middle of the **s** on dry
Deut 30:13	not kept beyond the **s,**
1 Kgs 7:23	rim to rim, called the **S.**
Job 11:9	and wider than the **s.**
Ps 93:4	violent raging of the **s-s,**
Ps 95:5	The **s** belongs to him,
Eccl 11:1	your grain across the **s-s,**
Isa 57:20	like the restless **s,** which
Jonah 1:4	wind over the **s,** causing a
Hab 2:14	waters fill the **s,** the earth
Matt 18:6	in the depths of the **s.**
Jas 1:6	wave of the **s** that is blown
Jude 1:13	waves of the **s,** churning up
Rev 10:2	right foot on the **s** and
Rev 13:1	rising up out of the **s.**
Rev 20:13	The **s** gave up its dead,
Rev 21:1	And the **s** was also gone.

SEAL, SEALS (n)
a piece of wax or clay impressed with a device such as a signet ring or cylinder engraved with the owner's name, a design, or both that certifies or authenticates a document

Rev 5:2	break the **s-s** on this scroll
Rev 6:1	the seven **s-s** on the scroll.
Rev 6:3	broke the second **s,** I heard
Rev 6:5	broke the third **s,** I heard
Rev 6:7	broke the fourth **s,** I heard
Rev 6:9	Lamb broke the fifth **s,** I saw
Rev 6:12	broke the sixth **s,** and there
Rev 8:1	broke the seventh **s** on the
Rev 9:4	did not have the **s** of God

SEAL, SEALED (v)
to confirm or make secure by or as if by a seal

Dan 12:4	secret; **s** up the book until
Rev 5:1	and it was **s-ed** with seven
Rev 22:10	Do not **s** up the prophetic

SEARCH, SEARCHES (v)
to investigate or examine thoroughly in an effort to find or verify something

Ps 34:14	**S** for peace, and work
Ps 139:23	**S** me, O God, and know
Eccl 3:6	A time to **s** and a time to

Jer 17:10 I, the LORD, **s** all hearts
1 Cor 2:10 Spirit **s-es** out everything
1 Pet 3:11 **S** for peace, and work

SEASHORE (n)
land adjacent to the sea
Josh 11:4 like the sand on the **s.**
1 Kgs 4:29 vast as the sands of the **s.**

SEASON, SEASONS (n)
the period normally characterized by a particular kind of weather; a period associated with some phase or activity of agriculture (as growth or harvesting)
Gen 1:14 signs to mark the **s-s,** days,
Ps 1:3 bearing fruit each **s.**
Gal 4:10 or months or **s-s** or years.

SEASONAL (adj)
of, relating to, or varying in occurrence according to the season
Lev 26:4 send you the **s** rains.

SEAT, SEATS (n)
a chair, stool, or bench intended to be sat in or on
Luke 11:43 to sit in the **s-s** of honor
Luke 14:9 to take whatever **s** is left

SEATED (v)
to put into a sitting position; to take one's seat or place
Matt 26:64 Son of Man **s** in the place
Luke 22:69 of Man will be **s** in the place
Eph 1:20 the dead and **s** him in the
Eph 2:6 with Christ and **s** us with him
Heb 12:2 Now he is **s** in the place of
Rev 14:14 a white cloud, and **s** on the

SECOND (adj)
next to the first in place or time
Job 42:12 Job in the **s** half of his life
Rev 20:14 lake of fire is the **s** death.

SECRET (adj)
kept from knowledge or view; hidden
Ps 90:8 before you—our **s** sins—
Jer 23:24 from me in a **s** place?
Matt 10:26 all that is **s** will be
Rom 2:16 judge everyone's **s** life.
Rom 16:25 a plan kept **s** from the
1 Cor 13:2 all of God's **s** plans
1 Cor 14:25 their **s** thoughts will be
Col 1:26 was kept **s** for centuries and

SECRET, SECRETS (n)
something kept hidden or unexplained; something kept from the knowledge of others or shared only confidentially with a few
see also MYSTERY
Deut 29:29 God has **s-s** known to no
Judg 16:15 don't share your **s-s** with
Ps 44:21 he knows the **s-s** of every
Prov 11:13 goes around telling **s-s,**
Dan 2:28 heaven who reveals **s-s,** and
Dan 2:29 who reveals **s-s** has shown
Mark 4:11 to understand the **s**
Mark 4:22 and every **s** will be brought
Luke 8:10 to understand the **s-s** of
1 Cor 15:51 reveal to you a wonderful **s.**
Phil 4:12 have learned the **s** of living
Col 1:27 the **s:** Christ lives in you.

SECURE (adj)
easy in mind; free from danger or the risk of loss; trustworthy, dependable
Job 31:24 felt **s** because of my gold?
Ps 30:7 made me as **s** as a mountain.
Prov 14:26 fear the LORD are **s;**
1 Thes 5:3 is peaceful and **s,**" then
2 Pet 3:17 your own **s** footing.

SECURE, SECURED (v)
to make fast, safe, or steady
Matt 27:65 Take guards and **s** it the
Heb 9:12 and **s-d** our redemption

SECURITY (n)
something given, deposited, or pledged to make certain the fulfillment of an obligation; freedom from danger; protection
Deut 24:17 widow's garment as **s** for
Ezra 9:8 has given us **s** in this holy
Prov 3:26 the LORD is your **s.**
Prov 19:23 bringing **s** and protection

SEDUCE, SEDUCED (v)
to persuade to disobedience or disloyalty; to entice
Deut 4:19 don't be **s-d** into
Job 31:9 has been **s-d** by a woman,
Job 36:18 you may be **s-d** by wealth.
Prov 6:25 her coy glances **s** you.

SEE, SEEING, SEES (v)
to perceive by the eye; to understand or recognize; to come to know
see also SAW
Ps 34:8 Taste and **s** that the
Ps 36:2 they cannot **s** how wicked
Ps 90:8 sins—and you **s** them
Ps 119:82 straining to **s** your promises
Prov 5:21 For the LORD **s-s** clearly
Prov 13:19 pleasant to **s** dreams come
Eccl 3:11 people cannot **s** the whole
Matt 6:18 Father, who **s-s** everything,

John 12:45	you are **s-ing** the one who
Rom 1:20	can clearly **s** his invisible
Rom 7:13	So we can **s** how terrible sin
1 Cor 13:12	we will **s** everything with
2 Cor 4:18	things we cannot **s** will last
2 Cor 5:7	by believing and not by **s-ing.**
2 Cor 8:21	everyone else to **s** that we
Phil 4:5	Let everyone **s** that you are
Col 1:16	things we can't **s**—such as
Rev 1:7	everyone will **s** him—even

SEED, SEEDS (n)
the grains of plants used for sowing

Gen 1:11	These **s-s** will then produce
Prov 11:30	The **s-s** of good deeds
Matt 13:3	went out to plant some **s-s.**
Matt 13:31	like a mustard **s** planted in
Matt 17:20	as a mustard **s,** you could say
Mark 4:15	The **s** that fell on
Luke 8:12	The **s-s** that fell on
1 Cor 3:6	I planted the **s** in your
2 Cor 9:6	few **s-s** will get a small
2 Cor 9:10	one who provides **s** for the

SEED-BEARING (adj)
a plant that produces seeds

Gen 1:11	every sort of **s** plant,

SEEK, SEEKING, SEEKS (v)
to go in search of; to try to acquire or gain
see also SOUGHT

2 Chr 7:14	pray and **s** my face and
2 Chr 15:2	Whenever you **s** him,
Prov 3:6	**S** his will in all you do,
Prov 25:27	not good to **s** honors
Prov 29:26	Many **s** the ruler's favor,
Isa 55:6	**S** the LORD while you can
Hos 10:12	time to **s** the LORD,
Zeph 2:3	**S** the LORD, all who are
Matt 6:33	**S** the Kingdom of God above
Matt 7:7	Keep on **s-ing,** and you
Matt 7:8	Everyone who **s-s,** finds.
Luke 12:31	**S** the Kingdom of God
Luke 19:10	Son of Man came to **s** and
Rom 3:11	no one is **s-ing** God.
1 Cor 7:27	have a wife, do not **s** to get
Heb 11:6	those who sincerely **s** him.

SEER (n)
one who practices divination and predicts events or developments

1 Sam 9:9	ask the **s,**" for prophets

SELF-CONTROL (n)
restraint exercised over one's own impulses, emotions, or desires

Prov 5:23	He will die for lack of **s;**
Prov 16:32	better to have **s** than to
Acts 24:25	righteousness and **s** and the
Gal 5:23	gentleness, and **s.** There is no
1 Tim 3:2	must exercise **s,** live wisely,
1 Tim 3:11	They must exercise **s** and be
Titus 2:2	older men to exercise **s,**
1 Pet 1:13	think clearly and exercise **s.**
2 Pet 1:6	and knowledge with **s,** and

SELF-DENIAL (n)
a restraint or limitation of one's own desires or interests

Col 2:18	insisting on pious **s** or the
Col 2:23	devotion, pious **s,** and severe

SELF-DISCIPLINE (n)
correction or regulation of oneself for the sake of improvement

2 Tim 1:7	but of power, love, and **s.**

SELF-INDULGENCE (n)
excessive or unrestrained gratification of one's own appetites, desires, or whims

Matt 23:25	full of greed and **s!**

SELFISH (adj)
seeking or concentrating on one's own advantage, pleasure, or well-being without regard for others

Matt 16:24	turn from your **s** ways,
Luke 9:23	turn from your **s** ways,
Gal 5:20	of anger, **s** ambition,
Phil 1:17	They preach with **s** ambition,
Jas 3:14	and there is **s** ambition in
Jas 3:16	is jealousy and **s** ambition,

SELFISHNESS (n)
the act of being concerned only with oneself

2 Cor 12:20	jealousy, anger, **s,** slander
Jas 3:15	jealousy and **s** are not God's

SELL, SELLING (v)
to give up (property) to another for something of value (as money)
see also SOLD

Prov 23:23	truth and never **s** it;
Prov 31:24	and sashes to **s** to the
Mark 10:21	and **s** all your possessions
Luke 17:28	buying and **s-ing,** farming and
Rev 13:17	could buy or **s** anything

SEND, SENDING (v)
to direct, order, or request to go
see also SENT

Isa 6:8	Here I am. **S** me.
Isa 55:11	with my word. I **s** it out,

Mal 3:1 I am **s-ing** my messenger,
Matt 9:38 ask him to **s** more workers
Mark 1:2 I am **s-ing** my messenger
1 Cor 1:17 For Christ didn't **s** me to

SENSE (n)
sound and prudent judgment based on a simple perception of the situation or facts; intelligence
Prov 3:21 common **s** and discernment.
Prov 8:14 Common **s** and success
Prov 12:11 chases fantasies has no **s.**
Prov 15:21 brings joy to those with no **s;**
Prov 18:1 they lash out at common **s.**
Prov 24:30 of one with no common **s.**

SENSIBLE (adj)
having, containing, or indicative of good sense or reason; rational, reasonable
Prov 10:23 brings pleasure to the **s.**
Prov 11:12 a **s** person keeps quiet.
Prov 15:21 **s** person stays on the right
Matt 24:45 A faithful, **s** servant is one

SENSITIVE (adj)
highly responsive or susceptible
Rom 15:1 those who are **s** about things

SENT (v)
to direct, order, or request to go
see also SEND
Exod 3:14 I Am has **s** me
Matt 10:40 the Father who **s** me.
Luke 10:16 God, who **s** me.
John 3:17 God **s** his Son into the
John 20:21 As the Father has **s** me, so
Rom 8:3 He **s** his own Son in a
Rom 10:15 them without being **s?**
Gal 4:4 time came, God **s** his Son,

SEPARATE, SEPARATED, SEPARATES (v)
to set or keep apart; to sort
Prov 17:9 on it **s-s** close friends.
Matt 25:32 a shepherd **s-s** the sheep
Rom 8:35 Can anything ever **s** us
Eph 2:14 of hostility that **s-d** us.
Col 1:21 his enemies, **s-d** from him

SERAPHIM (n)
six-winged angels standing in God's presence
Isa 6:2 were mighty **s,** each having
Isa 6:6 Then one of the **s** flew to me

SERIOUSNESS (n)
a sober attitude
Titus 2:7 the integrity and **s** of your

SERPENT (n)
a snake or crawling reptile often associated with temptation, sin, and evil; Satan
Gen 3:1 The **s** was the shrewdest of
Isa 27:1 **s,** the coiling, writhing **s.**
2 Cor 11:3 the cunning ways of the **s.**
Rev 12:9 the ancient **s** called the devil,
Rev 20:2 that old **s,** who is the devil,

SERVANT, SERVANTS (n)
one who performs tasks under the direction of another
see also SLAVE(S)
Exod 14:31 Lord and in his **s** Moses.
Lev 25:55 They are my **s-s,** whom I
1 Sam 3:10 Speak, your **s** is listening.
2 Kgs 17:13 my **s-s** the prophets.
Job 1:8 Have you noticed my **s** Job?
Ps 19:13 Keep your **s** from deliberate
Ps 31:16 your favor shine on your **s.**
Ps 89:3 with David, my chosen **s.**
Ps 104:4 flames of fire are your **s-s.**
Prov 14:35 king rejoices in wise **s-s**
Prov 17:2 A wise **s** will rule
Prov 22:7 so the borrower is **s** to the
Prov 31:15 work for her **s** girls.
Eccl 7:21 may hear your **s** curse you.
Eccl 10:7 seen **s-s** riding horseback
Isa 53:11 my righteous **s** will make it
Isa 65:8 I still have true **s-s** there.
Zech 3:8 to bring my **s,** the Branch.
Mal 1:6 father, and a **s** respects his
Matt 20:26 among you must be your **s,**
Matt 24:45 faithful, sensible **s** is one
Luke 1:48 of his lowly **s** girl, and
Luke 17:10 We are unworthy **s-s** who
Luke 22:26 leader should be like a **s.**
John 12:26 because my **s-s** must be
Rom 13:4 authorities are God's **s-s,**
1 Cor 3:5 are only God's **s-s** through
Col 1:23 God's **s** to proclaim it.
1 Tim 4:6 be a worthy **s** of Christ
Heb 1:7 his **s-s** like flames of fire.
Heb 1:14 angels are only **s-s**—spirits

SERVE, SERVED, SERVES, SERVING (v)
to meet the needs of and subject one's will to that of another
Deut 10:12 love him and **s** him with
Deut 11:13 your God and **s** him with
Deut 28:47 If you do not **s** the Lord
Deut 30:17 drawn away to **s** and
Josh 24:15 family, we will **s** the Lord.
2 Chr 12:8 between **s-ing** me and
Ps 34:22 redeem those who **s** him.
Ps 101:6 be allowed to **s** me.

Ps 103:21	of angels who **s** him and do
Isa 38:3	have **s-d** you single-mindedly
Dan 3:17	the God whom we **s** is able to
Matt 4:10	your God and **s** only him.
Matt 6:24	No one can **s** two masters.
Matt 20:28	not to be **s-d** but to **s**
Luke 22:27	among you as one who **s-s.**
John 12:2	Martha **s-d,** and Lazarus was
John 12:26	honor anyone who **s-s** me.
Acts 17:25	hands can't **s** his needs—
Rom 1:25	worshiped and **s-d** the things
Rom 12:7	your gift is **s-ing** others, **s**
Rom 12:11	work hard and **s** the Lord
Rom 13:6	They are **s-ing** God in what
Rom 14:18	If you **s** Christ with
Rom 16:18	people are not **s-ing** Christ
1 Cor 16:18	to all who **s** so well.
Gal 5:13	your freedom to **s** one another
Col 3:24	Master you are **s-ing** is Christ.
1 Tim 5:10	kind to strangers and **s-d** other
1 Pet 5:5	all of you, **s** each other in

SERVICE (n)
employment as a servant; the work performed by one that serves

Num 8:11	dedicating them to the LORD's **s.**
Luke 12:35	Be dressed for **s** and keep
Rom 15:17	through me in my **s** to God.
1 Cor 12:5	different kinds of **s,** but we

SET APART (v)
to designate or preserve for a particular use

Exod 16:23	holy Sabbath day **s** for the Lord
Deut 14:2	**s** as holy to the Lord
Heb 7:26	been **s** from sinners

SEVEN (adj)
of or relating to the number 7

Josh 6:4	around the town **s** times, with
Prov 6:16	LORD hates—no, **s** things
Prov 24:16	godly may trip **s** times,
Isa 4:1	so few men will be left that **s**
Luke 11:26	spirit finds **s** other spirits
Rev 1:4	John to the **s** churches in the
Rev 6:1	first of the **s** seals on the
Rev 8:2	were given **s** trumpets.
Rev 10:4	what the **s** thunders said,
Rev 15:7	handed each of the **s** angels

SEVEN (n)
the number 7

Dan 9:26	period of sixty-two sets of **s,**

SEVENFOLD (adj)
having seven units or members

Rev 4:5	This is the **s** Spirit of God.

SEVENTH (adj)
of or relating to the position of the number seven

Gen 2:2	On the **s** day God
Exod 20:10	the **s** day is a Sabbath day
Exod 23:11	uncultivated during the **s**
Exod 23:12	but on the **s** day you must
Heb 4:4	On the **s** day God rested

SEVENTY (adj)
of or relating to the number 70

Dan 9:24	A period of **s** sets of seven
Matt 18:22	Jesus replied, "but **s** times

SEVERE (adj)
strict in judgment, discipline, or government; inflicting physical discomfort or hardship

Rom 11:22	God is both kind and **s.**
1 Thes 1:6	in spite of the **s** suffering

SEWED (v)
to unite or fasten by stitches

Gen 3:7	So they **s** fig leaves together

SEXUAL (adj)
of, relating to, or associated with sex or the sexes; having or involving sex

Exod 22:19	who has **s** relations with
Lev 18:6	never have **s** relations with
Num 25:1	by having **s** relations with
Matt 1:25	did not have **s** relations with
Matt 15:19	adultery, all **s** immorality,
Acts 15:20	to idols, from **s** immorality,
1 Cor 5:1	about the **s** immorality going
1 Cor 5:11	yet indulges in **s** sin
1 Cor 6:9	who indulge in **s** sin, or who
1 Cor 6:18	Run from **s** sin! No other
1 Cor 7:1	to abstain from **s** relations.
1 Cor 10:8	not engage in **s** immorality
2 Cor 12:21	impurity, **s** immorality,
Eph 5:3	be no **s** immorality, impurity,
Col 3:5	to do with **s** immorality,
1 Thes 4:3	stay away from all **s** sin
2 Pet 2:10	own twisted **s** desire, and
2 Pet 2:18	to twisted **s** desires,
Rev 2:14	and by committing **s** sin.
Rev 2:20	teaches them to commit **s** sin

SEXUALLY (adv)

1 Tim 1:10	is for people who are **s** immoral
Rev 22:15	the sorcerers, the **s** immoral,

SHADE (n)
a place sheltered from the sun

Ps 121:5	you as your protective **s.**

SHADOW, SHADOWS (n)
shelter from danger or observation; an imperfect and faint representation; partial darkness or obscurity within a part of space
Ps 17:8 me in the **s** of your wings.
Ps 36:7 shelter in the **s** of your
Ps 39:6 are merely moving **s-s,** and
Ps 91:1 find rest in the **s** of the
Col 2:17 these rules are only **s-s** of
Heb 8:5 only a copy, a **s** of the real
Heb 10:1 was only a **s,** a dim preview

SHADOWBOXING (v)
to box with an imaginary opponent especially as a form of training
1 Cor 9:26 I am not just **s.**

SHAKE, SHAKEN, SHAKING (v)
to move to and fro or up and down; to cause to quake, quiver, or tremble; to weaken
Ps 16:8 I will not be **s-n,** for he
Ps 22:7 They sneer and **s** their heads,
Ps 62:2 where I will never be **s-n.**
Ps 64:8 see them will **s** their heads
Isa 28:16 believes need never be **s-n.**
Ezek 38:19 I promise a mighty **s-ing** in the
Hag 2:6 I will again **s** the heavens
Matt 24:29 the heavens will be **s-n.**
Mark 15:29 abuse, **s-ing** their heads
Luke 6:38 pressed down, **s-n** together to
Acts 2:25 I will not be **s-n,** for he is
2 Thes 2:2 be so easily **s-n** or alarmed
Heb 12:26 again I will **s** not only
Heb 12:27 will be **s-n** and removed,

SHAME (n)
a condition or feeling of humiliating disgrace or disrepute; something that brings censure and reproach
Lev 19:12 Do not bring **s** on the name
Ps 34:5 no shadow of **s** will darken
Prov 28:7 wild friends bring **s** to
Dan 12:2 some to **s** and everlasting
Titus 2:5 not bring **s** on the word
Heb 6:6 holding him up to public **s.**
1 Jn 2:28 shrink back from him in **s.**

SHAME (v)
to disgrace
1 Cor 1:27 in order to **s** those who
1 Cor 11:22 church and **s** the poor?

SHAMEFUL (adj)
bringing shame
Prov 18:13 facts is both **s** and foolish.
Hab 2:15 over their **s** nakedness.
Rom 1:24 do whatever **s** things their
Rom 1:27 Men did **s** things with
2 Cor 4:2 We reject all **s** deeds
2 Pet 2:2 teaching and **s** immorality.

SHARE (n)
a portion belonging to or due to
Deut 10:9 Levites have no **s** of property
2 Kgs 2:9 inherit a double **s** of your
Matt 21:34 to collect his **s** of the crop.
Rev 22:19 remove that person's **s** in

SHARE, SHARED, SHARING (v)
to grant or give a share in; to partake of, use, experience, occupy, or enjoy with others; to have in common
Gen 21:10 to **s** the inheritance
1 Sam 30:24 We **s** and **s** alike—
Ps 41:9 the one who **s-d** my food,
Luke 3:11 If you have food, **s** it with
Acts 2:42 fellowship, and to **s-ing** in
Acts 2:45 possessions and **s-d** the
Rom 8:17 we must also **s** his suffering.
Rom 11:31 they, too, will **s** in God's
1 Cor 10:16 aren't we **s-ing** in the blood
1 Cor 12:13 we all **s** the same Spirit.
2 Cor 1:7 as you **s** in our sufferings,
2 Cor 9:8 left over to **s** with others.
Gal 4:30 will not **s** the inheritance
Gal 6:6 teachers, **s-ing** all good things
Phil 3:10 suffer with him, **s-ing** in his
Col 1:12 has enabled you to **s** in the
1 Thes 2:8 much that we **s-d** with you
2 Thes 2:14 you can **s** in the glory
1 Tim 6:18 ready to **s** with others.
Heb 6:4 and **s-d** in the Holy Spirit,
Heb 12:10 we might **s** in his holiness.
Heb 13:16 to **s** with those in need.
Rev 3:20 and we will **s** a meal together

SHARPENS (v)
to make sharp or sharper
Prov 27:17 As iron **s** iron, so a

SHAVED, SHAVING (v)
to sever the hair from (the skin) close to the roots
Judg 16:17 my head were **s,** my strength
1 Cor 11:5 the same as **s-ing** her head.
1 Cor 11:6 her hair cut or her head **s,**

SHEARERS (n)
those who cut or clip (as hair or wool) from someone or something
Isa 53:7 silent before the **s,** he did
Acts 8:32 silent before the **s,** he did

SHED, SHEDDING (v)
to spill; to cause to flow

1 Chr 22:8 you have **s** so much blood
Ps 106:38 They **s** innocent blood,
Rom 3:25 his life, **s-ding** his blood.
Heb 9:22 without the **s-ding** of blood,
1 Jn 5:6 by **s-ding** his blood on the cross
Rev 16:6 they **s** the blood of your holy people

SHEEP (n)
a small domesticated animal, representing wealth and livelihood for many Israelites; figurative of God's people
Gen 22:8 God will provide a **s** for
Num 27:17 not be like **s** without a
Deut 17:1 defective cattle, **s,** or
1 Sam 15:14 bleating of **s** and goats
Ps 44:22 being slaughtered like **s.**
Ps 78:52 people like a flock of **s,**
Ps 100:3 We are his people, the **s**
Ps 119:176 wandered away like a lost **s;**
Isa 53:7 as a **s** is silent before
Jer 50:6 people have been lost **s.**
Matt 7:15 disguised as harmless **s** but
Matt 9:36 like **s** without a shepherd.
Matt 10:16 you out as **s** among wolves.
Matt 12:11 a **s** that fell into a well
Matt 25:32 separates the **s** from the
John 10:3 calls his own **s** by name
John 10:7 I am the gate for the **s.**
John 10:15 sacrifice my life for the **s.**
John 21:17 Then feed my **s.**
1 Pet 2:25 were like **s** who wandered

SHEEPFOLD (n)
a pen or shelter for sheep
John 10:1 sneaks over the wall of a **s,**

SHELTER, SHELTERS (n)
something that covers or affords protection
see also REFUGE
Lev 23:34 the Festival of **S-s** on the
Deut 16:16 the Festival of **S-s.**
Ps 9:9 LORD is a **s** for the
Ps 31:20 hide them in the **s** of your
Ps 36:7 All humanity finds **s** in the
Ps 61:4 safe beneath the **s** of your
Isa 4:6 will be a **s** from daytime heat
Isa 32:2 be like a **s** from the wind
Isa 58:7 give **s** to the homeless.
Zech 14:16 the Festival of **S-s.**

SHEPHERD, SHEPHERDS (n)
a person who tends sheep; figurative of political and religious leaders, especially those who care for God's people
Gen 48:15 has been my **s** all my life,
Gen 49:24 by the **S,** the Rock of Israel.
Num 27:17 be like sheep without a **s.**
2 Sam 7:7 tribal leaders, the **s-s** of my
1 Kgs 22:17 like sheep without a **s.**
Ps 23:1 The LORD is my **s;**
Ps 28:9 Lead them like a **s,** and
Isa 40:11 feed his flock like a **s.**
Jer 23:1 my people—the **s-s** of my
Jer 31:10 as a **s** does his flock.
Ezek 34:5 scattered without a **s,** and
Ezek 34:8 you were my **s-s,** you didn't
Ezek 34:12 like a **s** looking for his
Zech 11:9 won't be your **s** any longer.
Zech 13:7 Strike down the **s,** and
Matt 2:6 will be the **s** for my people
Matt 9:36 like sheep without a **s.**
Matt 26:31 God will strike the **S,**
John 10:11 I am the good **s.**
Acts 20:28 Feed and **s** God's flock—
Heb 13:20 Jesus, the great **S** of the
Jude 1:12 are like shameless **s-s** who care
Rev 7:17 on the throne will be their **S.**

SHEWBREAD (KJV)
Exod 25:30 Place the *Bread of the Presence*
Num 4:7 the *Bread of the Presence* is
1 Chr 23:29 in charge of the *sacred bread*
Matt 12:4 the *sacred loaves of bread*
Heb 9:2 and *sacred loaves of bread*

SHIELD (n)
a broad piece of defensive armor carried on the arm; one who protects or defends
2 Sam 22:3 He is my **s,** the power that
2 Sam 22:36 me your **s** of victory;
Ps 3:3 LORD, are a **s** around me;
Ps 5:12 them with your **s** of love.
Ps 7:10 God is my **s,** saving those
Ps 18:2 He is my **s,** the power that
Ps 28:7 LORD is my strength and **s.**
Ps 33:20 is our help and our **s.**
Ps 35:2 armor, and take up your **s.**
Ps 84:11 God is our sun and our **s.**
Ps 119:114 are my refuge and my **s;**
Ps 144:2 He is my **s,** and I take refuge
Prov 2:7 He is a **s** to those who walk
Eph 6:16 hold up the **s** of faith

SHINE, SHINES, SHINING (v)
to emit rays of light; to be eminent, conspicuous, or distinguished; to have a bright, glowing appearance
see also SHONE
Ps 37:6 of your cause will **s** like
Ps 50:2 God **s-s** in glorious radiance.
Ps 112:4 Light **s-s** in the darkness for
Ps 118:27 LORD is God, **s-ing** upon us.
Isa 60:1 Let your light **s** for all

Ezek 1:27	like a burning flame, **s-ing**
Dan 12:3	righteousness will **s** like
Matt 13:43	the righteous will **s** like
John 1:5	The light **s-s** in the darkness,
2 Cor 4:6	has made this light **s** in
Phil 2:15	of God, **s-ing** like bright lights

SHIP (n)

a large seagoing vessel

Prov 31:14	a merchant's **s,** bringing

SHIPWRECK, SHIPWRECKED (v)

to destroy (a ship) by grounding or foundering

2 Cor 11:25	Three times I was **s-ed.**
1 Tim 1:19	their faith has been **s-ed.**
Jude 1:12	reefs that can **s** you.

SHONE (v)

to have a bright, glowing appearance

see also SHINE

Matt 17:2	his face **s** like the sun,
Rev 21:11	It **s** with the glory of God

SHOP (n)

a handicraft establishment; workshop

Jer 18:2	Go down to the potter's **s,**

SHORT (adj)

brief; not coming up to a measure or requirement

Ps 89:47	Remember how **s** my life is,
Rom 3:23	all fall **s** of God's glorious
1 Cor 7:29	time that remains is very **s.**

SHORT-LIVED (adj)

not living or lasting long

Job 20:5	of the wicked has been **s**

SHORT-TEMPERED (adj)

having a quick temper

Prov 14:17	**S** people do foolish things,

SHOULDERS (n)

the place on the human body where the arm is joined to the trunk

Isa 9:6	government will rest on his **s.**
Luke 15:5	carry it home on his **s.**

SHOUT, SHOUTED, SHOUTING (v)

to utter a loud cry or in a loud voice

Job 38:7	all the angels **s-ed** for joy?
Ps 95:1	Let us **s** joyfully to
Ps 100:1	**S** with joy to the Lord,
Isa 12:6	people of Jerusalem **s** his
Isa 40:3	someone **s-ing,** "Clear the way
Isa 40:9	**s** from the mountaintops!
Isa 42:2	He will not **s** or raise his
Zech 9:9	people of Zion! **S** in triumph,
Matt 3:3	a voice **s-ing** in the wilderness,
Matt 10:27	**s** from the housetops for

SHOW (n)

an impressive display

Matt 23:5	Everything they do is for **s.**

SHOW, SHOWED, SHOWN, SHOWS (v)

to cause or permit to be seen; to point out; to reveal or demonstrate; to bestow

Exod 33:18	Then **s** me your glorious
2 Sam 22:26	To the faithful you **s**
Neh 9:19	pillar of fire **s-ed** them the
Ps 4:6	Who will **s** us better times?
Ps 16:11	You will **s** me the way
Ps 119:132	Come and **s** me your
Prov 3:6	he will **s** you which path
Prov 24:23	wrong to **s** favoritism
Eccl 9:1	God will **s** them favor.
Isa 30:18	so he can **s** you his love
Hos 6:6	I want you to **s** love, not
Zech 7:9	Judge fairly, and **s** mercy
Luke 24:40	**s-ed** them his hands and his
Acts 2:28	You have **s-n** me the way
Acts 10:34	that God **s-s** no favoritism.
Rom 3:20	The law simply **s-s** us how
Rom 3:21	But now God has **s-n** us a way
Rom 5:8	God **s-ed** his great love for us
Rom 9:22	the right to **s** his anger
Eph 2:7	as **s-n** in all he has done
Jas 2:18	I will **s** you my faith
1 Jn 4:9	God **s-ed** how much he loved

SHOWER, SHOWERED (v)

to give in abundance

Hos 10:12	come and **s** righteousness
2 Cor 1:5	more God will **s** us with
Eph 1:8	He has **s-ed** his kindness

SHOWERS (n)

something resembling a rain shower

Ezek 34:26	will be **s** of blessing.

SHREWD, SHREWDEST (adj)

marked by clever discerning awareness and hardheaded acumen

Gen 3:1	serpent was the **s-est** of all
Matt 10:16	So be as **s** as snakes

SHRINK (v)

to become smaller or more compacted

Matt 9:16	new patch would **s** and rip

SHUT (v)

to close

Isa 6:10	their ears and **s** their eyes.	
Dan 6:22	his angel to **s** the lions'	
Amos 5:13	keep their mouths **s**, for it	
Heb 11:33	They **s** the mouths of lions,	

SICK (adj)
affected with disease or ill health; lacking vigor

Ps 41:3	when they are **s** and restores
Prov 13:12	deferred makes the heart **s**,
Matt 9:12	need a doctor—**s** people do.
Matt 10:8	Heal the **s**, raise the dead,
Matt 25:36	I was **s**, and you cared for
Mark 3:10	all the **s** people eagerly
1 Cor 11:30	many of you are weak and **s**
Jas 5:14	Are any of you **s?**

SICKLE (n)
a small hand tool with a curved metal blade used for cutting stalks of grain

Joel 3:13	Swing the **s**, for the
Rev 14:14	a sharp **s** in his hand.

SICKNESS, SICKNESSES (n)
a disordered, weakened, or unsound condition; illness

Matt 4:24	whatever their **s** or disease,
Matt 8:17	He took our **s-es** and removed

SIDE (n)
the right or left part of the trunk of the body

John 20:20	in his hands and his **s**.

SIGHT (n)
mental or spiritual perception

Ps 51:4	done what is evil in your **s**.
Hab 1:13	cannot stand the **s** of evil.
Jas 1:27	religion in the **s** of God

SIGN, SIGNS (n)
something indicating the presence or existence of something else; something material or external that stands for or signifies something spiritual

Gen 9:12	you a **s** of my covenant
Gen 17:11	your foreskin as a **s** of
Ps 105:27	performed miraculous **s-s**
Isa 55:13	be an everlasting **s** of
Dan 6:27	he performs miraculous **s-s**
Matt 12:38	a miraculous **s** to prove
Matt 24:3	What **s** will signal your
Matt 24:30	the **s** that the Son of Man
Mark 16:17	These miraculous **s-s** will
Luke 11:29	them is the **s** of Jonah.
John 3:2	Your miraculous **s-s** are
John 20:30	do many other miraculous **s-s**
1 Cor 14:22	in tongues is a **s**, not for
2 Cor 12:12	did many **s-s** and wonders
2 Thes 2:9	counterfeit power and **s-s**

SIGNAL (n)
something (as a sound, gesture, or object) that conveys notice or warning

Num 10:5	you sound the **s** to move on,

SILENCE (n)
absence of speech, sound, or noise

Ps 39:2	I stood there in **s**—not even
Rev 8:1	there was **s** throughout heaven

SILENCE, SILENCED, SILENCING (v)
to compel or reduce to silence; to cause to cease criticism

Ps 8:2	strength, **s-ing** your enemies
Titus 1:11	They must be **s-d**, because they
1 Pet 2:15	honorable lives should **s**

SILENT (adj)
mute, speechless; still

Ps 30:12	praises to you and not be **s**.
Isa 53:7	as a sheep is **s** before the
Isa 62:1	Jerusalem, I cannot remain **s**.
Hab 2:20	the earth be **s** before him.
Acts 8:32	And as a lamb is **s** before
Acts 18:9	Speak out! Don't be **s!**
1 Cor 14:34	Women should be **s** during

SILVER (adj)
made of silver

Prov 25:11	apples in a **s** basket.
Dan 2:32	and arms were **s**, its belly

SILVER (n)
a shiny gray metal valued next to gold, capable of a high polish; coin made of silver

Ps 66:10	have purified us like **s**.
Prov 3:14	is more profitable than **s**,
Prov 8:10	instruction rather than **s**,
Prov 22:1	is better than **s** or gold.
Isa 48:10	but not as **s** is refined.
Zech 11:12	wages thirty pieces of **s**.
Zech 13:9	refine them like **s** and
Matt 25:15	two bags of **s** to another,
Matt 26:15	gave him thirty pieces of **s**.
Luke 7:41	500 pieces of **s** to one
Acts 3:6	don't have any **s** or gold
1 Cor 3:12	materials—gold, **s**, jewels,

SILVERSMITH (n)
an artisan who makes articles of silver

Acts 19:24	with Demetrius, a **s** who had

SIMON
1. One of the twelve disciples, Simon Peter (Matt 16:16); *see* PETER.

2. One of the twelve disciples, Simon the Zealot (Matt 10:4; Mark 3:18; Luke 6:15; Acts 1:13).
3. Simon the sorcerer, rebuked by Peter (Acts 8:9-24).
4. Simon who had leprosy (Matt 26:6; Mark 14:3).

SIMPLE (n)
a person lacking in knowledge or expertise
Ps 19:7 trustworthy, making wise the **s.**

SIMPLEMINDED (adj)
foolish
Prov 19:25 the s will learn a lesson;

SIN, SINS (n)
moral evil; transgression of or rebellion against God's laws
Gen 4:7 **S** is crouching at the door,
Lev 5:5 ways, you must confess your **s.**
Num 32:23 be sure that your **s** will find
Deut 24:16 to death for the **s-s** of their
Ps 19:13 servant from deliberate **s-s!**
Ps 32:1 whose **s** is put out of sight!
Ps 38:18 I confess my **s-s;** I am deeply
Ps 51:1 blot out the stain of my **s-s.**
Ps 51:2 Purify me from my **s.**
Ps 65:3 are overwhelmed by our **s-s,**
Ps 79:9 Save us and forgive our **s-s**
Ps 103:12 removed our **s-s** as far from
Prov 5:22 held captive by his own **s-s;**
Prov 10:19 Too much talk leads to **s.**
Prov 14:21 **s** to belittle one's neighbor;
Prov 17:19 who loves to quarrel loves **s;**
Prov 28:13 who conceal their **s-s** will
Prov 29:22 commits all kinds of **s.**
Isa 1:18 your **s-s** are like scarlet,
Isa 53:6 laid on him the **s-s** of us all.
Isa 59:2 Because of your **s-s,** he has
Jer 31:30 die for their own **s-s**—
Jer 31:34 again remember their **s-s.**
Ezek 18:19 pay for the parent's **s-s?**
Matt 1:21 save his people from their **s-s.**
Matt 6:12 forgive us our **s-s,** as we
Matt 26:28 to forgive the **s-s** of many.
Mark 3:29 This is a **s** with eternal
Luke 5:24 on earth to forgive **s-s.**
John 1:29 takes away the **s** of the world!
John 20:23 forgive anyone's **s-s,** they
Acts 2:38 repent of your **s-s** and turn
Rom 4:25 because of our **s-s,** and he
Rom 6:2 we have died to **s,** how can
Rom 6:11 the power of **s** and alive to
Rom 6:23 the wages of **s** is death,
Rom 7:7 law that showed me my **s.**
Rom 7:25 nature I am a slave to **s.**
1 Cor 6:18 is a **s** against your own body.
1 Cor 15:3 died for our **s-s,** just as
1 Cor 15:56 the law gives **s** its power.
Gal 1:4 gave his life for our **s-s,** just
Gal 6:1 believer is overcome by some **s,**
Eph 2:5 were dead because of our **s-s,**
1 Tim 5:22 share in the **s-s** of others.
Heb 2:17 would take away the **s-s** of
Heb 9:28 to take away the **s-s** of many
Heb 10:12 sacrifice for **s-s,** good for
Heb 12:1 the **s** that so easily trips
Jas 1:15 when **s** is allowed to grow,
Jas 4:17 is **s** to know what you ought
Jas 5:16 Confess your **s-s** to each other
1 Pet 2:24 carried our **s-s** in his body
1 Pet 3:18 suffered for our **s-s** once for
1 Jn 1:8 claim we have no **s,** we are
1 Jn 1:9 to forgive us our **s-s** and to
1 Jn 2:1 if anyone does **s,** we have
1 Jn 3:5 take away our **s-s,** and
1 Jn 3:5 there is no **s** in him.
1 Jn 5:16 a **s** that leads to death,
Rev 1:5 from our **s-s** by shedding his

SIN, SINNED, SINNING, SINS (v)
to commit an offense or fault against God; to break God's law
Exod 20:20 will keep you from **s-ning!**
2 Sam 12:13 I have **s-ned** against the
2 Chr 6:37 We have **s-ned,** done evil,
Job 1:5 my children have **s-ned**
Ps 51:4 and you alone, have I **s-ned;**
Ps 119:11 I might not **s** against you.
Jer 14:20 all have **s-ned** against you.
Dan 9:5 have **s-ned** and done wrong.
Mark 9:43 causes you to **s,** cut it off.
Luke 15:18 I have **s-ned** against both
Luke 17:3 another believer **s-s,** rebuke
John 8:7 who has never **s-ned** throw
John 8:11 Go and **s** no more.
Rom 1:30 invent new ways of **s-ning,**
Rom 3:23 everyone has **s-ned;** we all
Rom 5:12 When Adam **s-ned,** sin entered
Rom 14:23 is not right, you are **s-ning.**
1 Cor 15:34 is right, and stop **s-ning.**
Heb 4:15 we do, yet he did not **s.**
Heb 10:26 deliberately continue **s-ning**
1 Pet 2:22 He never **s-ned,** nor ever
1 Jn 1:10 we have not **s-ned,** we are
1 Jn 3:6 who keeps on **s-ning** does not
1 Jn 5:18 not make a practice of **s-ning,**

SINCERE (adj)
genuine, having no intention to deceive
Prov 27:6 Wounds from a **s** friend are
2 Cor 6:6 within us, and by our **s** love.
Jas 3:17 no favoritism and is always **s.**
1 Pet 1:22 show **s** love to each other

SINFUL (adj)
tainted with, marked by, or full of sin; wicked
Lev 5:1 is **s** to refuse to testify,
1 Sam 15:23 is as **s** as witchcraft,
Luke 11:13 So if you **s** people know
Rom 5:20 could see how **s** they were.
Rom 7:5 harvest of **s** deeds, resulting
Rom 7:18 is, in my **s** nature.
Rom 7:25 because of my **s** nature I am
Rom 8:4 follow our **s** nature but
Rom 8:13 deeds of your **s** nature,
Gal 5:13 to satisfy your **s** nature.
Col 2:11 away of your **s** nature.

SINLESS (adj)
having no moral blemish; having done nothing to incur the wrath of God
1 Pet 1:19 the **s,** spotless Lamb of God.

SING, SINGING (v)
to produce musical tones by means of the voice
Exod 15:1 I will **s** to the LORD,
Ps 5:11 let them **s** joyful praises
Ps 13:6 I will **s** to the LORD
Ps 47:6 to our King, **s** praises!
Ps 51:14 I will joyfully **s** of
Ps 63:7 my helper, I **s** for joy
Ps 69:30 praise God's name with **s-ing,**
Ps 89:1 I will **s** of the LORD's unfailing
Ps 95:1 let us **s** to the LORD!
Ps 96:1 **S** a new song to the LORD!
Ps 98:4 praise and **s** for joy!
Ps 100:2 Come before him, **s-ing** with
Ps 101:1 I will **s** of your love
Ps 108:1 can **s** your praises with all
Ps 147:1 How good to **s** praises to
Isa 35:10 enter Jerusalem **s-ing**
Jer 16:9 to the happy **s-ing** and laughter
Acts 16:25 praying and **s-ing** hymns
1 Cor 14:15 I will also **s** in words
1 Cor 14:26 one will **s,** another will
Col 3:16 **S** psalms and hymns and
Rev 15:3 And they were **s-ing** the song

SINGERS (n)
those who sing
2 Chr 5:13 trumpeters and **s** performed
Rev 18:22 of harps, **s,** flutes,

SINNER, SINNERS (n)
those guilty of sin
Ps 51:5 I was born a **s**—yes,
Prov 1:10 if **s-s** entice you, turn
Prov 23:17 Don't envy **s-s,** but
Eccl 9:18 one **s** can destroy much that
Isa 59:12 we know what **s-s** we are.
Isa 64:5 We are constant **s-s;** how
Matt 9:13 who know they are **s-s.**
Luke 5:8 I'm too much of a **s** to be
Luke 15:7 over one lost **s** who repents
Luke 18:13 to me, for I am a **s.**
Rom 4:5 faith in God who forgives **s-s.**
Rom 5:6 time and died for us **s-s.**
1 Tim 1:15 into the world to save **s-s**
Jas 5:20 whoever brings the **s** back
1 Pet 3:18 he died for **s-s** to bring

SISTER, SISTERS (n)
a female who has one or both parents in common with another; a female fellow Christian
Lev 18:9 relations with your **s** or half
Matt 19:29 or brothers or **s-s** or father
Mark 3:35 my brother and **s** and
1 Tim 5:2 as you would your own **s-s.**
Jas 2:1 dear brothers and **s-s,** how can

SIT, SITS, SITTING (v)
to place (the buttocks) on or in a seat
Ps 110:1 to my Lord, "**S** in the place
Matt 19:28 Son of Man **s-s** upon his
Matt 20:23 to say who will **s** on my right
Col 3:1 heaven, where Christ **s-s** in
Rev 3:21 are victorious will **s** with me
Rev 4:9 to the one **s-ting** on the throne

SKILL (n)
a developed aptitude or ability
Heb 5:14 have the **s** to recognize

SKILLED (adj)
having acquired mastery of or skill in something
Ps 71:15 I am not **s** with words.

SKILLFUL (adj)
possessed of or displaying skill
1 Kgs 7:14 was extremely **s** and talented
Ps 45:1 the pen of a **s** poet.
Ps 78:72 led them with **s** hands.

SKY, SKIES (n)
the upper atmosphere appearing as a great vault or arch above the earth
Gen 1:8 God called the space "**s.**"
Deut 33:26 across the **s-ies** in majestic
Ps 19:1 **s-ies** display his craftsmanship.
Prov 30:19 eagle glides through the **s,**
Isa 34:4 fall from the **s** like withered
Jer 33:22 the stars of the **s** cannot
Matt 24:29 will fall from the **s,**
Rev 20:11 The earth and **s** fled from

SLANDER (n)
the utterance of false charges or misrepresentations that defame and damage another's reputation
Matt 15:19 theft, lying, and **s.**
Mark 7:22 desires, envy, **s,** pride,
2 Cor 12:20 selfishness, **s,** gossip,
Eph 4:31 harsh words, and **s,** as
Col 3:8 malicious behavior, **s,**

SLANDER, SLANDERED, SLANDERING (v)
to utter slander; to malign or defame
Prov 10:18 **s-ing** others makes you a
1 Tim 3:11 must not **s** others.
2 Tim 3:3 they will **s** others
Titus 2:3 They must not **s** others
Titus 3:2 They must not **s** anyone
2 Pet 2:2 way of truth will be **s-ed.**

SLANDEROUS (adj)
of, relating to, or marked by slander
Lev 19:16 Do not spread **s** gossip

SLAUGHTER (n)
the butchering of livestock for market or sacrifice
Isa 53:7 led like a lamb to the **s.**
Jer 11:19 lamb being led to the **s.**
Acts 8:32 led like a sheep to the **s.**

SLAUGHTER, SLAUGHTERED (v)
to discredit, defeat, or demolish completely; to kill in a bloody or violent manner
Hos 6:5 to **s** you with my words,
Rev 5:6 looked as if it had been **s-ed,**
Rev 5:12 is the Lamb who was **s-ed**

SLAVE, SLAVES (n)
a person bound in servitude; one who has lost his liberty and has no rights
see also SERVANT(S)
Matt 20:27 must become your **s.**
John 8:34 who sins is a **s** of sin.
John 15:15 longer call you **s-s,** because
Rom 1:1 is from Paul, a **s** of Christ
Rom 6:6 are no longer **s-s** to sin.
Rom 6:16 you become the **s** of whatever
Rom 6:22 and have become **s-s** of God.
Rom 7:23 makes me a **s** to the sin
1 Cor 6:12 not become a **s** to anything.
1 Cor 9:19 have become a **s** to all
1 Cor 12:13 some are **s-s,** and some
Gal 3:28 Jew or Gentile, **s** or free,
Gal 4:7 no longer a **s** but God's own
Gal 4:8 you were **s-s** to so-called gods
Gal 4:30 rid of the **s** and her son,
Eph 6:5 **S-s,** obey your earthly masters
Phil 2:7 position of a **s** and was born
Col 3:11 barbaric, uncivilized, **s,** or
Col 4:1 be just and fair to your **s-s.**
1 Tim 1:10 or are **s** traders, liars,
Titus 3:3 became **s-s** to many lusts
Phlm 1:16 no longer like a **s** to you.
2 Pet 2:19 For you are a **s** to whatever

SLAVERY (n)
submission to a dominating influence; the practice of slaveholding
Exod 2:23 under their burden of **s.**
Rom 6:19 the illustration of **s** to help

SLEEP (n)
natural or induced state of rest; a state of lazy inactivity
Gen 2:21 man to fall into a deep **s.**
Gen 15:12 Abram fell into a deep **s,**
Prov 20:13 If you love **s,** you will
Prov 23:21 too much **s** clothes them
Rom 11:8 has put them into a deep **s.**

SLEEP, SLEEPING, SLEEPS (v)
to rest in a state of natural unconsciousness
Gen 28:11 against and lay down to **s.**
Ps 4:8 peace I will lie down and **s,**
Ps 121:4 Israel never slumbers or **s-s.**
Prov 6:9 how long will you **s?**
Eccl 5:12 who work hard **s** well,
Mark 13:36 find you **s-ing** when he

SLEEPER (n)
one that sleeps
Eph 5:14 said, "Awake, O **s,** rise up

SLEEPLESS (adj)
affording no sleep
2 Cor 6:5 exhaustion, endured **s** nights,

SLING (n)
an instrument for throwing stones; slingshot
1 Sam 17:50 with only a **s** and a stone,

SLOTHFUL(NESS) (KJV)
Prov 15:19 *lazy* person's way is blocked
Prov 21:25 the *lazy* will come to ruin,
Eccl 10:18 *Laziness* leads to a sagging roof
Rom 12:11 Never be *lazy,* but work hard
Heb 6:12 *spiritually dull and indifferent*

SLUGGARD (KJV)
Prov 6:6 a lesson from the ants, you *lazybones*
Prov 10:26 *Lazy people* irritate their employers
Prov 13:4 *Lazy people* want much but
Prov 20:4 *Those too lazy* to plow

Prov 26:16 *Lazy people* consider themselves smarter

SLUMBER (n)
sleep
Prov 6:10 a little more **s,** a little

SLY (adj)
clever in concealing one's aims or ends
Prov 7:10 dressed and **s** of heart.

SMALLEST (adj)
of little consequence
Matt 5:18 not even the **s** detail

SMASH, SMASHES (v)
to break or crush by violence
Ps 2:9 rod and **s** them like clay
Jer 23:29 hammer that **s-es** a rock

SMILE (v)
to bestow approval
Num 6:25 May the LORD **s** on you and
Ps 4:6 Let your face **s** on us, LORD.
Ps 67:1 May his face **s** with favor on

SMOKE (n)
the gaseous products of burning materials
Exod 19:18 The **s** billowed into the sky
Isa 6:4 building was filled with **s.**
Joel 2:30 and fire and columns of **s.**
Acts 2:19 and fire and clouds of **s.**
Rev 9:2 air turned dark from the **s.**
Rev 15:8 filled with **s** from God's

SMOKE (v)
to emit smoke
Ps 104:32 the mountains **s** at his touch.

SMOOTH (adj)
having a continuous, even surface
Jer 31:9 **s** paths where they will not
Luke 3:5 and the rough places made **s.**

SMOOTH (v)
to make smooth
Isa 26:7 you **s** out the path ahead
Isa 40:4 and **s** out the rough places.

SNAKE, SNAKES (n)
any of numerous limbless scaled reptiles
Num 21:8 replica of a poisonous **s** and
Prov 23:32 it bites like a poisonous **s;**
Matt 10:16 shrewd as **s-s** and harmless
Luke 3:7 You brood of **s-s!** Who warned
John 3:14 lifted up the bronze **s** on a

Rom 3:13 **S** venom drips from their

SNARE, SNARES (n)
something by which one is entangled, involved in difficulties, or impeded
Josh 23:13 they will be a **s** and a trap
Eccl 7:26 passion is a **s,** and her soft
Lam 4:20 was caught in their **s-s.**
Rom 11:9 table become a **s,** a trap that

SNOUT (n)
a long projecting nose (as of swine)
Prov 11:22 gold ring in a pig's **s.**

SNOW (n)
precipitation in the form of small white ice crystals
Prov 25:13 refresh like **s** in summer.
Isa 1:18 will make them as white as **s.**
Dan 7:9 clothing was as white as **s,**

SNUFFED (v)
to extinguish
Prov 13:9 wicked will be **s** out.

SOAP (n)
a cleansing and emulsifying agent
Mal 3:2 like a strong **s** that bleaches

SOAR, SOARING (v)
to sail or hover in the air often at a great height
2 Sam 22:11 flew, **s-ing** on the wings
Isa 40:31 will **s** high on wings

SODOM (n)
a city at the southern end of the Dead Sea destroyed because of its wickedness
Gen 13:12 to a place near **S** and settled
Gen 19:24 the sky on **S** and Gomorrah.
Isa 1:9 have been wiped out like **S,**
Luke 10:12 you, even wicked **S** will be
Rom 9:29 have been wiped out like **S,**
Rev 11:8 figuratively called "**S**"

SOIL (n)
firm land, earth
Matt 13:23 on good **s** represents those

SOJOURN (KJV)
Gen 12:10 where he *lived as a foreigner*
Acts 7:6 descendants would *live in a foreign land*

SOJOURNER (KJV)
Gen 23:4 a stranger and a *foreigner*
Num 35:15 *foreigners* living among you
Ps 39:12 a *traveler* passing through

SOLD (v)
to give up (property) to another in exchange for something of value
see also SELL

1 Kgs 21:25	**s** himself to what was evil
Matt 13:44	and **s** everything he owned

SOLDIER (n)
one engaged in military service

1 Cor 9:7	What **s** has to pay his own
2 Tim 2:3	a good **s** of Christ Jesus.

SOLID (adj)
firm; not liquid

Ps 40:2	set my feet on **s** ground
Heb 5:12	and cannot eat **s** food.

SOLOMON
King of Israel (united kingdom), second son of David and Bathsheba (2 Sam 12:24-25); chosen as successor by David (1 Kgs 1:28-40); given final advice by David (1 Kgs 2:1-9); enemies of his rule removed (1 Kgs 2:13-46); prayed for wisdom (1 Kgs 3:3-15; 4:29-34); demonstrated wisdom (1 Kgs 3:16-28); built and dedicated the Temple (1 Kgs 5–8); the LORD's second appearance (1 Kgs 9:1-9); became famous and powerful (9:10–10:29); visited by the queen of Sheba (1 Kgs 10:1-13); practiced idolatry and warned by God (1 Kgs 11:1-13); troubled by enemies (1 Kgs 11:14-40); died (1 Kgs 11:41-43); wrote many things (1 Kgs 4:32; Ps 72; 127; Prov 1:1; 10:1; 25:1; Eccl 1:1; Song 1:1); often mentioned in NT (Matt 6:29; 12:42; Luke 11:31; 12:27; Acts 7:47).

SON, SONS (n)
a parent's male child or descendant further removed; spiritual heir; relationship of Jesus to the heavenly Father
see also CHILD(REN), DESCENDANT(S)

Gen 17:19	birth to a **s** for you.
Gen 21:10	slave-woman and her **s.**
Gen 22:2	Take your **s,** your only
Ruth 4:15	better to you than seven **s-s!**
Ps 2:7	You are my **s.** Today I have
Isa 7:14	birth to a **s** and will call
Dan 7:13	someone like a **s** of man
Hos 11:1	I called my **s** out of Egypt.
Joel 2:28	**s-s** and daughters will
Matt 1:21	will have a **s,** and you are
Matt 2:15	I called my **S** out of Egypt.
Matt 3:17	my dearly loved **S,** who brings
Matt 4:3	you are the **S** of God, tell
Matt 11:27	truly knows the **S** except the
Matt 13:55	the carpenter's **s,** and we
Matt 14:33	really are the **S** of God!
Matt 16:16	are the Messiah, the **S** of
Matt 17:5	my dearly loved **S,** who brings
Matt 21:9	God for the **S** of David!
Matt 27:54	truly was the **S** of God!
Matt 28:19	Father and the **S** and the
Mark 14:62	will see the **S** of Man seated
Luke 1:32	be called the **S** of the Most
Luke 2:7	first child, a **s.** She wrapped
Luke 9:35	This is my **S,** my Chosen One.
Luke 12:8	on earth, the **S** of Man will
Luke 15:20	ran to his **s,** embraced him,
John 3:16	his one and only **S,** so that
John 3:36	doesn't obey the **S** will never
John 17:1	Glorify your **S** so he
Acts 13:33	You are my **S.** Today I have
Rom 1:4	shown to be the **S** of God
Rom 5:10	death of his **S** while we
Rom 8:3	He sent his own **S** in a body
Rom 8:29	to become like his **S,** so
Rom 8:32	even his own **S** but gave him
1 Cor 15:28	who gave his **S** authority
2 Cor 6:18	be my **s-s** and daughters,
Gal 4:4	God sent his **S,** born of a
Gal 4:30	slave and her **s,** for the **s**
Heb 1:2	and through the **S** he created
Heb 1:5	You are my **S.** Today I have
Heb 7:28	God appointed his **S** with an
Heb 10:29	trampled on the **S** of God,
1 Jn 2:23	acknowledges the **S** has the
1 Jn 4:9	one and only **S** into the world
1 Jn 5:5	Jesus is the **S** of God.
Rev 1:13	someone like the **S** of Man.

SONG, SONGS (n)
a short musical composition of words and music; the act of singing

Exod 15:2	my strength and my **s;**
Job 35:10	who gives **s-s** in the night?
Ps 40:3	given me a new **s** to sing,
Ps 63:5	praise you with **s-s** of joy.
Ps 96:1	Sing a new **s** to the LORD!
Ps 119:54	theme of my **s-s** wherever
Ps 137:3	of those **s-s** of Jerusalem!
Ps 149:1	Sing to the LORD a new **s.**
Isa 49:13	Burst into **s,** O mountains!
Isa 55:12	and hills will burst into **s,**
Rev 5:9	they sang a new **s** with these
Rev 15:3	God, and the **s** of the Lamb:

SOON (adv)
before long

John 13:32	Son, he will **s** give glory to
2 Cor 4:18	see now will **s** be gone,

SORCERER, SORCERERS (n)
a person who practices sorcery

Exod 7:11	his own wise men and **s-s,**

Acts 8:9 a **s** there for many years,
Acts 13:6 a Jewish **s,** a false prophet
Rev 22:15 the dogs—the **s,** the sexually

SORCERY (n)
the use of power gained from the assistance or control of evil spirits, especially for divining
Gal 5:20 idolatry, **s,** hostility, quarreling,

SORROW, SORROWS (n)
deep distress, sadness, or regret
Ps 116:3 I saw only trouble and **s.**
Isa 65:14 will cry in **s** and despair.
Jer 31:12 all their **s-s** will be gone.
Ezek 34:2 What **s** awaits you
Amos 5:18 What **s** awaits you
Matt 18:7 What **s** awaits the
Matt 23:13 What **s** awaits you
Luke 11:46 what **s** also awaits
Rom 9:2 with bitter **s** and unending
2 Cor 7:10 the kind of **s** God wants
Eph 4:30 do not bring **s** to God's Holy
1 Tim 6:10 themselves with many **s-s.**
Heb 13:17 with joy and not with **s.**
Jude 1:11 What **s** awaits them!
Rev 21:4 more death or **s** or crying

SORRY (adj)
feeling sorrow, regret, or penitence; inspiring pity
Gen 6:6 So the Lord was **s** he had
2 Chr 21:20 No one was **s** when he died.
Ps 38:18 I am deeply **s** for what I have
Mal 3:14 that we are **s** for our sins?
Matt 15:32 I feel **s** for these people.
Matt 20:34 Jesus felt **s** for them and
Mark 8:2 I feel **s** for these people.

SOUGHT (v)
to search or look for
see also SEEK
2 Chr 26:5 the king **s** guidance from
2 Chr 31:21 Hezekiah **s** his God
2 Chr 33:12 Manasseh **s** the Lord
Eccl 12:10 The Teacher **s** to find just
1 Thes 2:6 we have never **s** it from

SOUL, SOULS (n)
the inner life of a human being, the seat of emotions, and the center of human personality
Deut 6:5 heart, all your **s,** and all
Deut 28:65 fail, and your **s** to despair.
Deut 30:6 your heart and **s** and so you
Josh 22:5 all your heart and all your **s.**
2 Kgs 23:25 heart and **s** and strength,
Prov 3:22 for they will refresh your **s.**
Prov 16:24 sweet to the **s** and healthy
Jer 6:16 you will find rest for your **s-s.**
Matt 10:28 can destroy both **s** and body
Matt 11:29 you will find rest for your **s-s.**
Matt 22:37 all your heart, all your **s,**
Mark 8:37 worth more than your **s?**
Mark 12:30 heart, all your **s,** all your
Luke 16:23 his **s** went to the place of
Luke 21:19 firm, you will win your **s-s.**
John 12:27 my **s** is deeply troubled.
Heb 4:12 cutting between **s** and spirit,

SOUND (adj)
free from error, fallacy, or misapprehension
see also WHOLESOME
2 Tim 4:3 listen to **s** and wholesome

SOUND (n)
a particular auditory impression
Job 39:25 snorts at the **s** of the horn.
Ps 98:6 trumpets and the **s** of the
Dan 3:10 they hear the **s** of the horn,
Acts 2:2 there was a **s** from heaven

SOUND (v)
to give a summons by sound
Num 10:6 When you **s** the signal a
1 Cor 14:8 the bugler doesn't **s** a clear

SOUR (adj)
having an unpleasant, acidic taste
Ezek 18:2 parents have eaten **s** grapes,

SOVEREIGN (adj)
possessed of supreme power; unlimited in extent
Ps 71:16 your mighty deeds, O **S** Lord.
Isa 25:8 **S** Lord will wipe away all
Isa 40:10 the **S** Lord is coming
Isa 50:4 **S** Lord has given me his
Isa 61:1 Spirit of the **S** Lord is upon

SOVEREIGNTY (n)
supreme power especially over a body politic
Dan 5:18 God gave **s,** majesty, glory,
Dan 7:27 the **s,** power, and greatness

SOW(ED), SOWING (KJV)
Lev 25:3 you may *plant* your fields
Ps 126:5 Those who *plant* in tears
Matt 13:4 As he *scattered* them across
Luke 12:24 the ravens. They don't *plant*
Luke 19:21 crops you didn't *plant*

SOWER (KJV)
Isa 55:10 producing seed for the *farmer*
Jer 50:16 all *those who plant crops*
Matt 13:18 the *farmer planting seeds*

2 Cor 9:10 provides seed for the *farmer*

SPACE (n)
a blank or empty area; expanse
Gen 1:8 God called the **s** "sky."

SPANK (v)
to strike especially on the buttocks with the open hand
Prov 23:13 won't die if you **s** them.

SPARE, SPARED, SPARES (v)
to hold back from destroying, punishing, or harming; to have left over or as margin; to rescue from the necessity of doing or undergoing something
Esth 7:3 lives of my people will be **s-d.**
Prov 13:24 Those who **s** the rod of
Isa 54:2 your home, and **s** no expense!
Mal 3:17 as a father **s-s** an obedient
Rom 8:32 did not **s** even his own Son
Rom 11:21 if God did not **s** the original
2 Pet 2:4 God did not **s** even the angels
2 Pet 2:5 And God did not **s** the ancient

SPARKLED (v)
to glitter or shine
Rev 21:11 **s** like a precious stone—

SPARROW, SPARROWS (n)
any of several species of birds that eat grain and insects and gather in noisy flocks
Ps 84:3 Even the **s** finds a home,
Matt 10:31 than a whole flock of **s-s.**
Luke 12:6 What is the price of five **s-s**

SPEAK, SPEAKING, SPEAKS (v)
to express thoughts, opinions, or feelings orally; to talk
see also SPOKE
Deut 18:22 If the prophet **s-s** in the
Ps 15:3 or **s** evil of their friends.
Ps 78:2 will **s** to you in a parable.
Isa 3:8 because they **s** out against
Isa 32:4 stammer will **s** out plainly.
Matt 12:34 men like you **s** what is good
Matt 15:18 the words you **s** come from
Acts 2:11 hear these people **s-ing** in our
1 Cor 14:2 ability to **s** in tongues,
1 Cor 14:19 I would rather **s** five
1 Pet 3:16 if people **s** against you,

SPEAKERS (n)
one who makes a public speech
2 Cor 8:7 in your faith, your gifted **s,**

SPECK (n)
a small particle
Matt 7:3 why worry about a **s** in your

SPEECH (n)
the communication of thoughts in spoken words
Prov 16:23 a wise mind comes wise **s;**
Prov 22:11 gracious **s** will have the king
Prov 25:15 soft **s** can break bones.
Zeph 3:9 I will purify the **s** of all
1 Cor 1:17 not with clever **s,** for

SPELL (n)
a state of enchantment
Gal 3:1 cast an evil **s** on you?

SPEND, SPENT (v)
to use up or pay out; to exhaust or wear out
Prov 21:20 but fools **s** whatever they
Isa 55:2 Why **s** your money on food
Mark 5:26 she had **s-t** everything she had
2 Cor 12:15 I will gladly **s** myself

SPINS (v)
to draw out and twist into yarns or threads
Prov 31:13 flax and busily **s** it.

SPIRIT, SPIRITS (n)
"wind" or "breath"; a supernatural being; the third member of the Trinity, with God the Father and Jesus the Son; an attitude, mood, or disposition; an evil presence that can possess or influence a person; invisible, nonmaterial part of humans (as opposed to body or flesh)
see also ADVOCATE, HOLY SPIRIT
Gen 1:2 the **S** of God was hovering
Gen 6:3 My **S** will not put up with
Exod 31:3 filled him with the **S** of God,
Num 11:25 **S** rested upon them, they
Deut 34:9 full of the **s** of wisdom,
Judg 13:25 And the **S** of the Lord
1 Sam 16:13 And the **S** of the Lord
1 Sam 16:14 a tormenting **s** that filled
2 Kgs 2:9 double share of your **s** and
Job 33:4 the **S** of God has made me,
Ps 31:5 I entrust my **s** into your
Ps 34:18 those whose **s-s** are crushed.
Ps 51:10 Renew a loyal **s** within me.
Ps 51:17 you desire is a broken **s.**
Ps 139:7 can never escape from your **S!**
Isa 11:2 **S** of the Lord will rest
Isa 44:3 I will pour out my **S** on your
Isa 63:10 him and grieved his Holy **S.**
Ezek 11:19 put a new **s** within them.
Joel 2:28 I will pour out my **S** upon all
Zech 4:6 by my **S,** says the Lord

Matt 3:11	baptize you with the Holy **S**
Matt 3:16	and he saw the **S** of God
Matt 4:1	was led by the **S** into the
Matt 28:19	and the Son and the Holy **S.**
Mark 1:8	baptize you with the Holy **S!**
Mark 5:12	pigs," the **s-s** begged.
Luke 1:35	The Holy **S** will come upon
John 3:5	born of water and the **S.**
John 6:63	**S** alone gives eternal life.
John 14:26	the Holy **S**—he will teach
John 16:13	When the **S** of truth comes,
Acts 1:8	when the Holy **S** comes
Acts 2:4	as the Holy **S** gave them this
Acts 2:17	will pour out my **S** upon all
Acts 5:3	You lied to the Holy **S,** and
Acts 6:3	full of the **S** and wisdom.
Acts 8:15	to receive the Holy **S.**
Acts 9:17	and be filled with the Holy **S.**
Acts 11:16	be baptized with the Holy **S.**
Acts 19:2	receive the Holy **S** when you
Rom 8:5	controlled by the Holy **S** think
Rom 8:9	do not have the **S** of Christ
Rom 8:26	the Holy **S** prays for us
1 Cor 2:10	For his **S** searches out
1 Cor 12:1	abilities the **S** gives us.
1 Cor 12:13	one body by one **S,** and we
1 Cor 14:1	abilities the **S** gives—
2 Cor 3:6	covenant, the **S** gives life.
2 Cor 3:17	and wherever the **S** of the
2 Cor 5:3	not be **s-s** without bodies.
Gal 3:2	receive the Holy **S** by obeying
Gal 5:22	But the Holy **S** produces this
Eph 4:4	body and one **S,** just as you
Eph 4:30	to God's Holy **S** by the way
Eph 6:12	and against evil **s-s** in the
Eph 6:17	sword of the **S,** which is the
1 Thes 5:19	Do not stifle the Holy **S.**
1 Tim 3:16	vindicated by the **S.**
2 Tim 1:7	not given us a **s** of fear
1 Pet 3:4	gentle and quiet **s,** which
1 Jn 4:1	who claims to speak by the **S.**

SPIRITUAL (adj)
having to do with the spirit, usually God's Spirit

Jonah 4:11	living in **s** darkness, not
Rom 7:14	for it is **s** and good.
1 Cor 2:14	who are **s** can understand
1 Cor 14:37	think you are **s,** you should
1 Cor 15:44	there are also **s** bodies.
Eph 5:19	and hymns and **s** songs among
1 Pet 2:5	you offer **s** sacrifices that

SPIT (v)
to eject (as saliva) from the mouth

Matt 27:30	And they **s** on him and
Rev 3:16	I will **s** you out of my mouth

SPLENDOR (n)
great brightness or luster; magnificence

2 Chr 20:21	him for his holy **s.**
Ps 29:2	the LORD in the **s** of
Ps 145:5	majestic, glorious **s** and
Prov 20:29	experience is the **s** of
Isa 33:17	see the king in all his **s,**
Hab 3:3	brilliant **s** fills the heavens,

SPLINTERS (n)
thin pieces split or broken off lengthwise; slivers

Num 33:55	will be like **s** in your eyes

SPLIT (v)
to tear or rend apart

Matt 19:6	let no one **s** apart what God

SPOKE, SPOKEN (v)
to orally express thoughts, opinions, or feeling
see also SPEAK

Isa 40:5	The LORD has **s-n!**
Acts 19:37	and have not **s-n** against our
2 Pet 1:21	Spirit, and they **s** from God.

SPOT, SPOTS (n)
a small area visibly different (as in color, finish, or material) from the surrounding area; a taint on character or reputation

Jer 13:23	leopard take away its **s-s?**
Eph 5:27	church without a **s** or wrinkle

SPOTLESS (adj)
free from impurity; unblemished

1 Pet 1:19	the sinless, **s** Lamb of God.

SPREAD (v)
to stretch out; to become distributed, dispersed, or scattered

Isa 25:6	Armies will **s** a wonderful
Acts 6:7	God's message continued to **s.**
Acts 13:49	Lord's message **s** throughout
Acts 19:20	about the Lord **s** widely and
Phil 1:12	helped to **s** the Good News.
2 Thes 3:1	message will **s** rapidly and

SPRING, SPRINGS (n)
a source of water issuing from the ground

Ps 107:33	and **s-s** of water into dry,
Jas 3:12	fresh water from a salty **s.**
2 Pet 2:17	useless as dried-up **s-s** or

SPRINKLE, SPRINKLED (v)
to scatter in drops or particles

Lev 8:30	and he **s-d** them on Aaron
Lev 16:14	He must **s** blood seven
Heb 10:22	have been **s-d** with Christ's

STAFF (n)
a long stick used for walking or a weapon, often a symbol of authority and protection
see also ROD
Gen 49:10 nor the ruler's **s** from his
Exod 7:12 then Aaron's **s** swallowed up
Num 17:6 Aaron, brought Moses a **s.**
2 Kgs 4:29 travel; take my **s** and go!
Ps 23:4 Your rod and your **s** protect

STAGGER (v)
to totter
Isa 63:6 and made them **s** and fall

STAIN (n)
a soiled or discolored spot
2 Pet 2:13 disgrace and a **s** among you.

STAINED (v)
to discolor, soil
Isa 63:1 with his clothing **s** red?

STAIRWAY (n)
one or more flights of stairs
Gen 28:12 dreamed of a **s** that reached

STAND, STANDING, STANDS (v)
to remain stationary; to remain erect; to maintain one's position; to endure successfully
see also STOOD
Exod 3:5 you are **s-ing** on holy ground.
Josh 5:15 where you are **s-ing** is holy.
Josh 10:12 Let the sun **s** still
2 Chr 20:17 then **s** still and
Ps 24:3 Who may **s** in his holy
Ps 33:11 LORD's plans **s** firm
Ps 76:7 Who can **s** before you
Ps 119:89 word, O LORD, **s-s** firm
Prov 12:7 family of the godly **s-s** firm.
Isa 40:8 word of our God **s-s** forever.
Mal 3:2 be able to **s** and face him
Luke 6:48 that house, it **s-s** firm because
Rom 14:10 all **s** before the judgment
1 Cor 10:12 think you are **s-ing** strong,
1 Cor 10:13 to be more than you can **s.**
2 Cor 5:10 we must all **s** before Christ
Eph 6:14 **S** your ground, putting on the
Phil 1:27 you are **s-ing** together with
2 Tim 2:19 But God's truth **s-s** firm like
1 Pet 5:9 **S** firm against him, and
Rev 3:20 I **s** at the door and knock.

STANDARD, STANDARDS (n)
something established by authority, custom, or general consent as a model or example; criterion
Lev 24:22 This same **s** applies both to
Prov 20:23 LORD detests double **s-s;**

STANDING (n)
a position or condition
Rom 8:33 us right **s** with himself.

STAR, STARS (n)
a natural luminous body visible in the sky especially at night; sometimes symbolic for angels
Gen 1:16 He also made the **s-s.**
Num 24:17 A **s** will rise from Jacob;
Job 38:7 morning **s-s** sang together
Isa 14:12 O shining **s,** son of the
Dan 12:3 shine like the **s-s** forever.
Matt 2:2 We saw his **s** as it rose,
2 Pet 1:19 the Morning **S** shines in
Rev 2:28 also give them the morning **s!**
Rev 22:16 I am the bright morning **s.**

STARLIGHT (n)
light given by the stars
Ps 74:16 you made the **s** and the sun.

STARVE, STARVING (v)
to suffer extreme hunger
Job 24:10 they themselves are **s-ing.**
Prov 6:30 who steals because he is **s-ing.**
Luke 15:14 the land, and he began to **s.**

STATUE (n)
a three-dimensional representation usually of a person, animal, or mythical being that is produced by sculpturing, modeling, or casting
Dan 3:1 made a gold **s** ninety feet
Rev 13:14 make a great **s** of the

STATURE (n)
quality or status gained by growth, development, or achievement
Luke 2:52 wisdom and in **s** and in favor

STATUTES (KJV)
Exod 15:26 keeping all his *decrees*
Deut 4:40 If you obey all the *decrees* and
1 Kgs 3:14 *decrees* and my commands
Ps 19:8 *commandments* of the LORD
Ps 119:112 to keep your *decrees*

STAY, STAYED (v)
to continue in a place or condition
Ps 119:9 can a young person **s** pure?
Luke 2:43 but Jesus **s-ed** behind in
Luke 22:28 You have **s-ed** with me
Gal 5:1 make sure that you **s** free,

STEAL, STEALING, STEALS (v)
to take the property of another wrongfully
see also STOLE

Exod 20:15	You must not **s.**
Lev 19:11	Do not **s.**
Deut 5:19	You must not **s.**
Prov 28:24	who **s-s** from his father
Matt 19:18	You must not **s.**
Matt 27:64	coming and **s-ing** his body
Rom 13:9	You must not **s.**
Eph 4:28	If you are a thief, quit **s-ing.**
1 Pet 4:15	not be for murder, **s-ing,**

STEDFAST (KJV)

Ps 78:37	They did not *keep* his covenant
1 Cor 15:58	be *strong* and immovable.
Heb 3:14	if we are *faithful* to the end,
1 Pet 5:9	and be *strong* in your faith

STEPS (n)
course, way

Ps 37:23	LORD directs the **s** of
Prov 20:24	LORD directs our **s,**
1 Pet 2:21	you must follow in his **s.**

STIFFNECKED (KJV)

Exod 32:9	how *stubborn and rebellious*
Exod 34:9	*stubborn and rebellious* people
Deut 10:16	stop being *stubborn*
2 Chr 30:8	not be *stubborn,* as they
Acts 7:51	You *stubborn* people! You are

STIFFHEARTED (KJV)

Ezek 2:4	stubborn and *hard-hearted*

STILL (adj)
devoid of or abstaining from motion; quiet, calm

Ps 46:10	Be **s,** and know that I am
Isa 57:20	never **s** but continually
Mark 4:39	Silence! Be **s!**

STILL (adv)
without motion

Exod 14:13	Just stand **s** and watch
Josh 10:13	sun stood **s** and the moon
2 Chr 20:17	then stand **s** and watch

STILLNESS (n)
the quality or state of being still

Ps 107:30	What a blessing was that **s**

STING (n)
a wound or pain caused by or as if by stinging

1 Cor 15:55	where is your **s?**

STIRS (v)
to provoke

Prov 10:12	Hatred **s** up quarrels,

STOLE (v)
to wrongfully take the property of another
see also STEAL

Lev 6:4	give back whatever you **s,**

STOMACH (n)
the digestive tract of the body

1 Cor 6:13	**s,** and the **s** for food.
Phil 4:12	with a full **s** or empty,

STONE (adj)
of, relating to, or made of stone

Deut 4:13	he wrote on two **s** tablets.

STONE, STONES (n)
hardened mineral or rock; figurative of Christ or of hardened hearts

Exod 28:10	Six names will be on each **s,**
Josh 4:3	Take twelve **s-s** from the very
1 Sam 17:40	picked up five smooth **s-s**
Ps 91:12	even hurt your foot on a **s.**
Ps 118:22	**s** that the builders rejected
Isa 8:14	a **s** that makes people stumble,
Isa 28:16	a foundation **s** in Jerusalem,
Isa 50:7	face like a **s,** determined to
Jer 51:26	Even your **s-s** will never again
Matt 3:9	Abraham from these very **s-s.**
Matt 7:9	give them a **s** instead?
Matt 21:42	**s** that the builders rejected
Matt 24:2	Not one **s** will be left
Mark 16:3	roll away the **s** for us from
Luke 4:3	tell this **s** to become a loaf
John 8:7	sinned throw the first **s!**
1 Pet 2:5	you are living **s-s** that God

STONED, STONING (v)
to kill by pelting with stones

2 Cor 11:25	with rods. Once I was **s-d.**
Heb 11:37	Some died by **s-ing,** some were

STONY (adj)
insensitive to pity or human feeling

Ezek 11:19	away their **s,** stubborn heart

STOOD (v)
to maintain one's position
see also STAND

Josh 10:13	So the sun **s** still and
2 Tim 4:17	But the Lord **s** with me

STOP, STOPS (v)
to cease activity or operation; to pause or hesitate; to restrain or prevent
Job 37:14 **S** and consider the wonderful
Prov 15:18 cool-tempered person **s-s**
Jer 7:5 only if you **s** your evil
Jer 32:40 I will never **s** doing good
Lam 3:49 flow endlessly; they will not **s**
Dan 4:35 No one can **s** him or say to
Matt 19:14 come to me. Don't **s** them!
Eph 6:16 shield of faith to **s** the

STORE (n)
a large quantity, supply, or number
Isa 33:6 a rich **s** of salvation,

STORE, STORED (v)
to lay away; to accumulate
Matt 6:19 Don't **s** up treasures
Matt 6:26 plant or harvest or **s** food
Luke 2:51 And his mother **s-d** all these

STORIES (n)
fictional narratives
2 Pet 1:16 making up clever **s** when

STORM (n)
a heavy fall of rain, snow, or hail sometimes accompanied by thunder and lightning; a disturbed or agitated state
see also WHIRLWIND, WIND
Ps 50:3 and a great **s** rages around
Ps 55:8 from this wild **s** of hatred.
Ps 107:29 He calmed the **s** to a whisper
Luke 8:24 **s** stopped and all was calm.

STRAIN (v)
to exert (as oneself) to the utmost; to filter
Ps 119:123 My eyes **s** to see your
Jer 14:6 They **s** their eyes
Matt 23:24 You **s** your water so

STRANGE (adj)
foreign; not before known, heard, or seen
see also FOREIGN
Isa 28:11 who speak a **s** language!
1 Cor 14:21 people through **s** languages
1 Pet 4:12 something **s** were happening

STRANGER, STRANGERS (n)
a person who is unknown or with whom one is unacquainted
see also FOREIGNER(S)
Job 31:32 turned away a **s** but have
Matt 25:35 I was a **s**, and you invited
John 10:5 They won't follow a **s**;
1 Tim 5:10 been kind to **s-s** and served
Heb 13:2 to show hospitality to **s-s**, for

STRANGLED (adj)
characterized by choking to death
Acts 15:29 or the meat of **s** animals,

STRATEGIES (n)
a careful and clever plan or method
Eph 6:11 against all **s** of the devil.

STRAW (n)
stalks of grain after threshing
1 Cor 3:12 jewels, wood, hay, or **s**.

STRAYED (v)
to wander
Isa 53:6 like sheep, have **s** away.
Ezek 34:16 lost ones who **s** away, and

STREAMS (n)
bodies of running water (as a river or brook)
Ps 23:2 leads me beside peaceful **s**.
Jer 31:9 walk beside quiet **s** and

STRENGTH (n)
capacity for exertion or endurance; support; the power of a person or of God, measured variously in terms of wealth, wisdom, military might, or physical prowess
Exod 15:2 LORD is my **s** and my
Deut 6:5 your soul, and all your **s**.
2 Kgs 23:25 his heart and soul and **s**,
1 Chr 16:11 LORD and for his **s**;
Neh 8:10 of the LORD is your **s**!
Ps 23:3 He renews my **s**. He guides me
Ps 28:7 LORD is my **s** and shield.
Ps 33:16 nor is great **s** enough to save
Ps 46:1 God is our refuge and **s**,
Ps 59:17 O my **S**, to you I sing
Ps 65:6 armed yourself with mighty **s**.
Ps 84:5 for those whose **s** comes from
Ps 139:10 your **s** will support me.
Isa 31:1 depending on the **s** of human
Isa 40:26 power and incomparable **s**,
Jer 27:5 With my great **s** and powerful
Mic 5:4 with the LORD's **s**, in
Hab 3:19 LORD is my **s**!
Zech 4:6 nor by **s**, but by my Spirit,
Mark 12:30 your mind, and all your **s**.
1 Cor 1:25 the greatest of human **s**.
Phil 4:13 Christ, who gives me **s**.
Heb 11:34 weakness was turned to **s**.
Heb 13:9 Your **s** comes from God's

STRENGTHEN, STRENGTHENED, STRENGTHENS (v)
to make or become stronger
2 Chr 16:9 in order to **s** those whose
Isa 41:10 I will **s** you and help you.
1 Cor 8:1 is love that **s-s** the church.
1 Cor 14:4 in tongues is **s-ed** personally,
1 Cor 14:4 word of prophecy **s-s** the
1 Cor 14:5 whole church will be **s-ed.**
1 Cor 14:12 seek those that will **s** the
1 Cor 14:17 but it won't **s** the people
1 Cor 14:26 is done must **s** all of you.
2 Cor 13:10 has given me to **s** you, not
Heb 12:12 tired hands and **s** your weak
1 Pet 5:10 support, and **s** you, and he

STRIKE (v)
to aim and deliver a blow, stroke, or thrust (as with the hand, a weapon, or a tool); to inflict
see also STRUCK
Zech 13:7 **S** down the shepherd, and
Matt 26:31 God will **s** the Shepherd,
Rev 19:15 sword to **s** down the nations.

STRIP (v)
to remove extraneous or superficial matter from
Heb 12:1 let us **s** off every weight

STRIPS (n)
Long, narrow pieces of a material
Luke 2:12 wrapped snugly in **s** of cloth,

STRIPES (KJV)
Acts 16:33 washed their *wounds*
2 Cor 11:24 gave me thirty-nine *lashes*
1 Pet 2:24 By his *wounds* you are healed

STRONG, STRONGER, STRONGEST (adj)
having or marked by great physical power, moral or intellectual power, or great resources (as of wealth or talent); firm
Exod 6:1 force of my **s** hand, he
Deut 5:15 you out with his **s** hand
Deut 7:8 with such a **s** hand from your
Deut 31:6 So be **s** and courageous!
Josh 1:6 Be **s** and courageous,
Judg 16:5 makes him so **s** and how he
2 Sam 22:33 God is my **s** fortress, and
1 Kgs 8:42 and your **s** hand and your
1 Chr 28:20 Be **s** and courageous, and
Ezra 10:4 so be **s** and take action.
Ps 24:8 The LORD, **s** and mighty;
Ps 96:7 LORD is glorious and **s.**
Prov 18:10 LORD is a **s** fortress;
Prov 24:5 wise are mightier than the **s,**
Prov 30:25 Ants—they aren't **s**, but
Prov 31:17 She is energetic and **s**, a
Eccl 9:11 **s-est** warrior doesn't always
Isa 35:4 Be **s**, and do not fear,
Jer 50:34 one who redeems them is **s.**
Zeph 1:14 when even **s** men will cry
Luke 1:80 and became **s** in spirit.
Luke 2:40 grew up healthy and **s.**
Luke 11:22 someone even **s-er** attacks
1 Cor 1:8 keep you **s** to the end
1 Cor 1:25 God's weakness is **s-er** than
1 Cor 16:13 Be courageous. Be **s.**
Eph 6:10 final word: Be **s** in the Lord
1 Thes 3:13 your hearts **s,** blameless,
2 Tim 2:1 dear son, be **s** through the

STRUCK (v)
to inflict
see also STRIKE
Job 2:7 presence, and he **s** Job with
Isa 53:8 But he was **s** down for the

STRUGGLE (n)
strife; a violent effort or exertion
Rom 15:30 to join in my **s** by praying
Heb 12:4 lives in your **s** against sin.

STRUGGLE (v)
to proceed with difficulty or with great effort; to make strenuous or violent efforts in the face of difficulties or opposition
Gen 3:17 will **s** to scratch a living
Col 1:29 why I work and **s** so hard,
1 Tim 4:10 and continue to **s,** for our

STUBBORN (adj)
unreasonably or perversely unyielding
Exod 33:5 You are a **s** and rebellious
Exod 34:9 this is a **s** and rebellious
Lev 26:41 at last their **s** hearts will
Deut 10:16 hearts and stop being **s.**
2 Chr 36:13 a hard and **s** man, refusing
Ps 78:8 ancestors—**s**, rebellious,
Prov 28:14 the **s** are headed for serious
Ezek 36:26 out your stony, **s** heart and
Rom 2:5 because you are **s** and refuse

STUDENTS (n)
those who study
Matt 10:24 **S** are not greater than

STUDY (n)
application of the mental faculties to the acquisition of knowledge
Eccl 12:12 and much **s** wears you

STUDY (v)
to read in detail, especially with the intention of learning
Josh 1:8 **S** this Book of Instruction
Ezra 7:10 had determined to **s** and obey

STUMBLE, STUMBLES, STUMBLING (v)
to trip or walk unsteadily; to fall into sin or waywardness
Lev 19:14 or cause the blind to **s.**
Ps 37:24 Though they **s,** they will
Ps 66:9 he keeps our feet from **s-ing.**
Ps 119:165 great peace and do not **s.**
Ps 121:3 He will not let you **s;**
Prov 3:23 and your feet will not **s.**
Prov 24:17 don't be happy when they **s.**
Isa 8:14 stone that makes people **s,**
Jer 13:16 causing you to **s** and fall
Hos 14:9 paths sinners **s** and fall.
Mal 2:8 caused many to **s** into sin.
Matt 21:44 Anyone who **s-s** over that
John 11:10 is danger of **s-ing** because
Rom 9:33 that makes people **s,**
Rom 14:13 believer to **s** and fall.
Rom 14:20 makes another person **s.**
1 Cor 8:9 weaker conscience to **s.**
2 Cor 6:3 no one will **s** because of us,
1 Jn 2:10 does not cause others to **s.**

STUMP (n)
the part of a tree remaining attached to the root after the trunk is cut
Isa 6:13 so Israel's **s** will be a
Isa 11:1 Out of the **s** of David's

STUPID (adj)
lacking intelligence or reason
Ps 119:70 hearts are dull and **s,**
Prov 12:1 is **s** to hate correction.

STUPIDITY (n)
the quality or state of being stupid
Jer 31:19 kicked myself for my **s!**

SUBMISSION (n)
the condition of being submissive, humble, or compliant
1 Sam 15:22 **s** is better than offering

SUBMISSIVE (adj)
submitting to others
1 Cor 14:34 They should be **s,** just
Titus 2:5 be **s** to their husbands.

SUBMIT, SUBMITS (v)
to yield to authority or be accountable to another—God, society, or fellow believers
Ps 2:12 **S** to God's royal son,
Rom 13:1 Everyone must **s** to governing
Rom 13:5 So you must **s** to them, not
Eph 5:21 **s** to one another out of
Eph 5:24 As the church **s-s** to Christ,
Col 3:18 Wives, **s** to your husbands,
Heb 12:9 shouldn't we **s** even more

SUBTRACT (v)
to take away
Deut 4:2 Do not add to or **s** from
Deut 12:32 to them or **s** anything

SUBVERT (KJV)
Lam 3:36 they *twist* justice in the courts
Titus 1:11 *turning* whole families *away from the truth*

SUCCEED (v)
to turn out well; to attain a desired end
Gen 39:23 everything he did to **s.**
Josh 1:8 prosper and **s** in all you
1 Sam 2:9 No one will **s** by strength
1 Sam 18:14 continued to **s** in
2 Chr 20:20 prophets, and you will **s.**
Ps 20:4 and make all your plans **s.**
Prov 11:10 celebrates when the godly **s;**
Prov 13:13 respect a command will **s.**
Prov 16:3 and your plans will **s.**
Prov 20:18 Plans **s** through good
Prov 28:12 When the godly **s,** everyone
Eccl 10:10 wisdom; it helps you **s.**

SUCCESS (n)
the attainment of wealth, favor, or eminence; favorable or desired outcome
1 Chr 12:18 and **s** to all who help
2 Chr 26:5 LORD, God gave him **s.**
Prov 15:22 many advisers bring **s.**

SUCCESSFUL (adj)
resulting or terminating in success; gaining or having gained success
Deut 8:18 gives you power to be **s,**
Deut 30:9 make you **s** in everything
1 Kgs 2:3 that you will be **s** in all
2 Kgs 18:7 Hezekiah was **s** in
1 Chr 22:13 For you will be **s** if you
2 Chr 31:21 result, he was very **s.**
Ps 90:17 and make our efforts **s.**
Prov 1:3 disciplined and **s** lives,
Eccl 9:11 don't always lead **s** lives.

SUES (v)
to seek justice or right from (a person) by legal process

1 Cor 6:6	one believer **s** another—

SUFFER, SUFFERED, SUFFERING, SUFFERS (v)
to endure death, pain, distress, or loss

Job 36:15	rescues those who **s.**
Mark 8:31	Son of Man must **s** many
Luke 24:26	would have to **s** all these
Luke 24:46	Messiah would **s** and die
Rom 8:18	Yet what we **s** now is nothing
1 Cor 12:26	If one part **s-s,** all the parts
2 Cor 1:5	the more we **s** for Christ,
2 Cor 12:10	troubles that I **s** for Christ.
Phil 3:10	I want to **s** with him, sharing
2 Thes 1:4	and hardships you are **s-ing.**
Heb 11:26	better to **s** for the sake
1 Pet 2:21	just as Christ **s-ed** for you.
1 Pet 4:1	since Christ **s-ed** physical pain,
1 Pet 4:16	is no shame to **s** for being
1 Pet 5:10	So after you have **s-ed** a little
Rev 2:3	You have patiently **s-ed** for me

SUFFERING, SUFFERINGS (n)
the state or experience of one that suffers; pain, distress

Deut 16:3	the bread of **s**—so that
Job 36:15	means of their **s,** he rescues
Ps 119:71	My **s** was good for me,
Isa 48:10	you in the furnace of **s.**
Isa 49:13	on them in their **s.**
Lam 1:12	if there is any **s** like mine,
Luke 22:15	you before my **s** begins.
2 Cor 1:7	as you share in our **s-s,** you
Phil 1:29	the privilege of **s** for him.
Col 1:24	participating in the **s-s** of
2 Tim 2:3	Endure **s** along with me,
2 Tim 4:5	afraid of **s** for the Lord.
Heb 2:10	through his **s,** a perfect
Heb 2:18	gone through **s** and testing,
1 Pet 1:11	about Christ's **s** and his
1 Pet 4:13	Christ in his **s,** so that

SUMMED (v)
to summarize

Rom 13:9	commandments—are **s** up in
Gal 5:14	whole law can be **s** up in this

SUN (n)
the star that sustains life on the earth, being the source of heat and light

Josh 10:13	So the **s** stood still and
Judg 5:31	rise like the **s** in all its
Ps 84:11	God is our **s** and our shield.
Ps 121:6	The **s** will not harm you
Ps 136:8	the **s** to rule the day,
Eccl 1:9	Nothing under the **s** is truly
Isa 60:19	you need the **s** to shine by
Mal 4:2	name, the **S** of Righteousness
Matt 13:43	shine like the **s** in their
Matt 17:2	shone like the **s,** and his
Luke 23:45	light from the **s** was gone.
Eph 4:26	Don't let the **s** go down while
Rev 1:16	was like the **s** in all its
Rev 21:23	has no need of **s** or moon,

SUNDAY (n)
the first day of the week

Matt 28:1	Early on **S** morning, as

SUNLIGHT (n)
the light of the sun; sunshine

Matt 5:45	he gives his **s** to both the

SUPERIOR (adj)
of higher rank, quality, or importance

Heb 8:6	that is far **s** to the old

SUPERNATURAL (adj)
of or relating to God, a spirit, or the devil

2 Pet 2:10	scoff at **s** beings without
Jude 1:8	and scoff at **s** beings.

SUPPER (n)
meal eaten toward the end of the day; communion (i.e., Lord's Supper)

Luke 22:20	After **S** he took another cup of
Acts 2:42	meals (including the Lord's **S**)
1 Cor 11:33	gather for the Lord's **S,**

SUPPORT, SUPPORTS (v)
to pay the costs of; to assist or help

Lev 25:35	and cannot **s** himself, **s**
Ps 18:35	Your right hand **s-s** me;
Ps 139:10	your strength will **s** me.
Ps 147:6	The LORD **s-s** the humble,
1 Pet 5:10	he will restore, **s,** and
3 Jn 1:8	we ourselves should **s** them

SUPPRESS (v)
to stop or prohibit the revelation of

Rom 1:18	wicked people who **s** the truth

SUPREME (adj)
highest in rank, authority, degree, or quality

Col 1:15	was created and is **s** over all
Col 1:18	is the beginning, **s** over all

SURE (adj)
admitting of no doubt; careful to remember, attend to, or find out something

Num 32:23	you may be **s** that your sin
1 Sam 12:24	But be **s** to fear the
2 Cor 1:15	Since I was so **s** of your
2 Cor 9:5	of me to make **s** the gift you
Eph 5:5	You can be **s** that no immoral,
2 Tim 1:12	trust, and I am **s** that he is

SURETY (KJV)

Gen 43:9	I *personally guarantee* his safety
Prov 17:18	*put up security* for a friend
Heb 7:22	Jesus is the one who *guarantees*

SURFACE (n)
the external or superficial aspect of something

John 7:24	Look beneath the **s** so you can

SURGING (adj)
characterized by tossing and swelling

Ps 42:7	your waves and **s** tides sweep

SURPASS (v)
to become better, greater, or stronger than

Prov 31:29	world, but you **s** them all!

SURPLUS (n)
the amount that remains when use or need is satisfied

Luke 21:4	part of their **s,** but she,

SURPRISED (v)
to take unawares; to strike with wonder or amazement especially because it is unexpected

1 Thes 5:4	you won't be **s** when the day
1 Pet 4:4	former friends are **s** when you
1 Jn 3:13	So don't be **s,** dear brothers

SURRENDERED (v)
to yield to the power, control, or possession of another upon compulsion or demand

2 Sam 10:19	by Israel, they **s** to Israel
1 Chr 19:19	by Israel, they **s** to David

SURROUND, SURROUNDED, SURROUNDS (v)
to envelop; to encircle

Deut 33:12	He **s-s** them continuously
Ps 5:12	O Lord; you **s** them with
Ps 32:10	unfailing love **s-s** those who
Ps 33:22	unfailing love **s** us, Lord,
Ps 89:7	than all who **s** his throne.
Ps 125:2	the mountains **s** Jerusalem,
Ps 125:2	the Lord **s-s** his people,
Heb 12:1	we are **s-ed** by such a huge

SUSTAINS (v)
to keep up or prolong

Heb 1:3	God, and he **s** everything by

SWADDLED, SWADDLING (KJV)

Ezek 16:4	salt, and *wrapped in cloth*
Luke 2:7	wrapped him *snugly in strips of cloth*
Luke 2:12	baby *wrapped snugly* in strips

SWALLOW, SWALLOWED (v)
to take through the mouth and esophagus into the stomach; to envelop or absorb

Isa 25:8	He will **s** up death
Jonah 1:17	a great fish to **s** Jonah.
Hab 1:13	while the wicked **s** up people
Matt 23:24	a gnat, but you **s** a camel!
1 Cor 15:54	fulfilled: "Death is **s-ed** up
2 Cor 5:4	bodies will be **s-ed** up by life.

SWEAR (v)
to affirm by a solemn oath or binding commitment
see also SWORE, SWORN

Lev 19:12	using it to **s** falsely.
Isa 54:9	earth, so now I **s** that I will
Heb 6:13	one greater to **s** by, God took

SWEET, SWEETER (adj)
pleasing to the taste; agreeable, gratifying

Job 20:12	They enjoyed the **s** taste of
Ps 19:10	They are **s-er** than honey,
Ps 119:103	How **s** your words taste
Ps 119:103	they are **s-er** than honey.
Prov 20:17	Stolen bread tastes **s,** but
Prov 24:14	wisdom is **s** to your soul.
Prov 27:9	friend is as **s** as perfume
Song 1:2	your love is **s-er** than wine.
Song 4:11	lips are as **s** as nectar,
Isa 5:20	bitter is **s** and **s** is bitter.
Ezek 3:3	it tasted as **s** as honey in my

SWEET-SMELLING (adj)
of or relating to a pleasant scent

Phil 4:18	They are a **s** sacrifice that

SWEETNESS (n)
the quality or state of being sweet

Song 5:16	His mouth is **s** itself;

SWEPT (adj)
cleaned with a broom or brush

Matt 12:44	former home empty, **s,** and in

SWORD, SWORDS (n)
a handheld weapon with a long blade; figurative of war or persecution by government, also of God's word in spiritual warfare

Gen 3:24	a flaming **s** that flashed
Deut 32:41	my flashing **s** and begin
1 Sam 17:45	come to me with **s,** spear,
1 Sam 31:4	Take your **s** and kill me
2 Sam 12:10	live by the **s** because you
1 Kgs 20:11	putting on his **s** for battle
Ps 44:6	not count on my **s** to save me.
Ps 45:3	Put on your **s,** O mighty
Ps 64:3	their tongues like **s-s** and aim
Joel 3:10	plowshares into **s-s** and your
Amos 9:4	I will command the **s** to kill
Mic 4:3	will hammer their **s-s** into
Matt 10:34	not to bring peace, but a **s.**
Matt 26:52	who use the **s** will die by
Luke 2:35	a **s** will pierce your very
Eph 6:17	take the **s** of the Spirit,
Heb 4:12	sharpest two-edged **s,** cutting
Rev 1:16	sharp two-edged **s** came
Rev 19:15	came a sharp **s** to strike

SWORE, SWORN (v)

to affirm by a solemn oath or binding commitment

see also SWEAR

Exod 33:1	up to the land I **s** to give
Deut 7:8	the oath he had **s-n** to your
Deut 30:20	land the LORD **s** to give
Isa 45:23	I have **s-n** by my own

SYCAMORE-FIG (n)

a fig tree that has edible fruit similar but inferior to the common fig

Amos 7:14	take care of **s** trees.
Luke 19:4	and climbed a **s** tree beside

SYMBOL (n)

something that stands for or suggests something else

Rom 5:14	Adam is a **s,** a representation

SYMPATHIZE (v)

to share in suffering or grief

1 Pet 3:8	**S** with each other. Love each

SYNAGOGUE (n)

the house of worship and communal center of a Jewish congregation

Luke 4:16	to the **s** on the Sabbath
John 12:42	expel them from the **s.**
Acts 17:2	he went to the **s** service,
Rev 3:9	who belong to Satan's **s**—

T

TABERNACLE (n)

portable shrine or tent designated for the worship of God; metaphor for God dwelling among his people

see also SANCTUARY, TEMPLE

Exod 27:21	stand in the **T,** in front of
Exod 40:2	Set up the **T** on the first
Exod 40:34	cloud covered the **T,** and
Exod 40:34	of the LORD filled the **T.**
Num 3:29	area south of the **T** for their
Heb 8:5	to build the **T,** God gave him
Heb 9:11	more perfect **T** in heaven,
Heb 9:21	blood on the **T** and on
Rev 15:5	heaven, God's **T,** was thrown

TABLE, TABLES (n)

a piece of furniture consisting of a smooth flat slab fixed on legs

Exod 25:23	Then make a **t** of acacia
John 2:15	and turned over their **t-s.**

TABLETS (n)

flat slabs or plaques suited for or bearing an inscription

Exod 31:18	two stone **t** inscribed with
Deut 10:5	and placed the **t** in the Ark
2 Cor 3:3	carved not on **t** of stone,

TAKE, TAKEN, TAKES (v)

to exploit; to seize or capture physically; to remove; to move onto or into; to feel or experience; to lead, carry, or cause to go along to another place; to grasp or grip; to accept; to derive

see also TOOK

Gen 2:23	she was **t-n** from 'man.'
Gen 9:6	life will also be **t-n** by human
Lev 25:14	you must not **t** advantage of
Num 13:30	go at once to **t** the land,
Num 19:3	it will be **t-n** outside the camp
1 Chr 17:13	I will never **t** my favor
Ps 2:12	for all who **t** refuge in him!
Ps 5:4	O God, you **t** no pleasure in
Ps 49:17	they die, they **t** nothing with
Ps 51:11	and don't **t** your Holy Spirit
Prov 3:6	show you which path to **t.**
Jer 25:10	I will **t** away your happy
Zech 3:4	See, I have **t-n** away your sins,
Matt 10:38	refuse to **t** up your cross
Matt 11:29	**T** my yoke upon you. Let me
Matt 16:24	selfish ways, **t** up your cross,
Matt 24:40	one will be **t-n,** the other
Matt 26:26	**T** this and eat it, for this
Matt 26:39	cup of suffering be **t-n** away
Mark 14:36	Please **t** this cup of suffering
Mark 16:19	he was **t-n** up into heaven
John 1:29	Lamb of God who **t-s** away the
John 10:18	No one can **t** my life from me.
Acts 1:9	he was **t-n** up into a cloud
1 Tim 3:16	and **t-n** to heaven in glory.

TALK (n)
speech; pointless or fruitless discussion
Ps 5:9 Their **t** is foul, like
Prov 10:19 Too much **t** leads to
2 Tim 2:16 worthless, foolish **t** that

TALK BACK (v)
to answer impertinently
Titus 2:9 They must not **t**

TALL, TALLER (adj)
of a specified or considerable height
1 Sam 2:26 boy Samuel grew **t-er** and
1 Sam 9:2 and shoulders **t-er** than anyone
1 Sam 17:4 He was over nine feet **t**!
1 Chr 11:23 was 7½ feet **t** and whose

TAME (v)
to domesticate; to harness
Jas 3:7 People can **t** all kinds of
Jas 3:8 no one can **t** the tongue.

TANGLED (v)
to involve so as to hamper, obstruct, or embarrass; to entrap
Exod 4:10 and my words get **t.**
2 Pet 2:20 Christ and then get **t** up and

TASK (n)
duty, function
2 Cor 2:16 for such a **t** as this?
2 Cor 5:18 us this **t** of reconciling

TASTE (n)
the act of tasting; a sample experience
Prov 24:13 honeycomb is sweet to the **t.**
1 Pet 2:3 a **t** of the Lord's kindness.

TASTE, TASTED, TASTES (v)
to become acquainted with by experience; to ascertain the flavor of by taking a little into the mouth
Ps 34:8 **T** and see that the LORD
Prov 9:17 eaten in secret **t-s** the best!
Song 2:3 and **t** his delicious fruit.
Ezek 3:3 I ate it, it **t-d** as sweet as
Col 2:21 Don't handle! Don't **t**!

TATTOOS (n)
indelible marks or figures fixed upon the body
Lev 19:28 not mark your skin with **t.**

TAX, TAXES (n)
a charge usually of money imposed by authority on persons or property for public purposes
Matt 17:24 teacher pay the Temple **t**?
Matt 22:17 right to pay **t-es** to Caesar
Rom 13:7 Pay your **t-es** and

TAX COLLECTOR, TAX COLLECTORS (n)
one who collects tax or custom on behalf of the government
Matt 5:46 corrupt **t-s** do that
Matt 9:10 along with many **t-s** and
Matt 11:19 a friend of **t-s** and other sinners
Matt 21:31 **t-s** and prostitutes will get
Luke 5:27 he saw a **t** named Levi
Luke 18:11 I'm certainly not like that **t**!

TEACH, TEACHES, TEACHING (v)
to cause to know something; to instruct by precept, example, or experience
see also INSTRUCT, PREACH, TRAIN
Lev 10:11 you must **t** the Israelites
Deut 6:1 commanded me to **t** you.
2 Chr 17:9 of Judah, **t-ing** the people.
Job 21:22 who can **t** a lesson to God,
Ps 37:30 they **t** right from wrong.
Ps 51:13 Then I will **t** your ways
Prov 15:33 the LORD **t-es** wisdom;
Isa 2:3 he will **t** us his ways,
Matt 5:19 obeys God's laws and **t-es**
Matt 11:29 Let me **t** you, because
Matt 15:9 they **t** man-made ideas
Matt 22:16 You **t** the way of God
Matt 28:20 **T** these new disciples to
Mark 10:1 as usual he was **t-ing** them.
Luke 11:1 Lord, **t** us to pray,
Luke 12:12 Holy Spirit will **t** you
John 14:26 he will **t** you everything
Acts 6:4 in prayer and **t-ing** the word.
Rom 15:4 Scriptures long ago to **t**
Rom 15:14 you can **t** each other all
1 Cor 2:16 knows enough to **t** him?
1 Cor 14:26 another will **t,** another
1 Tim 2:12 do not let women **t** men
1 Tim 3:2 he must be able to **t.**
2 Tim 3:16 is useful to **t** us what
2 Tim 3:16 **t-es** us to do what is right.
Titus 2:15 You must **t** these things
Heb 5:12 you ought to be **t-ing** others.
1 Jn 2:27 need anyone to **t** you what

TEACHER, TEACHERS (n)
one who teaches
Job 36:22 Who is a **t** like him?
Prov 5:13 didn't I listen to my **t-s**?
Eccl 1:1 words of the **T,** King David's
Matt 10:24 not greater than their **t,**
Matt 23:10 only one **t,** the Messiah.
Luke 6:40 will become like the **t.**
Luke 20:46 these **t-s** of religious law!
John 13:14 Lord and **T,** have washed

Rom 12:7 If you are a **t**, teach well.
1 Cor 12:28 third are **t-s**, then those
Gal 6:6 should provide for their **t-s**,
Eph 4:11 and the pastors and **t-s**.
2 Tim 4:3 look for **t-s** who will tell
Jas 3:1 of you should become **t-s**
3 Jn 1:10 the traveling **t-s**, he also

TEACHING, TEACHINGS (n)
something taught; doctrine
see also INSTRUCTION(S), LAW(S)
Isa 8:20 to God's instructions and **t-s**!
Luke 6:47 listens to my **t**, and then
John 7:17 whether my **t** is from God
John 8:31 remain faithful to my **t-s**.
Acts 2:42 themselves to the apostles' **t**,
Eph 4:14 about by every wind of new **t**.
1 Thes 4:8 not disobeying human **t** but
2 Thes 2:15 grip on the **t** we passed on
1 Tim 1:3 those whose **t** is contrary to
1 Tim 1:10 contradicts the wholesome **t**
1 Tim 4:6 and the good **t** you have
1 Tim 4:16 how you live and on your **t**.
1 Tim 6:3 people may contradict our **t**,
2 Tim 4:2 your people with good **t**.
Titus 1:9 with wholesome **t** and show
Titus 3:8 insist on these **t-s** so that
Heb 6:1 stop going over the basic **t-s**

TEAR, TEARS (n)
a drop of clear saline fluid secreted from the eye
Job 16:20 I pour out my **t-s** to God.
Isa 25:8 will wipe away all **t-s**.
Rev 7:17 will wipe every **t** from their
Rev 21:4 will wipe every **t** from their

TELL, TELLING, TELLS (v)
to divulge or reveal; to give information to
Ps 26:7 thanksgiving and **t-ing** of all
Ps 71:16 I will **t** everyone that
Ps 118:17 live to **t** what the LORD
Jer 1:7 and say whatever I **t** you.
Jer 1:17 Go out and **t** them everything
John 2:25 No one needed to **t** him what
Acts 20:20 shrank back from **t-ing** you
Rom 10:14 him unless someone **t-s** them?
2 Cor 10:12 these other men who **t** you

TEMPER (n)
disposition; characteristic state of mind or of emotion; proneness to anger
Ps 37:8 Do not lose your **t**—it only
Prov 14:29 **t** shows great foolishness.
Prov 19:11 people control their **t**;
Eccl 7:9 Control your **t**, for anger

TEMPLE, TEMPLES (n)
first built in Solomon's reign as a permanent worship center, which was destroyed then rebuilt under Herod's reign; figurative of the human body and of Christ
see also HOUSE, SANCTUARY, TABERNACLE
1 Kgs 6:1 to construct the **T** of the
1 Kgs 8:10 cloud filled the **T** of the
1 Chr 29:16 to build a **T** to honor your
2 Chr 36:19 his army burned the **T**
Ps 27:4 meditating in his **T**.
Isa 6:1 train of his robe filled the **T**.
Jer 7:8 suffer because the **T** is here.
Joel 3:18 forth from the LORD's **T**,
Hab 2:20 LORD is in his holy **T**.
Hag 2:18 of the LORD's **T** began.
Matt 12:6 is even greater than the **T**!
Matt 26:61 able to destroy the **T** of God
Matt 27:51 sanctuary of the **T** was torn
Luke 21:5 stonework of the **T** and the
John 2:14 the **T** area he saw merchants
Acts 5:20 Go to the **T** and give the
Acts 17:24 live in man-made **t-s**,
1 Cor 3:16 together are the **t** of God
1 Cor 6:19 body is the **t** of the Holy
Eph 2:21 becoming a holy **t** for the
1 Pet 2:5 building into his spiritual **t**.
Rev 21:22 and the Lamb are its **t**.

TEMPT, TEMPTED, TEMPTING (v)
to entice to do wrong by promise of pleasure or gain; to test
Isa 13:17 They cannot be **t-ed** by silver
Matt 4:1 wilderness to be **t-ed** there by
Luke 4:2 where he was **t-ed** by the devil
Luke 4:13 finished **t-ing** Jesus, he left
1 Cor 7:5 be able to **t** you because
1 Cor 10:13 When you are **t-ed**, he will
Jas 1:13 you are being **t-ed**, do not say,
Jas 1:13 God is never **t-ed** to do wrong,

TEMPTATION, TEMPTATIONS (n)
a cause or occasion of enticement
Matt 6:13 don't let us yield to **t**,
Matt 18:7 **T-s** are inevitable, but what
Matt 26:41 will not give in to **t**.
Luke 8:13 fall away when they face **t**.
1 Cor 10:13 The **t-s** in your life are
1 Cor 10:13 not allow the **t** to be
Gal 6:1 fall into the same **t** yourself.
1 Tim 6:9 to be rich fall into **t** and
Jas 1:12 endure testing and **t**.

TEN (n)
the number 10
Exod 34:28 the **T** Commandments—
Deut 10:4 wrote the **T** Commandments

Luke 15:8 a woman has **t** silver coins
Rev 12:3 seven heads and **t** horns, with

TENDERHEARTED (adj)
easily moved to love, pity, or sorrow; compassionate
Deut 28:54 The most **t** man among you
Eph 4:32 each other, **t,** forgiving one
Col 3:12 yourselves with **t** mercy,

TENDERNESS (n)
the quality or state of being gentle, fond, or loving
Jas 5:11 is full of **t** and mercy.

TENTH (n)
one-tenth of any property or produce
see also TITHE
Gen 14:20 gave Melchizedek a **t** of all
Heb 7:2 Abraham took a **t** of all he

TENTMAKERS (n)
those who make tents
Acts 18:3 for they were **t** just as he

TENTS (n)
portable housing made of cloth or skins
see also TABERNACLE
Gen 13:12 Lot moved his **t** to a place

TERRIBLE (adj)
extremely bad; terrifying
Jer 8:6 What a **t** thing I have done
Zeph 1:15 a day of **t** distress and
Heb 10:31 It is a **t** thing to fall into

TERRIFY, TERRIFIED, TERRIFIES (v)
to scare, deter, or intimidate; to fill with terror
Deut 2:25 the earth **t-ied** because of you.
Deut 28:67 you will be **t-ied** by the awful
1 Sam 12:18 were **t-ied** of the LORD
Prov 21:15 but it **t-ies** evildoers.
Isa 13:8 and people are **t-ied.** Pangs of
Zeph 2:11 The LORD will **t** them
Matt 14:26 on the water, they were **t-ied.**
Matt 17:6 disciples were **t-ied** and fell
Matt 27:54 the crucifixion were **t-ied**
Mark 4:41 disciples were absolutely **t-ied.**
Luke 21:26 will be **t-ied** at what they

TERRIFYING (adj)
causing terror or apprehension
Deut 4:34 powerful arm, and **t** acts?
Deut 34:12 Moses performed **t** acts in the
Judg 13:6 of God's angels, **t** to see.

TERRITORY (n)
an indeterminate geographic area
2 Cor 10:16 done in someone else's **t.**

TERROR, TERRORS (n)
a state of intense fear; a frightening aspect
Deut 7:19 Remember the great **t-s** the
Job 9:34 no longer live in **t** of his
Ps 53:5 will grip them, **t** like they
Ps 91:5 afraid of the **t-s** of the night,
Prov 22:8 their reign of **t** will come to
Isa 51:17 the cup of **t,** tipping out its
Mic 7:17 trembling in **t** at his
Luke 9:34 them, and **t** gripped them
Acts 7:32 Moses shook with **t** and did

TEST, TESTINGS, TESTS (n)
a critical examination, observation, or evaluation
see also TRIAL(S), TROUBLE(S)
Deut 29:3 all the great **t-s** of strength,
1 Cor 10:9 should we put Christ to the **t,**
1 Tim 3:10 If they pass the **t,** then let
Heb 4:15 of the same **t-ings** we do, yet

TEST, TESTED, TESTING, TESTS (v)
to put to test or proof
Gen 22:1 God **t-ed** Abraham's faith.
Deut 6:16 You must not **t** the LORD your
Judg 3:1 land to **t** those Israelites
1 Kgs 10:1 she came to **t** him with hard
Job 23:10 when he **t-s** me, I will come
Ps 17:3 You have **t-ed** my thoughts
Ps 66:10 You have **t-ed** us,
Ps 78:18 They stubbornly **t-ed** God in
Ps 106:14 ran wild, **t-ing** God's patience
Ps 139:23 **t** me and know my anxious
Prov 17:3 the LORD **t-s** the heart.
Luke 4:12 You must not **t** the LORD your
Acts 5:9 of conspiring to **t** the Spirit
1 Thes 5:21 but **t** everything that is said.
Heb 2:18 suffering and **t-ing,** he is able
Heb 2:18 us when we are being **t-ed.**
Heb 3:8 they **t-ed** me in the wilderness.
Heb 11:17 when God was **t-ing** him.
Jas 1:3 when your faith is **t-ed,** your
Jas 1:12 who patiently endure **t-ing** and
1 Pet 1:7 It is being **t-ed** as fire tests
1 Jn 4:1 You must **t** them to see if
Rev 2:10 you into prison to **t** you.
Rev 3:10 great time of **t-ing** that will

TESTIFY, TESTIFIED, TESTIFIES, TESTIFYING (v)
to make a statement based on personal knowledge or belief; to give evidence or proof
Exod 20:16 must not **t** falsely against
Deut 5:20 must not **t** falsely against
Prov 24:28 Don't **t** against your

Luke 18:20 You must not **t** falsely.
John 1:34 Jesus, so I **t** that he is
John 5:32 else is also **t-ing** about me,
John 15:26 Father and will **t** all about
John 18:37 the world to **t** to the truth.
John 21:24 one who **t-ies** to these events
Acts 4:33 The apostles **t-ied** powerfully
Acts 10:43 the prophets **t-ied** about,
1 Jn 4:14 own eyes and now **t** that the

TESTIMONY (n)
the evidence given by a witness
see also TESTIFY
Num 35:30 to death on the **t** of only
John 1:7 might believe because of his **t.**
1 Tim 6:13 gave a good **t** before Pontius
1 Jn 5:9 Since we believe human **t,**
Rev 12:11 of the Lamb and by their **t.**

THANK, THANKING (v)
to express gratitude to; to acknowledge God's goodness
Ps 35:18 Then I will **t** you in front
Ps 79:13 pasture, will **t** you forever
Ps 145:10 works will **t** you, LORD,
Isa 12:4 sing: "**T** the LORD!
1 Cor 10:30 If I can **t** God for the food
Phil 4:6 and **t** him for all he has done.
1 Thes 2:13 we never stop **t-ing** God
1 Thes 3:9 How we **t** God for you!

THANKFUL (adj)
conscious of benefit received; expressive of thanks
Col 3:15 And always be **t.**
Col 3:16 to God with **t** hearts.
1 Thes 5:18 Be **t** in all circumstances,
Heb 12:28 let us be **t** and please God by

THANKFULNESS (n)
the quality or state of being thankful
Col 2:7 you will overflow with **t.**

THANKS (n)
kindly or grateful thoughts; gratitude
1 Chr 16:4 to give **t,** and to praise
Ps 30:12 I will give you **t** forever!
Ps 107:1 Give **t** to the LORD,
Rom 1:21 as God or even give him **t.**
1 Cor 11:24 gave **t** to God for it.
Phil 1:3 of you, I give **t** to my God.
1 Tim 2:1 behalf, and give **t** for them.
1 Tim 4:3 be eaten with **t** by faithful
Rev 4:9 and honor and **t** to the one

THANKSGIVING (n)
a prayer expressing gratitude; a public acknowledgment or celebration of God's goodness
Ps 26:7 singing a song of **t** and telling
Ps 28:7 I burst out in songs of **t.**
Ps 100:4 Enter his gates with **t;** go
Isa 51:3 Songs of **t** will fill the air.

THIEF, THIEVES (n)
one who steals, especially stealthily or secretly
Prov 6:30 might be found for a **t**
Prov 29:24 If you assist a **t,** you only
Jer 7:11 has become a den of **t-ves?**
Matt 6:19 where **t-ves** break in and steal.
Luke 19:46 turned it into a den of **t-ves.**
John 10:1 surely be a **t** and a robber!
John 10:8 me were **t-ves** and robbers.
1 Cor 6:10 or are **t-ves,** or greedy people,
1 Thes 5:2 unexpectedly, like a **t** in the
Rev 16:15 as unexpectedly as a **t!**

THINK, THINKING, THINKS (v)
to reflect, ponder, or remember; to subject to the processes of logical thought; to have as an opinion; to conceive or reason
see also MEDITATE, THOUGHT
1 Sam 12:24 **T** of all the wonderful
2 Chr 19:6 Always **t** carefully before
Ps 8:4 you should **t** about them,
Ps 63:6 I lie awake **t-ing** of you,
Ps 77:12 I cannot stop **t-ing** about your
Ps 119:97 I **t** about them all day long.
Ps 119:148 the night, **t-ing** about your
Prov 13:16 Wise people **t** before they
Prov 15:28 godly **t-s** carefully before
Prov 21:29 the virtuous **t** before they
Prov 23:7 are always **t-ing** about how
Prov 29:20 who speaks without **t-ing.**
Isa 44:18 are shut, and they cannot **t.**
Matt 22:42 What do you **t** about the
Rom 11:20 So don't **t** highly of
Phil 1:3 Every time I **t** of you, I give
Phil 2:3 Be humble, **t-ing** of others as
Phil 3:19 they **t** only about this life
Heb 10:24 Let us **t** of ways to motivate
1 Pet 1:13 So **t** clearly and exercise

THINKING (n)
opinion, judgment
Rom 1:28 them to their foolish **t**
2 Pet 3:1 wholesome **t** and refresh

THIRST (v)
to crave vehemently and urgently
Ps 42:2 I **t** for God, the living God.
Matt 5:6 who hunger and **t** for justice,

THIRSTY (adj)
feeling a desire for liquids; having a strong desire
Ps 107:9 he satisfies the **t** and fills
Prov 25:21 If they are **t,** give them
Isa 55:1 Is anyone **t?** Come and drink—
Matt 25:35 I was **t,** and you gave
John 4:14 will never be **t** again.
John 19:28 Scripture he said, "I am **t.**"
Rom 12:20 If they are **t,** give them
2 Cor 11:27 been hungry and **t** and
Rev 7:16 never again be hungry or **t;**
Rev 22:17 Let anyone who is **t** come.

THOMAS
One of the twelve disciples, also known as "the Twin" (Matt 10:3; Mark 3:18; Luke 6:15; Acts 1:13); willing to die with Jesus (John 11:16); queried Jesus (John 14:5); doubted Jesus' resurrection but was convinced by his appearance (John 20:24-28).

THORN, THORNS (n)
a woody plant bearing sharp impeding prickles or spines; something that causes distress or irritation
Gen 3:18 It will grow **t-s** and thistles
Num 33:55 in your eyes and **t-s** in your
Matt 13:7 seeds fell among **t-s** that
Matt 27:29 wove **t** branches into a
2 Cor 12:7 I was given a **t** in my flesh,
Heb 6:8 a field bears **t-s** and thistles,

THORNBUSHES (n)
any of various spiny or thorny shrubs or small trees
Luke 6:44 never gathered from **t,** nor

THOUGHT, THOUGHTS (n)
the action or process of thinking; a developed intention or plan; recollection, remembrance
Ps 77:12 They are constantly in my **t-s.**
Ps 92:5 And how deep are your **t-s.**
Ps 94:11 LORD knows people's **t-s;**
Ps 104:34 May all my **t-s** be pleasing
Ps 139:23 and know my anxious **t-s.**
Ps 142:4 no one gives me a passing **t!**
Isa 26:3 whose **t-s** are fixed on you!
Isa 55:8 My **t-s** are nothing like your
Matt 9:4 you have such evil **t-s** in your
Matt 15:19 heart come evil **t-s,** murder,
1 Cor 14:25 their secret **t-s** will be
Eph 4:23 renew your **t-s** and attitudes.
Rev 2:23 searches out the **t-s** and

THOUGHT (v)
to reflect, ponder, or remember
see also THINK
Ps 39:3 The more I **t** about it,
Luke 2:19 in her heart and **t** about them
1 Cor 13:11 I spoke and **t** and reasoned

THOUSAND (adj)
of the number 1,000
Ps 90:4 For you, a **t** years are as
Rev 20:7 When the **t** years come to an

THOUSANDS (n)
a very large number
Joel 3:14 **T** upon **t** are waiting

THREATS (n)
expressions of intention to inflict evil, injury, or damage
Matt 24:6 of wars and **t** of wars,

THREE (adj)
the number 3
Deut 19:15 of two or **t** witnesses.
Jonah 1:17 **t** days and **t** nights.
Matt 12:40 **t** days and **t** nights,
Matt 18:20 where two or **t** gather
Matt 26:34 you will deny **t** times that
Mark 8:31 but **t** days later he would rise
1 Jn 5:7 have these **t** witnesses—

THRILL (v)
to cause to experience a sudden sharp feeling of excitement
Ps 92:4 You **t** me, LORD,
Isa 60:5 your heart will **t** with joy,

THRIVING (adj)
characterized by success, prosperity, or growth
Ps 52:8 olive tree, **t** in the house

THROAT (n)
the front part of the neck
Prov 23:2 put a knife to your **t;**

THRONE, THRONES (n)
seat of power for a king or deity; symbolic of royal authority and the king's role as a judge
Deut 17:18 he sits on the **t** as king,
2 Sam 7:16 and your **t** will be secure
1 Chr 17:12 will secure his **t** forever.
Job 36:7 sets them on **t-s** with kings
Ps 45:6 Your **t,** O God, endures
Ps 47:8 nations, sitting on his holy **t.**
Ps 89:14 are the foundation of your **t.**
Ps 99:1 He sits on his **t** between the
Ps 102:12 sit on your **t** forever.
Ps 103:19 has made the heavens his **t;**
Isa 6:1 He was sitting on a lofty **t,**
Isa 66:1 Heaven is my **t,** and the
Dan 7:9 on a fiery **t** with wheels

Matt 19:28 upon his glorious **t**, you who
Matt 19:28 sit on twelve **t-s**, judging
Acts 7:49 Heaven is my **t**, and the
Rom 15:12 heir to David's **t** will come,
Col 1:16 such as **t-s**, kingdoms, rulers,
Heb 12:2 place of honor beside God's **t.**
Rev 3:21 sat with my Father on his **t.**
Rev 4:2 and I saw a **t** in heaven
Rev 4:4 Twenty-four **t-s** surrounded
Rev 5:5 heir to David's **t**, has won
Rev 20:11 a great white **t** and the
Rev 22:3 the **t** of God and of the Lamb

THROUGH (prep)
by way of
Eph 2:18 to the Father **t** the same Holy

THROUGHOUT (prep)
in or to every part of; during the whole course or period of
Gen 1:29 seed-bearing plant **t** the
Jer 23:40 be infamous **t** the ages.
Rom 10:18 message has gone **t** the earth,

THROW, THROWING (v)
to propel through the air by a forward motion of the hand or arm; to discard
Ps 22:18 themselves and **t** dice for my
Prov 16:33 We may **t** the dice,
Isa 41:9 and will not **t** you away.
Matt 27:35 his clothes by **t-ing** dice.
John 8:7 has never sinned **t** the first
John 19:24 apart, let's **t** dice for it.
Heb 10:35 do not **t** away this confident

THUNDER, THUNDERS (n)
the sound that follows a flash of lightning
Job 37:5 voice is glorious in the **t.**
Mark 3:17 nicknamed them "Sons of **T**"
Rev 10:3 the seven **t-s** answered.

THUNDER, THUNDERS (v)
to give forth a sound that resembles thunder
Ps 29:3 The God of glory **t-s.**
Amos 1:2 from Zion and **t** from Jerusalem

TIE, TIED (v)
to fasten, attach, or close by means of a tie
Prov 3:3 **T** them around your neck as
Matt 18:6 large millstone **t-d** around your

TIES (n)
bonds of kinship or affection
Col 2:2 together by strong **t** of love.

TIME, TIMES (n)
occasion; an opportune or suitable moment; an appointed, fixed, or customary moment or hour for something to happen, begin, or end; duration; conditions at present or at some specified period; added or accumulated quantities or instances
Esth 4:14 just such a **t** as this?"
Ps 9:9 a refuge in **t-s** of trouble.
Ps 62:8 trust in him at all **t-s.**
Eccl 3:1 a **t** for every activity under
Eccl 7:14 when hard **t-s** strike,
Eccl 8:5 wise will find a **t** and a way
Dan 12:7 at **t, t-s,** and half a **t.**
Hos 10:12 for now is the **t** to seek the
Amos 5:13 shut, for it is an evil **t.**
Matt 16:3 interpret the signs of the **t-s!**
Matt 18:21 sins against me? Seven **t-s?**
Luke 12:40 ready all the **t**, for the Son
John 4:53 was the very **t** Jesus had told
John 12:23 the **t** has come for the Son
Acts 1:7 those dates and **t-s**, and they
Acts 18:5 spent all his **t** preaching
1 Cor 7:29 The **t** that remains is very
2 Cor 6:2 the "right **t**" is now.
Gal 6:9 just the right **t** we will reap
2 Tim 1:9 the beginning of **t**—to show
Heb 9:28 once for all **t** as a sacrifice
Heb 10:12 for sins, good for all **t.**
1 Pet 4:17 For the **t** has come for
Rev 12:14 for a time, **t-s**, and half a

TIMID (adj)
lacking in courage or self-confidence
1 Thes 5:14 Encourage those who are **t.**

TIMIDITY (n)
the quality or state of being timid
2 Tim 1:7 of fear and **t**, but of power,

TIMOTHY
Paul's student and traveling companion from Lystra (Acts 16:1-3); raised by devout Jewish mother (2 Tim 1:5; 3:15); joined Paul on second missionary journey (Acts 16–20); sent to serve NT churches (1 Cor 4:17; 16:10; Phil 2:19; 1 Thes 3:5-6; 1 Tim 1:3); wrote letters with Paul (2 Cor 1:1; Phil 1:1; Col 1:1; 1 Thes 1:1; 2 Thes 1:1; Phlm 1:1); letters written to him by Paul (1 Tim 1:2; 2 Tim 1:2).

TIRED (adj)
drained of strength and energy
Exod 17:12 became so **t** he could no
Isa 35:3 those who have **t** hands,
Gal 6:9 let's not get **t** of doing what
2 Thes 3:13 never get **t** of doing good.
Heb 12:12 new grip with your **t** hands

TITHE, TITHES (n)
one-tenth of any property or produce
see also TENTH
Num 18:21 give them the **t-s** from the
Deut 12:17 neither the **t** of your grain
2 Chr 31:12 brought all the **t-s** and
Amos 4:4 bring your **t-s** every three
Mal 3:8 of the **t-s** and offerings due
Mal 3:10 Bring all the **t-s** into the

TITHE (v)
to pay or give a tenth of as an offering to God
Matt 23:23 You should **t,** yes,
Luke 11:42 you are careful to **t** even the

TITTLE (KJV)
Matt 5:18 the *smallest detail* of God's law
Luke 16:17 the *smallest point* of God's law

TITUS
Young Gentile pastor and helper of Paul (Gal 2:1-3; 2 Tim 4:10); sent to Corinth (2 Cor 2:13; 7:6-14; 8:6-23; 12:18); sent to Crete (Titus 1:4-5).

TODAY (adv)
on or for this day; at the present time
Ps 2:7 **T** I have become your Father.
Ps 95:7 listen to his voice **t!**
Matt 6:11 Give us **t** the food we
Luke 2:11 born **t** in Bethlehem,
Luke 23:43 I assure you, **t** you will be
Heb 1:5 **T** I have become your Father.
Heb 3:7 **T** when you hear his voice,
Heb 13:8 is the same yesterday, **t,** and

TOGETHER (adv)
with each other; as a unit; in or into one place, mass, collection, or group
Ps 133:1 brothers live **t** in harmony!
Jer 3:18 will return **t** from exile
Zeph 3:9 can worship the LORD **t.**
Acts 1:14 They all met **t** and were
Rom 1:12 When we get **t,** I want to
Eph 1:10 bring everything **t** under the

TOLERANT (adj)
marked by forbearance and endurance
Rom 2:4 how wonderfully kind, **t,** and

TOLERATE (v)
to put up with
Rev 2:2 know you don't **t** evil people.

TOMORROW (n)
the day after the present; the future
Prov 27:1 Don't brag about **t,** since you
Isa 22:13 and drink, for **t** we die!
Rom 8:38 our worries about **t**—not even
1 Cor 15:32 and drink, for **t** we die!

TONGUE, TONGUES (n)
part of the mouth that enables speech; dialect or language of a people; a special gift of speech given by the Holy Spirit
see also LANGUAGE(S)
Ps 5:9 Their **t-s** are filled
Ps 34:13 keep your **t** from speaking
Ps 39:1 I will hold my **t** when
Ps 45:1 king, for my **t** is like
Ps 78:36 lied to him with their **t-s.**
Ps 119:172 Let my **t** sing about
Ps 137:6 May my **t** stick to the
Prov 13:3 who control their **t** will have
Prov 15:4 a deceitful **t** crushes the
Prov 17:20 the lying **t** tumbles into
Prov 21:23 Watch your **t** and keep
Luke 16:24 in water and cool my **t.**
Acts 2:3 like flames or **t-s** of fire
Acts 10:46 speaking in other **t-s** and
Acts 19:6 in other **t-s** and prophesied.
Rom 14:11 me, and every **t** will confess
1 Cor 14:2 to speak in **t-s,** you will
1 Cor 14:4 speaks in **t-s** is strengthened
1 Cor 14:5 speak in **t-s,** but even more
1 Cor 14:13 speaks in **t-s** should pray
1 Cor 14:18 I speak in **t-s** more than
1 Cor 14:27 three should speak in **t-s.**
1 Cor 14:39 forbid speaking in **t-s.**
Phil 2:11 and every **t** confess that
Jas 3:2 if we could control our **t-s,** we
Jas 3:5 same way, the **t** is a small

TOOK (v)
to seize, grasp, or carry
see also TAKE
Matt 8:17 He **t** our sicknesses and
Matt 26:26 eating, Jesus **t** some bread and
Matt 26:27 And he **t** a cup of wine and
1 Cor 11:23 the Lord Jesus **t** some bread
1 Cor 11:25 the same way, he **t** the cup of
Phil 2:7 he **t** the humble position of

TOOTH (n)
a bonelike structure in the mouth used for chewing
Exod 21:24 eye for an eye, a **t** for a **t,**
Matt 5:38 eye for an eye, and a **t** for a **t.**

TORMENT (n)
extreme pain or anguish of body or mind
Luke 16:28 end up in this place of **t.**

TORMENT, TORMENTED (v)
to cause severe usually persistent or recurrent distress of body or mind

2 Cor 12:7	messenger from Satan to **t**
Rev 20:10	they will be **t-ed** day and night

TORMENTORS (n)
those who torment

Ps 137:3	Our **t** insisted on a joyful

TORTURED (v)
to punish or coerce by inflicting excruciating pain

Matt 18:34	prison to be **t** until he
Heb 11:35	others were **t**, refusing to

TOSSED (v)
to fling or heave continuously about

Jas 1:6	blown and **t** by the wind.

TOUCH, TOUCHED, TOUCHES (v)
to reach out or come in contact with; to lay hands upon; to have an influence upon

Gen 3:3	must not eat it or even **t** it;
Exod 19:12	or even **t** its boundaries.
Exod 19:12	Anyone who **t-es** the mountain
Isa 6:7	this coal has **t-ed** your lips.
Matt 9:21	If I can just **t** his robe,
Matt 14:36	who **t-ed** him were healed.
Luke 8:45	"Who **t-ed** me?" Jesus asked.
Luke 18:15	so he could **t** and bless
Luke 24:39	**T** me and make sure that
2 Cor 6:17	Don't **t** their filthy things,
Col 2:21	Don't taste! Don't **t**!"?
1 Jn 1:1	**t-ed** him with our own hands.
1 Jn 5:18	evil one cannot **t** them.

TOWER (n)
a tall building or structure typically higher than its surroundings

Gen 11:4	with a **t** that reaches into

TRADE, TRADED (v)
to give one thing in exchange for another

Gen 25:31	Jacob replied, "but **t** me your
Ps 106:20	They **t-d** their glorious God
Rom 1:25	They **t-d** the truth about God

TRADERS (n)
persons whose business is buying and selling

1 Tim 1:10	are slave **t**, liars, promise

TRADITION, TRADITIONS (n)
an inherited, customary, or established pattern of thought, action, or behavior

Matt 15:6	for the sake of your own **t**.
Mark 7:5	disciples follow our age-old **t**?
Mark 7:8	law and substitute your own **t**.
Mark 7:13	to hand down your own **t**.
Gal 1:14	in my zeal for the **t-s** of my

TRAGEDY (n)
a disastrous event; misfortune

Eccl 9:12	are caught by sudden **t**.

TRAGIC (adj)
of, marked by, or expressive of tragedy

Eccl 1:13	has dealt a **t** existence to

TRAIN (n)
a part of a gown that trails behind the wearer

Isa 6:1	throne, and the **t** of his robe

TRAIN, TRAINED (v)
to form by or undergo instruction or discipline
see also TEACH

Isa 2:4	against nation, nor **t** for war
Luke 6:40	who is fully **t-ed** will become
John 7:15	when he hasn't been **t-ed**?
Acts 22:3	I was carefully **t-ed** in our
1 Tim 4:7	**t** yourself to be godly.
Titus 2:4	women must **t** the younger
Heb 12:11	those who are **t-ed** in this way.

TRAINING (n)
acquired skill, knowledge, or experience; the act, process, or method of one who trains

Acts 4:13	men with no special **t** in the
1 Tim 4:8	Physical **t** is good, but

TRAITORS (n)
those who betray another's trust, are false to an obligation or duty, or commit treason

Ps 59:5	Show no mercy to wicked **t**.
Ps 119:158	Seeing these **t** makes me

TRAMPLE, TRAMPLED (v)
to crush, injure, or destroy by or as if by treading

Ps 60:12	for he will **t** down our foes.
Ps 91:13	You will **t** upon lions
Amos 5:11	You **t** the poor,
Amos 8:4	rob the poor and **t** down the
Mic 4:13	so you can **t** many nations to
Mic 7:19	You will **t** our sins under
Matt 7:6	They will **t** the pearls,
Luke 21:24	Jerusalem will be **t-d** down
Heb 10:29	who have **t-d** on the Son
Rev 14:20	The grapes were **t-d** in the

TRANCE (n)
a sleeplike state (as of deep hypnosis)

Acts 10:10	prepared, he fell into a **t**.
Acts 11:5	I went into a **t** and saw a

Acts 22:17 the Temple and fell into a **t.**

TRANSFIGURED (KJV)
Matt 17:2 Jesus' appearance was *transformed*
Mark 9:2 Jesus' appearance was *transformed*

TRANSFORM, TRANSFORMED (v)
to change the outward appearance of; to change in character or condition
see also CHANGE(D)
Matt 17:2 appearance was **t-ed** so that
Rom 12:2 let God **t** you into a new
1 Cor 15:51 but we will all be **t-ed!**

TRANSGRESSED, TRANSGRESSION (KJV)
Josh 7:11 and *broken* my covenant
1 Chr 5:25 tribes were *unfaithful*
1 Chr 10:13 because he was *unfaithful*
Rom 4:15 to avoid *breaking* the law
1 Jn 3:4 sin is *contrary to* the law

TRAP, TRAPS (n)
something by which one is caught or stopped unawares; a position or situation from which it is difficult or impossible to escape; a device for taking game or other animals
Deut 7:25 will become a **t** to you,
Deut 12:30 fall into the **t** of following
Ps 91:3 you from every **t** and protect
Prov 1:17 a bird sees a **t** being set,
Prov 3:26 foot from being caught in a **t.**
Prov 28:10 into their own **t,** but the
Prov 29:5 is to lay a **t** for their feet.
Prov 29:25 a dangerous **t,** but trusting
Isa 8:14 he will be a **t** and a snare.
Isa 24:17 Terror and **t-s** and snares will
Matt 16:23 are a dangerous **t** to me.
Rom 11:9 a snare, a **t** that makes them
1 Tim 3:7 into the devil's **t.**
2 Tim 2:26 from the devil's **t.**

TRAP, TRAPPED, TRAPS (v)
to catch or take in or as if in a trap
Ps 7:15 a deep pit to **t** others, then
Ps 9:16 wicked are **t-ped** by their own
Prov 6:2 if you have **t-ped** yourself by
Prov 12:13 wicked are **t-ped** by their
Prov 18:7 they **t** themselves with
Matt 22:15 to plot how to **t** Jesus into
1 Cor 3:19 He **t-s** the wise in the snare
1 Tim 6:9 temptation and are **t-ped** by

TREACHEROUS (adj)
characterized by or manifesting treachery
Prov 11:6 ambition of **t** people traps
Prov 13:2 but **t** people have an appetite
Prov 13:15 a **t** person is headed for
Prov 22:12 ruins the plans of the **t.**
Jer 3:8 But that **t** sister Judah had

TREACHERY (n)
violation of allegiance or of faith and confidence
Acts 1:18 he received for his **t.**

TREAD, TREADING, TREADS (v)
to beat or press with the feet
Deut 25:4 eating as it **t-s** out the grain.
Isa 63:2 have been **t-ing** out grapes?
Joel 3:13 Come, **t** the grapes,
1 Cor 9:9 from eating as it **t-s** out
1 Tim 5:18 from eating as it **t-s** out

TREASURE, TREASURES (n)
wealth or a collection of precious things; something of great value
Exod 19:5 my own special **t** from
Deut 7:6 to be his own special **t.**
1 Chr 29:3 my own private **t-s** of gold
Ps 119:111 Your laws are my **t;** they
Ps 135:4 Israel for his own special **t.**
Prov 2:4 seek them like hidden **t-s.**
Prov 18:22 finds a wife finds a **t,**
Song 4:10 delights me, my **t,** my bride.
Isa 10:3 Where will your **t-s** be safe?
Hag 2:7 the **t-s** of all the nations
Mal 3:17 they will be my own special **t.**
Matt 6:19 Don't store up **t-s** here on
Matt 6:21 Wherever your **t** is, there the
Matt 13:44 Heaven is like a **t** that a man
Luke 12:33 will store up **t** for you in
2 Cor 4:7 jars containing this great **t.**
Eph 3:8 the endless **t-s** available to
Col 2:3 hidden all the **t-s** of wisdom
1 Tim 6:19 storing up their **t** as a good
Heb 11:26 to own the **t-s** of Egypt, for

TREASURE, TREASURED (v)
to hold or keep as precious
Job 23:12 but have **t-d** his words more
Prov 2:1 I say, and **t** my commands.
Prov 7:1 always **t** my commands.
Prov 10:14 Wise people **t** knowledge,

TREASURY (n)
a place in which stores of wealth are kept
Deut 28:12 time from his rich **t** in the
Luke 6:45 things from the **t** of a good

TREAT, TREATED, TREATING (v)
to regard and deal with in a specified manner
Gen 18:25 **t-ing** the righteous
Eccl 8:14 people are often **t-ed** as though

Matt 18:17 **t** that person as a pagan
Eph 6:9 Masters, **t** your slaves in the
Heb 10:29 God, and have **t-ed** the blood
Heb 12:7 God is **t-ing** you as his own
1 Pet 3:7 **T** your wife with understanding

TREATY, TREATIES (n)
an agreement or arrangement made by negotiation
Exod 34:12 to make a **t** with the people
Deut 7:2 Make no **t-ies** with them and
Dan 9:27 will make a **t** with the people

TREE, TREES (n)
woody perennial plants, many of which produce crops; highly treasured natural resource; often linked with worship of pagan gods; symbolic of a growing believer
Gen 2:9 he placed the **t** of life and
Deut 21:23 from the **t** overnight.
Judg 9:8 the **t-s** decided to choose
2 Sam 18:9 got caught in the **t.**
1 Kgs 14:23 and under every green **t.**
Ps 1:3 They are like **t-s** planted along
Ps 52:8 like an olive **t,** thriving in
Ps 92:12 like palm **t-s** and grow
Ps 96:12 Let the **t-s** of the forest
Prov 3:18 Wisdom is a **t** of life to
Prov 11:30 deeds become a **t** of life;
Isa 55:12 and the **t-s** of the field
Isa 65:22 people will live as long as **t-s,**
Jer 17:8 They are like **t-s** planted along
Dan 4:10 saw a large **t** in the middle
Mic 4:4 and fig **t-s,** for there will be
Matt 3:10 sever the roots of the **t-s.**
Matt 3:10 every **t** that does not produce
Matt 12:33 **t** is identified by its fruit.
Mark 8:24 look like **t-s** walking
Luke 19:4 a sycamore-fig **t** beside the
Rom 11:24 cut from a wild olive **t.**
Gal 3:13 everyone who is hung on a **t.**
Jas 3:12 Does a fig **t** produce olives,
Jude 1:12 They are like **t-s** in autumn
Rev 22:2 the river grew a **t** of life,
Rev 22:14 the fruit from the **t** of life.
Rev 22:19 share in the **t** of life and

TREMBLE, TREMBLED, TREMBLES, TREMBLING (v)
to be affected with great fear or anxiety; to shake involuntarily
Exod 15:14 hear and **t;** anguish grips
Exod 19:16 horn, and all the people **t-d.**
Exod 20:18 a distance, **t-ing** with fear.
2 Sam 22:8 the earth quaked and **t-d.**
1 Chr 16:30 all the earth **t** before him.
Ps 2:11 fear, and rejoice with **t-ing.**
Ps 97:4 The earth sees and **t-s.**
Ps 102:15 the earth will **t** before his
Ps 104:32 The earth **t-s** at his glance;
Isa 66:2 contrite hearts, who **t** at my
Jer 10:10 whole earth **t-s** at his anger.
Dan 10:10 and lifted me, still **t-ing,**
Joel 2:1 Let everyone **t** in fear
Nah 1:5 hills melt away; the earth **t-s,**
Hab 3:6 the nations **t.** He shatters
Heb 4:1 we ought to **t** with fear that
Heb 12:21 I am terrified and **t-ing.**

TRESPASS(ES) (KJV)
Lev 19:21 a ram as a *guilt* offering
2 Chr 24:18 Because of this *sin,* divine
Matt 6:15 Father will not forgive your *sins*
Matt 18:15 . believer *sins* against you,
Eph 2:1 because of your *disobedience*

TRIAL, TRIALS (n)
a legal proceeding based in court; a test of faith, patience, or stamina through subjection to suffering or temptation
see also TEMPTATION(S), TEST(S), TROUBLE(S)
Job 42:11 all the **t-s** the LORD had
Ps 26:2 Put me on **t,** LORD,
Ps 37:33 when they are put on **t.**
Ps 143:2 Don't put your servant on **t,**
Mark 13:11 and stand **t,** don't worry in
Luke 22:28 with me in my time of **t.**
John 16:33 have many **t-s** and sorrows.
Rom 5:3 into problems and **t-s,** for we
1 Pet 1:7 through many **t-s,** it will
1 Pet 4:12 the fiery **t-s** you are going
2 Pet 2:9 from their **t-s,** even while

TRIBE, TRIBES (n)
family divisions, usually within Israel, but also of other ethnic peoples
Gen 49:28 are the twelve **t-s** of Israel,
Matt 19:28 the twelve **t-s** of Israel.
Heb 7:13 a different **t,** whose members
Rev 5:5 Lion of the **t** of Judah,
Rev 5:9 God from every **t** and language
Rev 11:9 all peoples, **t-s,** languages,
Rev 14:6 to every nation, **t,** language,

TRIBULATION (n)
a period of unparalleled suffering in the last days
Rev 7:14 who died in the great **t.**

TRIBUTE (n)
a gift or service showing respect, gratitude, or affection
Ps 76:11 Let everyone bring **t** to the

TRICK, TRICKED (v)
to deceive or cheat
Gen 27:35 and he **t-ed** me
Gen 29:25 Why have you **t-ed** me
Jer 29:31 has **t-ed** you into believing
2 Cor 4:2 We don't try to **t** anyone
Eph 4:14 people try to **t** us with lies

TRICKERY (n)
deception
Isa 29:21 those who use **t** to pervert
2 Cor 12:16 advantage of you by **t.**

TRIED (v)
to make an attempt at; to put to test
Ps 73:16 So I **t** to understand
Ps 95:9 tested and **t** my patience,
Ps 119:10 I have **t** hard to find
Heb 3:9 tested and **t** my patience,

TRIUMPH (n)
the joy or exultation of victory or success
Ps 118:7 I will look in **t** at those

TRIUMPH, TRIUMPHED (v)
to obtain victory
1 Sam 17:50 So David **t-ed** over the
Ps 54:7 and helped me to **t** over my

TRIUMPHAL (adj)
of, relating to, or marked by triumph
2 Cor 2:14 in Christ's **t** procession.

TRIUMPHANT (adj)
victorious, conquering
Deut 33:29 shield and your **t** sword!

TROUBLE, TROUBLES (n)
a state, condition, or cause of distress, annoyance, difficulty, or inconvenience
see also TEST(S), TRIAL(S)
Gen 41:51 made me forget all my **t-s**
Josh 7:25 have you brought **t** on us?
2 Chr 15:4 they were in **t** and turned
Job 5:7 are born for **t** as readily as
Ps 7:14 they are pregnant with **t**
Ps 9:9 a refuge in times of **t.**
Ps 10:14 you see the **t** and grief
Ps 22:11 from me, for **t** is near,
Ps 27:5 me there when **t-s** come;
Ps 32:7 you protect me from **t.**
Ps 34:17 them from all their **t-s.**
Ps 37:39 their fortress in times of **t.**
Ps 40:12 For **t-s** surround me—
Ps 41:1 them when they are in **t.**
Ps 46:1 ready to help in times of **t.**
Ps 49:5 I fear when **t** comes, when
Ps 50:15 when you are in **t,** and I will
Ps 54:7 have rescued me from my **t-s**
Ps 55:3 They bring **t** on me
Ps 66:14 I was in deep **t.**
Ps 81:7 cried to me in **t,** and
Ps 86:7 whenever I'm in **t,** and
Ps 91:15 I will be with them in **t.**
Ps 107:6 they cried in their **t,**
Ps 107:41 rescues the poor from **t**
Ps 116:3 I saw only **t** and sorrow.
Ps 120:1 took my **t-s** to the LORD;
Ps 138:7 I am surrounded by **t-s,** you
Prov 6:14 they constantly stir up **t.**
Prov 10:10 who wink at wrong cause **t,**
Prov 11:8 godly are rescued from **t,**
Prov 11:29 Those who bring **t** on their
Prov 12:13 the godly escape such **t.**
Prov 12:21 wicked have their fill of **t.**
Prov 13:20 with fools and get in **t.**
Prov 25:19 in times of **t** is like chewing
Eccl 4:10 falls alone is in real **t.**
Isa 38:14 I am in **t,** LORD. Help me!
Isa 53:4 And we thought his **t-s** were
Isa 58:10 and help those in **t.**
Hos 5:15 as soon as **t** comes, they
Nah 1:7 strong refuge when **t** comes.
Matt 6:34 Today's **t** is enough
Rom 8:35 if we have **t** or calamity,
1 Cor 7:28 at this time will have **t-s,**
2 Cor 4:17 our present **t-s** are small
2 Cor 6:4 We patiently endure **t-s** and
2 Cor 7:4 me happy despite all our **t-s.**
2 Cor 8:2 being tested by many **t-s,**
1 Thes 3:3 shaken by the **t-s** you were
1 Tim 6:5 These people always cause **t.**
Jas 1:2 when **t-s** come your way,
Jas 5:1 all the terrible **t-s** ahead

TROUBLE (v)
to worry or disturb
Luke 7:6 Lord, don't **t** yourself by

TROUBLED (adj)
concerned, worried
Dan 6:14 the king was deeply **t,** and he
Mark 14:33 and he became deeply **t** and
John 14:1 Don't let your hearts be **t.**
John 14:27 So don't be **t** or afraid.

TROUBLEMAKERS (n)
those who consciously or unconsciously causes trouble
Judg 19:22 crowd of **t** from the town

TRUE (adj)
fully realized or fulfilled; accurate; properly so called; steadfast, loyal, honest, and just; ideal, essential; being in accordance with the actual state of affairs; legitimate, rightful

Num 11:23 my word comes **t**!
Deut 18:22 does not happen or come **t**,
Josh 23:14 your God has come **t**.
1 Sam 9:6 everything he says comes **t**.
1 Kgs 10:6 and wisdom is **t**!
2 Chr 15:3 without the **t** God,
Ps 7:10 hearts are **t** and right.
Ps 19:9 laws of the LORD are **t**;
Ps 119:142 instructions are perfectly **t**.
Ps 119:151 your commands are **t**.
Isa 45:19 speak only what is **t** and
Jer 10:10 is the only **t** God.
Jer 26:15 it is absolutely **t** that
Jer 28:9 when his predictions come **t**
Luke 16:11 the **t** riches of heaven?
Luke 18:31 Son of Man will come **t**.
John 1:9 one who is the **t** light,
John 3:33 can affirm that God is **t**.
John 4:23 **t** worshipers will worship
John 6:32 offers you the **t** bread
John 6:55 my flesh is **t** food, and
John 7:28 one who sent me is **t**,
John 15:1 I am the **t** grapevine,
John 17:3 know you, the only **t** God,
Rom 3:4 else is a liar, God is **t**.
Rom 15:8 God is **t** to the promises
Eph 5:9 is good and right and **t**.
Phil 4:1 stay **t** to the Lord.
Phil 4:8 thoughts on what is **t**,
Jas 1:18 giving us his **t** word.
1 Jn 2:8 the **t** light is already
1 Jn 2:27 to teach you what is **t**.
1 Jn 5:20 He is the only **t** God,
Rev 19:9 These are **t** words that come
Rev 22:6 seen is trustworthy and **t**.

TRUMPET, TRUMPETS (n)
a wind instrument made of metal or an animal horn used to rally troops on the battlefield or by priests during sacrifices

Isa 27:13 the great **t** will sound.
Matt 24:31 blast of a **t**, and they will
1 Cor 15:52 when the last **t** is blown.
1 Thes 4:16 with the **t** call of God.
Rev 8:2 they were given seven **t-s**.
Rev 8:7 angel blew his **t**, and hail
Rev 18:22 flutes, and **t-s** will never

TRUST (n)
assured reliance on the character, ability, strength, or truth of someone or something; hope
see also BELIEVE, FAITH

Job 31:24 Have I put my **t** in money
Ps 40:3 put their **t** in the LORD.
Ps 56:3 I will put my **t** in you.
Isa 2:22 Don't put your **t** in mere
Jer 13:25 putting your **t** in false
Jer 17:5 who put their **t** in mere
John 12:46 who put their **t** in me
Heb 2:13 will put my **t** in him,
1 Jn 4:16 have put our **t** in his love.

TRUST, TRUSTED, TRUSTING, TRUSTS (v)
to place confidence or depend; to commit or place in one's care or keeping; to rely on the truthfulness or accuracy of
see also BELIEVE, FAITH

Gen 39:8 master **t-s** me with everything
Deut 1:32 refused to **t** the LORD
Deut 28:52 walls you **t-ed** to protect
2 Kgs 18:5 Hezekiah **t-ed** in the
2 Kgs 18:19 What are you **t-ing** in that
1 Chr 5:20 because they **t-ed** in him.
2 Chr 13:18 they **t-ed** in the LORD,
Job 4:18 God does not **t** his own angels
Job 15:31 fool themselves by **t-ing** in
Ps 13:5 I **t** in your unfailing love.
Ps 21:7 the king **t-s** in the LORD.
Ps 25:2 I **t** in you, my God!
Ps 25:3 No one who **t-s** in you will
Ps 31:14 I am **t-ing** you, O LORD,
Ps 33:4 we can **t** everything he
Ps 37:3 **T** in the LORD and do
Ps 41:9 the one I **t-ed** completely,
Ps 44:6 I do not **t** in my bow;
Ps 55:23 but I am **t-ing** you to save
Ps 62:8 O my people, **t** in him at
Ps 71:5 I've **t-ed** you, O LORD,
Ps 84:12 for those who **t** in you.
Ps 86:2 serve you and **t** you.
Ps 112:7 confidently **t** the LORD
Ps 115:8 as are all who **t** in them.
Ps 118:8 LORD than to **t** in
Ps 119:42 for I **t** in your word.
Prov 3:5 **T** in the LORD with
Prov 21:22 fortress in which they **t**.
Prov 28:25 **t-ing** the LORD leads to
Prov 28:26 who **t** their own insight
Prov 29:25 **t-ing** the LORD means safety.
Prov 31:11 Her husband can **t** her,
Isa 12:2 I will **t** in him and
Isa 25:9 We **t-ed** in him, and he saved
Isa 26:3 peace all who **t** in you,
Isa 31:1 for help, **t-ing** their horses,
Isa 40:31 who **t** in the LORD
Jer 7:14 this Temple that you **t** in
Jer 12:6 Do not **t** them, no matter

Jer 48:7 Because you have **t-ed** in your
Dan 3:28 his servants who **t-ed** in him.
Dan 6:23 for he had **t-ed** in his God.
Nah 1:7 to those who **t** in him.
Hab 2:4 They **t** in themselves,
Hab 2:18 foolish to **t** in your own
Matt 18:6 little ones who **t-s** in me to
John 2:24 Jesus didn't **t** them,
John 12:44 you are **t-ing** not only me,
John 14:1 in God, and **t** also in me.
Rom 9:32 instead of by **t-ing** in him.
Rom 9:33 But anyone who **t-s** in him will
Rom 10:11 Anyone who **t-s** in him will
Rom 15:13 peace because you **t** in
1 Cor 2:5 so you would **t** not in
1 Cor 7:25 wisdom that can be **t-ed,**
Eph 3:17 hearts as you **t** in him.
Phil 1:29 the privilege of **t-ing** in Christ
Col 2:12 because you **t-ed** the mighty
1 Tim 6:17 not to **t** in their money,
2 Tim 1:12 the one in whom I **t,**
2 Tim 3:15 that comes by **t-ing** in Christ
Heb 10:22 hearts fully **t-ing** him.
Heb 10:23 God can be **t-ed** to keep his
1 Pet 1:9 reward for **t-ing** him will be
1 Pet 2:6 anyone who **t-s** in him will
1 Pet 2:7 you who **t** him recognize

TRUSTWORTHY (adj)
worthy of confidence; dependable
see also FAITHFUL, LOYAL
2 Kgs 22:7 honest and **t** men.
Ps 19:7 of the LORD are **t,**
Ps 119:86 All your commands are **t.**
Ps 119:138 perfect and completely **t.**
Prov 11:13 those who are **t** can keep
Dan 6:4 responsible, and completely **t.**
Titus 2:10 to be entirely **t** and good.
Heb 6:19 a strong and **t** anchor

TRUTH, TRUTHS (n)
the property (as of a statement) of being in accord with fact or reality (natural and spiritual); sincerity in action, character, and utterance
Ps 15:2 speaking the **t** from sincere
Ps 25:5 Lead me by your **t** and teach
Ps 26:3 lived according to your **t.**
Ps 43:3 light and your **t;** let them
Ps 45:4 defending **t,** humility, and
Ps 86:11 live according to your **t!**
Ps 119:160 essence of your words is **t;**
Prov 8:7 for I speak the **t** and detest
Prov 12:17 honest witness tells the **t;**
Prov 12:22 in those who tell the **t.**
Prov 23:23 Get the **t** and never sell
Isa 45:23 I have spoken the **t,**
Isa 59:15 Yes, **t** is gone,
Jer 4:2 do so with **t,** justice,
Jer 9:3 to stand up for the **t.**
Dan 10:21 written in the Book of **T.**
Dan 11:2 I will reveal the **t** to you.
Amos 5:10 people who tell the **t!**
Zech 8:16 Tell the **t** to each other.
Zech 8:19 So love **t** and peace.
Luke 1:4 can be certain of the **t**
John 4:23 Father in spirit and in **t.**
John 7:18 him speaks **t,** not lies.
John 8:32 the **t** will set you free.
John 8:44 there is no **t** in him.
John 14:6 way, the **t,** and the life.
John 14:17 who leads into all **t.**
John 15:26 Advocate—the Spirit of **t.**
John 16:13 the Spirit of **t** comes,
John 17:17 your word, which is **t.**
John 18:37 to testify to the **t.**
Acts 20:30 distort the **t** in order
Acts 21:34 find out the **t** in all
Acts 24:8 can find out the **t** of our
Rom 1:18 who suppress the **t** by their
Rom 1:25 They traded the **t** about God
Rom 2:8 to obey the **t** and instead
Rom 2:20 complete knowledge and **t.**
1 Cor 2:13 to explain spiritual **t-s.**
2 Cor 6:7 We faithfully preach the **t.**
2 Cor 13:8 always stand for the **t.**
Gal 2:5 wanted to preserve the **t**
Gal 5:7 back from following the **t?**
Eph 1:13 also heard the **t,** the Good
Eph 4:15 will speak the **t** in love,
Eph 6:14 the belt of **t** and the body
2 Thes 2:10 **t** that would save them.
2 Thes 2:12 rather than believing the **t.**
1 Tim 2:4 and to understand the **t.**
1 Tim 3:15 and foundation of the **t.**
1 Tim 4:3 people who know the **t.**
1 Tim 6:5 their backs on the **t.**
2 Tim 2:15 explains the word of **t.**
2 Tim 3:7 able to understand the **t.**
Titus 1:14 turned away from the **t.**
Heb 10:26 received knowledge of the **t,**
Jas 3:14 don't cover up the **t** with
Jas 5:19 wanders away from the **t**
1 Pet 1:22 you obeyed the **t,** so now
2 Pet 1:12 standing firm in the **t**
2 Pet 2:2 the way of **t** will be
1 Jn 1:8 and not living in the **t.**
1 Jn 2:20 all of you know the **t.**
1 Jn 3:19 belong to the **t,** so we
1 Jn 4:6 Spirit of **t** or the spirit
1 Jn 5:6 Spirit, who is **t,** confirms
2 Jn 1:2 because the **t** lives
2 Jn 1:3 who live in **t** and love.

3 Jn 1:3	living according to the **t.**
3 Jn 1:8	partners as they teach the **t.**

TRUTHFUL (adj)
telling or disposed to tell the truth

Ps 5:9	cannot speak a **t** word.
Prov 12:19	**T** words stand the test
John 8:26	and he is completely **t.**

TRUTHFULNESS (n)
the quality or state of being truthful

Rom 3:7	highlights his **t** and brings
Rom 9:1	I speak with utter **t.**

TURMOIL (n)
a state or condition of extreme confusion, agitation, or commotion

Prov 15:16	treasure and inner **t.**

TURN, TURNED, TURNING, TURNS (v)
to convert or change allegiance; to return or change direction; to face toward or away; to divert one's attention from; to become or transform; to shape or bend

Deut 28:14	You must not **t** away from
Deut 30:10	if you **t** to the LORD
1 Kgs 11:4	old age, they **t-ed** his heart
2 Chr 7:14	seek my face and **t** from
2 Chr 34:33	they did not **t** away from
Esth 9:22	sorrow was **t-ed** into gladness
Ps 14:3	no, all have **t-ed** away; all
Ps 30:11	You have **t-ed** my mourning
Ps 40:1	and he **t-ed** to me and
Ps 119:59	I **t-ed** to follow your
Ps 119:102	I haven't **t-ed** away from
Prov 3:7	fear the LORD and **t** away
Prov 28:13	confess and **t** from them,
Isa 17:7	Creator and **t** their eyes to
Isa 54:8	anger I **t-ed** my face away
Isa 55:7	Let them **t** to the LORD
Isa 59:2	he has **t-ed** away and will
Jer 14:7	We have **t-ed** away from you
Jer 31:13	I will **t** their mourning into
Jer 31:19	I **t-ed** away from God,
Lam 3:40	Let us **t** back to the LORD.
Mal 4:6	preaching will **t** the hearts
Matt 3:8	your sins and **t-ed** to God.
Matt 18:3	truth, unless you **t** from your
Mark 4:12	Otherwise, they will **t** to me
Mark 8:34	must **t** from your selfish
Luke 1:17	He will **t** the hearts of
Luke 17:4	**t-s** again and asks forgiveness
Luke 22:32	you have repented and **t-ed**
John 12:40	and they cannot **t** to me
John 16:20	will suddenly **t** to wonderful
Acts 3:19	of your sins and **t** to God,
Acts 7:42	Then God **t-ed** away from
Acts 26:18	so they may **t** from darkness
Rom 1:26	Even the women **t-ed** against
Rom 2:4	to **t** you from your sin?
Rom 3:12	All have **t-ed** away;
Gal 1:6	that you are **t-ing** away so
2 Tim 2:19	LORD must **t** away from
Titus 2:12	instructed to **t** from godless
Heb 10:38	in anyone who **t-s** away.
1 Pet 2:25	But now you have **t-ed** to

TURTLEDOVES (n)
any of several small wild pigeons noted for plaintive cooing

Lev 12:8	must bring two **t** or two young
Luke 2:24	a pair of **t** or two young

TWELVE (adj)
of or relating to the number 12

Gen 35:22	names of the **t** sons of Jacob:
Gen 49:28	These are the **t** tribes of
Matt 10:1	Jesus called his **t** disciples
Luke 9:17	picked up **t** baskets of
Rev 21:12	names of the **t** tribes of
Rev 21:14	names of the **t** apostles of
Rev 21:21	The **t** gates were made of

TWINS (n)
two offspring produced at a birth

Gen 25:24	she did indeed have **t!**
Luke 17:4	**t-s** again and asks forgiveness

TWIST, TWISTED (v)
to distort or pervert

Exod 14:25	He **t-ed** their chariot wheels,
Exod 23:8	righteous person **t** the truth.
Deut 16:19	You must never **t** justice or
Job 34:12	will not **t** justice.
Isa 24:5	have **t-ed** God's instructions,
Lam 3:36	if they **t** justice in the courts—
Ezek 7:13	whose life is **t-ed** by sin
Gal 1:7	who deliberately **t** the truth
2 Pet 3:16	unstable have **t-ed** his letters

TWO-EDGED (adj)
marked by having two cutting edges

Heb 4:12	sharpest **t** sword, cutting
Rev 1:16	a sharp **t** sword came from
Rev 2:12	with the sharp **t** sword:

U

UNAFRAID (adv)
in a manner not filled with fear

Hos 2:18	you can live **u** in peace

UNBELIEF (n)
incredulity or skepticism in matters of religious truth
see also UNFAITHFUL

Matt 13:58	there because of their **u.**
Mark 6:6	he was amazed at their **u.**
Mark 9:24	help me overcome my **u!**
Mark 16:14	them for their stubborn **u**
Rom 11:23	Israel turn from their **u,**
1 Tim 1:13	it in ignorance and **u.**
Heb 3:19	because of their **u** they

UNBELIEVER, UNBELIEVERS (n)
one who does not believe; a non-Christian

Matt 6:32	dominate the thoughts of **u-s,**
Luke 12:30	the thoughts of **u-s** all over
1 Cor 6:6	right in front of **u-s!**
1 Cor 14:22	for believers, but for **u-s.**
2 Cor 6:15	a partner with an **u?**
1 Tim 5:8	people are worse than **u-s.**
Rev 21:8	But cowards, **u-s,** the corrupt,

UNBELIEVING (adj)
marked by unbelief

1 Pet 2:12	among your **u** neighbors.

UNBREAKABLE (adj)
not capable of being broken

Num 18:19	an eternal and **u** covenant

UNCHANGEABLE (adj)
not changing or to be changed; immutable

Heb 6:18	two things are **u** because

UNCIRCUMCISED (adj)
not circumcised; spiritually impure

Jer 9:26	of Israel also have **u** hearts.
1 Cor 7:18	man who was **u** when he
Gal 5:6	being circumcised or being **u.**
Col 3:11	circumcised or **u,** barbaric,

UNCLEAN (adj)
morally or spiritually impure; prohibited by ritual law for use or contact

Lev 10:10	is ceremonially **u** and what is
Lev 11:4	it is ceremonially **u** for you.
Lev 17:15	remain ceremonially **u** until
Lev 27:11	vow involves an **u** animal—
Isa 52:11	everything you touch is **u.**
Acts 10:14	have declared impure and **u.**
Acts 10:15	not call something **u** if God

UNDERGROUND (adj)
beneath the surface of the earth

Gen 8:2	The **u** waters stopped

UNDERMINE (v)
to weaken or ruin by degrees

Jer 38:4	will **u** the morale of
Ezek 13:11	A heavy rainstorm will **u** it

UNDERSTAND (v)
to grasp the meaning or reasonableness of; to be thoroughly familiar with
see also UNDERSTOOD

Job 5:9	things too marvelous to **u.**
Job 36:26	is greater than we can **u.**
Ps 73:16	tried to **u** why the wicked
Ps 119:27	Help me **u** the meaning of
Ps 119:125	then I will **u** your laws.
Ps 119:130	so even the simple can **u.**
Prov 2:5	will **u** what it means to fear
Prov 2:9	you will **u** what is right,
Prov 28:5	the LORD **u** completely.
Prov 30:18	things that I don't **u:**
Eccl 7:25	and to **u** the reason
Isa 6:9	carefully, but do not **u.**
Isa 40:21	you heard? Don't you **u?**
Jer 9:24	truly know me and **u** that
Hos 14:9	who are wise **u** these things.
Matt 13:11	permitted to **u** the secrets
Matt 13:23	truly hear and **u** God's
Luke 19:42	people would **u** the way
Luke 24:45	minds to **u** the Scriptures.
Acts 8:30	Do you **u** what you are
Rom 7:15	I don't really **u** myself,
Rom 15:21	never heard of him will **u.**
1 Cor 2:14	and they can't **u** it,
1 Cor 14:14	but I don't **u** what I am
2 Cor 3:14	they cannot **u** the truth.
Gal 1:11	you to **u** that the gospel
Eph 1:18	you can **u** the confident
Eph 5:17	thoughtlessly, but **u** what
Phil 1:10	want you to **u** what really
Phil 4:7	exceeds anything we can **u.**
Col 2:2	that they **u** God's mysterious
1 Tim 2:4	saved and to **u** the truth.
2 Tim 2:7	will help you **u** all these
Heb 11:3	By faith we **u** that the entire
2 Pet 3:16	are hard to **u,** and those

UNDERSTANDABLE (adj)
marked by being able to understand; comprehendible

1 Cor 14:19	rather speak five **u** words

UNDERSTANDING (n)
comprehension; explanation, interpretation; sympathy

Job 28:12	Where can they find **u?**
Job 28:28	to forsake evil is real **u.**
Ps 119:32	for you expand my **u.**
Ps 119:34	Give me **u** and I will
Ps 119:104	commandments give me **u;**

Prov 3:5 not depend on your own **u**.
Prov 10:13 lips of people with **u,**
Prov 14:29 People with **u** control
Prov 15:32 correction, you grow in **u.**
Prov 16:21 wise are known for their **u,**
Prov 18:2 Fools have no interest in **u;**
Prov 19:8 who cherish **u** will prosper.
Prov 20:5 a person with **u** will draw
Prov 28:16 ruler with no **u** will oppress
Isa 40:28 the depths of his **u.**
Isa 50:4 opens my **u** to his will.
Jer 10:12 With his own **u** he stretched
Mark 12:33 heart and all my **u** and all
Luke 2:47 were amazed at his **u** and his
1 Cor 14:20 but be mature in **u** matters
2 Cor 6:6 purity, our **u,** our patience,
Eph 1:8 along with all wisdom and **u.**
Phil 1:9 growing in knowledge and **u.**
Col 1:9 you spiritual wisdom and **u.**
2 Thes 3:5 a full **u** and expression
1 Tim 6:4 is arrogant and lacks **u.**
1 Pet 3:7 your wife with **u** as you live
2 Pet 1:20 from the prophet's own **u,**
1 Jn 5:20 he has given us **u** so that

UNDERSTOOD (v)
to comprehend the meaning of
see also UNDERSTAND
Neh 8:12 God's words and **u** them.
Ps 73:17 I finally **u** the destiny
1 Cor 13:2 and if I **u** all of God's

UNDERWORLD (n)
place of destruction (Hebrew *Sheol*)
see also HELL
Job 26:6 The **u** is naked in God's

UNDESERVED (adj)
of, relating to, or being that which one does not deserve
Rom 5:2 place of **u** privilege where

UNDISCIPLINED (adj)
marked by or possessing no discipline
Prov 29:15 disgraced by an **u** child.

UNDIVIDED (adj)
not directed or moved toward conflicting interests, states, or objects
2 Chr 19:9 faithfulness and an **u** heart.
2 Cor 11:3 your pure and **u** devotion

UNFADING (adj)
not losing freshness, value, or effectiveness
1 Pet 3:4 the **u** beauty of a gentle

UNFAILING (adj)
constant, everlasting, inexhaustible, sure
see also FAITHFUL
Exod 15:13 With your **u** love you
Ps 6:4 because of your **u** love.
Ps 13:5 trust in your **u** love.
Ps 17:7 Show me your **u** love in
Ps 18:50 you show **u** love to your
Ps 25:6 compassion and **u** love,
Ps 31:16 In your **u** love, rescue
Ps 32:10 but **u** love surrounds
Ps 33:5 the **u** love of the LORD
Ps 33:22 Let your **u** love surround
Ps 36:7 precious is your **u** love,
Ps 36:10 Pour out your **u** love
Ps 48:9 meditate on your **u** love
Ps 51:1 because of your **u** love.
Ps 52:8 trust in God's **u** love.
Ps 57:10 For your **u** love is
Ps 85:7 Show us your **u** love,
Ps 90:14 morning with your **u** love,
Ps 117:2 he loves us with **u** love;
Ps 119:41 give me your **u** love,
Ps 119:76 let your **u** love comfort
Ps 143:8 me hear of your **u** love
Ps 147:11 hope in his **u** love.
Isa 55:3 the **u** love I promised
Isa 63:7 the LORD's **u** love.
Lam 3:32 greatness of his **u** love.
Mic 7:18 in showing **u** love.

UNFAIR (adj)
marked by injustice, partiality, or deception
Job 31:13 If I have been **u** to my male
Rom 3:5 Isn't it **u,** then, for him
Rom 9:14 then, that God was **u?**
1 Pet 2:19 endure **u** treatment.

UNFAITHFUL (adj)
marked by stubborn disbelief and disloyalty; adulterous
see also TREACHEROUS, UNBELIEF
Ps 78:8 rebellious, and **u,** refusing
Prov 23:28 eager to make more men **u.**
Jer 3:20 you have been **u** to me,
Matt 5:32 unless she has been **u,**
Rom 3:3 some of them were **u;** but
2 Tim 2:13 If we are **u,** he remains

UNFORGIVING (adj)
unwilling or unable to forgive
2 Tim 3:3 will be unloving and **u;**

UNGODLY (adj)
sinful, wicked
see also GODLESS, WICKED

Eph 5:12 the things that **u** people do
2 Pet 2:6 will happen to **u** people.
Jude 1:15 of all the **u** things they

UNHOLY (adj)
showing disregard for what is holy; wicked
Matt 7:6 people who are **u.** Don't throw
Heb 10:29 were common and **u,** and have

UNION (n)
an act or instance of uniting two or more things into one
2 Cor 6:16 And what **u** can there be
Col 2:10 through your **u** with Christ,

UNITED (v)
to become one or as if one; in one accord or spirit
Gen 2:24 the two are **u** into one.
Mark 10:8 the two are **u** into one.
Rom 6:5 we have been **u** with him
Rom 7:4 now you are **u** with the one
1 Cor 6:16 The two are **u** into one.
Eph 4:3 to keep yourselves **u** in the
Eph 5:31 the two are **u** into one."

UNITY (n)
the quality or state of oneness or harmony
John 17:23 perfect **u** that the world
Eph 4:13 come to such **u** in our faith

UNIVERSE (n)
the whole body of things created; cosmos
Eph 4:10 the entire **u** with himself.
Heb 1:2 the Son he created the **u.**
Heb 11:3 the entire **u** was formed at

UNJUST (adj)
characterized by injustice
Ps 82:2 you hand down **u** decisions
Matt 5:45 the just and the **u** alike.

UNKIND (adj)
harsh, cruel
1 Pet 2:1 and all **u** speech.

UNKNOWN (adj)
not known or well-known
1 Cor 12:28 who speak in **u** languages.

UNLEAVENED (adj)
characterized by being without yeast
Exod 12:17 this Festival of **U** Bread,
Deut 16:16 the Festival of **U** Bread,

UNLOVING (adj)
characterized by lack of affection
2 Tim 3:3 be **u** and unforgiving;

UNMARRIED (adj)
not married
1 Cor 7:8 it's better to stay **u,**
1 Cor 7:32 An **u** man can spend his

UNPUNISHED (adj)
to not pay the consequences for a fault, offense, or violation
Exod 20:7 let you go **u** if you misuse
Deut 5:11 let you go **u** if you misuse
Prov 6:29 embraces her will not go **u.**
Prov 19:5 false witness will not go **u,**
Jer 49:12 You will not go **u!**
Amos 1:3 will not let them go **u!**

UNRELIABLE (adj)
not dependable
Prov 25:19 confidence in an **u** person
1 Tim 6:17 money, which is so **u.**

UNSTABLE (adj)
not firm, fixed, or constant; unsteady
2 Pet 2:14 They lure **u** people into sin,
2 Pet 3:16 ignorant and **u** have twisted

UNTHANKFUL (adj)
showing no gratitude
Luke 6:35 those who are **u** and wicked.

UNTHINKING (adj)
not having the power of thought
2 Pet 2:12 like **u** animals, creatures

UNTIE (v)
to free from something that ties, fastens, or restrains
Mark 1:7 a slave and **u** the straps
Luke 13:15 Don't you **u** your ox or

UNTRUSTWORTHY (adj)
not worthy of confidence; undependable
Luke 16:11 if you are **u** about worldly

UNWORTHILY (adv)
in an undeserving manner
1 Cor 11:27 this cup of the Lord **u**

UPHOLD (v)
to give support to
Ps 82:3 **u** the rights of the oppressed

UPRIGHT (adj)
marked by strong moral integrity
see also GODLY, RIGHT, RIGHTEOUS
Deut 32:4 how just and **u** he is!

Prov 3:33	blesses the home of the **u.**
Prov 15:8	in the prayers of the **u.**

UPROOT (v)
to displace from a country or traditional habitat

Ps 52:5	and **u** you from the land of
Matt 13:29	'you'll **u** the wheat if you do.

UPSET (adj)
emotionally disturbed or agitated

Prov 3:11	and don't be **u** when he
Luke 10:41	worried and **u** over all

URGE (n)
a continuing impulse

Deut 12:20	you have the **u** to eat meat,

URGE, URGED, URGES (v)
to solicit or entreat; to impel

Job 32:18	spirit within me **u-s** me on.
Matt 15:23	**u-d** him to send here away.
Rom 15:30	I **u** you in the name of our
1 Cor 4:16	I **u** you to imitate me.
1 Thes 2:12	encouraged you, and **u-d** you
2 Tim 4:1	I solemnly **u** you in the

URGENCY (n)
a force or impulse that impels

Exod 12:11	meal with **u,** for this is

USE (v)
to put into action or service

2 Tim 2:21	for the Master to **u** you
1 Pet 2:16	don't **u** your freedom as an

USEFUL (adj)
serviceable for an end or purpose

2 Tim 3:16	inspired by God and is **u** to
2 Pet 1:8	productive and **u** you will be

USELESS (adj)
having or being of no use; ineffectual, inept

John 15:6	thrown away like a **u** branch
Acts 26:14	It is **u** for you to fight
1 Cor 13:8	knowledge will become **u.**
1 Cor 15:14	**u,** and your faith is **u.**
1 Cor 15:58	do for the Lord is ever **u.**
2 Tim 2:14	Such arguments are **u,** and
Titus 1:10	who engage in **u** talk and
Heb 7:18	because it was weak and **u.**

UTTERMOST (KJV)

Isa 24:16	songs of praise from the *ends of the earth*
Acts 1:8	and to the *ends of the earth*

V

VAIN (adj)
marked by futility or ineffectualness

Isa 65:23	will not work in **v,** and

VALID (adj)
well-grounded or justifiable

John 8:14	claims are **v** even though

VALLEY, VALLEYS (n)
a depression in the earth's surface between ranges of mountains, hills, or other uplands

Ps 23:4	through the darkest **v,** I will
Song 2:1	lily of the **v.**
Isa 40:4	Fill in the **v-s,** and level
Joel 3:14	waiting in the **v** of decision.
Luke 3:5	The **v-s** will be filled, and

VALUABLE (adj)
having desirable or esteemed characteristics or qualities; of great use or service

Job 28:17	Wisdom is more **v** than gold
Ps 119:72	instructions are more **v**
Prov 8:11	is far more **v** than rubies.
Prov 20:15	words are more **v** than
Matt 10:31	you are more **v** to God than
Luke 12:24	are far more **v** to him than
Phil 3:7	these things were **v,** but now

VALUE (n)
monetary worth of something; relative worth, utility, or importance

Matt 13:46	a pearl of great **v,** he sold
1 Cor 3:13	a person's work has any **v.**
Phil 3:8	the infinite **v** of knowing

VALUED (v)
to estimate or assign the monetary worth of

Zech 11:13	sum at which they **v** me!

VANISHING (adj)
disappearing

Prov 21:6	lying tongue is a **v** mist

VANITY, VANITIES (KJV)

Deut 32:21	with their *useless idols*
Ps 144:4	For we are like *a breath of air*
Eccl 12:8	Everything is *meaningless*
Acts 14:15	turn from these *worthless things*
Eph 4:17	they are *hopelessly confused*

VEGETABLES (n)
a plant or its edible part

Rom 14:2	conscience will eat only **v.**

VEIL (n)
a facial covering
Exod 34:33 covered his face with a **v.**
2 Cor 3:14 same **v** covers their minds
2 Cor 3:18 have had that **v** removed can

VENGEANCE (n)
punishment inflicted in retaliation for an injury or offense
1 Sam 25:26 taking **v** into your own
1 Sam 25:33 carrying out **v** with my
Ps 94:1 O LORD, the God of **v,**
Isa 66:6 the LORD taking **v** against
Luke 21:22 be days of God's **v,** and the

VENOM (n)
poisonous matter secreted by some animals
Ps 140:3 a snake; the **v** of a viper
Rom 3:13 Snake **v** drips from their

VERILY (KJV)
Ps 58:11 There *truly* is a reward
John 16:20 *I tell you the truth*

VICIOUS (adj)
dangerously aggressive
Matt 7:15 but are really **v** wolves.
Acts 20:29 teachers, like **v** wolves,

VICTORIOUS (adj)
of, relating to, or characteristic of victory; having won a victory
see also OVERCOME
2 Sam 8:6 made David **v** wherever he
Isa 53:12 of a **v** soldier, because he
Matt 12:20 cause justice to be **v.**
Rev 2:11 Whoever is **v** will not be
Rev 2:17 everyone who is **v** I will give
Rev 2:26 To all who are **v,** who obey
Rev 3:5 All who are **v** will be clothed
Rev 3:21 Those who are **v** will sit with
Rev 21:7 All who are **v** will inherit

VICTORY, VICTORIES (n)
the overcoming of an enemy, antagonist, or struggle
see also OVERCOME
Exod 15:2 he has given me **v.**
2 Sam 22:51 You give great **v-ies** to your
Ps 18:50 You give great **v-ies** to your
Ps 20:5 we hear of your **v** and
Ps 21:1 because you give him **v.**
Ps 35:3 I will give you **v!**
Ps 44:4 You command **v-ies** for Israel.
Ps 45:4 majesty, ride out to **v,**
Ps 48:10 right hand is filled with **v.**
Ps 62:1 for my **v** comes from him.
Ps 98:3 have seen the **v** of our God.
Ps 118:14 he has given me **v.**
Ps 149:4 crowns the humble with **v.**
Isa 12:2 he has given me **v.**
Isa 52:10 see the **v** of our God.
Rom 8:37 overwhelming **v** is ours
1 Cor 15:54 Death is swallowed up in **v.**
Col 2:15 publicly by his **v** over them
Rev 5:5 David's throne, has won the **v.**

VILLAGE (n)
a settlement usually smaller than a town
Mark 6:6 Jesus went from **v** to **v,**

VINDICATED (v)
shown to be without blame; prove right
1 Tim 3:16 body and **v** by the Spirit.

VINE (KJV)
Gen 49:11 He ties his foal to a *grapevine*
Deut 8:8 and barley; of *grapevines*
Ps 80:8 from Egypt like a *grapevine*
John 15:5 I am the *vine;* you are the branches

VINEGAR (n)
a liquid made from wine that has been soured or overfermented
Prov 10:26 employers, like **v** to the

VINEYARD (n)
a plantation of grapevines
1 Kgs 21:1 who owned a **v** in Jezreel
Prov 31:16 earnings she plants a **v.**
Song 1:6 for myself—my own **v.**
Isa 5:1 beloved had a **v** on a rich
1 Cor 9:7 farmer plants a **v** and

VIOLATE, VIOLATED, VIOLATES, VIOLATING (v)
to do harm to the person or especially the chastity of; to fail to show proper respect for; to break or disregard
Lev 18:7 Do not **v** your father
Lev 18:8 for this would **v** your father.
Lev 18:10 this would **v** yourself.
Lev 18:14 Do not **v** your uncle,
Lev 18:16 this would **v** your brother.
Lev 20:11 If a man **v-s** his father by
Lev 20:20 he has **v-d** his uncle.
Lev 20:21 He has **v-d** his brother, and
Num 15:30 who brazenly **v** the LORD's
Deut 22:30 for this would **v** his father.
Deut 27:20 for he has **v-d** his father.
Isa 24:5 instructions, **v-d** his laws,
Mal 2:10 each other, **v-ing** the covenant

VIOLATION (n)
infringement, transgression
Heb 2:2 — firm, and every **v** of the law

VIOLENCE (n)
exertion of physical force so as to injure or abuse
Gen 6:11 — and was filled with **v.**
Ps 12:5 — I have seen **v** done to the
Ps 72:14 — them from oppression and **v,**
Isa 60:18 — **V** will disappear from your
Jonah 3:8 — and stop all their **v.**
Mic 2:2 — take it by fraud and **v.**

VIOLENT (adj)
emotionally agitated to the point of loss of self-control
1 Tim 3:3 — a heavy drinker or be **v.**
Titus 1:7 — not be a heavy drinker, **v,**

VIPER (n)
a particular species of venomous snakes
Ps 140:3 — venom of a **v** drips from

VIRGIN (n)
an unmarried woman who has not had sexual intercourse
Gen 24:16 — but she was still a **v.**
Isa 7:14 — The **v** will conceive a child!
Matt 1:18 — while she was still a **v,** she
Matt 1:23 — The **v** will conceive a child!
Luke 1:34 — this happen? I am a **v.**

VIRGINITY (n)
the quality or state of being virgin
Deut 22:15 — proof of her **v** to the elders

VIRTUE (KJV)
Phil 4:8 — things that are *excellent*
2 Pet 1:5 — provision of *moral excellence*

VIRTUOUS (adj)
morally excellent; righteous
Ruth 3:11 — you are a **v** woman.
Prov 31:10 — Who can find a **v** and
Prov 31:29 — There are many **v** and

VISION, VISIONS (n)
a visual form of divine revelation, including dreams, that consists of symbolic images, often accompanied by their interpretation
Num 12:6 — would reveal myself in **v-s.**
2 Sam 7:17 — LORD had said in this **v.**
Dan 9:24 — the prophetic **v,** and to
Dan 10:1 — that the **v** concerned events
Joel 2:28 — your young men will see **v-s.**
Hab 2:3 — This **v** is for a future time.
Acts 2:17 — Your young men will see **v-s,**
Acts 26:19 — I obeyed that **v** from heaven.
Col 2:18 — they have had **v-s** about these

VOICE (n)
verbal communication by human and divine means
Isa 40:3 — the **v** of someone shouting,
Mark 1:3 — He is a **v** shouting in the
John 10:3 — sheep recognize his **v** and
John 12:28 — a **v** spoke from heaven,
Rev 3:20 — If you hear my **v** and open

VOMIT (n)
matter disgorged from the stomach
Prov 26:11 — returns to its **v,** so a fool
2 Pet 2:22 — A dog returns to its **v.**

VOMIT (v)
to eject violently or abundantly
Lev 18:28 — it will **v** out the people

VOW, VOWS (n)
a binding promise or pledge
see also COVENANT, PROMISE
Num 6:2 — the special **v** of a Nazirite,
Judg 11:30 — Jephthah made a **v** to the
Ps 110:4 — and will not break his **v:**
Matt 5:34 — do not make any **v-s!**
Heb 7:21 — and will not break his **v:**

VOWED (v)
to promise solemnly
Eccl 8:2 — since you **v** to God that
Mark 7:11 — For I have **v** to give to

VULGAR (adj)
lewdly or profanely indecent
Ps 101:3 — at anything vile and **v.**

VULNERABLE (adj)
capable of being physically or emotionally wounded
2 Tim 3:6 — the confidence of **v** women

VULTURES (n)
any of various large birds that subsist chiefly or entirely on dead flesh
Matt 24:28 — gathering of **v** shows there
Rev 19:17 — shouting to the **v** flying high

W

WAGE, WAGES (n)
payment for labor or services; compensation
Hag 1:6 — Your **w-s** disappear as though
Zech 11:12 — give me my **w-s,** whatever
Mal 3:5 — cheat employees of their **w-s,**

Matt 20:2 the normal daily **w** and
Rom 4:4 their **w-s** are not a gift,
Rom 6:23 For the **w-s** of sin is death,

WAGE (v)
to engage in or carry on
2 Cor 10:3 but we don't **w** war

WAILING (v)
the act of expressing sorrow audibly
Amos 5:17 There will be **w** in every

WAIT, WAITED, WAITING (v)
to look forward expectantly; to stay in place in expectation of
Ps 40:1 I **w-ed** patiently for the LORD
Ps 62:5 that I am **w** quietly before
Ps 69:3 **w-ing** for my God to help me.
Isa 30:18 Blessed are those who **w** for
Mic 7:7 I **w** confidently for God to
Hab 3:16 I will **w** quietly for the
Luke 12:37 who are ready and **w-ing**
Rom 8:19 all creation is **w-ing** eagerly
Rom 8:23 We, too, **w** with eager hope
Heb 9:28 are eagerly **w-ing** for him.

WAKE (v)
to rouse from or as if from sleep
see also AWAKE
Prov 6:22 When you **w** up, they will
Rev 3:3 If you don't **w** up, I will

WAKENS (v)
to wake
Isa 50:4 by morning he **w** me and

WALK, WALKED, WALKING (v)
to roam, traverse, or advance by steps; to pursue a course of action or way of life
Gen 3:8 God **w-ing** about in the garden.
Lev 26:12 I will **w** among you;
Deut 11:22 God by **w-ing** in his ways
Deut 26:17 promised to **w** in his ways,
Josh 22:5 God, **w** in all his ways,
Ps 23:4 when I **w** through the
Ps 89:15 they will **w** in the light
Prov 4:12 When you **w**, you won't
Prov 6:22 When you **w**, their counsel
Isa 2:3 we will **w** in his paths.
Isa 40:31 They will **w** and not
Isa 43:2 When you **w** through the
Jer 6:16 godly way, and **w** in it.
Dan 3:25 **w-ing** around in the fire
Amos 3:3 two people **w** together
Mic 6:8 to **w** humbly with your God.
Mal 2:6 they **w-ed** with me, living good
Matt 14:29 boat and **w-ed** on the water
Mark 2:9 pick up your mat, and **w**
John 8:12 have to **w** in darkness,

WALL, WALLS (n)
a thick, high, continuous structure of stones or brick that formed a defensive barricade around an ancient city
Josh 6:20 Suddenly, the **w-s** of Jericho
Neh 2:17 rebuild the **w** of Jerusalem
Isa 58:12 as a rebuilder of **w-s** and
Heb 11:30 and the **w-s** came crashing
Rev 21:12 city **w** was broad and high,

WANDER, WANDERED, WANDERS (v)
to follow a winding course; to stray
Num 32:13 them **w** in the wilderness
Ps 119:10 don't let me **w** from your
Ps 119:67 I used to **w** off until you
Ps 119:176 I have **w-ed** away like a
Matt 18:12 one of them **w-s** away
Eph 4:18 **w** far from the life God
1 Tim 6:10 have **w-ed** from the true
Jas 5:19 someone among you **w-s**
1 Pet 2:25 like sheep who **w-ed** away.
2 Pet 2:15 They have **w-ed** off the

WANT, WANTED, WANTS (v)
to desire or wish
Gen 3:6 she **w-ed** the wisdom it would
Job 23:13 Whatever he **w-s** to do,
Ps 51:16 do not **w** a burnt offering.
Ps 119:58 heart I **w** your blessings.
Prov 13:4 Lazy people **w** much but
Eccl 6:2 they could ever **w**, but then
Mic 7:3 get what they **w**, and together
Matt 5:42 from those who **w** to borrow.
Matt 14:20 as they **w-ed**, and afterward,
Matt 19:21 If you **w** to be perfect,
Matt 23:37 I have **w-ed** to gather your
Luke 19:14 We do not **w** him to be
John 3:8 blows wherever it **w-s.**
John 7:17 Anyone who **w-s** to do the
John 15:7 ask for anything you **w**,
Acts 20:27 all that God **w-s** you to know.
Rom 7:15 I **w** to do what is right,
1 Cor 12:18 part just where he **w-s** it.
2 Cor 8:5 just as God **w-ed** them to do.
2 Cor 8:10 the first who **w-ed** to give,
2 Cor 12:14 you have—I **w** you.
Eph 1:5 This is what he **w-ed** to do,
Eph 5:17 what the Lord **w-s** you to do.
1 Tim 2:4 who **w-s** everyone to be saved
Heb 10:5 did not **w** animal sacrifices
Heb 13:18 is clear and we **w** to live
1 Pet 1:10 the prophets **w-ed** to know

1 Pet 3:17 — if that is what God **w-s,**

WAR, WARS (n)

armed conflict with an opposing military force; a state of hostility, conflict, or antagonism

Josh 11:23 — finally had rest from **w.**
Ps 46:9 — He causes **w-s** to end
Ps 68:30 — nations that delight in **w.**
Ps 120:7 — peace, they want **w!**
Ps 144:1 — He trains my hands for **w**
Isa 2:4 — nor train for **w** anymore.
2 Cor 10:3 — we don't wage **w** as humans
1 Pet 2:11 — that wage **w** against your
Rev 12:7 — Then there was **w** in heaven.
Rev 19:11 — and wages a righteous **w.**

WARN, WARNED, WARNING (v)

to give notice to beforehand especially of danger or evil; to counsel

Gen 2:16 — God **w-ed** him, "You may
Gen 31:24 — told him, "I'm **w-ing** you—
Gen 31:29 — to me last night and **w-ed** me,
Exod 19:21 — down and **w** the people
Num 16:40 — This would **w** the Israelites
1 Sam 8:9 — but solemnly **w** them about
1 Kgs 2:42 — LORD and **w** you not to
2 Kgs 17:13 — and seers to **w** both Israel
2 Chr 19:10 — must **w** them not to sin
Ezek 3:18 — If I **w** the wicked,
Ezek 33:3 — the alarm to **w** the people.
Matt 16:6 — "Watch out!" Jesus **w-ed** them.
Luke 16:28 — I want him to **w** them so
Acts 4:17 — must **w** them not to speak
1 Cor 4:14 — to **w** you as my beloved
1 Cor 10:11 — written down to **w** us who
Col 1:28 — **w-ing** everyone and teaching
1 Thes 4:6 — solemnly **w-ed** you before.
1 Thes 5:14 — urge you to **w** those who
2 Thes 3:15 — but **w** them as you would
Heb 3:13 — You must **w** each other

WARNING, WARNINGS (n)

something that warns or serves to warn; the act of warning

Ps 19:11 — They are a **w** to your servant,
Ps 81:8 — while I give you stern **w-s.**
Jer 6:8 — Listen to this **w,** Jerusalem,
Jer 42:19 — Don't forget this **w** I have
Zeph 3:7 — they will listen to my **w-s.**
1 Cor 10:6 — happened as a **w** to us,
1 Tim 5:20 — as a strong **w** to others.
Titus 3:10 — give a first and second **w.**

WARRIOR, WARRIORS (n)

a man engaged or experienced in warfare

Gen 6:4 — and famous **w-s** of ancient
Exod 15:3 — LORD is a **w;** Yahweh
Josh 1:14 — strong **w-s,** fully armed,
1 Chr 28:3 — for you are a **w** and
Ps 45:3 — your sword, O mighty **w!**
Jer 20:11 — beside me like a great **w.**

WASH, WASHED (v)

to cleanse—of physical, ceremonial, or spiritual significance

see also BAPTIZE(D), CLEANSE

Ps 51:7 — **w** me, and I will be whiter
John 13:5 — he began to **w** the disciples'
John 13:10 — does not need to **w,** except
Acts 22:16 — Have your sins **w-ed** away
Eph 5:26 — holy and clean, **w-ed** by the
Titus 3:5 — He **w-ed** away our sins,
Heb 10:22 — bodies have been **w-ed**
Jas 4:8 — **W** your hands, you sinners;
2 Pet 2:22 — **w-ed** pig returns to the mud.
Rev 7:14 — They have **w-ed** their robes in
Rev 22:14 — those who **w** their robes.

WASHBASIN (n)

a large bowl for water that is used to wash

Exod 30:18 — Make a bronze **w** with a

WASTE, WASTED (v)

to spend or use carelessly or inefficiently

Ps 127:1 — work of the builders is **w-d.**
Prov 29:3 — prostitutes, his wealth is **w-d.**
Prov 31:3 — do not **w** your strength
Luke 15:13 — there he **w-d** all his money
John 6:12 — so that nothing is **w-d.**
Gal 2:2 — all my efforts had been **w-d**

WATCH (n)

the act of keeping awake to guard, protect, or attend

Matt 24:42 — you, too, must keep **w!**
Acts 20:31 — my constant **w** and care

WATCH, WATCHES, WATCHING (v)

to diligently wait or keep guard; to observe closely

Judg 18:6 — the LORD is **w-ing** over
Job 14:16 — my steps, instead of **w-ing**
Job 34:21 — God **w-es** how people live;
Ps 1:6 — For the LORD **w-es** over the
Ps 17:11 — and surround me, **w-ing** for
Ps 61:7 — faithfulness **w** over him.
Ps 121:3 — one who **w-es** over you will
Prov 2:11 — Wise choices will **w** over
Prov 31:27 — carefully **w-es** everything
Eccl 11:4 — If they **w** every cloud,
Jer 24:6 — I will **w** over and care for
Jer 31:10 — gather them and **w** over
Acts 1:9 — while they were **w-ing,** and
Eph 6:6 — just when they are **w-ing** you.

Heb 13:17	is to **w** over your souls,
1 Pet 1:12	eagerly **w-ing** these things
1 Pet 3:12	eyes of the Lord **w** over

WATCHER (n)
one who watches

Job 7:20	you, O **w** of all humanity?

WATCHMAN (n)
a person who keeps watch; guard

Ezek 3:17	you as a **w** for Israel.
Ezek 33:6	hold the **w** responsible
Ezek 33:7	you a **w** for the people

WATER, WATERS (n)
precious resource for drink and irrigation, usually associated with blessing; a body of water

Exod 7:20	struck the **w** of the Nile.
Exod 17:1	there was no **w** there for
Num 20:2	was no **w** for the people
2 Sam 23:15	good **w** from the well
Ps 42:1	streams of **w,** so I long
Prov 25:21	give them **w** to drink.
Song 8:7	Many **w-s** cannot quench
Isa 11:9	for as the **w-s** fill the sea,
Isa 32:2	like streams of **w** in the
Isa 43:2	through deep **w-s,** I will be
Isa 49:10	lead them beside cool **w-s.**
Jer 17:8	reach deep into the **w.**
Jonah 2:3	The mighty **w-s** engulfed me;
Hab 2:14	For as the **w-s** fill the sea,
Zech 14:8	life-giving **w-s** will flow
Matt 14:25	them, walking on the **w.**
John 3:5	born of **w** and the Spirit.
John 4:10	would give you living **w.**
John 7:38	Rivers of living **w** will
1 Jn 5:6	his baptism in **w** and by
Rev 7:17	springs of life-giving **w.**
Rev 21:6	springs of the **w** of life.

WATERED, WATERING (v)
to moisten, sprinkle, or soak with water

Joel 3:18	**w-ing** the arid valley of acacias.
1 Cor 3:6	hearts, and Apollos **w-ed** it,
1 Cor 3:7	planting, or who does the **w-ing.**

WATERPROOF (v)
to cover or treat with a material to prevent permeation by water

Gen 6:14	cypress wood and **w** it with

WAVE, WAVES (n)
a moving ridge or swell on the surface of a liquid (as of the sea)

Matt 8:27	the winds and **w-s** obey him!
Jas 1:6	unsettled as a **w** of the

WAVER, WAVERED, WAVERING (v)
to fluctuate in opinion, allegiance, or direction

Rom 4:20	Abraham never **w-ed** in believing
Jude 1:22	to those whose faith is **w-ing.**

WAY, WAYS (n)
characteristic, regular, or habitual manner or mode of being, behaving, or happening; manner or method of doing or happening; a course of action; route

Exod 33:13	let me know your **w-s**
Deut 26:17	to walk in his **w-s,** and
Deut 30:16	by walking in his **w-s.**
Josh 22:5	walk in all his **w-s,** obey
2 Sam 22:31	God's **w** is perfect.
Ps 77:13	O God, your **w-s** are holy.
Ps 86:11	Teach me your **w-s,** O LORD,
Prov 2:9	find the right **w** to go.
Prov 4:11	teach you wisdom's **w-s**
Eccl 8:6	and a **w** for everything,
Isa 2:3	teach us his **w-s,** and we will
Isa 40:3	Clear the **w** through the
Jer 6:16	old, godly **w,** and walk in
Mic 4:2	teach us his **w-s,** and we will
Mal 3:1	prepare the **w** before me.
Matt 3:3	Prepare the **w** for the
Matt 3:8	Prove by the **w** you live
Luke 7:27	prepare your **w** before you.
John 14:6	I am the **w,** the truth,
Acts 9:2	followers of the **W** he
Acts 24:14	I follow the **W,** which
Rom 1:30	invent new **w-s** of sinning,
1 Cor 10:13	will show you a **w** out
1 Cor 12:31	show you a **w** of life
Col 1:10	Then the **w** you live will
Heb 10:20	and life-giving **w** through

WAYWARD (adj)
following one's own capricious, wanton, or depraved inclinations

Jer 3:14	Return home, you **w** children,
Jer 3:22	will heal your **w** hearts.

WEAK, WEAKER, WEAKEST (adj)
lacking strength; not able to withstand temptation or persuasion

Ps 72:13	pity for the **w** and the
Ps 103:14	he knows how **w** we are;
Isa 59:1	arm is not too **w** to save
Matt 12:20	will not crush the **w-est** reed
Matt 26:41	but the body is **w!**
Rom 14:1	who are **w** in faith,
1 Cor 8:9	others with a **w-er** conscience
1 Cor 9:22	bring the **w** to Christ.
1 Cor 11:30	many of you are **w** and
1 Cor 12:22	of the body that seem **w-est**
2 Cor 12:10	For when I am **w,** then

1 Thes 5:14 care of those who are **w.**

WEAKNESS, WEAKNESSES (n)
the quality or state of being weak
Ps 136:23 He remembered us in our **w.**
Isa 53:4 it was our **w-es** he carried;
Rom 8:3 the **w** of our sinful nature.
Rom 8:26 Spirit helps us in our **w.**
1 Cor 1:25 God's **w** is stronger than
1 Cor 2:3 I came to you in **w**—timid
2 Cor 12:5 boast only about my **w-es.**
2 Cor 12:10 take pleasure in my **w-es,**
2 Cor 13:4 he was crucified in **w,**
Heb 5:2 is subject to the same **w-es.**

WEALTH (n)
abundance of valuable material possessions or resources
see also MONEY, POSSESSIONS, RICHES, TREASURE(S)
2 Chr 1:11 not ask for **w,** riches,
Job 36:18 you may be seduced by **w.**
Ps 39:6 We heap up **w,** not knowing
Ps 62:10 if your **w** increases, don't
Prov 3:9 the LORD with your **w**
Prov 10:2 Tainted **w** has no lasting
Prov 13:11 **w** from hard work grows
Prov 21:20 wise have **w** and luxury,
Prov 29:3 prostitutes, his **w** is wasted.
Eccl 4:8 gain as much **w** as he can.
Luke 19:8 give half my **w** to the poor,
Eph 2:7 of the incredible **w** of his
1 Tim 6:6 contentment is itself great **w.**
Jas 5:3 The very **w** you were counting

WEALTHY (adj)
characterized by abundance
Prov 11:24 freely and become more **w;**
Eccl 2:26 sinner becomes **w,** God takes
1 Cor 1:26 or **w** when God called you.

WEAPON, WEAPONS (n)
something used to injure, defeat, or destroy
Prov 26:18 shooting a deadly **w**
Eccl 9:18 have wisdom than **w-s** of war,
2 Cor 6:7 use the **w-s** of righteousness

WEARY (adj)
exhausted in strength, endurance, or vigor
Isa 40:31 They will run and not grow **w.**
Isa 50:4 know how to comfort the **w.**
Matt 11:28 you who are **w** and carry
2 Cor 5:2 We grow **w** in our present
Heb 12:3 won't become **w** and give up.

WEDDING, WEDDINGS (n)
a marriage ceremony usually with its accompanying festivities
Matt 11:17 We played **w** songs, and
Matt 22:11 the proper clothes for a **w.**
Matt 24:38 parties and **w-s** right up
Rev 19:7 for the **w** feast of the Lamb,

WEEDS (n)
undesirable growth surrounding a plant
Matt 13:25 and planted **w** among the

WEEK (n)
a seven-day cycle
1 Cor 16:2 of each **w,** you should

WEEPING (n)
shedding of tears out of grief or sadness
Jer 31:15 deep anguish and bitter **w.**
Matt 2:18 heard in Ramah—**w** and
Matt 8:12 will be **w** and gnashing

WEEP, WEEPING (v)
to cry aloud, often linked with prayer and repentance
2 Sam 1:26 How I **w** for you,
Ps 126:6 They **w** as they go to
Jer 31:16 Do not **w** any longer,
Jer 50:4 will come **w-ing** and seeking
Matt 2:18 heard in Ramah—**w-ing** and
Matt 8:12 will be **w-ing** and gnashing
Luke 6:21 blesses you who **w** now,
Luke 22:62 the courtyard, **w-ing** bitterly.
Luke 23:28 don't **w** for me, but **w**
Rom 12:15 and **w** with those who **w.**

WEIGHED, WEIGHS (v)
to oppress or depress; to measure weight
Ps 146:8 up those who are **w-ed** down.
Prov 12:25 Worry **w-s** a person down;
Isa 53:4 our sorrows that **w-ed** him
Dan 5:27 *Tekel* means '**w-ed**'—you

WEIGHT, WEIGHTS (n)
a piece of material (as metal) of known specified weight for use in weighing articles; burden, hindrance
Lev 19:36 Your scales and **w-s** must be
Prov 11:1 he delights in accurate **w-s.**
Heb 12:1 strip off every **w** that slows

WELCOME (n)
the state of being accepted with pleasure
Prov 25:17 you will wear out your **w.**

WELCOMED, WELCOMES, WELCOMING (v)
to greet hospitably and with courtesy or cordiality
Matt 18:5 And anyone who **w-s** a little

Mark 9:37 Anyone who **w-s** a little child
John 13:20 who **w-s** my messenger
John 13:20 **w-s** me is **w-ing** the Father
Acts 28:7 He **w-d** us and treated us

WELL (adj)
completely cured or healed (physically or spiritually)
Isa 38:9 King Hezekiah was **w** again,
Matt 15:31 the crippled were made **w,**
Matt 17:18 that moment the boy was **w.**
Mark 5:34 your faith has made you **w.**
Jas 5:15 the Lord will make you **w.**

WELL (adv)
in a prosperous or affluent manner; in a kindly or friendly manner
Deut 6:18 all will go **w** with you.
Eph 6:3 things will go **w** for you,
1 Tim 3:7 church must speak **w** of him

WEPT (v)
to cry aloud
see also WEEP
Ps 137:1 we sat and **w** as we thought
John 11:35 Then Jesus **w.**

WEST (n)
the general direction of the sunset
Ps 103:12 as the east is from the **w.**
Ps 107:3 from east and **w,** from north

WHEAT (n)
a cereal grain that yields a fine white flour
Matt 3:12 gathering the **w** into his barn
Matt 13:25 among the **w,** then slipped
Mark 4:28 the heads of **w** are formed,
Luke 22:31 sift each of you like **w.**
John 12:24 a kernel of **w** is planted in

WHEELS (n)
circular frames of hard material capable of turning on an axle
Ezek 1:16 All four **w** looked alike

WHIPPED (v)
to strike with a lash or rod
2 Cor 11:23 been **w** times without

WHIRLWIND (n)
a small rotating windstorm, sometimes violent and destructive
see also STORM, WIND
2 Kgs 2:1 to heaven in a **w,**
Job 38:1 answered Job from the **w:**
Hos 8:7 and will harvest the **w.**
Nah 1:3 in the **w** and the storm.

WHISPER (n)
a minor or softer reflection of the original noise; hint, trace
1 Kgs 19:12 sound of a gentle **w.**
Job 26:14 merely a **w** of his power.
Ps 107:29 calmed the storm to a **w**

WHISPER (v)
to speak softly with little or no vibration of the vocal cords
Matt 10:27 What I **w** in your ear,

WHITE, WHITER (adj)
free from color; of the color white
Ps 51:7 I will be **w-r** than snow.
Isa 1:18 make them as **w** as snow.
Dan 7:9 clothing was as **w** as snow,
Matt 28:3 clothing was as **w** as snow.
Rev 1:14 like wool, as **w** as snow.
Rev 6:2 saw a **w** horse standing
Rev 19:11 a **w** horse was standing
Rev 20:11 saw a great **w** throne

WHITE (n)
the absence of color; free from spot or blemish
Rev 3:4 will walk with me in **w,**
Rev 7:13 who are clothed in **w?**

WHITEWASHED (adj)
glossed over with whitewash
Matt 23:27 are like **w** tombs—

WHOLE (adj)
entire; complete, unmodified; undivided
1 Sam 1:28 LORD his **w** life.
1 Sam 17:46 the **w** world will know
1 Chr 28:9 him with your **w** heart
Ps 72:19 Let the **w** earth be filled
Ps 103:1 with my **w** heart, I will
Prov 4:22 healing to their **w** body.
Eccl 12:13 That's the **w** story.
Isa 6:3 The **w** earth is filled
Isa 14:26 plan for the **w** earth,
Dan 2:35 covered the **w** earth.
Zeph 1:18 For the **w** land will be
Matt 6:22 eye is good, your **w** body
Matt 16:26 gain the **w** world but lose
Matt 24:14 throughout the **w** world,
John 21:25 I suppose the **w** world
Acts 17:26 throughout the **w** earth.
1 Cor 12:17 Or if your **w** body were
Gal 5:3 regulation in the **w** law of

WHOLEHEARTEDLY (adv)
in a completely and sincerely devoted, determined, or enthusiastic manner

Num 32:11 they have not obeyed me **w.**
Deut 11:18 commit yourselves **w** to
Deut 26:16 careful to obey them **w.**
Josh 14:8 For my part, I **w** followed
Josh 24:14 LORD and serve him **w.**
1 Chr 29:9 had given freely and **w**
2 Chr 25:2 sight, but not **w.**
2 Chr 31:21 sought his God **w.**
Jer 29:13 look for me **w,** you will
Jer 32:41 faithfully and **w** replant
Phil 2:2 happy by agreeing **w** with

WHOLESOME (adj)
promoting health or well-being of mind or spirit
see also SOUND
1 Tim 1:10 contradicts the **w** teaching
1 Tim 6:3 these are the **w** teachings
Titus 1:9 others with **w** teaching and
Titus 2:1 that reflects **w** teaching.
2 Pet 3:1 stimulate your **w** thinking

WHORE (KJV)
Lev 21:7 woman *defiled by prostitution*
Deut 23:18 the earnings of a *prostitute*
Prov 23:27 *prostitute* is a dangerous trap
Hos 4:14 sinning with *whores*
Rev 17:1 *prostitute,* who rules over

WICKED (adj)
morally very bad
Gen 13:13 area were extremely **w** and
Ps 7:9 those who are **w,** and defend
Prov 10:7 name of a **w** person rots
Prov 26:23 may hide a **w** heart, just
Jer 35:15 Turn from your **w** ways,
Ezek 18:21 But if **w** people turn away
Ezek 21:25 you corrupt and **w** prince
Ezek 33:8 that some **w** people are sure
Hos 10:9 not right that the **w** men of
Jonah 1:2 I have seen how **w** its people
Luke 6:35 who are unthankful and **w.**
1 Jn 5:17 All **w** actions are sin,

WICKED (n)
those who practice evil
2 Sam 22:27 but to the **w** you show
Ps 1:1 the advice of the **w,** or stand
Ps 10:13 Why do the **w** get away with
Ps 12:8 though the **w** strut about,
Ps 14:6 The **w** frustrate the plans
Ps 18:26 but to the **w** you show
Ps 37:1 worry about the **w** or envy
Ps 82:2 by favoring the **w?**
Ps 101:8 ferret out the **w** and free
Ps 139:19 you would destroy the **w!**
Ps 146:9 the plans of the **w.**
Prov 4:14 Don't do as the **w** do,
Prov 9:7 who corrects the **w** will
Prov 10:28 expectations of the **w** come
Prov 12:5 of the **w** is treacherous.
Prov 29:7 the **w** don't care at all.
Isa 5:23 to let the **w** go free,
Isa 11:4 mouth will destroy the **w.**
Isa 26:10 the **w** keep doing wrong
Isa 48:22 no peace for the **w,**
Mal 4:1 arrogant and the **w** will be

WICKEDNESS (n)
the quality or state of being wicked; something wicked
Lev 16:21 it all the **w,** rebellion,
Lev 19:29 with prostitution and **w.**
Deut 9:4 because of the **w** of the other
Ps 73:3 them prosper despite their **w.**
Jer 3:2 your prostitution and your **w.**
Jer 14:16 out their own **w** on them.
Jer 14:20 we confess our **w** and that
Ezek 33:19 turn from their **w** and do
Luke 11:39 of greed and **w!**
Rom 1:18 the truth by their **w.**
Rom 1:29 every kind of **w,** sin, greed,
Rom 2:8 and instead live lives of **w.**
2 Cor 6:14 be a partner with **w?**
Heb 8:12 I will forgive their **w,**

WIDE-OPEN (adj)
having virtually no limits or restrictions
1 Cor 16:9 a **w** door for a great

WIDE (adj)
fully opened; having great extent
Ps 81:10 Open your mouth **w,** and I
Matt 7:13 its gate is **w** for the
Eph 3:18 should, how **w,** how long,

WIDOW, WIDOWS (n)
a woman whose husband has died
Deut 10:18 orphans and **w-s** receive
Ps 68:5 defender of **w-s**—this is God,
Ps 146:9 for the orphans and **w-s,** but
Isa 1:17 Fight for the rights of **w-s.**
Luke 21:2 Then a poor **w** came by and
Acts 6:1 that their **w-s** were being
1 Cor 7:8 aren't married and to **w-s**—
1 Tim 5:3 Take care of any **w** who
1 Tim 5:16 care for the **w-s** who are
Jas 1:27 for orphans and **w-s** in their

WIFE (n)
the female partner in a marriage
see also WIVES
Gen 2:24 and is joined to his **w,**
Gen 19:26 But Lot's **w** looked back

Exod 20:17	covet your neighbor's **w**,	
Lev 20:10	his neighbor's **w**, both	
Deut 5:21	not covet your neighbor's **w**.	
Deut 24:5	happiness to the **w** he has	
Prov 5:18	Rejoice in the **w** of your	
Prov 12:4	A worthy **w** is a crown	
Prov 18:22	man who finds a **w**	
Prov 19:13	a quarrelsome **w** is as	
Prov 21:9	a quarrelsome **w** in a	
Prov 31:10	a virtuous and capable **w**?	
Mal 2:14	vows you and your **w** made	
Matt 1:20	to take Mary as your **w**.	
Matt 19:3	to divorce his **w** for just	
Luke 17:32	happened to Lot's **w**!	
Luke 18:29	up house or **w** or brothers	
1 Cor 7:2	should have his own **w**,	
1 Cor 7:15	the husband or **w** who isn't	
1 Cor 7:33	and how to please his **w**.	
Eph 5:23	head of his **w** as Christ	
Eph 5:33	love his **w** as he loves	
1 Tim 3:12	be faithful to his **w**,	
Titus 1:6	be faithful to his **w**,	
1 Pet 3:7	Treat your **w** with	
Rev 21:9	bride, the **w** of the Lamb.	

WILD (adj)
not tame or domesticated; growing without human aid; uncontrolled, unruly

Gen 1:25	made all sorts of **w** animals,
Gen 8:1	and all the **w** animals
Luke 15:13	his money in **w** living.
Rom 11:17	branches from a **w** olive

WILDERNESS (n)
any desolate, barren, or unpopulated area, usually linked with danger
see also DESERT

Num 16:13	kill us here in this **w**,
Num 26:65	all die in the **w**.
Num 32:13	wander in the **w** for forty
Deut 8:16	manna in the **w**, a food
Deut 29:5	led you through the **w**,
Ps 78:19	give us food in the **w**.
Ps 78:52	safely through the **w**.
Isa 32:15	**w** will become a fertile
Isa 35:6	will gush forth in the **w**,
Matt 3:3	the **w**, 'Prepare the way
Luke 5:16	withdrew to the **w** for
Rev 12:6	fled into the **w**, where God

WILDFLOWERS (n)
the flower of a wild or uncultivated plant

Ps 103:15	like grass; like **w**, we bloom
Matt 6:30	so wonderfully for **w** that are

WILL (n)
desire, wish

Ps 40:8	in doing your **w**, my God,
Ps 143:10	me to do your **w**, for you
Prov 3:6	Seek his **w** in all you do,
Matt 6:10	May your **w** be done on
Matt 7:21	who actually do the **w**
Matt 12:50	does the **w** of my Father
Matt 18:14	heavenly Father's **w** that
Matt 26:39	want your **w** to be done,
Matt 26:42	I drink it, your **w** be done.
John 5:30	carry out the **w** of the one
John 6:38	heaven to do the **w** of God
Rom 12:2	learn to know God's **w**
1 Thes 5:18	this is God's **w** for you
Heb 10:7	come to do your **w**, O God—
Heb 13:21	need for doing his **w**.
1 Pet 4:2	to do the **w** of God.

WILLING (adj)
inclined or favorably disposed in mind; done, borne, or accepted by choice or without reluctance

1 Chr 28:9	heart and a **w** mind.
Ps 51:12	and make me **w** to obey you.
Dan 3:28	command and were **w** to die
Matt 26:41	spirit is **w**, but the body
Rom 9:3	I would be **w** to be forever

WIN (v)
to be the victor in

1 Jn 5:5	who can **w** this battle
Rev 6:2	rode out to **w** many battles

WIND, WINDS (n)
a natural movement of air
see also STORM, WHIRLWIND

Ps 1:4	chaff, scattered by the **w**.
Eccl 2:11	like chasing the **w**.
Hos 8:7	have planted the **w** and
Mark 4:41	Even the **w** and waves
John 3:8	The **w** blows wherever
Eph 4:14	blown about by every **w**
Heb 1:7	his angels like the **w-s**,
Jas 1:6	and tossed by the **w**.

WINDOW, WINDOWS (n)
an opening in the wall of a building

Josh 2:21	rope hanging from the **w**.
Mal 3:10	will open the **w-s** of heaven
2 Cor 11:33	a basket through a **w**

WINDOWSILL (n)
the edge at the bottom of a window opening

Acts 20:9	sitting on the **w**, became

WINE (n)
the fermented juice of grapes, linked positively with blessings and negatively with drunkeness
Ps 104:15 **w** to make them glad,
Prov 31:6 and **w** for those in bitter
Song 1:2 love is sweeter than **w.**
Isa 28:7 who reel with **w** and stagger
Mark 15:36 with sour **w**, holding it
John 2:3 The **w** supply ran out
Rom 14:21 to eat meat or drink **w**
Eph 5:18 Don't be drunk with **w**,
1 Tim 5:23 drink a little **w** for
Rev 16:19 was filled with the **w**

WINEBIBBER(S) (KJV)
Prov 23:20 not carouse with *drunkards*
Matt 11:19 glutton and a *drunkard*, and
Luke 7:34 glutton and a *drunkard*, and

WINEPRESS (n)
a vat in which the juice from grapes is pressed in the process of making wine
Rev 19:15 juice flowing from a **w.**

WINESKINS (n)
a bag used for holding wine, made from the skin of an animal
Matt 9:17 stored in new **w** so that
Luke 5:37 new wine into old **w.**

WINGS (n)
feathered appendages of a bird, figurative of freedom, strength, and protection from God
Exod 19:4 carried you on eagles' **w**
Ps 17:8 in the shadow of your **w.**
Ps 91:4 shelter you with his **w.**
Isa 6:2 each having six **w.**
Isa 40:31 high on **w** like eagles.
Mal 4:2 rise with healing in his **w.**
Luke 13:34 chicks beneath her **w**,
Rev 4:8 living beings had six **w**,

WIPE, WIPED (v)
to clean or dry by rubbing; to expunge completely
Isa 25:8 will **w** away all tears.
Luke 7:38 she **w-d** them off with her
Acts 3:19 your sins may be **w-d** away.
Rev 7:17 And God will **w** every tear
Rev 21:4 He will **w** every tear

WISDOM (n)
knowledge, insight, judgment
Gen 3:6 she wanted the **w** it would
1 Kgs 4:29 gave Solomon very great **w**
1 Kgs 10:24 to hear the **w** God had
2 Chr 1:10 Give me the **w** and
Job 11:6 **w**, for true **w** is not
Job 42:3 that questions my **w** with such
Ps 51:6 teaching me **w** even there.
Prov 2:6 the LORD grants **w!**
Prov 3:13 the person who finds **w**,
Prov 8:11 **w** is far more valuable
Prov 11:2 with humility comes **w.**
Prov 16:16 better to get **w** than gold,
Prov 23:23 also get **w**, discipline,
Prov 29:3 man who loves **w** brings joy
Eccl 10:10 the value of **w**; it helps
Isa 11:2 on him—the Spirit of **w**
Isa 50:4 me his words of **w**, so that
Luke 2:52 Jesus grew in **w** and in
Acts 6:3 full of the Spirit and **w.**
1 Cor 1:21 him through human **w**, he
Eph 1:17 you spiritual **w** and insight
Col 2:3 treasures of **w** and knowledge.
Col 3:16 with all the **w** he gives.
2 Tim 3:15 given you the **w** to receive
Titus 2:12 world with **w**, righteousness,
Jas 1:5 If you need **w**, ask our
Rev 5:12 riches and **w** and strength

WISE, WISER, WISEST (adj)
marked by deep understanding, keen discernment, and a capacity for sound judgment
1 Kgs 3:12 you a **w** and understanding
Job 9:4 God is so **w** and so mighty.
Ps 14:2 anyone is truly **w**, if anyone
Ps 19:7 are trustworthy, making **w** the
Ps 119:100 I am even **w-r** than my
Prov 4:7 wisdom is the **w-st** thing
Prov 9:8 correct the **w**, and they
Prov 10:1 A **w** child brings joy to
Prov 11:30 a **w** person wins friends.
Prov 12:16 a **w** person stays calm
Prov 12:18 of the **w** bring healing.
Prov 13:1 A **w** child accepts a parent's
Prov 13:10 who take advice are **w.**
Prov 13:20 Walk with the **w** and
Prov 15:5 learns from correction is **w.**
Prov 16:23 From a **w** mind comes **w**
Prov 18:4 wisdom flows from the **w**
Prov 19:25 they will be all the **w-r.**
Prov 24:5 **w** are mightier than the
Prov 28:7 who obey the law are **w**;
Eccl 8:5 who are **w** will find a time
Eccl 9:17 quiet words of a **w** person
Matt 2:1 some **w** men from eastern
Matt 11:25 who think themselves **w**
Matt 25:2 foolish, and five were **w.**
Rom 3:11 No one is truly **w**; no one
1 Cor 1:19 wisdom of the **w** and
1 Cor 1:25 plan of God is **w-r** than
1 Cor 12:8 ability to give **w** advice;

Jas 3:13 If you are **w** and understand

WITCHCRAFT (n)
the use of sorcery or magic
Lev 19:26 practice fortune-telling or **w.**
Deut 18:10 omens, or engage in **w,**
Rev 21:8 those who practice **w,** idol

WITHDRAW, WITHDREW (v)
to remove; to retreat
Ps 66:20 or **w** his unfailing love from
Luke 5:16 But Jesus often **w-ew** to the

WITHER, WITHERS (v)
to shrivel and lose vitality, force, or freshness
Job 14:2 like a flower and then **w.**
Ps 1:3 leaves never **w,** and they
Isa 40:7 grass **w-s** and the flowers
Isa 64:6 autumn leaves, we **w** and fall,
1 Pet 1:24 grass **w-s** and the flower

WITHHELD (v)
to refrain from granting, giving, or allowing
Gen 22:12 You have not **w** from me

WITNESS, WITNESSES (n)
a person who gives testimony; one asked to be present at a transaction so as to be able to testify to its having taken place
Deut 19:15 of two or three **w-es.**
Prov 19:5 A false **w** will not go
Prov 21:28 but a credible **w** will be
Matt 18:16 by two or three **w-es.**
John 1:8 simply a **w** to tell about
Acts 1:8 will be my **w-es,** telling people
1 Tim 5:19 by two or three **w-es.**
1 Jn 5:7 we have these three **w-es**—

WITNESSED (v)
to have personal or direct cognizance of
Mal 2:14 the Lord **w** the vows

WIVES (n)
the female partner in marriage
see also WIFE
Eph 5:22 For **w,** this means submit
Eph 5:25 this means love your **w,**
1 Pet 3:1 way, you **w** must accept

WOE (KJV)
Isa 6:5 *It's all over!* I am doomed
Matt 18:7 *What sorrow awaits* the world
Matt 23:13 *What sorrow awaits* you
1 Cor 9:16 *How terrible* for me if I didn't
Rev 8:13 *Terror, terror, terror* to all who

WOLVES (n)
any of several wild, predatory animals that resemble large dogs
Matt 7:15 but are really vicious **w.**
Matt 10:16 you out as sheep among **w.**

WOMAN (n)
an adult female person
see also WOMEN
Gen 2:22 God made a **w** from the rib,
Gen 3:6 The **w** was convinced.
Gen 3:12 It was the **w** you gave me
Gen 3:16 he said to the **w,** "I will
Exod 3:22 Every Israelite **w** will ask
Lev 12:2 If a **w** becomes pregnant
Lev 15:19 a **w** has her menstrual
Lev 15:25 a **w** has a flow of blood
Num 5:29 If a **w** goes astray and defiles
Judg 4:9 be at the hands of a **w.**
Judg 16:4 love with a **w** named Delilah,
Ruth 3:11 knows you are a virtuous **w.**
2 Sam 11:2 he noticed a **w** of unusual
2 Sam 20:16 But a wise **w** in the town
Prov 11:16 A gracious **w** gains respect,
Prov 11:22 A beautiful **w** who lacks
Prov 14:1 A wise **w** builds her
Prov 30:19 how a man loves a **w.**
Prov 30:23 a bitter **w** who finally gets
Prov 31:30 **w** who fears the Lord
Matt 5:28 looks at a **w** with lust
Matt 9:20 Just then a **w** who had
Matt 26:7 was eating, a **w** came in
Mark 7:25 Right away a **w** who had
Luke 7:39 what kind of **w** is touching
John 4:7 Soon a Samaritan **w** came to
John 8:3 Pharisees brought a **w** who
Rom 7:2 when a **w** marries, the law
1 Cor 7:2 and each **w** should have
1 Cor 7:34 a married **w** has to think
1 Cor 11:3 the head of **w** is man, and
1 Cor 11:6 shameful for a **w** to have
1 Cor 11:13 it right for a **w** to pray
Gal 4:4 born of a **w,** subject to the
Gal 4:31 are children of the free **w.**
Rev 12:1 I saw a **w** clothed with the
Rev 12:13 he pursued the **w** who had
Rev 17:3 There I saw a **w** sitting on a

WOMB (n)
uterus
Ps 139:13 together in my mother's **w.**
Prov 31:2 O son of my **w,** O son
Jer 1:5 you in your mother's **w.**
Luke 1:44 baby in my **w** jumped for joy.
John 3:4 into his mother's **w** and be

WOMEN (n)
adult female persons
see also WOMAN

Gen 6:2	saw the beautiful **w** and took
Song 1:3	all the young **w** love you!
Mark 15:41	Many other **w** who had
Luke 1:42	you above all **w**, and your
Luke 23:27	many grief-stricken **w**.
Rom 1:26	Even the **w** turned against
1 Cor 7:25	the young **w** who are not
1 Tim 2:9	I want **w** to be modest in
2 Tim 3:6	of vulnerable **w** who are
Titus 2:3	teach the older **w** to live in
Titus 2:4	train the younger **w** to love
1 Pet 3:5	how the holy **w** of old made

WON (v)
to gain victory
see also WIN

1 Kgs 20:11	warrior who has already **w**.
1 Pet 3:1	They will be **w** over
1 Jn 2:13	you have **w** your battle

WONDERFUL (adj)
marked by a marvelous, amazing, or extraordinary quality

1 Chr 16:9	about his **w** deeds.
Job 37:14	consider the **w** miracles
Ps 16:6	What a **w** inheritance!
Ps 17:7	unfailing love in **w** ways.
Ps 71:17	about the **w** things you
Ps 72:18	does such **w** things.
Ps 75:1	tell of your **w** deeds.
Ps 105:2	about his **w** deeds.
Ps 118:23	it is **w** to see.
Ps 119:18	to see the **w** truths in
Ps 119:27	meditate on your **w** deeds.
Ps 119:129	Your laws are **w**.
Ps 139:6	knowledge is too **w** for
Ps 145:5	and your **w** miracles.
Eccl 11:9	Young people, it's **w** to be
Isa 9:6	be called: **W** Counselor,
Isa 12:5	he has done **w** things.
Isa 25:1	You do such **w** things!
Matt 21:15	saw these **w** miracles
Matt 21:42	and it is **w** to see.
Luke 13:17	rejoiced at the **w** things
Acts 2:11	about the **w** things God has
Acts 20:24	News about the **w** grace of
2 Cor 10:12	we are as **w** as these
Titus 2:13	hope to that **w** day when

WONDERS (n)
mighty works, miracles

1 Chr 16:12	Remember the **w** he has
Ps 26:7	and telling of all your **w**.
Ps 31:21	has shown me the **w** of his
Ps 77:14	are the God of great **w**!
Ps 89:5	your great **w**, Lord;
Mark 13:22	perform signs and **w** so
Acts 2:19	will cause **w** in the heavens
Acts 5:12	signs and **w** among the people.
2 Cor 12:12	signs and **w** and miracles
Heb 2:4	signs and **w** and various

WORD, WORDS (n)
something that is said; special revelation from God; commands

Deut 8:3	live by every **w** that comes
Deut 11:18	to these **w-s** of mine. Tie
Job 38:2	with such ignorant **w-s**?
Ps 19:3	speak without a sound or **w**;
Ps 52:4	others with your **w-s**, you liar!
Ps 119:9	pure? By obeying your **w**.
Ps 119:11	hidden your **w** in my heart,
Ps 119:103	How sweet your **w-s** taste
Ps 119:160	essence of your **w-s** is
Ps 119:162	I rejoice in your **w** like
Prov 12:19	Truthful **w-s** stand the test
Prov 12:25	an encouraging **w** cheers
Prov 16:24	Kind **w-s** are like honey—
Prov 17:27	wise person uses few **w-s**;
Prov 26:23	Smooth **w-s** may hide a
Isa 40:21	deaf to the **w-s** of God—
Jer 15:16	your **w-s**, I devoured
Jer 23:29	Does not my **w** burn like
Amos 8:13	for the Lord's **w**.
Matt 4:4	but by every **w** that comes
Matt 15:6	you cancel the **w** of God
Matt 24:35	**w-s** will never disappear.
John 1:1	the beginning the **W** already
John 6:68	the **w-s** that give eternal life.
John 15:7	and my **w-s** remain in you,
John 17:17	teach them your **w**, which
Rom 10:18	the **w-s** to all the world.
1 Cor 2:1	use lofty **w-s** and impressive
1 Cor 2:13	do not use **w-s** that come
1 Cor 14:9	to people in **w-s** they don't
1 Cor 14:19	than ten thousand **w-s** in
2 Cor 2:17	We preach the **w** of God
2 Cor 4:2	or distort the **w** of God.
Eph 6:17	which is the **w** of God.
Phil 2:16	firmly to the **w** of life;
2 Tim 2:15	explains the **w** of truth.
Titus 2:5	shame on the **w** of God.
Heb 4:12	For the **w** of God is
Heb 5:12	things about God's **w**.
Jas 1:22	listen to God's **w**.
1 Pet 1:23	eternal, living **w** of God.
1 Pet 2:8	not obey God's **w**, and so
1 Pet 3:1	to them without any **w-s**.
2 Pet 3:5	the heavens by the **w** of

Rev 19:13 title was the **W** of God.
Rev 22:19 of the **w-s** from this book

WORK, WORKS (n)
one's occupation; physical or creative effort
see also DEEDS
Gen 2:2 finished his **w** of creation,
Exod 20:9 week for your ordinary **w,**
Deut 5:13 week for your ordinary **w,**
Ps 77:12 about your mighty **w-s.**
Ps 107:24 impressive **w-s** on the
Ps 127:1 **w** of the builders is wasted.
Ps 150:2 Praise him for his mighty **w-s;**
Prov 21:5 planning and hard **w** lead
Eccl 2:19 my skill and hard **w** under
Eccl 5:19 To enjoy your **w** and accept
John 4:34 and from finishing his **w.**
John 5:36 Father gave me these **w-s** to
John 10:32 have done many good **w-s.**
Acts 13:2 for the special **w** to which
Acts 20:24 finishing the **w** assigned
Rom 4:5 not because of their **w,** but
1 Cor 3:5 the **w** the Lord gave us.
Gal 6:4 attention to your own **w,** for
Eph 4:12 people to do his **w** and build
Eph 4:16 part does its own special **w,**
Eph 4:28 your hands for good hard **w,**
Phil 1:6 began the good **w** within you,
1 Tim 6:18 rich in good **w-s** and
2 Tim 3:17 people to do every good **w.**
Heb 10:24 acts of love and good **w-s.**
Jas 2:26 faith is dead without good **w-s.**
Rev 15:3 marvelous are your **w-s,**

WORK, WORKED, WORKING (v)
to exert oneself physically or mentally
Prov 13:4 but those who **w** hard will
Eccl 5:12 who **w** hard sleep well,
Matt 6:28 They don't **w** or make their
Matt 12:30 anyone who isn't **w-ing** with
Luke 10:7 who **w** deserve their pay.
Luke 13:24 **W** hard to enter the narrow
Rom 4:6 righteous without **w-ing** for
Rom 8:28 to **w** together for the good
Rom 12:11 Never be lazy, but **w** hard
1 Cor 15:10 I have **w-ed** harder than
1 Cor 15:58 Always **w** enthusiastically
2 Cor 11:27 I have **w-ed** hard and
Eph 6:7 you were **w-ing** for the Lord
1 Thes 4:11 and **w-ing** with your hands,
2 Thes 3:10 unwilling to **w** will not
1 Tim 5:18 Those who **w** deserve their
1 Tim 6:2 slaves should **w** all the harder
Heb 6:10 how hard you have **w-ed** for
2 Pet 1:10 **w** hard to prove that you

WORKER, WORKERS (n)
one who works; laborer
Prov 10:4 poor; hard **w-s** get rich.
Prov 12:11 A hard **w** has plenty of
Prov 22:29 see any truly competent **w-s?**
Prov 27:18 **w-s** who protect
Prov 31:17 and strong, a hard **w.**
Matt 9:37 great, but the **w-s** are few.
Matt 20:1 one morning to hire **w-s** for
1 Cor 3:9 For we are both God's **w-s.**
2 Tim 2:15 Be a good **w,** one who does

WORLD (n)
the earth and its inhabitants; the human race; the current age and its value system
Ps 33:9 he spoke, the **w** began!
Ps 50:12 for all the **w** is mine
Ps 96:13 judge the **w** with justice,
Isa 13:11 will punish the **w** for its
Matt 16:26 you gain the whole **w** but
John 1:29 away the sin of the **w!**
John 3:16 God loved the **w** so much
John 8:12 I am the light of the **w.**
John 13:35 prove to the **w** that you
John 16:33 I have overcome the **w.**
John 17:5 shared before the **w** began.
John 17:14 And the **w** hates them
John 18:36 Kingdom is not of this **w.**
Rom 3:19 the entire **w** is guilty
1 Cor 1:27 things the **w** considers
1 Cor 2:7 glory before the **w** began.
1 Cor 3:1 you belonged to this **w** or
1 Cor 3:19 of this **w** is foolishness
1 Cor 6:2 to judge the **w,** can't you
2 Cor 5:19 reconciling the **w** to himself,
Eph 2:12 lived in this **w** without God
Eph 4:9 also descended to our lowly **w.**
Phil 2:15 lights in a **w** full of crooked
Titus 1:2 them before the **w** began.
Heb 9:26 ever since the **w** began.
Jas 2:5 poor in this **w** to be rich
Jas 4:4 a friend of the **w,** you make
1 Jn 2:2 the sins of all the **w.**
1 Jn 2:15 Do not love this **w** nor
1 Jn 5:4 defeats this evil **w,** and

WORLDLY (adj)
belonging to the sphere of human existence only; affected by sin; corrupt
Luke 16:9 Use your **w** resources to benefit
2 Cor 7:10 **w** sorrow, which lacks repentance,
2 Cor 10:4 not **w** weapons, to knock down
1 Pet 2:11 **w** desires that wage war

WORRY, WORRIES (n)
mental distress or agitation resulting from concern; anxiety
Prov 12:25 **W** weighs a person down;
Matt 6:27 Can all your **w-ies** add a single
Luke 21:34 and by the **w-ies** of this life.
1 Pet 5:7 Give all your **w-ies** and cares

WORRY, WORRIED, WORRYING (v)
to feel or experience concern or anxiety
Deut 20:8 anyone here afraid or **w-ied?**
Ps 37:1 Don't **w** about the wicked
Isa 7:4 Tell him to stop **w-ing.**
Matt 6:25 I tell you not to **w** about
Matt 10:19 don't **w** about how to
Luke 6:41 And why **w** about a speck in
Acts 27:33 You have been so **w-ied** that
Phil 4:6 Don't **w** about anything;

WORSE (adj)
of more inferior condition
Matt 12:45 that person is **w** off than
2 Pet 2:20 they are **w** off than

WORSHIP (n)
reverent devotion and allegiance pledged to God or a god
1 Cor 10:14 flee from the **w** of idols.

WORSHIP, WORSHIPED, WORSHIPING, WORSHIPS (v)
to regard with great respect, honor, or devotion
Gen 12:8 and he **w-ed** the LORD.
Gen 13:4 and there he **w-ed** the LORD
Gen 21:33 and there he **w-ed** the LORD,
Gen 26:25 there and **w-ed** the LORD.
Deut 12:30 and **w-ing** their gods.
2 Kgs 17:36 But **w** only the LORD,
Ps 29:2 **W** the LORD in the splendor
Ps 95:6 Come, let us **w** and bow down.
Ps 105:3 rejoice, you who **w** the LORD.
Isa 44:19 bow down to **w** a piece of
Jer 16:11 **w-ed** other gods and served
Dan 3:28 die rather than serve or **w** any
Hos 9:1 like prostitutes, **w-ing** other
Hos 9:10 as vile as the god they **w-ed.**
Hos 13:1 Ephraim sinned by **w-ing** Baal
Zeph 3:9 everyone can **w** the LORD
Zech 14:17 to Jerusalem to **w** the King,
Matt 2:2 we have come to **w** him.
Matt 4:9 kneel down and **w** me.
Matt 15:25 she came and **w-ed** him,
Matt 28:9 grasped his feet, and **w-ed**
Luke 23:47 he **w-ed** God and said,
John 4:24 **w** in spirit and in truth.
1 Cor 5:11 is greedy, or **w-s** idols,
Heb 9:14 we can **w** the living God.

WORST (adj)
most corrupt, bad, or evil
1 Tim 1:15 I am the **w** of them all.

WORTHLESS (adj)
valueless, useless, contemptible
1 Sam 12:21 worshiping **w** idols that
Prov 6:12 **w** and wicked people
1 Cor 3:20 he knows they are **w.**
Eph 5:11 part in the **w** deeds of evil
Titus 1:16 **w** for doing anything good.
Jas 5:3 and silver have become **w.**

WORTHY (adj)
having sufficient merit or importance; estimable, honorable
Gen 32:10 I am not **w** of all the
Prov 12:4 A **w** wife is a crown
Matt 8:8 Lord, I am not **w** to have
Matt 10:37 are not **w** of being mine;
Matt 22:8 I invited aren't **w** of the
Luke 15:19 I am no longer **w** of being
1 Cor 15:9 I'm not even **w** to be called
Eph 4:1 lead a life **w** of your calling,
Phil 1:27 a manner **w** of the Good News
Rev 5:5 He is **w** to open the scroll

WOUNDS (n)
injuries to the body
Isa 30:26 and cure the **w** he gave them.
Zech 13:6 what about those **w** on your
John 20:20 he showed them the **w** in
1 Pet 2:24 By his **w** you are healed.

WRAP (v)
to fold cloth, paper, etc. around something, especially in order to cover it
Exod 29:9 **W** the sashes around
Num 4:12 **w** them in a blue cloth

WRAPPINGS (n)
something used to wrap an object
John 20:5 saw the linen **w** lying there,

WRATH (n)
extreme displeasure, anger, or hostility; God's response to sin
Isa 13:13 Armies displays his **w** in
Rev 6:16 and from the **w** of the Lamb.
Rev 16:19 the wine of his fierce **w.**

WREATH (n)
a band of intertwined flowers or leaves worn as a mark of honor or victory

Prov 4:9 will place a lovely **w** on your

WRESTLED (v)

to engage in a violent or determined struggle

Gen 32:24 man came and **w** with him

WRITE, WRITING (v)

to inscribe or engrave; to record

see also WRITTEN

Deut 10:2 I will **w** on the tablets

Prov 3:3 **W** them deep within your

Prov 7:3 **W** them deep within your

Eccl 12:12 for **w-ing** books is endless,

Jer 31:33 I will **w** them on their hearts.

1 Tim 3:14 I am **w-ing** these things to

Heb 8:10 I will **w** them on their hearts.

Rev 3:12 I will **w** on them the name of

WRITHE (v)

to twist (the body or body part) in pain

Jer 4:19 my heart—I **w** in pain!

WRITTEN (v)

to enscribe or engrave; to record

see also WRITE

Deut 28:58 that are **w** in this book,

Josh 1:8 to obey everything **w** in it.

Isa 49:16 See, I have **w** your name

Dan 12:1 whose name is **w** in the book

Mal 3:16 scroll of remembrance was **w**

Luke 24:44 everything **w** about me in

John 20:31 these are **w** so that you

John 21:25 the books that would be **w.**

Rom 2:15 law is **w** in their hearts,

1 Cor 10:11 They were **w** down to warn

Heb 12:23 names are **w** in heaven.

Rev 21:27 whose names are **w** in the

WRONG (adj)

incorrect, sinful, immoral, or improper

Prov 14:2 who take the **w** path

Rom 7:19 don't want to do what is **w,**

Rom 12:9 Hate what is **w.** Hold tightly

Rom 14:14 of itself, is **w** to eat.

2 Tim 3:16 make us realize what is **w**

WRONG (adv)

in an unsuccessful or unfortunate way

Prov 15:22 Plans go **w** for lack

WRONG (n)

an injurious, unfair, or unjust act; something wrong, immoral, or unethical

Exod 23:2 the crowd in doing **w.**

Deut 32:4 faithful God who does no **w;**

Job 34:10 The Almighty can do no **w.**

Ps 141:9 snares of those who do **w.**

Isa 53:9 done no **w** and had never

Rom 13:10 Love does no **w** to others,

Rom 16:19 to stay innocent of any **w.**

1 Cor 6:9 those who do **w** will not

Jas 1:13 God is never tempted to do **w,**

1 Pet 3:17 to suffer for doing **w!**

WRONGDOING (n)

evil or improper behavior or action

Prov 26:26 their **w** will be exposed

Isa 61:8 justice. I hate robbery and **w.**

Acts 18:14 some **w** or serious crime,

Gal 3:13 the curse for our **w.**

WRONGED (v)

to injure or harm; to malign or discredit

Num 5:7 to the person who was **w.**

Isa 42:3 to all who have been **w.**

1 Cor 13:5 keeps no record of being **w.**

X

XERXES

Persian king (486–465 b.c.); mentioned in the books of Ezra, Esther, and Daniel (9:1, where he is called Ahasuerus)

Ezra 4:6 later when **X** began his reign,

Esth 1:1 in the days of King **X,** who

Esth 1:9 in the royal palace of King **X.**

Esth 1:19 from the presence of King **X,**

Esth 2:16 Esther was taken to King **X**

Esth 3:1 later King **X** promoted Haman

Esth 6:2 plotted to assassinate King **X.**

Esth 8:7 King **X** said to Queen Eshter

Esth 10:3 with authority next to that of King **X** himself

Y

YAHWEH (n)

"I Am Who I Am" or "I Will Be What I Will Be"; the personal name of God revealed to Moses in the burning bush

see also Lord

Gen 22:14 named the place **Y**-Yireh

Exod 3:15 **Y,** the God of your ancestors

Exod 6:2 I am **Y**—'the Lord'

Exod 15:3 warrior; **Y** is his name!

Exod 17:15 there and named it **Y**-nissi

Exod 33:19 I will call out my name, **Y,**

Exod 34:5 called out his own name, **Y.**

Judg 6:24 there and named it **Y**-Shalom

YEAR, YEARS (n)
the period of about 365 days; a period having special significance; a measure of age or duration
Gen 1:14 the seasons, days, and **y-s.**
Exod 12:40 lived in Egypt for 430 **y-s.**
Exod 16:35 manna for forty **y-s** until
Exod 34:23 Three times each **y** every
Lev 16:34 the LORD once each **y.**
Lev 25:11 During that **y** you must
Job 36:26 His **y-s** cannot be counted.
Ps 90:4 a thousand **y-s** are as a
Luke 3:23 about thirty **y-s** old when
Heb 10:1 again and again, **y** after **y,**
Heb 10:3 of their sins **y** after **y.**
2 Pet 3:8 like a thousand **y-s** to the
Rev 20:2 in chains for a thousand **y-s.**

YEAST (n)
a fungus used for making alcohol and bread
Exod 12:8 and bread made without **y.**
Exod 12:15 bread made with **y** during
Matt 16:6 Beware of the **y** of the
1 Cor 5:6 a little **y** that spreads

YESTERDAY (adv)
on the day preceding today
Heb 13:8 same **y,** today, and forever.

YIELD, YIELDS (v)
to produce; to surrender or submit
Prov 30:33 beating of cream **y-s** butter
Matt 6:13 don't let us **y** to temptation,
Luke 11:4 don't let us **y** to temptation.
Jas 3:17 willing to **y** to others.

YOKE (n)
a wooden crossbar linking two load-pulling animals together; figurative of bondage or linkage between people
Hos 11:4 lifted the **y** from his neck,
Matt 11:29 Take my **y** upon you.

YOUNG, YOUNGER (adj)
being in the first or an early stage of life, growth, or development
2 Chr 10:14 counsel of his **y-er** advisers.
Ps 119:9 How can a **y** person stay pure?
Prov 20:29 The glory of the **y** is their
Joel 2:28 your **y** men will see visions.
Acts 2:17 Your **y** men will see visions,
Acts 7:58 feet of a **y** man named Saul.
1 Tim 5:1 Talk to **y-er** men as you
Titus 2:4 must train the **y-er** women to
Titus 2:6 encourage the **y** men to live
1 Pet 5:5 same way, you **y-er** men must
1 Jn 2:13 you who are **y** in the faith

YOUTH (n)
the period between childhood and maturity
Ps 103:5 My **y** is renewed like the
Eccl 12:1 Honor him in your **y** before

YOUTHFUL (adj)
of, relating to, or characteristic of youth
2 Tim 2:22 that stimulates **y** lusts.

Z

ZEAL (n)
eagerness and ardent interest in pursuit of something
Num 25:13 in his **z** for me, his God,
Rom 10:2 but it is misdirected **z.**
Gal 1:14 **z** for the traditions of my ancestors

ZEALOT (n)
a Jewish revolutionary who sought liberation from Roman rule near and during the time of Christ
Matt 10:4 Simon (the **z**), Judas Iscariot,
Mark 3:18 Thaddaeus, Simon (the **z**),
Acts 1:13 Simon (the **Z**), and Judas (son

THE

NEW OXFORD BIBLE MAPS

INDEX TO MAPS

A

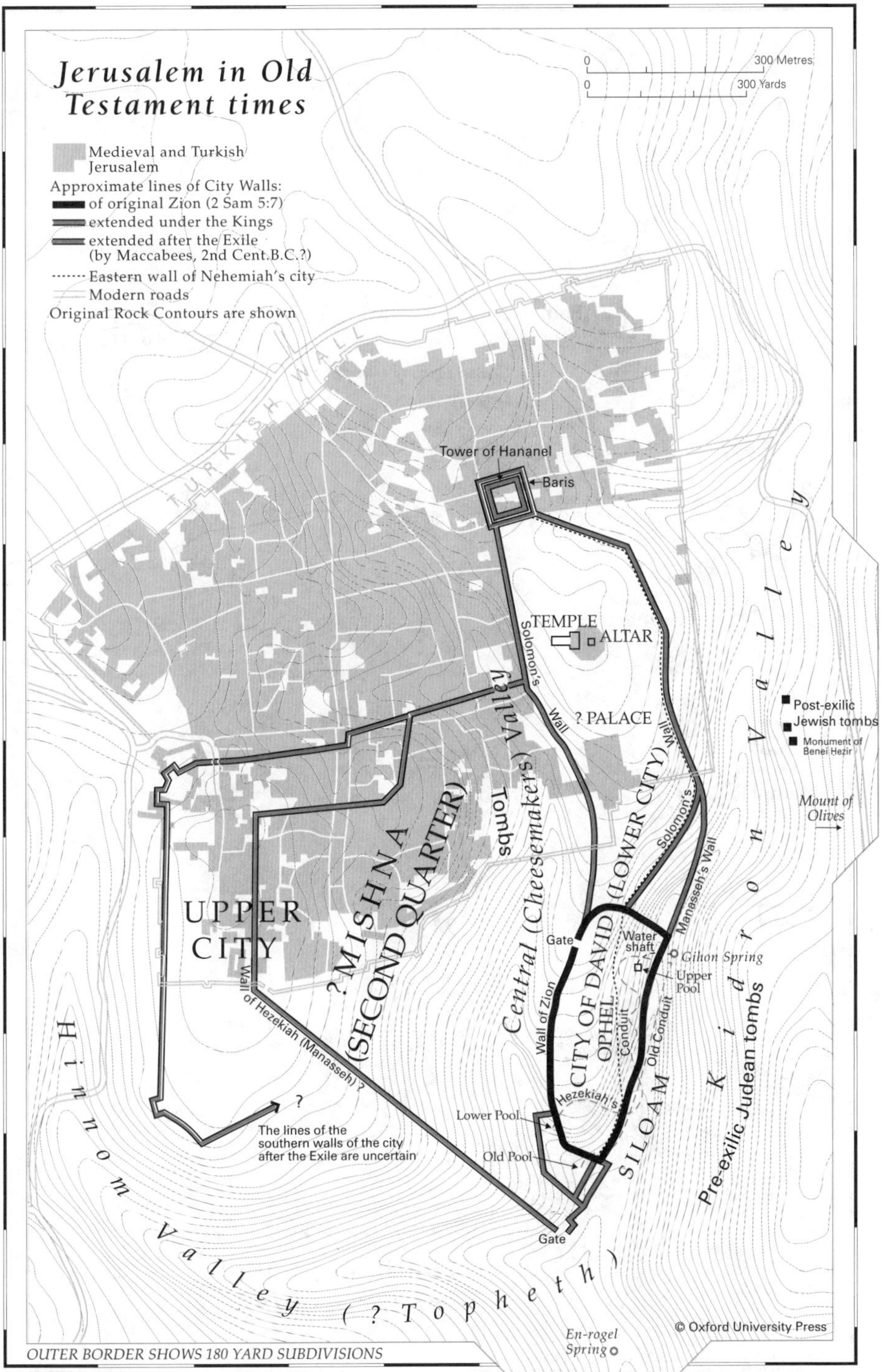
Jerusalem in Old Testament times
Medieval and Turkish Jerusalem
Approximate lines of City Walls:
of original Zion (2 Sam 5:7)
extended under the Kings
extended after the Exile (by Maccabees, 2nd Cent.B.C.?)
Eastern wall of Nehemiah's city
Modern roads
Original Rock Contours are shown
0 300 Metres
0 300 Yards
TURKISH WALL
Tower of Hananel
Baris
TEMPLE
ALTAR
? PALACE
Solomon's Wall
Solomon's Wall
Manasseh's Wall
Post-exilic Jewish tombs
Monument of Benei Hezir
Mount of Olives
Central (Cheesemakers') Valley
Tombs
?MISHNA (SECOND QUARTER)
UPPER CITY
CITY OF DAVID (LOWER CITY)
OPHEL
Gate
Water shaft
Gihon Spring
Upper Pool
Wall of Zion
Conduit
Old Conduit
Hezekiah's
Wall of Hezekiah (Manasseh) ?
?
The lines of the southern walls of the city after the Exile are uncertain
Lower Pool
Old Pool
SILOAM
Kidron Valley
Pre-exilic Judean tombs
Hinnom Valley (?Topheth)
Gate
En-rogel Spring
© Oxford University Press
OUTER BORDER SHOWS 180 YARD SUBDIVISIONS

MAP 2

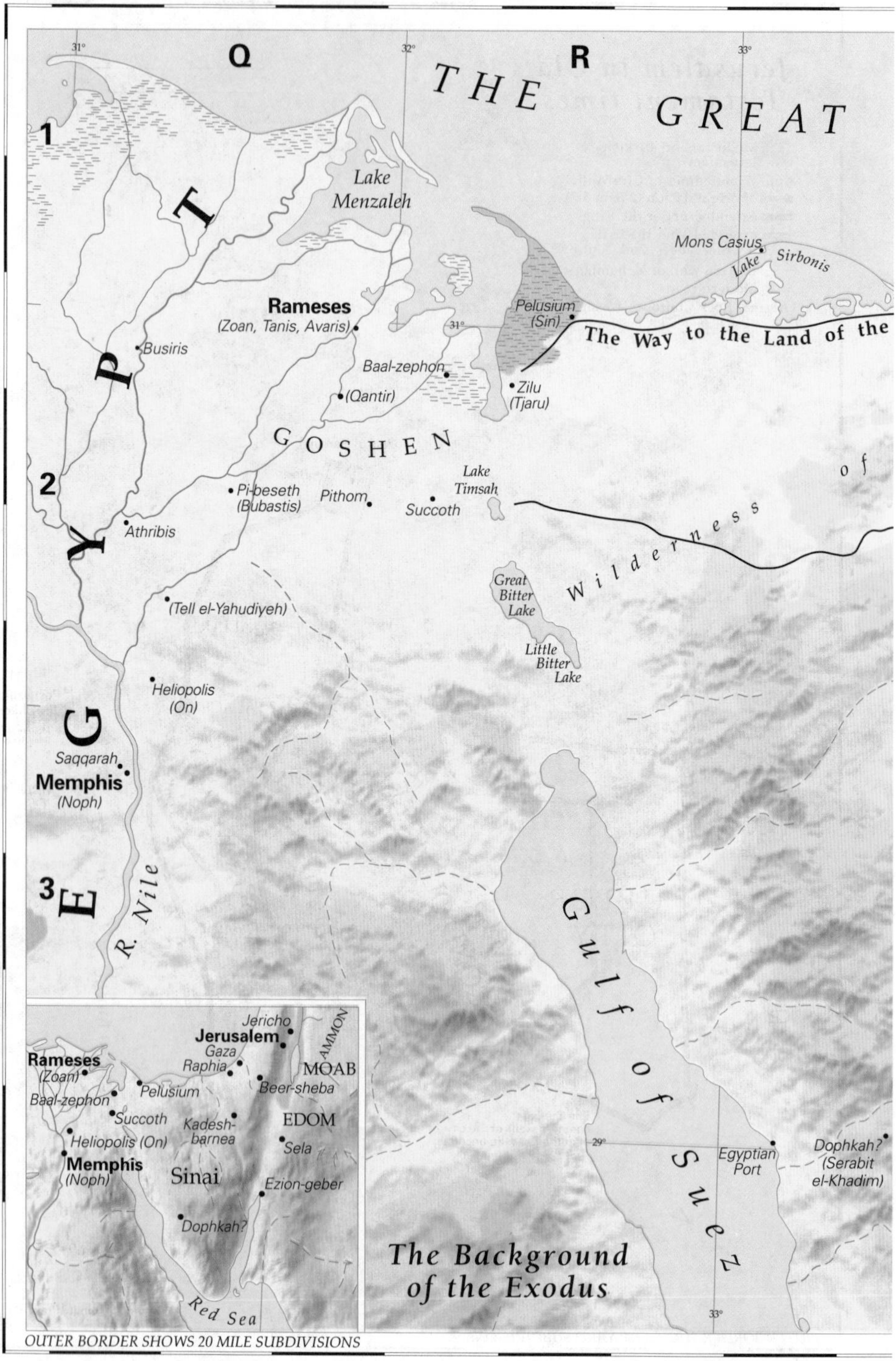

The Background of the Exodus
THE GREAT
EGYPT
Q
R
1
2
3
31°
32°
33°
29°
Lake Menzaleh
Mons Casius
Lake Sirbonis
Pelusium (Sin)
The Way to the Land of the
Rameses
(Zoan, Tanis, Avaris)
Busiris
Baal-zephon
(Qantir)
Zilu (Tjaru)
GOSHEN
Pi-beseth (Bubastis)
Pithom
Succoth
Lake Timsah
Athribis
Wilderness of
Great Bitter Lake
Little Bitter Lake
(Tell el-Yahudiyeh)
Heliopolis (On)
Saqqarah
Memphis
(Noph)
R. Nile
Gulf of Suez
Egyptian Port
Dophkah? (Serabit el-Khadim)
Jericho
AMMON
Jerusalem
Gaza
Raphia
MOAB
Rameses
(Zoan)
Pelusium
Beer-sheba
Baal-zephon
Succoth
Kadesh-barnea
EDOM
Heliopolis (On)
Sela
Memphis
(Noph)
Sinai
Ezion-geber
Dophkah?
Red Sea

OUTER BORDER SHOWS 20 MILE SUBDIVISIONS

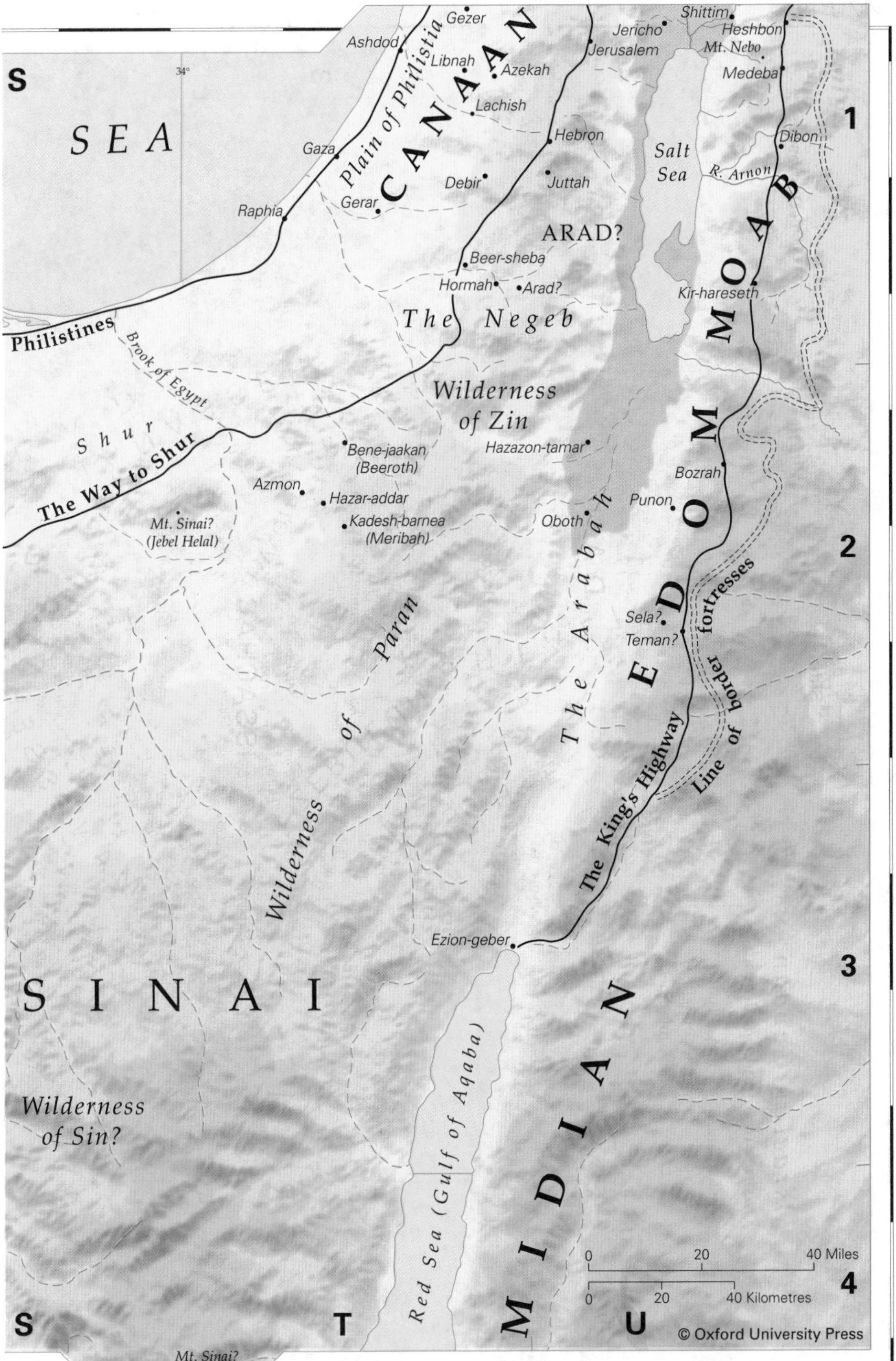

S
SEA
34°
Gezer
Ashdod
Plain of Philistia
CANAAN
Libnah
Azekah
Lachish
Gaza
Hebron
Debir
Juttah
Gerar
Raphia
ARAD?
Beer-sheba
Hormah
Arad?
The Negeb
Philistines
Brook of Egypt
Wilderness of Zin
Shur
The Way to Shur
Bene-jaakan (Beeroth)
Hazazon-tamar
Azmon
Hazar-addar
Kadesh-barnea (Meribah)
Mt. Sinai? (Jebel Helal)
Oboth
Wilderness of Paran
The Arabah
Shittim
Jericho
Heshbon
Jerusalem
Mt. Nebo
Medeba
1
Salt Sea
Dibon
R. Arnon
MOAB
Kir-hareseth
EDOM
Bozrah
Punon
2
Sela?
Teman?
Line of border fortresses
The King's Highway
Ezion-geber
3
SINAI
MIDIAN
Red Sea (Gulf of Aqaba)
Wilderness of Sin?
0 20 40 Miles
0 20 40 Kilometres
4
S
T
U
Mt. Sinai? (Mt. Horeb)

MAP 3

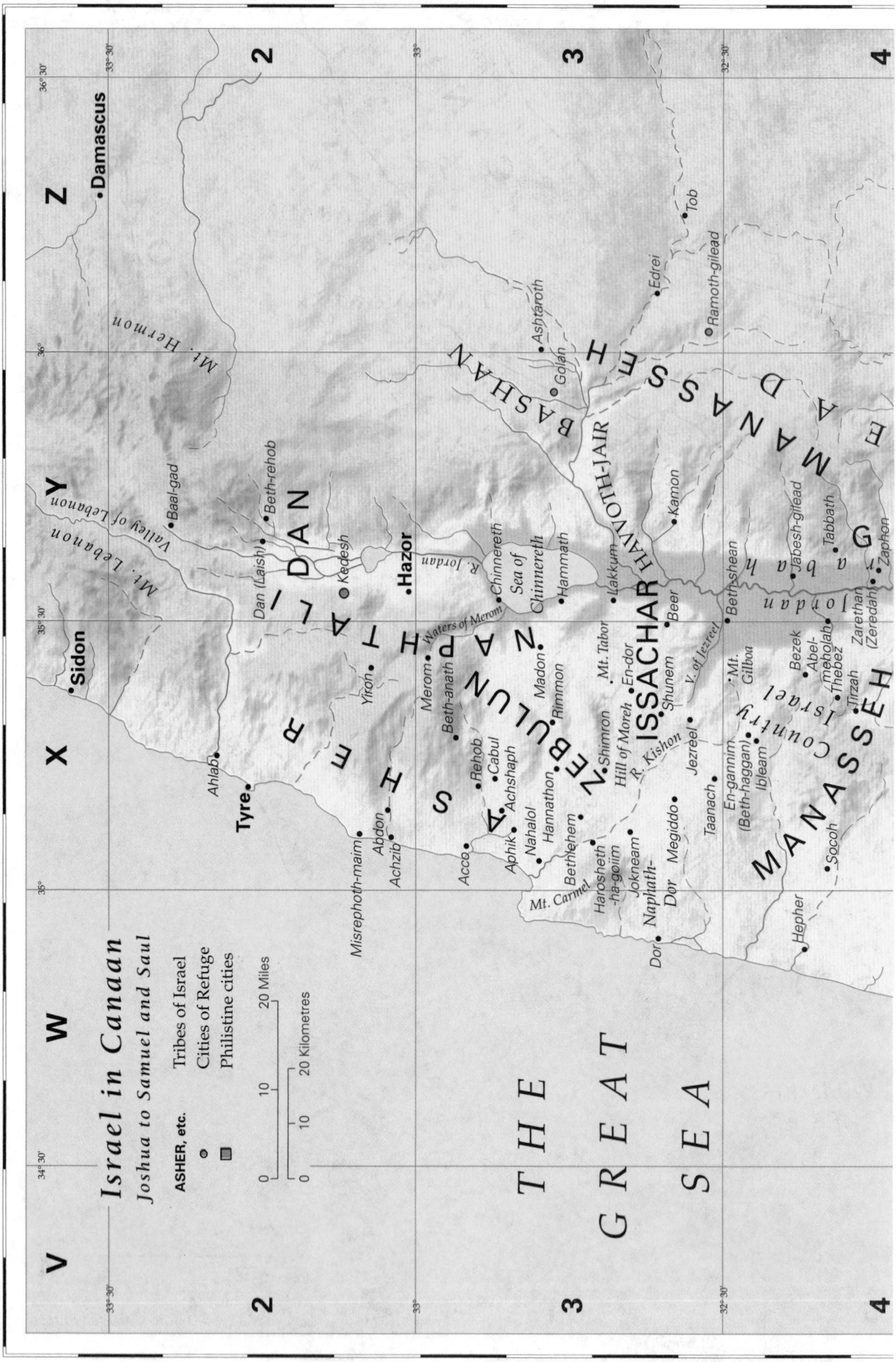
Israel in Canaan
Joshua to Samuel and Saul
ASHER, etc. Tribes of Israel
Cities of Refuge
Philistine cities
0 10 20 Miles
0 10 20 Kilometres
THE GREAT SEA
V
W
X
Y
Z
2
3
4
Damascus
Sidon
Tyre
Ahlab
Mt. Hermon
Mt. Lebanon
Valley of Lebanon
Baal-gad
Beth-rehob
Dan (Laish)
DAN
Kedesh
Hazor
R. Jordan
Waters of Merom
Chinnereth
Sea of Chinnereth
Hammath
Yiron
Merom
Beth-anath
Misrephoth-maim
Abdon
Achzib
Acco
Aphik
Rehob
Cabul
Achshaph
Nahalol
Hannathon
Bethlehem
Rimmon
Madon
Mt. Carmel
Harosheth-ha-goiim
Jokneam
Naphath-Dor
Dor
Megiddo
Shimron
Hill of Moreh
R. Kishon
Mt. Tabor
En-dor
Shunem
Jezreel
V. of Jezreel
Taanach
En-gannim (Beth-haggan)
Ibleam
Mt. Gilboa
Beth-shean
Beer
Lakkum
ISSACHAR
ZEBULUN
NAPHTALI
ASHER
MANASSEH
Israel Country
Bezek
Abel-meholah
Thebez
Tirzah
Zarethan (Zeredah)
Jordan
Arabah
Jabesh-gilead
Tabbath
Zaphon
Kamon
HAVVOTH-JAIR
BASHAN
Golan
Ashtaroth
Edrei
Ramoth-gilead
Tob
MANASSEH
GAD
Hepher
Socoh

MAP 3

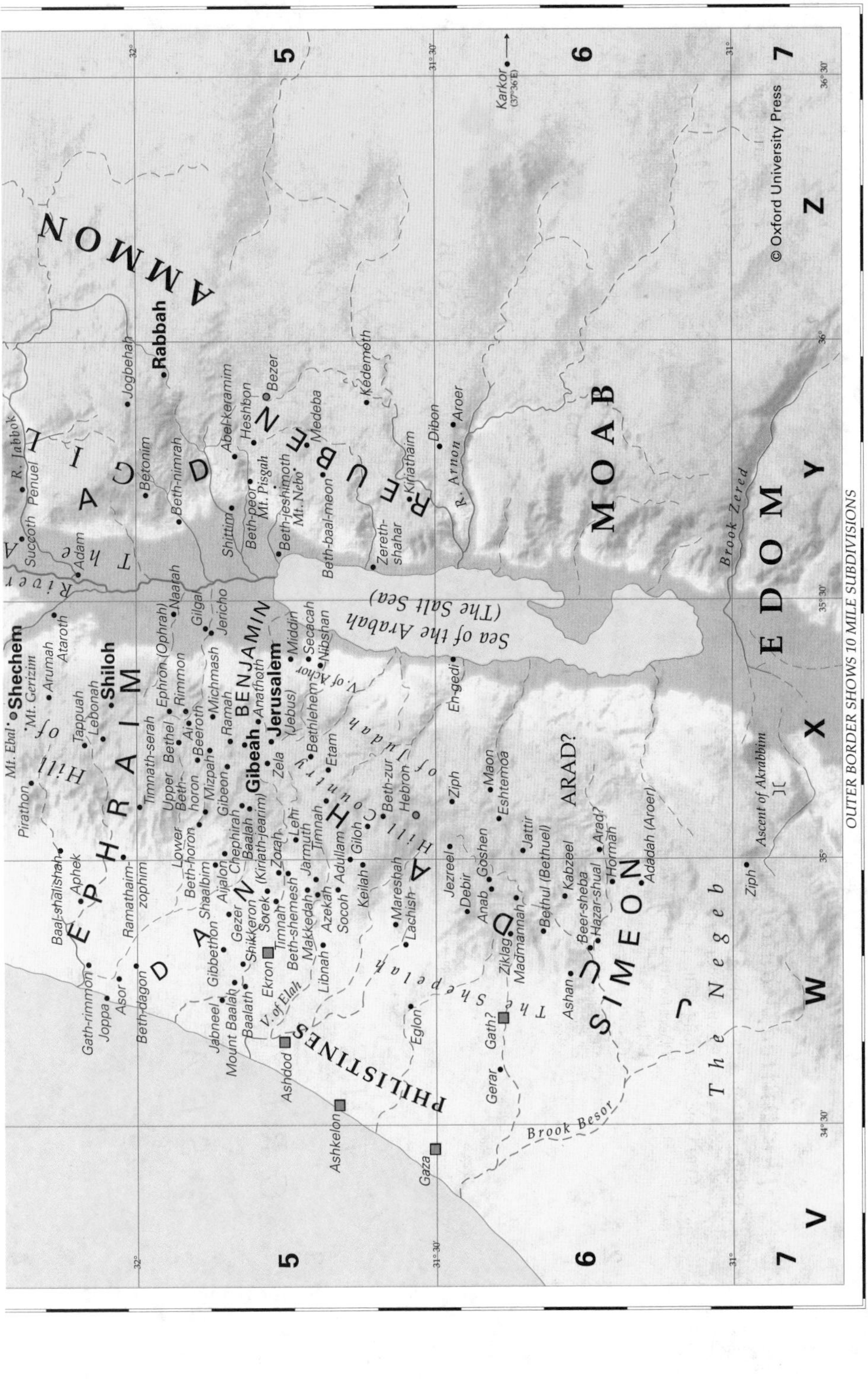
AMMON
GILEAD
EPHRAIM
DAN
BENJAMIN
JUDAH
REUBEN
SIMEON
PHILISTINES
MOAB
EDOM
Hill of Ephraim
The River Jordan
Hill Country of Judah
The Shephelah
The Negeb
Sea of the Arabah (The Salt Sea)
Shechem
Shiloh
Jerusalem
(Jebus)
Gibeah
Rabbah
Mt. Ebal
Mt. Gerizim
Arumah
Ataroth
Tappuah
Lebonah
Pirathon
Baal-shalishah
Aphek
Gath-rimmon
Joppa
Asor
Beth-dagon
Ramathaim-zophim
Timnath-serah
Upper Beth-horon
Lower Beth-horon
Bethel
Ai
Ephron (Ophrah)
Rimmon
Michmash
Beeroth
Mizpah
Ramah
Gibeon
Anathoth
Zela
Chephirah
Baalah (Kiriath-jearim)
Aijalon
Shaalbim
Gezer
Gibbethon
Jabneel
Mount Baalah
Baalath
Shikkeron
Ekron
Sorek
Zorah
Timnah
Beth-shemesh
Lehi
Jarmuth
Makkedah
Azekah
Libnah
Socoh
Adullam
V. of Elah
Keilah
Giloh
Bethlehem
Etam
Beth-zur
Hebron
Mareshah
Lachish
Eglon
Ashdod
Ashkelon
Gaza
Gerar
Gath?
Ziklag
Madmannah
Anab
Debir
Goshen
Jezreel
Ziph
Maon
Eshtemoa
Jattir
Bethul (Bethuel)
Kabzeel
Beer-sheba
Hazar-shual
Hormah
Arad?
ARAD?
Adadah (Aroer)
Ashan
Ziph
Ascent of Akrabbim
Brook Besor
Brook Zered
En-gedi
Middin
Secacah
Nibshan
V. of Achor
Jericho
Gilgal
Naarah
Adam
Succoth
Penuel
R. Jabbok
Betonim
Jogbehah
Beth-nimrah
Shittim
Abel-keramim
Heshbon
Beth-peor
Mt. Pisgah
Mt. Nebo
Beth-jeshimoth
Bezer
Medeba
Beth-baal-meon
Kedemoth
Zereth-shahar
Kiriathaim
Dibon
Aroer
R. Arnon
Karkor
(37°36'E)
32°
31° 30'
31°
34° 30'
35°
35° 30'
36°
36° 30'
V
W
X
Y
Z
5
6
7
OUTER BORDER SHOWS 10 MILE SUBDIVISIONS
© Oxford University Press

MAP 4

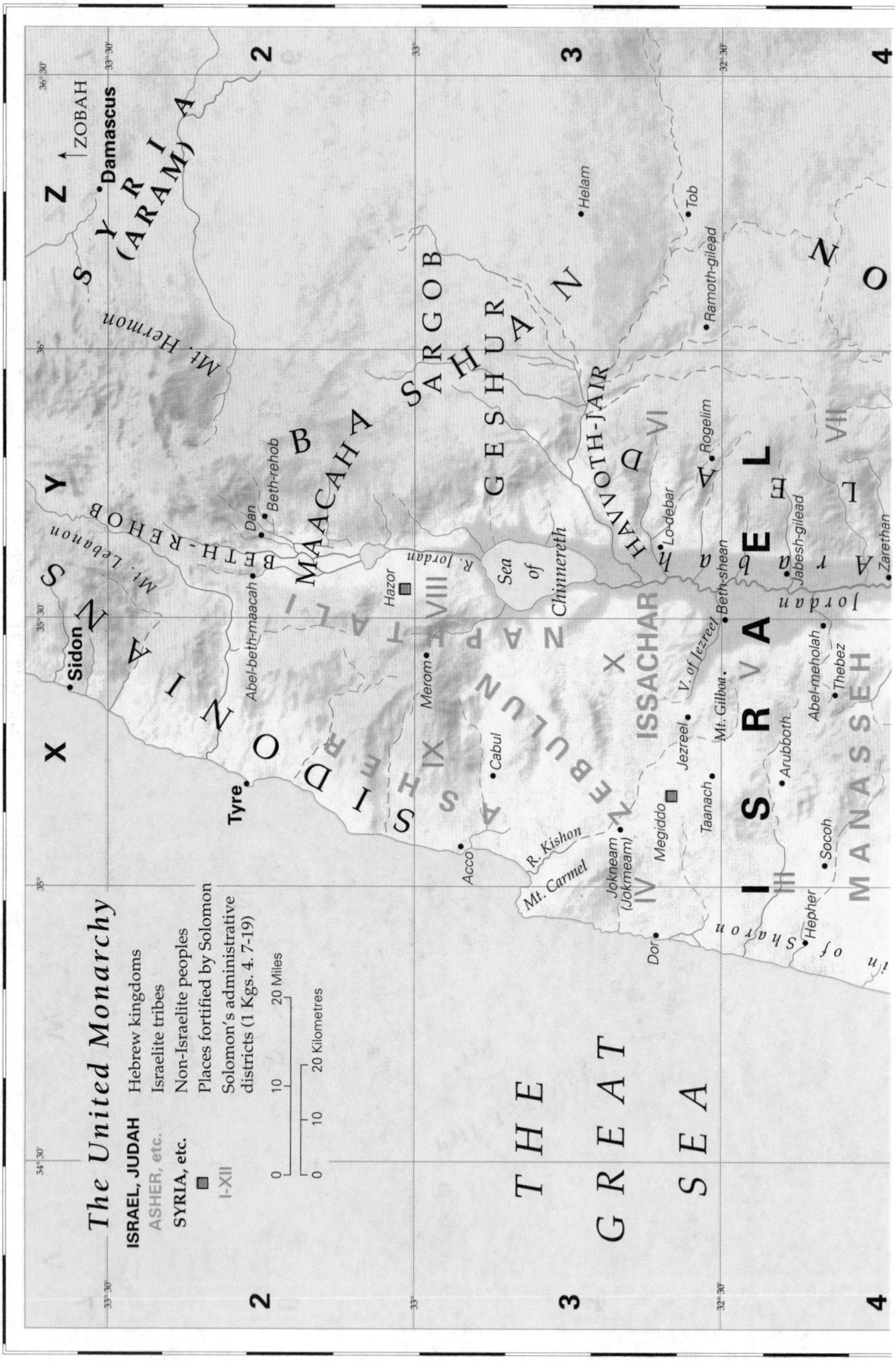

The United Monarchy
ISRAEL, JUDAH Hebrew kingdoms
ASHER, etc. Israelite tribes
SYRIA, etc. Non-Israelite peoples
Places fortified by Solomon
I-XII Solomon's administrative districts (1 Kgs. 4. 7-19)
0 10 20 Miles
0 10 20 Kilometres
THE GREAT SEA
SIDONIANS
SYRIA (ARAM)
ZOBAH
Damascus
Sidon
Tyre
Mt. Lebanon
Mt. Hermon
BETH-REHOB
Beth-rehob
Dan
Abel-beth-maacah
MAACAH
ARGOB
GESHUR
HAVOTH-JAIR
BASHAN
Helam
Tob
Ramoth-gilead
Rogelim
Lo-debar
Jabesh-gilead
Zarethan
Hazor
R. Jordan
Sea of Chinnereth
NAPHTALI
VIII
Merom
ASHER
IX
Cabul
Acco
ZEBULUN
R. Kishon
Mt. Carmel
Jokneam (Jokmeam)
IV
Dor
Megiddo
Taanach
Jezreel
V. of Jezreel
ISSACHAR
Mt. Gilboa
Beth-shean
Arubboth
Socoh
III
Hepher
Plain of Sharon
Abel-meholah
Thebez
Jordan
MANASSEH
ISRAEL
VI
VII
GILEAD
AMMON
Arabah
2
3
4
33° 30'
33°
32° 30'
34° 30'
35°
35° 30'
36°
36° 30'

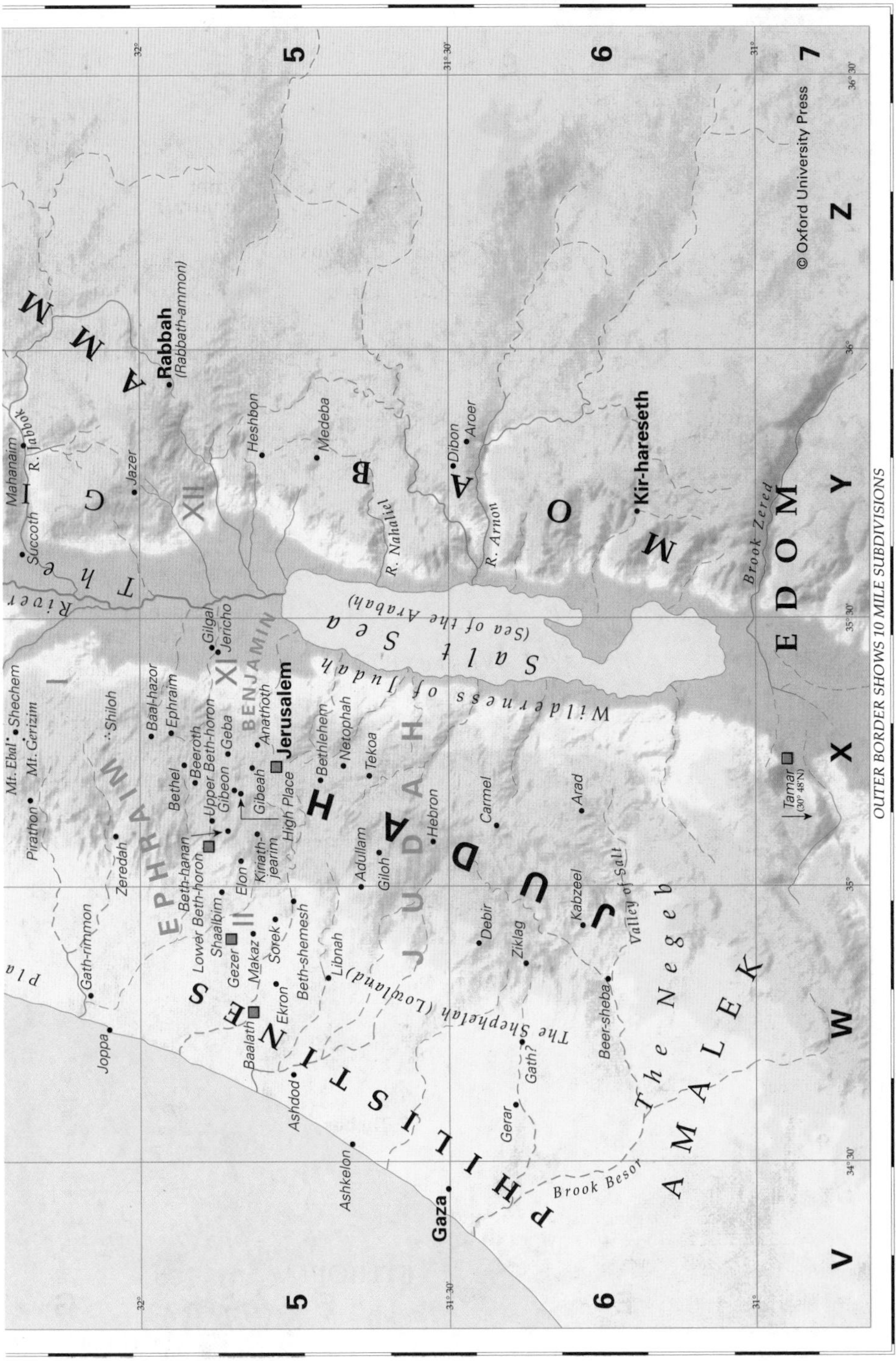

AMMON
GILEAD
MOAB
EDOM
JUDAH
EPHRAIM
BENJAMIN
PHILISTINES
AMALEK
The River Jordan
Salt Sea
(Sea of the Arabah)
Wilderness of Judah
The Shephelah (Lowland)
The Negeb
Valley of Salt
Brook Besor
Brook Zered
R. Arnon
R. Nahaliel
R. Jabbok
Rabbah
(Rabbath-ammon)
Mahanaim
Succoth
Jazer
Heshbon
Medeba
Dibon
Aroer
Kir-hareseth
Mt. Ebal
Shechem
Mt. Gerizim
Pirathon
Shiloh
Baal-hazor
Ephraim
Zeredah
Bethel
Beeroth
Upper Beth-horon
Gibeon
Geba
Gibeah
Anathoth
Jerusalem
High Place
Gilgal
Jericho
Beth-hanan
Lower Beth-horon
Shaalbim
Elon
Kiriath-jearim
Gezer
Makaz
Sorek
Baalath
Ekron
Beth-shemesh
Bethlehem
Netophah
Tekoa
Hebron
Carmel
Adullam
Giloh
Libnah
Debir
Ziklag
Kabzeel
Arad
Tamar
(30° 48'N)
Beer-sheba
Gath?
Gerar
Gath-rimmon
Joppa
Ashdod
Ashkelon
Gaza
Pla
II
XI
XII
V
W
X
Y
Z
5
6
7
32°
31° 30'
31°
34° 30'
35°
35° 30'
36°
36° 30'
© Oxford University Press
OUTER BORDER SHOWS 10 MILE SUBDIVISIONS

MAP 5

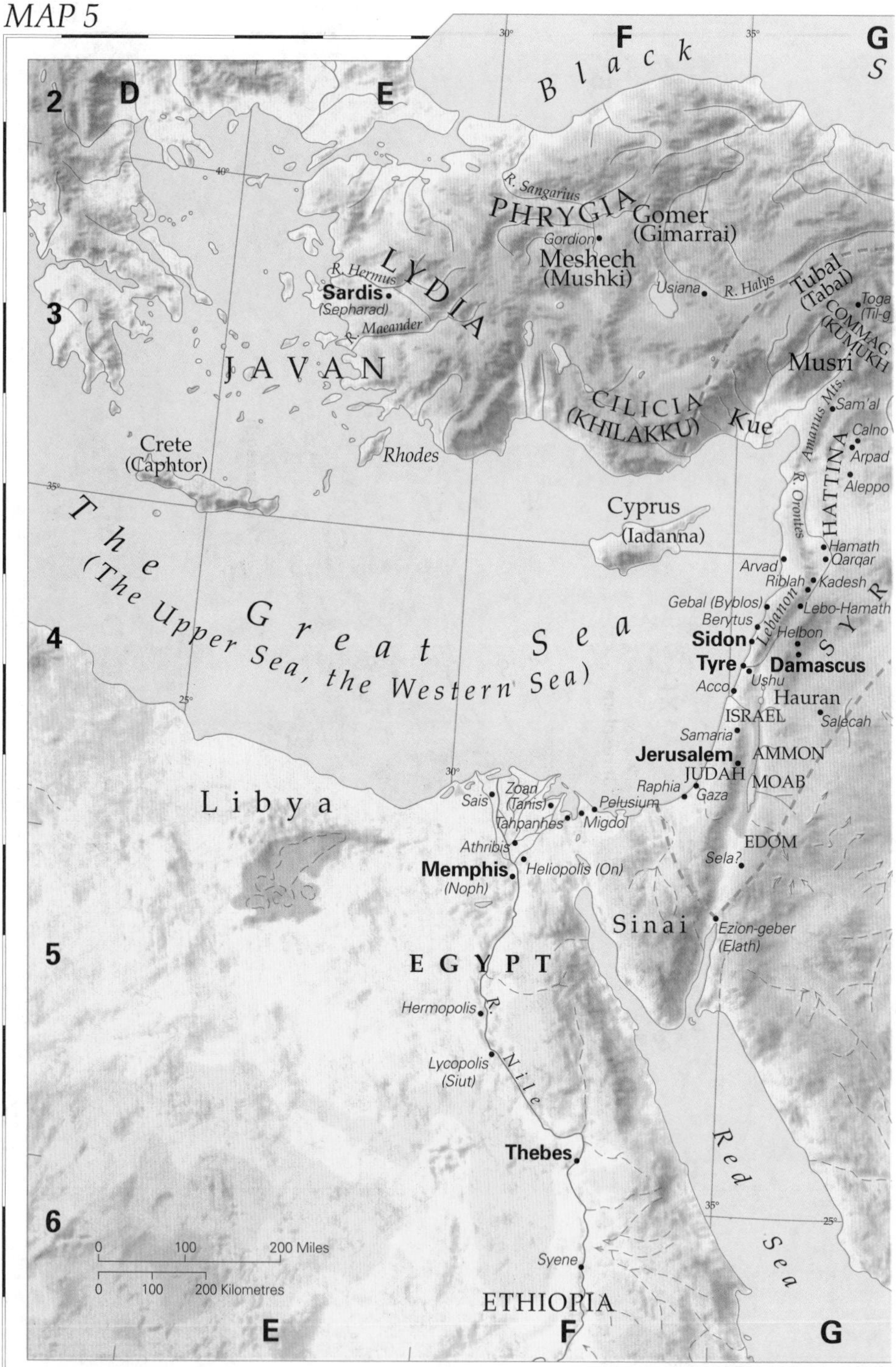

OUTER BORDER SHOWS

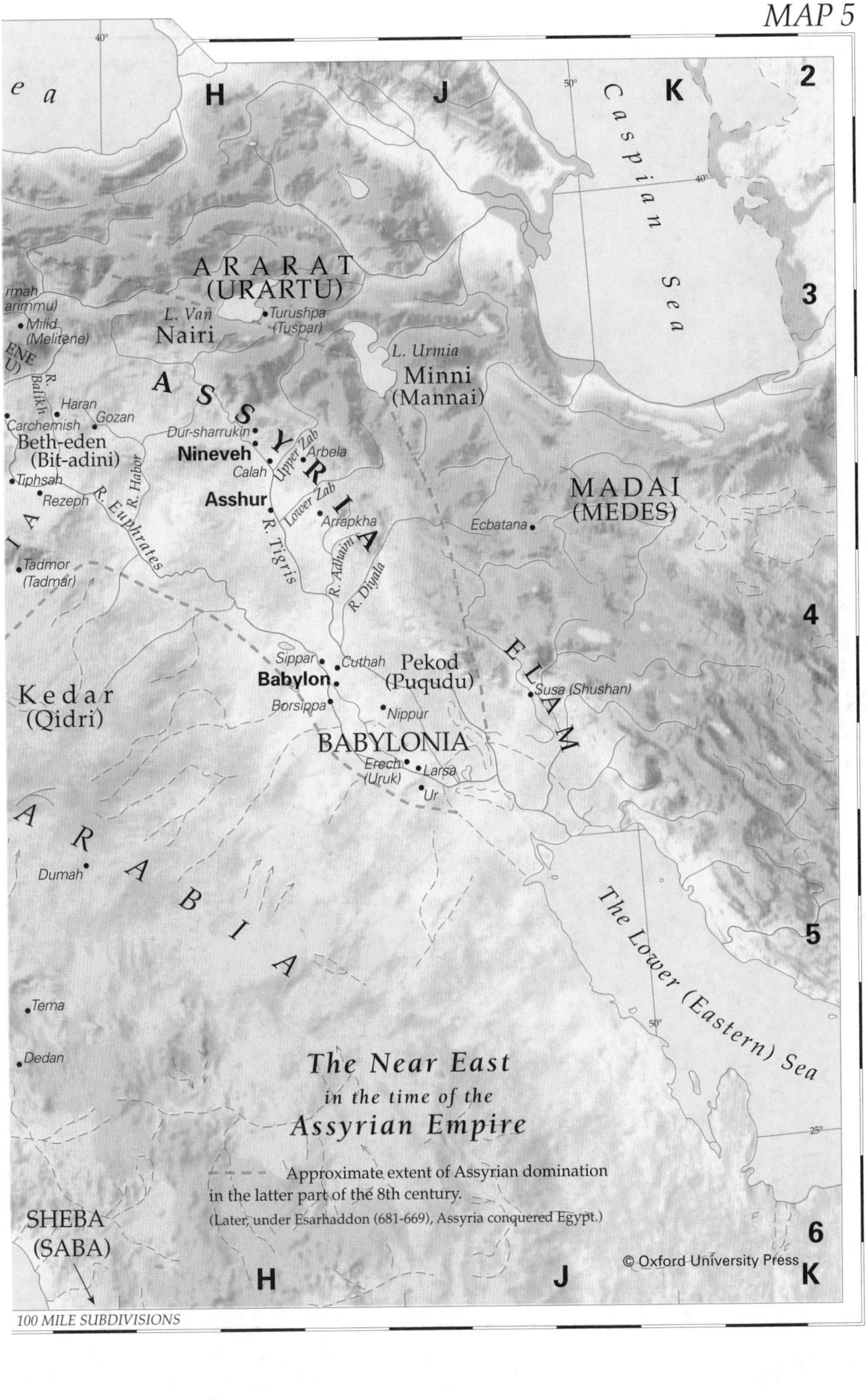

The Near East in the time of the Assyrian Empire

Approximate extent of Assyrian domination in the latter part of the 8th century.
(Later, under Esarhaddon (681-669), Assyria conquered Egypt.)

MAP 6

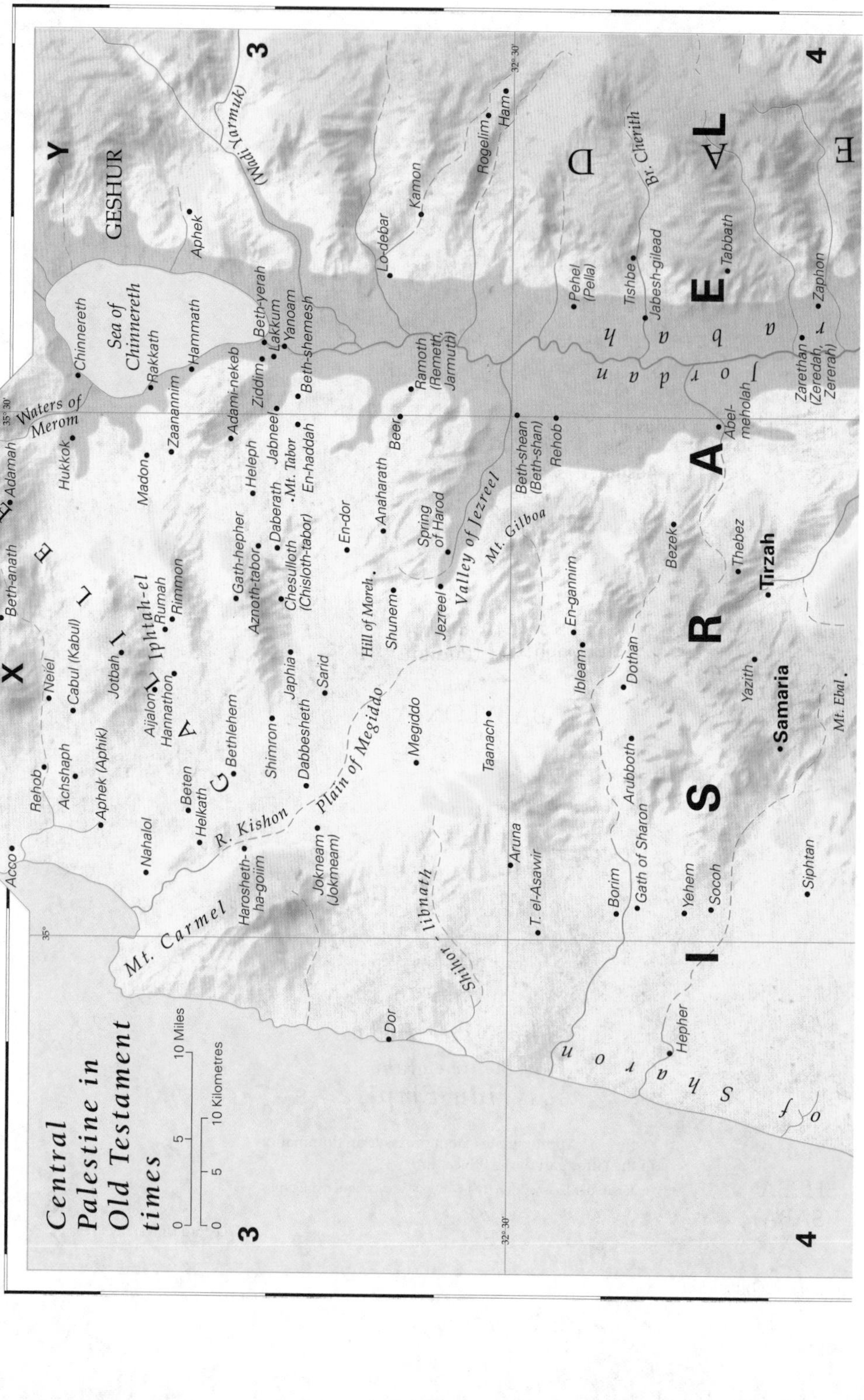

Central Palestine in Old Testament times
0 5 10 Miles
0 5 10 Kilometres
3
4
35°
35° 30'
32° 30'
Mt. Carmel
Dor
Shihor-libnath
Sharon
Hepher
Acco
Harosheth-ha-goiim
R. Kishon
Jokneam (Jokmeam)
Plain of Megiddo
Megiddo
Taanach
Aruna
T. el-Asawir
Borim
Gath of Sharon
Yehem
Socoh
Siphtan
Arubboth
Ibleam
Dothan
Samaria
Yazith
Mt. Ebal
Tirzah
Thebez
Bezek
En-gannim
Mt. Gilboa
Jezreel
Shunem
Hill of Moreh
Valley of Jezreel
Spring of Harod
Beth-shean (Beth-shan)
Rehob
Anaharath
En-dor
Nahalol
Helkath
Beten
Achshaph
Aphek (Aphik)
Rehob
Bethlehem
Shimron
Dabbesheth
Japhia
Sarid
Aijalon
Hannathon
Jotbah
Cabul (Kabul)
Neiel
Beth-anath
Iphtah-el
Rumah
Rimmon
Gath-hepher
Aznoth-tabor
Chesulloth (Chisloth-tabor)
Daberath
Mt. Tabor
En-haddah
Heleph
Jabneel
Adami-nekeb
Madon
Zaanannim
Hukkok
Adamah
Waters of Merom
Chinnereth
Rakkath
Sea of Chinnereth
Hammath
Ziddim
Lakkum
Beth-yerah
Yanoam
Beth-shemesh
Beer
Ramoth (Remeth, Jarmuth)
Lo-debar
Kamon
Rogelim
Ham
Aphek
GESHUR
Wadi Yarmuk
Pehel (Pella)
Tishbe
Jabesh-gilead
Tabbath
Br. Cherith
Zaphon
Zarethan (Zeredah, Zererah)
Abel-meholah
Jordan
ISRAEL
GALILEE
GILEAD

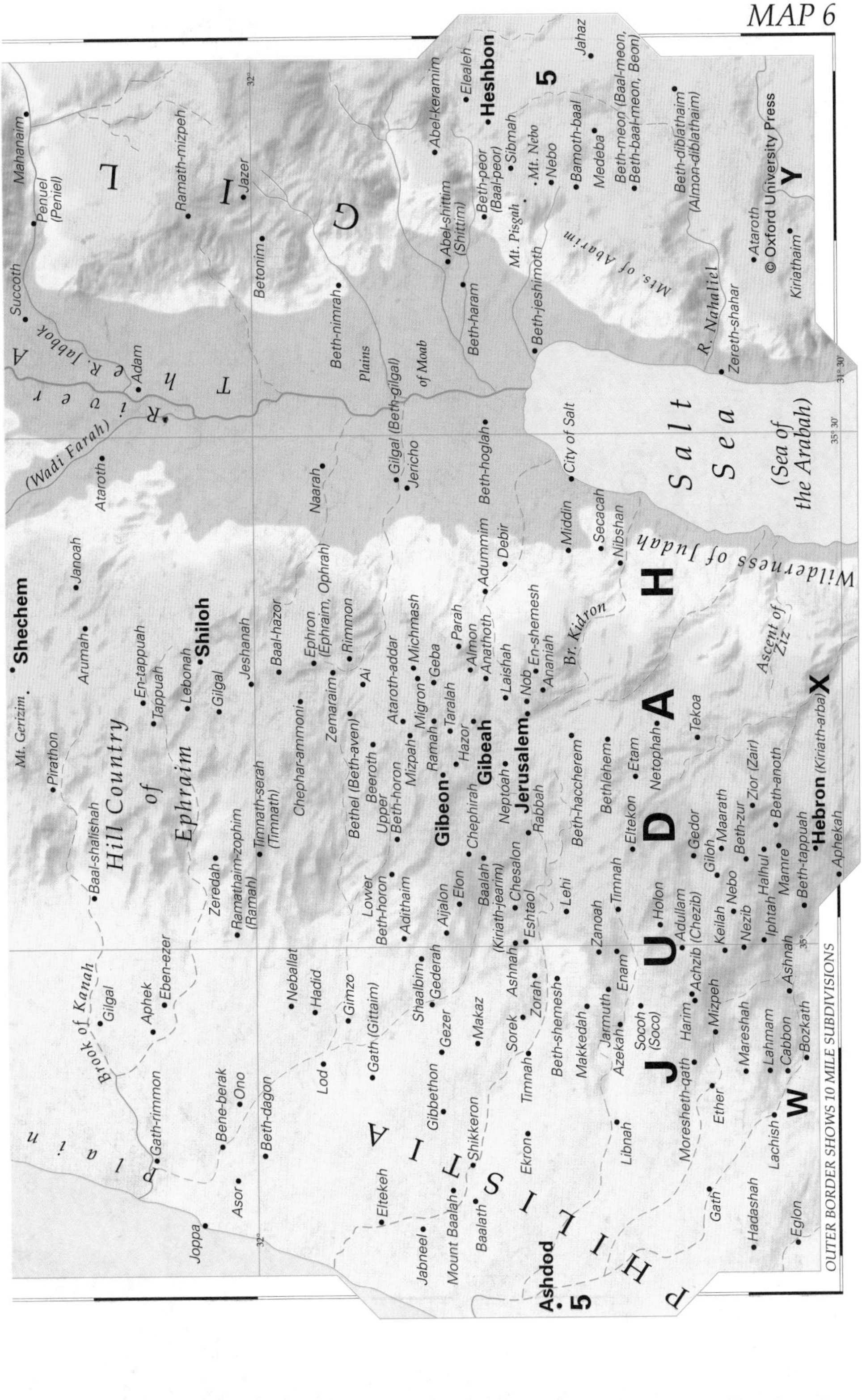
Hill Country of Ephraim
Salt Sea (Sea of the Arabah)
Wilderness of Judah
Mts. of Abarim
Plains of Moab
R. Jabbok
River Jordan
(Wadi Farah)
R. Nahaliel
Br. Kidron
Ascent of Ziz
Brook of Kanah
Plain
PHILISTIA
JUDAH
GILEAD
Shechem
Shiloh
Gibeon
Gibeah
Jerusalem
Hebron (Kiriath-arba)
Heshbon
Ashdod
Mahanaim
Penuel (Peniel)
Succoth
Adam
Ramath-mizpeh
Jazer
Betonim
Beth-nimrah
Abel-keramim
Elealeh
Jahaz
Beth-peor (Baal-peor)
Sibmah
Mt. Nebo
Nebo
Mt. Pisgah
Abel-shittim (Shittim)
Beth-haram
Beth-jeshimoth
Bamoth-baal
Medeba
Beth-meon (Baal-meon, Beth-baal-meon, Beon)
Beth-diblathaim (Almon-diblathaim)
Ataroth
Kiriathaim
Zereth-shahar
City of Salt
Beth-hoglah
Gilgal (Beth-gilgal)
Jericho
Naarah
Ataroth
Janoah
Arumah
Mt. Gerizim
Pirathon
En-tappuah
Tappuah
Lebonah
Gilgal
Jeshanah
Baal-hazor
Ephron (Ephraim, Ophrah)
Rimmon
Zemaraim
Ai
Ataroth-addar
Michmash
Geba
Parah
Almon
Anathoth
Adummim
Debir
Migron
Taralah
Hazor
Ramah
Mizpah
Bethel (Beth-aven)
Beeroth
Upper Beth-horon
Lower Beth-horon
Chephar-ammoni
Timnath-serah (Timnath)
Ramathaim-zophim (Ramah)
Zeredah
Baal-shalishah
Chephirah
Neptoah
Rabbah
Nob
Laishah
En-shemesh
Ananiah
Middin
Secacah
Nibshan
Beth-haccherem
Bethlehem
Etam
Netophah
Tekoa
Eltekon
Gedor
Maarath
Giloh
Beth-zur
Zior (Zair)
Beth-anoth
Halhul
Mamre
Beth-tappuah
Aphekah
Adithaim
Aijalon
Elon
Baalah (Kiriath-jearim)
Chesalon
Eshtaol
Lehi
Timnah
Holon
Adullam
Achzib (Chezib)
Keilah
Nebo
Nezib
Iphtah
Ashnah
Zanoah
Enam
Jarmuth
Socoh (Soco)
Azekah
Harim
Mizpeh
Mareshah
Lahmam
Cabbon
Bozkath
Ashnah
Makkedah
Beth-shemesh
Zorah
Sorek
Timnah
Makaz
Gezer
Gederah
Shaalbim
Gibbethon
Gimzo
Gath (Gittaim)
Hadid
Neballat
Lod
Ekron
Shikkeron
Libnah
Moresheth-gath
Ether
Lachish
Gath
Hadashah
Eglon
Elteke
Baalath
Mount Baalah
Jabneel
Joppa
Asor
Bene-berak
Ono
Gath-rimmon
Beth-dagon
Aphek
Eben-ezer
Gilgal
32°
31° 30'
35°
35° 30'
5
W
X
Y
© Oxford University Press
OUTER BORDER SHOWS 10 MILE SUBDIVISIONS

MAP 7

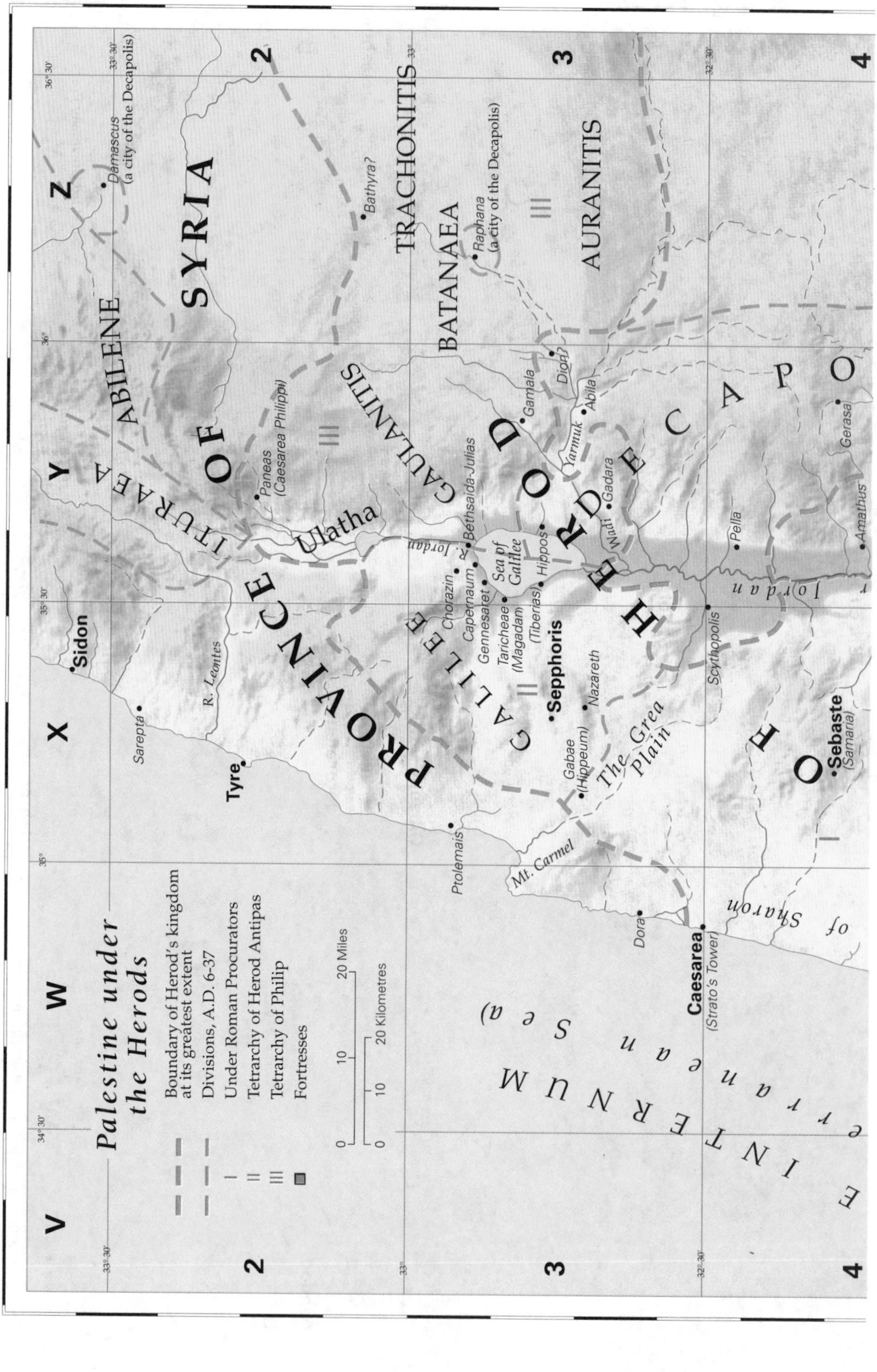

Palestine under the Herods
Boundary of Herod's kingdom at its greatest extent
Divisions, A.D. 6-37
I Under Roman Procurators
II Tetrarchy of Herod Antipas
III Tetrarchy of Philip
Fortresses
0 10 20 Miles
0 10 20 Kilometres
V
W
X
Y
Z
2
3
4
33° 30'
33°
32° 30'
34° 30'
35°
35° 30'
36°
36° 30'
PROVINCE OF SYRIA
ABILENE
ITURAEA
TRACHONITIS
BATANAEA
AURANITIS
GAULANITIS
GALILEE
DECAPOLIS
HERODS
Sidon
Sarepta
Tyre
R. Leontes
Damascus
(a city of the Decapolis)
Bathyra?
Raphana
(a city of the Decapolis)
Paneas
(Caesarea Philippi)
Ulatha
R. Jordan
Bethsaida-Julias
Chorazin
Capernaum
Gennesaret
Sea of Galilee
Taricheae
(Magadan)
(Tiberias)
Hippos
Gamala
Dion?
Abila
Yarmuk
Gadara
Wadi
Sepphoris
Nazareth
Gabae
(Hippeum)
The Great Plain
Scythopolis
Pella
Jordan
Gerasa
Amathus
Ptolemais
Mt. Carmel
Dora
Caesarea
(Strato's Tower)
Sebaste
(Samaria)
of Sharon
INTERNUM
Mediterranean Sea

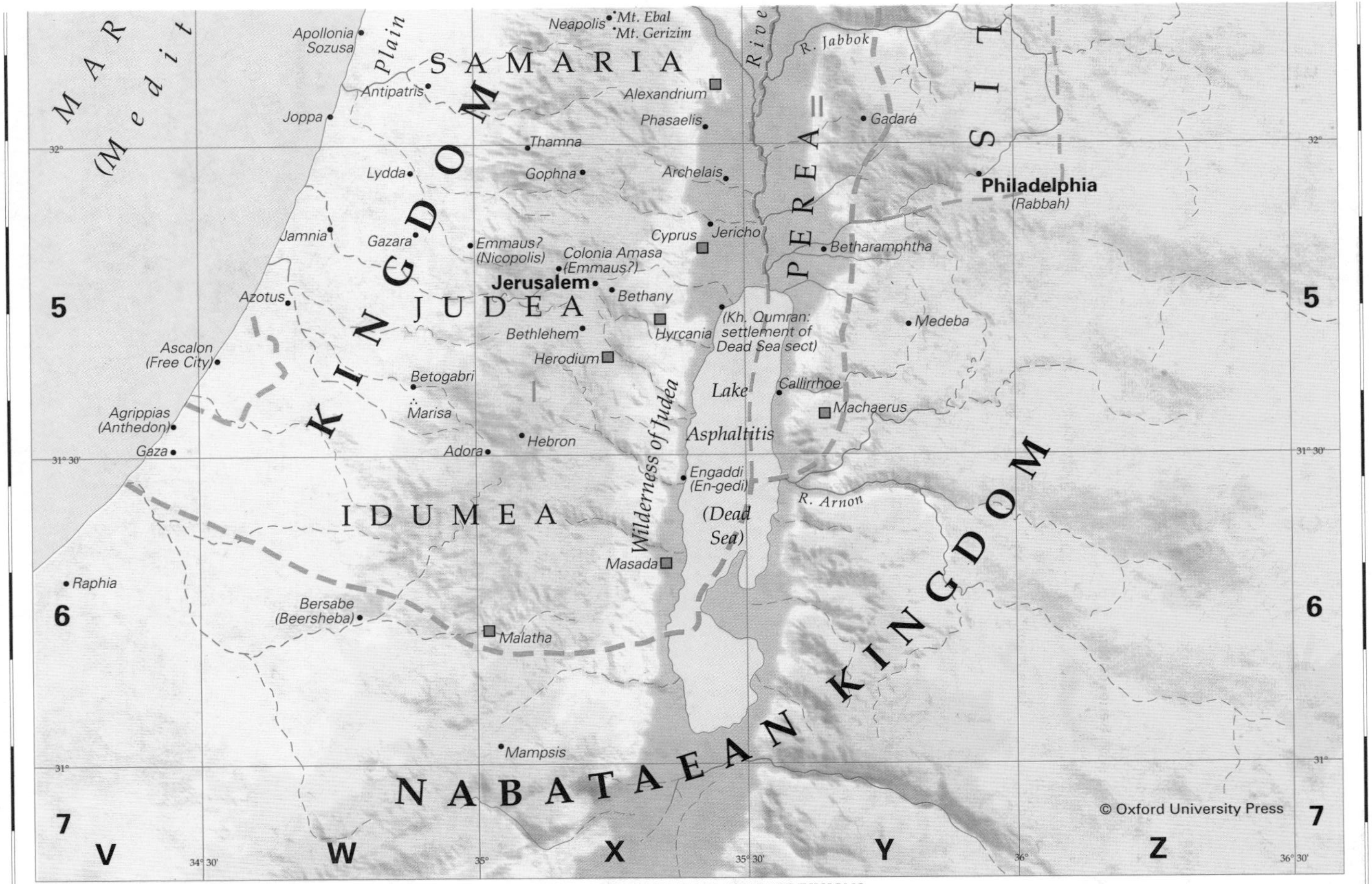

OUTER BORDER SHOWS 10 MILE SUBDIVISIONS

MAP 8

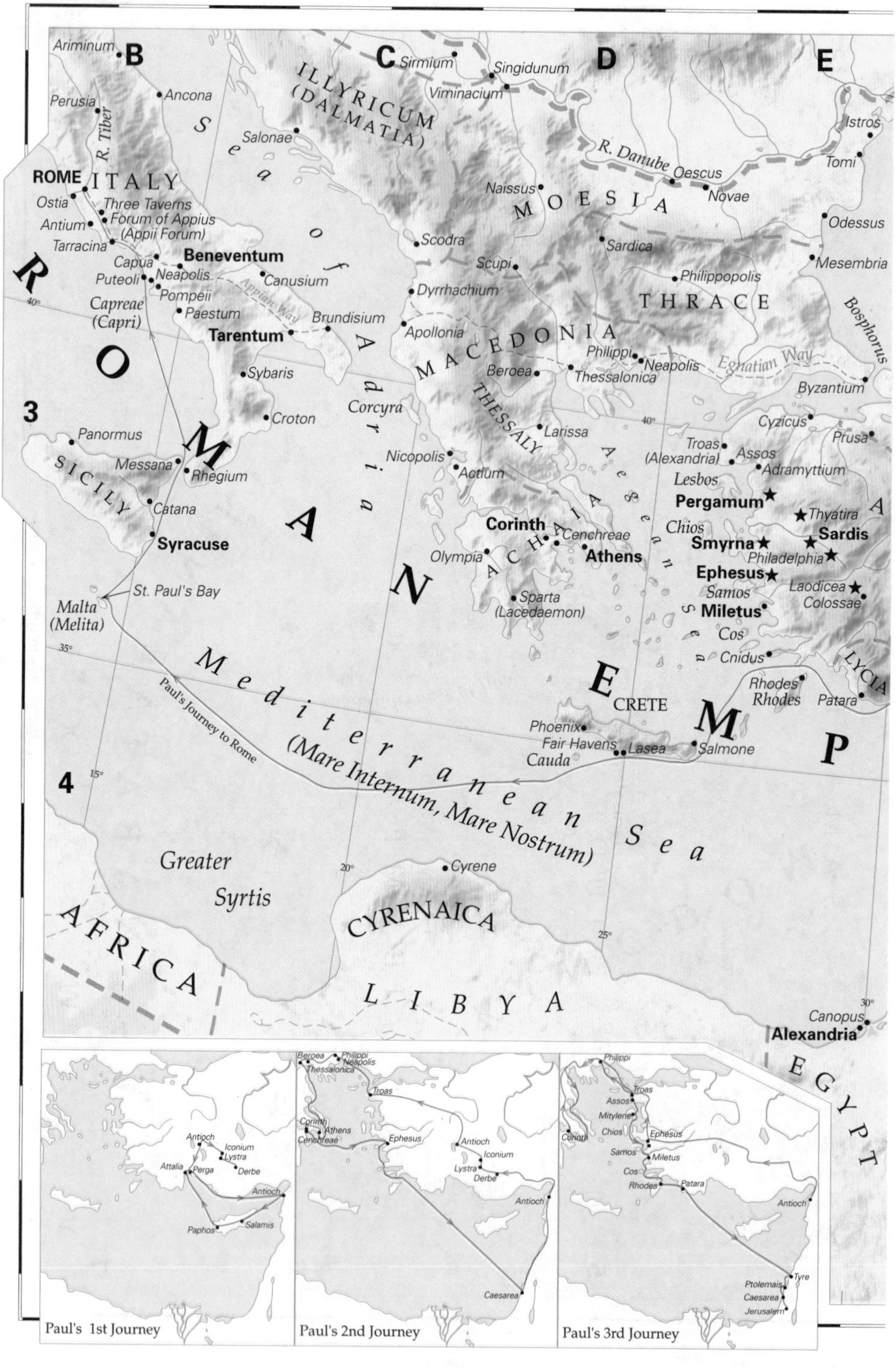

B
C
D
E
3
4
ROMAN EMPIRE
Ariminum
Ancona
Perusia
R. Tiber
ROME
ITALY
Ostia
Three Taverns
Antium
Forum of Appius
(Appii Forum)
Tarracina
Capua
Beneventum
Puteoli
Neapolis
Canusium
Pompeii
Appian Way
Capreae
(Capri)
Paestum
Brundisium
Tarentum
Sybaris
Croton
Panormus
Messana
Rhegium
SICILY
Catana
Syracuse
St. Paul's Bay
Malta
(Melita)
Sea of Adria
Corcyra
Sirmium
Singidunum
Viminacium
ILLYRICUM
(DALMATIA)
Salonae
R. Danube
Oescus
Novae
Istros
Tomi
Naissus
MOESIA
Odessus
Scodra
Sardica
Scupi
Mesembria
Philippopolis
Dyrrhachium
THRACE
Bosphorus
Apollonia
MACEDONIA
Philippi
Neapolis
Egnatian Way
Beroea
Thessalonica
Byzantium
THESSALY
Cyzicus
Larissa
Prusa
Nicopolis
Troas
(Alexandria)
Assos
Actium
Adramyttium
Aegean Sea
Lesbos
Pergamum
Thyatira
Corinth
Cenchreae
Chios
Smyrna
Sardis
Olympia
ACHAIA
Athens
Philadelphia
Ephesus
Laodicea
Samos
Colossae
Sparta
(Lacedaemon)
Miletus
Cos
Cnidus
LYCIA
Rhodes
Rhodes
Patara
CRETE
Phoenix
Fair Havens
Lasea
Salmone
Cauda
Mediterranean Sea
(Mare Internum, Mare Nostrum)
Paul's Journey to Rome
Greater
Syrtis
Cyrene
CYRENAICA
AFRICA
LIBYA
Canopus
Alexandria
EGYPT
40°
35°
15°
20°
25°
30°
Antioch
Iconium
Lystra
Derbe
Attalia
Perga
Antioch
Paphos
Salamis
Paul's 1st Journey
Beroea
Philippi
Neapolis
Thessalonica
Troas
Corinth
Athens
Cenchreae
Ephesus
Antioch
Iconium
Lystra
Derbe
Antioch
Caesarea
Paul's 2nd Journey
Philippi
Troas
Assos
Mitylene
Chios
Corinth
Ephesus
Samos
Miletus
Cos
Rhodes
Patara
Antioch
Tyre
Ptolemais
Caesarea
Jerusalem
Paul's 3rd Journey

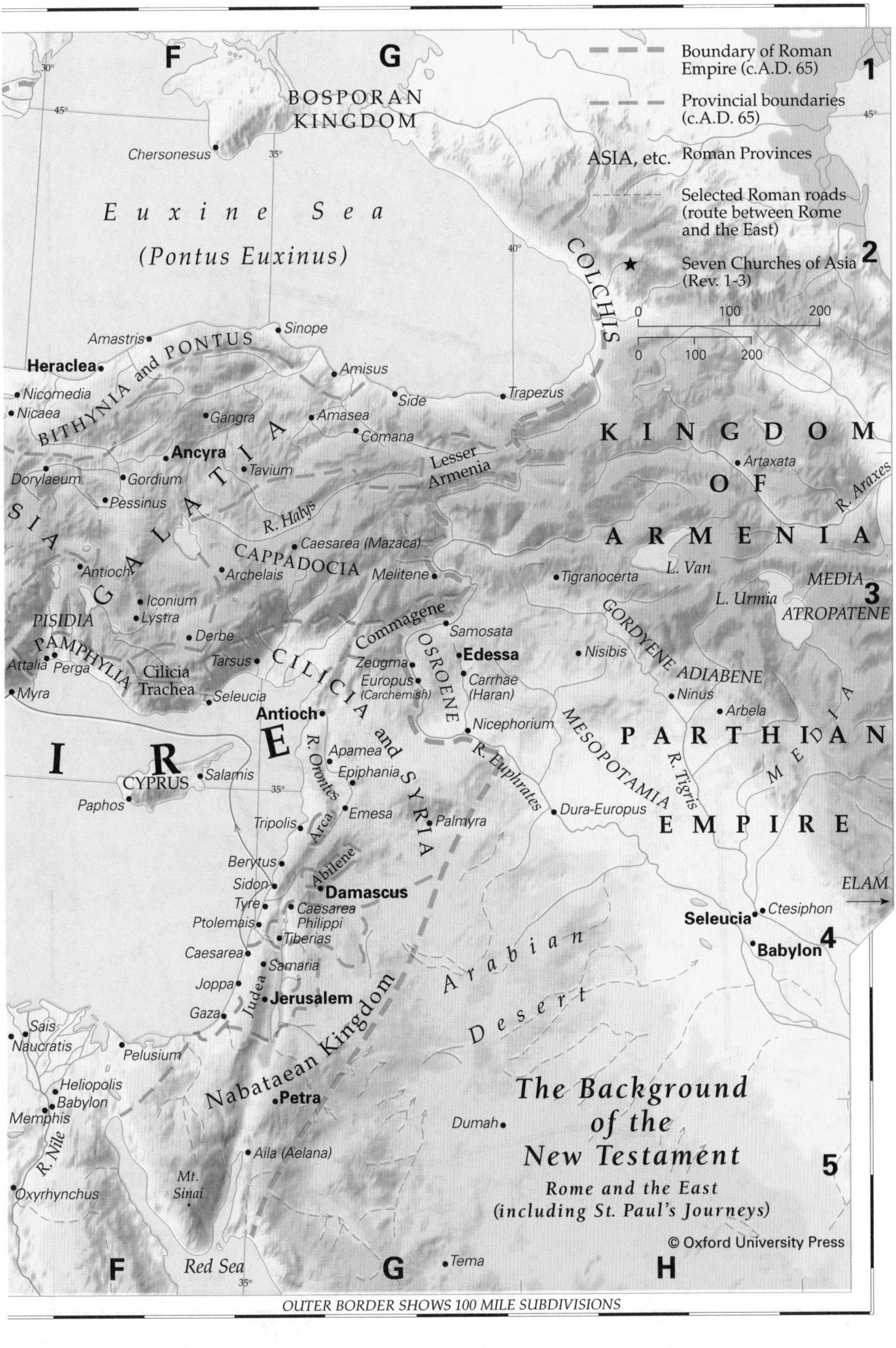

OUTER BORDER SHOWS 100 MILE SUBDIVISIONS

MAP 9

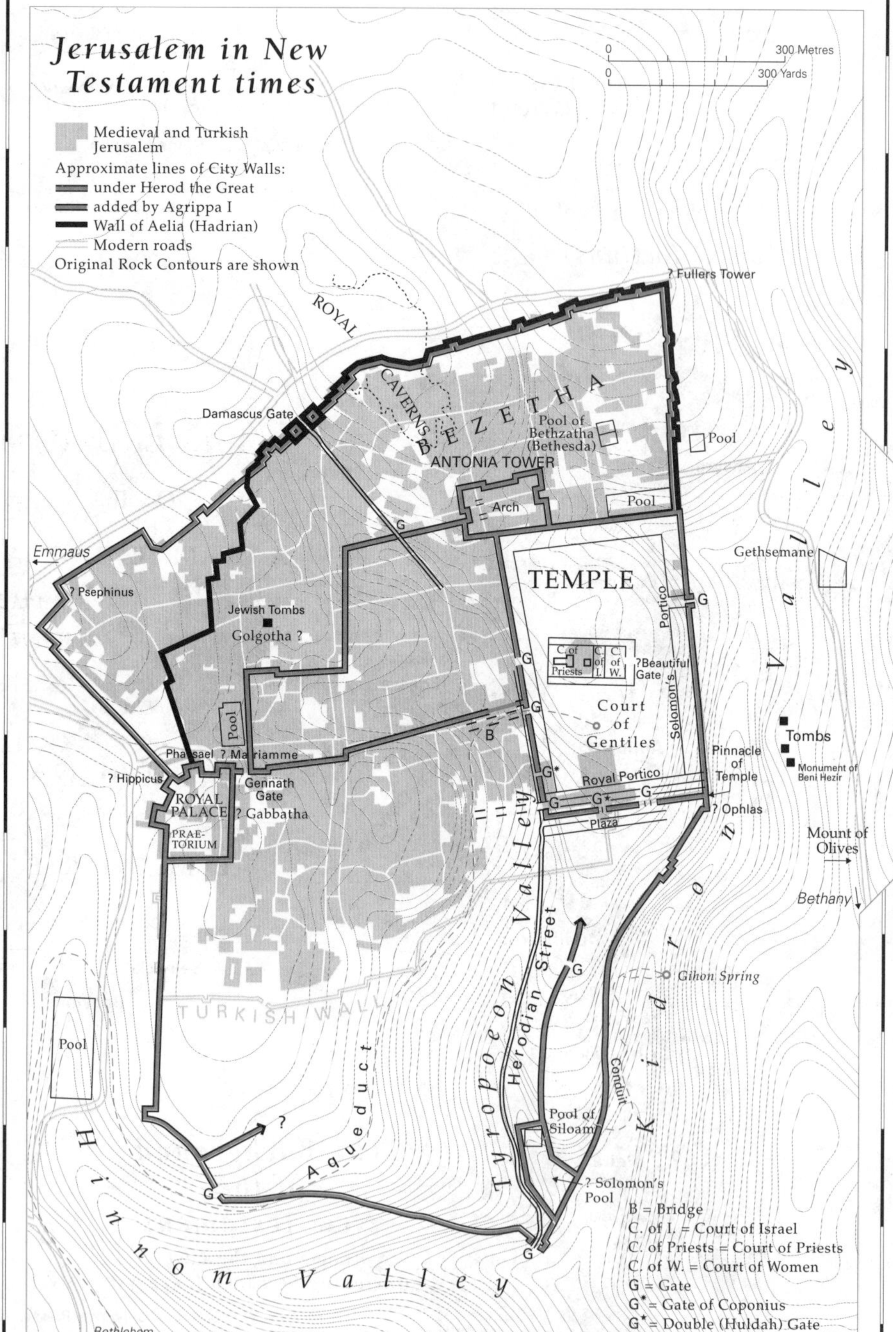
Jerusalem in New Testament times
Medieval and Turkish Jerusalem
Approximate lines of City Walls:
under Herod the Great
added by Agrippa I
Wall of Aelia (Hadrian)
Modern roads
Original Rock Contours are shown
0
300 Metres
0
300 Yards
? Fullers Tower
ROYAL
CAVERNS
BEZETHA
Damascus Gate
Pool of Bethzatha (Bethesda)
Pool
ANTONIA TOWER
Arch
Pool
G
Emmaus
Gethsemane
TEMPLE
Portico
G
? Psephinus
Jewish Tombs
Golgotha ?
G
C. of Priests
C. of I.
C. of W.
?Beautiful Gate
Court of Gentiles
Solomon's
G
Pool
B
Tombs
Monument of Beni Hezir
Phasael
? Mariamme
? Hippicus
Gennath Gate
? Gabbatha
ROYAL PALACE
PRAETORIUM
G*
Royal Portico
G
G
G
Pinnacle of Temple
? Ophlas
Plaza
Mount of Olives
Bethany
Kidron Valley
Tyropoeon Valley
Herodian Street
G
Gihon Spring
TURKISH WALL
Pool
Aqueduct
Conduit
?
Pool of Siloam
? Solomon's Pool
G
G
Hinnom Valley
B = Bridge
C. of I. = Court of Israel
C. of Priests = Court of Priests
C. of W. = Court of Women
G = Gate
G* = Gate of Coponius
G* = Double (Huldah) Gate
Bethlehem
© Oxford University Press

OUTER BORDER SHOWS 180 YARD SUBDIVISIONS